FOOTBALL YEARBOOK 2020-2021

Compiled by
John Anderson

First published in 2020
by HEADLINE PUBLISHING GROUP

1

Front cover photographs:
(left) Raul Jimenez (Wolverhampton Wanderers) – *David Davies/EMPICS SPORT/PA Images*; (centre and background) Virgil van Dijk (Liverpool) – *Visionhaus/Getty Images Sport*; (right) Raheem Sterling (Manchester City) – *Martin Rickett/PA Wire/PA Images*

Spine photograph:
Liverpool captain Jordan Henderson with the Premier League trophy, July 2020 – *Phil Noble/PA Wire/PA Images*

Cataloguing in Publication Data is available from the British Library

ISBN 9781472277213 (Hardback)
ISBN 9781472277220 (Trade Paperback)

Typeset by Wearset Ltd, Boldon, Tyne and Wear

Printed and bound by Clays Ltd, Elcograf S.p.A.

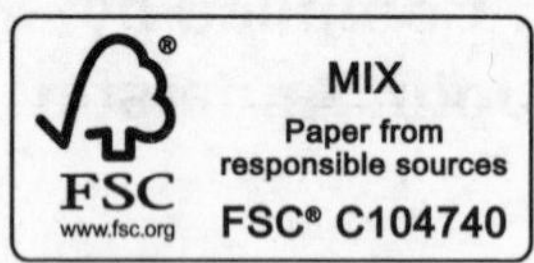

Headline's policy is to use papers that are natural, renewable and recyclable products and made from wood grown in sustainable forests. The logging and manufacturing processes are expected to conform to the environmental regulations of the country of origin.

HEADLINE PUBLISHING GROUP
An Hachette UK Company
Carmelite House
50 Victoria Embankment
London EC4Y 0DZ

www.headline.co.uk
www.hachette.co.uk

CONTENTS

INTRODUCTION

The 51st edition of the *Football Yearbook* is the first time it has been published without a sponsor. In a truly extraordinary season affected dramatically and drastically by the COVID-19 pandemic we have had curtailments, postponements, games behind closed doors and declarations of null-and-void competitions. Even so, the coverage in this edition is once again full and comprehensive.

Full coverage of the European Qualifying campaign for Euro 2020 including match line-ups and league tables is included. Due to the COVID-19 pandemic the Euro 2020 finals have been re-arranged for 2021. Other international football at various levels is well covered in this edition.

The concise feature entitled Cups and Ups and Downs Diary is included with dates of those events affecting cup finals, promotion and relegation issues. The Managers In and Out section is once again included, with a diary of the many managerial changes throughout the year.

At European level, the Champions League, with an unusal end to the competition, has its usual comprehensive details included, with results, goalscorers, attendances, full line-ups and formations from the qualifying rounds onwards and also including all the league tables from the respective group stages. The Europa League includes full line-ups, formations and league tables from the group stage onwards.

The 2019–20 Premier League season saw Liverpool's quest for glory interrupted, but eventually fulfilled late in June. The top two divisions in England did not complete until the end of July whilst The Championship season ended with Leeds United and West Bromwich Albion promoted automatically, and they were joined by Fulham who won the Championship Play-Off 2-1 against west London rivals Brentford at Wembley. Leagues One and Two ended prematurely and were decided on a points-per-game basis. Coventry City and Rotherham United were promoted automatically from League One with Wycombe Wanderers the big winners in the points-per-game issue, overcoming Oxford United in the play-off final. Tranmere Rovers, the big losers on points-per-game, were relegated to League Two along with Southend United and Bolton Wanderers who started the season with a 12-point deduction. League Two saw Swindon Town, Crewe Alexandra and Plymouth Argyle achieve automatic promotion and joining them in League One was Northampton Town with a comprehensive 4-0 final win over Exeter City.

Jordan Henderson of Liverpool and England won the Football Writers' Footballer of the Year award. Due to the COVID-19 pandemic the PFA Player of the Year award was cancelled.

All of these statistics are reproduced in the pages devoted not only to the Premier League, but the three Football League competitions too, as well as all major allied cup competitions.

In women's football, the UEFA Women's Euro 2021 Qualifying is covered up-to-date. The Women's Super League, Championship and National Leagues are included, together with the domestic cup competitions: Women's FA Cup and League Cup. The Women's UEFA Champions League is also covered. England Women's Internationals since 1974 and all of the 2019–20 season's games are included.

In an age where transfer fees are frequently undisclosed and rarely given as official figures, the edition reflects those listed at the time.

In the club-by-club pages that contain the line-ups of all league matches, appearances are split into starting and substitute appearances. In the Players Directory the totals show figures combined.

The Players Directory and its accompanying A to Z index enables the reader to quickly find the club of any specific player.

Throughout the book players sent off are designated with ■; substitutes in the club pages are 12, 13 and 14. From June onwards in the Premier League and Championship additional substitutes were allowed and these are shown as 15 and 16.

In addition to competitions already mentioned there is full coverage of Scottish Premiership, Scottish Football League and Scottish domestic cup competitions. There are also sections devoted to Welsh and Irish football, Under-21s and various other UEFA youth levels, schools, reserve team, academies, referees and the leading non-league competitions as well as the work of club chaplains. The chief tournaments outside the UK at club and national level are not forgotten. The International Directory itself features Europe in some depth as well as every FIFA-affiliated country's international results for the year since July 2019; every reigning league and cup champion worldwide is listed.

Naturally there are international appearances and goals scored by players for England, Scotland, Northern Ireland, Wales and the Republic of Ireland. For easy reference, those players making appearances and scoring goals in the season covered are picked out in bold type.

The *Football Yearbook* would like to extend its appreciation to the publishers Headline for excellent support in the preparation of this edition, particularly Graham Green for his continued help and Jonathan Taylor for the photographic selection throughout the book and his selection of the Team of the Season.

ACKNOWLEDGEMENTS

In addition the *Football Yearbook* is also keen to thank the following individuals and organisations for their co-operation. Special thanks to Jonathan Wilson for his Review of the Season.

Thanks are also due to Ian Nannestad for the Obituaries and the Did You Know? and Fact File features in the club section. Many thanks also to John English for his conscientious proof reading and compilation of the International Directory.

The *Football Yearbook* is grateful to the Football Association, the Scottish Professional Football League, the Football League, Rev. Nigel Sands for his contribution to the Chaplain's page and Bob Bannister, Paul Anderson, Kenny Holmes, Martin Cooper and Phil Harrison for their help.

Sincere thanks to George Schley and Simon Dunnington for their excellent work on the database, and to Andy Cordiner, Geoff Turner, Brian Tait, Robin Middlemiss and the staff at Wearset for their much appreciated efforts in the production of the book throughout the year.

TEAM OF THE SEASON 2019–20

JONATHAN TAYLOR

Alisson Becker
(Liverpool)

Trent Alexander-Arnold *(Liverpool)* | **Virgil van Dijk** *(Liverpool)* | **Caglar Sojuncu** *(Leicester C)* | **Andy Robertson** *(Liverpool)*

Raheem Sterling *(Manchester C)* | **Kevin De Bruyne** *(Manchester C)* | **Jordan Henderson** *(Liverpool)* | **Sadio Mané** *(Liverpool)*

Danny Ings *(Southampton)* | **Jamie Vardy** *(Leicester C)*

Manager: Jurgen Klopp
(Liverpool)

Alisson Becker: the Brazilian's resilience and consistency between the posts were major factors in helping to drive Liverpool to the title. Compatriot Ederson may have registered more clean sheets in the Premier League, but Alisson's all-round excellence makes him one of the very best keepers in the world.

Trent Alexander-Arnold: fast establishing himself as one of Europe's most exciting full-backs, and a vital cog in the Liverpool machine. Quick feet, a quick brain, and a spectacular range of set pieces and long passing give him an incredible array of offensive weapons. Now has both a Champions League and a Premier League medal at the age of 21.

Virgil van Dijk: perhaps not the almost flawless campaign of the previous season, but mightily impressive nonetheless. The Dutch colossus is a defensive thoroughbred and surely on-track to be one of Europe's most celebrated and coveted centre-halves.

Caglar Sojuncu: the Turkish international has cemented his reputation as one of the best central defenders in the league. As Leicester City maintained a Champions League push for much of the season, Sojuncu stood out with his first-rate tackling, heading and reading of the game.

Andy Robertson: another hugely productive season for the Scottish left-back: 36 league appearances, 12 assists and two goals speak volumes about Robertson's consistency, dynamism, output and – ultimately – undoubted value to his club side.

Raheem Sterling: a trailblazer both on and off the pitch, Sterling was an eloquent and inspirational figure in the age of Black Lives Matter. He scored 20 times in the Premier League and a remarkable 31 times in all competitions. City may have only finished with the League Cup to show for their efforts, but Sterling continues to tear defences apart with his pace, skill and football acumen.

Kevin De Bruyne: is there a better, more visionary passer in world football? The Belgian took his game to the next level, expertly pulling City's strings in midfield and facilitating nearly all their attacking menace with his intelligence, technique and extraordinary range of passing. A Premier League return of 13 goals and 20 assists tells its own story.

Jordan Henderson: the FWA Footballer of the Year ended his season by lifting Liverpool's first league title since 1990. Leads by example and provides the vital glue that binds his team together so effectively. So much to admire in this occasionally underrated midfield dynamo and genuine leader.

Sadio Mané: although Liverpool's front three didn't quite enjoy the same output as they did in the previous season, Mané remained one of the most potent attacking threats in the league. The Senegalese international grabbed 18 goals in the Reds' title-winning campaign and continued to cause Premier League defences a major headache with his fearless running, incisiveness and frequent goal threat.

Danny Ings: when Southampton lost 9-0 at home to Leicester City in October and dropped to eighteenth in the table, very few would have believed the Saints could finish in a comfortable eleventh spot with 52 points. Ings' endless energy and astuteness in the box were huge factors in that resurgence: he finished with 22 goals, just one shy of claiming a share of the Golden Boot. It would not have gone unnoticed by Gareth Southgate.

Jamie Vardy: the evergreen striker enjoyed one of his most productive seasons, scoring just one fewer (23) than he did in Leicester City's title-winning campaign of 2015–16, and recording his hundredth Premier League goal in the process. His eye for goal, speed and intense workrate made him a defender's nightmare and helped to sustain the Foxes' challenge at the business end of the table until the last few weeks.

Manager, Jurgen Klopp: it's impossible to look beyond the charismatic maestro. It would've been understandable if the Reds had struggled to kick on from their stellar 2018–19 campaign, but Klopp confidently delivered Liverpool's first title for three decades. The stats are extraordinary: 32 wins out of 38; 18 wins at home out of 19; 85 goals; and 99 points – a club record and the second highest points tally in the history of England's top division. A virtuoso performance, masterminded by a modern managerial genius.

FOREWORD

A new coronavirus (COVID-19) was to shake the world in early 2020. Football was not to be exempt. The disease was to claim many lives and affect our whole way of life. Lockdown came to many countries, the UK following the lead of Italy, France and others. Life as we knew it was suspended. Our magnificent health and key workers fought so bravely to keep the virus at bay and to allow us some semblance of normality. Schools were closed, those who could worked from home. Many workers were furloughed, many lost their jobs. The fight goes on.

Late in January football in China had been affected by the spread of the virus. By late February, matches in northern Italy were postponed. The start of South Korea's K-league was postponed, and games in Japan's J-league were also postponed. The top two divisions in Switzerland suspended matches. Other nations were to follow suit: Germany, Spain, Denmark, France and USA. The football world was in the grip of the virus.

On 10 March, it was announced that Olympiacos owner Evangelos Marinakis had tested positive for COVID-19. Several Arsenal players were forced to self-isolate after coming into contact with Marinakis at the clubs' Europa League clash at the Emirates on 27 February. The following day Arsenal's league clash with Manchester City was postponed as a precautionary measure. On 12 March Mikel Arteta tested positive for COVID-19 and their fixture at Brighton & HA that weekend was postponed.

By 13 March, the Football Association, Premier League, EFL and Women's Leagues had agreed to postpone football in England until at least 3 April. On the same day Scottish football was postponed indefinitely and Welsh football until 4 April at least. Extensions to these dates would come and go, as governments and authorities tried to understand the implications of the virus. However, the resolve to restart and finish the season was seemingly unwavering.

International football suffered the same fate. On 17 March, Euro 2020 was suspended until 2021. By 1 April, UEFA postponed all international matches until at least the end of June. On the same day the European Champions League and Europa League were suspended until further notice.

The Football Association announced on 26 March that all football below the three leagues of the National League would end immediately with all results expunged. No promotion or relegation would happen in any of these leagues. The women's game below the Women's Super League and Championship were also ended with the same conclusion.

Football was in either a suspended or curtailed state. In the UK, stadiums were given over to the NHS as testing stations or rest and relaxation areas for staff.

On 28 April, France banned all sporting events and therefore Ligues 1 and 2 were curtailed. Final league positions were calculated on a points-per-game basis. The decision would lead to legal proceedings.

After much debate in the EFL, Leagues One and Two were ended on 15 May. The league positions were decided on a points-per-game basis with play-offs to be played and relegations to be made. The National League voted to end the season on 22 April, but the decision to decide league positions on points-per-game was not made until 17 June. That decision meant that Barrow were promoted back to the Football League after 48 years in non-league. Play-offs were to be played.

With even more debate and votes behind them the SPFL ended the Scottish Premier League season on 18 May, positions calculated on a points-per-game basis. Celtic were champions for a ninth season in succession and Hearts relegated.

Football needed to return and the fans needed football to return. Salvation came from Germany who announced on 7 May that the Bundesliga would resume on 16 May. As matches began, the whole of Europe looked on in anticipation. Spain's La Liga would resume on 8 June and Serie A in Italy on 20 June.

The English Premier League and Championship remained committed to finishing the season and Project Restart was born. Many virtual meetings and votes were held. Non-contact training and then eventually full-contact training resumed and finally it was decided that the Premier League would restart on 17 June. The opening match would be the first one postponed due to the virus, Manchester City at home to Arsenal. City would prevail 3-0 in an error-strewn match. The Championship resumed on 20 June with the first game back a London derby between Fulham and Brentford at Craven Cottage. Brentford won 2-0 with two late goals.

Football was back. Played behind closed doors. Hand-shaking banned, face masks worn. Balls and goal-frames sanitised and cleaned at regular intervals. Social distancing, in near-empty stadiums, observed. Five substitutes allowed and drinks breaks in both halves, but football was back. Every Premier League match televised, with Saturday 3 o'clock kick-offs included – a sign of things to come?

Liverpool had to wait until 25 June to finally be crowned champions. They had been magnificent. Manchester City's 1-2 defeat at Chelsea sealed the title for the Reds and their 30-year wait was ended. The trophy was lifted by captain Jordan Henderson in an empty Anfield after their final home game of the season against Chelsea.

This is football – but not as we know it! Plans are being drawn up for the 2020–21 season. We wait in anticipation.

FOOTBALL AWARDS 2019–20

THE FOOTBALL WRITERS' FOOTBALLER OF THE YEAR 2020

The Football Writers' Association Sir Stanley Matthews Trophy for the Footballer of the Year was awarded to Jordan Henderson of Liverpool and England. Kevin De Bruyne (Manchester C and Belgium) was runner-up and Marcus Rashford (Manchester U and England) came third.

Past Winners
1947–48 Stanley Matthews (Blackpool), 1948–49 Johnny Carey (Manchester U), 1949–50 Joe Mercer (Arsenal), 1950–51 Harry Johnston (Blackpool), 1951–52 Billy Wright (Wolverhampton W), 1952–53 Nat Lofthouse (Bolton W), 1953–54 Tom Finney (Preston NE), 1954–55 Don Revie (Manchester C), 1955–56 Bert Trautmann (Manchester C), 1956–57 Tom Finney (Preston NE), 1957–58 Danny Blanchflower (Tottenham H), 1958–59 Syd Owen (Luton T), 1959–60 Bill Slater (Wolverhampton W), 1960–61 Danny Blanchflower (Tottenham H), 1961–62 Jimmy Adamson (Burnley), 1962–63 Stanley Matthews (Stoke C), 1963–64 Bobby Moore (West Ham U), 1964–65 Bobby Collins (Leeds U), 1965–66 Bobby Charlton (Manchester U), 1966–67 Jackie Charlton (Leeds U), 1967–68 George Best (Manchester U), 1968–69 Dave Mackay (Derby Co) shared with Tony Book (Manchester C), 1969–70 Billy Bremner (Leeds U), 1970–71 Frank McLintock (Arsenal), 1971–72 Gordon Banks (Stoke C), 1972–73 Pat Jennings (Tottenham H), 1973–74 Ian Callaghan (Liverpool), 1974–75 Alan Mullery (Fulham), 1975–76 Kevin Keegan (Liverpool), 1976–77 Emlyn Hughes (Liverpool), 1977–78 Kenny Burns (Nottingham F), 1978–79 Kenny Dalglish (Liverpool), 1979–80 Terry McDermott (Liverpool), 1980–81 Frans Thijssen (Ipswich T), 1981–82 Steve Perryman (Tottenham H), 1982–83 Kenny Dalglish (Liverpool), 1983–84 Ian Rush (Liverpool), 1984–85 Neville Southall (Everton), 1985–86 Gary Lineker (Everton), 1986–87 Clive Allen (Tottenham H), 1987–88 John Barnes (Liverpool), 1988–89 Steve Nicol (Liverpool), 1989–90 John Barnes (Liverpool), 1990–91 Gordon Strachan (Leeds U), 1991–92 Gary Lineker (Tottenham H), 1992–93 Chris Waddle (Sheffield W), 1993–94 Alan Shearer (Blackburn R), 1994–95 Jurgen Klinsmann (Tottenham H), 1995–96 Eric Cantona (Manchester U), 1996–97 Gianfranco Zola (Chelsea), 1997–98 Dennis Bergkamp (Arsenal), 1998–99 David Ginola (Tottenham H), 1999–2000 Roy Keane (Manchester U), 2000–01 Teddy Sheringham (Manchester U), 2001–02 Robert Pires (Arsenal), 2002–03 Thierry Henry (Arsenal), 2003–04 Thierry Henry (Arsenal), 2004–05 Frank Lampard (Chelsea), 2005–06 Thierry Henry (Arsenal), 2006–07 Cristiano Ronaldo (Manchester U), 2007–08 Cristiano Ronaldo (Manchester U), 2008–09 Ryan Giggs (Manchester U), 2009–10 Wayne Rooney (Manchester U), 2010–11 Scott Parker (West Ham U), 2011–12 Robin van Persie (Arsenal), 2012–13 Gareth Bale (Tottenham H), 2013–14 Luis Suárez (Liverpool), 2014–15 Eden Hazard (Chelsea), 2015–16 Jamie Vardy (Leicester C), 2016–17 N'Golo Kanté (Chelsea and France), 2017–18 Mohamed Salah (Liverpool and Egypt), 2018–19 Raheem Sterling (Manchester C and England), 2019–20 Jordan Henderson (Liverpool and England).

THE FOOTBALL WRITERS' WOMEN'S FOOTBALLER OF THE YEAR 2020

Vivienne Miedema (Arsenal and Netherlands)

THE PFA AWARDS 2020

Player of the Year: Kevin de Bruyne, Manchester C and Belgium.
Young Player of the Year: Trent Alexander-Arnold, Liverpool and England.
Women's Player of the Year: Beth England, Chelsea and England.
Women's Young Player of the Year: Lauren Hemp, Manchester C and England.
PFA Merit Award: Marcus Rashford, Manchester U and England.

PFA Premier League Team of the Year 2020
Nick Pope (Burnley), Trent Alexander-Arnold (Liverpool), Virgil van Dijk (Liverpool), Caglar Soyuncu (Leicester C), Andrew Robertson (Liverpool), David Silva (Manchester C), Jordan Henderson (Liverpool), Kevin de Bruyne (Manchester C), Jamie Vardy (Leicester C), Pierre-Emerick Aubameyang (Arsenal), Sadio Mane (Liverpool).

PFA Championship Team of the Year 2020
Brice Samba (Nottingham Forest), Luke Ayling (Leeds U), Ben White (Leeds U), Liam Cooper (Leeds U), Joe Bryan (Fulham), Eberechi Eze (QPR), Kalvin Phillips (Leeds U), Romaine Sawyers (WBA), Aleksandar Mitrovic (Fulham), Ollie Watkins (Brentford), Said Benrahma (Brentford).

PFA League One Team of the Year 2020
Marko Marosi (Coventry C), Fankaty Dabo (Coventry C), Michael Ihiekwe (Rotherham U), Rob Dickie (Oxford U), Joe Jacobsen (Wycombe W), Cameron Brannagan (Oxford U), Liam Walsh (Coventry C), Matt Crooks (Rotherham U), Armand Gnanduillet (Blackpool), Ivan Toney (Peterborough U), Matt Godden (Coventry C).

PFA League Two Team of the Year 2020
Alex Palmer (Plymouth Arg), Perry Ng (Crewe Alex), Ben Tozer (Cheltenham T), Charlie Goode (Northampton T), Randell Williams (Exeter C), Antoni Sarcevic (Plymouth Arg), Danny Mayor (Plymouth Arg), Nicky Adams (Northampton T), Charlie Kirk (Crewe Alex), Eoin Doyle (Swindon T), Jerry Yates (Swindon T).

SCOTTISH AWARDS 2019–20

SCOTTISH PFA PLAYER OF THE YEAR AWARDS 2020

Due to the COVID-19 pandemic the Scottish PFA Awards 2020 were cancelled.

SCOTTISH FOOTBALL WRITERS' ASSOCIATION AWARDS 2020

Player of the Year: Odsonne Edouard, Celtic and France U21
Young Player of the Year: Lewis Ferguson, Aberdeen and Scotland U21
International Player of the Year: John McGinn, Aston Villa and Scotland
Manager of the Year: Neil Lennon, Celtic

PREMIER LEAGUE AWARDS 2019–20

	PLAYER OF THE MONTH AWARDS 2019–20	MANAGER OF THE MONTH AWARDS 2019–20
August	Teemu Pukki (Norwich C)	Jurgen Klopp (Liverpool)
September	Pierre-Emerick Aubameyang (Arsenal)	Jurgen Klopp (Liverpool)
October	Jamie Vardy (Leicester C)	Frank Lampard (Chelsea)
November	Sadio Mane (Liverpool)	Jurgen Klopp (Liverpool)
December	Trent Alexander-Arnold (Liverpool)	Jurgen Klopp (Liverpool)
January	Sergio Aguero (Manchester C)	Jurgen Klopp (Liverpool)
February	Bruno Fernandes (Manchester U)	Sean Dyche (Burnley)
June	Bruno Fernandes (Manchester U)	Nuno Espirito Santo (Wolverhampton W)
July	Michael Antonio (West Ham U)	Ralph Hassenhuttl (Southampton)

SKY BET LEAGUE AWARDS 2019–20

SKY BET FOOTBALL LEAGUE PLAYER OF THE MONTH AWARDS 2019–20

	Championship	*League One*	*League Two*
August	Daniel Johnson (Preston NE)	Marcus Maddison (Peterborough U)	James Hanson (Grimsby T)
September	Chey Dunkley (Wigan Ath)	Jonson Clarke-Harris (Bristol R)	James Clarke (Walsall)
October	Aleksandar Mitrovic (Fulham)	Ian Henderson (Rochdale)	Eoin Doyle (Swindon T)
November	Jarrod Bowen (Hull C)	Joe Jacobson (Wycombe W)	Eoin Doyle (Swindon T)
December	Conor Chaplin (Barnsley)	Ivan Toney (Peterborough U)	Eoin Doyle (Swindon T)
January	Nahki Wells (QPR/Bristol C)	Alex Gilbey (MK Dons)	Luke Jephcott (Plymouth Arg)
February	Scott Hogan (Birmingham C)	Matty Taylor (Oxford U)	Callum Morton (Northampton T)
June	Jason Pearce (Charlton Ath)		
July	Said Benrahma (Brentford)		

SKY BET FOOTBALL LEAGUE MANAGER OF THE MONTH AWARDS 2019–20

	Championship	*League One*	*League Two*
August	Steve Cooper (Swansea C)	Paul Lambert (Ipswich T)	Matt Taylor (Exeter C)
September	Sabri Lamouchi (Nottingham F)	Joey Barton (Fleetwood T)	Michael Duff (Cheltenham T)
October	Danny Cowley (Huddersfield T)	Darren Ferguson (Peterborough U)	Graham Alexander (Salford C)
November	Marcelo Bielsa (Leeds U)	Gareth Ainsworth (Wycombe W)	Richie Wellens (Swindon T)
December	Jonathan Woodgate (Middlesbrough)	John Coleman (Accrington S)	Matt Taylor (Exeter C)
January	Sabri Lamouchi (Nottingham F)	Phil Parkinson (Sunderland)	Ryan Lowe (Plymouth Arg)
February	Slaven Bilic (WBA)	Mark Robins (Coventry C)	Michael Duff (Cheltenham T)
June	Thomas Frank (Brentford)		
July	Marcelo Bielsa (Leeds U)		

LEAGUE MANAGERS ASSOCIATION AWARDS 2019–20

SIR ALEX FERGUSON TROPHY FOR LMA MANAGER OF THE YEAR
Jurgen Klopp (Liverpool)

SKY BET FOOTBALL LEAGUE CHAMPIONSHIP MANAGER OF THE YEAR
Marcelo Bielsa (Leeds U)

SKY BET FOOTBALL LEAGUE ONE MANAGER OF THE YEAR
Mark Robins (Coventry C)

SKY BET FOOTBALL LEAGUE TWO MANAGER OF THE YEAR
David Artell (Crewe Alex)

BARCLAYS FA WOMEN'S SUPER LEAGUE MANAGER OF THE YEAR
Emma Hayes MBE (Chelsea)

FA WOMEN'S CHAMPIONSHIP MANAGER OF THE YEAR
Gemma Davies (Aston Villa)

OTHER AWARDS

EUROPEAN FOOTBALLER OF THE YEAR 2019
Virgil van Dijk, Liverpool and Netherlands

EUROPEAN WOMEN'S PLAYER OF THE YEAR 2019
Lucy Bronze, Lyon and England

FIFA BALLON D'OR PLAYER OF THE YEAR 2019
Lionel Messi, Barcelona and Argentina

FIFA BALLON D'OR WOMEN'S PLAYER OF THE YEAR 2019
Megan Rapinoe, OL Reign and USA

FIFA PUSKAS AWARD GOAL OF THE YEAR 2019
Daniel Zsori, Debrecen v Ferencvaros, NB 1, 16 February 2019

PREMIER LEAGUE 2019–20

(P) *Promoted into division at end of 2018–19 season.*

			Home					*Away*					*Total*						
		P	*W*	*D*	*L*	*F*	*A*	*W*	*D*	*L*	*F*	*A*	*W*	*D*	*L*	*F*	*A*	*GD*	*Pts*
1	Liverpool	38	18	1	0	52	16	14	2	3	33	17	32	3	3	85	33	52	99
2	Manchester C	38	15	2	2	57	13	11	1	7	45	22	26	3	9	102	35	67	81
3	Manchester U	38	10	7	2	40	17	8	5	6	26	19	18	12	8	66	36	30	66
4	Chelsea	38	11	3	5	30	16	9	3	7	39	38	20	6	12	69	54	15	66
5	Leicester C	38	11	4	4	35	17	7	4	8	32	24	18	8	12	67	41	26	62
6	Tottenham H	38	12	3	4	36	17	4	8	7	25	30	16	11	11	61	47	14	59
7	Wolverhampton W	38	8	7	4	27	19	7	7	5	24	21	15	14	9	51	40	11	59
8	Arsenal	38	10	6	3	36	24	4	8	7	20	24	14	14	10	56	48	8	56
9	Sheffield U (P)	38	10	3	6	24	15	4	9	6	15	24	14	12	12	39	39	0	54
10	Burnley	38	8	4	7	24	23	7	5	7	19	27	15	9	14	43	50	–7	54
11	Southampton	38	6	3	10	21	35	9	4	6	30	25	15	7	16	51	60	–9	52
12	Everton	38	8	7	4	24	21	5	3	11	20	35	13	10	15	44	56	–12	49
13	Newcastle U	38	6	8	5	20	21	5	3	11	18	37	11	11	16	38	58	–20	44
14	Crystal Palace	38	6	5	8	15	20	5	5	9	16	30	11	10	17	31	50	–19	43
15	Brighton & HA	38	5	7	7	20	27	4	7	8	19	27	9	14	15	39	54	–15	41
16	West Ham U	38	6	4	9	30	33	4	5	10	19	29	10	9	19	49	62	–13	39
17	Aston Villa (P)	38	7	3	9	22	30	2	5	12	19	37	9	8	21	41	67	–26	35
18	Bournemouth	38	5	6	8	22	30	4	1	14	18	35	9	7	22	40	65	–25	34
19	Watford	38	6	6	7	22	27	2	4	13	14	37	8	10	20	36	64	–28	34
20	Norwich C (P)	38	4	3	12	19	37	1	3	15	7	38	5	6	27	26	75	–49	21

PREMIER LEAGUE LEADING GOALSCORERS 2019–20

Qualification 8 league goals	*League*	*FA Cup*	*EFL Cup*	*Other*	*Total*
Raheem Sterling *(Manchester C)*	20	1	3	6	30
Pierre-Emerick Aubameyang *(Arsenal)*	22	4	0	3	29
Raul Jimenez *(Wolverhampton W)*	17	0	0	10	27
Danny Ings *(Southampton)*	22	1	2	0	25
Harry Kane *(Tottenham H)*	18	0	0	6	24
Jamie Vardy *(Leicester C)*	23	0	0	0	23
Mohamed Salah *(Liverpool)*	19	0	0	4	23
Anthony Martial *(Manchester U)*	17	1	1	4	23
Sergio Aguero *(Manchester C)*	16	2	3	2	23
Gabriel Jesus *(Manchester C)*	14	2	1	6	23
Sadio Mane *(Liverpool)*	18	0	0	4	22
Marcus Rashford *(Manchester U)*	17	0	4	1	22
Tammy Abraham *(Chelsea)*	15	0	0	3	18
Heung-Min Son *(Tottenham H)*	11	2	0	5	18
Mason Greenwood *(Manchester U)*	10	1	1	5	17
Kevin De Bruyne *(Manchester C)*	13	1	0	2	16
Dominic Calvert-Lewin *(Everton)*	13	0	2	0	15
Richarlison *(Everton)*	13	0	2	0	15
Chris Wood *(Burnley)*	14	0	0	0	14
Riyad Mahrez *(Manchester C)*	11	0	1	1	13
Alexandre Lacazette *(Arsenal)*	10	0	0	2	12
Bruno Fernandes *(Manchester U)*	8	1	0	3	12
Olivier Giroud *(Chelsea)*	8	1	0	3	12
Teemu Pukki *(Norwich C)*	11	0	0	0	11
Christian Pulisic *(Chelsea)*	9	1	0	1	11
Willian *(Chelsea)*	9	1	0	1	11
Jay Rodriguez *(Burnley)*	8	2	1	0	11
Michail Antonio *(West Ham U)*	10	0	0	0	10
Troy Deeney *(Watford)*	10	0	0	0	10
Neal Maupay *(Brighton & HA)*	10	0	0	0	10
Roberto Firmino *(Liverpool)*	9	0	0	1	10
Jack Grealish *(Aston Villa)*	8	0	2	0	10
Jordan Ayew *(Crystal Palace)*	9	0	0	0	9
Callum Wilson *(Bournemouth)*	8	1	0	0	9
Delle Alli *(Tottenham H)*	8	0	0	1	9
Ayoze Perez *(Leicester C)*	8	0	0	0	8

Other matches consist of UEFA Champions League, UEFA Europa League, FIFA Club World Cup, European Super Cup, Community Shield, Football League Trophy.

PREMIER LEAGUE – RESULTS 2019–20

	Arsenal	Aston Villa	Bournemouth	Brighton & HA	Burnley	Chelsea	Crystal Palace	Everton	Leicester C	Liverpool	Manchester C	Manchester U	Newcastle U	Norwich C	Sheffield U	Southampton	Tottenham H	Watford	West Ham U	Wolverhampton W
Arsenal	—	3-2	1-0	1-2	2-1	1-2	2-2	3-2	1-1	2-1	0-3	2-0	4-0	4-0	1-1	2-2	2-2	3-2	1-0	1-1
Aston Villa	1-0	—	1-2	2-1	2-2	1-2	2-0	2-0	1-4	1-2	1-6	0-3	2-0	1-0	0-0	1-3	2-3	2-1	0-0	0-1
Bournemouth	1-1	2-1	—	3-1	0-1	2-2	0-2	3-1	4-1	0-3	1-3	1-0	1-4	0-0	1-1	0-2	0-0	0-3	2-2	1-2
Brighton & HA	2-1	1-1	2-0	—	1-1	1-1	0-1	3-2	0-2	1-3	0-5	0-3	0-0	2-0	0-1	0-2	3-0	1-1	1-1	2-2
Burnley	0-0	1-2	3-0	1-2	—	2-4	0-2	1-0	2-1	0-3	1-4	0-2	1-0	2-0	1-1	3-0	1-1	1-0	3-0	1-1
Chelsea	2-2	2-1	0-1	2-0	3-0	—	2-0	4-0	1-1	1-2	2-1	0-2	1-0	1-0	2-2	0-2	2-1	3-0	0-1	2-0
Crystal Palace	1-1	1-0	1-0	1-1	0-1	2-3	—	0-0	0-2	1-2	0-2	0-2	1-0	2-0	0-1	0-2	1-1	1-0	2-1	1-1
Everton	0-0	1-1	1-3	1-0	1-0	3-1	3-1	—	2-1	0-0	1-3	1-1	2-2	0-2	0-2	1-1	1-1	1-0	2-0	3-2
Leicester C	2-0	4-0	3-1	0-0	2-1	2-2	3-0	2-1	—	0-4	0-1	0-2	5-0	1-1	2-0	1-2	2-1	2-0	4-1	0-0
Liverpool	3-1	2-0	2-1	2-1	1-1	5-3	4-0	5-2	2-1	—	3-1	2-0	3-1	4-1	2-0	4-0	2-1	2-0	3-2	1-0
Manchester C	3-0	3-0	2-1	4-0	5-0	2-1	2-2	2-1	3-1	4-0	—	1-2	5-0	5-0	2-0	2-1	2-2	8-0	2-0	0-2
Manchester U	1-1	2-2	5-2	3-1	0-2	4-0	1-2	1-1	1-0	1-1	2-0	—	4-1	4-0	3-0	2-2	2-1	3-0	1-1	0-0
Newcastle U	0-1	1-1	2-1	0-0	0-0	1-0	1-0	1-2	0-3	1-3	2-2	1-0	—	0-0	3-0	2-1	1-3	1-1	2-2	1-1
Norwich C	2-2	1-5	1-0	0-1	0-2	2-3	1-1	0-1	1-0	0-1	3-2	1-3	3-1	—	1-2	0-3	2-2	0-2	0-4	1-2
Sheffield U	1-0	2-0	2-1	1-1	3-0	3-0	1-0	0-1	1-2	0-1	0-1	3-3	0-2	1-0	—	0-1	3-1	1-1	1-0	1-0
Southampton	0-2	2-0	1-3	1-1	1-2	1-4	1-1	1-2	0-9	1-2	1-0	1-1	0-1	2-1	3-1	—	1-0	2-1	0-1	2-3
Tottenham H	2-1	3-1	3-2	2-1	5-0	0-2	4-0	1-0	3-0	0-1	2-0	1-1	0-1	2-1	1-1	2-1	—	1-1	2-0	2-3
Watford	2-2	3-0	0-0	0-3	0-3	1-2	0-0	2-3	1-1	3-0	0-4	2-0	2-1	2-1	0-0	1-3	0-0	—	1-3	2-1
West Ham U	1-3	1-1	4-0	3-3	0-1	3-2	1-2	1-1	1-2	0-2	0-5	2-0	2-3	2-0	1-1	3-1	2-3	3-1	—	0-2
Wolverhampton W	0-2	2-1	1-0	0-0	1-1	2-5	2-0	3-0	0-0	1-2	3-2	1-1	1-1	3-0	1-1	1-1	1-2	2-0	2-0	—

SKY BET CHAMPIONSHIP 2019–20

(P) *Promoted into division at end of 2018–19 season.* (R) *Relegated into division at end of 2018–19 season.*

			Home					*Away*					*Total*						
		P	*W*	*D*	*L*	*F*	*A*	*W*	*D*	*L*	*F*	*A*	*W*	*D*	*L*	*F*	*A*	*GD*	*Pts*
1	Leeds U	46	15	5	3	40	14	13	4	6	37	21	28	9	9	77	35	42	93
2	WBA	46	10	10	3	44	27	12	7	4	33	18	22	17	7	77	45	32	83
3	Brentford	46	14	5	4	44	18	10	4	9	36	20	24	9	13	80	38	42	81
4	Fulham (R)¶	46	15	2	6	40	26	8	10	5	24	22	23	12	11	64	48	16	81
5	Cardiff C (R)	46	11	9	3	35	21	8	7	8	33	37	19	16	11	68	58	10	73
6	Swansea C	46	10	5	8	27	23	8	11	4	35	30	18	16	12	62	53	9	70
7	Nottingham F	46	10	5	8	27	27	8	11	4	31	23	18	16	12	58	50	8	70
8	Millwall	46	10	8	5	33	25	7	9	7	24	26	17	17	12	57	51	6	68
9	Preston NE	46	12	4	7	39	29	6	8	9	20	25	18	12	16	59	54	5	66
10	Derby Co	46	11	8	4	33	21	6	5	12	29	43	17	13	16	62	64	–2	64
11	Blackburn R	46	10	9	4	33	24	7	3	13	33	39	17	12	17	66	63	3	63
12	Bristol C	46	8	7	8	30	33	9	5	9	30	32	17	12	17	60	65	–5	63
13	QPR	46	9	5	9	42	42	7	5	11	25	34	16	10	20	67	76	–9	58
14	Reading	46	7	4	12	26	34	8	7	8	33	24	15	11	20	59	58	1	56
15	Stoke C	46	11	3	9	36	26	5	5	13	26	42	16	8	22	62	68	–6	56
16	Sheffield W	46	7	7	9	19	30	8	4	11	39	36	15	11	20	58	66	–8	56
17	Middlesbrough	46	6	8	9	20	29	7	6	10	28	32	13	14	19	48	61	–13	53
18	Huddersfield T (R)	46	8	6	9	26	30	5	6	12	26	40	13	12	21	52	70	–18	51
19	Luton T (P)	46	8	7	8	33	37	6	2	15	21	45	14	9	23	54	82	–28	51
20	Birmingham C	46	6	7	10	33	42	6	7	10	21	33	12	14	20	54	75	–21	50
21	Barnsley (P)	46	7	9	7	29	33	5	4	14	20	36	12	13	21	49	69	–20	49
22	Charlton Ath (P)	46	8	6	9	28	27	4	6	13	22	38	12	12	22	50	65	–15	48
23	Wigan Ath*	46	10	7	6	33	23	5	7	11	24	33	15	14	17	57	56	1	47
24	Hull C	46	7	3	13	29	37	5	6	12	28	50	12	9	25	57	87	–30	45

**Wigan Ath deducted 12 pts for entering administration.*
¶Fulham promoted via play-offs.

SKY BET CHAMPIONSHIP LEADING GOALSCORERS 2019–20

Qualification 11 League Goals	*League*	*FA Cup*	*EFL Cup*	*Play-Offs*	*Total*
Aleksandar Mitrovic *(Fulham)*	26	0	0	0	26
Ollie Watkins *(Brentford)*	25	0	0	1	26
Lewis Grabban *(Nottingham F)*	20	0	0	0	20
Nahki Wells *(Bristol C)*	18	1	1	0	20
Includes 13 League, 1 FA Cup and 1 League Cup goals for QPR.					
Karlan Ahearne-Grant *(Huddersfield T)*	19	0	0	0	19
Jarrod Bowen *(Hull C)*	17	0	1	0	18
Includes 1 League goal for West Ham U.					
Andre Ayew *(Swansea C)*	15	0	2	1	18
Said Benrahma *(Brentford)*	17	0	0	0	17
Adam Armstrong *(Blackburn R)*	16	1	0	0	17
Yakou Meite *(Reading)*	13	2	2	0	17
Patrick Bamford *(Leeds U)*	16	0	0	0	16
Bryan Mbeumo *(Brentford)*	15	0	0	1	16
Lukas Jutkiewicz *(Birmingham C)*	15	0	0	0	15
Cauley Woodrow *(Barnsley)*	14	1	0	0	15
Jordan Hugill *(QPR)*	13	2	0	0	15
James Collins *(Luton T)*	14	0	0	0	14
Eberechi Eze *(QPR)*	14	0	0	0	14
Matt Smith *(Millwall)*	13	1	0	0	14
Famara Diedhiou *(Bristol C)*	12	1	1	0	14
George Puscas *(Reading)*	12	1	1	0	14
Steven Fletcher *(Sheffield W)*	13	0	0	0	13
Conor Chaplin *(Barnsley)*	11	2	0	0	13
Ashley Fletcher *(Middlesbrough)*	11	1	1	0	13
Martyn Waghorn *(Derby Co)*	12	0	0	0	12
Daniel Johnson *(Preston NE)*	12	0	0	0	12
Chris Martin *(Derby Co)*	11	1	0	0	12
Lyle Taylor *(Charlton Ath)*	11	0	0	0	11
Macauley Bonne *(Charlton Ath)*	11	0	0	0	11
Britt Assombalonga *(Middlesbrough)*	11	0	0	0	11
Sam Clucas *(Stoke C)*	11	0	0	0	11

SKY BET CHAMPIONSHIP – RESULTS 2019–20

	Barnsley	Birmingham C	Blackburn R	Brentford	Bristol C	Cardiff C	Charlton Ath	Derby Co	Fulham	Huddersfield T	Hull C	Leeds U	Luton T	Middlesbrough	Millwall	Nottingham F	Preston NE	QPR	Reading	Sheffield W	Stoke C	Swansea C	WBA	Wigan Ath
Barnsley	—	0-1	2-0	1-3	2-2	0-2	2-2	2-2	1-0	2-1	3-1	0-2	1-3	1-0	0-0	1-0	0-3	5-3	1-1	1-1	2-4	1-1	1-1	0-0
Birmingham C	2-0	—	1-0	1-1	1-1	1-1	1-1	1-3	0-1	0-3	3-3	4-5	2-1	2-1	1-1	2-1	0-1	0-2	1-3	3-3	2-1	1-3	2-3	2-3
Blackburn R	3-2	1-1	—	1-0	3-1	0-0	1-2	1-0	0-1	2-2	3-0	1-3	1-2	1-0	2-0	1-1	1-1	2-1	4-3	2-1	0-0	2-2	1-1	0-0
Brentford	1-2	0-1	2-2	—	1-1	2-1	2-1	3-0	1-0	0-1	1-1	1-1	7-0	3-2	3-2	0-1	1-0	3-1	1-0	5-0	0-0	3-1	1-0	3-0
Bristol C	1-0	1-3	0-2	0-4	—	0-1	2-1	3-2	1-1	5-2	2-1	1-3	3-0	2-2	1-2	0-0	1-1	2-0	1-0	1-2	1-1	0-0	0-3	2-2
Cardiff C	3-2	4-2	2-3	2-2	0-1	—	0-0	2-1	1-1	2-1	3-0	2-0	2-1	1-0	1-1	0-1	0-0	3-0	1-1	1-1	1-0	0-0	2-1	2-2
Charlton Ath	2-1	0-1	0-2	1-0	3-2	2-2	—	3-0	0-0	0-1	2-2	1-0	3-1	0-1	0-1	1-1	0-1	1-0	0-1	1-3	3-1	1-2	2-2	2-2
Derby Co	2-1	3-2	3-0	1-3	1-2	1-1	2-1	—	1-1	1-1	1-0	1-3	2-0	2-0	0-1	1-1	1-0	1-1	2-1	1-1	4-0	0-0	1-1	1-0
Fulham	0-3	1-0	2-0	0-2	1-2	2-0	2-2	3-0	—	3-2	0-3	2-1	3-2	1-0	4-0	1-2	2-0	2-1	1-2	5-3	1-0	1-0	1-1	2-0
Huddersfield T	2-1	1-1	2-1	0-0	2-1	0-3	4-0	1-2	1-2	—	3-0	0-2	0-2	0-0	1-1	2-1	0-0	2-0	0-2	0-2	2-5	1-1	2-1	0-2
Hull C	0-1	3-0	0-1	1-5	1-3	2-2	0-1	2-0	0-1	1-2	—	0-4	0-1	2-1	0-1	0-2	4-0	2-3	2-1	1-0	2-1	4-4	0-1	2-2
Leeds U	1-0	1-0	2-1	1-0	1-0	3-3	4-0	1-1	3-0	2-0	2-0	—	1-1	4-0	3-2	1-1	1-1	2-0	1-0	0-2	5-0	0-1	1-0	0-1
Luton T	1-1	1-2	3-2	2-1	3-0	0-1	2-1	3-2	3-3	2-1	0-3	1-2	—	3-3	1-1	1-2	1-1	1-1	0-5	1-0	1-1	0-1	1-2	2-1
Middlesbrough	1-0	1-1	1-1	0-1	1-3	1-3	1-0	2-2	0-0	1-0	2-2	0-1	0-1	—	1-1	2-2	1-1	0-1	1-0	1-4	2-1	0-3	0-1	1-0
Millwall	1-2	0-0	1-0	1-0	1-1	2-2	2-1	2-3	1-1	4-1	1-1	2-1	3-1	0-2	—	2-2	1-0	1-2	2-0	1-0	2-0	1-1	0-2	2-2
Nottingham F	1-0	3-0	3-2	1-0	1-0	0-1	0-1	1-0	0-1	3-1	1-2	2-0	3-1	1-1	0-3	—	1-1	0-0	1-1	0-4	1-4	2-2	1-2	1-0
Preston NE	5-1	2-0	3-2	2-0	3-3	1-3	2-1	0-1	2-1	3-1	2-1	1-1	2-1	0-2	0-1	1-1	—	1-3	0-2	2-1	3-1	1-1	0-1	3-0
QPR	0-1	2-2	4-2	1-3	0-1	6-1	2-2	2-1	1-2	1-1	1-2	1-0	3-2	2-2	4-3	0-4	2-0	—	2-2	0-3	4-2	1-3	0-2	3-1
Reading	2-0	2-3	1-2	0-3	0-1	3-0	0-2	3-0	1-4	0-0	1-1	0-1	3-0	1-2	2-1	1-1	1-0	1-0	—	1-3	1-1	1-4	1-2	0-3
Sheffield W	2-0	1-1	0-5	2-1	1-0	1-2	1-0	1-3	1-1	0-0	0-1	0-0	1-0	1-2	0-0	1-1	1-3	1-2	0-3	—	1-0	2-2	0-3	1-0
Stoke C	4-0	2-0	1-2	1-0	1-2	2-0	3-1	2-2	2-0	0-1	5-1	0-3	3-0	0-2	0-0	2-3	0-2	1-2	0-0	3-2	—	2-0	0-2	2-1
Swansea C	0-0	3-0	1-1	0-3	1-0	1-0	1-0	2-3	1-2	3-1	2-1	0-1	0-1	3-1	0-1	0-1	3-2	0-0	1-1	2-1	1-2	—	0-0	2-1
WBA	2-2	0-0	3-2	1-1	4-1	4-2	2-2	2-0	0-0	4-2	4-2	1-1	2-0	0-2	1-1	2-2	2-0	2-2	1-1	2-1	0-1	5-1	—	0-1
Wigan Ath	0-0	1-0	2-0	0-3	0-2	3-2	2-0	1-1	1-1	1-1	8-0	0-2	0-0	2-2	1-0	1-0	1-2	1-0	1-3	2-1	3-0	1-2	1-1	—

SKY BET LEAGUE ONE 2019–20

(P) Promoted into division at end of 2018–19 season. (R) Relegated into division at end of 2018–19 season.

			Home					Away					Total							
		P	*W*	*D*	*L*	*F*	*A*	*W*	*D*	*L*	*F*	*A*	*W*	*D*	*L*	*F*	*A*	*GD*	*Pts*	*PPG*
1	Coventry C	34	11	5	1	22	11	7	8	2	26	19	18	13	3	48	30	18	67	1.97
2	Rotherham U (R)	35	8	5	4	31	16	10	3	5	30	22	18	8	9	61	38	23	62	1.77
3	Wycombe W¶	34	13	3	2	34	20	4	5	7	11	20	17	8	9	45	40	5	59	1.74
4	Oxford U	35	11	3	3	33	13	6	6	6	28	24	17	9	9	61	37	24	60	1.71
5	Portsmouth	35	12	6	0	36	15	5	3	9	17	21	17	9	9	53	36	17	60	1.71
6	Fleetwood T	35	10	7	1	25	13	6	5	6	26	25	16	12	7	51	38	13	60	1.71
7	Peterborough U	35	12	3	2	41	13	5	5	8	27	27	17	8	10	68	40	28	59	1.69
8	Sunderland	36	10	8	1	35	13	6	3	8	13	19	16	11	9	48	32	16	59	1.64
9	Doncaster R	34	10	5	4	30	19	5	4	6	21	14	15	9	10	51	33	18	54	1.59
10	Gillingham	35	9	3	5	27	17	3	12	3	15	17	12	15	8	42	34	8	51	1.46
11	Ipswich T (R)	36	6	5	6	23	18	8	5	6	23	18	14	10	12	46	36	10	52	1.44
12	Burton Alb	35	6	8	3	19	14	6	4	8	31	36	12	12	11	50	50	0	48	1.37
13	Blackpool	35	9	2	6	27	23	2	10	6	17	20	11	12	12	44	43	1	45	1.29
14	Bristol R	35	7	6	5	23	19	5	3	9	15	30	12	9	14	38	49	−11	45	1.29
15	Shrewsbury T	34	6	5	6	21	24	4	6	7	10	18	10	11	13	31	42	−11	41	1.21
16	Lincoln C (P)	35	10	3	4	28	18	2	3	13	16	28	12	6	17	44	46	−2	42	1.20
17	Accrington S	35	7	2	8	33	27	3	8	7	14	26	10	10	15	47	53	−6	40	1.14
18	Rochdale	34	5	4	7	19	22	5	2	11	20	35	10	6	18	39	57	−18	36	1.06
19	Milton Keynes D (P)	35	9	1	8	20	21	1	6	10	16	26	10	7	18	36	47	−11	37	1.06
20	AFC Wimbledon	35	5	9	4	18	18	3	2	12	21	34	8	11	16	39	52	−13	35	1.00
21	Tranmere R (P)	34	3	6	8	19	26	5	2	10	17	34	8	8	18	36	60	−24	32	0.94
22	Southend U	35	2	4	11	18	42	2	3	13	21	43	4	7	24	39	85	−46	19	0.54
23	Bolton W (R)	34	4	8	5	17	23	1	3	13	10	43	5	11	18	27	66	−39	14	0.41

PPG = Points-per-game. ¶Wycombe W promoted via play-offs. Bury expelled from the Football League, so only three clubs relegated.

SKY BET LEAGUE ONE LEADING GOALSCORERS 2019–20

Qualification 8 League Goals	*League*	*FA Cup*	*EFL Cup*	*EFL Trophy*	*Play-Offs*	*Total*
Ivan Toney *(Peterborough U)*	24	2	0	0	0	26
Paddy Madden *(Fleetwood T)*	15	1	0	3	0	19
Armand Gnanduillet *(Blackpool)*	15	2	1	0	0	18
Freddie Ladapo *(Rotherham U)*	14	2	1	0	0	17
Matt Taylor *(Oxford U)*	13	1	2	1	0	17
On loan from Bristol C.						
Ian Henderson *(Rochdale)*	15	0	1	0	0	16
Tyler Walker *(Lincoln C)*	14	1	0	1	0	16
On loan from Nottingham F.						
Mohamed Eisa *(Peterborough U)*	14	2	0	0	0	16
Jonson Clarke-Harris *(Bristol R)*	13	2	1	0	0	16
Liam Boyce *(Burton Alb)*	10	1	5	0	0	16
Includes 2 League goals for Hearts.						
Matt Godden *(Coventry C)*	14	0	1	0	0	15
James Henry *(Oxford U)*	12	1	1	0	0	14
Ronan Curtis *(Portsmouth)*	11	2	0	0	1	14
John Marquis *(Portsmouth)*	8	2	1	3	0	14
Kieran Sadlier *(Doncaster R)*	11	0	0	1	0	12
Rhys Healey *(Milton Keynes D)*	11	0	1	0	0	12
Marcus Forss *(AFC Wimbledon)*	11	0	1	0	0	12
On loan from Brentford. Includes 1 EFL Cup goal for Brentford.						
Colby Bishop *(Accrington S)*	10	0	1	1	0	12
Michael Smith *(Rotherham U)*	9	3	0	0	0	12
Ched Evans *(Fleetwood T)*	9	1	0	0	2	12
Kayden Jackson *(Ipswich T)*	11	0	0	0	0	11
James Norwood *(Ipswich T)*	11	0	0	0	0	11
Chris Maguire *(Sunderland)*	10	0	0	1	0	11
Marcus Maddison *(Peterborough U)*	10	1	0	0	0	11
Includes 1 League goal on loan at Hull C.						
Matty Crooks *(Rotherham U)*	9	1	1	0	0	11
Tarique Fosu *(Oxford U)*	9	1	1	0	0	11
Includes 1 League goal for Brentford.						
Adebayo Akinfenwa *(Wycombe W)*	10	0	0	0	0	10
Lynden Gooch *(Sunderland)*	10	0	0	0	0	10
Lucas Akins *(Burton Alb)*	9	1	0	1	0	10
Dion Charles *(Accrington S)*	8	0	0	1	0	9
Daryl Murphy *(Bolton W)*	8	0	0	0	0	8

SKY BET LEAGUE ONE – RESULTS 2019–20

	Accrington S	AFC Wimbledon	Blackpool	Bolton W	Bristol R	Burton Alb	Coventry C	Doncaster R	Fleetwood T	Gillingham	Ipswich T	Lincoln C	Milton Keynes D	Oxford U	Peterborough U	Portsmouth	Rochdale	Rotherham U	Shrewsbury T	Southend U	Sunderland	Tranmere R	Wycombe W
Accrington S	—	2-1	1-1	7-1	PP	2-0	PP	PP	PP	0-1	2-0	4-3	2-1	2-2	0-2	4-1	1-2	1-2	2-3	1-2	1-3	1-2	PP
AFC Wimbledon	1-1	—	0-0	0-0	1-3	2-2	PP	2-1	1-2	1-0	0-0	1-1	PP	1-2	1-0	1-0	3-2	1-2	1-1	1-1	PP	PP	0-0
Blackpool	0-1	2-0	—	2-1	2-0	PP	PP	PP	3-1	2-3	2-1	2-1	0-3	2-1	4-3	1-1	PP	1-2	0-1	2-1	PP	1-2	1-1
Bolton W	0-0	2-2	0-0	—	1-1	3-4	0-0	PP	2-1	PP	0-5	PP	1-0	0-0	PP	0-1	1-3	PP	1-1	3-2	1-1	2-0	0-2
Bristol R	3-3	1-2	2-1	0-2	—	PP	1-2	0-2	0-0	1-1	PP	PP	1-0	3-1	0-0	2-2	PP	1-0	0-1	4-2	2-0	2-0	0-0
Burton Alb	1-1	1-0	0-0	2-2	2-0	—	0-0	PP	1-0	0-0	0-1	0-2	1-0	2-2	1-1	PP	3-1	0-1	PP	1-1	PP	4-2	PP
Coventry C	0-0	2-1	3-2	2-1	2-0	PP	—	1-1	2-1	1-0	1-1	1-0	1-1	PP	PP	1-0	2-1	1-1	PP	1-0	1-0	0-1	PP
Doncaster R	1-1	PP	0-1	2-1	2-0	2-2	0-1	—	3-2	1-1	PP	2-1	1-1	1-0	2-0	1-2	1-1	2-1	2-0	3-1	1-2	PP	3-1
Fleetwood T	2-0	2-1	0-0	PP	0-0	4-1	0-0	2-1	—	1-1	0-1	PP	1-0	2-1	2-1	1-0	2-1	PP	2-2	PP	1-1	2-1	1-1
Gillingham	PP	1-2	2-2	5-0	PP	1-2	PP	2-1	PP	—	0-1	1-0	3-1	1-1	1-2	1-1	1-0	0-3	2-0	3-1	1-0	PP	2-0
Ipswich T	4-1	2-1	2-2	PP	1-2	4-1	0-1	0-0	0-1	0-0	—	1-0	PP	0-1	1-4	PP	PP	0-2	3-0	PP	1-1	4-1	0-0
Lincoln C	2-0	PP	1-0	5-1	0-1	3-2	PP	PP	2-0	0-0	5-3	—	1-1	0-6	2-1	0-2	PP	0-1	0-0	4-0	2-0	1-0	PP
Milton Keynes D	PP	2-1	PP	1-0	3-0	0-3	0-0	0-1	PP	PP	0-1	2-1	—	1-0	0-4	3-1	2-1	2-3	1-0	0-1	0-1	1-3	2-0
Oxford U	3-0	5-0	2-1	PP	PP	2-4	3-3	3-0	PP	3-0	0-0	1-0	PP	—	1-0	PP	3-0	1-3	0-0	2-1	0-1	3-0	1-0
Peterborough U	4-0	3-2	PP	1-0	PP	1-0	2-2	0-3	1-3	0-0	2-2	2-0	PP	4-0	—	2-0	6-0	2-1	PP	4-0	3-0	PP	4-0
Portsmouth	PP	2-1	PP	1-0	PP	2-2	3-3	PP	2-2	0-0	1-0	1-0	3-1	1-1	2-2	—	3-0	3-2	2-0	4-1	2-0	2-0	2-0
Rochdale	2-1	PP	0-0	2-0	1-2	PP	1-2	1-1	2-3	2-2	0-1	1-1	2-0	PP	PP	0-3	—	3-1	1-0	PP	1-2	PP	0-3
Rotherham U	1-0	2-2	2-1	6-1	3-0	3-2	4-0	PP	2-2	PP	1-0	0-2	1-1	1-2	4-0	PP	0-1	—	0-0	PP	PP	1-1	0-1
Shrewsbury T	0-2	PP	PP	PP	3-4	0-0	2-1	1-0	0-3	1-1	PP	1-1	1-1	2-3	1-0	1-0	0-0	1-2	—	4-3	1-0	2-3	PP
Southend U	0-1	1-4	1-3	PP	3-1	2-3	0-2	1-7	3-3	0-1	1-3	2-1	2-2	0-4	0-2	PP	0-3	2-2	PP	—	PP	0-0	PP
Sunderland	PP	3-1	1-1	0-0	3-0	1-2	1-1	0-0	1-1	2-2	1-0	3-1	2-1	1-1	PP	2-1	3-0	1-1	PP	1-0	—	5-0	4-0
Tranmere R	1-1	1-0	1-1	5-0	0-0	2-1	1-4	0-3	PP	2-2	1-2	PP	PP	PP	2-2	0-2	2-3	PP	0-1	1-1	0-1	—	0-2
Wycombe W	1-1	PP	2-1	2-0	3-1	2-0	1-4	1-0	0-1	PP	1-1	3-1	3-2	PP	3-3	1-0	2-1	PP	1-0	4-3	1-0	3-1	—

SKY BET LEAGUE TWO 2019–20

(P) *Promoted into division at end of 2018–19 season.* (R) *Relegated into division at end of 2018–19 season.*

			Home					*Away*					*Total*							
		P	*W*	*D*	*L*	*F*	*A*	*W*	*D*	*L*	*F*	*A*	*W*	*D*	*L*	*F*	*A*	*GD*	*Pts*	*PPG*
1	Swindon T	36	13	2	4	34	17	8	4	5	28	22	21	6	9	62	39	23	69	1.92
2	Crewe Alex	37	13	3	3	38	17	7	6	5	29	26	20	9	8	67	43	24	69	1.86
3	Plymouth Arg (R)	37	12	5	2	38	16	8	3	7	23	23	20	8	9	61	39	22	68	1.84
4	Cheltenham T	36	11	5	2	35	17	6	8	4	17	10	17	13	6	52	27	25	64	1.78
5	Exeter C	37	10	7	1	31	15	8	4	7	22	28	18	11	8	53	43	10	65	1.76
6	Colchester U	37	9	5	4	28	17	6	8	5	24	20	15	13	9	52	37	15	58	1.57
7	Northampton T¶	37	11	2	6	31	14	6	5	7	23	26	17	7	13	54	40	14	58	1.57
8	Port Vale	37	9	8	1	28	15	5	7	7	22	29	14	15	8	50	44	6	57	1.54
9	Bradford C (R)	37	11	5	2	29	14	3	7	9	15	26	14	12	11	44	40	4	54	1.46
10	Forest Green R	36	5	4	8	16	22	8	6	5	27	18	13	10	13	43	40	3	49	1.36
11	Salford C (P)	37	5	6	8	20	24	8	5	5	29	22	13	11	13	49	46	3	50	1.35
12	Walsall (R)	36	6	5	8	21	26	7	3	7	19	23	13	8	15	40	49	–9	47	1.31
13	Crawley T	37	10	5	4	30	19	1	10	7	21	28	11	15	11	51	47	4	48	1.30
14	Newport Co	36	9	7	3	20	13	3	3	11	12	26	12	10	14	32	39	–7	46	1.28
15	Grimsby T	37	6	5	7	22	27	6	6	7	23	24	12	11	14	45	51	–6	47	1.27
16	Cambridge U	37	7	3	8	23	27	5	6	8	17	21	12	9	16	40	48	–8	45	1.22
17	Leyton Orient (P)	36	5	8	6	26	30	5	4	8	21	25	10	12	14	47	55	–8	42	1.17
18	Carlisle U	37	5	7	7	17	26	5	5	8	22	30	10	12	15	39	56	–17	42	1.14
19	Oldham Ath	37	6	7	5	28	21	3	7	9	16	36	9	14	14	44	57	–13	41	1.11
20	Scunthorpe U (R)	37	6	6	7	24	25	4	4	10	20	31	10	10	17	44	56	–12	40	1.08
21	Mansfield T	36	4	5	8	27	29	5	6	8	21	26	9	11	16	48	55	–7	38	1.06
22	Morecambe	37	4	8	6	20	23	3	3	13	15	37	7	11	19	35	60	–25	32	0.86
23	Stevenage	36	2	6	9	10	22	1	7	11	14	28	3	13	20	24	50	–26	22	0.61
24	Macclesfield T*	37	5	9	4	19	17	2	6	11	13	30	7	15	15	32	47	–15	19	0.51

*PPG = Points-per-game. ¶Northampton T promoted via play-offs. *Macclesfield T deducted 17 points. Stevenage reprieved from relegation.*

SKY BET LEAGUE TWO LEADING GOALSCORERS 2019–20

Qualification 7 league goals	*League*	*FA Cup*	*EFL Cup*	*EFL Trophy*	*Play-Offs*	*Total*
Eoin Doyle *(Swindon T)*	25	0	0	0	0	25
Nicky Maynard *(Mansfield T)*	14	1	0	0	0	15
Ryan Bowman *(Exeter C)*	13	1	0	0	1	15
Kevin van Veen *(Scunthorpe U)*	10	0	0	5	0	15
Jerry Yates *(Swindon T)*	13	1	0	0	0	14
Chris Porter *(Crewe Alex)*	12	1	1	0	0	14
Ollie Palmer *(Crawley T)*	13	1	0	0	0	14
James Vaughan *(Bradford C)*	14	0	0	0	0	14
Includes 3 League goals for Tranmere R.						
Beryly Lubala *(Crawley T)*	12	0	1	0	0	13
Danny Rose *(Mansfield T)*	11	0	1	1	0	13
Padraig Amond *(Newport Co)*	8	3	1	1	0	13
Theo Robinson *(Colchester U)*	11	0	0	1	0	12
On loan from Southend U.						
Josh Gordon *(Walsall)*	9	0	0	3	0	12
Sam Hoskins *(Northampton T)*	8	2	0	1	1	12
Antoni Sarcevic *(Plymouth Arg)*	10	1	0	0	0	11
Johnny Smith *(Oldham Ath)*	9	1	0	1	0	11
On loan from Bristol C.						
Luke Norris *(Colchester U)*	9	0	1	1	0	11
James Hanson *(Grimsby T)*	9	0	0	0	0	9
Daniel Powell *(Crewe Alex)*	9	0	0	0	0	9
Andrew Williams *(Northampton T)*	8	0	0	0	1	9
Adam Rooney *(Salford C)*	8	0	0	1	0	9
Chuma Anene *(Crewe Alex)*	7	2	0	0	0	9
Elijah Adebayo *(Walsall)*	8	0	0	0	0	8
Ryan Broom *(Cheltenham T)*	8	0	0	0	0	8
Josh Wright *(Leyton Orient)*	8	0	0	0	0	8
Ryan Hardie *(Plymouth Arg)*	7	0	0	1	0	8
IncluDes 1 EFL Trophy goal for Blackpool.						
Joseph Mills *(Forest Green R)*	7	1	0	0	0	8
Luke Jephcott *(Plymouth Arg)*	7	0	0	0	0	7
Charles Vernam *(Grimsby T)*	7	0	0	0	0	7
Nicky Law *(Exeter C)*	7	0	0	0	0	7

SKY BET LEAGUE TWO – RESULTS 2019–20

	Bradford C	Cambridge U	Carlisle U	Cheltenham T	Colchester U	Crawley T	Crewe Alex	Exeter C	Forest Green R	Grimsby T	Leyton Orient	Macclesfield T	Mansfield T	Morecambe	Newport Co	Northampton T	Oldham Ath	Plymouth Arg	Port Vale	Salford C	Scunthorpe U	Stevenage	Swindon T	Walsall
Bradford C	—	0-0	3-1	1-1	PP	2-1	PP	2-0	0-1	1-1	PP	PP	2-0	1-0	1-0	2-1	3-0	2-1	1-2	1-1	2-2	3-1	2-1	PP
Cambridge U	2-1	—	1-2	PP	2-1	2-1	PP	4-0	0-1	0-0	2-3	2-2	2-3	1-0	0-0	PP	1-2	1-0	PP	0-4	3-2	0-4	0-1	PP
Carlisle U	0-0	0-0	—	0-1	0-3	2-1	2-4	1-3	0-0	0-0	PP	2-1	0-2	2-2	2-0	0-2	1-0	0-3	PP	2-2	PP	PP	1-1	2-1
Cheltenham T	3-2	1-1	2-0	—	1-1	PP	1-1	PP	1-2	PP	2-1	3-0	1-0	2-1	PP	2-1	3-0	0-1	0-0	PP	4-1	4-2	2-2	3-1
Colchester U	0-0	1-2	3-0	0-2	—	1-1	PP	2-2	PP	2-3	2-1	2-1	PP	0-1	3-1	1-0	PP	3-0	1-1	1-0	PP	3-1	3-1	0-0
Crawley T	2-1	PP	0-0	1-0	2-1	—	1-2	0-1	1-1	3-2	PP	PP	1-0	1-1	PP	4-0	3-0	2-2	0-0	2-0	3-1	2-0	0-4	2-3
Crewe Alex	2-1	2-3	4-1	1-0	0-0	2-1	—	1-1	PP	PP	2-0	2-0	1-1	5-0	PP	PP	2-1	0-3	0-1	4-1	3-1	3-1	3-1	1-0
Exeter C	PP	2-0	PP	0-0	0-0	1-1	1-1	—	1-0	1-3	2-2	1-0	1-0	PP	1-0	3-2	5-1	4-0	2-0	PP	PP	2-1	1-1	3-3
Forest Green R	PP	PP	1-4	PP	1-0	3-1	0-0	0-1	—	1-0	PP	1-0	2-2	PP	0-2	PP	1-0	0-1	2-3	1-2	0-2	0-0	2-2	1-2
Grimsby T	1-1	PP	PP	0-0	2-2	1-1	0-2	0-1	2-2	—	0-4	1-0	0-1	2-1	4-2	0-3	PP	PP	5-2	1-0	0-1	3-1	0-3	PP
Leyton Orient	0-0	2-1	1-1	1-0	1-3	2-3	1-2	PP	2-4	1-1	—	1-1	2-1	PP	2-1	1-1	2-2	PP	3-3	PP	0-2	0-0	1-3	3-1
Macclesfield T	1-1	1-0	PP	PP	1-1	1-1	1-1	2-3	2-1	1-1	3-0	—	0-0	0-1	1-1	0-1	1-1	1-1	2-1	0-2	1-0	PP	PP	PP
Mansfield T	3-0	0-4	2-2	0-3	2-3	PP	PP	PP	3-4	0-1	2-3	PP	—	2-2	1-0	1-1	6-1	0-1	2-2	1-2	2-0	0-0	PP	PP
Morecambe	1-2	1-1	1-1	0-0	1-1	PP	1-1	2-3	0-2	0-2	1-0	2-0	1-1	—	2-1	2-2	1-2	PP	2-1	2-2	PP	PP	PP	0-1
Newport Co	2-1	0-1	1-0	1-1	PP	1-1	1-0	1-1	PP	PP	1-1	1-0	2-2	1-0	—	PP	0-1	1-0	1-0	1-2	2-1	1-1	2-0	0-0
Northampton T	PP	2-0	PP	1-1	PP	2-2	4-1	2-0	1-0	2-0	0-1	1-2	1-2	4-1	2-0	—	PP	3-1	0-1	2-0	3-0	1-0	0-1	0-1
Oldham Ath	3-0	PP	1-1	1-1	0-1	2-1	1-2	0-0	1-1	2-2	1-1	0-1	3-1	3-1	5-0	2-2	—	PP	PP	1-4	0-2	PP	PP	2-0
Plymouth Arg	2-1	0-0	2-0	0-2	1-0	2-2	2-1	PP	PP	3-0	4-0	3-0	3-1	3-0	1-0	PP	2-2	—	PP	2-2	2-2	2-1	1-2	3-0
Port Vale	PP	1-0	2-1	1-1	3-0	PP	PP	3-1	2-1	PP	1-0	2-2	2-2	3-1	PP	1-1	0-0	1-0	—	1-1	2-2	1-1	2-0	0-1
Salford C	2-0	1-0	PP	0-2	1-2	0-0	3-1	0-1	0-4	1-0	1-1	0-0	PP	PP	PP	1-2	1-1	2-3	1-1	—	1-1	2-0	2-3	1-2
Scunthorpe U	1-1	0-2	0-1	1-0	2-2	2-2	2-2	3-1	1-0	0-2	PP	PP	PP	3-0	1-2	3-0	2-2	1-3	2-1	PP	—	0-0	0-2	0-2
Stevenage	0-1	1-1	2-3	PP	0-0	0-0	1-5	0-1	0-0	2-1	0-3	2-2	PP	1-0	PP	0-1	0-0	1-2	0-1	0-1	PP	—	PP	PP
Swindon T	1-1	4-0	3-2	PP	0-3	PP	3-1	2-1	0-2	3-1	PP	3-0	1-0	3-1	0-2	0-1	2-0	1-1	3-0	PP	2-0	1-0	—	2-1
Walsall	0-1	2-1	1-2	1-2	PP	2-1	1-2	3-1	1-1	1-3	1-0	1-1	1-2	0-2	0-0	3-2	PP	PP	2-2	0-3	1-0	0-0	PP	—

FOOTBALL LEAGUE PLAY-OFFS 2019–20

■ *Denotes player sent off.*

SKY BET CHAMPIONSHIP SEMI-FINALS FIRST LEG

Sunday, 26 July 2020

Swansea C (0) 1 *(Ayew 81)*

Brentford (0) 0 0

Swansea C: (3412) Mulder; Cabango, van der Hoorn, Guehi; Roberts, Fulton, Grimes, Bidwell; Gallagher; Ayew, Brewster.
Brentford: (433) Raya; Dalsgaard, Jansson, Pinnock, Henry■; Jensen (Baptiste 85), Norgaard, Da Silva (Roerslev Rasmussen 70); Mbeumo (Marcondes 70), Benrahma (Valencia 85), Watkins.
Referee: Keith Stroud.

Monday, 27 July 2020

Cardiff C (0) 0

Fulham (0) 2 *(Onomah 49, Kebano 90)* 0

Cardiff C: (4231) Smithies; Bacuna, Morrison, Nelson, Bennett; Pack, Ralls; Mendez-Laing (Murphy J 70), Tomlin, Hoilett (Vaulks 70); Glatzel (Ward 70).
Fulham: (4231) Rodak; Christie, Hector, Ream, Bryan; Reed, Cairney; Knockaert (Kamara 81), Onomah, Kebano (Odoi 90); Reid.
Referee: Geoff Eltringham.

SKY BET CHAMPIONSHIP SEMI-FINALS SECOND LEG

Wednesday, 29 July 2020

Brentford (2) 3 *(Watkins 11, Marcondes 15, Mbeumo 46)*

Swansea C (0) 1 *(Brewster 78)* 0

Brentford: (433) Raya; Dalsgaard, Jansson, Pinnock, Henry; Marcondes (Da Silva 77), Norgaard, Jensen; Mbeumo (Canos 76), Watkins, Benrahma.
Swansea C: (3412) Mulder; Naughton (Celina 77), van der Hoorn (Cabango 46), Guehi; Roberts, Fulton (Dhanda 46), Grimes, Bidwell; Gallagher; Ayew, Brewster.
Brentford won 3-2 on aggregate. Referee: Chris Kavanagh.

Thursday, 30 July 2020

Fulham (1) 1 *(Kebano 9)*

Cardiff C (1) 2 *(Nelson 8, Tomlin 47)* 0

Fulham: (4231) Rodak; Christie, Hector, Ream, Bryan (Le Marchand 90); Reed, Cairney; Knockaert (Odoi 76), Onomah, Kebano (Kamara 46); Reid.
Cardiff C: (4231) Smithies; Bacuna, Morrison, Nelson, Bennett; Vaulks, Pack (Tomlin 46 (Whyte 84)); Hoilett (Mendez-Laing 46), Ralls, Murphy J (Paterson 81); Ward (Glatzel 71).
Fulham won 3-2 on aggregate. Referee: Paul Tierney.

SKY BET CHAMPIONSHIP FINAL

Wembley, Tuesday, 4 August 2020

Brentford (0) 1 *(Dalsgaard 120)*

Fulham (0) 2 *(Bryan 105, 117)* 0

Brentford: (433) Raya; Dalsgaard, Jansson, Pinnock, Henry (Fosu 106); Jensen (Dervisoglu 105), Norgaard, Da Silva (Canos 83); Mbeumo (Marcondes 61), Watkins, Benrahma.
Fulham: (4231) Rodak; Odoi (Christie 110), Hector, Ream, Bryan; Reed, Cairney; Kebano (Knockaert 81), Onomah (Le Marchand 110), Reid (Mitrovic 90); Kamara (Ivan Cavaleiro 105).
aet.
Referee: Martin Atkinson.

SKY BET LEAGUE ONE SEMI-FINALS FIRST LEG

Friday, 3 July 2020

Fleetwood T (1) 1 *(Evans 4 (pen))*

Wycombe W (3) 4 *(Ofoborh 2, Jacobson 6, Wheeler 45, Samuel 57)* 0

Fleetwood T: (343) Cairns; Connolly (Dempsey 46), Souttar, Gibson; Burns, Coutts (Madden■ 65), Whelan, Coyle■; Morris J (Andrew 36), Evans, McKay (Saunders 77).
Wycombe W: (4231) Allsop; Grimmer, Stewart, Charles, Jacobson; Gape, Ofoborh (Thompson 87); Wheeler (Freeman 90), Bloomfield (Pattison 80), Onyedinma (Akinfenwa 87); Samuel (Kashket 81).
Referee: Tony Harrington.

Portsmouth (1) 1 *(Curtis 32)*

Oxford U (1) 1 *(Browne 43)* 0

Portsmouth: (4231) Bass; McCrorie (Bolton 63), Burgess, Raggett, Brown; McGeehan, Morris; Harness, Cannon (Williams 62), Curtis; Harrison (Marquis 73).
Oxford U: (433) Eastwood; Long, Dickie, Moore, Ruffels; Woodburn (Sykes 55), Gorrin, Brannagan (Forde 81); Henry, Taylor (Mackie 73), Browne (Agyei 81).
Referee: Gavin Ward.

SKY BET LEAGUE ONE SEMI-FINALS SECOND LEG

Monday, 6 July 2020

Oxford U (1) 1 *(Harrison 45 (og))*

Portsmouth (1) 1 *(Harness 38)* 0

Oxford U: (433) Eastwood; Long (Woodburn 120), Dickie, Moore, Ruffels; Henry (Forde 100), Gorrin (Mousinho 120), Brannagan; Sykes (Agyei 85), Mackie (Taylor 63), Browne (Hanson 86).

Fulham captain Tom Cairney lifts the Championship Play-Off trophy after his side's win over west London rivals Brentford at Wembley in August. (Mike Egerton/PA Wire/PA Images)

Joe Jacobson, with Adebayo Akinfenwa in hot pursuit, celebrates scoring his penalty and Wycombe Wanderers' second goal in their 2-1 victory over Oxford United in the League One Play-Off Final at Wembley in July. (Action Images/Andrew Couldridge)

Portsmouth: (4231) Bass; Bolton (Evans 120), Burgess, Raggett, Seddon (Brown 60); Morris, McGeehan; Williams (Hawkins 114), Harness (Cannon 81), Curtis; Harrison (Marquis 60).
aet; Oxford U won 5-4 on penalties.
Referee: Darren England.

Wycombe W (0) 2 *(Onyedinma 47, 90)*

Fleetwood T (1) 2 *(Andrew 22, Evans 60 (pen))* 0

Wycombe W: (433) Allsop; Grimmer, Stewart, Charles, Jacobson; Ofoborh (Freeman 84), Gape, Bloomfield (Thompson 38); Wheeler (Pattison 58), Samuel (Akinfenwa 46), Onyedinma.
Fleetwood T: (4231) Cairns; Burns (Southam-Hales 90), Souttar, Gibson, Andrew; Whelan, Coutts; Morris J (Saunders 80), Connolly (Dempsey 72), McKay; Evans.
Wycombe W won 6-3 on aggregate.
Referee: Darren Bond.

SKY BET LEAGUE ONE FINAL

Wembley, Monday, 13 July 2020

Oxford U (0) 1 *(Sykes 57)*

Wycombe W (1) 2 *(Stewart 9, Jacobson 79 (pen))* 0

Oxford U: (433) Eastwood; Long (Forde 79), Dickie, Moore, Ruffels; Sykes, Gorrin (Kelly 46), Brannagan; Henry (Agyei 79), Taylor, Browne (Woodburn 89).
Wycombe W: (433) Allsop; Grimmer, Stewart, Charles, Jacobson; Wheeler, Gape, Ofoborh (Thompson 62); Bloomfield (Pattison 46), Samuel (Akinfenwa 62), Onyedinma (Freeman 90).
Referee: Rob Jones.

SKY BET LEAGUE TWO SEMI-FINALS FIRST LEG

Thursday, 18 June 2020

Colchester U (0) 1 *(Bramall 81)*

Exeter C (0) 0 0

Colchester U: (442) Gerken; Jackson, Eastman, Prosser, Bramall; Adubofour-Poku (Cowan-Hall 89), Pell, Stevenson (Lapslie 77), Senior (Gambin 68); Nouble, Norris (Robinson 77).
Exeter C: (352) Ward; Sweeney, Martin A, Moxey (Parkes 77); Williams, Taylor, Atangana, Law (Collins 67), Sparkes (Dickenson 77); Bowman, Martin L (Jay 38).
Referee: Josh Smith.

Northampton T (0) 0

Cheltenham T (1) 2 *(Raglan 26, Thomas 86)* 0

Northampton T: (352) Arnold; Goode, Turnbull, Wharton; Harriman, McCormack (Anderson 67), Watson, Olayinka, Adams; Morton (Williams A 67), Oliver (Smith 76).
Cheltenham T: (352) Evans; Raglan, Tozer, Boyle; Long, Broom (Ince 81), Thomas, Doyle-Hayes, Hussey; Reid (Smith 74), Nichols (May 74).
Referee: Marc Edwards.

SKY BET LEAGUE TWO SEMI-FINALS SECOND LEG

Monday, 22 June 2020

Cheltenham T (0) 0

Northampton T (1) 3 *(Oliver 9, Morton 57, 77)* 0

Cheltenham T: (352) Evans; Raglan (Nichols 81), Tozer, Boyle; Long, Broom (Addai 62), Thomas, Doyle-Hayes (Ince 62), Hussey; May, Smith (Reid 46).
Northampton T: (352) Arnold; Goode, Turnbull, Wharton; Harriman, McCormack (Olayinka 71), Watson, Hoskins, Adams (Martin 86); Morton, Oliver (Smith 84).
Northampton T won 3-2 on aggregate.
Referee: Leigh Doughty.

Exeter C (1) 3 *(Martin A 10, Richardson 58, Bowman 111)*

Colchester U (0) 1 *(Senior 78)* 0

Exeter C: (352) Maxted; Sweeney, Martin A, Moxey (Parkes 93); Williams, Collins, Law (Dickenson 93), Taylor (Atangana 82), Richardson; Bowman, Fisher (Seymour 75).
Colchester U: (4231) Gerken; Jackson (Welch-Hayes 99), Eastman, Prosser, Bramall; Pell, Stevenson (Lapslie 99); Adubofour-Poku (Cowan-Hall 118), Nouble, Gambin (Senior 56); Norris (Robinson 71).
aet; Exeter C won 3-2 on aggregate.
Referee: Charles Breakspear.

SKY BET LEAGUE TWO FINAL

Wembley, Monday, 29 June 2020

Exeter C (0) 0

Northampton T (2) 4 *(Watson 11, Morton 31, Hoskins 80, Williams A 89)* 0

Exeter C: (3412) Maxted; Sweeney (Dickenson 82), Martin A, Moxey■; Williams, Taylor, Atangana (Sparkes 61), Richardson (Parkes 51); Law; Bowman, Fisher (Collins 52).
Northampton T: (3412) Arnold; Goode, Turnbull, Wharton; Adams (Marshall 31), McCormack (Olayinka 74), Hoskins, Harriman; Watson (Anderson 88); Oliver (Smith 74), Morton (Williams A 88).
Referee: Michael Salisbury.

REVIEW OF THE SEASON 2019–20

It was the longest season, and also the shortest one. If you went by the calendar, Liverpool won the title later than any side ever had before; if you went by the fixture list, they won it earlier. Whatever the disruption caused by the COVID-19 pandemic, Liverpool were one of the most dominant champions the Premier League has known, at one stage a record 23 points clear of Manchester City in second.

After coming so close in 2018–19, totalling 97 points (at the time, the third-highest tally in history) and yet still coming second, there were doubts about whether Liverpool would be able to pick themselves up and go again. But if anything they were even better than they had been, tighter defensively and more ruthless, while it was City who faltered: they could have won every game from 8 October onwards and they still wouldn't have caught Liverpool.

The departure of their captain Vincent Kompany left City without a leader at the back and, when Aymeric Laporte suffered a serious knee injury at the end of August, they were left without a commanding figure in the centre of their defence, while the redeployment of Fernandinho to cover in the back line left them without their craftiest holding midfielder. The result was the frequent exposure of a glass jaw that had previously been glimpsed only occasionally by sides who have been able to play through City's press. City may have scored four or more on eleven occasions in the league, but they also lost nine times.

They did lift the Carabao Cup for the third successive year, beating Aston Villa in the final, but that will mean little beside an FA Cup semi-final exit to Arsenal and yet another mystifying Champions League failure. It's nine years since Pep Guardiola last won the Champions League, and over that period a clear pattern has emerged. Lyon may be a rather better side than a seventh-placed finish in Ligue Un made them seem. Still, to be so intimidated by their potency on the counter that you change your entire approach felt like a manager who has begun to over-complicate big European games. It is as though his 4-0 home defeat to Real Madrid when Bayern manager in 2014 continues to haunt him. Having adopted a back three to try to stifle

Trent Alexander-Arnold gilded his reputation with another fine season: four goals and 13 assists helped Liverpool to their first league title in 30 years. Here he is scoring direct from a free kick against Chelsea in July. (Pool via REUTERS/Laurence Griffiths)

Bruno Fernandes slots home a penalty for Manchester United against Tottenham Hotspur. This Premier League match finished 1-1 in June. (REUTERS / Matthew Childs)

Lyon's counter, City, without their usual width, were not merely inhibited going forward but ended up conceding three on the break anyway. As aggressive counter-pressing supplants possession as football's dominant mode – a priority on regaining rather than retaining the ball – for the first time questions have begun to be asked about Guardiola's method.

Liverpool, meanwhile, as the champions of the press, were relentless. Mohamed Salah, Roberto Firmino and Sadio Mané form arguably the best-balanced and most coherent attacking unit the Premier League has known; a blend of pace, guile and finishing ability combined with the tactical intelligence and industry to lead the press. Trent Alexander-Arnold and Andy Robertson were again potent creative forces from full-back, while Virgil van Dijk and Alisson proved themselves the best defender and goalkeeper in the league once again. That it was the captain, Jordan Henderson, who won the FWA Footballer of the Year award, though, suggested the extent to which Liverpool's success was less about individuals than the team.

After a 30-year wait for their nineteenth league title, Liverpool fans were understandably adamant there had been no anti-climax about the way the title was won, but Liverpool did suffer an odd stutter just before lockdown, losing four games out of six – a run that saw them lose their unbeaten league record at Watford, go out of the FA Cup at Chelsea and, most consequentially, exit the Champions League in thrillingly chaotic circumstances against Atletico Madrid.

They never quite regained their winter form, and as a consequence missed out on becoming only the second side to achieve 100 points, and the second to complete a season with a 100 per cent home record. They did, though, pick up the Club World Cup in December, beating Flamengo in the final. Their participation in that tournament in Qatar effectively forced them to field a youth team in the Carabao Cup – a worrying indication of the demands of the current calendar.

The drop from second to third was steep. Not since 1997–98 has 66 points been enough to take third. At the end of January, Manchester United were fifth and seemed in serious danger of missing out on Champions League qualification, but they went unbeaten after the arrival of Bruno Fernandes to finish ahead of Chelsea on goal difference. The season ended in frustration, though, as they were beaten by the eventual champions Sevilla in the Europa League semi-final.

Chelsea, despite accruing six points fewer than the previous season, were widely perceived to have had a good year. Hampered by a transfer ban and the sale of Eden Hazard, their new manager Frank Lampard blooded a number of promising young players and brought a more attacking style, but they were regularly undone by their defensive shortcomings, particularly against the counter-attack.

United and Chelsea both benefited from Leicester City's late-season collapse. Although a fifth-placed finish probably exceeded pre-season expectations, there was frustration on the final day as they ceded a Champions League slot with defeat to United, having been second at Christmas. Jamie Vardy's 23 goals, though, did make him the top scorer in the Premier League.

Tottenham took sixth and Europa League qualification with a surge over the final month. They had begun the season miserably, leading to Mauricio Pochettino departing in November to be replaced by Jose Mourinho. There has been all the usual discord, and nobody seems quite sure the extent to which the rise to sixth is Mourinho's doing.

There was a second successive seventh-placed finish for Wolves, although any frustration at missing out on European qualification was probably mitigated by the fact their season lasted 13 months, beginning in the second qualification round of the Europa League and culminating in a quarter-final. A slightly reduced schedule next season may not do anybody any harm.

Arsenal ended the season with glory at Wembley, beating Chelsea in the FA Cup final after overcoming City in the semi. That gave almost instant validation to Mikel Arteta and the project he embarked upon after replacing Unai Emery, who was sacked in November. But while Arteta has brought intensity and a clear sense of purpose, serious concerns remain about the make-up of the squad and the influence of certain agents.

Norwich beat Manchester City in September but that was a rare high point. For a time, they had a reputation for not quite getting due reward having played reasonably well but ten straight defeats at the end of the season told its own story and they were relegated 14 points adrift.

Aston Villa survived by taking 10 points from their final four games, condemning Watford, who went through four managers in an increasingly desperate attempt to generate a reaction, and Bournemouth. The Cherries parted company with Eddie Howe, who had been in charge for all but one season since 2008, soon after the end of the campaign.

Jamie Vardy heads home for Leicester City against Norwich City in the Premier League in December.
His 23 goals during the season won him the Golden Boot for the first time.
(Action Images via Reuters/Andrew Boyers)

Southampton's marksman Danny Ings enjoyed the most productive top-flight season of his career, scoring 22 goals in the Premier League and finishing joint-second in the race for the Golden Boot. Here he's firing home against Burnley in February. (REUTERS/David Klein)

Amid the gloomy sense that money dictates everything were three notable exceptions. Sheffield United, under Chris Wilder with his overlapping centre-backs, enjoyed a remarkable first season back in the top flight to finish ninth. Burnley again defied gravity, while Southampton overcame the embarrassment of losing 9-0 to Leicester in October, the biggest home defeat in top-flight history, to end up eleventh.

Their manager, Ralph Hasenhuttl, is part of a growing coterie of hard-pressing Austrians and Germans: Barnsley survived in the Championship in part because of Wigan's baffling lurch into administration, but also because of their charismatic Austrian coach Gerhard Struber.

The Championship was won, though, by the hardest presser of them all, Marcelo Bielsa, who in two years has transformed Leeds United. Slavan Bilic took West Bromwich Albion up in second, while Scott Parker's Fulham beat Brentford, pressing furiously and defying their relatively meagre budget under the Dane Thomas Frank, in the play-off final.

Charlton Athletic and Hull City, two clubs blighted by ownership problems, joined Wigan in being relegated, their places being taken – after the controversial decision was made to abandon the season and determine positions on a points-per-game basis – by Coventry City and Rotherham United. Gareth Ainsworth's direct Wycombe Wanderers were the improbable winners of the play-offs.

With Bury going out of business and Bolton Wanderers being docked 12 points after administration, the bottom of League One was a sad glimpse into the financial realities of the lower divisions. Southend United and Tranmere Rovers joined them in relegation on a points-per-game basis, with Swindon, Crewe, Plymouth and Northampton coming up.

Stevenage survived at the bottom of League Two as Macclesfield were relegated after being deducted 17 points in total. Barrow, another team adopting a rigorous pressing approach, returned to the league after a 48-year absence, and they were joined by Harrogate Town who beat Notts County in the play-off final to become a league club for the first time.

Jonathan Wilson

CUPS AND UPS AND DOWNS DIARY

AUGUST 2019

4 FA Community Shield: Manchester C 1 Liverpool 1 *(aet; Manchester C won 5-4 on penalties).*
14 European Super Cup 2019: Liverpool 2 Chelsea 2 *(aet; Liverpool won 5-4 on penalties).*

DECEMBER 2019

8 Betfred Scottish League Cup Final: Celtic 1 Rangers 0.
21 FIFA Club World Cup Final: Liverpool 1 Flamengo 0 *(aet).*

FEBRUARY 2020

1 Nathaniel MG Welsh League Cup Final: Connah's Quay Nomads 3 STM Sports 0.
15 BetMcLean Northern Irish League Cup Final: Coleraine 2 Crusaders 1.
29 Women's Continental Tyres League Cup Final: Chelsea 2 Arsenal 1.

MARCH 2020

1 Carabao Cup Final: Manchester C 2 Aston Villa 1.
13 All professional football in England and Scotland including the Premier League, EFL Leagues, all Scottish Leagues, FA Women's Super League and FA Women's Championship suspended due to COVID-19 pandemic).
15 University Football 2020: Cambridge v Oxford (postponed due to COVID-19 pandemic).

APRIL 2020

15 SPFL end the season for the Scottish Championship, Scottish League One and Scottish League Two. Dundee U declared champions of the Scottish Championship and promoted to the Scottish Premiership. Falkirk relegated from the Scottish Championship to Scottish League One. Raith R declared champions of Scottish League One and promoted to the Scottish Championship. Cove Rangers declared champions of Scottish League Two and promoted to Scottish League One.
22 National League clubs vote to end the season immediately.

MAY 2020

18 The Scottish Premiership ended and final league positions decided on a points-per-game basis: Celtic declared champions. Runners-up Rangers, third-placed Motherwell and fourth-placed Aberdeen qualify for the 2020–21 Europa League. Hearts relegated from the Scottish Premiership to the Scottish Championship.

JUNE 2020

9 EFL League One season ended and final league positions decided on a points-per-game basis: Coventry C declared champions and Rotherham U runners-up both promoted from EFL League One to EFL Championship. Tranmere R, Southend U and Bolton W relegated from EFL League One to EFL League Two.
9 EFL League Two season ended and final league positions decided on a points-per-game basis: Swindon T declared champions, Crewe Alex runners-up and Plymouth Arg all promoted from EFL League Two to EFL League One. Stevenage relegated from EFL League Two to the National League.
17 Premier League resumes after suspension of the season due to COVID-19 pandemic.
17 National League final positions decided on a points-per-game basis: Barrow declared champions and promoted from the National League to EFL League Two. Chorley, AFC Fylde and Ebbsfleet U relegated to either National League North or South.
20 EFL Championship resumes after suspension of the season due to COVID-19 pandemic.
25 Liverpool champions of the Premier League.
29 EFL League Two Play-Off Final: Northampton T 4 Exeter C 0 (*Northampton T promoted to EFL League One*).

JULY 2020

11 Norwich C relegated from the Premier League to EFL Championship.
13 EFL League One Play-Off Final: Wycombe W 2 Oxford U 1 (*Wycombe W promoted to EFL Championship*)
18 Leeds U champions of EFL Championship and promoted to the Premier League.
22 WBA runners-up and promoted from EFL Championship to the Premier League.
22 Charlton Ath, Wigan Ath (after 12 points deduction) and Hull C relegated from EFL Championship to EFL League One.
26 Qualification for European competitions for 2020–21 season – Champions League: Liverpool, Manchester C, Manchester U and Chelsea. Europa League: Leicester C and Tottenham H.
26 Bournemouth and Watford relegated from the Premier League to EFL Championship.
31 Tennent's Irish FA Cup Final: Glentoran 2 Ballymena U 1.

AUGUST 2020

1 The Emirates FA Cup Final: Arsenal 2 Chelsea 1.
1 National League North Play-Off Final: Boston U 0 Altrincham 1 *(Altrincham promoted to National League).*
1 National League South Play-Off Final: Weymouth 0 Dartford 0 (*aet; Weymouth won 3-0 on penalties and promoted to National League*).
2 National League Play-Off Final: Harrogate T 3 Notts Co 1 (*Harrogate T promoted to EFL League Two*).
4 EFL Championship Play-Off Final: Fulham 2 Brentford 1 (*Fulham promoted to the Premier League*).
11 Macclesfield T deducted 17 points for various breaches of league rules. As a result they are relegated from EFL League Two to the National League and Stevenage reprieved.
21 UEFA Europa League Final: Sevilla 3 Inter Milan 2.
23 UEFA Champions League Final: Bayern Munich 1 Paris Saint-Germain 0.
30 UEFA Women's Champions League Final: Lyon 3 Wolfsburg 0

THE FA COMMUNITY SHIELD WINNERS 1908–2019

CHARITY SHIELD 1908–2001

1908	Manchester U v QPR	1-1
Replay	Manchester U v QPR	4-0
1909	Newcastle U v Northampton T	2-0
1910	Brighton v Aston Villa	1-0
1911	Manchester U v Swindon T	8-4
1912	Blackburn R v QPR	2-1
1913	Professionals v Amateurs	7-2
1920	WBA v Tottenham H	2-0
1921	Tottenham H v Burnley	2-0
1922	Huddersfield T v Liverpool	1-0
1923	Professionals v Amateurs	2-0
1924	Professionals v Amateurs	3-1
1925	Amateurs v Professionals	6-1
1926	Amateurs v Professionals	6-3
1927	Cardiff C v Corinthians	2-1
1928	Everton v Blackburn R	2-1
1929	Professionals v Amateurs	3-0
1930	Arsenal v Sheffield W	2-1
1931	Arsenal v WBA	1-0
1932	Everton v Newcastle U	5-3
1933	Arsenal v Everton	3-0
1934	Arsenal v Manchester C	4-0
1935	Sheffield W v Arsenal	1-0
1936	Sunderland v Arsenal	2-1
1937	Manchester C v Sunderland	2-0
1938	Arsenal v Preston NE	2-1
1948	Arsenal v Manchester U	4-3
1949	Portsmouth v Wolverhampton W	1-1*
1950	English World Cup XI v FA Canadian Touring Team	4-2
1951	Tottenham H v Newcastle U	2-1
1952	Manchester U v Newcastle U	4-2
1953	Arsenal v Blackpool	3-1
1954	Wolverhampton W v WBA	4-4*
1955	Chelsea v Newcastle U	3-0
1956	Manchester U v Manchester C	1-0
1957	Manchester U v Aston Villa	4-0
1958	Bolton W v Wolverhampton W	4-1
1959	Wolverhampton W v Nottingham F	3-1
1960	Burnley v Wolverhampton W	2-2*
1961	Tottenham H v FA XI	3-2
1962	Tottenham H v Ipswich T	5-1
1963	Everton v Manchester U	4-0
1964	Liverpool v West Ham U	2-2*
1965	Manchester U v Liverpool	2-2*
1966	Liverpool v Everton	1-0
1967	Manchester U v Tottenham H	3-3*
1968	Manchester C v WBA	6-1
1969	Leeds U v Manchester C	2-1
1970	Everton v Chelsea	2-1
1971	Leicester C v Liverpool	1-0
1972	Manchester C v Aston Villa	1-0
1973	Burnley v Manchester C	1-0
1974	Liverpool v Leeds U	1-1
	Liverpool won 6-5 on penalties.	
1975	Derby Co v West Ham U	2-0
1976	Liverpool v Southampton	1-0
1977	Liverpool v Manchester U	0-0*
1978	Nottingham F v Ipswich T	5-0
1979	Liverpool v Arsenal	3-1
1980	Liverpool v West Ham U	1-0
1981	Aston Villa v Tottenham H	2-2*
1982	Liverpool v Tottenham H	1-0
1983	Manchester U v Liverpool	2-0
1984	Everton v Liverpool	1-0
1985	Everton v Manchester U	2-0
1986	Everton v Liverpool	1-1*
1987	Everton v Coventry C	1-0
1988	Liverpool v Wimbledon	2-1
1989	Liverpool v Arsenal	1-0
1990	Liverpool v Manchester U	1-1*
1991	Arsenal v Tottenham H	0-0*
1992	Leeds U v Liverpool	4-3
1993	Manchester U v Arsenal	1-1
	Manchester U won 5-4 on penalties.	
1994	Manchester U v Blackburn R	2-0
1995	Everton v Blackburn R	1-0
1996	Manchester U v Newcastle U	4-0
1997	Manchester U v Chelsea	1-1
	Manchester U won 4-2 on penalties.	
1998	Arsenal v Manchester U	3-0
1999	Arsenal v Manchester U	2-1
2000	Chelsea v Manchester U	2-0
2001	Liverpool v Manchester U	2-1

COMMUNITY SHIELD 2002–19

2002	Arsenal v Liverpool	1-0
2003	Manchester U v Arsenal	1-1
	Manchester U won 4-3 on penalties.	
2004	Arsenal v Manchester U	3-1
2005	Chelsea v Arsenal	2-1
2006	Liverpool v Chelsea	2-1
2007	Manchester U v Chelsea	1-1
	Manchester U won 3-0 on penalties.	
2008	Manchester U v Portsmouth	0-0
	Manchester U won 3-1 on penalties.	
2009	Chelsea v Manchester U	2-2
	Chelsea won 4-1 on penalties.	
2010	Manchester U v Chelsea	3-1
2011	Manchester U v Manchester C	3-2
2012	Manchester C v Chelsea	3-2
2013	Manchester U v Wigan Ath	2-0
2014	Arsenal v Manchester C	3-0
2015	Arsenal v Chelsea	1-0
2016	Manchester U v Leicester C	2-1
2017	Arsenal v Chelsea	1-1
	Arsenal won 4-1 on penalties.	
2018	Manchester C v Chelsea	2-0
2019	Manchester C v Liverpool	1-1
	Manchester C won 5-4 on penalties.	

** Each club retained shield for six months.* ▪ *Denotes player sent off.*

THE FA COMMUNITY SHIELD 2019

Manchester C (1) 1 Liverpool (0) 1

at Wembley, Sunday 4 August 2019, attendance 77,565

Manchester C: Bravo; Walker, Stones, Otamendi, Zinchenko, de Bruyne (Foden 89), Rodrigo, David Silva (Gundogan 61), Bernardo Silva, Sterling, Sane (Gabriel Jesus 13).
Scorer: Sterling 12.

Liverpool: Alisson; Alexander-Arnold (Matip 67), Gomez, van Dijk, Robertson, Wijnaldum, Fabinho (Keita 67), Henderson (Lallana 79), Salah, Firmino (Shaqiri 79), Origi (Oxlade-Chamberlain 79).
Scorer: Matip 77.

Manchester C won 5-4 on penalties.

Referee: Martin Atkinson.

ACCRINGTON STANLEY

FOUNDATION

Accrington Football Club, founder members of the Football League in 1888, were not connected with Accrington Stanley. In fact both clubs ran concurrently between 1891 when Stanley were formed and 1895 when Accrington FC folded. Actually Stanley Villa was the original name, those responsible for forming the club living in Stanley Street and using the Stanley Arms as their meeting place. They became Accrington Stanley in 1893. In 1894–95 they joined the Accrington & District League, playing at Moorhead Park. Subsequently they played in the North-East Lancashire Combination and the Lancashire Combination before becoming founder members of the Third Division (North) in 1921, two years after moving to Peel Park. In 1962 they resigned from the Football League, were wound up, re-formed in 1963, disbanded in 1966 only to restart as Accrington Stanley (1968), returning to the Lancashire Combination in 1970.

Wham Stadium, Livingstone Road, Accrington, Lancashire BB5 5BX.

Telephone: (01254) 356 950.

Website: www.accringtonstanley.co.uk

Email: via website.

Ground Capacity: 5,278.

Record Attendance: 13,181 v Hull C, Division 3 (N), 28 September 1948 (at Peel Park); 5,397 v Derby Co, FA Cup 4th rd, 26 January 2019.

Pitch Measurements: 102m × 66m (111.5yd × 72yd).

Chairman: Andy Holt.

Managing Director: David Burgess.

Manager: John Coleman.

Assistant Manager: Jimmy Bell.

Colours: Red shirts with white trim, red shorts with white trim, red socks with white trim.

Year Formed: 1891, reformed 1968.

Turned Professional: 1919.

Club Nickname: 'The Reds', 'Stanley'.

Previous Names: 1891, Stanley Villa; 1893, Accrington Stanley.

Grounds: 1891, Moorhead Park; 1897, Bell's Ground; 1919, Peel Park; 1970, Crown Ground (renamed Interlink Express Stadium, Fraser Eagle Stadium, Store First Stadium 2013, Wham Stadium 2015).

First Football League Game: 27 August 1921, Division 3 (N), v Rochdale (a) L 3-6 – Tattersall; Newton, Baines, Crawshaw, Popplewell, Burkinshaw, Oxley, Makin, Green (1), Hosker (2), Hartles.

Record League Victory: 8–0 v New Brighton, Division 3 (N), 17 March 1934 – Maidment; Armstrong (pen), Price, Dodds, Crawshaw, McCulloch, Wyper, Lennox (2), Cheetham (4), Leedham (1), Watson.

Record Cup Victory: 7–0 v Spennymoor U, FA Cup 2nd rd, 8 December 1938 – Tootill; Armstrong, Whittaker, Latham, Curran, Lee, Parry (2), Chadwick, Jepson (3), McLoughlin (2), Barclay.

Record Defeat: 1–9 v Lincoln C, Division 3 (N), 3 March 1951.

HONOURS

League Champions: FL 2 – 2017–18; Conference – 2005–06.

Runners-up: Division 3N – 1954–55, 1957–58.

FA Cup: 4th rd – 1927, 1937, 1959, 2010, 2017, 2019.

League Cup: 3rd rd – 2016–17.

FOOTBALL YEARBOOK FACT FILE

In 1999–2000 Accrington Stanley were one of three teams to finish level on 84 points at the top of the first division of the Unibond League. Stanley won the title thanks to their superior goal difference which edged them ahead of rivals Burscough and Witton Albion. The season was the first campaign that John Coleman, with Jimmy Bell as his assistant, was in charge of the club.

Most League Points (2 for a win): 61, Division 3 (N), 1954–55.

Most League Points (3 for a win): 93, FL 2, 2017–18.

Most League Goals: 96, Division 3 (N), 1954–55.

Highest League Scorer in Season: George Stewart, 35, Division 3 (N), 1955–56; George Hudson, 35, Division 4, 1960–61.

Most League Goals in Total Aggregate: George Stewart, 136, 1954–58.

Most League Goals in One Match: 5, Billy Harker v Gateshead, Division 3 (N), 16 November 1935; George Stewart v Gateshead, Division 3 (N), 27 November 1954.

Most Capped Player: Romuald Boco, 19 (51), Benin.

Most League Appearances: Andy Procter, 275, 2006–12, 2014–16.

Youngest League Player: Ian Gibson, 15 years 358 days, v Norwich C, 23 March 1959.

Record Transfer Fee Received: £1,000,000 from Ipswich T for Kayden Jackson, August 2018.

Record Transfer Fee Paid: £85,000 (rising to £150,000) to Swansea C for Ian Craney, January 2008.

Football League Record: 1921 Original Member of Division 3 (N); 1958–60 Division 3; 1960–62 Division 4; 2006–18 FL 2; 2018– FL 1.

LATEST SEQUENCES

Longest Sequence of League Wins: 7, 24.2.2018 – 7.4.2018.

Longest Sequence of League Defeats: 9, 8.3.1930 – 21.4.1930.

Longest Sequence of League Draws: 4, 25.8.2018 – 15.9.2018.

Longest Sequence of Unbeaten League Matches: 15, 3.2.2018 – 21.4.2018.

Longest Sequence Without a League Win: 18, 17.9.1938 – 31.12.1938.

Successive Scoring Runs: 24 from 23.12.2017.

Successive Non-scoring Runs: 6 from 29.12.2018.

MANAGERS

William Cronshaw *c.*1894
John Haworth 1897–1910
Johnson Haworth *c.*1916
Sam Pilkingson 1919–24
(*Tommy Booth p-m 1923–24*)
Ernie Blackburn 1924–32
Amos Wade 1932–35
John Hacking 1935–49
Jimmy Porter 1949–51
Walter Crook 1951–53
Walter Galbraith 1953–58
George Eastham Snr 1958–59
Harold Bodle 1959–60
James Harrower 1960–61
Harold Mather 1962–63
Jimmy Hinksman 1963–64
Terry Neville 1964–65
Ian Bryson 1965
Danny Parker 1965–66
Gerry Keenan
Gary Pierce
Dave Thornley
Phil Staley
Eric Whalley
Stan Allen 1995–96
Tony Greenwood 1996–98
Billy Rodaway 1998
Wayne Harrison 1998–99
John Coleman 1999–2012
Paul Cook 2012
Leam Richardson 2012–13
James Beattie 2013–14
John Coleman September 2014–

TEN YEAR LEAGUE RECORD

		P	*W*	*D*	*L*	*F*	*A*	*Pts*	*Pos*
2010-11	FL 2	46	18	19	9	73	55	73	5
2011-12	FL 2	46	14	15	17	54	66	57	14
2012-13	FL 2	46	14	12	20	51	68	54	18
2013-14	FL 2	46	14	15	17	54	56	57	15
2014-15	FL 2	46	15	11	20	58	77	56	17
2015-16	FL 2	46	24	13	9	74	48	85	4
2016-17	FL 2	46	17	14	15	59	56	65	13
2017-18	FL 2	46	29	6	11	76	46	93	1
2018-19	FL 1	46	14	13	19	51	67	55	14
2019-20	FL 1	35	10	10	15	47	53	40	17§

§Decided on points-per-game (1.14)

DID YOU KNOW ?

Accrington Stanley, then members of the Football Conference, knocked out two future Premier League clubs in their 2003–04 FA Cup campaign before going out to Colchester United in a third round replay. They defeated Huddersfield Town in the first round and followed up by beating AFC Bournemouth on penalties. It was their best FA Cup run as a non-league club.

ACCRINGTON STANLEY – SKY BET LEAGUE ONE 2019–20 LEAGUE RECORD

Match No.	*Date*	*Venue*	*Opponents*	*Result*		*H/T Score*	*Lg Pos.*	*Goalscorers*	*Attendance*
1	Aug 3	A	Lincoln C	L	0-2	0-1	20		8668
2	17	A	AFC Wimbledon	D	1-1	0-1	19	Bishop [64]	3979
3	20	H	Shrewsbury T	L	2-3	0-0	21	Bishop (pen) [67], Charles [72]	2284
4	24	A	Fleetwood T	L	0-2	0-1	21		2802
5	31	H	Milton Keynes D	W	2-1	0-1	20	Bishop [52], Hughes [59]	2218
6	Sept 7	A	Bristol R	D	3-3	2-2	19	Clark [18], Finley [19], Charles (pen) [77]	6524
7	14	H	Sunderland	L	1-3	1-3	20	Clark [5]	4164
8	17	A	Wycombe W	D	1-1	1-0	20	Charles [40]	3566
9	21	H	Blackpool	D	1-1	1-0	19	Tilt (og) [16]	4054
10	28	A	Southend U	W	1-0	0-0	17	Bishop [52]	5643
11	Oct 5	H	Oxford U	D	2-2	0-1	18	Clark [59], Zanzala [73]	2590
12	12	A	Rochdale	L	1-2	0-1	19	Pritchard [53]	3508
13	20	H	Ipswich T	W	2-0	2-0	17	Bishop 2 (1 pen) [17, 41 (p)]	3567
14	23	A	Peterborough U	L	0-4	0-0	18		5843
15	26	H	Gillingham	L	0-1	0-0	18		2102
16	Nov 2	A	Coventry C	D	0-0	0-0	19		5455
17	16	A	Rotherham U	L	0-1	0-1	19		8430
18	23	H	Bolton W	W	7-1	3-1	17	Bishop 2 (1 pen) [15 (p), 27], McConville 2 [33, 53], Charles [75], Zanzala 2 [80, 90]	5034
19	Dec 7	A	Tranmere R	D	1-1	1-1	18	McConville [18]	5751
20	14	H	Portsmouth	W	4-1	1-1	17	Harrison (og) [44], Charles [62], Bishop 2 [69, 77]	2429
21	21	A	Doncaster R	D	1-1	0-0	17	Zanzala [82]	7444
22	26	A	Blackpool	W	1-0	0-0	16	McConville [90]	9517
23	29	H	Burton Alb	W	2-0	1-0	15	McConville [39], Sykes [65]	2449
24	Jan 1	H	Rochdale	L	1-2	0-1	17	Zanzala [90]	2975
25	11	A	Ipswich T	L	1-4	0-3	17	Zanzala (pen) [86]	17,536
26	18	H	Southend U	L	1-2	1-1	17	Charles [17]	2146
27	25	A	Burton Alb	D	1-1	1-1	17	Charles [15]	2759
28	28	H	Peterborough U	L	0-2	0-1	17		1816
29	Feb 1	H	AFC Wimbledon	W	2-1	2-0	17	Clark [14], Charles [21]	2224
30	11	A	Shrewsbury T	W	2-0	1-0	16	Grant [13], Clark [71]	4699
31	15	H	Lincoln C	W	4-3	1-1	14	Shackell (og) [36], Pritchard [70], Conneely [78], Finley [90]	2279
32	22	H	Rotherham U	L	1-2	0-0	14	Clark [65]	3447
33	25	A	Oxford U	L	0-3	0-1	16		5622
34	29	A	Bolton W	D	0-0	0-0	16		12,011
35	Mar 7	H	Tranmere R	L	1-2	0-1	17	Woodyard (og) [82]	2881
36	14	A	Portsmouth	Cancelled					
37	21	H	Doncaster R	Cancelled					
38	28	H	Coventry C	Cancelled					
39	Apr 4	A	Gillingham	Cancelled					
40	10	H	Fleetwood T	Cancelled					
41	13	A	Milton Keynes D	Cancelled					
42	18	H	Bristol R	Cancelled					
43	25	A	Sunderland	Cancelled					
44	May 3	H	Wycombe W	Cancelled					

Final League Position: 17 (on points-per-game basis)

GOALSCORERS

League (47): Bishop 10 (3 pens), Charles 8 (1 pen), Clark 6, Zanzala 6 (1 pen), McConville 5, Finley 2, Pritchard 2, Conneely 1, Grant 1, Hughes 1, Sykes 1, own goals 4.
FA Cup (0).
Carabao Cup (1): Bishop 1 (1 pen).
Leasing.com Trophy (15): Clark 2, Sykes 2, Zanzala 2 (1 pen), Baker-Richardson 1, Bishop 1, Carvalho 1, Charles 1, Diallo 1, Finley 1, McConville 1, Pritchard 1, Simpson 1.

Evtimov D 19	Johnson C 32 + 1	Hughes M 31	Sykes R 31	Maguire J 10 + 1	Conneely S 30 + 1	Finley S 29 + 2	Clark J 34	Pritchard J 20 + 10	McConville S 15 + 3	Bishop C 24 + 3	Carvalho W 1 + 7	Sheriff L 2 + 6	Francis-Angol Z 5	Baker-Richardson C 2	Charles D 26 + 7	Zanzala O 7 + 17	Edwards P — + 4	Opoku J 19 + 2	Diallo S 6 + 3	Alese A 6 + 4	Simpson C 1 + 1	Rodgers H 5 + 1	Barclay B 8	Bursik J 16	Grant B 3 + 2	Ashley-Seal B 3 + 2	*Match No.*
1	2	3	4	5	6^2	7	8	9^1	10	11	12	13															1
1	2	4	3		7	8	6		9	11			5■	10^1	12												2
1	2	4	3	5^2	7	8	6		9	10				11^1	12	13											3
1	2	4	3		8	7	6	13	9■	11			5^2		10^1	12											4
1	2	4	3		8	7	6	9^2		10	12		5		11^1		13										5
1	2^2	4	3		6■	8	7	9		10		12	5^1		11			13									6
1	2	4^2	3			8	7	9^1		11	14	6^3			10			5	12	13							7
1	2	4	3		6	8	7		9	11^1					10			5			12						8
1	2	4	3		6	8	7	12	9						11			5			10^1						9
1	2	4	3		6	9	7	13	8	10^1					11^2	12		5									10
1	2	4	3		6	9	7	8		10					11^1	12		5									11
1		3	2		7	8	5	4		10	14	6^2			13	11^3	12	9^1									12
1	2	4	3■		6	9	7	14	8^3	11					13	10^1		5^2		12							13
1	2	3		12^3	6	9	7		8	11^1			5^2		14	10	13			4							14
1	2^2	3			8	7	6	12	9^3	11	14				13	10^1		5		4							15
1	2	3			6	9	7	8^1	10	11						12		5		4							16
1	2		3	5^1	7	9	6	10^3	12	13	14				11							4	8^2				17
1		4	3	5	6	9	7	13	8	10^3					11^1	12	14					2^2					18
1	13	4	3	5^3			6	12	9^1	10		14			11				8			2^2	7				19
	2	4	3		6	9^1	7	8		10^2					11	12		5	13					1			20
	2	4	3		6	9	7	8^1	12	10^2					11	13		5						1			21
	2	4	3			9	7	8^1	12						10	11		5					6	1			22
	2	4	3			9	7	12	8						10^1	11		5					6	1			23
	2^2	4	3		12	9	7	13	8^3		14				11	10		5					6^1	1			24
	2	4	3		6	9		8^2		11	7^1				10	12		5		13				1			25
	2^2	4	3		7^1	8	6	9		11					10	12			13	5				1			26
	2	4	3		7		8	10				12			11^2	13		5	9^1				6	1			27
	2	4	3		7		8	10				13			11	12		5^1	9				6^2	1			28
	2	4	3	5^2	7		8	10■							11	13			9^1	12			6	1			29
	2	4	3	5	7^1	13	8					14			10	12			6					1	9^3	11^2	30
	2	4	3	5	6	12	8	13		14					10^1				7^2					1	9	11^3	31
	2	3	4		6	7	8	10^3		13					9^2	14				5				1	12	11^1	32
	2		3		7	8	6	9		11^1					10^2	13		5		4^3		14		1		12	33
	2		3^1	5	6	7	8	10		11^3					12			13				4		1	9^2	14	34
	2			5^2	6	7	8	10		11^1					9	12		4				3■		1	13		35
																											36
																											37
																											38
																											39
																											40
																											41
																											42
																											43
																											44

FA Cup

First Round	Crewe Alex	(h)	0-2

Carabao Cup

First Round	Sunderland	(h)	1-3

Leasing.com Trophy

Group B (N)	Fleetwood T	(h)	2-1
Group B (N)	Oldham Ath	(a)	3-0
Group B (N)	Liverpool U21	(h)	5-2
Second Round (N)	Bolton W	(h)	2-0
Third Round (N)	Fleetwood T	(a)	2-2
(Accrington S won 5-3 on penalties)			
Quarter-Final	Salford C	(a)	1-2

AFC WIMBLEDON

FOUNDATION

While the history of AFC Wimbledon is straightforward since it was a new club formed in 2002, there were in effect two clubs operating for two years with Wimbledon connections. The other club was MK Dons, of course. In August 2001, the Football League had rejected the existing Wimbledon's application to move to Milton Keynes. In May 2002, they rejected local sites and were given permission to move by an independent commission set up by the Football League. AFC Wimbledon was founded in the summer of 2002 and held its first trials on Wimbledon Common. In subsequent years, there was considerable debate over the rightful home of the trophies obtained by the former Wimbledon football club. In October 2006, an agreement was reached between Milton Keynes Dons, its Supporters Association, the Wimbledon Independent Supporters Association and the Football Supporters Federation to transfer such trophies and honours to the London Borough of Merton.

The Cherry Red Records Stadium, Kingsmeadow, Jack Goodchild Way, 422a Kingston Road, Kingston-upon-Thames, Surrey KT1 3PB.

Telephone: (0208) 547 3528.

Website: www.afcwimbledon.co.uk

Email: info@afcwimbledon.co.uk

Ground Capacity: 4,850.

Record Attendance: 4,870 v Accrington S, FL 2 Play-Offs, 14 May 2016.

Pitch Measurements: 104m × 66m (114yd × 72yd).

President: Dickie Guy.

Chief Executive: Joe Palmer.

Manager: Glyn Hodges.

Assistant Manager: Nick Daws.

First-Team Coach: Vaughan Ryan.

Club Nickname: 'The Dons'.

Colours: Blue shirts with yellow trim, blue shorts with yellow trim, blue socks with yellow trim.

Year Formed: 2002.

Turned Professional: 2002.

HONOURS

League: *Runners-up:* FL 2 – (7th) 2015–16 *(promoted via play-offs)*; Conference – (2nd) 2010–11 *(promoted via play-offs)*.
FA Cup: 5th rd – 2019.
League Cup: never past 1st rd.

FOOTBALL YEARBOOK FACT FILE

AFC Wimbledon reached the first round proper of the FA Cup for the first time in 2008–09. The Dons, then members of Conference South, defeated Bedford Town, Dover Athletic and Maidstone United, to earn a home tie against Wycombe Wanderers. The game at Kingsmeadow attracted an attendance of 4,528 who saw Wycombe go through 4-1.

Grounds: 2002, Kingsmeadow (renamed The Cherry Red Records Stadium).

First Football League Game: 6 August 2011, FL 2 v Bristol R (h) L 2–3 – Brown; Hatton, Gwillim (Bush), Porter (Minshull), Stuart (1), Johnson B, Moore L, Wellard, Jolley (Ademeno (1)), Midson, Yussuff.

Record League Victory: 5–1 v Bury, FL 2, 19 November 2016 – Shea; Fuller, Robertson, Robinson (Taylor), Owens, Francomb (2 (1 pen)), Reeves, Parrett, Whelpdale (1), Elliott (1) (Nightingale), Poleon (1), (Barrett).

MANAGERS

Terry Eames 2002–04
Nicky English *(Caretaker)* 2004
Dave Anderson 2004–07
Terry Brown 2007–12
Neal Ardley 2012–18
Wally Downes 2018–19
Glyn Hodges September 2019–

Record Cup Victory: 5–0 v Bury, FA Cup 1st rd replay, 5 November 2016 – Shea; Fuller (Owens), Robertson, Robinson (1), Francomb. Parrett (1), Reeves, Bulman (Beere), Whelpdale, Barcham (Poleon (2)), Taylor (1).

Record Defeat: 0–5 v Oxford U, FL 2, 18 February 2020.

Most League Points (3 for a win): 75, FL 2, 2015–16.

Most League Goals: 64, FL 2, 2015–16.

Highest League Scorer in Season: Lyle Taylor, 20, 2015–16.

Most League Goals in Total Aggregate: Kevin Cooper, 107, 2002–04.

Most League Goals in One Match: 3, Lyle Taylor v Rotherham U, FL 1, 17 October 2017; 3, Joe Pigott v Rochdale, FL 1, 19 February 2019; 3, Marcus Foss v Southend U, FL 1, 12 October 2019.

Most Capped Player: Shane Smeltz, 5 (58), New Zealand.

Most League Appearances: Barry Fuller, 205, 2013–18.

Youngest League Player: Jack Madelin, 17 years 186 days v Burton Alb, 22 October 2019.

Record Transfer Fee Received: £150,000 from Bradford C for Jake Reeves, July 2017.

Record Transfer Fee Paid: £25,000 (in excess of) to Stevenage for Byron Harrison, January 2012.

Football League Record: 2011 Promoted from Conference Premier; 2011–16 FL 2; 2016– FL 1.

LATEST SEQUENCES

Longest Sequence of League Wins: 5, 2.4.2016 – 23.4.2016.

Longest Sequence of League Defeats: 8, 2.10.2018 – 17.11.2018.

Longest Sequence of League Draws: 4, 6.4.2019 – 23.4.2019.

Longest Sequence of Unbeaten League Matches: 10, 7.4.2018 – 18.8.2018.

Longest Sequence Without a League Win: 12, 4.5.2019 – 28.9.2019.

Successive Scoring Runs: 10 from 28.12.2016.

Successive Non-scoring Runs: 6 from 1.4.2017.

TEN YEAR LEAGUE RECORD

		P	*W*	*D*	*L*	*F*	*A*	*Pts*	*Pos*
2010-11	Conf P	46	27	9	10	83	47	90	2
2011-12	FL 2	46	15	9	22	62	78	54	16
2012-13	FL 2	46	14	11	21	54	76	53	20
2013-14	FL 2	46	14	14	18	49	57	53*	20
2014-15	FL 2	46	14	16	16	54	60	58	15
2015-16	FL 2	46	21	12	13	64	50	75	7
2016-17	FL 1	46	13	18	15	52	55	57	15
2017-18	FL 1	46	13	14	19	47	58	53	18
2018-19	FL 1	46	13	11	22	42	63	50	20
2019-20	FL 1	35	8	11	16	39	52	35	20§

** 3 pts deducted. §Decided on points-per-game (1.00)*

DID YOU KNOW ?

Ally Russell scored AFC Wimbledon's first-ever hat-trick when he netted three goals in their 4-0 home win over Cobham in October 2002. The victory was the Dons' seventh consecutive win. They finished their Combined Counties League campaign with 111 points from 46 games but still finished only third in the table.

AFC WIMBLEDON – SKY BET LEAGUE ONE 2019–20 LEAGUE RECORD

Match No.	*Date*	*Venue*	*Opponents*	*Result*	*H/T Score*	*Lg Pos.*	*Goalscorers*	*Attendance*
1	Aug 3	H	Rotherham U	L 1-2	0-1	15	Pigott [50]	4657
2	10	A	Fleetwood T	L 1-2	1-0	18	Appiah [26]	2684
3	17	H	Accrington S	D 1-1	1-0	18	O'Neill [42]	3979
4	20	A	Ipswich T	L 1-2	1-0	20	Guinness-Walker [41]	18,778
5	24	A	Sunderland	L 1-3	1-1	20	Appiah [34]	29,725
6	31	H	Wycombe W	D 0-0	0-0	21		4521
7	Sept 7	A	Milton Keynes D	L 1-2	0-2	21	Forss [83]	8627
8	14	H	Shrewsbury T	D 1-1	1-0	21	Ebanks-Landell (og) [31]	4084
9	17	A	Coventry C	L 1-2	1-1	21	Forss (pen) [8]	5239
10	21	H	Bristol R	L 1-3	1-1	22	Forss [20]	4268
11	28	A	Peterborough U	L 2-3	0-2	22	Pinnock [52], Wordsworth [78]	6744
12	Oct 5	H	Rochdale	W 3-2	3-0	21	Forss [2], Osew [16], Pinnock [28]	4068
13	12	A	Southend U	W 4-1	2-1	20	Forss 3 (1 pen) [5, 11, 52 (p)], Delaney [72]	6420
14	19	H	Portsmouth	W 1-0	0-0	20	Thomas [90]	4525
15	22	A	Burton Alb	L 0-1	0-1	21		2223
16	Nov 2	H	Lincoln C	D 1-1	0-1	20	Appiah [90]	4378
17	16	A	Blackpool	L 0-2	0-0	20		7588
18	23	H	Gillingham	W 1-0	1-0	19	Wagstaff [19]	4554
19	Dec 7	A	Bolton W	D 2-2	1-0	19	Forss 2 [41, 81]	11,501
20	14	H	Doncaster R	W 2-1	0-1	19	Forss (pen) [56], Reilly [70]	4311
21	21	A	Tranmere R	L 0-1	0-1	19		6285
22	26	A	Bristol R	W 2-1	0-1	18	Forss [70], Pigott [84]	9096
23	29	H	Oxford U	L 1-2	0-1	18	Pigott [47]	4763
24	Jan 1	H	Southend U	D 1-1	1-0	19	Reilly [23]	4422
25	11	A	Portsmouth	L 1-2	0-1	20	Pigott [62]	18,417
26	18	H	Peterborough U	W 1-0	0-0	19	Pigott [58]	4453
27	28	H	Burton Alb	D 2-2	1-2	19	Pinnock [16], Reilly [59]	3674
28	Feb 1	A	Accrington S	L 1-2	0-2	20	Pigott [73]	2224
29	8	H	Fleetwood T	L 1-2	1-1	20	McLoughlin [34]	4097
30	11	H	Ipswich T	D 0-0	0-0	20		4745
31	15	A	Rotherham U	D 2-2	1-0	20	Sanders [30], Appiah (pen) [90]	8626
32	18	A	Oxford U	L 0-5	0-2	20		6155
33	22	H	Blackpool	D 0-0	0-0	20		4593
34	29	A	Gillingham	W 2-1	0-0	19	Pigott [49], Reilly [90]	4893
35	Mar 7	H	Bolton W	D 0-0	0-0	20		4804
36	14	A	Doncaster R	Cancelled				
37	21	H	Tranmere R	Cancelled				
38	24	A	Rochdale	Cancelled				
39	28	A	Lincoln C	Cancelled				
40	Apr 10	H	Sunderland	Cancelled				
41	13	A	Wycombe W	Cancelled				
42	18	H	Milton Keynes D	Cancelled				
43	25	A	Shrewsbury T	Cancelled				
44	May 3	H	Coventry C	Cancelled				

Final League Position: 20 (on points-per-game basis)

GOALSCORERS

League (39): Forss 11 (3 pens), Pigott 7, Appiah 4 (1 pen), Reilly 4, Pinnock 3, Delaney 1, Guinness-Walker 1, McLoughlin 1, O'Neill 1, Osew 1, Sanders 1, Thomas 1, Wagstaff 1, Wordsworth 1, own goal 1.
FA Cup (1): Pigott 1.
Carabao Cup (2): O'Neill 1, Wagstaff 1.
Leasing.com Trophy (4): Folivi 1, Pigott 1 (1 pen), Reilly 1, Wood 1.

Tzanev N 2	Thomas T 31	Kalambayi P 16	McDonald R 11 + 4	O'Neill L 30 + 1	Hartigan A 20 + 7	Nightingale W 8 + 1	Reilly C 28 + 2	Guinness-Walker N 19 + 4	Folivi M 6 + 4	Pigott J 31 + 3	McLoughlin S 14 + 9	Connolly D — + 3	Appiah K 9 + 10	Pinnock M 17 + 8	Trott N 23	Wagstaff S 23 + 3	Osew P 15 + 3	Roscrow A — + 10	McDonnell J 1	Delaney R 13 + 1	Sanders M 18 + 2	Forss M 17 + 1	Wordsworth A 6 + 4	Madelin J — + 1	Rudoni J 8 + 3	Wood T — + 2	Sorensen M 9	Day J 9	Lamy J 1 + 1	*Match No.*
1	2^{3}	3	4	5	6^{1}	7	8	9	10^{2}	11	12	13	14																	1
1	4	2	3^{1}	5	6^{2}		7	9	14	11	12	13	10	8^{3}																2
	3	2	4	5	7		8^{1}	9^{2}	10	11	14			12	1	6^{3}	13													3
	3	2	4	5	7		8	9	11^{2}	13			10^{1}	12	1	6														4
	3	2^{2}	4	5	7	12	8^{3}	9	11^{1}			13	10	14	1	6														5
	4	2		5	7^{1}	3	8	9		11			10^{2}	13	1	6		12												6
	3^{3}	2		5		7	8	9	13	10			11^{1}			6^{2}			1	4	12	14								7
		2		5	7	3	8^{1}	9	13	10^{3}					1	6		14		4	12	11^{2}								8
		2^{3}		5	7	3	8	9	10^{1}	14			13		1	6		12		4		11^{2}								9
	2^{2}			5	7^{3}	3	8	9	11^{1}	13					1	6		14		4		10■	12							10
	2^{2}			5		3	8^{1}			10			11	12	1	6	9			4	7		13							11
	4	2			13	3	14		12	11				8^{2}	1	5	9				7	10^{3}	6^{1}							12
	4	2			13					11	14		12	6^{2}	1	5	9			3	7	10^{3}	8^{1}							13
	2	4			12					11			13	8^{1}	1	5	9			3	7	10^{2}	6							14
	4	2^{1}						12		10			13	6	1	5	9^{2}			3^{3}	7	11	8	14						15
	4	2		12	7^{1}					10	13		14	8^{3}	1	5	9			3^{2}		11	6							16
	4			2	12		13			10	7^{3}		14	8^{1}	1	5	9			3	6^{2}	11								17
		3		2			8	13		11^{1}			12	7	1	5	9			4	6	10^{2}								18
		3		2			8	13		11	12			7^{1}	1	5	9			4	6	10^{2}								19
	3		4	2	14		8	12		11	5			7^{1}	1		9^{2}				6	10^{3}			13					20
	3		4	2	12		8	9^{1}		11	5			6^{2}	1						7	10				13				21
	3		4	2			8	9		11	5			12	1						7	10^{1}			6					22
	3^{1}		4	2			8	9		11	5^{2}				1					12	7	10			6	13				23
	3			2	12		8	9		11	5				1					4	7	10			6^{1}					24
	3		4	2	6		8	9		11	5^{2}			12	1	13■					7	10^{1}								25
	3			2	7		8	9^{2}		11	5			10	1		13				6^{1}		12				4			26
	3			2	7		8			10	13			11		5	9^{2}						12		6^{1}		4	1		27
	3			2^{2}	7		6			10	13			11		5	12	14					9^{3}		8^{1}		4	1		28
	3		12	2	7		8			11	5^{3}			10			9	14							6^{1}		4^{2}	1	13	29
	3		4	2	7		8^{1}			11	5			10		12	9				6^{2}				13			1		30
	3		14	2			9			11	6^{1}		13	12		7^{3}	5				8				10^{2}		4	1		31
	4			3	9			6		11^{1}	2		12	7^{2}		13		14			8^{3}						5	1	10	32
	3^{1}		14	2	7		8^{2}			11	13		10^{3}			5	9	12							6		4	1		33
	3		13	2	7		8	9		11	5^{1}		10^{2}			6		12									4	1		34
	3			2	7		8^{1}	9		11	6		10^{2}			5		12							13		4	1		35
																														36
																														37
																														38
																														39
																														40
																														41
																														42
																														43
																														44

FA Cup

First Round	Doncaster R	(h)	1-1
Replay	Doncaster R	(a)	0-2

Carabao Cup

First Round	Milton Keynes D	(h)	2-2

(Milton Keynes D won 4-2 on penalties)

Leasing.com Trophy

Group C (S)	Brighton & HA U21	(h)	0-2
Group C (S)	Leyton Orient	(h)	3-0
Group C (S)	Southend U	(a)	1-3

ARSENAL

FOUNDATION

Formed by workers at the Royal Arsenal, Woolwich in 1886, they began as Dial Square (name of one of the workshops), and included two former Nottingham Forest players, Fred Beardsley and Morris Bates. Beardsley wrote to his old club seeking help and they provided the new club with a full set of red jerseys and a ball. The club became known as the 'Woolwich Reds' although their official title soon after formation was Woolwich Arsenal.

Emirates Stadium, Highbury House, 75 Drayton Park, Islington, London N5 1BU.

Telephone: (020) 7619 5003.

Ticket Office: (020) 7619 5000.

Website: www.arsenal.com

Email: ask@arsenal.co.uk

Ground Capacity: 60,704.

Record Attendance: 73,295 v Sunderland, Div 1, 9 March 1935 (at Highbury); 73,707 v RC Lens, UEFA Champions League, 25 November 1998 (at Wembley); 60,383 v Wolverhampton W, Premier League, 2 November 2019 (at Emirates).

Pitch Measurements: 105m × 68m (115yd × 74.5yd).

Chairman: Sir John 'Chips' Keswick.

Manager: Mikel Arteta.

Assistant Manager: Freddie Ljungberg.

Colours: Red shirts with white sleeves, white shorts with red trim, red socks with white trim.

Year Formed: 1886.

Turned Professional: 1891.

Previous Names: 1886, Dial Square; 1886, Royal Arsenal; 1891, Woolwich Arsenal; 1914, Arsenal.

Club Nickname: 'The Gunners'.

Grounds: 1886, Plumstead Common; 1887, Sportsman Ground; 1888, Manor Ground; 1890, Invicta Ground; 1893, Manor Ground; 1913, Highbury; 2006, Emirates Stadium.

HONOURS

League Champions: Premier League – 1997–98, 2001–02, 2003–04; Division 1 – 1930–31, 1932–33, 1933–34, 1934–35, 1937–38, 1947–48, 1952–53, 1970–71, 1988–89, 1990–91.
Runners-up: Premier League – 1998–99, 1999–2000, 2000–01, 2002–03, 2004–05, 2015–16; Division 1 – 1925–26, 1931–32, 1972–73; Division 2 – 1903–04.

FA Cup Winners: 1930, 1936, 1950, 1971, 1979, 1993, 1998, 2002, 2003, 2005, 2014, 2015, 2017, 2020.
Runners-up: 1927, 1932, 1952, 1972, 1978, 1980, 2001.

League Cup Winners: 1987, 1993.
Runners-up: 1968, 1969, 1988, 2007, 2011, 2018.

Double performed: 1970–71, 1997–98, 2001–02.

European Competitions
European Cup: 1971–72 *(qf)*, 1991–92.
UEFA Champions League: 1998–99, 1999–2000, 2000–01, 2001–02, 2002–03, 2003–04, 2004–05, 2005–06 *(runners-up)*, 2006–07, 2007–08 *(qf)*, 2008–09 *(sf)*, 2009–10 *(qf)*, 2010–11, 2011–12, 2012–13, 2013–14, 2014–15, 2015–16, 2016–17.
Fairs Cup: 1963–64, 1969–70 *(winners)*, 1970–71.
UEFA Cup: 1978–79, 1981–82, 1982–83, 1996–97, 1997–98, 1999–2000 *(runners-up)*.
Europa League: 2017–18 *(sf)*, 2018–19 *(runners-up)*, 2019–20.
European Cup-Winners' Cup: 1979–80 *(runners-up)*, 1993–94 *(winners)*, 1994–95 *(runners-up)*.
Super Cup: 1994 *(runners-up)*.

FOOTBALL YEARBOOK FACT FILE

Theo Walcott netted an unusual hat-trick for Arsenal in their amazing 7-5 Football League Cup win over Reading in October 2012. His goals were all scored in added time: one each at the end of the first half, the second half and the second period of extra time.

First Football League Game: 2 September 1893, Division 2, v Newcastle U (h) D 2–2 – Williams; Powell, Jeffrey; Devine, Buist, Howat; Gemmell, Henderson, Shaw (1), Elliott (1), Booth.

Record League Victory: 12–0 v Loughborough T, Division 2, 12 March 1900 – Orr; McNichol, Jackson; Moir, Dick (2), Anderson (1); Hunt, Cottrell (2), Main (2), Gaudie (3), Tennant (2).

Record Cup Victory: 11–1 v Darwen, FA Cup 3rd rd, 9 January 1932 – Moss; Parker, Hapgood; Jones, Roberts, John; Hulme (2), Jack (3), Lambert (2), James, Bastin (4).

Record Defeat: 0–8 v Loughborough T, Division 2, 12 December 1896.

Most League Points (2 for a win): 66, Division 1, 1930–31.

Most League Points (3 for a win): 90, Premier League, 2003–04.

Most League Goals: 127, Division 1, 1930–31.

Highest League Scorer in Season: Ted Drake, 42, 1934–35.

Most League Goals in Total Aggregate: Thierry Henry, 175, 1999–2007; 2011–12.

Most League Goals in One Match: 7, Ted Drake v Aston Villa, Division 1, 14 December 1935.

Most Capped Player: Thierry Henry, 81 (123), France.

Most League Appearances: David O'Leary, 558, 1975–93.

Youngest League Player: Jack Wilshere, 16 years 256 days v Blackburn R, 13 September 2008.

Record Transfer Fee Received: £40,000,000 from Liverpool for Alex Oxlade-Chamberlain, August 2017.

Record Transfer Fee Paid: £72,000,000 to Lille for Nicolas Pepe, August 2019.

Football League Record: 1893 Elected to Division 2; 1904–13 Division 1; 1913–19 Division 2; 1919–92 Division 1; 1992– Premier League.

MANAGERS

Sam Hollis 1894–97
Tom Mitchell 1897–98
George Elcoat 1898–99
Harry Bradshaw 1899–1904
Phil Kelso 1904–08
George Morrell 1908–15
Leslie Knighton 1919–25
Herbert Chapman 1925–34
George Allison 1934–47
Tom Whittaker 1947–56
Jack Crayston 1956–58
George Swindin 1958–62
Billy Wright 1962–66
Bertie Mee 1966–76
Terry Neill 1976–83
Don Howe 1984–86
George Graham 1986–95
Bruce Rioch 1995–96
Arsène Wenger 1996–2018
Unai Emery 2018–19
Mikel Arteta December 2019–

LATEST SEQUENCES

Longest Sequence of League Wins: 14, 10.2.2002 – 18.8.2002.

Longest Sequence of League Defeats: 7, 12.2.1977 – 12.3.1977.

Longest Sequence of League Draws: 6, 4.3.1961 – 1.4.1961.

Longest Sequence of Unbeaten League Matches: 49, 7.5.2003 – 24.10.2004.

Longest Sequence Without a League Win: 23, 28.9.1912 – 1.3.1913.

Successive Scoring Runs: 55 from 19.5.2001.

Successive Non-scoring Runs: 6 from 25.2.1987.

TEN YEAR LEAGUE RECORD

		P	W	D	L	F	A	Pts	Pos
2010-11	PR Lge	38	19	11	8	72	43	68	4
2011-12	PR Lge	38	21	7	10	74	49	70	3
2012-13	PR Lge	38	21	10	7	72	37	73	4
2013-14	PR Lge	38	24	7	7	68	41	79	4
2014-15	PR Lge	38	22	9	7	71	36	75	3
2015-16	PR Lge	38	20	11	7	65	36	71	2
2016-17	PR Lge	38	23	6	9	77	44	75	5
2017-18	PR Lge	38	19	6	13	74	51	63	6
2018-19	PR Lge	38	21	7	10	73	51	70	5
2019-20	PR Lge	38	14	14	10	56	48	56	8

DID YOU KNOW?

Arsenal featured in the first-ever BBC *Match of the Day* programme on 22 August 1964. Despite scoring twice within a minute through Geoff Strong and Joe Baker, the Gunners went down 3-2 away to Liverpool, Football League champions the previous season.

ARSENAL – PREMIER LEAGUE 2019–20 LEAGUE RECORD

Match No.	*Date*	*Venue*	*Opponents*	*Result*	*H/T Score*	*Lg Pos.*	*Goalscorers*	*Atten-dance*
1	Aug 11	A	Newcastle U	W 1-0	0-0	7	Aubameyang 58	47,635
2	17	H	Burnley	W 2-1	1-1	2	Lacazette 13, Aubameyang 64	60,214
3	24	A	Liverpool	L 1-3	0-1	2	Torreira 85	53,298
4	Sept 1	H	Tottenham H	D 2-2	1-2	5	Lacazette 45, Aubameyang 71	60,333
5	15	A	Watford	D 2-2	2-0	7	Aubameyang 2 21, 32	21,360
6	22	H	Aston Villa	W 3-2	0-1	4	Pepe (pen) 59, Chambers 81, Aubameyang 84	60,331
7	30	A	Manchester U	D 1-1	0-1	4	Aubameyang 58	73,201
8	Oct 6	H	Bournemouth	W 1-0	1-0	3	Luiz 9	60,326
9	21	A	Sheffield U	L 0-1	0-1	5		30,775
10	27	H	Crystal Palace	D 2-2	2-1	5	Papastathopoulos 7, Luiz 9	60,345
11	Nov 2	H	Wolverhampton W	D 1-1	1-0	5	Aubameyang 21	60,383
12	9	A	Leicester C	L 0-2	0-0	6		32,209
13	23	H	Southampton	D 2-2	1-1	7	Lacazette 2 18, 90	60,295
14	Dec 1	A	Norwich C	D 2-2	1-2	8	Aubameyang 2 (1 pen) 29 (p), 57	27,067
15	5	H	Brighton & HA	L 1-2	0-1	10	Lacazette 50	60,164
16	9	A	West Ham U	W 3-1	0-1	9	Martinelli 60, Pepe 66, Aubameyang 69	59,936
17	15	H	Manchester C	L 0-3	0-3	9		60,031
18	21	A	Everton	D 0-0	0-0	11		39,336
19	26	A	Bournemouth	D 1-1	0-1	11	Aubameyang 63	10,234
20	29	H	Chelsea	L 1-2	1-0	12	Aubameyang 13	60,309
21	Jan 1	H	Manchester U	W 2-0	2-0	10	Pepe 8, Papastathopoulos 42	60,328
22	11	A	Crystal Palace	D 1-1	1-0	10	Aubameyang 12	25,468
23	18	H	Sheffield U	D 1-1	1-0	10	Martinelli 45	60,310
24	21	A	Chelsea	D 2-2	0-1	10	Martinelli 63, Bellerin 87	40,577
25	Feb 2	A	Burnley	D 0-0	0-0	10		21,048
26	16	H	Newcastle U	W 4-0	0-0	10	Aubameyang 54, Pepe 57, Ozil 90, Lacazette 90	60,188
27	23	H	Everton	W 3-2	2-2	9	Nketiah 27, Aubameyang 2 33, 46	60,296
28	Mar 7	H	West Ham U	W 1-0	0-0	9	Lacazette 78	60,335
29	June 17	A	Manchester C	L 0-3	0-1	9		0
30	20	A	Brighton & HA	L 1-2	0-0	10	Pepe 68	0
31	25	A	Southampton	W 2-0	1-0	9	Nketiah 20, Willock 86	0
32	July 1	H	Norwich C	W 4-0	2-0	7	Aubameyang 2 33, 67, Xhaka 37, Cedric Soares 81	0
33	4	A	Wolverhampton W	W 2-0	1-0	7	Saka 43, Lacazette 86	0
34	7	H	Leicester C	D 1-1	1-0	7	Aubameyang 21	0
35	12	A	Tottenham H	L 1-2	1-1	9	Lacazette 16	0
36	15	H	Liverpool	W 2-1	2-1	9	Lacazette 32, Nelson 44	0
37	21	A	Aston Villa	L 0-1	0-1	10		0
38	26	H	Watford	W 3-2	3-1	8	Aubameyang 2 (1 pen) 5 (p), 33, Tierney 24	0

Final League Position: 8

GOALSCORERS

League (56): Aubameyang 22 (2 pens), Lacazette 10, Pepe 5 (1 pen), Martinelli 3, Luiz 2, Nketiah 2, Papastathopoulos 2, Bellerin 1, Cedric Soares 1, Chambers 1, Nelson 1, Ozil 1, Saka 1, Tierney 1, Torreira 1, Willock 1, Xhaka 1.
FA Cup (11): Aubameyang 4 (1 pen), Nketiah 2, Ceballos 1, Nelson 1, Papastathopoulos 1, Pepe 1 (1 pen), Saka 1.
Carabao Cup (10): Martinelli 4, Willock 2, Holding 1, Maitland-Niles 1, Nelson 1, Torreira 1.
UEFA Europa League (16): Aubameyang 3, Martinelli 3, Lacazette 2, Pepe 2, Saka 2, Willock 2, Ceballos 1, Mustafi 1.
Leasing.com Trophy (2): John-Jules 1, Olayinka 1.

Leno B 30	Maitland-Niles A 15 + 5	Chambers C 13 + 1	Papastathopoulos S 19	Monreal N 3	Guendouzi M 19 + 5	Xhaka G 30 + 1	Mkhitaryan H 1 + 2	Willock J 8 + 21	Nelson R 7 + 10	Aubameyang P 35 + 1	Ceballos D 18 + 6	Pepe N 22 + 9	Martinelli G 6 + 8	Luiz D 32 + 1	Lacazette A 22 + 8	Kolasinac S 19 + 7	Torreira L 17 + 12	Ozil M 18	Saka B 19 + 7	Tierney K 12 + 3	Holding R 6 + 2	Bellerin H 13 + 2	Mustafi S 13 + 2	Smith-Rowe E 1 + 1	Nketiah E 7 + 6	Pablo Mari V 2	Martinez D 8 + 1	Cedric Soares R 3 + 2	Match No.
1	2	3	4	5	6	7	8³	9¹	10²	11	12	13	14																1
1	2		3	5	7			6	10¹	8	9³	12		4	11²	13	14												2
1	2		3	5	6³	7	14	8²		11	9¹	10		4	13		12												3
1	2		3		8	7	13			11	12	9		4	10²	5	6¹												4
1	2		3		7²	6		12	14	11	8¹	10		4		5	13	9³											5
1	2▮	12	3		6	7³		14		11	9²	8		4		5	13		10¹										6
1		2	3		8	7		14	13	10	12	9²		4		5	6¹		11³										7
1		2	3		6	7		13		11	9²	8¹	12	4		5	14		10³										8
1		2	3		6	7²		9¹		11	12	8³	14	4	13	5			10										9
1		2	3		7	8¹				10	9	6		4	11	13			12	5²									10
1		2	3		7					11	8		12	4	10¹	14	6²	9	13	5³									11
1		2			7			13		11		12		3	10	8	6²	9			4¹	5							12
1		2¹	4		7			14		11		12	13	3	10		6³	9		8		5²							13
1		2			7²	6		9¹		8			14	4	11	5	12	10³	13				3						14
1			3			6		9¹		8		12	14	4	11³	5²	7	10		13		2							15
1	2	3	4		13	6²			14	11		8³	10			12	7	9		5¹									16
1	2	3	4		6			14		11		8	10			5¹	7³	9²	12					13					17
1	2	3				6		12	8	11²			10	4	13		7		5					9¹					18
1	2		3²			7		12	8³	10		14		4	11		6	9¹	5				13						19
1	2	3¹			7			13	8³	10		14		4	11		6	9²	5				12						20
1	2		3		14	7			12	10		8¹		4	11³	5²	6	9	13										21
1	2		3		12	7			14	10▮		8	13	4	11³	5	6¹	9²											22
1	2					7						8	10	4	11¹		6	9	5				3		12				23
1					12	7		14				8²	10³	4▮	11		6	9¹	5		13	2	3						24
1					6	7		13		10			8	4	11³		12	9²	5¹			2	3		14				25
1						7		14		10	6¹	8		4	13		12	9³	5			2	3		11²				26
1					14	7				10	6²	8		4		5¹	13	9³	12			2	3		11				27
1			2			7			13	10	6	8²		3	12			9³	5			14			11¹	4			28
1	15				7⁵	8¹		6⁴	16	10	12			13▮	14				9	5		2	3		11³	4²			29
1¹					8			15	16	11	7³	6⁵			10²	5			9⁴	14	4	2	3		13		12		30
	15					7		12		11	6⁴	9¹			14	13			8	5²	4	2	3		10³		1		31
						7		13	9²	11⁵	6	16		3	10³	4				8	12	5⁴	2¹		14		1	15	32
	12					7		14		11	6⁵			3	15	4	16		9³	8¹		13	2		10⁴		1	5²	33
	15					7		13		11⁴	6³			3	10²	4	14		9¹	8		5	2		12▮		1		34
						7		14	15	11	6	9¹		3	10	4⁴			12	8³		5²	2				1	13	35
	15					7		13	9³	14	12	11		3	10²	16	6¹		8⁵	4	2						1	5⁴	36
						12		15		11	6	14		3²	10	4	7¹		8³	13	2				9		1	5⁴	37
	2					7		9²	15	10	6³	8⁴		4	11¹	12	14			5	3				13		1		38

FA Cup

Third Round	Leeds U	(h)	1-0
Fourth Round	Bournemouth	(a)	2-1
Fifth Round	Portsmouth	(a)	2-0
Sixth Round	Sheffield U	(a)	2-1
Semi-Final	Manchester C	(Wembley)	2-0
Final	Chelsea	(Wembley)	2-1

Carabao Cup

Third Round	Nottingham F	(h)	5-0
Fourth Round	Liverpool	(a)	5-5

(Liverpool won 5-4 on penalties)

UEFA Europa League

Group F	Eintracht Frankfurt	(a)	3-0
Group F	Standard Liege	(h)	4-0
Group F	Vitoria de Guimaraes	(h)	3-2
Group F	Vitoria de Guimaraes	(a)	1-1
Group F	Eintracht Frankfurt	(h)	1-2
Group F	Standard Liege	(a)	2-2
Round of 32	Olympiacos	(a)	1-0
Round of 32	Olympiacos	(h)	1-2

Leasing.com Trophy (Arsenal U21)

Group H (S) Northampton T (a) 1-1

(Northampton T won 4-3 on penalties)

Group H (S) Peterborough U (a) 0-1

Group H (S) Cambridge U (a) 1-1

(Arsenal U21 won 4-3 on penalties)

ASTON VILLA

FOUNDATION

Cricketing enthusiasts of Villa Cross Wesleyan Chapel, Aston, Birmingham decided to form a football club during the winter of 1874–75. Football clubs were few and far between in the Birmingham area and in their first game against Aston Brook St Mary's rugby team they played one half rugby and the other soccer. In 1876 they were joined by Scottish soccer enthusiast George Ramsay who was immediately appointed captain and went on to lead Aston Villa from obscurity to one of the country's top clubs in a period of less than ten years.

Villa Park, Trinity Road, Birmingham B6 6HE.

Telephone: (0121) 327 2299.

Ticket Office: (0333) 323 1874.

Website: www.avfc.co.uk

Email: postmaster@avfc.co.uk

Ground Capacity: 42,095.

Record Attendance: 76,588 v Derby Co, FA Cup 6th rd, 2 March 1946.

Pitch Measurements: 105m × 68m (115yd × 74.5yd).

Executive Chairman: Nassef Sawiris.

Co-Chairman: Wes Edens.

Chief Executive: Christian Purslow.

Head Coach: Dean Smith.

Assistant Head Coaches: Richard O'Kelly, John Terry.

Colours: Claret shirts with sky blue sleeves, white shorts with sky blue trim, sky blue socks with claret trim.

Year Formed: 1874.

Turned Professional: 1885.

Club Nickname: 'The Villans'.

Grounds: 1874, Wilson Road and Aston Park (also used Aston Lower Grounds for some matches); 1876, Wellington Road, Perry Barr; 1897, Villa Park.

First Football League Game: 8 September 1888, Football League, v Wolverhampton W (a) D 1–1 – Warner; Cox, Coulton; Yates, Harry Devey, Dawson; Albert Brown, Green (1), Allen, Garvey, Hodgetts.

Record League Victory: 12–2 v Accrington S, Division 1, 12 March 1892 – Warner; Evans, Cox; Harry Devey, Jimmy Cowan, Baird; Athersmith (1), Dickson (2), John Devey (4), Lewis Campbell (4), Hodgetts (1).

HONOURS

League Champions: Division 1 – 1893–94, 1895–96, 1896–97, 1898–99, 1899–1900, 1909–10, 1980–81; Division 2 – 1937–38, 1959–60; Division 3 – 1971–72.
Runners-up: Premier League – 1992–93; Division 1 – 1902–03, 1907–08, 1910–11, 1912–13, 1913–14, 1930–31, 1932–33, 1989–90; Football League 1888–89; Division 2 – 1974–75, 1987–88.

FA Cup Winners: 1887, 1895, 1897, 1905, 1913, 1920, 1957.
Runners-up: 1892, 1924, 2000, 2015.

League Cup Winners: 1961, 1975, 1977, 1994, 1996.
Runners-up: 1963, 1971, 2010, 2020.

Double Performed: 1896–97.

European Competitions
European Cup: 1981–82 *(winners)*, 1982–83 *(qf)*.
UEFA Cup: 1975–76, 1977–78 *(qf)*, 1983–84, 1990–91, 1993–94, 1994–95, 1996–97, 1997–98 *(qf)*, 1998–99, 2001–02, 2008–09.
Europa League: 2009–10, 2010–11.
Intertoto Cup: 2000, 2001 *(winners)*, 2002 *(sf)*, 2008 *(qualified for UEFA Cup)*.
Super Cup: 1982 *(winners)*.
World Club Championship: 1982.

FOOTBALL YEARBOOK FACT FILE

The first named substitute for Aston Villa in a Football League game was Lew Chatterley who sat on the bench for the opening game of the 1965–66 season. The first substitute used by Villa was Graham Parker who replaced the injured Tony Hateley after eight minutes of the home game with Tottenham Hotspur on 25 September 1965.

Record Cup Victory: 13–0 v Wednesbury Old Ath, FA Cup 1st rd, 30 October 1886 – Warner; Coulton, Simmonds; Yates, Robertson, Burton (2); Richard Davis (1), Albert Brown (3), Hunter (3), Loach (2), Hodgetts (2).

Record Defeat: 0–8 v Chelsea, Premier League, 23 December 2012.

Most League Points (2 for a win): 70, Division 3, 1971–72.

Most League Points (3 for a win): 83, FL C, 2017–18.

Most League Goals: 128, Division 1, 1930–31.

Highest League Scorer in Season: 'Pongo' Waring, 49, Division 1, 1930–31.

Most League Goals in Total Aggregate: Harry Hampton, 215, 1904–15.

Most League Goals in One Match: 5, Harry Hampton v Sheffield W, Division 1, 5 October 1912; 5, Harold Halse v Derby Co, Division 1, 19 October 1912; 5, Len Capewell v Burnley, Division 1, 29 August 1925; 5, George Brown v Leicester C, Division 1, 2 January 1932; 5, Gerry Hitchens v Charlton Ath, Division 2, 18 November 1959.

Most Capped Player: Steve Staunton, 64 (102), Republic of Ireland.

Most League Appearances: Charlie Aitken, 561, 1961–76.

Youngest League Player: Jimmy Brown, 15 years 349 days v Bolton W, 17 September 1969.

Record Transfer Fee Received: £32,500,000 from Liverpool for Christian Benteke, July 2015.

Record Transfer Fee Paid: £22,500,000 to Club Brugge for Wesley Moraes, June 2019.

Football League Record: 1888 Founder Member of the League; 1936–38 Division 2; 1938–59 Division 1; 1959–60 Division 2; 1960–67 Division 1; 1967–70 Division 2; 1970–72 Division 3; 1972–75 Division 2; 1975–87 Division 1; 1987–88 Division 2; 1988–92 Division 1; 1992–2016 Premier League; 2016–19 FL C; 2019– Premier League.

MANAGERS

George Ramsay 1884–1926
(*Secretary-Manager*)
W. J. Smith 1926–34
(*Secretary-Manager*)
Jimmy McMullan 1934–35
Jimmy Hogan 1936–44
Alex Massie 1945–50
George Martin 1950–53
Eric Houghton 1953–58
Joe Mercer 1958–64
Dick Taylor 1964–67
Tommy Cummings 1967–68
Tommy Docherty 1968–70
Vic Crowe 1970–74
Ron Saunders 1974–82
Tony Barton 1982–84
Graham Turner 1984–86
Billy McNeill 1986–87
Graham Taylor 1987–90
Dr Jozef Venglos 1990–91
Ron Atkinson 1991–94
Brian Little 1994–98
John Gregory 1998–2002
Graham Taylor OBE 2002–03
David O'Leary 2003–06
Martin O'Neill 2006–10
Gerard Houllier 2010–11
Alex McLeish 2011–12
Paul Lambert 2012–15
Tim Sherwood 2015
Remi Garde 2015–16
Roberto Di Matteo 2016
Steve Bruce 2016–18
Dean Smith October 2018–

LATEST SEQUENCES

Longest Sequence of League Wins: 10, 2.3.2019 – 22.4.2019.

Longest Sequence of League Defeats: 11, 14.2.2016 – 30.4.2016.

Longest Sequence of League Draws: 6, 12.9.1981 – 10.10.1981.

Longest Sequence of Unbeaten League Matches: 15, 12.3.1949 – 27.8.1949.

Longest Sequence Without a League Win: 19, 14.8.2015 – 2.1.2016.

Successive Scoring Runs: 35 from 10.11.1895.

Successive Non-scoring Runs: 6 from 26.12.2014.

TEN YEAR LEAGUE RECORD

		P	*W*	*D*	*L*	*F*	*A*	*Pts*	*Pos*
2010-11	PR Lge	38	12	12	14	48	59	48	9
2011-12	PR Lge	38	7	17	14	37	53	38	16
2012-13	PR Lge	38	10	11	17	47	69	41	15
2013-14	PR Lge	38	10	8	20	39	61	38	15
2014-15	PR Lge	38	10	8	20	31	57	38	17
2015-16	PR Lge	38	3	8	27	27	76	17	20
2016-17	FL C	46	16	14	16	47	48	62	13
2017-18	FL C	46	24	11	11	72	42	83	4
2018-19	FL C	46	20	16	10	82	61	76	5
2019-20	PR Lge	38	9	8	21	41	67	35	17

DID YOU KNOW ?

When Aston Villa won the Football League title in 1980–81 they used just 14 players during the season, seven of whom were ever-present throughout the campaign. The number 3 shirt was the most used, being taken by three different players during the season.

ASTON VILLA – PREMIER LEAGUE 2019–20 LEAGUE RECORD

Match No.	Date	Venue	Opponents	Result		H/T Score	Lg Pos.	Goalscorers	Attendance
1	Aug 10	A	Tottenham H	L	1-3	1-0	16	McGinn [9]	60,407
2	17	H	Bournemouth	L	1-2	0-2	16	Douglas Luiz [71]	40,996
3	23	H	Everton	W	2-0	1-0	11	Wesley [21], El Ghazi [90]	41,922
4	31	A	Crystal Palace	L	0-1	0-0	18		25,248
5	Sept 16	H	West Ham U	D	0-0	0-0	17		42,010
6	22	A	Arsenal	L	2-3	1-0	18	McGinn [20], Wesley [60]	60,331
7	28	H	Burnley	D	2-2	1-0	18	El Ghazi [33], McGinn [79]	41,546
8	Oct 5	A	Norwich C	W	5-1	2-0	14	Wesley 2 [14, 30], Grealish [49], Hourihane [61], Douglas Luiz [83]	27,045
9	19	H	Brighton & HA	W	2-1	1-1	11	Grealish [45], Targett [90]	41,826
10	26	A	Manchester C	L	0-3	0-0	14		54,506
11	Nov 2	H	Liverpool	L	1-2	1-0	16	Trezeguet [21]	41,878
12	10	A	Wolverhampton W	L	1-2	0-1	17	Trezeguet [90]	31,607
13	25	H	Newcastle U	W	2-0	2-0	15	Hourihane [32], El Ghazi [36]	41,821
14	Dec 1	A	Manchester U	D	2-2	1-1	15	Grealish [11], Mings [66]	73,381
15	4	A	Chelsea	L	1-2	1-1	15	Trezeguet [41]	40,628
16	8	H	Leicester C	L	1-4	1-2	17	Grealish [45]	41,908
17	14	A	Sheffield U	L	0-2	0-0	17		30,396
18	21	H	Southampton	L	1-3	0-2	18	Grealish [75]	41,834
19	26	H	Norwich C	W	1-0	0-0	18	Hourihane [64]	41,289
20	28	A	Watford	L	0-3	0-1	18		21,348
21	Jan 1	A	Burnley	W	2-1	2-0	17	Wesley [27], Grealish [41]	19,561
22	12	H	Manchester C	L	1-6	0-4	18	El Ghazi (pen) [90]	41,823
23	18	A	Brighton & HA	D	1-1	0-1	18	Grealish [75]	30,551
24	21	H	Watford	W	2-1	0-1	16	Douglas Luiz [68], Mings [90]	40,867
25	Feb 1	A	Bournemouth	L	1-2	0-2	17	Samatta [70]	10,722
26	16	H	Tottenham H	L	2-3	1-2	17	Alderweireld (og) [9], Engels [53]	41,874
27	22	A	Southampton	L	0-2	0-1	17		31,478
28	Mar 9	A	Leicester C	L	0-4	0-1	19		32,125
29	June 17	H	Sheffield U	D	0-0	0-0	19		0
30	21	H	Chelsea	L	1-2	1-0	19	Hause [43]	0
31	24	A	Newcastle U	D	1-1	0-0	19	Elmohamady [83]	0
32	27	H	Wolverhampton W	L	0-1	0-0	19		0
33	July 5	A	Liverpool	L	0-2	0-0	18		0
34	9	H	Manchester U	L	0-3	0-2	19		0
35	12	H	Crystal Palace	W	2-0	1-0	19	Trezeguet 2 [45, 59]	0
36	16	A	Everton	D	1-1	0-0	19	Konsa [72]	0
37	21	H	Arsenal	W	1-0	1-0	17	Trezeguet [27]	0
38	26	A	West Ham U	D	1-1	0-0	17	Grealish [84]	0

Final League Position: 17

GOALSCORERS

League (41): Grealish 8, Trezeguet 6, Wesley 5, El Ghazi 4 (1 pen), Douglas Luiz 3, Hourihane 3, McGinn 3, Mings 2, Elmohamady 1, Engels 1, Hause 1, Konsa 1, Samatta 1, Targett 1, own goal 1.
FA Cup (1): El Ghazi 1.
Carabao Cup (20): Hourihane 4, Grealish 2, Guilbert 2, Kodjia 2, Davis 1, El Ghazi 1, Elmohamady 1, Jota 1, Konsa 1, Samatta 1, Targett 1, Trezeguet 1, Wesley 1, own goal 1.
Leasing.com Trophy (1): Archer 1.

Heaton T 20	Elmohamady A 11 + 7	Engels B 15 + 2	Mings T 33	Taylor N 11 + 3	Hourihane C 18 + 9	Trezeguet M 20 + 14	McGinn J 27 + 1	Grealish J 36	El Ghazi A 26 + 8	Wesley M 21	Jota R 4 + 6	Kodjia J — + 6	Douglas Luiz 28 + 8	Davis K 4 + 14	Guilbert F 22 + 3	Lansbury H 2 + 8	Nakamba M 19 + 10	Targett M 27 + 1	Konsa E 24 + 1	Steer J 1	Nyland O 5 + 2	Hause K 17 + 1	Drinkwater D 4	Reina J 12	Vassilev I — + 4	Samatta M 11 + 3	Borja Baston G — + 2	*Match No.*
1	2	3	4	5	6^{3}	7^{1}	8	9	10	11^{2}	12	13	14															1
1	2	3	4	5		9^{2}	6	8	11^{1}	10	12		7	13														2
1	13	3	4	5		10^{2}	8	9	12	11	7^{1}		6		2													3
1		3	4	5	13	11■	6	8		10^{3}	9^{1}		7^{2}	12	2	14												4
1	12	3	4	5			8	6	11	10	9^{1}		13	14	2^{3}		7^{2}											5
1	12	3	4	5	13	9^{1}	6	8	11^{3}	10					2	14	7^{2}											6
1		3	4	12	8	13	6	11	9^{2}	10^{3}				14	2		7	5^{1}										7
1		3^{2}	4		8^{3}	12	6	11	9^{1}	10			14		2		7	5	13									8
1		3	4		8^{1}	12	6	11	9^{3}	10^{2}			14	13	2		7	5										9
1		3	4			7	8	10^{2}	13	11^{1}			9	12	2		6	5										10
1	12	3	4		13	11	6		9	10^{3}		14	8^{2}		2^{1}		7	5										11
			4	13		11	6		9	10			8		2	14	7^{3}	5^{2}	3	1^{1}	12							12
1			4		8^{1}		6	11	9	10			7		2	12		5	3									13
1			4		8^{2}	12	6	11	9^{1}	10			7		2	13		5	3									14
1	2		4		8^{1}	9^{2}	6	11		10	13		12				7	5	3									15
1	2	12	4^{1}			13	8	10	7	11			9		14		6^{2}	5^{3}	3									16
1		3				14	6	11	9^{3}	10^{2}		13	12		2	8^{1}	7	5				4						17
1		3			8^{2}	14	6^{1}	11	9^{3}	10		13	7		2		12	5				4						18
1	2				12	10^{2}		9	8^{3}	11	13		7			14	6^{1}	5	3			4						19
1	2				7			10	12	11	8^{1}	14	6		13	9^{3}		5^{2}	3			4						20
1^{3}			3	8	13	9^{2}		11		10^{1}		12	6		5		7		2		14	4						21
	2		4	6	9^{2}	13		11	10				7^{1}			14	12		3		1	5	8^{3}					22
			3		14	9^{1}		11	10				13		5		7^{3}	8	2			4	6^{2}	1	12			23
			3			9^{2}		11	10				12		5		7	8	2			4	6^{1}	1	13			24
		12	3			14		11	9^{2}				7	13	5		6^{3}	8	2^{1}			4		1		10		25
		3				13		11	9^{2}				7		5		12	8	2			4	6^{1}	1		10^{3}	14	26
			3		13	12		10	9^{1}				7		5		6^{3}	8	2^{2}			4		1		11	14	27
	7^{1}	3	4		9^{2}			10	12				8	13	2		6	5						1		11		28
	14		4		6	12	8^{4}	11	9^{2}				7	10^{1}			15	5	2^{3}		1	3				13		29
			4		8^{3}	13	6^{4}	11	9^{2}		15		7	10^{1}			14	5	2		1	3				12		30
	14		4		13	11^{1}	6^{3}	8	9^{2}				7	12			15	5	2^{4}		1	3				10		31
	13		4	12	7^{2}	15	14	9	16				6	11^{5}			8^{4}	5^{1}	2^{3}		1	3				10		32
			4	5		11^{3}	8	6	9^{1}		13		7	10^{2}					2			3		1	14	12		33
			4	5	12	9	8^{2}	10	6^{1}				7^{4}	13			14		2			3		1	15	11^{3}		34
	2		4	5^{1}	8^{2}	9^{4}	6	11	15				7	13			14	12	3					1		10^{3}		35
	2		4		8	9^{1}	6	11	13				7	12				5	3					1		10^{2}		36
	2^{1}		4		8^{3}	9	6^{4}	11					7	13	12	15	14	5	3					1		10^{2}		37
			4		9^{2}	7^{4}	8	10	15				6	12	2^{3}		13	5	3			14		1		11^{1}		38

FA Cup

Third Round	Fulham	(a)	1-2

Carabao Cup

Second Round	Crewe Alex	(a)	6-1
Third Round	Brighton & HA	(a)	3-1
Fourth Round	Wolverhampton W	(h)	2-1
Quarter-Final	Liverpool	(h)	5-0
Semi-Final 1st leg	Leicester C	(a)	1-1
Semi-Final 2nd leg	Leicester C	(h)	2-1
Final	Manchester C	(Wembley)	1-2

Leasing.com Trophy (Aston Villa U21)

Group C (N)	Salford C	(a)	0-2
Group C (N)	Tranmere R	(a)	1-2

BARNSLEY

FOUNDATION

Many clubs owe their inception to the Church and Barnsley are among them, for they were formed in 1887 by the Rev. T. T. Preedy, curate of Barnsley St Peter's, and went under that name until it was dropped in 1897 a year before being admitted to the Second Division of the Football League.

Oakwell Stadium, Grove Street, Barnsley, South Yorkshire S71 1ET.

Telephone: (01226) 211 211.

Ticket Office: (01226) 211 183.

Website: www.barnsleyfc.co.uk

Email: administration@barnsleyfc.co.uk

Ground Capacity: 23,287.

Record Attendance: 40,255 v Stoke C, FA Cup 5th rd, 15 February 1936.

Pitch Measurements: 100.5m × 67m (110yd × 73.5yd).

Co-Chairmen: Chien Lee, Paul Conway.

Chief Executive: Dane Murphy.

Head Coach: Gerhard Struber.

First-Team Coaches: Matt Rose, Max Senft, Adam Murray.

Colours: Red shirts with white trim, white shorts with red trim, red socks with white trim.

Year Formed: 1887.

Turned Professional: 1888.

Previous Name: 1887, Barnsley St Peter's; 1897, Barnsley.

Club Nickname: 'The Tykes', 'The Reds', 'The Colliers'.

Ground: 1887, Oakwell.

First Football League Game: 1 September 1898, Division 2, v Lincoln C (a) L 0–1 – Fawcett; McArtney, Nixon; King, Burleigh, Porteous; Davis, Lees, Murray, McCullough, McGee.

Record League Victory: 9–0 v Loughborough T, Division 2, 28 January 1899 – Greaves; McArtney, Nixon; Porteous, Burleigh, Howard; Davis (4), Hepworth (1), Lees (1), McCullough (1), Jones (2). 9–0 v Accrington S, Division 3 (N), 3 February 1934 – Ellis; Cookson, Shotton; Harper, Henderson, Whitworth; Spence (2), Smith (1), Blight (4), Andrews (1), Ashton (1).

Record Cup Victory: 6–0 v Blackpool, FA Cup 1st rd replay, 20 January 1910 – Mearns; Downs, Ness; Glendinning, Boyle (1), Utley; Bartrop, Gadsby (1), Lillycrop (2), Tufnell (2), Forman. 6–0 v Peterborough U, League Cup 1st rd 2nd leg, 15 September 1981 – Horn; Joyce, Chambers, Glavin (2), Banks, McCarthy, Evans, Parker (2), Aylott (1), McHale, Barrowclough (1).

Record Defeat: 0–9 v Notts Co, Division 2, 19 November 1927.

Most League Points (2 for a win): 67, Division 3 (N), 1938–39.

Most League Points (3 for a win): 91, FL 1, 2018–19.

HONOURS

League Champions: Division 3N – 1933–34, 1938–39, 1954–55.
Runners-up: First Division – 1996–97; FL 1 – 2018–19; Division 3 – 1980–81; Division 3N – 1953–54; Division 4 – 1967–68.

FA Cup Winners: 1912.
Runners-up: 1910.

League Cup: quarter-final – 1982.

League Trophy Winners: 2016.

FOOTBALL YEARBOOK FACT FILE

Barnsley had their first taste of football abroad when they embarked on a 25-day tour of Europe following their FA Cup final defeat in 1910. The Reds began in Paris against Swindon Town and went on to play 11 fixtures in Central Europe, winning eight including a 12-2 victory over Graz. The tour was blamed for their poor form the following season when they finished second to bottom of Division Two and had to seek re-election.

Most League Goals: 118, Division 3 (N), 1933–34.

Highest League Scorer in Season: Cecil McCormack, 33, Division 2, 1950–51.

Most League Goals in Total Aggregate: Ernest Hine, 123, 1921–26 and 1934–38.

Most League Goals in One Match: 5, Frank Eaton v South Shields, Division 3 (N), 9 April 1927; 5, Peter Cunningham v Darlington, Division 3 (N), 4 February 1933; 5, Beau Asquith v Darlington, Division 3 (N), 12 November 1938; 5, Cecil McCormack v Luton T, Division 2, 9 September 1950.

Most Capped Player: Gerry Taggart, 35 (51), Northern Ireland.

Most League Appearances: Barry Murphy, 514, 1962–78.

Youngest League Player: Reuben Noble-Lazarus, 15 years 45 days v Ipswich T, 30 September 2008.

Record Transfer Fee Received: £3,000,000 (rising to £10,125,000) from Everton for John Stones, January 2013.

Record Transfer Fee Paid: £1,500,000 to Partizan Belgrade for Georgi Hristov, July 1997; £1,500,000 to QPR for Mike Sheron, January 1999.

Football League Record: 1898 Elected to Division 2; 1932–34 Division 3 (N); 1934–38 Division 2; 1938–39 Division 3 (N); 1946–53 Division 2; 1953–55 Division 3 (N); 1955–59 Division 2; 1959–65 Division 3; 1965–68 Division 4; 1968–72 Division 3; 1972–79 Division 4; 1979–81 Division 3; 1981–92 Division 2; 1992–97 Division 1; 1997–98 Premier League; 1998–2002 Division 1; 2002–04 Division 2; 2004–06 FL 1; 2006–14 FL C; 2014–16 FL 1; 2016–18 FL C; 2018–19 FL 1; 2019– FL C.

LATEST SEQUENCES

Longest Sequence of League Wins: 10, 5.3.1955 – 23.4.1955.

Longest Sequence of League Defeats: 9, 14.3.1953 – 25.4.1953.

Longest Sequence of League Draws: 7, 28.3.1911 – 22.4.1911.

Longest Sequence of Unbeaten League Matches: 21, 1.1.1934 – 5.5.1934.

Longest Sequence Without a League Win: 26, 13.12.1952 – 26.8.1953.

Successive Scoring Runs: 44 from 2.10.1926.

Successive Non-scoring Runs: 6 from 27.11.1971.

MANAGERS

Arthur Fairclough 1898–1901 (*Secretary-Manager*)
John McCartney 1901–04 (*Secretary-Manager*)
Arthur Fairclough 1904–12
John Hastie 1912–14
Percy Lewis 1914–19
Peter Sant 1919–26
John Commins 1926–29
Arthur Fairclough 1929–30
Brough Fletcher 1930–37
Angus Seed 1937–53
Tim Ward 1953–60
Johnny Steele 1960–71 (*continued as General Manager*)
John McSeveney 1971–72
Johnny Steele (*General Manager*) 1972–73
Jim Iley 1973–78
Allan Clarke 1978–80
Norman Hunter 1980–84
Bobby Collins 1984–85
Allan Clarke 1985–89
Mel Machin 1989–93
Viv Anderson 1993–94
Danny Wilson 1994–98
John Hendrie 1998–99
Dave Bassett 1999–2000
Nigel Spackman 2001
Steve Parkin 2001–02
Glyn Hodges 2002–03
Gudjon Thordarson 2003–04
Paul Hart 2004–05
Andy Ritchie 2005–06
Simon Davey 2007–09 (*Caretaker from November 2006*)
Mark Robins 2009–11
Keith Hill 2011–12
David Flitcroft 2012–13
Danny Wilson 2013–15
Lee Johnson 2015–16
Paul Heckingbottom 2016–18
Jose Morais 2018
Daniel Stendel 2018–19
Gerhard Struber November 2019–

TEN YEAR LEAGUE RECORD

		P	W	D	L	F	A	Pts	Pos
2010-11	FL C	46	14	14	18	55	66	56	17
2011-12	FL C	46	13	9	24	49	74	48	21
2012-13	FL C	46	14	13	19	56	70	55	21
2013-14	FL C	46	9	12	25	44	77	39	23
2014-15	FL 1	46	17	11	18	62	61	62	11
2015-16	FL 1	46	22	8	16	70	54	74	6
2016-17	FL C	46	15	13	18	64	67	58	14
2017-18	FL C	46	9	14	23	48	72	41	22
2018-19	FL 1	46	26	13	7	80	39	91	2
2019-20	FL C	46	12	13	21	49	69	49	21

DID YOU KNOW ?

In November 1954 Lol Chappell scored a hat-trick in two successive League games to equal a 34-year-old club record. He finished the season with a total of 21 League goals as the Reds won the Division Three North championship.

BARNSLEY – SKY BET CHAMPIONSHIP 2019–20 LEAGUE RECORD

Match No.	Date	Venue	Opponents	Result	H/T Score	Lg Pos.	Goalscorers	Attendance
1	Aug 3	H	Fulham	W 1-0	1-0	7	Thomas 13	14,823
2	10	A	Sheffield W	L 0-2	0-1	15		28,028
3	17	H	Charlton Ath	D 2-2	1-1	13	Woodrow 34, Chaplin 48	13,006
4	20	A	Birmingham C	L 0-2	0-0	17		20,061
5	24	H	Luton T	L 1-3	0-3	21	Wilks 72	13,250
6	31	A	Wigan Ath	D 0-0	0-0	21		23,792
7	Sept 15	H	Leeds U	L 0-2	0-0	22		17,598
8	21	A	Nottingham F	L 0-1	0-0	22		29,202
9	29	H	Brentford	L 1-3	1-1	22	Woodrow 1	12,188
10	Oct 2	H	Derby Co	D 2-2	1-2	22	Halme 13, Woodrow 90	13,634
11	5	A	Preston NE	L 1-5	1-1	23	McGeehan 43	12,431
12	19	H	Swansea C	D 1-1	0-0	24	Mowatt 70	12,424
13	22	A	WBA	D 2-2	2-0	24	Woodrow 2 18, 24	22,086
14	26	A	Huddersfield T	L 1-2	0-1	24	Brown 79	22,718
15	Nov 1	H	Bristol C	D 2-2	0-1	23	Halme 77, Woodrow 90	12,178
16	9	H	Stoke C	L 2-4	0-2	24	McGeehan 47, Schmidt 82	14,891
17	23	A	Blackburn R	L 2-3	0-1	24	Chaplin 48, Woodrow 82	13,781
18	27	A	Middlesbrough	L 0-1	0-0	24		18,043
19	30	H	Hull C	W 3-1	1-0	24	Mowatt 23, Bahre 75, Chaplin 90	13,598
20	Dec 7	A	Cardiff C	L 2-3	1-1	24	Chaplin 17, Peltier (og) 48	21,380
21	11	H	Reading	D 1-1	0-0	24	Woodrow 58	11,510
22	14	H	QPR	W 5-3	2-1	24	Chaplin 3 7, 18, 52, Woodrow (pen) 60, Diaby 82	12,212
23	21	A	Millwall	W 2-1	1-0	22	Chaplin 39, Schmidt 90	12,682
24	26	H	WBA	D 1-1	0-1	23	Halme 90	17,049
25	29	A	Swansea C	D 0-0	0-0	22		17,097
26	Jan 2	A	Derby Co	L 1-2	0-1	23	Simoes 50	27,782
27	11	H	Huddersfield T	W 2-1	1-0	22	Mowatt 14, Chaplin 65	17,158
28	18	A	Bristol C	L 0-1	0-0	22		20,570
29	21	H	Preston NE	L 0-3	0-3	22		12,207
30	Feb 1	A	Charlton Ath	L 1-2	0-2	23	Woodrow 71	19,870
31	8	H	Sheffield W	D 1-1	1-1	23	Woodrow 24	17,789
32	11	H	Birmingham C	L 0-1	0-0	23		12,788
33	15	A	Fulham	W 3-0	1-0	24	Woodrow 2 (1 pen) 24 (p), 79, Brown 51	18,516
34	22	H	Middlesbrough	W 1-0	0-0	23	Chaplin 73	16,106
35	26	A	Hull C	W 1-0	1-0	23	Woodrow 42	10,272
36	29	A	Reading	L 0-2	0-1	23		13,263
37	Mar 7	H	Cardiff C	L 0-2	0-0	24		12,751
38	June 20	A	QPR	W 1-0	1-0	23	Simoes 7	0
39	27	H	Millwall	D 0-0	0-0	24		0
40	30	H	Blackburn R	W 2-0	0-0	23	Chaplin 58, Brown 76	0
41	July 4	A	Stoke C	L 0-4	0-3	23		0
42	7	A	Luton T	D 1-1	0-1	23	Halme 84	0
43	11	H	Wigan Ath	D 0-0	0-0	24		0
44	16	A	Leeds U	L 0-1	0-1	24		0
45	19	H	Nottingham F	W 1-0	0-0	23	Schmidt 90	0
46	22	A	Brentford	W 2-1	1-0	22	Styles 41, Odour 90	0

Final League Position: 21

GOALSCORERS

League (49): Woodrow 14 (2 pens), Chaplin 11, Halme 4, Brown 3, Mowatt 3, Schmidt 3, McGeehan 2, Simoes 2, Bahre 1, Diaby 1, Odour 1, Styles 1, Thomas 1, Wilks 1, own goal 1.
FA Cup (5): Chaplin 2, Brown 1, Thomas 1, Woodrow 1.
Carabao Cup (0).

Radlinger S 18	Sibbick T 17 + 1	Diaby B 21	Andersen M 37 + 1	Cavare D 11	McGeehan C 10 + 3	Mowatt A 44	Thomas L 24 + 15	Bahre M 20 + 6	Wilks M 8 + 7	Woodrow C 37 + 3	Chaplin C 36 + 8	Thiam M 3 + 5	Miller G — + 1	Styles C 5 + 12	Williams B 16 + 4	Schmidt P 2 + 27	Halme A 26 + 6	Pinillos D 2 + 2	Green J — + 2	Collins B 19	Williams J 29 + 1	Brown J 39 + 1	Dougall K 9 + 3	Simoes E 6 + 11	Odour C 12 + 4	Ritzmaier M 13 + 2	Ludewig K 13 + 5	Sollbauer M 17	Walton J 9	Palmer R 3	Wolfe M — + 1	*Match No.*
1	2	3	4	5	6	7	8^1	9	10^2	11^3	12	13	14																			1
1	2	3	4	5	6	7^3	8	9^1	10^2	11	12	13		14																		2
1	2	3	4		8		6	7	9^2	11	10^1	12		13	5																	3
1	2	3	4		6	7	8^3	9^1	13		11	10^2			5	12	14															4
1	2	3^3	4^1		6	7	10	9	8			11			12		14	5^2	13													5
	6		3	2			8^2	7	9^3		11^1	10		14	5■	12	4	13		1												6
	6		3	2		7	10^1	14	11	9		12					4	13		1	5^2	8^3										7
	6		3		14	7	9		10	11^2	13					12	4^3	5		1	2^1	8										8
	6		3	2^3		7	10^2		13	11	9^1	14				12	4			1	5	8										9
	6		3^3			7	12	9	13	11	10			14	5		4			1	2^1	8^2										10
	3				6	7		10^2	12	11	9			13	5		4		14	1	2^3	8^1										11
	4	2^3	14	6^2	7^1	8				10	11				13		3			1		9	5	12								12
	4	2	3	6	7	8			12	10^2	11				13					1		9	5^1									13
	4	2	3	6^2	7^1	8	13		12	10	11									1		9	5									14
	4	2		6		8	12		10^1	11	7^2					13	3			1		9^3	5	14								15
	4^1	2		6	7^2	8	12		13	10	11^3					14	3			1		9	5									16
1	6	2	3			9	14	7^3		8	13				4	11^2	5^1					10	12									17
1		3	4	2	12	7	9^2	6^1		10	8				5	13						11										18
1		3	4			8	12	7^1		9^2	11				5	13	6				2	10										19
1		3	4			8		7^2		9	11				5	12	6				2	10^1			13							20
1	12	3	4			8		7		9	11				5^1	13					2	10^2	6									21
1		3	4		13	8	12	7^1		9	10										2	11	6		5^2							22
1		3	4			8	12	7^1		9^2	11					13	6				2	10			5							23
1		3	4			8^2	6	13		9	11					12	7				2	10^1			5							24
1		3	4			8^1	6	12		9	11					13	7				2	10^2			5							25
1		3	4			8	9	6^1			10					11^2	7				2	13		12	5							26
1		3	4			9	6^1				11^2					12	7				2	10		13	5	8						27
			4			9	6^2				11				5^1		3			1	2	10	7	13		8	12					28
1			4			9	6^2			12	11^3			13		14	3				2	10	7^1			8	5					29
1			4			8	6			10	11^3					14	7				2^2	9		12	5^1		13	3				30
			4			7	6^1	13		9	10^2			12		14				1	2	11		8^3	5			3				31
			4			7	14	13		9	11			6^2						1	2	10		8^3	5^1		12	3				32
						6	7^1	8		9^3	11^2					13	4			1	5	10	12	14			2	3				33
						7	12	6^2		9	11^1						3			1	4	10			8	13	5	2				34
						7	6^3	8^2		9	11				14		4			1	2	10			5^1	13	12	3				35
						7	12	14		9	11^3					13	3			1	4	10			8^1	6^2	5	2				36
						7	6			9	11^2				5	13	4			1		10^1		12		8	2	3				37
			3			7	15			11^3	12			14	4							9	13	10^1		8	5^4	2	1	6^2		38
			3			7	14			11^3	12			13	4		15					10		9^1		8^2	5	2	1	6^4		39
			3			7	13			11^5	15			12	4	16					5^2	10		9^4		8^3	14	2	1	6^1		40
			3			6	7			9^5	11			14	4^3	16					13	10^2		12	15	8^1	5^4	2	1			41
			3			6		7^1		9^4	11^3			13		15	14				4^2	10		12		8	5	2	1			42
			4			6				11^1	12			8		13	14				5	10		9		7^3	2^2	3	1			43
			4			6	12			9	11			8		13	7^1				5^3	10^2			14		2	3	1			44
			3			7	9^2			12	11			8		14	15				4^4	10				6^3	5^1	2	1		13	45
			3			7	9^1			13	11^2			8		15					4	10		12	14	6^3	5^4	2	1			46

FA Cup

Third Round	Crewe Alex	(a)	3-1
Fourth Round	Portsmouth	(a)	2-4

Carabao Cup

First Round	Carlisle U	(h)	0-3

BARROW

FOUNDATION

Barrow was home to a number of junior soccer clubs at the start of the twentieth century before a public meeting was called to set up a senior team in the town. Almost 800 people attended the meeting held in the Drill Hall on the night of Tuesday 16 July 1901 which resulted in the formation of Barrow Association Football Club. A team was put together made up, in the main, of seasoned professionals, some of whom were described as "bordering the veteran stage" and £300 was spent on laying out the club's new ground. The newly formed Barrow AFC were elected to the Lancashire League for the 1901–02 season and after making a promising start they eventually finished 10th out of 14 clubs.

The Progression Solicitors Stadium, Wilkie Road, Barrow-in-Furness, Cumbria LA14 5UW.

Telephone: (01229) 666010.

Website: www.barrowafc.com

Email: office@barrowafc.com

Ground Capacity: 5,916.

Record Attendance: 16,854 v Swansea T, FA Cup 3rd rd, 9 January 1954.

Pitch Measurements: 100.5m × 67.5m (110yd × 74yd).

Chairman: Paul Hornby.

Directors: Tony Shearer, Kristian Wilkes, Mark Hetherington.

Manager: David Dunn.

Assistant Manager: Rob Kelly.

Colours: Blue shirts with white trim, blue shorts with white trim, white socks with blue trim.

Year Formed: 1901.

Turned Professional: 1908.

Club Nickname: 'The Bluebirds'.

HONOURS

League Champions: National League – 2019–20; National League North – 2014–15. Lancashire Combination – 1920–21.
Runners-up: Lancashire Combination Division 2 – 1904–05.

FA Cup: Never past 3rd rd.

League Cup: Never past 2nd rd.

FA Trophy Winners: 1989–90, 2009–10.

Lancashire Senior Cup Winners: 1954–55.

FOOTBALL YEARBOOK FACT FILE

Barrow led Gillingham 7-0 in their Fourth Division match in October 1961 when the game was abandoned due to bad light. The Monday night game, played before floodlights were installed at Holker Street, started half an hour after the scheduled 5.15 p.m. kick-off because Gillingham missed their train out of Euston and had to make the 330-mile journey by plane and car. The Football League management committee decided that the result should stand and the Gills, who spent an extra £600 on their travelling costs, escaped without a fine.

Grounds: 1901, The Strawberry Ground; 1904, Ainslie Street; 1905, Little Park, Roose; 1909, Holker Street (renamed The Progression Solicitors Stadium 2019).

Record League Victory: 12–1 v Gateshead, Division 3(N), 5 May 1934.

Record League Defeat: 1–10 v Hartlepools U, Division 4, 4 April 1966–67.

Most League Points (2 for a win): 59, Division 4, 1966–67.

Most League Goals: 116, Division 3(N), 1933–34.

Highest League Scorer in Season: 39, Jimmy Shankly, Division 3(N), 1933–34.

Highest League Goals in One Match: 5, Jimmy Shankly v Gateshead, Division 3(N), 5 May 1934.

Most League Goals in Total Aggregate: Billy Gordon, 145, 1949–58.

Most Capped Player: Willie Millar, 2, Northern Ireland.

Most League Appearances: Brian Arrowsmith, 378, 1952–71.

Football League Record: 1921 Original Member of Division 3 (N); 1958–67 Division 4; 1967–70 Division 3; 1970–72 Division 4; 1972 Failed to gain re-election to Football League; 2020 Promoted from National League; 2020– FL 2.

MANAGERS

Jacob Fletcher 1901–04; **E. Freeland** 1904–05; **W. Smith** 1905–06; **Alec Craig** 1906–07; **Roger Charnley** 1907–08; **Jacob Fletcher** 1908–09; **Jas P. Phillips** 1909–13; **John Parker** 1913–20; **William Dickinson** 1920–22; **Jimmy Atkinson** 1922–23; **J. E. Moralee** 1923–26; **Robert Greenhalgh** 1926; **William Dickinson** 1926–27; **John S. Maconnachie** 1927–28; **Andrew Walker** 1929–30; **Thomas Miller** 1930; **John Commins** 1930–32; **Tommy Lowes** 1932–37; **James Y. Bissett** 1937; **Fred Pentland** 1938–40; **John Commins** 1945–47; **Andy Beattie** 1947–49; **Jack Hacking** 1949–55; **Joe Harvey** 1955–57; **Norman Dodgin** 1957–58; **Willie Brown** 1958–59; **Bill Rogers** 1959; **Ron Staniforth** 1959–64; **Don McEvoy** 1964–67; **Colin Appleton** 1967–69; **Fred Else** 1969; **Norman Bodell** 1969–70; **Don McEvoy** 1970–71; **Bill Rogers** 1971; **Jack Crompton** 1971–72; **Peter Kane** 1972–74; **Brian Arrowsmith** 1974–75; **Ron Yeats** 1975–77; **Alan Coglan and Billy McAdams** 1977; **David Hughes** 1977; **Brian McManus** 1977–79; **Micky Taylor** 1979–83; **Vic Halom** 1983–84; **Peter McDonnell** 1984; **Joe Wojciechowicz** 1984; **Brian Kidd** 1984–85; **John Cooke** 1985; **Bob Murphy** 1985; **Maurice Whittle** 1985; **David Johnson** 1985–86; **Glenn Skivington and Neil McDonald** 1986; **Ray Wilkie** 1986; **Neil McDonald** 1991; **John King** 1991–92; **Graham Heathcote** 1992; **Richard Dinnis** 1992–93; **Mick Cloudsdale** 1993–94; **Tony Hesketh** 1994–96; **Neil McDonald and Franny Ventre** 1996; **Mike Walsh** 1996; **Owen Brown** 1996–99; **Shane Westley** 1999; **Greg Challender** 1999; **Kenny Lowe** 1999–2003; **Lee Turnbull** 2003–05; **Darren Edmondson** 2005; **Phil Wilson** 2005–07; **Darren Sheridan and David Bayliss** 2007–12; **David Bayliss** 2012–13; **Alex Meechan** 2013; **Darren Edmondson** 2013–15; **Paul Cox** 2015–17; **Micky Moore** 2017; **Neill Hornby** 2017; **Ady Pennock** 2017–18; **Ian Evatt** 2018–20; **David Dunn** July 2020–

TEN YEAR LEAGUE RECORD

		P	*W*	*D*	*L*	*F*	*A*	*Pts*	*Pos*
2010-11	NL	46	12	14	20	52	67	50	18
2011-12	NL	46	17	9	20	62	76	60	13
2012-13	NL	46	11	13	22	45	83	46	22
2013-14	NLN	42	14	14	14	50	56	56	11
2014-15	NLN	42	26	9	7	81	43	87	1
2015-16	NL	46	17	14	15	64	71	65	11
2016-17	NL	46	20	15	11	72	53	75	7
2017-18	NL	46	11	16	19	51	63	49	20
2018-19	NL	46	17	13	16	52	51	64	11
2019-20	NL	37	21	7	9	68	39	70	1§

§Decided on points-per-game (1.89)

DID YOU KNOW ?

Centre-forward George Munro was the first Barrow player to score a hat-trick in a Football League game when he netted three goals in a 5-2 win over Wrexham on New Year's Eve 1921. It was Barrow's highest score in their opening season in Division Three North and the victory lifted them off the bottom of the table.

BIRMINGHAM CITY

FOUNDATION

In 1875, cricketing enthusiasts who were largely members of Trinity Church, Bordesley, determined to continue their sporting relationships throughout the year by forming a football club which they called Small Heath Alliance. For their earliest games played on waste land in Arthur Street, the team included three Edden brothers and two James brothers.

St Andrew's Trillion Trophy Stadium, Cattell Road, Birmingham B9 4RL.

Telephone: (0121) 772 0101.

Ticket Office: (0121) 772 0101 (option 2).

Website: www.bcfc.com

Email: reception@bcfc.com

Ground Capacity: 29,805.

Record Attendance: 66,844 v Everton, FA Cup 5th rd, 11 February 1939.

Pitch Measurements: 100m × 65m (109.5yd × 71yd).

Directors: Wenqing Zhao, Chun Kong Yiu, Gannan Zheng, Yao Wang, Xuandong Ren.

Head Coach: Aitor Karanka.

Assistant Head Coach: Alberto Escobar.

Colours: Blue shirts with white sleeves, white shorts with blue trim, blue socks.

Year Formed: 1875.

Turned Professional: 1885.

Previous Names: 1875, Small Heath Alliance; 1888, dropped 'Alliance'; 1905, Birmingham; 1945, Birmingham City.

Club Nickname: 'Blues'.

Grounds: 1875, waste ground near Arthur St; 1877, Muntz St, Small Heath; 1906, St Andrew's (renamed St Andrew's Trillion Trophy Stadium 2018).

First Football League Game: 3 September 1892, Division 2, v Burslem Port Vale (h) W 5–1 – Charsley; Bayley, Speller; Ollis, Jenkyns, Devey; Hallam (1), Edwards (1), Short (1), Wheldon (2), Hands.

Record League Victory: 12–0 v Walsall T Swifts, Division 2, 17 December 1892 – Charsley; Bayley, Jones; Ollis, Jenkyns, Devey; Hallam (2), Walton (3), Mobley (3), Wheldon (2), Hands (2). 12–0 v Doncaster R, Division 2, 11 April 1903 – Dorrington; Goldie, Wassell; Beer, Dougherty (1), Howard; Athersmith, Leonard (4), McRoberts (1), Wilcox (4), Field (1), (1 og).

Record Cup Victory: 9–2 v Burton W, FA Cup 1st rd, 31 October 1885 – Hedges; Jones, Evetts (1); Fred James, Felton, Arthur James (1); Davenport (2), Stanley (4), Simms, Figures, Morris (1).

Record Defeat: 1–9 v Blackburn R, Division 1, 5 January 1895; 1–9 v Sheffield W, Division 1, 13 December 1930; 0–8 v Bournemouth, FLC, 25 October 2014.

HONOURS

League Champions: Division 2 – 1892–93, 1920–21, 1947–48, 1954–55; Second Division – 1994–95.
Runners-up: FL C – 2006–07, 2008–09; Division 2 – 1893–94, 1900–01, 1902–03; 1971–72, 1984–85; Division 3 – 1991–92.

FA Cup: *Runners-up:* 1931, 1956.

League Cup Winners: 1963, 2011.
Runners-up: 2001.

League Trophy Winners: 1991, 1995.

European Competitions
Fairs Cup: 1955–58, 1958–60 *(runners-up)*, 1960–61 *(runners-up)*, 1961–62.
Europa League: 2011–12.

FOOTBALL YEARBOOK FACT FILE

In 1955–56 Birmingham City reached the FA Cup final without playing a single tie at their home ground. After a 7-1 third round win at Torquay United they followed with victories at Leyton Orient, West Bromwich Albion and Arsenal before defeating Sunderland 3-0 in the semi-final at Hillsborough. They went on to lose 3-1 to Manchester City in the Wembley final.

Most League Points (2 for a win): 59, Division 2, 1947–48.

Most League Points (3 for a win): 89, Division 2, 1994–95.

Most League Goals: 103, Division 2, 1893–94 (only 28 games).

Highest League Scorer in Season: Walter Abbott, 34, Division 2, 1898–99 (Small Heath); Joe Bradford, 29, Division 1, 1927–28 (Birmingham City).

Most League Goals in Total Aggregate: Joe Bradford, 249, 1920–35.

Most League Goals in One Match: 5, Walter Abbott v Darwen, Division 2, 26 November, 1898; 5, John McMillan v Blackpool, Division 2, 2 March 1901; 5, James Windridge v Glossop, Division 2, 23 January 1915.

Most Capped Player: Maik Taylor, 58 (including 8 on loan at Fulham) (88), Northern Ireland.

Most League Appearances: Frank Womack, 491, 1908–28.

Youngest League Player: Jude Bellingham, 16 years 57 days v Swansea C, 25 August 2019.

Record Transfer Fee Received: £20,000,000 from Borussia Dortmund for Jude Bellingham, July 2020.

Record Transfer Fee Paid: £7,000,000 to Dinamo Zagreb for Ivan Sunjic, July 2019.

Football League Record: 1892 Elected to Division 2; 1894–96 Division 1; 1896–1901 Division 2; 1901–02 Division 1; 1902–03 Division 2; 1903–08 Division 1; 1908–21 Division 2; 1921–39 Division 1; 1946–48 Division 2; 1948–50 Division 1; 1950–55 Division 2; 1955–65 Division 1; 1965–72 Division 2; 1972–79 Division 1; 1979–80 Division 2; 1980–84 Division 1; 1984–85 Division 2; 1985–86 Division 1; 1986–89 Division 2; 1989–92 Division 3; 1992–94 Division 1; 1994–95 Division 2; 1995–2002 Division 1; 2002–06 Premier League; 2006–07 FL C; 2007–08 Premier League; 2008–09 FL C; 2009–11 Premier League; 2011– FL C.

LATEST SEQUENCES

Longest Sequence of League Wins: 13, 17.12.1892 – 16.9.1893.

Longest Sequence of League Defeats: 8, 28.9.1985 – 23.11.1985.

Longest Sequence of League Draws: 8, 18.9.1990 – 23.10.1990.

Longest Sequence of Unbeaten League Matches: 20, 3.9.1994 – 2.1.1995.

Longest Sequence Without a League Win: 17, 28.9.1985 – 18.1.1986.

Successive Scoring Runs: 24 from 24.9.1892.

Successive Non-scoring Runs: 6 from 11.2.1989.

MANAGERS

Alfred Jones 1892–1908 (*Secretary-Manager*)
Alec Watson 1908–10
Bob McRoberts 1910–15
Frank Richards 1915–23
Billy Beer 1923–27
William Harvey 1927–28
Leslie Knighton 1928–33
George Liddell 1933–39
William Camkin and Ted Goodier 1939–45
Harry Storer 1945–48
Bob Brocklebank 1949–54
Arthur Turner 1954–58
Pat Beasley 1959–60
Gil Merrick 1960–64
Joe Mallett 1964–65
Stan Cullis 1965–70
Fred Goodwin 1970–75
Willie Bell 1975–77
Sir Alf Ramsay 1977–78
Jim Smith 1978–82
Ron Saunders 1982–86
John Bond 1986–87
Garry Pendrey 1987–89
Dave Mackay 1989–91
Lou Macari 1991
Terry Cooper 1991–93
Barry Fry 1993–96
Trevor Francis 1996–2001
Steve Bruce 2001–07
Alex McLeish 2007–11
Chris Hughton 2011–12
Lee Clark 2012–14
Gary Rowett 2014–16
Gianfranco Zola 2016–17
Harry Redknapp 2017
Steve Cotterill 2017–18
Garry Monk 2018–19
Pep Clotet 2019–20
Aitor Karanka July 2020–

TEN YEAR LEAGUE RECORD

		P	*W*	*D*	*L*	*F*	*A*	*Pts*	*Pos*
2010-11	PR Lge	38	8	15	15	37	58	39	18
2011-12	FL C	46	20	16	10	78	51	76	4
2012-13	FL C	46	15	16	15	63	69	61	12
2013-14	FL C	46	11	11	24	58	74	44	21
2014-15	FL C	46	16	15	15	54	64	63	10
2015-16	FL C	46	16	15	15	53	49	63	10
2016-17	FL C	46	13	14	19	45	64	53	19
2017-18	FL C	46	13	7	26	38	68	46	19
2018-19	FL C	46	14	19	13	64	58	52*	17
2019-20	FL C	46	12	14	20	54	75	50	20

** 9 pts deducted.*

DID YOU KNOW ?

Birmingham City became the first Football League club to introduce a mascot for marketing purposes. Beau Brummie was introduced to the fans on 29 October 1966 when the Blues met Blackburn Rovers at St Andrew's. The initial slogan used was 'Let's Go With Beau'.

BIRMINGHAM CITY – SKY BET CHAMPIONSHIP 2019–20 LEAGUE RECORD

Match No.	*Date*	*Venue*	*Opponents*	*Result*		*H/T Score*	*Lg Pos.*	*Goalscorers*	*Attendance*
1	Aug 3	A	Brentford	W	1-0	1-0	7	Pedersen 18	11,332
2	10	H	Bristol C	D	1-1	0-0	6	Jutkiewicz 64	21,808
3	17	A	Nottingham F	L	0-3	0-2	15		27,281
4	20	H	Barnsley	W	2-0	0-0	8	Jutkiewicz 69, Alvaro Gimenez 77	20,061
5	25	A	Swansea C	L	0-3	0-0	15		17,277
6	31	H	Stoke C	W	2-1	0-0	9	Jutkiewicz 73, Bellingham 76	20,652
7	Sept 14	A	Charlton Ath	W	1-0	0-0	8	Bellingham 52	18,752
8	21	H	Preston NE	L	0-1	0-1	11		20,806
9	28	A	Derby Co	L	2-3	0-1	13	Gardner, G 56, Sunjic 59	28,454
10	Oct 1	A	Wigan Ath	L	0-1	0-0	14		9244
11	4	H	Middlesbrough	W	2-1	1-0	12	Villalba 33, Bailey 89	19,703
12	19	A	Leeds U	L	0-1	0-0	12		35,731
13	22	H	Blackburn R	W	1-0	1-0	11	Colin 31	18,561
14	26	H	Luton T	W	2-1	1-0	11	Pedersen 45, Jutkiewicz 82	21,799
15	Nov 2	A	Cardiff C	L	2-4	1-2	12	Pedersen 3, Sunjic 89	23,778
16	9	H	Fulham	L	0-1	0-0	13		21,334
17	23	A	Huddersfield T	D	1-1	0-0	14	Jutkiewicz 78	22,573
18	27	A	Sheffield W	D	1-1	0-0	15	Alvaro Gimenez 48	22,059
19	30	H	Millwall	D	1-1	0-0	15	Clarke-Salter 79	19,715
20	Dec 7	A	Reading	W	3-2	1-1	13	Morrison (og) 41, Bela 59, Alvaro Gimenez 88	14,103
21	11	H	QPR	L	0-2	0-1	15		18,161
22	14	H	WBA	L	2-3	1-1	15	Jutkiewicz 3, Dean 47	20,796
23	21	A	Hull C	L	0-3	0-1	15		11,334
24	26	A	Blackburn R	D	1-1	0-0	16	Mrbati (pen) 63	15,887
25	29	H	Leeds U	L	4-5	1-2	17	Bellingham 27, Jutkiewicz 2 61, 90, Bela 83	22,059
26	Jan 1	H	Wigan Ath	L	2-3	1-1	18	Mrbati 39, Maghoma 81	18,616
27	11	A	Luton T	W	2-1	1-0	18	Jutkiewicz 4, Gardner, G 69	10,062
28	18	H	Cardiff C	D	1-1	1-0	18	Bellingham 4	20,482
29	21	A	Middlesbrough	D	1-1	1-0	18	Jutkiewicz 27	18,350
30	Feb 1	H	Nottingham F	W	2-1	1-1	17	Hogan 42, Pedersen 74	20,837
31	7	A	Bristol C	W	3-1	2-1	14	Hogan 23, Weimann (og) 30, Jutkiewicz 90	22,065
32	11	A	Barnsley	W	1-0	0-0	14	Hogan 76	12,788
33	15	H	Brentford	D	1-1	1-1	14	Jutkiewicz 13	20,379
34	22	H	Sheffield W	D	3-3	2-2	14	Murphy (og) 6, Jutkiewicz 30, Hogan 90	22,120
35	26	A	Millwall	D	0-0	0-0	14		11,209
36	29	A	QPR	D	2-2	1-0	15	Hogan 2 24, 81	14,113
37	Mar 7	H	Reading	L	1-3	1-0	16	Hogan 6	19,525
38	June 20	A	WBA	D	0-0	0-0	16		0
39	27	H	Hull C	D	3-3	0-2	16	Gardner, G 2 47, 88, Crowley 60	0
40	July 1	H	Huddersfield T	L	0-3	0-1	17		0
41	4	A	Fulham	L	0-1	0-0	17		0
42	8	H	Swansea C	L	1-3	1-2	17	Jutkiewicz 5	0
43	12	A	Stoke C	L	0-2	0-2	18		0
44	15	H	Charlton Ath	D	1-1	0-0	19	Jutkiewicz 90	0
45	18	A	Preston NE	L	0-2	0-1	20		0
46	22	H	Derby Co	L	1-3	0-1	21	Sunjic 56	0

Final League Position: 20

GOALSCORERS

League (54): Jutkiewicz 15, Hogan 7, Bellingham 4, Gardner, G 4, Pedersen 4, Alvaro Gimenez 3, Sunjic 3, Bela 2, Mrbati 2 (1 pen), Bailey 1, Clarke-Salter 1, Colin 1, Crowley 1, Dean 1, Maghoma 1, Villalba 1, own goals 3.
FA Cup (4): Bela 2, Crowley 1, Dean 1.
Carabao Cup (0).

Camp L 36	Colin M 44	Dean H 34 + 5	Roberts M 33 + 1	Pedersen K 44	Seddon S 3 + 1	Maghoma J 7 + 11	Gardner G 27 + 8	Davis D 13 + 2	Crowley D 29 + 9	Jutkiewicz L 42 + 4	Harding W 7 + 8	Sunjic I 37 + 3	Mrbati K 12 + 3	Villalba F 15 + 2	Medina A — + 1	Alvaro Gimenez C 12 + 12	Montero J 2 + 12	Bailey O — + 6	Bellingham J 32 + 9	Clarke-Salter J 19	McEachran J 5 + 3	Bela J 22 + 8	Trueman C 10	Bajrami G 2	Hogan S 16 + 1	Boyd-Munce C — + 6	Kieftenbeld M 2 + 6	Gordon N 1 + 1	Reid J — + 4	Burke R — + 1	Fernandez M — + 1	Match No.
1	2	3	4	5	6^{1}	7^{3}	8	9	10^{2}	11	12	13	14																			1
1	2	3	4	5			8	9	10^{1}	11	12	7		6^{2}	13																	2
1	2	4	3	5	13		6^{1}	7	10^{2}	11		8		9		12																3
1		3	4	5	6		12	9		11^{3}	2	8		7^{1}		10^{2}	13	14														4
1		3	4	5	6^{2}		12	7^{3}	13	11	2	8		9		10^{1}			14													5
1	2	4	3	5			14	7	13	11^{3}		8		6^{2}		10	9^{1}		12													6
1	2	4	3	5		12	14	8	6^{3}	11		7	10^{1}			13			9^{2}													7
1	2	4	3	5		12		7^{3}	6	11		8	10^{2}	14		13			9^{1}													8
1	2	4	3	5		9^{2}	7^{1}		6	11		8		12		10			13													9
1	2	4		5			7		6^{1}	10		8	12	9^{2}		11		13	14	3^{3}												10
1	2	4	3	5		13	12		6	11^{3}		7		9^{2}		10		14	8^{1}													11
1	2	4	3	5		12	14		6^{1}	11^{3}		8		9		10		13	7^{2}													12
1	2	4	3	5		13		7	6^{2}	11			10^{3}	9		14			8^{1}		12											13
1	2	3	4	5		13		14	6^{2}	11		7	10^{1}	9		12			8^{3}													14
1	2	4■	3	5		12			6^{3}	10		8	11^{1}	9		13		14	7^{2}													15
1	2		3	5					8^{2}	11		6	9^{1}	10^{3}		13	14		7	4		12										16
	2		3	5		9^{1}			6	11		7				13	12		8^{3}	4	14	10^{2}	1									17
	2		3	5				14	6	12		7		9		11^{1}	13		8^{3}	4		10^{2}	1									18
	2	12	3^{1}	5					6	11		7		9^{2}		10^{3}	14		8	4		13	1									19
	2	3		5		13			6^{2}	14	12	7				10			11	4^{1}	8^{3}	9	1									20
	2	3		5		10				12	4	6				11^{1}	14	13	9^{3}		7	8^{2}	1									21
	2	4		5			12	8		11		7^{2}				10	13		9^{1}		14	6^{3}	1	3								22
	2	3		5					14	11		7		9^{2}		12	13		10^{1}		6^{3}	8	1	4								23
	2	3		5		10^{3}	7	6		11	4	14	9^{2}			13			12			8^{1}	1									24
	2	3		5			8		9^{1}	11	4	7	10^{3}			13	14		6^{2}			12	1									25
	2	4		5		12	3			10		7	11^{2}			14	13		6		8^{1}	9^{3}	1									26
1	2	3■		5		6	8^{2}	7	14	11	13		10^{1}						12	4		9^{3}										27
1	2		3	5		12	13		8	11		7	9^{1}						6^{2}	4		10										28
1	2		3	5		10	7	6	12	11			9^{1}						13	4		8^{2}										29
1	2	3	14	5		13	7			11		12							9^{2}	4	8^{1}	6			10^{3}							30
1	2	13	3	5			8			10	12	7							9^{3}	4		6^{1}			11^{2}	14						31
1	2	13	3	5			7			11^{2}	14	8					9^{1}		6^{3}	4		12			10							32
1	2		3	5			7		12	11	13	8							9	4		6^{2}			10^{1}							33
1	2	13	3	5			7		12	11		8^{1}					14		9	4^{2}		6^{3}			10							34
1	2	4	3	5			7		12	11		8							9^{2}			6^{1}			10		13					35
1	2	4	3	5			7		9^{2}	10		8					12					6^{1}			11		13					36
1	2	4	3	5			8		6	11		7^{2}	12						9^{1}						10		13					37
1	2	3					9		6^{2}	10	5								8^{1}	4		12			11	13	7					38
1	2	3		5			8		6	10									9	4^{2}		12			11		7^{1}	13				39
1	2	3		5			7		6	10									8	4		9			11							40
1	2	15	3	5			7		8^{4}	13	14	6							9^{1}	4		10^{3}			11^{2}		12					41
1	2		3	5			7		6	10		8							12	4		9^{2}			11^{1}				13			42
1	5	3	2				8		16	10	9^{1}	7^{3}							6^{5}			12			11^{2}	14		4^{4}	13	15		43
1	2	4	3	5			8		6^{4}	10		7^{3}							12			9^{1}			11^{2}	15	14		13			44
1	2	4	3	5			9		6^{2}	10		7^{1}							8			12			11^{3}	13			14			45
1	2	4	3	5			8^{4}		6^{2}	11		7							10^{1}			9^{3}			15	12	13				14	46

FA Cup

Third Round	Blackburn R	(h)	2-1
Fourth Round	Coventry C	(a)	0-0
Replay	Coventry C	(h)	2-2
(aet; Birmingham C won 4-1 on penalties)			
Fifth Round	Leicester C	(a)	0-1

Carabao Cup

First Round	Portsmouth	(a)	0-3

BLACKBURN ROVERS

FOUNDATION

It was in 1875 that some public school old boys called a meeting at which the Blackburn Rovers club was formed and the colours blue and white adopted. The leading light was John Lewis, later to become a founder of the Lancashire FA, a famous referee who was in charge of two FA Cup finals, and a vice-president of both the FA and the Football League.

Ewood Park, Blackburn, Lancashire BB2 4JF.

Telephone: (01254) 372 001.

Ticket Office: (01254) 372 000.

Website: www.rovers.co.uk

Email: enquiries@rovers.co.uk

Ground Capacity: 31,367.

Record Attendance: 62,522 v Bolton W, FA Cup 6th rd, 2 March 1929.

Pitch Measurements: 105m × 66m (115yd × 72yd).

Chief Executive: Steve Waggott.

Manager: Tony Mowbray.

Assistant Manager: Mark Venus.

Colours: Light blue and white halved shirts, white shorts, light blue socks with white trim.

Year Formed: 1875.

Turned Professional: 1880.

Club Nickname: 'Rovers'.

HONOURS

League Champions: Premier League – 1994–95; Division 1 – 1911–12, 1913–14; Division 2 – 1938–39; Division 3 – 1974–75.
Runners-up: Premier League – 1993–94; FL 1 – 2017–18; First Division – 2000–01; Division 2 – 1957–58; Division 3 – 1979–80.

FA Cup Winners: 1884, 1885, 1886, 1890, 1891, 1928.
Runners-up: 1882, 1960.

League Cup Winners: 2002.

Full Members' Cup Winners: 1987.

European Competitions
European Cup: 1995–96.
UEFA Cup: 1994–95, 1998–99, 2002–03, 2003–04, 2006–07, 2007–08.
Intertoto Cup: 2007.

Grounds: 1875, all matches played away; 1876, Oozehead Ground; 1877, Pleasington Cricket Ground; 1878, Alexandra Meadows; 1881, Leamington Road; 1890, Ewood Park.

First Football League Game: 15 September 1888, Football League, v Accrington (h) D 5–5 – Arthur; Beverley, James Southworth; Douglas, Almond, Forrest; Beresford (1), Walton, John Southworth (1), Fecitt (1), Townley (2).

Record League Victory: 9–0 v Middlesbrough, Division 2, 6 November 1954 – Elvy; Suart, Eckersley; Clayton, Kelly, Bell; Mooney (3), Crossan (2), Briggs, Quigley (3), Langton (1).

Record Cup Victory: 11–0 v Rossendale, FA Cup 1st rd, 13 October 1884 – Arthur; Hopwood, McIntyre; Forrest, Blenkhorn, Lofthouse; Sowerbutts (2), Jimmy Brown (1), Fecitt (4), Barton (3), Birtwistle (1).

Record Defeat: 0–8 v Arsenal, Division 1, 25 February 1933; 0-8 v Lincoln C, Division 2, 29 August 1953.

FOOTBALL YEARBOOK FACT FILE

On 6 November 1965 John Byrom became the first substitute to be used by Blackburn Rovers in a Football League game when he replaced Mick McGrath against Manchester United in a First Division game at Old Trafford. The following week he came off the bench against Newcastle United and became the club's first substitute to score, helping Rovers to a 4-2 victory.

Most League Points (2 for a win): 60, Division 3, 1974–75.

Most League Points (3 for a win): 96, FL 1, 2017–18.

Most League Goals: 114, Division 2, 1954–55.

Highest League Scorer in Season: Ted Harper, 43, Division 1, 1925–26.

Most League Goals in Total Aggregate: Simon Garner, 168, 1978–92.

Most League Goals in One Match: 7, Tommy Briggs v Bristol R, Division 2, 5 February 1955.

Most Capped Player: Morten Gamst Pedersen, 70 (83), Norway.

Most League Appearances: Derek Fazackerley, 596, 1970–86.

Youngest League Player: Harry Dennison, 16 years 155 days v Bristol C, 8 April 1911.

Record Transfer Fee Received: £18,000,000 from Manchester C for Roque Santa Cruz, June 2009.

Record Transfer Fee Paid: £3,000,000 (rising to £10,000,000) to Arsenal for David Bentley, January 2006.

Football League Record: 1888 Founder Member of the League; 1936–39 Division 2; 1946–48 Division 1; 1948–58 Division 2; 1958–66 Division 1; 1966–71 Division 2; 1971–75 Division 3; 1975–79 Division 2; 1979–80 Division 3; 1980–92 Division 2; 1992–99 Premier League; 1999–2001 Division 1; 2001–12 Premier League; 2012–17 FL C; 2017–18 FL 1; 2018– FL C.

LATEST SEQUENCES

Longest Sequence of League Wins: 8, 1.3.1980 – 7.4.1980.

Longest Sequence of League Defeats: 7, 12.3.1966 – 16.4.1966.

Longest Sequence of League Draws: 5, 11.10.1975 – 1.11.1975.

Longest Sequence of Unbeaten League Matches: 23, 30.9.1987 – 27.2.1988.

Longest Sequence Without a League Win: 16, 11.11.1978 – 24.3.1979.

Successive Scoring Runs: 32 from 24.4.1954.

Successive Non-scoring Runs: 4 from 14.12.2015.

MANAGERS

Thomas Mitchell 1884–96 (*Secretary-Manager*)
J. Walmsley 1896–1903 (*Secretary-Manager*)
R. B. Middleton 1903–25
Jack Carr 1922–26 (*Team Manager under Middleton to 1925*)
Bob Crompton 1926–31 (*Hon. Team Manager*)
Arthur Barritt 1931–36 (*had been Secretary from 1927*)
Reg Taylor 1936–38
Bob Crompton 1938–41
Eddie Hapgood 1944–47
Will Scott 1947
Jack Bruton 1947–49
Jackie Bestall 1949–53
Johnny Carey 1953–58
Dally Duncan 1958–60
Jack Marshall 1960–67
Eddie Quigley 1967–70
Johnny Carey 1970–71
Ken Furphy 1971–73
Gordon Lee 1974–75
Jim Smith 1975–78
Jim Iley 1978
John Pickering 1978–79
Howard Kendall 1979–81
Bobby Saxton 1981–86
Don Mackay 1987–91
Kenny Dalglish 1991–95
Ray Harford 1995–96
Roy Hodgson 1997–98
Brian Kidd 1998–99
Graeme Souness 2000–04
Mark Hughes 2004–08
Paul Ince 2008
Sam Allardyce 2008–10
Steve Kean 2010–12
Henning Berg 2012
Michael Appleton 2013
Gary Bowyer 2013–15
Paul Lambert 2015–16
Owen Coyle 2016–17
Tony Mowbray February 2017–

TEN YEAR LEAGUE RECORD

		P	*W*	*D*	*L*	*F*	*A*	*Pts*	*Pos*
2010-11	PR Lge	38	11	10	17	46	59	43	15
2011-12	PR Lge	38	8	7	23	48	78	31	19
2012-13	FL C	46	14	16	16	55	62	58	17
2013-14	FL C	46	18	16	12	70	62	70	8
2014-15	FL C	46	17	16	13	66	59	67	9
2015-16	FL C	46	13	16	17	46	46	55	15
2016-17	FL C	46	12	15	19	53	65	51	22
2017-18	FL 1	46	28	12	6	82	40	96	2
2018-19	FL C	46	16	12	18	64	69	60	15
2019-20	FL C	46	17	12	17	66	63	63	11

DID YOU KNOW ?

Blackburn Rovers goalkeeper Bobby Mimms kept more clean sheets in 1992–93 than any other keeper in the Premier League. He played in all 42 of Rovers' games and equalled the club record by preventing the opposition from scoring on 19 occasions.

BLACKBURN ROVERS – SKY BET CHAMPIONSHIP 2019–20 LEAGUE RECORD

Match No.	Date	Venue	Opponents	Result		H/T Score	Lg Pos.	Goalscorers	Attendance
1	Aug 3	H	Charlton Ath	L	1-2	0-1	17	Phillips (og) 54	14,184
2	10	A	Fulham	L	0-2	0-1	24		17,987
3	17	H	Middlesbrough	W	1-0	1-0	18	Graham (pen) 25	14,012
4	20	A	Hull C	W	1-0	0-0	10	Williams 62	10,240
5	24	H	Cardiff C	D	0-0	0-0	14		13,291
6	31	A	WBA	L	2-3	2-3	17	Dack 1, Johnson 45	23,792
7	Sept 14	H	Millwall	W	2-0	1-0	11	Williams 18, Dack 74	11,873
8	21	A	Reading	W	2-1	1-0	10	Armstrong 8, Dack 48	16,906
9	28	H	Luton T	L	1-2	1-1	11	Travis 37	15,319
10	Oct 1	H	Nottingham F	D	1-1	0-0	11	Armstrong 63	12,521
11	5	A	QPR	L	2-4	0-1	14	Dack (pen) 57, Armstrong 86	13,560
12	19	H	Huddersfield T	D	2-2	2-1	14	Holtby 20, Dack 33	13,761
13	22	A	Birmingham C	L	0-1	0-1	15		18,561
14	26	A	Preston NE	L	2-3	2-0	17	Rudd (og) 1, Gallagher 11	19,165
15	Nov 2	H	Sheffield W	W	2-1	0-0	16	Adarabioyo 88, Buckley 90	14,147
16	9	A	Leeds U	L	1-2	1-2	18	Williams 40	35,567
17	23	H	Barnsley	W	3-2	1-0	17	Dack 2 24, 86, Downing 69	13,781
18	27	H	Brentford	W	1-0	1-0	13	Dack 11	11,401
19	30	A	Stoke C	W	2-1	1-0	11	Dack 13, Gallagher 84	22,292
20	Dec 7	H	Derby Co	W	1-0	0-0	11	Armstrong 57	12,800
21	11	A	Swansea C	D	1-1	1-1	10	Graham 4	14,162
22	14	A	Bristol C	W	2-0	1-0	9	Johnson 2, Armstrong 77	21,180
23	23	H	Wigan Ath	D	0-0	0-0	8		18,726
24	26	H	Birmingham C	D	1-1	0-0	9	Armstrong (pen) 55	15,887
25	29	A	Huddersfield T	L	1-2	1-1	13	Graham 7	22,859
26	Jan 1	A	Nottingham F	L	2-3	1-2	13	Downing 39, Worrall (og) 71	27,073
27	11	H	Preston NE	D	1-1	1-1	12	Armstrong 3	19,963
28	18	A	Sheffield W	W	5-0	3-0	11	Holtby 2 19, 45, Dawson (og) 36, Lenihan 48, Gallagher 90	23,504
29	28	H	QPR	W	2-1	2-1	10	Armstrong 10, Lenihan 30	11,505
30	Feb 1	A	Middlesbrough	D	1-1	0-0	10	Travis 57	19,937
31	8	H	Fulham	L	0-1	0-0	12		13,087
32	11	H	Hull C	W	3-0	0-0	8	Lenihan 73, Armstrong 79, Samuel 80	11,888
33	15	A	Charlton Ath	W	2-0	2-0	8	Buckley 29, Adarabioyo 37	25,363
34	22	A	Brentford	D	2-2	1-0	8	Armstrong 2 (1 pen) 11, 54 (p)	12,082
35	26	H	Stoke C	D	0-0	0-0	8		12,343
36	29	H	Swansea C	D	2-2	1-1	8	Gallagher 25, Johnson 90	13,099
37	Mar 8	A	Derby Co	L	0-3	0-2	10		26,590
38	June 20	H	Bristol C	W	3-1	1-1	7	Evans 37, Adarabioyo 60, Armstrong 71	0
39	27	A	Wigan Ath	L	0-2	0-0	9		0
40	30	A	Barnsley	L	0-2	0-0	10		0
41	July 4	H	Leeds U	L	1-3	0-2	11	Armstrong 48	0
42	7	A	Cardiff C	W	3-2	1-2	9	Graham 22, Samuel 46, Armstrong 70	0
43	11	H	WBA	D	1-1	0-1	12	Rothwell 63	0
44	14	A	Millwall	L	0-1	0-1	12		0
45	18	H	Reading	W	4-3	2-1	10	Brereton 3, Armstrong 6, Rothwell 56, Gallagher 87	0
46	22	A	Luton T	L	2-3	1-2	11	Armstrong 10, Gallagher 75	0

Final League Position: 11

GOALSCORERS

League (66): Armstrong 16 (2 pens), Dack 9 (1 pen), Gallagher 6, Graham 4 (1 pen), Adarabioyo 3, Holtby 3, Johnson 3, Lenihan 3, Williams 3, Buckley 2, Downing 2, Rothwell 2, Samuel 2, Travis 2, Brereton 1, Evans 1, own goals 4.
FA Cup (1): Armstrong 1 (1 pen).
Carabao Cup (4): Dack 1, Downing 1, Gallagher 1, Rothwell 1.

Walton C 46	Bennett E 29 + 12	Lenihan D 37	Mulgrew C 2	Bell A 19 + 2	Johnson B 25 + 9	Travis L 41 + 2	Downing S 38 + 3	Dack B 22	Armstrong A 40 + 6	Gallagher S 28 + 14	Graham D 14 + 24	Rothwell J 21 + 15	Buckley J 5 + 15	Adarabioyo T 33 + 1	Williams D 17	Brereton B 7 + 8	Cunningham G 8	Nyambe R 30 + 1	Evans C 11 + 2	Holtby L 16 + 11	Samuel D 7 + 8	Chapman H — + 5	Rankin-Costello J 8 + 3	Davenport J — + 9	Carter H 2	Vale J — + 1	*Match No.*
1	2	3	4	5	6	7^{3}	8^{2}	9	10^{1}	11	12	13	14														1
1	2			5^{2}	6	7^{3}	13	9	10	11	14	8^{1}		3	4	12											2
1	2	3			7	6	10^{3}	9^{2}	12	8	11^{1}	14	13		4		5										3
1	2	3			6	7	10	9^{2}	11^{3}	8^{1}	12	13	14		4		5										4
1	2	3		5	7	6	10^{3}	9^{1}	12	8	11^{2}	13			4			14									5
1	2	3			7^{2}	6	8	9	10^{3}	11^{1}	14	13	12		4		5										6
1	8	3			6	14	10^{3}	9	11	12		13	7^{1}	2^{2}	4		5										7
1	2	3			13	6	8	9	10^{1}	11^{3}	14				4		5		7^{2}	12							8
1	2^{3}	3			7^{1}	6	8	9	10	11^{2}	13				4		5			12	14						9
1	2	3				8	9	7^{2}	6	11^{1}	10^{3}	12			4		5			14	13						10
1	2	3^{3}		12			7	9	8		11^{2}	10		14	4		5^{1}		6	13							11
1	5				7	6^{2}	8^{3}	11	10	12		13		3	4			2	14	9^{1}							12
1	5				7^{2}	6	10^{3}	9	8	11^{1}	12	13	14	3	4			2									13
1	8			5				9	7	11	12	10^{1}		3	4			2	6								14
1	2					6	7^{3}	9	10	11^{1}	12	13	14	4	5			3		8^{2}							15
1	2					6	10	9	8^{1}	11^{2}	12		13	4	5			3	14	7^{3}							16
1	2	4		5		6	13	9	11	8^{2}	12	10^{3}	14	3						7^{1}							17
1	12	4				6	5	9	8^{2}		11^{3}	10		3		14		2^{1}	7	13							18
1	12	3				7	5	9	8^{1}	13	11^{2}	10^{3}		4				2	6	14							19
1	13	3				6	5	9	8^{3}	12	11^{1}	10^{2}	14	4				2	7								20
1	12	3				6	5	9■	8	14	11^{3}	10^{1}		4				2	7^{2}	13							21
1	9	3		5	8	7			12	10		13		4		11^{1}		2		6^{2}							22
1		3			12	7	5	9^{2}	8^{3}	14	11	10			4			2	6^{1}	13							23
1	8	3		5	7	12			10	11	13	14	6^{2}		4			2^{1}		9^{3}							24
1	2	3		12	8^{3}	7	5		13	10	11^{2}	9^{1}	6	4								14					25
1	2^{3}	3		5		6^{2}	9		7	13	14	10		4		11^{1}			8			12					26
1	13	3		5	12	6	10		8	11	14			4				2^{2}	7^{1}	9^{3}							27
1		3		5		6^{2}	7		11^{3}	8		10^{1}		4		14		2		9			12	13			28
1	12	3		5	14	6	7^{3}		11	8		10^{1}		4				2		9^{2}			13				29
1	12	3		5	14	6	7^{3}		11	8	13			4				2		9^{1}			10^{2}				30
1		3		5	7^{2}	6	10		11^{3}	8	13			4		14		2			12		9^{1}				31
1	10^{2}	3		5	7	6	8^{3}		9		11^{1}		14	4		13		2			12						32
1	14	3		5	7	6	8		10^{1}				9^{3}	4		13		2			11^{2}	12					33
1	13	4		6	9	7	8		11	12			2^{1}	5				3			10^{2}						34
1		3		5	7^{3}	6	9		11	8^{1}	14	10^{2}		4				2			12		13				35
1	2			5	14	6^{3}	7		9	11	13	10^{2}		4		12		3			8^{1}						36
1	2			5	12	7^{1}	8		10	6^{3}	13	9	14■	4		11^{2}		3									37
1	2	3			15	7	9		12	10^{3}	13			4		11^{2}			8^{5}	6^{1}	14		5^{4}	16			38
1	5	3			14	7^{3}	9		13	11^{1}	15	8^{5}		4		10^{4}		2		6^{2}	12			16			39
1	5^{5}		4		7		6		11^{3}	14	13	8^{2}		3		12■		2		10^{4}	9^{1}	16		15			40
1	5^{1}	3			7	6^{4}	12		11	9^{3}	14	8^{5}	16	4				2		10^{2}	13			15			41
1	12	3			8	6	7		11^{3}	15	10^{2}	13		4				2		14	9^{4}		5^{1}				42
1	14	3			8^{2}	6	7^{5}		11^{1}	13	10	15		4				2^{3}		12	9^{4}		5	16			43
1	2	3			7^{5}	6^{3}	8^{4}		11	12	10^{1}	13	16	4						14	9^{2}		5	15			44
1		3			8^{3}	7			11^{5}	13		9^{4}	12			10^{2}		2		6^{1}		15	5	14	4	16	45
1	16	3			8	7^{1}			10^{4}	15	14	9^{5}	13			11^{3}		2		6^{2}			5	12	4		46

FA Cup
Third Round Birmingham C (a) 1-2

Carabao Cup
First Round Oldham Ath (h) 3-2
Second Round Sheffield U (a) 1-2

BLACKPOOL

FOUNDATION

Old boys of St John's School, who had formed themselves into a football club, decided to establish a club bearing the name of their town and Blackpool FC came into being at a meeting at the Stanley Arms Hotel in the summer of 1887. In their first season playing at Raikes Hall Gardens, the club won both the Lancashire Junior Cup and the Fylde Cup.

Bloomfield Road, Seasiders Way, Blackpool, Lancashire FY1 6JJ.

Telephone: (01253) 599 344.

Ticket Office: (01253) 599 745.

Website: www.blackpoolfc.co.uk

Email: via website.

Ground Capacity: 16,616.

Record Attendance: 38,098 v Wolverhampton W, Division 1, 17 September 1955.

Pitch Measurements: 100m × 64m (109.5yd × 70yd).

Owner: Simon Sadler.

Managing Director: Ben Hatton.

Head Coach: Neil Critchley.

First-Team Coach: Mike Garrity.

HONOURS

League Champions: Division 2 – 1929–30.
Runners-up: Division 1 – 1955–56; Division 2 – 1936–37, 1969–70; Division 4 – 1984–85.

FA Cup Winners: 1953.
Runners-up: 1948, 1951.

League Cup: semi-final – 1962.

League Trophy Winners: 2002, 2004.

Anglo-Italian Cup Winners: 1971.
Runners-up: 1972.

Colours: Tangerine shirts with white trim, white shorts with tangerine trim, tangerine socks with white trim.

Year Formed: 1887.

Turned Professional: 1887.

Previous Name: 'South Shore' combined with Blackpool in 1899, twelve years after the latter had been formed on the breaking up of the old 'Blackpool St John's' club.

Club Nickname: 'The Seasiders'.

Grounds: 1887, Raikes Hall Gardens; 1897, Athletic Grounds; 1899, Raikes Hall Gardens; 1899, Bloomfield Road.

First Football League Game: 5 September 1896, Division 2, v Lincoln C (a) L 1–3 – Douglas; Parr, Bowman; Stuart, Stirzaker, Norris; Clarkin, Donnelly, Robert Parkinson, Mount (1), Jack Parkinson.

Record League Victory: 7–0 v Reading, Division 2, 10 November 1928 – Mercer; Gibson, Hamilton, Watson, Wilson, Grant, Ritchie, Oxberry (2), Hampson (5), Tufnell, Neal. 7–0 v Preston NE (away), Division 1, 1 May 1948 – Robinson; Shimwell, Crosland; Buchan, Hayward, Kelly; Hobson, Munro (1), McIntosh (5), McCall, Rickett (1). 7–0 v Sunderland, Division 1, 5 October 1957 – Farm; Armfield, Garrett, Kelly J, Gratrix, Kelly H, Matthews, Taylor (2), Charnley (2), Durie (2), Perry (1).

Record Cup Victory: 7–1 v Charlton Ath, League Cup 2nd rd, 25 September 1963 – Harvey; Armfield, Martin; Crawford, Gratrix, Cranston; Lea, Ball (1), Charnley (4), Durie (1), Oates (1).

FOOTBALL YEARBOOK FACT FILE

Blackpool adopted their famous tangerine shirts in 1923 after a recommendation from club director Albert Hargreaves. Hargreaves had officiated at a game between Belgium and the Netherlands and was impressed with the orange shirts worn by the Dutch team. The Seasiders adopted the new colours and, apart from a short spell in the 1930s, have retained tangerine shirts as their first-choice strip.

Record Defeat: 1–10 v Small Heath, Division 2, 2 March 1901 and v Huddersfield T, Division 1, 13 December 1930.

Most League Points (2 for a win): 58, Division 2, 1929–30 and Division 2, 1967–68.

Most League Points (3 for a win): 86, Division 4, 1984–85.

Most League Goals: 98, Division 2, 1929–30.

Highest League Scorer in Season: Jimmy Hampson, 45, Division 2, 1929–30.

Most League Goals in Total Aggregate: Jimmy Hampson, 248, 1927–38.

Most League Goals in One Match: 5, Jimmy Hampson v Reading, Division 2, 10 November 1928; 5, Jimmy McIntosh v Preston NE, Division 1, 1 May 1948.

Most Capped Player: Jimmy Armfield, 43, England.

Most League Appearances: Jimmy Armfield, 568, 1952–71.

Youngest League Player: Matty Kay, 16 years 32 days v Scunthorpe U, 13 November 2005.

Record Transfer Fee Received: £6,750,000 from Liverpool for Charlie Adam, July 2011.

Record Transfer Fee Paid: £1,250,000 to Leicester C for D.J. Campbell, August 2010.

Football League Record: 1896 Elected to Division 2; 1899 Failed re-election; 1900 Re-elected; 1900–30 Division 2; 1930–33 Division 1; 1933–37 Division 2; 1937–67 Division 1; 1967–70 Division 2; 1970–71 Division 1; 1971–78 Division 2; 1978–81 Division 3; 1981–85 Division 4; 1985–90 Division 3; 1990–92 Division 4; 1992–2000 Division 2; 2000–01 Division 3; 2001–04 Division 2; 2004–07 FL 1; 2007–10 FL C; 2010–11 Premier League; 2011–15 FL C; 2015–16 FL 1; 2016–17 FL 2; 2017– FL 1.

MANAGERS

Tom Barcroft 1903–33
(*Secretary-Manager*)
John Cox 1909–11
Bill Norman 1919–23
Maj. Frank Buckley 1923–27
Sid Beaumont 1927–28
Harry Evans 1928–33
(*Hon. Team Manager*)
Alex 'Sandy' Macfarlane 1933–35
Joe Smith 1935–58
Ronnie Suart 1958–67
Stan Mortensen 1967–69
Les Shannon 1969–70
Bob Stokoe 1970–72
Harry Potts 1972–76
Allan Brown 1976–78
Bob Stokoe 1978–79
Stan Ternent 1979–80
Alan Ball 1980–81
Allan Brown 1981–82
Sam Ellis 1982–89
Jimmy Mullen 1989–90
Graham Carr 1990
Bill Ayre 1990–94
Sam Allardyce 1994–96
Gary Megson 1996–97
Nigel Worthington 1997–99
Steve McMahon 2000–04
Colin Hendry 2004–05
Simon Grayson 2005–08
Ian Holloway 2009–12
Michael Appleton 2012–13
Paul Ince 2013–14
José Riga 2014
Lee Clark 2014–15
Neil McDonald 2015–16
Gary Bowyer 2016–18
Terry McPhillips 2018–19
Simon Grayson 2019–20
Neil Critchley March 2020–

LATEST SEQUENCES

Longest Sequence of League Wins: 9, 21.11.1936 – 1.1.1937.

Longest Sequence of League Defeats: 8, 26.11.1898 – 7.1.1899.

Longest Sequence of League Draws: 5, 4.12.1976 – 1.1.1977.

Longest Sequence of Unbeaten League Matches: 17, 6.4.1968 – 21.9.1968.

Longest Sequence Without a League Win: 23, 7.2.2015 – 29.8.2015.

Successive Scoring Runs: 33 from 23.2.1929.

Successive Non-scoring Runs: 5 from 25.11.1989.

TEN YEAR LEAGUE RECORD

		P	*W*	*D*	*L*	*F*	*A*	*Pts*	*Pos*
2010-11	PR Lge	38	10	9	19	55	78	39	19
2011-12	FL C	46	20	15	11	79	59	75	5
2012-13	FL C	46	14	17	15	62	63	59	15
2013-14	FL C	46	11	13	22	38	66	46	20
2014-15	FL C	46	4	14	28	36	91	26	24
2015-16	FL 1	46	12	10	24	40	63	46	22
2016-17	FL 2	46	18	16	12	69	46	70	7
2017-18	FL 1	46	15	15	16	60	55	60	12
2018-19	FL 1	46	15	17	14	50	52	62	10
2019-20	FL 1	35	11	12	12	44	43	45	13§

§*Decided on points-per-game (1.29)*

DID YOU KNOW ?

Blackpool were the first team to take advantage of a rule change after the Football League lifted its ban on flying to matches. After drawing 1-1 at Arsenal on Good Friday morning in April 1957 they flew back with the aim of being less tired for their game at Preston North End the following day. The Seasiders were rewarded with a point from a 0-0 draw at Deepdale.

BLACKPOOL – SKY BET LEAGUE ONE 2019–20 LEAGUE RECORD

Match No.	Date	Venue	Opponents	Result		H/T Score	Lg Pos.	Goalscorers	Attendance
1	Aug 3	H	Bristol R	W	2-0	1-0	2	Spearing (pen) 28, Gnanduillet 46	11,359
2	10	A	Southend U	W	3-1	3-0	1	Lennon (og) 9, Delfouneso 2 12, 37	6823
3	17	H	Oxford U	W	2-1	2-1	2	Edwards 5, Gnanduillet (pen) 45	9104
4	20	A	Gillingham	D	2-2	2-2	1	KaiKai 41, Gnanduillet 45	4390
5	24	A	Rochdale	D	0-0	0-0	2		4664
6	31	H	Portsmouth	D	1-1	0-1	3	Gnanduillet 58	10,605
7	Sept 7	A	Coventry C	L	2-3	2-2	6	KaiKai 2 1, 38	6637
8	14	H	Milton Keynes D	L	0-3	0-1	9		8283
9	17	A	Doncaster R	W	1-0	0-0	5	Gnanduillet 90	6964
10	21	A	Accrington S	D	1-1	0-1	6	Virtue 90	4054
11	27	H	Lincoln C	W	2-1	2-1	4	Scannell 11, Thompson 21	9203
12	Oct 7	A	Bolton W	D	0-0	0-0	4		14,003
13	12	H	Rotherham U	L	1-2	0-0	6	Gnanduillet (pen) 90	9932
14	22	H	Wycombe W	D	1-1	0-1	8	Heneghan 51	7298
15	26	A	Burton Alb	D	0-0	0-0	9		3012
16	Nov 2	H	Peterborough U	W	4-3	2-2	8	Mason (og) 27, Gnanduillet 2 (1 pen) 41, 48 (p), Butler (og) 74	7619
17	16	H	AFC Wimbledon	W	2-0	0-0	5	Gnanduillet 2 51, 81	7588
18	23	A	Ipswich T	D	2-2	1-1	8	Nuttall 22, Spearing (pen) 53	19,503
19	Dec 7	H	Fleetwood T	W	3-1	1-0	4	Feeney 11, KaiKai 47, Gnanduillet 65	10,355
20	14	A	Sunderland	D	1-1	1-1	5	Virtue 4	30,595
21	21	H	Shrewsbury T	L	0-1	0-0	7		7695
22	26	H	Accrington S	L	0-1	0-0	10		9517
23	29	A	Tranmere R	D	1-1	1-1	10	Heneghan 9	8487
24	Jan 1	A	Rotherham U	L	1-2	1-1	10	Gnanduillet 34	8689
25	18	A	Lincoln C	L	0-1	0-0	15		8929
26	28	A	Wycombe W	L	1-2	0-2	15	Dewsbury-Hall 86	3684
27	Feb 1	A	Oxford U	L	1-2	1-2	15	Madine 10	10,525
28	8	H	Southend U	W	2-1	1-0	14	Gnanduillet 2 (1 pen) 37, 64 (p)	7870
29	11	H	Gillingham	L	2-3	1-0	15	Gnanduillet 7, Delfouneso 90	6816
30	15	A	Bristol R	L	1-2	1-0	16	Madine 2	6631
31	22	A	AFC Wimbledon	D	0-0	0-0	16		4593
32	25	H	Bolton W	W	2-1	1-0	14	Ronan 13, Dewsbury-Hall 90	8116
33	29	H	Ipswich T	W	2-1	1-0	13	Dewsbury-Hall 26, Nuttall 90	9500
34	Mar 7	A	Fleetwood T	D	0-0	0-0	13		4884
35	10	H	Tranmere R	L	1-2	0-2	13	Dewsbury-Hall 58	8235
36	14	H	Sunderland	Cancelled					
37	21	A	Shrewsbury T	Cancelled					
38	29	A	Peterborough U	Cancelled					
39	Apr 4	H	Burton Alb	Cancelled					
40	10	H	Rochdale	Cancelled					
41	13	A	Portsmouth	Cancelled					
42	18	H	Coventry C	Cancelled					
43	25	A	Milton Keynes D	Cancelled					
44	May 3	H	Doncaster R	Cancelled					

Final League Position: 13 (on points-per-game basis)

GOALSCORERS

League (44): Gnanduillet 15 (4 pens), Dewsbury-Hall 4, KaiKai 4, Delfouneso 3, Heneghan 2, Madine 2, Nuttall 2, Spearing 2 (2 pens), Virtue 2, Edwards 1, Feeney 1, Ronan 1, Scannell 1, Thompson 1, own goals 3.
FA Cup (9): Delfouneso 4, Gnanduillet 2, KaiKai 1, Virtue 1, own goal 1.
Carabao Cup (2): Gnanduillet 1 (1 pen), Turton 1.
Leasing.com Trophy (8): Nuttall 2, Bushiri 1, Hardie 1, Heneghan 1, KaiKai 1, Nottingham 1, own goal 1.

Alnwick J 22	Turton O 26 + 4	Tilt C 17 + 3	Edwards R 19 + 2	Husband J 28	KaiKai S 17 + 5	Spearing J 28 + 2	Thompson J 15 + 3	Feeney L 33 + 2	Delfouneso N 21 + 7	Gnanduillet A 25 + 5	Nuttall J 9 + 18	Pritchard H — + 2	Bushiri R 2 + 2	Nottingham M — + 3	Anderton N 1 + 1	Guy C 6 + 9	Hardie R 2 + 5	Heneghan B 24 + 2	Virtue M 20 + 4	Scannell S 3 + 5	MacDonald C 9 + 3	Sims J — + 1	Howard M 4	Bola M 5	Ward G 2 + 3	Madine G 9 + 1	Thorniley J 2	Ronan C 10	Dewsbury-Hall K 9 + 1	Maxwell C 9	Moore T 8	Match No.
1	2	3	4	5[3]	6	7	8	9	10[2]	11[1]	12	13	14																			1
1	2	4	3	5■	11	7	8	6[2]	9[3]	10[1]	13		14	12																		2
1	7	4	3		9		8[2]	6	11[3]	10		12	2[1]	13	5	14																3
1	8	4	3		11	7	6	5[1]	9[2]	10			2[3]	13	14	12																4
1	2	4	3	9	10[3]	7	6	5[2]		11[1]	12					8	13	14														5
1	2	4	3	5	9[1]	7[2]	8	6		11	10					12			13													6
1	2[1]	4	3	5	9	7		6	13	11[2]	10[3]					8	14	12														7
1		4[1]	2	9	8	7	6	5		11	10[2]						12	3		13												8
1		4	2	9	12	7	8	5		13	10[1]					14	11[3]	3	6[2]													9
1	12	4	2[2]	9	13	7	8[3]	5			10						11[1]	3	6	14												10
1	2	4		5		7	8	6		10						12		3	9[2]	11[1]	13											11
1	2	4		5		7		9		10						8	12	3	6	11[1]												12
1	2	4		5[3]		7[2]		9	12	10						8	13	3	6	11[1]	14											13
1	2	4		5	9	7	8[2]	6[3]	11[1]	10	12					13		3		14												14
1	2	4■	12	5	9	7	8	6[1]	11	13								3	10[2]													15
1	13		2	4	7	6		5[2]	10	11[1]	14					12		3	8[3]		9											16
1		14	2	4	10	6		5	9	11[1]	13					12		3	7[3]		8[2]											17
1	12		2	4	9[1]	6	14	5	11		10					13		3	7[3]		8[2]											18
1	2	14	4	5	11[3]	7	12	6	9[1]	10[2]	13							3	8													19
1	3	5	4	6	10[2]	8	14	2	9[3]	11	13								7[1]	12												20
1	2[1]		4	5	12	7	8	6	11[3]	10	13							3	9[2]		14											21
1[3]	2		4	5	9[1]	7	8	6[2]	10	11	14							3		13		12										22
	2		4	5	12	7		6[2]	13	10[1]	11					8		3	9				1									23
	2[3]	13	4	5	10[2]	6	9[1]	14	8	11	12							3	7				1									24
	2	4			14	6		7[2]	11	10[1]	13					9		3					1	5	8[3]	12						25
	2					6		14	7[2]	13	10							3					1	5	8[3]	11	4	9[1]	12			26
	2					6[1]		5	12	10[2]	14							3	13					9		11	4	8[3]	7	1		27
	3					7[3]		2	12	10								4	13					6	14	11[1]		9[2]	8	1	5	28
	3					7[2]		2	13	10								4	12					6	14	11[1]		9[3]	8	1	5	29
	12			5				2	13	11[1]	14							4■	7		6					10[3]		9[2]	8	1	3	30
	2			4				5	11		12								7		6					10[1]		9	8	1	3	31
	2		14	4		12		5[2]	10		13								7		9					11[3]		6[1]	8	1	3	32
	2			4				5	10		12								6		9					11		7[1]	8	1	3	33
				4				5	10[2]	13	12							3	6		9					11[1]		7	8	1	2	34
				4		13		5	10[3]	12	11[1]							3	6[2]		9				14			8	7	1	2	35
																																36
																																37
																																38
																																39
																																40
																																41
																																42
																																43
																																44

FA Cup

First Round	Morecambe	(h)	4-1
Second Round	Maidstone U	(h)	3-1
Third Round	Reading	(a)	2-2
Replay	Reading	(h)	0-2

Carabao Cup

First Round	Macclesfield T	(h)	2-2

(Macclesfield T won 4-2 on penalties)

Leasing.com Trophy

Group G (N)	Morecambe	(h)	5-1
Group G (N)	Carlisle U	(a)	1-2
Group G (N)	Wolverhampton W U21	(h)	1-0
Second Round (N)	Scunthorpe U	(h)	1-3

BOLTON WANDERERS

FOUNDATION

In 1874 boys of Christ Church Sunday School, Blackburn Street, led by their master Thomas Ogden, established a football club which went under the name of the school and whose president was vicar of Christ Church. Membership was 6d (two and a half pence). When their president began to lay down too many rules about the use of church premises, the club broke away and formed Bolton Wanderers in 1877, holding their earliest meetings at the Gladstone Hotel.

University of Bolton Stadium, Burnden Way, Lostock, Bolton BL6 6JW.

Telephone: (01204) 673 673.

Ticket Office: (0844) 871 2932.

Website: www.bwfc.co.uk

Email: reception@bwfc.co.uk (or via website).

Ground Capacity: 28,018.

Record Attendance: 69,912 v Manchester C, FA Cup 5th rd, 18 February 1933 (at Burnden Park); 28,353 v Leicester C, Premier League, 23 December 2003 (at The Reebok Stadium).

Pitch Measurements: 102m × 65m (111.5yd × 71yd).

Chairman: Sharon Brittan.

Director: Michael James.

Manager: Ian Evatt.

Assistant Manager: Peter Atherton.

Colours: White shirts with blue sleeves and blue and red trim, blue shorts with white and red trim, white socks with red and blue trim.

Year Formed: 1874.

Turned Professional: 1880.

Previous Name: 1874, Christ Church FC; 1877, Bolton Wanderers.

Club Nickname: 'The Trotters'.

Grounds: Park Recreation Ground and Cockle's Field before moving to Pike's Lane ground 1881; 1895, Burnden Park; 1997, Reebok Stadium (renamed Macron Stadium 2014; University of Bolton Stadium 2018).

First Football League Game: 8 September 1888, Football League, v Derby Co (h) L 3–6 – Harrison; Robinson, Mitchell; Roberts, Weir, Bullough, Davenport (2), Milne, Coupar, Barbour, Brogan (1).

Record League Victory: 8–0 v Barnsley, Division 2, 6 October 1934 – Jones; Smith, Finney; Goslin, Atkinson, George Taylor; George T. Taylor (2), Eastham, Milsom (1), Westwood (4), Cook, (1 og).

Record Cup Victory: 13–0 v Sheffield U, FA Cup 2nd rd, 1 February 1890 – Parkinson; Robinson (1), Jones; Bullough, Davenport, Roberts; Rushton, Brogan (3), Cassidy (5), McNee, Weir (4).

HONOURS

League Champions: First Division – 1996–97; Division 2 – 1908–09, 1977–78; Division 3 – 1972–73.
Runners-up: Division 2 – 1899–1900, 1904–05, 1910–11, 1934–35; Second Division – 1992–93; FL 1 – 2016–17.

FA Cup Winners: 1923, 1926, 1929, 1958.
Runners-up: 1894, 1904, 1953.

League Cup: *Runners-up:* 1995, 2004.

League Trophy Winners: 1989.
Runners-up: 1986.

European Competitions
UEFA Cup: 2005–06, 2007–08.

FOOTBALL YEARBOOK FACT FILE

Bolton Wanderers' FA Cup third round tie against Stoke City in January 1974 attracted the biggest attendance of the round after being switched to a Sunday due to the power crisis at the time. It was the first time the FA had sanctioned Cup ties on a Sunday and 39,138 were at Burnden Park to see Wanderers defeat Stoke thanks to a hat-trick from John Byrom. The gate was three times the attendance for Bolton's previous home match.

Record Defeat: 1–9 v Preston NE, FA Cup 2nd rd, 5 November 1887.

Most League Points (2 for a win): 61, Division 3, 1972–73.

Most League Points (3 for a win): 98, Division 1, 1996–97.

Most League Goals: 100, Division 1, 1996–97.

Highest League Scorer in Season: Joe Smith, 38, Division 1, 1920–21.

Most League Goals in Total Aggregate: Nat Lofthouse, 255, 1946–61.

Most League Goals in One Match: 5, Tony Caldwell v Walsall, Division 3, 10 September 1983.

Most Capped Player: Ricardo Gardner, 72 (112), Jamaica.

Most League Appearances: Eddie Hopkinson, 519, 1956–70.

Youngest League Player: Ray Parry, 15 years 267 days v Wolverhampton W, 13 October 1951.

Record Transfer Fee Received: £15,000,000 from Chelsea for Nicolas Anelka, January 2008.

Record Transfer Fee Paid: £8,250,000 to Toulouse for Johan Elmander, June 2008.

Football League Record: 1888 Founder Member of the League; 1899–1900 Division 2; 1900–03 Division 1; 1903–05 Division 2; 1905–08 Division 1; 1908–09 Division 2; 1909–10 Division 1; 1910–11 Division 2; 1911–33 Division 1; 1933–35 Division 2; 1935–64 Division 1; 1964–71 Division 2; 1971–73 Division 3; 1973–78 Division 2; 1978–80 Division 1; 1980–83 Division 2; 1983–87 Division 3; 1987–88 Division 4; 1988–92 Division 3; 1992–93 Division 2; 1993–95 Division 1; 1995–96 Premier League; 1996–97 Division 1; 1997–98 Premier League; 1998–2001 Division 1; 2001–12 Premier League; 2012–16 FL C; 2016–17 FL 1; 2017–19 FL C; 2019–20 FL 1; 2020– FL 2.

LATEST SEQUENCES

Longest Sequence of League Wins: 11, 5.11.1904 – 2.1.1905.

Longest Sequence of League Defeats: 11, 7.4.1902 – 18.10.1902.

Longest Sequence of League Draws: 6, 25.1.1913 – 8.3.1913.

Longest Sequence of Unbeaten League Matches: 23, 13.10.1990 – 9.3.1991.

Longest Sequence Without a League Win: 26, 7.4.1902 – 10.1.1903.

Successive Scoring Runs: 24 from 22.11.1996.

Successive Non-scoring Runs: 11 from 9.4.2019.

MANAGERS

Tom Rawthorne 1874–85 (*Secretary*)
J. J. Bentley 1885–86 (*Secretary*)
W. G. Struthers 1886–87 (*Secretary*)
Fitzroy Norris 1887 (*Secretary*)
J. J. Bentley 1887–95 (*Secretary*)
Harry Downs 1895–96 (*Secretary*)
Frank Brettell 1896–98 (*Secretary*)
John Somerville 1898–1910
Will Settle 1910–15
Tom Mather 1915–19
Charles Foweraker 1919–44
Walter Rowley 1944–50
Bill Ridding 1951–68
Nat Lofthouse 1968–70
Jimmy McIlroy 1970
Jimmy Meadows 1971
Nat Lofthouse 1971 (*then Admin. Manager to 1972*)
Jimmy Armfield 1971–74
Ian Greaves 1974–80
Stan Anderson 1980–81
George Mulhall 1981–82
John McGovern 1982–85
Charlie Wright 1985
Phil Neal 1985–92
Bruce Rioch 1992–95
Roy McFarland 1995–96
Colin Todd 1996–99
Roy McFarland and Colin Todd 1995–96
Sam Allardyce 1999–2007
Sammy Lee 2007
Gary Megson 2007–09
Owen Coyle 2010–12
Dougie Freedman 2012–14
Neil Lennon 2014–16
Phil Parkinson 2016–19
Keith Hill 2019–20
Ian Evatt July 2020–

TEN YEAR LEAGUE RECORD

		P	*W*	*D*	*L*	*F*	*A*	*Pts*	*Pos*
2010-11	PR Lge	38	12	10	16	52	56	46	14
2011-12	PR Lge	38	10	6	22	46	77	36	18
2012-13	FL C	46	18	14	14	69	61	68	7
2013-14	FL C	46	14	17	15	59	60	59	14
2014-15	FL C	46	13	12	21	54	67	51	18
2015-16	FL C	46	5	15	26	41	81	30	24
2016-17	FL 1	46	25	11	10	68	36	86	2
2017-18	FL C	46	10	13	23	39	74	43	21
2018-19	FL C	46	8	8	30	29	78	32	23
2019-20	FL 1	34	5	11	18	27	66	14	23§

§Decided on points-per-game (0.41)

DID YOU KNOW ?

The first competitive game played by Bolton Wanderers at their current stadium ended in a goalless draw. Wanderers, who had just been promoted to the Premier League, met Everton on 1 September 1997 at what was then known as the Reebok Stadium.

BOLTON WANDERERS – SKY BET LEAGUE ONE 2019–20 LEAGUE RECORD

Match No.	Date	Venue	Opponents	Result		H/T Score	Lg Pos.	Goalscorers	Attendance
1	Aug 3	A	Wycombe W	L	0-2	0-0	22		6454
2	10	H	Coventry C	D	0-0	0-0	23		8901
3	17	A	Tranmere R	L	0-5	0-2	23		8568
4	24	H	Ipswich T	L	0-5	0-1	23		5454
5	31	A	Gillingham	L	0-5	0-2	23		5065
6	Sept 14	A	Rotherham U	L	1-6	1-3	23	Verlinden 4	10,088
7	17	H	Oxford U	D	0-0	0-0	23		6786
8	21	H	Sunderland	D	1-1	0-0	23	Hobbs 50	12,026
9	28	A	Portsmouth	L	0-1	0-0	23		18,382
10	Oct 7	H	Blackpool	D	0-0	0-0	23		14,003
11	19	H	Rochdale	L	1-3	0-0	23	Verlinden 56	13,828
12	22	A	Bristol R	W	2-0	1-0	23	Murphy, L 15, Murphy, D 68	7244
13	Nov 2	H	Fleetwood T	W	2-1	2-0	23	O'Grady 28, Murphy, D 33	12,756
14	16	H	Milton Keynes D	W	1-0	0-0	23	Murphy, D 90	11,819
15	23	A	Accrington S	L	1-7	1-3	23	Murphy, D 4	5034
16	Dec 7	H	AFC Wimbledon	D	2-2	0-1	23	Murphy, D 56, Dodoo 90	11,501
17	14	A	Peterborough U	L	0-1	0-1	23		6965
18	21	H	Southend U	W	3-2	2-1	23	Dodoo 36, Murphy, L 45, Murphy, D 64	12,055
19	26	A	Sunderland	D	0-0	0-0	23		33,821
20	29	H	Shrewsbury T	D	1-1	1-0	23	Verlinden 34	13,788
21	Jan 1	H	Burton Alb	L	3-4	2-3	23	Dodoo 5, Murphy, D 11, Politic 84	11,918
22	11	A	Rochdale	L	0-2	0-1	23		5560
23	14	A	Lincoln C	L	1-5	0-1	23	Darcy 47	8882
24	18	H	Portsmouth	L	0-1	0-1	23		13,407
25	28	H	Bristol R	D	1-1	0-0	23	Murphy, D 82	10,657
26	Feb 1	H	Tranmere R	W	2-0	1-0	23	Politic 2, O'Grady 64	13,044
27	8	A	Coventry C	L	1-2	0-1	23	Politic 77	6623
28	11	A	Doncaster R	L	1-2	0-1	23	Dodoo 57	7097
29	15	H	Wycombe W	L	0-2	0-1	23		11,737
30	22	A	Milton Keynes D	L	0-1	0-0	23		8539
31	25	A	Blackpool	L	1-2	0-1	23	Bryan 88	8116
32	29	H	Accrington S	D	0-0	0-0	23		12,011
33	Mar 7	A	AFC Wimbledon	D	0-0	0-0	23		4804
34	10	A	Burton Alb	D	2-2	2-1	23	Delaney 20, Hamilton 38	2034
35	14	H	Peterborough U	Cancelled					
36	21	A	Southend U	Cancelled					
37	24	H	Doncaster R	Cancelled					
38	28	A	Fleetwood T	Cancelled					
39	Apr 4	H	Lincoln C	Cancelled					
40	10	A	Ipswich T	Cancelled					
41	14	H	Gillingham	Cancelled					
42	21	A	Shrewsbury T	Cancelled					
43	25	H	Rotherham U	Cancelled					
44	May 3	A	Oxford U	Cancelled					

Final League Position: 23 (on points-per-game basis)

GOALSCORERS

League (27): Murphy, D 8, Dodoo 4, Politic 3, Verlinden 3, Murphy, L 2, O'Grady 2, Bryan 1, Darcy 1, Delaney 1, Hamilton 1, Hobbs 1.
FA Cup (0).
Carabao Cup (2): Darcy 1, Politic 1.
Leasing.com Trophy (5): Crawford 2, O'Grady 2, Politic 1.

Matthews R 33	Brockbank H 5+1	Edwards L 6	Zouma Y 14+3	Earl J 9	Murphy L 26+3	Lowe J 28+1	Weir J 7+1	Oztumer E 1	Politic D 19+5	Brown E 4+1 / Delaney R 2+2	White J 3+1	Darcy R 14+5	King-Harmes C 3+2	Alexander M 1 / Mellis J 1+5	Graham S 6+7	Hurford-Lockett F —+2	Boon J 1+2	Brown-Sterling D 1+1	Riley R —+1	Hobbs J 11	Senior A 1+1	Emmanuel J 25+2	Wright J 11	Chicksen A 14+2 / Bunney J 1+1	Bridcutt L 11	Verlinden T 12+3 / Georgiou A —+2	Crawford A 12	Buckley W 3+2	Murphy D 23+1	Dodoo J 16+8	O'Grady C 10+10	Nsiala A 12	Hamilton E 12	Faal M —+2	Fleming B 10	Hall C —+1	Bryan K 6	*Match No.*
1	2	3	4^{3}	5^{2}	6	7	8	9^{1}	10	11	12	13	14																									1
	2	3	4				8		9	10	5	11	6^{1}	1	7	12																						2
1	2		4		8	3	9			10^{3}	5^{2}	11	6^{1}		7		12	13	14																			3
1	2		4		7	3	9			14	5^{1}	10	8		6^{3}	12	13	11^{2}																				4
1	2		4		6	8	9		10^{1}	11		7^{3}	12		14		5			3^{2}	13																	5
1					8^{1}	12	9^{2}		7			13								3		2	4	5	6	10	11											6
1						8	12		7											3		2	4	5	6	10^{1}	9	11										7
1			12		13	8			7											3		2	4^{2}	5	6	10^{1}	9	11										8
1			4		13	8			12											3		2^{2}		5	6	10^{1}	9	7	11									9
1			4			8			7^{1}						12					3		2		5	6^{2}	10	9		11	13								10
1			4		13	6			7^{2}						9^{3}						3	2		5		10	8^{1}		11	12	14							11
1			3	4	6	7																2		5			9		11	8	10							12
1			3		7	8			12^{2}						13							2	4	5		9^{1}			11	6	10							13
1				4	9	8			13													2	3	5	6	12			11	7^{1}	10^{2}							14
1			12	4■	9	8									14							2	3	5	6^{3}	7^{1}			11	13	10^{2}							15
1			3			8			13			10			7^{2}							2	4	5		12			11	6	9^{1}							16
1			2^{2}	4	7	6						11^{1}										5		9	3	12			10	8	13							17
1				5	8	7						10^{1}			13							2	4		3	6^{2}			11	9	12							18
1				5	8	7						10^{2}										2	4	13	3	9^{1}			11	6	12							19
1				5	8	7■						10			13							2	4	12	3^{1}	9^{3}			11	6^{2}	14							20
1				4	7■		8		14			10										2	3	5		9^{1}		12	11^{2}	6^{3}	13							21
1		5	3									8			9^{2}							2		6					11	10^{1}	13	4	7	12				22
1	13	5	3^{2}		6				10^{1}			8^{3}										2							11	7	12	4	9	14				23
1		4^{1}			9	6			10			8^{2}										2								11	12	3	7		5	13		24
1		4			9	6			10			8^{1}										2^{2}						13^{3}	11	12	14	3	7		5			25
1					8	7			6^{1}			12										2							11		10	3	9		5		4	26
1					8^{3}	7			9	12				14								2							11	13	10	3^{2}	6^{1}		5		4	27
1					8	7				13				12						3^{1}		2							11	6	10		9		5		4^{2}	28
1					8	7			9					14						4		2^{3}		13					11	12	10^{1}	3	6		5^{2}			29
1					8	2			9					6^{1}	12					3		13					10^{3}		11	14		4	7^{2}		5			30
1					8	2			10					14						4				6^{1}			7^{3}		12	13	11^{2}	3	9				5	31
1			12		7	2			6											4^{1}							10		11	9		3			5		8	32
1					7	2^{2}			6	4		13										12				14	10^{3}		11^{1}	9		3	8		5			33
1					6				8^{1}	4		13		14								2				12	9^{3}			11		3	10^{2}		5		7	34
																																						35
																																						36
																																						37
																																						38
																																						39
																																						40
																																						41
																																						42
																																						43
																																						44

FA Cup

First Round	Plymouth Arg	(h)	0-1

Carabao Cup

First Round	Rochdale	(a)	2-5

Leasing.com Trophy

Group F (N)	Bradford C	(h)	1-1
(Bradford C won 4-3 on penalties)			
Group F (N)	Rochdale	(a)	1-1
(Rochdale won 5-3 on penalties)			
Group F (N)	Manchester C U21	(h)	3-1
Second Round (N)	Accrington S	(a)	0-2

AFC BOURNEMOUTH

FOUNDATION

There was a Bournemouth FC as early as 1875, but the present club arose out of the remnants of the Boscombe St John's club (formed 1890). The meeting at which Boscombe FC came into being was held at a house in Gladstone Road in 1899. They began by playing in the Boscombe and District Junior League.

Vitality Stadium, Dean Court, Kings Park, Bournemouth, Dorset BH7 7AF.

Telephone: (0344) 576 1910.

Ticket Office: (0344) 576 1910.

Website: www.afcb.co.uk

Email: enquiries@afcb.co.uk

Ground Capacity: 11,364.

Record Attendance: 28,799 v Manchester U, FA Cup 6th rd, 2 March 1957.

Pitch Measurements: 105m × 68m (115yd × 74.5yd).

Chairman: Jeff Mostyn.

Chief Executive: Neill Blake.

Manager: Jason Tindall.

Assistant Manager: Stephen Purches.

Colours: Red and black striped shirts, black shorts with red trim, black socks with red trim.

Year Formed: 1899.

Turned Professional: 1910.

Previous Names: 1890, Boscombe St John's; 1899, Boscombe FC; 1923, Bournemouth & Boscombe Ath FC; 1972, AFC Bournemouth.

Club Nickname: 'Cherries'.

Grounds: 1899, Castlemain Road, Pokesdown; 1910, Dean Court (renamed Fitness First Stadium 2001, Seward Stadium 2011, Goldsands Stadium 2012, Vitality Stadium 2015).

First Football League Game: 25 August 1923, Division 3 (S), v Swindon T (a) L 1–3 – Heron; Wingham, Lamb; Butt, Charles Smith, Voisey; Miller, Lister (1), Davey, Simpson, Robinson.

Record League Victory: 8–0 v Birmingham C, FL C, 25 October 2014 – Boruc; Francis, Elphick, Cook, Daniels; Ritchie (1), Arter (Gosling), Surman, Pugh (3); Pitman (1) (Rantie 2 (1 pen)), Wilson (1) (Fraser). 10–0 win v Northampton T at start of 1939–40 expunged from the records on outbreak of war.

Record Cup Victory: 11–0 v Margate, FA Cup 1st rd, 20 November 1971 – Davies; Machin (1), Kitchener, Benson, Jones, Powell, Cave (1), Boyer, MacDougall (9 incl. 1p), Miller, Scott (De Garis).

Record Defeat: 0–9 v Lincoln C, Division 3, 18 December 1982.

HONOURS

League Champions: FL C – 2014–15; Division 3 – 1986–87.
Runners-up: FL 1 – 2012–13; Division 3S – 1947–48; FL 2 – 2009–10; Division 4 – 1970–71.

FA Cup: 6th rd – 1957.

League Cup: quarter-final – 2015, 2018, 2019.

League Trophy Winners: 1984.
Runners-up: 1998.

FOOTBALL YEARBOOK FACT FILE

AFC Bournemouth's redeveloped Fitness First Stadium was not completed in time for the start of the 2001–02 campaign and as a result the team played their home games at The Avenue Stadium, home of Dorchester Town, for the first three months of the season. The first home game at the redeveloped ground was not until 10 November when the Cherries defeated Wrexham 3-0.

Most League Points (2 for a win): 62, Division 3, 1971–72.

Most League Points (3 for a win): 97, Division 3, 1986–87.

Most League Goals: 98, FL C, 2014–15.

Highest League Scorer in Season: Ted MacDougall, 42, 1970–71.

Most League Goals in Total Aggregate: Ron Eyre, 202, 1924–33.

Most League Goals in One Match: 4, Jack Russell v Clapton Orient, Division 3 (S), 7 January 1933; 4, Jack Russell v Bristol C, Division 3 (S), 28 January 1933; 4, Harry Mardon v Southend U, Division 3 (S), 1 January 1938; 4, Jack McDonald v Torquay U, Division 3 (S), 8 November 1947; 4, Ted MacDougall v Colchester U, 18 September 1970; 4, Brian Clark v Rotherham U, 10 October 1972; 4, Luther Blissett v Hull C, 29 November 1988; 4, James Hayter v Bury, Division 2, 21 October 2000.

Most Capped Player: Josh King, 29 (46), Norway.

Most League Appearances: Steve Fletcher, 628, 1992–2007; 2008–13.

Youngest League Player: Jimmy White, 15 years 321 days v Brentford, 30 April 1958.

Record Transfer Fee Received: £41,000,000 from Manchester C for Nathan Aké, August 2020.

Record Transfer Fee Paid: £25,200,000 to Levante for Jefferson Lerma, August 2018.

Football League Record: 1923 Elected to Division 3 (S) and remained a Third Division club for record number of years until 1970; 1970–71 Division 4; 1971–75 Division 3; 1975–82 Division 4; 1982–87 Division 3; 1987–90 Division 2; 1990–92 Division 3; 1992–2002 Division 2; 2002–03 Division 3; 2003–04 Division 2; 2004–08 FL 1; 2008–10 FL 2; 2010–13 FL 1; 2013–15 FL C; 2015–20 Premier League; 2020– FL C.

MANAGERS

Vincent Kitcher 1914–23
(*Secretary-Manager*)
Harry Kinghorn 1923–25
Leslie Knighton 1925–28
Frank Richards 1928–30
Billy Birrell 1930–35
Bob Crompton 1935–36
Charlie Bell 1936–39
Harry Kinghorn 1939–47
Harry Lowe 1947–50
Jack Bruton 1950–56
Fred Cox 1956–58
Don Welsh 1958–61
Bill McGarry 1961–63
Reg Flewin 1963–65
Fred Cox 1965–70
John Bond 1970–73
Trevor Hartley 1974–75
John Benson 1975–78
Alec Stock 1979–80
David Webb 1980–82
Don Megson 1983
Harry Redknapp 1983–92
Tony Pulis 1992–94
Mel Machin 1994–2000
Sean O'Driscoll 2000–06
Kevin Bond 2006–08
Jimmy Quinn 2008
Eddie Howe 2008–11
Lee Bradbury 2011–12
Paul Groves 2012
Eddie Howe 2012–20
Jason Tindall August 2020–

LATEST SEQUENCES

Longest Sequence of League Wins: 8, 12.3.2013 – 20.4.2013.

Longest Sequence of League Defeats: 7, 13.8.1994 – 13.9.1994.

Longest Sequence of League Draws: 5, 25.4.2000 – 19.8.2000.

Longest Sequence of Unbeaten League Matches: 18, 6.3.1982 – 28.8.1982.

Longest Sequence Without a League Win: 14, 6.3.1974 – 27.4.1974.

Successive Scoring Runs: 31 from 28.10.2000.

Successive Non-scoring Runs: 6 from 1.2.1975.

TEN YEAR LEAGUE RECORD

		P	W	D	L	F	A	Pts	Pos
2010-11	FL 1	46	19	14	13	75	54	71	6
2011-12	FL 1	46	15	13	18	48	52	58	11
2012-13	FL 1	46	24	11	11	76	53	83	2
2013-14	FL C	46	18	12	16	67	66	66	10
2014-15	FL C	46	26	12	8	98	45	90	1
2015-16	PR Lge	38	11	9	18	45	67	42	16
2016-17	PR Lge	38	12	10	16	55	67	46	9
2017-18	PR Lge	38	11	11	16	45	61	44	12
2018-19	PR Lge	38	13	6	19	56	70	45	14
2019-20	PR Lge	38	9	7	22	40	65	34	18

DID YOU KNOW ?

Despite recording an 11-0 win over Margate in the first round of the FA Cup in 1971–72, AFC Bournemouth generally had a dismal record in the Cup during the 1970s. They failed to win a game against teams from a higher division, while twice being eliminated from the competition by non-league opposition.

AFC BOURNEMOUTH – PREMIER LEAGUE 2019–20 LEAGUE RECORD

Match No.	Date	Venue	Opponents	Result		H/T Score	Lg Pos.	Goalscorers	Attendance
1	Aug 10	H	Sheffield U	D	1-1	0-0	6	Mepham 62	10,714
2	17	A	Aston Villa	W	2-1	2-0	6	King (pen) 2, Wilson, H 12	40,996
3	25	H	Manchester C	L	1-3	1-2	11	Wilson, H 45	10,486
4	31	A	Leicester C	L	1-3	1-2	15	Wilson, C 15	31,613
5	Sept 15	H	Everton	W	3-1	1-1	8	Wilson, C 2 23, 72, Fraser 67	10,416
6	20	A	Southampton	W	3-1	2-0	3	Ake 10, Wilson, H 35, Wilson, C 90	30,168
7	28	H	West Ham U	D	2-2	1-1	7	King 17, Wilson, C 46	10,729
8	Oct 6	A	Arsenal	L	0-1	0-1	10		60,326
9	19	H	Norwich C	D	0-0	0-0	9		10,669
10	26	A	Watford	D	0-0	0-0	8		20,821
11	Nov 2	H	Manchester U	W	1-0	1-0	7	King 45	10,669
12	9	A	Newcastle U	L	1-2	1-1	7	Wilson, H 14	44,424
13	23	H	Wolverhampton W	L	1-2	0-2	11	Cook, S 59	10,539
14	30	A	Tottenham H	L	2-3	0-1	12	Wilson, H 2 73, 90	59,626
15	Dec 3	A	Crystal Palace	L	0-1	0-0	12		23,497
16	7	H	Liverpool	L	0-3	0-2	15		10,832
17	14	A	Chelsea	W	1-0	0-0	14	Gosling 84	40,243
18	21	H	Burnley	L	0-1	0-0	14		10,020
19	26	H	Arsenal	D	1-1	1-0	16	Gosling 35	10,234
20	28	A	Brighton & HA	L	0-2	0-1	16		30,441
21	Jan 1	A	West Ham U	L	0-4	0-3	18		59,917
22	12	H	Watford	L	0-3	0-1	19		10,384
23	18	A	Norwich C	L	0-1	0-1	19		26,781
24	21	H	Brighton & HA	W	3-1	2-0	18	Wilson, H 36, Gross (og) 41, Wilson, C 74	10,065
25	Feb 1	H	Aston Villa	W	2-1	2-0	16	Billing 37, Ake 44	10,722
26	9	A	Sheffield U	L	1-2	1-1	16	Wilson, C 13	30,361
27	22	A	Burnley	L	0-3	0-0	16		18,227
28	29	H	Chelsea	D	2-2	0-1	18	Lerma 54, King 57	10,667
29	Mar 7	A	Liverpool	L	1-2	1-2	18	Wilson, C 9	53,323
30	June 20	H	Crystal Palace	L	0-2	0-2	18		0
31	24	A	Wolverhampton W	L	0-1	0-0	18		0
32	July 1	H	Newcastle U	L	1-4	0-2	19	Gosling 90	0
33	4	A	Manchester U	L	2-5	1-3	19	Stanislas 15, King (pen) 49	0
34	9	H	Tottenham H	D	0-0	0-0	18		0
35	12	H	Leicester C	W	4-1	0-1	18	Stanislas (pen) 66, Solanke 2 67, 87, Evans (og) 83	0
36	15	A	Manchester C	L	1-2	0-2	18	Brooks 88	0
37	19	H	Southampton	L	0-2	0-1	19		0
38	26	A	Everton	W	3-1	2-1	18	King (pen) 13, Solanke 45, Stanislas 80	0

Final League Position: 18

GOALSCORERS

League (40): Wilson, C 8, Wilson, H 7, King 6 (3 pens), Gosling 3, Solanke 3, Stanislas 3 (1 pen), Ake 2, Billing 1, Brooks 1, Cook, S 1, Fraser 1, Lerma 1, Mepham 1, own goals 2.
FA Cup (5): Billing 2, Solanke 1, Surridge 1, Wilson C 1.
Carabao Cup (0).

Ramsdale A 37	Mepham C 10 + 2	Cook S 28 + 1	Ake N 29	Smith A 24	Billing P 29 + 5	Lerma J 31 + 2	Rico D 27	King J 24 + 2	Fraser R 21 + 7	Wilson C 32 + 3	Solanke D 17 + 15	Daniels C 2	Wilson H 20 + 11	Surman A 2 + 3	Ibe J — + 2	Stacey J 17 + 2	Cook L 14 + 13	Danjuma A 6 + 8	Francis S 10 + 5	Gosling D 14 + 10	Simpson J 1 + 3	Stanislas J 7 + 8	Travers M 1	Surridge S — + 4	Brooks D 8 + 1	Kelly L 7 + 1	Match No.
1	2	3	4	5	6	7	8	9	10	11[1]	12																1
1		3	4	2	7[1]	8		10	9	11	13	5	6[2]	12													2
1	3	4	5	2[2]	9	8		7	10	11[3]	14	6[1]	12		13												3
1	3	4	5	2[2]	7	8		10[3]	9	11	13		6[1]	14	12												4
1	14	3	4		7	13	5[3]	9	12	11	10		6[1]			2	8[2]										5
1		3	4		8	7	5	9[3]	12	10	11[2]		6[1]	14		2	13										6
1		3	4		7[3]	8	5	9		10	11		6[1]			2[2]	14	12	13								7
1		3	4		8	7	5	9	12	11	10[1]		6[2]			2[3]		14	13								8
1		3	4	2	8		5	12	9	10	11[1]		6[2]				7	13									9
1		3	4	2	8	7	5	11	6	10[2]	13		12					9[1]									10
1		3	4	2	8	7	5	11	9	10			6[1]				12										11
1		3	4	2[3]	8		5[1]	11	9	10	13		6[2]				7	14	12								12
1		3	4	5	7[2]	12	8		11	10			9[1]				6[3]	13	2■	14							13
1		3	4			8	5		9[1]	11	10		12			2	7[2]	6		13							14
1	3		4	2	8[3]	7	5[2]		13	11	10		6				14	9[1]	12								15
1	3		4[1]		8[2]	7	5		9	11[3]	10						13	6	2	14	12						16
1	4				7	8	5	11[1]	10		12					2	6		3	9							17
1	4				7[2]	8	5	11	10	12	13					2	6[1]		3	9							18
1	4	3			13	8		10[1]	6	11			12			2	7			9[2]	5						19
1	4	3			7		5	11[3]	12	13	10		6[1]			2	14			8		9[2]					20
1	4	3				7	5[2]		13	10	11		9[1]				6		2	8[3]	14	12					21
		4	5	2	12	8[1]			9	10	11		6[3]				13		3	7[2]			1	14			22
1		3■	4	2	6	7[2]	5		11	10	13		9[1]				14		12	8[3]							23
1			4	2	8	7	5		9	11	10[1]		6[2]				13		3	12							24
1			4	2	8	7■	5		11	10			9						3	6							25
1			4	2	7		5	12	10[2]	11	14		6[1]	8[3]					3	9		13					26
1		4		5	6			11[2]	13	10	14		9[3]	7		2			3	8[1]		12					27
1		3	4	5	6	7		11[1]	9	10						2	8[2]			13		12					28
1		3[1]	4	5	8	6[3]			7	11	13					2	9			14	12	10[2]					29
1		3	4	5		6		10[2]		11	13		7[1]			2	9	12				14			8[3]		30
1		3	4	5	9[1]	8[2]				11	13		14			2[5]	7	15		12		10[4]			6[3]	16	31
1	16	3[5]	4	2	7[1]	8[4]		10			11		14				12	9[2]		15		13			6[3]	5	32
1			3	2[5]	13	8	5	11			10[2]		15			16	7[3]	12		14		9[4]			6[1]	4	33
1			3	2[1]		8	5	10		11			13			12				7		9			6[2]	4	34
1		12	3[1]		14	8	5			11[5]	10					2	15	9[2]		7[3]		13		16	6[4]	4	35
1		4			7[5]	8	6	10[4]		13	11[2]		15			3	14			9[3]		2[1]		16	12	5	36
1		3			8[5]	7[4]	5	11[2]		10	14		12			2	13			16		9[3]		15	6[1]	4	37
1		3		2	13	8	5	9[3]		10	11[1]		14							7		12			6[2]	4	38

FA Cup

Third Round	Luton T	(h)	4-0
Fourth Round	Arsenal	(h)	1-2

Carabao Cup

Second Round	Forest Green R	(h)	0-0
(Bournemouth won 3-0 on penalties)			
Third Round	Burton Alb	(a)	0-2

BRADFORD CITY

FOUNDATION

Bradford was a rugby stronghold around the turn of the 20th century but after Manningham RFC held an archery contest to help them out of financial difficulties in 1903, they were persuaded to give up the handling code and turn to soccer. So they formed Bradford City and continued at Valley Parade. Recognising this as an opportunity to spread the dribbling code in this part of Yorkshire, the Football League immediately accepted the new club's first application for membership of the Second Division.

The Utilita Energy Stadium, Valley Parade, Bradford, West Yorkshire BD8 7DY.

Telephone: (01274) 773 355.

Ticket Office: (01274) 770 012.

Website: www.bradfordcityfc.co.uk

Email: support@bradfordcityfc.co.uk

Ground Capacity: 24,433.

Record Attendance: 39,146 v Burnley, FA Cup 4th rd, 11 March 1911.

Pitch Measurements: 103.5m × 64m (113yd × 70yd).

Chairman: Stephan Rudd.

Manager: Stuart McCall.

Assistant Manager: Kenny Black.

HONOURS

League Champions: Division 2 – 1907–08; Division 3 – 1984–85; Division 3N – 1928–29.

Runners-up: First Division – 1998–99; Division 4 – 1981–82.

FA Cup Winners: 1911.

League Cup: *Runners-up:* 2013.

European Competitions

Intertoto Cup: 2000.

Colours: Claret shirts with amber stripes, black shorts with amber and claret trim, black socks with amber and claret trim.

Year Formed: 1903.

Turned Professional: 1903.

Club Nickname: 'The Bantams'.

Ground: 1903, Valley Parade (renamed Bradford & Bingley Stadium 1999, Intersonic Stadium 2007, Coral Windows Stadium 2007, Northern Commercials Stadium 2016, The Utilita Energy Stadium 2019).

First Football League Game: 1 September 1903, Division 2, v Grimsby T (a) L 0–2 – Seymour; Wilson, Halliday; Robinson, Millar, Farnall; Guy, Beckram, Forrest, McMillan, Graham.

Record League Victory: 11–1 v Rotherham U, Division 3 (N), 25 August 1928 – Sherlaw; Russell, Watson; Burkinshaw (1), Summers, Bauld; Harvey (2), Edmunds (3), White (3), Cairns, Scriven (2).

Record Cup Victory: 11–3 v Walker Celtic, FA Cup 1st rd (replay), 1 December 1937 – Parker; Rookes, McDermott; Murphy, Mackie, Moore; Bagley (1), Whittingham (1), Deakin (4 incl. 1p), Cooke (1), Bartholomew (4).

Record Defeat: 1–9 v Colchester U, Division 4, 30 December 1961.

Most League Points (2 for a win): 63, Division 3 (N), 1928–29.

FOOTBALL YEARBOOK FACT FILE

In 2012–13 Bradford City were the first fourth-tier team for 51 years to reach the final of the Football League Cup. The Bantams knocked out Premier League teams Wigan Athletic, Arsenal and Aston Villa on their way to Wembley only to go down to another Premier League outfit, Swansea City, in the final. It was the first time a fourth-tier team had reached the final since 1962.

Most League Points (3 for a win): 94, Division 3, 1984–85.

Most League Goals: 128, Division 3 (N), 1928–29.

Highest League Scorer in Season: David Layne, 34, Division 4, 1961–62.

Most League Goals in Total Aggregate: Bobby Campbell, 121, 1981–84, 1984–86.

Most League Goals in One Match: 7, Albert Whitehurst v Tranmere R, Division 3 (N), 6 March 1929.

Most Capped Player: Jamie Lawrence, 19 (24), Jamaica.

Most League Appearances: Cec Podd, 502, 1970–84.

Youngest League Player: Robert Cullingford, 16 years 141 days v Mansfield T, 22 April 1970.

Record Transfer Fee Received: £2,000,000 from Newcastle U for Des Hamilton, March 1997; £2,000,000 from Newcastle U for Andrew O'Brien, March 2001.

Record Transfer Fee Paid: £2,500,000 to Leeds U for David Hopkin, July 2000.

Football League Record: 1903 Elected to Division 2; 1908–22 Division 1; 1922–27 Division 2; 1927–29 Division 3 (N); 1929–37 Division 2; 1937–61 Division 3; 1961–69 Division 4; 1969–72 Division 3; 1972–77 Division 4; 1977–78 Division 3; 1978–82 Division 4; 1982–85 Division 3; 1985–90 Division 2; 1990–92 Division 3; 1992–96 Division 2; 1996–99 Division 1; 1999–2001 Premier League; 2001–04 Division 1; 2004–07 FL 1; 2007–13 FL 2; 2013–19 FL 1; 2019– FL 2.

LATEST SEQUENCES

Longest Sequence of League Wins: 10, 26.11.1983 – 3.2.1984.

Longest Sequence of League Defeats: 8, 21.1.1933 – 11.3.1933.

Longest Sequence of League Draws: 6, 30.1.1976 – 13.3.1976.

Longest Sequence of Unbeaten League Matches: 21, 11.1.1969 – 2.5.1969.

Longest Sequence Without a League Win: 16, 28.8.1948 – 20.11.1948.

Successive Scoring Runs: 30 from 26.12.1961.

Successive Non-scoring Runs: 7 from 18.4.1925.

MANAGERS

Robert Campbell 1903–05
Peter O'Rourke 1905–21
David Menzies 1921–26
Colin Veitch 1926–28
Peter O'Rourke 1928–30
Jack Peart 1930–35
Dick Ray 1935–37
Fred Westgarth 1938–43
Bob Sharp 1943–46
Jack Barker 1946–47
John Milburn 1947–48
David Steele 1948–52
Albert Harris 1952
Ivor Powell 1952–55
Peter Jackson 1955–61
Bob Brocklebank 1961–64
Bill Harris 1965–66
Willie Watson 1966–69
Grenville Hair 1967–68
Jimmy Wheeler 1968–71
Bryan Edwards 1971–75
Bobby Kennedy 1975–78
John Napier 1978
George Mulhall 1978–81
Roy McFarland 1981–82
Trevor Cherry 1982–87
Terry Dolan 1987–89
Terry Yorath 1989–90
John Docherty 1990–91
Frank Stapleton 1991–94
Lennie Lawrence 1994–95
Chris Kamara 1995–98
Paul Jewell 1998–2000
Chris Hutchings 2000
Jim Jefferies 2000–01
Nicky Law 2001–03
Bryan Robson 2003–04
Colin Todd 2004–07
Stuart McCall 2007–10
Peter Taylor 2010–11
Peter Jackson 2011
Phil Parkinson 2011–16
Stuart McCall 2016–18
Simon Grayson 2018
Michael Collins 2018–19
David Hopkin 2019
Gary Bowyer 2019–20
Stuart McCall February 2020–

TEN YEAR LEAGUE RECORD

		P	*W*	*D*	*L*	*F*	*A*	*Pts*	*Pos*
2010-11	FL 2	46	15	7	24	43	68	52	18
2011-12	FL 2	46	12	14	20	54	59	50	18
2012-13	FL 2	46	18	15	13	63	52	69	7
2013-14	FL 1	46	14	17	15	57	54	59	11
2014-15	FL 1	46	17	14	15	55	55	65	7
2015-16	FL 1	46	23	11	12	55	40	80	5
2016-17	FL 1	46	20	19	7	62	43	79	5
2017-18	FL 1	46	18	9	19	57	67	63	11
2018-19	FL 1	46	11	8	27	49	77	41	24
2019-20	FL 2	37	14	12	11	44	40	54	9§

§Decided on points-per-game (1.46)

DID YOU KNOW ?

Bradford City had a dismal start to 1983–84, winning just one of their opening 15 games before transforming their season with a club record run of 10 consecutive League wins. The record was achieved with a 2-0 win at Exeter City with Terry Gray and John Hawley scoring the goals.

BRADFORD CITY – SKY BET LEAGUE TWO 2019–20 LEAGUE RECORD

Match No.	Date	Venue	Opponents	Result	H/T Score	Lg Pos.	Goalscorers	Attendance
1	Aug 3	H	Cambridge U	D 0-0	0-0	14		14,810
2	10	A	Grimsby T	D 1-1	0-0	17	Vaughan 53	6882
3	17	H	Oldham Ath	W 3-0	2-0	7	Vaughan 4, Donaldson 32, Scannell 72	14,447
4	20	A	Stevenage	W 1-0	1-0	2	Soares (og) 42	2833
5	24	H	Forest Green R	L 0-1	0-0	9		13,504
6	31	A	Crewe Alex	L 1-2	1-1	12	Vaughan 32	4459
7	Sept 7	H	Northampton T	W 2-1	0-1	10	Donaldson 77, O'Connor, P 88	13,678
8	14	A	Walsall	W 1-0	0-0	7	Kinsella (og) 83	4649
9	17	A	Cheltenham T	L 2-3	0-0	9	Anderson 51, Richards-Everton 76	2702
10	21	H	Carlisle U	W 3-1	2-1	6	Pritchard 30, Mellor 40, Ismail 90	14,217
11	28	A	Scunthorpe U	D 1-1	0-1	8	O'Connor, P 56	4554
12	Oct 5	H	Swindon T	W 2-1	0-0	6	Akpan 69, McCartan 79	14,136
13	12	A	Morecambe	W 2-1	0-0	3	Akpan 47, Oteh 78	3899
14	19	H	Crawley T	W 2-1	1-0	2	Pritchard 18, Devine 49	13,813
15	22	H	Port Vale	L 1-2	1-1	4	Vaughan (pen) 45	14,345
16	Nov 2	H	Exeter C	W 2-0	2-0	2	Oteh 31, Vaughan 45	14,002
17	23	A	Plymouth Arg	L 1-2	0-2	7	Canavan (og) 51	9645
18	30	A	Macclesfield T	D 1-1	0-1	7	Vaughan 73	2751
19	Dec 7	H	Newport Co	W 1-0	0-0	6	Vaughan (pen) 58	14,016
20	14	A	Leyton Orient	D 0-0	0-0	5		6015
21	21	H	Salford C	D 1-1	0-0	5	Pritchard 53	14,642
22	26	A	Carlisle U	D 0-0	0-0	5		6039
23	29	H	Mansfield T	W 2-0	1-0	4	Vaughan 2 (2 pens) 13, 83	15,197
24	Jan 1	H	Morecambe	W 1-0	0-0	4	Oteh 80	14,111
25	4	A	Swindon T	D 1-1	0-1	4	McCartan 89	8407
26	11	A	Crawley T	L 1-2	0-2	6	Vaughan 84	2361
27	18	H	Scunthorpe U	D 2-2	2-1	5	Akpan 17, Vaughan 19	14,176
28	21	A	Colchester U	D 0-0	0-0	5		3022
29	25	A	Mansfield T	L 0-3	0-2	7		5537
30	28	H	Cheltenham T	D 1-1	1-0	7	Donaldson (pen) 11	12,731
31	Feb 1	A	Oldham Ath	L 0-3	0-3	8		5198
32	8	H	Grimsby T	D 1-1	0-0	8	Novak 80	17,668
33	11	H	Stevenage	W 3-1	0-1	8	McCartan 2 49, 54, Novak 90	12,845
34	15	A	Cambridge U	L 1-2	1-0	9	Reeves 17	4541
35	22	A	Newport Co	L 1-2	1-2	9	Donaldson 26	3439
36	29	H	Plymouth Arg	W 2-1	2-0	9	Richards-Everton 6, Connolly 45	15,225
37	Mar 7	A	Salford C	L 0-2	0-1	9		3443
38	14	H	Leyton Orient	Cancelled				
39	17	A	Port Vale	Cancelled				
40	21	H	Macclesfield T	Cancelled				
41	28	A	Exeter C	Cancelled				
42	Apr 4	H	Colchester U	Cancelled				
43	10	A	Forest Green R	Cancelled				
44	13	H	Crewe Alex	Cancelled				
45	18	A	Northampton T	Cancelled				
46	25	H	Walsall	Cancelled				

Final League Position: 9 (on points-per-game basis)

GOALSCORERS

League (44): Vaughan 11 (4 pens), Donaldson 4 (1 pen), McCartan 4, Akpan 3, Oteh 3, Pritchard 3, Novak 2, O'Connor, P 2, Richards-Everton 2, Anderson 1, Connolly 1, Devine 1, Ismail 1, Mellor 1, Reeves 1, Scannell 1, own goals 3.
FA Cup (1): Oteh 1.
Carabao Cup (0).
Leasing.com Trophy (3): Akpan 1, French 1, O'Connor, P 1.

O'Donnell R 33	Mellor K 22 + 3	O'Connor A 34 + 2	Richards-Everton B 32	Henley A 22 + 2	Anderson J 3 + 2	Palmer M 17 + 1	Gibson J 3 + 3	Doyle E 6	Vaughan J 23 + 2	Donaldson C 18 + 2	Devine D 6 + 7	Scannell S 2 + 3	Longridge J — + 1	Wood C 35	McCartan S 8 + 13	Patrick O — + 2	Akpan H 13 + 6	Devitt J 3 + 2	Cooke C 18 + 7	O'Connor P 16 + 3	Pritchard H 14 + 7	Connolly D 22 + 5	Ismail Z 6 + 5	Oteh A 8 + 10	French T — + 2	Taylor C 9 + 5	Reeves J 17 + 1	McGee L 4	Mottley-Henry D 4 + 3	Novak L 6	Guthrie K 1 + 1	Middleton G 2 + 1	*Match No.*
1	2	3	4	5^3	6^2	7	8	9^1	10	11	12	13	14																				1
1	2	3	4	5	6^1	7	8	9^2	10	11	13	12																					2
1	2	3	4	5		8			11^1	10	7^3	6^2		9	12	13	14																3
1	2	3	4	5^1		8			11	10	7	6^2		9		13	12																4
1	2	3	4			8^3	11^1		10	9	7^2	13		5			6	12	14														5
1	5	2	4			8^1	14		11	10				9^2			6	7^3	13	3	12												6
1	2	14	4			7			11^2	10	8^1			5					13	3	9	6^3	12■										7
1	2		4			8			11	10	7^2			5	13				12	3	9	6^1											8
1	2	3	4		8^1	7			11	10^3				5					13		9	6^2	12	14									9
1	2	12	4■			7			11^1	10				5					8	3	9^2	6^3	13	14									10
1	2	4				8^3			11	10^2				5	14		12		7	3	9	6^1		13									11
1	2	4								11	13			5	12		8^1		6	3^2	9	10	7^3		14								12
1		4		2					14	11^1	13			5			8^3		6	3	9	10	7^2	12									13
1	14	3	4	2					10		12			5	13		6		7		8^1		9^2	11^3									14
1	2	3	4						10		6^1			5			8		7	12			9	11									15
1		3	4	2	14				10		12			5			6^2		7■		8^3	13	9^1	11									16
1	13	3	4	2					10		14			5			6^2		7^1		8	9	12	11^3									17
1		3	4	2					10					5			13				8	9	11^1	12		6	7^2						18
1	2	4		6	14				11					9					7^3	3		12		10^2	13	8^1	5						19
1	2	4		6		13			11					9	14				7	3	12			10^2		8^3	5^1						20
1	6	2	4											9	12				7	3	8^1	11^2		10		13	5						21
1	6	2	4			7	13		14					9	12				5	3		10^2		11^1		8^3							22
1		2	4	5		7			11^1					8	9^3				13	3		10		14		12	6^2						23
1		2	4	5^1		7			11					8	9^2					3		10	13	12		14	6^3						24
1		3	4	2		6			10					5	13				8			9		12		11^2	7^1						25
1		3	4	2		8		10	11					5	14		12					6^1		13		9^3	7^2						26
	5	2	4			6		10	11^3					9	13		8^2		7^1	3		12					14	1					27
	2	3	4	5				11						9	10^1						12	6				8	7	1					28
	12	3	4	2^1				11		14				5	10			13			9^2	6				8	7^3	1					29
	5^2	2	4	12						11^1				8	9^3			7■	6	3		10		13		14		1					30
1		3	5	2			14			11^2				6	12				7	4^3		10				8	9^1		13				31
1		3	4	2						11^3				5			14		7		9^1	6^2					8		13	10	12		32
1		3	4	2										5	9^3		8^1				12	13				14	7		6	10	11^2		33
1		3	4	2										5	11^3		8^1			12	14	13					7		6	10		9^2	34
1		3	4	2^2						10				5	13		8^3			12	14						7		6	11		9^1	35
1	2^2	3	4	12						11				5	9^1		8^3		14			6					7		13	10			36
1	2^2	3	4							14				5				10^3	8		13	9					7		6^1	11		12	37
																																	38
																																	39
																																	40
																																	41
																																	42
																																	43
																																	44
																																	45
																																	46

FA Cup

First Round	Shrewsbury T	(a)	1-1
Replay	Shrewsbury T	(h)	0-1

Carabao Cup

First Round	Preston NE	(h)	0-4

Leasing.com Trophy

Group F (N)	Bolton W	(a)	1-1
(Bradford C won 4-3 on penalties)			
Group F (N)	Manchester C U21	(h)	1-2
Group F (N)	Rochdale	(h)	1-2

BRENTFORD

FOUNDATION

Formed as a small amateur concern in 1889 they were very successful in local circles. They won the championship of the West London Alliance in 1893 and a year later the West Middlesex Junior Cup before carrying off the Senior Cup in 1895. After winning both the London Senior Amateur Cup and the Middlesex Senior Cup in 1898 they were admitted to the Second Division of the Southern League.

Brentford Community Stadium, 166 Lionel Road North, Brentford, Middlesex TW8 9QT (new stadium for start of 2020–21 season).

Telephone: (0208) 847 2511.

Ticket Office: (0333) 005 8521.

Website: www.brentfordfc.com

Email: enquiries@brentfordfc.com

Ground Capacity: 17,250.

Record Attendance: 38,678 v Leicester C, FA Cup 6th rd, 26 February 1949 (at Griffin Park).

Pitch Measurements: 100m × 67m (109.5yd × 73.5yd).

Chairman: Cliff Crown.

Chief Executive: Jon Varney.

Head Coach: Thomas Frank.

Assistant Head Coach: Brian Riemer.

Colours: Red and white striped shirts with black trim, black shorts with white trim, black socks with white trim.

Year Formed: 1889.

Turned Professional: 1899.

Club Nickname: 'The Bees'.

Grounds: 1889, Clifden Road; 1891, Benns Fields, Little Ealing; 1895, Shotters Field; 1898, Cross Road, S. Ealing; 1900, Boston Park; 1904, Griffin Park; 2020, Brentford Community Stadium.

First Football League Game: 28 August 1920, Division 3, v Exeter C (a) L 0–3 – Young; Hodson, Rosier, Jimmy Elliott, Levitt, Amos, Smith, Thompson, Spreadbury, Morley, Henery.

Record League Victory: 9–0 v Wrexham, Division 3, 15 October 1963 – Cakebread; Coote, Jones; Slater, Scott, Higginson; Summers (1), Brooks (2), McAdams (2), Ward (2), Hales (1), (1 og).

Record Cup Victory: 7–0 v Windsor & Eton (away), FA Cup 1st rd, 20 November 1982 – Roche; Rowe, Harris (Booker), McNichol (1), Whitehead, Hurlock (2), Kamara, Joseph (1), Mahoney (3), Bowles, Roberts. *N.B.* 8–0 v Uxbridge: Frail, Jock Watson, Caie, Bellingham, Parsonage (1), Jay, Atherton, Leigh (1), Bell (2), Buchanan (2), Underwood (2), FA Cup, 3rd Qual rd, 31 October 1903.

Record Defeat: 0–7 v Swansea T, Division 3 (S), 8 November 1924; v Walsall, Division 3 (S), 19 January 1957; v Peterborough U, 24 November 2007.

HONOURS

League Champions: Division 2 – 1934–35; Division 3 – 1991–92; Division 3S – 1932–33; FL 2 – 2008–09; Third Division – 1998–99; Division 4 – 1962–63.
Runners-up: FL 1 – 2013–14; Second Division – 1994–95; Division 3S – 1929–30, 1957–58.

FA Cup: 6th rd – 1938, 1946, 1949, 1989.

League Cup: 4th rd – 1983, 2011.

League Trophy: *Runners-up:* 1985, 2001, 2011.

FOOTBALL YEARBOOK FACT FILE

Brentford's first game at their Griffin Park ground was a Western League fixture against Plymouth Argyle on 1 September 1904. The main stand was not allowed to be used for the fixture as it had still to be passed by the authorities and the players had to change at nearby public baths. The game ended in a 1-1 draw.

Most League Points (2 for a win): 62, Division 3 (S), 1932–33 and Division 4, 1962–63.

Most League Points (3 for a win): 94, FL 1, 2013–14.

Most League Goals: 98, Division 4, 1962–63.

Highest League Scorer in Season: Jack Holliday, 38, Division 3 (S), 1932–33.

Most League Goals in Total Aggregate: Jim Towers, 153, 1954–61.

Most League Goals in One Match: 5, Jack Holliday v Luton T, Division 3 (S), 28 January 1933; 5, Billy Scott v Barnsley, Division 2, 15 December 1934; 5, Peter McKennan v Bury, Division 2, 18 February 1949.

Most Capped Player: John Buttigieg, 22 (98), Malta.

Most League Appearances: Ken Coote, 514, 1949–64.

Youngest League Player: Danis Salman, 15 years 248 days v Watford, 15 November 1975.

Record Transfer Fee Received: £20,000,000 from Brighton & HA for Neal Maupay, August 2019.

Record Transfer Fee Paid: £5,800,000 to Troyes for Bryan Mbeumo, July 2019.

Football League Record: 1920 Original Member of Division 3; 1921–33 Division 3 (S); 1933–35 Division 2; 1935–47 Division 1; 1947–54 Division 2; 1954–62 Division 3 (S); 1962–63 Division 4; 1963–66 Division 3; 1966–72 Division 4; 1972–73 Division 3; 1973–78 Division 4; 1978–92 Division 3; 1992–93 Division 1; 1993–98 Division 2; 1998–99 Division 3; 1999–2004 Division 2; 2004–07 FL 1; 2007–09 FL 2; 2009–14 FL 1; 2014– FL C.

LATEST SEQUENCES

Longest Sequence of League Wins: 9, 30.4.1932 – 24.9.1932.

Longest Sequence of League Defeats: 9, 20.10.1928 – 25.12.1928.

Longest Sequence of League Draws: 5, 16.3.1957 – 6.4.1957.

Longest Sequence of Unbeaten League Matches: 26, 20.2.1999 – 16.10.1999.

Longest Sequence Without a League Win: 18, 9.9.2006 – 26.12.2006.

Successive Scoring Runs: 26 from 4.3.1963.

Successive Non-scoring Runs: 7 from 7.3.2000.

MANAGERS

Will Lewis 1900–03
(*Secretary-Manager*)
Dick Molyneux 1902–06
W. G. Brown 1906–08
Fred Halliday 1908–12, 1915–21, 1924–26
(*only Secretary to 1922*)
Ephraim Rhodes 1912–15
Archie Mitchell 1921–24
Harry Curtis 1926–49
Jackie Gibbons 1949–52
Jimmy Bain 1952–53
Tommy Lawton 1953
Bill Dodgin Snr 1953–57
Malcolm Macdonald 1957–65
Tommy Cavanagh 1965–66
Billy Gray 1966–67
Jimmy Sirrel 1967–69
Frank Blunstone 1969–73
Mike Everitt 1973–75
John Docherty 1975–76
Bill Dodgin Jnr 1976–80
Fred Callaghan 1980–84
Frank McLintock 1984–87
Steve Perryman 1987–90
Phil Holder 1990–93
David Webb 1993–97
Eddie May 1997
Micky Adams 1997–98
Ron Noades 1998–2000
Ray Lewington 2000–01
Steve Coppell 2001–02
Wally Downes 2002–04
Martin Allen 2004–06
Leroy Rosenior 2006
Scott Fitzgerald 2006–07
Terry Butcher 2007
Andy Scott 2007–11
Nicky Forster 2011
Uwe Rosler 2011–13
Mark Warburton 2013–15
Marinus Dijkhuizen 2015
Dean Smith 2015–18
Thomas Frank October 2018–

TEN YEAR LEAGUE RECORD

		P	W	D	L	F	A	Pts	Pos
2010-11	FL 1	46	17	10	19	55	62	61	11
2011-12	FL 1	46	18	13	15	63	52	67	9
2012-13	FL 1	46	21	16	9	62	47	79	3
2013-14	FL 1	46	28	10	8	72	43	94	2
2014-15	FL C	46	23	9	14	78	59	78	5
2015-16	FL C	46	19	8	19	72	67	65	9
2016-17	FL C	46	18	10	18	75	65	64	10
2017-18	FL C	46	18	15	13	62	52	69	9
2018-19	FL C	46	17	13	16	73	59	64	11
2019-20	FL C	46	24	9	13	80	38	81	3

DID YOU KNOW ?

Having played in white shirts during their first few years as a League club, Brentford switched to their familiar red and white stripes for the start of the 1925–26 season, a change sanctioned by the Football League. Apart from one season the Bees have retained the shirts ever since.

BRENTFORD – SKY BET CHAMPIONSHIP 2019–20 LEAGUE RECORD

Match No.	*Date*	*Venue*	*Opponents*	*Result*	*H/T Score*	*Lg Pos.*	*Goalscorers*	*Attendance*
1	Aug 3	H	Birmingham C	L 0-1	0-1	21		11,332
2	10	A	Middlesbrough	W 1-0	0-0	14	Watkins [54]	21,911
3	17	H	Hull C	D 1-1	0-0	12	Watkins [72]	11,000
4	21	A	Leeds U	L 0-1	0-0	18		35,004
5	24	A	Charlton Ath	L 0-1	0-1	19		16,771
6	31	H	Derby Co	W 3-0	3-0	14	Mbeumo [17], Watkins 2 [18, 45]	11,055
7	Sept 14	A	Preston NE	L 0-2	0-1	18		12,873
8	21	H	Stoke C	D 0-0	0-0	17		11,870
9	29	A	Barnsley	W 3-1	1-1	14	Watkins 3 [35, 46, 68]	12,188
10	Oct 2	H	Bristol C	D 1-1	0-0	15	Da Silva [64]	11,433
11	5	A	Nottingham F	L 0-1	0-0	17		27,598
12	19	H	Millwall	W 3-2	0-1	13	Da Silva [84], Mbeumo [88], Watkins [90]	10,886
13	22	A	Swansea C	W 3-0	2-0	12	Benrahma [30], Bidwell (og) [36], Mbeumo [56]	15,875
14	28	A	QPR	W 3-1	1-0	12	Watkins 2 [23, 90], Benrahma (pen) [60]	15,562
15	Nov 2	H	Huddersfield T	L 0-1	0-0	13		11,727
16	9	A	Wigan Ath	W 3-0	1-0	9	Mbeumo [5], Mokotjo [70], Da Silva [83]	9260
17	23	H	Reading	W 1-0	0-0	8	Watkins [62]	11,892
18	27	A	Blackburn R	L 0-1	0-1	8		11,401
19	30	H	Luton T	W 7-0	5-0	7	Mbeumo [6], Watkins [29], Jensen [33], Da Silva 3 (1 pen) [40, 45, 87 (p)], Benrahma (pen) [71]	11,287
20	Dec 7	A	Sheffield W	L 1-2	1-0	9	Mbeumo [29]	22,475
21	11	H	Cardiff C	W 2-1	1-0	7	Mbeumo [25], Watkins [46]	10,417
22	14	H	Fulham	W 1-0	1-0	4	Mbeumo [22]	12,305
23	21	A	WBA	D 1-1	1-1	5	Dalsgaard [43]	24,961
24	26	H	Swansea C	W 3-1	2-0	3	Mbeumo [20], Watkins 2 [25, 88]	11,848
25	29	A	Millwall	L 0-1	0-1	4		15,464
26	Jan 1	A	Bristol C	W 4-0	2-0	3	Mbeumo [6], Benrahma [26], Watkins 2 [82, 90]	20,858
27	11	H	QPR	W 3-1	3-0	3	Benrahma [19], Mbeumo [23], Watkins [33]	12,324
28	18	A	Huddersfield T	D 0-0	0-0	4		20,874
29	28	H	Nottingham F	L 0-1	0-1	5		12,274
30	Feb 1	A	Hull C	W 5-1	2-1	5	Benrahma 3 [12, 63, 85], Burke (og) [20], Watkins [58]	10,034
31	8	H	Middlesbrough	W 3-2	1-0	5	Jeanvier [24], Mbeumo [60], Watkins [87]	12,285
32	11	H	Leeds U	D 1-1	1-1	4	Benrahma [25]	12,294
33	15	A	Birmingham C	D 1-1	1-1	4	Pinnock [17]	20,379
34	22	H	Blackburn R	D 2-2	0-1	4	Watkins [62], Benrahma (pen) [71]	12,082
35	25	A	Luton T	L 1-2	0-2	5	Watkins [83]	10,008
36	29	A	Cardiff C	D 2-2	2-2	5	Racic [5], Mbeumo [21]	22,393
37	Mar 7	H	Sheffield W	W 5-0	3-0	4	Da Silva 2 [10, 73], Marcondes [18], Mbeumo [40], Fosu [82]	12,273
38	June 20	A	Fulham	W 2-0	0-0	4	Benrahma [88], Marcondes [90]	0
39	26	H	WBA	W 1-0	1-0	3	Watkins [16]	0
40	30	A	Reading	W 3-0	1-0	3	Mbeumo [23], Da Silva [64], Valencia [90]	0
41	July 4	H	Wigan Ath	W 3-0	1-0	3	Benrahma 3 [19, 57, 66]	0
42	7	H	Charlton Ath	W 2-1	0-1	3	Benrahma (pen) [75], Pinnock [85]	0
43	11	A	Derby Co	W 3-1	1-1	3	Watkins [3], Benrahma 2 [49, 64]	0
44	15	H	Preston NE	W 1-0	1-0	3	Watkins [4]	0
45	18	A	Stoke C	L 0-1	0-1	3		0
46	22	H	Barnsley	L 1-2	0-1	3	Da Silva [73]	0

Final League Position: 3

GOALSCORERS

League (80): Watkins 25, Benrahma 17 (4 pens), Mbeumo 15, Da Silva 10 (1 pen), Marcondes 2, Pinnock 2, Dalsgaard 1, Fosu 1, Jeanvier 1, Jensen 1, Mokotjo 1, Racic 1, Valencia 1, own goals 2.
FA Cup (1): Marcondes 1.
Carabao Cup (1): Forss 1.
Championship Play-Offs (4): Dalsgaard 1, Marcondes 1, Mbeumo 1, Watkins 1.

Raya D 46	Jeanvier J 25 + 1	Jansson P 34	Pinnock E 34 + 2	Dalsgaard H 42 + 1	Da Silva J 34 + 8	Jensen M 30 + 9	Henry R 46	Canos S 11 + 2	Watkins O 46	Marcondes E 13 + 12	Forss M — + 2	Zamburek J 1 + 15	Racic L 3 + 1	Mbeumo B 36 + 6	Yearwood D — + 2	Norgaard C 40 + 2	Benrahma S 39 + 4	Mokotjo K 14 + 11	Valencia J 1 + 18	Karelis N 1 + 3	Clarke J — + 1	Thompson D — + 2	Oksanen J — + 1	Roerslev Rasmussen M 5 + 6	Sorensen M — + 1	Dervisoglu H — + 4	Baptiste S 3 + 9	Fosu T 2 + 8	Match No.
1	2[2]	3	4	5	6	7	8	9	10	11[1]	12	13																	1
1	2	3	4[1]	5	6[3]	7	8	9[2]	10	11			12	13	14														2
1	2	3		5	13	7	8	9	10		14		4[1]	11[3]		6[2]	12												3
1	2	3	4[3]	5	12	6	8	11[2]	10	14				9[1]		7	13												4
1		3	4	5		7	8[3]	11	10	9			2[2]	14		6[1]	12	13											5
1	4	3		2		6[1]	8	5	10			13		9[2]		7	11[3]	12	14										6
1	4	3		2	13	7[2]	8	5	10					9[1]		6	11	12											7
1	4	3		2		7[2]	8	5[3]	10					9[1]		6	11	13		12	14								8
1	4	3	12	2	13	6[2]	5	9[1]	10[3]							7	11	8		14									9
1	4	3	13	2	6[3]	12	5	9[2]	10					14		7	11	8[1]											10
1	4	3		2	8[2]	6[3]	5	9	10					11[1]		7	12	13		14									11
1	4	3		2	13	6[3]	5		9					12		7[2]	11	8	14	10[1]									12
1	4	3		2	6[2]	13	5		10			14		9[1]		7	11[3]	8	12										13
1	4	3		2	8[2]	13	5		10					9[1]		7	11	6	12										14
1	4	3		2	8[1]	12	5		10			14		9[3]		7	11	6[2]	13										15
1	4■	3		2	8	13	5[3]		10			12		9[2]		7		6	11[1]			14							16
1		3	4	2	8[2]	6	5		10			12		9			11[1]	7					13						17
1		3	4	2	13	6	5[3]		10			9[1]		12		7	11	8[2]						14					18
1		3[1]	4	2[3]	8	6[2]	5		10			13		9		7	11							14	12				19
1	3		4		8	12	5		10					9		7	11	6[1]						2					20
1	13	3	4	2	8	6	5		10					9[2]		7[1]	11	12											21
1		3	4	2	6[1]	8	5		10					9[2]		12	11	7						13					22
1	3		4	2	8[3]	6[1]	5		10			14		9[2]		7	11	12	13										23
1		3	4	2	8	6[2]	5		10			14		9[1]		13	11[3]	7	12										24
1		3	4	2	8	6[1]	5[2]		10			12		9			11	7	13										25
1		3	4		8[1]	6[3]	5		10	13		14		9[2]		7	11	12						2					26
1		3	4	2	8[3]	6[1]	5		10	14				9[2]		7	11	12	13										27
1	3		4	2	8		5		10	13				9[1]		7	11	6[2]	12										28
1	3		4	2	8	6[1]	5		10	12				9		7	11												29
1	3		4	2	8[2]	6	5		10[3]	12				9[1]		7	11		13							14			30
1	3		4	2	8	6[1]	5		10	12				9[2]		7	11							13					31
1	3		4	2	8[1]	6[2]	5		10	12				9[3]		7	11										13	14	32
1	3		4	2		6[1]	5		10	9					12[2]	7	11										8	13	33
1	3[1]		4	2	8		5[3]		10	6[2]				9		7	11							12		14	13		34
1			4	2	6		8		10	12				9[2]		3[1]	11		14					5			7[3]	13	35
1			4	2	8		5		10	6[1]		13	3	9		7	11										12[2]		36
1	3		4	2	8[3]		5		10	6				9[2]		7[1]	11		14								12	13	37
1		3	4	2	8[3]	6[1]	5		10	13						7	11		14								12	9[2]	38
1		3	4	2	8[3]		5		10	6[1]				13		7	11	14									12	9[2]	39
1		3	4	2[3]	8[2]		5		10	6[4]				9[1]		7	11	15	12					14			13		40
1		3	4	2	12	13	5		10	6[2]		16		9[3]		7[5]	11[4]		14								8[1]	15	41
1		3	4	12	8	6[1]	5		10	13				9[3]		7	11							2[2]		14			42
1		3	4		8[2]	13	5[5]		10	6		12		9[4]		7[1]	11[3]		15			16		2				14	43
1		3	4	2	12	8[1]	5		10	6[3]		14		9[2]		7	11		13										44
1		3	4	2[4]	8[1]	6[3]	5[2]	14	10	12				9[5]		7	11									13	15	16	45
1		3	4[3]	2	8	12	5[1]	14	10	6[2]				9[4]		7	11										15	13	46

FA Cup

Third Round	Stoke C	(h)	1-0
Fourth Round	Leicester C	(h)	0-1

Carabao Cup

First Round	Cambridge U	(h)	1-1

(Cambridge U won 5-4 on penalties)

Championship play-offs

Semi-Finals 1st leg	Swansea C	(a)	0-1
Semi-Finals 2nd leg	Swansea C	(h)	3-1
Final	Fulham	(Wembley)	1-2

(*aet*)

BRIGHTON & HOVE ALBION

FOUNDATION

A professional club Brighton United was formed in November 1897 at the Imperial Hotel, Queen's Road, but folded in March 1900 after less than two seasons in the Southern League at the County Ground. An amateur team Brighton & Hove Rangers was then formed by some prominent United supporters and after one season at Withdean, decided to turn semi-professional and play at the County Ground. Rangers were accepted into the Southern League but folded in June 1901. John Jackson, the former United manager, organised a meeting at the Seven Stars public house, Ship Street on 24 June 1901 at which a new third club Brighton & Hove United was formed. They took over Rangers' place in the Southern League and pitch at County Ground. The name was changed to Brighton & Hove Albion before a match was played because of objections by Hove FC.

American Express Community Stadium, Village Way, Falmer, Brighton BN1 9BL.

Telephone: (0344) 324 6282.

Ticket Office: (0844) 327 1901.

Website: www.brightonandhovealbion.com

Email: supporter.services@bhafc.co.uk

Ground Capacity: 30,750.

Record Attendance: 36,747 v Fulham, Division 2, 27 December 1958 (at Goldstone Ground); 8,691 v Leeds U, FL 1, 20 October 2007 (at Withdean); 30,682 v Liverpool, Premier League, 12 January 2019 (at Amex).

Pitch Measurements: 105m × 68m (115yd × 74.5yd).

Chairman: Tony Bloom.

Chief Executive: Paul Barber.

Head Coach: Graham Potter.

Assistant Head Coach: Billy Reid.

Colours: Blue and white striped shirts with blue sleeves, white shorts, blue socks.

Year Formed: 1901.

Turned Professional: 1901.

Club Nickname: 'The Seagulls'.

Grounds: 1901, County Ground; 1902, Goldstone Ground; 1997, groundshare at Gillingham FC; 1999, Withdean Stadium; 2011, American Express Community Stadium.

First Football League Game: 28 August 1920, Division 3, v Southend U (a) L 0–2 – Hayes; Woodhouse, Little; Hall, Comber, Bentley; Longstaff, Ritchie, Doran, Rodgerson, March.

Record League Victory: 9–1 v Newport Co, Division 3 (S), 18 April 1951 – Ball; Tennant (1p), Mansell (1p); Willard, McCoy, Wilson; Reed, McNichol (4), Garbutt, Bennett (2), Keene (1). 9–1 v Southend U, Division 3, 27 November 1965 – Powney; Magill, Baxter; Leck, Gall, Turner; Gould (1), Collins (1), Livesey (2), Smith (3), Goodchild (2).

HONOURS

League Champions: FL 1 – 2010–11; Second Division – 2001–02; Division 3S – 1957–58; Third Division – 2000–01; Division 4 – 1964–65.
Runners-up: FL C – 2016–17; Division 2 – 1978–79; Division 3 – 1971–72, 1976–77, 1987–88; Division 3S – 1953–54, 1955–56.

FA Cup: *Runners-up:* 1983.

League Cup: 5th rd – 1979.

FOOTBALL YEARBOOK FACT FILE

After beating both Wisbech Town (10-1) and Southend United (9-1) in recent weeks Brighton & Hove Albion would have been hot favourites to beat Southern League club Bedford Town in their FA Cup second round tie in December 1965. However, after drawing 1-1 at the Goldstone Ground, they went down to a 2-1 defeat in the replay.

Record Cup Victory: 10–1 v Wisbech, FA Cup 1st rd, 13 November 1965 – Powney; Magill, Baxter; Collins (1), Gall, Turner; Gould, Smith (2), Livesey (3), Cassidy (2), Goodchild (1), (1 og).

Record Defeat: 0–9 v Middlesbrough, Division 2, 23 August 1958.

Most League Points (2 for a win): 65, Division 3 (S), 1955–56 and Division 3, 1971–72.

Most League Points (3 for a win): 95, FL 1, 2010–11.

Most League Goals: 112, Division 3 (S), 1955–56.

Highest League Scorer in Season: Peter Ward, 32, Division 3, 1976–77.

Most League Goals in Total Aggregate: Tommy Cook, 114, 1922–29.

Most League Goals in One Match: 5, Jack Doran v Northampton T, Division 3 (S), 5 November 1921; 5, Adrian Thorne v Watford, Division 3 (S), 30 April 1958.

Most Capped Player: Shane Duffy, 28 (33), Republic of Ireland.

Most League Appearances: Ernie 'Tug' Wilson, 509, 1922–36.

Youngest League Player: Ian Chapman, 16 years 259 days v Birmingham C, 14 February 1987.

Record Transfer Fee Received: £8,000,000 from Leicester C for Leonardo Ulloa, July 2014.

Record Transfer Fee Paid: £20,000,000 to Bristol C for Adam Webster, August 2019.

Football League Record: 1920 Original Member of Division 3; 1921–58 Division 3 (S); 1958–62 Division 2; 1962–63 Division 3; 1963–65 Division 4; 1965–72 Division 3; 1972–73 Division 2; 1973–77 Division 3; 1977–79 Division 2; 1979–83 Division 1; 1983–87 Division 2; 1987–88 Division 3; 1988–96 Division 2; 1996–2001 Division 3; 2001–02 Division 2; 2002–03 Division 1; 2003–04 Division 2; 2004–06 FL C; 2006–11 FL 1; 2011–17 FL C; 2017– Premier League.

MANAGERS

John Jackson 1901–05
Frank Scott-Walford 1905–08
John Robson 1908–14
Charles Webb 1919–47
Tommy Cook 1947
Don Welsh 1947–51
Billy Lane 1951–61
George Curtis 1961–63
Archie Macaulay 1963–68
Fred Goodwin 1968–70
Pat Saward 1970–73
Brian Clough 1973–74
Peter Taylor 1974–76
Alan Mullery 1976–81
Mike Bailey 1981–82
Jimmy Melia 1982–83
Chris Cattlin 1983–86
Alan Mullery 1986–87
Barry Lloyd 1987–93
Liam Brady 1993–95
Jimmy Case 1995–96
Steve Gritt 1996–98
Brian Horton 1998–99
Jeff Wood 1999
Micky Adams 1999–2001
Peter Taylor 2001–02
Martin Hinshelwood 2002
Steve Coppell 2002–03
Mark McGhee 2003–06
Dean Wilkins 2006–08
Micky Adams 2008–09
Russell Slade 2009
Gus Poyet 2009–13
Óscar Garcia 2013–14
Sammi Hyypia 2014
Chris Hughton 2014–19
Graham Potter May 2019–

LATEST SEQUENCES

Longest Sequence of League Wins: 9, 2.10.1926 – 20.11.1926.

Longest Sequence of League Defeats: 12, 17.8.2002 – 26.10.2002.

Longest Sequence of League Draws: 6, 16.2.1980 – 15.3.1980.

Longest Sequence of Unbeaten League Matches: 22, 2.5.2015 – 15.12.2015.

Longest Sequence Without a League Win: 15, 21.10.1972 – 27.1.1973.

Successive Scoring Runs: 31 from 4.2.1956.

Successive Non-scoring Runs: 6 from 30.3.2019.

TEN YEAR LEAGUE RECORD

		P	W	D	L	F	A	Pts	Pos
2010-11	FL 1	46	28	11	7	85	40	95	1
2011-12	FL C	46	17	15	14	52	52	66	10
2012-13	FL C	46	19	18	9	69	43	75	4
2013-14	FL C	46	19	15	12	55	40	72	6
2014-15	FL C	46	10	17	19	44	54	47	20
2015-16	FL C	46	24	17	5	72	42	89	3
2016-17	FL C	46	28	9	9	74	40	93	2
2017-18	PR Lge	38	9	13	16	34	54	40	15
2018-19	PR Lge	38	9	9	20	35	60	36	17
2019-20	PR Lge	38	9	14	15	39	54	41	15

DID YOU KNOW ?

The actor and comedian Norman Wisdom was a director of Brighton & Hove Albion from 1964 to 1970. He rewrote the song 'Good Old Sussex by the Sea' inserting lyrics appropriate to Albion and this quickly became a great favourite of the club's supporters.

BRIGHTON & HOVE ALBION – PREMIER LEAGUE 2019–20 LEAGUE RECORD

Match No.	Date	Venue	Opponents	Result		H/T Score	Lg Pos.	Goalscorers	Attendance
1	Aug 10	A	Watford	W	3-0	1-0	3	Doucoure (og) 28, Andone 65, Maupay 77	20,245
2	17	H	West Ham U	D	1-1	0-0	4	Trossard 65	30,459
3	24	H	Southampton	L	0-2	0-0	7		30,019
4	31	A	Manchester C	L	0-4	0-2	16		54,386
5	Sept 14	H	Burnley	D	1-1	0-0	15	Maupay 51	29,398
6	21	A	Newcastle U	D	0-0	0-0	15		43,360
7	28	A	Chelsea	L	0-2	0-0	16		40,683
8	Oct 5	H	Tottenham H	W	3-0	2-0	13	Maupay 3, Connolly 2 32, 65	30,610
9	19	A	Aston Villa	L	1-2	1-1	16	Webster 21	41,826
10	26	H	Everton	W	3-2	1-1	12	Gross 15, Maupay (pen) 80, Digne (og) 90	30,529
11	Nov 2	H	Norwich C	W	2-0	0-0	8	Trossard 68, Duffy 84	30,539
12	10	A	Manchester U	L	1-3	0-2	11	Dunk 64	73,556
13	23	H	Leicester C	L	0-2	0-0	12		30,640
14	30	A	Liverpool	L	1-2	0-2	15	Dunk 79	53,319
15	Dec 5	A	Arsenal	W	2-1	1-0	13	Webster 36, Maupay 80	60,164
16	8	H	Wolverhampton W	D	2-2	2-2	12	Maupay 34, Propper 36	30,189
17	16	A	Crystal Palace	D	1-1	0-0	13	Maupay 54	24,175
18	21	H	Sheffield U	L	0-1	0-1	13		30,505
19	26	A	Tottenham H	L	1-2	1-0	15	Webster 37	56,308
20	28	H	Bournemouth	W	2-0	1-0	14	Jahanbakhsh 3, Mooy 79	30,441
21	Jan 1	H	Chelsea	D	1-1	0-1	14	Jahanbakhsh 84	30,559
22	11	A	Everton	L	0-1	0-1	14		38,772
23	18	H	Aston Villa	D	1-1	1-0	14	Trossard 38	30,551
24	21	A	Bournemouth	L	1-3	0-2	15	Mooy 81	10,065
25	Feb 1	A	West Ham U	D	3-3	0-2	15	Ogbonna (og) 47, Gross 75, Murray 79	59,952
26	8	H	Watford	D	1-1	0-1	15	Mariappa (og) 78	30,443
27	22	A	Sheffield U	D	1-1	1-1	15	Maupay 30	31,888
28	29	H	Crystal Palace	L	0-1	0-0	15		30,124
29	Mar 7	A	Wolverhampton W	D	0-0	0-0	15		31,490
30	June 20	H	Arsenal	W	2-1	0-0	15	Dunk 75, Maupay 90	0
31	23	A	Leicester C	D	0-0	0-0	15		0
32	30	H	Manchester U	L	0-3	0-2	15		0
33	July 4	A	Norwich C	W	1-0	1-0	15	Trossard 25	0
34	8	H	Liverpool	L	1-3	1-2	15	Trossard 45	0
35	11	H	Manchester C	L	0-5	0-2	15		0
36	16	A	Southampton	D	1-1	1-0	15	Maupay 17	0
37	20	H	Newcastle U	D	0-0	0-0	15		0
38	26	A	Burnley	W	2-1	1-1	15	Bissouma 20, Connolly 50	0

Final League Position: 15

GOALSCORERS

League (39): Maupay 10 (1 pen), Trossard 5, Connolly 3, Dunk 3, Webster 3, Gross 2, Jahanbakhsh 2, Mooy 2, Andone 1, Bissouma 1, Duffy 1, Murray 1, Propper 1, own goals 4.
FA Cup (0).
Carabao Cup (3): Connolly 1, Murray 1, Roberts 1.
Leasing.com Trophy (5): Cashman 1, O'Hora 1, Radulovic 1, Richards 1, own goal 1.

Ryan M 38	Montoya M 23 + 4	Duffy S 12 + 7	Dunk L 36	Burn D 33 + 1	March S 11 + 8	Gross P 22 + 7	Propper D 32 + 3	Stephens D 28 + 5	Locadia J 1 + 1	Murray G 7 + 16	Andone F 1 + 2	Maupay N 30 + 7	Bernardo J 7 + 7	Trossard L 22 + 9	Mooy A 25 + 6	Webster A 31	Connolly A 14 + 10	Bong G — + 4	Alzate S 12 + 7	Bissouma Y 15 + 7	Schelotto E 4 + 4	Jahanbakhsh A 3 + 7	Mac Allister A 4 + 5	Lamptey T 7 + 1	*Match No.*
1	2	3	4	5	6^3	7	8	9	10^1	11^2	12	13	14												1
1	5	2	3	4	8	9^1	6	7		10^2	13	12		11^3	14										2
1	5	2	3	4	8^1	14	7	6^3	12	13	10■	9^2		11											3
1	5		3	4	9	14	7	6		13		10^1	8^2	11^3		2	12								4
1		2	3	8	5^3	9	7	6		11^1		10^2			12	4	13	14							5
1	5		3	4		9^2	7	6				10^3			11^1	2	12	13	8	14					6
1	5		3	4		9		7		14		10^3			11^2	2	13	12	8	6^1					7
1	2		4	5		6		8^3		14		10			9	3	11^1	13	7^2	12					8
1	2^2	13	4	5	12	6	7	8				11^3			9■	3	10^1		14						9
1	2^1		4	5		9^2	6	8		14		11		13		3	10^3		7		12				10
1	2	12	4	5		6^2	7	8				10		13		3^1	11^3		9		14				11
1	2^1	4	3	5	13	14	7	8		12		10		9^3			11^2		6						12
1	2^2	3		5	8^3		6	7^1		14		10		11	9	4				13	12				13
1	2^2		4	5		9	6	7				14		12	11	3	10^3		13	8^1					14
1	12	14	4	5		9^2	7	6				10		13	8	3	11^1		2^3						15
1			4	5		9^1	6	7		12		10		11^2	8	3			2			13			16
1	2	13	4	5		8^3	6					10	14	11^1	9	3			12	7^2					17
1	2^3		4	5		9^2	6	7		12		11		10^1	8	3	13			14					18
1		3		4		9		7				12	8^2	13	10	2	11^1		6	14	5^3				19
1	2	3	4	5			6	12		14		11		10	9^1				13	7^3		8^2			20
1	2		4	5^1			6					11	12	10	9^3	3	13		7	8^2		14			21
1	5^2	3	4			12	6	7^3		14		10	8	11		2			13			9^1			22
1	12		4			13	7	8		14		10	5	9^2	6^3	3	11^1		2						23
1			4		14	10^1	8	7				11	5^2	13	9	3	12		2			6^3			24
1	2^2		4		13	8	6	7		11			5	10	9^1	3					12				25
1		3	4	5^1	8	9^2	6			11		12		10	7				13		2^3	14			26
1		4	5	6			7			11^2		10^3	14	13	9	3	12			8	2^1				27
1	2^2		4	5	10^1		6			12		11		9	8	3			14	7^3		13			28
1	2		4	5	9^1		7	14				10		11^2	8^3	3				6		13	12		29
1	13		4	5	12	8^2	6	15				11		9^4	10^1	3	14			7^5	2^3		16		30
1		12	4	5	14		15	7		16		11^2		13	8	3^1	10^5			6^4			9^3	2	31
1	2	3	4^4	5	16		7^1	8				12	15	13	14		11^5			9			10^3	6^2	32
1		16	4	5		12	6	14				10	13	9^4	8^2	3	11^1			7^3			15	2^5	33
1			4	5		8^1	6^3	7				11		10	13	3	12			14			9^2	2	34
1	2^2		4	16		11^5	7^3	13				12	5	9^4	6	3	10^1			8		15		14	35
1	13		3	4	9^4	15	8^3	7		10^1		11		6^5	12	2				14			16	5^2	36
1		16	4	5	13	8^1	15	7		14		11^4		9	10^2	3				6^3			12	2^5	37
1			3	4	8^2		13	7		15		11^4	12		14	2	10^5			6^1		16	9^3	5	38

FA Cup

Third Round	Sheffield W	(h)	0-1

Carabao Cup

Second Round	Bristol R	(a)	2-1
Third Round	Aston Villa	(h)	1-3

Leasing.com Trophy (Brighton & HA U21)

Group C (S)	AFC Wimbledon	(a)	2-0
Group C (S)	Southend U	(a)	2-0
Group C (S)	Leyton Orient	(a)	1-1

(Leyton Orient won 4-2 on penalties)

Second Round (S)	Newport Co	(h)	0-0

(Newport Co won 5-4 on penalties)

BRISTOL CITY

FOUNDATION

The name Bristol City came into being in 1897 when the Bristol South End club, formed three years earlier, decided to adopt professionalism and apply for admission to the Southern League after competing in the Western League. The historic meeting was held at the Albert Hall, Bedminster. Bristol City employed Sam Hollis from Woolwich Arsenal as manager and gave him £40 to buy players. In 1900 they merged with Bedminster, another leading Bristol club.

Ashton Gate Stadium, Ashton Road, Bristol BS3 2EJ.

Telephone: (0117) 963 0600.

Ticket Office: (0117) 963 0600 (option 1).

Website: www.bcfc.co.uk

Email: supporterservices@bristol-sport.co.uk

Ground Capacity: 26,459.

Record Attendance: 43,335 v Preston NE, FA Cup 5th rd, 16 February 1935.

Pitch Measurements: 105m × 67m (115yd × 73.5yd).

Chairman: Jon Lansdown.

Chief Executive Officer: Mark Ashton.

Head Coach: Dean Holden.

Assistant Head Coaches: Keith Downing, Paul Simpson.

Colours: Red shirts with white trim, white shorts with red trim, red socks with white trim.

Year Formed: 1894.

Turned Professional: 1897.

Previous Name: 1894, Bristol South End; 1897, Bristol City.

Club Nickname: 'Robins'.

Grounds: 1894, St John's Lane; 1904, Ashton Gate.

First Football League Game: 7 September 1901, Division 2, v Blackpool (a) W 2–0 – Moles; Tuft, Davies; Jones, McLean, Chambers; Bradbury, Connor, Boucher, O'Brien (2), Flynn.

Record League Victory: 9–0 v Aldershot, Division 3 (S), 28 December 1946 – Eddols; Morgan, Fox; Peacock, Roberts, Jones (1); Chilcott, Thomas, Clark (4 incl. 1p), Cyril Williams (1), Hargreaves (3).

Record Cup Victory: 11–0 v Chichester C, FA Cup 1st rd, 5 November 1960 – Cook; Collinson, Thresher; Connor, Alan Williams, Etheridge; Tait (1), Bobby Williams (1), Atyeo (5), Adrian Williams (3), Derrick, (1 og).

Record Defeat: 0–9 v Coventry C, Division 3 (S), 28 April 1934.

Most League Points (2 for a win): 70, Division 3 (S), 1954–55.

HONOURS

League Champions: Division 2 – 1905–06; FL 1 – 2014–15; Division 3S – 1922–23, 1926–27, 1954–55.
Runners-up: Division 1 – 1906–07; Division 2 – 1975–76; FL 1 – 2006–07; Second Division – 1997–98; Division 3 – 1964–65, 1989–90; Division 3S – 1937–38.

FA Cup: *Runners-up:* 1909.

League Cup: semi-final – 1971, 1989, 2018.

League Trophy Winners: 1986, 2003, 2015.
Runners-up: 1987, 2000.

Welsh Cup Winners: 1934.

Anglo-Scottish Cup Winners: 1978.

FOOTBALL YEARBOOK FACT FILE

In October 1983 Terry Cooper became the Football League's first player-director when he was appointed to the board of Bristol City. Cooper was player-manager of the club at the time. The move came two years after the League gave permission to clubs to appoint a paid director.

Most League Points (3 for a win): 99, FL 1, 2014–15.

Most League Goals: 104, Division 3 (S), 1926–27.

Highest League Scorer in Season: Don Clark, 36, Division 3 (S), 1946–47.

Most League Goals in Total Aggregate: John Atyeo, 314, 1951–66.

Most League Goals in One Match: 6, Tommy 'Tot' Walsh v Gillingham, Division 3 (S), 15 January 1927.

Most Capped Player: Billy Wedlock, 26, England.

Most League Appearances: John Atyeo, 596, 1951–66.

Youngest League Player: Marvin Brown, 16 years 105 days v Bristol R, 17 October 1999.

Record Transfer Fee Received: £20,000,000 from Brighton & HA for Adam Webster, August 2019.

Record Transfer Fee Paid: £8,000,000 to Chelsea for Tomas Kalas, July 2019.

Football League Record: 1901 Elected to Division 2; 1906–11 Division 1; 1911–22 Division 2; 1922–23 Division 3 (S); 1923–24 Division 2; 1924–27 Division 3 (S); 1927–32 Division 2; 1932–55 Division 3 (S); 1955–60 Division 2; 1960–65 Division 3; 1965–76 Division 2; 1976–80 Division 1; 1980–81 Division 2; 1981–82 Division 3; 1982–84 Division 4; 1984–90 Division 3; 1990–92 Division 2; 1992–95 Division 1; 1995–98 Division 2; 1998–99 Division 1; 1999–2004 Division 2; 2004–07 FL 1; 2007–13 FL C; 2013–15 FL 1; 2015– FL C.

LATEST SEQUENCES

Longest Sequence of League Wins: 14, 9.9.1905 – 2.12.1905.

Longest Sequence of League Defeats: 8, 10.12.2016 – 21.1.2017.

Longest Sequence of League Draws: 4, 6.11.1999 – 27.11.1999.

Longest Sequence of Unbeaten League Matches: 24, 9.9.1905 – 10.2.1906.

Longest Sequence Without a League Win: 21, 16.3.2013 – 22.10.2013.

Successive Scoring Runs: 25 from 26.12.1905.

Successive Non-scoring Runs: 6 from 20.12.1980.

MANAGERS

Sam Hollis 1897–99
Bob Campbell 1899–1901
Sam Hollis 1901–05
Harry Thickett 1905–10
Frank Bacon 1910–11
Sam Hollis 1911–13
George Hedley 1913–17
Jack Hamilton 1917–19
Joe Palmer 1919–21
Alex Raisbeck 1921–29
Joe Bradshaw 1929–32
Bob Hewison 1932–49 (*under suspension 1938–39*)
Bob Wright 1949–50
Pat Beasley 1950–58
Peter Doherty 1958–60
Fred Ford 1960–67
Alan Dicks 1967–80
Bobby Houghton 1980–82
Roy Hodgson 1982
Terry Cooper 1982–88 (*Director from 1983*)
Joe Jordan 1988–90
Jimmy Lumsden 1990–92
Denis Smith 1992–93
Russell Osman 1993–94
Joe Jordan 1994–97
John Ward 1997–98
Benny Lennartsson 1998–99
Tony Pulis 1999–2000
Tony Fawthrop 2000
Danny Wilson 2000–04
Brian Tinnion 2004–05
Gary Johnson 2005–10
Steve Coppell 2010
Keith Millen 2010–11
Derek McInnes 2011–13
Sean O'Driscoll 2013
Steve Cotterill 2013–16
Lee Johnson 2016–20
Dean Holden August 2020–

TEN YEAR LEAGUE RECORD

		P	*W*	*D*	*L*	*F*	*A*	*Pts*	*Pos*
2010-11	FL C	46	17	9	20	62	65	60	15
2011-12	FL C	46	12	13	21	44	68	49	20
2012-13	FL C	46	11	8	27	59	84	41	24
2013-14	FL 1	46	13	19	14	70	67	58	12
2014-15	FL 1	46	29	12	5	96	38	99	1
2015-16	FL C	46	13	13	20	54	71	52	18
2016-17	FL C	46	15	9	22	60	66	54	17
2017-18	FL C	46	17	16	13	67	58	67	11
2018-19	FL C	46	19	13	14	59	53	70	8
2019-20	FL C	46	17	12	17	60	65	63	12

DID YOU KNOW ?

In early 1941 the main stand at Bristol City's Ashton Gate ground was destroyed in German air raids. City continued to use the ground during the war and received money towards rebuilding costs from the War Damages Commission. A replacement stand was eventually built in the 1950s.

BRISTOL CITY – SKY BET CHAMPIONSHIP 2019–20 LEAGUE RECORD

Match No.	Date	Venue	Opponents	Result	H/T Score	Lg Pos.	Goalscorers	Attendance
1	Aug 4	H	Leeds U	L 1-3	0-1	23	Weimann [79]	23,553
2	10	A	Birmingham C	D 1-1	0-0	21	Rowe [83]	21,808
3	17	H	QPR	W 2-0	1-0	10	Nagy [35], Afobe [59]	21,654
4	20	A	Derby Co	W 2-1	2-0	7	Weimann [16], Brownhill [45]	25,546
5	24	A	Hull C	W 3-1	1-1	4	Afobe 2 (1 pen) [41 (p), 80], Burke (og) [78]	10,458
6	31	H	Middlesbrough	D 2-2	1-0	5	Palmer [44], Rowe [81]	20,757
7	Sept 14	A	Stoke C	W 2-1	0-1	3	Diedhiou [55], Edwards (og) [62]	22,357
8	21	H	Swansea C	D 0-0	0-0	6		22,885
9	28	A	Preston NE	D 3-3	2-1	8	Moore [29], Weimann [36], Baker [60]	12,005
10	Oct 2	A	Brentford	D 1-1	0-0	7	Weimann [87]	11,433
11	5	H	Reading	W 1-0	1-0	6	Diedhiou [12]	21,419
12	19	A	Luton T	L 0-3	0-0	9		10,064
13	23	H	Charlton Ath	W 2-1	0-0	4	Diedhiou [75], Brownhill [90]	20,916
14	27	H	Wigan Ath	D 2-2	1-1	6	Weimann [39], Pereira [86]	22,246
15	Nov 1	A	Barnsley	D 2-2	1-0	5	Williams [43], Weimann [71]	12,178
16	10	A	Cardiff C	W 1-0	0-0	6	Brownhill [67]	23,846
17	23	H	Nottingham F	D 0-0	0-0	7		23,573
18	27	A	WBA	L 1-4	0-2	7	Diedhiou [80]	22,197
19	30	H	Huddersfield T	W 5-2	4-1	5	Brownhill [11], Kongolo (og) [30], Eliasson [36], Williams [40], Weimann [49]	20,762
20	Dec 7	A	Fulham	W 2-1	1-0	4	Brownhill [26], Diedhiou [76]	18,779
21	10	H	Millwall	L 1-2	0-1	4	O'Dowda [84]	19,742
22	14	H	Blackburn R	L 0-2	0-1	7		21,180
23	22	A	Sheffield W	L 0-1	0-0	8		23,180
24	26	A	Charlton Ath	L 2-3	0-1	10	Weimann [46], Eliasson [60]	18,058
25	29	H	Luton T	W 3-0	2-0	8	Watkins [4], Diedhiou (pen) [44], Weimann [66]	22,216
26	Jan 1	H	Brentford	L 0-4	0-2	11		20,858
27	11	A	Wigan Ath	W 2-0	0-0	9	Paterson [77], Diedhiou [79]	9074
28	18	H	Barnsley	W 1-0	0-0	8	Eliasson [87]	20,570
29	28	A	Reading	W 1-0	0-0	6	Paterson [62]	11,633
30	Feb 1	A	QPR	W 1-0	1-0	6	Diedhiou [16]	13,713
31	7	H	Birmingham C	L 1-3	1-2	6	Paterson [1]	22,065
32	12	H	Derby Co	W 3-2	2-0	7	Wells [38], Benkovic [44], Diedhiou [58]	20,368
33	15	A	Leeds U	L 0-1	0-1	7		35,819
34	22	H	WBA	L 0-3	0-2	7		24,022
35	25	A	Huddersfield T	L 1-2	0-1	7	Diedhiou [88]	19,703
36	29	A	Millwall	D 1-1	1-0	7	Pereira [10]	13,584
37	Mar 7	H	Fulham	D 1-1	0-0	7	Wells [70]	23,796
38	June 20	A	Blackburn R	L 1-3	1-1	9	Paterson [34]	0
39	28	H	Sheffield W	L 1-2	0-1	12	Wells [68]	0
40	July 1	A	Nottingham F	L 0-1	0-0	12		0
41	4	H	Cardiff C	L 0-1	0-0	12		0
42	8	H	Hull C	W 2-1	1-0	12	Diedhiou [41], Paterson [53]	0
43	11	A	Middlesbrough	W 3-1	2-0	11	Wells 2 [6, 79], Paterson [42]	0
44	15	H	Stoke C	D 1-1	1-0	10	Benkovic [45]	0
45	18	A	Swansea C	L 0-1	0-1	11		0
46	22	H	Preston NE	D 1-1	0-1	12	Diedhiou [48]	0

Final League Position: 12

GOALSCORERS

League (60): Diedhiou 12 (1 pen), Weimann 9, Paterson 6, Brownhill 5, Wells 5, Afobe 3 (1 pen), Eliasson 3, Benkovic 2, Pereira 2, Rowe 2, Williams 2, Baker 1, Moore 1, Nagy 1, O'Dowda 1, Palmer 1, Watkins 1, own goals 3.
FA Cup (1): Diedhiou 1.
Carabao Cup (3): Diedhiou 1, Hunt 1, Walsh 1.

Bentley D 42 + 1	Hunt J 29 + 6	Kalas T 23	Moore T 16 + 5	Dasilva J 22 + 2	Pack M 1	Brownhill J 28	Weimann A 42 + 3	Palmer K 11 + 14	O'Dowda C 17 + 15	Diedhiou F 29 + 12	Paterson J 15 + 6	Eliasson N 18 + 19	Taylor M — + 1	Wright B 3	Baker N 33 + 1	Pereira P 14 + 7	Nagy A 16 + 7	Rowe T 24 + 5	Afobe B 8 + 4	Massengo H 23 + 2	Semenyo A 3 + 6	Williams A 32	Szmidics S 1 + 2	Watkins M 5 + 4	Rodri L 1 + 5	Smith K 19 + 3	Wells N 13 + 4	Benkovic F 6 + 4	Henriksen M 4	Maenpaa N 4	Vyner Z 4 + 4	*Match No.*
1	2	3	4	5	6	7	8	9^2	10^1	11^3	12	13	14																			1
1	12	3				6	9^3	10		13		14		2^2	4	5^1	7	8	11													2
1	5^2	3	2			6	10	9^3				14			4	13	7^1	8	11	12												3
1	5^3	3	2			6	10	9^1	12	13					4	14		8	11^2	7												4
1	13	3^1	2			6	9	12		11^3					4	5^2		8	10	7	14											5
1	2^2		3			7	10	9^1	12			6			4	13		5	11	8^3	14											6
1	5		2^1			6	10	9^2		11		13			4			8		7	12	3										7
1	5		2			6	11	13	8^3	12		14			4^1			9		7		3	10^2									8
1	5		2^1			6	10	8^3	14	12					4			9		7	11^2	3		13								9
1	5		2^1			6	10	9	14	12		13			4			8		7^3	11^2	3										10
1	12		4			7	10	14	9^3	11^2		6^1				2		5		8	13	3										11
1	5		2^1			7	10	6^2	12	11^3		13			4			9		8		3			14							12
1			4			7	10	14	9	12■		6^2				2		5		8^3	11^1	3			13							13
1			2^1			7	10	6^2	8			12			4	5		9		13		3	14		11^3							14
1		2	4^2			6^1	11		8			12			13	5		9		7	14	3		10^3								15
1		2	13			6	11	12	8						4	5^2	7	9				3		10^1								16
1						6	11^3	12	8^1	10		13		2^2	4	5	7	9				3			14							17
1						6	11	10^3	9^1	13		14		2^2	4	5	7	12				3				8						18
1	2^2		12			6	10			11		9			4^1	13	8^3	5		7		3				14						19
1	2^3		14			6	10		12	11		9^1			4		8^2	5		7		3				13						20
1	2^3					6	10	12	13	11		9			4	14	8	5^2		7^1		3										21
1	12	3				6	10		13	11		9				2^2	8^1	5^3		7		4	14									22
1	5^1	2	4			6	10^2	12	8	11		13						9^3			14	3				7						23
1	5^1	2	4	12		6	11		14	10		13					8	9^2		7^3		3										24
1	2	3		5^1		6	9			11^3		10					7	12				4		8^2	14	13						25
1	2	3	12	5		7	10^3			11		9^1					13					4■		6^2	14	8						26
1	2			5			10			11	12	9			4		13	14		7^2		3		6^1		8^3						27
1	2			5		8	7		12	11	9^1	10			4							3				6						28
1	2		13	5		8	10		12	11	9^1	7^2			4							3				6						29
1	2^1			5			10			11	9^2	7			4	12		14		8^3		3				6	13					30
1	2^1			5^2			10			11	9	7			4		14			8^3		3				6	12	13				31
1	2			5			14		13	10	9	6^3						12				3				7^2	11^1	4	8			32
1		2		5			10^1	14	12	13	9^2	6^3			4					7		3					11		8			33
1	2			5			13	14	6^1	11	12	9^2					7^3					3					10	4	8			34
1	5	2		9			14			11	6	12			4		13	8^3									10	3^1	7^2			35
		3		5			10		9^2	11	6^1	13			4	2	8									7	12			1		36
		3		5			10		9	13	6^2	14			4^1	2				8						7	11^3	12		1		37
1	12	4		14				16	10	11^4	9	6^3			3	2^2		5^5	15	7^1						8	13					38
	2^4			5			6^3		9^5	13	16	12			4		14		10^2	7^1		3				8	11			1	15	39
12				5			9^4	14	8^3	13	15				4		6		11			3■				7	10^2			1^1	2	40
1	13	3		5			6^1		9^2	10	12				4		7		14							8	11^3	15			2^4	41
1	5	3		9			6^2			11^4	8				4^1		14		13					15		7	10^3	2			12	42
1	5^4	3		9			7		13	10^1	6^3				4		15							12		8	11^2	2			14	43
1	5^2	3		9			6^3		14	11	8	13			4^1											7	10	2			12	44
1	5^1	4		9^3			7	13		14	8	15				12			11			3^4		16		6^2	10^5				2	45
1		4		9			8	13		11	7^3					5^1	6		14			3					10^2	12			2	46

FA Cup

Third Round	Shrewsbury T	(h)	1-1
Replay	Shrewsbury T	(a)	0-1

Carabao Cup

First Round	QPR	(a)	3-3
(QPR won 5-4 on penalties)			

BRISTOL ROVERS

FOUNDATION

Bristol Rovers were formed at a meeting in Stapleton Road, Eastville, in 1883. However, they first went under the name of the Black Arabs (wearing black shirts). Changing their name to Eastville Rovers in their second season in 1888–89, they won the Gloucestershire Senior Cup. Original members of the Bristol & District League in 1892, this eventually became the Western League and Eastville Rovers adopted professionalism in 1897.

The Memorial Stadium, Filton Avenue, Horfield, Bristol BS7 0BF.

Telephone: (0117) 909 6648.

Ticket Office: (0117) 909 8848.

Website: www.bristolrovers.co.uk

Email: via website.

Ground Capacity: 11,796.

Record Attendance: 38,472 v Preston NE, FA Cup 4th rd, 30 January 1960 (at Eastville); 9,464 v Liverpool, FA Cup 4th rd, 8 February 1992 (at Twerton Park); 12,011 v WBA, FA Cup 6th rd, 9 March 2008 (at Memorial Stadium).

Pitch Measurements: 100m × 68m (109.5yd × 74.5yd).

Chairman: Steve Hamer.

Manager: Ben Garner.

First-Team Coach: Kevin Maher.

Colours: Blue and white quartered shirts, blue shorts with white trim, blue socks with white trim.

Year Formed: 1883.

Turned Professional: 1897.

Previous Names: 1883, Black Arabs; 1884, Eastville Rovers; 1897, Bristol Eastville Rovers; 1898, Bristol Rovers. ***Club Nicknames:*** 'The Pirates', 'The Gas'.

Grounds: 1883, Purdown; Three Acres, Ashley Hill; Rudgeway, Fishponds; 1897, Eastville; 1986, Twerton Park; 1996, The Memorial Stadium.

First Football League Game: 28 August 1920, Division 3, v Millwall (a) L 0–2 – Stansfield; Bethune, Panes; Boxley, Kenny, Steele; Chance, Bird, Sims, Bell, Palmer.

Record League Victory: 7–0 v Brighton & HA, Division 3 (S), 29 November 1952 – Hoyle; Bamford, Fox; Pitt, Warren, Sampson; McIlvenny, Roost (2), Lambden (1), Bradford (1), Petherbridge (2), (1 og). 7–0 v Swansea T, Division 2, 2 October 1954 – Radford; Bamford, Watkins; Pitt, Muir, Anderson; Petherbridge, Bradford (2), Meyer, Roost (1), Hooper (2), (2 og). 7–0 v Shrewsbury T, Division 3, 21 March 1964 – Hall; Hillard, Gwyn Jones; Oldfield, Stone (1), Mabbutt; Jarman (2), Brown (1), Biggs (1p), Hamilton, Bobby Jones (2).

Record Cup Victory: 7–1 v Dorchester, FA Cup 4th qualifying rd, 25 October 2014 – Midenhall; Locyer, Trotman (McChrystal), Parkes, Monkhouse (2), Clarke, Mansell (1) (Thomas), Brown, Gosling, Harrison (3), Taylor (1) (White).

Record Defeat: 0–12 v Luton T, Division 3 (S), 13 April 1936.

HONOURS

League Champions: Division 3 – 1989–90; Division 3S – 1952–53.
Runners-up: Division 3 – 1973–74; Conference – (2nd) 2014–15 *(promoted via play-offs)*.

FA Cup: 6th rd – 1951, 1958, 2008.

League Cup: 5th rd – 1971, 1972.

League Trophy: *Runners-up:* 1990, 2007.

FOOTBALL YEARBOOK FACT FILE

In September 1932 Bristol Rovers arranged for centre-forward Vivian Gibbins to be flown to their Division Three South home game against Southend. At the time Gibbins was a school teacher in East London and was unable to leave work until 4 p.m. He was driven to Romford Aerodrome from where he flew to Filton, arriving half an hour before kick-off. Gibbins went on to score in Rovers' 3-1 victory.

Most League Points (2 for a win): 64, Division 3 (S), 1952–53.

Most League Points (3 for a win): 93, Division 3, 1989–90.

Most League Goals: 92, Division 3 (S), 1952–53.

Highest League Scorer in Season: Geoff Bradford, 33, Division 3 (S), 1952–53.

Most League Goals in Total Aggregate: Geoff Bradford, 242, 1949–64.

Most League Goals in One Match: 4, Sidney Leigh v Exeter C, Division 3 (S), 2 May 1921; 4, Jonah Wilcox v Bournemouth, Division 3 (S), 12 December 1925; 4, Bill Culley v QPR, Division 3 (S), 5 March 1927; 4, Frank Curran v Swindon T, Division 3 (S), 25 March 1939; 4, Vic Lambden v Aldershot, Division 3 (S), 29 March 1947; 4, George Petherbridge v Torquay U, Division 3 (S), 1 December 1951; 4, Vic Lambden v Colchester U, Division 3 (S), 14 May 1952; 4, Geoff Bradford v Rotherham U, Division 2, 14 March 1959; 4, Robin Stubbs v Gillingham, Division 2, 10 October 1970; 4, Alan Warboys v Brighton & HA, Division 3, 1 December 1973; 4, Jamie Cureton v Reading, Division 2, 16 January 1999; 4, Ellis Harrison v Northampton T, FL 1, 7 January 2017.

Most Capped Player: Vitalijs Astafjevs, 31 (167), Latvia.

Most League Appearances: Stuart Taylor, 546, 1966–80.

Youngest League Player: Ronnie Dix, 15 years 173 days v Charlton Ath, 25 February 1928.

Record Transfer Fee Received: £2,000,000 from Fulham for Barry Hayles, November 1998; £2,000,000 from WBA for Jason Roberts, July 2000.

Record Transfer Fee Paid: £370,000 to QPR for Andy Tillson, November 1992.

Football League Record: 1920 Original Member of Division 3; 1921–53 Division 3 (S); 1953–62 Division 2; 1962–74 Division 3; 1974–81 Division 2; 1981–90 Division 3; 1990–92 Division 2. 1992–93 Division 1; 1993–2001 Division 2; 2001–04 Division 3; 2004–07 FL 2; 2007–11 FL 1; 2011–14 FL 2; 2014–15 Conference Premier; 2015–16 FL 2; 2016– FL 1.

MANAGERS

Alfred Homer 1899–1920 (*continued as Secretary to 1928*)
Ben Hall 1920–21
Andy Wilson 1921–26
Joe Palmer 1926–29
Dave McLean 1929–30
Albert Prince-Cox 1930–36
Percy Smith 1936–37
Brough Fletcher 1938–49
Bert Tann 1950–68 (*continued as General Manager to 1972*)
Fred Ford 1968–69
Bill Dodgin Snr 1969–72
Don Megson 1972–77
Bobby Campbell 1978–79
Harold Jarman 1979–80
Terry Cooper 1980–81
Bobby Gould 1981–83
David Williams 1983–85
Bobby Gould 1985–87
Gerry Francis 1987–91
Martin Dobson 1991
Dennis Rofe 1992
Malcolm Allison 1992–93
John Ward 1993–96
Ian Holloway 1996–2001
Garry Thompson 2001
Gerry Francis 2001
Garry Thompson 2001–02
Ray Graydon 2002–04
Ian Atkins 2004–05
Paul Trollope 2005–10
Dave Penney 2011
Paul Buckle 2011–12
Mark McGhee 2012
John Ward 2012–14
Darrell Clarke 2014–18
Graham Coughlan 2018–19
Ben Garner December 2019–

LATEST SEQUENCES

Longest Sequence of League Wins: 12, 18.10.1952 – 17.1.1953.

Longest Sequence of League Defeats: 8, 26.10.2002 – 21.12.2002.

Longest Sequence of League Draws: 6, 4.2.2017 – 28.2.2017.

Longest Sequence of Unbeaten League Matches: 32, 7.4.1973 – 27.1.1974.

Longest Sequence Without a League Win: 20, 5.4.1980 – 1.11.1980.

Successive Scoring Runs: 26 from 26.3.1927.

Successive Non-scoring Runs: 6 from 14.10.1922.

TEN YEAR LEAGUE RECORD

		P	W	D	L	F	A	Pts	Pos
2010-11	FL 1	46	11	12	23	48	82	45	22
2011-12	FL 2	46	15	12	19	60	70	57	13
2012-13	FL 2	46	16	12	18	60	69	60	14
2013-14	FL 2	46	12	14	20	43	54	50	23
2014-15	Conf P	46	25	16	5	73	34	91	2
2015-16	FL 2	46	26	7	13	77	46	85	3
2016-17	FL 1	46	18	12	16	68	70	66	10
2017-18	FL 1	46	16	11	19	60	66	59	13
2018-19	FL 1	46	13	15	18	47	50	54	15
2019-20	FL 1	35	12	9	14	38	49	45	14§

§Decided on points-per-game (1.29)

DID YOU KNOW ?

The only occasion that two Bristol Rovers players have scored a hat-trick in the same Football League game was on 1 December 1973 when Rovers won 8-2 at Brighton. Alan Warboys scored four and his strike partner Bruce Bannister got three. The result extended Rovers' unbeaten start to the season to 19 games and left them top of the Third Division table.

BRISTOL ROVERS – SKY BET LEAGUE ONE 2019–20 LEAGUE RECORD

Match No.	*Date*	*Venue*	*Opponents*	*Result*	*H/T Score*	*Lg Pos.*	*Goalscorers*	*Attendance*
1	Aug 3	A	Blackpool	L 0-2	0-1	20		11,359
2	10	H	Wycombe W	D 0-0	0-0	17		7668
3	17	A	Coventry C	L 0-2	0-1	21		6976
4	20	H	Tranmere R	W 2-0	1-0	17	Clarke-Harris [38], Smith (pen) [88]	6802
5	24	H	Oxford U	W 3-1	2-1	12	Upson [37], Clarke-Harris [45], Nichols [77]	7871
6	31	A	Burton Alb	L 0-2	0-0	14		2831
7	Sept 7	H	Accrington S	D 3-3	2-2	13	Rodman [4], Clarke-Harris 2 [41, 63]	6524
8	14	A	Lincoln C	W 1-0	0-0	12	Clarke-Harris (pen) [66]	8712
9	17	H	Gillingham	D 1-1	1-0	12	Smith [38]	6370
10	21	A	AFC Wimbledon	W 3-1	1-1	8	Ogogo [29], Clarke-Harris [75], Craig [87]	4268
11	28	H	Rotherham U	W 1-0	0-0	7	Clarke-Harris [48]	7321
12	Oct 12	H	Milton Keynes D	W 1-0	0-0	4	Davies [49]	7864
13	19	A	Doncaster R	L 0-2	0-1	7		7659
14	22	H	Bolton W	L 0-2	0-1	10		7244
15	26	H	Portsmouth	D 2-2	0-1	10	Rodman [78], MacGillivray (og) [90]	8648
16	Nov 2	A	Rochdale	W 2-1	2-1	9	Adeboyejo [8], O'Connell (og) [11]	3038
17	23	A	Shrewsbury T	W 4-3	2-1	9	Craig [11], Clarke, O [27], Sercombe [47], Ogogo [87]	6235
18	Dec 7	H	Southend U	W 4-2	0-2	5	Clarke-Harris (pen) [48], Ogogo [56], Upson [75], Kilgour [81]	6797
19	14	A	Ipswich T	W 2-1	2-1	4	Smith [4], Nichols [23]	18,806
20	21	H	Peterborough U	D 0-0	0-0	4		8030
21	26	H	AFC Wimbledon	L 1-2	1-0	6	Clarke-Harris (pen) [43]	9096
22	29	A	Fleetwood T	D 0-0	0-0	7		2848
23	Jan 1	A	Milton Keynes D	L 0-3	0-1	8		8236
24	11	H	Doncaster R	L 0-2	0-0	12		6834
25	18	A	Rotherham U	L 0-3	0-0	13		8287
26	25	H	Fleetwood T	D 0-0	0-0	13		6469
27	28	A	Bolton W	D 1-1	0-0	12	Clarke-Harris [63]	10,657
28	Feb 1	H	Coventry C	L 1-2	1-2	13	Clarke-Harris [23]	7859
29	8	A	Wycombe W	L 1-3	1-3	13	Mitchell-Lawson [27]	5769
30	11	A	Tranmere R	D 0-0	0-0	13		5026
31	15	H	Blackpool	W 2-1	0-1	13	Kilgour [73], Ginnelly [84]	6631
32	22	A	Sunderland	L 0-3	0-0	13		31,541
33	29	H	Shrewsbury T	L 0-1	0-0	14		6954
34	Mar 7	A	Southend U	L 1-3	0-1	15	Mitchell-Lawson [46]	5806
35	10	H	Sunderland	W 2-0	1-0	14	Clarke-Harris 2 (1 pen) [39, 75 (p)]	7281
36	14	H	Ipswich T	Cancelled				
37	21	A	Peterborough U	Cancelled				
38	28	H	Rochdale	Cancelled				
39	Apr 10	A	Oxford U	Cancelled				
40	13	H	Burton Alb	Cancelled				
41	18	A	Accrington S	Cancelled				
42	21	A	Portsmouth	Cancelled				
43	25	H	Lincoln C	Cancelled				
44	May 3	A	Gillingham	Cancelled				

Final League Position: 14 (on points-per-game basis)

GOALSCORERS

League (38): Clarke-Harris 13 (4 pens), Ogogo 3, Smith 3 (1 pen), Craig 2, Kilgour 2, Mitchell-Lawson 2, Nichols 2, Rodman 2, Upson 2, Adeboyejo 1, Clarke, O 1, Davies 1, Ginnelly 1, Sercombe 1, own goals 2.
FA Cup (6): Clarke-Harris 2 (1 pen), Craig 1, Leahy 1, Rodman 1, Sercombe 1.
Carabao Cup (4): Smith 2, Clarke-Harris 1, Nichols 1.
Leasing.com Trophy (5): Adeboyejo 1, Kilgour 1, Little 1, Nichols 1, Sercombe 1.

Jaakkola A 21	Little M 9 + 2	Davies T 18 + 1	Craig T 34	Leahy L 31 + 1	Upson E 32 + 1	Clarke O 26 + 1	Sercombe L 20 + 2	Rodman A 23 + 6	Adeboyejo V 6 + 12	Bennett K 2 + 10	Smith T 11 + 9	Nichols T 12 + 7	Ogogo A 25 + 2	Hare J 7 + 3	Clarke-Harris J 24 + 2	Kilgour A 33	van Stappershoef J 4 + 1	Kelly M 2 + 3	Menayese R 10 + 3	Hargreaves C 3 + 3	Holmes-Dennis T 2 + 2	Tomlinson L — + 1	Barrett J 3 + 4	Reilly G 1 + 3	Mitchell-Lawson J 8 + 2	Ginnelly J 5 + 4	Blackman J 10	Abraham T — + 4	Harries C 2 + 1	Daly J 1 + 2	Match No.
1	2	3	4	5	6	7	8	9²	10¹	11	12	13																			1
1	2²	3	4	5	7¹	8	9		11	14		10³	6	12	13																2
1		3		5	12	6	8³		14	9²	11	13	7	2	10¹	4															3
1		3	4	6	8	7			13	12	11²	14	9³	2	10¹	5															4
1		3	4	6	8	7¹		14	12		11³	13	9	2	10²	5															5
1		3	4	6	8²	7			13		10¹	12	9	2	11	5															6
		2	3	9		8		6¹		12	13	10²	7	5	11	4	1														7
1	5²	2	3	9	7	6					12	10¹	8	13	11	4															8
1	13	2	3	9	7	6³	12		14		10²		8	5¹	11	4															9
1		2	3	9	7		6	5¹			12	10²	8		11	4³		13	14												10
1		2	3	9	7		8	5³	12		11¹	13	6		10²	4			14												11
		2	3	9	7³		8¹	5	14	12	10	11²	6			4	1			13											12
1		2	3	9	6	7¹		5	12	13	10	11²	8			4															13
1		2	3		7	8		5	10	13	12	11²	6¹			4		9													14
1	13	2	3²	9	7¹	6³	12	5	10	14	11		8			4															15
1	2		4	12	8³	9	10	6¹	11²		13		7			3		5	14												16
1	5¹		3	8	6	9³	10	13	11²		12		7			4			2		14										17
1	2		3	5	7³		9	6	12		13	10²	8		11¹	4				14											18
1			3	9	7	6■	8	5	12		11²	10¹				4			2			13									19
1			3	9	7	6	8	5	13		11²	10¹			12	4			2												20
1			3	9	7		8	5	12	14	13	10³	6²		11¹	4			2												21
1			4	6	8		10	2				12	7²		11	5		13	3	9¹											22
1²			3	9	7		8	5		14		11	6¹		10	4	12		2³	13											23
			3	9¹	6		8	5							10	4	1		2	7³	13		11²	12	14						24
		14	3	9	6	12	8³	5							11	4¹	1		2				7²	10		13					25
		3	4		6¹	7	8²	14					12		10	2					5		11³	13		9	1				26
		3	4	5	7	8		11					6		10	2									12	9¹	1				27
		4	3		6³	7		5					13		10	2					8²		12	14	11¹	9	1				28
	2		3	5	6³	8		9²					7		10	4							14		11¹	12	1	13			29
	2		4	5	6	8		9					7		10	3									11¹	12	1				30
	2		4	5	7	6		9³					8²		10	3							14		11¹	12	1	13			31
			4	5	6¹	8		12					7■		10	2			3				13		11²	9³	1		14		32
			4	5	7	8	6³	14							10²	2			3¹						11	9	1	12		13	33
			3	9	7²	8	6	13		12				5¹		2									11		1	14	4	10³	34
			3	9		8	7	5						13	10¹	2		14		6²					11³		1		4	12	35
																															36
																															37
																															38
																															39
																															40
																															41
																															42
																															43
																															44

FA Cup

First Round	Bromley	(h)	1-1
Replay	Bromley	(a)	1-0
Second Round	Plymouth Arg	(h)	1-1
Replay	Plymouth Arg	(a)	1-0
Third Round	Coventry C	(h)	2-2
Replay	Coventry C	(a)	0-3

Carabao Cup

First Round	Cheltenham T	(h)	3-0
Second Round	Brighton & HA	(h)	1-2

Leasing.com Trophy

Group F (S)	Plymouth Arg	(a)	1-1
(Plymouth Arg won 5-3 on penalties)			
Group F (S)	Chelsea U21	(h)	2-1
Group F (S)	Swindon T	(h)	1-0
Second Round (S)	Leyton Orient	(h)	1-1
(Bristol R won 4-2 on penalties)			
Third Round (S)	Stevenage	(h)	0-1

BURNLEY

FOUNDATION

On 18 May 1882 Burnley (Association) Football Club was still known as Burnley Rovers as members of that rugby club had decided on that date to play Association Football in the future. It was only a matter of days later that the members met again and decided to drop Rovers from the club's name.

Turf Moor, Harry Potts Way, Burnley, Lancashire BB10 4BX.

Telephone: (01282) 446 800.

Ticket Office: (0844) 807 1882.

Website: www.burnleyfc.com

Email: info@burnleyfc.com

Ground Capacity: 21,944.

Record Attendance: 54,775 v Huddersfield T, FA Cup 3rd rd, 23 February 1924.

Pitch Measurements: 105m × 68m (115yd × 74.5yd).

Chairman: Mike Garlick.

Chief Executive: Dave Baldwin.

Manager: Sean Dyche.

Assistant Manager: Ian Woan.

Colours: Claret shirts with sky blue sleeves, white shorts with claret trim, claret socks with sky blue and white trim.

Year Formed: 1882.

Turned Professional: 1883.

Previous Name: 1882, Burnley Rovers; 1882, Burnley.

Club Nickname: 'The Clarets'.

Grounds: 1882, Calder Vale; 1883, Turf Moor.

First Football League Game: 8 September 1888, Football League, v Preston NE (a) L 2–5 – Smith; Lang, Bury, Abrahams, Friel, Keenan, Brady, Tait, Poland (1), Gallocher (1), Yates.

Record League Victory: 9–0 v Darwen, Division 1, 9 January 1892 – Hillman; Walker, McFettridge, Lang, Matthews, Keenan, Nicol (3), Bowes, Espie (1), McLardie (3), Hill (2).

Record Cup Victory: 9–0 v Crystal Palace, FA Cup 2nd rd (replay), 10 February 1909 – Dawson; Barron, McLean; Cretney (2), Leake, Moffat; Morley, Ogden, Smith (3), Abbott (2), Smethams (1). 9–0 v New Brighton, FA Cup 4th rd, 26 January 1957 – Blacklaw; Angus, Winton; Seith, Adamson, Miller; Newlands (1), McIlroy (3), Lawson (3), Cheesebrough (1), Pilkington (1). 9–0 v Penrith, FA Cup 1st rd, 17 November 1984 – Hansbury; Miller, Hampton, Phelan, Overson (Kennedy), Hird (3 incl. 1p), Grewcock (1), Powell (2), Taylor (3), Biggins, Hutchison.

Record Defeat: 0–11 v Darwen, FA Cup 1st rd, 17 October 1885.

Most League Points (2 for a win): 62, Division 2, 1972–73.

HONOURS

League Champions: Division 1 – 1920–21, 1959–60; FL C – 2015–16; Division 2 – 1897–98, 1972–73; Division 3 – 1981–82; Division 4 – 1991–92.
Runners-up: Division 1 – 1919–20, 1961–62; FL C – 2013–14; Division 2 – 1912–13, 1946–47; Second Division – 1999–2000.

FA Cup Winners: 1914.
Runners-up: 1947, 1962.

League Cup: semi-final – 1961, 1969, 1983, 2009.

League Trophy: *Runners-up:* 1988.

Anglo-Scottish Cup Winners: 1979.

European Competitions
European Cup: 1960–61 *(qf)*.
Fairs Cup: 1966–67.
Europa League: 2018–19.

FOOTBALL YEARBOOK FACT FILE

Burnley were one of the first clubs in the Football League to develop a separate training ground away from their home stadium. In April 1955 the Clarets purchased the 79-acre Home Farm at Gawthorpe. The premises were completely revamped in more modern times and are now known as the Barnfield Training Centre.

Most League Points (3 for a win): 93, FL C, 2013–14; FL C, 2015–16.

Most League Goals: 102, Division 1, 1960–61.

Highest League Scorer in Season: George Beel, 35, Division 1, 1927–28.

Most League Goals in Total Aggregate: George Beel, 179, 1923–32.

Most League Goals in One Match: 6, Louis Page v Birmingham C, Division 1, 10 April 1926.

Most Capped Player: Jimmy McIlroy, 51 (55), Northern Ireland.

Most League Appearances: Jerry Dawson, 522, 1907–28.

Youngest League Player: Tommy Lawton, 16 years 174 days v Doncaster R, 28 March 1936.

Record Transfer Fee Received: £25,000,000 (rising to £30,000,000) from Everton for Michael Keane, July 2017.

Record Transfer Fee Paid: £15,000,000 to Leeds U for Chris Wood, August 2017; £15,000,000 to Middlesbrough for Ben Gibson, August 2018.

Football League Record: 1888 Original Member of the Football League; 1897–98 Division 2; 1898–1900 Division 1; 1900–13 Division 2; 1913–30 Division 1; 1930–47 Division 2; 1947–71 Division 1; 1971–73 Division 2; 1973–76 Division 1; 1976–80 Division 2; 1980–82 Division 3; 1982–83 Division 2; 1983–85 Division 3; 1985–92 Division 4; 1992–94 Division 2; 1994–95 Division 1; 1995–2000 Division 2; 2000–04 Division 1; 2004–09 FL C; 2009–10 Premier League; 2010–14 FL C; 2014–15 Premier League; 2015–16 FL C; 2016– Premier League.

LATEST SEQUENCES

Longest Sequence of League Wins: 10, 16.11.1912 – 18.1.1913.

Longest Sequence of League Defeats: 8, 2.1.1995 – 25.2.1995.

Longest Sequence of League Draws: 6, 21.2.1931 – 28.3.1931.

Longest Sequence of Unbeaten League Matches: 30, 6.9.1920 – 25.3.1921.

Longest Sequence Without a League Win: 24, 16.4.1979 – 17.11.1979.

Successive Scoring Runs: 27 from 13.2.1926.

Successive Non-scoring Runs: 6 from 21.3.2015.

MANAGERS

Harry Bradshaw 1894–99
(*Secretary-Manager from 1897*)
Club Directors 1899–1900
J. Ernest Mangnall 1900–03
(*Secretary-Manager*)
Spen Whittaker 1903–10
(*Secretary-Manager*)
John Haworth 1910–24
(*Secretary-Manager*)
Albert Pickles 1925–31
(*Secretary-Manager*)
Tom Bromilow 1932–35
Selection Committee 1935–45
Cliff Britton 1945–48
Frank Hill 1948–54
Alan Brown 1954–57
Billy Dougall 1957–58
Harry Potts 1958–70
(*General Manager to 1972*)
Jimmy Adamson 1970–76
Joe Brown 1976–77
Harry Potts 1977–79
Brian Miller 1979–83
John Bond 1983–84
John Benson 1984–85
Martin Buchan 1985
Tommy Cavanagh 1985–86
Brian Miller 1986–89
Frank Casper 1989–91
Jimmy Mullen 1991–96
Adrian Heath 1996–97
Chris Waddle 1997–98
Stan Ternent 1998–2004
Steve Cotterill 2004–07
Owen Coyle 2007–10
Brian Laws 2010
Eddie Howe 2011–12
Sean Dyche October 2012–

TEN YEAR LEAGUE RECORD

		P	*W*	*D*	*L*	*F*	*A*	*Pts*	*Pos*
2010-11	FL C	46	18	14	14	65	61	68	8
2011-12	FL C	46	17	11	18	61	58	62	13
2012-13	FL C	46	16	13	17	62	60	61	11
2013-14	FL C	46	26	15	5	72	37	93	2
2014-15	PR Lge	38	7	12	19	28	53	33	19
2015-16	FL C	46	26	15	5	72	35	93	1
2016-17	PR Lge	38	11	7	20	39	55	40	16
2017-18	PR Lge	38	14	12	12	36	39	54	7
2018-19	PR Lge	38	11	7	20	45	68	40	15
2019-20	PR Lge	38	15	9	14	43	50	54	10

DID YOU KNOW ?

In January 1921 Burnley introduced a live monkey as a mascot. The monkey, dressed in the club colours, was subsequently presented to centre-forward Joe Anderson. There was significant criticism in the local press and the monkey quickly disappeared.

BURNLEY – PREMIER LEAGUE 2019–20 LEAGUE RECORD

Match No.	Date	Venue	Opponents	Result		H/T Score	Lg Pos.	Goalscorers	Attendance
1	Aug 10	H	Southampton	W	3-0	0-0	3	Barnes 2 [63, 70], Gudmundsson [75]	19,784
2	17	A	Arsenal	L	1-2	1-1	9	Barnes [43]	60,214
3	25	A	Wolverhampton W	D	1-1	1-0	6	Barnes [13]	30,522
4	31	H	Liverpool	L	0-3	0-2	11		21,762
5	Sept 14	A	Brighton & HA	D	1-1	0-0	13	Hendrick [90]	29,398
6	21	H	Norwich C	W	2-0	2-0	7	Wood 2 [10, 14]	19,712
7	28	A	Aston Villa	D	2-2	0-1	10	Rodriguez [68], Wood [81]	41,546
8	Oct 5	H	Everton	W	1-0	0-0	5	Hendrick [72]	20,650
9	19	A	Leicester C	L	1-2	1-1	8	Wood [26]	32,105
10	26	H	Chelsea	L	2-4	0-2	11	Rodriguez [86], McNeil [89]	20,975
11	Nov 2	A	Sheffield U	L	0-3	0-3	14		31,131
12	9	H	West Ham U	W	3-0	2-0	9	Barnes [11], Wood [44], Roberto (og) [54]	20,255
13	23	A	Watford	W	3-0	0-0	6	Wood [53], Barnes (pen) [82], Tarkowski [88]	19,711
14	30	H	Crystal Palace	L	0-2	0-1	8		19,818
15	Dec 3	H	Manchester C	L	1-4	0-1	11	Brady [89]	20,101
16	7	A	Tottenham H	L	0-5	0-3	13		58,401
17	14	H	Newcastle U	W	1-0	0-0	12	Wood [58]	19,798
18	21	A	Bournemouth	W	1-0	0-0	10	Rodriguez [89]	10,020
19	26	A	Everton	L	0-1	0-0	12		39,177
20	28	H	Manchester U	L	0-2	0-1	13		21,924
21	Jan 1	H	Aston Villa	L	1-2	0-2	15	Wood [80]	19,561
22	11	A	Chelsea	L	0-3	0-2	15		40,396
23	19	H	Leicester C	W	2-1	0-1	14	Wood [56], Westwood [79]	19,788
24	22	A	Manchester U	W	2-0	1-0	13	Wood [39], Rodriguez [56]	73,198
25	Feb 2	H	Arsenal	D	0-0	0-0	11		21,048
26	15	A	Southampton	W	2-1	1-1	10	Westwood [2], Vydra [60]	26,302
27	22	H	Bournemouth	W	3-0	0-0	8	Vydra [53], Rodriguez (pen) [61], McNeil [87]	18,227
28	29	A	Newcastle U	D	0-0	0-0	9		52,219
29	Mar 7	H	Tottenham H	D	1-1	1-0	10	Wood [13]	20,496
30	June 22	A	Manchester C	L	0-5	0-3	11		0
31	25	H	Watford	W	1-0	0-0	11	Rodriguez [73]	0
32	29	A	Crystal Palace	W	1-0	0-0	8	Mee [62]	0
33	July 5	H	Sheffield U	D	1-1	1-0	9	Tarkowski [43]	0
34	8	A	West Ham U	W	1-0	1-0	9	Rodriguez [38]	0
35	11	A	Liverpool	D	1-1	0-1	9	Rodriguez [69]	0
36	15	H	Wolverhampton W	D	1-1	0-0	10	Wood (pen) [90]	0
37	18	A	Norwich C	W	2-0	1-0	9	Wood [45], Godfrey (og) [80]	0
38	26	H	Brighton & HA	L	1-2	1-1	10	Wood [44]	0

Final League Position: 10

GOALSCORERS

League (43): Wood 14 (1 pen), Rodriguez 8 (1 pen), Barnes 6 (1 pen), Hendrick 2, McNeil 2, Tarkowski 2, Vydra 2, Westwood 2, Brady 1, Gudmundsson 1, Mee 1, own goals 2.
FA Cup (5): Pieters 2, Rodriguez 2, Hendrick 1.
Carabao Cup (1): Rodriguez 1.

Pope N 38	Lowton M 17	Tarkowski J 38	Mee B 32	Pieters E 21 + 3	Gudmundsson J 6 + 6	Cork J 30	Westwood A 35	McNeil D 38	Wood C 29 + 3	Barnes A 17 + 2	Lennon A 4 + 12	Rodriguez J 20 + 16	Hendrick J 22 + 2	Vydra M 7 + 12	Brady R 5 + 12	Taylor C 22 + 2	Bardsley P 21	Drinkwater D 1	Long K 6 + 2	Brownhill J 9 + 1	Thompson M — + 1	*Match No.*
1	2	3	4	5	6	7	8	9^{1}	10	11^{2}	12	13										1
1	2	3	4	5	6^{2}	8	7	9	10^{1}	11	13	12										2
1	2	3	4	5	6^{1}	7	8	9^{3}	10	11^{2}	12	13	14									3
1	2	3	4	5		8	7	9	11	10^{1}	6	12										4
1	2	3	4	5		8^{3}	7	9	11^{2}	10	6^{1}	13	12	14								5
1	2	3	4	5		8	7	9^{2}	11	10^{1}	12	13	6^{3}		14							6
1	2	3	4	5		8^{1}	7	9	10	11^{2}		12	6		13							7
1	2	3	4	5^{1}	6^{3}		8	9	10	11^{2}	14	13	7			12						8
1	2	3	4	5			7	6	10		12	11^{2}	8	13	9^{1}							9
1	2	3	4	5		8	7	9		11^{1}		10	6^{2}	12	13							10
1	2	3	4	5^{1}		8	7	9^{2}		10		11^{3}	6	14	13	12						11
1		3	4			7	8	9	10^{2}	11^{1}		12	6		13	5	2					12
1		3	4			8	7	9	10^{1}	11		12	6			5	2					13
1		3	4	12		8		9	10	11^{2}	14	13	7		6^{3}	5^{1}	2					14
1		3	4	5		8		9^{3}	11^{2}	12	6	13	10		14		2	7^{1}				15
1	2	3	4	5		8		6	11^{1}		13	10	7	12	9^{2}							16
1		3	4	5		8	7	9	11^{1}	10		12	6				2					17
1		3	4			8	7	9^{3}	10	11^{2}	12	13	6^{1}		14	5	2					18
1		3	4		12	8^{3}	7	9	10^{2}	13		11			6^{1}	5	2		14			19
1		3	4		13	8^{3}	7	9	10	11^{2}		12	6^{1}		14	5	2					20
1		3	4		12	8	7	9	10	11^{1}		13			6^{2}	5	2					21
1	2	3	4			8	7	9	11		6		10^{1}	12		5						22
1		3	4			8	7	9	10^{1}		12	11	6			5	2					23
1	2	3	4			8	7	9	10			11	6			5						24
1	2	3	4			8	7	9	10			11	6			5						25
1		3	4			8	7	9	10^{1}			11	6	12		5	2					26
1		3	4			8^{2}	7	9^{3}			12	10	6	11^{1}	14	5	2			13		27
1		3	4			7	8	9	12			11	6	10^{1}		5	2					28
1		3	4			8	7	9	10		13	11^{1}	6^{2}	12		5	2					29
1	2	3	4	12		8	7	9				10^{1}		11^{2}		5				6	13	30
1	2	3	4	12		8	7	9				10^{1}		11		5				6		31
1		3	4	9		8^{1}	7	10						11		5	2		12	6		32
1		4		9^{2}	13		7	6	12			10		11^{1}		5	2		3	8		33
1		4		6			7	9	12			10		11^{1}		5	2		3	8		34
1		4		6^{1}	13		7	9	10^{2}			11		12		5	2		3	8		35
1		4		6	12		7	9	10			11^{2}		13	14	5^{1}	2		3	8^{3}		36
1		4		5	6^{1}		7	9	10^{2}			11		13	12		2		3	8		37
1		4		5	6^{1}		7	9	10			11^{2}		13	12		2		3	8		38

FA Cup

Third Round	Peterborough U	(h)	4-2
Fourth Round	Norwich C	(h)	1-2

Carabao Cup

Second Round	Sunderland	(h)	1-3

BURTON ALBION

FOUNDATION

Once upon a time there were three Football League clubs bearing the name Burton. Then there were none. In reality it had been two. Originally Burton Swifts and Burton Wanderers competed in it until 1901 when they amalgamated to form Burton United. This club disbanded in 1910. There was no senior club representing the town until 1924 when Burton Town, formerly known as Burton All Saints, played in the Birmingham & District League, subsequently joining the Midland League in 1935–36. When the Second World War broke out the club fielded a team in a truncated version of the Birmingham & District League taking over from the club's reserves. But it was not revived in peacetime. So it was not until a further decade that a club bearing the name of Burton reappeared. Founded in 1950 Burton Albion made progress from the Birmingham & District League, too, then into the Southern League and because of its geographical situation later had spells in the Northern Premier League. In April 2009 Burton Albion restored the name of the town to the Football League competition as champions of the Blue Square Premier League.

Pirelli Stadium, Princess Way, Burton-on-Trent, Staffordshire DE13 0AR.

Telephone: (01283) 565 938.

Ticket Office: (01283) 565 938.

Website: www.burtonalbionfc.co.uk

Email: bafc@burtonalbionfc.co.uk

Ground Capactiy: 7,088.

Record Attendance: 5,806 v Weymouth, Southern League Cup final 2nd leg, 1964 (at Eton Park); 6,746 v Derby Co, FL C, 26 August 2016 (at Pirelli Stadium).

Pitch Measurements: 100m × 67m (109.5yd × 73.5yd).

Chairman: Ben Robinson.

Manager: Jake Buxton.

Assistant Manager: Gary Crosby.

Colours: Yellow shirts with black trim, black shorts with yellow trim, yellow socks with black trim.

Year Formed: 1950.

Turned Professional: 1950.

Club Nickname: 'The Brewers'.

Grounds: 1950, Eton Park; 2005, Pirelli Stadium.

First Football League Game: 8 August 2009, FL 2, v Shrewsbury T (a) L 1–3 – Redmond; Edworthy, Boertien, Austin, Branston, McGrath, Maghoma, Penn, Phillips (Stride), Walker, Shroot (Pearson) (1).

HONOURS

League Champions: FL 2 – 2014–15; Conference – 2008–09.
Runners-up: FL 1 – 2015–16.

FA Cup: 4th rd – 2011.

League Cup: semi-final 2019.

FOOTBALL YEARBOOK FACT FILE

Full-back Ron Edwards was an instant success when he was switched to play at centre-forward in Burton Albion's inaugural season in 1950–51. Ron scored after just four minutes of his first game in his new position and went on to net five goals in Albion's 7-2 demolition of Kidderminster Reserves in the Birmingham & District League. It was the first hat-trick to be scored by an Albion player since their formation.

Record League Victory: 6-1 v Aldershot T, FL 2, 12 December 2009 – Krysiak; James, Boertien, Stride, Webster, McGrath, Jackson, Penn, Kabba (2), Pearson (3) (Harrad) (1), Gilroy (Maghoma).

Record Cup Victory: 12–1 v Coalville T, Birmingham Senior Cup, 6 September 1954.

Record Defeat: 0–10 v Barnet, Southern League, 7 February 1970.

Most League Points (3 for a win): 94, FL 2, 2014–15.

Most League Goals: 71, FL 2, 2009–10; 2012–13.

Highest League Scorer in Season: Shaun Harrad, 21, 2009–10.

Most League Goals in Total Aggregate: Lucas Akins, 53, 2014–20.

Most League Goals in One Match: 3, Greg Pearson v Aldershot T, FL 2, 12 December 2009; 3, Shaun Harrad v Rotherham U, FL 2, 11 September 2010; 3, Lucas Akins v Colchester U, FL 1, 23 April 2016; 3, Marcus Harness v Rochdale, FL 1, 5 January 2019; 3, Scott Fraser v Oxford U, FL 1, 20 August 2019.

Most Capped Player: Liam Boyce, 11 (21), Northern Ireland.

Most League Appearances: Lucas Akins, 240, 2014–20.

Youngest League Player: Sam Austin, 17 years 310 days v Stevenage, 25 October 2014.

Record Transfer Fee Received: £2,000,000 from Hull C for Jackson Irvine, August 2017.

Record Transfer Fee Paid: £500,000 to Ross Co for Liam Boyce, June 2017.

Football League Record: 2009 Promoted from Blue Square Premier; 2009–15 FL 2; 2015–16 FL 1; 2016–18 FL C; 2018– FL 1.

MANAGERS

Reg Weston 1953–57
Sammy Crooks 1957
Eddie Shimwell 1958
Bill Townsend 1959–62
Peter Taylor 1962–65
Alex Tait 1965–70
Richie Norman 1970–73
Ken Gutteridge 1973–74
Harold Bodle 1974–76
Ian Storey-Moore 1978–81
Neil Warnock 1981–86
Brian Fidler 1986–88
Vic Halom 1988
Bobby Hope 1988
Chris Wright 1988–89
Ken Blair 1989–90
Steve Powell 1990–91
Brian Fidler 1991–92
Brian Kenning 1992–94
John Barton 1994–98
Nigel Clough 1998–2009
Roy McFarland 2009
Paul Peschisolido 2009–12
Gary Rowett 2012–14
Jimmy Floyd Hasselbaink 2014–15
Nigel Clough 2015–20
Jake Buxton May 2020–

LATEST SEQUENCES

Longest Sequence of League Wins: 4, 24.11.2015 – 12.12.2015.

Longest Sequence of League Defeats: 8, 25.2.2012 – 24.3.2012.

Longest Sequence of League Draws: 6, 25.4.2011 – 16.8.2011.

Longest Sequence of Unbeaten League Matches: 13, 7.3.2015 – 8.8.2015.

Longest Sequence Without a League Win: 16, 31.12.2011 – 24.3.2012.

Successive Scoring Runs: 18 from 16.4.2011 – 8.10.2011.

Successive Non-scoring Runs: 5 from 23.9.2017.

TEN YEAR LEAGUE RECORD

		P	*W*	*D*	*L*	*F*	*A*	*Pts*	*Pos*
2010-11	FL 2	46	12	15	19	56	70	51	19
2011-12	FL 2	46	14	12	20	54	81	54	17
2012-13	FL 2	46	22	10	14	71	65	76	4
2013-14	FL 2	46	19	15	12	47	42	72	6
2014-15	FL 2	46	28	10	8	69	39	94	1
2015-16	FL 1	46	25	10	11	57	37	85	2
2016-17	FL C	46	13	13	20	49	63	52	20
2017-18	FL C	46	10	11	25	38	81	41	23
2018-19	FL 1	46	17	12	17	66	57	63	9
2019-20	FL 1	35	12	12	11	50	50	48	12§

§*Decided on points-per-game (1.37)*

DID YOU KNOW ?

Burton Albion's first ever win in the Football League Cup came at Sheffield United in August 2012 when they entered the second round thanks to a 5-4 win on penalties. The Brewers had lost in the first round of each of their previous seasons in the competition.

BURTON ALBION – SKY BET LEAGUE ONE 2019–20 LEAGUE RECORD

Match No.	*Date*	*Venue*	*Opponents*	*Result*		*H/T Score*	*Lg Pos.*	*Goalscorers*	*Attendance*
1	Aug 3	H	Ipswich T	L	0-1	0-1	16		4565
2	10	A	Gillingham	W	2-1	2-1	11	Broadhead 2 [42, 44]	4682
3	17	H	Rotherham U	L	0-1	0-1	16		3822
4	20	A	Oxford U	W	4-2	1-0	9	Buxton [30], Fraser 3 [61, 70, 84]	6111
5	24	A	Shrewsbury T	D	0-0	0-0	11		5553
6	31	H	Bristol R	W	2-0	0-0	8	Akins [87], Edwards [90]	2831
7	Sept 14	H	Coventry C	D	0-0	0-0	11		4409
8	17	A	Portsmouth	D	2-2	2-1	9	Sbarra [3], Wallace [6]	16,610
9	21	A	Tranmere R	L	1-2	0-0	14	Akins (pen) [66]	6235
10	Oct 5	A	Milton Keynes D	W	3-0	1-0	14	Boyce 2 [32, 90], Sarkic [54]	9111
11	19	A	Fleetwood T	L	1-4	1-1	15	Sarkic [45]	3098
12	22	H	AFC Wimbledon	W	1-0	1-0	13	Templeton [31]	2223
13	26	H	Blackpool	D	0-0	0-0	13		3012
14	Nov 2	A	Doncaster R	D	2-2	1-1	13	Templeton [36], Akins (pen) [53]	7492
15	23	A	Peterborough U	L	0-1	0-0	15		6462
16	26	A	Sunderland	W	2-1	1-1	14	Edwards [20], Boyce [68]	26,538
17	Dec 3	H	Southend U	D	1-1	0-1	12	Fraser [49]	1880
18	7	H	Lincoln C	L	0-2	0-1	15		3782
19	14	A	Wycombe W	L	0-2	0-1	15		5448
20	21	H	Rochdale	W	3-1	2-1	14	Edwards [11], Akins (pen) [18], Boyce [82]	2298
21	26	H	Tranmere R	W	4-2	1-1	12	Fraser [12], Akins [50], Boyce 2 [60, 86]	3970
22	29	A	Accrington S	L	0-2	0-1	14		2449
23	Jan 1	A	Bolton W	W	4-3	3-2	12	Templeton [13], Akins 2 [26, 45], Boyce [81]	11,918
24	11	H	Fleetwood T	W	1-0	0-0	11	Edwards [89]	2354
25	14	H	Milton Keynes D	W	1-0	1-0	6	Boyce [20]	2005
26	25	H	Accrington S	D	1-1	1-1	9	Brayford [30]	2759
27	28	A	AFC Wimbledon	D	2-2	2-1	10	Powell [7], Murphy [41]	3674
28	Feb 1	A	Rotherham U	L	2-3	1-1	11	Murphy [7], Sarkic [47]	8563
29	8	H	Gillingham	D	0-0	0-0	11		2750
30	11	H	Oxford U	D	2-2	1-0	12	Akins [20], Murphy [71]	2278
31	15	A	Ipswich T	L	1-4	1-2	12	Murphy [6]	19,922
32	22	A	Southend U	W	3-2	1-1	12	Akins [5], Edwards [49], Murphy [74]	5571
33	29	H	Peterborough U	D	1-1	0-0	12	Brayford [65]	3795
34	Mar 7	A	Lincoln C	L	2-3	2-2	12	Powell 2 [6, 30]	8474
35	10	H	Bolton W	D	2-2	1-2	12	Murphy 2 [28, 65]	2034
36	14	H	Wycombe W	Cancelled					
37	21	A	Rochdale	Cancelled					
38	28	H	Doncaster R	Cancelled					
39	Apr 4	A	Blackpool	Cancelled					
40	10	H	Shrewsbury T	Cancelled					
41	13	A	Bristol R	Cancelled					
42	18	H	Sunderland	Cancelled					
43	25	A	Coventry C	Cancelled					
44	May 3	H	Portsmouth	Cancelled					

Final League Position: 12 (on points-per-game basis)

GOALSCORERS

League (50): Akins 9 (3 pens), Boyce 8, Murphy 7, Edwards 5, Fraser 5, Powell 3, Sarkic 3, Templeton 3, Brayford 2, Broadhead 2, Buxton 1, Sbarra 1, Wallace 1.
FA Cup (8): Fraser 2, Akins 1, Boyce 1, Brayford 1, Edwards 1, Sarkic 1, Templeton 1.
Carabao Cup (9): Boyce 5, Broadhead 1, Edwards 1, Fraser 1, Sarkic 1.
Leasing.com Trophy (4): Akins 1, Fraser 1, Quinn 1, Templeton 1.

O'Hara K 33	Brayford J 29 + 3	O'Toole J 25	Buxton J 20 + 4	Daniel C 19 + 5	Edwards R 33	Quinn S 27 + 2	Wallace K 20 + 6	Fraser S 25 + 5	Akins L 35	Boyce L 17 + 8	Broadhead N 12 + 7	Sarkic O 24 + 4	Hutchinson R 8 + 9	Templeton D 7 + 11	Nartey R 20 + 5	Sbarra J 6 + 16	Dyer L — + 5	Anderson J — + 1	Hart B — + 3	Shaughnessy C 6 + 2	Murphy J 10	Powell J 7 + 3	Thomas K — + 2	Garratt B 2 + 1	*Match No.*
1	2	3	4	5²	6	7■	8³	9	10¹	11	12	13	14												1
1	2	3	4	5	7		8	6	11	10	9¹		12												2
1	2²	3	4	5	6	7¹	13	8³	9	10	11	12		14											3
1	2		3	5	7²	8	4	9³	6	11	10¹	12			13	14									4
1	2	3¹	4	5	6	7³	8	11	10	12		9²			14	13									5
1	2	3	4²		6	7	5	8	9	10¹		11³		14	12	13									6
1	2	3			6	7	5	8¹	9	10³	12	11²		14	4	13									7
1	2	3■	14	12	6	7	5		9	13	10³	11¹			4	8²									8
1	2³		13	5	6	7¹	4		10	12	11	9²	14		3	8									9
1		3			6		7	8	2	10	11²	9¹	5³		4	13	12	14							10
1	2	3			6³		7	8	10	13	9¹	11	5²		4	14	12								11
1	13	3	14		6		7	8²	2	10³	9		5	11¹	4		12								12
1	2	3			6	7²	5	8	10	13	11	9¹		14	4³		12								13
1	2	3				13	7	8	5	10	12	9³		11²	4¹	6	14								14
1	2	3		14	6	7	5	8	10	13	12³	9¹		11²	4										15
1	14	3	4	13	6	7	5	8	10	11¹		9³		12	2²										16
1		3■	4	5	6²	7¹	13	8	9	10			12	11³	2	14									17
1			4	5	6	8	7²	9	2	10	11¹			12	3	13									18
1	12		4	5²		7	8	9	2	11		14	13	6¹	3	10³									19
1	2		4	5	6¹		7	8²	11	10		9³	13		3	12			14						20
1	2¹		4	5	6	7		9²	10	11		8³		14	3	12			13						21
1	2²		4	5	6	7¹		9	10	11		8³		13	3	12			14						22
1	2		4	14	7	12		8	10	13		9²	5	11¹	3	6³									23
1	2	3	4	5³	7	6		8	11	13		10¹	12	9²		14									24
1	2	3	4		7	8³		9²	5	11	10¹			14	13	6				12					25
1	2	3	4	5	6	7		8²	10			9¹		14						12	11³	13			26
1	2	3	14	5	6	8³		12	10					13	4					7	11²	9¹			27
1	2	3	4	5³	9¹	7		12	11			8²	14							6	10	13			28
1	2	3		5	6	7³	13		11			8■			14					4	10²	9¹	12		29
1	2				6		7	8¹	10		9²		5³		3	12				4	11	13	14		30
1²	2				6	7	13		10		14	9	5		3¹					4	11³	8		12	31
1	2	3		9	6²	7¹	14		5		12	11³				13				4	10	8			32
1	2	3		9³	6²	7	4	13	5		14	10¹	12								11	8			33
	2	4	3³	12	6¹	7		13	5			11	9²			14					10	8		1	34
	2	4	3		6	7¹	14	12	5			10²	9			13					11	8³		1	35
																									36
																									37
																									38
																									39
																									40
																									41
																									42
																									43
																									44

FA Cup

First Round	Salford C	(a)	1-1
Replay	Salford C	(h)	4-1
Second Round	Oldham Ath	(a)	1-0
Third Round	Northampton T	(h)	2-4

Carabao Cup

First Round	Port Vale	(a)	2-1
Second Round	Morecambe	(h)	4-0
Third Round	Bournemouth	(h)	2-0
Fourth Round	Leicester C	(h)	1-3

Leasing.com Trophy

Group E (N)	Crewe Alex	(a)	3-1
Group E (N)	Everton U21	(h)	0-2
Group E (N)	Mansfield T	(h)	1-2

CAMBRIDGE UNITED

FOUNDATION

The football revival in Cambridge began soon after World War II when the Abbey United club (formed 1912) decided to turn professional in 1949. In 1951 they changed their name to Cambridge United. They were competing in the United Counties League before graduating to the Eastern Counties League in 1951 and the Southern League in 1958.

The Abbey Stadium, Newmarket Road, Cambridge CB5 8LN.

Telephone: (01223) 566 500.

Ticket Office: (01223) 566 500 (option 1).

Website: www.cambridge-united.co.uk

Email: info@cambridge-united.co.uk

Ground Capacity: 8,127.

Record Attendance: 14,000 v Chelsea, Friendly, 1 May 1970.

Pitch Measurements: 100.5m × 67.5m (110yd × 74yd).

Vice-Chairman: Eddie Clark.

Chief Executive: Ian Mather.

Head Coach: Mark Bonner.

HONOURS

League Champions: Division 3 – 1990–91; Division 4 – 1976–77.
Runners-up: Division 3 – 1977–78; Fourth Division – (6th) 1989–90 *(promoted via play-offs)*; Third Division – 1998–99; Conference – (2nd) 2013–14 *(promoted via play-offs)*.

FA Cup: 6th rd – 1990, 1991.

League Cup: quarter-final – 1993.

League Trophy: *Runners-up:* 2002.

Colours: Amber and black striped shirts, black shorts with amber trim, black socks with amber trim.

Year Formed: 1912.

Turned Professional: 1949.

Ltd Co.: 1948.

Previous Name: 1919, Abbey United; 1951, Cambridge United.

Club Nickname: The 'U's'.

Grounds: 1932, Abbey Stadium (renamed R Costings Abbey Stadium 2009, Cambs Glass Stadium 2016, The Abbey Stadium 2017).

First Football League Game: 15 August 1970, Division 4, v Lincoln C (h) D 1–1 – Roberts; Thompson, Meldrum (1), Slack, Eades, Hardy, Leggett, Cassidy, Lindsey, McKinven, Harris.

Record League Victory: 7–0 v Morecambe, FL 2, 19 April 2016 – Norris; Roberts (1), Coulson, Clark, Dunne (Williams), Ismail (1), Berry (2 pens), Ledson (Spencer), Dunk (2), Williamson (1) (Simpson).

Record Cup Victory: 5–1 v Bristol C, FA Cup 5th rd second replay, 27 February 1990 – Vaughan; Fensome, Kimble, Bailie (O'Shea), Chapple, Daish, Cheetham (Robinson), Leadbitter (1), Dublin (2), Taylor (1), Philpott (1).

Record Defeat: 0–7 v Sunderland, League Cup 2nd rd, 1 October 2002; 0–7 v Luton T, FL 2, 18 November 2017.

Most League Points (2 for a win): 65, Division 4, 1976–77.

FOOTBALL YEARBOOK FACT FILE

Abbey United, as the U's were then known, competed in the FA Cup for the first time in 1927–28. It was an inauspicious start for United, who at the time were members of the Cambridgeshire League. They were drawn away to Great Yarmouth Town in the extra preliminary round and lost 3-1. The attendance of 3,000 was the largest the team had played in front of at that time.

Most League Points (3 for a win): 86, Division 3, 1990–91.

Most League Goals: 87, Division 4, 1976–77.

Highest League Scorer in Season: David Crown, 24, Division 4, 1985–86.

Most League Goals in Total Aggregate: John Taylor, 86, 1988–92; 1996–2001.

Most League Goals in One Match: 5, Steve Butler v Exeter C, Division 2, 4 April 1994.

Most Capped Player: Reggie Lambe, 12 (41), Bermuda.

Most League Appearances: Steve Spriggs, 416, 1975–87.

Youngest League Player: Andy Sinton, 16 years 228 days v Wolverhampton W, 2 November 1982.

Record Transfer Fee Received: £1,300,000 from Leicester C for Trevor Benjamin, July 2000.

Record Transfer Fee Paid: £190,000 to Luton T for Steve Claridge, November 1992.

Football League Record: 1970 Elected to Division 4; 1973–74 Division 3; 1974–77 Division 4; 1977–78 Division 3; 1978–84 Division 2; 1984–85 Division 3; 1985–90 Division 4; 1990–91 Division 3; 1991–92 Division 2; 1992–93 Division 1; 1993–95 Division 2; 1995–99 Division 3; 1999–2002 Division 2; 2002–04 Division 3; 2004–05 FL2; 2005–14 Conference Premier; 2014– FL 2.

MANAGERS

Bill Whittaker 1949–55
Gerald Williams 1955
Bert Johnson 1955–59
Bill Craig 1959–60
Alan Moore 1960–63
Roy Kirk 1964–66
Bill Leivers 1967–74
Ron Atkinson 1974–78
John Docherty 1978–83
John Ryan 1984–85
Ken Shellito 1985
Chris Turner 1985–90
John Beck 1990–92
Ian Atkins 1992–93
Gary Johnson 1993–95
Tommy Taylor 1995–96
Roy McFarland 1996–2001
John Beck 2001
John Taylor 2001–04
Claude Le Roy 2004
Herve Renard 2004
Steve Thompson 2004–05
Rob Newman 2005–06
Jimmy Quinn 2006–08
Gary Brabin 2008–09
Martin Ling 2009–11
Jez George 2011–12
Richard Money 2012–15
Shaun Derry 2015–18
Joe Dunne 2018
Colin Calderwood 2018–20
Mark Bonner March 2020–

LATEST SEQUENCES

Longest Sequence of League Wins: 7, 19.2.1977 – 1.4.1977.

Longest Sequence of League Defeats: 7, 8.4.1985 – 30.4.1985.

Longest Sequence of League Draws: 6, 6.9.1986 – 30.9.1986.

Longest Sequence of Unbeaten League Matches: 14, 9.9.1972 – 10.11.1972.

Longest Sequence Without a League Win: 31, 8.10.1983 – 23.4.1984.

Successive Scoring Runs: 26 from 9.4.2002.

Successive Non-scoring Runs: 5 from 29.9.1973.

TEN YEAR LEAGUE RECORD

		P	W	D	L	F	A	Pts	Pos
2010-11	Conf P	46	11	17	18	53	61	50	17
2011-12	Conf P	46	19	14	13	57	41	71	9
2012-13	Conf P	46	15	14	17	68	69	59	14
2013-14	Conf P	46	23	13	10	72	35	82	2
2014-15	FL 2	46	13	12	21	61	66	51	19
2015-16	FL 2	46	18	14	14	66	55	68	9
2016-17	FL 2	46	19	9	18	58	50	66	11
2017-18	FL 2	46	17	13	16	56	60	64	12
2018-19	FL 2	46	12	11	23	40	66	47	21
2019-20	FL 2	37	12	9	16	40	48	45	16§

§Decided on points-per-game (1.22)

DID YOU KNOW ?

In 1962–63 Cambridge United and their neighbours Cambridge City were the two leading teams in the Southern League. City just pipped United to the title with the crucial fixture between the clubs in April attracting 11,574 fans to watch City win 2-1.

CAMBRIDGE UNITED – SKY BET LEAGUE TWO 2019–20 LEAGUE RECORD

Match No.	Date	Venue	Opponents	Result	H/T Score	Lg Pos.	Goalscorers	Attendance
1	Aug 3	A	Bradford C	D 0-0	0-0	14		14,810
2	10	H	Newport Co	D 0-0	0-0	18		3949
3	17	A	Colchester U	W 2-1	0-1	10	Richards 54, Darling 86	4148
4	20	H	Scunthorpe U	W 3-2	0-1	3	Knibbs 2 52, 54, Lewis 73	3917
5	24	H	Oldham Ath	L 1-2	1-1	11	Richards 35	4004
6	31	A	Port Vale	L 0-1	0-0	13		4874
7	Sept 7	H	Forest Green R	L 0-1	0-0	16		3784
8	14	A	Crewe Alex	W 3-2	1-0	12	Smith 2 (1 pen) 12, 72 (p), Lewis 69	3568
9	17	A	Mansfield T	W 4-0	0-0	8	Roles 74, Smith 86, Maris 90, Lambe (pen) 90	3567
10	21	H	Swindon T	L 0-1	0-1	11		4443
11	28	A	Stevenage	D 1-1	0-1	11	Smith 83	3452
12	Oct 5	H	Macclesfield T	D 2-2	1-0	11	Roles 13, Smith 78	3678
13	12	A	Salford C	L 0-1	0-0	16		3026
14	19	H	Exeter C	W 4-0	1-0	10	Hannant 38, Roles 57, Taft 72, Dallas 87	3816
15	22	H	Grimsby T	D 0-0	0-0	11		4898
16	26	A	Northampton T	L 0-2	0-2	13		5221
17	Nov 2	H	Crawley T	W 2-1	0-0	12	Smith 83, Lewis 86	3538
18	16	A	Walsall	L 1-2	0-2	13	Knibbs 90	5429
19	23	A	Carlisle U	D 0-0	0-0	13		4041
20	Dec 7	H	Plymouth Arg	W 1-0	1-0	11	Knoyle 18	4492
21	14	A	Cheltenham T	D 1-1	1-0	11	Lewis 27	2813
22	21	H	Leyton Orient	L 2-3	0-3	11	Roles 69, Smith (pen) 82	5408
23	26	A	Swindon T	L 0-4	0-3	13		8211
24	29	H	Morecambe	W 1-0	0-0	12	Roles 57	4086
25	Jan 1	H	Mansfield T	L 2-3	2-1	13	Knibbs 3, Taylor, G 44	3848
26	4	A	Macclesfield T	L 0-1	0-1	13		1454
27	11	A	Exeter C	L 0-2	0-0	16		4517
28	18	H	Stevenage	L 0-4	0-1	16		4228
29	25	A	Morecambe	D 1-1	0-0	17	Knibbs 68	2019
30	28	H	Salford C	L 0-4	0-1	19		3444
31	Feb 1	H	Colchester U	W 2-1	0-0	16	Dallas 85, Knibbs 86	5015
32	8	A	Newport Co	W 1-0	0-0	15	O'Neil 68	3336
33	11	A	Scunthorpe U	W 2-0	1-0	12	El Mizouni 16, Mullin 61	2746
34	15	H	Bradford C	W 2-1	0-1	12	Darling 84, Knibbs 90	4541
35	22	A	Plymouth Arg	D 0-0	0-0	11		11,597
36	29	H	Carlisle U	L 1-2	0-1	13	Lambe 82	4122
37	Mar 7	A	Leyton Orient	L 1-2	0-2	16	Mullin 63	5813
38	14	H	Cheltenham T	Cancelled				
39	17	A	Grimsby T	Cancelled				
40	21	H	Northampton T	Cancelled				
41	28	A	Crawley T	Cancelled				
42	Apr 4	H	Walsall	Cancelled				
43	10	A	Oldham Ath	Cancelled				
44	13	H	Port Vale	Cancelled				
45	18	A	Forest Green R	Cancelled				
46	25	H	Crewe Alex	Cancelled				

Final League Position: 16 (on points-per-game basis)

GOALSCORERS

League (40): Knibbs 7, Smith 7 (2 pens), Roles 5, Lewis 4, Dallas 2, Darling 2, Lambe 2 (1 pen), Mullin 2, Richards 2, El Mizouni 1, Hannant 1, Knoyle 1, Maris 1, O'Neil 1, Taft 1, Taylor, G 1.
FA Cup (1): Smith 1.
Carabao Cup (1): Richards 1.
Leasing.com Trophy (2): Knibbs 2.

Mitov D 27	Knoyle K 26	Taylor G 29 + 1	Taft G 25 + 2	Jones D 10 + 4	Lambe R 14 + 9	O'Neil L 23 + 5	Lewis P 35 + 1	Hannant L 23 + 4	Dallas A 2 + 20	Ibehre J 2 + 2	Smith S 25 + 3	Maris G 24 + 6	Dunk H 20 + 9	Davies L 14 + 2	Richards M 14 + 4	Knibbs H 12 + 12	Darling H 23 + 1	Roles J 12 + 11	Carruthers S 7 + 3	Ward E 13	Norville-Williams J — + 5	Burton C 10	Adeboyejo V 7 + 1	El Mizouni I 5 + 2	Mullin P 5 + 1	Match No.
1	2	3	4	5^{3}	6^{1}	7■	8	9	10^{2}	11	12	13	14													1
1	2^{1}	4	3	5	6		8	9	13	11^{2}	10^{3}	7		12	14											2
1		3	4		6		7	9	10^{1}		13	8^{3}	5	2	11^{2}	12	14									3
1		3	4			6^{2}	7	12			11	13	8^{1}	5	14	10^{3}	2	9								4
1		3	4		13	7^{2}	6	9			11^{3}	8^{1}		5	10	14	2	12								5
1		3	4		13	7^{3}	6	9^{1}			11		5	2	10	14		12	8^{2}							6
1		3	4			7^{1}	6	8	14	13	11^{2}	12		5	10^{3}		2		9							7
1	5		4		13	8^{2}	6	9			11	12			10^{3}		2	14	7^{1}	3						8
1	5	3	4		8		6^{1}	9^{3}	14		11^{2}	7	12		10		2	13								9
1	5	2	4		9	7	6		14	12	11^{3}	13			10			8^{1}		3^{2}						10
1	5	2^{2}	4		13	7^{1}	12	9			10	8	14		11			6^{3}		3						11
1	5		4		7		6	9	13		11		12		10^{1}		2	8		3^{2}						12
1	5^{1}		4			7^{2}	6	9	13		11	8	12		10		2			3						13
1	2		3		9		6	8	14		11^{3}	7^{1}	5	12	13			10^{2}		4						14
1	2		4		7		6	5	13		11^{2}		9		10	12		8^{1}		3						15
1	5		4		8	14	7	6	13		11^{2}		9		10^{1}	12	2			3^{3}						16
1	2		4	14	8^{3}	12	6	5			11	7	9^{2}		10^{1}	13				3						17
1		2	4^{3}	8		6	7^{1}				11	9	13	5^{2}		10		12		3	14					18
1	2	14	4^{2}	5		13	9	6^{1}	12		11	8	10				3	7^{3}								19
1	2	5			9^{1}	7^{3}	6	8	13		10					11^{2}	4	14	12	3						20
1	2	4		5	9	12	6	7^{2}	14		11^{3}					10		13	8^{1}	3						21
1	2^{2}	4		5	9■		6	7^{1}			11		13		14	10^{3}		12	8	3						22
1		3	4			8	6	5^{1}	13		11	7^{2}	9			14	2	10^{3}			12					23
		3	4	5	12	6^{2}	8				11	9	13		10^{3}	14	2	7^{1}				1				24
		3	4^{2}	13	7■		8	6^{3}	14		11	12	5			10^{1}	2	9				1				25
		3	4	5^{2}		6^{3}	7	12	13		11	9				10	2	8^{1}			14	1				26
1		3		14		6^{3}	8	9^{1}	12		10^{2}	7	5	2		11	4				13					27
1	2	3	4	5		9	7	6^{3}	13			8^{2}	10^{1}			11		12			14					28
1	2	3		14		7^{3}	8	12				6	5^{1}			10	4	9^{2}					11	13		29
1	2	3		5^{1}	14	7^{2}	8	13				6^{3}	12			11	4						10	9		30
	2^{1}	3	14			8	7		13			9	5	6		12	4					1	11^{2}	10^{3}		31
	2	3	12			8	7		14			9	5	6		10^{2}	4^{1}					1	11^{3}		13	32
	2	3	4		12	8^{3}	7					9	5	6		14						1	13	10^{1}	11^{2}	33
	2^{1}	4				7^{3}	8					9	5	6		13	3		12			1	10^{2}	14	11	34
	2	3			13	8^{2}	7^{1}					9	5	6		14	4		12			1		10	11^{3}	35
	2	3			12				14			8	5	6^{2}			4	13	7			1	11^{3}	9^{1}	10	36
	2	3				12	7^{1}				14	9	5	6^{3}			4	13	8^{2}			1	10		11	37
																										38
																										39
																										40
																										41
																										42
																										43
																										44
																										45
																										46

FA Cup

First Round	Exeter C	(h)	1-1
Replay	Exeter C	(a)	0-1

Carabao Cup

First Round	Brentford	(a)	1-1
(Cambridge U won 5-4 on penalties)			
Second Round	Swansea C	(a)	0-6

Leasing.com Trophy

Group H (S)	Northampton T	(h)	0-1
Group H (S)	Arsenal U21	(h)	1-1
(Arsenal U21 won 4-3 on penalties)			
Group H (S)	Peterborough U	(a)	1-2

CARDIFF CITY

FOUNDATION

Credit for the establishment of a first class professional football club in such a rugby stronghold as Cardiff is due to members of the Riverside club formed in 1899 out of a cricket club of that name. Cardiff became a city in 1905 and in 1908 the South Wales and Monmouthshire FA granted Riverside permission to call themselves Cardiff City. The club turned professional under that name in 1910.

Cardiff City Stadium, Leckwith Road, Cardiff CF11 8AZ.

Telephone: (0845) 345 1400.

Ticket Office: (0845) 345 1400.

Website: www.cardiffcityfc.co.uk

Email: club@cardiffcityfc.co.uk

Ground Capacity: 33,280.

Record Attendance: 57,893 v Arsenal, Division 1, 22 April 1953 (at Ninian Park); 32,478 v Reading, FL C, 6 May 2018 (at Cardiff City Stadium).

Ground Record Attendance: 62,634, Wales v England, 17 October 1959 (at Ninian Park); 33,280, Wales v Belgium, 12 June 2015 (at Cardiff City Stadium).

Pitch Measurements: 105m × 68m (115yd × 74.5yd).

Chairman: Mehmet Dalman.

Chief Executive: Ken Choo.

Manager: Neil Harris.

Assistant Manager: David Livermore.

Colours: Blue shirts with white trim, white shorts with blue trim, blue socks with white trim.

Year Formed: 1899.

Turned Professional: 1910.

Previous Names: 1899, Riverside; 1902, Riverside Albion; 1908, Cardiff City.

Club Nickname: 'The Bluebirds'.

Grounds: Riverside, Sophia Gardens, Old Park and Fir Gardens; 1910, Ninian Park; 2009, Cardiff City Stadium.

First Football League Game: 28 August 1920, Division 2, v Stockport Co (a) W 5–2 – Kneeshaw; Brittan, Leyton; Keenor (1), Smith, Hardy; Grimshaw (1), Gill (2), Cashmore, West, Evans (1).

Record League Victory: 9–2 v Thames, Division 3 (S), 6 February 1932 – Farquharson; Eric Morris, Roberts; Galbraith, Harris, Ronan; Emmerson (1), Keating (1), Jones (1), McCambridge (1), Robbins (5).

Record Cup Victory: 8–0 v Enfield, FA Cup 1st rd, 28 November 1931 – Farquharson; Smith, Roberts; Harris (1), Galbraith, Ronan; Emmerson (2), Keating (3); O'Neill (2), Robbins, McCambridge.

HONOURS

League Champions: FL C – 2012–13; Division 3S – 1946–47; Third Division – 1992–93.
Runners-up: FL C – 2017–18; Division 1 – 1923–24; Division 2 – 1920–21, 1951–52, 1959–60; Division 3 – 1975–76, 1982–83; Third Division – 2000–01; Division 4 – 1987–88.

FA Cup Winners: 1927.
Runners-up: 1925, 2008.

League Cup: *Runners-up:* 2012.

Welsh Cup Winners: 22 times.

European Competitions
European Cup-Winners' Cup: 1964–65 *(qf)*, 1965–66, 1967–68 *(sf)*, 1968–69, 1969–70, 1970–71 *(qf)*, 1971–72, 1973–74, 1974–75, 1976–77, 1977–78, 1988–89, 1992–93, 1993–94.

FOOTBALL YEARBOOK FACT FILE

In 1909 Cardiff City, then members of the South Wales League, played two friendly matches at Cardiff Arms Park, home of the city's rugby union club. They attracted a crowd of 1,000 to see a 3-3 draw with Crystal Palace in October and the following month a larger attendance watched them lose 7-0 to First Division club Bristol City.

Record Defeat: 2–11 v Sheffield U, Division 1, 1 January 1926.
Most League Points (2 for a win): 66, Division 3 (S), 1946–47.
Most League Points (3 for a win): 90, FL C, 2017–18.
Most League Goals: 95, Division 3, 2000–01.
Highest League Scorer in Season: Robert Earnshaw, 31, Division 2, 2002–03.
Most League Goals in Total Aggregate: Len Davies, 128, 1920–31.
Most League Goals in One Match: 5, Hugh Ferguson v Burnley, Division 1, 1 September 1928; 5, Walter Robbins v Thames, Division 3 (S), 6 February 1932; 5, William Henderson v Northampton T, Division 3 (S), 22 April 1933.
Most Capped Player: Aron Gunnarsson, 59 (87), Iceland.
Most League Appearances: Phil Dwyer, 471, 1972–85.
Youngest League Player: Bob Adams, 15 years 355 days v Southend U, 18 February 1933.
Record Transfer Fee Received: £10,000,000 from Internazionale for Gary Medel, August 2014.
Record Transfer Fee Paid: £15,000,000 to Nantes for Emiliano Sala, January 2019.
Football League Record: 1920 Elected to Division 2; 1921–29 Division 1; 1929–31 Division 2; 1931–47 Division 3 (S); 1947–52 Division 2; 1952–57 Division 1; 1957–60 Division 2; 1960–62 Division 1; 1962–75 Division 2; 1975–76 Division 3; 1976–82 Division 2; 1982–83 Division 3; 1983–85 Division 2; 1985–86 Division 3; 1986–88 Division 4; 1988–90 Division 3; 1990–92 Division 4; 1992–93 Division 3; 1993–95 Division 2; 1995–99 Division 3; 1999–2000 Division 2; 2000–01 Division 3; 2001–03 Division 2; 2003–04 Division 1; 2004–13 FL C; 2013–14 Premier League; 2014–18 FL C; 2018–19 Premier League; 2019– FL C.

MANAGERS

Davy McDougall 1910–11
Fred Stewart 1911–33
Bartley Wilson 1933–34
B. Watts-Jones 1934–37
Bill Jennings 1937–39
Cyril Spiers 1939–46
Billy McCandless 1946–48
Cyril Spiers 1948–54
Trevor Morris 1954–58
Bill Jones 1958–62
George Swindin 1962–64
Jimmy Scoular 1964–73
Frank O'Farrell 1973–74
Jimmy Andrews 1974–78
Richie Morgan 1978–81
Graham Williams 1981–82
Len Ashurst 1982–84
Jimmy Goodfellow 1984
Alan Durban 1984–86
Frank Burrows 1986–89
Len Ashurst 1989–91
Eddie May 1991–94
Terry Yorath 1994–95
Eddie May 1995
Kenny Hibbitt (*Chief Coach*) 1995–96
Phil Neal 1996
Russell Osman 1996–97
Kenny Hibbitt 1997–98
Frank Burrows 1998–2000
Billy Ayre 2000
Bobby Gould 2000
Alan Cork 2000–02
Lennie Lawrence 2002–05
Dave Jones 2005–11
Malky Mackay 2011–13
Ole Gunnar Solskjaer 2014
Russell Slade 2014–16
Paul Trollope 2016
Neil Warnock 2016–19
Neil Harris November 2019–

LATEST SEQUENCES

Longest Sequence of League Wins: 9, 26.10.1946 – 28.12.1946.
Longest Sequence of League Defeats: 7, 4.11.1933 – 25.12.1933.
Longest Sequence of League Draws: 6, 29.11.1980 – 17.1.1981.
Longest Sequence of Unbeaten League Matches: 21, 21.9.1946 – 1.3.1947.
Longest Sequence Without a League Win: 15, 21.11.1936 – 6.3.1937.
Successive Scoring Runs: 24 from 25.8.2012.
Successive Non-scoring Runs: 8 from 20.12.1952.

TEN YEAR LEAGUE RECORD

		P	W	D	L	F	A	Pts	Pos
2010-11	FL C	46	23	11	12	76	54	80	4
2011-12	FL C	46	19	18	9	66	53	75	6
2012-13	FL C	46	25	12	9	72	45	87	1
2013-14	PR Lge	38	7	9	22	32	74	30	20
2014-15	FL C	46	16	14	16	57	61	62	11
2015-16	FL C	46	17	17	12	56	51	68	8
2016-17	FL C	46	17	11	18	60	61	62	12
2017-18	FL C	46	27	9	10	69	39	90	2
2018-19	PR Lge	38	10	4	24	34	69	34	18
2019-20	FL C	46	19	16	11	68	58	73	5

DID YOU KNOW ?

Striker Alan Warboys scored a hat-trick in the first 10 minutes of Cardiff City's game against Carlisle United on 6 March 1971. He went on to score another goal two minutes before half-time as the Bluebirds won the top of the table clash to leave them at the head of the Second Division.

CARDIFF CITY – SKY BET CHAMPIONSHIP 2019–20 LEAGUE RECORD

Match No.	Date	Venue	Opponents	Result	H/T Score	Lg Pos.	Goalscorers	Attendance
1	Aug 3	A	Wigan Ath	L 2-3	1-0	16	Ralls [20], Bogle [70]	12,169
2	10	H	Luton T	W 2-1	0-0	12	Flint [52], Vassell [90]	24,724
3	18	A	Reading	L 0-3	0-2	19		14,252
4	21	H	Huddersfield T	W 2-1	1-0	12	Ralls [42], Hoilett [88]	21,821
5	24	A	Blackburn R	D 0-0	0-0	15		13,291
6	30	H	Fulham	D 1-1	1-1	10	Murphy, J [42]	22,631
7	Sept 13	A	Derby Co	D 1-1	1-1	12	Glatzel (pen) [19]	25,873
8	21	H	Middlesbrough	W 1-0	1-0	13	Fletcher (og) [2]	23,141
9	28	A	Hull C	D 2-2	0-1	12	Glatzel [55], Ward [90]	10,756
10	Oct 2	H	QPR	W 3-0	2-0	10	Morrison [11], Pack [45], Paterson [72]	21,387
11	5	A	WBA	L 2-4	0-2	11	Ward 2 [75, 86]	25,140
12	18	H	Sheffield W	D 1-1	0-1	11	Tomlin [87]	22,486
13	22	A	Millwall	D 2-2	1-1	13	Ward [12], Hoilett [57]	11,769
14	27	A	Swansea C	L 0-1	0-1	14		20,270
15	Nov 2	H	Birmingham C	W 4-2	2-1	14	Ralls 3 (2 pens) [30 (p), 69, 90 (p)], Nelson [38]	23,778
16	10	H	Bristol C	L 0-1	0-0	14		23,846
17	23	A	Charlton Ath	D 2-2	0-2	16	Mendez-Laing [52], Tomlin [73]	16,011
18	26	H	Stoke C	W 1-0	1-0	10	Bacuna [11]	20,884
19	30	A	Nottingham F	W 1-0	1-0	10	Mendez-Laing [14]	28,209
20	Dec 7	H	Barnsley	W 3-2	1-1	8	Flint [20], Ward [68], Tomlin [90]	21,380
21	11	A	Brentford	L 1-2	0-1	9	Pack [64]	10,417
22	14	A	Leeds U	D 3-3	0-2	12	Tomlin [60], Morrison [82], Glatzel [88]	34,552
23	21	H	Preston NE	D 0-0	0-0	12		22,625
24	26	H	Millwall	D 1-1	0-0	11	Flint [59]	23,583
25	29	A	Sheffield W	W 2-1	2-1	10	Glatzel [5], Hoilett [8]	25,385
26	Jan 1	A	QPR	L 1-6	0-3	12	Vaulks [90]	12,355
27	12	H	Swansea C	D 0-0	0-0	12		28,529
28	18	A	Birmingham C	D 1-1	0-1	13	Tomlin [63]	20,482
29	28	H	WBA	W 2-1	0-0	12	Paterson [46], Tomlin [76]	22,516
30	31	H	Reading	D 1-1	0-1	11	Paterson [70]	22,518
31	Feb 8	A	Luton T	W 1-0	0-0	8	Tomlin [73]	10,041
32	12	A	Huddersfield T	W 3-0	2-0	8	Murphy, J [28], Vaulks [33], Paterson [69]	20,238
33	15	H	Wigan Ath	D 2-2	1-2	9	Murphy, J [8], Naismith (og) [55]	21,287
34	22	A	Stoke C	L 0-2	0-1	10		25,436
35	25	H	Nottingham F	L 0-1	0-0	10		21,273
36	29	H	Brentford	D 2-2	2-2	11	Hoilett [34], Ralls [45]	22,393
37	Mar 7	A	Barnsley	W 2-0	0-0	9	Vaulks [65], Paterson [66]	12,751
38	June 21	H	Leeds U	W 2-0	1-0	7	Hoilett [35], Glatzel [71]	0
39	27	A	Preston NE	W 3-1	0-0	6	Ralls [69], Mendez-Laing [82], Glatzel [90]	0
40	30	H	Charlton Ath	D 0-0	0-0	6		0
41	July 4	A	Bristol C	W 1-0	0-0	6	Ward [85]	0
42	7	H	Blackburn R	L 2-3	2-1	6	Vaulks [14], Glatzel [41]	0
43	10	A	Fulham	L 0-2	0-1	6		0
44	14	H	Derby Co	W 2-1	1-1	6	Hoilett [17], Tomlin [59]	0
45	18	A	Middlesbrough	W 3-1	1-0	6	Morrison [4], Murphy, J 2 [47, 81]	0
46	22	H	Hull C	W 3-0	2-0	5	Hoilett [20], Morrison [34], Ward [83]	0

Final League Position: 5

GOALSCORERS

League (68): Tomlin 8, Glatzel 7 (1 pen), Hoilett 7, Ralls 7 (2 pens), Ward 7, Murphy, J 5, Paterson 5, Morrison 4, Vaulks 4, Flint 3, Mendez-Laing 3, Pack 2, Bacuna 1, Bogle 1, Nelson 1, Vassell 1, own goals 2.
FA Cup (10): Murphy, J 3, Flint 2, Paterson 2, Glatzel 1, Ward 1, Whyte 1.
Carabao Cup (0).
Championship Play-Offs (2): Nelson 1, Tomlin 1.

Etheridge N 16	Peltier L 24 + 1	Flint A 26	Morrison S 35 + 1	Bennett J 44	Bacuna L 35 + 6	Ralls J 25 + 2	Mendez-Laing N 21 + 6	Reid B 1	Murphy J 16 + 11	Madine G 5 + 3	Day J — + 1	Bogle O 2 + 9	Whyte G 15 + 9	Smithies A 30	Pack M 32 + 5	Paterson C 18 + 18	Glatzel R 23 + 7	Hoilett J 29 + 12	Vaulks W 18 + 9	Vassell I — + 2	Nelson C 31 + 2	Tomlin L 24 + 9	Ward D 7 + 21	Bamba S 1 + 5	Richards A 10 + 1	Adomah A 9	Sanderson D 9 + 1	Smith B — + 3	*Match No.*
1^{1}	2	3	4	5	6	7	8	9	10^{3}	11^{2}	12	13	14																1
	2	4	3	5		6			10^{1}				8^{2}	1	7	9	11^{3}	12	13	14									2
		4	3	5	2	7	8							1	6^{1}	14	11	10^{3}	9^{2}	13	12								3
	2	4	3	5	6	7			10			12	8^{3}	1			11^{1}	13	14			9^{2}							4
	2	4	3	5	6	7			10			13	8	1			11^{2}	12				9^{1}							5
	2	4	3	5	6	7	14		10^{3}				8^{1}	1		13	11	12				9^{2}							6
	2	4	3	5	6	7	13		10^{2}			14	8^{1}	1		9	11^{3}	12											7
	2	4	3	5	6	7			10^{1}			11^{2}	8	1		9		12					13						8
	2	4	3	5	6	8	12		14				9^{1}	1	7		10^{2}	11^{3}					13						9
	2	4	3	5	6				10				8^{3}	1	7	12	11^{2}	14				9^{1}	13						10
	2	4	3	5	6		12		14				8^{3}	1	7	9^{1}	11^{2}	10					13						11
1	2	4	3	5	6^{1}	8	9^{3}		11				13		7		10^{2}					14	12						12
1	2	4	3	5		7			12			13	8		6	14		10^{1}				9^{2}	11^{3}						13
1	2	4	3	5		8	9^{2}		14			12	6^{3}		7	13	10^{1}						11						14
1	2	4		5	6	8	9^{2}					12			7	13		11^{1}			3^{3}		10■	14					15
1	2	4		5	6		8			13		11^{2}	12		7	14		10^{3}			3	9^{1}							16
1	2	4		5	6		8			11^{1}		12			7	9^{3}		10^{2}	14		3	13							17
1	2	4		5	6		8^{2}			11^{1}		12			7	13		10	14		3	9^{3}							18
1	2	3	14	5	6		8^{2}			11^{1}					7	13		10^{3}			4	9	12						19
1	2	3		5	6^{3}		8		12	11^{2}					7			10^{1}	14		4	9	13						20
1	2	3		5	6		8^{2}		12	13					7	14		10^{1}			4	9	11^{3}						21
1	2	3^{1}	4■	5		9	6						13		8		14		7^{2}		12	11	10^{3}						22
1	2	3			6		8^{3}		10^{1}	12					7	14	11^{2}				4	9	13		5				23
1	2^{1}	3		5	6		8						14		7		11^{2}	10^{3}			4	9	13		12				24
1		3		5^{1}	6		8^{2}								7	14	11	10	12		4	9^{3}		13	2				25
1	13	4			2^{1}								14		9		11^{3}	10	8		5	7	12	3^{2}	6				26
	2		3	5	6				13				8^{1}	1	7	12	11^{2}	10			4	9							27
			3	5	6	13							8	1	7	12	14	10^{2}			4	9^{3}	11^{1}		2				28
			3	5	13								8^{2}	1	6	9	11^{1}	10^{3}	7		4	12		14	2				29
			3	5	12								8^{1}	1	7	11		10^{2}	6		4	9	13		2				30
			3	5	13				10^{1}				14	1	7	11		12	6		4	9^{2}			2	8^{3}			31
			3	5	12				10^{1}					1	7	11^{3}		13	6		4	9	14		2	8^{2}			32
			3	5^{1}	12				10^{3}					1	7	11^{2}		13	6		4	9	14		2	8			33
			3	5					10^{1}				14	1	7	11	13	12	6		4		9^{2}		2^{3}	8			34
			3	5	14	12			10^{2}					1	7^{1}	9	11	8	6		4		13				2^{3}		35
			3	5	8	7^{1}								1		10		11	6		4		12			9	2		36
			3	5	6	8^{1}			13					1	12	10^{3}	14	11^{2}	7		4					9	2		37
			3	5	6	8^{3}	13							1	14	10^{1}	12	11^{4}	7^{5}		4	16				9^{2}	2	15	38
			3	5	7	9^{3}	13							1	15	11^{1}	12	10^{4}	6		4	14				8^{2}	2		39
			3	5	6^{3}	8^{4}	11^{2}							1	7	12	10^{1}	13	15		4	14				9	2		40
			3	5	7	9	8^{1}							1		11^{2}		10^{3}	6		4	12	13	14			2		41
			3	5	6	9			10^{3}				15	1	16	13	11^{2}	8^{4}	7^{1}		4	12	14				2^{5}		42
			3	5	6	9	8^{4}		15					1		11^{2}	13	10^{3}	7		4	12	14				2^{1}		43
			3	5	2	6	8^{3}							1	7^{4}	15	11^{2}	10	12		4	9^{1}	13					14	44
			3	5	2	7^{5}	8^{4}		12					1	13		11^{3}	10^{1}	6		4	9^{2}	14	15			16		45
			3	5	2	7^{4}	8^{2}		13					1	6	16	11^{3}	10^{1}	12		4	9^{5}	14					15	46

FA Cup

Third Round	Carlisle U	(h)	2-2
Replay	Carlisle U	(a)	4-3
Fourth Round	Reading	(a)	1-1
Replay	Reading	(h)	3-3

(*aet; Reading won 4-1 on penalties*)

Carabao Cup

Second Round	Luton T	(h)	0-3

Championship Play-Offs

Semi-Finals 1st leg	Fulham	(h)	0-2
Semi-Finals 2nd leg	Fulham	(a)	2-1

CARLISLE UNITED

FOUNDATION

Carlisle United came into being when members of Shaddongate United voted to change its name on 17 May 1904. The new club was admitted to the Second Division of the Lancashire Combination in 1905–06, winning promotion the following season. Devonshire Park was officially opened on 2 September 1905, when St Helens Town were the visitors. Despite defeat in a disappointing 3–2 start, a respectable mid-table position was achieved.

Brunton Park, Warwick Road, Carlisle, Cumbria CA1 1LL.

Telephone: (01228) 526 237.

Ticket Office: (0330) 094 5930 (option 1).

Website: www.carlisleunited.co.uk

Email: enquiries@carlisleunited.co.uk

Ground Capacity: 17,030.

Record Attendance: 27,500 v Birmingham C, FA Cup 3rd rd, 5 January 1957 and v Middlesbrough, FA Cup 5th rd, 7 February 1970.

Pitch Measurements: 102m × 68m (111.5yd × 74.5yd).

Chairman: Andrew Jenkins.

Chief Executive: Nigel Clibbens.

Head Coach: Chris Beech.

Assistant Head Coach: Gavin Skelton.

Colours: Blue shirts with dark blue sleeves and red trim, blue shorts with dark blue trim, blue socks with dark blue and red trim.

Year Formed: 1904. ***Turned Professional:*** 1921.

Previous Name: 1904, Shaddongate United; 1904, Carlisle United.

Club Nicknames: 'The Cumbrians', 'The Blues'.

Grounds: 1904, Milholme Bank; 1905, Devonshire Park; 1909, Brunton Park.

First Football League Game: 25 August 1928, Division 3 (N), v Accrington S (a) W 3–2 – Prout; Coulthard, Cook; Harrison, Ross, Pigg; Agar (1), Hutchison, McConnell (1), Ward (1), Watson.

Record League Victory: 8–0 v Hartlepool U, Division 3 (N), 1 September 1928 – Prout; Smiles, Cook; Robinson (1) Ross, Pigg; Agar (1), Hutchison (1), McConnell (4), Ward (1), Watson. 8–0 v Scunthorpe U, Division 3 (N), 25 December 1952 – MacLaren; Hill, Scott; Stokoe, Twentyman, Waters; Harrison (1), Whitehouse (5), Ashman (2), Duffett, Bond.

Record Cup Victory: 6–0 v Shepshed Dynamo, FA Cup 1st rd, 16 November 1996 – Caig; Hopper, Archdeacon (pen), Walling, Robinson, Pounewatchy, Peacock (1), Conway (1) (Jansen), Smart (McAlindon (1)), Hayward, Aspinall (Thorpe), (2 og). 6–0 v Tipton T, FA Cup 1st rd, 6 November 2010 – Collin; Simek, Murphy, Chester, Cruise, Robson (McKenna), Berrett, Taiwo (Hurst), Marshall, Zoko (Curran) (2), Madine (4).

HONOURS

League Champions: Division 3 – 1964–65; FL 2 – 2005–06; Third Division – 1994–95.
Runners-up: Division 3 – 1981–82; Division 4 – 1963–64; Conference – (3rd) 2004–05 *(promoted via play-offs)*.

FA Cup: 6th rd – 1975.

League Cup: semi-final – 1970.

League Trophy Winners: 1997, 2011.
Runners-up: 1995, 2003, 2006, 2010.

FOOTBALL YEARBOOK FACT FILE

In November 1955 Carlisle United featured in a historic FA Cup tie when they met Darlington in a first round replay at Brunton Park in the first competitive floodlit fixture between two Football League teams. The teams drew 0-0 after extra time and went on to a second replay at Newcastle United, again played under lights. Darlington won 3-1 in front of a crowd of 34,230.

Record Defeat: 1–11 v Hull C, Division 3 (N), 14 January 1939.

Most League Points (2 for a win): 62, Division 3 (N), 1950–51.

Most League Points (3 for a win): 91, Division 3, 1994–95.

Most League Goals: 113, Division 4, 1963–64.

Highest League Scorer in Season: Jimmy McConnell, 42, Division 3 (N), 1928–29.

Most League Goals in Total Aggregate: Jimmy McConnell, 124, 1928–32.

Most League Goals in One Match: 5, Hugh Mills v Halifax T, Division 3 (N), 11 September 1937; 5, Jim Whitehouse v Scunthorpe U, Division 3 (N), 25 December 1952.

Most Capped Player: Reggie Lambe, 6 (41), Bermuda; Hallam Hope, 6, Barbados.

Most League Appearances: Allan Ross, 466, 1963–79.

Youngest League Player: John Slaven, 16 years 162 days v Scunthorpe U, 16 March 2002.

Record Transfer Fee Received: £1,000,000 from Crystal Palace for Matt Jansen, February 1998.

Record Transfer Fee Paid: £140,000 to Blackburn R for Joe Garner, August 2007.

Football League Record: 1928 Elected to Division 3 (N); 1958–62 Division 4; 1962–63 Division 3; 1963–64 Division 4; 1964–65 Division 3; 1965–74 Division 2; 1974–75 Division 1; 1975–77 Division 2; 1977–82 Division 3; 1982–86 Division 2; 1986–87 Division 3; 1987–92 Division 4; 1992–95 Division 3; 1995–96 Division 2; 1996–97 Division 3; 1997–98 Division 2; 1998–2004 Division 3; 2004–05 Conference; 2005–06 FL 2; 2006–14 FL 1; 2014– FL 2.

LATEST SEQUENCES

Longest Sequence of League Wins: 7, 18.2.2006 – 8.4.2006.

Longest Sequence of League Defeats: 12, 27.9.2003 – 13.12.2003.

Longest Sequence of League Draws: 6, 11.2.1978 – 11.3.1978.

Longest Sequence of Unbeaten League Matches: 19, 1.10.1994 – 11.2.1995.

Longest Sequence Without a League Win: 15, 12.4.2014 – 20.9.2014.

Successive Scoring Runs: 26 from 23.8.1947.

Successive Non-scoring Runs: 7 from 25.2.2017.

MANAGERS

Harry Kirkbride 1904–05 (*Secretary-Manager*)
McCumiskey 1905–06 (*Secretary-Manager*)
Jack Houston 1906–08 (*Secretary-Manager*)
Bert Stansfield 1908–10
Jack Houston 1910–12
Davie Graham 1912–13
George Bristow 1913–30
Billy Hampson 1930–33
Bill Clarke 1933–35
Robert Kelly 1935–36
Fred Westgarth 1936–38
David Taylor 1938–40
Howard Harkness 1940–45
Bill Clark 1945–46 (*Secretary-Manager*)
Ivor Broadis 1946–49
Bill Shankly 1949–51
Fred Emery 1951–58
Andy Beattie 1958–60
Ivor Powell 1960–63
Alan Ashman 1963–67
Tim Ward 1967–68
Bob Stokoe 1968–70
Ian MacFarlane 1970–72
Alan Ashman 1972–75
Dick Young 1975–76
Bobby Moncur 1976–80
Martin Harvey 1980
Bob Stokoe 1980–85
Bryan 'Pop' Robson 1985
Bob Stokoe 1985–86
Harry Gregg 1986–87
Cliff Middlemass 1987–91
Aidan McCaffery 1991–92
David McCreery 1992–93
Mick Wadsworth (*Director of Coaching*) 1993–96
Mervyn Day 1996–97
David Wilkes and John Halpin (*Directors of Coaching*), and **Michael Knighton** 1997–99
Nigel Pearson 1998–99
Keith Mincher 1999
Martin Wilkinson 1999–2000
Ian Atkins 2000–01
Roddy Collins 2001–02; 2002–03
Paul Simpson 2003–06
Neil McDonald 2006–07
John Ward 2007–08
Greg Abbott 2008–13
Graham Kavanagh 2013–14
Keith Curle 2014–18
John Sheridan 2018–19
Steven Pressley 2019
Chris Beech November 2019–

TEN YEAR LEAGUE RECORD

		P	W	D	L	F	A	Pts	Pos
2010-11	FL 1	46	16	11	19	60	62	59	12
2011-12	FL 1	46	18	15	13	65	66	69	8
2012-13	FL 1	46	14	13	19	56	77	55	17
2013-14	FL 1	46	11	12	23	43	76	45	22
2014-15	FL 2	46	14	8	24	56	74	50	20
2015-16	FL 2	46	17	16	13	67	62	67	10
2016-17	FL 2	46	18	17	11	69	68	71	6
2017-18	FL 2	46	17	16	13	62	54	67	10
2018-19	FL 2	46	20	8	18	67	62	68	11
2019-20	FL 2	37	10	12	15	39	56	42	18§

§Decided on points-per-game (1.14)

DID YOU KNOW ?

Carlisle United set a new club record when they were undefeated in the opening 10 games of the 1989–90 season. The run eventually came to an end when they lost at home to Scunthorpe United in October. The Cumbrians kept pace with the leading clubs for the remainder of the season only to miss out on a play-off place on goal difference.

CARLISLE UNITED – SKY BET LEAGUE TWO 2019–20 LEAGUE RECORD

Match No.	Date	Venue	Opponents	Result	H/T Score	Lg Pos.	Goalscorers	Attendance
1	Aug 3	H	Crawley T	W 2-1	2-1	5	McKirdy [6], Scougall [32]	4833
2	10	A	Swindon T	L 2-3	0-0	10	Olomola [52], Sagaf [90]	7024
3	17	H	Mansfield T	L 0-2	0-2	18		4576
4	20	A	Cheltenham T	L 0-2	0-2	20		2634
5	24	H	Salford C	D 2-2	2-2	21	Olomola [7], Scougall [43]	4806
6	31	A	Scunthorpe U	W 1-0	0-0	18	Loft [60]	3359
7	Sept 7	H	Exeter C	L 1-3	0-1	19	Olomola [61]	4167
8	14	A	Stevenage	W 3-2	1-1	15	McKirdy 2 [38, 83], Thomas [52]	2616
9	17	H	Forest Green R	D 0-0	0-0	17		3219
10	21	A	Bradford C	L 1-3	1-2	18	Olomola [14]	14,217
11	28	H	Oldham Ath	W 1-0	1-0	16	Olomola [3]	4321
12	Oct 5	A	Newport Co	L 0-1	0-0	18		3681
13	12	H	Crewe Alex	L 2-4	0-2	20	Hope [59], Elliot [84]	4521
14	19	A	Plymouth Arg	L 0-2	0-1	20		8446
15	22	H	Northampton T	L 0-2	0-0	21		3324
16	26	A	Leyton Orient	D 1-1	0-1	20	Iredale [48]	5765
17	Nov 2	H	Macclesfield T	W 2-1	1-1	19	McKirdy [45], Loft [82]	3880
18	16	A	Port Vale	L 1-2	1-0	20	Loft [1]	4783
19	23	H	Cambridge U	D 0-0	0-0	21		4041
20	Dec 7	A	Morecambe	D 1-1	0-0	22	Hope [47]	3126
21	14	H	Grimsby T	D 0-0	0-0	21		3653
22	21	A	Colchester U	L 0-3	0-2	22		3164
23	26	H	Bradford C	D 0-0	0-0	22		6039
24	29	A	Walsall	W 2-1	0-0	20	Thomas [52], McKirdy [90]	4794
25	Jan 1	A	Crewe Alex	L 1-4	0-4	22	Iredale [56]	4316
26	11	H	Plymouth Arg	L 0-3	0-1	22		4212
27	18	A	Oldham Ath	D 1-1	1-1	22	Webster [25]	3977
28	25	H	Walsall	W 2-1	2-0	22	Anderton [21], Loft [42]	4097
29	28	A	Forest Green R	W 4-1	2-0	20	Thomas 3 (1 pen) [23, 26, 47 (p)], Kayode [49]	1514
30	Feb 1	A	Mansfield T	D 2-2	0-0	21	Watt [81], Kayode [90]	4272
31	8	H	Swindon T	D 1-1	0-1	21	Hayden [62]	4620
32	11	H	Cheltenham T	L 0-1	0-1	21		3088
33	15	A	Crawley T	D 0-0	0-0	22		2114
34	22	H	Morecambe	D 2-2	1-2	21	Patrick [45], Hayden [65]	4679
35	29	A	Cambridge U	W 2-1	1-0	20	Alessandra [27], Anderton [73]	4122
36	Mar 7	H	Colchester U	L 0-3	0-2	20		3769
37	10	H	Newport Co	W 2-0	2-0	18	Patrick [5], Kayode (pen) [33]	2822
38	14	A	Grimsby T	Cancelled				
39	17	A	Northampton T	Cancelled				
40	21	H	Leyton Orient	Cancelled				
41	28	A	Macclesfield T	Cancelled				
42	Apr 4	H	Port Vale	Cancelled				
43	10	A	Salford C	Cancelled				
44	13	H	Scunthorpe U	Cancelled				
45	18	A	Exeter C	Cancelled				
46	25	H	Stevenage	Cancelled				

Final League Position: 18 (on points-per-game basis)

GOALSCORERS

League (39): McKirdy 5, Olomola 5, Thomas 5 (1 pen), Loft 4, Kayode 3 (1 pen), Anderton 2, Hayden 2, Hope 2, Iredale 2, Patrick 2, Scougall 2, Alessandra 1, Elliot 1, Sagaf 1, Watt 1, Webster 1.
FA Cup (12): McKirdy 5, Thomas 3, Bridge 1, Hayden 1, Jones, M 1, Olomola 1.
Carabao Cup (4): Bridge 2 (2 pens), McKirdy 1, Thomas 1.
Leasing.com Trophy (5): Loft 2, Branthwaite 1, Carroll 1, Hope 1.

Collin A 37	Elliot C 13 + 3	Mellish J 13 + 2	Knight-Percival N 14 + 1	Webster B 32	Thomas N 31 + 2	Scougall S 14 + 6	Jones M 37	Bridge J 20 + 8	Olomola O 14 + 13	McKirdy H 21 + 7	Loft R 9 + 17	Carroll C 6 + 3	Iredale J 18 + 4	Sagaf M 11 + 6	Sorensen E 1 + 7	Hope H 13 + 10	Jones G 30	Branthwaite J 9	Hayden A 18	Birch C — + 1	Charters T — + 7	Watt E 12	Hunt M 3 + 1	Kayode J 3 + 2	Anderton N 10	Alessandra L 10	Guy C 2 + 1	Patrick O 6 + 1	*Match No.*
1	2	3	4	5	6^{2}	7	8	9	10^{1}	11^{3}	12	13	14																1
1	2	5	4	3	9	6^{1}	7	8	10^{3}	11^{2}	13	12■		14															2
1	2		4	3	9^{2}	8^{1}	7	6	13	11^{3}	10		5		12	14													3
1	2		4	3	9	8	7	6^{1}	12	11^{3}	10^{2}		5	14		13													4
1	2	14	4	3	9	8	7	6	10^{1}		13		5^{2}		12	11^{3}													5
1	2		4	3	9		8	6		11^{2}	12	7^{3}	5	13	10^{1}	14													6
1	2^{1}		4	3	9		8^{2}	6	10	12	13	7^{3}	5	11	14														7
1	2^{2}		4	3	9^{3}		7	6	10^{1}	11	14		5	12		13	8												8
1	13		4	3	9^{1}		7	6	10	11^{2}	14		5	2^{3}		12	8												9
1	12		5	4	10		8	7■	11	9^{2}			6^{3}	2^{1}	14	13	3												10
1	2		4	3	9^{2}		7		10	11^{1}	13		5	6		12	8												11
1	2		4	3			7	9	10^{1}	12	13		5	6		11^{2}	8												12
1	2	12	5^{1}	4		13	8	7^{2}	11	14			6	9^{3}		10	3												13
1		4		3	14	8^{1}	7	6^{2}	11^{3}				9	13	12	10	5	2											14
1	5	4		3	10^{2}	8	7^{3}	6	14	13	12					11^{1}	9	2											15
1		4	14	3	10^{1}		7	6	12	11			9	8^{2}		13	5	2^{3}											16
1		4			9		8	7^{3}	10^{1}	11^{2}	13	14	5	6		12	2	3											17
1				4	6		8	12	10^{1}	9	11	7^{2}	5		13		2	3											18
1		4			9	12	8		10^{2}	6^{1}	11	7	5			13	2	3											19
1		8		2	11	7^{2}	6		12		10^{1}				13	9	5	3	4										20
1	12				6	8^{3}	7		14	9^{2}	10	2^{1}		13		11	5	4	3										21
1	8^{2}		4	3	9^{1}	7	6	13	12		11^{3}					10	5		2	14									22
1				4	10^{3}	9	7		14	12	13	6^{1}		8^{2}		11	5	3	2										23
1				3	11^{2}	6^{1}	7		13	9	12		5	8		10	2		4										24
1				4	9		7	12	13	6	11^{1}		5	8^{3}		10^{2}	2		3		14								25
1		3		4	9^{1}	12	7	6^{2}		11	13					10	5		2■			8							26
1				3	9^{2}	7	6			11^{3}	14					10	5		2		13	8^{1}	4	12					27
1				4	9	8^{2}	6	12			10^{1}		13				2		3		14	7			5	11^{3}			28
1				3	11	13	7	6			14						2		5^{2}			8	12	10^{1}	4	9^{3}			29
1				3	9^{2}	14	7	6^{1}		12							2		4			8		11	5	10^{3}	13		30
1				4	9		6	13		11^{3}							2		3		14	7			5	10^{1}	8^{2}	12	31
1				3	11		6^{1}		14		13		12				2		4			7			5^{2}	10	8^{3}	9	32
1		6		3	9	13	7^{1}										2		4		12	8			5	11^{2}		10	33
1		8		3	9^{1}		6^{2}	13	14	12							2		4			7			5	10		11^{3}	34
1		6		3			7	14	13	11^{1}							2		4		12	8^{3}			5	10^{2}		9	35
1		8					6	13		9							2		3			7^{2}	4	12	5	10		11^{1}	36
1					12		8	6^{2}					14				2		3		13	7	4	10^{1}	5	9		11^{3}	37
																													38
																													39
																													40
																													41
																													42
																													43
																													44
																													45
																													46

FA Cup

First Round	Dulwich	(a)	4-1
Second Round	Forest Green R	(a)	2-2
Replay	Forest Green R	(h)	1-0
Third Round	Cardiff C	(a)	2-2
Replay	Cardiff C	(h)	3-4

Carabao Cup

First Round	Barnsley	(a)	3-0
Second Round	Rochdale	(a)	1-2

Leasing.com Trophy

Group G (N)	Wolverhampton W U21	(h)	2-4
Group G (N)	Blackpool	(h)	2-1
Group G (N)	Morecambe	(a)	1-3

CHARLTON ATHLETIC

FOUNDATION

The club was formed on 9 June 1905, by a group of 14- and 15-year-old youths living in streets by the Thames in the area which now borders the Thames Barrier. The club's progress through local leagues was so rapid that after the First World War they joined the Kent League where they spent a season before turning professional and joining the Southern League in 1920. A year later they were elected to the Football League's Division 3 (South).

The Valley, Floyd Road, Charlton, London SE7 8BL.

Telephone: (020) 8333 4000.

Ticket Office: (03330) 144 444.

Website: www.cafc.co.uk

Email: info@cafc.co.uk

Ground Capacity: 27,111.

Record Attendance: 75,031 v Aston Villa, FA Cup 5th rd, 12 February 1938 (at The Valley).

Pitch Measurements: 102.5m × 67.5m (112yd × 74yd).

Owner: East Street Investments.

Chief Operating Officer: Tony Keohane.

Manager: Lee Bowyer.

Assistant Manager: Johnnie Jackson.

Colours: Red shirts with thin white stripes, white shorts with red trim, red socks with white trim.

Year Formed: 1905.

Turned Professional: 1920.

Club Nickname: 'The Addicks'.

Grounds: 1906, Siemen's Meadow; 1907, Woolwich Common; 1909, Pound Park; 1913, Horn Lane; 1920, The Valley; 1923, Catford (The Mount); 1924, The Valley; 1985, Selhurst Park; 1991, Upton Park; 1992, The Valley.

First Football League Game: 27 August 1921, Division 3 (S), v Exeter C (h) W 1–0 – Hughes; Johnny Mitchell, Goodman; Dowling (1), Hampson, Dunn; Castle, Bailey, Halse, Green, Wilson.

Record League Victory: 8–1 v Middlesbrough, Division 1, 12 September 1953 – Bartram; Campbell, Ellis; Fenton, Ufton, Hammond; Hurst (2), O'Linn (2), Leary (1), Firmani (3), Kiernan.

Record Cup Victory: 8–0 v Stevenage, FL Trophy, 9 October 2018 – Phillips; Marshall, Dijksteel, Sarr, Stevenson (3) (Reeves), Lapslie (1), Maloney, Ward (Morgan), Pratley (1), Vetokele (2), Ajose (1).

Record Defeat: 1–11 v Aston Villa, Division 2, 14 November 1959.

Most League Points (2 for a win): 61, Division 3 (S), 1934–35.

Most League Points (3 for a win): 101, FL 1, 2011–12.

HONOURS

League Champions: First Division – 1999–2000; FL 1 – 2011–12; Division 3S – 1928–29, 1934–35.
Runners-up: Division 1 – 1936–37; Division 2 – 1935–36, 1985–86.

FA Cup Winners: 1947.
Runners-up: 1946.

League Cup: quarter-final – 2007.

Full Members' Cup:
Runners-up 1987.

FOOTBALL YEARBOOK FACT FILE

Charlton Athletic struggled to raise a team during the 1940–41 season with few of their signed players available for matches. When they played West Ham United at The Valley on 30 November they had just 10 men on the pitch with an outfield player in goal. The Addicks, not surprisingly, lost 2-1.

Most League Goals: 107, Division 2, 1957–58.

Highest League Scorer in Season: Ralph Allen, 32, Division 3 (S), 1934–35.

Most League Goals in Total Aggregate: Stuart Leary, 153, 1953–62.

Most League Goals in One Match: 5, Wilson Lennox v Exeter C, Division 3 (S), 2 February 1929; 5, Eddie Firmani v Aston Villa, Division 1, 5 February 1955; 5, John Summers v Huddersfield T, Division 2, 21 December 1957; 5, John Summers v Portsmouth, Division 2, 1 October 1960.

Most Capped Player: Jonatan Johansson, 42 (106), Finland.

Most League Appearances: Sam Bartram, 579, 1934–56.

Youngest League Player: Jonjo Shelvey, 16 years 59 days v Burnley, 26 April 2008.

Record Transfer Fee Received: £16,500,000 from Tottenham H for Darren Bent, June 2007.

Record Transfer Fee Paid: £4,750,000 to Wimbledon for Jason Euell, January 2001.

Football League Record: 1921 Elected to Division 3 (S); 1929–33 Division 2; 1933–35 Division 3 (S); 1935–36 Division 2; 1936–57 Division 1; 1957–72 Division 2; 1972–75 Division 3; 1975–80 Division 2; 1980–81 Division 3; 1981–86 Division 2; 1986–90 Division 1; 1990–92 Division 2; 1992–98 Division 1; 1998–99 Premier League; 1999–2000 Division 1; 2000–07 Premier League; 2007–09 FL C; 2009–12 FL 1; 2012–16 FL C; 2016–19 FL 1; 2019–20 FL C; 2020– FL 1.

MANAGERS

Walter Rayner 1920–25
Alex Macfarlane 1925–27
Albert Lindon 1928
Alex Macfarlane 1928–32
Albert Lindon 1932–33
Jimmy Seed 1933–56
Jimmy Trotter 1956–61
Frank Hill 1961–65
Bob Stokoe 1965–67
Eddie Firmani 1967–70
Theo Foley 1970–74
Andy Nelson 1974–79
Mike Bailey 1979–81
Alan Mullery 1981–82
Ken Craggs 1982
Lennie Lawrence 1982–91
Steve Gritt and Alan Curbishley 1991–95
Alan Curbishley 1995–2006
Iain Dowie 2006
Les Reed 2006
Alan Pardew 2006–08
Phil Parkinson 2008–11
Chris Powell 2011–14
José Riga 2014
Bob Peeters 2014–15
Guy Luzon 2015
Karel Fraeye 2015–16
José Riga 2016
Russell Slade 2016
Karl Robinson 2016–18
Lee Bowyer September 2018–

LATEST SEQUENCES

Longest Sequence of League Wins: 12, 26.12.1999 – 7.3.2000.

Longest Sequence of League Defeats: 10, 11.4.1990 – 15.9.1990.

Longest Sequence of League Draws: 6, 13.12.1992 – 16.1.1993.

Longest Sequence of Unbeaten League Matches: 15, 4.10.1980 – 20.12.1980.

Longest Sequence Without a League Win: 18, 18.10.2008 – 17.1.2009.

Successive Scoring Runs: 25 from 26.12.1935.

Successive Non-scoring Runs: 5 from 17.10.2015.

TEN YEAR LEAGUE RECORD

		P	W	D	L	F	A	Pts	Pos
2010-11	FL 1	46	15	14	17	62	66	59	13
2011-12	FL 1	46	30	11	5	82	36	101	1
2012-13	FL C	46	17	14	15	65	59	65	9
2013-14	FL C	46	13	12	21	41	61	51	18
2014-15	FL C	46	14	18	14	54	60	60	12
2015-16	FL C	46	9	13	24	40	80	40	22
2016-17	FL 1	46	14	18	14	60	53	60	13
2017-18	FL 1	46	20	11	15	58	51	71	6
2018-19	FL 1	46	26	10	10	73	40	88	3
2019-20	FL C	46	12	12	22	50	65	48	22

DID YOU KNOW ?

The first player to score a Football League hat-trick for Charlton Athletic was Harold Miller who netted after 13, 65 and 79 minutes of the 6-0 win over Newport County at The Valley on 14 April 1923. At the time this was also the Addicks' record League victory.

CHARLTON ATHLETIC – SKY BET CHAMPIONSHIP 2019–20 LEAGUE RECORD

Match No.	Date	Venue	Opponents	Result		H/T Score	Lg Pos.	Goalscorers	Attendance
1	Aug 3	A	Blackburn R	W	2-1	1-0	3	Purrington 43, Taylor 77	14,184
2	10	H	Stoke C	W	3-1	1-1	2	Taylor 25, Aneke 75, Gallagher 83	17,848
3	17	A	Barnsley	D	2-2	1-1	2	Gallagher 40, Taylor (pen) 89	13,006
4	21	H	Nottingham F	D	1-1	1-0	5	Taylor 18	17,204
5	24	H	Brentford	W	1-0	1-0	2	Gallagher 41	16,771
6	31	A	Reading	W	2-0	0-0	2	Leko 51, Taylor (pen) 80	16,906
7	Sept 14	H	Birmingham C	L	0-1	0-0	2		18,752
8	21	A	Wigan Ath	L	0-2	0-1	7		9567
9	28	H	Leeds U	W	1-0	1-0	6	Bonne 32	21,808
10	Oct 2	H	Swansea C	L	1-2	1-1	8	Leko 2	15,741
11	5	A	Fulham	D	2-2	1-0	10	Gallagher 41, Bonne 57	18,654
12	19	H	Derby Co	W	3-0	1-0	7	Bonne 6, Sarr 48, Gallagher 67	19,408
13	23	A	Bristol C	L	1-2	0-0	10	Bonne 65	20,916
14	26	A	WBA	D	2-2	0-1	8	Bonne 60, Cullen (pen) 90	25,356
15	Nov 3	H	Preston NE	L	0-1	0-0	10		16,027
16	9	A	Millwall	L	1-2	0-1	11	Leko 51	17,109
17	23	H	Cardiff C	D	2-2	2-0	13	Gallagher 13, Leko 42	16,011
18	26	A	Luton T	L	1-2	1-1	14	Leko 7	10,004
19	30	H	Sheffield W	L	1-3	1-1	17	Bonne 26	18,338
20	Dec 7	A	Middlesbrough	L	0-1	0-1	17		18,681
21	10	H	Huddersfield T	L	0-1	0-0	17		13,488
22	13	H	Hull C	D	2-2	1-0	17	Pratley 34, Sarr 50	14,447
23	21	A	QPR	D	2-2	0-1	18	Taylor 56, Sarr 90	16,166
24	26	H	Bristol C	W	3-2	1-0	17	Bonne 2 40, 77, Doughty 82	18,058
25	30	A	Derby Co	L	1-2	0-1	19	Taylor (pen) 83	26,058
26	Jan 2	A	Swansea C	L	0-1	0-1	19		15,352
27	11	H	WBA	D	2-2	1-1	19	Davison 28, Lockyer 76	19,720
28	18	A	Preston NE	L	1-2	1-1	19	Green 5	12,358
29	22	H	Fulham	D	0-0	0-0	19		16,424
30	Feb 1	H	Barnsley	W	2-1	2-0	19	Taylor 9, Green 45	19,870
31	8	A	Stoke C	L	1-3	1-1	21	Purrington 45	23,508
32	11	A	Nottingham F	W	1-0	1-0	19	Taylor 24	28,029
33	15	H	Blackburn R	L	0-2	0-2	19		25,363
34	22	H	Luton T	W	3-1	1-1	18	Taylor 2 (1 pen) 34, 61 (p), Lapslie 87	18,969
35	26	A	Sheffield W	L	0-1	0-0	18		21,370
36	29	A	Huddersfield T	L	0-4	0-1	20		21,539
37	Mar 7	H	Middlesbrough	L	0-1	0-1	22		18,080
38	June 20	A	Hull C	W	1-0	1-0	19	Pearce 18	0
39	27	H	QPR	W	1-0	1-0	18	Pratley 12	0
40	30	A	Cardiff C	D	0-0	0-0	18		0
41	July 3	H	Millwall	L	0-1	0-0	18		0
42	7	A	Brentford	L	1-2	1-0	20	Bonne 8	0
43	11	H	Reading	L	0-1	0-1	20		0
44	15	A	Birmingham C	D	1-1	0-0	21	Bonne 58	0
45	18	H	Wigan Ath	D	2-2	1-2	21	Doughty 11, Bonne 90	0
46	22	A	Leeds U	L	0-4	0-2	23		0

Final League Position: 22

GOALSCORERS

League (50): Bonne 11, Taylor 11 (4 pens), Gallagher 6, Leko 5, Sarr 3, Doughty 2, Green 2, Pratley 2, Purrington 2, Aneke 1, Cullen 1 (1 pen), Davison 1, Lapslie 1, Lockyer 1, Pearce 1.
FA Cup (0).
Carabao Cup (0).

Phillips D 46	Lockyer T 43	Pearce J 35 + 4	Sarr N 26 + 3	Dijksteel A 1	Lapslie G 4 + 6	Forster-Caskey J 7 + 4	Pratley D 30 + 6	Purrington B 24 + 7	Williams J 15 + 11	Taylor L 17 + 5	Gallagher C 25 + 1	Morgan A 11 + 10	Oshilaja A 19 + 6	Solly C 12 + 2	Leko J 19 + 2	Cullen J 34	Aneke C 2 + 18	Bonne M 26 + 7	Field S 10 + 7	Oztumer E 11 + 3	Hemed T 9 + 9	Kayal B 2 + 4	Matthews A 28 + 1	Davison J 5 + 4	Doughty A 20 + 9	Vennings J — + 3	Ledley J 1	Dempsey B 3 + 1	Green A 8 + 5	Davis D 5	McGeady A 8 + 2	Smith M — + 2	*Match No.*
1	2	3	4^1	5	6^3	7	8	9	10^2	11	12	13	14																				1
1	3	4			13		8	5	9^2	11	10			2	6^1	7	12																2
1	3	4					6^3	5	9	10	8		12	2^1	11^2	7	13	14															3
1	3		4				13	5	12	10	8		2		11^3	7	14		6^2	9^1													4
1	3	4			12		6	5	9^3	10	8		2^1		11^2	7			14		13												5
1	3	4					13	5	9^1	10	8			2	11^3	7	12		6^2		14												6
1	3	4						5	12		8			2	11^3	7	13		6^2	9^1	10	14											7
1	3		4				6^2	5	9		8		2		11	7	13	12			10^1												8
1	3	14	4				6	5	9^1		10^3			2	8	7	12	11^2	13														9
1	3	4				14		5^3	13		10				8^1	7	12	11	6	9^2			2										10
1	2	3	4			9^2	7		10^1		8			5	12	6		11^3	13				14										11
1	3		5			6	4		10^1		9^3			2	7	8		11^2	12		13	14											12
1	3	4				5^2	12				9		2	13	11	7	14	10	6^1			8^3											13
1	2	3^3	4				7^2	9			8			5		6	12	11		10^1		13		14									14
1	3	4	5^1				6^2	10			9			2	12	7	13	11		14		8^3											15
1	2	3	4		13		7^1	9			8				10^2	6		11				12	5										16
1	3	4						5			8	12	6		10^2	7^1		11		9			2		13								17
1	2	3	4^1				7	9^2			8	6		5	10			11						13	12								18
1	3		4				7					8^1	6		10			11		9^2			2	13	5	12							19
1		4					7	5^2		13	6	12	3		9			10					2		11		8^1						20
1	2	3	4				7	9		12	6			5	10^1			11							8^2	13							21
1	2	3	4				5	9		13	8	7^1	12		10			11^2					6										22
1	3	13	4				6	5^2		10	9	12	14		7^1			11					2		8^3								23
1	2	13	4				3	12		10	8^1	6^2	7	14				11					5		9^3								24
1	3		5^2				4	6		12	7	8	9^3	2				11^1						13	10			14					25
1	3	4	14				6	5^3		10^1	9	8^2											2	11	12	13		7					26
1	2		4			13	6		12		9		3^2								14		5	11^3	8			7^1	10				27
1	3		5				8		9^2			13	4^1							12	14		2	10	6			7	11^3				28
1	3	4					6	5	12	13		10^1				7				9^3	11^2		2		8				14				29
1	3	4	5			12	9	14	8^1	11^2						7					13		2		6^3				10				30
1	3	4					7	5^1	9^2	10						6				13			2		12				11	8			31
1	3	4	5					13		10						9				8^1	11^3		2		6^2					7	12	14	32
1	3	4^1	5							10						8		14			11^2		2		6				13	7	9^3	12	33
1	3	14	4		12					11			6^1			7		13		9^2			2		5				10^3	8			34
1	3	4			12					11			5			7		10^2		8^1			2		6				13	9			35
1		4			8^3				12	11			3			6		13		7^1	14		2		5				10		9^2		36
1		4			9^1		6	5^3	10^2	11			3			8		12			14		2		13				7				37
1	3	4					7	13	15			9^1	5^2			8	14	10^4	16		11^3		2		12						6^5		38
1	4	3					7	14				9^5	5^3			8	13	10^4	16		11^2		2		12				15		6^1		39
1	3	2	4		5^3	6^4	12	16				15	14			7	11^2	13	8^1						9				10^5				40
1	3	4	16				7^5		14			9^1	5^3			8	13	10^2	12		11		2		15						6^4		41
1	2	3	4		13	8^4	12		10^1			15	14			6	16	11^5	7^2				5		9^3								42
1	3	4				15	8^4		12			9^2	5^1			7	11	10			14		2		13						6^3		43
1	3	4	16				15	14	9^3			13				7	12	10	8^4		11^1		2		5^2						6^5		44
1	2	3^4	4			9^1			13			12				6	14	11	7^2				5	10^3	8						15		45
1	3	4^3	5						14			12				7	13	11^4	9				2	10^2	6				15		8^1		46

FA Cup
Third Round WBA (h) 0-1

Carabao Cup
First Round Forest Green R (h) 0-0
(Forest Green R won 5-3 on penalties)

CHELSEA

FOUNDATION

Chelsea may never have existed but for the fact that Fulham rejected an offer to rent the Stamford Bridge ground from Mr H. A. Mears who had owned it since 1904. Fortunately he was determined to develop it as a football stadium rather than sell it to the Great Western Railway and got together with Frederick Parker, who persuaded Mears of the financial advantages of developing a major sporting venue. Chelsea FC was formed in 1905 and applications made to join both the Southern League and Football League. The latter competition was decided upon because of its comparatively meagre representation in the south of England.

Stamford Bridge, Fulham Road, London SW6 1HS.

Telephone: (0371) 811 1955.

Ticket Office: (0371) 811 1905.

Website: www.chelseafc.com

Email: enquiries@chelseafc.com

Ground Capacity: 40,834.

Record Attendance: 82,905 v Arsenal, Division 1, 12 October 1935.

Pitch Measurements: 103m × 67.5m (112.5yd × 74yd).

Chairman: Bruce Buck.

Chief Executive: Guy Laurence.

Manager: Frank Lampard.

Assistant Manager: Jody Morris.

Colours: Blue shirts with black trim, blue shorts, white socks.

Year Formed: 1905. ***Turned Professional:*** 1905.

Club Nickname: 'The Blues'.

Ground: 1905, Stamford Bridge.

First Football League Game: 2 September 1905, Division 2, v Stockport Co (a) L 0–1 – Foulke; Mackie, McEwan; Key, Harris, Miller; Moran, Jack Robertson, Copeland, Windridge, Kirwan.

Record League Victory: 8–0 v Wigan Ath, Premier League, 9 May 2010 – Cech; Ivanovic (Belletti), Ashley Cole (1), Ballack (Matic), Terry, Alex, Kalou (1) (Joe Cole), Lampard (pen), Anelka (2), Drogba (3, 1 pen), Malouda; 8–0 v Aston Villa, Premier League, 23 December 2012 – Cech; Azpilicueta, Ivanovic (1), Cahill, Cole, Luiz (1), Lampard (1) (Ramirez (2)), Moses, Mata (Piazon), Hazard (1), Torres (1) (Oscar (1)).

HONOURS

League Champions: Premier League – 2004–05, 2005–06, 2009–10, 2014–15, 2016–17; Division 1 – 1954–55; Division 2 – 1983–84, 1988–89.
Runners-up: Premier League – 2003–04, 2006–07, 2007–08, 2010–11; Division 2 – 1906–07, 1911–12, 1929–30, 1962–63, 1976–77.

FA Cup Winners: 1970, 1997, 2000, 2007, 2009, 2010, 2012, 2018.
Runners-up: 1915, 1967, 1994, 2002, 2017, 2020.

League Cup Winners: 1965, 1998, 2005, 2007, 2015.
Runners-up: 1972, 2008, 2019.

Full Members' Cup Winners: 1986, 1990.

European Competitions

Champions League: 1999–2000, 2003–04 *(sf)*, 2004–05 *(sf)*, 2005–06, 2006–07 *(sf)*, 2007–08 *(runners-up)*, 2008–09 *(sf)*, 2009–10, 2010–11 *(qf)*, 2011–12 *(winners)*, 2012–13, 2013–14 *(sf)*, 2014–15, 2015–16, 2017–18, 2019–20.
Fairs Cup: 1958–60, 1965–66, 1968–69.
UEFA Cup: 2000–01, 2001–02, 2002–03.
Europa League: 2012–13 *(winners)*, 2018–19 *(winners)*.
European Cup-Winners' Cup: 1970–71 *(winners)*, 1971–72, 1994–95 *(sf)*, 1997–98 *(winners)*, 1998–99 *(sf)*.
Super Cup: 1998 *(winners)*, 2012, 2013, 2019.
Club World Cup: 2012 *(runners-up)*.

FOOTBALL YEARBOOK FACT FILE

Chelsea were the last winners of the League South War Cup, defeating Millwall in the final at Wembley in April 1945 in front of 90,000 fans, the largest attendance at a wartime match in England. Those present included King George VI and Queen Elizabeth, Princesses Elizabeth and Margaret, and King Haakon of Norway.

Record Cup Victory: 13–0 v Jeunesse Hautcharage, ECWC, 1st rd 2nd leg, 29 September 1971 – Bonetti; Boyle, Harris (1), Hollins (1p), Webb (1), Hinton, Cooke, Baldwin (3), Osgood (5), Hudson (1), Houseman (1).

Record Defeat: 1–8 v Wolverhampton W, Division 1, 26 September 1953; 0–7 v Nottingham F, Division 1, 20 April 1991.

Most League Points (2 for a win): 57, Division 2, 1906–07.

Most League Points (3 for a win): 99, Division 2, 1988–89.

Most League Goals: 103, Premier League, 2009–10.

Highest League Scorer in Season: Jimmy Greaves, 41, 1960–61.

Most League Goals in Total Aggregate: Bobby Tambling, 164, 1958–70.

Most League Goals in One Match: 5, George Hilsdon v Glossop, Division 2, 1 September 1906; 5, Jimmy Greaves v Wolverhampton W, Division 1, 30 August 1958; 5, Jimmy Greaves v Preston NE, Division 1, 19 December 1959; 5, Jimmy Greaves v WBA, Division 1, 3 December 1960; 5, Bobby Tambling v Aston Villa, Division 1, 17 September 1966; 5, Gordon Durie v Walsall, Division 2, 4 February 1989.

Most Capped Player: Frank Lampard, 104 (106), England.

Most League Appearances: Ron Harris, 655, 1962–80.

Youngest League Player: Ian Hamilton, 16 years 138 days v Tottenham H, 18 March 1967.

Record Transfer Fee Received: £88,500,000 from Real Madrid for Eden Hazard, June 2019.

Record Transfer Fee Paid: £71,600,000 to Athletic Bilbao for Kepa Arrizabalaga, August 2018.

Football League Record: 1905 Elected to Division 2; 1907–10 Division 1; 1910–12 Division 2; 1912–24 Division 1; 1924–30 Division 2; 1930–62 Division 1; 1962–63 Division 2; 1963–75 Division 1; 1975–77 Division 2; 1977–79 Division 1; 1979–84 Division 2; 1984–88 Division 1; 1988–89 Division 2; 1989–92 Division 1; 1992– Premier League.

MANAGERS

John Tait Robertson 1905–07
David Calderhead 1907–33
Leslie Knighton 1933–39
Billy Birrell 1939–52
Ted Drake 1952–61
Tommy Docherty 1961–67
Dave Sexton 1967–74
Ron Suart 1974–75
Eddie McCreadie 1975–77
Ken Shellito 1977–78
Danny Blanchflower 1978–79
Geoff Hurst 1979–81
John Neal 1981–85 (*Director to 1986*)
John Hollins 1985–88
Bobby Campbell 1988–91
Ian Porterfield 1991–93
David Webb 1993
Glenn Hoddle 1993–96
Ruud Gullit 1996–98
Gianluca Vialli 1998–2000
Claudio Ranieri 2000–04
Jose Mourinho 2004–07
Avram Grant 2007–08
Luiz Felipe Scolari 2008–09
Guus Hiddink 2009
Carlo Ancelotti 2009–11
Andre Villas-Boas 2011–12
Roberto Di Matteo 2012
Rafael Benitez 2012–13
Jose Mourinho 2013–15
Guus Hiddink 2015–16
Antonio Conte 2016–18
Maurizio Sarri 2018–19
Frank Lampard July 2019–

LATEST SEQUENCES

Longest Sequence of League Wins: 13, 1.10.2016 – 31.12.2016.

Longest Sequence of League Defeats: 7, 1.11.1952 – 20.12.1952.

Longest Sequence of League Draws: 6, 20.8.1969 – 13.9.1969.

Longest Sequence of Unbeaten League Matches: 40, 23.10.2004 – 29.10.2005.

Longest Sequence Without a League Win: 21, 3.11.1987 – 2.4.1988.

Successive Scoring Runs: 27 from 29.10.1988.

Successive Non-scoring Runs: 9 from 14.3.1981.

TEN YEAR LEAGUE RECORD

		P	W	D	L	F	A	Pts	Pos
2010-11	PR Lge	38	21	8	9	69	33	71	2
2011-12	PR Lge	38	18	10	10	65	46	64	6
2012-13	PR Lge	38	22	9	7	75	39	75	3
2013-14	PR Lge	38	25	7	6	71	27	82	3
2014-15	PR Lge	38	26	9	3	73	32	87	1
2015-16	PR Lge	38	12	14	12	59	53	50	10
2016-17	PR Lge	38	30	3	5	85	33	93	1
2017-18	PR Lge	38	21	7	10	62	38	70	5
2018-19	PR Lge	38	21	9	8	63	39	72	3
2019-20	PR Lge	38	20	6	12	69	54	66	4

DID YOU KNOW?

Chelsea's Stamford Bridge ground hosted a professional baseball match in February 1914. An estimated crowd of 18,000, including King George V, turned out to witness the Chicago White Sox beat the New York Giants 5-4, the final match of a world tour carried out by the two teams.

CHELSEA – PREMIER LEAGUE 2019–20 LEAGUE RECORD

Match No.	*Date*	*Venue*	*Opponents*	*Result*		*H/T Score*	*Lg Pos.*	*Goalscorers*	*Attendance*
1	Aug 11	A	Manchester U	L	0-4	0-1	19		73,620
2	18	H	Leicester C	D	1-1	1-0	15	Mount [7]	40,629
3	24	A	Norwich C	W	3-2	2-2	12	Abraham 2 [3, 68], Mount [17]	27,032
4	31	H	Sheffield U	D	2-2	2-0	9	Abraham 2 [19, 43]	40,560
5	Sept 14	A	Wolverhampton W	W	5-2	3-0	6	Tomori [31], Abraham 3 [34, 41, 55], Mount [90]	31,534
6	22	H	Liverpool	L	1-2	0-2	11	Kante [71]	40,638
7	28	H	Brighton & HA	W	2-0	0-0	6	Jorginho (pen) [50], Willian [76]	40,683
8	Oct 6	A	Southampton	W	4-1	3-1	5	Abraham [17], Mount [24], Kante [40], Batshuayi [89]	31,473
9	19	H	Newcastle U	W	1-0	0-0	4	Alonso [73]	40,513
10	26	A	Burnley	W	4-2	2-0	4	Pulisic 3 [21, 45, 56], Willian [58]	20,975
11	Nov 2	A	Watford	W	2-1	1-0	3	Abraham [5], Pulisic [55]	21,011
12	9	H	Crystal Palace	W	2-0	0-0	3	Abraham [52], Pulisic [79]	40,525
13	23	A	Manchester C	L	1-2	1-2	4	Kante [21]	54,486
14	30	H	West Ham U	L	0-1	0-0	4		40,595
15	Dec 4	H	Aston Villa	W	2-1	1-1	4	Abraham [24], Mount [48]	40,628
16	7	A	Everton	L	1-3	0-1	4	Kovacic [52]	39,114
17	14	H	Bournemouth	L	0-1	0-0	4		40,243
18	22	A	Tottenham H	W	2-0	2-0	4	Willian 2 (1 pen) [12, 45 (p)]	61,104
19	26	H	Southampton	L	0-2	0-1	4		40,651
20	29	A	Arsenal	W	2-1	0-1	4	Jorginho [83], Abraham [87]	60,309
21	Jan 1	A	Brighton & HA	D	1-1	1-0	4	Azpilicueta [10]	30,559
22	11	H	Burnley	W	3-0	2-0	4	Jorginho (pen) [27], Abraham [38], Hudson-Odoi [49]	40,396
23	18	A	Newcastle U	L	0-1	0-0	4		52,217
24	21	H	Arsenal	D	2-2	1-0	4	Jorginho (pen) [28], Azpilicueta [84]	40,577
25	Feb 1	A	Leicester C	D	2-2	0-0	4	Rudiger 2 [46, 71]	32,186
26	17	H	Manchester U	L	0-2	0-1	4		40,504
27	22	H	Tottenham H	W	2-1	1-0	4	Giroud [15], Alonso [48]	40,608
28	29	A	Bournemouth	D	2-2	1-0	4	Alonso 2 [33, 85]	10,667
29	Mar 8	H	Everton	W	4-0	2-0	4	Mount [14], Pedro [21], Willian [51], Giroud [54]	40,694
30	June 21	A	Aston Villa	W	2-1	0-1	4	Pulisic [60], Giroud [62]	0
31	25	H	Manchester C	W	2-1	1-0	4	Pulisic [36], Willian (pen) [78]	0
32	July 1	A	West Ham U	L	2-3	1-1	4	Willian 2 (1 pen) [42 (p), 72]	0
33	4	H	Watford	W	3-0	2-0	4	Giroud [28], Willian (pen) [43], Barkley [90]	0
34	7	A	Crystal Palace	W	3-2	2-1	3	Giroud [6], Pulisic [27], Abraham [71]	0
35	11	A	Sheffield U	L	0-3	0-2	3		0
36	14	H	Norwich C	W	1-0	1-0	3	Giroud [45]	0
37	22	A	Liverpool	L	3-5	1-3	4	Giroud [45], Abraham [61], Pulisic [73]	0
38	26	H	Wolverhampton W	W	2-0	2-0	4	Mount [45], Giroud [45]	0

Final League Position: 4

GOALSCORERS

League (69): Abraham 15, Pulisic 9, Willian 9 (4 pens), Giroud 8, Mount 7, Alonso 4, Jorginho 4 (3 pens), Kante 3, Azpilicueta 2, Rudiger 2, Barkley 1, Batshuayi 1, Hudson-Odoi 1, Kovacic 1, Pedro 1, Tomori 1.
FA Cup (11): Barkley 3, Batshuayi 1, Giroud 1, Hudson-Odoi 1, Mount 1, Pulisic 1, Tomori 1, Willian 1, own goal 1.
Carabao Cup (8): Batshuayi 3, Barkley 1, Hudson-Odoi 1, James 1, Pedro 1 (1 pen), Zouma 1.
UEFA Champions League (12): Abraham 3, Azpilicueta 2, Jorginho 2 (2 pens), Batshuayi 1, James 1, Kovacic 1, Pulisic 1, Willian 1.
European Super Cup (2): Giroud 1, Jorginho 1 (1 pen).
Leasing.com Trophy (7): Anjorin 2, Brown 2, Lamptey 2, Russell 1.

Arrizabalaga K 33	Azpilicueta C 36	Christensen A 21	Zouma K 25 + 3	Emerson 13 + 2	Jorginho F 27 + 4	Kovacic M 23 + 8	Pedro R 8 + 3	Mount M 32 + 5	Barkley R 13 + 8	Abraham T 25 + 9	Pulisic C 19 + 6	Giroud O 12 + 6	Kante N 20 + 2	Willian 29 + 7	Alonso M 15 + 3	Tomori F 15	Batshuayi M 1 + 15	Gilmour B 2 + 4	Rudiger A 19 + 1	Hudson-Odoi C 7 + 15	James R 16 + 8	Lamptey T — + 1	Caballero W 5	Anjorin F — + 1	Broja A — + 1	Loftus-Cheek R 2 + 5	*Match No.*
1	2	3	4	5	6[3]	7	8	9	10[1]	11[2]	12	13	14														1
1	2	3	4	5	7[2]	14	8	9		12	10[3]	11[1]	6	13													2
1	2	3	4	5	7	6		11[3]	8	10[1]	9[2]	12		13	14												3
1	2		4	5	7	8[2]		11	6[1]	10[3]	9			12		3	13	14									4
1	5	3	12		6	7[2]		10	13	11[3]				9	8	4	14		2[1]								5
1	2	3[2]	13	5[1]	7	8		11		10[3]			6	9	12	4	14										6
1	2	3			7	13	9[1]	8	6[2]	10[3]				11	5	4	14			12							7
1	2		3		7	13		9[2]		11[3]	12		6	8	5	4	14			10[1]							8
1	2		3		7	12		8[2]	6[1]	10	13			9	5	4				11[3]	14						9
1	2		3		6	7		9		11[2]	10	13		8[3]	5[1]	4				14	12						10
1	2		3	5	6	7		9		11[2]	10[1]			8[3]		4	13			12	14						11
1			3	5		7		9[3]		11[1]	10[2]		6	8		4	12	14		13	2						12
1	2		3	5[1]	7[3]	8		14		10[2]	11		6	9		4	13				12						13
1			3	5	6[2]	7	8[1]	9			10	11[3]	13	12		4				14	2						14
1	5	3	4		14	7		9		11[1]	10[2]		6	8[3]			12			13	2						15
1	5	3	4			7		9		11	10		6	8[1]			13			12	2[2]						16
1	2		4	5	7[3]	13		9		11	10[2]		6	8[1]			14		3	12							17
1	5[3]		3		12	7[1]		9		11[2]			6	10	8	4	14		2		13						18
1	5		3[1]	8	7		14	12		11	13		6	10[3]		4			2	9[2]							19
1	5		3	8[1]	12	7[3]		9		11			6	10		4[2]			2	14		13					20
1	5		4		7	13		9[2]		11	10[1]		6	8					3	12	2						21
1	5	3			7			9	6	11				10					4	8	2						22
1	5	3		13	7			8[1]	12	10[3]			6	11			14		4	9	2[2]						23
1	2	3		5	7	8[1]		13	12	10			6[2]	11[3]			14		4	9							24
	5	3			7[2]	13	10[1]	9	14	11[3]			6	12					4	8	2		1				25
	5	3[2]	13		7	8	9	12				14	6[1]	11			10[3]		4		2		1				26
	2	3			6	7		9	10[2]	12		11[1]		13	8				4		5		1				27
	2	3			6[1]	7	10	9	13			11[3]		12	8	4[2]	14				5		1				28
1	2		4				11	8[1]	6			10[3]		9[2]	5			7	3		12			13	14		29
1	2	3				6[2]		8	13	14	12	10[3]	7	9[4]	5				4		15					11[1]	30
1	2	3				13	14	8[4]	6[2]	12	11[3]	10[1]	7	9	5			15	4								31
1	2	3				8[1]		12	6[3]	10[2]	11	13	7	9	5				4							14	32
1	5	3	4					8[1]	6	14	11	10[2]	7[4]	9[3]				15		12	2					13	33
1	5	3	4		14			8	6[1]	13	11	10[2]		9				7[3]			2					12	34
1	5	3[1]	4		7			8[2]	6[5]	10	11[3]	14		9	13				12	15	2[4]					16	35
1	2		4		7	8			12	15	11[3]	10[4]		9	5[2]				3	14	13					6[1]	36
1	2		3	15	6	7		10[2]		14	13	11[3]		9[1]	8[4]				4	12	5						37
	2		3		6[5]	7[4]	15	9[3]	16	13	11[1]	10[2]			8				4	12	5		1			14	38

FA Cup

Third Round	Nottingham F	(h)	2-0
Fourth Round	Hull C	(a)	2-1
Fifth Round	Liverpool	(h)	2-0
Sixth Round	Leicester C	(a)	1-0
Semi-Final	Manchester U	(Wembley)	3-1
Final	Arsenal	(Wembley)	1-2

Carabao Cup

Third Round	Grimsby T	(h)	7-1
Fourth Round	Manchester U	(h)	1-2

Leasing.com Trophy (Chelsea U21)

Group F (S)	Swindon T	(a)	3-2
Group F (S)	Bristol R	(a)	1-2
Group F (S)	Plymouth Arg	(a)	1-0
Second Round (S)	Walsall	(a)	2-3

European Super Cup

Final	Liverpool	(Istanbul)	2-2

aet; Liverpool won 5-4 on penalties.

UEFA Champions League

Group H	Valencia	(h)	0-1
Group H	Lille OSC	(a)	2-1
Group H	Ajax	(a)	1-0
Group H	Ajax	(h)	4-4
Group H	Valencia	(a)	2-2
Group H	Lille OSC	(h)	2-1
Round of 16	Bayern Munich	(h)	0-3
Round of 16	Bayern Munich	(a)	1-4

CHELTENHAM TOWN

FOUNDATION

Although a scratch team representing Cheltenham played a match against Gloucester in 1884, the earliest recorded match for Cheltenham Town FC was a friendly against Dean Close School on 12 March 1892. The School won 4–3 and the match was played at Prestbury (half a mile from Whaddon Road). Cheltenham Town played Wednesday afternoon friendlies at a local cricket ground until entering the Mid Gloucester League. In those days the club played in deep red coloured shirts and were nicknamed 'the Rubies'. The club moved to Whaddon Lane for season 1901–02 and changed to red and white colours two years later.

The Jonny-Rocks Stadium, Whaddon Road, Cheltenham, Gloucestershire GL52 5NA.

Telephone: (01242) 573 558.

Ticket Office: (01242) 573 558 (option 1).

Website: www.ctfc.com

Email: info@ctfc.com

Ground Capacity: 7,036.

Record Attendance: 10,389 v Blackpool, FA Cup 3rd rd, 13 January 1934 (at Cheltenham Athletic Ground); 8,326 v Reading, FA Cup 1st rd, 17 November 1956 (at Whaddon Road).

Pitch Measurements: 102m × 65m (111.5yd × 71yd).

Chairman: Andy Wilcox.

Vice-Chairman: David Bloxham.

Manager: Michael Duff.

Assistant Manager: Russell Milton.

Colours: Red shirts with thin white stripes and white sleeves, white shorts with red trim, red socks with white trim.

Year Formed: 1892.

Turned Professional: 1932.

Club Nickname: 'The Robins'.

Grounds: Pre-1932, Agg-Gardner's Recreation Ground; Whaddon Lane; Carter's Lane; 1932, Whaddon Road (renamed The Abbey Business Stadium 2009, World of Smile Stadium 2015, LCI Rail Stadium 2016, Jonny-Rocks Stadium 2019).

First Football League Game: 7 August 1999, Division 3, v Rochdale (h) L 0–2 – Book; Griffin, Victory, Banks, Freeman, Brough (Howarth), Howells, Bloomer (Devaney), Grayson, Watkins (McAuley), Yates.

Record League Victory: 5–0 v Mansfield T, FL 2, 6 May 2006 – Higgs; Gallinagh, Bell, McCann (1) (Connolly), Caines, Duff, Wilson, Bird (1p), Gillespie (1) (Spencer), Guinan (Odejayi (1)), Vincent (1).

Record Cup Victory: 12–0 v Chippenham R, FA Cup 3rd qual. rd, 2 November 1935 – Bowles; Whitehouse, Williams; Lang, Devonport (1), Partridge (2); Perkins, Hackett, Jones (4), Black (4), Griffiths (1).

HONOURS

League Champions: Conference – 1998–99, 2015–16.
Runners-up: Conference – 1997–98.

FA Cup: 5th rd – 2002.

League Cup: never past 2nd rd.

FOOTBALL YEARBOOK FACT FILE

When Cheltenham Town won the Football Conference title in 1998–99 they failed to win any of their opening three games but then won seven in a row at the start of a run that saw them lose just two out of 30 matches. From early September until the end of the season the club were always in the top two and sealed the title and promotion to the Football League with a 3-2 win over Yeovil Town in April.

Record Defeat: 1–8 v Crewe Alex, FL 2, 2 April 2011; 0–7 v Crystal Palace, League Cup 2nd rd, 2 October 2002.
N.B. 1–10 v Merthyr T, Southern League, 8 March 1952.

Most League Points (2 for a win): 60, Southern League Division 1, 1963–64.

Most League Points (3 for a win): 78, Division 3, 2001–02.

Most League Goals: 67, FL 2, 2017–18.

Highest League Scorer in Season: Mo Eisa, 23, FL 2, 2017–18.

Most League Goals in Total Aggregate: Julian Alsop, 39, 2000–03; 2009–10.

Most League Goals in One Match: 3, Martin Devaney v Plymouth Arg, Division 3, 23 September 2000; 3, Neil Grayson v Cardiff C, Division 3, 1 April 2001; 3, Damien Spencer v Hull C, Division 3, 23 August 2003; 3, Damien Spencer v Milton Keynes D, FL 1, 31 January 2009; 3, Michael Pook v Burton Alb, FL 2, 13 March 2010; 3, Mohamed Eisa v Port Vale, FL 2, 10 February 2018.

Most Capped Player: Grant McCann, 7 (40), Northern Ireland.

Most League Appearances: David Bird, 288, 2001–11.

Youngest League Player: Kyle Haynes, 17 years 85 days v Oldham Ath, 24 March 2009.

Record Transfer Fee Received: £1,400,000 from Bristol C for Mo Eisa, July 2018.

Record Transfer Fee Paid: £60,000 to Aldershot T for Jermaine McGlashan, January 2012.

Football League Record: 1999 Promoted to Division 3; 2002 Division 2; 2003–04 Division 3; 2004–06 FL 2; 2006–09 FL 1; 2009–15 FL 2; 2015–16 National League; 2016– FL 2.

MANAGERS

George Blackburn 1932–34
George Carr 1934–37
Jimmy Brain 1937–48
Cyril Dean 1948–50
George Summerbee 1950–52
William Raeside 1952–53
Arch Anderson 1953–58
Ron Lewin 1958–60
Peter Donnelly 1960–61
Tommy Cavanagh 1961
Arch Anderson 1961–65
Harold Fletcher 1965–66
Bob Etheridge 1966–73
Willie Penman 1973–74
Dennis Allen 1974–79
Terry Paine 1979
Alan Grundy 1979–82
Alan Wood 1982–83
John Murphy 1983–88
Jim Barron 1988–90
John Murphy 1990
Dave Lewis 1990–91
Ally Robertson 1991–92
Lindsay Parsons 1992–95
Chris Robinson 1995–97
Steve Cotterill 1997–2002
Graham Allner 2002–03
Bobby Gould 2003
John Ward 2003–07
Keith Downing 2007–08
Martin Allen 2008–09
Mark Yates 2009–14
Paul Buckle 2014–15
Gary Johnson 2015–18
Michael Duff September 2018–

LATEST SEQUENCES

Longest Sequence of League Wins: 5, 11.2.2020 – 29.2.2020.

Longest Sequence of League Defeats: 7, 14.4.2018 – 18.8.2018.

Longest Sequence of League Draws: 5, 5.4.2003 – 21.4.2003.

Longest Sequence of Unbeaten League Matches: 16, 1.12.2001 – 12.3.2002.

Longest Sequence Without a League Win: 14, 20.12.2008 – 7.3.2009.

Successive Scoring Runs: 17 from 16.2.2008.

Successive Non-scoring Runs: 5 from 10.3.2012 – 30.3.2012.

TEN YEAR LEAGUE RECORD

		P	W	D	L	F	A	Pts	Pos
2010-11	FL 2	46	13	13	20	56	77	52	17
2011-12	FL 2	46	23	8	15	66	50	77	6
2012-13	FL 2	46	20	15	11	58	51	75	5
2013-14	FL 2	46	13	16	17	53	63	55	17
2014-15	FL 2	46	9	14	23	40	67	41	23
2015-16	NL	46	30	11	5	87	30	101	1
2016-17	FL 2	46	12	14	20	49	69	50	21
2017-18	FL 2	46	13	12	21	67	73	51	17
2018-19	FL 2	46	15	12	19	57	68	57	16
2019-20	FL 2	36	17	13	6	52	27	64	4§

§*Decided on points-per-game (1.78)*

Cheltenham Town played Wolverhampton Wanderers in a friendly to mark the first occasion floodlights were used at Whaddon Road. The game, played in October 1951, was also the first time Wolves had played under lights. Wolves led 3-1 but the Robins fought back to draw 3-3.

CHELTENHAM TOWN – SKY BET LEAGUE TWO 2019–20 LEAGUE RECORD

Match No.	Date	Venue	Opponents	Result		H/T Score	Lg Pos.	Goalscorers	Attendance
1	Aug 3	A	Leyton Orient	L	0-1	0-0	17		6534
2	10	H	Scunthorpe U	W	4-1	0-0	7	Broom 68, Raglan 71, Addai 73, Thomas (pen) 90	2742
3	17	A	Morecambe	D	0-0	0-0	11		1692
4	20	H	Carlisle U	W	2-0	2-0	5	Reilly 15, Varney 45	2634
5	24	H	Swindon T	D	2-2	2-2	8	Hussey 19, Varney 41	4401
6	31	A	Crawley T	L	0-1	0-0	11		2095
7	Sept 7	H	Stevenage	W	4-2	1-0	6	Reilly 22, Long 57, Broom 80, Addai 90	2708
8	14	A	Salford C	W	2-0	1-0	6	Broom 2 32, 82	2389
9	17	H	Bradford C	W	3-2	0-0	3	Reilly 59, Doyle-Hayes 69, Tozer 80	2702
10	21	A	Plymouth Arg	W	2-0	1-0	3	Varney 40, Aimson (og) 90	8956
11	28	H	Crewe Alex	D	1-1	1-1	3	Reilly 9	3549
12	Oct 5	A	Oldham Ath	D	1-1	0-1	5	Broom 71	3496
13	19	A	Walsall	W	2-1	1-0	5	Tozer 35, Varney 58	4494
14	22	H	Macclesfield T	W	3-0	1-0	2	Varney 45, Thomas 59, Broom 76	2632
15	Nov 2	H	Forest Green R	L	1-2	0-2	6	Varney 67	5788
16	16	A	Exeter C	D	0-0	0-0	6		4956
17	23	H	Colchester U	D	1-1	0-1	6	Thomas (pen) 70	3045
18	26	A	Grimsby T	D	0-0	0-0	5		2508
19	Dec 7	A	Mansfield T	W	3-0	1-0	4	Smith 32, Boyle 52, Addai 86	3715
20	14	H	Cambridge U	D	1-1	0-1	3	Boyle 53	2813
21	21	A	Port Vale	D	1-1	1-1	4	Addai 24	4404
22	26	H	Plymouth Arg	L	0-1	0-1	7		1222
23	29	A	Northampton T	D	1-1	1-1	8	Thomas (pen) 3	5090
24	Jan 1	A	Newport Co	D	1-1	0-0	8	Tozer 86	3913
25	4	H	Oldham Ath	W	3-0	1-0	5	Sheaf 32, May 76, Broom 90	3029
26	11	H	Walsall	W	3-1	1-0	3	Sheaf 18, Thomas 48, May 71	3868
27	18	A	Crewe Alex	L	0-1	0-0	7		4478
28	28	A	Bradford C	D	1-1	0-1	8	May 84	12,731
29	Feb 1	H	Morecambe	W	2-1	2-0	7	Thomas (pen) 32, May 35	3044
30	8	A	Scunthorpe U	L	0-1	0-1	7		3159
31	11	A	Carlisle U	W	1-0	1-0	7	Reid 26	3088
32	15	H	Leyton Orient	W	2-1	1-1	5	May 18, Reid 88	3527
33	22	H	Mansfield T	W	1-0	0-0	5	Reid 65	3274
34	25	H	Northampton T	W	2-1	1-1	5	Broom 19, Varney 85	2934
35	29	A	Colchester U	W	2-0	1-0	4	May 39, Hussey 79	3698
36	Mar 7	H	Port Vale	D	0-0	0-0	5		3741
37	14	A	Cambridge U	Cancelled					
38	17	A	Macclesfield T	Cancelled					
39	21	H	Grimsby T	Cancelled					
40	24	H	Newport Co	Cancelled					
41	28	A	Forest Green R	Cancelled					
42	Apr 4	H	Exeter C	Cancelled					
43	10	A	Swindon T	Cancelled					
44	13	H	Crawley T	Cancelled					
45	18	A	Stevenage	Cancelled					
46	25	H	Salford C	Cancelled					

Final League Position: 4 (on points-per-game basis)

GOALSCORERS

League (52): Broom 8, Varney 7, May 6, Thomas 6 (4 pens), Addai 4, Reilly 4, Reid 3, Tozer 3, Boyle 2, Hussey 2, Sheaf 2, Doyle-Hayes 1, Long 1, Raglan 1, Smith 1, own goal 1.
FA Cup (3): Addai 2, Reid 1 (1 pen).
Carabao Cup (0).
Leasing.com Trophy (8): Smith 3, Addai 1, Lloyd 1, Long 1, Sheaf 1, Tozer 1.
League Two Play-offs (2): Raglan 1, Thomas 1.

Flinders S 25	Raglan C 35	Tozer B 34	Boyle W 11 + 2	Long S 31 + 3	Broom R 33 + 1	Ince R 1 + 8	Sheaf M 14 + 5	Debayo J 3 + 4	Campbell T 6 + 5	Varney L 18 + 3	Hussey C 31 + 2	Reilly G 18 + 3	Addai A 7 + 18	Clements C 16 + 6	Doyle-Hayes J 28 + 2	Thomas C 22 + 4	Greaves J 29	Lloyd G 3 + 10	Smith J 2 + 10	Bowry D — + 1	Reid R 5 + 4	Horton G — + 1	May A 12	Lovett R — + 1	Evans O 11	Nichols T 1 + 4	Match No.
1	2	3	4	5	6	7■	8¹	9²	10³	11■	12	13	14														1
1	2	3		5	6		8	12	11¹		9³	10	13	4²	7	14											2
1	2	3		5	6		8¹	9		10		11²			7	12	4	13									3
1	2	3		5	6			9³	14	11¹	12	10²		7	8		4	13									4
1	2	3		5	6			13	14	10¹	9³	11²		7	8		4	12									5
1	2	3		5	6				12		9	11¹	13	7	8		4	10²									6
1	2	3		5	6					10²	9	11¹	12	7		8	4		13								7
1	3	4		2	7					11¹	6	10²	12		9	8	5		13								8
1	2	3		5	6³					11	9	10²	13	12	8	7¹	4			14							9
1	2	3		5	6					11³	9	10¹	13	12	8²	7	4		14								10
1	2	3		5	6					11¹	9	10²	12	13	8³	7	4	14									11
1	2³	3		5	6						9	11²	10	12	8¹	7	4	14	13								12
1	2	3		5	9	13				10¹	8	11²	12		7³	6	4		14								13
1	2	3		5	6¹	14				11²	9	10³	13		8	7	4		12								14
1	2¹	3		5	6	12				11	9	10²		13	8³	7	4		14								15
1	2	3		5	6					10	9	11¹	12		8	7	4										16
1	2²	3			6		14				9	13	10¹	7	8	5	4		11³		12						17
1		2	3	12	8		14				9	11²	13	7³	6	5	4				10¹						18
1	2		3	5¹	9						8		10	6	7		4		11			12					19
1	2	3	4	5	6		12	14					11¹	7	8		9²		13		10³						20
1	2	3		5	9		6³	13				10¹	11	8²	7	14	4	12									21
1	2	3	14	5	6		13				9	11³	10¹	7²	8		4	12									22
1	2	3		5	10	12	6²		14		9		13■		8¹	7	4	11³									23
1	2	3	4	6	7		12		10²		9	13				8	5¹	11									24
1³	2	3		13	5		8¹		10²		9			7		6	4	14					11	12			25
	2	3		12	5³		8		10²		9			7¹	14	6	4	13					11		1		26
	2	3		5			6²		13		9		11¹	7		8	4	12					10		1		27
	2	3	14	5³			7		10¹	12	9		13		8	6²	4						11		1		28
	2	3		5	12	14	6³			11²	9				8	7¹	4						10		1	13	29
	2	3		5	6					11²	9		14		8¹	7³	4				13		10		1	12	30
	2	3	4	5	6	14	8³			12	9		13		7						10²		11¹		1		31
	2	3	4	5²	6		7³			10¹	9			12	8						13		11		1	14	32
	2	3	4		5					11¹	8		14	6²	7	13					12		10		1	9³	33
	2	3	4	5	6					12	9		13		8	7					10²		11¹		1		34
	2	3	4	5	8	12	6			11²	9			7³					13				10¹		1	14	35
	2		3	5	8	13	6³				9				12	7¹	4		14		11²		10		1		36
																											37
																											38
																											39
																											40
																											41
																											42
																											43
																											44
																											45
																											46

FA Cup

First Round	Swindon T	(h)	1-1
Replay	Swindon T	(a)	1-0
Second Round	Port Vale	(h)	1-3

Carabao Cup

First Round	Bristol R	(a)	0-3

Leasing.com Trophy

Group E (S)	Exeter C	(a)	0-1
Group E (S)	West Ham U U21	(h)	4-3
Group E (S)	Newport Co	(h)	4-7

League Two Play-Offs

Semi-Final 1st leg	Northampton T	(a)	2-0
Semi-Final 2nd leg	Northampton T	(h)	0-3

COLCHESTER UNITED

FOUNDATION

Colchester United was formed in 1937 when a number of enthusiasts of the much older Colchester Town club decided to establish a professional concern as a limited liability company. The new club continued at Layer Road which had been the amateur club's home since 1909.

JobServe Community Stadium, United Way, Colchester, Essex CO4 5UP.

Telephone: (01206) 755 100.

Ticket Office: (01206) 755 161.

Website: www.cu-fc.com

Email: media@colchesterunited.net

Ground Capacity: 10,105.

Record Attendance: 19,072 v Reading, FA Cup 1st rd, 27 November 1948 (at Layer Road); 10,064 v Norwich C, FL 1, 16 January 2010 (at Community Stadium).

Pitch Measurements: 100m × 65m (109.5yd × 71yd).

Executive Chairman: Robbie Cowling.

Head Coach: Steve Ball.

Colours: Royal blue shirts with white trim, royal blue shorts with white trim, white socks with royal blue trim.

Year Formed: 1937.

Turned Professional: 1937.

Club Nickname: 'The U's'.

Grounds: 1937, Layer Road; 2008, Weston Homes Community Stadium (renamed JobServe Community Stadium 2018).

First Football League Game: 19 August 1950, Division 3 (S), v Gillingham (a) D 0–0 – Wright; Kettle, Allen; Bearryman, Stewart, Elder; Jones, Curry, Turner, McKim, Church.

Record League Victory: 9–1 v Bradford C, Division 4, 30 December 1961 – Ames; Millar, Fowler; Harris, Abrey, Ron Hunt; Foster, Bobby Hunt (4), King (4), Hill (1), Wright.

Record Cup Victory: 9-1 v Leamington, FA Cup 1st rd, 5 November 2005 – Davison; Stockley (Garcia), Duguid, Brown (1), Chilvers, Watson (1), Halford (1), Izzet (Danns) (2), Iwelumo (1) (Williams), Cureton (2), Yeates (1).

Record Defeat: 0–8 v Leyton Orient, Division 4, 15 October 1988.

Most League Points (2 for a win): 60, Division 4, 1973–74.

HONOURS

League Champions: Conference – 1991–92.
Runners-up: FL 1 – 2005–06; Division 4 – 1961–62; Conference – 1990–91.

FA Cup: 6th rd – 1971.

League Cup: 5th rd – 1975.

League Trophy: *Runners-up:* 1997.

FOOTBALL YEARBOOK FACT FILE

Colchester United were top of the Division Three South table on goal average after defeating Watford 2-0 in their final fixture of the 1956–57 season. United's nearest rivals both still had a match left to play with the U's needing each to lose to give them the title and promotion. However, both Ipswich Town and Torquay United avoided defeat in their last games leaving the U's in third place.

Most League Points (3 for a win): 81, Division 4, 1982–83.

Most League Goals: 104, Division 4, 1961–62.

Highest League Scorer in Season: Bobby Hunt, 38, Division 4, 1961–62.

Most League Goals in Total Aggregate: Martyn King, 130, 1956–64.

Most League Goals in One Match: 4, Bobby Hunt v Bradford C, Division 4, 30 December 1961; 4, Martyn King v Bradford C, Division 4, 30 December 1961; 4, Bobby Hunt v Doncaster R, Division 4, 30 April 1962.

Most Capped Player: Brandon Comley, 9, Montserrat.

Most League Appearances: Micky Cook, 613, 1969–84.

Youngest League Player: Todd Miller, 16 years 166 days v Exeter C, 16 March 2019.

Record Transfer Fee Received: £2,500,000 from Reading for Greg Halford, January 2007.

Record Transfer Fee Paid: £400,000 to Cheltenham T for Steve Gillespie, July 2008.

Football League Record: 1950 Elected to Division 3 (S); 1958–61 Division 3; 1961–62 Division 4; 1962–65 Division 3; 1965–66 Division 4; 1966–68 Division 3; 1968–74 Division 4; 1974–76 Division 3, 1976–77 Division 4; 1977–81 Division 3; 1981–90 Division 4; 1990–92 Conference; 1992–98 Division 3; 1998–2004 Division 2; 2004–06 FL 1; 2006–08 FL C; 2008–16 FL 1; 2016– FL 2.

MANAGERS

Ted Fenton 1946–48
Jimmy Allen 1948–53
Jack Butler 1953–55
Benny Fenton 1955–63
Neil Franklin 1963–68
Dick Graham 1968–72
Jim Smith 1972–75
Bobby Roberts 1975–82
Allan Hunter 1982–83
Cyril Lea 1983–86
Mike Walker 1986–87
Roger Brown 1987–88
Jock Wallace 1989
Mick Mills 1990
Ian Atkins 1990–91
Roy McDonough 1991–94
George Burley 1994
Steve Wignall 1995–99
Mick Wadsworth 1999
Steve Whitton 1999–2003
Phil Parkinson 2003–06
Geraint Williams 2006–08
Paul Lambert 2008–09
Aidy Boothroyd 2009–10
John Ward 2010–12
Joe Dunne 2012–14
Tony Humes 2014–15
Kevin Keen 2015–16
John McGreal 2016–20
Steve Ball July 2020–

LATEST SEQUENCES

Longest Sequence of League Wins: 7, 31.12.2005 – 7.2.2006.

Longest Sequence of League Defeats: 9, 31.10.2015 – 28.12.2015.

Longest Sequence of League Draws: 6, 21.3.1977 – 11.4.1977.

Longest Sequence of Unbeaten League Matches: 20, 22.12.1956 – 19.4.1957.

Longest Sequence Without a League Win: 20, 2.3.1968 – 31.8.1968.

Successive Scoring Runs: 24 from 15.9.1962.

Successive Non-scoring Runs: 5 from 11.2.2006.

TEN YEAR LEAGUE RECORD

		P	*W*	*D*	*L*	*F*	*A*	*Pts*	*Pos*
2010-11	FL 1	46	16	14	16	57	63	62	10
2011-12	FL 1	46	13	20	13	61	66	59	10
2012-13	FL 1	46	14	9	23	47	68	51	20
2013-14	FL 1	46	13	14	19	53	61	53	16
2014-15	FL 1	46	14	10	22	58	77	52	19
2015-16	FL 1	46	9	13	24	57	99	40	23
2016-17	FL 2	46	19	12	15	67	57	69	8
2017-18	FL 2	46	16	14	16	53	52	62	13
2018-19	FL 2	46	20	10	16	65	53	70	8
2019-20	FL 2	37	15	13	9	52	37	58	6§

§Decided on points-per-game (1.57)

DID YOU KNOW ?

In 1976–77 Colchester United won their opening 12 home games in Division Four, scoring 39 goals and conceding just eight goals during the run. The U's went on to win 19 of their 23 fixtures at Layer Road and finished the season in third place to earn promotion.

COLCHESTER UNITED – SKY BET LEAGUE TWO 2019–20 LEAGUE RECORD

Match No.	Date	Venue	Opponents	Result	H/T Score	Lg Pos.	Goalscorers	Attendance
1	Aug 3	H	Port Vale	D 1-1	1-1	12	Norris 45	3729
2	10	A	Plymouth Arg	L 0-1	0-0	19		10,542
3	17	H	Cambridge U	L 1-2	1-0	20	Norris (pen) 9	4148
4	20	A	Grimsby T	D 2-2	2-0	21	Nouble 25, Norris 45	4103
5	24	H	Northampton T	W 1-0	0-0	17	Norris (pen) 66	3164
6	31	A	Oldham Ath	W 1-0	1-0	13	Nouble 45	3091
7	Sept 7	H	Walsall	D 0-0	0-0	13		3265
8	14	A	Forest Green R	L 0-1	0-1	17		2758
9	17	A	Swindon T	W 3-0	1-0	13	Eastman 45, Robinson 2 55, 75	6634
10	21	H	Leyton Orient	W 2-1	2-1	10	Adubofour-Poku 3, Jackson 28	5519
11	28	A	Macclesfield T	D 1-1	1-1	9	Robinson 45	1532
12	Oct 5	H	Stevenage	W 3-1	0-1	8	Eastman 48, Nouble (pen) 82, Adubofour-Poku 83	3331
13	12	A	Crawley T	L 1-2	1-0	8	Prosser 35	2636
14	19	H	Morecambe	L 0-1	0-0	11		3011
15	22	A	Crewe Alex	D 0-0	0-0	12		3659
16	26	H	Newport Co	W 3-1	2-1	9	Jackson 33, Stevenson 42, Senior 75	2955
17	Nov 2	A	Mansfield T	W 3-2	1-1	8	Comley 8, Senior 74, Gambin 87	4125
18	23	A	Cheltenham T	D 1-1	1-0	10	Norris 28	3045
19	Dec 7	H	Salford C	W 1-0	0-0	8	Pell 90	3713
20	14	A	Scunthorpe U	D 2-2	0-1	9	Norris 58, Prosser 62	3081
21	21	H	Carlisle U	W 3-0	2-0	8	Knight-Percival (og) 26, Harriott 41, Bramall 52	3164
22	26	A	Leyton Orient	W 3-1	1-0	4	Robinson 2 41, 90, Pell 64	5648
23	29	H	Exeter C	D 2-2	1-1	6	Pell 16, Robinson 59	4739
24	Jan 1	H	Crawley T	D 1-1	0-0	6	Nouble 64	3729
25	4	A	Stevenage	D 0-0	0-0	8		3027
26	11	A	Morecambe	D 1-1	1-0	9	Nouble 35	1593
27	18	H	Macclesfield T	W 2-1	2-0	8	Harriott 14, Kelleher (og) 16	3252
28	21	H	Bradford C	D 0-0	0-0	7		3022
29	25	A	Exeter C	D 0-0	0-0	5		4745
30	28	H	Swindon T	W 3-1	0-0	5	Norris 74, Robinson 2 85, 89	3258
31	Feb 1	A	Cambridge U	L 1-2	0-0	6	Norris 67	5015
32	8	H	Plymouth Arg	W 3-0	3-0	5	Stevenson 14, Robinson 2 30, 36	4768
33	11	H	Grimsby T	L 2-3	2-1	5	Prosser 17, Robinson 42	2954
34	15	A	Port Vale	L 0-3	0-1	7		5199
35	22	A	Salford C	W 2-1	2-1	6	Adubofour-Poku 27, Harriott 41	2589
36	29	H	Cheltenham T	L 0-2	0-1	8		3698
37	Mar 7	A	Carlisle U	W 3-0	2-0	6	Adubofour-Poku 2 41, 59, Norris 43	3769
38	14	H	Scunthorpe U	Cancelled				
39	17	H	Crewe Alex	Cancelled				
40	21	A	Newport Co	Cancelled				
41	28	H	Mansfield T	Cancelled				
42	Apr 4	A	Bradford C	Cancelled				
43	10	A	Northampton T	Cancelled				
44	13	H	Oldham Ath	Cancelled				
45	18	A	Walsall	Cancelled				
46	25	H	Forest Green R	Cancelled				

Final League Position: 6 (on points-per-game basis)

GOALSCORERS

League (52): Robinson 11, Norris 9 (2 pens), Adubofour-Poku 5, Nouble 5 (1 pen), Harriott 3, Pell 3, Prosser 3, Eastman 2, Jackson 2, Senior 2, Stevenson 2, Bramall 1, Comley 1, Gambin 1, own goals 2.
FA Cup (0).
Carabao Cup (6): Comley 1, Eastman 1, Gambin 1, Norris 1, Senior 1, own goal 1.
Leasing.com Trophy (6): Cowan-Hall 2, Clampin 1, Norris 1, Robinson 1, own goal 1.
League Two Play-offs (2): Brammall 1, Senior 1.

Gerken D 36	Vincent-Young K 2	Eastman T 35 + 1	Prosser L 35	Bramall C 24	Lapslie T 7 + 10	Pell H 21 + 1	Senior C 19 + 10	Brown J 5 + 6	Nouble F 30 + 6	Norris L 19 + 13	Gambin L 9 + 19	Stevenson B 24 + 4	Hasanally A — + 2	Jackson R 33 + 1	Clampin R 13	Comley B 22 + 2	James C — + 3	Sowunmi O 5 + 2	Cowan-Hall P 2 + 3	Robinson T 19 + 9	Adubofour-Poku K 23 + 6	Sarpeng-Wiredu B 5 + 2	Harriott C 17 + 5	Ross E 1	Kensadale O — + 1	Ogedi-Uzokwe J — + 2	Moore T 1	Match No.
1	2	3	4	5	6	7^2	8^3	9^1	10	11	12	13	14															1
1	2	3	4	5^1	6^3		8^2	9	10	11	12	7	14	13														2
1		3	4				8^2	9	10	11	12	7		2	5^1	6	13											3
1		3	4				8^1	9	10	11^2	12	7		2	5	6		13										4
1		3	4				9^1	6^3	11	10	12	8^2		2	5	7	14		13									5
1		3	4				8^2	13	9	11^3	10^1	7		2	5	6			14	12								6
1		3	4		7		9^1	12	11	10^2		8		2	5				6^3	13	14							7
1		3	4		7		8		10^3	11	9^2	6		2	5^1					13	14	12						8
1		3	4	5	12		8	13	9		14			2		7				11^3	10^2	6^1						9
1		3	4	5	12		8^3		9	14				2		7			13	11^2	10	6^1						10
1		3	5	6	8		12		10^3	14		13				9		4	7^2	11		2^1						11
1		3	4	5				14	6^1	11^2	12	8^3		2		7				10	9	13						12
1		3	4		7		8^3	12	9	14		13		2	5					11^2	10	6^1						13
1		3	4	5	7^1		13		10	12	14			2						11^3	6	8	9^2					14
1		3	4	5			8^1		10	11^3	12	6		2		7				14▪	9^2		13					15
1		3	4	5			8^3	14	10^1	11	12	6		2		7					9^2		13					16
1		3	4	5	12	14	8		11		13	7^1		2		6					9^3		10^2					17
1		3	4	5	14	7^1	8^3		10	11	13			2		6					9^2		12					18
1		3	4	5	12	7	8		10	11^1	13			2^2		6				14	9^3							19
1		3	4	5		7	8^1		10	11^2				2		6				13	9		12					20
		3	4^2	5	12	6			13		9	7		2				14		11^3	8		10^1	1				21
1		4		5	13	6	14		12		9^3	7		2				3		11	8^1		10^2					22
1		4		5^1	12▪	6			13		9	7		2				3^3		11	8^2		10		14			23
1		3	4			6			10	12	9^1	7		2	5^2		14			11^3	13		8					24
1		3	4			6			8	11^3	9^2	7		2	5					13	12		10^1			14		25
1		3	4		14	6			8	11	12^3	7		2▪	5						9^1		10^2			13		26
1		3	4		13	6			10	14		7^2			5	12				11^3	9		8				2^1	27
1		3	4			6	12		10^1	14	13			2	5	7				11^2	9		8^3					28
1		3	4			6	12			14	9^1	13		2	5	7				11^2	8		10^3					29
1		3	4	5		6	14		12	13	9^1			2		7				11	8^2		10^3					30
1		3	4	5		6	8^2		10	11^3	13			2		7				14	9^1		12					31
1		3	4	5		6^1	13		10	14	12	9		2		7				11^2			8^3					32
1		3	4	5		6^1	14		10	12		9		2		7^2				11	13		8^3					33
1		3	4	5		6^1	8^3		10	13	14	9		2		7^2				11	12							34
1		14	4	5		7			12	10		8		2^3		13		3		11^2	6		9^1					35
1			4	5		6	14		12	13		9		2		7^2		3▪		11	8^3		10^1					36
1		3	4	5		6	12		10	11^2	14	7		2						13	9^3		8^1					37
																												38
																												39
																												40
																												41
																												42
																												43
																												44
																												45
																												46

FA Cup

First Round	Coventry C	(h)	0-2

Carabao Cup

First Round	Swindon T	(h)	3-0
Second Round	Crystal Palace	(a)	0-0
(Colchester U won 5-4 on penalties)			
Third Round	Tottenham H	(h)	0-0
(Colchester U won 4-3 on penalties)			
Fourth Round	Crawley T	(a)	3-1
Quarter-Final	Manchester U	(a)	0-3

Leasing.com Trophy

Group A (S)	Gillingham	(a)	3-2
Group A (S)	Tottenham H U21	(h)	1-1
(Tottenham H U21 won 6-5 on penalties)			
Group A (S)	Ipswich T	(h)	1-0
Second Round (S)	Stevenage	(h)	1-2

League Two Play-Offs

Semi-Final 1st leg	Exeter C	(h)	1-0
Semi-Final 2nd leg	Exeter C	(a)	1-3
(aet.)			

COVENTRY CITY

FOUNDATION

Workers at Singers' cycle factory formed a club in 1883. The first success of Singers FC was to win the Birmingham Junior Cup in 1891 and this led in 1894 to their election to the Birmingham & District League. Four years later they changed their name to Coventry City and joined the Southern League in 1908 at which time they were playing in blue and white quarters.

Groundsharing with Birmingham C for 2020–21 season.

Sky Blue Lodge, Leamington Road, Coventry CV8 3FL.

Telephone: (02476) 991 987.

Ticket Office: (02476) 991 987.

Website: www.ccfc.co.uk

Email: info@ccfc.co.uk

Ground Capacity: 29,400.

Record Attendance: 51,455 v Wolverhampton W, Division 2, 29 April 1967 (at Highfield Road); 31,407 v Chelsea, FA Cup 6th rd, 7 March 2009 (at Ricoh Arena).

Pitch Measurements: 100m × 68m (109.5yd × 74.5yd).

Chairman: Tim Fisher.

Chief Executive: David Boddy.

Manager: Mark Robins.

Assistant Manager: Adi Viveash.

Colours: Sky blue shirts with white trim, sky blue shorts, sky blue socks with white trim.

Year Formed: 1883.

Turned Professional: 1893.

Previous Name: 1883, Singers FC; 1898, Coventry City.

Club Nickname: 'Sky Blues'.

Grounds: 1883, Binley Road; 1887, Stoke Road; 1899, Highfield Road; 2005, Ricoh Arena; 2013, Sixfields Stadium (groundshare with Northampton T); 2014, Ricoh Arena; 2019, St Andrew's Trillion Trophy Stadium (groundshare with Birmingham C).

First Football League Game: 30 August 1919, Division 2, v Tottenham H (h) L 0–5 – Lindon; Roberts, Chaplin, Allan, Hawley, Clarke, Sheldon, Mercer, Sambrooke, Lowes, Gibson.

Record League Victory: 9–0 v Bristol C, Division 3 (S), 28 April 1934 – Pearson; Brown, Bisby; Perry, Davidson, Frith; White (2), Lauderdale, Bourton (5), Jones (2), Lake.

Record Cup Victory: 8–0 v Rushden & D, League Cup 2nd rd, 2 October 2002 – Debec; Caldwell, Quinn, Betts (1p), Konjic (Shaw), Davenport, Pipe, Safri (Stanford), Mills (2) (Bothroyd (2)), McSheffery (3), Partridge.

Record Defeat: 2–10 v Norwich C, Division 3 (S), 15 March 1930.

HONOURS

League Champions: Division 2 – 1966–67; FL 1 – 2019–20.
Division 3 – 1963–64; Division 3S – 1935–36.
Runners-up: Division 3S – 1933–34; Division 4 – 1958–59.

FA Cup Winners: 1987.

League Cup: semi-final – 1981, 1990.

League Trophy Winners: 2017.

European Competitions
Fairs Cup: 1970–71.

FOOTBALL YEARBOOK FACT FILE

Coventry City were the first football club to have their catering facilities included in the prestigious Egon Ronay Guide. The club's Grandstand Restaurant, described as 'airy, spacious and unusually situated high above the football ground', was first included in the 1972 guide and regularly appeared in the following years.

Most League Points (2 for a win): 60, Division 4, 1958–59 and Division 3, 1963–64.

Most League Points (3 for a win): 75, FL 2, 2017–18.

Most League Goals: 108, Division 3 (S), 1931–32.

Highest League Scorer in Season: Clarrie Bourton, 49, Division 3 (S), 1931–32.

Most League Goals in Total Aggregate: Clarrie Bourton, 173, 1931–37.

Most League Goals in One Match: 5, Clarrie Bourton v Bournemouth, Division 3 (S), 17 October 1931; 5, Arthur Bacon v Gillingham, Division 3 (S), 30 December 1933.

Most Capped Player: Magnus Hedman, 44 (58), Sweden.

Most League Appearances: Steve Ogrizovic, 507, 1984–2000.

Youngest League Player: Ben Mackey, 16 years 167 days v Ipswich T, 12 April 2003.

Record Transfer Fee Received: £13,000,000 from Internazionale for Robbie Keane, July 2000.

Record Transfer Fee Paid: £6,500,000 to Norwich C for Craig Bellamy, August 2000.

Football League Record: 1919 Elected to Division 2; 1925–26 Division 3 (N); 1926–36 Division 3 (S); 1936–52 Division 2; 1952–58 Division 3 (S); 1958–59 Division 4; 1959–64 Division 3; 1964–67 Division 2; 1967–92 Division 1; 1992–2001 Premier League; 2001–04 Division 1; 2004–12 FL C; 2012–17 FL 1; 2017–18 FL 2; 2018–20 FL 1; 2020– FL C.

LATEST SEQUENCES

Longest Sequence of League Wins: 6, 25.4.1964 – 5.9.1964.

Longest Sequence of League Defeats: 9, 30.8.1919 – 11.10.1919.

Longest Sequence of League Draws: 6, 1.11.2003 – 29.11.2003.

Longest Sequence of Unbeaten League Matches: 25, 26.11.1966 – 13.5.1967.

Longest Sequence Without a League Win: 19, 30.8.1919 – 20.12.1919.

Successive Scoring Runs: 25 from 10.9.1966.

Successive Non-scoring Runs: 11 from 11.10.1919.

MANAGERS

H. R. Buckle 1909–10
Robert Wallace 1910–13
(Secretary-Manager)
Frank Scott-Walford 1913–15
William Clayton 1917–19
H. Pollitt 1919–20
Albert Evans 1920–24
Jimmy Kerr 1924–28
James McIntyre 1928–31
Harry Storer 1931–45
Dick Bayliss 1945–47
Billy Frith 1947–48
Harry Storer 1948–53
Jack Fairbrother 1953–54
Charlie Elliott 1954–55
Jesse Carver 1955–56
George Raynor 1956
Harry Warren 1956–57
Billy Frith 1957–61
Jimmy Hill 1961–67
Noel Cantwell 1967–72
Bob Dennison 1972
Joe Mercer 1972–75
Gordon Milne 1972–81
Dave Sexton 1981–83
Bobby Gould 1983–84
Don Mackay 1985–86
George Curtis 1986–87
(became Managing Director)
John Sillett 1987–90
Terry Butcher 1990–92
Don Howe 1992
Bobby Gould 1992–93
(with Don Howe, June 1992)
Phil Neal 1993–95
Ron Atkinson 1995–96
(became Director of Football)
Gordon Strachan 1996–2001
Roland Nilsson 2001–02
Gary McAllister 2002–04
Eric Black 2004
Peter Reid 2004–05
Micky Adams 2005–07
Iain Dowie 2007–08
Chris Coleman 2008–10
Aidy Boothroyd 2010–11
Andy Thorn 2011–12
Mark Robins 2012–13
Steven Pressley 2013–15
Tony Mowbray 2015–16
Russell Slade 2016–17
Mark Robins March 2017–

TEN YEAR LEAGUE RECORD

		P	W	D	L	F	A	Pts	Pos
2010-11	FL C	46	14	13	19	54	58	55	18
2011-12	FL C	46	9	13	24	41	65	40	23
2012-13	FL 1	46	18	11	17	66	59	55*	15
2013-14	FL 1	46	16	13	17	74	77	51*	18
2014-15	FL 1	46	13	16	17	49	60	55	17
2015-16	FL 1	46	19	12	15	67	49	69	8
2016-17	FL 1	46	9	12	25	37	68	39	23
2017-18	FL 2	46	22	9	15	64	47	75	6
2018-19	FL 1	46	18	11	17	54	54	65	8
2019-20	FL 1	34	18	13	3	48	30	67	1§

** 10 pts deducted. §Decided on points-per-game (1.97)*

DID YOU KNOW ?

In 1909–10 Coventry City, then playing in the Southern League, reached the quarter-finals of the FA Cup. City defeated Wrexham and Kettering in the qualifying rounds and wins over Preston, Portsmouth and Nottingham Forest took them into the last eight where they were defeated by Everton.

COVENTRY CITY – SKY BET LEAGUE ONE 2019–20 LEAGUE RECORD

Match No.	Date	Venue	Opponents	Result		H/T Score	Lg Pos.	Goalscorers	Attendance
1	Aug 3	H	Southend U	W	1-0	0-0	7	Westbrooke 51	6534
2	10	A	Bolton W	D	0-0	0-0	8		8901
3	17	H	Bristol R	W	2-0	1-0	4	Shipley 45, Kastaneer 81	6976
4	20	A	Portsmouth	D	3-3	1-2	3	Hiwula 3, Godden (pen) 75, Rose 86	18,748
5	24	H	Gillingham	W	1-0	1-0	5	Hyam 26	5624
6	31	A	Oxford U	D	3-3	1-0	4	Westbrooke 35, Godden 56, O'Hare 90	8080
7	Sept 7	H	Blackpool	W	3-2	2-2	2	Godden 41, Jobello 45, O'Hare 90	6637
8	14	A	Burton Alb	D	0-0	0-0	1		4409
9	17	H	AFC Wimbledon	W	2-1	1-1	1	Hiwula 27, Walsh 90	5239
10	28	H	Doncaster R	D	1-1	0-1	4	Bakayoko 89	7010
11	Oct 5	A	Rotherham U	L	0-4	0-2	4		10,337
12	13	H	Tranmere R	L	0-1	0-0	7		5658
13	19	A	Milton Keynes D	D	0-0	0-0	6		13,621
14	23	H	Fleetwood T	W	2-1	0-1	4	Bakayoko 59, Westbrooke (pen) 68	4672
15	26	A	Peterborough U	D	2-2	1-0	6	Bakayoko 12, Biamou 85	8005
16	Nov 2	H	Accrington S	D	0-0	0-0	6		5455
17	16	H	Rochdale	W	2-1	1-1	3	Shipley 42, Walsh 72	5433
18	23	A	Sunderland	D	1-1	1-0	5	Hyam 26	29,809
19	Dec 7	H	Ipswich T	D	1-1	0-1	6	Biamou 56	8085
20	14	A	Shrewsbury T	L	1-2	1-0	7	Shipley 26	7336
21	21	H	Lincoln C	W	1-0	1-0	5	Westbrooke 32	6863
22	29	A	Wycombe W	W	4-1	3-1	5	McCallum 3, Godden 3 (1 pen) 16 (p), 44, 50	7533
23	Jan 1	A	Tranmere R	W	4-1	2-1	3	Godden 3 (1 pen) 3, 67, 90 (p), Shipley 17	7828
24	11	H	Milton Keynes D	D	1-1	1-0	4	McCallum 1	6666
25	18	A	Doncaster R	W	1-0	1-0	4	Shipley 26	9537
26	28	A	Fleetwood T	D	0-0	0-0	5		2506
27	Feb 1	A	Bristol R	W	2-1	2-1	5	Allen 38, Walsh 45	7859
28	8	H	Bolton W	W	2-1	1-0	4	Bakayoko 3, Biamou 90	6623
29	11	H	Portsmouth	W	1-0	0-0	3	Godden 84	6983
30	15	A	Southend U	W	2-0	0-0	2	O'Hare 60, Biamou 79	7278
31	22	A	Rochdale	W	2-1	1-0	2	Rose 4, Godden 71	4356
32	25	H	Rotherham U	D	1-1	0-1	2	Godden 47	8990
33	Mar 1	H	Sunderland	W	1-0	1-0	1	Godden 2	10,055
34	7	A	Ipswich T	W	1-0	1-0	1	Godden 16	18,825
35	14	H	Shrewsbury T	Cancelled					
36	21	A	Lincoln C	Cancelled					
37	24	H	Wycombe W	Cancelled					
38	28	A	Accrington S	Cancelled					
39	Apr 4	H	Peterborough U	Cancelled					
40	10	A	Gillingham	Cancelled					
41	13	H	Oxford U	Cancelled					
42	18	A	Blackpool	Cancelled					
43	25	H	Burton Alb	Cancelled					
44	May 3	A	AFC Wimbledon	Cancelled					

Final League Position: 1 (on points-per-game basis)

GOALSCORERS

League (48): Godden 14 (3 pens), Shipley 5, Bakayoko 4, Biamou 4, Westbrooke 4 (1 pen), O'Hare 3, Walsh 3, Hiwula 2, Hyam 2, McCallum 2, Rose 2, Allen 1, Jobello 1, Kastaneer 1.
FA Cup (12): Biamou 4, Shipley 2, McCallum 1, O'Hare 1, Pask 1, Walsh 1, own goals 2.
Carabao Cup (4): Hiwula 2, Bakayoko 1, Godden 1.
Leasing.com Trophy (3): Biamou 3 (1 pen).

Marosi M 34	Dabo F 32	Rose M 30 + 1	McFadzean K 28 + 2	Mason B 10 + 1	Shipley J 24 + 7	Kelly L 25 + 2	Westbrooke Z 22 + 3	Hiwula J 14 + 1	Jobello W 10	Bakayoko A 11 + 12	Eccles J 1 + 2	Biamou M 5 + 13	Godden M 22 + 4	Bapaga W — + 1	Kastaneer G 1 + 9	McCallum S 25 + 1	Hyam D 28 + 1	O'Hare C 18 + 11	Wakefield C — + 1	Watson T 1 + 2	Walsh L 25 + 1	Drysdale D 1	Allen J 7 + 4	Pask J — + 2	Giles R — + 1	Match No.
1	2	3	4	5	6^1	7	8	9	10	11	12															1
1	2	4	3	5	8	7	6^2	11^1	9	10^3		12	13	14												2
1	2	4	3	5	6^3	7	8	11	9^2	12	14		10^1		13											3
1	2■	4	3	5	8	7	6^3	11^2	9^1	14			10		13■	12										4
1		3		5	8	7	6^1	11	9^3	13			10^2			2	4	12	14							5
1	2	3	14		8	7	6	11^3	9^2				10			5^1	4	12		13						6
1	2	4^1	3		8		6^3	11	9^2				10		14	5	13	12			7					7
1	2		3		8		6^1	11	9^2				10		13	5	4	12			7					8
1	2		3	5	8			11^2	9^1			13	10		12		4	6			7					9
1	2		3	5	8			11^2	9^1	13			10		12		4	6			7					10
1	2	14	3■	5	8	13		11^1		12			10		9^2		4	6			7^3					11
1	2	3		13	8		6^3	11^2		14			10		12	5^1	4	9			7					12
1	2	3			8		6	11^2		10^1		12			13	5	4	9			7					13
1	2	3	12		8^3	14	6	9^2		10		13				5	4	11			7^1					14
1	5^1	2	3		13	7	6			11^2		10				9	4	8		12						15
1		2	3		12	7	6^1			10		11■				9	4	8		5^2	13					16
1	5	2		8	11		9			10	6^1						3	12			7	4				17
1	5	2	3	8	10^1	6	9^3	12		11^2							4	13			7		14			18
1	2	3	4		12	8	9^3			11		10^1	14			6	5^2	7					13			19
1	2	4	3		10^3	7				13		11^2	12		14	5		8^1			6		9			20
1	5	2	3		10^1	6	9					12	11			8	4				7					21
1	5	2	3		10^3	7	9^2			12			11^1			8	4	13			6		14			22
1	5	2	3		10^1	7	9^2			12			11			8	4	13			6					23
1	2	3	4		10^2	9	7^1					13	11			6	5	12			8					24
1	5	2	3		10^3	7	13					14	11^1			8	4	9^2			6		12			25
1	5	2	3		10^1	6	9^2					13	11			8	4	12			7					26
1	5	2	3		12	6	14					13	11^3			9	4	10^1			8		7^2			27
1	5	2	3^2			6				11^1		12				9	4	10			8		7	13		28
1	5	2	3			6				11^2		12	13			8	4	10			7		9^1			29
1	5^3	2	3		10^2	6	9^1					13	11			8	4	12			7			14		30
1	5	2	3		12	6						13	11^1			8	4	10			7		9^2			31
1	5	2	3			6				12		9^1	11			8^2	4	10			7				13	32
1	5	2	3		13	6				12			11^2			8	4	10			7		9^1			33
1	5	2	3		12	6	14			13			11^3			8	4	10^2			7		9^1			34
																										35
																										36
																										37
																										38
																										39
																										40
																										41
																										42
																										43
																										44

FA Cup

First Round	Colchester U	(a)	2-0
Second Round	Ipswich T	(h)	1-1
Replay	Ipswich T	(a)	2-1
Third Round	Bristol R	(a)	2-2
Replay	Bristol R	(h)	3-0
Fourth Round	Birmingham C	(h)	0-0
Replay	Birmingham C	(a)	2-2

(aet; Birmingham C won 4-1 on penalties.)

Carabao Cup

First Round	Exeter C	(h)	4-1
Second Round	Watford	(a)	0-3

Leasing.com Trophy

Group D (S)	Walsall	(h)	0-0
(Coventry C won 5-4 on penalties)			
Group D (S)	Forest Green R	(a)	0-0
(Forest Green R won 8-7 on penalties)			
Group D (S)	Southampton U21	(h)	3-2
Second Round (S)	Milton Keynes D	(a)	0-2

CRAWLEY TOWN

FOUNDATION

Formed in 1896, Crawley Town initially entered the West Sussex League before switching to the mid-Sussex League in 1901, winning the Second Division in its second season. The club remained at such level until 1951 when it became members of the Sussex County League and five years later moved to the Metropolitan League while remaining as an amateur club. It was not until 1962 that the club turned semi-professional and a year later, joined the Southern League. Many honours came the club's way, but the most successful run was achieved in 2010–11 when they reached the fifith round of the FA Cup and played before a crowd of 74,778 spectators at Old Trafford against Manchester United. Crawley Town spent 48 years at the Town Mead ground before a new site was occupied at Broadfield in 1997, ideally suited to access from the neighbouring motorway. History was also made on 9 April when the team won promotion to the Football League after beating Tamworth 3-0 to stretch their unbeaten League record to 26 games. They finished the season with a Conference record points total of 105 and at the same time, established another milestone for the longest unbeaten run, having extended it to 30 matches by the end of the season.

The People's Pension Stadium, Winfield Way, Crawley, West Sussex RH11 9RX.

Telephone: (01293) 410 000.

Ticket Office: (01293) 410 005.

Website: www.crawleytownfc.com

Email: feedback@crawleytownfc.com

Ground Capacity: 5,907.

Record Attendance: 5,880 v Reading, FA Cup 3rd rd, 5 January 2013.

Pitch Measurements: 103.5m × 66m (113yd × 72yd).

Chairman: Ziya Eren.

Managing Director: Selim Gaygusuz.

Head Coach: John Yems.

Assistant Head Coaches: Lee Bradbury, Edu Rubio.

Colours: Red shirts with white trim, red shorts with white trim, red socks with white trim.

Year Formed: 1896. ***Turned Professional:*** 1962.

Club Nickname: 'The Red Devils'.

Grounds: Up to 1997, Town Mead; 1997 Broadfield Stadium (renamed Checkatrade.com Stadium 2013; The People's Pension Stadium 2018).

HONOURS

League Champions: Conference – 2010–11.
FL 2 – (3rd) 2011–12 *(promoted)*.

FA Cup: 5th rd – 2011, 2012.

League Cup: 3rd rd – 2013.

FOOTBALL YEARBOOK FACT FILE

Crawley Town were elected to the Metropolitan League in 1956 after finishing as runners-up in the Second Division of the Sussex County League. Town, who were then an amateur club, found it tough going in their new league and lost their opening four matches before getting their first victory when they defeated West Ham United 'A' team 2-1 at Town Mead.

First Football League Game: 6 August 2011, FL 2 v Port Vale (a) D 2-2 – Shearer; Hunt, Howell, Bulman, McFadzean (1), Dempster (Thomas), Simpson, Torres, Tubbs (Neilson), Barnett (1) (Wassmer), Smith.

Record League Victory: 5–1 v Barnsley, FL 1, 14 February 2015 – Price; Dickson, Bradley (1), Ward, Fowler (Smith); Young, Elliott (1), Edwards, Wordsworth (Morgan), Pogba (Tomlin); McLeod (3).

Record League Defeat: 6-0 v Morecambe, FL 2, 10 September 2011.

Most League Points (3 for a win): 84, FL 2, 2011–12.

Most League Goals: 76, FL 2, 2011–12.

Highest League Scorer in Season: James Collins, 20, FL 2, 2016–17.

Most League Goals in Total Aggregate: Billy Clarke, 20, 2011–14; Matt Tubbs, 20, 2011–12, 2013–14; James Collins, 20, 2016–17.

Most League Goals in One Match: 3, Izale McLeod v Barnsley, FL 1, 14 February 2015; 3, Jimmy Smith v Colchester U, FL 2, 14 February 2017.

Most Capped Player: Dean Morgan, 1 (3), Montserrat.

Most League Appearances: Dannie Bulman, 218, 2006–09; 2010–14; 2017–20.

Youngest League Player: Brian Galach, 17 years 353 days v Tranmere R, 4 May 2019.

Record Transfer Fee Received: £1,100,000 from Peterborough U for Tyrone Barnett, July 2012.

Record Transfer Fee Paid: £220,000 to York C for Richard Brodie, August 2010.

Football League Record: 2011 Promoted from Conference Premier; 2011–12 FL 2; 2012–15 FL 1; 2015– FL 2.

MANAGERS

John Maggs 1978–90
Brian Sparrow 1990–92
Steve Wicks 1992–93
Ted Shepherd 1993–95
Colin Pates 1995–96
Billy Smith 1997–99
Cliff Cant 1999–2000
Billy Smith 2000–03
Francis Vines 2003–05
John Hollins 2005–06
David Woozley, Ben Judge and John Yems 2006–07
Steve Evans 2007–12
Sean O'Driscoll 2012
Richie Barker 2012–13
John Gregory 2013–14
Dean Saunders 2014–15
Mark Yates 2015–16
Dermot Drummy 2016–17
Harry Kewell 2017–18
Gabriele Cioffi 2018–19
John Yems December 2019–

LATEST SEQUENCES

Longest Sequence of League Wins: 7, 17.9.2011 – 25.10.2011.

Longest Sequence of League Defeats: 8, 28.3.2016 – 7.5.2016.

Longest Sequence of League Draws: 5, 25.10.2014 – 29.11.2014.

Longest Sequence of Unbeaten League Matches: 13, 17.9.2011 – 17.12.2011.

Longest Sequence Without a League Win: 13, 25.10.2014 – 27.1.2015.

Successive Scoring Runs: 21 from 6.4.2019.

Successive Non-scoring Runs: 4 from 14.10.2017.

TEN YEAR LEAGUE RECORD

		P	*W*	*D*	*L*	*F*	*A*	*Pts*	*Pos*
2010-11	Conf P	46	31	12	3	93	50	105	1
2011-12	FL 2	46	23	15	8	76	54	84	3
2012-13	FL 1	46	18	14	14	59	58	68	10
2013-14	FL 1	46	14	15	17	48	54	57	14
2014-15	FL 1	46	13	11	22	53	79	50	22
2015-16	FL 2	46	13	8	25	45	78	47	20
2016-17	FL 2	46	13	12	21	53	71	51	19
2017-18	FL 2	46	16	11	19	58	66	59	14
2018-19	FL 2	46	15	8	23	51	68	53	19
2019-20	FL 2	37	11	15	11	51	47	48	13§

§Decided on points-per-game (1.30)

DID YOU KNOW ?

Crawley Town had one of their most successful pre-war seasons in 1927–28. The team led the West Sussex League table in late April but lost 5-0 to their nearest rivals and finished the season as runners-up. They went one better in the Sussex Intermediate Cup, winning the trophy by defeating Hailsham 6-1 in the final.

CRAWLEY TOWN – SKY BET LEAGUE TWO 2019–20 LEAGUE RECORD

Match No.	Date	Venue	Opponents	Result	H/T Score	Lg Pos.	Goalscorers	Attendance
1	Aug 3	A	Carlisle U	L 1-2	1-2	16	Lubula 16	4833
2	10	H	Salford C	W 2-0	1-0	9	Lubula (pen) 36, Ferguson 55	2400
3	17	A	Scunthorpe U	D 2-2	1-1	12	Lubula 16, Ferguson 74	3186
4	20	H	Crewe Alex	L 1-2	1-1	18	Lubula 16	2006
5	24	A	Leyton Orient	W 3-2	1-1	12	Ferguson 30, Palmer 2 69, 71	4905
6	31	H	Cheltenham T	W 1-0	0-0	8	Palmer 90	2095
7	Sept 7	A	Macclesfield T	D 1-1	0-1	11	Lubula 73	1788
8	14	H	Mansfield T	W 1-0	0-0	8	Lubula 53	2068
9	17	H	Plymouth Arg	D 2-2	1-0	7	Grego-Cox 9, Palmer (pen) 85	2501
10	21	A	Northampton T	D 2-2	0-1	8	Nathaniel-George 70, Martin (og) 90	5121
11	28	H	Walsall	L 2-3	1-3	10	Nathaniel-George (pen) 42, Payne 90	2275
12	Oct 5	A	Forest Green R	L 1-3	0-1	13	Enigbokan-Bloomfield 58	2136
13	12	H	Colchester U	W 2-1	0-1	9	Grego-Cox 55, Enigbokan-Bloomfield 80	2636
14	19	A	Bradford C	L 1-2	0-1	13	Grego-Cox 81	13,813
15	22	A	Newport Co	D 1-1	1-0	13	Nathaniel-George (pen) 35	3119
16	26	H	Swindon T	L 0-4	0-2	17		2601
17	Nov 2	A	Cambridge U	L 1-2	0-0	17	Lubula 79	3538
18	16	H	Morecambe	D 1-1	1-0	16	Lubula (pen) 44	2079
19	23	H	Exeter C	L 0-1	0-0	17		2170
20	Dec 7	A	Stevenage	D 0-0	0-0	16		2780
21	14	H	Port Vale	D 0-0	0-0	16		1944
22	21	A	Oldham Ath	L 1-2	1-0	19	Young 17	2737
23	26	H	Northampton T	W 4-0	1-0	16	Ferguson 27, Lubula 62, Palmer 80, Enigbokan-Bloomfield 84	2190
24	29	A	Grimsby T	D 1-1	1-1	15	Nadesan 37	3612
25	Jan 1	A	Colchester U	D 1-1	0-0	16	Palmer 72	3729
26	4	H	Forest Green R	D 1-1	1-0	16	Lubula 45	2082
27	11	H	Bradford C	W 2-1	2-0	13	Palmer 2 21, 40	2361
28	18	A	Walsall	L 1-2	1-0	15	Camara 27	4011
29	25	H	Grimsby T	W 3-2	1-2	14	Palmer 2 16, 70, Nadesan 77	2480
30	28	A	Plymouth Arg	D 2-2	1-1	13	Palmer 2 27, 90	9184
31	Feb 1	H	Scunthorpe U	W 3-1	3-0	13	Tunnicliffe 6, Grego-Cox 24, Palmer 45	2130
32	8	A	Salford C	D 0-0	0-0	12		2385
33	11	A	Crewe Alex	L 1-2	0-0	14	Ferguson (pen) 84	3314
34	15	H	Carlisle U	D 0-0	0-0	14		2114
35	22	H	Stevenage	W 2-0	1-0	12	Lubula 21, Nadesan 90	2232
36	29	A	Exeter C	D 1-1	1-0	12	Nadesan 34	5404
37	Mar 7	H	Oldham Ath	W 3-0	1-0	12	German 36, Nadesan 70, Lubula (pen) 76	2037
38	14	A	Port Vale	Cancelled				
39	17	H	Newport Co	Cancelled				
40	21	A	Swindon T	Cancelled				
41	28	H	Cambridge U	Cancelled				
42	Apr 4	A	Morecambe	Cancelled				
43	10	H	Leyton Orient	Cancelled				
44	13	A	Cheltenham T	Cancelled				
45	18	H	Macclesfield T	Cancelled				
46	25	A	Mansfield T	Cancelled				

Final League Position: 13 (on points-per-game basis)

GOALSCORERS

League (51): Palmer 13 (1 pen), Lubula 12 (3 pens), Ferguson 5 (1 pen), Nadesan 5, Grego-Cox 4, Enigbokan-Bloomfield 3, Nathaniel-George 3 (2 pens), Camara 1, German 1, Payne 1, Tunnicliffe 1, Young 1, own goal 1.
FA Cup (5): Grego-Cox 2, Nadesan 1, Nathaniel-George 1, Palmer 1.
Carabao Cup (6): Bulman 1, Dallison 1, Ferguson 1, Lubala 1, Morais 1, Nadesan 1.
Leasing.com Trophy (2): Enigbokan-Bloomfield 1, Nathaniel-George 1.

Morris G 37	Young L 13 + 2	Tunnicliffe J 37	Dallison T 20 + 1	Sesay D 18 + 7	Ferguson N 29 + 2	Bulman D 28 + 1	Camara P 23 + 6	Morais F 2 + 3	Lubula B 32 + 2	Palmer O 22 + 6	Grego-Cox R 24 + 4	Enigbokan-Bloomfield M 10 + 11	Nathaniel-George A 7 + 9	Doherty J 30 + 1	Francomb G 10 + 5	Dacres-Cogley J 15 + 1	Nadesan A 22 + 3	Payne J 1 + 1	Sendles-White J 12 + 2	Allarakhia T 7 + 12	Van Velzen G — + 4	McNerney J 6	German R 1 + 7	Powell J — + 6	Adebowale E 1	*Match No.*
1	2■	3	4	5	6	7[3]	8	9	10[1]	11[2]	12	13	14													1
1		3	4	2	7[3]	6	9	13	10	12	8[2]	11[1]		5	14											2
1		3	4	5[1]	7	6	9[3]	14	10	12	8			13		2	11[2]									3
1		3	4	2[3]	13		7		10	11	12		8[2]	5		14	9[1]	6								4
1		3	4	12	7[1]	6	9	14	10	13	8			5		2[2]	11[3]									5
1		3	4	2	7[1]	6[3]		9	10	11	8[2]	14		5	12		13									6
1	13	3	4	2[2]	9[1]	6	7		10	11	8	12		5												7
1	13	4		2[3]	7[2]	6	9		10	11[1]	8	12		5					3	14						8
1		4		2	7[1]	6[3]	9[2]		10	13	8	11		5	12				3	14						9
1	2[3]	3	4	13	7[1]	12			10[2]	11	8	9	14	5	6											10
1	5	4	3	2	7[3]	6[2]	9		12		8	11	10[1]					13		14						11
1		3	4	2	8	6[2]	9[1]		10		7	11[3]	13	5						12	14					12
1	2	3	4		7		6		10		9[2]	11	12	5						8[1]	13					13
1	2	3	4	13	7		6[2]		10		9	11[1]	12	5[3]						8	14					14
1		3	4	2	8		12		9		10[2]	11	6[1]	5			13			7						15
1		3	4	2	8		7[1]			14	6	10	9[3]	5			11[2]			12	13					16
1	2	3	4		9	6	8		10		11[1]		7[2]	5			12			13						17
1	2	3	4	5	9[1]	6	8		10[3]	13	7	14	12				11[2]									18
1	2	3	4	5	8[1]		9		10	11			12		6		7									19
1	2	3			7	6			10	11	8	12		5			9[1]					4				20
1	2	3			8	7	13		6	10	11[1]	12	9[2]	5								4				21
1	2	3			8	7	13		9	10		12	6[2]	5						11[1]		4				22
1	2	3			8	7	9		6	10		12		5			11[1]					4				23
1	2	3		12	8	7[3]	9[1]		6[2]	10			13	5	14		11					4				24
1		3	4[2]	13	6	7[1]			9	10			14	8		5[3]	11		12			2				25
1		3	4		8[2]	7	6		9[1]	10		13		5		2	11[3]		14	12						26
1		4		13	8	7	6		9	10[1]				5		2	11[2]		3				12			27
1		3	12			7	6		10	11				5	13	2	9[2]		4	8[1]						28
1		3	4			8	6[2]		9	11[3]	12			5	7[1]	2	10			13			14			29
1		4				8			9[1]	10	12			5	7[3]	2	11		3	6[2]			13	14		30
1		3		12		8[2]			9	10	6[1]			5	7[3]	2	11		4	13				14		31
1		2		8		7				11	9[3]				6[2]	5	10		3	12			14	13	4[1]	32
1		4		5	14	8				11[1]	6[2]	12			7	2	10[3]		3	9			13			33
1		3			8[1]		9[2]		12	11	6			5	7	2	10		4	13						34
1		3			7[2]	8	14		9		6[1]	10[3]		5		2	11		4				12	13		35
1		4		9[3]		8	14		6		10[2]			5	7	2	11[1]		3				12	13		36
1		4		9[2]	7[3]		14		6					5	8	2	10		3	13			11[1]	12		37
																										38
																										39
																										40
																										41
																										42
																										43
																										44
																										45
																										46

FA Cup

First Round	Scunthorpe U	(h)	4-1
Second Round	Fleetwood T	(h)	1-2

Leasing.com Trophy

Group B (S)	Portsmouth	(a)	0-1
Group B (S)	Norwich C U21	(h)	1-2
Group B (S)	Oxford U	(h)	1-4

Carabao Cup

First Round	Walsall	(a)	3-2
Second Round	Norwich C	(h)	1-0
Third Round	Stoke C	(h)	1-1
(Crawley T won 5-3 on penalties)			
Fourth Round	Colchester U	(h)	1-3

CREWE ALEXANDRA

FOUNDATION

The first match played at Crewe was on 1 December 1877 against Basford, the leading North Staffordshire team of that time. During the club's history they have also played in a number of other leagues including the Football Alliance, Football Combination, Lancashire League, Manchester League, Central League and Lancashire Combination. Two former players, Aaron Scragg in 1899 and Jackie Pearson in 1911, had the distinction of refereeing FA Cup finals. Pearson was also capped for England against Ireland in 1892.

The Alexandra Stadium, Gresty Road, Crewe, Cheshire CW2 6EB.

Telephone: (01270) 213 014.

Ticket Office: (01270) 252 610.

Website: www.crewealex.net

Email: info@crewealex.net

Ground Capacity: 10,109.

Record Attendance: 20,000 v Tottenham H, FA Cup 4th rd, 30 January 1960.

Pitch Measurements: 100.5m × 67m (110yd × 73.5yd).

Chairman: John Bowler MBE.

Manager: David Artell.

Assistant Manager: Kenny Lunt.

Colours: Red shirts with black trim, white shorts, red socks.

Year Formed: 1877. ***Turned Professional:*** 1893. ***Club Nickname:*** 'The Railwaymen'.

Ground: 1898, Gresty Road.

First Football League Game: 3 September 1892, Division 2, v Burton Swifts (a) L 1–7 – Hickton; Moore, Cope; Linnell, Johnson, Osborne; Bennett, Pearson (1), Bailey, Barnett, Roberts.

Record League Victory: 8–0 v Rotherham U, Division 3 (N), 1 October 1932 – Foster; Pringle, Dawson; Ward, Keenor (1), Turner (1); Gillespie, Swindells (1), McConnell (2), Deacon (2), Weale (1).

Record Cup Victory: 8–0 v Hartlepool U, Auto Windscreens Shield 1st rd, 17 October 1995 – Gayle; Collins (1), Booty, Westwood (Unsworth), Macauley (1), Whalley (1), Garvey (1), Murphy (1), Savage (1) (Rivers (1p)), Lennon, Edwards, (1 og). 8–0 v Doncaster R, LDV Vans Trophy 3rd rd, 10 November 2002 – Bankole; Wright, Walker, Foster, Tierney; Lunt (1), Brammer, Sorvel, Vaughan (1) (Bell); Ashton (3) (Miles), Jack (2) (Jones (1)).

Record Defeat: 2–13 v Tottenham H, FA Cup 4th rd replay, 3 February 1960.

HONOURS

League: *Runners-up:* Second Division – 2002–03; FL 2 – 2019–20.

FA Cup: semi-final – 1888.

League Cup: never past 3rd rd.

League Trophy Winners: 2013.

Welsh Cup Winners: 1936, 1937.

FOOTBALL YEARBOOK FACT FILE

After Crewe Alexandra lost their FA Cup fourth round replay to Swifts in December 1887 they successfully protested that the goal posts were the wrong height. The game was ordered to be replayed on a neutral ground, which Alex won 2-1. They went on to knock out both Derby County and Middlesbrough to reach the semi-finals of the competition for the only time in their history.

Most League Points (2 for a win): 59, Division 4, 1962–63.

Most League Points (3 for a win): 86, Division 2, 2002–03.

Most League Goals: 95, Division 3 (N), 1931–32.

Highest League Scorer in Season: Terry Harkin, 35, Division 4, 1964–65.

Most League Goals in Total Aggregate: Bert Swindells, 126, 1928–37.

Most League Goals in One Match: 5, Tony Naylor v Colchester U, Division 3, 24 April 1993.

Most Capped Player: Clayton Ince, 38 (79), Trinidad & Tobago.

Most League Appearances: Tommy Lowry, 436, 1966–78.

Youngest League Player: Steve Walters, 16 years 119 days v Peterborough U, 6 May 1988.

Record Transfer Fee Received: £3,000,000 (rising to £6,000,000) from Manchester U for Nick Powell, June 2012.

Record Transfer Fee Paid: £650,000 to Torquay U for Rodney Jack, July 1998.

Football League Record: 1892 Original Member of Division 2; 1896 Failed re-election; 1921 Re-entered Division (N); 1958–63 Division 4; 1963–64 Division 3; 1964–68 Division 4; 1968–69 Division 3; 1969–89 Division 4; 1989–91 Division 3; 1991–92 Division 4; 1992–94 Division 3; 1994–97 Division 2; 1997–2002 Division 1; 2002–03 Division 2; 2003–04 Division 1; 2004–06 FL C; 2006–09 FL 1; 2009–12 FL 2; 2012–16 FL 1; 2016–20 FL 2; 2020– FL 1.

LATEST SEQUENCES

Longest Sequence of League Wins: 7, 30.4.1994 – 3.9.1994.

Longest Sequence of League Defeats: 10, 16.4.1979 – 22.8.1979.

Longest Sequence of League Draws: 5, 18.9.2010 – 9.10.2010.

Longest Sequence of Unbeaten League Matches: 17, 25.3.1995 – 16.9.1995.

Longest Sequence Without a League Win: 30, 22.9.1956 – 6.4.1957.

Successive Scoring Runs: 26 from 7.4.1934.

Successive Non-scoring Runs: 9 from 6.11.1974.

MANAGERS

W. C. McNeill 1892–94 (*Secretary-Manager*)
J. G. Hall 1895–96 (*Secretary-Manager*)
R. Roberts (*1st team Secretary-Manager*) 1897
J. B. Blomerley 1898–1911 (*Secretary-Manager, continued as Hon. Secretary to 1925*)
Tom Bailey (*Secretary only*) 1925–38
George Lillycrop (*Trainer*) 1938–44
Frank Hill 1944–48
Arthur Turner 1948–51
Harry Catterick 1951–53
Ralph Ward 1953–55
Maurice Lindley 1956–57
Willie Cook 1957–58
Harry Ware 1958–60
Jimmy McGuigan 1960–64
Ernie Tagg 1964–71 (*continued as Secretary to 1972*)
Dennis Viollet 1971
Jimmy Melia 1972–74
Ernie Tagg 1974
Harry Gregg 1975–78
Warwick Rimmer 1978–79
Tony Waddington 1979–81
Arfon Griffiths 1981–82
Peter Morris 1982–83
Dario Gradi 1983–2007
Steve Holland 2007–08
Gudjon Thordarson 2008–09
Dario Gradi 2009–11
Steve Davis 2011–17
David Artell January 2017–

TEN YEAR LEAGUE RECORD

		P	W	D	L	F	A	Pts	Pos
2010-11	FL 2	46	18	11	17	87	65	65	10
2011-12	FL 2	46	20	12	14	67	59	72	7
2012-13	FL 1	46	18	10	18	54	62	64	13
2013-14	FL 1	46	13	12	21	54	80	51	19
2014-15	FL 1	46	14	10	22	43	75	52	20
2015-16	FL 1	46	7	13	26	46	83	34	24
2016-17	FL 2	46	14	13	19	58	67	55	17
2017-18	FL 2	46	17	5	24	62	75	56	15
2018-19	FL 2	46	19	8	19	60	59	65	12
2019-20	FL 2	37	20	9	8	67	43	69	2§

§Decided on points-per-game (1.86)

DID YOU KNOW ?

Crewe's Gresty Road ground staged its first game under floodlights in September 1958 when Alex defeated Workington 2-0 in a Division Three North fixture watched by an attendance of 8,980. It was the club's first home win of the season. The lights were bought from Coventry City and the £3,000 cost was funded by the club's Supporters' Association.

CREWE ALEXANDRA – SKY BET LEAGUE TWO 2019–20 LEAGUE RECORD

Match No.	Date	Venue	Opponents	Result	H/T Score	Lg Pos.	Goalscorers	Attendance
1	Aug 3	H	Plymouth Arg	L 0-3	0-2	24		5273
2	10	A	Oldham Ath	W 2-1	2-1	12	Porter 2 (1 pen) 21, 41 (p)	3884
3	17	H	Walsall	W 1-0	0-0	6	Nolan 61	4629
4	20	A	Crawley T	W 2-1	1-1	1	Wintle 29, Green 55	2006
5	24	A	Newport Co	L 0-1	0-0	6		3712
6	31	H	Bradford C	W 2-1	1-1	3	Kirk 42, Lowery 60	4459
7	Sept 7	A	Grimsby T	W 2-0	0-0	3	Lowery 46, Kirk 90	4679
8	14	H	Cambridge U	L 2-3	0-1	5	Nolan 63, Anene 67	3568
9	17	A	Leyton Orient	W 2-1	1-1	2	Nolan 32, Jones 90	4289
10	21	H	Salford C	W 4-1	0-1	2	Porter 50, Lowery 2 57, 82, Pickering 62	4714
11	28	A	Cheltenham T	D 1-1	1-1	2	Porter 45	3549
12	Oct 5	H	Exeter C	D 1-1	0-1	4	Anene 76	5131
13	12	A	Carlisle U	W 4-2	2-0	1	Hunt 7, Powell 27, Porter 78, Jones, G (og) 85	4521
14	19	H	Swindon T	W 3-1	0-1	1	Porter 2 59, 90, Kirk 90	4792
15	22	H	Colchester U	D 0-0	0-0	1		3659
16	Nov 2	H	Port Vale	L 0-1	0-0	4		7705
17	16	A	Northampton T	L 1-4	1-3	4	Porter 37	5236
18	23	H	Morecambe	W 5-0	3-0	3	Finney 2 22, 90, Lowery 31, Kirk 38, Wintle 58	4149
19	26	A	Forest Green R	D 0-0	0-0	3		2192
20	Dec 14	H	Mansfield T	D 1-1	1-1	4	Anene 8	4060
21	21	A	Stevenage	W 5-1	2-0	3	Anene 2 29, 65, Finney 32, Powell 57, Cuthbert (og) 70	2993
22	26	A	Salford C	L 1-3	0-2	3	Pickering 82	3031
23	29	H	Scunthorpe U	W 3-1	2-0	3	Powell 2 20, 83, Green 40	4578
24	Jan 1	H	Carlisle U	W 4-1	4-0	3	Ainley 17, Powell 2 26, 31, Anene 34	4316
25	11	A	Swindon T	L 1-3	0-1	4	Anene 61	7601
26	18	H	Cheltenham T	W 1-0	0-0	3	Ng 69	4478
27	21	A	Macclesfield T	D 1-1	0-1	3	Ainley 90	2435
28	25	A	Scunthorpe U	D 2-2	0-1	4	Powell 46, Finney 69	3139
29	28	H	Leyton Orient	W 2-0	1-0	3	Kirk 2, Powell 88	3249
30	Feb 1	A	Walsall	W 2-1	0-1	2	Powell 50, Finney 67	4610
31	8	H	Oldham Ath	W 2-1	0-0	2	Jones 55, Kirk 90	5271
32	11	H	Crawley T	W 2-1	0-0	2	Porter 2 (1 pen) 72 (p), 90	3314
33	15	A	Plymouth Arg	L 1-2	0-0	3	Pickering 52	11,567
34	22	H	Macclesfield T	W 2-0	2-0	2	Porter (pen) 11, Walker 35	5413
35	29	A	Morecambe	D 1-1	0-0	2	Ng 47	2872
36	Mar 3	A	Exeter C	D 1-1	0-1	2	Nottingham 61	4221
37	7	H	Stevenage	W 3-1	1-0	1	Porter 15, Kirk 63, Wintle 67	4263
38	14	A	Mansfield T	Cancelled				
39	17	A	Colchester U	Cancelled				
40	21	H	Forest Green R	Cancelled				
41	28	A	Port Vale	Cancelled				
42	Apr 4	H	Northampton T	Cancelled				
43	10	H	Newport Co	Cancelled				
44	13	A	Bradford C	Cancelled				
45	18	H	Grimsby T	Cancelled				
46	25	A	Cambridge U	Cancelled				

Final League Position: 2 (on points-per-game basis)

GOALSCORERS

League (67): Porter 12 (3 pens), Powell 9, Anene 7, Kirk 7, Finney 5, Lowery 5, Nolan 3, Pickering 3, Wintle 3, Ainley 2, Green 2, Jones 2, Ng 2, Hunt 1, Nottingham 1, Walker 1, own goals 2.
FA Cup (7): Anene 2, Dale 1, Green 1, Kirk 1, Porter 1 (1 pen), own goal 1.
Carabao Cup (3): Kirk 1, Porter 1, Wintle 1.
Leasing.com Trophy (4): Ainley 1, Dale 1, Finney 1, Green 1.

Jaaskelainen W 35	Ng P 36	Wintle R 37	Nolan E 19	Pickering H 35	Lowery T 28 + 1	Jones J 13 + 10	Green P 22 + 4	Powell D 24 + 6	Porter C 25 + 1	Kirk C 35 + 1	Ainley C 6 + 19	Finney O 11 + 7	Lancashire O 7 + 2	Dale O 7 + 20	Hunt N 22 + 3	Anene C 12 + 16	Richards D 2	Mbulu C 3 + 1	Adebisi R 1 + 1	Johnson T — + 1	Nottingham M 12	Offord L 9	Walker S 6	*Match No.*
1	2	3	4	5	6	7[1]	8[2]	9	10	11	12	13												1
1	2	7	4	5	6[3]	13	8	9[2]	10	11[1]	14		3	12										2
1	2	6	4	5	8		7	9[1]	10	11[2]			3■	12	13									3
1	2	7	4	5[1]	8		6	9[2]	10	11		13		12	3									4
1	2	7	4		6		8	9	10	11			3		5									5
1	2	7	4	5	8		6	9[2]	10[1]	11			3	12		13								6
	2	7	4	5	8		6	9	10[1]	11[2]			3		13	12	1							7
1	2	7	4	5	8		6■	9[1]	10[2]	11[3]	14		3	12		13								8
1	2	7	4	5	8	6		9[3]	10[2]	11[1]	13			12	3	14								9
1	2	7	4	5	8	6		12	10[3]	11[1]	14			9[2]	3	13								10
1	2■	7	4	5	8	6		9[3]	10[1]	11[2]			13	12	3	14								11
1		7	4	5	8	6[2]	14	12	10[1]	11			3	9[3]	2	13								12
	2	7	4	5	8	12	6[2]	9[1]	10	11				13	3		1							13
1	2	7	4	5	8	13	6[1]		10	11	14		12	9[2]	3[3]									14
1	2	7	4	5	8	12	6[2]		10[3]	11	13			9[1]	3	14								15
1	2	7	4	5	8[2]	14	6[3]		10	11	9[1]			12	3	13								16
1	2	7		5	8		6[3]	12	10	11[2]	13			9[1]	3	14		4						17
1	2	6		5	8[2]	12			10[3]	11	14	7		9[1]	3	13		4						18
1	2	7	4	5	8[2]	14	6	13	10	11[1]				9	3[3]			12						19
1	2	6	4	5	8[2]	12		9[1]		11	13	7[3]		14	3	10								20
1	2	7	4	5	6[1]		13	9[2]		11	12	8[3]		14	3	10								21
1	2	6		5	8	12		9		11[1]	14	7[2]		13	4	10		3[3]						22
1	2	3		5[1]	8		7	9		11	6[2]	13			4	10			12					23
1	2	3			8		7	9		11[1]	6[2]	13		12	4	10			5					24
1	2	3		5	8[3]		7	9		11	6[2]	14		13	4[1]	10				12				25
1	2	7		5	6		8	9		11[1]				12	4	10					3			26
1	2	7		5	6		8[2]	9[3]		11[1]	14	12		13	4	10					3			27
1	2	7		5	6		12	9			11[1]	8			4	10					3			28
1	2	8		5	12	13	7[3]	9		11	14	6[1]				10					3	4[2]		29
1	2	7		5		6		9		11	12	8[1]				10					3	4		30
1	2	8		5		7			12	11	14	6[2]		13		10[1]					3	4	9[3]	31
1	2	7		5		8			10	11	12	6[2]		13							3	4	9[1]	32
1	2	8		5		7	6[3]		10	11[2]	13			12		14					3	4	9[1]	33
1	2	6		5		7		14	10[3]	11[2]	13	8[1]				12					3	4	9	34
1	2	7		5		6	13	14	10[2]	11[3]		8[1]				12					3	4	9	35
1	2	8		5		7	6	11	10[1]	13					14	12					3[2]	4	9[3]	36
1	2	6		5		8[1]		9	10[3]	11[2]	7	13		12		14					3	4		37
																								38
																								39
																								40
																								41
																								42
																								43
																								44
																								45
																								46

FA Cup

First Round	Accrington S	(a)	2-0
Second Round	Eastleigh	(a)	1-1
Replay	Eastleigh	(h)	3-1
Third Round	Barnsley	(h)	1-3

Carabao Cup

First Round	Middlesbrough	(a)	2-2

(Crewe Alex won 4-2 on penalties)

Second Round	Aston Villa	(h)	1-6

Leasing.com Trophy

Group E (N)	Burton Alb	(h)	1-3
Group E (N)	Mansfield T	(a)	1-1

(Crewe Alex won 4-3 on penalties)

Group E (N)	Everton U21	(h)	2-2

(Crewe Alex won 5-4 on penalties)

CRYSTAL PALACE

FOUNDATION

There was a Crystal Palace club as early as 1861 but the present organisation was born in 1905 after the formation of a club by the company that controlled the Crystal Palace (building) had been rejected by the FA, who did not like the idea of the Cup Final hosts running their own club. A separate company had to be formed and they had their home on the old Cup Final ground until 1915.

Selhurst Park Stadium, Whitehorse Lane, London SE25 6PU.

Telephone: (020) 8768 6000.

Ticket Office: (0871) 200 0071.

Website: www.cpfc.co.uk

Email: info@cpfc.co.uk

Ground Capacity: 25,486.

Record Attendance: 51,482 v Burnley, Division 2, 11 May 1979 (at Selhurst Park).

Pitch Measurements: 101m × 68m (110.5yd × 74.5yd).

Chairman: Steve Parish.

Chief Executive: Phil Alexander.

Manager: Roy Hodgson.

Assistant Manager: Ray Lewington.

Colours: Red and blue striped shirts, blue shorts, blue socks with red trim.

Year Formed: 1905.

Turned Professional: 1905.

Club Nickname: 'The Eagles'.

Grounds: 1905, Crystal Palace; 1915, Herne Hill; 1918, The Nest; 1924, Selhurst Park.

First Football League Game: 28 August 1920, Division 3, v Merthyr T (a) L 1–2 – Alderson; Little, Rhodes; McCracken, Jones, Feebury; Bateman, Conner, Smith, Milligan (1), Whibley.

Record League Victory: 9–0 v Barrow, Division 4, 10 October 1959 – Rouse; Long, Noakes; Truett, Evans, McNichol; Gavin (1), Summersby (4 incl. 1p), Sexton, Byrne (2), Colfar (2).

Record Cup Victory: 8–0 v Southend U, Rumbelows League Cup 2nd rd (1st leg), 25 September 1990 – Martyn; Humphrey (Thompson (1)), Shaw, Pardew, Young, Thorn, McGoldrick, Thomas, Bright (3), Wright (3), Barber (Hodges (1)).

Record Defeat: 0–9 v Burnley, FA Cup 2nd rd replay, 10 February 1909; 0–9 v Liverpool, Division 1, 12 September 1990.

HONOURS

League Champions: First Division – 1993–94; Division 2 – 1978–79; Division 3S – 1920–21.
Runners-up: Division 2 – 1968–69; Division 3 – 1963–64; Division 3S – 1928–29, 1930–31, 1938–39; Division 4 – 1960–61.

FA Cup: ***Runners-up:*** 1990, 2016.

League Cup: semi-final – 1993, 1995, 2001, 2012.

Full Members' Cup Winners: 1991.

European Competition
Intertoto Cup: 1998.

FOOTBALL YEARBOOK FACT FILE

Crystal Palace played at The Nest, former home of Croydon Common, from 1918 until 1924. One of the terms of the lease was that the club could not host matches on either Christmas Day or Good Friday. It was not until 1931, by which time the club had moved to Selhurst Park, that Palace played a Football League match at home on 25 December.

Most League Points (2 for a win): 64, Division 4, 1960–61.

Most League Points (3 for a win): 90, Division 1, 1993–94.

Most League Goals: 110, Division 4, 1960–61.

Highest League Scorer in Season: Peter Simpson, 46, Division 3 (S), 1930–31.

Most League Goals in Total Aggregate: Peter Simpson, 153, 1930–36.

Most League Goals in One Match: 6, Peter Simpson v Exeter C, Division 3 (S), 4 October 1930.

Most Capped Player: Wayne Hennessey, 48 (89), Wales.

Most League Appearances: Jim Cannon, 571, 1973–88.

Youngest League Player: John Bostock, 15 years 287 days v Watford, 29 October 2007.

Record Transfer Fee Received: £45,000,000 from Manchester U for Aaron Wan-Bissaka, July 2019.

Record Transfer Fee Paid: £27,000,000 to Liverpool for Christian Benteke, August 2016.

Football League Record: 1920 Original Members of Division 3; 1921–25 Division 2; 1925–58 Division 3 (S); 1958–61 Division 4; 1961–64 Division 3; 1964–69 Division 2; 1969–73 Division 1; 1973–74 Division 2; 1974–77 Division 3; 1977–79 Division 2; 1979–81 Division 1; 1981–89 Division 2; 1989–92 Division 1; 1992–93 Premier League; 1993–94 Division 1; 1994–95 Premier League; 1995–97 Division 1; 1997–98 Premier League; 1998–2004 Division 1; 2004–05 Premier League; 2005–13 FL C; 2013– Premier League.

LATEST SEQUENCES

Longest Sequence of League Wins: 8, 21.5.2017 – 30.9.2017.

Longest Sequence of League Defeats: 8, 10.1.1998 – 14.3.1998.

Longest Sequence of League Draws: 5, 21.9.2002 – 19.10.2002.

Longest Sequence of Unbeaten League Matches: 18, 22.2.1969 – 13.8.1969.

Longest Sequence Without a League Win: 20, 3.3.1962 – 8.9.1962.

Successive Scoring Runs: 24 from 27.4.1929.

Successive Non-scoring Runs: 9 from 19.11.1994.

MANAGERS

John T. Robson 1905–07
Edmund Goodman 1907–25 (*Secretary 1905–33*)
Alex Maley 1925–27
Fred Mavin 1927–30
Jack Tresadern 1930–35
Tom Bromilow 1935–36
R. S. Moyes 1936
Tom Bromilow 1936–39
George Irwin 1939–47
Jack Butler 1947–49
Ronnie Rooke 1949–50
Charlie Slade and Fred Dawes (*Joint Managers*) 1950–51
Laurie Scott 1951–54
Cyril Spiers 1954–58
George Smith 1958–60
Arthur Rowe 1960–62
Dick Graham 1962–66
Bert Head 1966–72 (*continued as General Manager to 1973*)
Malcolm Allison 1973–76
Terry Venables 1976–80
Ernie Walley 1980
Malcolm Allison 1980–81
Dario Gradi 1981
Steve Kember 1981–82
Alan Mullery 1982–84
Steve Coppell 1984–93
Alan Smith 1993–95
Steve Coppell (*Technical Director*) 1995–96
Dave Bassett 1996–97
Steve Coppell 1997–98
Attilio Lombardo 1998
Terry Venables (*Head Coach*) 1998–99
Steve Coppell 1999–2000
Alan Smith 2000–01
Steve Bruce 2001
Trevor Francis 2001–03
Steve Kember 2003
Iain Dowie 2003–06
Peter Taylor 2006–07
Neil Warnock 2007–10
Paul Hart 2010
George Burley 2010–11
Dougie Freedman 2011–12
Ian Holloway 2012–13
Tony Pulis 2013–14
Neil Warnock 2014
Alan Pardew 2015–16
Sam Allardyce 2016–17
Frank de Boer 2017
Roy Hodgson September 2017–

TEN YEAR LEAGUE RECORD

		P	W	D	L	F	A	Pts	Pos
2010-11	FL C	46	12	12	22	44	69	48	20
2011-12	FL C	46	13	17	16	46	51	56	17
2012-13	FL C	46	19	15	12	73	62	72	5
2013-14	PR Lge	38	13	6	19	33	48	45	11
2014-15	PR Lge	38	13	9	16	47	51	48	10
2015-16	PR Lge	38	11	9	18	39	51	42	15
2016-17	PR Lge	38	12	5	21	50	63	41	14
2017-18	PR Lge	38	11	11	16	45	55	44	11
2018-19	PR Lge	38	14	7	17	51	53	49	12
2019-20	PR Lge	38	11	10	17	31	50	43	14

DID YOU KNOW ?

Crystal Palace played their first-ever game in top flight football on 9 August 1969 when they drew 2-2 at home to Manchester United in front of a crowd of 48,610, a new record for Selhurst Park. It was also the first time that Palace appeared on the BBC's *Match of the Day* programme.

CRYSTAL PALACE – PREMIER LEAGUE 2019–20 LEAGUE RECORD

Match No.	Date	Venue	Opponents	Result	H/T Score	Lg Pos.	Goalscorers	Attendance
1	Aug 10	H	Everton	D 0-0	0-0	8		25,151
2	18	A	Sheffield U	L 0-1	0-0	14		30,197
3	24	A	Manchester U	W 2-1	1-0	10	Ayew 32, Van Aanholt 90	73,454
4	31	H	Aston Villa	W 1-0	0-0	4	Ayew 73	25,248
5	Sept 14	A	Tottenham H	L 0-4	0-4	11		59,812
6	22	H	Wolverhampton W	D 1-1	0-0	12	Dendoncker (og) 46	25,122
7	28	H	Norwich C	W 2-0	1-0	9	Milivojevic (pen) 21, Townsend 90	25,477
8	Oct 5	A	West Ham U	W 2-1	0-0	4	Van Aanholt (pen) 63, Ayew 87	59,912
9	19	H	Manchester C	L 0-2	0-2	6		25,480
10	27	A	Arsenal	D 2-2	1-2	6	Milivojevic (pen) 32, Ayew 52	60,345
11	Nov 3	H	Leicester C	L 0-2	0-0	9		25,480
12	9	A	Chelsea	L 0-2	0-0	10		40,525
13	23	H	Liverpool	L 1-2	0-0	13	Zaha 82	25,486
14	30	A	Burnley	W 2-0	1-0	10	Zaha 45, Schlupp 78	19,818
15	Dec 3	H	Bournemouth	W 1-0	0-0	5	Schlupp 76	23,497
16	7	A	Watford	D 0-0	0-0	8		20,070
17	16	H	Brighton & HA	D 1-1	0-0	9	Zaha 76	24,175
18	21	A	Newcastle U	L 0-1	0-0	12		45,453
19	26	H	West Ham U	W 2-1	0-0	9	Kouyate 68, Ayew 90	25,462
20	28	A	Southampton	D 1-1	0-0	9	Tomkins 50	31,108
21	Jan 1	A	Norwich C	D 1-1	0-1	9	Wickham 85	27,021
22	11	H	Arsenal	D 1-1	0-1	9	Ayew 54	25,468
23	18	A	Manchester C	D 2-2	1-0	9	Tosun 39, Fernandinho (og) 90	54,439
24	21	H	Southampton	L 0-2	0-1	11		23,739
25	Feb 1	H	Sheffield U	L 0-1	0-0	13		25,170
26	8	A	Everton	L 1-3	0-1	14	Benteke 51	38,987
27	22	H	Newcastle U	W 1-0	1-0	13	Van Aanholt 44	25,486
28	29	A	Brighton & HA	W 1-0	0-0	12	Ayew 70	30,124
29	Mar 7	H	Watford	W 1-0	1-0	11	Ayew 28	25,461
30	June 20	A	Bournemouth	W 2-0	2-0	9	Milivojevic 12, Ayew 23	0
31	24	A	Liverpool	L 0-4	0-2	9		0
32	29	H	Burnley	L 0-1	0-0	11		0
33	July 4	A	Leicester C	L 0-3	0-0	13		0
34	7	H	Chelsea	L 2-3	1-2	14	Zaha 34, Benteke 72	0
35	12	A	Aston Villa	L 0-2	0-1	14		0
36	16	H	Manchester U	L 0-2	0-1	14		0
37	20	A	Wolverhampton W	L 0-2	0-1	14		0
38	26	H	Tottenham H	D 1-1	0-1	14	Schlupp 53	0

Final League Position: 14

GOALSCORERS

League (31): Ayew 9, Zaha 4, Milivojevic 3 (2 pens), Schlupp 3, Van Aanholt 3 (1 pen), Benteke 2, Kouyate 1, Tomkins 1, Tosun 1, Townsend 1, Wickham 1, own goals 2.
FA Cup (0).
Carabao Cup (0).

Guaita V 35	Ward J 27 + 2	Kelly M 17 + 2	Dann S 14 + 2	Van Aanholt P 29	Townsend A 14 + 10	McArthur J 37	Milivojevic L 28 + 3	Meyer M 6 + 11	Benteke C 13 + 11	Ayew J 37	Zaha W 37 + 1	Wickham C — + 6	Schlupp J 11 + 6	McCarthy J 16 + 17	Cahill G 25	Kouyate C 29 + 6	Sakho M 11 + 3	Victor Camarasa — + 1	Hennessey W 3	Tomkins J 18	Riedewald J 7 + 10	Pierrick B — + 2	Tosun C 2 + 3	Mitchell T 2 + 2	*Match No.*
1	2	3	4	5	6	7	8	9	10^{2}	11^{1}	12	13													1
1	2	3	4	5	6^{2}	7^{3}	8	9^{1}	10		11	14	12	13											2
1	2	3		5	13	7	8		12	11^{1}	6		10^{2}	14	4	9^{3}									3
1	2	3^{1}		5	13	6	7		14	10^{3}	9		11^{2}		4	8	12								4
1	2			5	10^{3}		8		12	11^{1}	6		9	13	3	7^{2}	4	14							5
1	2			5		7^{2}	8		12	11^{1}	6		10	13	3	9	4								6
1	2	3		5	12	7^{2}	8	14		11^{3}	6		10	13	4	9^{1}									7
1	2	3		5	12	8			13	11^{2}	6		10	7^{1}	4	9									8
	2		14	5	12	9	8^{2}		13	11	6		10^{1}		4	7			1	3^{3}					9
	2			5	6	9	8		12	11^{1}	10			13	4	7^{2}			1	3					10
1	2			5		6^{2}	8	12	13	11^{3}	10		9	14	4	7^{1}				3					11
1	2^{1}	12		5	6	9^{2}	8			11	10		13	14	4	7^{3}				3					12
1	2^{1}	12		5	6	9	8		14	11^{3}	10		13		4	7^{2}				3					13
1		2	4^{1}	5	6^{2}	9	8		14	11^{3}	10		13			7	12			3					14
1		2		5^{1}	6^{2}	9	8			11	10		12	13		7	4■			3					15
1		2			6^{2}	9	8		13	11	10		5^{1}	14	4	7^{3}				3	12				16
1		2	4			8	7	13	10	9	11			12		6^{2}				3	5^{1}				17
1		2		5		8^{1}	7	12	10	9	11			6		4				3					18
1		2		5^{1}		8	7	9^{2}		10	11	13		14		6^{3}	4			3	12				19
1		2				9	8	6^{1}		11	10			7		12	4			3	5				20
1		2^{3}				9	8	6^{2}		11	10	13		7		12	4^{1}			3	5	14			21
1		2				8		6^{1}		11	10			9	4	7				3	5		12		22
1	13	2				8				6	10	12		9	4	7				3	5^{2}		11^{1}		23
1	13	2^{1}				8		12		6	10	14		9	4	7^{2}				3	5		11^{3}		24
1	2			5	12	9^{3}	8	13	11^{1}	6	10			7^{2}	4	14				3					25
1	2^{3}		12	5		9	6	13	11	7	10			8^{2}	4	14				3^{1}					26
1	2		3	5		8			10^{1}	9	11			7	4	6^{2}					13		12		27
1	2		3	5		9			11^{2}	10	7			6^{1}	4	8					12		13		28
1	2		3	5		8^{1}	12		10	9	11			7	4	6									29
1	2		3	5	13	8^{3}	7^{1}		10^{2}	9	11			12	4	6					14				30
	2			5	7	9^{2}	13	12		11^{4}	10^{1}			6	3	8^{3}	4		1		14	15			31
1	2		3	5	6^{2}	9	8	13		11	10			12	4	7^{1}									32
1	2			5^{4}	14	7^{2}	8		11^{3}	6	10			13	3	12	4				9^{1}			15	33
1	2		3	5	14	9^{2}	7^{4}	15	11	10^{3}	6			13	4^{1}	8	12								34
1	2		3	5	13	8^{1}	6^{4}	15	11■	10^{2}	7			12		9^{3}	4				14				35
1	2		3	5^{3}	6	9^{1}	8			10	11		12	7^{2}			4				13			14	36
1	2		3		6	8				10	11		9^{2}	7		12	4^{1}				13			5	37
1	2		4		6	8^{1}	13			10	11		9^{2}	7		3					12			5	38

FA Cup
Third Round Derby Co (h) 0-1

Carabao Cup
Second Round Colchester U (h) 0-0
(Colchester U won 5-4 on penalties)

DERBY COUNTY

FOUNDATION

Derby County was formed by members of the Derbyshire County Cricket Club in 1884, when football was booming in the area and the cricketers thought that a football club would help boost finances for the summer game. To begin with, they sported the cricket club's colours of amber, chocolate and pale blue, and went into the game at the top immediately entering the FA Cup.

Pride Park Stadium, Pride Park, Derby DE24 8XL.

Telephone: (0871) 472 1884.

Ticket Office: (0871) 472 1884 (option 1).

Website: www.dcfc.co.uk

Email: derby.county@dcfc.co.uk

Ground Capacity: 32,956.

Record Attendance: 41,826 v Tottenham H, Division 1, 20 September 1969 (at Baseball Ground); 33,378 v Liverpool, Premier League, 18 March 2000 (at Pride Park).

Stadium Record Attendance: 33,597, England v Mexico, 25 May 2001 (at Pride Park).

Pitch Measurements: 105m × 68m (115yd × 74.5yd).

Executive Chairman: Mel Morris CBE.

Chief Executive Officer: Stephen Pearce.

Manager: Phillip Cocu.

Assistant Manager: Chris van der Weerden.

Colours: White shirts with black trim, black shorts with white trim, white socks with black trim.

Year Formed: 1884.

Turned Professional: 1884.

Club Nickname: 'The Rams'.

Grounds: 1884, Racecourse Ground; 1895, Baseball Ground; 1997, Pride Park (renamed The iPro Stadium 2013; Pride Park Stadium 2016).

First Football League Game: 8 September 1888, Football League, v Bolton W (a) W 6–3 – Marshall; Latham, Ferguson, Williamson; Monks, Walter Roulstone; Bakewell (2), Cooper (2), Higgins, Harry Plackett, Lol Plackett (2).

Record League Victory: 9–0 v Wolverhampton W, Division 1, 10 January 1891 – Bunyan; Archie Goodall, Roberts; Walker, Chalmers, Walter Roulstone (1); Bakewell, McLachlan, Johnny Goodall (1), Holmes (2), McMillan (5). 9–0 v Sheffield W, Division 1, 21 January 1899 – Fryer; Methven, Staley; Cox, Archie Goodall, May; Oakden (1), Bloomer (6), Boag, McDonald (1), Allen, (1 og).

HONOURS

League Champions: Division 1 – 1971–72, 1974–75; Division 2 – 1911–12, 1914–15, 1968–69, 1986–87; Division 3N – 1956–57.
Runners-up: Division 1 – 1895–96, 1929–30, 1935–36; First Division – 1995–96; Division 2 – 1925–26; Division 3N – 1955–56.

FA Cup Winners: 1946.
Runners-up: 1898, 1899, 1903.

League Cup: semi-final – 1968, 2009.

Texaco Cup Winners: 1972.

Anglo-Italian Cup: *Runners-up:* 1993–94, 1994–95.

European Competitions
European Cup: 1972–73 (*sf*), 1975–76.
UEFA Cup: 1974–75, 1976–77.

FOOTBALL YEARBOOK FACT FILE

Derby County played at the County Ground, situated in the middle of a racecourse, until switching to the Baseball Ground in 1895. The County Ground, which was under the control of the local Race Committee, was not always available for football and the club played a number of games at the Baseball Ground before making a permanent move.

Record Cup Victory: 12–0 v Finn Harps, UEFA Cup 1st rd 1st leg, 15 September 1976 – Moseley; Thomas, Nish, Rioch (1), McFarland, Todd (King), Macken, Gemmill, Hector (5), George (3), James (3).

Record Defeat: 2–11 v Everton, FA Cup 1st rd, 1889–90.

Most League Points (2 for a win): 63, Division 2, 1968–69 and Division 3 (N), 1955–56 and 1956–57.

Most League Points (3 for a win): 85, FL C, 2013–14.

Most League Goals: 111, Division 3 (N), 1956–57.

Highest League Scorer in Season: Jack Bowers, 37, Division 1, 1930–31; Ray Straw, 37 Division 3 (N), 1956–57.

Most League Goals in Total Aggregate: Steve Bloomer, 292, 1892–1906 and 1910–14.

Most League Goals in One Match: 6, Steve Bloomer v Sheffield W, Division 1, 2 January 1899.

Most Capped Player: Deon Burton, 42 (59), Jamaica.

Most League Appearances: Kevin Hector, 486, 1966–78 and 1980–82.

Youngest League Player: Mason Bennett, 15 years 99 days v Middlesbrough 22 October 2011.

Record Transfer Fee Received: £8,500,000 (rising to £11,000,000) from Huddersfield T for Tom Ince, July 2017.

Record Transfer Fee Paid: £7,500,000 (rising to £10,000,000) to Arsenal for Krystian Bielik, August 2019.

Football League Record: 1888 Founder Member of the Football League; 1907–12 Division 2; 1912–14 Division 1; 1914–15 Division 2; 1915–21 Division 1; 1921–26 Division 2; 1926–53 Division 1; 1953–55 Division 2; 1955–57 Division 3 (N); 1957–69 Division 2; 1969–80 Division 1; 1980–84 Division 2; 1984–86 Division 3; 1986–87 Division 2; 1987–91 Division 1; 1991–92 Division 2; 1992–96 Division 1; 1996–2002 Premier League; 2002–04 Division 1; 2004–07 FL C; 2007–08 Premier League; 2008– FL C.

MANAGERS

W. D. Clark 1896–1900
Harry Newbould 1900–06
Jimmy Methven 1906–22
Cecil Potter 1922–25
George Jobey 1925–41
Ted Magner 1944–46
Stuart McMillan 1946–53
Jack Barker 1953–55
Harry Storer 1955–62
Tim Ward 1962–67
Brian Clough 1967–73
Dave Mackay 1973–76
Colin Murphy 1977
Tommy Docherty 1977–79
Colin Addison 1979–82
Johnny Newman 1982
Peter Taylor 1982–84
Roy McFarland 1984
Arthur Cox 1984–93
Roy McFarland 1993–95
Jim Smith 1995–2001
Colin Todd 2001–02
John Gregory 2002–03
George Burley 2003–05
Phil Brown 2005–06
Billy Davies 2006–07
Paul Jewell 2007–08
Nigel Clough 2009–13
Steve McClaren 2013–15
Paul Clement 2015–16
Darren Wassall 2016
Nigel Pearson 2016
Steve McClaren 2016–17
Gary Rowett 2017–18
Frank Lampard 2018–19
Phillip Cocu July 2019–

LATEST SEQUENCES

Longest Sequence of League Wins: 9, 15.3.1969 – 19.4.1969.

Longest Sequence of League Defeats: 8, 12.12.1987 – 10.2.1988.

Longest Sequence of League Draws: 6, 26.3.1927 – 18.4.1927.

Longest Sequence of Unbeaten League Matches: 22, 8.3.1969 – 20.9.1969.

Longest Sequence Without a League Win: 36, 22.9.2007 – 30.8.2008.

Successive Scoring Runs: 29 from 3.12.1960.

Successive Non-scoring Runs: 8 from 30.10.1920.

TEN YEAR LEAGUE RECORD

		P	*W*	*D*	*L*	*F*	*A*	*Pts*	*Pos*
2010-11	FL C	46	13	10	23	58	71	49	19
2011-12	FL C	46	18	10	18	50	58	64	12
2012-13	FL C	46	16	13	17	65	62	61	10
2013-14	FL C	46	25	10	11	84	52	85	3
2014-15	FL C	46	21	14	11	85	56	77	8
2015-16	FL C	46	21	15	10	66	43	78	5
2016-17	FL C	46	18	13	15	54	50	67	9
2017-18	FL C	46	20	15	11	70	48	75	6
2018-19	FL C	46	20	14	12	69	54	74	6
2019-20	FL C	46	17	13	16	62	64	64	10

DID YOU KNOW ?

Bobby Saxton was the first Derby County player to appear as a substitute in a Football League match. Selected for the number 12 shirt for the opening game of the 1965–66 season, Saxton came on the field after just 21 minutes, replacing the injured Geoff Barrowcliffe.

DERBY COUNTY – SKY BET CHAMPIONSHIP 2019–20 LEAGUE RECORD

Match No.	Date	Venue	Opponents	Result		H/T Score	Lg Pos.	Goalscorers	Attendance
1	Aug 5	A	Huddersfield T	W	2-1	2-1	4	Lawrence 2 [22, 25]	22,596
2	10	H	Swansea C	D	0-0	0-0	6		27,337
3	17	A	Stoke C	D	2-2	1-1	8	Waghorn 2 (1 pen) [2, 70 (p)]	23,863
4	20	H	Bristol C	L	1-2	0-2	11	Marriott [85]	25,546
5	24	H	WBA	D	1-1	1-0	16	Waghorn (pen) [6]	26,718
6	31	A	Brentford	L	0-3	0-3	19		11,055
7	Sept 13	H	Cardiff C	D	1-1	1-1	18	Malone [6]	25,873
8	21	A	Leeds U	D	1-1	0-1	18	Martin [90]	34,741
9	28	H	Birmingham C	W	3-2	1-0	14	Martin [2], Waghorn [50], Paterson [74]	28,454
10	Oct 2	A	Barnsley	D	2-2	2-1	16	Martin [34], Huddlestone (pen) [43]	13,634
11	5	H	Luton T	W	2-0	1-0	13	Pearson (og) [11], Lawrence [70]	27,944
12	19	A	Charlton Ath	L	0-3	0-1	15		19,408
13	23	H	Wigan Ath	W	1-0	0-0	14	Shinnie [90]	24,697
14	26	A	Hull C	L	0-2	0-0	16		16,326
15	Nov 2	H	Middlesbrough	W	2-0	1-0	15	Lawrence 2 [22, 84]	26,293
16	9	A	Nottingham F	L	0-1	0-0	16		29,314
17	23	H	Preston NE	W	1-0	1-0	11	Waghorn [33]	27,417
18	26	A	Fulham	L	0-3	0-2	13		16,856
19	30	H	QPR	D	1-1	1-1	14	Waghorn [23]	26,289
20	Dec 7	A	Blackburn R	L	0-1	0-0	16		12,800
21	11	H	Sheffield W	D	1-1	0-1	16	Martin (pen) [82]	26,203
22	14	H	Millwall	L	0-1	0-1	16		26,272
23	21	A	Reading	L	0-3	0-1	17		14,831
24	26	A	Wigan Ath	D	1-1	0-0	18	Waghorn [90]	14,211
25	30	H	Charlton Ath	W	2-1	1-0	17	Knight 2 [10, 77]	26,058
26	Jan 2	H	Barnsley	W	2-1	1-0	17	Marriott [45], Waghorn [57]	27,782
27	11	A	Middlesbrough	D	2-2	0-1	17	Knight [54], Holmes [90]	19,706
28	18	H	Hull C	W	1-0	0-0	15	Clarke [64]	27,412
29	28	A	Luton T	L	2-3	0-0	16	Rooney [63], Martin [85]	10,057
30	31	H	Stoke C	W	4-0	2-0	13	Waghorn [21], Martin [24], Rooney [67], Bogle [74]	27,984
31	Feb 8	A	Swansea C	W	3-2	1-0	13	Waghorn [8], Holmes [64], Lawrence [80]	16,230
32	12	A	Bristol C	L	2-3	0-2	13	Waghorn [61], Martin [82]	20,368
33	15	H	Huddersfield T	D	1-1	0-0	13	Lawrence [61]	27,502
34	21	H	Fulham	D	1-1	0-0	12	Rooney (pen) [55]	25,442
35	25	A	QPR	L	1-2	1-1	14	Waghorn [43]	11,669
36	29	A	Sheffield W	W	3-1	3-0	13	Lawrence 2 [7, 24], Knight [30]	25,148
37	Mar 8	H	Blackburn R	W	3-0	2-0	12	Sibley [26], Martin 2 (1 pen) [41, 85 (p)]	26,590
38	June 20	A	Millwall	W	3-2	1-1	12	Sibley 3 [26, 71, 90]	0
39	27	H	Reading	W	2-1	2-0	8	Lawrence [44], Rooney (pen) [45]	0
40	July 1	A	Preston NE	W	1-0	1-0	7	Rooney [18]	0
41	4	H	Nottingham F	D	1-1	0-1	7	Martin [90]	0
42	8	A	WBA	L	0-2	0-1	9		0
43	11	H	Brentford	L	1-3	1-1	10	Knight [29]	0
44	14	A	Cardiff C	L	1-2	1-1	10	Knight [30]	0
45	19	H	Leeds U	L	1-3	0-0	12	Martin [54]	0
46	22	A	Birmingham C	W	3-1	1-0	10	Shinnie [6], Whittaker [87], Sibley [90]	0

Final League Position: 10

GOALSCORERS

League (62): Waghorn 12 (2 pens), Martin 11 (2 pens), Lawrence 10, Knight 6, Rooney 5 (2 pens), Sibley 5, Holmes 2, Marriott 2, Shinnie 2, Bogle 1, Clarke 1, Huddlestone 1 (1 pen), Malone 1, Paterson 1, Whittaker 1, own goal 1.
FA Cup (5): Holmes 1, Marriott 1, Martin 1, Rooney 1 (1 pen), Wisdom 1.
Carabao Cup (1): Buchanan 1.

Roos K 22	Bogle J 33 + 4	Keogh R 8	Clarke M 34 + 1	Malone S 15 + 3	Evans G 11 + 6	Huddlestone T 11	Dowell K 8 + 2	Jozefzoon F 6 + 8	Waghorn M 36 + 7	Lawrence T 37	Bennett M 2 + 5	Knight J 20 + 11	Paterson J 5 + 5	Lowe M 24 + 5	Marriott J 10 + 22	Bielik K 19 + 1	Buchanan L 3 + 2	Holmes D 29 + 4	Martin C 25 + 10	Davies C 25 + 7	Shinnie G 12 + 11	Wisdom A 16 + 2	Whittaker M 1 + 15	Forsyth C 20 + 2	Hamer B 24 + 1	Sibley L 9 + 2	Bird M 21 + 1	Rooney W 20	Brown J — + 1	Hector-Ingram J — + 1	Match No.
1	2	3	4	5	6	7	8^{2}	9^{1}	10	11	12	13																			1
1	2^{2}	3	4	5	8^{1}	7	6	9^{3}	10	11			12	13	14																2
1		3	4	5^{1}	6^{3}	7	9	8	11	10^{2}		14		2	13	12															3
1		3	4^{3}	5^{1}		7	9	12	11	10	8^{2}	14		2	13	6															4
1		3			13	7	9		8^{2}	10	12	6^{3}	14	2	11^{1}	4	5														5
1		3				7	8^{2}		10	11	13	6	14	2	9^{3}	4	5^{1}	12													6
1		3	4	5		6		12	8	10				2	11^{2}	7		9^{1}	13												7
1		3	4	5		6		10^{3}	8			14	12	2	11^{2}	7^{1}		9	13												8
1	13			5		6		10^{2}	8			14	9	2	12	3		7^{3}	11^{1}	4											9
1	2		12			6^{1}			8	10	14	13	9	5		3		7^{3}	11^{2}	4											10
1	2		4	5				8	12	9			10^{2}			7^{3}		13	11^{1}	3	6	14									11
1	2		4	5				12	8^{2}	10	14		9^{3}			7^{1}		13	11	3	6										12
1	2		4	5^{3}					11^{2}	10			9^{1}	14	13	7		8	12	3	6										13
1	2		4				9^{1}		14	10				5	13	7		8	11^{2}	3	6^{3}		12								14
1	2		4	5^{3}	12				13	10				14	8	7^{1}		9	11^{2}	3	6										15
1	2		4^{1}		12				14	10			13	5	8	7		9^{2}	11	3	6^{3}										16
1	2				12				13	10	8^{2}			5		7		9	11^{3}	3	6^{1}	14		4							17
1	2				6^{2}		13		8	10				5	14	7		9^{3}	11^{1}	3			12	4							18
	5^{1}			9	8				10^{2}	7		13			11^{3}			6	14	3		2	12	4	1						19
	9^{2}			5			8		10^{3}	11					14	7^{1}		6	12	3		2	13	4	1						20
	2			5	7				13	10		6^{2}			12			9	11	3			8^{1}	4	1						21
	2				7		12	13	8	10		6^{1}		5				9^{3}	11	3			14	4^{2}	1						22
	2			5▮					8^{3}	10		6		12	14	7^{2}		9	11^{1}	3				4	1	13					23
	2								9	10		8^{3}		5	13	6^{1}		7	11^{2}	3			14	4	1		12				24
			4						8^{2}			9		5	11^{1}	6▮		10		3		2	12	13	1		7				25
			4	12					11^{1}			9		5	10^{2}			6		3		2	13		1		8	7			26
	2		4						11	9^{2}		10^{1}		5				8	12	3			13		1		6	7			27
	2		4			7			11	10		8		5				6				3			1			9			28
	2		4						11	10		7^{2}		5▮	12			8^{1}	13			3			1		6	9			29
	2		4						7^{2}	10					14			8	11^{1}	13	12	3		5	1		6	9^{3}			30
	2^{2}		4						11	10^{3}		7^{1}			14			8		13	12	3		5	1		6	9			31
	2		4						8	10				5	12			7	11			3			1		6^{1}	9			32
1	14		4						10	9					13			6^{1}	11^{2}	3	12	2^{3}		5			7	8			33
			4					12	11^{1}	10		8^{2}			13					3	7	2		5	1		6	9			34
	12		4						8	10				5	11^{2}				13	3^{1}	7^{3}	2	14		1		6	9			35
	2		4						8^{3}	9		10^{1}			14				11^{2}	12	13	3		5	1		6	7			36
	2^{3}		4						8^{1}			10			12				11	13	6	3	14	5	1	9^{2}	7				37
	2^{2}		4		15				11^{3}	10		12						8^{1}	16	14	13	3		5	1	9	7^{4}	6^{5}			38
	2		4						8^{2}	10▮		14						13	11^{3}	15	12	3		5	1	9^{1}	7	6^{4}			39
	2^{1}		4	16	3^{4}				11			10		5				8^{3}	14	15	12			13	1	9^{2}	7	6^{5}			40
	2		4		3			12	13▮			10^{1}		14				8^{2}	11		15		16	5^{3}	1	9^{4}	7^{5}	6			41
	2		4		3							14					13	10^{1}	11^{5}		7^{2}		12	5^{3}	1	8▮	6	9^{4}	15	16	42
	2		4		3			12		10		8^{1}		5					11		14		13		1	9^{2}	7^{3}	6			43
1	12		4	16				13		10		8^{2}		2^{1}	14				11	3	15			5^{5}		9^{3}	7^{4}	6			44
1	2		4						8	10^{1}		12			15		13		11	3	14			5^{2}		9^{3}	7^{4}	6			45
1^{1}	2		4		13				8^{2}			10^{5}			16		5		11	3	9^{4}		15		12	14	6	7^{3}			46

FA Cup

Third Round	Crystal Palace	(a)	1-0
Fourth Round	Northampton T	(a)	0-0
Replay	Northampton T	(h)	4-2
Fifth Round	Manchester U	(h)	0-3

Carabao Cup

First Round	Scunthorpe U	(a)	1-0
Second Round	Nottingham F	(a)	0-3

DONCASTER ROVERS

FOUNDATION

In 1879, Mr Albert Jenkins assembled a team to play a match against the Yorkshire Institution for the Deaf. The players remained together as Doncaster Rovers, joining the Midland Alliance in 1889 and the Midland Counties League in 1891.

Keepmoat Stadium, Stadium Way, Lakeside, Doncaster, South Yorkshire DN4 5JW.

Telephone: (01302) 764 664.

Ticket Office: (01302) 762 576.

Website: www.doncasterroversfc.co.uk

Email: info@clubdoncaster.co.uk

Ground Capacity: 15,148.

Record Attendance: 37,149 v Hull C, Division 3 (N), 2 October 1948 (at Belle Vue); 15,001 v Leeds U, FL 1, 1 April 2008 (at Keepmoat Stadium).

Pitch Measurements: 100m × 66m (109.5yd × 72yd).

Chairman: David Blunt.

Chief Executive: Gavin Baldwin.

Manager: Darren Moore.

Assistant Manager: Jamie Smith.

Colours: Red and white hooped shirts, red shorts with black trim, red socks with black and white trim.

Year Formed: 1879.

Turned Professional: 1885.

Club Nickname: 'Rovers', 'Donny'.

Grounds: 1880–1916, Intake Ground; 1920, Benetthorpe Ground; 1922, Low Pasture, Belle Vue; 2007, Keepmoat Stadium.

First Football League Game: 7 September 1901, Division 2, v Burslem Port Vale (h) D 3–3 – Eggett; Simpson, Layton; Longden, Jones, Wright, Langham, Murphy, Price, Goodson (2), Bailey (1).

Record League Victory: 10–0 v Darlington, Division 4, 25 January 1964 – Potter; Raine, Meadows, Windross (1), White, Ripley (2), Robinson, Booth (2), Hale (4), Jeffrey, Broadbent (1).

Record Cup Victory: 7–0 v Blyth Spartans, FA Cup 1st rd, 27 November 1937 – Imrie; Shaw, Rodgers, McFarlane, Bycroft, Cyril Smith, Burton (1), Killourhy (4), Morgan (2), Malam, Dutton; 7–0 v Chorley, FA Cup 1st rd replay, 20 November 2018 – Lawlor; Mason, Butler, Anderson T■, Andrew, Whiteman (Rowe), Coppinger (Taylor), Kane (1) (Crawford), May (4), Marquis (1), Blair (1).

Record Defeat: 0–12 v Small Heath, Division 2, 11 April 1903.

HONOURS

League Champions: FL 1 – 2012–13; Division 3N – 1934–35, 1946–47, 1949–50; Third Division – 2003–04; Division 4 – 1965–66, 1968–69.
Runners-up: Division 3N – 1937–38, 1938–39; Division 4 – 1983–84; Conference – (3rd) 2002–03 *(promoted via play-offs (and golden goal)).*

FA Cup: 5th rd – 1952, 1954, 1955, 1956, 2019.

League Cup: 5th rd – 1976, 2006.

League Trophy Winners: 2007.

FOOTBALL YEARBOOK FACT FILE

On 24 August 1976 Doncaster Rovers became the first team to win a Football League Cup tie on a penalty shoot-out. Both legs of Rovers' first round tie against Lincoln City ended 1-1 and the replay at Nottingham Forest's City Ground ended 2-2 after extra time. Rovers eventually went through 3-2 on penalties.

Most League Points (2 for a win): 72, Division 3 (N), 1946–47.

Most League Points (3 for a win): 92, Division 3, 2003–04.

Most League Goals: 123, Division 3 (N), 1946–47.

Highest League Scorer in Season: Clarrie Jordan, 42, Division 3 (N), 1946–47.

Most League Goals in Total Aggregate: Tom Keetley, 180, 1923–29.

Most League Goals in One Match: 6, Tom Keetley v Ashington, Division 3 (N), 16 February 1929.

Most Capped Player: Len Graham, 14, Northern Ireland.

Most League Appearances: James Coppinger, 582, 2004–20.

Youngest League Player: Alick Jeffrey, 15 years 229 days v Fulham, 15 September 1954.

Record Transfer Fee Received: £2,000,000 from Reading for Matthew Mills, July 2009.

Record Transfer Fee Paid: £1,150,000 to Sheffield U for Billy Sharp, August 2010.

Football League Record: 1901 Elected to Division 2; 1903 Failed re-election; 1904 Re-elected; 1905 Failed re-election; 1923 Re-elected to Division 3 (N); 1935–37 Division 2; 1937–47 Division 3 (N); 1947–48 Division 2; 1948–50 Division 3 (N); 1950–58 Division 2; 1958–59 Division 3; 1959–66 Division 4; 1966–67 Division 3; 1967–69 Division 4; 1969–71 Division 3; 1971–81 Division 4; 1981–83 Division 3; 1983–84 Division 4; 1984–88 Division 3; 1988–92 Division 4; 1992–98 Division 3; 1998–2003 Conference; 2003–04 Division 3; 2004–08 FL 1; 2008–12 FL C; 2012–13 FL 1; 2013–14 FL C; 2014–16 FL 1; 2016–17 FL 2; 2017– FL 1.

LATEST SEQUENCES

Longest Sequence of League Wins: 10, 22.1.1947 – 4.4.1947.

Longest Sequence of League Defeats: 9, 14.1.1905 – 1.4.1905.

Longest Sequence of League Draws: 4, 1.1.2018 – 23.1.2018.

Longest Sequence of Unbeaten League Matches: 20, 26.12.1968 – 12.4.1969.

Longest Sequence Without a League Win: 20, 9.8.1997 – 29.11.1997.

Successive Scoring Runs: 27 from 10.11.1934.

Successive Non-scoring Runs: 7 from 27.9.1947.

MANAGERS

Arthur Porter 1920–21
Harry Tufnell 1921–22
Arthur Porter 1922–23
Dick Ray 1923–27
David Menzies 1928–36
Fred Emery 1936–40
Bill Marsden 1944–46
Jackie Bestall 1946–49
Peter Doherty 1949–58
Jack Hodgson and Sid Bycroft (*Joint Managers*) 1958
Jack Crayston 1958–59 (*continued as Secretary-Manager to 1961*)
Jackie Bestall 1959–60
Norman Curtis 1960–61
Danny Malloy 1961–62
Oscar Hold 1962–64
Bill Leivers 1964–66
Keith Kettleborough 1966–67
George Raynor 1967–68
Lawrie McMenemy 1968–71
Maurice Setters 1971–74
Stan Anderson 1975–78
Billy Bremner 1978–85
Dave Cusack 1985–87
Dave Mackay 1987–89
Billy Bremner 1989–91
Steve Beaglehole 1991–93
Ian Atkins 1994
Sammy Chung 1994–96
Kerry Dixon (*Player-Manager*) 1996–97
Dave Cowling 1997
Mark Weaver 1997–98
Ian Snodin 1998–99
Steve Wignall 1999–2001
Dave Penney 2002–06
Sean O'Driscoll 2006–11
Dean Saunders 2011–13
Brian Flynn 2013
Paul Dickov 2013–15
Darren Ferguson 2015–18
Grant McCann 2018–19
Darren Moore July 2019–

TEN YEAR LEAGUE RECORD

		P	W	D	L	F	A	Pts	Pos
2010-11	FL C	46	11	15	20	55	81	48	21
2011-12	FL C	46	8	12	26	43	80	36	24
2012-13	FL 1	46	25	9	12	62	44	84	1
2013-14	FL C	46	11	11	24	39	70	44	22
2014-15	FL 1	46	16	13	17	58	62	61	13
2015-16	FL 1	46	11	13	22	48	64	46	21
2016-17	FL 2	46	25	10	11	85	55	85	3
2017-18	FL 1	46	13	17	16	52	52	56	15
2018-19	FL 1	46	20	13	13	76	58	73	6
2019-20	FL 1	34	15	9	10	51	33	54	9§

§Decided on points-per-game (1.59)

DID YOU KNOW ?

Doncaster Rovers met foreign opposition for the first time on 9 December 1935 when they played a friendly against FC Austria, losing 2-1 after missing a penalty. The game, played on a Monday afternoon at Belle Vue, attracted an attendance of 4,000.

DONCASTER ROVERS – SKY BET LEAGUE ONE 2019–20 LEAGUE RECORD

Match No.	*Date*	*Venue*	*Opponents*	*Result*	*H/T Score*	*Lg Pos.*	*Goalscorers*	*Attendance*
1	Aug 3	H	Gillingham	D 1-1	1-1	10	Sadlier [45]	7939
2	10	A	Rochdale	D 1-1	0-0	14	Sadlier [90]	3587
3	17	H	Fleetwood T	W 3-2	2-1	7	John [19], Coppinger [39], Burns (og) [90]	6740
4	24	H	Lincoln C	W 2-1	1-0	8	Ennis [13], Taylor, J [83]	10,177
5	Sept 7	H	Rotherham U	W 2-1	0-1	7	Coppinger [66], Whiteman (pen) [88]	11,407
6	14	A	Ipswich T	D 0-0	0-0	8		18,928
7	17	H	Blackpool	L 0-1	0-0	10		6964
8	21	H	Peterborough U	W 2-0	2-0	7	Coppinger [30], Sadlier [39]	8940
9	28	A	Coventry C	D 1-1	1-0	9	Whiteman [41]	7010
10	Oct 5	H	Portsmouth	L 1-2	0-0	10	James [82]	8962
11	12	A	Oxford U	L 0-3	0-1	11		6861
12	19	H	Bristol R	W 2-0	1-0	9	Sadlier [39], Taylor, J [56]	7659
13	22	A	Southend U	W 7-1	2-1	6	Thomas 2 [23, 52], Ralph (2 ogs) [26, 90], Whiteman [70], Sadlier [82], May [89]	5066
14	Nov 2	H	Burton Alb	D 2-2	1-1	11	Taylor, J [39], Sadlier [57]	7492
15	23	A	Wycombe W	L 0-1	0-0	13		4875
16	Dec 7	H	Milton Keynes D	D 1-1	0-0	13	John [85]	7193
17	14	A	AFC Wimbledon	L 1-2	1-0	14	Thomas [12]	4311
18	21	H	Accrington S	D 1-1	0-0	15	Taylor, J [57]	7444
19	26	A	Peterborough U	W 3-0	1-0	14	Sadlier 2 [17, 61], Whiteman [82]	6786
20	29	H	Sunderland	L 1-2	1-1	16	Taylor, J [40]	12,432
21	Jan 1	H	Oxford U	W 1-0	1-0	15	James [34]	7524
22	7	H	Shrewsbury T	W 2-0	1-0	11	Ennis [4], Anderson, T [75]	7054
23	11	A	Bristol R	W 2-0	0-0	8	Whiteman [86], Bingham [90]	6834
24	18	H	Coventry C	L 0-1	0-1	9		9537
25	24	A	Sunderland	D 0-0	0-0	10		30,251
26	28	H	Southend U	W 3-1	2-0	9	Ennis [24], Sadlier 2 [41, 55]	7063
27	Feb 1	A	Fleetwood T	L 1-2	0-1	10	Ennis [55]	3008
28	4	A	Tranmere R	W 3-0	0-0	9	Ramsey 2 [54, 75], Okenabirhie [84]	5464
29	8	H	Rochdale	D 1-1	1-0	8	Taylor, J [1]	7638
30	11	H	Bolton W	W 2-1	1-0	8	Okenabirhie [40], Ennis [48]	7097
31	15	A	Gillingham	L 1-2	1-1	9	Sheaf [13]	4754
32	22	A	Shrewsbury T	L 0-1	0-0	11		5672
33	29	H	Wycombe W	W 3-1	1-0	10	Ennis [45], Sadlier [71], McCarthy (og) [83]	7522
34	Mar 7	A	Milton Keynes D	W 1-0	0-0	9	Ramsey [67]	7880
35	14	H	AFC Wimbledon	Cancelled				
36	17	A	Portsmouth	Cancelled				
37	21	A	Accrington S	Cancelled				
38	24	A	Bolton W	Cancelled				
39	28	A	Burton Alb	Cancelled				
40	Apr 4	H	Tranmere R	Cancelled				
41	10	A	Lincoln C	Cancelled				
42	18	A	Rotherham U	Cancelled				
43	25	H	Ipswich T	Cancelled				
44	May 3	A	Blackpool	Cancelled				

Final League Position: 9 (on points-per-game basis)

GOALSCORERS

League (51): Sadlier 11, Ennis 6, Taylor, J 6, Whiteman 5 (1 pen), Coppinger 3, Ramsey 3, Thomas 3, James 2, John 2, Okenabirhie 2, Anderson, T 1, Bingham 1, May 1, Sheaf 1, own goals 4.
FA Cup (3): Anderson, T 1, Bingham 1, Coppinger 1.
Carabao Cup (0).
Leasing.com Trophy (6): May 2, John 1, Sadlier 1, Sterling 1, Wright 1.

Lawlor I 7	Halliday B 34	Baptiste A 2	Anderson T 32	James R 26+1	Whiteman B 33	Sheaf B 29+3	May A 7+8	Coppinger J 24+5	Gomes M 13+10	Sadlier K 28+5	Ennis N 22+7	Crawford A —+1	Blair M 3+9	Taylor J 22+6	John C 17+1	Sterling K 1+2	Kiwomya A —+1	Dieng T 27	Daniels D 8+2	Wright J 16+4	Thomas K 5+5	Bingham R 3+5	Watters M —+5	Cole D 5+4	Okenabirhie F 2+3	Ramsey J 6+1	Amos D 2	Lokilo J —+1	Match No.
1	2	3	4	5	6	7	8	9^{2}	10^{1}	11	12	13																	1
1	2	3^{2}	4	5	7	6	8	9^{1}	10^{3}	11	13		12	14															2
1	2		3	5	7	6	10^{3}	9^{2}	14	8	11^{1}			13	4	12													3
1	2		3	5	7		10^{2}	9^{1}	6^{3}	8	11		14	13	4	12													4
1	2		3	5	6	7	10^{3}	9		13	12		14	8^{1}	4	11^{2}													5
1	2		3	5	6	7	12	9^{1}		13	11^{3}		8^{2}	10	4		14												6
1	2		3	5	6	7	12	13		9^{1}	11		10^{2}	8	4														7
	2		3	5	6	7	12	9^{2}	14	8^{1}	11			10^{3}	4			1	13										8
	2		3	5	6	7	12	9	13	8^{1}	11^{2}			10				1	4										9
	2		3	5	6	7	8^{1}	9		11				10				1	4	12									10
	2		3	5	6	7		9		8	12			10				1	4		11^{1}								11
	2		3	5	7	6	14	9^{2}		10	11^{1}			8				1	4^{3}	12	13								12
	2		3	5	7	6	13	9^{2}	14	10				8				1	4^{1}	12	11^{3}								13
	2		3	5	6	7^{3}	14	9^{1}	12	10				8^{2}				1	4		11	13							14
	2		4■	5	7	6	14	9^{2}	10^{3}	13				8^{1}				1	12	3		11							15
	2			5	7	6^{2}	8^{3}	9	13	10					4			1	3		14	11^{1}	12						16
	2			5^{1}	6	7		9		10	13			12	4			1	3		11	8^{2}							17
	2		3	5^{2}		6		9^{3}	7	10	13			8	4			1		12	11^{1}	14							18
	2		4	12	6	9^{1}		13	7	10	11^{3}			8^{2}	5			1		3	14								19
	2		3		6			9^{2}	7	8	11			10	5^{1}			1		4	12		13						20
	2		4	5	6	7		9^{3}	13	10	11^{1}			8^{2}				1		3	14		12						21
	2		4	5	6	7		9^{2}	12	10	11^{3}			8^{1}				1		3		14	13						22
	2		4	5	6	7		12	9^{1}	10^{3}	11		14	8^{2}				1		3		13							23
	2		4	5	6	7		9		10^{1}	11			8				1		3		12							24
	2		4	10^{1}	6	7		13	9		11^{3}		12	8^{2}	5			1		3			14						25
	2		3	5	7	6		9		10	11^{1}		12	8^{2}	4			1						13					26
	2		4		6	7^{3}		13	9	10^{1}	11			8^{2}	5			1		3				12	14				27
	2		4		6	13			9	7	10^{2}		14		5			1		3				11^{1}	12	8^{3}			28
	2		4	5	6	14			9^{2}	10	13			7^{3}				1		3				11^{1}	12	8			29
	2		4	5^{3}	6	7		9^{2}		8	10				12			1		3				13	11^{1}	14			30
	2		4		7	6				12	10^{1}		8^{2}		5			1		3				13	11■	9			31
	2		4		7	6^{1}		10^{2}	14	13	11^{3}			12	5			1		3				9		8			32
	2		4		6	14			9^{3}	7	10^{2}		13					1		3				11		8^{1}	5	12	33
	2		4		7	6^{1}			13	8	10^{2}		14	12				1		3				11		9^{3}	5		34
																													35
																													36
																													37
																													38
																													39
																													40
																													41
																													42
																													43
																													44

FA Cup

First Round	AFC Wimbledon	(a)	1-1
Replay	AFC Wimbledon	(h)	2-0
Second Round	Gillingham	(a)	0-3

Carabao Cup

First Round	Grimsby T	(a)	0-1

Leasing.com Trophy

Group H (N)	Lincoln C	(h)	3-1
Group H (N)	Rotherham U	(a)	2-3
Group H (N)	Manchester U U21	(h)	1-2
Second Round (N)	Leicester C U21	(h)	0-3

EVERTON

FOUNDATION

St Domingo Church Sunday School formed a football club in 1878 which played at Stanley Park. Enthusiasm was so great that in November 1879 they decided to expand membership and changed the name to Everton, playing in black shirts with a scarlet sash and nicknamed the 'Black Watch'. After wearing several other colours, royal blue was adopted in 1901.

Goodison Park, Goodison Road, Liverpool L4 4EL.

Telephone: (0151) 556 1878.

Ticket Office: (0151) 556 1878.

Website: www.evertonfc.com

Email: everton@evertonfc.com

Ground Capacity: 39,414.

Record Attendance: 78,299 v Liverpool, Division 1, 18 September 1948.

Pitch Measurements: 100.48m × 68m (110yd × 74.5yd).

Chairman: Bill Kenwright CBE.

Chief Executive: Dr Denise Barrett-Baxendale MBE.

Manager: Carlo Ancelotti.

Assistant Manager: Duncan Ferguson.

Colours: Blue shirts with white trim, white shorts with blue trim, white socks with blue trim.

Year Formed: 1878.

Turned Professional: 1885.

Previous Name: 1878, St Domingo FC; 1879, Everton.

Club Nickname: 'The Toffees'.

Grounds: 1878, Stanley Park; 1882, Priory Road; 1884, Anfield Road; 1892, Goodison Park.

First Football League Game: 8 September 1888, Football League, v Accrington (h) W 2–1 – Smalley; Dick, Ross; Holt, Jones, Dobson; Fleming (2), Waugh, Lewis, Edgar Chadwick, Farmer.

HONOURS

League Champions: Division 1 – 1914–15, 1927–28, 1931–32, 1938–39, 1962–63, 1969–70, 1984–85, 1986–87; Football League 1890–91; Division 2 – 1930–31.
Runners-up: Division 1 – 1894–95, 1901–02, 1904–05, 1908–09, 1911–12, 1985–86; Football League 1889–90; Division 2 – 1953–54.

FA Cup Winners: 1906, 1933, 1966, 1984, 1995.
Runners-up: 1893, 1897, 1907, 1968, 1985, 1986, 1989, 2009.

League Cup: *Runners-up:* 1977, 1984.

League Super Cup: *Runners-up:* 1986.

Full Members' Cup: *Runners-up:* 1989, 1991.

European Competitions
European Cup: 1963–64, 1970–71 *(qf)*.
Champions League: 2005–06.
Fairs Cup: 1962–63, 1964–65, 1965–66.
UEFA Cup: 1975–76, 1978–79, 1979–80, 2005–06, 2007–08, 2008–09.
Europa League: 2009–10, 2014–15, 2017–18.
European Cup-Winners' Cup: 1966–67, 1984–85 *(winners)*, 1995–96.

Record League Victory: 9–1 v Manchester C, Division 1, 3 September 1906 – Scott; Balmer, Crelley; Booth, Taylor (1), Abbott (1); Sharp, Bolton (1), Young (4), Settle (2), George Wilson; 9–1 v Plymouth Arg, Division 2, 27 December 1930 – Coggins; Williams, Cresswell; McPherson, Griffiths, Thomson; Critchley, Dunn, Dean (4), Johnson (1), Stein (4).

FOOTBALL YEARBOOK FACT FILE

Everton played a match under artificial illumination at Anfield in January 1890. The ground was lit up by 15 paraffin-fuelled Wells Lights and a crowd estimated at 12,000 saw the Toffees defeat Sheffield United 5-2 in a friendly fixture.

Record Cup Victory: 11–2 v Derby Co, FA Cup 1st rd, 18 January 1890 – Smalley; Hannah, Doyle (1); Kirkwood, Holt (1), Parry; Latta, Brady (3), Geary (3), Edgar Chadwick, Millward (3).

Record Defeat: 4–10 v Tottenham H, Division 1, 11 October 1958.

Most League Points (2 for a win): 66, Division 1, 1969–70.

Most League Points (3 for a win): 90, Division 1, 1984–85.

Most League Goals: 121, Division 2, 1930–31.

Highest League Scorer in Season: William Ralph 'Dixie' Dean, 60, Division 1, 1927–28 (All-time League record).

Most League Goals in Total Aggregate: William Ralph 'Dixie' Dean, 349, 1925–37.

Most League Goals in One Match: 6, Jack Southworth v WBA, Division 1, 30 December 1893.

Most Capped Player: Tim Howard, 93 (121), USA.

Most League Appearances: Neville Southall, 578, 1981–98.

Youngest League Player: Jose Baxter, 16 years 191 days v Blackburn R, 16 August 2008.

Record Transfer Fee Received: £75,000,000 from Manchester U for Romelu Lukaku, July 2017.

Record Transfer Fee Paid: £40,000,000 (rising to £45,000,000) to Swansea C for Gylfi Sigurdsson, August 2017.

Football League Record: 1888 Founder Member of the Football League; 1930–31 Division 2; 1931–51 Division 1; 1951–54 Division 2; 1954–92 Division 1; 1992– Premier League.

MANAGERS

W. E. Barclay 1888–89 *(Secretary-Manager)*
Dick Molyneux 1889–1901 *(Secretary-Manager)*
William C. Cuff 1901–18 *(Secretary-Manager)*
W. J. Sawyer 1918–19 *(Secretary-Manager)*
Thomas H. McIntosh 1919–35 *(Secretary-Manager)*
Theo Kelly 1936–48
Cliff Britton 1948–56
Ian Buchan 1956–58
Johnny Carey 1958–61
Harry Catterick 1961–73
Billy Bingham 1973–77
Gordon Lee 1977–81
Howard Kendall 1981–87
Colin Harvey 1987–90
Howard Kendall 1990–93
Mike Walker 1994
Joe Royle 1994–97
Howard Kendall 1997–98
Walter Smith 1998–2002
David Moyes 2002–13
Roberto Martinez 2013–16
Ronald Koeman 2016–17
Sam Allardyce 2017–18
Marco Silva 2018–19
Carlo Ancelotti December 2019–

LATEST SEQUENCES

Longest Sequence of League Wins: 12, 24.3.1894 – 13.10.1894.

Longest Sequence of League Defeats: 6, 27.8.2005– 15.10.2005.

Longest Sequence of League Draws: 5, 4.5.1977 – 16.5.1977.

Longest Sequence of Unbeaten League Matches: 20, 29.4.1978 – 16.12.1978.

Longest Sequence Without a League Win: 14, 6.3.1937 – 4.9.1937.

Successive Scoring Runs: 40 from 15.3.1930.

Successive Non-scoring Runs: 6 from 27.8.2005.

TEN YEAR LEAGUE RECORD

		P	*W*	*D*	*L*	*F*	*A*	*Pts*	*Pos*
2010-11	PR Lge	38	13	15	10	51	45	54	7
2011-12	PR Lge	38	15	11	12	50	40	56	7
2012-13	PR Lge	38	16	15	7	55	40	63	6
2013-14	PR Lge	38	21	9	8	61	39	72	5
2014-15	PR Lge	38	12	11	15	48	50	47	11
2015-16	PR Lge	38	11	14	13	59	55	47	11
2016-17	PR Lge	38	17	10	11	62	44	61	7
2017-18	PR Lge	38	13	10	15	44	58	49	8
2018-19	PR Lge	38	15	9	14	54	46	54	8
2019-20	PR Lge	38	13	10	15	44	56	49	12

DID YOU KNOW ?

Everton's FA Cup fifth round tie at Goodison Park against Liverpool in March 1967 was watched by over 100,000 spectators. The match attendance was 64,851 while another 40,149 watched the game on closed circuit television at Anfield.

EVERTON – PREMIER LEAGUE 2019–20 LEAGUE RECORD

Match No.	Date	Venue	Opponents	Result		H/T Score	Lg Pos.	Goalscorers	Attendance
1	Aug 10	A	Crystal Palace	D	0-0	0-0	8		25,151
2	17	H	Watford	W	1-0	1-0	7	Bernard [10]	39,066
3	23	A	Aston Villa	L	0-2	0-1	9		41,922
4	Sept 1	H	Wolverhampton W	W	3-2	2-1	6	Richarlison 2 [5, 80], Iwobi [12]	39,374
5	15	A	Bournemouth	L	1-3	1-1	11	Calvert-Lewin [44]	10,416
6	21	H	Sheffield U	L	0-2	0-1	14		39,354
7	28	H	Manchester C	L	1-3	1-1	15	Calvert-Lewin [33]	39,222
8	Oct 5	A	Burnley	L	0-1	0-0	17		20,650
9	19	H	West Ham U	W	2-0	1-0	13	Bernard [17], Sigurdsson [90]	39,263
10	26	A	Brighton & HA	L	2-3	1-1	16	Webster (og) [20], Calvert-Lewin [74]	30,529
11	Nov 3	H	Tottenham H	D	1-1	0-0	17	Tosun [90]	39,001
12	9	A	Southampton	W	2-1	1-0	13	Davies [4], Richarlison [75]	29,754
13	23	H	Norwich C	L	0-2	0-0	15		39,241
14	Dec 1	A	Leicester C	L	1-2	1-0	17	Richarlison [23]	32,144
15	4	A	Liverpool	L	2-5	2-4	18	Keane [21], Richarlison [45]	53,094
16	7	H	Chelsea	W	3-1	1-0	14	Richarlison [5], Calvert-Lewin 2 [49, 84]	39,114
17	15	A	Manchester U	D	1-1	1-0	16	Lindelof (og) [36]	63,328
18	21	H	Arsenal	D	0-0	0-0	15		39,336
19	26	H	Burnley	W	1-0	0-0	13	Calvert-Lewin [80]	39,177
20	28	A	Newcastle U	W	2-1	1-0	10	Calvert-Lewin 2 [13, 64]	52,211
21	Jan 1	A	Manchester C	L	1-2	0-0	11	Richarlison [71]	54,407
22	11	H	Brighton & HA	W	1-0	1-0	11	Richarlison [38]	38,772
23	18	A	West Ham U	D	1-1	1-1	11	Calvert-Lewin [44]	59,915
24	21	H	Newcastle U	D	2-2	1-0	12	Kean [30], Calvert-Lewin [54]	38,822
25	Feb 1	A	Watford	W	3-2	2-2	9	Mina 2 [45, 45], Walcott [90]	21,229
26	8	H	Crystal Palace	W	3-1	1-0	7	Bernard [18], Richarlison [58], Calvert-Lewin [88]	38,987
27	23	A	Arsenal	L	2-3	2-2	11	Calvert-Lewin [1], Richarlison [45]	60,296
28	Mar 1	H	Manchester U	D	1-1	1-1	11	Calvert-Lewin [3]	39,374
29	8	A	Chelsea	L	0-4	0-2	12		40,694
30	June 21	H	Liverpool	D	0-0	0-0	12		0
31	24	A	Norwich C	W	1-0	0-0	10	Keane [55]	0
32	July 1	H	Leicester C	W	2-1	2-0	11	Richarlison [10], Sigurdsson (pen) [16]	0
33	6	A	Tottenham H	L	0-1	0-1	11		0
34	9	H	Southampton	D	1-1	1-1	11	Richarlison [44]	0
35	12	A	Wolverhampton W	L	0-3	0-1	11		0
36	16	H	Aston Villa	D	1-1	0-0	11	Walcott [87]	0
37	20	A	Sheffield U	W	1-0	0-0	11	Richarlison [46]	0
38	26	H	Bournemouth	L	1-3	1-2	12	Kean [41]	0

Final League Position: 12

GOALSCORERS

League (44): Calvert-Lewin 13, Richarlison 13, Bernard 3, Kean 2, Keane 2, Mina 2, Sigurdsson 2 (1 pen), Walcott 2, Davies 1, Iwobi 1, Tosun 1, own goals 2.
FA Cup (0).
Carabao Cup (10): Calvert-Lewin 2, Richarlison 2, Baines 1, Davies 1, Digne 1, Holgate 1, Iwobi 1, Sigurdsson 1 (1 pen).
Leasing.com Trophy (5): Niasse 2, Evans 1, Gordon 1, Simms 1.

Pickford J 38	Coleman S 21 + 6	Keane M 28 + 3	Mina Y 25 + 4	Digne L 35	Schneiderlin M 12 + 3	Andre Gomes F 17 + 2	Richarlison 36	Sigurdsson G 28 + 7	Bernard C 15 + 12	Calvert-Lewin D 30 + 6	Gbamin J 1 + 1	Kean M 6 + 23	Davies T 23 + 7	Walcott T 17 + 8	Holgate M 24 + 3	Iwobi A 19 + 6	Delph F 13 + 3	Tosun C 2 + 3	Sidibe D 18 + 7	Baines L 4 + 4	Niasse O — + 3	Gordon A 4 + 7	Branthwaite J 2 + 2	Match No.
1	2	3	4	5	6■	7^{1}	8	9^{3}	10	11^{2}	12	13	14											1
1	2	3	4	5^{3}		7	8^{1}	9	10	11^{2}	6	13		12	14									2
1	2	3	4	5	6	7	8^{3}	9^{1}	10^{2}	11		13		14		12								3
1	2	3	4	5		6	8	9	12	13		11^{2}				10^{1}	7							4
1	2	3	4	5	6		8^{3}	9^{1}	13	11^{2}		12		14		10	7							5
1	2^{3}	3	4	5	6^{2}		8	9	10^{1}			11		14		13	7	12						6
1	2	3	4	5	6^{3}		10	9		11		13	14	8^{1}		12^{2}	7							7
1	2■	3	4	5	6^{3}	14	8	9^{1}		11^{2}		13				10	7		12					8
1		3	4^{3}	5		6	11	13	10			12	7	8^{1}	14	9^{2}			2					9
1		3		5		7	11	12	10^{1}	14			6	8^{3}	4	9^{2}	13		2					10
1			3	5		9^{3}	11	14		13			8^{2}	7^{1}	4	10	6	12	2					11
1		14	3	5	7		10^{3}	9		13			6	8^{2}	4	12		11^{1}	2					12
1	13		3	5	7^{1}		10	9		14			6	8^{3}	4	12		11	2^{2}					13
1		4	3	8	13		11	7		10^{1}		12	6		2	9^{2}			5					14
1		4	5	6	14		10	9	12	11^{2}		13	8^{3}		3	7			2^{1}					15
1		3		5^{2}	7		11^{1}	8	14	10			12	6^{3}	4	9			2	13				16
1	2	3	4	5^{1}			10		9^{2}	11		13^{3}	7		8	6				12	14			17
1		13	3	5			10	7		11		14	6		4	9^{1}	8^{2}	12^{3}	2					18
1	2		3	8			10^{2}	6	9^{1}	11		12	13	14	4		7		5^{3}					19
1	13	3	14				9	7		11		10^{1}	8	6^{2}	4		12		2	5^{3}				20
1	2^{1}		3	9			10	6^{2}		11		13	8	12	4		7		5					21
1	13	3	14	5^{3}			11	8	9^{1}	10			7	6^{2}	4		12		2					22
1	2		3	5					9^{1}	11		10^{3}	7	6^{2}	4		8		13		14	12		23
1	12		3	5	7				9^{2}	10		11^{1}	13	6^{3}	4		8		2		14			24
1		14	3	5	13		11	7^{2}		10^{3}		12		6	4	9^{1}	8■		2					25
1	2	4	3	5	7		11	8^{3}	9^{2}	10			13	6^{1}	14				12					26
1			3		7^{1}	12	11	9	13	10		14			4	6^{2}	8^{3}		2	5				27
1	2^{1}	3				8^{3}	11	9	13	10		14	7	6^{2}	4				12	5				28
1		3		5		7	11	9	6^{1}	10^{3}		13	8^{2}	12	4				2			14		29
1	2	4		5		8	11	12	13	10^{3}		14	7		3	6^{2}						9^{1}		30
1	2	3		5		8	11^{2}	12	9^{3}	10		13	7^{1}		4	6^{4}				14		15		31
1	2	3	13	5		7	11^{1}	8	14	10			12		4	6^{2}						9^{3}		32
1	2^{5}	3	12	5		8	10	7^{3}	14	11		16	6^{4}		4^{1}	9^{2}			15			13		33
1	2	4	3	5		8^{1}	11	12	15	10^{3}		14	7			6^{2}			13			9^{4}		34
1	12	2	3^{1}	4			10^{5}	7	15	11		16	6	5^{3}		14				9^{2}		8^{4}	13	35
1	2	3		5		8	11^{5}	15	9^{3}	10		16	7^{4}	13	4^{1}	6^{2}						14	12	36
1	13	3		5		7	11	9^{2}		10			8	6^{1}					2			12	4	37
1	2^{2}	3		5^{3}		6	10	9	15	16		11^{4}	7^{5}	8^{1}					12	14		13	4	38

FA Cup

Third Round	Liverpool	(a)	0-1

Carabao Cup

Second Round	Lincoln C	(a)	4-2
Third Round	Sheffield W	(a)	2-0
Fourth Round	Watford	(h)	2-0
Quarter-Final	Leicester C	(h)	2-2

(Leicester C won 4-2 on penalties)

Leasing.com Trophy (Everton U21)

Group E (N)	Mansfield T	(a)	1-1

(Everton U21 won 4-1 on penalties)

Group E (N)	Burton Alb	(a)	2-0
Group E (N)	Crewe Alex	(a)	2-2

(Crewe Alex won 5-4 on penalties)

Second Round (N)	Fleetwood T	(h)	0-4

EXETER CITY

FOUNDATION

Exeter City was formed in 1904 by the amalgamation of St Sidwell's United and Exeter United. The club first played in the East Devon League and then the Plymouth & District League. After an exhibition match between West Bromwich Albion and Woolwich Arsenal, which was held to test interest as Exeter was then a rugby stronghold, it was decided to form Exeter City. At a meeting at the Red Lion Hotel in 1908, the club turned professional.

St James Park, Stadium Way, Exeter, Devon EX4 6PX.

Telephone: (01392) 411 243.

Ticket Office: (01392) 413 952.

Website: www.exetercityfc.co.uk

Email: reception@ecfc.co.uk

Ground Capacity: 8,541.

Record Attendance: 20,984 v Sunderland, FA Cup 6th rd (replay), 4 March 1931.

Pitch Measurements: 103m × 64m (112.5yd × 70yd).

Chairman: Julian Tagg.

Chief Operating Officer: Justin Quick.

Manager: Matt Taylor.

Assistant Manager: Wayne Carlisle.

Colours: Red and white striped shirts with white sleeves, black shorts with white trim, white socks with black hoops.

Year Formed: 1904.

Turned Professional: 1908.

Club Nickname: 'The Grecians'.

Ground: 1904, St James Park.

First Football League Game: 28 August 1920, Division 3, v Brentford (h) W 3–0 – Pym; Coleburne, Feebury (1p); Crawshaw, Carrick, Mitton; Appleton, Makin, Wright (1), Vowles (1), Dockray.

Record League Victory: 8–1 v Coventry C, Division 3 (S), 4 December 1926 – Bailey; Pollard, Charlton; Pullen, Pool, Garrett; Purcell (2), McDevitt, Blackmore (2), Dent (2), Compton (2). 8–1 v Aldershot, Division 3 (S), 4 May 1935 – Chesters; Gray, Miller; Risdon, Webb, Angus; Jack Scott (1), Wrightson (1), Poulter (3), McArthur (1), Dryden (1), (1 og).

Record Cup Victory: 14–0 v Weymouth, FA Cup 1st qual rd, 3 October 1908 – Fletcher; Craig, Bulcock; Ambler, Chadwick, Wake; Parnell (1), Watson (1), McGuigan (4), Bell (6), Copestake (2).

Record Defeat: 0–9 v Notts Co, Division 3 (S), 16 October 1948. 0–9 v Northampton T, Division 3 (S), 12 April 1958.

HONOURS

League Champions: Division 4 – 1989–90.

Runners-up: Division 3S – 1932–33; FL 2 – 2008–09; Division 4 – 1976–77; Conference – (4th) 2007–08 *(promoted via play-offs)*.

FA Cup: 6th rd replay – 1931; 6th rd – 1981.

League Cup: never past 4th rd.

FOOTBALL YEARBOOK FACT FILE

In 1910–11 Exeter City were unable to play their home FA Cup ties at their St James Park ground because the pitch was less than the minimum regulation length of 100 yards. Their fourth qualifying round replay against Reading was played at the County Ground, home of the city's rugby club, but the Grecians were forced to concede home advantage to their next two opponents, Nelson and Burnley.

Most League Points (2 for a win): 62, Division 4, 1976–77.

Most League Points (3 for a win): 89, Division 4, 1989–90.

Most League Goals: 88, Division 3 (S), 1932–33.

Highest League Scorer in Season: Fred Whitlow, 33, Division 3 (S), 1932–33.

Most League Goals in Total Aggregate: Tony Kellow, 129, 1976–78, 1980–83, 1985–88.

Most League Goals in One Match: 4, Harold 'Jazzo' Kirk v Portsmouth, Division 3 (S), 3 March 1923; 4, Fred Dent v Bristol R, Division 3 (S), 5 November 1927; 4, Fred Whitlow v Watford, Division 3 (S), 29 October 1932.

Most Capped Player: Joel Grant, 2 (14), Jamaica.

Most League Appearances: Arnold Mitchell, 495, 1952–66.

Youngest League Player: Ethan Ampadu, 15 years 337 days v Crawley T, 16 August 2016.

Record Transfer Fee Received: £1,800,000 from Brentford for Ollie Watkins, July 2017.

Record Transfer Fee Paid: £100,000 to Aberdeen for Jayden Stockley, August 2017.

Football League Record: 1920 Elected to Division 3; 1921–58 Division 3 (S); 1958–64 Division 4; 1964–66 Division 3; 1966–77 Division 4; 1977–84 Division 3; 1984–90 Division 4; 1990–92 Division 3; 1992–94 Division 2; 1994–2003 Division 3; 2003–08 Conference; 2008–09 FL 2; 2009–12 FL 1; 2012– FL 2.

LATEST SEQUENCES

Longest Sequence of League Wins: 7, 31.12.2016 – 4.2.2017.

Longest Sequence of League Defeats: 7, 14.1.1984 – 25.2.1984.

Longest Sequence of League Draws: 6, 13.9.1986 – 4.10.1986.

Longest Sequence of Unbeaten League Matches: 13, 22.4.2019 – 21.9.2019.

Longest Sequence Without a League Win: 18, 21.2.1995 – 19.8.1995.

Successive Scoring Runs: 22 from 15.9.1958.

Successive Non-scoring Runs: 6 from 17.1.1986.

MANAGERS

Arthur Chadwick 1910–22
Fred Mavin 1923–27
Dave Wilson 1928–29
Billy McDevitt 1929–35
Jack English 1935–39
George Roughton 1945–52
Norman Kirkman 1952–53
Norman Dodgin 1953–57
Bill Thompson 1957–58
Frank Broome 1958–60
Glen Wilson 1960–62
Cyril Spiers 1962–63
Jack Edwards 1963–65
Ellis Stuttard 1965–66
Jock Basford 1966–67
Frank Broome 1967–69
Johnny Newman 1969–76
Bobby Saxton 1977–79
Brian Godfrey 1979–83
Gerry Francis 1983–84
Jim Iley 1984–85
Colin Appleton 1985–87
Terry Cooper 1988–91
Alan Ball 1991–94
Terry Cooper 1994–95
Peter Fox 1995–2000
Noel Blake 2000–01
John Cornforth 2001–02
Neil McNab 2002–03
Gary Peters 2003
Eamonn Dolan 2003–04
Alex Inglethorpe 2004–06
Paul Tisdale 2006–18
Matt Taylor June 2018–

TEN YEAR LEAGUE RECORD

		P	*W*	*D*	*L*	*F*	*A*	*Pts*	*Pos*
2010-11	FL 1	46	20	10	16	66	73	70	8
2011-12	FL 1	46	10	12	24	46	75	42	23
2012-13	FL 2	46	18	10	18	63	62	64	10
2013-14	FL 2	46	14	13	19	54	57	55	16
2014-15	FL 2	46	17	13	16	61	65	64	10
2015-16	FL 2	46	17	13	16	63	65	64	14
2016-17	FL 2	46	21	8	17	75	56	71	5
2017-18	FL 2	46	24	8	14	64	54	80	4
2018-19	FL 2	46	19	13	14	60	49	70	9
2019-20	FL 2	37	18	11	8	53	43	65	5§

§Decided on points-per-game (1.76)

DID YOU KNOW ?

At the end of the 1950–51 season Exeter City went on a four-match tour of the Netherlands, playing some of the leading Dutch sides of the era. They began by defeating DOS Utrecht followed by a 5-3 win against a Haarlem team that included seven full internationals. The Grecians then lost 4-2 to BVV before completing the trip with a 2-0 victory over Den Haag.

EXETER CITY – SKY BET LEAGUE TWO 2019–20 LEAGUE RECORD

Match No.	*Date*	*Venue*	*Opponents*	*Result*	*H/T Score*	*Lg Pos.*	*Goalscorers*	*Atten-dance*
1	Aug 3	H	Macclesfield T	W 1-0	0-0	6	Bowman [88]	4502
2	10	A	Stevenage	W 1-0	0-0	3	Law [89]	2398
3	17	H	Swindon T	D 1-1	0-0	2	Jay [72]	5435
4	20	A	Oldham Ath	D 0-0	0-0	4		2805
5	24	A	Morecambe	W 3-2	2-1	1	Taylor [21], Martin, L [25], Law [85]	1517
6	31	H	Mansfield T	W 1-0	1-0	1	Bowman [5]	4316
7	Sept 7	A	Carlisle U	W 3-1	1-0	1	Martin, L [36], Martin, A [67], Law [90]	4167
8	14	H	Leyton Orient	D 2-2	1-1	1	Sweeney [41], Law (pen) [90]	4933
9	17	H	Port Vale	W 2-0	0-0	1	Bowman [81], Martin, L [89]	3765
10	21	A	Newport Co	D 1-1	1-0	1	Martin, L [15]	4762
11	28	H	Grimsby T	L 1-3	0-1	1	Bowman [90]	4973
12	Oct 5	A	Crewe Alex	D 1-1	1-0	2	Moxey [2]	5131
13	12	H	Forest Green R	W 1-0	1-0	2	Bowman [11]	5312
14	19	A	Cambridge U	L 0-4	0-1	4		3816
15	22	A	Scunthorpe U	L 1-3	1-2	6	Jay [27]	3055
16	26	H	Plymouth Arg	W 4-0	1-0	2	Law 2 (1 pen) [42 (p), 83], Parkes [49], Williams [67]	7924
17	Nov 2	A	Bradford C	L 0-2	0-2	5		14,002
18	16	H	Cheltenham T	D 0-0	0-0	5		4956
19	23	A	Crawley T	W 1-0	0-0	4	Moxey [77]	2170
20	Dec 7	H	Northampton T	W 3-2	1-1	2	Williams [38], Martin, A [64], Fisher [66]	3971
21	14	A	Salford C	W 1-0	1-0	2	Bowman [33]	2922
22	21	H	Walsall	D 3-3	2-3	2	Bowman 2 [32, 41], Martin, L [64]	4323
23	26	H	Newport Co	W 1-0	1-0	2	Martin, L [14]	5968
24	29	A	Colchester U	D 2-2	1-1	2	Taylor [8], Bowman (pen) [77]	4739
25	Jan 1	A	Forest Green R	W 1-0	1-0	2	Atangana [5]	3012
26	11	H	Cambridge U	W 2-0	0-0	2	Bowman [53], Williams [81]	4517
27	18	A	Grimsby T	W 1-0	0-0	2	Law [67]	6021
28	25	H	Colchester U	D 0-0	0-0	2		4745
29	28	A	Port Vale	L 1-3	1-0	2	Ajose [22]	3347
30	Feb 1	A	Swindon T	L 1-2	1-2	4	Williams [34]	13,095
31	8	H	Stevenage	W 2-1	1-0	3	Williams [36], Jay [81]	4458
32	11	H	Oldham Ath	W 5-1	2-1	3	Richardson [20], Jay (pen) [43], Collins [51], Bowman [61], Dickenson [90]	3527
33	15	A	Macclesfield T	W 3-2	2-1	2	Ajose [11], Sweeney [17], Bowman [86]	1389
34	22	A	Northampton T	L 0-2	0-1	3		5046
35	29	H	Crawley T	D 1-1	0-1	3	Dickenson [82]	5404
36	Mar 3	H	Crewe Alex	D 1-1	1-0	4	Parkes [32]	4221
37	7	A	Walsall	L 1-3	0-1	4	Bowman [51]	5521
38	14	H	Salford C	Cancelled				
39	17	H	Scunthorpe U	Cancelled				
40	23	A	Plymouth Arg	Cancelled				
41	28	H	Bradford C	Cancelled				
42	Apr 4	A	Cheltenham T	Cancelled				
43	10	H	Morecambe	Cancelled				
44	13	A	Mansfield T	Cancelled				
45	18	H	Carlisle U	Cancelled				
46	25	A	Leyton Orient	Cancelled				

Final League Position: 5 (on points-per-game basis)

GOALSCORERS

League (53): Bowman 13 (1 pen), Law 7 (2 pens), Martin, L 6, Williams 5, Jay 4 (1 pen), Ajose 2, Dickenson 2, Martin, A 2, Moxey 2, Parkes 2, Sweeney 2, Taylor 2, Atangana 1, Collins 1, Fisher 1, Richardson 1.
FA Cup (4): Fisher 2, Atangana 1, Bowman 1.
Carabao Cup (1): Sweeney 1.
Leasing.com Trophy (13): Jay 4, Ajose 3, Randall 2, Martin, L 1, Taylor 1, Tillson 1, own goal 1.
League Two Play-offs (3): Bowman 1, Martin, A 1, Richardson 1.

Ward L 20	Sweeney P 35 + 1	Martin A 32 + 3	Parkes T 25 + 6	Moxey D 21 + 3	Williams R 33 + 4	Taylor J 24 + 9	Collins A 33 + 3	Law N 28 + 4	Ajose N 10 + 3	Bowman R 36 + 1	Martin L 21 + 7	Warren G — + 1	Woodman C 4 + 2	Jay M 9 + 5	Richardson J 10 + 8	Sparkes J 17	Fisher A 3 + 13	Seymour B 3 + 8	Atangana N 18 + 4	Maxted J 17	Tillson J — + 2	Randall J — + 2	Chrisene B — + 1	Dickenson B 8 + 2	Match No.
1	2	3	4	5	6^{1}	7	8	9	10^{2}	11	12	13													1
1	2		3	4	6	8	7	9	10^{1}	11	12		5												2
1	2	3		4	6	7^{1}	8	9	10^{2}	11	13		5	12											3
1	2	3		4	13	12	7	6	14	10	11^{2}			9^{3}	5^{1}	8									4
1	2	3	14	4	5^{3}	6	7	9		10	11^{2}				13	8^{1}	12								5
1	2	3		4	5	7	8			10	11		12	6^{1}		9									6
1	2	3	12	4	5	6	7	9		10^{2}	11^{1}			14		8^{3}	13								7
1	2	3^{1}	13	4	5	6	7^{2}	9		11	10^{3}					8	12	14							8
1	2	14	3	4	13	6	7	9		10	12				5^{2}	8^{1}		11^{3}							9
1	2	13	3	4	5^{1}	6	7	9^{2}		11	10				12	8									10
1	2		3	4	5	6	7^{3}	9		10	11^{1}				12	8^{2}	13	14							11
1	2	12	3	4	5	6	7	9		11^{3}	10^{2}					8^{1}	13		14						12
	2	3	4		5	6	7^{1}	9		11	10^{2}					8	13		12	1					13
	2^{2}	3	4		5	7	12	9		11	10^{3}			14		8	13		6^{1}	1					14
		2	3	4	13	14	7	12		10				9	5	8^{3}		11^{2}	6^{1}	1					15
	2	3	4		5	6	7	9^{1}		10^{3}	11^{2}		8	13				14	12	1					16
	2	3	4▪		5	6▪	7	9		11	10^{1}		8^{2}		13			12		1					17
	2	3		4	5		7			10	12		14	9^{2}		8	11^{3}		6^{1}	1	13				18
	2	3	14	4	5	13	7	9		11	10^{2}					8^{3}		12	6^{1}	1					19
	2	3	13	4	5	14	7^{3}	9		10						8^{2}	11^{1}	12	6	1					20
	2	3	4	8	5	9^{1}	7	12		10	13						11^{2}		6	1					21
	2	3	12	4^{1}	5	13	7^{3}	9		11	10^{2}					8		14	6	1					22
	2	3	4		5	7	12	9		11	10^{1}					8^{2}		13	6	1					23
	2	3	4		5	6	7		14	12	11^{1}			9^{2}	8			10^{3}	13	1					24
	2	3	4		5	12	6	9^{2}		10	11^{1}				8				7▪	1	13				25
	2	3	4	12	5^{2}	6	7	8		10	11^{1}				9^{3}					1		13	14		26
	2	3	4	13	5	6	7	8		10	11^{1}									1		12		9^{2}	27
	3	4	5		2	7	8	9	11^{1}	10					6		12			1					28
	3	4	5		12	7^{2}	9	13	11^{3}	10					6		14		8	1				2^{1}	29
1	3	4	5^{1}	6	2	8^{2}	12	9	14	11	7^{3}								10					13	30
1	2	3	4		5		7	8^{3}	11^{2}	10				12	13		14		6					9^{1}	31
1	3	4	5^{2}	12	2^{1}		7		11	10^{3}				9	6		13		8					14	32
1	2	3		4	5	12	6		11^{2}	10				8^{1}	13				7					9	33
1	2	3	4		5		7	12	11^{2}	10				8^{3}	13		14		6					9^{1}	34
1	3^{2}	4		5	2	7		9	11^{1}	10	12				13				8					6	35
1	2	3	4		5	12	7	8		10	11^{1}								6					9	36
1	13	3	4		8	12	7	10^{2}		11				9	2		14		6^{3}					5^{1}	37
																									38
																									39
																									40
																									41
																									42
																									43
																									44
																									45
																									46

FA Cup

First Round	Cambridge U	(a)	1-1
Replay	Cambridge U	(h)	1-0
Second Round	Hartlepool U	(h)	2-2
Replay (aet)	Hartlepool U	(a)	0-1

League Two Play-Offs

Semi-Final 1st leg	Colchester U	(a)	0-1
Semi-Final 2nd leg	Colchester U	(h)	3-1
Final	Northampton T	(Wembley)	0-4

Carabao Cup

First Round	Coventry C	(a)	1-4

Leasing.com Trophy

Group E (S)	Cheltenham T	(h)	1-0
Group E (S)	Newport Co	(a)	2-0
Group E (S)	West Ham U U21	(h)	3-1
Second Round (S)	Oxford U	(h)	0-0
(Exeter C won 3-0 on penalties)			
Third Round (S)	Ipswich T	(h)	2-1
Quarter-Final	Stevenage	(h)	3-0
Semi-Final	Portsmouth	(a)	2-3

FLEETWOOD TOWN

FOUNDATION

Originally formed in 1908 as Fleetwood FC, it was liquidated in 1976. Re-formed as Fleetwood Town in 1977, it folded again in 1996. Once again, it was re-formed a year later as Fleetwood Wanderers, but a sponsorship deal saw the club's name immediately changed to Fleetwood Freeport through the local retail outlet centre. This sponsorship ended in 2002, but since then local energy businessman Andy Pilley took charge and the club has risen through the non-league pyramid until finally achieving Football League status in 2012 as Fleetwood Town.

Highbury Stadium, Park Avenue, Fleetwood, Lancashire FY7 6TX.

Telephone: (01253) 775 080.

Ticket Office: (01253) 775 080.

Website: www.fleetwoodtownfc.com

Email: info@fleetwoodtownfc.com

Ground Capacity: 5,103.

Record Attendance: (Before 1997) 6,150 v Rochdale, FA Cup 1st rd, 13 November 1965; (Since 1997) 5,194 v York C, FL 2 Play-Off semi-final 2nd leg, 16 May 2014.

Pitch Measurements: 100m × 65m (109.5yd × 71yd).

Chairman: Andy Pilley.

Chief Executive: Steve Curwood.

Head Coach: Joey Barton.

Assistant Head Coach: Clint Hill.

Colours: Red shirts with white sleeves and red trim, white shorts with red trim, red socks with white trim.

Year Formed: 1908 (re-formed 1997).

Previous Names: 1908, Fleetwood FC; 1977, Fleetwood Town; 1997, Fleetwood Wanderers; 2002 Fleetwood Town.

Club Nicknames: 'The Trawlermen', 'The Cod Army'.

Grounds: 1908, North Euston Hotel; 1934, Memorial Park (now Highbury Stadium).

First Football League Game: 18 August 2012, FL 2, v Torquay U (h) D 0–0 – Davies; Beeley, Mawene, McNulty, Howell, Nicolson, Johnson, McGuire, Ball, Parkin, Mangan.

HONOURS

League Champions: Conference – 2011–12.

FA Cup: 3rd rd – 2012, 2017, 2018, 2019.

League Cup: never past 2nd rd.

FOOTBALL YEARBOOK FACT FILE

Future England striker Jamie Vardy was Fleetwood Town's leading scorer in 2011–12 when the club won the Football Conference title to earn promotion to the Football League. Vardy netted 31 goals including two hat-tricks in Conference games and added another three in the FA Cup. At the end of the season he was sold to Leicester City for a club record fee.

Record League Victory: 13–0 v Oldham T, North West Counties Div 2, 5 December 1998.

Record Defeat: 0–7 v Billingham T, FA Cup 1st qual rd, 15 September 2001.

Most League Points (3 for a win): 82, FL 1, 2016–17.

Most League Goals: 66, FL 2, 2013–14.

Highest League Scorer in Season: Ched Evans, 17, FL 1, 2018–19.

Most League Goals in Total Aggregate: David Ball, 41, 2012–17.

Most League Goals in One Match: 3, Steven Schumacher v Newport Co, FL 2, 2 November 2013; 3, Paddy Madden v Burton Alb, FL 1, 19 October 2019.

Most Capped Player: Conor McLaughlin, 25 (38), Northern Ireland.

Most League Appearances: Ashley Hunter, 181, 2015–20.

Youngest League Player: Barry Baggley, 17 years 26 days v Walsall, 9 March 2019.

Record Transfer Fee Received: £1,000,000 (rising to £1,700,000) from Leicester C for Jamie Vardy, May 2012.

Record Transfer Fee Paid: £300,000 to Kidderminster H for Jamille Matt, January 2013; £300,000 to Huddersfield T for Kyle Dempsey, May 2017.

Football League Record: 2012 Promoted from Conference Premier; 2012–14 FL 2; 2014– FL 1.

MANAGER

Alan Tinsley 1997
Mark Hughes 1998
Brian Wilson 1998–99
Mick Hoyle 1999–2001
Les Attwood 2001
Mark Hughes 2001
Alan Tinsley 2001–02
Mick Hoyle 2002–03
Tony Greenwood 2003–08
Micky Mellon 2008–12
Graham Alexander 2012–15
Steven Pressley 2015–16
Uwe Rosler 2016–18
John Sheridan 2018
Joey Barton June 2018–

LATEST SEQUENCES

Longest Sequence of League Wins: 5, 1.2.2020 – 22.2.2020.

Longest Sequence of League Defeats: 6, 20.1.2018 – 20.2.2018.

Longest Sequence of League Draws: 3, 18.1.2020 – 28.1.2020.

Longest Sequence of Unbeaten League Matches: 18, 19.11.2016 – 4.3.2017.

Longest Sequence Without a League Win: 9, 20.1.2018 – 17.3.2018.

Successive Scoring Runs: 24 from 2.5.2016.

Successive Non-scoring Runs: 4 from 22.2.2014.

TEN YEAR LEAGUE RECORD

		P	*W*	*D*	*L*	*F*	*A*	*Pts*	*Pos*
2010-11	Conf P	46	22	12	12	68	42	78	5
2011-12	Conf P	46	31	10	5	102	48	103	1
2012-13	FL 2	46	15	15	16	55	57	60	13
2013-14	FL 2	46	22	10	14	66	52	76	4
2014-15	FL 1	46	17	12	17	49	52	63	10
2015-16	FL 1	46	12	15	19	52	56	51	19
2016-17	FL 1	46	23	13	10	64	43	82	4
2017-18	FL 1	46	16	9	21	59	68	57	14
2018-19	FL 1	46	16	13	17	58	52	61	11
2019-20	FL 1	35	16	12	7	51	38	60	6§

§Decided on points-per-game (1.71)

DID YOU KNOW ?

Fleetwood Town are one of only two current Football League clubs to have played in an FA Vase final. The Cod Army started off in the preliminary round of the 1984–85 competition with a 3-2 win at Maghull and went on to win the following seven rounds to earn a place in the final where they went down to Halesowen Town.

FLEETWOOD TOWN – SKY BET LEAGUE ONE 2019–20 LEAGUE RECORD

Match No.	*Date*	*Venue*	*Opponents*	*Result*		*H/T Score*	*Lg Pos.*	*Goalscorers*	*Attendance*
1	Aug 3	A	Peterborough U	W	3-1	2-0	1	Soutar ^{4}, Morris, J ^{13}, Andrew ^{81}	7958
2	10	H	AFC Wimbledon	W	2-1	0-1	3	Madden ^{56}, Morris, J ^{65}	2684
3	17	A	Doncaster R	L	2-3	1-2	5	McAleny ^{10}, Madden ^{56}	6740
4	20	H	Wycombe W	D	1-1	0-0	7	Madden ^{90}	2319
5	24	H	Accrington S	W	2-0	1-0	6	Madden ^{28}, Evans (pen) ^{71}	2802
6	31	A	Lincoln C	L	0-2	0-2	9		8361
7	Sept 7	H	Oxford U	W	2-1	1-1	4	Madden ^{15}, Clarke, P ^{79}	2672
8	14	A	Southend U	D	3-3	2-1	4	Dunne ^{34}, Morris, J ^{45}, Dempsey ^{52}	5236
9	21	H	Rochdale	W	2-1	1-1	4	Andrew ^{22}, Evans ^{87}	3229
10	28	A	Shrewsbury T	W	3-0	1-0	3	Lang (og) ^{36}, Morris, J ^{56}, Madden ^{81}	5888
11	Oct 5	H	Ipswich T	L	0-1	0-0	3		4312
12	19	H	Burton Alb	W	4-1	1-1	4	Evans ^{38}, Madden 3 $^{58, 68, 90}$	3098
13	23	A	Coventry C	L	1-2	1-0	5	Madden ^{9}	4672
14	26	H	Milton Keynes D	W	1-0	0-0	4	Evans ^{85}	2722
15	Nov 2	A	Bolton W	L	1-2	0-2	5	Morris, J ^{85}	12,756
16	23	H	Tranmere R	W	2-1	1-0	7	Morris, J ^{15}, Madden ^{82}	3811
17	Dec 7	A	Blackpool	L	1-3	0-1	9	McAleny ^{80}	10,355
18	14	H	Gillingham	D	1-1	0-0	9	Madden ^{56}	2468
19	21	A	Rotherham U	D	2-2	1-0	9	Evans 2 $^{26, 63}$	7883
20	26	A	Rochdale	W	3-2	0-1	7	Madden ^{53}, Dempsey ^{65}, Burns ^{89}	3167
21	29	H	Bristol R	D	0-0	0-0	8		2848
22	Jan 1	H	Sunderland	D	1-1	1-0	7	Evans (pen) ^{13}	4011
23	11	A	Burton Alb	L	0-1	0-0	10		2354
24	18	H	Shrewsbury T	D	2-2	0-1	11	Coyle ^{49}, Morris, J ^{87}	2797
25	25	A	Bristol R	D	0-0	0-0	11		6469
26	28	H	Coventry C	D	0-0	0-0	11		2506
27	Feb 1	H	Doncaster R	W	2-1	1-0	9	Evans ^{35}, Soutar ^{49}	3008
28	8	A	AFC Wimbledon	W	2-1	1-1	9	O'Neill (og) ^{22}, Madden ^{81}	4097
29	11	A	Wycombe W	W	1-0	0-0	9	Madden ^{75}	3286
30	15	H	Peterborough U	W	2-1	1-0	8	Connolly ^{15}, Burns ^{76}	2801
31	22	H	Portsmouth	W	1-0	1-0	6	Connolly ^{12}	3370
32	25	A	Sunderland	D	1-1	1-0	7	McKay ^{5}	28,255
33	Mar 3	A	Ipswich T	W	1-0	1-0	6	Evans ^{40}	15,678
34	7	H	Blackpool	D	0-0	0-0	7		4884
35	10	A	Portsmouth	D	2-2	1-1	5	McKay ^{19}, Soutar ^{55}	16,775
36	14	A	Gillingham	Cancelled					
37	21	H	Rotherham U	Cancelled					
38	28	H	Bolton W	Cancelled					
39	Apr 4	A	Milton Keynes D	Cancelled					
40	10	A	Accrington S	Cancelled					
41	13	H	Lincoln C	Cancelled					
42	18	A	Oxford U	Cancelled					
43	21	A	Tranmere R	Cancelled					
44	25	H	Southend U	Cancelled					

Final League Position: 6 (on points-per-game basis)

GOALSCORERS

League (51): Madden 15, Evans 9 (2 pens), Morris, J 7, Soutar 3, Andrew 2, Burns 2, Connolly 2, Dempsey 2, McAleny 2, McKay 2, Clarke, P 1, Coyle 1, Dunne 1, own goals 2.
FA Cup (5): Evans 1, Hunter 1, Madden 1, McAleny 1, Morris, J 1.
Carabao Cup (0).
Leasing.com Trophy (13): Madden 3 (1 pen), Andrew 2, Burns 2, Clarke, P 2, Morris, J 2, Coutts 1, Sowerby 1.
League One Play-offs (3): Evans 2 (2 pens), Andrew 1.

Cairns A 25	Coyle L 34	Soutar H 33 + 1	Clarke P 11 + 1	Andrew D 35	Coutts P 28 + 4	Rossiter J 15	Biggins H 5 + 5	Burns W 31 + 3	McAleny C 4 + 8	Morris J 23 + 10	Madden P 25 + 10	Hunter A 1 + 13	Sowerby J 13 + 11	Wallace R — + 3	Gilks M 5	Eastham A 5 + 4	Evans C 19 + 9	Dempsey K 19 + 2	Dunne J 9	Mooney D — + 1	Southam M — + 1	Crellin B 5	Saunders H — + 6	Connolly C 13	Whelan G 11	Gibson L 9	McKay B 7 + 1	Thorvaldsson I — + 2	*Match No.*
1	2	3	4	5	6^{1}	7	8	9	10^{3}	11^{2}	12	13	14																1
1	2	4	3	5	6	7	8^{2}	9	10^{3}	11^{1}	12	13	14																2
1	2	3	4	5	7	8^{1}	14	9	10^{2}	11	12		6^{3}	13															3
	2	3	4^{2}	5^{1}	6			8	9	10	11	14	7^{3}	12	1	13													4
	2	3	4	5	6	7	13	9^{2}		8	10^{1}	11^{3}		14	1		12												5
	2	4	3^{3}	5	6	7^{2}	8^{1}	9		11	10	13			1		12	14											6
	2		3	5	6	7	14	9^{3}		11^{1}	10	13			1		12	8^{2}	4										7
	2	14	3	5	6	7^{3}	12	9		11^{2}	10^{1}				1		13	8	4										8
1	2	3		5	7	6		9^{1}		11^{3}	12	13					10	8^{2}	4	14									9
1	2	3	14	5	6	7		9		11^{2}	12	13					10^{3}	8^{1}	4										10
1	2	3		5	6	7		9		11^{1}	12	13					10	8^{2}	4										11
1	2	3		5	6	7		11^{3}		12	9	13					10^{1}	8^{2}	4		14								12
1	2	3		5		7		12	14	9^{1}	11^{2}	13	6^{3}				10	8	4										13
1	2	3		5^{3}	7	6^{1}		9	14	11^{2}	10	13					12	8	4										14
1	2	3		5	6	7^{2}		9^{3}	13	14	11^{1}	12					10	8	4										15
	2	4		5	6^{2}	7^{1}		9^{3}		11	10	13	14			3	12	8				1							16
	2	4		5	6			9^{1}	13	11	10		7^{2}			3	12	8				1							17
	2	4	3	5				6		9	11		8				10^{1}	7				1	12						18
	2	3	4	9	7			5		13	10		6^{1}			12	11^{2}	8				1							19
	2	4		5	7		8^{3}	12	14	9^{2}	11		6^{1}			3	10	13				1							20
1	2	4	3	5	8			6	12	9^{1}	10						11	7											21
1	2	4		5	7^{1}		14	8		9^{2}	10		12			3	11^{3}	6					13						22
1	2	4		5	6			11^{3}	14	9	12		13			3	10	8^{2}						7^{1}					23
1	2	3		5	6			9		12	11		7^{1}				10	8						4					24
1	2	4		5	13			9^{2}		12	11^{3}		7			14	10	8^{1}						3	6				25
1	2	3		5			7^{2}		14	12	11^{1}		8			13	10	9^{3}						4	6				26
1	2^{3}	4		6	12			7		10^{2}	13		9				11^{1}						14	3	8	5			27
1	2^{2}	4		6	14			7		10^{1}	13		9				11							3^{3}	8	5	12		28
1		3		9	7			5			10		13				11■						12	2^{2}	6	4	8^{1}		29
1	5^{3}	3		8	6			9		13	10		12											2^{1}	7	4	11^{2}	14	30
1	2	3		5	8			9		12	10^{1}		13										14	7^{2}	6	4	11^{3}		31
1	2	3		5	6^{1}			9^{2}		12	10		13										14	7	8	4	11^{3}		32
1	2	3		5	6^{3}			9			10		13				12							7^{1}	8	4	11^{2}	14	33
1	2	3		5	6			9^{1}		13	10		14				12							7^{2}	8	4	11^{3}		34
1	2	4		6^{1}	13			12		7^{2}	14		9^{3}				11							3	8	5	10		35
																													36
																													37
																													38
																													39
																													40
																													41
																													42
																													43
																													44

FA Cup

First Round	Barnet	(a)	2-0
Second Round	Crawley T	(a)	2-1
Third Round	Portsmouth	(h)	1-2

Carabao Cup

First Round	Nottingham F	(a)	0-1

League One Play-Offs

Semi-Final 1st leg	Wycombe W	(h)	1-4
Semi-Final 2nd leg	Wycombe W	(a)	2-2

Leasing.com Trophy

Group B (N)	Accrington S	(a)	1-2
Group B (N)	Liverpool U21	(h)	1-1
(Fleetwood T won 4-3 on penalties)			
Group B (N)	Oldham Ath	(h)	5-2
Second Round (N)	Everton U21	(a)	4-0
Third Round (N)	Accrington S	(h)	2-2
(Accrington S won 5-3 on penalties)			

FOREST GREEN ROVERS

FOUNDATION

A football club was recorded at Forest Green as early as October 1889, established by Rev Edward Peach, a local Congregationalist minister. This club joined the Mid-Gloucestershire League for 1894–95 but disappeared around 1896 and was reformed as Forest Green Rovers in 1898. Rovers affiliated to the Gloucestershire county FA from 1899–1900 and competed in local leagues, mostly the Stroud & District and Dursley & District Leagues before joining the Gloucestershire Senior League North in 1937, where they remained until 1968. They became founder members of the Gloucestershire County League in 1968 and progressed to the Hellenic League in 1975. Success over Rainworth MW in the 1982 FA Vase final at Wembley was the start of the club's rise up the pyramid, firstly to the Southern League for the 1982–83 season and then the Football Conference from 1998–99. Rovers reached the play-offs in 2014–15 and 2015–16, losing to Bristol Rovers and Grimsby Town respectively, before finally achieving their goal of a place in the Football League with their 3-1 Play-Off victory over Tranmere Rovers on 14 May 2017.

The New Lawn Stadium, Another Way, Nailsworth, GL6 0FG.

Telephone: (0333) 123 1889.

Ticket Office: (0333) 123 1889.

Website: fgr.co.uk

Email: reception@fgr.co.uk

Ground Capacity: 5,009.

Record Attendance: 4,836 v Derby Co, FA Cup 3rd rd, 3 January 2009.

Pitch Measurements: 100m × 66m (109.5yd × 72yd).

Chairman: Dale Vince.

Chief Executive: Henry Staelens.

Manager: Mark Cooper.

Colours: Green and black patterned shirts, green shorts with black trim, green and black hooped socks.

Year Formed: 1889.

Previous Names: 1889, Forest Green; 1898, Forest Green Rovers; 1911, Nailsworth & Forest Green United; 1919 Forest Green Rovers; 1989, Stroud; 1992, Forest Green Rovers.

HONOURS

League Champions: Southern League – 1997–98.

FA Cup: 3rd rd – 2009, 2010.

League Cup: never past 2nd rd.

FA Trophy: *Runners-up:* 1998–99, 2000–01.

FA Vase: *Winners:* 1981–82.

FOOTBALL YEARBOOK FACT FILE

In 1925–26 Forest Green Rovers were promoted from the Stroud & District League into the Gloucestershire Northern Senior League via an early version of the play-offs. Rovers defeated local rivals Viney Hill and Rodborough Old Boys in 'Test' matches to gain their place in the higher league.

Club Nicknames: Rovers, The Green, FGR, The Little Club on the Hill, Green Army, The Green Devils.

Grounds: 1890, The Lawn Ground; 2006, The New Lawn.

Record Victory: 8–0 v Fareham T, Southern League Southern Division, 1996–97; 8–0 v Hyde U, Football Conference, 10 August 2013.

Record Defeat: 0–10 v Gloucester, Mid-Gloucestershire League, 13 January 1900.

Most League Points (3 for a win): 74, FL 2, 2018–19.

Most League Goals: 68, FL 2, 2018–19.

Highest League Scorer in Season: Christian Doidge, 20, FL 2, 2017–18.

Most League Goals in Total Aggregate: Christian Doidge, 34, 2017–19.

Most League Goals in One Match: 3, George Williams v Newport Co, FL 2, 26 December 2018.

Most Capped Player: Omar Bugiel, 1 (7), Lebanon.

Most League Appearances: Carl Winchester, 80, 2018–20.

Youngest League Player: Vaughan Covil, 16 years 159 days v Exeter C, 1 January 2020.

Record Transfer Fee Received: £500,000 from Barnsley for Ethan Pinnock, June 2017.

Record Transfer Fee Paid: £25,000 to Bury for Adrian Randall, August 1999.

Football League Record: 2017 Promoted from National League; 2017– FL 2.

MANAGERS

Bill Thomas 1955–56
Eddie Cowley 1957–58
Don Cowley 1958–60
Jimmy Sewell 1966–67
Alan Morris 1967–68
Peter Goring 1968–79
Tony Morris 1979–80
Bob Mursell 1980–82
Roy Hillman 1982
Steve Millard 1983–87
John Evans 1987–90
Jeff Evans 1990
Bobby Jones 1990–91
Tim Harris 1991–92
Pat Casey 1992–94
Frank Gregan 1994–2000
Nigel Spink and David Norton 2000–01
Nigel Spink 2001–02
Colin Addison 2002–03
Tim Harris 2003–04
Alan Lewer 2004–05
Gary Owers 2005–06
Jim Harvey 2006–09
Dave Hockaday 2009–13
Adrian Pennock 2013–16
Mark Cooper May 2016–

LATEST SEQUENCES

Longest Sequence of League Wins: 4, 6.4.2019 – 22.4.2019.

Longest Sequence of League Defeats: 5, 9.12.2017 – 1.1.2018.

Longest Sequence of League Draws: 4, 11.8.2018 – 25.8.2018.

Longest Sequence of Unbeaten League Matches: 12, 4.8.2018 – 6.10.2018.

Longest Sequence Without a League Win: 10, 26.8.2017 – 14.10.2017.

Successive Scoring Runs: 13 from 25.8.2018.

Successive Non-scoring Runs: 3 from 26.11.2019.

TEN YEAR LEAGUE RECORD

		P	W	D	L	F	A	Pts	Pos
2010-11	Conf	46	10	16	20	53	72	46	20
2011-12	Conf	46	19	13	14	66	45	70	10
2012-13	Conf	46	18	11	17	63	49	65	10
2013-14	Conf	46	19	10	17	80	66	67	10
2014-15	Conf	46	22	16	8	80	54	79*	5
2015-16	NL	46	26	11	9	69	42	89	2
2016-17	NL	46	25	11	10	88	56	86	3
2017-18	FL 2	46	13	8	25	54	77	47	21
2018-19	FL 2	46	20	14	12	68	47	74	5
2019-20	FL 2	36	13	10	13	43	40	49	10§

**3 pts deducted. §Decided on points-per-game (1.36)*

DID YOU KNOW ?

Forest Green Rovers defeated Avon Bradford 12-1 in their FA Vase preliminary round tie in 1978–79, setting a new record score for the competition. Striker Kenny Gill scored a double hat-trick in the game. Rovers also won their first round match before going out to eventual finalists Almondsbury Greenway.

FOREST GREEN ROVERS – SKY BET LEAGUE TWO 2019–20 LEAGUE RECORD

Match No.	Date	Venue	Opponents	Result		H/T Score	Lg Pos.	Goalscorers	Attendance
1	Aug 3	H	Oldham Ath	W	1-0	0-0	6	Allen [72]	2541
2	10	A	Walsall	D	1-1	1-0	5	Mills, J (pen) [45]	5205
3	17	H	Grimsby T	W	1-0	0-0	2	Mondal [75]	2152
4	20	A	Port Vale	L	1-2	1-2	8	Mills, J [6]	4010
5	24	A	Bradford C	W	1-0	0-0	3	Mills, J [90]	13,504
6	31	H	Newport Co	L	0-2	0-1	9		2897
7	Sept 7	A	Cambridge U	W	1-0	0-0	5	Aitchison [78]	3784
8	14	H	Colchester U	W	1-0	1-0	3	Prosser (og) [31]	2758
9	17	A	Carlisle U	D	0-0	0-0	5		3219
10	21	H	Stevenage	D	0-0	0-0	5		1881
11	28	A	Salford C	W	4-0	3-0	4	Stevens 2 [3, 59], Collins [16], Adams [31]	2561
12	Oct 5	H	Crawley T	W	3-1	1-0	1	Mills, J 2 (1 pen) [24, 55 (p)], Collins [52]	2136
13	12	A	Exeter C	L	0-1	0-1	4		5312
14	19	H	Mansfield T	D	2-2	1-0	6	Collins [30], Aitchison [61]	2276
15	22	A	Morecambe	W	2-0	0-0	3	Aitchison [75], Shephard [90]	1658
16	Nov 2	A	Cheltenham T	W	2-1	2-0	1	Aitchison [15], Frear [40]	5788
17	16	H	Plymouth Arg	L	0-1	0-1	2		3897
18	23	A	Leyton Orient	W	4-2	3-0	2	Adams 2 [15, 33], Stevens [43], Mondal [88]	4614
19	26	H	Crewe Alex	D	0-0	0-0	2		2192
20	Dec 7	H	Scunthorpe U	L	0-2	0-0	3		2060
21	14	A	Northampton T	L	0-1	0-1	6		4534
22	21	H	Swindon T	D	2-2	0-2	6	Mills, J 2 [55, 90]	4216
23	26	A	Stevenage	D	0-0	0-0	6		2388
24	29	H	Macclesfield T	W	1-0	0-0	5	Rawson [74]	2155
25	Jan 1	H	Exeter C	L	0-1	0-1	5		3012
26	4	A	Crawley T	D	1-1	0-1	7	Tunnicliffe (og) [63]	2082
27	11	A	Mansfield T	W	4-3	1-2	7	Rawson 2 [45, 52], Winchester [60], Collins [90]	3956
28	18	H	Salford C	L	1-2	1-1	9	March [11]	2707
29	25	A	Macclesfield T	L	1-2	1-0	9	Winchester [17]	1653
30	28	H	Carlisle U	L	1-4	0-2	9	Winchester (pen) [59]	1514
31	Feb 1	A	Grimsby T	D	2-2	1-1	9	Bailey [32], Aitchison [50]	4675
32	8	H	Walsall	L	1-2	0-0	10	March [87]	3136
33	11	H	Port Vale	L	2-3	0-2	10	Winchester 2 (1 pen) [78 (p), 90]	1682
34	15	A	Oldham Ath	D	1-1	0-0	10	Williams [88]	2720
35	22	A	Scunthorpe U	L	0-1	0-0	10		3706
36	Mar 7	A	Swindon T	W	2-0	1-0	11	Stevens [4], Adams [50]	9257
37	14	H	Northampton T	Cancelled					
38	17	H	Morecambe	Cancelled					
39	21	A	Crewe Alex	Cancelled					
40	28	H	Cheltenham T	Cancelled					
41	31	H	Leyton Orient	Cancelled					
42	Apr 4	A	Plymouth Arg	Cancelled					
43	10	H	Bradford C	Cancelled					
44	13	A	Newport Co	Cancelled					
45	18	H	Cambridge U	Cancelled					
46	25	A	Colchester U	Cancelled					

Final League Position: 10 (on points-per-game basis)

GOALSCORERS

League (43): Mills, J 7 (2 pens), Aitchison 5, Winchester 5 (2 pens), Adams 4, Collins 4, Stevens 4, Rawson 3, March 2, Mondal 2, Allen 1, Bailey 1, Frear 1, Shephard 1, Williams 1, own goals 2.
FA Cup (6): Aitchison 1, Collins 1, Mills, J 1, Shephard 1, Stevens 1, own goal 1.
Carabao Cup (0).
Leasing.com Trophy (3): Stevens 2, Grubb 1.

Thomas L 14 + 1	Rawson F 28 + 2	Mills M 17 + 2	McGinley N 14 + 6	Bernard D 25 + 3	Dawson K 12 + 3	Morton J 7 + 5	Mills J 24	Collins A 14 + 14	McCoulsky S 4 + 2	Williams G 2 + 2	Mondal J 7 + 14	Allen T 2 + 3	Stevens M 21 + 8	Winchester C 35	Kitching L 27 + 2	Adams E 30 + 4	Wollacott J 9 + 1	Godwin-Malife U 11 + 1	Grubb D 3 + 4	Taylor K 5	Aitchison J 23 + 5	Shephard L 17 + 2	Frear E 7 + 7	Smith A 8	Covil V — + 2	Brown J 5	March J 7 + 3	Logan C 5	Hall R 3 + 3	Bailey O 5	Stokes C 5	Match No.
1	2	3	4	5	6	7	8	9^{3}	10^{2}	11^{1}	12	13	14																			1
1	2^{3}	3	4	5	7	6^{2}	8	10^{1}	11				13	9	12	14																2
		3	4	7	8^{2}		5		11		13		10^{1}	6		9	1	2	12													3
		3	4	5^{3}		7	8	11^{1}			10^{2}	12	14	9		6	1	2	13													4
	3	4■	13	12	6		11		10^{1}				14	7	5^{2}	8	1	2^{3}	9													5
12	2	3	4^{2}	5			8	14			13	10^{3}		7		6	1■		9	11^{1}												6
1	4				6	12	8				14	11^{3}	10	7	3			2	9^{2}	5^{1}	13											7
1	4			2		7^{1}	8				12		11	6	3	14		5^{3}		9^{2}	10	13										8
1	3			2		7■	8				14		11	6	4	13		5^{2}		9^{1}	10^{3}	12										9
1	3^{1}		12	2			8				9^{3}		11	6	4	13			14	7■	10	5^{2}										10
1		3		2			8	9^{3}			13		11	6	4	7		12	14		10^{1}	5^{2}										11
1	12	3^{2}		2		14	8	10^{3}				13	11	6	4	7					9	5^{1}										12
1^{1}	3			2		13	8	10			14		11	6	4	7	12	5^{3}			9^{2}											13
1	3			2^{1}		14	8	10^{3}			13		11	6	4	7^{2}					9	5	12									14
	3			2		7^{1}	8	13					10	6	4	9	1				12	5	11^{2}									15
	3			2			5	12					11	7	4	6	1				9	8	10^{1}									16
	3	13	12	2^{2}			5^{1}	11					9	7	4	6	1				10	8										17
	4	3	14	2	13		5	10^{1}			12		11^{2}	8		7	1				9^{3}	6										18
	3	4^{2}		2			9	13			12		10	8	5	7	1				11^{1}	6										19
1	3	4	12	2^{2}	8^{3}			14			13		10	7	9	6					11^{1}	5										20
		3		2			5	10^{1}			13		11^{2}	7	4	8					9	6	12	1								21
		3	14			12	5	13					11^{1}	8	4^{3}	7		2			10	6	9^{2}	1								22
	12	3	8			7^{3}	4	14					13	6		9		2^{1}			11	5	10^{2}	1								23
	4	3^{2}	5		14			13			6		11^{1}	8	12	7					10^{3}	2	9	1								24
	2	3^{2}	8		9^{1}						10		11^{3}	7	4	6					12	5	13	1	14							25
	3	13	5	12				11			8			7	4	6					10^{3}	2^{2}		1	14	9^{1}						26
	3			2			5	14	12		8			7	4	6					10^{2}		13	1		9^{3}	11^{1}					27
	3			2			5	13	14		8			7	4	6					10^{1}		12	1		9^{3}	11^{2}					28
	3		5	2				13			12		14	7	4	6										9^{1}	11^{3}	1	8^{2}	10		29
	3	4		12				10^{2}					14	8	5	7						2^{1}	13				11	1	6^{3}	9		30
	3		5	2	8^{3}			13					14	9	4	6					10^{1}						11^{2}	1	12	7		31
	3				2^{2}			12		13				7	4	6^{3}					10		14				11	1	9^{1}	8	5	32
	3			2^{3}	13			14					10^{1}	7	4	8					12		9				11	1		6^{2}	5	33
1	2		8		5			11^{1}		13				7	4	6					10^{3}					9^{2}	14		12		3	34
1	2		8		9			10^{3}		11^{1}				6	4	7		5^{2}			12						13		14		3	35
1			8	2	7								4	3		5		9			10^{1}		6				12				11	36
																																37
																																38
																																39
																																40
																																41
																																42
																																43
																																44
																																45
																																46

FA Cup

First Round	Billericay T	(h)	4-0
Second Round	Carlisle U	(h)	2-2
Replay	Carlisle U	(a)	0-1

Carabao Cup

First Round	Charlton Ath	(a)	0-0
(Forest Green R won 5-3 on penalties)			
Second Round	Bournemouth	(a)	0-0
(Bournemouth won 3-0 on penalties)			

Leasing.com Trophy

Group D (S)	Southampton U21	(h)	3-2
Group D (S)	Coventry C	(h)	0-0
(Forest Green R won 8-7 on penalties)			
Group D (S)	Walsall	(a)	0-6

FULHAM

FOUNDATION

Churchgoers were responsible for the foundation of Fulham, which first saw the light of day as Fulham St Andrew's Church Sunday School FC in 1879. They won the West London Amateur Cup in 1887 and the championship of the West London League in its initial season of 1892–93. The name Fulham had been adopted in 1888.

Craven Cottage, Stevenage Road, London SW6 6HH.

Telephone: (0843) 208 1222.

Ticket Office: (0203) 871 0810.

Website: www.fulhamfc.com

Email: enquiries@fulhamfc.com

Ground Capacity: 25,700 (temporarily 19,000).

Record Attendance: 49,335 v Millwall, Division 2, 8 October 1938.

Pitch Measurements: 100m × 65m (109.5yd × 71yd).

Chairman: Shahid Khan.

Chief Executive: Alistair Mackintosh.

Head Coach: Scott Parker.

Assistant Head Coach: Stuart Gray.

Colours: White shirts with black trim, black shorts with white trim, white socks with black trim.

Year Formed: 1879.

Turned Professional: 1898.

Reformed: 1987.

Previous Name: 1879, Fulham St Andrew's; 1888, Fulham.

Club Nickname: 'The Cottagers'.

Grounds: 1879, Star Road, Fulham; c.1883, Eel Brook Common, 1884, Lillie Road; 1885, Putney Lower Common; 1886, Ranelagh House, Fulham; 1888, Barn Elms, Castelnau; 1889, Purser's Cross (Roskell's Field), Parsons Green Lane; 1891, Eel Brook Common; 1891, Half Moon, Putney; 1895, Captain James Field, West Brompton; 1896, Craven Cottage.

First Football League Game: 3 September 1907, Division 2, v Hull C (h) L 0–1 – Skene; Ross, Lindsay; Collins, Morrison, Goldie; Dalrymple, Freeman, Bevan, Hubbard, Threlfall.

Record League Victory: 10–1 v Ipswich T, Division 1, 26 December 1963 – Macedo; Cohen, Langley; Mullery (1), Keetch, Robson (1); Key, Cook (1), Leggat (4), Haynes, Howfield (3).

Record Cup Victory: 7–0 v Swansea C, FA Cup 1st rd, 11 November 1995 – Lange; Jupp (1), Herrera, Barkus (Brooker (1)), Moore, Angus, Thomas (1), Morgan, Brazil (Hamill), Conroy (3) (Bolt), Cusack (1).

Record Defeat: 0–10 v Liverpool, League Cup 2nd rd 1st leg, 23 September 1986.

HONOURS

League Champions: First Division – 2000–01; Division 2 – 1948–49; Second Division – 1998–99; Division 3S – 1931–32.
Runners-up: Division 2 – 1958–59; Division 3 – 1970–71; Third Division – 1996–97.

FA Cup: *Runners-up:* 1975.

League Cup: quarter-final – 1968, 1971, 2000, 2005.

European Competitions
UEFA Cup: 2002–03.
Europa League: 2009–10 *(runners-up)*, 2011–12.
Intertoto Cup: 2002 *(winners)*.

FOOTBALL YEARBOOK FACT FILE

In 1974–75 Fulham reached the FA Cup final after playing a record 11 games. They began by defeating Hull City in a second replay and their fourth round tie against Nottingham Forest went to a third replay. The next two rounds were negotiated at the first attempt but the semi-final against Birmingham City went to a replay. The Cottagers went down 2-0 to West Ham United in the final.

Most League Points (2 for a win): 60, Division 2, 1958–59 and Division 3, 1970–71.

Most League Points (3 for a win): 101, Division 2, 1998–99. 101, Division 1, 2000–01.

Most League Goals: 111, Division 3 (S), 1931–32.

Highest League Scorer in Season: Frank Newton, 43, Division 3 (S), 1931–32.

Most League Goals in Total Aggregate: Gordon Davies, 159, 1978–84, 1986–91.

Most League Goals in One Match: 5, Fred Harrison v Stockport Co, Division 2, 5 September 1908; 5, Bedford Jezzard v Hull C, Division 2, 8 October 1955; 5, Jimmy Hill v Doncaster R, Division 2, 15 March 1958; 5, Steve Earle v Halifax T, Division 3, 16 September 1969.

Most Capped Player: Johnny Haynes, 56, England.

Most League Appearances: Johnny Haynes, 594, 1952–70.

Youngest League Player: Harvey Elliott, 16 years 30 days v Wolverhampton W, 4 May 2019.

Record Transfer Fee Received: £25,000,000 from Tottenham H for Ryan Sessegnon, August 2019.

Record Transfer Fee Paid: £22,800,000 to Marseille for André-Frank Zambo Anguissa, August 2018.

Football League Record: 1907 Elected to Division 2; 1928–32 Division 3 (S); 1932–49 Division 2; 1949–52 Division 1; 1952–59 Division 2; 1959–68 Division 1; 1968–69 Division 2; 1969–71 Division 3; 1971–80 Division 2; 1980–82 Division 3; 1982–86 Division 2; 1986–92 Division 3; 1992–94 Division 2; 1994–97 Division 3; 1997–99 Division 2; 1999–2001 Division 1; 2001–14 Premier League; 2014–18 FL C; 2018–19 Premier League; 2019–20 FL C; 2020– Premier League.

LATEST SEQUENCES

Longest Sequence of League Wins: 12, 7.5.2000 – 18.10.2000.

Longest Sequence of League Defeats: 11, 2.12.1961 – 24.2.1962.

Longest Sequence of League Draws: 6, 23.12.2006 – 20.1.2007.

Longest Sequence of Unbeaten League Matches: 23, 23.12.2017 – 27.4.2018.

Longest Sequence Without a League Win: 15, 25.2.1950 – 23.8.1950.

Successive Scoring Runs: 26 from 28.3.1931.

Successive Non-scoring Runs: 6 from 21.8.1971.

MANAGERS

Harry Bradshaw 1904–09
Phil Kelso 1909–24
Andy Ducat 1924–26
Joe Bradshaw 1926–29
Ned Liddell 1929–31
Jim McIntyre 1931–34
Jimmy Hogan 1934–35
Jack Peart 1935–48
Frank Osborne 1948–64
(was Secretary-Manager or General Manager for most of this period and Team Manager 1953–56)
Bill Dodgin Snr 1949–53
Duggie Livingstone 1956–58
Bedford Jezzard 1958–64
(General Manager for last two months)
Vic Buckingham 1965–68
Bobby Robson 1968
Bill Dodgin Jnr 1968–72
Alec Stock 1972–76
Bobby Campbell 1976–80
Malcolm Macdonald 1980–84
Ray Harford 1984–96
Ray Lewington 1986–90
Alan Dicks 1990–91
Don Mackay 1991–94
Ian Branfoot 1994–96
(continued as General Manager)
Micky Adams 1996–97
Ray Wilkins 1997–98
Kevin Keegan 1998–99
(Chief Operating Officer)
Paul Bracewell 1999–2000
Jean Tigana 2000–03
Chris Coleman 2003–07
Lawrie Sanchez 2007
Roy Hodgson 2007–10
Mark Hughes 2010–11
Martin Jol 2011–13
Rene Muelenstein 2013–14
Felix Magath 2014
Kit Symons 2014–15
Slavisa Jokanovic 2015–18
Claudio Ranieri 2018–19
Scott Parker February 2019–

TEN YEAR LEAGUE RECORD

		P	*W*	*D*	*L*	*F*	*A*	*Pts*	*Pos*
2010-11	PR Lge	38	11	16	11	49	43	49	8
2011-12	PR Lge	38	14	10	14	48	51	52	9
2012-13	PR Lge	38	11	10	17	50	60	43	12
2013-14	PR Lge	38	9	5	24	40	85	32	19
2014-15	FL C	46	14	10	22	62	83	52	17
2015-16	FL C	46	12	15	19	66	79	51	20
2016-17	FL C	46	22	14	10	85	57	80	6
2017-18	FL C	46	25	13	8	79	46	88	3
2018-19	PR Lge	38	7	5	26	34	81	26	19
2019-20	FL C	46	23	12	11	64	48	81	4

DID YOU KNOW ?

Fulham's game against Luton Town on Saturday 2 September 1939 was the final Football League game to be played before the season was abandoned due to the outbreak of war. The Cottagers switched the kick-off time to 6 p.m. with the Second Division match ending in a 1-1 draw.

FULHAM – SKY BET CHAMPIONSHIP 2019–20 LEAGUE RECORD

Match No.	Date	Venue	Opponents	Result	H/T Score	Lg Pos.	Goalscorers	Attendance
1	Aug 3	A	Barnsley	L 0-1	0-1	21		14,823
2	10	H	Blackburn R	W 2-0	1-0	11	Cairney 34, Mitrovic 81	17,987
3	16	A	Huddersfield T	W 2-1	0-0	3	Mitrovic 51, Ivan Cavaleiro 80	20,775
4	21	H	Millwall	W 4-0	2-0	3	Ivan Cavaleiro 2 15, 63, Knockaert 32, Mitrovic (pen) 56	17,066
5	24	H	Nottingham F	L 1-2	0-1	5	Mitrovic 83	18,186
6	30	A	Cardiff C	D 1-1	1-1	4	Mitrovic 45	22,631
7	Sept 14	H	WBA	D 1-1	0-0	10	Knockaert 49	17,770
8	21	A	Sheffield W	D 1-1	1-0	12	Cairney 42	23,342
9	27	H	Wigan Ath	W 2-0	0-0	7	Bryan 47, Cairney 83	18,253
10	Oct 1	A	Reading	W 4-1	3-0	4	Cairney 2 13, 67, Mitrovic 2 26, 29	13,809
11	5	H	Charlton Ath	D 2-2	0-1	7	Ivan Cavaleiro 55, Mitrovic 63	18,654
12	19	A	Stoke C	L 0-2	0-1	10		23,189
13	23	H	Luton T	W 3-2	1-0	7	Mitrovic 3 16, 53, 67	18,082
14	26	A	Middlesbrough	D 0-0	0-0	5		19,101
15	Nov 2	H	Hull C	L 0-3	0-1	8		18,168
16	9	A	Birmingham C	W 1-0	0-0	6	Mitrovic 52	21,334
17	22	H	QPR	W 2-1	1-1	4	Kamara 2 27, 64	18,320
18	26	H	Derby Co	W 3-0	2-0	3	Reid 7, Mitrovic 40, Cairney 89	16,856
19	29	A	Swansea C	W 2-1	2-0	3	Mitrovic 2 22, 43	16,024
20	Dec 7	H	Bristol C	L 1-2	0-1	3	Kamara 86	18,779
21	10	A	Preston NE	L 1-2	0-1	3	Mitrovic 81	10,093
22	14	A	Brentford	L 0-1	0-1	6		12,305
23	21	H	Leeds U	W 2-1	1-0	3	Mitrovic (pen) 7, Onomah 69	18,878
24	26	A	Luton T	D 3-3	1-2	5	Reid 2 9, 90, Mitrovic 77	10,068
25	29	H	Stoke C	W 1-0	1-0	3	Reid 26	18,747
26	Jan 1	H	Reading	L 1-2	0-1	5	Ivan Cavaleiro 61	18,575
27	11	A	Hull C	W 1-0	1-0	4	Ivan Cavaleiro 29	11,347
28	17	H	Middlesbrough	W 1-0	1-0	3	Knockaert 6	18,375
29	22	A	Charlton Ath	D 0-0	0-0	3		16,424
30	Feb 1	H	Huddersfield T	W 3-2	3-2	3	Reid 10, Cairney 15, Mitrovic 31	18,013
31	8	A	Blackburn R	W 1-0	0-0	3	Mitrovic 65	13,087
32	12	A	Millwall	D 1-1	1-1	3	Mitrovic 3	12,870
33	15	H	Barnsley	L 0-3	0-1	3		18,516
34	21	A	Derby Co	D 1-1	0-0	3	Mitrovic 71	25,442
35	26	H	Swansea C	W 1-0	0-0	3	Mitrovic 90	17,626
36	29	H	Preston NE	W 2-0	0-0	3	Nugent (og) 58, Kamara 90	19,020
37	Mar 7	A	Bristol C	D 1-1	0-0	3	Cairney 84	23,796
38	June 20	H	Brentford	L 0-2	0-0	3		0
39	27	A	Leeds U	L 0-3	0-1	4		0
40	30	A	QPR	W 2-1	1-1	4	Arter 21, Christie 75	0
41	July 4	H	Birmingham C	W 1-0	0-0	4	Onomah 90	0
42	7	A	Nottingham F	W 1-0	1-0	4	Arter 45	0
43	10	H	Cardiff C	W 2-0	1-0	3	Mitrovic (pen) 35, Onomah 66	0
44	14	A	WBA	D 0-0	0-0	4		0
45	18	H	Sheffield W	W 5-3	3-0	4	Kebano 2 11, 73, Mitrovic 2 (1 pen) 26, 41 (p), Reid 90	0
46	22	A	Wigan Ath	D 1-1	0-1	4	Kebano 49	0

Final League Position: 4

GOALSCORERS

League (64): Mitrovic 26 (4 pens), Cairney 8, Ivan Cavaleiro 6, Reid 6, Kamara 4, Kebano 3, Knockaert 3, Onomah 3, Arter 2, Bryan 1, Christie 1, own goal 1.
FA Cup (2): Arter 1, Knockaert 1.
Carabao Cup (0).
Leasing.com Trophy (3): Abraham 2, Harris 1.
Championship Play-Offs (5): Bryan 2, Kebano 2, Onomah 1.

Bettinelli M 13 + 1	Odoi D 30 + 4	Mawson A 25 + 2	Le Marchand M 3 + 9	Bryan J 39 + 4	McDonald K 7 + 9	Johansen S 19 + 14	Cairney T 38 + 1	Kamara A 8 + 17	Mitrovic A 40	Ivan Cavaleiro R 36 + 7	Christie C 13 + 11	Knockaert A 32 + 10	Ayite F — + 1	Ream T 44	Arter H 21 + 7	Reid B 30 + 11	Reed H 21 + 4	Sessegnon S 9 + 5	Onomah J 20 + 11	Kebano N 5 + 11	Rodak M 33	De La Torre L — + 2	O'Riley M — + 1	Hector M 20	Stansfield J — + 1	Kongolo T — + 1	Jasper S — + 2	*Match No.*
1	2	3	4^{1}	5	6	7^{2}	8	9	10	11^{3}	12	13	14															1
1	2	3	14	5		8^{1}	6		10	11^{2}		9^{3}		4	7	12	13											2
1		3	14	5		8^{1}	6		10	11^{2}		9^{3}		4	7	12	13	2										3
1		3		5	13	8	6^{1}	14	10	11^{3}		9		4	7^{2}	12		2										4
1		3^{3}		5		8^{1}	6	13	10	11	14	9		4	7	12		2^{2}										5
1		3	14	5		12	9^{3}	13	11	10^{2}		8^{1}		4	7▪		6	2										6
1	13	3		5			8		10	11		9		4		6^{1}	7	2^{2}	12									7
1	13	3		5			8	14	10	11^{1}		9^{3}		4	12	6	7	2^{2}										8
1		3		5		6^{2}	9		11	10^{1}		8^{3}		4	13	12	7	2	14									9
1	2	3	14	5^{3}		8	9^{2}	13	11			7^{1}		4	6	10			12									10
1		3		5		8^{3}	9		11	10		7		4	6^{2}	13	12	2^{1}	14									11
1		2		4			9		11	8		5^{2}		3	6^{1}	10	7		12	13								12
	2	3		5	14	13	8		10	11		9^{1}		4		6^{2}	7^{3}		12		1							13
12	2	3	14	5			8		10	9^{3}		13		4		11^{2}	7		6^{1}		1▪							14
1	2^{3}	3	12	5^{1}		6	8	14	10	11		13		4		9^{2}	7											15
	2	3	5^{1}			8		14	10	11^{2}	12	9		4		6^{3}	7		13		1							16
	2	3		5	14	6	8	10		11^{3}	13	9^{2}		4		12	7^{1}				1							17
	2	3		5		6	7	8^{1}	11	10^{3}	14	12		4		9^{2}			13		1							18
	2	3		5	12	6	7	8^{1}	11	10^{3}	13	14		4					9^{2}		1							19
	2^{3}	3		5		6	7	12	11	10^{2}	14	8		4					9^{1}	13	1							20
	5▪	3^{2}		12		7		10	11	9^{1}	2	8^{3}		4					6	13	1	14						21
		3		5		6^{1}	8	12	10	9^{3}	2	13		4		14			7	11^{2}	1							22
		3		5		13	6		10	9^{3}	2	14		4		11^{1}	7^{2}	12	8		1							23
		3		5^{3}			8	14	10	9^{2}	2	12		4		11	7^{1}		6	13	1							24
	13	3^{2}		5			8^{3}		10	12	2	9		4		11	7	14	6^{1}		1							25
	3			5^{2}		8		11	10	13	2	9		4		6	7^{1}				1	14	12^{3}					26
	5	14		12	7				10^{1}	11^{2}	2	9^{3}		4	13	8			6		1			3				27
	2	14		5	7	12	6^{1}			11		9^{3}		4	13	10			8^{2}		1			3				28
	2			5	7	13	8^{2}			9	12			4	6^{1}	10			11^{3}		1			3	14			29
	4			5	7^{2}	14	8^{3}	12	10	9^{1}	2				13	11			6		1			3				30
	2			5	7	13	8^{2}	14	10	9^{3}				4		11			6^{1}		1			3		12		31
	2			5			6	8^{1}	11	12				4	7^{2}	10			9	13	1			3				32
				5	7^{1}		6^{2}	14	10	11		9		4	13	12		2^{3}	8		1			3				33
	2			5	14	6^{1}	8	12	10	13		9^{2}		4	7^{3}	11					1			3				34
	2			5	14		7	13	11	10^{1}		8^{2}		4	6^{3}	9				12	1			3				35
	2			5^{1}	14		8	13	10	11	12	9^{2}		4	7^{3}	6					1			3				36
	5					14	8	9	10	11^{1}	2	13		4^{2}	7	6^{3}				12	1			3				37
	2			5		14	7		11	12		8^{3}		4	13	9^{4}	6^{2}			10^{1}	1			3			15	38
	2		15	5^{4}		16	9^{5}		11	13		8^{2}		4	7^{1}	10^{3}	6		14	12▪	1			3				39
	5		14	13	16		6^{5}			9^{4}	2	11^{2}		4	8^{1}	10^{3}	7	15	12		1			3				40
	5^{1}			12			8			11^{3}	2	9^{4}		4	6^{2}	10	7		13	14	1			3			15	41
	2		14	5		13				8		12		4	6^{2}	11^{3}	7		9	10^{1}	1			3				42
				5	16	12			11	13	2	8^{2}		4	6^{1}	10^{3}	7^{4}	15	9^{5}	14	1			3				43
	2			5		13			11	10^{1}	14	8		4^{3}		9	6		7^{2}	12	1			3				44
	16		5			7^{1}	14		11		2	8^{5}		4	6^{4}	13	12▪	15	9^{3}	10^{2}	1			3				45
	2^{3}			5		13	7^{4}	14	11		15	8^{1}		4	6^{2}	12			9	10	1			3				46

FA Cup

Third Round	Aston Villa	(h)	2-1
Fourth Round	Manchester C	(a)	0-4

Championship Play-Offs

Semi-Finals 1st leg	Cardiff C	(a)	2-0
Semi-Finals 2nd leg	Cardiff C	(h)	1-2
Final	Brentford	(Wembley)	2-1

(aet)

Carabao Cup

Second Round	Southampton	(h)	0-1

Leasing.com Trophy (Fulham U21)

Group G (S)	Milton Keynes D	(a)	0-1
Group G (S)	Stevenage	(a)	1-1

(Stevenage won 4-2 on penalties)

Group G (S)	Wycombe W	(a)	2-1

GILLINGHAM

FOUNDATION

The success of the pioneering Royal Engineers of Chatham excited the interest of the residents of the Medway Towns and led to the formation of many clubs including Excelsior. After winning the Kent Junior Cup and the Chatham District League in 1893, Excelsior decided to go for bigger things and it was at a meeting in the Napier Arms, Brompton, in 1893 that New Brompton FC came into being, buying and developing the ground which is now Priestfield Stadium. They changed their name to Gillingham in 1913, when they also changed their strip from black and white stripes to predominantly blue.

MEMS Priestfield Stadium, Redfern Avenue, Gillingham, Kent ME7 4DD.

Telephone: (01634) 300 000.

Ticket Office: (01634) 300 000 (option 1).

Website: www.gillinghamfootballclub.com

Email: via website.

Ground Capacity: 11,582.

Record Attendance: 23,002 v QPR, FA Cup 3rd rd, 10 January 1948.

Pitch Measurements: 100.5m × 64m (110yd × 70yd).

Chairman: Paul Scally.

Manager: Steve Evans.

Assistant Manager: Paul Raynor.

Colours: Blue shirts with white trim, blue shorts with white trim, blue socks with white trim.

Year Formed: 1893.

Turned Professional: 1894.

Previous Name: 1893, New Brompton; 1913, Gillingham.

Club Nickname: 'The Gills'.

Ground: 1893, Priestfield Stadium (renamed KRBS Priestfield Stadium 2009, MEMS Priestfield Stadium 2011).

First Football League Game: 28 August 1920, Division 3, v Southampton (h) D 1–1 – Branfield; Robertson, Sissons; Battiste, Baxter, Wigmore; Holt, Hall, Gilbey (1), Roe, Gore.

Record League Victory: 10–0 v Chesterfield, Division 3, 5 September 1987 – Kite; Haylock, Pearce, Shipley (2) (Lillis), West, Greenall (1), Pritchard (2), Shearer (2), Lovell, Elsey (2), David Smith (1).

Record Cup Victory: 10–1 v Gorleston, FA Cup 1st rd, 16 November 1957 – Brodie; Parry, Hannaway; Riggs, Boswell, Laing; Payne, Fletcher (2), Saunders (5), Morgan (1), Clark (2).

Record Defeat: 2–9 v Nottingham F, Division 3 (S), 18 November 1950.

HONOURS

League Champions: FL 2 – 2012–13; Division 4 – 1963–64.
Runners-up: Third Division – 1995–96; Division 4 – 1973–74.

FA Cup: 6th rd – 2000.

League Cup: 4th rd – 1964, 1997.

FOOTBALL YEARBOOK FACT FILE

In 1946–47 Gillingham had one of their most successful seasons as a non-league club. A 6-0 win over Bedford Town in their final game of the season earned them the Southern League title and they also won the League Cup, defeating Yeovil Town over two legs. They were defeated in the semi-finals of the Kent Senior Cup but lifted the Kent Senior Shield, winning 7-0 in the final.

Most League Points (2 for a win): 62, Division 4, 1973–74.

Most League Points (3 for a win): 85, Division 2, 1999–2000.

Most League Goals: 90, Division 4, 1973–74.

Highest League Scorer in Season: Ernie Morgan, 31, Division 3 (S), 1954–55; Brian Yeo, 31, Division 4, 1973–74.

Most League Goals in Total Aggregate: Brian Yeo, 135, 1963–75.

Most League Goals in One Match: 6, Fred Cheesmur v Merthyr T, Division 3 (S), 26 April 1930.

Most Capped Player: Andrew Crofts, 13 (includes 1 on loan from Brighton & HA) (29), Wales.

Most League Appearances: John Simpson, 571, 1957–72.

Youngest League Player: Luke Freeman, 15 years 247 days v Hartlepool U, 24 November 2007.

Record Transfer Fee Received: £1,500,000 from Manchester C for Robert Taylor, November 1999.

Record Transfer Fee Paid: £600,000 to Reading for Carl Asaba, August 1998.

Football League Record: 1920 Original Member of Division 3; 1921 Division 3 (S); 1938 Failed re-election; Southern League 1938–44; Kent League 1944–46; Southern League 1946–50; 1950 Re-elected to Division 3 (S); 1958–64 Division 4; 1964–71 Division 3; 1971–74 Division 4; 1974–89 Division 3; 1989–92 Division 4; 1992–96; Division 3; 1996–2000 Division 2; 2000–04 Division 1; 2004–05 FL C; 2005–08 FL 1; 2008–09 FL 2; 2009–10 FL 1; 2010–13 FL 2; 2013– FL 1.

LATEST SEQUENCES

Longest Sequence of League Wins: 7, 18.12.1954 – 29.1.1955.

Longest Sequence of League Defeats: 10, 20.9.1988 – 5.11.1988.

Longest Sequence of League Draws: 5, 21.1.2017 – 14.2.2017.

Longest Sequence of Unbeaten League Matches: 20, 13.10.1973 – 10.2.1974.

Longest Sequence Without a League Win: 15, 1.4.1972 – 2.9.1972.

Successive Scoring Runs: 20 from 31.10.1959.

Successive Non-scoring Runs: 6 from 11.2.1961.

MANAGERS

W. Ironside Groombridge 1896–1906 *(Secretary-Manager)* *(previously Financial Secretary)*
Steve Smith 1906–08
W. I. Groombridge 1908–19 *(Secretary-Manager)*
George Collins 1919–20
John McMillan 1920–23
Harry Curtis 1923–26
Albert Hoskins 1926–29
Dick Hendrie 1929–31
Fred Mavin 1932–37
Alan Ure 1937–38
Bill Harvey 1938–39
Archie Clark 1939–58
Harry Barratt 1958–62
Freddie Cox 1962–65
Basil Hayward 1966–71
Andy Nelson 1971–74
Len Ashurst 1974–75
Gerry Summers 1975–81
Keith Peacock 1981–87
Paul Taylor 1988
Keith Burkinshaw 1988–89
Damien Richardson 1989–92
Glenn Roeder 1992–93
Mike Flanagan 1993–95
Neil Smillie 1995
Tony Pulis 1995–99
Peter Taylor 1999–2000
Andy Hessenthaler 2000–04
Stan Ternent 2004–05
Neale Cooper 2005
Ronnie Jepson 2005–07
Mark Stimson 2007–10
Andy Hessenthaler 2010–12
Martin Allen 2012–13
Peter Taylor 2013–14
Justin Edinburgh 2015–17
Adrian Pennock 2017
Steve Lovell 2017–19
Steve Evans May 2019–

TEN YEAR LEAGUE RECORD

		P	W	D	L	F	A	Pts	Pos
2010-11	FL 2	46	17	17	12	67	57	68	8
2011-12	FL 2	46	20	10	16	79	62	70	8
2012-13	FL 2	46	23	14	9	66	39	83	1
2013-14	FL 1	46	15	8	23	60	79	53	17
2014-15	FL 1	46	16	14	16	65	66	62	12
2015-16	FL 1	46	19	12	15	71	56	69	9
2016-17	FL 1	46	12	14	20	59	79	50	20
2017-18	FL 1	46	13	17	16	50	55	56	17
2018-19	FL 1	46	15	10	21	61	72	55	13
2019-20	FL 1	35	12	15	8	42	34	51	10§

§Decided on points-per-game (1.46)

DID YOU KNOW ?

Gillingham narrowly missed out on promotion to the second tier of English football in 1986–87 after finishing fifth in Division Three to make the Football League's first-ever play-offs. They defeated Sunderland in the semi-finals but then drew with Swindon Town in the final played over two legs. Promotion was decided by a replay at Selhurst Park which saw Swindon win 2-0.

GILLINGHAM – SKY BET LEAGUE ONE 2019–20 LEAGUE RECORD

Match No.	*Date*		*Venue*	*Opponents*	*Result*		*H/T Score*	*Lg Pos.*	*Goalscorers*	*Atten-dance*
1	Aug	3	A	Doncaster R	D	1-1	1-1	10	Jakubiak ^{30}	7939
2		10	H	Burton Alb	L	1-2	1-2	16	Cisse ^{7}	4682
3		20	H	Blackpool	D	2-2	2-2	19	Jakubiak 2 $^{9, 37}$	4390
4		24	A	Coventry C	L	0-1	0-1	19		5624
5		31	H	Bolton W	W	5-0	2-0	16	Ogilvie ^{27}, Lee 2 $^{39, 57}$, Hanlan ^{54}, Boon (og) ^{76}	5065
6	Sept	7	A	Tranmere R	D	2-2	2-0	16	Jakubiak ^{16}, Jones ^{36}	6687
7		14	H	Wycombe W	W	2-0	0-0	14	Ndjoli 2 (1 pen) $^{59, 73 (p)}$	4814
8		17	A	Bristol R	D	1-1	0-1	15	O'Connor ^{83}	6370
9		21	H	Ipswich T	L	0-1	0-1	16		7214
10		28	A	Oxford U	L	0-3	0-3	16		6553
11	Oct	5	H	Southend U	W	3-1	1-0	15	Jones ^{43}, O'Keefe ^{46}, Hanlan ^{87}	5091
12		12	A	Portsmouth	D	0-0	0-0	15		18,036
13		19	H	Peterborough U	L	1-2	0-1	16	Mandron ^{80}	6269
14		22	A	Shrewsbury T	D	1-1	1-0	17	O'Keefe (pen) ^{43}	5076
15		26	A	Accrington S	W	1-0	0-0	15	Charles ^{59}	2102
16	Nov	2	H	Rotherham U	L	0-3	0-2	16		4893
17		16	H	Lincoln C	W	1-0	1-0	14	Mandron ^{24}	5567
18		23	A	AFC Wimbledon	L	0-1	0-1	14		4554
19	Dec	7	H	Sunderland	W	1-0	0-0	14	Ogilvie ^{89}	5401
20		14	A	Fleetwood T	D	1-1	0-0	13	Jakubiak ^{82}	2468
21		21	H	Milton Keynes D	W	3-1	2-0	12	Mandron ^{31}, Hanlan ^{33}, Ehmer ^{57}	4739
22		26	A	Ipswich T	D	0-0	0-0	13		22,082
23		29	H	Rochdale	W	1-0	0-0	11	Ogilvie ^{86}	4761
24	Jan	1	H	Portsmouth	D	1-1	0-1	11	Jakubiak ^{80}	5724
25		11	A	Peterborough U	D	0-0	0-0	14		6696
26		18	H	Oxford U	D	1-1	0-1	14	Lee (pen) ^{61}	5051
27		25	A	Rochdale	D	2-2	1-1	14	Roberts 2 $^{32, 59}$	3084
28		29	H	Shrewsbury T	W	2-0	2-0	12	O'Keefe ^{26}, Lee (pen) ^{40}	4212
29	Feb	8	A	Burton Alb	D	0-0	0-0	12		2750
30		11	A	Blackpool	W	3-2	0-1	11	Akinde ^{73}, Charles ^{76}, Hanlan ^{90}	6816
31		15	H	Doncaster R	W	2-1	1-1	10	John (2 ogs) $^{44, 67}$	4754
32		18	A	Southend U	W	1-0	0-0	9	Ogilvie ^{67}	6021
33		22	A	Lincoln C	D	0-0	0-0	10		8950
34		29	H	AFC Wimbledon	L	1-2	0-0	11	Charles ^{87}	4893
35	Mar	7	A	Sunderland	D	2-2	0-0	11	Mandron 2 $^{74, 90}$	29,872
36		14	H	Fleetwood T	Cancelled					
37		21	A	Milton Keynes D	Cancelled					
38		29	A	Rotherham U	Cancelled					
39	Apr	4	H	Accrington S	Cancelled					
40		10	H	Coventry C	Cancelled					
41		14	A	Bolton W	Cancelled					
42		18	H	Tranmere R	Cancelled					
43		25	A	Wycombe W	Cancelled					
44	May	3	H	Bristol R	Cancelled					

Final League Position: 10 (on points-per-game basis)

GOALSCORERS

League (42): Jakubiak 6, Mandron 5, Hanlan 4, Lee 4 (2 pens), Ogilvie 4, Charles 3, O'Keefe 3 (1 pen), Jones 2, Ndjoli 2 (1 pen), Roberts 2, Akinde 1, Cisse 1, Ehmer 1, O'Connor 1, own goals 3.
FA Cup (5): Hanlan 2, Lee 2, Byrne 1.
Carabao Cup (2): Hanlan 1 (1 pen), Ndjoli 1 (1 pen).
Leasing.com Trophy (4): Jakubiak 1, Mandron 1, O'Keefe 1, Tucker 1.

Bonham J 35	Hodson L 4 + 3	Ehmer M 35	Jones A 30	Fuller B 30	Cisse O 2	O'Keefe S 26 + 4	Jakubiak A 12 + 12	Charles R 5 + 10	Ndjoli M 7 + 5	Hanlan B 31 + 4	Marshall M 3 + 15	List E 1 + 3	Byrne M 16 + 2	Mandron M 13 + 10	Ogilvie C 33	O'Connor T 26 + 2	Willock M 3 + 4	Lee O 22 + 6	Pringle B 6 + 4	Tucker J 26 + 2	Roberts J 10	Akinde J 7 + 2	Graham J 2 + 5	Match No.
1	2	3	4	5	6	7	8^1	9^3	10^2	11	12	13	14											1
1	2	3	4	5	8^3	7	10^1		9^2	11	6	14	12	13										2
1	2	3	8	5		7	11^1			10	12	9^2	6	13	4									3
1	2	3	8	5		7^2	9	11^1	12	10^3		13	6	14	4									4
1		3	7	2			11	13		10^2	12		8	14	4	5	6^1	9^3						5
1		3	6	2		12	10		14	13			7	11^3	4	5		9^1	8^2					6
1		3	7	2		14			11^2	12	9		6	10^1	4	5		8^3	13					7
1		3	7	2^2			11		9^3	10^1	13		6	14	4	5		8		12				8
1	12	3		5		7	11^2			10			6	14	4	8^3		9	13	2^1				9
1		3	6	5		14	11^2			10	13		7		4	8		12	9^1	2^3				10
1		3	7	2^3		6	13		11	10^1	12		8		4	5		9^2		14				11
1	14	3	8			7	10^3		6^1	11^2	12		9	13	4	5				2				12
1		3	6			7^1	12		11^3	10	14		8	13	4	5		9^2		2				13
1	14	3	6			7	10^3	9^2	13	11	8^1				4	5		12		2				14
1		3	6			8	12	10^1	14	11^3			7	9^2	4	5		13		2				15
1		3	6			7	11^2	9^3	12	10	14		8		4	5		13		2^1				16
1		3	6	5		7	12	13		10^2			8	11	4			9^1		2				17
1		3	7	2^2		8^1				11	13		6	10	5	12		9^3	14■	4				18
1		3	6	2						10	12		7^1	11	5	8		9		4				19
1		3	6	2^3		7^2	12			10	13			11	5	8^1		9	14	4				20
1		3	6	2		7	14	12		10^2	13			11	5	8^1		9^3		4				21
1		3	6	2		7	12			10				11^1	5	8		9		4				22
1		3	6	2		7	13	14		10	12			11^1	5	8^3		9^2		4				23
1		3	6	2		7^1	12			10	13			11^2	5	8		9		4				24
1		3	6	2		7	12			10					5	8		9		4	11^1			25
1		3	6	2		7	12			10					5	8		9		4	11^1			26
1		4	7	2		6	14			9				12	5		13	8^1		3	11^3	10^2		27
1		3	6	2		7^3		14		13					5		12	9	8	4	11^1	10^2		28
1		3		2						13					5	8	6^2	9	7	4	11	10^1	12	29
1		3		2		12		13		9				14	5	6			7^3	4	11^1	10	8^2	30
1		3		2		7^2		14		11					5	6	12		8^1	4	9^3	10	13	31
1		3		2				14		9				10^1	5	6	7^2	13		4	8^3	11	12	32
1		3	6	2		7^2		14		10					5	8		9^1		4	11^3	12	13	33
1		3	6^1	2		7		14		11					5	8^3	13	9^2		4		10	12	34
1		3	8	2		7^2				10				11	5	13		12		4	9^1	14	6^3	35
																								36
																								37
																								38
																								39
																								40
																								41
																								42
																								43
																								44

FA Cup

First Round	Sunderland	(a)	1-1
Replay	Sunderland	(h)	1-0
(aet)			
Second Round	Doncaster R	(h)	3-0
Third Round	West Ham U	(h)	0-2

Carabao Cup

First Round	Newport Co	(h)	2-2

(Newport Co won 4-1 on penalties)

Leasing.com Trophy

Group A (S)	Colchester U	(h)	2-3
Group A (S)	Ipswich T	(a)	0-4
Group A (S)	Tottenham H U21	(h)	2-0

GRIMSBY TOWN

FOUNDATION

Grimsby Pelham FC, as they were first known, came into being at a meeting held at the Wellington Arms in September 1878. Pelham is the family name of big landowners in the area, the Earls of Yarborough. The receipts for their first game amounted to 6s. 9d. (equivalent to approx. £25 today). After a year, the club name was changed to Grimsby Town.

Blundell Park, Cleethorpes, North East Lincolnshire DN35 7PY.

Telephone: (01472) 605 050.

Ticket Office: (01472) 605 050 (option 4).

Website: www.grimsby-townfc.co.uk

Email: enquiries@gtfc.co.uk

Ground Capacity: 8,916.

Record Attendance: 31,651 v Wolverhampton W, FA Cup 5th rd, 20 February 1937.

Pitch Measurements: 101.5m × 68.5m (111yd × 75yd).

Chairman: Philip Day.

Chief Executive: Ian Fleming.

Manager: Ian Holloway.

Assistant Manager: Anthony Limbrick.

HONOURS

League Champions: Division 2 – 1900–01, 1933–34; Division 3 – 1979–80; Division 3N – 1925–26, 1955–56; Division 4 – 1971–72.
Runners-up: Division 2 – 1928–29; Division 3 – 1961–62; Division 3N – 1951–52; Division 4 – 1978–79, 1989–90. Conference – (4th) 2015–16 *(promoted via play-offs)*.

FA Cup: semi-final – 1936, 1939.

League Cup: 5th rd – 1980, 1985.

League Trophy Winners: 1998.
Runners-up: 2008.

Colours: Black and white striped shirts with red trim, black shorts with white trim, black socks with red and white trim.

Year Formed. 1878. ***Turned Professional:*** 1890. ***Ltd Co.:*** 1890.

Previous Name: 1878, Grimsby Pelham; 1879, Grimsby Town.

Club Nickname: 'The Mariners'.

Grounds: 1880, Clee Park; 1889, Abbey Park; 1899, Blundell Park.

First Football League Game: 3 September 1892, Division 2, v Northwich Victoria (h) W 2–1 – Whitehouse; Lundie, T. Frith; C. Frith, Walker, Murrell; Higgins, Henderson, Brayshaw, Riddoch (2), Ackroyd.

Record League Victory: 9–2 v Darwen, Division 2, 15 April 1899 – Bagshaw; Lockie, Nidd; Griffiths, Bell (1), Nelmes; Jenkinson (3), Richards (1), Cockshutt (3), Robinson, Chadburn (1).

Record Cup Victory: 8–0 v Darlington, FA Cup 2nd rd, 21 November 1885 – G. Atkinson; J. H. Taylor, H. Taylor; Hall, Kimpson, Hopewell; H. Atkinson (1), Garnham, Seal (3), Sharman, Monument (4).

Record Defeat: 1–9 v Arsenal, Division 1, 28 January 1931.

Most League Points (2 for a win): 68, Division 3 (N), 1955–56.

Most League Points (3 for a win): 83, Division 3, 1990–91.

FOOTBALL YEARBOOK FACT FILE

Grimsby Town installed their first set of floodlights in March 1953, marking the occasion with a friendly against Blackburn Rovers. However, the lights, which were mounted on short concrete towers, were ruled to be inadequate to stage competitive first-team games. It was only after new lights were added in 1960 that Town were able to play Football League fixtures under the lights.

Most League Goals: 103, Division 2, 1933–34.

Highest League Scorer in Season: Pat Glover, 42, Division 2, 1933–34.

Most League Goals in Total Aggregate: Pat Glover, 180, 1930–39.

Most League Goals in One Match: 6, Tommy McCairns v Leicester Fosse, Division 2, 11 April 1896.

Most Capped Player: Pat Glover, 7, Wales.

Most League Appearances: John McDermott, 647, 1987–2007.

Youngest League Player: Tony Ford, 16 years 143 days v Walsall, 4 October 1975.

Record Transfer Fee Received: £1,500,000 from Everton for John Oster, July 1997.

Record Transfer Fee Paid: £500,000 to Preston NE for Lee Ashcroft, August 1998.

Football League Record: 1892 Original Member of Division 2; 1901–03 Division 1; 1903 Division 2; 1910 Failed re-election; 1911 re-elected Division 2; 1920–21 Division 3; 1921–26 Division 3 (N); 1926–29 Division 2; 1929–32 Division 1; 1932–34 Division 2; 1934–48 Division 1; 1948–51 Division 2; 1951–56 Division 3 (N); 1956–59 Division 2; 1959–62 Division 3; 1962–64 Division 2; 1964–68 Division 3; 1968–72 Division 4; 1972–77 Division 3; 1977–79 Division 4; 1979–80 Division 3; 1980–87 Division 2; 1987–88 Division 3; 1988–90 Division 4; 1990–91 Division 3; 1991–92 Division 2; 1992–97 Division 1; 1997–98 Division 2; 1998–2003 Division 1; 2003–04 Division 2; 2004–10 FL 2; 2010–16 Conference National League; 2016– FL 2.

LATEST SEQUENCES

Longest Sequence of League Wins: 11, 19.1.1952 – 29.3.1952.

Longest Sequence of League Defeats: 9, 30.11.1907 – 18.1.1908.

Longest Sequence of League Draws: 5, 6.2.1965 – 6.3.1965.

Longest Sequence of Unbeaten League Matches: 19, 16.2.1980 – 30.8.1980.

Longest Sequence Without a League Win: 22, 24.3.2008 – 1.11.2008.

Successive Scoring Runs: 33 from 6.10.1928.

Successive Non-scoring Runs: 7 from 19.10.2019.

MANAGERS

H. N. Hickson 1902–20 *(Secretary-Manager)*
Haydn Price 1920
George Fraser 1921–24
Wilf Gillow 1924–32
Frank Womack 1932–36
Charles Spencer 1937–51
Bill Shankly 1951–53
Billy Walsh 1954–55
Allenby Chilton 1955–59
Tim Ward 1960–62
Tom Johnston 1962–64
Jimmy McGuigan 1964–67
Don McEvoy 1967–68
Bill Harvey 1968–69
Bobby Kennedy 1969–71
Lawrie McMenemy 1971–73
Ron Ashman 1973–75
Tom Casey 1975–76
Johnny Newman 1976–79
George Kerr 1979–82
David Booth 1982–85
Mike Lyons 1985–87
Bobby Roberts 1987–88
Alan Buckley 1988–94
Brian Laws 1994–96
Kenny Swain 1997
Alan Buckley 1997–2000
Lennie Lawrence 2000–01
Paul Groves 2001–04
Nicky Law 2004
Russell Slade 2004–06
Graham Rodger 2006
Alan Buckley 2006–08
Mike Newell 2008–09
Neil Woods 2009–11
Rob Scott and Paul Hurst 2011–13
Paul Hurst 2013–16
Marcus Bignot 2016–17
Russell Slade 2017–18
Michael Jolley 2018–19
Ian Holloway December 2019–

TEN YEAR LEAGUE RECORD

		P	W	D	L	F	A	Pts	Pos
2010-11	Conf	46	15	17	14	72	62	62	11
2011-12	Conf	46	19	13	14	79	60	70	11
2012-13	Conf	46	23	14	9	70	38	83	4
2013-14	Conf	46	22	12	12	65	46	78	4
2014-15	Conf	46	25	11	10	74	40	86	3
2015-16	NL	46	22	14	10	82	45	80	4
2016-17	FL 2	46	17	11	18	59	63	62	14
2017-18	FL 2	46	13	12	21	42	66	51	18
2018-19	FL 2	46	16	8	22	45	56	56	17
2019-20	FL 2	37	12	11	14	45	51	47	15§

§Decided on points-per-game (1.27)

DID YOU KNOW ?

Grimsby Town's all-time record goalscorer Pat Glover played as a goalkeeper for the Mariners in their First Division game at Charlton Athletic in March 1939. Regular keeper George Tweedy was ruled out with 'flu and second choice George Moulson was in hospital after suffering a head injury in the previous game. Town lost the match 3-1.

GRIMSBY TOWN – SKY BET LEAGUE TWO 2019–20 LEAGUE RECORD

Match No.	*Date*	*Venue*	*Opponents*	*Result*	*H/T Score*	*Lg Pos.*	*Goalscorers*	*Atten-dance*
1	Aug 3	A	Morecambe	W 2-0	0-0	2	Whitehouse [68], Wright [90]	2872
2	10	H	Bradford C	D 1-1	0-0	4	Hanson [66]	6882
3	17	A	Forest Green R	L 0-1	0-0	13		2152
4	20	H	Colchester U	D 2-2	0-2	14	Hanson (pen) [48], Green [87]	4103
5	24	H	Port Vale	W 5-2	1-1	7	Cook [20], Ogbu [51], Green [57], Waterfall [80], Hanson [86]	4290
6	31	A	Walsall	W 3-1	1-1	4	Whitehouse [41], Hanson 2 (1 pen) [68, 81 (p)]	4812
7	Sept 7	H	Crewe Alex	L 0-2	0-0	7		4679
8	14	A	Oldham Ath	D 2-2	0-1	9	Cook [81], Ohman [90]	3789
9	17	A	Salford C	L 0-1	0-1	11		2782
10	21	H	Macclesfield T	W 1-0	0-0	9	Robson [56]	3794
11	28	A	Exeter C	W 3-1	1-0	7	Robson 2 [23, 67], Ogbu (pen) [59]	4973
12	Oct 5	H	Mansfield T	L 0-1	0-0	9		5087
13	12	A	Stevenage	L 1-2	0-2	10	Rose, A [80]	3220
14	19	H	Leyton Orient	L 0-4	0-2	14		4132
15	22	A	Cambridge U	D 0-0	0-0	16		4898
16	Nov 23	A	Northampton T	L 0-2	0-2	19		5211
17	26	H	Cheltenham T	D 0-0	0-0	18		2508
18	Dec 7	H	Swindon T	L 0-3	0-2	20		3723
19	14	A	Carlisle U	D 0-0	0-0	20		3653
20	21	H	Scunthorpe U	L 0-1	0-0	21		7385
21	26	A	Macclesfield T	D 1-1	0-0	21	Vernam [59]	1991
22	29	H	Crawley T	D 1-1	1-1	22	Hessenthaler [2]	3612
23	Jan 1	H	Salford C	W 1-0	0-0	19	Rose, A [83]	4555
24	4	A	Mansfield T	W 1-0	0-0	18	Benning (og) [66]	5848
25	11	A	Leyton Orient	D 1-1	0-0	18	Clarke [74]	6248
26	18	H	Exeter C	L 0-1	0-0	18		6021
27	25	A	Crawley T	L 2-3	2-1	20	Whitehouse [21], Hanson [32]	2480
28	28	H	Stevenage	W 3-1	1-0	16	Nugent (og) [16], Clarke (pen) [63], Vernam [72]	4175
29	Feb 1	H	Forest Green R	D 2-2	1-1	17	Vernam [19], Driscoll-Glennon [53]	4675
30	8	A	Bradford C	D 1-1	0-0	18	Hendrie [90]	17,668
31	11	A	Colchester U	W 3-2	1-2	16	Vernam 3 [21, 66, 69]	2954
32	15	H	Morecambe	W 2-1	0-0	15	Hanson [69], Benson [86]	4704
33	22	A	Swindon T	L 1-3	0-0	16	Hanson [59]	8180
34	25	H	Newport Co	W 4-2	2-1	14	Garmston [1], Benson [40], Hanson [61], Wright [84]	3578
35	29	H	Northampton T	L 0-3	0-2	14		4879
36	Mar 3	A	Plymouth Arg	L 0-3	0-3	14		9327
37	7	A	Scunthorpe U	W 2-0	0-0	13	Vernam [52], Waterfall [61]	6855
38	14	H	Carlisle U	Cancelled				
39	17	H	Cambridge U	Cancelled				
40	21	A	Cheltenham T	Cancelled				
41	28	H	Plymouth Arg	Cancelled				
42	Apr 4	A	Newport Co	Cancelled				
43	10	A	Port Vale	Cancelled				
44	13	H	Walsall	Cancelled				
45	18	A	Crewe Alex	Cancelled				
46	25	H	Oldham Ath	Cancelled				

Final League Position: 15 (on points-per-game basis)

GOALSCORERS

League (45): Hanson 9 (2 pens), Vernam 7, Robson 3, Whitehouse 3, Benson 2, Clarke 2 (1 pen), Cook 2, Green 2, Ogbu 2 (1 pen), Rose, A 2, Waterfall 2, Wright 2, Driscoll-Glennon 1, Garmston 1, Hendrie 1, Hessenthaler 1, Ohman 1, own goals 2.
FA Cup (1): Waterfall 1.
Carabao Cup (2): Cook 1, Green 1.
Leasing.com Trophy (4): Ogbu 2, Cardwell 1, Green 1.

McKeown J 36	Hewitt E 18 + 2	Ohman L 14 + 1	Davis H 19 + 2	Hendrie L 32	Hessenthaler J 28	Clifton H 22 + 3	Whitehouse E 25 + 8	Green M 19 + 10	Hanson J 26 + 3	Rose A 7 + 11	Wright M 12 + 13	Pollock M 11 + 8	Ogbu M 11 + 9	Waterfall L 30	Cook J 10 + 4	Ring S 1 + 1	Vernam C 19 + 8	Gibson L 16 + 1	Robson E 11 + 5	Cardwell H — + 2	Driscoll-Glennon A 11 + 1	Clarke B 10 + 3	Tilley J 3 + 7	Benson J 8 + 3	Grandin E 4 + 1	Garmston B 3 + 2	Russell S 1	Match No.
1	2	3	4	5	6	7	8	9^{3}	10^{1}	11^{2}	12	13	14															1
1	2	3^{2}	4	5	7	6	8	9	10	11^{1}		13	12															2
1	2		4	5	7	6^{2}	8	9^{3}	10				11^{1}	3	12	13	14											3
1	6^{1}		4	2	7		8^{2}	9	10		13		11^{3}	3	14	5	12											4
1	2		4^{2}	5	7	13	8^{1}	9^{3}	10		14	12	11	3	6													5
1	2	4		5	7		8	9^{3}	10		12	14	11^{2}	3	6^{1}			13										6
1	2	4		5^{3}	7		8^{2}	9	10		12		11	3	6^{1}		14		13									7
1	6^{3}	4		2	7		8		10		9^{1}		11	3	12		13	5^{2}	14									8
1	12	4^{1}		2	7		8^{2}	9	10				11	3	6^{3}		14	5	13									9
1	2			5	7	13	14	9	10	11^{3}	12			3	6^{1}			4	8^{2}									10
1			13	2	7		14		12	9^{1}	11	4	10^{2}	3	6			5^{3}	8									11
1			4	2	7		14	12	10	13	9^{1}		11^{2}	3	6^{3}			5	8									12
1	2		4	5	8		6^{3}	10^{2}	11	13			12	3	9^{1}		14		7									13
1	6^{3}	4		2	7	8^{1}	14	12	10	11			13	3			9^{2}	5										14
1	7	4	13	2^{1}	8		9	10^{2}	11	12		5		3				6										15
1	2		4		6	7	12	9^{1}	10	13			14	3	11^{2}			5	8^{3}									16
1	2		4		8	7	6^{3}	9	10^{2}	11^{1}			12	3				5	13	14								17
1	2		4		8	7	6^{1}	9^{3}	10	13	14			3			11^{2}	5	12									18
1			4	2	6	7	14	11^{2}	10^{1}	13	9^{3}			3			12	5	8									19
1			4	2	6	7^{1}		10^{2}		12	9		13	3			11	5	8									20
1			4	2	6^{2}	7	14			12	9	13	10^{1}	3			11	5^{3}	8									21
1			4	2	6	7^{2}		10^{1}		12	9^{3}		13	3	14		11	5	8									22
1			4	2	6	7^{2}				13	9^{1}		12	3	10^{3}		11	5	8	14								23
1			4	2	6	7	14			13	9^{3}	12	10^{1}	3■			11	5^{2}	8									24
1	14	12	4^{3}	2	6	7	8			10^{1}	9^{2}	3					11				5	13						25
1		3		2	6^{1}	7	8^{2}		13		9^{3}	4					11				5	10	12	14				26
1		3		2^{1}	6	7	8^{2}		10		12	4					11				5	9^{3}	13	14				27
1		3		2	6^{1}	7	8	13	10^{2}			4					11				5	9^{3}	14	12				28
1		3		2		6^{3}	8^{2}	13	10^{1}		14	4					11				5	9	12	7				29
1				2		6^{1}	8^{3}	14	10			4		3			11				5	9^{2}	13	7	12			30
1	2	4					6	10^{2}	13		14			3			11				8	12	9^{1}	7		5^{3}		31
1				2		13	8^{3}	12	10			4		3			11				5	9^{2}	14	7	6^{1}			32
1				2			8	12	10		13	4^{3}		3			11				5	9^{1}		7	6^{2}	14		33
1	2					6	8^{1}	12	10^{3}		13	4		3			11^{2}					14	9	7		5		34
		4^{1}		2		6		12	11^{2}					3			14				5	8	10	7	9^{3}	13	1	35
1			4^{1}	2		6	8	10			14	13		3			11				12	9		7^{2}		5^{3}		36
1	7		4^{1}	2			8	14			9	12		3			11				5^{3}	10^{2}	13		6			37
																												38
																												39
																												40
																												41
																												42
																												43
																												44
																												45
																												46

FA Cup

First Round	Newport Co	(h)	1-1
Replay	Newport Co	(a)	0-2

Carabao Cup

First Round	Doncaster R	(h)	1-0
Second Round	Macclesfield T	(h)	0-0
(Grimsby T won 5-4 on penalties)			
Third Round	Chelsea	(a)	1-7

Leasing.com Trophy

Group A (N)	Scunthorpe U	(h)	1-2
Group A (N)	Sunderland	(a)	2-3
Group A (N)	Leicester C U21	(h)	1-2

HARROGATE TOWN

FOUNDATION

An earlier club, Harrogate AFC, was formed in 1914, but did not start the 1914–15 season and was reformed in 1919. They competed in the Midland, Yorkshire and Northern Leagues before folding in 1932. The current club was established in the summer of 1935 as Harrogate Hotspurs, several of the players having previously played for Harrogate YMCA. Harry Lunn, the club's first secretary, had previously been secretary of the YMCA team. Hotspurs began life in the Harrogate & District League in 1935–36 when they finished in fourth position, gaining their first trophy when they won the Harrogate Charity Cup. By 1948 they had reached the West Yorkshire League and they changed their name to Harrogate Town to reflect their status as the town's leading club.

CNG Stadium, Wetherby Road, Harrogate HG2 7SA.

Telephone: (01423) 210 600.

Ticket Office: (01423) 210 600.

Website: harrogatetownafc.com

Email: enquiries@harrogatetownafc.com

Ground Capacity: 5,000.

Record Attendance: 4,280 v Harrogate Railway, Whitworth Cup Final, May 1950.

Pitch Measurements: 100m × 66m (109.5yd × 72yd).

Chairman: Irving Weaver.

Vice-Chairman: Howard Matthews.

Managing Director: Garry Plant.

Manager: Simon Weaver.

Assistant Manager: Paul Thirlwell.

Colours: Yellow shirts with black trim, black shorts, yellow socks with black trim.

Year Formed: 1914. ***Turned Professional:*** 2017.

Previous Names: 1914, Harrogate AFC; 1935, Harrogate Hotspurs; 1948, Harrogate Town.

Club Nickname: 'Town', 'Sulphurites'.

Grounds: 1919, Starbeck Lane; 1920, Wetherby Lane; 1935, Christ Church Stray; 1937, Old Showground; 1946, Wetherby Road.

First League Game: (As Harrogate AFC) 30 August 1919, West Riding League v Horsforth (h) (at Starbeck Lane) W 1–0 – Middleton; Deans, Bell, Goodall, Carroll, Jenkinson, H (Capt), Day, O'Rourke, Priestley, Craven (1), Codd.

HONOURS

League Champions: Northern Premier League Division One – 2001–02.
Yorkshire League Division One – 1926–27.
Yorkshire League Division Two – 1981–82.

FA Cup: Second Round – 2012–13.

FA Trophy: Semi-Final – 2019–20.

FA Vase: Fourth Round – 1989–90.

Northern Premier League Division One Cup Winners: 1989–90.

West Riding County Challenge Cup Winners: 1924–25, 1926–27.

West Riding County Cup Winners: 1962–63, 1972–73, 1985–86, 2001–02, 2002–03, 2007–08.

Whitworth Cup Winners: 1919–20, 1924–25, 1931–32, 1946–47, 1947–48, 1950–51, 1954–55, 1959–60, 1961–62, 1972–73, 1977–78, 1983–84, 1995–96.

FOOTBALL YEARBOOK FACT FILE

Although Harrogate Town entered the FA Cup for the first time in 1950–51 it was not until 2002–03 that they reached the first round proper. On that occasion Town defeated Great Harwood, Accrington Stanley and Wisbech Town in the qualifying rounds only to lose 5-1 away to Farnborough Town in a match attended by 1,090.

Record League Victory: 13–0 v Micklefield Welfare, Yorkshire League Division 2, 5 April 1969 – Fountain; Wilkinson, Askew K, Sanderson, Langlands, Crowther, Whiteley, Troughton (3), Foxton (6), Knapton (3), Nottingham (13th goalscorer not known).

Record Cup Victory: 11–2 v Yeadon Celtic, West Riding County Challenge Cup, 5 November 1938 – McLaren; Hebblethwaite, Keogan, Atha, Harker, Clelland, Annakin (4), Sibson, Stanley (7), Everitt C, Richardson.

Record Defeat: 1–10, v Methley U (h), West Yorkshire League Division One, 20 August 1956.

Most League Points in a Season: 86, Northern Premier League Division One, 2001–02.

Most League Goals in a Season: 100, National League North, 2017–18.

Highest League Scorer in Season: Les Liggins, 37, West Yorkshire League, 1946–47.

Most League and Cup Appearances: Paul Williamson, 447 (including 12 as substitute), 1980–85, 1986–93.

Youngest Player: Jim Hague, 14 years v Holmefield, 3 November 1956, West Riding County Challenge Cup.

Most League Goals in One Match: 7, Arthur Stanley v Yeadon Celtic, West Riding County Challenge Cup, 5 November 1938.

Most League and Cup Goals: Jim Hague, 135, 1956–58, 1961–74, 1975–79.

Football League Record: 2020 Promoted from National League; 2020– FL 2.

LATEST SEQUENCES

Longest Sequence of League Wins: 11, 27.12.1926 – 19.4.1927 (Yorkshire League Division One); 11, 7.3.1981 – 12.5.1981 (Yorkshire League Division Three).

Longest Sequence of League Defeats: 8, 15.4.1967 – 7.5.1967 (Yorkshire League Division One).

Longest Sequence of League Draws: 5, 5.10.1991 – 22.10.1991 (Northern Premier League Division One).

Longest Sequence of Unbeaten League Matches: 24, 21.8.2001 – 2.3.2002 (Northern Premier League Division One).

Longest Sequence Without a League Win: 23, 3.12.1966 – 7.5.1967 (Yorkshire League Division One).

MANAGERS

Tommy Codd 1919–20
J. C. Field 1920–21
Jimmy Dyer 1921–23
Mr Gill 1923–24
Mr Sixton 1924–29
C. Edwards 1929–30
Selection Committee 1930–31
Tom Bell 1931–32
Eddie Smith 1935–46
Selection Committee 1946–50
Walter Cook 1950–53
Bernard Cross 1953–55
Jack (Boss) Townrow 1955–67
Selection Committee 1967–69
Stan Hall 1969–70
Thomas (Chick) Farr 1970–71
Peter Gunby 1971–77
Alan Milburn 1977–78
Reg Taylor 1978–79
Alan Smith 1979–88
Denis Metcalf 1988–89
Alan Smith 1989–90
John Reed 1990–91
Alan Smith 1991–93
Mick Doig and John Deacey 1993
Frank Gray 1994
John Deacey then Alan Smith 1994–96
Mick Doig 1996–97
Paul Marshall 1997–98
Gavin Liddle 1998–99
Alan Smith (caretaker) 1999
Paul Ward 1999
Dave Fell 1999–2000
Mick Hennigan 2000–01
John Reed 2001–05
Neil Aspin 2005–09
Simon Weaver 2009–

TEN YEAR LEAGUE RECORD

		P	W	D	L	F	A	Pts	Pos
2010-11	NLN	40	13	11	16	52	66	50	12
2011-12	NLN	42	14	10	18	59	69	52	15
2012-13	NLN	42	20	9	13	72	50	69	6
2013-14	NLN	42	19	9	14	75	59	63*	9
2014-15	NLN	42	14	10	18	50	62	52	15
2015-16	NLN	42	21	9	12	73	46	72	4
2016-17	NLN	42	16	11	15	71	63	59	11
2017-18	NLN	42	26	7	9	100	49	85	2
2018-19	NL	46	21	11	14	78	57	74	6
2019-20	NL	37	19	9	9	61	44	66	2§

**3 pts deducted. §Decided on points-per-game (1.78).*

DID YOU KNOW ?

Floodlights were installed at Harrogate Town's Wetherby Road ground in 1982 and were used for the first time on 21 September 1982 when Accrington Stanley were the visitors for an FA Cup first qualifying round replay. Town won 3-1 in front of a crowd of 2,000 only to go out to Frickley Athletic in the next round.

HUDDERSFIELD TOWN

FOUNDATION

A meeting, attended largely by members of the Huddersfield & District FA, was held at the Imperial Hotel in 1906 to discuss the feasibility of establishing a football club in this rugby stronghold. However, it was not until a man with both the enthusiasm and the money to back the scheme came on the scene that real progress was made. This benefactor was Mr Hilton Crowther and it was at a meeting at the Albert Hotel in 1908 that the club formally came into existence with an investment of £2,000 and joined the North-Eastern League.

The John Smith's Stadium, Stadium Way, Leeds Road, Huddersfield, West Yorkshire HD1 6PX.

Telephone: (01484) 960 600.

Ticket Office: (01484) 960 606.

Website: www.htafc.com

Email: info@htafc.com

Ground Capacity: 24,329.

Record Attendance: 67,037 v Arsenal, FA Cup 6th rd, 27 February 1932 (at Leeds Road); 24,169 v Tottenham H, Premier League, 30 September 2017; 24,169 v Manchester U, Premier League, 21 October 2017; 24,169 v WBA, Premier League, 4 November 2017; 24,169 v Chelsea, Premier League, 12 December 2017 (at John Smith's Stadium).

Pitch Measurements: 106m × 68m (116yd × 74.5yd).

Chairman: Paul Hodgkinson.

Chief Executive: Mark Devlin.

Head Coach: Carlos Corberán.

Assistant Head Coaches: Jorge Alarcón, Narcís Pèlach.

Colours: Blue and white striped shirts, white shorts with blue trim, white socks with blue trim.

Year Formed: 1908.

Turned Professional: 1908.

Club Nickname: 'The Terriers'.

Grounds: 1908, Leeds Road; 1994, The Alfred McAlpine Stadium (renamed the Galpharm Stadium 2004, John Smith's Stadium 2012).

First Football League Game: 3 September 1910, Division 2, v Bradford PA (a) W 1–0 – Mutch; Taylor, Morris; Beaton, Hall, Bartlett; Blackburn, Wood, Hamilton (1), McCubbin, Jee.

Record League Victory: 10–1 v Blackpool, Division 1, 13 December 1930 – Turner; Goodall, Spencer; Redfern, Wilson, Campbell; Bob Kelly (1), McLean (4), Robson (3), Davies (1), Smailes (1).

Record Cup Victory: 7–0 v Lincoln U, FA Cup 1st rd, 16 November 1991 – Clarke; Trevitt, Charlton, Donovan (2), Mitchell, Doherty, O'Regan (1), Stapleton (1) (Wright), Roberts (2), Onuora (1), Barnett (Ireland). *N.B.* 11–0 v Heckmondwike (a), FA Cup pr rd, 18 September 1909 – Doggart; Roberts, Ewing; Hooton, Stevenson, Randall; Kenworthy (2), McCreadie (1), Foster (4), Stacey (4), Jee.

Record Defeat: 1–10 v Manchester C, Division 2, 7 November 1987.

HONOURS

League Champions: Division 1 – 1923–24, 1924–25, 1925–26; Division 2 – 1969–70; Division 4 – 1979–80.
Runners-up: Division 1 – 1926–27, 1927–28, 1933–34; Division 2 – 1919–20, 1952–53.

FA Cup Winners: 1922.
Runners-up: 1920, 1928, 1930, 1938.

League Cup: semi-final – 1968.

League Trophy: *Runners-up:* 1994.

FOOTBALL YEARBOOK FACT FILE

Huddersfield Town were the first Football League team to win a match under the 'Golden Goal' rule which was introduced for the Auto Windscreens Shield for the 1994–95 season. Town's second round tie at home to Lincoln City was tied at 2-2 and the teams went into extra time. Iain Dunne netted after 106 minutes and the game came to an abrupt end.

Most League Points (2 for a win): 66, Division 4, 1979–80.

Most League Points (3 for a win): 87, FL 1, 2010–11.

Most League Goals: 101, Division 4, 1979–80.

Highest League Scorer in Season: Sam Taylor, 35, Division 2, 1919–20; George Brown, 35, Division 1, 1925–26; Jordan Rhodes, 35, 2011–12.

Most League Goals in Total Aggregate: George Brown, 142, 1921–29; Jimmy Glazzard, 142, 1946–56.

Most League Goals in One Match: 5, Dave Mangnall v Derby Co, Division 1, 21 November 1931; 5, Alf Lythgoe v Blackburn R, Division 1, 13 April 1935; 5, Jordan Rhodes v Wycombe W, FL 1, 6 January 2012.

Most Capped Player: Jimmy Nicholson, 31 (41), Northern Ireland.

Most League Appearances: Billy Smith, 521, 1914–34.

Youngest League Player: Denis Law, 16 years 303 days v Notts Co, 24 December 1956.

Record Transfer Fee Received: £15,000,000 from AFC Bournemouth for Philip Billing, July 2019.

Record Transfer Fee Paid: £17,500,000 to Monaco for Terence Kongolo, June 2018.

Football League Record: 1910 Elected to Division 2; 1920–52 Division 1; 1952–53 Division 2; 1953–56 Division 1; 1956–70 Division 2; 1970–72 Division 1; 1972–73 Division 2; 1973–75 Division 3; 1975–80 Division 4; 1980–83 Division 3; 1983–88 Division 2; 1988–92 Division 3; 1992–95 Division 2; 1995–2001 Division 1; 2001–03 Division 2; 2003–04 Division 3; 2004–12 FL 1; 2012–17 FL C; 2017–19 Premier League; 2019– FL C.

LATEST SEQUENCES

Longest Sequence of League Wins: 11, 5.4.1920 – 4.9.1920.

Longest Sequence of League Defeats: 8, 2.3.2019 – 26.4.2019.

Longest Sequence of League Draws: 6, 3.3.1987 – 3.4.1987.

Longest Sequence of Unbeaten League Matches: 43, 1.1.2011 – 19.11.2011.

Longest Sequence Without a League Win: 22, 4.12.1971 – 29.4.1972.

Successive Scoring Runs: 27 from 12.3.2005.

Successive Non-scoring Runs: 7 from 14.10.2000.

MANAGERS

Fred Walker 1908–10
Richard Pudan 1910–12
Arthur Fairclough 1912–19
Ambrose Langley 1919–21
Herbert Chapman 1921–25
Cecil Potter 1925–26
Jack Chaplin 1926–29
Clem Stephenson 1929–42
Ted Magner 1942–43
David Steele 1943–47
George Stephenson 1947–52
Andy Beattie 1952–56
Bill Shankly 1956–59
Eddie Boot 1960–64
Tom Johnston 1964–68
Ian Greaves 1968–74
Bobby Collins 1974
Tom Johnston 1975–78
(had been General Manager since 1975)
Mike Buxton 1978–86
Steve Smith 1986–87
Malcolm Macdonald 1987–88
Eoin Hand 1988–92
Ian Ross 1992–93
Neil Warnock 1993–95
Brian Horton 1995–97
Peter Jackson 1997–99
Steve Bruce 1999–2000
Lou Macari 2000–02
Mick Wadsworth 2002–03
Peter Jackson 2003–07
Andy Ritchie 2007–08
Stan Ternent 2008
Lee Clark 2008–12
Simon Grayson 2012–13
Mark Robins 2013–14
Chris Powell 2014–15
David Wagner 2015–19
Jan Siewert 2019
Danny Cowley 2019–20
Carlos Corberán July 2020–

TEN YEAR LEAGUE RECORD

		P	W	D	L	F	A	Pts	Pos
2010-11	FL 1	46	25	12	9	77	48	87	3
2011-12	FL 1	46	21	18	7	79	47	81	4
2012-13	FL C	46	15	13	18	53	73	58	19
2013-14	FL C	46	14	11	21	58	65	53	17
2014-15	FL C	46	13	16	17	58	75	55	16
2015-16	FL C	46	13	12	21	59	70	51	19
2016-17	FL C	46	25	6	15	56	58	81	5
2017-18	PR Lge	38	9	10	19	28	58	37	16
2018-19	PR Lge	38	3	7	28	22	76	16	20
2019-20	FL C	46	13	12	21	52	70	51	18

DID YOU KNOW ?

Huddersfield Town wore red shirts in their first season, leading to the local press giving them the nickname 'the Scarlet Runners'. The club colours changed to light blue for 1909–10 and the club then became 'Town' before adopting the name 'the Terriers' at the start of the 1969–70 season.

HUDDERSFIELD TOWN – SKY BET CHAMPIONSHIP 2019–20 LEAGUE RECORD

Match No.	Date	Venue	Opponents	Result		H/T Score	Lg Pos.	Goalscorers	Atten-dance
1	Aug 5	H	Derby Co	L	1-2	1-2	15	Ahearne-Grant (pen) 30	22,596
2	10	A	QPR	D	1-1	0-0	19	Ahearne-Grant (pen) 49	14,377
3	16	H	Fulham	L	1-2	0-0	20	Ahearne-Grant 57	20,775
4	21	A	Cardiff C	L	1-2	0-1	23	Chalobah 50	21,821
5	24	H	Reading	L	0-2	0-0	23		21,847
6	31	A	Luton T	L	1-2	0-0	23	Ahearne-Grant 47	10,062
7	Sept 15	H	Sheffield W	L	0-2	0-1	23		22,754
8	22	A	WBA	L	2-4	2-1	24	O'Brien 16, Ahearne-Grant 35	23,577
9	28	H	Millwall	D	1-1	1-1	23	Campbell 24	20,781
10	Oct 1	A	Stoke C	W	1-0	0-0	22	Bacuna 82	20,372
11	5	H	Hull C	W	3-0	0-0	21	Ahearne-Grant 68, Bacuna 74, Kachunga 82	21,702
12	19	A	Blackburn R	D	2-2	1-2	22	Ahearne-Grant (pen) 13, Bacuna 63	13,761
13	23	H	Middlesbrough	D	0-0	0-0	22		22,839
14	26	H	Barnsley	W	2-1	1-0	20	Schindler 30, Ahearne-Grant 53	22,718
15	Nov 2	A	Brentford	W	1-0	0-0	18	Ahearne-Grant 62	11,727
16	9	A	Preston NE	L	1-3	0-2	19	Bacuna 74	16,038
17	23	H	Birmingham C	D	1-1	0-0	19	Campbell 55	22,573
18	26	H	Swansea C	D	1-1	1-1	19	Ahearne-Grant 41	20,062
19	30	A	Bristol C	L	2-5	1-4	19	Ahearne-Grant 35, Bacuna 57	20,762
20	Dec 7	H	Leeds U	L	0-2	0-0	21		23,805
21	10	A	Charlton Ath	W	1-0	0-0	19	Daly 90	13,488
22	14	A	Wigan Ath	D	1-1	0-1	19	Ahearne-Grant 70	10,383
23	21	H	Nottingham F	W	2-1	1-0	19	Schindler 32, Mounie 49	22,529
24	26	A	Middlesbrough	L	0-1	0-1	20		25,313
25	29	H	Blackburn R	W	2-1	1-1	19	Stankovic 25, Mounie 71	22,859
26	Jan 1	H	Stoke C	L	2-5	0-1	20	Mounie 48, Batth (og) 50	21,933
27	11	A	Barnsley	L	1-2	0-1	20	O'Brien 66	17,158
28	18	H	Brentford	D	0-0	0-0	20		20,874
29	28	A	Hull C	W	2-1	1-0	19	Ahearne-Grant 24, Mounie 90	10,474
30	Feb 1	A	Fulham	L	2-3	2-3	20	Smith-Rowe 35, Mounie 39	18,013
31	8	H	QPR	W	2-0	0-0	19	Kachunga 57, Mounie (pen) 61	21,083
32	12	H	Cardiff C	L	0-3	0-2	20		20,238
33	15	A	Derby Co	D	1-1	0-0	20	Toffolo 81	27,502
34	22	A	Swansea C	L	1-3	0-1	21	Mounie 78	15,148
35	25	H	Bristol C	W	2-1	1-0	19	Willock 39, Ahearne-Grant (pen) 63	19,703
36	29	H	Charlton Ath	W	4-0	1-0	17	Ahearne-Grant 2 25, 90, Mounie 75, Bacuna 90	21,539
37	Mar 7	A	Leeds U	L	0-2	0-1	18		36,514
38	June 20	H	Wigan Ath	L	0-2	0-1	20		0
39	28	A	Nottingham F	L	1-3	0-1	22	Ahearne-Grant (pen) 90	0
40	July 1	A	Birmingham C	W	3-0	1-0	19	Ahearne-Grant (pen) 10, Campbell 51, Kachunga 72	0
41	4	H	Preston NE	D	0-0	0-0	20		0
42	7	A	Reading	D	0-0	0-0	18		0
43	10	H	Luton T	L	0-2	0-0	19		0
44	14	A	Sheffield W	D	0-0	0-0	20		0
45	17	H	WBA	W	2-1	1-1	17	Willock 4, Smith-Rowe 86	0
46	22	A	Millwall	L	1-4	1-1	19	Ahearne-Grant 36	0

Final League Position: 18

GOALSCORERS

League (52): Ahearne-Grant 19 (6 pens), Mounie 8 (1 pen), Bacuna 6, Campbell 3, Kachunga 3, O'Brien 2, Schindler 2, Smith-Rowe 2, Willock 2, Chalobah 1, Daly 1, Stankovic 1, Toffolo 1, own goal 1.
FA Cup (0).
Carabao Cup (0).

Grabara K 28	Hadergjonaj F 14 + 7	Elphick T 14	Schindler C 45	Kongolo T 10 + 1	Bacuna J 25 + 13	Hogg J 37	Mooy A 1	Diakhaby A 9 + 9	Ahearne-Grant K 42 + 1	Pritchard A 10 + 8	Mbenza I 1 + 4	Kachunga E 30 + 6	Quaner C — + 5	O'Brien L 36 + 2	Stankovic J 13 + 6	Chalobah T 30 + 6	Mounie S 12 + 18	van La Parra R 3 + 1	Campbell F 21 + 12	Brown J 12 + 3	Koroma J 3 + 4	Simpson D 23 + 1	Schofield R 1	Daly M — + 4	Duhaney D 4 + 2	Harratt K — + 1 / High S — + 1	Edmonds-Green R 1 + 1	Stearman R 17	Toffolo H 19	Smith-Rowe E 13 + 6	King A 6 + 8	Coleman J 2 + 1	Pyke R — + 1	Lossl J 15	Willock C 8 + 6	Rowe A 1	Bryant M — + 1	*Match No.*
1	2	3	4	5	6^1	7	8	9^2	10^3	11	12	13	14																									1
1	2	3	4	5	6^1	7		9^2	10	11^3		12	13	8	14																							2
1	2	3	4	5	6^1	7			10	11^3		9^2		8		12	13	14																				3
1	2	3	4	5	13	6		12	11	9	8^1					7^2		10^3	14																			4
1	2		3	4		7		8^3	11	9^2	12					6		10^1	13	5	14																	5
1	2		3	4		6^3		8	9	12		13				7	14	10^2	11^1	5																		6
1	2	3	4	5	13	7		9^1	11		12			8^2		6	14		10^3																			7
1	2	3	4	5^1		7		14	11			9		8^3		6	13		10^2	12																		8
1		3	4		13	7		12	10			8^1		9^2		6			11	5		2																9
1		3	4		14	7		12	10		13	8^1		9		6^3			11^2	5		2																10
1		3	4		12	7^1		8^3	11			10		9	13	6^2			14	5		2																11
1	14	3	4		12	7		8^3	11^2			10		9		6^1			13	5		2																12
		3	4		12	7		9^2	10			11		6		8^1			13	5		2	1															13
1		3	4		6^1	7		13	11			9		8		12			10^2	5		2																14
1	12	3	4		6^3	7		13	10			8		9		14			11^2	5^1		2																15
1		3^1	4	5	6			10^2	11	14		8		9	12	7	13					2^3																16
1			3	13	2	6		12	10	9^2		8		5	4	7			11^1																			17
1	14		3		2	7		13	10^3	9^2		8		5	4	6■	12		11^1																			18
1	2		3	4^3	10	8		12^2	9			6		5	7				11^1		13			14														19
1	5		3		8	7			10			6			4		11^2				9^1			13	2	12												20
1	5		3		8	7			11			6			4		10^2				9^1	12		13			2											21
1	5		3		9	7			11			8			4	6	12				10^1	2																22
1	5		3		9^2	7			11			6^1			4	8	10			13	12	2																23
1	5		3		9	6^1			10			8		12	4	7	11					2																24
1	13		3		7				10			8^1		9	4	6	11^3		12	5^2		2					14											25
1	13		3		6	8^1			10					9	4	7	11		12	5		2^2																26
1	12		3		6				10^2			8		9	4	7	13		11	5^1	14	2^3																27
1	12		4		13				10			8^1		7		6			11^2			2						3	5	9^3	14							28
1^2			4		2				10			8		7		6	12		11^1									3	5	9^3	14	13						29
			4		2				10			8		7		6^2	11^1		12									3	5	9^3	13	1	14					30
			4		10^2	6						8^3		7			11^1		12			2						3	5	9	13			1	14			31
			4		10	6^2						8		7			11^1		13			2						3	5	9^3	12			1	14			32
			4		10	7						8		9			12		11^2			2^3						3	5	13	6^1			1	14			33
			4		10^1	7			11			8^3		9			12					2						3	5	13	6^2			1	14			34
			4		13	6^1			10					7		12	14		11^3			2						3	5	9				1	8^2			35
			4		12				10	13				7		6	14		11^3			2						3	5	9^2				1	8^1			36
			4		14				10	13				7		6	12		11^1			2						3	5	9^3				1	8^2			37
			4		10	6^4			11	12		13		7^2	14							2^5			15			3^3	5	9^1	16			1	8			38
			4		16■	6^2			11	9^1				10	14	12			15						2^5			3^3	5	13	8			1	7^4			39
			4			6			10^2	14		8^4	15	7		16	12		11^1						2^5			3	5	9^3	13			1				40
			4			6			10^4	9^3		8^2	12	7	16	2^5	13		11^1									3	5	14				1	15			41
			4			6^1			10	14		13	16	12	3	2	11^2								15				5	9^3	7^5			1	8^4			42
			4		14	6^2			10	15				7^3	3	2	12		11^1										5	9	13			1	8^4			43
			4			6			10			8^1		7		2	11^2		13									3	5	9				1	12			44
			4		10^3	7			13			15		9		2	12		11^1									3	5	14	6^2			1	8^4			45
									10^5	9^3				7		4	11^2			16				13	2	15		3	5	14	6^4	1				8^1	12	46

FA Cup
Third Round Southampton (a) 0-2

Carabao Cup
First Round Lincoln C (h) 0-1

HULL CITY

FOUNDATION

The enthusiasts who formed Hull City in 1904 were brave men indeed. More than that, they were audacious for they immediately put the club on the map in this Rugby League fortress by obtaining a three-year agreement with the Hull Rugby League club to rent their ground! They had obtained quite a number of conversions to the dribbling code, before the Rugby League forbade the use of any of their club grounds by Association Football clubs. By that time, Hull City were well away, having entered the FA Cup in their initial season and the Football League, Second Division after only a year.

The KCOM Stadium, West Park, Hull, East Yorkshire HU3 6HU.

Telephone: (01482) 504 600.

Ticket Office: (01482) 505 600.

Website: www.hullcitytigers.com

Email: info@hulltigers.com

Ground Capacity: 24,983.

Record Attendance: 55,019 v Manchester U, FA Cup 6th rd, 26 February 1949 (at Boothferry Park); 25,512 v Sunderland, FL C, 28 October 2007 (at KC Stadium).

Pitch Measurements: 105m × 68m (115yd × 74.5yd).

Chairman: Dr Assem Allam.

Vice-Chairman: Ehab Allam.

Manager: Grant McCann.

Assistant Manager: Cliff Byrne.

HONOURS

League Champions: Division 3 – 1965–66; Division 3N – 1932–33, 1948–49.

Runners-up: FL C – 2012–13; FL 1 – 2004–05; Division 3 – 1958–59; Third Division – 2003–04; Division 4 – 1982–83.

FA Cup: *Runners-up:* 2014.

League Cup: semi-final – 2017.

League Trophy: *Runners-up:* 1984.

European Competitions

Europa League: 2014–15.

Colours: Amber shirts with black trim, black shorts with amber trim, amber socks with black trim.

Year Formed: 1904.

Turned Professional: 1905.

Club Nickname: 'The Tigers'.

Grounds: 1904, Boulevard Ground (Hull RFC); 1905, Anlaby Road (Hull CC); 1944, Boulevard Ground; 1946, Boothferry Park; 2002, Kingston Communications Stadium; 2016, renamed KCOM Stadium.

First Football League Game: 2 September 1905, Division 2, v Barnsley (h) W 4–1 – Spendiff; Langley, Jones; Martin, Robinson, Gordon (2); Rushton, Spence (1), Wilson (1), Howe, Raisbeck.

Record League Victory: 11–1 v Carlisle U, Division 3 (N), 14 January 1939 – Ellis; Woodhead, Dowen; Robinson (1), Blyth, Hardy; Hubbard (2), Richardson (2), Dickinson (2), Davies (2), Cunliffe (2).

Record Cup Victory: 8–2 v Stalybridge Celtic (a), FA Cup 1st rd, 26 November 1932 – Maddison; Goldsmith, Woodhead; Gardner, Hill (1), Denby; Forward (1), Duncan, McNaughton (1), Wainscoat (4), Sargeant (1).

Record Defeat: 0–8 v Wolverhampton W, Division 2, 4 November 1911; 0–8 v Wigan Ath, FL C, 14 July 2020.

FOOTBALL YEARBOOK FACT FILE

Ray Henderson became the first substitute to be used by Hull City in a Football League game when he replaced Dennis Butler in the Second Division game at Brighton on 28 August 1965. He also became the first substitute to score for the Tigers, netting what proved to be the winner after 51 minutes.

Most League Points (2 for a win): 69, Division 3, 1965–66.

Most League Points (3 for a win): 90, Division 4, 1982–83.

Most League Goals: 109, Division 3, 1965–66.

Highest League Scorer in Season: Bill McNaughton, 39, Division 3 (N), 1932–33.

Most League Goals in Total Aggregate: Chris Chilton, 193, 1960–71.

Most League Goals in One Match: 5, Ken McDonald v Bristol C, Division 2, 17 November 1928; 5, Simon 'Slim' Raleigh v Halifax T, Division 3 (N), 26 December 1930.

Most Capped Player: Theo Whitmore, 28 (105), Jamaica.

Most League Appearances: Andy Davidson, 520, 1952–67.

Youngest League Player: Matthew Edeson, 16 years 63 days v Fulham, 10 October 1992.

Record Transfer Fee Received: £22,000,000 from West Ham U for Jarrod Bowen, January 2020.

Record Transfer Fee Paid: £13,000,000 to Tottenham H for Ryan Mason, August 2016.

Football League Record: 1905 Elected to Division 2; 1930–33 Division 3 (N); 1933–36 Division 2; 1936–49 Division 3 (N); 1949–56 Division 2; 1956–58 Division 3 (N); 1958–59 Division 3; 1959–60 Division 2; 1960–66 Division 3; 1966–78 Division 2; 1978–81 Division 3; 1981–83 Division 4; 1983–85 Division 3; 1985–91 Division 2; 1991–92 Division 3; 1992–96 Division 2; 1996–2004 Division 3; 2004–05 FL 1; 2005–08 FL C; 2008–10 Premier League; 2010–13 FL C; 2013–15 Premier League; 2015–16 FL C; 2016–17 Premier League; 2017–20 FL C; 2020– FL 1.

LATEST SEQUENCES

Longest Sequence of League Wins: 10, 23.2.1966 – 20.4.1966.

Longest Sequence of League Defeats: 8, 7.4.1934 – 8.9.1934.

Longest Sequence of League Draws: 5, 14.2.2012 – 10.3.2012.

Longest Sequence of Unbeaten League Matches: 19, 13.3.2001 – 22.9.2001.

Longest Sequence Without a League Win: 27, 27.3.1989 – 4.11.1989.

Successive Scoring Runs: 26 from 10.4.1990.

Successive Non-scoring Runs: 6 from 13.11.1920.

MANAGERS

James Ramster 1904–05 *(Secretary-Manager)*
Ambrose Langley 1905–13
Harry Chapman 1913–14
Fred Stringer 1914–16
David Menzies 1916–21
Percy Lewis 1921–23
Bill McCracken 1923–31
Haydn Green 1931–34
John Hill 1934–36
David Menzies 1936
Ernest Blackburn 1936–46
Major Frank Buckley 1946–48
Raich Carter 1948–51
Bob Jackson 1952–55
Bob Brocklebank 1955–61
Cliff Britton 1961–70 *(continued as General Manager to 1971)*
Terry Neill 1970–74
John Kaye 1974–77
Bobby Collins 1977–78
Ken Houghton 1978–79
Mike Smith 1979–82
Bobby Brown 1982
Colin Appleton 1982–84
Brian Horton 1984–88
Eddie Gray 1988–89
Colin Appleton 1989
Stan Ternent 1989–91
Terry Dolan 1991–97
Mark Hateley 1997–98
Warren Joyce 1998–2000
Brian Little 2000–02
Jan Molby 2002
Peter Taylor 2002–06
Phil Parkinson 2006
Phil Brown *(after caretaker role December 2006)* 2007–10
Ian Dowie *(consultant)* 2010
Nigel Pearson 2010–11
Nick Barmby 2011–12
Steve Bruce 2012–16
Mike Phelan 2016–17
Marco Silva 2017
Leonid Slutsky 2017
Nigel Adkins 2017–19
Grant McCann June 2019–

TEN YEAR LEAGUE RECORD

		P	*W*	*D*	*L*	*F*	*A*	*Pts*	*Pos*
2010-11	FL C	46	16	17	13	52	51	65	11
2011-12	FL C	46	19	11	16	47	44	68	8
2012-13	FL C	46	24	7	15	61	52	79	2
2013-14	PR Lge	38	10	7	21	38	53	37	16
2014-15	PR Lge	38	8	11	19	33	51	35	18
2015-16	FL C	46	24	11	11	69	35	83	4
2016-17	PR Lge	38	9	7	22	37	80	34	18
2017-18	FL C	46	11	16	19	70	70	49	18
2018-19	FL C	46	17	11	18	66	68	62	13
2019-20	FL C	46	12	9	25	57	87	45	24

DID YOU KNOW ?

It took Hull City five matches and 510 minutes to defeat Darlington in their FA Cup second round tie in 1960–61. It was only in the fourth replay at Ayresome Park that the teams were separated, the Tigers winning 3-0 with goals from Dave King, Ralph Gubbins and Doug Clarke.

HULL CITY – SKY BET CHAMPIONSHIP 2019–20 LEAGUE RECORD

Match No.	Date	Venue	Opponents	Result		H/T Score	Lg Pos.	Goalscorers	Attendance
1	Aug 3	A	Swansea C	L	1-2	1-0	17	Batty [3]	15,741
2	10	H	Reading	W	2-1	2-0	13	Bowen [6], Irvine [16]	10,673
3	17	A	Brentford	D	1-1	0-0	10	Bowen [53]	11,000
4	20	H	Blackburn R	L	0-1	0-0	15		10,240
5	24	H	Bristol C	L	1-3	1-1	20	Bowen [44]	10,458
6	31	A	Millwall	D	1-1	1-1	20	Grosicki [18]	12,495
7	Sept 14	H	Wigan Ath	D	2-2	2-1	20	Bowen [10], Grosicki [20]	10,069
8	21	A	Luton T	W	3-0	0-0	14	Stewart 2 [63, 90], Grosicki [87]	10,066
9	28	H	Cardiff C	D	2-2	1-0	15	Grosicki [44], De Wijs [89]	10,756
10	Oct 1	H	Sheffield W	W	1-0	0-0	12	Eaves [72]	11,590
11	5	A	Huddersfield T	L	0-3	0-0	16		21,702
12	19	H	QPR	L	2-3	1-1	18	Bowen [29], Magennis [90]	10,285
13	23	A	Nottingham F	W	2-1	1-0	15	Magennis [38], Bowen [48]	27,624
14	26	H	Derby Co	W	2-0	0-0	12	Bowen 2 [74, 80]	16,326
15	Nov 2	A	Fulham	W	3-0	1-0	11	Bowler [9], Bowen [57], Eaves [84]	18,168
16	9	H	WBA	L	0-1	0-1	12		13,866
17	24	A	Middlesbrough	D	2-2	0-2	14	Eaves [71], Bowen [75]	18,596
18	27	H	Preston NE	W	4-0	1-0	9	Bowen 2 [30, 77], Magennis (pen) [48], Grosicki [51]	9826
19	30	A	Barnsley	L	1-3	0-1	12	Lewis-Potter [81]	13,598
20	Dec 7	H	Stoke C	W	2-1	0-1	12	Bowen 2 [49, 56]	11,019
21	10	A	Leeds U	L	0-2	0-0	13		35,200
22	13	A	Charlton Ath	D	2-2	0-1	13	Bowen [47], Phillips (og) [90]	14,447
23	21	H	Birmingham C	W	3-0	1-0	11	Eaves [45], Grosicki [58], Lewis-Potter [88]	11,334
24	26	H	Nottingham F	L	0-2	0-1	13		15,001
25	29	A	QPR	W	2-1	1-1	12	Honeyman [32], Irvine [89]	13,814
26	Jan 1	A	Sheffield W	W	1-0	0-0	8	Bowen [61]	24,842
27	11	H	Fulham	L	0-1	0-1	11		11,347
28	18	A	Derby Co	L	0-1	0-0	12		27,412
29	28	H	Huddersfield T	L	1-2	0-1	13	Tafazolli [66]	10,474
30	Feb 1	H	Brentford	L	1-5	1-2	14	Tafazolli [29]	10,034
31	8	A	Reading	D	1-1	0-0	14	Wilks [82]	13,393
32	11	A	Blackburn R	L	0-3	0-0	15		11,888
33	14	H	Swansea C	D	4-4	1-1	15	Da Silva Lopes [6], Maddison [50], Wilks [61], Eaves [90]	9757
34	22	A	Preston NE	L	1-2	1-0	17	Wilks [40]	12,342
35	26	H	Barnsley	L	0-1	0-1	17		10,272
36	29	H	Leeds U	L	0-4	0-1	18		16,178
37	Mar 7	A	Stoke C	L	1-5	0-3	21	Da Silva Lopes [73]	23,126
38	June 20	H	Charlton Ath	L	0-1	0-1	22		0
39	27	A	Birmingham C	D	3-3	2-0	21	Magennis [2], Scott [16], Kane [67]	0
40	July 2	H	Middlesbrough	W	2-1	1-1	19	Kane [8], Wilks [90]	0
41	5	A	WBA	L	2-4	1-2	21	Stewart [24], Wilks [48]	0
42	8	A	Bristol C	L	1-2	0-1	22	De Wijs [60]	0
43	11	H	Millwall	L	0-1	0-1	22		0
44	14	A	Wigan Ath	L	0-8	0-7	22		0
45	18	H	Luton T	L	0-1	0-0	23		0
46	22	A	Cardiff C	L	0-3	0-2	24		0

Final League Position: 24

GOALSCORERS

League (57): Bowen 16, Grosicki 6, Eaves 5, Wilks 5, Magennis 4 (1 pen), Stewart 3, Da Silva Lopes 2, De Wijs 2, Irvine 2, Kane 2, Lewis-Potter 2, Tafazolli 2, Batty 1, Bowler 1, Honeyman 1, Maddison 1, Scott 1, own goal 1.
FA Cup (4): Eaves 3, Grosicki 1.
Carabao Cup (5): Bowen 1, Magennis 1 (1 pen), Milinkovic 1, Tafazolli 1, Toral 1.

Long G 45	Lichaj E 29	Burke R 36	De Wijs J 35	Kingsley S 7 + 1	Bowen J 29	Batty D 19 + 11	Stewart K 21 + 6	Grosicki K 28	Irvine J 34 + 1	Dicko N 1 + 1	Tafazolli R 7 + 8	Eaves T 22 + 18	Bowler J 11 + 17	Toral J 8 + 6	Honeyman G 21 + 21	Da Silva Lopes L 33 + 7	Magennis J 20 + 9	McKenzie R 8	Fleming B 4	Pennington M 13 + 1	Elder C 30	Balogh N — + 3	Lewis-Potter K 1 + 20	Kane H 6 + 1	Samuelsen M 3 + 4	Wilks M 16 + 2	Maddison M 4 + 3	McLoughlin S 5 + 2	Berry J — + 1	MacDonald A 5	Scott J 4 + 3	Ingram M 1	Match No.
1	2	3	4^{1}	5	6	7	8	9^{3}	10	11^{2}	12	13	14																				1
1	2	3	4	5	6	7^{1}	8	9^{3}	10	13		11^{2}		12	14																		2
1	2^{1}	3	4	5	7	13	6	10	9			11^{3}			8^{2}	12	14																3
1		3	4	5	6	7^{2}	8	9	10			11^{1}	12			14	13	2^{3}															4
1		3	4^{1}		6		8	9	10^{3}		12	11	13		7^{2}	2	14		5														5
1	5	3^{2}	4		6		7	9	8		13			14	10^{3}	12	11▪			2^{1}													6
1	2		3		6		7	9	10		4	11^{2}	13		8^{1}	12					5												7
1	2	3	4	5	7	14	6	10	9^{3}			11^{1}			13	8^{2}	12																8
1	2	3	4		7		6	10^{3}	9			13	12		14	8^{1}	11^{2}		5														9
1	2	3	4		7	13	6	10^{3}	9			12	14		8^{2}		11^{1}		5														10
1	2	3	4		7	8^{2}	6	10^{3}				11	12		9^{1}	13	14		5														11
1	2	3			7		6	10^{3}	9		4	11^{1}	14	13	8^{2}		12				5												12
1	2	3	4^{1}		6			9^{3}	8		12			10^{2}	13	7	11▪				5	14											13
1	2	3	4		11		13	9^{3}	8			12	6^{1}	10^{2}	14	7					5												14
1	2	3	4		11		13	10	7^{3}			12	8^{1}	9^{2}	14	6					5												15
1	2	3	4		11		7^{2}	10	9			12	8^{1}		13	6^{3}					5		14										16
1	2	3	4		9	13	7	11^{3}	8			10	12			6^{2}					5^{1}		14										17
1	2	3	4		9	6		10^{2}	7			14	8^{1}		12		11^{3}				5		13										18
1	2	3	4		11	7^{2}		9	8			12	6		10^{1}	13					5^{3}		14										19
1	2	3	4		6	7		9^{1}	10		13	11^{2}	12			8					5												20
1	2	3	4		6	7^{1}		9^{3}	10			11	12		14	8					5^{2}		13										21
1	2	3	4		6	7^{1}		9	10			11^{3}	12		14	8					5^{2}		13										22
1	2	3	4		9	12		10^{3}	6			11^{2}	8^{1}		14	7					5		13										23
1	2	3	4	12	8	6^{2}		10	9			11	13		14	7^{3}					5^{1}												24
1	2	3	4	5^{1}	11	14		10^{2}	6			13	8		9^{3}	7				12													25
1	5	3	4		8	7		10^{2}	6			11^{3}	14		9^{1}	12				2			13										26
1	5	3^{2}	4		8			10	9^{3}			11	14		12	6				2			13	7^{1}									27
1	2	3			8				9^{2}		4		10^{1}		13	6	11^{3}				5			7	12	14							28
1	5	3			9			10	13		4	12			14	6	11	2^{2}						7^{3}		8^{1}							29
1	2	3		5					7^{3}		4	13			9	6	11^{2}						10	14		8^{1}	12						30
1	3^{2}					8^{1}			10			11^{3}			9	7	12	2			5		14			13	6	4					31
1						6^{3}			9			13			7	2	11^{2}	3			5		12			10^{1}	8	4	14				32
1						7^{1}			10		13	14			12	6	11	2		3	5					8^{3}	9^{2}	4					33
1		3	4						7			11^{1}		12	9^{2}	6	10			2	5^{3}	13				8	14						34
1			4^{3}				7		10					9^{2}	13	6	11	2		3	5				12		8^{1}	14					35
1						13	6								10	7^{1}	11^{2}	2		3	5	12			9^{3}	8	14	4					36
1						12	7^{1}		9						14	6	11	2		3	5		13		10^{3}	8^{2}		4					37
1			4			6^{4}						11^{1}	8^{3}	9^{2}	13		14			2	5		15	7	16	10^{5}				3	12		38
1		3	4			7	16					14	13		15	6^{4}	10^{1}			2	5		12	8^{5}		9^{2}					11^{3}		39
1		3	4			6^{5}	13					16		15	12	9	11^{4}			2	5^{2}		14	7^{1}		8					10^{3}		40
1		3	4			14	7^{3}					13		9^{4}	6	5	11^{2}			2			12		10^{1}	8					15		41
1		3	4				12					13	14	9^{1}	6	7	11^{2}				5					8				2	10^{3}		42
1		2	4			13	6^{2}				15	11^{1}	7^{3}		9	8	12				5		14			10				3^{4}			43
1		3	4			12	13				14	15	8^{1}	9^{2}	7	6	11^{5}			2^{3}	5		16			10^{4}							44
						8^{2}	7				4	11^{1}			9	2	10				5		13			6				3	12	1	45
1						6	7				4	11^{1}		13	9^{3}	2					5^{4}		14		12	8		15		3	10^{2}		46

FA Cup

Third Round	Rotherham U	(a)	3-2
Fourth Round	Chelsea	(h)	1-2

Carabao Cup

First Round	Tranmere R	(a)	3-0
Second Round	Preston NE	(a)	2-2

(Preston NE won 5-4 on penalties)

IPSWICH TOWN

FOUNDATION

Considering that Ipswich Town only reached the Football League in 1938, many people outside of East Anglia may be surprised to learn that this club was formed at a meeting held in the Town Hall as far back as 1878 when Mr T. C. Cobbold, MP, was voted president. Originally it was the Ipswich Association FC to distinguish it from the older Ipswich Football Club which played rugby. These two amalgamated in 1888 and the handling game was dropped in 1893.

Portman Road, Ipswich, Suffolk IP1 2DA.

Telephone: (01473) 400 500.

Ticket Office: (03330) 050 503.

Website: www.itfc.co.uk

Email: enquiries@itfc.co.uk

Ground Capacity: 30,311.

Record Attendance: 38,010 v Leeds U, FA Cup 6th rd, 8 March 1975.

Pitch Measurements: 102.5m × 66m (112yd × 72yd).

Chairman: Marcus Evans.

Director: Mark Andrews.

Manager: Paul Lambert.

Assistant Manager: Stuart Taylor.

Colours: Blue shirts with white trim, blue shorts with white trim, blue socks with white trim.

Year Formed: 1878.

Turned Professional: 1936.

Previous Name: 1878, Ipswich Association FC; 1888, Ipswich Town.

Club Nicknames: 'The Blues', 'Town', 'The Tractor Boys'.

Grounds: 1878, Broom Hill and Brook's Hall; 1884, Portman Road.

First Football League Game: 27 August 1938, Division 3 (S), v Southend U (h) W 4–2 – Burns; Dale, Parry; Perrett, Fillingham, McLuckie; Williams, Davies (1), Jones (2), Alsop (1), Little.

Record League Victory: 7–0 v Portsmouth, Division 2, 7 November 1964 – Thorburn; Smith, McNeil; Baxter, Bolton, Thompson; Broadfoot (1), Hegan (2), Baker (1), Leadbetter, Brogan (3). 7–0 v Southampton, Division 1, 2 February 1974 – Sivell; Burley, Mills (1), Morris, Hunter, Beattie (1), Hamilton (2), Viljoen, Johnson, Whymark (2), Lambert (1) (Woods). 7–0 v WBA, Division 1, 6 November 1976 – Sivell; Burley, Mills, Talbot, Hunter, Beattie (1), Osborne, Wark (1), Mariner (1) (Bertschin), Whymark (4), Woods.

HONOURS

League Champions: Division 1 – 1961–62; Division 2 – 1960–61, 1967–68, 1991–92; Division 3S – 1953–54, 1956–57.
Runners-up: Division 1 – 1980–81, 1981–82.

FA Cup Winners: 1978.

League Cup: semi-final – 1982, 1985, 2001, 2011.

Texaco Cup Winners: 1973.

European Competitions
European Cup: 1962–63.
UEFA Cup: 1973–74, 1974–75, 1975–76, 1977–78, 1979–80, 1980–81 *(winners)*, 1981–82, 1982–83, 2001–02, 2002–03.
European Cup-Winners' Cup: 1978–79 *(qf)*.

FOOTBALL YEARBOOK FACT FILE

In 1972–73 Kevin Beattie was the first winner of Ipswich Town's Player of the Year Award. He won again the following season when he was also voted as the PFA Young Player of the Year. He went on to win nine England caps and was selected in the PFA First Division Team of the Year on three occasions.

Record Cup Victory: 10–0 v Floriana, European Cup prel. rd, 25 September 1962 – Bailey; Malcolm, Compton; Baxter, Laurel, Elsworthy (1); Stephenson, Moran (2), Crawford (5), Phillips (2), Blackwood.

Record Defeat: 1–10 v Fulham, Division 1, 26 December 1963.

Most League Points (2 for a win): 64, Division 3 (S), 1953–54 and 1955–56.

Most League Points (3 for a win): 87, Division 1, 1999–2000.

Most League Goals: 106, Division 3 (S), 1955–56.

Highest League Scorer in Season: Ted Phillips, 41, Division 3 (S), 1956–57.

Most League Goals in Total Aggregate: Ray Crawford, 204, 1958–63 and 1966–69.

Most League Goals in One Match: 5, Alan Brazil v Southampton, Division 1, 16 February 1981.

Most Capped Player: Allan Hunter, 47 (53), Northern Ireland.

Most League Appearances: Mick Mills, 591, 1966–82.

Youngest League Player: Connor Wickham, 16 years 11 days, v Doncaster R, 11 April 2009.

Record Transfer Fee Received: £8,000,000 (rising to £12,000,000) from Sunderland for Connor Wickham, June 2011.

Record Transfer Fee Paid: £4,800,000 to Sampdoria for Matteo Sereni, August 2001.

Football League Record: 1938 Elected to Division 3 (S); 1954–55 Division 2; 1955–57 Division 3 (S); 1957–61 Division 2; 1961–64 Division 1; 1964–68 Division 2; 1968–86 Division 1; 1986–92 Division 2; 1992–95 Premier League; 1995–2000 Division 1; 2000–02 Premier League; 2002–04 Division 1; 2004–19 FL C; 2019– FL 1.

MANAGERS

Mick O'Brien 1936–37
Scott Duncan 1937–55
(continued as Secretary)
Alf Ramsey 1955–63
Jackie Milburn 1963–64
Bill McGarry 1964–68
Bobby Robson 1969–82
Bobby Ferguson 1982–87
Johnny Duncan 1987–90
John Lyall 1990–94
George Burley 1994–2002
Joe Royle 2002–06
Jim Magilton 2006–09
Roy Keane 2009–11
Paul Jewell 2011–12
Mick McCarthy 2012–18
Paul Hurst 2018
Paul Lambert October 2018–

LATEST SEQUENCES

Longest Sequence of League Wins: 8, 23.9.1953 – 31.10.1953.

Longest Sequence of League Defeats: 10, 4.9.1954 – 16.10.1954.

Longest Sequence of League Draws: 7, 10.11.1990 – 21.12.1990.

Longest Sequence of Unbeaten League Matches: 23, 8.12.1979 – 26.4.1980.

Longest Sequence Without a League Win: 21, 28.8.1963 – 14.12.1963.

Successive Scoring Runs: 31 from 7.3.2004.

Successive Non-scoring Runs: 7 from 28.2.1995.

TEN YEAR LEAGUE RECORD

		P	W	D	L	F	A	Pts	Pos
2010-11	FL C	46	18	8	20	62	68	62	13
2011-12	FL C	46	17	10	19	69	77	61	15
2012-13	FL C	46	16	12	18	48	61	60	14
2013-14	FL C	46	18	14	14	60	54	68	9
2014-15	FL C	46	22	12	12	72	54	78	6
2015-16	FL C	46	18	15	13	53	51	69	7
2016-17	FL C	46	13	16	17	48	58	55	16
2017-18	FL C	46	17	9	20	57	60	60	12
2018-19	FL C	46	5	16	25	36	77	31	24
2019-20	FL 1	36	14	10	12	46	36	52	11§

§Decided on points-per-game (1.44)

DID YOU KNOW ?

Full-back Ossie Parry was Ipswich Town's first professional player. Parry signed from Crystal Palace in June 1936 and made his debut in the club's first Southern League game. He kept his place in the team when Town joined the Football League two years later and remained at Portman Road until June 1950.

IPSWICH TOWN – SKY BET LEAGUE ONE 2019–20 LEAGUE RECORD

Match No.	Date	Venue	Opponents	Result	H/T Score	Lg Pos.	Goalscorers	Attendance
1	Aug 3	A	Burton Alb	W 1-0	1-0	7	Garbutt [11]	4565
2	10	H	Sunderland	D 1-1	1-0	6	Garbutt [15]	24,051
3	17	A	Peterborough U	D 2-2	1-1	8	Norwood [4], Chambers [90]	10,071
4	20	H	AFC Wimbledon	W 2-1	0-1	5	Norwood [81], Jackson [90]	18,778
5	24	A	Bolton W	W 5-0	1-0	1	Norwood 2 (1 pen) [19 (p), 72], Edwards [50], Jackson 2 [60, 64]	5454
6	31	H	Shrewsbury T	W 3-0	2-0	1	Jackson [2], Norwood (pen) [10], Downes [69]	19,161
7	Sept 14	H	Doncaster R	D 0-0	0-0	2		18,928
8	17	A	Milton Keynes D	W 1-0	1-0	2	Nolan [12]	10,167
9	21	A	Gillingham	W 1-0	1-0	1	Vincent-Young [32]	7214
10	28	H	Tranmere R	W 4-1	1-1	1	Garbutt [35], Jackson [48], Nolan [62], Vincent-Young [70]	19,785
11	Oct 5	A	Fleetwood T	W 1-0	0-0	1	Jackson [58]	4312
12	20	A	Accrington S	L 0-2	0-2	1		3567
13	23	H	Rotherham U	L 0-2	0-1	2		20,550
14	26	A	Southend U	W 3-1	1-0	1	Norwood 2 [8, 70], Jackson [76]	8632
15	Nov 5	A	Rochdale	W 1-0	0-0	1	Rowe [53]	3150
16	23	H	Blackpool	D 2-2	1-1	2	Edwards [8], Garbutt (pen) [58]	19,503
17	26	H	Wycombe W	D 0-0	0-0	2		19,215
18	Dec 7	A	Coventry C	D 1-1	1-0	2	Keane [31]	8085
19	14	H	Bristol R	L 1-2	1-2	2	Norwood [37]	18,806
20	21	A	Portsmouth	L 0-1	0-0	3		18,801
21	26	H	Gillingham	D 0-0	0-0	2		22,082
22	29	A	Lincoln C	L 3-5	1-2	4	Garbutt [32], Toffolo (og) [59], Keane [83]	10,012
23	Jan 1	A	Wycombe W	D 1-1	0-0	5	Norwood [54]	8523
24	11	H	Accrington S	W 4-1	3-0	3	Jackson [12], Norwood [29], Judge [44], Keane [90]	17,536
25	14	A	Oxford U	D 0-0	0-0	3		8191
26	18	A	Tranmere R	W 2-1	0-1	3	Downes [55], Jackson [79]	7921
27	25	H	Lincoln C	W 1-0	1-0	1	Woolfenden [44]	18,795
28	28	A	Rotherham U	L 0-1	0-1	3		9327
29	Feb 1	H	Peterborough U	L 1-4	0-2	4	Norwood (pen) [79]	21,351
30	8	A	Sunderland	L 0-1	0-0	7		32,726
31	11	A	AFC Wimbledon	D 0-0	0-0	7		4745
32	15	H	Burton Alb	W 4-1	2-1	7	Judge 2 [29, 63], Jackson 2 [45, 52]	19,922
33	22	H	Oxford U	L 0-1	0-1	8		19,363
34	29	A	Blackpool	L 1-2	0-1	9	Sears [54]	9500
35	Mar 3	H	Fleetwood T	L 0-1	0-1	9		15,678
36	7	H	Coventry C	L 0-1	0-1	10		18,825
37	14	A	Bristol R	Cancelled				
38	21	H	Portsmouth	Cancelled				
39	Apr 4	H	Southend U	Cancelled				
40	10	H	Bolton W	Cancelled				
41	13	A	Shrewsbury T	Cancelled				
42	18	H	Rochdale	Cancelled				
43	25	A	Doncaster R	Cancelled				
44	May 3	H	Milton Keynes D	Cancelled				

Final League Position: 11 (on points-per-game basis)

GOALSCORERS

League (46): Jackson 11, Norwood 11 (3 pens), Garbutt 5 (1 pen), Judge 3, Keane 3, Downes 2, Edwards 2, Nolan 2, Vincent-Young 2, Chambers 1, Rowe 1, Sears 1, Woolfenden 1, own goal 1.
FA Cup (4): Dozzell 1, Garbutt 1, Judge 1, Keane 1.
Carabao Cup (1): Dobra 1.
Leasing.com Trophy (8): Roberts 3, Keane 2, El Mizouni 1, Huws 1, own goal 1.

Holy T 21	Donacien J 12 + 1	Woolfenden L 31	Wilson J 21 + 2	Kenlock M 8 + 1	Rowe D 9 + 5	Skuse C 25 + 4	Downes F 29	Garbutt L 28	Norwood J 22 + 6	Jackson K 28 + 4	Judge A 21 + 9	Huws E 11 + 6	El Mizouni I 1 + 2	Chambers L 31	Dozzell A 8 + 2	Roberts J — + 1	Edwards G 22 + 5	Georgiou A — + 10	Vincent-Young K 9	Nolan J 17 + 5	Keane W 14 + 9	Nsiala A 3	Dobra A — + 3	Norris W 15	Sears F 2 + 9	Bishop T 2 + 7	Earl J 5 + 2	Simpson T — + 3	McGavin B 1	*Match No.*
1	2	3	4^{1}	5	6^{2}	7	8	9	10	11^{3}	12	13	14																	1
1	2	3		5	6^{2}	7	8	9^{1}	10	11^{3}	12			4	13	14														2
1	2	3		5	6^{2}	7	8		10	11	12		13	4			9^{1}													3
1	2	3	4	5	9^{1}	7	8		10	13	14		11^{2}		6^{3}			12												4
1			4	5	14	7^{2}	8		10^{1}	11	9	12		3			6^{3}	13	2											5
1		3		5	6^{3}	7	8		10	11^{2}	9^{1}			4			13	12	2	14										6
1		3		5		7	8^{3}		10	11^{2}	9			4			6^{1}	13	2	12	14									7
1			4			3	6	8	11^{3}	10^{1}		7^{2}		2			14	13	5	9	12									8
1		2	4			7	6^{2}		14	11^{3}	10	13		3	9^{1}		8		5	12										9
1			4		12	3	6	8	10^{2}	11	9^{1}	13		2					5	7										10
1		2	4▮		13	7	6	8	10^{3}	11^{2}		14		3			12		5^{1}	9										11
1		2			13	6		8		11	10^{2}			3	7^{3}		5	14		9		4^{1}	12▮							12
1			4		7^{2}	6		5	13	10		8^{1}		3			14	12	2	9	11^{3}									13
		3	13		6^{2}	8^{1}	7	5	10	11	14			4			9		2^{3}	12				1						14
		3			6^{2}	7		5	11^{3}	10	9^{1}			4	14		2	13		8	12			1						15
	2	3			10^{2}	7	6^{1}	5		11	14			4			8^{3}	12		9	13			1						16
1	5	2	4^{1}		12	6		8	10^{2}	11		7^{3}		3			13			9	14									17
	2	3	4			12	6	5		13	10^{2}				7		8^{1}			9	11			1						18
1		3	4			2	7	5	9	11	12				6^{2}			13		8^{1}	10									19
	13	3				5^{2}	8	9	11	14	12			4▮			6^{1}			7	10	2^{3}		1						20
	2^{1}	3				8		5	10	11	9						6			7		4		1	12					21
	2^{3}	4	13				7	5	10^{1}	11	9			3	8		6^{2}				14			1	12					22
		4	2				6	8	10^{1}	11	9^{2}	7		3			5				12			1		13				23
		4	3			12	6	8	10	11^{1}	9^{2}	7^{3}		2			5				14			1		13				24
		4	3				6	8	10^{1}		9	7		2			5				11			1	12					25
		4	3			14	6	8	13	10	9^{2}	7^{1}		2			5				11^{3}			1		12				26
		4	3				6	8	13	11	9^{2}	7		2			5				10^{1}			1		12				27
		4	3				6	8	12	11	9^{2}	7^{3}		2			5			13	10^{1}			1	14					28
		4	3	12		7	6	8^{2}	13	10	9^{1}			2			5				11^{3}			1	14					29
1	6^{3}	4	3	9		5	8		11^{2}	12		13		2						7^{1}	10						14			30
1	6	4	3			5	7		10^{2}	11		8		2							12				13		9^{1}			31
1		2				12	7	8		10	9^{2}			3			5			6^{3}	11^{1}				14	13	4			32
1		2					6	8		11▮	9^{2}			3			5^{1}			7	10				13	12	4			33
1		2				7	6^{2}	5			12	9		3							11^{3}		13		10	8^{1}	4	14		34
1	5		2					9			10			3	8					6^{3}	11^{2}				12	14	4	13	7^{1}	35
		4				7		5^{1}			9			3	6		2			8			14	1	10^{2}	11^{3}	12	13		36
																														37
																														38
																														39
																														40
																														41
																														42
																														43
																														44

FA Cup

First Round	Lincoln C	(h)	1-1
Replay	Lincoln C	(a)	1-0
Second Round	Coventry C	(a)	1-1
Replay	Coventry C	(h)	1-2

Carabao Cup

First Round	Luton T	(a)	1-3

Leasing.com Trophy

Group A (S)	Tottenham H U21	(h)	2-1
Group A (S)	Gillingham	(h)	4-0
Group A (S)	Colchester U	(a)	0-1
Second Round (S)	Peterborough U	(a)	1-1

(Ipswich T won 6-5 on penalties)

Third Round (S)	Exeter C	(a)	1-2

LEEDS UNITED

FOUNDATION

Immediately the Leeds City club (founded in 1904) was wound up by the FA in October 1919, following allegations of illegal payments to players, a meeting was called by a Leeds solicitor, Mr Alf Masser, at which Leeds United was formed. They joined the Midland League, playing their first game in that competition in November 1919. It was in this same month that the new club had discussions with the directors of a virtually bankrupt Huddersfield Town who wanted to move to Leeds in an amalgamation. But Huddersfield survived even that crisis.

Elland Road Stadium, Elland Road, Leeds, West Yorkshire LS11 0ES.

Telephone: (0871) 334 1919.

Ticket Office: (0371) 334 1992.

Website: www.leedsunited.com

Email: reception@leedsunited.com

Ground Capacity: 37,890.

Record Attendance: 57,892 v Sunderland, FA Cup 5th rd (replay), 15 March 1967.

Pitch Measurements: 105m × 68m (115yd × 74.5yd).

Chairman: Andrea Radrizzani.

Managing Director: Angus Kinnear.

Head Coach: Marcelo Bielsa.

Assistant Head Coaches: Pablo Quiroga, Diego Flores, Diego Reyes.

Colours: White shirts with blue trim, white shorts with blue trim, white socks with blue trim.

Year Formed: 1919, as Leeds United after disbandment (by FA order) of Leeds City (formed in 1904).

Turned Professional: 1920.

Club Nickname: 'The Whites'.

Ground: 1919, Elland Road.

First Football League Game: 28 August 1920, Division 2, v Port Vale (a) L 0–2 – Down; Duffield, Tillotson; Musgrove, Baker, Walton; Mason, Goldthorpe, Thompson, Lyon, Best.

Record League Victory: 8–0 v Leicester C, Division 1, 7 April 1934 – Moore; George Milburn, Jack Milburn; Edwards, Hart, Copping; Mahon (2), Firth (2), Duggan (2), Furness (2), Cochrane.

HONOURS

League Champions: Division 1 – 1968–69, 1973–74, 1991–92; FL C – 2019–20. Division 2 – 1923–24, 1963–64, 1989–90.
Runners-up: Division 1 – 1964–65, 1965–66, 1969–70, 1970–71, 1971–72; Division 2 – 1927–28, 1931–32, 1955–56; FL 1 – 2009–10.

FA Cup Winners: 1972.
Runners-up: 1965, 1970, 1973.

League Cup Winners: 1968.
Runners-up: 1996.

European Competitions
European Cup: 1969–70 *(sf)*, 1974–75 *(runners-up)*.
Champions League: 1992–93, 2000–01 *(sf)*.
Fairs Cup: 1965–66 *(sf)*, 1966–67 *(runners-up)*, 1967–68 *(winners)*, 1968–69 *(qf)*, 1970–71 *(winners)*.
UEFA Cup: 1971–72, 1973–74, 1979–80, 1995–96, 1998–99, 1999–2000 *(sf)*, 2001–02, 2002–03.
European Cup-Winners' Cup: 1972–73 *(runners-up)*.

FOOTBALL YEARBOOK FACT FILE

When Leeds United joined the Football League for the 1920–21 season they were required to play in the qualifying rounds of the FA Cup. In the extra preliminary round they fielded a reserve team which comfortably beat Booth Town of the Bradford & District League. Their opponents protested to the FA that United had fielded a weakened team and the club were fined £50.

Record Cup Victory: 10–0 v Lyn (Oslo), European Cup 1st rd 1st leg, 17 September 1969 – Sprake; Reaney, Cooper, Bremner (2), Charlton, Hunter, Madeley, Clarke (2), Jones (3), Giles (2) (Bates), O'Grady (1).

Record Defeat: 1–8 v Stoke C, Division 1, 27 August 1934.

Most League Points (2 for a win): 67, Division 1, 1968–69.

Most League Points (3 for a win): 93, FL C, 2019–20.

Most League Goals: 98, Division 2, 1927–28.

Highest League Scorer in Season: John Charles, 42, Division 2, 1953–54.

Most League Goals in Total Aggregate: Peter Lorimer, 168, 1965–79 and 1983–86.

Most League Goals in One Match: 5, Gordon Hodgson v Leicester C, Division 1, 1 October 1938.

Most Capped Player: Lucas Radebe, 58 (70), South Africa.

Most League Appearances: Jack Charlton, 629, 1953–73.

Youngest League Player: Peter Lorimer, 15 years 289 days v Southampton, 29 September 1962.

Record Transfer Fee Received: £30,800,000 from Manchester U for Rio Ferdinand, July 2002.

Record Transfer Fee Paid: £30,000,000 to Valencia for Rodrigo, August 2020.

Football League Record: 1920 Elected to Division 2; 1924–27 Division 1; 1927–28 Division 2; 1928–31 Division 1; 1931–32 Division 2; 1932–47 Division 1; 1947–56 Division 2; 1956–60 Division 1; 1960–64 Division 2; 1964–82 Division 1; 1982–90 Division 2; 1990–92 Division 1; 1992–2004 Premier League; 2004–07 FL C; 2007–10 FL 1; 2010–20 FL C; 2020– Premier League.

MANAGERS

Dick Ray 1919–20
Arthur Fairclough 1920–27
Dick Ray 1927–35
Bill Hampson 1935–47
Willis Edwards 1947–48
Major Frank Buckley 1948–53
Raich Carter 1953–58
Bill Lambton 1958–59
Jack Taylor 1959–61
Don Revie OBE 1961–74
Brian Clough 1974
Jimmy Armfield 1974–78
Jock Stein CBE 1978
Jimmy Adamson 1978–80
Allan Clarke 1980–82
Eddie Gray MBE 1982–85
Billy Bremner 1985–88
Howard Wilkinson 1988–96
George Graham 1996–98
David O'Leary 1998–2002
Terry Venables 2002–03
Peter Reid 2003
Eddie Gray *(Caretaker)* 2003–04
Kevin Blackwell 2004–06
Dennis Wise 2006–08
Gary McAllister 2008
Simon Grayson 2008–12
Neil Warnock 2012–13
Brian McDermott 2013–14
Dave Hockaday 2014
Darko Milanic 2014
Neil Redfearn 2014–15
Uwe Rosler 2015
Steve Evans 2015–16
Garry Monk 2016–17
Thomas Christiansen 2017–18
Paul Heckingbottom 2018
Marcelo Bielsa June 2018–

LATEST SEQUENCES

Longest Sequence of League Wins: 9, 18.4.2009 – 5.9.2009.

Longest Sequence of League Defeats: 6, 28.12.2003 – 7.2.2004.

Longest Sequence of League Draws: 5, 2.5.2015 – 22.8.2015.

Longest Sequence of Unbeaten League Matches: 34, 26.10.1968 – 26.8.1969.

Longest Sequence Without a League Win: 17, 1.2.1947 – 26.5.1947.

Successive Scoring Runs: 30 from 27.8.1927.

Successive Non-scoring Runs: 6 from 30.1.1982.

TEN YEAR LEAGUE RECORD

		P	W	D	L	F	A	Pts	Pos
2010-11	FL C	46	19	15	12	81	70	72	7
2011-12	FL C	46	17	10	19	65	68	61	14
2012-13	FL C	46	17	10	19	57	66	61	13
2013-14	FL C	46	16	9	21	59	67	57	15
2014-15	FL C	46	15	11	20	50	61	56	15
2015-16	FL C	46	14	17	15	50	58	59	13
2016-17	FL C	46	22	9	15	61	47	75	7
2017-18	FL C	46	17	9	20	59	64	60	13
2018-19	FL C	46	25	8	13	73	50	83	3
2019-20	FL C	46	28	9	9	77	35	93	1

DID YOU KNOW ?

Leeds United have lost to non-league opposition in the FA Cup on two occasions. In 2008–09 they went down 1-0 away to Histon in a second round tie, while in 2016–17 they lost by the same margin at Sutton United in the fourth round.

LEEDS UNITED – SKY BET CHAMPIONSHIP 2019–20 LEAGUE RECORD

Match No.	*Date*	*Venue*	*Opponents*	*Result*	*H/T Score*	*Lg Pos.*	*Goalscorers*	*Attendance*
1	Aug 4	A	Bristol C	W 3-1	1-0	1	Hernandez [26], Bamford [57], Harrison [72]	23,553
2	10	H	Nottingham F	D 1-1	0-0	3	Hernandez [59]	35,453
3	17	A	Wigan Ath	W 2-0	1-0	1	Bamford 2 [34, 65]	14,819
4	21	H	Brentford	W 1-0	0-0	1	Nketiah [81]	35,004
5	24	A	Stoke C	W 3-0	1-0	1	Dallas [42], Alioski [50], Bamford [66]	24,090
6	31	H	Swansea C	L 0-1	0-0	3		34,935
7	Sept 15	A	Barnsley	W 2-0	0-0	1	Nketiah [84], Klich (pen) [89]	17,598
8	21	H	Derby Co	D 1-1	1-0	1	Lowe (og) [20]	34,741
9	28	A	Charlton Ath	L 0-1	0-1	4		21,808
10	Oct 1	H	WBA	W 1-0	1-0	1	Bartley (og) [38]	34,648
11	5	A	Millwall	L 1-2	0-2	5	Alioski [46]	16,311
12	19	H	Birmingham C	W 1-0	0-0	2	Philips [65]	35,731
13	22	A	Preston NE	D 1-1	0-0	2	Nketiah [87]	18,275
14	26	A	Sheffield W	D 0-0	0-0	3		27,516
15	Nov 2	H	QPR	W 2-0	1-0	1	Roberts [39], Harrison [82]	35,284
16	9	H	Blackburn R	W 2-1	2-1	3	Bamford (pen) [30], Harrison [35]	35,567
17	23	A	Luton T	W 2-1	0-0	2	Bamford [51], Pearson (og) [90]	10,068
18	26	A	Reading	W 1-0	0-0	1	Harrison [87]	16,918
19	30	H	Middlesbrough	W 4-0	2-0	1	Bamford [3], Klich 2 [45, 73], Helder Costa [67]	35,626
20	Dec 7	A	Huddersfield T	W 2-0	0-0	1	Alioski [50], Hernandez [78]	23,805
21	10	H	Hull C	W 2-0	0-0	1	De Wijs (og) [73], Alioski [82]	35,200
22	14	H	Cardiff C	D 3-3	2-0	2	Helder Costa [6], Bamford 2 (1 pen) [8, 52 (p)]	34,552
23	21	A	Fulham	L 1-2	0-1	2	Bamford [54]	18,878
24	26	H	Preston NE	D 1-1	0-1	2	Dallas [89]	35,638
25	29	A	Birmingham C	W 5-4	2-1	1	Helder Costa [15], Harrison [21], Ayling [69], Dallas [84], Harding (og) [90]	22,059
26	Jan 1	A	WBA	D 1-1	0-1	1	Ajayi (og) [52]	25,618
27	11	H	Sheffield W	L 0-2	0-0	2		36,422
28	18	A	QPR	L 0-1	0-1	2		16,049
29	28	H	Millwall	W 3-2	0-2	1	Bamford 2 [48, 66], Hernandez [62]	34,006
30	Feb 1	H	Wigan Ath	L 0-1	0-0	2		35,162
31	8	A	Nottingham F	L 0-2	0-1	2		29,455
32	11	A	Brentford	D 1-1	1-1	2	Cooper [38]	12,294
33	15	H	Bristol C	W 1-0	1-0	2	Ayling [16]	35,819
34	22	H	Reading	W 1-0	0-0	2	Hernandez [57]	35,483
35	26	A	Middlesbrough	W 1-0	1-0	2	Klich [45]	24,647
36	29	A	Hull C	W 4-0	1-0	2	Ayling [5], Hernandez [47], Roberts 2 [81, 84]	16,178
37	Mar 7	H	Huddersfield T	W 2-0	1-0	1	Ayling [3], Bamford [51]	36,514
38	June 21	A	Cardiff C	L 0-2	0-1	2		0
39	27	H	Fulham	W 3-0	1-0	1	Bamford [10], Alioski [56], Harrison [71]	0
40	30	H	Luton T	D 1-1	0-0	1	Dallas [63]	0
41	July 4	A	Blackburn R	W 3-1	2-0	1	Bamford [7], Philips [40], Klich [53]	0
42	9	H	Stoke C	W 5-0	1-0	1	Klich (pen) [45], Helder Costa [47], Cooper [57], Hernandez [72], Bamford [90]	0
43	12	A	Swansea C	W 1-0	0-0	1	Hernandez [89]	0
44	16	H	Barnsley	W 1-0	1-0	1	Sollbauer (og) [28]	0
45	19	A	Derby Co	W 3-1	0-0	1	Hernandez [56], Shackleton [75], Clarke (og) [84]	0
46	22	H	Charlton Ath	W 4-0	2-0	1	White [13], Dallas [28], Roberts [51], Shackleton [66]	0

Final League Position: 1

GOALSCORERS

League (77): Bamford 16 (2 pens), Hernandez 9, Harrison 6, Klich 6 (2 pens), Alioski 5, Dallas 5, Ayling 4, Helder Costa 4, Roberts 4, Nketiah 3, Cooper 2, Philips 2, Shackleton 2, White 1, own goals 8.
FA Cup (0).
Carabao Cup (5): Nketiah 2, Berardi 1, Helder Costa 1, Klich 1.

Casilla F 36	Dallas S 45	White B 46	Cooper L 36 + 2	Douglas B 6 + 9	Philips K 37	Hernandez P 27 + 9	Forshaw A 6 + 1	Klich M 45	Harrison J 45 + 1	Bamford P 43 + 2	Helder Costa W 33 + 10	Alioski E 21 + 18	Davis L — + 3	Shackleton J 5 + 17	Nketiah E 2 + 15	Berardi G 13 + 9	Roberts T 12 + 11	Ayling L 35 + 2	Clarke J — + 1	Casey O — + 1	Struijk P 2 + 3	Stevens J — + 4	Augustin J — + 3	Meslier I 10	Poveda-Ocampo I 1 + 3	Gotts R — + 1	Bogusz M — + 1	Match No.
1	2	3	4	5^{2}	6	7	8	9^{1}	10^{3}	11	12	13	14															1
1	2	3	4	5	6	7	8	9^{2}	10^{1}	11	13	12																2
1	2	3	4	5	6	7	8^{2}	9^{1}	10	11	12			13														3
1	2^{3}	3	4		6	7^{2}	8	9	10^{1}	11	12	5			13	14												4
1	5	2			3	9^{2}	7	6^{3}	11	10^{1}	13	8		14	12	4												5
1	2	3	4	14	6	7	9	8^{2}	10	11^{1}	13	5^{3}			12													6
1	2	3	4		6	7		9^{3}	10^{1}	11^{2}	12	5		8	13	14												7
1	2	3	4	13	6	7^{2}		9	10^{1}	11^{3}	12	5		8	14													8
1	2	3	4		6		12	9	10	11^{3}	7	5^{2}		8^{1}	13		14											9
1	2	3	4^{1}		6			9	10	11	7	5		8^{2}		12	13^{3}	14										10
1	9	3		12	6^{3}			8	10	11^{2}	7^{1}	5			13	4■	14	2										11
1	5	3		14	6			7^{2}	11	10^{1}	9^{3}	8			12	4	13	2										12
1	8	3			6			9	10	11^{1}	7	5			13	4^{2}	12	2										13
1	5	3	13		6			7	11	10^{1}	9^{2}	8			12	4		2										14
1	5	3	4		6	12		7	10^{2}	11	8^{1}		13				9	2										15
1	5	3	4^{1}		6	13		8	10^{3}	11	7^{2}		14			12	9	2										16
1	5	3	12		6	7		8	10^{2}	11	13					4^{1}	9^{3}	2	14									17
1	5	3	4		6	8		7^{2}	10^{3}	11	12	13		14			9^{1}	2										18
1	5	3	4		6^{3}	9		7	10	11^{2}	8^{1}	12			13	14		2										19
1	5	3		14		9		6^{2}	10	11^{1}	8^{3}	7			12	4		2		13								20
1	5	3		14	6	8		9^{2}	10^{1}	11	7^{3}	12				4		2			13							21
1	5	3			6	8		9	10^{2}	11^{1}	7	13			12	4^{3}		2			14							22
1	5	3	4		6	9^{1}		8	10	11	7^{2}	12			13			2^{3}				14						23
1	8	3	4		6			9	10	11^{1}	7	5			12			2										24
1	5	3	4		6			9^{2}	10		8	7			11^{1}	13	12	2										25
1	9	3	4	12	6			8	10	13	7	5^{2}			11^{1}			2										26
1	8	3	4	5^{1}	6	13		9^{2}	10	11	7^{3}	12						2				14						27
1	5^{1}	3	4		6■	8		9^{2}	10	11	7	12						2				13						28
1	8	3	4			9^{1}		6	10	11	7	5		12				2										29
1	8	3	4			9		6	10	11	7	5^{1}					12	2										30
1	2	6	4			8^{1}		9	10	11^{3}	7	5^{2}		13			12	3					14					31
1	5	3	4		6	8		9	10	11^{1}	7							2					12					32
1	5	3	4		6	8^{2}		9	10	11^{1}	7			13				2					12					33
1	5	3	4		6^{1}	9^{2}		8	10	11	7	12		13				2										34
1	5	6	4			9^{1}		8	10	11	7			12		3		2										35
	5	3	4		6	8^{3}		9	10^{2}	11^{1}	7	13		14			12	2						1				36
	5	6	4			8		9^{2}	10^{3}	11^{1}	7	14		13		3	12	2						1				37
	5	3	4		6			9^{3}	10	11	7^{2}	12					8	2^{1}						1	13	14		38
	5	3	4	14	6	13^{5}		8^{3}	10^{4}	11^{1}	7^{2}	12		16			9	2						1	15			39
	5^{4}	3	4^{1}		6	14		8^{3}	10	11	7	13		15		12^{2}	9	2						1				40
		3	4	5	6	12		9^{2}	7	11		10		13			8^{1}	2						1				41
	5^{2}	3	4^{5}	13	6	12		9^{3}	10^{4}	11	7	14		15		16	8^{1}	2						1				42
	5^{1}	3	4		6	13		8	10^{4}	11	7^{3}	12		15		14	9^{2}	2						1				43
	5	7	4			12^{4}		6	8^{3}	11	9^{2}	13		15		2	10^{1}	3			14			1				44
1	2	3		5		8			13	14		10		9		4^{1}	11^{3}	12			6				7^{2}			45
	7	3	4			9^{3}		5^{5}	8^{4}	11^{1}		10^{2}		14			12	2			6	15		1	13		16	46

FA Cup

Third Round	Arsenal	(a)	0-1

Carabao Cup

First Round	Salford C	(a)	3-0
Second Round	Stoke C	(h)	2-2

(Stoke C won 5-4 on penalties)

LEICESTER CITY

FOUNDATION

In 1884 a number of young footballers, who were mostly old boys of Wyggeston School, held a meeting at a house on the Roman Fosse Way and formed Leicester Fosse FC. They collected 9d (less than 4p) towards the cost of a ball, plus the same amount for membership. Their first professional, Harry Webb from Stafford Rangers, was signed in 1888 for 2s 6d (12p) per week, plus travelling expenses.

King Power Stadium, Filbert Way, Leicester LE2 7FL.

Telephone: (0344) 815 5000.

Ticket Office: (0344) 815 5000 (option 1).

Website: www.lcfc.com

Email: lcfchelp@lcfc.co.uk

Ground Capacity: 32,261.

Record Attendance: 47,298 v Tottenham H, FA Cup 5th rd, 18 February 1928 (at Filbert Street); 32,242 v Sunderland, Premier League, 8 August 2015 (at King Power Stadium).

Pitch Measurements: 105m × 68m (115yd × 74.5yd).

Chairman: Aiyawatt Srivaddhanaprabha.

Chief Executive: Susan Whelan.

Manager: Brendan Rodgers.

Assistant Manager: Chris Davies.

Colours: Blue shirts with white trim, blue shorts with white trim, blue socks with white trim.

Year Formed: 1884.

Turned Professional: 1888.

Previous Name: 1884, Leicester Fosse; 1919, Leicester City.

Club Nickname: 'The Foxes'.

Grounds: 1884, Victoria Park; 1887, Belgrave Road; 1888, Victoria Park; 1891, Filbert Street; 2002, Walkers Stadium (now known as King Power Stadium from 2011).

First Football League Game: 1 September 1894, Division 2, v Grimsby T (a) L 3–4 – Thraves; Smith, Bailey; Seymour, Brown, Henrys; Hill, Hughes, McArthur (1), Skea (2), Priestman.

Record League Victory: 10–0 v Portsmouth, Division 1, 20 October 1928 – McLaren; Black, Brown; Findlay, Carr, Watson; Adcock, Hine (3), Chandler (6), Lochhead, Barry (1).

Record Cup Victory: 8–1 v Coventry C (a), League Cup 5th rd, 1 December 1964 – Banks; Sjoberg, Norman (2); Roberts, King, McDerment; Hodgson (2), Cross, Goodfellow, Gibson (1), Stringfellow (2), (1 og).

Record Defeat: 0–12 (as Leicester Fosse) v Nottingham F, Division 1, 21 April 1909.

HONOURS

League Champions: Premier League – 2015–16; FL C – 2013–14; Division 2 – 1924–25, 1936–37, 1953–54, 1956–57, 1970–71, 1979–80; FL 1 – 2008–09.
Runners-up: Division 1 – 1928–29; First Division – 2002–03; Division 2 – 1907–08.

FA Cup: *Runners-up:* 1949, 1961, 1963, 1969.

League Cup Winners: 1964, 1997, 2000.
Runners-up: 1965, 1999.

European Competitions
UEFA Champions League: 2016–17 (*qf*).

UEFA Cup: 1997–98, 2000–01.
European Cup-Winners' Cup: 1961–62.

FOOTBALL YEARBOOK FACT FILE

Leicester Fosse, as the club was then known, were awarded a penalty in their seventh Football League game at home to Newcastle United in October 1894. However, the spot-kick was entrusted to 'Tout' Miller whose shot went wide of the goal. Fosse scored their first League goal from the penalty spot in the 5-1 win over Notts County on 1 December 1894.

Most League Points (2 for a win): 61, Division 2, 1956–57.

Most League Points (3 for a win): 102, FL C, 2013–14.

Most League Goals: 109, Division 2, 1956–57.

Highest League Scorer in Season: Arthur Rowley, 44, Division 2, 1956–57.

Most League Goals in Total Aggregate: Arthur Chandler, 259, 1923–35.

Most League Goals in One Match: 6, John Duncan v Port Vale, Division 2, 25 December 1924; 6, Arthur Chandler v Portsmouth, Division 1, 20 October 1928.

Most Capped Player: Kasper Schmeichel, 53, Denmark.

Most League Appearances: Adam Black, 528, 1920–35.

Youngest League Player: Dave Buchanan, 16 years 192 days v Oldham Ath, 1 January 1979.

Record Transfer Fee Received: £80,000,000 from Manchester U for Harry Maguire, August 2019.

Record Transfer Fee Paid: £40,000,000 to Monaco for Youri Tielemans, July 2019.

Football League Record: 1894 Elected to Division 2; 1908–09 Division 1; 1909–25 Division 2; 1925–35 Division 1; 1935–37 Division 2; 1937–39 Division 1; 1946–54 Division 2; 1954–55 Division 1; 1955–57 Division 2; 1957–69 Division 1; 1969–71 Division 2; 1971–78 Division 1; 1978–80 Division 2; 1980–81 Division 1; 1981–83 Division 2; 1983–87 Division 1; 1987–92 Division 2; 1992–94 Division 1; 1994–95 Premier League; 1995–96 Division 1; 1996–2002 Premier League; 2002–03 Division 1; 2003–04 Premier League; 2004–08 FL C; 2008–09 FL 1; 2009–14 FL C; 2014– Premier League.

LATEST SEQUENCES

Longest Sequence of League Wins: 9, 21.12.2013 – 1.2.2014.

Longest Sequence of League Defeats: 8, 17.3.2001 – 28.4.2001.

Longest Sequence of League Draws: 6, 2.10.2004 – 2.11.2004.

Longest Sequence of Unbeaten League Matches: 23, 1.11.2008 – 7.3.2009.

Longest Sequence Without a League Win: 18, 12.4.1975 – 1.11.1975.

Successive Scoring Runs: 32 from 23.11.2013.

Successive Non-scoring Runs: 7 from 21.11.1987.

MANAGERS

Frank Gardner 1884–92
Ernest Marson 1892–94
J. Lee 1894–95
Henry Jackson 1895–97
William Clark 1897–98
George Johnson 1898–1912
Jack Bartlett 1912–14
Louis Ford 1914–15
Harry Linney 1915–19
Peter Hodge 1919–26
Willie Orr 1926–32
Peter Hodge 1932–34
Arthur Lochhead 1934–36
Frank Womack 1936–39
Tom Bromilow 1939–45
Tom Mather 1945–46
John Duncan 1946–49
Norman Bullock 1949–55
David Halliday 1955–58
Matt Gillies 1958–68
Frank O'Farrell 1968–71
Jimmy Bloomfield 1971–77
Frank McLintock 1977–78
Jock Wallace 1978–82
Gordon Milne 1982–86
Bryan Hamilton 1986–87
David Pleat 1987–91
Gordon Lee 1991
Brian Little 1991–94
Mark McGhee 1994–95
Martin O'Neill 1995–2000
Peter Taylor 2000–01
Dave Bassett 2001–02
Micky Adams 2002–04
Craig Levein 2004–06
Robert Kelly 2006–07
Martin Allen 2007
Gary Megson 2007
Ian Holloway 2007–08
Nigel Pearson 2008–10
Paulo Sousa 2010
Sven-Göran Eriksson 2010–11
Nigel Pearson 2011–15
Claudio Ranieri 2015–17
Craig Shakespeare 2017
Claude Puel 2017–19
Brendan Rodgers February 2019–

TEN YEAR LEAGUE RECORD

		P	*W*	*D*	*L*	*F*	*A*	*Pts*	*Pos*
2010-11	FL C	46	19	10	17	76	71	67	10
2011-12	FL C	46	18	12	16	66	55	66	9
2012-13	FL C	46	19	11	16	71	48	68	6
2013-14	FL C	46	31	9	6	83	43	102	1
2014-15	PR Lge	38	11	8	19	46	55	41	14
2015-16	PR Lge	38	23	12	3	68	36	81	1
2016-17	PR Lge	38	12	8	18	48	63	44	12
2017-18	PR Lge	38	12	11	15	56	60	47	9
2018-19	PR Lge	38	15	7	16	51	48	52	9
2019-20	PR Lge	38	18	8	12	67	41	62	5

DID YOU KNOW ?

Leicester City defender Graham Cross scored an unusual hat-trick during a 20-minute spell of the First Division game against Nottingham Forest at Filbert Street in April 1966. Firstly, he slammed a cross into his own goal to put the visitors 1-0 up and then made amends by equalising two minutes later, before netting the winner after 37 minutes.

LEICESTER CITY – PREMIER LEAGUE 2019–20 LEAGUE RECORD

Match No.	Date	Venue	Opponents	Result		H/T Score	Lg Pos.	Goalscorers	Attendance
1	Aug 11	H	Wolverhampton W	D	0-0	0-0	10		32,015
2	18	A	Chelsea	D	1-1	0-1	12	Ndidi [67]	40,629
3	24	A	Sheffield U	W	2-1	1-0	3	Vardy [38], Barnes [70]	30,079
4	31	H	Bournemouth	W	3-1	2-1	3	Vardy 2 [12, 73], Tielemans [41]	31,613
5	Sept 14	A	Manchester U	L	0-1	0-1	5		73,689
6	21	H	Tottenham H	W	2-1	0-1	3	Ricardo Pereira [69], Maddison [85]	32,129
7	29	H	Newcastle U	W	5-0	1-0	3	Ricardo Pereira [16], Vardy 2 [54, 64], Dummett (og) [57], Ndidi [90]	32,168
8	Oct 5	A	Liverpool	L	1-2	0-1	3	Maddison [80]	53,322
9	19	H	Burnley	W	2-1	1-1	3	Vardy [45], Tielemans [74]	32,105
10	25	A	Southampton	W	9-0	5-0	2	Chilwell [10], Tielemans [17], Perez 3 [19, 39, 57], Vardy 3 (1 pen) [45, 58, 90 (p)], Maddison [85]	28,762
11	Nov 3	A	Crystal Palace	W	2-0	0-0	3	Soyuncu [57], Vardy [88]	25,480
12	9	H	Arsenal	W	2-0	0-0	2	Vardy [68], Maddison [75]	32,209
13	23	A	Brighton & HA	W	2-0	0-0	2	Perez [64], Vardy (pen) [82]	30,640
14	Dec 1	H	Everton	W	2-1	0-1	2	Vardy [68], Iheanacho [90]	32,144
15	4	H	Watford	W	2-0	0-0	2	Vardy (pen) [55], Maddison [90]	31,763
16	8	A	Aston Villa	W	4-1	2-1	2	Vardy 2 [20, 75], Iheanacho [41], Evans [49]	41,908
17	14	H	Norwich C	D	1-1	1-1	2	Krul (og) [38]	32,101
18	21	A	Manchester C	L	1-3	1-2	2	Vardy [22]	54,415
19	26	H	Liverpool	L	0-4	0-1	2		32,211
20	28	A	West Ham U	W	2-1	1-1	2	Iheanacho [40], Gray [56]	59,519
21	Jan 1	A	Newcastle U	W	3-0	2-0	2	Perez [36], Maddison [39], Choudhury [87]	52,178
22	11	H	Southampton	L	1-2	1-1	2	Praet [14]	32,115
23	19	A	Burnley	L	1-2	1-0	3	Barnes [33]	19,788
24	22	H	West Ham U	W	4-1	2-0	3	Barnes [24], Ricardo Pereira [45], Perez 2 (1 pen) [81 (p), 88]	31,968
25	Feb 1	H	Chelsea	D	2-2	0-0	3	Barnes [54], Chilwell [64]	32,186
26	14	A	Wolverhampton W	D	0-0	0-0	3		31,682
27	22	H	Manchester C	L	0-1	0-0	3		32,068
28	28	A	Norwich C	L	0-1	0-0	3		27,010
29	Mar 9	H	Aston Villa	W	4-0	1-0	3	Barnes 2 [40, 85], Vardy 2 (1 pen) [63 (p), 79]	32,125
30	June 20	A	Watford	D	1-1	0-0	3	Chilwell [90]	0
31	23	H	Brighton & HA	D	0-0	0-0	3		0
32	July 1	A	Everton	L	1-2	0-2	3	Iheanacho [51]	0
33	4	H	Crystal Palace	W	3-0	0-0	3	Iheanacho [49], Vardy 2 [77, 90]	0
34	7	A	Arsenal	D	1-1	0-1	4	Vardy [84]	0
35	12	A	Bournemouth	L	1-4	1-0	4	Vardy [23]	0
36	16	H	Sheffield U	W	2-0	1-0	4	Perez [29], Gray [79]	0
37	19	A	Tottenham H	L	0-3	0-3	4		0
38	26	H	Manchester U	L	0-2	0-0	5		0

Final League Position: 5

GOALSCORERS

League (67): Vardy 23 (4 pens), Perez 8 (1 pen), Barnes 6, Maddison 6, Iheanacho 5, Chilwell 3, Ricardo Pereira 3, Tielemans 3, Gray 2, Ndidi 2, Choudhury 1, Evans 1, Praet 1, Soyuncu 1, own goals 2.
FA Cup (4): Barnes 1, Iheanacho 1, Ricardo Pereira 1, own goal 1.
Carabao Cup (12): Iheanacho 4, Maddison 3, Tielemans 2, Evans 1, Gray 1, Justin 1.
Leasing.com Trophy (10): Hirst 3 (1 pen), Muskwe 3, Dewsbury-Hall 2, Eppiah 2.

Schmeichel K 38	Ricardo Pereira D 28	Evans J 38	Soyuncu C 34	Chilwell B 27	Ndidi O 29 + 3	Perez A 26 + 7	Tielemans Y 32 + 5	Choudhury H 10 + 10	Maddison J 29 + 2	Vardy J 34 + 1	Barnes H 24 + 12	Albrighton M 9 + 11	Fuchs C 8 + 3	Praet D 12 + 15	Morgan W 4 + 7	Mendy N 4 + 3	Gray D 3 + 18	Iheanacho K 12 + 8	Justin J 11 + 2	James M — + 1	Bennett R 3 + 2	Thomas L 3	Hirst G — + 2	*Match No.*
1	2	3	4	5	6	7^{2}	8	9^{1}	10	11	12	13												1
1	2	3	4		6	7^{2}	8	9^{1}	10	11		13	5	12										2
1	2	3	4			10^{2}	7^{3}	6	9	11	12		5	8^{1}	13	14								3
1	2	3	4	5	6		8	13	9^{3}	11	10^{2}	7^{1}	14				12							4
1	2	3	4	5	6	12	8	9^{1}	10	11	13						7^{2}							5
1	2	3	4	5	6	7^{1}	8^{3}	14	9	11	10^{2}			12			13							6
1	2	3	4	5	6	7^{3}	9	13		11	10^{1}	12		8^{2}			14							7
1	2	3	4	5	6	13	9	14	10^{3}	11	7^{1}	12		8^{2}										8
1	2	3	4	5	6	7^{1}	8		9^{2}	11	10^{3}			13	14		12							9
1	2	3	4	5	6	7^{2}	8		9	11	10^{1}	12					13							10
1	2	3	4	5	6	7^{1}	8		9^{3}	11	10^{2}			14	13		12							11
1	2	3	4	5	6	7^{1}	8		9	11	10^{2}			13			12							12
1	2	3^{1}	4	5	6	7^{2}	8		9	11	10^{3}			13	12		14							13
1	2	3	4	5	6	7^{1}	8		9	11	10^{2}	13						12						14
1	2	3	4		6	7^{1}	8^{2}	13	9	11	10^{3}		5	12					14					15
1	2	3	4	5^{3}	6		8		9	11	12	13		7^{2}				10^{1}	14					16
1	2	3	4	5	6		8		9	11	13			7^{2}			12	10^{1}						17
1	2	3	4	5	6	7^{2}	8^{3}		9	11	10^{1}	12		14			13							18
1	2	3	4	5	6	13	9	14	10^{3}	11	7^{1}	12		8^{2}										19
1		4			13	10^{1}		7	12		14	9	5		3	8^{2}	6^{3}	11	2					20
1	6	3^{3}	2	9	5	11	7	13	8^{2}				4		14		12	10^{1}						21
1	2	4	3	5		7^{2}	14	6	9	11	10^{1}			8^{3}			13	12						22
1	2	3	4			7^{2}	13		9	11	10		5	8^{1}		6		12						23
1	2	3	4	5	12	7	8		9	11^{2}	10^{3}				14	6^{1}		13						24
1	2	3	4	5		7	8^{1}	6	9	11^{2}	10			13				12						25
1	2	3	4	5		7^{1}	8^{2}	6■	9	11	10^{3}	12		13	14									26
1	5	3	2	9		14	6		8	11	12		4^{3}	7^{2}				10^{1}		13				27
1	2	3	4	5	12	7^{3}	13	6^{1}	9		10	14		8^{2}				11						28
1	2	3	4		6^{3}		13		9	12	10	7		8^{2}		14		11^{1}	5					29
1		3	4	5	6		8^{2}	13	9	11	10^{1}	7^{3}					12	14	2					30
1		3	4	5	6	14	12		9	11	13					7^{1}	8^{3}	10^{2}	2					31
1		3	4	5	6	14	9^{3}		13	11	10^{1}	7^{4}		8^{2}			15	12	2					32
1		3	4	5^{1}	8	6^{3}	7^{5}	16		11	15	9^{4}	14	13				10^{2}	2		12			33
1		3	4		6^{4}	11	7			10	13	8^{1}	12	15			14	9^{2}	5		2^{3}			34
1		3	4■		6	9^{3}	7			11	14	5^{1}	8	13				10^{2}	2		12			35
1		4			6	9^{1}	7	12		10	11^{2}				3		13		5		2	8		36
1		4			6^{3}	9^{2}	7^{4}			10	11^{5}			14	3	15	12	13	5		2^{1}	8	16	37
1		4■			7	12	8^{3}	6^{4}		11	13	5^{2}		14	3		15	10^{1}	2			9^{5}	16	38

FA Cup

Third Round	Wigan Ath	(h)	2-0
Fourth Round	Brentford	(a)	1-0
Fifth Round	Birmingham C	(h)	1-0
Sixth Round	Chelsea	(h)	0-1

Carabao Cup

Second Round	Newcastle U	(a)	1-1
(Leicester C won 4-2 on penalties)			
Third Round	Luton T	(a)	4-0
Fourth Round	Burton Alb	(a)	3-1
Quarter-Final	Everton	(a)	2-2
(Leicester C won 4-2 on penalties)			
Semi-Final 1st leg	Aston Villa	(h)	1-1
Semi-Final 2nd leg	Aston Villa	(a)	1-2

Leasing.com Trophy (Leicester C U21)

Group A (N)	Scunthorpe U	(a)	1-1
(Leicester C U21 won 3-1 on penalties)			
Group A (N)	Grimsby T	(a)	2-1
Group A (N)	Sunderland	(a)	2-1
Second Round (N)	Doncaster R	(a)	3-0
Third Round (N)	Tranmere R	(a)	2-1
Quarter-Final	Newport Co	(a)	0-1

LEYTON ORIENT

FOUNDATION

There is some doubt about the foundation of Leyton Orient, and, indeed, some confusion with clubs like Leyton and Clapton over their early history. As regards the foundation, the most favoured version is that Leyton Orient was formed originally by members of Homerton Theological College who established Glyn Cricket Club in 1881 and then carried on through the following winter playing football. Eventually many employees of the Orient Shipping Line became involved and so the name Orient was chosen in 1888.

The Breyer Group Stadium, Brisbane Road, Leyton, London E10 5NF.

Telephone: (0208) 926 1111.

Ticket Office: (0208) 926 1010.

Website: www.leytonorient.com

Email: info@leytonorient.net

Ground Capacity: 9,241.

Record Attendance: 34,345 v West Ham U, FA Cup 4th rd, 25 January 1964.

Pitch Measurements: 100.5m × 65m (110yd × 71yd).

Chairman: Nigel Travis.

Chief Executive: Danny Macklin.

Director of Football: Martin Ling.

Head Coach: Ross Embleton.

Colours: Red shirts with white trim, red shorts, red socks.

Year Formed: 1881. ***Turned Professional:*** 1903.

Previous Names: 1881, Glyn Cricket and Football Club; 1886, Eagle Football Club; 1888, Orient Football Club; 1898, Clapton Orient; 1946, Leyton Orient; 1966, Orient; 1987, Leyton Orient.

Club Nickname: 'The O's'.

Grounds: 1884, Glyn Road; 1896, Whittles Athletic Ground; 1900, Millfields Road; 1930, Lea Bridge Road; 1937, Brisbane Road (renamed Matchroom Stadium; 2018, The Breyer Group Stadium).

First Football League Game: 2 September 1905, Division 2, v Leicester Fosse (a) L 1–2 – Butler; Holmes, Codling; Lamberton, Boden, Boyle; Kingaby (1), Wootten, Leigh, Evenson, Bourne.

Record League Victory: 8–0 v Crystal Palace, Division 3 (S), 12 November 1955 – Welton; Lee, Earl; Blizzard, Aldous, McKnight; White (1), Facey (3), Burgess (2), Heckman, Hartburn (2). 8–0 v Rochdale, Division 4, 20 October 1987 – Wells; Howard, Dickenson (1), Smalley (1), Day, Hull, Hales (2), Castle (Sussex), Shinners (2), Godfrey (Harvey), Comfort (2). 8–0 v Colchester U, Division 4, 15 October 1988 – Wells; Howard, Dickenson, Hales (1p), Day (1), Sitton (1), Baker (1), Ward, Hull (3), Juryeff, Comfort (1). 8–0 v Doncaster R, Division 3, 28 December 1997 – Hyde; Channing, Naylor, Smith (1p), Hicks, Clark, Ling, Roger Joseph, Griffiths (3) (Harris), Richards (2) (Baker (1)), Inglethorpe (1) (Simpson).

HONOURS

League Champions: Division 3 – 1969–70; Division 3S – 1955–56.
Runners-up: Division 2 – 1961–62; Division 3S – 1954–55.

FA Cup: semi-final – 1978.

League Cup: 5th rd – 1963.

FOOTBALL YEARBOOK FACT FILE

In 1973–74 Orient missed out on promotion to the top flight by a single point. The O's were in the top three of Division Two for most of the season but went into the final fixture against Aston Villa having won just two of their previous 14 games. Victory would have sent Orient up but they missed out when the game ended in a 1-1 draw in front of an attendance of 29,766.

Record Cup Victory: 9–2 v Chester, League Cup 3rd rd, 15 October 1962 – Robertson; Charlton, Taylor; Gibbs, Bishop, Lea; Deeley (1), Waites (3), Dunmore (2), Graham (3), Wedge.

Record Defeat: 0–8 v Aston Villa, FA Cup 4th rd, 30 January 1929.

Most League Points (2 for a win): 66, Division 3 (S), 1955–56.

Most League Points (3 for a win): 86, FL 1, 2013–14.

Most League Goals: 106, Division 3 (S), 1955–56.

Highest League Scorer in Season: Tom Johnston, 35, Division 2, 1957–58.

Most League Goals in Total Aggregate: Tom Johnston, 121, 1956–58, 1959–61.

Most League Goals in One Match: 4, Wally Leigh v Bradford C, Division 2, 13 April 1906; 4, Albert Pape v Oldham Ath, Division 2, 1 September 1924; 4, Peter Kitchen v Millwall, Division 3, 21 April 1984.

Most Capped Player: Jobi McAnuff, 22 (32), Jamaica.

Most League Appearances: Peter Allen, 432, 1965–78.

Youngest League Player: Paul Went, 15 years 327 days v Preston NE, 4 September 1965.

Record Transfer Fee Received: £1,000,000 (rising to £1,500,000) from Fulham for Gabriel Zakuani, July 2006.

Record Transfer Fee Paid: £200,000 to Oldham Ath for Liam Kelly, July 2016.

Football League Record: 1905 Elected to Division 2; 1929–56 Division 3 (S); 1956–62 Division 2; 1962–63 Division 1; 1963–66 Division 2; 1966–70 Division 3; 1970–82 Division 2; 1982–85 Division 3; 1985–89 Division 4; 1989–92 Division 3; 1992–95 Division 2; 1995–2004 Division 3; 2004–06 FL 2; 2006–15 FL 1; 2015–17 FL 2; 2017–19 National League; 2019– FL 2.

LATEST SEQUENCES

Longest Sequence of League Wins: 10, 21.1.1956 – 30.3.1956.

Longest Sequence of League Defeats: 9, 1.4.1995 – 6.5.1995.

Longest Sequence of League Draws: 6, 30.11.1974 – 28.12.1974.

Longest Sequence of Unbeaten League Matches: 15, 13.4.2013 – 19.10.2013.

Longest Sequence Without a League Win: 23, 6.10.1962 – 13.4.1963.

Successive Scoring Runs: 22 from 12.3.1927.

Successive Non-scoring Runs: 8 from 19.11.1994.

MANAGERS

Sam Omerod 1905–06
Ike Ivenson 1906
Billy Holmes 1907–22
Peter Proudfoot 1922–29
Arthur Grimsdell 1929–30
Peter Proudfoot 1930–31
Jimmy Seed 1931–33
David Pratt 1933–34
Peter Proudfoot 1935–39
Tom Halsey 1939
Bill Wright 1939–45
Willie Hall 1945
Bill Wright 1945–46
Charlie Hewitt 1946–48
Neil McBain 1948–49
Alec Stock 1949–59
Les Gore 1959–61
Johnny Carey 1961–63
Benny Fenton 1963–64
Dave Sexton 1965
Dick Graham 1966–68
Jimmy Bloomfield 1968–71
George Petchey 1971–77
Jimmy Bloomfield 1977–81
Paul Went 1981
Ken Knighton 1981–83
Frank Clark 1983–91 *(Managing Director)*
Peter Eustace 1991–94
Chris Turner and John Sitton 1994–95
Pat Holland 1995–96
Tommy Taylor 1996–2001
Paul Brush 2001–03
Martin Ling 2003–09
Geraint Williams 2009–10
Russell Slade 2010–14
Kevin Nugent 2014
Mauro Milanese 2014
Fabio Liverani 2014–15
Ian Hendon 2015–16
Kevin Nolan 2016
Andy Hessenthaler 2016
Alberto Cavasin 2016
Andy Edwards 2016–17
Danny Webb 2017
Martin Ling 2017
Omer Riza 2017
Steve Davis 2017
Justin Edinburgh 2017–19
Ross Embleton June 2019–

TEN YEAR LEAGUE RECORD

		P	*W*	*D*	*L*	*F*	*A*	*Pts*	*Pos*
2010-11	FL 1	46	19	13	14	71	62	70	7
2011-12	FL 1	46	13	11	22	48	75	50	20
2012-13	FL 1	46	21	8	17	55	48	71	7
2013-14	FL 1	46	25	11	10	85	45	86	3
2014-15	FL 1	46	12	13	21	59	69	49	23
2015-16	FL 2	46	19	12	15	60	61	69	8
2016-17	FL 2	46	10	6	30	47	87	36	24
2017-18	NL	46	16	12	18	58	56	60	13
2018-19	NL	46	25	14	7	73	35	89	1
2019-20	FL 2	36	10	12	14	47	55	42	17§

§Decided on points-per-game (1.17)

DID YOU KNOW ?

On 7 February 1925 Albert Pape travelled with the Clapton Orient team to play at Manchester United only to find himself sold to United 90 minutes before kick-off. Pape, who was Orient's leading scorer at the time, played in the game for United and scored the third of his new team's goals in their 4-2 win.

LEYTON ORIENT – SKY BET LEAGUE TWO 2019–20 LEAGUE RECORD

Match No.	Date	Venue	Opponents	Result		H/T Score	Lg Pos.	Goalscorers	Attendance
1	Aug 3	H	Cheltenham T	W	1-0	0-0	6	Wright 68	6534
2	10	A	Macclesfield T	L	0-3	0-1	13		2167
3	17	H	Stevenage	D	0-0	0-0	16		5104
4	20	A	Mansfield T	W	3-2	0-2	9	Wilkinson 64, Angol 78, Maguire-Drew 90	4128
5	24	H	Crawley T	L	2-3	1-1	13	Wright 22, Angol (pen) 53	4905
6	31	A	Salford C	D	1-1	0-1	15	Neal (og) 87	3154
7	Sept 7	H	Swindon T	L	1-3	0-3	17	Maguire-Drew 74	7042
8	14	A	Exeter C	D	2-2	1-1	18	Angol 44, Dennis 51	4933
9	17	H	Crewe Alex	L	1-2	1-1	19	Maguire-Drew 42	4289
10	21	A	Colchester U	L	1-2	1-2	21	Wilkinson 44	5519
11	28	H	Port Vale	D	3-3	1-2	21	Wright 2 3, 90, Wilkinson 59	5490
12	Oct 5	A	Northampton T	W	1-0	0-0	20	Brophy 57	5419
13	12	H	Walsall	W	3-1	0-1	17	Widdowson 48, Harrold 60, Wilkinson 75	6951
14	19	A	Grimsby T	W	4-0	2-0	12	Happe 11, Coulson 21, Alabi 80, Wright (pen) 85	4132
15	22	A	Plymouth Arg	L	0-4	0-4	17		8810
16	26	H	Carlisle U	D	1-1	1-0	16	Wright (pen) 7	5765
17	Nov 2	A	Morecambe	L	0-1	0-0	16		2691
18	16	H	Scunthorpe U	L	0-2	0-1	17		6670
19	23	H	Forest Green R	L	2-4	0-3	18	Harrold 54, Maguire-Drew 78	4614
20	Dec 7	A	Oldham Ath	D	1-1	1-1	19	Maguire-Drew 25	3121
21	14	H	Bradford C	D	0-0	0-0	19		6015
22	21	A	Cambridge U	W	3-2	3-0	15	Turley 29, Wright 36, Maguire-Drew 45	5408
23	26	H	Colchester U	L	1-3	0-1	19	Sotiriou 86	5648
24	29	A	Newport Co	D	1-1	1-0	17	Sotiriou 2	4447
25	Jan 1	A	Walsall	L	0-1	0-1	20		4263
26	11	H	Grimsby T	D	1-1	0-0	20	Angol (pen) 90	6248
27	18	A	Port Vale	L	0-1	0-0	21		5047
28	21	H	Northampton T	D	1-1	0-1	20	Wright (pen) 86	3774
29	25	H	Newport Co	W	2-1	0-0	18	Haynes (og) 81, Sotiriou 89	5084
30	28	A	Crewe Alex	L	0-2	0-1	21		3249
31	Feb 1	A	Stevenage	W	3-0	1-0	19	Sotiriou 2 19, 62, Cisse 59	4357
32	8	H	Macclesfield T	D	1-1	0-0	20	Brophy 75	5708
33	11	H	Mansfield T	W	2-1	1-0	17	Dayton 45, Benning (og) 74	3587
34	15	A	Cheltenham T	L	1-2	1-1	17	Wilkinson 17	3527
35	22	H	Oldham Ath	D	2-2	1-2	18	Haymer (og) 13, Johnson 54	5334
36	Mar 7	H	Cambridge U	W	2-1	2-0	17	Maguire-Drew 17, Johnson 45	5813
37	14	A	Bradford C	Cancelled					
38	17	H	Plymouth Arg	Cancelled					
39	21	A	Carlisle U	Cancelled					
40	28	H	Morecambe	Cancelled					
41	31	A	Forest Green R	Cancelled					
42	Apr 4	A	Scunthorpe U	Cancelled					
43	10	A	Crawley T	Cancelled					
44	13	H	Salford C	Cancelled					
45	18	A	Swindon T	Cancelled					
46	25	H	Exeter C	Cancelled					

Final League Position: 17 (on points-per-game basis)

GOALSCORERS

League (47): Wright 8 (3 pens), Maguire-Drew 7, Sotiriou 5, Wilkinson 5, Angol 4 (2 pens), Brophy 2, Harrold 2, Johnson 2, Alabi 1, Cisse 1, Coulson 1, Dayton 1, Dennis 1, Happe 1, Turley 1, Widdowson 1, own goals 4.
FA Cup (1): Dayton 1.
Carabao Cup (0).
Leasing.com Trophy (4): Angol 1, Dennis 1, Gorman 1, Happe 1.

Brill D 19	Coulson J 26 + 2	Ekpiteta M 26 + 1	Happe D 32	Ling S 15	Maguire-Drew J 21 + 12	Clay C 30 + 5	Wright J 33 + 2	Brophy J 29 + 5	Angol L 20 + 6	Wilkinson C 23 + 3	Sargeant S 11 + 1	Alabi J — + 10	Dennis L 7 + 9	Harrold M 9 + 15	Widdowson J 14 + 2	Gorman D 7 + 6	Judd M 6 + 3	Marsh G 23 + 3	Dayton J 8 + 3	Turley J 8	Kyprianou H 3 + 3	Sotiriou R 7 + 3	Cisse O 9 + 1	Vigouroux L 6	Johnson D 4 + 2	McAnuff J — + 1	*Match No.*
1^{2}	2	3	4	5	6^{3}	7	8	9	10	11^{1}	12	13	14														1
1	3^{2}	2	4	5	9^{1}	6	7	8	10^{3}	11		14	12	13													2
1	3	2	4^{2}	5		6^{1}	7	9	11	10^{3}			13	14	8	12											3
1	3	2	4^{2}	5	14	7	6	9	10	11^{3}			12		8^{1}	13											4
1	4	3		2^{3}	9^{2}	6^{1}	7	5	10	11		13	8			14	12										5
1	2^{1}	3	4	5	12	7	6	8^{3}	11	10			9^{2}	13			14										6
1	3	2	4^{3}	5	12	7^{2}	6	9	11^{1}	10			14		8	13											7
1	4	3		2	9^{3}	12	6		10	13		14	11^{1}		5	7^{2}		8									8
1	4	3		2	9	13	6		10^{2}	12			11^{1}	14	5	7^{3}		8									9
1	4	3		2	8^{2}	12	7	10^{3}		11		14	9^{1}	13	5			6									10
1	3	2^{3}	4	5	14	7^{2}	9	13		11			10^{1}	12	8			6									11
1	3	12	4	2^{3}	13	8	9	6		10				11^{1}	5	7^{2}		14									12
1	3		4			6	7	9^{3}		11■		13		10^{2}	5	8^{1}	2	12	14								13
1	3	2	4			8	7	9				13	12	11^{1}	5	10^{3}		14	6^{2}								14
1	3	2	4		14	8	7	9				13	12	11^{2}	5	10^{3}			6^{1}								15
1	3	2	4		12	9	8	10					13	11^{1}	5	14		7^{2}	6^{3}								16
1	3	2^{1}	4		14	6	8	11		12^{3}				10	5	13		7	9^{2}								17
1	4	3	5^{1}	2	6	8	7	9	12			13	10^{2}	11													18
1	3		4	5^{2}	12	9	6	10	7			13		11		8^{1}				2							19
			4	2	7^{2}		8	12	10^{3}	11^{1}	1			13	5			9	14	3	6						20
		4	5		10^{1}	8	6	12	11	7	1						2	9		3							21
	14	4	5		7^{1}	8	6	10^{3}	11		1			12			2■	9^{2}		3	13						22
		4	5^{2}		7	8	6	10	11		1			12				2	9^{1}	3		13					23
		3	5		7^{2}	8	6	12	10		1			13			2	9		4		11^{1}					24
		4	5		8	6	7^{3}	12	11^{1}		1		14	13			2	9		3^{2}		10					25
	3		4		10	13	6	5	11	8	1			14			12	9^{1}		2^{2}	7^{3}						26
	3		4		8	13	7	5	11^{1}	10	1			14			2^{2}	9			6^{3}		12				27
	2^{2}	3	4		13	6	8	9		10	1			11^{3}				5	14■			12	7^{1}				28
		3	4		11^{2}	6	8	5	12	10	1			13				2			14	9^{1}	7^{3}				29
		3	4		11	6	8	5	12	10	1			13				2^{1}				9	7^{2}				30
		3	4		11^{3}	8^{1}	6	5	13	10								2			14	9^{2}	7	1	12		31
	12	3	4^{1}		11^{2}	8	6	5	14	10^{3}								2				9	7	1	13		32
	3		4		13	8	12	5	10	9								2	6^{2}				7	1	11^{1}		33
	3		4		13	8	14	5	10^{1}	11^{2}					12			2	6^{3}				7	1	9		34
	3		4		11	8	6	5		9^{1}								2				12	7	1	10		35
	3		4		9^{3}	8		5	14						13			2	6^{1}			11	7	1	10^{2}	12	36
																											37
																											38
																											39
																											40
																											41
																											42
																											43
																											44
																											45
																											46

FA Cup
First Round Maldon & Tiptree (h) 1-2

Carabao Cup
First Round Plymouth Arg (a) 0-2

Leasing.com Trophy
Group C (S) Southend U (h) 2-0
Group C (S) AFC Wimbledon (a) 0-3
Group C (S) Brighton & HA U21 (h) 1-1
(Leyton Orient won 4-2 on penalties)
Second Round (S) Bristol R (a) 1-1
(Bristol R won 4-2 on penalties)

LINCOLN CITY

FOUNDATION

The original Lincoln Football Club was established in the early 1860s and was one of the first provisional clubs to affiliate to the Football Association. In their early years, they regularly played matches against the famous Sheffield Football Club and later became known as Lincoln Lindum. The present organisation was formed at a public meeting held in the Monson Arms Hotel in June 1884 and won the Lincolnshire Cup in only their third season. They were founder members of the Midland League in 1889 and that competition's first champions.

LNER Stadium, Sincil Bank, Lincoln LN5 8LD.

Telephone: (01522) 880 011.

Ticket Office: (01522) 880 011.

Website: www.redimps.com

Email: admin@theredimps.com

Ground Capacity: 10,653.

Record Attendance: 23,196 v Derby Co, League Cup 4th rd, 15 November 1967.

Pitch Measurements: 100m × 65m (109.5yd × 71yd).

Chairman: Clive Nates.

Chief Executive Officer: Liam Scully.

Manager: Michael Appleton.

Assistant Manager: David Kerslake.

Colours: Red and white striped shirts with black trim, black shorts with red trim, red socks with black and white trim.

Year Formed: 1884.

Turned Professional: 1892.

Ltd Co.: 1895.

Club Nickname: 'The Red Imps'.

Grounds: 1883, John O'Gaunt's; 1894, Sincil Bank (renamed LNER Stadium 2019).

First Football League Game: 3 September 1892, Division 2, v Sheffield U (a) L 2–4 – William Gresham; Coulton, Neill; Shaw, Mettam, Moore; Smallman, Irving (1), Cameron (1), Kelly, James Gresham.

Record League Victory: 11–1 v Crewe Alex, Division 3 (N), 29 September 1951 – Jones; Green (1p), Varney; Wright, Emery, Grummett (1); Troops (1), Garvey, Graver (6), Whittle (1), Johnson (1).

Record Cup Victory: 8–1 v Bromley, FA Cup 2nd rd, 10 December 1938 – McPhail; Hartshorne, Corbett; Bean, Leach, Whyte (1); Hancock, Wilson (1), Ponting (3), Deacon (1), Clare (2).

Record Defeat: 3–11 v Manchester C, Division 2, 23 March 1895.

Most League Points (2 for a win): 74, Division 4, 1975–76.

Most League Points (3 for a win): 85, FL 2, 2018–19.

HONOURS

League Champions: Division 3 (N) – 1931–32, 1947–48, 1951–52; FL 2 – 2018–19; Division 4 – 1975–76; National League – 1987–88, 2016–17.
Runners-up: Division 3 (N) – 1927–28, 1930–31, 1936–37; Division 4 – 1980–81.

FA Cup: quarter-final – 2017.

League Cup: 4th rd – 1968.

League Trophy Winners: 2018.

FOOTBALL YEARBOOK FACT FILE

When Lincoln City moved from John O'Gaunt's to Sincil Bank they transferred the original stand to the new ground. A further stand was then built on the Sincil Bank side in 1897 with the architect being Kenny Bayne who had been the club's goalkeeper in their very first match against Sleaford in October 1884.

Most League Goals: 121, Division 3 (N), 1951–52.

Highest League Scorer in Season: Allan Hall, 41, Division 3 (N), 1931–32.

Most League Goals in Total Aggregate: Andy Graver, 143, 1950–55 and 1958–61.

Most League Goals in One Match: 6, Frank Keetley v Halifax T, Division 3 (N), 16 January 1932; 6, Andy Graver v Crewe Alex, Division 3 (N), 29 September 1951.

Most Capped Player: Gareth McAuley, 5 (80), Northern Ireland; Joe Morrell, 5, Wales.

Most League Appearances: Grant Brown, 407, 1989–2002.

Youngest League Player: Shane Nicholson, 16 years 172 days v Burnley, 22 November 1986.

Record Transfer Fee Received: £750,000 from Liverpool for Jack Hobbs, August 2005.

Record Transfer Fee Paid: £100,000 to Barnet for John Akinde, July 2018.

Football League Record: 1892 Founder member of Division 2. Remained in Division 2 until 1920 when they failed re-election but also missed seasons 1908–09 and 1911–12 when not re-elected. 1921–32 Division 3 (N); 1932–34 Division 2; 1934–48 Division 3 (N); 1948–49 Division 2; 1949–52 Division 3 (N); 1952–61 Division 2; 1961–62 Division 3; 1962–76 Division 4; 1976–79 Division 3; 1979–81 Division 4; 1981–86 Division 3; 1986–87 Division 4; 1987–88 GM Vauxhall Conference; 1988–92 Division 4; 1992–98 Division 3; 1998–99 Division 2; 1999–2004 Division 3; 2004–11 FL 2; 2011–17 Conference National League; 2017–19 FL 2; 2019– FL 1.

LATEST SEQUENCES

Longest Sequence of League Wins: 10, 1.9.1930 – 18.10.1930.

Longest Sequence of League Defeats: 12, 21.9.1896 – 9.1.1897.

Longest Sequence of League Draws: 5, 21.2.1981 – 7.3.1981.

Longest Sequence of Unbeaten League Matches: 19, 29.12.2018 – 13.4.2019.

Longest Sequence Without a League Win: 19, 22.8.1978 – 23.12.1978.

Successive Scoring Runs: 37 from 1.3.1930.

Successive Non-scoring Runs: 5 from 15.11.1913.

MANAGERS

Alf Martin 1896–97 *(Secretary/Manager)*
David Calderhead 1900–07
John Henry Strawson 1907–14 *(had been Secretary)*
George Fraser 1919–21
David Calderhead Jnr. 1921–24
Horace Henshall 1924–27
Harry Parkes 1927–36
Joe McClelland 1936–46
Bill Anderson 1946–65 *(General Manager to 1966)*
Roy Chapman 1965–66
Ron Gray 1966–70
Bert Loxley 1970–71
David Herd 1971–72
Graham Taylor 1972–77
George Kerr 1977–78
Willie Bell 1977–78
Colin Murphy 1978–85
John Pickering 1985
George Kerr 1985–87
Peter Daniel 1987
Colin Murphy 1987–90
Allan Clarke 1990
Steve Thompson 1990–93
Keith Alexander 1993–94
Sam Ellis 1994–95
Steve Wicks *(Head Coach)* 1995
John Beck 1995–98
Shane Westley 1998
John Reames 1998–2000
Phil Stant 2000–01
Alan Buckley 2001–02
Keith Alexander 2002–06
John Schofield 2006–07
Peter Jackson 2007–09
Chris Sutton 2009–10
Steve Tilson 2010–11
David Holdsworth 2011–13
Gary Simpson 2013–14
Chris Moyses 2014–16
Danny Cowley 2016–19
Michael Appleton September 2019–

TEN YEAR LEAGUE RECORD

		P	*W*	*D*	*L*	*F*	*A*	*Pts*	*Pos*
2010-11	FL 2	46	13	8	25	45	81	47	23
2011-12	Conf	46	13	10	23	56	66	49	17
2012-13	Conf	46	15	11	20	72	86	54	16
2013-14	Conf	46	17	14	15	60	59	65	14
2014-15	Conf	46	16	10	20	62	71	58	15
2015-16	NL	46	16	13	17	69	68	61	13
2016-17	NL	46	30	9	7	83	40	99	1
2017-18	FL 2	46	20	15	11	64	48	75	7
2018-19	FL 2	46	23	16	7	73	43	85	1
2019-20	FL 1	35	12	6	17	44	46	42	16§

§Decided on points-per-game (1.20)

DID YOU KNOW ?

After drawing 0-0 at home to Bury on 26 August 1953 Lincoln City played a further 236 games before their next goalless draw, which came at Leyton Orient on 21 February 1959. This remains an all-time Football League record.

LINCOLN CITY – SKY BET LEAGUE ONE 2019–20 LEAGUE RECORD

Match No.	Date	Venue	Opponents	Result	H/T Score	Lg Pos.	Goalscorers	Attendance
1	Aug 3	H	Accrington S	W 2-0	1-0	2	O'Connor 35, Akinde (pen) 81	8668
2	10	A	Rotherham U	W 2-0	1-0	2	MacDonald (og) 42, Anderson 48	10,706
3	17	H	Southend U	W 4-0	2-0	1	Shackell 31, Toffolo 40, Walker (pen) 48, Andrade 81	9016
4	20	A	Milton Keynes D	L 1-2	1-2	2	Walker 11	8166
5	24	A	Doncaster R	L 1-2	0-1	7	Grant 57	10,177
6	31	H	Fleetwood T	W 2-0	2-0	2	Walker 2 34, 35	8361
7	Sept 7	A	Wycombe W	L 1-3	0-2	5	Akinde 50	5562
8	14	H	Bristol R	L 0-1	0-0	7		8712
9	17	A	Rochdale	D 1-1	0-1	8	Walker 86	2659
10	21	H	Oxford U	L 0-6	0-2	10		8746
11	27	A	Blackpool	L 1-2	1-2	11	Payne 24	9203
12	Oct 5	H	Sunderland	W 2-0	1-0	11	Walker 2 17, 59	10,264
13	12	A	Peterborough U	L 0-2	0-0	12		9872
14	18	H	Shrewsbury T	D 0-0	0-0	11		8710
15	22	A	Portsmouth	L 0-1	0-1	15		17,266
16	Nov 2	A	AFC Wimbledon	D 1-1	1-0	17	Payne 31	4378
17	16	A	Gillingham	L 0-1	0-1	17		5567
18	Dec 7	A	Burton Alb	W 2-0	1-0	17	Anderson 2, Walker 90	3782
19	14	H	Tranmere R	W 1-0	0-0	16	Akinde 77	8369
20	21	A	Coventry C	L 0-1	0-1	16		6863
21	26	A	Oxford U	L 0-1	0-1	17		10,115
22	29	H	Ipswich T	W 5-3	2-1	17	Anderson 7, Walker 2 45, 72, Bostwick 79, Hesketh 90	10,012
23	Jan 1	H	Peterborough U	W 2-1	0-1	16	Walker 67, Grant 90	10,025
24	4	A	Sunderland	L 1-3	0-3	16	Walker 66	31,748
25	11	A	Shrewsbury T	D 1-1	0-1	16	Walker (pen) 48	6275
26	14	H	Bolton W	W 5-1	1-0	15	Anderson 7, Walker 61, Emmanuel (og) 85, Akinde 2 86, 90	8882
27	18	H	Blackpool	W 1-0	0-0	12	John-Jules 63	8929
28	25	A	Ipswich T	L 0-1	0-1	12		18,795
29	28	H	Portsmouth	L 0-2	0-1	13		8983
30	Feb 1	A	Southend U	L 1-2	0-0	14	Anderson 89	6605
31	7	H	Rotherham U	L 0-1	0-0	14		9876
32	11	H	Milton Keynes D	D 1-1	1-1	14	Bridcutt 22	7783
33	15	A	Accrington S	L 3-4	1-1	15	Scully 30, Shackell 76, Lewis 53	2279
34	22	H	Gillingham	D 0-0	0-0	15		8950
35	Mar 7	H	Burton Alb	W 3-2	2-2	14	Hopper 2 21, 38, Scully 62	8474
36	14	A	Tranmere R	Cancelled				
37	21	H	Coventry C	Cancelled				
38	28	H	AFC Wimbledon	Cancelled				
39	Apr 4	A	Bolton W	Cancelled				
40	10	H	Doncaster R	Cancelled				
41	13	A	Fleetwood T	Cancelled				
42	18	H	Wycombe W	Cancelled				
43	25	A	Bristol R	Cancelled				
44	May 3	H	Rochdale	Cancelled				

Final League Position: 16 (on points-per-game basis)

GOALSCORERS

League (44): Walker 14 (2 pens), Akinde 5 (1 pen), Anderson 5, Grant 2, Hopper 2, Payne 2, Scully 2, Shackell 2, Andrade 1, Bostwick 1, Bridcutt 1, Hesketh 1, John-Jules 1, Lewis 1, O'Connor 1, Toffolo 1, own goals 2.
FA Cup (1): Walker 1.
Carabao Cup (3): Anderson 2, Andrade 1.
Leasing.com Trophy (4): Akinde 3 (1 pen), Walker 1.

Vickers J 35	Eardley N 35	Bolger C 25 + 3	Bostwick M 16 + 2	Toffolo H 26	O'Connor M 14 + 3	Morrell J 29	Anderson H 24 + 6	Payne J 18 + 5	Grant J 29 + 3	Walker T 26 + 3	Akinde J 3 + 20	Andrade B 11 + 6	Chapman E 5 + 6	Shackell J 26	Connolly C 9 + 2	Hesketh J 14 + 6	Pett T 1 + 1	Melbourne M 6 + 2	Elbouzedi Z 1 + 4	Coventry C 5 + 2	John-Jules T 7	Lewis A — + 2	Edun T 6	Hopper T 5 + 3	Bridcutt L 5	Scully A 3 + 2	Sheehan A 1	*Match No.*
1	2	3	4	5	6^1	7	8^3	9	10	11^2	12	13	14															1
1	2	3	4	5	6^2	7	8	9	10^3	11^1	13	12	14															2
1	2	3	6^2	5	12	7	8^3	9	10	11^1	13	14		4														3
1	2		3	5	6^2	7	8	9	10	11^1	12	13		4														4
1	2		3	5	6^1	7	8^3	9	10	11^2	13	12	14	4														5
1	2		3	5	14	7	8	9	10^3	11^1	12	13		4	6^2													6
1	2		3	5	7^2		13	9^1	10	11	12	8^3	14	4	6													7
1	2	12	3^2	5	13	7	8	9		11^1	14	10		4	6^3													8
1	2	3		5		7	8^1	9		11	12	10		4	6													9
1	2	3		5		7	8^1	9^2	12	11	13	10		4	6													10
1	2	3		5		7	8^1	9	12	11		10		4	6													11
1	2	3		5	6^1	7		9	10	11		8^2		4	12	13												12
1	2	3		5	7^3			9^1	10^2	11	14	8	6	4		13	12											13
1	2	3■		5	6	7		9^2	10^1	11	12	8		4	13													14
1	2			5	7^1	8	12	9	13	10	11^2	6^3		4	3	14												15
1	2			5	6	7		9^2	10^1	11	13	8		4	3	12												16
1	2	12		5			14	8^2		11	13	10	7	4	3^3	9^1	6											17
1	2	3	12	5		7	8		10	13	11^1		6	4^2		9^3		14										18
1	2	4	3	5		7^3	8^2	13	10	12	11^1		6			9		14										19
1	2	4	3	5	6^2		8^1	13	10	11	12		7			9												20
1	2	4	3	5	7^1	6	8	13	10	11	12					9^2												21
1	2	4	3	5	6^1	7	8		10	11			12			9												22
1	2	4	3	5	6^1	7	8	12	10	11	13					9^2												23
1	2	12	3^2	5		7	6	9^1	8	11	13			4		10^3			14									24
1	2	3		5		8			9	10	13			4		6^2			12	7	11^1							25
1	2	3		5		7	8^2		10	11	12			4		9^1			13	6^3		14						26
1	2	3				8	6		9	10				4				5			11		7					27
1	2	3				7	6^3		9	11				4				5	14	13	10^2		8^1	12				28
1	2	3				7	6^2		9	12				4		13		5		8^1	10			11				29
1	2	3				7	12	14	9					4		13		5	6^3		10		8^2	11^1				30
1	2	3				7	8^1		10					4		9^2		5			11			13	6	12		31
1	2	3				7^2	8^3		10					4		9^1				13	11		5	12	6	14		32
1	2	3	14				6^3		8^1				13	4		10						12	5	11^2	7	9		33
1	2	3	4				12		10							9^1				7			5■	11	6	8		34
1	2		3			9	12		10^1									5		7				11	6	8	4	35
																												36
																												37
																												38
																												39
																												40
																												41
																												42
																												43
																												44

FA Cup

First Round	Ipswich T	(a)	1-1
Replay	Ipswich T	(h)	0-1

Carabao Cup

First Round	Huddersfield T	(a)	1-0
Second Round	Everton	(h)	2-4

Leasing.com Trophy

Group H (N)	Doncaster R	(a)	1-3
Group H (N)	Manchester U U21	(h)	0-1
Group H (N)	Rotherham U	(h)	3-0

LIVERPOOL

FOUNDATION

But for a dispute between Everton FC and their landlord at Anfield in 1892, there may never have been a Liverpool club. This dispute persuaded the majority of Evertonians to quit Anfield for Goodison Park, leaving the landlord, Mr John Houlding, to form a new club. He originally tried to retain the name 'Everton' but when this failed, he founded Liverpool Association FC on 15 March 1892.

Anfield Stadium, Anfield Road, Anfield, Liverpool L4 0TH.

Telephone: (0151) 263 2361.

Ticket Office: (0843) 170 5555.

Website: www.liverpoolfc.com

Email: customerservices@liverpoolfc.com

Ground Capacity: 53,394.

Record Attendance: 61,905 v Wolverhampton W, FA Cup 4th rd, 2 February 1952.

Pitch Measurements: 101m × 68m (110.5yd × 74.5yd).

Chairman: Tom Werner.

Chief Executive: Peter Moore.

Manager: Jürgen Klopp.

Assistant Managers: Peter Krawietz, Pepijn Lijnders.

Colours: Red shirts with white and teal trim, red shorts with white trim, red socks with white and teal trim.

Year Formed: 1892.

Turned Professional: 1892.

Club Nicknames: 'The Reds', 'Pool'.

Ground: 1892, Anfield.

First Football League Game: 2 September 1893, Division 2, v Middlesbrough Ironopolis (a) W 2–0 – McOwen; Hannah, McLean; Henderson, McQue (1), McBride; Gordon, McVean (1), Matt McQueen, Stott, Hugh McQueen.

HONOURS

League Champions: Premier League – 2019–20; Division 1 – 1900–01, 1905–06, 1921–22, 1922–23, 1946–47, 1963–64, 1965–66, 1972–73, 1975–76, 1976–77, 1978–79, 1979–80, 1981–82, 1982–83, 1983–84, 1985–86, 1987–88, 1989–90; Division 2 – 1893–94, 1895–96, 1904–05, 1961–62.
Runners-up: Premier League – 2001–02, 2008–09, 2013–14, 2018–19; Division 1 – 1898–99, 1909–10, 1968–69, 1973–74, 1974–75, 1977–78, 1984–85, 1986–87, 1988–89, 1990–91.

FA Cup Winners: 1965, 1974, 1986, 1989, 1992, 2001, 2006.
Runners-up: 1914, 1950, 1971, 1977, 1988, 1996, 2012.

League Cup Winners: 1981, 1982, 1983, 1984, 1995, 2001, 2003, 2012.
Runners-up: 1978, 1987, 2005, 2016.

League Super Cup Winners: 1986.

European Competitions

European Cup: 1964–65 *(sf)*, 1966–67, 1973–74, 1976–77 *(winners)*, 1977–78 *(winners)*, 1978–79, 1979–80, 1980–81 *(winners)*, 1981–82 *(qf)*, 1982–83 *(qf)*, 1983–84 *(winners)*, 1984–85 *(runners-up)*.
Champions League: 2001–02 *(qf)*, 2002–03, 2004–05 *(winners)*, 2005–06, 2006–07 *(runners-up)*, 2007–08 *(sf)*, 2008–09 *(qf)*, 2009–10, 2014–15, 2017–18 *(runners-up)*, 2018–19 *(winners)*, 2019–20.
Fairs Cup: 1967–68, 1968–69, 1969–70, 1970–71 *(sf)*.
UEFA Cup: 1972–73 *(winners)*, 1975–76 *(winners)*, 1991–92 *(qf)*, 1995–96, 1997–98, 1998–99, 2000–01 *(winners)*, 2002–03 *(qf)*, 2003–04.
Europa League: 2009–10 *(sf)*, 2010–11, 2012–13, 2014–15, 2015–16 *(runners-up)*.
European Cup-Winners' Cup: 1965–66 *(runners-up)*, 1971–72, 1974–75, 1992–93, 1996–97 *(sf)*.
Super Cup: 1977 *(winners)*, 1978, 1984, 2001 *(winners)*, 2005 *(winners)*, 2019 *(winners)*.
World Club Championship: 1981, 1984.
FIFA Club World Cup: 2005, 2019 *(winners)*.

FOOTBALL YEARBOOK FACT FILE

Liverpool created a club record of 85 unbeaten matches at home between 21 January 1978 and 31 January 1981. The sequence, which included 63 Football League games, was finally broken by Leicester City. Despite their win at Anfield, the Foxes were relegated from the top flight at the end of the season.

Record League Victory: 10–1 v Rotherham T, Division 2, 18 February 1896 – Storer; Goldie, Wilkie; McCartney, McQue, Holmes; McVean (3), Ross (2), Allan (4), Becton (1), Bradshaw.

Record Cup Victory: 11–0 v Stromsgodset Drammen, ECWC 1st rd 1st leg, 17 September 1974 – Clemence; Smith (1), Lindsay (1p), Thompson (2), Cormack (1), Hughes (1), Boersma (2), Hall, Heighway (1), Kennedy (1), Callaghan (1).

Record Defeat: 1–9 v Birmingham C, Division 2, 11 December 1954.

Most League Points (2 for a win): 68, Division 1, 1978–79.

Most League Points (3 for a win): 99, Premier League, 2019–20.

Most League Goals: 106, Division 2, 1895–96.

Highest League Scorer in Season: Roger Hunt, 41, Division 2, 1961–62.

Most League Goals in Total Aggregate: Roger Hunt, 245, 1959–69.

Most League Goals in One Match: 5, Andy McGuigan v Stoke C, Division 1, 4 January 1902; 5, John Evans v Bristol R, Division 2, 15 September 1954; 5, Ian Rush v Luton T, Division 1, 29 October 1983.

Most Capped Player: Steven Gerrard, 114, England.

Most League Appearances: Ian Callaghan, 640, 1960–78.

Youngest League Player: Jack Robinson, 16 years 250 days v Hull C, 9 May 2010.

Record Transfer Fee Received: £142,000,000 from Barcelona for Philippe Coutinho, January 2018.

Record Transfer Fee Paid: £75,000,000 to Southampton for Virgil van Dijk, January 2018.

Football League Record: 1893 Elected to Division 2; 1894–95 Division 1; 1895–96 Division 2; 1896–1904 Division 1; 1904–05 Division 2; 1905–54 Division 1; 1954–62 Division 2; 1962–92 Division 1; 1992– Premier League.

MANAGERS

W. E. Barclay 1892–96
Tom Watson 1896–1915
David Ashworth 1920–23
Matt McQueen 1923–28
George Patterson 1928–36
(continued as Secretary)
George Kay 1936–51
Don Welsh 1951–56
Phil Taylor 1956–59
Bill Shankly 1959–74
Bob Paisley 1974–83
Joe Fagan 1983–85
Kenny Dalglish 1985–91
Graeme Souness 1991–94
Roy Evans 1994–98
(then Joint Manager)
Gerard Houllier 1998–2004
Rafael Benitez 2004–10
Roy Hodgson 2010–11
Kenny Dalglish 2011–12
Brendan Rodgers 2012–15
Jürgen Klopp October 2015–

LATEST SEQUENCES

Longest Sequence of League Wins: 18, 27.10.2019 – 24.2.2020.

Longest Sequence of League Defeats: 9, 29.4.1899 – 14.10.1899.

Longest Sequence of League Draws: 6, 19.2.1975 – 19.3.1975.

Longest Sequence of Unbeaten League Matches: 44, 12.1.2019 – 24.2.2020.

Longest Sequence Without a League Win: 14, 12.12.1953 – 20.3.1954.

Successive Scoring Runs: 36 from 10.3.2019.

Successive Non-scoring Runs: 5 from 21.4.2000.

TEN YEAR LEAGUE RECORD

		P	W	D	L	F	A	Pts	Pos
2010-11	PR Lge	38	17	7	14	59	44	58	6
2011-12	PR Lge	38	14	10	14	47	40	52	8
2012-13	PR Lge	38	16	13	9	71	43	61	7
2013-14	PR Lge	38	26	6	6	101	50	84	2
2014-15	PR Lge	38	18	8	12	52	48	62	6
2015-16	PR Lge	38	16	12	10	63	50	60	8
2016-17	PR Lge	38	22	10	6	78	42	76	4
2017-18	PR Lge	38	21	12	5	84	38	75	4
2018-19	PR Lge	38	30	7	1	89	22	97	2
2019-20	PR Lge	38	32	3	3	85	33	99	1

DID YOU KNOW ?

Liverpool FC appeared in a BBC *Panorama* programme about the culture of Liverpool shown on BBC2 on 22 April 1964. The feature included film of the fans singing and thus introduced the now legendary Kop Choir to a national audience.

LIVERPOOL – PREMIER LEAGUE 2019–20 LEAGUE RECORD

Match No.	*Date*	*Venue*	*Opponents*	*Result*	*H/T Score*	*Lg Pos.*	*Goalscorers*	*Attendance*
1	Aug 9	H	Norwich C	W 4-1	4-0	1	Hanley (og) [7], Salah [19], van Dijk [28], Origi [42]	53,333
2	17	A	Southampton	W 2-1	1-0	1	Mane [45], Firmino [71]	31,712
3	24	H	Arsenal	W 3-1	1-0	1	Matip [41], Salah 2 (1 pen) [49 (p), 58]	53,298
4	31	A	Burnley	W 3-0	2-0	1	Wood (og) [33], Mane [37], Firmino [80]	21,762
5	Sept 14	H	Newcastle U	W 3-1	2-1	1	Mane 2 [28, 40], Salah [72]	51,430
6	22	A	Chelsea	W 2-1	2-0	1	Alexander-Arnold [14], Firmino [30]	40,638
7	28	A	Sheffield U	W 1-0	0-0	1	Wijnaldum [70]	31,774
8	Oct 5	H	Leicester C	W 2-1	1-0	1	Mane [40], Milner (pen) [90]	53,322
9	20	A	Manchester U	D 1-1	0-1	1	Lallana [85]	73,737
10	27	H	Tottenham H	W 2-1	0-1	1	Henderson [52], Salah (pen) [75]	53,222
11	Nov 2	A	Aston Villa	W 2-1	0-1	1	Robertson [87], Mane [90]	41,878
12	10	H	Manchester C	W 3-1	2-0	1	Fabinho [6], Salah [13], Mane [51]	53,324
13	23	A	Crystal Palace	W 2-1	0-0	1	Mane [49], Firmino [85]	25,486
14	30	H	Brighton & HA	W 2-1	2-0	1	van Dijk 2 [18, 24]	53,319
15	Dec 4	H	Everton	W 5-2	4-2	1	Origi 2 [6, 31], Shaqiri [17], Mane [45], Wijnaldum [90]	53,094
16	7	A	Bournemouth	W 3-0	2-0	1	Oxlade-Chamberlain [35], Keita [44], Salah [54]	10,832
17	14	H	Watford	W 2-0	1-0	1	Salah 2 [38, 90]	53,311
18	26	A	Leicester C	W 4-0	1-0	1	Firmino 2 [31, 74], Milner (pen) [71], Alexander-Arnold [78]	32,211
19	29	H	Wolverhampton W	W 1-0	1-0	1	Mane [42]	53,326
20	Jan 2	H	Sheffield U	W 2-0	1-0	1	Salah [4], Mane [64]	53,321
21	11	A	Tottenham H	W 1-0	1-0	1	Firmino [37]	61,023
22	19	H	Manchester U	W 2-0	1-0	1	van Dijk [14], Salah [90]	52,916
23	23	A	Wolverhampton W	W 2-1	1-0	1	Henderson [8], Firmino [84]	31,746
24	29	A	West Ham U	W 2-0	1-0	1	Salah (pen) [35], Oxlade-Chamberlain [52]	59,959
25	Feb 1	H	Southampton	W 4-0	0-0	1	Oxlade-Chamberlain [47], Henderson [60], Salah 2 [71, 90]	53,291
26	15	A	Norwich C	W 1-0	0-0	1	Mane [78]	27,110
27	24	H	West Ham U	W 3-2	1-1	1	Wijnaldum [9], Salah [68], Mane [81]	53,313
28	29	A	Watford	L 0-3	0-0	1		21,634
29	Mar 7	H	Bournemouth	W 2-1	2-1	1	Salah [24], Mane [33]	53,323
30	June 21	A	Everton	D 0-0	0-0	1		0
31	24	H	Crystal Palace	W 4-0	2-0	1	Alexander-Arnold [23], Salah [44], Fabinho [55], Mane [69]	0
32	July 2	A	Manchester C	L 0-4	0-3	1		0
33	5	H	Aston Villa	W 2-0	0-0	1	Mane [71], Jones [89]	0
34	8	A	Brighton & HA	W 3-1	2-1	1	Salah 2 [6, 76], Henderson [8]	0
35	11	H	Burnley	D 1-1	1-0	1	Robertson [34]	0
36	15	A	Arsenal	L 1-2	1-2	1	Mane [20]	0
37	22	H	Chelsea	W 5-3	3-1	1	Keita [23], Alexander-Arnold [38], Wijnaldum [43], Firmino [54], Oxlade-Chamberlain [84]	0
38	26	A	Newcastle U	W 3-1	1-1	1	van Dijk [38], Origi [59], Mane [89]	0

Final League Position: 1

GOALSCORERS

League (85): Salah 19 (3 pens), Mane 18, Firmino 9, van Dijk 5, Alexander-Arnold 4, Henderson 4, Origi 4, Oxlade-Chamberlain 4, Wijnaldum 4, Fabinho 2, Keita 2, Milner 2 (2 pens), Robertson 2, Jones 1, Lallana 1, Matip 1, Shaqiri 1, own goals 2.
FA Cup (4): Jones 2, own goals 2.
Carabao Cup (7): Milner 2 (1 pen), Origi 2, Hoever 1, Oxlade-Chamberlain 1, own goal 1.
UEFA Champions League (17): Salah 4, Oxlade-Chamberlain 3, Mane 2, Minamino 2, Wijnaldum 2, Firmino 1, Keita 1, Lovren 1, Robertson 1.
FIFA World Club Cup (3): Firmino 2, Keita 1.
European Super Cup (2): Mane 2.
Leasing.com Trophy (5): Williams 2, Dixon-Bonner 1, Elliott 1, Stewart 1.

Alisson R 29	Alexander-Arnold T 35 + 3	Gomez J 22 + 6	van Dijk V 38	Robertson A 34 + 2	Henderson J 26 + 4	Fabinho H 22 + 6	Wijnaldum G 35 + 2	Salah M 33 + 1	Firmino R 34 + 4	Origi D 7 + 21	Adrian 9 + 2	Mane S 31 + 4	Milner J 9 + 13	Matip J 8 + 1	Oxlade-Chamberlain A 17 + 13	Lallana A 3 + 12	Shaqiri X 2 + 5	Lovren D 9 + 1	Keita N 9 + 9	Jones C 1 + 5	Elliott H — + 2	Minamino T 2 + 8	Williams N 3 + 3	Match No.
1^{1}	2	3	4	5	6	7	8	9	10^{3}	11^{2}	12	13	14											1
	2		4	5	14	12	7	9^{2}	10	13	1	11	8^{1}	3	6^{3}									2
	2		4	5	6	7	8^{1}	9	10^{3}		1	11^{2}	12	3	13	14								3
	2		4	5	6^{1}	7	8	9	10^{2}	13	1	11^{3}		3	12		14							4
	2		4	5		7	8^{3}	9	12	11^{1}	1	10	13	3	6^{2}		14							5
	2	14	4	5	6^{2}	7	8	9^{3}	10		1	11^{1}	12	3		13								6
	2		4	5	6^{1}	7	8	9	10^{2}	12	1	11^{3}	13	3	14									7
	2		4	5	12	7	6^{2}	10^{3}	11^{1}	13	1	9	8			14		3						8
1	2		4	5	6^{2}	7	8^{3}		10	11^{1}		9		3	12	13			14					9
1	2	13	4	5	6	7	8^{1}	9^{2}	10^{3}	14		11	12					3						10
1	2		4	5	6		8^{2}	9^{1}	10	12		11			13	7^{3}		3	14					11
1	2	14	4	5	6^{1}	7	8	9^{3}	10^{2}			11	12		13			3						12
1	2	14	4	5	6^{2}	7	8		10^{3}	12		9	13		11^{1}			3						13
1■	2		4	5	7		8	9^{1}	10^{2}	13	14	11			6^{3}	12		3						14
	2^{3}	14	4	5	12		6		13	11^{2}	1	10	7			9^{1}	8	3						15
1	12	2	4	5^{2}	7			9	10				8		11^{3}		14	3^{1}	6	13				16
1	2	3	4	12	6		7^{1}	11	9^{3}	14		10	5		13		8^{2}							17
1	2	3	4	5	7^{3}		8	9^{2}	10	12		11	13			14			6^{1}					18
1	2	3	4	5	6		7^{2}	11	9^{3}	13		10	14			8^{1}			12					19
1	2	3	4	5^{2}	7		8	9^{3}	10	12		11^{1}	6			13					14			20
1	2	3	4	5	7		8	9^{3}	10	13		11^{2}			6^{1}	12	14							21
1	2	3	4	5	7	14	8	9	10^{2}	13		11^{3}			6^{1}	12								22
1	2	3	4	5	7	13	8	9^{3}	10	14		11^{1}			6^{2}							12		23
1	2^{2}	3	4	5	7	12	8	9	10	11^{1}					6^{3}				13	14				24
1	2	3	4	5	6^{3}	7	8^{2}	9	10						11^{1}	14			12			13		25
1	2	3	4	5	7	13	8^{2}	9	10			12	14		11^{1}				6^{3}					26
1	2	3	4	5		7	8	9	10			11^{2}		13	12				6^{1}					27
1	2		4	5		7	8^{1}	9	10^{3}	13		11			6^{2}	12		3				14		28
	2	3	4			7	8	9	10^{2}	13	1	11	5		6^{1}	12								29
1	2	12	4		6	7	14		10^{4}	15		11	5^{1}	3^{5}	13			16	8^{3}			9^{2}		30
1	2^{2}	3	4	5^{5}	6^{1}	7	8	9	10^{3}			11^{4}			12				16		15	13	14	31
1	2^{4}	3^{1}	4	5	6	7	8^{2}	9	10^{3}	14		11^{5}			12				13			16	15	32
1	2	3	4	5^{5}	12	7^{1}	13	9	14	10^{2}		11			6^{3}				8^{4}	15			16	33
1	2	3	4	12	7^{4}	14	8	9	10^{5}			13	15		11^{2}				6^{3}			16	5^{1}	34
1	13	3	4	5		7	6^{3}	9	10			11			14				12	8^{1}			2^{2}	35
1	2	3	4	5		7	8^{4}	9^{3}	10^{2}	14		11			6^{1}		15		12			13		36
1	2	3	4	5		7	8^{2}	9^{3}	10^{5}	16		11^{4}	13		14				6^{1}	12		15		37
1	15	3	4	5			7	12	14	10^{3}		13	8		9^{1}				6^{5}	16		11^{2}	2^{4}	38

FA Cup

Third Round	Everton	(h)	1-0
Fourth Round	Shrewsbury T	(a)	2-2
Replay	Shrewsbury T	(h)	1-0
Fifth Round	Chelsea	(a)	0-2

Carabao Cup

Third Round	Milton Keynes D	(a)	2-0
Fourth Round	Arsenal	(h)	5-5
(Liverpool won 5-4 on penalties)			
Quarter-Final	Aston Villa	(a)	0-5

Leasing.com Trophy (Liverpool U21)

Group B (N)	Oldham Ath	(a)	2-3
Group B (N)	Fleetwood T	(a)	1-1
(Fleetwood T won 4-3 on penalties)			
Group B (N)	Accrington S	(a)	2-5

FIFA Club World Cup

Semi-Final	Monterrey	(Doha)	2-1
Final	Flamengo	(Doha)	1-0

aet.

European Super Cup

Final	Chelsea	(Istanbul)	2-2

aet; Liverpool won 5-4 on penalties.

UEFA Champions League

Group E	Napoli	(a)	0-2
Group E	Red Bull Salzburg	(h)	4-3
Group E	Genk	(a)	4-1
Group E	Genk	(h)	2-1
Group E	Napoli	(h)	1-1
Group E	Red Bull Salzburg	(a)	2-0
Round of 16	Atletico Madrid	(a)	0-1
Round of 16	Atletico Madrid	(h)	2-3

LUTON TOWN

FOUNDATION

Formed by an amalgamation of two leading local clubs, Wanderers and Excelsior a works team, at a meeting in Luton Town Hall in April 1885. The Wanderers had three months earlier changed their name to Luton Town Wanderers and did not take too kindly to the formation of another Town club but were talked around at this meeting. Wanderers had already appeared in the FA Cup and the new club entered in its inaugural season.

Kenilworth Road Stadium, 1 Maple Road, Luton, Bedfordshire LU4 8AW.

Telephone: (01582) 411 622.

Ticket Office: (01582) 416 976.

Website: www.lutontown.co.uk

Email: info@lutontown.co.uk

Ground Capacity: 10,265.

Record Attendance: 30,069 v Blackpool, FA Cup 6th rd replay, 4 March 1959.

Pitch Measurements: 101m × 66m (110.5yd × 72yd).

Chairman: David Wilkinson.

Chief Executive: Gary Sweet.

Manager: Nathan Jones.

Chief Recruitment Officer: Mick Harford.

HONOURS

League Champions: Division 2 – 1981–82; FL 1 – 2004–05, 2018–19; Division 3S – 1936–37; Division 4 – 1967–68; Conference – 2013–14.
Runners-up: FL 2 – 2017–18; Division 2 – 1954–55, 1973–74; Division 3 – 1969–70; Division 3S – 1935–36; Third Division – 2001–02.

FA Cup: *Runners-up:* 1959.

League Cup Winners: 1988.
Runners-up: 1989.

League Trophy Winners: 2009.

Full Members' Cup: *Runners-up:* 1988.

Colours: Orange shirts with navy blue trim, navy blue shorts, orange socks with navy blue trim.

Year Formed: 1885.

Turned Professional: 1890.

Ltd Co.: 1897.

Club Nickname: 'The Hatters'.

Grounds: 1885, Excelsior, Dallow Lane; 1897, Dunstable Road; 1905, Kenilworth Road.

First Football League Game: 4 September 1897, Division 2, v Leicester Fosse (a) D 1–1 – Williams; McCartney, McEwen; Davies, Stewart, Docherty; Gallacher, Coupar, Birch, McInnes, Ekins (1).

Record League Victory: 12–0 v Bristol R, Division 3 (S), 13 April 1936 – Dolman; Mackey, Smith; Finlayson, Nelson, Godfrey; Rich, Martin (1), Payne (10), Roberts (1), Stephenson.

Record Cup Victory: 9–0 v Clapton, FA Cup 1st rd (replay after abandoned game), 30 November 1927 – Abbott; Kingham, Graham; Black, Rennie, Fraser; Pointon, Yardley (4), Reid (2), Woods (1), Dennis (2).

Record Defeat: 0–9 v Small Heath, Division 2, 12 November 1898.

Most League Points (2 for a win): 66, Division 4, 1967–68.

FOOTBALL YEARBOOK FACT FILE

Luton Town got off to a great start in the 1939–40 season, winning both their opening matches 3-0, against Sheffield Wednesday and Bradford Park Avenue, then drawing 1-1 at Fulham. After three games they were at the top of the table for the first time in the club's history only for the campaign to be abandoned when the Second World War broke out.

Most League Points (3 for a win): 98, FL 1 2004–05.

Most League Goals: 103, Division 3 (S), 1936–37.

Highest League Scorer in Season: Joe Payne, 55, Division 3 (S), 1936–37.

Most League Goals in Total Aggregate: Gordon Turner, 243, 1949–64.

Most League Goals in One Match: 10, Joe Payne v Bristol R, Division 3 (S), 13 April 1936.

Most Capped Player: Mal Donaghy, 58 (91), Northern Ireland.

Most League Appearances: Bob Morton, 495, 1948–64.

Youngest League Player: Mike O'Hara, 16 years 32 days v Stoke C, 1 October 1960.

Record Transfer Fee Received: £6,000,000 from Leicester C for James Justin, June 2019.

Record Transfer Fee Paid: £1,340,000 to HNK Rijeka for Simon Sluga, July 2019.

Football League Record: 1897 Elected to Division 2; 1900 Failed re-election; 1920 Division 3; 1921–37 Division 3 (S); 1937–55 Division 2; 1955–60 Division 1; 1960–63 Division 2; 1963–65 Division 3; 1965–68 Division 4; 1968–70 Division 3; 1970–74 Division 2; 1974–75 Division 1; 1975–82 Division 2; 1982–96 Division 1; 1996–2001 Division 2; 2001–02 Division 3; 2002–04 Division 2; 2004–05 FL 1; 2005–07 FL C; 2007–08 FL 1; 2008–09 FL 2; 2009–14 Conference Premier; 2014–18 FL 2; 2018–19 FL 1; 2019– FL C.

LATEST SEQUENCES

Longest Sequence of League Wins: 12, 19.2.2002 – 6.4.2002.

Longest Sequence of League Defeats: 8, 11.11.1899 – 6.1.1900.

Longest Sequence of League Draws: 5, 28.8.1971 – 18.9.1971.

Longest Sequence of Unbeaten League Matches: 28, 20.10.2018 – 6.4.2019.

Longest Sequence Without a League Win: 16, 9.9.1964 – 6.11.1964.

Successive Scoring Runs: 25 from 24.10.1931.

Successive Non-scoring Runs: 5 from 10.4.1973.

MANAGERS

Charlie Green 1901–28 *(Secretary-Manager)*
George Thomson 1925
John McCartney 1927–29
George Kay 1929–31
Harold Wightman 1931–35
Ted Liddell 1936–38
Neil McBain 1938–39
George Martin 1939–47
Dally Duncan 1947–58
Syd Owen 1959–60
Sam Bartram 1960–62
Bill Harvey 1962–64
George Martin 1965–66
Allan Brown 1966–68
Alec Stock 1968–72
Harry Haslam 1972–78
David Pleat 1978–86
John Moore 1986–87
Ray Harford 1987–89
Jim Ryan 1990–91
David Pleat 1991–95
Terry Westley 1995
Lennie Lawrence 1995–2000
Ricky Hill 2000
Lil Fuccillo 2000
Joe Kinnear 2001–03
Mike Newell 2003–07
Kevin Blackwell 2007–08
Mick Harford 2008–09
Richard Money 2009–11
Gary Brabin 2011–12
Paul Buckle 2012–13
John Still 2013–15
Nathan Jones 2016–19
Mick Harford 2019 *(caretaker)*
Graeme Jones 2019–20
Nathan Jones May 2020–

TEN YEAR LEAGUE RECORD

		P	W	D	L	F	A	Pts	Pos
2010-11	Conf P	46	23	15	8	85	37	84	3
2011-12	Conf P	46	22	15	9	78	42	81	5
2012-13	Conf P	46	18	13	15	70	62	67	7
2013-14	Conf P	46	30	11	5	102	35	101	1
2014-15	FL 2	46	19	11	16	54	44	68	8
2015-16	FL 2	46	19	9	18	63	61	66	11
2016-17	FL 2	46	20	17	9	70	43	77	4
2017-18	FL 2	46	25	13	8	94	46	88	2
2018-19	FL 1	46	27	13	6	90	42	94	1
2019-20	FL C	46	14	9	23	54	82	51	19

DID YOU KNOW ?

In January 1956 Luton Town made a mid-season visit to Spain where they played a Catalonian Select XI at the Camp de Les Corts, then home of FC Barcelona. The Hatters went down to a 3-1 defeat and reports state they were jeered by the home fans for what was perceived as rough play.

LUTON TOWN – SKY BET CHAMPIONSHIP 2019–20 LEAGUE RECORD

Match No.	Date	Venue	Opponents	Result		H/T Score	Lg Pos.	Goalscorers	Attendance
1	Aug 2	H	Middlesbrough	D	3-3	2-2	1	Bradley 17, Cranie 24, Collins 85	10,053
2	10	A	Cardiff C	L	1-2	0-0	17	Pearson 86	24,724
3	17	H	WBA	L	1-2	1-0	20	Cornick 15	10,059
4	20	A	Sheffield W	L	0-1	0-0	23		23,353
5	24	A	Barnsley	W	3-1	3-0	18	Butterfield 2, Collins 4, Cornick 31	13,250
6	31	H	Huddersfield T	W	2-1	0-0	15	Collins (pen) 57, Shinnie 66	10,062
7	Sept 14	A	QPR	L	2-3	1-3	16	Cornick 36, Collins 48	16,186
8	21	H	Hull C	L	0-3	0-0	21		10,066
9	28	A	Blackburn R	W	2-1	1-1	16	Collins 17, Pearson 57	15,319
10	Oct 2	H	Millwall	D	1-1	0-0	17	McManaman 86	10,049
11	5	A	Derby Co	L	0-2	0-1	18		27,944
12	19	H	Bristol C	W	3-0	0-0	16	Ruddock 56, Cornick 62, Williams (og) 90	10,064
13	23	A	Fulham	L	2-3	0-1	18	Potts 60, LuaLua 90	18,082
14	26	A	Birmingham C	L	1-2	0-1	18	Cornick 67	21,799
15	Nov 2	H	Nottingham F	L	1-2	0-1	21	McManaman 87	10,053
16	9	A	Reading	L	0-3	0-2	21		15,251
17	23	H	Leeds U	L	1-2	0-0	21	Collins 54	10,068
18	26	H	Charlton Ath	W	2-1	1-1	20	Ruddock 19, Brown 53	10,004
19	30	A	Brentford	L	0-7	0-5	21		11,287
20	Dec 7	H	Wigan Ath	W	2-1	0-1	20	McManaman 87, Moncur 90	10,011
21	10	A	Stoke C	L	0-3	0-2	21		20,216
22	14	A	Preston NE	L	1-2	1-1	21	Collins (pen) 43	12,083
23	21	H	Swansea C	L	0-1	0-0	21		10,062
24	26	H	Fulham	D	3-3	2-1	22	LuaLua 5, Collins 28, Cornick 84	10,068
25	29	A	Bristol C	L	0-3	0-2	23		22,216
26	Jan 1	A	Millwall	L	1-3	1-0	24	Bradley 41	12,134
27	11	H	Birmingham C	L	1-2	0-1	24	Collins (pen) 62	10,062
28	19	A	Nottingham F	L	1-3	1-1	24	Cornick 23	27,081
29	28	H	Derby Co	W	3-2	0-0	24	Ruddock 67, Daniels 73, Bogle (og) 86	10,057
30	Feb 1	A	WBA	L	0-2	0-1	24		25,141
31	8	H	Cardiff C	L	0-1	0-0	24		10,041
32	12	H	Sheffield W	W	1-0	1-0	23	Collins 23	10,001
33	15	A	Middlesbrough	W	1-0	1-0	23	Tunnicliffe 17	19,734
34	22	A	Charlton Ath	L	1-3	1-1	24	Cornick 36	18,969
35	25	H	Brentford	W	2-1	2-0	23	Baptiste (og) 9, Cranie 45	10,008
36	29	H	Stoke C	D	1-1	0-1	24	Collins (pen) 90	10,070
37	Mar 7	A	Wigan Ath	D	0-0	0-0	23		10,292
38	June 20	H	Preston NE	D	1-1	0-0	24	McManaman 87	0
39	27	A	Swansea C	W	1-0	0-0	23	Collins 72	0
40	30	A	Leeds U	D	1-1	0-0	24	Cornick 50	0
41	July 4	H	Reading	L	0-5	0-3	24		0
42	7	H	Barnsley	D	1-1	1-0	24	Berry 13	0
43	10	A	Huddersfield T	W	2-0	0-0	23	Bradley 49, Lee 71	0
44	14	H	QPR	D	1-1	1-0	23	Collins (pen) 20	0
45	18	A	Hull C	W	1-0	0-0	22	LuaLua 85	0
46	22	H	Blackburn R	W	3-2	2-1	20	Carter (og) 28, Johnson (og) 35, Collins (pen) 60	0

Final League Position: 19

GOALSCORERS

League (54): Collins 14 (6 pens), Cornick 9, McManaman 4, Bradley 3, LuaLua 3, Ruddock 3, Cranie 2, Pearson 2, Berry 1, Brown 1, Butterfield 1, Daniels 1, Lee 1, Moncur 1, Potts 1, Shinnie 1, Tunnicliffe 1, own goals 5.
FA Cup (0).
Carabao Cup (6): Jervis 1, Jones 1, Lee 1 (1 pen), Sheehan 1, Shinnie 1, own goal 1.

Sluga S 33	Cranie M 19 + 5	Pearson M 41 + 1	Bradley S 39 + 1	Potts D 31 + 2	Ruddock P 40 + 4	Shinnie A 16 + 5	Tunnicliffe R 37 + 3	Lee E 8 + 3	McManaman C 10 + 13	Collins J 44 + 2	Butterfield J 11 + 4	Cornick H 37 + 8	Moncur G 1 + 16	Bree J 34 + 5	Berry L 15 + 6	LuaLua K 15 + 14	Brown I 17 + 8	Bolton L 10 + 14	Galloway B — + 3	Jones L 1 + 3	Shea J 13	Sheehan A 2 + 2	Rea G 13 + 2	Daniels D 2 + 1	Carter-Vickers C 15 + 1	Hylton D 2 + 9	Kioso P — + 1	Match No.
1	2	3	4	5	6	7²	8	9¹	10³	11	12	13	14															1
1	2²	3	4	5	6		7		10	11	8³	12	9¹	13	14													2
1	2	3	4	5	6³	14	7		9¹	10	8	11²				12	13											3
1	2¹	3	4		14	7	8			9	6³	10		5		11²	13	12										4
1		3	4		12	7	8	13		9	6	10²		5³		11¹		2	14									5
1		3	4		13	7	6			9	8¹	10²		5		11³	12	2		14								6
1		3	4			7	6	14		9		10³	13	2		11²	8	5¹	12									7
1		3	4	14	12	7	6			9		10	13	5		11²	8¹	2³										8
1		3	4	5	7		8		12	11	6²	10³		2	13		9¹			14								9
1		3	4	5	7		8		12	11	6²	10¹		2		13	9³	14										10
1		3	4	5	7	6³	8		9¹	11		10²		2		13	12	14										11
	6	3	4	5	7		8		13	11		10³		2¹		14	9²	12			1							12
	7	3	4	5	6		8		13	10²		9³		2¹		14	11	12			1							13
	2	3	4	5	8		6²		10¹	12	14	13				11	9	7³			1							14
	6	3	4	5	7		8		13	11		10²		2³		12	9¹	14			1							15
	6	3		5		13	7		10	9	8³	11²				14		2¹		4	1	12						16
		3	4	5	6	7³	8		12	11		10²		2		13	9¹	14			1							17
		3	4	5	7	6	8¹			11		10		2			9	12			1							18
		3	4	5	6	7²	8			11	14	10¹		2			9³	13	12		1							19
		3	4	5¹	6	7²	8		14	10		11	13	2	9³			12			1							20
		3	4		6	7¹	8			10	14	11	13	2	9²						1	5³	12					21
		3	4		7		12		8²	11	6¹	13	14	5	9³	10		2			1							22
1		3	4		8	7	13		14	11	6¹	10³	12	5	9²			2										23
1		3	4		7		6		8¹	11		12		5	9	10²		2		13								24
	12	3	4		8		6²			10		9	13	5	7	11³		2¹			1	14						25
	3	2	4		6		7		9¹	10		13		5	12	11²		14			1	8³						26
1		3	4	12	6	7²	14			9		10	13	5¹	8³	11								2				27
1		3	4	5	8		9	13		11		7¹	12	2		10							6²					28
1		3¹	4	5	6		8			10		9³		2	14	11²	13						7	12				29
1		3		5	8		6¹		13	9		10		2		11³	12						7	4²	14			30
1		3		5	8		7²			11		10	13	2	12	14	9¹						6³		4			31
1		3	4	5	8	13	7			11		10¹		2			9²						6			12		32
1	6²	2	4	5¹	7		9			11				12	8	10³	14						13		3			33
1		3		5	8		7		12	11		10¹	13	2³	9			14					6²		4			34
1	2	3		5	7		8			11		10¹			9								6		4	12		35
1	2	3		5³	7		8		14	11		10	12				9²	13					6¹		4			36
1	5	2	4		7		8			11		10¹				12	9						6		3			37
1	2²	3⁴	15	5	8		7		12	10⁵		11	14	13			9³						6¹		4	16		38
1	14	2	4	5³	6			9²		11	8¹	10⁴		13			12						7		3	15		39
1	8³	3	5	6	9		7		11¹	13		12		2				14							4	10²		40
1	14	2	4	5	7⁵	16	8²	9⁴		11		6³		12	13		10¹								3	15		41
1	6		4	5	8	12		9¹		11		13		2	7										3	10²		42
1	15		4	5	6	7⁴		9³	12	10²		11¹		2	8	13									3	14		43
1	12		4	5	6	7³		9¹		11²		10⁴	14	2	8	15									3	13		44
1	5⁴		4		7			10³		11¹		8²	14	2	9	12							6		3	13	15	45
1	5	14	4		8			9³		11²		6¹		2	10	12							7		3	13		46

FA Cup

Third Round	Bournemouth	(a)	0-4

Carabao Cup

First Round	Ipswich T	(h)	3-1
Second Round	Cardiff C	(a)	3-0
Third Round	Leicester C	(h)	0-4

MACCLESFIELD TOWN

FOUNDATION

From the mid-19th century until 1874, Macclesfield Town FC played under rugby rules. In 1891 they moved to the Moss Rose ground and finished champions of the Manchester & District League in 1906 and 1908. By 1911, they had carried off the Cheshire Senior Cup five times. Macclesfield were founder members of the Cheshire County League in 1919.

Moss Rose Stadium, London Road, Macclesfield, Cheshire SK11 7SP.

Telephone: (01625) 264 686.

Ticket Office: (01625) 264 686.

Website: www.mtfc.co.uk

Email: reception@mtfc.co.uk

Ground Capacity: 6,355.

Record Attendance: 9,008 v Winsford U, Cheshire Senior Cup 2nd rd, 4 February 1948.

Pitch Measurements: 101m × 67m (110.5yd × 73.5yd).

Majority Shareholder: Amar Alkadhi.

Head Coach: Tim Flowers.

Assistant Head Coaches: Danny Whitaker and Gary Whild.

Colours: Blue shirts with white trim, white shorts with blue trim, blue socks with white trim.

Year Formed: 1874.

Turned Professional: 1886.

Club Nickname: 'The Silkmen'.

Grounds: 1874, Rostron Field; 1891, Moss Rose.

First Football League Game: 9 August 1997, Division 3, v Torquay U (h) W 2–1 – Price; Tinson, Rose, Payne (Edey), Howarth, Sodje (1), Askey, Wood, Landon (1) (Power), Mason, Sorvel.

Record League Victory: 6–0 v Stockport Co, FL 1, 26 December 2005 – Fettis; Harsley, Sandwith, Morley, Swailes (Teague), Navarro, Whitaker (Miles (1)), Bullock (1), Parkin (2), Wijnhard (2) (Townson), McIntyre.

Record Cup Victory: 15–0 v Chester St Mary's, Cheshire Senior Cup 3rd rd, 6 February 1886; 15–0 v Barnton Rovers, Cheshire Senior Cup 1st rd, 12 November 1887.

HONOURS

League Champions: Vauxhall Conference – 1994–95, 1996–97; National League – 2017–18.
Runners-up: Division 3 – 1997–98.

FA Cup: 4th rd – 2013.

League Cup: 3rd rd – 2019.

FA Trophy Winners: 1969–70, 1995–96.
Runners-up: 1988–89.

FOOTBALL YEARBOOK FACT FILE

In 1986–87 Macclesfield Town completed a Northern Premier League treble, winning all three trophies in the space of a fortnight. They started off by defeating Burton Albion at Maine Road to win the League Challenge Cup and two days later a goal in the last minute of extra time in the second leg of the President's Cup defeated Marine. Finally, they clinched the League title with a 3-1 victory at Hyde United.

Record Defeat: 1–13 v Tranmere R reserves, 3 May 1929.

Most League Points (3 for a win): 82, Division 3, 1997–98.

Most League Goals: 66, Division 3, 1999–2000.

Highest League Scorer in Season: Jon Parkin, 22, FL 2, 2004–05.

Most League Goals in Total Aggregate: Matt Tipton, 50, 2002–05; 2006–07; 2009–10.

Most League Goals in One Match: 3, Rickie Lambert v Luton T, Division 3, 24 November 2001; 3, Jonathan Parkin v Notts Co, FL 2, 25 January 2005; 3, Matt Tipton v Rochdale, FL 2, 19 February 2005.

Most Capped Player: George Abbey, 10 (18), Nigeria.

Most League Appearances: Darren Tinson, 263, 1997–2003.

Youngest League Player: Elliott Hewitt, 16 years 342 days v Hereford U, 7 May 2011.

Record Transfer Fee Received: £300,000 from Stockport Co for Rickie Lambert, April 2002.

Record Transfer Fee Paid: £40,000 to Bury for Danny Swailes, January 2005.

Football League Record: 1997 Promoted to Division 3; 1998–99 Division 2; 1999–2004 Division 3; 2004–12 FL 2; 2012–17 National League; 2018–20 FL2; 2020– National League.

MANAGERS

Since 1967
Keith Goalen 1967–68
Frank Beaumont 1968–72
Billy Haydock 1972–74
Eddie Brown 1974
John Collins 1974
Willie Stevenson 1974
John Collins 1975–76
Tony Coleman 1976
John Barnes 1976
Brian Taylor 1976
Dave Connor 1976–78
Derek Partridge 1978
Phil Staley 1978–80
Jimmy Williams 1980–81
Brian Booth 1981–85
Neil Griffiths 1985–86
Roy Campbell 1986
Peter Wragg 1986–93
Sammy McIlroy 1993–2000
Peter Davenport 2000
Gil Prescott 2000–01
David Moss 2001–03
John Askey 2003–04
Brian Horton 2004–06
Paul Ince 2006–07
Ian Brightwell 2007–08
Keith Alexander 2008–10
Gary Simpson 2010–12
Steve King 2012–13
John Askew 2013–18
Mark Yates 2018
Sol Campbell 2018–19
Daryl McMahon 2019–20
Mark Kennedy 2020
Tim Flowers August 2020–

LATEST SEQUENCES

Longest Sequence of League Wins: 6, 25.1.2005 – 26.2.2005.

Longest Sequence of League Defeats: 8, 2.1.2012 – 21.2.2012.

Longest Sequence of League Draws: 5, 16.11.2019 – 26.12.2019.

Longest Sequence of Unbeaten League Matches: 8, 16.10.1999 – 27.11.1999.

Longest Sequence Without a League Win: 36, 2.1.2012 – 12.10.2018 over 2 spells in League.

Successive Scoring Runs: 14 from 11.10.2003.

Successive Non-scoring Runs: 5 from 18.12.1998.

TEN YEAR LEAGUE RECORD

		P	W	D	L	F	A	Pts	Pos
2010-11	FL 2	46	14	13	19	59	73	55	15
2011-12	FL 2	46	8	13	25	39	64	37	24
2012-13	Conf	46	17	12	17	65	70	63	11
2013-14	Conf	46	18	7	21	62	63	61	15
2014-15	Conf	46	21	15	10	60	46	78	6
2015-16	NL	46	19	9	18	60	48	66	10
2016-17	NL	46	20	8	18	64	57	68	9
2017-18	NL	46	27	11	8	67	46	92	1
2018-19	FL 2	46	10	14	22	48	74	44	22
2019-20	FL 2	37	7	15	15	32	47	19*	24§

**17 pts deducted. §Decided on points-per-game (0.51)*

DID YOU KNOW ?

Macclesfield Town reached the first round proper of the FA Cup for the first time in their history in 1960–61 as a result of winning each of their four qualifying round games away from their Moss Rose home. They were drawn away to Fourth Division Southport where they finally went out of the competition, losing 7-2.

MACCLESFIELD TOWN – SKY BET LEAGUE TWO 2019–20 LEAGUE RECORD

Match No.	Date	Venue	Opponents	Result	H/T Score	Lg Pos.	Goalscorers	Attendance
1	Aug 3	A	Exeter C	L 0-1	0-0	17		4502
2	10	H	Leyton Orient	W 3-0	1-0	8	Archibald 30, Osaoabe 68, Vassell 83	2167
3	17	A	Northampton T	W 2-1	1-0	4	Stephens 39, Archibald 90	4319
4	20	H	Morecambe	L 0-1	0-0	10		1862
5	24	H	Scunthorpe U	W 1-0	0-0	4	Ironside (pen) 54	1860
6	31	A	Stevenage	D 2-2	1-0	7	Stephens 27, Ironside (pen) 85	2504
7	Sept 7	H	Crawley T	D 1-1	1-0	9	Vassell 21	1788
8	14	A	Swindon T	L 0-3	0-2	13		7055
9	17	H	Newport Co	D 1-1	1-1	14	Osaoabe 19	1435
10	21	A	Grimsby T	L 0-1	0-0	15		3794
11	28	H	Colchester U	D 1-1	1-1	17	Osaoabe 13	1532
12	Oct 5	A	Cambridge U	D 2-2	0-1	16	Archibald 65, Gnahoua 68	3678
13	12	H	Port Vale	W 2-1	1-1	12	Gnahoua 39, Osaoabe 64	3467
14	19	A	Oldham Ath	W 1-0	0-0	9	McCourt 86	4428
15	22	A	Cheltenham T	L 0-3	0-1	14		2632
16	Nov 2	A	Carlisle U	L 1-2	1-1	15	Archibald 25	3880
17	16	H	Mansfield T	D 0-0	0-0	15		2055
18	23	A	Salford C	D 0-0	0-0	14		2484
19	30	H	Bradford C	D 1-1	1-0	14	McCourt (pen) 32	2751
20	Dec 14	A	Walsall	D 1-1	1-0	15	Welch-Hayes 8	3846
21	26	H	Grimsby T	D 1-1	0-0	18	Ironside (pen) 49	1991
22	29	A	Forest Green R	L 0-1	0-0	19		2155
23	Jan 1	A	Port Vale	D 2-2	0-1	18	Harris 56, Ironside 57	5350
24	4	H	Cambridge U	W 1-0	1-0	17	Gnahoua 5	1454
25	11	H	Oldham Ath	D 1-1	0-0	17	Ironside (pen) 90	2205
26	18	A	Colchester U	L 1-2	0-2	17	Stephens 72	3252
27	21	H	Crewe Alex	D 1-1	1-0	16	Green (og) 44	2435
28	25	H	Forest Green R	W 2-1	0-1	15	Ironside 74, Gnahoua 83	1653
29	28	A	Newport Co	L 0-1	0-1	15		3354
30	Feb 1	H	Northampton T	L 0-1	0-0	18		1712
31	8	A	Leyton Orient	D 1-1	0-0	19	Blyth 90	5708
32	11	A	Morecambe	L 0-2	0-2	20		1611
33	15	H	Exeter C	L 2-3	1-2	21	Kirby 40, Kelleher 63	1389
34	18	H	Plymouth Arg	D 1-1	1-0	19	Tracey 33	1887
35	22	A	Crewe Alex	L 0-2	0-2	20		5413
36	29	H	Salford C	L 0-2	0-2	21		2317
37	Mar 7	A	Plymouth Arg	L 0-3	0-1	22		12,310
38	14	H	Walsall	Cancelled				
39	17	H	Cheltenham T	Cancelled				
40	21	A	Bradford C	Cancelled				
41	28	H	Carlisle U	Cancelled				
42	Apr 4	A	Mansfield T	Cancelled				
43	10	A	Scunthorpe U	Cancelled				
44	13	H	Stevenage	Cancelled				
45	18	A	Crawley T	Cancelled				
46	25	H	Swindon T	Cancelled				

Final League Position: 24 (on points-per-game basis)

GOALSCORERS

League (32): Ironside 6 (4 pens), Archibald 4, Gnahoua 4, Osaoabe 4, Stephens 3, McCourt 2 (1 pen), Vassell 2, Blyth 1, Harris 1, Kelleher 1, Kirby 1, Tracey 1, Welch-Hayes 1, own goal 1.
FA Cup (0).
Carabao Cup (2): Gomis 1, own goal 1.
Leasing.com Trophy (5): Archibald 2, Fitzpatrick 1, Gomis 1, Ironside 1.

Evans O 24	Welch-Hayes M 24	Kelleher F 37	Vassell T 17	Archibald T 23 + 5	McCourt J 18 + 3	Harris J 25	Clarke E 5 + 1	Osaoabe E 22 + 3	Stephens B 13 + 10	Ironside J 25 + 8	Blyth J — + 19	Fitzpatrick D 17 + 4	Horsfall F 21 + 5	Gomis V 4 + 7	Kirby C 29 + 5	O'Keeffe C 28 + 3	Gnahoua A 26 + 3	Ntambwe B — + 3	Cameron N 12 + 4	Charles-Cook R 2	Mitchell J 11	Whitehead D 10	Hamblin H 3 + 1	Rose M — + 1	Tracey S 6 + 1	Wilson D 1 + 4	Tollitt B 4 + 1	*Match No.*
1	2	3	4^{1}	5	6	7	8	9	10^{3}	11^{2}	12	13	14															1
1	2	3	4	5	6^{1}	7	8	9	10^{2}	11^{3}	12			13	14													2
1	2	3	4	5	7^{1}	6	8^{2}	9	11^{3}	10				12	14	13												3
1	2	3	4	5	7^{2}	6	8^{3}	9	11^{1}	10				14	13	12												4
1	2	3	4	8	6	7	12	9	10^{2}	11^{1}	14				13	5^{3}												5
1	2	3	4	8	6^{2}	7		9	10^{1}	11			13		12	5^{3}	14											6
1	2	3	4	5		7		9	10^{1}	11^{3}			13	14	6	8^{2}	12											7
1	2	4	5	8^{1}		6		9		11^{2}			3	14	7^{3}	10	13	12										8
1	2	3	4	5		6		9	12					11^{1}	7	8	10											9
1	2	3	4	5		6		9	13	12				11^{1}	7	8	10^{2}											10
1	2	3	4	5		6		9		13			14	10^{3}	7	8^{1}	11^{2}	12										11
1	2	3	4	5		6	8^{2}	9	13	12		14		11^{3}	7		10^{1}											12
1	2	3	4	5	12	7		9		10					6	8	11^{1}											13
1	2	3	4	5	12	6		9		11			13		7^{2}	8	10^{1}											14
1	2	3	4	5	6			9		10				12	7	8	11^{1}											15
1	5	3	4	8				9	10	11^{1}				12	6	7			2									16
1	5	3	4	11^{1}		7			10^{2}	12	13	8			6		9		2									17
1	5	3			9	7		12	11^{1}		13	8	4		6		10^{2}		2									18
1		3			6	7		11^{2}	13^{3}		12	8	4		10■	5	9^{1}	14	2									19
1	6	3			8	7		10		12		5	2			9	11^{1}		4									20
1	5	3			6	7		11	13	12		8^{2}	4			9^{1}	10		2									21
1	5	3				7		9		11	13	12	4		6	8^{1}	10		2^{2}									22
1	2	3			6^{1}	7		9		11^{2}	13	8	4		5	12	10											23
1	2	3			10	7			14	11^{3}	13	8	4		6	5^{1}	9^{2}		12									24
	2^{2}	3			9	7				11	13	8	4		6^{1}	5	10		12	1								25
		4		12	7			13	9^{3}	10^{2}	14	5	2		8	6^{1}	11		3	1								26
		3		6^{1}	8^{2}				12	11^{3}	14	5	4		7	2	10		13		1	9						27
		3		7		8^{3}		12	13	11^{2}	14	5	4		9^{1}	2■	10				1	6						28
		3		12		8^{2}		9	7^{1}	11	13	5	4		2		10				1	6						29
		3							9^{1}	10	13	5	4		6^{3}	2	11		12		1	8^{2}	7	14				30
		3		12						11^{2}	14	5	4		8^{1}	2	10				1	9	6		7^{3}	13		31
		3		12						11		5	4		9	2	10^{1}				1	8	6^{3}		7^{2}	14	13	32
		3		13						11^{1}	14	5^{2}	4		9	2			6		1	8			12	10^{3}	7	33
		3		9								12	4		8	5	10		2		1	7	13		11^{2}		6^{1}	34
		3		9	12				14	13			4		8	5	10^{3}		2		1	6^{1}			11		7^{2}	35
		3		9	6^{2}					12	14		4		8	5	10		2		1				11^{1}	13	7^{3}	36
		3		10	8				12	11^{3}	14	5	4		9^{2}	2					1	6			7^{1}	13		37
																												38
																												39
																												40
																												41
																												42
																												43
																												44
																												45
																												46

FA Cup

First Round	Kingstonian	(h)	0-4

Carabao Cup

First Round	Blackpool	(a)	2-2
(Macclesfield T won 4-2 on penalties)			
Second Round	Grimsby T	(a)	0-0
(Grimsby T won 5-4 on penalties)			

Leasing.com Trophy

Group D (N)	Newcastle U U21	(h)	2-1
Group D (N)	Port Vale	(h)	2-3
Group D (N)	Shrewsbury T	(a)	1-3

MANCHESTER CITY

FOUNDATION

Manchester City was formed as a limited company in 1894 after their predecessors Ardwick had been forced into bankruptcy. However, many historians like to trace the club's lineage as far back as 1880 when St Mark's Church, West Gorton added a football section to their cricket club. They amalgamated with Belle Vue for one season before splitting again under the name Gorton Association FC in 1884–85. In 1887 Gorton AFC turned professional and moved ground to Hyde Road under the new name Ardwick AFC.

Etihad Stadium, Etihad Campus, Manchester M11 3FF.

Telephone: (0161) 444 1894.

Ticket Office: (0161) 444 1894.

Website: www.mancity.com

Email: mancity@mancity.com

Ground Capacity: 55,017.

Record Attendance: 84,569 v Stoke C, FA Cup 6th rd, 3 March 1934 (at Maine Road; British record for any game outside London or Glasgow); 54,693 v Leicester C, Premier League, 6 February 2016 (at Etihad Stadium).

Pitch Measurements: 105m × 68m (115yd × 74.5yd).

Chairman: Khaldoon Al Mubarak.

Chief Executive: Ferran Soriano.

Manager: Pep Guardiola.

Assistant Managers: Juan Manuel Lillo, Rodolfo Borrell, Brian Kidd.

Colours: Light blue shirts, white shorts, light blue socks.

Year Formed: 1887 as Ardwick FC; 1894 as Manchester City.

Turned Professional: 1887 as Ardwick FC.

Previous Names: 1880, St Mark's Church, West Gorton; 1884, Gorton; 1887, Ardwick; 1894, Manchester City.

Club Nicknames: 'The Blues', 'The Citizens'.

Grounds: 1880, Clowes Street; 1881, Kirkmanshulme Cricket Ground; 1882, Queens Road; 1884, Pink Bank Lane; 1887, Hyde Road (1894–1923 as City); 1923, Maine Road; 2003, City of Manchester Stadium (renamed Etihad Stadium 2011).

First Football League Game: 3 September 1892, Division 2, v Bootle (h) W 7–0 – Douglas; McVickers, Robson; Middleton, Russell, Hopkins; Davies (3), Morris (2), Angus (1), Weir (1), Milarvie.

HONOURS

League Champions: Premier League – 2011–12, 2013–14, 2017–18, 2018–19; Division 1 – 1936–37, 1967–68; First Division – 2001–02; Division 2 – 1898–99, 1902–03, 1909–10, 1927–28, 1946–47, 1965–66.
Runners-up: Premier League – 2012–13, 2014–15, 2019–20; Division 1 – 1903–04, 1920–21, 1976–77; First Division – 1999–2000; Division 2 – 1895–96, 1950–51, 1988–89.

FA Cup Winners: 1904, 1934, 1956, 1969, 2011, 2019.
Runners-up: 1926, 1933, 1955, 1981, 2013.

League Cup Winners: 1970, 1976, 2014, 2016, 2018, 2019, 2020.
Runners-up: 1974.

Full Members Cup: *Runners-up:* 1986.

European Competitions
European Cup: 1968–69.
Champions League: 2011–12, 2012–13, 2013–14, 2014–15, 2015–16 *(sf)*, 2016–17, 2017–18 *(qf)*, 2018–19 *(sf)*, 2019–20 *(qf)*.
UEFA Cup: 1972–73, 1976–77, 1977–78, 1978–79 *(qf)*, 2003–04, 2008–09 *(qf)*.
Europa League: 2010–11, 2011–12.
European Cup-Winners' Cup: 1969–70 *(winners)*, 1970–71 *(sf)*.

Record League Victory: 10–1 v Huddersfield T, Division 2, 7 November 1987 – Nixon; Gidman, Hinchcliffe, Clements, Lake, Redmond, White (3), Stewart (3), Adcock (3), McNab (1), Simpson.

Record Cup Victory: 10–1 v Swindon T, FA Cup 4th rd, 29 January 1930 – Barber; Felton, McCloy; Barrass, Cowan, Heinemann; Toseland, Marshall (5), Tait (3), Johnson (1), Brook (1).

Record Defeat: 1–9 v Everton, Division 1, 3 September 1906.

FOOTBALL YEARBOOK FACT FILE

Centre-forward Jimmy Currier scored 84 goals from 113 appearances for Manchester City in the emergency competitions during the Second World War. Currier, who was a guest from Bolton Wanderers, netted 47 times during the 1940–41 season including five goals in each of two consecutive games against Rochdale in January 1941.

Most League Points (2 for a win): 62, Division 2, 1946–47.

Most League Points (3 for a win): 100, Premier League, 2017–18.

Most League Goals: 108, Division 2, 1926–27, 108, Division 1, 2001–02.

Highest League Scorer in Season: Tommy Johnson, 38, Division 1, 1928–29.

Most League Goals in Total Aggregate: Sergio Aguero, 180, 2011–20.

Most League Goals in One Match: 5, Fred Williams v Darwen, Division 2, 18 February 1899; 5, Tom Browell v Burnley, Division 2, 24 October 1925; 5, Tom Johnson v Everton, Division 1, 15 September 1928; 5, George Smith v Newport Co, Division 2, 14 June 1947; 5, Sergio Aguero v Newcastle U, Premier League, 3 October 2015.

Most Capped Player: David Silva, 87 (125), Spain.

Most League Appearances: Alan Oakes, 564, 1959–76.

Youngest League Player: Glyn Pardoe, 15 years 314 days v Birmingham C, 11 April 1962.

Record Transfer Fee Received: £34,000,000 from Juventus for Danilo, August 2019.

Record Transfer Fee Paid: £62,500,000 to Atletico Madrid for Rodrigo Hernandez Cascant, July 2019.

Football League Record: 1892 Ardwick elected founder member of Division 2; 1894 Newly-formed Manchester C elected to Division 2; Division 1 1899–1902, 1903–09, 1910–26, 1928–38, 1947–50, 1951–63, 1966–83, 1985–87, 1989–92; Division 2 1902–03, 1909–10, 1926–28, 1938–47, 1950–51, 1963–66, 1983–85, 1987–89; 1992–96 Premier League; 1996–98 Division 1; 1998–99 Division 2; 1999–2000 Division 1; 2000–01 Premier League; 2001–02 Division 1; 2002– Premier League.

LATEST SEQUENCES

Longest Sequence of League Wins: 18, 26.8.2017 – 27.12.2017.

Longest Sequence of League Defeats: 8, 23.8.1995 – 14.10.1995.

Longest Sequence of League Draws: 7, 5.10.2009 – 28.11.2009.

Longest Sequence of Unbeaten League Matches: 30, 8.4.2017 – 2.1.2018.

Longest Sequence Without a League Win: 17, 26.12.1979 – 7.4.1980.

Successive Scoring Runs: 44 from 3.10.1936.

Successive Non-scoring Runs: 6 from 30.1.1971.

MANAGERS

Joshua Parlby 1893–95
(Secretary-Manager)
Sam Omerod 1895–1902
Tom Maley 1902–06
Harry Newbould 1906–12
Ernest Magnall 1912–24
David Ashworth 1924–25
Peter Hodge 1926–32
Wilf Wild 1932–46
(continued as Secretary to 1950)
Sam Cowan 1946–47
John 'Jock' Thomson 1947–50
Leslie McDowall 1950–63
George Poyser 1963–65
Joe Mercer 1965–71
(continued as General Manager to 1972)
Malcolm Allison 1972–73
Johnny Hart 1973
Ron Saunders 1973–74
Tony Book 1974–79
Malcolm Allison 1979–80
John Bond 1980–83
John Benson 1983
Billy McNeill 1983–86
Jimmy Frizzell 1986–87
(continued as General Manager)
Mel Machin 1987–89
Howard Kendall 1989–90
Peter Reid 1990–93
Brian Horton 1993–95
Alan Ball 1995–96
Steve Coppell 1996
Frank Clark 1996–98
Joe Royle 1998–2001
Kevin Keegan 2001–05
Stuart Pearce 2005–07
Sven-Göran Eriksson 2007–08
Mark Hughes 2008–09
Roberto Mancini 2009–13
Manuel Pellegrini 2013–16
Pep Guardiola June 2016–

TEN YEAR LEAGUE RECORD

		P	W	D	L	F	A	Pts	Pos
2010-11	PR Lge	38	21	8	9	60	33	71	3
2011-12	PR Lge	38	28	5	5	93	29	89	1
2012-13	PR Lge	38	23	9	6	66	34	78	2
2013-14	PR Lge	38	27	5	6	102	37	86	1
2014-15	PR Lge	38	24	7	7	83	38	79	2
2015-16	PR Lge	38	19	9	10	71	41	66	4
2016-17	PR Lge	38	23	9	6	80	39	78	3
2017-18	PR Lge	38	32	4	2	106	27	100	1
2018-19	PR Lge	38	32	2	4	95	23	98	1
2019-20	PR Lge	38	26	3	9	102	35	81	2

DID YOU KNOW ?

In 1971–72 Francis Lee created a new British record for penalties scored in a season when he netted 15 times in all games from the spot for Manchester City, including 13 in Football League games. He scored a career total of 148 goals for City, of which 47 were from penalty kicks.

MANCHESTER CITY – PREMIER LEAGUE 2019–20 LEAGUE RECORD

Match No.	*Date*	*Venue*	*Opponents*	*Result*	*H/T Score*	*Lg Pos.*	*Goalscorers*	*Attendance*
1	Aug 10	A	West Ham U	W 5-0	1-0	1	Gabriel Jesus [25], Sterling 3 [51, 75, 90], Aguero (pen) [86]	59,870
2	17	H	Tottenham H	D 2-2	2-1	3	Sterling [20], Aguero [35]	54,503
3	25	A	Bournemouth	W 3-1	2-1	2	Aguero 2 [15, 64], Sterling [43]	10,486
4	31	H	Brighton & HA	W 4-0	2-0	2	De Bruyne [2], Aguero 2 [42, 55], Bernardo Silva [79]	54,386
5	Sept 14	A	Norwich C	L 2-3	1-2	2	Aguero [45], Rodri [88]	27,035
6	21	H	Watford	W 8-0	5-0	2	Silva [1], Aguero (pen) [7], Mahrez [12], Bernardo Silva 3 [15, 48, 60], Otamendi [18], De Bruyne [85]	54,273
7	28	A	Everton	W 3-1	1-1	2	Gabriel Jesus [24], Mahrez [71], Sterling [84]	39,222
8	Oct 6	H	Wolverhampton W	L 0-2	0-0	2		54,435
9	19	A	Crystal Palace	W 2-0	2-0	2	Gabriel Jesus [39], Silva [41]	25,480
10	26	H	Aston Villa	W 3-0	0-0	2	Sterling [46], Silva [65], Gundogan [70]	54,506
11	Nov 2	H	Southampton	W 2-1	0-1	2	Aguero [70], Walker [86]	53,922
12	10	A	Liverpool	L 1-3	0-2	4	Bernardo Silva [78]	53,324
13	23	H	Chelsea	W 2-1	2-1	3	De Bruyne [29], Mahrez [37]	54,486
14	30	A	Newcastle U	D 2-2	1-1	2	Sterling [22], De Bruyne [82]	49,937
15	Dec 3	A	Burnley	W 4-1	1-0	2	Gabriel Jesus 2 [24, 50], Rodri [68], Mahrez [87]	20,101
16	7	H	Manchester U	L 1-2	0-2	3	Otamendi [85]	54,403
17	15	A	Arsenal	W 3-0	3-0	3	De Bruyne 2 [2, 40], Sterling [15]	60,031
18	21	H	Leicester C	W 3-1	2-1	3	Mahrez [30], Gundogan (pen) [43], Gabriel Jesus [69]	54,415
19	27	A	Wolverhampton W	L 2-3	1-0	3	Sterling 2 [25, 50]	31,737
20	29	H	Sheffield U	W 2-0	0-0	3	Aguero [52], De Bruyne [82]	54,512
21	Jan 1	H	Everton	W 2-1	0-0	3	Gabriel Jesus 2 [51, 58]	54,407
22	12	A	Aston Villa	W 6-1	4-0	2	Mahrez 2 [18, 24], Aguero 3 [28, 57, 81], Gabriel Jesus [45]	41,823
23	18	H	Crystal Palace	D 2-2	0-1	2	Aguero 2 [82, 87]	54,439
24	21	A	Sheffield U	W 1-0	0-0	2	Aguero [73]	31,285
25	Feb 2	A	Tottenham H	L 0-2	0-0	2		61,022
26	19	H	West Ham U	W 2-0	1-0	2	Rodri [30], De Bruyne [62]	54,000
27	22	A	Leicester C	W 1-0	0-0	2	Gabriel Jesus [80]	32,068
28	Mar 8	A	Manchester U	L 0-2	0-1	2		73,288
29	June 17	H	Arsenal	W 3-0	1-0	2	Sterling [45], De Bruyne (pen) [51], Foden [90]	0
30	22	H	Burnley	W 5-0	3-0	2	Foden 2 [22, 63], Mahrez 2 (1 pen) [43, 45 (p)], Silva [51]	0
31	25	A	Chelsea	L 1-2	0-1	2	De Bruyne [55]	0
32	July 2	H	Liverpool	W 4-0	3-0	2	De Bruyne (pen) [25], Sterling [35], Foden [45], Oxlade-Chamberlain (og) [66]	0
33	5	A	Southampton	L 0-1	0-1	2		0
34	8	H	Newcastle U	W 5-0	2-0	2	Gabriel Jesus [10], Mahrez [21], Fernandez (og) [58], Silva [65], Sterling [90]	0
35	11	A	Brighton & HA	W 5-0	2-0	2	Sterling 3 [21, 53, 81], Gabriel Jesus [44], Bernardo Silva [56]	0
36	15	H	Bournemouth	W 2-1	2-0	2	Silva [6], Gabriel Jesus [39]	0
37	21	A	Watford	W 4-0	2-0	2	Sterling 2 [31, 40], Foden [63], Laporte [66]	0
38	26	H	Norwich C	W 5-0	2-0	2	Gabriel Jesus [11], De Bruyne 2 [45, 90], Sterling [79], Mahrez [83]	0

Final League Position: 2

GOALSCORERS

League (102): Sterling 20, Aguero 16 (2 pens), Gabriel Jesus 14, De Bruyne 13 (2 pens), Mahrez 11 (1 pen), Bernardo Silva 6, Silva 6, Foden 5, Rodri 3, Gundogan 2 (1 pen), Otamendi 2, Laporte 1, Walker 1, own goals 2.
FA Cup (11): Aguero 2, Gabriel Jesus 2, Bernardo Silva 1, De Bruyne 1 (1 pen), Foden 1, Gundogan 1 (1 pen), Harwood-Bellis 1, Sterling 1, Zinchenko 1.
Carabao Cup (14): Aguero 3, Sterling 3, Bernardo Silva 1, Gabriel Jesus 1, Joao Cancelo 1, Mahrez 1, Otamendi 1, Rodri 1, own goals 2.
UEFA Champions League (21): Gabriel Jesus 6, Sterling 6, Aguero 2 (1 pen), De Bruyne 2 (1 pen), Foden 2, Gundogan 2, Mahrez 1.
Leasing.com Trophy (7): Doyle 3 (1 pen), Bernabe 1, Braaf 1, Rogers 1, own goal 1.

Ederson 35	Walker K 28 + 1	Stones J 12 + 4	Laporte A 14 + 1	Zinchenko A 13 + 6	De Bruyne K 32 + 3	Rodri R 29 + 6	Silva D 22 + 5	Mahrez R 21 + 12	Gabriel Jesus F 21 + 13	Sterling R 30 + 3	Aguero S 18 + 6	Gundogan I 21 + 10	Foden P 9 + 14	Otamendi N 18 + 6	Bernardo Silva M 23 + 11	Joao Cancelo C 13 + 4	Fernandinho L 26 + 4	Mendy B 18 + 1	Tasende J 4 + 2	Garcia E 8 + 5	Bravo C 3 + 1	Sane L — + 1	Doyle T — + 1	*Match No.*
1	2	3	4	5	6^{2}	7	8^{3}	9	10^{1}	11	12	13	14											1
1	2		4	5	6	7^{2}	13	14	12	11	10^{1}	8		3	9^{3}									2
1	2^{3}		4	5	6	12	8	13		11	10	7^{1}		3	9^{2}	14								3
1	2		4^{1}	5	6^{2}	7	8^{3}	9		11	10	13		3	14		12							4
1	2	3		5	12	7	9^{2}	14	13	10	11	6^{1}		4	8^{3}									5
1	2^{2}				6	7	8	9			10			3^{3}	11	13	4	5^{1}	12	14				6
1	2			5	6^{2}	7	14	9	10^{1}	11^{3}	12	8		3	13		4							7
1	2^{1}			12		7	9^{3}	8^{2}	14	10	11	6		3	13	5	4							8
1		12			6^{2}	4	8^{1}		10	11		7	13		9	2	3	5						9
1		4			6^{2}		8		10	11^{3}	13	7	14		9	2	3■	5^{1}	12					10
1	2	4			6		8^{1}		12	11	10^{3}	7	13	14	9^{2}		3		5					11
	2	3			9	6			12	10	11^{1}	7			8		4		5		1			12
1		3			6	7^{1}	8^{2}	9	14	11	10^{3}	12	13			2	4	5						13
1	2	3			6	14	8^{2}	9^{1}	10^{3}	11		7	13		12		4	5						14
1	2				6^{2}	7	8	12	10	11^{1}			13	3	9		4^{3}		5	14				15
1	2	3^{1}			6	7^{3}	8	13	10	11		14		12	9^{2}		4		5					16
1	2			14	9	6		13	11	8		7^{2}	10^{1}	3	12		4	5^{3}						17
1	2				6^{3}	12		9	10	11^{2}	14	7^{1}	13	4	8		3	5						18
1■	2				9^{3}	6		8^{2}		10	11^{1}	14		3	7		4	5		13	12			19
	2			5	6	7		9	14	11^{3}	10^{2}	12	13		8^{1}		3			4	1			20
					6	2	12	9^{2}	11	13		7	10^{1}			5	3	8		4	1			21
1		3			6^{2}	7^{3}	8	9	11		10	14	12	13		2	4^{1}	5						22
1		3			6	14	8^{1}	13	12	9^{3}	10	7			11^{2}	2	4	5						23
1	5		4^{2}	8	6	7		9	11^{1}	10^{3}	12			3	14		2			13				24
1	2			5■	6	7		9^{2}	13	11^{3}	10^{1}	8		3	14	12	4							25
1	2	12	4^{1}		6^{2}	7	8^{3}		11		10	13	14	3	9			5						26
1	2		4^{1}		8	7		9	13		10^{2}	6		12	11		3	5						27
1				5^{3}		7		12	13	11	10^{2}	8	9	4	6^{1}	2	3	14						28
1	2		4^{3}		8^{4}	15	6^{2}	9^{1}	10^{5}	11	16	7	13		12		14	5		3				29
1			14	5	13	7	8	9^{2}	12		10^{1}		11^{4}	3	6	2	4^{3}					15		30
1	2		4^{4}	14	6	7^{2}	12	9	13	11		8		15	10^{1}		3■	5^{3}						31
1	2^{2}		4^{3}		9	7		12	11^{1}	10^{4}		6	8	15	14	13		5		3				32
1			4	5	12		8	9^{2}	10	11^{1}			13		6	2	7			3				33
1	12	3		5	6	7^{1}	8	9^{5}	10^{4}	15		13	11^{3}	4	14	2^{2}							16	34
1	2	16	4	14	6^{3}	7^{5}	13	9	10^{1}	11			12		8		15	5^{2}		3^{4}				35
1	2^{1}	3		15		14	9	16	11^{5}	12		7^{3}	10	4	8^{2}		6	5^{4}		13				36
1	2^{2}	14	4^{3}	12	6	7		13	10	11^{1}			9		8	5				3				37
1	2		4		6	7^{3}	8^{4}	14	10	9		13	11^{2}		15	5	12			3^{1}				38

FA Cup

Third Round	Port Vale	(h)	4-1
Fourth Round	Fulham	(h)	4-0
Fifth Round	Sheffield W	(a)	1-0
Sixth Round	Newcastle U	(a)	2-0
Semi-Final	Arsenal	(Wembley)	0-2

Carabao Cup

Third Round	Preston NE	(a)	3-0
Fourth Round	Southampton	(h)	3-1
Quarter-Final	Oxford U	(a)	3-1
Semi-Final 1st leg	Manchester U	(a)	3-1
Semi-Final 2nd leg	Manchester U	(h)	0-1
Final	Aston Villa	(Wembley)	2-1

UEFA Champions League

Group C	Shakhtar Donetsk	(a)	3-0
Group C	Dinamo Zagreb	(h)	2-0
Group C	Atalanta	(h)	5-1
Group C	Atalanta	(a)	1-1
Group C	Shakhtar Donetsk	(h)	1-1
Group C	Dinamo Zagreb	(a)	4-1
Round of 16	Real Madrid	(a)	2-1
Round of 16	Real Madrid	(h)	2-1
Quarter-Finals	Lyon	(Lisbon)	1-3

Leasing.com Trophy (Manchester C U21)

Group F (N)	Rochdale	(a)	2-0
Group F (N)	Bradford C	(a)	2-1
Group F (N)	Bolton W	(a)	1-3
Second Round (N)	Shrewsbury T	(a)	1-1

(Manchester C U21 won 6-5 on penalties)

Third Round (N)	Scunthorpe U	(a)	1-3

MANCHESTER UNITED

FOUNDATION

Manchester United was formed as comparatively recently as 1902 after their predecessors, Newton Heath, went bankrupt. However, it is usual to give the date of the club's foundation as 1878 when the dining room committee of the carriage and waggon works of the Lancashire and Yorkshire Railway Company formed Newton Heath L and YR Cricket and Football Club. They won the Manchester Cup in 1886 and as Newton Heath FC were admitted to the Second Division in 1892.

Old Trafford, Sir Matt Busby Way, Manchester M16 0RA.

Telephone: (0161) 868 8000.

Ticket Office: (0161) 868 8000 (option 1).

Website: www.manutd.co.uk

Email: enquiries@manutd.co.uk

Ground Capacity: 74,879.

Record Attendance: 76,098 v Blackburn R, Premier League, 31 March 2007. 83,260 v Arsenal, First Division, 17 January 1948 (at Maine Road – United shared City's ground after Old Trafford suffered World War II bomb damage).

Ground Record Attendance: 76,962 Wolverhampton W v Grimsby T, FA Cup semi-final, 25 March 1939.

Pitch Measurements: 105m × 68m (115yd × 74.5yd).

Co-Chairmen: Joel Glazer, Avram Glazer.

Chief Executive: Edward Woodward.

Manager: Ole Gunnar Solskjaer.

Assistant Manager: Mike Phelan.

Colours: Red shirts with white trim, white shorts with red trim, black socks with white trim.

Year Formed: 1878 as Newton Heath LYR; 1902, Manchester United.

Turned Professional: 1885.

Previous Name: 1880, Newton Heath; 1902, Manchester United.

Club Nickname: 'Red Devils'.

Grounds: 1880, North Road, Monsall Road; 1893, Bank Street; 1910, Old Trafford (played at Maine Road 1941–49).

HONOURS

League Champions: Premier League – 1992–93, 1993–94, 1995–96, 1996–97, 1998–99, 1999–2000, 2000–01, 2002–03, 2006–07, 2007–08, 2008–09, 2010–11, 2012–13; Division 1 – 1907–08, 1910–11, 1951–52, 1955–56, 1956–57, 1964–65, 1966–67; Division 2 – 1935–36, 1974–75.
Runners-up: Premier League – 1994–95, 1997–98, 2005–06, 2009–10, 2011–12, 2017–18; Division 1 – 1946–47, 1947–48, 1948–49, 1950–51, 1958–59, 1963–64, 1967–68, 1979–80, 1987–88, 1991–92; Division 2 – 1896–97, 1905–06, 1924–25, 1937–38.

FA Cup Winners: 1909, 1948, 1963, 1977, 1983, 1985, 1990, 1994, 1996, 1999, 2004, 2016.
Runners-up: 1957, 1958, 1976, 1979, 1995, 2005, 2007, 2018.

League Cup Winners: 1992, 2006, 2009, 2010, 2017.
Runners-up: 1983, 1991, 1994, 2003.

European Competitions
European Cup: 1956–57 *(sf)*, 1957–58 *(sf)*, 1965–66 *(sf)*, 1967–68 *(winners)*, 1968–69 *(sf)*.
Champions League: 1993–94, 1994–95, 1996–97 *(sf)*, 1997–98 *(qf)*, 1998–99 *(winners)*, 1999–2000 *(qf)*, 2000–01 *(qf)*, 2001–02 *(sf)*, 2002–03 *(qf)*, 2003–04, 2004–05, 2005–06, 2006–07 *(sf)*, 2007–08 *(winners)*, 2008–09 *(runners-up)*, 2009–10 *(qf)*, 2010–11 *(runners-up)*, 2011–12, 2012–13, 2013–14 *(qf)*, 2015–16, 2017–18, 2018–19.
Fairs Cup: 1964–65.
UEFA Cup: 1976–77, 1980–81, 1982–83, 1984–85 *(qf)*, 1992–93, 1995–96.
Europa League: 2011–12, 2015–16, 2016–17 *(winners)*, 2019–20.
European Cup-Winners' Cup: 1963–64 *(qf)*, 1977–78, 1983–84 *(sf)*, 1990–91 *(winners)*. 1991–92.
Super Cup: 1991 *(winners)*, 1999, 2008.
World Club Championship: 1968, 1999 *(winners)*, 2000.
FIFA Club World Cup: 2008 *(winners)*.
NB: In 1958–59 FA refused permission to compete in European Cup.

FOOTBALL YEARBOOK FACT FILE

Manchester United played their home games at Maine Road, home of rivals Manchester City, in the 1947–48 season as Old Trafford was unavailable due to bomb damage sustained during the war. When both clubs were drawn at home in the FA Cup, United were forced to play elsewhere, their 'home' ties with Liverpool and Charlton Athletic being played at the grounds of Everton and Huddersfield Town.

First Football League Game: 3 September 1892, Division 1, v Blackburn R (a) L 3–4 – Warner; Clements, Brown; Perrins, Stewart, Erentz; Farman (1), Coupar (1), Donaldson (1), Carson, Mathieson.

Record League Victory (as Newton Heath): 10–1 v Wolverhampton W, Division 1, 15 October 1892 – Warner; Mitchell, Clements; Perrins, Stewart (3), Erentz; Farman (1), Hood (1), Donaldson (3), Carson (1), Hendry (1).

Record League Victory (as Manchester U): 9–0 v Ipswich T, Premier League, 4 March 1995 – Schmeichel; Keane (1) (Sharpe), Irwin, Bruce (Butt), Kanchelskis, Pallister, Cole (5), Ince (1), McClair, Hughes (2), Giggs.

Record Cup Victory: 10–0 v RSC Anderlecht, European Cup prel. rd 2nd leg, 26 September 1956 – Wood; Foulkes, Byrne; Colman, Jones, Edwards; Berry (1), Whelan (2), Taylor (3), Viollet (4), Pegg.

Record Defeat: 0–7 v Blackburn R, Division 1, 10 April 1926; 0–7 v Aston Villa, Division 1, 27 December 1930; 0–7 v Wolverhampton W, Division 2, 26 December 1931.

Most League Points (2 for a win): 64, Division 1, 1956–57.

Most League Points (3 for a win): 92, Premier League, 1993–94.

Most League Goals: 103, Division 1, 1956–57 and 1958–59.

Highest League Scorer in Season: Dennis Viollet, 32, 1959–60.

Most League Goals in Total Aggregate: Bobby Charlton, 199, 1956–73.

Most League Goals in One Match: 5, Andrew Cole v Ipswich T, Premier League, 3 March 1995; 5, Dimitar Berbatov v Blackburn R, Premier League, 27 November 2010.

Most Capped Player: Bobby Charlton, 106, England.

Most League Appearances: Ryan Giggs, 672, 1991–2014.

Youngest League Player: Jeff Whitefoot, 16 years 105 days v Portsmouth, 15 April 1950.

Record Transfer Fee Received: £80,000,000 from Real Madrid for Cristiano Ronaldo, July 2009.

Record Transfer Fee Paid: £89,300,000 to Juventus for Paul Pogba, August 2016.

Football League Record: 1892 Newton Heath elected to Division 1; 1894–1906 Division 2; 1906–22 Division 1; 1922–25 Division 2; 1925–31 Division 1; 1931–36 Division 2; 1936–37 Division 1; 1937–38 Division 2; 1938–74 Division 1; 1974–75 Division 2; 1975–92 Division 1; 1992– Premier League.

MANAGERS

J. Ernest Mangnall 1903–12
John Bentley 1912–14
John Robson 1914–21
(Secretary-Manager from 1916)
John Chapman 1921–26
Clarence Hilditch 1926–27
Herbert Bamlett 1927–31
Walter Crickmer 1931–32
Scott Duncan 1932–37
Walter Crickmer 1937–45
(Secretary-Manager)
Matt Busby 1945–69
(continued as General Manager then Director)
Wilf McGuinness 1969–70
Sir Matt Busby 1970–71
Frank O'Farrell 1971–72
Tommy Docherty 1972–77
Dave Sexton 1977–81
Ron Atkinson 1981–86
Sir Alex Ferguson 1986–2013
David Moyes 2013–14
Louis van Gaal 2014–16
Jose Mourinho 2016–18
Ole Gunnar Solskjaer December 2018–

LATEST SEQUENCES

Longest Sequence of League Wins: 14, 15.10.1904 – 3.1.1905.

Longest Sequence of League Defeats: 14, 26.4.1930 – 25.10.1930.

Longest Sequence of League Draws: 6, 30.10.1988 – 27.11.1988.

Longest Sequence of Unbeaten League Matches: 29, 11.4.2010 – 1.2.2011.

Longest Sequence Without a League Win: 16, 19.4.1930 – 25.10.1930.

Successive Scoring Runs: 36 from 3.12.2007.

Successive Non-scoring Runs: 5 from 7.2.1981.

TEN YEAR LEAGUE RECORD

		P	W	D	L	F	A	Pts	Pos
2010-11	PR Lge	38	23	11	4	78	37	80	1
2011-12	PR Lge	38	28	5	5	89	33	89	2
2012-13	PR Lge	38	28	5	5	86	43	89	1
2013-14	PR Lge	38	19	7	12	64	43	64	7
2014-15	PR Lge	38	20	10	8	62	37	70	4
2015-16	PR Lge	38	19	9	10	49	35	66	5
2016-17	PR Lge	38	18	15	5	54	29	69	6
2017-18	PR Lge	38	25	6	7	68	28	81	2
2018-19	PR Lge	38	19	9	10	65	54	66	6
2019-20	PR Lge	38	18	12	8	66	36	66	3

DID YOU KNOW?

Manchester United first appeared on the BBC's iconic *Match of the Day* programme on 5 September 1964, the third edition of the new highlights show. On that occasion United lost 2-1 to Fulham at Craven Cottage. The Red Devils were struggling in the lower half of the First Division table at the time but went on to win the title.

MANCHESTER UNITED – PREMIER LEAGUE 2019–20 LEAGUE RECORD

Match No.	*Date*	*Venue*	*Opponents*	*Result*		*H/T Score*	*Lg Pos.*	*Goalscorers*	*Atten-dance*
1	Aug 11	H	Chelsea	W	4-0	1-0	2	Rashford 2 (1 pen) [18 (p), 67], Martial [65], James [81]	73,620
2	19	A	Wolverhampton W	D	1-1	1-0	4	Martial [27]	31,314
3	24	H	Crystal Palace	L	1-2	0-1	5	James [89]	73,454
4	31	A	Southampton	D	1-1	1-0	7	James [10]	30,499
5	Sept 14	H	Leicester C	W	1-0	1-0	4	Rashford (pen) [8]	73,689
6	22	A	West Ham U	L	0-2	0-1	8		59,936
7	30	H	Arsenal	D	1-1	1-0	10	McTominay [45]	73,201
8	Oct 6	A	Newcastle U	L	0-1	0-0	12		51,198
9	20	H	Liverpool	D	1-1	1-0	13	Rashford [36]	73,737
10	27	A	Norwich C	W	3-1	2-0	7	McTominay [21], Rashford [30], Martial [73]	27,108
11	Nov 2	A	Bournemouth	L	0-1	0-1	10		10,669
12	10	H	Brighton & HA	W	3-1	2-0	7	Pereira [17], McTominay [19], Rashford [66]	73,556
13	24	A	Sheffield U	D	3-3	0-1	9	Williams [72], Greenwood [77], Rashford [79]	32,024
14	Dec 1	H	Aston Villa	D	2-2	1-1	9	Heaton (og) [42], Lindelof [64]	73,381
15	4	H	Tottenham H	W	2-1	1-1	6	Rashford 2 (1 pen) [6, 49 (p)]	73,252
16	7	A	Manchester C	W	2-1	2-0	5	Rashford (pen) [23], Martial [29]	54,403
17	15	H	Everton	D	1-1	0-1	6	Greenwood [77]	63,328
18	22	A	Watford	L	0-2	0-0	8		21,488
19	26	H	Newcastle U	W	4-1	3-1	7	Martial 2 [24, 51], Greenwood [36], Rashford [41]	73,206
20	28	A	Burnley	W	2-0	1-0	5	Martial [44], Rashford [90]	21,924
21	Jan 1	A	Arsenal	L	0-2	0-2	5		60,328
22	11	H	Norwich C	W	4-0	1-0	5	Rashford 2 (1 pen) [27, 52 (p)], Martial [54], Greenwood [76]	73,271
23	19	A	Liverpool	L	0-2	0-1	5		52,916
24	22	H	Burnley	L	0-2	0-1	5		73,198
25	Feb 1	H	Wolverhampton W	D	0-0	0-0	6		73,363
26	17	A	Chelsea	W	2-0	1-0	7	Martial [45], Maguire [66]	40,504
27	23	H	Watford	W	3-0	1-0	5	Bruno Fernandes (pen) [42], Martial [58], Greenwood [75]	73,347
28	Mar 1	A	Everton	D	1-1	1-1	5	Bruno Fernandes [31]	39,374
29	8	H	Manchester C	W	2-0	1-0	5	Martial [30], McTominay [90]	73,288
30	June 19	A	Tottenham H	D	1-1	0-1	5	Bruno Fernandes (pen) [81]	0
31	24	H	Sheffield U	W	3-0	2-0	5	Martial 3 [7, 44, 74]	0
32	30	A	Brighton & HA	W	3-0	2-0	5	Greenwood [16], Bruno Fernandes 2 [29, 50]	0
33	July 4	H	Bournemouth	W	5-2	3-1	5	Greenwood 2 [29, 54], Rashford (pen) [35], Martial [45], Bruno Fernandes [59]	0
34	9	A	Aston Villa	W	3-0	2-0	5	Bruno Fernandes (pen) [27], Greenwood [45], Pogba [58]	0
35	13	H	Southampton	D	2-2	2-1	5	Rashford [20], Martial [23]	0
36	16	A	Crystal Palace	W	2-0	1-0	5	Rashford [45], Martial [78]	0
37	22	H	West Ham U	D	1-1	0-1	3	Greenwood [51]	0
38	26	A	Leicester C	W	2-0	0-0	3	Bruno Fernandes (pen) [71], Lingard [90]	0

Final League Position: 3

GOALSCORERS

League (66): Martial 17, Rashford 17 (6 pens), Greenwood 10, Bruno Fernandes 8 (4 pens), McTominay 4, James 3, Lindelof 1, Lingard 1, Maguire 1, Pereira 1, Pogba 1, Williams 1, own goal 1.
FA Cup (13): Ighalo 3, Maguire 2, Bruno Fernandes 1 (1 pen), Dalot 1, Greenwood 1 (1 pen), Jones 1, Lingard 1, Martial 1, Mata 1, Shaw 1.
Carabao Cup (8): Rashford 4 (1 pen), Greenwood 1, Martial 1, Matic 1, own goal 1.
UEFA Europa League (25): Greenwood 5, Martial 4 (1 pen), Bruno Fernandes 3 (3 pens), Fred 2, Ighalo 2, Lingard 2, Mata 2 (1 pen), Andreas Pereira 1, James 1, McTominay 1, Rashford 1, Young 1.
Leasing.com Trophy (7): Chong 2, Galbraith 1, Garner 1, Greenwood 1, Laird 1, Ramazani 1.

De Gea D 38	Wan Bissaka A 34 + 1	Maguire H 38	Lindelof V 35	Shaw L 20 + 4	McTominay S 20 + 7	Pogba P 13 + 3	Lingard J 9 + 13	Pereira A 18 + 7	Rashford M 31	Martial A 31 + 1	James D 26 + 7	Greenwood M 12 + 19	Mata J 8 + 11	Young A 10 + 2	Matic N 18 + 3	Fred F 23 + 6	Chong T — + 3	Tuanzebe A 2 + 3	Gomes A — + 2	Dalot D 1 + 3	Rojo M 1 + 2	Williams B 11 + 6	Garner J — + 1	Jones P 2	Bruno Fernandes M 14	Bailly E 1 + 3	Ighalo O — + 11	Fosu-Mensah T 2 + 1	*Match No.*
1	2	3	4	5	6	7	8^{3}	9^{1}	10^{2}	11	12	13	14																1
1	2	4	3	5	7	6	9^{1}	13	10^{3}	11	8^{2}	14	12																2
1	2	4	3	5^{1}	7^{3}	6	9^{2}		10	11	8	13	14	12															3
1	2	4	3		7^{3}	6	12	8^{1}	11		10	14	9^{2}	5	13														4
1	2	4	3		6			8	11		10^{3}		9^{2}	5	7^{1}	12	13	14											5
1	2	4	3		6		12	8	11^{1}		10		9^{3}	5	7^{2}	13			14										6
1		4	3		6	7	9^{1}	8^{2}	11		10	12		2		13		5											7
1		4			6			8	11		10	13	9^{2}	5^{3}		7	14	3		2^{1}	12								8
1	5	3	2		6			9^{2}	11^{1}	12	10			8		7					4	13							9
1	2	4	3		6		13	9^{3}	10	11^{1}	8^{2}	12		5		7							14						10
1	2^{3}	4	3		6		12	9^{1}	10	11	8^{2}	13		5		7						14							11
1	2	4	3		6		12	9^{1}	10^{3}	11	8	13				7					14	5^{2}							12
1	5	3	2				12	6^{2}	10	11^{3}	9	13				7		14				8		4^{1}					13
1	2	4	3	13			12	6	10	11^{3}	8	14	9^{1}			7						5^{2}							14
1	2	4	3	13	6		9^{2}	12	10		8	11^{1}		5		7													15
1	2	4	3	5^{2}	6		9^{3}	12	10	11^{1}	8			13		7		14											16
1	2	4	3	5	6		9^{1}		10	11	8^{2}	12	13			7													17
1	2	4	3	5	6^{3}	13	9^{2}		10	11	8^{1}	12	14			7													18
1	2	4	3	5	6^{1}	12	13	9	10^{2}	11^{3}		8	14			7													19
1		4	3	13			12	9^{1}	10	11^{2}	8			2	7	6						5							20
1	2	4	3	5			9^{1}	12	10	11	8^{2}	13	14		7^{3}	6													21
1	2	4	3					9^{2}	10^{1}	11^{3}	12	13	8		7	6			14			5							22
1	5	3	2	4^{3}				9^{2}		11	10	12	13		7	6				14		8^{1}							23
1	2	4		14			13	8^{1}		11	10^{2}	12	9		7	6						5^{3}		3					24
1	2	4	3	5			13	6^{1}		11	10^{2}	12	8^{3}			7				14					9				25
1	5	3		4				12		11^{3}	10^{1}				7	6				13		8			9^{2}	2	14		26
1	2	4	3	5	12					11^{3}	10	8^{2}			7	6^{1}	13								9		14		27
1	2	4	3	5	7^{2}					11^{3}		10^{1}	13		6	8						14			9		12		28
1	5	3	2	4	12					11^{2}	10				7	6						8^{1}			9^{3}	13	14		29
1	2	4	3^{3}	5	6^{5}	13			10	11^{4}	8^{1}	12			15	7^{2}									9	16	14		30
1	2	4	3	5	13	6^{1}		12	10^{2}	11^{4}	14	8^{3}	16		7										9^{5}		15		31
1	2	4	3	5^{3}	12	6^{1}		14	10^{5}	11^{4}	15	8			7							13			9^{2}		16		32
1	2	4	3^{1}	5		6			10^{5}	11^{4}	14	8^{3}	16		7^{2}	13									9	12	15		33
1	2^{1}	4	3	5	12	6			10	11^{5}	15	8^{4}			7^{2}	14						13			9^{3}		16		34
1	2	4	3	5^{2}	14	6^{1}			10	11	15	8^{4}			7	12						13			9^{3}				35
1	2	4	3		6^{2}	7	12		10	11		8^{1}			13										9			5	36
1	12	4	3			6			10^{2}	11		8			7							5			9		13	2^{1}	37
1	2	4	3		13	6	12		10^{3}	11^{4}		8^{1}			7							5			9^{2}		14	15	38

FA Cup

Third Round	Wolverhampton W	(a)	0-0
Replay	Wolverhampton W	(h)	1-0
Fourth Round	Tranmere R	(a)	6-0
Fifth Round	Derby Co	(a)	3-0
Sixth Round	Norwich C	(a)	2-1
(*aet*)			
Semi-Final	Chelsea	(Wembley)	1-3

Carabao Cup

Third Round	Rochdale	(h)	1-1
(Manchester U won 5-3 on penalties)			
Fourth Round	Chelsea	(a)	2-1
Quarter-Final	Colchester U	(h)	3-0
Semi-Final 1st leg	Manchester C	(h)	1-3
Semi-Final 2nd leg	Manchester C	(a)	1-0

Leasing.com Trophy (Manchester U U21)

Group H (N)	Rotherham U	(a)	2-0
Group H (N)	Lincoln C	(a)	1-0
Group H (N)	Doncaster R	(a)	2-1
Second Round (N)	Tranmere R	(a)	2-3

UEFA Europa League

Group L	Astana	(h)	1-0
Group L	AZ Alkmaar	(a)	0-0
Group L	Partizan Belgrade	(a)	1-0
Group L	Partizan Belgrade	(h)	3-0
Group L	Astana	(a)	1-2
Group L	AZ Alkmaar	(h)	4-0
Round of 32	Club Brugge	(a)	1-1
Round of 32	Club Brugge	(h)	5-0
Round of 16	LASK	(a)	5-0
Round of 16	LASK	(h)	2-1
Quarter-Finals	FC Copenhagen	(Cologne)	1-0
(*aet.*)			
Semi-Finals	Sevilla	(Cologne)	1-2

MANSFIELD TOWN

FOUNDATION

The club was formed as Mansfield Wesleyans in 1897, and changed their name to Mansfield Wesley in 1906 and Mansfield Town in 1910. This was after the Mansfield Wesleyan Chapel trustees had requested that the club change its name as 'it has no longer had any connection with either the chapel or school'. The new club participated in the Notts and Derby District League, but in the following season 1911–12 joined the Central Alliance.

One Call Stadium, Quarry Lane, Mansfield, Nottinghamshire NG18 5DA.

Telephone: (01623) 482 482.

Ticket Office: (01623) 482 482.

Website: www.mansfieldtown.net

Email: info@mansfieldtown.net

Ground Capacity: 9,376.

Record Attendance: 24,467 v Nottingham F, FA Cup 3rd rd, 10 January 1953.

Pitch Measurements: 100.5m × 64m (110yd × 70yd).

Chairman: John Radford.

Chief Executive: Carolyn Radford.

Manager: Graham Coughlan.

Assistant Manager: Joe Dunne.

Colours: Yellow shirts with blue trim, blue shorts with yellow trim, yellow socks with blue trim.

Year Formed: 1897.

Turned Professional: 1906.

Ltd Co.: 1922.

Previous Name: 1897, Mansfield Wesleyans; 1906, Mansfield Wesley; 1910, Mansfield Town.

Grounds: 1897–99, Westfield Lane; 1899–1901, Ratcliffe Gate; 1901–12, Newgate Lane; 1912–16, Ratcliffe Gate; 1916, Field Mill (renamed One Call Stadium 2012).

Club Nickname: 'The Stags'.

First Football League Game: 29 August 1931, Division 3 (S), v Swindon T (h) W 3–2 – Wilson; Clifford, England; Wake, Davis, Blackburn; Gilhespy, Readman (1), Johnson, Broom (2), Baxter.

Record League Victory: 9–2 v Rotherham U, Division 3 (N), 27 December 1932 – Wilson; Anthony, England; Davies, S. Robinson, Slack; Prior, Broom, Readman (3), Hoyland (3), Bowater (3).

Record Cup Victory: 8–0 v Scarborough (a), FA Cup 1st rd, 22 November 1952 – Bramley; Chessell, Bradley; Field, Plummer, Lewis; Scott, Fox (3), Marron (2), Sid Watson (1), Adam (2).

Record Defeat: 1–8 v Walsall, Division 3 (N), 19 January 1933.

Most League Points (2 for a win): 68, Division 4, 1974–75.

Most League Points (3 for a win): 81, Division 4, 1985–86.

HONOURS

League Champions: Division 3 – 1976–77; Division 4 – 1974–75; Conference – 2012–13.
Runners-up: Division 3N – 1950–51, Third Division – (3rd) 2001–02 *(promoted to Second Division)*.

FA Cup: 6th rd – 1969.

League Cup: 5th rd – 1976.

League Trophy Winners: 1987.

FOOTBALL YEARBOOK FACT FILE

Mansfield Town played at home against Halifax Town on 22 occasions in Football League matches without suffering a defeat, including a spell of 16 consecutive victories. The Stags lost to the West Yorkshire club at Field Mill for the first time in November 1980, almost 48 years after their initial encounter.

Most League Goals: 108, Division 4, 1962–63.

Highest League Scorer in Season: Ted Harston, 55, Division 3 (N), 1936–37.

Most League Goals in Total Aggregate: Harry Johnson, 104, 1931–36.

Most League Goals in One Match: 7, Ted Harston v Hartlepools U, Division 3N, 23 January 1937.

Most Capped Player: John McClelland, 6 (53), Northern Ireland; Reggie Lambe, 6 (41), Bermuda; Omari Sterling-James, 6 (8), Saint Kitts & Nevis.

Most League Appearances: Rod Arnold, 440, 1970–83.

Youngest League Player: Cyril Poole, 15 years 351 days v New Brighton, 27 February 1937.

Record Transfer Fee Received: £30,000 (rising to £655,000) from Swindon T for Colin Calderwood, July 1985.

Record Transfer Fee Paid: £150,000 to Peterborough U for Lee Angol, May 2017.

Football League Record: 1931 Elected to Division 3 (S); 1932–37 Division 3 (N); 1937–47 Division 3 (S); 1947–58 Division 3 (N); 1958–60 Division 3; 1960–63 Division 4; 1963–72 Division 3; 1972–75 Division 4; 1975–77 Division 3; 1977–78 Division 2; 1978–80 Division 3; 1980–86 Division 4; 1986–91 Division 3; 1991–92 Division 4; 1992–93 Division 2; 1993–2002 Division 3; 2002–03 Division 2; 2003–04 Division 3; 2004–08 FL 2; 2008–13 Conference Premier; 2013– FL 2.

LATEST SEQUENCES

Longest Sequence of League Wins: 7, 13.9.1991 – 26.10.1991.

Longest Sequence of League Defeats: 7, 18.1.1947 – 15.3.1947.

Longest Sequence of League Draws: 5, 18.10.1986 – 22.11.1986.

Longest Sequence of Unbeaten League Matches: 20, 14.2.1976 – 21.8.1976.

Longest Sequence Without a League Win: 14, 25.3.2000 – 2.9.2000.

Successive Scoring Runs: 27 from 1.10.1962.

Successive Non-scoring Runs: 8 from 25.3.2000.

MANAGERS

John Baynes 1922–25
Ted Davison 1926–28
Jack Hickling 1928–33
Henry Martin 1933–35
Charlie Bell 1935
Harold Wightman 1936
Harold Parkes 1936–38
Jack Poole 1938–44
Lloyd Barke 1944–45
Roy Goodall 1945–49
Freddie Steele 1949–51
George Jobey 1952–53
Stan Mercer 1953–55
Charlie Mitten 1956–58
Sam Weaver 1958–60
Raich Carter 1960–63
Tommy Cummings 1963–67
Tommy Eggleston 1967–70
Jock Basford 1970–71
Danny Williams 1971–74
Dave Smith 1974–76
Peter Morris 1976–78
Billy Bingham 1978–79
Mick Jones 1979–81
Stuart Boam 1981–83
Ian Greaves 1983–89
George Foster 1989–93
Andy King 1993–96
Steve Parkin 1996–99
Billy Dearden 1999–2002
Stuart Watkiss 2002
Keith Curle 2002–04
Carlton Palmer 2004–05
Peter Shirtliff 2005–06
Billy Dearden 2006–08
Paul Holland 2008
Billy McEwan 2008
David Holdsworth 2008–10
Duncan Russell 2010–11
Paul Cox 2011–14
Adam Murray 2014–16
Steve Evans 2016–18
David Flitcroft 2018–19
John Dempster 2019
Graham Coughlan December 2019–

TEN YEAR LEAGUE RECORD

		P	*W*	*D*	*L*	*F*	*A*	*Pts*	*Pos*
2010-11	Conf P	46	17	10	19	73	75	61	13
2011-12	Conf P	46	25	14	7	87	48	89	3
2012-13	Conf P	46	30	5	11	92	52	95	1
2013-14	FL 2	46	15	15	16	49	58	60	11
2014-15	FL 2	46	13	9	24	38	62	48	21
2015-16	FL 2	46	17	13	16	61	53	64	12
2016-17	FL 2	46	17	15	14	54	50	66	12
2017-18	FL 2	46	18	18	10	67	52	72	8
2018-19	FL 2	46	20	16	10	69	41	76	4
2019-20	FL 2	36	9	11	16	48	55	38	21§

§*Decided on points-per-game (1.06)*

DID YOU KNOW ?

The highest attendance for a Mansfield Town Football League match during the regular season was 37,726 for the game at Ninian Park, Cardiff, on 27 December 1937. Having beaten Cardiff City 3-0 at Field Mill on Christmas Day they went down to a 4-1 defeat two days later.

MANSFIELD TOWN – SKY BET LEAGUE TWO 2019–20 LEAGUE RECORD

Match No.	Date	Venue	Opponents	Result		H/T Score	Lg Pos.	Goalscorers	Attendance
1	Aug 3	A	Newport Co	D	2-2	0-2	10	Pearce [47], Rose [49]	4481
2	10	H	Morecambe	D	2-2	1-2	14	Maynard [39], Rose [72]	4465
3	17	A	Carlisle U	W	2-0	2-0	8	Rose [28], Maynard [45]	4576
4	20	H	Leyton Orient	L	2-3	2-0	13	Rose 2 (2 pens) [12, 29]	4128
5	24	H	Stevenage	D	0-0	0-0	14		3982
6	31	A	Exeter C	L	0-1	0-1	19		4316
7	Sept 7	H	Scunthorpe U	W	2-0	1-0	12	Preston [31], Rose [54]	4772
8	14	A	Crawley T	L	0-1	0-0	16		2068
9	17	H	Cambridge U	L	0-4	0-0	18		3567
10	21	A	Port Vale	D	2-2	1-1	20	Gordon [14], Rose (pen) [75]	5109
11	28	H	Plymouth Arg	L	0-1	0-1	20		4499
12	Oct 5	A	Grimsby T	W	1-0	0-0	19	Pearce [90]	5087
13	12	H	Oldham Ath	W	6-1	3-1	15	Maynard 3 [31, 34, 45], Wheater (og) [56], Afolayan [66], Knowles (pen) [83]	4368
14	19	A	Forest Green R	D	2-2	0-1	17	Cook 2 [63, 74]	2276
15	22	H	Salford C	L	1-2	0-0	18	Maynard [77]	4170
16	26	A	Walsall	W	2-1	1-1	14	Cook [30], MacDonald [68]	4521
17	Nov 2	H	Colchester U	L	2-3	1-1	14	Sweeney [45], Sterling-James [90]	4125
18	16	A	Macclesfield T	D	0-0	0-0	14		2055
19	23	A	Swindon T	L	0-1	0-1	15		6741
20	Dec 7	H	Cheltenham T	L	0-3	0-1	18		3715
21	14	A	Crewe Alex	D	1-1	1-1	18	Cook [27]	4060
22	21	H	Northampton T	D	1-1	0-0	18	Cook [74]	4496
23	26	H	Port Vale	D	2-2	0-0	20	Maynard [81], Hamilton [90]	5565
24	29	A	Bradford C	L	0-2	0-1	21		15,197
25	Jan 1	A	Cambridge U	W	3-2	1-2	17	Maynard 3 [36, 71, 81]	3848
26	4	H	Grimsby T	L	0-1	0-0	19		5848
27	11	H	Forest Green R	L	3-4	2-1	19	Hamilton [3], Rose [40], Maynard [90]	3956
28	18	A	Plymouth Arg	L	1-3	0-1	20	Cook [66]	10,523
29	25	H	Bradford C	W	3-0	2-0	19	Rose [7], Maynard [43], Cook [77]	5537
30	28	A	Oldham Ath	L	1-3	0-2	22	Khan [90]	2961
31	Feb 1	H	Carlisle U	D	2-2	0-0	22	Maynard 2 [58, 72]	4272
32	8	A	Morecambe	D	1-1	0-0	22	Riley [60]	1965
33	11	A	Leyton Orient	L	1-2	0-1	22	Watts [60]	3587
34	15	H	Newport Co	W	1-0	1-0	20	Rose [29]	3653
35	22	A	Cheltenham T	L	0-1	0-0	22		3274
36	Mar 7	A	Northampton T	W	2-1	1-0	21	Rose (pen) [12], Tomlinson [74]	5666
37	14	H	Crewe Alex	Cancelled					
38	17	A	Salford C	Cancelled					
39	21	H	Walsall	Cancelled					
40	28	A	Colchester U	Cancelled					
41	31	H	Swindon T	Cancelled					
42	Apr 4	H	Macclesfield T	Cancelled					
43	10	A	Stevenage	Cancelled					
44	13	H	Exeter C	Cancelled					
45	18	A	Scunthorpe U	Cancelled					
46	25	H	Crawley T	Cancelled					

Final League Position: 21 (on points-per-game basis)

GOALSCORERS

League (48): Maynard 14, Rose 11 (4 pens), Cook 7, Hamilton 2, Pearce 2, Afolayan 1, Gordon 1, Khan 1, Knowles 1 (1 pen), MacDonald 1, Preston 1, Riley 1, Sterling-James 1, Sweeney 1, Tomlinson 1, Watts 1, own goal 1.
FA Cup (1): Maynard 1.
Carabao Cup (2): Pearce 1, Sterling-James 1.
Leasing.com Trophy (6): Sterling-James 2, Hamilton 1, Knowles 1, Rose 1, Sweeney 1.

Logan C 22	Preston M 20 + 2	Sweeney R 32 + 1	Pearce K 28 + 1	Hamilton C 25 + 9	MacDonald A 27 + 2	Bishop N 27 + 1	Mellis J 9 + 4	Benning M 30 + 3	Maynard N 29 + 4	Rose D 28 + 3	Gordon K 17 + 1	Khan O 12 + 9	Cook A 10 + 13	White H 9 + 1	Tomlinson W 15 + 3	Smith A 1 + 4	Clarke J 6 + 6	Sterling-James O 1 + 7	Knowles J — + 5	Shaughnessy C 14 + 1	Afolayan O — + 6	Olejnik R 11	Davies C — + 5	Charsley H 7 + 2	Riley J 6	Watts K 7	Stone A 3	*Match No.*
1	2	3[3]	4	5[1]	6	7	8■	9	10[2]	11	12	13	14															1
1	4■	12	3	6	8	7		5	10[1]	11[2]	2	9	13															2
1		4	3	12	7[2]	6[1]		9	11[3]	10	5	14		2	8	13												3
1		4	3	13	6			8	11[1]	10	5	9[3]		2[2]	7	12	14											4
1	3	4		9	6[2]		8	5		11		10[1]			7		2	12	13									5
1	2[1]	4■	3	13	6		9	8	10	11	5				7[2]			12										6
1	2	4	3	8	6	12	9[2]	13	11[1]	10	5									7								7
1	2	4[2]	3	8	6[1]		9	12	10[3]	11	5							14		7	13							8
1	2■	4	3	11	12	6		8[1]		10	5[3]	14	13					9[2]		7								9
1		4	3	11	12	7		8		10	5	9[1]		2						6								10
1		4	3	11[2]	6	7		8	14	10	5	9[3]	13							2[1]	12							11
1		4	3	12	6	7		8	11[3]	10[2]	5	9[1]	13	2■						14								12
1		4	3		6[3]	7		8	10[1]	11[2]	5	9	12						14	2	13							13
1	4		3	9[1]		7		5	10[2]		2	11	12		8[3]				14	6	13							14
1		4	3		6[1]	7		8	11		5	9	10							2	12							15
1	12	4	3[3]	13	6	8		5	11[2]		2	9	10[1]							7	14							16
1	3	4		13	8[2]	7[1]	12	5	10		2	9[3]	11					14		6								17
1	2	4	3	14	9		12	8	11[2]	13	5		10[1]		7[3]					6								18
1	2	4	3	9			7[2]		10		5[1]	13	11			8		12	14	6[3]								19
	3	4		5	6	7[1]	8	9[3]	11	13		12	10[2]					14		2		1						20
	3	4		9	6	7		5	11[3]	13		14	10[1]				2	12		8[2]		1						21
	3	4		9	6	7		5	12	11[2]			10[1]		8[3]	13	2					1	14					22
	3	4		9	6[3]	7[1]	14	5	13	10[2]		12	11		8		2					1						23
1	3	4[1]	12	6	8		13	5	14	11[3]		9[2]	10		7		2											24
1	4		3	9	6	7[2]	8	5	11	10			13	2[1]			12											25
1	3		4	9	6	7[3]	8	5	11	10[1]			12	2[2]			13						14					26
	3	4		9	6[2]	7		5	10	11[1]		14	13		8[3]	12	2					1						27
	3	4	2	9	7	6[1]		8	10	11[3]			13	5[2]			12					1		14				28
		4	3	9	6	7		5	11[2]	10[3]			13		14				12			1		8[1]	2			29
		4	3	9	6			5	11[2]	10[3]		14	13		12							1		8[1]	2	7		30
	14	4	3	13	7[2]	6		8	11[1]	10					12							1		9[3]	5	2		31
		4	3	12		6		8	11[3]	10[1]					7		13					1	14	9	5[2]	2		32
		2	3	9		6		8[2]	11	10					7		12					1		13	5[1]	4		33
		3	2	9		6			10	11				5	7									8		4	1	34
		2	3	8		7		12	11	10				5	6								13	9[1]		4[2]	1	35
		2	3	9		7			11[2]	10				13	6								12	8	5	4[1]	1	36
																												37
																												38
																												39
																												40
																												41
																												42
																												43
																												44
																												45
																												46

FA Cup

First Round	Chorley	(h)	1-0
Second Round	Shrewsbury T	(a)	0-2

Carabao Cup

First Round	Morecambe	(h)	2-2

(Morecambe won 6-5 on penalties)

Leasing.com Trophy

Group E (N)	Everton U21	(h)	1-1

(Everton U21 won 4-1 on penalties)

Group E (N)	Crewe Alex	(h)	1-1

(Crewe Alex won 4-3 on penalties)

Group E (N)	Burton Alb	(a)	2-1
Second Round (N)	Port Vale	(a)	2-2

(Port Vale won 4-2 on penalties)

MIDDLESBROUGH

FOUNDATION

A previous belief that Middlesbrough Football Club was founded at a tripe supper at the Corporation Hotel has proved to be erroneous. In fact, members of Middlesbrough Cricket Club were responsible for forming it at a meeting in the gymnasium of the Albert Park Hotel in 1875.

Riverside Stadium, Middlehaven Way, Middlesbrough TS3 6RS.

Telephone: (01642) 929 420.

Ticket Office: (01642) 929 421.

Website: www.mfc.co.uk

Email: via website.

Ground Capacity: 33,570.

Record Attendance: 53,802 v Newcastle U, Division 1, 27 December 1949 (at Ayresome Park); 34,814 v Newcastle U, Premier League, 5 March 2003 (at Riverside Stadium); 35,000, England v Slovakia, Euro 2004 qualifier, 11 June 2003.

Pitch Measurements: 105m × 68m (115yd × 74.5yd).

Chairman: Steve Gibson.

Chief Executive: Neil Bausor.

Manager: Neil Warnock.

Assistant Manager: Kevin Blackwell.

Colours: Red shirts with white trim, white shorts with red trim, white socks with red trim.

HONOURS

League Champions: First Division – 1994–95; Division 2 – 1926–27, 1928–29, 1973–74.
Runners-up: FL C – 2015–16; First Division – 1997–98; Division 2 – 1901–02, 1991–92; Division 3 – 1966–67, 1986–87.

FA Cup: *Runners-up:* 1997.

League Cup Winners: 2004.
Runners-up: 1997, 1998.

Amateur Cup Winners: 1895, 1898.

Anglo-Scottish Cup Winners: 1976.

Full Members' Cup: *Runners-up:* 1990.

European Competitions
UEFA Cup: 2004–05, 2005–06 *(runners-up).*

Year Formed: 1876; re-formed 1986.

Turned Professional: 1889; became amateur 1892, and professional again, 1899.

Club Nickname: 'Boro'.

Grounds: 1877, Old Archery Ground, Albert Park; 1879, Breckon Hill; 1882, Linthorpe Road Ground; 1903, Ayresome Park; 1995, Riverside Stadium.

First Football League Game: 2 September 1899, Division 2, v Lincoln C (a) L 0–3 – Smith; Shaw, Ramsey; Allport, McNally, McCracken; Wanless, Longstaffe, Gettins, Page, Pugh.

Record League Victory: 9–0 v Brighton & HA, Division 2, 23 August 1958 – Taylor; Bilcliff, Robinson; Harris (2p), Phillips, Walley; Day, McLean, Clough (5), Peacock (2), Holliday.

Record Cup Victory: 7–0 v Hereford U, Coca-Cola Cup 2nd rd, 1st leg, 18 September 1996 – Miller; Fleming (1), Branco (1), Whyte, Vickers, Whelan, Emerson (1), Mustoe, Stamp, Juninho, Ravanelli (4).

Record Defeat: 0–9 v Blackburn R, Division 2, 6 November 1954.

FOOTBALL YEARBOOK FACT FILE

After relegation from the Second Division in 1965–66, Middlesbrough struggled in their first season in the third tier and by mid-September the team were second to bottom of the table. Results slowly improved and remarkably they finished the campaign as runners-up. The only time in the season that they were in the top two places was after their 4-1 victory over Oxford United in their final match.

Most League Points (2 for a win): 65, Division 2, 1973–74.

Most League Points (3 for a win): 94, Division 3, 1986–87.

Most League Goals: 122, Division 2, 1926–27.

Highest League Scorer in Season: George Camsell, 59, Division 2, 1926–27 (Second Division record).

Most League Goals in Total Aggregate: George Camsell, 325, 1925–39.

Most League Goals in One Match: 5, John Wilkie v Gainsborough T, Division 2, 2 March 1901; 5, Andy Wilson v Nottingham F, Division 1, 6 October 1923; 5, George Camsell v Manchester C, Division 2, 25 December 1926; 5, George Camsell v Aston Villa, Division 1, 9 September 1935; 5, Brian Clough v Brighton & HA, Division 2, 22 August 1958.

Most Capped Player: Mark Schwarzer, 52 (109), Australia.

Most League Appearances: Tim Williamson, 563, 1902–23.

Youngest League Player: Luke Williams, 16 years 200 days v Barnsley, 18 December 2009.

Record Transfer Fee Received: £18,000,000 from Wolverhampton W for Adama Traore, August 2019.

Record Transfer Fee Paid: £15,000,000 to Nottingham F for Britt Assombalonga, July 2017.

Football League Record: 1899 Elected to Division 2; 1902–24 Division 1; 1924–27 Division 2; 1927–28 Division 1; 1928–29 Division 2; 1929–54 Division 1; 1954–66 Division 2; 1966–67 Division 3; 1967–74 Division 2; 1974–82 Division 1; 1982–86 Division 2; 1986–87 Division 3; 1987–88 Division 2; 1988–89 Division 1; 1989–92 Division 2; 1992–93 Premier League; 1993–95 Division 1; 1995–97 Premier League; 1997–98 Division 1; 1998–2009 Premier League; 2009–16 FL C; 2016–17 Premier League; 2017– FL C.

MANAGERS

John Robson 1899–1905
Alex Mackie 1905–06
Andy Aitken 1906–09
J. Gunter 1908–10 *(Secretary-Manager)*
Andy Walker 1910–11
Tom McIntosh 1911–19
Jimmy Howie 1920–23
Herbert Bamlett 1923–26
Peter McWilliam 1927–34
Wilf Gillow 1934–44
David Jack 1944–52
Walter Rowley 1952–54
Bob Dennison 1954–63
Raich Carter 1963–66
Stan Anderson 1966–73
Jack Charlton 1973–77
John Neal 1977–81
Bobby Murdoch 1981–82
Malcolm Allison 1982–84
Willie Maddren 1984–86
Bruce Rioch 1986–90
Colin Todd 1990–91
Lennie Lawrence 1991–94
Bryan Robson 1994–2001
Steve McClaren 2001–06
Gareth Southgate 2006–09
Gordon Strachan 2009–10
Tony Mowbray 2010–13
Aitor Karanka 2013–17
Garry Monk 2017
Tony Pulis 2017–19
Jonathan Woodgate 2019–20
Neil Warnock June 2020–

LATEST SEQUENCES

Longest Sequence of League Wins: 9, 16.2.1974 – 6.4.1974.

Longest Sequence of League Defeats: 8, 26.12.1995 – 17.2.1996.

Longest Sequence of League Draws: 8, 3.4.1971 – 1.5.1971.

Longest Sequence of Unbeaten League Matches: 24, 8.9.1973 – 19.1.1974.

Longest Sequence Without a League Win: 19, 3.10.1981 – 6.3.1982.

Successive Scoring Runs: 26 from 21.9.1946.

Successive Non-scoring Runs: 7, 25.1.2014 – 1.3.2014.

TEN YEAR LEAGUE RECORD

		P	W	D	L	F	A	Pts	Pos
2010-11	FL C	46	17	11	18	68	68	62	12
2011-12	FL C	46	18	16	12	52	51	70	7
2012-13	FL C	46	18	5	23	61	70	59	16
2013-14	FL C	46	16	16	14	62	50	64	12
2014-15	FL C	46	25	10	11	68	37	85	4
2015-16	FL C	46	26	11	9	63	31	89	2
2016-17	PR Lge	38	5	13	20	27	53	28	19
2017-18	FL C	46	22	10	14	67	45	76	5
2018-19	FL C	46	20	13	13	49	41	73	7
2019-20	FL C	46	13	14	19	48	61	53	17

DID YOU KNOW ?

Ayresome Park, Middlesbrough's home for 90 years, was built in 1903 at a cost of £6,000. The ground was formally opened on 1 September 1903 when Boro defeated Celtic 1-0 in a friendly match in front of an estimated crowd of 8,000.

MIDDLESBROUGH – SKY BET CHAMPIONSHIP 2019–20 LEAGUE RECORD

Match No.	Date	Venue	Opponents	Result		H/T Score	Lg Pos.	Goalscorers	Attendance
1	Aug 2	A	Luton T	D	3-3	2-2	1	Fletcher [7], Assombalonga [37], Wing [68]	10,053
2	10	H	Brentford	L	0-1	0-0	18		21,911
3	17	A	Blackburn R	L	0-1	0-1	21		14,012
4	20	H	Wigan Ath	W	1-0	1-0	14	Assombalonga [23]	18,649
5	24	H	Millwall	D	1-1	0-0	17	McNair [70]	19,279
6	31	A	Bristol C	D	2-2	0-1	18	Moore (og) [64], Assombalonga [68]	20,757
7	Sept 14	H	Reading	W	1-0	0-0	13	Johnson [60]	19,414
8	21	A	Cardiff C	L	0-1	0-1	15		23,141
9	28	H	Sheffield W	L	1-4	1-4	18	McNair [19]	22,075
10	Oct 1	H	Preston NE	D	1-1	1-1	19	Assombalonga [42]	17,961
11	4	A	Birmingham C	L	1-2	0-1	20	Ayala [87]	19,703
12	19	H	WBA	L	0-1	0-0	21		20,174
13	23	A	Huddersfield T	D	0-0	0-0	21		22,839
14	26	H	Fulham	D	0-0	0-0	22		19,101
15	Nov 2	A	Derby Co	L	0-2	0-1	22		26,293
16	9	A	QPR	D	2-2	1-2	22	Assombalonga 2 [23, 69]	14,404
17	24	H	Hull C	D	2-2	2-0	21	Tavernier [7], Fletcher [26]	18,596
18	27	H	Barnsley	W	1-0	0-0	20	Fletcher [54]	18,043
19	30	A	Leeds U	L	0-4	0-2	20		35,626
20	Dec 7	H	Charlton Ath	W	1-0	1-0	19	Saville [1]	18,681
21	10	A	Nottingham F	D	1-1	0-0	20	McNair (pen) [81]	24,577
22	14	A	Swansea C	L	1-3	0-1	20	Tavernier [59]	14,625
23	20	H	Stoke C	W	2-1	0-0	18	Fletcher [57], Wing [71]	18,270
24	26	H	Huddersfield T	W	1-0	1-0	19	Spence [37]	25,313
25	29	A	WBA	W	2-0	1-0	16	Ayala [17], Fletcher [90]	25,077
26	Jan 1	A	Preston NE	W	2-0	1-0	16	Gestede [40], Fletcher [62]	13,824
27	11	H	Derby Co	D	2-2	1-0	16	Wing [16], McNair (pen) [67]	19,706
28	17	A	Fulham	L	0-1	0-1	16		18,375
29	21	H	Birmingham C	D	1-1	0-1	17	Fletcher [81]	18,350
30	Feb 1	H	Blackburn R	D	1-1	0-0	18	Coulson [75]	19,937
31	8	A	Brentford	L	2-3	0-1	18	Wing [58], Fletcher [63]	12,285
32	11	A	Wigan Ath	D	2-2	0-1	18	Wing 2 [64, 68]	9023
33	15	H	Luton T	L	0-1	0-1	18		19,734
34	22	A	Barnsley	L	0-1	0-0	20		16,106
35	26	H	Leeds U	L	0-1	0-1	21		24,647
36	Mar 2	H	Nottingham F	D	2-2	2-1	22	Gestede [40], Wing [44]	18,884
37	7	A	Charlton Ath	W	1-0	1-0	19	McNair [17]	18,080
38	June 20	H	Swansea C	L	0-3	0-3	21		0
39	27	A	Stoke C	W	2-0	1-0	19	Fletcher [29], Tavernier [62]	0
40	July 2	A	Hull C	L	1-2	1-1	21	Assombalonga (pen) [4]	0
41	5	H	QPR	L	0-1	0-1	22		0
42	8	A	Millwall	W	2-0	0-0	18	Assombalonga [68], Fletcher (pen) [87]	0
43	11	H	Bristol C	L	1-3	0-2	18	Assombalonga [82]	0
44	14	A	Reading	W	2-1	1-1	17	Fletcher [45], Roberts [82]	0
45	18	H	Cardiff C	L	1-3	0-1	19	Assombalonga [85]	0
46	22	A	Sheffield W	W	2-1	1-1	18	McNair [22], Assombalonga [90]	0

Final League Position: 17

GOALSCORERS

League (48): Assombalonga 11 (1 pen), Fletcher 11 (1 pen), Wing 7, McNair 6 (2 pens), Tavernier 3, Ayala 2, Gestede 2, Coulson 1, Johnson 1, Roberts 1, Saville 1, Spence 1, own goal 1.
FA Cup (2): Fletcher 1, Saville 1.
Carabao Cup (2): Bola 1, Fletcher 1.

Randolph D 14	Howson J 41	Ayala D 23 + 2	Shotton R 20 + 1	Coulson H 20 + 9	Wing L 28 + 12	Clayton A 21 + 6	McNair P 36 + 5	Johnson M 29 + 9	Assombalonga B 27 + 8	Fletcher A 37 + 6	Browne M 5 + 8	Saville G 31 + 6	Dijksteel A 12 + 4	Gestede R 5 + 14	Friend G 14	Tavernier M 27 + 10	Walker S 1 + 6	Bola M 6 + 1	Fry D 36	Pears A 24	Liddle B — + 1	O'Neill T — + 1	Spence D 18 + 4	Roberts P 8 + 2	Nmecha L 4 + 7	Wood-Gordon N — + 1	Moukoudi H 8	Morrison R 3	Stojanovic D 8	*Match No.*
1	2	3	4	5	6	7	8[2]	9[1]	10	11	12	13																		1
1	2	3	4	5	6	7[2]	8	9[1]	10	11[3]	13		12	14																2
1	9	3	4		7		6	8[2]	11	10	13		2[1]		5[3]	12	14													3
1	2	3	4		8	7	6	12	10	9[3]	11[1]	13		14				5[2]												4
1	2	3	4		13	7[2]	6	12	10	9	11[1]	8						5												5
1			4		8	7	6	9[1]	10	11[2]		12	2	13				5	3											6
1		12	4		8[2]	7	6	9[3]	10	11		13	2			14		5[1]	3											7
1		3	4		13	7[2]	6	9[3]	10	11	12	8[1]	5			14			2											8
1		13	4		8	7[1]	6	9[3]	10	11	12		2				14	5[2]	3											9
1	8	3	5			7	6	13	10[2]	12	11[1]		2			9			4											10
1	8	3	5		13	7[1]	6		10	12	11[2]		2[3]	14		9			4											11
1	5	3	4		7		6	9	11	12	13	8[2]				10[1]			2											12
	5	3	4	13	7	14	6	9[2]	12	11[1]		8[3]				10			2	1										13
	5	3		9[2]	7		2	13	10	11	12	8[1]				6			4	1										14
	5	3		13	7[3]		2	9[2]	11		10[1]	8■	12			6	14		4	1										15
1	5[1]	3			7	13	6	9	11	10			12		4	8[2]			2											16
1	2	3			7	12	6	9■	10	11[1]			5			8			4											17
	2	3		9	7	13	6[2]		11	10			5[1]			8		12	4	1										18
	5	3			6[1]		2		11[2]	10[3]		8				7	14	9	4	1	12	13								19
	2	3		9		7			10[1]	11		6				8	12		4	1			5							20
	3	4		6		8[2]	7	12		11		9				10	13		5	1			2[1]							21
	2	3		5	14	7[1]	6■	9[3]		10	12■	8[2]		13		11			4	1										22
	2	3		9	12	7[1]		14		10		6		13		8	11[2]		4	1			5[3]							23
	3	4		6	8			7[1]		11		9		12		10			5	1			2							24
	2	3		5	9[2]	6		12		11		7		13		10			4	1			8[1]							25
	2	3[1]		13	14	6	12	8		11		7		10		9[3]			4	1			5[2]							26
	2			8	6		3			11[2]		7		13		10			4	1			5	9[1]	12					27
	2			8	12	6[2]	3			13		7[3]		11		10[1]			4	1			5	9	14					28
	2				6		3	8		10		7[3]		14		12			4[2]	1			5	9[1]	11	13				29
	2			13	6		3	8	12	11		7[2]		14		9[1]			4	1			5		10[3]					30
	2			5	9		6	10[1]	12	11[3]		7		14		8[2]			4	1					13		3			31
	2			5	8		6		11[1]	10		7				13			4[3]	1			14		12		3	9[2]		32
	2			9	8		6		12	10		7[1]		13	4					1			5[2]		11		3			33
	5		3	13	6		14	9	11[1]	10		7[2]		12	4					1							2	8[3]		34
	2		3	10	9	6		12	14	11[3]		7[2]			5[1]	8				1					13		4			35
	2		3	10	9[1]	6	7	5				12		11		8[2]				1			13				4			36
	2		3	10	9	6	7[1]	5				12		11		8[2]							13				4		1	37
	2		3[1]	11[3]	8	7[2]	6	14	16	15				10[4]	5				4				13	12	9[5]				1	38
	7		14		13		6[2]	5	11	10		8[3]			4	12			3				2	9[1]					1	39
	7			11	12		6	5	10[3]	14		8			4	13			3				2[1]	9[2]					1	40
	2			15	12		14	5[4]	11	10[3]		9[1]			4	16			3					7[5]	13		6	8[2]	1	41
	8		4			13	7[2]	6	11[1]	10		9	14		5	12			3				2[3]						1	42
	8[5]		4[2]	15	12	16	7[4]	6	11	10[3]		9[1]			5	14			3				2	13					1	43
	6			14			13	5	12	11[1]		7	2[2]		4	10			3	1			8	9[3]						44
	7■			12			13	5	14	11[4]		6[3]	2[1]		4	10			3	1			8	9[2]	15					45
					12		7	9	11	10		8	2		3	6[1]			4				5						1	46

FA Cup
Third Round Tottenham H (h) 1-1
Replay Tottenham H (a) 1-2

Carabao Cup
First Round Crewe Alex (h) 2-2
(Crewe Alex won 4-2 on penalties)

MILLWALL

FOUNDATION

Formed in 1885 as Millwall Rovers by employees of Morton & Co, a jam and marmalade factory in West Ferry Road. The founders were predominantly Scotsmen. Their first headquarters was The Islanders pub in Tooke Street, Millwall. Their first trophy was the East End Cup in 1887.

The Den, Zampa Road, Bermondsey, London SE16 3LN.

Telephone: (020) 7232 1222.

Ticket Office: (0844) 826 2004.

Website: www.millwallfc.co.uk

Email: questions@millwallplc.com

Ground Capacity: 19,734.

Record Attendance: 48,672 v Derby Co, FA Cup 5th rd, 20 February 1937 (at The Den, Cold Blow Lane); 20,093 v Arsenal, FA Cup 3rd rd, 10 January 1994 (at The Den, Bermondsey).

Pitch Measurements: 106m × 68m (116yd × 74.5yd).

Chairman: John Berylson.

Chief Executive: Steve Kavanagh.

Manager: Gary Rowett.

Assistant Manager: Callum Davidson.

HONOURS

League Champions: Division 2 – 1987–88; Second Division – 2000–01; Division 3S – 1927–28, 1937–38; Division 4 – 1961–62.
Runners-up: Division 3 – 1965–66, 1984–85; Division 3S – 1952–53; Division 4 – 1964–65.

FA Cup: *Runners-up:* 2004.

League Cup: 5th rd – 1974, 1977, 1995.

League Trophy: *Runners-up:* 1999.

European Competitions
UEFA Cup: 2004–05.

Colours: Blue shirts with white trim, white shorts with blue trim, blue socks with white trim.

Year Formed: 1885.

Turned Professional: 1893.

Previous Names: 1885, Millwall Rovers; 1889, Millwall Athletic; 1899, Millwall; 1985, Millwall Football & Athletic Company.

Club Nickname: 'The Lions'.

Grounds: 1885, Glengall Road, Millwall; 1886, Back of 'Lord Nelson'; 1890, East Ferry Road; 1901, North Greenwich; 1910, The Den, Cold Blow Lane; 1993, The Den, Bermondsey.

First Football League Game: 28 August 1920, Division 3, v Bristol R (h) W 2–0 – Lansdale; Fort, Hodge; Voisey (1), Riddell, McAlpine; Waterall, Travers, Broad (1), Sutherland, Dempsey.

Record League Victory: 9–1 v Torquay U, Division 3 (S), 29 August 1927 – Lansdale, Tilling, Hill, Amos, Bryant (3), Graham, Chance, Hawkins (3), Landells (1), Phillips (2), Black. 9–1 v Coventry C, Division 3 (S), 19 November 1927 – Lansdale, Fort, Hill, Amos, Collins (1), Graham, Chance, Landells (4), Cock (2), Phillips (2), Black.

Record Cup Victory: 7–0 v Gateshead, FA Cup 2nd rd, 12 December 1936 – Yuill; Ted Smith, Inns; Brolly, Hancock, Forsyth; Thomas (1), Mangnall (1), Ken Burditt (2), McCartney (2), Thorogood (1).

Record Defeat: 1–9 v Aston Villa, FA Cup 4th rd, 28 January 1946.

Most League Points (2 for a win): 65, Division 3 (S), 1927–28 and Division 3, 1965–66.

FOOTBALL YEARBOOK FACT FILE

The original nickname for Millwall was 'the Dockers' on account of the club's location on the Isle of Dogs in London's docklands. After defeating Aston Villa over three games in an FA Cup tie in March 1900 the club were described as 'the Lions of the South', and following the move to New Cross in 1910 'the Dockers' fell out of usage and the club became 'the Lions'.

Most League Points (3 for a win): 93, Division 2, 2000–01.

Most League Goals: 127, Division 3 (S), 1927–28.

Highest League Scorer in Season: Richard Parker, 37, Division 3 (S), 1926–27.

Most League Goals in Total Aggregate: Neil Harris, 124, 1995–2004; 2006–11.

Most League Goals in One Match: 5, Richard Parker v Norwich C, Division 3 (S), 28 August 1926.

Most Capped Player: David Forde, 24, Republic of Ireland; Shane Ferguson, 24 (including 4 whilst on loan from Newcastle U) (43), Northern Ireland.

Most League Appearances: Barry Kitchener, 523, 1967–82.

Youngest League Player: Moses Ashikodi, 15 years 240 days v Brighton & HA, 22 February 2003.

Record Transfer Fee Received: £8,000,000 from Middlesbrough for George Saville, January 2019.

Record Transfer Fee Paid: £1,000,000 (rising to £1,500,000) to Sheffield U for Ryan Leonard, August 2018.

Football League Record: 1920 Original Members of Division 3; 1921 Division 3 (S); 1928–34 Division 2; 1934–38 Division 3 (S); 1938–48 Division 2; 1948–58 Division 3 (S); 1958–62 Division 4; 1962–64 Division 3; 1964–65 Division 4; 1965–66 Division 3; 1966–75 Division 2; 1975–76 Division 3; 1976–79 Division 2; 1979–85 Division 3; 1985–88 Division 2; 1988–90 Division 1; 1990–92 Division 2; 1992–96 Division 1; 1996–2001 Division 2; 2001–04 Division 1; 2004–06 FL C; 2006–10 FL 1; 2010–15 FL C; 2015–17 FL 1; 2017– FL C.

LATEST SEQUENCES

Longest Sequence of League Wins: 10, 10.3.1928 – 25.4.1928.

Longest Sequence of League Defeats: 11, 10.4.1929 – 16.9.1929.

Longest Sequence of League Draws: 5, 22.12.1973 – 12.1.1974.

Longest Sequence of Unbeaten League Matches: 19, 22.8.1959 – 31.10.1959.

Longest Sequence Without a League Win: 20, 26.12.1989 – 5.5.1990.

Successive Scoring Runs: 22 from 27.11.1954.

Successive Non-scoring Runs: 6 from 27.4.2013.

MANAGERS

F. B. Kidd 1894–99
(Hon. Treasurer/Manager)
E. R. Stopher 1899–1900
(Hon. Treasurer/Manager)
George Saunders 1900–11
(Hon. Treasurer/Manager)
Herbert Lipsham 1911–19
Robert Hunter 1919–33
Bill McCracken 1933–36
Charlie Hewitt 1936–40
Bill Voisey 1940–44
Jack Cock 1944–48
Charlie Hewitt 1948–56
Ron Gray 1956–57
Jimmy Seed 1958–59
Reg Smith 1959–61
Ron Gray 1961–63
Billy Gray 1963–66
Benny Fenton 1966–74
Gordon Jago 1974–77
George Petchey 1978–80
Peter Anderson 1980–82
George Graham 1982–86
John Docherty 1986–90
Bob Pearson 1990
Bruce Rioch 1990–92
Mick McCarthy 1992–96
Jimmy Nicholl 1996–97
John Docherty 1997
Billy Bonds 1997–98
Keith Stevens 1998–2000
(then Joint Manager)
(*plus* **Alan McLeary** 1999–2000)
Mark McGhee 2000–03
Dennis Wise 2003–05
Steve Claridge 2005
Colin Lee 2005
David Tuttle 2005–06
Nigel Spackman 2006
Willie Donachie 2006–07
Kenny Jackett 2007–13
Steve Lomas 2013
Ian Holloway 2014–15
Neil Harris 2015–19
Gary Rowett October 2019–

TEN YEAR LEAGUE RECORD

		P	W	D	L	F	A	Pts	Pos
2010-11	FL C	46	18	13	15	62	48	67	9
2011-12	FL C	46	15	12	19	55	57	57	16
2012-13	FL C	46	15	11	20	51	62	56	20
2013-14	FL C	46	11	15	20	46	74	48	19
2014-15	FL C	46	9	14	23	42	76	41	22
2015-16	FL 1	46	24	9	13	73	49	81	4
2016-17	FL 1	46	20	13	13	66	57	73	6
2017-18	FL C	46	19	15	12	56	45	72	8
2018-19	FL C	46	10	14	22	48	64	44	21
2019-20	FL C	46	17	17	12	57	51	68	8

DID YOU KNOW ?

Millwall's ground at The Den suffered bomb damage in April 1943 and shortly afterwards the grandstand was gutted by fire. As a result the Lions began the 1943–44 season playing at The Valley, also playing occasional games at Crystal Palace and West Ham, before returning home in February 1944.

MILLWALL – SKY BET CHAMPIONSHIP 2019–20 LEAGUE RECORD

Match No.	Date	Venue	Opponents	Result	H/T Score	Lg Pos.	Goalscorers	Attendance
1	Aug 3	H	Preston NE	W 1-0	1-0	7	Wallace, J [33]	14,923
2	10	A	WBA	D 1-1	0-0	6	Smith [75]	24,305
3	17	H	Sheffield W	W 1-0	1-0	5	Smith [37]	15,017
4	21	A	Fulham	L 0-4	0-2	9		17,066
5	24	A	Middlesbrough	D 1-1	0-0	10	Bradshaw [76]	19,279
6	31	H	Hull C	D 1-1	1-1	12	Wallace, J (pen) [10]	12,495
7	Sept 14	A	Blackburn R	L 0-2	0-1	15		11,873
8	21	H	QPR	L 1-2	0-0	16	Hutchinson [71]	16,808
9	28	A	Huddersfield T	D 1-1	1-1	17	Smith [41]	20,781
10	Oct 2	A	Luton T	D 1-1	0-0	18	Bradshaw [60]	10,049
11	5	H	Leeds U	W 2-1	2-0	15	Wallace, J (pen) [16], Bradshaw [45]	16,311
12	19	A	Brentford	L 2-3	1-0	17	Bradshaw [45], Wallace, J (pen) [55]	10,886
13	22	H	Cardiff C	D 2-2	1-1	16	Bradshaw 2 [45, 77]	11,769
14	26	H	Stoke C	W 2-0	1-0	15	Thompson [28], Wallace, J (pen) [75]	14,008
15	Nov 2	A	Reading	L 1-2	0-2	17	Wallace, J [63]	14,485
16	9	H	Charlton Ath	W 2-1	1-0	15	Hutchinson [6], Smith [90]	17,109
17	23	A	Swansea C	W 1-0	0-0	10	Wallace, J [65]	16,840
18	26	H	Wigan Ath	D 2-2	1-1	11	Hutchinson [24], Smith [60]	10,021
19	30	A	Birmingham C	D 1-1	0-0	13	Williams [61]	19,715
20	Dec 6	H	Nottingham F	D 2-2	1-0	12	Williams [15], O'Brien [90]	12,976
21	10	A	Bristol C	W 2-1	1-0	12	Wallace, J [11], Cooper [70]	19,742
22	14	A	Derby Co	W 1-0	1-0	11	Bradshaw [25]	26,272
23	21	H	Barnsley	L 1-2	0-1	13	O'Brien [85]	12,682
24	26	A	Cardiff C	D 1-1	0-0	12	Wallace, J [63]	23,583
25	29	H	Brentford	W 1-0	1-0	11	O'Brien [8]	15,464
26	Jan 1	H	Luton T	W 3-1	0-1	6	Bradshaw [69], Mahoney [78], Smith [81]	12,134
27	11	A	Stoke C	D 0-0	0-0	7		22,515
28	18	H	Reading	W 2-0	0-0	7	Smith [71], Bodvarsson [82]	14,011
29	28	A	Leeds U	L 2-3	2-0	9	Hutchinson [4], Wallace, J (pen) [23]	34,006
30	Feb 1	A	Sheffield W	D 0-0	0-0	9		23,052
31	9	H	WBA	L 0-2	0-1	10		13,818
32	12	H	Fulham	D 1-1	1-1	11	Bodvarsson [7]	12,870
33	15	A	Preston NE	W 1-0	0-0	10	Hutchinson [78]	12,468
34	22	A	Wigan Ath	L 0-1	0-0	11		9639
35	26	H	Birmingham C	D 0-0	0-0	10		11,209
36	29	H	Bristol C	D 1-1	0-1	10	Smith [51]	13,584
37	Mar 6	A	Nottingham F	W 3-0	3-0	7	Smith 3 [20, 26, 33]	27,307
38	June 20	H	Derby Co	L 2-3	1-1	10	Smith [15], Bodvarsson [90]	0
39	27	A	Barnsley	D 0-0	0-0	11		0
40	30	H	Swansea C	D 1-1	1-0	11	Bennett [21]	0
41	July 3	A	Charlton Ath	W 1-0	0-0	8	Cooper [81]	0
42	8	H	Middlesbrough	L 0-2	0-0	11		0
43	11	A	Hull C	W 1-0	1-0	9	Leonard [2]	0
44	14	H	Blackburn R	W 1-0	1-0	7	Bennett [20]	0
45	18	A	QPR	L 3-4	0-1	9	Smith [49], Hutchinson [67], Molumby [90]	0
46	22	H	Huddersfield T	W 4-1	1-1	8	Mahoney [4], Cooper [47], Skalak [63], Bodvarsson [79]	0

Final League Position: 8

GOALSCORERS

League (57): Smith 13, Wallace, J 10 (5 pens), Bradshaw 8, Hutchinson 6, Bodvarsson 4, Cooper 3, O'Brien 3, Bennett 2, Mahoney 2, Williams 2, Leonard 1, Molumby 1, Skalak 1, Thompson 1.
FA Cup (3): Bradshaw 1, Mahoney 1 (1 pen), Smith 1.
Carabao Cup (4): Bodvarsson 2, Bradshaw 1, O'Brien 1.

Fielding F 1	Romeo M 43	Pearce A 28 + 1	Cooper J 46	Wallace M 38 + 5	Wallace J 43	Williams S 28 + 4	Thompson B 20 + 8	Mahoney C 14 + 24	O'Brien A 8 + 10	Smith M 20 + 21	Bialkowski B 45 + 1	Leonard R 13 + 4	Bradshaw T 29 + 16	Ferguson S 19 + 10	Bodvarsson J 13 + 18	Skalak J 4 + 8	Molumby J 31 + 5	McCarthy J 1 + 1	Hutchinson S 36	Mitchell B 1 + 6	Woods R 17 + 1	Bennett M 7 + 2	Brown J 1	Muller H — + 1	Burey T — + 1	*Match No.*
1[1]	2	3	4	5	6	7	8	9	10[2]	11[3]	12	13	14													1
	2[1]	3	4	5[2]	9	8	10	6		13	1	7	11[3]	12	14											2
	2	3	4	5	9■	8	7	6[2]	10[3]	11[1]	1	13	12	14												3
	2	3	4	5		8[2]	10[3]	6		13	1	7	11	12		9[1]	14									4
	2	3	4	5		8[2]	10	9[3]	6[1]	11	1	7	13	12				14								5
	2	3	4	5[3]	6		8	9[2]	14	10	1	7	11[1]	13	12											6
	2	3	4	5[3]	6		8	10[1]		12	1	9[2]	13	14	11		7									7
		4[2]	5		7		9	13	14	10	1		12	6	11[1]		8	2[3]	3							8
	2	3	4	13	9	8	14	6[3]	10[1]	11[2]	1	7	12	5■												9
	2		4	5	6		12	9[1]	13	11[2]	1	7	10				8		3							10
	2		4	5	6	12	10[2]				1	7[1]	11	9	13		8		3							11
	2		4	5	6	8	10				1		11	9	12		7[1]		3							12
	2		3	5	9	8	7	13	6[2]	11[1]	1		10		12				4							13
	2		4	5	6	8	10	12			1		11[2]	9[1]	13		7		3							14
	2		4	5	6	8[2]	10	14		13	1		11[3]	9[1]	12		7		3							15
	2		4	5	6	8	9[2]	12	14	13	1		10[3]		11[1]		7		3							16
	5	3	4	8	9[3]	7	6	11[1]		12	1		14		10[2]	13			2							17
	2		4	5	6	8	10[2]	9[1]	14	12	1		11[3]			13	7		3							18
	2	3	4	5	10	8	6[3]		14	11[1]	1		13		12	9[2]	7									19
	2	3	4	5	6	8	10[3]	14	13	11[1]	1		12			9[2]	7									20
	5	3	4	8	9[3]	7	12	14		13	1		10[2]		11[1]		6		2							21
	5	3	4	8	9	7	12[3]		13	14	1		10[2]		11[1]		6		2							22
	2		4		6	8		14	13	12	1		10[3]	5	11[1]	9[2]	7		3							23
	5	3	4	12	9	7		13		14	1		10[3]	8[1]	11[2]		6		2							24
	5	3	4	8	9[3]	7			11[2]		1		10[1]	13	12	14	6		2							25
	5	3[1]	4	14	9[3]	7		13	11[2]	10	1		12	8			6		2							26
	5	3	4	8	9[3]	6■		11[1]		13	1		10[2]	12			7		2	14						27
	2		4	5	6			12		11[2]	1		10	9[1]	13		8		3	14	7[3]					28
	5	3[2]	4	8	9			13		14	1		10[3]	12	11[1]		6		2		7					29
	2		4	5	6	7		13		10[1]	1		11[3]	9[2]	12		14		3		8					30
	2		4	5	8	6[3]		13	10[2]	11[1]	1		14		12		9		3		7					31
	5	3[2]	4	8	9					14	1	12	10[1]		11	13	6		2		7[3]					32
	5	3	4	8	9[3]			12		14	1	13	10[1]		11[2]		6		2		7					33
	5	3[1]	4	8	9			14		13	1		10[3]		11[2]		6		2		7	12				34
	5	3[1]	4	8	9			14		12	1		13		10[3]		7		2		6	11[2]				35
	2		4	5	9			6[1]	14	10[2]	1		11[3]		13		7		3		8	12				36
	2	13	4	5	8					11[2]	1		12	10[3]	14		6		3		7	9[1]				37
	2		4	5[4]	6[3]	16		15		11[1]	1	10[2]	13	9	12	14	7		3		8[5]					38
	5		3	4	9[5]	7	16	14		12	1		10[1]	8[4]		15	6[3]		2		13	11[2]				39
	5		3	4	9	7		12		13	1		10[2]	8					2		6	11[1]				40
	5[4]	3	4	8	9[5]	16	12	14		11[2]	1	10[3]	13				6[1]		2	15	7					41
	5[4]	3[1]	4	8[5]	9	7[3]	10[2]	14		11	1		13	16			12		2	15	6					42
		3	4	13	9[4]	14	15			16	1	7	11[5]	8[3]		12			2	5[2]	6	10[1]				43
	5[2]	3	4	13	9[5]		14	15			1	6	10[3]	8[4]	12		16		2		7	11[1]				44
	5[2]	3[5]	4		9			15		13	1	6[4]	11[3]	8	12		14		2	16	7	10[1]				45
			4	5		8	10[4]	6		11[5]	1			9[1]	15	12	7[3]		3	14			2[2]	13	16	46

FA Cup

Third Round	Newport Co	(h)	3-0
Fourth Round	Sheffield U	(h)	0-2

Carabao Cup

First Round	WBA	(a)	2-1
Second Round	Oxford U	(a)	2-2

(Oxford U won 4-2 on penalties)

MILTON KEYNES DONS

FOUNDATION

In July 2004 Wimbledon became MK Dons and relocated to Milton Keynes. In 2007 it recognised itself as a new club with no connection to the old Wimbledon FC. In August of that year the replica trophies and other Wimbledon FC memorabilia were returned to the London Borough of Merton.

Stadium MK, Stadium Way West, Milton Keynes, Buckinghamshire MK1 1ST.

Telephone: (01908) 622 922.

Ticket Office: (01908) 622 933.

Website: www.mkdons.com

Email: info@mkdons.com

Ground Capacity: 30,303.

Record Attendance: 28,521 v Liverpool, EFL Cup 3rd rd, 25 September 2019.

Pitch Measurements: 105m × 68m (115yd × 74.5yd).

Chairman: Pete Winkelman.

Executive Director: Andrew Cullen.

Manager: Russell Martin.

Assistant Manager: Luke Williams.

Colours: White shirts with gold and black trim, white shorts with gold and black trim, white socks with gold and black trim.

Year Formed: 2004.

Turned Professional: 2004.

Club Nickname: 'The Dons'.

Grounds: 2004, The National Hockey Stadium; 2007, Stadium MK.

First Football League Game: 7 August 2004, FL 1, v Barnsley (h) D 1–1 – Rachubka; Palmer, Lewington, Harding, Williams, Oyedele, Kamara, Smith, Smart (Herve), McLeod (1) (Hornuss), Small.

Record League Victory: 7–0 v Oldham Ath, FL 1, 20 December 2014 – Martin; Spence, McFadzean, Kay (Baldock), Lewington; Potter (1), Alli (1); Baker C (1), Carruthers (Green), Bowditch (1) (Afobe (1)); Grigg (2).

Record Cup Victory: 6–0 v Nantwich T, FA Cup 1st rd, 12 November 2011 – Martin; Chicksen, Baldock G, Doumbe (1), Flanagan, Williams S, Powell (1) (O'Shea (1), Chadwick (Galloway), Bowditch (2), MacDonald (Williams G (1)), Balanta.

HONOURS

League Champions: FL 2 – 2007–08.
Runners-up: FL 1 – 2014–15.

FA Cup: 5th rd – 2013.

League Cup: 4th rd – 2015.

League Trophy Winners: 2008.

FOOTBALL YEARBOOK FACT FILE

The record attendance for a football match at Stadium MK, home of Milton Keynes Dons, is 29,669 for the international fixture between Brazil and Cameroon in November 2018. The match, which was part of the Brasil Global Tour series, was won 1-0 by Brazil with a goal from Everton's Richarlison. The overall stadium record attendance is 30,048 for a 2015 Rugby World Cup match between Fiji and Uruguay.

MANAGERS

Stuart Murdock 2004
Danny Wilson 2004–06
Martin Allen 2006–07
Paul Ince 2007–08
Roberto Di Matteo 2008–09
Paul Ince 2009–10
Karl Robinson 2010–16
Robbie Neilson 2016–18
Dan Micciche 2018
Paul Tisdale 2018–19
Russell Martin November 2019–

Record Defeat: 0–6 v Southampton, Capital One Cup 3rd rd, 23 September 2015.

Most League Points (3 for a win): 97, FL 2, 2007–08.

Most League Goals: 101, FL 1, 2014–15.

Highest League Scorer in Season: Izale McLeod, 21, 2006–07.

Most League Goals in Total Aggregate: Izale McLeod, 62, 2004–07; 2012–14.

Most Capped Player: Lee Hodson, 7 (24), Northern Ireland.

Most League Goals in One Match: 3, Clive Platt v Barnet, FL 2, 20 January 2007; 3, Mark Wright v Bury, FL 2, 2 February 2008; 3, Aaron Wilbraham v Cheltenham T, FL 1, 31 January 2009; 3, Sam Baldock v Colchester U, FL 1, 12 March 2011; 3, Sam Baldock v Chesterfield, FL 1, 20 August 2012; 3, Dean Bowditch v Bury, FL 1, 22 September 2012; 3, Dele Alli v Notts Co, FL 1, 11 March 2014; 3, Dele Alli v Crewe Alex, FL 1, 20 September 2014; 3, Benik Afobe v Colchester U, FL 1, 29 November 2014; 3, Robert Hall v Leyton Orient, FL 1, 18 April 2015; 3, Ryan Colclough v Fleetwood T, FL 1, 9 September 2016.

Most League Appearances: Dean Lewington, 652, 2004–20.

Youngest League Player: Brendon Galloway, 16 years 42 days v Rochdale, 28 April 2012.

Record Transfer Fee Received: £5,000,000 from Tottenham H for Dele Alli, February 2015.

Record Transfer Fee Paid: £400,000 to Bristol C for Kieran Agard, August 2016.

Football League Record: 2004–06 FL 1; 2006–08 FL 2; 2008–15 FL 1; 2015–16 FL C; 2016–18 FL 1; 2018–19 FL 2; 2019– FL 1.

LATEST SEQUENCES

Longest Sequence of League Wins: 8, 7.9.2007 – 20.10.2007.

Longest Sequence of League Defeats: 6, 2.4.2018 – 28.4.2018.

Longest Sequence of League Draws: 4, 12.2.2013 – 2.3.2013.

Longest Sequence of Unbeaten League Matches: 18, 29.1.2008 – 3.5.2008.

Longest Sequence Without a League Win: 12, 17.9.2019 – 7.12.2019.

Successive Scoring Runs: 18 from 21.8.2018.

Successive Non-scoring Runs: 5 from 5.10.2019.

TEN YEAR LEAGUE RECORD

		P	W	D	L	F	A	Pts	Pos
2010-11	FL 1	46	23	8	15	67	60	77	5
2011-12	FL 1	46	22	14	10	84	47	80	5
2012-13	FL 1	46	19	13	14	62	45	70	8
2013-14	FL 1	46	17	9	20	63	65	60	10
2014-15	FL 1	46	27	10	9	101	44	91	2
2015-16	FL C	46	9	12	25	39	69	39	23
2016-17	FL 1	46	16	13	17	60	58	61	12
2017-18	FL 1	46	11	12	23	43	69	45	23
2018-19	FL 2	46	23	10	13	71	49	79	3
2019-20	FL 1	35	10	7	18	36	47	37	19§

§Decided on points-per-game (1.06)

DID YOU KNOW ?

The first Milton Keynes Dons player to win a full international cap was defender Craig Morgan who appeared for Wales against Cyprus in October 2006. He never actually played for the Dons after this as within a matter of days he was loaned to Wrexham, then to Peterborough before joining Posh on a permanent basis.

MILTON KEYNES DONS – SKY BET LEAGUE ONE 2019–20 LEAGUE RECORD

Match No.	Date	Venue	Opponents	Result		H/T Score	Lg Pos.	Goalscorers	Attendance
1	Aug 10	H	Shrewsbury T	W	1-0	0-0	10	Healey 90	7967
2	17	A	Wycombe W	L	2-3	1-2	14	Bowery 32, Houghton (pen) 51	5243
3	20	H	Lincoln C	W	2-1	2-1	10	Brittain 2, Williams 22	8166
4	24	H	Peterborough U	L	0-4	0-3	15		9402
5	31	A	Accrington S	L	1-2	1-0	15	Agard 18	2218
6	Sept 7	H	AFC Wimbledon	W	2-1	2-0	12	Nombe 10, Healey 26	8627
7	14	A	Blackpool	W	3-0	1-0	10	Martin 5, Houghton 62, Kasumu 75	8283
8	17	H	Ipswich T	L	0-1	0-1	11		10,167
9	21	H	Southend U	L	0-1	0-1	15		7493
10	28	A	Sunderland	L	1-2	0-2	15	Bowery 55	29,954
11	Oct 5	H	Burton Alb	L	0-3	0-1	17		9111
12	12	A	Bristol R	L	0-1	0-0	18		7864
13	19	H	Coventry C	D	0-0	0-0	19		13,621
14	22	A	Rochdale	L	0-2	0-1	19		2286
15	26	A	Fleetwood T	L	0-1	0-0	20		2722
16	Nov 2	H	Tranmere R	L	1-3	1-1	21	Reeves 42	7171
17	16	A	Bolton W	L	0-1	0-0	21		11,819
18	23	H	Rotherham U	L	2-3	2-0	21	Gilbey 4, Mason 13	7811
19	Dec 7	A	Doncaster R	D	1-1	0-0	21	Gilbey 51	7193
20	14	H	Oxford U	W	1-0	0-0	21	Mason 59	10,031
21	21	A	Gillingham	L	1-3	0-2	21	Gilbey 52	4739
22	26	A	Southend U	D	2-2	1-1	21	Mason 13, Healey 64	6189
23	29	H	Portsmouth	W	3-1	2-0	21	Healey 35, McGrandles 42, Gilbey 84	12,788
24	Jan 1	H	Bristol R	W	3-0	1-0	20	Healey 16, Nombe 60, Agard 84	8236
25	11	A	Coventry C	D	1-1	0-1	19	Morris 75	6666
26	14	A	Burton Alb	L	0-1	0-1	19		2005
27	18	H	Sunderland	L	0-1	0-0	20		13,327
28	28	H	Rochdale	W	2-1	0-1	20	Morris 49, Healey (pen) 90	6393
29	Feb 1	H	Wycombe W	W	2-0	0-0	19	Healey 68, Gladwin 86	9699
30	8	A	Shrewsbury T	D	1-1	0-0	19	Healey 77	5791
31	11	A	Lincoln C	D	1-1	1-1	18	Healey 3	7783
32	22	H	Bolton W	W	1-0	0-0	18	Healey 68	8539
33	25	A	Portsmouth	L	1-3	1-1	18	Gilbey 45	16,577
34	29	A	Rotherham U	D	1-1	1-1	18	Healey 22	8883
35	Mar 7	H	Doncaster R	L	0-1	0-0	18		7880
36	14	A	Oxford U	Cancelled					
37	21	H	Gillingham	Cancelled					
38	28	A	Tranmere R	Cancelled					
39	Apr 4	H	Fleetwood T	Cancelled					
40	10	A	Peterborough U	Cancelled					
41	13	H	Accrington S	Cancelled					
42	18	A	AFC Wimbledon	Cancelled					
43	25	H	Blackpool	Cancelled					
44	May 3	A	Ipswich T	Cancelled					

Final League Position: 19 (on points-per-game basis)

GOALSCORERS

League (36): Healey 11 (1 pen), Gilbey 5, Mason 3, Agard 2, Bowery 2, Houghton 2 (1 pen), Morris 2, Nombe 2, Brittain 1, Gladwin 1, Kasumu 1, Martin 1, McGrandles 1, Reeves 1, Williams 1.
FA Cup (0).
Carabao Cup (6): Boateng 1, Brittain 1, Healey 1, Kasumu 1, McGrandles 1, Nombe 1.
Leasing.com Trophy (7): Agard 2, Nombe 2, Dickenson 1, Mason 1, McGrandles 1.

Nicholls L 35	Williams G 28	Martin R 11	Walsh J 23 + 1	Brittain C 28 + 3	Houghton J 30	McGrandles C 25 + 6	Lewington D 32 + 1	Boateng H 14 + 6	Agard K 11 + 8	Bowery J 10 + 6	Reeves B 4 + 13	Healey R 15 + 4	Cargill B 7 + 5	Poole R 17 + 2	Gilbey A 27 + 3	Harley R 2 + 1	Dickenson B 2 + 5	Nombe S 11 + 10	Kasumu D 14 + 7	Asonganyi D — + 3	Moore-Taylor J 13 + 1	Mason J 10 + 3	Morris C 9 + 1	Gladwin B — + 9	Thompson L 7 + 2	Match No.
1	2	3^3	4	5	6	7^1	8	9	10	11^2	12	13	14													1
1	5	3		14	6	7	8^3	9^2	10^1	11		13	4	2	12											2
1	8	3		5	7^2	13	14	6^3	11	10			4	2	12	9^1										3
1	2	3		5	7^1		8^2	9	10	11		12	4		6^3	13	14									4
1	2		3	5		14	8	6	11^1	12		10	4		9^2	7^3		13								5
1	2	3	4		6	5	9	12	14	13		11^1			8^3			10^2	7							6
1	5	3	4	13	7^2	6	8	12	11^1					2				10	9							7
1	5	3	4^1	13	6	8		7^3	14	12				2			9^2	11	10							8
1		3	4	5	8^1	6	9^2	10^3	12					2	14		13	11	7							9
1	4	3		5	8^2	6	9	14	13	11^1				2	7^3			10	12							10
1		3^2	4	5		6	9^3	8		11			13	2	7^1				10	12	14					11
1	5	3^1	2	10		7	8	9^3		11^2	13		4				12		6	14						12
1	2		3	8	7	6	5	11^2	13		12				10^1				9		4					13
1	2			5		6	9	14	13	11^2	12		4		8		10^3		7^1		3					14
1	2		3	6^1	7	12	5^3	9^2	11	13			14	8	10						4					15
1	2^1		3	6	7^3	9	5		11■		10^2		14	13	8					12	4					16
1	2■		3	8		6	5	13		11	10^1		12		7		14				4^2	9^3				17
1			3	7^1	6	9^3	5	12		10^2	13		4■	2	8		14					11				18
1			4	2	6	7	5	9^3	10^1		12			3	8			13	14			11^2				19
1			4	2	6	7^1	5	9^2	10^3	13	12			3	8				14			11				20
1			4	2	6	7^3	5	9^2	11^1	13	14			3	8			12				10				21
1			4	2	6	7	5				9^2	12		3	8			10^1	13			11				22
1	3		4	2	6	7	5		13		14	11^1			9^3			12	8			10^2				23
1	3		4	2	6	7^2	5		14		12	10^3			9^1			11	8			13				24
1	3		4	2	6	7	5					10			9^1			13	8^2			11^3	12	14		25
1	3		4	2	7^2	6^1	5					11			8			12				9	10	13		26
1	3		4	2	7	6^1	5					11						14	8^3			9	10^2	13	12	27
1	3		14	2	6		5					11^3			9			12	7^1		4		10	13	8^2	28
1	3			2	6	12	5					11^1			9			7	14		4		10^2	13	8^3	29
1	3			2^1	7	12	5					11		13	8			10			4		9		6^2	30
1	3				8	7^3	5				13	11		2	6			9^2	14		4		10^1		12	31
1	3				6	13	5				9^3	11		2	8			12			4		10^1	14	7^2	32
1	3				6^3	9^2	5				14	11		2	8			13			4		10■	12	7^1	33
1	5		3	9^1	6							11		2	8			10^2	12		4	14		13	7^3	34
1	3			2	6		5				14	11			9				8^1		4^3	12	10	13	7^2	35
																										36
																										37
																										38
																										39
																										40
																										41
																										42
																										43
																										44

FA Cup

First Round	Port Vale	(h)	0-1

Carabao Cup

First Round	AFC Wimbledon	(a)	2-2
(Milton Keynes D won 4-2 on penalties)			
Second Round	Southend U	(a)	4-1
Third Round	Liverpool	(h)	0-2

Leasing.com Trophy

Group G (S)	Stevenage	(a)	3-0
Group G (S)	Fulham U21	(h)	1-0
Group G (S)	Wycombe W	(h)	1-2
Second Round (S)	Coventry C	(h)	2-0
Third Round (S)	Newport Co	(a)	0-3

MORECAMBE

FOUNDATION

Several attempts to start a senior football club in a rugby stronghold finally succeeded on 7 May 1920 at the West View Hotel, Morecambe and a team competed in the Lancashire Combination for 1920–21. The club shared with a local cricket club at Woodhill Lane for the first season and a crowd of 3,000 watched the first game. The club moved to Roseberry Park, the name of which was changed to Christie Park after J.B. Christie who as President had purchased the ground.

Mazuma Stadium, Christie Way, Westgate, Morecambe, Lancashire LA4 4TB.

Telephone: (01524) 411 797.

Ticket Office: (01524) 411 797.

Website: www.morecambefc.com

Email: office@morecambefc.com

HONOURS

League: *Runners-up:* Conference – (3rd) 2006–07 *(promoted via play-offs).*

FA Cup: 3rd rd – 1962, 2001, 2003.

League Cup: 3rd rd – 2008.

Ground Capacity: 6,241.

Record Attendance: 9,383 v Weymouth, FA Cup 3rd rd, 6 January 1962 (at Christie Park); 5,375 v Newcastle U, League Cup, 28 August 2013 (at Globe Arena).

Pitch Measurements: 103m × 71m (112.5yd × 77.5yd).

Co-Chairmen: Graham Howse, Rod Taylor.

Manager: Derek Adams.

Assistant Manager: John McMahon.

Colours: Red shirts with white trim, red shorts with white trim, red socks with black trim.

Year Formed: 1920.

Turned Professional: 1920.

Club Nickname: 'The Shrimps'.

Grounds: 1920, Woodhill Lane; 1921, Christie Park; 2010, Globe Arena (renamed Mazuma Stadium 2020).

First Football League game: 11 August 2007, FL 2, v Barnet (h) D 0–0 – Lewis; Yates, Adams, Artell, Bentley, Stanley, Baker (Burns), Sorvel, Twiss (Newby), Curtis, Hunter (Thompson).

FOOTBALL YEARBOOK FACT FILE

Morecambe entered the EFL Trophy (then known as the LDV Vans Trophy) on five occasions between 2000 and 2006 when a number of clubs from the Football Conference were permitted to enter. Their only victory came in a first round tie at Blundell Park in 2005–06 when the Shrimps drew 1-1 with Grimsby Town and then edged the following penalty shoot-out 4-3.

Record League Victory: 6–0 v Crawley T, FL 2, 10 September 2011 – Roche; Reid, Wilson (pen), McCready, Haining (Parrish), Fenton (1), Drummond, McDonald, Price (Jevons), Carlton (3) (Alessandra), Ellison (1).

Record Cup Victory: 6–2 v Nelson (a), Lancashire Trophy, 27 January 2004.

Record Defeat: 0–7 v Cambridge U, FL 2, 19 April 2016.

Most League Points (3 for a win): 73, FL 2, 2009–10.

Most League Goals: 73, FL 2, 2009–10.

Highest League Scorer in Season: Phil Jevons, 18, 2009–10.

Most League Goals in Total Aggregate: Kevin Ellison, 81, 2011–20.

Most League Goals in One Match: 3, Jon Newby v Rotherham U, FL 2, 29 March 2008.

Most League Appearances: Barry Roche, 436, 2008–20.

Youngest League Player: Aaron McGowan, 16 years 263 days, 20 April 2013.

Record Transfer Fee Received: £225,000 from Stockport Co for Carl Baker, July 2008.

Record Transfer Fee Paid: £50,000 to Southport for Carl Baker, July 2007.

Football League Record: 2006–07 Promoted from Conference; 2007– FL 2.

MANAGERS

Jimmy Milne 1947–48
Albert Dainty 1955–56
Ken Horton 1956–61
Joe Dunn 1961–64
Geoff Twentyman 1964–65
Ken Waterhouse 1965–69
Ronnie Clayton 1969–70
Gerry Irving and Ronnie Mitchell 1970
Ken Waterhouse 1970–72
Dave Roberts 1972–75
Alan Spavin 1975–76
Johnny Johnson 1976–77
Tommy Ferber 1977–78
Mick Hogarth 1978–79
Don Curbage 1979–81
Jim Thompson 1981
Les Rigby 1981–84
Sean Gallagher 1984–85
Joe Wojciechowicz 1985–88
Eric Whalley 1988
Billy Wright 1988–89
Lawrie Milligan 1989
Bryan Griffiths 1989–93
Leighton James 1994
Jim Harvey 1994–2006
Sammy McIlroy 2006–11
Jim Bentley 2011–19
Derek Adams November 2019–

LATEST SEQUENCES

Longest Sequence of League Wins: 7, 31.10.2009 – 12.12.2009.

Longest Sequence of League Defeats: 7, 4.3.2017 – 1.4.2017.

Longest Sequence of League Draws: 5, 3.1.2015 – 31.1.2015.

Longest Sequence of Unbeaten League Matches: 12, 31.1.2009 – 21.3.2009.

Longest Sequence Without a League Win: 13, 20.3.2018 – 18.8.2018.

Successive Scoring Runs: 17 from 13.8.2011.

Successive Non-scoring Runs: 7 from 21.4.2018.

TEN YEAR LEAGUE RECORD

		P	*W*	*D*	*L*	*F*	*A*	*Pts*	*Pos*
2010-11	FL 2	46	13	12	21	54	73	51	20
2011-12	FL 2	46	14	14	18	63	57	56	15
2012-13	FL 2	46	15	13	18	55	61	58	16
2013-14	FL 2	46	13	15	18	52	64	54	18
2014-15	FL 2	46	17	12	17	53	52	63	11
2015-16	FL 2	46	12	10	24	69	91	46	21
2016-17	FL 2	46	14	10	22	53	73	52	18
2017-18	FL 2	46	9	19	18	41	56	46	22
2018-19	FL 2	46	14	12	20	54	70	54	18
2019-20	FL 2	37	7	11	19	35	60	32	22§

§Decided on points-per-game (0.86)

DID YOU KNOW ?

Morecambe were known as 'the Seasiders' for many years due to the town's popularity as a seaside resort. It is only in relatively recent years that they have become 'the Shrimps', taking their new title from the local potted delicacy.

MORECAMBE – SKY BET LEAGUE TWO 2019–20 LEAGUE RECORD

Match No.	Date	Venue	Opponents	Result		H/T Score	Lg Pos.	Goalscorers	Attendance
1	Aug 3	H	Grimsby T	L	0-2	0-0	21		2872
2	10	A	Mansfield T	D	2-2	2-1	21	Lavelle [4], Alessandra [21]	4465
3	17	H	Cheltenham T	D	0-0	0-0	19		1692
4	20	A	Macclesfield T	W	1-0	0-0	17	Sutton [65]	1862
5	24	H	Exeter C	L	2-3	1-2	18	Alessandra 2 [45, 63]	1517
6	31	A	Swindon T	L	1-3	1-3	20	Alessandra [13]	6877
7	Sept 7	H	Salford C	D	2-2	0-1	20	Miller [48], Alessandra [50]	2778
8	14	A	Scunthorpe U	L	0-3	0-3	22		3017
9	17	H	Walsall	L	0-1	0-1	22		1616
10	21	A	Oldham Ath	L	1-3	0-1	22	Miller [78]	3305
11	28	H	Northampton T	D	2-2	0-2	22	Buxton [72], Ellison [90]	2245
12	Oct 5	A	Port Vale	L	1-3	1-0	23	O'Sullivan [18]	4485
13	12	H	Bradford C	L	1-2	0-0	24	Brewitt [90]	3899
14	19	A	Colchester U	W	1-0	0-0	23	Stockton [66]	3011
15	22	H	Forest Green R	L	0-2	0-0	23		1658
16	26	A	Stevenage	L	0-1	0-0	24		2288
17	Nov 2	H	Leyton Orient	W	1-0	0-0	24	Leitch-Smith [74]	2691
18	16	A	Crawley T	D	1-1	0-1	23	Stockton [81]	2079
19	23	A	Crewe Alex	L	0-5	0-3	24		4149
20	Dec 7	H	Carlisle U	D	1-1	0-0	24	O'Sullivan [50]	3126
21	14	A	Plymouth Arg	L	0-3	0-2	24		9174
22	21	H	Newport Co	W	2-1	0-1	23	Stockton [68], O'Sullivan [80]	2161
23	26	H	Oldham Ath	L	1-2	0-1	23	Mendes Gomes [47]	2797
24	29	A	Cambridge U	L	0-1	0-0	23		4086
25	Jan 1	A	Bradford C	L	0-1	0-0	23		14,111
26	11	H	Colchester U	D	1-1	0-1	23	Phillips [69]	1593
27	14	H	Port Vale	W	2-1	2-0	23	Old [6], Stockton [12]	1639
28	18	A	Northampton T	L	1-4	0-2	24	Phillips [64]	4761
29	25	H	Cambridge U	D	1-1	0-0	23	Phillips [46]	2019
30	28	A	Walsall	W	2-0	0-0	23	Old [68], Mendes Gomes [90]	3554
31	Feb 1	A	Cheltenham T	L	1-2	0-2	23	Leitch-Smith [84]	3044
32	8	H	Mansfield T	D	1-1	0-0	23	Kenyon [85]	1965
33	11	H	Macclesfield T	W	2-0	2-0	23	Diagouraga [18], Wildig [35]	1611
34	15	A	Grimsby T	L	1-2	0-0	23	Phillips [90]	4704
35	22	A	Carlisle U	D	2-2	2-1	23	Stockton [18], Wildig [24]	4679
36	29	H	Crewe Alex	D	1-1	0-0	23	Wildig [68]	2872
37	Mar 7	A	Newport Co	L	0-1	0-0	23		3048
38	14	H	Plymouth Arg	Cancelled					
39	17	A	Forest Green R	Cancelled					
40	21	H	Stevenage	Cancelled					
41	28	A	Leyton Orient	Cancelled					
42	Apr 4	H	Crawley T	Cancelled					
43	10	A	Exeter C	Cancelled					
44	13	H	Swindon T	Cancelled					
45	18	A	Salford C	Cancelled					
46	25	H	Scunthorpe U	Cancelled					

Final League Position: 22 (on points-per-game basis)

GOALSCORERS

League (35): Alessandra 5, Stockton 5, Phillips 4, O'Sullivan 3, Wildig 3, Leitch-Smith 2, Mendes Gomes 2, Miller 2, Old 2, Brewitt 1, Buxton 1, Diagouraga 1, Ellison 1, Kenyon 1, Lavelle 1, Sutton 1.
FA Cup (1): Stockton 1.
Carabao Cup (2): Old 2.
Leasing.com Trophy (6): Brewitt 1, Conlan 1, Ellison 1, Howard 1, Tutte 1 (1 pen), Wildig 1.

Roche B 16	Buxton A 9 + 4	Lavelle S 31	Old S 37	Conlan L 19 + 1	Kenyon A 22 + 5	Wildig A 21 + 7	O'Sullivan J 27 + 7	Alessandra L 21 + 1	Oates R 2 + 3	Miller S 10 + 8	Stockton C 23 + 7	Tutte A 10 + 2	Ellison K 8 + 13	Cranston J 12 + 12	Tanner G 23	Sutton R 11 + 4	Brewitt T 17 + 5	Leitch-Smith A 8 + 15	Howard M — + 1	Halstead M 12	Mendes Gomes C 15 + 1	Cooney R 11	Phillips A 11	Diagouraga T 12	Slew J 9 + 2	Mafoumbi C 9	Mbulu C 1 + 2	Bradbury H — + 3	*Match No.*
1	2	3	4	5	6^{1}	7	8	9^{3}	10^{2}	11	12	13	14																1
1	2	3	4	5	14	7	8^{3}	9		13	11^{2}	6^{1}	10	12															2
1	2	3	4		6^{3}		8	9		13	11	7	10^{2}	12	5^{1}	14													3
1	6	3	4				7	8^{1}	13	11^{2}	10^{3}	12	14	9		2	5												4
1	5^{3}	3■	4^{2}				9	12		10	11^{1}	7	14	8		2	6	13											5
1		3	4	8		7^{2}	9	10		11^{3}	14	6		13	5	2^{1}		12											6
1	12	3	4	8^{1}		6^{2}	9	11^{3}		10		7	14	13	5	2													7
1	12	2	4			7	9	11		10^{3}	13	6	14	8^{2}	5	3^{1}													8
1	5	3	4			7^{3}	8	9	14	11^{1}	13	6	10^{2}		2			12											9
1	2	3	4			7	6	11	9^{2}	13	10^{1}	8^{3}		14	5			12											10
1	12	3	4	5^{2}	8^{3}	13	6^{1}	9		10		7	14		2			11											11
1	5	3	4		8		6	10^{1}		13			12	9■	2		7^{2}	11^{3}	14										12
1	5^{3}	3	4		7	13	8	10^{1}		11	14		12		2		6	9^{2}											13
1		3	4	5	8	12	6^{1}	11^{3}		13	10^{2}		9		2	14	7												14
1		3	4	5	8^{2}	12	6	10■		13	11		9		2		7^{1}												15
1	14	3	4	5^{3}	8	12	6			10	11^{2}		9^{1}	13	2		7												16
		3	4	5	14	7^{2}	9	11			10^{3}	6^{1}		12	2		8	13		1									17
		3	4^{2}	9	5	8^{1}	13	11			10^{3}		14		6	2	7	12		1									18
		3■	4	9	7^{1}	8^{3}	13	10^{2}			11		14	12	5	2	6			1									19
			4	5	7	8^{2}	9^{3}	11		14	10^{1}			13	2	3	6	12		1									20
			4	5	7		8	11^{1}			13		14	12	2	3■	6	10^{3}		1	9^{2}								21
			3	5	4	8^{1}	7	11^{3}			12		13	14	2		6	10		1	9^{2}								22
			3	5	4		7			12	11		10		2	13	6^{1}	9		1	8^{2}								23
			4	5	7	14	8	11^{1}					10^{3}	12	2	3	6^{2}	13		1	9								24
			4	5	7	8^{1}	9						12		2	3	6	10		1	11								25
		4	3	5	7		12				10^{2}							13		1	9	2	6	8	11^{1}				26
		4	3		7		12				10^{2}				5		13	14		1	9	2	6^{3}	8	11^{1}				27
		4	3^{3}		7^{2}		14				10				5	12		13		1	9	2	6^{1}	8	11				28
		4	3	5	7^{3}	12					10						13	14			9	2	6^{2}	8	11^{1}	1			29
		4	3			7					10			5			14	13			9	2^{3}	6^{1}	8	11^{2}	1	12		30
		4	3		12	7					10			5				13			9^{1}		6	8^{3}	11^{2}	1	2	14	31
		4	3		12	7^{2}	9^{1}				10			5							11^{3}	2	6	8	14	1	13		32
		4	3	12	7	11^{1}	9				10			5								2	6	8		1			33
		4	3			11^{3}	9^{2}				10			5			7	12			13	2	6	8^{1}	14	1			34
		4	3		13	6	12				10			5							9^{2}	2	7	8	11^{1}	1			35
		4	3			8^{3}	12							5			14	10^{1}			9	2	6■	7	11^{2}	1		13	36
		4	3		7^{2}	8	9		13					5			14				11^{1}	2		6	10^{3}	1		12	37
																													38
																													39
																													40
																													41
																													42
																													43
																													44
																													45
																													46

FA Cup

First Round	Blackpool	(a)	1-4

Carabao Cup

First Round	Mansfield T	(a)	2-2
Second Round	Burton Alb	(a)	0-4

Leasing.com Trophy

Group G (N)	Blackpool	(a)	1-5
Group G (N)	Wolverhampton W U21	(h)	2-2
(Wolverhampton W U21 won 5-4 on penalties)			
Group G (N)	Carlisle U	(h)	3-1

NEWCASTLE UNITED

FOUNDATION

In October 1882 a club called Stanley, which had been formed in 1881, changed its name to Newcastle East End to avoid confusion with two other local clubs, Stanley Nops and Stanley Albion. Shortly afterwards another club, Rosewood, merged with them. Newcastle West End had been formed in August 1882 and they played on a pitch which was part of the Town Moor. They moved to Brandling Park in 1885 and St James' Park 1886 (home of Newcastle Rangers). West End went out of existence after a bad run and the remaining committee men invited East End to move to St James' Park. They accepted and, at a meeting in Bath Lane Hall in 1892, changed their name to Newcastle United.

St James' Park, Newcastle-upon-Tyne NE1 4ST.

Telephone: (0344) 372 1892.

Ticket Office: (0344) 372 1892 (option 1).

Website: www.nufc.co.uk

Email: admin@nufc.com

Ground Capacity: 52,305.

Record Attendance: 68,386 v Chelsea, Division 1, 3 September 1930.

Pitch Measurements: 105m × 68m (115yd × 74.5yd).

Managing Director: Lee Charnley.

Head Coach: Steve Bruce.

First-Team Coaches: Steve Agnew, Stephen Clemence.

Colours: Black and white striped shirts, black shorts, black socks with white trim.

Year Formed: 1881.

Turned Professional: 1889.

Previous Names: 1881, Stanley; 1882, Newcastle East End; 1892, Newcastle United.

Club Nickname: 'The Magpies', 'The Toon'.

Grounds: 1881, South Byker; 1886, Chillingham Road, Heaton; 1892, St James' Park.

First Football League Game: 2 September 1893, Division 2, v Royal Arsenal (a) D 2–2 – Ramsay; Jeffery, Miller; Crielly, Graham, McKane; Bowman, Crate (1), Thompson, Sorley (1), Wallace. Graham not Crate scored according to some reports.

Record League Victory: 13–0 v Newport Co, Division 2, 5 October 1946 – Garbutt; Cowell, Graham; Harvey, Brennan, Wright; Milburn (2), Bentley (1), Wayman (4), Shackleton (6), Pearson.

HONOURS

League Champions: Division 1 – 1904–05, 1906–07, 1908–09, 1926–27; FL C – 2009–10, 2016–17; First Division – 1992–93; Division 2 – 1964–65.
Runners-up: Premier League – 1995–96, 1996–97; Division 2 – 1897–98, 1947–48.

FA Cup Winners: 1910, 1924, 1932, 1951, 1952, 1955.
Runners-up: 1905, 1906, 1908, 1911, 1974, 1998, 1999.

League Cup: *Runners-up:* 1976.

Texaco Cup Winners: 1974, 1975.
Anglo-Italian Cup Winners: 1972–73.

European Competitions
Champions League: 1997–98, 2002–03, 2003–04.
Fairs Cup: 1968–69 *(winners)*, 1969–70 *(qf)*, 1970–71.
UEFA Cup: 1977–78, 1994–95, 1996–97 *(qf)*, 1999–2000, 2003–04 *(sf)*, 2004–05 *(qf)*, 2006–07.
Europa League: 2012–13 *(qf)*.
European Cup Winners' Cup: 1998–99.
Intertoto Cup: 2001 *(runners-up)*, 2005, 2006 *(winners)*.

FOOTBALL YEARBOOK FACT FILE

In March 1909, Newcastle United were presented with a Great Dane for a mascot. Named 'Rex', he was described as 'a handsome fellow, with [an] excellent black and white coat'. However, they lost in the FA Cup semi-final that season and Rex appears to have been discarded to be replaced by a figure of a magpie wearing football boots and smoking a cigar.

Record Cup Victory: 9–0 v Southport (at Hillsborough), FA Cup 4th rd, 1 February 1932 – McInroy; Nelson, Fairhurst; McKenzie, Davidson, Weaver (1); Boyd (1), Jimmy Richardson (3), Cape (2), McMenemy (1), Lang (1).

Record Defeat: 0–9 v Burton Wanderers, Division 2, 15 April 1895.

Most League Points (2 for a win): 57, Division 2, 1964–65.

Most League Points (3 for a win): 102, FL C, 2009–10.

Most League Goals: 98, Division 1, 1951–52.

Highest League Scorer in Season: Hughie Gallacher, 36, Division 1, 1926–27.

Most League Goals in Total Aggregate: Jackie Milburn, 177, 1946–57.

Most League Goals in One Match: 6, Len Shackleton v Newport Co, Division 2, 5 October 1946.

Most Capped Player: Shay Given, 82 (134), Republic of Ireland.

Most League Appearances: Jim Lawrence, 432, 1904–22.

Youngest League Player: Steve Watson, 16 years 223 days v Wolverhampton W, 10 November 1990.

Record Transfer Fee Received: £35,000,000 from Liverpool for Andy Carroll, January 2011.

Record Transfer Fee Paid: £40,000,000 to TSG 1899 Hoffenheim for Joelinton, July 2019.

Football League Record: 1893 Elected to Division 2; 1898–1934 Division 1; 1934–48 Division 2; 1948–61 Division 1; 1961–65 Division 2; 1965–78 Division 1; 1978–84 Division 2; 1984–89 Division 1; 1989–92 Division 2; 1992–93 Division 1; 1993–2009 Premier League; 2009–10 FL C; 2010–16 Premier League; 2016–17 FL C; 2017– Premier League.

MANAGERS

Frank Watt 1895–32
(Secretary-Manager)
Andy Cunningham 1930–35
Tom Mather 1935–39
Stan Seymour 1939–47
(Hon. Manager)
George Martin 1947–50
Stan Seymour 1950–54
(Hon. Manager)
Duggie Livingstone 1954–56
Stan Seymour 1956–58
(Hon. Manager)
Charlie Mitten 1958–61
Norman Smith 1961–62
Joe Harvey 1962–75
Gordon Lee 1975–77
Richard Dinnis 1977
Bill McGarry 1977–80
Arthur Cox 1980–84
Jack Charlton 1984
Willie McFaul 1985–88
Jim Smith 1988–91
Ossie Ardiles 1991–92
Kevin Keegan 1992–97
Kenny Dalglish 1997–98
Ruud Gullit 1998–99
Sir Bobby Robson 1999–2004
Graeme Souness 2004–06
Glenn Roeder 2006–07
Sam Allardyce 2007–08
Kevin Keegan 2008
Joe Kinnear 2008–09
Alan Shearer 2009
Chris Hughton 2009–10
Alan Pardew 2010–15
John Carver 2015
Steve McClaren 2015–16
Rafael Benitez 2016–19
Steve Bruce July 2019–

LATEST SEQUENCES

Longest Sequence of League Wins: 13, 25.4.1992 – 18.10.1992.

Longest Sequence of League Defeats: 10, 23.8.1977 – 15.10.1977.

Longest Sequence of League Draws: 4, 15.11.2008 – 6.12.2008.

Longest Sequence of Unbeaten League Matches: 17, 13.2.2010 – 2.5.2010.

Longest Sequence Without a League Win: 21, 14.1.1978 – 23.8.1978.

Successive Scoring Runs: 25 from 15.4.1939.

Successive Non-scoring Runs: 6 from 29.10.1988.

TEN YEAR LEAGUE RECORD

		P	W	D	L	F	A	Pts	Pos
2010-11	PR Lge	38	11	13	14	56	57	46	12
2011-12	PR Lge	38	19	8	11	56	51	65	5
2012-13	PR Lge	38	11	8	19	45	68	41	16
2013-14	PR Lge	38	15	4	19	43	59	49	10
2014-15	PR Lge	38	10	9	19	40	63	39	15
2015-16	PR Lge	38	9	10	19	44	65	37	18
2016-17	FL C	46	29	7	10	85	40	94	1
2017-18	PR Lge	38	12	8	18	39	47	44	10
2018-19	PR Lge	38	12	9	17	42	48	45	13
2019-20	PR Lge	38	11	11	16	38	58	44	13

DID YOU KNOW ?

It was not until November 2007 that Newcastle United won a penalty shoot-out in a senior competitive match. The Magpies, who had previously recorded seven consecutive defeats in games decided by spot-kicks, finally broke their drought with a 5-4 victory over Watford to decide their Carling Cup fourth round tie.

NEWCASTLE UNITED – PREMIER LEAGUE 2019–20 LEAGUE RECORD

Match No.	Date	Venue	Opponents	Result		H/T Score	Lg Pos.	Goalscorers	Attendance
1	Aug 11	H	Arsenal	L	0-1	0-0	14		47,635
2	17	A	Norwich C	L	1-3	0-1	17	Shelvey 90	27,059
3	25	A	Tottenham H	W	1-0	1-0	19	Joelinton 27	59,245
4	31	H	Watford	D	1-1	1-1	14	Schar 41	44,157
5	Sept 14	A	Liverpool	L	1-3	1-2	17	Willems 7	51,430
6	21	H	Brighton & HA	D	0-0	0-0	17		43,360
7	29	A	Leicester C	L	0-5	0-1	19		32,168
8	Oct 6	H	Manchester U	W	1-0	0-0	16	Longstaff, M 72	51,198
9	19	A	Chelsea	L	0-1	0-0	18		40,513
10	27	H	Wolverhampton W	D	1-1	1-0	17	Lascelles 37	46,019
11	Nov 2	A	West Ham U	W	3-2	2-0	15	Clark 16, Fernandez 22, Shelvey 51	59,907
12	9	H	Bournemouth	W	2-1	1-1	11	Yedlin 42, Clark 52	44,424
13	25	A	Aston Villa	L	0-2	0-2	14		41,821
14	30	H	Manchester C	D	2-2	1-1	14	Willems 25, Shelvey 88	49,937
15	Dec 5	A	Sheffield U	W	2-0	1-0	11	Saint-Maximin 15, Shelvey 70	30,409
16	8	H	Southampton	W	2-1	0-0	10	Shelvey 68, Fernandez 87	42,303
17	14	A	Burnley	L	0-1	0-0	11		19,798
18	21	H	Crystal Palace	W	1-0	0-0	9	Almiron 83	45,453
19	26	A	Manchester U	L	1-4	1-3	10	Longstaff, M 17	73,206
20	28	H	Everton	L	1-2	0-1	11	Schar 56	52,211
21	Jan 1	H	Leicester C	L	0-3	0-2	13		52,178
22	11	A	Wolverhampton W	D	1-1	1-1	13	Almiron 7	31,570
23	18	H	Chelsea	W	1-0	0-0	12	Hayden 90	52,217
24	21	A	Everton	D	2-2	0-1	13	Lejeune 2 90, 90	38,822
25	Feb 1	H	Norwich C	D	0-0	0-0	10		52,204
26	16	A	Arsenal	L	0-4	0-0	13		60,188
27	22	A	Crystal Palace	L	0-1	0-1	14		25,486
28	29	H	Burnley	D	0-0	0-0	14		52,219
29	Mar 7	A	Southampton	W	1-0	0-0	13	Saint-Maximin 79	30,096
30	June 21	H	Sheffield U	W	3-0	0-0	13	Saint-Maximin 55, Ritchie 69, Joelinton 78	0
31	24	H	Aston Villa	D	1-1	0-0	13	Gayle 68	0
32	July 1	A	Bournemouth	W	4-1	2-0	13	Gayle 5, Longstaff, S 30, Almiron 57, Lazaro 77	0
33	5	H	West Ham U	D	2-2	1-1	12	Almiron 17, Shelvey 67	0
34	8	A	Manchester C	L	0-5	0-2	13		0
35	11	A	Watford	L	1-2	1-0	13	Gayle 23	0
36	15	H	Tottenham H	L	1-3	0-1	13	Ritchie 56	0
37	20	A	Brighton & HA	D	0-0	0-0	13		0
38	26	H	Liverpool	L	1-3	1-1	13	Gayle 1	0

Final League Position: 13

GOALSCORERS

League (38): Shelvey 6, Almiron 4, Gayle 4, Saint-Maximin 3, Clark 2, Fernandez 2, Joelinton 2, Lejeune 2, Longstaff, M 2, Ritchie 2, Schar 2, Willems 2, Hayden 1, Lascelles 1, Lazaro 1, Longstaff, S 1, Yedlin 1.
FA Cup (11): Almiron 4, Joelinton 2, Lazaro 1, Longstaff, M 1, Longstaff, S 1, Saint-Maximin 1, own goal 1.
Carabao Cup (1): Muto 1.
Leasing.com Trophy (2): Anderson 1, Charman 1.

Dubravka M 38	Schar F 18 + 4	Lascelles J 24	Dummett P 14 + 2	Manquillo J 18 + 3	Hayden I 26 + 3	Shelvey J 25 + 1	Longstaff S 14 + 9	Ritchie M 14 + 4	Almiron M 35 + 1	Joelinton 32 + 6	Willems J 18 + 1	Saint-Maximin A 23 + 3	Krafth E 11 + 6	Ki S 1 + 2	Muto Y 2 + 6	Atsu C 6 + 13	Fernandez F 29 + 3	Carroll A 4 + 15	Yedlin D 10 + 6	Clark C 14	Longstaff M 6 + 3	Gayle D 10 + 10	Lejeune F 4 + 2	Bentaleb N 8 + 4	Lazaro V 4 + 9	Rose D 10 + 1	Watts K — + 1	*Match No.*
1	2	3	4	5	6	7^1	8^2	9	10	11	12	13																1
1	2	3	4		6	7	13	9	10	11^1			5	8^2	12													2
1	3	4^2	5		8		9	6	7	11^3		10^1	2		14	12	13											3
1	3^3	4	5	12	8		9		7	11	6		2^1		13	10^2	14											4
1	3^3	4	5	12	8	9			7^2	11	6		2^1		13	10	14											5
1	3	4	5	2	8	9^1			7^2	11	6^3	13		12		10		14										6
1	4	3	5		6■		7		8^3	11^2			2	12	9^1	10		13	14									7
1	3	4					9		7^3	11^1	6	10^2	14			13		12	2	5	8							8
1	3	4					9		7^1	11^2	6	10^3				13		12	2	5	8	14						9
1		4				12	8■		7	11^1	6	10^2				14	3		2	5	9^3	13						10
1		4	13		8	9			7	11^3	6^2	10^1				12	3	14	2	5								11
1		4^1	12		8	9			7	11^2	6	10^3				14	3	13	2	5								12
1			5^1		8	9			7^3	11^2	6	10				14	3	12	2	4		13						13
1			5	2	8	9			7	11^1	6	10^2				13	3			4		12						14
1			5	2	8	9			7^3	12	6	10^2	14			13	3	11^1		4								15
1	12		5	2	8	9	14		7^3	11^2	6	10					3	13		4^1								16
1	3		5	2	9		8			10	6^1				13	7^2	4	11				12						17
1	2		9^3	5	6^1	7	12		8	11^2							3	10	14			13	4					18
1	2^3			5			7		8^2	10	9		14			12	3		13		6	11^1	4					19
1	2				6	7	14		8	11^1	9^3					13	3	10	5			12	4^2					20
1	2			5^2	6	7^3	14		10	11	8^1		12		9		3		13				4					21
1			5^1		2		8		10	7^3	6					13	3	14		4	9	11^2	12					22
1		4			8	9^3	13	12	7	11	6^1	10	2^2				3			5	14							23
1	14	4			2		8	6	7	11^3			12			10^1	3			5^2	9		13					24
1		4			8^2		13	6	7	11		10^3					3		2^1	5				9	12	14		25
1	14	4			12		8	13	7	11		10					3^2			5^3				9	2^1	6		26
1	5	4					8	13	7^2	11		10					3					12		9	2■	6^1		27
1		4		2	7	8		6	10	9^1		12					3					11				5		28
1		3		2^2	7^3	8	14	6^1	11	12		9					4					10			13	5		29
1	15	3		2	8	7^4		6^5	10^3	11^2		9^1					4	13	16					12	14	5		30
1		3		2	8^4	7		6^2	10^3	11^1		9					4	12				13		14	15	5		31
1		3		5^5	15	6	9^1		12	10^4		8^3	2				4	13	16			11^2		7	14			32
1		3		5	7^1	6		14	9	10^4		8^2	2				4	15				11^3		12	13			33
1	4			12		8^3		10^5		11^2			3^4		15	16	5		2		14	13		9	7^1	6		34
1	7	3^4		2		8		9^1	10	12		6	14				4					11^2		13	15	5^3		35
1	4					9		6	10	13		7	3				5		2^1		14	11^2		8^3	12			36
1				5		6		9	8^3	13		10^1	2				3	12				11^2		7	14	4		37
1				2	14	6	13	9	8^3	12		10^1					3	15				11^4		7^2	5	4^5	16	38

FA Cup

Third Round	Rochdale	(a)	1-1
Replay	Rochdale	(h)	4-1
Fourth Round	Oxford U	(h)	0-0
Replay	Oxford U	(a)	3-2
(*aet*)			
Fifth Round	WBA	(a)	3-2
Sixth Round	Manchester C	(h)	0-2

Carabao Cup

Second Round	Leicester C	(h)	1-1

(Leicester C won 4-2 on penalties)

Leasing.com Trophy (Newcastle U U21)

Group D (N)	Macclesfield T	(a)	1-2
Group D (N)	Shrewsbury T	(a)	0-3
Group D (N)	Port Vale	(a)	1-2

NEWPORT COUNTY

FOUNDATION

In 1912 Newport County were formed following a meeting at The Tredegar Arms Hotel. A professional football club had existed in the town called Newport FC, but they ceased to exist in 1907. The first season as Newport County was in the second division of the Southern League. They started life playing at Somerton Park where they remained through their League years. They were elected to the Football League for the beginning of the 1920–21 season as founder members of Division 3. At the end of the 1987–88 season, they were relegated from the Football League and replaced by Lincoln City. On February 27 1989, Newport County went out of business and from the ashes Newport AFC was born. Starting down the pyramid in the Hellenic League, they eventally gained promotion to the Conference in 2011 and were promoted to the Football League after a play-off with Wrexham in 2013.

Rodney Parade, Rodney Road, Newport, South Wales NP19 0UU.

Telephone: (01633) 415 376.

Ticket Office: (01633) 415 374.

Website: www.newport-county.co.uk

Email: office@newport-county.co.uk

Ground Capacity: 8,700.

Record Attendance: 24,268 v Cardiff C, Division 3 (S), 16 October 1937 (Somerton Park); 4,660 v Swansea C, FA Cup 1st rd, 11 November 2006 (Newport Stadium); 9,836 v Tottenham H, FA Cup 4th rd, 27 January 2018 (Rodney Parade).

Pitch Measurements: 100m × 68m (109.5yd × 74.5yd).

Chairman: Gavin Foxall.

Manager: Michael Flynn.

Assistant Manager: Wayne Hatswell.

Colours: Amber shirts with black trim, amber shorts with black trim, amber socks with black trim.

Year Formed: 1912.

Turned Professional: 1912.

Previous Names: Newport County, 1912; Newport AFC, 1989; Newport County, 1999.

Club Nicknames: 'The Exiles', 'The Ironsides', 'The Port', 'The County'.

Grounds: 1912–89, 1990–92, Somerton Park; 1992–94, Meadow Park Stadium; 1994, Newport Stadium; 2012, Rodney Parade.

First Football League Game: 28 August 1920, Division 3, v Reading (h) L 0–1.

HONOURS

League Champions: Division 3S – 1938–39.
Runners-up: Conference – (3rd) 2012–13 *(promoted via play-offs)*.

FA Cup: 5th rd – 1949, 2019.

League Cup: never past 3rd rd.

Welsh Cup Winners: 1980.
Runners-up: 1963, 1987.

European Competitions
European Cup Winners' Cup: 1980–81 *(qf)*.

FOOTBALL YEARBOOK FACT FILE

Although most clubs chose to kick off Saturday afternoon games at 3.00 p.m. following the introduction of floodlighting systems, Newport matches started at 3.15 p.m. to allow workers from the local steelworks to attend. It was only in the mid-1980s, shortly before the club was relegated to the Conference, that County switched to 3.00 p.m. kick-offs.

Record League Victory: 10-0 v Merthyr T, Division 3(S), 10 April 1930 – Martin (5), Gittins (2), Thomas (1), Bagley (1), Lawson (1).

Record Cup Victory: 7-0 v Working, FA Cup 1st rd, 24 November 1928 – Young (3), Pugh (2) Gittins (1), Reid (1).

Record Defeat: 0–13 v Newcastle U, Division 2, 5 October 1946.

Most League Points (2 for a win): 61, Division 4, 1979–80.

Most League Points (3 for a win): 78, Division 3, 1982–83.

Most League Goals: 85, Division 4, 1964–65.

Highest League Scorer in Season: Tudor Martin, 34, Division 3 (S), 1929–30.

Most League Goals in Total Aggregate: Reg Parker, 99, 1948–54.

Most League Goals in One Match: 5, Tudor Martin v Merthyr T, Dvision 3 (S), 10 April 1930.

Most Capped Player: Keanu Marsh Brown, 10, Guyana.

Most League Appearances: Len Weare, 527, 1955–70.

Youngest League Player: Regan Poole, 16 years 94 days v Shrewsbury T, 20 September 2014.

Record Transfer Fee Received: £500,000 (rising to £1,000,000) from Peterborough U for Conor Washington, January 2014.

Record Transfer Fee Paid: £80,000 to Swansea C for Alan Waddle, January 1981.

Football League Record: 1920 Original member of Division 3; 1921–31 Division 3 (S) – dropped out of Football League; 1932 Re-elected to Division 3 (S); 1932–39 Division 3 (S); 1946–47 Division 2; 1947–58 Division 3 (S); 1958–62 Division 3; 1962–80 Division 4; 1980–87 Division 3; 1987–88 Division 4 (relegated from Football League); 2011 Promoted to Conference; 2011–13 Conference Premier; 2013– FL 2.

LATEST SEQUENCES

Longest Sequence of League Wins: 4, 21.8.2018 – 8.9.2018.

Longest Sequence of League Defeats: 8, 22.11.2016 – 7.1.2017.

Longest Sequence of League Draws: 4, 31.10.2015 – 24.11.2015.

Longest Sequence of Unbeaten League Matches: 17, 15.3.2019 – 7.9.2019.

Longest Sequence Without a League Win: 12, 15.3.2016 – 6.8.2017.

Successive Scoring Runs: 16 from 11.3.2017.

Successive Non-scoring Runs: 4 from 1.2.2020.

MANAGERS

Davy McDougle 1912–13 *(Player-Manager)*
Sam Hollis 1913–17
Harry Parkes 1919–22
Jimmy Hindmarsh 1922–35
Louis Page 1935–36
Tom Bromilow 1936–37
Billy McCandless 1937–45
Tom Bromilow 1945–50
Fred Stansfield 1950–53
Billy Lucas 1953–61
Bobby Evans 1961–62
Billy Lucas 1962–67
Leslie Graham 1967–69
Bobby Ferguson 1969–70 *(Player-Manager)*
Billy Lucas 1970–74
Brian Harris 1974–75
Dave Elliott 1975–76 *(Player-Manager)*
Jimmy Scoular 1976–77
Colin Addison 1977–78
Len Ashurst 1978–82
Colin Addison 1982–85
Bobby Smith 1985–86
John Relish 1986
Jimmy Mullen 1986–87
John Lewis 1987
Brian Eastick 1987–88
David Williams 1988
Eddie May 1988
John Mahoney 1988–89
John Relish 1989–93
Graham Rogers 1993–96
Chris Price 1997
Tim Harris 1997–2002
Peter Nicholas 2002–04
John Cornforth 2004–05
Peter Beadle 2005–08
Dean Holdsworth 2008–11
Anthony Hudson 2011
Justin Edinburgh 2011–15
Jimmy Dack 2015
Terry Butcher 2015
John Sheridan 2015–16
Warren Feeney 2016
Graham Westley 2016–17
Michael Flynn May 2017–

TEN YEAR LEAGUE RECORD

		P	*W*	*D*	*L*	*F*	*A*	*Pts*	*Pos*
2010-11	Conf P	46	18	15	13	78	60	69	9
2011-12	Conf P	46	11	14	21	53	65	47	19
2012-13	Conf P	46	25	10	11	85	60	85	3
2013-14	FL 2	46	14	16	16	56	59	58	14
2014-15	FL 2	46	18	11	17	51	54	65	9
2015-16	FL 2	46	10	13	23	43	64	43	22
2016-17	FL 2	46	12	12	22	51	73	48	22
2017-18	FL 2	46	16	16	14	56	58	64	11
2018-19	FL 2	46	20	11	15	59	59	71	7
2019-20	FL 2	36	12	10	14	32	39	46	14§

§Decided on points-per-game (1.28)

DID YOU KNOW ?

Newport County's Rodney Parade ground has hosted sporting activities since 1877, making it the second oldest sports stadium in the EFL. Like Preston North End's Deepdale ground (which dates back to 1875), it was first used to host rugby and cricket matches rather than football.

NEWPORT COUNTY – SKY BET LEAGUE TWO 2019–20 LEAGUE RECORD

Match No.	Date	Venue	Opponents	Result		H/T Score	Lg Pos.	Goalscorers	Attendance
1	Aug 3	H	Mansfield T	D	2-2	2-0	10	Labadie 6, Amond (pen) 34	4481
2	10	A	Cambridge U	D	0-0	0-0	15		3949
3	17	H	Plymouth Arg	W	1-0	0-0	9	Howkins 81	5048
4	20	A	Walsall	D	0-0	0-0	12		4337
5	24	H	Crewe Alex	W	1-0	0-0	5	Amond 90	3712
6	31	A	Forest Green R	W	2-0	1-0	2	Amond 4, Haynes 90	2897
7	Sept 7	H	Port Vale	W	1-0	0-0	2	Matt 77	3913
8	14	A	Northampton T	L	0-2	0-1	4		4616
9	17	A	Macclesfield T	D	1-1	1-1	6	Amond 1	1435
10	21	H	Exeter C	D	1-1	0-1	7	Abrahams (pen) 64	4762
11	28	A	Swindon T	W	2-0	1-0	6	O'Brien 38, Matt 82	7843
12	Oct 5	H	Carlisle U	W	1-0	0-0	3	Nurse 90	3681
13	19	H	Scunthorpe U	W	2-1	1-0	3	Amond 45, Sheehan 56	3936
14	22	H	Crawley T	D	1-1	0-1	5	Abrahams (pen) 74	3119
15	26	A	Colchester U	L	1-3	1-2	7	Abrahams 5	2955
16	Nov 2	H	Salford C	L	1-2	1-1	7	Pond (og) 45	3947
17	23	H	Oldham Ath	L	0-1	0-1	11		3748
18	Dec 7	A	Bradford C	L	0-1	0-0	12		14,016
19	14	H	Stevenage	D	1-1	0-1	12	Matt 90	3556
20	21	A	Morecambe	L	1-2	1-0	13	Labadie 14	2161
21	26	A	Exeter C	L	0-1	0-1	14		5968
22	29	H	Leyton Orient	D	1-1	0-1	13	Amond 81	4447
23	Jan 1	H	Cheltenham T	D	1-1	0-0	14	Abrahams 47	3913
24	11	A	Scunthorpe U	W	2-1	0-1	11	Matt 72, Amond 76	3001
25	18	H	Swindon T	W	2-0	1-0	11	Sheehan 1, Matt 49	4981
26	25	A	Leyton Orient	L	1-2	0-0	11	Matt 90	5084
27	28	H	Macclesfield T	W	1-0	1-0	11	Labadie 34	3354
28	Feb 1	A	Plymouth Arg	L	0-1	0-1	12		10,956
29	8	H	Cambridge U	L	0-1	0-0	13		3336
30	11	H	Walsall	D	0-0	0-0	13		3049
31	15	A	Mansfield T	L	0-1	0-1	16		3653
32	22	H	Bradford C	W	2-1	2-1	15	Inniss 28, Bennett 33	3439
33	25	A	Grimsby T	L	2-4	1-2	16	Green 10, Amond 68	3578
34	29	A	Oldham Ath	L	0-5	0-2	16		2912
35	Mar 7	H	Morecambe	W	1-0	0-0	15	Gorman 69	3048
36	10	A	Carlisle U	L	0-2	0-2	15		2822
37	14	A	Stevenage	Cancelled					
38	17	A	Crawley T	Cancelled					
39	21	H	Colchester U	Cancelled					
40	24	A	Cheltenham T	Cancelled					
41	28	A	Salford C	Cancelled					
42	Apr 4	H	Grimsby T	Cancelled					
43	10	A	Crewe Alex	Cancelled					
44	13	H	Forest Green R	Cancelled					
45	18	A	Port Vale	Cancelled					
46	25	H	Northampton T	Cancelled					

Final League Position: 14 (on points-per-game basis)

GOALSCORERS

League (32): Amond 8 (1 pen), Matt 6, Abrahams 4 (2 pens), Labadie 3, Sheehan 2, Bennett 1, Gorman 1, Green 1, Haynes 1, Howkins 1, Inniss 1, Nurse 1, O'Brien 1, own goal 1.
FA Cup (4): Amond 3 (1 pen), Labadie 1.
Carabao Cup (2): Abrahams 1, Amond 1 (1 pen).
Leasing.com Trophy (15): Abrahams 5, Maloney 3, Amond 1, Bennett 1, Collins 1, Dolan 1 (1 pen), Hillier 1, Whitely 1, own goal 1.

King T 31	Howkins K 10 + 6	Demetriou M 21	Haynes R 32	Willmott R 26 + 1	Sheehan J 33	Dolan M 13 + 9	Labadie J 24 + 3	McNamara D 20 + 1	Matt J 26 + 7	Amond P 26 + 7	Whitely C 3 + 7	Abrahams T 17 + 16	Bennett S 25 + 3	O'Brien M 21	Maloney T 5 + 5	Nurse G 9 + 8	Collins L — + 6	Inniss R 21 + 1	Leadbitter D 3	Poleon D — + 5	Townsend N 5	Baker A 4	Green J 8 + 3	Waters B 2 + 4	Gorman D 7 + 1	Khan O 4 + 1	Match No.
1	2	3	4	5	6	7^2	8	9^1	10	11	12	13															1
1	3	4	5	6	7	8^2	9	2	11	10^1		12	13														2
1	12	3^1	5	7	8		9	2	11	10		13	6^2	4													3
1	3		5	7	6		8^1	2	10	9		11		4	12												4
1	3		5	6^3	9	7^2		2		10	8^1	11		4	13	12	14										5
1	12		5	6	9	8^1	7^3	2		11	14	10		3^2	13			4									6
1	14		5	8	9	7	6^3		12	11	13	10^2		3				4	2^1								7
1	3		5	7	6	8^3	9	2^1	12■	10^2	13	11		4						14							8
1	3		5	11	7	12	8	2		10		9^2	6^1	4						13							9
1	3		8	5	6	13	7		11^3	10^2	9^1	12	4	2						14							10
1	3		5	7	8	13	9^2	2	11	12		10^1	6	4													11
1	3		5	6	8	9^3		2^1	11	10^2	13	12	7	4		14											12
1			6	7	8		9^1	2	11	10^2		12	5	3		13		4									13
1			5	7	8		9^2	2^3	11^1	10	13	14	6	4		12		3									14
1			5	7^1	8	14	13	2	12	11^2		10	6	4		9^3		3									15
1			9	5^2	7	8^1		12	11	10	14	13	4	3	6^3			2									16
			5			12	6^1	2^2	11	10	9^3	8	7	4	13	14		3			1						17
			5		7	8^2		2^3	12	10^1		11		4	6	9	14	3		13	1						18
		4	5		6	7^3		2^2	11	10		13	12	3^1	9	8	14				1						19
		4	5		6		9	2	11	10		14	12	3^3	7^2	8^1		13			1						20
		4	8		7		9	5^3	10	11^1		13	3		6^2	12	14	2			1						21
1		4	5^2		7		9	2	10	12		11	6			8		3^1		13							22
1		3^3	5		8	12	9^1	2	10	14		11^2	6		13	7		4									23
1		4	9		7		8		12	11		10	5	3^1		6		2									24
1		4	9		7		8		10^1			11^3	5^2	3				2				6	12	13	14		25
1		4	5	7	8	9^3			10	14		11^2	6	3		13						2^1	12				26
1		4	5	8	6		9		10	11^1		13	3									2	7^2	12			27
1	13	2	8^1	5	7		6		10	9^2			3			12						4^3	11	14			28
1	4^2	5		8	9^3		7		10	12		14	6					3	2^1				11			13	29
1		5		12			6		11	13		14	4					3	2^3				8^1	9^2	7	10	30
1		5		2		14	6		13	9		11^2	4				12	3					8	10^3	7^1		31
1	13	4	9	5	6	14			11			12	3					2					10^3		7^1	8^2	32
1		4		5	7		12		11^3	13		14	3			9		2^1					10^2		6	8	33
1	13	4	5	2^2	6	14			11^3	9						8	12	3							7	10^1	34
1		4	9	6	7	8			10			11^1	3					2					12		5		35
1		4	8	5	9	7^1	12		13	11^3			3					2■					10^2	14	6		36
																											37
																											38
																											39
																											40
																											41
																											42
																											43
																											44
																											45
																											46

FA Cup

First Round	Grimsby T	(a)	1-1
Replay	Grimsby T	(h)	2-0
Second Round	Maldon & Tiptree	(a)	1-0
Third Round	Millwall	(a)	0-3

Carabao Cup

First Round	Gillingham	(a)	2-2
(Newport Co won 4-1 on penalties)			
Second Round	West Ham U	(h)	0-2

Leasing.com Trophy

Group E (S)	West Ham U U21	(h)	4-5
Group E (S)	Exeter C	(h)	0-2
Group E (S)	Cheltenham T	(a)	7-4
Second Round (S)	Brighton & HA U21	(a)	0-0
(Newport Co won 5-4 on penalties)			
Third Round (S)	Milton Keynes D	(h)	3-0
Quarter-Final	Leicester C U21	(h)	1-0
Semi-Final	Salford C	(h)	0-0
(Salford C won 6-5 on penalties)			

NORTHAMPTON TOWN

FOUNDATION

Formed in 1897 by schoolteachers connected with the Northampton & District Elementary Schools' Association, they survived a financial crisis at the end of their first year when they were £675 in the red and became members of the Midland League – a fast move indeed for a new club. They achieved Southern League membership in 1901.

PTS Academy Stadium, Upton Way, Northampton NN5 5QA.

Telephone: (01604) 683 700.

Ticket Office: (01604) 683 777.

Website: www.ntfc.co.uk

Email: wendy.lambell@ntfc.co.uk

Ground Capacity: 7,798.

Record Attendance: 24,523 v Fulham, Division 1, 23 April 1966 (at County Ground); 7,798 v Manchester U, EFL Cup 3rd rd, 21 September 2016; 7,798 v Derby Co, FA Cup 4th rd, 24 January 2019 (at Sixfields Stadium).

Pitch Measurements: 106m × 66m (116yd × 72yd).

Chairman: Kelvin Thomas.

Chief Executive: James Whiting.

Manager: Keith Curle.

Assistant Manager: Colin West.

Colours: Claret shirts with white sleeves, white shorts, claret socks with white trim.

Year Formed: 1897.

Turned Professional: 1901.

Grounds: 1897, County Ground; 1994, Sixfields Stadium (renamed PTS Academy Stadium 2018).

Club Nickname: 'The Cobblers'.

First Football League Game: 28 August 1920, Division 3, v Grimsby T (a) L 0–2 – Thorpe; Sproston, Hewison; Jobey, Tomkins, Pease; Whitworth, Lockett, Thomas, Freeman, MacKechnie.

Record League Victory: 10–0 v Walsall, Division 3 (S), 5 November 1927 – Hammond; Watson, Jeffs; Allen, Brett, Odell; Daley, Smith (3), Loasby (3), Hoten (1), Wells (3).

Record Cup Victory: 10–0 v Sutton T, FA Cup prel rd, 7 December 1907 – Cooch; Drennan, Lloyd Davies, Tirrell (1), McCartney, Hickleton, Badenock (3), Platt (3), Lowe (1), Chapman (2), McDiarmid.

Record Defeat: 0–11 v Southampton, Southern League, 28 December 1901.

HONOURS

League Champions: Division 3 – 1962–63; FL 2 – 2015–16; Division 4 – 1986–87.
Runners-up: Division 2 – 1964–65; Division 3S – 1927–28, 1949–50; FL 2 – 2005–06; Division 4 – 1975–76.

FA Cup: 5th rd – 1934, 1950, 1970.

League Cup: 5th rd – 1965, 1967.

FOOTBALL YEARBOOK FACT FILE

Northampton Town were reported to have paid their first-ever transfer fee when they bought defender Edwin Lloyd Davies from Stoke in November 1907. He proved a real bargain and continued to play for the Cobblers well past his 40th birthday, making a total of over 300 appearances. The 12 caps he won for Wales while at the County Ground remain a club record.

Most League Points (2 for a win): 68, Division 4, 1975–76.

Most League Points (3 for a win): 99, Division 4, 1986–87; FL 2, 2015–16.

Most League Goals: 109, Division 3, 1962–63 and Division 3 (S), 1952–53.

Highest League Scorer in Season: Cliff Holton, 36, Division 3, 1961–62.

Most League Goals in Total Aggregate: Jack English, 135, 1947–60.

Most League Goals in One Match: 5, Ralph Hoten v Crystal Palace, Division 3 (S), 27 October 1928.

Most Capped Player: Edwin Lloyd Davies, 12 (16), Wales.

Most League Appearances: Tommy Fowler, 521, 1946–61.

Youngest League Player: Adrian Mann, 16 years 297 days v Bury, 5 May 1984.

Record Transfer Fee Received: £470,000 from Blackburn R for Mark Bunn, September 2008.

Record Transfer Fee Paid: £165,000 to Oldham Ath for Josh Low, July 2003.

Football League Record: 1920 Original Member of Division 3; 1921 Division 3 (S); 1958–61 Division 4; 1961–63 Division 3; 1963–65 Division 2; 1965–66 Division 1; 1966–67 Division 2; 1967–69 Division 3; 1969–76 Division 4; 1976–77 Division 3; 1977–87 Division 4; 1987–90 Division 3; 1990–92 Division 4; 1992–97 Division 3; 1997–99 Division 2; 1999–2000 Division 3; 2000–03 Division 2; 2003–04 Division 3; 2004–06 FL 2; 2006–09 FL 1; 2009–16 FL 2; 2016–18 FL 1; 2018–20 FL 2; 2020– FL 1.

LATEST SEQUENCES

Longest Sequence of League Wins: 10, 28.12.2015 – 23.2.2016.

Longest Sequence of League Defeats: 8, 26.10.1935 – 21.12.1935.

Longest Sequence of League Draws: 6, 5.2.2011 – 26.2.2011.

Longest Sequence of Unbeaten League Matches: 31, 28.12.2015 – 10.9.2016.

Longest Sequence Without a League Win: 18, 5.2.2011 – 25.4.2011.

Successive Scoring Runs: 28 from 29.8.2015.

Successive Non-scoring Runs: 7 from 7.4.1939.

MANAGERS

Arthur Jones 1897–1907
(Secretary-Manager)
Herbert Chapman 1907–12
Walter Bull 1912–13
Fred Lessons 1913–19
Bob Hewison 1920–25
Jack Tresadern 1925–30
Jack English 1931–35
Syd Puddefoot 1935–37
Warney Cresswell 1937–39
Tom Smith 1939–49
Bob Dennison 1949–54
Dave Smith 1954–59
David Bowen 1959–67
Tony Marchi 1967–68
Ron Flowers 1968–69
Dave Bowen 1969–72
(continued as General Manager and Secretary 1972–85 when joined the board)
Billy Baxter 1972–73
Bill Dodgin Jnr 1973–76
Pat Crerand 1976–77
By committee 1977
Bill Dodgin Jnr 1977
John Petts 1977–78
Mike Keen 1978–79
Clive Walker 1979–80
Bill Dodgin Jnr 1980–82
Clive Walker 1982–84
Tony Barton 1984–85
Graham Carr 1985–90
Theo Foley 1990–92
Phil Chard 1992–93
John Barnwell 1993–94
Ian Atkins 1995–99
Kevin Wilson 1999–2001
Kevan Broadhurst 2001–03
Terry Fenwick 2003
Martin Wilkinson 2003
Colin Calderwood 2003–06
John Gorman 2006
Stuart Gray 2007–09
Ian Sampson 2009–11
Gary Johnson 2011
Aidy Boothroyd 2011–13
Chris Wilder 2014–16
Rob Page 2016–17
Justin Edinburgh 2017
Jimmy Floyd Hasselbaink 2017–18
Dean Austin 2018
Keith Curle October 2018–

TEN YEAR LEAGUE RECORD

		P	*W*	*D*	*L*	*F*	*A*	*Pts*	*Pos*
2010-11	FL 2	46	11	19	16	63	71	52	16
2011-12	FL 2	46	12	12	22	56	79	48	20
2012-13	FL 2	46	21	10	15	64	55	73	6
2013-14	FL 2	46	13	14	19	42	57	53	21
2014-15	FL 2	46	18	7	21	67	62	61	12
2015-16	FL 2	46	29	12	5	82	46	99	1
2016-17	FL 1	46	14	11	21	60	73	53	16
2017-18	FL 1	46	12	11	23	43	77	47	22
2018-19	FL 2	46	14	19	13	64	63	61	15
2019-20	FL 2	37	17	7	13	54	40	58	7§

§Decided on points-per-game (1.57)

DID YOU KNOW ?

Northampton Town were one of many Football League clubs to travel to the Netherlands in the period between the wars to play against the host's national team. On 9 November 1932 the Cobblers defeated the Dutch National XI 4-0 in a match held at the Sparta Stadium in Rotterdam.

NORTHAMPTON TOWN – SKY BET LEAGUE TWO 2019–20 LEAGUE RECORD

Match No.	*Date*	*Venue*	*Opponents*	*Result*		*H/T Score*	*Lg Pos.*	*Goalscorers*	*Attendance*
1	Aug 3	H	Walsall	L	0-1	0-1	17		6260
2	10	A	Port Vale	D	1-1	1-1	19	Watson [45]	5931
3	17	H	Macclesfield T	L	1-2	0-1	20	Turnbull [72]	4319
4	20	A	Swindon T	W	1-0	0-0	19	Williams, A [67]	7203
5	24	A	Colchester U	L	0-1	0-0	20		3164
6	31	H	Plymouth Arg	W	3-1	3-1	17	Watson (pen) [7], Williams, A 2 [21, 41]	5535
7	Sept 7	A	Bradford C	L	1-2	1-0	18	Goode [20]	13,678
8	14	H	Newport Co	W	2-0	1-0	14	Williams, A [5], Hoskins [72]	4616
9	17	A	Stevenage	W	1-0	0-0	10	Smith [56]	2877
10	21	H	Crawley T	D	2-2	1-0	12	Lines (pen) [15], McWilliams, S [64]	5121
11	28	A	Morecambe	D	2-2	2-0	13	Turnbull 2 [21, 37]	2245
12	Oct 5	H	Leyton Orient	L	0-1	0-0	14		5419
13	12	A	Scunthorpe U	L	0-3	0-3	18		3377
14	19	H	Salford C	W	2-0	1-0	15	Hoskins (pen) [35], Turnbull [66]	4886
15	22	A	Carlisle U	W	2-0	0-0	9	Pollock [51], Hoskins [90]	3324
16	26	H	Cambridge U	W	2-0	2-0	8	Smith [26], Taft (og) [45]	5221
17	Nov 2	A	Oldham Ath	D	2-2	1-0	9	Warburton [6], Williams, A [80]	3274
18	16	H	Crewe Alex	W	4-1	3-1	7	Wharton 2 [10, 18], Hoskins (pen) [24], Williams, A [56]	5236
19	23	H	Grimsby T	W	2-0	2-0	5	Wharton [25], Oliver [41]	5211
20	Dec 7	A	Exeter C	L	2-3	1-1	7	Goode [33], Hoskins [79]	3971
21	14	H	Forest Green R	W	1-0	1-0	7	Mills, M (og) [45]	4534
22	21	A	Mansfield T	D	1-1	0-0	7	Smith [84]	4496
23	26	A	Crawley T	L	0-4	0-1	9		2190
24	29	H	Cheltenham T	D	1-1	1-1	9	Turnbull [38]	5090
25	Jan 1	H	Stevenage	W	1-0	0-0	7	Williams, A [90]	4613
26	11	A	Salford C	W	2-1	1-1	8	Hoskins [29], Williams, A [63]	2919
27	18	H	Morecambe	W	4-1	2-0	6	Anderson [28], Watson [45], Adams [55], Lines [75]	4761
28	21	A	Leyton Orient	D	1-1	1-0	6	Watson [43]	3774
29	28	H	Scunthorpe U	W	3-0	1-0	6	Oliver 2 [7, 62], Hoskins (pen) [70]	4038
30	Feb 1	A	Macclesfield T	W	1-0	0-0	5	Morton [59]	1712
31	8	H	Port Vale	L	0-1	0-0	6		5583
32	11	H	Swindon T	L	0-1	0-0	6		5759
33	15	A	Walsall	L	2-3	2-0	8	Morton 2 [21, 39]	4541
34	22	H	Exeter C	W	2-0	1-0	7	Oliver [1], Hoskins (pen) [81]	5046
35	25	A	Cheltenham T	L	1-2	1-1	7	Watson [3]	2934
36	29	A	Grimsby T	W	3-0	2-0	6	Goode [9], Morton 2 [26, 82]	4879
37	Mar 7	H	Mansfield T	L	1-2	0-1	7	Smith [90]	5666
38	14	A	Forest Green R	Cancelled					
39	17	H	Carlisle U	Cancelled					
40	21	A	Cambridge U	Cancelled					
41	28	H	Oldham Ath	Cancelled					
42	Apr 4	A	Crewe Alex	Cancelled					
43	10	H	Colchester U	Cancelled					
44	13	A	Plymouth Arg	Cancelled					
45	18	H	Bradford C	Cancelled					
46	25	A	Newport Co	Cancelled					

Final League Position: 7 (on points-per-game basis)

GOALSCORERS

League (54): Hoskins 8 (4 pens), Williams, A 8, Morton 5, Turnbull 5, Watson 5 (1 pen), Oliver 4, Smith 4, Goode 3, Wharton 3, Lines 2 (1 pen), Adams 1, Anderson 1, McWilliams, S 1, Pollock 1, Warburton 1, own goals 2.
FA Cup (12): Oliver 3, Adams 2, Hoskins 2 (1 pen), Smith 2, Goode 1, Watson 1, Wharton 1.
Carabao Cup (1): Warburton 1.
Leasing.com Trophy (3): Harriman 1, Hoskins 1, Smith 1.
League Two Play-offs (7): Morton 3, Hoskins 1, Oliver 1, Watson 1, Williams, A 1.

Cornell D 33 + 1	Hall-Johnson R 4 + 1	Goode C 36	Wharton S 30 + 2	Martin J 13 + 4	McCormack A 11 + 4	Lines C 25 + 6	Hoskins S 36 + 1	Warburton M 8 + 10	Adams N 37	Smith H 7 + 12	McWilliams S 13 + 4	Williams A 20 + 12	Watson R 21 + 4	Arnold S 4	Bunney J 3 + 1	Morias J — + 2	Turnbull J 31	Oliver V 19 + 11	Waters B 2 + 5	Pollock S 3 + 8	Harriman M 15 + 6	Kaja E — + 4	Anderson P 17 + 1	Roberts M — + 1	Olayinka J 1	Morton C 7 + 2	Marshall M 5 + 2	Jones L 6 + 1	Match No.
1	2^1	3	4	5	6^2	7	8	9^3	10	11	12	13	14																1
13	2	3	4	5^1		7	10	9^3	8	11			6	1^2	12	14													2
1		2	4	8^3			11	9^1	5	10^2	7	13	6			14	3	12											3
1		3	4^1			6	11		9		2	10^2	8		5		7	13	12										4
1		3				8^3	9		6	13	2	11^2	7		5		4	10^1	12	14									5
1		3		13		6	10	9^1	8^3		2	11^2	7		5		4	14	12										6
1		3	14	5		7	10	9^1	8^3		6	11^2					4	12	13		2								7
1		3	4	5		8	10	14	7^3	13	9^2	11^1					6				2	12							8
1		3	4	5		9	10		7^2	12■	8	11^1					6^3	13			2	14							9
1		3	4	5		9^1	7	14	10^2		8	11^3					6	12			2	13							10
1	13	3	4	5		8	7	14	10	12	9^2	11^1					6				2^3								11
1	3		4	5	12	8	6	14	9	11^2	7^3	10^1						13			2								12
1	2	3	4	5^2	12		8	9	10	14	7^3	13					6^1	11■											13
1		3	5		6^2	7	8		10^1		14	11					4		9^3	12	2		13						14
1		3	5			13	9		10	12	6	11^2					4	14	8^3	7	2^1								15
1		2	4		7^1	13	10		9	11^3	6	14					3		12	8			5^2						16
1		3	5		9^3	8	2	11	6	10^2		12					4	13			14		7^1						17
1		2	3		7^2	6	5	14	8	12		10					4	11^1		13			9^3						18
1		2	3		6	7	5		8	12		10^2	13				4	11^1		14			9^3						19
1		2	4		6^1	7	8		5	12		10^2	13				3	11				14	9^3						20
1		2	4			7^2	10		8	13	12	14	6				3	11^1			5		9^3						21
1		2	3	14	6^3		10		8	12		13	7				4	11			5^1		9^2						22
		2	3	9^1	8^3	6^2	10		5	11	12	13	7	1			4	14											23
1		2	3				9^1		8			11	7				4	10		12	5		6						24
1		2	3			12	10	14	8			13	7^3				4	11		6^2	5^1		9						25
1		2	3			6	5	12	8^1			10^2	7				4	11			13		9^3	14					26
1		2	3	14		6	5	13	8^1			10	7				4	11^2			12		9^3						27
1		2	4■	13		6	12	10	8^1			14	7				3	11^3			5		9^2						28
1		3		4		14	5		8^3			11^2	7					10			2		9^1		6	12	13		29
1		3		4		6	9		8			12	7					11								10^1	5	2	30
1		3	4			14	9	13	8			12	7^2					11					6^3			10^1	5	2	31
1		3	4			6^1	9		8			10	13				7	11^2								12	5	2	32
1		3	4				8	12	5			11^3	6				7	14			13		9^2			10^1		2	33
1		2			14	7	8		5				6^3				4	11^1		12	13		9^2			10		3	34
1		2	12		14	7	10^2		8^3				6				4				5		9^1			11	13	3	35
		2	4		6^2	12	9		8				7	1			3	11^1		13	14					10	5^3		36
		2	4		6^3		9■		8	12			7	1			3	11		14						10^2	5^1	13	37
																													38
																													39
																													40
																													41
																													42
																													43
																													44
																													45
																													46

FA Cup

First Round	Chippenham T	(a)	3-0
Second Round	Notts Co	(h)	3-1
Third Round	Burton Alb	(a)	4-2
Fourth Round	Derby Co	(h)	0-0
Replay	Derby Co	(a)	2-4

Carabao Cup

First Round	Swansea C	(a)	1-3

Leasing.com Trophy

Group H (S)	Arsenal U21	(h)	1-1
(Northampton T won 4-3 on penalties)			
Group H (S)	Peterborough U	(h)	0-2
Group H (S)	Cambridge U	(a)	1-0
Second Round (S)	Portsmouth	(a)	1-2

League Two Play-Offs

Semi-Final 1st leg	Cheltenham T	(h)	0-2
Semi-Final 2nd leg	Cheltenham T	(a)	3-0
Final	Exeter C	(Wembley)	4-0

NORWICH CITY

FOUNDATION

Formed in 1902, largely through the initiative of two local schoolmasters who called a meeting at the Criterion Cafe, they were shocked by an FA Commission which in 1904 declared the club professional and ejected them from the FA Amateur Cup. However, this only served to strengthen their determination. New officials were appointed and a professional club established at a meeting in the Agricultural Hall in March 1905.

Carrow Road, Norwich, Norfolk NR1 1JE.

Telephone: (01603) 760 760.

Ticket Office: (01603) 721 902 (option 1).

Website: www.canaries.co.uk

Email: reception@canaries.co.uk

Ground Capacity: 27,329.

Record Attendance: 25,037 v Sheffield W, FA Cup 5th rd, 16 February 1935 (at The Nest); 43,984 v Leicester C, FA Cup 6th rd, 30 March 1963 (at Carrow Road).

Pitch Measurements: 105.2m × 68m (115yd × 74.5yd).

Joint Majority Shareholders: Delia Smith, Michael Wynn-Jones.

Chief Operating Officer: Ben Kensell.

Head Coach: Daniel Farke.

Assistant Head Coach: Edmund Riemer.

HONOURS

League Champions: FL C – 2018–19; First Division – 2003–04; Division 2 – 1971–72, 1985–86; FL 1 – 2009–10; Division 3S – 1933–34.
Runners-up: FL C – 2010–11; Division 3 – 1959–60; Division 3S – 1950–51.

FA Cup: semi-final – 1959, 1989, 1992.

League Cup Winners: 1962, 1985.
Runners-up: 1973, 1975.

European Competitions
UEFA Cup: 1993–94.

Colours: Yellow shirts with green trim, green shorts with yellow trim, yellow socks with green trim.

Year Formed: 1902.

Turned Professional: 1905.

Club Nickname: 'The Canaries'.

Grounds: 1902, Newmarket Road; 1908, The Nest, Rosary Road; 1935, Carrow Road.

First Football League Game: 28 August 1920, Division 3, v Plymouth Arg (a) D 1–1 – Skermer; Gray, Gadsden; Wilkinson, Addy, Martin; Laxton, Kidger, Parker, Whitham (1), Dobson.

Record League Victory: 10–2 v Coventry C, Division 3 (S), 15 March 1930 – Jarvie; Hannah, Graham; Brown, O'Brien, Lochhead (1); Porter (1), Anderson, Hunt (5), Scott (2), Slicer (1).

Record Cup Victory: 8–0 v Sutton U, FA Cup 4th rd, 28 January 1989 – Gunn; Culverhouse, Bowen, Butterworth, Linighan, Townsend (Crook), Gordon, Fleck (3), Allen (4), Phelan, Putney (1).

Record Defeat: 2–10 v Swindon T, Southern League, 5 September 1908.

Most League Points (2 for a win): 64, Division 3 (S), 1950–51.

Most League Points (3 for a win): 95, FL 1, 2009–10.

Most League Goals: 99, Division 3 (S), 1952–53.

Highest League Scorer in Season: Ralph Hunt, 31, Division 3 (S), 1955–56.

FOOTBALL YEARBOOK FACT FILE

Norwich City fought their way through five rounds to reach the last eight of the FA Amateur Cup in 1903–04 before losing out to Ealing in a replay. When the Canaries entered the following season, however, an FA Commission concluded the club had breached the rules for amateur clubs. As a result several club officials were suspended by the FA and City withdrew from the competition.

Most League Goals in Total Aggregate: Johnny Gavin, 122, 1945–54, 1955–58.

Most League Goals in One Match: 5, Tommy Hunt v Coventry C, Division 3 (S), 15 March 1930; 5, Roy Hollis v Walsall, Division 3 (S), 29 December 1951.

Most Capped Player: Wes Hoolahan, 42 (43), Republic of Ireland.

Most League Appearances: Ron Ashman, 592, 1947–64.

Youngest League Player: Ryan Jarvis, 16 years 282 days v Walsall, 19 April 2003.

Record Transfer Fee Received: £22,000,000 (rising to £24,000,000) from Leicester C for James Maddison, June 2018.

Record Transfer Fee Paid: £8,500,000 to Sporting Lisbon for Ricky van Wolfswinkel, July 2013; £8,500,000 to Everton for Steven Naismith, January 2016.

Football League Record: 1920 Original Member of Division 3; 1921 Division 3 (S); 1934–39 Division 2; 1946–58 Division 3 (S); 1958–60 Division 3; 1960–72 Division 2; 1972–74 Division 1; 1974–75 Division 2; 1975–81 Division 1; 1981–82 Division 2; 1982–85 Division 1; 1985–86 Division 2; 1986–92 Division 1; 1992–95 Premier League; 1995–2004 Division 1; 2004–05 Premier League; 2005–09 FL C; 2009–10 FL 1; 2010–11 FL C; 2011–14 Premier League; 2014–15 FL C; 2015–16 Premier League; 2016–19 FL C; 2019–20 Premier League; 2020– FL C.

LATEST SEQUENCES

Longest Sequence of League Wins: 10, 23.11.1985 – 25.1.1986.

Longest Sequence of League Defeats: 10, 7.3.2020 – 26.7.2020.

Longest Sequence of League Draws: 7, 15.1.1994 – 26.2.1994.

Longest Sequence of Unbeaten League Matches: 20, 31.8.1950 – 30.12.1950.

Longest Sequence Without a League Win: 25, 22.9.1956 – 23.2.1957.

Successive Scoring Runs: 30 from 1.12.2018.

Successive Non-scoring Runs: 5 from 7.3.2020.

MANAGERS

John Bowman 1905–07
James McEwen 1907–08
Arthur Turner 1909–10
Bert Stansfield 1910–15
Major Frank Buckley 1919–20
Charles O'Hagan 1920–21
Albert Gosnell 1921–26
Bert Stansfield 1926
Cecil Potter 1926–29
James Kerr 1929–33
Tom Parker 1933–37
Bob Young 1937–39
Jimmy Jewell 1939
Bob Young 1939–45
Duggie Lochhead 1945–46
Cyril Spiers 1946–47
Duggie Lochhead 1947–50
Norman Low 1950–55
Tom Parker 1955–57
Archie Macaulay 1957–61
Willie Reid 1961–62
George Swindin 1962
Ron Ashman 1962–66
Lol Morgan 1966–69
Ron Saunders 1969–73
John Bond 1973–80
Ken Brown 1980–87
Dave Stringer 1987–92
Mike Walker 1992–94
John Deehan 1994–95
Martin O'Neill 1995
Gary Megson 1995–96
Mike Walker 1996–98
Bruce Rioch 1998–2000
Bryan Hamilton 2000
Nigel Worthington 2000–06
Peter Grant 2006–07
Glenn Roeder 2007–09
Bryan Gunn 2009
Paul Lambert 2009–12
Chris Hughton 2012–14
Neil Adams 2014–15
Alex Neil 2015–17
Daniel Farke May 2017–

TEN YEAR LEAGUE RECORD

		P	*W*	*D*	*L*	*F*	*A*	*Pts*	*Pos*
2010-11	FL C	46	23	15	8	83	58	84	2
2011-12	PR Lge	38	12	11	15	52	66	47	12
2012-13	PR Lge	38	10	14	14	41	58	44	11
2013-14	PR Lge	38	8	9	21	28	62	33	18
2014-15	FL C	46	25	11	10	88	48	86	3
2015-16	PR Lge	38	9	7	22	39	67	34	19
2016-17	FL C	46	20	10	16	85	69	70	8
2017-18	FL C	46	15	15	16	49	60	60	14
2018-19	FL C	46	27	13	6	93	57	94	1
2019-20	PR Lge	38	5	6	27	26	75	21	20

DID YOU KNOW ?

Norwich City struggled badly when they first joined the Football League in the 1920–21 season. The Canaries played 502 minutes before Bob Dennison netted the first home goal for the club, while it was not until their 14th match that they were able to record their first victory.

NORWICH CITY – PREMIER LEAGUE 2019–20 LEAGUE RECORD

Match No.	Date	Venue	Opponents	Result		H/T Score	Lg Pos.	Goalscorers	Attendance
1	Aug 9	A	Liverpool	L	1-4	0-4	20	Pukki 64	53,333
2	17	H	Newcastle U	W	3-1	1-0	10	Pukki 3 32, 63, 75	27,059
3	24	H	Chelsea	L	2-3	2-2	16	Cantwell 6, Pukki 30	27,032
4	31	A	West Ham U	L	0-2	0-1	19		59,950
5	Sept 14	H	Manchester C	W	3-2	2-1	12	McLean 18, Cantwell 28, Pukki 50	27,035
6	21	A	Burnley	L	0-2	0-2	16		19,712
7	28	A	Crystal Palace	L	0-2	0-1	17		25,477
8	Oct 5	H	Aston Villa	L	1-5	0-2	18	Drmic 87	27,045
9	19	A	Bournemouth	D	0-0	0-0	19		10,669
10	27	H	Manchester U	L	1-3	0-2	19	Hernandez 88	27,108
11	Nov 2	A	Brighton & HA	L	0-2	0-0	19		30,539
12	8	H	Watford	L	0-2	0-1	20		27,074
13	23	A	Everton	W	2-0	0-0	18	Cantwell 54, Srbeny 90	39,241
14	Dec 1	H	Arsenal	D	2-2	2-1	19	Pukki 21, Cantwell 45	27,067
15	4	A	Southampton	L	1-2	0-2	19	Pukki 65	27,019
16	8	H	Sheffield U	L	1-2	1-0	19	Tettey 27	26,881
17	14	A	Leicester C	D	1-1	1-1	19	Pukki 26	32,101
18	21	H	Wolverhampton W	L	1-2	1-0	19	Cantwell 17	27,053
19	26	A	Aston Villa	L	0-1	0-0	20		41,289
20	28	H	Tottenham H	D	2-2	1-0	20	Vrancic 18, Aurier (og) 61	27,072
21	Jan 1	H	Crystal Palace	D	1-1	1-0	20	Cantwell 4	27,021
22	11	A	Manchester U	L	0-4	0-1	20		73,271
23	18	H	Bournemouth	W	1-0	1-0	20	Pukki (pen) 33	26,781
24	22	A	Tottenham H	L	1-2	0-1	20	Pukki (pen) 70	58,182
25	Feb 1	A	Newcastle U	D	0-0	0-0	20		52,204
26	15	H	Liverpool	L	0-1	0-0	20		27,110
27	23	A	Wolverhampton W	L	0-3	0-2	20		31,046
28	28	H	Leicester C	W	1-0	0-0	20	Lewis 70	27,010
29	Mar 7	A	Sheffield U	L	0-1	0-1	20		31,379
30	June 19	H	Southampton	L	0-3	0-0	20		0
31	24	H	Everton	L	0-1	0-0	20		0
32	July 1	A	Arsenal	L	0-4	0-2	20		0
33	4	H	Brighton & HA	L	0-1	0-1	20		0
34	7	A	Watford	L	1-2	1-1	20	Emi 4	0
35	11	H	West Ham U	L	0-4	0-2	20		0
36	14	A	Chelsea	L	0-1	0-1	20		0
37	18	H	Burnley	L	0-2	0-1	20		0
38	26	A	Manchester C	L	0-5	0-2	20		0

Final League Position: 20

GOALSCORERS

League (26): Pukki 11 (2 pens), Cantwell 6, Drmic 1, Emi 1, Hernandez 1, Lewis 1, McLean 1, Srbeny 1, Tettey 1, Vrancic 1, own goal 1.
FA Cup (8): Idah 3 (1 pen), Drmic 2, Cantwell 1, Hanley 1, Hernandez 1.
Carabao Cup (0).
Leasing.com Trophy (4): Ahadme 1, Hutchinson 1, Lomas 1, Scully 1.

Krul T 36	Aarons M 36	Hanley G 14 + 1	Godfrey B 30	Lewis J 25 + 3	McLean K 32 + 5	Trybull T 14 + 2	Emi B 28 + 8	Stiepermann M 14 + 10	Cantwell T 30 + 7	Pukki T 33 + 3	Leitner M 7 + 2	Hernandez O 14 + 12	Drmic J 5 + 16	Vrancic M 6 + 14	Tettey A 28 + 2	Byram S 15 + 2	Srbeny D — + 8	Zimmermann C 16 + 1	Amadou I 8 + 3	Roberts P — + 3	Fahrmann R 1	McGovern M 1 + 1	Idah A 1 + 11	Duda O 9 + 1	Rupp L 8 + 4	Klose T 7	Martin J — + 5	Famewo A — + 1	Thomas J — + 1	Match No.
1	2	3	4	5	6	7^{2}	8	9^{1}	10	11^{3}	12	13	14																	1
1	2	3	4	5^{3}		6^{2}	10	9^{1}	8	11	7			12	13	14														2
1	2	3	4	5	13	7^{2}	8	9^{3}	10	11	6^{1}			14			12													3
1	2		4	5	14	6	8	9^{2}	10^{3}	11	7		13					3^{1}	12											4
1			4	5	7		8^{1}	9^{2}	10	11			12		6	2	13		3											5
1			4	5	7		8	9^{2}	10^{3}	11	12		13		6^{1}	2			3	14										6
	2		4	5	7		8	9^{2}	10^{3}	11	6		13						3	14	1^{1}	12								7
	2		4	5	7		8	9^{1}	10^{2}	11^{3}	6		14				13		3	12		1								8
1	2		4^{1}	5	9	12	7		10^{2}	11	8^{3}	13			6		14		3											9
1	2		4	5^{3}	9		7	13	10^{1}	11	8^{2}	12			6	14			3											10
1	2		4	5	7	6^{3}	8	9^{1}	14	11		10	12		3^{2}		13													11
1	2		4	5^{3}	7	6	8^{2}	9^{1}	12	11		10	13	14	3															12
1	2		4		9^{2}	7	12		8^{1}	11^{3}		10			6	5	14	3	13											13
1	2		4		9	7	12		8^{1}	11		10				5		3	6											14
1	2		4		9	7^{1}	14	13	8^{3}	11		10			12	5		3	6^{2}											15
1	2		4	12	9		8		13	11		10^{1}		7^{3}	6	5^{2}	14	3												16
1	2		4		9	7^{2}	8^{3}	13	10^{1}	11		12		14	6	5		3												17
1	2	4			9	7^{1}	8		10^{2}	11		14		13	6^{3}	5	12	3												18
1	2	4			9	7^{1}	8^{3}	13	10	11		14		12	6^{2}	5		3												19
1	2	4		5	12	13	8	9^{1}	14	11		10		7^{2}	6^{3}			3												20
1	2	4			9		8	13	10^{1}	11^{2}		12		7	6^{3}	5		3					14							21
1	2	4^{3}		14	9		8		10			12		7^{2}	6	5		3	13				11^{1}							22
1	2	12	4■		7		8^{3}		10	11^{2}			13		6	5		3						9^{1}	14					23
1	2	4			7^{3}			14	10	11		12	13		6^{1}	5		3						9	8^{2}					24
1	2	4			7		12		10^{1}	11		13		14	6^{2}	5		3						9	8^{3}					25
1	2	4		12	7		13		10	11			14		6^{3}	5^{1}		3						9	8^{2}					26
1	2	4	3	5	7		13	14	10^{3}	11			12		6									9^{1}	8^{2}					27
1	2	3	4	5	7		8	14	10^{1}	11^{2}			13		6									9^{3}	12					28
1	2	3	4	5	7		8		10^{1}	11			12	13	6^{2}								14	9^{3}						29
1	2		3	5	7	8^{2}	6^{4}		9^{1}	10^{3}		12	11^{5}	13									15	14		4	16			30
1	2		3	5^{5}	6		13		16	12		10^{3}	11	15	7^{4}								14	9^{1}	8^{2}	4				31
1	2		3	5	9	6^{2}	7^{3}	15	10^{5}	11^{1}		12	14	16	4								13		8^{4}					32
1	2		3	5	7		8		14	13		10^{1}	11^{3}	15	6^{4}								12	9^{2}		4				33
1	2		3	5	12		8	9^{2}		11^{4}		10^{3}	15	6	7^{1}								13			4	14			34
1	2		3	5	16		8^{3}	9^{1}	12	11^{2}		10^{4}		7^{5}	6								13		14	4	15			35
1	2		3	5	9		12	13	7^{1}	15		10^{2}	11^{4}		6^{3}								14		8^{5}	4	16			36
1	2		3	5	7		8■		9^{2}			10^{3}	11■	15	6^{4}			12					14		13	4^{1}				37
1	2		4	5	7^{5}			9^{1}	8^{4}	11^{2}		10^{3}		13				3					12		6		14	15	16	38

FA Cup

Third Round	Preston NE	(a)	4-2
Fourth Round	Burnley	(a)	2-1
Fifth Round	Tottenham H	(a)	1-1

(*aet; Norwich C won 3-2 on penalties.*)

Sixth Round	Manchester U	(h)	1-2

(*aet*)

Carabao Cup

Second Round	Crawley T	(a)	0-1

Leasing.com Trophy (Norwich C U21)

Group B (S)	Oxford U	(a)	1-2
Group B (S)	Portsmouth	(a)	1-3
Group B (S)	Crawley T	(a)	2-1

NOTTINGHAM FOREST

FOUNDATION

One of the oldest football clubs in the world, Nottingham Forest was formed at a meeting in the Clinton Arms in 1865. Known originally as the Forest Football Club, the game which first drew the founders together was 'shinney', a form of hockey. When they determined to change to football in 1865, one of their first moves was to buy a set of red caps to wear on the field.

The City Ground, Pavilion Road, Nottingham NG2 5FJ.

Telephone: (0115) 982 4444.

Ticket Office: (0115) 982 4388.

Website: www.nottinghamforest.co.uk

Email: reception@nottinghamforest.co.uk

Ground Capacity: 30,332.

Record Attendance: 49,946 v Manchester U, Division 1, 28 October 1967.

Pitch Measurements: 102.5m × 67.5m (112yd × 74yd).

Chairman: Nicholas Randall QC.

Chief Executive: Ioannis Vrentzos.

Head Coach: Sabri Lamouchi.

Assistant Head Coaches: Bruno Baltazar, David Barriac, Jean-Paul Ancian.

Colours: Red shirts with white trim, white shorts with red trim, red socks.

Year Formed: 1865.

Turned Professional: 1889.

Previous Name: Forest Football Club.

Club Nickname: 'The Reds'.

Grounds: 1865, Forest Racecourse; 1879, The Meadows; 1880, Trent Bridge Cricket Ground; 1882, Parkside, Lenton; 1885, Gregory, Lenton; 1890, Town Ground; 1898, City Ground.

First Football League Game: 3 September 1892, Division 1, v Everton (a) D 2–2 – Brown; Earp, Scott; Hamilton, Albert Smith, McCracken; McCallum, 'Tich' Smith, Higgins (2), Pike, McInnes.

Record League Victory: 12–0 v Leicester Fosse, Division 1, 12 April 1909 – Iremonger; Dudley, Maltby; Hughes (1), Needham, Armstrong; Hooper (3), Marrison, West (3), Morris (2), Spouncer (3 incl. 1p).

Record Cup Victory: 14–0 v Clapton (away), FA Cup 1st rd, 17 January 1891 – Brown; Earp, Scott; Albert Smith, Russell, Jeacock; McCallum (2), 'Tich' Smith (1), Higgins (5), Lindley (4), Shaw (2).

Record Defeat: 1–9 v Blackburn R, Division 2, 10 April 1937.

Most League Points (2 for a win): 70, Division 3 (S), 1950–51.

Most League Points (3 for a win): 94, Division 1, 1997–98.

Most League Goals: 110, Division 3 (S), 1950–51.

HONOURS

League Champions: Division 1 – 1977–78; First Division – 1997–98; Division 2 – 1906–07, 1921–22; Division 3S – 1950–51.
Runners-up: Division 1 – 1966–67, 1978–79; First Division – 1993–94; Division 2 – 1956–57; FL 1 – 2007–08.

FA Cup Winners: 1898, 1959.
Runners-up: 1991.

League Cup Winners: 1978, 1979, 1989, 1990.
Runners-up: 1980, 1992.
Anglo-Scottish Cup Winners: 1977.

Full Members' Cup Winners: 1989, 1992.

European Competitions
European Cup: 1978–79 *(winners)*, 1979–80 *(winners)*, 1980–81.
Fairs Cup: 1961–62, 1967–68.
UEFA Cup: 1983–84 *(sf)*, 1984–85, 1995–96 *(qf)*.
Super Cup: 1979 *(winners)*, 1980.
World Club Championship: 1980.

FOOTBALL YEARBOOK FACT FILE

Nottingham Forest were 3-1 up in their FA Cup quarter-final tie at Newcastle United in February 1974 when home fans invaded the pitch and delayed the match. The disruption aided the Magpies who won 4-3. The FA ordered the game to be replayed at Goodison Park and the teams drew 0-0 in the first game before Newcastle eventually won through with a 1-0 victory in the replay.

Highest League Scorer in Season: Wally Ardron, 36, Division 3 (S), 1950–51.

Most League Goals in Total Aggregate: Grenville Morris, 199, 1898–1913.

Most League Goals in One Match: 4, Enoch West v Sunderland, Division 1, 9 November 1907; 4, Tommy Gibson v Burnley, Division 2, 25 January 1913; 4, Tom Peacock v Port Vale, Division 2, 23 December 1933; 4, Tom Peacock v Barnsley, Division 2, 9 November 1935; 4, Tom Peacock v Port Vale, Division 2, 23 November 1935; 4, Tom Peacock v Doncaster R, Division 2, 26 December 1935; 4, Tommy Capel v Gillingham, Division 3 (S), 18 November 1950; 4, Wally Ardron v Hull C, Division 2, 26 December 1952; 4, Tommy Wilson v Barnsley, Division 2, 9 February 1957; 4, Peter Withe v Ipswich T, Division 1, 4 October 1977; 4, Marlon Harewood v Stoke C, Division 1, 22 February 2003; Gareth McCleary v Leeds U, FL C, 20 March 2012.

Most Capped Player: Stuart Pearce, 76 (78), England.

Most League Appearances: Bob McKinlay, 614, 1951–70.

Youngest League Player: Craig Westcarr, 16 years 257 days v Burnley, 13 October 2001.

Record Transfer Fee Received: £15,000,000 from Middlesbrough for Britt Assombalonga, July 2017.

Record Transfer Fee Paid: £13,200,000 to Benfica for João Carvalho, June 2018.

Football League Record: 1892 Elected to Division 1; 1906–07 Division 2; 1907–11 Division 1; 1911–22 Division 2; 1922–25 Division 1; 1925–49 Division 2; 1949–51 Division 3 (S); 1951–57 Division 2; 1957–72 Division 1; 1972–77 Division 2; 1977–92 Division 1; 1992–93 Premier League; 1993–94 Division 1; 1994–97 Premier League; 1997–98 Division 1; 1998–99 Premier League; 1999–2004 Division 1; 2004–05 FL C; 2005–08 FL 1; 2008– FL C.

MANAGERS

Harry Radford 1889–97 *(Secretary-Manager)*
Harry Haslam 1897–1909 *(Secretary-Manager)*
Fred Earp 1909–12
Bob Masters 1912–25
John Baynes 1925–29
Stan Hardy 1930–31
Noel Watson 1931–36
Harold Wightman 1936–39
Billy Walker 1939–60
Andy Beattie 1960–63
Johnny Carey 1963–68
Matt Gillies 1969–72
Dave Mackay 1972
Allan Brown 1973–75
Brian Clough 1975–93
Frank Clark 1993–96
Stuart Pearce 1996–97
Dave Bassett 1997–99 *(previously General Manager)*
Ron Atkinson 1999
David Platt 1999–2001
Paul Hart 2001–04
Joe Kinnear 2004
Gary Megson 2005–06
Colin Calderwood 2006–08
Billy Davies 2009–11
Steve McClaren 2011
Steve Cotterill 2011–12
Sean O'Driscoll 2012
Alex McLeish 2012–13
Billy Davies 2013–14
Stuart Pearce 2014–15
Dougie Freedman 2015–16
Philippe Montanier 2016–17
Mark Warburton 2017
Aitor Karanka 2018–19
Martin O'Neill 2019
Sabri Lamouchi June 2019–

LATEST SEQUENCES

Longest Sequence of League Wins: 7, 9.5.1979 – 1.9.1979.

Longest Sequence of League Defeats: 14, 21.3.1913 – 27.9.1913.

Longest Sequence of League Draws: 7, 29.4.1978 – 2.9.1978.

Longest Sequence of Unbeaten League Matches: 42, 26.11.1977 – 25.11.1978.

Longest Sequence Without a League Win: 19, 8.9.1998 – 16.1.1999.

Successive Scoring Runs: 22 from 28.3.1931.

Successive Non-scoring Runs: 7 from 26.11.2011.

TEN YEAR LEAGUE RECORD

		P	W	D	L	F	A	Pts	Pos
2010-11	FL C	46	20	15	11	69	50	75	6
2011-12	FL C	46	14	8	24	48	63	50	19
2012-13	FL C	46	17	16	13	63	59	67	8
2013-14	FL C	46	16	17	13	67	64	65	11
2014-15	FL C	46	15	14	17	71	69	59	14
2015-16	FL C	46	13	16	17	43	47	55	16
2016-17	FL C	46	14	9	23	62	72	51	21
2017-18	FL C	46	15	8	23	51	65	53	17
2018-19	FL C	46	17	15	14	61	54	66	9
2019-20	FL C	46	18	16	12	58	50	70	7

DID YOU KNOW ?

Nottingham Forest first appeared on the BBC *Match of the Day* programme on 17 October 1964 when highlights of their match at Leicester City were shown. In a tightly fought encounter, Forest went down to a 3-2 defeat in the East Midlands derby fixture.

NOTTINGHAM FOREST – SKY BET CHAMPIONSHIP 2019–20 LEAGUE RECORD

Match No.	Date	Venue	Opponents	Result		H/T Score	Lg Pos.	Goalscorers	Attendance
1	Aug 3	H	WBA	L	1-2	1-2	17	Cash [8]	27,592
2	10	A	Leeds U	D	1-1	0-0	19	Grabban [77]	35,453
3	17	H	Birmingham C	W	3-0	2-0	9	Lolley [15], Grabban [22], Dawson [65]	27,281
4	21	A	Charlton Ath	D	1-1	0-1	13	Adomah [78]	17,204
5	24	A	Fulham	W	2-1	1-0	9	Grabban 2 [4, 61]	18,186
6	31	H	Preston NE	D	1-1	0-1	10	Adomah [79]	27,249
7	Sept 14	A	Swansea C	W	1-0	0-0	9	Semedo [85]	17,102
8	21	H	Barnsley	W	1-0	0-0	5	Watson [56]	29,202
9	27	A	Stoke C	W	3-2	1-1	1	Lolley [36], Ameobi [47], Grabban [61]	23,800
10	Oct 1	A	Blackburn R	D	1-1	0-0	3	Lolley [65]	12,521
11	5	H	Brentford	W	1-0	0-0	2	Watson [56]	27,598
12	20	A	Wigan Ath	L	0-1	0-1	4		13,077
13	23	H	Hull C	L	1-2	0-1	8	Cash [52]	27,624
14	Nov 2	A	Luton T	W	2-1	1-0	5	Grabban [39], Ameobi [58]	10,053
15	9	H	Derby Co	W	1-0	0-0	5	Grabban [56]	29,314
16	23	A	Bristol C	D	0-0	0-0	5		23,573
17	27	A	QPR	W	4-0	1-0	4	Tobias Figueiredo [15], Grabban [81], Joao Carvalho [88], Semedo [90]	12,937
18	30	H	Cardiff C	L	0-1	0-1	4		28,209
19	Dec 6	A	Millwall	D	2-2	0-1	4	Grabban 2 [63, 88]	12,976
20	10	H	Middlesbrough	D	1-1	0-0	5	Yates [63]	24,577
21	14	H	Sheffield W	L	0-4	0-4	8		28,002
22	21	A	Huddersfield T	L	1-2	0-1	9	Worrall [74]	22,529
23	26	A	Hull C	W	2-0	1-0	7	Grabban 2 (1 pen) [11 (p), 82]	15,001
24	29	H	Wigan Ath	W	1-0	0-0	5	Tobias Figueiredo [60]	27,844
25	Jan 1	H	Blackburn R	W	3-2	2-1	4	Lolley [22], Grabban 2 (1 pen) [25 (p), 55]	27,073
26	11	A	Reading	D	1-1	0-0	5	Watson [90]	16,602
27	19	H	Luton T	W	3-1	1-1	5	Lolley 2 [36, 57], Grabban (pen) [90]	27,081
28	22	H	Reading	D	1-1	0-0	4	Grabban [80]	26,840
29	28	A	Brentford	W	1-0	1-0	3	Lolley [14]	12,274
30	Feb 1	A	Birmingham C	L	1-2	1-1	4	Tiago Silva [18]	20,837
31	8	H	Leeds U	W	2-0	1-0	4	Ameobi [31], Walker [90]	29,455
32	11	H	Charlton Ath	L	0-1	0-1	5		28,029
33	15	A	WBA	D	2-2	1-1	5	Bartley (og) [45], Cash [90]	25,117
34	22	H	QPR	D	0-0	0-0	5		28,750
35	25	A	Cardiff C	W	1-0	0-0	3	Tiago Silva [49]	21,273
36	Mar 2	A	Middlesbrough	D	2-2	1-2	4	Yates [29], Grabban [86]	18,884
37	6	H	Millwall	L	0-3	0-3	4		27,307
38	June 20	A	Sheffield W	D	1-1	0-0	5	Lolley [69]	0
39	28	H	Huddersfield T	W	3-1	1-0	4	Grabban 2 [43, 46], Yates [85]	0
40	July 1	H	Bristol C	W	1-0	0-0	4	Tiago Silva [62]	0
41	4	A	Derby Co	D	1-1	1-0	5	Lolley [12]	0
42	7	H	Fulham	L	0-1	0-1	5		0
43	11	A	Preston NE	D	1-1	1-1	5	Grabban (pen) [5]	0
44	15	H	Swansea C	D	2-2	1-2	5	Ameobi 2 [20, 55]	0
45	19	A	Barnsley	L	0-1	0-0	5		0
46	22	H	Stoke C	L	1-4	0-1	7	Tobias Figueiredo [61]	0

Final League Position: 7

GOALSCORERS

League (58): Grabban 20 (4 pens), Lolley 9, Ameobi 5, Cash 3, Tiago Silva 3, Tobias Figueiredo 3, Watson 3, Yates 3, Adomah 2, Semedo 2, Dawson 1, Joao Carvalho 1, Walker 1, Worrall 1, own goal 1.
FA Cup (0).
Carabao Cup (4): Adomah 1, Joao Carvalho 1, Lolley 1, Tiago Silva 1.

Muric A 4	Cash M 40 + 2	Dawson M 16 + 2	Worrall J 46	Robinson J 16 + 2	Watson B 45	Adomah A 5 + 19	Tiago Silva R 34 + 10	Semedo A 10 + 14	Lolley J 37 + 5	Grabban L 43 + 2	Mir R 2 + 9	Ameobi S 37 + 8	Johnson B 2 + 2	Sow S 22 + 3	Jenkinson C 7 + 1	Bostock J 1 + 6	Samba B 40	Joao Carvalho A 9 + 14	Yuri Ribeiro O 27	Chema R 7 + 1	Tobias Figueiredo P 30	Yates R 16 + 11	Diakhaby A 2 + 12	Walker T 1 + 6	Bong G 1	Nuno Da Costa J 4 + 6	Mighten A — + 8	Smith J 2	Benalouane Y — + 1	Match No.
1	2	3	4	5	6	7	8^1	9^3	10^2	11	12	13	14																	1
1	2	3	4	5	6^3	7^2	8^1	9	10	11	14	13		12																2
1	2	3	4	5	6	13	12	9^1	7	11	14	10^3		8^2																3
1	7^2	3	4	5	6	13	8	9^1		11	14	10^3			2	12														4
	14	3	4	5	6	13	9^1	12	7^2	11		10		8	2^3		1													5
		3	4	5	6^2	14	8	9^1	7	11		10^3		12	2		1	13												6
	2	3	4		6	7^1	14	13	12	11		10^2		8			1	9^3	5											7
	2	3	4		6	12	9^1	14	8^3	11		13		7			1	10^2	5											8
	2	3^1	4	5	7	14	13		8^3	11		10		6			1	9^2		12										9
	2		4	5	8	13	14		6	10		11^1		7^3			1	12	9^2		3									10
	2		3		6	13	9		8	11^3	14	12		7^2			1	10^1	5	4										11
	2		4	5^3	8		13		9	12	10^1	11				7^2	1	14	6		3									12
	2		3	5^3	7	13	6		8	11	14	10^2					1	9^1		4		12								13
	2		3	13	6	12	7		9^2	10^3	14	11^1					1		5		4	8								14
	2		4		6	13	9^3		7^2	11		10^1	14				1	12	5		3	8								15
	2		4	5	7	12	8		9^2	10^3	14	11^1					1	13			3	6■								16
	2		4	5	6	8^1	7	14	9^2	11^3		10				13	1	12			3									17
	2		4	5^3	6	13	7	12	8	11	14	10^2					1	9^1			3									18
	5	3	4	9	7	14	6	8^3	12	13	10^2	11					1				2^1									19
	2	3	4	5	7	14	9^2	13	8	11		10^1					1	12				6^3								20
	2	3	4	5	7		9			11		8					1	10				6								21
	2		4		7^3		9	12	8	11		10^2		6^1			1	13		5	3	14								22
	2		4		7		9	10^2	8^3	11		12		6^1			1	14		5	3	13								23
	2		4		7	14	12	9	13	11^3		8					1	10^2		5	3	6^1								24
	2		4	12	7	14	9	13	8^3	11		10		6^2			1			5^1	3									25
	2		4		7		9^2		13	11		8		6	14		1		10^1	5^3	3	12								26
	2	3	4		7	10^1	9^3		8^2	11		12		6			1	14	5			13								27
	2	3	4		6	13	9		8^2	11		10		7^1			1	12	5											28
	2		4		6	14	10		9^1	11^2		8^3		7			1		5		3	13	12							29
	2		4		6		9^3	13	8	11		10^1					1		5		3	7^2	12	14						30
	2		4		7		10^2		9	11^3		8^1		6			1		5		3	13	12	14						31
	12		4		6		9^2	13	8						2		1				3	7^3	10	11	5^1	14				32
	2		4		6		10^3	13	9	11		8^1		7^2			1		5		3		12	14						33
	2		4		6		7^3		9	11		8^1					1	14	5		3	12	10^2				13			34
	2		4		6		9^3	12	10	11		8^2					1		5		3	7^1	13	14						35
	2		4		6			9^1	10	11		7^2				14	1	13	5		3	8^3	12							36
	2		4		6			7^1	8^3	11		10				12	1	9^2	5		3		14	13						37
	2		4				9^3	13	8	11^4		10^2	7^1			14	1		5		3	6	15			12				38
	2		4		6^4		9^2		7^5	11		10^3	8^1			16	1	14	5		3	12				13	15			39
	2	14	4		7		9^3		8^1	11^4		10		13			1		5		3	6^2		15		12				40
	2		4		6		13		9^3	10^4		12		8^2			1		5		3	7	14			11^1	15			41
	2		4		7^5		10^4	15	9^2	11		8^3		6^1			1		5		3	12	14			13	16			42
		3	4		7		12			10		9^3		8^1	2		1		5			6	14			11^2	13			43
		14	4		6		12		13	11		10^4		9^1	2		1		5		3^2	8^5	16			7^3	15			44
		2	4		6		9^2			11		13		7	5^3				8		3^4	12				10^1	15	1	14	45
	2		4		6		12		10	11		7		8^1					5^3		3	9^2				13	14	1		46

FA Cup
Third Round Chelsea (a) 0-2

Carabao Cup
First Round Fleetwood T (h) 1-0
Second Round Derby Co (h) 3-0
Third Round Arsenal (a) 0-5

OLDHAM ATHLETIC

FOUNDATION

It was in 1895 that John Garland, the landlord of the Featherstall and Junction Hotel, decided to form a football club. As Pine Villa they played in the Oldham Junior League. In 1899 the local professional club, Oldham County, went out of existence and one of the liquidators persuaded Pine Villa to take over their ground at Sheepfoot Lane and change their name to Oldham Athletic.

Boundary Park, Furtherwood Road, Oldham, Lancashire OL1 2PB.

Telephone: (0161) 624 4972.

Ticket Office: (0161) 785 5150.

Website: www.oldhamathletic.co.uk

Email: enquiries@oldhamathletic.co.uk

Ground Capacity: 13,513.

Record Attendance: 47,671 v Sheffield W, FA Cup 4th rd, 25 January 1930.

Pitch Measurements: 100m × 68m (109.5yd × 74.5yd).

Chairman: Abdallah Lemsagam.

Managing Director: Natalie Atkinson.

Head Coach: Harry Kewell.

Assistant Head Coach: Alan Maybury.

Colours: Blue shirts with white and red trim, white shorts with blue and red trim, blue socks with white trim.

Year Formed: 1895.

Turned Professional: 1899.

Previous Name: 1895, Pine Villa; 1899, Oldham Athletic.

Club Nickname: 'The Latics'.

Grounds: 1895, Sheepfoot Lane; 1900, Hudson Field; 1906, Sheepfoot Lane; 1907, Boundary Park (renamed SportsDirect.com Park 2014, Boundary Park 2018).

First Football League Game: 9 September 1907, Division 2, v Stoke (a) W 3–1 – Hewitson; Hodson, Hamilton; Fay, Walders, Wilson; Ward, Billy Dodds (1), Newton (1), Hancock, Swarbrick (1).

Record League Victory: 11–0 v Southport, Division 4, 26 December 1962 – Bollands; Branagan, Marshall; McCall, Williams, Scott; Ledger (1), Johnstone, Lister (6), Colquhoun (1), Whitaker (3).

Record Cup Victory: 10–1 v Lytham, FA Cup 1st rd, 28 November 1925 – Gray; Wynne, Grundy; Adlam, Heaton, Naylor (1), Douglas, Pynegar (2), Ormston (2), Barnes (3), Watson (2).

Record Defeat: 4–13 v Tranmere R, Division 3 (N), 26 December 1935.

HONOURS

League Champions: Division 2 – 1990–91; Division 3 – 1973–74; Division 3N – 1952–53.
Runners-up: Division 1 – 1914–15; Division 2 – 1909–10; Division 4 – 1962–63.

FA Cup: semi-final – 1913, 1990, 1994.

League Cup: *Runners-up:* 1990.

FOOTBALL YEARBOOK FACT FILE

Oldham Athletic's Boundary Park ground is the second highest stadium in senior English football. Standing at 526 feet above sea level it is slightly lower than The Hawthorns, home of West Bromwich Albion, although many fans feel the Latics' ground is the coldest in the country as it is more exposed to the elements.

Most League Points (2 for a win): 62, Division 3, 1973–74.

Most League Points (3 for a win): 88, Division 2, 1990–91.

Most League Goals: 95, Division 4, 1962–63.

Highest League Scorer in Season: Tom Davis, 33, Division 3 (N), 1936–37.

Most League Goals in Total Aggregate: Roger Palmer, 141, 1980–94.

Most League Goals in One Match: 7, Eric Gemmell v Chester, Division 3 (N), 19 January 1952.

Most Capped Player: Gunnar Halle, 24 (64), Norway.

Most League Appearances: Ian Wood, 525, 1966–80.

Youngest League Player: Wayne Harrison, 16 years 347 days v Notts Co, 27 October 1984.

Record Transfer Fee Received: £1,700,000 from Aston Villa for Earl Barrett, February 1992.

Record Transfer Fee Paid: £750,000 to Aston Villa for Ian Olney, June 1992.

Football League Record: 1907 Elected to Division 2; 1910–23 Division 1; 1923–35 Division 2; 1935–53 Division 3 (N); 1953–54 Division 2; 1954–58 Division 3 (N); 1958–63 Division 4; 1963–69 Division 3; 1969–71 Division 4; 1971–74 Division 3; 1974–91 Division 2; 1991–92 Division 1; 1992–94 Premier League; 1994–97 Division 1; 1997–2004 Division 2; 2004–18 FL 1; 2018– FL 2.

LATEST SEQUENCES

Longest Sequence of League Wins: 10, 12.1.1974 – 12.3.1974.

Longest Sequence of League Defeats: 8, 15.12.1934 – 2.2.1935.

Longest Sequence of League Draws: 5, 7.4.2018 – 21.4.2018.

Longest Sequence of Unbeaten League Matches: 20, 1.5.1990 – 10.11.1990.

Longest Sequence Without a League Win: 17, 4.9.1920 – 18.12.1920.

Successive Scoring Runs: 25 from 25.8.1962.

Successive Non-scoring Runs: 6 from 12.2.2011.

MANAGERS

David Ashworth 1906–14
Herbert Bamlett 1914–21
Charlie Roberts 1921–22
David Ashworth 1923–24
Bob Mellor 1924–27
Andy Wilson 1927–32
Bob Mellor 1932–33
Jimmy McMullan 1933–34
Bob Mellor 1934–45
(continued as Secretary to 1953)
Frank Womack 1945–47
Billy Wootton 1947–50
George Hardwick 1950–56
Ted Goodier 1956–58
Norman Dodgin 1958–60
Danny McLennan 1960
Jack Rowley 1960–63
Les McDowall 1963–65
Gordon Hurst 1965–66
Jimmy McIlroy 1966–68
Jack Rowley 1968–69
Jimmy Frizzell 1970–82
Joe Royle 1982–94
Graeme Sharp 1994–97
Neil Warnock 1997–98
Andy Ritchie 1998–2001
Mick Wadsworth 2001–02
Iain Dowie 2002–03
Brian Talbot 2004–05
Ronnie Moore 2005–06
John Sheridan 2006–09
Joe Royle 2009
Dave Penney 2009–10
Paul Dickov 2010–13
Lee Johnson 2013–15
Dean Holden 2015
Darren Kelly 2015
David Dunn 2015–16
John Sheridan 2016
Stephen Robinson 2016–17
John Sheridan 2017
Richie Wellens 2017–18
Frankie Bunn 2018
Paul Scholes 2019
Laurent Banide 2019
Dino Maamria 2019–20
Harry Kewell August 2020–

TEN YEAR LEAGUE RECORD

		P	W	D	L	F	A	Pts	Pos
2010-11	FL 1	46	13	17	16	53	60	56	17
2011-12	FL 1	46	14	12	20	50	66	54	16
2012-13	FL 1	46	14	9	23	46	59	51	19
2013-14	FL 1	46	14	14	18	50	59	56	15
2014-15	FL 1	46	14	15	17	54	67	57	15
2015-16	FL 1	46	12	18	16	44	58	54	17
2016-17	FL 1	46	12	17	17	31	44	53	17
2017-18	FL 1	46	11	17	18	58	75	50	21
2018-19	FL 2	46	16	14	16	67	60	62	14
2019-20	FL 2	37	9	14	14	44	57	41	19§

§Decided on points-per-game (1.11)

DID YOU KNOW ?

Kenny Chaytor became the youngest-ever scorer of a Football League hat-trick when he netted a treble for Oldham Athletic against Mansfield Town in January 1955 at the age of 17 years and 72 days. His record stood for 16 years before being broken by the Birmingham City prodigy Trevor Francis.

OLDHAM ATHLETIC – SKY BET LEAGUE TWO 2019–20 LEAGUE RECORD

Match No.	Date	Venue	Opponents	Result		H/T Score	Lg Pos.	Goalscorers	Attendance
1	Aug 3	A	Forest Green R	L	0-1	0-0	17		2541
2	10	H	Crewe Alex	L	1-2	1-2	22	Missilou 2	3884
3	17	A	Bradford C	L	0-3	0-2	24		14,447
4	20	H	Exeter C	D	0-0	0-0	23		2805
5	24	A	Cambridge U	W	2-1	1-1	22	Vera 28, Wheater 67	4004
6	31	H	Colchester U	L	0-1	0-1	22		3091
7	Sept 7	A	Plymouth Arg	D	2-2	1-1	22	Branger 27, Wheater 77	9061
8	14	H	Grimsby T	D	2-2	1-0	20	Missilou 19, Morais 66	3789
9	17	A	Scunthorpe U	D	2-2	0-0	21	Missilou 62, Branger 64	3020
10	21	H	Morecambe	W	3-1	1-0	19	Maouche 33, Azankpo 51, Smith 89	3305
11	28	A	Carlisle U	L	0-1	0-1	19		4321
12	Oct 5	H	Cheltenham T	D	1-1	1-0	21	Morais 9	3496
13	12	A	Mansfield T	L	1-6	1-3	21	Haymer 43	4368
14	19	H	Macclesfield T	L	0-1	0-0	21		4428
15	22	H	Walsall	W	2-0	0-0	20	Wilson 55, Azankpo 69	2438
16	26	A	Port Vale	D	0-0	0-0	19		4301
17	Nov 2	H	Northampton T	D	2-2	0-1	20	Wilson 85, Smith 89	3274
18	23	A	Newport Co	W	1-0	1-0	20	Mills 45	3748
19	Dec 7	H	Leyton Orient	D	1-1	1-1	21	Smith 2	3121
20	14	A	Swindon T	L	0-2	0-1	22		6825
21	21	H	Crawley T	W	2-1	0-1	20	Wheater 49, Maouche 58	2737
22	26	A	Morecambe	W	2-1	1-0	17	Azankpo 30, Sylla 75	2797
23	29	H	Salford C	L	1-4	0-3	18	Azankpo 58	5278
24	Jan 1	H	Scunthorpe U	L	0-2	0-1	21		2972
25	4	A	Cheltenham T	L	0-3	0-1	21		3029
26	11	A	Macclesfield T	D	1-1	0-0	21	Smith 85	2205
27	14	A	Stevenage	D	0-0	0-0	19		2156
28	18	H	Carlisle U	D	1-1	1-1	19	Smith 42	3977
29	25	A	Salford C	D	1-1	0-1	21	Rowe 83	3646
30	28	H	Mansfield T	W	3-1	2-0	18	Smith 23, Haymer 43, Nepomuceno 58	2961
31	Feb 1	H	Bradford C	W	3-0	3-0	14	Dearnley 11, Smith 20, Maouche 45	5198
32	8	A	Crewe Alex	L	1-2	0-0	17	Smith 48	5271
33	11	A	Exeter C	L	1-5	1-2	19	Wheater 23	3527
34	15	H	Forest Green R	D	1-1	0-0	18	Nepomuceno 56	2720
35	22	A	Leyton Orient	D	2-2	2-1	19	Dearnley 2 15, 18	5334
36	29	H	Newport Co	W	5-0	2-0	17	Rowe 2 25, 52, Dearnley 27, Haymer 62, Smith 83	2912
37	Mar 7	A	Crawley T	L	0-3	0-1	18		2037
38	14	H	Swindon T	Cancelled					
39	17	A	Walsall	Cancelled					
40	21	H	Port Vale	Cancelled					
41	28	A	Northampton T	Cancelled					
42	Apr 4	H	Stevenage	Cancelled					
43	10	H	Cambridge U	Cancelled					
44	13	A	Colchester U	Cancelled					
45	18	H	Plymouth Arg	Cancelled					
46	25	A	Grimsby T	Cancelled					

Final League Position: 19 (on points-per-game basis)

GOALSCORERS

League (44): Smith 9, Azankpo 4, Dearnley 4, Wheater 4, Haymer 3, Maouche 3, Missilou 3, Rowe 3, Branger 2, Morais 2, Nepomuceno 2, Wilson 2, Mills 1, Sylla 1, Vera 1.
FA Cup (2): Morais 1, Smith 1.
Carabao Cup (2): Maouche 1, Nepomuceno 1.
Leasing.com Trophy (5): Azankpo 2, Iacovitti 1, Smith 1, Stott 1.

Woods G 15	Mills Z 19 + 6	Wheater D 34	Haymer T 36 + 1	Iacovitti A 24	Missilou C 27 + 3	Maouche M 20 + 11	Sefil S 3 + 1	Sylla M 25 + 5	Branger J 9 + 7	Wilson S 8 + 13	Azankpo D 22 + 6	Nepomuceno G 12 + 3	Vera U 3 + 2	Stott J 8 + 1	Smith-Brown A 5 + 1	Eagles C 5 + 10	Fage D 7 + 5	Morais F 14 + 2	McHale D — + 1	Smith J 25 + 3	de la Paz Z 22 + 1	Egert T 3 + 3	Adams K — + 1	McCann C 15 + 1	Mckinney L — + 2	Emmerson Z — + 2	Gaskell R — + 1	Jones D 6	Akpa Akpro J 3	Piergianni C 11	Dieseruvwe E 1 + 3	N'Guessan C 3 + 5	Rowe D 10	Dearnley Z 6 + 2	Borthwick-Jackson C 6	*Match No.*
1	2	3	4	5	6	7	8	9^{2}	10^{3}	11^{1}	12	13	14																							1
1	6^{1}		2		8	7	3		9	11^{2}	13	12	10^{3}	4	5	14																				2
1	2		13	4	9^{1}	7	3	8		12	11^{2}	10			5^{3}	14	6																			3
1	13	3	2	4			14	6	8^{2}	12	11	7^{3}			5	10^{1}	9																			4
1		3	2	4	8	7		12	14		13	6^{2}	11^{3}		5	10^{1}	9																			5
1		3	2	4	9^{2}	8		6	12	11^{1}	13		14		5^{3}	7	10																			6
1	14	3	2	4	8	9^{1}		6	10	11^{2}	12						5	7^{3}	13																	7
1	13	3	2	4	6	9		8	10^{1}		11						5	7^{2}		12																8
1	14	3	2	4	7	6^{1}		12	8^{2}		11					10^{3}	5	9		13																9
	2	3	4	5	9	8		6	10		11							7^{1}		12	1															10
1	2	4	3	5	8	9		6	7^{1}	12	11^{3}					13	14	10^{2}																		11
		4	2	5	9	8		6		13	11						14	10^{1}		7^{3}	1	3^{2}	12													12
1		4	2	5	8	6^{2}		7					10^{1}	12	14		13^{3}	9■		11		3■														13
		3	2	5	8	9^{3}		6^{2}		12	10^{1}			4		14				11	1			7	13											14
		3	2	5	8					10^{3}	11^{1}			4		12		6^{2}		9	1			7		13	14									15
		3	2	5	8					10^{1}	11			4		13		6^{2}		9	1			7	12											16
		3	2	5	7^{1}	13				12	11^{3}			4		8		9^{2}		10	1			6		14										17
	2	4	3	6	9						11			5				7		10	1			8												18
	6	3	2	5^{2}		12				11^{1}	14			4				13		9	1			8				7	10^{3}							19
	5	3	2	8		9					10			4^{2}			14	13		11	1	12^{3}		6				7^{1}								20
	2	4	3	5		10^{1}		8		12	9^{3}					13				6	1	14		7					11^{2}							21
	2	4	3	5		11^{3}		8		12	9^{2}					13		10^{1}		6	1	14		7												22
	5	4	2			10		7		13	11					14	12	9^{1}		6	1	3^{2}		8^{3}												23
	2	4	3	5	14	13		7		12	11							6^{2}		9	1							8^{3}	10^{1}							24
	5	3	2	4^{1}	8^{2}	13		7	14	11	10	9				12					1							6^{3}								25
1		3■	2		6^{3}	14		8		12	11	5								9								7^{1}		4	10^{2}	13				26
1^{3}	5	3	2		9			13		14	11	7^{2}								10	12							6^{1}		4		8				27
	5	3	2		7^{1}	9		13		12^{3}	10^{2}									8	1									4		6	11	14		28
	2	4	3	5	13	9^{3}		7			10^{1}	14								8	1											6^{2}	11	12		29
		3	2		8^{3}	12		7	14			6^{2}								9	1									4		13	10	11^{1}	5	30
	13	3	2		8^{1}	12		7				6^{2}								9	1			14						4			10	11^{3}	5	31
	5^{1}	3	2		8	10^{2}		7	12			6								9	1									4	13		11			32
	12	3■	2		9			7^{3}	10^{2}											6	1			8						4	14	13	11^{1}		5	33
1	2		3		8^{2}	12		13	14			6								9^{1}				7						4			10	11^{3}	5	34
1	5	3	2		9^{2}	12		8												6				7						4	13		11	10^{1}		35
		3	2		13	12		7^{3}				6								9	1			8^{1}						4		14	10	11^{2}	5	36
		3^{1}	2			13		8	14			6								9	1			7						4		12	10	11^{2}	5^{3}	37
																																				38
																																				39
																																				40
																																				41
																																				42
																																				43
																																				44
																																				45
																																				46

FA Cup

First Round	Gateshead	(a)	2-1
Second Round	Burton Alb	(h)	0-1

Carabao Cup

First Round	Blackburn R	(a)	2-3

Leasing.com Trophy

Group B (N)	Liverpool U21	(h)	3-2
Group B (N)	Accrington S	(h)	0-3
Group B (N)	Fleetwood T	(a)	2-5

OXFORD UNITED

FOUNDATION

There had been an Oxford United club around the time of World War I but only in the Oxfordshire Thursday League and there is no connection with the modern club which began as Headington in 1893, adding 'United' a year later. Playing first on Quarry Fields and subsequently Wootten's Fields, they owe much to a Dr Hitchings for their early development.

The Kassam Stadium, Grenoble Road, Oxford OX4 4XP.

Telephone: (01865) 337 500.

Ticket Office: (01865) 337 533.

Website: www.oufc.co.uk

Email: admin@oufc.co.uk

Ground Capacity: 12,537.

Record Attendance: 22,750 v Preston NE, FA Cup 6th rd, 29 February 1964 (at Manor Ground); 12,243 v Leyton Orient, FL 2, 6 May 2006 (at The Kassam Stadium).

Pitch Measurements: 100.5m × 67m (110yd × 73.5yd).

Chairman: Sumrith 'Tiger' Thanakarnjanasuth.

Head Coach: Karl Robinson.

Assistant Head Coach: Derek Fazackerley.

HONOURS

League Champions: Division 2 – 1984–85; Division 3 – 1967–68, 1983–84.
Runners-up: Second Division – 1995–96; FL 2 – 2015–16; Conference – (3rd) 2009–10 *(promoted via play-offs).*

FA Cup: 6th rd – 1964.

League Cup Winners: 1986.

League Trophy: *Runners-up:* 2016, 2017.

Colours: Yellow shirts with blue trim, blue shorts with yellow trim, yellow socks with blue trim.

Year Formed: 1893.

Turned Professional: 1949.

Previous Names: 1893, Headington; 1894, Headington United; 1960, Oxford United.

Club Nickname: 'The U's'.

Grounds: 1893, Headington Quarry; 1894, Wootten's Fields; 1898, Sandy Lane Ground; 1902, Britannia Field; 1909, Sandy Lane; 1910, Quarry Recreation Ground; 1914, Sandy Lane; 1922, The Paddock Manor Road; 1925, Manor Ground; 2001, The Kassam Stadium.

First Football League Game: 18 August 1962, Division 4, v Barrow (a) L 2–3 – Medlock; Beavon, Quartermain; Ron Atkinson, Kyle, Jones; Knight, Graham Atkinson (1), Houghton (1), Cornwell, Colfar.

Record League Victory: 7–0 v Barrow, Division 4, 19 December 1964 – Fearnley; Beavon, Quartermain; Ron Atkinson (1), Kyle, Jones; Morris, Booth (3), Willey (1), Graham Atkinson (1), Harrington (1).

Record Cup Victory: 9–1 v Dorchester T, FA Cup 1st rd, 11 November 1995 – Whitehead; Wood (2), Mike Ford (1), Smith, Elliott, Gilchrist, Rush (1), Massey (Murphy), Moody (3), Bobby Ford (1), Angel (Beauchamp (1)).

Record Defeat: 0–7 v Sunderland, Division 1, 19 September 1998; 0–7 v Wigan Ath, FL 1, 23 December 2017.

Most League Points (2 for a win): 61, Division 4, 1964–65.

FOOTBALL YEARBOOK FACT FILE

Headington United (as Oxford United were then called) beat Wycombe Wanderers 3-2 in an FA Cup second qualifying round tie in October 1951. However, their opponents protested that future England goalkeeper Colin McDonald was ineligible as he was a Burnley player turning out for Headington during his National Service. The appeal was upheld and Headington were expelled from the competition.

Most League Points (3 for a win): 95, Division 3, 1983–84.

Most League Goals: 91, Division 3, 1983–84.

Highest League Scorer in Season: John Aldridge, 30, Division 2, 1984–85.

Most League Goals in Total Aggregate: Graham Atkinson, 77, 1962–73.

Most League Goals in One Match: 4, Tony Jones v Newport Co, Division 4, 22 September 1962; 4, Arthur Longbottom v Darlington, Division 4, 26 October 1963; 4, Richard Hill v Walsall, Division 2, 26 December 1988; 4, John Durnin v Luton T, 14 November 1992; 4, Tom Craddock v Accrington S, FL 2, 20 October 2011.

Most Capped Player: Jim Magilton, 18 (52), Northern Ireland.

Most League Appearances: John Shuker, 478, 1962–77.

Youngest League Player: Jason Seacole, 16 years 149 days v Mansfield T, 7 September 1976.

Record Transfer Fee Received: £3,000,000 from Leeds U for Kemar Roofe, July 2016.

Record Transfer Fee Paid: £470,000 to Aberdeen for Dean Windass, July 1998.

Football League Record: 1962 Elected to Division 4; 1965–68 Division 3; 1968–76 Division 2; 1976–84 Division 3; 1984–85 Division 2; 1985–88 Division 1; 1988–92 Division 2; 1992–94 Division 1; 1994–96 Division 2; 1996–99 Division 1; 1999–2001 Division 2; 2001–04 Division 3; 2004–06 FL 2; 2006–10 Conference; 2010–16 FL 2; 2016– FL 1.

MANAGERS

Harry Thompson 1949–58
(Player-Manager) 1949-51
Arthur Turner 1959–69
(continued as General Manager to 1972)
Ron Saunders 1969
Gerry Summers 1969–75
Mick Brown 1975–79
Bill Asprey 1979–80
Ian Greaves 1980–82
Jim Smith 1982–85
Maurice Evans 1985–88
Mark Lawrenson 1988
Brian Horton 1988–93
Denis Smith 1993–97
Malcolm Crosby 1997–98
Malcolm Shotton 1998–99
Micky Lewis 1999–2000
Denis Smith 2000
David Kemp 2000–01
Mark Wright 2001
Ian Atkins 2001–04
Graham Rix 2004
Ramon Diaz 2004–05
Brian Talbot 2005–06
Darren Patterson 2006
Jim Smith 2006–07
Darren Patterson 2007–08
Chris Wilder 2008–14
Gary Waddock 2014
Michael Appleton 2014–17
Pep Clotet 2017–18
Karl Robinson March 2018–

LATEST SEQUENCES

Longest Sequence of League Wins: 6, 13.4.2013 – 17.8.2013.

Longest Sequence of League Defeats: 8, 18.4.2014 – 23.8.2014.

Longest Sequence of League Draws: 5, 7.10.1978 – 28.10.1978.

Longest Sequence of Unbeaten League Matches: 20, 17.3.1984 – 29.9.1984.

Longest Sequence Without a League Win: 27, 14.11.1987 – 27.8.1988.

Successive Scoring Runs: 17 from 22.4.2006.

Successive Non-scoring Runs: 6 from 26.3.1988.

TEN YEAR LEAGUE RECORD

		P	W	D	L	F	A	Pts	Pos
2010-11	FL 2	46	17	12	17	58	60	63	12
2011-12	FL 2	46	17	17	12	59	48	68	9
2012-13	FL 2	46	19	8	19	60	61	65	9
2013-14	FL 2	46	16	14	16	53	50	62	8
2014-15	FL 2	46	15	16	15	50	49	61	13
2015-16	FL 2	46	24	14	8	84	41	86	2
2016-17	FL 1	46	20	9	17	65	52	69	8
2017-18	FL 1	46	15	11	20	61	66	56	16
2018-19	FL 1	46	15	15	16	58	64	60	12
2019-20	FL 1	35	17	9	9	61	37	60	4§

§Decided on points-per-game (1.71)

DID YOU KNOW ?

When Harvey Bradbury came off the bench for Oxford United in their Checkatrade Trophy game at Wycombe Wanderers in November 2018 he created a new first for the club. His father Lee Bradbury had made over 60 appearances for the U's between July 2004 and January 2006 and they thus became the first father and son to have appeared for the club in senior football.

OXFORD UNITED – SKY BET LEAGUE ONE 2019–20 LEAGUE RECORD

Match No.	*Date*	*Venue*	*Opponents*	*Result*	*H/T Score*	*Lg Pos.*	*Goalscorers*	*Attendance*
1	Aug 3	A	Sunderland	D 1-1	1-0	10	Fosu [14]	33,498
2	10	H	Peterborough U	W 1-0	1-0	6	Brannagan [12]	6959
3	17	A	Blackpool	L 1-2	1-2	11	Ruffels [45]	9104
4	20	H	Burton Alb	L 2-4	0-1	16	Brannagan [47], Forde [56]	6111
5	24	A	Bristol R	L 1-3	1-2	17	Woodburn [27]	7871
6	31	H	Coventry C	D 3-3	0-1	18	Mackie [64], Dabo (2 ogs) [85, 90]	8080
7	Sept 7	A	Fleetwood T	L 1-2	1-1	20	Moore [33]	2672
8	14	H	Tranmere R	W 3-0	1-0	17	Henry 2 (2 pens) [23, 90], Brannagan [70]	6294
9	17	A	Bolton W	D 0-0	0-0	17		6786
10	21	A	Lincoln C	W 6-0	2-0	12	Fosu 3 [5, 40, 70], Mackie [48], Henry [54], Taylor [79]	8746
11	28	H	Gillingham	W 3-0	3-0	10	Henry 2 [10, 34], Taylor [30]	6553
12	Oct 5	A	Accrington S	D 2-2	1-0	9	Fosu [28], Brannagan [70]	2590
13	12	H	Doncaster R	W 3-0	1-0	8	Henry 2 (1 pen) [45, 78 (p)], Brannagan [47]	6861
14	19	A	Rotherham U	W 2-1	1-1	5	Fosu [23], Taylor [57]	8837
15	26	H	Rochdale	W 3-0	2-0	5	Ruffels [20], Fosu [27], Long [86]	6666
16	Nov 2	A	Portsmouth	D 1-1	0-0	4	Taylor [90]	18,528
17	23	A	Southend U	W 4-0	2-0	6	Taylor 2 [1, 84], Henry [33], Agyei [86]	6835
18	Dec 7	H	Shrewsbury T	D 0-0	0-0	7		6931
19	14	A	Milton Keynes D	L 0-1	0-0	8		10,031
20	21	H	Wycombe W	W 1-0	1-0	6	Henry [23]	10,123
21	26	H	Lincoln C	W 1-0	1-0	3	Baptiste [36]	10,115
22	29	A	AFC Wimbledon	W 2-1	1-0	2	McLoughlin (og) [26], Sykes [61]	4763
23	Jan 1	A	Doncaster R	L 0-1	0-1	4		7524
24	11	H	Rotherham U	L 1-3	0-3	5	Browne [71]	8077
25	14	H	Ipswich T	D 0-0	0-0	5		8191
26	18	A	Gillingham	D 1-1	1-0	5	Fosu [16]	5051
27	Feb 1	H	Blackpool	W 2-1	2-1	8	Browne 2 [18, 40]	10,525
28	8	A	Peterborough U	L 0-4	0-1	10		8363
29	11	A	Burton Alb	D 2-2	0-1	10	Agyei [63], Taylor [90]	2278
30	15	H	Sunderland	L 0-1	0-1	11		9105
31	18	H	AFC Wimbledon	W 5-0	2-0	10	Taylor 2 [32, 90], Holland 2 [34, 55], Henry [50]	6155
32	22	A	Ipswich T	W 1-0	1-0	9	Taylor [44]	19,363
33	25	H	Accrington S	W 3-0	1-0	8	Henry [13], Taylor 2 [50, 72]	5622
34	29	H	Southend U	W 2-1	1-1	6	Henry (pen) [17], Taylor [84]	7451
35	Mar 7	A	Shrewsbury T	W 3-2	1-2	3	Browne [45], Agyei [59], Ruffels [88]	6474
36	14	H	Milton Keynes D	Cancelled				
37	21	A	Wycombe W	Cancelled				
38	28	H	Portsmouth	Cancelled				
39	Apr 4	A	Rochdale	Cancelled				
40	10	H	Bristol R	Cancelled				
41	13	A	Coventry C	Cancelled				
42	18	H	Fleetwood T	Cancelled				
43	25	A	Tranmere R	Cancelled				
44	May 3	H	Bolton W	Cancelled				

Final League Position: 4 (on points-per-game basis)

GOALSCORERS

League (61): Taylor 13, Henry 12 (4 pens), Fosu 8, Brannagan 5, Browne 4, Agyei 3, Ruffels 3, Holland 2, Mackie 2, Baptiste 1, Forde 1, Long 1, Moore 1, Sykes 1, Woodburn 1, own goals 3.
FA Cup (9): Hall 2, Baptiste 1, Fosu 1, Henry 1, Holland 1, Kelly 1, Long 1, Taylor 1 (1 pen).
Carabao Cup (9): Taylor 2, Baptiste 1, Brannagan 1, Fosu 1, Hall 1, Henry 1 (1 pen), Moore 1, Sykes 1.
Leasing.com Trophy (8): Hall 3 (2 pens), Baptiste 1, Brannagan 1, Dickie 1, Forde 1 (1 pen), Taylor 1.
League One Play-offs (3): Browne 1, Sykes 1, own goal 1.

Eastwood S 29	Cadden C 21	Dickie R 34	Mousinho J 25 + 1	Ruffels J 35	Brannagan C 29 + 1	Gorrin A 29 + 2	Woodburn B 11	Henry J 30	Fosu T 21 + 4	Mackie J 15 + 17	Hanson J 2 + 3	Hall R 3 + 10	Moore E 12 + 8	Forde A 9 + 9	Taylor M 20 + 6	Baptiste S 9 + 8	Long S 10 + 6	Agyei D 1 + 12	Thorne G 1 + 3	Sykes M 17 + 6	Archer J 6	Browne M 8 + 3	Holland N 7 + 3	Kelly L 1 + 2	Match No.
1	2	3	4	5	6^2	7	8^1	9	10^3	11	12	13	14												1
1	2	3	4	5	7^2	6	9^1	8	10^3	11	12	14		13											2
1	2	3	4	5	7	6^1	9^3	10		8	11^2	12	14	13											3
1	2	3	4	5	7	6^3	9^1	8	12	13		14		10^2	11										4
1	2	3		5	7^2		9^3	8	10	12	6	14	4	13	11^1										5
1	2	3		5^3	7	6	9^2	8	13	11			4	10^1		12	14								6
1	2^1	3		5	7	6^3		9	14	11	12		4	8		10^2	13								7
1	2	3	4	5	7	6	9^2	8	10^1	11^3				14	13	12									8
1	2	3	4	5	7	6	9^3	8	10^1			14		12	11^2			13							9
1	2	3	4	5	7	6	9	8^1	10^2	11^3				12	13				14						10
1	2	3^2	4	5	7	6^3	8	9	11	14			12		10^1	13									11
1	2	3	4	5	7	13	9^2	8	10	11^1				12^3	14	6									12
1	2	3	4	5	8	7		6	11^1	10^2		13				12		14		9^3					13
1	2		4	5	8	7		6^3	11	13			3		10^2	12	14			9^1					14
1	2^3	3	4	5	8^1	7		6	11^2	10		14				12	13			9					15
1		3	4	5^1		7		8	9^3	11^2			12	14	10	13	2			6					16
1	2	3	4	5		7^2		6	11^1			12	13	8^3	10			14		9					17
	2	3	4	5				7^2	11	13		9^1	12	6^3	10		14			8	1				18
	2	3	4	5	8^2	7			11	12		9^1			10	13		14		6^3	1				19
	2	3	4	5	6^2	7^3		9	11	10^1			14		13	8				12	1				20
	2	3	4	5	8	7		9^1	11^3	13			14		10^2	6				12	1				21
		3	13	5	6^2	7			12	11^3		9^1	4		14	10	2			8	1				22
	2	3	4	5		7^3		6	11^1	13		12			10	8		14		9^2	1				23
1		3		5	8^1	7^3			11	10^2			4		14	6	2			9		12	13		24
1		3	4	5	12	7			11	14					10^3	8	2			13		6^2	9^1		25
1		3	4	5		7			11	10^1						8	2	12		6		13	9^2		26
1		3	4	5	8	7		6^3		13							2		14	9^2		10	11^1	12	27
1		3	4	5	8	7^1		6^2		14					10		2			9^3		11	13	12	28
1		3	4	5	8	12		9						14	10		2^1	13		6^2			11	7^3	29
1		3	4	6	8			7^2		14			5	2	11			10^3		9^1		12	13		30
1		3		5	7			9		14			4	2	10			13	12	6^1		8^2	11^3		31
1		3		5	8	7		9^1		13			4	2	10^2			14		12		6	11^3		32
1		3		5	8	6		9^1		14			4		10		2	13	7^2	12		11^3			33
1		3		5	8	7^3		9		14			4	2^1	10		13	12		6^2		11			34
1		3		5	8	7^3		9		14			4		10^2		2	13		12		6	11^1		35
																									36
																									37
																									38
																									39
																									40
																									41
																									42
																									43
																									44

FA Cup

First Round	Hayes & Yeading U	(a)	2-0
Second Round	Walsall	(a)	1-0
Third Round	Hartlepool U	(h)	4-1
Fourth Round	Newcastle U	(a)	0-0
Replay(aet)	Newcastle U	(h)	2-3

Carabao Cup

First Round	Peterborough U	(h)	1-0
Second Round	Millwall	(h)	2-2
(Oxford U won 4-2 on penalties)			
Third Round	West Ham U	(h)	4-0
Fourth Round	Sunderland	(h)	1-1
(Oxford U won 4-2 on penalties)			
Quarter-Final	Manchester C	(h)	1-3

Leasing.com Trophy

Group B (S)	Norwich C U21	(h)	2-1
Group B (S)	Portsmouth	(h)	2-2
(Portsmouth won 5-4 on penalties)			
Group B (S)	Crawley T	(a)	4-1
Second Round (S)	Exeter C	(a)	0-0
(Exeter C won 3-0 on penalties)			

League One Play-Offs

Semi-Final 1st leg	Portsmouth	(a)	1-1
Semi-Final 2nd leg	Portsmouth	(h)	1-1
(aet; Oxford U won 5-4 on penalties)			
Final	Wycombe W	(Wembley)	1-2

PETERBOROUGH UNITED

FOUNDATION

The old Peterborough & Fletton club, founded in 1923, was suspended by the FA during season 1932–33 and disbanded. Local enthusiasts determined to carry on and in 1934 a new professional club, Peterborough United, was formed and entered the Midland League the following year. Peterborough's first success came in 1939–40, but from 1955–56 to 1959–60 they won five successive titles. During the 1958–59 season they were undefeated in the Midland League. They reached the third round of the FA Cup, won the Northamptonshire Senior Cup, the Maunsell Cup and were runners-up in the East Anglian Cup.

Weston Homes Stadium, London Road, Peterborough PE2 8AL.

Telephone: (01733) 563 947.

Ticket Office: (0844) 847 1934.

Website: www.theposh.com

Email: via website.

Ground Capacity: 15,314.

Record Attendance: 30,096 v Swansea T, FA Cup 5th rd, 20 February 1965.

Pitch Measurements: 102.5m × 64m (112yd × 70yd).

Chairman: Darragh MacAnthony.

Chief Executive: Bob Symns.

Manager: Darren Ferguson.

First-Team Coach: Gavin Strachan.

Colours: Blue shirts with white sleeves, white shorts with blue trim, blue socks with white trim.

Year Formed: 1934.

Turned Professional: 1934.

Club Nickname: 'The Posh'.

Ground: 1934, London Road Stadium (renamed ABAX Stadium 2014; Weston Homes Stadium 2019).

First Football League Game: 20 August 1960, Division 4, v Wrexham (h) W 3–0 – Walls; Stafford, Walker; Rayner, Rigby, Norris; Hails, Emery (1), Bly (1), Smith, McNamee (1).

Record League Victory: 9–1 v Barnet (a) Division 3, 5 September 1998 – Griemink; Hooper (1), Drury (Farell), Gill, Bodley, Edwards, Davies, Payne, Grazioli (5), Quinn (2) (Rowe), Houghton (Etherington) (1).

Record Cup Victory: 9–1 v Rushden T, FA Cup 1st qual rd, 6 October 1945 – Hilliard; Bryan, Parrott, Warner, Hobbs, Woods, Polhill (1), Fairchild, Laxton (6), Tasker (1), Rodgers (1); 9–1 v Kingstonian, FA Cup 1st rd, 25 November 1992. Match ordered to be replayed by FA. Peterborough won replay 1–0.

Record Defeat: 1–8 v Northampton T, FA Cup 2nd rd (2nd replay), 18 December 1946.

HONOURS

League Champions: Division 4 – 1960–61, 1973–74.
Runners-up: FL 1 – 2008–09; FL 2 – 2007–08.

FA Cup: 6th rd – 1965.

League Cup: semi-final – 1966.

League Trophy Winners: 2014.

FOOTBALL YEARBOOK FACT FILE

The first Peterborough United player to win a full international cap was Ollie Conmy who made his debut for the Republic of Ireland against Belgium in March 1965 and went on to appear five times for his country during his stay at London Road. Born in County Mayo, he moved with his family to West Yorkshire as a youngster, joining Posh from Huddersfield Town.

Most League Points (2 for a win): 66, Division 4, 1960–61.

Most League Points (3 for a win): 92, FL 2, 2007–08.

Most League Goals: 134, Division 4, 1960–61.

Highest League Scorer in Season: Terry Bly, 52, Division 4, 1960–61.

Most League Goals in Total Aggregate: Jim Hall, 122, 1967–75.

Most League Goals in One Match: 5, Guiliano Grazioli v Barnet, Division 3, 5 September 1998.

Most Capped Player: Gabriel Zakuani, 17 (29), DR Congo.

Most League Appearances: Tommy Robson, 482, 1968–81.

Youngest League Player: Matthew Etherington, 15 years 262 days v Brentford, 3 May 1997.

Record Transfer Fee Received: £5,500,000 from Nottingham F for Britt Assombalonga, August 2014.

Record Transfer Fee Paid: £1,250,000 (in excess of) to Bristol C for Mo Eisa, June 2019.

Football League Record: 1960 Elected to Division 4; 1961–68 Division 3, when they were demoted for financial irregularities; 1968–74 Division 4; 1974–79 Division 3; 1979–91 Division 4; 1991–92 Division 3; 1992–94 Division 1; 1994–97 Division 2; 1997–2000 Division 3; 2000–04 Division 2; 2004–05 FL 1; 2005–08 FL 2; 2008–09 FL 1; 2009–10 FL C; 2010–11 FL 1; 2011–13 FL C; 2013– FL 1.

LATEST SEQUENCES

Longest Sequence of League Wins: 9, 1.2.1992 – 14.3.1992.

Longest Sequence of League Defeats: 8, 16.12.2006 – 27.1.2007.

Longest Sequence of League Draws: 8, 18.12.1971 – 12.2.1972.

Longest Sequence of Unbeaten League Matches: 17, 15.1.2008 – 5.4.2008.

Longest Sequence Without a League Win: 17, 23.9.1978 – 30.12.1978.

Successive Scoring Runs: 33 from 20.9.1960.

Successive Non-scoring Runs: 6 from 13.8.2002.

MANAGERS

Jock Porter 1934–36
Fred Taylor 1936–37
Vic Poulter 1937–38
Sam Haden 1938–48
Jack Blood 1948–50
Bob Gurney 1950–52
Jack Fairbrother 1952–54
George Swindin 1954–58
Jimmy Hagan 1958–62
Jack Fairbrother 1962–64
Gordon Clark 1964–67
Norman Rigby 1967–69
Jim Iley 1969–72
Noel Cantwell 1972–77
John Barnwell 1977–78
Billy Hails 1978–79
Peter Morris 1979–82
Martin Wilkinson 1982–83
John Wile 1983–86
Noel Cantwell 1986–88 *(continued as General Manager)*
Mick Jones 1988–89
Mark Lawrenson 1989–90
Dave Booth 1990–91
Chris Turner 1991–92
Lil Fuccillo 1992–93
Chris Turner 1993–94
John Still 1994–95
Mick Halsall 1995–96
Barry Fry 1996–2005
Mark Wright 2005–06
Steve Bleasdale 2006
Keith Alexander 2006–07
Darren Ferguson 2007–09
Mark Cooper 2009–10
Jim Gannon 2010
Gary Johnson 2010–11
Darren Ferguson 2011–15
Dave Robertson 2015
Graham Westley 2015–16
Grant McCann 2016–18
Steve Evans 2018–19
Darren Ferguson January 2019–

TEN YEAR LEAGUE RECORD

		P	*W*	*D*	*L*	*F*	*A*	*Pts*	*Pos*
2010-11	FL 1	46	23	10	13	106	75	79	4
2011-12	FL C	46	13	11	22	67	77	50	18
2012-13	FL C	46	15	9	22	66	75	54	22
2013-14	FL 1	46	23	5	18	72	58	74	6
2014-15	FL 1	46	18	9	19	53	56	63	9
2015-16	FL 1	46	19	6	21	82	73	63	13
2016-17	FL 1	46	17	11	18	62	62	62	11
2017-18	FL 1	46	17	13	16	68	60	64	9
2018-19	FL 1	46	20	12	14	71	62	72	7
2019-20	FL 1	35	17	8	10	68	40	59	7§

§Decided on points-per-game (1.69)

DID YOU KNOW ?

Peterborough United were elected as members of the Football League in May 1960, replacing Gateshead. The three teams that were re-elected in the voting were Oldham, Southport and Hartlepools United. The first letter of the four teams successful in the process spelled the word 'Posh', Peterborough's nickname.

PETERBOROUGH UNITED – SKY BET LEAGUE ONE 2019–20 LEAGUE RECORD

Match No.	*Date*	*Venue*	*Opponents*	*Result*	*H/T Score*	*Lg Pos.*	*Goalscorers*	*Attendance*
1	Aug 3	H	Fleetwood T	L 1-3	0-2	19	Toney [67]	7958
2	10	A	Oxford U	L 0-1	0-1	21		6959
3	17	H	Ipswich T	D 2-2	1-1	20	Toney [29], Eisa [62]	10,071
4	20	A	Southend U	W 2-0	0-0	15	Eisa [55], Toney [57]	5890
5	24	A	Milton Keynes D	W 4-0	3-0	10	Maddison [21], Toney [28], Eisa 2 [40, 72]	9402
6	31	H	Sunderland	W 3-0	1-0	7	Maddison 2 [36, 64], Knight [52]	10,005
7	Sept 14	H	Rochdale	W 6-0	3-0	6	Toney 3 [18, 45, 58], Eisa [34], Maddison 2 (1 pen) [51, 62 (p)]	5733
8	17	A	Tranmere R	D 2-2	0-0	6	Eisa [54], Toney [56]	5243
9	21	A	Doncaster R	L 0-2	0-2	9		8940
10	28	H	AFC Wimbledon	W 3-2	2-0	8	Maddison [29], Eisa 2 [41, 66]	6744
11	Oct 5	A	Wycombe W	D 3-3	2-0	7	Eisa [10], Knight [38], Toney [70]	5083
12	12	H	Lincoln C	W 2-0	0-0	3	Reed [82], Toney [88]	9872
13	19	A	Gillingham	W 2-1	1-0	3	Ward [40], Eisa (pen) [51]	6269
14	23	H	Accrington S	W 4-0	0-0	1	Maddison [56], Toney [69], Kent [85], Dembele [90]	5843
15	26	H	Coventry C	D 2-2	0-1	3	Maddison (pen) [52], Eisa [90]	8005
16	Nov 2	A	Blackpool	L 3-4	2-2	3	Eisa [13], Toney [45], Maddison (pen) [71]	7619
17	5	A	Shrewsbury T	L 0-1	0-1	3		4890
18	23	H	Burton Alb	W 1-0	0-0	3	Ward [90]	6462
19	Dec 7	A	Portsmouth	D 2-2	1-1	3	Toney [10], Eisa [72]	17,643
20	14	H	Bolton W	W 1-0	1-0	3	Toney [23]	6965
21	21	A	Bristol R	D 0-0	0-0	2		8030
22	26	H	Doncaster R	L 0-3	0-1	4		6786
23	29	A	Rotherham U	L 0-4	0-0	6		9019
24	Jan 1	A	Lincoln C	L 1-2	1-0	6	Toney [28]	10,025
25	11	H	Gillingham	D 0-0	0-0	9		6696
26	18	A	AFC Wimbledon	L 0-1	0-0	10		4453
27	21	H	Wycombe W	W 4-0	2-0	8	Toney 2 (1 pen) [23 (p), 73], Dembele [44], Taylor [56]	3851
28	25	H	Rotherham U	W 2-1	2-1	5	Toney [2], Szmidics [22]	7495
29	28	A	Accrington S	W 2-0	1-0	4	Szmidics [11], Ward [51]	1816
30	Feb 1	A	Ipswich T	W 4-1	2-0	3	Toney (pen) [23], Szmidics 2 [33, 74], Dembele [50]	21,351
31	8	H	Oxford U	W 4-0	1-0	3	Dembele [36], Toney 2 [56, 77], Knight [90]	8363
32	11	H	Southend U	W 4-0	0-0	2	Dembele [50], Taylor [57], Toney 2 [70, 74]	5036
33	15	A	Fleetwood T	L 1-2	0-1	4	Butler [54]	2801
34	29	A	Burton Alb	D 1-1	0-0	7	Eisa [52]	3795
35	Mar 7	H	Portsmouth	W 2-0	1-0	4	Butler [32], Toney [86]	9414
36	14	A	Bolton W	Cancelled				
37	21	H	Bristol R	Cancelled				
38	29	H	Blackpool	Cancelled				
39	Apr 4	A	Coventry C	Cancelled				
40	10	H	Milton Keynes D	Cancelled				
41	13	A	Sunderland	Cancelled				
42	18	H	Shrewsbury T	Cancelled				
43	25	A	Rochdale	Cancelled				
44	May 3	H	Tranmere R	Cancelled				

Final League Position: 7 (on points-per-game basis)

GOALSCORERS

League (68): Toney 24 (2 pens), Eisa 14 (1 pen), Maddison 9 (3 pens), Dembele 5, Szmidics 4, Knight 3, Ward 3, Butler 2, Taylor 2, Kent 1, Reed 1.
FA Cup (8): Eisa 2, Jade-Jones 2, Toney 2, Kent 1, Maddison 1.
Carabao Cup (0).
Leasing.com Trophy (6): Jade-Jones 2, Ward 2, Dembele 1, Kanu 1.

Pym C 35	Mason N 25 + 5	Kent F 28	Beevers M 32	Butler D 26 + 3	Ward J 18 + 10	Woodyard A 8 + 6	Boyd G 17 + 5	Dembele S 12 + 13	Toney I 32	Eisa M 27 + 2	Maddison M 19 + 3	Blake-Tracy F 11 + 3	Knight J 16 + 8	Reed L 23 + 1	Tasdemir S 1 + 9	Burrows H 2 + 2	Thompson N 12 + 3	Kanu I 1 + 5	Bennett R 7 + 6	Jade-Jones R 2 + 9	Brown R 10	Taylor J 11	Szmidics S 10	*Match No.*
1	2	3	4	5	6^{1}	7	8	9	10	11	12													1
1	2	3	4	5^{3}		7^{2}	8	9	10	11^{1}	6	12	13	14										2
1	2	3	4		13		8		10	11^{2}	9^{1}	5	7	6	12									3
1	2	3	4		14		8	13	10	11^{1}	9^{3}	5	7^{2}	6	12									4
1	2	4	3		12		7	14	10	11^{2}	9^{1}	5	8^{3}	6		13								5
1	2^{2}	3	4	5			8	12	10	11^{3}	9		7^{1}	6		13	14							6
1	2^{3}	3	4	5	7			13	10^{1}	11	9^{2}		8	6	14		12							7
1	2	3	4	5	8			13	11	10^{1}	9^{2}		7	6	12									8
1	2^{1}	3	4	5^{3}	8^{2}			12	10	11	9		7	6			13	14						9
1	2	3	4			13	8		10	11	9^{2}	5	7	6^{1}	12									10
1	2	3	4	14		13	8		11	10	9^{3}	5^{1}	7^{2}	6	12									11
1	2	3	4			13	8	12	11	10^{2}	9^{1}	5	7	6■										12
1	6		4	12	2^{2}	13	8	9^{1}	11	10^{3}		5	7					14	3					13
1	2	3	4		13	14	8	12	11	10^{1}	9^{2}	5	7	6^{3}										14
1	2^{3}	3	4	13	14		8	12	11	10	9	5^{2}	7	6^{1}										15
1	2^{2}	3	4	5			8^{1}	12	11	10	9		7	6	13									16
1			4	5	14		8^{2}	13	10	11	9^{1}		7	6			2^{3}	12	3					17
1		3	4	5	7	14		12		11	9^{1}	13		6		8^{3}	2			10^{2}				18
1	2^{2}	4	3	8		7			11	10^{1}				6	12		5	9		13				19
1	12	4	3	8	5	7			11	10^{1}	13			6	9^{3}		2^{2}			14				20
1	2	4		8	5	6			11	10^{2}	9^{1}			7	13				3	12				21
1	2	4		8	5^{3}	6	12		11	10^{2}	9	14		7					3^{1}	13				22
1	2	3■	4	5	12	7	9		10^{1}	14				6^{3}		8^{2}			13	11				23
1	2		4	5	12	7	8^{1}	13■	11	10^{2}	9			6					3					24
1	2	3	4■	5	14		8^{2}		10	11^{3}	12			6					13		7^{1}	9		25
1	2	3		5	12				11	10^{2}				6^{1}					4	13	7	8	9	26
1		4	3	8	5		14	11^{3}	10								2^{2}		12	13	6	7	9^{1}	27
1		4	3	8	5^{3}			11^{2}	10				12				2		14	13	7^{1}	6	9	28
1	13	4	3	8	5			11^{2}	10				12				2^{3}			14	6	7	9^{1}	29
1	13	4	3	8	5^{2}			10	11				12				2^{3}		14		6^{1}	7	9	30
1	12	4^{1}	3	8	5			11^{2}	10				14				2■		13		6^{3}	7	9	31
1	4		3	8	5		12	11	10^{2}	14			13						2		6^{1}	7	9^{3}	32
1	4^{2}		3	8	5			10		11^{1}			6				2	12		13		7	9	33
1			3	8	5^{1}		13	10		11		4	12				2	14			6^{2}	7	9^{3}	34
1	12		3	8	5		14	11	10			4	13				2^{3}				6^{2}	7	9^{1}	35
																								36
																								37
																								38
																								39
																								40
																								41
																								42
																								43
																								44

FA Cup

First Round	Stevenage	(a)	1-1
Replay	Stevenage	(h)	2-0
Second Round	Dover Ath	(h)	3-0
Third Round	Burnley	(a)	2-4

Carabao Cup

First Round	Oxford U	(a)	0-1

Leasing.com Trophy

Group H (S)	Northampton T	(a)	2-0
Group H (S)	Arsenal U21	(h)	1-0
Group H (S)	Cambridge U	(h)	2-1
Second Round (S)	Ipswich T	(h)	1-1

(Ipswich T won 6-5 on penalties)

PLYMOUTH ARGYLE

FOUNDATION

The club was formed in September 1886 as the Argyle Athletic Club by former public and private school pupils who wanted to continue playing the game. The meeting was held in a room above the Borough Arms (a coffee house), Bedford Street, Plymouth. It was common then to choose a local street/terrace as a club name and Argyle or Argyll was a fashionable name throughout the land due to Queen Victoria's great interest in Scotland.

Home Park, Plymouth, Devon PL2 3DQ.

Telephone: (01752) 562 561.

Ticket Office: (01752) 907 700.

Website: www.pafc.co.uk

Email: argyle@pafc.co.uk

Ground Capacity: 18,050.

Record Attendance: 43,596 v Aston Villa, Division 2, 10 October 1936.

Pitch Measurements: 103m × 66m (112.5yd × 72yd).

Chairman: Simon Hallett.

Chief Executive: Andrew Parkinson.

Manager: Ryan Lowe.

Assistant Manager: Steven Schumacher.

Colours: Dark green shirts with black trim, black shorts, white socks with dark green trim.

Year Formed: 1886.

Turned Professional: 1903.

Previous Name: 1886, Argyle Athletic Club; 1903, Plymouth Argyle.

Club Nickname: 'The Pilgrims'.

Ground: 1886, Home Park.

First Football League Game: 28 August 1920, Division 3, v Norwich C (h) D 1–1 – Craig; Russell, Atterbury; Logan, Dickinson, Forbes; Kirkpatrick, Jack, Bowler, Heeps (1), Dixon.

Record League Victory: 8–1 v Millwall, Division 2, 16 January 1932 – Harper; Roberts, Titmuss; Mackay, Pullan, Reed; Grozier, Bowden (2), Vidler (3), Leslie (1), Black (1), (1 og). 8–1 v Hartlepool U (a), Division 2, 7 May 1994 – Nicholls; Patterson (Naylor), Hill, Burrows, Comyn, McCall (1), Barlow, Castle (1), Landon (3), Marshall (1), Dalton (2).

Record Cup Victory: 6–0 v Corby T, FA Cup 3rd rd, 22 January 1966 – Leiper; Book, Baird; Williams, Nelson, Newman; Jones (1), Jackson (1), Bickle (3), Piper (1), Jennings.

Record Defeat: 0–9 v Stoke C, Division 2, 17 December 1960.

Most League Points (2 for a win): 68, Division 3 (S), 1929–30.

HONOURS

League Champions: Second Division – 2003–04; Division 3 – 1958–59; Division 3S – 1929–30, 1951–52; Third Division – 2001–02.
Runners-up: FL 2 – 2016–17; Division 3 – 1974–75, 1985–86; Division 3S – 1921–22, 1922–23, 1923–24, 1924–25, 1925–26, 1926–27.

FA Cup: semi-final – 1984.

League Cup: semi-final – 1965, 1974.

FOOTBALL YEARBOOK FACT FILE

The highest attendance to watch a Plymouth Argyle match was for the FA Cup fourth round tie away to Arsenal in January 1932. The game attracted 65,386 fans and at the time it was also a ground record for Highbury. Argyle scored after just four minutes through Jack Vidler, but eventually lost 4-2.

Most League Points (3 for a win): 102, Division 3, 2001–02.

Most League Goals: 107, Division 3 (S), 1925–26 and 1951–52.

Highest League Scorer in Season: Jack Cock, 32, Division 3 (S), 1926–27.

Most League Goals in Total Aggregate: Sammy Black, 174, 1924–38.

Most League Goals in One Match: 5, Wilf Carter v Charlton Ath, Division 2, 27 December 1960.

Most Capped Player: Moses Russell, 20 (23), Wales.

Most League Appearances: Kevin Hodges, 530, 1978–92.

Youngest League Player: Lee Phillips, 16 years 43 days v Gillingham, 29 October 1996.

Record Transfer Fee Received: £2,000,000 from Hull C for Peter Halmosi, July 2008.

Record Transfer Fee Paid: £500,000 to Cardiff C for Steve MacLean, January 2008.

Football League Record: 1920 Original Member of Division 3; 1921–30 Division 3 (S); 1930–50 Division 2; 1950–52 Division 3 (S); 1952–56 Division 2; 1956–58 Division 3 (S); 1958–59 Division 3; 1959–68 Division 2; 1968–75 Division 3; 1975–77 Division 2; 1977–86 Division 3; 1986–95 Division 2; 1995–96 Division 3; 1996–98 Division 2; 1998–2002 Division 3; 2002–04 Division 2; 2004–10 FL C; 2010–11 FL 1; 2011–17 FL 2; 2017–19 FL 1; 2019–20 FL 2; 2020– FL 1.

LATEST SEQUENCES

Longest Sequence of League Wins: 9, 8.3.1986 – 12.4.1986.

Longest Sequence of League Defeats: 9, 12.10.1963 – 7.12.1963.

Longest Sequence of League Draws: 5, 26.2.2000 – 14.3.2000.

Longest Sequence of Unbeaten League Matches: 22, 20.4.1929 – 21.12.1929.

Longest Sequence Without a League Win: 13, 1.5.2018 – 2.10.2018.

Successive Scoring Runs: 39 from 15.4.1939.

Successive Non-scoring Runs: 5 from 21.11.2009.

MANAGERS

Frank Brettell 1903–05
Bob Jack 1905–06
Bill Fullerton 1906–07
Bob Jack 1910–38
Jack Tresadern 1938–47
Jimmy Rae 1948–55
Jack Rowley 1955–60
Neil Dougall 1961
Ellis Stuttard 1961–63
Andy Beattie 1963–64
Malcolm Allison 1964–65
Derek Ufton 1965–68
Billy Bingham 1968–70
Ellis Stuttard 1970–72
Tony Waiters 1972–77
Mike Kelly 1977–78
Malcolm Allison 1978–79
Bobby Saxton 1979–81
Bobby Moncur 1981–83
Johnny Hore 1983–84
Dave Smith 1984–88
Ken Brown 1988–90
David Kemp 1990–92
Peter Shilton 1992–95
Steve McCall 1995
Neil Warnock 1995–97
Mick Jones 1997–98
Kevin Hodges 1998–2000
Paul Sturrock 2000–04
Bobby Williamson 2004–05
Tony Pulis 2005–06
Ian Holloway 2006–07
Paul Sturrock 2007–09
Paul Mariner 2009–10
Peter Reid 2010–11
Carl Fletcher 2011–13
John Sheridan 2013–15
Derek Adams 2015–19
Ryan Lowe June 2019–

TEN YEAR LEAGUE RECORD

		P	*W*	*D*	*L*	*F*	*A*	*Pts*	*Pos*
2010-11	FL 1	46	15	7	24	51	74	42*	23
2011-12	FL 2	46	10	16	20	47	64	46	21
2012-13	FL 2	46	13	13	20	46	55	52	21
2013-14	FL 2	46	16	12	18	51	58	60	10
2014-15	FL 2	46	20	11	15	55	37	71	7
2015-16	FL 2	46	24	9	13	72	46	81	5
2016-17	FL 2	46	26	9	11	71	46	87	2
2017-18	FL 1	46	19	11	16	58	59	68	7
2018-19	FL 1	46	13	11	22	56	80	50	21
2019-20	FL 2	37	20	8	9	61	39	68	3§

** 10 pts deducted. §Decided on points-per-game (1.84)*

DID YOU KNOW ?

Club captain John Newman was the first winner of Plymouth Argyle's 'Player of the Year' award in 1965–66. Newman played over 300 first-team games for the club before moving on to Exeter City in November 1967.

PLYMOUTH ARGYLE – SKY BET LEAGUE TWO 2019–20 LEAGUE RECORD

Match No.	Date	Venue	Opponents	Result		H/T Score	Lg Pos.	Goalscorers	Attendance
1	Aug 3	A	Crewe Alex	W	3-0	2-0	1	McFadzean 2 [4, 90], Joel Grant [26]	5273
2	10	H	Colchester U	W	1-0	0-0	1	Sarcevic [57]	10,542
3	17	A	Newport Co	L	0-1	0-0	5		5048
4	20	H	Salford C	D	2-2	1-1	6	Mayor [43], Telford (pen) [89]	11,405
5	24	H	Walsall	W	3-0	1-0	2	Taylor 2 [13, 89], Sarcevic [82]	9337
6	31	A	Northampton T	L	1-3	1-3	6	Riley [10]	5535
7	Sept 7	H	Oldham Ath	D	2-2	1-1	8	Wootton [31], Moore, B [74]	9061
8	14	A	Port Vale	L	0-1	0-0	11		5275
9	17	A	Crawley T	D	2-2	0-1	12	Edwards 2 [73, 79]	2501
10	21	H	Cheltenham T	L	0-2	0-1	14		8956
11	28	A	Mansfield T	W	1-0	1-0	12	Grant, C [13]	4499
12	Oct 5	H	Scunthorpe U	D	2-2	1-1	12	Aimson 2 [18, 76]	8800
13	12	A	Swindon T	D	1-1	0-1	11	Joel Grant [76]	9548
14	19	H	Carlisle U	W	2-0	1-0	8	Joel Grant [22], Sarcevic [90]	8446
15	22	H	Leyton Orient	W	4-0	4-0	8	Joel Grant [14], Rudden [17], McFadzean [34], Widdowson (og) [45]	8810
16	26	A	Exeter C	L	0-4	0-1	10		7924
17	Nov 16	A	Forest Green R	W	1-0	1-0	11	Sarcevic [24]	3897
18	23	H	Bradford C	W	2-1	2-0	8	Moore, B [5], Edwards [25]	9645
19	Dec 7	A	Cambridge U	L	0-1	0-1	9		4492
20	14	H	Morecambe	W	3-0	2-0	8	Cooper, G [44], Sarcevic (pen) [45], Grant, C [90]	9174
21	26	A	Cheltenham T	W	1-0	1-0	8	Rudden [33]	1222
22	29	H	Stevenage	W	2-1	1-0	7	Denton (og) [23], Canavan [90]	11,719
23	Jan 1	H	Swindon T	L	1-2	1-1	9	Telford [22]	15,062
24	4	A	Scunthorpe U	W	3-1	1-0	6	Jephcott 2 [12, 56], Moore, B [50]	3450
25	11	A	Carlisle U	W	3-0	1-0	5	Jephcott 2 [33, 49], Hardie [75]	4212
26	18	H	Mansfield T	W	3-1	1-0	4	Canavan [43], Sarcevic (pen) [61], Hardie [90]	10,523
27	25	A	Stevenage	W	2-1	0-0	3	Moore, B [47], Hardie [85]	3627
28	28	H	Crawley T	D	2-2	1-1	4	Sarcevic (pen) [44], Jephcott [83]	9184
29	Feb 1	H	Newport Co	W	1-0	1-0	3	Bakinson [5]	10,956
30	8	A	Colchester U	L	0-3	0-3	4		4768
31	11	A	Salford C	W	3-2	1-0	4	Moore, B [19], Sarcevic [67], Hardie [90]	2297
32	15	H	Crewe Alex	W	2-1	0-0	4	Jephcott [57], Sarcevic (pen) [71]	11,567
33	18	A	Macclesfield T	D	1-1	0-1	4	Sarcevic [84]	1887
34	22	H	Cambridge U	D	0-0	0-0	4		11,597
35	29	A	Bradford C	L	1-2	0-2	5	Hardie [87]	15,225
36	Mar 3	H	Grimsby T	W	3-0	3-0	3	Bakinson [22], Hardie [30], Jephcott [40]	9327
37	7	H	Macclesfield T	W	3-0	1-0	3	Hardie [33], Cooper, G 2 [62, 77]	12,310
38	14	A	Morecambe	Cancelled					
39	17	A	Leyton Orient	Cancelled					
40	23	H	Exeter C	Cancelled					
41	28	A	Grimsby T	Cancelled					
42	Apr 4	H	Forest Green R	Cancelled					
43	10	A	Walsall	Cancelled					
44	13	H	Northampton T	Cancelled					
45	18	A	Oldham Ath	Cancelled					
46	25	H	Port Vale	Cancelled					

Final League Position: 3 (on points-per-game basis)

GOALSCORERS

League (61): Sarcevic 10 (4 pens), Hardie 7, Jephcott 7, Moore, B 5, Joel Grant 4, Cooper, G 3, Edwards 3, McFadzean 3, Aimson 2, Bakinson 2, Canavan 2, Grant, C 2, Rudden 2, Taylor 2, Telford 2 (1 pen), Mayor 1, Riley 1, Wootton 1, own goals 2.
FA Cup (2): McFadzean 1, Sarcevic 1 (1 pen).
Carabao Cup (4): Baxter 1, McFadzean 1, Taylor 1, Telford 1.
Leasing.com Trophy (4): Joel Grant 1, Moore, B 1, Riley 1, Rudden 1.

Palmer A 37	Wootton S 34 + 1	Canavan N 32 + 1	Sawyer G 28	Edwards J 31 + 3	Riley J 11 + 4	Sarcevic A 30 + 2	Mayor D 31 + 3	McFadzean C 24 + 1	Grant Joel 14 + 10	Moore B 26 + 4	Baxter J 3 + 6	Grant C 10 + 7	Taylor R 7 + 10	Telford D 7 + 12	Lolos K — + 4	Rudden Z 7 + 7	Grant Joshua 17 + 5	Cooper G 21 + 6	Randell A — + 4	Aimson W 5	Clarke B 2 + 7	Bakinson T 12 + 2	Jephcott L 13 + 1	Hardie R 5 + 8	Cleal J — + 1	Match No.
1	2	3	4	5[1]	6	7[3]	8	9	10	11[2]	12	13	14													1
1	2	3	4	5[3]	6	7	8	9	11[2]	10[1]	13		14	12												2
1	2	3	4	5[1]	6	7[3]	8	9			12	13	11	10[2]	14											3
1	2	3	4	5	6[3]	14	8	9			12	7[1]	10[2]	11	13											4
1	2	3	4	5	6[1]	14▮	8	9			13	7[2]	11	10[3]		12										5
1	2	3	4[2]	5	6		8	9		12		7	11[3]			10[1]	13	14								6
1	2	3		5[3]	6		8	9		10	7[2]		11[1]			12	4	13	14							7
1	2	3		6[2]		7	8	9[1]		11	5		10[3]	12		13	4	14								8
1	13		4	6		7	8	9	11[2]	10[3]	5[1]			12		14	2			3						9
1			4	5		7	8	9	11[1]				12	10[2]	14		2	6[3]	13	3						10
1	2		4	5	14	6	10[2]	8	11[1]			7	12		13			9[3]		3						11
1	2		4	5[3]	12	7	11[1]	8	9			6	10[2]			13	14			3						12
1	2	12	4	5	6[3]	7	8	9[1]	10		13					11		14		3[2]						13
1	3	4	5	8	2	7		6	11[3]	12						10[2]	14	9[1]			13					14
1	2	3	4	5	6	7	12	9	11[2]	13						10[3]		8[1]			14					15
1		3	4	7[1]	5	6	13	9[3]	10	12						11[2]	2	8			14					16
1	2	3	4	6	12[3]	7	8	9[1]	10[2]	11			14	13			5									17
1	2	3	4	6		7	8	9	11[2]	10[1]			13	12			5									18
1	2	3	4	5[3]		6	8		12	11		9[2]		10[1]			7	13			14					19
1	3	4	5			7[3]	9		11[1]	6		13		10[2]		12	8	2			14					20
1	2	3	4	14		7	8		13	6				12		11[3]	5	9[1]			10[2]					21
1	2	3		5		7	8		13	6		14		12		10[2]	4	9[3]			11[1]					22
1	2	3		7		6	14		10[2]	5		8[3]		11[1]		13	4	9			12					23
1	2	3	4	5		6	7		12	10[2]		14						9[1]			13	8	11[3]			24
1	2	3	4	5[3]	14	6[1]	7			10		13						9[2]				8	11	12		25
1	2	3	4	5		6	8[3]		13	10							14	9[1]				7	11[2]	12		26
1	2	3	4	5		6			13	10							8	9[1]				7	11[2]	12		27
1	3	4	5	2[2]		7			14	10		13					8	6				9[1]	12	11[3]		28
1	2	3	4▮	12			8			5		6[2]	13					9	14			7	11[1]	10[3]		29
1	2	3				7	8	13	14	6			12				4	9[2]				5	11[3]	10[1]		30
1	2	3		5		6	8[2]	4	12	10							14	9[3]				7	11[1]	13		31
1	2	3		5		6	8	4[1]	14	10							7	9[2]				12	11[3]	13		32
1	2	3	4	5[2]		6	8			10				14			7[3]	9[1]				12	11	13		33
1	3	4	5	2[1]		7	9	6[2]		10				12				13				8	11[3]	14		34
1	3	4	5▮	2[2]		7▮	9	6		10			12	14								8[3]	11[1]	13		35
1	3	4		12			9	5		2		7	13	14				6[1]				8	11[2]	10[3]		36
1	3	4					9	5		2[1]		7		12				6[2]	13			8	11[3]	10	14	37
																										38
																										39
																										40
																										41
																										42
																										43
																										44
																										45
																										46

FA Cup

First Round	Bolton W	(a)	1-0
Second Round	Bristol R	(a)	1-1
Replay	Bristol R	(h)	0-1

Carabao Cup

First Round	Leyton Orient	(h)	2-0
Second Round	Reading	(h)	2-4

Leasing.com Trophy

Group F (S)	Bristol R	(h)	1-1
(Plymouth Arg won 5-3 on penalties)			
Group F (S)	Swindon T	(a)	3-0
Group F (S)	Chelsea U21	(h)	0-1

PORT VALE

FOUNDATION

Port Vale Football Club was formed in 1876 and took its name from the venue of the inaugural meeting at 'Port Vale House' situated in a suburb of Stoke-on-Trent. Upon moving to Burslem in 1884 the club changed its name to 'Burslem Port Vale' and after several seasons in the Midland League became founder members of the Football League Division Two in 1892. The prefix 'Burslem' was dropped from the name as a new ground several miles away was acquired.

Vale Park, Hamil Road, Burslem, Stoke-on-Trent, Staffordshire ST6 1AW.

Telephone: (01782) 655 800.

Ticket Office: (01782) 655 800 (option 1).

Website: www.port-vale.co.uk

Email: enquiries@port-vale.co.uk

Ground Capacity: 19,052.

Record Attendance: 22,993 v Stoke C, Division 2, 6 March 1920 (at Recreation Ground); 49,768 v Aston Villa, FA Cup 5th rd, 20 February 1960 (at Vale Park).

Pitch Measurements: 104m × 70m (114yd × 76.5yd).

Co-Chair: Kevin Shanahan, Carol Shanahan.

Chief Executive: Colin Garlick.

Manager: John Askey.

Assistant Manager: Dave Kevan.

Colours: White shirts with black features and yellow trim, black shorts with white trim, white socks with black trim.

Year Formed: 1876.

Turned Professional: 1885.

Previous Names: 1876, Port Vale; 1884, Burslem Port Vale; 1909, Port Vale.

Club Nickname: 'Valiants'.

Grounds: 1876, Limekin Lane, Longport; 1881, Westport; 1884, Moorland Road, Burslem; 1886, Athletic Ground, Cobridge; 1913, Recreation Ground, Hanley; 1950, Vale Park.

First Football League Game: 3 September 1892, Division 2, v Small Heath (a) L 1–5 – Frail; Clutton, Elson; Farrington, McCrindle, Delves; Walker, Scarratt, Bliss (1), Jones. (Only 10 men).

Record League Victory: 9–1 v Chesterfield, Division 2, 24 September 1932 – Leckie; Shenton, Poyser; Sherlock, Round, Jones; McGrath, Mills, Littlewood (6), Kirkham (2), Morton (1).

Record Cup Victory: 7–1 v Irthlingborough, FA Cup 1st rd, 12 January 1907 – Matthews; Dunn, Hamilton; Eardley, Baddeley, Holyhead; Carter, Dodds (2), Beats, Mountford (2), Coxon (3).

Record Defeat: 0–10 v Sheffield U, Division 2, 10 December 1892. 0–10 v Notts Co, Division 2, 26 February 1895.

HONOURS

League Champions: Division 3N – 1929–30, 1953–54; Division 4 – 1958–59.
Runners-up: Second Division – 1993–94; Division 3N – 1952–53.

FA Cup: semi-final – 1954.

League Cup: 4th rd – 2007.

League Trophy Winners: 1993, 2001.

Anglo-Italian Cup: *Runners-up:* 1996.

FOOTBALL YEARBOOK FACT FILE

Port Vale were originally known as 'the Valeites', but towards the end of the First World War the local press began referring to them as 'the Colliers'. This was quickly dropped and 'the Valeites' came back into use before the modern nickname 'the Valiants' was adopted.

Most League Points (2 for a win): 69, Division 3 (N), 1953–54.

Most League Points (3 for a win): 89, Division 2, 1992–93.

Most League Goals: 110, Division 4, 1958–59.

Highest League Scorer in Season: Wilf Kirkham 38, Division 2, 1926–27.

Most League Goals in Total Aggregate: Wilf Kirkham, 153, 1923–29, 1931–33.

Most League Goals in One Match: 6, Stewart Littlewood v Chesterfield, Division 2, 24 September 1922.

Most Capped Player: Chris Birchall, 24 (43), Trinidad & Tobago.

Most League Appearances: Roy Sproson, 760, 1950–72.

Youngest League Player: Malcolm McKenzie, 15 years 347 days v Newport Co, 12 April 1966.

Record Transfer Fee Received: £2,000,000 from Wimbledon for Gareth Ainsworth, October 1998.

Record Transfer Fee Paid: £500,000 to Lincoln C for Gareth Ainsworth, September 1997.

Football League Record: 1892 Original Member of Division 2. Failed re-election in 1896; Re-elected 1898; Resigned 1907; Returned in Oct, 1919, when they took over the fixtures of Leeds City; 1929–30 Division 3 (N); 1930–36 Division 2; 1936–38 Division 3 (N); 1938–52 Division 3 (S); 1952–54 Division 3 (N); 1954–57 Division 2; 1957–58 Division 3 (S); 1958–59 Division 4; 1959–65 Division 3; 1965–70 Division 4; 1970–78 Division 3; 1978–83 Division 4; 1983–84 Division 3; 1984–86 Division 4; 1986–89 Division 3; 1989–94 Division 2; 1994–2000 Division 1; 2000–04 Division 2; 2004–08 FL 1; 2008–13 FL 2; 2013–17 FL 1; 2017– FL 2.

LATEST SEQUENCES

Longest Sequence of League Wins: 8, 8.4.1893 – 30.9.1893.

Longest Sequence of League Defeats: 9, 9.3.1957 – 20.4.1957.

Longest Sequence of League Draws: 6, 26.4.1981 – 12.9.1981.

Longest Sequence of Unbeaten League Matches: 19, 5.5.1969 – 8.11.1969.

Longest Sequence Without a League Win: 17, 7.12.1991 – 21.3.1992.

Successive Scoring Runs: 22 from 12.9.1992.

Successive Non-scoring Runs: 5 from 19.8.2017.

MANAGERS

Sam Gleaves 1896–1905 *(Secretary-Manager)*
Tom Clare 1905–11
A. S. Walker 1911–12
H. Myatt 1912–14
Tom Holford 1919–24 *(continued as Trainer)*
Joe Schofield 1924–30
Tom Morgan 1930–32
Tom Holford 1932–35
Warney Cresswell 1936–37
Tom Morgan 1937–38
Billy Frith 1945–46
Gordon Hodgson 1946–51
Ivor Powell 1951
Freddie Steele 1951–57
Norman Low 1957–62
Freddie Steele 1962–65
Jackie Mudie 1965–67
Sir Stanley Matthews *(General Manager)* 1965–68
Gordon Lee 1968–74
Roy Sproson 1974–77
Colin Harper 1977
Bobby Smith 1977–78
Dennis Butler 1978–79
Alan Bloor 1979
John McGrath 1980–83
John Rudge 1983–99
Brian Horton 1999–2004
Martin Foyle 2004–07
Lee Sinnott 2007–08
Dean Glover 2008–09
Micky Adams 2009–10
Jim Gannon 2011
Micky Adams 2011–14
Robert Page 2014–16
Bruno Ribeiro 2016
Michael Brown 2017
Neil Aspin 2017–19
John Askey February 2019–

TEN YEAR LEAGUE RECORD

		P	W	D	L	F	A	Pts	Pos
2010-11	FL 2	46	17	14	15	54	49	65	11
2011-12	FL 2	46	20	9	17	68	60	59*	12
2012-13	FL 2	46	21	15	10	87	52	78	3
2013-14	FL 1	46	18	7	21	59	73	61	9
2014-15	FL 1	46	15	9	22	55	65	54	18
2015-16	FL 1	46	18	11	17	56	58	65	12
2016-17	FL 1	46	12	13	21	45	70	49	21
2017-18	FL 2	46	11	14	21	49	67	47	20
2018-19	FL 2	46	12	13	21	39	55	49	20
2019-20	FL 2	37	14	15	8	50	44	57	8§

**10 pts deducted. §Decided on points-per-game (1.54)*

DID YOU KNOW ?

Port Vale were one of several clubs to introduce mascots for marketing purposes in the 1960s in the wake of the success of World Cup Willie. Prince Val wore a cloak and a crown with the initials 'PV' but the concept was not a great success and he was quickly forgotten.

PORT VALE – SKY BET LEAGUE TWO 2019–20 LEAGUE RECORD

Match No.	Date	Venue	Opponents	Result		H/T Score	Lg Pos.	Goalscorers	Attendance
1	Aug 3	A	Colchester U	D	1-1	1-1	12	Pope (pen) [5]	3729
2	10	H	Northampton T	D	1-1	1-1	16	Amoo [26]	5931
3	17	A	Salford C	D	1-1	0-0	17	Bennett [81]	3770
4	20	H	Forest Green R	W	2-1	2-1	11	Bennett [4], Amoo [34]	4010
5	24	A	Grimsby T	L	2-5	1-1	16	Whitehouse (og) [13], Smith [62]	4290
6	31	H	Cambridge U	W	1-0	0-0	10	Bennett [84]	4874
7	Sept 7	A	Newport Co	L	0-1	0-0	14		3913
8	14	H	Plymouth Arg	W	1-0	0-0	10	Smith [76]	5275
9	17	A	Exeter C	L	0-2	0-0	15		3765
10	21	H	Mansfield T	D	2-2	1-1	13	Cullen [45], Smith [90]	5109
11	28	A	Leyton Orient	D	3-3	2-1	15	Burgess [23], Legge [27], Jake Taylor [85]	5490
12	Oct 5	H	Morecambe	W	3-1	0-1	10	Joyce [49], Pope 2 [68, 90]	4485
13	12	A	Macclesfield T	L	1-2	1-1	13	Bennett [12]	3467
14	19	H	Stevenage	D	1-1	1-1	16	Jake Taylor [8]	4429
15	22	A	Bradford C	W	2-1	1-1	10	Worrall [18], Atkinson [90]	14,345
16	26	H	Oldham Ath	D	0-0	0-0	11		4301
17	Nov 2	A	Crewe Alex	W	1-0	0-0	10	Jake Taylor [61]	7705
18	16	H	Carlisle U	W	2-1	0-1	8	Worrall [60], Cullen [83]	4783
19	23	A	Scunthorpe U	L	1-2	1-1	9	Jake Taylor [30]	3391
20	Dec 7	H	Walsall	L	0-1	0-0	10		5079
21	14	A	Crawley T	D	0-0	0-0	10		1944
22	21	H	Cheltenham T	D	1-1	1-1	10	Tozer (og) [39]	4404
23	26	A	Mansfield T	D	2-2	0-0	10	Smith [53], Legge [66]	5565
24	29	H	Swindon T	W	2-0	1-0	10	Burgess [13], Jake Taylor [52]	5495
25	Jan 1	H	Macclesfield T	D	2-2	1-0	10	Worrall [18], Amoo [62]	5350
26	11	A	Stevenage	W	1-0	0-0	10	Pope (pen) [88]	2646
27	14	A	Morecambe	L	1-2	0-2	10	Gibbons [71]	1639
28	18	H	Leyton Orient	W	1-0	0-0	10	Amoo [71]	5047
29	25	A	Swindon T	L	0-3	0-2	10		7343
30	28	H	Exeter C	W	3-1	0-1	10	Bennett 2 (1 pen) [50 (p), 70], Legge [64]	3347
31	Feb 1	H	Salford C	D	1-1	0-0	10	Burgess, C (og) [55]	5281
32	8	A	Northampton T	W	1-0	0-0	9	Worrall [72]	5583
33	11	A	Forest Green R	W	3-2	2-0	9	Brisley [14], Pope 2 (1 pen) [38, 70 (p)]	1682
34	15	H	Colchester U	W	3-0	1-0	6	Conlon [14], Cullen 2 [54, 72]	5199
35	22	A	Walsall	D	2-2	2-1	8	Legge [12], Burgess [36]	6301
36	29	H	Scunthorpe U	D	2-2	1-0	7	Cullen [16], Smith [78]	5121
37	Mar 7	A	Cheltenham T	D	0-0	0-0	8		3741
38	14	H	Crawley T	Cancelled					
39	17	H	Bradford C	Cancelled					
40	21	A	Oldham Ath	Cancelled					
41	28	H	Crewe Alex	Cancelled					
42	Apr 4	A	Carlisle U	Cancelled					
43	10	H	Grimsby T	Cancelled					
44	13	A	Cambridge U	Cancelled					
45	18	H	Newport Co	Cancelled					
46	25	A	Plymouth Arg	Cancelled					

Final League Position: 8 (on points-per-game basis)

GOALSCORERS

League (50): Bennett 6 (1 pen), Pope 6 (3 pens), Cullen 5, Smith 5, Jake Taylor 5, Amoo 4, Legge 4, Worrall 4, Burgess 3, Atkinson 1, Brisley 1, Conlon 1, Gibbons 1, Joyce 1, own goals 3.
FA Cup (5): Pope 4, Worrall 1.
Carabao Cup (1): Cullen 1 (1 pen).
Leasing.com Trophy (9): Cullen 2, Jake Taylor 2, Amoo 1 (1 pen), Archer 1, Bennett 1, Browne 1, Burgess, C 1.

Brown S 37	Gibbons J 31 + 1	Legge L 37	Smith N 33 + 1	Crookes A 14	Oyeleke E 3 + 3	Joyce L 36	Conlon T 19 + 3	Worrall D 34	Pope T 15 + 17	Amoo D 30 + 2	Cullen M 7 + 11	Bennett R 17 + 9	Montano C 29 + 1	Lloyd R 1 + 5	Campbell-Gordon R — + 1	Archer J — + 3	Evans C 1 + 4	Browne R 6 + 5	Kennedy K 1	Taylor Jake 16	Burgess S 23 + 1	Atkinson W 7 + 4	Brisley S 6 + 3	Clark M 4	*Match No.*
1	2	3	4	5	6	7	8	9^{1}	10^{2}	11^{3}	12	13	14												1
1	2	3	4	5	6^{1}	7	8	9	10	11	12														2
1	2	3	4	5		7	8	6	10^{1}	9^{2}		12	11	13											3
1	2	3	4	5		7	8	6	13	9		10^{2}	11^{1}	12											4
1	2	3	4	5		6	9	8^{2}	13	7	12	11^{1}		10^{3}	14										5
1	2	3	4	5		7	8	6	12	9		10^{2}	11^{1}												6
1	2	3	4	5		7	8^{3}	6	12	9		10^{1}	11^{2}			13	14								7
1	2	3	4	5		7	8^{1}	6		9^{2}		10	11				12^{3}	13							8
1		3	4	5		7		6	13		14	10^{2}	11	12				9^{3}	2	8^{1}					9
1	2	3	4	5		8		6	11		10	13	9^{1}	12^{2}						7					10
1	2	3	4	5	8^{3}	7		9	10^{2}	11^{1}		13		14						6	12				11
1		3	4	5		7		9	10	11		12								8	6^{1}	2			12
1	2^{2}	3	4	5		7		9	10^{1}	12		11				13				6		8			13
1	13	3	4	5		7		6	12	9		10	11^{2}							8		2^{1}			14
1	2	3	4			7		11		9		10	5							8^{2}	6^{1}	12	13		15
1	2	3	4			7			13	9	14	10^{3}	5					11		8^{2}	6^{1}	12			16
1	2	3	4			7		11	12	9		10^{2}	5^{1}				13			8	6				17
1	2	3	4			7		11^{1}	12	9	13	10^{3}	5					14		6	8^{2}				18
1	2	3	4			7^{2}	13	11▮		9^{3}	12	10	5					14		8	6^{1}				19
1	2	3	4				8▮		10	9	12	13	11				5^{1}			6		7^{2}			20
1	2	3	4			7			10	9			5					11		8	6				21
1	2	3	4			7		11	10	9	12		5							8	6^{1}				22
1	2	3	4			7		11	10^{1}	9			5			12					6	8			23
1	2	3	4			7		11	10^{1}	9	12		5							6	8				24
1	2	3	4			7		11	13	9^{1}		10^{3}	5					14		6^{2}	8	12			25
1	2	3	4			7	8	11	10	9			5								6^{1}		12		26
1	2	3	4			7	8	11	10^{1}	9	13	12	5								6^{2}				27
1	2	3	4			7	13	11	12	9	10^{1}		5^{3}				14				6	8^{2}			28
1	2	3	4^{3}			7^{1}	14	11		9	10^{2}	13	5								6	8	12		29
1	2	3				7	8	11	12	9		10^{1}	5								6		4		30
1	2	3				7	8	11	12	9		10^{1}									6		4	5	31
1	2	3	13			7	8	9	12			10^{2}	11								6^{1}		4	5	32
1		3			13	7	8^{1}	9	10▮				5					11			6^{2}	12	4	2▮	33
1		3	2			7	8	9			10^{1}	12	5					11			6		4		34
1		3	2		13	7	8^{3}	9	14	12	10^{2}		5					11^{1}			6		4		35
1	2	3	4		13	7	8^{1}	11	12	9	10^{2}		5								6				36
1	2	3	4			7	8	11	12	9^{1}	10^{2}							13			6			5	37
																									38
																									39
																									40
																									41
																									42
																									43
																									44
																									45
																									46

FA Cup

First Round	Milton Keynes D	(a)	1-0
Second Round	Cheltenham T	(a)	3-1
Third Round	Manchester C	(a)	1-4

Carabao Cup

First Round	Burton Alb	(h)	1-2

Leasing.com Trophy

Group D (N)	Shrewsbury T	(h)	2-1
Group D (N)	Macclesfield T	(a)	3-2
Group D (N)	Newcastle U U21	(h)	2-1
Second Round (N)	Mansfield T	(h)	2-2
(Port Vale won 4-2 on penalties)			
Third Round (N)	Salford C	(a)	0-3

PORTSMOUTH

FOUNDATION

At a meeting held in his High Street, Portsmouth offices in 1898, solicitor Alderman J. E. Pink and five other business and professional men agreed to buy some ground close to Goldsmith Avenue for £4,950 which they developed into Fratton Park in record breaking time. A team of professionals was signed up by manager Frank Brettell and entry to the Southern League obtained for the new club's September 1899 kick-off.

Fratton Park, Frogmore Road, Portsmouth, Hampshire PO4 8RA.

Telephone: (0345) 646 1898.

Ticket Office: (0345) 646 1898.

Website: www.portsmouthfc.co.uk

Email: info@pompeyfc.co.uk

Ground Capacity: 18,948.

Record Attendance: 51,385 v Derby Co, FA Cup 6th rd, 26 February 1949.

Pitch Measurements: 100m × 66m (109.5yd × 72yd).

Chairman: Michael Eisner.

Chief Executive: Mark Catlin.

Manager: Kenny Jackett.

Assistant Manager: Joe Gallen.

Colours: Blue shirts with white and red trim, white shorts with blue trim, red socks.

Year Formed: 1898.

Turned Professional: 1898.

Club Nickname: 'Pompey'.

Ground: 1898, Fratton Park.

First Football League Game: 28 August 1920, Division 3, v Swansea T (h) W 3–0 – Robson; Probert, Potts; Abbott, Harwood, Turner; Thompson, Stringfellow (1), Reid (1), James (1), Beedie.

Record League Victory: 9–1 v Notts Co, Division 2, 9 April 1927 – McPhail; Clifford, Ted Smith; Reg Davies (1), Foxall, Moffat; Forward (1), Mackie (2), Haines (3), Watson, Cook (2).

Record Cup Victory: 7–0 v Stockport Co, FA Cup 3rd rd, 8 January 1949 – Butler; Rookes, Ferrier; Scoular, Flewin, Dickinson; Harris (3), Barlow, Clarke (2), Phillips (2), Froggatt.

Record Defeat: 0–10 v Leicester C, Division 1, 20 October 1928.

Most League Points (2 for a win): 65, Division 3, 1961–62.

HONOURS

League Champions: Division 1 – 1948–49, 1949–50; First Division – 2002–03; Division 3 – 1961–62, 1982–83; Division 3S – 1923–24; FL 2 – 2016–17.
Runners-up: Division 2 – 1926–27, 1986–87.

FA Cup Winners: 1939, 2008.
Runners-up: 1929, 1934, 2010.

League Cup: 5th rd – 1961, 1986, 1994, 2005, 2010.

League Trophy Winners: 2019.
Finalists: 2020.

European Competitions
UEFA Cup: 2008–09.

FOOTBALL YEARBOOK FACT FILE

Portsmouth have suffered many financial crises over the years. The club was initially incorporated as the Portsmouth Football and Athletic Company Limited in 1898. Due to financial difficulties arising from relegation to the Southern League Second Division, this company was voluntarily wound up in May 1912 to be succeeded by the Portsmouth Football Company Limited.

Most League Points (3 for a win): 98, Division 1, 2002–03.

Most League Goals: 97, Division 1, 2002–03.

Highest League Scorer in Season: Guy Whittingham, 42, Division 1, 1992–93.

Most League Goals in Total Aggregate: Peter Harris, 194, 1946–60.

Most League Goals in One Match: 5, Alf Strange v Gillingham, Division 3, 27 January 1923; 5, Peter Harris v Aston Villa, Division 1, 3 September 1958.

Most Capped Player: Jimmy Dickinson, 48, England.

Most League Appearances: Jimmy Dickinson, 764, 1946–65.

Youngest League Player: Clive Green, 16 years 259 days v Wrexham, 21 August 1976.

Record Transfer Fee Received: £18,800,000 from Real Madrid for Lassana Diarra, January 2009.

Record Transfer Fee Paid: £9,000,000 (rising to £11,000,000) to Liverpool for Peter Crouch, July 2008.

Football League Record: 1920 Original Member of Division 3; 1921 Division 3 (S); 1924–27 Division 2; 1927–59 Division 1; 1959–61 Division 2; 1961–62 Division 3; 1962–76 Division 2; 1976–78 Division 3; 1978–80 Division 4; 1980–83 Division 3; 1983–87 Division 2; 1987–88 Division 1; 1988–92 Division 2; 1992–2003 Division 1; 2003–10 Premier League; 2010–12 FL C; 2012–13 FL 1; 2013–17 FL 2; 2017– FL 1.

LATEST SEQUENCES

Longest Sequence of League Wins: 7, 12.3.2019 – 22.4.2019.

Longest Sequence of League Defeats: 9, 26.12.2012 – 9.2.2013.

Longest Sequence of League Draws: 5, 2.2.2019 – 23.2.2019.

Longest Sequence of Unbeaten League Matches: 15, 18.4.1924 – 18.10.1924.

Longest Sequence Without a League Win: 25, 29.11.1958 – 22.8.1959.

Successive Scoring Runs: 23 from 30.8.1930.

Successive Non-scoring Runs: 6 from 27.12.1993.

MANAGERS

Frank Brettell 1898–1901
Bob Blyth 1901–04
Richard Bonney 1905–08
Bob Brown 1911–20
John McCartney 1920–27
Jack Tinn 1927–47
Bob Jackson 1947–52
Eddie Lever 1952–58
Freddie Cox 1958–61
George Smith 1961–70
Ron Tindall 1970–73
(General Manager to 1974)
John Mortimore 1973–74
Ian St John 1974–77
Jimmy Dickinson 1977–79
Frank Burrows 1979–82
Bobby Campbell 1982–84
Alan Ball 1984–89
John Gregory 1989–90
Frank Burrows 1990–91
Jim Smith 1991–95
Terry Fenwick 1995–98
Alan Ball 1998–99
Tony Pulis 2000
Steve Claridge 2000–01
Graham Rix 2001–02
Harry Redknapp 2002–04
Velimir Zajec 2004–05
Alain Perrin 2005
Harry Redknapp 2005–08
Tony Adams 2008–09
Paul Hart 2009
Avram Grant 2009–10
Steve Cotterill 2010–11
Michael Appleton 2011–12
Guy Whittingham 2012–13
Richie Barker 2013–14
Andy Awford 2014–15
Paul Cook 2015–17
Kenny Jackett June 2017–

TEN YEAR LEAGUE RECORD

		P	W	D	L	F	A	Pts	Pos
2010-11	FL C	46	15	13	18	53	60	58	16
2011-12	FL C	46	13	11	22	50	59	40*	22
2012-13	FL 1	46	10	12	24	51	69	32*	24
2013-14	FL 2	46	14	17	15	56	66	59	13
2014-15	FL 2	46	14	15	17	52	54	57	16
2015-16	FL 2	46	21	15	10	75	44	78	6
2016-17	FL 2	46	26	9	11	79	40	87	1
2017-18	FL 1	46	20	6	20	57	56	66	8
2018-19	FL 1	46	25	13	8	83	51	88	4
2019-20	FL 1	35	17	9	9	53	36	60	5§

** 10 pts deducted. §Decided on points-per-game (1.71)*

DID YOU KNOW ?

Portsmouth's Fratton Park ground hosted a baseball match in June 1918 between teams representing the United States and Canadian armies. The USA won 4-3 in front of a large attendance with proceeds going to the British Red Cross.

PORTSMOUTH – SKY BET LEAGUE ONE 2019–20 LEAGUE RECORD

Match No.	Date	Venue	Opponents	Result		H/T Score	Lg Pos.	Goalscorers	Attendance
1	Aug 3	A	Shrewsbury T	L	0-1	0-0	16		7880
2	10	H	Tranmere R	W	2-0	1-0	9	Close [27], Naylor [75]	18,575
3	17	A	Sunderland	L	1-2	1-2	15	Harness [22]	29,140
4	20	H	Coventry C	D	3-3	2-1	14	Curtis [10], Marquis [43], Evans [56]	18,748
5	31	A	Blackpool	D	1-1	1-0	17	Harness [17]	10,605
6	Sept 17	H	Burton Alb	D	2-2	1-2	18	Curtis [39], Pitman (pen) [90]	16,610
7	21	A	Wycombe W	L	0-1	0-0	20		7688
8	28	H	Bolton W	W	1-0	0-0	19	Pitman [66]	18,382
9	Oct 5	A	Doncaster R	W	2-1	0-0	16	Evans [60], Harrison [90]	8962
10	12	H	Gillingham	D	0-0	0-0	16		18,036
11	19	A	AFC Wimbledon	L	0-1	0-0	17		4525
12	22	H	Lincoln C	W	1-0	1-0	16	Marquis [28]	17,266
13	26	A	Bristol R	D	2-2	1-0	16	Evans (pen) [9], Curtis [70]	8648
14	Nov 2	H	Oxford U	D	1-1	0-0	15	Evans (pen) [58]	18,528
15	5	H	Southend U	W	4-1	1-0	13	Marquis [45], Harrison 2 (1 pen) [50, 80 (p)], Harness [84]	16,995
16	23	A	Rochdale	W	3-0	1-0	11	Curtis 2 [15, 47], Williams [88]	3789
17	26	H	Rotherham U	W	3-2	2-1	10	Curtis [1], Marquis [37], Close [66]	16,355
18	Dec 7	H	Peterborough U	D	2-2	1-1	10	Brown [26], Harrison [52]	17,643
19	14	A	Accrington S	L	1-4	1-1	10	Curtis [35]	2429
20	21	H	Ipswich T	W	1-0	0-0	10	Curtis [50]	18,801
21	26	H	Wycombe W	W	2-0	0-0	8	Close [66], Curtis [73]	18,419
22	29	A	Milton Keynes D	L	1-3	0-2	9	Curtis [90]	12,788
23	Jan 1	A	Gillingham	D	1-1	1-0	9	Evans [36]	5724
24	11	H	AFC Wimbledon	W	2-1	1-0	7	Harness [20], Marquis [79]	18,417
25	18	A	Bolton W	W	1-0	1-0	7	Burgess [42]	13,407
26	28	A	Lincoln C	W	2-0	1-0	6	Curtis [45], Marquis (pen) [86]	8983
27	Feb 1	H	Sunderland	W	2-0	1-0	6	Burgess [25], Bolton [52]	18,531
28	8	A	Tranmere R	W	2-0	1-0	5	Raggett [13], Williams [51]	6985
29	11	A	Coventry C	L	0-1	0-0	6		6983
30	15	H	Shrewsbury T	W	2-0	0-0	6	Harrison [64], Marquis [82]	18,214
31	22	A	Fleetwood T	L	0-1	0-1	7		3370
32	25	H	Milton Keynes D	W	3-1	1-1	5	Cannon [4], Marquis [49], Harness [90]	16,577
33	28	H	Rochdale	W	3-0	1-0	3	Williams [45], Seddon [78], Burgess [84]	17,600
34	Mar 7	A	Peterborough U	L	0-2	0-1	6		9414
35	10	H	Fleetwood T	D	2-2	1-1	4	Raggett [36], Soutar (og) [48]	16,775
36	14	H	Accrington S	Cancelled					
37	17	H	Doncaster R	Cancelled					
38	21	A	Ipswich T	Cancelled					
39	28	A	Oxford U	Cancelled					
40	Apr 10	A	Rotherham U	Cancelled					
41	13	H	Blackpool	Cancelled					
42	18	A	Southend U	Cancelled					
43	21	H	Bristol R	Cancelled					
44	May 3	A	Burton Alb	Cancelled					

Final League Position: 5 (on points-per-game basis)

GOALSCORERS

League (53): Curtis 11, Marquis 8 (1 pen), Evans 5 (2 pens), Harness 5, Harrison 5 (1 pen), Burgess 3, Close 3, Williams 3, Pitman 2 (1 pen), Raggett 2, Bolton 1, Brown 1, Cannon 1, Naylor 1, Seddon 1, own goal 1.
FA Cup (10): Close 2, Curtis 2, Marquis 2, Bolton 1, Burgess 1, Haunstrup 1, Pitman 1.
Carabao Cup (5): Harrison 2, Close 1, Harness 1, Marquis 1 (1 pen).
Leasing.com Trophy (15): Harrison 3, Marquis 3, Harness 2, McGeehan 2, Flint 1, Lethbridge 1, Maloney 1, Pitman 1, Walkes 1.
League One Play-offs (2): Curtis 1, Harness 1.

MacGillivray C 20	Walkes A 10 + 1	Downing P 6	Burgess C 31 + 1	Brown L 16	Naylor T 33	McCrorie R 12 + 5	Curtis R 31 + 2	Evans G 10 + 7	Harness M 16 + 9	Marquis J 25 + 8	Bolton J 20 + 3	Pitman B 4 + 7	Harrison E 17 + 11	Close B 27 + 2	Cannon A 13 + 5	Raggett S 26	Haunstrup B 7 + 3	Williams R 20 + 6	Hawkins O 5 + 2	Bass A 15	Seddon S 10 + 2	McGeehan C 10 + 2	Whatmough J 1	Match No.
1	2^{1}	3	4	5	6	7■	8	9^{3}	10^{2}	11	12	13	14											1
1	2	3	4	5	6		10		8	12		13	11^{1}	7	9^{2}									2
1	2^{1}	3	4	5	7	14	11^{3}	13	9	10			12	6	8^{2}									3
1		4	13	5^{3}	7	2	11	8^{1}	9	10		14		6		3^{2}	12							4
1	14	3	2		4	7^{2}	11	12^{3}	9^{1}	10			13	8	6		5							5
1		4	2		3	6^{2}	10	12		11		9	14	7	13		5^{1}	8^{3}						6
1			4		7		10			11	2^{1}	12	8■	6	9		5		3					7
1			3		6		10^{2}	13	12	11	2	9		7		4	5	8^{1}						8
1			3	5	7			9	6^{1}	10^{2}	2	11	12	8		4		13						9
			3	5	7			9^{3}	6	12	2	10^{1}	11	8^{2}	14	4		13		1				10
1			3	5	6		13	9	8^{3}	11^{2}	2		12	7	14	4		10^{1}						11
1			3	5	6	2	12	9	10^{1}	11				7		4		8						12
1			3	5	7	2	10	9		11^{1}			12	6		4		8						13
1			3	5	6	2^{1}	10	9^{2}		11	12		13	7		4		8						14
			3	5	7	2^{1}	9		13	10			11	8		4	12	6^{2}		1				15
1	6		3	5			10^{1}		13	9		12	11^{2}	7			2	8	4					16
1	6		3	5			10		12	9			11	7			2	8^{1}	4					17
1			3	5	6	13	10		12	9			11	7			2^{2}	8^{1}	4					18
1	5				3	6	10		8^{2}	9^{1}	2	13	11	7		4		12						19
1	5		3		6	2^{1}	10	13			12		11	7	9^{2}	4		8						20
1	5		3		6		10^{1}	13	12	14	2		11	7	9^{3}	4		8^{2}						21
1	5		3		6		10	13	9^{1}	12	2	14	11^{3}	7	8^{2}	4								22
	5		3		6		10	9^{2}	8	12	2		11^{1}	7		4			13	1				23
			3		6		10		8	12	2^{2}		11		9^{1}	4	13			1	5	7		24
			3		7		10		8^{1}	9	2		11^{2}		12	4		13		1	5	6		25
			3		6		10			11	2			7	9^{1}	4		8		1	5	12		26
			3		6		10			11^{2}	2		12	13	9^{1}	4		8		1	5	7		27
			3		6		10				2		11	7		4		8		1	5	9		28
			3		6		10		12	11^{2}	2		13	7		4		8^{1}		1	5	9		29
			3		6	13	10^{3}	9^{1}	8	12	2^{2}		11			4		14		1	5	7		30
			3		6	13	10		8	9	2^{2}					4		12	11^{1}	1	5	7		31
			3	5	6	2	10^{2}		12	11				7	9^{1}	4		8^{3}		1	14	13		32
			3	5^{3}	6		10			11^{2}	2		14	13	9^{1}	4		8		1	12	7		33
					6	12	10			11	2			7^{2}	13	4		8	14	1	5	9^{1}	3^{3}	34
					7	2	10		12	13	3		11		9	4		8^{1}		1	5	6^{2}		35
																								36
																								37
																								38
																								39
																								40
																								41
																								42
																								43
																								44

FA Cup

First Round	Harrogate T	(a)	2-1
Second Round	Altrincham	(h)	2-1
Third Round	Fleetwood T	(a)	2-1
Fourth Round	Barnsley	(h)	4-2
Fifth Round	Arsenal	(h)	0-2

League One Play-Offs

Semi-Final 1st leg	Oxford U	(h)	1-1
Semi-Final 2nd leg	Oxford U	(a)	1-1

(aet; Oxford U won 5-4 on penalties)

Carabao Cup

First Round	Birmingham C	(h)	3-0
Second Round	QPR	(a)	2-0
Third Round	Southampton	(h)	0-4

Leasing.com Trophy

Group B (S)	Crawley T	(h)	1-0
Group B (S)	Norwich C U21	(h)	3-1
Group B (S)	Oxford U	(a)	2-2

(Portsmouth won 5-4 on penalties)

Second Round (S)	Northampton T	(h)	2-1
Third Round (S)	Walsall	(a)	2-1
Quarter-Final	Scunthorpe U	(h)	2-1
Semi-Final	Exeter C	(h)	3-2
Final	Salford C	(Wembley)	P-P

PRESTON NORTH END

FOUNDATION

North End Cricket and Rugby Club, which was formed in 1863, indulged in most sports before taking up soccer in about 1879. In 1881 they decided to stick to football to the exclusion of other sports and even a 16–0 drubbing by Blackburn Rovers in an invitation game at Deepdale, a few weeks after taking this decision, did not deter them for they immediately became affiliated to the Lancashire FA.

Deepdale Stadium, Sir Tom Finney Way, Deepdale, Preston, Lancashire PR1 6RU.

Telephone: (0344) 856 1964.

Ticket Office: (0344) 856 1966.

Website: www.pnefc.net

Email: enquiries@pne.co.uk

Ground Capacity: 23,404.

Record Attendance: 42,684 v Arsenal, Division 1, 23 April 1938.

Pitch Measurements: 100m × 67m (109.5yd × 73.5yd).

Chairman: Craig Hemmings.

Chief Executive: John Kay.

Manager: Alex Neil.

First-Team Coaches: Steve Thompson, Frankie McAvoy.

Colours: White shirts with blue sleeves, blue shorts with white trim, white socks with blue trim.

Year Formed: 1880.

Turned Professional: 1885.

Club Nicknames: 'The Lilywhites', 'North End'.

Ground: 1881, Deepdale.

First Football League Game: 8 September 1888, Football League, v Burnley (h) W 5–2 – Trainer; Howarth, Holmes; Robertson, William Graham, Johnny Graham; Gordon (1), Jimmy Ross (2), Goodall, Dewhurst (2), Drummond.

Record League Victory: 10–0 v Stoke, Division 1, 14 September 1889 – Trainer; Howarth, Holmes; Kelso, Russell (1), Johnny Graham; Gordon, Jimmy Ross (2), Nick Ross (3), Thomson (2), Drummond (2).

Record Cup Victory: 26–0 v Hyde, FA Cup 1st rd, 15 October 1887 – Addision; Howarth, Nick Ross; Russell (1), Thomson (5), Johnny Graham (1); Gordon (5), Jimmy Ross (8), John Goodall (1), Dewhurst (3), Drummond (2).

Record Defeat: 0–7 v Nottingham F, Division 2, 9 April 1927; 0–7 v Blackpool, Division 1, 1 May 1948.

Most League Points (2 for a win): 61, Division 3, 1970–71.

Most League Points (3 for a win): 95, Division 2, 1999–2000.

Most League Goals: 100, Division 2, 1927–28 and Division 1, 1957–58.

HONOURS

League Champions: Football League 1888–89, 1889–90; Division 2 – 1903–04, 1912–13, 1950–51; Second Division – 1999–2000; Division 3 – 1970–71; Third Division – 1995–96.
Runners-up: Football League 1890–91, 1891–92; Division 1 – 1892–93, 1905–06, 1952–53, 1957–58; Division 2 – 1914–15, 1933–34; Division 4 – 1986–87.

FA Cup Winners: 1889, 1938.
Runners-up: 1888, 1922, 1937, 1954, 1964.

League Cup: 4th rd – 1963, 1966, 1972, 1981, 2003, 2017.

Double Performed: 1888–89.

FOOTBALL YEARBOOK FACT FILE

Preston North End enjoyed one of the most successful seasons in their history in the emergency wartime competitions in 1940–41. They comfortably topped the League North table, which was decided on goal average, and after drawing 1-1 at Wembley defeated Arsenal 2-0 at Ewood Park to win the League War Cup.

Highest League Scorer in Season: Ted Harper, 37, Division 2, 1932–33.

Most League Goals in Total Aggregate: Tom Finney, 187, 1946–60.

Most League Goals in One Match: 4, Jimmy Ross v Stoke, Division 1, 6 October 1888; 4, Nick Ross v Derby Co, Division 1, 11 January 1890; 4, George Drummond v Notts Co, Division 1, 12 December 1891; 4, Frank Becton v Notts Co, Division 1, 31 March 1893; 4, George Harrison v Grimsby T, Division 2, 3 November 1928; 4, Alex Reid v Port Vale, Division 2, 23 February 1929; 4, James McClelland v Reading, Division 2, 6 September 1930; 4, Dick Rowley v Notts Co, Division 2, 16 April 1932; 4, Ted Harper v Burnley, Division 2, 29 August 1932; 4, Ted Harper v Lincoln C, Division 2, 11 March 1933; 4, Charlie Wayman v QPR, Division 2, 25 December 1950; 4, Alex Bruce v Colchester U, Division 3, 28 February 1978; 4, Joe Garner v Crewe Alex, FL 1, 14 March 2015.

Most Capped Player: Tom Finney, 76, England.

Most League Appearances: Alan Kelly, 447, 1961–75.

Youngest League Player: Ethan Walker, 16 years 154 days v Aston Villa, 29 December 2018.

Record Transfer Fee Received: £10,000,000 from West Ham U for Jordan Hugill, January 2018.

Record Transfer Fee Paid: £1,500,000 to Manchester U for David Healy, January 2001.

Football League Record: 1888 Founder Member of League; 1901–04 Division 2; 1904–12 Division 1; 1912–13 Division 2; 1913–14 Division 1; 1914–15 Division 2; 1919–25 Division 1; 1925–34 Division 2; 1934–49 Division 1; 1949–51 Division 2; 1951–61 Division 1; 1961–70 Division 2; 1970–71 Division 3; 1971–74 Division 2; 1974–78 Division 3; 1978–81 Division 2; 1981–85 Division 3; 1985–87 Division 4; 1987–92 Division 3; 1992–93 Division 2; 1993–96 Division 3; 1996–2000 Division 2; 2000–04 Division 1; 2004–11 FL C; 2011–15 FL 1; 2015– FL C.

LATEST SEQUENCES

Longest Sequence of League Wins: 14, 25.12.1950 – 27.3.1951.

Longest Sequence of League Defeats: 8, 22.9.1984 – 27.10.1984.

Longest Sequence of League Draws: 6, 24.2.1979 – 20.3.1979.

Longest Sequence of Unbeaten League Matches: 23, 8.9.1888 – 14.9.1889.

Longest Sequence Without a League Win: 15, 14.4.1923 – 20.10.1923.

Successive Scoring Runs: 30 from 15.11.1952.

Successive Non-scoring Runs: 6 from 19.11.1960.

MANAGERS

Charlie Parker 1906–15
Vincent Hayes 1919–23
Jim Lawrence 1923–25
Frank Richards 1925–27
Alex Gibson 1927–31
Lincoln Hayes 1931–32
Run by committee 1932–36
Tommy Muirhead 1936–37
Run by committee 1937–49
Will Scott 1949–53
Scot Symon 1953–54
Frank Hill 1954–56
Cliff Britton 1956–61
Jimmy Milne 1961–68
Bobby Seith 1968–70
Alan Ball Snr 1970–73
Bobby Charlton 1973–75
Harry Catterick 1975–77
Nobby Stiles 1977–81
Tommy Docherty 1981
Gordon Lee 1981–83
Alan Kelly 1983–85
Tommy Booth 1985–86
Brian Kidd 1986
John McGrath 1986–90
Les Chapman 1990–92
Sam Allardyce 1992 (*Caretaker*)
John Beck 1992–94
Gary Peters 1994–98
David Moyes 1998–2002
Kelham O'Hanlon 2002 (*Caretaker*)
Craig Brown 2002–04
Billy Davies 2004–06
Paul Simpson 2006–07
Alan Irvine 2007–09
Darren Ferguson 2010
Phil Brown 2011
Graham Westley 2012–13
Simon Grayson 2013–17
Alex Neil July 2017–

TEN YEAR LEAGUE RECORD

		P	W	D	L	F	A	Pts	Pos
2010-11	FL C	46	10	12	24	54	79	42	22
2011-12	FL 1	46	13	15	18	54	68	54	15
2012-13	FL 1	46	14	17	15	54	49	59	14
2013-14	FL 1	46	23	16	7	72	46	85	5
2014-15	FL 1	46	25	14	7	79	40	89	3
2015-16	FL C	46	15	17	14	45	45	62	11
2016-17	FL C	46	16	14	16	64	63	62	11
2017-18	FL C	46	19	16	11	57	46	73	7
2018-19	FL C	46	16	13	17	67	67	61	14
2019-20	FL C	46	18	12	16	59	54	66	9

DID YOU KNOW ?

Preston North End hold the record for the number of Football League games played by any club. Their 1-1 draw with Blackburn Rovers on 11 January 2020 was the club's 4,987th match in the competition, overtaking the previous record held by Notts County.

PRESTON NORTH END – SKY BET CHAMPIONSHIP 2019–20 LEAGUE RECORD

Match No.	Date	Venue	Opponents	Result		H/T Score	Lg Pos.	Goalscorers	Attendance
1	Aug 3	A	Millwall	L	0-1	0-1	21		14,923
2	10	H	Wigan Ath	W	3-0	2-0	10	Maguire 6, Moult 39, Gallagher 54	14,789
3	17	A	Swansea C	L	2-3	1-1	16	Rafferty 11, Johnson (pen) 67	15,250
4	21	H	Stoke C	W	3-1	2-0	10	Johnson 7, Bodin 25, Harrop 69	11,973
5	24	H	Sheffield W	W	2-1	1-0	6	Johnson 2 (2 pens) 32, 65	15,715
6	31	A	Nottingham F	D	1-1	1-0	7	Bodin 40	27,249
7	Sept 14	H	Brentford	W	2-0	1-0	5	Maguire 4, Barkhuizen 70	12,873
8	21	A	Birmingham C	W	1-0	1-0	3	Maguire 23	20,806
9	28	H	Bristol C	D	3-3	1-2	5	Gallagher (pen) 45, Johnson (pen) 51, Bauer 70	12,005
10	Oct 1	A	Middlesbrough	D	1-1	1-1	5	Harrop 40	17,961
11	5	H	Barnsley	W	5-1	1-1	3	Johnson 2 31, 61, Barkhuizen 50, Pearson 63, Harrop 77	12,431
12	19	A	Reading	L	0-1	0-0	6		14,135
13	22	H	Leeds U	D	1-1	0-0	5	Barkhuizen 74	18,275
14	26	H	Blackburn R	W	3-2	0-2	2	Barkhuizen 2 53, 82, Johnson (pen) 65	19,165
15	Nov 3	A	Charlton Ath	W	1-0	0-0	1	Gallagher (pen) 58	16,027
16	9	H	Huddersfield T	W	3-1	2-0	2	Stockley 4, Browne 33, Gallagher (pen) 50	16,038
17	23	A	Derby Co	L	0-1	0-1	3		27,417
18	27	A	Hull C	L	0-4	0-1	5		9826
19	Dec 2	H	WBA	L	0-1	0-0	6		13,015
20	7	A	QPR	L	0-2	0-1	7		12,179
21	10	H	Fulham	W	2-1	1-0	6	Maguire 23, Nugent 52	10,093
22	14	H	Luton T	W	2-1	1-1	3	Gallagher 5, Stockley 84	12,083
23	21	A	Cardiff C	D	0-0	0-0	4		22,625
24	26	A	Leeds U	D	1-1	1-0	6	Browne 22	35,638
25	29	H	Reading	L	0-2	0-2	7		13,680
26	Jan 1	H	Middlesbrough	L	0-2	0-1	9		13,824
27	11	A	Blackburn R	D	1-1	1-1	10	Harrop 17	19,963
28	18	H	Charlton Ath	W	2-1	1-1	9	Harrop 31, Bauer 52	12,358
29	21	A	Barnsley	W	3-0	3-0	6	Barkhuizen 2 19, 45, Johnson 34	12,207
30	Feb 1	H	Swansea C	D	1-1	1-1	7	Sinclair 28	12,502
31	8	A	Wigan Ath	W	2-1	1-0	6	Barkhuizen 7, Johnson 48	12,439
32	12	A	Stoke C	W	2-0	0-0	6	Browne 58, Barkhuizen 75	20,418
33	15	H	Millwall	L	0-1	0-0	6		12,468
34	22	H	Hull C	W	2-1	0-1	6	Gallagher (pen) 67, Browne 71	12,342
35	25	A	WBA	L	0-2	0-2	6		22,150
36	29	A	Fulham	L	0-2	0-0	6		19,020
37	Mar 7	H	QPR	L	1-3	1-0	6	Johnson (pen) 19	12,378
38	June 20	A	Luton T	D	1-1	0-0	6	Sinclair 52	0
39	27	H	Cardiff C	L	1-3	0-0	7	Johnson 73	0
40	July 1	H	Derby Co	L	0-1	0-1	9		0
41	4	A	Huddersfield T	D	0-0	0-0	9		0
42	8	A	Sheffield W	W	3-1	0-0	8	Sinclair 78, Stockley 87, Potts 90	0
43	11	H	Nottingham F	D	1-1	1-1	8	Stockley 15	0
44	15	A	Brentford	L	0-1	0-1	9		0
45	18	H	Birmingham C	W	2-0	1-0	8	Bauer 43, Potts 87	0
46	22	A	Bristol C	D	1-1	1-0	9	Maguire 16	0

Final League Position: 9

GOALSCORERS

League (59): Johnson 12 (6 pens), Barkhuizen 9, Gallagher 6 (4 pens), Harrop 5, Maguire 5, Browne 4, Stockley 4, Bauer 3, Sinclair 3, Bodin 2, Potts 2, Moult 1, Nugent 1, Pearson 1, Rafferty 1.
FA Cup (2): Bodin 1, Harrop 1.
Carabao Cup (6): Barkhuizen 2, Harrop 2, Green 1, Huntington 1.

Rudd D 46	Clarke T 7 + 3	Bauer P 41	Davies B 36	Hughes A 28	Pearson B 38	Gallagher P 22 + 11	Barkhuizen T 35 + 9	Browne A 35 + 8	Potts B 14 + 18	Maguire S 36 + 8	Stockley J 9 + 23	Bodin B 11 + 7	Green A — + 4	Fisher D 26 + 2	Johnson D 32 + 1	Moult L 2	Rafferty J 28 + 1	Harrop J 15 + 17	Storey J 7 + 3	Ledson R 8 + 5	Nugent D 11 + 13	Ginnelly J — + 1	Huntington P 8 + 1	Sinclair S 11 + 7	Bayliss T — + 1	*Match No.*
1	2	3	4	5	6	7^{3}	8^{2}	9	10^{1}	11	12	13	14													1
1	13	3	4	5	6	8^{1}		12		10	14	7		2^{2}	9	11^{3}										2
1		3	4		6	8	14	13		10		7^{3}	12	2	9^{2}	11^{1}	5									3
1	2^{1}	3	4		6	7^{3}	11	14	13			8^{2}		12	9		5	10								4
1		3^{2}	4		6	14	12	7		10	11	8^{1}		2	9^{3}		5		13							5
1		3	4		6	7^{2}		2	8		12	11^{1}	14		9^{3}		5	10		13						6
1		3	4			12	11^{3}	6	14	10		8^{2}		2	9		5	13		7^{1}						7
1		3	4	5	6	7^{1}	11^{2}	12	13	10				2^{3}	9		14	8								8
1		3	4		6	7^{1}	11	12		8^{3}				2	9		5	10^{2}			13	14				9
1		3	4		6	14	11^{3}	9	13	10				2	7^{2}		5	8^{1}			12					10
1		3	4		6	7	8^{3}	2	14	10^{2}	13				9		5	12			11^{1}					11
1		3	4	5	6	7^{1}	8^{3}	12		10	14			2	9			13			11^{2}					12
1		3	4		6		10^{2}	7	8	12			13	2	9		5				11^{1}					13
1		3		4	6	7^{1}	11	8	13	10^{2}	12			2	9		5									14
1		3	4		6	12	8	7		10	11			2	9^{1}		5									15
1		3	4			7^{1}	8	9	12	10	11^{2}			2			5			6	13					16
1		3	4^{3}		6	12	8	7		10	11^{1}	13		2^{2}	9		5		14							17
1		3			6	7	11		14	10^{3}		8^{2}			9		5	12	4	2^{1}	13					18
1					6		8^{3}	2	9^{1}	10^{2}	11	14			7		5	12	4		13		3			19
1				5	6		8^{2}	7	9^{3}	10	11^{1}	12					2	14	4		13		3			20
1	13	3		5	6^{2}		12	8	9	10		7^{3}					$2^{\blacksquare}$	14			11^{1}		4			21
1		3		5	6	7	13	9^{2}		10	14	8^{3}		2				12			11^{1}		4			22
1	2	3		5	6	7^{2}	11^{1}	9	13	10	14	8^{3}									12		4			23
1	2		4	5	6		10^{2}	7	9	8^{3}	13							14		12	11^{1}		3			24
1	2^{3}		4	5	6	13	12	7	9^{1}	11	14	8						10^{2}					3			25
1		3^{1}	4	5	6	7	8	9^{2}		10	13			2				14			11^{3}		12			26
1	2	3	4		6	7^{3}	8^{1}	9	14	11	12						5	10^{2}						13		27
1		3	4				8	6	14	11^{1}				2	7^{2}		5	9^{3}		13	12			10		28
1		3	4		7		10^{3}	6	12	13				2	8^{2}		5	9			14			11^{1}		29
1		3	4		6		11^{2}	7		13				2	9		5	10^{1}			12			8		30
1	13	3	4	5^{2}	6		8	7		11^{3}	14			2	9			12						10^{1}		31
1		3	4	5	6	13	8	7		11^{1}				2	9						12			10^{2}		32
1	2	3	4	5	6	13	8	7^{1}		14					9			12			11^{3}			10^{2}		33
1		3	4	5	6	7^{3}	8	12	14	11^{2}	13			2				9						10^{1}		34
1		3	4	5	6		8^{2}	7	14	10^{3}	13			$2^{\blacksquare}$	9						11^{1}			12		35
1		3	4	5			8	6	9^{3}	10^{2}	12			2	7			14			11^{1}			13		36
1		3	4	5		7^{1}	8^{2}	6		11	12			2	9			10^{3}		13				14		37
1		3	4	5	6	7^{2}	8^{5}	2	13	11^{1}	15	16		14	9^{4}						12			10^{3}		38
1		3	4	5	6	13	8^{1}	7	14	12	11^{5}			2^{2}	9^{3}			16			15			10^{4}		39
1			4	5	6^{4}	10^{3}	14	8	9	12	15						2	13			11^{1}		3	7^{2}		40
1		3	4	5	6		11^{4}	7^{1}	8	13	12	15					2	10^{2}		9^{3}				14		41
1		3	4	8^{3}	6^{2}	16	10^{5}	9	12	11^{4}	14				13		5		2	7^{1}				15		42
1		3	4^{1}	5	6^{2}	16	14		8	9	11^{4}				7^{5}		2	15	12	13				10^{3}		43
1		4		5			10^{3}	9^{2}	12	11^{4}	13	16		2^{1}	7		8	15	3	6^{5}				14		44
1		3		5		7	13		8	12	11				9^{2}		2	10^{1}	4	6						45
1		3		5		7^{4}	13	12	8	11^{3}	14				9		2	10^{2}	4	6^{1}					15	46

FA Cup

Third Round	Norwich C	(h)	2-4

Carabao Cup

First Round	Bradford C	(a)	4-0
Second Round	Hull C	(h)	2-2
(Preston NE won 5-4 on penalties)			
Third Round	Manchester C	(h)	0-3

QUEENS PARK RANGERS

FOUNDATION

There is an element of doubt about the date of the foundation of this club, but it is believed that in either 1885 or 1886 it was formed through the amalgamation of Christchurch Rangers and St Jude's Institute FC. The leading light was George Wodehouse, whose family maintained a connection with the club until comparatively recent times. Most of the players came from the Queen's Park district so this name was adopted after a year as St Jude's Institute.

The Kiyan Prince Foundation Stadium, South Africa Road, Shepherds Bush, London W12 7PJ.

Telephone: (020) 8743 0262.

Ticket Office: (08444) 777 007.

Website: www.qpr.co.uk

Email: boxoffice@qpr.co.uk

Ground Capacity: 18,181.

Record Attendance: 41,097 v Leeds U, FA Cup 3rd rd, 9 January 1932 (at White City); 35,353 v Leeds U, Division 1, 27 April 1974 (at Loftus Road).

Pitch Measurements: 100m × 66m (109.5yd × 72yd).

Chairman: Amit Bhatia.

Chief Executive: Lee Hoos.

Manager: Mark Warburton.

Assistant Manager: John Eustace.

Colours: Blue and white hooped shirts with red trim, white shorts with blue trim, white socks with blue trim.

Year Formed: 1885* (*see Foundation*).

Turned Professional: 1898.

Previous Name: 1885, St Jude's; 1887, Queens Park Rangers. ***Club Nicknames:*** 'Rangers', 'The Hoops', 'R's'.

Grounds: 1885* (*see Foundation*), Welford's Fields; 1888–99, London Scottish Ground, Brondesbury, Home Farm, Kensal Rise Green, Gun Club Wormwood Scrubs, Kilburn Cricket Ground; 1899, Kensal Rise Athletic Ground; 1901, Latimer Road, Notting Hill; 1904, Agricultural Society, Park Royal; 1907, Park Royal Ground; 1917, Loftus Road; 1931, White City; 1933, Loftus Road; 1962, White City; 1963, Loftus Road (renamed The Kiyan Prince Foundation Stadium 2019).

First Football League Game: 28 August 1920, Division 3, v Watford (h) L 1–2 – Price; Blackman, Wingrove; McGovern, Grant, O'Brien; Faulkner, Birch (1), Smith, Gregory, Middlemiss.

Record League Victory: 9–2 v Tranmere R, Division 3, 3 December 1960 – Drinkwater; Woods, Ingham; Keen, Rutter, Angell; Lazarus (2), Bedford (2), Evans (2), Andrews (1), Clark (2).

Record Cup Victory: 8–1 v Bristol R (a), FA Cup 1st rd, 27 November 1937 – Gilfillan; Smith, Jefferson; Lowe, James, March; Cape, Mallett, Cheetham (3), Fitzgerald (3) Bott (2). 8–1 v Crewe Alex, Milk Cup 1st rd, 3 October 1983 – Hucker; Neill, Dawes, Waddock (1), McDonald (1), Fenwick, Micklewhite (1), Stewart (1), Allen (1), Stainrod (3), Gregory.

HONOURS

League Champions: FL C – 2010–11; Division 2 – 1982–83; Division 3 – 1966–67; Division 3S – 1947–48.
Runners-up: Division 1 – 1975–76; Division 2 – 1967–68, 1972–73; Second Division – 2003–04; Division 3S – 1946–47.

FA Cup: *Runners-up:* 1982.

League Cup Winners: 1967.
Runners-up: 1986.

European Competitions
UEFA Cup: 1976–77 *(qf)*, 1984–85.

FOOTBALL YEARBOOK FACT FILE

Queens Park Rangers' FA Cup tie against Everton in February 1915 was switched from their usual ground at Park Royal to Chelsea's Stamford Bridge. The loop line of the Great Western Railway, which took fans to Park Royal, was closed for military usage and the switch was made to ensure a healthy attendance. Rangers lost the match 2-1 in front of a 33,000 crowd.

Record Defeat: 1–8 v Mansfield T, Division 3, 15 March 1965. 1–8 v Manchester U, Division 1, 19 March 1969.

Most League Points (2 for a win): 67, Division 3, 1966–67.

Most League Points (3 for a win): 88, FL C, 2010–11.

Most League Goals: 111, Division 3, 1961–62.

Highest League Scorer in Season: George Goddard, 37, Division 3 (S), 1929–30.

Most League Goals in Total Aggregate: George Goddard, 174, 1926–34.

Most League Goals in One Match: 4, George Goddard v Merthyr T, Division 3 (S), 9 March 1929; 4, George Goddard v Swindon T, Division 3 (S), 12 April 1930; 4, George Goddard v Exeter C, Division 3 (S), 20 December 1930; 4, George Goddard v Watford, Division 3 (S), 19 September 1931; 4, Tom Cheetham v Aldershot, Division 3 (S), 14 September 1935; 4, Tom Cheetham v Aldershot, Division 3 (S), 12 November 1938.

Most Capped Player: Alan McDonald, 52, Northern Ireland.

Most League Appearances: Tony Ingham, 514, 1950–63.

Youngest League Player: Frank Sibley, 16 years 97 days v Bristol C, 10 March 1964.

Record Transfer Fee Received: £19,500,000 from Crystal Palace for Eberechi Eze, August 2020.

Record Transfer Fee Paid: £12,500,000 to Anzhi Makhachkala for Chris Samba, January 2013.

Football League Record: 1920 Original Members of Division 3; 1921–48 Division 3 (S); 1948–52 Division 2; 1952–58 Division 3 (S); 1958–67 Division 3; 1967–68 Division 2; 1968–69 Division 1; 1969–73 Division 2; 1973–79 Division 1; 1979–83 Division 2; 1983–92 Division 1; 1992–96 Premier League; 1996–2001 Division 1; 2001–04 Division 2; 2004–11 FL C; 2011–13 Premier League; 2013–14 FL C; 2014–15 Premier League; 2015– FL C.

LATEST SEQUENCES

Longest Sequence of League Wins: 8, 7.11.1931 – 28.12.1931.

Longest Sequence of League Defeats: 9, 25.2.1969 – 5.4.1969.

Longest Sequence of League Draws: 6, 29.1.2000 – 5.3.2000.

Longest Sequence of Unbeaten League Matches: 20, 11.3.1972 – 23.9.1972.

Longest Sequence Without a League Win: 20, 7.12.1968 – 7.4.1969.

Successive Scoring Runs: 33 from 9.12.1961.

Successive Non-scoring Runs: 6 from 18.3.1939.

MANAGERS

James Cowan 1906–13
Jimmy Howie 1913–20
Ned Liddell 1920–24
Will Wood 1924–25
(had been Secretary since 1903)
Bob Hewison 1925–31
John Bowman 1931
Archie Mitchell 1931–33
Mick O'Brien 1933–35
Billy Birrell 1935–39
Ted Vizard 1939–44
Dave Mangnall 1944–52
Jack Taylor 1952–59
Alec Stock 1959–65
(General Manager to 1968)
Bill Dodgin Jnr 1968
Tommy Docherty 1968
Les Allen 1968–71
Gordon Jago 1971–74
Dave Sexton 1974–77
Frank Sibley 1977–78
Steve Burtenshaw 1978–79
Tommy Docherty 1979–80
Terry Venables 1980–84
Gordon Jago 1984
Alan Mullery 1984
Frank Sibley 1984–85
Jim Smith 1985–88
Trevor Francis 1988–89
Don Howe 1989–91
Gerry Francis 1991–94
Ray Wilkins 1994–96
Stewart Houston 1996–97
Ray Harford 1997–98
Gerry Francis 1998–2001
Ian Holloway 2001–06
Gary Waddock 2006
John Gregory 2006–07
Luigi Di Canio 2007–08
Iain Dowie 2008
Paulo Sousa 2008–09
Jim Magilton 2009
Paul Hart 2009–10
Neil Warnock 2010–12
Mark Hughes 2012
Harry Redknapp 2012–15
Chris Ramsey 2015
Jimmy Floyd Hasselbaink 2015–16
Ian Holloway 2016–18
Steve McClaren 2018–19
Mark Warburton May 2019–

TEN YEAR LEAGUE RECORD

		P	W	D	L	F	A	Pts	Pos
2010-11	FL C	46	24	16	6	71	32	88	1
2011-12	PR Lge	38	10	7	21	43	66	37	17
2012-13	PR Lge	38	4	13	21	30	60	25	20
2013-14	FL C	46	23	11	12	60	44	80	4
2014-15	PR Lge	38	8	6	24	42	73	30	20
2015-16	FL C	46	14	18	14	54	54	60	12
2016-17	FL C	46	15	8	23	52	66	53	18
2017-18	FL C	46	15	11	20	58	70	56	16
2018-19	FL C	46	14	9	23	53	71	51	19
2019-20	FL C	46	16	10	20	67	76	58	13

DID YOU KNOW ?

Queens Park Rangers recorded their first-ever away victory in a Football League Cup tie in the first leg of their semi-final with Birmingham City in January 1967. The R's won 4-1 and went on to win the tie 7-2 on aggregate before sensationally defeating West Bromwich Albion in the final at Wembley.

QUEENS PARK RANGERS – SKY BET CHAMPIONSHIP 2019–20 LEAGUE RECORD

Match No.	Date	Venue	Opponents	Result		H/T Score	Lg Pos.	Goalscorers	Attendance
1	Aug 3	A	Stoke C	W	2-1	1-0	3	Hugill [8], Eze [53]	24,004
2	10	H	Huddersfield T	D	1-1	0-0	4	Hall [83]	14,377
3	17	A	Bristol C	L	0-2	0-1	14		21,654
4	21	H	Swansea C	L	1-3	0-1	19	Hugill [66]	12,287
5	24	H	Wigan Ath	W	3-1	0-1	13	Wells [48], Eze [61], Hugill [81]	11,921
6	31	A	Sheffield W	W	2-1	0-1	8	Hugill 2 [60, 64]	23,446
7	Sept 14	H	Luton T	W	3-2	3-1	7	Eze [3], Wells 2 [20, 28]	16,186
8	21	A	Millwall	W	2-1	0-0	4	Wells 2 [56, 72]	16,808
9	28	H	WBA	L	0-2	0-0	9		13,959
10	Oct 2	A	Cardiff C	L	0-3	0-2	11		21,387
11	5	H	Blackburn R	W	4-2	1-0	9	Wells [30], Eze [49], Samuel [60], Hugill [77]	13,560
12	19	A	Hull C	W	3-2	1-1	5	Manning [44], Eze 2 (2 pens) [78, 88]	10,285
13	22	H	Reading	D	2-2	1-1	4	Wells [29], Hugill [58]	12,330
14	28	H	Brentford	L	1-3	0-1	8	Hall [48]	15,562
15	Nov 2	A	Leeds U	L	0-2	0-1	9		35,284
16	9	H	Middlesbrough	D	2-2	2-1	10	Wells [25], Howson (og) [44]	14,404
17	22	A	Fulham	L	1-2	1-1	10	Hugill [3]	18,320
18	27	H	Nottingham F	L	0-4	0-1	16		12,937
19	30	A	Derby Co	D	1-1	1-1	16	Eze (pen) [45]	26,289
20	Dec 7	H	Preston NE	W	2-0	1-0	14	Eze 2 (1 pen) [17, 67 (p)]	12,179
21	11	A	Birmingham C	W	2-0	1-0	12	Hall [45], Samuel [67]	18,161
22	14	A	Barnsley	L	3-5	1-2	13	Amos 2 [12, 54], Chair [90]	12,212
23	21	H	Charlton Ath	D	2-2	1-0	14	Cameron [6], Pugh [70]	16,166
24	26	A	Reading	L	0-1	0-0	14		12,495
25	29	H	Hull C	L	1-2	1-1	15	Chair [20]	13,814
26	Jan 1	H	Cardiff C	W	6-1	3-0	15	Wells 3 [9, 48, 64], Samuel 2 [27, 41], Eze [57]	12,355
27	11	A	Brentford	L	1-3	0-3	15	Wells [62]	12,324
28	18	H	Leeds U	W	1-0	1-0	14	Wells [20]	16,049
29	28	A	Blackburn R	L	1-2	1-2	14	Hugill [22]	11,505
30	Feb 1	H	Bristol C	L	0-1	0-1	16		13,713
31	8	A	Huddersfield T	L	0-2	0-0	17		21,083
32	11	A	Swansea C	D	0-0	0-0	17		14,778
33	15	H	Stoke C	W	4-2	2-2	16	Hugill [34], Eze [38], Samuel [71], Chair [90]	13,125
34	22	A	Nottingham F	D	0-0	0-0	15		28,750
35	25	H	Derby Co	W	2-1	1-1	12	Hall [34], Chair [75]	11,669
36	29	H	Birmingham C	D	2-2	0-1	14	Pugh [51], Hugill [55]	14,113
37	Mar 7	A	Preston NE	W	3-1	0-1	12	Hall [61], Manning [78], Eze [84]	12,378
38	June 20	H	Barnsley	L	0-1	0-1	13		0
39	27	A	Charlton Ath	L	0-1	0-1	13		0
40	30	H	Fulham	L	1-2	1-1	15	Hugill [1]	0
41	July 5	A	Middlesbrough	W	1-0	1-0	13	Hugill [32]	0
42	8	A	Wigan Ath	L	0-1	0-1	14		0
43	11	H	Sheffield W	L	0-3	0-2	16		0
44	14	A	Luton T	D	1-1	0-1	16	Ball [65]	0
45	18	H	Millwall	W	4-3	1-0	14	Masterson [43], Manning [52], Eze [62], Kane [73]	0
46	22	A	WBA	D	2-2	1-1	14	Manning [34], Eze [61]	0

Final League Position: 13

GOALSCORERS

League (67): Eze 14 (4 pens), Hugill 13, Wells 13, Hall 5, Samuel 5, Chair 4, Manning 4, Amos 2, Pugh 2, Ball 1, Cameron 1, Kane 1, Masterson 1, own goal 1.
FA Cup (6): Hugill 2, Samuel 1, Scowen 1, Wallace 1, Wells 1.
Carabao Cup (3): Chair 1, Manning 1 (1 pen), Wells 1.

Lumley J 27	Rangel A 21	Hall G 30	Barbet Y 27	Manning R 41	Cameron G 36	Amos L 26 + 8	Samuel B 34 + 3	Scowen J 8 + 10	Eze E 46	Hugill J 30 + 9	Pugh M 12 + 15	Shodipo O 2 + 10	Leistner T 20 + 2	Chair I 26 + 15	Kane T 21 + 11	Wells N 20 + 6	Smith M 2 + 6	Ball D 30 + 1	Mlakar J — + 6	Kelly L 19	Wallace L 10 + 1	Masterson C 10 + 2	Clarke J — + 6	Oteh A 1 + 8	Bettache F — + 3	Kakay O 7	Ramkilde M — + 1	Gubbins J — + 1	*Match No.*
1	2	3	4	5	6	7^1	8^2	9	10	11^3	12	13	14																1
1	2^2	3	4	5	7	6^3	8	9^1	10	11				12	13	14													2
1	2^2	3	4	5	7	6	8		10^3	11				12	14	13	9^1												3
1		3	4	5	7^2	6^1	8	12	10	11	14			13	2		9^3												4
1	2	3	4	5				6^1	8	13	10^2		12	9		11	14	7^3											5
1	2^3	3	5	6				13	7^2	10			4	9	14	11^1		8	12										6
1		3	5	6		13			7	10	14		4	9^3	2^2	11^1		8	12										7
1			5	6	3			12	9	10	13		4	7^2	2	11^1		8											8
1			5■	6	3		12		7^1	10	13		4	9	2	11^2	14	8^3											9
	2^2			5	4		8	7	10	11	14		3	9^3	13	12		6^1		1									10
	2		4	5	6		8^1	7	10	12	13		3	9^2		11^3			14	1									11
	2		4	5	7	14	8^1	6	10	12	13		3	9^3		11^2				1									12
	2^1		4	5	8	13		7	9	10	14		3	6^3	12	11^2				1									13
	2	4		5	7^1		9	8	6				3	10		11			12	1									14
	2	3		6					9	11	13		4^1	7^2	12	10^3		8	14	1	5								15
1		3		6	4	9^2		13	7	12				10^1	2	11		8			5								16
1		3		6		9^2		12	7	10			4	13	2	11^1		8^3	14		5								17
1		3		6		7^1	14	13	9	12			4	10^2	2	11^3		8			5■								18
1	2	3		5	7	8^1	6	12	9	11	10^2		4			13													19
1		3		5	6	13	7	12	9^2	10	8		4		2	11^1													20
1		3		5	6	7^3	8		10	12	9^2		4		2	11^1	14	13											21
1		3		8	6^2	7	11		9	10			4	13	2	12					5^1								22
1		3		5	6	7^2	12	13	8	11	9^3		4	14	2	10^1													23
1		3		5	7^2	6	10^3		9	11	8^1		4	12	2	14	13												24
1	2	3		5		6^1	8		10	13			4	9^2		11	12	7											25
1		3			2	6	8^3		10	13	12		4	9^1		11^2	14	7			5								26
1		3		5	4	6	8		10	13		14		9^3	2	11^2		7^1				12							27
		3			6	7^2	8	12	10		14			9^1	2	11^3				1	5	4	13						28
		3			6	7^1	8		10	11	12	13		9^2	2					1	5	4							29
		3				7^1	8		10	11	12	14		9^2	2			6^3		1	5	4	13						30
		3				6^2	8^3		9	11	13			10^1	2			7		1	5	4	12	14					31
	2^1	3	4	5	7		8		9	11	10				12			6		1									32
	2	3	4	5	7		8		9	11^2	10^1			12				6		1				13					33
	2	3	4	5	7	13	8		9^2	11	10^1			12				6		1									34
		3	4	5	6		8		9	11^1	10^2			13	2			7		1			12						35
	2		4	5	7		8		9	11	10^1			12				6		1		3							36
	2	3	4	5	6■	13	8		9	11	10^1			12				7^2		1									37
	2^3		4	5		7^1	8		10	11		12		9	14			6^2		1	13	3							38
	2^2		4	5	7^4	14	8^3		10	11		12		9^1	15			6^5		1		3		13	16				39
			4	8	3	7	10^1		9	11		12		14	5^2			6^3		1				13		2			40
1			4	8	3	6	9		10^2	11^1				12	5			7						13		2			41
1			4	5	6	12	11		10			13		9^4	2^3			7^1					14	8^2	15	3			42
1			4	8	3	6	11		9			10^3		14				7^2				2^1	13	12		5			43
1	2^1		4	5	7	6^2	9^3		11			14		10				8				12		13		3			44
1			4	5	7	9^3			10			8^1		11^2	12			6				3		13	14	2			45
1			4	5^4	7^1	8	11^2		10			14		9	13			6				3				2^3	12	15	46

FA Cup

Third Round	Swansea C	(h)	5-1
Fourth Round	Sheffield W	(h)	1-2

Carabao Cup

First Round	Bristol C	(h)	3-3
(QPR won 5-4 on penalties)			
Second Round	Portsmouth	(h)	0-2

READING

FOUNDATION

Reading was formed as far back as 1871 at a public meeting held at the Bridge Street Rooms. They first entered the FA Cup as early as 1877 when they amalgamated with the Reading Hornets. The club was further strengthened in 1889 when Earley FC joined them. They were the first winners of the Berks & Bucks Cup in 1878–79.

Madejski Stadium, Junction 11, M4, Reading, Berkshire RG2 0FL.

Telephone: (0118) 968 1100.

Ticket Office: (0118) 968 1313.

Website: www.readingfc.co.uk

Email: supporterservice@readingfc.co.uk

Ground Capacity: 24,162.

Record Attendance: 33,042 v Brentford, FA Cup 5th rd, 19 February 1927 (at Elm Park); 24,184 v Everton, Premier League, 17 November 2012 (at Madejski Stadium).

Pitch Measurements: 103m × 68m (112.5yd × 74.5yd).

Vice-Chairman: Sir John Madejski.

Chief Executive: Nigel Howe.

Manager: Veljko Paunović.

Assistant Manager: Eddie Niedzwiecki.

Colours: Blue and white hooped shirts with red trim, white shorts with blue and red trim, white socks with blue and red trim.

Year Formed: 1871.

Turned Professional: 1895.

Club Nickname: 'The Royals'.

Grounds: 1871, Reading Recreation; Reading Cricket Ground; 1882, Coley Park; 1889, Caversham Cricket Ground; 1896, Elm Park; 1998, Madejski Stadium.

First Football League Game: 28 August 1920, Division 3, v Newport Co (a) W 1–0 – Crawford; Smith, Horler; Christie, Mavin, Getgood; Spence, Weston, Yarnell, Bailey (1), Andrews.

Record League Victory: 10–2 v Crystal Palace, Division 3 (S), 4 September 1946 – Groves; Glidden, Gulliver; McKenna, Ratcliffe, Young; Chitty, Maurice Edelston (3), McPhee (4), Barney (1), Deverell (2).

Record Cup Victory: 6–0 v Leyton, FA Cup 2nd rd, 12 December 1925 – Duckworth; Eggo, McConnell; Wilson, Messer, Evans; Smith (2), Braithwaite (1), Davey (1), Tinsley, Robson (2).

Record Defeat: 0–18 v Preston NE, FA Cup 1st rd, 1893–94.

Most League Points (2 for a win): 65, Division 4, 1978–79.

HONOURS

League Champions: FL C – 2005–06, 2011–12; Second Division – 1993–94; Division 3 – 1985–86; Division 3S – 1925–26; Division 4 – 1978–79.
Runners-up: First Division – 1994–95; Second Division – 2001–02; Division 3S – 1931–32, 1934–35, 1948–49, 1951–52.

FA Cup: semi-final – 1927, 2015.

League Cup: 5th rd – 1996, 1998.

Full Members' Cup Winners: 1988.

FOOTBALL YEARBOOK FACT FILE

Reading's 'Player of the Year' award dates back to the 1963–64 season with the winner on the first two occasions being full-back Colin Meldrum. The player with most wins in the history of the award is goalkeeper Steve Death with four (1969–70, 1972–73, 1973–74 and 1976–77).

Most League Points (3 for a win): 106, Championship, 2005–06 (Football League Record).

Most League Goals: 112, Division 3 (S), 1951–52.

Highest League Scorer in Season: Ronnie Blackman, 39, Division 3 (S), 1951–52.

Most League Goals in Total Aggregate: Ronnie Blackman, 158, 1947–54.

Most League Goals in One Match: 6, Arthur Bacon v Stoke C, Division 2, 3 April 1931.

Most Capped Player: Chris Gunter, 59 (96), Wales.

Most League Appearances: Martin Hicks, 500, 1978–91.

Youngest League Player: Peter Castle, 16 years 49 days v Watford, 30 April 2003.

Record Transfer Fee Received: £7,000,000 from TSG 1899 Hoffenheim for Gylfi Sigurdsson, August 2010.

Record Transfer Fee Paid: £7,500,000 to Internazionale for George Puscas, August 2019.

Football League Record: 1920 Original Member of Division 3; 1921–26 Division 3 (S); 1926–31 Division 2; 1931–58 Division 3 (S); 1958–71 Division 3; 1971–76 Division 4; 1976–77 Division 3; 1977–79 Division 4; 1979–83 Division 3; 1983–84 Division 4; 1984–86 Division 3; 1986–88 Division 2; 1988–92 Division 3; 1992–94 Division 2; 1994–98 Division 1; 1998–2002 Division 2; 2002–04 Division 1; 2004–06 FL C; 2006–08 Premier League; 2008–12 FL C; 2012–13 Premier League; 2013– FL C.

MANAGERS

Thomas Sefton 1897–1901
(Secretary-Manager)
James Sharp 1901–02
Harry Matthews 1902–20
Harry Marshall 1920–22
Arthur Chadwick 1923–25
H. S. Bray 1925–26
(Secretary only since 1922 and 1926–35)
Andrew Wylie 1926–31
Joe Smith 1931–35
Billy Butler 1935–39
John Cochrane 1939
Joe Edelston 1939–47
Ted Drake 1947–52
Jack Smith 1952–55
Harry Johnston 1955–63
Roy Bentley 1963–69
Jack Mansell 1969–71
Charlie Hurley 1972–77
Maurice Evans 1977–84
Ian Branfoot 1984–89
Ian Porterfield 1989–91
Mark McGhee 1991–94
Jimmy Quinn and Mick Gooding 1994–97
Terry Bullivant 1997–98
Tommy Burns 1998–99
Alan Pardew 1999–2003
Steve Coppell 2003–09
Brendan Rodgers 2009
Brian McDermott 2009–13
Nigel Adkins 2013–14
Steve Clarke 2014–15
Brian McDermott 2015–16
Jaap Stam 2016–18
Paul Clement 2018
José Gomes 2018–19
Mark Bowen 2019–20
Veljko Paunović August 2020–

LATEST SEQUENCES

Longest Sequence of League Wins: 13, 17.8.1985 – 19.10.1985.

Longest Sequence of League Defeats: 8, 29.12.2007 – 24.2.2008.

Longest Sequence of League Draws: 6, 23.3.2002 – 20.4.2002.

Longest Sequence of Unbeaten League Matches: 33, 9.8.2005 – 14.2.2006.

Longest Sequence Without a League Win: 14, 30.4.1927 – 29.10.1927.

Successive Scoring Runs: 32 from 1.10.1932.

Successive Non-scoring Runs: 6 from 29.3.2008.

TEN YEAR LEAGUE RECORD

		P	*W*	*D*	*L*	*F*	*A*	*Pts*	*Pos*
2010-11	FL C	46	20	17	9	77	51	77	5
2011-12	FL C	46	27	8	11	69	41	89	1
2012-13	PR Lge	38	6	10	22	43	73	28	19
2013-14	FL C	46	19	14	13	70	56	71	7
2014-15	FL C	46	13	11	22	48	69	50	19
2015-16	FL C	46	13	13	20	52	59	52	17
2016-17	FL C	46	26	7	13	68	64	85	3
2017-18	FL C	46	10	14	22	48	70	44	20
2018-19	FL C	46	10	17	19	49	66	47	20
2019-20	FL C	46	15	11	20	59	58	56	14

DID YOU KNOW ?

Reading were 4-0 up after 37 minutes of their Football League Cup fourth round tie against Arsenal in October 2012. However, the Gunners fought back to equalise deep into added time and went on to win the match 7-5.

READING – SKY BET CHAMPIONSHIP 2019–20 LEAGUE RECORD

Match No.	Date	Venue	Opponents	Result	H/T Score	Lg Pos.	Goalscorers	Attendance
1	Aug 3	H	Sheffield W	L 1-3	0-1	24	Meite [54]	16,319
2	10	A	Hull C	L 1-2	0-2	22	Lucas Joao [66]	10,673
3	18	H	Cardiff C	W 3-0	2-0	17	Puscas 2 [25, 40], Swift [83]	14,252
4	21	A	WBA	D 1-1	0-0	15	Ejaria [71]	21,803
5	24	A	Huddersfield T	W 2-0	0-0	11	Ejaria [71], Morrison [84]	21,847
6	31	H	Charlton Ath	L 0-2	0-0	16		16,906
7	Sept 14	A	Middlesbrough	L 0-1	0-0	17		19,414
8	21	H	Blackburn R	L 1-2	0-1	20	Swift [57]	16,906
9	28	A	Swansea C	D 1-1	0-1	20	Yiadom [90]	16,036
10	Oct 1	H	Fulham	L 1-4	0-3	21	Meite [89]	13,809
11	5	A	Bristol C	L 0-1	0-1	22		21,419
12	19	H	Preston NE	W 1-0	0-0	19	Miazga [90]	14,135
13	22	A	QPR	D 2-2	1-1	20	Puscas [31], Baldock [74]	12,330
14	Nov 2	H	Millwall	W 2-1	2-0	19	Obita [9], Baldock [37]	14,485
15	9	H	Luton T	W 3-0	2-0	17	Morrison [22], Ejaria [30], McCleary [79]	15,251
16	23	A	Brentford	L 0-1	0-0	18		11,892
17	26	H	Leeds U	L 0-1	0-0	18		16,918
18	30	A	Wigan Ath	W 3-1	0-1	18	Puscas 3 (1 pen) [79 (p), 80, 84]	8965
19	Dec 7	H	Birmingham C	L 2-3	1-1	18	Meite [45], Lucas Joao [90]	14,103
20	11	A	Barnsley	D 1-1	0-0	18	Lucas Joao [76]	11,510
21	14	A	Stoke C	D 0-0	0-0	18		21,701
22	21	H	Derby Co	W 3-0	1-0	16	Adam (pen) [5], Lucas Joao [58], Meite (pen) [86]	14,831
23	26	H	QPR	W 1-0	0-0	15	Swift [52]	12,495
24	29	A	Preston NE	W 2-0	2-0	14	Swift [12], Lucas Joao [16]	13,680
25	Jan 1	A	Fulham	W 2-1	1-0	14	Swift [14], Adam [48]	18,575
26	11	H	Nottingham F	D 1-1	0-0	14	Tobias Figueiredo (og) [90]	16,602
27	18	A	Millwall	L 0-2	0-0	16		14,011
28	22	A	Nottingham F	D 1-1	0-0	15	Baldock [83]	26,840
29	28	H	Bristol C	L 0-1	0-0	15		11,633
30	31	A	Cardiff C	D 1-1	1-0	15	Meite [8]	22,518
31	Feb 8	H	Hull C	D 1-1	0-0	16	Obita [56]	13,393
32	12	H	WBA	L 1-2	1-1	16	Puscas (pen) [11]	13,942
33	15	A	Sheffield W	W 3-0	1-0	15	Meite [21], Puscas [72], Baldock (pen) [90]	22,199
34	22	A	Leeds U	L 0-1	0-0	16		35,483
35	26	H	Wigan Ath	L 0-3	0-1	16		10,088
36	29	H	Barnsley	W 2-0	1-0	16	Meite [17], Puscas [60]	13,263
37	Mar 7	A	Birmingham C	W 3-1	0-1	13	Miazga [51], Meite [56], Pele [87]	19,525
38	June 20	H	Stoke C	D 1-1	1-0	14	Lucas Joao [7]	0
39	27	A	Derby Co	L 1-2	0-2	14	Rinomhota [62]	0
40	30	H	Brentford	L 0-3	0-1	16		0
41	July 4	A	Luton T	W 5-0	3-0	13	Meite 4 [17, 18, 35, 62], Puscas [57]	0
42	7	H	Huddersfield T	D 0-0	0-0	13		0
43	11	A	Charlton Ath	W 1-0	1-0	13	Puscas (pen) [3]	0
44	14	H	Middlesbrough	L 1-2	1-1	14	Moore [33]	0
45	18	A	Blackburn R	L 3-4	1-2	15	Swift [15], Baldock [64], Meite [68]	0
46	22	H	Swansea C	L 1-4	1-1	15	Puscas (pen) [43]	0

Final League Position: 14

GOALSCORERS

League (59): Meite 13 (1 pen), Puscas 12 (4 pens), Lucas Joao 6, Swift 6, Baldock 5 (1 pen), Ejaria 3, Adam 2 (1 pen), Miazga 2, Morrison 2, Obita 2, McCleary 1, Moore 1, Pele 1, Rinomhota 1, Yiadom 1, own goal 1.
FA Cup (9): Meite 2, Baldock 1, Boye 1, Loader 1, Obita 1, Puscas 1 (1 pen), Richards 1, Rinomhota 1.
Carabao Cup (6): Barrett 2, Meite 2 (1 pen), Boye 1, Puscas 1.

Virginia J 2	Yiadom A 24	Miazga M 19 + 1	Moore L 40 + 3	Richards O 23 + 5	Loader D 1 + 6	Rinomhota A 28 + 9	Swift J 40 + 1	Barrett J 2 + 3	Barrow M 1	Meite Y 32 + 8	Olise M 13 + 6	Adam C 8 + 13	Novakovich A — + 1	Pele J 26 + 5	Boye L 5 + 14	Lucas Joao E 12 + 7	Puscas G 30 + 8	Morrison M 43 + 1	Rafael Cabral B 44	Ejaria O 36	McIntyre T 9 + 1	Obita J 14 + 7	Blackett T 16 + 4	Baldock S 12 + 12	McCleary G 2 + 17	Gunter C 18 + 2	Aluko S — + 2	Felipe Araruna H 2 + 1	Masika A — + 5	Osho G 4 + 1	Match No.
1	2	3	4	5	6^{1}	7	8^{3}	9^{2}	10	11	12	13	14																		1
1	2^{3}	3	4	5		7	9			8		13		6^{2}	10^{1}	11	12	14													2
	6	2	4	9		14	7			12				5	13	11^{1}	10^{2}	3	1	8^{3}											3
	5	2	4	9		13	7^{3}					14		8	10^{1}	12	11^{2}	3	1	6											4
	5	2^{1}	4	9		14	6							7	10^{2}	11	13	3	1	8^{3}	12										5
	5^{1}		2	9^{2}			6	14		13				7^{3}	12	11	10	3	1	8	4										6
	5		2	9	14	8^{1}	7			11					10^{3}	13	12	3	1	6	4^{2}										7
	5		2				6			12				7	14	11^{3}	10	3^{2}	1	8	4^{1}	9	13								8
	5		2	14		7	6	13							11^{2}	12	10	3	1	8		9^{3}	4^{1}								9
	2		4	5		7	6■	11^{1}		9	14				12	13	10^{2}	3	1	8^{3}											10
	5	2	4	9		7		13		11				6^{2}	12	14	10^{1}	3^{3}	1	8											11
	5	2	4		12		6			11^{1}		14		7^{3}			10^{2}	3	1	8		9		13							12
	5	2	4	9		7^{1}	6							13			10	3	1	8^{2}				11	12						13
	5	2	4^{1}			7	6			13				14			11^{2}	3	1	8		9	12	10^{3}							14
	5	2	4	9	14	7	6			13							11^{2}	3	1	8^{1}				10^{3}	12						15
	5	2	4	9		7^{3}	6			12					14		10^{2}	3	1	8				11^{1}	13						16
		3	5	6	13	8^{3}	7			10^{2}					12		11^{1}	4	1	9					14	2					17
	5	2	4	9		7				10^{2}		14		6^{3}	13	12	11	3^{1}	1						8						18
	5	2^{1}	4	9		7				10		14		6^{3}	12	13	11	3	1						8^{2}						19
		2	4			7				13		6				10	11^{1}	3^{2}	1	8		9^{3}	14	12		5					20
			4		14	7						9^{1}		8	13	10^{2}		3	1	6			5	11^{3}	12	2					21
			4			7^{1}	12			6		8^{2}		13	14	10		3	1	9			5	11^{3}		2					22
			4			12	6^{2}			9	13	8^{1}		7	14	10		3	1	11^{3}			5			2					23
			4			12	6^{2}			9^{3}		7^{1}		8		10		3	1	11		14	5		13	2					24
		13	4			12	9			8^{2}		7^{1}		6		11^{3}		3	1	10			5	14		2					25
			4			14	9			8		7^{2}		6			12	3	1	10^{3}		13	5	11^{1}		2					26
			4				9			8		7^{1}		6^{3}			13	3	1	10		12	5	11^{2}	14	2					27
			4		13		7				8^{2}			6			11^{1}	3	1	9		10	5	12		2					28
			4				7^{3}			13	8			6			11^{1}	3	1	9		10	5^{2}	12		2	14				29
			4	14			6^{1}			11		12		7			13	3	1	8	5	9^{3}		10^{2}		2					30
			2	13			6			10				7				3	1	8		9^{2}	4	11^{3}		5^{1}	14	12			31
	2		4			12	9^{3}			6		13		8^{2}			11	3	1	10		5		14				7^{1}			32
	2		4	5		6	7			8	9^{1}	12					11^{2}	3	1	10^{3}				13					14		33
	2		4	5		7	9^{1}			8	10	12		6			11	3	1												34
	2		4	5			8			10	12	13		7^{2}				3	1	9				11				6^{1}			35
	2	3				7	8^{3}			6^{1}	10^{2}			14			11	4	1	9		5			12				13		36
	2	3	14	5		6	7^{3}			8	10^{2}			12			11	4	1	9^{1}					13						37
			4	5		13	7			8^{4}	6^{2}	14				11^{1}	12	3	1	10^{3}		9			15	2					38
		3■	4	5^{4}		6	7			8	9^{2}						11^{1}		1	10^{3}		15		12	13	2			14		39
			4			6	7^{3}			8	9^{2}	14					12	3	1	10		5		11^{1}	13	2					40
				15		6	7^{5}			8^{3}	14			9^{1}			11^{4}	3	1	10^{2}	4		5	16	13				12	2	41
						9	8			7	12			6^{2}	13		11^{1}	3	1		4	10^{3}	5		15	14				2^{4}	42
			16	14		8	9^{4}			7	10^{3}			6^{1}			11^{2}	3	1		4	12	5	13		15				2^{5}	43
			6^{3}			8	9			7	10^{1}						11^{2}	3	1		4	14	5^{4}	13	15				12	2	44
			12	9^{3}		8	7^{5}			10	6						11^{4}	3	1		4^{1}	15	5^{2}	14	13	2				16	45
		3^{2}	4	8		7	6^{1}			10■	9				14		11^{3}	2	1				13		12	5					46

FA Cup

Third Round	Blackpool	(h)	2-2
Replay	Blackpool	(a)	2-0
Fourth Round	Cardiff C	(h)	1-1
Replay	Cardiff C	(a)	3-3
(*aet; Reading won 4-1 on penalties.*)			
Fifth Round	Sheffield U	(h)	1-2
(*aet*)			

Carabao Cup

First Round	Wycombe W	(a)	1-1
(Reading won 4-2 on penalties)			
Second Round	Plymouth Arg	(a)	4-2
Third Round	Wolverhampton W	(a)	1-1
(Wolverhampton W won 4-2 on penalties)			

ROCHDALE

FOUNDATION

Considering the love of rugby in their area, it is not surprising that Rochdale had difficulty in establishing an Association Football club. The earlier Rochdale Town club formed in 1900 went out of existence in 1907 when the present club was immediately established and joined the Manchester League, before graduating to the Lancashire Combination in 1908.

Crown Oil Arena, Sandy Lane, Rochdale, Lancashire OL11 5DR.

Telephone: (01706) 644 648.

Ticket Office: (01706) 644 648 (option 3).

Website: www.rochdaleafc.co.uk

Email: office@rochdaleafc.co.uk

Ground Capacity: 9,507.

Record Attendance: 24,231 v Notts Co, FA Cup 2nd rd, 10 December 1949.

Pitch Measurements: 104m × 69.5m (114yd × 76yd).

Chairman: Andrew Kilpatrick.

Chief Executive: David Bottomley.

Manager: Brian Barry-Murphy.

First-Team Coach: Lee Riley.

Colours: Blue shirts with black stripes, black shorts with blue trim, blue socks.

Year Formed: 1907.

Turned Professional: 1907.

Club Nickname: 'The Dale'.

Ground: 1907, St Clements Playing Fields (renamed Spotland, 1921; renamed Crown Oil Arena, 2016).

First Football League Game: 27 August 1921, Division 3 (N), v Accrington Stanley (h) W 6–3 – Crabtree; Nuttall, Sheehan; Hill, Farrer, Yarwood; Hoad, Sandiford, Dennison (2), Owens (3), Carney (1).

Record League Victory: 8–1 v Chesterfield, Division 3 (N), 18 December 1926 – Hill; Brown, Ward; Hillhouse, Parkes, Braidwood; Hughes, Bertram, Whitehurst (5), Schofield (2), Martin (1).

Record Cup Victory: 8–2 v Crook T, FA Cup 1st rd, 26 November 1927 – Moody; Hopkins, Ward; Braidwood, Parkes, Barker; Tompkinson, Clennell (3) Whitehurst (4), Hall, Martin (1).

Record Defeat: 1–9 v Tranmere R, Division 3 (N), 25 December 1931.

HONOURS

League: *Runners-up:* Division 3N – 1923–24, 1926–27.

FA Cup: 5th rd – 1990, 2003, 2018.

League Cup: *Runners-up:* 1962.

FOOTBALL YEARBOOK FACT FILE

Rochdale won their first trophy of any significance in March 1910 when they defeated Eccles Borough in the final of the Lancashire Junior Cup in a match played at Burnden Park, Bolton. Dale were 2-0 down after 50 minutes but fought back to equalise and then grabbed a late winner.

Most League Points (2 for a win): 62, Division 3 (N), 1923–24.

Most League Points (3 for a win): 82, FL 2, 2009–10.

Most League Goals: 105, Division 3 (N), 1926–27.

Highest League Scorer in Season: Albert Whitehurst, 44, Division 3 (N), 1926–27.

Most League Goals in Total Aggregate: Reg Jenkins, 119, 1964–73.

Most League Goals in One Match: 6, Tommy Tippett v Hartlepools U, Division 3 (N), 21 April 1930.

Most Capped Player: Leo Bertos, 6 (56), New Zealand.

Most League Appearances: Gary Jones, 470, 1998–2001; 2003–12.

Youngest League Player: Zac Hughes, 16 years 105 days v Exeter C, 19 September 1987.

Record Transfer Fee Received: £1,000,000 from Wolverhampton W for Luke Matheson, January 2020.

Record Transfer Fee Paid: £150,000 to Stoke C for Paul Connor, March 2001.

Football League Record: 1921 Elected to Division 3 (N); 1958–59 Division 3; 1959–69 Division 4; 1969–74 Division 3; 1974–92 Division 4; 1992–2004 Division 3; 2004–10 FL 2; 2010–12 FL 1; 2012–14 FL 2; 2014– FL 1.

LATEST SEQUENCES

Longest Sequence of League Wins: 8, 29.9.1969 – 3.11.1969.

Longest Sequence of League Defeats: 17, 14.11.1931 – 12.3.1932.

Longest Sequence of League Draws: 6, 17.8.1968 – 14.9.1968.

Longest Sequence of Unbeaten League Matches: 20, 15.9.1923 – 19.1.1924.

Longest Sequence Without a League Win: 28, 14.11.1931 – 29.8.1932.

Successive Scoring Runs: 29 from 10.10.2008.

Successive Non-scoring Runs: 9 from 14.3.1980.

MANAGERS

Billy Bradshaw 1920
Run by committee 1920–22
Tom Wilson 1922–23
Jack Peart 1923–30
Will Cameron 1930–31
Herbert Hopkinson 1932–34
Billy Smith 1934–35
Ernest Nixon 1935–37
Sam Jennings 1937–38
Ted Goodier 1938–52
Jack Warner 1952–53
Harry Catterick 1953–58
Jack Marshall 1958–60
Tony Collins 1960–68
Bob Stokoe 1967–68
Len Richley 1968–70
Dick Conner 1970–73
Walter Joyce 1973–76
Brian Green 1976–77
Mike Ferguson 1977–78
Doug Collins 1979
Bob Stokoe 1979–80
Peter Madden 1980–83
Jimmy Greenhoff 1983–84
Vic Halom 1984–86
Eddie Gray 1986–88
Danny Bergara 1988–89
Terry Dolan 1989–91
Dave Sutton 1991–94
Mick Docherty 1994–96
Graham Barrow 1996–99
Steve Parkin 1999–2001
John Hollins 2001–02
Paul Simpson 2002–03
Alan Buckley 2003
Steve Parkin 2003–06
Keith Hill 2007–11
(Caretaker from December 2006)
Steve Eyre 2011
John Coleman 2012–13
Keith Hill 2013–19
Brian Barry-Murphy April 2019–

TEN YEAR LEAGUE RECORD

		P	W	D	L	F	A	Pts	Pos
2010-11	FL 1	46	18	14	14	63	55	68	9
2011-12	FL 1	46	8	14	24	47	81	38	24
2012-13	FL 2	46	16	13	17	68	70	61	12
2013-14	FL 2	46	24	9	13	69	48	81	3
2014-15	FL 1	46	19	6	21	72	66	63	8
2015-16	FL 1	46	19	12	15	68	61	69	10
2016-17	FL 1	46	19	12	15	71	62	69	9
2017-18	FL 1	46	11	18	17	49	57	51	20
2018-19	FL 1	46	15	9	22	54	87	54	16
2019-20	FL 1	34	10	6	18	39	57	36	18§

§Decided on points-per-game (1.06)

DID YOU KNOW ?

Rochdale have played Coventry City at home in cup ties on five occasions and have yet to lose. Their 2-1 victory over the Sky Blues in January 1971 was played on a Monday afternoon after the First Division club refused to appear under the lights at Spotland.

ROCHDALE – SKY BET LEAGUE ONE 2019–20 LEAGUE RECORD

Match No.	Date	Venue	Opponents	Result		H/T Score	Lg Pos.	Goalscorers	Attendance
1	Aug 3	A	Tranmere R	W	3-2	1-0	5	Henderson 2 (1 pen) [12 (p), 48], Norrington-Davies [69]	8032
2	10	H	Doncaster R	D	1-1	0-0	5	Morley [66]	3587
3	17	A	Shrewsbury T	D	0-0	0-0	8		5641
4	20	H	Sunderland	L	1-2	1-1	13	Camps [33]	5258
5	24	H	Blackpool	D	0-0	0-0	13		4664
6	31	A	Southend U	W	3-0	2-0	10	Henderson [35], Morley [37], Camps [77]	5614
7	Sept 14	A	Peterborough U	L	0-6	0-3	16		5733
8	17	H	Lincoln C	D	1-1	1-0	16	Dooley [13]	2659
9	21	A	Fleetwood T	L	1-2	1-1	17	Pyke [8]	3229
10	28	H	Wycombe W	L	0-3	0-2	18		3039
11	Oct 5	A	AFC Wimbledon	L	2-3	0-3	19	Henderson 2 [66, 90]	4068
12	12	H	Accrington S	W	2-1	1-0	17	Henderson 2 [40, 49]	3508
13	19	A	Bolton W	W	3-1	0-0	14	Camps [65], Rathbone [70], Tavares [84]	13,828
14	22	H	Milton Keynes D	W	2-0	1-0	11	Camps [3], Henderson [60]	2286
15	26	A	Oxford U	L	0-3	0-2	14		6666
16	Nov 2	H	Bristol R	L	1-2	1-2	14	Camps [43]	3038
17	5	H	Ipswich T	L	0-1	0-0	15		3150
18	16	A	Coventry C	L	1-2	1-1	16	Henderson [28]	5433
19	23	H	Portsmouth	L	0-3	0-1	16		3789
20	Dec 7	A	Rotherham U	W	1-0	1-0	16	Morley [42]	8313
21	21	A	Burton Alb	L	1-3	1-2	18	Camps [2]	2298
22	26	H	Fleetwood T	L	2-3	1-0	19	Wilbraham 2 [41, 60]	3167
23	29	A	Gillingham	L	0-1	0-0	19		4761
24	Jan 1	A	Accrington S	W	2-1	1-0	18	Henderson [45], Dooley [64]	2975
25	11	H	Bolton W	W	2-0	1-0	18	Matheson [44], Ryan [80]	5560
26	18	A	Wycombe W	L	1-2	1-1	18	Henderson [18]	4498
27	25	H	Gillingham	D	2-2	1-1	18	Henderson (pen) [28], Dooley [68]	3084
28	28	A	Milton Keynes D	L	1-2	1-0	18	Henderson [16]	6393
29	Feb 1	H	Shrewsbury T	W	1-0	0-0	18	Smith [88]	2829
30	8	A	Doncaster R	D	1-1	0-1	18	Rathbone [81]	7638
31	11	A	Sunderland	L	0-3	0-3	19		27,401
32	22	H	Coventry C	L	1-2	0-1	19	Wilbraham [72]	4356
33	28	A	Portsmouth	L	0-3	0-1	19		17,600
34	Mar 7	H	Rotherham U	W	3-1	1-0	19	Henderson 2 [28, 70], Lund [75]	4142
35	17	H	Tranmere R	Cancelled					
36	21	H	Burton Alb	Cancelled					
37	24	H	AFC Wimbledon	Cancelled					
38	28	A	Bristol R	Cancelled					
39	Apr 4	H	Oxford U	Cancelled					
40	10	A	Blackpool	Cancelled					
41	13	H	Southend U	Cancelled					
42	18	A	Ipswich T	Cancelled					
43	25	H	Peterborough U	Cancelled					
44	May 3	A	Lincoln C	Cancelled					

Final League Position: 18 (on points-per-game basis)

GOALSCORERS

League (39): Henderson 15 (2 pens), Camps 6, Dooley 3, Morley 3, Wilbraham 3, Rathbone 2, Lund 1, Matheson 1, Norrington-Davies 1, Pyke 1, Ryan 1, Smith 1, Tavares 1.
FA Cup (5): McShane 1, Morley 1 (1 pen), Wilbraham 1, Williams, MJ 1, own goal 1.
Carabao Cup (8): Camps 2, Done 1, Henderson 1 (1 pen), Matheson 1, Morley 1, Pyke 1, Rathbone 1.
Leasing.com Trophy (3): Pyke 1, Tavares 1, Wilbraham 1.

Sanchez R 26	Keohane J 26 + 2	O'Connell E 31	McNulty J 13 + 1	Norrington-Davies R 27	Williams MJ 28	Camps C 28	Rathbone O 19 + 5	Pyke R 11 + 2	Henderson I 29 + 2	Dooley S 19 + 3	Morley A 18 + 5	Done M 14 + 10	Ryan J 16 + 8	Andrew C 3 + 17	Matheson L 18 + 2	Wilbraham A 11 + 8	Tavares F 1 + 13	McShane P 15 + 1	Lynch J 8	Bradley L — + 2	Hopper H — + 1	Gillam M — + 2	Baah K 4 + 3	Magliore T 2	McLaughlin R — + 3	Smith T 2 + 2	Lund M 5	Match No.
1	2	3³	4	5	6	7	8¹	9²	10	11	12	13	14															1
1	2	3	4	5	7	9		8²	11	10	6¹	12		13														2
1	2	3	4	5	8	9	7		11	10¹	12	6²		13														3
1		3	4	5	6¹	11	9²		10	7	8³	14	12	13	2													4
1		3	4	5	6	9	10²	12	11	8¹		14	7³	13	2													5
1	2	3	4	5	6	11²	12	9³	10¹	7	8	13	14															6
1	2	3	4	5	6	9	12	10²	11³	8	7¹		13	14														7
1	2	3	4	5	7	9	6	10¹	11	8			12															8
1		4³	3	5	6	9	7	10¹	11²	8	13		12	14	2													9
1	2		4	5	3	7	10¹		8	12	14		6³	9		11²	13											10
1	3			5	6	8	9		12		7¹		13	4	2	10	11²											11
1	2	3			7	11	6		9²		14	5	8¹	13		10³	12	4										12
	2²	3		5	7¹	9	6		10		8	11³			12	13	14	4	1									13
	2	3		5	7³	9	6		10¹		8	11²		14		13	12	4	1									14
	2	3		5	7	9	6¹		12		8²	11³		14		10■	13	4	1									15
		3		5	7¹	9	6³	12	10		8	11²		14	2		13	4	1									16
	5	3			6	11		7²	10		8³	9	12	14	2		13	4¹	1									17
1	2	3			4	6		11	10		8	5	7²	13		9¹	12											18
1	3¹	4		5	7	9		8	11		6²	10³			2		12			13	14							19
1	5	3		4		8		11²	10¹		7	9	6³		2		14					12	13					20
1	5	3		4	7	9	6³	10¹		12		11	8²		2	13							14					21
1	5	3		4	7	9	12			8³		10¹	6²	14	2	11							13					22
1	5¹	3			7■	8	6			9				14	13	10²		4³				12	11	2				23
1	5	3				6	8		10²	9			7	13			14	4³					11¹	2	12			24
1	5	3			4	8			10²	6			7	13	2	11¹	12			14			9³					25
	9	3		5	6				10	8			7¹	11	2		12	4	1									26
	9²	3		5	7³		12		11	6		14	8		2	13		4	1							10¹		27
	2	4	3²	5	7		9		11	6		13	8¹			12		14	1							10³		28
1	2	3		5			9		11	6²	7¹	12	8			10³		4							14	13		29
1		3		5			9		10	14	8	11¹	7²		2	13		4								12	6³	30
1	12	3	4	5²					10	9	8¹	11³	7		2	13									14		6	31
1		3³	13	5		10			11	9¹		12	7		2	14		4					6²				8	32
1	12		4	5¹	7³	9			11		6²	13		14	2	10		3									8	33
1	5	3			6	9	12		10		8¹				2	11		4									7	34
																												35
																												36
																												37
																												38
																												39
																												40
																												41
																												42
																												43
																												44

FA Cup

First Round	Wrexham	(a)	0-0
Replay	Wrexham	(h)	1-0
Second Round	Boston U	(h)	0-0
Replay	Boston U	(a)	2-1
Third Round	Newcastle U	(h)	1-1
Replay	Newcastle U	(a)	1-4

Carabao Cup

First Round	Bolton W	(h)	5-2
Second Round	Carlisle U	(h)	2-1
Third Round	Manchester U	(a)	1-1

(Manchester U won 5-3 on penalties)

Leasing.com Trophy

Group F (N)	Manchester C U21	(h)	0-2
Group F (N)	Bolton W	(h)	1-1

(Rochdale won 5-3 on penalties)

Group F (N)	Bradford C	(a)	2-1

ROTHERHAM UNITED

FOUNDATION

Rotherham were formed in 1870 before becoming Town in the late 1880s. Thornhill United were founded in 1877 and changed their name to Rotherham County in 1905. The Town amalgamated with Rotherham County to form Rotherham United in 1925.

The AESSEAL New York Stadium, New York Way, Rotherham, South Yorkshire S60 1AH.

Telephone: (0170) 9827 760.

Ticket Office: (0170) 982 7768.

Website: www.themillers.co.uk

Email: office@rotherhamunited.net

Ground Capacity: 12,088.

Record Attendance: 25,170 v Sheffield U, Division 2, 13 December 1952 (at Millmoor); 7,082 v Aldershot T, FL 2 Play-offs semi-final 2nd leg, 19 May 2010 (at Don Valley); 11,758 v Sheffield U, FL 1, 7 September 2013 (at New York Stadium).

Pitch Measurements: 102m × 64m (111.5yd × 70yd).

Chairman: Tony Stewart OBE.

Chief Operating Officer: Paul Douglas.

Manager: Paul Warne.

Assistant Manager: Richie Barker.

Colours: Red shirts with white sleeves, white shorts with red trim, red socks.

Year Formed: 1870. ***Turned Professional:*** 1905. ***Club Nickname:*** 'The Millers'.

Previous Names: 1877, Thornhill United; 1905, Rotherham County; 1925, amalgamated with Rotherham Town under Rotherham United.

Grounds: 1870, Red House Ground; 1907, Millmoor; 2008, Don Valley Stadium; 2012, New York Stadium (renamed The AESSEAL New York Stadium, 2014).

First Football League Game: 2 September 1893, Division 2, Rotherham T v Lincoln C (a) D 1–1 – McKay; Thickett, Watson; Barr, Brown, Broadhead; Longden, Cutts, Leatherbarrow, McCormick, Pickering, (1 og). 30 August 1919, Division 2, Rotherham Co v Nottingham F (h) W 2–0 – Branston; Alton, Baines; Bailey, Coe, Stanton; Lee (1), Cawley (1), Glennon, Lees, Lamb.

Record League Victory: 8–0 v Oldham Ath, Division 3 (N), 26 May 1947 – Warnes; Selkirk, Ibbotson; Edwards, Horace Williams, Danny Williams; Wilson (2), Shaw (1), Ardron (3), Guest (1), Hainsworth (1).

Record Cup Victory: 6–0 v Spennymoor U, FA Cup 2nd rd, 17 December 1977 – McAlister; Forrest, Breckin, Womble, Stancliffe, Green, Finney, Phillips (3), Gwyther (2) (Smith), Goodfellow, Crawford (1). 6–0 v Wolverhampton W, FA Cup 1st rd, 16 November 1985 – O'Hanlon; Forrest, Dungworth, Gooding (1), Smith (1), Pickering, Birch (2), Emerson, Tynan (1), Simmons (1), Pugh. 6–0 v King's Lynn, FA Cup 2nd rd, 6 December 1997 – Mimms; Clark, Hurst (Goodwin), Garner (1) (Hudson) (1), Warner (Bass), Richardson (1), Berry (1), Thompson, Druce (1), Glover (1), Roscoe.

Record Defeat: 1–11 v Bradford C, Division 3 (N), 25 August 1928.

HONOURS

League Champions: Division 3 – 1980–81; Division 3N – 1950–51; Division 4 – 1988–89.
Runners-up: Second Division – 2000–01; FL 1 – 2019–20; Division 3N – 1946–47, 1947–48, 1948–49; FL 2 – 2012–13; Third Division – 1999–2000; Division 4 – 1991–92.

FA Cup: 5th rd – 1953, 1968.

League Cup: *Runners-up:* 1961.

League Trophy Winners: 1996.

FOOTBALL YEARBOOK FACT FILE

Rotherham United's Millmoor stadium hosted greyhound racing between 1931 and 1933. The racing was organised by an independent company who sublet the premises from the football club. Around 2,000 attended the opening night and at one point racing took place on five nights a week. It proved a useful source of revenue to the club before the venture moved on to a different venue in the town.

Most League Points (2 for a win): 71, Division 3 (N), 1950–51.

Most League Points (3 for a win): 91, Division 2, 2000–01.

Most League Goals: 114, Division 3 (N), 1946–47.

Highest League Scorer in Season: Wally Ardron, 38, Division 3 (N), 1946–47.

Most League Goals in Total Aggregate: Gladstone Guest, 130, 1946–56.

Most League Goals in One Match: 4, Roland Bastow v York C, Division 3 (N), 9 November 1935; 4, Roland Bastow v Rochdale, Division 3 (N), 7 March 1936; 4, Wally Ardron v Crewe Alex, Division 3 (N), 5 October 1946; 4, Wally Ardron v Carlisle U, Division 3 (N), 13 September 1947; 4, Wally Ardron v Hartlepools U, Division 3 (N), 13 October 1948; 4, Ian Wilson v Liverpool, Division 2, 2 May 1955; 4, Carl Gilbert v Swansea C, Division 3, 28 September 1971; 4, Carl Airey v Chester, Division 3, 31 August 1987; 4, Shaun Goater v Hartlepool U, Division 3, 9 April 1994; 4, Lee Glover v Hull C, Division 3, 28 December 1997; 4, Darren Byfield v Millwall, Division 1, 10 August 2002; 4, Adam Le Fondre v Cheltenham T, FL 2, 21 August 2010.

Most Capped Player: Kari Arnason, 20 (83), Iceland.

Most League Appearances: Danny Williams, 461, 1946–62.

Youngest League Player: Kevin Eley, 16 years 72 days v Scunthorpe U, 15 May 1984.

Record Transfer Fee Received: £2,100,000 (rising to £3,500,000) from Cardiff C for Will Vaulks, June 2019.

Record Transfer Fee Paid: £500,000 (in excess of) to Plymouth Arg for Freddie Ladapo, June 2019.

Football League Record: 1893 Rotherham Town elected to Division 2; 1896 Failed re-election; 1919 Rotherham County elected to Division 2; 1923–51 Division 3 (N); 1951–68 Division 2; 1968–73 Division 3; 1973–75 Division 4; 1975–81 Division 3; 1981–83 Division 2; 1983–88 Division 3; 1988–89 Division 4; 1989–91 Division 3; 1991–92 Division 4; 1992–97 Division 2; 1997–2000 Division 3; 2000–01 Division 2; 2001–04 Division 1; 2004–05 FL C; 2005–07 FL 1; 2007–13 FL 2; 2013–14 FL 1; 2014–17 FL C; 2017–18 FL 1; 2018–19 FL C; 2019–20 FL 1; 2020– FL C.

MANAGERS

Billy Heald 1925–29 *(Secretary only for several years)*
Stanley Davies 1929–30
Billy Heald 1930–33
Reg Freeman 1934–52
Andy Smailes 1952–58
Tom Johnston 1958–62
Danny Williams 1962–65
Jack Mansell 1965–67
Tommy Docherty 1967–68
Jimmy McAnearney 1968–73
Jimmy McGuigan 1973–79
Ian Porterfield 1979–81
Emlyn Hughes 1981–83
George Kerr 1983–85
Norman Hunter 1985–87
Dave Cusack 1987–88
Billy McEwan 1988–91
Phil Henson 1991–94
Archie Gemmill and John McGovern 1994–96
Danny Bergara 1996–97
Ronnie Moore 1997–2005
Mick Harford 2005
Alan Knill 2005–07
Mark Robins 2007–09
Ronnie Moore 2009–11
Andy Scott 2011–12
Steve Evans 2012–15
Neil Redfearn 2015–16
Neil Warnock 2016
Alan Stubbs 2016
Kenny Jackett 2016
Paul Warne November 2016–

LATEST SEQUENCES

Longest Sequence of League Wins: 9, 2.2.1982 – 6.3.1982.

Longest Sequence of League Defeats: 10, 14.2.2017 – 8.4.2017.

Longest Sequence of League Draws: 6, 13.10.1969 – 22.11.1969.

Longest Sequence of Unbeaten League Matches: 18, 13.10.1969 – 7.2.1970.

Longest Sequence Without a League Win: 21, 9.5.2004 – 20.11.2004.

Successive Scoring Runs: 30 from 3.4.1954.

Successive Non-scoring Runs: 6 from 21.8.2004.

TEN YEAR LEAGUE RECORD

		P	W	D	L	F	A	Pts	Pos
2010-11	FL 2	46	17	15	14	75	60	66	9
2011-12	FL 2	46	18	13	15	67	63	67	10
2012-13	FL 2	46	24	7	15	74	59	79	2
2013-14	FL 1	46	24	14	8	86	58	86	4
2014-15	FL C	46	11	16	19	46	67	46*	21
2015-16	FL C	46	13	10	23	53	71	49	21
2016-17	FL C	46	5	8	33	40	98	23	24
2017-18	FL 1	46	24	7	15	73	53	79	4
2018-19	FL C	46	8	16	22	52	83	40	22
2019-20	FL 1	35	18	8	9	61	38	62	2§

**3 pts deducted. §Decided on points-per-game (1.77)*

DID YOU KNOW ?

Rotherham United played three games against Dutch team Amersfoort in the immediate post-war years as part of a series of encounters arranged between sporting organisations from the two towns. United won 5-2 in Amersfoort in May 1948, drew 2-2 at Millmoor in September of that year and won 4-0 again in the Netherlands in May 1949.

ROTHERHAM UNITED – SKY BET LEAGUE ONE 2019–20 LEAGUE RECORD

Match No.	*Date*		*Venue*	*Opponents*	*Result*		*H/T Score*	*Lg Pos.*	*Goalscorers*	*Attendance*
1	Aug	3	A	AFC Wimbledon	W	2-1	1-0	6	Ladapo [29], Robertson [84]	4657
2		10	H	Lincoln C	L	0-2	0-1	13		10,706
3		17	A	Burton Alb	W	1-0	1-0	6	O'Hara (og) [24]	3822
4		31	H	Tranmere R	D	1-1	0-0	13	Wiles [73]	8691
5	Sept	7	A	Doncaster R	L	1-2	1-0	15	Hastie [37]	11,407
6		14	H	Bolton W	W	6-1	3-1	13	Wiles [14], Ladapo 2 [28, 53], Morris 2 [40, 55], Hastie [65]	10,088
7		17	A	Sunderland	D	1-1	0-1	14	Hastie [66]	29,078
8		21	H	Shrewsbury T	D	0-0	0-0	13		8380
9		28	A	Bristol R	L	0-1	0-0	13		7321
10	Oct	5	H	Coventry C	W	4-0	2-0	13	Crooks 2 [13, 75], Smith 2 (2 pens) [19, 58]	10,337
11		12	A	Blackpool	W	2-1	0-0	10	Smith [51], Robertson [87]	9932
12		19	H	Oxford U	L	1-2	1-1	11	Ihiekwe [35]	8837
13		23	A	Ipswich T	W	2-0	1-0	9	Crooks 2 [11, 48]	20,550
14		26	H	Wycombe W	L	0-1	0-1	11		8337
15	Nov	2	A	Gillingham	W	3-0	2-0	10	Smith [19], Crooks 2 [43, 88]	4893
16		16	H	Accrington S	W	1-0	1-0	6	Morris [30]	8430
17		23	A	Milton Keynes D	W	3-2	0-2	4	Barlaser [66], Ladapo 2 [71, 86]	7811
18		26	A	Portsmouth	L	2-3	1-2	4	Ladapo 2 (1 pen) [15, 62 (p)]	16,355
19	Dec	7	H	Rochdale	L	0-1	0-1	8		8313
20		14	A	Southend U	D	2-2	1-0	6	Kiernan (og) [29], Ladapo [60]	5652
21		21	H	Fleetwood T	D	2-2	0-1	8	Ladapo [62], Crooks [80]	7883
22		26	A	Shrewsbury T	W	2-1	0-0	5	Mattock [60], Smith [90]	7555
23		29	H	Peterborough U	W	4-0	0-0	3	Wood [50], Butler (og) [68], Ward (og) [77], Vassell [90]	9019
24	Jan	1	H	Blackpool	W	2-1	1-1	2	Smith [21], Barlaser [85]	8689
25		11	A	Oxford U	W	3-1	3-0	1	Vassell 2 [16, 33], Wood [45]	8077
26		18	H	Bristol R	W	3-0	0-0	1	Vassell [51], Smith [53], Ogbene [88]	8287
27		25	A	Peterborough U	L	1-2	1-2	2	Ihiekwe [35]	7495
28		28	H	Ipswich T	W	1-0	1-0	1	Wood [42]	9327
29	Feb	1	H	Burton Alb	W	3-2	1-1	1	Smith 2 [9, 46], Ladapo [71]	8563
30		7	A	Lincoln C	W	1-0	0-0	1	Crooks [47]	9876
31		15	H	AFC Wimbledon	D	2-2	0-1	1	Crooks [60], Ladapo [81]	8626
32		22	A	Accrington S	W	2-1	0-0	1	Ladapo [64], Wiles [90]	3447
33		25	A	Coventry C	D	1-1	1-0	1	Ladapo [23]	8990
34		29	H	Milton Keynes D	D	1-1	1-1	1	Ladapo [10]	8883
35	Mar	7	A	Rochdale	L	1-3	0-1	2	Lindsay [90]	4142
36		14	H	Southend U	Cancelled					
37		21	A	Fleetwood T	Cancelled					
38		29	H	Gillingham	Cancelled					
39	Apr	4	A	Wycombe W	Cancelled					
40		10	H	Portsmouth	Cancelled					
41		13	A	Tranmere R	Cancelled					
42		18	H	Doncaster R	Cancelled					
43		25	A	Bolton W	Cancelled					
44	May	3	H	Sunderland	Cancelled					

Final League Position: 2 (on points-per-game basis)

GOALSCORERS

League (61): Ladapo 14 (1 pen), Crooks 9, Smith 9 (2 pens), Vassell 4, Hastie 3, Morris 3, Wiles 3, Wood 3, Barlaser 2, Ihiekwe 2, Robertson 2, Lindsay 1, Mattock 1, Ogbene 1, own goals 4.
FA Cup (9): Smith 3, Ihiekwe 2, Ladapo 2, Crooks 1, Vassell 1.
Carabao Cup (4): Crooks 1, Ladapo 1, Vassell 1, Wood 1.
Leasing.com Trophy (3): Clarke 1, Morris 1, own goal 1.

Iversen D 34	Olosunde M 27 + 5	Ihiekwe M 33	Robertson C 17	Mattock J 22 + 2	Barlaser D 24 + 3	MacDonald S 3 + 10	Crooks M 31 + 2	Vassell K 13 + 7	Smith M 26 + 8	Ladapo F 20 + 11	Wiles B 28 + 5	Morris C 11 + 10	Proctor J — + 3	Wood R 21 + 2	Lindsay J 14 + 8	Ogbene C 19 + 6	Price L 1	Hastie J 10 + 4	Jones B 9 + 1	Clarke T 4 + 4	Lamy J — + 3	Thompson A 9 + 1	Adelakun H 8 + 1	Yates J — + 1	Koroma J — + 5	Tilt C 1	Match No.
1	2	3	4	5	6^{2}	7	8	9^{3}	10	11^{1}	12	13	14														1
1	2	3	4	5	8^{1}	7	6	9^{3}	10^{2}	11	12	13	14														2
1	2	3	5		7^{1}	12	8	9	11^{2}	10^{3}	6		14	4	13												3
1	2	3	5	14	7^{2}		8	11^{3}	10	9^{1}	6			4	13	12											4
	2	3	5	13		7^{2}	12		14	10	8	11^{3}		4	6		1	9^{1}									5
1	2	3	4	5	14	12	8		13	9	6	10^{3}			7^{1}			11^{2}									6
1	2	3	4	5	14	13	8		12	9^{2}	6	10^{3}			7			11^{1}									7
1		3	4	5		13	8		12	9^{2}	6	10			7			11^{1}	2								8
1	12	3	4	5		14	8		13	9	6^{1}	10^{3}			7			11	2^{2}								9
1	2	3		5	6^{2}	12	9		11^{1}	14	8	13		4	7			10^{3}									10
1	2^{1}	3	5		8		7^{2}		10		6			4	9	12		11^{3}	14	13							11
1	2	3		5	7^{1}		6^{2}		10		9	13		4	8	12		11^{3}			14						12
1	6^{2}	3		5	13		10^{3}		11		7	14		4	8	12			2	9^{1}							13
1	9^{1}	3		5			8		10		6	14		4^{3}	7	11		12	2^{2}	13							14
1	13	3		5^{1}			9		11	14	7	12		4	6	8^{2}			2	10^{3}							15
1	2	3	4		7		8^{3}		10^{2}	12	6	11^{1}			13	9■			5			14					16
1	2	3	4		6		9^{2}	13	11^{3}	12	7	8						10^{1}	5	14							17
1	2^{3}	3	4		6^{2}		14	10^{1}		11	8	7			13	12			5	9							18
1	2^{2}	3	4	5			8	14	12	10	6	11^{3}			7^{1}	9		13									19
1	2	3	4	5	7				11^{1}	10	8	12				6		9									20
1	5			4	8		3	7	11^{1}	10	6^{2}	14				12		13		9^{3}		2					21
1	6	3	4	5^{1}	7		8	12	13	11		10^{3}		14		9^{2}						2					22
1	9	3	4^{1}	5■	8		7	13	14	10^{3}		11^{2}		12		6						2					23
1	5	3			8		7	12	10^{2}	11^{1}	9^{3}	14		4		6		13				2					24
1	5	3			8^{2}		7	10^{3}	11	13	2			4	12	6				14			9^{1}				25
1	2	3			8		7^{2}	11^{3}	10	12	5			4	13	6					14		9^{1}				26
1	2^{1}	3		5	8	13			11	10	7^{3}			4		6					12		9^{2}	14			27
1	14	3		5	8		7^{2}	11^{3}	10	13	12			4		6						2	9^{1}				28
1	14	3		5	8^{3}		7	11^{2}	10	13	12			4		6						2	9^{1}				29
1		3			8	14	7	10^{1}	11	12	5			4		6^{3}						2	9^{2}		13		30
1		3			8		7	10^{2}	11	12	5			4	14	6^{1}						2	9^{3}		13		31
1	2	3		5	8		7	10^{2}	11^{1}	12	13			4		6							9^{3}		14		32
1	2	3		5	8^{1}	13	7^{3}		11	10	9^{2}			4	14	6							12				33
1	2^{3}	3		5		14	7	12	10^{2}	11	9			4	8^{1}	6									13		34
1	14						8	12	10	11^{3}	9			3	7	6			5^{2}			2			13	4^{1}	35
																											36
																											37
																											38
																											39
																											40
																											41
																											42
																											43
																											44

FA Cup

First Round	Maidenhead U	(a)	3-1
Second Round	Solihull Moors	(a)	4-3
Third Round	Hull C	(h)	2-3

Carabao Cup

First Round	Shrewsbury T	(a)	4-0
Second Round	Sheffield W	(h)	0-1

Leasing.com Trophy

Group H (N)	Manchester U U21	(h)	0-2
Group H (N)	Doncaster R	(h)	3-2
Group H (N)	Lincoln C	(a)	0-3

SALFORD CITY

FOUNDATION

The origins of Salford City are obscure, the club having been established as Salford Central in 1940 and remained in minor competitions until 1963 when the name was changed to Salford Amateurs and they entered the Manchester League. In 1980 this club merged with another local club, Anson Villa, and adopted the name Salford. They were members of the Cheshire County League and then the North West Counties League. In 1990 Salford became Salford City and after gaining promotion to the Northern Premier League for 2008–09 they have since made rapid progress to achieve Football League status.

The Peninsula Stadium, Moor Lane, Salford, Greater Manchester M7 3PZ.

Telephone: (0161) 241 9772.

Ticket Office: (0845) 847 2252.

Website: salfordcityfc.co.uk

Email: enquiries@salfordcityfc.co.uk

Ground Capacity: 5,032.

Record Attendance: 4,518 v Leeds U, EFL Cup 1st rd, 13 August 2019.

Chairman: Karen Baird.

President: Dave Russell.

Manager: Graham Alexander.

Assistant Manager: Chris Lucketti.

Colours: Red shirts with white trim, white shorts, white socks.

Year Formed: 1940.

Turned Professional: 2017.

Previous Names: 1940, Salford Central; 1963, Salford Amateurs; 1989, Salford City.

Club Nickname: 'The Ammies'.

Grounds: 1979, Moor Lane (renamed The Peninsula Stadium 2017).

HONOURS

League Champions: National League North – 2017–18; Northern Premier League Division One North – 2014–15.
Runners-up: North West Counties League Premier Division – 2007–08.
Play-Off Winners: National League – 2018–19 (*promoted to FL 2*); Northern Premier League Premier Division – 2015–16 (*promoted to National League North*).

FA Cup: 2nd rd – 2015–16.

League Trophy: *Finalists:* 2020.

Manchester Premier Cup Winners: 1977–78, 1978–79.
Runners-up: 1989–90, 2001–02, 2012–13.

North West Counties League Challenge Cup Winners: 2005–06.

Lancashire Amateur Cup Winners: 1973, 1975, 1977.

FOOTBALL YEARBOOK FACT FILE

Salford City made their first-ever appearance in the FA Cup in the 1990–91 season when they took part in the preliminary round of the competition. City lost 3-0 at home to Warrington Town on that occasion and a short feature on the match was filmed for BBC Television.

MANAGERS

Anthony Johnson and Bernard Morley 2015–18
Graham Alexander May 2018–

First Football League Game: 3 August 2019, FL 2, v AFC Wimbledon (a) W 2–1 – Neal; Maynard, Pond, Piergianni, Wiseman, Towell (Armstrong), Smith, Shelton, Touray, Rooney (Beesley), Dieseruwe (2) (Threlkeld).

Record League Victory: 4–0 v Cambridge U (a), FL 2, 28 January 2020 – Letheren; Wiseman, Pond (Towell), Burgess, Touray (1), Andrade, O'Connor (Armstrong), Baldwin, Hunter (1), Thomas-Asante (Hogan), Rooney (2).

Record Cup Victory: 5–0 v Kennek Ryhope, FA Cup Preliminary rd, 2000–01; 5–0 v Atherton Laburnum R, FA Cup 1st Qualifying rd, 2008–09; 5–0 v Whitby T, FA Cup 1st Qualifying rd, 2015–16.

Record Cup Defeat: 1–7 v St Helen's T, FA Cup prel rd, 2001–02.

Most League Points (3 for a win): 50, FL 2, 2019–20.

Most League Goals: 49, FL 2, 2019–20.

Highest League Scorer in Season: Adam Rooney, 8, FL 2, 2019–20.

Most League Goals in Total Aggregate: Adam Rooney, 8, FL 2, 2019–20.

Most League Goals in One Match: No more than 2 goals.

Most Capped Player: Nathan Pond, 4, Montserrat.

Most League Appearances: Ibou Touray, 35, 2019–20.

Youngest League Player: Brandon Thomas-Assante, 20 years 259 days v Cheltenham T, 14 September 2019.

Football League Record: 2019 Promoted from National League; 2019– FL 2.

LATEST SEQUENCES

Longest Sequence of League Wins: 2, 29.2.2020 – 7.3.2020.

Longest Sequence of League Defeats: 3, 1.1.2020 – 11.1.2020.

Longest Sequence of League Draws: 5, 17.8.2019 – 7.9.2019.

Longest Sequence of Unbeaten League Matches: 5, 18.1.2020 – 8.2.2019.

Longest Sequence Without a League Win: 7, 10.8.2019 – 14.9.2019.

Successive Scoring Runs: 6 from 4.1.2020.

Successive Non-scoring Runs: 3 from 23.11.2019.

TEN YEAR LEAGUE RECORD

		P	*W*	*D*	*L*	*F*	*A*	*Pts*	*Pos*
2010–11	NPL1N	44	17	11	16	68	73	62	12
2011–12	NPL1N	42	14	10	18	69	71	52	13
2012–13	NPL1N	42	11	13	18	65	79	46	16
2013–14	NPL1N	42	15	7	20	68	80	52	12
2014–15	NPL1N	42	30	5	7	92	42	95	1
2015–16	NPLP	46	27	9	10	94	48	90	3
2016–17	NLN	42	22	11	9	79	44	77	4
2017–18	NLN	42	28	7	7	80	45	91	1
2018–19	NL	46	25	10	11	77	45	85	3
2019-20	FL 2	37	13	11	13	49	46	50	11§

§Decided on points-per-game (1.35)

DID YOU KNOW ?

Salford City joined the North West Counties League in 1982–83 but were initially perennial strugglers. It was not until their 10th season in the competition, 1991–92, that they finished in the top half of the table.

SALFORD CITY – SKY BET LEAGUE TWO 2019–20 LEAGUE RECORD

Match No.	Date	Venue	Opponents	Result		H/T Score	Lg Pos.	Goalscorers	Attendance
1	Aug 3	H	Stevenage	W	2-0	1-0	2	Dieseruvwe 2 [29, 48]	3416
2	10	A	Crawley T	L	0-2	0-1	11		2400
3	17	H	Port Vale	D	1-1	0-0	14	Beesley [90]	3770
4	20	A	Plymouth Arg	D	2-2	1-1	15	Beesley [37], Touray [79]	11,405
5	24	A	Carlisle U	D	2-2	2-2	15	Dieseruvwe [28], Whitehead (pen) [33]	4806
6	31	H	Leyton Orient	D	1-1	1-0	16	Towell [13]	3154
7	Sept 7	A	Morecambe	D	2-2	1-0	15	Lloyd 2 [15, 66]	2778
8	14	H	Cheltenham T	L	0-2	0-1	19		2389
9	17	H	Grimsby T	W	1-0	1-0	16	Shelton [21]	2782
10	21	A	Crewe Alex	L	1-4	1-0	17	Rooney [39]	4714
11	28	H	Forest Green R	L	0-4	0-3	18		2561
12	Oct 5	A	Walsall	W	3-0	1-0	17	Armstrong [21], Jervis [49], Touray [72]	4751
13	12	H	Cambridge U	W	1-0	0-0	14	Rooney [77]	3026
14	19	A	Northampton T	L	0-2	0-1	18		4886
15	22	A	Mansfield T	W	2-1	0-0	15	Jervis [48], Rooney [65]	4170
16	26	H	Scunthorpe U	D	1-1	1-1	12	Burgess, C [45]	3448
17	Nov 2	A	Newport Co	W	2-1	1-1	11	Burgess, C [40], Maynard [54]	3947
18	16	H	Swindon T	L	2-3	1-1	12	Rooney 2 (2 pens) [4, 90]	3509
19	23	H	Macclesfield T	D	0-0	0-0	12		2484
20	Dec 7	A	Colchester U	L	0-1	0-0	13		3713
21	14	H	Exeter C	L	0-1	0-1	14		2922
22	21	A	Bradford C	D	1-1	0-0	14	Rooney [79]	14,642
23	26	H	Crewe Alex	W	3-1	2-0	11	Towell [7], Thomas-Asante [12], Wintle (og) [85]	3031
24	29	A	Oldham Ath	W	4-1	3-0	11	Jervis 2 [15, 36], Thomas-Asante 2 [16, 48]	5278
25	Jan 1	A	Grimsby T	L	0-1	0-0	11		4555
26	4	H	Walsall	L	1-2	0-1	12	Thomas-Asante [62]	3173
27	11	H	Northampton T	L	1-2	1-1	14	Baldwin [20]	2919
28	18	A	Forest Green R	W	2-1	1-1	13	Touray [3], O'Connor [55]	2707
29	25	H	Oldham Ath	D	1-1	1-0	12	Thomas-Asante [15]	3646
30	28	A	Cambridge U	W	4-0	1-0	12	Rooney 2 (1 pen) [32, 52 (p)], Hunter [55], Touray [88]	3444
31	Feb 1	A	Port Vale	D	1-1	0-0	11	Elliott [75]	5281
32	8	H	Crawley T	D	0-0	0-0	11		2385
33	11	H	Plymouth Arg	L	2-3	0-1	11	Wilson 2 [62, 69]	2297
34	15	A	Stevenage	W	1-0	1-0	11	Thomas-Asante [32]	3246
35	22	H	Colchester U	L	1-2	1-2	13	Hunter [43]	2589
36	29	A	Macclesfield T	W	2-0	2-0	10	Hunter [30], Towell [37]	2317
37	Mar 7	H	Bradford C	W	2-0	1-0	10	Hunter 2 [10, 47]	3443
38	14	A	Exeter C	Cancelled					
39	17	H	Mansfield T	Cancelled					
40	21	A	Scunthorpe U	Cancelled					
41	24	A	Swindon T	Cancelled					
42	28	H	Newport Co	Cancelled					
43	Apr 10	H	Carlisle U	Cancelled					
44	13	A	Leyton Orient	Cancelled					
45	18	H	Morecambe	Cancelled					
46	25	A	Cheltenham T	Cancelled					

Final League Position: 11 (on points-per-game basis)

GOALSCORERS

League (49): Rooney 8 (3 pens), Thomas-Asante 6, Hunter 5, Jervis 4, Touray 4, Dieseruvwe 3, Towell 3, Beesley 2, Burgess, C 2, Lloyd 2, Wilson 2, Armstrong 1, Baldwin 1, Elliott 1, Maynard 1, O'Connor 1, Shelton 1, Whitehead 1 (1 pen), own goal 1.
FA Cup (2): Touray 1, Towell 1.
Carabao Cup (0).
Leasing.com Trophy (12): Armstrong 3, Burgess, C 2, Elliott 1, Hogan 1, Jervis 1, Lloyd 1 (1 pen), Rooney 1, Threlkeld 1, Towell 1.

Neal C 15	Maynard L 21 + 1	Pond N 19 + 3	Piergianni C 11 + 2	Wiseman S 25	Towell R 22 + 4	Smith M 3 + 1	Shelton M 5	Touray I 35	Rooney A 24 + 8	Dieseruvwe E 10 + 10	Beesley J 4 + 3	Armstrong L 12 + 9	Threlkeld O 12 + 6	Jones J 15 + 5	Whitehead D 7 + 5	Gaffney R 1 + 1	Walker T — + 4	Lloyd D 4 + 5	Letheren K 19	Baldwin J 10 + 3	Jones D 3	Jervis J 19 + 1	Rodney D 1 + 2	Hughes S 4 + 4	Doyle A — + 1	Burgess C 26 + 3	Thomas-Asante B 15 + 5	Conway C 15 + 5	Howard M 3	Hogan L 11 + 1	Hunter A 9 + 2	O'Connor M 8	Andrade B 6 + 1	Elliott T 3 + 5	Wilson J 4 + 1	Eastham A 4	Gibson D 2 + 1	*Match No.*
1	2	3	4	5	6^2	7	8	9	10^1	11^3	12	13	14																									1
1	2	3	4	6	7	5^3	8^1	9	10^2	11	13	14		12																								2
1	5^3	3	4	6	7			9	10^1	11	14			2^2	8	12	13																					3
1	2	3	4	5	7^1	13		8		12	11			6	9^3	10^2	14																					4
1	2^1	3	4	6		5^3		9	13	10	11		12	7	8^2		14																					5
1	7	3^1	4	2	8			5	11^3	10	6		12	13			14	9^2																				6
	6		4	2	7^2				11^1	9^3				13				10	1	3	5	8	12	14														7
	6		3		7^1						8			2				9	1	4^2	5	11^3	10		12	13	14											8
	5	13	4	6			7	9	10^1	11		12			8^2				1					3		2												9
	5		4^1	6			7	9	11	10^2		12			8^3			14	1				13	2		3												10
	7^1	2	3	6			8^3	9	14	11		10		5				13	1			12				4^2												11
	7	4		2				5	11^2	13		10^1	12	8	14				1			9				3		6^3										12
	6			2	8^1			5	10^2	13		9	12	7					1					4		3		11										13
	8	3		2				5	11^1	12		10		7^2	14			13	1			9				4		6^3										14
	7	3		2				5	11^2	12		10^1	13	8								9		14		4		6^3	1									15
	7	4		2				5	11	12		10^1		8								9				3		6	1									16
	7	3	14		6^3			5	10^2	12			2	8								11		13		4		9^1	1									17
1				2	8			5	10	11^2		12	7	6^1								9				4	13			3								18
1	8	3			6^1			5	10			9^2	2		7			13				11				4	12											19
1	8				7			9		13		11^2	2		14			6^3			5	10^1				3		12		4								20
1	8^3				7			5	13			11^2	2	12				14				6				4	10^1	9		3								21
1	7^1				8			5	12			10^2	2	13								9				3	11	6		4								22
1			14		7			9	10^3			13	2	5^2	12							6				3	11^1	8		4								23
1	12				7			5	11^2			14	2	8^1	13							9				4	10	6^3		3								24
1					7			5	10^1	12		13	2		8^2							6				4	11	9		3								25
1					7			5	13	14		10^3	2^1	8								9^2				4	11	6		3	12							26
		14		2^2	8			5	12			11^3							1	7		6		3		4	10	9^1			13							27
		3		2	7■			5	11^1										1	13		9^2		14		4	10^3				6■	8	12					28
		3		2				5	11^2										1	8		9^1				4	10	12				7	6	13				29
		3^3		2	14			5	11			13							1	8						4	10^1			12	9	7^2	6					30
				2	13			5	11										1	8						3	10^2	14		4	9^3	7^1	6	12				31
				2	14			5	11^3										1	8						3	13	12		4	9^2	7^1	6	10				32
				2				5	11^1										1	7						4	12	14		3	9	8	6^2	10^3	13			33
		14		2	12			5											1	8						4	10	9^2			6^1	7		13	11^3	3		34
		3		2				5	14										1	8							11	6			9	7^1		13	10^2	4^3	12	35
		3			7			5					2						1	13						14	11^1				9^2		6^3	12	10	4	8	36
		4			8			5	12				2						1	13						14	6^2				9			11^1	10^3	3	7	37
																																						38
																																						39
																																						40
																																						41
																																						42
																																						43
																																						44
																																						45
																																						46

FA Cup

First Round	Burton Alb	(h)	1-1
Replay	Burton Alb	(a)	1-4

Carabao Cup

First Round	Leeds U	(h)	0-3

Leasing.com Trophy

Group C (N)	Aston Villa U21	(h)	2-0
Group C (N)	Tranmere R	(a)	2-0
Second Round (N)	Wolverhampton W U21	(h)	3-0
Third Round (N)	Port Vale	(h)	3-0
Quarter-Final	Accrington S	(h)	2-1
Semi-Final	Newport Co	(a)	0-0

(Salford C won 6-5 on penalties)

Final	Portsmouth	(Wembley)	P-P

SCUNTHORPE UNITED

FOUNDATION

The year of foundation for Scunthorpe United has often been quoted as 1910, but the club can trace its history back to 1899 when Brumby Hall FC, who played on the Old Showground, consolidated their position by amalgamating with some other clubs and changing their name to Scunthorpe United. The year 1910 was when that club amalgamated with North Lindsey United as Scunthorpe and Lindsey United. The link is Mr W. T. Lockwood whose chairmanship covers both years.

The Sands Venue Stadium, Jack Brownsword Way, Scunthorpe, North Lincolnshire DN15 8TD.

Telephone: (01724) 840 139.

Ticket Office: (01724) 747 670.

Website: www.scunthorpe-united.co.uk

Email: feedback@scunthorpe-united.co.uk

Ground Capacity: 9,088.

Record Attendance: 23,935 v Portsmouth, FA Cup 4th rd, 30 January 1954 (at Old Showground); 9,077 v Manchester U, League Cup 3rd rd, 22 September 2010 (at Glanford Park).

Pitch Measurements: 102.5m × 66m (112yd × 72yd).

Chairman: Peter Swann.

President: Sir Ian Botham.

Manager: Neil Cox.

Assistant Manager: Mark Lillis.

Colours: Claret shirts with light blue trim and sleeves, claret shorts with light blue trim, light blue socks with claret trim.

Year Formed: 1899.

Turned Professional: 1912.

Previous Names: Amalgamated first with Brumby Hall then North Lindsey United to become Scunthorpe and Lindsey United, 1910; 1958, Scunthorpe United.

Club Nickname: 'The Iron'.

Grounds: 1899, Old Showground; 1988, Glanford Park (renamed The Sands Venue Stadium 2019).

First Football League Game: 19 August 1950, Division 3 (N), v Shrewsbury T (h) D 0–0 – Thompson; Barker, Brownsword; Allen, Taylor, McCormick; Mosby, Payne, Gorin, Rees, Boyes.

Record League Victory: 8–1 v Luton T (h), Division 3, 24 April 1965 – Sidebottom; Horstead, Hemstead; Smith, Neale, Lindsey; Bramley (1), Scott, Thomas (5), Mahy (1), Wilson (1). 8–1 v Torquay U (a), Division 3, 28 October 1995 – Samways; Housham, Wilson, Ford (1), Knill (1), Hope (Nicholson), Thornber, Bullimore (Walsh), McFarlane (4) (Young), Eyre (2), Paterson.

Record Cup Victory: 9–0 v Boston U, FA Cup 1st rd, 21 November 1953 – Malan; Hubbard, Brownsword; Sharpe, White, Bushby; Mosby (1), Haigh (3), Whitfield (2), Gregory (1), Mervyn Jones (2).

HONOURS

League Champions: FL 1 – 2006–07; Division 3N – 1957–58.
Runners-up: FL 2 – 2004–05, 2013–14.

FA Cup: 5th rd – 1958, 1970.

League Cup: 4th rd – 2010.

League Trophy: *Runners-up:* 2009.

FOOTBALL YEARBOOK FACT FILE

Ted Gorin became the first Scunthorpe United player to score a hat-trick in a Football League match when he netted all three in the home win over Accrington Stanley on 30 September 1950. It was the only treble of his senior career and three months later he was transferred to Shrewsbury Town.

Record Defeat: 0–8 v Carlisle U, Division 3 (N), 25 December 1952.

Most League Points (2 for a win): 66, Division 3 (N), 1956–57, 1957–58.

Most League Points (3 for a win): 91, FL 1, 2006–07.

Most League Goals: 88, Division 3 (N), 1957–58.

Highest League Scorer in Season: Barrie Thomas, 31, Division 2, 1961–62.

Most League Goals in Total Aggregate: Steve Cammack, 110, 1979–81, 1981–86.

Most League Goals in One Match: 5, Barrie Thomas v Luton T, Division 3, 24 April 1965.

Most Capped Player: Grant McCann, 12 (40), Northern Ireland.

Most League Appearances: Jack Brownsword, 597, 1950–65.

Youngest League Player: Hakeeb Adelakun, 16 years 201 days v Tranmere R, 29 December 2012.

Record Transfer Fee Received: £2,400,000 from Celtic for Gary Hooper, July 2010.

Record Transfer Fee Paid: £700,000 to Hibernian for Rob Jones, July 2009.

Football League Record: 1950 Elected to Division 3 (N); 1958–64 Division 2; 1964–68 Division 3; 1968–72 Division 4; 1972–73 Division 3; 1973–83 Division 4; 1983–84 Division 3; 1984–92 Division 4; 1992–99 Division 3; 1999–2000 Division 2; 2000–04 Division 3; 2004–05 FL 2; 2005–07 FL 1; 2007–08 FL C; 2008–09 FL 1; 2009–11 FL C; 2011–13 FL 1; 2013–14 FL 2; 2014–19 FL 1; 2019– FL 2.

LATEST SEQUENCES

Longest Sequence of League Wins: 7, 9.4.2016 – 6.8.2017.

Longest Sequence of League Defeats: 8, 29.11.1997 – 20.1.1998.

Longest Sequence of League Draws: 6, 2.1.1984 – 25.2.1984.

Longest Sequence of Unbeaten League Matches: 28, 23.11.2013 – 21.4.2014.

Longest Sequence Without a League Win: 16, 16.3.2019 – 7.9.2019.

Successive Scoring Runs: 24 from 13.1.2007.

Successive Non-scoring Runs: 7 from 19.4.1975.

MANAGERS

Harry Allcock 1915–53
(Secretary-Manager)
Tom Crilly 1936–37
Bernard Harper 1946–48
Leslie Jones 1950–51
Bill Corkhill 1952–56
Ron Suart 1956–58
Tony McShane 1959
Bill Lambton 1959
Frank Soo 1959–60
Dick Duckworth 1960–64
Fred Goodwin 1964–66
Ron Ashman 1967–73
Ron Bradley 1973–74
Dick Rooks 1974–76
Ron Ashman 1976–81
John Duncan 1981–83
Allan Clarke 1983–84
Frank Barlow 1984–87
Mick Buxton 1987–91
Bill Green 1991–93
Richard Money 1993–94
David Moore 1994–96
Mick Buxton 1996–97
Brian Laws 1997–2004; 2004–06
Nigel Adkins 2006–10
Ian Baraclough 2010–11
Alan Knill 2011–12
Brian Laws 2012–13
Russ Wilcox 2013–14
Mark Robins 2014–16
Nick Daws 2016
Graham Alexander 2016–18
Nick Daws 2018
Stuart McCall 2018–19
Paul Hurst 2019–20
Neil Cox August 2020–

TEN YEAR LEAGUE RECORD

		P	W	D	L	F	A	Pts	Pos
2010-11	FL C	46	12	6	28	43	87	42	24
2011-12	FL 1	46	10	22	14	55	59	52	18
2012-13	FL 1	46	13	9	24	49	73	48	21
2013-14	FL 2	46	20	21	5	68	44	81	2
2014-15	FL 1	46	14	14	18	62	75	56	16
2015-16	FL 1	46	21	11	14	60	47	74	7
2016-17	FL 1	46	24	10	12	80	54	82	3
2017-18	FL 1	46	19	17	10	65	50	74	5
2018-19	FL 1	46	12	10	24	53	83	46	23
2019-20	FL 2	37	10	10	17	44	56	40	20§

§Decided on points-per-game (1.08)

DID YOU KNOW ?

Scunthorpe United's FA Cup third round tie at Sunderland in January 1953 was watched by 56,507 fans, a club record for matches played on domestic grounds. The League One play-off final against Millwall in May 2009 attracted a higher gate (59,661) but this was played at Wembley Stadium.

SCUNTHORPE UNITED – SKY BET LEAGUE TWO 2019–20 LEAGUE RECORD

Match No.	Date	Venue	Opponents	Result		H/T Score	Lg Pos.	Goalscorers	Attendance
1	Aug 3	H	Swindon T	L	0-2	0-0	21		4135
2	10	A	Cheltenham T	L	1-4	0-0	24	Novak [55]	2742
3	17	H	Crawley T	D	2-2	1-1	23	McArdle [33], Lund [54]	3186
4	20	A	Cambridge U	L	2-3	1-0	24	McArdle 2 [41, 60]	3917
5	24	A	Macclesfield T	L	0-1	0-0	24		1860
6	31	H	Carlisle U	L	0-1	0-0	24		3359
7	Sept 7	A	Mansfield T	L	0-2	0-1	24		4772
8	14	H	Morecambe	W	3-0	3-0	23	Proctor [25], van Veen [33], Lund [40]	3017
9	17	H	Oldham Ath	D	2-2	0-0	23	Lund [68], van Veen [77]	3020
10	21	A	Walsall	L	0-1	0-0	23		4037
11	28	H	Bradford C	D	1-1	1-0	23	Ward (pen) [13]	4554
12	Oct 5	A	Plymouth Arg	D	2-2	1-1	22	Gilliead [7], Eisa [90]	8800
13	12	H	Northampton T	W	3-0	3-0	22	Novak 2 [11, 14], van Veen [31]	3377
14	19	A	Newport Co	L	1-2	0-1	22	O'Brien (og) [49]	3936
15	22	H	Exeter C	W	3-1	2-1	22	Perch [24], Ward [37], Gilliead [75]	3055
16	26	A	Salford C	D	1-1	1-1	22	van Veen [34]	3448
17	Nov 2	H	Stevenage	D	0-0	0-0	21		3309
18	16	A	Leyton Orient	W	2-0	1-0	19	Gilliead [4], Novak [79]	6670
19	23	H	Port Vale	W	2-1	1-1	16	van Veen [37], Ntlhe [51]	3391
20	Dec 7	A	Forest Green R	W	2-0	0-0	14	Gilliead [57], Eisa [71]	2060
21	14	H	Colchester U	D	2-2	1-0	13	Eisa [42], van Veen [47]	3081
22	21	A	Grimsby T	W	1-0	0-0	12	van Veen [62]	7385
23	26	H	Walsall	L	0-2	0-1	12		3842
24	29	A	Crewe Alex	L	1-3	0-2	14	Novak [81]	4578
25	Jan 1	A	Oldham Ath	W	2-0	1-0	12	Eisa [35], Lund [83]	2972
26	4	H	Plymouth Arg	L	1-3	0-1	14	van Veen [65]	3450
27	11	H	Newport Co	L	1-2	1-0	15	Eisa [38]	3001
28	18	A	Bradford C	D	2-2	1-2	14	Gilliead [33], McAtee [74]	14,176
29	25	H	Crewe Alex	D	2-2	1-0	16	Bedeau [15], van Veen [73]	3139
30	28	A	Northampton T	L	0-3	0-1	17		4038
31	Feb 1	A	Crawley T	L	1-3	0-3	20	van Veen (pen) [57]	2130
32	8	H	Cheltenham T	W	1-0	1-0	16	McAtee [17]	3159
33	11	H	Cambridge U	L	0-2	0-1	18		2746
34	22	H	Forest Green R	W	1-0	0-0	17	McAtee [46]	3706
35	29	A	Port Vale	D	2-2	0-1	18	Gilliead [71], Miller [90]	5121
36	Mar 3	A	Swindon T	L	0-2	0-1	18		7583
37	7	H	Grimsby T	L	0-2	0-0	19		6855
38	14	A	Colchester U	Cancelled					
39	17	A	Exeter C	Cancelled					
40	21	H	Salford C	Cancelled					
41	28	A	Stevenage	Cancelled					
42	Apr 4	H	Leyton Orient	Cancelled					
43	10	H	Macclesfield T	Cancelled					
44	13	A	Carlisle U	Cancelled					
45	18	H	Mansfield T	Cancelled					
46	25	A	Morecambe	Cancelled					

Final League Position: 20 (on points-per-game basis)

GOALSCORERS

League (44): van Veen 10 (1 pen), Gilliead 6, Eisa 5, Novak 5, Lund 4, McArdle 3, McAtee 3, Ward 2 (1 pen), Bedeau 1, Miller 1, Ntlhe 1, Perch 1, Proctor 1, own goal 1.
FA Cup (1): Colclough 1.
Carabao Cup (0).
Leasing.com Trophy (13): van Veen 5, Eisa 4, Novak 2 (1 pen), Colclough 1, Lund 1.

Eastwood J 10 + 1	Clarke J 11 + 1	McGahey H 31 + 1	Butler A 16 + 2	Ntlhe K 14 + 4	Songo'o Y 16	Gilliead A 33 + 2	Lund M 22	Slater R 7 + 5	Hammill A 3	Novak L 18 + 1	Wootton K 4 + 1	Colclough R 8 + 12	van Veen K 23 + 4	McAtee J 11 + 8	Watson R 23	McArdle R 26	Eisa A 24 + 4	Perch J 30	Miller G 7 + 8	Brown J 20	Proctor J 4 + 9	Ward J 3 + 3	Dales A — + 3	Sutton L 13 + 3	Bedeau J 11	Beestin A — + 3	Lawrence-Gabriel J 8 + 1	Lawlor I 4	Liddle B 2 + 2	Butroid L 4	Green D — + 2	Rowe J 1	El-Mhanni Y — + 1	Pugh T — + 1	Match No.
1	2	3	4	5	6¹	7	8	9³	10²	11	12	13	14																						1
1	2	3	4	5	6²	7	8	9¹		11	10	12		13																					2
		2	4	5		6	7	8	9¹		10			12	1	3	11																		3
	13	2²	4	5		6	7	12	9¹		10				1	3	11	8■																	4
	2		4	5		6	7	8			11¹	12			1	3	9		10																5
	2	12	4²		6	8³	7	9¹				13		14	1	3	10		11	5															6
	2	3	4		7		6	8²				13	12		1		9		11¹	5	10														7
		3			8	6	7	12					11²	13	1	4	9¹	2		5	10														8
		3			8	6	7					12	11		1	4	9¹	2		5	10														9
		3		14	8³	6	7	13				9	11		1	4	12	2	10²	5¹															10
		3		12	7	6	8■	10²		13		9¹			1	4		2		5		11³	14												11
		3		12	8	6				11		9²	10¹		1	4	14	2³		5	13			7											12
13		3		2	8	6		14		11		9	10²		1¹	4				5	12			7³											13
		3			7	6²		12		10		9	14		1	4		2		5	11³	13		8¹											14
		3			8	12	7			10³		6	11¹		1	4		2		5	13	9²		14											15
		3			7	13	8			10		6³	11¹		1	4	12	2		5	14	9²													16
1		3	4		7	6²				11		9	10¹				13	2		5	12			8											17
1	2	3	13	5		6	8			11			10²	12		4	9¹	7																	18
1	2	3	12	5		6	8■			11			10¹			4	9²	7					13												19
1	2	3		5		6				11			10¹			4	9	7			12			8■											20
1	2	3		5	8	6				11			10	12		4	9	7¹																	21
1		3		5	7¹	6				11			10	13		4		2		9²	14	12³		8											22
		2				5				9			10		1	3	11	6		8¹	12	13		7²	4										23
		3				6	8			11			10²		1	4	9¹	7	13	5			12	2											24
1		3		2		6	7			11³		13		10¹		4	9²	8		5	14			12											25
1		3		2		9¹	8			10		13	12			4	11	7		5				6²											26
	2	3	4	5			6			10■		12		9	1		11	7		8¹															27
	2²	3		12³		6	7					13		10	1		9	8	11¹	5					4	14									28
		3				6	8						11²	10¹	1		9	7	13	5					4	12	2								29
		3	4			6	8						11■	10¹			9	7	12						5		2	1							30
		3	4			6³						14	11	10²			9	8	13					2	5		12	1	7¹						31
		3	4			6							11¹	10²			9	8	12					7	5	13	2	1							32
		3	4			6						13	11	10			9³	8¹	12					7²	5		2	1	14						33
			3			9							10¹	7	1	2	11	6	12						4		5			8					34
			4			8							11²	7	1	3	10¹	9	13						5		2		14	6³	12				35
						10								12	1	3		7¹	11					8	4		2		9²	5		6³	13	14	36
			4			7							11	8	1	3²		9	10					13■	5		2			6¹	12				37
																																			38
																																			39
																																			40
																																			41
																																			42
																																			43
																																			44
																																			45
																																			46

FA Cup

First Round	Crawley T	(a)	1-4

Carabao Cup

First Round	Derby Co	(h)	0-1

Leasing.com Trophy

Group A (N)	Grimsby T	(a)	2-1
Group A (N)	Leicester C U21	(h)	1-1
(Leicester C U21 won 3-1 on penalties)			
Group A (N)	Sunderland	(h)	3-0
Second Round (N)	Blackpool	(a)	3-1
Third Round (N)	Manchester C U21	(h)	3-1
Quarter-Final	Portsmouth	(a)	1-2

SHEFFIELD UNITED

FOUNDATION

In March 1889, Yorkshire County Cricket Club formed Sheffield United six days after an FA Cup semi-final between Preston North End and West Bromwich Albion had finally convinced Charles Stokes, a member of the cricket club, that the formation of a professional football club would prove successful at Bramall Lane. The United's first secretary, Mr J. B. Wostinholm, was also secretary of the cricket club.

Bramall Lane Ground, Cherry Street, Bramall Lane, Sheffield, South Yorkshire S2 4SU.

Telephone: (01142) 537 200.

Ticket Office: (01142) 537 200 (option 1).

Website: www.sufc.co.uk

Email: info@sufc.co.uk

Ground Capacity: 32,125.

Record Attendance: 68,287 v Leeds U, FA Cup 5th rd, 15 February 1936.

Pitch Measurements: 100m × 64m (109.5yd × 70yd).

Chairman: H.H. Prince Musa'ad bin Khalid Al Saud.

Chief Executive Officer: Stephen Bettis.

Manager: Chris Wilder.

Assistant Manager: Alan Knill.

HONOURS

League Champions: Division 1 – 1897–98; Division 2 – 1952–53; FL 1 – 2016–17; Division 4 – 1981–82.
Runners-up: Division 1 – 1896–97, 1899–1900; FL C – 2005–06, 2018–19; Division 2 – 1892–93, 1938–39, 1960–61, 1970–71, 1989–90; Division 3 – 1988–89.

FA Cup Winners: 1899, 1902, 1915, 1925.
Runners-up: 1901, 1936.

League Cup: semi-final – 2003, 2015.

Colours: Red and white striped shirts with black trim, black shorts with white trim, red socks with white trim.

Year Formed: 1889.

Turned Professional: 1889.

Club Nickname: 'The Blades'.

Ground: 1889, Bramall Lane.

First Football League Game: 3 September 1892, Division 2, v Lincoln C (h) W 4–2 – Lilley; Witham, Cain; Howell, Hendry, Needham (1); Wallace, Dobson, Hammond (3), Davies, Drummond.

Record League Victory: 10–0 v Burslem Port Vale (a), Division 2, 10 December 1892 – Howlett; Witham, Lilley; Howell, Hendry, Needham; Drummond (1), Wallace (1), Hammond (4), Davies (2), Watson (2). 10-0 v Burnley, Division 1 (h), 19 January 1929.

Record Cup Victory: 6–0 v Leyton Orient (h), FA Cup 1st rd, 6 November 2016 – Ramsdale; Basham (1), O'Connell, Wright, Freeman (1), Coutts (Whiteman), Duffy (Brooks), Fleck, Lafferty, Scougall (1) (Lavery), Chapman (3).

Record Defeat: 0–13 v Bolton W, FA Cup 2nd rd, 1 February 1890.

Most League Points (2 for a win): 60, Division 2, 1952–53.

FOOTBALL YEARBOOK FACT FILE

Alan Woodward was a talented winger for Sheffield United, making over 600 first-team appearances between 1964 and 1978. He was also a more than capable goalkeeper and on five occasions took over in goal in an emergency. He conceded just once during this time, with his longest appearance being for 80 minutes against Leeds United in November 1967.

Most League Points (3 for a win): 100, FL 1, 2016–17.

Most League Goals: 102, Division 1, 1925–26.

Highest League Scorer in Season: Jimmy Dunne, 41, Division 1, 1930–31.

Most League Goals in Total Aggregate: Harry Johnson, 201, 1919–30.

Most League Goals in One Match: 5, Harry Hammond v Bootle, Division 2, 26 November 1892; 5, Harry Johnson v West Ham U, Division 1, 26 December 1927.

Most Capped Player: Billy Gillespie, 25, Northern Ireland.

Most League Appearances: Joe Shaw, 632, 1948–66.

Youngest League Player: Louis Reed, 16 years 257 days v Rotherham U, 8 April 2014.

Record Transfer Fee Received: £12,000,000 from Bournemouth for David Brooks, July 2018.

Record Transfer Fee Paid: £22,000,000 to Genk for Sander Berge, January 2020.

Football League Record: 1892 Elected to Division 2; 1893–1934 Division 1; 1934–39 Division 2; 1946–49 Division 1; 1949–53 Division 2; 1953–56 Division 1; 1956–61 Division 2; 1961–68 Division 1; 1968–71 Division 2; 1971–76 Division 1; 1976–79 Division 2; 1979–81 Division 3; 1981–82 Division 4; 1982–84 Division 3; 1984–88 Division 2; 1988–89 Division 3; 1989–90 Division 2; 1990–92 Division 1; 1992–94 Premier League; 1994–2004 Division 1; 2004–06 FL C; 2006–07 Premier League; 2007–11 FL C; 2011–17 FL 1; 2017–19 FL C; 2019– Premier League.

LATEST SEQUENCES

Longest Sequence of League Wins: 8, 28.3.2017 – 5.8.2017.

Longest Sequence of League Defeats: 7, 19.8.1975 – 20.9.1975.

Longest Sequence of League Draws: 6, 6.5.2001 – 8.9.2001.

Longest Sequence of Unbeaten League Matches: 22, 2.9.1899 – 13.1.1900.

Longest Sequence Without a League Win: 19, 27.9.1975 – 7.2.1976.

Successive Scoring Runs: 34 from 30.3.1956.

Successive Non-scoring Runs: 6 from 4.12.1993.

MANAGERS

J. B. Wostinholm 1889–99
(Secretary-Manager)
John Nicholson 1899–1932
Ted Davison 1932–52
Reg Freeman 1952–55
Joe Mercer 1955–58
Johnny Harris 1959–68
(continued as General Manager to 1970)
Arthur Rowley 1968–69
Johnny Harris *(General Manager resumed Team Manager duties)* 1969–73
Ken Furphy 1973–75
Jimmy Sirrel 1975–77
Harry Haslam 1978–81
Martin Peters 1981
Ian Porterfield 1981–86
Billy McEwan 1986–88
Dave Bassett 1988–95
Howard Kendall 1995–97
Nigel Spackman 1997–98
Steve Bruce 1998–99
Adrian Heath 1999
Neil Warnock 1999–2007
Bryan Robson 2007–08
Kevin Blackwell 2008–10
Gary Speed 2010
Micky Adams 2010–11
Danny Wilson 2011–13
David Weir 2013
Nigel Clough 2013–15
Nigel Adkins 2015–16
Chris Wilder May 2016–

TEN YEAR LEAGUE RECORD

		P	*W*	*D*	*L*	*F*	*A*	*Pts*	*Pos*
2010-11	FL C	46	11	9	26	44	79	42	23
2011-12	FL 1	46	27	9	10	92	51	90	3
2012-13	FL 1	46	19	18	9	56	42	75	5
2013-14	FL 1	46	18	13	15	48	46	67	7
2014-15	FL 1	46	19	14	13	66	53	71	5
2015-16	FL 1	46	18	12	16	64	59	66	11
2016-17	FL 1	46	30	10	6	92	47	100	1
2017-18	FL C	46	20	9	17	62	55	69	10
2018-19	FL C	46	26	11	9	78	41	89	2
2019-20	PR Lge	38	14	12	12	39	39	54	9

DID YOU KNOW ?

In the 1914–15 season Sheffield United used just 18 players in their Football League campaign, the fewest in the club's history. Two of those players made only a single appearance, but none of the remaining 16 played in all 38 matches.

SHEFFIELD UNITED – PREMIER LEAGUE 2019–20 LEAGUE RECORD

Match No.	Date	Venue	Opponents	Result		H/T Score	Lg Pos.	Goalscorers	Attendance
1	Aug 10	A	Bournemouth	D	1-1	0-0	6	Sharp [88]	10,714
2	18	H	Crystal Palace	W	1-0	0-0	7	Lundstram [47]	30,197
3	24	H	Leicester C	L	1-2	0-1	9	McBurnie [62]	30,079
4	31	A	Chelsea	D	2-2	0-2	8	Robinson, C [46], Zouma (og) [89]	40,560
5	Sept 14	H	Southampton	L	0-1	0-0	14		30,985
6	21	A	Everton	W	2-0	1-0	8	Mina (og) [40], Mousset [79]	39,354
7	28	H	Liverpool	L	0-1	0-0	12		31,774
8	Oct 5	A	Watford	D	0-0	0-0	12		20,811
9	21	H	Arsenal	W	1-0	1-0	9	Mousset [30]	30,775
10	26	A	West Ham U	D	1-1	0-1	7	Mousset [69]	59,878
11	Nov 2	H	Burnley	W	3-0	3-0	6	Lundstram 2 [17, 43], Fleck [44]	31,131
12	9	A	Tottenham H	D	1-1	0-0	5	Baldock [78]	59,781
13	24	H	Manchester U	D	3-3	1-0	6	Fleck [19], Mousset [52], McBurnie [90]	32,024
14	Dec 1	A	Wolverhampton W	D	1-1	1-0	7	Mousset [2]	31,642
15	5	H	Newcastle U	L	0-2	0-1	9		30,409
16	8	A	Norwich C	W	2-1	0-1	8	Stevens [49], Baldock [52]	26,881
17	14	H	Aston Villa	W	2-0	0-0	5	Fleck 2 [50, 73]	30,396
18	21	A	Brighton & HA	W	1-0	1-0	5	McBurnie [23]	30,505
19	26	H	Watford	D	1-1	1-1	6	Norwood (pen) [36]	30,222
20	29	A	Manchester C	L	0-2	0-0	8		54,512
21	Jan 2	A	Liverpool	L	0-2	0-1	8		53,321
22	10	H	West Ham U	W	1-0	0-0	5	McBurnie [53]	30,124
23	18	A	Arsenal	D	1-1	0-1	7	Fleck [83]	60,310
24	21	H	Manchester C	L	0-1	0-0	7		31,285
25	Feb 1	A	Crystal Palace	W	1-0	0-0	5	Guaita (og) [58]	25,170
26	9	H	Bournemouth	W	2-1	1-1	5	Sharp [45], Lundstram [84]	30,361
27	22	H	Brighton & HA	D	1-1	1-1	6	Stevens [26]	31,888
28	Mar 7	H	Norwich C	W	1-0	1-0	6	Sharp [36]	31,379
29	June 17	A	Aston Villa	D	0-0	0-0	6		0
30	21	A	Newcastle U	L	0-3	0-0	7		0
31	24	A	Manchester U	L	0-3	0-2	8		0
32	July 2	H	Tottenham H	W	3-1	1-0	7	Berge [31], Mousset [69], McBurnie [84]	0
33	5	A	Burnley	D	1-1	0-1	8	Egan [80]	0
34	8	H	Wolverhampton W	W	1-0	0-0	7	Egan [90]	0
35	11	H	Chelsea	W	3-0	2-0	6	McGoldrick 2 [18, 77], McBurnie [33]	0
36	16	A	Leicester C	L	0-2	0-1	8		0
37	20	H	Everton	L	0-1	0-0	8		0
38	26	A	Southampton	L	1-3	1-0	9	Lundstram [26]	0

Final League Position: 9

GOALSCORERS

League (39): McBurnie 6, Mousset 6, Fleck 5, Lundstram 5, Sharp 3, Baldock 2, Egan 2, McGoldrick 2, Stevens 2, Berge 1, Norwood 1 (1 pen), Robinson, C 1, own goals 3.
FA Cup (7): McGoldrick 2, Besic 1, Clarke 1, Norwood 1, Robinson C 1, Sharp 1.
Carabao Cup (2): Norwood 1, Stearman 1.

Henderson D 36	Basham C 38	Egan J 36	O'Connell J 32 + 1	Baldock G 38	Lundstram J 26 + 8	Norwood O 37 + 1	Fleck J 28 + 2	Stevens E 38	Robinson C 9 + 7	McGoldrick D 22 + 6	McBurnie O 24 + 12	Freeman L 3 + 8	Sharp B 10 + 15	Jagielka P 2 + 4	Morrison R — + 1	Mousset L 11 + 19	Osborn B 6 + 7	Clarke L — + 2	Besic M 2 + 7	Moore S 2	Berge S 12 + 2	Robinson J 6	Zivkovic R — + 5	Freeman K — + 2	Rodwell J — + 1	*Match No.*
1	2^3	3	4	5	6^2	7	8	9	10	11^1	12	13	14													1
1	2	3	4	5	6	7	8^1	9	11^2	10^3	13	12		14												2
1	2^3	3	4	5	6	7		9	11^1	10^2	13	8	12		14											3
1	2^3	3	4	5	6	7		9	10	12	11^1	8^2				13	14									4
1	2^3	3	4	5	6^2	7	8	9	14	10	11^1		12■			13										5
1	2	3	4	5	6	7^2	8	9	11^1		10^3			13		12	14									6
1	2	3	4	5	6	7^2	8	9	10^1		11					12		13								7
1	2	3	4	5	6	7	8	9	11^2		10^1		13			12										8
1	2	3	4	5	6	7^3	8	9		10^2	14	13	12			11^1										9
1	2	3	4	5	6	7^2	8	9	11^1	10^3			12			13			14							10
1	2	3^3	4	5	6	7	8	9		10^2	13		12	14		11^1										11
1	2	3	4	5	6	7	8	9	12	11^2		13				10^1										12
	2^3		4	5	6	7	8	9	14	10^2	12		13	3		11^1				1						13
1	2	3	4	5	6^3	7	8	9	13	11^1	12	14				10^2										14
1	2^3	3	4	5	6	7^2	8	9		13	10	14	11^1			12										15
1	2	3	4	5	6	7^2	8	9	13	10^3	14					11^1			12							16
1	2	3	4	5	6	7^2	8	9		10^3	12					11^1	14		13							17
1	2	3	4	5	6	7^3		9		11	10^2	8^1				13	12		14							18
1	2	3	4	5	6	7	8	9		11	10^1					12										19
1	2	3	4	5		7	8	9	11^1	12	13		14			10^3			6^2							20
1	2	3	4	5	6	7^3	8	9		10^2	12		13			11^1			14							21
1	2	3	4	5	6^2	7	8	9		11^1	10^3		14			12			13							22
1	2^3	3	4	5	6^2	7	8	9	13		10		12			11^1			14							23
1	2^3	3	4	5	13	7	8	9	14		11		10^1			12			6^2							24
1	2	3	4	5	13	7	8	9			10^3		11^1			12	14				6^2					25
1	2	3	4	5	12	7	8	9			10		11^2			13					6^1					26
1	2	3	4	5	14	7	8	9^1		13	10		11^2				12				6^3					27
1	2	3	4	5	6	7	8	9^1		13	10^3		11^2				12				14					28
1	2	3		5	8	7		9		12	10^3	13	11^2			14					6^1	4				29
1	2	3■		5	12	7	8^2	9			10^4	13	11^3								6^1	4	14	15		30
	2			5	6	7^2	8	9		10^3	13			3		11^1				1	12	4	14			31
1	2	3		5		7		9		11^1	10^2					12	8				6	4		13		32
1	2^4	3	13	5		7^1		9		11	10^3		12			14	8				6	4^2			15	33
1	2	3	4	5		7		9			10^1		11^2			12	8				6		13			34
1	2^3	3	4	5	13	7		9		11	10^1			14		12	8				6^2					35
1	2^4	3	4	5	13	7	14	9		11^3	10		15			12	8^2				6^1					36
1	2^4	3	4	5	14	7^3	12	9		11	10^1		13				8^2				6		15			37
1	2^3	3		5	6	14	8	9			10^1		11^2					13			7	4	12			38

FA Cup

Third Round	AFC Fylde	(h)	2-1
Fourth Round	Millwall	(a)	2-0
Fifth Round (*aet*)	Reading	(a)	2-1
Sixth Round	Arsenal	(h)	1-2

Carabao Cup

Second Round	Blackburn R	(h)	2-1
Third Round	Sunderland	(h)	0-1

SHEFFIELD WEDNESDAY

FOUNDATION

Sheffield being one of the principal centres of early Association Football, this club was formed as long ago as 1867 by the Sheffield Wednesday Cricket Club (formed 1825) and their colours from the start were blue and white. The inaugural meeting was held at the Adelphi Hotel and the original committee included Charles Stokes who was subsequently a founder member of Sheffield United.

Hillsborough Stadium, Hillsborough, Sheffield, South Yorkshire S6 1SW.

Telephone: (0370) 020 1867.

Ticket Office: (0370) 020 1867 (option 1).

Website: www.swfc.co.uk

Email: footballenquiries@swfc.co.uk

Ground Capacity: 39,732.

Record Attendance: 72,841 v Manchester C, FA Cup 5th rd, 17 February 1934.

Pitch Measurements: 105m × 68m (115yd × 74.5yd).

Chairman: Dejphon Chansiri.

Manager: Garry Monk.

Coach: Lee Bullen.

Colours: Blue and white striped shirts with black trim, black shorts with blue trim, black socks with blue trim.

Year Formed: 1867 (fifth oldest League club).

Turned Professional: 1887.

Previous Name: The Wednesday until 1929.

Club Nickname: 'The Owls'.

Grounds: 1867, Highfield; 1869, Myrtle Road; 1877, Sheaf House; 1887, Olive Grove; 1899, Owlerton (since 1912 known as Hillsborough). Some games were played at Endcliffe in the 1880s. Until 1895 Bramall Lane was used for some games.

First Football League Game: 3 September 1892, Division 1, v Notts Co (a) W 1–0 – Allan; Tom Brandon (1), Mumford; Hall, Betts, Harry Brandon; Spiksley, Brady, Davis, Bob Brown, Dunlop.

Record League Victory: 9–1 v Birmingham, Division 1, 13 December 1930 – Brown; Walker, Blenkinsop; Strange, Leach, Wilson; Hooper (3), Seed (2), Ball (2), Burgess (1), Rimmer (1).

Record Cup Victory: 12–0 v Halliwell, FA Cup 1st rd, 17 January 1891 – Smith; Thompson, Brayshaw; Harry Brandon (1), Betts, Cawley (2); Winterbottom, Mumford (2), Bob Brandon (1), Woolhouse (5), Ingram (1).

Record Defeat: 0–10 v Aston Villa, Division 1, 5 October 1912.

Most League Points (2 for a win): 62, Division 2, 1958–59.

Most League Points (3 for a win): 93, FL 1, 2011–12.

HONOURS

League Champions: Division 1 – 1902–03, 1903–04, 1928–29, 1929–30; Division 2 – 1899–1900, 1925–26, 1951–52, 1955–56, 1958–59.
Runners-up: Division 1 – 1960–61; Division 2 – 1949–50, 1983–84; FL 1 – 2011–12.

FA Cup Winners: 1896, 1907, 1935.
Runners-up: 1890, 1966, 1993.

League Cup Winners: 1991.
Runners-up: 1993.

European Competitions
Fairs Cup: 1961–62 *(qf)*, 1963–64.
UEFA Cup: 1992–93.
Intertoto Cup: 1995.

FOOTBALL YEARBOOK FACT FILE

Sheffield Wednesday were one of the three Premier League clubs to enter the Intertoto Cup in the summer of 1995, the first time English teams had entered the competition. Wednesday won two of their four matches but failed to progress to the second round. The Owls played their home games at Rotherham's Millmoor as Hillsborough was being refurbished in preparation for the Euro '96 finals the following year.

Most League Goals: 106, Division 2, 1958–59.

Highest League Scorer in Season: Derek Dooley, 46, Division 2, 1951–52.

Most League Goals in Total Aggregate: Andrew Wilson, 199, 1900–20.

Most League Goals in One Match: 6, Doug Hunt v Norwich C, Division 2, 19 November 1938.

Most Capped Player: Nigel Worthington, 50 (66), Northern Ireland.

Most League Appearances: Andrew Wilson, 501, 1900–20.

Youngest League Player: Peter Fox, 15 years 269 days v Orient, 31 March 1973.

Record Transfer Fee Received: £5,000,000 from Reading for Lucas Joao, August 2019.

Record Transfer Fee Paid: £10,000,000 to Middlesbrough for Jordan Rhodes, July 2017.

Football League Record: 1892 Elected to Division 1; 1899–1900 Division 2; 1900–20 Division 1; 1920–26 Division 2; 1926–37 Division 1; 1937–50 Division 2; 1950–51 Division 1; 1951–52 Division 2; 1952–55 Division 1; 1955–56 Division 2; 1956–58 Division 1; 1958–59 Division 2; 1959–70 Division 1; 1970–75 Division 2; 1975–80 Division 3; 1980–84 Division 2; 1984–90 Division 1; 1990–91 Division 2; 1991–92 Division 1; 1992–2000 Premier League; 2000–03 Division 1; 2003–04 Division 2; 2004–05 FL 1; 2005–10 FL C; 2010–12 FL 1; 2012– FL C.

LATEST SEQUENCES

Longest Sequence of League Wins: 9, 23.4.1904 – 15.10.1904.

Longest Sequence of League Defeats: 8, 9.9.2000 – 17.10.2000.

Longest Sequence of League Draws: 7, 15.3.2008 – 14.4.2008.

Longest Sequence of Unbeaten League Matches: 19, 10.12.1960 – 8.4.1961.

Longest Sequence Without a League Win: 20, 11.1.1975 – 30.8.1975.

Successive Scoring Runs: 40 from 14.11.1959.

Successive Non-scoring Runs: 8 from 8.3.1975.

MANAGERS

Arthur Dickinson 1891–1920 *(Secretary-Manager)*
Robert Brown 1920–33
Billy Walker 1933–37
Jimmy McMullan 1937–42
Eric Taylor 1942–58 *(continued as General Manager to 1974)*
Harry Catterick 1958–61
Vic Buckingham 1961–64
Alan Brown 1964–68
Jack Marshall 1968–69
Danny Williams 1969–71
Derek Dooley 1971–73
Steve Burtenshaw 1974–75
Len Ashurst 1975–77
Jackie Charlton 1977–83
Howard Wilkinson 1983–88
Peter Eustace 1988–89
Ron Atkinson 1989–91
Trevor Francis 1991–95
David Pleat 1995–97
Ron Atkinson 1997–98
Danny Wilson 1998–2000
Peter Shreeves *(Acting)* 2000
Paul Jewell 2000–01
Peter Shreeves 2001
Terry Yorath 2001–02
Chris Turner 2002–04
Paul Sturrock 2004–06
Brian Laws 2006–09
Alan Irvine 2010–11
Gary Megson 2011–12
Dave Jones 2012–13
Stuart Gray 2013–15
Carlos Carvalhal 2015–18
Jos Luhukay 2018
Steve Bruce 2019
Garry Monk September 2019–

TEN YEAR LEAGUE RECORD

		P	*W*	*D*	*L*	*F*	*A*	*Pts*	*Pos*
2010-11	FL 1	46	16	10	20	67	67	58	15
2011-12	FL 1	46	28	9	9	81	48	93	2
2012-13	FL C	46	16	10	20	53	61	58	18
2013-14	FL C	46	13	14	19	63	65	53	16
2014-15	FL C	46	14	18	14	43	49	60	13
2015-16	FL C	46	19	17	10	66	45	74	6
2016-17	FL C	46	24	9	13	60	45	81	4
2017-18	FL C	46	14	15	17	59	60	57	15
2018-19	FL C	46	16	16	14	60	62	64	12
2019-20	FL C	46	15	11	20	58	66	56	16

DID YOU KNOW ?

Sheffield Wednesday's home game against Aston Villa in the 1888–89 season began on 26 November and finished on 13 March. The original match was abandoned after 79 minutes due to poor light and the Football League Management Committee instructed the two clubs to play the remaining time later in the season.

SHEFFIELD WEDNESDAY – SKY BET CHAMPIONSHIP 2019–20 LEAGUE RECORD

Match No.	Date	Venue	Opponents	Result		H/T Score	Lg Pos.	Goalscorers	Attendance
1	Aug 3	A	Reading	W	3-1	1-0	1	Harris 30, Hutchinson 56, Lucas Joao 90	16,319
2	10	H	Barnsley	W	2-0	1-0	1	Murphy 2, Fletcher 60	28,028
3	17	A	Millwall	L	0-1	0-1	6		15,017
4	20	H	Luton T	W	1-0	0-0	1	Harris 54	23,353
5	24	A	Preston NE	L	1-2	0-1	7	Fletcher 78	15,715
6	31	H	QPR	L	1-2	1-0	11	Fletcher (pen) 23	23,446
7	Sept 15	A	Huddersfield T	W	2-0	1-0	10	Fletcher 10, Winnall 72	22,754
8	21	H	Fulham	D	1-1	0-1	8	Nuhiu 90	23,342
9	28	A	Middlesbrough	W	4-1	4-1	7	Clayton (og) 5, Iorfa 6, Reach 23, Fletcher 34	22,075
10	Oct 1	A	Hull C	L	0-1	0-0	8		11,590
11	5	H	Wigan Ath	W	1-0	0-0	8	Luongo 57	22,753
12	18	A	Cardiff C	D	1-1	1-0	6	Borner 19	22,486
13	22	H	Stoke C	W	1-0	1-0	3	Luongo 43	22,460
14	26	H	Leeds U	D	0-0	0-0	4		27,516
15	Nov 2	A	Blackburn R	L	1-2	0-0	7	Murphy 83	14,147
16	9	H	Swansea C	D	2-2	0-1	7	Forestieri 81, Fox 90	23,073
17	23	A	WBA	L	1-2	0-1	9	Fletcher (pen) 58	25,566
18	27	H	Birmingham C	D	1-1	0-0	10	Harris 81	22,059
19	30	A	Charlton Ath	W	3-1	1-1	9	Fletcher 2 (1 pen) 17, 80 (p), Nuhiu 90	18,338
20	Dec 7	H	Brentford	W	2-1	0-1	6	Fletcher 2 (1 pen) 69 (p), 73	22,475
21	11	A	Derby Co	D	1-1	1-0	8	Fletcher 23	26,203
22	14	A	Nottingham F	W	4-0	4-0	5	Rhodes 3 9, 13, 37, Fletcher 45	28,002
23	22	H	Bristol C	W	1-0	0-0	3	Bannan (pen) 85	23,180
24	26	A	Stoke C	L	2-3	0-1	4	Fox 67, Lees 74	25,359
25	29	H	Cardiff C	L	1-2	1-2	6	Lees 18	25,385
26	Jan 1	H	Hull C	L	0-1	0-0	7		24,842
27	11	A	Leeds U	W	2-0	0-0	6	Murphy 87, Nuhiu 90	36,422
28	18	H	Blackburn R	L	0-5	0-3	10		23,504
29	28	A	Wigan Ath	L	1-2	1-0	11	Murphy 32	9759
30	Feb 1	H	Millwall	D	0-0	0-0	11		23,052
31	8	A	Barnsley	D	1-1	1-1	11	Windass 16	17,789
32	12	A	Luton T	L	0-1	0-1	12		10,001
33	15	H	Reading	L	0-3	0-1	12		22,199
34	22	A	Birmingham C	D	3-3	2-2	12	Murphy 65, Bannan 20, Forestieri (pen) 34	22,120
35	26	H	Charlton Ath	W	1-0	0-0	12	Fletcher 90	21,370
36	29	H	Derby Co	L	1-3	0-3	12	Windass 74	25,148
37	Mar 7	A	Brentford	L	0-5	0-3	15		12,273
38	June 20	H	Nottingham F	D	1-1	0-0	15	Wickham 90	0
39	28	A	Bristol C	W	2-1	1-0	13	Wickham 13, Luongo 59	0
40	July 1	H	WBA	L	0-3	0-1	13		0
41	5	A	Swansea C	L	1-2	0-0	15	Nuhiu 90	0
42	8	H	Preston NE	L	1-3	0-0	16	Murphy 58	0
43	11	A	QPR	W	3-0	2-0	14	Iorfa 5, Windass 45, Murphy 78	0
44	14	H	Huddersfield T	D	0-0	0-0	15		0
45	18	A	Fulham	L	3-5	0-3	16	Nuhiu 2 (1 pen) 49 (p), 89, Murphy 78	0
46	22	H	Middlesbrough	L	1-2	1-1	17	Murphy 10	0

Final League Position: 16

GOALSCORERS

League (58): Fletcher 13 (4 pens), Murphy 9, Nuhiu 6 (1 pen), Harris 3, Luongo 3, Rhodes 3, Windass 3, Bannan 2 (1 pen), Forestieri 2 (1 pen), Fox 2, Iorfa 2, Lees 2, Wickham 2, Borner 1, Hutchinson 1, Lucas Joao 1, Reach 1, Winnall 1, own goal 1.
FA Cup (3): Fox 1, Reach 1, Winnall 1.
Carabao Cup (1): Nuhiu 1.

Westwood K 14	Odubajo M 19 + 3	Lees T 24 + 3	Borner J 34 + 3	Palmer L 33	Lee K 20 + 8	Hutchinson S 20 + 3	Bannan B 42 + 2	Reach A 26 + 11	Fletcher S 23 + 4	Harris K 40 + 3	Forestieri F 8 + 9	Lucas Joao E — + 1	Dawson C 23 + 1	Murphy J 24 + 15	Pelupessy J 11 + 6	Rhodes J 7 + 9	Luongo M 17 + 10	Iorfa D 40 + 1	Fox M 24 + 3	Winnall S 6 + 7	Nuhiu A 14 + 24	Urhoghide O 3	Da Cruz A 8 + 6	Windass J 6 + 3	Wickham C 8 + 5	Wildsmith J 9	Hunt A 2 + 4	Shaw L 1 + 1	*Match No.*
1■	2	3	4	5	6^{1}	7	8	9	10^{3}	11^{2}	12	13	14																1
	2	3	4	5	6^{3}	7		8	10^{2}	11			1	9^{1}	12	13	14												2
1		3	4	5^{2}	8^{3}	7	12	6	10	11				9		14	13	2^{1}											3
1	2	3	4		14	6	7	9^{1}	11^{2}	10^{3}				8			13		5	12									4
1	2^{2}	3	4		6^{3}	7	8	13	10	11	12			9^{1}					5		14								5
1			4	2^{2}		7	8	6^{3}	11	9	10			13			12	3	5^{1}		14								6
1	2		4	5	14	6	7	9	11^{2}	10^{3}				8^{1}				3		12	13								7
1	2		4	5	8^{2}	6	9	7^{1}	11^{3}	10				12				3		13	14								8
1	2		4	5		7^{1}	8	6	10	9^{3}							12	3	14	13	11^{2}								9
1	2		4	5	14	7^{3}	8	6		9^{1}				12		13		3		10^{2}	11								10
1	2		4	5	12		9	7^{2}	11^{3}	10				13	6		8^{1}	3			14								11
			4	2		6	9^{1}	7	11	10^{2}			1	13			8	3	5		12								12
			4	2	12	6	9	7	11^{3}	10^{2}	13		1				8^{1}	3	5		14								13
1				2	12	4	8	6	11	9	13				7^{1}			3	5		10^{2}								14
1			4	2	8	6		7^{2}	11	10^{3}	12			13	9^{1}			3	5		14								15
1		4		2	7		8	13	11	9^{3}	12			6^{2}		14		3	5		10^{1}								16
1			4	2■	8^{2}	6^{3}	9	12	11	10^{1}				7			13	3	5		14								17
	2	12	4^{1}		7^{2}		8	6^{3}	11	10	13		1				9	3	5		14								18
	2	4				7^{2}	8	14	10	6^{3}	9^{1}		1	12			13	3	5		11								19
	2	4				7^{3}	8	13	11	9			1	6^{2}		12	14	3	5		10^{1}								20
	2■	4				7	8	6	11^{3}	9^{1}			1	12		10^{2}	14	3	5		13								21
		4^{1}	12	2			8	6	11^{2}	9			1			10^{3}	7	3	5	14	13								22
		4	12	2			8	6		9			1		14	10^{2}	7^{3}	3	5^{1}	13	11								23
		4		2		12	8	6		9			1	14		10^{2}	7^{1}	3	5	13	11^{3}								24
		4	13	2^{2}		6	7	9		10			1	8^{3}		12		3^{1}	5	11	14								25
		3	4			7	8	6^{3}	12	9			1	14		13		2	5	11^{2}	10^{1}								26
			4		6	14	9	10					1	7	13		8^{2}	3	5	11^{1}	12	2^{3}							27
		14	4		8^{3}	13	6	10					1	7			9■	3	5	11^{1}	12	2^{2}							28
	2	12	4				8	14		9^{3}			1	6	7	13		3	5^{1}	10^{2}	11								29
	5		4	2			8	10		9^{1}	12		1	6^{2}	7			3			11		13						30
		3	4	5	12		7				10^{2}		1	13	6^{1}			2			14		8	9	11^{3}				31
		3	5	2^{3}	8		9			12	6^{1}		1	14				4			13		11	7^{2}	10				32
			4	5	7		12			10	9		1	13	6^{1}			3			11^{3}	2■	8^{2}		14				33
		3	5	6	8		9		14	10	11^{3}		1	7	2^{2}			4^{1}	12						13				34
		3	4	2	7		8		12	9^{1}	10^{3}		1	6					5		13		14		11^{2}				35
		3^{3}	4	2	7		8		11^{2}	9^{1}	10		1	6				14	5					13	12				36
		4		2			8		11^{3}	14	12		1	6	7			3	5				9^{2}	10^{1}	13				37
	13		4	2	6^{3}		7	15	12^{4}	9				5^{2}		10^{1}	8^{5}	3					14		11	1	16		38
	14		4^{1}	2	6		7			9				5^{3}	15	10^{2}	8^{4}	3	12		16		13		11^{5}	1			39
	4			2	14		6^{4}	9^{2}		8				5		11^{1}	7^{3}	3			13		12		10	1	15		40
			4	2	6^{1}		7	9^{2}		13				5		15	8^{3}	3			14		11^{4}		10	1	12		41
	12		4	2			8	14		9^{3}				6^{1}	5		7	3			11		10^{2}	13		1			42
	5	3^{3}	4				7			9				12	13		8	2			15		11^{1}	10^{4}		1	6^{2}	14	43
	5	3	4				7	15		9				11^{1}	13		8^{3}	2			14		12	10^{4}		1	6^{2}		44
	5^{1}	3	4				8	15		9				14	7^{5}		6^{4}	2			13		11^{2}	10^{3}	12	1	16		45
		3		4	8^{3}		7	14		9				5			12	2			10^{2}			13	11	1		6^{1}	46

FA Cup

Third Round	Brighton & HA	(a)	1-0
Fourth Round	QPR	(a)	2-1
Fifth Round	Manchester C	(h)	0-1

Carabao Cup

Second Round	Rotherham U	(a)	1-0
Third Round	Everton	(h)	0-2

SHREWSBURY TOWN

FOUNDATION

Shrewsbury School having provided a number of the early England and Wales international players it is not surprising that there was a Town club as early as 1876 which won the Birmingham Senior Cup in 1879. However, the present Shrewsbury Town club was formed in 1886 and won the Welsh FA Cup as early as 1891.

Montgomery Waters Meadow, Oteley Road, Shrewsbury, Shropshire SY2 6ST.

Telephone: (01743) 289 177.

Ticket Office: (01743) 273 943.

Website: www.shrewsburytown.com

Email: info@shrewsburytown.co.uk

Ground Capacity: 9,875.

Record Attendance: 18,917 v Walsall, Division 3, 26 April 1961 (at Gay Meadow); 10,210 v Chelsea, League Cup 4th rd, 28 October 2014 (at New Meadow).

Pitch Measurements: 105m × 68.5m (115yd × 75yd).

Chairman: Roland Wycherley.

Chief Executive: Brian Caldwell.

Manager: Sam Ricketts.

Assistant Manager: Graham Barrow.

Colours: Blue and yellow striped shirts, blue shorts with yellow trim, blue socks with yellow trim.

Year Formed: 1886.

Turned Professional: 1896.

Club Nicknames: 'Town', 'Blues', 'Salop'. The name 'Salop' is a colloquialism for the county of Shropshire. Since Shrewsbury is the only club in Shropshire, cries of 'Come on Salop' are frequently used!

Grounds: 1886, Old Racecourse Ground; 1889, Ambler's Field; 1893, Sutton Lane; 1895, Barracks Ground; 1910, Gay Meadow; 2007, New Meadow (renamed ProStar Stadium 2008; Greenhous Meadow 2010; Montgomery Waters Meadow 2017).

First Football League Game: 19 August 1950, Division 3 (N), v Scunthorpe U (a) D 0–0 – Egglestone; Fisher, Lewis; Wheatley, Depear, Robinson; Griffin, Hope, Jackson, Brown, Barker.

Record League Victory: 7–0 v Swindon T, Division 3 (S), 6 May 1955 – McBride; Bannister, Skeech; Wallace, Maloney, Candlin; Price, O'Donnell (1), Weigh (4), Russell, McCue (2); 7-0 v Gillingham, FL 2, 13 September 2008 – Daniels; Herd, Tierney, Davies (2), Jackson (1) (Langmead), Coughlan (1), Cansdell-Sherriff (1), Thornton, Hibbert (1) (Hindmarch), Holt (pen), McIntyre (Ashton).

Record Cup Victory: 11–2 v Marine, FA Cup 1st rd, 11 November 1995 – Edwards; Seabury (Dempsey (1)), Withe (1), Evans (1), Whiston (2), Scott (1), Woods, Stevens (1), Spink (3) (Anthrobus), Walton, Berkley, (1 og).

HONOURS

League Champions: Division 3 – 1978–79; Third Division – 1993–94.
Runners-up: FL 2 – 2011–12, 2014–15; Division 4 – 1974–75; Conference – (3rd) 2003–04 *(promoted via play-offs).*

FA Cup: 6th rd – 1979, 1982.

League Cup: semi-final – 1961.

League Trophy: *Runners-up:* 1996, 2018.

Welsh Cup Winners: 1891, 1938, 1977, 1979, 1984, 1985.
Runners-up: 1931, 1948, 1980.

FOOTBALL YEARBOOK FACT FILE

Shrewsbury Town played in the FA Amateur Cup for the first three seasons of the competition before turning professional in August 1896. Their best performance came in the 1895–96 season when they defeated Casuals, Old Brightonians and Marlow, only to fall to a 2-0 defeat to Royal Artillery (Portsmouth) in the semi-final at Reading.

Record Defeat: 1–8 v Norwich C, Division 3 (S), 13 September 1952; 1–8 v Coventry C, Division 3, 22 October 1963.

Most League Points (2 for a win): 62, Division 4, 1974–75.

Most League Points (3 for a win): 89, FL 2, 2014–15.

Most League Goals: 101, Division 4, 1958–59.

Highest League Scorer in Season: Arthur Rowley, 38, Division 4, 1958–59.

Most League Goals in Total Aggregate: Arthur Rowley, 152, 1958–65 (thus completing his League record of 434 goals).

Most League Goals in One Match: 5, Alf Wood v Blackburn R, Division 3, 2 October 1971.

Most Capped Player: Jimmy McLaughlin, 5 (12), Northern Ireland; Bernard McNally, 5, Northern Ireland; Aaron Pierre, 5 (10), Grenada.

Most League Appearances: Mickey Brown, 418, 1986–91; 1992–94; 1996–2001.

Youngest League Player: Graham French, 16 years 177 days v Reading, 30 September 1961.

Record Transfer Fee Received: £600,000 (rising to £1,500,000) from Manchester C for Joe Hart, May 2006.

Record Transfer Fee Paid: £200,000 to Tranmere R for Oliver Norburn, August 2018.

Football League Record: 1950 Elected to Division 3 (N); 1951–58 Division 3 (S); 1958–59 Division 4; 1959–74 Division 3; 1974–75 Division 4; 1975–79 Division 3; 1979–89 Division 2; 1989–94 Division 3; 1994–97 Division 2; 1997–2003 Division 3; 2003–04 Conference; 2004–12 FL 2; 2012–14 FL 1; 2014–15 FL 2; 2015– FL 1.

MANAGERS

W. Adams 1905–12
(Secretary-Manager)
A. Weston 1912–34
(Secretary-Manager)
Jack Roscamp 1934–35
Sam Ramsey 1935–36
Ted Bousted 1936–40
Leslie Knighton 1945–49
Harry Chapman 1949–50
Sammy Crooks 1950–54
Walter Rowley 1955–57
Harry Potts 1957–58
Johnny Spuhler 1958
Arthur Rowley 1958–68
Harry Gregg 1968–72
Maurice Evans 1972–73
Alan Durban 1974–78
Richie Barker 1978
Graham Turner 1978–84
Chic Bates 1984–87
Ian McNeill 1987–90
Asa Hartford 1990–91
John Bond 1991–93
Fred Davies 1994–97
(previously Caretaker-Manager 1993–94)
Jake King 1997–99
Kevin Ratcliffe 1999–2003
Jimmy Quinn 2003–04
Gary Peters 2004–08
Paul Simpson 2008–10
Graham Turner 2010–14
Mike Jackson 2014
Micky Mellon 2014–16
Paul Hurst 2016–18
John Askey 2018
Sam Ricketts December 2018–

LATEST SEQUENCES

Longest Sequence of League Wins: 7, 28.10.1995 – 16.12.1995.

Longest Sequence of League Defeats: 11, 9.4.2003 – 14.8.2004. (Spread over 2 periods in Football League. 2003–04 season in Conference.)

Longest Sequence of League Draws: 6, 30.10.1963 – 14.12.1963.

Longest Sequence of Unbeaten League Matches: 16, 30.10.1993 – 26.2.1994.

Longest Sequence Without a League Win: 18, 8.3.2003 – 14.8.2004.

Successive Scoring Runs: 28 from 7.9.1960.

Successive Non-scoring Runs: 6 from 1.1.1991.

TEN YEAR LEAGUE RECORD

		P	*W*	*D*	*L*	*F*	*A*	*Pts*	*Pos*
2010-11	FL 2	46	22	13	11	72	49	79	4
2011-12	FL 2	46	26	10	10	66	41	88	2
2012-13	FL 1	46	13	16	17	54	60	55	16
2013-14	FL 1	46	9	15	22	44	65	42	23
2014-15	FL 2	46	27	8	11	67	31	89	2
2015-16	FL 1	46	13	11	22	58	79	50	20
2016-17	FL 1	46	13	12	21	46	63	51	18
2017-18	FL 1	46	25	12	9	60	39	87	3
2018-19	FL 1	46	12	16	18	51	59	52	18
2019-20	FL 1	34	10	11	13	31	42	41	15§

§Decided on points-per-game (1.21)

DID YOU KNOW ?

Shrewsbury Town's former ground at Gay Meadow bordered the River Severn and during matches a local man, Fred Davies, would wait in his coracle on the river to retrieve any stray footballs that might be kicked out of the ground.

SHREWSBURY TOWN – SKY BET LEAGUE ONE 2019–20 LEAGUE RECORD

Match No.	Date	Venue	Opponents	Result	H/T Score	Lg Pos.	Goalscorers	Attendance
1	Aug 3	H	Portsmouth	W 1-0	0-0	7	Giles 68	7880
2	10	A	Milton Keynes D	L 0-1	0-0	12		7967
3	17	H	Rochdale	D 0-0	0-0	12		5641
4	20	A	Accrington S	W 3-2	0-0	8	Hughes (og) 77, Okenabirhie 85, Udoh 89	2284
5	24	H	Burton Alb	D 0-0	0-0	9		5553
6	31	A	Ipswich T	L 0-3	0-2	12		19,161
7	Sept 14	A	AFC Wimbledon	D 1-1	0-1	15	Cummings 73	4084
8	17	H	Southend U	W 4-3	2-1	13	Beckles 19, Cummings 27, Norburn 61, Lang 83	4909
9	21	A	Rotherham U	D 0-0	0-0	11		8380
10	28	H	Fleetwood T	L 0-3	0-1	12		5888
11	Oct 5	A	Tranmere R	W 1-0	1-0	12	Pierre 20	7314
12	18	A	Lincoln C	D 0-0	0-0	12		8710
13	22	H	Gillingham	D 1-1	0-1	14	Beckles 64	5076
14	26	H	Sunderland	W 1-0	1-0	12	Cummings 22	8117
15	Nov 2	A	Wycombe W	L 0-1	0-0	12		4826
16	5	H	Peterborough U	W 1-0	1-0	11	Ebanks-Landell 45	4890
17	23	H	Bristol R	L 3-4	1-2	12	Laurent 2 37, 67, Norburn 62	6235
18	Dec 7	A	Oxford U	D 0-0	0-0	12		6931
19	14	H	Coventry C	W 2-1	0-1	11	Golbourne 68, Whalley 90	7336
20	21	A	Blackpool	W 1-0	0-0	11	Okenabirhie (pen) 56	7695
21	26	H	Rotherham U	L 1-2	0-0	11	Pierre 66	7555
22	29	A	Bolton W	D 1-1	0-1	12	Udoh 53	13,788
23	Jan 7	A	Doncaster R	L 0-2	0-1	15		7054
24	11	H	Lincoln C	D 1-1	1-0	15	Norburn (pen) 36	6275
25	18	A	Fleetwood T	D 2-2	1-0	16	Whalley 38, Cummings 81	2797
26	29	A	Gillingham	L 0-2	0-2	16		4212
27	Feb 1	A	Rochdale	L 0-1	0-0	16		2829
28	8	H	Milton Keynes D	D 1-1	0-0	16	Beckles 62	5791
29	11	H	Accrington S	L 0-2	0-1	17		4699
30	15	A	Portsmouth	L 0-2	0-0	17		18,214
31	22	H	Doncaster R	W 1-0	0-0	17	Edwards 76	5672
32	25	H	Tranmere R	L 2-3	0-2	17	Pierre 56, Lang 61	5009
33	29	A	Bristol R	W 1-0	0-0	15	Udoh 69	6954
34	Mar 7	H	Oxford U	L 2-3	2-1	16	Udoh 12, Lang 34	6474
35	14	A	Coventry C	Cancelled				
36	21	H	Blackpool	Cancelled				
37	28	H	Wycombe W	Cancelled				
38	Apr 4	A	Sunderland	Cancelled				
39	10	A	Burton Alb	Cancelled				
40	13	H	Ipswich T	Cancelled				
41	18	A	Peterborough U	Cancelled				
42	21	H	Bolton W	Cancelled				
43	25	H	AFC Wimbledon	Cancelled				
44	May 3	A	Southend U	Cancelled				

Final League Position: 15 (on points-per-game basis)

GOALSCORERS

League (31): Cummings 4, Udoh 4, Beckles 3, Lang 3, Norburn 3 (1 pen), Pierre 3, Laurent 2, Okenabirhie 2 (1 pen), Whalley 2, Ebanks-Landell 1, Edwards 1, Giles 1, Golbourne 1, own goal 1.
FA Cup (8): Cummings 2 (1 pen), Laurent 2, Edwards 1, Goss 1, Pierre 1, Walker 1.
Carabao Cup (0).
Leasing.com Trophy (8): Edwards 2, Cummings 1, Golbourne 1, Okenabirhie 1, Thompson 1, Walker 1, own goal 1.

O'Leary M 30	Williams R 24+1	Ebanks-Landell E 28	Pierre A 29+1	Love D 26+2	Edwards D 24+5	Vincelot R 2	McCormick L 4+1	Giles R 15+4	Okenabirhie F 6+11	Morison S 6+1	Laurent J 30+1	Whalley S 15+8	Eisa A —+1	Beckles O 25+3	Walker B 4+11	Goss S 15+7	Thompson L 1+9	Udoh D 12+13	Norburn O 17	Lang C 14+2	Cummings J 13+11	Golbourne S 14+1	Murphy J 4	John-Lewis L —+2	Sears R 2	Hart S 2+2	McAleny C 5	Ramsey K 3+2	Vela J 4	*Match No.*
1	2	3	4	5	6	7	8^2	9	10^3	11^1	12	13	14																	1
1	3^1	4	5	2	7	8	9^2	6	13	11^3		10		12	14															2
1		3	4	5	7		9^1	8	13	10^3		11		2	14	6^2	12													3
1		3	4	5	8		6^2	9	13	11^1		10^3		2		7	12	14												4
1		3	4	5	6			9	12	10^1	8^2	11^3		2	7		13	14												5
1		3	4	5	7		14	9^1		11^3	8^2	10■		2		6	12	13												6
1	3	4	5	2				6		14	7				13	8		10^3	9^1	11^2	12									7
1	2	3		5	13			9			6	12		4		7		14	8^2	11^3	10^1									8
1	2	3		5	13			9			8^2	11^3		4	14	7			6	10^1	12									9
1	2^3	3^1	12	5				9			6	13		4		7		14	8	10	11^2									10
1	2		3	5				9	12		6			4	14	7	13	11^1	8^3	10^2										11
1	2		3	5				9	10^1		6	13		4		7^3	14	12	8		11^2									12
1	2		3	5	14			9	12		6^3	13		4		7		10^1	8		11^2									13
1	2		3	5	11^1				12		7	9^2		4		14	13		6		10^3	8								14
1	2■		3	5^2	11^3				13		6^1	9		4		12	14		7		10	8								15
		2	3	5	11^3				12		6	9^2		4	14		13		7		10^1	8	1							16
	2		3	5	11			12	13		6			4^1			9^3		7		10^2	8	1	14						17
1	2	3	4	5	11^1			13	10^3		6				14	8^2		12	7			9								18
1	2^2	3	4	5	11			13	10^1		9	12				6^3			7		14	8								19
1		2	3	5	10				11^1		6	9^2		4	7^3	14		12				8		13						20
1	14	2	3	5^2	9^1			13	10^3		6	11		4	7			12				8								21
1	2	3	4	5^2				11	13		7	9						10^1	6		12	8								22
1	2	3	4	5^1	13			11			9	12				6^3		10	7		14	8^2								23
1	2	3	4^3		7^2						6	10		12				13	8	11^1	14	9			5					24
1	2	3	4	5	11^1						7	9		12				13	6	10^3	14	8^2								25
1		2	3	14	13						7	9		4	6			10^1		11^3	12				5^2	8				26
1	2	3		5	7						6	12		4		14		13		9^2	10^1	8					11^3			27
	2	3	4		6						7			8		12		10		13	11^2		1				9	5^1		28
	2	3		5^1	7						6			4		14		13		9^2	10	8^3	1			12	11			29
1	2	3	4		8						6			5		7		11^3		14	13					9^1	10^2	12		30
1		3	4		7^1						10			5	14	12		11		6	13						9^3	2	8^2	31
1		3	4		9^3						10			5	13	7		11^2		8	12					14		2	6^1	32
1	2	3	4		7						8			5	13			10		11^2	9^1							12	6	33
1	2	3	4^3	14	7						8			5	13			9		11^1	6^2	12							10■	34
																														35
																														36
																														37
																														38
																														39
																														40
																														41
																														42
																														43
																														44

FA Cup

First Round	Bradford C	(h)	1-1
Replay	Bradford C	(a)	1-0
Second Round	Mansfield T	(h)	2-0
Third Round	Bristol C	(a)	1-1
Replay	Bristol C	(h)	1-0
Fourth Round	Liverpool	(h)	2-2
Replay	Liverpool	(a)	0-1

Carabao Cup

First Round	Rotherham U	(h)	0-4

Leasing.com Trophy

Group D (N)	Port Vale	(a)	1-2
Group D (N)	Newcastle U U21	(h)	3-0
Group D (N)	Macclesfield T	(h)	3-1
Second Round (N)	Manchester C U21	(h)	1-1

(Manchester C U21 won 6-5 on penalties)

SOUTHAMPTON

FOUNDATION

The club was formed by members of the St Mary's Church of England Young Men's Association at a meeting of the Y.M.A. in November 1885 and it was named as such. For the sake of brevity this was usually shortened to St Mary's Y.M.A. The rector Canon Albert Basil Orme Wilberforce was elected president. The name was changed to plain St Mary's during 1887–88 and did not become Southampton St Mary's until 1894, the inaugural season in the Southern League.

St Mary's Stadium, Britannia Road, Southampton, Hampshire SO14 5FP.

Telephone: (0845) 688 9448.

Ticket Office: (0845) 688 9288.

Website: www.southamptonfc.com

Email: sfc@southamptonfc.com

Ground Capacity: 32,384.

Record Attendance: 31,044 v Manchester U, Division 1, 8 October 1969 (at The Dell); 32,363 v Coventry C, FL C, 28 April 2012 (at St Mary's).

Pitch Measurements: 105m × 68m (115yd × 74.5yd).

Chairman: Gao Jisheng.

Chief Executive: Martin Semmens.

Manager: Ralph Hasenhüttl.

Assistant Manager: Danny Röhl.

Colours: Red shirt with white sash and black trim, black shorts with red and white trim, red socks with white hoop.

Year Formed: 1885. ***Turned Professional:*** 1894.

Previous Names: 1885, St Mary's Young Men's Association; 1887–88, St Mary's; 1894–95, Southampton St Mary's; 1897, Southampton.

Club Nickname: 'Saints'.

Grounds: 1885, 'The Common' (from 1887 also used the County Cricket Ground and Antelope Cricket Ground); 1889, Antelope Cricket Ground; 1896, The County Cricket Ground; 1898, The Dell; 2001, St Mary's.

First Football League Game: 28 August 1920, Division 3, v Gillingham (a) D 1–1 – Allen; Parker, Titmuss; Shelley, Campbell, Turner; Barratt, Dominy (1), Rawlings, Moore, Foxall.

Record League Victory: 8–0 v Sunderland, Premier League, 18 October 2014 – Forster; Clyne, Fonte, Alderweireld, Bertrand; Davis S (Mané), Schneiderlin, Cork (1); Long (Wanyama (1)), Pelle (2) (Mayuka), Tadic (1) (plus 3 Sunderland own goals).

Record Cup Victory: 7–1 v Ipswich T, FA Cup 3rd rd, 7 January 1961 – Reynolds; Davies, Traynor, Conner, Page, Huxford, Paine (1), O'Brien (3 incl. 1p), Reeves, Mulgrew (2), Penk (1).

HONOURS

League Champions: Division 3 – 1959–60; Division 3S – 1921–22.
Runners-up: Division 1 – 1983–84; FL C – 2011–12; Division 2 – 1965–66, 1977–78; FL 1 – 2010–11; Division 3 – 1920–21.

FA Cup Winners: 1976.
Runners-up: 1900, 1902, 2003.

League Cup: *Runners-up:* 1979, 2017.

League Trophy Winners: 2010.

Full Members' Cup: *Runners-up:* 1992.

European Competitions
Fairs Cup: 1969–70.
UEFA Cup: 1971–72, 1981–82, 1982–83, 1984–85, 2003–04.
Europa League: 2015–16, 2016–17.
European Cup-Winners' Cup: 1976–77 *(qf)*.

FOOTBALL YEARBOOK FACT FILE

After defeating Millwall 2-0 at The Dell in an FA Cup quarter-final replay in March 1927, Southampton fans had to wait almost 20 years for the next home win in the competition. It was on 5 January 1946 that Saints finally ended the sequence with a 4-3 victory over Newport County.

Record Defeat: 0–9 v Leicester C, Premier League, 25 October 2019.

Most League Points (2 for a win): 61, Division 3 (S), 1921–22 and Division 3, 1959–60.

Most League Points (3 for a win): 92, FL 1, 2010–11.

Most League Goals: 112, Division 3 (S), 1957–58.

Highest League Scorer in Season: Derek Reeves, 39, Division 3, 1959–60.

Most League Goals in Total Aggregate: Mike Channon, 185, 1966–77, 1979–82.

Most League Goals in One Match: 5, Charlie Wayman v Leicester C, Division 2, 23 October 1948.

Most Capped Player: Maya Yoshida, 83 (100), Japan.

Most League Appearances: Terry Paine, 713, 1956–74.

Youngest League Player: Theo Walcott, 16 years 143 days v Wolverhampton W, 6 August 2005.

Record Transfer Fee Received: £75,000,000 from Liverpool for Virgil van Dijk, January 2018.

Record Transfer Fee Paid: £19,000,000 to Monaco for Guido Carrillo, January 2018.

Football League Record: 1920 Original Member of Division 3; 1921–22 Division 3 (S); 1922–53 Division 2; 1953–58 Division 3 (S); 1958–60 Division 3; 1960–66 Division 2; 1966–74 Division 1; 1974–78 Division 2; 1978–92 Division 1; 1992–2005 Premier League; 2005–09 FL C; 2009–11 FL 1; 2011–12 FL C; 2012– Premier League.

LATEST SEQUENCES

Longest Sequence of League Wins: 10, 16.4.2011 – 20.8.2011.

Longest Sequence of League Defeats: 5, 16.8.1998 – 12.9.1998.

Longest Sequence of League Draws: 8, 29.8.2005 – 15.10.2005.

Longest Sequence of Unbeaten League Matches: 19, 5.9.1921 – 31.12.1921.

Longest Sequence Without a League Win: 20, 30.8.1969 – 27.12.1969.

Successive Scoring Runs: 28 from 10.2.2008.

Successive Non-scoring Runs: 5 from 22.9.2018.

MANAGERS

Cecil Knight 1894–95
(Secretary-Manager)
Charles Robson 1895–97
Ernest Arnfield 1897–1911
(Secretary-Manager)
(continued as Secretary)
George Swift 1911–12
Ernest Arnfield 1912–19
Jimmy McIntyre 1919–24
Arthur Chadwick 1925–31
George Kay 1931–36
George Gross 1936–37
Tom Parker 1937–43
J. R. Sarjantson stepped down from the board to act as Secretary-Manager 1943–47 with the next two listed being Team Managers during this period
Arthur Dominy 1943–46
Bill Dodgin Snr 1946–49
Sid Cann 1949–51
George Roughton 1952–55
Ted Bates 1955–73
Lawrie McMenemy 1973–85
Chris Nicholl 1985–91
Ian Branfoot 1991–94
Alan Ball 1994–95
Dave Merrington 1995–96
Graeme Souness 1996–97
Dave Jones 1997–2000
Glenn Hoddle 2000–01
Stuart Gray 2001
Gordon Strachan 2001–04
Paul Sturrock 2004
Steve Wigley 2004
Harry Redknapp 2004–05
George Burley 2005–08
Nigel Pearson 2008
Jan Poortvliet 2008–09
Mark Wotte 2009
Alan Pardew 2009–10
Nigel Adkins 2010–13
Mauricio Pochettino 2013–14
Ronald Koeman 2014–16
Claude Puel 2016–17
Mauricio Pellegrino 2017–18
Mark Hughes 2018
Ralph Hasenhüttl December 2018–

TEN YEAR LEAGUE RECORD

		P	W	D	L	F	A	Pts	Pos
2010-11	FL 1	46	28	8	10	86	38	92	2
2011-12	FL C	46	26	10	10	85	46	88	2
2012-13	PR Lge	38	9	14	15	49	60	41	14
2013-14	PR Lge	38	15	11	12	54	46	56	8
2014-15	PR Lge	38	18	6	14	54	33	60	7
2015-16	PR Lge	38	18	9	11	59	41	63	6
2016-17	PR Lge	38	12	10	16	41	48	46	8
2017-18	PR Lge	38	7	15	16	37	56	36	17
2018-19	PR Lge	38	9	12	17	45	65	39	16
2019-20	PR Lge	38	15	7	16	51	60	52	11

DID YOU KNOW ?

The first time Southampton appeared on the BBC's flagship programme *Match of the Day* was on 29 October 1966. Viewers were able to see highlights of Saints' 1-0 win at Leeds United, with the winning goal coming from Ron Davies in the second half.

SOUTHAMPTON – PREMIER LEAGUE 2019–20 LEAGUE RECORD

Match No.	Date	Venue	Opponents	Result		H/T Score	Lg Pos.	Goalscorers	Attendance
1	Aug 10	A	Burnley	L	0-3	0-0	18		19,784
2	17	H	Liverpool	L	1-2	0-1	18	Ings 83	31,712
3	24	A	Brighton & HA	W	2-0	0-0	17	Djenepo 55, Redmond 90	30,019
4	31	H	Manchester U	D	1-1	0-1	13	Vestergaard 58	30,499
5	Sept 14	A	Sheffield U	W	1-0	0-0	10	Djenepo 66	30,985
6	20	H	Bournemouth	L	1-3	0-2	11	Ward-Prowse (pen) 53	30,168
7	28	A	Tottenham H	L	1-2	1-2	14	Ings 39	59,645
8	Oct 6	H	Chelsea	L	1-4	1-3	17	Ings 30	31,473
9	19	A	Wolverhampton W	D	1-1	0-0	17	Ings 53	30,915
10	25	H	Leicester C	L	0-9	0-5	18		28,762
11	Nov 2	A	Manchester C	L	1-2	1-0	18	Ward-Prowse 13	53,922
12	9	H	Everton	L	1-2	0-1	19	Ings 50	29,754
13	23	A	Arsenal	D	2-2	1-1	19	Ings 8, Ward-Prowse 71	60,295
14	30	H	Watford	W	2-1	0-1	18	Ings 78, Ward-Prowse 83	26,929
15	Dec 4	H	Norwich C	W	2-1	2-0	17	Ings 22, Bertrand 43	27,019
16	8	A	Newcastle U	L	1-2	0-0	18	Ings 52	42,303
17	14	H	West Ham U	L	0-1	0-1	18		27,701
18	21	A	Aston Villa	W	3-1	2-0	17	Ings 2 21, 51, Stephens 31	41,834
19	26	A	Chelsea	W	2-0	1-0	14	Obafemi 31, Redmond 73	40,651
20	28	H	Crystal Palace	D	1-1	0-0	15	Ings 74	31,108
21	Jan 1	H	Tottenham H	W	1-0	1-0	12	Ings 17	30,976
22	11	A	Leicester C	W	2-1	1-1	12	Armstrong 19, Ings 81	32,115
23	18	H	Wolverhampton W	L	2-3	2-0	13	Bednarek 15, Long 35	31,152
24	21	A	Crystal Palace	W	2-0	1-0	9	Redmond 22, Armstrong 48	23,739
25	Feb 1	A	Liverpool	L	0-4	0-0	11		53,291
26	15	H	Burnley	L	1-2	1-1	13	Ings 18	26,302
27	22	H	Aston Villa	W	2-0	1-0	12	Long 8, Armstrong 90	31,478
28	29	A	West Ham U	L	1-3	1-2	13	Obafemi 31	59,962
29	Mar 7	H	Newcastle U	L	0-1	0-0	14		30,096
30	June 19	A	Norwich C	W	3-0	0-0	13	Ings 49, Armstrong 54, Redmond 79	0
31	25	H	Arsenal	L	0-2	0-1	14		0
32	28	A	Watford	W	3-1	1-0	13	Ings 2 16, 70, Ward-Prowse 82	0
33	July 5	H	Manchester C	W	1-0	1-0	13	Adams 16	0
34	9	A	Everton	D	1-1	1-1	12	Ings 31	0
35	13	A	Manchester U	D	2-2	1-2	12	Armstrong 12, Obafemi 90	0
36	16	H	Brighton & HA	D	1-1	0-1	12	Ings 66	0
37	19	A	Bournemouth	W	2-0	1-0	11	Ings 41, Adams 90	0
38	26	H	Sheffield U	W	3-1	0-1	11	Adams 2 50, 71, Ings (pen) 84	0

Final League Position: 11

GOALSCORERS

League (51): Ings 22 (1 pen), Armstrong 5, Ward-Prowse 5 (1 pen), Adams 4, Redmond 4, Obafemi 3, Djenepo 2, Long 2, Bednarek 1, Bertrand 1, Stephens 1, Vestergaard 1.
FA Cup (5): Boufal 1, Ings 1, Long 1, Smallbone 1, Vokins 1.
Carabao Cup (6): Ings 2, Cedric 1, Obafemi 1, Redmond 1, Stephens 1.
Leasing.com Trophy (4): Slattery 2 (1 pen), Hale 1, N'Lundulu 1.

Gunn A 10	Bednarek J 34	Stephens J 27 + 1	Vestergaard J 17 + 2	Valery Y 10 + 1	Romeu O 20 + 10	Ward-Prowse J 38	Bertrand R 31 + 1	Ings D 32 + 6	Redmond N 32	Adams C 12 + 18	Obafemi M 8 + 13	Hojbjerg P 30 + 3	Boufal S 8 + 12	Yoshida M 6 + 2	Armstrong S 19 + 11	Djenepo M 10 + 8	Danso K 3 + 3	Cedric Soares R 16	Long S 15 + 11	McCarthy A 28	Walker-Peters K 7 + 3	Smallbone W 4 + 5	Tella N — + 1	Vokins J 1	*Match No.*
1	2	3^{2}	4	5	6	7	8	9^{1}	10	11^{3}	12	13	14												1
1	2		4	5	7^{1}	6	9^{3}	12	11	10^{2}		8		3	13	14									2
1	3		4	2^{1}	6	8		11^{3}	9	10^{2}		7	13		14	12	5								3
1	3		4		6	8		11^{3}		10^{1}		7	9^{2}	14	13		5■	2	12						4
1	2		4		6	9		12		11^{3}		7	10^{2}	3	13	8^{1}		5	14						5
1	3		4		6	8	12	13	10^{3}	11^{2}		7	9		14		2^{1}	5							6
1	2		4^{1}		6	5	8	11^{2}	10		13	7	9^{3}	3	12				14						7
1	3			2	7	6	5	10^{2}	9^{3}	13	12	8	14	4					11^{1}						8
1	2		4	5^{1}	6^{2}	9	8	11	10			7	12	3			13								9
1	2	12	4^{1}	5^{3}	7	6	9■	10^{2}	11			8		3	14		13								10
	3^{3}	4	5	2^{1}	8	7		10^{2}	11	14		6			9	13	12			1					11
	2	3	4		7	6		10	9^{2}	13	14		12		5^{3}	11		8^{1}		1					12
	4	3				7	5	11^{1}	9		10^{2}	8	14		6^{3}	13		2	12	1					13
	4	3		14		7	5	10	9^{1}		11^{2}	8	13			6		2^{3}	12	1					14
	4	3			12	7	5	10^{2}	9	13		8		14		6^{1}		2	11^{3}	1					15
	4	3				7	5	11^{2}	9	13		8	12			6^{1}		2	10	1					16
	4	3			12	7	5	11	9^{1}	14		8			13	6		2^{3}	10^{2}	1					17
	4	3			12	7	5	11^{3}	9	14	13	8			6^{1}			2	10^{2}	1					18
	4	3			14	7	5	12	9	11^{2}	10^{1}	8	13		6^{3}			2		1					19
	4	3				7	5	11	9	10^{1}		8	6^{2}		13	12		2		1					20
	4	3			14	7	5	10^{2}	11		13	8			6^{3}	9^{1}		2	12	1					21
	4	3			14	7	5	11	9^{3}	12		8			6^{2}	13		2	10^{1}	1					22
	4	3				7	5	11	9^{3}	12		8	14		6^{1}	13		2	10^{2}	1					23
		3	4		12	7	5	13	9	14	11^{3}	8			6			2^{1}	10^{2}	1					24
	4	3			7	2	5	11^{2}	9	12	13	8	14			6^{3}			10^{1}	1					25
		3	4			6	5	10		14	13	7	9^{1}		8	12			11^{3}	1	2^{2}				26
	4	3			14	2	5	11^{1}		12	13	8			6	9			10^{2}	1		7^{3}			27
	4	3	13		14	2	5	12			11^{2}	8	9^{1}		6				10	1		7^{3}			28
	4	3		2		7	5	11		12	13	8	6^{2}			9■			10^{1}	1					29
	4	3		2^{5}		7	5	10^{3}	9^{4}	12	11^{2}	8	16		6^{1}					1	15	13	14		30
	4	3■	14	2^{1}	15	7	5	10^{4}	9		11^{2}	8^{3}			6				13	1	12				31
	3		4		8	7	5	11	9	13					12				10^{2}	1	2	6^{1}			32
	4	3			8	7	5	10	9	11^{1}					6^{2}				12	1	2	13			33
	4	3			8^{1}	7	5	11	9	10^{2}		12			6^{3}				13	1	2	14			34
	4	3			8^{3}	7	5	10	9	11^{1}	14				6^{2}				12	1	2	13			35
	3		4		8^{1}	7		10	9	12	11^{2}	2			14					1	13	6^{3}		5	36
		3	4		8^{2}	7	5	11^{3}	9	12	14	13			6				10^{1}	1	2				37
		3	4		8^{3}	7	5	11	9	10^{2}	14				6^{1}				13	1	2	12			38

FA Cup

Third Round	Huddersfield T	(h)	2-0
Fourth Round	Tottenham H	(h)	1-1
Replay	Tottenham H	(a)	2-3

Carabao Cup

Second Round	Fulham	(a)	1-0
Third Round	Portsmouth	(a)	4-0
Fourth Round	Manchester C	(a)	1-3

Leasing.com Trophy (Southampton U21)

Group D (S)	Forest Green R	(a)	2-3
Group D (S)	Walsall	(a)	0-1
Group D (S)	Coventry C	(a)	2-3

SOUTHEND UNITED

FOUNDATION

The leading club in Southend around the turn of the 20th century was Southend Athletic, but they were an amateur concern. Southend United was a more ambitious professional club when they were founded in 1906, employing Bob Jack as secretary-manager and immediately joining the Second Division of the Southern League.

Roots Hall Stadium, Victoria Avenue, Southend-on-Sea, Essex SS2 6NQ.

Telephone: (01702) 304 050.

Ticket Office: (08444) 770 077.

Website: www.southendunited.co.uk

Email: info@southend-united.co.uk

Ground Capacity: 12,055.

Record Attendance: 22,862 v Tottenham H, FA Cup 3rd rd replay, 11 January 1936 (at Southend Stadium); 31,090 v Liverpool, FA Cup 3rd rd, 10 January 1979 (at Roots Hall).

Pitch Measurements: 100.5m × 67.5m (110yd × 74yd).

Chairman: Ron Martin.

Manager: Mark Molesley.

Assistant Manager: Tom Prodomo.

Colours: Navy blue shirts with white trim, navy blue shorts, white socks.

Year Formed: 1906.

Turned Professional: 1906.

Club Nicknames: 'The Blues', 'The Shrimpers'.

Grounds: 1906, Roots Hall, Prittlewell; 1920, Kursaal; 1934, Southend Stadium; 1955, Roots Hall Football Ground.

First Football League Game: 28 August 1920, Division 3, v Brighton & HA (a) W 2–0 – Capper; Reid, Newton; Wileman, Henderson, Martin; Nicholls, Nuttall, Fairclough (2), Myers, Dorsett.

Record League Victory: 9–2 v Newport Co, Division 3 (S), 5 September 1936 – McKenzie; Nelson, Everest (1); Deacon, Turner, Carr; Bolan, Lane (1), Goddard (4), Dickinson (2), Oswald (1).

Record Cup Victory: 10–1 v Golders Green, FA Cup 1st rd, 24 November 1934 – Moore; Morfitt, Kelly; Mackay, Joe Wilson, Carr (1); Lane (1), Johnson (5), Cheesmuir (2), Deacon (1), Oswald. 10–1 v Brentwood, FA Cup 2nd rd, 7 December 1968 – Roberts; Bentley, Birks; McMillan (1) Beesley, Kurila; Clayton, Chisnall, Moore (4), Best (5), Hamilton. 10–1 v Aldershot, Leyland DAF Cup prel rd, 6 November 1990 – Sansome; Austin, Powell, Cornwell, Prior (1), Tilson (3), Cawley, Butler, Ansah (1), Benjamin (1), Angell (4).

Record Defeat: 1–9 v Brighton & HA, Division 3, 27 November 1965; 0–8 v Crystal Palace, League Cup 2nd rd (1st leg), 25 September 1990.

HONOURS

League Champions: FL 1 – 2005–06; Division 4 – 1980–81.
Runners-up: Division 3 – 1990–91; Division 4 – 1971–72, 1977–78.

FA Cup: 3rd rd – 1921; 5th rd – 1926, 1952, 1976, 1993.

League Cup: quarter-final – 2007.

League Trophy: *Runners-up:* 2004, 2005, 2013.

FOOTBALL YEARBOOK FACT FILE

Southend United changed their colours to red and yellow hooped shirts for the 1910–11 season, hoping this would bring the team good fortune. However, the new strip was unpopular and the team were dubbed 'the Beef and Mustards'. United finished second bottom of the table and were relegated to the Second Division of the Southern League, with the traditional blue shirts being quickly restored.

Most League Points (2 for a win): 67, Division 4, 1980–81.

Most League Points (3 for a win): 85, Division 3, 1990–91.

Most League Goals: 92, Division 3 (S), 1950–51.

Highest League Scorer in Season: Jim Shankly, 31, 1928–29; Sammy McCrory, 1957–58, both in Division 3 (S).

Most League Goals in Total Aggregate: Roy Hollis, 122, 1953–60.

Most League Goals in One Match: 5, Jim Shankly v Merthyr T, Division 3 (S), 1 March 1930.

Most Capped Player: Jason Demetriou, 20 (51), Cyprus.

Most League Appearances: Sandy Anderson, 452, 1950–63.

Youngest League Player: Phil O'Connor, 16 years 76 days v Lincoln C, 26 December 1969.

Record Transfer Fee Received: £2,000,000 (rising to £2,750,000) from Nottingham F for Stan Collymore, June 1993.

Record Transfer Fee Paid: £500,000 to Galatasaray for Mike Marsh, September 1995.

Football League Record: 1920 Original Member of Division 3; 1921–58 Division 3 (S); 1958–66 Division 3; 1966–72 Division 4; 1972–76 Division 3; 1976–78 Division 4; 1978–80 Division 3; 1980–81 Division 4; 1981–84 Division 3; 1984–87 Division 4; 1987–89 Division 3; 1989–90 Division 4; 1990–91 Division 3; 1991–92 Division 2; 1992–97 Division 1; 1997–98 Division 2; 1998–2004 Division 3; 2004–05 FL 2; 2005–06 FL 1; 2006–07 FL C; 2007–10 FL 1; 2010–15 FL 2; 2015–20 FL 1; 2020– FL 2.

LATEST SEQUENCES

Longest Sequence of League Wins: 8, 29.8.2005 – 9.10.2005.

Longest Sequence of League Defeats: 7, 16.4.2016 – 13.8.2016.

Longest Sequence of League Draws: 6, 30.1.1982 – 19.2.1982.

Longest Sequence of Unbeaten League Matches: 16, 20.2.1932 – 29.8.1932.

Longest Sequence Without a League Win: 17, 26.8.2006 – 2.12.2006.

Successive Scoring Runs: 24 from 23.3.1929.

Successive Non-scoring Runs: 6 from 6.4.1979.

MANAGERS

Bob Jack 1906–10
George Molyneux 1910–11
O. M. Howard 1911–12
Joe Bradshaw 1912–19
Ned Liddell 1919–20
Tom Mather 1920–21
Ted Birnie 1921–34
David Jack 1934–40
Harry Warren 1946–56
Eddie Perry 1956–60
Frank Broome 1960
Ted Fenton 1961–65
Alvan Williams 1965–67
Ernie Shepherd 1967–69
Geoff Hudson 1969–70
Arthur Rowley 1970–76
Dave Smith 1976–83
Peter Morris 1983–84
Bobby Moore 1984–86
Dave Webb 1986–87
Dick Bate 1987
Paul Clark 1987–88
Dave Webb *(General Manager)* 1988–92
Colin Murphy 1992–93
Barry Fry 1993
Peter Taylor 1993–95
Steve Thompson 1995
Ronnie Whelan 1995–97
Alvin Martin 1997–99
Alan Little 1999–2000
David Webb 2000–01
Rob Newman 2001–03
Steve Wignall 2003
Steve Tilson 2003–10
Paul Sturrock 2010–13
Phil Brown 2013–18
Chris Powell 2018–19
Kevin Bond 2019
Sol Campbell 2019–20
Mark Molesley August 2020–

TEN YEAR LEAGUE RECORD

		P	*W*	*D*	*L*	*F*	*A*	*Pts*	*Pos*
2010-11	FL 2	46	16	13	17	62	56	61	13
2011-12	FL 2	46	25	8	13	77	48	83	4
2012-13	FL 2	46	16	13	17	61	55	61	11
2013-14	FL 2	46	19	15	12	56	39	72	5
2014-15	FL 2	46	24	12	10	54	38	84	5
2015-16	FL 1	46	16	11	19	58	64	59	14
2016-17	FL 1	46	20	12	14	70	53	72	7
2017-18	FL 1	46	17	12	17	58	62	63	10
2018-19	FL 1	46	14	8	24	55	68	50	19
2019-20	FL 1	35	4	7	24	39	85	19	22§

§Decided on points-per-game (0.54)

DID YOU KNOW ?

Southend United's Roots Hall ground hosted rugby league in the 1984–85 season when Kent Invicta moved in and rebranded under the name Southend Invicta. The move was not a success and the highest crowd attracted was 504 for the New Year's Day game against Fulham. The team finished second from bottom of the Second Division table and folded shortly afterwards.

SOUTHEND UNITED – SKY BET LEAGUE ONE 2019–20 LEAGUE RECORD

Match No.	*Date*	*Venue*	*Opponents*	*Result*	*H/T Score*	*Lg Pos.*	*Goalscorers*	*Attendance*
1	Aug 3	A	Coventry C	L 0-1	0-0	16		6534
2	10	H	Blackpool	L 1-3	0-3	21	Turton (og) [75]	6823
3	17	A	Lincoln C	L 0-4	0-2	22		9016
4	20	H	Peterborough U	L 0-2	0-0	22		5890
5	24	A	Wycombe W	L 3-4	2-1	22	Goodship [11], Humphrys 2 [30, 47]	4196
6	31	H	Rochdale	L 0-3	0-2	22		5614
7	Sept 14	H	Fleetwood T	D 3-3	1-2	22	McLaughlin [17], Humphrys 2 [48, 87]	5236
8	17	A	Shrewsbury T	L 3-4	1-2	22	McLaughlin [29], Humphrys [77], Cox [90]	4909
9	21	A	Milton Keynes D	W 1-0	1-0	21	Kelman [4]	7493
10	28	H	Accrington S	L 0-1	0-0	21		5643
11	Oct 5	A	Gillingham	L 1-3	0-1	22	Cox [58]	5091
12	12	H	AFC Wimbledon	L 1-4	1-2	22	Dieng [13]	6420
13	18	A	Tranmere R	D 1-1	1-0	22	Hopper [9]	7066
14	22	H	Doncaster R	L 1-7	1-2	22	Hutchinson [11]	5066
15	26	H	Ipswich T	L 1-3	0-1	22	Acquah [83]	8632
16	Nov 2	A	Sunderland	L 0-1	0-1	22		30,407
17	5	A	Portsmouth	L 1-4	0-1	22	Goodship [69]	16,995
18	23	H	Oxford U	L 0-4	0-2	22		6835
19	Dec 3	A	Burton Alb	D 1-1	1-0	22	McLaughlin [21]	1880
20	7	A	Bristol R	L 2-4	2-0	22	Hopper [13], Goodship [36]	6797
21	14	H	Rotherham U	D 2-2	0-1	22	Demetriou (pen) [49], Mantom [52]	5652
22	21	A	Bolton W	L 2-3	1-2	22	Lennon [10], Dieng [81]	12,055
23	26	H	Milton Keynes D	D 2-2	1-1	22	Demetriou (pen) [32], Kiernan [66]	6189
24	Jan 1	A	AFC Wimbledon	D 1-1	0-1	22	Kelman (pen) [90]	4422
25	11	H	Tranmere R	D 0-0	0-0	22		5988
26	18	A	Accrington S	W 2-1	1-1	22	Kelman [11], Demetriou (pen) [51]	2146
27	28	A	Doncaster R	L 1-3	0-2	22	Phillips [69]	7063
28	Feb 1	H	Lincoln C	W 2-1	0-0	22	Kelman [63], Bwomono [90]	6605
29	8	A	Blackpool	L 1-2	0-1	22	McLaughlin [72]	7870
30	11	A	Peterborough U	L 0-4	0-0	22		5036
31	15	H	Coventry C	L 0-2	0-0	22		7278
32	18	H	Gillingham	L 0-1	0-0	22		6021
33	22	H	Burton Alb	L 2-3	1-1	22	Mantom [29], O'Toole (og) [90]	5571
34	29	A	Oxford U	L 1-2	1-1	22	Gard [45]	7451
35	Mar 7	H	Bristol R	W 3-1	1-0	22	Kelman [18], Egbri [55], Kilgour (og) [79]	5806
36	14	A	Rotherham U	Cancelled				
37	21	H	Bolton W	Cancelled				
38	28	H	Sunderland	Cancelled				
39	Apr 4	A	Ipswich T	Cancelled				
40	10	H	Wycombe W	Cancelled				
41	13	A	Rochdale	Cancelled				
42	18	H	Portsmouth	Cancelled				
43	25	A	Fleetwood T	Cancelled				
44	5 3	H	Shrewsbury T	Cancelled				

Final League Position: 22 (on points-per-game basis)

GOALSCORERS

League (39): Humphrys 5, Kelman 5 (1 pen), McLaughlin 4, Demetriou 3 (3 pens), Goodship 3, Cox 2, Dieng 2, Hopper 2, Mantom 2, Acquah 1, Bwomono 1, Egbri 1, Gard 1, Hutchinson 1, Kiernan 1, Lennon 1, Phillips 1, own goals 3.
FA Cup (0).
Carabao Cup (3): Kelman 2, Goodship 1.
Leasing.com Trophy (3): Hamilton 1, Hopper 1, Ralph 1.

Oxley M 19	Bwomono E 34	Shaughnessy J 14 + 2	Lennon H 15 + 1	Ralph N 17	Mantom S 21 + 1	Milligan M 30	Hyam L 2 + 3	McLaughlin S 27	Robinson T 1 + 2	Goodship B 14 + 9	Hutchinson I 12 + 10	Humphrys S 14 + 7	Gunnarsson P 3	Cox S 16 + 3	Ridgewell L 1	Gard L 2	Ndukwu L — + 7	Kelman C 12 + 6	Bishop N 12	White J 9 + 2	Hamilton E 12 + 2	Blackman A 1 + 2	Demetriou J 15 + 5	Kiernan R 17 + 2	Acquah E — + 7	Dieng T 21	Hopper T 12 + 2	Rush M 1 + 6	Taylor R 2	Kinali E 3 + 3	Barratt S 3 + 6	Phillips H 2	Clifford T 8	Mitchell-Nelson M 5 + 1	Coker K — + 2	Egbri T 6	Taylor C — + 1	Seaden H 1	Kyprianou H 1	Match No.
1	2	3	4	5	6	7	8^{2}	9^{1}	10^{3}	11	12	13		14																										1
1	5	2	3	9	8^{2}	7			13		6	11^{3}		10	4^{1}		12	14																						2
	2	3		5	8^{1}	7		9^{3}			6	13		10			14	11^{2}	1	4	12																			3
	8	3	4	5^{1}	9	6				10^{2}		12		11			14		1	2^{3}	7	13																		4
	5^{2}	3	4	9	6	7			13	11^{1}		10^{3}					12		1	2	8	14																		5
1			4	5		6	7			10^{1}		11		9			12	14		3^{3}	8^{2}		2	13																6
1	2		4		7			9^{2}		12	6^{1}	11		10			14				8	5^{3}	13	3																7
1	2		4	5^{2}	6		12	8		10		9		11							7^{1}		13	3																8
1	2		4	5		7	13	9^{3}		11^{1}	12			10				6		14	8^{2}			3																9
1	2		4	5■	13	8		9		12	14	10		11^{3}				6^{1}			7^{2}			3																10
1	5	12	3			8		9			6^{1}	11		10							7		2^{2}	4	13■															11
1	2^{3}	3	4^{2}	5^{1}				9		11	12			10							8		14	7		6	13													12
	2^{3}	3		5		4		9			6^{1}	12		10					1		7		13		14	8	11^{2}													13
	2	4	13	5		3		10■			8	12		9					1		7■					6^{2}	11^{1}													14
1	5	3		8		6^{1}					7	10		9									13	2	12	4	11^{2}													15
	5	2	4	8		6^{2}	14			9^{3}	7			10					1						12	3	11^{1}	13												16
	2	3	5^{2}	6		7				8	9			10^{1}					1					13	12	4	11^{3}	14												17
	2			6		7		9		13	12			10					1		8^{1}			3		4	11		5^{2}											18
	2			5	8^{3}			9^{1}		6^{2}	11	12		13					1				7	4		3	10			14										19
	2				8	9		10		6^{3}		12							1		13		7^{1}	4	14	3	11^{2}		5											20
	2		5		8^{3}	9		6^{1}		10^{2}	12	11		13			14		1				7	3		4														21
	2		5^{2}		9	6		7		10^{3}		11							1	12			8^{1}	4		3	13	14												22
1	5				8	7		9^{1}		13		11^{2}						12		2			6	4		3	10													23
1	2				8	7		9			12	10^{2}						13					6^{3}	4		3	11			5^{1}	14									24
1	5				8	7		9				11^{1}						12		4			6^{2}	2		3	10				13									25
1	5				8	7		9		12								10^{1}		2			6	4		3^{2}	11				13									26
1	3				8^{2}	7		6		14	13	10^{3}						11		4			2^{1}	5							12	9								27
1	3					8		10		12	9^{3}							11		4^{2}			2								6	7^{1}	5	13	14					28
1	3				11	7		9		12	8^{3}							10^{2}					2			4		14		13	6^{1}		5							29
1	3				9^{1}	8		10										12					7		13	4		11^{2}					5	2		6				30
1^{3}	2				8	7				10^{2}	13							11								4					9^{1}		5	3	12	6	14			31
	2	12			7	8		11										10								4		13					9	3		6^{1}		1	5^{2}	32
	2	3			6^{1}	8		11					1					10								7				12	13		5	4		9^{2}				33
	2	4				7		8^{2}		14	13		1			6^{1}		10								3				11	12		5			9^{3}				34
	3	4						10					1			9^{1}		11					8					12		7			5	2		6				35
																																								36
																																								37
																																								38
																																								39
																																								40
																																								41
																																								42
																																								43
																																								44

FA Cup

First Round	Dover Ath	(a)	0-1

Carabao Cup

First Round	Stevenage	(a)	2-1
Second Round	Milton Keynes D	(h)	1-4

Leasing.com Trophy

Group C (S)	Leyton Orient	(a)	0-2
Group C (S)	Brighton & HA U21	(h)	0-2
Group C (S)	AFC Wimbledon	(h)	3-1

STEVENAGE

FOUNDATION

There have been several clubs associated with the town of Stevenage. Stevenage Town was formed in 1884. They absorbed Stevenage Rangers in 1955 and later played at Broadhall Way. The club went into liquidation in 1968 and Stevenage Athletic was formed, but they, too, followed a similar path in 1976. Then Stevenage Borough was founded. The Broadhall Way pitch was dug up and remained unused for three years. Thus the new club started its life in the modest surrounds of the King George V playing fields with a roped-off ground in the Chiltern League. A change of competition followed to the Wallspan Southern Combination and by 1980 the club returned to the council-owned Broadhall Way when "Borough" was added to the name. Entry into the United Counties League was so successful the league and cup were won in the first season. On to the Isthmian League Division Two and the climb up the pyramid continued. In 1995–96 Stevenage Borough won the Conference but was denied a place in the Football League as the ground did not measure up to the competition's standards. Subsequent improvements changed this and the 7,100 capacity venue became one of the best appointed grounds in non-league football. After winning elevation to the Football League the club dropped Borough from its title.

Lamex Stadium, Broadhall Way, Stevenage, Hertfordshire SG2 8RH.

Telephone: (01438) 223 223.

Ticket Office: (01438) 223 223.

Website: stevenagefc.com

Email: info@stevenagefc.com

Ground Capacity: 7,800.

Record Attendance: 8,040 v Newcastle U, FA Cup 4th rd, 25 January 1998.

Pitch Measurements: 104m × 64m (114yd × 70yd).

Chairman: Phil Wallace.

Chief Executive Officer: Alex Tunbridge.

Manager: Alex Revell.

First-Team Coaches: Ronnie Henry, Mark Sampson.

Colours: Red and white striped shirts, white shorts with red trim, white socks with red trim.

Year Formed: 1976.

Turned Professional: 1976.

Nickname: 'The Boro'.

Previous Name: 1976, Stevenage Borough; 2010, Stevenage.

HONOURS

League Champions: Conference – 1995–96, 2009–10.

FA Cup: 5th rd – 2012.

League Cup: 2nd rd – 2012, 2017.

FOOTBALL YEARBOOK FACT FILE

When Stevenage were drawn at home to Newcastle United in the FA Cup fourth round in January 1998 the Magpies tried, unsuccessfully, to have the game switched to an alternative venue. The Borough installed a temporary stand which raised the capacity from 6,500 and were rewarded with a record attendance of 8,040 and a 1-1 draw to earn a lucrative replay at St James' Park.

Grounds: 1976, King George V playing fields; 1980, Broadhall Way (renamed Lamex Stadium 2009).

First Football League Game: 7 August 2010, FL 2, v Macclesfield T (h) D 2–2 – Day; Henry, Laird, Bostwick, Roberts, Foster, Wilson (Sinclair), Byrom, Griffin (1), Winn (Odubade), Vincenti (1) (Beardsley).

Record League Victory: 6–0 v Yeovil T, FL 2, 14 April 2012 – Day; Lascelles (1), Laird, Roberts (1), Ashton (1), Shroot (Mousinho), Wilson (Myrie-Williams), Long, Agyemang (1), Reid (Slew), Freeman (2).

Record Victory: 11–1 v British Timken Ath 1980–81.

Record Defeat: 0–8 v Charlton Ath, FL Trophy, 9 October 2018.

Most League Points (3 for a win): 73, FL 1, 2011–12.

Most League Goals: 69, FL 1, 2011–12.

Highest League Scorer in Season: Matthew Godden, 20, FL 2, 2016–17.

Most League Goals in Total Aggregate: Matthew Godden, 30, 2016–18.

Most League Goals in One Match: 3, Chris Holroyd v Hereford U, FL 2, 28 September 2010; 3, Dani Lopez v Sheffield U, FL 1, 16 March 2013; 3, Chris Whelpdale v Morecambe, FL 2, 28 November 2015; 3, Matthew Godden v Newport Co, FL 2, 7 January 2017; 3, Alex Revell v Exeter C, FL 2, 28 April 2018.

Most Capped Player: Terence Vancooten, 11, Guyana.

Most League Appearances: Ronnie Henry, 230, 2014–19.

Youngest League Player: Liam Smyth, 17 years 47 days v Port Vale, 23 October 2018.

Record Transfer Fee Received: £1,500,000 from Watford for Ben Wilmot, May 2018.

Record Transfer Fee Paid: £125,000 to Exeter C for James Dunne, May 2012.

Football League Record: 2011 Promoted from Conference Premier; 2010–11 FL 2; 2011–14 FL 1; 2014– FL 2.

MANAGERS

Derek Montgomery 1976–83
Frank Cornwell 1983–87
John Bailey 1987–88
Brian Wilcox 1988–90
Paul Fairclough 1990–98
Richard Hill 1998–2000
Steve Wignall 2000
Paul Fairclough 2000–02
Wayne Turner 2002–03
Graham Westley 2003–06
Mark Stimson 2006–07
Peter Taylor 2007–08
Graham Westley 2008–12
Gary Smith 2012–13
Graham Westley 2013–15
Teddy Sheringham 2015–16
Darren Sarll 2016–18
Dino Maamria 2018–19
Graham Westley 2019–20
Alex Revell February 2020–

LATEST SEQUENCES

Longest Sequence of League Wins: 6, 12.3.2011 – 2.4.2011.

Longest Sequence of League Defeats: 8, 25.1.2020 – 7.3.2020.

Longest Sequence of League Draws: 5, 17.3.2012 – 31.3.2012.

Longest Sequence of Unbeaten League Matches: 17, 9.4.2012 – 5.10.2012.

Longest Sequence Without a League Win: 12, 3.8.2019 – 5.10.2019.

Successive Scoring Runs: 17 from 9.4.2012.

Successive Non-scoring Runs: 5 from 3.8.2019.

TEN YEAR LEAGUE RECORD

		P	W	D	L	F	A	Pts	Pos
2010-11	FL 2	46	18	15	13	62	45	69	6
2011-12	FL 1	46	18	19	9	69	44	73	6
2012-13	FL 1	46	15	9	22	47	64	54	18
2013-14	FL 1	46	11	9	26	46	72	42	24
2014-15	FL 2	46	20	12	14	62	54	72	6
2015-16	FL 2	46	11	15	20	52	67	48	18
2016-17	FL 2	46	20	7	19	67	63	67	10
2017-18	FL 2	46	14	13	19	60	65	55	16
2018-19	FL 2	46	20	10	16	59	55	70	10
2019-20	FL 2	36	3	13	20	24	50	22	23§

§Decided on points-per-game (0.61)

DID YOU KNOW ?

Stevenage Borough took part in the FA Vase between 1982–83 and 1990–91. Their best performance came in 1985–86 when they battled their way through six rounds only to fall to Southall in the quarter-finals.

STEVENAGE – SKY BET LEAGUE TWO 2019–20 LEAGUE RECORD

Match No.	Date	Venue	Opponents	Result	H/T Score	Lg Pos.	Goalscorers	Attendance
1	Aug 3	A	Salford C	L 0-2	0-1	21		3416
2	10	H	Exeter C	L 0-1	0-0	23		2398
3	17	A	Leyton Orient	D 0-0	0-0	22		5104
4	20	H	Bradford C	L 0-1	0-1	22		2833
5	24	A	Mansfield T	D 0-0	0-0	23		3982
6	31	H	Macclesfield T	D 2-2	0-1	23	Guthrie [68], Wildin [72]	2504
7	Sept 7	A	Cheltenham T	L 2-4	0-1	23	Newton 2 [48, 72]	2708
8	14	H	Carlisle U	L 2-3	1-1	24	Guthrie 2 [25, 54]	2616
9	17	H	Northampton T	L 0-1	0-0	24		2877
10	21	A	Forest Green R	D 0-0	0-0	24		1881
11	28	H	Cambridge U	D 1-1	1-0	24	Cowley [9]	3452
12	Oct 5	A	Colchester U	L 1-3	1-0	24	Cowley [17]	3331
13	12	H	Grimsby T	W 2-1	2-0	23	Guthrie [17], Carter [44]	3220
14	19	A	Port Vale	D 1-1	1-1	24	Guthrie (pen) [23]	4429
15	22	A	Swindon T	L 0-1	0-0	24		5524
16	26	H	Morecambe	W 1-0	0-0	23	Cuthbert [82]	2288
17	Nov 2	A	Scunthorpe U	D 0-0	0-0	23		3309
18	23	A	Walsall	D 0-0	0-0	23		4938
19	Dec 7	H	Crawley T	D 0-0	0-0	23		2780
20	14	A	Newport Co	D 1-1	1-0	23	Sonupe [12]	3556
21	21	H	Crewe Alex	L 1-5	0-2	24	Cuthbert [84]	2993
22	26	H	Forest Green R	D 0-0	0-0	24		2388
23	29	A	Plymouth Arg	L 1-2	0-1	24	List [60]	11,719
24	Jan 1	A	Northampton T	L 0-1	0-0	24		4613
25	4	H	Colchester U	D 0-0	0-0	23		3027
26	11	H	Port Vale	L 0-1	0-0	24		2646
27	14	H	Oldham Ath	D 0-0	0-0	24		2156
28	18	A	Cambridge U	W 4-0	1-0	23	List [36], Cassidy [59], Carter [87], Lakin [90]	4228
29	25	H	Plymouth Arg	L 1-2	0-0	24	Carter [89]	3627
30	28	A	Grimsby T	L 1-3	0-1	24	Lakin [90]	4175
31	Feb 1	H	Leyton Orient	L 0-3	0-1	24		4357
32	8	A	Exeter C	L 1-2	0-1	24	Kemp [79]	4458
33	11	A	Bradford C	L 1-3	1-0	24	Carter [26]	12,845
34	15	H	Salford C	L 0-1	0-1	24		3246
35	22	A	Crawley T	L 0-2	0-1	24		2232
36	Mar 7	A	Crewe Alex	L 1-3	0-1	24	Carter [90]	4263
37	14	H	Newport Co	Cancelled				
38	17	H	Swindon T	Cancelled				
39	21	A	Morecambe	Cancelled				
40	28	H	Scunthorpe U	Cancelled				
41	31	H	Walsall	Cancelled				
42	Apr 4	A	Oldham Ath	Cancelled				
43	10	H	Mansfield T	Cancelled				
44	13	A	Macclesfield T	Cancelled				
45	18	H	Cheltenham T	Cancelled				
46	25	A	Carlisle U	Cancelled				

Final League Position: 23 (on points-per-game basis)

GOALSCORERS

League (24): Carter 5, Guthrie 5 (1 pen), Cowley 2, Cuthbert 2, Lakin 2, List 2, Newton 2, Cassidy 1, Kemp 1, Sonupe 1, Wildin 1.
FA Cup (1): List 1.
Carabao Cup (1): Parrett 1.
Leasing.com Trophy (5): Cowley 3 (1 pen), Carter 1, Mackail-Smith 1.

Farman P 35	Vancooten T 12 + 4	Cuthbert S 21	Fielding J 1 + 2	Wildin L 21	Parrett D 11 + 6	Soares T 14 + 1	Iontton A 4 + 3	Stokes C 25	Sonupe E 5 + 4	Guthrie K 18 + 4 / Kemp D 5 + 1	Taylor P 5 + 5	Newton D 6 + 4 / Carroll C 2 + 2	Husin N 6 + 4	Cowley J 11 + 7 / Reading P 1	Watts K 14 + 2	Carter C 25 + 4	Fernandez L 2 + 2	Byrom J 5 + 1 / Folami B — + 2	Kennedy B 12 + 6	Smith J — + 1	Rollinson J — + 1	Lakin C 18 + 2	List E 19 + 2	El-Abd A 1 + 1	Mackail-Smith C 6 + 12	Denton T 13 + 2	Timlin M 11 + 6	Nugent B 23	Bastien S 1	Digby P 16 + 1	Smyth L — + 1	Revell A — + 2	Leesley J 7 + 1	Dabo D 8	Cassidy J 8 + 1	Jackson S 2 + 2	Parkhouse D 2 + 2	Match No.
1	2	3	4^{3}	5	6^{2}	7	8^{1}	9	10	11	12	13	14																									1
1	4	3		2	12	8^{2}	7	5	6	13	11	10^{3}	9^{1}	14																								2
1	3^{3}	4^{2}		2		8	13	6		10	9^{1}	11		14	5	7	12																					3
1				5		3		8		10	11^{1}	9	7		4		2^{2}	6^{3}	12	13	14																	4
1			14	2		3	13	8			10^{1}	11	6^{3}		4	5^{2}		7	12			9																5
1				2		3	8^{3}	5		10		13	12	14	4	6^{2}		7	9				11^{1}															6
1		2^{3}		5				9		10^{2}		12		14	4	8		7	6				11^{1}	3	13													7
1				2				5		10		9	8^{3}	14	4	7	3^{1}		6				13		11^{2}	12												8
1		3		2				5		10	13	9	8		4	7^{1}			6				11^{2}		12													9
1		3		2			9^{2}	4		10		13	14	11^{1}	12	7			6							5^{3}	8											10
1		3		2^{3}			12	5^{1}		10			8	9	13	6			14				11^{2}				7	4										11
1		3				6^{1}		5	12	10			14	11^{2}	2	7			9						13		8^{3}	4										12
1		2	12	5^{3}				4	14	10				11^{2}	8	6^{1}		13								9	7	3										13
1	13	2		5^{2}				4		10				11^{1}	8	6									12	9	7	3										14
1	2^{2}	3			12			5	11^{3}	10					9	7^{1}		8							14	6	13	4										15
	2	3			7^{3}			5		10				11	9	12						8^{1}			14	6	13	4^{2}	1									16
1	2	4			9			3		11					10	8						6				5	7											17
1	3			2^{3}				5	14					9		6	13					8	11^{1}		10		7	4^{2}		12								18
1	2	3			13			4		12				10		14						8^{1}	5		11^{3}	9	6			7^{2}								19
1	2	3							9^{2}	11						7						10	6^{1}		13	5	12	4		8								20
1	2	3				13			9		11^{2}			14		7^{3}			6			12	10			5	8^{1}	4										21
1		3			9					14	13			11^{1}		6^{3}			10			7	8^{2}		12	5		4		2								22
1		3			7				12		14			10^{3}					6			8	11^{2}		9	5^{1}	13	4		2								23
1	14				10	6		3^{1}						11^{2}					9			8	5^{3}		12		7	4		2	13							24
1					9^{2}	6		5							11^{3}				8			7	2		10^{1}	13	12	4		3		14						25
1	7				13			5		11									6			8^{3}	2		10^{2}		12	4		3		14	9^{1}					26
1	13			2^{2}				5		11				12		7			14			9	6^{3}				8^{1}	4		3			10					27
1				2	7^{3}			5			14					12			13			9	6^{1}					4		3			10^{2}	8	11			28
1				2		7^{1}		5		12						8						13	9^{3}					4		3			10^{2}	6	11	14		29
1	14	3		2												9						10	13			5^{2}		4		6				7^{1}	11	8^{3}	12	30
1	3^{1}	4^{2}			8					12						7						6						5		2			13	9	11	14	10^{3}	31
1					7	3^{2}				9		5		8		12		13										4		2				6	10	11^{1}		32
1		4^{1}				8				7		2^{3}				10		13						12		6		5		3				9	14		11^{2}	33
1				2	13	4				10^{2}						7						9^{1}	6^{3}		12					3			5	8	11		14	34
1				2	12	3				10		13				7						9	6^{3}		14			4					5^{1}	8^{2}	11			35
1				2	7^{2}					11		14				6			13			8	9^{3}		12			4		3			5		10^{1}			36
																																						37
																																						38
																																						39
																																						40
																																						41
																																						42
																																						43
																																						44
																																						45
																																						46

FA Cup

First Round	Peterborough U	(h)	1-1
Replay	Peterborough U	(a)	0-2

Carabao Cup

First Round	Southend U	(h)	1-2

Leasing.com Trophy

Group G (S)	Milton Keynes D	(h)	0-3
Group G (S)	Wycombe W	(a)	1-0
Group G (S)	Fulham U21	(h)	1-1
(Stevenage won 4-2 on penalties)			
Second Round (S)	Colchester U	(a)	2-1
Third Round (S)	Bristol R	(a)	1-0
Quarter-Final	Exeter C	(a)	0-3

STOKE CITY

FOUNDATION

The date of the formation of this club has long been in doubt. The year 1863 was claimed, but more recent research by local club historian Wade Martin has uncovered nothing earlier than 1868, when a couple of Old Carthusians, who were apprentices at the local works of the old North Staffordshire Railway Company, met with some others from that works, to form Stoke Ramblers. It should also be noted that the old Stoke club went bankrupt in 1908 when a new club was formed.

bet365 Stadium, Stanley Matthews Way, Stoke-on-Trent, Staffordshire ST4 4EG.

Telephone: (01782) 367 598.

Ticket Office: (01782) 367 599.

Website: www.stokecityfc.com

Email: info@stokecityfc.com

Ground Capacity: 30,089.

Record Attendance: 51,380 v Arsenal, Division 1, 29 March 1937 (at Victoria Ground); 30,022 v Everton, Premier League, 17 March 2018 (at bet365 Stadium).

Pitch Measurements: 105m × 68m (115yd × 74.5yd).

Chairman: Peter Coates.

Chief Executive: Tony Scholes.

Manager: Michael O'Neill.

Assistant Manager: Billy McKinley.

HONOURS

League Champions: Division 2 – 1932–33, 1962–63; Second Division – 1992–93; Division 3N – 1926–27.
Runners-up: FL C – 2007–08; Division 2 – 1921–22.

FA Cup: *Runners-up:* 2011.

League Cup Winners: 1972.
Runners-up: 1964.

League Trophy Winners: 1992, 2000.

European Competitions
UEFA Cup: 1972–73, 1974–75.
Europa League: 2011–12.

Colours: Red and white striped shirts, white shorts with red trim, white socks with red trim.

Year Formed: 1863* (*see Foundation*).

Turned Professional: 1885.

Previous Names: 1868, Stoke Ramblers; 1870, Stoke; 1925, Stoke City.

Club Nickname: 'The Potters'.

Grounds: 1875, Sweeting's Field; 1878, Victoria Ground (previously known as the Athletic Club Ground); 1997, Britannia Stadium (renamed bet365 Stadium, 2016).

First Football League Game: 8 September 1888, Football League, v WBA (h) L 0–2 – Rowley; Clare, Underwood; Ramsey, Shutt, Smith; Sayer, McSkimming, Staton, Edge, Tunnicliffe.

Record League Victory: 10–3 v WBA, Division 1, 4 February 1937 – Doug Westland; Brigham, Harbot; Tutin, Turner (1p), Kirton; Matthews, Antonio (2), Freddie Steele (5), Jimmy Westland, Johnson (2).

Record Cup Victory: 7–1 v Burnley, FA Cup 2nd rd (replay), 20 February 1896 – Clawley; Clare, Eccles; Turner, Grewe, Robertson; Willie Maxwell, Dickson, Alan Maxwell (3), Hyslop (4), Schofield.

Record Defeat: 0–10 v Preston NE, Division 1, 14 September 1889.

Most League Points (2 for a win): 63, Division 3 (N), 1926–27.

Most League Points (3 for a win): 93, Division 2, 1992–93.

FOOTBALL YEARBOOK FACT FILE

Stoke City produced two pop singles in the 1971–72 season to celebrate reaching the Football League Cup final and the FA Cup semi-finals. 'We'll Be with You' (attributed to 'Potters') and 'We'll Be Together' ('Gordon Banks and his Friends') were both written by local songwriter Jackie Trent and her husband Tony Hatch. 'We'll Be with You' reached number 34 in the pop charts in April 1972.

Most League Goals: 92, Division 3 (N), 1926–27.

Highest League Scorer in Season: Freddie Steele, 33, Division 1, 1936–37.

Most League Goals in Total Aggregate: Freddie Steele, 142, 1934–49.

Most League Goals in One Match: 7, Neville Coleman v Lincoln C, Division 2, 23 February 1957.

Most Capped Player: Glenn Whelan, 81 (91), Republic of Ireland.

Most League Appearances: Eric Skeels, 507, 1958–76.

Youngest League Player: Peter Bullock, 16 years 163 days v Swansea C, 19 April 1958.

Record Transfer Fee Received: £20,000,000 (rising to £25,000,000) from West Ham U for Marko Arnautovic, July 2017.

Record Transfer Fee Paid: £18,300,000 to Porto for Giannelli Imbula, February 2016.

Football League Record: 1888 Founder Member of Football League; 1890 Not re-elected; 1891 Re-elected; relegated in 1907, and after one year in Division 2, resigned for financial reasons; 1919 re-elected to Division 2; 1922–23 Division 1; 1923–26 Division 2; 1926–27 Division 3 (N); 1927–33 Division 2; 1933–53 Division 1; 1953–63 Division 2; 1963–77 Division 1; 1977–79 Division 2; 1979–85 Division 1; 1985–90 Division 2; 1990–92 Division 3; 1992–93 Division 2; 1993–98 Division 1; 1998–2002 Division 2; 2002–04 Division 1; 2004–08 FL C; 2008–18 Premier League; 2018– FL C.

LATEST SEQUENCES

Longest Sequence of League Wins: 8, 30.3.1895 – 21.9.1895.

Longest Sequence of League Defeats: 11, 6.4.1985 – 17.8.1985.

Longest Sequence of League Draws: 5, 13.5.2012 – 15.9.2012.

Longest Sequence of Unbeaten League Matches: 25, 5.9.1992 – 20.2.1993.

Longest Sequence Without a League Win: 17, 22.4.1989 – 14.10.1989.

Successive Scoring Runs: 21 from 24.12.1921.

Successive Non-scoring Runs: 8 from 29.12.1984.

MANAGERS

Tom Slaney 1874–83
(Secretary-Manager)
Walter Cox 1883–84
(Secretary-Manager)
Harry Lockett 1884–90
Joseph Bradshaw 1890–92
Arthur Reeves 1892–95
William Rowley 1895–97
H. D. Austerberry 1897–1908
A. J. Barker 1908–14
Peter Hodge 1914–15
Joe Schofield 1915–19
Arthur Shallcross 1919–23
John 'Jock' Rutherford 1923
Tom Mather 1923–35
Bob McGrory 1935–52
Frank Taylor 1952–60
Tony Waddington 1960–77
George Eastham 1977–78
Alan A'Court 1978
Alan Durban 1978–81
Richie Barker 1981–83
Bill Asprey 1984–85
Mick Mills 1985–89
Alan Ball 1989–91
Lou Macari 1991–93
Joe Jordan 1993–94
Lou Macari 1994–97
Chic Bates 1997–98
Chris Kamara 1998
Brian Little 1998–99
Gary Megson 1999
Gudjon Thordarson 1999–2002
Steve Cotterill 2002
Tony Pulis 2002–05
Johan Boskamp 2005–06
Tony Pulis 2006–13
Mark Hughes 2013–18
Paul Lambert 2018
Gary Rowett 2018–19
Nathan Jones 2019
Michael O'Neill November 2019–

TEN YEAR LEAGUE RECORD

		P	W	D	L	F	A	Pts	Pos
2010-11	PR Lge	38	13	7	18	46	48	46	13
2011-12	PR Lge	38	11	12	15	36	53	45	14
2012-13	PR Lge	38	9	15	14	34	45	42	13
2013-14	PR Lge	38	13	11	14	45	52	50	9
2014-15	PR Lge	38	15	9	14	48	45	54	9
2015-16	PR Lge	38	14	9	15	41	55	51	9
2016-17	PR Lge	38	11	11	16	41	56	44	13
2017-18	PR Lge	38	7	12	19	35	68	33	19
2018-19	FL C	46	11	22	13	45	52	55	16
2019-20	FL C	46	16	8	22	62	68	56	15

DID YOU KNOW ?

Stoke City took part in an early game under artificial lights on 27 February 1890 when they defeated Crewe Alexandra 3-1 at the Victoria Ground. The ground was illuminated with Wells Lights and a luminous ball was used to help fans follow the proceedings.

STOKE CITY – SKY BET CHAMPIONSHIP 2019–20 LEAGUE RECORD

Match No.	Date	Venue	Opponents	Result		H/T Score	Lg Pos.	Goalscorers	Attendance
1	Aug 3	H	QPR	L	1-2	0-1	17	Clucas ^{78}	24,004
2	10	A	Charlton Ath	L	1-3	1-1	22	Ince ^{37}	17,848
3	17	H	Derby Co	D	2-2	1-1	23	Hogan 2 $^{32, 55}$	23,863
4	21	A	Preston NE	L	1-3	0-2	24	McClean ^{89}	11,973
5	24	H	Leeds U	L	0-3	0-1	24		24,090
6	31	A	Birmingham C	L	1-2	0-0	24	Lindsay ^{58}	20,652
7	Sept 14	H	Bristol C	L	1-2	1-0	24	Clucas ^{4}	22,357
8	21	A	Brentford	D	0-0	0-0	23		11,870
9	27	H	Nottingham F	L	2-3	1-1	23	Gregory ^{10}, McClean ^{84}	23,800
10	Oct 1	H	Huddersfield T	L	0-1	0-0	24		20,372
11	5	A	Swansea C	W	2-1	1-1	24	Clucas ^{22}, Hogan ^{90}	16,612
12	19	H	Fulham	W	2-0	1-0	23	Campbell ^{16}, Gregory (pen) ^{80}	23,189
13	22	A	Sheffield W	L	0-1	0-1	23		22,460
14	26	A	Millwall	L	0-2	0-1	23		14,008
15	Nov 4	H	WBA	L	0-2	0-1	24		22,360
16	9	A	Barnsley	W	4-2	2-0	23	Clucas 2 $^{8, 67}$, Gregory (pen) ^{30}, Allen ^{64}	14,891
17	23	H	Wigan Ath	W	2-1	0-1	22	Batth ^{55}, Diouf ^{90}	22,530
18	26	A	Cardiff C	L	0-1	0-1	23		20,884
19	30	H	Blackburn R	L	1-2	0-1	23	Evans (og) ^{80}	22,292
20	Dec 7	A	Hull C	L	1-2	1-0	23	Vokes ^{7}	11,019
21	10	H	Luton T	W	3-0	2-0	22	McClean ^{35}, Allen 2 $^{45, 50}$	20,216
22	14	H	Reading	D	0-0	0-0	22		21,701
23	20	A	Middlesbrough	L	1-2	0-0	22	Clucas ^{53}	18,270
24	26	H	Sheffield W	W	3-2	1-0	21	McClean ^{11}, Campbell ^{90}, Vokes ^{90}	25,359
25	29	A	Fulham	L	0-1	0-1	21		18,747
26	Jan 1	A	Huddersfield T	W	5-2	1-0	21	Vokes ^{15}, Powell ^{57}, Campbell 2 $^{66, 70}$, Gregory ^{90}	21,933
27	11	H	Millwall	D	0-0	0-0	21		22,515
28	20	A	WBA	W	1-0	1-0	21	Campbell ^{9}	23,199
29	25	H	Swansea C	W	2-0	0-0	19	Clucas ^{55}, McClean ^{90}	22,593
30	31	A	Derby Co	L	0-4	0-2	20		27,984
31	Feb 8	H	Charlton Ath	W	3-1	1-1	20	McClean ^{28}, Ince ^{47}, Powell ^{66}	23,508
32	12	H	Preston NE	L	0-2	0-0	21		20,418
33	15	A	QPR	L	2-4	2-2	21	Clucas ^{27}, Campbell ^{31}	13,125
34	22	H	Cardiff C	W	2-0	1-0	19	Paterson (og) ^{25}, Allen ^{72}	25,436
35	26	A	Blackburn R	D	0-0	0-0	20		12,343
36	29	A	Luton T	D	1-1	1-0	21	Vokes ^{9}	10,070
37	Mar 7	H	Hull C	W	5-1	3-0	17	Powell 2 $^{11, 86}$, Campbell (pen) ^{16}, Clucas 2 $^{18, 50}$	23,126
38	June 20	A	Reading	D	1-1	0-1	18	Powell ^{90}	0
39	27	H	Middlesbrough	L	0-2	0-1	20		0
40	30	A	Wigan Ath	L	0-3	0-1	20		0
41	July 4	H	Barnsley	W	4-0	3-0	18	Vokes ^{8}, Campbell 2 $^{10, 38}$, Ince ^{87}	0
42	9	A	Leeds U	L	0-5	0-1	21		0
43	12	H	Birmingham C	W	2-0	2-0	17	Batth ^{12}, Clucas ^{45}	0
44	15	A	Bristol C	D	1-1	0-1	17	Batth ^{64}	0
45	18	H	Brentford	W	1-0	1-0	17	Gregory ^{38}	0
46	22	A	Nottingham F	W	4-1	1-0	16	Batth ^{19}, McClean ^{73}, Gregory ^{78}, Nuno Da Costa (og) ^{90}	0

Final League Position: 15

GOALSCORERS

League (62): Clucas 11, Campbell 9 (1 pen), McClean 7, Gregory 6 (2 pens), Powell 5, Vokes 5, Allen 4, Batth 4, Hogan 3, Ince 3, Diouf 1, Lindsay 1, own goals 3.
FA Cup (0).
Carabao Cup (4): Vokes 3, Batth 1.

Butland J 35	Smith T 27 + 3	Batth D 40 + 3	Collins N 6 + 8	McClean J 33 + 3	Cousins J 15 + 5	Clucas S 44	Allen J 34 + 1	Powell N 22 + 7	Vokes S 18 + 18	Afobe B 1	Gregory L 22 + 18	Campbell T 18 + 15	Ince T 31 + 7	Lindsay L 17 + 3	Ward S 15	Woods R 8	Hogan S 4 + 9	Duffy M 1 + 5	Verlinden T — + 5	Etebo P 8 + 3	Edwards T 13	Federici A 7	Carter-Vickers C 12	Martins Indi B 31 + 2	Ndiaye P 10 + 3	Diouf M — + 8	Shawcross R 5	Tymon J 1 + 1	Thompson J 8 + 7	Chester J 13 + 3	Ngoy J — + 1	Oakley-Boothe T 1 + 1	Sorenson L 2 + 4	Davies A 4	Match No.
1	2	3	4	5	6	7	8	9^{2}	10^{1}	11^{3}	12	13	14																						1
1	2	3				8	7				11^{3}	12	9	4	5	6^{2}	10^{1}	13	14																2
1	2	3	12	5		8^{3}	7				11	13	9^{1}	4		6	10^{2}			14															3
1		3	12	5		8	7		14		11		9^{3}	4		6^{1}	10^{2}			13	2														4
			2	9	6	8	13				11^{2}		14	4			12	10^{1}		7	5	1	3^{3}												5
	2	3		10		9	7				11^{3}	14	6^{2}	4	5^{1}		12	13		8		1													6
1				9^{2}		8	7■				11^{3}	13	10^{1}	3			14			12	5		2	4	6										7
1		12		9		8			14		11^{3}	13	10^{2}	3^{1}						7	5		2	4	6										8
1				5		9		10^{2}	13		11^{3}	14	6	12						7	2		3	4	8^{1}										9
		3		5		7	9^{3}	13			11^{2}	12	10^{1}					14		8		1	2	4	6										10
		3				8	7		12		11^{1}	10^{2}					13			9	2	1	4	5	6										11
		4				8^{3}	6		13		10^{2}	11^{1}		14			12			9	2	1	3	5	7										12
		4				8	9				11	10^{3}		13	5		14	12		6^{1}	2	1	3^{2}		7										13
		3		12		7	8		13		11	14	9^{3}	4			10^{1}					1	2	5^{2}	6										14
1	2	4		12		9	8		11			10^{2}	13	5^{1}	6			14					3		7^{3}										15
1		3		11		8^{1}	6		14		10^{3}		9^{2}		5	7					2			4	12	13									16
1		3		11			6	8^{3}	12		10^{1}		9		5	7^{2}					2			4	13	14									17
1		3				10^{3}	9	13	12		11^{1}		6		5	8	14						2	4	7^{2}										18
1		3		11		8	6	14	10				9^{2}		5^{3}	7^{1}	13						2	4		12									19
1		3		10^{1}		9	6	14	11		12		8^{3}		5	7^{2}					2			4	13										20
1		12		11	7	8^{3}	6	14	10^{2}				9	4	5						2					13	3^{1}								21
1	12	3		11	7	8^{3}	6	14	10^{2}				9	4	5		13				2^{1}														22
1	2	3		11^{2}	7	8	6	12	13		10		9^{3}	4	5^{1}											14									23
1	2	4		11	7	8	6		13		10^{1}	12	9		5^{2}												3								24
1	2	4		11	7^{3}	8	6		13		10^{2}	14	9		5^{1}									12			3								25
1	2	3		11		8	6	7^{1}	10		12	9		4										5											26
1	2	3		11^{1}		8	6	7	10		13	9		4					12					5^{2}											27
1	2	3	14	10	13	7	6	9^{2}			12	11^{1}	8^{3}	4										5											28
1	2	3	13	10		7	6	9^{3}	11^{1}		12		8^{2}	4										5		14									29
1	2	3		10		7	6	9^{3}	11^{2}		14		8	4					12									5^{1}	13						30
1	2	3		10		7	6	9^{1}	13			11^{2}	8^{3}						14					5					12	4					31
1	2	3		10^{1}		7	6	9	12		14	11	8						13^{3}					5^{2}						4					32
1	2	3			12	7	6^{3}	9	13			11^{2}	8											5					10^{1}	4	14				33
1	2	3	13		12	9	8	10^{1}			14	11^{3}	7											5					6^{2}	4					34
1	2	3	4		13	9	7	10^{3}			12	11^{1}	6											5					8^{2}	14					35
1	2	3	14		7	10	6	9^{2}	11^{1}		12		8^{3}											5					13	4					36
1	2	3				9	6^{1}	10^{3}	13		14	11^{2}	8											5					7	4		12			37
1	15	12	2^{4}	13		9		10	14		16	11	8^{3}											5^{5}			3^{1}		7^{2}	4			6		38
1	2	3		8	14	10		9■	13		15	11^{4}	12											5^{2}					7^{3}	4			6^{1}		39
1	16	4	2^{4}	10	7	9			11		12	13	8^{2}		5^{3}									14			3^{5}		6^{1}	15					40
1	2	3		10^{4}	6	7^{5}		9^{3}	11^{2}		12	8^{1}	13											5		15			16	4			14		41
1	2	4	3^{1}	10	7	6^{5}		9^{4}	11^{3}		13	8^{2}												5		14			16	12			15		42
	2	3		10	6	7		9^{3}	11^{2}		13	8^{1}	12											5					14	4				1	43
	2	4	14	10	7	6^{3}		9^{1}	11		8^{2}	13												5					12	3				1	44
	2	4	14	10	6	7		9^{3}	11^{1}		8^{2}	12												5						3			13	1	45
	5	3		8	6				10^{3}		11^{4}	14	15											4				13	7^{1}	2		9^{2}	12	1	46

FA Cup

Third Round	Brentford	(a)	0-1

Carabao Cup

First Round	Wigan Ath	(a)	1-0
Second Round	Leeds U	(a)	2-2
(Stoke C won 5-4 on penalties)			
Third Round	Crawley T	(a)	1-1
(Crawley T won 5-3 on penalties)			

SUNDERLAND

FOUNDATION

A Scottish schoolmaster named James Allan, working at Hendon Board School, took the initiative in the foundation of Sunderland in 1879 when they were formed as The Sunderland and District Teachers' Association FC at a meeting in the Adults School, Norfolk Street. Due to financial difficulties, they quickly allowed members from outside the teaching profession and so became Sunderland AFC in October 1880.

Stadium of Light, Sunderland, Tyne and Wear SR5 1SU.

Telephone: (0371) 911 1200.

Ticket Office: (0371) 911 1973.

Website: www.safc.com

Email: enquiries@safc.com

Ground Capacity: 48,095.

Record Attendance: 75,118 v Derby Co, FA Cup 6th rd replay, 8 March 1933 (at Roker Park); 48,335 v Liverpool, Premier League, 13 April 2002 (at Stadium of Light).

Pitch Measurements: 105m × 68m (115yd × 74.5yd).

Owner: Stewart Donald.

Chief Executive: Jim Rodwell.

Manager: Phil Parkinson.

Assistant Manager: Steve Parkin.

Colours: Red and white striped shirts, black shorts with white trim, red socks.

Year Formed: 1879.

Turned Professional: 1886.

Previous Names: 1879, Sunderland and District Teachers AFC; 1880, Sunderland.

Club Nickname: 'The Black Cats'.

Grounds: 1879, Blue House Field, Hendon; 1882, Groves Field, Ashbrooke; 1883, Horatio Street; 1884, Abbs Field, Fulwell; 1886, Newcastle Road; 1898, Roker Park; 1997, Stadium of Light.

First Football League Game: 13 September 1890, Football League, v Burnley (h) L 2–3 – Kirtley; Porteous, Oliver; Wilson, Auld, Gibson; Spence (1), Miller, Campbell (1), Scott, Davy Hannah.

Record League Victory: 9–1 v Newcastle U (a), Division 1, 5 December 1908 – Roose; Forster, Melton; Daykin, Thomson, Low; Mordue (1), Hogg (3), Brown, Holley (3), Bridgett (2).

Record Cup Victory: 11–1 v Fairfield, FA Cup 1st rd, 2 February 1895 – Doig; McNeill, Johnston; Dunlop, McCreadie (1), Wilson; Gillespie (1), Millar (5), Campbell, Jimmy Hannah (3), Scott (1).

HONOURS

League Champions: Division 1 – 1892–93, 1894–95, 1901–02, 1912–13, 1935–36; Football League 1891–92; FL C – 2004–05, 2006–07; First Division – 1995–96, 1998–99; Division 2 – 1975–76; Division 3 – 1987–88.
Runners-up: Division 1 – 1893–94, 1897–98, 1900–01, 1922–23, 1934–35; Division 2 – 1963–64, 1979–80.

FA Cup Winners: 1937, 1973.
Runners-up: 1913, 1992.

League Cup: *Runners-up:* 1985, 2014.

League Trophy: *Runners-up:* 2019.

European Competitions
European Cup-Winners' Cup: 1973–74.

FOOTBALL YEARBOOK FACT FILE

Sunderland were lined up to undertake an extensive tour of the United States of America in the summer of 1894. This was to be linked to the newly formed professional soccer organisation, the American League of Professional Football. However, the ALPF collapsed within weeks of starting its schedule and the Black Cats had to wait another 60 years before they finally played a match in the USA.

Record Defeat: 0–8 v Sheff Wed, Division 1, 26 December 1911; 0–8 v West Ham U, Division 1, 19 October 1968; 0–8 v Watford, Division 1, 25 September 1982; 0–8 v Southampton, Premier League, 18 October 2014.

Most League Points (2 for a win): 61, Division 2, 1963–64.

Most League Points (3 for a win): 105, Division 1, 1998–99.

Most League Goals: 109, Division 1, 1935–36.

Highest League Scorer in Season: Dave Halliday, 43, Division 1, 1928–29.

Most League Goals in Total Aggregate: Charlie Buchan, 209, 1911–25.

Most League Goals in One Match: 5, Charlie Buchan v Liverpool, Division 1, 7 December 1919; 5, Bobby Gurney v Bolton W, Division 1, 7 December 1935; 5, Dominic Sharkey v Norwich C, Division 2, 20 February 1962.

Most Capped Player: Seb Larsson, 59 (118), Sweden.

Most League Appearances: Jim Montgomery, 537, 1962–77.

Youngest League Player: Derek Forster, 15 years 184 days v Leicester C, 22 August 1964.

Record Transfer Fee Received: £25,000,000 (rising to £30,000,000) from Everton for Jordan Pickford, June 2017.

Record Transfer Fee Paid: £13,800,000 (rising to £17,100,000) to FC Lorient for Didier Ndong, August 2016.

Football League Record: 1890 Elected to Division 1; 1958–64 Division 2; 1964–70 Division 1; 1970–76 Division 2; 1976–77 Division 1; 1977–80 Division 2; 1980–85 Division 1; 1985–87 Division 2; 1987–88 Division 3; 1988–90 Division 2; 1990–91 Division 1; 1991–92 Division 2; 1992–96 Division 1; 1996–97 Premier League; 1997–99 Division 1; 1999–2003 Premier League; 2003–04 Division 1; 2004–05 FL C; 2005–06 Premier League; 2006–07 FL C; 2007–17 Premier League; 2017–18 FL C: 2018– FL 1.

MANAGERS

Tom Watson 1888–96
Bob Campbell 1896–99
Alex Mackie 1899–1905
Bob Kyle 1905–28
Johnny Cochrane 1928–39
Bill Murray 1939–57
Alan Brown 1957–64
George Hardwick 1964–65
Ian McColl 1965–68
Alan Brown 1968–72
Bob Stokoe 1972–76
Jimmy Adamson 1976–78
Ken Knighton 1979–81
Alan Durban 1981–84
Len Ashurst 1984–85
Lawrie McMenemy 1985–87
Denis Smith 1987–91
Malcolm Crosby 1991–93
Terry Butcher 1993
Mick Buxton 1993–95
Peter Reid 1995–2002
Howard Wilkinson 2002–03
Mick McCarthy 2003–06
Niall Quinn 2006
Roy Keane 2006–08
Ricky Sbragia 2008–09
Steve Bruce 2009–11
Martin O'Neill 2011–13
Paolo Di Canio 2013
Gus Poyet 2013–15
Dick Advocaat 2015
Sam Allardyce 2015–16
David Moyes 2016–17
Simon Grayson 2017
Chris Coleman 2017–18
Jack Ross 2018–19
Phil Parkinson October 2019–

LATEST SEQUENCES

Longest Sequence of League Wins: 13, 14.11.1891 – 2.4.1892.

Longest Sequence of League Defeats: 17, 18.1.2003 – 16.8.2003.

Longest Sequence of League Draws: 6, 26.3.1949 – 19.4.1949.

Longest Sequence of Unbeaten League Matches: 19, 26.12.2018 – 9.4.2019

Longest Sequence Without a League Win: 22, 21.12.2002 – 16.8.2003.

Successive Scoring Runs: 43 from 30.3.2018.

Successive Non-scoring Runs: 10 from 27.11.1976.

TEN YEAR LEAGUE RECORD

		P	*W*	*D*	*L*	*F*	*A*	*Pts*	*Pos*
2010-11	PR Lge	38	12	11	15	45	56	47	10
2011-12	PR Lge	38	11	12	15	45	46	45	13
2012-13	PR Lge	38	9	12	17	41	54	39	17
2013-14	PR Lge	38	10	8	20	41	60	38	14
2014-15	PR Lge	38	7	17	14	31	53	38	16
2015-16	PR Lge	38	9	12	17	48	62	39	17
2016-17	PR Lge	38	6	6	26	29	69	24	20
2017-18	FL C	46	7	16	23	52	80	37	24
2018-19	FL 1	46	22	19	5	80	47	85	5
2019-20	FL 1	36	16	11	9	48	32	59	8§

§Decided on points-per-game (1.64)

DID YOU KNOW ?

Winger Arthur Bridgett made over 300 appearances for Sunderland between 1903 and 1912 and was capped 11 times for England. He later moved to live in the Potteries and became manager of the Stoke United Ladies team that won the English Ladies Cup in 1922 and travelled to Barcelona where they defeated a team from Paris in September 1923.

SUNDERLAND – SKY BET LEAGUE ONE 2019–20 LEAGUE RECORD

Match No.	Date	Venue	Opponents	Result		H/T Score	Lg Pos.	Goalscorers	Attendance
1	Aug 3	H	Oxford U	D	1-1	0-1	10	Gooch (pen) [49]	33,498
2	10	A	Ipswich T	D	1-1	0-1	14	Gooch [64]	24,051
3	17	H	Portsmouth	W	2-1	2-1	8	Willis [27], Maguire [39]	29,140
4	20	A	Rochdale	W	2-1	1-1	5	McGeady [28], Wyke [56]	5258
5	24	H	AFC Wimbledon	W	3-1	1-1	4	Maguire 3 [8, 53, 79]	29,725
6	31	A	Peterborough U	L	0-3	0-1	6		10,005
7	Sept 14	A	Accrington S	W	3-1	3-1	5	Gooch [7], McGeady [25], McNulty [36]	4164
8	17	H	Rotherham U	D	1-1	1-0	4	McNulty [1]	29,078
9	21	A	Bolton W	D	1-1	0-0	5	McGeady (pen) [90]	12,026
10	28	H	Milton Keynes D	W	2-1	2-0	5	Power [24], O'Nien [28]	29,954
11	Oct 5	A	Lincoln C	L	0-2	0-1	6		10,264
12	19	A	Wycombe W	L	0-1	0-1	10		8395
13	22	H	Tranmere R	W	5-0	3-0	7	Watmore [24], Maguire [26], Gooch [39], Grigg [83], O'Nien [90]	28,551
14	26	A	Shrewsbury T	L	0-1	0-1	8		8117
15	Nov 2	H	Southend U	W	1-0	1-0	7	O'Nien [20]	30,407
16	23	H	Coventry C	D	1-1	0-1	10	Mgunga-Kimpioka [90]	29,809
17	26	H	Burton Alb	L	1-2	1-1	11	McGeady (pen) [19]	26,538
18	Dec 7	A	Gillingham	L	0-1	0-0	11		5401
19	14	H	Blackpool	D	1-1	1-1	12	Wyke [37]	30,595
20	26	H	Bolton W	D	0-0	0-0	15		33,821
21	29	A	Doncaster R	W	2-1	1-1	13	Gooch [6], Maguire [61]	12,432
22	Jan 1	A	Fleetwood T	D	1-1	0-1	13	Maguire (pen) [86]	4011
23	4	H	Lincoln C	W	3-1	3-0	9	Flanagan [19], Bostwick (og) [23], Gooch [29]	31,748
24	11	H	Wycombe W	W	4-0	3-0	6	Wyke [6], Hume [16], Maguire 2 (1 pen) [21 (p), 78]	29,331
25	18	A	Milton Keynes D	W	1-0	0-0	6	Gooch [79]	13,327
26	24	H	Doncaster R	D	0-0	0-0	5		30,251
27	29	A	Tranmere R	W	1-0	0-0	5	Wyke [60]	6850
28	Feb 1	A	Portsmouth	L	0-2	0-1	7		18,531
29	8	H	Ipswich T	W	1-0	0-0	6	Maguire [81]	32,726
30	11	H	Rochdale	W	3-0	3-0	5	Gooch 2 [11, 32], O'Connell (og) [15]	27,401
31	15	A	Oxford U	W	1-0	1-0	5	Willis [2]	9105
32	22	H	Bristol R	W	3-0	0-0	4	Gooch [71], Wyke [73], O'Nien [82]	31,541
33	25	H	Fleetwood T	D	1-1	0-1	4	Power [90]	28,255
34	Mar 1	A	Coventry C	L	0-1	0-1	5		10,055
35	7	H	Gillingham	D	2-2	0-0	5	Lafferty 2 [64, 83]	29,872
36	10	A	Bristol R	L	0-2	0-1	7		7281
37	14	A	Blackpool	Cancelled					
38	28	A	Southend U	Cancelled					
39	Apr 4	H	Shrewsbury T	Cancelled					
40	10	A	AFC Wimbledon	Cancelled					
41	13	H	Peterborough U	Cancelled					
42	18	A	Burton Alb	Cancelled					
43	25	H	Accrington S	Cancelled					
44	May 3	A	Rotherham U	Cancelled					

Final League Position: 8 (on points-per-game basis)

GOALSCORERS

League (48): Gooch 10 (1 pen), Maguire 10 (2 pens), Wyke 5, McGeady 4 (2 pens), O'Nien 4, Lafferty 2, McNulty 2, Power 2, Willis 2, Flanagan 1, Grigg 1, Hume 1, Mgunga-Kimpioka 1, Watmore 1, own goals 2.
FA Cup (1): McGeady 1.
Carabao Cup (8): McNulty 2, Dobson 1, Flanagan 1, Grigg 1, McGeady 1, Power 1, Wyke 1.
Leasing.com Trophy (4): Grigg 1, Maguire 1, McNulty 1, Watmore 1.

McLaughlin J 31 + 1	McLaughlin C 12 + 3	Willis J 35	Flanagan T 16 + 2	Hume D 30 + 2	Gooch L 28 + 2	Dobson G 26 + 3	McGeouch D 5 + 3	Embleton E 1 + 2	Grigg W 8 + 12	McNulty M 7 + 8	Watmore D 6 + 11	McGeady A 13 + 2	Maguire C 28 + 7	O'Nien L 35	Ozturk A 20 + 2	Leadbitter G 11 + 3	Power M 30 + 1	Wyke C 22 + 5	Lynch J 14 + 2	De Bock L 4 + 1	Burge L 5	Mgunga-Kimpioka B — + 4	Lafferty K 2 + 9	Wright B 5	Scowen J 1 + 3	Semenyo A 1 + 6	*Match No.*
1	2	3	4	5	6^1	7	8	9^3	10^2	11	12	13	14														1
1	2	3^2	4	5^3	9	7	8		13	10		11^1	12	6	14												2
1	5	4		14	8				13	11^1		10^3	9^2	2	3	6	7	12									3
1	5	4			8^2		13	14	12			10	9^3	2	3	7	6^1	11									4
1		4		5	8^3	14	13		12			10	9^1	2	3	7	6^2	11									5
1	5	4	13		8^2	14			12	9^3		10^1		2■	3	7	6	11■									6
1		4		5	8	6	12	14	13	11^1		10	9^2	2	3	7^3											7
1	2^3	4		5	8^2	7	6		14	11^1		10	13	9	3			12									8
1	12	4	3	5^2	8	6			11			10	9^1	2		7^3	14	13									9
1	2	3		12	10^1	14	6		13				8	9			7	11^2	4	5^3							10
1	2	3			10^3		6		14	13		12	8^1	9			7	11	4	5^2							11
	2	3		5					12	14	8^1	10	13	9		7^3	6	11^2	4		1						12
	13	3		5	10^1	6			11^3	12	8^2		9	2			7		4		1	14					13
12		3		5		6			11^2	13	8^1	10	9	2			7		4		1^3	14					14
1	2	3		5		6			11^2	13	12	10^1	9^3	8		14	7		4								15
		3^2	13	5		6			10^1		12	11	9	2		7	8^3		4		1	14					16
	2^1	3		5					11		8	10	12	9		7^2	6		4		1	13					17
1	5^1	2	4			6			10	11^2			13	9	3	7		12		8							18
1			2	8	12	6■			13		9^1		11^3	5	3	14	7	10^2		4							19
1		2	4^3	8	11^1					14	9^2		12	5	3	7	6	10		13							20
1		2		8	11^1	6					12		9	5	3		7	10	4								21
1		2^2		8	11	6^1				13	12		9	5	3		7	10	4								22
1		2	4	8	11^1	6					12		9^2	5	3	13	7	10									23
1		2	4^1	8	11^2	6				13			9	5	3		7	10	12								24
1		2		8	11	6							9	5	3		7	10^1	4				12				25
1		2		8	11	6					13		9^2	5	3		7	10^1	4				12				26
1		2		8	11	6							9^1	5			7	10	4					3	12		27
1		2		8^3	11	6					13		9^2	5			7	10^1	4				12	3		14	28
1	13	2	4	8^1	11^2	6							9	5			7	10					12	3			29
1		2	4	8	11^1	6					13		9^3	5			7	10^2					14	3		12	30
1		2	4	8	11^3	6							9^2	5	13		7	10					14	3^1	12		31
1		2	4	8	11^2	6					14		9^3	5	3		7	10^1					13			12	32
1		2^2	4	8^3	11	6^1					14		9	5	3		7	10					13			12	33
1		2^2	4	8^1	11	6							9	5	3		7	10					12			13	34
1		2	4	8^3	11	6							9^2	5	3^1		7		14				10		13	12	35
1		2	4	8	13				14				9	5	3^1		7	12					10^3		6^2	11	36
																											37
																											38
																											39
																											40
																											41
																											42
																											43
																											44

FA Cup

First Round	Gillingham	(h)	1-1
Replay	Gillingham	(a)	0-1
(aet)			

Carabao Cup

First Round	Accrington S	(a)	3-1
Second Round	Burnley	(a)	3-1
Third Round	Sheffield U	(a)	1-0
Fourth Round	Oxford U	(a)	1-1

(Oxford U won 4-2 on penalties)

Leasing.com Trophy

Group A (N)	Grimsby T	(h)	3-2
Group A (N)	Leicester C U21	(h)	1-2
Group A (N)	Scunthorpe U	(a)	0-3

SWANSEA CITY

FOUNDATION

The earliest Association Football in Wales was played in the northern part of the country and no international took place in the south until 1894, when a local paper still thought it necessary to publish an outline of the rules and an illustration of the pitch markings. There had been an earlier Swansea club, but this has no connection with Swansea Town (now City) formed at a public meeting in June 1912.

Liberty Stadium, Morfa, Landore, Swansea SA1 2FA.

Telephone: (01792) 616 400.

Ticket Office: (01792) 616 400.

Website: www.swanseacity.com

Email: info@swanseacityfc.com

Ground Capacity: 21,088.

Record Attendance: 32,796 v Arsenal, FA Cup 4th rd, 17 February 1968 (at Vetch Field); 20,972 v Liverpool, Premier League, 1 May 2016 (at Liberty Stadium).

Pitch Measurements: 105m × 68m (115yd × 74.5yd).

Executive Chairman: Trevor Birch.

Head Coach: Steve Cooper.

Assistant Coach: Mike Marsh.

Colours: White shirts with black trim, black shorts with white trim, white socks with black trim.

Year Formed: 1912.

Turned Professional: 1912.

Previous Name: 1912, Swansea Town; 1970, Swansea City.

Club Nicknames: 'The Swans', 'The Jacks'.

Grounds: 1912, Vetch Field; 2005, Liberty Stadium.

First Football League Game: 28 August 1920, Division 3, v Portsmouth (a) L 0–3 – Crumley; Robson, Evans; Smith, Holdsworth, Williams; Hole, Ivor Jones, Edmundson, Rigsby, Spottiswood.

Record League Victory: 8–0 v Hartlepool U, Division 4, 1 April 1978 – Barber; Evans, Bartley, Lally (1) (Morris), May, Bruton, Kevin Moore, Robbie James (3 incl. 1p), Curtis (3), Toshack (1), Chappell.

Record Cup Victory: 12–0 v Sliema W (Malta), ECWC 1st rd 1st leg, 15 September 1982 – Davies; Marustik, Hadziabdic (1), Irwin (1), Kennedy, Rajkovic (1), Loveridge (2) (Leighton James), Robbie James, Charles (2), Stevenson (1), Latchford (1) (Walsh (3)).

Record Defeat: 0–8 v Liverpool, FA Cup 3rd rd, 9 January 1990; 0–8 v Monaco, ECWC, 1st rd 2nd leg, 1 October 1991.

Most League Points (2 for a win): 62, Division 3 (S), 1948–49.

Most League Points (3 for a win): 92, FL 1, 2007–08.

Most League Goals: 90, Division 2, 1956–57.

HONOURS

League Champions: FL 1 – 2007–08; Division 3S – 1924–25, 1948–49; Third Division – 1999–2000.

FA Cup: semi-final – 1926, 1964.

League Cup Winners: 2013.

League Trophy Winners: 1994, 2006.

Welsh Cup Winners: 11 times; *Runners-up:* 8 times.

European Competitions
Europa League: 2013–14.
European Cup-Winners' Cup: 1961–62, 1966–67, 1981–82, 1982–83, 1983–84, 1989–90, 1991–92.

FOOTBALL YEARBOOK FACT FILE

Swansea City goalkeeper Nico Schroeder became the first European player to appear in the Football League following the UK's entry to the then Common Market and the relaxation of rules on the employment of professionals in the 1970s. Schroeder, who was a non-contract player with the Swans, made a single first-team appearance as deputy for Steve Potter at Stockport County in August 1976.

Highest League Scorer in Season: Cyril Pearce, 35, Division 2, 1931–32.

Most League Goals in Total Aggregate: Ivor Allchurch, 166, 1949–58, 1965–68.

Most League Goals in One Match: 5, Jack Fowler v Charlton Ath, Division 3S, 27 December 1924.

Most Capped Player: Ashley Williams, 64 (86), Wales.

Most League Appearances: Wilfred Milne, 587, 1919–37.

Youngest League Player: Nigel Dalling, 15 years 289 days v Southport, 6 December 1974.

Record Transfer Fee Received: £40,000,000 (rising to £45,000,000) from Everton for Gylfi Sigurdsson, August 2017.

Record Transfer Fee Paid: £18,000,000 to West Ham U for André Ayew, January 2018.

Football League Record: 1920 Original Member of Division 3; 1921–25 Division 3 (S); 1925–47 Division 2; 1947–49 Division 3 (S); 1949–65 Division 2; 1965–67 Division 3; 1967–70 Division 4; 1970–73 Division 3; 1973–78 Division 4; 1978–79 Division 3; 1979–81 Division 2; 1981–83 Division 1; 1983–84 Division 2; 1984–86 Division 3; 1986–88 Division 4; 1988–92 Division 3; 1992–96 Division 2; 1996–2000 Division 3; 2000–01 Division 2; 2001–04 Division 3; 2004–05 FL 2; 2005–08 FL 1; 2008–11 FL C; 2011–18 Premier League; 2018– FL C.

LATEST SEQUENCES

Longest Sequence of League Wins: 9, 27.11.1999 – 22.1.2000.

Longest Sequence of League Defeats: 9, 26.1.1991 – 19.3.1991.

Longest Sequence of League Draws: 8, 25.11.2008 – 28.12.2008.

Longest Sequence of Unbeaten League Matches: 19, 19.10.1970 – 9.3.1971.

Longest Sequence Without a League Win: 15, 25.3.1989 – 2.9.1989.

Successive Scoring Runs: 27 from 28.8.1947.

Successive Non-scoring Runs: 6 from 6.2.1996.

MANAGERS

Walter Whittaker 1912–14
William Bartlett 1914–15
Joe Bradshaw 1919–26
Jimmy Thomson 1927–31
Neil Harris 1934–39
Haydn Green 1939–47
Bill McCandless 1947–55
Ron Burgess 1955–58
Trevor Morris 1958–65
Glyn Davies 1965–66
Billy Lucas 1967–69
Roy Bentley 1969–72
Harry Gregg 1972–75
Harry Griffiths 1975–77
John Toshack 1978–83
(resigned October re-appointed in December) 1983–84
Colin Appleton 1984
John Bond 1984–85
Tommy Hutchison 1985–86
Terry Yorath 1986–89
Ian Evans 1989–90
Terry Yorath 1990–91
Frank Burrows 1991–95
Bobby Smith 1995
Kevin Cullis 1996
Jan Molby 1996–97
Micky Adams 1997
Alan Cork 1997–98
John Hollins 1998–2001
Colin Addison 2001–02
Nick Cusack 2002
Brian Flynn 2002–04
Kenny Jackett 2004–07
Roberto Martinez 2007–09
Paulo Sousa 2009–10
Brendan Rodgers 2010–12
Michael Laudrup 2012–14
Garry Monk 2014–15
Francesco Guidolin 2016
Bob Bradley 2016
Paul Clement 2017
Carlos Carvalhal 2017–18
Graham Potter 2018–19
Steve Cooper June 2019–

TEN YEAR LEAGUE RECORD

		P	W	D	L	F	A	Pts	Pos
2010-11	FL C	46	24	8	14	69	42	80	3
2011-12	PR Lge	38	12	11	15	44	51	47	11
2012-13	PR Lge	38	11	13	14	47	51	46	9
2013-14	PR Lge	38	11	9	18	54	54	42	12
2014-15	PR Lge	38	16	8	14	46	49	56	8
2015-16	PR Lge	38	12	11	15	42	52	47	12
2016-17	PR Lge	38	12	5	21	45	70	41	15
2017-18	PR Lge	38	8	9	21	28	56	33	18
2018-19	FL C	46	18	11	17	65	62	65	10
2019-20	FL C	46	18	16	12	62	53	70	6

DID YOU KNOW ?

Swansea Town changed their name to Swansea City in February 1970 following an announcement by Prince Charles, newly appointed as Prince of Wales, to grant the town city status the previous summer. The first competitive game played under the new title was a 0-0 draw at home to Exeter City on 24 February 1970.

SWANSEA CITY – SKY BET CHAMPIONSHIP 2019–20 LEAGUE RECORD

Match No.	Date	Venue	Opponents	Result	H/T Score	Lg Pos.	Goalscorers	Attendance
1	Aug 3	H	Hull C	W 2-1	0-1	3	Borja Baston [47], van der Hoorn [49]	15,741
2	10	A	Derby Co	D 0-0	0-0	6		27,337
3	17	H	Preston NE	W 3-2	1-1	3	Borja Baston 2 [45, 69], Byers [63]	15,250
4	21	A	QPR	W 3-1	1-0	2	Celina [29], Borja Baston (pen) [70], Surridge [80]	12,287
5	25	H	Birmingham C	W 3-0	0-0	2	Naughton [63], Celina [68], Borja Baston (pen) [75]	17,277
6	31	A	Leeds U	W 1-0	0-0	1	Routledge [90]	34,935
7	Sept 14	H	Nottingham F	L 0-1	0-0	1		17,102
8	21	A	Bristol C	D 0-0	0-0	2		22,885
9	28	H	Reading	D 1-1	1-0	2	Borja Baston [3]	16,036
10	Oct 2	A	Charlton Ath	W 2-1	1-1	1	Dhanda [17], Ayew [65]	15,741
11	5	H	Stoke C	L 1-2	1-1	4	Ayew [1]	16,612
12	19	A	Barnsley	D 1-1	0-0	3	Ayew [67]	12,424
13	22	H	Brentford	L 0-3	0-2	7		15,875
14	27	H	Cardiff C	W 1-0	1-0	4	Wilmot [24]	20,270
15	Nov 2	A	Wigan Ath	W 2-1	1-1	2	Dyer [12], Surridge [90]	9080
16	9	A	Sheffield W	D 2-2	1-0	4	Ayew [32], Wilmot [90]	23,073
17	23	H	Millwall	L 0-1	0-0	6		16,840
18	26	A	Huddersfield T	D 1-1	1-1	5	Fulton [18]	20,062
19	29	H	Fulham	L 1-2	0-2	6	Byers [65]	16,024
20	Dec 8	A	WBA	L 1-5	1-3	11	Surridge [39]	22,927
21	11	H	Blackburn R	D 1-1	1-1	11	Ayew [10]	14,162
22	14	H	Middlesbrough	W 3-1	1-0	10	Ayew 2 (1 pen) [22 (p), 71], Surridge [73]	14,625
23	21	A	Luton T	W 1-0	0-0	6	Ayew [82]	10,062
24	26	A	Brentford	L 1-3	0-2	8	Ayew [65]	11,848
25	29	H	Barnsley	D 0-0	0-0	9		17,097
26	Jan 2	H	Charlton Ath	W 1-0	1-0	6	Dhanda [14]	15,352
27	12	A	Cardiff C	D 0-0	0-0	7		28,529
28	18	H	Wigan Ath	W 2-1	1-1	5	Brewster [19], Ayew [67]	15,659
29	25	A	Stoke C	L 0-2	0-0	7		22,593
30	Feb 1	A	Preston NE	D 1-1	1-1	8	Brewster [33]	12,502
31	8	H	Derby Co	L 2-3	0-1	9	Dhanda [56], Naughton [58]	16,230
32	11	H	QPR	D 0-0	0-0	9		14,778
33	14	A	Hull C	D 4-4	1-1	9	Routledge [13], Naughton [55], Garrick [77], Brewster [84]	9757
34	22	H	Huddersfield T	W 3-1	1-0	9	Ayew [28], Fulton [80], Garrick [90]	15,148
35	26	A	Fulham	L 0-1	0-0	9		17,626
36	29	A	Blackburn R	D 2-2	1-1	9	Brewster [45], Ayew (pen) [48]	13,099
37	Mar 7	H	WBA	D 0-0	0-0	11		16,788
38	June 20	A	Middlesbrough	W 3-0	3-0	8	Brewster 2 [18, 21], Ayew (pen) [34]	0
39	27	H	Luton T	L 0-1	0-0	10		0
40	30	A	Millwall	D 1-1	0-1	8	Bialkowski (og) [66]	0
41	July 5	H	Sheffield W	W 2-1	0-0	8	Brewster [52], Ayew (pen) [66]	0
42	8	A	Birmingham C	W 3-1	2-1	7	Brewster [12], Cabango [45], Fulton [52]	0
43	12	H	Leeds U	L 0-1	0-0	7		0
44	15	A	Nottingham F	D 2-2	2-1	8	Brewster [8], Ayew (pen) [45]	0
45	18	H	Bristol C	W 1-0	1-0	7	Roberts [45]	0
46	22	A	Reading	W 4-1	1-1	6	Brewster [17], Routledge 2 [66, 90], Cullen [84]	0

Final League Position: 6

GOALSCORERS

League (62): Ayew 15 (5 pens), Brewster 10, Borja Baston 6 (2 pens), Routledge 4, Surridge 4, Dhanda 3, Fulton 3, Naughton 3, Byers 2, Celina 2, Garrick 2, Wilmot 2, Cabango 1, Cullen 1, Dyer 1, Roberts 1, van der Hoorn 1, own goal 1.
FA Cup (1): Byers 1.
Carabao Cup (10): Surridge 3, Ayew 2, Byers 2, Garrick 1, Peterson 1, Routledge 1.
Championship Play-Offs (2): Ayew 1, Brewster 1.

Woodman F 43	Roberts C 32 + 6	van der Hoorn M 27 + 1	Rodon J 20 + 1	Bidwell J 36 + 1	Fulton J 29 + 7	Grimes M 46	Dyer N 7 + 3	Byers G 22 + 13	Celina B 28 + 7	Borja Baston G 15 + 5	Peterson K 4 + 3	Naughton K 28 + 4	Kalulu A 7 + 4	Dhanda Y 9 + 7	Surridge S 7 + 13	Ayew A 43 + 1	Garrick J 1 + 10	Routledge W 10 + 11	Carroll T 5 + 3	Wilmot B 16 + 5	Cabango B 19 + 2	McKay B — + 4	John D — + 1	Brewster R 19 + 1	Gallagher C 19	Guehi M 11 + 1	Cullen L — + 6	Mulder E 3 + 1	Match No.
1	2	3	4	5	6	7	8^{2}	9^{1}	10	11	12	13																	1
1	2	3	4	5	6	7	8^{1}		9	11^{3}	12		10^{2}	13	14														2
1	2	3	4	5	6	7	8^{1}	13	9	11^{3}			10^{2}		14	12													3
1	2	3	4	5	6	7		9^{1}	10	11^{2}		14			13	8^{3}	12												4
1	2	3	4	5^{1}	6	7		13	9^{3}	11		12		10^{2}		8	14												5
1	2	3	4	5	6	7		14	10	11^{1}				9^{2}	12	8^{3}		13											6
1	2	3	4	5	6	7	13	12	9^{1}	11^{2}					14	8		10^{3}											7
1	13	3	4	5■	6	7		9^{2}	10	11^{1}		2			12	8													8
1	2	3	4		6^{3}	7		9	10^{1}	11^{2}		5			13	8	12		14										9
1	2	3	4		6	7			10^{2}	11		5		9^{1}		8			12	13									10
1	2	3	4	12	6^{2}	7		13	10^{3}	11		5^{1}		9		8		14											11
1		3	4^{1}	5		7		9^{3}	10	13		2			11^{2}	8	14		6	12									12
1	2	3	4	5	6^{2}	7		12	13	11^{3}	10			9^{1}	14	8													13
1		4		5		7	8^{1}	6	9			2			12	11		10		3									14
1	12	4		5	14	7	8^{1}	6	9^{3}			2			13	11		10^{2}		3									15
1	12	4		5	13	7	8^{1}	6	9^{2}			2			14	11		10^{3}		3									16
1		4		5		7	8^{2}	6	9^{3}	13	12	2			14	11		10^{1}		3									17
1	2	4^{1}		5	6	7		13	9^{2}	11	10^{3}				14	8				3	12								18
1	2	4			6^{2}	7		9		14	10^{1}	5			11^{3}	8			13	3		12							19
1	2	4			6	7	12	9^{2}			10^{1}	5	14		11	8^{3}				3		13							20
1	2	4		5		7		6	11^{1}				12		10	9			8■		3								21
1	2	4		5	12	7		6^{1}	11^{3}					8^{2}	10	9					3	13	14						22
1	2	4		5	12	7		6	11^{3}	10^{2}		14				9		13	8^{1}	3									23
1	2			5		7		6^{3}	11	12			13		10^{2}	9			8^{1}	4	3	14							24
1				5	6	7		12	11			2			10^{2}	9		13	8^{1}	4	3								25
1	2	4^{1}			14	7		6	13	10^{3}		5		8^{2}		9		11		12	3								26
1	2					7		6	9			5				8		10		4	3			11					27
1	2				12	7		6^{1}	10			5				8		13		4	3			11^{2}	9				28
1	2^{1}		12	5^{3}		7		6^{2}	10	14				13		8					3			11	9	4			29
1			3	5	12	7		6^{1}	10			2				8								11^{2}	9	4	13		30
1	2		4			6		9^{1}				5		12		7		10^{2}						11	8	3	13		31
1	2		3			6			10			5	12	9^{1}		7								11	8	4			32
1				5	6^{2}	7			10^{3}			2		12		11	14	8^{1}		3				13	9	4			33
1	14		4	5	6^{2}	7						2	8^{1}			10	12			13	3			11^{3}	9				34
1	13		4	5	6	7						2^{2}	8^{1}			10	12				3			11	9				35
1	12		4	5	6	7						2				10	8^{1}			13	3			11	9^{2}				36
1			4	5	6	7	12					2	8^{1}			10					3			11	9				37
1	2			5	7^{2}	6		13	16				8^{1}	15		10^{4}	12	14		4	3			11^{3}	9^{5}				38
1	2			5	6^{2}	7		13					8^{1}			10	12■	14		4	3^{3}			11	9				39
1				5		7		6	12			2		10^{1}		8				4^{2}	3			11	9	13			40
1	2	12		5	6	7		13				3				8		10^{1}						11^{3}	9^{2}	4	14		41
1	5			8	6	7						2				9		12			3			10^{1}	11	4			42
1^{3}	5			8^{4}	6^{2}	7		13	16			2				10		12			3			11^{1}	9	4^{5}	15	14	43
	5	3^{1}		8	6^{2}	7		14	13			2■				11	15				12			10^{4}	9^{3}	4		1	44
	5	3^{2}		8	6	7								14		10		13			2			11^{1}	9^{3}	4	12	1	45
	5	3^{2}		8	6^{1}	7			15					12		10		13^{4}			2^{3}			11	9	4	14	1	46

FA Cup

Third Round	QPR	(a)	1-5

Carabao Cup

First Round	Northampton T	(h)	3-1
Second Round	Cambridge U	(h)	6-0
Third Round	Watford	(a)	1-2

Championship Play-Offs

Semi-Finals 1st leg	Brentford	(h)	1-0
Semi-Finals 2nd leg	Brentford	(a)	1-3

SWINDON TOWN

FOUNDATION

It is generally accepted that Swindon Town came into being in 1881, although there is no firm evidence that the club's founder, Rev. William Pitt, captain of the Spartans (an offshoot of a cricket club), changed his club's name to Swindon Town before 1883, when the Spartans amalgamated with St Mark's Young Men's Friendly Society.

The Energy Check County Ground, County Road, Swindon, Wiltshire SN1 2ED.

Telephone: (0330) 002 1879.

Ticket Office: (0330) 002 1879.

Website: www.swindontownfc.co.uk

Email: reception@swindontownfc.co.uk

Ground Capacity: 15,547.

Record Attendance: 32,000 v Arsenal, FA Cup 3rd rd, 15 January 1972.

Pitch Measurements: 100m × 68m (109.5yd × 74.5yd).

Chairman: Lee Power.

Chief Executive: Steve Anderson.

Manager: Richie Wellens.

Assistant Manager: Noel Hunt.

Colours: Red shirts with white trim, white shorts with red trim, red socks with white trim.

Year Formed: 1881* (*see Foundation*).

Turned Professional: 1894.

Club Nickname: 'The Robins'.

Grounds: 1881, The Croft; 1896, County Ground (renamed The Energy Check County Ground 2017).

First Football League Game: 28 August 1920, Division 3, v Luton T (h) W 9–1 – Nash; Kay, Macconachie; Langford, Hawley, Wareing; Jefferson (1), Fleming (4), Rogers, Batty (2), Davies (1), (1 og).

Record League Victory: 9–1 v Luton T, Division 3 (S), 28 August 1920 – Nash; Kay, Macconachie; Langford, Hawley, Wareing; Jefferson (1), Fleming (4), Rogers, Batty (2), Davies (1), (1 og).

Record Cup Victory: 10–1 v Farnham U Breweries (a), FA Cup 1st rd (replay), 28 November 1925 – Nash; Dickenson, Weston, Archer, Bew, Adey; Denyer (2), Wall (1), Richardson (4), Johnson (3), Davies.

Record Defeat: 1–10 v Manchester C, FA Cup 4th rd (replay), 25 January 1930.

Most League Points (2 for a win): 64, Division 3, 1968–69.

HONOURS

League Champions: Second Division – 1995–96; FL 2 – 2011–12, 2019–20; Division 4 – 1985–86.
Runners-up: Division 3 – 1962–63, 1968–69.

FA Cup: semi-final – 1910, 1912.

League Cup Winners: 1969.

League Trophy: *Runners-up:* 2012.

Anglo-Italian Cup Winners: 1970.

FOOTBALL YEARBOOK FACT FILE

Unusually, Swindon Town switched to professional status during the middle of a season. At a meeting in January 1895 it was resolved that the club would begin to pay their players from the beginning of the following month. The Robins had been due to play Old Carthusians in an FA Amateur Cup tie but after the original fixture was postponed due to frost they withdrew from the competition.

Most League Points (3 for a win): 102, Division 4, 1985–86.

Most League Goals: 100, Division 3 (S), 1926–27.

Highest League Scorer in Season: Harry Morris, 47, Division 3 (S), 1926–27.

Most League Goals in Total Aggregate: Harry Morris, 216, 1926–33.

Most League Goals in One Match: 5, Harry Morris v QPR, Division 3 (S), 18 December 1926; 5, Harry Morris v Norwich C, Division 3 (S), 26 April 1930; 5, Keith East v Mansfield T, Division 3, 20 November 1965.

Most Capped Player: Rod Thomas, 30 (50), Wales.

Most League Appearances: John Trollope, 770, 1960–80.

Youngest League Player: Paul Rideout, 16 years 107 days v Hull C, 29 November 1980.

Record Transfer Fee Received: A combined £4,000,000 from QPR for Ben Gladwin and Massimo Luongo, May 2015.

Record Transfer Fee Paid: £800,000 to West Ham U for Joey Beauchamp, August 1994.

Football League Record: 1920 Original Member of Division 3; 1921–58 Division 3 (S); 1958–63 Division 3; 1963–65 Division 2; 1965–69 Division 3; 1969–74 Division 2; 1974–82 Division 3; 1982–86 Division 4; 1986–87 Division 3; 1987–92 Division 2; 1992–93 Division 1; 1993–94 Premier League; 1994–95 Division 1; 1995–96 Division 2; 1996–2000 Division 1; 2000–04 Division 2; 2004–06 FL 1; 2006–07 FL 2; 2007–11 FL 1; 2011–12 FL 2; 2012–17 FL 1; 2017–20 FL 2; 2020– FL 1.

MANAGERS

Sam Allen 1902–33
Ted Vizard 1933–39
Neil Harris 1939–41
Louis Page 1945–53
Maurice Lindley 1953–55
Bert Head 1956–65
Danny Williams 1965–69
Fred Ford 1969–71
Dave Mackay 1971–72
Les Allen 1972–74
Danny Williams 1974–78
Bobby Smith 1978–80
John Trollope 1980–83
Ken Beamish 1983–84
Lou Macari 1984–89
Ossie Ardiles 1989–91
Glenn Hoddle 1991–93
John Gorman 1993–94
Steve McMahon 1994–98
Jimmy Quinn 1998–2000
Colin Todd 2000
Andy King 2000–01
Roy Evans 2001
Andy King 2001–05
Iffy Onuora 2005–06
Dennis Wise 2006
Paul Sturrock 2006–07
Maurice Malpas 2008
Danny Wilson 2008–11
Paul Hart 2011
Paolo Di Canio 2011–13
Kevin MacDonald 2013
Mark Cooper 2013–15
Martin Ling 2015
Luke Williams 2015–17
David Flitcroft 2017–18
Phil Brown 2018
Richie Wellens November 2018–

LATEST SEQUENCES

Longest Sequence of League Wins: 10, 31.12.2011 – 28.2.2012.

Longest Sequence of League Defeats: 8, 29.8.2005 – 8.10.2005.

Longest Sequence of League Draws: 6, 22.11.1991 – 28.12.1991.

Longest Sequence of Unbeaten League Matches: 22, 12.1.1986 – 23.8.1986.

Longest Sequence Without a League Win: 19, 30.10.1999 – 4.3.2000.

Successive Scoring Runs: 31 from 17.4.1926.

Successive Non-scoring Runs: 5 from 5.4.1997.

TEN YEAR LEAGUE RECORD

		P	W	D	L	F	A	Pts	Pos
2010-11	FL 1	46	9	14	23	50	72	41	24
2011-12	FL 2	46	29	6	11	75	32	93	1
2012-13	FL 1	46	20	14	12	72	39	74	6
2013-14	FL 1	46	19	9	18	63	59	66	8
2014-15	FL 1	46	23	10	13	76	57	79	4
2015-16	FL 1	46	16	11	19	64	71	59	15
2016-17	FL 1	46	11	11	24	44	66	44	22
2017-18	FL 2	46	20	8	18	67	65	68	9
2018-19	FL 2	46	16	16	14	59	56	64	13
2019-20	FL 2	36	21	6	9	62	39	69	1§

§Decided on points-per-game (1.92)

DID YOU KNOW?

Swindon Town were one of the earliest teams to arrange a former players' match for charitable purposes. In September 1899 a team of former Swindon players faced their counterparts from Reading in a match to raise funds for the widow of club skipper Jimmy Munro who had died suddenly from meningitis earlier in the year. Reading won the match 3-2.

SWINDON TOWN – SKY BET LEAGUE TWO 2019–20 LEAGUE RECORD

Match No.	Date	Venue	Opponents	Result		H/T Score	Lg Pos.	Goalscorers	Attendance
1	Aug 3	A	Scunthorpe U	W	2-0	0-0	2	Yates [59], Anderson [70]	4135
2	10	H	Carlisle U	W	3-2	0-0	2	Yates [56], Fryers [70], Woolery [90]	7024
3	17	A	Exeter C	D	1-1	0-0	1	Doyle [88]	5435
4	20	H	Northampton T	L	0-1	0-0	7		7203
5	24	A	Cheltenham T	D	2-2	2-2	10	Doyle 2 [6, 33]	4401
6	31	H	Morecambe	W	3-1	3-1	5	Doyle 2 [5, 21], Yates [17]	6877
7	Sept 7	A	Leyton Orient	W	3-1	3-0	4	Anderson [23], Widdowson (og) [43], Yates [45]	7042
8	14	H	Macclesfield T	W	3-0	2-0	2	Anderson [37], Doyle 2 [45, 76]	7055
9	17	H	Colchester U	L	0-3	0-1	4		6634
10	21	A	Cambridge U	W	1-0	1-0	4	Yates [27]	4443
11	28	H	Newport Co	L	0-2	0-1	5		7843
12	Oct 5	A	Bradford C	L	1-2	0-0	7	Yates [74]	14,136
13	12	H	Plymouth Arg	D	1-1	1-0	7	Doyle [45]	9548
14	19	A	Crewe Alex	L	1-3	1-0	7	Doyle [37]	4792
15	22	H	Stevenage	W	1-0	0-0	7	Doyle [90]	5524
16	26	A	Crawley T	W	4-0	2-0	5	Doyle 3 [5, 44, 61], Yates [87]	2601
17	Nov 2	H	Walsall	W	2-1	1-0	3	Doyle [5], Jaiyesimi [47]	7014
18	16	A	Salford C	W	3-2	1-1	1	Doyle 2 (1 pen) [10, 54 (p)], Yates [78]	3509
19	23	H	Mansfield T	W	1-0	1-0	1	Doyle [23]	6741
20	Dec 7	A	Grimsby T	W	3-0	2-0	1	Doyle [10], Yates 2 [24, 52]	3723
21	14	H	Oldham Ath	W	2-0	1-0	1	Woolery [45], Doyle [85]	6825
22	21	A	Forest Green R	D	2-2	2-0	1	Doyle 2 [16, 35]	4216
23	26	H	Cambridge U	W	4-0	3-0	1	Doyle (pen) [5], Anderson 3 [40, 45, 66]	8211
24	29	A	Port Vale	L	0-2	0-1	1		5495
25	Jan 1	A	Plymouth Arg	W	2-1	1-1	1	Jaiyesimi [35], Doyle [77]	15,062
26	4	H	Bradford C	D	1-1	1-0	1	Yates (pen) [11]	8407
27	11	H	Crewe Alex	W	3-1	1-0	1	Hunt [32], Yates [69], Rose [72]	7601
28	18	A	Newport Co	L	0-2	0-1	1		4981
29	25	H	Port Vale	W	3-0	2-0	1	Jaiyesimi [41], Hope [45], Doughty [60]	7343
30	28	A	Colchester U	L	1-3	0-0	1	Jaiyesimi [48]	3258
31	Feb 1	H	Exeter C	W	2-1	2-1	1	Collins (og) [20], Hope [45]	13,095
32	8	A	Carlisle U	D	1-1	1-0	1	Edmonds-Green [11]	4620
33	11	A	Northampton T	W	1-0	0-0	1	Lyden [77]	5759
34	22	H	Grimsby T	W	3-1	0-0	1	Yates [46], Jaiyesimi [49], Hendrie (og) [57]	8180
35	Mar 3	H	Scunthorpe U	W	2-0	1-0	1	Doyle 2 [41, 77]	7583
36	7	H	Forest Green R	L	0-2	0-1	2		9257
37	14	A	Oldham Ath	Cancelled					
38	17	A	Stevenage	Cancelled					
39	21	H	Crawley T	Cancelled					
40	24	H	Salford C	Cancelled					
41	28	A	Walsall	Cancelled					
42	31	A	Mansfield T	Cancelled					
43	Apr 10	H	Cheltenham T	Cancelled					
44	13	A	Morecambe	Cancelled					
45	18	H	Leyton Orient	Cancelled					
46	25	A	Macclesfield T	Cancelled					

Final League Position: 1 (on points-per-game basis)

GOALSCORERS

League (62): Doyle 25 (2 pens), Yates 13 (1 pen), Anderson 6, Jaiyesimi 5, Hope 2, Woolery 2, Doughty 1, Edmonds-Green 1, Fryers 1, Hunt 1, Lyden 1, Rose 1, own goals 3.
FA Cup (1): Yates 1.
Carabao Cup (0).
Leasing.com Trophy (2): Ballard 1, May 1.

McCormick L 12	Hunt R 33 + 1	Conroy D 11	Baudry M 24	Fryers Z 22	Isgrove L 24 + 5	Doughty M 24 + 7	Lyden J 17 + 4	Woolery K 20 + 14	Anderson K 17 + 3	Yates J 30 + 1	Ballard D — + 1	Jaiyesimi D 15 + 6	Twine S — + 6	Doyle E 28	May A 1 + 8	Reid T 1 + 3	Iandolo E 10 + 3	Rose D 10 + 9	Grant A 29 + 1	Broadbent T 3 + 6	Zakuani G 5 + 1	Benda S 24	Donohue D 5	Caddis P 18 + 1	Curran T — + 2	McGilp C — + 2	Edmonds-Green R 9	Hope H 4 + 1	Muskwe A — + 5	Palmer M — + 1	Match No.
1	2	3	4	5	6^{2}	7	8	9	10^{1}	11	12	13																			1
1	2	4	3	5	8^{1}	6	7	10	9	11			12																		2
1	2	3	4	5	8^{2}	7	6	10	9^{1}				12	11	13																3
1	2	3	4	5^{2}	8	6	9	10					13	11	7^{1}	12															4
1	5	4	3		8^{2}	7■	6	10	9					11		2^{1}	12	13													5
1	5	4	3		6		8	12	9^{2}	11^{1}				10	13	14	2^{3}	7													6
1	2	3	4		6^{1}		8^{3}	13	9^{2}	11				10	14		5	7	12												7
1	2	3^{2}	4		6^{1}			13	9	11				10	12		5	7	8^{3}	14											8
1	2	4	3^{2}		6	13		14	9^{3}	10				11			5	7^{1}	8	12											9
1	2	3		4	6^{3}	13		12	9^{2}	10				11	14		5	7^{1}	8												10
1	2	3^{2}		4	6	13		9^{3}		11				10	12	14	5	8^{1}	7												11
1	2			4	8^{3}	12	7^{1}	10	9^{2}	11			13		14		5		6		3										12
	2		3		6^{1}	12	7	13	9^{2}	11				10					8		4	1	5								13
	2		3		6^{2}		7	13	9^{1}	11^{3}		14		10				12	8		4	1	5								14
	2		3	4	6^{1}	8		9^{2}		10		12		11					7		13	1	5								15
	2		3	4	6^{3}	8	13	14	12	10		9^{2}		11^{1}					7			1	5								16
	2		3	4		8	12	13	9^{1}	10		6^{2}		11					7			1	5								17
	2		3	4		9^{2}	7	8		10		12		11^{3}			5	14	6^{1}			1		13							18
	5		3	4		9^{3}	7^{2}	8^{1}		10				11			14	12	6	13		1		2							19
	5		3	4		9	7^{3}	8		10^{2}		12		11^{1}				13	6			1		2	14						20
	5		3	4	14	8^{2}		9	12	11^{1}		6^{3}		10				13	7			1		2							21
	5		3	4		9^{2}		6^{1}	7^{3}	10		13		11			14	12	8			1		2							22
			3		12	9		6^{1}	7	10^{3}				11			5	13	8^{2}		4	1		2	14						23
	12		3^{3}		14	9^{2}	13	6	7	10				11			5^{1}		8		4	1		2							24
	5			4	8^{2}	13	6	12		10^{3}		9^{1}		11				7	3			1		2		14					25
	5			4^{3}	8^{2}	13	6■	10		11		9^{1}			14			7	3	12		1		2							26
	5				8	7		10		11		9						6	3	4		1		2							27
	5				8^{2}			10		11		9	12					7^{1}	6	3		1		2		13	4				28
	5		3^{1}		8^{3}	7		10				9^{2}	14					13	6	12		1		2			4	11			29
	5		3			8	6	10				9							7			1		2			4	11			30
	5		3			7		12		10		6		11^{1}					8			1		2			4	9^{2}	13		31
	5			4	14	8		13		11		6^{2}		10^{1}					7			1		2			3	9^{3}	12		32
	5			4	9^{3}	8	6	14		13		11^{1}		10					7	12		1		2^{2}			3				33
	5			4	6^{1}	8	12	14		11		9^{2}		10^{3}					7			1		2			3		13		34
				5	9^{2}	8			13	11		7^{1}		10					6^{3}	4		1		2			3		12	14	35
	5			4	14	8			7^{3}	11^{1}		9^{2}		10					6			1		2			3	13	12		36
																															37
																															38
																															39
																															40
																															41
																															42
																															43
																															44
																															45
																															46

FA Cup

First Round	Cheltenham T	(a)	1-1
Replay	Cheltenham T	(h)	0-1

Carabao Cup

First Round	Colchester U	(a)	0-3

Leasing.com Trophy

Group F (S)	Chelsea U21	(h)	2-3
Group F (S)	Plymouth Arg	(h)	0-3
Group F (S)	Bristol R	(a)	0-1

TOTTENHAM HOTSPUR

FOUNDATION

The Hotspur Football Club was formed from an older cricket club in 1882. Most of the founders were old boys of St John's Presbyterian School and Tottenham Grammar School. The Casey brothers were well to the fore as the family provided the club's first goalposts (painted blue and white) and their first ball. They soon adopted the local YMCA as their meeting place, but after a couple of moves settled at the Red House.

Tottenham Hotspur Stadium, Lilywhite House, 782 High Road, Tottenham, London N17 0BX.

Telephone: (0344) 499 5000.

Ticket Office: (0344) 844 0102.

Website: www.tottenhamhotspur.com

Email: supporterservices@tottenhamhotspur.com

Ground Capacity: 62,062.

Record Attendance: 75,038 v Sunderland, FA Cup 6th rd, 5 March 1938 (at White Hart Lane); 85,512 v Bayer Leverkusen, UEFA Champions League Group E, 2 November 2016 (at Wembley); 61,104 v Chelsea, Premier League, 22 December 2019 (at Tottenham Hotspur Stadium).

Pitch Measurements: 105m × 68m (115yd × 74.5yd).

Executive Chairman: Daniel Levy.

Head Coach: Jose Mourinho.

Assistant Head Coach: Joao Sacramento.

Colours: White shirts with navy blue and yellow trim, navy blue shorts with yellow trim, white socks with navy blue and yellow trim.

Year Formed: 1882. ***Turned Professional:*** 1895.

Previous Names: 1882, Hotspur Football Club; 1884, Tottenham Hotspur.

Club Nickname: 'Spurs'.

Grounds: 1882, Tottenham Marshes; 1888, Northumberland Park; 1899, White Hart Lane; 2018, Tottenham Hotspur Stadium.

First Football League Game: 1 September 1908, Division 2, v Wolverhampton W (h) W 3–0 – Hewitson; Coquet, Burton; Morris (1), Danny Steel, Darnell; Walton, Woodward (2), Macfarlane, Bobby Steel, Middlemiss.

HONOURS

League Champions: Division 1 – 1950–51, 1960–61; Division 2 – 1919–20, 1949–50.
Runners-up: Premier League – 2016–17; Division 1 – 1921–22, 1951–52, 1956–57, 1962–63; Division 2 – 1908–09, 1932–33.

FA Cup Winners: 1901 (as non-league club), 1921, 1961, 1962, 1967, 1981, 1982, 1991.
Runners-up: 1987.

League Cup Winners: 1971, 1973, 1999, 2008.
Runners-up: 1982, 2002, 2009, 2015.

European Competitions
European Cup: 1961–62 *(sf)*.
Champions League: 2010–11 *(qf)*, 2016–17, 2017–18, 2018–19 *(runners-up)*, 2019–20.
UEFA Cup: 1971–72 *(winners)*, 1972–73 *(sf)*, 1973–74 *(runners-up)*, 1983–84 *(winners)*, 1984–85 *(qf)*, 1999–2000, 2006–07 *(qf)*, 2007–08, 2008–09.
Europa League: 2011–12, 2012–13 *(qf)*, 2013–14, 2014–15, 2015–16, 2016–17.
European Cup-Winners' Cup: 1962–63 *(winners)*, 1963–64, 1967–68, 1981–82 *(sf)*, 1982–83, 1991–92 *(qf)*.
Intertoto Cup: 1995.

Record League Victory: 9–0 v Bristol R, Division 2, 22 October 1977 – Daines; Naylor, Holmes, Hoddle (1), McAllister, Perryman, Pratt, McNab, Moores (3), Lee (4), Taylor (1).

FOOTBALL YEARBOOK FACT FILE

Roy Low became the first substitute to appear for Tottenham Hotspur in a Football League match when he replaced Derek Possee during the 1-1 draw with Arsenal at White Hart Lane on 11 September 1965. He was one of just two substitutes used by Spurs in League games during the 1965–66 season.

Record Cup Victory: 13–2 v Crewe Alex, FA Cup 4th rd (replay), 3 February 1960 – Brown; Hills, Henry; Blanchflower, Norman, Mackay; White, Harmer (1), Smith (4), Allen (5), Jones (3 incl. 1p).

Record Defeat: 0–8 v Cologne, UEFA Intertoto Cup, 22 July 1995.

Most League Points (2 for a win): 70, Division 2, 1919–20.

Most League Points (3 for a win): 86, Premier League, 2016–17.

Most League Goals: 115, Division 1, 1960–61.

Highest League Scorer in Season: Jimmy Greaves, 37, Division 1, 1962–63.

Most League Goals in Total Aggregate: Jimmy Greaves, 220, 1961–70.

Most League Goals in One Match: 5, Ted Harper v Reading, Division 2, 30 August 1930; 5, Alf Stokes v Birmingham C, Division 1, 18 September 1957; 5, Bobby Smith v Aston Villa, Division 1, 29 March 1958; 5, Jermain Defoe v Wigan Ath, Premier League, 22 November 2009.

Most Capped Player: Hugo Lloris, 76 (114), France.

Most League Appearances: Steve Perryman, 655, 1969–86.

Youngest League Player: Ally Dick, 16 years 301 days v Manchester C, 20 February 1982.

Record Transfer Fee Received: £85,300,000 from Real Madrid for Gareth Bale, September 2013.

Record Transfer Fee Paid: £55,500,000 (rising to £63,000,000) to Lyon for Tanguy Ndombele, July 2019.

Football League Record: 1908 Elected to Division 2; 1909–15 Division 1; 1919–20 Division 2; 1920–28 Division 1; 1928–33 Division 2; 1933–35 Division 1; 1935–50 Division 2; 1950–77 Division 1; 1977–78 Division 2; 1978–92 Division 1; 1992– Premier League.

MANAGERS

Frank Brettell 1898–99
John Cameron 1899–1906
Fred Kirkham 1907–08
Peter McWilliam 1912–27
Billy Minter 1927–29
Percy Smith 1930–35
Jack Tresadern 1935–38
Peter McWilliam 1938–42
Arthur Turner 1942–46
Joe Hulme 1946–49
Arthur Rowe 1949–55
Jimmy Anderson 1955–58
Bill Nicholson 1958–74
Terry Neill 1974–76
Keith Burkinshaw 1976–84
Peter Shreeves 1984–86
David Pleat 1986–87
Terry Venables 1987–91
Peter Shreeves 1991–92
Doug Livermore 1992–93
Ossie Ardiles 1993–94
Gerry Francis 1994–97
Christian Gross *(Head Coach)* 1997–98
George Graham 1998–2001
Glenn Hoddle 2001–03
David Pleat (*Caretaker*) 2003–04
Jacques Santini 2004
Martin Jol 2004–07
Juande Ramos 2007–08
Harry Redknapp 2008–12
Andre Villas-Boas 2012–13
Tim Sherwood 2013–14
Mauricio Pochettino 2014–19
Jose Mourinho November 2019–

LATEST SEQUENCES

Longest Sequence of League Wins: 13, 23.4.1960 – 1.10.1960.

Longest Sequence of League Defeats: 7, 1.1.1994 – 27.2.1994.

Longest Sequence of League Draws: 6, 9.1.1999 – 27.2.1999.

Longest Sequence of Unbeaten League Matches: 22, 31.8.1949 – 31.12.1949.

Longest Sequence Without a League Win: 16, 29.12.1934 – 13.4.1935.

Successive Scoring Runs: 32 from 24.2.1962.

Successive Non-scoring Runs: 6 from 28.12.1985.

TEN YEAR LEAGUE RECORD

		P	*W*	*D*	*L*	*F*	*A*	*Pts*	*Pos*
2010-11	PR Lge	38	16	14	8	55	46	62	5
2011-12	PR Lge	38	20	9	9	66	41	69	4
2012-13	PR Lge	38	21	9	8	66	46	72	5
2013-14	PR Lge	38	21	6	11	55	51	69	6
2014-15	PR Lge	38	19	7	12	58	53	64	5
2015-16	PR Lge	38	19	13	6	69	35	70	3
2016-17	PR Lge	38	26	8	4	86	26	86	2
2017-18	PR Lge	38	23	8	7	74	36	77	3
2018-19	PR Lge	38	23	2	13	67	39	71	4
2019-20	PR Lg	38	16	11	11	61	47	59	6

DID YOU KNOW ?

Goalkeeper Paul Robinson became only the third goalkeeper to score a goal in the history of the Premier League when he netted for Tottenham Hotspur against Watford in March 2007. His 80-yard strike directly from a free kick was also the first time a keeper had scored from his own half in the competition.

TOTTENHAM HOTSPUR – PREMIER LEAGUE 2019–20 LEAGUE RECORD

Match No.	*Date*	*Venue*	*Opponents*	*Result*		*H/T Score*	*Lg Pos.*	*Goalscorers*	*Attendance*
1	Aug 10	H	Aston Villa	W	3-1	0-1	5	Ndombele [73], Kane 2 [86, 90]	60,407
2	17	A	Manchester C	D	2-2	1-2	5	Lamela [23], Lucas Moura [56]	54,503
3	25	H	Newcastle U	L	0-1	0-1	7		59,245
4	Sept 1	A	Arsenal	D	2-2	2-1	9	Eriksen [10], Kane (pen) [40]	60,333
5	14	H	Crystal Palace	W	4-0	4-0	3	Son 2 [10, 23], Van Aanholt (og) [21], Lamela [42]	59,812
6	21	A	Leicester C	L	1-2	1-0	5	Kane [29]	32,129
7	28	H	Southampton	W	2-1	2-1	4	Ndombele [24], Kane [43]	59,645
8	Oct 5	A	Brighton & HA	L	0-3	0-2	8		30,610
9	19	H	Watford	D	1-1	0-1	7	Alli [86]	58,754
10	27	A	Liverpool	L	1-2	1-0	11	Kane [1]	53,222
11	Nov 3	A	Everton	D	1-1	0-0	11	Alli [63]	39,001
12	9	H	Sheffield U	D	1-1	0-0	12	Son [58]	59,781
13	23	A	West Ham U	W	3-2	2-0	9	Son [36], Lucas Moura [43], Kane [49]	59,930
14	30	H	Bournemouth	W	3-2	1-0	5	Alli 2 [21, 50], Sissoko [69]	59,626
15	Dec 4	A	Manchester U	L	1-2	1-1	8	Alli [39]	73,252
16	7	H	Burnley	W	5-0	3-0	6	Kane 2 [5, 54], Lucas Moura [9], Son [32], Sissoko [74]	58,401
17	15	A	Wolverhampton W	W	2-1	1-0	5	Lucas Moura [8], Vertonghen [90]	31,674
18	22	H	Chelsea	L	0-2	0-2	7		61,104
19	26	H	Brighton & HA	W	2-1	0-1	5	Kane [53], Alli [72]	56,308
20	28	A	Norwich C	D	2-2	0-1	6	Eriksen [55], Kane (pen) [83]	27,072
21	Jan 1	A	Southampton	L	0-1	0-1	6		30,976
22	11	H	Liverpool	L	0-1	0-1	8		61,023
23	18	A	Watford	D	0-0	0-0	8		21,366
24	22	H	Norwich C	W	2-1	1-0	6	Alli [38], Son [79]	58,182
25	Feb 2	H	Manchester C	W	2-0	0-0	5	Bergwijn [63], Son [71]	61,022
26	16	A	Aston Villa	W	3-2	2-1	5	Alderweireld [27], Son 2 [45, 90]	41,874
27	22	A	Chelsea	L	1-2	0-1	5	Rudiger (og) [89]	40,608
28	Mar 1	H	Wolverhampton W	L	2-3	2-1	7	Bergwijn [13], Aurier [45]	58,064
29	7	A	Burnley	D	1-1	0-1	8	Alli (pen) [50]	20,496
30	June 19	H	Manchester U	D	1-1	1-0	8	Bergwijn [27]	0
31	23	H	West Ham U	W	2-0	0-0	7	Soucek (og) [64], Kane [82]	0
32	July 2	A	Sheffield U	L	1-3	0-1	9	Kane [90]	0
33	6	H	Everton	W	1-0	1-0	8	Keane (og) [24]	0
34	9	A	Bournemouth	D	0-0	0-0	9		0
35	12	H	Arsenal	W	2-1	1-1	8	Son [19], Alderweireld [81]	0
36	15	A	Newcastle U	W	3-1	1-0	7	Son [27], Kane 2 [60, 90]	0
37	19	H	Leicester C	W	3-0	3-0	6	Justin (og) [6], Kane 2 [37, 40]	0
38	26	A	Crystal Palace	D	1-1	1-0	6	Kane [13]	0

Final League Position: 6

GOALSCORERS

League (61): Kane 18 (2 pens), Son 11, Alli 8 (1 pen), Lucas Moura 4, Bergwijn 3, Alderweireld 2, Eriksen 2, Lamela 2, Ndombele 2, Sissoko 2, Aurier 1, Vertonghen 1, own goals 5.
FA Cup (8): Lucas Moura 2, Son 2 (1 pen), Lamela 1, Lo Celso 1, Vertonghen 1, own goal 1.
Carabao Cup (0).
UEFA Champions League (18): Kane 6 (2 pens), Son 5, Alli 1, Aurier 1, Eriksen 1, Lamela 1, Lo Celso 1, Lucas Moura 1, Sessegnon 1.
Leasing.com Trophy (2): Oakley-Boothe 1, Shashoua 1.

Lloris H 21	Walker-Peters K 3	Alderweireld T 33	Sanchez D 27 + 2	Rose D 10 + 2	Ndombele T 12 + 9	Winks H 26 + 5	Sissoko M 28 + 1	Lamela E 12 + 13	Lucas Moura R 25 + 10	Kane H 29	Eriksen C 10 + 10	Nkoudou G — + 1	Skipp O 1 + 6	Lo Celso G 15 + 13	Son H 28 + 2	Davies B 16 + 2	Vertonghen J 19 + 4	Alli B 21 + 4	Aurier S 31 + 2	Gazzaniga P 17 + 1	Wanyama V — + 2	Dier E 15 + 4	Foyth J 1 + 3	Sessegnon R 4 + 2	Parrott T — + 2	Tanganga J 6	Fernandes G — + 7	Bergwijn S 8 + 6	Match No.
1	2	3	4	5	6^3	7^1	8	9^2	10	11	12	13	14																1
1	2	3	4	5	7	6^1	8	9^2	12	11	10^3		14	13															2
1	2^2	3	4	5^3		7	6	9^1	8	11	12			13	10	14													3
1		3	2	5		7	6	8^1		11	10			13	9^2		4	12											4
1		3		5^2	12	7^1	6	8	14	11^3	9				10	13	4		2										5
		3		5	8^3	6	7^1	9^2	14	10	13				11		4		2	1	12								6
1		3		5	8^2	6^3	7	12		10	9				11^1		4		2■		14	13							7
1^1		3			6^2	13	2	8	14	11	9				10^3	5	4			12		7							8
		2	3^1	8	14	7^3	6	13	9^2	11					12		4	10	5	1									9
		3	4	5	12	7^1	6		13	10	9^3			14	11			8	2^2	1									10
		3	4		7^1		6		11		9^3			12	8■	5		10	2^2	1			13	14					11
			3		7^1	12	6		14	11				8	10	5		9^2	2^3	1		4	13						12
		4	3	12		7	14		8^3	11	13				10	5^1		9^2	2	1		6							13
		4	3		6^1	14	8		12	11				13	10^2		5	9^3	2	1		7							14
		4	3		13	7^2	6^3		8^1	11	12			14	10		5	9	2	1									15
		4	3				6		8^1	11			13		10		5	9^3	2^2	1		7		12	14				16
		4	3			13	6		8^1	11	12				10^3		5	9^2	2	1		7	14						17
		4	3	14	13		7		8^2	11	12				10■		5^3	9	2	1		6^1							18
		3	2			6^2	7		9^3	11	13			12			4	10	5	1		14		8^1					19
		3	13		5			14	12	10	8			7^3			4^1	11	6	1			2^2	9					20
		3			7^1		6	13	10	11^2	8			12			4	9	2	1				5					21
		3	4	5^1		8		12	10		7^2			13	9			11	6	1						2			22
		3				7		9	10		12			6^2	11		4	8^1	2	1						5	13		23
1		3				7^1		8^2	11		13			6	10		4^3	9	2			12		5			14		24
1		3	4		12	7		13	11^3					6	8			9^1	2			14				5		10^2	25
1		3	4			7			8					12	11	5	14	9^2	2			6^1					13	10^3	26
1		4^2	3		8^1	9		12	10					7		6	5	14	13							2		11^3	27
			2		12	7			9					6		8^3		10	5^2	1		3			14	4^1	13	11	28
1		4	2		7^2			9^3	12				6^1	13			8	11	14			3				5		10	29
1			3			7	6	9^1		11				13	10	5			2			4					12	8^2	30
1			3			14	6	12	8^2	11				7	10^3	5		9^1	2			4						13	31
1			3		13		6^2	12	8	11				7	10	5^4	15	14	2^3			4						9^1	32
1		3				7	6	13	9^2	10				8^3	11^1	5	14		2			4						12	33
1		3			12	7	6^3	9	14	10				8^2	13	5	4		2^4								15	11^1	34
1		4	3			8	6	14	9^1	11			13	7^2	10^3	5			2									12	35
1		4	3			7	6	13	8^1	11^3				9^2	10	5	14		2									12	36
1		4	3			7^4	6	12	9^1	10			15	8^2	11^3	5			2								14	13	37
1		3	15			7	6^2		8^4	11			14	9^1	10^3	5		13	2			4						12	38

FA Cup

Third Round	Middlesbrough	(a)	1-1
Replay	Middlesbrough	(h)	2-1
Fourth Round	Southampton	(a)	1-1
Replay	Southampton	(h)	3-2
Fifth Round	Norwich C	(h)	1-1

(*aet; Norwich C won 3-2 on penalties.*)

Carabao Cup

Third Round	Colchester U	(a)	0-0

(Colchester U won 4-3 on penalties)

UEFA Champions League

Group B	Olympiacos	(a)	2-2
Group B	Bayern Munich	(h)	2-7
Group B	Red Star Belgrade	(h)	5-0
Group B	Red Star Belgrade	(a)	4-0
Group B	Olympiacos	(h)	4-2
Group B	Bayern Munich	(a)	1-3
Round of 16	RB Leipzig	(h)	0-1
Round of 16	RB Leipzig	(a)	0-3

Leasing.com Trophy (Tottenham H U21)

Group A (S)	Ipswich T	(a)	1-2
Group A (S)	Colchester U	(a)	1-1

(Tottenham H U21 won 6-5 on penalties)

Group A (S)	Gillingham	(a)	0-2

TRANMERE ROVERS

FOUNDATION

Formed in 1884 as Belmont they adopted their present title the following year and eventually joined their first league, the West Lancashire League, in 1889–90, the same year as their first success in the Wirral Challenge Cup. The club almost folded in 1899–1900 when all the players left en bloc to join a rival club, but they survived the crisis and went from strength to strength, winning the 'Combination' title in 1907–08 and the Lancashire Combination in 1913–14. They joined the Football League in 1921 from the Central League.

Prenton Park, Prenton Road West, Birkenhead, Merseyside CH42 9PY.

Telephone: (0333) 014 4452.

Ticket Office: (0333) 014 4452 (Option 2).

Website: www.tranmererovers.co.uk

Email: customerservice@tranmererovers.co.uk

Ground Capacity: 15,012.

Record Attendance: 24,424 v Stoke C, FA Cup 4th rd, 5 February 1972.

Pitch Measurements: 100m × 64m (109.5yd × 70yd).

Chairman: Mark Palios.

Vice-Chairman: Nicola Palios.

Managing Director: Dawn Tolcher.

Manager: Mike Jackson.

Assistant Manager: Ian Dawes.

Colours: White shirts with blue trim, white shorts with blue trim, white socks with blue trim.

Year Formed: 1884.

Turned Professional: 1912.

Previous Name: 1884, Belmont AFC; 1885, Tranmere Rovers.

Club Nickname: 'Rovers'.

Grounds: 1884, Steeles Field; 1887, Ravenshaws Field/Old Prenton Park; 1912, Prenton Park.

First Football League Game: 27 August 1921, Division 3 (N), v Crewe Alex (h) W 4–1 – Bradshaw; Grainger, Stuart (1); Campbell, Milnes (1), Heslop; Moreton, Groves (1), Hyam, Ford (1), Hughes.

Record League Victory: 13–4 v Oldham Ath, Division 3 (N), 26 December 1935 – Gray; Platt, Fairhurst; McLaren, Newton, Spencer; Eden, MacDonald (1), Bell (9), Woodward (2), Urmson (1).

Record Cup Victory: 13–0 v Oswestry U, FA Cup 2nd prel rd, 10 October 1914 – Ashcroft; Stevenson, Bullough, Hancock, Taylor, Holden (1), Moreton (1), Cunningham (2), Smith (5), Leck (3), Gould (1).

HONOURS

League Champions: Division 3 (N) – 1937–38.
Runners-up: Division 4 – 1988–89.

FA Cup: quarter-final – 2000, 2001, 2004.

League Cup: *Runners-up:* 2000.

Welsh Cup Winners: 1935.
Runners-up: 1934.

Leyland DAF Cup Winners: 1990.
Runners-up: 1991.

FOOTBALL YEARBOOK FACT FILE

The first Englishman to play in the World Cup finals was George Moorhouse who appeared for the United States in the 1930 tournament in Uruguay. George was on the books of Tranmere Rovers in the early 1920s and made two first-team appearances at outside-left in the 1921–22 season before emigrating to North America.

Record Defeat: 1–9 v Tottenham H, FA Cup 3rd rd (replay), 14 January 1953.

Most League Points (2 for a win): 60, Division 4, 1964–65.

Most League Points (3 for a win): 80, Division 4, 1988–89; Division 3, 1989–90; Division 2, 2002–03.

Most League Goals: 111, Division 3 (N), 1930–31.

Highest League Scorer in Season: Bunny Bell, 35, Division 3 (N), 1933–34.

Most League Goals in Total Aggregate: Ian Muir, 142, 1985–95.

Most League Goals in One Match: 9, Bunny Bell v Oldham Ath, Division 3 (N), 26 December 1935.

Most Capped Player: John Aldridge, 30 (69), Republic of Ireland.

Most League Appearances: Harold Bell, 595, 1946–64 (incl. League record 401 consecutive appearances).

Youngest League Player: Iain Hume, 16 years 167 days v Swindon T, 15 April 2000.

Record Transfer Fee Received: £2,250,000 from WBA for Jason Koumas, August 2002.

Record Transfer Fee Paid: £450,000 to Aston Villa for Shaun Teale, August 1995.

Football League Record: 1921 Original Member of Division 3 (N): 1938–39 Division 2; 1946–58 Division 3 (N); 1958–61 Division 3; 1961–67 Division 4; 1967–75 Division 3; 1975–76 Division 4; 1976–79 Division 3; 1979–89 Division 4; 1989–91 Division 3; 1991–92 Division 2; 1992–2001 Division 1; 2001–04 Division 2; 2004–14 FL 1; 2014–15 FL 2; 2015–18 National League; 2018–19 FL 2; 2019–20 FL 1; 2020– FL 2.

MANAGERS

Bert Cooke 1912–35
Jackie Carr 1935–36
Jim Knowles 1936–39
Bill Ridding 1939–45
Ernie Blackburn 1946–55
Noel Kelly 1955–57
Peter Farrell 1957–60
Walter Galbraith 1961
Dave Russell 1961–69
Jackie Wright 1969–72
Ron Yeats 1972–75
John King 1975–80
Bryan Hamilton 1980–85
Frank Worthington 1985–87
Ronnie Moore 1987
John King 1987–96
John Aldridge 1996–2001
Dave Watson 2001–02
Ray Mathias 2002–03
Brian Little 2003–06
Ronnie Moore 2006–09
John Barnes 2009
Les Parry 2009–12
Ronnie Moore 2012–14
Robert Edwards 2014
Micky Adams 2014–15
Gary Brabin 2015–16
Paul Cardin 2016
Micky Mellon 2016–20
Mike Jackson July 2020–

LATEST SEQUENCES

Longest Sequence of League Wins: 9, 9.2.1990 – 19.3.1990.

Longest Sequence of League Defeats: 8, 29.10.1938 – 17.12.1938.

Longest Sequence of League Draws: 5, 26.12.1997 – 31.1.1998.

Longest Sequence of Unbeaten League Matches: 18, 16.3.1970 – 4.9.1970.

Longest Sequence Without a League Win: 16, 8.11.1969 – 14.3.1970.

Successive Scoring Runs: 32 from 24.2.1934.

Successive Non-scoring Runs: 7 from 20.12.1997.

TEN YEAR LEAGUE RECORD

		P	*W*	*D*	*L*	*F*	*A*	*Pts*	*Pos*
2010-11	FL 1	46	15	11	20	53	60	56	17
2011-12	FL 1	46	14	14	18	49	53	56	12
2012-13	FL 1	46	19	10	17	58	48	67	11
2013-14	FL 1	46	12	11	23	52	79	47	21
2014-15	FL 2	46	9	12	25	45	67	39	24
2015-16	NL	46	22	12	12	61	44	78	6
2016-17	NL	46	29	8	9	79	39	95	2
2017-18	NL	46	24	10	12	78	46	82	2
2018-19	FL 2	46	20	13	13	63	50	73	6
2019-20	FL 1	34	8	8	18	36	60	32	21§

§*Decided on points-per-game (0.94)*

DID YOU KNOW ?

Tranmere Rovers first took part in league competition in the 1889–90 season as members of the West Lancashire Association League. They then played in the Liverpool & District League before joining the Lancashire Combination for 1892–93.

TRANMERE ROVERS – SKY BET LEAGUE ONE 2019–20 LEAGUE RECORD

Match No.	Date	Venue	Opponents	Result	H/T Score	Lg Pos.	Goalscorers	Attendance
1	Aug 3	H	Rochdale	L 2-3	0-1	14	Dooley (og) [89], Jennings [90]	8032
2	10	A	Portsmouth	L 0-2	0-1	20		18,575
3	17	H	Bolton W	W 5-0	2-0	13	Banks [38], Ferrier 2 [40, 46], Jennings [63], Payne [75]	8568
4	20	A	Bristol R	L 0-2	0-1	18		6802
5	31	A	Rotherham U	D 1-1	0-0	19	Payne [90]	8691
6	Sept 7	H	Gillingham	D 2-2	0-2	17	Jennings [67], Mullin [70]	6687
7	14	A	Oxford U	L 0-3	0-1	19		6294
8	17	H	Peterborough U	D 2-2	0-0	19	Ridehalgh [65], Banks [70]	5243
9	21	H	Burton Alb	W 2-1	0-0	18	Banks [90], Payne [90]	6235
10	28	A	Ipswich T	L 1-4	1-1	20	Payne [39]	19,785
11	Oct 5	H	Shrewsbury T	L 0-1	0-1	20		7314
12	13	A	Coventry C	W 1-0	0-0	18	Taylor [83]	5658
13	18	H	Southend U	D 1-1	0-1	17	Mullin (pen) [85]	7066
14	22	A	Sunderland	L 0-5	0-3	20		28,551
15	Nov 2	A	Milton Keynes D	W 3-1	1-1	18	Hepburn-Murphy 3 [19, 53, 69]	7171
16	17	H	Wycombe W	L 0-2	0-2	18		5460
17	23	A	Fleetwood T	L 1-2	0-1	20	Mullin [87]	3811
18	Dec 7	H	Accrington S	D 1-1	1-1	20	Morris [38]	5751
19	14	A	Lincoln C	L 0-1	0-0	20		8369
20	21	H	AFC Wimbledon	W 1-0	1-0	20	Hepburn-Murphy [26]	6285
21	26	A	Burton Alb	L 2-4	1-1	20	Ferrier [26], Morris [64]	3970
22	29	H	Blackpool	D 1-1	1-1	20	Ferrier [43]	8487
23	Jan 1	H	Coventry C	L 1-4	1-2	21	Jennings [34]	7828
24	11	A	Southend U	D 0-0	0-0	21		5988
25	18	H	Ipswich T	L 1-2	1-0	21	Monthe [32]	7921
26	29	H	Sunderland	L 0-1	0-0	21		6850
27	Feb 1	A	Bolton W	L 0-2	0-1	21		13,044
28	4	H	Doncaster R	L 0-3	0-0	21		5464
29	8	H	Portsmouth	L 0-2	0-1	21		6985
30	11	H	Bristol R	D 0-0	0-0	21		5026
31	22	A	Wycombe W	L 1-3	0-1	21	Vaughan [63]	4756
32	25	A	Shrewsbury T	W 3-2	2-0	21	Ellis [9], Woodyard [14], Taylor [90]	5009
33	Mar 7	A	Accrington S	W 2-1	1-0	21	Vaughan [8], Ellis [77]	2881
34	10	A	Blackpool	W 2-1	2-0	21	Ferrier [37], Vaughan [45]	8235
35	14	H	Lincoln C	Cancelled				
36	17	A	Rochdale	Cancelled				
37	21	A	AFC Wimbledon	Cancelled				
38	28	H	Milton Keynes D	Cancelled				
39	Apr 4	A	Doncaster R	Cancelled				
40	13	H	Rotherham U	Cancelled				
41	18	A	Gillingham	Cancelled				
42	21	H	Fleetwood T	Cancelled				
43	25	H	Oxford U	Cancelled				
44	May 3	A	Peterborough U	Cancelled				

Final League Position: 21 (on points-per-game basis)

GOALSCORERS

League (36): Ferrier 5, Hepburn-Murphy 4, Jennings 4, Payne 4, Banks 3, Mullin 3 (1 pen), Vaughan 3, Ellis 2, Morris 2, Taylor 2, Monthe 1, Ridehalgh 1, Woodyard 1, own goal 1.
FA Cup (14): Ferrier 4, Morris 3, Blackett-Taylor 2, Monthe 2, Mullin 2 (1 pen), Jennings 1.
Carabao Cup (0).
Leasing.com Trophy (6): Jennings 2, Blackett-Taylor 1, Hepburn-Murphy 1, Payne 1, Ray 1.

Davies S 28	Nelson S 16 + 3	Ray G 15	Monthe E 30 + 1	Ridehalgh L 27 + 2	Banks O 8 + 3	Perkins D 23 + 4	Morris K 33 + 1	Ponticelli J 1	Jennings C 23 + 6	Payne S 11 + 4	Hepburn-Murphy R 8 + 9	Ferrier M 15 + 5	Mullin P 9 + 11	Wilson K 13	Potter D 11 + 1	Taylor C 13 + 11	Woods C 9 + 4	Borthwick-Jackson C 1 + 2	Danns N 13 + 5	Caprice J 19 + 1	Gilmour H 2 + 2	Pilling L — + 1	Chapman A 6	Clarke P 6	Woodyard A 11	Feeney M 1	Vaughan J 8	McCullough L 6	Cook A 5	Ellis M 3	*Match No.*
1	2^{3}	3	4	5	6	7	8	9^{1}	10	11^{2}	$12^{\blacksquare}$	13	14																		1
1		3	4	5	6	7	8		10^{2}	13		11^{1}		2	9	12															2
1	14	3	4	5	6	7	8		10	13		11^{2}	12	2^{1}		9^{3}															3
1		3	4	5	$6^{\blacksquare}$	7	8		9		12	11		2^{1}		$10^{\blacksquare}$															4
1	2^{1}	3	4	5		8	9		6	11	12		10^{2}		7		13														5
1	2^{1}	3	4	5	12	8	6^{3}		9	11	14		10^{2}		7		13														6
1	3		4	5	14	7^{3}	13		8	11^{2}	9		10		6		2^{1}	12													7
1	2	3	4	9	6	8	5		13	11^{1}			10		7^{2}	12															8
1	2	3^{1}	4	9	6	8^{3}	5			11			10		7^{2}	14		13	12												9
1	3		4	5	8		9^{3}		13	10	14		11^{1}		7^{2}	12			6	2											10
1			3	4	7^{1}		5^{2}		$11^{\blacksquare}$	10	14		9		6^{3}	13			8	2	12										11
1		3	4	5			6			10	12		11^{1}		8	9				2	7										12
1		3	4	5		8	6		12	11	9^{2}		13			10^{1}			7	2											13
1		3	4	5		8	6		9	10	12		11^{1}						7	2											14
1	2		3	4		6	9		11		10^{2}		13	8		12			7	5^{1}											15
1	2		3	4^{3}		7^{2}	9		11		10^{1}	13	14	8	6	12				5											16
1	3	2^{2}	4			13	11		7		9^{1}	10	14		6^{3}	12		8		5											17
1^{2}	3		4	5		7	8^{3}		9		14	11^{1}				10	13		6	2		12									18
	3		4	5		7	8		9	12	11^{1}					$10^{\blacksquare}$			6	2			1								19
	3		2	4		8	9^{3}		7		11	10^{1}	12		13		14		6^{2}	5			1								20
	2		3	4		8	9		7^{1}		11	10	12						6	5			1								21
	3		4			6	8		9			11				10	5		7	2			1								22
	3	4				6	8		9			11	12			10^{1}	5		7	2			1								23
			4	14		7	9		10^{3}			11	12			13	2^{2}		6^{1}	5			1	3	8						24
1			3	4	12	7^{1}	8		11			10				13			9^{2}	5				2	6						25
1			$3^{\blacksquare}$	4^{3}		7^{1}	9		11	13		10^{2}	12	8			2			5	14				6						26
1	13						6		9^{1}			10		5			4		12	2	7				8	3^{2}	11				27
1			3	4		13	8		12			11		5			2^{3}			14					7		9^{1}	6^{2}	10		28
1		3	4	12			6					13		2^{2}		9	5^{1}		14						7		10^{3}	8	11		29
1	12	3^{2}	4	5			6					13				9				2					7		10^{1}	8	11		30
1			4	5			9					12		2		6								3	8		10	7	11^{1}		31
1				5		12	6		13					2		9^{2}			14					4	7		11^{3}	8^{1}	10	3	32
1			14	5		12	6		10^{2}					2		9^{3}			13					4	8		11	7^{1}		3	33
1			4			7	9		13			11		5		12	8^{1}							3	6		10^{2}			2	34
																															35
																															36
																															37
																															38
																															39
																															40
																															41
																															42
																															43
																															44

FA Cup

First Round	Wycombe W	(h)	2-2
Replay (*aet*)	Wycombe W	(a)	2-1
Second Round	Chichester C	(h)	5-1
Third Round	Watford	(a)	3-3
Replay (*aet*)	Watford	(h)	2-1
Fourth Round	Manchester U	(h)	0-6

Carabao Cup

First Round	Hull C	(h)	0-3

Leasing.com Trophy

Group C (N)	Aston Villa U21	(h)	2-1
Group C (N)	Salford C	(h)	0-2
Second Round (N)	Manchester U U21	(h)	3-2
Third Round (N)	Leicester C U21	(h)	1-2

WALSALL

FOUNDATION

Two of the leading clubs around Walsall in the 1880s were Walsall Swifts (formed 1877) and Walsall Town (formed 1879). The Swifts were winners of the Birmingham Senior Cup in 1881, while the Town reached the 4th round (5th round modern equivalent) of the FA Cup in 1883. These clubs amalgamated as Walsall Town Swifts in 1888, becoming simply Walsall in 1895.

Banks's Stadium, Bescot Crescent, Walsall WS1 4SA.
Telephone: (01922) 622 791.
Ticket Office: (01922) 651 414/416.
Website: www.saddlers.co.uk
Email: info@walsallfc.co.uk
Ground Capacity: 10,862.
Record Attendance: 25,453 v Newcastle U, Division 2, 29 August 1961 (at Fellows Park); 11,049 v Rotherham U, Division 1, 9 May 2004 (at Bescot Stadium).
Pitch Measurements: 100.5m × 67m (110yd × 73.5yd).
Chairman: Lee Pomlett.
Chief Executive: Stefan Gamble.
Manager: Darrell Clarke.
Assistant Manager: Brian Dutton.
Colours: Red shirts with white and green trim, white shorts with red and green trim, green socks with red trim.
Year Formed: 1888.
Turned Professional: 1888.
Previous Names: Walsall Swifts (founded 1877) and Walsall Town (founded 1879) amalgamated in 1888 as Walsall Town Swifts; 1895, Walsall.
Club Nickname: 'The Saddlers'.
Grounds: 1888, Fellows Park; 1990, Bescot Stadium (renamed Banks's Stadium 2007).
First Football League Game: 3 September 1892, Division 2, v Darwen (h) L 1–2 – Hawkins; Withington, Pinches; Robinson, Whitrick, Forsyth; Marshall, Holmes, Turner, Gray (1), Pangbourn.
Record League Victory: 10–0 v Darwen, Division 2, 4 March 1899 – Tennent; Ted Peers (1), Davies; Hickinbotham, Jenkyns, Taggart; Dean (3), Vail (2), Aston (4), Martin, Griffin.
Record Cup Victory: 7–0 v Macclesfield T (a), FA Cup 2nd rd, 6 December 1997 – Walker; Evans, Marsh, Viveash (1), Ryder, Peron, Boli (2 incl. 1p) (Ricketts), Porter (2), Keates, Watson (Platt), Hodge (2 incl. 1p).
Record Defeat: 0–12 v Small Heath, 17 December 1892; 0–12 v Darwen, 26 December 1896, both Division 2.
Most League Points (2 for a win): 65, Division 4, 1959–60.
Most League Points (3 for a win): 89, FL 2, 2006–07.
Most League Goals: 102, Division 4, 1959–60.

HONOURS

League Champions: FL 2 – 2006–07; Division 4 – 1959–60.
Runners-up: Second Division – 1998–99; Division 3 – 1960–61; Third Division – 1994–95; Division 4 – 1979–80.

FA Cup: last 16 – 1889; 5th rd – 1939, 1975, 1978, 1987, 2002, 2003.

League Cup: semi-final – 1984.

League Trophy: *Runners-up:* 2015.

FOOTBALL YEARBOOK FACT FILE

Following the postponement of four consecutive home games due to a waterlogged pitch, Walsall staged their home fixture with Brighton & Hove Albion at The Hawthorns, ground of their neighbours West Bromwich Albion. The game attracted 7,535 fans and was the Saddlers' second highest home attendance of the season.

Highest League Scorer in Season: Gilbert Alsop, 40, Division 3 (N), 1933–34 and 1934–35.

Most League Goals in Total Aggregate: Tony Richards, 184, 1954–63; Colin Taylor, 184, 1958–63, 1964–68, 1969–73.

Most League Goals in One Match: 5, Gilbert Alsop v Carlisle U, Division 3 (N), 2 February 1935; 5, Bill Evans v Mansfield T, Division 3 (N), 5 October 1935; 5, Johnny Devlin v Torquay U, Division 3 (S), 1 September 1949.

Most Capped Player: Mick Kearns, 15 (18), Republic of Ireland.

Most League Appearances: Colin Harrison, 473, 1964–82.

Youngest League Player: Geoff Morris, 16 years 218 days v Scunthorpe U, 14 September 1965.

Record Transfer Fee Received: £1,500,000 (rising to £5,000,000) from Brentford for Rico Henry, August 2016.

Record Transfer Fee Paid: £300,000 to Anorthosis Famagusta for Andreas Makris, August 2016.

Football League Record: 1892 Elected to Division 2; 1895 Failed re-election; 1896–1901 Division 2; 1901 Failed re-election; 1921 Original Member of Division 3 (N); 1927–31 Division 3 (S); 1931–36 Division 3 (N); 1936–58 Division 3 (S); 1958–60 Division 4; 1960–61 Division 3; 1961–63 Division 2; 1963–79 Division 3; 1979–80 Division 4; 1980–88 Division 3; 1988–89 Division 2; 1989–90 Division 3; 1990–92 Division 4; 1992–95 Division 3; 1995–99 Division 2; 1999–2000 Division 1; 2000–01 Division 2; 2001–04 Division 1; 2004–06 FL 1; 2006–07 FL 2; 2007–19 FL 1; 2019– FL 2.

LATEST SEQUENCES

Longest Sequence of League Wins: 7, 9.4.2005 – 9.8.2005.

Longest Sequence of League Defeats: 15, 29.10.1988 – 4.2.1989.

Longest Sequence of League Draws: 5, 7.5.1988 – 17.9.1988.

Longest Sequence of Unbeaten League Matches: 21, 6.11.1979 – 22.3.1980.

Longest Sequence Without a League Win: 18, 15.10.1988 – 4.2.1989.

Successive Scoring Runs: 27 from 6.11.1979.

Successive Non-scoring Runs: 5 from 10.4.2004.

TEN YEAR LEAGUE RECORD

		P	W	D	L	F	A	Pts	Pos
2010-11	FL 1	46	12	12	22	56	75	48	20
2011-12	FL 1	46	10	20	16	51	57	50	19
2012-13	FL 1	46	17	17	12	65	58	68	9
2013-14	FL 1	46	14	16	16	49	49	58	13
2014-15	FL 1	46	14	17	15	50	54	59	14
2015-16	FL 1	46	24	12	10	71	49	84	3
2016-17	FL 1	46	14	16	16	51	58	58	14
2017-18	FL 1	46	13	13	20	53	66	52	19
2018-19	FL 1	46	12	11	23	49	71	47	22
2019-20	FL 2	36	13	8	15	40	49	47	12§

§Decided on points-per-game (1.31)

MANAGERS

H. Smallwood 1888–91 *(Secretary-Manager)*
A. G. Burton 1891–93
J. H. Robinson 1893–95
C. H. Ailso 1895–96 *(Secretary-Manager)*
A. E. Parsloe 1896–97 *(Secretary-Manager)*
L. Ford 1897–98 *(Secretary-Manager)*
G. Hughes 1898–99 *(Secretary-Manager)*
L. Ford 1899–1901 *(Secretary-Manager)*
J. E. Shutt 1908–13 *(Secretary-Manager)*
Haydn Price 1914–20
Joe Burchell 1920–26
David Ashworth 1926–27
Jack Torrance 1927–28
James Kerr 1928–29
Sid Scholey 1929–30
Peter O'Rourke 1930–32
Bill Slade 1932–34
Andy Wilson 1934–37
Tommy Lowes 1937–44
Harry Hibbs 1944–51
Tony McPhee 1951
Brough Fletcher 1952–53
Major Frank Buckley 1953–55
John Love 1955–57
Billy Moore 1957–64
Alf Wood 1964
Reg Shaw 1964–68
Dick Graham 1968
Ron Lewin 1968–69
Billy Moore 1969–72
John Smith 1972–73
Ronnie Allen 1973
Doug Fraser 1973–77
Dave Mackay 1977–78
Alan Ashman 1978
Frank Sibley 1979
Alan Buckley 1979–86
Neil Martin *(Joint Manager with Buckley)* 1981–82
Tommy Coakley 1986–88
John Barnwell 1989–90
Kenny Hibbitt 1990–94
Chris Nicholl 1994–97
Jan Sorensen 1997–98
Ray Graydon 1998–2002
Colin Lee 2002–04
Paul Merson 2004–06
Kevin Broadhurst 2006
Richard Money 2006–08
Jimmy Mullen 2008–09
Chris Hutchings 2009–11
Dean Smith 2011–15
Sean O'Driscoll 2015–16
Jon Whitney 2016–18
Dean Keates 2018–19
Martin O'Connor 2019
Darrell Clarke May 2019–

DID YOU KNOW ?

Injuries to the club's two regular goalkeepers, Peter McSevich and Billy Bryan, led Walsall to include 44-year-old Harry Wait between the sticks for the final five fixtures of the 1935–36 season. Wait, who had been the club's trainer since February 1930, had not played a League match for over six years prior to this.

WALSALL – SKY BET LEAGUE TWO 2019–20 LEAGUE RECORD

Match No.	Date	Venue	Opponents	Result		H/T Score	Lg Pos.	Goalscorers	Attendance
1	Aug 3	A	Northampton T	W	1-0	1-0	6	Clarke [13]	6260
2	10	H	Forest Green R	D	1-1	0-1	5	Hardy [86]	5205
3	17	A	Crewe Alex	L	0-1	0-0	15		4629
4	20	H	Newport Co	D	0-0	0-0	16		4337
5	24	A	Plymouth Arg	L	0-3	0-1	19		9337
6	31	H	Grimsby T	L	1-3	1-1	21	Lavery [5]	4812
7	Sept 7	A	Colchester U	D	0-0	0-0	21		3265
8	14	H	Bradford C	L	0-1	0-0	21		4649
9	17	A	Morecambe	W	1-0	1-0	20	Sinclair [4]	1616
10	21	H	Scunthorpe U	W	1-0	0-0	16	Clarke [65]	4037
11	28	A	Crawley T	W	3-2	3-1	14	Clarke [14], Adebayo [27], McDonald [44]	2275
12	Oct 5	H	Salford C	L	0-3	0-1	15		4751
13	12	A	Leyton Orient	L	1-3	1-0	19	Sinclair [21]	6951
14	19	H	Cheltenham T	L	1-2	0-1	19	Gordon (pen) [52]	4494
15	22	A	Oldham Ath	L	0-2	0-0	19		2438
16	26	H	Mansfield T	L	1-2	1-1	21	Adebayo [45]	4521
17	Nov 2	A	Swindon T	L	1-2	0-1	22	Gaffney [54]	7014
18	16	H	Cambridge U	W	2-1	2-0	21	Gordon [1], Sadler [10]	5429
19	23	H	Stevenage	D	0-0	0-0	22		4938
20	Dec 7	A	Port Vale	W	1-0	0-0	17	Adebayo [46]	5079
21	14	H	Macclesfield T	D	1-1	0-1	17	McDonald [74]	3846
22	21	A	Exeter C	D	3-3	3-2	17	Sweeney (og) [13], Lavery [18], Gordon [31]	4323
23	26	A	Scunthorpe U	W	2-0	1-0	15	McDonald [43], Bates [84]	3842
24	29	H	Carlisle U	L	1-2	0-0	16	Adebayo [70]	4794
25	Jan 1	H	Leyton Orient	W	1-0	1-0	15	Gordon [43]	4263
26	4	A	Salford C	W	2-1	1-0	11	Lavery [27], Gordon [51]	3173
27	11	A	Cheltenham T	L	1-3	0-1	12	Adebayo [78]	3868
28	18	H	Crawley T	W	2-1	0-1	12	Gordon [72], McDonald [88]	4011
29	25	A	Carlisle U	L	1-2	0-2	13	Sadler [50]	4097
30	28	H	Morecambe	L	0-2	0-0	14		3554
31	Feb 1	H	Crewe Alex	L	1-2	1-0	15	Lavery [15]	4610
32	8	A	Forest Green R	W	2-1	0-0	14	Gordon (pen) [52], McDonald [73]	3136
33	11	A	Newport Co	D	0-0	0-0	15		3049
34	15	H	Northampton T	W	3-2	0-2	13	Gordon [55], Guthrie [77], Holden [90]	4541
35	22	H	Port Vale	D	2-2	1-2	14	Adebayo [15], Gordon [58]	6301
36	Mar 7	H	Exeter C	W	3-1	1-0	14	Holden [3], Adebayo 2 [71, 90]	5521
37	14	A	Macclesfield T	Cancelled					
38	17	H	Oldham Ath	Cancelled					
39	21	A	Mansfield T	Cancelled					
40	28	H	Swindon T	Cancelled					
41	31	A	Stevenage	Cancelled					
42	Apr 4	A	Cambridge U	Cancelled					
43	10	H	Plymouth Arg	Cancelled					
44	13	A	Grimsby T	Cancelled					
45	18	H	Colchester U	Cancelled					
46	25	A	Bradford C	Cancelled					

Final League Position: 12 (on points-per-game basis)

GOALSCORERS

League (40): Gordon 9 (2 pens), Adebayo 8, McDonald 5, Lavery 4, Clarke 3, Holden 2, Sadler 2, Sinclair 2, Bates 1, Gaffney 1, Guthrie 1, Hardy 1, own goal 1.
FA Cup (3): Lavery 2, Bates 1.
Carabao Cup (2): Lavery 2 (1 pen).
Leasing.com Trophy (11): Gordon 3 (1 pen), Lavery 2 (2 pens), McDonald 2, Scarr 2, Kinsella 1, Norman 1.

Roberts L 32	Scarr D 32 + 1	Clarke J 27	Sadler M 24 + 3	Norman C 12 + 6	Kinsella L 28 + 3	Guthrie D 17 + 8	Sinclair S 22 + 4	Pring C 20 + 1	Gordon J 26 + 8	Adebayo E 15 + 15	Liddle G 10 + 2	Jules Z 13 + 4	Holden R 23 + 6	Hardy J 2 + 9	Lavery C 22 + 5	Kiersey J 1 + 1	McDonald W 21 + 7	Cockerill-Mollett C 6 + 3	Gaffney R 11 + 4	Bates A 9 + 4	Rose J 4	Facey S 12 + 1	Roberts K 1 + 1	Nolan J — + 4	Sheron N 6 + 1	Match No.
1	2	3^{1}	4	5	6	7^{3}	8	9	10^{2}	11	12	13	14													1
1	3	2	4^{1}	6^{2}	7		8	9	11	10	5^{3}		12	13	14											2
1	3	2		5^{2}	7		6	9	11^{3}	14		4		13	10	8^{1}	12									3
1	3	2	4	5	7		6	9	12	10				8^{2}	11^{1}	13										4
1	3	2	4	5	8^{1}		6		10^{2}	11	7			14	12		13	9^{3}								5
1	3	2	4^{3}			14	8	5	12	10	7		6	9^{2}	11^{1}		13									6
1	12	3		2	9	8^{1}	13	6^{2}		14	4	5	7^{3}		11				10							7
1	5	4			9	8	7		14		3	6^{1}	2^{3}	13	10^{2}			12	11							8
1	3	4	13		8	7	6		12		2	9	5^{2}		10^{1}				11							9
1	3	2		14	13	6^{3}	8		12		7	4	5		10^{2}		9^{1}		11							10
1	3	2	4		12	7^{3}	8		13	10^{2}	14	5	6				9^{1}		11							11
1	3	2	4^{2}				7		11	10	8	5^{1}	6	13			9^{3}	14		12						12
1	3	4		12	6	7^{3}	9		13	14	2	5	8^{1}				10^{2}		11							13
1		3			6^{1}		8	5	9	13	2^{3}	4	12	14			11		10^{2}	7						14
	3	2	4■	13			8	5^{1}	9	10		12^{3}	6						11^{2}	7	1	14				15
	4			2	9	13	7		10^{3}	12			6^{1}				14	5	11	8^{2}	1		3			16
	2		3		8	7^{2}		9		10^{1}		4^{3}	6	14	13				11	12	1	5				17
1		3	4		8				11^{1}	13			6		10^{2}		9	5	12	7		2				18
1	3	4			8^{2}	12			11	14			6^{3}	13	10		9^{1}	5		7		2				19
1	3	5	4		6	7^{3}	8		10^{2}	11^{1}			12		13		9		14			2				20
1	3	5	4		6^{2}	7	8	12	11	13					10^{3}		9		14			2^{1}				21
1	3	4	12		7	8^{2}	9	5	6^{3}						11		10^{1}		14	13		2				22
1	3	2	4		6	12	8	5	13	14					11^{3}		9^{2}		10^{1}	7						23
1		3■	4			8			11	13^{3}		14	6^{2}	12	10^{1}		9	5		7		2				24
1	3		4	12	8	7^{1}		5■	11				6		10		9^{3}	14		13		2^{2}				25
1	4	3	12	2	7				6			13	10		11		9^{1}	5^{2}		8						26
1	4	3	2	13	7				6	12		5^{1}	10		11		9			8^{2}						27
1	3	5	4	2	8	13			6^{1}	11^{2}			7^{3}		10		9						14	12		28
1	3	2^{2}	4	13	9^{3}	12		5	6	11			7^{1}				10							14	8	29
1	3		4	2		8^{2}	14	5	6^{1}	11^{3}			13		10		9							12	7	30
1	3		4		8	13		5	10	14			6^{2}		11		9^{3}					2		12	7^{1}	31
1	3		4		9		7	5	6^{2}	13			10^{1}		11		12					2			8	32
1	2		3	5	6	8^{3}	12	9	10^{1}	13		4^{2}			11		14								7	33
1	2		3		8	13	6^{2}	9	10	11		4^{1}	14				12					5			7^{3}	34
	3		4		7	8^{1}	13	5	10^{2}	11			6		12		9				1	2				35
1	4	3		2	13	8^{1}	7^{3}	5	11	12			6		10^{2}		9								14	36
																										37
																										38
																										39
																										40
																										41
																										42
																										43
																										44
																										45
																										46

FA Cup

First Round	Darlington	(h)	2-2
Replay	Darlington	(a)	1-0
Second Round	Oxford U	(h)	0-1

Carabao Cup

First Round	Crawley T	(h)	2-3

Leasing.com Trophy

Group D (S)	Coventry C	(a)	0-0
(Coventry C won 5-4 on penalties)			
Group D (S)	Southampton U21	(h)	1-0
Group D (S)	Forest Green R	(h)	6-0
Second Round (S)	Chelsea U21	(h)	3-2
Third Round (S)	Portsmouth	(h)	1-2

WATFORD

FOUNDATION

The club was formed as Watford Rovers in 1881. The name was changed to West Herts in 1893 and then the name Watford was adopted after rival club Watford St Mary's was absorbed in 1898.

Vicarage Road Stadium, Vicarage Road, Watford, Hertfordshire WD18 0ER.

Telephone: (01923) 496 000.

Ticket Office: (01923) 223 023.

Website: www.watfordfc.com

Email: yourvoice@watfordfc.com

Ground Capacity: 22,200.

Record Attendance: 34,099 v Manchester U, FA Cup 4th rd (replay), 3 February 1969.

Pitch Measurements: 105m × 68m (115yd × 74.5yd).

Chairman and Chief Executive: Scott Duxbury.

Head Coach: Vladimir Ivić.

Assistant Head Coach: Miloš Veselinović.

Colours: Yellow and black shirts, black shorts, black socks.

Year Formed: 1881.

Turned Professional: 1897.

Previous Names: 1881, Watford Rovers; 1893, West Herts; 1898, Watford.

Club Nickname: 'The Hornets'.

Grounds: 1883, Vicarage Meadow, Rose and Crown Meadow; 1889, Colney Butts; 1890, Cassio Road; 1922, Vicarage Road.

First Football League Game: 28 August 1920, Division 3, v QPR (a) W 2–1 – Williams; Horseman, Fred Gregory; Bacon, Toone, Wilkinson; Bassett, Ronald (1), Hoddinott, White (1), Waterall.

Record League Victory: 8–0 v Sunderland, Division 1, 25 September 1982 – Sherwood; Rice, Rostron, Taylor, Terry, Bolton, Callaghan (2), Blissett (4), Jenkins (2), Jackett, Barnes.

Record Cup Victory: 10–1 v Lowestoft T, FA Cup 1st rd, 27 November 1926 – Yates; Prior, Fletcher (1); Frank Smith, Bert Smith, Strain; Stephenson, Warner (3), Edmonds (3), Swan (1), Daniels (1), (1 og).

Record Defeat: 0–10 v Wolverhampton W, FA Cup 1st rd (replay), 24 January 1912.

Most League Points (2 for a win): 71, Division 4, 1977–78.

Most League Points (3 for a win): 89, FL C, 2014–15.

Most League Goals: 92, Division 4, 1959–60.

HONOURS

League Champions: Second Division – 1997–98; Division 3 – 1968–69; Division 4 – 1977–78.
Runners-up: Division 1 – 1982–83; FL C – 2014–15; Division 2 – 1981–82; Division 3 – 1978–79.

FA Cup: *Runners-up:* 1984, 2019.

League Cup: semi-final – 1979, 2005.

European Competitions
UEFA Cup: 1983–84.

FOOTBALL YEARBOOK FACT FILE

Watford reached the final of the short-lived Division Three South Cup on two occasions. They lost 3-2 to Bristol Rovers at The Den in 1934–35, while they shared the trophy in 1936–37 after drawing 3-3 on aggregate with Millwall, both games being played during the following season.

Highest League Scorer in Season: Cliff Holton, 42, Division 4, 1959–60.

Most League Goals in Total Aggregate: Luther Blissett, 148, 1976–83, 1984–88, 1991–92.

Most League Goals in One Match: 5, Eddie Mummery v Newport Co, Division 3 (S), 5 January 1924.

Most Capped Players: Craig Cathcart, 32 (50), Northern Ireland.

Most League Appearances: Luther Blissett, 415, 1976–83, 1984–88, 1991–92.

Youngest League Player: Keith Mercer, 16 years 125 days v Tranmere R, 16 February 1973.

Record Transfer Fee Received: £35,000,000 from Everton for Richarlison, July 2018.

Record Transfer Fee Paid: £30,000,000 to Rennes for Ismaila Sarr, August 2019.

Football League Record: 1920 Original Member of Division 3; 1921–58 Division 3 (S); 1958–60 Division 4; 1960–69 Division 3; 1969–72 Division 2; 1972–75 Division 3; 1975–78 Division 4; 1978–79 Division 3; 1979–82 Division 2; 1982–88 Division 1; 1988–92 Division 2; 1992–96 Division 1; 1996–98 Division 2; 1998–99 Division 1; 1999–2000 Premier League; 2000–04 Division 1; 2004–06 FL C; 2006–07 Premier League; 2007–15 FL C; 2015–20 Premier League; 2020– FL C.

LATEST SEQUENCES

Longest Sequence of League Wins: 7, 28.8.2000 – 14.10.2000.

Longest Sequence of League Defeats: 9, 26.12.1972 – 27.2.1973.

Longest Sequence of League Draws: 7, 16.2.2008 – 22.3.2008.

Longest Sequence of Unbeaten League Matches: 22, 1.10.1996 – 1.3.1997.

Longest Sequence Without a League Win: 19, 27.11.1971 – 8.4.1972.

Successive Scoring Runs: 22 from 20.8.1985.

Successive Non-scoring Runs: 7 from 18.12.1971.

MANAGERS

John Goodall 1903–10
Harry Kent 1910–26
Fred Pagnam 1926–29
Neil McBain 1929–37
Bill Findlay 1938–47
Jack Bray 1947–48
Eddie Hapgood 1948–50
Ron Gray 1950–51
Haydn Green 1951–52
Len Goulden 1952–55
(General Manager to 1956)
Johnny Paton 1955–56
Neil McBain 1956–59
Ron Burgess 1959–63
Bill McGarry 1963–64
Ken Furphy 1964–71
George Kirby 1971–73
Mike Keen 1973–77
Graham Taylor 1977–87
Dave Bassett 1987–88
Steve Harrison 1988–90
Colin Lee 1990
Steve Perryman 1990–93
Glenn Roeder 1993–96
Graham Taylor 1996
Kenny Jackett 1996–97
Graham Taylor 1997–2001
Gianluca Vialli 2001–02
Ray Lewington 2002–05
Adrian Boothroyd 2005–08
Brendan Rodgers 2008–09
Malky Mackay 2009–11
Sean Dyche 2011–12
Gianfranco Zola 2012–13
Beppe Sannino 2013–14
Oscar Garcia 2014
Billy McKinlay 2014
Slavisa Jokanovic 2014–15
Quique Sanchez Flores 2015–16
Walter Mazzarri 2016–17
Marco Silva 2017–18
Javi Gracia 2018–19
Quique Sanchez Flores 2019
Nigel Pearson 2019–20
Vladimir Ivić August 2020–

TEN YEAR LEAGUE RECORD

		P	*W*	*D*	*L*	*F*	*A*	*Pts*	*Pos*
2010-11	FL C	46	16	13	17	77	71	61	14
2011-12	FL C	46	16	16	14	56	64	64	11
2012-13	FL C	46	23	8	15	85	58	77	3
2013-14	FL C	46	15	15	16	74	64	60	13
2014-15	FL C	46	27	8	11	91	50	89	2
2015-16	PR Lge	38	12	9	17	40	50	45	13
2016-17	PR Lge	38	11	7	20	40	68	40	17
2017-18	PR Lge	38	11	8	19	44	64	41	14
2018-19	PR Lge	38	14	8	16	52	59	50	11
2019-20	PR Lge	38	8	10	20	36	64	34	19

DID YOU KNOW ?

Watford had to apply for re-election to the Football League on two occasions after finishing in the bottom two of Division Three South. Fortunately for the Hornets they topped the poll in both 1926–27 and 1950–51 and comfortably retained their membership of the competition.

WATFORD – PREMIER LEAGUE 2019–20 LEAGUE RECORD

Match No.	*Date*	*Venue*	*Opponents*	*Result*	*H/T Score*	*Lg Pos.*	*Goalscorers*	*Attendance*
1	Aug 10	H	Brighton & HA	L 0-3	0-1	18		20,245
2	17	A	Everton	L 0-1	0-1	19		39,066
3	24	H	West Ham U	L 1-3	1-1	20	Gray [17]	20,035
4	31	A	Newcastle U	D 1-1	1-1	20	Hughes [2]	44,157
5	Sept 15	H	Arsenal	D 2-2	0-2	20	Cleverley [53], Pereyra (pen) [81]	21,360
6	21	A	Manchester C	L 0-8	0-5	20		54,273
7	28	A	Wolverhampton W	L 0-2	0-1	20		30,711
8	Oct 5	H	Sheffield U	D 0-0	0-0	20		20,811
9	19	A	Tottenham H	D 1-1	1-0	20	Doucoure [6]	58,754
10	26	H	Bournemouth	D 0-0	0-0	20		20,821
11	Nov 2	H	Chelsea	L 1-2	0-1	20	Deulofeu (pen) [80]	21,011
12	8	A	Norwich C	W 2-0	1-0	18	Deulofeu [2], Gray [52]	27,074
13	23	H	Burnley	L 0-3	0-0	20		19,711
14	30	A	Southampton	L 1-2	1-0	20	Sarr [24]	26,929
15	Dec 4	A	Leicester C	L 0-2	0-0	20		31,763
16	7	H	Crystal Palace	D 0-0	0-0	20		20,070
17	14	A	Liverpool	L 0-2	0-1	20		53,311
18	22	H	Manchester U	W 2-0	0-0	20	Sarr [50], Deeney (pen) [54]	21,488
19	26	A	Sheffield U	D 1-1	1-1	19	Deulofeu [27]	30,222
20	28	H	Aston Villa	W 3-0	1-0	19	Deeney 2 (1 pen) [42, 67 (p)], Sarr [71]	21,348
21	Jan 1	H	Wolverhampton W	W 2-1	1-0	19	Deulofeu [30], Doucoure [49]	20,584
22	12	A	Bournemouth	W 3-0	1-0	17	Doucoure [42], Deeney [65], Pereyra [90]	10,384
23	18	H	Tottenham H	D 0-0	0-0	17		21,366
24	21	A	Aston Villa	L 1-2	1-0	19	Deeney [38]	40,867
25	Feb 1	H	Everton	L 2-3	2-2	19	Masina [10], Pereyra [42]	21,229
26	8	A	Brighton & HA	D 1-1	1-0	19	Doucoure [19]	30,443
27	23	A	Manchester U	L 0-3	0-1	19		73,347
28	29	H	Liverpool	W 3-0	0-0	17	Sarr 2 [54, 60], Deeney [72]	21,634
29	Mar 7	A	Crystal Palace	L 0-1	0-1	17		25,461
30	June 20	H	Leicester C	D 1-1	0-0	16	Dawson [90]	0
31	25	A	Burnley	L 0-1	0-0	16		0
32	28	H	Southampton	L 1-3	0-1	16	Bednarek (og) [79]	0
33	July 4	A	Chelsea	L 0-3	0-2	17		0
34	7	H	Norwich C	W 2-1	1-1	17	Dawson [10], Welbeck [55]	0
35	11	H	Newcastle U	W 2-1	0-1	17	Deeney 2 (2 pens) [52, 82]	0
36	17	A	West Ham U	L 1-3	0-3	17	Deeney [49]	0
37	21	H	Manchester C	L 0-4	0-2	18		0
38	26	A	Arsenal	L 2-3	1-3	19	Deeney (pen) [43], Welbeck [66]	0

Final League Position: 19

GOALSCORERS

League (36): Deeney 10 (5 pens), Sarr 5, Deulofeu 4 (1 pen), Doucoure 4, Pereyra 3 (1 pen), Dawson 2, Gray 2, Welbeck 2, Cleverley 1, Hughes 1, Masina 1, own goal 1.
FA Cup (4): Chalobah 1, Dele-Bashiru 1, Hinds 1, Pereyra 1.
Carabao Cup (5): Janmaat 1, Penaranda 1, Pereyra 1, Sarr 1, Welbeck 1.

Foster B 38	Femenia K 26 + 2	Dawson C 26 + 3	Cathcart C 28 + 1	Holebas J 11 + 3	Doucoure A 36 + 1	Capoue E 30	Hughes W 27 + 3	Deulofeu G 25 + 3	Gray A 7 + 16	Deeney T 26 + 1	Pereyra R 17 + 11	Success I — + 5	Welbeck D 8 + 10	Cleverley T 11 + 7	Sarr I 22 + 6	Quina D — + 4	Kabasele C 26 + 1	Janmaat D 7 + 1	Chalobah N 10 + 12	Mariappa A 15 + 5	Foulquier D 1 + 2	Prodl S 1	Masina A 20 + 6	Pussetto I — + 7	Joao Pedro — + 3	Match No.
1	2	3	4	5	6	7	8	9^{1}	10^{2}	11	12	13														1
1	2	3	4	5	6	7^{3}	8^{1}	10^{2}	14	11	9		12	13												2
1	2	3	4	5	7	6	8^{2}	10^{1}	11				12	9^{3}	13	14										3
1	8	2	4		6^{2}		9^{1}	14	11^{3}		10	12		7			3	5	13							4
1	2	3		5^{3}	6	7	8^{2}	10	11^{1}		13			9	12		4	14								5
1	2	3		5	8	7	9^{2}	11^{3}	14		12			10	13					4	6^{1}					6
1		3	4	5	7	8		11^{1}	13		12		10	6	9^{2}			2								7
1		12	3	6	8			13	11^{2}		9		10^{3}	7	14		5	2				4^{1}				8
1	13	4	5	6	9		14	12			11^{3}		10^{1}	7			3	2^{2}	8							9
1		4	5		9		12	10	13		11			7^{1}			3	2	8^{2}		14		6^{3}			10
1	14	4	5^{1}		7		13	10	11		9						3	2^{3}	8^{2}	12			6			11
1		4	5	6^{3}	7	8	9	10^{2}	12		11^{1}						3■	2		13			14			12
1	2	4^{1}	5	6	7	8	9^{3}	10	11^{2}	13					14					3			12			13
1	2^{3}		3	6	7	8	9^{2}	11^{1}	12						10				13	4	14		5			14
1	2		4		7	8	9^{2}	11^{1}	14	10^{3}		12			6	13				3			5			15
1	2		4		7^{2}	8		11	12	10	9^{1}				6		3		13				5			16
1	5		4		9^{2}	6	7	10	12	11^{1}					8	13	3			2						17
1	5		4		9^{1}	6^{2}	7	10		11	13	14			8^{3}		3		12	2						18
1	5	14	4			6	7	10	13	11^{2}	12				8^{1}		3		9^{3}	2						19
1	5	13	4^{3}		9	6	7^{1}	10		11					8		3		12^{2}	2■			14			20
1	5^{1}	2	4	12	9	7		10^{2}		11	14				8^{3}		3■		6				13			21
1		3	4		9^{2}	7		10^{3}	14	11	12				8^{1}	13			6	2			5			22
1		3	4		9	7		10		11	12				8^{2}				6^{1}	2			5	13		23
1		3	4		9	7		10^{3}	13	11	8^{2}						14		6^{1}	2			5	12		24
1			4		9	7		10^{3}		11	8^{2}	13	12				3		6^{1}	2			5	14		25
1			4		9	6	7	10^{2}		11	8^{1}		13				3			2			5	12		26
1		2	4		9^{3}	7	6	10		11^{2}	8^{1}		13	14	12		3						5			27
1	2		4		9^{3}	7	6	10^{1}		11	12				8^{2}		3		14				5	13		28
1	2		4		9	7	6^{3}		14	11^{2}	10^{1}		12		8		3						5	13		29
1	2^{4}	4		16	9^{3}	6^{2}	7			11	10^{1}		12	13	8		3		15	14			5^{5}			30
1	2	4	12		13	8	7^{3}		15	10^{4}			11	9^{1}	6		3^{2}		14				5			31
1	2^{4}	4	3	13	9	7	6^{1}			11	10^{2}		12		8								5^{3}	15	14	32
1	5^{3}	4			9	7^{1}	10			11^{2}	15		12	13	8^{4}		3		6	2			14			33
1	2	4			9	6^{2}	7^{1}			11			10	12	8		3		13				5			34
1	2	4			9	6	7		13	11^{1}			10^{2}	12	8		3						5			35
1	2	4			7^{3}		6		13	11^{2}			10^{4}	9	8		3		14	12			5^{1}		15	36
1	5	4			7^{2}		9			11^{1}	10^{3}		12	8	6		3		13	2			14			37
1	2^{1}	3			7^{2}		6^{3}			11	9^{4}		10	13	8		4		14	12			5		15	38

FA Cup

Third Round	Tranmere R	(h)	3-3
Replay	Tranmere R	(a)	1-2
(*aet*)			

Carabao Cup

Second Round	Coventry C	(h)	3-0
Third Round	Swansea C	(h)	2-1
Fourth Round	Everton	(a)	0-2

WEST BROMWICH ALBION

FOUNDATION

There is a well known story that when employees of Salter's Spring Works in West Bromwich decided to form a football club, they had to send someone to the nearby Association Football stronghold of Wednesbury to purchase a football. A weekly subscription of 2d (less than 1p) was imposed and the name of the new club was West Bromwich Strollers.

The Hawthorns, West Bromwich, West Midlands B71 4LF.

Telephone: (0871) 271 1100.

Ticket Office: (0121) 227 2227.

Website: www.wba.co.uk

Email: via website.

Ground Capacity: 26,850.

Record Attendance: 64,815 v Arsenal, FA Cup 6th rd, 6 March 1937.

Pitch Measurements: 105m × 68m (115yd × 74.5yd).

Chairman: Li Piyue.

Chief Executive: Xu Ke.

Head Coach: Slaven Bilic.

Assistant Coaches: Dean Racunica, Danillo Butorovic.

Colours: Navy blue and white striped shirts, white shorts with navy blue trim, navy blue socks with white trim.

Year Formed: 1878.

Turned Professional: 1885.

Previous Name: 1878, West Bromwich Strollers; 1881, West Bromwich Albion.

Club Nicknames: 'The Throstles', 'The Baggies', 'Albion'.

Grounds: 1878, Coopers Hill; 1879, Dartmouth Park; 1881, Bunns Field, Walsall Street; 1882, Four Acres (Dartmouth Cricket Club); 1885, Stoney Lane; 1900, The Hawthorns.

First Football League Game: 8 September 1888, Football League, v Stoke (a) W 2–0 – Roberts; Jack Horton, Green; Ezra Horton, Perry, Bayliss; Bassett, Woodhall (1), Hendry, Pearson, Wilson (1).

Record League Victory: 12–0 v Darwen, Division 1, 4 April 1892 – Reader; Jack Horton, McCulloch; Reynolds (2), Perry, Groves; Bassett (3), McLeod, Nicholls (1), Pearson (4), Geddes (1), (1 og).

Record Cup Victory: 10–1 v Chatham (away), FA Cup 3rd rd, 2 March 1889 – Roberts; Jack Horton, Green; Timmins (1), Charles Perry, Ezra Horton; Bassett (2), Walter Perry (1), Bayliss (2), Pearson, Wilson (3), (1 og).

Record Defeat: 3–10 v Stoke C, Division 1, 4 February 1937.

League Champions: Division 1 – 1919–20; FL C – 2007–08; Division 2 – 1901–02, 1910–11.
Runners-up: Division 1 – 1924–25, 1953–54; FL C – 2009–10, 2019–20; First Division – 2001–02, 2003–04; Division 2 – 1930–31, 1948–49.

FA Cup Winners: 1888, 1892, 1931, 1954, 1968.
Runners-up: 1886, 1887, 1895, 1912, 1935.

League Cup Winners: 1966.
Runners-up: 1967, 1970.

European Competitions
Fairs Cup: 1966–67.
UEFA Cup: 1978–79 *(qf)*, 1979–80, 1981–82.
European Cup-Winners' Cup: 1968–69 *(qf)*.

FOOTBALL YEARBOOK FACT FILE

West Bromwich Albion have reached the final of the FA Youth Cup three times with their only success coming in 1975–76. On that occasion they defeated local rivals Wolverhampton Wanderers 5-0 on aggregate, with a bumper crowd of 15,758 in attendance at The Hawthorns to see the Baggies clinch the trophy.

Most League Points (2 for a win): 60, Division 1, 1919–20.

Most League Points (3 for a win): 91, FL C, 2009–10.

Most League Goals: 105, Division 2, 1929–30.

Highest League Scorer in Season: William 'Ginger' Richardson, 39, Division 1, 1935–36.

Most League Goals in Total Aggregate: Tony Brown, 218, 1963–79.

Most League Goals in One Match: 6, Jimmy Cookson v Blackpool, Division 2, 17 September 1927.

Most Capped Player: James Morrison, 46, Scotland.

Most League Appearances: Tony Brown, 574, 1963–80.

Youngest League Player: Charlie Wilson, 16 years 73 days v Oldham Ath, 1 October 1921.

Record Transfer Fee Received: £16,500,000 from Dalian Yifang for Salomon Rondon, July 2019.

Record Transfer Fee Paid: £15,000,000 to RB Leipzig for Oliver Burke, August 2017.

Football League Record: 1888 Founder Member of Football League; 1901–02 Division 2; 1902–04 Division 1; 1904–11 Division 2; 1911–27 Division 1; 1927–31 Division 2; 1931–38 Division 1; 1938–49 Division 2; 1949–73 Division 1; 1973–76 Division 2; 1976–86 Division 1; 1986–91 Division 2; 1991–92 Division 3; 1992–93 Division 2; 1993–2002 Division 1; 2002–03 Premier League; 2003–04 Division 1; 2004–06 Premier League; 2006–08 FL C; 2008–09 Premier League; 2009–10 FL C; 2010–18 Premier League; 2018–20 FL C; 2020– Premier League.

LATEST SEQUENCES

Longest Sequence of League Wins: 11, 5.4.1930 – 8.9.1930.

Longest Sequence of League Defeats: 11, 28.10.1995 – 26.12.1995.

Longest Sequence of League Draws: 5, 30.8.1999 – 3.10.1999.

Longest Sequence of Unbeaten League Matches: 17, 7.9.1957 – 7.12.1957.

Longest Sequence Without a League Win: 20, 27.8.2017 – 2.1.2018.

Successive Scoring Runs: 36 from 26.4.1958.

Successive Non-scoring Runs: 5 from 1.4.2017.

MANAGERS

Louis Ford 1890–92
(Secretary-Manager)
Henry Jackson 1892–94
(Secretary-Manager)
Edward Stephenson 1894–95
(Secretary-Manager)
Clement Keys 1895–96
(Secretary-Manager)
Frank Heaven 1896–1902
(Secretary-Manager)
Fred Everiss 1902–48
Jack Smith 1948–52
Jesse Carver 1952
Vic Buckingham 1953–59
Gordon Clark 1959–61
Archie Macaulay 1961–63
Jimmy Hagan 1963–67
Alan Ashman 1967–71
Don Howe 1971–75
Johnny Giles 1975–77
Ronnie Allen 1977
Ron Atkinson 1978–81
Ronnie Allen 1981–82
Ron Wylie 1982–84
Johnny Giles 1984–85
Nobby Stiles 1985–86
Ron Saunders 1986–87
Ron Atkinson 1987–88
Brian Talbot 1988–91
Bobby Gould 1991–92
Ossie Ardiles 1992–93
Keith Burkinshaw 1993–94
Alan Buckley 1994–97
Ray Harford 1997
Denis Smith 1997–1999
Brian Little 1999–2000
Gary Megson 2000–04
Bryan Robson 2004–06
Tony Mowbray 2006–09
Roberto Di Matteo 2009–11
Roy Hodgson 2011–12
Steve Clarke 2012–13
Pepe Mel 2014
Alan Irvine 2014
Tony Pulis 2015–17
Alan Pardew 2017–18
Darren Moore 2018–19
Slaven Bilic June 2019–

TEN YEAR LEAGUE RECORD

		P	W	D	L	F	A	Pts	Pos
2010-11	PR Lge	38	12	11	15	56	71	47	11
2011-12	PR Lge	38	13	8	17	45	52	47	10
2012-13	PR Lge	38	14	7	17	53	57	49	8
2013-14	PR Lge	38	7	15	16	43	59	36	17
2014-15	PR Lge	38	11	11	16	38	51	44	13
2015-16	PR Lge	38	10	13	15	34	48	43	14
2016-17	PR Lge	38	12	9	17	43	51	45	10
2017-18	PR Lge	38	6	13	19	31	56	31	20
2018-19	FL C	46	23	11	12	87	62	80	4
2019-20	FL C	46	22	17	7	77	45	83	2

DID YOU KNOW ?

West Bromwich Albion featured in the first-ever FA Cup final to be televised in colour. Their 1968 Wembley victory over Everton was shown live on all three channels, with BBC 2 showing the match in colour and BBC 1 and ITV coverage in black and white.

WEST BROMWICH ALBION – SKY BET CHAMPIONSHIP 2019–20 LEAGUE RECORD

Match No.	Date	Venue	Opponents	Result	H/T Score	Lg Pos.	Goalscorers	Attendance
1	Aug 3	A	Nottingham F	W 2-1	2-1	3	Edwards [15], Phillips [26]	27,592
2	10	H	Millwall	D 1-1	0-0	4	Bartley [57]	24,305
3	17	A	Luton T	W 2-1	0-1	3	Diangana 2 [48, 51]	10,059
4	21	H	Reading	D 1-1	0-0	6	Zohore (pen) [88]	21,803
5	24	A	Derby Co	D 1-1	0-1	8	Zohore (pen) [84]	26,718
6	31	H	Blackburn R	W 3-2	3-2	4	Phillips [22], Livermore [31], Diangana [40]	23,792
7	Sept 14	A	Fulham	D 1-1	0-0	6	Ajayi [80]	17,770
8	22	H	Huddersfield T	W 4-2	1-2	4	Phillips 2 [19, 74], Furlong [70], Ajayi [89]	23,577
9	28	A	QPR	W 2-0	0-0	1	Ferguson [53], Matheus Pereira [84]	13,959
10	Oct 1	A	Leeds U	L 0-1	0-1	2		34,648
11	5	H	Cardiff C	W 4-2	2-0	1	Matheus Pereira [20], Diangana [42], Austin [71], Sawyers [90]	25,140
12	19	A	Middlesbrough	W 1-0	0-0	1	Robson-Kanu [82]	20,174
13	22	H	Barnsley	D 2-2	0-2	1	Diaby (og) [68], Matheus Pereira [81]	22,086
14	26	H	Charlton Ath	D 2-2	1-0	1	Phillips [10], Robson-Kanu [81]	25,356
15	Nov 4	A	Stoke C	W 2-0	1-0	1	Phillips [8], Robson-Kanu (pen) [69]	22,360
16	9	A	Hull C	W 1-0	1-0	1	Livermore [28]	13,866
17	23	H	Sheffield W	W 2-1	1-0	1	Robson-Kanu [10], Austin (pen) [88]	25,566
18	27	H	Bristol C	W 4-1	2-0	1	Gibbs [10], Matheus Pereira [39], Robson-Kanu [82], Austin [87]	22,197
19	Dec 2	A	Preston NE	W 1-0	0-0	1	Austin (pen) [90]	13,015
20	8	H	Swansea C	W 5-1	3-1	1	Ajayi [25], Matheus Pereira [34], Robson-Kanu [44], Phillips [70], Edwards [74]	22,927
21	11	A	Wigan Ath	D 1-1	0-0	2	Austin [59]	9444
22	14	A	Birmingham C	W 3-2	1-1	1	Diangana [10], Austin 2 [73, 81]	20,796
23	21	H	Brentford	D 1-1	1-1	1	Furlong [45]	24,961
24	26	A	Barnsley	D 1-1	1-0	1	Krovinovic [5]	17,049
25	29	H	Middlesbrough	L 0-2	0-1	2		25,077
26	Jan 1	H	Leeds U	D 1-1	1-0	2	Ajayi [2]	25,618
27	11	A	Charlton Ath	D 2-2	1-1	1	Zohore [22], Robson-Kanu [46]	19,720
28	20	H	Stoke C	L 0-1	0-1	1		23,199
29	28	A	Cardiff C	L 1-2	0-0	2	Austin (pen) [61]	22,516
30	Feb 1	H	Luton T	W 2-0	1-0	1	Daniels (og) [14], Ajayi [70]	25,141
31	9	A	Millwall	W 2-0	1-0	1	Krovinovic [42], O'Shea [84]	13,818
32	12	A	Reading	W 2-1	1-1	1	Matheus Pereira [26], Bartley [49]	13,942
33	15	H	Nottingham F	D 2-2	1-1	1	Robinson [37], Tobias Figueiredo (og) [65]	25,117
34	22	A	Bristol C	W 3-0	2-0	1	Robinson [32], Robson-Kanu 2 [36, 79]	24,022
35	25	H	Preston NE	W 2-0	2-0	1	Robson-Kanu [6], Livermore [45]	22,150
36	29	H	Wigan Ath	L 0-1	0-0	1		24,942
37	Mar 7	A	Swansea C	D 0-0	0-0	2		16,788
38	June 20	H	Birmingham C	D 0-0	0-0	1		0
39	26	A	Brentford	L 0-1	0-1	1		0
40	July 1	A	Sheffield W	W 3-0	1-0	2	Austin (pen) [37], Matheus Pereira 2 [58, 85]	0
41	5	H	Hull C	W 4-2	2-1	2	Austin [4], Hegazi [37], Grosicki [49], Diangana [76]	0
42	8	H	Derby Co	W 2-0	1-0	1	Diangana [11], O'Shea [76]	0
43	11	A	Blackburn R	D 1-1	1-0	2	Krovinovic [41]	0
44	14	H	Fulham	D 0-0	0-0	2		0
45	17	A	Huddersfield T	L 1-2	1-1	2	O'Shea [42]	0
46	22	H	QPR	D 2-2	1-1	2	Diangana [44], Robinson [49]	0

Final League Position: 2

GOALSCORERS

League (77): Austin 10 (4 pens), Robson-Kanu 10 (1 pen), Diangana 8, Matheus Pereira 8, Phillips 7, Ajayi 5, Krovinovic 3, Livermore 3, O'Shea 3, Robinson 3, Zohore 3 (2 pens), Bartley 2, Edwards 2, Furlong 2, Ferguson 1, Gibbs 1, Grosicki 1, Hegazi 1, Sawyers 1, own goals 3.
FA Cup (4): Zohore 2, Phillips 1, Townsend 1.
Carabao Cup (1): Austin 1.

Johnstone S 46	Ferguson N 21	Ajayi S 42 + 1	Bartley K 37 + 1	Gibbs K 14	Livermore J 43 + 2	Sawyers R 42	Phillips M 30 + 9	Krovinovic F 24 + 16	Edwards K 9 + 17	Zohore K 5 + 12	Burke O — + 2	Townsend C 19 + 8	Harper R 4 + 6	Robson-Kanu H 24 + 15	Brunt C — + 7	Diangana G 23 + 7	Matheus Pereira F 38 + 4	Austin C 18 + 16	Furlong D 22 + 9	Hegazi A 14 + 2	Barry G 1 + 2	O'Shea D 16 + 1	Robinson C 10 + 6	Grosicki K 4 + 10	Match No.
1	2	3	4	5^{2}	6	7	8	9	10^{3}	11^{1}	12	13	14												1
1	2	3	4	5	6^{2}	7	8^{3}	9	10	11^{1}	13			12	14										2
1	2	3	4	5	7	6	8^{2}	9	10^{1}	11^{3}						12	13	14							3
1		3	4	5	7^{3}	6	8	9	14	13						10^{1}	12	11^{2}	2						4
1	2	3	4	5^{1}	7	6	8^{3}	9	10^{2}	11						13	14		12						5
1	5	3	4		7	6	8	13	14	12						10^{2}	9^{3}	11^{1}	2						6
1	5	3	4		6^{2}	7	8^{1}	12	13					14		10^{3}	9	11	2						7
1	5	3	4		6	7	8^{3}	9^{1}		13				14		12	10	11^{2}	2						8
1	5	3	4		6	7	8^{2}	14	13					12		10	9^{3}	11^{1}	2						9
1	5	3	4		7^{3}	6	8^{2}	12	14	13				11^{1}		10	9		2						10
1	5	3	4		6	7	8^{2}	13	12	14						10^{1}	9	11^{3}	2						11
1	5	3	4		6^{3}	7		9^{2}	13					12		10	8	11^{1}	2	14					12
1	5^{1}	3	4		7	6		12	8^{2}			13		14		10^{3}	9	11	2						13
1	5■	3	4		7	6	8^{1}					12		13	14	10^{3}	9	11^{2}	2						14
1		3	4		6	7	8^{3}	12				5		13	14	10	9^{1}	11^{2}	2						15
1		3	4		6	7	8^{1}	12	13	14		5		11^{3}		10^{2}	9		2						16
1		7	3				8	6^{3}				5		11^{2}	14	10	9	13	2	4^{1}	12				17
1	2	4	3	5^{1}	7	6	8		13					11		10^{2}	9^{3}	14	12						18
1	2	4	3	5	7	6	8^{1}	14	12					11^{3}		10^{2}	9	13							19
1	2	4	3^{2}	5^{1}	7	6	8		14					11		10^{3}	9		12	13					20
1	2^{3}	4	3		6	7	8^{1}	9	10			5		12			13	11^{2}	14						21
1	2	4	3		6	7	8^{3}		12			5^{2}		11		10^{1}	9	14	13						22
1	5	3	4^{1}		7	6	8^{2}	14	10^{3}					11			9	13	2			12			23
1		3		5^{3}	7	6		8^{2}		12		14		11			9	10^{1}	2	4	13				24
1	5^{2}	3			7		8	14	10^{1}			13		11			9	12	2	4	6^{3}				25
1		3	4	5^{1}	6	7	8^{3}	10^{2}	13	14		12		11			9		2						26
1		3	4		6	7	8^{3}		14	11^{1}		5		9^{2}		12	10	13	2						27
1			4		7	6	8			12		5^{2}		11^{3}	14	10^{1}	9	13	2	3					28
1	5		3^{3}		6	7	8	9	10^{2}	13				11^{1}				12	14	4		2			29
1		3	4		7	6	8^{2}	9^{3}				5	14	12				11^{1}	13			2	10		30
1		3	4		6	7	13	9				5		11^{3}			8^{2}	14				2	10^{1}	12	31
1		3	4		6	7	12	8^{1}				5		10^{3}			9	14				2	11^{2}	13	32
1		3	4		8	7	12	6^{3}				5	14	10^{2}			9^{1}					2	11	13	33
1		3			6	7■	14	8^{2}				5	13	10			9^{3}			4		2	11^{1}	12	34
1		3			7		12	8				5	6	10^{3}			9^{1}	14		4		2	11^{2}	13	35
1		3	12		7		13	8				5	6^{2}	10			9			4^{1}		2	11^{3}	14	36
1		3	4^{2}		7	6		8	14			5		10			9^{3}		13			2	11^{1}	12	37
1		3		5	7^{4}	6	8^{1}	15	13	16				11^{3}		12	9^{5}	14	2	4			10^{2}		38
1		3		5	6^{3}	7	8^{1}	12	16	13			14	11^{2}		10^{4}	9^{5}		2	4			15		39
1		16	3	5	15	7		8^{3}					6^{5}	14		11^{1}	9^{4}	10^{2}		4		2	12	13	40
1			3	5^{1}	13	7^{2}		9^{5}				12	6^{4}	14	15	16	8	11^{3}		4■		2		10	41
1		3	4		6	7	15	14				5		13		8^{1}	9^{3}	11^{2}				2	12	10^{4}	42
1		3	4		6^{3}	7		9^{4}				5	14	12		13	8	11^{1}				2	15	10^{2}	43
1		3			6	7	12	15				5		13		8^{3}	9^{4}	11^{2}		4		2	14	10^{1}	44
1		3			6^{2}	7	8^{1}	12				5^{4}		11^{3}		10^{5}	9	14	15	4		2	16	13	45
1		3	4		6^{5}	7^{2}	16	9				15			13	10^{1}	8^{3}	12	2^{4}			5	11	14	46

FA Cup

Third Round	Charlton Ath	(a)	1-0
Fourth Round	West Ham U	(a)	1-0
Fifth Round	Newcastle U	(h)	2-3

Carabao Cup

First Round	Millwall	(h)	1-2

WEST HAM UNITED

FOUNDATION

Thames Ironworks FC was formed by employees of this famous shipbuilding company in 1895 and entered the FA Cup in their initial season at Chatham and the London League in their second. The committee wanted to introduce professional players, so Thames Ironworks was wound up in June 1900 and relaunched a month later as West Ham United.

London Stadium, Queen Elizabeth Olympic Park, London E20 2ST.

Telephone: (020) 8548 2748.

Ticket Office: (0333) 030 1966.

Website: www.whufc.com

Email: supporterservices@westhamunited.co.uk

Ground Capacity: 60,000.

Record Attendance: 42,322 v Tottenham H, Division 1, 17 October 1970 (at Boleyn Ground); 59,988 v Everton, Premier League, 30 March 2019 (at London Stadium).

Pitch Measurements: 105m × 68m (115yd × 74.5yd).

Joint Chairmen: David Sullivan and David Gold.

Vice-Chairman: Baroness Karren Brady CBE.

Manager: David Moyes.

Assistant Manager: Alan Irvine.

HONOURS

League Champions: Division 2 – 1957–58, 1980–81.
Runners-up: First Division – 1992–93; Division 2 – 1922–23, 1990–91.

FA Cup Winners: 1964, 1975, 1980.
Runners-up: 1923, 2006.

League Cup: *Runners-up:* 1966, 1981.

European Competitions
UEFA Cup: 1999–2000; 2006–07.
Europa League: 2015–16, 2016–17.
European Cup-Winners' Cup: 1964–65 *(winners)*, 1965–66 *(sf)*, 1975–76 *(runners-up)*, 1980–81 *(qf)*.
Intertoto Cup: 1999 *(winners)*.

Colours: Claret shirts with sky blue sleeves, white shorts with claret and sky blue trim, white socks with claret and sky blue trim.

Year Formed: 1895.

Turned Professional: 1900.

Previous Name: 1895, Thames Ironworks FC; 1900, West Ham United.

Club Nicknames: 'The Hammers', 'The Irons'.

Grounds: 1895, Memorial Recreation Ground, Canning Town; 1904, Boleyn Ground; 2016, London Stadium.

First Football League Game: 30 August 1919, Division 2, v Lincoln C (h) D 1–1 – Hufton; Cope, Lee; Lane, Fenwick, McCrae; David Smith, Moyes (1), Puddefoot, Morris, Bradshaw.

Record League Victory: 8–0 v Rotherham U, Division 2, 8 March 1958 – Gregory; Bond, Wright; Malcolm, Brown, Lansdowne; Grice, Smith (2), Keeble (2), Dick (4), Musgrove. 8–0 v Sunderland, Division 1, 19 October 1968 – Ferguson; Bonds, Charles; Peters, Stephenson, Moore (1); Redknapp, Boyce, Brooking (1), Hurst (6), Sissons.

Record Cup Victory: 10–0 v Bury, League Cup 2nd rd (2nd leg), 25 October 1983 – Parkes; Stewart (1), Walford, Bonds (Orr), Martin (1), Devonshire (2), Allen, Cottee (4), Swindlehurst, Brooking (2), Pike.

FOOTBALL YEARBOOK FACT FILE

Goalkeeper George Kitchen was a versatile sportsman and took penalty kicks for West Ham United, scoring on his club debut against Swindon Town. He was also a very useful golfer who was a professional at the Queen's Park Links in Bournemouth during the summer and competed in the Open championship on a number of occasions while on the club's books.

Record Defeat: 2–8 v Blackburn R, Division 1, 26 December 1963; 0–6 v Oldham Ath, League Cup semi-final (1st leg), 14 February 1990.

Most League Points (2 for a win): 66, Division 2, 1980–81.

Most League Points (3 for a win): 88, Division 1, 1992–93.

Most League Goals: 101, Division 2, 1957–58.

Highest League Scorer in Season: Vic Watson, 42, Division 1, 1929–30.

Most League Goals in Total Aggregate: Vic Watson, 298, 1920–35.

Most League Goals in One Match: 6, Vic Watson v Leeds U, Division 1, 9 February 1929; 6, Geoff Hurst v Sunderland, Division 1, 19 October 1968.

Most Capped Player: Bobby Moore, 108, England.

Most League Appearances: Billy Bonds, 663, 1967–88.

Youngest League Player: Billy Williams, 16 years 221 days v Blackpool, 6 May 1922.

Record Transfer Fee Received: £25,000,000 from Marseille for Dmitri Payet, January 2017.

Record Transfer Fee Paid: £45,000,000 to Eintracht Frankfurt for Sebastien Haller, July 2019.

Football League Record: 1919 Elected to Division 2; 1923–32 Division 1; 1932–58 Division 2; 1958–78 Division 1; 1978–81 Division 2; 1981–89 Division 1; 1989–91 Division 2; 1991–93 Division 1; 1993–2003 Premier League; 2003–04 Division 1; 2004–05 FL C; 2005–11 Premier League; 2011–12 FL C; 2012– Premier League.

MANAGERS

Syd King 1902–32
Charlie Paynter 1932–50
Ted Fenton 1950–61
Ron Greenwood 1961–74
(continued as General Manager to 1977)
John Lyall 1974–89
Lou Macari 1989–90
Billy Bonds 1990–94
Harry Redknapp 1994–2001
Glenn Roeder 2001–03
Alan Pardew 2003–06
Alan Curbishley 2006–08
Gianfranco Zola 2008–10
Avram Grant 2010–11
Sam Allardyce 2011–15
Slaven Bilic 2015–17
David Moyes 2017–18
Manuel Pellegrini 2018–19
David Moyes December 2019–

LATEST SEQUENCES

Longest Sequence of League Wins: 9, 19.10.1985 – 14.12.1985.

Longest Sequence of League Defeats: 9, 28.3.1932 – 29.8.1932.

Longest Sequence of League Draws: 5, 29.11.2015 – 26.12.2015.

Longest Sequence of Unbeaten League Matches: 27, 27.12.1980 – 10.10.1981.

Longest Sequence Without a League Win: 17, 31.1.1976 – 21.8.1976.

Successive Scoring Runs: 27 from 5.10.1957.

Successive Non-scoring Runs: 5 from 17.9.2006.

TEN YEAR LEAGUE RECORD

		P	*W*	*D*	*L*	*F*	*A*	*Pts*	*Pos*
2010-11	PR Lge	38	7	12	19	43	70	33	20
2011-12	FL C	46	24	14	8	81	48	86	3
2012-13	PR Lge	38	12	10	16	45	53	46	10
2013-14	PR Lge	38	11	7	20	40	51	40	13
2014-15	PR Lge	38	12	11	15	44	47	47	12
2015-16	PR Lge	38	16	14	8	65	51	62	7
2016-17	PR Lge	38	12	9	17	47	64	45	11
2017-18	PR Lge	38	10	12	16	48	68	42	13
2018-19	PR Lge	38	15	7	16	52	55	52	10
2019-20	PR Lge	38	10	9	19	49	62	39	16

DID YOU KNOW ?

West Ham United won the inaugural Football League War Cup in 1939–40, defeating Blackburn Rovers 1-0 in the final at Wembley in front of a crowd of 42,339. The match kicked off at 6.30 p.m. so as not to affect factory production during the daytime.

WEST HAM UNITED – PREMIER LEAGUE 2019–20 LEAGUE RECORD

Match No.	*Date*	*Venue*	*Opponents*	*Result*		*H/T Score*	*Lg Pos.*	*Goalscorers*	*Attendance*
1	Aug 10	H	Manchester C	L	0-5	0-1	20		59,870
2	17	A	Brighton & HA	D	1-1	0-0	15	Hernandez ^{61}	30,459
3	24	A	Watford	W	3-1	1-1	13	Noble (pen) ^{3}, Haller 2 $^{64, 73}$	20,035
4	31	H	Norwich C	W	2-0	1-0	5	Haller ^{24}, Yarmolenko ^{56}	59,950
5	Sept 16	A	Aston Villa	D	0-0	0-0	8		42,010
6	22	H	Manchester U	W	2-0	1-0	5	Yarmolenko ^{44}, Cresswell ^{84}	59,936
7	28	A	Bournemouth	D	2-2	1-1	3	Yarmolenko ^{10}, Cresswell ^{74}	10,729
8	Oct 5	H	Crystal Palace	L	1-2	0-0	7	Haller ^{54}	59,912
9	19	A	Everton	L	0-2	0-1	10		39,263
10	26	H	Sheffield U	D	1-1	1-0	9	Snodgrass ^{44}	59,878
11	Nov 2	H	Newcastle U	L	2-3	0-2	12	Balbuena ^{73}, Snodgrass ^{90}	59,907
12	9	A	Burnley	L	0-3	0-2	16		20,255
13	23	H	Tottenham H	L	2-3	0-2	16	Antonio ^{73}, Ogbonna ^{90}	59,930
14	30	A	Chelsea	W	1-0	0-0	13	Cresswell ^{48}	40,595
15	Dec 4	A	Wolverhampton W	L	0-2	0-1	13		31,217
16	9	H	Arsenal	L	1-3	1-0	16	Ogbonna ^{38}	59,936
17	14	A	Southampton	W	1-0	1-0	15	Haller ^{37}	27,701
18	26	A	Crystal Palace	L	1-2	0-0	17	Snodgrass ^{57}	25,462
19	28	H	Leicester C	L	1-2	1-1	17	Fornals ^{45}	59,519
20	Jan 1	H	Bournemouth	W	4-0	3-0	16	Noble 2 (1 pen) $^{17, 35 (p)}$, Haller ^{25}, Felipe Anderson ^{66}	59,917
21	10	A	Sheffield U	L	0-1	0-0	16		30,124
22	18	H	Everton	D	1-1	1-1	16	Diop ^{40}	59,915
23	22	A	Leicester C	L	1-4	0-2	17	Noble (pen) ^{50}	31,968
24	29	H	Liverpool	L	0-2	0-1	17		59,959
25	Feb 1	H	Brighton & HA	D	3-3	2-0	18	Diop ^{30}, Snodgrass 2 $^{45, 57}$	59,952
26	19	A	Manchester C	L	0-2	0-1	18		54,000
27	24	A	Liverpool	L	2-3	1-1	18	Diop ^{12}, Fornals ^{54}	53,313
28	29	H	Southampton	W	3-1	2-1	16	Bowen ^{15}, Haller ^{40}, Antonio ^{54}	59,962
29	Mar 7	A	Arsenal	L	0-1	0-0	16		60,335
30	June 20	H	Wolverhampton W	L	0-2	0-0	17		0
31	23	A	Tottenham H	L	0-2	0-0	17		0
32	July 1	H	Chelsea	W	3-2	1-1	16	Soucek ^{45}, Antonio ^{51}, Yarmolenko ^{89}	0
33	5	A	Newcastle U	D	2-2	1-1	16	Antonio ^{4}, Soucek ^{65}	0
34	8	H	Burnley	L	0-1	0-1	16		0
35	11	A	Norwich C	W	4-0	2-0	16	Antonio 4 $^{11, 45, 54, 74}$	0
36	17	H	Watford	W	3-1	3-0	15	Antonio ^{6}, Soucek ^{10}, Rice ^{36}	0
37	22	A	Manchester U	D	1-1	1-0	15	Antonio (pen) ^{45}	0
38	26	H	Aston Villa	D	1-1	0-0	16	Yarmolenko ^{85}	0

Final League Position: 16

GOALSCORERS

League (49): Antonio 10 (1 pen), Haller 7, Snodgrass 5, Yarmolenko 5, Noble 4 (3 pens), Cresswell 3, Diop 3, Soucek 3, Fornals 2, Ogbonna 2, Balbuena 1, Bowen 1, Felipe Anderson 1, Hernandez 1, Rice 1.
FA Cup (2): Fornals 1, Zabaleta 1.
Carabao Cup (2): Fornals 1, Wilshere 1.
Leasing.com Trophy (9): Kemp 2, Powell 2 (2 pens), Scully 2, Corbett 1, Costa Da Rosa 1, Parkes 1.

Fabianski L 25	Fredericks R 25 + 2	Balbuena F 13 + 4	Diop I 31 + 1	Cresswell A 31	Wilshere J 2 + 6	Rice D 38	Felipe Anderson G 20 + 5	Lanzini M 14 + 10	Antonio M 19 + 5	Haller S 24 + 8	Fornals P 24 + 12	Snodgrass R 17 + 7	Hernandez J 1 + 1	Ogbonna A 31	Masuaku A 10 + 7	Yarmolenko A 10 + 13	Sanchez C 1 + 5	Noble M 32 + 1	Zabaleta P 6 + 4	Roberto J 7 + 1	Ajeti A — + 9	Martin D 4 + 1	Holland N — + 2	Randolph D 2	Ngakia J 5	Soucek T 12 + 1	Bowen J 11 + 2	Johnson B 3	*Match No.*
1	2	3	4	5	6^{2}	7	8^{3}	9	10^{1}	11	12	13	14																1
1	2		3		8^{1}	6		10	12		9^{2}	7	11^{3}	4	5	13	14												2
1	2		3			6	10^{2}	9^{3}	12	11	13			4	5	8^{1}	14	7											3
1	2		3			6	10^{3}	9		11	14	12		4	5	7^{1}	13	8^{2}											4
1	2	14	3			6	10^{2}	9		11	12			4	5■	7^{1}		8^{3}	13										5
1	2^{2}		3	5	12	6	10^{1}			11	9	14		4		7^{3}		8	13										6
1^{1}	2		3	5	14	6	10	13		11	9^{2}			4		7		8^{3}		12									7
	2		3	5^{3}	13	6	10	9^{1}		11	12			4		7^{2}		8	14	1									8
	2		3		13	6	10^{1}	9		11	7^{2}			4	5	12		8^{3}		1	14								9
		3	4	5		6	10^{1}	12		11	13	9^{3}				7		8^{2}	2	1	14								10
	14	3	4	5		6	10	13		11		9				7^{2}		8^{1}	2^{3}	1	12								11
	2	3	4	5		7	9^{2}	13		11	10^{3}	6				12		8^{1}		1	14								12
	2		3^{3}	5		8	9^{1}		12	11	13	10		4		6^{2}	14	7		1									13
	2	3		5		8	10^{1}		11^{2}	13	9^{3}	6		4	14	12		7				1							14
	2	3		5		8	10			11^{3}	9	6^{1}		4		12		7^{2}			14	1	13						15
	2	3		5^{1}		8	10^{2}		11	13	9	6^{3}		4	12			7				1	14						16
	2	3	14	5		8			10	11^{2}	9	6^{1}		4		12	13	7^{3}				1							17
		3		5		8	13	12	10	11^{2}	9^{1}	6^{3}		4				7	2	1	14								18
1	2	3	4			6	10	9^{3}	12	11^{1}	8	13			5		7^{2}				14								19
1	2	3		5		7	10^{1}	12		11	9	6^{2}		4	13			8											20
1^{1}		2		4		7	10	9^{3}		11	14	13		3	8^{2}			6	5			12							21
			3	5		7		10^{2}		11	9^{1}	6		4	12			8	2		13			1					22
			3	5		8		10	12	11	13	7^{1}		4	6^{2}			9	2					1					23
1			3	5		8		10^{1}		11	12	7		4	6			9							2				24
1	2		3	5		6		14	10^{1}	11	13	7^{3}		4	12			9								8^{2}			25
1	2^{1}		3	5		7			11			10^{2}		4	6			9	12							8	13		26
1			3	5		6	10^{2}		11	13	12	8^{3}		4				9							2	7^{1}	14		27
1			3	5		7	13		10	11	9^{2}	12		4				6							2		8^{1}		28
1			3	5		8	13		10	11	9^{2}	14		4				7^{1}							2	12	6^{3}		29
1	14		3	5		4	10^{1}	12	11		9^{2}					13		6							2^{3}	7	8		30
1	2	3	4	5		7	13	12	11		10^{2}							9^{1}								6	8		31
1	2	14	3	5	12	6		10^{1}	11		9^{3}			4		13										7	8^{2}		32
1	2		3	5		7		10^{1}	11		9^{2}			4		13		12								6	8		33
1	2		3	5		7			11	12	9^{2}			4		8^{1}					13					6	10		34
1	2	16	3	5	12	7			11^{2}	13	10^{4}			4^{5}	15	14		9^{1}								6	8^{3}		35
1		14	3	5		6			11^{3}	12	10^{1}			4		13		9								7	8^{2}	2	36
1			3	5^{1}		6			11^{2}	13	10			4	12	14		9								7	8^{3}	2	37
1	2		3			7	15	14	11^{2}	12	10^{3}			4		13		9^{4}								6	8^{1}	5	38

FA Cup

Third Round	Gillingham	(a)	2-0
Fourth Round	WBA	(h)	0-1

Carabao Cup

Second Round	Newport Co	(a)	2-0
Third Round	Oxford U	(a)	0-4

Leasing.com Trophy (West Ham U U21)

Group E (S)	Newport Co	(a)	5-4
Group E (S)	Cheltenham T	(a)	3-4
Group E (S)	Exeter C	(a)	1-3

WIGAN ATHLETIC

FOUNDATION

Following the demise of Wigan Borough and their resignation from the Football League in 1931, a public meeting was called in Wigan at the Queen's Hall in May 1932 at which a new club, Wigan Athletic, was founded in the hope of carrying on in the Football League. With this in mind, they bought Springfield Park for £2,250, but failed to gain admission to the Football League until 46 years later.

DW Stadium, Loire Drive, Newtown, Wigan, Lancashire WN5 0UZ.

Telephone: (01942) 774 000.

Ticket Office: (01942) 311 111.

Website: www.wiganathletic.com

Email: feedback@wiganathletic.com

Ground Capacity: 25,113.

Record Attendance: 27,526 v Hereford U, 12 December 1953 (at Springfield Park); 25,133 v Manchester U, Premier League, 11 May 2008 (at DW Stadium).

Pitch Measurements: 105m × 68m (115yd × 74.5yd).

Executive Chairman: Darren Royle.

Chief Executive: Jonathan Jackson.

Caretaker Manager: Leam Richardson.

First-Team Coaches: Anthony Barry, Nick Colgan.

Colours: Blue shirts with thin white stripes and green trim, blue shorts, blue socks with green trim.

Year Formed: 1932.

Turned Professional: 1932.

Club Nickname: 'The Latics'.

Grounds: 1932, Springfield Park; 1999, JJB Stadium (renamed DW Stadium, 2009).

First Football League Game: 19 August 1978, Division 4, v Hereford U (a) D 0–0 – Brown; Hinnigan, Gore, Gillibrand, Ward, Davids, Corrigan, Purdie, Houghton, Wilkie, Wright.

Record League Victory: 8–0 v Hull C, FL C, 14 July 2020 – Marshall; Byrne, Kipre, Balogun (Dobre), Robinson (Evans), Williams (1) (Massey), Morsy, Naismith (1), Dowell (3) (Roberts), Lowe (1), Moore (2) (Pearce).

Record Cup Victory: 6–0 v Carlisle U (a), FA Cup 1st rd, 24 November 1934 – Caunce; Robinson, Talbot; Paterson, Watson, Tufnell; Armes (2), Robson (1), Roberts (2), Felton, Scott (1).

Record Defeat: 1–9 v Tottenham H, Premier League, 22 November 2009; 0–8 v Chelsea, Premier League, 9 May 2010.

HONOURS

League Champions: FL 1 – 2015–16, 2017–18; Second Division – 2002–03; Third Division – 1996–97.
Runners-up: FL C – 2004–05.

FA Cup Winners: 2013.

League Cup: *Runners-up:* 2006.

League Trophy Winners: 1985, 1999.

European Competitions
Europa League: 2013–14.

FOOTBALL YEARBOOK FACT FILE

Wigan Athletic were one of the top non-league clubs in the country for much of the post-war period before their election to the Football League in 1978. However, in 1946–47 they finished bottom of the Cheshire League and were not re-elected at the end of the season. Fortunately for the Latics, a subsequent application to the Lancashire Combination was successful.

Most League Points (2 for a win): 55, Division 4, 1978–79 and 1979–80.

Most League Points (3 for a win): 100, Division 2, 2002–03.

Most League Goals: 89, FL 1, 2017–18.

Highest League Scorer in Season: Graeme Jones, 31, Division 3, 1996–97.

Most League Goals in Total Aggregate: Andy Liddell, 70, 1998–2004.

Most League Goals in One Match: Not more than three goals by one player.

Most Capped Players: Kevin Kilbane, 22 (110), Republic of Ireland; Henri Camara, 22 (99), Senegal.

Most League Appearances: Kevin Langley, 317, 1981–86, 1990–94.

Youngest League Player: Steve Nugent, 16 years 132 days v Leyton Orient, 16 September 1989.

Record Transfer Fee Received: £15,250,000 from Manchester U for Antonio Valencia, June 2009.

Record Transfer Fee Paid: £7,000,000 to Newcastle U for Charles N'Zogbia, January 2009.

Football League Record: 1978 Elected to Division 4; 1982–92 Division 3; 1992–93 Division 2; 1993–97 Division 3; 1997–2003 Division 2; 2003–04 Division 1; 2004–05 FL C; 2005–13 Premier League; 2013–15 FL C; 2015–16 FL 1; 2016–17 FL C; 2017–18 FL 1; 2018–20 FL C; 2020– FL 1.

LATEST SEQUENCES

Longest Sequence of League Wins: 11, 2.11.2002 – 18.1.2003.

Longest Sequence of League Defeats: 8, 10.9.2011 – 6.11.2011.

Longest Sequence of League Draws: 6, 11.12.2001 – 5.1.2002.

Longest Sequence of Unbeaten League Matches: 25, 8.5.1999 – 3.1.2000.

Longest Sequence Without a League Win: 14, 9.5.1989 – 17.10.1989.

Successive Scoring Runs: 24 from 27.4.1996.

Successive Non-scoring Runs: 4 from 8.12.2018.

MANAGERS

Charlie Spencer 1932–37
Jimmy Milne 1946–47
Bob Pryde 1949–52
Ted Goodier 1952–54
Walter Crook 1954–55
Ron Suart 1955–56
Billy Cooke 1956
Sam Barkas 1957
Trevor Hitchen 1957–58
Malcolm Barrass 1958–59
Jimmy Shirley 1959
Pat Murphy 1959–60
Allenby Chilton 1960
Johnny Ball 1961–63
Allan Brown 1963–66
Alf Craig 1966–67
Harry Leyland 1967–68
Alan Saunders 1968
Ian McNeill 1968–70
Gordon Milne 1970–72
Les Rigby 1972–74
Brian Tiler 1974–76
Ian McNeill 1976–81
Larry Lloyd 1981–83
Harry McNally 1983–85
Bryan Hamilton 1985–86
Ray Mathias 1986–89
Bryan Hamilton 1989–93
Dave Philpotts 1993
Kenny Swain 1993–94
Graham Barrow 1994–95
John Deehan 1995–98
Ray Mathias 1998–99
John Benson 1999–2000
Bruce Rioch 2000–01
Steve Bruce 2001
Paul Jewell 2001–07
Chris Hutchings 2007
Steve Bruce 2007–09
Roberto Martinez 2009–13
Owen Coyle 2013
Uwe Rosler 2013–14
Malky Mackay 2014–15
Gary Caldwell 2015–16
Warren Joyce 2016–17
Paul Cook 2017–20

TEN YEAR LEAGUE RECORD

		P	W	D	L	F	A	Pts	Pos
2010-11	PR Lge	38	9	15	14	40	61	42	16
2011-12	PR Lge	38	11	10	17	42	62	43	15
2012-13	PR Lge	38	9	9	20	47	73	36	18
2013-14	FL C	46	21	10	15	61	48	73	5
2014-15	FL C	46	9	12	25	39	64	39	23
2015-16	FL 1	46	24	15	7	82	45	87	1
2016-17	FL C	46	10	12	24	40	57	42	23
2017-18	FL 1	46	29	11	6	89	29	98	1
2018-19	FL C	46	13	13	20	51	64	52	18
2019-20	FL C	46	15	14	17	57	56	47	23*

** 12 pts deducted.*

DID YOU KNOW ?

Wigan Athletic were one of just a handful of non-league clubs to appear on the BBC *Match of the Day* programme in the 1970s when highlights of their FA Cup third round tie against Manchester City were screened in January 1971. The Latics went down to a 1-0 defeat at Maine Road in front of a crowd of 46,212.

WIGAN ATHLETIC – SKY BET CHAMPIONSHIP 2019–20 LEAGUE RECORD

Match No.	Date	Venue	Opponents	Result		H/T Score	Lg Pos.	Goalscorers	Attendance
1	Aug 3	H	Cardiff C	W	3-2	0-1	2	Jacobs [59], Windass [63], Evans, L [75]	12,169
2	10	A	Preston NE	L	0-3	0-2	16		14,789
3	17	H	Leeds U	L	0-2	0-1	19		14,819
4	20	A	Middlesbrough	L	0-1	0-1	21		18,649
5	24	A	QPR	L	1-3	1-0	22	Kipre [2]	11,921
6	31	H	Barnsley	D	0-0	0-0	22		23,792
7	Sept 14	A	Hull C	D	2-2	1-2	22	Dunkley [8], Gelhardt [75]	10,069
8	21	H	Charlton Ath	W	2-0	1-0	19	Dunkley 2 [22, 70]	9567
9	27	A	Fulham	L	0-2	0-0	19		18,253
10	Oct 1	H	Birmingham C	W	1-0	0-0	17	Pilkington [76]	9244
11	5	A	Sheffield W	L	0-1	0-0	19		22,753
12	20	H	Nottingham F	W	1-0	1-0	18	Lowe [35]	13,077
13	23	A	Derby Co	L	0-1	0-0	19		24,697
14	27	A	Bristol C	D	2-2	1-1	18	Dunkley 2 [44, 53]	22,246
15	Nov 2	H	Swansea C	L	1-2	1-1	20	Moore (pen) [21]	9080
16	9	H	Brentford	L	0-3	0-1	20		9260
17	23	A	Stoke C	L	1-2	1-0	20	Morsy [39]	22,530
18	26	A	Millwall	D	2-2	1-1	21	Pilkington [3], Robinson [56]	10,021
19	30	H	Reading	L	1-3	1-0	22	Garner [34]	8965
20	Dec 7	A	Luton T	L	1-2	1-0	22	Moore [35]	10,011
21	11	H	WBA	D	1-1	0-0	23	Johnstone (og) [50]	9444
22	14	H	Huddersfield T	D	1-1	1-0	23	Windass [43]	10,383
23	23	A	Blackburn R	D	0-0	0-0	23		18,726
24	26	H	Derby Co	D	1-1	0-0	24	Garner [81]	14,211
25	29	A	Nottingham F	L	0-1	0-0	24		27,844
26	Jan 1	A	Birmingham C	W	3-2	1-1	22	Windass 2 [9, 50], Kipre [73]	18,616
27	11	H	Bristol C	L	0-2	0-0	23		9074
28	18	A	Swansea C	L	1-2	1-1	23	Byrne [16]	15,659
29	28	H	Sheffield W	W	2-1	0-1	22	Moore [56], Lowe [90]	9759
30	Feb 1	A	Leeds U	W	1-0	0-0	22	Hernandez (og) [59]	35,162
31	8	H	Preston NE	L	1-2	0-1	22	Dunkley [57]	12,439
32	11	H	Middlesbrough	D	2-2	1-0	22	Morsy [29], Moukoudi (og) [76]	9023
33	15	A	Cardiff C	D	2-2	2-1	22	Moore 2 (1 pen) [5, 45 (p)]	21,287
34	22	H	Millwall	W	1-0	0-0	22	Hutchinson (og) [57]	9639
35	26	A	Reading	W	3-0	1-0	22	Moore [23], Lowe [67], Jacobs [90]	10,088
36	29	A	WBA	W	1-0	0-0	19	Morsy [73]	24,942
37	Mar 7	H	Luton T	D	0-0	0-0	20		10,292
38	June 20	A	Huddersfield T	W	2-0	1-0	17	Lowe [26], Pilkington [48]	0
39	27	H	Blackburn R	W	2-0	0-0	17	Evans, L [80], Jacobs [90]	0
40	30	H	Stoke C	W	3-0	1-0	14	Dowell [40], Naismith 2 [65, 68]	0
41	July 4	A	Brentford	L	0-3	0-1	16		0
42	8	H	QPR	W	1-0	1-0	15	Moore [33]	0
43	11	A	Barnsley	D	0-0	0-0	15		0
44	14	H	Hull C	W	8-0	7-0	13	Naismith [1], Moore 2 [27, 40], Dowell 3 [32, 42, 65], Lowe [37], Williams [45]	0
45	18	A	Charlton Ath	D	2-2	2-1	13	Lowe [9], Dowell [40]	0
46	22	H	Fulham	D	1-1	1-0	13	Moore [32]	0

Final League Position: 23

GOALSCORERS

League (57): Moore 10 (2 pens), Dunkley 6, Lowe 6, Dowell 5, Windass 4, Jacobs 3, Morsy 3, Naismith 3, Pilkington 3, Evans, L 2, Garner 2, Kipre 2, Byrne 1, Gelhardt 1, Robinson 1, Williams 1, own goals 4.
FA Cup (0).
Carabao Cup (0).

Marshall D 39	Byrne N 39	Dunkley C 22 + 4	Fox D 9 + 2	Robinson A 38	Macleod L 11 + 1	Evans L 18 + 14	Pilkington A 9 + 7	Windass J 12 + 3	Jacobs M 19 + 13	Garner J 9 + 19	Lowe J 40 + 6	Kipre C 32 + 4	Naismith K 22 + 15	Moore K 32 + 4	Williams J 34 + 4	Morsy S 43	Massey G 21 + 10	Enobakhare B — + 2	Lang C — + 1	Mulgrew C 12	Gelhardt J 2 + 16	Sterling D 7 + 1	Jones J 7	Roberts G 3 + 6	Dowell K 12	Pearce T 4 + 3	Balogun L 10 + 1	Mlakar J — + 1	Dobre M — + 1	*Match No.*
1	2	3	4	5	6^{2}	7	8^{1}	9	10	11^{3}	12	13	14																	1
1	2		4^{2}	5	6	7		9	8^{3}	11^{1}	13	3	10	12	14															2
1	2	3	4	5		9			10^{2}		12		14	11^{3}	7■	6	8^{1}	13												3
1	5	3	4	8^{2}		6			14		10^{3}	2	12	11		7	9^{1}	13												4
1	5	3	4	8		6			10^{1}	11	9^{2}	2^{3}	12			7	14		13											5
1	2	3		5		14			10^{2}	12	9			11^{1}	6	7	8^{3}			4	13									6
1	2	3		5					10^{3}	12	9		14	11^{2}	6	7	8^{1}			4	13									7
1	2	3		5		12			10	14	9^{2}		13	11^{3}	7	6	8^{1}			4										8
1	2	3		5		9			10^{1}	13	8^{3}		12	11^{2}	6	7				4	14									9
1	2	3		5		14	13	9		12	10^{2}			11^{1}	6	7	8^{3}			4										10
1	2	3		5			12	9		11^{2}	10^{3}			13	6	7	8^{1}			4	14									11
1	2	3		5	6		14	13	10		8^{1}		12	11^{3}	7		9^{2}			4										12
1		3		5	7					13	9	12	14	10^{2}	6	8	11^{3}			4^{1}		2								13
1		3		5	7				12		9	4	13	10	6^{2}	8	11^{1}					2								14
1		3		5	7^{1}		14		12		11^{3}	4		10	6	8	9^{2}				13	2								15
1		3	14	5	7^{1}			13	11^{2}		9	4■		10	6	8					12	2^{3}								16
1	2	3		5	8^{1}				13	10^{3}	9		14	12	7	6	11^{2}			4										17
1		3		5	7		9^{1}	14		11^{3}	6	12		10^{2}		8	13			4		2								18
1		3		5	6		8^{1}	9^{3}	10^{2}	11	13		12			7				4	14	2								19
		3■		5	7		9^{1}			11^{2}	6	14		10		8	12			4^{3}	13	2	1							20
	2^{3}			5		6		11^{2}	10^{1}	13	9	3	4			7	8					14	1	12						21
	2			5		6	12	9	10	13	11^{1}	3	4			7	8^{2}						1							22
	2	13		5		6		11	10^{2}		9	3	4		12	7	8^{1}						1							23
	2	14		5		7	8^{2}	11^{1}	10^{3}	13	9	3	4		12	6							1							24
	2			5		6^{2}		10		14	9^{3}	3	4		7	8	11^{1}				13		1	12						25
	2	12		5		6		11	10^{2}		8	3	4^{1}		9	7							1	13						26
1	2			5	14	6^{3}		11^{2}		12	8	3	4		9^{1}	7					13				10					27
1	2			5		6^{3}				11^{1}	8^{2}	3	4	12	9	7	13							14	10					28
1	2			5		7^{3}			13	14	10	3	4	11	12	6					9^{1}				8^{2}					29
1	2	4				7			13		12	3	5	10	9	8	11^{1}									6^{2}				30
1	2	4				7^{2}			13	14	11	3	5	10^{3}	9	8					12					6^{1}				31
1	2	4■					8^{2}		10^{3}		13	3	5	11	7	6	14				9^{1}						12			32
1	2					8^{2}	12		14		9^{3}	3	5	10	6	7	11^{1}				13						4			33
1	2					13	8^{1}		10		9^{2}	3	5	11	6	7					12						4			34
1	2	14				12			13		8	3		11	7^{3}	6	10^{2}							9^{1}		5	4			35
1	2					14			12		8	3	13	11	6	7	10^{1}							9^{3}		5	4^{2}			36
1	2						12		13	14	8^{3}	3	5	11	7	6	10^{2}							9^{1}			4			37
1	2		4^{4}	5^{5}		13	6^{1}		12	14	11	3	16	9^{3}	7	8									10^{2}	15				38
1	2		4	5		12	8^{1}		13	14	10	3		11^{3}	6	7									9^{2}					39
1	2			5		14			8^{1}	15	10^{2}	3	12	11^{4}	6^{5}	7	13				16				9^{3}		4			40
1	2^{5}		14	5		16				13■	8^{3}	3	10	11^{2}	6	7	12								9^{4}		4^{1}	15		41
1	2		4	5		12					10	3	8^{2}	11	6	7	13								9^{1}					42
1	2		4■	5^{3}							10^{2}	3	8	11	6	7	13				12				9^{1}	14				43
1	2			5^{3}		14					10	3	8	11^{1}	6^{2}	7	13							15	9^{4}	12	4^{5}		16	44
1	2			5		12					10^{2}	3	8	11	6	7								13	9^{1}		4			45
1	2			5		14				13	10	3	8	11	6^{2}	7					12				9^{1}		4^{3}			46

FA Cup
Third Round Leicester C (a) 0-2

Carabao Cup
First Round Stoke C (h) 0-1

WOLVERHAMPTON WANDERERS

FOUNDATION

Enthusiasts of the game at St Luke's School, Blakenhall formed a club in 1877. In the same neighbourhood a cricket club called Blakenhall Wanderers had a football section. Several St Luke's footballers played cricket for them and shortly before the start of the 1879–80 season the two amalgamated and Wolverhampton Wanderers FC was brought into being.

Molineux Stadium, Waterloo Road, Wolverhampton, West Midlands WV1 4QR.

Telephone: (0371) 222 2220.

Ticket Office: (0371) 222 1877.

Website: wolves.co.uk

Email: info@wolves.co.uk

Ground Capacity: 32,050.

Record Attendance: 61,315 v Liverpool, FA Cup 5th rd, 11 February 1939.

Pitch Measurements: 105m × 68m (115yd × 74.5yd).

Executive Chairman: Jeff Shi.

Head Coach: Nuno Espírito Santo.

Assistant Head Coach: Rui Pedro Silva.

Colours: Gold shirts with black trim, black shorts with gold trim, gold socks.

Year Formed: 1877* (*see Foundation*).

Turned Professional: 1888.

Previous Names: 1879, St Luke's combined with Wanderers Cricket Club to become Wolverhampton Wanderers (1923) Ltd. New limited companies followed in 1982 and 1986 (current).

Club Nickname: 'Wolves'.

Grounds: 1877, Windmill Field; 1879, John Harper's Field; 1881, Dudley Road; 1889, Molineux.

First Football League Game: 8 September 1888, Football League, v Aston Villa (h) D 1–1 – Baynton; Baugh, Mason; Fletcher, Allen, Lowder; Hunter, Cooper, Anderson, White, Cannon, (1 og).

Record League Victory: 10–1 v Leicester C, Division 1, 15 April 1938 – Sidlow; Morris, Dowen; Galley, Cullis, Gardiner; Maguire (1), Horace Wright, Westcott (4), Jones (1), Dorsett (4).

Record Cup Victory: 14–0 v Crosswell's Brewery, FA Cup 2nd rd, 13 November 1886 – Ike Griffiths; Baugh, Mason; Pearson, Allen (1), Lowder; Hunter (4), Knight (2), Brodie (4), Bernie Griffiths (2), Wood. Plus one goal 'scrambled through'.

Record Defeat: 1–10 v Newton Heath, Division 1, 15 October 1892.

Most League Points (2 for a win): 64, Division 1, 1957–58.

HONOURS

League Champions: Division 1 – 1953–54, 1957–58, 1958–59; FL C – 2008–09, 2017–18; Division 2 – 1931–32, 1976–77; FL 1 – 2013–14; Division 3 – 1988–89; Division 3N – 1923–24; Division 4 – 1987–88.
Runners-up: Division 1 – 1937–38, 1938–39, 1949–50, 1954–55, 1959–60; Division 2 – 1966–67, 1982–83.

FA Cup Winners: 1893, 1908, 1949, 1960.
Runners-up: 1889, 1896, 1921, 1939.

League Cup Winners: 1974, 1980.

League Trophy Winners: 1988.

Texaco Cup Winners: 1971.

European Competitions
European Cup: 1958–59, 1959–60 *(qf)*.
UEFA Cup: 1971–72 (*runners-up*), 1973–74, 1974–75, 1980–81.
Europa League: 2019–20.
European Cup-Winners' Cup: 1960–61 *(sf)*.

FOOTBALL YEARBOOK FACT FILE

Wolverhampton Wanderers travelled to Ireland twice during the Big Freeze of 1962–63 to get some match action, playing Coventry City on both occasions. Wolves won 3-0 at Flower Lodge, home of Cork Hibernians, on 9 February and then 6-3 at Celtic Park, home of defunct club Belfast Celtic, on 20 February.

Most League Points (3 for a win): 103, FL 1, 2013–14.

Most League Goals: 115, Division 2, 1931–32.

Highest League Scorer in Season: Dennis Westcott, 38, Division 1, 1946–47.

Most League Goals in Total Aggregate: Steve Bull, 250, 1986–99.

Most League Goals in One Match: 5, Joe Butcher v Accrington, Division 1, 19 November 1892; 5, Tom Phillipson v Barnsley, Division 2, 26 April 1926; 5, Tom Phillipson v Bradford C, Division 2, 25 December 1926; 5, Billy Hartill v Notts Co, Division 2, 12 October 1929; 5, Billy Hartill v Aston Villa, Division 1, 3 September 1934.

Most Capped Player: Billy Wright, 105, England (70 consecutive).

Most League Appearances: Derek Parkin, 501, 1967–82.

Youngest League Player: Jimmy Mullen, 16 years 43 days v Leeds U, 18 February 1939.

Record Transfer Fee Received: £15,000,000 from Leeds U for Helder Costa, July 2020.

Record Transfer Fee Paid: £30,000,000 to Benfica for Raúl Jimenez, April 2019.

Football League Record: 1888 Founder Member of Football League: 1906–23 Division 2; 1923–24 Division 3 (N); 1924–32 Division 2; 1932–65 Division 1; 1965–67 Division 2; 1967–76 Division 1; 1976–77 Division 2; 1977–82 Division 1; 1982–83 Division 2; 1983–84 Division 1; 1984–85 Division 2; 1985–86 Division 3; 1986–88 Division 4; 1988–89 Division 3; 1989–92 Division 2; 1992–2003 Division 1; 2003–04 Premier League; 2004–09 FL C; 2009–12 Premier League; 2012–13 FL C; 2013–14 FL 1; 2014–18 FL C; 2018– Premier League.

LATEST SEQUENCES

Longest Sequence of League Wins: 9, 11.1.2014 – 11.3.2014.

Longest Sequence of League Defeats: 8, 5.12.1981 – 13.2.1982.

Longest Sequence of League Draws: 6, 22.4.1995 – 20.8.1995.

Longest Sequence of Unbeaten League Matches: 21, 15.1.2005 – 13.8.2005.

Longest Sequence Without a League Win: 19, 1.12.1984 – 6.4.1985.

Successive Scoring Runs: 41 from 20.12.1958.

Successive Non-scoring Runs: 7 from 2.2.1985.

MANAGERS

George Worrall 1877–85 *(Secretary-Manager)*
John Addenbrooke 1885–1922
George Jobey 1922–24
Albert Hoskins 1924–26 *(had been Secretary since 1922)*
Fred Scotchbrook 1926–27
Major Frank Buckley 1927–44
Ted Vizard 1944–48
Stan Cullis 1948–64
Andy Beattie 1964–65
Ronnie Allen 1966–68
Bill McGarry 1968–76
Sammy Chung 1976–78
John Barnwell 1978–81
Ian Greaves 1982
Graham Hawkins 1982–84
Tommy Docherty 1984–85
Bill McGarry 1985
Sammy Chapman 1985–86
Brian Little 1986
Graham Turner 1986–94
Graham Taylor 1994–95
Mark McGhee 1995–98
Colin Lee 1998–2000
Dave Jones 2001–04
Glenn Hoddle 2004–06
Mick McCarthy 2006–12
Stale Solbakken 2012–13
Dean Saunders 2013
Kenny Jackett 2013–16
Walter Zenga 2016
Paul Lambert 2016–17
Nuno Espírito Santo May 2017–

TEN YEAR LEAGUE RECORD

		P	*W*	*D*	*L*	*F*	*A*	*Pts*	*Pos*
2010-11	PR Lge	38	11	7	20	46	66	40	17
2011-12	PR Lge	38	5	10	23	40	82	25	20
2012-13	FL C	46	14	9	23	55	69	51	23
2013-14	FL 1	46	31	10	5	89	31	103	1
2014-15	FL C	46	22	12	12	70	56	78	7
2015-16	FL C	46	14	16	16	53	58	58	14
2016-17	FL C	46	16	10	20	54	58	58	15
2017-18	FL C	46	30	9	7	82	39	99	1
2018-19	PR Lge	38	16	9	13	47	46	57	7
2019-20	PR Lge	38	15	14	9	51	40	59	7

DID YOU KNOW ?

Tom Phillipson established a club record, yet to be broken, by scoring in 13 consecutive Football League games for Wolverhampton Wanderers during the 1926–27 season. In 1933 he became a councillor in Wolverhampton and served as mayor of the town from 1944–45.

WOLVERHAMPTON WANDERERS – PREMIER LEAGUE 2019–20 LEAGUE RECORD

Match No.	*Date*	*Venue*	*Opponents*	*Result*	*H/T Score*	*Lg Pos.*	*Goalscorers*	*Attendance*
1	Aug 11	A	Leicester C	D 0-0	0-0	10		32,015
2	19	H	Manchester U	D 1-1	0-1	12	Neves [55]	31,314
3	25	H	Burnley	D 1-1	0-1	15	Jimenez (pen) [90]	30,522
4	Sept 1	A	Everton	L 2-3	1-2	17	Saiss [9], Jimenez [75]	39,374
5	14	H	Chelsea	L 2-5	0-3	19	Abraham (og) [69], Cutrone [85]	31,534
6	22	A	Crystal Palace	D 1-1	0-0	19	Jota [90]	25,122
7	28	H	Watford	W 2-0	1-0	13	Doherty [18], Janmaat (og) [61]	30,711
8	Oct 6	A	Manchester C	W 2-0	0-0	11	Traore 2 [80, 90]	54,435
9	19	H	Southampton	D 1-1	0-0	12	Jimenez (pen) [61]	30,915
10	27	A	Newcastle U	D 1-1	0-1	12	Jonny [73]	46,019
11	Nov 2	A	Arsenal	D 1-1	0-1	11	Jimenez [76]	60,383
12	10	H	Aston Villa	W 2-1	1-0	8	Neves [41], Jimenez [84]	31,607
13	23	A	Bournemouth	W 2-1	2-0	5	Joao Moutinho [21], Jimenez [31]	10,539
14	Dec 1	H	Sheffield U	D 1-1	0-1	6	Doherty [64]	31,642
15	4	H	West Ham U	W 2-0	1-0	5	Dendoncker [23], Cutrone [86]	31,217
16	8	A	Brighton & HA	D 2-2	2-2	6	Jota 2 [28, 44]	30,189
17	15	H	Tottenham H	L 1-2	0-1	8	Traore [67]	31,674
18	21	A	Norwich C	W 2-1	0-1	6	Saiss [60], Jimenez [81]	27,053
19	27	H	Manchester C	W 3-2	0-1	5	Traore [55], Jimenez [82], Doherty [89]	31,737
20	29	A	Liverpool	L 0-1	0-1	7		53,326
21	Jan 1	A	Watford	L 1-2	0-1	7	Pedro Neto [60]	20,584
22	11	H	Newcastle U	D 1-1	1-1	7	Dendoncker [14]	31,570
23	18	A	Southampton	W 3-2	0-2	6	Pedro Neto [53], Jimenez 2 (1 pen) [65 (p), 76]	31,152
24	23	H	Liverpool	L 1-2	0-1	7	Jimenez [51]	31,746
25	Feb 1	A	Manchester U	D 0-0	0-0	7		73,363
26	14	H	Leicester C	D 0-0	0-0	7		31,682
27	23	H	Norwich C	W 3-0	2-0	8	Jota 2 [19, 30], Jimenez [50]	31,046
28	Mar 1	A	Tottenham H	W 3-2	1-2	6	Doherty [27], Jota [57], Jimenez [73]	58,064
29	7	H	Brighton & HA	D 0-0	0-0	5		31,490
30	June 20	A	West Ham U	W 2-0	0-0	6	Jimenez [73], Pedro Neto [84]	0
31	24	H	Bournemouth	W 1-0	0-0	6	Jimenez [60]	0
32	27	A	Aston Villa	W 1-0	0-0	5	Dendoncker [62]	0
33	July 4	H	Arsenal	L 0-2	0-1	6		0
34	8	A	Sheffield U	L 0-1	0-0	6		0
35	12	H	Everton	W 3-0	1-0	6	Jimenez (pen) [45], Dendoncker [46], Jota [74]	0
36	15	A	Burnley	D 1-1	0-0	6	Jimenez [76]	0
37	20	H	Crystal Palace	W 2-0	1-0	6	Daniel Podence [41], Jonny [68]	0
38	26	A	Chelsea	L 0-2	0-2	7		0

Final League Position: 7

GOALSCORERS

League (51): Jimenez 17 (4 pens), Jota 7, Dendoncker 4, Doherty 4, Traore 4, Pedro Neto 3, Cutrone 2, Jonny 2, Neves 2, Saiss 2, Daniel Podence 1, Joao Moutinho 1, own goals 2.
FA Cup (0).
Carabao Cup (2): Bruno Jordao 1, Cutrone 1.
UEFA Europa League (38): Jimenez 10 (2 pens), Jota 9, Doherty 3, Dendoncker 2, Neves 2 (1 pen), Pedro Neto 2, Ruben Vinagre 2, Traore 2, Bennett 1, Boly 1, Gibbs-White 1, Saiss 1, own goals 2.
Leasing.com Trophy (6): Ashley-Seal 3 (1 pen), Dai 1, Samuels 1, Watt 1.

Rui Patricio P 38	Bennett R 7 + 4	Coady C 38	Boly W 22	Doherty M 32 + 4	Dendoncker L 32 + 6	Neves R 35 + 3	Joao Moutinho F 34 + 4	Jonny C 33 + 2	Jimenez R 37 + 1	Jota D 27 + 7	Cutrone P 3 + 9	Saiss R 31 + 2	Traore A 27 + 10	Pedro Neto L 9 + 20	White M 1 + 6	Ruben Vinagre G 6 + 10	Vallejo J 1 + 1	Kilman M 2 + 1	Daniel Podence C 3 + 6	Bruno Jordao A — + 1	Match No.
1	2	3	4	5	6	7^{2}	8	9	10	11^{1}	12	13									1
1	2	3	4	5^{1}	6	7	8	9	10^{3}	11^{2}	14		12	13							2
1	2	3	4	5^{3}	12	7	8^{1}	9	10	11			14	13	6^{2}						3
1	2	3	4■		6	7^{3}	12		10	13	11^{2}	8^{1}	5	14		9					4
1		3		13	6^{1}	7	8	9	10^{3}	11	12	4	5^{2}		14		2				5
1		3	2	5^{1}	6^{2}	12	7	8	10^{3}	11	14	4■	9	13							6
1		3	2	5	6	14	7	8	11^{2}		13	4	9^{3}	10^{1}	12						7
1	12	3	2	13	6	7	8	14	10		11^{2}	4^{1}	5			9^{3}					8
1	2^{1}	3	4	13	6	7^{2}	8	9	10	14	11^{3}		5				12				9
1		3		2	6	7	8	9^{2}	11	10^{1}		4	5	12		13					10
1		3		5^{1}	2	6	7	8	10	11^{2}		4	9	13		12					11
1	13	3		5	2	6^{2}	7	8	10^{3}	11^{1}	14	4	9	12							12
1		3		5	2	6	7	8	10	11^{1}		4	9			12					13
1		3		5	2	6	7	8	10	11			9					4			14
1	14	3		5	2	6	7	8	10^{2}	11^{1}	13	4	9^{3}	12							15
1		3		5	2	6	7	8	10^{2}	11^{1}	13	4	9^{3}	12		14					16
1		3		5	2	6	7	8	10	11		4	9								17
1		3		5	2	6	7	8	10^{2}	11^{1}	13	4	9	12							18
1	14	3		5	2	6	7	8^{1}	10^{3}	11^{2}		4	9	13		12					19
1	2	3			6^{1}	7^{2}	8	5	14	11^{3}		12	13	10		9		4			20
1	2^{2}	3		5	6	12	7	8^{1}	10	14		4	9	11^{3}		13					21
1		3		5	2	6	7	8	10			4	9	11^{1}		12					22
1		3		5	2	7	6	8	10			4	11	9^{1}				12			23
1		3		5	2	6	7^{2}	8	11	12		4	10	9^{1}	13						24
1		3	2	5	14	6	7	8	10^{3}	11^{1}		4	9^{2}	12					13		25
1		3	2	5	6	7^{3}	14	8	11	10^{2}		4	12	9^{1}					13		26
1		3	2	5	6	7	8	9^{3}	10^{2}	11^{1}		4	13	12		14					27
1		3	2	5	13	6	7		10^{3}	11^{2}		4	9^{1}	12		8			14		28
1		3	2	5	6	7^{1}	8		10	11^{2}		4	12			9			13		29
1		3	2	5	6^{2}	7	8	9^{4}	10^{3}	11^{1}		4	12	13	14	15					30
1		3	2	5	13	6	7^{4}	8	10^{3}	11^{1}		4	9^{2}	12	14				15		31
1		3	2	5	6	7	8	9	10^{2}	11^{1}		4	12	13							32
1		3	2	5^{2}	6^{1}	7	8^{3}	9	11	12		4	10	13	14						33
1		3	2	5	12	6	7	8	10	11		4	9^{1}								34
1		3	2	5	6	7	14	8	10^{3}	12		4	13	9^{1}					11^{2}		35
1		3	2	12	14	6	7	15	10^{3}	11^{2}		4	5	13		8^{4}			9^{1}		36
1		3	4	5	2	6	7	8	10	12			9^{2}	13					11^{1}		37
1		3	2	5^{3}	6	7^{4}	14	8^{2}	10	11^{5}		4	12	9^{1}		13			15	16	38

FA Cup

Third Round	Manchester U	(h)	0-0
Replay	Manchester U	(a)	0-1

Carabao Cup

Third Round	Reading	(h)	1-1
(Wolverhampton W won 4-2 on penalties)			
Fourth Round	Aston Villa	(a)	1-2

Leasing.com Trophy (Wolverhampton W U21)

Group G (N)	Carlisle U	(a)	4-2
Group G (N)	Morecambe	(a)	2-2
(Wolverhampton W U21 won 5-4 on penalties)			
Group G (N)	Blackpool	(a)	0-1
Second Round (N)	Salford C	(a)	0-3

UEFA Europa League

Second Qualifying Round	Crusaders	(h)	2-0
Second Qualifying Round	Crusaders	(a)	4-1
Third Qualifying Round	Pyunik	(a)	4-0
Third Qualifying Round	Pyunik	(h)	4-0
Play-off Round	Torino	(a)	3-2
Play-off Round	Torino	(h)	2-1
Group K	Braga	(h)	0-1
Group K	Besiktas	(a)	1-0
Group K	Slovan Bratislava	(a)	2-1
Group K	Slovan Bratislava	(h)	1-0
Group K	Braga	(a)	3-3
Group K	Besiktas	(h)	4-0
Round of 32	Espanyol	(h)	4-0
Round of 32	Espanyol	(a)	2-3
Round of 16	Olympiacos	(a)	1-1
Round of 16	Olympiacos	(h)	1-0
Quarter-Finals	Sevilla	(Duisburg)	0-1

WYCOMBE WANDERERS

FOUNDATION

In 1887 a group of young furniture trade workers called a meeting at the Steam Engine public house with the aim of forming a football club and entering junior football. It is thought that they were named after the famous FA Cup winners, The Wanderers, who had visited the town in 1877 for a tie with the original High Wycombe club. It is also possible that they played informally before their formation, although there is no proof of this.

Adams Park, Hillbottom Road, High Wycombe, Buckinghamshire HP12 4HJ.

Telephone: (01494) 472 100.

Ticket Office: (01494) 441 118.

Website: www.wycombewanderers.co.uk

Email: wwfc@wwfc.com

Ground Capacity: 9,558.

Record Attendance: 15,850 v St Albans C, FA Amateur Cup 4th rd, 25 February 1950 (at Loakes Park); 9,921 v Fulham, FA Cup 3rd rd, 9 January 2002 (at Adams Park).

Pitch Measurements: 100m × 64m (109.5yd × 70yd).

Chairman: Rob Couhig.

Manager: Gareth Ainsworth.

Assistant Manager: Richard Dobson.

Colours: Light blue and dark blue quartered shirts, dark blue shorts with light blue trim, dark blue socks.

Year Formed: 1887. ***Turned Professional:*** 1974.

Club Nicknames: 'The Chairboys' (after High Wycombe's tradition of furniture making), 'The Blues'.

Grounds: 1887, The Rye; 1893, Spring Meadow; 1895, Loakes Park; 1899, Daws Hill Park; 1901, Loakes Park; 1990, Adams Park.

First Football League Game: 14 August 1993, Division 3 v Carlisle U (a) D 2–2: Hyde; Cousins, Horton (Langford), Kerr, Crossley, Ryan, Carroll, Stapleton, Thompson, Scott, Guppy (1) (Hutchinson), (1 og).

Record League Victory: 5–0 v Burnley, Division 2, 15 April 1997 – Parkin; Cousins, Bell, Kavanagh, McCarthy, Forsyth, Carroll (2p) (Simpson), Scott (Farrell), Stallard (1), McGavin (1) (Read (1)), Brown. 5–0 v Northampton T, Division 2, 4 January 2003 – Talia; Senda, Ryan, Thomson, McCarthy, Johnson, Bulman, Simpson (1), Faulconbridge (Harris), Dixon (1) (Roberts 3), Brown (Currie). 5–0 v Hartlepool U, FL 1, 25 February 2012 – Bull; McCoy, Basey, Eastmond (Bloomfield), Laing, Doherty (1), Hackett, Lewis, Bevon (2) (Strevons), Hayes (2) (McClure), McNamee.

Record Cup Victory: 5–0 v Hitchin T (a), FA Cup 2nd rd, 3 December 1994 – Hyde; Cousins, Brown, Crossley, Evans, Ryan (1), Carroll, Bell (1), Thompson, Garner (3) (Hemmings), Stapleton (Langford). 5–0 v Chesterfield (a), FA Cup 2nd rd, 3 December 2017 – Blackman; Harriman, Stewart (1), Pierre, Jacobson, Bloomfield (Wood), O'Nien, Gape (Bean), Kashket (3) (Cowan-Hall), Hayes (1), Akinfenwa.

Record Defeat: 0–7 v Shrewsbury T, Johnstone's Paint Trophy, 7 October 2008.

HONOURS

League Champions: Conference – 1992–93.
Runners-up: FL 2 – (3rd) 2008–09, 2010–11 *(promoted to FL 1)*; Conference – 1991–92.

FA Cup: semi-final – 2001.

League Cup: semi-final – 2007.

FA Amateur Cup Winners: 1931.

FOOTBALL YEARBOOK FACT FILE

Wycombe Wanderers were winners of the Anglo Italian Semi Professional Cup in 1975. Wanderers, who were selected as the Isthmian League Division One champions, played AC Monza, winners of the Coppa Italia Serie C, over two legs. The Chairboys lost 1-0 in Italy but came back to win 2-0 in the home leg in front of a crowd of 3,351.

Most League Points (3 for a win): 84, FL 2, 2014–15; 84, FL 2, 2017–18.

Most League Goals: 79, FL 2, 2017–18.

Highest League Scorer in Season: Scott McGleish, 25, 2007–08.

Most League Goals in Total Aggregate: Nathan Tyson, 51, 2004–06, 2017–19.

Most League Goals in One Match: 3, Miquel Desouza v Bradford C, Division 2, 2 September 1995; 3, John Williams v Stockport Co, Division 2, 24 February 1996; 3, Mark Stallard v Walsall, Division 2, 21 October 1997; 3, Sean Devine v Reading, Division 2, 2 October 1999; 3, Sean Divine v Bury, Division 2, 26 February 2000; 3, Stuart Roberts v Northampton T, Division 2, 4 January 2003; 3, Nathan Tyson v Lincoln C, FL 2, 5 March 2005; 3, Nathan Tyson v Kidderminster H, FL 2, 2 April 2005; 3, Nathan Tyson v Stockport Co, FL 2, 10 September 2005; 3, Kevin Betsy v Mansfield T, FL 2, 24 September 2005; 3, Scott McGleish v Mansfield T, FL 2, 8 January 2008; 3, Stuart Beavon v Bury, FL 1, 17 March 2012; 3, Craig Mackail-Smith v Crawley T, FL 2, 18 November 2017; 3, Joe Jacobson v Lincoln C, FL 1, 7 September 2019.

Most Capped Player: Mark Rogers, 7, Canada; Marvin McCoy, 7 (8), Antigua and Barbuda.

Most League Appearances: Matt Bloomfield, 470, 2003–20.

Youngest League Player: Jordon Ibe, 15 years 311 days v Hartlepool U, 15 October 2011.

Record Transfer Fee Received: £675,000 from Nottingham F for Nathan Tyson, January 2006.

Record Transfer Fee Paid: £200,000 to Barnet for Sean Devine, April 1999; £200,000 to Barnet for Darren Currie, July 2001.

Football League Record: 1993 Promoted to Division 3 from Conference; 1993–94 Division 3; 1994–2004 Division 2; 2004–09 FL 2; 2009–10 FL 1; 2010–11 FL 2; 2011–12 FL 1; 2012–18 FL 2; 2018–20 FL 1; 2020– FL C.

MANAGERS

First coach appointed 1951.
Prior to Brian Lee's appointment in 1969 the team was selected by a Match Committee which met every Monday evening.

James McCormack 1951–52
Sid Cann 1952–61
Graham Adams 1961–62
Don Welsh 1962–64
Barry Darvill 1964–68
Brian Lee 1969–76
Ted Powell 1976–77
John Reardon 1977–78
Andy Williams 1978–80
Mike Keen 1980–84
Paul Bence 1984–86
Alan Gane 1986–87
Peter Suddaby 1987–88
Jim Kelman 1988–90
Martin O'Neill 1990–95
Alan Smith 1995–96
John Gregory 1996–98
Neil Smillie 1998–99
Lawrie Sanchez 1999–2003
Tony Adams 2003–04
John Gorman 2004–06
Paul Lambert 2006–08
Peter Taylor 2008–09
Gary Waddock 2009–12
Gareth Ainsworth November 2012–

LATEST SEQUENCES

Longest Sequence of League Wins: 6, 12.11.2016 – 17.12.2016.

Longest Sequence of League Defeats: 6, 18.3.2006 – 17.4.2006.

Longest Sequence of League Draws: 5, 24.1.2004 – 21.2.2004.

Longest Sequence of Unbeaten League Matches: 21, 6.8.2005 – 10.12.2005.

Longest Sequence Without a League Win: 13, 10.1.2004 – 20.3.2004.

Successive Scoring Runs: 16 from 13.9.2014.

Successive Non-scoring Runs: 5 from 15.10.1996.

TEN YEAR LEAGUE RECORD

		P	*W*	*D*	*L*	*F*	*A*	*Pts*	*Pos*
2010-11	FL 2	46	22	14	10	69	50	80	3
2011-12	FL 1	46	11	10	25	65	88	43	21
2012-13	FL 2	46	17	9	20	50	60	60	15
2013-14	FL 2	46	12	14	20	46	54	50	22
2014-15	FL 2	46	23	15	8	67	45	84	4
2015-16	FL 2	46	17	13	16	45	44	64	13
2016-17	FL 2	46	19	12	15	58	53	69	9
2017-18	FL 2	46	24	12	10	79	60	84	3
2018-19	FL 1	46	14	11	21	55	67	53	17
2019-20	FL 1	34	17	8	9	45	40	59	3§

§*Decided on points-per-game (1.74)*

DID YOU KNOW ?

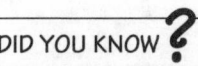

Wycombe Wanderers made their first Wembley appearance in the FA Amateur Cup final against Bishop Auckland in April 1957. Wanderers went down to a 3-1 defeat with around 90,000 fans in attendance, still an all-time record number of spectators at a Chairboys match.

WYCOMBE WANDERERS – SKY BET LEAGUE ONE 2019–20 LEAGUE RECORD

Match No.	Date	Venue	Opponents	Result	H/T Score	Lg Pos.	Goalscorers	Attendance
1	Aug 3	H	Bolton W	W 2-0	0-0	2	Smyth [56], Onyedinma [82]	6454
2	10	A	Bristol R	D 0-0	0-0	4		7668
3	17	H	Milton Keynes D	W 3-2	2-1	3	Jacobson (pen) [12], Onyedinma [37], Wheeler [90]	5243
4	20	A	Fleetwood T	D 1-1	0-0	3	Akinfenwa [57]	2319
5	24	H	Southend U	W 4-3	1-2	3	Milligan (og) [36], Kashket 2 [55, 90], Stewart [89]	4196
6	31	A	AFC Wimbledon	D 0-0	0-0	4		4521
7	Sept 7	H	Lincoln C	W 3-1	2-0	1	Jacobson 3 [5, 36, 75]	5562
8	14	A	Gillingham	L 0-2	0-0	3		4814
9	17	H	Accrington S	D 1-1	0-1	3	Freeman (pen) [72]	3566
10	21	H	Portsmouth	W 1-0	0-0	3	Akinfenwa (pen) [82]	7688
11	28	A	Rochdale	W 3-0	2-0	2	Onyedinma 2 [16, 77], Akinfenwa [26]	3039
12	Oct 5	H	Peterborough U	D 3-3	0-2	2	Akinfenwa 2 (1 pen) [56, 90 (p)], Pym (og) [63]	5083
13	19	H	Sunderland	W 1-0	1-0	2	Charles [28]	8395
14	22	A	Blackpool	D 1-1	1-0	2	Kashket [8]	7298
15	26	A	Rotherham U	W 1-0	1-0	2	Kashket [5]	8337
16	Nov 2	H	Shrewsbury T	W 1-0	0-0	1	Aarons [57]	4826
17	17	A	Tranmere R	W 2-0	2-0	1	Akinfenwa [43], Jacobson (pen) [45]	5460
18	23	H	Doncaster R	W 1-0	0-0	1	Jacobson (pen) [90]	4875
19	26	A	Ipswich T	D 0-0	0-0	1		19,215
20	Dec 14	H	Burton Alb	W 2-0	1-0	1	Wheeler [24], Bloomfield [90]	5448
21	21	A	Oxford U	L 0-1	0-1	1		10,123
22	26	A	Portsmouth	L 0-2	0-0	1		18,419
23	29	H	Coventry C	L 1-4	1-3	1	Akinfenwa [14]	7533
24	Jan 1	H	Ipswich T	D 1-1	0-0	1	Wheeler [66]	8523
25	11	A	Sunderland	L 0-4	0-3	2		29,331
26	18	H	Rochdale	W 2-1	1-1	2	McCarthy [31], Jacobson (pen) [90]	4498
27	21	A	Peterborough U	L 0-4	0-2	2		3851
28	28	H	Blackpool	W 2-1	2-0	2	Freeman [5], Samuel [9]	3684
29	Feb 1	A	Milton Keynes D	L 0-2	0-0	2		9699
30	8	H	Bristol R	W 3-1	3-1	2	Akinfenwa [9], Charles [39], Bloomfield [41]	5769
31	11	H	Fleetwood T	L 0-1	0-0	4		3286
32	15	A	Bolton W	W 2-0	1-0	3	Nsiala (og) [44], Jacobson (pen) [62]	11,737
33	22	H	Tranmere R	W 3-1	1-0	3	Stewart [45], Akinfenwa [71], Jacobson (pen) [90]	4756
34	29	A	Doncaster R	L 1-3	0-1	4	Akinfenwa [67]	7522
35	14	A	Burton Alb	Cancelled				
36	21	H	Oxford U	Cancelled				
37	24	A	Coventry C	Cancelled				
38	28	A	Shrewsbury T	Cancelled				
39	Apr 4	H	Rotherham U	Cancelled				
40	10	A	Southend U	Cancelled				
41	13	H	AFC Wimbledon	Cancelled				
42	18	A	Lincoln C	Cancelled				
43	25	H	Gillingham	Cancelled				
44	May 3	A	Accrington S	Cancelled				

Final League Position: 3 (on points-per-game basis)

GOALSCORERS

League (45): Akinfenwa 10 (2 pens), Jacobson 9 (6 pens), Kashket 4, Onyedinma 4, Wheeler 3, Bloomfield 2, Charles 2, Freeman 2 (1 pen), Stewart 2, Aarons 1, McCarthy 1, Samuel 1, Smyth 1, own goals 3.
FA Cup (3): Jacobson 1, Samuel 1, Stewart 1.
Carabao Cup (1): Samuel 1.
Leasing.com Trophy (3): Aarons 1, Ofoborh 1, Parker 1.
League One Play-offs (8): Jacobson 2 (1 pen), Onyedinma 2, Ofoborh 1, Samuel 1, Stewart 1, Wheeler 1.

Allsop R 32	Grimmer J 18	El-Abd A 2	Stewart A 34	Jacobson J 30	Bloomfield M 22 + 4	Gape D 28	Pattison A 8 + 9	Smyth P 13 + 6	Akinfenwa A 20 + 12	Samuel A 15 + 6	Wheeler D 25 + 6	Onyedinma F 11 + 2	Freeman N 16 + 10	Phillips G 10 + 1	Charles D 25	Parker J 3 + 10	Kashket S 11 + 8	Ofoborh N 7 + 11	Aarons R 5 + 5	Mascoll J 2 + 2	Thompson C 20 + 1	Jombati S 6 + 1	McCarthy J 9	Stockdale D 2	Match No.
1	2	3	4	5	6³	7	8	9¹	10	11²	12	13	14												1
1	2	3	4	5	6	7	8	11¹	10	12		9²	13												2
1	2		3	5	6¹	7	8	9³	14	10²	12	11	13	4											3
1			3	5	13	7	6		10²	12	11	9³	8¹	2	4	14									4
1	2		3	5	8	7	6¹		13	10³	12	11²	14		4		9								5
1	2		3	5	8²	7	13		10		11		6		4	12	9¹								6
1	2		3	5	6³	7			13	10²	9		8		4		11¹	12	14						7
1	2²		3	5³		7	8		10	11¹	13		9	14	4		12	6							8
1	2		3		8	7			12		10	11¹	6	4		13	9²			5					9
1	2		3	5²	6³	7	14		10			11¹	8		4		9	12■		13					10
1	2		3			7	8¹		10³		9	11		5²	4	13	12			14	6				11
1	2		3			7			10		9¹	11²	8	5	4		13		12		6■				12
1	2		3	5	6²	8	12		10		9		7		4	13			11¹						13
1	2		3	5	14	7			10		9		8¹	4			11³	13	12		6²				14
1	2		3	5	9	7¹	12		13		10				4		11³	14	6²		8				15
1	2		3	5	8²	7	13		10		12		14		4		9³		11¹		6				16
1	2		3	5	9³	8			10	13	6²		12		4		11¹	14			7				17
1	2		3	5	6¹			11³	12	10²	9				4		14	7	13		8				18
1	2		3	5	6¹	7		11²	10		9		13		4		12				8				19
1			3	5	7		14		12	10¹	9				4		13	6	11³		8²	2			20
1			3	5	6¹	7²		13	10■		9				4		11³	12	14		8	2			21
1			3	5			12	11¹		10	13		8		4		14	7	9²		6³	2			22
1			3	5	7			13	10		11¹		12	4		14	9³	8			6²	2			23
1			3	5	6			11¹	12	10²	9		8	2	4		13	7							24
1			3	5	8	7³	13	11²	12	10	9			2¹	4	14					6				25
1			4	5		7¹		12	10		9²		8		3	11		13			6		2		26
1			3	5²	8			13	11	14			9	4■		10³		6¹			7	12	2		27
			3		6²	7³		11	13	10	9¹		8		4			14		5	12		2	1	28
			4	5	14	7²	13	11¹		10³	9		8			12					6	3	2	1	29
1			3	5	8¹	7		13	10²	9	11		12		4			14			6³		2		30
1			3	5		7	6¹	12	13	10²	9	14	8			11³						4	2		31
1			3	5		7		6³	10²	13	9	11¹			4	14		12			8		2		32
1			3	5	14	7		11	10¹	13	8	9³			4			12			6²		2		33
1			3	5		6		8¹	12	11³	9	10²	13		4	14					7		2		34
																									35
																									36
																									37
																									38
																									39
																									40
																									41
																									42
																									43
																									44

FA Cup

First Round	Tranmere R	(a)	2-2
Replay	Tranmere R	(h)	1-2
(aet)			

Carabao Cup

First Round	Reading	(h)	1-1
(Reading won 4-2 on penalties)			

Leasing.com Trophy

Group G (S)	Stevenage	(h)	0-1
Group G (S)	Fulham U21	(h)	1-2
Group G (S)	Milton Keynes D	(a)	2-1

League One Play-Offs

Semi-Final 1st leg	Fleetwood T	(a)	4-1
Semi-Final 2nd leg	Fleetwood T	(h)	2-2
Final	Oxford U	(Wembley)	2-1

ENGLISH LEAGUE PLAYERS DIRECTORY

Players listed represent those with their clubs during the 2019–20 season.

Club names in *italic* indicate loans.

Players are listed alphabetically on pages 537–543 where the number alongside each player corresponds to the team number heading. (Aarons, Maximillian 58 = team 58 (Norwich C)).

ACCRINGTON S (1)

BARCLAY, Ben (D) 21 1
b. 7-10-96
2018–19 Brighton & HA 0 0
2018–19 *Notts Co* 13 1 **13 1**
2019–20 Accrington S 8 0 **8 0**

BISHOP, Colby (M) 31 10
H: 5 11 W: 11 05 b. 14-11-94
2013–14 Notts Co 0 0
2014–15 Notts Co 3 0
2015–16 Notts Co 1 0 **4 0**
From Gloucester C, Worcester C, Boston U.
2019–20 Accrington S 27 10 **27 10**

BOLTON, Jack (D) 0 0
2019–20 Accrington S 0 0

CARVALHO, Wilson (M) 8 0
b. 4-7-93
2013–14 Port Vale 0 0
2014–15 Port Vale 0 0
From Corby T, Kettering T, Oxford C, Stratford T.
2019–20 Accrington S 8 0 **8 0**

CHARLES, Dion (M) 33 8
H: 5 10 W: 10 08 b.Preston 7-10-95
Internationals: Northern Ireland U21.
2013–14 Blackpool 0 0
From AFC Fylde.
2016–17 Fleetwood T 0 0
From Southport.
2019–20 Accrington S 33 8 **33 8**

CLARK, Jordan (F) 218 25
H: 6 0 W: 11 07 b.Barnsley 22-9-93
2010–11 Barnsley 4 0
2011–12 Barnsley 2 0
2012–13 Barnsley 0 0
2012–13 *Chesterfield* 2 0 **2 0**
2013–14 Barnsley 0 0 **6 0**
2013–14 *Scunthorpe U* 1 0 **1 0**
2014–15 Shrewsbury T 27 3
2015–16 Shrewsbury T 20 2 **47 5**
2016–17 Accrington S 42 1
2017–18 Accrington S 43 8
2018–19 Accrington S 43 5
2019–20 Accrington S 34 6 **162 20**

CONNEELY, Seamus (D) 277 13
H: 5 9 W: 10 10 b.Galway 9-7-88
Internationals: Republic of Ireland U21, U23.
2008 Galway U 20 0
2009 Galway U 34 2
2010 Galway U 32 0 **86 2**
2010–11 Sheffield U 0 0
2011–12 Sheffield U 0 0
From Sligo R.
2014–15 Accrington S 16 3
2015–16 Accrington S 46 3
2016–17 Accrington S 38 1
2017–18 Accrington S 33 2
2018–19 Accrington S 27 1
2019–20 Accrington S 31 1 **191 11**

EDWARDS, Phil (D) 480 34
H: 5 8 W: 11 03 b.Bootle 8-11-85
2005–06 Wigan Ath 0 0
2006–07 Accrington S 33 1
2007–08 Accrington S 31 1
2008–09 Accrington S 46 0
2009–10 Accrington S 46 8
2010–11 Accrington S 44 13
2011–12 Stevenage 22 0 **22 0**
2011–12 *Rochdale* 3 0
2012–13 Rochdale 44 0 **47 0**
2013–14 Burton Alb 41 2
2014–15 Burton Alb 45 6
2015–16 Burton Alb 46 0
2016–17 Burton Alb 0 0 **132 8**
2016–17 *Oxford U* 38 3 **38 3**
2017–18 Bury 37 0
2018–19 Bury 0 0 **37 0**
2019–20 Accrington S 4 0 **204 23**

EVTIMOV, Dimitar (G) 60 0
H: 6 3 W: 13 00 b.Plevan 7-9-93
Internationals: Bulgaria U19, U21, Full caps.
2012–13 Nottingham F 0 0
2013–14 Nottingham F 1 0
2014–15 Nottingham F 0 0
2014–15 *Mansfield T* 10 0 **10 0**
2015–16 Nottingham F 1 0
2016–17 Nottingham F 0 0
2016–17 *Olhanense* 10 0 **10 0**
2017–18 Port Vale 1 0 **1 0**
2017–18 Nottingham F 0 0
2018–19 Nottingham F 0 0 **2 0**
2018–19 Burton Alb 7 0 **7 0**
2018–19 Accrington S 11 0
2019–20 Accrington S 19 0 **30 0**

FINLEY, Sam (M) 68 3
H: 5 7 W: 10 10 b.Liverpool 4-8-92
From Southport, Warrington T, The New Saints, AFC Fylde.
2018–19 Accrington S 37 1
2019–20 Accrington S 31 2 **68 3**

FRANCIS-ANGOL, Zaine (D) 71 3
b.Walthamstow 30-6-93
Internationals: Antiqua and Barbuda Full caps.
2012–13 Motherwell 22 0
2013–14 Motherwell 33 3
2014–15 Motherwell 11 0 **66 3**
From Kidderminster H, AFC Fylde.
2019–20 Accrington S 5 0 **5 0**

GILBOY, Lewis (M) 0 0
2018–19 Accrington S 0 0
2019–20 Accrington S 0 0

GRANT, Bobby (M) 336 71
H: 5 11 W: 12 00 b.Liverpool 1-7-90
2006–07 Accrington S 1 0
2007–08 Accrington S 7 0
2008–09 Accrington S 15 1
2009–10 Accrington S 42 14
2010–11 Scunthorpe U 27 0
2010–11 *Rochdale* 6 2
2011–12 Scunthorpe U 29 7
2011–12 *Accrington S* 8 3
2012–13 Scunthorpe U 3 0 **59 7**
2012–13 Rochdale 36 15 **42 17**
2013–14 Blackpool 6 0
2013–14 *Fleetwood T* 1 0
2014–15 Blackpool 0 0 **6 0**
2014–15 *Shrewsbury T* 33 6 **33 6**
2015–16 Fleetwood T 38 10
2016–17 Fleetwood T 46 9
2017–18 Fleetwood T 29 3
2018–19 Fleetwood T 4 0 **118 22**
On loan from Wrexham.
2019–20 Accrington S 5 1 **78 19**

HUGHES, Mark (D) 488 28
H: 6 1 W: 13 03 b.Liverpool 9-12-86
2004–05 Everton 0 0
2005–06 Everton 0 0
2005–06 *Stockport Co* 3 1 **3 1**
2006–07 Everton 1 0 **1 0**
2006–07 Northampton T 17 2
2007–08 Northampton T 35 1
2008–09 Northampton T 41 1 **93 4**
2009–10 Walsall 26 1 **26 1**
2010–11 N Queensland F 30 4 **30 4**
2011–12 Bury 25 0
2012–13 Bury 27 0 **52 0**
2012–13 *Accrington S* 5 0
2013–14 Morecambe 44 5
2014–15 Morecambe 40 3 **84 8**
2015–16 Stevenage 20 1 **20 1**
2015–16 Accrington S 15 1
2016–17 Accrington S 36 2
2017–18 Accrington S 46 4
2018–19 Accrington S 46 1
2019–20 Accrington S 31 1 **179 9**

JOHNSON, Callum (M) 105 1
b. 23-10-97
From Middlesbrough.
2017–18 Accrington S 31 1
2018–19 Accrington S 41 0
2019–20 Accrington S 33 0 **105 1**

MAGUIRE, Joe (D) 43 1
H: 5 10 W: 11 00 b.Manchester 18-1-96
2015–16 Liverpool 0 0
2015–16 *Leyton Orient* 0 0
2016–17 Liverpool 0 0
2016–17 Fleetwood T 3 0
2017–18 Fleetwood T 2 0
2018–19 Fleetwood T 0 0 **5 0**
2018–19 *Crawley T* 27 1 **27 1**
2019–20 Accrington S 11 0 **11 0**

MARTIN, Dan (M) 0 0
2019–20 Accrington S 0 0

McCONVILLE, Sean (M) 269 56
H: 5 8 W: 11 07 b.Liverpool 6-3-89
2008–09 Accrington S 5 0
2009–10 Accrington S 28 1
2010–11 Accrington S 43 13
2011–12 Rochdale 4 0 **4 0**
From Barrow, Stalybridge Celtic, Chester.
2015–16 Accrington S 42 5
2016–17 Accrington S 41 5
2017–18 Accrington S 43 12
2018–19 Accrington S 45 15
2019–20 Accrington S 18 5 **265 56**

MOHAMMED, Zehn (D) 0 0
b. 28-2-00
2017–18 Accrington S 0 0
2018–19 Accrington S 0 0
2019–20 Accrington S 0 0

OGLE, Reagan (D) 4 0
H: 5 8 W: 10 06 b. 29-3-99
2016–17 Accrington S 1 0
2017–18 Accrington S 3 0
2018–19 Accrington S 0 0
2019–20 Accrington S 0 0 **4 0**

PERRITT, Harry (M) 0 0
2018–19 Accrington S 0 0
2019–20 Accrington S 0 0

PRITCHARD, Joe (M) 34 2
H: 5 8 W: 10 06 b.Watford 10-9-96
From Tottenham H.
2018–19 Bolton W 4 0 **4 0**
2019–20 Accrington S 30 2 **30 2**

RODGERS, Harvey (M) 36 1
H: 5 10 W: 12 06 b.York 20-10-96
2016–17 Hull C 0 0
2016–17 *Accrington S* 19 1
2017–18 Fleetwood T 0 0
2017–18 Accrington S 5 0
2018–19 Accrington S 6 0
2019–20 Accrington S 6 0 **36 1**

SAVIN, Toby (G) 0 0
2017–18 Accrington S 0 0
2018–19 Accrington S 0 0
2019–20 Accrington S 0 0

SCOTT, Andrew (M) 0 0
b. 19-6-00
Internationals: Northern Ireland U17.
From Maiden C.
2018–19 Accrington S 0 0
2019–20 Accrington S 0 0

SHERIFF, Lamine (M) 8 0
b. 27-1-99
2019–20 Accrington S 8 0 **8 0**

SIMMONDS, Okera (F) 0 0
H: 6 2 W: 12 04 b.Manchester 25-12-99
Internationals: England U16.
2018–19 Accrington S 0 0
2019–20 Accrington S 0 0

SOUSA, Erico (M) **10 0**
b. 12-3-95
2013–14 Barnsley 0 0
From Hyde U, Celje, Tadcaster Alb.
2017–18 Accrington S 6 0
2018–19 Accrington S 4 0
2019–20 Accrington S 0 0 **10 0**

SYKES, Ross (D) **53 4**
H: 6 5 W: 11 07 b.Burnley 26-3-99
2016–17 Accrington S 0 0
2017–18 Accrington S 2 0
2018–19 Accrington S 20 3
2019–20 Accrington S 31 1 **53 4**

WATSON, Niall (M) **2 0**
b. 15-6-00
2017–18 Accrington S 2 0
2018–19 Accrington S 0 0
2019–20 Accrington S 0 0 **2 0**

ZANZALA, Offrande (F) **59 11**
b. 13-12-97
2015–16 Derby Co 0 0
2015–16 *Stevenage* 2 0 **2 0**
2016–17 Derby Co 0 0
2017–18 Derby Co 0 0
2017–18 *Accrington S* 6 1
2018–19 Accrington S 27 4
2019–20 Accrington S 24 6 **57 11**

Scholars
Bowe, Adam; Buckley, Jack Joseph; Doherty, Jack Edward; Ellis, Gabriel David; Evans, Jack Robert Matthew; Graham, Ryan Richard; Kasongo, Guelor Bukomo; Madzura, Rigobert; McKinlay, Jak Thomas; Muldoon, Ryan Paul; Nolan, Mitchell Arron; Ridge, Charles Disney; Spinelli, Lorenzo Kevin; Stowe, Luke Dean; Sung, Warren James.

AFC WIMBLEDON (2)

APPIAH, Kwesi (F) **123 24**
H: 5 11 W: 12 08 b.Thamesmead 12-8-90
Internationals: Ghana Full caps.
2008–09 Peterborough U 0 0
From Brackley T, Thurrock, Margate.
2011–12 Crystal Palace 4 0
2012–13 Crystal Palace 2 0
2012–13 *Aldershot T* 2 0 **2 0**
2012–13 *Yeovil T* 5 0 **5 0**
2013–14 Crystal Palace 0 0
2013–14 *Notts Co* 7 0 **7 0**
2013–14 *AFC Wimbledon* 7 3
2014–15 Crystal Palace 0 0
2014–15 *Cambridge U* 19 6 **19 6**
2014–15 *Reading* 6 1 **6 1**
2015–16 Crystal Palace 0 0
2016–17 Crystal Palace 0 0
2017–18 Crystal Palace 0 0 **6 0**
2017–18 *Viking FK* 12 2
2017–18 AFC Wimbledon 14 3
2018–19 AFC Wimbledon 26 4
2019–20 AFC Wimbledon 19 4 **66 14**

ASHLEY, Ossama (M) **0 0**
2017–18 AFC Wimbledon 0 0
2018–19 AFC Wimbledon 0 0
2019–20 AFC Wimbledon 0 0

ASSAL, Ayoub (M) **0 0**
b. 21-1-02
2019–20 AFC Wimbledon 0 0

AWOYEJO, Jamil (D) **0 0**
2019–20 AFC Wimbledon 0 0

BILER, Huseyin (D) **0 0**
2019–20 AFC Wimbledon 0 0

COLLINS, Reuben (D) **0 0**
b. 16-12-00
2019–20 AFC Wimbledon 0 0

CONNOLLY, Dylan (F) **42 1**
H: 5 9 W: 10 12 b.Dublin 2-5-95
Internationals: Republic of Ireland U17, U21.
2014–15 Ipswich T 0 0
2015–16 Ipswich T 0 0
From Bray W, Dundalk.
2018–19 AFC Wimbledon 12 0
2019–20 AFC Wimbledon 3 0 **15 0**
2019–20 *Bradford C* 27 1 **27 1**

COX, Matthew (G) **0 0**
Internationals: England U17.
2019–20 AFC Wimbledon 0 0

FISHER, David (F) **0 0**
2019–20 AFC Wimbledon 0 0

GUINNESS-WALKER, Nesta (D) **23 1**
b.Hounslow 30-11-99
From Metropolitan Police.
2019–20 AFC Wimbledon 23 1 **23 1**

HARTIGAN, Anthony (M) **69 0**
H: 5 10 W: 10 10 b.Kingston upon Thames 27-1-00
2017–18 AFC Wimbledon 11 0
2018–19 AFC Wimbledon 31 0
2019–20 AFC Wimbledon 27 0 **69 0**

KALAMBAYI, Paul (D) **33 0**
b. 28-7-99
2015–16 AFC Wimbledon 0 0
2016–17 AFC Wimbledon 0 0
2017–18 AFC Wimbledon 0 0
2018–19 AFC Wimbledon 17 0
2019–20 AFC Wimbledon 16 0 **33 0**

MADELIN, Jack (D) **1 0**
b. 19-4-02
Internationals: Wales U16, U17.
2019–20 AFC Wimbledon 1 0 **1 0**

McDONALD, Rod (D) **105 3**
H: 6 3 W: 12 13 b.Crewe 11-4-92
2010–11 Oldham Ath 0 0
From Colwyn Bay, Nantwich T, Hereford U, AFC Telford U.
2015–16 Northampton T 23 3
2016–17 Northampton T 7 0 **30 3**
2016–17 Coventry C 0 0
2017–18 Coventry C 37 0 **37 0**
2018–19 AFC Wimbledon 23 0
2019–20 AFC Wimbledon 15 0 **38 0**

McDONNELL, Joe (G) **23 0**
H: 5 10 W: 9 13 b.Basingstoke 19-5-94
2014–15 AFC Wimbledon 4 0
2015–16 AFC Wimbledon 0 0
2016–17 AFC Wimbledon 3 0
2017–18 AFC Wimbledon 1 0
2018–19 AFC Wimbledon 14 0
2019–20 AFC Wimbledon 1 0 **23 0**

McLOUGHLIN, Shane (D) **34 2**
b.Castleisland 1-3-97
Internationals: Republic of Ireland U16, U18.
2014–15 Ipswich T 0 0
2015–16 Ipswich T 0 0
2016–17 Ipswich T 0 0
2017–18 Ipswich T 1 0
2018–19 Ipswich T 0 0 **1 0**
2018–19 AFC Wimbledon 10 1
2019–20 AFC Wimbledon 23 1 **33 2**

McNAB, Finlay (M) **0 0**
b. 27-12-00
2019–20 AFC Wimbledon 0 0

NIGHTINGALE, Will (M) **86 1**
H: 6 1 W: 13 03 b.Wandsworth 2-7-95
2013–14 AFC Wimbledon 0 0
2014–15 AFC Wimbledon 4 0
2015–16 AFC Wimbledon 4 0
2016–17 AFC Wimbledon 12 0
2017–18 AFC Wimbledon 18 1
2018–19 AFC Wimbledon 39 0
2019–20 AFC Wimbledon 9 0 **86 1**

O'NEILL, Luke (D) **181 7**
H: 6 0 W: 11 04 b.Slough 20-8-91
Internationals: England U17.
2009–10 Leicester C 1 0 **1 0**
2009–10 *Tranmere R* 4 0 **4 0**
From Kettering T, Mansfield T
2012–13 Burnley 1 0
2013–14 Burnley 0 0
2013–14 *York C* 15 1 **15 1**
2013–14 *Southend U* 1 0
2014–15 Burnley 0 0 **1 0**
2014–15 *Scunthorpe U* 13 0 **13 0**
2014–15 *Leyton Orient* 8 0 **8 0**
2015–16 Southend U 14 0
2016–17 Southend U 17 1 **32 1**
2017–18 Gillingham 38 1
2018–19 Gillingham 38 3 **76 4**
2019–20 AFC Wimbledon 31 1 **31 1**

OSEW, Paul (D) **18 1**
b. 25-11-00
2019–20 AFC Wimbledon 18 1 **18 1**

PIGOTT, Joe (F) **189 44**
H: 6 0 W: 9 05 b.London 24-11-93
2012–13 Charlton Ath 0 0
2013–14 Charlton Ath 11 0
2013–14 *Gillingham* 7 1 **7 1**
2014–15 Charlton Ath 1 0
2014–15 *Newport Co* 10 3 **10 3**
2014–15 *Southend U* 20 6
2015–16 Charlton Ath 0 0 **12 0**
2015–16 *Southend U* 23 3 **43 9**
2015–16 *Luton T* 15 4 **15 4**
2016–17 Cambridge U 10 0 **10 0**
From Maidstone U.
2017–18 AFC Wimbledon 18 5
2018–19 AFC Wimbledon 40 15
2019–20 AFC Wimbledon 34 7 **92 27**

PINNOCK, Mitch (M) **61 6**
H: 5 10 b. 12-12-94
Internationals: England C.
2012–13 Southend U 2 0
2013–14 Southend U 0 0 **2 0**
From Bromley, Maidstone U, Dover Ath, Kingstonian, Dover Ath.
2018–19 AFC Wimbledon 34 3
2019–20 AFC Wimbledon 25 3 **59 6**

PROCTER, Archie (D) **0 0**
b. 13-11-01
2019–20 AFC Wimbledon 0 0

REILLY, Callum (M) **182 11**
H: 6 1 W: 12 03 b.Warrington 3-10-93
Internationals: Republic of Ireland U21.
2012–13 Birmingham C 18 1
2013–14 Birmingham C 25 0
2014–15 Birmingham C 17 1 **60 2**
2014–15 *Burton Alb* 2 0
2015–16 Burton Alb 14 0
2016–17 Burton Alb 0 0 **16 0**
2016–17 *Coventry C* 18 0 **18 0**
2017–18 Bury 18 0 **18 0**
2017–18 *Gillingham* 15 0
2018–19 Gillingham 25 5 **40 5**
2019–20 AFC Wimbledon 30 4 **30 4**

ROBINSON, Zach (F) **0 0**
2019–20 AFC Wimbledon 0 0

ROSCROW, Adam (F) **10 0**
b. 17-2-95
Internationals: Wales C.
From Cardiff Metropolitan University.
2019–20 AFC Wimbledon 10 0 **10 0**

RUDONI, Jack (M) **11 0**
2018–19 AFC Wimbledon 0 0
2019–20 AFC Wimbledon 11 0 **11 0**

STABANA, Kyron (D) **0 0**
b.Leicester 27-8-98
Internationals: England U17.
2016–17 Derby Co 0 0
2017–18 Derby Co 0 0
2018–19 AFC Wimbledon 0 0
2019–20 AFC Wimbledon 0 0

THOMAS, Terell (D) **57 1**
H: 6 0 b. 13-10-97
2014–15 Charlton Ath 0 0
2015–16 Charlton Ath 0 0
2016–17 Charlton Ath 0 0
2017–18 Wigan Ath 3 0 **3 0**
2018–19 AFC Wimbledon 23 0
2019–20 AFC Wimbledon 31 1 **54 1**

TZANEV, Nikola (G) **2 0**
Internationals: New Zealand U20, Full caps.
From Brentford.
2016–17 AFC Wimbledon 0 0
2017–18 AFC Wimbledon 0 0
2018–19 AFC Wimbledon 0 0
2019–20 AFC Wimbledon 2 0 **2 0**

WAGSTAFF, Scott (M) **319 29**
H: 5 10 W: 10 03 b.Maidstone 31-3-90
2007–08 Charlton Ath 2 0
2008–09 Charlton Ath 2 0
2008–09 *Bournemouth* 5 0 **5 0**
2009–10 Charlton Ath 30 4
2010–11 Charlton Ath 40 8
2011–12 Charlton Ath 34 4
2012–13 Charlton Ath 9 1 **117 17**
2012–13 *Leyton Orient* 7 0 **7 0**
2013–14 Bristol C 37 5
2014–15 Bristol C 26 2
2015–16 Bristol C 9 1 **72 8**
2016–17 Gillingham 26 1
2017–18 Gillingham 31 0 **57 1**
2018–19 AFC Wimbledon 35 2
2019–20 AFC Wimbledon 26 1 **61 3**

WOOD, Tommy (F) **3 0**
b. 26-11-98
From Burnley.
2018–19 AFC Wimbledon 1 0
2019–20 AFC Wimbledon 2 0 **3 0**

WORDSWORTH, Anthony (M) **345 63**
H: 6 1 W: 12 00 b.Camden 3-1-89

2007–08	Colchester U	3	0		
2008–09	Colchester U	30	3		
2009–10	Colchester U	41	11		
2010–11	Colchester U	35	5		
2011–12	Colchester U	44	13		
2012–13	Colchester U	24	3	**177**	**35**
2012–13	Ipswich T	7	1		
2013–14	Ipswich T	10	1		
2014–15	Ipswich T	1	0	**18**	**2**
2014–15	*Rotherham U*	6	1	**6**	**1**
2014–15	*Crawley T*	18	4	**18**	**4**
2015–16	Southend U	21	4		
2016–17	Southend U	34	11		
2017–18	Southend U	24	3	**79**	**18**
2018–19	AFC Wimbledon	37	2		
2019–20	AFC Wimbledon	10	1	**47**	**3**

Scholars
Adje, Hersey Dylan Francis; Awoyejo, Jamil Tyrique Daniel; Chiabi, Muumbe Troy Makowani; Currie, Jack Alexander; Frimpong, Kwaku Amponsah; Jenkins, Luke; Mbele, Richie Bless; Ogundere, Isaac Ifeoluwa Foloronso; Olaniyan, Isaac Humayun Kola; Osu, Olukayode Jacomo Maria; Sarmient-Ramirez, Julian Andres; White, Albert James; Biler, Huseyin.

ARSENAL (3)

AUBAMEYANG, Pierre-Emerick (F) **369 199**
H: 6 2 W: 11 09 b.Bitam 18-6-89
Internationals: France U21. Gabon U23, Full caps.

2008–09	AC Milan	0	0		
2008–09	*Dijon*	34	8	**34**	**8**
2009–10	AC Milan	0	0		
2009–10	*Lille*	14	2	**14**	**2**
2010–11	AC Milan	0	0		
2010–11	*Monaco*	19	2	**19**	**2**
2010–11	*Saint-Etienne*	17	10		
2011–12	Saint-Etienne	19	6		
2012–13	Saint-Etienne	37	19	**73**	**35**
2013–14	Borussia Dortmund	32	13		
2014–15	Borussia Dortmund	33	16		
2015–16	Borussia Dortmund	31	25		
2016–17	Borussia Dortmund	32	31		
2017–18	Borussia Dortmund	16	13	**144**	**98**
2017–18	Arsenal	13	10		
2018–19	Arsenal	36	22		
2019–20	Arsenal	36	22	**85**	**54**

AZEEZ, Miguel (M) **0 0**
b. 20-9-02
Internationals: England U16, U17, U18.

2019–20	Arsenal	0	0

BALLARD, Daniel (D) **1 0**
b. 22-9-99
Internationals: Northern Ireland U18, U21.

2019–20	Arsenal	0	0		
2019–20	*Swindon T*	1	0	**1**	**0**

BALOGUN, Folarin (M) **0 0**
b. 3-7-01
Internationals: England U17, U18. USA U18.

2019–20	Arsenal	0	0

BELLERIN, Hector (D) **166 7**
H: 5 10 W: 11 09 b.Barcelona 19-3-95
Internationals: Spain U16, U17, U19, U21, Full caps.

2012–13	Arsenal	0	0		
2013–14	Arsenal	0	0		
2013–14	*Watford*	8	0	**8**	**0**
2014–15	Arsenal	20	2		
2015–16	Arsenal	36	1		
2016–17	Arsenal	33	1		
2017–18	Arsenal	35	2		
2018–19	Arsenal	19	0		
2019–20	Arsenal	15	1	**158**	**7**

BOLA, Tolaji (D) **0 0**
b. 4-1-99
Internationals: England U16, U17, U18.

2019–20	Arsenal	0	0

BURTON, Robbie (M) **0 0**
b.Gravesend 26-12-99
Internationals: Wales U16, U17, U19, U21.

2019–20	Arsenal	0	0

Transferred to Dinamo Zagreb, February 2020.

CEBALLOS, Dani (M) **157 12**
b.Seville 7-8-96
Internationals: Spain U19, U21, Full caps.

2013–14	Real Betis	1	0		
2014–15	Real Betis	33	5		
2015–16	Real Betis	34	0		
2016–17	Real Betis	30	2	**98**	**7**
2017–18	Real Madrid	12	2		
2018–19	Real Madrid	23	3	**35**	**5**

On loan from Real Madrid.

2019–20	Arsenal	24	0	**24**	**0**

CEDRIC SOARES, Ricardo (D) **220 4**
H: 5 8 W: 10 08 b.Gelsenkirchen, Germany 31-8-91
Internationals: Portugal U16, U17, U18, U19, U20, U21, Full caps.

2010–11	Sporting Lisbon	2	0		
2011–12	Sporting Lisbon	0	0		
2011–12	*Academica*	24	0	**24**	**0**
2012–13	Sporting Lisbon	13	1		
2013–14	Sporting Lisbon	28	1		
2014–15	Sporting Lisbon	24	0	**67**	**2**
2015–16	Southampton	24	0		
2016–17	Southampton	30	0		
2017–18	Southampton	32	0		
2018–19	Southampton	18	1		
2018–19	*Inter Milan*	4	0	**4**	**0**
2019–20	Southampton	16	0	**120**	**1**
2019–20	Arsenal	5	1	**5**	**1**

CHAMBERS, Calum (M) **139 6**
H: 6 0 W: 10 05 b.Petersfield 20-1-95
Internationals: England U17, U19, U21, Full caps.

2011–12	Southampton	0	0		
2012–13	Southampton	0	0		
2013–14	Southampton	22	0	**22**	**0**
2014–15	Arsenal	23	1		
2015–16	Arsenal	12	0		
2016–17	Arsenal	1	1		
2016–17	*Middlesbrough*	24	1	**24**	**1**
2017–18	Arsenal	12	0		
2018–19	Arsenal	0	0		
2018–19	*Fulham*	31	2	**31**	**2**
2019–20	Arsenal	14	1	**62**	**3**

CLARKE, Harrison (D) **0 0**
b.Ipswich 2-3-01
Internationals: England U17.

2019–20	Arsenal	0	0

COTTERELL, Ben (M) **0 0**
b. 31-1-01
Internationals: England U18.

2019–20	Arsenal	0	0

COYLE, Trae (F) **0 0**
b. 11-1-01
Internationals: England U16, U17.

2019–20	Arsenal	0	0

ELNENY, Mohamed (M) **199 8**
H: 5 11 W: 11 00 b.Al-Mahalla Al-Kubra 11-7-92
Internationals: Egypt U20, U23, Full caps.

2010–11	El Mokawloon	21	2		
2011–12	El Mokawloon	14	0	**35**	**2**
2012–13	Basel	15	0		
2013–14	Basel	32	1		
2014–15	Basel	28	2	**75**	**3**
2015–16	Basle	16	2	**16**	**2**
2015–16	Arsenal	11	0		
2016–17	Arsenal	14	0		
2017–18	Arsenal	13	0		
2018–19	Arsenal	8	0		
2019–20	Arsenal	0	0	**46**	**0**
2019–20	*Besiktas*	27	1	**27**	**1**

GREENWOOD, Sam (F) **0 0**
b.Sunderland 26-1-02
Internationals: England U16, U17, U18.

2019–20	Arsenal	0	0

GUENDOUZI, Matteo (M) **83 0**
H: 5 11 W: 10 10 b.Poissy 14-4-99
Internationals: France U18, U19, U20, U21.

2015–16	Lorient	0	0		
2016–17	Lorient	8	0		
2017–18	Lorient	18	0	**26**	**0**
2018–19	Arsenal	33	0		
2019–20	Arsenal	24	0	**57**	**0**

HEIN, Karl Jakob (G) **0 0**
b. 13-4-02
Internationals: Estonia U16, U17, U19, U21.
From Nomme U.

2019–20	Arsenal	0	0

HILLSON, James Andrew (G) **0 0**
b. 14-1-01
From Reading.

2019–20	Arsenal	0	0

HOLDING, Rob (D) **66 1**
b.Tameside 20-9-95
Internationals: England U21.

2014–15	Bolton W	0	0		
2014–15	*Bury*	1	0	**1**	**0**
2015–16	Bolton W	26	1	**26**	**1**
2016–17	Arsenal	9	0		
2017–18	Arsenal	12	0		
2018–19	Arsenal	10	0		
2019–20	Arsenal	8	0	**39**	**0**

ILIEV, Dejan (G) **22 0**
H: 6 5 b.Strumica 25-2-95
Internationals: Macedonia U17, U19, U21.

2012–13	Arsenal	0	0		
2013–14	Arsenal	0	0		
2014–15	Arsenal	0	0		
2015–16	Arsenal	0	0		
2016–17	Arsenal	0	0		
2017–18	Arsenal	0	0		
2018–19	Arsenal	0	0		
2019–20	Arsenal	0	0		
2019–20	*Clinic Sered*	18	0	**18**	**0**
2019–20	*Jagiellonia*	4	0	**4**	**0**

JOHN-JULES, Tyreece (F) **7 1**
H: 6 0 b. 14-2-01
Internationals: England U16, U17, U18, U19.

2018–19	Arsenal	0	0		
2019–20	Arsenal	0	0		
2019–20	*Lincoln C*	7	1	**7**	**1**

KOLASINAC, Sead (D) **171 6**
H: 6 0 W: 12 13 b.Karlsruhe 20-6-93
Internationals: Germany U18, U19, U20. Bosnia and Herzegovina Full caps.

2012–13	Schalke 04	16	0		
2013–14	Schalke 04	24	0		
2014–15	Schalke 04	6	0		
2015–16	Schalke 04	23	1		
2016–17	Schalke 04	25	3	**94**	**4**
2017–18	Arsenal	27	2		
2018–19	Arsenal	24	0		
2019–20	Arsenal	26	0	**77**	**2**

LACAZETTE, Alexandre (F) **300 137**
H: 5 9 W: 10 12 b.Lyon 28-5-91
Internationals: France U16, U17, U18, U19, U20, U21, Full caps.

2009–10	Lyon	1	0		
2010–11	Lyon	9	1		
2011–12	Lyon	29	5		
2012–13	Lyon	31	3		
2013–14	Lyon	36	15		
2014–15	Lyon	33	27		
2015–16	Lyon	34	21		
2016–17	Lyon	30	28	**203**	**100**
2017–18	Arsenal	32	14		
2018–19	Arsenal	35	13		
2019–20	Arsenal	30	10	**97**	**37**

LENO, Bernd (G) **295 0**
H: 6 3 W: 12 06 b.Bietigheim-Bissingen 4-3-92
Internationals: Germany, U17, U18, U19, U21, Full caps.
From Stuttgart.

2011–12	Bayer Leverkusen	33	0		
2012–13	Bayer Leverkusen	32	0		
2013–14	Bayer Leverkusen	34	0		
2014–15	Bayer Leverkusen	34	0		
2015–16	Bayer Leverkusen	33	0		
2016–17	Bayer Leverkusen	34	0		
2017–18	Bayer Leverkusen	33	0	**233**	**0**
2018–19	Arsenal	32	0		
2019–20	Arsenal	30	0	**62**	**0**

LOPEZ SALGUERO, Joel (D) **0 0**
b.Barcelona 31-3-02
Internationals: Spain U17.
From Barcelona.

2019–20	Arsenal	0	0

LUIZ, David (D) **357 21**
H: 6 2 W: 13 03 b.Sao Paulo 22-4-87
Internationals: Brazil U20, Full caps.

2005	Vitoria	0	0		
2006	Vitoria	26	1	**26**	**1**
2006–07	Benfica	10	0		
2007–08	Benfica	8	0		
2008–09	Benfica	19	2		
2009–10	Benfica	29	2		
2010–11	Benfica	16	0	**82**	**4**
2010–11	Chelsea	12	2		

2011–12 Chelsea 20 2
2012–13 Chelsea 30 2
2013–14 Chelsea 19 0
2014–15 Paris Saint-Germain 28 2
2015–16 Paris Saint-Germain 25 1
2016–17 Paris Saint-Germain 3 0 **56 3**
2016–17 Chelsea 33 1
2017–18 Chelsea 10 1
2018–19 Chelsea 36 3
2019–20 Chelsea 0 0 **160 11**
2019–20 Arsenal 33 2 **33 2**

MACEY, Matt (G) 49 0
H: 6 6 W: 14 05 b.Bristol 9-9-94
2011–12 Bristol R 0 0
2012–13 Bristol R 0 0
2013–14 Arsenal 0 0
2014–15 Arsenal 0 0
2014–15 *Accrington S* 4 0 **4 0**
2015–16 Arsenal 0 0
2016–17 Arsenal 0 0
2016–17 *Luton T* 11 0 **11 0**
2017–18 Arsenal 0 0
2018–19 Arsenal 0 0
2018–19 *Plymouth Arg* 34 0 **34 0**
2019–20 Arsenal 0 0

MAITLAND-NILES, Ainsley (F) 83 2
H: 5 10 W: 11 05 b.Goodmayes 29-8-97
Internationals: England U17, U18, U19, U20, U21.
2014–15 Arsenal 1 0
2015–16 Arsenal 0 0
2015–16 *Ipswich T* 30 1 **30 1**
2016–17 Arsenal 1 0
2017–18 Arsenal 15 0
2018–19 Arsenal 16 1
2019–20 Arsenal 20 0 **53 1**

MARTINELLI, Gabriel (F) 14 3
b.Guarulhos 18-6-01
Internationals: Brazil U23.
From Ituano.
2019–20 Arsenal 14 3 **14 3**

MARTINEZ, Damian (G) 66 0
H: 6 3 W: 13 05 b.Mar del Plata 2-9-92
Internationals: Argentina U17, U20.
2010–11 Arsenal 0 0
2011–12 Arsenal 0 0
2011–12 *Oxford U* 1 0 **1 0**
2012–13 Arsenal 0 0
2013–14 Arsenal 0 0
2013–14 *Sheffield W* 11 0 **11 0**
2014–15 Arsenal 4 0
2014–15 *Rotherham U* 8 0 **8 0**
2015–16 Arsenal 0 0
2015–16 *Wolverhampton W* 13 0 **13 0**
2016–17 Arsenal 2 0
2017–18 Arsenal 0 0
2018–19 Arsenal 0 0
2018–19 *Reading* 18 0
2019–20 Arsenal 9 0 **15 0**
2019–20 *Reading* 0 0 **18 0**

MAVROPANOS, Konstantinos (D) 34 3
H: 6 4 W: 12 08 b.Athens 11-12-97
Internationals: Greece U21.
2016–17 PAS Giannina 2 0
2017–18 PAS Giannina 14 3 **16 3**
2017–18 Arsenal 3 0
2018–19 Arsenal 4 0
2019–20 Arsenal 0 0 **7 0**
2019–20 *Nurnberg* 11 0 **11 0**
2019–20 *Stuttgart* 0 0

McENEFF, Jordan John (F) 0 0
b.Londonderry 8-1-01
Internationals: Republic of Ireland U17.
2019–20 Arsenal 0 0

MEDLEY, Zechariah (D) 0 0
b. 7-7-00
Internationals: England U16.
2018–19 Arsenal 0 0
2019–20 Arsenal 0 0

MKHITARYAN, Henrikh (M) 369 125
H: 5 10 W: 12 00 b.Yerevan 21-1-89
Internationals: Armenia U17, U19, U21, Full caps.
2006 Pyunik 12 1
2007 Pyunik 24 12
2008 Pyunik 24 6
2009 Pyunik 10 11 **70 30**
2009–10 Metalurg Donetsk 29 9
2010–11 Metalurg Donetsk 8 3 **37 12**
2010–11 Shakhtar Donetsk 17 3
2011–12 Shakhtar Donetsk 26 10
2012–13 Shakhtar Donetsk 29 25 **72 38**
2013–14 Borussia Dortmund 31 9
2014–15 Borussia Dortmund 28 3
2015–16 Borussia Dortmund 31 11 **90 23**
2016–17 Manchester U 24 4
2017–18 Manchester U 15 1 **39 5**
2017–18 Arsenal 11 2
2018–19 Arsenal 25 6
2019–20 Arsenal 3 0 **39 8**
2019–20 *Roma* 22 9 **22 9**

MONREAL, Nacho (D) 360 10
H: 5 10 W: 11 04 b.Pamplona 26-2-86
Internationals: Spain U19, U21, Full caps.
2006–07 Osasuna 11 0
2007–08 Osasuna 27 0
2008–09 Osasuna 28 0
2009–10 Osasuna 31 1
2010–11 Osasuna 31 1 **128 2**
2011–12 Malaga 31 0
2012–13 Malaga 14 1 **45 1**
2012–13 Arsenal 10 1
2013–14 Arsenal 23 0
2014–15 Arsenal 28 0
2015–16 Arsenal 37 0
2016–17 Arsenal 36 0
2017–18 Arsenal 28 5
2018–19 Arsenal 22 1
2019–20 Arsenal 3 0 **187 7**
Transferred to Real Sociedad, August 2019.

MUSTAFI, Shkodran (D) 213 14
H: 6 0 W: 11 07 b.Bad Hersfeld 17-4-92
Internationals: Germany U16, U17, U18, U19, U20, U21, Full caps.
2009–10 Everton 0 0
2010–11 Everton 0 0
2011–12 Everton 0 0
2011–12 Sampdoria 1 0
2012–13 Sampdoria 17 0
2013–14 Sampdoria 33 1 **51 1**
2014–15 Valencia 33 4
2015–16 Valencia 30 2 **63 6**
2016–17 Arsenal 26 2
2017–18 Arsenal 27 3
2018–19 Arsenal 31 2
2019–20 Arsenal 15 0 **99 7**

NELSON, Reiss (F) 43 8
H: 5 9 W: 11 00 b.London 10-12-99
Internationals: England U16, U17, U18, U19, U20, U21.
From Lewisham Bor.
2017–18 Arsenal 3 0
2018–19 Arsenal 0 0
2018–19 *Hoffenheim* 23 7 **23 7**
2019–20 Arsenal 17 1 **20 1**

NKETIAH, Eddie (F) 38 6
b.Lewisham 30-5-99
Internationals: England U18, U19, U20, U21.
2017–18 Arsenal 3 0
2018–19 Arsenal 5 1
2019–20 Arsenal 13 2 **21 3**
2019–20 *Leeds U* 17 3 **17 3**

OKONKWO, Arthur (G) 0 0
b. 9-9-01
Internationals: England U16, U17, U18.
2019–20 Arsenal 0 0

OLAYINKA, James (M) 1 0
b. 5-10-00
2019–20 Arsenal 0 0
2019–20 *Northampton T* 1 0 **1 0**

OLOWU, Joseph Olugbenga (D) 0 0
b. 27-11-99
2018–19 Arsenal 0 0
2019–20 Arsenal 0 0

OSEI-TUTU, Jordi (D) 21 5
b.Slough 2-10-98
2017–18 Arsenal 0 0
2018–19 Arsenal 0 0
2019–20 Arsenal 0 0
2019–20 *Bochum* 21 5 **21 5**

OZIL, Mesut (M) 389 65
H: 5 11 W: 11 06 b.Gelsenkirchen 15-10-88
Internationals: Germany U19, U21, Full caps.
2005–06 Schalke 04 0 0
2006–07 Schalke 04 19 0
2007–08 Schalke 04 11 0 **30 0**
2007–08 Werder Bremen 12 1
2008–09 Werder Bremen 27 3
2009–10 Werder Bremen 31 9
2010–11 Werder Bremen 0 0 **70 13**
2010–11 Real Madrid 36 6
2011–12 Real Madrid 35 4
2012–13 Real Madrid 32 9
2013–14 Real Madrid 2 0 **105 19**
2013–14 Arsenal 26 5
2014–15 Arsenal 22 4
2015–16 Arsenal 35 6
2016–17 Arsenal 33 8
2017–18 Arsenal 26 4
2018–19 Arsenal 24 5
2019–20 Arsenal 18 1 **184 33**

PABLO MARI, Villar (M) 183 11
b.Almussafes 31-8-93
2011–12 Real Mallorca 2 0
2012–13 Real Mallorca 0 0 **2 0**
2013–14 Gimnastic 29 2
2014–15 Gimnastic 37 3
2015–16 Gimnastic 25 1 **91 6**
2016–17 Manchester C 0 0
2016–17 *Girona* 8 0 **8 0**
2017–18 Manchester C 0 0
2017–18 NAC Breda 20 1 **20 1**
2018–19 Manchester C 0 0
2018–19 *Deportivo la Coruna* 38 2 **38 2**
2019 Flamengo 22 2 **22 2**
2019–20 Arsenal 2 0 **2 0**

PAPASTATHOPOULOS, Sokratis (D) 338 15
H: 6 1 W: 12 13 b.Kalamata 9-6-88
Internationals: Greece U17, U19, U21, Full caps.
2005–06 AEK Athens 0 0
2005–06 *Niki Volou* 11 0 **11 0**
2006–07 AEK Athens 14 0
2007–08 AEK Athens 24 1 **38 1**
2008–09 Genoa 21 2
2009–10 Genoa 30 0 **51 2**
2010–11 AC Milan 5 0
2010–11 AC Milan 0 0
2011–12 AC Milan 0 0
2012–13 AC Milan 0 0 **5 0**
2012–13 *Werder Bremen* 30 1
2012–13 Werder Bremen 29 1 **59 2**
2013–14 Borussia Dortmund 28 1
2014–15 Borussia Dortmund 21 1
2015–16 Borussia Dortmund 25 1
2016–17 Borussia Dortmund 26 2
2017–18 Borussia Dortmund 30 2 **130 7**
2018–19 Arsenal 25 1
2019–20 Arsenal 19 2 **44 3**

PEPE, Nicolas (M) 158 30
b.Mantes la Jolie 29-5-95
Internationals: Ivory Coast Full caps.
2014–15 Angers 7 0
2015–16 Angers 0 0
2015–16 *Orleans* 29 7 **29 7**
2016–17 Angers 33 3 **40 3**
2017–18 Lille 36 13
2018–19 Lille 22 2 **58 15**
2019–20 Arsenal 31 5 **31 5**

SAKA, Bukayo (M) 27 1
H: 5 10 b.London 5-9-01
Internationals: England U16, U17, U18, U19.
2018–19 Arsenal 1 0
2019–20 Arsenal 26 1 **27 1**

SALIBA, William Alain Andre Gabriel (D) 12 0
b.Bondy 24-3-01
Internationals: France U16, U17, U18, U19, U20.
2018–19 Saint-Etienne 0 0
2019–20 Arsenal 0 0
2019–20 *Saint-Etienne* 12 0 **12 0**

SHEAF, Ben (M) 42 1
H: 5 10 W: 10 01 b.Dartford 5-2-98
Internationals: England U16, U18.
2015–16 Arsenal 0 0
2016–17 Arsenal 0 0
2017–18 Arsenal 0 0
2017–18 *Stevenage* 10 0 **10 0**
2018–19 Arsenal 0 0
2019–20 Arsenal 0 0
2019–20 *Doncaster R* 32 1 **32 1**

SMITH, Matthew (D) 0 0
b. 5-10-00
2019–20 Arsenal 0 0

SMITH, Tom (G) 0 0
b. 30-1-02
Internationals: England U16.
2019–20 Arsenal 0 0

SMITH-ROWE, Emile (M) 24 2
H: 6 0 W: 11 07 b.London 28-6-00
Internationals: England U16, U17, U18, U19, U20.
2017–18 Arsenal 0 0
2018–19 Arsenal 0 0
2018–19 *RB Leipzig* 3 0 **3 0**

2019–20 Arsenal 2 0 **2 0**
2019–20 *Huddersfield T* 19 2 **19 2**

SWANSON, Zak (D) 0 0
b. 28-9-00
2019–20 Arsenal 0 0

TIERNEY, Kieran (D) 117 6
b.Douglas 5-6-97
Internationals: Scotland U18, U19, Full caps.
2014–15 Celtic 2 0
2015–16 Celtic 23 1
2016–17 Celtic 24 1
2017–18 Celtic 32 3
2018–19 Celtic 21 0
2019–20 Celtic 0 0 **102 5**
2019–20 Arsenal 15 1 **15 1**

TORMEY, Nathan Alexander (M) 0 0
b.Hatfield 25-5-00
2019–20 Arsenal 0 0

TORREIRA, Lucas (M) 168 11
H: 5 5 W: 9 06 b.Fray Bentos 11-2-96
Internationals: Uruguay Full caps.
2014–15 Pescara 5 0
2015–16 Sampdoria 0 0
2015–16 *Pescara* 29 4 **34 4**
2016–17 Sampdoria 35 0
2017–18 Sampdoria 36 4 **71 4**
2018–19 Arsenal 34 2
2019–20 Arsenal 29 1 **63 3**

WILLOCK, Chris (M) 14 2
H: 5 10 W: 10 08 b.London 31-1-98
Internationals: England U16, U17, U18, U19, U20.
2015–16 Arsenal 0 0
2016–17 Arsenal 0 0
2017–18 Arsenal 0 0
2018–19 Arsenal 0 0
2019–20 Arsenal 0 0
2019–20 *WBA* 0 0
2019–20 *Huddersfield T* 14 2 **14 2**

WILLOCK, Joe (M) 33 1
b.Waltham Forest 20-8-99
Internationals: England U16, U19, U20, U21.
2017–18 Arsenal 2 0
2018–19 Arsenal 2 0
2019–20 Arsenal 29 1 **33 1**

XHAKA, Granit (M) 280 15
H: 6 0 W: 11 00 b.Gnjilane 27-9-92
Internationals: Switzerland U17, U18, U19, U21, Full caps.
2010–11 Basel 19 1
2011–12 Basel 23 0 **42 1**
2012–13 Borussia M'gladbach 22 1
2013–14 Borussia M'gladbach 28 0
2014–15 Borussia M'gladbach 30 2
2015–16 Borussia M'gladbach 28 3 **108 6**
2016–17 Arsenal 32 2
2017–18 Arsenal 38 1
2018–19 Arsenal 29 4
2019–20 Arsenal 31 1 **130 8**

Scholars
Alebiosu, Ryan; Butler-Oyedeji, Nathan Jerome Chatoyer; Dennis, Matthew; Ejeheri, Ovie Prince; Graczyk, Hubert; Kirk, Alexander Michael; Laing, Levi Alexander; Matthews, Alfie; Ogungbo, Mazeed; Oyegoke, Daniel Oladele Akinbiyi; Plange, Luke Elliot; Sraha, Jason Robert Osei; Taylor-Hart, Kido.

ASTON VILLA (4)

ARCHER, Cameron (F) 0 0
b.Walsall 21-7-01
2019–20 Aston Villa 0 0

BORJA BASTON, Gonzalez (F) 239 74
H: 6 3 W: 12 13 b. 25-8-92
Internationals: Spain U16, U17, U19.
2009–10 Atletico Madrid 1 0
2010–11 Atletico Madrid 0 0
2011–12 Atletico Madrid 0 0
2011–12 *Murcia* 20 4 **20 4**
2012–13 Atletico Madrid 0 0
2012–13 *Huesca* 31 9 **31 9**
2013–14 Atletico Madrid 0 0
2013–14 *Deportivo La Coruna* 33 10 **33 10**
2014–15 Atletico Madrid 0 0
2014–15 *Zaragoza* 38 22 **38 22**
2015–16 Atletico Madrid 0 0 **1 0**
2015–16 *Eibar* 36 18 **36 18**
2016–17 Swansea C 18 1
2017–18 Swansea C 0 0
2017–18 *Malaga* 20 2 **20 2**
2018–19 Swansea C 0 0
2018–19 *Alaves* 20 0 **20 0**
2019–20 Swansea C 20 6 **38 7**
2019–20 Aston Villa 2 0 **2 0**

BREE, James (D) 124 0
H: 5 10 W: 11 09 b.Wakefield 11-10-97
2013–14 Barnsley 1 0
2014–15 Barnsley 11 0
2015–16 Barnsley 19 0
2016–17 Barnsley 19 0 **50 0**
2016–17 Aston Villa 7 0
2017–18 Aston Villa 6 0
2018–19 Aston Villa 8 0
2018–19 *Ipswich T* 14 0 **14 0**
2019–20 Aston Villa 0 0 **21 0**
2019–20 *Luton T* 39 0 **39 0**

CHESTER, James (D) 330 21
H: 5 11 W: 11 04 b.Warrington 23-1-89
Internationals: Wales Full caps.
2007–08 Manchester U 0 0
2008–09 Manchester U 0 0
2008–09 *Peterborough U* 5 0 **5 0**
2009–10 Manchester U 0 0
2009–10 *Plymouth Arg* 3 0 **3 0**
2010–11 Manchester U 0 0
2010–11 *Carlisle U* 18 2 **18 2**
2010–11 Hull C 21 1
2011–12 Hull C 44 2
2012–13 Hull C 44 1
2013–14 Hull C 24 1
2014–15 Hull C 23 2 **156 7**
2015–16 WBA 13 0 **13 0**
2016–17 Aston Villa 45 3
2017–18 Aston Villa 46 4
2018–19 Aston Villa 28 5
2019–20 Aston Villa 0 0 **119 12**
2019–20 *Stoke C* 16 0 **16 0**

DAVIS, Keinan (M) 57 2
H: 5 6 W: 10 10 b.Stevenage 13-2-98
Internationals: England U20.
2015–16 Aston Villa 0 0
2016–17 Aston Villa 6 0
2017–18 Aston Villa 28 2
2018–19 Aston Villa 5 0
2019–20 Aston Villa 18 0 **57 2**

DOUGLAS LUIZ, de Paulo (M) 99 6
b.Rio 9-5-98
Internationals: Brazil U20, U23, Full caps.
2016 Vasco da Gama 14 2
2017 Vasco da Gama 11 1 **25 3**
2017–18 Manchester C 0 0
2017–18 *Girona* 15 0
2018–19 Manchester C 0 0
2018–19 *Girona* 23 0 **38 0**
2019–20 Aston Villa 36 3 **36 3**

DOYLE-HAYES, Jake (M) 36 1
b.Ballyjamesduff 30-12-98
Internationals: Republic of Ireland U17, U18, U19.
2017–18 Aston Villa 0 0
2018–19 Aston Villa 0 0
2018–19 *Cambridge U* 6 0 **6 0**
2019–20 Aston Villa 0 0
2019–20 *Cheltenham T* 30 1 **30 1**

EL GHAZI, Anwar (F) 174 34
H: 6 2 W: 12 00 b.Barendrecht 3-5-95
Internationals: Netherlands U17, U18, U21, Full caps.
2014–15 Ajax 31 9
2015–16 Ajax 27 11
2016–17 Ajax 12 0 **70 20**
2016–17 Lille 12 1
2017–18 Lille 27 4 **39 5**
2018–19 *Aston Villa* 31 5
2019–20 Aston Villa 34 4 **65 9**

ELMOHAMADY, Ahmed (M) 421 28
H: 5 11 W: 12 10 b.El Mahalla El-Kubra 9-9-87
Internationals: Egypt Full caps.
2003–04 Ghazi Al-Mehalla 0 0
2004–05 Ghazi Al-Mehalla 14 4
2005–06 Ghazi Al-Mehalla 3 0 **17 4**
2006–07 ENPPI 12 2
2007–08 ENPPI 6 1
2008–09 ENPPI 28 6
2009–10 ENPPI 12 1 **58 10**
2010–11 Sunderland 36 0
2011–12 Sunderland 18 1
2012–13 Sunderland 2 0 **56 1**
2012–13 *Hull C* 41 3
2013–14 Hull C 38 2
2014–15 Hull C 38 2
2015–16 Hull C 41 3
2016–17 Hull C 33 0 **191 10**
2017–18 Aston Villa 43 0
2018–19 Aston Villa 38 2
2019–20 Aston Villa 18 1 **99 3**

ENGELS, Bjorn (D) 124 16
b.Kaprijke 15-9-94
Internationals: Belgium U17, U18, U19, U21.
2012–13 Club Brugge 0 0
2013–14 Club Brugge 23 4
2014–15 Club Brugge 7 3
2015–16 Club Brugge 10 2
2016–17 Club Brugge 15 2
2017–18 Club Brugge 2 0 **57 11**
2017–18 Olympiacos 17 3 **17 3**
2018–19 Reims 33 1 **33 1**
2019–20 Aston Villa 17 1 **17 1**

GREALISH, Jack (M) 196 28
H: 5 9 W: 10 10 b.Birmingham 10-9-95
Internationals: Republic of Ireland U17, U18, U21. England U21.
2012–13 Aston Villa 0 0
2013–14 Aston Villa 1 0
2013–14 *Notts Co* 37 5 **37 5**
2014–15 Aston Villa 17 0
2015–16 Aston Villa 16 1
2016–17 Aston Villa 31 5
2017–18 Aston Villa 27 3
2018–19 Aston Villa 31 6
2019–20 Aston Villa 36 8 **159 23**

GREEN, Andre (F) 63 5
H: 5 11 W: 11 03 b.Solihull 2-5-98
Internationals: England U16, U17, U18, U19, U20.
2014–15 Aston Villa 0 0
2015–16 Aston Villa 2 0
2016–17 Aston Villa 15 0
2017–18 Aston Villa 5 1
2018–19 Aston Villa 18 1
2018–19 *Portsmouth* 6 1 **6 1**
2019–20 Aston Villa 0 0 **40 2**
2019–20 *Preston NE* 4 0 **4 0**
2019–20 *Charlton Ath* 13 2 **13 2**

GUILBERT, Frederic (D) 182 2
b.Valognes 24-12-94
Internationals: France U21.
2011–12 Caen 0 0
2012–13 Caen 0 0
2013–14 Cherbourg 28 0 **28 0**
2014–15 Bordeaux 3 0
2015–16 Bordeaux 30 0
2016–17 Bordeaux 3 0 **36 0**
2016–17 *Caen* 23 0
2017–18 Caen 36 1
2018–19 Caen 34 1 **93 2**
2019–20 Aston Villa 25 0 **25 0**

HAUSE, Kortney (D) 133 7
H: 6 2 W: 13 03 b.Goodmayes 16-7-95
Internationals: England U20, U21.
2012–13 Wycombe W 9 1
2013–14 Wycombe W 14 1 **23 2**
2013–14 Wolverhampton W 0 0
2014–15 Wolverhampton W 17 0
2014–15 *Gillingham* 14 1 **14 1**
2015–16 Wolverhampton W 25 0
2016–17 Wolverhampton W 24 2
2017–18 Wolverhampton W 1 0
2018–19 Wolverhampton W 0 0 **67 2**
2018–19 *Aston Villa* 11 1
2019–20 Aston Villa 18 1 **29 2**

HAYDEN, Kaine (D) 0 0
2019–20 Aston Villa 0 0

HEATON, Tom (G) 343 0
H: 6 1 W: 13 12 b.Chester 15-4-86
Internationals: England 16, U17, U18, U19, U21, Full caps.
2003–04 Manchester U 0 0
2004–05 Manchester U 0 0
2005–06 Manchester U 0 0
2005–06 *Swindon T* 14 0 **14 0**
2006–07 Manchester U 0 0
2007–08 Manchester U 0 0
2008–09 Manchester U 0 0
2008–09 *Cardiff C* 21 0
2009–10 Manchester U 0 0
2009–10 *Rochdale* 12 0 **12 0**
2009–10 *Wycombe W* 16 0 **16 0**
2010–11 Cardiff C 27 0
2011–12 Cardiff C 2 0 **50 0**
2012–13 Bristol C 43 0 **43 0**
2013–14 Burnley 46 0
2014–15 Burnley 38 0
2015–16 Burnley 46 0
2016–17 Burnley 35 0
2017–18 Burnley 4 0
2018–19 Burnley 19 0 **188 0**
2019–20 Aston Villa 20 0 **20 0**

HEPBURN-MURPHY, Rushian (F) 46 6
H: 5 8 W: 9 04 b.Birmingham 19-9-98
Internationals: England U16, U17, U18, U19, U20.
2014–15 Aston Villa 1 0
2015–16 Aston Villa 1 0
2016–17 Aston Villa 3 0
2017–18 Aston Villa 3 0
2018–19 Aston Villa 5 0
2018–19 *Cambridge U* 16 2 **16 2**
2019–20 Aston Villa 0 0 **13 0**
2019–20 *Tranmere R* 17 4 **17 4**
2019–20 *Derby Co* 0 0

HOGAN, Scott (F) 160 57
H: 5 11 W: 10 01 b.Salford 13-4-92
Internationals: Republic of Ireland Full caps.
2009–10 Rochdale 0 0
From FC Halifax T, Stocksbridge PS, Ashton U, Hyde.
2013–14 Rochdale 33 17 **33 17**
2014–15 Brentford 1 0
2015–16 Brentford 7 7
2016–17 Brentford 25 14 **33 21**
2016–17 Aston Villa 13 1
2017–18 Aston Villa 37 6
2018–19 Aston Villa 6 0
2018–19 *Sheffield U* 8 2 **8 2**
2019–20 Aston Villa 0 0 **56 7**
2019–20 *Stoke C* 13 3 **13 3**
2019–20 *Birmingham C* 17 7 **17 7**

HOURIHANE, Conor (M) 365 66
H: 5 11 W: 9 11 b.Cork 2-2-91
Internationals: Republic of Ireland U19, U21, Full caps.
2008–09 Sunderland 0 0
2009–10 Sunderland 0 0
2010–11 Ipswich T 0 0
2011–12 Plymouth Arg 38 2
2012–13 Plymouth Arg 42 5
2013–14 Plymouth Arg 45 8 **125 15**
2014–15 Barnsley 46 13
2015–16 Barnsley 41 10
2016–17 Barnsley 25 6 **112 29**
2016–17 Aston Villa 17 1
2017–18 Aston Villa 41 11
2018–19 Aston Villa 43 7
2019–20 Aston Villa 27 3 **128 22**

JOTA, Ramallo (M) 211 42
H: 5 11 W: 10 08 b.A Coruna 16-6-91
2010–11 Celta Vigo 4 0
2011–12 Celta Vigo 0 0
2012–13 Celta Vigo 0 0
2013–14 Celta Vigo 0 0 **4 0**
2013–14 *Eibar* 35 11
2014–15 Brentford 42 11
2015–16 Brentford 5 0
2015–16 *Eibar* 13 0
2016–17 Brentford 21 12
2016–17 *Eibar* 5 0 **53 11**
2017–18 Brentford 4 0 **72 23**
2017–18 Birmingham C 32 5
2018–19 Birmingham C 40 3 **72 8**
2019–20 Aston Villa 10 0 **10 0**

KALINIC, Lovre (G) 219 0
H: 6 7 W: 12 06 b.Split 3-4-90
Internationals: Croatia U16, U17, U21, Full caps.
2008–09 Hadjuk Split 0 0
2008–09 *Junak Sinj* 4 0 **4 0**
2009–10 Hadjuk Split 0 0
2009–10 *Novalja* 23 0 **23 0**
2010–11 Hadjuk Split 1 0
2011–12 Hadjuk Split 1 0
2011–12 *Karlovac* 11 0 **11 0**
2012–13 Hadjuk Split 4 0
2013–14 Hadjuk Split 24 0
2014–15 Hadjuk Split 28 0
2015–16 Hadjuk Split 31 0
2016–17 Hadjuk Split 13 0 **102 0**
2016–17 Gent 19 0
2017–18 Gent 35 0
2018–19 Gent 14 0 **68 0**
2018–19 Aston Villa 7 0
2019–20 Aston Villa 0 0 **7 0**
2019–20 *Toulouse* 4 0 **4 0**

KODJIA, Jonathan (F) 259 81
H: 6 2 W: 12 02 b.Saint-Denis 22-10-89
Internationals: Ivory Coast Full caps.
2008–09 Reims 2 0
2009–10 Reims 0 0
2010–11 Reims 5 0
2011–12 Reims 2 0
2011–12 *Cherbourg* 16 4 **16 4**
2012–13 Reims 0 0
2012–13 *Amiens SC* 34 9 **34 9**
2013–14 Reims 0 0 **9 0**
2013–14 *Caen* 27 5 **27 5**
2014–15 Angers SCO 28 15 **28 15**
2015–16 Bristol C 45 19
2016–17 Bristol C 4 0 **49 19**
2016–17 Aston Villa 36 19
2017–18 Aston Villa 15 1
2018–19 Aston Villa 39 9
2019–20 Aston Villa 6 0 **96 29**
Transferred to Al-Gharafa, January 2020.

KONSA, Ezri (D) 138 2
H: 6 0 W: 12 02 b. 23-10-97
Internationals: England U20, U21.
2015–16 Charlton Ath 0 0
2016–17 Charlton Ath 32 0
2017–18 Charlton Ath 39 0 **71 0**
2018–19 Brentford 42 1 **42 1**
2019–20 Aston Villa 25 1 **25 1**

LANSBURY, Henri (M) 287 48
H: 6 0 W: 13 06 b.Enfield 12-10-90
Internationals: England U16, U17, U19, U21.
2007–08 Arsenal 0 0
2008–09 Arsenal 0 0
2008–09 *Scunthorpe U* 16 4 **16 4**
2009–10 Arsenal 1 0
2009–10 *Watford* 37 5 **37 5**
2010–11 Arsenal 0 0
2010–11 *Norwich C* 23 4 **23 4**
2011–12 Arsenal 2 0
2011–12 *West Ham U* 22 1 **22 1**
2012–13 Arsenal 0 0 **3 0**
2012–13 Nottingham F 32 5
2013–14 Nottingham F 29 7
2014–15 Nottingham F 39 10
2015–16 Nottingham F 28 4
2016–17 Nottingham F 17 6 **145 32**
2016–17 Aston Villa 18 0
2017–18 Aston Villa 10 2
2018–19 Aston Villa 3 0
2019–20 Aston Villa 10 0 **41 2**

McGINN, John (M) 256 25
H: 5 8 W: 10 08 b.Glasgow 18-10-94
Internationals: Scotland U19, U21, Full caps.
2012–13 St Mirren 22 1
2013–14 St Mirren 35 3
2014–15 St Mirren 30 0 **87 4**
2015–16 Hibernian 36 3
2016–17 Hibernian 29 4
2017–18 Hibernian 35 5
2018–19 Hibernian 1 0 **101 12**
2018–19 Aston Villa 40 6
2019–20 Aston Villa 28 3 **68 9**

MINGS, Tyrone (D) 122 5
H: 6 3 W: 12 00 b.Bath 19-3-93
Internationals: England Full caps.
2012–13 Ipswich T 1 0
2013–14 Ipswich T 16 0
2014–15 Ipswich T 40 1 **57 1**
2015–16 Bournemouth 1 0
2016–17 Bournemouth 7 0
2017–18 Bournemouth 4 0
2018–19 Bournemouth 5 0 **17 0**
2018–19 *Aston Villa* 15 2
2019–20 Aston Villa 33 2 **48 4**

NAKAMBA, Marvelous (M) 151 2
b.Hwange 19-1-94
Internationals: Zimbabwe U20, Full caps.
2012–13 Nancy 0 0
2013–14 Nancy 2 0 **2 0**
2014–15 Vitesse 6 0
2015–16 Vitesse 30 1
2016–17 Vitesse 31 1 **67 2**
2017–18 Club Brugge 35 0
2018–19 Club Brugge 18 0 **53 0**
2019–20 Aston Villa 29 0 **29 0**

NYLAND, Orjan (G) 195 0
H: 6 4 W: 12 04 b.Volda 10-9-90
Internationals: Norway U18, U21, Full caps.
2011 Hodd 28 0
2012 Hodd 28 0 **56 0**
2013 Molde 20 0
2014 Molde 28 0
2015 Molde 13 0 **61 0**
2015–16 Ingolstadt 6 0
2016–17 Ingolstadt 12 0
2017–18 Ingolstadt 30 0 **48 0**
2018–19 Aston Villa 23 0
2019–20 Aston Villa 7 0 **30 0**

O'HARE, Callum (F) 49 6
b.Solihull 1-5-98
Internationals: England U20.
2016–17 Aston Villa 0 0
2017–18 Aston Villa 4 0
2018–19 Aston Villa 0 0
2018–19 *Carlisle U* 16 3 **16 3**
2019–20 Aston Villa 0 0 **4 0**
2019–20 *Coventry C* 29 3 **29 3**

RAMSEY, Jacob (M) 8 3
b. 28-5-01
Internationals: England U18, U19.
2018–19 Aston Villa 1 0
2019–20 Aston Villa 0 0 **1 0**
2019–20 *Doncaster R* 7 3 **7 3**

REINA, Jose (G) 585 0
H: 6 2 W: 14 06 b.Madrid 31-8-82
Internationals: Spain U16, U17, U18, U21, Full caps.
2000–01 Barcelona 19 0
2001–02 Barcelona 11 0 **30 0**
2002–03 Villarreal 33 0
2003–04 Villarreal 38 0
2004–05 Villarreal 38 0 **109 0**
2005–06 Liverpool 33 0
2006–07 Liverpool 35 0
2007–08 Liverpool 38 0
2008–09 Liverpool 38 0
2009–10 Liverpool 38 0
2010–11 Liverpool 38 0
2011–12 Liverpool 34 0
2012–13 Liverpool 31 0
2013–14 Liverpool 0 0 **285 0**
2013–14 *Napoli* 30 0
2014–15 Bayern Munich 3 0 **3 0**
2015–16 Napoli 37 0
2016–17 Napoli 37 0
2017–18 Napoli 37 0 **141 0**
2018–19 AC Milan 4 0
2019–20 AC Milan 1 0 **5 0**
On loan from AC Milan.
2019–20 Aston Villa 12 0 **12 0**

SAMATTA, Mbwana (F) 271 107
b.Salaam 23-12-92
Internationals: Tanzania Full caps.
2010–11 Simba 25 13 **25 13**
2011 TP Mazembe 8 2
2012 TP Mazembe 29 3
2013 TP Mazembe 37 20
2013–14 TP Mazembe 29 15
2014–15 TP Mazembe 0 0
2015–16 TP Mazembe 0 0 **103 40**
2015–16 Genk 16 4
2016–17 Genk 35 12
2017–18 Genk 30 7
2018–19 Genk 28 23
2019–20 Genk 20 7 **129 53**
2019–20 Aston Villa 14 1 **14 1**

SARKIC, Matija (G) 14 0
H: 6 4 W: 11 07 b.Podgorica 23-6-97
Internationals: Montenegro U17, U19, U21, Full caps.
2014–15 Anderlecht 0 0
2015–16 Aston Villa 0 0
2016–17 Aston Villa 0 0
2017–18 Aston Villa 0 0
2017–18 *Wigan Ath* 0 0
2018–19 Aston Villa 0 0
2019–20 Aston Villa 0 0
2019–20 *Livingston* 14 0 **14 0**

STEER, Jed (G) 112 0
H: 6 2 W: 14 00 b.Norwich 23-9-92
Internationals: England U16, U17, U19.
2009–10 Norwich C 0 0
2010–11 Norwich C 0 0
2011–12 Norwich C 0 0
2011–12 *Yeovil T* 12 0
2012–13 Cambridge U 0 0
2012–13 Norwich C 0 0
2013–14 Aston Villa 0 0
2014–15 Aston Villa 1 0
2014–15 *Doncaster R* 13 0 **13 0**
2014–15 *Yeovil T* 12 0 **24 0**
2015–16 Aston Villa 0 0
2015–16 *Huddersfield T* 38 0 **38 0**
2016–17 Aston Villa 0 0
2017–18 Aston Villa 0 0
2018–19 Aston Villa 16 0
2018–19 *Charlton Ath* 19 0 **19 0**
2019–20 Aston Villa 1 0 **18 0**

TARGETT, Matt (D) 89 3
H: 6 0 W: 12 11 b.Edinburgh 18-9-95
Internationals: Scotland U19, England U19, U20, U21.
2013–14 Southampton 0 0
2014–15 Southampton 6 0
2015–16 Southampton 14 0

2016–17 Southampton 5 0
2017–18 Southampton 2 0
2017–18 *Fulham* 18 1 **18 1**
2018–19 Southampton 16 1 **43 1**
2019–20 Aston Villa 28 1 **28 1**

TAYLOR, Neil (D) 274 0
H: 5 9 W: 10 02 b.Ruthin 7-2-89
Internationals: Wales U17, U19, U21, C, Full caps. Great Britain.
2007–08 Wrexham 26 0 **26 0**
From Wrexham.
2010–11 Swansea C 29 0
2011–12 Swansea C 36 0
2012–13 Swansea C 6 0
2013–14 Swansea C 10 0
2014–15 Swansea C 34 0
2015–16 Swansea C 34 0
2016–17 Swansea C 11 0 **160 0**
2016–17 Aston Villa 14 0
2017–18 Aston Villa 29 0
2018–19 Aston Villa 31 0
2019–20 Aston Villa 14 0 **88 0**

TREZEGUET, Mahmoud (M) 185 39
b.Kafr el-Sheikh 1-10-94
Internationals: Egypt U20, U23, Full caps.
2012–13 Al Ahly 7 0
2013–14 Al Ahly 20 2
2014–15 Al Ahly 31 5
2015–16 Al Ahly 0 0 **58 7**
2015–16 *Anderlecht* 7 0
2016–17 Anderlecht 1 0
2016–17 *Royal Excel Mouscron* 20 4 **20 4**
2017–18 Anderlecht 0 0 **8 0**
2017–18 *Kasimpasa* 31 13
2018–19 Kasimpasa 34 9 **65 22**
2019–20 Aston Villa 34 6 **34 6**

TSHIBOLA, Aaron (M) 99 2
H: 6 3 W: 11 01 b.Newham 2-1-95
Internationals: England U18. DR Congo Full caps.
2011–12 Reading 0 0
2012–13 Reading 0 0
2013–14 Reading 0 0
2014–15 Reading 1 0
2014–15 *Hartlepool U* 23 0 **23 0**
2015–16 Reading 12 0 **13 0**
2016–17 Aston Villa 8 1
2016–17 *Nottingham F* 4 0 **4 0**
2017–18 Aston Villa 0 0
2017–18 *Milton Keynes D* 12 0 **12 0**
2017–18 *Kilmarnock* 12 0
2018–19 Aston Villa 0 0
2017–18 *Kilmarnock* 27 1 **39 1**
2019–20 Aston Villa 0 0 **8 1**
Transferred to Waasland Beveren, August 2019.

VASSILEV, Indiana (M) 4 0
b.Georgia 16-2-01
Internationals: USA U17, U18, U20.
2019–20 Aston Villa 4 0 **4 0**

WESLEY, Moraes (F) 146 43
b.Juiz de Fora 26-11-96
Internationals: Brazil Full caps.
2015–16 Trencin 18 6 **18 6**
2015–16 Club Brugge 6 2
2016–17 Club Brugge 25 6
2017–18 Club Brugge 38 11
2018–19 Club Brugge 38 13 **107 32**
2019–20 Aston Villa 21 5 **21 5**

Players retained or with offer of contract
Appiah, Paul Nana Akwashi; Bridge, Mungo Olayipo Oladapo; Brunt, Lewis; Campton-Sturridge, Dj; Clarke, Jack Aidan; Guy, Ben Tyler; Hassan, Mahmoud Ahmed Ibrahim; Onodi, Akos Sandor; Peleteiro Ramallo, Jose Ignacio; Revan, Dominic; Rowe, Callum Miles; Sinisalo, Viljami Kari Veikko; Tait Moran, Michael; Walker, Jake; Wright, Tyreik Samuel.

Scholars
Ableen-Goodridge, Tristan Kareem; Archer, Cameron Desmond; Barry, Louie Mark; Burton, Bradley; Farr, Charlie Edward James; Hayden, Kaine Kesler; Lindley, Hayden Taylor; Marschall, Filip; Philogene-Bidace, Jaden; Raikhy, Arjan Singh; Ramsey, Aaron James; Revan, Sebastian Emmanuel; Sohna, Harrison Sheriff; Sohna, Myles Baboucarr; Sylla Diallo, Mamadou; Young, Bradley Jamie Ethan; Zito, Patrick Tchuako.

BARNSLEY (5)

ADEBOYEJO, Victor (F) 66 4
b. 12-1-98
2014–15 Leyton Orient 1 0
2015–16 Leyton Orient 1 0
2016–17 Leyton Orient 13 1 **15 1**
2017–18 Barnsley 0 0
2018–19 Barnsley 25 2 **25 2**
2019–20 *Bristol R* 18 1 **18 1**
2019–20 *Cambridge U* 8 0 **8 0**

ANDERSEN, Mads (D) 91 6
b. 27-12-97
Internationals: Denmark U19.
2016–17 Brondy 0 0
2016–17 *Koge* 25 2 **25 2**
2017–18 Horsens 8 1
2018–19 Horsens 20 3 **28 4**
2019–20 Barnsley 38 0 **38 0**

BAHRE, Mike-Steven (M) 86 3
H: 5 10 W: 11 00 b.Garbsen 10-8-95
2014–15 Hannover 96 0 0
2015–16 Hannover 96 1 0
2015–16 *Hallescher* 6 0 **6 0**
2016–17 Hannover 96 2 0
2017–18 *Meppen* 16 1 **16 1**
2017–18 Hannover 96 0 0
2018–19 Hannover 96 0 0 **3 0**
2018–19 *Barnsley* 35 1
2019–20 Barnsley 26 1 **61 2**

BIRD, Jared (M) 14 0
H: 5 9 W: 9 11 b.Nottingham 21-8-97
From Derby Co.
2016–17 Barnsley 0 0
2017–18 Barnsley 3 0
2017–18 *Yeovil T* 11 0 **11 0**
2018–19 Barnsley 0 0
2019–20 Barnsley 0 0 **3 0**

BROWN, Jacob (M) 87 11
H: 5 10 W: 9 11 b. 10-4-98
2014–15 Barnsley 0 0
2015–16 Barnsley 0 0
2016–17 Barnsley 2 0
2017–18 Barnsley 0 0
2017–18 *Chesterfield* 13 0 **13 0**
2018–19 Barnsley 32 8
2019–20 Barnsley 40 3 **74 11**

CAVARE, Dimitri (D) 84 3
H: 6 1 W: 13 03 b.Pointe-‡-Pitre 5-2-95
Internationals: France U20. Guadeloupe Full caps.
2013–14 Lens 1 0
2014–15 Lens 20 0 **21 0**
2015–16 Rennes 0 0
2016–17 Rennes 2 0
2017–18 Rennes 0 0 **2 0**
2017–18 Barnsley 9 1
2018–19 Barnsley 41 2
2019–20 Barnsley 11 0 **61 3**
Transferred to Sion, February 2020.

CHAPLIN, Conor (M) 179 41
H: 5 10 W: 10 12 b.Worthing 16-2-97
2014–15 Portsmouth 9 1
2015–16 Portsmouth 30 8
2016–17 Portsmouth 39 8
2017–18 Portsmouth 26 5 **104 22**
2018–19 Coventry C 31 8 **31 8**
2019–20 Barnsley 44 11 **44 11**

COLLINS, Bradley (G) 89 0
H: 6 0 W: 10 12 b. 18-2-97
2017–18 Chelsea 0 0
2017–18 *Forest Green R* 39 0 **39 0**
2018–19 Chelsea 0 0
2018–19 *Burton Alb* 31 0 **31 0**
2019–20 Barnsley 19 0 **19 0**

DIABY, Bambo (D) 81 6
b.Mataro 17-12-97
2015–16 Cornelia 1 0 **1 0**
2016–17 Sampdoria 0 0
2016–17 *Mantova* 7 0 **7 0**
2017–18 Sampdoria 0 0
2017–18 *Peralada* 34 4 **34 4**
2017–18 *Girona* 0 0
2018–19 Lokeren 18 1 **18 1**
2019–20 Barnsley 21 1 **21 1**

DOUGALL, Kenneth (M) 183 13
H: 6 0 W: 12 06 b.Brisbane 7-5-93
Internationals: Australia U23.
2013–14 Brisbane C 34 10 **34 10**
2014–15 Telstar 29 1 **29 1**
2015–16 Sparta Rotterdam 32 0
2016–17 Sparta Rotterdam 20 1
2017–18 Sparta Rotterdam 29 1 **81 2**
2018–19 Barnsley 27 0
2019–20 Barnsley 12 0 **39 0**

FIELDING, Sam (D) 0 0
b.Burton upon Trent 2-11-99
From York C.
2018–19 Barnsley 0 0
2019–20 Barnsley 0 0

GREATOREX, Jake (G) 0 0
H: 6 1 b.Pontefract 7-9-99
2018–19 Barnsley 0 0
2019–20 Barnsley 0 0

GREEN, Jordan (F) 89 8
H: 5 6 W: 10 03 b.London 22-2-95
2015–16 Bournemouth 0 0
2016–17 Bournemouth 0 0
2016–17 *Newport Co* 10 0
2017–18 Yeovil T 37 2
2018–19 Yeovil T 19 4 **56 6**
2018–19 Barnsley 10 1
2019–20 Barnsley 2 0 **12 1**
2019–20 *Newport Co* 11 1 **21 1**

HALME, Aapo (D) 81 5
b.Helsinki 22-5-98
Internationals: Finland U16, U17, U18, U19, U21.
2014 Honka 1 0 **1 0**
2015 Klubi 04 15 1 **15 1**
2015 HJK 2 0
2016 HJK 14 0
2017 HJK 13 0 **29 0**
2018–19 Leeds U 4 0 **4 0**
2019–20 Barnsley 32 4 **32 4**

HELLIWELL, Jordan (D) 0 0
H: 5 7 b.Wakefield 23-9-01
2018–19 Barnsley 0 0
2019–20 Barnsley 0 0

KENDRICK, Henry (G) 0 0
H: 6 3 b.Barnsley 3-12-00
2018–19 Barnsley 0 0
2019–20 Barnsley 0 0

LUDEWIG, Kilian (D) 36 1
b. 5-3-00
Internationals: Germany U16, U17, U18.
2018–19 Liefering 18 1 **18 1**
2019–20 Red Bull Salzburg 0 0
On loan from Red Bull Salzburg.
2019–20 Barnsley 18 0 **18 0**

MARSH, Aiden (F) 0 0
b. 5-5-13
2019–20 Barnsley 0 0

McGEEHAN, Cameron (M) 170 37
H: 5 11 W: 11 03 b.Kingston upon Thames 6-4-95
Internationals: Northern Ireland U17, U19, U21.
2013–14 Norwich C 0 0
2014–15 Norwich C 0 0
2014–15 *Luton T* 15 3
2014–15 *Cambridge U* 4 3 **4 3**
2015–16 Luton T 41 12
2016–17 Luton T 24 10 **80 25**
2017–18 Barnsley 9 1
2017–18 *Scunthorpe U* 13 0 **13 0**
2018–19 Barnsley 39 6
2019–20 Barnsley 13 2 **61 9**
2019–20 *Portsmouth* 12 0 **12 0**

MILLER, George (F) 103 19
H: 5 10 W: 10 01 b.Bolton 11-8-98
2015–16 Bury 1 0
2016–17 Bury 28 7
2017–18 Middlesbrough 0 0
2017–18 *Bury* 19 8 **48 15**
2018–19 Middlesbrough 0 0
2018–19 *Bradford C* 39 3 **39 3**
2018–19 Barnsley 0 0
2019–20 Barnsley 1 0 **1 0**
2019–20 *Scunthorpe U* 15 1 **15 1**

MOON, Jasper (M) 0 0
H: 6 1 b.Coventry 24-11-00
2018–19 Barnsley 0 0
2019–20 Barnsley 0 0

MOWATT, Alex (D) 248 26
H: 5 10 W: 11 03 b.Doncaster 13-2-95
Internationals: England U19, U20.
2013–14 Leeds U 29 1

2014–15	Leeds U	38	9		
2015–16	Leeds U	34	2		
2016–17	Leeds U	15	0	**116**	**12**
2016–17	Barnsley	11	1		
2017–18	Barnsley	1	0		
2017–18	*Oxford U*	30	2	**30**	**2**
2018–19	Barnsley	46	8		
2019–20	Barnsley	44	3	**102**	**12**

ODOUR, Clarke (F) **16** **1**

b. 25-6-99

2018–19	Leeds U	0	0		
2019–20	Leeds U	0	0		
2019–20	Barnsley	16	1	**16**	**1**

OMAR, Ali (D) **0** **0**

b. 14-9-99

2018–19	QPR	0	0		
2019–20	Barnsley	0	0		

PALMER, Romal (M) **3** **0**

From Manchester C.

2019–20	Barnsley	3	0	**3**	**0**

PINILLOS, Daniel (D) **131** **2**

H: 6 0 W: 11 09 b.Logrono 22-10-92

2013–14	Ourense	21	0	**21**	**0**
2013–14	Cordoba	16	1		
2014–15	Cordoba	12	0		
2015–16	Nottingham F	19	0		
2016–17	Nottingham F	16	1	**35**	**1**
2017–18	Cordoba	0	0	**28**	**1**
2017–18	Barnsley	8	0		
2018–19	Barnsley	35	0		
2019–20	Barnsley	4	0	**47**	**0**

RADLINGER, Samuel (G) **69** **0**

b.Ried im Innkreis 7-11-92

Internationals: Austria U18, U19, U20, U21.

2010–11	Reid	0	0		
2010–11	*Union St Florian*	25	0	**25**	**0**
2011–12	Hannover 96	0	0		
2012–13	Hannover 96	0	0		
2013–14	Hannover 96	0	0		
2013–14	*Rapid Vienna*	1	0	**1**	**0**
2014–15	Hannover 96	0	0		
2014–15	*Nuremberg*	0	0		
2015–16	Hannover 96	2	0		
2016–17	Hannover 96	0	0		
2017–18	Hannover 96	1	0		
2018–19	Hannover 96	0	0	**3**	**0**
2018–19	Brann	22	0	**22**	**0**
2019–20	Barnsley	18	0	**18**	**0**

RITZMAIER, Marcel (M) **151** **9**

b.Knittelfeld 22-4-93

Internationals: Austria U16, U17, U18, U19, U21.

2009–10	Austria Karnten	1	0	**1**	**0**
2010–11	PSV Eindhoven	0	0		
2011–12	PSV Eindhoven	0	0		
2012–13	PSV Eindhoven	4	0		
2013–14	PSV Eindhoven	0	0		
2013–14	*Cambuur*	31	3	**31**	**3**
2014–15	PSV Eindhoven	5	0		
2015–16	PSV Eindhoven	0	0		
2015–16	*NEC*	20	1	**20**	**1**
2016–17	PSV Eindhoven	0	0		
2016–17	*Go Ahead Eagles*	28	2	**28**	**2**
2017–18	PSV Eindhoven	0	0	**9**	**0**
2018–19	Wolfsburg	29	1		
2019–20	Wolfsburg	18	2	**47**	**3**
2019–20	Barnsley	15	0	**15**	**0**

SANG, Chris (F) **2** **0**

H: 6 2 b.Liverpool 26-6-98

From Wigan Ath.

2017–18	Bury	2	0		
2018–19	Bury	0	0	**2**	**0**
2019–20	Barnsley	0	0		

SCHMIDT, Patrick (F) **93** **18**

b.Eisenstadt 22-7-98

Internationals: Austria U16, U17, U18, U19, U21.

2016–17	Admira Wacker	15	1		
2017–18	Admira Wacker	20	6		
2018–19	Admira Wacker	27	8		
2019–20	Admira Wacker	2	0	**64**	**15**
2019–20	Barnsley	29	3	**29**	**3**

SIBBICK, Toby (D) **46** **0**

H: 6 0 W: 10 12 b.Isleworth 23-5-99

2016–17	AFC Wimbledon	2	0		
2017–18	AFC Wimbledon	1	0		
2018–19	AFC Wimbledon	23	0	**26**	**0**
2019–20	Barnsley	18	0	**18**	**0**
2019–20	*Hearts*	2	0	**2**	**0**

SIMOES, Elliot (F) **17** **2**

b. 20-12-99

From FC United of Manchester.

2019–20	Barnsley	17	2	**17**	**2**

SOLLBAUER , Michael (D) **315** **7**

b. 15-5-90

2009–10	Austria Karnten	18	0	**18**	**0**
2010–11	Wolfsburg	29	1		
2011–12	Wolfsburg	31	3		
2012–13	Wolfsburg	34	0		
2013–14	Wolfsburg	34	0		
2014–15	Wolfsburg	32	0		
2015–16	Wolfsburg	25	0		
2016–17	Wolfsburg	23	1		
2017–18	Wolfsburg	24	1		
2018–19	Wolfsburg	30	1	**262**	**7**
2019–20	Wolfsberg	18	0	**18**	**0**
2019–20	Barnsley	17	0	**17**	**0**

STYLES, Callum (F) **65** **1**

b. 28-3-00

2015–16	Bury	1	0		
2016–17	Bury	13	0		
2017–18	Bury	11	0		
2018–19	Bury	16	0	**41**	**0**
2018–19	Barnsley	7	0		
2019–20	Barnsley	17	1	**24**	**1**

THIAM, Mamadou (F) **142** **19**

H: 6 0 W: 12 13 b.Aubervilliers 20-3-95

Internationals: Senegal U20.

2013–14	Dijon	0	0		
2014–15	Dijon	8	0		
2015–16	Dijon	17	3		
2016–17	Dijon	0	0	**25**	**3**
2016–17	*Clermont*	34	8	**34**	**8**
2017–18	Barnsley	29	1		
2018–19	Barnsley	46	7		
2019–20	Barnsley	8	0	**83**	**8**

THOMAS, Luke (F) **84** **5**

H: 5 7 W: 10 08 b. 19-2-99

Internationals: England U20.

2015–16	Derby Co	0	0		
2016–17	Derby Co	0	0		
2017–18	Derby Co	2	0		
2018–19	Derby Co	0	0	**2**	**0**
2018–19	*Coventry C*	43	4	**43**	**4**
2019–20	Barnsley	39	1	**39**	**1**

WALTON, Jack (G) **15** **0**

H: 6 0 W: 12 02 b.Bury 23-4-98

2014–15	Barnsley	0	0		
2015–16	Barnsley	0	0		
2016–17	Barnsley	0	0		
2017–18	Barnsley	3	0		
2018–19	Barnsley	3	0		
2019–20	Barnsley	9	0	**15**	**0**

WILKS, Mallik (F) **104** **23**

b.Leeds 15-12-98

2016–17	Leeds U	0	0		
2017–18	Leeds U	0	0		
2017–18	*Accrington S*	19	3	**19**	**3**
2017–18	*Grimsby T*	6	0	**6**	**0**
2018–19	Leeds U	0	0		
2018–19	*Doncaster R*	46	14	**46**	**14**
2019–20	Barnsley	15	1	**15**	**1**
2019–20	*Hull C*	18	5	**18**	**5**

WILLIAMS, Ben (D) **31** **0**

H: 5 10 W: 11 00 b. 31-3-99

Internationals: Wales U17, U19, U21.

From Blackburn R.

2017–18	Barnsley	0	0		
2018–19	Barnsley	11	0		
2019–20	Barnsley	20	0	**31**	**0**

WILLIAMS, Jordan (D) **50** **0**

b. 22-10-99

Internationals: England U17, U18.

2017–18	Huddersfield T	0	0		
2017–18	*Bury*	9	0	**9**	**0**
2018–19	Barnsley	11	0		
2019–20	Barnsley	30	0	**41**	**0**

WOLFE, Matthew (M) **1** **0**

2017–18	Barnsley	0	0		
2018–19	Barnsley	0	0		
2019–20	Barnsley	1	0	**1**	**0**

WOODROW, Cauley (F) **172** **47**

H: 6 0 W: 12 04 b.Hemel Hempstead 2-12-94

Internationals: England U17, U20, U21.

2011–12	Fulham	0	0		
2012–13	Fulham	0	0		
2013–14	Fulham	6	1		
2013–14	*Southend U*	19	2	**19**	**2**
2014–15	Fulham	29	3		
2015–16	Fulham	14	4		
2016–17	Fulham	5	0		
2016–17	*Burton Alb*	14	5	**14**	**5**
2017–18	Fulham	0	0	**54**	**8**
2017–18	*Bristol C*	14	2	**14**	**2**
2018–19	Barnsley	31	16		
2019–20	Barnsley	40	14	**71**	**30**

Players retained or with offer of contract

Ward, Keaton.

Scholars

Ackroyd, Joe; Aleksiev, Sezgin Seher; Ariely, Amir Moshe; Binns, Bradley; Birks, Jack; Brown, Archie Myles; Calligan, William Marcus; Chapman, Angus Charles; Hassa-Smith, Kareem David; Hassell, Bayley Robert John; Hodgson, Connor James; Lancaster, William Jack; Marsh, Aiden Levi; Nicholson, Sam Oliver; Olatubosun, Joshua Oluwaferanmi Paul; Pache, Rudi; Sherlock, Jack Edward; Sil-Conde, Newton; Walmsley, Callum Richard; Widdop, Harry Jacob; Winfield, Charlie James.

BIRMINGHAM C (6)

ALVARO GIMENEZ, Candela (F) **215** **36**

b.Elche 19-5-91

2007–08	Elche	7	0		
2008–09	Elche	0	0		
2009–10	Elche	0	0		
2009–10	Valencia	0	0		

From Torrellano Illice.

2011–12	Real Mallorca	12	2		
2012–13	Real Mallorca	1	0	**13**	**2**
2013–14	Elche	2	0		
2014–15	Elche	17	0		
2015–16	Elche	39	2	**65**	**2**
2016–17	Alcorcon	32	2		
2017–18	Alcorcon	29	6	**61**	**8**
2018–19	Almira	39	20	**39**	**20**
2019–20	Birmingham C	24	3	**24**	**3**
2019–20	*Cadiz*	13	1	**13**	**1**

BAILEY, Odin (M) **11** **2**

b. 8-12-99

Internationals: England U16.

2017–18	Birmingham C	0	0		
2018–19	Birmingham C	0	0		
2019–20	Birmingham C	6	1	**6**	**1**
2019–20	*Forest Green R*	5	1	**5**	**1**

BAJRAMI, Geraldo (D) **2** **0**

b.Birmingham 24-9-99

Internationals: Albania U21.

2019–20	Birmingham C	2	0	**2**	**0**

BELA, Jeremie (M) **188** **29**

b.Melun 8-4-93

Internationals: France U16.

2010–11	Lens	0	0		
2011–12	Lens	0	0		
2012–13	Lens	16	1		
2013–14	Lens	1	0	**17**	**1**
2013–14	Djon	4	0		
2014–15	Djon	33	6		
2015–16	Djon	23	4		
2016–17	Djon	14	0	**74**	**10**
2017–18	Albacete	33	5		
2018–19	Albacete	34	11		
2019–20	Albacete	0	0	**67**	**16**
2019–20	Birmingham C	30	2	**30**	**2**

BELLINGHAM, Jude (M) **41** **4**

b.Stourbridge 29-6-03

Internationals: England U16, U17.

2019–20	Birmingham C	41	4	**41**	**4**

Transferred to Borussia Dortmund, July 2019.

BOYD-MUNCE, Caolan (M) **6** **0**

b.Belfast 26-1-00

Internationals: Northern Ireland U16, U17, U19, U21.

From Glentoran.

2018–19	Birmingham C	0	0		
2019–20	Birmingham C	6	0	**6**	**0**

BURKE, Ryan (D) **1** **0**

b. 23-11-00

Internationals: Republic of Ireland U16.

From St Patrick's.

2019–20	Birmingham C	1	0	**1**	**0**

CAMP, Lee (G) **539** **0**

H: 5 11 W: 11 11 b.Derby 22-8-84

Internationals: England U21. Northern Ireland Full caps.

2002–03	Derby Co	1	0		

2003–04 Derby Co 0 0
2003–04 *QPR* 12 0
2004–05 Derby Co 45 0
2005–06 Derby Co 40 0
2006–07 Derby Co 3 0 **89 0**
2006–07 *Norwich C* 3 0
2006–07 *QPR* 11 0
2007–08 QPR 46 0
2008–09 QPR 4 0 **73 0**
2008–09 *Nottingham F* 15 0
2009–10 Nottingham F 45 0
2010–11 Nottingham F 46 0
2011–12 Nottingham F 46 0
2012–13 Nottingham F 26 0 **178 0**
2012–13 Norwich C 3 0 **6 0**
2013–14 WBA 0 0
2013–14 Bournemouth 33 0
2014–15 Bournemouth 9 0
2015–16 Bournemouth 0 0 **42 0**
2015–16 Rotherham U 41 0
2016–17 Rotherham U 18 0 **59 0**
2017–18 Cardiff C 0 0
2017–18 *Sunderland* 12 0 **12 0**
2018–19 Birmingham C 44 0
2019–20 Birmingham C 36 0 **80 0**

COLIN, Maxime (D) 310 8
H: 5 11 W: 12 00 b.Arras 15-11-91
Internationals: France U20.
2010–11 Boulogne 26 0
2011–12 Boulogne 23 0
2012–13 Boulogne 4 0 **53 0**
2012–13 Troyes 18 0
2013–14 Troyes 35 0
2014–15 Troyes 2 0 **55 0**
2014–15 Anderlecht 17 1
2015–16 Anderlecht 1 0 **18 1**
2015–16 Brentford 21 0
2016–17 Brentford 38 4
2017–18 Brentford 3 0 **62 4**
2017–18 Birmingham C 35 2
2018–19 Birmingham C 43 0
2019–20 Birmingham C 44 1 **122 3**

CONCANNON, Jack (M) 0 0
2019–20 Birmingham C 0 0

CROWLEY, Daniel (M) 115 10
H: 5 9 W: 10 10 b.Coventry 3-8-97
Internationals: Republic of Ireland U16, U17. England U16, U17, U19.
2015–16 Arsenal 0 0
2015–16 *Barnsley* 11 0 **11 0**
2016–17 Arsenal 0 0
2016–17 *Oxford U* 6 2 **6 2**
2016–17 *Go Ahead Eagles* 16 2 **16 2**
2017–18 Willem II 10 0
2018–19 Willem II 34 5 **44 5**
2019–20 Birmingham C 38 1 **38 1**

DACRES-COGLEY, Josh (D) 34 0
H: 5 9 W: 10 10 b.Coventry 12-3-96
2016–17 Birmingham C 14 0
2017–18 Birmingham C 3 0
2018–19 Birmingham C 1 0
2019–20 Birmingham C 0 0 **18 0**
2019–20 *Crawley T* 16 0 **16 0**

DAVIS, David (M) 280 12
H: 5 8 W: 12 03 b.Smethwick 20-2-91
2009–10 Wolverhampton W 0 0
2009–10 *Darlington* 5 0 **5 0**
2010–11 Wolverhampton W 0 0
2010–11 *Walsall* 7 0 **7 0**
2010–11 *Shrewsbury T* 19 2 **19 2**
2011–12 Wolverhampton W 7 0
2011–12 *Chesterfield* 9 0 **9 0**
2012–13 Wolverhampton W 28 0
2013–14 Wolverhampton W 18 0 **53 0**
2014–15 Birmingham C 42 3
2015–16 Birmingham C 35 1
2016–17 Birmingham C 41 4
2017–18 Birmingham C 38 2
2018–19 Birmingham C 11 0
2019–20 Birmingham C 15 0 **182 10**
2019–20 *Charlton Ath* 5 0 **5 0**

DEAN, Harlee (M) 342 11
H: 6 0 W: 11 10 b.Basingstoke 26-7-91
2008–09 Dagenham & R 0 0
2009–10 Dagenham & R 1 0 **1 0**
2010–11 Southampton 0 0
2011–12 Southampton 0 0
2011–12 *Brentford* 26 1
2012–13 Brentford 44 3
2013–14 Brentford 32 0
2014–15 Brentford 35 1
2015–16 Brentford 42 0
2016–17 Brentford 42 3
2017–18 Brentford 3 0 **224 8**
2017–18 Birmingham C 34 1
2018–19 Birmingham C 44 1
2019–20 Birmingham C 39 1 **117 3**

FERNANDEZ, Miguel (M) 1 0
b. 12-8-00
From Cornella.
2019–20 Birmingham C 1 0 **1 0**

GARDNER, Craig (M) 327 36
H: 5 10 W: 11 13 b.Solihull 25-11-86
Internationals: England U21.
2004–05 Aston Villa 0 0
2005–06 Aston Villa 8 0
2006–07 Aston Villa 13 2
2007–08 Aston Villa 23 3
2008–09 Aston Villa 14 0
2009–10 Aston Villa 1 0 **59 5**
2009–10 Birmingham C 13 1
2010–11 Birmingham C 29 8
2011–12 Sunderland 30 3
2012–13 Sunderland 33 6
2013–14 Sunderland 18 2 **81 11**
2014–15 WBA 35 3
2015–16 WBA 34 3
2016–17 WBA 9 0 **78 6**
2016–17 *Birmingham C* 20 2
2017–18 Birmingham C 26 2
2018–19 Birmingham C 21 1
2019–20 Birmingham C 0 0 **109 14**

GARDNER, Gary (M) 208 18
H: 6 2 W: 12 13 b.Solihull 29-6-92
Internationals: England U17, U19, U20, U21.
2009–10 Aston Villa 0 0
2010–11 Aston Villa 0 0
2011–12 Aston Villa 14 0
2011–12 *Coventry C* 4 1 **4 1**
2012–13 Aston Villa 2 0
2013–14 Aston Villa 0 0
2013–14 *Sheffield W* 3 0 **3 0**
2014–15 Aston Villa 0 0
2014–15 *Brighton & HA* 17 2 **17 2**
2014–15 Nottingham F 18 4
2015–16 Aston Villa 0 0
2015–16 *Nottingham F* 20 2 **38 6**
2016–17 Aston Villa 26 1
2017–18 Aston Villa 0 0
2017–18 *Barnsley* 29 2 **29 2**
2018–19 Aston Villa 0 0 **42 1**
2018–19 *Birmingham C* 40 2
2019–20 Birmingham C 35 4 **75 6**

GORDON, Nico (D) 2 0
2019–20 Birmingham C 2 0 **2 0**

GROUNDS, Jonathan (D) 336 11
H: 6 1 W: 13 10 b.Thornaby 2-2-88
2007–08 Middlesbrough 5 0
2008–09 Middlesbrough 2 0
2008–09 *Norwich C* 16 3 **16 3**
2009–10 Middlesbrough 20 0
2010–11 Middlesbrough 6 1
2011–12 Middlesbrough 0 0 **33 1**
2011–12 *Chesterfield* 13 0 **13 0**
2011–12 *Yeovil T* 14 0 **14 0**
2012–13 Oldham Ath 44 1
2013–14 Oldham Ath 45 2 **89 3**
2014–15 Birmingham C 45 1
2015–16 Birmingham C 45 1
2016–17 Birmingham C 42 2
2017–18 Birmingham C 26 0
2018–19 Birmingham C 0 0
2018–19 *Bolton W* 13 0 **13 0**
2019–20 Birmingham C 0 0 **158 4**

HARDING, Wes (D) 51 0
H: 5 11 W: 12 06 b.Leicester 20-10-96
2017–18 Birmingham C 9 0
2018–19 Birmingham C 27 0
2019–20 Birmingham C 15 0 **51 0**

JUTKIEWICZ, Lucas (F) 431 98
H: 6 1 W: 12 11 b.Southampton 20-3-89
2005–06 Swindon T 5 0
2006–07 Swindon T 33 5 **38 5**
2006–07 Everton 0 0
2007–08 Everton 0 0
2007–08 *Plymouth Arg* 3 0 **3 0**
2008–09 Everton 1 0
2008–09 *Huddersfield T* 7 0 **7 0**
2009–10 Everton 0 0 **1 0**
2009–10 *Motherwell* 33 12 **33 12**
2010–11 Coventry C 42 9
2011–12 Coventry C 25 9 **67 18**
2011–12 Middlesbrough 19 2
2012–13 Middlesbrough 24 8
2013–14 Middlesbrough 22 1 **65 11**
2013–14 *Bolton W* 20 7 **20 7**
2014–15 Burnley 25 0
2015–16 Burnley 5 0
2016–17 Burnley 2 0 **32 0**
2016–17 Birmingham C 38 11
2017–18 Birmingham C 35 5
2018–19 Birmingham C 46 14
2019–20 Birmingham C 46 15 **165 45**

KEITA, Cheick (D) 83 2
H: 5 7 W: 12 00 b.Paris 16-7-96
Internationals: Mali U20.
From Monaco.
2014–15 Virtus Entella 0 0
2015–16 Virtus Entella 31 0
2016–17 Virtus Entella 14 0 **45 0**
2016–17 Birmingham C 10 0
2017–18 Birmingham C 1 0
2017–18 *Bologna* 3 0 **3 0**
2018–19 Birmingham C 0 0
2019–20 *Eupen* 24 2 **24 2**
2019–20 Birmingham C 0 0 **11 0**

KIEFTENBELD, Maikel (M) 375 10
H: 5 10 W: 11 11 b.Lemelerveld 26-6-90
Internationals: Netherlands U21.
2008–09 Go Ahead Eagles 30 1
2009–10 Go Ahead Eagles 33 2 **63 3**
2010–11 Groningen 33 0
2011–12 Groningen 26 1
2012–13 Groningen 29 1
2013–14 Groningen 31 0
2014–15 Groningen 33 0 **152 2**
2015–16 Birmingham C 42 3
2016–17 Birmingham C 39 1
2017–18 Birmingham C 35 0
2018–19 Birmingham C 36 1
2019–20 Birmingham C 8 0 **160 5**

LAKIN, Charlie (M) 30 2
b.Solihull 8-5-99
2017–18 Birmingham C 0 0
2018–19 Birmingham C 10 0
2019–20 Birmingham C 0 0 **10 0**
2019–20 *Stevenage* 20 2 **20 2**

LUYAMBULA, Michael (G) 0 0
b. 8-6-19
From Borussia Dortmund.
2019–20 Birmingham C 0 0
2019–20 *Crawley T* 0 0
Transferred to VfB Lubeck, June 2020.

MAGHOMA, Jacques (M) 380 48
H: 5 9 W: 11 06 b.Lubumbashi 23-10-87
Internationals: DR Congo Full caps.
2005–06 Tottenham H 0 0
2006–07 Tottenham H 0 0
2007–08 Tottenham H 0 0
2008–09 Tottenham H 0 0
2009–10 Burton Alb 35 3
2010–11 Burton Alb 41 4
2011–12 Burton Alb 36 4
2012–13 Burton Alb 43 15 **155 26**
2013–14 Sheffield W 25 2
2014–15 Sheffield W 32 0 **57 2**
2015–16 Birmingham C 40 5
2016–17 Birmingham C 27 3
2017–18 Birmingham C 41 5
2018–19 Birmingham C 42 6
2019–20 Birmingham C 18 1 **168 20**

McEACHRAN, Josh (D) 185 1
H: 5 10 W: 10 03 b.Oxford 1-3-93
Internationals: England U16, U17, U19, U20, U21.
2010–11 Chelsea 9 0
2011–12 Chelsea 2 0
2011–12 *Swansea C* 4 0 **4 0**
2012–13 Chelsea 0 0
2012–13 *Middlesbrough* 38 0 **38 0**
2013–14 Chelsea 0 0
2013–14 *Watford* 7 0 **7 0**
2013–14 *Wigan Ath* 8 0 **8 0**
2014–15 Chelsea 0 0 **11 0**
2014–15 *Vitesse* 19 0 **19 0**
2015–16 Brentford 14 0
2016–17 Brentford 27 0
2017–18 Brentford 25 0
2018–19 Brentford 24 1 **90 1**
2019–20 Birmingham C 8 0 **8 0**

MEDINA, Agus (M) 108 9
b.Barbera del Valles 8-9-94
2014–15 Sabadell 7 0
2015–16 Sabadell 30 3 **37 3**
2016–17 Celta Vigo 0 0
2017–18 Celta Vigo 0 0
2018–19 Cornella 35 3
2019–20 Birmingham C 1 0 **1 0**
2019–20 *Cornella* 35 3 **70 6**

MRBATI, Kerim (F) **166 28**
b. 20-5-94
Internationals: Sweden U19, U21, Full caps.

2012	Enkoping	16	2	**16**	**2**
2013	Sirius	23	2		
2014	Sirius	23	3	**46**	**5**
2015	Djurgarden	28	4		
2016	Djurgarden	0	0		
2017	Djurgarden	25	8		
2018	Djurgarden	24	6	**77**	**18**
2018–19	Birmingham C	12	1		
2019–20	Birmingham C	15	2	**27**	**3**

O'KEEFFE, Corey (M) **32 0**
H: 6 1 W: 11 00 b.Birmingham 5-6-88
Internationals: Republic of Ireland U17, U18, U19.

2016–17	Birmingham C	1	0		
2017–18	Birmingham C	0	0		
2018–19	Birmingham C	0	0		
2019–20	Birmingham C	0	0	**1**	**0**
2019–20	*Macclesfield T*	31	0	**31**	**0**

PEDERSEN, Kristian (D) **202 8**
H: 6 2 W: 13 01 b.Ringsted 4-8-94
Internationals: Denmark U21.

2014–15	HB Koge	28	1		
2015–16	HB Koge	30	1	**58**	**2**
2016–17	Union Berlin	29	0		
2017–18	Union Berlin	32	1	**61**	**1**
2018–19	Birmingham C	39	1		
2019–20	Birmingham C	44	4	**83**	**5**

RAMOS, Mohamed (G) **0 0**
b.Santa Cruz de Tenerife 13-4-00
Internationals: Spain U17.

2019–20	Real Madrid	0	0		

On loan from Real Madrid.

2019–20	Birmingham C	0	0		

REDMOND, Joe (D) **0 0**
b.Dublin 23-1-00
Internationals: Republic of Ireland U16, U17, U18.
From St Joseph's.

2019–20	Birmingham C	0	0		

REID, Jayden (F) **4 0**
From Swansea C.

2019–20	Birmingham C	4	0	**4**	**0**

ROBERTS, Marc (D) **144 6**
H: 6 0 W: 12 11 b.Wakefield 26-7-90
Internationals: England C.

2014–15	Barnsley	0	0		
2015–16	Barnsley	32	1		
2016–17	Barnsley	40	4	**72**	**5**
2017–18	Birmingham C	30	1		
2018–19	Birmingham C	8	0		
2019–20	Birmingham C	34	0	**72**	**1**

SEDDON, Steve (D) **57 7**
b.Reading 25-12-97

2017–18	Birmingham C	0	0		
2018–19	Birmingham C	0	0		
2018–19	*Stevenage*	23	3	**23**	**3**
2018–19	*AFC Wimbledon*	18	3	**18**	**3**
2019–20	Birmingham C	4	0	**4**	**0**
2019–20	*Portsmouth*	12	1	**12**	**1**

STIRK, Ryan (M) **0 0**
b. 25-9-00
Internationals: Wales U17, U19.

2019–20	Birmingham C	0	0		

STOCKDALE, David (G) **344 0**
H: 6 3 W: 13 04 b.Leeds 20-9-85
Internationals: England C.

2002–03	York C	1	0		
2003–04	York C	0	0	**1**	**0**
2004–05	York C	0	0		
2005–06	York C	0	0		
2006–07	Darlington	6	0		
2007–08	Darlington	41	0	**47**	**0**
2008–09	Fulham	0	0		
2008–09	*Rotherham U*	8	0	**8**	**0**
2008–09	*Leicester C*	8	0	**8**	**0**
2009–10	Fulham	1	0		
2009–10	*Plymouth Arg*	21	0	**21**	**0**
2010–11	Fulham	7	0		
2011–12	Fulham	8	0		
2011–12	*Ipswich T*	18	0	**18**	**0**
2012–13	Fulham	2	0		
2012–13	*Hull C*	24	0	**24**	**0**
2013–14	Fulham	21	0	**39**	**0**
2014–15	Brighton & HA	42	0		
2015–16	Brighton & HA	46	0		
2016–17	Brighton & HA	45	0	**133**	**0**
2017–18	Birmingham C	36	0		
2018–19	Birmingham C	0	0		
2018–19	*Southend U*	3	0	**3**	**0**
2018–19	*Wycombe W*	2	0		
2018–19	*Coventry C*	2	0	**2**	**0**
2019–20	Birmingham C	0	0	**36**	**0**
2019–20	*Wycombe W*	2	0	**4**	**0**

SUNJIC, Ivan (M) **127 10**
b.Zenica 9-10-96
Internationals: Croatia U16, U17, U18, U19, U21, Full caps.

2013–14	Dinamo Zagreb	1	0		
2014–15	Dinamo Zagreb	0	0		
2015–16	Dinamo Zagreb	0	0		
2015–16	Lokomativa	10	0		
2016–17	Lokomativa	23	1		
2017–18	Lokomativa	29	6	**62**	**7**
2018–19	Dinamo Zagreb	24	0	**25**	**0**
2019–20	Birmingham C	40	3	**40**	**3**

TRUEMAN, Connal (G) **12 0**
H: 6 1 W: 11 10 b.Birmingham 26-3-96

2014–15	Birmingham C	0	0		
2014–15	*Oldham Ath*	0	0		
2015–16	Birmingham C	0	0		
2016–17	Birmingham C	0	0		
2017–18	Birmingham C	0	0		
2018–19	Birmingham C	2	0		
2019–20	Birmingham C	10	0	**12**	**0**

VILLALBA, Fran (M) **73 7**
b.Valencia 11-5-98
Internationals: Spain U16, U17, U18, U19.

2014–15	Valencia	0	0		
2015–16	Valencia	1	0		
2016–17	Valencia	0	0		
2017–18	Valencia	0	0		
2018–19	Valencia	0	0		
2018–19	*Numancia*	39	4	**39**	**4**
2019–20	Valencia	0	0	**1**	**0**
2019–20	Birmingham C	17	1	**17**	**1**
2019–20	*Almeria*	16	2	**16**	**2**

WEAVER, Jake (G) **0 0**
b.Redditch 8-5-97

2018–19	Birmingham C	0	0		
2019–20	Birmingham C	0	0		

Players retained or with offer of contract
Gimenez, Candela Allvaro; Guzman, Garcia Ivan; Hutton, Remeao; Jeacock, Zachary Anton John; Roberts, Mitchell Anthony; Sun, Bernard Yipeng; Thompson-Sommers, Kane Angleis Gavin.

Scholars
Andrews, Joshua Matthew; Bellingham, Jude Victor William; Bradle-Hurst, Joshua; Campbell, Tate Lucas; Chang, Alfie James; Clayton, Aaron Edwin Thomas; Craig, Kade Elliott James; Djurovic, Daniel Ray; Dugmore, Joshua Wayne; George, Kai Adan; Gordon, Nico Diago; Hurst, Kyle Christopher; Kinina, Nicholas Peter; Knight, Kai George; Miller, Amari Miquel; Noakes, Charlie Andrew John; Oakley, Marcel Errol Emmanuel; Powell, Lucas Stefan; Rouse, Elias James; Traore, Oumar; Walker, Remi Ian; Williams, Joshua Aaron; Zohore, Yoane.

BLACKBURN R (7)

ARMSTRONG, Adam (F) **222 57**
H: 5 8 W: 10 12 b.Newcastle upon Tyne 10-2-97
Internationals: England U16, U17, U18, U19, U20, U21.

2013–14	Newcastle U	4	0		
2014–15	Newcastle U	11	0		
2015–16	Newcastle U	0	0		
2015–16	*Coventry C*	40	20	**40**	**20**
2016–17	Newcastle U	2	0		
2016–17	*Barnsley*	34	6	**34**	**6**
2017–18	Newcastle U	0	0	**17**	**0**
2017–18	*Bolton W*	20	1	**20**	**1**
2017–18	*Blackburn R*	21	9		
2018–19	Blackburn R	44	5		
2019–20	Blackburn R	46	16	**111**	**30**

BELL, Amari (D) **204 9**
H: 5 11 W: 12 00 b.Burton-upon-Trent 5-5-94

2012–13	Birmingham C	0	0		
2013–14	Birmingham C	1	0		
2014–15	Birmingham C	0	0	**1**	**0**
2014–15	*Swindon T*	10	0	**10**	**0**
2014–15	*Gillingham*	7	0	**7**	**0**
2015–16	Fleetwood T	44	0		
2016–17	Fleetwood T	44	2		
2017–18	Fleetwood T	27	4	**115**	**6**
2017–18	Blackburn R	12	0		
2018–19	Blackburn R	38	3		
2019–20	Blackburn R	21	0	**71**	**3**

BENNETT, Elliott (M) **421 28**
H: 5 9 W: 10 11 b.Telford 18-12-88

2006–07	Wolverhampton W	0	0		
2007–08	Wolverhampton W	0	0		
2007–08	*Crewe Alex*	9	1	**9**	**1**
2007–08	*Bury*	19	1		
2008–09	Wolverhampton W	0	0		
2008–09	*Bury*	46	3	**65**	**4**
2009–10	Wolverhampton W	0	0		
2009–10	*Brighton & HA*	43	7		
2010–11	Brighton & HA	46	6		
2011–12	Norwich C	33	1		
2012–13	Norwich C	24	1		
2013–14	Norwich C	2	0		
2014–15	Norwich C	9	0		
2014–15	*Brighton & HA*	7	0	**96**	**13**
2015–16	Norwich C	0	0	**68**	**2**
2015–16	*Bristol C*	15	0	**15**	**0**
2015–16	Blackburn R	21	2		
2016–17	Blackburn R	25	3		
2017–18	Blackburn R	41	2		
2018–19	Blackburn R	40	1		
2019–20	Blackburn R	41	0	**168**	**8**

BRERETON, Ben (F) **93 10**
b.Stoke-on-Trent 18-4-99
Internationals: England U19, U20.
From Stoke C.

2016–17	Nottingham F	18	3		
2017–18	Nottingham F	35	5	**53**	**8**
2018–19	Blackburn R	25	1		
2019–20	Blackburn R	15	1	**40**	**2**

BUCKLEY, John (M) **22 2**
b. 13-10-99

2018–19	Blackburn R	2	0		
2019–20	Blackburn R	20	2	**22**	**2**

BUTTERWORTH, Daniel (F) **1 0**
H: 5 11 W: 10 12 b.Manchester 14-9-94
From Manchester U.

2017–18	Blackburn R	0	0		
2018–19	Blackburn R	1	0		
2019–20	Blackburn R	0	0	**1**	**0**

CARTER, Hayden (D) **2 0**
b. 17-12-99

2019–20	Blackburn R	2	0	**2**	**0**

CHAPMAN, Harry (M) **42 3**
H: 5 10 W: 11 00 b.Hartlepool 5-11-97
Internationals: England U18, U20.

2015–16	Middlesbrough	0	0		
2015–16	*Barnsley*	11	1	**11**	**1**
2016–17	Middlesbrough	0	0		
2016–17	*Sheffield U*	12	1	**12**	**1**
2017–18	Middlesbrough	0	0		
2017–18	*Blackburn R*	12	1		
2018–19	Middlesbrough	0	0		
2018–19	*Blackburn R*	2	0		
2019–20	Blackburn R	5	0	**19**	**1**

DACK, Bradley (M) **266 73**
H: 5 9 b.Greenwich 31-12-93

2012–13	Gillingham	16	1		
2013–14	Gillingham	28	3		
2014–15	Gillingham	42	9		
2015–16	Gillingham	40	13		
2016–17	Gillingham	34	5	**160**	**31**
2017–18	Blackburn R	42	18		
2018–19	Blackburn R	42	15		
2019–20	Blackburn R	22	9	**106**	**42**

DAVENPORT, Jacob (M) **27 1**
b.Manchester 28-12-98

2017–18	Manchester C	0	0		
2017–18	*Burton Alb*	17	1	**17**	**1**
2018–19	Blackburn R	1	0		
2019–20	Blackburn R	9	0	**10**	**0**

DOWNING, Stewart (M) **579 50**
H: 5 11 W: 10 04 b.Middlesbrough 22-7-84
Internationals: England U21, B, Full caps.

2001–02	Middlesbrough	3	0		
2002–03	Middlesbrough	2	0		
2003–04	Middlesbrough	20	0		
2003–04	*Sunderland*	7	3	**7**	**3**
2004–05	Middlesbrough	35	5		
2005–06	Middlesbrough	12	1		
2006–07	Middlesbrough	34	2		
2007–08	Middlesbrough	38	9		
2008–09	Middlesbrough	37	0		
2009–10	Aston Villa	25	2		
2010–11	Aston Villa	38	7	**63**	**9**
2011–12	Liverpool	36	0		
2012–13	Liverpool	29	3		

2013–14 Liverpool 0 0 **65 3**
2013–14 West Ham U 32 1
2014–15 West Ham U 37 6 **69 7**
2015–16 Middlesbrough 45 3
2016–17 Middlesbrough 30 1
2017–18 Middlesbrough 40 3
2018–19 Middlesbrough 38 2 **334 26**
2019–20 Blackburn R 41 2 **41 2**

EASTHAM, Jordan (G) 0 0
b. 8-9-01
2019–20 Blackburn R 0 0

EVANS, Corry (M) 282 10
H: 5 8 W: 10 12 b.Belfast 30-7-90
Internationals: Northern Ireland U16, U17, U19, U21, B, Full caps.
2007–08 Manchester U 0 0
2008–09 Manchester U 0 0
2009–10 Manchester U 0 0
2010–11 Manchester U 0 0
2010–11 *Carlisle U* 1 0 **1 0**
2010–11 *Hull C* 18 3
2011–12 Hull C 43 2
2012–13 Hull C 32 1
2013–14 Hull C 0 0 **93 6**
2013–14 Blackburn R 21 1
2014–15 Blackburn R 38 1
2015–16 Blackburn R 30 1
2016–17 Blackburn R 19 0
2017–18 Blackburn R 32 0
2018–19 Blackburn R 35 0
2019–20 Blackburn R 13 1 **188 4**

FISHER, Andy (G) 0 0
b. 12-2-98
2016–17 Blackburn R 0 0
2017–18 Blackburn R 0 0
2018–19 Blackburn R 0 0
2019–20 Blackburn R 0 0
2019–20 *Northampton T* 0 0
2019–20 *Milton Keynes D* 0 0

GALLAGHER, Sam (F) 153 24
H: 6 4 W: 11 11 b.Crediton 15-9-95
Internationals: Scotland U19, England U19, U20.
2013–14 Southampton 18 1
2014–15 Southampton 0 0
2015–16 Southampton 0 0
2015–16 *Milton Keynes D* 13 0 **13 0**
2016–17 Southampton 0 0
2016–17 *Blackburn R* 43 11
2017–18 Southampton 0 0
2017–18 *Birmingham C* 33 6 **33 6**
2018–19 Southampton 4 0 **22 1**
2019–20 Blackburn R 42 6 **85 17**

GRAHAM, Danny (F) 544 153
H: 5 11 W: 12 05 b.Gateshead 12-8-85
Internationals: England U20.
2003–04 Middlesbrough 0 0
2003–04 *Darlington* 9 2 **9 2**
2004–05 Middlesbrough 11 1
2005–06 Middlesbrough 3 0
2005–06 *Derby Co* 14 0 **14 0**
2005–06 *Leeds U* 3 0 **3 0**
2006–07 Middlesbrough 1 0
2006–07 *Blackpool* 4 1 **4 1**
2006–07 *Carlisle U* 11 7
2007–08 Carlisle U 45 14
2008–09 Carlisle U 44 15 **100 36**
2009–10 Watford 46 14
2010–11 Watford 45 23 **91 37**
2011–12 Swansea C 36 12
2012–13 Swansea C 18 3 **54 15**
2012–13 Sunderland 13 0
2013–14 Sunderland 0 0
2013–14 *Hull C* 18 1 **18 1**
2013–14 *Middlesbrough* 18 6 **33 7**
2014–15 Sunderland 14 1
2014–15 *Wolverhampton W* 5 1 **5 1**
2015–16 Sunderland 10 0 **37 1**
2015–16 *Blackburn R* 18 7
2016–17 Blackburn R 35 12
2017–18 Blackburn R 42 14
2018–19 Blackburn R 43 15
2019–20 Blackburn R 38 4 **176 52**

GRAYSON, Joe (M) 8 2
H: 5 10 W: 11 09 b. 26-3-99
2018–19 Blackburn R 0 0
2018–19 *Grimsby T* 8 2 **8 2**
2019–20 Blackburn R 0 0

HART, Sam (D) 50 1
b. 10-9-96
2016–17 Liverpool 0 0
2016–17 *Port Vale* 11 1
2017–18 Port Vale 0 0 **11 1**
2017–18 Blackburn R 3 0
2017–18 *Rochdale* 3 0
2018–19 Blackburn R 0 0
2018–19 *Rochdale* 11 0 **14 0**
2018–19 *Southend U* 18 0 **18 0**
2019–20 Blackburn R 0 0 **3 0**
2019–20 *Shrewsbury T* 4 0 **4 0**

HOLTBY, Lewis (M) 324 43
H: 5 8 W: 10 04 b.Erkelenz 18-9-90
Internationals: Germany U18, U19, U20, U21, Full caps.
2007–08 Alemania Aachen 2 0
2008–09 Alemania Aachen 31 7 **33 7**
2009–10 Schalke 04 9 0
2009–10 *VfL Bochum* 14 2 **14 2**
2010–11 *Mainz* 30 5 **30 5**
2011–12 Schalke 04 27 6
2012–13 Schalke 04 19 4 **55 10**
2012–13 Tottenham H 11 0
2013–14 Tottenham H 13 1
2013–14 *Fulham* 13 1 **13 1**
2014–15 Tottenham H 1 0 **25 1**
2014–15 *Hamburg* 22 0
2015–16 Hamburg 34 3
2016–17 Hamburg 29 1
2017–18 Hamburg 16 6
2018–19 Hamburg 26 4 **127 14**
2019–20 Blackburn R 27 3 **27 3**

JOHNSON, Brad (M) 482 65
H: 6 0 W: 12 10 b.Hackney 28-4-87
2004–05 Cambridge U 1 0 **1 0**
2005–06 Northampton T 3 0
2006–07 Northampton T 27 5
2007–08 Northampton T 23 2 **53 7**
2007–08 Leeds U 21 3
2008–09 Leeds U 15 1
2008–09 *Brighton & HA* 10 4 **10 4**
2009–10 Leeds U 36 7
2010–11 Leeds U 45 5 **117 16**
2011–12 Norwich C 28 2
2012–13 Norwich C 37 1
2013–14 Norwich C 32 3
2014–15 Norwich C 41 15
2015–16 Norwich C 4 0 **142 21**
2015–16 Derby Co 31 5
2016–17 Derby Co 33 3
2017–18 Derby Co 33 4
2018–19 Derby Co 28 2 **125 14**
2019–20 Blackburn R 34 3 **34 3**

LENIHAN, Darragh (M) 168 7
H: 5 10 W: 12 00 b.Dublin 16-3-94
Internationals: Republic of Ireland U17, U19, U21, Full caps.
2011–12 Blackburn R 0 0
2012–13 Blackburn R 0 0
2013–14 Blackburn R 0 0
2014–15 Blackburn R 3 0
2014–15 *Burton Alb* 17 1 **17 1**
2015–16 Blackburn R 23 0
2016–17 Blackburn R 40 0
2017–18 Blackburn R 14 1
2018–19 Blackburn R 34 2
2019–20 Blackburn R 37 3 **151 6**

LEUTWILER, Jayson (G) 127 0
H: 6 3 W: 12 07 b.Basel 25-4-89
Internationals: Switzerland U16, U17, U18, U19, U20, U21. Canada Full caps.
2012–13 Middlesbrough 0 0
2013–14 Middlesbrough 3 0 **3 0**
2014–15 Shrewsbury T 46 0
2015–16 Shrewsbury T 29 0
2016–17 Shrewsbury T 43 0 **118 0**
2017–18 Blackburn R 1 0
2018–19 Blackburn R 5 0
2019–20 Blackburn R 0 0 **6 0**

MAGLIORE, Tyler (D) 4 0
b. 21-12-98
2018–19 Blackburn R 2 0
2019–20 Blackburn R 0 0 **2 0**
2019–20 *Rochdale* 2 0 **2 0**

MOLS, Stefan (M) 0 0
H: 5 11 W: 11 11 b. 31-1-99
2017–18 Blackburn R 0 0
2018–19 Blackburn R 0 0
2019–20 Blackburn R 0 0

MULGREW, Charlie (D) 353 59
H: 6 3 W: 13 01 b.Glasgow 6-3-86
Internationals: Scotland U21, Full caps.
2002–03 Celtic 0 0
2003–04 Celtic 0 0
2004–05 Celtic 0 0
2005–06 Celtic 0 0
2005–06 *Dundee U* 13 2 **13 2**
2006–07 Wolverhampton W 6 0
2007–08 *Southend U* 18 1 **18 1**
2007–08 Wolverhampton W 0 0 **6 0**
2008–09 Aberdeen 35 5
2009–10 Aberdeen 37 4 **72 9**
2010–11 Celtic 23 0
2011–12 Celtic 30 8
2012–13 Celtic 30 5
2013–14 Celtic 28 6
2014–15 Celtic 10 0
2015–16 Celtic 11 1 **132 20**
2016–17 Blackburn R 28 3
2017–18 Blackburn R 41 14
2018–19 Blackburn R 29 10
2019–20 Blackburn R 2 0 **100 27**
2019–20 *Wigan Ath* 12 0 **12 0**

NYAMBE, Ryan (D) 114 0
H: 6 0 W: 12 00 b.Katima Mulilo 4-12-97
Internationals: Namibia Full caps.
2014–15 Blackburn R 0 0
2015–16 Blackburn R 0 0
2016–17 Blackburn R 25 0
2017–18 Blackburn R 29 0
2018–19 Blackburn R 29 0
2019–20 Blackburn R 31 0 **114 0**

PLATT, Matt (D) 0 0
b. 3-10-97
2016–17 Blackburn R 0 0
2017–18 Blackburn R 0 0
2018–19 Blackburn R 0 0
2018–19 *Accrington S* 0 0
2019–20 Blackburn R 0 0

RANKIN-COSTELLO, Joe (M) 11 0
H: 5 10 W: 11 00 b.Stockport 26-7-99
From Manchester U.
2017–18 Blackburn R 0 0
2018–19 Blackburn R 0 0
2019–20 Blackburn R 11 0 **11 0**

ROTHWELL, Joe (M) 145 10
H: 6 1 W: 12 02 b.Manchester 11-1-95
Internationals: England U16, U17, U19, U20.
2014–15 Manchester U 0 0
2014–15 *Blackpool* 3 0 **3 0**
2015–16 Manchester U 0 0
2015–16 *Barnsley* 4 0 **4 0**
2016–17 Oxford U 33 1
2017–18 Oxford U 36 5 **69 6**
2018–19 Blackburn R 33 2
2019–20 Blackburn R 36 2 **69 4**

SAMUEL, Dominic (F) 111 22
H: 6 0 W: 14 00 b.Southwark 1-4-94
Internationals: England U19.
2011–12 Reading 0 0
2012–13 Reading 1 0
2012–13 *Colchester U* 2 0 **2 0**
2013–14 Reading 0 0
2013–14 *Dagenham & R* 1 0 **1 0**
2014–15 Reading 0 0
2014–15 *Coventry C* 13 6 **13 6**
2015–16 Reading 1 0
2015–16 *Gillingham* 25 7 **25 7**
2016–17 Reading 9 2 **11 2**
2016–17 *Ipswich T* 6 0 **6 0**
2017–18 Blackburn R 36 5
2018–19 Blackburn R 2 0
2019–20 Blackburn R 15 2 **53 7**

SMALLWOOD, Richard (M) 282 9
H: 5 11 W: 11 05 b.Redcar 29-12-90
Internationals: England U18.
2008–09 Middlesbrough 0 0
2009–10 Middlesbrough 0 0
2010–11 Middlesbrough 13 1
2011–12 Middlesbrough 13 0
2012–13 Middlesbrough 22 2
2013–14 Middlesbrough 13 0
2013–14 *Rotherham U* 18 0
2014–15 Middlesbrough 0 0 **61 3**
2014–15 *Rotherham U* 41 1
2015–16 Rotherham U 43 1
2016–17 *Scunthorpe U* 16 1 **16 1**
2016–17 Rotherham U 25 1 **127 3**
2017–18 Blackburn R 46 2
2018–19 Blackburn R 32 0
2019–20 Blackburn R 0 0 **78 2**

TRAVIS, Lewis (D) 74 3
b. 16-10-97
2016–17 Blackburn R 0 0
2017–18 Blackburn R 5 0
2018–19 Blackburn R 26 1
2019–20 Blackburn R 43 2 **74 3**

VALE, Jack (F) 1 0
b. 3-3-01
Internationals: Wales U17, U19, U21.
2019–20 Blackburn R 1 0 **1 0**

WHARTON, Scott (D) **83** **9**
b.Blackburn 3-10-97

2015–16	Blackburn R	0	0		
2016–17	Blackburn R	2	0		
2016–17	*Cambridge U*	9	1	**9**	**1**
2017–18	Blackburn R	0	0		
2017–18	*Lincoln C*	14	2		
2018–19	Blackburn R	0	0		
2018–19	*Lincoln C*	11	1	**25**	**3**
2018–19	*Bury*	15	2	**15**	**2**
2019–20	Blackburn R	0	0	**2**	**0**
2019–20	*Northampton T*	32	3	**32**	**3**

WILLIAMS, Derrick (D) **240** **9**
H: 5 11 W: 11 11 b.Waterford 17-1-93
Internationals: Republic of Ireland U19, U21, Full caps.

2009–10	Aston Villa	0	0		
2010–11	Aston Villa	0	0		
2011–12	Aston Villa	0	0		
2012–13	Aston Villa	1	0	**1**	**0**
2013–14	Bristol C	43	1		
2014–15	Bristol C	44	2		
2015–16	Bristol C	24	1	**111**	**4**
2016–17	Blackburn R	39	1		
2017–18	Blackburn R	45	1		
2018–19	Blackburn R	27	0		
2019–20	Blackburn R	17	3	**128**	**5**

Players retained or with offer of contract
Annesley, Louie John; Barnes, Samuel Peter; Burns, Samuel Gordon; Durrant, Samuel Joseph David; Garrett, Jake Joseph; Lyons, Brad Joseph; Paton, Benjamin Alan; Pike, Daniel Christopher; Saadi, Jalil; Thompson, Lewis; White, Thomas Alan; Whitehall, Isaac Ben.

Scholars
Baker, Alexander John William; Boyomo, Flavien Enzo Thiedort; Brennan, Luke; Cirino, Lenni Rae Rowan; Connolly, James Alfred; Dowling, Aidan Paul Harvey; Ferguson, Joseph Martua; Gilsenan, Zak Thomas; Harlock, Jared Alan; Lonsdale, Brandon Lee James; Pleavin, Ben Spencer; Wyatt, George Ray; Zimba, Chanka Solomon.

BLACKPOOL (8)

ALNWICK, Jak (G) **143** **0**
H: 6 2 W: 12 13 b.Hexham 17-6-93
Internationals: England U17, U18, U19, U20.

2010–11	Newcastle U	0	0		
2011–12	Newcastle U	0	0		
2012–13	Newcastle U	0	0		
2013–14	Newcastle U	0	0		
2014–15	Newcastle U	6	0	**6**	**0**
2014–15	*Bradford C*	1	0	**1**	**0**
2015–16	Port Vale	41	0		
2016–17	Port Vale	26	0	**67**	**0**
2016–17	Rangers	1	0		
2017–18	Rangers	5	0		
2018–19	Rangers	0	0		
2018–19	*Scunthorpe U*	41	0	**41**	**0**
2019–20	Rangers	0	0	**6**	**0**

On loan from Rangers.

2019–20	Blackpool	22	0	**22**	**0**

BANGE, Ewan (M) **0** **0**

2019–20	Blackpool	0	0		

BONEY, Myles (G) **2** **0**
H: 5 11 W: 11 09 b.Blackpool 1-2-98

2014–15	Blackpool	0	0		
2015–16	Blackpool	0	0		
2016–17	Blackpool	1	0		
2017–18	Blackpool	0	0		
2018–19	Blackpool	1	0		
2019–20	Blackpool	0	0	**2**	**0**

DELFOUNESO, Nathan (F) **311** **41**
H: 6 1 W: 12 04 b.Birmingham 2-2-91
Internationals: England U16, U17, U19, U21.

2007–08	Aston Villa	0	0		
2008–09	Aston Villa	4	0		
2009–10	Aston Villa	9	1		
2010–11	Aston Villa	11	1		
2010–11	*Burnley*	11	1	**11**	**1**
2011–12	Aston Villa	6	0		
2011–12	*Leicester C*	4	0	**4**	**0**
2012–13	Aston Villa	1	0		
2012–13	*Blackpool*	40	6		
2013–14	Aston Villa	0	0	**31**	**2**
2013–14	*Blackpool*	11	0		
2013–14	*Coventry C*	14	3	**14**	**3**
2014–15	Blackpool	38	3		
2015–16	Blackburn R	15	1	**15**	**1**
2015–16	*Bury*	4	0	**4**	**0**
2016–17	Swindon T	18	1	**18**	**1**
2016–17	Blackpool	18	5		
2017–18	Blackpool	40	9		
2018–19	Blackpool	39	7		
2019–20	Blackpool	28	3	**214**	**33**

DEVITT, Jamie (F) **281** **43**
H: 5 10 W: 10 05 b.Dublin 6-7-90
Internationals: Republic of Ireland U21.

2007–08	Hull C	0	0		
2008–09	Hull C	0	0		
2009–10	Hull C	0	0		
2009–10	*Darlington*	6	1	**6**	**1**
2009–10	*Shrewsbury T*	9	2	**9**	**2**
2009–10	*Grimsby T*	15	5	**15**	**5**
2010–11	Hull C	16	0		
2011–12	Hull C	0	0		
2011–12	*Bradford C*	7	1		
2011–12	*Accrington S*	16	2	**16**	**2**
2012–13	Hull C	0	0	**16**	**0**
2012–13	*Rotherham U*	1	0	**1**	**0**
2013–14	Chesterfield	7	0	**7**	**0**
2013–14	*Morecambe*	14	2		
2014–15	Morecambe	36	3		
2015–16	Morecambe	39	6	**89**	**11**
2016–17	Carlisle U	35	0		
2017–18	Carlisle U	40	10		
2018–19	Carlisle U	35	11	**110**	**21**
2019–20	Blackpool	0	0		
2019–20	*Bradford C*	5	0	**12**	**1**

EDWARDS, Ryan (D) **242** **10**
b.Liverpool 7-10-93

2011–12	Blackburn R	0	0		
2012–13	Rochdale	26	0	**26**	**0**
2012–13	Blackburn R	0	0		
2012–13	*Fleetwood T*	9	0	**9**	**0**
2013–14	Blackburn R	0	0		
2013–14	*Chesterfield*	5	0	**5**	**0**
2013–14	*Tranmere R*	0	0		
2013–14	*Morecambe*	9	0		
2014–15	Morecambe	31	0		
2015–16	Morecambe	37	0		
2016–17	Morecambe	43	1	**120**	**1**
2017–18	Plymouth Arg	25	3		
2018–19	Plymouth Arg	36	5	**61**	**8**
2019–20	Blackpool	21	1	**21**	**1**

FEENEY, Liam (M) **399** **27**
H: 5 10 W: 12 02 b.Hammersmith 21-1-87

2008–09	Southend U	1	0	**1**	**0**
2008–09	Bournemouth	14	3		
2009–10	Bournemouth	44	5		
2010–11	Bournemouth	46	4		
2011–12	Bournemouth	5	0	**109**	**12**
2011–12	Millwall	34	4		
2012–13	Millwall	22	1		
2013–14	Millwall	17	0	**73**	**5**
2013–14	*Bolton W*	4	0		
2013–14	*Blackburn R*	6	0		
2014–15	Bolton W	41	3		
2015–16	Bolton W	37	5	**82**	**8**
2015–16	*Ipswich T*	9	1	**9**	**1**
2016–17	Blackburn R	34	0		
2017–18	Blackburn R	1	0	**41**	**0**
2017–18	*Cardiff C*	15	0	**15**	**0**
2018–19	Blackpool	34	0		
2019–20	Blackpool	35	1	**69**	**1**

GARRITY, Ben (M) **0** **0**
From Warrington T.

2019–20	Blackpool	0	0		

GNANDUILLET, Armand (F) **240** **53**
H: 6 4 W: 13 12 b.Angers 13-2-92
Internationals: Ivory Coast U20.

2012–13	Chesterfield	13	3		
2013–14	Chesterfield	34	5		
2014–15	Chesterfield	26	2		
2014–15	*Tranmere R*	4	2	**4**	**2**
2014–15	*Oxford U*	4	0	**4**	**0**
2015–16	Chesterfield	9	0	**82**	**10**
2015–16	*Stevenage*	14	5	**14**	**5**
2015–16	Leyton Orient	17	4		
2016–17	Leyton Orient	1	0	**18**	**4**
2016–17	Blackpool	19	3		
2017–18	Blackpool	26	4		
2018–19	Blackpool	43	10		
2019–20	Blackpool	30	15	**118**	**32**

HAMILTON, CJ (M) **142** **15**
H: 5 7 W: 11 09 b.Harrow 23-3-95

2015–16	Sheffield U	0	0		
2016–17	Mansfield T	29	0		
2017–18	Mansfield T	33	2		
2018–19	Mansfield T	46	11		
2019–20	Mansfield T	34	2	**142**	**15**
2019–20	Blackpool	0	0		

HARDIE, Ryan (F) **114** **39**
b.Stranraer 4-3-97
Internationals: Scotland U16, U17, U19, U20, U21.

2014–15	Rangers	5	2		
2015–16	Rangers	1	0		
2015–16	*Raith R*	10	6		
2016–17	Rangers	0	0		
2016–17	*St Mirren*	16	3	**16**	**3**
2016–17	*Raith R*	18	6	**28**	**12**
2017–18	Rangers	7	0		
2017–18	*Livingston*	16	8		
2018–19	Rangers	0	0	**13**	**2**
2018–19	Livingston	21	7	**37**	**15**
2019–20	Blackpool	7	0	**7**	**0**
2019–20	*Plymouth Arg*	13	7	**13**	**7**

HOWARD, Mark (G) **220** **0**
H: 6 0 W: 11 13 b.Southwark 21-9-86

2005–06	Falkirk	8	0	**8**	**0**
2006–07	Cardiff C	0	0		
2006–07	Swansea C	0	0		
2007–08	St Mirren	10	0		
2008–09	St Mirren	33	0		
2009–10	St Mirren	2	0	**45**	**0**
2010–11	Aberdeen	9	0	**9**	**0**
2011–12	Blackpool	4	0		
2011–12	Sheffield U	0	0		
2012–13	Sheffield U	11	0		
2013–14	Sheffield U	19	0		
2014–15	Sheffield U	35	0		
2015–16	Sheffield U	15	0	**80**	**0**
2016–17	Bolton W	27	0		
2017–18	Bolton W	8	0	**35**	**0**
2018–19	Blackpool	32	0		
2019–20	*Salford C*	3	0	**3**	**0**
2019–20	Blackpool	4	0	**40**	**0**

HOWE, Teddy (D) **1** **0**
b. 9-10-98

2018–19	Reading	1	0		
2019–20	Reading	0	0	**1**	**0**
2019–20	Blackpool	0	0		

HUSBAND, James (D) **176** **5**
H: 5 10 W: 10 00 b.Leeds 3-1-94

2011–12	Doncaster R	3	0		
2012–13	Doncaster R	33	3		
2013–14	Doncaster R	28	1	**64**	**4**
2014–15	Middlesbrough	3	0		
2014–15	*Fulham*	5	0		
2015–16	Middlesbrough	0	0		
2015–16	*Fulham*	12	0	**17**	**0**
2015–16	*Huddersfield T*	11	0	**11**	**0**
2016–17	Middlesbrough	1	0	**4**	**0**
2017–18	Norwich C	18	0		
2018–19	Norwich C	1	0	**19**	**0**
2018–19	*Fleetwood T*	33	1	**33**	**1**
2019–20	Blackpool	28	0	**28**	**0**

KAIKAI, Sullay (F) **113** **24**
H: 6 0 W: 11 07 b.London 26-8-95

2013–14	Crystal Palace	0	0		
2013–14	*Crawley T*	5	0	**5**	**0**
2014–15	Crystal Palace	0	0		
2014–15	*Cambridge U*	25	5	**25**	**5**
2015–16	Crystal Palace	1	0		
2015–16	*Shrewsbury T*	26	12	**26**	**12**
2016–17	Brentford	18	3	**18**	**3**
2016–17	Crystal Palace	1	0		
2017–18	Crystal Palace	1	0		
2017–18	*Charlton Ath*	14	0	**14**	**0**
2018–19	Crystal Palace	0	0	**3**	**0**
2019–20	Blackpool	22	4	**22**	**4**

Transferred to NAC Breda January 2019.

MACDONALD, Calum (D) **12** **0**
Internationals: Scotland U21.

2016–17	Derby Co	0	0		
2017–18	Derby Co	0	0		
2018–19	Derby Co	0	0		
2019–20	Derby Co	0	0		
2019–20	Blackpool	12	0	**12**	**0**

MADINE, Gary (F) **362** **76**
H: 6 1 W: 12 00 b.Gateshead 24-8-90

2007–08	Carlisle U	11	0		
2008–09	Carlisle U	14	1		
2008–09	*Rochdale*	3	0	**3**	**0**
2009–10	Carlisle U	20	4		
2009–10	*Coventry C*	9	0		
2009–10	*Chesterfield*	4	0	**4**	**0**
2010–11	Carlisle U	21	8		
2010–11	Sheffield W	22	5		
2011–12	Sheffield W	38	18		
2012–13	Sheffield W	30	3		

2013–14	Sheffield W	1	0		
2013–14	*Carlisle U*	5	2	**71**	**15**
2014–15	Sheffield W	10	0	**101**	**26**
2014–15	*Coventry C*	11	3	**20**	**3**
2014–15	*Blackpool*	15	3		
2015–16	Bolton W	32	5		
2016–17	Bolton W	36	9		
2017–18	Bolton W	28	10	**96**	**24**
2017–18	Cardiff C	13	0		
2018–19	Cardiff C	5	0		
2018–19	*Sheffield U*	16	3	**16**	**3**
2019–20	Cardiff C	8	0	**26**	**0**
2019–20	Blackpool	10	2	**25**	**5**

MAFOUMBI, Christoffer (G) **46** **0**
H: 6 5 W: 12 08 b. 3-3-94
Internationals: Congo Full caps.

2011–12	Lens	0	0		
2012–13	Lens	0	0		
2013–14	Lens	0	0		
2014–15	Le Ponet	12	0	**12**	**0**
2015–16	Vereya Stara Zagora	3	0	**3**	**0**
2016–17	Free State Stars	4	0	**4**	**0**
2017–18	Blackpool	4	0		
2018–19	Blackpool	14	0		
2019–20	Blackpool	0	0	**18**	**0**
2019–20	*Morecambe*	9	0	**9**	**0**

MAXWELL, Chris (G) **195** **0**
H: 6 0 W: 11 07 b.Wrexham 30-7-90
Internationals: Wales U17, U19, U21, U23.

2012–13	Fleetwood T	0	0		
2013–14	Fleetwood T	18	0		
2014–15	Fleetwood T	46	0		
2015–16	Fleetwood T	46	0	**110**	**0**
2016–17	Preston NE	38	0		
2017–18	Preston NE	30	0		
2018–19	Preston NE	8	0		
2018–19	*Charlton Ath*	0	0		
2019–20	Preston NE	0	0	**76**	**0**
2019–20	*Hibernian*	0	0		
2019–20	Blackpool	9	0	**9**	**0**

NOTTINGHAM, Michael (D) **44** **3**
b.Birmingham 14-4-89
Internationals: Saint Kitts and Nevis Full caps.
From Gresley, Solihull Moors, Salford C.

2018–19	Blackpool	29	2		
2019–20	Blackpool	3	0	**32**	**2**
2019–20	*Crewe Alex*	12	1	**12**	**1**

NUTTALL, Joe (F) **68** **8**
H: 6 0 W: 11 05 b.Bury 27-1-97

2015–16	Aberdeen	2	0		
2016–17	Aberdeen	0	0	**2**	**0**
2016–17	*Stranraer*	9	2	**9**	**2**
2016–17	*Dumbarton*	2	0	**2**	**0**
2017–18	Blackburn R	13	2		
2018–19	Blackburn R	15	2	**28**	**4**
2019–20	Blackpool	27	2	**27**	**2**

SARKIC, Oliver (F) **58** **6**

2014–15	Benfica	0	0		
2015–16	Benfica	0	0		
2016–17	Benfica	0	0		
2016–17	*Fafe*	18	2	**18**	**2**
2017–18	Benfica	0	0		
2018–19	Leeds U	0	0		
2018–19	*Barakaldo*	12	1	**12**	**1**
2019–20	Burton Alb	28	3	**28**	**3**
2019–20	Blackpool	0	0		

SCANNELL, Sean (F) **335** **22**
H: 5 9 W: 11 07 b.Croydon 19-9-90
Internationals: Republic of Ireland U17, U18, U19, U21, B.

2007–08	Crystal Palace	23	2		
2008–09	Crystal Palace	25	2		
2009–10	Crystal Palace	26	2		
2010–11	Crystal Palace	19	2		
2011–12	Crystal Palace	37	4	**130**	**12**
2012–13	Huddersfield T	34	2		
2013–14	Huddersfield T	38	1		
2014–15	Huddersfield T	42	4		
2015–16	Huddersfield T	29	1		
2016–17	Huddersfield T	15	0		
2017–18	Burton Alb	18	0	**18**	**0**
2017–18	Huddersfield T	0	0	**158**	**8**
2018–19	Bradford C	16	0		
2019–20	Bradford C	5	1	**21**	**1**
2019–20	Blackpool	8	1	**8**	**1**

SHAW, Nathan (M) **0** **0**

2018–19	Blackpool	0	0		
2019–20	Blackpool	0	0		

SIMS, Jack (G) **1** **0**
H: 6 2 W: 11 07 b.Southend-on-Sea 10-3-00

2018–19	Blackpool	0	0		
2019–20	Blackpool	1	0	**1**	**0**

SPEARING, Jay (M) **319** **18**
H: 5 6 W: 11 01 b.Wallasey 25-11-88

2006–07	Liverpool	0	0		
2007–08	Liverpool	0	0		
2008–09	Liverpool	0	0		
2009–10	Liverpool	3	0		
2009–10	*Leicester C*	7	1	**7**	**1**
2010–11	Liverpool	11	0		
2011–12	Liverpool	16	0		
2012–13	Liverpool	0	0		
2012–13	*Bolton W*	37	2		
2013–14	Liverpool	0	0	**30**	**0**
2013–14	Bolton W	45	2		
2014–15	Bolton W	21	1		
2014–15	*Blackburn R*	15	1	**15**	**1**
2015–16	Bolton W	22	2		
2016–17	Bolton W	37	3		
2017–18	Bolton W	0	0	**162**	**10**
2017–18	Blackpool	33	0		
2018–19	Blackpool	42	4		
2019–20	Blackpool	30	2	**105**	**6**

THORNILEY, Jordan (D) **47** **0**
b.Warrington 24-11-96
From Everton.

2016–17	Sheffield W	0	0		
2017–18	Sheffield W	11	0		
2017–18	*Accrington S*	14	0	**14**	**0**
2018–19	Sheffield W	20	0		
2019–20	Sheffield W	0	0	**31**	**0**
2019–20	Blackpool	2	0	**2**	**0**

TURTON, Oliver (D) **273** **6**
H: 5 11 W: 11 11 b.Manchester 6-12-92

2010–11	Crewe Alex	1	0		
2011–12	Crewe Alex	2	0		
2012–13	Crewe Alex	20	0		
2013–14	Crewe Alex	12	1		
2014–15	Crewe Alex	44	1		
2015–16	Crewe Alex	46	1		
2016–17	Crewe Alex	45	1	**170**	**4**
2017–18	Blackpool	41	1		
2018–19	Blackpool	32	1		
2019–20	Blackpool	30	0	**103**	**2**

VIRTUE, Matthew (M) **50** **5**
b.Epsom 2-5-97

2017–18	Liverpool	0	0		
2017–18	*Notts Co*	13	0	**13**	**0**
2018–19	Blackpool	13	3		
2019–20	Blackpool	24	2	**37**	**5**

WARD, Grant (M) **173** **11**
H: 5 10 W: 11 07 b.Lewisham 5-12-94

2013–14	Tottenham H	0	0		
2014	*Chicago Fire*	23	1	**23**	**1**
2014–15	Tottenham H	0	0		
2014–15	*Coventry C*	11	0	**11**	**0**
2015–16	Tottenham H	0	0		
2015–16	*Rotherham U*	40	2	**40**	**2**
2016–17	Ipswich T	43	6		
2017–18	Ipswich T	37	2		
2018–19	Ipswich T	14	0	**94**	**8**
2019–20	Blackpool	5	0	**5**	**0**

WESTON, Tony (F) **0** **0**
b. 17-9-03

2019–20	Blackpool	0	0		

YUSSUF, Abdi (F) **78** **10**
H: 6 1 W: 11 13 b.Zanzibar 3-10-92
Internationals: Tanzania Full caps.

2010–11	Leicester C	0	0		
2011–12	Burton Alb	17	1		
2012–13	Burton Alb	8	0	**25**	**1**

From Lincoln C, Oxford C.

2015–16	Mansfield T	26	5	**26**	**5**
2016–17	Crawley T	16	2	**16**	**2**
2016–17	Grimsby T	11	2	**11**	**2**

From Barrow, Solihull Moors.

2019–20	Blackpool	0	0		

Scholars
Adarkwa, Nana Kwabena Sarpong; Antwi, Cameron Akwasi; Apter, Robert Julian; Bange, Ewan; Beaumont, Tyrese; Goumou, Perez Julius Oluwaseyi; Kellett, Samuel Robert; Liptrott, Matthew Benjamin; Mandjoba, Andy Kanga Shalom; McGladdery, William; Monks, Charles George; Ravenscroft, Hayden James Joseph; Rogers, Max; Sinclair, Sky; Smith, Ryley; Turner, Aaron Harry; Wilson, Ellis; Winstanley, Harry George; Wood, Jak Daniel.

BOLTON W (9)

ALEXANDER, Matthew (G) **1** **0**

2019–20	Bolton W	1	0	**1**	**0**

ALNWICK, Ben (G) **239** **0**
H: 6 2 W: 13 12 b.Prudhoe 1-1-87
Internationals: England U16, U17, U18, U19, U21.

2003–04	Sunderland	0	0		
2004–05	Sunderland	3	0		
2005–06	Sunderland	5	0		
2006–07	Sunderland	11	0	**19**	**0**
2006–07	Tottenham H	0	0		
2007–08	Tottenham H	0	0		
2007–08	*Luton T*	4	0	**4**	**0**
2007–08	*Leicester C*	8	0	**8**	**0**
2008–09	Tottenham H	0	0		
2008–09	*Carlisle U*	6	0	**6**	**0**
2009–10	Tottenham H	1	0		
2009–10	*Norwich C*	3	0	**3**	**0**
2010–11	Tottenham H	0	0		
2010–11	*Leeds U*	0	0		
2010–11	*Doncaster R*	0	0		
2011–12	Tottenham H	0	0		
2011–12	*Leyton Orient*	6	0		
2012–13	Tottenham H	0	0	**1**	**0**
2012–13	Barnsley	10	0		
2013–14	Barnsley	0	0	**10**	**0**
2013–14	Charlton Ath	10	0	**10**	**0**
2013–14	Leyton Orient	1	0	**7**	**0**
2014–15	Peterborough U	41	0		
2015–16	Peterborough U	39	0		
2016–17	Peterborough U	4	0	**84**	**0**
2016–17	Bolton W	21	0		
2017–18	Bolton W	39	0		
2018–19	Bolton W	27	0		
2019–20	Bolton W	0	0	**87**	**0**

BOON, Jordan (D) **3** **0**

2018–19	Bolton W	0	0		
2019–20	Bolton W	3	0	**3**	**0**

Transferred to Ostersund, March 2020.

BROCKBANK, Harry (F) **9** **0**
H: 5 11 W: 12 08 b.Bolton 26-9-98

2017–18	Bolton W	0	0		
2018–19	Bolton W	3	0		
2019–20	Bolton W	6	0	**9**	**0**

BROWN, Eddie (F) **5** **0**

2019–20	Bolton W	5	0	**5**	**0**

BROWN-STERLING, De'Marlio (M) **2** **0**
b. 12-9-01

2019–20	Bolton W	2	0	**2**	**0**

BUCKLEY, Will (F) **303** **44**
H: 6 0 W: 13 00 b.Oldham 12-8-88

2007–08	Rochdale	7	0		
2008–09	Rochdale	37	10		
2009–10	Rochdale	15	3	**59**	**13**
2009–10	Watford	6	1		
2010–11	Watford	33	4	**39**	**5**
2011–12	Brighton & HA	29	8		
2012–13	Brighton & HA	36	8		
2013–14	Brighton & HA	30	3		
2014–15	Brighton & HA	1	0	**96**	**19**
2014–15	Sunderland	22	0		
2015–16	Sunderland	0	0		
2015–16	*Leeds U*	4	0	**4**	**0**
2015–16	*Birmingham C*	10	1	**10**	**1**
2016–17	Sunderland	0	0	**22**	**0**
2016–17	*Sheffield W*	11	0	**11**	**0**
2017–18	Bolton W	24	2		
2018–19	Bolton W	33	4		
2019–20	Bolton W	5	0	**62**	**6**

BUNNEY, Joe (F) **161** **16**
H: 6 1 W: 11 00 b.Manchester 26-9-93

2012–13	Rochdale	1	1		
2013–14	Rochdale	21	3		
2014–15	Rochdale	19	2		
2015–16	Rochdale	32	9		
2016–17	Rochdale	29	1		
2017–18	Rochdale	20	0		
2017–18	Northampton T	12	0		
2018–19	Northampton T	0	0		
2018–19	*Blackpool*	5	0	**5**	**0**
2018–19	*Rochdale*	16	0	**138**	**16**
2019–20	Northampton T	4	0	**16**	**0**
2019–20	Bolton W	2	0	**2**	**0**

CHICKSEN, Adam (D) **194** **3**
H: 5 8 W: 11 09 b.Milton Keynes 27-9-91
Internationals: Zimbabwe Full caps.

2008–09	Milton Keynes D	1	0		
2009–10	Milton Keynes D	6	0		

2010–11 Milton Keynes D 14 0
2011–12 Milton Keynes D 20 0
2011–12 *Leyton Orient* 3 0
2012–13 Milton Keynes D 32 2
2013–14 Milton Keynes D 0 0 **73 2**
2013–14 Brighton & HA 1 0
2014–15 Brighton & HA 5 0
2014–15 *Gillingham* 3 0
2014–15 *Fleetwood T* 13 0 **13 0**
2015–16 Brighton & HA 1 0 **7 0**
2015–16 *Leyton Orient* 6 0 **9 0**
2015–16 *Gillingham* 6 0 **9 0**
2016–17 Charlton Ath 21 1 **21 1**
2017–18 Bradford C 18 0
2018–19 Bradford C 28 0 **46 0**
2019–20 Bolton W 16 0 **16 0**

CRAWFORD, Ali (M) 275 34
H: 5 7 W: 9 09 b.Lanark 30-7-91
2009–10 Hamilton A 7 0
2010–11 Hamilton A 14 0
2011–12 Hamilton A 19 2
2012–13 Hamilton A 33 3
2013–14 Hamilton A 36 2
2014–15 Hamilton A 38 10
2015–16 Hamilton A 33 5
2016–17 Hamilton A 33 8
2017–18 Hamilton A 14 1 **227 31**
2018–19 Doncaster R 35 3
2019–20 Doncaster R 1 0 **36 3**
2019–20 Bolton W 12 0 **12 0**

DARCY, Ronan (M) 20 1
b. 20-8-00
2018–19 Bolton W 1 0
2019–20 Bolton W 19 1 **20 1**

DELANEY, Ryan (D) 96 11
H: 6 0 W: 11 05 b.Wexford 6-9-96
Internationals: Republic of Ireland U21.
From Wexford.
2016–17 Burton Alb 0 0
2017 *Cork C* 30 6 **30 6**
2017–18 Rochdale 18 2
2018–19 Rochdale 30 1
2019–20 AFC Wimbledon 14 1 **14 1**
2019–20 Rochdale 0 0 **48 3**
2019–20 Bolton W 4 1 **4 1**

DODOO, Joseph (F) 72 11
H: 6 0 W: 12 08 b.Nottingham 6-1-95
Internationals: England U18.
2013–14 Leicester C 0 0
2014–15 Leicester C 0 0
2015–16 Leicester C 1 0 **1 0**
2015–16 *Bury* 4 1 **4 1**
2016–17 Rangers 20 3
2017–18 Rangers 0 0
2017–18 *Charlton Ath* 5 1 **5 1**
2018–19 Rangers 0 0 **20 3**
On loan from Rangers.
2018–19 Blackpool 18 2 **18 2**
2019–20 Bolton W 24 4 **24 4**

EDMONDSON, Myles (D) 0 0
2019–20 Bolton W 0 0

EDWARDS, Liam (D) 6 0
b. 2-10-96
From Stoke C.
2018–19 Birmingham C 0 0
2019–20 Bolton W 6 0 **6 0**

EMMANUEL, Josh (D) 97 0
H: 5 11 W: 11 00 b.London 18-8-97
2015–16 Ipswich T 4 0
2015–16 *Crawley T* 2 0 **2 0**
2016–17 Ipswich T 15 0
2017–18 Ipswich T 0 0
2017–18 *Rotherham U* 31 0 **31 0**
2018–19 Ipswich T 4 0
2018–19 *Shrewsbury T* 14 0 **14 0**
2019–20 Ipswich T 0 0 **23 0**
2019–20 Bolton W 27 0 **27 0**

FAAL, Muhammadu (F) 2 0
b.London 1-7-97
From L'Aquilla, Waltham Forest, Dulwich Hamlet, Kingstonian, Enfield T.
2019–20 Bolton W 2 0 **2 0**

FITZMARTIN, Jay (M) 0 0
2019–20 Bolton W 0 0

GRAHAM, Sonny (M) 13 0
2019–20 Bolton W 13 0 **13 0**

HALL, Connor (F) 14 0
H: 5 11 W: 12 02 b.Slough 18-2-98
2017–18 Bolton W 0 0
2018–19 Bolton W 0 0
2018–19 *Accrington S* 13 0 **13 0**
2019–20 Bolton W 1 0 **1 0**

HOBBS, Jack (D) 312 6
H: 6 3 W: 13 05 b.Portsmouth 18-8-88
Internationals: England U19.
2004–05 Lincoln C 1 0 **1 0**
2005–06 Liverpool 0 0
2006–07 Liverpool 0 0
2007–08 Liverpool 2 0
2007–08 *Scunthorpe U* 9 1 **9 1**
2008–09 Liverpool 0 0 **2 0**
2008–09 Leicester C 44 1
2009–10 Leicester C 44 0
2010–11 Leicester C 26 0 **114 1**
2010–11 *Hull C* 13 0
2011–12 Hull C 40 1
2012–13 Hull C 22 0 **75 1**
2013–14 Nottingham F 27 1
2014–15 Nottingham F 17 0
2015–16 Nottingham F 20 0
2016–17 Nottingham F 9 0
2017–18 Nottingham F 2 0 **75 1**
2018–19 Bolton W 25 1
2019–20 Bolton W 11 1 **36 2**

HURFORD-LOCKETT, Finlay (M) 2 0
2019–20 Bolton W 2 0 **2 0**

HUTCHINSON, Luke (G) 0 0
2019–20 Bolton W 0 0

KING-HARMES, Callum (M) 5 0
Internationals: Wales U16.
From Wolverhampton W.
2019–20 Bolton W 5 0 **5 0**

MATTHEWS, Remi (G) 105 0
H: 6 0 W: 12 04 b.Gorleston 10-2-94
2014–15 Norwich C 0 0
2014–15 *Burton Alb* 0 0
2015–16 Norwich C 0 0
2015–16 *Burton Alb* 2 0 **2 0**
2015–16 *Doncaster R* 9 0 **9 0**
2016–17 Norwich C 0 0
2016–17 *Hamilton A* 17 0 **17 0**
2017–18 Norwich C 0 0
2017–18 *Plymouth Arg* 26 0 **26 0**
2018–19 Bolton W 18 0
2019–20 Bolton W 33 0 **51 0**

MELLIS, Jacob (M) 261 17
H: 5 11 W: 10 11 b.Nottingham 8-1-91
Internationals: England U16, U17, U19.
2009–10 Chelsea 0 0
2009–10 *Southampton* 12 0 **12 0**
2010–11 Chelsea 0 0
2010–11 *Barnsley* 15 2
2011–12 Chelsea 0 0
2012–13 Barnsley 36 6
2013–14 Barnsley 30 2 **81 10**
2014–15 Blackpool 13 0 **13 0**
2014–15 *Oldham Ath* 7 0 **7 0**
2015–16 Bury 23 0
2016–17 Bury 35 3 **58 3**
2017–18 Mansfield T 30 1
2018–19 Mansfield T 41 3
2019–20 Mansfield T 13 0 **84 4**
2019–20 Bolton W 6 0 **6 0**

MURPHY, Daryl (F) 444 108
H: 6 2 W: 13 12 b.Waterford 15-3-83
Internationals: Republic of Ireland U21, Full caps.
2000–01 Luton T 0 0
2001–02 Luton T 0 0
From Waterford U.
2005–06 Sunderland 18 1
2005–06 *Sheffield W* 4 0 **4 0**
2006–07 Sunderland 38 10
2007–08 Sunderland 28 3
2008–09 Sunderland 23 0
2009–10 Sunderland 3 0 **110 14**
2009–10 *Ipswich T* 18 6
2010–11 Celtic 18 3
2011–12 Ipswich T 33 4
2012–13 Celtic 1 0 **19 3**
2012–13 *Ipswich T* 39 7
2013–14 Ipswich T 45 13
2014–15 Ipswich T 44 27
2015–16 Ipswich T 34 10
2016–17 Ipswich T 4 0 **217 67**
2016–17 Newcastle U 15 5 **15 5**
2017–18 Nottingham F 27 7
2018–19 Nottingham F 28 4
2019–20 Nottingham F 0 0 **55 11**
2019–20 Bolton W 24 8 **24 8**

MURPHY, Luke (M) 361 32
H: 6 1 W: 11 05 b.Alsager 21-10-89
2008–09 Crewe Alex 9 1
2009–10 Crewe Alex 32 3
2010–11 Crewe Alex 39 3
2011–12 Crewe Alex 42 8
2012–13 Crewe Alex 39 6 **161 21**
2013–14 Leeds U 37 3
2014–15 Leeds U 30 3
2015–16 Leeds U 36 1
2016–17 Leeds U 0 0
2016–17 *Burton Alb* 19 1
2017–18 Leeds U 0 0
2017–18 *Burton Alb* 38 1 **57 2**
2018–19 Leeds U 0 0 **103 7**
2018–19 Bolton W 11 0
2019–20 Bolton W 29 2 **40 2**

O'GRADY, Chris (F) 519 96
H: 6 3 W: 12 04 b.Nottingham 25-1-86
2002–03 Leicester C 1 0
2003–04 Leicester C 0 0
2004–05 Leicester C 0 0
2004–05 *Notts Co* 9 0 **9 0**
2005–06 Leicester C 13 1
2005–06 *Rushden & D* 22 4 **22 4**
2006–07 Leicester C 10 0 **24 1**
2006–07 Rotherham U 13 4
2007–08 Rotherham U 38 9 **51 13**
2008–09 Oldham Ath 13 0
2008–09 *Bury* 6 0 **6 0**
2008–09 *Bradford C* 2 0 **2 0**
2008–09 *Stockport Co* 18 2 **18 2**
2009–10 Rochdale 43 22
2010–11 Rochdale 46 9
2011–12 Rochdale 1 0 **90 31**
2011–12 Sheffield W 32 5
2012–13 Sheffield W 21 4 **53 9**
2012–13 *Barnsley* 16 5
2013–14 Barnsley 40 15 **56 20**
2014–15 Brighton & HA 28 1
2014–15 *Sheffield U* 4 1 **4 1**
2015–16 Brighton & HA 3 0
2015–16 *Nottingham F* 21 2 **21 2**
2016–17 Brighton & HA 0 0 **31 1**
2016–17 *Burton Alb* 26 1 **26 1**
2017–18 Chesterfield 35 2 **35 2**
2018–19 Oldham Ath 38 7
2019–20 Oldham Ath 0 0 **51 7**
2019–20 Bolton W 20 2 **20 2**

OSIGWE, Kwame (M) 0 0
b. 11-1-02
2019–20 Bolton W 0 0

POLITIC, Dennis (M) 24 3
Internationals: Romania U17.
2019–20 Bolton W 24 3 **24 3**

RICHARDS, D'Neal (D) 0 0
2019–20 Bolton W 0 0

RILEY, Regan (M) 1 0
2019–20 Bolton W 1 0 **1 0**

SENIOR, Adam (D) 2 0
2019–20 Bolton W 2 0 **2 0**

THOMASON, George (M) 0 0
From Longridge.
2019–20 Bolton W 0 0

WEIR, James (M) 16 0
H: 5 10 W: 11 03 b.Preston 4-8-95
Internationals: England U18, U19.
2014–15 Manchester U 0 0
2015–16 Manchester U 1 0
2016–17 Manchester U 0 0 **1 0**
2016–17 Hull C 0 0
2016–17 *Wigan Ath* 4 0 **4 0**
2017–18 Hull C 3 0
2018–19 Hull C 0 0 **3 0**
2019–20 Bolton W 8 0 **8 0**
Transferred to Pohromie, March 2020.

WHALLEY, Nathan (D) 0 0
2019–20 Bolton W 0 0

WHITE, Joe (D) 4 0
2019–20 Bolton W 4 0 **4 0**

ZOUMA, Yoan (D) 17 0
2017–18 Angers 0 0
2018–19 Angers 0 0
2019–20 Bolton W 17 0 **17 0**

Scholars
Alexander, Matthew; Assarsson, Markus Daniel Bernard; Brown, Edward James; Brow-Sterling, De' Marlio Shakie; Colvin, Ryan Taylor Thomas Lee; Darcy, Ronan Thomas; Edmondson, Myles Gregory; Fitzmartin, Jay Leon; Graham, Sonny; Hurfor-Lockett, Finlay; Hutchinson, Luke;

Kin-Harmes, Callum; Osigwe, Kwame Kelechi Okechukwu; Richards, D'Neal Demareo; Riley, Regan David; Senior, Adam Nicholas; Whalley, Nathan Mark; White, Joseph Anthony.

BOURNEMOUTH (10)

AKE, Nathan (M) 151 12
H: 5 11 W: 11 01 b.Den Haag 18-2-95
Internationals: Netherlands U15, U16, U17, U19, U21, Full caps.
2012–13 Chelsea 3 0
2013–14 Chelsea 1 0
2014–15 Chelsea 1 0
2014–15 *Reading* 5 0 **5 0**
2015–16 Chelsea 0 0
2015–16 *Watford* 24 1 **24 1**
2016–17 Chelsea 2 0 **7 0**
2016–17 *Bournemouth* 10 3
2017–18 Bournemouth 38 2
2018–19 Bournemouth 38 4
2019–20 Bournemouth 29 2 **115 11**

ANTHONY, Jaidon (F) 0 0
b. 1-12-99
2019–20 Bournemouth 0 0

ARTER, Harry (M) 290 31
H: 5 9 W: 11 07 b.Sidcup 28-12-89
Internationals: Republic of Ireland U17, U19, Full caps.
2007–08 Charlton Ath 0 0
2008–09 Charlton Ath 0 0
From Woking.
2010–11 Bournemouth 18 0
2010–11 *Carlisle U* 5 1 **5 1**
2011–12 Bournemouth 34 5
2012–13 Bournemouth 37 8
2013–14 Bournemouth 31 3
2014–15 Bournemouth 43 9
2015–16 Bournemouth 21 1
2016–17 Bournemouth 35 1
2017–18 Bournemouth 13 1
2018–19 Bournemouth 0 0
2018–19 *Cardiff C* 25 0 **25 0**
2019–20 Bournemouth 0 0 **232 28**
2019–20 *Fulham* 28 2 **28 2**

BEGOVIC, Asmir (G) 297 1
H: 6 5 W: 13 01 b.Trebinje 20-6-87
Internationals: Canada U20. Bosnia & Herzogovina Full caps.
2006–07 Portsmouth 0 0
2006–07 *Macclesfield T* 3 0 **3 0**
2007–08 Portsmouth 0 0
2007–08 *Bournemouth* 8 0
2007–08 *Yeovil T* 2 0
2008–09 Portsmouth 2 0
2008–09 *Yeovil T* 14 0 **16 0**
2009–10 Portsmouth 9 0 **11 0**
2009–10 *Ipswich T* 6 0 **6 0**
2009–10 Stoke C 4 0
2010–11 Stoke C 28 0
2011–12 Stoke C 23 0
2012–13 Stoke C 38 0
2013–14 Stoke C 32 1
2014–15 Stoke C 35 0 **160 1**
2015–16 Chelsea 17 0
2016–17 Chelsea 2 0 **19 0**
2017–18 Bournemouth 38 0
2018–19 Bournemouth 24 0
2019–20 Bournemouth 0 0 **70 0**
2019–20 *Qarabag* 10 0 **10 0**
2019–20 *AC Milan* 2 0 **2 0**

BILLING, Phillip (M) 115 6
H: 6 4 W: 12 08 b. 11-6-96
Internationals: Denmark U19, U21.
2013–14 Huddersfield T 1 0
2014–15 Huddersfield T 0 0
2015–16 Huddersfield T 13 1
2016–17 Huddersfield T 24 2
2017–18 Huddersfield T 16 0
2018–19 Huddersfield T 27 2 **81 5**
2019–20 Bournemouth 34 1 **34 1**

BORUC, Artur (G) 389 0
H: 6 4 W: 13 08 b.Siedlce 20-2-80
Internationals: Poland Full caps.
2005–06 Celtic 34 0
2006–07 Celtic 36 0
2007–08 Celtic 30 0
2008–09 Celtic 34 0
2009–10 Celtic 28 0 **162 0**
2010–11 Fiorentina 26 0
2011–12 Fiorentina 36 0 **62 0**
2012–13 Southampton 20 0
2013–14 Southampton 29 0
2014–15 Southampton 0 0 **49 0**
2014–15 *Bournemouth* 37 0
2015–16 Bournemouth 32 0
2016–17 Bournemouth 35 0
2017–18 Bournemouth 0 0
2018–19 Bournemouth 12 0
2019–20 Bournemouth 0 0 **116 0**

BROOKS, David (M) 69 11
b. 8-7-98
Internationals: England U20. Wales U21, Full caps.
2015–16 Sheffield U 0 0
2016–17 Sheffield U 0 0
2017–18 Sheffield U 30 3 **30 3**
2018–19 Bournemouth 30 7
2019–20 Bournemouth 9 1 **39 8**

BUTCHER, Matt (M) 40 2
H: 6 2 W: 12 13 b.Portsmouth 14-5-97
From Poole T.
2015–16 Bournemouth 0 0
2016–17 Bournemouth 0 0
2016–17 *Yeovil T* 34 2 **34 2**
2017–18 Bournemouth 0 0
2018–19 Bournemouth 0 0
2019–20 Bournemouth 0 0
2019–20 *St Johnstone* 6 0 **6 0**

CAMP, Brennan (D) 0 0
b.Portland 12-10-00
Internationals: Scotland U19.
2019–20 Bournemouth 0 0

COOK, Lewis (M) 155 1
H: 5 9 W: 11 03 b.York 3-2-97
Internationals: England U16, U17, U18, U19, U20, U21, Full caps.
2014–15 Leeds U 37 0
2015–16 Leeds U 43 1 **80 1**
2016–17 Bournemouth 6 0
2017–18 Bournemouth 29 0
2018–19 Bournemouth 13 0
2019–20 Bournemouth 27 0 **75 0**

COOK, Steve (D) 314 19
H: 6 1 W: 12 13 b.Hastings 19-4-91
2008–09 Brighton & HA 2 0
2009–10 Brighton & HA 0 0
2010–11 Brighton & HA 0 0
2011–12 Brighton & HA 1 0 **3 0**
2011–12 Bournemouth 26 0
2012–13 Bournemouth 33 1
2013–14 Bournemouth 38 3
2014–15 Bournemouth 46 5
2015–16 Bournemouth 36 4
2016–17 Bournemouth 38 2
2017–18 Bournemouth 34 2
2018–19 Bournemouth 31 1
2019–20 Bournemouth 29 1 **311 19**

DANIELS, Charlie (M) 404 21
H: 6 1 W: 12 12 b.Harlow 7-9-86
2005–06 Tottenham H 0 0
2006–07 Tottenham H 0 0
2006–07 *Chesterfield* 2 0 **2 0**
2007–08 Tottenham H 0 0
2007–08 *Leyton Orient* 31 2
2008–09 Tottenham H 0 0
2008–09 *Gillingham* 5 1 **5 1**
2008–09 Leyton Orient 21 2
2009–10 Leyton Orient 41 0
2010–11 Leyton Orient 42 0
2011–12 Leyton Orient 13 0 **148 4**
2011–12 Bournemouth 21 2
2012–13 Bournemouth 34 4
2013–14 Bournemouth 23 0
2014–15 Bournemouth 42 1
2015–16 Bournemouth 37 3
2016–17 Bournemouth 34 4
2017–18 Bournemouth 35 1
2018–19 Bournemouth 21 1
2019–20 Bournemouth 2 0 **249 16**

DANJUMA, Arnaut (F) 75 17
b.Oss 31-1-97
Internationals: Netherlands U21, Full caps.
2015–16 PSV Eindhoven 0 0
2016–17 NEC Nijmegen 12 1
2017–18 NEC Nijmegen 28 11 **40 12**
2018–19 Club Brugge 20 5
2019–20 Club Brugge 1 0 **21 5**
2019–20 Bournemouth 14 0 **14 0**

DEFOE, Jermain (F) 600 223
H: 5 7 W: 10 04 b.Beckton 7-10-82
Internationals: England U16, U18, U21, B, Full caps.
1999–2000 West Ham U 0 0
2000–01 West Ham U 1 0
2000–01 *Bournemouth* 29 18
2001–02 West Ham U 35 10
2002–03 West Ham U 38 8
2003–04 West Ham U 19 11 **93 29**
2003–04 Tottenham H 15 7
2004–05 Tottenham H 35 13
2005–06 Tottenham H 36 9
2006–07 Tottenham H 34 10
2007–08 Tottenham H 19 4
2007–08 Portsmouth 12 8
2008–09 Portsmouth 19 7 **31 15**
2008–09 Tottenham H 8 3
2009–10 Tottenham H 34 18
2010–11 Tottenham H 22 4
2011–12 Tottenham H 25 11
2012–13 Tottenham H 34 11
2013–14 Tottenham H 14 1 **276 91**
2014 Toronto 19 11 **19 11**
2014–15 Sunderland 17 4
2015–16 Sunderland 33 15
2016–17 Sunderland 37 15 **87 34**
2017–18 Bournemouth 24 4
2018–19 Bournemouth 4 0
2018–19 *Rangers* 17 8
2019–20 Bournemouth 0 0 **57 22**
2019–20 *Rangers* 20 13 **37 21**

DENNIS, William (G) 0 0
b.Watford 10-7-00
2019–20 Bournemouth 0 0

DOBRE, Mihai (M) 37 2
b. 30-8-98
Internationals: Romania U17, U21.
2017–18 Bournemouth 0 0
2017–18 *Bury* 10 0 **10 0**
2017–18 *Rochdale* 5 1 **5 1**
2018–19 Bournemouth 0 0
2018–19 *Yeovil T* 21 1 **21 1**
2019–20 Bournemouth 0 0
2019–20 *Wigan Ath* 1 0 **1 0**

FRANCIS, Simon (D) 575 9
H: 6 0 W: 12 06 b.Nottingham 16-2-85
Internationals: England U18, U20.
2002–03 Bradford C 25 1
2003–04 Bradford C 30 0 **55 1**
2003–04 Sheffield U 5 0
2004–05 Sheffield U 6 0
2005–06 Sheffield U 1 0 **12 0**
2005–06 *Grimsby T* 5 0 **5 0**
2005–06 *Tranmere R* 17 1 **17 1**
2006–07 Southend U 40 1
2007–08 Southend U 27 2
2008–09 Southend U 45 0
2009–10 Southend U 45 1 **157 4**
2010–11 Charlton Ath 34 0
2011–12 Charlton Ath 0 0 **34 0**
2011–12 Bournemouth 29 0
2012–13 Bournemouth 42 1
2013–14 Bournemouth 46 1
2014–15 Bournemouth 42 1
2015–16 Bournemouth 38 0
2016–17 Bournemouth 34 0
2017–18 Bournemouth 32 0
2018–19 Bournemouth 17 0
2019–20 Bournemouth 15 0 **295 3**

FRASER, Ryan (M) 222 24
H: 5 4 W: 10 13 b.Aberdeen 24-2-94
Internationals: Scotland U19, U21, Full caps.
2010–11 Aberdeen 2 0
2011–12 Aberdeen 3 0
2012–13 Aberdeen 16 0 **21 0**
2012–13 Bournemouth 5 0
2013–14 Bournemouth 37 3
2014–15 Bournemouth 21 1
2015–16 Bournemouth 0 0
2015–16 *Ipswich T* 18 4 **18 4**
2016–17 Bournemouth 28 3
2017–18 Bournemouth 26 5
2018–19 Bournemouth 38 7
2019–20 Bournemouth 28 1 **183 20**

GENESINI, Brooklyn (D) 0 0
b. 12-12-01
2019–20 Bournemouth 0 0

GILLELA, Dinesh (D) 0 0
b. 2-1-00
2019–20 Bournemouth 0 0

GOSLING, Dan (M) 238 21
H: 6 0 W: 11 00 b.Brixham 2-2-90
Internationals: England U17, U18, U19, U21.
2006–07 Plymouth Arg 12 2
2007–08 Plymouth Arg 10 0 **22 2**
2007–08 Everton 0 0
2008–09 Everton 11 2
2009–10 Everton 11 2 **22 4**
2010–11 Newcastle U 1 0
2011–12 Newcastle U 12 1
2012–13 Newcastle U 3 0
2013–14 Newcastle U 8 0 **24 1**
2013–14 *Blackpool* 14 2 **14 2**
2014–15 Bournemouth 18 0
2015–16 Bournemouth 34 3
2016–17 Bournemouth 27 2
2017–18 Bournemouth 28 2
2018–19 Bournemouth 25 2
2019–20 Bournemouth 24 3 **156 12**

HOBSON, Shaun (D) 0 0
2017–18 Bournemouth 0 0
2018–19 Bournemouth 0 0
2019–20 Bournemouth 0 0

IBE, Jordan (F) 157 11
H: 5 9 W: 11 00 b.Southwark 8-12-95
Internationals: England U18, U19, U20, U21.
2011–12 Wycombe W 7 1 **7 1**
2011–12 Liverpool 0 0
2012–13 Liverpool 1 0
2013–14 Liverpool 1 0
2013–14 *Birmingham C* 11 1 **11 1**
2014–15 Liverpool 12 0
2014–15 *Derby Co* 20 5 **20 5**
2015–16 Liverpool 27 1 **41 1**
2016–17 Bournemouth 25 0
2017–18 Bournemouth 32 2
2018–19 Bournemouth 19 1
2019–20 Bournemouth 2 0 **78 3**

JORDAN, Corey (D) 0 0
H: 6 1 W: 11 11 b.Bournemouth 4-3-99
2015–16 Bournemouth 0 0
2016–17 Bournemouth 0 0
2017–18 Bournemouth 0 0
2018–19 Bournemouth 0 0
2019–20 Bournemouth 0 0

KELLY, Lloyd (D) 51 2
H: 5 10 W: 11 00 b. 1-10-98
Internationals: England U20, U21.
2016–17 Bristol C 0 0
2017–18 Bristol C 11 1
2018–19 Bristol C 32 1 **43 2**
2019–20 Bournemouth 8 0 **8 0**

KILKENNY, Gavin (M) 0 0
b.Dublin 1-2-00
Internationals: Republic of Ireland U21.
2019–20 Bournemouth 0 0

KING, Josh (F) 253 54
H: 5 11 W: 11 09 b.Oslo 15-1-92
Internationals: Norway U15, U16, U18, U19, U21, Full caps.
2008–09 Manchester U 0 0
2009–10 Manchester U 0 0
2010–11 Manchester U 0 0
2010–11 *Preston NE* 8 0 **8 0**
2011–12 Manchester U 0 0
2011–12 *Borussia M'gladbach* 2 0 **2 0**
2011–12 *Hull C* 18 1 **18 1**
2012–13 Manchester U 0 0
2012–13 Blackburn R 16 2
2013–14 Blackburn R 32 2
2014–15 Blackburn R 16 1 **64 5**
2015–16 Bournemouth 31 6
2016–17 Bournemouth 36 16
2017–18 Bournemouth 33 8
2018–19 Bournemouth 35 12
2019–20 Bournemouth 26 6 **161 48**

LERMA, Jefferson (M) 230 12
H: 5 10 W: 11 00 b.El Cerrito 25-10-94
Internationals: Colombia Full caps.
2013 Atletico Huila 24 0
2014 Atletico Huila 32 4
2015 Atletico Huila 22 2 **78 6**
2015–16 *Levante* 33 1
2016–17 Levante 30 2
2017–18 Levante 26 0 **89 3**
2018–19 Bournemouth 30 2
2019–20 Bournemouth 33 1 **63 3**

MEPHAM, Chris (D) 68 2
H: 6 3 W: 11 11 b. 5-11-97
Internationals: Wales U20, U21, Full caps.
2016–17 Brentford 0 0
2017–18 Brentford 21 1
2018–19 Brentford 22 0 **43 1**
2018–19 Bournemouth 13 0
2019–20 Bournemouth 12 1 **25 1**

NDJOLI, Mikael (F) 37 4
b. 16-12-98
2017–18 Bournemouth 0 0
2018–19 Bournemouth 0 0
2018–19 *Kilmarnock* 24 2 **24 2**
2019–20 Bournemouth 0 0
2019–20 *Gillingham* 12 2 **12 2**
2019–20 *Motherwell* 1 0 **1 0**

O'CONNELL, Keelan (M) 6 0
b. 30-11-99
2017–18 Bournemouth 0 0
2018–19 Bournemouth 0 0
2018–19 *Greenock Morton* 6 0 **6 0**
2019–20 Bournemouth 0 0

OFOBORH, Nnamdi (F) 18 0
H: 6 0 W: 12 02 b.Southwark 7-11-99
Internationals: Nigeria U20.
2018–19 Bournemouth 0 0
2019–20 Bournemouth 0 0
2019–20 *Wycombe W* 18 0 **18 0**

RAMSDALE, Aaron (G) 76 0
b. 14-5-98
Internationals: England U18, U19, U20, U21.
2015–16 Sheffield U 0 0
2016–17 Sheffield U 0 0
2016–17 Bournemouth 0 0
2017–18 Bournemouth 0 0
2017–18 *Chesterfield* 19 0 **19 0**
2018–19 Bournemouth 0 0
2018–19 *AFC Wimbledon* 20 0 **20 0**
2019–20 Bournemouth 37 0 **37 0**

RICO, Diego (D) 196 8
H: 5 11 W: 11 11 b.Burgos 26-4-93
2011–12 Zaragoza 0 0
2012–13 Zaragoza 0 0
2013–14 Zaragoza 30 2
2014–15 Zaragoza 37 2
2015–16 Zaragoza 39 1 **106 5**
2016–17 Leganes 25 1
2017–18 Leganes 26 2 **51 3**
2018–19 Bournemouth 12 0
2019–20 Bournemouth 27 0 **39 0**

SAYDEE, Christian (F) 0 0
b.Hillingdon 10-5-02
2019–20 Bournemouth 0 0

SIMPSON, Jack (D) 11 0
H: 5 10 W: 13 01 b. 8-1-97
Internationals: England U21.
2015–16 Bournemouth 0 0
2016–17 Bournemouth 0 0
2017–18 Bournemouth 1 0
2018–19 Bournemouth 6 0
2019–20 Bournemouth 4 0 **11 0**

SMITH, Adam (D) 288 9
H: 5 8 W: 10 07 b.Leytonstone 29-4-91
Internationals: England U16, U17, U19, U20, U21.
2007–08 Tottenham H 0 0
2008–09 Tottenham H 0 0
2009–10 Tottenham H 0 0
2009–10 *Wycombe W* 3 0 **3 0**
2009–10 *Torquay U* 16 0 **16 0**
2010–11 Tottenham H 0 0
2010–11 *Bournemouth* 38 1
2011–12 Tottenham H 1 0
2011–12 *Milton Keynes D* 17 2 **17 2**
2011–12 *Leeds U* 3 0 **3 0**
2012–13 Tottenham H 0 0
2012–13 *Millwall* 25 1 **25 1**
2013–14 Tottenham H 0 0 **1 0**
2013–14 *Derby Co* 8 0 **8 0**
2013–14 Bournemouth 5 0
2014–15 Bournemouth 29 0
2015–16 Bournemouth 31 2
2016–17 Bournemouth 36 1
2017–18 Bournemouth 27 1
2018–19 Bournemouth 25 1
2019–20 Bournemouth 24 0 **215 6**

SMITH, Bradley (D) 51 0
H: 5 10 W: 11 00 b.New South Wales 9-4-94
Internationals: England U17, U19, U20. Australia U23, Full caps.
2011–12 Liverpool 0 0
2012–13 Liverpool 0 0
2013–14 Liverpool 1 0
2014–15 Liverpool 0 0
2014–15 *Swindon T* 7 0 **7 0**
2015–16 Liverpool 4 0 **5 0**
2016–17 Bournemouth 5 0
2017–18 Bournemouth 0 0
2018–19 *Seattle Sounders* 31 0 **31 0**
2019–20 Bournemouth 0 0 **5 0**
2019–20 *Cardiff C* 3 0 **3 0**

SOLANKE, Dominic (F) 88 11
H: 6 1 W: 11 11 b.Reading 14-9-97
Internationals: England U16, U17, U18, U19, U20, U21, Full caps.
2014–15 Chelsea 0 0
2015–16 Chelsea 0 0
2015–16 *Vitesse* 25 7 **25 7**
2016–17 Chelsea 0 0
2017–18 Liverpool 21 1
2018–19 Liverpool 0 0 **21 1**
2018–19 Bournemouth 10 0
2019–20 Bournemouth 32 3 **42 3**

STACEY, Jack (M) 156 7
H: 6 4 W: 13 05 b.Bracknell 6-4-96
2014–15 Reading 6 0
2015–16 Reading 0 0
2015–16 *Barnet* 2 0 **2 0**
2015–16 *Carlisle U* 9 2 **9 2**
2016–17 Reading 0 0 **6 0**
2016–17 *Exeter C* 34 0 **34 0**
2017–18 Luton T 41 1
2018–19 Luton T 45 4 **86 5**
2019–20 Bournemouth 19 0 **19 0**

STANISLAS, Junior (M) 253 35
H: 6 0 W: 12 00 b.Kidbrooke 26-11-89
Internationals: England U20, U21.
2007–08 West Ham U 0 0
2008–09 West Ham U 9 2
2008–09 *Southend U* 6 1 **6 1**
2009–10 West Ham U 26 3
2010–11 West Ham U 6 1
2011–12 West Ham U 1 0 **42 6**
2011–12 Burnley 31 0
2012–13 Burnley 35 5
2013–14 Burnley 27 2 **93 7**
2014–15 Bournemouth 13 1
2015–16 Bournemouth 21 3
2016–17 Bournemouth 21 7
2017–18 Bournemouth 19 5
2018–19 Bournemouth 23 2
2019–20 Bournemouth 15 3 **112 21**

SURMAN, Andrew (M) 414 35
H: 5 10 W: 11 06 b.Johannesburg 20-8-86
Internationals: England U21.
2003–04 Southampton 0 0
2004–05 Southampton 0 0
2004–05 *Walsall* 14 2 **14 2**
2005–06 Southampton 12 2
2005–06 *Bournemouth* 24 6
2006–07 Southampton 37 4
2007–08 Southampton 40 2
2008–09 Southampton 44 7
2009–10 Southampton 0 0 **133 15**
2009–10 Wolverhampton W 7 0 **7 0**
2010–11 Norwich C 22 3
2011–12 Norwich C 25 4
2012–13 Norwich C 4 0
2013–14 Norwich C 0 0
2013–14 *Bournemouth* 35 0
2014–15 Norwich C 1 0 **52 7**
2014–15 Bournemouth 41 3
2015–16 Bournemouth 38 0
2016–17 Bournemouth 22 0
2017–18 Bournemouth 25 2
2018–19 Bournemouth 18 0
2019–20 Bournemouth 5 0 **208 11**

SURRIDGE, Sam (F) 82 20
b.Wimborne 28-7-98
Internationals: England U21.
2015–16 Bournemouth 0 0
2016–17 Bournemouth 0 0
2017–18 Bournemouth 0 0
2017–18 *Yeovil T* 41 8 **41 8**
2018–19 Bournemouth 2 0
2018–19 *Oldham Ath* 15 8 **15 8**
2019–20 Bournemouth 4 0 **6 0**
2019–20 *Swansea C* 20 4 **20 4**

TAYLOR, Kyle (M) 5 0
b. 28-8-99
2017–18 Bournemouth 0 0
2018–19 Bournemouth 0 0
2019–20 Bournemouth 0 0
2019–20 *Forest Green R* 5 0 **5 0**

TRAVERS, Mark (G) 3 0
H: 6 3 W: 12 13 b. 18-5-99
Internationals: Republic of Ireland U16, U17, U18, U19, U21.
From Shamrock R.
2018–19 Bournemouth 2 0
2019–20 Bournemouth 1 0 **3 0**

WILSON, Callum (M) 220 83
H: 5 11 W: 10 06 b.Coventry 27-2-92
Internationals: England U21, Full caps.
2009–10 Coventry C 0 0
2010–11 Coventry C 1 0
2011–12 Coventry C 0 0
2012–13 Coventry C 11 1
2013–14 Coventry C 37 21 **49 22**
2014–15 Bournemouth 45 20
2015–16 Bournemouth 13 5
2016–17 Bournemouth 20 6
2017–18 Bournemouth 28 8
2018–19 Bournemouth 30 14
2019–20 Bournemouth 35 8 **171 61**

ZEMURA, Jordan (D) 0 0
2018–19 Charlton Ath 0 0
2019–20 Bournemouth 0 0

Players retained or with offer of contract
Cordner, Tyler Jack; Glover, Ryan; Groeneveld, Arnaut Danjuma; Scrimshaw, Jake; Sherring, Sam; Vincent, Francis William.

Scholars
Adams, Jake Norman; Bertrand, Harvey-Joe Edward; Besant, Joe Matthew; Burgess, Matthew Richard; Camp, Breenan; Channell, Brandon Anthony Emmanuel; Cope, Jake William; Dinsmore, Thomas Jack; Genesini, Brooklyn David Anthony; Gidaree, Tarik Andre Calvin; Gray, Luke Anthony; Greenwood, Benjamin Sean; Hanfrey, Thomas William; Hunt, George Elliott; Ibsen Rossi, Zeno; Kurran-Browne, Connor Chadney; Mohamed, Abdirahman Adan; Moriah-Welsh, Nathan Daniel; Murray, Jordan Kenneth; Nippard, Luke Ryan; Oliver, James Robert; Pardoe, Luke Daniel; Plain, Cameron Christopher; Pollock, Euan George; Roberts, Aaron Joseph; Saydee, Christian; Seddon, Jack; Terrell, Billy Edwards James; Torniainen, Jack Maurice; Wadham, Jack; Ward, Calum

BRADFORD C (11)

AKPAN, Hope (M) 240 17
H: 6 0 W: 10 08 b.Liverpool 14-8-91
Internationals: Nigeria Full caps.
2007–08 Everton 0 0
2008–09 Everton 0 0
2009–10 Everton 0 0
2010–11 Everton 0 0
2010–11 *Hull C* 2 0 **2 0**
2011–12 Crawley T 26 1
2012–13 Crawley T 21 4 **47 5**
2012–13 Reading 9 0
2013–14 Reading 29 1
2014–15 Reading 20 0 **58 1**
2015–16 Blackburn R 35 3
2016–17 Blackburn R 25 1 **60 4**
2017–18 Burton Alb 26 2 **26 2**
2018–19 Bradford C 28 2
2019–20 Bradford C 19 3 **47 5**

ANDERSON, Jermaine (M) 103 8
b. 16-5-96
Internationals: England U18, U20.
2012–13 Peterborough U 1 0
2013–14 Peterborough U 13 0
2014–15 Peterborough U 24 1
2015–16 Peterborough U 14 4
2016–17 Peterborough U 7 0
2017–18 Peterborough U 17 0
2018–19 Peterborough U 0 0 **76 5**
2018–19 *Doncaster R* 9 1 **9 1**
2018–19 Bradford C 13 1
2019–20 Bradford C 5 1 **18 2**

COLVILLE, Luca (M) 11 1
H: 6 1 W: 11 00 b.York 17-2-99
2018–19 Bradford C 11 1
2019–20 Bradford C 0 0 **11 1**
Transferred to Greenock Morton, August 2019.

COUSIN-DAWSON, Finn (D) 0 0
b. 10-5-01
2019–20 Bradford C 0 0

DEVINE, Daniel (M) 30 1
H: 5 11 W: 12 00 b.Bradford 4-9-97
2015–16 Bradford C 0 0
2016–17 Bradford C 11 0
2017–18 Bradford C 3 0
2018–19 Bradford C 3 0
2019–20 Bradford C 13 1 **30 1**

DONALDSON, Clayton (F) 462 140
H: 6 1 W: 11 07 b.Bradford 7-2-84
Internationals: England C. Jamaica Full caps.
2002–03 Hull C 2 0
2003–04 Hull C 0 0
2004–05 Hull C 0 0 **2 0**
From York C
2007–08 Hibernian 17 5 **17 5**
2008–09 Crewe Alex 37 6
2009–10 Crewe Alex 37 13
2010–11 Crewe Alex 43 28 **117 47**
2011–12 Brentford 46 11
2012–13 Brentford 44 18
2013–14 Brentford 46 17 **136 46**
2014–15 Birmingham C 46 15
2015–16 Birmingham C 40 11
2016–17 Birmingham C 23 6
2017–18 Birmingham C 4 0 **113 32**
2017–18 Sheffield U 26 5 **26 5**
2018–19 Bolton W 31 1 **31 1**
2019–20 Bradford C 20 4 **20 4**

FRENCH, Tyler (D) 2 0
b.Bury St Edmunds 12-2-99
From Long Melford, Hadleigh U, AFC Sudbury.
2019–20 Bradford C 2 0 **2 0**

GIBSON, Jordan (F) 28 2
b. 26-2-98
From Rangers.
2017–18 Bradford C 5 1
2018–19 Bradford C 11 0
2018–19 *Stevenage* 6 1 **6 1**
2019–20 Bradford C 6 0 **22 1**

GUTHRIE, Kurtis (F) 116 29
H: 5 11 W: 11 00 b.Jersey 21-4-93
Internationals: England C.
2011–12 Accrington S 13 0
2012–13 Accrington S 0 0 **13 0**
From Bath C, Welling U, Forest Green R.
2016–17 Colchester U 33 12
2017–18 Colchester U 12 1 **45 13**
2018–19 Stevenage 34 11
2019–20 Stevenage 22 5 **56 16**
2019–20 Bradford C 2 0 **2 0**

HENLEY, Adam (D) 109 1
H: 5 10 W: 12 02 b.Knoxville 14-6-94
Internationals: Wales U19, U21, Full caps.
2011–12 Blackburn R 7 0
2012–13 Blackburn R 15 0
2013–14 Blackburn R 14 0
2014–15 Blackburn R 18 1
2015–16 Blackburn R 24 0
2016–17 Blackburn R 2 0 **80 1**
2018–19 Real Salt Lake 5 0 **5 0**
2019–20 Bradford C 24 0 **24 0**

HORNBY, Sam (G) 11 0
b. 14-2-95
2015–16 Burton Alb 0 0
2016–17 Burton Alb 0 0
From Brackley T, Kidderminster H.
2017–18 Port Vale 11 0
2018–19 Port Vale 0 0 **11 0**
2019–20 Bradford C 0 0

ISMAIL, Zeli (M) 160 16
H: 5 8 W: 11 12 b.Kukes 12-12-93
Internationals: England U16, U17.
2010–11 Wolverhampton W 0 0
2011–12 Wolverhampton W 0 0
2012–13 Wolverhampton W 0 0
2012–13 *Milton Keynes D* 7 0 **7 0**
2013–14 Wolverhampton W 9 0
2013–14 *Burton Alb* 15 3
2014–15 Wolverhampton W 0 0
2014–15 *Notts Co* 14 4 **14 4**
2015–16 Wolverhampton W 0 0 **9 0**
2015–16 *Burton Alb* 3 0 **18 3**
2015–16 *Oxford U* 5 0 **5 0**
2015–16 *Cambridge U* 11 1 **11 1**
2016–17 Bury 16 3
2017–18 Bury 21 0 **37 3**
2017–18 *Walsall* 16 1
2018–19 Walsall 32 3 **48 4**
2019–20 Bradford C 11 1 **11 1**

LONGRIDGE, Jackson (D) 168 12
b.Glasgow 12-4-95
2011–12 Ayr U 2 0
2012–13 Ayr U 3 0
2013–14 Ayr U 4 0 **9 0**
2014–15 Stranraer 34 1 **34 1**
2015–16 Livingston 30 1
2016–17 Livingston 30 3
2017–18 Livingston 31 3 **91 7**
2018–19 Dunfermline Ath 33 4 **33 4**
2019–20 Bradford C 1 0 **1 0**

McCARTAN, Shay (M) 194 40
H: 5 10 W: 11 09 b.Newry 18-5-94
Internationals: Northern Ireland U17, U19, U21, Full caps.
2011–12 Burnley 1 0
2012–13 Burnley 0 0 **1 0**
2013–14 Accrington S 18 1
2014–15 Accrington S 31 6
2015–16 Accrington S 27 7
2016–17 Accrington S 34 11 **110 25**
2017–18 Bradford C 24 4
2018–19 Bradford C 0 0
2018–19 *Lincoln C* 38 7 **38 7**
2019–20 Bradford C 21 4 **45 8**

MELLOR, Kelvin (D) 272 16
H: 5 10 W: 11 09 b.Copenhagen 25-1-91
2007–08 Crewe Alex 0 0
2008–09 Crewe Alex 0 0
2009–10 Crewe Alex 0 0
2010–11 Crewe Alex 1 0
2011–12 Crewe Alex 12 1
2012–13 Crewe Alex 35 0
2013–14 Crewe Alex 28 1 **76 2**
2014–15 Plymouth Arg 37 1
2015–16 Plymouth Arg 41 1 **78 2**
2016–17 Blackpool 44 4
2017–18 Blackpool 29 6 **73 10**
2018–19 Bradford C 20 1
2019–20 Bradford C 25 1 **45 2**

MIDDLETON, Glenn (M) 24 2
Internationals: Scotland U16, U17, U19, U21.
2016–17 Norwich C 0 0
2017–18 Norwich C 0 0
2018–19 Rangers 15 2
2019–20 Rangers 0 0 **15 2**
2019–20 *Hibernian* 6 0 **6 0**
On loan from Rangers.
2019–20 Bradford C 3 0 **3 0**

MORRIS, Connor (F) 0 0
2019–20 Bradford C 0 0

MOTTLEY-HENRY, Dylan (F) 22 0
b. 2-8-97
2014–15 Bradford C 1 0
2015–16 Bradford C 1 0
From Altrincham, Bradford PA, Tranmere R.
2017–18 Barnsley 1 0
2018–19 Barnsley 0 0
2018–19 *Tranmere R* 12 0 **12 0**
2019–20 Barnsley 0 0 **1 0**
2019–20 Bradford C 7 0 **9 0**

NOVAK, Lee (F) 369 85
H: 6 0 W: 12 04 b.Newcastle upon Tyne 28-9-88
2008–09 Huddersfield T 0 0
2009–10 Huddersfield T 37 12
2010–11 Huddersfield T 31 5
2011–12 Huddersfield T 41 13
2012–13 Huddersfield T 35 4 **144 34**
2013–14 Birmingham C 38 9
2014–15 Birmingham C 21 1
2015–16 Birmingham C 0 0 **59 10**
2015–16 *Chesterfield* 35 14 **35 14**
2016–17 Charlton Ath 29 2
2017–18 Charlton Ath 2 0 **31 2**
2017–18 Scunthorpe U 32 6
2018–19 Scunthorpe U 43 12
2019–20 Scunthorpe U 19 5 **94 23**
2019–20 Bradford C 6 2 **6 2**

O'CONNOR, Anthony (D) 286 15
H: 6 2 W: 12 06 b.Cork 25-10-92
Internationals: Republic of Ireland U17, U19, U21.
2010–11 Blackburn R 0 0
2011–12 Blackburn R 0 0
2012–13 Blackburn R 0 0
2012–13 *Burton Alb* 46 0
2013–14 Blackburn R 0 0
2013–14 *Torquay U* 31 0 **31 0**

2014–15	Plymouth Arg	40	3	**40**	**3**
2015–16	Burton Alb	21	1	**67**	**1**
2016–17	Aberdeen	32	3		
2017–18	Aberdeen	38	2	**70**	**5**
2018–19	Bradford C	42	6		
2019–20	Bradford C	36	0	**78**	**6**

O'CONNOR, Paudie (D) 42 2
b.Limerick 14-7-97
From Limerick.

2017–18	Leeds U	4	0		
2018–19	Leeds U	0	0	**4**	**0**
2018–19	*Blackpool*	10	0	**10**	**0**
2018–19	*Bradford C*	9	0		
2019–20	Bradford C	19	2	**28**	**2**

O'DONNELL, Richard (G) 289 0
H: 6 2 W: 13 05 b.Sheffield 12-9-88

2007–08	Sheffield W	0	0		
2007–08	*Rotherham U*	0	0		
2007–08	*Oldham Ath*	4	0	**4**	**0**
2008–09	Sheffield W	0	0		
2009–10	Sheffield W	0	0		
2010–11	Sheffield W	9	0		
2011–12	Sheffield W	6	0	**15**	**0**
2011–12	*Macclesfield T*	11	0	**11**	**0**
2012–13	Chesterfield	14	0	**14**	**0**
2013–14	Walsall	46	0		
2014–15	Walsall	44	0	**90**	**0**
2015–16	Wigan Ath	10	0	**10**	**0**
2015–16	Bristol C	21	0		
2016–17	Bristol C	8	0	**29**	**0**
2016–17	Rotherham U	12	0		
2017–18	Rotherham U	10	0	**22**	**0**
2017–18	Northampton T	19	0	**19**	**0**
2018–19	Bradford C	42	0		
2019–20	Bradford C	33	0	**75**	**0**

PRITCHARD, Harry (M) 60 6
b.High Wycombe 14-9-92
From Flackwell Heath, Burnham, Maidenhead U.

2018–19	Blackpool	37	3		
2019–20	Blackpool	2	0	**39**	**3**
2019–20	Bradford C	21	3	**21**	**3**

REEVES, Jake (M) 202 6
H: 5 8 W: 11 11 b.Lewisham 30-6-93

2010–11	Brentford	1	0		
2011–12	Brentford	8	0		
2012–13	Brentford	6	0		
2012–13	*AFC Wimbledon*	5	0		
2013–14	Brentford	20	0	**35**	**0**
2014–15	Swindon T	10	1	**10**	**1**
2014–15	AFC Wimbledon	23	2		
2015–16	AFC Wimbledon	40	1		
2016–17	AFC Wimbledon	46	1	**114**	**4**
2017–18	Bradford C	25	0		
2018–19	Bradford C	0	0		
2019–20	Bradford C	18	1	**43**	**1**

RICHARDS-EVERTON, Ben (D) 131 5
H: 6 2 W: 14 00 b.Birmingham 17-10-92
Internationals: England C.
From Hinckley U, Tamworth.

2014–15	Partick Thistle	2	0	**2**	**0**
2014–15	*Airdrieonians*	18	0	**18**	**0**
2015–16	Dunfermline Ath	34	2		
2016–17	Dunfermline Ath	6	0	**40**	**2**
2017–18	Accrington S	22	1		
2018–19	Accrington S	17	0	**39**	**1**
2018–19	Bradford C	0	0		
2019–20	Bradford C	32	2	**32**	**2**

RILEY, Joe (D) 8 0
H: 6 0 W: 11 03 b.Blackpool 6-12-96

2016–17	Manchester U	0	0		
2016–17	*Sheffield U*	2	0	**2**	**0**
2017–18	Manchester u	0	0		
2018–19	Bradford C	6	0		
2019–20	Bradford C	0	0	**6**	**0**

SIKORA, Jorge (D) 0 0

2019–20	Bradford C	0	0		

STAUNTON, Reece (D) 1 0
b. 10-12-01
Internationals: Republic of Ireland U18.

2017–18	Bradford C	1	0		
2018–19	Bradford C	0	0		
2019–20	Bradford C	0	0	**1**	**0**

SUTTON, Levi (M) 58 1
b. 24-3-96

2014–15	Scunthorpe U	0	0		
2015–16	Scunthorpe U	1	0		
2016–17	Scunthorpe U	8	0		
2017–18	Scunthorpe U	15	0		
2018–19	Scunthorpe U	18	1		
2019–20	Scunthorpe U	16	0	**58**	**1**
2019–20	Bradford C	0	0		

SYKES-KENWORTHY, George (G) 0 0

2017–18	Bradford C	0	0		
2018–19	Bradford C	0	0		
2019–20	Bradford C	0	0		

TAYLOR, Chris (M) 406 41
H: 5 11 W: 11 00 b.Oldham 20-12-86

2005–06	Oldham Ath	14	0		
2006–07	Oldham Ath	44	4		
2007–08	Oldham Ath	42	5		
2008–09	Oldham Ath	42	10		
2009–10	Oldham Ath	32	1		
2010–11	Oldham Ath	42	11		
2011–12	Oldham Ath	38	2		
2012–13	Millwall	22	3		
2013–14	Blackburn R	34	0		
2014–15	Blackburn R	16	1		
2015–16	Blackburn R	12	0	**62**	**1**
2015–16	*Millwall*	10	3	**32**	**6**
2016–17	Bolton W	16	0		
2016–17	*Oldham Ath*	16	0	**270**	**33**
2017–18	Bolton W	0	0	**16**	**0**
2018–19	Blackpool	12	1	**12**	**1**
2019–20	Bradford C	14	0	**14**	**0**

VAUGHAN, James (F) 326 92
H: 5 11 W: 13 00 b.Birmingham 14-7-88
Internationals: England U17, U19, U21.

2004–05	Everton	2	1		
2005–06	Everton	1	0		
2006–07	Everton	14	4		
2007–08	Everton	8	1		
2008–09	Everton	13	0		
2009–10	Everton	8	1		
2009–10	*Derby Co*	2	0	**2**	**0**
2010–11	Everton	1	0	**47**	**7**
2010–11	*Crystal Palace*	30	9	**30**	**9**
2011–12	Norwich C	5	0		
2012–13	Norwich C	0	0	**5**	**0**
2012–13	*Huddersfield T*	33	14		
2013–14	Huddersfield T	23	10		
2014–15	Huddersfield T	26	7		
2015–16	Huddersfield T	4	0	**86**	**31**
2015–16	*Birmingham C*	15	0	**15**	**0**
2016–17	Bury	37	24	**37**	**24**
2017–18	Sunderland	23	2	**23**	**2**
2017–18	Wigan Ath	19	3		
2018–19	Wigan Ath	19	2	**38**	**5**
2018–19	*Portsmouth*	10	0	**10**	**0**
2019–20	Bradford C	25	11	**25**	**11**
2019–20	*Tranmere R*	8	3	**8**	**3**

WOOD, Connor (D) 57 1
b.Harlow 17-7-96
From Soham Town Rangers, Chesham U.

2017–18	Leicester C	0	0		
2018–19	Bradford C	22	1		
2019–20	Bradford C	35	0	**57**	**1**

Scholars
Cousi-Dawson, Finn; Donaghy, Thomas Patrick; Goldthorp, Eliot James; Morris, Connor Alan; Norman, Oliver Max; Ormerod, Harvey Steven; Ripley, Wade Owen; Scales, Kian; Shanks, Connor David; Sikora, Jorge Jack Antoni; Smethurst, Hayden; Sukiennicki, Olivier Mariusz; White, Jonathan Paul; Wood, Charles Hamilton.

BRENTFORD (12)

ADAMS, Joe (M) 3 0
b. 13-2-01
Internationals: Wales U17, U19.

2017–18	Bury	2	0		
2018–19	Bury	1	0	**3**	**0**
2019–20	Brentford	0	0		

BALCOMBE, Ellery (G) 8 0
b. 15-10-99
Internationals: England U18, U19, U20.

2016–17	Brentford	0	0		
2017–18	Brentford	0	0		
2018–19	Brentford	0	0		
2019–20	Brentford	0	0		
2019–20	*Viborg*	8	0	**8**	**0**

BAPTISTE, Shandon (M) 38 1
b. 8-4-98
Internationals: Grenada Full caps.

2017–18	Oxford U	0	0		
2018–19	Oxford U	9	0		
2019–20	Oxford U	17	1	**26**	**1**
2019–20	Brentford	12	0	**12**	**0**

BENRAHMA, Said (F) 156 43
H: 5 8 W: 10 08 b.Toulouse 10-8-95
Internationals: Algeria Full caps.

2013–14	Nice	5	0		
2014–15	Nice	3	1		
2015–16	Nice	9	2		
2015–16	*Angers*	12	1	**12**	**1**
2016–17	Nice	0	0		
2016–17	*Gazelec Ajaccio*	15	3	**15**	**3**
2017–18	Nice	0	0	**17**	**3**
2017–18	*Chateauroux*	31	9	**31**	**9**
2018–19	Brentford	38	10		
2019–20	Brentford	43	17	**81**	**27**

CANOS, Sergi (M) 147 21
H: 5 8 W: 11 11 b.Nules 2-2-97
Internationals: Spain U16, U17, U19, U20.

2015–16	Liverpool	1	0	**1**	**0**
2015–16	*Brentford*	38	7		
2016–17	Norwich C	3	0	**3**	**0**
2016–17	Brentford	18	4		
2017–18	Brentford	30	3		
2018–19	Brentford	44	7		
2019–20	Brentford	13	0	**143**	**21**

CLARKE, Josh (M) 89 6
H: 5 8 W: 11 00 b.Waltham Forest 5-7-95

2012–13	Brentford	0	0		
2013–14	Brentford	1	0		
2014–15	Brentford	0	0		
2014–15	*Dagenham & R*	0	0		
2014–15	*Stevenage*	1	0	**1**	**0**
2015–16	Brentford	11	0		
2015–16	*Barnet*	10	3	**10**	**3**
2016–17	Brentford	30	2		
2017–18	Brentford	28	1		
2018–19	Brentford	1	0		
2018–19	*Burton Alb*	6	0	**6**	**0**
2019–20	Brentford	1	0	**72**	**3**

COLE, Reece (M) 43 4
b. 17-2-98

2015–16	Brentford	0	0		
2016–17	Brentford	1	0		
2017–18	Brentford	0	0		
2017–18	*Newport Co*	4	1	**4**	**1**
2018–19	Brentford	0	0		
2018–19	*Yeovil T*	1	0	**1**	**0**
2018–19	*Macclesfield T*	18	1	**18**	**1**
2019–20	Brentford	0	0	**1**	**0**
2019–20	*Partick Thistle*	19	2	**19**	**2**

DA SILVA, Josh (M) 59 11
b. 23-10-98
Internationals: England U19, U20.

2016–17	Arsenal	0	0		
2017–18	Arsenal	0	0		
2018–19	Brentford	17	1		
2019–20	Brentford	42	10	**59**	**11**

DALSGAARD, Henrik (F) 313 22
H: 6 4 W: 12 11 b.Viborg 27-7-89
Internationals: Denmark U20, U21, Full caps.

2008–09	AaB	4	1		
2009–10	AaB	25	0		
2010–11	AaB	15	1		
2011–12	AaB	30	2		
2012–13	AaB	31	2		
2013–14	AaB	18	2		
2014–15	AaB	26	1		
2015–16	AaB	17	0	**166**	**9**
2015–16	Zulte Waregem	19	3		
2016–17	Zulte Waregem	16	6	**35**	**9**
2017–18	Brentford	29	1		
2018–19	Brentford	40	2		
2019–20	Brentford	43	1	**112**	**4**

DANIELS, Luke (G) 211 0
H: 6 1 W: 12 10 b.Bolton 5-1-88
Internationals: England U18, U19.

2006–07	WBA	0	0		
2007–08	*Motherwell*	2	0	**2**	**0**
2007–08	WBA	0	0		
2008–09	WBA	0	0		
2008–09	*Shrewsbury T*	38	0	**38**	**0**
2009–10	WBA	0	0		
2009–10	*Tranmere R*	37	0	**37**	**0**
2010–11	WBA	0	0		
2010–11	*Charlton Ath*	0	0		
2010–11	*Rochdale*	1	0	**1**	**0**
2010–11	*Bristol R*	9	0	**9**	**0**
2011–12	WBA	0	0		
2011–12	*Southend U*	9	0	**9**	**0**
2012–13	WBA	0	0		
2013–14	WBA	1	0		
2014–15	WBA	0	0	**1**	**0**
2014–15	Scunthorpe U	23	0		
2015–16	Scunthorpe U	39	0		

2016–17 Scunthorpe U 39 0 **101 0**
2016–17 Brentford 0 0
2017–18 Brentford 1 0
2018–19 Brentford 12 0
2019–20 Brentford 0 0 **13 0**

DERVISOGLU, Halil (F) 55 15
Internationals: Turkey U19, U21.
2017–18 Sparta Rotterdam 0 0
2018–19 Sparta Rotterdam 34 10
2019–20 Sparta Rotterdam 17 5 **51 15**
2019–20 Brentford 4 0 **4 0**

FORSS, Marcus (F) 26 12
H: 6 1 b. 18-6-99
Internationals: Finland U17, U18, U19, U21.
From WBA.
2018–19 Brentford 6 1
2019–20 Brentford 2 0 **8 1**
2019–20 *AFC Wimbledon* 18 11 **18 11**

FOSU, Tarique (M) 140 29
H: 5 7 W: 10 08 b. 5-11-95
Internationals: England U18.
2013–14 Reading 0 0
2014–15 Reading 1 0
2015–16 Reading 0 0
2015–16 *Fleetwood T* 6 1 **6 1**
2015–16 *Accrington S* 8 3 **8 3**
2016–17 Reading 0 0 **1 0**
2016–17 *Colchester U* 33 5 **33 5**
2017–18 Charlton Ath 30 9
2018–19 Charlton Ath 27 2 **57 11**
2019–20 Oxford U 25 8 **25 8**
2019–20 Brentford 10 1 **10 1**

GUNNARSSON, Patrik (G) 9 0
b. 15-11-00
Internationals: Iceland U16, U17, U18, U19, U21.
From Breidablik.
2018–19 Brentford 1 0
2018–19 *IR* 5 0 **5 0**
2019–20 Brentford 0 0 **1 0**
2019–20 *Southend U* 3 0 **3 0**

HAMMAR, Fredrik (M) 13 4
b. 26-2-01
Internationals: Sweden U17, U19.
2017 Brommapojkarna 1 0
2018 Brommapojkarna 0 0
2018 Akropolis 12 4 **12 4**
2019–20 Brommapojkarna 0 0 **1 0**
2019–20 Brentford 0 0

HENRY, Rico (D) 126 3
H: 5 7 W: 10 06 b.Birmingham 8-7-97
Internationals: England U19, U20.
2014–15 Walsall 9 0
2015–16 Walsall 35 2
2016–17 Walsall 2 0 **46 2**
2016–17 Brentford 12 0
2017–18 Brentford 8 0
2018–19 Brentford 14 1
2019–20 Brentford 46 0 **80 1**

JANSSON, Pontus (D) 272 20
H: 6 3 W: 13 08 b.Arlov 13-2-91
Internationals: Sweden U17, U19, U21, Full caps.
2009 Malmo 2 0
2009 *IFK Malmo* 9 4 **9 4**
2010 Malmo 18 1
2011 Malmo 15 2
2012 Malmo 30 1
2013 Malmo 24 1
2014 Malmo 9 1 **98 6**
2014–15 Torino 9 0
2015–16 Torino 7 1
2015–16 Torino 0 0 **16 1**
2016–17 *Leeds U* 34 3
2017–18 Leeds U 42 3
2018–19 Leeds U 39 3 **115 9**
2019–20 Brentford 34 0 **34 0**

JEANVIER, Julian (D) 159 10
H: 6 0 W: 12 04 b.Clichy 31-3-92
Internationals: Guinea Full caps.
2012–13 Nancy 6 0 **6 0**
2013–14 Lille 0 0
2014–15 Lille 0 0
2014–15 *Mouscron-Peruwelz* 17 0 **17 0**
2015–16 Lille 0 0
2015–16 *Red Star* 24 2 **24 2**
2016–17 Reims 29 3
2017–18 Reims 33 2 **62 5**
2018–19 Brentford 24 2
2019–20 Brentford 26 1 **50 3**

JENSEN, Mathias (M) 108 16
b. 1-1-96
Internationals: Denmark U18, U19, U20, U21.
2015–16 Nordsjaelland 5 1
2016–17 Nordsjaelland 22 2
2017–18 Nordsjaelland 35 12
2018–19 Nordsjaelland 1 0 **63 15**
2018–19 Celta Vigo 6 0 **6 0**
2019–20 Brentford 39 1 **39 1**

KARELIS, Nikolaos (F) 188 53
b.Rethymno 24-2-92
Internationals: Greece U17, U19, U21, Full caps.
2007–08 Ergotelis 1 0
2008–09 Ergotelis 2 0
2009–10 Ergotelis 6 0
2010–11 Ergotelis 12 1
2011–12 Ergotelis 9 0 **30 1**
2012–13 Amkar Perm 9 0 **9 0**
2013–14 Panathinaikos 32 5
2014–15 Panathinaikos 36 16
2015–16 Panathinaikos 16 8 **84 29**
2015–16 Genk 18 10
2016–17 Genk 18 9
2017–18 Genk 20 4 **56 23**
2018–19 PAOK 5 0 **5 0**
2019–20 Brentford 4 0 **4 0**

MARCONDES, Emiliano (M) 174 41
H: 6 0 W: 11 11 b.Hvidovre 9-3-95
Internationals: Denmark U17, U18, U19, U20, U21.
2012–13 Nordsjaelland 3 0
2013–14 Nordsjaelland 11 1
2014–15 Nordsjaelland 24 5
2015–16 Nordsjaelland 30 2
2016–17 Nordsjaelland 25 12
2017–18 Nordsjaelland 19 17 **112 37**
2017–18 Brentford 12 0
2018–19 Brentford 13 0
2019–20 Brentford 25 2 **50 2**
2019–20 *Midtjylland* 12 2 **12 2**

MBEUMO, Bryan (M) 83 26
b.Avallon 7-8-99
Internationals: France U17, U20, U21.
2016–17 Troyes 0 0
2017–18 Troyes 4 0
2018–19 Troyes 35 10
2019–20 Troyes 2 1 **41 11**
2019–20 Brentford 42 15 **42 15**

MOGENSEN, Gustav (F) 0 0
b. 19-4-01
Internationals: Denmark U16, U17, U18, U19.
From Aarhus.
2019–20 Brentford 0 0

MOKOTJO, Kamohelo (M) 279 11
H: 5 6 W: 9 13 b.Odendaalsrus 11-3-91
Internationals: South Africa U20, U23, Full caps.
2008–09 SuperSport U 1 0
2009–10 SuperSport U 0 0 **1 0**
2009–10 *Excelsior* 25 1 **25 1**
2010–11 Feyenoord 14 0
2011–12 Feyenoord 20 0
2012–13 Feyenoord 1 0 **35 0**
2013–14 PEC Zwolle 27 2
2014–15 PEC Zwolle 0 0 **27 2**
2014–15 FC Twente 33 1
2015–16 FC Twente 31 1
2016–17 FC Twente 33 1 **97 3**
2017–18 Brentford 35 1
2018–19 Brentford 34 3
2019–20 Brentford 25 1 **94 5**

NORGAARD, Christian (M) 165 8
b.Copenhagen 10-3-94
Internationals: Denmark U16, U17, U19, U20, U21.
2011–12 Lyngby 1 0 **1 0**
2012–13 Hamburg 0 0
2013–14 Brondby 13 0
2014–15 Brondby 21 3
2015–16 Brondby 16 0
2016–17 Brondby 31 4
2017–18 Brondby 34 1
2018–19 Brondby 1 0 **116 8**
2018–19 Fiorentina 6 0 **6 0**
2019–20 Brentford 42 0 **42 0**

OKSANEN, Jaako (D) 26 2
H: 6 0 W: 11 05 b.Helsinki 7-11-00
Internationals: Finland U16, U17, U18, U19, U21.
2016 Klubi 04 1 0
2017 Klubi 04 22 2 **23 2**
2017 HJK Helsinki 1 0 **1 0**
2018–19 Brentford 1 0
2019–20 Brentford 1 0 **2 0**

PINNOCK, Ethan (D) 94 5
H: 6 4 W: 12 06 b.Lambeth 29-5-93
Internationals: England C.
From Dulwich Hamlet.
2017–18 Barnsley 12 2
2018–19 Barnsley 46 1 **58 3**
2019–20 Brentford 36 2 **36 2**

RACIC, Luka (D) 6 1
b.Greve 8-5-99
Internationals: Denmark U16, U17, U18, U19, U20, U21.
2018–19 Brentford 2 0
2019–20 Brentford 4 1 **6 1**

RAYA, David (G) 144 0
H: 6 0 W: 12 08 b.Barcelona 15-9-95
2013–14 Blackburn R 0 0
2014–15 Blackburn R 2 0
2015–16 Blackburn R 5 0
2016–17 Blackburn R 5 0
2017–18 Blackburn R 45 0
2018–19 Blackburn R 41 0 **98 0**
2019–20 Brentford 46 0 **46 0**

READ, Arthur (M) 0 0
H: 5 10 W: 10 01 b.Leighton Buzzard 3-11-99
2018–19 Luton T 0 0
2019–20 Brentford 0 0

ROERSLEV RASMUSSEN, Mads (D) 21 0
b. 24-6-99
Internationals: Denmark U17, U18, U19, U20, U21.
2016–17 FC Copenhagen 3 0
2016–17 *Halmstads* 1 0 **1 0**
2017–18 FC Copenhagen 2 0
2018–19 FC Copenhagen 0 0
2018–19 *Vendsyssel* 4 0 **4 0**
2019–20 FC Copenhagen 0 0 **5 0**
2019–20 Brentford 11 0 **11 0**

SERY, Japhet (D) 0 0
b. 10-4-00
Internationals: Denmark U16, U17, U18, U19, U21.
2019–20 Midtylland 0 0
On loan from Midtylland.
2019–20 Brentford 0 0

SHAIBU, Justin (F) 40 0
H: 5 11 b. 28-10-97
Internationals: Denmark U17, U18, U20.
2014–15 HB Koge 8 0
2015–16 HB Koge 12 0 **20 0**
2016–17 Brentford 4 0
2017–18 Brentford 2 0
2017–18 *Walsall* 14 0 **14 0**
2018–19 Brentford 0 0
2019–20 Brentford 0 0 **6 0**

SORENSEN, Mads (D) 38 1
H: 6 1 W: 11 07 b. 7-1-99
Internationals: Denmark U18, U19, U21.
2014–15 Horsens 6 0
2015–16 Horsens 5 0
2016–17 Horsens 6 0
2017–18 Horsens 3 1 **20 1**
2017–18 Brentford 0 0
2018–19 Brentford 8 0
2019–20 Brentford 1 0 **9 0**
2019–20 *AFC Wimbledon* 9 0 **9 0**

THOMPSON, Dominic (M) 2 0
b.Barnet 26-7-00
2018–19 Arsenal 0 0
2019–20 Brentford 2 0 **2 0**

VALENCIA, Joel (F) 155 12
b.Esmeraldas 16-11-94
Internationals: Spain U17. Ecuador U17.
2011–12 Zaragoza 1 0
2012–13 Zaragoza 0 0
2013–14 Zaragoza 0 0 **1 0**
2014–15 Logrones 33 1
2015–16 Logrones 17 0 **50 1**
2015–16 Koper 13 1
2016–17 Koper 13 0 **26 1**
2017–18 Piast Gliwice 25 3
2018–19 Piast Gliwice 33 6
2019–20 Piast Gliwice 1 0 **59 9**
2019–20 Brentford 19 1 **19 1**

WATKINS, Ollie (F) 200 66
H: 5 10 W: 11 00 b.Torbay 30-12-95
2013–14 Exeter C 1 0

2014–15	Exeter C	2	0		
2015–16	Exeter C	20	8		
2016–17	Exeter C	45	13	**68**	**21**
2017–18	Brentford	45	10		
2018–19	Brentford	41	10		
2019–20	Brentford	46	25	**132**	**45**

YEARWOOD, Dru (M) 54 0
H: 5 9 W: 9 13 b. 17-2-00

2017–18	Southend U	25	0		
2018–19	Southend U	27	0		
2019–20	Southend U	0	0	**52**	**0**
2019–20	Brentford	2	0	**2**	**0**

ZAMBUREK, Jan (M) 17 0
H: 6 0 b. 13-2-01
Internationals: Czech Republic U16, U17, U18, U19.

2018–19	Brentford	1	0		
2019–20	Brentford	16	0	**17**	**0**

Players retained or with offer of contract
Andersson, Simon Leonard; Carre, Julien Serge; Dalsgaard, Henrik; Hansen, Emiliano Marcondes; Koutsimouka, Aubrel Fady Widel; Maghoma, Edmond-Paris; O'Connor, Kane; Pressley, Aaron Alex; Shepperd, Nathan.

BRIGHTON & HA (13)

AHANNACH, Soufyan (M) 99 29

2012–13	Almere C	2	0		
2013–14	Almere C	6	0		
2014–15	Almere C	13	3		
2015–16	Almere C	26	7		
2016–17	Almere C	38	18	**85**	**28**
2017–18	Brighton & HA	0	0		
2017–18	*Sparta Rotterdam*	12	1	**12**	**1**
2018–19	Brighton & HA	0	0		
2019–20	Brighton & HA	0	0		
2019–20	*Union Saint-Gilloise*	2	0	**2**	**0**

Transferred to Go Ahead Eagles, January 2020.

ALZATE, Steve (M) 53 3
H: 5 10 W: 10 03 b.Camden Town 1-9-98
Internationals: Colombia Full caps.

2016–17	Leyton Orient	12	1	**12**	**1**
2017–18	Brighton & HA	0	0		
2018–18	Brighton & HA	0	0		
2018–19	*Swindon T*	22	2	**22**	**2**
2019–20	Brighton & HA	19	0	**19**	**0**

ANDONE, Florin (F) 191 63
H: 6 0 W: 11 07 b.Botosani 5-1-94
Internationals: Romania U19, Full caps.

2012–13	Villarreal	0	0		
2013–14	Villarreal	0	0		
2013–14	*Atletico Baleares*	34	12	**34**	**12**
2014–15	Cordoba	20	5		
2015–16	Cordoba	36	21	**56**	**26**
2016–17	Deportivo la Coruna	37	12		
2017–18	Deportivo la Coruna	29	7	**66**	**19**
2018–19	Brighton & HA	23	3		
2019–20	Brighton & HA	3	1	**26**	**4**
2019–20	*Galatasaray*	9	2	**9**	**2**

ARCE, Billy (F) 68 21

2016	Independiente	0	0		
2017	Independiente	32	12		
2018	Independiente	20	6	**52**	**18**
2018–19	Brighton & HA	0	0		
2018–19	*Extramadura*	3	0	**3**	**0**
2019–20	Brighton & HA	0	0		
2019–20	*Emelec*	6	2	**6**	**2**
2019–20	*Barcelona*	7	1	**7**	**1**

BALUTA, Tudor (M) 57 2
b.Craiova 27-3-99
Internationals: Romania U19, U21, Full caps.

2015–16	Viitorul Constanta	2	0		
2016–17	Viitorul Constanta	0	0		
2017–18	Viitorul Constanta	24	0		
2018–19	Viitorul Constanta	27	2	**53**	**2**
2019–20	Brighton & HA	0	0		
2019–20	*Den Haag*	4	0	**4**	**0**

BERNARDO, Junior (D) 96 2
H: 6 1 W: 12 00 b.S„o Paulo 14-5-95

2014	Red Bull Brasil	0	0		
2015	Red Bull Brasil	3	0	**3**	**0**
2015–16	Liefering	1	0	**1**	**0**
2015–16	Red Bull Salzburg	13	0		
2016–17	Red Bull Salzburg	3	1	**16**	**1**
2016–17	RB Leipzig	22	0		
2017–18	RB Leipzig	18	1	**40**	**1**
2018–19	Brighton & HA	22	0		
2019–20	Brighton & HA	14	0	**36**	**0**

BISSOUMA, Yves (M) 97 4
H: 5 9 W: 12 04 b.Issia 30-8-96
Internationals: Mali Full caps.

2016–17	Lille	23	1		
2017–18	Lille	24	2	**47**	**3**
2018–19	Brighton & HA	28	0		
2019–20	Brighton & HA	22	1	**50**	**1**

BURN, Dan (D) 258 9
H: 6 6 W: 13 00 b.Blyth 1-5-92

2009–10	Darlington	4	0	**4**	**0**
2010–11	Fulham	0	0		
2011–12	Fulham	0	0		
2012–13	Fulham	0	0		
2012–13	*Yeovil T*	34	2	**34**	**2**
2013–14	Fulham	9	0		
2013–14	*Birmingham C*	24	0	**24**	**0**
2014–15	Fulham	20	1		
2015–16	Fulham	32	0	**61**	**1**
2016–17	Wigan Ath	42	1		
2017–18	Wigan Ath	45	5		
2018–19	Wigan Ath	14	0	**101**	**6**
2018–19	Brighton & HA	0	0		
2019–20	Brighton & HA	34	0	**34**	**0**

BUTTON, David (G) 293 0
H: 6 3 W: 13 00 b.Stevenage 27-2-89
Internationals: England U16, U17, U19, U20.

2005–06	Tottenham H	0	0		
2006–07	Tottenham H	0	0		
2007–08	*Rochdale*	0	0		
2007–08	Tottenham H	0	0		
2008–09	Tottenham H	0	0		
2008–09	*Bournemouth*	4	0	**4**	**0**
2008–09	*Luton T*	0	0		
2008–09	*Dagenham & R*	3	0	**3**	**0**
2009–10	Tottenham H	0	0		
2009–10	*Crewe Alex*	10	0	**10**	**0**
2009–10	*Shrewsbury T*	26	0	**26**	**0**
2010–11	Tottenham H	0	0		
2010–11	*Plymouth Arg*	30	0	**30**	**0**
2011–12	Tottenham H	0	0		
2011–12	*Leyton Orient*	1	0	**1**	**0**
2011–12	*Doncaster R*	7	0	**7**	**0**
2011–12	*Barnsley*	9	0	**9**	**0**
2012–13	Tottenham H	0	0		
2012–13	Charlton Ath	5	0	**5**	**0**
2013–14	Brentford	42	0		
2014–15	Brentford	46	0		
2015–16	Brentford	46	0	**134**	**0**
2016–17	Fulham	40	0		
2017–18	Fulham	20	0	**60**	**0**
2018–19	Brighton & HA	4	0		
2019–20	Brighton & HA	0	0	**4**	**0**

COCHRANE, Alex (M) 0 0
b. 21-4-00
Internationals: England U16, U20.

2019–20	Brighton & HA	0	0		

CONNOLLY, Aaron (F) 26 3
b. 28-1-00
Internationals: Republic of Ireland U17, U19, U21, Full caps.

2017–18	Brighton & HA	0	0		
2018–19	Brighton & HA	0	0		
2018–19	*Luton T*	2	0	**2**	**0**
2019–20	Brighton & HA	24	3	**24**	**3**

COX, George (M) 26 1
b. 14-1-98

2018–19	Brighton & HA	0	0		
2018–19	*Northampton T*	5	0	**5**	**0**
2019–20	Brighton & HA	0	0		
2019–20	*Fortuna Sittard*	21	1	**21**	**1**

DAVIES, Archie (M) 0 0
b. 7-10-98

2019–20	Brighton & HA	0	0		

DAVIES, Jordan (D) 0 0
b.Wrexham 18-8-98

2019–20	Brighton & HA	0	0		

DUFFY, Shane (D) 246 16
H: 6 4 W: 12 00 b.Derry 1-1-92
Internationals: Northern Ireland U16, U17, U19, U21, B. Republic of Ireland U19, U21, Full caps.

2008–09	Everton	0	0		
2009–10	Everton	0	0		
2010–11	Everton	0	0		
2010–11	*Burnley*	1	0	**1**	**0**
2011–12	Everton	4	0		
2011–12	*Scunthorpe U*	18	2	**18**	**2**
2012–13	Everton	1	0		
2013–14	Everton	0	0		
2013–14	*Yeovil T*	37	1	**37**	**1**
2014–15	Everton	0	0	**5**	**0**
2014–15	Blackburn R	19	1		
2015–16	Blackburn R	41	4		
2016–17	Blackburn R	3	0	**63**	**5**
2016–17	Brighton & HA	31	2		
2017–18	Brighton & HA	37	0		
2018–19	Brighton & HA	35	5		
2019–20	Brighton & HA	19	1	**122**	**8**

DUNK, Lewis (D) 282 16
H: 6 3 W: 12 02 b.Brighton 1-12-91
Internationals: England Full caps.

2009–10	Brighton & HA	1	0		
2010–11	Brighton & HA	5	0		
2011–12	Brighton & HA	31	0		
2012–13	Brighton & HA	8	0		
2013–14	Brighton & HA	6	0		
2013–14	*Bristol C*	2	0	**2**	**0**
2014–15	Brighton & HA	38	5		
2015–16	Brighton & HA	38	3		
2016–17	Brighton & HA	43	2		
2017–18	Brighton & HA	38	1		
2018–19	Brighton & HA	36	2		
2019–20	Brighton & HA	36	3	**280**	**16**

GROSS, Pascal (M) 280 32
H: 5 7 W: 10 06 b.Bad Salzungen 15-6-91
Internationals: Germany U18, U19.

2008–09	1899 Hoffenheim	4	0		
2009–10	1899 Hoffenheim	1	0		
2010–11	1899 Hoffenheim	0	0	**5**	**0**
2010–11	Karlsruher	3	1		
2011–12	Karlsruher	22	2	**25**	**3**
2012–13	Ingolstadt 04	30	2		
2013–14	Ingolstadt 04	29	2		
2014–15	Ingolstadt 04	34	7		
2015–16	Ingolstadt 04	32	1		
2016–17	Ingolstadt 04	33	5	**158**	**17**
2017–18	Brighton & HA	38	7		
2018–19	Brighton & HA	25	3		
2019–20	Brighton & HA	29	2	**92**	**12**

GWARGIS, Peter (M) 35 4
b.Sidney 4-9-00
Internationals: Sweden U17, U19.

2017	Husqvarna	19	1	**19**	**1**
2018	Jonkopings	16	3	**16**	**3**
2019–20	Brighton & HA	0	0		

IFILL, Markus (M) 0 0
b. 2-11-03

2019–20	Brighton & HA	0	0		

IZQUIERDO, Jose (D) 240 65
H: 5 7 W: 11 07 b.Pereira 7-7-92
Internationals: Colombia Full caps.

2010	Deportivo Pereira	9	1		
2011	Deportivo Pereira	21	1		
2012	Deportivo Pereira	24	10		
2013	Deportivo Pereira	15	2	**69**	**14**
2013	Once Caldas	16	3		
2014	Once Caldas	24	9	**40**	**12**
2014–15	Club Brugge	32	13		
2015–16	Club Brugge	24	7		
2016–17	Club Brugge	28	14		
2017–18	Club Brugge	0	0	**84**	**34**
2017–18	Brighton & HA	32	5		
2018–19	Brighton & HA	15	0		
2019–20	Brighton & HA	0	0	**47**	**5**

JAHANBAKHSH, Alireza (M) 225 63
H: 5 11 W: 12 02 b.Jirandeh 11-8-93
Internationals: Iran U20, U23, Full caps.

2010–11	Damash Tehran	12	0	**12**	**0**
2011–12	Damash Gilan	16	2		
2012–13	Damash Gilan	28	8	**44**	**10**
2013–14	NEC	27	5		
2014–15	NEC	28	12	**55**	**17**
2015–16	AZ Alkmaar	23	3		
2016–17	AZ Alkmaar	29	10		
2017–18	AZ Alkmaar	33	21	**85**	**34**
2018–19	Brighton & HA	19	0		
2019–20	Brighton & HA	10	2	**29**	**2**

JENKS, Teddy (M) 0 0
b. 12-3-02
Internationals: England U16, U17.

2019–20	Brighton & HA	0	0		

KAYAL, Beram (M) 267 8
H: 5 10 W: 11 09 b.Jadeidi 2-5-88
Internationals: Israel U17, U18, U19, U21, Full caps.

2008–09	Maccabi Haifa	30	1		
2009–10	Maccabi Haifa	27	1	**57**	**2**
2010–11	Celtic	21	2		
2011–12	Celtic	19	0		
2012–13	Celtic	27	0		
2013–14	Celtic	13	0		
2014–15	Celtic	6	0	**86**	**2**

2014–15	Brighton & HA	18	1		
2015–16	Brighton & HA	43	2		
2016–17	Brighton & HA	20	0		
2017–18	Brighton & HA	19	0		
2018–19	Brighton & HA	18	1		
2019–20	Brighton & HA	0	0	**118**	**4**
2019–20	*Charlton Ath*	6	0	**6**	**0**

KNOCKAERT, Anthony (M) 316 56
H: 5 8 W: 10 11 b.Lille 20-11-91
Internationals: France U20, U21.

2011–12	Guingamp	34	10	**34**	**10**
2012–13	Leicester C	42	8		
2013–14	Leicester C	42	5		
2014–15	Leicester C	9	0	**93**	**13**
2015–16	Standard Liege	20	5	**20**	**5**
2015–16	Brighton & HA	19	5		
2016–17	Brighton & HA	45	15		
2017–18	Brighton & HA	33	3		
2018–19	Brighton & HA	30	2	**127**	**25**
2019–20	*Fulham*	42	3	**42**	**3**

LAMPTEY, Tariq (M) 9 0
b.Hilingdon 30-9-00
Internationals: England U18, U19, U20.

2019–20	Chelsea	1	0	**1**	**0**
2019–20	Brighton & HA	8	0	**8**	**0**

LOCADIA, Jurgen (F) 175 54
H: 6 2 W: 12 04 b.Emmen 7-11-93
Internationals: Netherlands U17, U18, U19, U20, U21.

2011–12	PSV Eindhoven	0	0		
2012–13	PSV Eindhoven	15	6		
2013–14	PSV Eindhoven	31	13		
2014–15	PSV Eindhoven	23	6		
2015–16	PSV Eindhoven	29	8		
2016–17	PSV Eindhoven	14	3		
2017–18	PSV Eindhoven	15	9	**127**	**45**
2017–18	Brighton & HA	6	1		
2018–19	Brighton & HA	26	2		
2019–20	Brighton & HA	2	0	**34**	**3**
2019–20	*Hoffenheim*	11	4	**11**	**4**
2019–20	*Cincinnati*	3	2	**3**	**2**

LONGMAN, Ryan (M) 0 0
b. 6-11-00

2019–20	Brighton & HA	0	0		

MAC ALLISTER, Alexis (M) 88 11
Internationals: Argentina U23, Full caps.

2016–17	Argentinos Juniors	23	3		
2017–18	Argentinos Juniors	24	2		
2018–19	Argentinos Juniors	19	5	**66**	**10**
2019–20	Brighton & HA	9	0	**9**	**0**
2019–20	*Boca Juniors*	13	1	**13**	**1**

MARCH, Solly (M) 165 9
H: 6 1 W: 12 02 b.Lewes 26-7-94
Internationals: England U20, U21.

2012–13	Brighton & HA	0	0		
2013–14	Brighton & HA	23	0		
2014–15	Brighton & HA	11	1		
2015–16	Brighton & HA	16	3		
2016–17	Brighton & HA	25	3		
2017–18	Brighton & HA	36	1		
2018–19	Brighton & HA	35	1		
2019–20	Brighton & HA	19	0	**165**	**9**

MAUPAY, Neal (F) 209 65
H: 5 7 W: 10 12 b.Versailles 14-8-96
Internationals: France U16, U17, U19, U21.

2012–13	Nice	15	3		
2013–14	Nice	16	2		
2014–15	Nice	13	1	**44**	**6**
2015–16	Saint-Etienne	15	1		
2016–17	Saint-Etienne	0	0	**15**	**1**
2016–17	*Brest*	28	11	**28**	**11**
2017–18	Brentford	42	12		
2018–19	Brentford	43	25		
2019–20	Brentford	0	0	**85**	**37**
2019–20	Brighton & HA	37	10	**37**	**10**

McGILL, Thomas (G) 0 0
Internationals: England U16, U17, U19, U20.

2019–20	Brighton & HA	0	0		
2019–20	*Crawley T*	0	0		

MLAKAR, Jan (F) 49 16
b.Ljublijana 23-10-98
Internationals: Slovenia U17, U19, U21, B.

2016–17	Fiorentina	1	0		
2017–18	Fiorentina	0	0	**1**	**0**
2017–18	*Venezia*	3	0	**3**	**0**
2017–18	Maribor	12	3		
2018–19	Maribor	26	13	**38**	**16**
2019–20	Brighton & HA	0	0		
2019–20	Brighton & HA	0	0		
2019–20	*QPR*	6	0	**6**	**0**
2019–20	*Wigan Ath*	1	0	**1**	**0**

MOLUMBY, Jayson (M) 36 1
b. 6-8-99
Internationals: Republic of Ireland U16, U17, U19, U21.

2017–18	Brighton & HA	0	0		
2018–19	Brighton & HA	0	0		
2019–20	Brighton & HA	0	0		
2019–20	*Millwall*	36	1	**36**	**1**

MONTOYA, Martin (D) 167 3
H: 5 9 W: 11 09 b.Barcelona 14-4-91
Internationals: Spain U17, U18, U19, U21, U23.

2008–09	Barcelona	0	0		
2009–10	Barcelona	0	0		
2010–11	Barcelona	2	0		
2011–12	Barcelona	7	0		
2012–13	Barcelona	15	1		
2013–14	Barcelona	13	0		
2014–15	Barcelona	8	0		
2015–16	Barcelona	0	0	**45**	**1**
2015–16	*Inter Milan*	3	0	**3**	**0**
2015–16	*Real Betis*	13	0	**13**	**0**
2016–17	Valencia	29	2		
2017–18	Valencia	25	0	**54**	**2**
2018–19	Brighton & HA	25	0		
2019–20	Brighton & HA	27	0	**52**	**0**

MOOY, Aaron (M) 265 36
H: 5 9 W: 10 10 b.Sydney 15-9-90
Internationals: Australia U20, U23, Full caps.

2009–10	Bolton W	0	0		
2010–11	St Mirren	13	0		
2011–12	St Mirren	8	1	**21**	**1**
2012–13	Western Sydney W	23	1		
2013–14	Western Sydney W	26	3	**49**	**4**
2014–15	Melbourne C	27	7		
2015–16	Melbourne C	26	11	**53**	**18**
2016–17	Manchester C	0	0		
2016–17	*Huddersfield T*	45	4		
2017–18	Huddersfield T	36	4		
2018–19	Huddersfield T	29	3		
2019–20	Huddersfield T	1	0	**111**	**11**
2019–20	Brighton & HA	31	2	**31**	**2**

MURRAY, Glenn (F) 501 189
H: 6 1 W: 12 12 b.Maryport 25-9-83

2005–06	Carlisle U	26	3		
2006–07	Carlisle U	1	0	**27**	**3**
2006–07	*Stockport Co*	11	3	**11**	**3**
2006–07	Rochdale	31	16		
2007–08	Rochdale	23	9	**54**	**25**
2007–08	Brighton & HA	21	9		
2008–09	Brighton & HA	23	11		
2009–10	Brighton & HA	32	12		
2010–11	Brighton & HA	42	22		
2011–12	Crystal Palace	38	6		
2012–13	Crystal Palace	42	30		
2013–14	Crystal Palace	14	1		
2014–15	Crystal Palace	17	7		
2014–15	*Reading*	18	8	**18**	**8**
2015–16	Crystal Palace	2	0	**113**	**44**
2015–16	Bournemouth	19	3	**19**	**3**
2016–17	Brighton & HA	45	23		
2017–18	Brighton & HA	35	12		
2018–19	Brighton & HA	38	13		
2019–20	Brighton & HA	23	1	**259**	**103**

O'HORA, Warren (D) 0 0
b.Dublin 19-4-99
From Bohemians.

2019–20	Brighton & HA	0	0		

OSTIGARD, Leo (D) 40 1
Internationals: Norway U16, U17, U18, U19, U20, U21, U23.

2017–18	Molde	1	0	**1**	**0**
2017–18	*Viking*	11	0	**11**	**0**
2018–19	Brighton & HA	0	0		
2019–20	Brighton & HA	0	0		
2019–20	*St Pauli*	28	1	**28**	**1**

PROPPER, Davy (M) 309 36
H: 6 1 W: 11 05 b.Arnhem 2-9-91
Internationals: Netherlands U19, U21, Full caps.

2009–10	Vitesse	11	0		
2010–11	Vitesse	29	3		
2011–12	Vitesse	19	1		
2012–13	Vitesse	14	0		
2013–14	Vitesse	35	7		
2014–15	Vitesse	34	7	**142**	**18**
2015–16	PSV Eindhoven	33	10		
2016–17	PSV Eindhoven	34	6	**67**	**16**
2017–18	PSV	0	0		
2017–18	Brighton & HA	35	0		
2018–19	Brighton & HA	30	1		
2019–20	Brighton & HA	35	1	**100**	**2**

RADULOVIC, Bojan (F) 0 0
b.Lleida 1-1-99
Internationals: Serbia U19.
From Liedia.

2017–18	Brighton & HA	0	0		
2018–19	Brighton & HA	0	0		
2019–20	Brighton & HA	0	0		

RICHARDS, Taylor (M) 0 0
b.London 4-12-00
Internationals: England U17.

2018–19	Manchester C	0	0		
2019–20	Brighton & HA	0	0		

ROBERTS, Haydon (D) 0 0
b. 10-5-02
Internationals: England U17, U18.

2019–20	Brighton & HA	0	0		

RYAN, Mathew (G) 305 0
H: 6 0 W: 12 13 b.Plumpton 8-4-82
Internationals: Australia U23, Full caps.

2009	Blacktown C	0	0		
2009–10	Central Coast Mariners	0	0		
2010	Blacktown C	11	0	**11**	**0**
2010–11	Central Coast Mariners	31	0		
2011–12	Central Coast Mariners	24	0		
2012–13	Central Coast Mariners	25	0	**80**	**0**
2013–14	Club Brugge	40	0		
2014–15	Club Brugge	37	0	**77**	**0**
2015–16	Valencia	8	0		
2016–17	Valencia	2	0	**10**	**0**
2016–17	*Genk*	17	0	**17**	**0**
2017–18	Brighton & HA	38	0		
2018–19	Brighton & HA	34	0		
2019–20	Brighton & HA	38	0	**110**	**0**

SANCHEZ, Robert (G) 43 0
b. 18-11-97
From Levante.

2018–19	Brighton & HA	0	0		
2018–19	*Forest Green R*	17	0	**17**	**0**
2019–20	Brighton & HA	0	0		
2019–20	*Rochdale*	26	0	**26**	**0**

SANDERS, Max (M) 20 1
b. 4-1-99
Internationals: England U19.

2017–18	Brighton & HA	0	0		
2018–19	Brighton & HA	0	0		
2019–20	Brighton & HA	0	0		
2019–20	*AFC Wimbledon*	20	1	**20**	**1**

SCHELOTTO, Ezequiel (M) 261 15
H: 6 2 W: 12 00 b.Buenos Aires 23-5-89
Internationals: Italy U21, Full caps.

2008–09	Cesena	0	0		
2009–10	Cesena	40	6		
2010–11	Cesena	17	0		
2010–11	*Cesena*	14	1	**71**	**7**
2011–12	Atalanta	37	2		
2012–13	Atalanta	16	0	**53**	**2**
2012–13	Inter Milan	12	1		
2013–14	Inter Milan	0	0		
2013–14	*Sassuolo*	11	1	**11**	**1**
2013–14	*Parma*	16	4	**16**	**4**
2014–15	Inter Milan	0	0	**12**	**1**
2014–15	*Chievo*	29	0		
2015–16	Sporting Lisbon	14	0		
2016–17	Sporting Lisbon	23	0	**37**	**0**
2017–18	Sporting	0	0		
2017–18	Brighton & HA	20	0		
2018–19	Brighton & HA	0	0		
2018–19	*Chievo*	4	0	**33**	**0**
2019–20	Brighton & HA	8	0	**28**	**0**

SPONG, Jack (M) 0 0
b. 4-2-02

2019–20	Brighton & HA	0	0		

STEELE, Jason (G) 272 0
H: 6 2 W: 12 07 b.Newton Aycliffe 18-8-90
Internationals: England U16, U17, U19, U21. Great Britain.

2007–08	Middlesbrough	0	0		
2008–09	Middlesbrough	0	0		
2009–10	Middlesbrough	0	0		
2009–10	*Northampton T*	13	0	**13**	**0**
2010–11	Middlesbrough	35	0		
2011–12	Middlesbrough	34	0		
2012–13	Middlesbrough	46	0		
2013–14	Middlesbrough	16	0		
2014–15	Middlesbrough	0	0	**131**	**0**
2014–15	*Blackburn R*	31	0		
2015–16	Blackburn R	41	0		
2016–17	Blackburn R	41	0	**113**	**0**
2017–18	Sunderland	15	0	**15**	**0**
2018–19	Brighton & HA	0	0		
2019–20	Brighton & HA	0	0		

STEPHENS, Dale (M)				**378**	**37**
H: 5 7 W: 11 04 b.Bolton 12-6-89					
2006–07	Bury	3	0		
2007–08	Bury	6	1	**9**	**1**
2008–09	Oldham Ath	0	0		
2009–10	Oldham Ath	26	2		
2009–10	*Rochdale*	6	1	**6**	**1**
2010–11	Oldham Ath	34	9	**60**	**11**
2010–11	*Southampton*	6	0	**6**	**0**
2011–12	Charlton Ath	30	5		
2012–13	Charlton Ath	28	2		
2013–14	Charlton Ath	26	3	**84**	**10**
2013–14	Brighton & HA	14	2		
2014–15	Brighton & HA	16	2		
2015–16	Brighton & HA	45	7		
2016–17	Brighton & HA	39	2		
2017–18	Brighton & HA	36	0		
2018–19	Brighton & HA	30	1		
2019–20	Brighton & HA	33	0	**213**	**14**

TAU, Percy (F)				**117**	**30**
b.Witbank 13-5-94					
Internationals: South Africa Full caps.					
2013–14	Mamelodi Sundowns	1	0		
2014–15	Mamelodi Sundowns	5	0		
2015–16	Mamelodi Sundowns	0	0		
2015–16	*Witbank Spurs*	11	3	**11**	**3**
2016–17	Mamelodi Sundowns	29	7		
2017–18	Mamelodi Sundowns	30	11	**65**	**18**
2018–19	Brighton & HA	0	0		
2018–19	*Union*	23	6	**23**	**6**
2019–20	Brighton & HA	0	0		
2019–20	*Club Brugge*	18	3	**18**	**3**

TROSSARD, Leandro (M)				**203**	**66**
b.Waterschei 4-12-94					
Internationals: Belgium U16, U17, U18, U19, U21.					
2011–12	Genk	1	0		
2012–13	Genk	0	0		
2012–13	*Lommel U*	12	7		
2013–14	Genk	0	0		
2013–14	*Westerlo*	17	3	**17**	**3**
2014–15	Genk	0	0		
2014–15	*Lommel U*	30	16	**42**	**23**
2015–16	Genk	0	0		
2015–16	*OH Leuven*	30	8	**30**	**8**
2016–17	Genk	31	6		
2017–18	Genk	17	7		
2018–19	Genk	34	14	**83**	**27**
2019–20	Brighton & HA	31	5	**31**	**5**

WALTON, Christian (G)				**156**	**0**
H: 6 0 W: 11 11 b.Wadebridge 9-11-95					
Internationals: England U19, U20, U21.					
2011–12	Plymouth Arg	0	0		
2012–13	Plymouth Arg	0	0		
2013–14	Brighton & HA	0	0		
2014–15	Brighton & HA	3	0		
2015–16	Brighton & HA	0	0		
2015–16	*Bury*	4	0	**4**	**0**
2015–16	*Plymouth Arg*	4	0	**4**	**0**
2016–17	Brighton & HA	0	0		
2016–17	*Luton T*	27	0	**27**	**0**
2016–17	*Southend U*	7	0	**7**	**0**
2017–18	Brighton & HA	0	0		
2017–18	*Wigan Ath*	31	0		
2018–19	Brighton & HA	0	0		
2018–19	*Wigan Ath*	34	0	**65**	**0**
2019–20	Brighton & HA	0	0	**3**	**0**
2019–20	*Blackburn R*	46	0	**46**	**0**

WEBSTER, Adam (D)				**193**	**12**
H: 6 1 W: 11 11 b.West Wittering 4-1-95					
Internationals: England U18, U19.					
2011–12	Portsmouth	3	0		
2012–13	Portsmouth	18	0		
2013–14	Portsmouth	4	2		
2014–15	Portsmouth	15	1		
2015–16	Portsmouth	27	2	**67**	**5**
2016–17	Ipswich T	23	1		
2017–18	Ipswich T	28	0	**51**	**1**
2018–19	Bristol C	44	3		
2019–20	Bristol C	0	0	**44**	**3**
2019–20	Brighton & HA	31	3	**31**	**3**

WHITE, Ben (D)				**103**	**3**
b.Poole 8-11-97					
2016–17	Brighton & HA	0	0		
2017–18	Brighton & HA	0	0		
2017–18	*Newport Co*	42	1	**42**	**1**
2018–19	Brighton & HA	0	0		
2018–19	*Peterborough U*	15	1	**15**	**1**
2019–20	Brighton & HA	0	0		
2019–20	*Leeds U*	46	1	**46**	**1**

YAPI, Romaric (D)				**0**	**0**
b.Evry 13-7-00					
From Paris Saint-Germain.					
2019–20	Brighton & HA	0	0		

Players retained or with offer of contract
Byrne Furlong, Walter James; Cashman, Danny Christopher; Clarke, Matthew Edward Barkell; Desbois, Adam Jack; Kazukolovas, Kipras; Leonard, Marc Henry; Rushworth, Carl Andrew; Tolaj, Lorent; Tsoungui, Antef; Wilson, Benjamin John.

Scholars
Bull, Toby Graham; Clark-Eden, Ben; Dackers, Marcus Matthias; Everitt, Matthew; Jenkins, Nathan Euan; Leahy, Jack; Miller, Todd Owen; Offiah, Odeluga Joshua; Packham, Samuel James; Rees, Roco; Talley, Fynn Michael Cordell; Tanimowo, Ayobami Babatunde; Turns, Edward James; Vukoje, Stefan Charles.

BRISTOL C (14)

ADELAKUN, Hakeeb (F)				**153**	**16**
H: 6 3 W: 11 11 b.Hackney 11-6-96					
2012–13	Scunthorpe U	2	0		
2013–14	Scunthorpe U	28	2		
2014–15	Scunthorpe U	32	6		
2015–16	Scunthorpe U	21	2		
2016–17	Scunthorpe U	17	2		
2017–18	Scunthorpe U	39	4	**139**	**16**
2018–19	Bristol C	5	0		
2019–20	Bristol C	0	0	**5**	**0**
2019–20	*Rotherham U*	9	0	**9**	**0**

BAKER, Nathan (D)				**255**	**3**
H: 6 2 W: 11 11 b.Worcester 23-4-91					
Internationals: England U19, U20, U21.					
2008–09	Aston Villa	0	0		
2009–10	Aston Villa	0	0		
2009–10	*Lincoln C*	18	0	**18**	**0**
2010–11	Aston Villa	4	0		
2011–12	Aston Villa	8	0		
2011–12	*Millwall*	6	0	**6**	**0**
2012–13	Aston Villa	26	0		
2013–14	Aston Villa	30	0		
2014–15	Aston Villa	11	0		
2015–16	Aston Villa	0	0		
2015–16	*Bristol C*	36	1		
2016–17	Aston Villa	32	1	**111**	**1**
2017–18	Bristol C	34	0		
2018–19	Bristol C	16	0		
2019–20	Bristol C	34	1	**120**	**2**

BAKINSON, Tyreeq (M)				**45**	**3**
H: 6 1 W: 11 00 b.Camden 8-1-98					
2015–16	Luton T	1	0		
2016–17	Luton T	0	0		
2017–18	Luton T	0	0	**1**	**0**
2017–18	Bristol C	0	0		
2018–19	Bristol C	0	0		
2018–19	*Newport Co*	30	1	**30**	**1**
2019–20	Bristol C	0	0		
2019–20	*Plymouth Arg*	14	2	**14**	**2**

BALDWIN, Aden (D)				**4**	**0**
b. 10-6-97					
2018–19	Bristol C	0	0		
2018–19	*Cheltenham T*	4	0	**4**	**0**
2019–20	Bristol C	0	0		

BENTLEY, Daniel (G)				**307**	**0**
H: 6 2 W: 11 05 b.Wickford 13-7-93					
2011–12	Southend U	1	0		
2012–13	Southend U	9	0		
2013–14	Southend U	46	0		
2014–15	Southend U	42	0		
2015–16	Southend U	43	0	**141**	**0**
2016–17	Brentford	45	0		
2017–18	Brentford	45	0		
2018–19	Brentford	33	0	**123**	**0**
2019–20	Bristol C	43	0	**43**	**0**

CUNDY, Robbie (D)				**0**	**0**
b. 30-5-97					
2014–15	Oxford U	0	0		
2015–16	Oxford U	0	0		
2016–17	Oxford U	0	0		
From Gloucester C.					
2019–20	Bristol C	0	0		

DASILVA, Jay (D)				**100**	**0**
b. 22-4-98					
Internationals: England U16, U17, U18, U19, U20, U21.					
2016–17	Chelsea	0	0		
2016–17	*Charlton Ath*	10	0		
2017–18	Chelsea	0	0		
2017–18	*Charlton Ath*	38	0	**48**	**0**
2018–19	Chelsea	0	0		
2018–19	*Bristol C*	28	0		
2019–20	Bristol C	24	0	**52**	**0**

DIEDHIOU, Famara (F)				**282**	**98**
H: 6 4 W: 12 08 b.Saint-Louis 15-12-92					
Internationals: Senegal Full caps.					
2011–12	Belfort	11	3	**11**	**3**
2012–13	Epinal	30	12	**30**	**12**
2013–14	Ajaccio	33	13	**33**	**13**
2014–15	Sochaux	13	1		
2014–15	*Clermont*	14	2		
2015–16	Sochaux	0	0	**13**	**1**
2015–16	*Clermont*	36	21	**50**	**23**
2016–17	Angers	31	8	**31**	**8**
2017–18	Bristol C	32	13		
2018–19	Bristol C	41	13		
2019–20	Bristol C	41	12	**114**	**38**

EDWARDS, Opi (M)				**0**	**0**
b.Bristol 30-4-99					
2017–18	Bristol C	0	0		
2018–19	Bristol C	0	0		
2019–20	Bristol C	0	0		

ELIASSON, Niclas (M)				**173**	**11**
H: 5 9 W: 10 06 b.Varberg 7-12-95					
Internationals: Sweden U17, U19, U21.					
2012	Falkenberg	0	0		
2013	Falkenberg	29	1	**29**	**1**
2014	AIK Solna	16	1		
2015	AIK Solna	10	0		
2016	AIK Solna	5	0	**31**	**1**
2016	*Norrkoping*	13	1		
2017	Norrkoping	17	3	**30**	**4**
2017–18	IFK Norrkoping	0	0		
2017–18	Bristol C	13	0		
2018–19	Bristol C	33	2		
2019–20	Bristol C	37	3	**83**	**5**

GILMARTIN, Rene (G)				**86**	**0**
H: 6 5 W: 13 06 b.Dublin 31-5-87					
Internationals: Republic of Ireland U19, U21.					
2005–06	Walsall	2	0		
2006–07	Walsall	0	0		
2007–08	Walsall	0	0		
2008–09	Walsall	11	0		
2009–10	Walsall	22	0	**35**	**0**
2010–11	Watford	0	0		
2011–12	Watford	2	0		
2011–12	*Yeovil T*	8	0	**8**	**0**
2011–12	*Crawley T*	6	0	**6**	**0**
2012–13	Plymouth Arg	13	0		
2013–14	Plymouth Arg	0	0	**13**	**0**
2014–15	Watford	0	0		
2015–16	Watford	0	0		
2016–17	Watford	0	0	**2**	**0**
2017–18	Colchester U	0	0		
2018–19	Colchester U	22	0	**22**	**0**
2019–20	Bristol C	0	0		

HINDS, Freddy (F)				**13**	**0**
H: 5 9 W: 10 08 b.Potton 28-1-99					
2016–17	Luton T	0	0		
2017–18	Bristol C	1	0		
2017–18	*Cheltenham T*	12	0	**12**	**0**
2018–19	Bristol C	0	0		
2019–20	Bristol C	0	0	**1**	**0**
2019–20	*Colchester U*	0	0		

HOLDEN, Rory (F)				**35**	**2**
H: 5 7 W: 10 10 b.Derry 23-8-97					
Internationals: Northern Ireland U21.					
From Derry C.					
2017–18	Bristol C	0	0		
2018–19	Bristol C	0	0		
2018–19	*Rochdale*	6	0	**6**	**0**
2019–20	Bristol C	0	0		
2019–20	*Walsall*	29	2	**29**	**2**

HUNT, Jack (D)				**331**	**3**
H: 5 9 W: 11 02 b.Rothwell 6-12-90					
2009–10	Huddersfield T	0	0		
2010–11	Huddersfield T	19	1		
2010–11	*Chesterfield*	20	0	**20**	**0**
2011–12	Huddersfield T	43	1		
2012–13	Huddersfield T	40	0		
2013–14	Huddersfield T	2	0	**104**	**2**
2013–14	Crystal Palace	0	0		
2013–14	*Barnsley*	11	0	**11**	**0**
2014–15	Crystal Palace	0	0		
2014–15	*Nottingham F*	17	0	**17**	**0**
2014–15	*Rotherham U*	16	0	**16**	**0**
2015–16	Sheffield W	34	0		
2016–17	Sheffield W	32	0		
2017–18	Sheffield W	29	0	**95**	**0**
2018–19	Bristol C	33	1		
2019–20	Bristol C	35	0	**68**	**1**

JANNEH, Saikou (F)				**0**	**0**
From Clevedon T.					
2018–19	Bristol C	0	0		
2019–20	Bristol C	0	0		

KALAS, Tomas (D)				**214**	**2**
H: 6 0 W: 12 00 b.Olomouc 15-5-93					
Internationals: Czech Republic U17, U18, U19, U21, Full caps.					
2009–10	Sigma Olomouc	1	0		
2010–11	Chelsea	0	0		
2010–11	*Sigma Olomouc*	4	0	**5**	**0**
2011–12	Chelsea	0	0		
2012–13	Chelsea	0	0		
2012–13	*Vitesse*	34	1	**34**	**1**
2013–14	Chelsea	2	0		
2014–15	Chelsea	0	0		
2014–15	*Cologne*	0	0		
2014–15	*Middlesbrough*	17	0		
2015–16	Chelsea	0	0		
2015–16	*Middlesbrough*	26	0	**43**	**0**
2016–17	Chelsea	0	0		
2016–17	*Fulham*	36	1		
2017–18	Chelsea	0	0		
2017–18	*Fulham*	33	0	**69**	**1**
2018–19	Chelsea	0	0	**2**	**0**
2018–19	*Bristol C*	38	0		
2019–20	Bristol C	23	0	**61**	**0**

LEMONHEIGH-EVANS, Connor (F)				**0**	**0**
b. 24-1-97					
Internationals: Wales U16, U17, U18, U21.					
2013–14	Bristol C	0	0		
2014–15	Bristol C	0	0		
2015–16	Bristol C	0	0		
2016–17	Bristol C	0	0		
2017–18	Bristol C	0	0		
2018–19	Bristol C	0	0		
2019–20	Bristol C	0	0		

MAENPAA, Niki (G)				**217**	**0**
H: 6 3 W: 13 05 b.Espoo 23-1-85					
Internationals: Finland U18, U19, U21, Full caps.					
2006–07	Den Bosch	27	0		
2007–08	Den Bosch	33	0		
2008–09	Den Bosch	7	0	**67**	**0**
2009–10	Willem II	6	0		
2010–11	Willem II	12	0	**18**	**0**
2011–12	AZ Alkmaar	0	0		
2012–13	VVV-Venlo	33	0		
2013–14	VVV-Venlo	33	0		
2014–15	VVV-Venlo	35	0	**101**	**0**
2015–16	Brighton & HA	0	0		
2016–17	Brighton & HA	1	0		
2017–18	Brighton & HA	0	0	**1**	**0**
2018–19	Bristol C	26	0		
2019–20	Bristol C	4	0	**30**	**0**

MASSENGO, Han-Noah (M)				**28**	**0**
b.Villepinte 7-7-01					
Internationals: France U17, U18.					
2018–19	Monaco	3	0		
2019–20	Monaco	0	0	**3**	**0**
2019–20	Bristol C	25	0	**25**	**0**

MOORE, Taylor (D)				**132**	**2**
H: 6 0 W: 12 08 b.Walthamstow 12-5-97					
Internationals: England U17, U18, U19, U20.					
From West Ham U.					
2014–15	Lens	4	0		
2015–16	Lens	5	0	**9**	**0**
2016–17	Bristol C	5	0		
2016–17	*Bury*	19	0	**19**	**0**
2017–18	Bristol C	0	0		
2017–18	*Cheltenham T*	36	0	**36**	**0**
2018–19	Bristol C	0	0		
2018–19	*Southend U*	34	1	**34**	**1**
2019–20	Bristol C	21	1	**26**	**1**
2019–20	*Blackpool*	8	0	**8**	**0**

MORRELL, Joe (M)				**68**	**3**
H: 5 3 W: 11 04 b.Ipswich 3-1-97					
Internationals: Wales U17, U19, U21, Full caps.					
2013–14	Bristol C	0	0		
2014–15	Bristol C	0	0		
2015–16	Bristol C	0	0		
2016–17	Bristol C	0	0		
2017–18	Bristol C	0	0		
2017–18	*Cheltenham T*	38	3	**38**	**3**
2018–19	Bristol C	1	0		
2019–20	Bristol C	0	0	**1**	**0**
2019–20	*Lincoln C*	29	0	**29**	**0**

MORTON, James (M)				**12**	**0**
b. 22-4-99					
2019–20	Bristol C	0	0		
2019–20	*Forest Green R*	12	0	**12**	**0**

NAGY, Adam (F)				**100**	**2**
b.Budapest 17-6-95					
Internationals: Hungary U20, U21, Full caps.					
2013–14	Ferencvaros	0	0		
2014–15	Ferencvaros	1	0		
2015–16	Ferencvaros	25	0	**26**	**0**
2016–17	Bologna	25	0		
2017–18	Bologna	12	1		
2018–19	Bologna	14	0		
2019–20	Bologna	0	0	**51**	**1**
2019–20	Bristol C	23	1	**23**	**1**

NURSE, George (M)				**0**	**0**
2019–20	Bristol C	0	0		

O'DOWDA, Callum (M)				**208**	**18**
H: 5 11 W: 11 11 b.Oxford 23-4-95					
Internationals: Republic of Ireland U21, Full caps.					
2012–13	Oxford U	0	0		
2013–14	Oxford U	10	0		
2014–15	Oxford U	39	4		
2015–16	Oxford U	38	8	**87**	**12**
2016–17	Bristol C	34	0		
2017–18	Bristol C	24	1		
2018–19	Bristol C	31	4		
2019–20	Bristol C	32	1	**121**	**6**

O'LEARY, Max (G)				**45**	**0**
H: 6 1 W: 12 03 b.Bath 10-10-96					
2013–14	Bristol C	0	0		
2014–15	Bristol C	0	0		
2015–16	Bristol C	0	0		
2016–17	Bristol C	0	0		
2017–18	Bristol C	0	0		
2018–19	Bristol C	15	0	**15**	**0**
2019–20	*Shrewsbury T*	30	0	**30**	**0**

PALMER, Kasey (M)				**97**	**10**
H: 5 11 W: 10 10 b.London 9-11-96					
Internationals: England U17, U18, U20, U21.					
2015–16	Chelsea	0	0		
2016–17	Chelsea	0	0		
2016–17	*Huddersfield T*	24	4		
2017–18	Chelsea	0	0		
2017–18	*Huddersfield T*	4	0	**28**	**4**
2017–18	*Derby Co*	15	2	**15**	**2**
2018–19	Chelsea	0	0		
2018–19	*Blackburn R*	14	1	**14**	**1**
2018–19	*Bristol C*	15	2		
2019–20	Bristol C	25	1	**40**	**3**

PATERSON, Jamie (F)				**316**	**51**
H: 5 9 W: 10 07 b.Coventry 20-12-91					
2010–11	Walsall	14	0		
2011–12	Walsall	34	3		
2012–13	Walsall	46	12	**94**	**15**
2013–14	Nottingham F	32	8		
2014–15	Nottingham F	21	1		
2015–16	Nottingham F	1	0	**54**	**9**
2015–16	*Huddersfield T*	34	6	**34**	**6**
2016–17	Bristol C	22	4		
2017–18	Bristol C	41	5		
2018–19	Bristol C	40	5		
2019–20	*Derby Co*	10	1	**10**	**1**
2019–20	Bristol C	21	6	**124**	**20**

PEREIRA, Pedro (D)				**75**	**2**
b.Lisbon 22-1-98					
Internationals: Portugal U16, U17, U18, U19, U20.					
2015–16	Sampdoria	9	0		
2016–17	Sampdoria	12	0	**21**	**0**
2016–17	Benfica	1	0		
2017–18	Benfica	0	0		
2017–18	*Genoa*	6	0		
2018–19	Benfica	0	0		
2018–19	*Genoa*	26	0	**32**	**0**
2019–20	Benfica	0	0	**1**	**0**
On loan from Benfica.					
2019–20	Bristol C	21	2	**21**	**2**

PRING, Cameron (D)				**36**	**1**
b. 22-1-98					
2018–19	Bristol C	0	0		
2018–19	*Newport Co*	7	1	**7**	**1**
2018–19	*Cheltenham T*	8	0	**8**	**0**
2019–20	Bristol C	0	0		
2019–20	*Walsall*	21	0	**21**	**0**

RODRI, Lozano (F)				**226**	**51**
H: 5 8 W: 10 00 b.Soria 6-6-90					
Internationals: Spain U21.					
2011–12	Barcelona B	18	8	**18**	**8**
2012–13	Barcelona	0	0		
2012–13	*Sheffield W*	11	1	**11**	**1**
2012–13	*Real Zaragoza*	12	2	**12**	**2**
2013–14	Barcelona	0	0		
2013–14	*Almeria*	27	8	**27**	**8**
2014–15	1860 Munich	6	1		
2015–16	1860 Munich	0	0	**6**	**1**
2015–16	*Vallodolid*	34	4	**34**	**4**
2016–17	Cordoba	40	11	**40**	**11**
2017–18	Cultural Leonesa	39	11	**39**	**11**
2018–19	Granada	33	5	**33**	**5**
2019–20	Bristol C	6	0	**6**	**0**
Transferred to Real Oviedo, January 2020.					

ROWE, Tommy (M)				**435**	**64**
H: 5 11 W: 12 11 b.Manchester 1-5-89					
2006–07	Stockport Co	4	0		
2007–08	Stockport Co	24	6		
2008–09	Stockport Co	44	7	**72**	**13**
2008–09	Peterborough U	0	0		
2009–10	Peterborough U	32	2		
2010–11	Peterborough U	35	5		
2011–12	Peterborough U	43	4		
2012–13	Peterborough U	31	5		
2013–14	Peterborough U	34	7	**175**	**23**
2014–15	Wolverhampton W	14	0		
2015–16	Wolverhampton W	3	0	**17**	**0**
2015–16	*Scunthorpe U*	14	1	**14**	**1**
2015–16	*Doncaster R*	10	3		
2016–17	Doncaster R	46	13		
2017–18	Doncaster R	40	4		
2018–19	Doncaster R	32	5	**128**	**25**
2019–20	Bristol C	29	2	**29**	**2**

SEMENYO, Antoine (F)				**42**	**3**
b. 7-1-00					
2017–18	Bristol C	1	0		
2018–19	Newport Co	21	3	**21**	**3**
2018–19	Bristol C	4	0		
2019–20	Bristol C	9	0	**14**	**0**
2019–20	*Sunderland*	7	0	**7**	**0**

SMITH, Jonny (F)				**28**	**9**
2019–20	Bristol C	0	0		
2019–20	*Oldham Ath*	28	9	**28**	**9**

SMITH, Korey (M)				**323**	**6**
H: 5 9 W: 11 01 b.Hatfield 31-1-91					
2008–09	Norwich C	2	0		
2009–10	Norwich C	37	4		
2010–11	Norwich C	28	0		
2011–12	Norwich C	0	0		
2011–12	*Barnsley*	12	0	**12**	**0**
2012–13	Norwich C	0	0	**67**	**4**
2012–13	*Yeovil T*	17	0	**17**	**0**
2012–13	*Oldham Ath*	10	0		
2013–14	Oldham Ath	42	1	**52**	**1**
2014–15	Bristol C	44	0		
2015–16	Bristol C	36	0		
2016–17	Bristol C	23	0		
2017–18	Bristol C	45	1		
2018–19	Bristol C	5	0		
2019–20	Bristol C	22	0	**175**	**1**

SZMIDICS, Sammie (M)				**155**	**39**
H: 5 6 W: 10 01 b.Colchester 24-9-95					
2013–14	Colchester U	7	0		
2014–15	Colchester U	31	4		
2015–16	Colchester U	5	0		
2016–17	Colchester U	19	5		
2017–18	Colchester U	37	12		
2018–19	Colchester U	43	14	**142**	**35**
2019–20	Bristol C	3	0	**3**	**0**
2019–20	*Peterborough U*	10	4	**10**	**4**

TAYLOR, Matty (F)				**166**	**63**
H: 5 9 W: 11 05 b. 30-3-90					
Internationals: England C.					
From Oxford U, North Leigh, Forest Green R.					
2015–16	Bristol R	46	27		
2016–17	Bristol R	27	16	**73**	**43**
2016–17	Bristol C	15	2		
2017–18	Bristol C	18	1		
2018–19	Bristol C	33	4		
2019–20	Bristol C	1	0	**67**	**7**
2019–20	*Oxford U*	26	13	**26**	**13**

VYNER, Zak (D)				**80**	**1**
H: 5 10 W: 10 10 b.Bath 14-5-97					
2015–16	Bristol C	4	0		
2016–17	Bristol C	3	0		
2016–17	*Accrington S*	16	0	**16**	**0**
2017–18	Bristol C	1	0		
2017–18	*Plymouth Arg*	17	1	**17**	**1**
2018–19	Bristol C	0	0		
2018–19	*Rotherham U*	31	0		
2019–20	Rotherham U	0	0	**31**	**0**
2019–20	Aberdeen	0	0		
2019–20	Bristol C	8	0	**16**	**0**

WALSH, Liam (M) **59 4**
b. 15-9-97
Internationals: England U16, U18.
2015–16 Everton 0 0
2015–16 *Yeovil T* 15 1 **15 1**
2016–17 Everton 0 0
2017–18 Everton 0 0
2017–18 *Birmingham C* 3 0 **3 0**
2017–18 Bristol C 6 0
2018–19 Bristol C 9 0
2019–20 Bristol C 0 0 **15 0**
2019–20 *Coventry C* 26 3 **26 3**

WATKINS, Marley (M) **210 27**
H: 5 10 W: 10 03 b.London 17-10-90
Internationals: Wales Full caps.
2008–09 Cheltenham T 12 0
2009–10 Cheltenham T 13 1
2010–11 Cheltenham T 1 0 **26 1**
From Bath C, Hereford U
2013–14 Inverness CT 26 1
2014–15 Inverness CT 33 7 **59 8**
2015–16 Barnsley 34 5
2016–17 Barnsley 42 10 **76 15**
2017–18 Norwich C 24 0 **24 0**
2018–19 Bristol C 16 2
2019–20 Bristol C 9 1 **25 3**

WEIMANN, Andreas (F) **323 51**
H: 5 9 W: 11 09 b.Vienna 5-8-91
Internationals: Austria U17, U19, U20, U21, Full caps.
2008–09 Aston Villa 0 0
2009–10 Aston Villa 0 0
2010–11 Aston Villa 1 0
2010–11 *Watford* 18 4
2011–12 Aston Villa 14 2
2011–12 *Watford* 3 0 **21 4**
2012–13 Aston Villa 30 7
2013–14 Aston Villa 37 5
2014–15 Aston Villa 31 3 **113 17**
2015–16 Derby Co 30 4
2016–17 Derby Co 11 0
2016–17 *Wolverhampton W* 19 2 **19 2**
2017–18 Derby Co 40 5 **81 9**
2018–19 Bristol C 44 10
2019–20 Bristol C 45 9 **89 19**

WELLS, Nahki (F) **330 112**
H: 5 7 W: 11 00 b.Bermuda 1-6-90
Internationals: Bermuda Full caps.
2010–11 Carlisle U 3 0 **3 0**
2011–12 Bradford C 33 10
2012–13 Bradford C 39 18
2013–14 Bradford C 19 14 **91 42**
2013–14 Huddersfield T 22 7
2014–15 Huddersfield T 35 11
2015–16 Huddersfield T 44 17
2016–17 Huddersfield T 43 10
2017–18 Huddersfield T 0 0 **144 45**
2017–18 Burnley 9 0
2018–19 Burnley 0 0
2018–19 *QPR* 40 7
2019–20 Burnley 0 0 **9 0**
2019–20 *QPR* 26 13 **66 20**
2019–20 Bristol C 17 5 **17 5**

WILLIAMS, Ashley (D) **609 22**
H: 6 0 W: 11 02 b.Wolverhampton 23-8-84
Internationals: Wales Full caps.
2003–04 Stockport Co 10 0
2004–05 Stockport Co 44 1
2005–06 Stockport Co 36 1
2006–07 Stockport Co 46 1
2007–08 Stockport Co 26 0 **162 3**
2007–08 *Swansea C* 3 0
2008–09 Swansea C 46 2
2009–10 Swansea C 46 5
2010–11 Swansea C 46 3
2011–12 Swansea C 37 1
2012–13 Swansea C 37 0
2013–14 Swansea C 34 1
2014–15 Swansea C 37 0
2015–16 Swansea C 36 2 **322 14**
2016–17 Everton 36 1
2017–18 Everton 24 1
2018–19 Everton 0 0 **60 2**
2018–19 *Stoke C* 33 1 **33 1**
2019–20 Bristol C 32 2 **32 2**

WOLLACOTT, Jojo (G) **10 0**
b. 8-9-96
2015–16 Bristol C 0 0
2016–17 Bristol C 0 0
2017–18 Bristol C 0 0
2018–19 Bristol C 0 0
2019–20 Bristol C 0 0
2019–20 *Forest Green R* 10 0 **10 0**

WRIGHT, Bailey (D) **256 9**
H: 5 9 W: 13 05 b.Melbourne 28-7-92
Internationals: Australia U17, Full caps.
2010–11 Preston NE 2 0
2011–12 Preston NE 13 1
2012–13 Preston NE 38 2
2013–14 Preston NE 43 4
2014–15 Preston NE 27 1
2015–16 Preston NE 38 0
2016–17 Preston NE 18 0 **179 8**
2016–17 Bristol C 21 1
2017–18 Bristol C 36 0
2018–19 Bristol C 12 0
2019–20 Bristol C 3 0 **72 1**
2019–20 *Sunderland* 5 0 **5 0**

Players retained or with offer of contract
Britton, Louis Sidney; Edwards, Owura Nsiah; Harper, Vincent; Harrison, Tom Jack; Moir-Pring, Cameron Lewis; Robertson, Lochlan; Smith, Zachary William Pince; Webb, Bradley James.

Scholars
Allen, Khari Jarell Marlon; Backwell, Tommy George; Bell, Samuel John; Benarous, Ayman Omar; Buse, William Jack; Conway, Tommy Daniel John; Cray, Samuel David; Francois, Marlee Jean; Henry, Prince; Low, Joseph David; Owers, Joshua Gary; Pearson, Callum; Pearson, Samuel; Porton, Joseph John; Salmon, Cameron James; Scott, Alex Jay; Soady, Barnaby James; South, Thomas Jemar D'Andre; Swaby, Thierry John Paul; Taylor, James Edward; Taylor, James John; Thuo, Mark Williams; Towler, Ryley Ben; Williams, Nathaniel James.

BRISTOL R (15)

ANDRE, Alexis (G) **1 0**
b. 31-5-97
2017–18 Bristol R 1 0
2018–19 Bristol R 0 0
2019–20 Bristol R 0 0 **1 0**

BARRETT, Josh (F) **23 0**
b. 21-6-98
Internationals: Republic of Ireland U17, U19, U21.
2015–16 Reading 3 0
2016–17 Reading 0 0
2017–18 Reading 0 0
2017–18 *Coventry C* 6 0 **6 0**
2018–19 Reading 2 0
2019–20 Reading 5 0 **10 0**
2019–20 Bristol R 7 0 **7 0**

BENNETT, Kyle (F) **332 37**
H: 5 5 W: 9 08 b.Telford 9-9-90
Internationals: England U18.
2007–08 Wolverhampton W 0 0
2008–09 Wolverhampton W 0 0
2009–10 Wolverhampton W 0 0
2010–11 Bury 32 2 **32 2**
2011–12 Doncaster R 36 4
2012–13 Doncaster R 35 3
2013–14 Doncaster R 3 0
2013–14 *Crawley T* 4 0 **4 0**
2013–14 *Bradford C* 18 1 **18 1**
2014–15 Doncaster R 42 8 **116 15**
2015–16 Portsmouth 42 6
2016–17 Portsmouth 39 6
2017–18 Portsmouth 18 0 **99 12**
2017–18 Bristol R 17 3
2018–19 Bristol R 19 0
2018–19 *Swindon T* 15 4 **15 4**
2019–20 Bristol R 12 0 **48 3**

CLARKE-HARRIS, Jonson (F) **231 53**
H: 6 0 W: 11 01 b.Leicester 21-7-94
2012–13 Peterborough U 0 0
2012–13 *Southend U* 3 0 **3 0**
2012–13 *Bury* 12 4 **12 4**
2013–14 Oldham Ath 40 6
2014–15 Oldham Ath 5 1 **45 7**
2014–15 Rotherham U 15 3
2014–15 *Milton Keynes D* 5 0 **5 0**
2014–15 *Doncaster R* 9 1 **9 1**
2015–16 Rotherham U 35 6
2016–17 Rotherham U 7 0
2017–18 Rotherham U 14 0 **71 9**
2017–18 *Coventry C* 17 3
2018–19 Coventry C 27 5 **44 8**
2018–19 Bristol R 16 11
2019–20 Bristol R 26 13 **42 24**

CRAIG, Tony (D) **509 14**
H: 6 0 W: 10 03 b.Greenwich 20-4-85
2002–03 Millwall 2 1
2003–04 Millwall 9 0
2004–05 Millwall 10 0
2004–05 *Wycombe W* 14 0 **14 0**
2005–06 Millwall 28 0
2006–07 Millwall 30 1
2007–08 Crystal Palace 13 0 **13 0**
2007–08 *Millwall* 5 1
2008–09 Millwall 44 2
2009–10 Millwall 30 2
2010–11 Millwall 24 0
2011–12 Millwall 23 0
2011–12 *Leyton Orient* 4 0 **4 0**
2012–13 Brentford 44 0
2013–14 Brentford 44 0
2014–15 Brentford 23 0 **111 0**
2015–16 Millwall 18 1
2016–17 Millwall 43 1
2017–18 Millwall 4 0 **270 9**
2017–18 Bristol R 17 1
2018–19 Bristol R 46 2
2019–20 Bristol R 34 2 **97 5**

DALY, James (F) **3 0**
2017–18 Crystal Palace 0 0
2018–19 Crystal Palace 0 0
2019–20 Crystal Palace 0 0
2019–20 Bristol R 3 0 **3 0**

DAVIES, Tom (D) **107 2**
H: 5 11 W: 11 00 b.Warrington 18-4-92
2014–15 Fleetwood T 0 0
2015–16 Accrington S 32 1 **32 1**
2016–17 Portsmouth 12 0
2017–18 Portsmouth 0 0 **12 0**
2017–18 Coventry C 21 0
2018–19 Coventry C 23 0 **44 0**
2019–20 Bristol R 19 1 **19 1**

EHMER, Max (M) **298 13**
H: 6 2 W: 11 00 b.Frankfurt 3-2-92
2009–10 QPR 0 0
2010–11 QPR 0 0
2010–11 *Yeovil T* 27 0
2011–12 QPR 0 0
2011–12 *Yeovil T* 24 0 **51 0**
2011–12 *Preston NE* 9 0 **9 0**
2012–13 QPR 0 0
2012–13 *Stevenage* 6 1 **6 1**
2013–14 QPR 1 0
2013–14 *Carlisle U* 12 1 **12 1**
2014–15 QPR 0 0 **1 0**
2014–15 *Gillingham* 27 1
2015–16 Gillingham 30 0
2016–17 Gillingham 45 6
2017–18 Gillingham 42 2
2018–19 Gillingham 40 1
2019–20 Gillingham 35 1 **219 11**
2019–20 Bristol R 0 0

HARE, Josh (D) **12 0**
H: 6 0 W: 12 04 b.Cantebury 12-8-94
2012–13 Gillingham 0 0
2013–14 Gillingham 0 0
2014–15 Gillingham 2 0
2015–16 Gillingham 0 0 **2 0**
From Eastbourne Bor, Maidstone U, Eastleigh.
2019–20 Bristol R 10 0 **10 0**

HARGREAVES, Cameron (D) **6 0**
From Exeter C.
2017–18 Bristol R 0 0
2018–19 Bristol R 0 0
2019–20 Bristol R 6 0 **6 0**

HARRIES, Cian (D) **14 0**
H: 6 1 W: 12 02 b. 1-4-97
Internationals: Wales U17, U19, U20, U21.
2015–16 Coventry C 1 0
2016–17 Coventry C 8 0 **9 0**
2017–18 Swansea C 0 0
2018–19 Swansea C 2 0
2019–20 Swansea C 0 0 **2 0**
2019–20 *Fortuna Sittard* 0 0
2019–20 Bristol R 3 0 **3 0**

HOLMES-DENNIS, Tareiq (M) **85 2**
H: 5 9 W: 11 11 b.Farnborough 31-10-95
Internationals: England U18.
2012–13 Charlton Ath 0 0
2013–14 Charlton Ath 0 0
2014–15 Charlton Ath 0 0
2014–15 *Oxford U* 14 0 **14 0**
2014–15 *Plymouth Arg* 17 1 **17 1**
2015–16 Charlton Ath 11 0
2015–16 *Oldham Ath* 10 0 **10 0**

2016–17 Charlton Ath 1 0 **12 0**
2016–17 Huddersfield T 9 0
2017–18 Huddersfield T 0 0 **9 0**
2017–18 *Portsmouth* 1 0 **1 0**
2018–19 Bristol R 18 1
2019–20 Bristol R 4 0 **22 1**

HOOLE, Luca (D) 0 0
Internationals: Wales U19.
2019–20 Bristol R 0 0

JAAKKOLA, Anssi (G) 159 0
H: 6 4 W: 13 12 b.Kemi 13-3-87
Internationals: Finland U21, Full caps.
2005 TP-47 3 0
2006 TP-47 14 0 **17 0**
2006–07 Siena 0 0
2007–08 Siena 1 0
2008–09 Siena 0 0
2008–09 *Colligiana* 7 0 **7 0**
2009–10 Siena 0 0 **1 0**
2010–11 Slavia Prague 2 0 **2 0**
2010–11 Kilmarnock 8 0
2011–12 Kilmarnock 5 0
2012–13 Kilmarnock 0 0 **13 0**
2013–14 Ajax Cape Town 24 0
2014–15 Ajax Cape Town 28 0
2015–16 Ajax Cape Town 26 0 **78 0**
2016–17 Reading 0 0
2017–18 Reading 5 0
2018–19 Reading 15 0 **20 0**
2019–20 Bristol R 21 0 **21 0**

KAVANAGH, Rhys (F) 0 0
b. 29-9-98
From Newport Co.
2017–18 Bristol R 0 0
2018–19 Bristol R 0 0
2019–20 Bristol R 0 0

KELLY, Michael (D) 27 0
H: 5 11 b.Kilmarnock 3-11-97
Internationals: Scotland U16, U17.
2017–18 Bristol R 1 0
2018–19 Bristol R 21 0
2019–20 Bristol R 5 0 **27 0**

KILGOUR, Alfie (D) 37 2
b. 18-5-98
2015–16 Bristol R 0 0
2016–17 Bristol R 0 0
2017–18 Bristol R 0 0
2018–19 Bristol R 4 0
2019–20 Bristol R 33 2 **37 2**

LEAHY, Luke (M) 249 16
H: 5 10 W: 11 07 b.Coventry 19-11-92
2012–13 Falkirk 8 1
2013–14 Falkirk 19 1
2014–15 Falkirk 33 3
2015–16 Falkirk 36 3
2016–17 Falkirk 31 3 **127 11**
2017–18 Walsall 46 2
2018–19 Walsall 44 3 **90 5**
2019–20 Bristol R 32 0 **32 0**

LITTLE, Mark (D) 351 5
H: 6 1 W: 12 10 b.Worcester 20-8-88
Internationals: England U19.
2005–06 Wolverhampton W 0 0
2006–07 Wolverhampton W 26 0
2007–08 Wolverhampton W 1 0
2007–08 *Northampton T* 17 0
2008–09 Wolverhampton W 0 0
2008–09 *Northampton T* 9 0 **26 0**
2009–10 Wolverhampton W 0 0 **27 0**
2009–10 *Chesterfield* 12 0 **12 0**
2009–10 *Peterborough U* 9 0
2010–11 Peterborough U 35 0
2011–12 Peterborough U 35 1
2012–13 Peterborough U 40 1
2013–14 Peterborough U 38 1 **157 3**
2014–15 Bristol C 37 1
2015–16 Bristol C 23 0
2016–17 Bristol C 28 0 **88 1**
2017–18 Bolton W 28 1
2018–19 Bolton W 2 0 **30 1**
2019–20 Bristol R 11 0 **11 0**

MATTHEWS, Sam (M) 16 0
b. 1-3-97
2013–14 Bournemouth 0 0
2014–15 Bournemouth 0 0
2015–16 Bournemouth 0 0
2016–17 Bournemouth 0 0
2017–18 Bournemouth 0 0
From Braintree T, Eastleigh.
2018–19 Bristol R 16 0
2019–20 Bristol R 0 0 **16 0**

MENAYESE, Rollin (D) 30 0
H: 6 3 W: 12 08 b. 4-12-97
Internationals: Wales U17.
From Weston-super-Mare.
2017–18 Bristol R 3 0
2017–18 *Swindon T* 14 0 **14 0**
2018–19 Bristol R 0 0
2019–20 Bristol R 13 0 **16 0**

MOORE, Deon (F) 5 0
b.Croydon 14-5-99
From Carshalton Ath.
2016–17 Peterborough U 4 0 **4 0**
From Mersham.
2018–19 Bristol R 1 0
2019–20 Bristol R 0 0 **1 0**

MORGAN, Ben (D) 0 0
2018–19 Bristol R 0 0
2019–20 Bristol R 0 0

NICHOLS, Tom (F) 247 47
H: 5 10 W: 10 10 b.Wellington 1-9-93
2010–11 Exeter C 1 0
2011–12 Exeter C 7 1
2012–13 Exeter C 3 0
2013–14 Exeter C 28 6
2014–15 Exeter C 36 15
2015–16 Exeter C 23 10 **98 32**
2015–16 Peterborough U 7 1
2016–17 Peterborough U 43 10 **50 11**
2017–18 Bristol R 39 1
2018–19 Bristol R 36 1
2019–20 Bristol R 19 2 **94 4**
2019–20 *Cheltenham T* 5 0 **5 0**

OGOGO, Abu (D) 390 25
H: 5 8 W: 10 02 b.Epsom 3-11-89
2007–08 Arsenal 0 0
2008–09 Arsenal 0 0
2008–09 *Barnet* 9 1 **9 1**
2009–10 Dagenham & R 30 2
2010–11 Dagenham & R 33 1
2011–12 Dagenham & R 40 1
2012–13 Dagenham & R 46 1
2013–14 Dagenham & R 44 8
2014–15 Dagenham & R 32 4 **225 17**
2015–16 Shrewsbury T 42 2
2016–17 Shrewsbury T 26 0
2017–18 Shrewsbury T 35 2 **103 4**
2018–19 Coventry C 10 0 **10 0**
2018–19 Bristol R 16 0
2019–20 Bristol R 27 3 **43 3**

PHILLIPS, Kieran (F) 0 0
2019–20 Bristol R 0 0

REILLY, Gavin (F) 251 63
H: 5 9 W: 10 05 b.Dumfries 10-5-93
2010–11 Queen of the South 1 0
2011–12 Queen of the South 14 2
2012–13 Queen of the South 30 12
2013–14 Queen of the South 34 12
2014–15 Queen of the South 32 13 **111 39**
2015–16 Hearts 28 4
2016–17 Hearts 0 0 **28 4**
2016–17 *Dunfermline Ath* 22 1 **22 1**
2017–18 St Mirren 35 11 **35 11**
2018–19 Bristol R 30 4
2019–20 *Cheltenham T* 21 4 **21 4**
2019–20 Bristol R 4 0 **34 4**

RODMAN, Alex (F) 223 26
H: 6 2 W: 12 08 b.Sutton Coldfield 15-2-87
Internationals: England C.
2010–11 Aldershot T 14 5
2011–12 Aldershot T 18 1
2012–13 Aldershot T 11 1 **43 7**
2012–13 *York C* 18 1 **18 1**
From Grimsby T, Gateshead.
2015–16 Newport Co 29 4 **29 4**
2016–17 Notts Co 16 1 **16 1**
2016–17 Shrewsbury T 20 1
2017–18 Shrewsbury T 41 5 **61 6**
2018–19 Bristol R 27 5
2019–20 Bristol R 29 2 **56 7**

RUSSE, Luke (M) 3 0
b. 19-7-99
2017–18 Bristol R 3 0
2018–19 Bristol R 0 0
2019–20 Bristol R 0 0 **3 0**

SERCOMBE, Liam (M) 414 53
H: 5 10 W: 10 10 b.Exeter 25-4-90
2008–09 Exeter C 29 2
2009–10 Exeter C 28 1
2010–11 Exeter C 42 3
2011–12 Exeter C 33 7
2012–13 Exeter C 20 1
2013–14 Exeter C 44 5
2014–15 Exeter C 40 4 **236 23**
2015–16 Oxford U 45 14
2016–17 Oxford U 30 3 **75 17**
2017–18 Bristol R 42 8
2018–19 Bristol R 39 4
2019–20 Bristol R 22 1 **103 13**

TOMLINSON, Lucas (M) 1 0
2019–20 Bristol R 1 0 **1 0**

UPSON, Edward (M) 353 21
H: 5 10 W: 11 07 b.Bury St Edmunds 21-11-89
Internationals: England U17, U19.
2006–07 Ipswich T 0 0
2007–08 Ipswich T 0 0
2008–09 Ipswich T 0 0
2009–10 Ipswich T 0 0
2009–10 *Barnet* 9 1 **9 1**
2010–11 Yeovil T 23 0
2011–12 Yeovil T 41 3
2012–13 Yeovil T 41 2
2013–14 Yeovil T 24 4 **129 9**
2013–14 Millwall 10 0
2014–15 Millwall 26 2
2015–16 Millwall 32 0 **68 2**
2016–17 Milton Keynes D 42 3
2017–18 Milton Keynes D 37 3 **79 6**
2018–19 Bristol R 35 1
2019–20 Bristol R 33 2 **68 3**

VAN STAPPERSHOEF, Jordi (G) 28 0
2014–15 Volendam 1 0
2015–16 Volendam 0 0
2016–17 Volendam 2 0
2017–18 Volendam 0 0
2018–19 Volendam 20 0 **23 0**
2019–20 Bristol R 5 0 **5 0**

WARWICK, Harry (F) 0 0
2018–19 Bristol R 0 0
2019–20 Bristol R 0 0

WIDDRINGTON, Theo (M) 0 0
2017–18 Portsmouth 0 0
2018–19 Bristol R 0 0
2019–20 Bristol R 0 0

Players retained or with offer of contract
Armstrong, Liam James; Mehew, Thomas Samuel James.

Scholars
Biss, Adam David; Budd, Joseph William; Crawford, Isaiah Marco; Fowler, George James; Gorman, James Cameron; Heal, Samuel William; Hoole, Luca Anthony; Hulbert, Oliver George; Murray, Kinsly Lile; Njonjo, Henry Gichanga; Noble, Luc Joseph; Paul, Levi Anthony; Phillips, Kieran Lee; Raymond, Mason Stevie-Dean; Thoma-Barker, Harry Craig; Walker, Zain Alexander; Ward, Jed Macaulay.

BURNLEY (16)

BARDSLEY, Phillip (D) 326 8
H: 5 11 W: 11 13 b.Salford 28-6-85
Internationals: Scotland Full caps.
2003–04 Manchester U 0 0
2004–05 Manchester U 0 0
2005–06 Manchester U 8 0
2005–06 *Burnley* 6 0
2006–07 Manchester U 0 0
2006–07 *Rangers* 5 1 **5 1**
2006–07 *Aston Villa* 13 0 **13 0**
2007–08 Manchester U 0 0 **8 0**
2007–08 *Sheffield U* 16 0 **16 0**
2007–08 Sunderland 11 0
2008–09 Sunderland 28 0
2009–10 Sunderland 26 0
2010–11 Sunderland 34 3
2011–12 Sunderland 31 1
2012–13 Sunderland 18 1
2013–14 Sunderland 26 2 **174 7**
2014–15 Stoke C 25 0
2015–16 Stoke C 11 0
2016–17 Stoke C 15 0 **51 0**
2017–18 Burnley 13 0
2018–19 Burnley 19 0
2019–20 Burnley 21 0 **59 0**

BARNES, Ashley (F) 361 89
H: 6 0 W: 12 00 b.Bath 30-10-89
Internationals: Austria U20.
2006–07 Plymouth Arg 0 0
2007–08 Plymouth Arg 0 0
2008–09 Plymouth Arg 15 1
2009–10 Plymouth Arg 7 1 **22 2**

2009–10 *Torquay U* 6 0 **6 0**
2009–10 *Brighton & HA* 8 4
2010–11 Brighton & HA 42 18
2011–12 Brighton & HA 43 11
2012–13 Brighton & HA 34 8
2013–14 Brighton & HA 22 5 **149 46**
2013–14 Burnley 21 3
2014–15 Burnley 35 5
2015–16 Burnley 8 0
2016–17 Burnley 28 6
2017–18 Burnley 36 9
2018–19 Burnley 37 12
2019–20 Burnley 19 6 **184 41**

BENSON, Josh (M) 11 2
H: 5 9 W: 11 03 b. 5-12-99
From Arsenal.
2018–19 Burnley 0 0
2019–20 Burnley 0 0
2019–20 *Grimsby T* 11 2 **11 2**

BRADY, Robert (F) 235 20
H: 5 9 W: 10 12 b.Belfast 14-1-92
Internationals: Republic of Ireland Youth, U21, Full caps.
2008–09 Manchester U 0 0
2009–10 Manchester U 0 0
2010–11 Manchester U 0 0
2011–12 Manchester U 0 0
2011–12 *Hull C* 39 3
2012–13 Manchester U 0 0
2012–13 Hull C 32 4
2013–14 Hull C 16 3
2014–15 Hull C 27 0 **114 10**
2015–16 Norwich C 36 3
2016–17 Norwich C 23 4 **59 7**
2016–17 Burnley 14 1
2017–18 Burnley 15 1
2018–19 Burnley 16 0
2019–20 Burnley 17 1 **62 3**

BROWNHILL, Josh (M) 222 23
H: 5 10 W: 10 12 b.Warrington 19-12-95
2013–14 Preston NE 24 3
2014–15 Preston NE 18 2
2015–16 Preston NE 3 0 **45 5**
2015–16 *Barnsley* 22 2 **22 2**
2016–17 Bristol C 27 1
2017–18 Bristol C 45 5
2018–19 Bristol C 45 5
2019–20 Bristol C 28 5 **145 16**
2019–20 Burnley 10 0 **10 0**

COONEY, Ryan (M) 32 0
b. 26-2-00
2016–17 Bury 0 0
2017–18 Bury 12 0
2018–19 Bury 9 0 **21 0**
2019–20 Burnley 0 0
2019–20 *Morecambe* 11 0 **11 0**

CORK, Jack (D) 454 13
H: 6 0 W: 10 12 b.Carshalton 25-6-89
Internationals: England U16, U17, U18, U19, U20, U21, Full caps. Great Britain.
2006–07 Chelsea 0 0
2006–07 *Bournemouth* 7 0 **7 0**
2007–08 Chelsea 0 0
2007–08 *Scunthorpe U* 34 2 **34 2**
2008–09 Chelsea 0 0
2008–09 *Southampton* 23 0
2008–09 *Watford* 19 0 **19 0**
2009–10 Chelsea 0 0
2009–10 *Coventry C* 21 0 **21 0**
2009–10 *Burnley* 11 1
2010–11 Chelsea 0 0
2010–11 *Burnley* 40 3
2011–12 Southampton 46 0
2012–13 Southampton 28 0
2013–14 Southampton 28 0
2014–15 Southampton 12 2 **137 2**
2014–15 Swansea C 15 1
2015–16 Swansea C 35 1
2016–17 Swansea C 30 0 **80 2**
2017–18 Burnley 38 2
2018–19 Burnley 37 1
2019–20 Burnley 30 0 **156 7**

DRISCOLL-GLENNON, Anthony (D) 12 1
b.Bootle 26-11-99
2018–19 Burnley 0 0
2019–20 Burnley 0 0
2019–20 *Grimsby T* 12 1 **12 1**

DUNNE, Jimmy (D) 53 4
b.Drogheda 19-10-97
Internationals: Republic of Ireland U21.
2017–18 Burnley 0 0
2017–18 *Accrington S* 20 0 **20 0**
2018–19 Burnley 0 0
2018–19 *Hearts* 12 2 **12 2**
2018–19 *Sunderland* 12 1 **12 1**
2019–20 Burnley 0 0
2019–20 *Fleetwood T* 9 1 **9 1**

GIBSON, Ben (D) 227 6
H: 6 1 W: 12 04 b.Nunthorpe 15-1-93
Internationals: England U17, U18, U20, U21.
2010–11 Middlesbrough 1 0
2011–12 Middlesbrough 0 0
2011–12 *Plymouth Arg* 13 0 **13 0**
2012–13 Middlesbrough 1 0
2012–13 *Tranmere R* 28 1 **28 1**
2013–14 Middlesbrough 31 1
2014–15 Middlesbrough 36 0
2015–16 Middlesbrough 33 1
2016–17 Middlesbrough 38 1
2017–18 Middlesbrough 45 1 **185 4**
2018–19 Burnley 1 1
2019–20 Burnley 0 0 **1 1**

GOODRIDGE, Mace (M) 0 0
b. 13-9-99
From Newcastle U.
2019–20 Burnley 0 0

GUDMUNDSSON, Johann Berg (M) 296 32
H: 6 1 W: 12 06 b.Reykjavik 27-10-90
Internationals: Iceland U19, U21, Full caps.
2009–10 AZ Alkmaar 0 0
2010–11 AZ Alkmaar 23 1
2011–12 AZ Alkmaar 30 3
2012–13 AZ Alkmaar 31 2
2013–14 AZ Alkmaar 35 3 **119 9**
2014–15 Charlton Ath 41 10
2015–16 Charlton Ath 40 6 **81 16**
2016–17 Burnley 20 1
2017–18 Burnley 35 2
2018–19 Burnley 29 3
2019–20 Burnley 12 1 **96 7**

HARKER, Rob (F) 0 0
H: 6 2 b.Gargrave 6-3-00
2015–16 Bury 0 0
2016–17 Bury 0 0
2017–18 Bury 0 0
2018–19 Burnley 0 0
2019–20 Burnley 0 0

HART, Joe (G) 439 0
H: 6 3 W: 13 03 b.Shrewsbury 19-4-87
Internationals: England U19, U21, Full caps.
2004–05 Shrewsbury T 6 0
2005–06 Shrewsbury T 46 0 **52 0**
2006–07 Manchester C 1 0
2006–07 *Tranmere R* 6 0 **6 0**
2006–07 *Blackpool* 5 0 **5 0**
2007–08 Manchester C 26 0
2008–09 Manchester C 23 0
2009–10 Manchester C 0 0
2009–10 *Birmingham C* 36 0 **36 0**
2010–11 Manchester C 38 0
2011–12 Manchester C 38 0
2012–13 Manchester C 38 0
2013–14 Manchester C 31 0
2014–15 Manchester C 36 0
2015–16 Manchester C 35 0
2016–17 Manchester C 0 0
2016–17 *Torino* 36 0 **36 0**
2017–18 Manchester C 0 0 **266 0**
2017–18 *West Ham U* 19 0 **19 0**
2018–19 Burnley 19 0
2019–20 Burnley 0 0 **19 0**

HENDRICK, Jeff (M) 318 31
H: 6 1 W: 11 11 b.Dublin 31-1-92
Internationals: Republic of Ireland U17, U19, U21, Full caps.
2010–11 Derby Co 4 0
2011–12 Derby Co 42 3
2012–13 Derby Co 45 6
2013–14 Derby Co 30 4
2014–15 Derby Co 41 7
2015–16 Derby Co 32 2
2016–17 Derby Co 2 0 **196 22**
2016–17 Burnley 32 2
2017–18 Burnley 34 2
2018–19 Burnley 32 3
2019–20 Burnley 24 2 **122 9**

JENSEN, Lukas (G) 7 0
b. 8-10-94
2017–18 Helsingor 1 0
2018–19 Helsingor 0 0 **1 0**
2018–19 HIK 6 0 **6 0**
2019–20 Burnley 0 0

KOIKI, Ali (D) 15 0
b. 22-8-99
From Crystal Palace.
2018–19 Burnley 0 0
2018–19 *Swindon T* 15 0 **15 0**
2019–20 Burnley 0 0

LEGZDINS, Adam (G) 114 0
H: 6 1 W: 14 02 b.Penkridge 28-11-86
2006–07 Birmingham C 0 0
2007–08 Birmingham C 0 0
2008–09 Crewe Alex 0 0
2009–10 Crewe Alex 6 0 **6 0**
2010–11 Burton Alb 46 0
2011–12 Derby Co 4 0
2011–12 *Burton Alb* 1 0 **47 0**
2012–13 Derby Co 31 0
2013–14 Derby Co 0 0 **35 0**
2014–15 Leyton Orient 11 0 **11 0**
2015–16 Birmingham C 5 0
2016–17 Birmingham C 10 0 **15 0**
2017–18 Burnley 0 0
2018–19 Burnley 0 0
2019–20 Burnley 0 0

LENNON, Aaron (M) 415 35
H: 5 6 W: 10 03 b.Leeds 16-4-87
Internationals: England U17, U19, U21, B, Full caps.
2003–04 Leeds U 11 0
2004–05 Leeds U 27 1 **38 1**
2005–06 Tottenham H 27 2
2006–07 Tottenham H 26 3
2007–08 Tottenham H 29 2
2008–09 Tottenham H 35 5
2009–10 Tottenham H 22 3
2010–11 Tottenham H 34 3
2011–12 Tottenham H 23 3
2012–13 Tottenham H 34 4
2013–14 Tottenham H 27 1
2014–15 Tottenham H 9 0
2014–15 *Everton* 14 2
2015–16 Tottenham H 0 0 **266 26**
2015–16 Everton 25 5
2016–17 Everton 11 0
2017–18 Everton 15 0 **65 7**
2017–18 Burnley 14 0
2018–19 Burnley 16 1
2019–20 Burnley 16 0 **46 1**

LONG, Kevin (D) 144 7
H: 6 3 W: 13 01 b.Cork 18-8-90
Internationals: Republic of Ireland Full caps.
2009 Cork C 16 0 **16 0**
2009–10 Burnley 0 0
2010–11 Burnley 0 0
2010–11 *Accrington S* 15 0
2011–12 Burnley 0 0
2011–12 *Accrington S* 24 4 **39 4**
2011–12 *Rochdale* 16 0 **16 0**
2012–13 Burnley 14 0
2012–13 *Portsmouth* 5 0 **5 0**
2013–14 Burnley 7 0
2014–15 Burnley 1 0
2015–16 Burnley 0 0
2015–16 *Barnsley* 11 2 **11 2**
2015–16 *Milton Keynes D* 2 0 **2 0**
2016–17 Burnley 3 0
2017–18 Burnley 16 1
2018–19 Burnley 6 0
2019–20 Burnley 8 0 **55 1**

LOWTON, Matt (M) 282 13
H: 5 11 W: 12 04 b.Chesterfield 9-6-89
2008–09 Sheffield U 0 0
2009–10 Sheffield U 2 0
2009–10 *Ferencvaros* 5 0 **5 0**
2010–11 Sheffield U 32 4
2011–12 Sheffield U 44 6 **78 10**
2012–13 Aston Villa 37 2
2013–14 Aston Villa 23 0
2014–15 Aston Villa 12 0 **72 2**
2015–16 Burnley 27 1
2016–17 Burnley 36 0
2017–18 Burnley 26 0
2018–19 Burnley 21 0
2019–20 Burnley 17 0 **127 1**

McMAHON, George (G) 0 0
2016–17 Rotherham U 0 0
2017–18 Rotherham U 0 0
2018–19 Burnley 0 0
2019–20 Burnley 0 0

McNEIL, Dwight (F) 60 5
b. 22-11-99
Internationals: England U20, U21.
2017–18 Burnley 1 0

2018–19 Burnley 21 3
2019–20 Burnley 38 2 **60 5**

MEE, Ben (D) 315 7
H: 5 11 W: 11 09 b.Sale 21-9-89
Internationals: England U19, U20, U21.
2007–08 Manchester C 0 0
2008–09 Manchester C 0 0
2009–10 Manchester C 0 0
2010–11 Manchester C 0 0
2010–11 *Leicester C* 15 0 **15 0**
2011–12 Manchester C 0 0
2011–12 Burnley 31 0
2012–13 Burnley 19 1
2013–14 Burnley 38 0
2014–15 Burnley 33 2
2015–16 Burnley 46 2
2016–17 Burnley 34 1
2017–18 Burnley 29 0
2018–19 Burnley 38 0
2019–20 Burnley 32 1 **300 7**

MUMBONGO, Joel (F) 0 0
b. 9-1-99
Internationals: Sweden U17, U18, U19.
From Verona.
2019–20 Burnley 0 0

N'GUESSAN, Christian (M) 8 0
2016–17 Blackpool 0 0
2017–18 Burnley 0 0
2018–19 Burnley 0 0
2019–20 Burnley 0 0
2019–20 *Oldham Ath* 8 0 **8 0**

O'NEILL, Aiden (M) 79 5
H: 5 10 W: 11 00 b.Brisbane 4-7-98
Internationals: Australia U23.
From Brisbane Ath.
2016–17 Burnley 3 0
2016–17 *Oldham Ath* 15 0 **15 0**
2017–18 Burnley 0 0
2017–18 *Fleetwood T* 21 1 **21 1**
2018–19 Burnley 0 0
2018–19 *Central Coast Mariners* 23 4 **23 4**
2019–20 Burnley 0 0 **3 0**
2019–20 *Brisbane Roar* 17 0 **17 0**

PEACOCK-FARRELL, Bailey (G) 40 0
H: 6 2 W: 11 07 b.Darlington 29-10-96
Internationals: Northern Ireland U21, Full caps.
2015–16 Leeds U 1 0
2016–17 Leeds U 0 0
2017–18 Leeds U 11 0
2018–19 Leeds U 28 0
2019–20 Leeds U 0 0 **40 0**
2019–20 Burnley 0 0

PHILLIPS, Adam (M) 15 4
b.Garstang 15-1-98
Internationals: England U16, U17.
2014–15 Liverpool 0 0
2015–16 Liverpool 0 0
2016–17 Liverpool 0 0
2017–18 Norwich C 0 0
2017–18 *Cambridge U* 4 0 **4 0**
2018–19 Norwich C 0 0
2018–19 *Hamilton A* 0 0
2019–20 Burnley 0 0
2019–20 *Morecambe* 11 4 **11 4**

PIETERS, Erik (D) 373 6
H: 6 0 W: 13 00 b.Tiel 7-8-88
Internationals: Netherlands U17, U19, U21, Full caps.
2006–07 FC Utrecht 20 0
2007–08 FC Utrecht 31 2 **51 2**
2008–09 PSV Eindhoven 17 0
2009–10 PSV Eindhoven 27 0
2010–11 PSV Eindhoven 31 0
2011–12 PSV Eindhoven 16 0
2012–13 PSV Eindhoven 2 0 **93 0**
2013–14 Stoke C 36 1
2014–15 Stoke C 31 0
2015–16 Stoke C 35 0
2016–17 Stoke C 36 0
2017–18 Stoke C 31 0
2018–19 Stoke C 21 2 **190 3**
2018–19 *Amiens* 15 1 **15 1**
2019–20 Burnley 24 0 **24 0**

POPE, Nick (G) 150 0
H: 6 3 W: 11 13 b.Cambridge 19-4-92
Internationals: England Full caps.
2011–12 Charlton Ath 0 0
2012–13 Charlton Ath 1 0
2013–14 Charlton Ath 0 0
2013–14 *York C* 22 0 **22 0**
2014–15 Charlton Ath 8 0
2014–15 *Bury* 22 0 **22 0**
2015–16 Charlton Ath 24 0 **33 0**
2016–17 Burnley 0 0
2017–18 Burnley 35 0
2018–19 Burnley 0 0
2019–20 Burnley 38 0 **73 0**

RICHARDSON, Lewis (F) 0 0
b. 7-2-03
Internationals: England U16, U17.
2019–20 Burnley 0 0

RODRIGUEZ, Jay (F) 344 98
H: 6 0 W: 12 00 b.Burnley 29-7-89
Internationals: England U21, Full caps.
2007–08 Burnley 1 0
2007–08 *Stirling Alb* 11 3 **11 3**
2008–09 Burnley 25 2
2009–10 Burnley 0 0
2009–10 *Barnsley* 6 1 **6 1**
2010–11 Burnley 42 14
2011–12 Burnley 37 15
2012–13 Southampton 35 6
2013–14 Southampton 33 15
2014–15 Southampton 0 0
2015–16 Southampton 12 0
2016–17 Southampton 24 5 **104 26**
2017–18 WBA 37 7
2018–19 WBA 45 22 **82 29**
2019–20 Burnley 36 8 **141 39**

TARKOWSKI, James (D) 269 14
H: 6 1 W: 12 10 b.Manchester 19-11-92
Internationals: England Full caps.
2010–11 Oldham Ath 9 0
2011–12 Oldham Ath 16 1
2012–13 Oldham Ath 21 2
2013–14 Oldham Ath 26 2 **72 5**
2013–14 Brentford 13 2
2014–15 Brentford 34 1
2015–16 Brentford 23 1 **70 4**
2015–16 Burnley 4 0
2016–17 Burnley 19 0
2017–18 Burnley 31 0
2018–19 Burnley 35 3
2019–20 Burnley 38 2 **127 5**

TAYLOR, Charlie (D) 212 3
H: 5 9 W: 11 00 b.York 18-9-93
Internationals: England U19.
2011–12 Leeds U 2 0
2011–12 *Bradford C* 3 0 **3 0**
2012–13 Leeds U 0 0
2012–13 *York C* 4 0 **4 0**
2012–13 *Inverness CT* 7 0 **7 0**
2013–14 Leeds U 0 0
2013–14 *Fleetwood T* 32 0 **32 0**
2014–15 Leeds U 23 2
2015–16 Leeds U 39 1
2016–17 Leeds U 29 0 **93 3**
2017–18 Burnley 11 0
2018–19 Burnley 38 0
2019–20 Burnley 24 0 **73 0**

THOMAS, Bobby (D) 0 0
b. 30-1-01
2019–20 Burnley 0 0

THOMPSON, Max (F) 1 0
b. 9-2-02
From Everton.
2019–20 Burnley 1 0 **1 0**

VYDRA, Matej (F) 259 75
H: 5 10 W: 11 09 b.Chotebor 1-5-92
Internationals: Czech Republic U16, U17, U18, U19, U21, Full caps.
2009–10 Banik Ostrava 13 4 **13 4**
2010–11 Udinese 2 0
2011–12 Udinese 0 0
2011–12 *Club Brugge* 1 0 **1 0**
2012–13 Udinese 0 0
2012–13 *Watford* 41 20
2013–14 Udinese 0 0
2013–14 *WBA* 23 3 **23 3**
2014–15 Udinese 0 0 **2 0**
2014–15 *Watford* 42 16
2015–16 Watford 0 0
2015–16 *Reading* 31 3 **31 3**
2016–17 Watford 1 0 **84 36**
2016–17 Derby Co 33 5
2017–18 Derby Co 40 21 **73 26**
2018–19 Burnley 13 1
2019–20 Burnley 19 2 **32 3**

WESTWOOD, Ashley (M) 372 23
H: 5 10 W: 11 00 b.Nantwich 1-4-90
2008–09 Crewe Alex 2 0
2009–10 Crewe Alex 36 6
2010–11 Crewe Alex 46 5
2011–12 Crewe Alex 41 3
2012–13 Crewe Alex 3 0 **128 14**
2012–13 Aston Villa 30 0
2013–14 Aston Villa 35 3
2014–15 Aston Villa 27 0
2015–16 Aston Villa 32 2
2016–17 Aston Villa 23 0 **147 5**
2016–17 Burnley 9 0
2017–18 Burnley 19 0
2018–19 Burnley 34 2
2019–20 Burnley 35 2 **97 4**

WOOD, Chris (F) 356 121
H: 6 3 W: 12 10 b.Auckland 7-12-91
Internationals: New Zealand U17, U23, Full caps.
2008–09 WBA 2 0
2009–10 WBA 18 1
2010–11 WBA 1 0
2010–11 *Barnsley* 7 0 **7 0**
2010–11 *Brighton & HA* 29 8 **29 8**
2011–12 WBA 0 0
2011–12 *Birmingham C* 23 9 **23 9**
2011–12 *Bristol C* 19 3 **19 3**
2012–13 WBA 0 0 **21 1**
2012–13 *Millwall* 19 11 **19 11**
2012–13 Leicester C 20 9
2013–14 Leicester C 26 4
2014–15 Leicester C 7 1 **53 14**
2014–15 *Ipswich T* 8 0 **8 0**
2015–16 Leeds U 36 13
2016–17 Leeds U 44 27
2017–18 Leeds U 3 1 **83 41**
2017–18 Burnley 24 10
2018–19 Burnley 38 10
2019–20 Burnley 32 14 **94 34**

Players retained or with offer of contract
Cropper, Jordan Geoffrey.

Scholars
Allen, Harry George; Armstrong, Finlay Patric; Brennan, Corey Carl; Calderbank-Park, Kai; Carson, Matthew Alan; Chima, Udoka Godwill; Conley, Joseph Thomas; Conn, Christopher Seamus Michael; Connolly, Joel Alexander George; Eastmond, Tremaine Leroy Winston; Fenlon, Rhys-James Roy; George, Mitchell Colin; Harris, William; Major, Jayden Anthony; McGlynn, Joseph Peter; Moonan, Dylan; Patterson, Kane Mazo; Pruti, Edon; Rain, Matthew; Rooney, Jake Richard; Thomas, Lewis Luka; Thompson, Max; Tucker, Ne'Jai; Unwin, Samual Connor; Woods, Benjamin Jack.

BURTON ALB (17)

AKINS, Lucas (F) 419 74
H: 5 10 W: 11 07 b.Huddersfield 25-2-89
2006–07 Huddersfield T 2 0
2007–08 Huddersfield T 3 0 **5 0**
2008–09 Hamilton A 11 0
2008–09 *Partick Thistle* 9 1 **9 1**
2009–10 Hamilton A 0 0 **11 0**
2010–11 Tranmere R 33 2
2011–12 Tranmere R 44 5 **77 7**
2012–13 Stevenage 46 10
2013–14 Stevenage 31 3 **77 13**
2014–15 Burton Alb 35 9
2015–16 Burton Alb 44 12
2016–17 Burton Alb 38 5
2017–18 Burton Alb 42 5
2018–19 Burton Alb 46 13
2019–20 Burton Alb 35 9 **240 53**

ANDERSON, Jevan (D) 1 0
b. 3-3-00
From Aberdeen, Formartine U.
2019–20 Burton Alb 1 0 **1 0**

BEARDSLEY, Chris (F) 203 21
H: 6 0 W: 12 12 b.Derby 28-2-84
2002–03 Mansfield T 5 0
2003–04 Mansfield T 15 1
2004–05 Doncaster R 4 0 **4 0**
2004–05 Kidderminster H 25 5 **25 5**
2005–06 Mansfield T 3 0
2006–07 Mansfield T 10 0
From Rushden & D, York C, Kettering T.
2010–11 Stevenage 23 1
2011–12 Stevenage 31 7
2012–13 Preston NE 19 1
2013–14 Preston NE 0 0 **19 1**
2013–14 *Bristol R* 24 1 **24 1**

2014–15 Stevenage 29 4 **83 12**
2015–16 Mansfield T 14 1 **47 2**
2018–19 Burton Alb 1 0
2019–20 Burton Alb 0 0 **1 0**

BOYCE, Liam (F) 177 70
H: 6 0 W: 13 01 b.Belfast 8-4-91
Internationals: Northern Ireland U19, U21, Full caps.
From Cliftonville.
2014–15 Ross Co 30 10
2015–16 Ross Co 35 15
2016–17 Ross Co 34 23 **99 48**
2017–18 Burton Alb 16 3
2018–19 Burton Alb 37 11
2019–20 Burton Alb 25 8 **78 22**
Transferred to Hearts, January 2020.

BRAYFORD, John (D) 409 12
H: 5 8 W: 11 02 b.Stoke 29-12-87
Internationals: England C.
2008–09 Crewe Alex 36 2
2009–10 Crewe Alex 45 0 **81 2**
2010–11 Derby Co 46 1
2011–12 Derby Co 23 0
2012–13 Derby Co 40 1 **109 2**
2013–14 Cardiff C 0 0
2013–14 *Sheffield U* 15 1
2014–15 Cardiff C 26 0 **26 0**
2014–15 Sheffield U 22 1
2015–16 Sheffield U 19 1
2016–17 Sheffield U 3 0
2016–17 *Burton Alb* 33 0
2017–18 Sheffield U 0 0 **59 3**
2017–18 Burton Alb 28 0
2018–19 Burton Alb 41 3
2019–20 Burton Alb 32 2 **134 5**

BUXTON, Jake (D) 415 18
H: 6 1 W: 13 05 b.Sutton-in-Ashfield 4-3-85
2002–03 Mansfield T 3 0
2003–04 Mansfield T 9 1
2004–05 Mansfield T 30 1
2005–06 Mansfield T 39 0
2006–07 Mansfield T 30 1
2007–08 Mansfield T 40 2
2008–09 Mansfield T 0 0 **151 5**
From Burton Alb.
2008–09 Derby Co 0 0
2009–10 Derby Co 19 1
2010–11 Derby Co 1 0
2011–12 Derby Co 21 2
2012–13 Derby Co 31 3
2013–14 Derby Co 45 2
2014–15 Derby Co 19 3
2015–16 Derby Co 3 0 **139 11**
2016–17 Wigan Ath 39 1 **39 1**
2017–18 Burton Alb 32 0
2018–19 Burton Alb 30 0
2019–20 Burton Alb 24 1 **86 1**

BYWATER, Steve (G) 384 0
H: 6 2 W: 12 10 b.Manchester 7-6-81
Internationals: England U19, U21.
1997–98 Rochdale 0 0
1998–99 West Ham U 0 0
1999–2000 West Ham U 4 0
1999–2000 *Wycombe W* 2 0 **2 0**
1999–2000 *Hull C* 4 0 **4 0**
2000–01 West Ham U 1 0
2001–02 West Ham U 0 0
2001–02 *Wolverhampton W* 0 0
2001–02 *Cardiff C* 0 0
2002–03 West Ham U 0 0
2003–04 West Ham U 17 0
2004–05 West Ham U 36 0
2005–06 West Ham U 1 0 **59 0**
2005–06 *Coventry C* 14 0 **14 0**
2006–07 Derby Co 37 0
2007–08 Derby Co 18 0
2007–08 *Ipswich T* 17 0 **17 0**
2008–09 Derby Co 31 0
2009–10 Derby Co 42 0
2010–11 Derby Co 22 0 **150 0**
2010–11 *Cardiff C* 8 0 **8 0**
2011–12 Sheffield W 32 0
2012–13 Sheffield W 0 0 **32 0**
2013–14 Millwall 7 0
2014–15 Millwall 0 0 **7 0**
2014–15 *Gillingham* 13 0 **13 0**
2014–15 Doncaster R 21 0 **21 0**
2015–16 Burton Alb 0 0
2016–17 Burton Alb 5 0
2017–18 Burton Alb 44 0
2018–19 Burton Alb 8 0
2019–20 Burton Alb 0 0 **57 0**

DANIEL, Colin (M) 363 32
H: 5 11 W: 11 06 b.Eastwood 15-2-88
2006–07 Crewe Alex 0 0
2007–08 Crewe Alex 1 0
2008–09 Crewe Alex 13 1 **14 1**
2008–09 *Macclesfield T* 8 0
2009–10 Macclesfield T 38 3
2010–11 Macclesfield T 43 8
2011–12 Macclesfield T 36 2 **125 13**
2013–14 Mansfield T 28 2
2014–15 Port Vale 28 4
2015–16 Port Vale 20 2 **48 6**
2015–16 *Mansfield T* 9 2 **37 4**
2016–17 Blackpool 34 4
2017–18 Blackpool 44 4 **78 8**
2018–19 Peterborough U 20 0 **20 0**
2018–19 Burton Alb 17 0
2019–20 Burton Alb 24 0 **41 0**

DYER, Lloyd (M) 498 65
H: 5 8 W: 10 03 b.Birmingham 13-9-82
2001–02 WBA 0 0
2002–03 WBA 0 0
2003–04 WBA 17 2
2003–04 *Kidderminster H* 7 1 **7 1**
2004–05 WBA 4 0
2004–05 *Coventry C* 6 0 **6 0**
2005–06 WBA 0 0 **21 2**
2005–06 *QPR* 15 0 **15 0**
2005–06 Millwall 6 0 **6 0**
2006–07 Milton Keynes D 41 5
2007–08 Milton Keynes D 45 11 **86 16**
2008–09 Leicester C 44 10
2009–10 Leicester C 33 3
2010–11 Leicester C 35 3
2011–12 Leicester C 36 4
2012–13 Leicester C 42 3
2013–14 Leicester C 40 7 **230 30**
2014–15 Watford 14 1
2014–15 *Birmingham C* 18 1 **18 1**
2015–16 Watford 0 0 **14 1**
2015–16 Burnley 3 0 **3 0**
2016–17 Burton Alb 42 7
2017–18 Burton Alb 38 7
2018–19 Bolton W 7 0 **7 0**
2019–20 Burton Alb 5 0 **85 14**

EDWARDS, Ryan (M) 149 12
H: 5 7 W: 11 07 b.Sydney 17-11-93
Internationals: Australia U20, U23.
2011–12 Reading 0 0
2012–13 Reading 0 0
2012–13 *Rochdale* 0 0
2013–14 Reading 0 0
2014–15 Reading 7 0 **7 0**
2015–16 Partick Thistle 17 2
2016–17 Partick Thistle 38 1
2017–18 Partick Thistle 36 4 **91 7**
2018–19 Hearts 4 0 **4 0**
2018–19 *St Mirren* 14 0 **14 0**
2019–20 Burton Alb 33 5 **33 5**

FOX, Ben (M) 28 1
H: 5 11 W: 12 00 b.Burton upon Trent 1-2-98
2016–17 Burton Alb 1 0
2017–18 Burton Alb 0 0
2018–19 Burton Alb 27 1
2019–20 Burton Alb 0 0 **28 1**

FRASER, Scott (M) 191 25
H: 6 0 W: 10 12 b.Dundee 30-3-95
2013–14 Dundee U 1 0
2014–15 Dundee U 0 0
2014–15 *Airdrieonians* 38 5 **38 5**
2015–16 Dundee U 32 1
2016–17 Dundee U 25 4
2017–18 Dundee U 23 4 **81 9**
2018–19 Burton Alb 42 6
2019–20 Burton Alb 30 5 **72 11**

GARRATT, Ben (G) 226 0
H: 6 1 W: 10 06 b.Market Drayton 25-4-94
Internationals: England U17, U18, U19.
2011–12 Crewe Alex 0 0
2012–13 Crewe Alex 1 0
2013–14 Crewe Alex 26 0
2014–15 Crewe Alex 30 0
2015–16 Crewe Alex 46 0
2016–17 Crewe Alex 46 0
2017–18 Crewe Alex 36 0
2018–19 Crewe Alex 38 0 **223 0**
2019–20 Burton Alb 3 0 **3 0**

HART, Ben (D) 3 0
2018–19 Burton Alb 0 0
2019–20 Burton Alb 3 0 **3 0**

HAWKINS, Callum (G) 0 0
b.Rotherham 12-12-99
2018–19 Burton Alb 0 0
2019–20 Burton Alb 0 0

HUTCHINSON, Reece (D) 42 0
b. 14-4-00
2017–18 Burton Alb 0 0
2018–19 Burton Alb 25 0
2019–20 Burton Alb 17 0 **42 0**

LIVESEY, Jack (G) 0 0
b. 21-3-00
2019–20 Burton Alb 0 0

MURPHY, Jamie (F) 377 70
H: 6 0 W: 12 00 b.Glasgow 28-8-89
Internationals: Scotland U19, U21, Full caps.
2006–07 Motherwell 2 0
2007–08 Motherwell 16 1
2008–09 Motherwell 30 2
2009–10 Motherwell 35 6
2010–11 Motherwell 35 6
2011–12 Motherwell 36 9
2012–13 Motherwell 22 10 **176 34**
2012–13 Sheffield U 17 2
2013–14 Sheffield U 34 4
2014–15 Sheffield U 43 11
2015–16 Sheffield U 1 0 **95 17**
2015–16 Brighton & HA 37 6
2016–17 Brighton & HA 35 2
2017–18 Brighton & HA 4 0 **76 8**
2017–18 *Rangers* 16 4
2018–19 Rangers 2 0
2019–20 Rangers 2 0 **20 4**
On loan from Rangers.
2019–20 Burton Alb 10 7 **10 7**

O'TOOLE, John (M) 397 62
H: 6 2 W: 13 07 b.Harrow 30-9-88
Internationals: Republic of Ireland U21.
2007–08 Watford 35 3
2008–09 Watford 22 7
2008–09 *Sheffield U* 9 1 **9 1**
2009–10 Watford 0 0 **57 10**
2009–10 Colchester U 31 2
2010–11 Colchester U 11 0
2011–12 Colchester U 15 0
2012–13 Colchester U 15 0 **72 2**
2012–13 *Bristol R* 18 3
2013–14 Bristol R 41 13 **59 16**
2014–15 Northampton T 35 2
2014–15 *Southend U* 2 0 **2 0**
2015–16 Northampton T 38 12
2016–17 Northampton T 40 10
2017–18 Northampton T 29 6
2018–19 Northampton T 31 3 **173 33**
2019–20 Burton Alb 25 0 **25 0**

POWELL, Joe (F) 20 5
b. 30-10-98
2018–19 West Ham U 0 0
2018–19 *Northampton T* 10 2 **10 2**
2019–20 West Ham U 0 0
2019–20 Burton Alb 10 3 **10 3**

QUINN, Stephen (M) 427 26
H: 5 6 W: 9 08 b.Dublin 4-4-86
Internationals: Republic of Ireland U21, Full caps.
2005–06 Sheffield U 0 0
2005–06 *Milton Keynes D* 15 0 **15 0**
2005–06 *Rotherham U* 16 0 **16 0**
2006–07 Sheffield U 15 2
2007–08 Sheffield U 19 2
2008–09 Sheffield U 43 7
2009–10 Sheffield U 44 4
2010–11 Sheffield U 37 1
2011–12 Sheffield U 45 4
2012–13 Sheffield U 3 0 **206 20**
2012–13 Hull C 42 3
2013–14 Hull C 15 0
2014–15 Hull C 28 1 **85 4**
2015–16 Reading 27 1
2016–17 Reading 7 0
2017–18 Reading 0 0 **34 1**
2018–19 Burton Alb 42 1
2019–20 Burton Alb 29 0 **71 1**

SBARRA, Joe (M) 49 1
H: 5 10 W: 11 00 b.Lichfield 21-12-98
2016–17 Burton Alb 1 0
2017–18 Burton Alb 17 0
2018–19 Burton Alb 9 0
2019–20 Burton Alb 22 1 **49 1**

SHARMAN-LOWE, Teddy (G) 0 0
2019–20 Burton Alb 0 0

TEMPLETON, David (M) 269 65
H: 5 8 W: 8 12 b.Glasgow 7-1-89
Internationals: Scotland U19, U21.
2005–06 Stenhousemuir 17 8
2006–07 Stenhousemuir 13 3 **30 11**

2007–08 Hearts 0 0
2007–08 *Raith R* 15 4 **15 4**
2008–09 Hearts 3 0
2009–10 Hearts 16 2
2010–11 Hearts 33 7
2011–12 Hearts 27 1
2012–13 Hearts 2 1 **81 11**
2012–13 Rangers 24 16
2013–14 Rangers 20 3
2014–15 Rangers 22 3
2015–16 Rangers 1 0 **67 22**
2016–17 Hamilton A 3 1
2017–18 Hamilton A 27 8 **30 9**
2018–19 Burton Alb 28 5
2019–20 Burton Alb 18 3 **46 8**
Transferred to Hamilton A, January 2020.

THOMAS, Kwame (F) 53 6
H: 5 10 W: 12 00 b.Nottingham 28-9-95
Internationals: England U16, U17, U20.
2011–12 Derby Co 0 0
2012–13 Derby Co 0 0
2013–14 Derby Co 0 0
2014–15 Derby Co 4 0
2014–15 *Notts Co* 5 0 **5 0**
2015–16 Derby Co 0 0 **4 0**
2015–16 *Blackpool* 18 0 **18 0**
2016–17 Coventry C 14 3
2017–18 Coventry C 0 0 **14 3**
From Solihul Moors.
2019–20 Doncaster R 10 3 **10 3**
2019–20 Burton Alb 2 0 **2 0**

VALE, Ethan (M) 0 0
2019–20 Burton Alb 0 0

WALLACE, Kieran (M) 63 2
H: 6 1 W: 11 11 b.Nottingham 26-1-95
Internationals: England U16, U17.
2014–15 Sheffield U 4 0
2015–16 Sheffield U 11 0
2016–17 Sheffield U 0 0 **15 0**
2016–17 *Fleetwood T* 0 0
From Matlock T.
2018–19 Burton Alb 22 1
2019–20 Burton Alb 26 1 **48 2**

Scholars
Armitage, Thomas George; Carter, Tyo Kaden; Gilligan, Ciaran Patrick; Hewlett, Thomas Paul; Holmes, Jack Harry; Idouarab, Said Yussuf; Lal, Rueben Arun; Latt-Fairweather, Thierry Ricky Everton; McDonnell, Cael Liam; McLean, Ben Angus; Nyirenda, Yewo; Redfern, Luke Harry Michael; Richardson, Matthew James; Shittu, Akinola Emmanuel; Smith, Nathan John.

CAMBRIDGE U (18)

BURTON, Callum (G) 11 0
H: 6 2 W: 12 00 b.Newport, Shropshire 15-8-96
Internationals: England U16, U17, U18.
2013–14 Shrewsbury T 0 0
2014–15 Shrewsbury T 0 0
2015–16 Shrewsbury T 1 0
2016–17 Shrewsbury T 0 0 **1 0**
2017–18 Hull C 0 0
2017–18 Hull C 0 0
2019–20 Cambridge U 10 0 **10 0**

CARRUTHERS, Samir (F) 168 7
H: 5 8 W: 11 00 b.Islington 4-4-93
Internationals: Republic of Ireland U19, U21.
2011–12 Aston Villa 3 0
2012–13 Aston Villa 0 0
2013–14 Aston Villa 0 0 **3 0**
2013–14 *Milton Keynes D* 23 2
2014–15 Milton Keynes D 32 2
2015–16 Milton Keynes D 39 1
2016–17 Milton Keynes D 23 1 **117 6**
2016–17 Sheffield U 14 0
2017–18 Sheffield U 14 1
2018–19 Sheffield U 0 0 **28 1**
2018–19 *Oxford U* 10 0 **10 0**
2019–20 Cambridge U 10 0 **10 0**

DALLAS, Andrew (F) 40 5
b. 22-7-99
2017–18 Rangers 0 0
2017–18 *Stenhousemuir* 6 3 **6 3**
2018–19 Rangers 0 0
2018–19 *Greenock Morton* 12 0 **12 0**
2019–20 Cambridge U 22 2 **22 2**

DARLING, Harry (D) 39 2
H: 5 11 W: 11 11 b. 8-8-99
2016–17 Cambridge U 0 0
2017–18 Cambridge U 3 0
2018–19 Cambridge U 12 0
2019–20 Cambridge U 24 2 **39 2**

DAVIES, Leon (D) 31 0
b. 21-11-99
2015–16 Cambridge U 0 0
2016–17 Cambridge U 5 0
2017–18 Cambridge U 4 0
2018–19 Cambridge U 6 0
2019–20 Cambridge U 16 0 **31 0**

DEARMAN, Joe (D) 0 0
2019–20 Cambridge U 0 0

DICKENS, Tom (D) 0 0
2019–20 Cambridge U 0 0

DUNK, Harrison (M) 207 10
H: 6 0 W: 11 07 b. 25-10-90
2014–15 Cambridge U 32 2
2015–16 Cambridge U 45 4
2016–17 Cambridge U 38 2
2017–18 Cambridge U 37 2
2018–19 Cambridge U 26 0
2019–20 Cambridge U 29 0 **207 10**

HANNANT, Luke (M) 90 5
b. 4-11-93
From Dereham T, Team Northumbria, Gateshead.
2017–18 Port Vale 18 1
2018–19 Port Vale 45 3 **63 4**
2019–20 Cambridge U 27 1 **27 1**

IBEHRE, Jabo (F) 599 121
H: 6 2 W: 13 13 b.Islington 28-1-83
1999–2000 Leyton Orient 3 0
2000–01 Leyton Orient 5 2
2001–02 Leyton Orient 28 4
2002–03 Leyton Orient 25 5
2003–04 Leyton Orient 35 4
2004–05 Leyton Orient 19 2
2005–06 Leyton Orient 33 8
2006–07 Leyton Orient 30 4
2007–08 Leyton Orient 31 7 **209 36**
2008–09 Walsall 39 10 **39 10**
2009–10 Milton Keynes D 10 1
2009–10 *Southend U* 4 0 **4 0**
2009–10 *Stockport Co* 20 5 **20 5**
2010–11 Milton Keynes D 42 3
2011–12 Milton Keynes D 39 8
2012–13 Milton Keynes D 3 0 **94 12**
2012–13 Colchester U 30 8
2013–14 Colchester U 37 8
2014–15 Colchester U 5 0 **72 16**
2014–15 *Oldham Ath* 11 2 **11 2**
2014–15 *Barnsley* 9 2 **9 2**
2015–16 Carlisle U 36 15
2016–17 Carlisle U 38 12 **74 27**
2017–18 Cambridge U 27 7
2018–19 Cambridge U 36 4
2019–20 Cambridge U 4 0 **67 11**

IRON, Finley (G) 0 0
2016–17 Cambridge U 0 0
2017–18 Cambridge U 0 0
2018–19 Cambridge U 0 0
2019–20 Cambridge U 0 0

JOHN, Louis (D) 22 0
b. 20-11-92
2013–14 Crawley T 0 0
From Sutton U.
2018–19 Cambridge U 22 0
2019–20 Cambridge U 0 0 **22 0**

JONES, Daniel (D) 283 11
H: 6 2 W: 13 00 b.Rowley Regis 14-7-86
2005–06 Wolverhampton W 1 0
2006–07 Wolverhampton W 8 0
2007–08 Wolverhampton W 1 0
2007–08 *Northampton T* 33 3 **33 3**
2008–09 Wolverhampton W 0 0
2008–09 *Oldham Ath* 23 1 **23 1**
2009–10 Wolverhampton W 0 0 **10 0**
2009–10 *Notts Co* 7 0
2009–10 *Bristol R* 17 0 **17 0**
2010–11 Sheffield W 25 0
2011–12 Sheffield W 3 0
2012–13 Sheffield W 9 0 **37 0**
2012–13 Port Vale 16 1
2013–14 Port Vale 20 0 **36 1**
2014–15 Chesterfield 33 0
2015–16 Chesterfield 19 1
2016–17 Chesterfield 14 0 **66 1**
2017–18 Notts Co 27 4
2018–19 Notts Co 13 1 **47 5**
2019–20 Cambridge U 14 0 **14 0**

KNIBBS, Harvey (F) 24 7
b.Bristol 26-4-99
2017–18 Aston Villa 0 0
2018–19 Aston Villa 0 0
2019–20 Cambridge U 24 7 **24 7**

KNOWLES, Tom (M) 4 1
b. 27-9-98
2017–18 Cambridge U 1 0
2018–19 Cambridge U 3 1
2019–20 Cambridge U 0 0 **4 1**

KNOYLE, Kyle (D) 96 1
H: 5 10 W: 9 13 b.Newham 24-9-96
Internationals: England U18.
2015–16 West Ham U 0 0
2015–16 *Dundee U* 9 0 **9 0**
2016–17 West Ham U 0 0
2016–17 *Wigan Ath* 1 0 **1 0**
2017–18 Swindon T 18 0
2018–19 Swindon T 42 0 **60 0**
2019–20 Cambridge U 26 1 **26 1**

LAMBE, Reggie (M) 268 30
H: 5 7 W: 10 09 b.Bermuda 4-2-91
Internationals: Bermuda Full caps.
2009–10 Ipswich T 0 0
2010–11 Ipswich T 2 0 **2 0**
2010–11 *Bristol R* 7 0 **7 0**
2012 Toronto 27 2
2013 Toronto 27 0 **54 2**
2014 Nykoping 11 1 **11 1**
2014–15 Mansfield T 30 5
2015–16 Mansfield T 37 5 **67 10**
2016–17 Carlisle U 38 6
2017–18 Carlisle U 34 6 **72 12**
2018–19 Cambridge U 32 3
2019–20 Cambridge U 23 2 **55 5**

LEWIS, Paul (M) 84 9
H: 6 1 W: 11 00 b. 17-12-94
Internationals: England C.
From Macclesfield T.
2016–17 Cambridge U 13 0
2017–18 Cambridge U 12 1
2018–19 Cambridge U 23 4
2019–20 Cambridge U 36 4 **84 9**

MARIS, George (F) 135 20
b.Sheffield 6-3-96
2014–15 Barnsley 2 0
2015–16 Barnsley 1 0 **3 0**
2016–17 Cambridge U 23 4
2017–18 Cambridge U 40 10
2018–19 Cambridge U 39 5
2019–20 Cambridge U 30 1 **132 20**

MITOV, Dimitar (G) 51 0
H: 6 2 W: 12 00 b. 22-1-97
Internationals: Bulgaria U16, U17, U19, U21.
2014–15 Charlton Ath 0 0
2015–16 Charlton Ath 0 0
2016–17 Charlton Ath 0 0
2017–18 Cambridge U 3 0
2018–19 Cambridge U 21 0
2019–20 Cambridge U 27 0 **51 0**

NEAL, Joe (F) 0 0
2018–19 Cambridge U 0 0
2019–20 Cambridge U 0 0

NORVILLE-WILLIAMS, Jordan (D) 5 0
From Arsenal.
2017–18 Cambridge U 0 0
2018–19 Cambridge U 0 0
2019–20 Cambridge U 5 0 **5 0**

O'NEIL, Liam (D) 168 6
H: 6 0 W: 12 06 b.Cambridge 31-7-93
2011–12 WBA 0 0
2011–12 *VPS* 14 0 **14 0**
2012–13 WBA 0 0
2013–14 WBA 3 0
2014–15 WBA 0 0 **3 0**
2014–15 *Scunthorpe U* 22 2 **22 2**
2015–16 Chesterfield 26 0
2016–17 Chesterfield 17 2 **43 2**
2016–17 Cambridge U 13 1
2017–18 Cambridge U 26 0
2018–19 Cambridge U 19 0
2019–20 Cambridge U 28 1 **86 2**

RICHARDS, Marc (F) 602 186
H: 6 2 W: 12 06 b.Wolverhampton 8-7-82
Internationals: England U18, U20.
1999–2000 Blackburn R 0 0
2000–01 Blackburn R 0 0
2001–02 Blackburn R 0 0

2001–02 *Crewe Alex* 4 0 **4 0**
2001–02 *Oldham Ath* 5 0 **5 0**
2001–02 *Halifax T* 5 0 **5 0**
2002–03 Blackburn R 0 0
2002–03 *Swansea C* 17 7 **17 7**
2003–04 Northampton T 41 8
2004–05 Northampton T 12 2
2004–05 *Rochdale* 5 2 **5 2**
2005–06 Northampton T 0 0
2005–06 Barnsley 38 12
2006–07 Barnsley 31 6 **69 18**
2007–08 Port Vale 29 5
2008–09 Port Vale 30 10
2009–10 Port Vale 46 20
2010–11 Port Vale 40 16
2011–12 Port Vale 36 17 **181 68**
2012–13 Chesterfield 34 12
2013–14 Chesterfield 38 8 **72 20**
2013–14 Northampton T 0 0
2014–15 Northampton T 31 18
2015–16 Northampton T 31 15
2016–17 Northampton T 42 10
2017–18 Northampton T 19 1 **176 54**
2017–18 Swindon T 20 11
2018–19 Swindon T 30 4 **50 15**
2019–20 Cambridge U 18 2 **18 2**

SIMPER, Lewis (D) **0 0**
b. 7-4-01
2019–20 Cambridge U 0 0

TAFT, George (D) **149 6**
H: 5 9 W: 11 09 b.Leicester 29-7-93
Internationals: England U18, U19.
2010–11 Leicester C 0 0
2011–12 Leicester C 0 0
2012–13 Leicester C 0 0
2013–14 Leicester C 0 0
2013–14 *York C* 3 0 **3 0**
2014–15 Burton Alb 30 1
2015–16 Burton Alb 0 0 **30 1**
2015–16 *Cambridge U* 11 1
2016–17 Mansfield T 13 0
2017–18 Mansfield T 0 0 **13 0**
2017–18 *Cambridge U* 28 1
2018–19 Cambridge U 37 2
2019–20 Cambridge U 27 1 **103 5**
2019–20 Bolton W 0 0

TAYLOR, Greg (D) **207 6**
H: 6 1 W: 12 02 b.Bedford 15-1-90
Internationals: England C.
2008–09 Northampton T 0 0
From Kettering T, Darlington, Luton T.
2014–15 Cambridge U 43 0
2015–16 Cambridge U 16 0
2016–17 Cambridge U 36 2
2017–18 Cambridge U 43 1
2018–19 Cambridge U 39 2
2019–20 Cambridge U 30 1 **207 6**

WARD, Elliot (D) **341 22**
H: 6 2 W: 13 00 b.Harrow 19-1-85
2001–02 West Ham U 0 0
2002–03 West Ham U 0 0
2003–04 West Ham U 0 0
2004–05 West Ham U 11 0
2004–05 *Bristol R* 3 0 **3 0**
2005–06 West Ham U 4 0 **15 0**
2005–06 *Plymouth Arg* 16 1 **16 1**
2006–07 Coventry C 39 3
2007–08 Coventry C 37 6
2008–09 Coventry C 33 5
2009–10 Coventry C 8 0 **117 14**
2009–10 *Doncaster R* 6 1 **6 1**
2009–10 *Preston NE* 4 0 **4 0**
2010–11 Norwich C 39 1
2011–12 Norwich C 12 0
2012–13 Norwich C 0 0 **51 1**
2012–13 *Nottingham F* 31 3 **31 3**
2013–14 Bournemouth 23 0
2014–15 Bournemouth 2 0
2015–16 Bournemouth 0 0 **25 0**
2015–16 *Huddersfield T* 5 0 **5 0**
2015–16 Blackburn R 7 1
2016–17 Blackburn R 6 0
2017–18 Blackburn R 10 0 **23 1**
2017–18 *Milton Keynes D* 15 0 **15 0**
2018–19 Notts Co 17 1 **17 1**
2019–20 Cambridge U 13 0 **13 0**

WORMAN, Ben (M) **1 0**
b. 30-8-01
2017–18 Cambridge U 0 0
2018–19 Cambridge U 1 0
2019–20 Cambridge U 0 0 **1 0**

Scholars
Battersby, Jake Anthony; Brown, Nathaniel Gary; Chadwick, Louis; Cowling, Myles Alex Eddie; D'Arcy, Blake Lewis; Dearman, Joe Clive; Gill, Jonah James; Gray, Joshua Michael; Hasani, Inglian; Mansaray, Mustapha Alex; Maragh, Geneiro Dicaprio; Miller, Diego Lewis; Richar-Noel, Nehemiah Constantine; Rider, Joseph Anthony; Steel, Harvey James; Toyer, Daniel Charles.

CARDIFF C (19)

BACUNA, Leandro (M) **342 26**
H: 6 2 W: 12 00 b.Groningen 21-8-91
Internationals: Netherlands U19, U21. Curacao Full caps.
2009–10 FC Groningen 20 2
2010–11 FC Groningen 24 0
2011–12 FC Groningen 32 7
2012–13 FC Groningen 33 5 **109 14**
2013–14 Aston Villa 35 5
2014–15 Aston Villa 19 0
2015–16 Aston Villa 31 1
2016–17 Aston Villa 30 1
2017–18 Aston Villa 1 0 **116 7**
2017–18 Reading 33 1
2018–19 Reading 26 3 **59 4**
2018–19 Cardiff C 11 0
2019–20 Cardiff C 41 1 **52 1**

BAGAN, Joel (D) **0 0**
From Southampton.
2019–20 Cardiff C 0 0

BAMBA, Souleymane (D) **352 22**
H: 6 3 W: 14 02 b.Ivry-sur-Seine 13-1-85
Internationals: Ivory Coast Full caps.
2004–05 Paris Saint-Germain 1 0
2005–06 Paris Saint-Germain 0 0 **1 0**
2006–07 Dunfermline Ath 23 0
2007–08 Dunfermline Ath 15 0
2008–09 Dunfermline Ath 1 0 **39 0**
2008–09 Hibernian 29 0
2009–10 Hibernian 30 2
2010–11 Hibernian 16 2 **75 4**
2010–11 Leicester C 16 2
2011–12 Leicester C 36 1 **52 3**
2012–13 Trabzonspor 18 0
2013–14 Trabzonspor 9 0 **27 0**
2014–15 Palermo 1 0 **1 0**
2014–15 *Leeds U* 19 1
2015–16 Leeds U 30 4
2016–17 Leeds U 2 0 **51 5**
2016–17 Cardiff C 26 2
2017–18 Cardiff C 46 4
2018–19 Cardiff C 28 4
2019–20 Cardiff C 6 0 **106 10**

BENNETT, Joe (D) **295 6**
H: 5 10 W: 10 04 b.Rochdale 28-3-90
Internationals: England U19, U20, U21.
2008–09 Middlesbrough 1 0
2009–10 Middlesbrough 12 0
2010–11 Middlesbrough 31 0
2011–12 Middlesbrough 41 1
2012–13 Middlesbrough 0 0 **85 1**
2012–13 Aston Villa 25 0
2013–14 Aston Villa 5 0
2014–15 Brighton & HA 41 1 **41 1**
2015–16 Aston Villa 0 0
2015–16 *Bournemouth* 0 0
2015–16 *Sheffield W* 3 0 **3 0**
2016–17 Aston Villa 0 0 **30 0**
2016–17 Cardiff C 24 3
2017–18 Cardiff C 38 1
2018–19 Cardiff C 30 0
2019–20 Cardiff C 44 0 **136 4**

BODENHAM, Jack (D) **0 0**
Internationals: Wales U19.
2018–19 Cardiff C 0 0
2019–20 Cardiff C 0 0

BOGLE, Omar (F) **103 33**
H: 6 3 W: 12 08 b.Birmingham 26-7-92
Internationals: England C.
From Hinckley U, Solihull Moors.
2016–17 Grimsby T 27 19 **27 19**
2016–17 Wigan Ath 14 3 **14 3**
2017–18 Cardiff C 10 3
2017–18 *Peterborough U* 9 1 **9 1**
2018–19 Cardiff C 0 0
2018–19 *Birmingham C* 15 1 **15 1**
2018–19 *Portsmouth* 12 4 **12 4**
2019–20 Cardiff C 11 1 **21 4**
2019–20 *Den Haag* 5 1 **5 1**

BOWEN, Sam (M) **0 0**
Internationals: Wales U19.
2019–20 Cardiff C 0 0

BROWN, Ciaron (D) **15 0**
b. 1-1-01
Internationals: Northern Ireland U21, Full caps.
2018–19 Cardiff C 0 0
2018–19 *Livingston* 6 0
2019–20 Cardiff C 0 0
2019–20 *Livingston* 9 0 **15 0**

CONNOLLY, Matthew (D) **286 13**
H: 6 1 W: 11 03 b.Barnet 24-9-87
2005–06 Arsenal 0 0
2006–07 Arsenal 0 0
2006–07 *Bournemouth* 5 1 **5 1**
2007–08 Arsenal 0 0
2007–08 *Colchester U* 16 2 **16 2**
2007–08 QPR 20 0
2008–09 QPR 35 0
2009–10 QPR 19 2
2010–11 QPR 36 0
2011–12 QPR 6 0
2011–12 *Reading* 6 0 **6 0**
2012–13 QPR 0 0 **116 2**
2012–13 Cardiff C 36 5
2013–14 Cardiff C 3 0
2014–15 Cardiff C 23 0
2014–15 *Watford* 6 1 **6 1**
2015–16 Cardiff C 43 1
2016–17 Cardiff C 28 1
2017–18 Cardiff C 4 0
2018–19 Cardiff C 0 0
2019–20 Cardiff C 0 0 **137 7**

COXE, Cameron (D) **0 0**
b. 18-12-98
Internationals: Wales U17, U19, U20, U21.
2017–18 Cardiff C 0 0
2018–19 Cardiff C 0 0
2019–20 Cardiff C 0 0

CUNNINGHAM, Greg (D) **251 8**
H: 6 0 W: 11 00 b.Galway 31-1-91
Internationals: Republic of Ireland U17, U21, Full caps.
2008–09 Manchester C 0 0
2009–10 Manchester C 2 0
2010–11 Manchester C 0 0
2010–11 *Leicester C* 13 0 **13 0**
2011–12 Manchester C 0 0
2011–12 *Nottingham F* 27 0 **27 0**
2012–13 Manchester C 0 0 **2 0**
2012–13 Bristol C 30 1
2013–14 Bristol C 37 1
2014–15 Bristol C 24 2 **91 4**
2015–16 Preston NE 43 2
2016–17 Preston NE 40 1
2017–18 Preston NE 20 1 **103 4**
2018–19 Cardiff C 7 0
2019–20 Cardiff C 0 0 **7 0**
2019–20 *Blackburn R* 8 0 **8 0**

D'ALMEIDA, Tavio (D) **0 0**
b. 11-12-00
From Auxerre.
2019–20 Cardiff C 0 0

DAY, Joe (G) **225 0**
H: 6 1 W: 12 00 b.Brighton 13-8-90
2011–12 Peterborough U 0 0
2012–13 Peterborough U 0 0
2013–14 Peterborough U 4 0
2014–15 Peterborough U 0 0 **4 0**
2014–15 *Newport Co* 36 0
2015–16 Newport Co 41 0
2016–17 Newport Co 45 0
2017–18 Newport Co 46 0
2018–19 Newport Co 43 0 **211 0**
2019–20 Cardiff C 1 0 **1 0**
2019–20 *AFC Wimbledon* 9 0 **9 0**

ETHERIDGE, Neil (G) **200 0**
H: 6 3 W: 14 00 b.Enfield 7-2-90
Internationals: England U16. Philippines Full caps.
2008–09 Fulham 0 0
2009–10 Fulham 0 0
2010–11 Fulham 0 0
2011–12 Fulham 0 0
2012–13 Fulham 0 0
2012–13 *Bristol R* 12 0 **12 0**
2013–14 Fulham 0 0
2013–14 *Crewe Alex* 4 0 **4 0**
2014–15 Oldham Ath 0 0
2014–15 Charlton Ath 4 0 **4 0**
2015–16 Walsall 40 0
2016–17 Walsall 41 0 **81 0**
2017–18 Cardiff C 45 0
2018–19 Cardiff C 38 0
2019–20 Cardiff C 16 0 **99 0**

FLINT, Aiden (D)				**338**	**44**
H: 6 2 W: 12 00 b.Pinxton 11-7-89					
Internationals: England C.					
2010–11	Swindon T	3	0		
2011–12	Swindon T	32	2		
2012–13	Swindon T	29	2	**64**	**4**
2013–14	Bristol C	34	3		
2014–15	Bristol C	46	14		
2015–16	Bristol C	44	6		
2016–17	Bristol C	46	5		
2017–18	Bristol C	39	8	**209**	**36**
2018–19	Middlesbrough	39	1	**39**	**1**
2019–20	Cardiff C	26	3	**26**	**3**

GLATZEL, Robert (F)				**112**	**29**
b.Munich 8-1-94					
2012–13	1860 Munich	0	0		
2012–13	Heimstetten	4	1	**4**	**1**
2013–14	Wacker Burghasen	4	0	**4**	**0**
2014–15	1860 Munich	0	0		
2015–16	Kaiserslautern	0	0		
2016–17	Kaiserslautern	19	4	**19**	**4**
2017–18	Heidenheim	29	4		
2018–19	Heidenheim	26	13	**55**	**17**
2019–20	Cardiff C	30	7	**30**	**7**

HARRIS, Mark (M)				**24**	**2**
b. 29-12-98					
Internationals: Wales U17, U19, U20, U21.					
2016–17	Cardiff C	2	0		
2017–18	Cardiff C	0	0		
2018–19	Cardiff C	0	0		
2018–19	*Newport Co*	16	2	**16**	**2**
2018–19	*Port Vale*	6	0	**6**	**0**
2019–20	Cardiff C	0	0	**2**	**0**

HOILETT, Junior (M)				**378**	**51**
H: 5 8 W: 11 00 b.Ottawa 5-6-90					
Internationals: Canada Full caps.					
2007–08	Blackburn R	0	0		
2007–08	*Paderborn*	12	1	**12**	**1**
2008–09	Blackburn R	0	0		
2008–09	*St Pauli*	21	6	**21**	**6**
2009–10	Blackburn R	23	0		
2010–11	Blackburn R	24	5		
2011–12	Blackburn R	34	7	**81**	**12**
2012–13	QPR	26	1		
2013–14	QPR	35	4		
2014–15	QPR	22	0		
2015–16	QPR	29	6		
2016–17	QPR	0	0	**112**	**11**
2016–17	Cardiff C	33	2		
2017–18	Cardiff C	46	9		
2018–19	Cardiff C	32	3		
2019–20	Cardiff C	41	7	**152**	**21**

HUMPHRIES, Lloyd (M)				**0**	**0**
b. 3-10-97					
Internationals: Wales U19.					
2018–19	Cardiff C	0	0		
2019–20	Cardiff C	0	0		

MAYEMBE, Ntazana (M)				**0**	**0**
2019–20	Cardiff C	0	0		

MENDEZ-LAING, Nathaniel (M)				**274**	**39**
H: 5 10 W: 11 12 b.Birmingham 15-4-92					
Internationals: England U16, U17.					
2009–10	Wolverhampton W	0	0		
2010–11	Wolverhampton W	0	0		
2010–11	*Peterborough U*	33	5		
2011–12	Wolverhampton W	0	0		
2011–12	*Sheffield U*	8	1	**8**	**1**
2012–13	Peterborough U	21	3		
2012–13	*Portsmouth*	8	0	**8**	**0**
2013–14	Peterborough U	16	1		
2013–14	*Shrewsbury T*	6	0	**6**	**0**
2014–15	Peterborough U	14	0	**84**	**9**
2014–15	*Cambridge U*	11	1	**11**	**1**
2015–16	Rochdale	33	7		
2016–17	Rochdale	39	8	**72**	**15**
2017–18	Cardiff C	38	6		
2018–19	Cardiff C	20	4		
2019–20	Cardiff C	27	3	**85**	**13**

MOORE, Shamar (F)				**0**	**0**
b. 17-1-01					
From Reading.					
2019–20	Cardiff C	0	0		

MORRISON, Sean (D)				**339**	**36**
H: 6 4 W: 14 00 b.Plymouth 8-1-91					
2007–08	Swindon T	2	0		
2008–09	Swindon T	20	1		
2009–10	Swindon T	9	1		
2009–10	*Southend U*	8	0	**8**	**0**
2010–11	Swindon T	19	4	**50**	**6**
2010–11	Reading	0	0		
2010–11	*Huddersfield T*	0	0		
2011–12	Reading	0	0		
2011–12	*Huddersfield T*	19	1	**19**	**1**
2012–13	Reading	16	2		
2013–14	Reading	21	1		
2014–15	Reading	1	1	**38**	**4**
2014–15	Cardiff C	41	6		
2015–16	Cardiff C	30	3		
2016–17	Cardiff C	44	4		
2017–18	Cardiff C	39	7		
2018–19	Cardiff C	34	1		
2019–20	Cardiff C	36	4	**224**	**25**

MURPHY, Brian (G)				**160**	**0**
H: 6 0 W: 13 00 b.Waterford 7-5-83					
Internationals: Republic of Ireland U16.					
2000–01	Manchester C	0	0		
2001–02	Manchester C	0	0		
2002–03	Manchester C	0	0		
2002–03	*Oldham Ath*	0	0		
2002–03	*Peterborough U*	1	0	**1**	**0**
From Waterford					
2003–04	Swansea C	11	0		
2004–05	Swansea C	2	0		
2005–06	Swansea C	0	0		
2006–07	Swansea C	0	0	**13**	**0**
2007	Bohemians	29	0		
2008	Bohemians	33	0		
2009	Bohemians	35	0	**97**	**0**
2009–10	Ipswich T	16	0		
2010–11	Ipswich T	4	0		
2011–12	Ipswich T	0	0	**20**	**0**
2011–12	QPR	0	0		
2012–13	QPR	0	0		
2013–14	QPR	2	0		
2014–15	QPR	0	0	**2**	**0**
2015–16	Portsmouth	21	0		
2016–17	Portsmouth	0	0	**21**	**0**
2016–17	Cardiff C	5	0		
2017–18	Cardiff C	1	0		
2018–19	Cardiff C	0	0		
2019–20	Cardiff C	0	0	**6**	**0**
Transferred to Waterford, February 2020.					

MURPHY, Josh (F)				**193**	**25**
H: 5 8 W: 10 07 b.Wembley 24-2-95					
Internationals: England U18, U19, U20.					
2012–13	Norwich C	0	0		
2013–14	Norwich C	9	0		
2014–15	Norwich C	13	1		
2014–15	*Wigan Ath*	5	0	**5**	**0**
2015–16	Norwich C	0	0		
2015–16	*Milton Keynes D*	42	5	**42**	**5**
2016–17	Norwich C	27	4		
2017–18	Norwich C	41	7	**90**	**12**
2018–19	Cardiff C	29	3		
2019–20	Cardiff C	27	5	**56**	**8**

NELSON, Curtis (D)				**343**	**16**
H: 6 0 W: 11 07 b.Newcastle-under-Lyme 21-5-93					
Internationals: England U18.					
2010–11	Plymouth Arg	35	0		
2011–12	Plymouth Arg	17	0		
2012–13	Plymouth Arg	27	3		
2013–14	Plymouth Arg	44	1		
2014–15	Plymouth Arg	42	1		
2015–16	Plymouth Arg	46	3	**211**	**8**
2016–17	Oxford U	33	2		
2017–18	Oxford U	20	1		
2018–19	Oxford U	46	4	**99**	**7**
2019–20	Cardiff C	33	1	**33**	**1**

PACK, Marlon (M)				**431**	**28**
H: 6 2 W: 11 09 b.Portsmouth 25-3-91					
2008–09	Portsmouth	0	0		
2009–10	Portsmouth	0	0		
2009–10	*Wycombe W*	8	0	**8**	**0**
2009–10	*Dagenham & R*	17	1	**17**	**1**
2010–11	Portsmouth	1	0	**1**	**0**
2010–11	*Cheltenham T*	38	2		
2011–12	Cheltenham T	43	5		
2012–13	Cheltenham T	43	7		
2013–14	Cheltenham T	0	0	**124**	**14**
2013–14	Bristol C	43	0		
2014–15	Bristol C	34	3		
2015–16	Bristol C	45	1		
2016–17	Bristol C	33	2		
2017–18	Bristol C	42	3		
2018–19	Bristol C	46	2		
2019–20	Bristol C	1	0	**244**	**11**
2019–20	Cardiff C	37	2	**37**	**2**

PATERSON, Callum (D)				**232**	**52**
H: 6 0 W: 12 00 b.London 13-10-94					
Internationals: Scotland U18, U19, U21, Full caps.					
2012–13	Hearts	22	3		
2013–14	Hearts	37	11		
2014–15	Hearts	29	6		
2015–16	Hearts	29	5		
2016–17	Hearts	20	8	**137**	**33**
2017–18	Cardiff C	32	10		
2018–19	Cardiff C	27	4		
2019–20	Cardiff C	36	5	**95**	**19**

RALLS, Joe (M)				**256**	**27**
H: 5 10 W: 11 00 b.Farnborough 13-10-93					
Internationals: England U19.					
2011–12	Cardiff C	10	1		
2012–13	Cardiff C	4	0		
2013–14	Cardiff C	0	0		
2013–14	*Yeovil T*	37	3	**37**	**3**
2014–15	Cardiff C	28	2		
2015–16	Cardiff C	43	1		
2016–17	Cardiff C	42	6		
2017–18	Cardiff C	37	7		
2018–19	Cardiff C	28	0		
2019–20	Cardiff C	27	7	**219**	**24**

RICHARDS, Ashley (M)				**142**	**0**
H: 6 1 W: 12 04 b.Swansea 12-4-91					
Internationals: Wales U17, U19, U21, Full caps.					
2009–10	Swansea C	15	0		
2010–11	Swansea C	6	0		
2011–12	Swansea C	8	0		
2012–13	Swansea C	0	0		
2012–13	*Crystal Palace*	11	0	**11**	**0**
2013–14	Swansea C	0	0		
2013–14	*Huddersfield T*	9	0	**9**	**0**
2014–15	Swansea C	10	0	**39**	**0**
2014–15	*Fulham*	14	0		
2015–16	Fulham	22	0	**36**	**0**
2016–17	Cardiff C	26	0		
2017–18	Cardiff C	6	0		
2018–19	Cardiff C	4	0		
2019–20	Cardiff C	11	0	**47**	**0**

SANG, Tom (M)				**0**	**0**
b. 29-6-99					
From Bolton W, Manchester U.					
2019–20	Cardiff C	0	0		

SMITHIES, Alex (G)				**384**	**0**
H: 6 1 W: 10 01 b.Huddersfield 25-3-90					
Internationals: England U16, U17, U18, U19.					
2006–07	Huddersfield T	0	0		
2007–08	Huddersfield T	2	0		
2008–09	Huddersfield T	27	0		
2009–10	Huddersfield T	46	0		
2010–11	Huddersfield T	22	0		
2011–12	Huddersfield T	13	0		
2012–13	Huddersfield T	46	0		
2013–14	Huddersfield T	46	0		
2014–15	Huddersfield T	44	0		
2015–16	Huddersfield T	1	0	**247**	**0**
2015–16	QPR	18	0		
2016–17	QPR	46	0		
2017–18	QPR	43	0	**107**	**0**
2018–19	Cardiff C	0	0		
2019–20	Cardiff C	30	0	**30**	**0**

TOMLIN, Lee (F)				**333**	**70**
H: 5 11 W: 11 09 b.Leicester 12-1-89					
Internationals: England C.					
2010–11	Peterborough U	37	8		
2011–12	Peterborough U	37	8		
2012–13	Peterborough U	42	11		
2013–14	Peterborough U	19	5		
2013–14	Middlesbrough	14	4		
2014–15	Middlesbrough	42	7	**56**	**11**
2015–16	Bournemouth	6	0	**6**	**0**
2015–16	*Bristol C*	18	6		
2016–17	Bristol C	38	6	**56**	**12**
2017–18	Cardiff C	13	1		
2017–18	*Nottingham F*	15	4	**15**	**4**
2018–19	Cardiff C	0	0		
2018–19	*Peterborough U*	19	2	**154**	**34**
2019–20	Cardiff C	33	8	**46**	**9**

VASSELL, Isaac (F)				**73**	**12**
H: 5 7 W: 11 02 b.Newquay 9-9-93					
2011–12	Plymouth Arg	6	0		
2012–13	Plymouth Arg	0	0		
2013–14	Plymouth Arg	0	0	**6**	**0**
From Truro C.					
2016–17	Luton T	40	8		
2017–18	Luton T	2	2	**42**	**10**
2017–18	Birmingham C	9	1		
2018–19	Birmingham C	14	0		
2019–20	Birmingham C	0	0	**23**	**1**
2019–20	Cardiff C	2	1	**2**	**1**

VAULKS, Will (D) 260 27
H: 5 11 b.Birkenhead 13-9-93
Internationals: Wales Full caps.
2012–13 Tranmere R 0 0
2012–13 Falkirk 6 0
2013–14 Falkirk 33 1
2014–15 Falkirk 34 3
2015–16 Falkirk 35 6 **108 10**
2016–17 Rotherham U 40 1
2017–18 Rotherham U 44 5
2018–19 Rotherham U 41 7 **125 13**
2019–20 Cardiff C 27 4 **27 4**

WAITE, James (M) 0 0
b.Monmouth 11-5-91
Internationals: Wales U19.
2019–20 Cardiff C 0 0

WARD, Danny (M) 310 55
H: 5 11 W: 12 05 b.Bradford 11-12-91
2008–09 Bolton W 0 0
2009–10 Bolton W 2 0
2009–10 *Swindon T* 28 7 **28 7**
2010–11 Bolton W 0 0 **2 0**
2010–11 *Coventry C* 5 0 **5 0**
2010–11 *Huddersfield T* 7 3
2011–12 Huddersfield T 39 4
2012–13 Huddersfield T 28 2
2013–14 Huddersfield T 38 10
2014–15 Huddersfield T 12 0 **124 19**
2014–15 *Rotherham U* 16 3
2015–16 Rotherham U 34 4
2016–17 Rotherham U 41 10 **91 17**
2017–18 Cardiff C 18 4
2018–19 Cardiff C 14 1
2019–20 Cardiff C 28 7 **60 12**

WHYTE, Gavin (F) 60 7
b.Belfast 31-1-96
Internationals: Northern Ireland U21, Full caps.
From Crusaders.
2018–19 Oxford U 36 7 **36 7**
2019–20 Cardiff C 24 0 **24 0**

Players retained or with offer of contract
Bolger, Aaron Nigel; Griffiths, Daniel Lawrence; Martin, Daniel John; Patten, Keenan; Ratcliffe, George; Reynolds, Ryan Michael; Williams, Jack Daniel; Williams-Margetson, Ben; Wootton, Laurence Thomas.

Scholars
Chiabi, Mweembe Thomas Dimba; Cogman, Jaimie Michael; Colwill, Rubin; Davies, Isaak James; Evans, Kieron Thomas; Jones, Taylor Kian; Kavanagh, Ryan William; King, Eli Josef; Ligendza, Siyabonga Wes-Lee; Masrani, Jack Michael; Parsons, Samuel Steven; Pinchard, Harry Matthew; Pritchard, Owen Robert; Stewart, Bradley Luke; Thomas, Frazer Lee; Vaughan, Ethan Rhys; Yanko, Nativ.

CARLISLE U (20)

ALESSANDRA, Lewis (F) 397 60
H: 5 9 W: 11 07 b.Heywood 8-2-89
2007–08 Oldham Ath 15 2
2008–09 Oldham Ath 32 5
2009–10 Oldham Ath 1 0
2010–11 Oldham Ath 19 1 **67 8**
2011–12 Morecambe 42 4
2012–13 Morecambe 40 3
2013–14 Plymouth Arg 42 7
2014–15 Plymouth Arg 44 11 **86 18**
2015–16 Rochdale 8 1 **8 1**
2015–16 *York C* 11 2 **11 2**
2016–17 Hartlepool U 46 9 **46 9**
2017–18 Notts Co 39 7
2018–19 Notts Co 26 2 **65 9**
2019–20 Morecambe 22 5 **104 12**
2019–20 Carlisle U 10 1 **10 1**

ANDERTON, Nick (D) 48 2
H: 6 2 W: 12 06 b. 22-4-96
2014–15 Preston NE 0 0
2015–16 Preston NE 0 0
From Aldershot T, Barrow.
2017–18 Blackpool 4 0
2018–19 Accrington S 22 0 **22 0**
2018–19 Blackpool 10 0
2019–20 Blackpool 2 0 **16 0**
2019–20 Carlisle U 10 2 **10 2**

BARNES, Charlie (D) 0 0
2019–20 Carlisle U 0 0

BIRCH, Charlie (M) 1 0
2018–19 Carlisle U 0 0
2019–20 Carlisle U 1 0 **1 0**

BRIDGE, Jack (M) 67 2
H: 5 10 W: 11 07 b. 21-9-95
2013–14 Southend U 0 0
2014–15 Southend U 0 0
2015–16 Southend U 2 0
2016–17 Southend U 4 0
2017–18 Southend U 1 0 **7 0**
2017–18 Northampton T 4 0
2018–19 Northampton T 28 2 **32 2**
2019–20 Carlisle U 28 0 **28 0**

CHARTERS, Taylor (M) 7 0
b.Whitehaven 2-10-01
2019–20 Carlisle U 7 0 **7 0**

COLLIN, Adam (G) 359 0
H: 6 2 W: 12 00 b.Penrith 9-12-84
2003–04 Newcastle U 0 0
2003–04 *Oldham Ath* 0 0
From Workington
2009–10 Carlisle U 29 0
2010–11 Carlisle U 46 0
2011–12 Carlisle U 46 0
2012–13 Carlisle U 12 0
2013–14 Rotherham U 34 0
2014–15 Rotherham U 36 0
2015–16 Rotherham U 1 0 **71 0**
2015–16 *Aberdeen* 3 0 **3 0**
2016–17 Notts Co 43 0
2017–18 Notts Co 30 0 **73 0**
2018–19 Carlisle U 42 0
2019–20 Carlisle U 37 0 **212 0**

ELLIOT, Christie (F) 222 13
b.South Shields 26-5-91
2011–12 Partick Thistle 29 5
2012–13 Partick Thistle 22 2
2012–13 *Albion R* 6 1 **6 1**
2013–14 Partick Thistle 30 1
2014–15 Partick Thistle 26 2
2015–16 Partick Thistle 12 0
2016–17 Partick Thistle 31 0
2017–18 Partick Thistle 17 0
2018–19 Partick Thistle 33 1 **200 11**
2019–20 Carlisle U 16 1 **16 1**
Transferred to Dundee, January 2020.

ETUHU, Kelvin (F) 233 11
H: 5 11 W: 11 02 b.Kano 30-5-88
2005–06 Manchester C 0 0
2006–07 Manchester C 0 0
2006–07 *Rochdale* 4 2 **4 2**
2007–08 Manchester C 6 1
2007–08 *Leicester C* 4 0 **4 0**
2008–09 Manchester C 4 0
2009–10 Manchester C 0 0
2009–10 *Cardiff C* 16 0 **16 0**
2010–11 Manchester C 0 0 **10 1**
2011–12 Kavala 0 0
2011–12 Portsmouth 13 1
2012–13 Portsmouth 0 0 **13 1**
2012–13 Barnsley 26 0
2013–14 Barnsley 20 0 **46 0**
2014–15 Bury 43 2
2015–16 Bury 18 0
2016–17 Bury 20 2 **81 4**
2017–18 Carlisle U 20 3
2018–19 Carlisle U 39 0
2019–20 Carlisle U 0 0 **59 3**

GRAY, Louis (G) 0 0
H: 6 1 W: 11 11 b.Wrexham 11-8-95
From Wrexham.
2017–18 Everton 0 0
2017–18 *Carlisle U* 0 0
2018–19 Carlisle U 0 0
2019–20 Carlisle U 0 0

GUY, Callum (M) 61 0
b. 25-11-96
2015–16 Derby Co 0 0
2016–17 Derby Co 0 0
2016–17 *Port Vale* 11 0 **11 0**
2017–18 Derby Co 0 0
2017–18 *Bradford C* 17 0 **17 0**
2018–19 Blackpool 15 0
2019–20 Blackpool 15 0 **30 0**
2019–20 Carlisle U 3 0 **3 0**

HAYDEN, Aaron (D) 23 2
b. 16-1-97
2015–16 Wolverhampton W 0 0
2015–16 *Newport Co* 5 0 **5 0**
2016–17 Wolverhampton W 0 0
2017–18 Wolverhampton W 0 0
2018–19 Wolverhampton W 0 0
2019–20 Carlisle U 18 2 **18 2**

HUNT, Max (D) 4 0
2017–18 Derby Co 0 0
2018–19 Derby Co 0 0
2019–20 Derby Co 0 0
2019–20 Carlisle U 4 0 **4 0**

IREDALE, Jack (D) 95 9
b.Greenock 2-5-96
Internationals: Australia U17.
2016–17 Perth Glory 23 2 **23 2**
2017 ECU Joondalup 4 1 **4 1**
2017–18 Greenock Morton 9 2
2017–18 *Queen's Park* 14 1 **14 1**
2018–19 Greenock Morton 23 1 **32 3**
2019–20 Carlisle U 22 2 **22 2**

JONES, Gethin (D) 81 0
H: 5 10 W: 11 09 b.Perth 13-10-95
Internationals: Wales U17, U19, U21.
2014–15 Everton 0 0
2014–15 *Plymouth Arg* 6 0 **6 0**
2015–16 Everton 0 0
2016–17 Everton 0 0
2016–17 *Barnsley* 17 0 **17 0**
2017–18 Fleetwood T 10 0
2018–19 Fleetwood T 3 0 **13 0**
2018–19 *Mansfield T* 15 0 **15 0**
2019–20 Carlisle U 30 0 **30 0**

JONES, Mike (M) 480 36
H: 5 11 W: 12 04 b.Birkenhead 15-8-87
2005–06 Tranmere R 1 0
2006–07 Tranmere R 0 0
2006–07 *Shrewsbury T* 13 1 **13 1**
2007–08 Tranmere R 9 1 **10 1**
2008–09 Bury 46 4
2009–10 Bury 41 5
2010–11 Bury 42 8
2011–12 Bury 24 3 **153 20**
2011–12 Sheffield W 10 0
2012–13 Sheffield W 0 0 **10 0**
2012–13 Crawley T 40 1
2013–14 Crawley T 42 3 **82 4**
2014–15 Oldham Ath 45 6
2015–16 Oldham Ath 35 3 **80 9**
2016–17 Carlisle U 28 0
2017–18 Carlisle U 43 0
2018–19 Carlisle U 24 1
2019–20 Carlisle U 37 0 **132 1**

KERR, Keighran (F) 0 0
2018–19 Carlisle U 0 0
2019–20 Carlisle U 0 0

KNIGHT-PERCIVAL, Nathaniel (M) 242 13
H: 6 0 W: 11 06 b.Cambridge 31-3-87
Internationals: England C.
2012–13 Peterborough U 31 0
2013–14 Peterborough U 15 1 **46 1**
2014–15 Shrewsbury T 28 1
2015–16 Shrewsbury T 35 5 **63 6**
2016–17 Bradford C 42 0
2017–18 Bradford C 41 4
2018–19 Bradford C 35 2 **118 6**
2019–20 Carlisle U 15 0 **15 0**

LIGHTFOOT, Liam (D) 0 0
b.Carlisle 2-10-01
2019–20 Carlisle U 0 0

McKIRDY, Harry (M) 67 10
H: 5 9 W: 11 00 b.Stoke-on-Trent 29-3-97
From Stoke C.
2016–17 Aston Villa 0 0
2016–17 *Stevenage* 11 1 **11 1**
2017–18 Aston Villa 0 0
2017–18 *Crewe Alex* 16 3 **16 3**
2018–19 Aston Villa 0 0
2018–19 *Newport Co* 12 1 **12 1**
2019–20 Carlisle U 28 5 **28 5**

MELLISH, Jon (D) 15 0
b.South Shields 19-9-19
From Gateshead.
2019–20 Carlisle U 15 0 **15 0**

PATRICK, Omari (F) 19 3
b. 26-5-96
From Kidderminster H.
2018–19 Bradford C 1 0
2018–19 *Yeovil T* 9 1 **9 1**
2019–20 Bradford C 2 0 **3 0**
2019–20 Carlisle U 7 2 **7 2**

ROBINSON, Isaac (G) 0 0
b. 11-9-02
2019–20 Carlisle U 0 0

SAGAF, Mohammed (M) **17 1**
b.Kismayo 12-11-97
From Ipswich T, Barking, Braintree T.

2019–20	Carlisle U	17	1	**17**	**1**

SCOUGALL, Stefan (M) **145 12**
H: 5 7 W: 8 13 b.Edinburgh 7-12-92
Internationals: Scotland U21.

2013–14	Sheffield U	15	2		
2014–15	Sheffield U	25	1		
2015–16	Sheffield U	11	0		
2015–16	*Fleetwood T*	10	1	**10**	**1**
2016–17	Sheffield U	25	4	**76**	**7**
2017–18	St Johnstone	24	1		
2018–19	St Johnstone	0	0	**24**	**1**
2018–19	Carlisle U	15	1		
2019–20	Carlisle U	20	2	**35**	**3**

WALTON, Adam (D) **0 0**

2019–20	Carlisle U	0	0		

WEBSTER, Byron (D) **307 21**
H: 6 5 W: 12 07 b.Sherburn-in-Elmet 31-3-87

2007–08	Siad Most	23	4		
2008–09	Siad Most	0	0	**23**	**4**
2009–10	Doncaster R	5	0		
2010–11	Doncaster R	7	0	**12**	**0**
2010–11	*Hereford U*	2	0	**2**	**0**
2010–11	*Northampton T*	8	0		
2011–12	Northampton T	13	0	**21**	**0**
2012–13	Yeovil T	44	5		
2013–14	Yeovil T	41	3		
2014–15	Millwall	11	0		
2014–15	*Yeovil T*	14	0	**99**	**8**
2015–16	Millwall	40	6		
2016–17	Millwall	44	2		
2017–18	Millwall	10	0		
2018–19	Millwall	4	0	**109**	**8**
2018–19	Scunthorpe U	9	0	**9**	**0**
2019–20	Carlisle U	32	1	**32**	**1**

Players retained or with offer of contract
Dixon, Joshua James.

Scholars
Armstrong, Jamie Peter; Barnes, Charlie George; Bell, Lewis James; Birch, Charlie Mark; Day, Elliott; Leslie, Keelan James; Lightfoot, Robert Liam; Robinson, Isaac John; Rooks, Lewis Jack; Soper, Kyle; Steele, Roan Oliver; Swailes, Ryan Lee; Walton, Adam Jack; Wilson, Thomas Jackson.

CHARLTON ATH (21)

AMOS, Ben (G) **167 0**
H: 6 1 W: 13 00 b.Macclesfield 10-4-90
Internationals: England U16, U17, U18, U19, U20, U21.

2007–08	Manchester U	0	0		
2008–09	Manchester U	0	0		
2009–10	Manchester U	0	0		
2009–10	*Peterborough U*	1	0	**1**	**0**
2010–11	Manchester U	0	0		
2010–11	*Oldham Ath*	16	0	**16**	**0**
2011–12	Manchester U	1	0		
2012–13	Manchester U	0	0		
2012–13	*Hull C*	17	0	**17**	**0**
2013–14	Manchester U	0	0		
2013–14	*Carlisle U*	9	0	**9**	**0**
2014–15	Manchester U	0	0	**1**	**0**
2014–15	*Bolton W*	9	0		
2015–16	Bolton W	40	0		
2016–17	Bolton W	0	0		
2016–17	*Cardiff C*	16	0	**16**	**0**
2017–18	Bolton W	0	0		
2017–18	*Charlton Ath*	46	0		
2018–19	Bolton W	0	0	**49**	**0**
2018–19	*Millwall*	12	0	**12**	**0**
2019–20	Charlton Ath	0	0	**46**	**0**

ANEKE, Chuks (M) **228 57**
H: 6 3 W: 13 01 b.Newham 3-7-93
Internationals: England U16, U17, U18, U19.

2010–11	Arsenal	0	0		
2011–12	Arsenal	0	0		
2011–12	*Stevenage*	6	0	**6**	**0**
2011–12	*Preston NE*	7	1	**7**	**1**
2012–13	Arsenal	0	0		
2012–13	*Crewe Alex*	30	6		
2013–14	Arsenal	0	0		
2013–14	*Crewe Alex*	40	15	**70**	**21**
2014–15	Arsenal	0	0		
2014–15	Zulte-Waregem	30	2		
2015–16	Zulte-Waregem	11	2	**41**	**4**
2016–17	Milton Keynes D	15	4		
2017–18	Milton Keynes D	31	9		
2018–19	Milton Keynes D	38	17	**84**	**30**
2019–20	Charlton Ath	20	1	**20**	**1**

BONNE, Macauley (F) **108 18**
H: 5 11 W: 12 00 b.Ipswich 26-10-95
Internationals: Zimbabwe U23, Full caps.

2013–14	Colchester U	14	2		
2014–15	Colchester U	10	1		
2015–16	Colchester U	33	3		
2016–17	Colchester U	18	1	**75**	**7**

From Leyton Orient.

2019–20	Charlton Ath	33	11	**33**	**11**

DAVISON, Joshua (F) **9 1**
From Peterborough U, Enfield T.

2019–20	Charlton Ath	9	1	**9**	**1**

DEMPSEY, Ben (M) **4 0**
b. 25-11-99

2018–19	Charlton Ath	0	0		
2019–20	Charlton Ath	4	0	**4**	**0**

DOUGHTY, Alfie (M) **29 2**

2018–19	Charlton Ath	0	0		
2019–20	Charlton Ath	29	2	**29**	**2**

FORSTER-CASKEY, Jake (M) **177 16**
H: 5 10 W: 10 00 b.Southend 25-4-94
Internationals: England U16, U17, U18, U20, U21.

2009–10	Brighton & HA	1	0		
2010–11	Brighton & HA	0	0		
2011–12	Brighton & HA	4	1		
2012–13	Brighton & HA	3	0		
2012–13	*Oxford U*	16	3	**16**	**3**
2013–14	Brighton & HA	28	3		
2014–15	Brighton & HA	29	1		
2015–16	Brighton & HA	2	0	**67**	**5**
2015–16	*Milton Keynes D*	20	1	**20**	**1**
2016–17	Charlton Ath	15	2		
2016–17	*Rotherham U*	6	0	**6**	**0**
2017–18	Charlton Ath	41	5		
2018–19	Charlton Ath	1	0		
2019–20	Charlton Ath	11	0	**68**	**7**

HARNESS, Nathan (G) **0 0**
b. 19-1-00
From Stevenage, Dunstable.

2019–20	Charlton Ath	0	0		

HEMED, Tomer (F) **394 94**
H: 6 0 W: 12 04 b.Haifa 2-5-87
Internationals: Israel U17, U18, U19, U21, Full caps.

2005–06	Maccabi Haifa	3	1		
2006–07	Maccabi Haifa	8	2		
2007–08	Maccabi Haifa	7	0		
2007–08	*Maccabi Herzliya*	17	3	**17**	**3**
2008–09	Maccabi Haifa	0	0		
2008–09	*Bnei Yehuda*	28	1	**28**	**1**
2009–10	Maccabi Haifa	0	0		
2009–10	*Maccabi Ahi Nazareth*	33	9	**33**	**9**
2010–11	Maccabi Haifa	31	13	**49**	**16**
2011–12	Mallorca	29	7		
2012–13	Mallorca	37	11		
2013–14	Mallorca	24	2	**90**	**20**
2014–15	Almeria	35	8	**35**	**8**
2015–16	Brighton & HA	44	17		
2016–17	Brighton & HA	37	11		
2017–18	Brighton & HA	16	2		
2018–19	Brighton & HA	0	0		
2018–19	*QPR*	27	7	**27**	**7**
2019–20	Brighton & HA	0	0	**97**	**30**
2019–20	Charlton Ath	18	0	**18**	**0**

HENRY, Aaron (M) **0 0**
b. 31-8-03
Internationals: England U16.

2019–20	Charlton Ath	0	0		

LAPSLIE, George (M) **38 1**
b. 5-9-97

2016–17	Charlton Ath	0	0		
2017–18	Charlton Ath	1	0		
2018–19	Charlton Ath	27	0		
2019–20	Charlton Ath	10	1	**38**	**1**

LEDLEY, Joe (M) **446 53**
H: 6 0 W: 11 06 b.Cardiff 23-1-87
Internationals: Wales U17, U19, U21, Full caps.

2004–05	Cardiff C	28	3		
2005–06	Cardiff C	42	3		
2006–07	Cardiff C	46	2		
2007–08	Cardiff C	41	10		
2008–09	Cardiff C	40	4		
2009–10	Cardiff C	29	3	**226**	**25**
2010–11	Celtic	29	2		
2011–12	Celtic	32	7		
2012–13	Celtic	25	7		
2013–14	Celtic	20	4	**106**	**20**
2013–14	Crystal Palace	14	2		
2014–15	Crystal Palace	32	2		
2015–16	Crystal Palace	19	1		
2016–17	Crystal Palace	18	1	**83**	**6**
2017–18	Derby Co	26	1		
2018–19	Derby Co	4	1	**30**	**2**
2019–20	Charlton Ath	1	0	**1**	**0**

Transferred to Newcastle Jets, February 2020.

LOCKYER, Tom (D) **254 6**
H: 6 0 W: 11 05 b.Bristol 30-12-94
Internationals: Wales U21, Full caps.

2012–13	Bristol R	4	0		
2013–14	Bristol R	41	1		
2015–16	Bristol R	43	0		
2016–17	Bristol R	46	0		
2017–18	Bristol R	37	1		
2018–19	Bristol R	40	3	**211**	**5**
2019–20	Charlton Ath	43	1	**43**	**1**

MALONEY, Taylor (M) **12 0**
H: 5 9 W: 10 03 b. 21-1-99

2017–18	Charlton Ath	1	0		
2018–19	Charlton Ath	1	0		
2019–20	Charlton Ath	0	0	**2**	**0**
2019–20	*Newport Co*	10	0	**10**	**0**

MATTHEWS, Adam (D) **249 7**
H: 5 10 W: 11 02 b.Swansea 13-1-92
Internationals: Wales U17, U19, U21, Full caps.

2008–09	Cardiff C	0	0		
2009–10	Cardiff C	32	1		
2010–11	Cardiff C	8	0	**40**	**1**
2011–12	Celtic	27	0		
2012–13	Celtic	22	2		
2013–14	Celtic	23	1		
2014–15	Celtic	29	1	**101**	**4**
2015–16	Sunderland	1	0		
2015–16	*Bristol C*	9	0		
2016–17	Sunderland	0	0		
2016–17	*Bristol C*	12	0	**21**	**0**
2017–18	Sunderland	34	1		
2018–19	Sunderland	23	1	**58**	**2**
2019–20	Charlton Ath	29	0	**29**	**0**

MAYNARD-BREWER, Ashley (G) **0 0**
b. 25-6-99
Internationals: Australia U23.

2017–18	Charlton Ath	0	0		
2018–19	Charlton Ath	0	0		
2019–20	Charlton Ath	0	0		

MORGAN, Albie (M) **29 0**
b.Portsmouth 2-2-00

2018–19	Charlton Ath	8	0		
2019–20	Charlton Ath	21	0	**29**	**0**

OCRAN, Wilberforce (F) **0 0**
b. 24-9-99
From Barnsley.

2018–19	Charlton Ath	0	0		
2019–20	Charlton Ath	0	0		

ODOH, Abraham (M) **0 0**
From Tooting & Mitcham U.

2019–20	Charlton Ath	0	0		

OSAGHAE, Joseph (G) **0 0**
b. 20-2-01

2018–19	Charlton Ath	0	0		
2019–20	Charlton Ath	0	0		

OSHILAJA, Adedeji (D) **180 9**
H: 5 11 W: 11 10 b.Bermondsey 16-7-93

2012–13	Cardiff C	0	0		
2013–14	Cardiff C	0	0		
2013–14	*Newport Co*	8	0	**8**	**0**
2013–14	*Sheffield W*	2	0	**2**	**0**
2014–15	Cardiff C	0	0		
2014–15	*AFC Wimbledon*	23	1		
2015–16	Cardiff C	0	0		
2015–16	*Gillingham*	22	3		
2016–17	Cardiff C	0	0		
2016–17	*Gillingham*	33	2	**55**	**5**
2017–18	AFC Wimbledon	42	2		
2018–19	AFC Wimbledon	25	1	**90**	**4**
2019–20	Charlton Ath	25	0	**25**	**0**

OZTUMER, Erhun (M) **168 37**
b.Greenwich 29-5-91

2014–15	Peterborough U	20	1		
2015–16	Peterborough U	30	6	**50**	**7**
2016–17	Walsall	41	15		
2017–18	Walsall	45	15	**86**	**30**
2018–19	Bolton W	17	0		
2019–20	Bolton W	1	0	**18**	**0**
2019–20	Charlton Ath	14	0	**14**	**0**

PAGE, Lewis (D) **55** **1**
b.London 20-5-96

2014–15	West Ham U	0	0		
2015–16	West Ham U	0	0		
2015–16	*Cambridge U*	6	0	**6**	**0**
2016–17	West Ham U	0	0		
2016–17	*Coventry C*	22	0	**22**	**0**
2016–17	Charlton Ath	8	0		
2017–18	Charlton Ath	8	1		
2018–19	Charlton Ath	11	0		
2019–20	Charlton Ath	0	0	**27**	**1**

PEARCE, Jason (D) **464** **21**
H: 5 11 W: 12 00 b.Hillingdon 6-12-87

2006–07	Portsmouth	0	0		
2007–08	Bournemouth	33	1		
2008–09	Bournemouth	44	2		
2009–10	Bournemouth	39	1		
2010–11	Bournemouth	46	3	**162**	**7**
2011–12	Portsmouth	43	2	**43**	**2**
2011–12	Leeds U	0	0		
2012–13	Leeds U	33	0		
2013–14	Leeds U	45	2		
2014–15	Leeds U	21	0	**99**	**2**
2014–15	Wigan Ath	16	2		
2015–16	Wigan Ath	31	2	**47**	**4**
2016–17	Charlton Ath	23	1		
2017–18	Charlton Ath	25	2		
2018–19	Charlton Ath	26	2		
2019–20	Charlton Ath	39	1	**113**	**6**

PHILLIPS, Dillon (M) **81** **0**
H: 6 2 W: 11 11 b. 11-6-95

2012–13	Charlton Ath	0	0		
2013–14	Charlton Ath	0	0		
2014–15	Charlton Ath	0	0		
2015–16	Charlton Ath	0	0		
2016–17	Charlton Ath	8	0		
2017–18	Charlton Ath	0	0		
2018–19	Charlton Ath	27	0		
2019–20	Charlton Ath	46	0	**81**	**0**

POWELL, Johl (D) **0** **0**

2019–20	Charlton Ath	0	0		

PRATLEY, Darren (M) **466** **47**
H: 6 1 W: 10 12 b.Barking 22-4-85

2001–02	Fulham	0	0		
2002–03	Fulham	0	0		
2003–04	Fulham	1	0		
2004–05	Fulham	0	0		
2004–05	*Brentford*	14	1		
2005–06	Fulham	0	0	**1**	**0**
2005–06	*Brentford*	32	4	**46**	**5**
2006–07	Swansea C	28	1		
2007–08	Swansea C	42	5		
2008–09	Swansea C	37	4		
2009–10	Swansea C	36	7		
2010–11	Swansea C	34	9	**177**	**26**
2011–12	Bolton W	25	1		
2012–13	Bolton W	31	2		
2013–14	Bolton W	20	2		
2014–15	Bolton W	22	4		
2015–16	Bolton W	36	1		
2016–17	Bolton W	12	0		
2017–18	Bolton W	32	2	**178**	**12**
2018–19	Charlton Ath	28	2		
2019–20	Charlton Ath	36	2	**64**	**4**

PURRINGTON, Ben (D) **147** **2**
H: 5 9 W: 11 07 b.Exeter 5-5-96

2013–14	Plymouth Arg	12	0		
2014–15	Plymouth Arg	8	0		
2015–16	Plymouth Arg	13	0		
2016–17	Plymouth Arg	19	0	**52**	**0**
2016–17	Rotherham U	10	0		
2017–18	Rotherham U	10	0		
2018–19	Rotherham U	0	0	**20**	**0**
2018–19	*AFC Wimbledon*	26	0	**26**	**0**
2018–19	*Charlton Ath*	18	0		
2019–20	Charlton Ath	31	2	**49**	**2**

QUITIRNA, Junior (M) **0** **0**
b. 1-1-01

2019–20	Charlton Ath	0	0		

SARPENG-WIREDU, Brendan (M) **7** **0**
b. 7-11-99

2018–19	Charlton Ath	0	0		
2019–20	Charlton Ath	0	0		
2019–20	*Colchester U*	7	0	**7**	**0**

SARR, Naby (D) **127** **8**
H: 6 5 W: 14 11 b.Marseille 13-8-93
Internationals: France U20, U21.

2012–13	Lyon	0	0		
2013–14	Lyon	2	0	**2**	**0**
2014–15	Sporting Lisbon	8	0	**8**	**0**
2015–16	Charlton Ath	12	1		
2016–17	Charlton Ath	0	0		
2016–17	*Red Star*	22	2	**22**	**2**
2017–18	Charlton Ath	18	0		
2018–19	Charlton Ath	36	2		
2019–20	Charlton Ath	29	3	**95**	**6**

SOLLY, Chris (D) **302** **3**
H: 5 8 W: 10 07 b.Rochester 20-1-91
Internationals: England U16, U17.

2008–09	Charlton Ath	1	0		
2009–10	Charlton Ath	9	0		
2010–11	Charlton Ath	14	1		
2011–12	Charlton Ath	44	0		
2012–13	Charlton Ath	45	1		
2013–14	Charlton Ath	12	0		
2014–15	Charlton Ath	38	0		
2015–16	Charlton Ath	34	0		
2016–17	Charlton Ath	27	0		
2017–18	Charlton Ath	27	0		
2018–19	Charlton Ath	37	1		
2019–20	Charlton Ath	14	0	**302**	**3**

STEVENSON, Toby (D) **3** **0**
b.Colchester 22-11-99
From Leyton Orient.

2018–19	Charlton Ath	3	0		
2019–20	Charlton Ath	0	0	**3**	**0**

TAYLOR, Lyle (F) **338** **117**
H: 6 2 W: 12 00 b.Greenwich 29-3-90
Internationals: Montserrat Full caps.

2007–08	Millwall	0	0		
2008–09	Millwall	0	0		
From Concord R					
2010–11	Bournemouth	11	0		
2011–12	Bournemouth	18	0	**29**	**0**
2011–12	*Hereford U*	8	2	**8**	**2**
2012–13	Falkirk	34	24	**34**	**24**
2013–14	Sheffield U	20	2	**20**	**2**
2013–14	*Partick Thistle*	20	7		
2014–15	Scunthorpe U	18	3	**18**	**3**
2014–15	*Partick Thistle*	15	3	**35**	**10**
2015–16	AFC Wimbledon	42	20		
2016–17	AFC Wimbledon	43	10		
2017–18	AFC Wimbledon	46	14	**131**	**44**
2018–19	Charlton Ath	41	21		
2019–20	Charlton Ath	22	11	**63**	**32**

VENNINGS, James (M) **3** **0**
b. 24-5-00

2019–20	Charlton Ath	3	0	**3**	**0**

WILLIAMS, Jon (M) **160** **3**
H: 5 6 W: 10 00 b.Tunbridge Wells 9-10-93
Internationals: Wales U17, U19, U21, Full caps.

2010–11	Crystal Palace	0	0		
2011–12	Crystal Palace	14	0		
2012–13	Crystal Palace	29	0		
2013–14	Crystal Palace	9	0		
2013–14	*Ipswich T*	13	1		
2014–15	Crystal Palace	2	0		
2014–15	*Ipswich T*	7	1		
2015–16	Crystal Palace	1	0		
2015–16	*Nottingham F*	10	0	**10**	**0**
2015–16	*Milton Keynes D*	13	0	**13**	**0**
2016–17	Crystal Palace	0	0		
2016–17	*Ipswich T*	8	0	**28**	**2**
2017–18	Crystal Palace	0	0		
2017–18	*Sunderland*	12	1	**12**	**1**
2018–19	Crystal Palace	0	0	**55**	**0**
2018–19	Charlton Ath	16	0		
2019–20	Charlton Ath	26	0	**42**	**0**

YAO, Kenneth (D) **0** **0**
b. 5-9-98

2018–19	Charlton Ath	0	0		
2019–20	Charlton Ath	0	0		

Players retained or with offer of contract
Aouachria, Wassim Chouaib; Clayden, Charles James; Mingi, Jade Jay; Vega, Luca.

Scholars
Afran-Kesey, Richard George Marcel; Agyemang, Terrell Nana Obeng; Aidoo, Kasim Ishmael Amu-Kadar; Albon, Luca James; Allsopp, Edward; Appiah, Jimmy Akumi; Bakrin, Nazir Oladayo Temitope; Barker, Charlie Mel; Barton, Frederick Joseph Terry; Buhari, Muhammad Ashraf Haroun; French, Billy; Garande, Kai Tapiwa Ocean; Gavin, Dylan John; Harvey, Nathan Michael; Henry, Aaron Lewis; Santos, Hurtado Jeremy Andres; Thompso-Fearon, Andre Anthony; Watkins, Joe Christopher.

CHELSEA (22)

ABRAHAM, Tammy (F) **145** **68**
H: 6 3 W: 12 13 b.London 2-10-97
Internationals: England U18, U19, U21, Full caps.

2015–16	Chelsea	2	0		
2016–17	Chelsea	0	0		
2016–17	*Bristol C*	41	23	**41**	**23**
2017–18	Chelsea	0	0		
2017–18	*Swansea C*	31	5	**31**	**5**
2018–19	Chelsea	0	0		
2018–19	*Aston Villa*	37	25	**37**	**25**
2019–20	Chelsea	34	15	**36**	**15**

ALONSO, Marcus (D) **262** **31**
H: 6 2 W: 13 05 b.Madrid 28-12-90
Internationals: Spain U19, Full caps.

2008–09	RM Castilla	11	0		
2009–10	RM Castilla	28	3	**39**	**3**
2009–10	Real Madrid	1	0	**1**	**0**
2010–11	Bolton W	4	0		
2011–12	Bolton W	5	1		
2012–13	Bolton W	26	4	**35**	**5**
2013–14	Fiorentina	3	0		
2013–14	*Sunderland*	16	0	**16**	**0**
2014–15	Fiorentina	22	1		
2015–16	Fiorentina	31	3		
2016–17	Fiorentina	2	0	**58**	**4**
2016–17	Chelsea	31	6		
2017–18	Chelsea	33	7		
2018–19	Chelsea	31	2		
2019–20	Chelsea	18	4	**113**	**19**

AMPADU, Ethan (M) **12** **0**
b.Exeter 14-9-00
Internationals: England U16, Wales U17, U19, Full caps.

2016–17	Exeter C	8	0	**8**	**0**
2017–18	Chelsea	1	0		
2018–19	Chelsea	0	0		
2019–20	Chelsea	0	0	**1**	**0**
2019–20	*RB Leipzig*	3	0	**3**	**0**

ANJORIN, Faustino (M) **1** **0**
b.Poole 23-11-01
Internationals: England U17, U18, U19.

2019–20	Chelsea	1	0	**1**	**0**

ARRIZABALAGA, Kepa (G) **212** **0**
H: 6 1 W: 12 11 b.Ondorroa 3-10-94
Internationals: Spain U18, U19, U21, Full caps.

2011–12	Basconia	12	0		
2012–13	Basconia	19	0	**31**	**0**
2013–14	Athletic Bilbao	0	0		
2014–15	Athletic Bilbao	0	0		
2014–15	*Ponferradina*	20	0	**20**	**0**
2015–16	Athletic Bilbao	0	0		
2015–16	*Vallodolid*	39	0	**39**	**0**
2016–17	Athletic Bilbao	23	0		
2017–18	Athletic Bilbao	30	0	**53**	**0**
2018–19	Chelsea	36	0		
2019–20	Chelsea	33	0	**69**	**0**

AZPILICUETA, Cesar (D) **417** **9**
H: 5 10 W: 10 13 b.Pamplona 28-8-89
Internationals: Spain U16, U17, U19, U20, U21, U23, Full caps.

2006–07	Osasuna	1	0		
2007–08	Osasuna	29	0		
2008–09	Osasuna	36	0		
2009–10	Osasuna	33	0	**99**	**0**
2010–11	Marseille	15	0		
2011–12	Marseille	30	1		
2012–13	Marseille	2	0	**47**	**1**
2012–13	Chelsea	27	0		
2013–14	Chelsea	29	0		
2014–15	Chelsea	29	0		
2015–16	Chelsea	37	2		
2016–17	Chelsea	38	1		
2017–18	Chelsea	37	2		
2018–19	Chelsea	38	1		
2019–20	Chelsea	36	2	**271**	**8**

BABA, Abdul Rahman (D) **144** **3**
H: 5 10 W: 12 00 b.Tamale 2-7-94
Internationals: Ghana U20, Full caps.

2011–12	Asante Kotoko	25	0	**25**	**0**
2012–13	Greuther Furth	20	0		
2013–14	Greuther Furth	22	0		
2014–15	Greuther Furth	2	2	**44**	**2**
2014–15	Augsburg	31	0	**31**	**0**
2015–16	Chelsea	15	0		
2016–17	Chelsea	0	0		
2016–17	*Schalke 04*	13	0		
2017–18	Chelsea	0	0		

2017–18 *Schalke 04* 1 0
2018–19 Chelsea 0 0
2018–19 *Schalke 04* 2 0 **16 0**
2018–19 *Reims* 11 1 **11 1**
2019–20 Chelsea 0 0 **15 0**
2019–20 *Mallorca* 2 0 **2 0**

BAKAYOKO, Tiemoue (M) 167 8
H: 6 1 W: 12 02 b.Paris 17-8-94
Internationals: France U16, U17, U18, U20, U21, Full caps.
2013–14 Rennes 24 1 **24 1**
2014–15 Monaco 12 0
2015–16 Monaco 19 1
2016–17 Monaco 32 2
2017–18 Chelsea 29 2
2018–19 Chelsea 0 0
2018–19 *AC Milan* 31 1 **31 1**
2019–20 Chelsea 0 0 **29 2**
2019–20 *Monaco* 20 1 **83 4**

BAKER, Lewis (M) 130 20
b.Luton 25-4-95
Internationals: England U17, U19, U20, U21.
2012–13 Chelsea 0 0
2013–14 Chelsea 0 0
2014–15 Chelsea 0 0
2014–15 *Sheffield W* 4 0 **4 0**
2014–15 *Milton Keynes D* 12 3 **12 3**
2015–16 Chelsea 0 0
2015–16 *Vitesse* 31 5
2016–17 Chelsea 0 0
2016–17 *Vitesse* 33 10 **64 15**
2017–18 Chelsea 0 0
2017–18 *Middlesbrough* 12 1 **12 1**
2018–19 Chelsea 0 0
2018–19 *Leeds U* 11 0 **11 0**
2018–19 *Reading* 19 1 **19 1**
2019–20 Chelsea 0 0
2019–20 *Fortuna Dusseldorf* 8 0 **8 0**

BARKLEY, Ross (M) 217 29
H: 6 2 W: 12 00 b.Liverpool 5-12-93
Internationals: England U16, U17, U19, U20, U21, Full caps.
2010–11 Everton 0 0
2011–12 Everton 6 0
2012–13 Everton 7 0
2012–13 *Sheffield W* 13 4 **13 4**
2012–13 *Leeds U* 4 0 **4 0**
2013–14 Everton 34 6
2014–15 Everton 29 2
2015–16 Everton 38 8
2016–17 Everton 36 5
2017–18 Everton 0 0 **150 21**
2017–18 Chelsea 2 0
2018–19 Chelsea 27 3
2019–20 Chelsea 21 1 **50 4**

BATE, Lewis (M) 0 0
b.London 29-10-02
Internationals: England U17, U18.
2019–20 Chelsea 0 0

BATSHUAYI, Michy (F) 243 86
H: 5 11 W: 12 04 b.Brussels 2-10-93
Internationals: Belgium U21, Full caps.
2010–11 Standard Liege 2 0
2011–12 Standard Liege 23 6
2012–13 Standard Liege 34 12
2013–14 Standard Liege 38 21 **97 39**
2014–15 Marseille 26 9
2015–16 Marseille 36 17 **62 26**
2016–17 Chelsea 20 5
2017–18 Chelsea 12 2
2017–18 *Borussia Dortmund* 10 7 **10 7**
2018–19 Chelsea 0 0
2018–19 *Valencia* 15 1 **15 1**
2018–19 *Crystal Palace* 11 5 **11 5**
2019–20 Chelsea 16 1 **48 8**

BAXTER, Nathan (G) 47 0
b.London 8-11-98
2018–19 Chelsea 0 0
2018–19 *Yeovil T* 34 0 **34 0**
2019–20 Chelsea 0 0
2019–20 *Ross Co* 13 0 **13 0**

BLACKMAN, Jamal (G) 95 0
H: 6 6 W: 14 09 b.Croydon 27-10-93
Internationals: England U16, U17, U18, U19.
2011–12 Chelsea 0 0
2012–13 Chelsea 0 0
2013–14 Chelsea 0 0
2014–15 Chelsea 0 0
2014–15 *Middlesbrough* 0 0
2015–16 Chelsea 0 0
2015–16 *Ostersunds FK* 12 0 **12 0**
2016–17 Chelsea 0 0
2016–17 *Wycombe W* 42 0 **42 0**
2017–18 Chelsea 0 0
2017–18 *Sheffield U* 31 0 **31 0**
2018–19 Chelsea 0 0
2018–19 *Leeds U* 0 0
2019–20 Chelsea 0 0
2019–20 *Vitesse* 0 0
2019–20 *Bristol R* 10 0 **10 0**

BROJA, Armando (F) 1 0
b.Slough 10-9-01
Internationals: Albania U19, U21.
2019–20 Chelsea 1 0 **1 0**

BROWN, Isaiah (M) 98 9
H: 6 0 W: 10 13 b.Peterborough 7-1-97
Internationals: England U16, U17, U19, U20.
2012–13 WBA 1 0 **1 0**
2013–14 Chelsea 0 0
2014–15 Chelsea 1 0
2015–16 Chelsea 0 0
2015–16 *Vitesse* 22 1 **22 1**
2016–17 Chelsea 0 0
2016–17 *Rotherham U* 20 3 **20 3**
2016–17 *Huddersfield T* 15 4 **15 4**
2017–18 Chelsea 0 0
2017–18 *Brighton & HA* 13 0 **13 0**
2018–19 Chelsea 0 0
2018–19 *Leeds U* 1 0 **1 0**
2019–20 Chelsea 0 0 **1 0**
2019–20 *Luton T* 25 1 **25 1**

CABALLERO, Willy (G) 341 0
H: 6 1 W: 12 08 b.Santa Elena 28-9-81
Internationals: Argentina U21, Full caps.
2001–02 Boca Juniors 4 0
2002–03 Boca Juniors 4 0
2003–04 Boca Juniors 1 0
2004–05 Boca Juniors 6 0 **15 0**
2005–06 Elche 10 0
2006–07 Elche 39 0
2007–08 Elche 38 0
2008–09 Elche 38 0
2009–10 Elche 39 0
2010–11 Elche 22 0 **166 0**
2010–11 Malaga 15 0
2011–12 Malaga 28 0
2012–13 Malaga 36 0
2013–14 Malaga 38 0 **117 0**
2014–15 Manchester C 2 0
2015–16 Manchester C 4 0
2016–17 Manchester C 17 0 **23 0**
2017–18 Chelsea 3 0
2018–19 Chelsea 2 0
2019–20 Chelsea 5 0 **10 0**

CHALOBAH, Trevoh (D) 79 3
H: 6 3 b.Freetown 5-7-99
Internationals: England U16, U17, U19, U20, U21.
2017–18 Chelsea 0 0
2018–19 Chelsea 0 0
2018–19 *Ipswich T* 43 2 **43 2**
2019–20 Chelsea 0 0
2019–20 *Huddersfield T* 36 1 **36 1**

CHRISTENSEN, Andreas (D) 119 5
H: 6 2 W: 11 09 b.Allerod 10-4-96
Internationals: Denmark U16, U17, U19, U21, Full caps.
2012–13 Chelsea 0 0
2013–14 Chelsea 0 0
2014–15 Chelsea 1 0
2015–16 Chelsea 0 0
2015–16 *Borussia M'gladbach* 31 3
2016–17 Chelsea 0 0
2016–17 Borussia M'gladbach 31 2 **62 5**
2017–18 Chelsea 27 0
2018–19 Chelsea 8 0
2019–20 Chelsea 21 0 **57 0**

CLARKE-SALTER, Jake (D) 71 3
H: 6 2 W: 11 00 b.Carshalton 22-9-97
Internationals: England U18, U19, U20, U21.
2015–16 Chelsea 1 0
2016–17 Chelsea 0 0
2016–17 *Bristol R* 12 1 **12 1**
2017–18 Chelsea 0 0
2017–18 *Sunderland* 11 0 **11 0**
2018–19 Chelsea 0 0
2018–19 *Vitesse* 28 1 **28 1**
2019–20 Chelsea 0 0 **1 0**
2019–20 *Birmingham C* 19 1 **19 1**

CUMMING, Jamie (G) 0 0
b.Winchester 4-9-99
Internationals: England U17, U19.
2018–19 Chelsea 0 0
2019–20 Chelsea 0 0

DRINKWATER, Daniel (M) 281 17
H: 5 10 W: 11 00 b.Manchester 5-3-90
Internationals: England U18, U19, Full caps.
2008–09 Manchester U 0 0
2009–10 Manchester U 0 0
2009–10 *Huddersfield T* 33 2 **33 2**
2010–11 Manchester U 0 0
2010–11 *Cardiff C* 9 0 **9 0**
2010–11 *Watford* 12 0 **12 0**
2011–12 Manchester U 0 0
2011–12 *Barnsley* 17 1 **17 1**
2011–12 Leicester C 19 2
2012–13 Leicester C 42 1
2013–14 Leicester C 45 7
2014–15 Leicester C 23 0
2015–16 Leicester C 35 2
2016–17 Leicester C 29 1
2017–18 Leicester C 0 0 **193 13**
2017–18 Chelsea 12 1
2018–19 Chelsea 0 0
2019–20 Chelsea 0 0 **12 1**
2019–20 *Burnley* 1 0 **1 0**
2019–20 *Aston Villa* 4 0 **4 0**

EMERSON, dos Santos (D) 91 2
H: 5 9 W: 9 13 b.Santos 13-3-94
Internationals: Brazil U17. Italy Full caps.
2011 Santos 0 0
2012 Santos 1 0
2013 Santos 14 1
2014 Santos 3 0 **18 1**
2014–15 *Palermo* 9 0 **9 0**
2015–16 Roma 8 1
2016–17 Roma 25 0
2017–18 Roma 1 0 **34 1**
2017–18 Chelsea 5 0
2018–19 Chelsea 10 0
2019–20 Chelsea 15 0 **30 0**

GALLAGHER, Conor (M) 45 6
b.Epsom 6-2-00
Internationals: England U17, U18, U19, U20, U21.
2019–20 Chelsea 0 0
2019–20 *Charlton Ath* 26 6 **26 6**
2019–20 *Swansea C* 19 0 **19 0**

GILMOUR, Billy (M) 6 0
b.glasgow 11-6-01
Internationals: Scotland U16, U17, U19, U21.
From Rangers.
2019–20 Chelsea 6 0 **6 0**

GIROUD, Olivier (F) 423 164
H: 6 3 W: 13 11 b.Chambery 30-9-86
Internationals: France Full caps.
2005–06 Grenoble 3 0
2006–07 Grenoble 15 2 **18 2**
2007–08 Grenoble 0 0
2007–08 *Istres* 33 14 **33 14**
2008–09 Tours 23 8
2009–10 Tours 38 21 **61 29**
2010–11 Montpellier 37 12
2011–12 Montpellier 36 21 **73 33**
2012–13 Arsenal 34 11
2013–14 Arsenal 36 16
2014–15 Arsenal 27 14
2015–16 Arsenal 38 16
2016–17 Arsenal 29 12
2017–18 Arsenal 16 4 **180 73**
2017–18 Chelsea 13 3
2018–19 Chelsea 27 2
2019–20 Chelsea 18 8 **58 13**

GRANT, Josh (D) 30 0
b. 11-10-98
Internationals: England U18, U20.
2018–19 Chelsea 0 0
2018–19 *Yeovil T* 8 0 **8 0**
2019–20 Chelsea 0 0
2019–20 *Plymouth Arg* 22 0 **22 0**

GUEHI, Marc (D) 12 0
Internationals: England U16, U17, U18, U19, U20, U21.
2018–19 Chelsea 0 0
2019–20 Chelsea 0 0
2019–20 *Swansea C* 12 0 **12 0**

HUDSON-ODOI, Callum (M) 34 1
H: 6 0 b.Wandsworth 7-11-00
Internationals: England U16, U17, U18, U19, Full caps.
2017–18 Chelsea 2 0
2018–19 Chelsea 10 0
2019–20 Chelsea 22 1 **34 1**

JAMES, Reece (D) 69 3
b.London 8-12-99
Internationals: England U18, U19, U20, U21.
2018–19 Chelsea 0 0
2018–19 *Wigan Ath* 45 3 **45 3**
2019–20 Chelsea 24 0 **24 0**

JORGINHO, Filho Jorge (M) 321 20
H: 5 11 W: 11 03 b.Imbituba 20-12-91
Internationals: Italy Full caps.
2010–11 Verona 0 0
2010–11 *Sambonifacese* 31 1 **31 1**
2011–12 Verona 30 2
2012–13 Verona 41 2
2013–14 Verona 18 7 **89 11**
2013–14 Napoli 15 0
2014–15 Napoli 23 0
2015–16 Napoli 35 0
2016–17 Napoli 27 0
2017–18 Napoli 33 2 **133 2**
2018–19 Chelsea 37 2
2019–20 Chelsea 31 4 **68 6**

KANTE, Ngolo (M) 277 17
H: 5 7 W: 11 00 b.Paris 29-3-91
Internationals: France Full caps.
2011–12 Boulogne 1 0
2012–13 Boulogne 37 3 **38 3**
2013–14 Caen 38 2
2014–15 Caen 37 2 **75 4**
2015–16 Leicester C 37 1 **37 1**
2016–17 Chelsea 35 1
2017–18 Chelsea 34 1
2018–19 Chelsea 36 4
2019–20 Chelsea 22 3 **127 9**

KENEDY, Robert (F) 103 7
H: 6 0 W: 12 08 b.Santa Rita do Sapucai 8-2-96
Internationals: Brazil U17, U20, U23.
2013 Fluminense 9 0
2014 Fluminense 20 2
2015 Fluminense 1 0 **30 2**
2015–16 Chelsea 14 1
2016–17 Chelsea 1 0
2016–17 *Watford* 1 0 **1 0**
2017–18 Chelsea 0 0
2017–18 *Newcastle U* 13 2
2018–19 Chelsea 0 0
2018–19 *Newcastle U* 25 1 **38 3**
2019–20 Chelsea 0 0 **15 1**
2019–20 *Getafe* 19 1 **19 1**

KOVACIC, Mateo (M) 259 13
H: 5 11 W: 11 07 b.Linz 6-5-94
Internationals: Croatia U17, U19, U21, Full caps.
2010–11 Dinamo Zagreb 7 1
2011–12 Dinamo Zagreb 25 4
2012–13 Dinamo Zagreb 11 1 **43 6**
2012–13 InterMilan 13 0
2013–14 InterMilan 32 0
2014–15 InterMilan 35 5 **80 5**
2015–16 Real Madrid 25 0
2016–17 Real Madrid 27 1
2017–18 Real Madrid 21 0
2018–19 Real Madrid 0 0 **73 1**
2018–19 *Chelsea* 32 0
2019–20 Chelsea 31 1 **63 1**

LOFTUS-CHEEK, Ruben (M) 77 9
H: 6 4 W: 11 03 b.Lewisham 23-1-96
Internationals: England U16, U17, U19, U21, Full caps.
2012–13 Chelsea 0 0
2013–14 Chelsea 0 0
2014–15 Chelsea 3 0
2015–16 Chelsea 13 1
2016–17 Chelsea 6 0
2017–18 Chelsea 0 0
2017–18 *Crystal Palace* 24 2 **24 2**
2018–19 Chelsea 24 6
2019–20 Chelsea 7 0 **53 7**

MAATSEN, Ian (D) 0 0
b.Vlaardingen 10-3-02
Internationals: Netherlands U16, U17, U18.
From PSV Eindhoven.
2019–20 Chelsea 0 0

MADDOX, Jacob (M) 38 1
b. 3-11-98
Internationals: England U16, U17, U19, U20.
2018–19 Chelsea 0 0
2018–19 *Cheltenham T* 38 1 **38 1**
2019–20 Chelsea 0 0
2019–20 *Tranmere R* 0 0
2019–20 *Southampton* 0 0

McCORMICK, Luke (M) 5 0
b. 21-1-99
2019–20 Chelsea 0 0
2019–20 *Shrewsbury T* 5 0 **5 0**

MIAZGA, Matt (D) 141 7
H: 6 4 W: 12 08 b.Clifton, NJ 19-7-95
Internationals: Poland U18. USA U18, U20, U23, Full caps.
2013 New York Red Bulls 1 0
2014 New York Red Bulls 7 0
2015 New York Red Bulls 26 1 **34 1**
2015–16 Chelsea 2 0
2016–17 Chelsea 0 0
2016–17 *Vitesse* 23 0
2017–18 Chelsea 0 0
2017–18 *Vitesse* 36 4 **59 4**
2018–19 Chelsea 0 0
2018–19 *Nantes* 8 0 **8 0**
2018–19 *Reading* 18 0
2019–20 Chelsea 0 0 **2 0**
2019–20 *Reading* 20 2 **38 2**

MOSES, Victor (M) 304 35
H: 5 10 W: 11 07 b.Lagos 12-12-90
Internationals: England U16, U17, U19, U21. Nigeria Full caps.
2007–08 Crystal Palace 13 3
2008–09 Crystal Palace 27 2
2009–10 Crystal Palace 18 6 **58 11**
2009–10 Wigan Ath 14 1
2010–11 Wigan Ath 21 1
2011–12 Wigan Ath 38 6
2012–13 Wigan Ath 1 0 **74 8**
2012–13 Chelsea 23 1
2013–14 Chelsea 0 0
2013–14 *Liverpool* 19 1 **19 1**
2014–15 Chelsea 0 0
2014–15 *Stoke C* 19 3 **19 3**
2015–16 Chelsea 0 0
2015–16 *West Ham U* 21 1 **21 1**
2016–17 Chelsea 34 3
2017–18 Chelsea 28 3
2018–19 Chelsea 2 0
2018–19 *Fenerbahce* 14 4 **14 4**
2019–20 Chelsea 0 0 **87 7**
2019–20 *Inter Milan* 12 0 **12 0**

MOUNT, Mason (M) 101 24
H: 5 10 b.Portsmouth 10-1-99
Internationals: England U16, U17, U18, U19, U21, Full caps.
2017–18 Chelsea 0 0
2017–18 *Vitesse* 29 9 **29 9**
2018–19 Chelsea 0 0
2018–19 *Derby Co* 35 8 **35 8**
2019–20 Chelsea 37 7 **37 7**

MUSONDA, Charly (M) 59 2
H: 5 8 W: 10 10 b.Brussels 15-10-96
Internationals: Belgium U16, U17, U19, U21.
2015–16 Chelsea 0 0
2015–16 *Real Betis* 16 1
2016–17 Chelsea 0 0
2016–17 Real Betis 8 0
2016–17 Chelsea 0 0
2016–17 *Real Betis* 24 1 **48 2**
2017–18 Chelsea 3 0
2017–18 *Celtic* 4 0 **4 0**
2018–19 Chelsea 0 0
2018–19 *Vitesse* 1 0
2019–20 Chelsea 0 0 **3 0**
2019–20 *Vitesse* 3 0 **4 0**

NARTEY, Richard (D) 25 0
b.London 6-9-98
2019–20 Chelsea 0 0
2019–20 *Burton Alb* 25 0 **25 0**

PANTIC, Danilo (M) 104 12
H: 5 11 b.Ruma 26-10-96
Internationals: Serbia, U17, U19, U21.
2012–13 Partizan Belgrade 1 0
2013–14 Partizan Belgrade 10 1
2014–15 Partizan Belgrade 7 1
2015–16 Chelsea 0 0
2015–16 *Vitesse* 6 0 **6 0**
2016–17 Chelsea 0 0
2016–17 *Excelsior* 9 0 **9 0**
2017–18 Chelsea 0 0
2017–18 *Partizan Belgrade* 31 4
2018–19 Chelsea 0 0
2018–19 *Partizan Belgrade* 32 6 **81 12**
2019–20 Chelsea 0 0
2019–20 *Fehervar* 8 0 **8 0**

PASALIC, Mario (M) 192 40
H: 6 1 W: 12 04 b.Mainz 9-2-95
Internationals: Croatia U16, U17, U19, U21, Full caps.
2012–13 Hajduk Split 2 0
2013–14 Hajduk Split 30 11 **32 11**
2014–15 Chelsea 0 0
2014–15 *Elche* 31 3 **31 3**
2015–16 Chelsea 0 0
2015–16 *Monaco* 16 3 **16 3**
2016–17 Chelsea 0 0
2016–17 *AC Milan* 24 5 **24 5**
2017–18 Chelsea 0 0
2017–18 *Spartak Moscow* 21 4 **21 4**
2018–19 Chelsea 0 0
2018–19 *Atalanta* 33 5
2019–20 Chelsea 0 0
2019–20 *Atalanta* 35 9 **68 14**

PEDRO, Rodriguez (F) 341 87
H: 5 7 W: 10 01 b.Santa Cruz de Tenerife 28-7-87
Internationals: Spain U21, Full caps.
2007–08 Barcelona 2 0
2008–09 Barcelona 6 0
2009–10 Barcelona 34 12
2010–11 Barcelona 33 13
2011–12 Barcelona 29 5
2012–13 Barcelona 28 7
2013–14 Barcelona 37 15
2014–15 Barcelona 35 6 **204 58**
2015–16 Chelsea 29 7
2016–17 Chelsea 35 9
2017–18 Chelsea 31 4
2018–19 Chelsea 31 8
2019–20 Chelsea 11 1 **137 29**

PIAZON, Lucas (M) 138 26
H: 6 0 W: 11 11 b.Curitiba 20-1-94
Internationals: Brazil U17, U20, U23.
2011–12 Chelsea 0 0
2012–13 Chelsea 1 0
2012–13 *Malaga* 11 0 **11 0**
2013–14 Chelsea 0 0
2013–14 *Vitesse* 29 11
2014–15 Chelsea 0 0
2014–15 Vitesse 0 0 **29 11**
2014–15 *Eintracht Frankfurt* 0 0
2015–16 Chelsea 0 0
2015–16 *Reading* 23 3 **23 3**
2016–17 Chelsea 0 0
2016–17 *Fulham* 29 5
2017–18 Chelsea 0 0
2017–18 *Fulham* 22 5 **51 10**
2018–19 Chelsea 0 0
2018–19 *Chievo* 4 0 **4 0**
2019–20 Chelsea 0 0 **1 0**
2019–20 *Rio Ave* 19 2 **19 2**

PULISIC, Christian (M) 115 22
b.Hershey 18-9-98
Internationals: USA U17, Full caps.
2015–16 Borussia Dortmund 9 2
2016–17 Borussia Dortmund 29 3
2017–18 Borussia Dortmund 32 4
2018–19 Borussia Dortmund 20 4 **90 13**
2019–20 Chelsea 25 9 **25 9**

RUDIGER, Antonio (D) 202 9
H: 6 3 W: 13 05 b.Berlin 3-3-93
Internationals: Germany U18, U19, U20, U21, Full caps.
2011–12 Stuttgart 1 0
2012–13 Stuttgart 16 0
2013–14 Stuttgart 30 2
2014–15 Stuttgart 19 0 **66 2**
2015–16 Roma 30 2
2016–17 Roma 26 0 **56 2**
2017–18 Chelsea 27 2
2018–19 Chelsea 33 1
2019–20 Chelsea 20 2 **80 5**

STERLING, Dujon (D) 46 0
H: 5 11 b.London 3-11-99
Internationals: England U16, U17, U19, U20.
2017–18 Chelsea 0 0
2018–19 Chelsea 0 0
2018–19 *Coventry C* 38 0 **38 0**
2019–20 Chelsea 0 0
2019–20 *Wigan Ath* 8 0 **8 0**

TOMORI, Fikayo (D) 94 2
H: 6 0 W: 11 11 b.Calgary 19-12-97
Internationals: Canada U20. England U19, U20, U21, Full caps.
2015–16 Chelsea 1 0
2016–17 Chelsea 0 0
2016–17 *Brighton & HA* 9 0 **9 0**
2017–18 Chelsea 0 0
2017–18 *Hull C* 25 0 **25 0**
2018–19 Chelsea 0 0
2018–19 *Derby Co* 44 1 **44 1**
2019–20 Chelsea 15 1 **16 1**

UGBO, Ike (F) **74** **17**
H: 6 1 W: 11 07 b.Lewisham 21-9-98
Internationals: England U17, U20.

2017–18	Chelsea	0	0		
2017–18	*Barnsley*	16	1	**16**	**1**
2017–18	*Milton Keynes D*	15	2	**15**	**2**
2018–19	Chelsea	0	0		
2018–19	*Scunthorpe U*	15	1	**15**	**1**
2019–20	Chelsea	0	0		
2019–20	*Roda*	28	13	**28**	**13**

VAN GINKEL, Marco (M) **160** **34**
H: 6 1 W: 12 11 b.Amersfoort 1-12-92
Internationals: Netherlands U15, U19, U21, Full caps

2009–10	Vitesse	3	0		
2010–11	Vitesse	26	5		
2011–12	Vitesse	34	5		
2012–13	Vitesse	33	8	**96**	**18**
2013–14	Chelsea	2	0		
2014–15	Chelsea	0	0		
2014–15	*AC Milan*	17	1	**17**	**1**
2015–16	Chelsea	0	0		
2015–16	*Stoke C*	17	0	**17**	**0**
2015–16	*PSV Eindhoven*	13	8		
2016–17	Chelsea	0	0		
2016–17	*PSV Eindhoven*	15	7	**28**	**15**
2017–18	Chelsea	0	0		
2018–19	Chelsea	0	0		
2019–20	Chelsea	0	0	**2**	**0**

WILLIAN, da Silva (M) **370** **58**
H: 5 9 W: 11 10 b.Ribeirao 9-8-88
Internationals: Brazil U20, Full caps.

2006	Corinthians	5	0		
2007	Corinthians	0	0	**5**	**0**
2008–09	Shakhtar Donetsk	29	5		
2009–10	Shakhtar Donetsk	22	5		
2010–11	Shakhtar Donetsk	28	3		
2011–12	Shakhtar Donetsk	27	5		
2012–13	Shakhtar Donetsk	14	2	**120**	**20**
2012–13	Anzhi Makhachkala	7	1		
2013–14	Anzhi Makhachkala	4	0	**11**	**1**
2013–14	Chelsea	25	4		
2014–15	Chelsea	36	2		
2015–16	Chelsea	35	5		
2016–17	Chelsea	34	8		
2017–18	Chelsea	36	6		
2018–19	Chelsea	32	3		
2019–20	Chelsea	36	9	**234**	**37**

ZAPPACOSTA, Davide (M) **216** **10**
H: 6 1 W: 11 00 b.Sora 11-6-92
Internationals: Italy U21, Full caps.

2009–10	Isola Liri	2	0		
2010–11	Isola Liri	11	1	**13**	**1**
2011–12	Avellino	27	0		
2012–13	Avellino	24	1		
2013–14	Avellino	32	2	**83**	**3**
2014–15	Atalanta	29	3	**29**	**3**
2015–16	Torino	25	1		
2016–17	Torino	29	1		
2017–18	Torino	2	0	**56**	**2**
2017–18	Chelsea	22	1		
2018–19	Chelsea	4	0		
2019–20	Chelsea	0	0	**26**	**1**
2019–20	*Roma*	9	0	**9**	**0**

ZOUMA, Kurt (D) **202** **7**
H: 6 2 W: 13 04 b.Lyon 27-10-94
Internationals: France U16, U17, U19, U20, U21, Full caps.

2011–12	Saint-Etienne	20	1		
2012–13	Saint-Etienne	18	2		
2013–14	Chelsea	0	0		
2013–14	*Saint-Etienne*	23	0	**61**	**3**
2014–15	Chelsea	15	0		
2015–16	Chelsea	23	1		
2016–17	Chelsea	9	0		
2017–18	Chelsea	0	0		
2017–18	*Stoke C*	34	1	**34**	**1**
2018–19	Chelsea	0	0		
2018–19	*Everton*	32	2	**32**	**2**
2019–20	Chelsea	28	0	**75**	**1**

Players retained or with offer of contract
Ballo, Thierno Mamadou; Bergstrom, Lucas Carl Edvard; Brown, Charlie; De Souza, Nathan Allan; Ekwah Elimby, Pierre Emmanuel; Elliott, Benjamin Njongoue; Familia-Castillo, Juan Carlos; Fiabema, Bryan Benjamin; Harris, Myles Spencer; Lawrence, Henry; Lewis, Marcel; Livramento, Valentino Francisco; McClelland, Sam; Nunn, George Johannes; Palmieri Dos Santos, Emerson; Rankine, Dion Joseph; Russell, Jonathan; Samuels Colwill, Levi Lemar; Simeu, Dynel Brown Kembo; Simons, Xavier Levi; Tie, Nicolas; Uwakwe, Tariq; Van Ginkel, Marco Wulfert Cornelius; Zappacosta, Davide; Zouma, Kurt Happy.

Scholars
Aina, Jordan; Askew, Jake; Brooking, Joshua Royston; Clark, James Robert; Haigh, Joe Samuel; Humphreys, Bashir.

CHELTENHAM T (23)

ADDAI, Alex (M) **46** **4**
b.Stepney 20-12-93

2011–12	Blackpool	0	0		
2012–13	Blackpool	0	0		
2013–14	Blackpool	0	0		

From Carshalton Ath, Whitehawk, Crawley Down Gatwick, Kingstonian, Grays Ath, Wingate & Finchley, Merstham.

2018–19	Cheltenham T	21	0		
2019–20	Cheltenham T	25	4	**46**	**4**

BOWRY, Dan (D) **1** **0**
b.Croydon 29-4-98
Internationals: Antigua and Barbuda Full caps.

2016–17	Charlton Ath	0	0		
2017–18	Charlton Ath	0	0		
2018–19	Charlton Ath	0	0		
2019–20	Cheltenham T	1	0	**1**	**0**

BOYLE, William (D) **131** **13**
H: 6 2 W: 11 00 b.Garforth 1-9-95

2014–15	Huddersfield T	1	0		
2015–16	Huddersfield T	1	0		
2015–16	*York C*	12	0	**12**	**0**
2016–17	Huddersfield T	0	0	**2**	**0**
2016–17	*Kilmarnock*	11	0	**11**	**0**
2016–17	Cheltenham T	21	2		
2017–18	Cheltenham T	34	5		
2018–19	Cheltenham T	38	4		
2019–20	Cheltenham T	13	2	**106**	**13**

BRENNAN, Archie (M) **0** **0**

2018–19	Cheltenham T	0	0		
2019–20	Alvechurch	0	0		
2019–20	Cheltenham T	0	0		

BROOM, Ryan (M) **82** **10**
H: 5 10 W: 12 08 b.Newport 4-9-96

2015–16	Bristol R	1	0		
2016–17	Bristol R	5	0		
2017–18	Bristol R	3	0	**9**	**0**
2018–19	Cheltenham T	39	2		
2019–20	Cheltenham T	34	8	**73**	**10**

CAMPBELL, Tahvon (F) **95** **7**
b. 10-1-97

2015–16	WBA	0	0		
2015–16	*Yeovil T*	17	1		
2016–17	WBA	0	0		
2016–17	*Yeovil T*	19	1	**36**	**2**
2016–17	*Notts Co*	11	0	**11**	**0**
2017–18	WBA	0	0		
2017–18	*Forest Green R*	14	2		
2018–19	Forest Green R	18	3	**32**	**5**
2018–19	*Gillingham*	5	0	**5**	**0**
2019–20	Cheltenham T	11	0	**11**	**0**

CHAMBERLAIN, Tom (M) **0** **0**

2019–20	Cheltenham T	0	0		

CLEMENTS, Chris (M) **212** **18**
H: 5 9 W: 10 04 b.Birmingham 6-2-90

2008–09	Crewe Alex	0	0		
2009	*IBV*	15	1	**15**	**1**
2009–10	Crewe Alex	0	0		
2010–11	Crewe Alex	0	0		

From Hednesford T.

2013–14	Mansfield T	23	1		
2014–15	Mansfield T	34	1		
2015–16	Mansfield T	38	5		
2016–17	Mansfield T	20	3	**115**	**10**
2016–17	Grimsby T	16	4		
2017–18	Grimsby T	0	0	**16**	**4**
2017–18	*Forest Green R*	14	1	**14**	**1**
2018–19	Cheltenham T	30	2		
2019–20	Cheltenham T	22	0	**52**	**2**

DEBAYO, Josh (D) **12** **0**
H: 6 0 W: 10 10 b.London 17-10-96

2015–16	Southampton	0	0		
2016–17	Leicester C	0	0		
2017–18	Leicester C	0	0		
2018–19	Cheltenham T	5	0		
2019–20	Cheltenham T	7	0	**12**	**0**

EBANKS, Callum (F) **0** **0**

2019–20	Cheltenham T	0	0		

FLINDERS, Scott (G) **459** **1**
H: 6 4 W: 13 00 b.Rotherham 12-6-86
Internationals: England U20.

2004–05	Barnsley	11	0		
2005–06	Barnsley	3	0	**14**	**0**
2006–07	Crystal Palace	8	0		
2006–07	*Gillingham*	9	0	**9**	**0**
2006–07	*Brighton & HA*	12	0	**12**	**0**
2007–08	Crystal Palace	0	0		
2007–08	*Yeovil T*	9	0	**9**	**0**
2008–09	Crystal Palace	0	0	**8**	**0**
2009–10	Hartlepool U	46	0		
2010–11	Hartlepool U	26	1		
2011–12	Hartlepool U	45	0		
2012–13	Hartlepool U	46	0		
2013–14	Hartlepool U	43	0		
2014–15	Hartlepool U	46	0	**252**	**1**
2015–16	York C	43	0	**43**	**0**

From Macclesfield T.

2017–18	Cheltenham T	41	0		
2018–19	Cheltenham T	46	0		
2019–20	Cheltenham T	25	0	**112**	**0**

HORTON, Grant (D) **1** **0**
b.Colchester 13-9-01

2019–20	Cheltenham T	1	0	**1**	**0**

HUSSEY, Chris (D) **286** **8**
H: 5 10 W: 10 03 b.Hammersmith 2-1-89

2009–10	Coventry C	8	0		
2010–11	Coventry C	11	0		
2010–11	*Crewe Alex*	0	0		
2011–12	Coventry C	29	0		
2012–13	Coventry C	10	0	**58**	**0**
2012–13	AFC Wimbledon	19	0		
2013–14	AFC Wimbledon	0	0	**19**	**0**
2013–14	Burton Alb	27	1	**27**	**1**
2013–14	*Bury*	11	2		
2014–15	Bury	38	0		
2015–16	Bury	41	1	**90**	**3**
2016–17	Sheffield U	7	0		
2017–18	Sheffield U	0	0	**7**	**0**
2017–18	*Swindon T*	18	1	**18**	**1**
2018–19	Cheltenham T	34	1		
2019–20	Cheltenham T	33	2	**67**	**3**

INCE, Rohan (D) **129** **4**
H: 6 3 W: 12 08 b.Whitechapel 8-11-92

2010–11	Chelsea	0	0		
2011–12	Chelsea	0	0		
2012–13	Chelsea	0	0		
2012–13	*Yeovil T*	2	0	**2**	**0**
2013–14	Brighton & HA	28	0		
2014–15	Brighton & HA	32	1		
2015–16	Brighton & HA	12	0		
2015–16	*Fulham*	10	1	**10**	**1**
2016–17	Brighton & HA	0	0		
2016–17	*Swindon T*	14	2	**14**	**2**
2017–18	Brighton & HA	0	0	**72**	**1**
2017–18	*Bury*	22	0	**22**	**0**
2019–20	Cheltenham T	9	0	**9**	**0**

LAPWORTH, Freddie (G) **0** **0**

2018–19	Cheltenham T	0	0		
2019–20	Cheltenham T	0	0		

LLOYD, George (M) **27** **3**
H: 5 8 W: 9 13 b. 11-2-00

2017–18	Cheltenham T	7	2		
2018–19	Cheltenham T	7	1		
2019–20	Cheltenham T	13	0	**27**	**3**

LONG, Sean (D) **72** **1**
H: 5 10 W: 11 00 b.Dublin 2-5-95
Internationals: Republic of Ireland U16, U17, U18, U19, U21.

2013–14	Reading	0	0		
2014–15	Reading	0	0		
2015–16	Reading	0	0		
2015–16	*Luton T*	9	0	**9**	**0**
2016–17	Reading	0	0		
2016–17	*Cambridge U*	7	0	**7**	**0**
2017–18	Lincoln C	17	0	**17**	**0**
2018–19	Cheltenham T	5	0		
2019–20	Cheltenham T	34	1	**39**	**1**

LOVETT, Rhys (G) **2** **0**
b. 15-5-97
From Rochdale.

2016–17	Cheltenham T	0	0		
2017–18	Cheltenham T	1	0		
2018–19	Cheltenham T	0	0		
2019–20	Cheltenham T	1	0	**2**	**0**

MAY, Alfie (F) **104** **16**
H: 5 9 W: 11 05 b. 2-7-93
From Hythe T.

2016–17	Doncaster R	16	3		
2017–18	Doncaster R	27	4		

2018–19	Doncaster R	34	2		
2019–20	Doncaster R	15	1	**92**	**10**
2019–20	Cheltenham T	12	6	**12**	**6**

RAGLAN, Charlie (D) **127 4**
H: 6 0 W: 11 13 b.Wythenshawe 28-4-93

2011–12	Port Vale	0	0		
2012–13	Port Vale	0	0		
2013–14	Port Vale	0	0		
2014–15	Chesterfield	18	1		
2015–16	Chesterfield	27	0		
2016–17	Chesterfield	1	0	**46**	**1**
2016–17	*Oxford U*	16	0		
2017–18	Oxford U	0	0		
2017–18	*Port Vale*	10	0	**10**	**0**
2018–19	Oxford U	1	0	**17**	**0**
2018–19	*Cheltenham T*	19	2		
2019–20	Cheltenham T	35	1	**54**	**3**

REID, Reuben (F) **422 116**
H: 6 0 W: 12 02 b.Bristol 26-7-88

2005–06	Plymouth Arg	1	0		
2006–07	Plymouth Arg	6	0		
2006–07	*Rochdale*	2	0	**2**	**0**
2006–07	*Torquay U*	7	2	**7**	**2**
2007–08	Plymouth Arg	0	0		
2007–08	*Wycombe W*	11	1	**11**	**1**
2007–08	Brentford	10	1	**10**	**1**
2008–09	Rotherham U	41	18	**41**	**18**
2009–10	WBA	4	0		
2009–10	*Peterborough U*	13	0	**13**	**0**
2010–11	WBA	0	0	**4**	**0**
2010–11	*Walsall*	18	3	**18**	**3**
2010–11	Oldham Ath	19	2		
2011–12	Oldham Ath	20	5	**39**	**7**
2012–13	Yeovil T	19	4	**19**	**4**
2012–13	*Plymouth Arg*	18	2		
2013–14	Plymouth Arg	46	17		
2014–15	Plymouth Arg	42	18		
2015–16	Plymouth Arg	29	7		
2016–17	Plymouth Arg	0	0	**142**	**44**
2016–17	Exeter C	36	13		
2017–18	Exeter C	21	7	**57**	**20**
2017–18	Forest Green R	21	6		
2018–19	Forest Green R	29	7	**50**	**13**
2019–20	Cheltenham T	9	3	**9**	**3**

SMITH, Jonte (F) **17 1**
H: 6 1 W: 10 12 b.Bermuda 10-7-94
Internationals: Bermuda U17, Full caps.

2012–13	Crawley T	4	0		
2013–14	Crawley T	0	0	**4**	**0**

From PS Kemi, Flekkeroy, Gloucester C, Lewes, Welling U, Lewes.

2018–19	Oxford U	1	0	**1**	**0**
2019–20	Cheltenham T	12	1	**12**	**1**

THOMAS, Conor (M) **193 14**
H: 6 1 W: 11 05 b.Coventry 29-10-93
Internationals: England U17, U18.

2010–11	*Liverpool*	0	0		
2010–11	Coventry C	0	0		
2011–12	Coventry C	27	1		
2012–13	Coventry C	11	0		
2013–14	Coventry C	43	0		
2014–15	Coventry C	16	0		
2015–16	Coventry C	3	0	**100**	**1**
2016–17	Swindon T	33	1		
2017–18	Swindon T	2	0	**35**	**1**
2018–19	Cheltenham T	32	6		
2019–20	Cheltenham T	26	6	**58**	**12**

TOZER, Ben (D) **336 14**
H: 6 1 W: 12 11 b.Plymouth 1-3-90

2007–08	Swindon T	2	0	**2**	**0**
2007–08	Newcastle U	0	0		
2008–09	Newcastle U	0	0		
2009–10	Newcastle U	1	0		
2010–11	Newcastle U	0	0	**1**	**0**
2010–11	*Northampton T*	31	3		
2011–12	Northampton T	45	3		
2012–13	Northampton T	46	0		
2013–14	Northampton T	29	0		
2013–14	*Colchester U*	1	0	**1**	**0**
2014–15	Northampton T	22	0	**173**	**6**
2015–16	Yeovil T	26	0	**26**	**0**
2016–17	Newport Co	23	1		
2017–18	Newport Co	39	3	**62**	**4**
2017–18	Cheltenham T	0	0		
2018–19	Cheltenham T	37	1		
2019–20	Cheltenham T	34	3	**71**	**4**

VARNEY, Luke (F) **467 93**
H: 5 11 W: 11 00 b.Leicester 28-9-82

2002–03	Crewe Alex	0	0		
2003–04	Crewe Alex	8	1		
2004–05	Crewe Alex	26	4		
2005–06	Crewe Alex	27	5		
2006–07	Crewe Alex	34	17	**95**	**27**
2007–08	Charlton Ath	39	8		
2008–09	Charlton Ath	18	2	**57**	**10**
2008–09	*Sheffield W*	4	2		
2008–09	Derby Co	10	1		
2009–10	Derby Co	1	0		
2009–10	*Sheffield W*	39	9	**43**	**11**
2010–11	Derby Co	1	0	**12**	**1**
2010–11	*Blackpool*	30	5	**30**	**5**
2011–12	Portsmouth	30	6	**30**	**6**
2012–13	Leeds U	34	4		
2013–14	Leeds U	11	2	**45**	**6**
2013–14	*Blackburn R*	12	0		
2014–15	Blackburn R	11	0	**23**	**0**
2014–15	*Ipswich T*	10	1		
2015–16	Ipswich T	18	1		
2016–17	Ipswich T	15	3	**43**	**5**
2016–17	Burton Alb	15	1		
2017–18	Burton Alb	18	0	**33**	**1**
2018–19	Cheltenham T	35	14		
2019–20	Cheltenham T	21	7	**56**	**21**

Scholars
Atwell, Liam Alfie; Basford, Aaron John; Bedford, Kian Leslie; Chamberlain, Thomas Jack; Clark, George Ian Hartley; Davis, Felix William; Ebanks, Callum Jerimiah; Horton, Grant Dean; Lapworth, Freddie James; Lawrence, Isaac Anthony; Lawrence, Toby Paul; Paterson, Charlie Jack; Stanton, Charles Matthew Shayne; Stevens, Daniel Lloyd.

COLCHESTER U (24)

ADUBOFOUR-POKU, Kwame (M) **29 5**
From Cray W, Worthing.

2019–20	Colchester U	29	5	**29**	**5**

BRAMALL, Cohen (D) **29 1**
H: 5 9 W: 11 00 b.Crewe 2-4-95
From Hednesford T.

2017–18	Arsenal	0	0		
2017–18	*Birmingham C*	5	0	**5**	**0**
2018–19	Arsenal	0	0		
2019–20	Colchester U	24	1	**24**	**1**

BROWN, Jevani (M) **100 13**
b. 16-10-94
Internationals: Jamaica U17.

2013–14	Peterborough U	0	0		
2014–15	Peterborough U	0	0		

From Barton R, Arlesey T, Kettering T, Stamford, St Neots T.

2017–18	Cambridge U	41	6		
2018–19	Cambridge U	43	7	**84**	**13**
2019–20	Colchester U	11	0	**11**	**0**
2019–20	*Forest Green R*	5	0	**5**	**0**

CHILVERS, Noah (M) **2 0**
b. 22-2-01

2018–19	Colchester U	2	0		
2019–20	Colchester U	0	0	**2**	**0**

CLAMPIN, Ryan (M) **13 0**
b. 29-1-99

2018–19	Colchester U	0	0		
2019–20	Colchester U	13	0	**13**	**0**

COLLINGE, Danny (D) **0 0**
H: 6 2 W: 13 03 b. 9-4-98
Internationals: England U16, U17.

2013–14	Milton Keynes D	0	0		
2014–15	Milton Keynes D	0	0		
2015–16	Stuttgart	0	0		
2016–17	Stuttgart	0	0		
2017–18	Stuttgart	0	0		
2018–19	Stuttgart	0	0		
2019–20	Colchester U	0	0		

COMLEY, Brandon (M) **122 2**
H: 5 11 W: 11 05 b.Islington 18-11-95
Internationals: Montserrat Full caps.

2014–15	QPR	1	0		
2015–16	QPR	0	0		
2015–16	*Carlisle U*	12	0	**12**	**0**
2016–17	QPR	1	0	**2**	**0**
2016–17	*Grimsby T*	33	0		
2017–18	Grimsby T	0	0	**33**	**0**
2017–18	Colchester U	38	1		
2018–19	Colchester U	13	0		
2019–20	Colchester U	24	1	**75**	**2**

COULTER, Callum (G) **0 0**

2019–20	Colchester U	0	0		

COWAN-HALL, Paris (F) **205 30**
H: 5 8 W: 11 08 b.Portsmouth 5-10-90

2008–09	Portsmouth	0	0		
2009–10	Portsmouth	0	0		
2009–10	*Grimsby T*	3	0	**3**	**0**
2010–11	Portsmouth	0	0		
2010–11	Scunthorpe U	1	0	**1**	**0**

From Woking.

2012–13	Plymouth Arg	40	3	**40**	**3**
2013–14	Wycombe W	25	4		
2014–15	Wycombe W	20	6		
2014–15	Millwall	5	0		
2015–16	Millwall	3	0	**8**	**0**
2015–16	*Bristol R*	3	0	**3**	**0**
2015–16	*Wycombe W*	5	1		
2016–17	Wycombe W	28	4		
2017–18	Wycombe W	34	8		
2018–19	Wycombe W	33	4	**145**	**27**
2019–20	Colchester U	5	0	**5**	**0**

DUNNE, Louis (M) **2 0**
b.Waltham Forest 7-9-98
Internationals: Republic of Ireland U17, U18.

2015–16	Colchester U	2	0		
2016–17	Colchester U	0	0		
2017–18	Colchester U	0	0		
2018–19	Colchester U	0	0		
2019–20	Colchester U	0	0	**2**	**0**

EASTMAN, Tom (D) **339 19**
H: 6 3 W: 13 12 b.Clacton 21-10-91

2009–10	Ipswich T	1	0		
2010–11	Ipswich T	9	0	**10**	**0**
2011–12	Colchester U	25	3		
2011–12	*Crawley T*	6	0	**6**	**0**
2012–13	Colchester U	29	2		
2013–14	Colchester U	36	0		
2014–15	Colchester U	46	1		
2015–16	Colchester U	43	2		
2016–17	Colchester U	35	3		
2017–18	Colchester U	42	3		
2018–19	Colchester U	31	3		
2019–20	Colchester U	36	2	**323**	**19**

ELIAS-FERNANDES, Michael (M) **0 0**
b.Hounslow 24-6-99

2019–20	Colchester U	0	0		

GAMBIN, Luke (M) **157 16**
H: 5 6 W: 11 00 b.Surrey 16-3-93
Internationals: Malta Full caps.

2011–12	Barnet	1	0		
2012–13	Barnet	10	2		
2015–16	Barnet	44	4		
2016–17	Barnet	19	4	**74**	**10**
2016–17	Luton T	16	1		
2017–18	Luton T	13	1		
2018–19	Luton T	0	0	**29**	**2**
2018–19	*Crawley T*	26	3	**26**	**3**
2019–20	Colchester U	28	1	**28**	**1**

GERKEN, Dean (G) **309 0**
H: 6 3 W: 12 08 b.Southend 22-5-85

2003–04	Colchester U	1	0		
2004–05	Colchester U	13	0		
2005–06	Colchester U	7	0		
2006–07	Colchester U	27	0		
2007–08	Colchester U	40	0		
2008–09	Colchester U	21	0		
2008–09	*Darlington*	7	0	**7**	**0**
2009–10	Bristol C	39	0		
2010–11	Bristol C	1	0		
2011–12	Bristol C	10	0		
2012–13	Bristol C	3	0	**53**	**0**
2013–14	Ipswich T	41	0		
2014–15	Ipswich T	16	0		
2015–16	Ipswich T	26	0		
2016–17	Ipswich T	2	0		
2017–18	Ipswich T	1	0		
2018–19	Ipswich T	18	0	**104**	**0**
2019–20	Colchester U	36	0	**145**	**0**

HARRIOTT, Callum (M) **152 21**
H: 5 5 W: 10 05 b.Norbury 4-3-94
Internationals: England U19. Guyana Full caps.

2010–11	Charlton Ath	3	0		
2011–12	Charlton Ath	0	0		
2012–13	Charlton Ath	14	2		
2013–14	Charlton Ath	28	5		
2014–15	Charlton Ath	21	1		
2015–16	Charlton Ath	20	3	**86**	**11**
2015–16	*Colchester U*	20	5		
2016–17	Reading	12	1		
2017–18	Reading	0	0		
2018–19	Reading	12	1	**24**	**2**
2019–20	Colchester U	22	3	**42**	**8**

HASANALLY, Andre (M) **2 0**
b.London 10-2-02

2019–20	Colchester U	2	0	**2**	**0**

ISSA, Tariq (M) **2 0**
H: 5 7 W: 10 08 b. 2-9-97

2016–17	Colchester U	0	0		
2017–18	Colchester U	2	0		
2018–19	Colchester U	0	0		
2019–20	Colchester U	0	0	**2**	**0**

JACKSON, Ryan (M) **263 9**
H: 5 9 W: 10 03 b.Streatham 31-7-90
Internationals: England C.
2011–12 AFC Wimbledon 7 0 **7 0**
2013–14 Newport Co 29 0
2014–15 Newport Co 34 0 **63 0**
2015–16 Gillingham 37 2
2016–17 Gillingham 34 1 **71 3**
2017–18 Colchester U 42 2
2018–19 Colchester U 46 2
2019–20 Colchester U 34 2 **122 6**

JAMES, Cameron (D) **25 0**
H: 6 0 W: 12 00 b.Chelmsford 11-2-98
2015–16 Colchester U 1 0
2016–17 Colchester U 14 0
2017–18 Colchester U 7 0
2018–19 Colchester U 0 0
2019–20 Colchester U 3 0 **25 0**

KENSADALE, Ollie (D) **3 0**
b. 20-4-00
2018–19 Colchester U 2 0
2019–20 Colchester U 1 0 **3 0**

LAPSLIE, Tom (M) **139 3**
H: 5 6 W: 10 12 b.Waltham Forest 5-5-95
2013–14 Colchester U 0 0
2014–15 Colchester U 11 1
2015–16 Colchester U 10 1
2016–17 Colchester U 37 0
2017–18 Colchester U 29 0
2018–19 Colchester U 35 1
2019–20 Colchester U 17 0 **139 3**

NORRIS, Luke (F) **241 55**
H: 6 1 W: 13 05 b.Stevenage 3-6-93
2011–12 Brentford 1 0
2012–13 Brentford 0 0
2013–14 Brentford 1 0 **2 0**
2013–14 *Northampton T* 10 4 **10 4**
2013–14 *Dagenham & R* 19 4 **19 4**
2014–15 Gillingham 37 6
2015–16 Gillingham 33 8 **70 14**
2016–17 Swindon T 39 4
2017–18 Swindon T 35 13 **74 17**
2018–19 Colchester U 34 7
2019–20 Colchester U 32 9 **66 16**

NOUBLE, Frank (F) **307 45**
H: 6 3 W: 12 08 b.Lewisham 24-9-91
Internationals: England U17, U19.
2009–10 West Ham U 8 0
2009–10 *WBA* 3 0 **3 0**
2009–10 *Swindon T* 8 0 **8 0**
2010–11 West Ham U 2 0
2010–11 *Swansea C* 6 1 **6 1**
2010–11 *Barnsley* 4 0
2010–11 *Charlton Ath* 9 1 **9 1**
2011–12 West Ham U 3 1 **13 1**
2011–12 *Gillingham* 13 5
2011–12 *Barnsley* 6 0 **10 0**
2012–13 Wolverhampton W 2 0 **2 0**
2012–13 Ipswich T 17 2
2013–14 Ipswich T 38 2
2014–15 Ipswich T 1 0 **56 4**
2014–15 Coventry C 31 6 **31 6**
2015 Tianjin Songjiang 15 3 **15 3**
2016–17 Gillingham 12 1 **25 6**
2016–17 Southend U 5 0 **5 0**
2017–18 Newport Co 45 9 **45 9**
2018–19 Colchester U 43 9
2019–20 Colchester U 36 5 **79 14**

OGEDI-UZOKWE, Junior (F) **12 1**
b. 20-3-94
From Maldon & Tiptree
2017–18 Colchester U 9 1
2018–19 Colchester U 1 0
2019–20 *Derry City* 0 0
2019–20 Colchester U 2 0 **12 1**
Transferred to Hapoel Hadera, February 2020.

PELL, Harry (M) **238 30**
H: 6 4 W: 13 05 b.Tilbury 21-10-91
2010–11 Bristol R 10 0 **10 0**
2010–11 *Hereford U* 7 0
2011–12 Hereford U 30 3 **37 3**
2012–13 AFC Wimbledon 17 2
2013–14 AFC Wimbledon 33 4
2014–15 AFC Wimbledon 9 0 **59 6**
2016–17 Cheltenham T 42 7
2017–18 Cheltenham T 37 5 **79 12**
2018–19 Colchester U 31 6
2019–20 Colchester U 22 3 **53 9**

PROSSER, Luke (D) **275 15**
H: 6 2 W: 12 04 b.Waltham Cross 28-5-88
2005–06 Port Vale 0 0
2006–07 Port Vale 0 0
2007–08 Port Vale 5 0
2008–09 Port Vale 26 1
2009–10 Port Vale 2 1 **33 2**
2010–11 Southend U 17 1
2011–12 Southend U 21 1
2012–13 Southend U 25 0
2013–14 Southend U 25 3
2014–15 Southend U 30 0
2015–16 Southend U 13 2 **131 7**
2015–16 *Northampton T* 8 0 **8 0**
2016–17 Colchester U 14 0
2017–18 Colchester U 16 1
2018–19 Colchester U 38 2
2019–20 Colchester U 35 3 **103 6**

ROSS, Ethan (G) **4 0**
b. 6-3-97
From WBA.
2018–19 Colchester U 3 0
2019–20 Colchester U 1 0 **4 0**

SCARLETT, Miquel (D) **0 0**
2017–18 Gillingham 0 0
2018–19 Gillingham 0 0
2019–20 Colchester U 0 0

SENIOR, Courtney (F) **90 12**
b. 30-6-97
2014–15 Wycombe W 1 0 **1 0**
2015–16 Brentford 0 0
2016–17 Colchester U 0 0
2017–18 Colchester U 18 4
2018–19 Colchester U 42 6
2019–20 Colchester U 29 2 **89 12**

SIMS, Oliver (F) **0 0**
2017–18 Colchester U 0 0
2018–19 Colchester U 0 0
2019–20 Colchester U 0 0

SOWUNMI, Omar (D) **76 3**
H: 6 6 W: 14 09 b.Colchester 7-11-95
2015–16 Yeovil T 5 1
2016–17 Yeovil T 11 0
2017–18 Yeovil T 36 2
2018–19 Yeovil T 17 0 **69 3**
2019–20 Colchester U 7 0 **7 0**

STEVENSON, Ben (M) **88 6**
H: 6 0 W: 10 08 b.Leicester 23-3-97
2015–16 Coventry C 0 0
2016–17 Coventry C 28 2
2017–18 Coventry C 5 0 **33 2**
2017–18 Wolverhampton W 0 0
2017–18 *Colchester U* 13 2
2018–19 Wolverhampton W 0 0
2018–19 Colchester U 14 0
2019–20 Colchester U 28 2 **55 4**

VOSE, Bailey (G) **0 0**
b. 11-5-98
From Brighton & HA.
2018–19 Colchester U 0 0
2019–20 Colchester U 0 0

WELCH-HAYES, Miles (D) **48 1**
b.Oxford 25-10-96
2016–17 Oxford U 1 0 **1 0**
Frm Bath C.
2018–19 Macclesfield T 23 0
2019–20 Macclesfield T 24 1 **47 1**
2019–20 Colchester U 0 0

WRIGHT, Diaz (M) **9 0**
b. 22-2-98
2016–17 Colchester U 0 0
2017–18 Colchester U 0 0
2018–19 Colchester U 9 0
2019–20 Colchester U 0 0 **9 0**

Players retained or with offer of contract
Hall, Paris Declan Joseph; McLeod, Sammie Thomas; Weaire, Matthew Steen.

Scholars
Akolbire, Lordon; Anderson, Callum George; Collins, Ted Jamie; Cornish, Sam David; Coulter, Callum Andrew Charles; Cracknell, William David; Fouche, Joshua Alexander; Freitas, Gouveia Diogo Manuel; Hallett, Chandler Lewis; Hutchinson, Jacob; Kazeem, Al-Amin Ayomide; Kennedy, Gene John; Marshall, Miranda Marley Zane; Sayer, Harvey Stephen; Stagg, Thomas Jack; Thomas, Donell Tyrell Arnold; Tricker, Matthew James Elliot.

COVENTRY C (25)

ALLASSANI, Reise (M) **5 0**
b.Wandsworth 3-1-96
Internationals: England U16, U17.
2013–14 Crystal Palace 0 0
2014–15 Crystal Palace 0 0
2015–16 Crystal Palace 0 0
From Dulwich Hamlet.
2018–19 Coventry C 5 0
2019–20 Coventry C 0 0 **5 0**

ALLEN, Jamie (M) **215 20**
H: 5 11 W: 11 05 b.Rochdale 29-1-95
2012–13 Rochdale 0 0
2013–14 Rochdale 25 6
2014–15 Rochdale 35 0
2015–16 Rochdale 38 3
2016–17 Rochdale 31 2
2017–18 Rochdale 4 0 **133 11**
2017–18 Burton Alb 29 1
2018–19 Burton Alb 42 7 **71 8**
2019–20 Coventry C 11 1 **11 1**

BAKAYOKO, Amadou (F) **147 20**
H: 6 4 W: 13 05 b. 1-1-96
2013–14 Walsall 6 0
2014–15 Walsall 7 0
2015–16 Walsall 0 0
2016–17 Walsall 39 4
2017–18 Walsall 41 5 **93 9**
2018–19 Coventry C 31 7
2019–20 Coventry C 23 4 **54 11**

BAPAGA, Will (F) **1 0**
2019–20 Coventry C 1 0 **1 0**

BARTLETT, Daniel (M) **0 0**
From Southampton.
2019–20 Coventry C 0 0

BIAMOU, Maxime (F) **106 18**
b. 13-11-90
2014–15 Villemobmble Sports 15 3 **15 3**
2015–16 Yzeure 30 6 **30 6**
From Sutton U.
2017–18 Coventry C 39 5
2018–19 Coventry C 4 0
2019–20 Coventry C 18 4 **61 9**

BREMANG, David (F) **0 0**
2018–19 Coventry C 0 0
2019–20 Coventry C 0 0

BROWN, Junior (D) **240 21**
H: 5 9 W: 10 09 b.Crewe 7-5-89
2006–07 Crewe Alex 0 0
2007–08 Crewe Alex 1 0 **1 0**
From Halifax T, Northwich Vic.
2012–13 Fleetwood T 43 11
2013–14 Fleetwood T 21 1 **64 12**
2013–14 *Tranmere R* 9 1 **9 1**
2014–15 Oxford U 11 0 **11 0**
2014–15 Mansfield T 24 2 **24 2**
2015–16 Shrewsbury T 31 0
2016–17 Shrewsbury T 43 5
2017–18 Shrewsbury T 15 1 **89 6**
2018–19 Coventry C 22 0
2019–20 Coventry C 0 0 **22 0**
2019–20 *Scunthorpe U* 20 0 **20 0**

BURROUGHS, Jack (M) **0 0**
Internationals: Scotland U19.
2018–19 Coventry C 0 0
2019–20 Coventry C 0 0

DABO, Fankaty (D) **94 1**
H: 5 11 W: 12 02 b.Southwark 11-10-95
Internationals: England U16, U17, U20.
2016–17 Chelsea 0 0
2016–17 *Swindon T* 15 1 **15 1**
2017–18 Chelsea 0 0
2017–18 *Vitesse* 26 0 **26 0**
2018–19 Chelsea 0 0
2018–19 *Sparta Rotterdam* 21 0 **21 0**
2019–20 Coventry C 32 0 **32 0**

DRYSDALE, Declan (D) **1 0**
2018–19 Tranmere R 0 0
2018–19 Coventry C 0 0
2019–20 Coventry C 1 0 **1 0**

ECCLES, Josh (D) **3 0**
2018–19 Coventry C 0 0
2019–20 Coventry C 3 0 **3 0**

EVANS-HARRIOT, Aaron (M) **0 0**
From Cheltenham T.
2019–20 Coventry C 0 0

GODDEN, Matthew (F) **158 58**
H: 6 1 W: 12 03 b.Canterbury 29-7-91
2009–10 Scunthorpe U 0 0
2010–11 Scunthorpe U 5 0

2011–12 Scunthorpe U 1 0
2012–13 Scunthorpe U 8 0
2013–14 Scunthorpe U 4 0
2014–15 Scunthorpe U 0 0 **18 0**
From Ebbsfleet U.
2016–17 Stevenage 38 20
2017–18 Stevenage 38 10 **76 30**
2018–19 Peterborough U 38 14
2019–20 Peterborough U 0 0 **38 14**
2019–20 Coventry C 26 14 **26 14**

HICKMAN, Jak (F) 0 0
b. 11-9-98
2017–18 Coventry C 0 0
2018–19 Coventry C 0 0
2019–20 Coventry C 0 0

HIWULA, Jordy (F) 192 45
H: 5 10 W: 11 12 b.Manchester 24-9-94
Internationals: England U18, U19.
2013–14 Manchester C 0 0
2014–15 Manchester C 0 0
2014–15 *Yeovil T* 8 0 **8 0**
2014–15 *Walsall* 19 9
2015–16 Huddersfield T 0 0
2015–16 *Wigan Ath* 14 2 **14 2**
2015–16 *Walsall* 13 3 **32 12**
2016–17 Huddersfield T 0 0
2016–17 *Bradford C* 41 9 **41 9**
2017–18 Huddersfield T 0 0
2017–18 *Fleetwood T* 43 8 **43 8**
2018–19 Coventry C 39 12
2019–20 Coventry C 15 2 **54 14**

HYAM, Dominic (D) 97 3
H: 6 2 W: 11 00 b.Leuchars 20-12-95
Internationals: Scotland U19, U21.
2014–15 Reading 0 0
2015–16 Reading 0 0
2015–16 *Dagenham & R* 16 0 **16 0**
2016–17 Reading 0 0
2016–17 *Portsmouth* 0 0
2017–18 Coventry C 14 0
2018–19 Coventry C 38 1
2019–20 Coventry C 29 2 **81 3**

JOBELLO, Wesley (M) 125 8
b.Gennevilliers 23-1-94
Internationals: France U18. Martinique Full caps.
2011–12 Marseille 1 0
2012–13 Marseille 0 0
2013–14 Marseille 0 0
2014–15 Marseille 0 0 **1 0**
2015–16 Clermont Foot 26 0
2016–17 Clermont Foot 27 3 **53 3**
2017–18 Gazelec Ajaccio 24 2
2018–19 Gazelec Ajaccio 37 2 **61 4**
2019–20 Coventry C 10 1 **10 1**

JONES, Jodi (F) 102 11
b.London 22-10-97
2014–15 Dagenham & R 8 1
2015–16 Dagenham & R 27 3 **35 4**
2015–16 Coventry C 6 0
2016–17 Coventry C 34 1
2017–18 Coventry C 19 5
2018–19 Coventry C 8 1
2019–20 Coventry C 0 0 **67 7**

KASTANEER, Gervane (F) 85 13
b.Rotterdam 9-6-96
Internationals: Netherlands U19, U20, U21. Curacao Full caps.
2012–13 Dordrecht 3 0 **3 0**
2013–14 ADO Den Haag 0 0
2014–15 ADO Den Haag 8 1
2015–16 ADO Den Haag 5 0
2015–16 *FC Eindhoven* 14 4 **14 4**
2016–17 ADO Den Haag 14 4 **27 5**
2017–18 Kaiserslautern 10 1 **10 1**
2018–19 NAC Breda 21 2 **21 2**
2019–20 Coventry C 10 1 **10 1**

KELLY, Liam (M) 310 27
H: 6 2 W: 13 11 b.Milton Keynes 10-2-90
Internationals: Scotland U18, U21, Full caps.
2009–10 Kilmarnock 15 1
2010–11 Kilmarnock 32 7
2011–12 Kilmarnock 34 1
2012–13 Kilmarnock 19 6 **100 15**
2012–13 Bristol C 19 0
2013–14 Bristol C 2 0 **21 0**
2014–15 Oldham Ath 37 1
2015–16 Oldham Ath 41 6 **78 7**
2016–17 Leyton Orient 21 4 **21 4**
2017–18 Coventry C 33 1
2018–19 Coventry C 30 0
2019–20 Coventry C 27 0 **90 1**

MAROSI, Marko (G) 112 0
H: 6 3 W: 12 08 b. 23-10-93
Internationals: Slovakia U21.
2013–14 Wigan Ath 0 0
2014–15 Doncaster R 3 0
2015–16 Doncaster R 1 0
2016–17 Doncaster R 25 0
2017–18 Doncaster R 13 0
2018–19 Doncaster R 36 0 **78 0**
2019–20 Coventry C 34 0 **34 0**

MASON, Brandon (M) 39 0
H: 5 9 W: 11 00 b.Westminster 30-9-97
2016–17 Watford 2 0
2017–18 Watford 0 0 **2 0**
2017–18 *Dundee U* 1 0 **1 0**
2018–19 Coventry C 25 0
2019–20 Coventry C 11 0 **36 0**

MAYCOCK, Callum (D) 31 0
b. 23-12-97
2016–17 Coventry C 3 0
2017–18 Coventry C 1 0
2018–19 Coventry C 0 0
2018–19 *Macclesfield T* 27 0 **27 0**
2019–20 Coventry C 0 0 **4 0**

McFADZEAN, Kyle (D) 314 14
H: 6 1 W: 13 04 b.Sheffield 20-2-87
Internationals: England C.
2004–05 Sheffield U 0 0
2005–06 Sheffield U 0 0
2006–07 Sheffield U 0 0
From Alfreton T
2011–12 Crawley T 37 2
2012–13 Crawley T 17 3
2013–14 Crawley T 42 1 **96 6**
2014–15 Milton Keynes D 41 3
2015–16 Milton Keynes D 39 0 **80 3**
2016–17 Burton Alb 31 1
2017–18 Burton Alb 42 0
2018–19 Burton Alb 35 4 **108 5**
2018–19 Coventry C 0 0
2019–20 Coventry C 30 0 **30 0**

NEWTON, Joe (D) 0 0
From Royston T.
2019–20 Coventry C 0 0

NGANDU, Jonny (F) 0 0
2018–19 Coventry C 0 0
2019–20 Coventry C 0 0

PASK, Josh (D) 17 0
b. 1-11-97
2015–16 West Ham U 0 0
2015–16 *Dagenham & R* 5 0 **5 0**
2016–17 West Ham U 0 0
2016–17 *Gillingham* 10 0 **10 0**
2017–18 West Ham U 0 0
2018–19 West Ham U 0 0
2019–20 Coventry C 2 0 **2 0**

PONTICELLI, Jordan (F) 28 3
b. 10-9-98
2017–18 Coventry C 19 3
2018–19 Coventry C 5 0
2018–19 *Macclesfield T* 3 0 **3 0**
2019–20 Coventry C 0 0 **24 3**
2019–20 *Tranmere R* 1 0 **1 0**

ROSE, Michael (D) 127 7
b.Aberdeen 11-10-95
2015–16 Aberdeen 1 0 **1 0**
2015–16 *Forfar Ath* 7 0 **7 0**
2016–17 Ayr U 20 1
2017–18 Ayr U 34 2
2018–19 Ayr U 34 2 **88 5**
2019–20 Coventry C 31 2 **31 2**

ROWE, Blaine (D) 0 0
2019–20 Coventry C 0 0

SHIPLEY, Jordan (M) 95 12
b. 26-6-97
Internationals: Republic of Ireland U21.
2016–17 Coventry C 1 0
2017–18 Coventry C 30 4
2018–19 Coventry C 33 3
2019–20 Coventry C 31 5 **95 12**

THOMPSON, Jordan (D) 4 0
b. 8-4-99
2016–17 Coventry C 0 0
2017–18 Coventry C 0 0
2018–19 Coventry C 4 0
2019–20 Coventry C 0 0 **4 0**

TYLER, Cian (G) 0 0
b. 22-3-02
Internationals: Wales U17.
2019–20 Coventry C 0 0

WAKEFIELD, Charlie (M) 11 0
b.Derby 23-5-00
From Chelsea.
2016–17 Chesterfield 1 0
2017–18 Chesterfield 1 0 **2 0**
2018–19 Coventry C 8 0
2019–20 Coventry C 1 0 **9 0**

WALTERS, Dexter (M) 0 0
2018–19 Coventry C 0 0
2019–20 Coventry C 0 0

WESTBROOKE, Zain (M) 33 4
b. 28-10-96
From Chelsea.
2016–17 Brentford 1 0
2017–18 Brentford 0 0 **1 0**
2017–18 Coventry C 0 0
2018–19 Coventry C 7 0
2019–20 Coventry C 25 4 **32 4**

WILLIAMS, Morgan (D) 1 0
b. 30-8-99
From Mickleover Sports.
2018–19 Coventry C 1 0
2019–20 Coventry C 0 0 **1 0**

WILSON, Ben (G) 28 0
H: 6 1 W: 11 09 b.Stanley 9-8-92
2010–11 Sunderland 0 0
2011–12 Sunderland 0 0
2012–13 Sunderland 0 0
2013–14 Accrington S 0 0
2013–14 Cardiff C 0 0
2014–15 Cardiff C 0 0
2015–16 Cardiff C 0 0
2015–16 *AFC Wimbledon* 8 0 **8 0**
2016–17 Cardiff C 3 0
2016–17 *Rochdale* 8 0 **8 0**
2017–18 Cardiff C 0 0 **3 0**
2017–18 *Oldham Ath* 5 0 **5 0**
2018–19 Bradford C 4 0 **4 0**
2019–20 Coventry C 0 0

YOUNG, Jordan (F) 5 1
b. 31-7-99
2015–16 Swindon T 3 1
2016–17 Swindon T 2 0
2017–18 Swindon T 0 0
2018–19 Swindon T 0 0 **5 1**
2019–20 Coventry C 0 0

Players retained or with offer of contract
Bannatyne-Billson, Thomas David.

Scholars
Burroughs, George Gilbert; Costa, Alexander; Fallows, Keelan Brian; Forsyth, Kai Joseph William; Harland, Matthew; Lafferty, Daniel Paul; Martin, Callum Paul; Nee, Harrison; Nightingale, Joseph; Pitt-Eckersall, Samuel; Purves, Hayden James; Rowe, Blaine Morgan Brian; Taylor, Adam Simon; Tyler, Cian Lee.

CRAWLEY T (26)

ADEBOWALE, Emmanuel (D) 1 0
From Sheffield U, Hayes & Yeading U, Bishop's Stortford, Dover Ath, Eastbourne Bor.
2019–20 Crawley T 1 0 **1 0**

ALLARAKHIA, Tarryn (M) 24 0
b. 17-10-97
From Leyton Orient, Aveley, Maldon and Tiptree.
2017–18 Colchester U 0 0
2018–19 Crawley T 5 0
2019–20 Crawley T 19 0 **24 0**

BOADU, Denzeil (F) 0 0
b.Islington 20-2-97
Internationals: England U16, U17.
2016–17 Manchester C 0 0
2017–18 Borussia Dortmund 0 0
2018–19 Borussia Dortmund 0 0
2019–20 Crawley T 0 0

BULMAN, Dannie (M) 546 25
H: 5 9 W: 11 12 b.Ashford 24-1-79
1998–99 Wycombe W 11 1
1999–2000 Wycombe W 29 1
2000–01 Wycombe W 36 4
2001–02 Wycombe W 46 5
2002–03 Wycombe W 42 3
2003–04 Wycombe W 38 0 **202 14**
From Stevenage, Crawley T.
2010–11 Oxford U 5 0 **5 0**
2011–12 Crawley T 41 3

2012–13	Crawley T	36	1		
2013–14	Crawley T	39	0		
2014–15	AFC Wimbledon	41	1		
2015–16	AFC Wimbledon	42	3		
2016–17	AFC Wimbledon	38	0	**121**	**4**
2017–18	Crawley T	37	0		
2018–19	Crawley T	36	3		
2019–20	Crawley T	29	0	**218**	**7**

CAMARA, Panutche (F) 104 6
H: 6 1 W: 9 13 b. 28-2-97
From Dulwich Hamlet.

2017–18	Crawley T	30	2		
2018–19	Crawley T	45	3		
2019–20	Crawley T	29	1	**104**	**6**

DALLISON, Tom (M) 60 0
H: 5 10 W: 14 01 b. 2-2-96

2012–13	Arsenal	0	0		
2013–14	Brighton & HA	0	0		
2014–15	Brighton & HA	0	0		
2015–16	Brighton & HA	0	0		
2015–16	*Crawley T*	1	0		
2016–17	Brighton & HA	0	0		
2016–17	*Cambridge U*	5	0	**5**	**0**
2017–18	Brighton & HA	0	0		
2017–18	*Accrington S*	2	0	**2**	**0**
2018–19	Falkirk	12	0	**12**	**0**
2018–19	Crawley T	19	0		
2019–20	Crawley T	21	0	**41**	**0**

DOHERTY, Josh (M) 65 0
H: 5 10 W: 11 00 b.Newtownards 15-3-96
Internationals: Northern Ireland U17, U19, U21.

2013–14	Watford	1	0		
2014–15	Watford	0	0		
2015–16	Watford	0	0	**1**	**0**

From Leyton Orient, Ards.

2017–18	Crawley T	15	0		
2018–19	Crawley T	18	0		
2019–20	Crawley T	31	0	**64**	**0**

FERGUSON, Nathan (M) 31 5
b. 12-10-95

2014–15	Dagenham & R	0	0		
2015–16	Burton Alb	0	0		
2016–17	Port Vale	0	0		

From Bromley, Dulwich Hamlet.

2019–20	Crawley T	31	5	**31**	**5**

FORREST, George (D) 0 0
From AFC Hornchurch.

2019–20	Crawley T	0	0		

FRANCOMB, George (D) 281 11
H: 5 11 W: 11 07 b.Hackney 8-9-91

2009–10	Norwich C	2	0		
2010–11	Norwich C	0	0		
2010–11	*Barnet*	13	0	**13**	**0**
2011–12	Norwich C	0	0		
2011–12	*Hibernian*	14	0	**14**	**0**
2012–13	Norwich C	0	0	**2**	**0**
2012–13	*AFC Wimbledon*	15	0		
2013–14	AFC Wimbledon	33	3		
2014–15	AFC Wimbledon	37	3		
2015–16	AFC Wimbledon	40	3		
2016–17	AFC Wimbledon	34	2		
2017–18	AFC Wimbledon	37	0	**196**	**11**
2018–19	Crawley T	41	0		
2019–20	Crawley T	15	0	**56**	**0**

GALACH, Brian (F) 1 0
H: 5 9 W: 10 03 b.Waltham Forest 16-5-01
From Leyton Orient, Aldershot T.

2018–19	Crawley T	1	0		
2019–20	Crawley T	0	0	**1**	**0**

GERMAN, Ricky (F) 21 1
H: 6 2 W: 12 08 b.Brent 13-1-99

2016–17	Chesterfield	7	0		
2017–18	Chesterfield	2	0	**9**	**0**
2018–19	Crawley T	4	0		
2019–20	Crawley T	8	1	**12**	**1**

GREGO-COX, Reece (F) 68 6
H: 5 7 W: 10 03 b.Hammersmith 12-11-96
Internationals: Republic of Ireland U17, U19, U21.

2014–15	QPR	4	0		
2015–16	QPR	0	0		
2016–17	Newport Co	7	0	**7**	**0**
2016–17	QPR	1	0		
2017–18	QPR	0	0	**5**	**0**
2018–19	Crawley T	28	2		
2019–20	Crawley T	28	4	**56**	**6**

JONES, Alfie (G) 0 0

2017–18	Milton Keynes D	0	0		
2018–19	Crawley T	0	0		
2019–20	Crawley T	0	0		

LUBULA, Beryl (F) 38 12
b. 8-1-98

2017–18	Birmingham C	1	0		
2018–19	Birmingham C	3	0	**4**	**0**
2019–20	Crawley T	34	12	**34**	**12**

McNERNEY, Joe (D) 96 6
H: 6 4 W: 13 03 b. 24-1-89
From Woking.

2015–16	Crawley T	11	1		
2016–17	Crawley T	34	3		
2017–18	Crawley T	16	1		
2018–19	Crawley T	29	1		
2019–20	Crawley T	6	0	**96**	**6**

MEITE, Ibrahim (F) 23 2
H: 6 1 W: 11 05 b.Wandsworth 1-6-96

2016–17	Cardiff C	1	0		
2017–18	Cardiff C	0	0		
2017–18	*Crawley T*	19	2		
2018–19	Cardiff C	0	0	**1**	**0**
2018–19	Crawley T	2	0		
2019–20	Crawley T	0	0	**21**	**2**
2019–20	*Pirin Blagoevgrad*	1	0	**1**	**0**

MORAIS, Filipe (M) 385 41
H: 5 9 W: 11 10 b.Lisbon 21-11-85
Internationals: Portugal U21.

2003–04	Chelsea	0	0		
2004–05	Chelsea	0	0		
2005–06	Chelsea	0	0		
2005–06	*Milton Keynes D*	13	0	**13**	**0**
2006–07	Millwall	12	1	**12**	**1**
2006–07	*St Johnstone*	13	1		
2007–08	Hibernian	28	1		
2008–09	Hibernian	2	0	**30**	**1**
2008–09	Inverness CT	12	3	**12**	**3**
2009–10	St Johnstone	30	2	**43**	**3**
2010–11	Oldham Ath	23	3		
2011–12	Oldham Ath	36	5		
2012–13	Oldham Ath	0	0		
2012–13	Stevenage	28	3		
2013–14	Stevenage	27	4	**55**	**7**
2014–15	Bradford C	30	3		
2015–16	Bradford C	7	1		
2016–17	Bradford C	17	1	**54**	**5**
2016–17	Bolton W	19	2		
2017–18	Bolton W	33	1	**52**	**3**
2018–19	Crawley T	34	8		
2019–20	*Oldham Ath*	16	2	**75**	**10**
2019–20	Crawley T	5	0	**39**	**8**

MORRIS, Glenn (G) 359 0
H: 6 0 W: 12 03 b.Woolwich 20-12-83

2001–02	Leyton Orient	2	0		
2002–03	Leyton Orient	23	0		
2003–04	Leyton Orient	27	0		
2004–05	Leyton Orient	12	0		
2005–06	Leyton Orient	4	0		
2006–07	Leyton Orient	3	0		
2007–08	Leyton Orient	16	0		
2008–09	Leyton Orient	26	0		
2009–10	Leyton Orient	11	0	**124**	**0**
2010–11	Southend U	33	0		
2011–12	Southend U	24	0		
2012–13	Southend U	0	0	**57**	**0**
2012–13	Aldershot T	2	0	**2**	**0**

From Woking, Eastleigh.

2014–15	Gillingham	10	0		
2015–16	Gillingham	0	0	**10**	**0**
2016–17	Crawley T	39	0		
2017–18	Crawley T	44	0		
2018–19	Crawley T	46	0		
2019–20	Crawley T	37	0	**166**	**0**

NADESAN, Ashley (F) 86 18
H: 6 2 W: 11 11 b. 9-9-94

2015–16	Fleetwood T	0	0		
2016–17	Fleetwood T	0	0		
2017–18	Fleetwood T	1	0		
2017–18	*Carlisle U*	15	4		
2018–19	Fleetwood T	20	1	**21**	**1**
2018–19	*Carlisle U*	25	8	**40**	**12**
2019–20	Crawley T	25	5	**25**	**5**

NATHANIEL-GEORGE, Ashley (M) 46 9
b. 14-6-95
From Wealdstone, Potters Bar T, Hendon.

2018–19	Crawley T	30	6		
2019–20	Crawley T	16	3	**46**	**9**

OKOYE, Paolo (M) 0 0

2019–20	Crawley T	0	0		

PALMER, Oliver (F) 249 55
b.London 21-1-92

2013–14	Mansfield T	38	4		
2014–15	Mansfield T	16	1	**54**	**5**
2015–16	Leyton Orient	45	7		
2016–17	Leyton Orient	20	5	**65**	**12**
2016–17	*Luton T*	17	3	**17**	**3**
2017–18	Lincoln C	45	8	**45**	**8**
2018–19	Crawley T	40	14		
2019–20	Crawley T	28	13	**68**	**27**

PAYNE, Josh (M) 181 14
H: 6 0 W: 11 09 b.Basingstoke 25-11-90
Internationals: England C.

2008–09	West Ham U	2	0		
2008–09	*Cheltenham T*	11	1	**11**	**1**
2009–10	West Ham U	0	0		
2009–10	*Colchester U*	3	0	**3**	**0**
2009–10	*Wycombe W*	3	1	**3**	**1**
2010–11	West Ham U	0	0	**2**	**0**
2010–11	Doncaster R	0	0		
2010–11	Oxford U	28	1		
2011–12	Oxford U	6	0	**34**	**1**
2011–12	Aldershot T	17	2		
2012–13	Aldershot T	15	1	**32**	**3**
2016–17	Crawley T	32	1		
2017–18	Crawley T	35	5		
2018–19	Crawley T	27	1		
2019–20	Crawley T	2	1	**96**	**8**

POWELL, Jack (M) 12 0
b. 29-1-94
Internationals: England C.

2013–14	Millwall	0	0		
2014–15	Millwall	5	0		
2015–16	Millwall	1	0	**6**	**0**

From Ebbsfleet U, Maidstone U.

2019–20	Crawley T	6	0	**6**	**0**

SENDLES-WHITE, Jamie (D) 43 0
H: 6 2 W: 13 05 b.Kingston 10-4-94
Internationals: Northern Ireland U19, U20, U21.

2011–12	QPR	0	0		
2012–13	QPR	0	0		
2013–14	QPR	0	0		
2013–14	*Colchester U*	0	0		
2014–15	QPR	0	0		
2014–15	*Mansfield T*	7	0	**7**	**0**
2015–16	Hamilton A	7	0	**7**	**0**
2015–16	Swindon T	10	0		
2016–17	Swindon T	5	0	**15**	**0**

From Leyton Orient, St Albans C, Torquay U.

2019–20	Crawley T	14	0	**14**	**0**

SESAY, David (D) 43 0
b. 18-9-98
From Watford.

2018–19	Crawley T	18	0		
2019–20	Crawley T	25	0	**43**	**0**

SMITH, Jimmy (M) 407 47
H: 6 0 W: 10 03 b.Newham 7-1-87
Internationals: England U16, U17, U19.

2004–05	Chelsea	0	0		
2005–06	Chelsea	1	0		
2006–07	Chelsea	0	0		
2006–07	*QPR*	29	6	**29**	**6**
2007–08	Chelsea	0	0		
2007–08	*Norwich C*	9	0	**9**	**0**
2008–09	Chelsea	0	0	**1**	**0**
2008–09	*Sheffield W*	12	0	**12**	**0**
2008–09	*Leyton Orient*	16	0		
2009–10	Leyton Orient	40	2		
2010–11	Leyton Orient	31	7		
2011–12	Leyton Orient	38	6		
2012–13	Leyton Orient	35	3		
2013–14	Leyton Orient	0	0	**160**	**18**
2013–14	Stevenage	42	3	**42**	**3**
2014–15	Crawley T	36	1		
2015–16	Crawley T	31	1		
2016–17	Crawley T	46	7		
2017–18	Crawley T	37	10		
2018–19	Crawley T	4	1		
2019–20	Crawley T	0	0	**154**	**20**

TUNNICLIFFE, Jordan (D) 37 1
b.Nuneaton 13-10-93

2013–14	Barnsley	0	0		
2014–15	Barnsley	0	0		

From Kidderminster H, AFC Fylde.

2019–20	Crawley T	37	1	**37**	**1**

VAN VELZEN, Gyliano (F) 128 14
b.Amsterdam 14-4-94
Internationals: Netherlands U16, U17, U21.

2010–11	Manchester U	0	0		
2011–12	Manchester U	0	0		
2012–13	Manchester U	0	0		
2012–13	*Royal Antwerp*	12	1	**12**	**1**
2013–14	Utrecht	5	0		
2014–15	Utrecht	2	0	**7**	**0**
2015–16	Volendam	30	3		
2016–17	Volendam	22	3	**52**	**6**
2016–17	Roda JC	12	1		
2017–18	Roda JC	22	0		
2018–19	Roda JC	29	6	**63**	**7**
2019–20	Crawley T	4	0	**4**	**0**

YOUNG, Lewis (M) **288 5**
H: 5 10 W: 11 02 b.Stevenage 27-9-89

2008–09	Watford	1	0		
2009–10	Watford	0	0	**1**	**0**
2009–10	*Hereford U*	6	0	**6**	**0**
2010–11	Burton Alb	19	0	**19**	**0**
2011–12	Northampton T	30	0	**30**	**0**
2012–13	Yeovil T	15	0		
2013–14	Yeovil T	0	0	**15**	**0**
2013–14	Bury	4	0	**4**	**0**
2014–15	Crawley T	38	0		
2015–16	Crawley T	38	0		
2016–17	Crawley T	43	0		
2017–18	Crawley T	41	3		
2018–19	Crawley T	38	1		
2019–20	Crawley T	15	1	**213**	**5**

CREWE ALEX (27)

ADEBISI, Rio (D) **2 0**
b.Croydon 27-9-00

2019–20	Crewe Alex	2	0	**2**	**0**

AINLEY, Callum (M) **156 14**
H: 5 8 W: 10 01 b.Middlewich 2-11-97

2015–16	Crewe Alex	16	1		
2016–17	Crewe Alex	27	1		
2017–18	Crewe Alex	45	4		
2018–19	Crewe Alex	43	6		
2019–20	Crewe Alex	25	2	**156**	**14**

ANENE, Chuma (M) **188 40**
b.Oslo 14-5-93
Internationals: Norway U16, U17, U19, U20.

2010	Valerenga	0	0		
2011	Valerenga	6	1		
2011	*Ullensaker/Kisa*	5	0		
2012	Valerenga	14	2		
2013	Valerenga	3	0	**23**	**3**
2013	*Stabaek*	12	4	**12**	**4**
2014	Ullensaker/Kisa	14	2	**19**	**2**
2014–15	Rabotnicki	27	7		
2015–16	Rabotnicki	2	2	**29**	**9**
2015–16	Amkar Perm	14	1		
2016–17	Amkar Perm	10	1	**24**	**2**
2017	Kairat	20	4		
2018	Kairat	9	4	**29**	**8**
2018	Fredericia	7	0	**7**	**0**
2019–20	Midtjylland	0	0		
2019–20	*Frederica*	2	0	**2**	**0**
2019–20	*Jerv*	15	5	**15**	**5**

On loan from Midtylland.

2019–20	Crewe Alex	28	7	**28**	**7**

BOOTH, Sam (G) **0 0**
b. 6-12-00

2019–20	Crewe Alex	0	0		

DALE, Owen (F) **47 1**
H: 5 9 W: 10 03 b.Warrington 1-11-98

2016–17	Crewe Alex	0	0		
2017–18	Crewe Alex	4	0		
2018–19	Crewe Alex	16	1		
2019–20	Crewe Alex	27	0	**47**	**1**

FINNEY, Oliver (M) **37 5**
b.Stoke-on-Trent 15-12-97

2015–16	Crewe Alex	0	0		
2016–17	Crewe Alex	1	0		
2017–18	Crewe Alex	1	0		
2018–19	Crewe Alex	17	0		
2019–20	Crewe Alex	18	5	**37**	**5**

GREEN, Paul (M) **558 47**
H: 5 9 W: 10 02 b.Pontefract 10-4-83
Internationals: Republic of Ireland Full caps.

2003–04	Doncaster R	43	8		
2004–05	Doncaster R	42	7		
2005–06	Doncaster R	34	3		
2006–07	Doncaster R	41	2		
2007–08	Doncaster R	38	5	**198**	**25**
2008–09	Derby Co	29	3		
2009–10	Derby Co	33	2		
2010–11	Derby Co	36	2		
2011–12	Derby Co	27	1	**125**	**8**
2012–13	Leeds U	32	4		
2013–14	Leeds U	9	0	**41**	**4**
2013–14	*Ipswich T*	14	2	**14**	**2**
2014–15	Rotherham U	37	3		
2015–16	Rotherham U	24	0	**61**	**3**
2016–17	Oldham Ath	41	1		
2017–18	Oldham Ath	6	0	**47**	**1**
2017–18	*Crewe Alex*	20	1		
2018–19	Crewe Alex	26	1		
2019–20	Crewe Alex	26	2	**72**	**4**

GRIFFITHS, Regan (M) **0 0**

2019–20	Crewe Alex	0	0		

HUNT, Nicky (D) **400 4**
H: 6 1 W: 13 07 b.Westhoughton 3-9-83
Internationals: England U21.

2000–01	Bolton W	1	0		
2001–02	Bolton W	0	0		
2002–03	Bolton W	0	0		
2003–04	Bolton W	31	1		
2004–05	Bolton W	29	0		
2005–06	Bolton W	20	0		
2006–07	Bolton W	33	0		
2007–08	Bolton W	14	0		
2008–09	Bolton W	0	0		
2008–09	*Birmingham C*	11	0	**11**	**0**
2009–10	Bolton W	0	0	**128**	**1**
2009–10	*Derby Co*	21	0	**21**	**0**
2010–11	Bristol C	7	0		
2011–12	Bristol C	0	0	**7**	**0**
2011–12	Preston NE	17	1	**17**	**1**
2012–13	Rotherham U	9	0	**9**	**0**
2012–13	Accrington S	11	0		
2013–14	Accrington S	37	0		
2014–15	Accrington S	29	0	**77**	**0**
2015–16	Mansfield T	19	0	**19**	**0**
2015–16	Leyton Orient	16	0		
2016–17	Leyton Orient	35	1	**51**	**1**
2017–18	Notts Co	13	0	**13**	**0**
2018–19	Crewe Alex	22	0		
2019–20	Crewe Alex	25	1	**47**	**1**

JAASKELAINEN, William (G) **39 0**
b. 25-7-98
Internationals: Finland U19.

2015–16	Bolton W	0	0		
2016–17	Bolton W	0	0		
2017–18	Bolton W	0	0		
2017–18	Crewe Alex	0	0		
2018–19	Crewe Alex	4	0		
2019–20	Crewe Alex	35	0	**39**	**0**

JOHNSON, Travis (D) **1 0**
b. 28-8-00

2018–19	Crewe Alex	0	0		
2019–20	Crewe Alex	1	0	**1**	**0**

KIRK, Charlie (M) **139 23**
H: 5 7 W: 11 00 b.Winsford 24-12-97

2015–16	Crewe Alex	14	0		
2016–17	Crewe Alex	22	0		
2017–18	Crewe Alex	25	5		
2018–19	Crewe Alex	42	11		
2019–20	Crewe Alex	36	7	**139**	**23**

LANCASHIRE, Oliver (D) **272 6**
H: 6 1 W: 11 10 b.Basingstoke 13-12-88

2006–07	Southampton	0	0		
2007–08	Southampton	0	0		
2008–09	Southampton	11	0		
2009–10	Southampton	2	0	**13**	**0**
2009–10	*Grimsby T*	25	1	**25**	**1**
2010–11	Walsall	29	0		
2011–12	Walsall	20	1	**49**	**1**
2012–13	Aldershot T	12	0	**12**	**0**
2013–14	Rochdale	38	0		
2014–15	Rochdale	21	0		
2015–16	Rochdale	34	2	**93**	**2**
2016–17	Shrewsbury T	16	1	**16**	**1**
2017–18	Swindon T	35	1		
2018–19	Swindon T	20	0	**55**	**1**
2019–20	Crewe Alex	9	0	**9**	**0**

LOWERY, Tom (M) **82 6**
b.Holmes Chapel 31-12-97

2016–17	Crewe Alex	7	0		
2017–18	Crewe Alex	31	0		
2018–19	Crewe Alex	15	1		
2019–20	Crewe Alex	29	5	**82**	**6**

LUNDSTRAM, Josh (M) **0 0**

2017–18	Crewe Alex	0	0		
2018–19	Crewe Alex	0	0		
2019–20	Crewe Alex	0	0		

MILLER, Shaun (F) **374 79**
H: 5 10 W: 11 08 b.Alsager 25-9-87

2006–07	Crewe Alex	7	3		
2007–08	Crewe Alex	15	1		
2008–09	Crewe Alex	33	4		
2009–10	Crewe Alex	33	7		
2010–11	Crewe Alex	42	18		
2011–12	Crewe Alex	33	5		
2012–13	Sheffield U	15	4		
2013–14	Sheffield U	13	0	**28**	**4**
2013–14	*Shrewsbury T*	8	3	**8**	**3**
2014–15	Coventry C	12	1	**12**	**1**
2014–15	*Crawley T*	5	0	**5**	**0**
2014–15	*York C*	6	0	**6**	**0**
2015–16	Morecambe	37	15		
2016–17	Carlisle U	30	4		
2017–18	Carlisle U	23	3	**53**	**7**
2017–18	*Crewe Alex*	15	6		
2018–19	Crewe Alex	29	3	**207**	**47**
2019–20	*Morecambe*	18	2	**55**	**17**

NG, Perry (D) **140 6**
H: 5 11 W: 12 02 b.Liverpool 24-6-94

2014–15	Crewe Alex	0	0		
2015–16	Crewe Alex	6	0		
2016–17	Crewe Alex	16	0		
2017–18	Crewe Alex	38	4		
2018–19	Crewe Alex	44	0		
2019–20	Crewe Alex	36	2	**140**	**6**

NOLAN, Eddie (D) **303 7**
H: 6 0 W: 13 05 b.Waterford 5-8-88
Internationals: Republic of Ireland U21, B, Full caps.

2005–06	Blackburn R	0	0		
2006–07	Blackburn R	0	0		
2006–07	*Stockport Co*	4	0	**4**	**0**
2007–08	Blackburn R	0	0		
2007–08	*Hartlepool U*	11	0	**11**	**0**
2008–09	Blackburn R	0	0		
2008–09	Preston NE	21	0		
2009–10	Preston NE	19	0		
2009–10	*Sheffield W*	14	1	**14**	**1**
2010–11	Preston NE	0	0	**40**	**0**
2010–11	Scunthorpe U	35	0		
2011–12	Scunthorpe U	30	1		
2012–13	Scunthorpe U	12	0		
2013–14	Scunthorpe U	39	0		
2014–15	Scunthorpe U	6	0	**122**	**1**
2015–16	York C	15	1	**15**	**1**
2016–17	Blackpool	3	0	**3**	**0**
2017–18	Crewe Alex	42	0		
2018–19	Crewe Alex	33	1		
2019–20	Crewe Alex	19	3	**94**	**4**

OFFORD, Luke (M) **9 0**
b.Chichester 19-11-99

2017–18	Crewe Alex	0	0		
2018–19	Crewe Alex	0	0		
2019–20	Crewe Alex	9	0	**9**	**0**

PICKERING, Harry (M) **102 6**
H: 6 1 W: 12 04 b. 29-12-98

2017–18	Crewe Alex	35	3		
2018–19	Crewe Alex	32	0		
2019–20	Crewe Alex	35	3	**102**	**6**

PORTER, Chris (F) **524 158**
H: 6 1 W: 12 09 b.Wigan 12-12-83

2002–03	Bury	2	0		
2003–04	Bury	37	9		
2004–05	Bury	32	9	**71**	**18**
2005–06	Oldham Ath	31	7		
2006–07	Oldham Ath	35	21	**66**	**28**
2007–08	Motherwell	37	14		
2008–09	Motherwell	22	9	**59**	**23**
2008–09	Derby Co	5	3		
2009–10	Derby Co	21	4		
2010–11	Derby Co	18	2	**44**	**9**
2011–12	Sheffield U	34	5		
2012–13	Sheffield U	21	3		
2012–13	*Shrewsbury T*	5	1	**5**	**1**
2013–14	Sheffield U	32	7		
2013–14	*Chesterfield*	3	0	**3**	**0**
2014–15	Sheffield U	1	0	**88**	**15**
2014–15	Colchester U	21	7		
2015–16	Colchester U	32	7		
2016–17	Colchester U	38	16	**91**	**30**
2017–18	Crewe Alex	31	9		
2018–19	Crewe Alex	40	13		
2019–20	Crewe Alex	26	12	**97**	**34**

POWELL, Daniel (F) **325 54**
H: 5 11 W: 13 03 b.Luton 12-3-91

2008–09	Milton Keynes D	7	1		
2009–10	Milton Keynes D	2	1		
2010–11	Milton Keynes D	29	9		
2011–12	Milton Keynes D	43	6		
2012–13	Milton Keynes D	34	7		
2013–14	Milton Keynes D	32	1		
2014–15	Milton Keynes D	42	8		
2015–16	Milton Keynes D	22	2		
2016–17	Milton Keynes D	20	2	**231**	**37**
2017–18	Northampton T	29	2		
2018–19	Northampton T	35	6	**64**	**8**
2019–20	Crewe Alex	30	9	**30**	**9**

REILLY, Lewis (F) **8 0**
b. 7-7-99

2017–18	Crewe Alex	5	0		
2018–19	Crewe Alex	3	0		
2019–20	Crewe Alex	0	0	**8**	**0**

RICHARDS, Dave (G) **17 0**
H: 5 11 W: 11 11 b.Abergavenny 31-12-93

2013–14	Cardiff C	0	0		
2013–14	Bristol C	0	0		
2014–15	Bristol C	0	0		
2015–16	Crewe Alex	0	0		
2016–17	Crewe Alex	0	0		

2017–18	Crewe Alex	11	0		
2018–19	Crewe Alex	4	0		
2019–20	Crewe Alex	2	0	**17**	**0**

SASS-DAVIES, Billy (D) — 2 0
b.Manchester 17-2-00
Internationals: Wales U19.

2017–18	Crewe Alex	0	0		
2018–19	Crewe Alex	2	0		
2019–20	Crewe Alex	0	0	**2**	**0**

VISSER, Dino (G) — 70 0
b.Johannesburg 10-7-89

2010–11	Platinum Stars	1	0		
2011–12	Platinum Stars	0	0		
2012–13	Bloemfontein Celtic	0	0		
2013–14	Bloemfontein Celtic	0	0		
2013–14	*Black Leopards*	1	0	**1**	**0**
2014–15	Polokwane City	10	0		
2015–16	Polokwane City	0	0	**10**	**0**
2016–17	Engen Santos	23	0	**23**	**0**
2017–18	Platinum Stars	15	0	**16**	**0**
2018–19	Cape Umoya U	20	0	**20**	**0**
2019–20	Exeter C	0	0		
2019–20	Crewe Alex	0	0		

WINTLE, Ryan (M) — 121 7
H: 5 5 W: 10 01 b.Newcastle-under-Lyme 13-6-97

2015–16	Crewe Alex	3	0		
2016–17	Crewe Alex	17	1		
2017–18	Crewe Alex	18	2		
2018–19	Crewe Alex	46	1		
2019–20	Crewe Alex	37	3	**121**	**7**

Scholars
Akpo, Jerry Le Grand; Allen, Luke; Djalo, Abdul Karimo; Goodrich, Jack David; Green, Fenton Lloyd; Hartshorn, Ethan James; Kennington, Liam Dean Kevin; Levey, Joseph Paul Michael; Lokko, Daniel Arvin Yaw Senyo; Marrow, Jack Robert David; Marsden, Bailey; McDonald, Matthew David; Onyeka, Tyreece Obiora; Priestman, Jakob Adam; Robbins, Joseph Aidan Thomas; Stubbs, Kyle; Walklate, Andrew Lawrence; Woodthorpe, Nathan John Edward; Wrench, Jamie Laurence.

CRYSTAL PALACE (28)

AYEW, Jordan (F) — 317 58
H: 6 0 W: 12 11 b.Marseille 11-9-91
Internationals: Ghana U20, Full caps.

2009–10	Marseille	4	1		
2010–11	Marseille	22	2		
2011–12	Marseille	34	3		
2012–13	Marseille	35	7		
2013–14	Marseille	16	1	**111**	**14**
2013–14	*Sochaux*	17	5	**17**	**5**
2014–15	Lorient	31	12	**31**	**12**
2015–16	Aston Villa	30	7		
2016–17	Aston Villa	21	2	**51**	**9**
2016–17	Swansea C	14	1		
2017–18	Swansea C	36	7		
2018–19	Swansea C	0	0	**50**	**8**
2018–19	*Crystal Palace*	20	1		
2019–20	Crystal Palace	37	9	**57**	**10**

BENTEKE, Christian (F) — 329 108
H: 6 3 W: 13 00 b.Kinshasa 3-12-90
Internationals: Belgium U17, U18, U19, U21, Full caps.

2007–08	Genk	7	0		
2008–09	Genk	3	0		
2008–09	Standard Liege	9	3		
2009–10	*KV Kortrijk*	24	9	**24**	**9**
2010–11	Standard Liege	5	0		
2010–11	*KV Mechelen*	15	5	**15**	**5**
2011–12	Standard Liege	4	0	**18**	**3**
2011–12	Genk	32	16		
2012–13	Genk	5	3	**47**	**19**
2012–13	Aston Villa	34	19		
2013–14	Aston Villa	26	10		
2014–15	Aston Villa	29	13	**89**	**42**
2015–16	Liverpool	29	9	**29**	**9**
2016–17	Crystal Palace	36	15		
2017–18	Crystal Palace	31	3		
2018–19	Crystal Palace	16	1		
2019–20	Crystal Palace	24	2	**107**	**21**

BOLASIE, Yannick (M) — 329 37
H: 6 2 W: 13 02 b.DR Congo 24-5-89
Internationals: DR Congo Full caps.

2008–09	Plymouth Arg	0	0		
2008–09	*Barnet*	20	3		
2009–10	Plymouth Arg	16	1		
2009–10	*Barnet*	22	2	**42**	**5**
2010–11	Plymouth Arg	35	7	**51**	**8**
2011–12	Bristol C	23	1		
2012–13	Bristol C	0	0	**23**	**1**
2012–13	Crystal Palace	43	3		
2013–14	Crystal Palace	29	0		
2014–15	Crystal Palace	34	4		
2015–16	Crystal Palace	26	5		
2016–17	Crystal Palace	1	0		
2016–17	Everton	13	1		
2017–18	Everton	16	1		
2018–19	Everton	0	0	**29**	**2**
2018–19	*Aston Villa*	21	2	**21**	**2**
2018–19	*Anderlecht*	17	6	**17**	**6**
2019–20	Crystal Palace	0	0	**133**	**12**
2019–20	*Sporting Lisbon*	13	1	**13**	**1**

CAHILL, Gary (D) — 417 30
H: 6 2 W: 12 06 b.Dronfield 19-12-85
Internationals: England U20, U21, Full caps.

2003–04	Aston Villa	0	0		
2004–05	Aston Villa	0	0		
2004–05	*Burnley*	27	1	**27**	**1**
2005–06	Aston Villa	7	1		
2006–07	Aston Villa	20	0		
2007–08	Aston Villa	1	0	**28**	**1**
2007–08	*Sheffield U*	16	2	**16**	**2**
2007–08	Bolton W	13	0		
2008–09	Bolton W	33	3		
2009–10	Bolton W	29	5		
2010–11	Bolton W	36	3		
2011–12	Bolton W	19	2	**130**	**13**
2011–12	Chelsea	10	1		
2012–13	Chelsea	26	2		
2013–14	Chelsea	30	1		
2014–15	Chelsea	36	1		
2015–16	Chelsea	23	2		
2016–17	Chelsea	37	6		
2017–18	Chelsea	27	0		
2018–19	Chelsea	2	0		
2019–20	Chelsea	0	0	**191**	**13**
2019–20	Crystal Palace	25	0	**25**	**0**

DANN, Scott (D) — 403 29
H: 6 2 W: 12 00 b.Liverpool 14-2-87
Internationals: England U21.

2004–05	Walsall	1	0		
2005–06	Walsall	0	0		
2006–07	Walsall	30	4		
2007–08	Walsall	28	3	**59**	**7**
2007–08	Coventry C	16	0		
2008–09	Coventry C	31	3	**47**	**3**
2009–10	Birmingham C	30	0		
2010–11	Birmingham C	20	2		
2011–12	Birmingham C	0	0	**50**	**2**
2011–12	Blackburn R	27	1		
2012–13	Blackburn R	46	4		
2013–14	Blackburn R	25	0	**98**	**5**
2013–14	Crystal Palace	14	1		
2014–15	Crystal Palace	34	2		
2015–16	Crystal Palace	35	5		
2016–17	Crystal Palace	23	3		
2017–18	Crystal Palace	17	1		
2018–19	Crystal Palace	10	0		
2019–20	Crystal Palace	16	0	**149**	**12**

DREHER, Luke (M) — 1 0
H: 6 1 W: 12 00 b.Epsom 27-11-98

2015–16	Crystal Palace	0	0		
2016–17	Crystal Palace	0	0		
2017–18	Crystal Palace	0	0		
2018–19	Crystal Palace	1	0		
2019–20	Crystal Palace	0	0	**1**	**0**

GORDON, John-Kymani (F) — 0 0
b.London 13-2-03
Internationals: England U16.

2019–20	Crystal Palace	0	0		

GUAITA, Vicente (G) — 269 0
H: 6 3 W: 12 08 b.Valencia 18-2-87

2006–07	Valencia	0	0		
2007–08	Valencia	0	0		
2008–09	Valencia	2	0		
2009–10	Valencia	0	0		
2009–10	*Recreativo*	30	0	**30**	**0**
2010–11	Valencia	21	0		
2011–12	Valencia	26	0		
2012–13	Valencia	14	0		
2013–14	Valencia	13	0	**76**	**0**
2014–15	Getafe	29	0		
2015–16	Getafe	38	0		
2016–17	Getafe	8	0		
2017–18	Getafe	33	0	**108**	**0**
2018–19	Crystal Palace	20	0		
2019–20	Crystal Palace	35	0	**55**	**0**

HENDERSON, Stephen (G) — 166 0
H: 6 3 W: 11 00 b.Dublin 2-5-88
Internationals: Republic of Ireland U16, U17, U19, U21.

2005–06	Aston Villa	0	0		
2006–07	Aston Villa	0	0		
2007–08	Bristol C	1	0		
2008–09	Bristol C	1	0		
2009–10	Bristol C	3	0		
2009–10	*Aldershot T*	8	0	**8**	**0**
2010–11	Bristol C	0	0	**5**	**0**
2010–11	*Yeovil T*	33	0	**33**	**0**
2011–12	Portsmouth	25	0		
2011–12	*West Ham U*	0	0		
2012–13	West Ham U	0	0		
2012–13	*Ipswich T*	24	0	**24**	**0**
2013–14	West Ham U	0	0		
2013–14	*Bournemouth*	2	0	**2**	**0**
2014–15	Charlton Ath	31	0		
2015–16	Charlton Ath	22	0	**53**	**0**
2016–17	Nottingham F	12	0		
2017–18	Nottingham F	0	0		
2017–18	*Portsmouth*	1	0	**26**	**0**
2018–19	Nottingham F	0	0	**12**	**0**
2018–19	*Wycombe W*	3	0	**3**	**0**
2019–20	Crystal Palace	0	0		

HENNESSEY, Wayne (G) — 289 0
H: 6 0 W: 11 06 b.Anglesey 24-1-87
Internationals: Wales U17, U19, U21, Full caps.

2004–05	Wolverhampton W	0	0		
2005–06	Wolverhampton W	0	0		
2006–07	Wolverhampton W	0	0		
2006–07	*Bristol C*	0	0		
2006–07	*Stockport Co*	15	0	**15**	**0**
2007–08	Wolverhampton W	46	0		
2008–09	Wolverhampton W	35	0		
2009–10	Wolverhampton W	13	0		
2010–11	Wolverhampton W	24	0		
2011–12	Wolverhampton W	34	0		
2012–13	Wolverhampton W	0	0		
2013–14	Wolverhampton W	0	0	**152**	**0**
2013–14	*Yeovil T*	12	0	**12**	**0**
2013–14	Crystal Palace	1	0		
2014–15	Crystal Palace	3	0		
2015–16	Crystal Palace	29	0		
2016–17	Crystal Palace	29	0		
2017–18	Crystal Palace	27	0		
2018–19	Crystal Palace	18	0		
2019–20	Crystal Palace	3	0	**110**	**0**

HENRY, Dion (G) — 1 0
H: 5 11 W: 10 03 b.Ipswich 12-9-97

2014–15	Peterborough U	0	0		
2015–16	Peterborough U	1	0		
2016–17	Peterborough U	0	0	**1**	**0**
2017–18	Crystal Palace	0	0		
2018–19	Crystal Palace	0	0		
2019–20	Crystal Palace	0	0		

INNISS, Ryan (D) — 92 1
H: 6 5 W: 13 02 b.Kent 5-6-95
Internationals: England U16, U17.

2012–13	Crystal Palace	0	0		
2013–14	Crystal Palace	0	0		
2013–14	*Cheltenham T*	2	0	**2**	**0**
2013–14	*Gillingham*	3	0	**3**	**0**
2014–15	Crystal Palace	0	0		
2014–15	*Yeovil T*	6	0	**6**	**0**
2014–15	*Port Vale*	5	0		
2015–16	Crystal Palace	0	0		
2015–16	*Port Vale*	15	0	**20**	**0**
2016–17	Crystal Palace	0	0		
2016–17	*Southend U*	10	0	**10**	**0**
2017–18	Crystal Palace	0	0		
2017–18	*Colchester U*	18	0	**18**	**0**
2018–19	Crystal Palace	0	0		
2018–19	*Dundee*	11	0	**11**	**0**
2019–20	Crystal Palace	0	0		
2019–20	*Newport Co*	22	1	**22**	**1**

JACH, Jaroslaw (D) — 99 4
H: 6 3 W: 12 11 b.Bielawa 17-2-94
Internationals: Poland U21, Full caps.

2013–14	Zagkebie Lubin	2	0		
2014–15	Zagkebie Lubin	13	0		
2015–16	Zagkebie Lubin	13	2		
2016–17	Zagkebie Lubin	23	1	**51**	**3**
2017–18	Zaglebie Lubin	17	1	**17**	**1**
2017–18	Crystal Palace	0	0		
2018–19	Crystal Palace	0	0		
2018–19	*Caykur Rizesport*	5	0	**5**	**0**
2018–19	*Sheriff Tiraspol*	14	0	**14**	**0**
2019–20	Crystal Palace	0	0		
2019–20	*Rakow Czestochowa*	12	0	**12**	**0**

KELLY, Martin (D) **160 1**
H: 6 3 W: 12 02 b.Bolton 27-4-90
Internationals: England U19, U20, U21, Full caps.

2007–08	Liverpool	0	0		
2008–09	Liverpool	0	0		
2008–09	*Huddersfield T*	7	1	**7**	**1**
2009–10	Liverpool	1	0		
2010–11	Liverpool	11	0		
2011–12	Liverpool	12	0		
2012–13	Liverpool	4	0		
2013–14	Liverpool	5	0	**33**	**0**
2014–15	Crystal Palace	31	0		
2015–16	Crystal Palace	13	0		
2016–17	Crystal Palace	29	0		
2017–18	Crystal Palace	15	0		
2018–19	Crystal Palace	13	0		
2019–20	Crystal Palace	19	0	**120**	**0**

KIRBY, Nya (M) **11 1**
H: 5 9 W: 10 06 b.Islington 31-1-00
Internationals: England U16, U17, U18, U19.
From Tottenham H.

2017–18	Crystal Palace	0	0		
2018–19	Crystal Palace	0	0		
2018–19	*Blackpool*	11	1	**11**	**1**
2019–20	Crystal Palace	0	0		

KOUYATE, Cheikhou (M) **384 20**
H: 6 3 W: 11 11 b.Dakar 21-12-89
Internationals: Senegal U20, Full caps.

2007–08	Brussels	10	0		
2008–09	Brussels	0	0	**10**	**0**
2008–09	*Kortrijk*	26	3	**26**	**3**
2009–10	Anderlecht	21	1		
2010–11	Anderlecht	23	1		
2011–12	Anderlecht	38	0		
2012–13	Anderlecht	33	1		
2013–14	Anderlecht	38	1	**153**	**4**
2014–15	West Ham U	31	4		
2015–16	West Ham U	34	5		
2016–17	West Ham U	31	1		
2017–18	West Ham U	33	2	**129**	**12**
2018–19	Crystal Palace	31	0		
2019–20	Crystal Palace	35	1	**66**	**1**

LOKILO, Jason (M) **5 0**
H: 5 9 b.Brussel 17-9-98
Internationals: DR Congo U20.

2014–15	Anderlecht	0	0		
2015–16	Crystal Palace	0	0		
2016–17	Crystal Palace	0	0		
2017–18	Crystal Palace	0	0		
2018–19	Crystal Palace	0	0		
2018–19	*Lorient*	4	0	**4**	**0**
2019–20	Crystal Palace	0	0		
2019–20	*Doncaster R*	1	0	**1**	**0**

McARTHUR, James (M) **494 37**
H: 5 6 W: 9 13 b.Glasgow 7-10-87
Internationals: Scotland U21, Full caps.

2004–05	Hamilton A	6	0		
2005–06	Hamilton A	20	1		
2006–07	Hamilton A	36	1		
2007–08	Hamilton A	34	4		
2008–09	Hamilton A	37	2		
2009–10	Hamilton A	35	1	**168**	**9**
2010–11	Wigan Ath	18	0		
2011–12	Wigan Ath	31	3		
2012–13	Wigan Ath	34	3		
2013–14	Wigan Ath	41	4		
2014–15	Wigan Ath	5	1	**129**	**11**
2014–15	Crystal Palace	32	2		
2015–16	Crystal Palace	28	2		
2016–17	Crystal Palace	29	5		
2017–18	Crystal Palace	33	5		
2018–19	Crystal Palace	38	3		
2019–20	Crystal Palace	37	0	**197**	**17**

McCARTHY, James (M) **356 27**
H: 5 11 W: 11 05 b.Glasgow 12-11-90
Internationals: Republic of Ireland U17, U18, U19, U21, Full caps.

2006–07	Hamilton A	23	1		
2007–08	Hamilton A	35	7		
2008–09	Hamilton A	37	6	**95**	**14**
2009–10	Wigan Ath	20	1		
2010–11	Wigan Ath	24	3		
2011–12	Wigan Ath	33	0		
2012–13	Wigan Ath	38	3		
2013–14	Wigan Ath	5	0	**120**	**7**
2013–14	Everton	34	1		
2014–15	Everton	28	2		
2015–16	Everton	29	2		
2016–17	Everton	12	1		
2017–18	Everton	4	0		
2018–19	Everton	1	0		
2019–20	Everton	0	0	**108**	**6**
2019–20	Crystal Palace	33	0	**33**	**0**

McGREGOR, Gio (M) **0 0**
b.Hammersmith 9-1-99

2018–19	Crystal Palace	0	0		
2019–20	Crystal Palace	0	0		

MEYER, Max (M) **192 18**
H: 5 7 W: 10 03 b.Oberhausen 18-9-95
Internationals: Germany U16, U17, U19, U21, U23, Full caps.

2012–13	Schalke 04	5	0		
2013–14	Schalke 04	30	6		
2014–15	Schalke 04	28	5		
2015–16	Schalke 04	32	5		
2016–17	Schalke 04	27	1		
2017–18	Schalke 04	24	0	**146**	**17**
2018–19	Crystal Palace	29	1		
2019–20	Crystal Palace	17	0	**46**	**1**

MILIVOJEVIC, Luka (M) **290 49**
H: 6 0 b.Kragujevac 7-4-91
Internationals: Serbia U21, Full caps.

2007–08	Radnicki Kraguejevac	5	1	**5**	**1**
2008–09	Rad Belgrade	1	0		
2009–10	Rad Belgrade	9	0		
2010–11	Rad Belgrade	26	0		
2011–12	Rad Belgrade	13	3	**49**	**3**
2011–12	Red Star Belgrade	11	1		
2012–13	Red Star Belgrade	25	6	**36**	**7**
2013–14	Anderlecht	16	0		
2014–15	Anderlecht	3	0	**19**	**0**
2014–15	Olympiacos	23	2		
2015–16	Olympiacos	22	3		
2016–17	Olympiacos	17	6	**62**	**11**
2016–17	Crystal Palace	14	2		
2017–18	Crystal Palace	36	10		
2018–19	Crystal Palace	38	12		
2019–20	Crystal Palace	31	3	**119**	**27**

MITCHELL, Tyrick (D) **4 0**
b. 1-9-99
From Brentford.

2019–20	Crystal Palace	4	0	**4**	**0**

PIERRICK, Brandon (M) **2 0**
b. 10-12-01

2019–20	Crystal Palace	2	0	**2**	**0**

RIEDEWALD, Jairo (D) **92 2**
H: 6 0 W: 12 06 b.Amsterdam 9-9-96
Internationals: Netherlands U16, U17, U19, U21, Full caps.

2013–14	Ajax	5	2		
2014–15	Ajax	19	0		
2015–16	Ajax	23	0		
2016–17	Ajax	16	0	**63**	**2**
2017–18	Crystal Palace	12	0		
2018–19	Crystal Palace	0	0		
2019–20	Crystal Palace	17	0	**29**	**0**

SAKHO, Mamadou (D) **275 10**
H: 6 2 W: 12 07 b.Paris 13-2-90
Internationals: France U16, U17, U18, U19, U21, Full caps.

2006–07	Paris Saint-Germain	0	0		
2007–08	Paris Saint-Germain	12	0		
2008–09	Paris Saint-Germain	23	1		
2009–10	Paris Saint-Germain	32	0		
2010–11	Paris Saint-Germain	35	4		
2011–12	Paris Saint-Germain	22	0		
2012–13	Paris Saint-Germain	27	2	**151**	**7**
2013–14	Liverpool	18	1		
2014–15	Liverpool	16	0		
2015–16	Liverpool	22	1		
2016–17	Liverpool	0	0		
2016–17	*Crystal Palace*	8	0		
2017–18	Liverpool	0	0	**56**	**2**
2017–18	Crystal Palace	19	1		
2018–19	Crystal Palace	27	0		
2019–20	Crystal Palace	14	0	**68**	**1**

SCHLUPP, Jeffrey (M) **221 23**
H: 5 8 W: 11 00 b.Hamburg 23-12-92
Internationals: Ghana Full caps.

2010–11	Leicester C	0	0		
2010–11	*Brentford*	9	6	**9**	**6**
2011–12	Leicester C	21	2		
2012–13	Leicester C	19	3		
2013–14	Leicester C	26	1		
2014–15	Leicester C	32	3		
2015–16	Leicester C	24	1		
2016–17	Leicester C	4	0	**126**	**10**
2016–17	Crystal Palace	15	0		
2017–18	Crystal Palace	24	0		
2018–19	Crystal Palace	30	4		
2019–20	Crystal Palace	17	3	**86**	**7**

SORLOTH, Alexander (F) **158 56**
H: 6 4 W: 14 02 b.Trondheim 5-12-95
Internationals: Norway U16, U17, U18, U19, U21, Full caps.

2013	Rosenborg	0	0		
2014	Rosenborg	6	0	**6**	**0**
2015	Bodo/Glimt	26	13	**26**	**13**
2015–16	Groningen	13	2		
2016–17	Groningen	25	3	**38**	**5**
2017–18	Midtjylland	19	10	**19**	**10**
2017–18	Crystal Palace	4	0		
2018–19	Crystal Palace	12	0		
2018–19	*Gent*	19	4	**19**	**4**
2019–20	Crystal Palace	0	0	**16**	**0**
2019–20	*Trabzonspor*	34	24	**34**	**24**

TAVARES, Nikola (D) **0 0**
Internationals: Croatia U18, U19.

2018–19	Crystal Palace	0	0		
2019–20	Crystal Palace	0	0		

TOMKINS, James (D) **314 16**
H: 6 3 W: 11 10 b.Basildon 29-3-89
Internationals: England U16, U17, U18, U19, U20, U21. Great Britain.

2005–06	West Ham U	0	0		
2006–07	West Ham U	0	0		
2007–08	West Ham U	6	0		
2008–09	West Ham U	12	1		
2008–09	*Derby Co*	7	0	**7**	**0**
2009–10	West Ham U	23	0		
2010–11	West Ham U	19	1		
2011–12	West Ham U	44	4		
2012–13	West Ham U	26	1		
2013–14	West Ham U	31	0		
2014–15	West Ham U	22	1		
2015–16	West Ham U	25	0	**208**	**8**
2016–17	Crystal Palace	24	3		
2017–18	Crystal Palace	28	3		
2018–19	Crystal Palace	29	1		
2019–20	Crystal Palace	18	1	**99**	**8**

TOWNSEND, Andros (M) **298 30**
H: 6 0 W: 12 00 b.Chingford 16-7-91
Internationals: England U16, U17, U19, U21, Full caps.

2008–09	Tottenham H	0	0		
2008–09	*Yeovil T*	10	1	**10**	**1**
2009–10	Tottenham H	0	0		
2009–10	*Leyton Orient*	22	2	**22**	**2**
2009–10	*Milton Keynes D*	9	2	**9**	**2**
2010–11	Tottenham H	0	0		
2010–11	*Ipswich T*	13	1	**13**	**1**
2010–11	*Watford*	3	0	**3**	**0**
2010–11	*Millwall*	11	2	**11**	**2**
2011–12	Tottenham H	0	0		
2011–12	*Leeds U*	6	1	**6**	**1**
2011–12	*Birmingham C*	15	0	**15**	**0**
2012–13	Tottenham H	5	0		
2012–13	*QPR*	12	2	**12**	**2**
2013–14	Tottenham H	25	1		
2014–15	Tottenham H	17	2		
2015–16	Tottenham H	3	0	**50**	**3**
2015–16	Newcastle U	13	4	**13**	**4**
2016–17	Crystal Palace	36	3		
2017–18	Crystal Palace	36	2		
2018–19	Crystal Palace	38	6		
2019–20	Crystal Palace	24	1	**134**	**12**

TUPPER, Joe (G) **0 0**
b. 15-11-97
From Reading.

2018–19	Crystal Palace	0	0		
2019–20	Crystal Palace	0	0		

VAN AANHOLT, Patrick (D) **297 26**
H: 5 9 W: 10 08 b.Den Bosch 3-7-88
Internationals: Netherlands U16, U17, U18, U19, U20, U21, Full caps.

2007–08	Chelsea	0	0		
2008–09	Chelsea	0	0		
2009–10	Chelsea	2	0		
2009–10	*Coventry C*	20	0	**20**	**0**
2009–10	*Newcastle U*	7	0	**7**	**0**
2010–11	Chelsea	0	0		
2010–11	*Leicester C*	12	1	**12**	**1**
2011–12	Chelsea	0	0		
2011–12	*Wigan Ath*	3	0	**3**	**0**
2011–12	*Vitesse*	9	0		
2012–13	Chelsea	0	0		
2012–13	*Vitesse*	31	1		
2013–14	Chelsea	0	0	**2**	**0**
2013–14	*Vitesse*	27	4	**67**	**5**
2014–15	Sunderland	28	0		
2015–16	Sunderland	33	4		
2016–17	Sunderland	21	3	**82**	**7**
2016–17	Crystal Palace	11	2		
2017–18	Crystal Palace	28	5		

2018–19 Crystal Palace 36 3
2019–20 Crystal Palace 29 3 **104 13**

VICTOR CAMARASA (M) 149 13
H: 6 0 W: 12 00 b.Meliana 28-5-94
Internationals: Spain U21.
2012–13 Levante 0 0
2013–14 Levante 3 0
2014–15 Levante 24 2
2015–16 Levante 34 2
2016–17 Levante 0 0 **61 4**
2016–17 *Alaves* 31 3 **31 3**
2017–18 Real Betis 24 1
2018–19 Real Betis 0 0
2018–19 *Cardiff C* 32 5 **32 5**
2019–20 Real Betis 0 0 **24 1**
On loan from Real Betis.
2019–20 Crystal Palace 1 0 **1 0**

WARD, Joel (D) 331 11
H: 6 2 W: 11 13 b.Emsworth 29-10-89
2008–09 Portsmouth 0 0
2008–09 *Bournemouth* 21 1 **21 1**
2009–10 Portsmouth 3 0
2010–11 Portsmouth 42 3
2011–12 Portsmouth 44 3 **89 6**
2012–13 Crystal Palace 25 0
2013–14 Crystal Palace 36 0
2014–15 Crystal Palace 37 1
2015–16 Crystal Palace 30 2
2016–17 Crystal Palace 38 0
2017–18 Crystal Palace 19 0
2018–19 Crystal Palace 7 1
2019–20 Crystal Palace 29 0 **221 4**

WICKHAM, Connor (F) 220 43
H: 6 0 W: 14 01 b.Hereford 31-3-93
Internationals: England U16, U17, U19, U21.
2008–09 Ipswich T 2 0
2009–10 Ipswich T 26 4
2010–11 Ipswich T 37 9 **65 13**
2011–12 Sunderland 16 1
2012–13 Sunderland 12 0
2012–13 *Sheffield W* 6 1
2013–14 Sunderland 15 5
2013–14 *Sheffield W* 11 8
2013–14 *Leeds U* 5 0 **5 0**
2014–15 Sunderland 36 5 **79 11**
2015–16 Crystal Palace 21 5
2016–17 Crystal Palace 8 2
2017–18 Crystal Palace 0 0
2018–19 Crystal Palace 6 0
2019–20 Crystal Palace 6 1 **41 8**
2019–20 *Sheffield W* 13 2 **30 11**

WOODS, Sam (D) 3 1
b.Bromley 11-9-98
2018–19 Crystal Palace 0 0
2019–20 Crystal Palace 0 0
2019–20 *Hamilton A* 3 1 **3 1**

ZAHA, Wilfried (F) 341 49
H: 5 11 W: 10 05 b.Ivory Coast 10-11-92
Internationals: England U19, U21, Full caps. Ivory Coast Full caps.
2009–10 Crystal Palace 1 0
2010–11 Crystal Palace 41 1
2011–12 Crystal Palace 41 6
2012–13 Crystal Palace 43 6
2012–13 Manchester U 0 0
2013–14 Manchester U 2 0 **2 0**
2013–14 *Cardiff C* 12 0 **12 0**
2014–15 Crystal Palace 31 4
2015–16 Crystal Palace 34 2
2016–17 Crystal Palace 35 7
2017–18 Crystal Palace 29 9
2018–19 Crystal Palace 34 10
2019–20 Crystal Palace 38 4 **327 49**

Players retained or with offer of contract
Akrobor-Boateng, David Lionel; Aveiro, Brandon Paulo Vale; Baghuelou-Rich, Jay Noah; Banks, Scott Brian; Boateng, Malachi; Bryon, Lewis; Gonzalez Quintero, Kevin; Hobbs, Lewis James; Robertson, Sean Dominic; Webber, Oliver Henry.

Scholars
Addy, Tetteh-Quaye; Ajayi, Joshua; Bello, Lion; Chamberlin-Gayle, Jashaun Deviente; Gordon, John-Kymani Linton Michael; Henderson, Kyran Kayode Gavin Tidoye; Jessup, Cameron Lewis; Luthra, Rohan; Olopade, Denzelle; Omilabu, David Oluwatimileyin; Parris, Kamari; Quick, Daniel James; Rak-Sakyi, Jesurun; Russell, Jacob Luke; Russell, Jude Thomas; Siddik, Cardo; Smith, Rowan Darren; Steele, Aidan Daniel; Street, Robert Nicholas; Thiselton, Dylan; Watson, Noah Christopher; Woodman, Deonysus Sangai; Wright, Ellison Paul.

DERBY CO (29)

ANYA, Ikechi (M) 190 12
H: 5 5 W: 11 04 b.Glasgow 3-1-88
Internationals: Scotland Full caps.
2004–05 Wycombe W 3 0
2005–06 Wycombe W 2 0
2006–07 Wycombe W 13 0
2007–08 Wycombe W 0 0 **18 0**
2008–09 Northampton T 14 3 **14 3**
From Sevilla Atletico.
2010–11 Celta Vigo 1 0 **1 0**
2011–12 Granada 0 0
2012–13 Watford 25 3
2013–14 Watford 35 5
2014–15 Watford 35 0
2015–16 Watford 28 0
2016–17 Watford 1 0 **124 8**
2016–17 Derby Co 26 1
2017–18 Derby Co 7 0
2018–19 Derby Co 0 0
2019–20 Derby Co 0 0 **33 1**

BENNETT, Mason (F) 115 9
H: 5 10 W: 10 02 b.Shirebrook 15-7-96
Internationals: England U16, U17, U19.
2011–12 Derby Co 9 0
2012–13 Derby Co 6 0
2013–14 Derby Co 13 1
2013–14 *Chesterfield* 5 0 **5 0**
2014–15 Derby Co 2 0
2014–15 *Bradford C* 11 1 **11 1**
2015–16 Derby Co 0 0
2015–16 *Burton Alb* 16 1 **16 1**
2016–17 Derby Co 2 0
2017–18 Derby Co 3 0
2017–18 *Notts Co* 2 1 **2 1**
2018–19 Derby Co 30 3
2019–20 Derby Co 7 0 **72 4**
2019–20 *Millwall* 9 2 **9 2**

BIELIK, Krystian (M) 66 3
H: 5 10 W: 11 00 b.Vrinnevi 4-1-98
Internationals: Poland U16, U17, U18, U19, U21, Full caps.
2014–15 Legia Warsaw 5 0 **5 0**
2014–15 Arsenal 0 0
2015–16 Arsenal 0 0
2016–17 Arsenal 0 0
2016–17 *Birmingham C* 10 0 **10 0**
2017–18 Arsenal 0 0
2017–18 *Walsall* 0 0
2018–19 Arsenal 0 0
2018–19 *Charlton Ath* 31 3 **31 3**
2019–20 Derby Co 20 0 **20 0**

BIRD, Max (M) 26 0
H: 6 0 W: 10 10 b.Burton 18-9-00
2017–18 Derby Co 0 0
2018–19 Derby Co 4 0
2019–20 Derby Co 22 0 **26 0**

BOGLE, Jayden (D) 77 3
b. 27-7-00
Internationals: England U20.
From Stoke C.
2017–18 Derby Co 0 0
2018–19 Derby Co 40 2
2019–20 Derby Co 37 1 **77 3**

BROWN, Jordan (D) 1 0
b. 21-6-01
2019–20 Derby Co 1 0 **1 0**

BUCHANAN, Lee (D) 5 0
b. 7-3-01
Internationals: England U19.
2018–19 Derby Co 0 0
2019–20 Derby Co 5 0 **5 0**

CARSON, Scott (G) 468 0
H: 6 0 W: 13 06 b.Whitehaven 3-9-85
Internationals: England U18, U21, B, Full caps.
2002–03 Leeds U 0 0
2003–04 Leeds U 3 0
2004–05 Leeds U 0 0 **3 0**
2004–05 Liverpool 4 0
2005–06 Liverpool 0 0
2005–06 *Sheffield W* 9 0 **9 0**
2006–07 Liverpool 0 0
2006–07 *Charlton Ath* 36 0 **36 0**
2007–08 Liverpool 0 0 **4 0**
2007–08 *Aston Villa* 35 0 **35 0**
2008–09 WBA 35 0
2009–10 WBA 43 0
2010–11 WBA 32 0 **110 0**
2011–12 Bursaspor 34 0
2012–13 Bursaspor 29 0 **63 0**
2013–14 Wigan Ath 16 0
2014–15 Wigan Ath 34 0 **50 0**
2015–16 Derby Co 36 0
2016–17 Derby Co 46 0
2017–18 Derby Co 46 0
2018–19 Derby Co 30 0
2019–20 Derby Co 0 0 **158 0**
2019–20 *Manchester C* 0 0

CLARKE, Matthew (M) 189 8
H: 5 11 W: 11 00 b.Ipswich 22-9-96
2013–14 Ipswich T 0 0
2014–15 Ipswich T 4 0
2015–16 Ipswich T 0 0 **4 0**
2015–16 *Portsmouth* 29 1
2016–17 Portsmouth 33 1
2017–18 Portsmouth 42 2
2018–19 Portsmouth 46 3 **150 7**
2019–20 Brighton & HA 0 0
2019–20 Derby Co 35 1 **35 1**

DAVIES, Curtis (D) 477 23
H: 6 2 W: 11 13 b.Waltham Forest 15-3-85
Internationals: England U21.
2003–04 Luton T 6 0
2004–05 Luton T 44 1
2005–06 Luton T 6 1 **56 2**
2005–06 WBA 33 2
2006–07 WBA 32 0
2007–08 WBA 0 0 **65 2**
2007–08 *Aston Villa* 12 1
2008–09 Aston Villa 35 1
2009–10 Aston Villa 2 1
2010–11 Aston Villa 0 0 **49 3**
2010–11 *Leicester C* 12 0 **12 0**
2010–11 Birmingham C 6 0
2011–12 Birmingham C 42 5
2012–13 Birmingham C 41 6 **89 11**
2013–14 Hull C 37 2
2014–15 Hull C 21 0
2015–16 Hull C 39 2
2016–17 Hull C 26 0 **123 4**
2017–18 Derby Co 46 1
2018–19 Derby Co 5 0
2019–20 Derby Co 32 0 **83 1**

EVANS, George (M) 138 8
H: 6 0 W: 11 12 b.Cheadle 13-12-94
Internationals: England U16, U17, U19.
2012–13 Manchester C 0 0
2013–14 Manchester C 0 0
2013–14 *Crewe Alex* 23 1 **23 1**
2014–15 Manchester C 0 0
2014–15 *Scunthorpe U* 16 1 **16 1**
2015–16 Manchester C 0 0
2015–16 *Walsall* 12 3 **12 3**
2015–16 Reading 6 0
2016–17 Reading 35 2
2017–18 Reading 18 1 **59 3**
2018–19 Derby Co 11 0
2019–20 Derby Co 17 0 **28 0**

FORSYTH, Craig (M) 304 19
H: 6 0 W: 12 00 b.Carnoustie 24-2-89
Internationals: Scotland Full caps.
2006–07 Dundee 1 0
2007–08 Dundee 0 0
2007–08 *Montrose* 9 0 **9 0**
2008–09 Dundee 1 0
2008–09 *Arbroath* 26 2 **26 2**
2009–10 Dundee 24 2
2010–11 Dundee 33 8 **59 10**
2011–12 Watford 20 3
2012–13 Watford 2 0 **22 3**
2012–13 *Bradford C* 7 0 **7 0**
2012–13 *Derby Co* 10 0
2013–14 Derby Co 46 2
2014–15 Derby Co 44 1
2015–16 Derby Co 12 0
2016–17 Derby Co 3 1
2017–18 Derby Co 31 0
2018–19 Derby Co 13 0
2019–20 Derby Co 22 0 **181 4**

FRENCH, Samuel (G) 0 0
b. 27-2-01
From Leicester C.
2019–20 Derby Co 0 0
2019–20 *Stevenage* 0 0

HECTOR-INGRAM, Jahmal (F) 1 0
Internationals: England U16, U17.
From West Ham U.
2019–20 Derby Co 1 0 **1 0**

HOLMES, Duane (M) 169 15
H: 5 8 W: 10 03 b.Wakefield 6-11-94
Internationals: USA Full caps.
2012–13 Huddersfield T 0 0
2013–14 Huddersfield T 16 0
2013–14 *Yeovil T* 5 0 **5 0**
2014–15 Huddersfield T 0 0
2014–15 *Bury* 6 0 **6 0**
2015–16 Huddersfield T 6 1 **22 1**
2016–17 Scunthorpe U 32 3
2017–18 Scunthorpe U 45 7
2018–19 Scunthorpe U 1 0 **78 10**
2018–19 Derby Co 25 2
2019–20 Derby Co 33 2 **58 4**

HUDDLESTONE, Tom (M) 459 18
H: 6 2 W: 11 02 b.Nottingham 28-12-86
Internationals: England U16, U17, U19, U20, U21, Full caps.
2003–04 Derby Co 43 0
2004–05 Derby Co 45 0
2005–06 Tottenham H 4 0
2005–06 *Wolverhampton W* 13 1 **13 1**
2006–07 Tottenham H 21 1
2007–08 Tottenham H 28 3
2008–09 Tottenham H 22 0
2009–10 Tottenham H 33 2
2010–11 Tottenham H 14 2
2011–12 Tottenham H 2 0
2012–13 Tottenham H 20 0
2013–14 Tottenham H 0 0 **144 8**
2013–14 Hull C 36 3
2014–15 Hull C 31 0
2015–16 Hull C 37 2
2016–17 Hull C 31 1 **135 6**
2017–18 Derby Co 44 2
2018–19 Derby Co 24 0
2019–20 Derby Co 11 1 **167 3**

JOZEFZOON, Florian (F) 198 22
H: 5 8 W: 11 00 b.Amsterdam 9-2-91
Internationals: Netherlands U19, U21.
2010–11 Ajax 4 0
2011–12 Ajax 0 0 **4 0**
2011–12 *NAC Breda* 16 0 **16 0**
2012–13 RKC Waalwijk 34 7 **34 7**
2013–14 PSV Eindhoven 16 2
2014–15 PSV Eindhoven 15 2
2015–16 PSV Eindhoven 9 1
2016–17 PSV Eindhoven 5 0 **45 5**
2016–17 Brentford 19 1
2017–18 Brentford 39 7 **58 8**
2018–19 Derby Co 27 2
2019–20 Derby Co 14 0 **41 2**

KEOGH, Richard (D) 549 19
H: 6 0 W: 11 02 b.Harlow 11-8-86
Internationals: Republic of Ireland U21, Full caps.
2004–05 Stoke C 0 0
2005–06 Bristol C 9 1
2005–06 *Wycombe W* 3 0 **3 0**
2006–07 Bristol C 31 2
2007–08 Bristol C 0 0 **40 3**
2007–08 *Huddersfield T* 9 1 **9 1**
2007–08 *Carlisle U* 7 0
2007–08 *Cheltenham T* 10 0 **10 0**
2008–09 Carlisle U 32 1
2009–10 Carlisle U 41 3 **80 4**
2010–11 Coventry C 46 1
2011–12 Coventry C 45 0 **91 1**
2012–13 Derby Co 46 4
2013–14 Derby Co 41 1
2014–15 Derby Co 45 0
2015–16 Derby Co 46 1
2016–17 Derby Co 42 0
2017–18 Derby Co 42 1
2018–19 Derby Co 46 3
2019–20 Derby Co 8 0 **316 10**

KNIGHT, Jason (M) 31 6
b. 13-2-01
Internationals: Republic of Ireland U17, U18, U19, U21.
2018–19 Derby Co 0 0
2019–20 Derby Co 31 6 **31 6**

LAWRENCE, Tom (F) 216 39
H: 5 9 W: 11 11 b.Wrexham 13-1-94
Internationals: Wales U17, U19, U21, Full caps.
2012–13 Manchester U 0 0
2013–14 Manchester U 1 0 **1 0**
2013–14 *Carlisle U* 9 3 **9 3**
2013–14 *Yeovil T* 19 2 **19 2**
2014–15 Leicester C 3 0
2014–15 *Rotherham U* 6 1 **6 1**
2015–16 Leicester C 0 0
2015–16 *Blackburn R* 21 2 **21 2**
2015–16 *Cardiff C* 14 0 **14 0**
2016–17 Leicester C 0 0 **3 0**
2016–17 *Ipswich T* 34 9 **34 9**
2017–18 Derby Co 39 6
2018–19 Derby Co 33 6
2019–20 Derby Co 37 10 **109 22**

LOWE, Max (D) 86 2
H: 5 9 W: 11 09 b.Birmingham 11-5-97
Internationals: England U16, U17, U18, U20.
2013–14 Derby Co 0 0
2014–15 Derby Co 0 0
2015–16 Derby Co 0 0
2016–17 Derby Co 9 0
2017–18 Derby Co 0 0
2017–18 *Shrewsbury T* 12 0 **12 0**
2018–19 Derby Co 3 0
2018–19 *Aberdeen* 33 2 **33 2**
2019–20 Derby Co 29 0 **41 0**

MALONE, Scott (D) 303 23
H: 6 2 W: 11 11 b.Rowley Regis 25-3-91
Internationals: England U19.
2008–09 Wolverhampton W 0 0
2008–09 *Ujpest* 7 1 **7 1**
2009–10 Wolverhampton W 0 0
2009–10 *Southend U* 17 0 **17 0**
2010–11 Wolverhampton W 0 0
2010–11 *Burton Alb* 22 1 **22 1**
2011–12 Wolverhampton W 0 0
2011–12 Bournemouth 32 5 **32 5**
2012–13 Millwall 15 1
2013–14 Millwall 33 3
2014–15 Millwall 20 1 **68 5**
2014–15 Cardiff C 13 0
2015–16 Cardiff C 41 2 **54 2**
2016–17 Fulham 36 6 **36 6**
2017–18 Huddersfield T 22 0 **22 0**
2018–19 Derby Co 27 2
2019–20 Derby Co 18 1 **45 3**

MARRIOTT, Jack (F) 200 59
H: 5 8 W: 11 03 b.Beverley 9-9-94
2012–13 Ipswich T 1 0
2013–14 Ipswich T 1 0
2013–14 *Gillingham* 1 0 **1 0**
2014–15 Ipswich T 0 0 **2 0**
2014–15 *Carlisle U* 4 0 **4 0**
2014–15 *Colchester U* 5 1 **5 1**
2015–16 Luton T 40 14
2016–17 Luton T 39 8 **79 22**
2017–18 Peterborough U 44 27 **44 27**
2018–19 Derby Co 33 7
2019–20 Derby Co 32 2 **65 9**

MARTIN, Chris (F) 451 124
H: 6 2 W: 12 06 b.Beccles 4-11-88
Internationals: England U19. Scotland Full caps.
2006–07 Norwich C 18 4
2007–08 Norwich C 7 0
2008–09 Norwich C 0 0
2008–09 *Luton T* 40 11 **40 11**
2009–10 Norwich C 42 17
2010–11 Norwich C 30 4
2011–12 Norwich C 4 0
2011–12 *Crystal Palace* 26 7 **26 7**
2012–13 Norwich C 1 0 **102 25**
2012–13 *Swindon T* 12 1 **12 1**
2012–13 *Derby Co* 13 2
2013–14 Derby Co 44 20
2014–15 Derby Co 35 18
2015–16 Derby Co 45 15
2016–17 Derby Co 5 0
2016–17 *Fulham* 31 10 **31 10**
2017–18 Derby Co 23 1
2017–18 *Reading* 10 1 **10 1**
2018–19 Derby Co 0 0
2018–19 *Hull C* 30 2 **30 2**
2019–20 Derby Co 35 11 **200 67**

MITCHELL, Jonathan (G) 35 0
H: 5 11 W: 13 08 b.Hartlepool 24-11-94
Internationals: England U21.
2014–15 Derby Co 0 0
2015–16 Derby Co 0 0
2015–16 *Luton T* 5 0 **5 0**
2016–17 Derby Co 0 0
2017–18 Derby Co 0 0
2018–19 Derby Co 0 0
2018–19 *Oxford U* 10 0 **10 0**
2018–19 *Shrewsbury T* 9 0 **9 0**
2019–20 Derby Co 0 0
2019–20 *Macclesfield T* 11 0 **11 0**

MITCHELL-LAWSON, Jayden (M) 11 2
b. 17-9-99
From Swindon T.
2018–19 Derby Co 1 0
2019–20 Derby Co 0 0 **1 0**
2019–20 *Bristol R* 10 2 **10 2**

RAVAS, Henrich (G) 0 0
From Boston U.
2018–19 Derby Co 0 0
2019–20 Derby Co 0 0

ROONEY, Wayne (F) 559 236
H: 5 10 W: 12 13 b.Liverpool 24-10-85
Internationals: England U15, U16, U19, Full caps.
2002–03 Everton 33 6
2003–04 Everton 34 9
2004–05 Manchester U 29 11
2005–06 Manchester U 36 16
2006–07 Manchester U 35 14
2007–08 Manchester U 27 12
2008–09 Manchester U 30 12
2009–10 Manchester U 32 26
2010–11 Manchester U 28 11
2011–12 Manchester U 34 27
2012–13 Manchester U 27 12
2013–14 Manchester U 29 17
2014–15 Manchester U 33 12
2015–16 Manchester U 28 8
2016–17 Manchester U 25 5 **393 183**
2017–18 Everton 31 10 **98 25**
2018 DC United 20 12
2019 DC United 28 11 **48 23**
2019–20 Derby Co 20 5 **20 5**

ROOS, Kelle (G) 87 0
H: 6 4 W: 14 02 b.Rijkevoort 31-5-92
2013–14 Derby Co 0 0
2014–15 Derby Co 0 0
2015–16 Derby Co 0 0
2015–16 *Rotherham U* 4 0 **4 0**
2015–16 *AFC Wimbledon* 17 0 **17 0**
2016–17 Derby Co 0 0
2016–17 *Bristol R* 16 0 **16 0**
2017–18 Derby Co 0 0
2017–18 *Port Vale* 8 0 **8 0**
2017–18 *Plymouth Arg* 4 0 **4 0**
2018–19 Derby Co 16 0
2019–20 Derby Co 22 0 **38 0**

SHINNIE, Graeme (D) 323 16
b.Aberdeen 4-8-91
Internationals: Scotland U21, Full caps.
2009–10 Inverness CT 1 0
2010–11 Inverness CT 19 0
2011–12 Inverness CT 26 1
2012–13 Inverness CT 37 0
2013–14 Inverness CT 36 3
2014–15 Inverness CT 37 2 **156 6**
2015–16 Aberdeen 37 1
2016–17 Aberdeen 36 2
2017–18 Aberdeen 35 2
2018–19 Aberdeen 36 3 **144 8**
2019–20 Derby Co 23 2 **23 2**

SIBLEY, Louie (M) 11 5
b. 1-9-01
Internationals: England U17, U18, U19.
2019–20 Derby Co 11 5 **11 5**

WAGHORN, Martyn (F) 353 97
H: 5 9 W: 13 01 b.South Shields 23-1-90
Internationals: England U19, U21.
2007–08 Sunderland 3 0
2008–09 Sunderland 1 0
2008–09 *Charlton Ath* 7 1 **7 1**
2009–10 Sunderland 0 0
2009–10 *Leicester C* 43 12
2010–11 Sunderland 2 0 **6 0**
2010–11 Leicester C 30 4
2011–12 Leicester C 4 1
2011–12 *Hull C* 5 1 **5 1**
2012–13 Leicester C 24 3
2013–14 Leicester C 2 0 **103 20**
2013–14 *Millwall* 14 3 **14 3**
2013–14 Wigan Ath 15 5
2014–15 Wigan Ath 23 3 **38 8**
2015–16 Rangers 25 20
2016–17 Rangers 32 7 **57 27**
2017–18 Ipswich T 44 16 **44 16**
2018–19 Derby Co 36 9
2019–20 Derby Co 43 12 **79 21**

WHITTAKER, Morgan (F) 16 1
b. 7-1-01
Internationals: England U16, U17, U18, U19.
2019–20 Derby Co 16 1 **16 1**

WILSON, Tyree (M) **0 0**
2018–19 Derby Co 0 0
2019–20 Derby Co 0 0

WISDOM, Andre (D) **157 0**
H: 6 1 W: 12 04 b.Leeds 9-5-93
Internationals: England U16, U17, U19, U21.
2009–10 Liverpool 0 0
2010–11 Liverpool 0 0
2011–12 Liverpool 0 0
2012–13 Liverpool 12 0
2013–14 Liverpool 2 0
2013–14 *Derby Co* 34 0
2014–15 Liverpool 0 0
2014–15 *WBA* 24 0 **24 0**
2015–16 Liverpool 0 0
2015–16 *Norwich C* 10 0 **10 0**
2016–17 Liverpool 0 0 **14 0**
2016–17 *Red Bull Salzburg* 16 0 **16 0**
2017–18 Derby Co 30 0
2018–19 Derby Co 11 0
2019–20 Derby Co 18 0 **93 0**

YATES, Matthew (G) **0 0**
Internationals: England U17.
2017–18 Derby Co 0 0
2018–19 Derby Co 0 0
2019–20 Derby Co 0 0

Players retained or with offer of contract
Aghatise, Osazee; Bateman, Joseph Joshua; Cresswell, Cameron Ian; Dixon, Connor Liam; Minkley, Callum; Shonibare, Joshua; Wassall, Ethan Luca.

Scholars
Bardell, Max James; Brown, Archibald Norman; Cashin, Eiran Joe; Charles, Jaden Gary; Cybulski, Bartosz Marcin; Ebosele, Festy Oseiwe; Foster, Bradley; Grewa-Pollard, William Michael; Halwax, Harry; Jinkinson, Hugo Raymond Junior; Matthews, Alexander Niall; McDonald, Kornell Mark Marshall; Perez, De Gracia Andres Alvaro; Rogers, Jack Aaron; Solomon, Harrison James; Stretton, Jack Kirk; Thompson, Liam Francis; Thompson, Sebastian Blake.

DONCASTER R (30)

AMOS, Danny (D) **6 0**
H: 5 11 W: 10 10 b.Sheffield 22-12-99
Internationals: Northern Ireland U19, U21.
2016–17 Doncaster R 0 0
2017–18 Doncaster R 3 0
2018–19 Doncaster R 1 0
2019–20 Doncaster R 2 0 **6 0**

ANDERSON, Thomas (M) **143 6**
H: 6 4 W: 13 01 b.Burnley 2-9-93
2012–13 Burnley 0 0
2013–14 Burnley 0 0
2014–15 Burnley 0 0
2014–15 *Carlisle U* 8 0 **8 0**
2015–16 Burnley 0 0
2015–16 *Chesterfield* 18 0
2016–17 Burnley 0 0
2016–17 *Chesterfield* 35 2 **53 2**
2017–18 Burnley 0 0
2017–18 *Port Vale* 20 0 **20 0**
2017–18 *Doncaster R* 7 2
2018–19 Doncaster R 23 1
2019–20 Doncaster R 32 1 **62 4**

BAPTISTE, Alex (D) **484 24**
H: 6 0 W: 11 11 b.Sutton-in-Ashfield 31-1-86
2002–03 Mansfield T 4 0
2003–04 Mansfield T 17 0
2004–05 Mansfield T 41 1
2005–06 Mansfield T 41 1
2006–07 Mansfield T 46 3
2007–08 Mansfield T 25 0 **174 5**
2008–09 Blackpool 21 1
2009–10 Blackpool 42 3
2010–11 Blackpool 21 2
2011–12 Blackpool 43 1
2012–13 Blackpool 43 1 **170 8**
2013–14 Bolton W 39 4
2014–15 Bolton W 0 0 **39 4**
2014–15 *Blackburn R* 32 3 **32 3**
2015–16 Middlesbrough 0 0
2015–16 *Sheffield U* 11 1 **11 1**
2016–17 Middlesbrough 0 0
2016–17 *Preston NE* 24 3 **24 3**
2017–18 QPR 26 0
2018–19 QPR 4 0 **30 0**
2018–19 *Luton T* 2 0 **2 0**
2019–20 Doncaster R 2 0 **2 0**

BINGHAM, Rakish (F) **146 22**
H: 6 0 W: 12 00 b.Newham 25-10-93
2011–12 Wigan Ath 0 0
2012–13 Wigan Ath 0 0
2013–14 Wigan Ath 0 0
2014–15 Mansfield T 28 6 **28 6**
2014–15 *Hartlepool U* 5 1
2015–16 Hartlepool U 31 4 **36 5**
2016–17 Hamilton A 30 5
2017–18 Hamilton A 32 5
2018–19 Hamilton A 2 0 **64 10**
2018–19 Cheltenham T 10 0 **10 0**
2019–20 Doncaster R 8 1 **8 1**
Transferred to Dundee U, February 2020.

BLAIR, Matty (M) **255 20**
H: 5 10 W: 11 09 b.Coventry 30-11-87
Internationals: England C.
2012–13 York C 44 6 **44 6**
2013–14 Fleetwood T 24 3
2013–14 *Northampton T* 3 1 **3 1**
2014–15 Fleetwood T 8 0 **32 3**
2014–15 *Cambridge U* 2 0 **2 0**
2014–15 Mansfield T 3 0
2015–16 Mansfield T 32 2 **35 2**
2016–17 Doncaster R 45 3
2017–18 Doncaster R 40 2
2018–19 Doncaster R 42 3
2019–20 Doncaster R 12 0 **139 8**

BLANEY, Shane (D) **0 0**
H: 6 3 W: 12 06 b.Letterkenny 20-1-99
From Finn Harps.
2018–19 Doncaster R 0 0
2019–20 Doncaster R 0 0

BOOCOCK, Rieves (F) **1 0**
b.Sheffield 22-9-00
2018–19 Doncaster R 1 0
2019–20 Doncaster R 0 0 **1 0**

COLE, Devante (F) **158 32**
H: 6 1 W: 11 06 b.Alderley Edge 10-5-95
Internationals: England U16, U17, U18, U19.
2013–14 Manchester C 0 0
2014–15 Manchester C 0 0
2014–15 *Barnsley* 19 5 **19 5**
2014–15 *Milton Keynes D* 15 3 **15 3**
2015–16 Bradford C 19 5 **19 5**
2015–16 Fleetwood T 14 2
2016–17 Fleetwood T 35 5
2017–18 Fleetwood T 28 10 **77 17**
2017–18 Wigan Ath 6 0
2018–19 Wigan Ath 0 0 **6 0**
2018–19 *Burton Alb* 13 2 **13 2**
2019–20 *Motherwell* 0 0
2019–20 Doncaster R 9 0 **9 0**

COPPINGER, James (F) **656 73**
H: 5 7 W: 10 03 b.Middlesbrough 10-1-81
Internationals: England U16.
1997–98 Newcastle U 0 0
1998–99 Newcastle U 0 0
1999–2000 Newcastle U 0 0
1999–2000 *Hartlepool U* 10 3
2000–01 Newcastle U 1 0
2001–02 Newcastle U 0 0 **1 0**
2001–02 *Hartlepool U* 14 2 **24 5**
2002–03 Exeter C 43 5 **43 5**
2004–05 Doncaster R 31 0
2005–06 Doncaster R 36 5
2006–07 Doncaster R 39 4
2007–08 Doncaster R 39 3
2008–09 Doncaster R 32 5
2009–10 Doncaster R 39 4
2010–11 Doncaster R 40 7
2011–12 Doncaster R 38 2
2012–13 Doncaster R 25 2
2012–13 *Nottingham F* 6 0 **6 0**
2013–14 Doncaster R 41 4
2014–15 Doncaster R 34 4
2015–16 Doncaster R 39 3
2016–17 Doncaster R 39 10
2017–18 Doncaster R 38 3
2018–19 Doncaster R 43 4
2019–20 Doncaster R 29 3 **582 63**

GIBBONS, Myron (F) **0 0**
b.Doncaster 15-11-00
2018–19 Doncaster R 0 0
2019–20 Doncaster R 0 0

GOMES, Madger (M) **28 0**
b.Alicante 1-2-97
Internationals: Spain U17, U18.
From Villareal, Liverpool.
2017–18 Leeds U 0 0
2018–19 Istra 1961 5 0 **5 0**
2019–20 Doncaster R 23 0 **23 0**

GREAVES, Anthony (M) **0 0**
b. 17-11-00
2018–19 Doncaster R 0 0
2019–20 Doncaster R 0 0

HALLIDAY, Bradley (M) **207 3**
H: 5 11 W: 10 10 b.Redcar 10-7-95
2013–14 Middlesbrough 0 0
2014–15 Middlesbrough 0 0
2014–15 *York C* 24 1 **24 1**
2015–16 Middlesbrough 0 0
2015–16 *Hartlepool U* 6 0 **6 0**
2015–16 *Accrington S* 32 0 **32 0**
2016–17 Middlesbrough 0 0
2016–17 Cambridge U 30 1
2017–18 Cambridge U 43 1
2018–19 Cambridge U 38 0 **111 2**
2019–20 Doncaster R 34 0 **34 0**

HASANI, Lirak (M) **2 0**
b.Doncaster 25-6-02
2018–19 Doncaster R 2 0
2019–20 Doncaster R 0 0 **2 0**

HORTON, Branden (D) **0 0**
b. 9-9-00
2017–18 Doncaster R 0 0
2018–19 Doncaster R 0 0
2019–20 Doncaster R 0 0

JAMES, Reece (D) **116 4**
H: 5 6 W: 11 03 b.Bacup 7-11-93
2012–13 Manchester U 0 0
2013–14 Manchester U 0 0
2013–14 *Carlisle U* 1 0 **1 0**
2014–15 Manchester U 0 0
2014–15 *Rotherham U* 7 0 **7 0**
2014–15 *Huddersfield T* 6 1 **6 1**
2015–16 Wigan Ath 26 1
2016–17 Wigan Ath 0 0
2017–18 Wigan Ath 22 0 **48 1**
2018–19 Sunderland 27 0 **27 0**
2019–20 Doncaster R 27 2 **27 2**

JONES, Louis (G) **0 0**
2015–16 Doncaster R 0 0
2016–17 Doncaster R 0 0
2017–18 Doncaster R 0 0
2018–19 Doncaster R 0 0
2019–20 Doncaster R 0 0

KIWOMYA, Alex (M) **59 8**
H: 5 10 W: 10 08 b.Sheffield 20-5-96
Internationals: England U16, U17, U18, U19.
2014–15 Chelsea 0 0
2014–15 *Barnsley* 5 0 **5 0**
2015–16 Chelsea 0 0
2015–16 *Fleetwood T* 4 0 **4 0**
2016–17 Chelsea 0 0
2016–17 *Crewe Alex* 34 7 **34 7**
2017–18 Doncaster R 12 1
2018–19 Doncaster R 3 0
2019–20 Doncaster R 1 0 **16 1**

LAWLOR, Ian (G) **91 0**
H: 6 4 W: 12 08 b.Dublin 27-10-94
Internationals: Republic of Ireland U17, U19, U21.
2011–12 Manchester C 0 0
2012–13 Manchester C 0 0
2013–14 Manchester C 0 0
2014–15 Manchester C 0 0
2015–16 Manchester C 0 0
2015–16 *Barnet* 5 0 **5 0**
2015–16 *Bury* 12 0 **12 0**
2016–17 Doncaster R 19 0
2017–18 Doncaster R 34 0
2018–19 Doncaster R 10 0
2019–20 Doncaster R 7 0 **70 0**
2019–20 *Scunthorpe U* 4 0 **4 0**

LONGBOTTOM, William (F) **4 0**
H: 5 9 W: 9 11 b.Leeds 12-12-98
2015–16 Doncaster R 1 0
2016–17 Doncaster R 3 0
2017–18 Doncaster R 0 0
2018–19 Doncaster R 0 0
2019–20 Doncaster R 0 0 **4 0**
Transferred to Waterford, January 2020.

OKENABIRHIE, Fejiri (F) **63 14**
H: 5 10 W: 11 09 b. 25-2-96
Internationals: England C.
2013–14 Stevenage 3 0
2014–15 Stevenage 0 0
2015–16 Stevenage 0 0 **3 0**
From Harrow Bor, Dagenham & R.
2018–19 Shrewsbury T 38 10
2019–20 Shrewsbury T 17 2 **55 12**
2019–20 Doncaster R 5 2 **5 2**

SADLIER, Kieran (F) 58 15
H: 5 10 W: 10 06 b. 14-9-94
Internationals: Republic of Ireland U17, U19, U21.
2013–14 West Ham U 0 0
2014–15 St Mirren 11 1 **11 1**
2015–16 Peterborough U 0 0
2015–16 *FC Halifax T* 0 0
From Sligo R, Cork C.
2018–19 Doncaster R 14 3
2019–20 Doncaster R 33 11 **47 14**

TAYLOR, Jon (M) 337 54
H: 5 11 W: 12 04 b.Liverpool 23-12-89
2009–10 Shrewsbury T 2 0
2010–11 Shrewsbury T 20 6
2011–12 Shrewsbury T 33 0
2012–13 Shrewsbury T 37 7
2013–14 Shrewsbury T 41 9 **133 22**
2014–15 Peterborough U 24 3
2015–16 Peterborough U 44 11 **68 14**
2016–17 Rotherham U 42 4
2017–18 Rotherham U 25 4
2018–19 Rotherham U 41 4
2019–20 Rotherham U 0 0 **108 12**
2019–20 Doncaster R 28 6 **28 6**

WATSON, Jack (F) 0 0
b. 4-7-02
2019–20 Doncaster R 0 0

WATTERS, Max (D) 5 0
2019–20 Doncaster R 5 0 **5 0**

WHITEMAN, Ben (M) 146 21
b.Rochdale 17-6-96
2014–15 Sheffield U 0 0
2015–16 Sheffield U 6 0
2016–17 Sheffield U 2 0 **8 0**
2016–17 *Mansfield T* 23 7 **23 7**
2017–18 Doncaster R 42 6
2018–19 Doncaster R 40 3
2019–20 Doncaster R 33 5 **115 14**

WRIGHT, Joe (D) 109 2
H: 6 4 W: 12 06 b. 26-2-95
Internationals: Wales U21.
2013–14 Huddersfield T 0 0
2014–15 Huddersfield T 0 0
2015–16 Huddersfield T 0 0
2015–16 *Accrington S* 20 0 **20 0**
2016–17 Doncaster R 22 0
2017–18 Doncaster R 33 0
2018–19 Doncaster R 14 2
2019–20 Doncaster R 20 0 **89 2**

Scholars
Bell, Charlie John; Blythe, Benjamin Elliot; Bojang, Ethan; Bottomley, Benjamin Phillip; Clemitson, Joshua Daniel; Conradi, Skar Marius; Cunningham, Lewis Thomas; Derrett, Owan Mackenzie; Dimou, Nathan; Jemson, Maxwell; McGowan, Will; Nelson, Luca David; Ravenhill, Liam; Smith, Martijn Earl; Walker, Elliott; Watson, Jack Charles.

EVERTON (31)

ADENIRAN, Dennis (M) 1 0
H: 5 11 b.London 2-1-99
Internationals: England U17, U18, U19.
2016–17 Fulham 1 0 **1 0**
2017–18 Everton 0 0
2018–19 Everton 0 0
2019–20 Everton 0 0

ANDRE GOMES, Filipe (M) 169 13
H: 6 2 W: 13 01 b.Porto 30-7-93
Internationals: Portugal U17, U28, U19, U20, U21, Full caps.
2012–13 Benfica 7 1
2013–14 Benfica 7 1 **14 2**
2014–15 Valencia 33 4
2015–16 Valencia 30 3 **63 7**
2016–17 Barcelona 30 3
2017–18 Barcelona 16 0 **46 3**
On loan from Barcelona.
2018–19 Everton 27 1
2019–20 Everton 19 0 **46 1**

BAINES, Leighton (D) 493 33
H: 5 8 W: 11 00 b.Liverpool 11-12-84
Internationals: England U21, Full caps.
2002–03 Wigan Ath 6 0
2003–04 Wigan Ath 26 0
2004–05 Wigan Ath 41 1
2005–06 Wigan Ath 37 0
2006–07 Wigan Ath 35 3
2007–08 Wigan Ath 0 0 **145 4**
2007–08 Everton 22 0
2008–09 Everton 31 1
2009–10 Everton 37 1
2010–11 Everton 38 5
2011–12 Everton 33 4
2012–13 Everton 38 5
2013–14 Everton 32 5
2014–15 Everton 31 2
2015–16 Everton 18 2
2016–17 Everton 32 2
2017–18 Everton 22 2
2018–19 Everton 6 0
2019–20 Everton 8 0 **348 29**

BANINGIME, Beni (M) 9 0
H: 5 10 W: 11 00 b.Kinshasa 9-9-98
2017–18 Everton 8 0
2018–19 Everton 0 0
2018–19 *Wigan Ath* 1 0 **1 0**
2019–20 Everton 0 0 **8 0**

BERNARD, Caldeira (M) 219 30
H: 5 4 W: 8 11 b.Belo Horizonte 8-9-92
Internationals: Brazil Full caps.
2011 Atletico Mineiro 23 0
2012 Atletico Mineiro 36 11
2013 Atletico Mineiro 3 1 **62 12**
2013–14 Shaktar Donetsk 18 2
2014–15 Shaktar Donetsk 14 0
2015–16 Shaktar Donetsk 21 2
2016–17 Shaktar Donetsk 24 4
2017–18 Shaktar Donetsk 19 6 **96 14**
2018–19 Everton 34 1
2019–20 Everton 27 3 **61 4**

BESIC, Muhamed (M) 148 4
H: 5 10 W: 11 11 b.Berlin 10-9-92
Internationals: Bosnia-Herzegovina U21, Full caps.
2010–11 Hamburg 3 0
2011–12 Hamburg 0 0
2012–13 Hamburg 0 0 **3 0**
2012–13 Ferencvaros 22 1
2013–14 Ferencvaros 25 0 **47 1**
2014–15 Everton 23 0
2015–16 Everton 12 0
2016–17 Everton 0 0
2017–18 Everton 2 0
2017–18 *Middlesbrough* 15 1
2018–19 Everton 0 0
2018–19 *Middlesbrough* 37 2 **52 3**
2019–20 Everton 0 0 **37 0**
2019–20 *Sheffield U* 9 0 **9 0**

BOWLER, Josh (M) 29 1
b. 5-3-99
2016–17 QPR 1 0 **1 0**
2017–18 Everton 0 0
2018–19 Everton 0 0
2019–20 Everton 0 0
2019–20 *Hull C* 28 1 **28 1**

BRANTHWAITE, Jarrad (M) 13 0
2018–19 Carlisle U 0 0
2019–20 Carlisle U 9 0 **9 0**
2019–20 Everton 4 0 **4 0**

BROADHEAD, Nathan (F) 19 2
H: 5 10 W: 11 07 b.Bangor 5-4-98
Internationals: Wales U17, U19, U20, U21.
2017–18 Everton 0 0
2018–19 Everton 0 0
2019–20 Everton 0 0
2019–20 *Burton Alb* 19 2 **19 2**

CALVERT-LEWIN, Dominic (M) 145 29
b. 16-3-97
Internationals: England U20, U21.
2013–14 Sheffield U 0 0
2014–15 Sheffield U 2 0
2015–16 Sheffield U 9 0
2015–16 *Northampton T* 20 5 **20 5**
2016–17 Sheffield U 0 0 **11 0**
2016–17 Everton 11 1
2017–18 Everton 32 4
2018–19 Everton 35 6
2019–20 Everton 36 13 **114 24**

COLEMAN, Seamus (D) 283 21
H: 6 4 W: 10 07 b.Donegal 11-10-88
Internationals: Republic of Ireland U21, U23, Full caps.
2008–09 Everton 0 0
2009–10 Everton 3 0
2009–10 *Blackpool* 9 1 **9 1**
2010–11 Everton 34 4
2011–12 Everton 18 0
2012–13 Everton 26 0
2013–14 Everton 36 6
2014–15 Everton 35 3
2015–16 Everton 28 1
2016–17 Everton 26 4
2017–18 Everton 12 0
2018–19 Everton 29 2
2019–20 Everton 27 0 **274 20**

CONNOLLY, Callum (D) 112 11
b.Liverpool 23-9-97
Internationals: England U17, U18, U19, U20, U21.
2015–16 Everton 1 0
2015–16 *Barnsley* 3 0 **3 0**
2016–17 Everton 0 0
2016–17 *Wigan Ath* 17 2
2017–18 Everton 0 0
2017–18 *Ipswich T* 34 4 **34 4**
2018–19 Everton 0 0
2018–19 *Wigan Ath* 17 1 **34 3**
2018–19 *Bolton W* 16 2 **16 2**
2019–20 Everton 0 0 **1 0**
2019–20 *Lincoln C* 11 0 **11 0**
2019–20 *Fleetwood T* 13 2 **13 2**

DAVIES, Tom (M) 105 5
b.Liverpool 30-6-98
Internationals: England U16, U17, U18, U19, U21.
2015–16 Everton 2 0
2016–17 Everton 24 2
2017–18 Everton 33 2
2018–19 Everton 16 0
2019–20 Everton 30 1 **105 5**

DELPH, Fabian (D) 234 13
H: 5 8 W: 11 00 b.Bradford 21-11-89
Internationals: England U19, U21, Full caps.
2006–07 Leeds U 1 0
2007–08 Leeds U 1 0
2008–09 Leeds U 42 6
2009–10 Aston Villa 8 0
2010–11 Aston Villa 7 0
2011–12 Aston Villa 11 0
2011–12 *Leeds U* 5 0 **49 6**
2012–13 Aston Villa 24 0
2013–14 Aston Villa 34 3
2014–15 Aston Villa 28 0 **112 3**
2015–16 Manchester C 17 2
2016–17 Manchester C 7 1
2017–18 Manchester C 22 1
2018–19 Manchester C 11 0 **57 4**
2019–20 Everton 16 0 **16 0**

DIGNE, Lucas (D) 211 9
H: 5 10 W: 11 11 b.Meaux 20-7-93
Internationals: France U16, U17, U18, U19, U21, Full caps.
2011–12 Lille 16 0
2012–13 Lille 33 2 **49 2**
2013–14 Paris Saint-Germain 15 0
2014–15 Paris Saint-Germain 15 0
2014–15 Paris Saint-Germain 0 0 **30 0**
2015–16 Roma 33 3 **33 3**
2016–17 Barcelona 17 0
2017–18 Barcelona 12 0 **29 0**
2018–19 Everton 35 4
2019–20 Everton 35 0 **70 4**

DOWELL, Kieran (F) 78 16
H: 5 9 W: 9 04 b.Ormskirk 10-10-97
Internationals: England U16, U17, U18, U20, U21.
2014–15 Everton 0 0
2015–16 Everton 2 0
2016–17 Everton 0 0
2017–18 Everton 0 0
2017–18 *Nottingham F* 38 9 **38 9**
2018–19 Everton 0 0
2018–19 *Sheffield U* 16 2 **16 2**
2019–20 Everton 0 0 **2 0**
2019–20 *Derby Co* 10 0 **10 0**
2019–20 *Wigan Ath* 12 5 **12 5**

FEENEY, Morgan (D) 1 0
H: 6 3 W: 12 02 b.Bootle 6-2-98
Internationals: England U17, U18, U19.
2017–18 Everton 0 0
2018–19 Everton 0 0
2019–20 Everton 0 0
2019–20 *Tranmere R* 1 0 **1 0**

GARBUTT, Luke (D) 144 14
H: 5 10 W: 11 07 b.Harrogate 21-5-93
Internationals: England U16, U17, U18, U19, U20, U21.
2010–11 Everton 0 0
2011–12 Everton 0 0
2011–12 *Cheltenham T* 34 2 **34 2**
2012–13 Everton 0 0
2013–14 Everton 1 0
2013–14 *Colchester U* 19 2 **19 2**
2014–15 Everton 4 0
2015–16 Everton 0 0

2015–16	*Fulham*	25	1	**25**	**1**
2016–17	Everton	0	0		
2016–17	*Wigan Ath*	8	0	**8**	**0**
2017–18	Everton	0	0		
2018–19	Everton	0	0		
2018–19	*Oxford U*	25	4	**25**	**4**
2019–20	Everton	0	0	**5**	**0**
2019–20	*Ipswich T*	28	5	**28**	**5**

GBAMIN, Jean-Philippe (M) 179 5
b.San Pedro 25-5-95
Internationals: France U18, U19, U20, U21. Ivory Coast Full caps.

2012–13	Lens	2	0		
2013–14	Lens	30	2		
2014–15	Lens	33	0		
2015–16	Lens	26	1	**91**	**3**
2016–17	Mainz 05	25	0		
2017–18	Mainz 05	30	1		
2018–19	Mainz 05	31	1	**86**	**2**
2019–20	Mainz	0	0		
2019–20	Everton	2	0	**2**	**0**

GIBSON, Lewis (D) 9 0
b. 19-7-00
Internationals: England U17, U18, U20.
From Newcastle U.

2019–20	Everton	0	0		
2019–20	*Fleetwood T*	9	0	**9**	**0**

GORDON, Anthony (M) 11 0
b. 24-2-01
Internationals: England U18, U19.

2017–18	Everton	0	0		
2018–19	Everton	0	0		
2019–20	Everton	11	0	**11**	**0**

HOLGATE, Mason (D) 104 2
H: 5 11 W: 11 11 b.Doncaster 22-10-96
Internationals: England U20, U21.

2014–15	Barnsley	20	1	**20**	**1**
2015–16	Everton	0	0		
2016–17	Everton	18	0		
2017–18	Everton	15	0		
2018–19	Everton	5	0		
2018–19	*WBA*	19	1	**19**	**1**
2019–20	Everton	27	0	**65**	**0**

HORNBY, Fraser (M) 12 3
H: 6 5 b.Northampton 13-9-99
Internationals: Scotland U17, U19, U21.
From Northampton T.

2017–18	Everton	0	0		
2018–19	Everton	0	0		
2018–19	Everton	0	0		
2019–20	*Kortrijk*	12	3	**12**	**3**

IWOBI, Alex (M) 125 12
H: 5 11 W: 11 11 b.Lagos 3-5-96
Internationals: England U16, U17, U18. Nigeria Full caps.

2012–13	Arsenal	0	0		
2013–14	Arsenal	0	0		
2014–15	Arsenal	0	0		
2015–16	Arsenal	13	2		
2016–17	Arsenal	26	3		
2017–18	Arsenal	26	3		
2018–19	Arsenal	35	3		
2019–20	Arsenal	0	0	**100**	**11**
2019–20	Everton	25	1	**25**	**1**

KEAN, Moise (F) 64 13
b.Vercelli 28-2-00
Internationals: Italy U16, U17, U19, U20, U21, Full caps.

2016–17	Juventus	3	1		
2017–18	Juventus	0	0		
2017–18	Verona	19	4	**19**	**4**
2018–19	Juventus	13	6		
2019–20	Juventus	0	0	**16**	**7**
2019–20	Everton	29	2	**29**	**2**

KEANE, Michael (D) 237 15
H: 5 7 W: 12 13 b.Stockport 11-1-93
Internationals: Republic of Ireland U17, U19. England U19, U20, U21, Full caps.

2011–12	Manchester U	0	0		
2012–13	Manchester U	0	0		
2012–13	*Leicester C*	22	2	**22**	**2**
2013–14	Manchester U	0	0		
2013–14	*Derby Co*	7	0	**7**	**0**
2013–14	*Blackburn R*	13	3	**13**	**3**
2014–15	Manchester U	1	0	**1**	**0**
2014–15	Burnley	21	0		
2015–16	Burnley	44	5		
2016–17	Burnley	35	2	**100**	**7**
2017–18	Everton	30	0		
2018–19	Everton	33	1		
2019–20	Everton	31	2	**94**	**3**

KENNY, Jonjoe (D) 86 2
H: 5 9 W: 10 08 b.Kirkdale 15-3-97
Internationals: England U16, U17, U18, U19, U20, U21.

2014–15	Everton	0	0		
2015–16	Everton	1	0		
2015–16	*Wigan Ath*	7	0	**7**	**0**
2015–16	*Oxford U*	17	0	**17**	**0**
2016–17	Everton	1	0		
2017–18	Everton	19	0		
2018–19	Everton	10	0		
2019–20	Everton	0	0	**31**	**0**
2019–20	*Schalke 04*	31	2	**31**	**2**

LOSSL, Jonas (G) 305 0
H: 6 5 W: 14 00 b.Kolding 1-2-89
Internationals: Denmark U17, U18, U19, U20, U21, Full caps.

2009–10	Midtjylland	12	0		
2010–11	Midtjylland	30	0		
2011–12	Midtjylland	25	0		
2012–13	Midtjylland	27	0		
2013–14	Midtjylland	33	0	**127**	**0**
2014–15	Guingamp	30	0		
2015–16	Guingamp	37	0	**67**	**0**
2016–17	Mainz	27	0		
2017–18	Mainz	0	0	**27**	**0**
2017–18	*Huddersfield T*	38	0		
2018–19	Huddersfield T	31	0		
2019–20	Everton	0	0		
2019–20	*Huddersfield T*	15	0	**84**	**0**

MARTINA, Cuco (D) 247 5
H: 6 1 W: 11 05 b.Rotterdam 25-9-89
Internationals: Curacao Full caps.

2008–09	Roosendaal	14	0		
2009–10	Roosendaal	23	1		
2010–11	Roosendaal	32	1	**69**	**2**
2011–12	Waalwijk	23	0		
2012–13	Waalwijk	34	1	**57**	**1**
2013–14	FC Twente	16	1		
2014–15	FC Twente	32	0	**48**	**1**
2015–16	Southampton	15	1		
2016–17	Southampton	9	0	**24**	**1**
2017–18	Everton	21	0		
2018–19	Everton	0	0		
2018–19	*Stoke C*	17	0	**17**	**0**
2018–19	*Feyenoord*	11	0	**11**	**0**
2019–20	Everton	0	0	**21**	**0**

MINA, Yerry (D) 141 16
H: 6 5 W: 11 11 b.Guachene 23-9-94
Internationals: Colombia U23, Full caps.

2013	Deportivo Pasto	10	1	**10**	**1**
2014	Santa Fe	23	2		
2015	Santa Fe	23	2		
2016	Santa Fe	10	2	**56**	**6**
2016	Palmeiras	13	4		
2017	Palmeiras	15	2	**28**	**6**
2017–18	Barcelona	5	0	**5**	**0**
2018–19	Everton	13	1		
2019–20	Everton	29	2	**42**	**3**

NIASSE, Oumar (F) 127 36
H: 6 0 b.Ouakam 18-4-90
Internationals: Senegal U23, Full caps.

2013–14	Akhisar Belediyespor	34	12	**34**	**12**
2014–15	Lokomotiv Moscow	13	4		
2015–16	Lokomotiv Moscow	15	8	**28**	**12**
2015–16	Everton	5	0		
2016–17	Everton	0	0		
2016–17	*Hull C*	17	4	**17**	**4**
2017–18	Everton	22	8		
2018–19	Everton	5	0		
2018–19	*Cardiff C*	13	0	**13**	**0**
2019–20	Everton	3	0	**35**	**8**

PENNINGTON, Matthew (D) 121 4
H: 6 1 W: 12 02 b.Warrington 6-10-94
Internationals: England U19.

2013–14	Everton	0	0		
2013–14	*Tranmere R*	17	2	**17**	**2**
2014–15	Everton	0	0		
2014–15	*Coventry C*	24	0	**24**	**0**
2015–16	Everton	4	0		
2015–16	*Walsall*	5	0	**5**	**0**
2016–17	Everton	3	1		
2017–18	Everton	0	0		
2017–18	*Leeds U*	24	0	**24**	**0**
2018–19	Everton	0	0		
2018–19	*Ipswich T*	30	1	**30**	**1**
2019–20	Everton	0	0	**7**	**1**
2019–20	*Hull C*	14	0	**14**	**0**

PICKFORD, Jordan (G) 232 0
H: 6 1 b.Washington 7-3-94
Internationals: England U16, U17, U18, U19, U20, U21, Full caps.

2010–11	Sunderland	0	0		
2011–12	Sunderland	0	0		
2012–13	Sunderland	0	0		
2013–14	Sunderland	0	0		
2013–14	*Burton Alb*	12	0	**12**	**0**
2013–14	*Carlisle U*	18	0	**18**	**0**
2014–15	Sunderland	0	0		
2014–15	*Bradford C*	33	0	**33**	**0**
2015–16	Sunderland	2	0		
2015–16	*Preston NE*	24	0	**24**	**0**
2016–17	Sunderland	29	0	**31**	**0**
2017–18	Everton	38	0		
2018–19	Everton	38	0		
2019–20	Everton	38	0	**114**	**0**

RICHARLISON, de Andrade (F) 175 49
H: 5 10 W: 11 03 b.Nova Venecia 10-5-97
Internationals: Brazil U20, Full caps.

2015	America Mineiro	24	9	**24**	**9**
2016	Fluminense	28	4		
2017	Fluminense	14	5		
2017–18	Fluminense	0	0	**42**	**9**
2017–18	Watford	38	5	**38**	**5**
2018–19	Everton	35	13		
2019–20	Everton	36	13	**71**	**26**

SANDRO, Ramirez (F) 116 19
H: 5 8 W: 11 03 b.Las Palmas 9-7-95
Internationals: Spain U16, U17, U18, U19, U21.

2014–15	Barcelona	7	2		
2015–16	Barcelona	10	0	**17**	**2**
2016–17	Malaga	30	14	**30**	**14**
2017–18	Everton	8	0		
2017–18	*Sevilla*	13	0	**13**	**0**
2018–19	Everton	0	0		
2018–19	*Real Sociedad*	24	0	**24**	**0**
2019–20	Everton	0	0	**8**	**0**
2019–20	*Vallodolid*	24	3	**24**	**3**

SCHNEIDERLIN, Morgan (M) 341 16
H: 5 11 W: 11 11 b.Obernai 8-11-89
Internationals: France U16, U17, U18, U19, U20, U21, Full caps.

2007–08	Strasbourg	5	0	**5**	**0**
2008–09	Southampton	30	0		
2009–10	Southampton	37	1		
2010–11	Southampton	27	0		
2011–12	Southampton	42	2		
2012–13	Southampton	36	5		
2013–14	Southampton	33	2		
2014–15	Southampton	26	4	**231**	**14**
2015–16	Manchester U	29	1		
2016–17	Manchester U	3	0	**32**	**1**
2016–17	Everton	14	1		
2017–18	Everton	30	0		
2018–19	Everton	14	0		
2019–20	Everton	15	0	**73**	**1**

SIDIBE, Djibril (D) 243 12
b.Troyes 29-7-92
Internationals: France U20, U21, Full caps.

2009–10	Troyes	1	0		
2010–11	Troyes	6	0		
2011–12	Troyes	34	1	**41**	**1**
2012–13	Lille	14	1		
2013–14	Lille	20	0		
2014–15	Lille	25	2		
2015–16	Lille	37	4	**96**	**7**
2016–17	Monaco	29	2		
2017–18	Monaco	27	2		
2018–19	Monaco	25	0		
2019–20	Monaco	0	0	**81**	**4**

On loan from Monaco.

2019–20	Everton	25	0	**25**	**0**

SIGURDSSON, Gylfi (M) 378 92
H: 6 1 W: 12 02 b.Reykjavik 9-9-89
Internationals: Iceland U17, U18, U19, U21, Full caps.

2007–08	Reading	0	0		
2008–09	Reading	0	0		
2008–09	*Shrewsbury T*	5	1	**5**	**1**
2008–09	*Crewe Alex*	15	3	**15**	**3**
2009–10	Reading	38	16		
2010–11	Reading	4	2	**42**	**18**
2010–11	Hoffenheim	28	9		
2011–12	Hoffenheim	6	0	**34**	**9**
2011–12	*Swansea C*	18	7		
2012–13	Tottenham H	33	3		
2013–14	Tottenham H	25	5	**58**	**8**
2014–15	Swansea C	32	7		
2015–16	Swansea C	36	11		
2016–17	Swansea C	38	9	**124**	**34**

2017–18	Everton	27	4		
2018–19	Everton	38	13		
2019–20	Everton	35	2	**100**	**19**

SIMMS, Ellis (F) **0** **0**
b.Oldham 5-1-01
From Manchester C.

2019–20	Everton	0	0		

STEKELENBURG, Maarten (G) **293** **0**
H: 6 6 W: 14 05 b.Haarlem 22-9-82
Internationals: Netherlands U21, Full caps.

2001–02	Ajax	0	0		
2002–03	Ajax	9	0		
2003–04	Ajax	10	0		
2004–05	Ajax	11	0		
2005–06	Ajax	27	0		
2006–07	Ajax	32	0		
2007–08	Ajax	31	0		
2008–09	Ajax	12	0		
2009–10	Ajax	33	0		
2010–11	Ajax	26	0	**191**	**0**
2011–12	Roma	29	0		
2012–13	Roma	18	0	**47**	**0**
2013–14	Fulham	19	0		
2014–15	Fulham	0	0		
2014–15	Monaco	0	0		
2015–16	Fulham	0	0	**19**	**0**
2015–16	*Southampton*	17	0	**17**	**0**
2016–17	Everton	19	0		
2017–18	Everton	0	0		
2018–19	Everton	0	0		
2019–20	Everton	0	0	**19**	**0**

TARASHAJ, Shani (F) **74** **13**
H: 5 9 b. 7-2-95
Internationals: Switzerland U17, U18, U19, U21, Full caps.

2014–15	Grasshoppers	19	1		
2015–16	Grasshoppers	18	8	**52**	**12**
2015–16	Everton	0	0		
2015–16	*Grasshoppers*	15	3		
2016–17	Everton	0	0		
2016–17	*Eintracht Frankfurt*	13	1	**13**	**1**
2017–18	Everton	0	0		
2018–19	Everton	0	0		
2018–19	*Grasshopper*	9	0	**9**	**0**
2019–20	Everton	0	0		
2019–20	*Emmen*	0	0		

TOSUN, Cenk (M) **255** **90**
H: 6 0 W: 12 04 b.Wetzlar 7-6-91
Internationals: Germany U16, U18, U19, U21. Turkey U21, Full caps.

2009–10	Eintracht Frankfurt	1	0	**1**	**0**
2010–11	Gaziantepspor	14	10		
2011–12	Gaziantepspor	32	6		
2012–13	Gaziantepspor	32	10		
2013–14	Gaziantepspor	31	13	**109**	**39**
2014–15	Besiktas	18	5		
2015–16	Besiktas	29	8		
2016–17	Besiktas	33	20		
2017–18	Besiktas	16	8	**96**	**41**
2017–18	Everton	14	5		
2018–19	Everton	25	3		
2019–20	Everton	5	1	**44**	**9**
2019–20	*Crystal Palace*	5	1	**5**	**1**

VIRGINIA, Joao (G) **2** **0**
H: 6 3 W: 13 01 b.Faro 10-10-99
Internationals: Portugal U16, U17, U18, U19, U20, U21.
From Benfica, Arsenal.

2018–19	Everton	0	0		
2019–20	*Reading*	2	0	**2**	**0**
2019–20	Everton	0	0		

WALCOTT, Theo (F) **367** **79**
H: 5 9 W: 11 01 b.Stanmore 16-3-89
Internationals: England U16, U17, U19, U21, Full caps.

2005–06	Southampton	21	4	**21**	**4**
2005–06	Arsenal	0	0		
2006–07	Arsenal	16	0		
2007–08	Arsenal	25	4		
2008–09	Arsenal	22	2		
2009–10	Arsenal	23	3		
2010–11	Arsenal	28	9		
2011–12	Arsenal	35	8		
2012–13	Arsenal	32	14		
2013–14	Arsenal	13	5		
2014–15	Arsenal	14	5		
2015–16	Arsenal	28	5		
2016–17	Arsenal	28	10		
2017–18	Arsenal	6	0	**270**	**65**
2017–18	Everton	14	3		
2018–19	Everton	37	5		
2019–20	Everton	25	2	**76**	**10**

Players retained or with offer of contract
Anderson, Joseph William; Astley, Ryan; Carroll, Bobby Lee; Dobbin, Lewis Norman; Garcia Ferreira, Rafael Isidro; Hansen, Nicolas Defreitas; Hughes, Rhys Alex; Hunt, MacKenzie James; Iversen, Einar Hjellestad; John, Kyle Alex; Leban, Zan Luk; Markelo, Nathangelo Alexandro; Ouzounidis, Con; Tyrer, Harry Alfred; Warrington, Lewis Wesley.

Scholars
Anderson Ogbomo, Jonathan Osazee; Barrett, Jack Joseph; Cannon, Thomas Christopher; Davidson, Joel; Hagan, Harry Paul; Higgins, Liam Thomas; Hosie, Joshua; Kristensen, Sebastian; Lowey, Daniel Harry; McAllister, Sean Paul; McIntyre, Jack Cameron; Onyango, Tyler Jaden Napier Edward; Quirk, Sebastian Anthony; Thompson, Dylan Isaac.

EXETER C (32)

AJOSE, Nicholas (F) **282** **83**
H: 5 8 W: 11 00 b.Bury 7-10-91
Internationals: England U16, U17.

2009–10	Manchester U	0	0		
2010–11	Manchester U	0	0		
2010–11	*Bury*	28	13		
2011–12	Peterborough U	2	0		
2011–12	*Scunthorpe U*	7	0	**7**	**0**
2011–12	*Chesterfield*	12	1	**12**	**1**
2012–13	*Crawley T*	19	2	**19**	**2**
2012–13	Peterborough U	0	0		
2012–13	*Bury*	19	4		
2013–14	Peterborough U	22	7	**24**	**7**
2013–14	*Swindon T*	16	6		
2014–15	Leeds U	3	0		
2014–15	*Crewe Alex*	27	8	**27**	**8**
2015–16	Leeds U	0	0	**3**	**0**
2015–16	Swindon T	38	24		
2016–17	Charlton Ath	21	6		
2016–17	*Swindon T*	15	5	**69**	**35**
2017–18	Charlton Ath	12	1		
2017–18	*Bury*	9	1	**56**	**18**
2018–19	Charlton Ath	9	1	**42**	**8**
2018–19	*Mansfield T*	10	2	**10**	**2**
2019–20	Exeter C	13	2	**13**	**2**

ARTHUR, Jack (G) **0** **0**

2019–20	Exeter C	0	0		

ATANGANA, Nigel (M) **168** **5**
H: 6 2 W: 11 05 b.Corbeil-Essonnes 9-9-89

2014–15	Portsmouth	30	1		
2015–16	Portsmouth	13	0	**43**	**1**
2015–16	Leyton Orient	16	0		
2016–17	Leyton Orient	29	0	**45**	**0**
2017–18	Cheltenham T	32	1		
2018–19	Cheltenham T	26	2	**58**	**3**
2019–20	Exeter C	22	1	**22**	**1**

BOWMAN, Ryan (F) **173** **36**
H: 6 2 W: 11 12 b.Carlisle 30-11-91

2009–10	Carlisle U	6	0		
2010–11	Carlisle U	3	0	**9**	**0**

From Darlington, Hereford U

2013–14	York C	37	8	**37**	**8**

From York C, Gateshead.

2016–17	Motherwell	24	2		
2017–18	Motherwell	32	7		
2018–19	Motherwell	16	1	**72**	**10**
2018–19	Exeter C	18	5		
2019–20	Exeter C	37	13	**55**	**18**

CHRISENE, Benjamin (M) **1** **0**
b. 12-1-04
Internationals: England U16.

2019–20	Exeter C	1	0	**1**	**0**

COLLINS, Archie (M) **62** **2**
b. 31-8-99

2016–17	Exeter C	0	0		
2017–18	Exeter C	0	0		
2018–19	Exeter C	26	1		
2019–20	Exeter C	36	1	**62**	**2**

DEAN, Will (M) **0** **0**
b. 7-8-00

2017–18	Exeter C	0	0		
2018–19	Exeter C	0	0		
2019–20	Exeter C	0	0		

DIABATE, Cheick (D) **0** **0**

2019–20	Exeter C	0	0		

DICKENSON, Brennan (F) **200** **23**
H: 6 0 W: 12 07 b.Ferndown 26-2-93

2012–13	Brighton & HA	0	0		
2012–13	*Chesterfield*	11	1	**11**	**1**
2012–13	*AFC Wimbledon*	7	2	**7**	**2**
2013–14	Brighton & HA	0	0		
2013–14	*Northampton T*	13	1	**13**	**1**
2014–15	Gillingham	34	1		
2015–16	Gillingham	33	1	**67**	**2**
2016–17	Colchester U	36	12		
2017–18	Colchester U	7	0		
2018–19	Colchester U	42	3	**85**	**15**
2019–20	Milton Keynes D	7	0	**7**	**0**
2019–20	Exeter C	10	2	**10**	**2**

DODD, James (M) **0** **0**

2018–19	Exeter C	0	0		
2019–20	Exeter C	0	0		

DYER, Jordan (D) **0** **0**

2018–19	Exeter C	0	0		
2019–20	Exeter C	0	0		

FISHER, Alex (F) **204** **46**
H: 6 2 W: 12 00 b. 30-6-90

2006–07	Oxford U	0	0		
2007–08	Oxford U	10	1		
2008–09	Oxford U	3	1	**13**	**2**
2009–10	Jerez Industrial	0	0		
2010–11	Jerez Industrial	21	11	**21**	**11**
2011–12	Tienen	7	1	**7**	**1**
2012–13	Racing Mechelen	27	7	**27**	**7**
2013–14	Heist	2	0	**2**	**0**
2013–14	Monza	14	2	**14**	**2**
2014–15	Mansfield T	14	1	**14**	**1**
2015–16	Inverness CT	1	0		
2016–17	Inverness CT	21	8	**22**	**8**
2017–18	Motherwell	11	0	**11**	**0**
2017–18	Yeovil T	17	6		
2018–19	Yeovil T	40	7	**57**	**13**
2019–20	Exeter C	16	1	**16**	**1**

HARTRIDGE, Alex (D) **3** **0**
b. 9-3-99

2017–18	Exeter C	0	0		
2018–19	Exeter C	3	0		
2019–20	Exeter C	0	0	**3**	**0**

HOLMES, Lee (M) **329** **29**
H: 5 8 W: 10 06 b.Mansfield 2-4-87
Internationals: England U16, U17, U19.

2002–03	Derby Co	2	0		
2003–04	Derby Co	23	2		
2004–05	Derby Co	3	0		
2004–05	*Swindon T*	15	1		
2005–06	Derby Co	18	0		
2006–07	Derby Co	0	0		
2006–07	*Bradford C*	16	0	**16**	**0**
2007–08	Derby Co	0	0	**46**	**2**
2007–08	*Walsall*	19	4	**19**	**4**
2008–09	Southampton	11	0		
2009–10	Southampton	5	0		
2010–11	Southampton	7	0		
2011–12	Southampton	6	1	**29**	**1**
2011–12	*Oxford U*	7	2	**7**	**2**
2011–12	*Swindon T*	10	1	**25**	**2**
2012–13	Preston NE	28	3		
2013–14	Preston NE	32	3		
2014–15	Preston NE	0	0	**60**	**6**
2014–15	*Portsmouth*	5	0	**5**	**0**
2014–15	*Exeter C*	8	0		
2015–16	Exeter C	37	2		
2016–17	Exeter C	16	5		
2017–18	Exeter C	27	2		
2018–19	Exeter C	34	3		
2019–20	Exeter C	0	0	**122**	**12**

JAY, Matt (D) **56** **9**
H: 5 10 W: 10 12 b.Torbay 27-2-96

2013–14	Exeter C	2	0		
2014–15	Exeter C	3	0		
2015–16	Exeter C	0	0		
2016–17	Exeter C	2	0		
2017–18	Exeter C	17	1		
2018–19	Exeter C	18	4		
2019–20	Exeter C	14	4	**56**	**9**

KEY, Josh (M) **0** **0**
b. 1-11-99

2017–18	Exeter C	0	0		
2018–19	Exeter C	0	0		
2019–20	Exeter C	0	0		

KITE, Harry (M) **0** **0**
b.Exeter 29-6-00

2017–18	Exeter C	0	0		
2018–19	Exeter C	0	0		
2019–20	Exeter C	0	0		

LAW, Nicky (M) 455 61
H: 5 10 W: 11 07 b.Nottingham 29-3-88
2005–06 Sheffield U 0 0
2006–07 Sheffield U 4 0
2006–07 *Yeovil T* 6 0 **6 0**
2007–08 Sheffield U 1 0
2007–08 *Bradford C* 10 2
2008–09 Sheffield U 0 0 **5 0**
2008–09 *Bradford C* 33 0
2009–10 Rotherham U 42 4
2010–11 Rotherham U 44 4 **86 8**
2011–12 Motherwell 38 4
2012–13 Motherwell 38 6 **76 10**
2013–14 Rangers 32 9
2014–15 Rangers 36 10
2015–16 Rangers 18 1 **86 20**
2016–17 Bradford C 40 4
2017–18 Bradford C 38 0 **121 6**
2018–19 Exeter C 43 10
2019–20 Exeter C 32 7 **75 17**

MARTIN, Aaron (D) 186 11
H: 6 3 W: 11 13 b.Newport (IW) 29-9-89
2009–10 Southampton 2 0
2010–11 Southampton 8 0
2011–12 Southampton 10 1
2012–13 Southampton 0 0
2012–13 *Crystal Palace* 4 0 **4 0**
2012–13 *Coventry C* 12 0
2013–14 Southampton 0 0 **20 1**
2013–14 Birmingham C 8 0 **8 0**
2014–15 Yeovil T 12 3 **12 3**
2014–15 Coventry C 27 0
2015–16 Coventry C 29 2 **68 2**
2016–17 Oxford U 4 0
2017–18 Oxford U 12 0 **16 0**
2018–19 Exeter C 23 3
2019–20 Exeter C 35 2 **58 5**

MARTIN, Lee (M) 358 27
H: 5 10 W: 10 03 b.Taunton 9-2-87
2004–05 Manchester U 0 0
2005–06 Manchester U 0 0
2006–07 Manchester U 0 0
2006–07 *Rangers* 7 0 **7 0**
2006–07 *Stoke C* 13 1 **13 1**
2007–08 Manchester U 0 0
2007–08 *Plymouth Arg* 12 2 **12 2**
2007–08 *Sheffield U* 6 0 **6 0**
2008–09 Manchester U 1 0
2008–09 *Nottingham F* 13 1 **13 1**
2009–10 Manchester U 0 0 **1 0**
2009–10 Ipswich T 16 1
2010–11 Ipswich T 16 0
2010–11 *Charlton Ath* 20 2 **20 2**
2011–12 Ipswich T 34 5
2012–13 Ipswich T 34 0
2013–14 Ipswich T 0 0 **100 6**
2013–14 Millwall 26 1
2014–15 Millwall 27 1
2015–16 Millwall 8 0 **61 2**
2015–16 *Northampton T* 10 0 **10 0**
2016–17 Gillingham 17 0
2017–18 Gillingham 35 6 **52 6**
2018–19 Exeter C 35 1
2019–20 Exeter C 28 6 **63 7**

MAXTED, Jonathan (G) 37 0
H: 6 0 W: 11 03 b. 26-10-93
2012–13 Doncaster R 0 0
2013–14 Doncaster R 0 0
2014–15 Hartlepool U 0 0
2017–18 Accrington S 1 0
2018–19 Accrington S 19 0 **20 0**
2019–20 Exeter C 17 0 **17 0**

MORISON, Louis (M) 0 0
2019–20 Exeter C 0 0

MOXEY, Dean (D) 354 16
H: 6 2 W: 11 00 b.Exeter 14-1-86
Internationals: England C.
2008–09 Exeter C 43 4
2009–10 Derby Co 30 0
2010–11 Derby Co 22 2 **52 2**
2010–11 Crystal Palace 17 1
2011–12 Crystal Palace 24 0
2012–13 Crystal Palace 30 0
2013–14 Crystal Palace 20 0 **91 1**
2014–15 Bolton W 20 1
2015–16 Bolton W 33 0
2016–17 Bolton W 19 0 **72 1**
2017–18 Exeter C 34 3
2018–19 Exeter C 38 3
2019–20 Exeter C 24 2 **139 12**

PARKES, Tom (D) 309 8
H: 6 3 W: 12 05 b.Sutton-in-Ashfield 15-1-92
Internationals: England U17. England C.
2008–09 Leicester C 0 0
2009–10 Leicester C 0 0
2009–10 *Burton Alb* 22 1
2010–11 Leicester C 0 0
2010–11 *Yeovil T* 1 0 **1 0**
2010–11 *Burton Alb* 5 0
2011–12 Leicester C 0 0
2011–12 *Burton Alb* 4 0 **31 1**
2011–12 *Bristol R* 14 0
2012–13 Leicester C 0 0
2012–13 Bristol R 40 1
2013–14 Bristol R 44 1
2015–16 Bristol R 31 0 **129 2**
2016–17 Leyton Orient 41 1 **41 1**
2017–18 Carlisle U 37 1
2018–19 Carlisle U 39 1 **76 2**
2019–20 Exeter C 31 2 **31 2**

RANDALL, Joel (M) 2 0
b.Salisbury 29-10-99
2017–18 Exeter C 0 0
2018–19 Exeter C 0 0
2019–20 Exeter C 2 0 **2 0**

SEYMOUR, Ben (F) 11 0
b.Watford 16-4-99
2019–20 Exeter C 11 0 **11 0**

SPARKES, Jack (M) 20 0
b.Exeter 29-9-00
2017–18 Exeter C 3 0
2018–19 Exeter C 0 0
2019–20 Exeter C 17 0 **20 0**

SWEENEY, Pierce (D) 148 14
H: 5 10 W: 12 07 b.Dublin 11-9-94
Internationals: Republic of Ireland U17, U19, U21.
2012–13 Reading 0 0
2013–14 Reading 0 0
2014–15 Reading 0 0
2015–16 Reading 0 0
2016–17 Exeter C 29 0
2017–18 Exeter C 40 8
2018–19 Exeter C 43 4
2019–20 Exeter C 36 2 **148 14**

TAYLOR, Jake (M) 268 27
H: 5 10 W: 12 01 b.Ascot 1-12-91
Internationals: Wales U17, U19, U21, Full caps.
2010–11 Reading 1 0
2011–12 Reading 0 0
2011–12 *Aldershot T* 3 0 **3 0**
2011–12 *Exeter C* 30 3
2012–13 Reading 0 0
2012–13 *Cheltenham T* 8 1 **8 1**
2012–13 *Crawley T* 4 0 **4 0**
2013–14 Reading 8 0
2014–15 Reading 22 2
2014–15 *Leyton Orient* 3 0 **3 0**
2015–16 Reading 0 0 **31 2**
2015–16 *Motherwell* 7 0 **7 0**
2015–16 Exeter C 16 4
2016–17 Exeter C 43 4
2017–18 Exeter C 44 8
2018–19 Exeter C 46 3
2019–20 Exeter C 33 2 **212 24**

THOMPSON, Jared (G) 0 0
b.Swindon 23-3-99
Internationals: England U16, U17, U18.
2018–19 Chelsea 0 0
2019–20 Exeter C 0 0

TILLSON, Jordan (D) 124 2
H: 6 0 W: 11 09 b.Bath 5-3-93
2012–13 Exeter C 0 0
2013–14 Exeter C 1 0
2014–15 Exeter C 3 0
2015–16 Exeter C 26 1
2016–17 Exeter C 20 0
2017–18 Exeter C 37 1
2018–19 Exeter C 21 0
2018–19 *Cheltenham T* 14 0 **14 0**
2019–20 Exeter C 2 0 **110 2**
Transferred to Ross County, January 2020.

WARD, Lewis (G) 32 0
b. 5-3-97
Internationals: England U16.
2014–15 Reading 0 0
2015–16 Reading 0 0
2016–17 Reading 0 0
2017–18 Reading 0 0
2018–19 Reading 0 0
2018–19 *Northampton T* 0 0
2018–19 *Forest Green R* 12 0 **12 0**
2019–20 Exeter C 20 0 **20 0**

WARREN, Gary (D) 208 13
H: 6 0 W: 11 11 b.Bristol 16-8-84
From Newport Co.
2012–13 Inverness CT 31 5
2013–14 Inverness CT 34 2
2014–15 Inverness CT 36 2
2015–16 Inverness CT 25 0
2016–17 Inverness CT 33 2
2017–18 Inverness CT 22 2 **181 13**
2018–19 Yeovil T 26 0 **26 0**
2019–20 Exeter C 1 0 **1 0**

WILLIAMS, Randell (F) 73 8
H: 6 3 b.London 30-12-96
From Tower Hamlets.
2016–17 Crystal Palace 0 0
2017–18 Watford 0 0
2017–18 *Wycombe W* 6 1
2018–19 Watford 0 0
2018–19 *Wycombe W* 20 2 **26 3**
2018–19 Exeter C 10 0
2019–20 Exeter C 37 5 **47 5**

WOODMAN, Craig (D) 546 7
H: 5 9 W: 10 11 b.Tiverton 22-12-82
1999–2000 Bristol C 0 0
2000–01 Bristol C 2 0
2001–02 Bristol C 6 0
2002–03 Bristol C 10 0
2003–04 Bristol C 21 0
2004–05 Bristol C 3 0
2004–05 *Mansfield T* 8 1 **8 1**
2004–05 *Torquay U* 22 1
2005–06 Bristol C 37 1
2005–06 *Torquay U* 2 0 **24 1**
2006–07 Bristol C 11 0 **90 1**
2007–08 Wycombe W 29 0
2008–09 Wycombe W 46 1
2009–10 Wycombe W 44 1 **119 2**
2010–11 Brentford 41 1
2011–12 Brentford 18 0 **59 1**
2012–13 Exeter C 44 0
2013–14 Exeter C 41 1
2014–15 Exeter C 32 0
2015–16 Exeter C 25 0
2016–17 Exeter C 33 0
2017–18 Exeter C 33 0
2018–19 Exeter C 32 0
2019–20 Exeter C 6 0 **246 1**

Players retained or with offer of contract
Smerdon, Noah John.

Scholars
Arthur, Jack Jamie; Clark, Max Harry; Diabate, Cheick Tiemoko; Ford, Harry Joseph; Iseguan, Chukwuka Nelson; Johnson, Ellis Oren; Lovett, Frank Eli; Morison, Louis; Moyse, Alexander George Heal; Simpson, Theo Jon; Stafford, Jack Elliot; Veale, Jack Lewis; Wilson, Lewis.

FLEETWOOD T (33)

ANDREW, Danny (D) 213 10
H: 5 11 W: 11 06 b.Holbeach 23-12-90
2009–10 Peterborough U 2 0 **2 0**
2009–10 *Cheltenham T* 10 0
2010–11 Cheltenham T 43 4
2011–12 Cheltenham T 10 0
2012–13 Cheltenham T 1 0 **64 4**
From Gloucester C, Macclesfield T.
2014–15 Fleetwood T 7 0
2015–16 Fleetwood T 9 0
2016–17 Grimsby T 46 0 **46 0**
2017–18 Doncaster R 4 0
2018–19 Doncaster R 46 4 **50 4**
2019–20 Fleetwood T 35 2 **51 2**

BAGGLEY, Barry (M) 3 0
b.Belfast 11-2-02
Internationals: Northern Ireland U17.
2018–19 Fleetwood T 3 0
2019–20 Fleetwood T 0 0 **3 0**

BIGGINS, Harrison (M) 40 1
b. 15-3-96
From Stocksbridge Park Steels.
2017–18 Fleetwood T 7 0
2018–19 Fleetwood T 23 1
2019–20 Fleetwood T 10 0 **40 1**

BURNS, Wes (F) 204 24
H: 5 8 W: 10 10 b.Cardiff 28-12-95
Internationals: Wales U21.
2012–13 Bristol C 6 0
2013–14 Bristol C 20 1
2014–15 Bristol C 3 1
2014–15 *Oxford U* 9 1 **9 1**
2014–15 *Cheltenham T* 14 4 **14 4**
2015–16 Bristol C 14 1 **43 3**
2015–16 *Fleetwood T* 14 5
2016–17 Fleetwood T 10 0
2016–17 *Aberdeen* 13 0 **13 0**
2017–18 Fleetwood T 28 2
2018–19 Fleetwood T 39 7
2019–20 Fleetwood T 34 2 **125 16**

CAIRNS, Alex (G) 140 0
H: 6 0 W: 11 05 b.Doncaster 4-1-93
2011–12 Leeds U 1 0
2012–13 Leeds U 0 0
2013–14 Leeds U 0 0
2014–15 Leeds U 0 0 **1 0**
2015–16 Chesterfield 0 0
2015–16 Rotherham U 0 0
2016–17 Fleetwood T 30 0
2017–18 Fleetwood T 38 0
2018–19 Fleetwood T 46 0
2019–20 Fleetwood T 25 0 **139 0**

CLARKE, Eddie (D) 8 0
b. 29-12-98
2018–19 Fleetwood T 2 0
2019–20 Fleetwood T 0 0 **2 0**
2019–20 *Macclesfield T* 6 0 **6 0**

COTTAM, James (G) 0 0
b.Preston 7-9-00
From Preston NE.
2019–20 Fleetwood T 0 0

COUTTS, Paul (M) 345 10
H: 5 9 W: 11 11 b.Aberdeen 22-7-88
Internationals: Scotland U21.
2008–09 Peterborough U 37 0
2009–10 Peterborough U 16 0 **53 0**
2009–10 Preston NE 13 1
2010–11 Preston NE 23 1
2011–12 Preston NE 41 2 **77 4**
2012–13 Derby Co 44 3
2013–14 Derby Co 8 0
2014–15 Derby Co 7 0 **59 3**
2014–15 Sheffield U 20 0
2015–16 Sheffield U 32 0
2016–17 Sheffield U 43 2
2017–18 Sheffield U 16 1
2018–19 Sheffield U 13 0 **124 3**
2019–20 Fleetwood T 32 0 **32 0**

COYLE, Lewie (M) 132 1
H: 5 8 W: 10 08 b.Hull 15-10-95
2015–16 Leeds U 11 0
2016–17 Leeds U 4 0
2017–18 Leeds U 0 0
2017–18 *Fleetwood T* 42 0
2018–19 Leeds U 0 0 **15 0**
2018–19 *Fleetwood T* 41 0
2019–20 Fleetwood T 34 1 **117 1**

CRELLIN, Billy (G) 5 0
Internationals: England U17, U18, U19, U20.
2017–18 Fleetwood T 0 0
2018–19 Fleetwood T 0 0
2019–20 Fleetwood T 5 0 **5 0**

DEMPSEY, Kyle (M) 197 16
b.Whitehaven 17-9-95
2013–14 Carlisle U 4 0
2014–15 Carlisle U 43 10 **47 10**
2015–16 Huddersfield T 21 1
2016–17 Huddersfield T 0 0 **21 1**
2016–17 *Fleetwood T* 38 2
2017–18 Fleetwood T 45 1
2018–19 Fleetwood T 14 0
2018–19 *Peterborough U* 11 0 **11 0**
2019–20 Fleetwood T 21 2 **118 5**

EVANS, Ched (F) 248 84
H: 6 0 W: 12 00 b.Rhyl 28-12-88
Internationals: Wales U21, Full caps.
2006–07 Manchester C 0 0
2007–08 Manchester C 0 0
2007–08 *Norwich C* 28 10 **28 10**
2008–09 Manchester C 16 1 **16 1**
2009–10 Sheffield U 33 4
2010–11 Sheffield U 34 9
2011–12 Sheffield U 36 29
2016–17 Chesterfield 25 5 **25 5**
2017–18 Sheffield U 9 0
2018–19 Sheffield U 0 0 **112 42**
2018–19 *Fleetwood T* 39 17
2019–20 Fleetwood T 28 9 **67 26**

GARNER, Gerard (F) 1 0
b.Liverpool 2-11-98
2017–18 Fleetwood 0 0
2018–19 Fleetwood T 1 0
2019–20 Fleetwood T 0 0 **1 0**

GILKS, Matthew (G) 435 0
H: 6 3 W: 13 12 b.Rochdale 4-6-82
Internationals: Scotland Full caps.
2000–01 Rochdale 3 0
2001–02 Rochdale 19 0
2002–03 Rochdale 20 0
2003–04 Rochdale 12 0
2004–05 Rochdale 30 0
2005–06 Rochdale 46 0
2006–07 Rochdale 46 0 **176 0**
2007–08 Norwich C 0 0
2008–09 Blackpool 5 0
2008–09 *Shrewsbury T* 4 0 **4 0**
2009–10 Blackpool 26 0
2010–11 Blackpool 18 0
2011–12 Blackpool 42 0
2012–13 Blackpool 45 0
2013–14 Blackpool 46 0 **182 0**
2014–15 Burnley 0 0
2015–16 Burnley 0 0
2016–17 Rangers 0 0
2016–17 Wigan Ath 14 0 **14 0**
2017–18 Scunthorpe U 42 0
2018–19 Scunthorpe U 0 0 **42 0**
2018–19 Lincoln C 12 0 **12 0**
2019–20 Fleetwood T 5 0 **5 0**

HAYES, Cian (F) 0 0
2019–20 Fleetwood T 0 0

HILL, James (D) 2 0
b. 10-1-02
2018–19 Fleetwood T 2 0
2019–20 Fleetwood T 0 0 **2 0**

HOLGATE, Harrison (D) 0 0
2018–19 Fleetwood T 0 0
2019–20 Fleetwood T 0 0

HUNTER, Ashley (F) 192 36
H: 5 10 W: 10 08 b.Derby 29-9-93
2014–15 Fleetwood T 12 1
2015–16 Fleetwood T 24 5
2016–17 Fleetwood T 44 8
2017–18 Fleetwood T 44 9
2018–19 Fleetwood T 43 8
2019–20 Fleetwood T 14 0 **181 31**
2019–20 *Salford C* 11 5 **11 5**

JOHNSTON, Carl (M) 0 0
b. 29-5-02
Internationals: Northern Ireland U17, U19.
From Linfield.
2019–20 Fleetwood T 0 0

MADDEN, Patrick (F) 409 132
H: 6 0 W: 11 13 b.Dublin 4-3-90
Internationals: Republic of Ireland U19, U21, U23, Full caps.
2008 Bohemians 18 4
2009 Bohemians 2 0
2009 Shelbourne 13 6 **13 6**
2010 Bohemians 34 10 **54 14**
2010–11 Carlisle U 13 0
2011–12 Carlisle U 18 1
2012–13 Carlisle U 1 1 **32 2**
2012–13 *Yeovil T* 35 22
2013–14 Yeovil T 9 0 **44 22**
2013–14 Scunthorpe U 21 5
2014–15 Scunthorpe U 46 14
2015–16 Scunthorpe U 46 20
2016–17 Scunthorpe U 34 11
2017–18 Scunthorpe U 20 2 **167 52**
2017–18 Fleetwood T 20 6
2018–19 Fleetwood T 44 15
2019–20 Fleetwood T 35 15 **99 36**

MARNEY, Dean (M) 378 21
H: 5 10 W: 11 09 b.Barking 31-1-84
Internationals: England U21.
2002–03 Tottenham H 0 0
2002–03 *Swindon T* 9 0 **9 0**
2003–04 Tottenham H 3 0
2003–04 *QPR* 2 0 **2 0**
2004–05 Tottenham H 5 2
2004–05 *Gillingham* 3 0 **3 0**
2005–06 Tottenham H 0 0 **8 2**
2005–06 *Norwich C* 13 0 **13 0**
2006–07 Hull C 37 2
2007–08 Hull C 41 6
2008–09 Hull C 31 0
2009–10 Hull C 16 1 **125 9**
2009–10 Burnley 0 0
2010–11 Burnley 36 3
2011–12 Burnley 37 0
2012–13 Burnley 38 2
2013–14 Burnley 38 3
2014–15 Burnley 20 0
2015–16 Burnley 12 0
2016–17 Burnley 21 1
2017–18 Burnley 0 0 **202 9**
2018–19 Fleetwood T 16 1
2019–20 Fleetwood T 0 0 **16 1**

MATETE, Jay (M) 0 0
From Reading.
2019–20 Fleetwood T 0 0

McALENY, Conor (F) 127 26
H: 5 10 W: 12 05 b.Liverpool 12-8-92
2009–10 Everton 0 0
2010–11 Everton 0 0
2011–12 Everton 2 0
2011–12 *Scunthorpe U* 3 0 **3 0**
2012–13 Everton 0 0
2013–14 Everton 0 0
2013–14 *Brentford* 4 0 **4 0**
2014–15 Everton 0 0
2014–15 *Cardiff C* 8 2 **8 2**
2015–16 Everton 0 0
2015–16 *Charlton Ath* 8 0 **8 0**
2015–16 *Wigan Ath* 13 4 **13 4**
2016–17 Everton 0 0 **2 0**
2016–17 *Oxford U* 18 10 **18 10**
2017–18 Fleetwood T 29 5
2018–19 Fleetwood T 14 0
2018–19 *Kilmarnock* 11 3 **11 3**
2019–20 Fleetwood T 12 2 **55 7**
2019–20 *Shrewsbury T* 5 0 **5 0**

MOONEY, Dan (F) 2 0
b. 3-7-99
Internationals: Wales U19, U21.
2018–19 Fleetwood T 1 0
2019–20 Fleetwood T 1 0 **2 0**

MORRIS, Josh (M) 248 53
H: 5 9 W: 10 00 b.Preston 30-9-91
Internationals: England U20.
2010–11 Blackburn R 4 0
2011–12 Blackburn R 2 0
2011–12 *Yeovil T* 5 0 **5 0**
2012–13 Blackburn R 10 0
2012–13 *Rotherham U* 5 0 **5 0**
2013–14 Blackburn R 4 0
2013–14 *Carlisle U* 6 0 **6 0**
2013–14 *Fleetwood T* 14 2
2014–15 Blackburn R 0 0 **20 0**
2014–15 *Fleetwood T* 45 8
2015–16 Bradford C 13 1 **13 1**
2016–17 Scunthorpe U 44 19
2017–18 Scunthorpe U 44 11
2018–19 Scunthorpe U 19 5 **107 35**
2019–20 Fleetwood T 33 7 **92 17**

MORRIS, Shayden (M) 0 0
2019–20 Fleetwood T 0 0

ROSSITER, Jordan (M) 42 1
H: 5 8 W: 10 10 b.Liverpool 24-3-97
Internationals: England U16, U17, U18, U19.
2013–14 Liverpool 0 0
2014–15 Liverpool 0 0
2015–16 Liverpool 1 0 **1 0**
2016–17 Rangers 4 0
2017–18 Rangers 2 0
2018–19 Rangers 4 0
2018–19 *Bury* 16 1 **16 1**
2019–20 Rangers 0 0 **10 0**
On loan from Rangers.
2019–20 Fleetwood T 15 0 **15 0**

RYDEL, Ryan (D) 5 0
b. 9-2-01
2018–19 Fleetwood T 5 0
2019–20 Fleetwood T 0 0 **5 0**

SAUNDERS, Harvey (M) 6 0
b. 20-7-97
From Darlington Railway Ath, Bishop Auckland, Durham C, Darlington.
2018–19 Fleetwood T 0 0
2019–20 Fleetwood T 6 0 **6 0**

SHERON, Nathan (D) 34 0
b.Whiston 4-10-97
2017–18 Fleetwood T 0 0
2018–19 Fleetwood T 26 0
2019–20 Fleetwood T 0 0 **26 0**
2019–20 *Walsall* 7 0 **7 0**
2019–20 *St Mirren* 1 0 **1 0**

SMITH, Lawrence (M) 0 0
2018–19 Fleetwood T 0 0
2019–20 Fleetwood T 0 0

SOUTHAM, Macauley (M) 2 0
b. 2-2-96
2014–15 Cardiff C 0 0
2015–16 Cardiff C 0 0
From Barry T.
2018–19 Fleetwood T 1 0
2019–20 Fleetwood T 1 0 **2 0**

SOWERBY, Jack (F) 102 7
b. 23-3-95
2014–15 Fleetwood T 0 0
2015–16 Fleetwood T 8 0
2016–17 Fleetwood T 8 1
2017–18 Fleetwood T 22 2
2018–19 Carlisle U 25 4 **25 4**
2018–19 Fleetwood T 15 0
2019–20 Fleetwood T 24 0 **77 3**

WALLACE, Ross (M) 466 45
H: 5 6 W: 9 12 b.Dundee 23-5-85
Internationals: Scotland U18, U19, U21, B, Full caps.
2001–02 Celtic 0 0
2002–03 Celtic 0 0
2003–04 Celtic 8 1
2004–05 Celtic 16 0
2005–06 Celtic 11 0
2006–07 Celtic 2 0 **37 1**
2006–07 Sunderland 32 6
2007–08 Sunderland 21 2
2008–09 Sunderland 0 0 **53 8**
2008–09 Preston NE 39 5
2009–10 Preston NE 41 7 **80 12**
2010–11 Burnley 40 3
2011–12 Burnley 44 5
2012–13 Burnley 36 3
2013–14 Burnley 14 0
2014–15 Burnley 15 1 **149 12**
2015–16 Sheffield W 40 4
2016–17 Sheffield W 41 5
2017–18 Sheffield W 27 2 **108 11**
2018–19 Fleetwood T 36 1
2019–20 Fleetwood T 3 0 **39 1**
Transferred to St Mirren, February 2020.

WHELAN, Glenn (M) 525 19
H: 5 11 W: 12 07 b.Dublin 13-1-84
Internationals: Republic of Ireland U16, U21, B, Full caps.
2000–01 Manchester C 0 0
2001–02 Manchester C 0 0
2002–03 Manchester C 0 0
2003–04 Manchester C 0 0
2003–04 *Bury* 13 0 **13 0**
2004–05 Sheffield W 36 2
2005–06 Sheffield W 43 1
2006–07 Sheffield W 38 7
2007–08 Sheffield W 25 2 **142 12**
2007–08 Stoke C 14 1
2008–09 Stoke C 26 1
2009–10 Stoke C 33 2
2010–11 Stoke C 29 0
2011–12 Stoke C 30 1
2012–13 Stoke C 32 0
2013–14 Stoke C 32 0
2014–15 Stoke C 28 0
2015–16 Stoke C 37 0
2016–17 Stoke C 30 0 **291 5**
2017–18 Aston Villa 33 1
2018–19 Aston Villa 35 1 **68 2**
2019–20 Hearts 0 0
2019–20 Fleetwood T 11 0 **11 0**

Players retained or with offer of contract
Crowe, Barry Thomas; Czajor, Szymon; Fowler, Michael.

Scholars
Barratt, Samuel Anthony William; Batch, Billy Thomas; Bird, Samuel David; Borwick, Johnathon Robert; Collins, Joseph Francis; Cooke, Jamie John; Edwards, Daniel John; Goldsborough, Liam Paul; Hayes, Cian Jude; Makepeace, Kian James Blackmore; Patterson, Lewis Thomas; Pengelly, Scott James; Raffie, Akiel; Sithole, Shaun Thabo; Steer, Kai Philip James; Takpe, Enoch Oluwakayode; Thompson, Ben Owen; Williams, Anthony Joseph.

FOREST GREEN R (34)

ADAMS, Ebou (M) 39 4
b. 15-1-96
Internationals: Gambia Full caps.
From Dartford.
2017–18 Norwich C 0 0
2017–18 *Shrewsbury T* 5 0 **5 0**
From Ebbsfleet U.
2019–20 Forest Green R 34 4 **34 4**

AITCHISON, Jack (F) 45 7
b.Fauldhouse 5-3-00
Internationals: Scotland U16, U17, U19.
2015–16 Celtic 1 1
2016–17 Celtic 2 0
2017–18 Celtic 0 0
2018–19 Celtic 0 0
2018–19 *Dumbarton* 4 0 **4 0**
2018–19 *Alloa Ath* 10 1 **10 1**
2019–20 Celtic 0 0 **3 1**
On loan from Celtic.
2019–20 Forest Green R 28 5 **28 5**

ALLEN, Taylor (F) 5 1
b. 16-6-00
From Romulus, Nuneaton Bor.
2019–20 Forest Green R 5 1 **5 1**

ARTWELL, Oliver (M) 0 0
2019–20 Forest Green R 0 0

BERNARD, Dominic (D) 28 0
b.Gloucester 29-3-97
Internationals: Republic of Ireland U17, U18.
2018–19 Birmingham C 0 0
2019–20 Forest Green R 28 0 **28 0**

BUNKER, Harvey (M) 0 0
2019–20 Forest Green R 0 0

COLLINS, Aaron (F) 98 16
b. 27-5-97
Internationals: Wales U19.
2014–15 Newport Co 2 0
2015–16 Newport Co 18 2
2015–16 Wolverhampton W 0 0
2016–17 Wolverhampton W 0 0
2016–17 *Notts Co* 18 2 **18 2**
2017–18 Wolverhampton W 0 0
2017–18 *Newport Co* 10 0 **30 2**
2018–19 Wolverhampton W 0 0
2018–19 *Colchester U* 7 0 **7 0**
2018–19 Morecambe 15 8 **15 8**
2019–20 Forest Green R 28 4 **28 4**

COVIL, Vaughn (M) 2 0
b. 26-7-03
Internationals: USA U16.
From Southampton.
2019–20 Forest Green R 2 0 **2 0**

DAWSON, Kevin (M) 253 19
H: 5 10 W: 12 08 b.Dublin 30-6-90
Internationals: Republic of Ireland U18.
2011 Shelbourne 26 2
2012 Shelbourne 25 2 **51 4**
2012–13 Yeovil T 20 2
2013–14 Yeovil T 35 1
2014–15 Yeovil T 17 1
2015–16 Yeovil T 10 0
2016–17 Yeovil T 39 2 **121 6**
2016–17 Cheltenham T 0 0
2017–18 Cheltenham T 34 5
2018–19 Cheltenham T 32 4 **66 9**
2019–20 Forest Green R 15 0 **15 0**

FREAR, Elliott (F) 86 4
H: 5 8 W: 10 01 b.Exeter 11-9-90
Internationals: England C.
2009–10 Exeter C 0 0
2010–11 Exeter C 0 0
2011–12 Exeter C 10 0
2012–13 Exeter C 2 0 **12 0**
From Salisbury C, Forest Green R.
2016–17 Motherwell 15 1
2017–18 Motherwell 23 1
2018–19 Motherwell 22 1 **60 3**
2019–20 Forest Green R 14 1 **14 1**

GODWIN-MALIFE, Udoka (D) 17 0
b. 9-5-00
From Oxford C.
2018–19 Forest Green R 5 0
2019–20 Forest Green R 12 0 **17 0**

GRUBB, Dayle (M) 56 8
H: 6 0 W: 12 13 b. 24-7-91
From Weston-super-Mare
2017–18 Forest Green R 21 5
2018–19 Forest Green R 28 3
2019–20 Forest Green R 7 0 **56 8**

HILL, Ethan (D) 0 0
2019–20 Forest Green R 0 0

JONES, Dan (M) 0 0
Internationals: Wales U17.
2019–20 Forest Green R 0 0

JONES, Isaiah (D) 0 0
From Tooting & Mitcham U.
2019–20 Forest Green R 0 0

KITCHING, Liam (D) 29 0
2017–18 Leeds U 0 0
2018–19 Leeds U 0 0
2019–20 Forest Green R 29 0 **29 0**

MARCH, Josh (M) 10 2
2019–20 Forest Green R 10 2 **10 2**

McCOULSKY, Shawn (F) 61 6
b.Lewisham 6-1-97
From Dulwich Hamlet.
2017–18 Bristol C 0 0
2017–18 *Newport Co* 27 6 **27 6**
2018–19 Bristol C 0 0
2018–19 *Southend U* 15 0 **15 0**
2018–19 Forest Green R 13 0
2019–20 Forest Green R 6 0 **19 0**

McGINLEY, Nathan (D) 69 0
b.Middlesbrough 15-9-96
2017–18 Middlesbrough 0 0
2017–18 *Wycombe W* 11 0 **11 0**
2018–19 Middlesbrough 0 0
2018–19 *Forest Green R* 38 0
2019–20 Forest Green R 20 0 **58 0**
Transferred to Motherwell, June 2020.

MILLS, Joseph (D) 264 15
H: 5 9 W: 11 00 b.Swindon 30-10-89
Internationals: England U17, U18.
2006–07 Southampton 0 0
2007–08 Southampton 0 0
2008–09 Southampton 8 0
2008–09 *Scunthorpe U* 14 0 **14 0**
2009–10 Southampton 16 0
2010–11 Southampton 2 0
2010–11 *Doncaster R* 18 2 **18 2**
2011–12 Southampton 0 0 **26 0**
2011–12 Reading 15 0
2012–13 Reading 0 0 **15 0**
2012–13 *Burnley* 10 0
2013–14 Burnley 0 0 **10 0**
2013–14 *Oldham Ath* 11 0
2013–14 *Shrewsbury T* 13 0 **13 0**
2014–15 Oldham Ath 30 0
2015–16 Oldham Ath 15 1 **56 1**
2016–17 Perth Glory 22 1
2017–18 Perth Glory 22 0 **44 1**
2018–19 Forest Green R 44 4
2019–20 Forest Green R 24 7 **68 11**

MILLS, Matthew (D) 391 23
H: 6 3 W: 12 12 b.Swindon 14-7-86
Internationals: England U19.
2004–05 Southampton 0 0
2004–05 *Coventry C* 4 0 **4 0**
2004–05 *Bournemouth* 12 3 **12 3**
2005–06 Southampton 4 0 **4 0**
2005–06 Manchester C 1 0
2006–07 Manchester C 1 0
2006–07 *Colchester U* 9 0 **9 0**
2007–08 Manchester C 0 0 **2 0**
2007–08 *Doncaster R* 34 3
2008–09 Doncaster R 41 0
2009–10 Doncaster R 0 0 **75 3**
2009–10 Reading 23 2
2010–11 Reading 38 2 **61 4**
2011–12 Leicester C 25 1 **25 1**
2012–13 Bolton W 18 1
2013–14 Bolton W 32 1
2014–15 Bolton W 37 4 **87 6**
2015–16 Nottingham F 42 5
2016–17 Nottingham F 27 1
2017–18 Nottingham F 13 0 **82 6**
2017–18 Barnsley 4 0 **4 0**
2018–19 Pune C 7 0 **7 0**
2019–20 Forest Green R 19 0 **19 0**

MONDAL, Junior (F) 39 5
b. 27-3-97
From Spennymoor T, Whitby T.
2018–19 Forest Green R 18 3
2019–20 Forest Green R 21 2 **39 5**

OGUNLEYE, Daniel (F) 0 0
b. 9-1-02
2019–20 Forest Green R 0 0

RAWSON, Farrend (D) 132 6
H: 6 1 W: 11 07 b.Nottingham 11-7-96
2014–15 Derby Co 0 0

2014–15 *Rotherham U* 4 0
2015–16 Derby Co 0 0
2015–16 *Rotherham U* 16 2 **20 2**
2016–17 Derby Co 0 0
2016–17 *Coventry C* 14 0 **14 0**
2017–18 Derby Co 0 0
2017–18 *Accrington S* 12 0 **12 0**
2017–18 Forest Green R 18 1
2018–19 Forest Green R 38 0
2019–20 Forest Green R 30 3 **86 4**

SAUNDERS, Alfie (D) 0 0
2019–20 Forest Green R 0 0

SHEPHARD, Liam (D) 146 7
H: 5 10 W: 10 08 b.Rhondda 22-11-94
Internationals: Wales U21.
2013–14 Swansea C 0 0
2014–15 Swansea C 0 0
2014–15 *Yeovil T* 20 0
2015–16 Swansea C 0 0
2015–16 *Yeovil T* 6 0
2016–17 Swansea C 0 0
2016–17 *Yeovil T* 38 1 **64 1**
2017–18 Peterborough U 24 0 **24 0**
2018–19 Forest Green R 39 5
2019–20 Forest Green R 19 1 **58 6**

SMITH, Adam (G) 126 0
H: 5 11 W: 11 00 b.Sunderland 23-11-92
2010–11 Leicester C 0 0
2011–12 Leicester C 0 0
2011–12 *Chesterfield* 0 0
2011–12 *Bristol R* 0 0
2012–13 Leicester C 0 0
2013–14 Leicester C 0 0
2013–14 *Stevenage* 0 0
2014–15 Leicester C 0 0
2014–15 *Mansfield T* 4 0 **4 0**
2015–16 Northampton T 46 0
2016–17 Northampton T 40 0 **86 0**
2017–18 Bristol R 23 0
2018–19 Bristol R 5 0 **28 0**
2019–20 Forest Green R 8 0 **8 0**

STEVENS, Mathew (F) 43 5
H: 5 11 W: 11 09 b. 12-2-98
2015–16 Barnet 10 1 **10 1**
2016–17 Peterborough U 1 0
2017–18 Peterborough U 0 0
2018–19 Peterborough U 3 0 **4 0**
2019–20 Forest Green R 29 4 **29 4**

STOKES, Chris (M) 157 7
H: 5 7 W: 10 04 b.Trowbridge 8-3-91
Internationals: England U17, C.
2009–10 Crewe Alex 2 0 **2 0**
From Forest Green R.
2014–15 Coventry C 16 1
2015–16 Coventry C 36 2
2016–17 Coventry C 7 0
2017–18 Coventry C 29 0 **88 3**
2018–19 Bury 37 4 **37 4**
2019–20 Stevenage 25 0 **25 0**
2019–20 Forest Green R 5 0 **5 0**

THOMAS, Lewis (G) 15 0
Internationals: Wales U17.
From Swansea C.
2018–19 Forest Green R 0 0
2019–20 Forest Green R 15 0 **15 0**

WILLIAMS, George C (F) 93 8
H: 5 10 W: 12 04 b.Milton Keynes 7-9-95
Internationals: Wales U17, U19, U21, Full caps.
2012–13 Fulham 0 0
2013–14 Fulham 0 0
2014–15 Fulham 14 0
2014–15 *Milton Keynes D* 4 0
2015–16 Fulham 1 0
2015–16 *Gillingham* 10 0 **10 0**
2016–17 Fulham 0 0
2016–17 *Milton Keynes D* 11 0 **15 0**
2017–18 Fulham 0 0 **15 0**
2017–18 *St Johnstone* 11 0 **11 0**
2018–19 Forest Green R 38 7
2019–20 Forest Green R 4 1 **42 8**

WINCHESTER, Carl (D) 264 22
H: 5 10 W: 11 08 b.Belfast 12-4-93
Internationals: Northern Ireland U16, U17, U18, U19, U21, Full caps.
2010–11 Oldham Ath 6 1
2011–12 Oldham Ath 12 0
2012–13 Oldham Ath 9 0
2013–14 Oldham Ath 12 1
2014–15 Oldham Ath 41 4
2015–16 Oldham Ath 31 1
2016–17 Oldham Ath 9 1 **120 8**
2016–17 Cheltenham T 20 1
2017–18 Cheltenham T 44 5 **64 6**
2018–19 Forest Green R 45 3
2019–20 Forest Green R 35 5 **80 8**

Scholars
Artwell, Oliver Joseph Robert; Bradshaw, Daniel William; Bunker, Harvey James; Covil, Vaughn Patrick; Hallett, Luke James; Hill, Ethan; Jeremiah, Joseph Kenneth; Jones, Daniel Owen; Jones, Isaiah Malchai Tayne; Morgan, Dylan James; Ogunleye, Daniel Oluwatomi Emeka; Oladipo, Destiny Olajuwon; Orford, Owen James; Owens, Louis Benjamin; Rees, Luc William; Thayer, Archie David; Turner, William; Yang, Seung Woo.

FULHAM (35)

ABRAHAM, Timmy (F) 4 0
From Charlton Ath.
2019–20 Fulham 0 0
2019–20 *Bristol R* 4 0 **4 0**

ARCHER, Jordan (G) 190 0
H: 6 1 W: 12 08 b.Walthamstow 12-4-93
Internationals: Scotland U19, U20, U21, Full caps.
2011–12 Tottenham H 0 0
2012–13 Tottenham H 0 0
2012–13 *Wycombe W* 27 0 **27 0**
2013–14 Tottenham H 0 0
2014–15 Tottenham H 0 0
2014–15 *Northampton T* 13 0 **13 0**
2014–15 *Millwall* 0 0
2015–16 Millwall 39 0
2016–17 Millwall 36 0
2017–18 Millwall 45 0
2018–19 Millwall 24 0 **144 0**
2019–20 Oxford U 6 0 **6 0**
2019–20 Fulham 0 0

AYITE, Floyd (M) 257 41
H: 5 9 W: 10 10 b.Bordeaux 15-12-88
Internationals: Togo Full caps.
2008–09 Bordeaux 0 0
2008–09 *Angers* 33 3 **33 3**
2009–10 Bordeaux 0 0
2009–10 *Nancy* 6 0 **6 0**
2010–11 Bordeaux 7 0
2011–12 Bordeaux 0 0 **7 0**
2011–12 Reims 18 3
2012–13 Reims 23 2
2013–14 Reims 32 5 **73 10**
2014–15 Bastia 30 6
2015–16 Bastia 32 8 **62 14**
2016–17 Fulham 31 9
2017–18 Fulham 28 4
2018–19 Fulham 16 1
2019–20 Fulham 1 0 **76 14**
Transferred to Genclerbirligi, September 2019.

BETTINELLI, Marcus (G) 142 0
H: 6 4 W: 12 13 b.Camberwell 24-5-92
Internationals: England U21.
2010–11 Fulham 0 0
2011–12 Fulham 0 0
2012–13 Fulham 0 0
2013–14 Fulham 0 0
2013–14 *Accrington S* 39 0 **39 0**
2014–15 Fulham 39 0
2015–16 Fulham 11 0
2016–17 Fulham 6 0
2017–18 Fulham 26 0
2018–19 Fulham 7 0
2019–20 Fulham 14 0 **103 0**

BRYAN, Joe (D) 284 18
H: 5 7 W: 11 05 b.Bristol 17-9-93
2011–12 Bristol C 1 0
2012–13 Bristol C 13 0
2012–13 *Plymouth Arg* 10 1 **10 1**
2013–14 Bristol C 21 2
2014–15 Bristol C 41 6
2015–16 Bristol C 39 2
2016–17 Bristol C 44 1
2017–18 Bristol C 43 5
2018–19 Bristol C 1 0 **203 16**
2018–19 Fulham 28 0
2019–20 Fulham 43 1 **71 1**

CAIRNEY, Tom (M) 334 44
H: 6 0 W: 11 05 b.Nottingham 20-1-91
Internationals: Scotland U19, U21, Full caps.
2009–10 Hull C 11 1
2010–11 Hull C 22 1
2011–12 Hull C 27 0
2012–13 Hull C 10 0
2013–14 Hull C 0 0 **70 2**
2013–14 Blackburn R 37 5
2014–15 Blackburn R 39 3 **76 8**
2015–16 Fulham 39 8
2016–17 Fulham 45 12
2017–18 Fulham 34 5
2018–19 Fulham 31 1
2019–20 Fulham 39 8 **188 34**

CHRISTIE, Cyrus (D) 291 6
H: 6 2 W: 12 03 b.Coventry 30-9-92
Internationals: Republic of Ireland Full caps.
2011–12 Coventry C 37 0
2012–13 Coventry C 31 2
2013–14 Coventry C 34 0 **102 2**
2014–15 Derby Co 38 0
2015–16 Derby Co 42 1
2016–17 Derby Co 27 1
2017–18 Derby Co 0 0 **107 2**
2017–18 Middlesbrough 25 1 **25 1**
2017–18 Fulham 5 0
2018–19 Fulham 28 0
2019–20 Fulham 24 1 **57 1**

DAVIS, Benjamin (M) 0 0
b.Phuket 24-11-00
Internationals: Singapore U16, U19. Thailand U23.
2019–20 Fulham 0 0

DE LA TORRE, Luca (M) 7 0
H: 5 9 W: 9 13 b.San Diego 23-5-98
Internationals: USA U17, U20, Full caps.
2016–17 Fulham 0 0
2017–18 Fulham 5 0
2018–19 Fulham 0 0
2019–20 Fulham 2 0 **7 0**

FRANCOIS, Tyrese (M) 0 0
b.Campbelltown 16-7-00
2019–20 Fulham 0 0

HARRIS, Jayden (M) 0 0
b.London 4-11-19
2019–20 Fulham 0 0

HECTOR, Michael (D) 287 15
H: 6 4 W: 12 13 b.Newham 19-7-92
Internationals: Jamaica Full caps.
2009–10 Reading 0 0
2010–11 Reading 0 0
2011 *Dundalk* 11 2 **11 2**
2011–12 Reading 0 0
2011–12 *Barnet* 27 2 **27 2**
2012–13 Reading 0 0
2012–13 *Shrewsbury T* 8 0 **8 0**
2012–13 *Aldershot T* 8 1 **8 1**
2012–13 *Cheltenham T* 18 1 **18 1**
2013–14 Reading 9 0
2013–14 *Aberdeen* 20 1 **20 1**
2014–15 Reading 41 3
2015–16 Chelsea 0 0
2015–16 *Reading* 30 1 **80 4**
2016–17 Chelsea 0 0
2016–17 *Ein Frankfurt* 22 1 **22 1**
2017–18 Chelsea 0 0
2017–18 *Hull C* 36 1 **36 1**
2018–19 Chelsea 0 0
2018–19 *Sheffield W* 37 2 **37 2**
2019–20 Fulham 20 0 **20 0**

IVAN CAVALEIRO, Ricardo (M) 193 27
H: 5 9 W: 11 07 b.Vialonga 18-10-93
Internationals: Portugal U17, U18, U19, U20, U21, Full caps.
2012–13 Benfica 0 0
2013–14 Benfica 8 0
2014–15 Benfica 0 0 **8 0**
2014–15 *Deportivo La Coruna* 34 3 **34 3**
2015–16 Monaco 12 1 **12 1**
2016–17 Wolverhampton W 31 5
2017–18 Wolverhampton W 42 9
2018–19 Wolverhampton W 23 3 **96 17**
2019–20 Fulham 43 6 **43 6**

JASPER, Sylvester (M) 2 0
2019–20 Fulham 2 0 **2 0**

JOHANSEN, Stefan (F) 307 41
H: 6 0 W: 12 04 b.Vardo 8-1-91
Internationals: Norway U16, U17, U18, U19, U21, U23, Full caps.
2007 Bodo/Glimt 4 0
2008 Bodo/Glimt 1 0
2009 Bodo/Glimt 4 0
2010 Bodo/Glimt 20 0 **29 0**
2011 Stromsgodset 13 1
2012 Stromsgodset 27 3
2013 Stromsgodset 27 4 **67 8**

2013–14 Celtic 16 2
2014–15 Celtic 34 9
2015–16 Celtic 23 1 **73 12**
2016–17 Fulham 36 11
2017–18 Fulham 45 8
2018–19 Fulham 12 0
2018–19 *WBA* 12 2 **12 2**
2019–20 Fulham 33 0 **126 19**

KAMARA, Aboubakar (F) 137 30
H: 5 10 W: 12 08 b.Gonesse 7-3-95
2013–14 Monaco 0 0
2014–15 Monaco 2 0 **2 0**
2015–16 Kortrijk 12 0 **12 0**
2015–16 Amiens 16 5
2016–17 Amiens 29 10 **45 15**
2017–18 Fulham 30 7
2018–19 Fulham 13 3
2018–19 *Yeni Malatyaspor* 10 1 **10 1**
2019–20 Fulham 25 4 **68 14**

KEBANO, Neeskens (M) 159 31
H: 5 11 W: 11 11 b.Montereau 10-3-92
Internationals: France U17, U18, U19, U20. DR Congo Full caps.
2010–11 Paris Saint-Germain 3 0
2011–12 Paris Saint-Germain 0 0
2012–13 Paris Saint-Germain 0 0 **3 0**
2012–13 *Caen* 12 1 **12 1**
2013–14 Charleroi 26 5
2014–15 Charleroi 33 12
2015–16 Charleroi 5 1 **64 18**
2016–17 Genk 3 0 **3 0**
2016–17 Fulham 28 6
2017–18 Fulham 26 3
2018–19 Fulham 7 0
2019–20 Fulham 16 3 **77 12**

LE MARCHAND, Maxime (M) 264 6
H: 5 11 W: 10 10 b.Saint Melo 10-11-89
2009–10 Rennes 0 0
2009–10 *Le Havre* 27 1
2010–11 Le Havre 22 0
2011–12 Le Havre 20 1
2012–13 Le Havre 28 0
2013–14 Le Havre 31 2
2014–15 Le Havre 33 1 **161 5**
2015–16 Nice 26 1
2016–17 Nice 10 0
2017–18 Nice 29 0 **65 1**
2018–19 Fulham 26 0
2019–20 Fulham 12 0 **38 0**

MAWSON, Alfie (D) 201 20
H: 5 8 W: 12 11 b.Hillingdon 19-1-94
Internationals: England U21.
2012–13 Brentford 0 0
2013–14 Brentford 0 0
2014–15 Brentford 0 0
2014–15 *Wycombe W* 45 6 **45 6**
2015–16 Barnsley 45 6
2016–17 Barnsley 4 2 **49 8**
2016–17 Swansea C 27 4
2017–18 Swansea C 38 2 **65 6**
2018–19 Fulham 15 0
2019–20 Fulham 27 0 **42 0**

McDONALD, Kevin (M) 471 36
H: 6 2 W: 13 03 b.Carnoustie 4-11-88
Internationals: Scotland U19, U21, Full caps.
2005–06 Dundee 26 3
2006–07 Dundee 31 2
2007–08 Dundee 34 9 **91 14**
2008–09 Burnley 25 1
2009–10 Burnley 26 1
2010–11 Burnley 0 0 **51 2**
2010–11 *Scunthorpe U* 5 1 **5 1**
2010–11 *Notts Co* 11 0 **11 0**
2011–12 Sheffield U 31 3
2012–13 Sheffield U 45 1
2013–14 Sheffield U 1 1 **77 5**
2013–14 Wolverhampton W 41 5
2014–15 Wolverhampton W 46 0
2015–16 Wolverhampton W 33 3 **120 8**
2016–17 Fulham 43 3
2017–18 Fulham 42 3
2018–19 Fulham 15 0
2019–20 Fulham 16 0 **116 6**

MITROVIC, Aleksandar (F) 281 119
H: 6 2 W: 13 10 b.Smederevo 16-9-94
Internationals: Serbia U19, U21, Full caps.
2011–12 Teleoptik 25 7 **25 7**
2012–13 Partizan Belgrade 25 10
2013–14 Partizan Belgrade 3 3 **28 13**
2013–14 Anderlecht 32 16
2014–15 Anderlecht 37 20 **69 36**
2015–16 Newcastle U 34 9
2016–17 Newcastle U 25 4
2017–18 Newcastle U 6 1 **65 14**
2017–18 *Fulham* 17 12
2018–19 Fulham 37 11
2019–20 Fulham 40 26 **94 49**

NORMAN, Magnus (G) 7 0
H: 6 3 W: 12 13 b.Kingston Upon Thames 19-1-97
Internationals: England U16, U18.
2017–18 Fulham 0 0
2018–19 Fulham 0 0
2018–19 *Rochdale* 7 0 **7 0**
2019–20 Fulham 0 0

O'RILEY, Matt (M) 1 0
H: 6 2 W: 12 02 b.Hounslow 21-11-00
Internationals: England U16, U18.
2017–18 Fulham 0 0
2018–19 Fulham 0 0
2019–20 Fulham 1 0 **1 0**

ODOI, Dennis (D) 389 11
H: 5 10 W: 11 09 b.Leuven 27-5-88
Internationals: Belgium U20, U21, Full caps.
2006–07 Oud-Heverlee Leuven 3 0
2007–08 Oud-Heverlee Leuven 21 0
2008–09 Oud-Heverlee Leuven 33 3 **57 3**
2009–10 Sint-Truiden 26 1
2010–11 Sint-Truiden 33 2 **59 3**
2011–12 Anderlecht 19 0
2012–13 Anderlecht 14 0 **33 0**
2013–14 Lokeren 37 1
2014–15 Lokeren 35 0
2015–16 Lokeren 35 1 **107 2**
2016–17 Fulham 30 2
2017–18 Fulham 38 1
2018–19 Fulham 31 0
2019–20 Fulham 34 0 **133 3**

ONOMAH, Joshua (M) 92 7
H: 5 11 W: 10 01 b.Enfield 27-4-97
Internationals: England U16, U17, U18, U19, U20, U21.
2013–14 Tottenham H 0 0
2014–15 Tottenham H 0 0
2015–16 Tottenham H 8 0
2016–17 Tottenham H 5 0
2017–18 Tottenham H 0 0
2017–18 *Aston Villa* 33 4 **33 4**
2018–19 Tottenham H 0 0 **13 0**
2018–19 *Sheffield W* 15 0 **15 0**
2019–20 Fulham 31 3 **31 3**

OPOKU, Jerome (D) 21 0
b.London 14-10-98
2019–20 Fulham 0 0
2019–20 *Accrington S* 21 0 **21 0**

RAMIREZ, Fabricio (G) 170 0
H: 6 1 W: 12 02 b.Las Palmas 31-12-87
Internationals: Spain U20.
2006–07 Deportivo La Coruna 0 0
2007–08 Deportivo La Coruna 6 0
2008–09 Deportivo La Coruna 0 0
2009–10 Valladolid 1 0
2010–11 Valladolid 0 0 **1 0**
2010–11 *Recreativo* 40 0 **40 0**
2011–12 Real Betis 15 0
2012–13 Real Betis 2 0 **17 0**
2013–14 Deportivo La Coruna 6 0
2014–15 Deportivo La Coruna 31 0
2015–16 Deportivo La Coruna 0 0 **43 0**
2016–17 Besiktas 32 0
2017–18 Besiktas 34 0 **66 0**
2018–19 Fulham 2 0
2019–20 Fulham 0 0 **2 0**
2019–20 *Mallorca* 1 0 **1 0**

REAM, Tim (D) 450 9
H: 6 1 W: 11 05 b.St Louis 5-10-87
Internationals: USA Full caps.
2006 St Louis Billikens 19 0
2007 St Louis Billikens 19 0
2008 St Louis Billikens 22 0
2008 Chicago Fire 12 0
2009 Chicago Fire 7 0 **19 0**
2009 St Louis Billikens 22 6 **82 6**
2010 New York RB 30 1
2011 New York RB 28 0 **58 1**
2011–12 Bolton W 13 0
2012–13 Bolton W 15 0
2013–14 Bolton W 42 0
2014–15 Bolton W 44 0 **114 0**
2015–16 Fulham 29 0
2016–17 Fulham 34 1
2017–18 Fulham 44 1
2018–19 Fulham 26 0
2019–20 Fulham 44 0 **177 2**

REID, Bobby (M) 245 40
H: 5 7 W: 10 10 b.Bristol 1-3-93
Internationals: Jamaica Full caps.
2010–11 Bristol C 1 0
2011–12 Bristol C 0 0
2011–12 *Cheltenham T* 1 0 **1 0**
2012–13 Bristol C 4 1
2012–13 *Oldham Ath* 7 0 **7 0**
2013–14 Bristol C 24 1
2014–15 Bristol C 2 0
2014–15 *Plymouth Arg* 33 3 **33 3**
2015–16 Bristol C 28 2
2016–17 Bristol C 30 3
2017–18 Bristol C 46 19 **135 26**
2018–19 Cardiff C 27 5
2019–20 Cardiff C 1 0 **28 5**
2019–20 Fulham 41 6 **41 6**

RODAK, Marek (G) 133 0
H: 6 2 W: 10 12 b. 13-12-96
Internationals: Slovakia U17, U19, U21.
2014–15 Fulham 0 0
2015–16 Fulham 0 0
2016–17 Fulham 0 0
2016–17 *Accrington S* 20 0 **20 0**
2017–18 Fulham 0 0
2017–18 *Rotherham U* 35 0
2018–19 Fulham 0 0
2018–19 *Rotherham U* 45 0 **80 0**
2019–20 Fulham 33 0 **33 0**

RUI FONTE, Pedro (F) 158 22
H: 6 0 W: 12 13 b.Lisbon 23-3-90
Internationals: Portugal U16, U17, U18, U19, U20, U21.
2008–09 Arsenal 0 0
2008–09 *Crystal Palace* 10 0 **10 0**
2009–10 Setubal 13 0 **13 0**
2010–11 Espanyol 11 0
2011–12 Espanyol 19 1
2012–13 Espanyol 10 0 **40 1**
2013–14 Benfica 0 0
2014–15 Benfica 0 0
2014–15 Belenenses 12 2 **12 2**
2015–16 Braga 15 4
2016–17 Braga 22 10
2017–18 Braga 2 1 **39 15**
2017–18 Fulham 27 3
2018–19 Fulham 0 0
2018–19 *Lille* 17 1 **17 1**
2019–20 Fulham 0 0 **27 3**
Transferred to Braga, August 2019.

SERI, Jean (M) 216 17
H: 5 5 W: 10 08 b.Grand-Bereby 19-7-91
Internationals: Ivory Coast U23, Full caps.
2013–14 Pacos de Ferreira 21 1
2014–15 Pacos de Ferreira 33 1 **54 2**
2015–16 Nice 38 3
2016–17 Nice 34 7
2017–18 Nice 31 2 **103 12**
2018–19 Fulham 32 1
2019–20 Fulham 0 0 **32 1**
2019–20 *Galatasaray* 27 2 **27 2**

SESSEGNON, Steven (D) 14 0
H: 5 8 W: 10 06 b.Roehampton 18-5-00
Internationals: England U16, U17, U18, U19, U20, U21.
2017–18 Fulham 0 0
2018–19 Fulham 0 0
2019–20 Fulham 14 0 **14 0**

STANSFIELD, Jay (F) 1 0
Internationals: England U18.
From Exeter C.
2019–20 Fulham 1 0 **1 0**

TAYLOR-CROSSDALE, Martell (F) 0 0
b.London 26-12-99
Internationals: England U16, U17, U18, U20.
From Chelsea.
2019–20 Fulham 0 0

ZAMBO, Andre-Franck (M) 137 2
H: 6 0 W: 11 09 b.Yaounde 16-11-95
Internationals: Cameroon Full caps.
2015–16 Marseille 9 0
2016–17 Marseille 33 0
2017–18 Marseille 37 0 **79 0**
2018–19 Fulham 22 0
2019–20 Fulham 0 0 **22 0**
2019–20 *Villarreal* 36 2 **36 2**

Scholars
Biereth, Mika Miles; Bowat, Ibane; Chisholm, Mac Lindsey; Cover, Tristan; D'Auri-Henry, Luciano Paul; Odutayo, Idris Adewale Olarewaju; Pajaziti, Adrion; Williams, Jay Terry.

GILLINGHAM (36)

AKINDE, John (F)				**303**	**89**
H: 6 2 W: 10 01 b.Camberwell 8-7-89					
2008–09	Bristol C	7	1		
2008–09	*Wycombe W*	11	7		
2009–10	Bristol C	7	0		
2009–10	*Wycombe W*	6	1	**17**	**8**
2009–10	*Brentford*	2	0	**2**	**0**
2010–11	Bristol C	2	0	**16**	**1**
2010–11	*Bristol R*	14	0	**14**	**0**
2010–11	*Dagenham & R*	9	2		
2011–12	Crawley T	25	1		
2011–12	*Dagenham & R*	5	0	**14**	**2**
2012–13	Crawley T	6	0	**31**	**1**
2012–13	Portsmouth	11	0		
2013–14	Portsmouth	0	0	**11**	**0**
From Alfreton T.					
2015–16	Barnet	43	23		
2016–17	Barnet	46	26		
2017–18	Barnet	32	7	**121**	**56**
2018–19	Lincoln C	45	15		
2019–20	Lincoln C	23	5	**68**	**20**
2019–20	Gillingham	9	1	**9**	**1**

BONHAM, Jack (G)				**120**	**0**
H: 6 4 W: 14 13 b.Stevenage 14-9-93					
Internationals: Republic of Ireland U17.					
2010–11	Watford	0	0		
2011–12	Watford	0	0		
2012–13	Watford	1	0	**1**	**0**
2013–14	Brentford	1	0		
2014–15	Brentford	0	0		
2015–16	Brentford	0	0		
2016–17	Brentford	1	0		
2017–18	Brentford	0	0		
2017–18	*Carlisle U*	42	0	**42**	**0**
2018–19	Brentford	0	0	**2**	**0**
2018–19	*Bristol R*	40	0	**40**	**0**
2019–20	Gillingham	35	0	**35**	**0**

BYRNE, Mark (M)				**337**	**28**
H: 5 9 W: 11 00 b.Dublin 9-11-88					
2006–07	Nottingham F	0	0		
2007–08	Nottingham F	1	0		
2008–09	Nottingham F	1	0		
2009–10	Nottingham F	0	0		
2010–11	Nottingham F	0	0	**2**	**0**
2010–11	*Barnet*	28	6		
2011–12	Barnet	43	5		
2012–13	Barnet	40	3	**111**	**14**
2014–15	Newport Co	42	4		
2015–16	Newport Co	46	2	**88**	**6**
2016–17	Gillingham	31	1		
2017–18	Gillingham	42	3		
2018–19	Gillingham	45	4		
2019–20	Gillingham	18	0	**136**	**8**

CHARLES, Regan (M)				**42**	**6**
H: 5 9 W: 10 12 b.London 1-3-97					
From Arsenal.					
2015–16	Charlton Ath	1	0		
2016–17	Charlton Ath	0	0		
2017–18	Charlton Ath	0	0	**1**	**0**
2018–19	Gillingham	26	3		
2019–20	Gillingham	15	3	**41**	**6**

CISSE, Ousseynou (D)				**238**	**11**
H: 6 5 W: 13 05 b.Dakar 6-4-91					
Internationals: Mali Full caps.					
2009–10	Amiens	9	0		
2010–11	Amiens	8	0		
2011–12	Amiens	19	0	**36**	**0**
2012–13	Dijon	24	0		
2013–14	Dijon	36	4		
2014–15	Dijon	35	1	**95**	**5**
2015–16	Rayo Vallecano	0	0		
2015–16	*Waasland-Beveren*	12	1	**12**	**1**
2016–17	Tours	25	1	**25**	**1**
2017–18	Milton Keynes D	32	0		
2018–19	Milton Keynes D	26	2	**58**	**2**
2019–20	Gillingham	2	1	**2**	**1**
2019–20	*Leyton Orient*	10	1	**10**	**1**

FULLER, Barry (D)				**462**	**3**
H: 5 10 W: 11 10 b.Ashford 25-9-84					
Internationals: England C.					
2004–05	Charlton Ath	0	0		
2005–06	Charlton Ath	0	0		
2005–06	*Barnet*	15	1		
From Stevenage B.					
2007–08	Gillingham	10	0		
2008–09	Gillingham	37	0		
2009–10	Gillingham	36	0		
2010–11	Gillingham	42	0		
2011–12	Gillingham	9	0		
2012–13	Gillingham	0	0		
2012–13	Barnet	39	0	**54**	**1**
2013–14	AFC Wimbledon	45	0		
2014–15	AFC Wimbledon	45	1		
2015–16	AFC Wimbledon	45	0		
2016–17	AFC Wimbledon	28	0		
2017–18	AFC Wimbledon	42	0	**205**	**1**
2018–19	Gillingham	39	1		
2019–20	Gillingham	30	0	**203**	**1**

HANLAN, Brandon (F)				**101**	**15**
H: 6 0 W: 11 07 b.Chelsea 31-5-97					
2016–17	Charlton Ath	9	0		
2017–18	Colchester U	18	2	**18**	**2**
2017–18	Charlton Ath	0	0	**9**	**0**
2018–19	Gillingham	39	9		
2019–20	Gillingham	35	4	**74**	**13**

HODSON, Lee (D)				**200**	**4**
H: 5 11 W: 11 02 b.Boreham Wood 2-10-91					
Internationals: Northern Ireland U19, U21, Full caps.					
2008–09	Watford	1	0		
2009–10	Watford	31	0		
2010–11	Watford	29	1		
2011–12	Watford	20	0		
2012–13	Watford	2	0	**83**	**1**
2012–13	*Brentford*	13	0	**13**	**0**
2013–14	Milton Keynes D	23	1		
2014–15	Milton Keynes D	14	1		
2015–16	Milton Keynes D	3	0	**40**	**2**
2015–16	*Kilmarnock*	13	0	**13**	**0**
2016–17	Rangers	11	1		
2017–18	Rangers	6	0		
2018–19	*St Mirren*	20	0		
2018–19	Rangers	0	0		
2019–20	Rangers	0	0	**17**	**1**
On loan from Rangers.					
2019–20	Gillingham	7	0	**7**	**0**
2019–20	*St Mirren*	7	0	**27**	**0**

LEE, Oliver (M)				**235**	**23**
H: 5 11 W: 12 07 b.Hornchurch 11-7-91					
2009–10	West Ham U	0	0		
2010–11	West Ham U	0	0		
2010–11	*Dagenham & R*	5	0		
2011–12	West Ham U	0	0		
2011–12	*Dagenham & R*	16	3	**21**	**3**
2011–12	*Gillingham*	8	0		
2012–13	Barnet	11	0	**11**	**0**
2012–13	Birmingham C	0	0		
2013–14	Birmingham C	16	1		
2014–15	Birmingham C	0	0	**16**	**1**
2014–15	*Plymouth Arg*	15	2	**15**	**2**
2015–16	Luton T	34	3		
2016–17	Luton T	33	1		
2017–18	Luton T	38	6	**105**	**10**
2018–19	Hearts	31	3	**31**	**3**
On loan from Hearts.					
2019–20	Gillingham	28	4	**36**	**4**

MANDRON, Mikael (F)				**133**	**18**
H: 6 3 W: 12 13 b.Boulogne 11-10-94					
Internationals: Scotland U20.					
2011–12	Sunderland	0	0		
2012–13	Sunderland	2	0		
2013–14	Sunderland	0	0		
2013–14	*Fleetwood T*	11	1	**11**	**1**
2014–15	Sunderland	1	0		
2014–15	*Shrewsbury T*	3	0	**3**	**0**
2015–16	Sunderland	0	0	**3**	**0**
2015–16	*Hartlepool U*	5	0	**5**	**0**
2016–17	Wigan Ath	3	0	**3**	**0**
2017–18	Colchester U	44	10		
2018–19	Colchester U	41	2	**85**	**12**
2019–20	Gillingham	23	5	**23**	**5**

O'KEEFE, Stuart (M)				**168**	**10**
H: 5 8 W: 10 00 b.Eye 4-3-91					
2008–09	Southend U	3	0		
2009–10	Southend U	7	0		
2010–11	Southend U	0	0	**10**	**0**
2010–11	Crystal Palace	4	0		
2011–12	Crystal Palace	13	0		
2012–13	Crystal Palace	5	0		
2013–14	Crystal Palace	12	1		
2014–15	Crystal Palace	2	0	**36**	**1**
2014–15	*Blackpool*	4	0	**4**	**0**
2014–15	Cardiff C	6	0		
2015–16	Cardiff C	24	2		
2016–17	Cardiff C	8	0		
2016–17	*Milton Keynes D*	18	4	**18**	**4**
2017–18	Cardiff C	0	0		
2017–18	*Portsmouth*	21	0	**21**	**0**
2018–19	Cardiff C	0	0	**38**	**2**
2018–19	*Plymouth Arg*	11	0	**11**	**0**
2019–20	Gillingham	30	3	**30**	**3**

OGILVIE, Connor (D)				**140**	**6**
H: 6 0 W: 12 08 b.Harlow 14-2-96					
Internationals: England U16, U17.					
2013–14	Tottenham H	0	0		
2014–15	Tottenham H	0	0		
2015–16	Tottenham H	0	0		
2015–16	*Stevenage*	21	1		
2016–17	Tottenham H	0	0		
2016–17	*Stevenage*	18	0	**39**	**1**
2017–18	Tottenham H	0	0		
2017–18	*Gillingham*	37	1		
2018–19	Tottenham H	0	0		
2018–19	*Gillingham*	31	0		
2019–20	Gillingham	33	4	**101**	**5**

PRINGLE, Ben (M)				**258**	**24**
H: 5 8 W: 11 10 b.Whitley Bay 25-7-88					
2009–10	Derby Co	5	0		
2010–11	Derby Co	15	0	**20**	**0**
2010–11	*Torquay U*	5	0	**5**	**0**
2011–12	Rotherham U	21	4		
2012–13	Rotherham U	41	7		
2013–14	Rotherham U	45	5		
2014–15	Rotherham U	40	3	**147**	**19**
2015–16	Fulham	15	2	**15**	**2**
2015–16	*Ipswich T*	10	2	**10**	**2**
2016–17	Preston NE	10	0		
2017–18	Preston NE	0	0		
2017–18	*Oldham Ath*	13	1	**13**	**1**
2018–19	Preston NE	0	0	**10**	**0**
2018–19	*Grimsby T*	15	0	**15**	**0**
2018–19	*Tranmere R*	13	0	**13**	**0**
2019–20	Gillingham	10	0	**10**	**0**

ROYCE, Simon (G)				**361**	**0**
b.Forest Gate 9-9-71					
1991–92	Southend U	1	0		
1992–93	Southend U	3	0		
1993–94	Southend U	6	0		
1994–95	Southend U	13	0		
1995–96	Southend U	46	0		
1996–97	Southend U	43	0		
1997–98	Southend U	37	0	**149**	**0**
1998–99	Charlton Ath	8	0		
1999–2000	Charlton Ath	0	0		
2000–01	Leicester C	19	0		
2001–02	Leicester C	0	0		
2001–02	*Brighton & HA*	6	0	**6**	**0**
2001–02	*Manchester C*	0	0		
2002–03	Leicester C	0	0	**19**	**0**
2002–03	*QPR*	16	0		
2003–04	Charlton Ath	1	0		
2004–05	Charlton Ath	0	0	**9**	**0**
2004–05	*Luton T*	2	0	**2**	**0**
2004–05	*QPR*	13	0		
2005–06	QPR	30	0		
2006–07	QPR	20	0	**79**	**0**
2006–07	Gillingham	3	0		
2007–08	Gillingham	33	0		
2008–09	Gillingham	42	0		
2009–10	Gillingham	17	0		
2010–11	Brentford	2	0		
2011–12	Brentford	0	0	**2**	**0**
2019–20	Gillingham	0	0	**95**	**0**

TUCKER, Jack (D)				**29**	**0**
b. 13-11-99					
2017–18	Gillingham	1	0		
2018–19	Gillingham	0	0		
2019–20	Gillingham	28	0	**29**	**0**

WALSH, Joe (G)				**0**	**0**
2019–20	Gillingham	0	0		

WILLOCK, Matthew (M)				**44**	**1**
b. 20-8-96					
2016–17	Manchester U	0	0		
2017–18	Manchester U	0	0		
2017–18	*Utrecht*	3	0	**3**	**0**
2017–18	*St Johnstone*	11	1	**11**	**1**
2018–19	Manchester U	0	0		
2018–19	*St Mirren*	12	0	**12**	**0**
2018–19	*Crawley T*	11	0	**11**	**0**
2019–20	Gillingham	7	0	**7**	**0**

WOODS, Henry (M)				**0**	**0**
2018–19	Gillingham	0	0		
2019–20	Gillingham	0	0		

Players retained or with offer of contract
Ablade, Terry; Ashby-Hammond, Luca; Ashby-Hammond, Taye; Carvalho, Fabio; De, Havilland Ryan James; Drameh, Cody Callum Pierre; Fossey, Marlon Joseph; Hilton, Sonny; Jenz, Moritz; Las, Damian Jan; McAvoy, Connor; Mundle-Smith, Jaydn Josiah; Murphy, Luca Michael; O'Neill, Oliver John; Page, Jonathon Charles; Tiehi, Jean-Pierre Alberic; Wickens, George Alexander.

Scholars
Allen, Ben James; Baker, Matthew; Bake-Moran, George Henry David Kevin; Bancroft, Toby William Day; Fernandez, Emmanuel Oluwasegun; Hards, Jay Scott; Laing, Harry Derek; Lamb, Thomas Jay; Lintott, Harvey Daniel; Maher, Harry; Medhurst, Vinnie Regan; Nelson, Ronny Alex Scott Hall; Sithole, Gerald Albert; Walker, Charlie Jack; Witt, James David.

GRIMSBY T (37)

ADLARD, Luis (F) 0 0
2019–20 Grimsby T 0 0

BATTERSBY, Ollie (G) 0 0
2018–19 Grimsby T 0 0
2019–20 Grimsby T 0 0

BUCKLEY, Brandon (F) 0 0
b. 21-9-00
2018–19 Grimsby T 0 0
2019–20 Grimsby T 0 0

CARDWELL, Harry (F) 37 1
b. 23-10-96
Internationals: Scotland U19, U21.
From Reading.
2017–18 Grimsby T 16 0
2018–19 Grimsby T 19 1
2019–20 Grimsby T 2 0 **37 1**

CLARKE, Billy (F) 361 71
H: 5 7 W: 10 01 b.Cork 13-12-87
Internationals: Republic of Ireland U17, U19, U21.
2004–05 Ipswich T 0 0
2005–06 Ipswich T 2 0
2005–06 *Colchester U* 6 0 **6 0**
2006–07 Ipswich T 27 3
2007–08 Ipswich T 20 0
2007–08 *Falkirk* 8 1 **8 1**
2008–09 Ipswich T 0 0 **49 3**
2008–09 *Darlington* 20 8 **20 8**
2008–09 *Northampton T* 5 3 **5 3**
2008–09 *Brentford* 8 6 **8 6**
2009–10 Blackpool 18 1
2010–11 Blackpool 0 0
2011–12 Blackpool 9 0 **27 1**
2011–12 *Sheffield U* 5 1 **5 1**
2011–12 Crawley T 17 3
2012–13 Crawley T 36 10
2013–14 Crawley T 29 7 **82 20**
2014–15 Bradford C 36 13
2015–16 Bradford C 29 4
2016–17 Bradford C 33 7
2017–18 Charlton Ath 17 1
2018–19 Charlton Ath 0 0 **17 1**
2018–19 Bradford C 14 1 **112 25**
2019–20 Plymouth Arg 9 0 **9 0**
2019–20 Grimsby T 13 2 **13 2**

CLIFTON, Harry (M) 74 2
H: 5 11 W: 13 12 b. 12-6-98
Internationals: Wales U21.
2016–17 Grimsby T 0 0
2017–18 Grimsby T 10 0
2018–19 Grimsby T 39 2
2019–20 Grimsby T 25 0 **74 2**

COOK, Jordan (F) 190 22
H: 5 10 W: 10 10 b.Hetton-le-Hole 20-3-90
2007–08 Sunderland 0 0
2008–09 Sunderland 0 0
2009–10 Sunderland 0 0
2009–10 *Darlington* 5 0 **5 0**
2010–11 Sunderland 3 0
2010–11 *Walsall* 8 1
2011–12 Sunderland 0 0 **3 0**
2011–12 *Carlisle U* 14 4 **14 4**
2012–13 Charlton Ath 7 0
2012–13 *Yeovil T* 1 0 **1 0**
2013–14 Charlton Ath 3 0 **10 0**
2014–15 Walsall 32 5
2015–16 Walsall 34 3 **74 9**
2016–17 Luton T 35 3
2017–18 Luton T 10 0 **45 3**
2018–19 Grimsby T 24 4
2019–20 Grimsby T 14 2 **38 6**

CURRAN, Jock (M) 0 0
2018–19 Grimsby T 0 0
2019–20 Grimsby T 0 0

DAVIS, Harry (D) 266 21
H: 6 2 W: 12 04 b.Burnley 24-9-91
2009–10 Crewe Alex 1 0
2010–11 Crewe Alex 1 0
2011–12 Crewe Alex 41 5
2012–13 Crewe Alex 42 1
2013–14 Crewe Alex 32 3
2014–15 Crewe Alex 31 1
2015–16 Crewe Alex 11 1
2016–17 Crewe Alex 25 1 **184 12**
2016–17 *St Mirren* 6 2
2017–18 St Mirren 20 3 **26 5**
2018–19 Grimsby T 35 4
2019–20 Grimsby T 21 0 **56 4**

GARMSTON, Bradley (D) 102 3
H: 5 9 W: 10 12 b.Greenwich 18-1-94
Internationals: Republic of Ireland U17, U9, U21.
2012–13 WBA 0 0
2012–13 *Colchester U* 13 0 **13 0**
2013–14 WBA 0 0
2014–15 WBA 0 0
2014–15 *Gillingham* 8 1
2015–16 Gillingham 33 0
2016–17 Gillingham 5 0
2017–18 Gillingham 19 1
2018–19 Gillingham 19 0
2019–20 Gillingham 0 0 **84 2**
2019–20 Grimsby T 5 1 **5 1**

GRANDIN, Elliot (F) 177 22
H: 5 10 W: 10 07 b.Caen 17-10-87
Internationals: France U21.
2004–05 Caen 1 0
2005–06 Caen 19 3
2006–07 Caen 23 2
2007–08 Caen 12 1 **55 6**
2007–08 Marseille 8 0
2008–09 Marseille 8 2 **16 2**
2008–09 *Grenoble* 8 0 **8 0**
2009–10 CSKA Sofia 10 4
2010–11 CSKA Sofia 1 0 **11 4**
2010–11 Blackpool 23 1
2011–12 Blackpool 7 2
2011–12 *Nice* 9 0 **9 0**
2012–13 Blackpool 12 3
2013–14 Crystal Palace 0 0
2013–14 Blackpool 7 1 **49 7**
2014–15 Astra Giurgiu 2 0 **2 0**
2015–16 Shrewsbury T 0 0
2016–17 Ermis Aradippou 13 3 **13 3**
2018–19 Freujus 9 0 **9 0**
2019–20 Saint-Pierroise 0 0
2019–20 Grimsby T 5 0 **5 0**

GREEN, Matt (F) 235 44
H: 6 0 W: 12 09 b.Bath 2-1-87
Internationals: England C.
2006–07 Cardiff C 6 0
2007–08 Cardiff C 0 0 **6 0**
2007–08 *Darlington* 4 0 **4 0**
From Torquay U
2010–11 Oxford U 17 0 **17 0**
2010–11 *Cheltenham T* 19 0 **19 0**
From Mansfield T
2013–14 Birmingham C 10 1
2014–15 Birmingham C 0 0 **10 1**
2015–16 Mansfield T 44 16
2016–17 Mansfield T 42 10 **86 26**
2017–18 Lincoln C 45 13
2018–19 Lincoln C 19 2 **64 15**
2019–20 Grimsby T 29 2 **29 2**

HANSON, James (F) 372 92
H: 6 4 W: 12 04 b.Bradford 9-11-87
2009–10 Bradford C 34 12
2010–11 Bradford C 36 6
2011–12 Bradford C 39 13
2012–13 Bradford C 43 10
2013–14 Bradford C 35 12
2014–15 Bradford C 38 9
2015–16 Bradford C 41 11
2016–17 Bradford C 17 4 **283 77**
2016–17 Sheffield U 13 1
2017–18 Sheffield U 1 0 **14 1**
2017–18 *Bury* 17 0 **17 0**
2018–19 AFC Wimbledon 29 5 **29 5**
2019–20 Grimsby T 29 9 **29 9**

HENDRIE, Luke (M) 149 3
b. 27-8-94
Internationals: England U16, U17.
2013–14 Derby Co 0 0
2014–15 Derby Co 0 0
2015–16 Burnley 0 0
2015–16 *Hartlepool U* 3 0 **3 0**
2015–16 *York C* 18 0 **18 0**
2016–17 Burnley 0 0
2016–17 *Kilmarnock* 32 0 **32 0**
2017–18 Burnley 0 0
2017–18 *Bradford C* 13 0 **13 0**
2017–18 Shrewsbury T 10 0 **10 0**
2018–19 Grimsby T 41 2
2019–20 Grimsby T 32 1 **73 3**

HESSENTHALER, Jake (M) 231 8
b.Gravesend 20-4-94
2012–13 Gillingham 0 0
2013–14 Gillingham 19 1
2014–15 Gillingham 37 1
2015–16 Gillingham 38 4
2016–17 Gillingham 28 1
2017–18 Gillingham 37 0 **159 7**
2018–19 Grimsby T 44 0
2019–20 Grimsby T 28 1 **72 1**

HEWITT, Elliott (D) 232 9
H: 5 11 W: 11 10 b.Rhyl 30-5-94
Internationals: Wales U17, U21.
2010–11 Macclesfield T 1 0
2011–12 Macclesfield T 21 0 **22 0**
2012–13 Ipswich T 7 0
2013–14 Ipswich T 4 0
2013–14 *Gillingham* 20 0 **20 0**
2014–15 Ipswich T 3 0 **14 0**
2014–15 *Colchester U* 21 1 **21 1**
2015–16 Notts Co 38 0
2016–17 Notts Co 29 2
2017–18 Notts Co 43 4
2018–19 Notts Co 25 2 **135 8**
2019–20 Grimsby T 20 0 **20 0**

HOPE, Joseph (D) 0 0
2019–20 Grimsby T 0 0

KHOURI, Evan (M) 0 0
From West Ham U.
2019–20 Grimsby T 0 0

McKEOWN, James (G) 161 0
H: 6 1 W: 14 00 b.Birmingham 24-7-89
Internationals: Republic of Ireland U19.
2005–06 Walsall 0 0
2006–07 Walsall 0 0
2007–08 Peterborough U 1 0
2008–09 Peterborough U 1 0
2009–10 Peterborough U 4 0 **6 0**
2016–17 Grimsby T 39 0
2017–18 Grimsby T 37 0
2018–19 Grimsby T 43 0
2019–20 Grimsby T 36 0 **155 0**

McPHERSON, Brandon (M) 0 0
2018–19 Grimsby T 0 0
2019–20 Grimsby T 0 0

OGBU, Moses (F) 213 66
b.Osogbo 7-2-91
2010 Sirius 3 0
2011 Sirius 18 1
2012 Sirius 21 8
2013 Sirius 25 18
2014 Sirius 28 8
2015 Sirius 29 5
2016 Sirius 14 3
2016 Jonkopings Sodra 12 0 **12 0**
2017 Sirius 15 14
2018 Sirius 28 7 **181 64**
2019–20 Grimsby T 20 2 **20 2**
Transferred to Mjallby, March 2020.

OHMAN, Ludvig (D) 142 3
H: 6 2 W: 12 08 b.Umea 9-10-91
Internationals: Sweden U17, U19.
2010 Kalmar 1 0
2011 Kalmar 0 0
2012 Kalmar 16 0
2013 Kalmar 15 0
2014 Kalmar 6 0
2015 Kalmar 19 0 **57 0**
2016 Nagoya Grampus 9 0 **9 0**
2017 Eskilstuna 26 2 **26 2**
2018 Brommapojkarna 22 0 **22 0**
2018–19 Grimsby T 13 0
2019–20 Grimsby T 15 1 **28 1**

PAINTER, Cameron (M) 0 0
2019–20 Grimsby T 0 0

POLLOCK, Matthew (D) 21 0
b. 28-9-01
2018–19 Grimsby T 2 0
2019–20 Grimsby T 19 0 **21 0**

RING, Sebastian (D) 118 5
b. 18-4-95
2013 Orebro SK 0 0
2013 BK Forward 9 1
2014 Orebro SK 0 0
2014 BK Forward 24 2 **33 3**
2015 Orebro SK 0 0

2016 Orebro SK 21 1
2017 Orebro SK 22 1
2018 Orebro SK 25 0 **68 2**
2018–19 Grimsby T 15 0
2019–20 Grimsby T 2 0 **17 0**
Transferred to Kalmar, January 2020.

ROSE, Ahkeem (F) 34 3
b. 27-11-98
2018–19 Grimsby T 16 1
2019–20 Grimsby T 18 2 **34 3**

RUSSELL, Sam (G) 11 0
H: 6 0 W: 10 12 b.Middlesbrough 4-10-82
From Middlesbrough, Rochdale, Wrexham, Darlington.
2017–18 Forest Green R 5 0 **5 0**
2018–19 Grimsby T 5 0
2019–20 Grimsby T 1 0 **6 0**

STARBUCK, Joseph (M) 0 0
2019–20 Grimsby T 0 0

TILLEY, James (F) 11 0
H: 5 6 W: 9 04 b.Billingshurt 13-6-98
2014–15 Brighton & HA 1 0
2015–16 Brighton & HA 0 0
2016–17 Brighton & HA 0 0
2017–18 Brighton & HA 0 0
2018–19 Brighton & HA 0 0
2019–20 Brighton & HA 0 0 **1 0**
2019–20 Grimsby T 10 0 **10 0**

VERNAM, Charles (F) 84 12
b. 8-10-96
2013–14 Derby Co 0 0
2014–15 Derby Co 0 0
2015–16 Derby Co 0 0
2016 *Vestmannaeyjar* 9 1 **9 1**
2016–17 Derby Co 0 0
2016–17 *Coventry C* 4 0 **4 0**
2017–18 Derby Co 0 0
2017–18 *Grimsby T* 9 1
2018–19 Grimsby T 35 3
2019–20 Grimsby T 27 7 **71 11**

WATERFALL, Luke (D) 119 10
H: 6 2 W: 13 02 b.Sheffield 30-7-90
2008–09 Tranmere R 0 0
From Ilkeston, Gainsborough T
2013–14 Scunthorpe U 9 1
2014–15 Scunthorpe U 0 0 **9 1**
2014–15 *Mansfield T* 5 0 **5 0**
2017–18 Lincoln C 30 2
2018–19 Lincoln C 1 0 **31 2**
2018–19 Shrewsbury T 44 5
2019–20 Shrewsbury T 0 0 **44 5**
2019–20 Grimsby T 30 2 **30 2**

WHITEHOUSE, Elliott (M) 90 6
H: 5 11 W: 12 08 b.Worksop 27-10-93
Internationals: England C.
2012–13 Sheffield U 3 0
2013–14 Sheffield U 0 0 **3 0**
2013–14 *York C* 15 0 **15 0**
2014–15 Notts Co 7 1 **7 1**
2017–18 Lincoln C 32 2 **32 2**
2019–20 Grimsby T 33 3 **33 3**

WRIGHT, Max (M) 27 2
b.Grimsby 6-4-98
2016–17 Grimsby T 0 0
2017–18 Grimsby T 0 0
2018–19 Grimsby T 2 0
2019–20 Grimsby T 25 2 **27 2**

Scholars
Adlard, Luis Samuel; Banks, Hugo James; Blakeley, Adam Thomas; Boyes, Patrick William; Davey, Owen Jay; Derrick, Lewis Jack; Drinkell, Harvey John; Goundry, Jaz Leo; Hope, Joseph Alexander; Idehen, Duncan Nosahaere; Khouri, Evan Marley; McPherson, Brandon Samuel; Owoeye, Ayodeji Abel Bamidele; Painter, Cameron Nathan; Potts, Jamie; Smaller, Joshua James; Stead, Lennon Oren; Walker, Aidan James.

HUDDERSFIELD T (38)

AHEARNE-GRANT, Karlan (F) 154 48
H: 6 0 b.London 19-12-97
Internationals: England U17, U18, U19.
2014–15 Charlton Ath 5 0
2015–16 Charlton Ath 17 1
2015–16 *Cambridge U* 3 0 **3 0**
2016–17 Charlton Ath 8 0
2017–18 Charlton Ath 22 1
2017–18 *Crawley T* 15 9 **15 9**
2018–19 Charlton Ath 28 14 **80 16**
2018–19 Huddersfield T 13 4
2019–20 Huddersfield T 43 19 **56 23**

AKINOLA, Tim (M) 0 0
2018–19 Lincoln C 0 0
2019–20 Huddersfield T 0 0

AUSTERFIELD, Joshua (M) 0 0
b. 2-11-01
2019–20 Huddersfield T 0 0

BACUNA, Juninho (F) 141 9
H: 6 1 W: 12 04 b.Groningen 7-8-97
Internationals: Netherlands U18, U20, U21. Curacao Full caps.
2014–15 Groningen 11 0
2015–16 Groningen 14 0
2016–17 Groningen 24 1
2017–18 Groningen 33 1 **82 2**
2018–19 Huddersfield T 21 1
2019–20 Huddersfield T 38 6 **59 7**

BOCKHORN, Herbert (D) 28 0
b.Kampala 31-1-95
2014–15 Werder Bremen 0 0
2015–16 Wiedenbruck 2000 28 0 **28 0**
2016–17 Borussia Dortmund 0 0
2017–18 Borussia Dortmund 0 0
2018–19 Borussia Dortmund 0 0
2019–20 Huddersfield T 0 0

BROWN, Jaden (D) 15 0
Internationals: England U16, U17, U18, U19.
From Tottenham H.
2018–19 Huddersfield T 0 0
2018–19 *Exeter C* 0 0
2019–20 Huddersfield T 15 0 **15 0**

BROWN, Reece (M) 109 13
H: 5 9 W: 12 04 b.Dudley 3-3-96
Internationals: England U16, U17, U18, U20.
2013–14 Birmingham C 6 0
2014–15 Birmingham C 1 0
2014–15 *Notts Co* 3 0 **3 0**
2015–16 Birmingham C 1 0
2016–17 Birmingham C 8 0 **16 0**
2016–17 *Chesterfield* 2 0 **2 0**
2017–18 Forest Green R 33 2
2018–19 Forest Green R 45 11 **78 13**
2019–20 Huddersfield T 0 0
2019–20 *Peterborough U* 10 0 **10 0**

BRYANT, Mitch (F) 1 0
2019–20 Huddersfield T 1 0 **1 0**

CAMPBELL, Frazier (F) 304 61
H: 5 11 W: 12 04 b.Huddersfield 13-9-87
Internationals: England U16, U17, U18, U21, Full caps.
2005–06 Manchester U 0 0
2006–07 Manchester U 0 0
2007–08 Manchester U 1 0
2007–08 *Hull C* 34 15
2008–09 Manchester U 1 0
2008–09 *Tottenham H* 10 1 **10 1**
2009–10 Manchester U 0 0 **2 0**
2009–10 Sunderland 31 4
2010–11 Sunderland 3 0
2011–12 Sunderland 12 1
2012–13 Sunderland 12 1 **58 6**
2012–13 Cardiff C 12 7
2013–14 Cardiff C 37 6 **49 13**
2014–15 Crystal Palace 20 4
2015–16 Crystal Palace 11 0
2016–17 Crystal Palace 12 1 **43 5**
2017–18 Hull C 36 6
2018–19 Hull C 39 12 **109 33**
2019–20 Huddersfield T 33 3 **33 3**

CHAPMAN, Jacob (G) 0 0
b. 22-10-00
2019–20 Huddersfield T 0 0

COLEMAN, Joel (G) 68 0
H: 6 6 W: 12 13 b.Bolton 26-9-95
2013–14 Oldham Ath 0 0
2014–15 Oldham Ath 11 0
2015–16 Oldham Ath 32 0 **43 0**
2016–17 Huddersfield T 5 0
2017–18 Huddersfield T 0 0
2018–19 Huddersfield T 1 0
2018–19 *Shrewsbury T* 16 0 **16 0**
2019–20 Huddersfield T 3 0 **9 0**

DALY, Matty (M) 6 1
H: 5 9 b. 10-3-01
Internationals: England U17, U18.
2018–19 Huddersfield T 2 0
2019–20 Huddersfield T 4 1 **6 1**

DIAKHABY, Adama (F) 91 6
H: 6 0 W: 10 03 b.Ajaccio 5-7-95
Internationals: France U21.
From Caen.
2015–16 Rennes 0 0
2016–17 Rennes 25 4 **25 4**
2017–18 Monaco 22 2 **22 2**
2018–19 Huddersfield T 12 0
2019–20 Huddersfield T 18 0 **30 0**
2019–20 *Nottingham F* 14 0 **14 0**

DUHANEY, Demeaco (D) 7 0
H: 5 11 W: 11 00 b.Manchester 13-10-98
Internationals: England U18, U20.
2017–18 Manchester C 0 0
2018–19 Huddersfield T 1 0
2019–20 Huddersfield T 6 0 **7 0**

EDMONDS-GREEN, Rarmani (D) 11 1
b.London 14-1-99
2019–20 Huddersfield T 2 0 **2 0**
2019–20 *Swindon T* 9 1 **9 1**

ELPHICK, Tommy (M) 360 14
H: 5 11 W: 11 07 b.Brighton 7-9-87
2005–06 Brighton & HA 1 0
2006–07 Brighton & HA 3 0
2007–08 Brighton & HA 39 2
2008–09 Brighton & HA 39 1
2009–10 Brighton & HA 44 3
2010–11 Brighton & HA 27 1
2011–12 Brighton & HA 0 0
2012–13 Brighton & HA 0 0 **153 7**
2012–13 Bournemouth 34 2
2013–14 Bournemouth 38 1
2014–15 Bournemouth 46 1
2015–16 Bournemouth 12 1 **130 5**
2016–17 Aston Villa 26 0
2017–18 Aston Villa 4 0
2017–18 *Reading* 4 0 **4 0**
2018–19 Aston Villa 11 1 **41 1**
2018–19 *Hull C* 18 1 **18 1**
2019–20 Huddersfield T 14 0 **14 0**

HADERGJONAJ, Florent (D) 179 2
H: 6 0 W: 11 11 b.Langnau 31-7-94
Internationals: Switzerland U20, U21, Full caps.
2013–14 Young Boys 11 1
2014–15 Young Boys 26 0
2015–16 Young Boys 32 0
2016–17 Young Boys 2 0 **71 1**
2016–17 Ingolstadt 04 25 1 **25 1**
2017–18 FC Ingolstadt 2 0 **2 0**
2017–18 *Huddersfield T* 23 0
2018–19 Huddersfield T 24 0
2019–20 Huddersfield T 21 0 **68 0**
2019–20 *Kasimpasa* 13 0 **13 0**

HAMER, Ben (G) 255 0
H: 5 11 W: 12 04 b.Chard 20-11-87
2006–07 Reading 0 0
2007–08 Reading 0 0
2007–08 *Brentford* 20 0
2008–09 Reading 0 0
2008–09 *Brentford* 45 0
2009–10 Reading 0 0
2010–11 Reading 0 0
2010–11 *Brentford* 10 0 **75 0**
2010–11 *Exeter C* 18 0 **18 0**
2011–12 Charlton Ath 41 0
2012–13 Charlton Ath 41 0
2013–14 Charlton Ath 32 0 **114 0**
2014–15 Leicester C 8 0
2015–16 Leicester C 0 0
2015–16 *Bristol C* 4 0 **4 0**
2016–17 Leicester C 0 0
2017–18 Leicester C 4 0 **12 0**
2018–19 Huddersfield T 7 0 **7 0**
2019–20 *Derby Co* 25 0 **25 0**

HARRATT, Kian (F) 1 0
b. 21-6-02
From Barnsley, Leeds U.
2019–20 Huddersfield T 1 0 **1 0**

HIGH, Scott (M) 1 0
b.Dewsbury 15-2-01
2019–20 Huddersfield T 1 0 **1 0**

HOGG, Jonathan (M) 322 2
H: 5 7 W: 10 05 b.Middlesbrough 6-12-88
2007–08 Aston Villa 0 0
2008–09 Aston Villa 0 0
2009–10 Aston Villa 0 0
2009–10 *Darlington* 5 1 **5 1**
2010–11 Aston Villa 5 0
2010–11 *Portsmouth* 19 0 **19 0**
2011–12 Aston Villa 0 0 **5 0**

2011–12 Watford 40 0
2012–13 Watford 38 0 **78 0**
2013–14 Huddersfield T 34 0
2014–15 Huddersfield T 26 0
2015–16 Huddersfield T 22 0
2016–17 Huddersfield T 37 1
2017–18 Huddersfield T 30 0
2018–19 Huddersfield T 29 0
2019–20 Huddersfield T 37 0 **215 1**

JACKSON, Ben (M) 0 0
2019–20 Huddersfield T 0 0

KACHUNGA, Elias (F) 226 41
H: 5 9 W: 10 01 b.Cologne 22-4-92
Internationals: Germany U19, U21, DR Congo Full caps.
2009–10 Borussia M'gladbach 0 0
2010–11 Borussia M'gladbach 2 0
2011–12 Borussia M'gladbach 0 0
2011–12 *Osnabruck* 17 10 **17 10**
2012–13 Borussia M'gladbach 0 0 **2 0**
2012–13 *Hertha Berlin* 2 0 **2 0**
2012–13 *Paderborn* 13 3
2013–14 Paderborn 33 6
2014–15 Paderborn 32 6 **78 15**
2015–16 Ingolstadt 10 0
2016–17 Ingolstadt 0 0 **10 0**
2016–17 *Huddersfield T* 42 12
2017–18 Huddersfield T 19 1
2018–19 Huddersfield T 20 0
2019–20 Huddersfield T 36 3 **117 16**

KONGOLO, Terence (D) 166 2
H: 6 0 W: 11 00 b.Rotterdam 14-2-94
Internationals: Netherlands U16, U17, U18, U19, U20, U21, Full caps.
2011–12 Feyenoord 1 0
2012–13 Feyenoord 5 0
2013–14 Feyenoord 17 0
2014–15 Feyenoord 31 0
2015–16 Feyenoord 29 0
2016–17 Feyenoord 23 1 **106 1**
2017–18 Monaco 3 0 **3 0**
2017–18 *Huddersfield T* 13 0
2018–19 Huddersfield T 32 1
2019–20 Huddersfield T 11 0 **56 1**
2019–20 *Fulham* 1 0 **1 0**

KOROMA, Josh (F) 37 3
H: 5 10 W: 10 06 b. 8-11-98
Internationals: England C.
2015–16 Leyton Orient 3 0
2016–17 Leyton Orient 22 3 **25 3**
2019–20 Huddersfield T 7 0 **7 0**
2019–20 *Rotherham U* 5 0 **5 0**

MBENZA, Isaac (F) 153 20
H: 6 2 W: 12 02 b.Saint-Denis 8-3-96
Internationals: Belgium U17, U19, U21.
2014–15 Valenciennes 13 1
2015–16 Valenciennes 35 6 **48 7**
2016–17 Standard Liege 21 1 **21 1**
2016–17 Montpellier 16 3
2017–18 Montpellier 38 8
2018–19 Montpellier 0 0 **54 11**
On loan from Montpellier.
2018–19 Huddersfield T 22 1
2019–20 Huddersfield T 5 0 **27 1**
2019–20 *Amiens* 3 0 **3 0**

MOUNIE, Steve (F) 158 42
H: 6 3 W: 12 08 b.Parakou 29-9-94
Internationals: Benin Full caps.
2014–15 Montpellier 0 0
2015–16 Montpellier 2 0
2015–16 *Nimes* 32 11 **32 11**
2016–17 Montpellier 35 14 **37 14**
2017–18 Huddersfield T 28 7
2018–19 Huddersfield T 31 2
2019–20 Huddersfield T 30 8 **89 17**

O'BRIEN, Lewis (M) 78 6
H: 5 8 W: 9 13 b.Colchester 14-10-98
2017–18 Huddersfield T 0 0
2018–19 Huddersfield T 0 0
2018–19 *Bradford C* 40 4 **40 4**
2019–20 Huddersfield T 38 2 **38 2**

PRITCHARD, Alex (M) 191 28
H: 5 7 W: 9 11 b.Grays 3-5-93
Internationals: England U20, U21.
2011–12 Tottenham H 0 0
2012–13 Tottenham H 0 0
2012–13 *Peterborough U* 6 0 **6 0**
2013–14 Tottenham H 1 0
2013–14 *Swindon T* 36 6 **36 6**
2014–15 Tottenham H 0 0
2014–15 *Brentford* 45 12 **45 12**
2015–16 Tottenham H 1 0 **2 0**
2015–16 *WBA* 2 0 **2 0**
2016–17 Norwich C 30 6
2017–18 Norwich C 8 1 **38 7**
2017–18 Huddersfield T 14 1
2018–19 Huddersfield T 30 2
2019–20 Huddersfield T 18 0 **62 3**

PYKE, Rekeil (F) 39 1
H: 5 10 W: 10 03 b. 1-9-97
2016–17 Huddersfield T 0 0
2016–17 *Colchester U* 12 0 **12 0**
2017–18 Huddersfield T 0 0
2017–18 *Port Vale* 7 0 **7 0**
2018–19 Huddersfield T 0 0
2018–19 *Rochdale* 6 0
2019–20 *Rochdale* 13 1 **19 1**
2019–20 Huddersfield T 1 0 **1 0**

QUANER, Collin (F) 172 23
H: 6 3 W: 12 11 b.Dusseldorf 18-6-91
Internationals: Germany U20.
From Fortuna Dusseldorf.
2010–11 Arminia Bielefeld 17 1 **17 1**
2011–12 Ingolstadt 04 15 1
2012–13 Ingolstadt 04 1 0
2013–14 Ingolstadt 04 11 1 **27 2**
2013–14 *Rostock* 7 0 **7 0**
2014–15 Aalen 27 6 **27 6**
2015–16 Union Berlin 15 1
2016–17 Union Berlin 14 7 **29 8**
2016–17 Huddersfield T 16 2
2017–18 Huddersfield T 26 0
2018–19 Huddersfield T 2 0
2018–19 *Ipswich T* 16 4 **16 4**
2019–20 Huddersfield T 5 0 **49 2**

ROWE, Aaron (M) 3 0
b. 7-9-00
2018–19 Huddersfield T 2 0
2019–20 Huddersfield T 1 0 **3 0**

SCHINDLER, Christopher (D) 315 9
H: 6 2 W: 12 02 b.Munich 29-4-90
Internationals: Germany U21.
2009–10 1860 Munich 0 0
2010–11 1860 Munich 16 1
2011–12 1860 Munich 30 1
2012–13 1860 Munich 18 0
2013–14 1860 Munich 26 0
2014–15 1860 Munich 29 1
2015–16 1860 Munich 33 1 **152 4**
2016–17 Huddersfield T 44 2
2017–18 Huddersfield T 37 0
2018–19 Huddersfield T 37 1
2019–20 Huddersfield T 45 2 **163 5**

SCHOFIELD, Ryan (G) 19 0
H: 6 3 W: 11 00 b.Huddersfield 11-12-99
Internationals: England U18, U19, U20.
2018–19 Huddersfield T 0 0
2018–19 *Notts Co* 17 0 **17 0**
2019–20 Huddersfield T 1 0 **1 0**
2019–20 *Livingston* 1 0 **1 0**

SIMPSON, Danny (D) 331 1
H: 5 9 W: 11 05 b.Eccles 4-1-87
2005–06 Manchester U 0 0
2006–07 Manchester U 0 0
2006–07 *Sunderland* 14 0 **14 0**
2007–08 Manchester U 3 0
2007–08 *Ipswich T* 8 0 **8 0**
2008–09 Manchester U 0 0
2008–09 *Blackburn R* 12 0 **12 0**
2009–10 Manchester U 0 0 **3 0**
2009–10 Newcastle U 39 1
2010–11 Newcastle U 30 0
2011–12 Newcastle U 35 0
2012–13 Newcastle U 19 0 **123 1**
2013–14 QPR 33 0
2014–15 QPR 1 0 **34 0**
2014–15 Leicester C 14 0
2015–16 Leicester C 30 0
2016–17 Leicester C 35 0
2017–18 Leicester C 28 0
2018–19 Leicester C 6 0 **113 0**
2019–20 Huddersfield T 24 0 **24 0**

SOBHI, Ramadan (F) 124 19
b.Cairo 27-1-97
Internationals: Egypt U17, U20, U23, Full caps.
2013–14 Al Ahly 3 1
2014–15 Al Ahly 24 5
2015–16 Al Ahly 28 5
2016–17 Stoke C 17 0
2017–18 Stoke C 24 2 **41 2**
2018–19 Huddersfield T 4 0
2018–19 *Al Ahly* 18 2
2019–20 Huddersfield T 0 0 **4 0**
2019–20 *Al Ahly* 6 4 **79 17**

STANKOVIC, Jon (M) 55 2
H: 6 3 W: 12 04 b.Ljubljana 14-1-96
Internationals: Slovenia U16, U17, U18, U19, U21.
2012–13 Domzale 6 0
2013–14 Domzale 12 0
2014–15 Domzale 0 0
2015–16 Domzale 0 0 **18 0**
2016–17 Huddersfield T 7 0
2017–18 Huddersfield T 0 0
2018–19 Huddersfield T 11 1
2019–20 Huddersfield T 19 1 **37 2**

STEARMAN, Richard (D) 451 15
H: 6 2 W: 10 08 b.Wolverhampton 19-8-87
Internationals: England U16, U17, U19, U21.
2004–05 Leicester C 8 1
2005–06 Leicester C 34 3
2006–07 Leicester C 35 1
2007–08 Leicester C 39 2 **116 7**
2008–09 Wolverhampton W 37 1
2009–10 Wolverhampton W 16 1
2010–11 Wolverhampton W 31 0
2011–12 Wolverhampton W 30 0
2012–13 Wolverhampton W 12 1
2012–13 *Ipswich T* 15 0 **15 0**
2013–14 Wolverhampton W 40 2
2014–15 Wolverhampton W 42 0
2015–16 Wolverhampton W 4 0
2015–16 Fulham 29 0
2016–17 Fulham 0 0 **29 0**
2016–17 *Wolverhampton W* 18 0 **230 5**
2017–18 Sheffield U 28 2
2018–19 Sheffield U 16 1
2019–20 Sheffield U 0 0 **44 3**
2019–20 Huddersfield T 17 0 **17 0**

TOFFOLO, Harry (D) 168 8
H: 6 0 W: 11 03 b. 19-8-95
Internationals: England U18, U19, U20.
2014–15 Norwich C 0 0
2014–15 *Swindon T* 28 1 **28 1**
2015–16 Norwich C 0 0
2015–16 *Rotherham U* 7 0 **7 0**
2015–16 *Peterborough U* 7 0 **7 0**
2016–17 Norwich C 0 0
2016–17 *Scunthorpe U* 22 2 **22 2**
2017–18 Norwich C 0 0
2017–18 *Doncaster R* 13 0 **13 0**
2017–18 Millwall 0 0
2018–19 Lincoln C 46 3
2019–20 Lincoln C 26 1 **72 4**
2019–20 Huddersfield T 19 1 **19 1**

VAN LA PARRA, Rajiv (M) 254 23
H: 5 11 W: 11 05 b.Rotterdam 4-6-91
Internationals: Netherlands, U17, U19, U21.
2008–09 Caan 2 0
2009–10 Caan 8 1
2010–11 Caan 6 0 **16 1**
2011–12 Heerenveen 23 4
2012–13 Heerenveen 31 5
2013–14 Heerenveen 32 5 **86 14**
2014–15 Wolverhampton W 40 1
2015–16 Wolverhampton W 13 0 **53 1**
2015–16 *Brighton & HA* 6 2 **6 2**
2015–16 Huddersfield T 8 0
2016–17 Huddersfield T 40 2
2017–18 Huddersfield T 33 3
2018–19 Huddersfield T 5 0
2018–19 *Middlesbrough* 3 0 **3 0**
2019–20 Huddersfield T 4 0 **90 5**
Transferred to Red Star Belgrade, August 2019.

Players retained or with offer of contract
Crichlow-Noble, Romoney; Elliott, Christopher Tchanga; McCamley, William David; Obiero, Micah; Olagunju, Mustapha Oluwatosin; Pata, Ilounga.

Scholars
Alfieri, George Anthony; Annakin, Taylor William Gerald; Ayina, Loick Denis Henry; Bamford, Thomas Samuel; Baxte-Alleyne, Darnel Darren; Bell, Thomas James; Bellagambi, Giosue Ebong; Billam, Luke Andrew; Bilokapic, Nicholas; Bright, Myles Iain Christian; Daley, Luke Steven; Diarra, Brahima; Edionhon, Andre Egbe Silveria; Headley, Jaheim Anthony; Ijiwole, Andrew Jose; Jones, Patrick Samuel; Kherbouche, Nasim; Krasniqi, Ernaldo; Meeson, Seth David; Midgley, Benjamin James; Mintus, Darnell Dantae Bowers; Okpolokpo, Joshua Melive Oghenrukewe; Roxburgh, Michael David; Sharroc-Peplow, Samuel Jacob; Shipley, Robson Leslie; Thompson, Remi Kai; Zunda, Gulutte.

HULL C (39)

BALOGH, Norbert (F) **81 9**
b.Debrecen 21-2-96
Internationals: Hungary U18, U19, U20, U21, Full caps.

2013–14	Letavertes	11	2	**11**	**2**
2014–15	Debrecen	15	2		
2015–16	Debrecen	18	3	**33**	**5**
2015–16	Palermo	4	0		
2016–17	Palermo	16	0		
2017–18	Palermo	2	0		
2018–19	Palermo	0	0	**22**	**0**
2018–19	*APOEL*	12	2	**12**	**2**
2019–20	Hull C	3	0	**3**	**0**

BATTY, Daniel (D) **58 1**
b.Featherstone 10-12-97

2016–17	Hull C	0	0		
2017–18	Hull C	1	0		
2018–19	Hull C	27	0		
2019–20	Hull C	30	1	**58**	**1**

BERRY, James (F) **1 0**
b.Wigan 10-2-00

2017–18	Wigan Ath	0	0		
2018–19	Wigan Ath	0	0		
2019–20	Hull C	1	0	**1**	**0**

BONDS, Elliott (M) **0 0**
b.London 23-3-00
Internationals: Guyana Full caps.
From Dagenham & R.

2019–20	Hull C	0	0		

BURKE, Reece (D) **144 4**
H: 6 2 W: 12 11 b.London 2-9-96
Internationals: England U18, U19, U20.

2013–14	West Ham U	0	0		
2014–15	West Ham U	5	0		
2015–16	West Ham U	0	0		
2015–16	*Bradford C*	34	2	**34**	**2**
2016–17	West Ham U	0	0		
2016–17	*Wigan Ath*	10	1	**10**	**1**
2017–18	West Ham U	0	0	**5**	**0**
2017–18	*Bolton W*	25	1	**25**	**1**
2018–19	Hull C	34	0		
2019–20	Hull C	36	0	**70**	**0**

DA SILVA LOPES, Leonardo (M) **142 5**
H: 5 6 W: 9 08 b.Lisbon 30-11-98
Internationals: Portugal U20.

2014–15	Peterborough U	2	0		
2015–16	Peterborough U	8	0		
2016–17	Peterborough U	38	2		
2017–18	Peterborough U	39	0	**87**	**2**
2018–19	Wigan Ath	1	0		
2018–19	*Gillingham*	14	1	**14**	**1**
2019–20	Wigan Ath	0	0	**1**	**0**
2019–20	Hull C	40	2	**40**	**2**

DE WIJS, Jordy (D) **103 3**
H: 6 2 W: 13 03 b.Vlijmen 8-1-95
Internationals: Netherlands U17, U18, U20, U21.

2014–15	PSV Eindhoven	0	0		
2015–16	PSV Eindhoven	1	0		
2016–17	PSV Eindhoven	0	0		
2016–17	*Excelsior*	15	0		
2017–18	PSV Eindhoven	1	0	**2**	**0**
2017–18	*Excelsior*	19	0	**34**	**0**
2018–19	Hull C	32	1		
2019–20	Hull C	35	2	**67**	**3**

DICKO, Nouha (M) **248 67**
H: 5 8 W: 11 00 b.Paris 14-5-92
Internationals: Mali Full caps.

2009–10	Strasbourg B	18	4		
2010–11	Strasbourg B	24	8	**42**	**12**
2010–11	Strasbourg	3	0	**3**	**0**
2011–12	Wigan Ath	0	0		
2011–12	*Blackpool*	10	4		
2012–13	Wigan Ath	0	0		
2012–13	*Blackpool*	22	5	**32**	**9**
2012–13	*Wolverhampton W*	4	1		
2013–14	Wigan Ath	0	0		
2013–14	*Rotherham U*	5	5	**5**	**5**
2013–14	Wolverhampton W	19	12		
2014–15	Wolverhampton W	37	14		
2015–16	Wolverhampton W	5	0		
2016–17	Wolverhampton W	30	3		
2017–18	Wolverhampton W	5	1	**100**	**31**
2017–18	Hull C	29	4		
2018–19	Hull C	16	2		
2019–20	Hull C	2	0	**47**	**6**
2019–20	*Vitesse*	19	4	**19**	**4**

EAVES, Tom (M) **256 63**
H: 6 3 W: 13 07 b.Liverpool 14-1-92

2009–10	Oldham Ath	15	0		
2010–11	Bolton W	0	0		
2010–11	*Oldham Ath*	0	0	**15**	**0**
2011–12	Bolton W	0	0		
2012–13	Bolton W	3	0		
2012–13	*Bristol R*	16	7	**16**	**7**
2012–13	*Shrewsbury T*	10	6		
2013–14	Bolton W	0	0		
2013–14	*Rotherham U*	8	0	**8**	**0**
2013–14	*Shrewsbury T*	25	2	**35**	**8**
2014–15	Bolton W	1	0		
2014–15	*Yeovil T*	5	0		
2014–15	*Bury*	9	1	**9**	**1**
2015–16	Bolton W	0	0	**4**	**0**
2016–17	Yeovil T	40	4	**45**	**4**
2017–18	Gillingham	41	17		
2018–19	Gillingham	43	21	**84**	**38**
2019–20	Hull C	40	5	**40**	**5**

ELDER, Callum (D) **111 1**
H: 5 11 W: 10 08 b.Sydney 27-1-95
Internationals: Australia U20.

2013–14	Leicester C	0	0		
2014–15	Leicester C	0	0		
2014–15	*Mansfield T*	21	0	**21**	**0**
2015–16	Leicester C	0	0		
2015–16	*Peterborough U*	18	1	**18**	**1**
2016–17	Leicester C	0	0		
2016–17	*Brentford*	6	0	**6**	**0**
2016–17	*Barnsley*	5	0	**5**	**0**
2017–18	Leicester C	0	0		
2017–18	*Wigan Ath*	27	0	**27**	**0**
2018–19	Leicester C	0	0		
2018–19	*Ipswich T*	4	0		
2019–20	Ipswich T	0	0	**4**	**0**
2019–20	Hull C	30	0	**30**	**0**

FLEMING, Brandon (D) **18 0**
b.Dewsbury 3-12-99

2017–18	Hull C	0	0		
2018–19	Hull C	4	0		
2019–20	Hull C	4	0	**8**	**0**
2019–20	*Bolton W*	10	0	**10**	**0**

GREAVES, Jacob (D) **29 0**
b.Cottingham 12-9-00

2019–20	Hull C	0	0		
2019–20	*Cheltenham T*	29	0	**29**	**0**

HENRIKSEN, Markus (M) **275 41**
H: 6 2 W: 13 05 b.Trondheim 25-7-92
Internationals: Norway U16, U17, U18, U19, U21, U23, Full caps.

2009	Rosenborg	3	0		
2010	Rosenborg	28	7		
2011	Rosenborg	29	3		
2012	Rosenborg	18	1	**78**	**11**
2012–13	AZ Alkmaar	29	3		
2013–14	AZ Alkmaar	26	2		
2014–15	AZ Alkmaar	22	7		
2015–16	AZ Alkmaar	28	12		
2016–17	AZ Alkmaar	3	2	**108**	**26**
2016–17	Hull C	15	0		
2017–18	Hull C	31	2		
2018–19	Hull C	39	2		
2019–20	Hull C	0	0	**85**	**4**
2019–20	*Bristol C*	4	0	**4**	**0**

HONEYMAN, George (M) **125 13**
H: 5 8 W: 11 05 b.Prudhoe 8-9-94

2014–15	Sunderland	0	0		
2015–16	Sunderland	1	0		
2016–17	Sunderland	5	0		
2017–18	Sunderland	42	6		
2018–19	Sunderland	35	6		
2019–20	Sunderland	0	0	**83**	**12**
2019–20	Hull C	42	1	**42**	**1**

INGRAM, Matt (G) **156 0**
H: 6 3 W: 12 13 b.Croydon 18-12-93

2011–12	Wycombe W	0	0		
2012–13	Wycombe W	8	0		
2013–14	Wycombe W	46	0		
2014–15	Wycombe W	46	0		
2015–16	Wycombe W	24	0		
2015–16	QPR	4	0		
2016–17	QPR	0	0		
2017–18	Northampton T	20	0	**20**	**0**
2017–18	QPR	2	0		
2018–19	Wycombe W	1	0	**125**	**0**
2018–19	QPR	4	0	**10**	**0**
2019–20	Hull C	1	0	**1**	**0**

IRVINE, Jackson (M) **244 26**
H: 5 10 W: 11 00 b.Melbourne 7-3-93
Internationals: Scotland U19. Australia U20, U23, Full caps.

2012–13	Celtic	1	0		
2013–14	Celtic	0	0		
2013–14	*Kilmarnock*	27	1	**27**	**1**
2014–15	Celtic	0	0	**1**	**0**
2014–15	*Ross Co*	28	2		
2015–16	Ross Co	36	2	**64**	**4**
2016–17	Burton Alb	42	10		
2017–18	Burton Alb	3	1	**45**	**11**
2017–18	Hull C	34	2		
2018–19	Hull C	38	6		
2019–20	Hull C	35	2	**107**	**10**

JONES, Callum (M) **0 0**
b. 5-4-01
From Bury.

2019–20	Hull C	0	0		

KINGSLEY, Stephen (D) **174 1**
H: 5 10 W: 10 09 b.Stirling 23-7-94
Internationals: Scotland U18, U19, U21, Full caps.

2010–11	Falkirk	3	0		
2011–12	Falkirk	15	0		
2012–13	Falkirk	35	0		
2013–14	Falkirk	35	1	**88**	**1**
2014–15	Swansea C	0	0		
2014–15	*Yeovil T*	12	0	**12**	**0**
2015–16	Swansea C	4	0		
2015–16	*Crewe Alex*	12	0	**12**	**0**
2016–17	Swansea C	13	0	**17**	**0**
2017–18	Hull C	11	0		
2018–19	Hull C	26	0		
2019–20	Hull C	8	0	**45**	**0**

LEWIS-POTTER, Keane (F) **21 2**
b. 22-2-01

2018–19	Hull C	0	0		
2019–20	Hull C	21	2	**21**	**2**

LICHAJ, Eric (D) **304 6**
H: 5 11 W: 12 07 b.Chicago 17-11-88
Internationals: USA U17, U20, Full caps.

2007–08	Aston Villa	0	0		
2008–09	Aston Villa	0	0		
2009–10	Aston Villa	0	0		
2009–10	*Lincoln C*	6	0	**6**	**0**
2009–10	*Leyton Orient*	9	1	**9**	**1**
2010–11	Aston Villa	5	0		
2010–11	*Leeds U*	16	0	**16**	**0**
2011–12	Aston Villa	10	1		
2012–13	Aston Villa	17	0	**32**	**1**
2013–14	Nottingham F	24	0		
2014–15	Nottingham F	42	0		
2015–16	Nottingham F	43	1		
2016–17	Nottingham F	41	2		
2017–18	Nottingham F	23	1	**173**	**4**
2018–19	Hull C	39	0		
2019–20	Hull C	29	0	**68**	**0**

LONG, George (G) **217 0**
H: 6 0 W: 12 05 b.Sheffield 5-11-93
Internationals: England U18, U20.

2010–11	Sheffield U	1	0		
2011–12	Sheffield U	2	0		
2012–13	Sheffield U	36	0		
2013–14	Sheffield U	27	0		
2014–15	Sheffield U	0	0		
2014–15	*Oxford U*	10	0	**10**	**0**
2014–15	*Motherwell*	13	0	**13**	**0**
2015–16	Sheffield U	31	0		
2016–17	Sheffield U	3	0		
2017–18	Sheffield U	0	0	**100**	**0**
2017–18	*AFC Wimbledon*	45	0	**45**	**0**
2018–19	Hull C	4	0		
2019–20	Hull C	45	0	**49**	**0**

MACDONALD, Angus (D) **88 1**
H: 6 0 W: 11 00 b.Winchester 15-10-92
Internationals: England U16, U19, C.

2011–12	Reading	0	0		
2011–12	*Torquay U*	2	0		
2012–13	Reading	0	0		
2012–13	*AFC Wimbledon*	4	0	**4**	**0**
2012–13	*Torquay U*	14	0	**16**	**0**

From Salisbury C, Torquay U.

2016–17	Barnsley	39	1		
2017–18	Barnsley	11	0	**50**	**1**
2017–18	Hull C	12	0		
2018–19	Hull C	1	0		
2019–20	Hull C	5	0	**18**	**0**

MAGENNIS, Josh (F) **353** **56**
H: 6 2 W: 14 07 b.Bangor 15-8-90
Internationals: Northern Ireland U17, U19, U21, Full caps.

2009–10	Cardiff C	9	0	**9**	**0**
2009–10	*Grimsby T*	2	0	**2**	**0**
2010–11	Aberdeen	29	3		
2011–12	Aberdeen	23	1		
2012–13	Aberdeen	35	5		
2013–14	Aberdeen	18	1	**105**	**10**
2013–14	*St Mirren*	13	0	**13**	**0**
2014–15	Kilmarnock	38	8		
2015–16	Kilmarnock	34	10	**72**	**18**
2016–17	Charlton Ath	39	10		
2017–18	Charlton Ath	42	10	**81**	**20**
2018–19	Bolton W	42	4		
2019–20	Bolton W	0	0	**42**	**4**
2019–20	Hull C	29	4	**29**	**4**

MANNION, Will (G) **0** **0**
H: 6 1 b. 5-5-98
Internationals: England U19.
From AFC Wimbledon.

2016–17	Hull C	0	0		
2017–18	Hull C	0	0		
2017–18	*Plymouth Arg*	0	0		
2018–19	Hull C	0	0		
2019–20	Hull C	0	0		

McKENZIE, Robbie (M) **26** **0**
b.Kingston upon Hull 25-9-98

2017–18	Hull C	0	0		
2018–19	Hull C	18	0		
2019–20	Hull C	8	0	**26**	**0**

McLOUGHLIN, Sean (D) **28** **1**
b.Cork 13-11-96
Internationals: Republic of Ireland U21.
From Cork C.

2019–20	Hull C	7	0	**7**	**0**
2019–20	*St Mirren*	21	1	**21**	**1**

MILINKOVIC, Manuel David (M) **87** **13**
H: 5 10 W: 11 00 b.Antibes 20-5-94

2014–15	Ternana	3	0	**3**	**0**
2015–16	Salernitana	9	0	**9**	**0**
2015–16	Genoa	0	0		
2015–16	*Virtus Lanciano*	7	0	**7**	**0**
2016–17	Genoa	0	0		
2016–17	*Messina*	34	7	**34**	**7**
2017–18	Genoa	0	0		
2017–18	*Hearts*	24	6	**24**	**6**
2018–19	Hull C	8	0		
2019–20	Hull C	0	0	**8**	**0**
2019–20	*Vancouver Whitecaps*	2	0	**2**	**0**

RITSON, Lewis (D) **0** **0**
b.South Shields 1-11-98

2017–18	Hull C	0	0		
2018–19	Hull C	0	0		
2019–20	Hull C	0	0		

SAMUELSEN, Martin (F) **75** **8**
H: 6 2 W: 11 05 b.Haugesund 17-4-97
Internationals: Norway U16, U17, U18, U21, Full caps.

2015–16	West Ham U	0	0		
2015–16	*Peterborough U*	17	1		
2016–17	West Ham U	0	0		
2016–17	*Blackburn R*	3	0	**3**	**0**
2016–17	*Peterborough U*	11	1		
2017–18	Peterborough U	0	0	**28**	**2**
2017–18	West Ham U	0	0		
2017–18	*Burton Alb*	9	0	**9**	**0**
2018–19	West Ham U	0	0		
2018–19	*Haugesund*	28	6	**28**	**6**
2019–20	Hull C	7	0	**7**	**0**

SCOTT, James (F) **43** **5**
Internationals: Scotland U21.

2016–17	Motherwell	0	0		
2017–18	Motherwell	2	0		
2018–19	Motherwell	12	1		
2019–20	Motherwell	22	3	**36**	**4**
2019–20	Hull C	7	1	**7**	**1**

SHEAF, Max (M) **20** **2**
b.Gravesend 10-3-00

2018–19	Hull C	1	0		
2019–20	Hull C	0	0	**1**	**0**
2019–20	*Cheltenham T*	19	2	**19**	**2**

SMITH, Andy (D) **0** **0**
b. 11-9-01

2019–20	Hull C	0	0		

STEWART, Kevin (D) **102** **6**
H: 5 7 W: 11 06 b.Enfield 7-9-93

2012–13	Tottenham H	0	0		
2012–13	*Crewe Alex*	4	0		
2013–14	Crewe Alex	0	0	**4**	**0**
2014–15	Liverpool	0	0		
2014–15	*Cheltenham T*	4	1	**4**	**1**
2014–15	*Burton Alb*	7	2	**7**	**2**
2015–16	Liverpool	7	0		
2015–16	*Swindon T*	5	0	**5**	**0**
2016–17	Liverpool	4	0	**11**	**0**
2017–18	Hull C	17	0		
2018–19	Hull C	27	0		
2019–20	Hull C	27	3	**71**	**3**

TAFAZOLLI, Ryan (D) **220** **15**
H: 6 5 W: 12 03 b.Sutton 28-9-91

2010–11	Southampton	0	0		

From Salisbury, Cambridge C, Carshalton Ath

2013–14	Mansfield T	24	2		
2014–15	Mansfield T	36	1		
2015–16	Mansfield T	44	5	**104**	**8**
2016–17	Peterborough U	31	3		
2017–18	Peterborough U	33	1		
2018–19	Peterborough U	37	1	**101**	**5**
2019–20	Hull C	15	2	**15**	**2**

TORAL, Jon (M) **131** **17**
H: 6 0 W: 12 07 b.Reus 5-2-95

2013–14	Arsenal	0	0		
2014–15	Arsenal	0	0		
2014–15	*Brentford*	34	6	**34**	**6**
2015–16	Arsenal	0	0		
2015–16	*Birmingham C*	36	8	**36**	**8**
2016–17	Arsenal	0	0		
2016–17	*Rangers*	12	2	**12**	**2**
2017–18	Hull C	27	1		
2018–19	Hull C	8	0		
2019–20	Hull C	14	0	**49**	**1**

Players retained or with offer of contract
Berry-McNally, James Jon; Cartwright, Harvey Jay; Chadwick, William Anthony; Foulkes, Harrison Andrew; Hanson, Ryan David; Hickey, Jordan; Jacob, Matthew James; Koy, Lupano Danny; Odunston, Lucas Thomas; Robson, David Leslie; Salam, Ahmed Mamdoh Abd.

Scholars
Bayram, Jake Thomas; Beckett, Louis George; Best, Thomas Steven Michael; Carew, Harvey James; Fisk, Harry Simon; Green, Oliver Jon Christopher; Guilfoyle, Robert Patrick; Hinds, Anthony Omarian Joshua; Jarvis, William Robert; Leake, Jake David; Lovick, Harry Oliver; Power, McCauley Thomas; Rees, Luke James; Snelgrove, McCauley James; Thompson, Quinn; Ward, Joshua Andrew.

IPSWICH T (40)

ALLEY, Jake (G) **0** **0**
b. 10-9-01

2019–20	Ipswich T	0	0		

BISHOP, Teddy (M) **87** **1**
H: 5 11 W: 10 03 b.Cambridge 15-7-96

2013–14	Ipswich T	0	0		
2014–15	Ipswich T	33	1		
2015–16	Ipswich T	4	0		
2016–17	Ipswich T	19	0		
2017–18	Ipswich T	4	0		
2018–19	Ipswich T	18	0		
2019–20	Ipswich T	9	0	**87**	**1**

BROWN, Kai (F) **0** **0**
b. 30-4-01

2018–19	Ipswich T	0	0		
2019–20	Ipswich T	0	0		

CHAMBERS, Luke (D) **666** **34**
H: 6 1 W: 11 13 b.Kettering 29-8-85

2002–03	Northampton T	1	0		
2003–04	Northampton T	24	0		
2004–05	Northampton T	27	0		
2005–06	Northampton T	43	0		
2006–07	Northampton T	29	1	**124**	**1**
2006–07	Nottingham F	14	0		
2007–08	Nottingham F	42	6		
2008–09	Nottingham F	39	2		
2009–10	Nottingham F	23	3		
2010–11	Nottingham F	44	6		
2011–12	Nottingham F	43	0	**205**	**17**
2012–13	Ipswich T	44	3		
2013–14	Ipswich T	46	3		
2014–15	Ipswich T	45	1		
2015–16	Ipswich T	45	3		
2016–17	Ipswich T	46	4		
2017–18	Ipswich T	37	1		
2018–19	Ipswich T	43	0		
2019–20	Ipswich T	31	1	**337**	**16**

CHIREWA, Tawanda (M) **0** **0**

2019–20	Ipswich T	0	0		

CLEMENTS, Bailey (D) **0** **0**
b. 15-11-00

2019–20	Ipswich T	0	0		

COTTER, Barry (D) **2** **0**
b. 4-12-98
Internationals: Republic of ireland U19.
From Limerick.

2017–18	Ipswich T	2	0		
2017–18	Ipswich T	0	0		
2019–20	Ipswich T	0	0	**2**	**0**

DOBRA, Armando (M) **3** **0**
b. 14-4-01
Internationals: Albania U19.

2019–20	Ipswich T	3	0	**3**	**0**

DONACIEN, Janoi (D) **184** **1**
H: 6 0 W: 11 11 b.St Lucia 3-11-93
Internationals: St Lucia Full caps.

2011–12	Aston Villa	0	0		
2012–13	Aston Villa	0	0		
2013–14	Aston Villa	0	0		
2014–15	Aston Villa	0	0		
2014–15	*Tranmere R*	31	0	**31**	**0**
2015–16	Aston Villa	0	0		
2015–16	*Wycombe W*	2	0	**2**	**0**
2015–16	*Newport Co*	29	0	**29**	**0**
2016–17	Accrington S	35	1		
2017–18	Accrington S	45	0		
2018–19	Ipswich T	10	0		
2018–19	*Accrington S*	19	0	**99**	**1**
2019–20	Ipswich T	13	0	**23**	**0**

DOWNES, Flynn (M) **78** **3**
H: 5 8 W: 11 00 b. 20-1-99
Internationals: England U19, U20.

2016–17	Ipswich T	0	0		
2017–18	Ipswich T	10	0		
2017–18	*Luton T*	10	0	**10**	**0**
2018–19	Ipswich T	29	1		
2019–20	Ipswich T	29	2	**68**	**3**

DOZZELL, Andre (M) **38** **2**
b.Ipswich 2-5-99
Internationals: England U16, U17, U18, U19, U20.

2015–16	Ipswich T	2	1		
2016–17	Ipswich T	6	0		
2017–18	Ipswich T	1	0		
2018–19	Ipswich T	19	1		
2019–20	Ipswich T	10	0	**38**	**2**

EDWARDS, Gwion (M) **223** **33**
H: 5 9 W: 12 00 b.Carmarthen 1-3-93
Internationals: Wales U19, U21.

2011–12	Swansea C	0	0		
2012–13	Swansea C	0	0		
2012–13	*St Johnstone*	6	0		
2013–14	Swansea C	0	0		
2013–14	*St Johnstone*	13	0	**19**	**0**
2013–14	*Crawley T*	6	2		
2014–15	Crawley T	37	4		
2015–16	Crawley T	42	8	**85**	**14**
2016–17	Peterborough U	33	7		
2017–18	Peterborough U	26	4	**59**	**11**
2018–19	Ipswich T	33	6		
2019–20	Ipswich T	27	2	**60**	**8**

EL MIZOUNI, Idris (M) **14** **1**
b. 26-9-00
Internationals: Tunisia U23, Tunisia Full caps.

2018–19	Ipswich T	4	0		
2019–20	Ipswich T	3	0	**7**	**0**
2019–20	*Cambridge U*	7	1	**7**	**1**

FOLAMI, Ben (F) **6** **0**
b.Sydney 8-6-99

2017–18	Ipswich T	4	0		
2017–18	Ipswich T	0	0		
2019–20	Ipswich T	0	0	**4**	**0**
2019–20	*Stevenage*	2	0	**2**	**0**

GIBBS, Liam (M) **0** **0**

2019–20	Ipswich T	0	0		

HENDERSON, Alex (D) **0** **0**

2019–20	Ipswich T	0	0		

HOLY, Tomas (G) **188** **0**
H: 6 9 W: 16 05 b.Rychnov nad Kneznou 10-12-91
Internationals: Czech Republic U16, U17, U18.

2010–11	Sparta Prague	0	0		
2011–12	Sparta Prague	0	0		
2012–13	Sparta Prague	0	0		
2013–14	Sparta Prague	0	0		
2013–14	*Vlasim*	9	0	**9**	**0**

2013–14 *Viktoria Zizkov* 14 0
2014–15 Sparta Prague 0 0
2014–15 *Viktoria Zizkov* 27 0 **41 0**
2015–16 Sparta Prague 0 0
2015–16 *Zlin* 20 0 **20 0**
2016–17 Fastav Zlin 0 0
2016–17 Gillingham 6 0
2017–18 Gillingham 45 0
2018–19 Gillingham 46 0 **97 0**
2019–20 Ipswich T 21 0 **21 0**

HUGHES, Thomas (F) 0 0
b. 21-10-00
2019–20 Ipswich T 0 0

HUWS, Emyr (M) 111 10
H: 5 10 W: 11 07 b.Llanelli 30-9-93
Internationals: Wales U17, U19, U21, Full caps.
2010–11 Manchester C 0 0
2011–12 Manchester C 0 0
2012–13 Manchester C 0 0
2012–13 *Northampton T* 10 0 **10 0**
2013–14 Manchester C 0 0
2013–14 *Birmingham C* 17 2 **17 2**
2014–15 Wigan Ath 16 0
2015–16 Wigan Ath 0 0 **16 0**
2015–16 *Huddersfield T* 30 5 **30 5**
2016–17 Cardiff C 3 0
2016–17 *Ipswich T* 13 3
2017–18 Cardiff C 0 0 **3 0**
2017–18 Ipswich T 5 0
2018–19 Ipswich T 0 0
2019–20 Ipswich T 17 0 **35 3**

JACKSON, Kayden (F) 133 31
H: 5 11 W: 11 07 b.Bradford 22-2-94
Internationals: England C.
2013–14 Swindon T 0 0
2014–15 Swindon T 0 0
From Oxford C, Tamworth, Wrexham.
2016–17 Barnsley 0 0
2016–17 *Grimsby T* 20 1 **20 1**
2017–18 Accrington S 44 16
2018–19 Accrington S 1 0 **45 16**
2018–19 Ipswich T 36 3
2019–20 Ipswich T 32 11 **68 14**

JUDGE, Alan (F) 345 51
H: 5 6 W: 11 03 b.Dublin 11-11-88
Internationals: Republic of Ireland U17, U8, U19, U21, U23, Full caps.
2006–07 Blackburn R 0 0
2007–08 Blackburn R 0 0
2008–09 Blackburn R 0 0
2008–09 *Plymouth Arg* 17 2
2009–10 Blackburn R 0 0
2009–10 *Plymouth Arg* 37 5 **54 7**
2010–11 Blackburn R 0 0
2010–11 Notts Co 19 1
2011–12 Notts Co 43 7
2012–13 Notts Co 39 8 **101 16**
2013–14 Blackburn R 11 0 **11 0**
2013–14 Brentford 22 7
2014–15 Brentford 37 3
2015–16 Brentford 38 14
2016–17 Brentford 0 0
2017–18 Brentford 13 0
2018–19 Brentford 20 1 **130 25**
2018–19 Ipswich T 19 0
2019–20 Ipswich T 30 3 **49 3**

KEANE, Will (F) 105 11
H: 6 2 W: 11 05 b.Stockport 11-1-93
Internationals: England U16, U17, U19, U20, U21.
2009–10 Manchester U 0 0
2010–11 Manchester U 0 0
2011–12 Manchester U 1 0
2012–13 Manchester U 0 0
2013–14 Manchester U 0 0
2013–14 *Wigan Ath* 4 0 **4 0**
2013–14 *QPR* 10 0 **10 0**
2014–15 Manchester U 0 0
2014–15 *Sheffield W* 13 3 **13 3**
2015–16 Manchester U 1 0
2015–16 *Preston NE* 20 1 **20 1**
2016–17 Manchester U 0 0 **2 0**
2016–17 Hull C 5 0
2017–18 Hull C 9 1
2018–19 Hull C 8 0 **22 1**
2018–19 *Ipswich T* 11 3
2019–20 Ipswich T 23 3 **34 6**

KENLOCK, Myles (D) 64 0
H: 6 1 W: 10 08 b.Croydon 29-11-96
2015–16 Ipswich T 2 0
2016–17 Ipswich T 18 0
2017–18 Ipswich T 16 0
2018–19 Ipswich T 19 0
2019–20 Ipswich T 9 0 **64 0**

LANKESTER, Jack (F) 11 1
b.Ipswich 19-1-00
2018–19 Ipswich T 11 1
2019–20 Ipswich T 0 0 **11 1**

McGAVIN, Brett (M) 1 0
b.Bury St Edmunds 21-12-99
2019–20 Ipswich T 1 0 **1 0**

MORRIS, Ben (F) 8 1
b. 6-6-99
Internationals: England U17, U18, U19.
2016–17 Ipswich T 0 0
2017–18 Ipswich T 3 0
2018–19 Ipswich T 1 0
2018–19 *Forest Green R* 4 1 **4 1**
2019–20 Ipswich T 0 0 **4 0**

NDABA, Corrie (D) 0 0
Internationals: Republic of Ireland U18.
2018–19 Ipswich T 0 0
2019–20 Ipswich T 0 0

NOLAN, Jon (M) 121 15
H: 5 11 W: 11 05 b.Huyton 22-4-92
Internationals: England C.
From Everton, Stockport Co, Lindoln C, Grimsby T.
2016–17 Chesterfield 30 1 **30 1**
2017–18 Shrewsbury T 43 9 **43 9**
2018–19 Ipswich T 26 3
2019–20 Ipswich T 22 2 **48 5**

NORWOOD, James (F) 77 40
H: 6 0 W: 12 13 b.Eastbourne 5-9-90
Internationals: England U18, C.
2009–10 Exeter C 3 0
2010–11 Exeter C 1 0 **4 0**
From Forest Green R.
2018–19 Tranmere R 45 29 **45 29**
2019–20 Ipswich T 28 11 **28 11**

NSIALA, Aristote (D) 169 6
H: 6 4 W: 14 09 b.DR Congo 25-3-92
Internationals: DR Congo Full caps.
2009–10 Everton 0 0
2010–11 Everton 0 0
2010–11 *Macclesfield T* 10 0 **10 0**
2011–12 Everton 0 0
2011–12 *Accrington S* 19 0
2012–13 Accrington S 17 0
2013–14 Accrington S 0 0 **36 0**
From Southport, Grimsby T.
2016–17 Hartlepool U 21 1 **21 1**
2016–17 Shrewsbury T 21 1
2017–18 Shrewsbury T 44 3 **65 4**
2018–19 Ipswich T 22 1
2019–20 Ipswich T 3 0 **25 1**
2019–20 *Bolton W* 12 0 **12 0**

NYDAM, Tristan (M) 24 0
H: 5 7 W: 9 06 b. 6-11-99
Internationals: England U18, U19.
2016–17 Ipswich T 0 0
2017–18 Ipswich T 18 0
2018–19 Ipswich T 1 0
2018–19 *St Johnstone* 5 0 **5 0**
2019–20 Ipswich T 0 0 **19 0**

PRZYBEK, Adam (G) 0 0
b. 2-4-00
Internationals: England U16. Wales U16, U17, U19, U21.
2018–19 WBA 0 0
2019–20 Ipswich T 0 0

ROBERTS, Jordan (M) 104 13
H: 5 11 W: 12 13 b.Watford 5-1-94
Internationals: England C.
2011–12 Aldershot T 4 0
2012–13 Aldershot T 5 0 **9 0**
From Havant & Waterlooville, Bishops Stortford, Aldershot T.
2015–16 Inverness CT 9 2 **9 2**
2016–17 Crawley T 23 3
2017–18 Crawley T 35 6 **58 9**
2018–19 Ipswich T 12 0
2018–19 *Lincoln C* 5 0 **5 0**
2019–20 Ipswich T 1 0 **13 0**
2019–20 *Gillingham* 10 2 **10 2**

ROWE, Danny (M) 52 6
H: 6 0 b.Wythenshawe 9-3-92
2016–17 Ipswich T 4 0
2017–18 Ipswich T 2 0
2017–18 *Lincoln C* 12 1
2018–19 Ipswich T 3 0
2018–19 *Lincoln C* 17 4 **29 5**
2019–20 Ipswich T 14 1 **23 1**

SEARS, Freddie (F) 362 64
H: 5 8 W: 10 01 b.Hornchurch 27-11-89
Internationals: England U19, U20, U21.
2007–08 West Ham U 7 1
2008–09 West Ham U 17 0
2009–10 West Ham U 1 0
2009–10 *Crystal Palace* 18 0 **18 0**
2009–10 *Coventry C* 10 0 **10 0**
2010–11 West Ham U 11 1
2010–11 *Scunthorpe U* 9 0 **9 0**
2011–12 West Ham U 10 0 **46 2**
2011–12 *Colchester U* 11 2
2012–13 Colchester U 35 7
2013–14 Colchester U 32 12
2014–15 Colchester U 24 10 **102 31**
2014–15 Ipswich T 21 9
2015–16 Ipswich T 45 6
2016–17 Ipswich T 40 7
2017–18 Ipswich T 36 2
2018–19 Ipswich T 24 6
2019–20 Ipswich T 11 1 **177 31**

SIMPSON, Tyreece (F) 3 0
2019–20 Ipswich T 3 0 **3 0**

SKUSE, Cole (M) 543 11
H: 6 1 W: 11 05 b.Bristol 29-3-86
2004–05 Bristol C 7 0
2005–06 Bristol C 38 2
2006–07 Bristol C 42 0
2007–08 Bristol C 25 0
2008–09 Bristol C 33 2
2009–10 Bristol C 43 2
2010–11 Bristol C 30 1
2011–12 Bristol C 36 2
2012–13 Bristol C 25 0 **279 9**
2013–14 Ipswich T 43 0
2014–15 Ipswich T 40 1
2015–16 Ipswich T 39 0
2016–17 Ipswich T 40 0
2017–18 Ipswich T 39 1
2018–19 Ipswich T 34 0
2019–20 Ipswich T 29 0 **264 2**

SMITH, Tommy (D) 294 25
b. 18-11-01
Internationals: England U17, U18. New Zealand U23, Full caps.
2007–08 Ipswich T 0 0
2008–09 Ipswich T 2 0
2009–10 Ipswich T 14 0
2009–10 *Brentford* 8 0 **8 0**
2010–11 Ipswich T 22 3
2010–11 *Colchester U* 6 0 **6 0**
2011–12 Ipswich T 26 3
2012–13 Ipswich T 38 3
2013–14 Ipswich T 45 6
2014–15 Ipswich T 42 4
2015–16 Ipswich T 45 2
2016–17 Ipswich T 10 0
2017–18 Ipswich T 3 0
2018 Colorado Rapids 33 4 **33 4**
2019–20 Ipswich T 0 0 **247 21**

VINCENT-YOUNG, Kane (D) 121 6
H: 5 11 W: 11 00 b.Camden Town 15-3-96
2014–15 Colchester U 0 0
2015–16 Colchester U 14 0
2016–17 Colchester U 18 0
2017–18 Colchester U 38 1
2018–19 Colchester U 40 3
2019–20 Colchester U 2 0 **112 4**
2019–20 Ipswich T 9 2 **9 2**

WILSON, James (D) 230 6
H: 6 2 W: 11 05 b.Chepstow 26-2-89
Internationals: Wales U19. U21, Full caps.
2005–06 Bristol C 0 0
2006–07 Bristol C 0 0
2007–08 Bristol C 0 0
2008–09 Bristol C 2 0
2008–09 *Brentford* 14 0
2009–10 Bristol C 0 0
2009–10 *Brentford* 13 0 **27 0**
2010–11 Bristol C 2 0
2011–12 Bristol C 21 0
2012–13 Bristol C 6 0
2013–14 Bristol C 0 0 **31 0**
2013–14 *Cheltenham T* 4 0 **4 0**
2013–14 Oldham Ath 16 1
2014–15 Oldham Ath 41 1
2015–16 Oldham Ath 43 0 **100 2**
2016–17 Sheffield U 7 1
2017–18 Sheffield U 0 0 **7 1**
2017–18 *Walsall* 19 1 **19 1**
2017–18 Lincoln C 8 1
2018–19 Lincoln C 11 1
2019–20 Lincoln C 0 0 **19 2**
2019–20 Ipswich T 23 0 **23 0**

WOOLFENDEN, Luke (D) **66 3**
b.Ipswich 21-10-98

2017–18	Ipswich T	2	0		
2018–19	Ipswich T	1	0		
2018–19	*Swindon T*	32	2	**32**	**2**
2019–20	Ipswich T	31	1	**34**	**1**

WRIGHT, Harry (G) **0 0**
b. 3-11-98

2018–19	Ipswich T	0	0		
2019–20	Ipswich T	0	0		

Players retained or with offer of contract
Andoh, Levi Leslie; Brown, Zak William; Crowe, Dylan; Drinan, Aaron John.

Scholars
Alexander, Fraser; Baggott, Elkan William Tio; Baker, Teddy James; Bareck, Michael Oluwasegun; Bello, Samson Olaoluwa; Bort, Antoni Krzysztof; Curtis, Harley William; Cutbush, Alfie; Edward-Alley, Jake Vintin; Egan, Toby Joe; Fehrenbach, Louie Oscar; Foudil, Lounes Mohamed; Healy, Matthew James; Henderson, Alexander; Hughes, Thomas; Kabongolo, Brooklyn Lukongola; O'Reilly, Connor Anthony; Oppong, Colin; Reed, Lewis John; Ruffles, Dylan Isaac; Siziba, Zandazenkosi Dumisle; Stewart, Cameron Jack; Viral, Allan Miloud Bernard; Wyss, Benjamin Robert.

LEEDS U (41)

ALIOSKI, Ezgjan (M) **262 42**
b.Prilep 12-2-92
Internationals: Macedonia U19, U21, Full caps.

2012–13	Young Boys	0	0		
2012–13	Schaffhausen	10	0		
2013–14	Schaffhausen	26	2		
2014–15	Schaffhausen	35	2		
2015–16	Schaffhausen	16	0	**87**	**4**
2015–16	Lugano	16	3		
2016–17	Lugano	34	16	**50**	**19**
2017–18	Leeds U	42	7		
2018–19	Leeds U	44	7		
2019–20	Leeds U	39	5	**125**	**19**

AUGUSTIN, Jean-Kevin (F) **78 14**
b.Paris 16-6-97
Internationals: France U16, U17, U18, U19, U20, U21.

2014–15	Paris Saint-Germain	0	0		
2015–16	Paris Saint-Germain	13	1		
2016–17	Paris Saint-Germain	10	1	**23**	**2**
2017–18	RB Leipzig	25	9		
2018–19	RB Leipzig	17	3		
2019–20	RB Leipzig	0	0	**42**	**12**
2019–20	*Monaco*	10	0	**10**	**0**

On loan from RB Leipzig.

2019–20	Leeds U	3	0	**3**	**0**

AYLING, Luke (D) **390 12**
H: 5 11 W: 10 08 b.Lambeth 25-8-91

2009–10	Arsenal	0	0		
2009–10	*Yeovil T*	4	0		
2010–11	Yeovil T	37	0		
2011–12	Yeovil T	44	0		
2012–13	Yeovil T	39	0		
2013–14	Yeovil T	42	2	**166**	**2**
2014–15	Bristol C	46	4		
2015–16	Bristol C	33	0		
2016–17	Bristol C	1	0	**80**	**4**
2016–17	Leeds U	42	0		
2017–18	Leeds U	27	0		
2018–19	Leeds U	38	2		
2019–20	Leeds U	37	4	**144**	**6**

BAMFORD, Patrick (F) **231 80**
H: 6 1 W: 11 02 b.Newark 5-9-93
Internationals: Republic of Ireland U18. England U18, U19, U21.

2010–11	Nottingham F	0	0		
2011–12	Nottingham F	2	0	**2**	**0**
2011–12	Chelsea	0	0		
2012–13	Chelsea	0	0		
2012–13	*Milton Keynes D*	14	4		
2013–14	Chelsea	0	0		
2013–14	*Milton Keynes D*	23	14	**37**	**18**
2013–14	*Derby Co*	21	8	**21**	**8**
2014–15	Chelsea	0	0		
2014–15	*Middlesbrough*	38	17		
2015–16	Chelsea	0	0		
2015–16	*Crystal Palace*	6	0	**6**	**0**
2015–16	*Norwich C*	7	0	**7**	**0**
2016–17	Chelsea	0	0		
2016–17	*Burnley*	6	0	**6**	**0**
2016–17	*Middlesbrough*	8	1		
2017–18	Middlesbrough	39	11	**85**	**29**
2018–19	Leeds U	22	9		
2019–20	Leeds U	45	16	**67**	**25**

BERARDI, Gaetano (D) **282 0**
H: 5 10 W: 11 00 b.Sorengo 21-8-88
Internationals: Switzerland U20, U21, Full caps.

2006–07	Brescia	1	0		
2007–08	Brescia	9	0		
2008–09	Brescia	26	0		
2009–10	Brescia	29	0		
2010–11	Brescia	27	0		
2011–12	Brescia	13	0	**105**	**0**
2011–12	Sampdoria	9	0		
2012–13	Sampdoria	21	0		
2013–14	Sampdoria	5	0	**35**	**0**
2014–15	Leeds U	22	0		
2015–16	Leeds U	28	0		
2016–17	Leeds U	26	0		
2017–18	Leeds U	31	0		
2018–19	Leeds U	13	0		
2019–20	Leeds U	22	0	**142**	**0**

BOGUSZ, Mateusz (M) **1 0**
H: 5 9 b.Ruda Slalka 22-8-01
Internationals: Poland U16, U17, U19, U20, U21.

2018–19	Leeds U	0	0		
2019–20	Leeds U	1	0	**1**	**0**

CAPRILE, Elia (G) **0 0**
b.Verona 25-8-01
Internationals: Italy U18.
From Verona.

2019–20	Leeds U	0	0		

CASEY, Oliver (D) **1 0**
b. 14-10-00

2019–20	Leeds U	1	0	**1**	**0**

CASILLA, Francisco (G) **294 0**
H: 6 4 W: 13 01 b.Alcocer 2-10-86
Internationals: Spain U19, U21, Full caps.

2004–05	Real Madrid	0	0		
2005–06	Real Madrid	0	0		
2006–07	Real Madrid	0	0		
2007–08	Espanyol	4	0		
2008–09	Cadiz	35	0		
2009–10	Cadiz	31	0	**66**	**0**
2010–11	Cartagena	35	0	**35**	**0**
2011–12	Espanyol	16	0		
2012–13	Espanyol	21	0		
2013–14	Espanyol	37	0		
2014–15	Espanyol	37	0	**115**	**0**
2015–16	Real Madrid	4	0		
2016–17	Real Madrid	11	0		
2017–18	Real Madrid	10	0	**25**	**0**
2018–19	Leeds U	17	0		
2019–20	Leeds U	36	0	**53**	**0**

COOPER, Liam (D) **275 14**
H: 6 2 W: 13 07 b.Hull 30-8-91
Internationals: Scotland U17, U19, Full caps.

2008–09	Hull C	0	0		
2009–10	Hull C	2	0		
2010–11	Hull C	2	0		
2010–11	*Carlisle U*	6	1	**6**	**1**
2011–12	Hull C	7	0		
2011–12	*Huddersfield T*	4	0	**4**	**0**
2012–13	Hull C	0	0	**11**	**0**
2012–13	Chesterfield	29	2		
2013–14	Chesterfield	41	3		
2014–15	Chesterfield	1	0	**71**	**5**
2014–15	Leeds U	29	1		
2015–16	Leeds U	39	1		
2016–17	Leeds U	11	0		
2017–18	Leeds U	30	1		
2018–19	Leeds U	36	3		
2019–20	Leeds U	38	2	**183**	**8**

DALLAS, Stuart (M) **272 51**
H: 6 0 W: 12 09 b.Cookstown 19-4-91
Internationals: Northern Ireland U21, U23, Full caps.

2010–11	Crusaders	13	16		
2011–12	Crusaders	8	8	**21**	**24**
2012–13	Brentford	7	0		
2013–14	Brentford	18	2		
2013–14	*Northampton T*	12	3	**12**	**3**
2014–15	Brentford	38	6	**63**	**8**
2015–16	Leeds U	45	5		
2016–17	Leeds U	31	2		
2017–18	Leeds U	29	2		
2018–19	Leeds U	26	2		
2019–20	Leeds U	45	5	**176**	**16**

DAVIS, Leif (D) **7 0**
b.Newcastle-upon-Tyne 12-1-00
From Morecambe.

2018–19	Leeds U	4	0		
2019–20	Leeds U	3	0	**7**	**0**

DE BOCK, Laurens (D) **248 3**
b. 7-11-92
Internationals: Belgium U16, U17, U18, U19, U21.

2009–10	Lokeren	5	0		
2010–11	Lokeren	25	0		
2011–12	Lokeren	29	1		
2012–13	Lokeren	21	0	**80**	**1**
2012–13	Club Brugge	11	0		
2013–14	Club Brugge	33	0		
2014–15	Club Brugge	36	0		
2015–16	Club Brugge	31	1		
2016–17	Club Brugge	18	0		
2017–18	Club Brugge	6	0	**135**	**1**
2017–18	Leeds U	7	0		
2018–19	Leeds U	0	0		
2018–19	*Oostende*	13	1	**13**	**1**
2019–20	Leeds U	0	0	**7**	**0**
2019–20	*Sunderland*	5	0	**5**	**0**
2019–20	*Den Haag*	8	0	**8**	**0**

DOUGLAS, Barry (D) **299 22**
H: 5 9 W: 10 00 b.Glasgow 4-9-89
Internationals: Scotland Full caps.

2008–09	Queen's Park	30	2		
2009–10	Queen's Park	35	8	**65**	**10**
2010–11	Dundee U	23	2		
2011–12	Dundee U	10	1		
2012–13	Dundee U	28	1	**61**	**4**
2013–14	Lech Poznan	18	0		
2014–15	Lech Poznan	27	3		
2015–16	Lech Poznan	13	0	**58**	**3**
2015–16	Konyaspor	12	0		
2016–17	Konyaspor	22	0	**34**	**0**
2017–18	Wolverhampton W	39	5	**39**	**5**
2018–19	Leeds U	27	0		
2019–20	Leeds U	15	0	**42**	**0**

EDMONDSON, Ryan (F) **2 0**
b. 20-5-01
Internationals: England U19.
From Leeds U.

2017–18	Leeds U	1	0		
2018–19	Leeds U	1	0		
2019–20	Leeds U	0	0	**2**	**0**

FORSHAW, Adam (M) **247 14**
H: 6 1 W: 11 02 b.Liverpool 8-10-91

2009–10	Everton	0	0		
2010–11	Everton	1	0		
2011–12	Everton	0	0	**1**	**0**
2011–12	*Brentford*	7	0		
2012–13	Brentford	43	3		
2013–14	Brentford	39	8	**89**	**11**
2014–15	Wigan Ath	16	1	**16**	**1**
2014–15	Middlesbrough	18	0		
2015–16	Middlesbrough	29	2		
2016–17	Middlesbrough	34	0		
2017–18	Middlesbrough	11	0	**92**	**2**
2017–18	Leeds U	12	0		
2018–19	Leeds U	30	0		
2019–20	Leeds U	7	0	**49**	**0**

GALLOWAY, Josh (M) **0 0**
b.Glasgow 21-1-02
From Carlisle U.

2019–20	Leeds U	0	0		

GOTTS, Robbie (D) **1 0**
b.Harrogate 9-11-99

2018–19	Leeds U	0	0		
2019–20	Leeds U	1	0	**1**	**0**

GROT, Jay-Roy (F) **84 12**
H: 6 4 W: 14 09 b.Arnhem 13-3-98
Internationals: Netherlands U17, U18, U19, U20, U21.

2015–16	NEC	10	0		
2016–17	NEC	20	5		
2017–18	NEC	1	0	**31**	**5**
2017–18	Leeds U	20	1		
2018–19	Leeds U	0	0		
2018–19	*VVV-Venlo*	33	6	**33**	**6**
2019–20	Leeds U	0	0	**20**	**1**
2019–20	*Vitesse*	0	0		

HERNANDEZ, Pablo (M) **413 75**
H: 5 8 W: 10 00 b.Castellon 11-4-85
Internationals: Spain Full caps.

2005–06	Valencia	1	0		
2006–07	*Cadiz*	14	4	**14**	**4**
2007–08	Getafe	28	3	**28**	**3**
2008–09	Valencia	21	4		

2009–10 Valencia 33 5
2010–11 Valencia 26 5
2011–12 Valencia 30 3 **111 17**
2012–13 Swansea C 30 3
2013–14 Swansea C 27 2 **57 5**
2014–15 Al Arabi 13 6
2014–15 *Al-Nasr* 12 3 **12 3**
2015–16 Al Arabi 0 0 **13 6**
2015–16 *Rayo Vallecano* 27 3 **27 3**
2016–17 Leeds U 35 6
2017–18 Leeds U 41 7
2018–19 Leeds U 39 12
2019–20 Leeds U 36 9 **151 34**

HOSANNAH, Bryce (D) 0 0
b. 8-4-99
From Crystal Palace.
2019–20 Leeds U 0 0

HUFFER, Will (G) 1 0
b.London 30-10-98
Internationals: England U17, U18.
2018–19 Leeds U 1 0
2019–20 Leeds U 0 0 **1 0**

KLICH, Mateusz (M) 257 38
H: 6 0 W: 10 10 b.Tarnow 13-6-90
Internationals: Poland U18, U19, U20, U21, Full caps.
2008–09 Cracovia 8 0
2009–10 Cracovia 21 1
2010–11 Cracovia 27 4 **56 5**
2011–12 Wolfsburg 0 0
2012–13 Wolfsburg 0 0
2012–13 *Zwolle* 13 2
2013–14 Zwolle 30 4 **43 6**
2014–15 Wolfsburg 0 0
2014–15 Kaiserslautern 5 1
2015–16 Kaiserslautern 16 3 **21 4**
2016–17 FC Twente 29 6 **29 6**
2017–18 Leeds U 4 0
2017–18 *FC Utrecht* 13 1 **13 1**
2018–19 Leeds U 46 10
2019–20 Leeds U 45 6 **95 16**

McCALMONT, Alfie (M) 0 0
b.Thirsk 25-3-00
Internationals: Northern Ireland U17, U19, U21, Full caps.
2019–20 Leeds U 0 0

MESLIER, Illan (G) 38 0
b.Lorient 2-3-00
Internationals: France U18, U19, U20.
2016–17 Lorient 0 0
2017–18 Lorient 0 0
2018–19 Lorient 28 0
2019–20 Lorient 0 0 **28 0**
On loan from Lorient.
2019–20 Leeds U 10 0 **10 0**

MIAZEK, Kamil (G) 4 0
b. 15-8-96
Internationals: Poland U19.
From Feyenoord.
2016–17 Chojniczanka Chojnice 4 0
2017–18 Chojniczanka Chojnice 0 0 **4 0**
2018–19 Leeds U 0 0
2019–20 Leeds U 0 0

O'KANE, Eunan (M) 279 18
H: 5 8 W: 13 04 b.Derry 10-7-90
Internationals: Northern Ireland U16, U17, U19, U20, U21. Republic of Ireland U21, Full caps.
2007–08 Everton 0 0
2008–09 Everton 0 0
2009–10 Coleraine 13 4 **13 4**
2009–10 Torquay U 16 1
2010–11 Torquay U 45 6
2011–12 Torquay U 45 5
2012–13 Torquay U 0 0 **106 12**
2012–13 Bournemouth 37 1
2013–14 Bournemouth 37 1
2014–15 Bournemouth 11 0
2015–16 Bournemouth 16 0 **101 2**
2016–17 Leeds U 24 0
2017–18 Leeds U 32 0
2018–19 Leeds U 0 0
2018–19 *Luton T* 3 0
2019–20 Leeds U 0 0 **56 0**
2019–20 *Luton T* 0 0 **3 0**

PHILIPS, Kalvin (M) 165 12
H: 5 10 W: 11 05 b.Leeds 2-12-95
2014–15 Leeds U 2 1
2015–16 Leeds U 10 0
2016–17 Leeds U 33 1
2017–18 Leeds U 41 7
2018–19 Leeds U 42 1
2019–20 Leeds U 37 2 **165 12**

POVEDA-OCAMPO, Ian (M) 4 0
b.London 9-2-00
Internationals: England U16, U17, U18, U19, U20.
From Chelsea, Arsenal, Barcelona, Brentford.
2018–19 Manchester C 0 0
2019–20 Manchester C 0 0
2019–20 Leeds U 4 0 **4 0**

ROBERTS, Tyler (F) 96 16
H: 5 11 W: 11 11 b.Gloucester 12-1-98
Internationals: Wales U16, U17, U19, U20, U21, Full caps.
2014–15 WBA 0 0
2015–16 WBA 1 0
2016–17 WBA 0 0 **1 0**
2016–17 *Oxford U* 14 0 **14 0**
2016–17 *Shrewsbury T* 13 4 **13 4**
2017–18 Leeds U 0 0
2017–18 *Walsall* 17 5 **17 5**
2018–19 Leeds U 28 3
2019–20 Leeds U 23 4 **51 7**

SHACKLETON, Jamie (M) 41 2
b.Leeds 8-10-99
Internationals: England U20.
2018–19 Leeds U 19 0
2019–20 Leeds U 22 2 **41 2**

SHAUGHNESSY, Conor (M) 42 0
H: 6 3 W: 11 09 b. 30-6-96
Internationals: Republic of Ireland U16, U17, U18, U21, Full caps.
2017–18 Leeds U 9 0
2018–19 Leeds U 0 0
2018–19 *Hearts* 10 0 **10 0**
2019–20 Leeds U 0 0 **9 0**
2019–20 *Mansfield T* 15 0 **15 0**
2019–20 *Burton Alb* 8 0 **8 0**

STEVENS, Jordan (M) 14 0
b. 25-3-00
2017–18 Forest Green R 9 0 **9 0**
2017–18 Leeds U 0 0
2018–19 Leeds U 1 0
2019–20 Leeds U 4 0 **5 0**

STRUIJK, Pascal (D) 5 0
Internationals: Netherlands U17.
From Ajax.
2017–18 Leeds U 0 0
2018–19 Leeds U 0 0
2019–20 Leeds U 5 0 **5 0**

Players retained or with offer of contract
Bouy, Ouasim; Cresswell, Charlie Richard; Huggins, Niall Joseph; Jenkins, Jack; Kamwa, Bobby-Emmanuel; Kenneh, Nohan; McCarron, Liam James; McKinstry, Stuart Adamson; Mihaylov, Dzhoshkun Temenuzhkov; Mujica, Garcia Rafael Sebastian; Shergill, Joshveer Singh.

Scholars
Amissah, Emmanuel Agyekum; Bray, Owen Anthony; Burlace, Dane Lee; Chikukwa, Jimiel Takunda; Edris, Niklas Haugland; Fewster, William Charles Storm; Gibbon, Cole Jay; Hughes, Alfie Thomas; Kachosa, Ethan Takudzwa; Kumwenda, Henri Mwayi; Leverett, Samuel George; Lyons, Luke Anthony; McMillan, Max Henry; Pilkington, Aaron Jon; Ragan, Taylor Peter; Rigby, Maximus Marlon William; Rubie, Mason; Skerry, Cooper Mark; Stanley, Joseph Thomas; Teale, Connor Derek; Thornton, Jamie William; Turner, Matthew David.

LEICESTER C (42)

ADRIEN SILVA, Sebastien (M) 255 36
H: 5 9 W: 11 11 b.Angouleme 15-3-89
Internationals: Portugal U16, U17, U18, U19, U21, Full caps.
2007–08 Sporting Lisbon 6 0
2008–09 Sporting Lisbon 13 0
2009–10 Sporting Lisbon 13 0
2010–11 Sporting Lisbon 0 0
2010–11 *Maccabi Haifa* 6 0 **6 0**
2010–11 *Academica* 6 1 **6 1**
2011–12 Sporting Lisbon 0 0
2011–12 *Academica* 28 4 **28 4**
2012–13 Sporting Lisbon 19 3
2013–14 Sporting Lisbon 28 8
2014–15 Sporting Lisbon 30 8
2015–16 Sporting Lisbon 29 8
2016–17 Sporting Lisbon 27 4
2017–18 Sporting Lisbon 3 0 **168 31**
2017–18 Leicester C 12 0
2018–19 Leicester C 2 0
2018–19 *Monaco* 15 0
2019–20 Leicester C 0 0 **14 0**
2019–20 *Monaco* 18 0 **33 0**

ALBRIGHTON, Marc (M) 260 17
H: 6 2 W: 12 06 b.Tamworth 18-11-89
Internationals: England U20, U21.
2008–09 Aston Villa 0 0
2009–10 Aston Villa 3 0
2010–11 Aston Villa 29 5
2011–12 Aston Villa 26 2
2012–13 Aston Villa 9 0
2013–14 Aston Villa 19 0 **86 7**
2013–14 *Wigan Ath* 4 0 **4 0**
2014–15 Leicester C 18 2
2015–16 Leicester C 38 2
2016–17 Leicester C 33 2
2017–18 Leicester C 34 2
2018–19 Leicester C 27 2
2019–20 Leicester C 20 0 **170 10**

AMARTEY, Daniel (M) 124 4
H: 6 0 W: 12 04 b.Accra 1-12-94
Internationals: Ghana U20, Full caps.
2013 Djurgardens 23 0
2014 Djurgardens 11 0 **34 0**
2014–15 Copenhagen 29 3
2015–16 Copenhagen 15 0 **44 3**
2015–16 Leicester C 5 0
2016–17 Leicester C 24 1
2017–18 Leicester C 8 0
2018–19 Leicester C 9 0
2019–20 Leicester C 0 0 **46 1**

BARNES, Harvey (M) 125 27
b. 8-12-97
Internationals: England U18, U20, U21.
2016–17 Leicester C 0 0
2016–17 *Milton Keynes D* 21 6 **21 6**
2017–18 Leicester C 3 0
2017–18 *Barnsley* 23 5 **23 5**
2018–19 Leicester C 16 1
2018–19 *WBA* 26 9 **26 9**
2019–20 Leicester C 36 6 **55 7**

BENKOVIC, Filip (D) 86 10
H: 6 4 W: 14 05 b.Zagreb 13-7-97
Internationals: Croatia U17, U19, U21, Full caps.
2015–16 Dinamo Zagreb 13 0
2016–17 Dinamo Zagreb 18 2
2017–18 Dinamo Zagreb 25 4 **56 6**
2018–19 Leicester C 0 0
2018–19 *Celtic* 20 2 **20 2**
2019–20 Leicester C 0 0
2019–20 *Bristol C* 10 2 **10 2**

CHILWELL, Ben (D) 107 4
H: 5 10 W: 11 03 b.Milton Keynes 21-12-96
Internationals: England U18, U19, U20, U21, Full caps.
2015–16 Leicester C 0 0
2015–16 *Huddersfield T* 8 0 **8 0**
2016–17 Leicester C 12 1
2017–18 Leicester C 24 0
2018–19 Leicester C 36 0
2019–20 Leicester C 27 3 **99 4**

CHOUDHURY, Hamza (M) 63 1
H: 5 10 W: 10 01 b.Loughborough 1-10-97
Internationals: England U21.
2015–16 Leicester C 0 0
2015–16 *Burton Alb* 13 0
2016–17 Leicester C 0 0
2016–17 *Burton Alb* 13 0 **26 0**
2017–18 Leicester C 8 0
2018–19 Leicester C 9 0
2019–20 Leicester C 20 1 **37 1**

CLARK, Mitchell (D) 44 0
b.Nuneaton 13-3-99
Internationals: Wales U17, U19.
2017–18 Aston Villa 0 0
2018–19 Aston Villa 0 0
2018–19 *Port Vale* 40 0
2019–20 Leicester C 0 0
2019–20 *Port Vale* 4 0 **44 0**

DEWSBURY-HALL, Kiernan (M) 10 4
b. 6-9-98
2019–20 Leicester C 0 0
2019–20 *Blackpool* 10 4 **10 4**

DIABATE, Fousseni (M) 52 17
H: 5 9 W: 10 06 b.Aubervilliers 18-10-95
Internationals: Mali U20, U23.
From Rennes, Reims.
2016–17 Guingamp 0 0
2017–18 Ajaccio GFCO 0 0
2017–18 Leicester C 14 0
2018–19 Leicester C 1 0
2018–19 *Sivasspor* 17 2 **17 2**
2019–20 Leicester C 0 0 **15 0**
2019–20 *Amiens* 20 15 **20 15**

EVANS, Jonny (D) 329 14
H: 6 2 W: 12 02 b.Belfast 3-1-88
Internationals: Northern Ireland U16, U17, U21, Full caps.
2004–05 Manchester U 0 0
2005–06 Manchester U 0 0
2006–07 Manchester U 0 0
2006–07 *Antwerp* 14 2 **14 2**
2006–07 *Sunderland* 18 1
2007–08 Manchester U 0 0
2007–08 *Sunderland* 15 0 **33 1**
2008–09 Manchester U 17 0
2009–10 Manchester U 18 0
2010–11 Manchester U 13 0
2011–12 Manchester U 29 1
2012–13 Manchester U 23 3
2013–14 Manchester U 17 0
2014–15 Manchester U 14 0
2015–16 Manchester U 0 0 **131 4**
2015–16 WBA 30 1
2016–17 WBA 31 2
2017–18 WBA 28 2 **89 5**
2018–19 Leicester C 24 1
2019–20 Leicester C 38 1 **62 2**

FUCHS, Christian (D) 442 24
H: 6 1 W: 12 08 b.Pitten 7-4-86
Internationals: Austria U17, U19, U21, Full caps.
2002–03 Wiener Neustadt 12 0 **12 0**
2003–04 Mattersburg 13 0
2004–05 Mattersburg 24 2
2005–06 Mattersburg 35 1
2006–07 Mattersburg 35 6
2007–08 Mattersburg 33 3 **140 12**
2008–09 Bochum 22 2
2009–10 Bochum 31 4
2010–11 Bochum 0 0 **53 6**
2010–11 *Mainz 05* 31 0 **31 0**
2011–12 Schalke 29 2
2012–13 Schalke 29 0
2013–14 Schalke 16 0
2014–15 Schalke 25 2 **99 4**
2015–16 Leicester C 32 0
2016–17 Leicester C 36 2
2017–18 Leicester C 25 0
2018–19 Leicester C 3 0
2019–20 Leicester C 11 0 **107 2**

GHEZZAL, Rachid (M) 151 15
H: 6 0 W: 10 03 b.Decines-Charpieu 9-5-92
Internationals: France U20. Algeria Full caps.
2012–13 Lyon 14 1
2013–14 Lyon 0 0
2014–15 Lyon 18 0
2015–16 Lyon 29 8
2016–17 Lyon 26 2 **87 11**
2017–18 Monaco 26 2 **26 2**
2018–19 Leicester C 19 1
2019–20 Leicester C 0 0 **19 1**
2019–20 *Fiorentina* 19 1 **19 1**

GRAY, Demarai (M) 204 18
H: 5 10 W: 10 04 b.Birmingham 28-6-96
Internationals: England U18, U19, U20, U21.
2013–14 Birmingham C 7 1
2014–15 Birmingham C 41 6
2015–16 Birmingham C 24 1 **72 8**
2015–16 Leicester C 12 0
2016–17 Leicester C 30 1
2017–18 Leicester C 35 3
2018–19 Leicester C 34 4
2019–20 Leicester C 21 2 **132 10**

HIRST, George (F) 25 3
b.Sheffield 15-2-99
Internationals: England U17, U18, U20.
2016–17 Sheffield W 1 0
2017–18 Sheffield W 0 0 **1 0**
2018–19 Oh Leuven 22 3 **22 3**
2019–20 Leicester C 2 0 **2 0**

HUGHES, Sam (M) 8 0
b.West Kirby 15-4-97
From Chester.
2017–18 Leicester C 0 0
2018–19 Leicester C 0 0
2019–20 Leicester C 0 0
2019–20 *Salford C* 8 0 **8 0**

HULME, Callum (M) 1 0
b. 10-11-00
From Manchester C.
2016–17 Bury 0 0
2017–18 Bury 0 0
2018–19 Bury 1 0 **1 0**
2019–20 Leicester C 0 0

IHEANACHO, Kelechi (M) 117 21
H: 6 2 W: 13 08 b.Imo 3-10-96
Internationals: Nigeria U17, U20, Full caps.
2014–15 Manchester C 0 0
2015–16 Manchester C 26 8
2016–17 Manchester C 20 4 **46 12**
2017–18 Leicester C 21 3
2018–19 Leicester C 30 1
2019–20 Leicester C 20 5 **71 9**

IVERSEN, Daniel (G) 76 0
b. 19-7-97
Internationals: Denmark U16, U17, U18, U19, U20, U21.
2014–15 Esbjerg 0 0
2015–16 Esbjerg 0 0
2015–16 Leicester C 0 0
2016–17 Leicester C 0 0
2017–18 Leicester C 0 0
2018–19 Leicester C 0 0
2018–19 *Oldham Ath* 42 0 **42 0**
2019–20 Leicester C 0 0
2019–20 *Rotherham U* 34 0 **34 0**

JAKUPOVIC, Eldin (G) 181 1
H: 6 3 W: 13 00 b.Kozarac 2-10-84
Internationals: Bosnia & Herzegovina U21, Switzerland U21, Full caps.
2004–05 Grasshoppers 8 0
2005–06 FC Thun 23 0 **23 0**
2006–07 Lokomotiv Moscow 20 0 **20 0**
2007–08 Grasshoppers 23 1
2008–09 Grasshoppers 32 0 **63 1**
2010–11 Olympiacos Volou 26 0 **26 0**
2011–12 Aris Salonika 1 0 **1 0**
2012–13 Hull C 5 0
2013–14 Hull C 1 0
2013–14 *Leyton Orient* 13 0 **13 0**
2014–15 Hull C 3 0
2015–16 Hull C 2 0
2016–17 Hull C 22 0 **33 0**
2017–18 Leicester C 2 0
2018–19 Leicester C 0 0
2019–20 Leicester C 0 0 **2 0**

JAMES, Matthew (M) 147 7
H: 6 0 W: 11 12 b.Bacup 22-7-91
Internationals: England U16, U17, U19, U20.
2007–08 Manchester U 0 0
2008–09 Manchester U 0 0
2009–10 Manchester U 0 0
2009–10 *Preston NE* 18 2
2010–11 Manchester U 0 0
2010–11 *Preston NE* 10 0 **28 2**
2011–12 Manchester U 0 0
2012–13 Leicester C 24 3
2013–14 Leicester C 35 1
2014–15 Leicester C 27 0
2015–16 Leicester C 0 0
2016–17 Leicester C 1 0
2016–17 *Barnsley* 18 1 **18 1**
2017–18 Leicester C 13 0
2018–19 Leicester C 0 0
2019–20 Leicester C 1 0 **101 4**

JOHNSON, Darnell (D) 1 0
b. 3-9-98
Internationals: England U16, U17, U18, U19, U20.
2019–20 Leicester C 0 0
2019–20 *Hibernian* 1 0 **1 0**

JUSTIN, James (F) 103 6
H: 6 0 W: 11 03 b.Luton 11-7-97
Internationals: England U20, U21.
2015–16 Luton T 1 0
2016–17 Luton T 29 1
2017–18 Luton T 17 2
2018–19 Luton T 43 3 **90 6**
2019–20 Leicester C 13 0 **13 0**

KING, Andy (M) 360 57
H: 6 0 W: 11 10 b.Barnstaple 29-10-88
Internationals: Wales U19, U21, Full caps.
2007–08 Leicester C 11 1
2008–09 Leicester C 45 9
2009–10 Leicester C 43 9
2010–11 Leicester C 45 15
2011–12 Leicester C 30 4
2012–13 Leicester C 42 7
2013–14 Leicester C 30 4
2014–15 Leicester C 24 2
2015–16 Leicester C 25 2
2016–17 Leicester C 23 1
2017–18 Leicester C 11 1
2017–18 *Swansea C* 11 2 **11 2**
2018–19 Leicester C 0 0
2018–19 *Derby Co* 4 0 **4 0**
2019–20 Leicester C 0 0 **329 55**
2019–20 *Rangers* 2 0 **2 0**
2019–20 *Huddersfield T* 14 0 **14 0**

KNIGHT, Josh (D) 32 3
b.Leicester 7-9-97
2017–18 Leicester C 0 0
2018–19 Leicester C 0 0
2018–19 *Peterborough U* 8 0
2019–20 Leicester C 0 0
2019–20 *Peterborough U* 24 3 **32 3**

LESHABELA, Thakgalo (M) 0 0
b. 18-9-99
Internationals: South Africa U20.
2018–19 Leicester C 0 0
2019–20 Leicester C 0 0

LOFT, Ryan (F) 36 4
H: 6 3 W: 11 07 b.Gravesend 14-9-97
2016–17 Tottenham H 0 0
2016–17 *Stevenage* 9 0 **9 0**
2017–18 Tottenham H 0 0
2017–18 *Exeter C* 1 0 **1 0**
2018–19 Leicester C 0 0
2019–20 Leicester C 0 0
2019–20 *Carlisle U* 26 4 **26 4**

MADDISON, James (M) 163 35
H: 5 10 W: 11 07 b.Coventry 23-11-96
Internationals: England U21, Full caps.
2013–14 Coventry C 0 0
2014–15 Coventry C 12 2
2015–16 Norwich C 0 0
2015–16 *Coventry C* 23 3 **35 5**
2016–17 Norwich C 3 1
2016–17 *Aberdeen* 14 2 **14 2**
2017–18 Norwich C 44 14 **47 15**
2018–19 Leicester C 36 7
2019–20 Leicester C 31 6 **67 13**

MENDY, Nampalys (D) 240 1
H: 5 6 W: 10 10 b.La Seyne-sur-Mer 9-6-92
Internationals: France U18, U19, U20, U21.
2010–11 Monaco 14 0
2011–12 Monaco 28 0
2012–13 Monaco 32 0 **74 0**
2013–14 Nice 36 0
2014–15 Nice 36 0
2015–16 Nice 38 1
2016–17 Leicester C 4 0
2017–18 Leicester C 0 0
2017–18 *Nice* 14 0 **124 1**
2018–19 Leicester C 31 0
2019–20 Leicester C 7 0 **42 0**

MORGAN, Wes (D) 631 24
H: 6 2 W: 14 00 b.Nottingham 21-1-84
Internationals: Jamaica Full caps.
2002–03 Nottingham F 0 0
2002–03 *Kidderminster H* 5 1 **5 1**
2003–04 Nottingham F 32 2
2004–05 Nottingham F 43 1
2005–06 Nottingham F 43 2
2006–07 Nottingham F 38 0
2007–08 Nottingham F 42 1
2008–09 Nottingham F 42 1
2009–10 Nottingham F 44 3
2010–11 Nottingham F 46 1
2011–12 Nottingham F 22 1 **352 12**
2011–12 Leicester C 17 0
2012–13 Leicester C 45 1
2013–14 Leicester C 45 2
2014–15 Leicester C 37 2
2015–16 Leicester C 38 2
2016–17 Leicester C 27 1
2017–18 Leicester C 32 0
2018–19 Leicester C 22 3
2019–20 Leicester C 11 0 **274 11**

MUSKWE, Admiral (F) 5 0
Internationals: England U17. Zimbabwe Full caps.
2019–20 Leicester C 0 0
2019–20 *Swindon T* 5 0 **5 0**

NDIDI, Onyinye (D) 181 10
b. 16-12-96
Internationals: Nigeria U20, Full caps.
2014–15 Genk 6 0
2015–16 Genk 36 4
2016–17 Genk 19 0 **61 4**

2016–17 Leicester C 17 2
2017–18 Leicester C 33 0
2018–19 Leicester C 38 2
2019–20 Leicester C 32 2 **120 6**

NDUKWU, Layton (F) 7 0
Internationals: England U16, U17.
2017–18 Leicester C 0 0
2018–19 Leicester C 0 0
2019–20 Leicester C 0 0
2019–20 *Southend U* 7 0 **7 0**

PEREZ, Ayoze (F) 258 67
H: 5 10 W: 10 06 b.Santa Cruz de Tenerife 23-7-93
Internationals: Spain U21.
2012–13 Tenerife 16 1
2013–14 Tenerife 30 16 **46 17**
2014–15 Newcastle U 36 7
2015–16 Newcastle U 34 6
2016–17 Newcastle U 36 9
2017–18 Newcastle U 36 8
2018–19 Newcastle U 37 12 **179 42**
2019–20 Leicester C 33 8 **33 8**

PRAET, Dennis (M) 264 25
b.Leuven 14-5-94
Internationals: Belgium U16, U17, U18, U19, U21, Full caps.
2011–12 Anderlecht 7 0
2012–13 Anderlecht 27 2
2013–14 Anderlecht 37 5
2014–15 Anderlecht 30 7
2015–16 Anderlecht 37 6
2016–17 Anderlecht 1 0 **139 20**
2016–17 Sampdoria 32 1
2017–18 Sampdoria 32 1
2018–19 Sampdoria 34 2
2019–20 Sampdoria 0 0 **98 4**
2019–20 Leicester C 27 1 **27 1**

RICARDO PEREIRA, Domingos (D) 189 11
H: 5 9 W: 11 00 b.Lisbon 6-10-93
Internationals: Portugal U19, U20, U21, Full caps.
2011–12 Vitoria Guimaraes 3 0
2012–13 Vitoria Guimaraes 27 0 **30 0**
2013–14 Porto 14 2
2014–15 Porto 5 0
2015–16 Porto 0 0
2015–16 *Nice* 26 0
2016–17 Porto 0 0
2016–17 *Nice* 24 2 **50 2**
2017–18 Porto 27 2 **46 4**
2018–19 Leicester C 35 2
2019–20 Leicester C 28 3 **63 5**

SCHMEICHEL, Kasper (G) 498 0
H: 6 1 W: 13 00 b.Copenhagen 5-11-86
Internationals: Denmark U19, U20, U21, Full caps.
2003–04 Manchester C 0 0
2004–05 Manchester C 0 0
2005–06 Manchester C 0 0
2005–06 *Darlington* 4 0 **4 0**
2005–06 *Bury* 15 0
2006–07 Manchester C 0 0
2006–07 *Falkirk* 15 0 **15 0**
2006–07 *Bury* 14 0 **29 0**
2007–08 Manchester C 7 0
2007–08 *Cardiff C* 14 0 **14 0**
2007–08 *Coventry C* 9 0 **9 0**
2008–09 Manchester C 1 0
2009–10 Manchester C 0 0 **8 0**
2009–10 Notts Co 43 0 **43 0**
2010–11 Leeds U 37 0 **37 0**
2011–12 Leicester C 46 0
2012–13 Leicester C 46 0
2013–14 Leicester C 46 0
2014–15 Leicester C 24 0
2015–16 Leicester C 38 0
2016–17 Leicester C 30 0
2017–18 Leicester C 33 0
2018–19 Leicester C 38 0
2019–20 Leicester C 38 0 **339 0**

SLIMANI, Islam (F) 272 116
H: 6 2 W: 12 06 b.Algiers 18-6-88
Internationals: Algeria Full caps.
2008–09 JSM Cheraga 20 18 **20 18**
2009–10 CR Belouizdad 30 8
2010–11 CR Belouizdad 27 10
2011–12 CR Belouizdad 26 10
2012–13 CR Belouizdad 15 4 **98 32**
2013–14 Sporting Lisbon 26 8
2014–15 Sporting Lisbon 21 12
2015–16 Sporting Lisbon 33 27
2016–17 Sporting Lisbon 2 1 **82 48**
2016–17 Leicester C 23 7
2017–18 Leicester C 12 1
2017–18 *Newcastle U* 4 0 **4 0**
2018–19 Leicester C 0 0
2018–19 *Fenerbahce* 15 1 **15 1**
2019–20 Leicester C 0 0 **35 8**
2019–20 *Monaco* 18 9 **18 9**

SOYUNCU, Caglar (D) 124 4
H: 6 2 W: 12 08 b.Izmir 23-5-96
Internationals: Turkey U18, U19, U20, U21, Full caps.
2014–15 Altinordu 4 0
2015–16 Altinordu 30 2 **34 2**
2016–17 Freiburg 24 0
2017–18 Freiburg 26 1 **50 1**
2018–19 Leicester C 6 0
2019–20 Leicester C 34 1 **40 1**

THOMAS, George (M) 86 8
H: 5 8 W: 12 00 b.Leicester 24-3-97
Internationals: Wales U17, U19, U20, U21, Full caps.
2013–14 Coventry C 1 0
2014–15 Coventry C 6 0
2015–16 Coventry C 7 0
2015–16 *Yeovil T* 5 0 **5 0**
2016–17 Coventry C 28 5 **42 5**
2017–18 Leicester C 0 0
2018–19 Leicester C 0 0
2018–19 *Scunthorpe U* 37 3 **37 3**
2019–20 Leicester C 0 0
2019–20 *Den Haag* 2 0 **2 0**

THOMAS, Luke (M) 3 0
Internationals: England U18, U19.
2019–20 Leicester C 3 0 **3 0**

TIELEMANS, Youri (M) 236 37
H: 5 9 W: 10 08 b.Sint-Pieters-Leeuw 7-5-97
Internationals: Belgium U16, U21, Full caps.
2013–14 Anderlecht 29 1
2014–15 Anderlecht 39 6
2015–16 Anderlecht 34 6
2016–17 Anderlecht 37 13 **139 26**
2017–18 Monaco 27 0
2018–19 Monaco 20 5 **47 5**
On loan from Monaco.
2018–19 Leicester C 13 3
2019–20 Leicester C 37 3 **50 6**

VARDY, Jamie (F) 274 123
H: 5 10 W: 11 12 b.Sheffield 11-1-87
Internationals: England Full caps.
2012–13 Leicester C 26 4
2013–14 Leicester C 37 16
2014–15 Leicester C 34 5
2015–16 Leicester C 36 24
2016–17 Leicester C 35 13
2017–18 Leicester C 37 20
2018–19 Leicester C 34 18
2019–20 Leicester C 35 23 **274 123**

WARD, Danny (G) 71 0
H: 5 11 W: 13 12 b.Wrexham 22-6-93
Internationals: Wales U17, U19, U21, Full caps.
2011–12 Liverpool 0 0
2012–13 Liverpool 0 0
2013–14 Liverpool 0 0
2014–15 Liverpool 0 0
2014–15 *Morecambe* 5 0 **5 0**
2015–16 Liverpool 2 0
2015–16 *Aberdeen* 21 0 **21 0**
2016–17 Liverpool 0 0
2016–17 *Huddersfield T* 43 0 **43 0**
2017–18 Liverpool 0 0 **2 0**
2018–19 Leicester C 0 0
2019–20 Leicester C 0 0

Players retained or with offer of contract
Daley-Campbell, Vontae Jason; Flynn, Shane Aidan Conor; O'Connor, Darragh; Okpoda Eppiah, Joshua Felix; Pennant, Terell Amari Leroy; Reghba, Ali; Shade, Tyrese; Sowah, Kamal; Stolarczyk, Jakub; Tavares, Sidnei Wilson Vieira David; Ughelumba, Calvin Chinedu; Wright, Callum.

Scholars
Aisthorpe, Bailey Trafford; Arlott-John, Dempsey Michael Asa; Barrett, Connor; Bosworth, Oliver Michael; Ewing, Oliver James; Fitzhugh, Ethan Michael; Gyamfi, Dennis; Gyamfi, Johnson Adu; Leathers, Adam James; Loughlan, Liam; Marcal-Madivadua, Wanya; Maswanhise, Tawanda Jethro; McAteer, Kasey; Murch, Oliver Edward; Obi, Daniel Iheukwu; Odunze, Chituru Ethan; Russ, Brian William James; Sams, Thomas James; Springer, Jahquan Aswad; Yfeko, Johnly Levi.

LEYTON ORIENT (43)

ALABI, James (F) 23 2
b.London 8-11-94
Internationals: England C.
2012–13 Stoke C 0 0
2012–13 *Scunthorpe U* 9 1
2013–14 Stoke C 0 0
2013–14 *Mansfield T* 1 0 **1 0**
2013–14 *Scunthorpe U* 1 0 **10 1**
2014–15 Stoke C 0 0
2014–15 *Accrington S* 2 0 **2 0**
2015–16 Ipswich T 0 0
From Chester, Tranmere R.
2019–20 Leyton Orient 10 1 **10 1**

ANGOL, Lee (M) 123 28
H: 5 10 W: 11 04 b. 4-8-94
2012–13 Wycombe W 3 0
2013–14 Wycombe W 0 0 **3 0**
2014–15 Luton T 0 0
2015–16 Peterborough U 33 11
2016–17 Peterborough U 13 1 **46 12**
2017–18 Mansfield T 29 9 **29 9**
2018–19 Shrewsbury T 17 3 **17 3**
2018–19 *Lincoln C* 2 0 **2 0**
2019–20 Leyton Orient 26 4 **26 4**

BRILL, Dean (G) 238 0
H: 6 2 W: 14 05 b.Luton 2-12-85
2003–04 Luton T 5 0
2004–05 Luton T 0 0
2005–06 Luton T 5 0
2006–07 Luton T 11 0
2006–07 *Gillingham* 8 0 **8 0**
2007–08 Luton T 37 0
2008–09 Luton T 23 0 **81 0**
2009–10 Oldham Ath 28 0
2010–11 Oldham Ath 30 0 **58 0**
2011–12 Barnet 36 0 **36 0**
From Luton T.
2013–14 Inverness CT 12 0
2014–15 Inverness CT 24 0
2015–16 Inverness CT 0 0 **36 0**
2016–17 Motherwell 0 0
2016–17 Colchester U 0 0
2017–18 Leyton Orient 0 0
2018–19 Leyton Orient 0 0
2019–20 Leyton Orient 19 0 **19 0**

BROPHY, James (D) 98 2
b. 25-7-94
From Harrow Bor, Woodlands U, Broadfields U.
2015–16 Swindon T 28 0
2016–17 Swindon T 30 0
2017–18 Swindon T 6 0 **64 0**
2018–19 Leyton Orient 0 0
2019–20 Leyton Orient 34 2 **34 2**

CLAY, Craig (M) 105 2
H: 5 11 W: 11 07 b.Nottingham 5-5-92
Internationals: England C.
2010–11 Chesterfield 3 1
2011–12 Chesterfield 5 0
2012–13 Chesterfield 19 0 **27 1**
2013–14 York C 8 0 **8 0**
From Grimsby T.
2016–17 Motherwell 35 1
2017–18 Motherwell 0 0 **35 1**
2019–20 Leyton Orient 35 0 **35 0**

COULSON, Josh (D) 104 3
H: 6 3 W: 11 11 b.Cambridge 28-1-89
2014–15 Cambridge U 46 1
2015–16 Cambridge U 23 1
2016–17 Cambridge U 7 0
2017–18 Cambridge U 0 0 **76 2**
2019–20 Leyton Orient 28 1 **28 1**

DAYTON, James (M) 171 15
H: 5 8 W: 10 00 b.Enfield 12-12-88
2007–08 Crystal Palace 0 0
2008–09 Crystal Palace 0 0
2008–09 *Yeovil T* 2 0 **2 0**
From Bishop's Stortford, Bromley
2010–11 Kilmarnock 10 2
2011–12 Kilmarnock 29 3
2012–13 Kilmarnock 27 1 **66 6**
2013–14 Oldham Ath 34 3
2014–15 Oldham Ath 17 1 **51 4**
2014–15 *St Mirren* 13 1 **13 1**
2016–17 Cheltenham T 28 3 **28 3**
2019–20 Leyton Orient 11 1 **11 1**

DENNIS, Louis (F) 25 1
H: 6 1 W: 10 12 b.Hendon 9-10-92
2011–12 Dagenham & R 0 0
2012–13 Dagenham & R 6 0
2013–14 Dagenham & R 2 0 **8 0**

From Bromley.
2018–19 Portsmouth 1 0 **1 0**
2019–20 Leyton Orient 16 1 **16 1**

EKPITETA, Marvin (D) 27 0
Internationals: Nigeria U20. England C.
2019–20 Leyton Orient 27 0 **27 0**

GORMAN, Dale (D) 83 4
H: 5 11 W: 11 00 b.Letterkenny 28-6-96
Internationals: Northern Ireland U17, U19, U21.
2014–15 Stevenage 0 0
2015–16 Stevenage 13 0
2016–17 Stevenage 25 1
2017–18 Stevenage 24 2 **62 3**
2019–20 Leyton Orient 13 0 **13 0**
2019–20 *Newport Co* 8 1 **8 1**

HAPPE, Daniel (D) 34 1
b.Tower Hamlets 28-9-98
Internationals: England C.
2016–17 Leyton Orient 2 0
2019–20 Leyton Orient 32 1 **34 1**

HARROLD, Matt (F) 428 77
H: 6 1 W: 11 10 b.Leyton 25-7-84
2003–04 Brentford 13 2
2004–05 Brentford 19 0 **32 2**
2004–05 *Grimsby T* 6 2 **6 2**
2005–06 Yeovil T 42 9
2006–07 Yeovil T 5 0 **47 9**
2006–07 Southend U 36 3
2007–08 Southend U 16 0
2008–09 Southend U 0 0 **52 3**
2008–09 Wycombe W 37 9
2009–10 Wycombe W 36 8 **73 17**
2010–11 Shrewsbury T 41 8 **41 8**
2011–12 Bristol R 40 16
2012–13 Bristol R 6 2
2013–14 Bristol R 30 6 **76 24**
2014–15 Crawley T 20 1
2014–15 *Cambridge U* 7 1 **7 1**
2015–16 Crawley T 37 8
2016–17 Crawley T 11 0
2017–18 Crawley T 2 0 **70 9**
2019–20 Leyton Orient 24 2 **24 2**

JANATA, Arthur (G) 0 0
2016–17 Leyton Orient 0 0
2019–20 Leyton Orient 0 0

JOHNSON, Danny (F) 14 13
b. 28-2-93
2014–15 Cardiff C 0 0
2014–15 *Tranmere R* 4 0 **4 0**
2014–15 *Stevenage* 4 0 **4 0**
From Gateshead
2018–19 Motherwell 22 6 **22 6**
2019–20 Dundee 19 5 **19 5**
2019–20 Leyton Orient 6 2 **6 2**

JUDD, Myles (D) 29 0
H: 5 10 W: 10 08 b.Redbridge 26-8-99
2015–16 Leyton Orient 0 0
2016–17 Leyton Orient 20 0
2019–20 Leyton Orient 9 0 **29 0**

KYPRIANOU, Hector (M) 6 0
Internationals: Cyprus U19.
2019–20 Leyton Orient 6 0 **6 0**

LING, Sam (D) 15 0
2013–14 Leyton Orient 0 0
2014–15 Leyton Orient 0 0
2015–16 Leyton Orient 0 0
2015–16 Histon 0 0
From Dagenham & R.
2019–20 Leyton Orient 15 0 **15 0**

MAGUIRE-DREW, Jordan (M) 47 7
b. 15-9-97
2017–18 Brighton & HA 0 0
2017–18 *Lincoln C* 11 0 **11 0**
2017–18 *Coventry C* 3 0 **3 0**
2018–19 Brighton & HA 0 0
2019–20 Leyton Orient 33 7 **33 7**

McANUFF, Jobi (M) 581 58
H: 5 11 W: 11 05 b.Edmonton 9-11-81
Internationals: Jamaica Full caps.
2000–01 Wimbledon 0 0
2001–02 Wimbledon 38 4
2002–03 Wimbledon 31 4
2003–04 Wimbledon 27 5 **96 13**
2003–04 West Ham U 12 1
2004–05 West Ham U 1 0 **13 1**
2004–05 Cardiff C 43 2 **43 2**
2005–06 Crystal Palace 41 8
2006–07 Crystal Palace 34 5 **75 13**
2007–08 Watford 39 2
2008–09 Watford 40 3
2009–10 Watford 3 0 **82 5**
2009–10 Reading 36 3
2010–11 Reading 40 4
2011–12 Reading 40 5
2012–13 Reading 38 0
2013–14 Reading 35 2 **189 14**
2014–15 Leyton Orient 34 3
2015–16 Leyton Orient 17 3
2016–17 Stevenage 31 4 **31 4**
2019–20 Leyton Orient 1 0 **52 6**

OGIE, Shadrach (D) 0 0
b.Limerick 26-8-01
Internationals: Republic of Ireland U18, U19.
From Hornchurch.
2019–20 Leyton Orient 0 0

SARGEANT, Sam (G) 28 0
H: 6 0 W: 10 08 b. 23-9-97
2014–15 Leyton Orient 0 0
2015–16 Leyton Orient 1 0
2016–17 Leyton Orient 15 0
2019–20 Leyton Orient 12 0 **28 0**

SHABANI, Brendon (M) 0 0
2019–20 Leyton Orient 0 0

SOTIRIOU, Ruel (F) 10 5
Internationals: Cyprus U19, U21.
2019–20 Leyton Orient 10 5 **10 5**

SWEENEY, Jayden (D) 0 0
2019–20 Leyton Orient 0 0

TURLEY, Jamie (D) 32 2
H: 6 1 W: 12 13 b.Reading 7-4-90
Internationals: England C.
2014–15 Swindon T 0 0
2015–16 Newport Co 0 0
2016–17 Newport Co 6 1 **6 1**
2018–19 Notts Co 18 0 **18 0**
2019–20 Leyton Orient 8 1 **8 1**

VIGOUROUX, Lawrence (G) 125 0
b.London 19-11-93
Internationals: Chile U20.
2012–13 Tottenham H 0 0
2013–14 Tottenham H 0 0
2014–15 Liverpool 0 0
2015–16 Liverpool 0 0
2015–16 *Swindon T* 33 0
2016–17 Swindon T 43 0
2017–18 Swindon T 14 0
2018–19 Swindon T 29 0 **119 0**
2019–20 Leyton Orient 6 0 **6 0**

WIDDOWSON, Joe (D) 268 2
H: 6 0 W: 12 00 b.Forest Gate 28-3-89
2007–08 West Ham U 0 0
2007–08 *Rotherham U* 3 0 **3 0**
2008–09 West Ham U 0 0
2008–09 *Grimsby T* 20 1
2009–10 Grimsby T 38 0 **58 1**
2010–11 Rochdale 34 0
2011–12 Rochdale 32 0 **66 0**
2012–13 Northampton T 39 0
2013–14 Northampton T 25 0 **64 0**
2014–15 Bury 1 0 **1 0**
2014–15 *Morecambe* 8 0 **8 0**
2014–15 Dagenham & R 21 0
2015–16 Dagenham & R 31 0 **52 0**
2019–20 Leyton Orient 16 1 **16 1**

WILKINSON, Conor (F) 133 17
H: 6 1 W: 12 02 b.Croydon 23-1-95
Internationals: Republic of Ireland U17, U19, U21.
2012–13 Millwall 0 0
2013–14 Bolton W 0 0
2013–14 *Torquay U* 3 0 **3 0**
2014–15 Bolton W 4 0
2014–15 *Oldham Ath* 17 3 **17 3**
2015–16 Bolton W 0 0
2015–16 *Barnsley* 8 1 **8 1**
2015–16 *Newport Co* 12 1 **12 1**
2015–16 *Portsmouth* 1 0 **1 0**
2016–17 Bolton W 9 0 **13 0**
2016–17 *Chesterfield* 12 4 **12 4**
2017–18 Gillingham 34 3
2018–19 Gillingham 7 0 **41 3**
2019–20 Leyton Orient 26 5 **26 5**

WRIGHT, Josh (M) 357 27
H: 6 1 W: 11 07 b.Bethnal Green 6-11-89
Internationals: England U16, U17, U18, U19.
2007–08 Charlton Ath 0 0
2007–08 *Barnet* 32 1 **32 1**
2008–09 Charlton Ath 2 0 **2 0**
2008–09 *Brentford* 5 0 **5 0**
2008–09 *Gillingham* 5 0
2009–10 Scunthorpe U 35 0
2010–11 Scunthorpe U 36 0 **71 0**
2011–12 Millwall 18 1
2012–13 Millwall 24 0
2013–14 Millwall 3 0
2013–14 *Leyton Orient* 2 0
2014–15 Millwall 1 0 **46 1**
2014–15 *Crawley T* 4 0 **4 0**
2014–15 Leyton Orient 29 2
2015–16 Gillingham 41 1
2016–17 Gillingham 41 13
2017–18 Gillingham 3 0 **90 14**
2017–18 Southend U 23 1 **23 1**
2018–19 Bradford C 18 0 **18 0**
2019–20 Leyton Orient 35 8 **66 10**

Scholars
Adeyemi, Prince Jordan Adetola; Byrne, Rhys John Howard; Campbell, Sean Kehinde Temitope; Dunba-Bonnie, Deago Michael-David; Francoi-Vernal, Tristan Dion; Frempong, Kevin Asante-Atta; Ifeanyi, Sharon; Lovatt, Finlay Dean; Marfo, Wynford Domfeh; McClenaghan, Bradley Michael; Mirza, Ahmad Reshad; Mullin-Hammond, Lawrence Miles; Palmer, Kyrell Lee; Papadopoulos, Antony; Sanders, William James; Sivi, Jeremie; Solomon, Alexander; Young, Jayden.

LINCOLN C (44)

ADEBAYO-SMITH, Jordan (F) 0 0
2018–19 Lincoln C 0 0
2019–20 Lincoln C 0 0

AL-OYOUNI, Ziyad (D) 0 0
2019–20 Lincoln C 0 0

ANDERSON, Harry (F) 129 16
H: 5 6 W: 9 11 b. 9-1-97
2014–15 Peterborough U 10 0
2015–16 Peterborough U 5 0
2016–17 Peterborough U 1 0 **16 0**
2017–18 Lincoln C 40 6
2018–19 Lincoln C 43 5
2019–20 Lincoln C 30 5 **113 16**

ANDREW, Charlie (G) 0 0
b.Hull 6-1-00
2017–18 Hull C 0 0
2018–19 Hull C 0 0
2019–20 Hull C 0 0
2019–20 Lincoln C 0 0

BOLGER, Cian (D) 236 13
H: 6 4 W: 12 05 b.Co. Kildare 12-3-92
Internationals: Republic of Ireland U19, U21.
2009–10 Leicester C 0 0
2010–11 Leicester C 0 0
2010–11 *Bristol R* 6 0
2011–12 Leicester C 0 0
2011–12 *Bristol R* 39 2
2012–13 Leicester C 0 0
2012–13 *Bristol R* 3 0 **48 2**
2012–13 Bolton W 0 0
2013–14 Bolton W 0 0
2013–14 *Colchester U* 4 0 **4 0**
2013–14 *Southend U* 1 0
2014–15 Southend U 23 1
2015–16 Southend U 22 0 **46 1**
2015–16 *Bury* 9 0 **9 0**
2016–17 Fleetwood T 32 5
2017–18 Fleetwood T 41 3
2018–19 Fleetwood T 11 1 **84 9**
2018–19 Lincoln C 17 1
2019–20 Lincoln C 28 0 **45 1**

BOSTWICK, Michael (D) 385 41
H: 6 4 W: 14 00 b.Eltham 17-5-88
Internationals: England C.
2006–07 Millwall 0 0
From Rushden & D, Ebbsfleet U
2010–11 Stevenage 41 2
2011–12 Stevenage 43 7 **84 9**
2012–13 Peterborough U 39 5
2013–14 Peterborough U 42 4
2014–15 Peterborough U 38 7
2015–16 Peterborough U 36 4
2016–17 Peterborough U 39 3 **194 23**
2017–18 Lincoln C 44 6
2018–19 Lincoln C 45 2
2019–20 Lincoln C 18 1 **107 9**

BRADLEY, Alex (M) 7 1
b.Worcester 27-1-99
Internationals: Finland U17, U19.
2018–19 WBA 0 0
2018–19 *Burton Alb* 7 1 **7 1**
2019–20 Lincoln C 0 0

BUCCI, Gianluca (D) **0** **0**

2019–20	Lincoln C	0	0		

CHAPMAN, Ellis (M) **16** **0**
b.Lincoln 8-1-01
From Leicester C.

2017–18	Lincoln C	0	0		
2018–19	Lincoln C	5	0		
2019–20	Lincoln C	11	0	**16**	**0**

COKER, Ben (D) **227** **4**
H: 5 11 W: 11 09 b.Hatfield 17-6-89

2010–11	Colchester U	20	0		
2011–12	Colchester U	20	0		
2012–13	Colchester U	1	0	**41**	**0**
2013–14	Southend U	45	2		
2014–15	Southend U	32	1		
2015–16	Southend U	40	1		
2016–17	Southend U	31	0		
2017–18	Southend U	22	0		
2018–19	Southend U	16	0	**186**	**4**
2019–20	Lincoln C	0	0		
2019–20	*Cambridge U*	0	0		

EARDLEY, Neal (M) **366** **15**
H: 5 11 W: 11 10 b.Llandudno 6-11-88
Internationals: Wales U17, U19, U21, Full caps.

2005–06	Oldham Ath	1	0		
2006–07	Oldham Ath	36	2		
2007–08	Oldham Ath	42	6		
2008–09	Oldham Ath	34	2		
2009–10	Oldham Ath	0	0	**113**	**10**
2009–10	Blackpool	24	0		
2010–11	Blackpool	31	1		
2011–12	Blackpool	26	1		
2012–13	Blackpool	23	0	**104**	**2**
2013–14	Birmingham C	5	0		
2014–15	Birmingham C	4	0		
2014–15	*Leyton Orient*	1	0	**1**	**0**
2015–16	Birmingham C	5	0	**14**	**0**
2016–17	Hibernian	2	0	**2**	**0**
2016–17	Northampton T	10	0	**10**	**0**
2017–18	Lincoln C	44	1		
2018–19	Lincoln C	43	2		
2019–20	Lincoln C	35	0	**122**	**3**

EDUN, Tayo (D) **14** **1**
H: 5 9 b.London 14-5-98
Internationals: England U17, U18, U19, U20.

2016–17	Fulham	0	0		
2017–18	Fulham	2	0		
2018–19	Fulham	0	0		
2018–19	*Ipswich T*	6	1	**6**	**1**
2019–20	Fulham	0	0	**2**	**0**
2019–20	Lincoln C	6	0	**6**	**0**

ELBOUZEDI, Zak (M) **12** **0**
Internationals: Republic of Ireland U16, U17, U18, U19, U21.

2016–17	WBA	0	0		
2017–18	Inverness CT	4	0		
2017–18	*Elgin C*	3	0	**3**	**0**
2018–19	Inverness CT	0	0	**4**	**0**

From Waterford.

2019–20	Lincoln C	5	0	**5**	**0**

FRECKLINGTON, Lee (M) **427** **64**
H: 5 8 W: 11 00 b.Lincoln 8-9-85
Internationals: Republic of Ireland B.

2003–04	Lincoln C	0	0		
2004–05	Lincoln C	3	0		
2005–06	Lincoln C	18	2		
2006–07	Lincoln C	42	8		
2007–08	Lincoln C	34	4		
2008–09	Lincoln C	27	7		
2008–09	Peterborough U	7	0		
2009–10	Peterborough U	35	2		
2010–11	Peterborough U	9	1		
2011–12	Peterborough U	37	5		
2012–13	Peterborough U	5	0	**93**	**8**
2012–13	*Rotherham U*	31	6		
2013–14	Rotherham U	39	10		
2014–15	Rotherham U	29	2		
2015–16	Rotherham U	27	5		
2016–17	Rotherham U	22	1		
2017–18	Rotherham U	19	4	**167**	**28**
2017–18	Lincoln C	16	4		
2018–19	Lincoln C	27	3		
2019–20	Lincoln C	0	0	**167**	**28**

GRANT, Jorge (M) **145** **29**
H: 5 9 W: 11 07 b.Oxford 26-9-94

2013–14	Nottingham F	0	0		
2014–15	Nottingham F	1	0		
2015–16	Nottingham F	10	0		
2016–17	Nottingham F	6	0		
2016–17	*Notts Co*	17	6		
2017–18	Nottingham F	0	0		
2017–18	*Notts Co*	45	15	**62**	**21**
2018–19	Nottingham F	0	0	**17**	**0**
2018–19	*Luton T*	17	2	**17**	**2**
2018–19	*Mansfield T*	17	4	**17**	**4**
2019–20	Lincoln C	32	2	**32**	**2**

HINDS, Akeem (D) **0** **0**

2017–18	Rotherham U	0	0		
2018–19	Rotherham U	0	0		
2019–20	Rotherham U	0	0		
2019–20	Lincoln C	0	0		

HOPPER, Tom (F) **173** **38**
H: 6 1 W: 12 00 b.Boston 14-12-93
Internationals: England U18.

2011–12	Leicester C	0	0		
2012–13	Leicester C	0	0		
2012–13	*Bury*	22	3	**22**	**3**
2013–14	Leicester C	0	0		
2014–15	Leicester C	0	0		
2014–15	*Scunthorpe U*	12	4		
2015–16	Scunthorpe U	34	8		
2016–17	Scunthorpe U	31	5		
2017–18	Scunthorpe U	38	7	**115**	**24**
2018–19	Southend U	14	7		
2019–20	Southend U	14	2	**28**	**9**
2019–20	Lincoln C	8	2	**8**	**2**

JONES, James (M) **167** **19**
H: 5 9 W: 10 10 b.Winsford 1-2-96
Internationals: Scotland U19, U21.

2014–15	Crewe Alex	24	1		
2015–16	Crewe Alex	31	0		
2016–17	Crewe Alex	45	10		
2017–18	Crewe Alex	6	1		
2018–19	Crewe Alex	38	5		
2019–20	Crewe Alex	23	2	**167**	**19**
2019–20	Lincoln C	0	0		

LEWIS, Aaron (D) **9** **1**
H: 6 0 W: 13 05 b.Swansea 26-6-98
Internationals: Wales U20, U21.

2018–19	Swansea C	0	0		
2018–19	*Doncaster R*	7	0	**7**	**0**
2019–20	Lincoln C	2	1	**2**	**1**

MELBOURNE, Max (D) **14** **0**
b.Solihull 24-10-98

2017–18	WBA	0	0		
2017–18	*Ross Co*	3	0	**3**	**0**
2018–19	WBA	0	0		
2018–19	*Partick Thistle*	3	0	**3**	**0**
2019–20	Lincoln C	8	0	**8**	**0**

PAYNE, Jack (M) **208** **32**
H: 5 5 W: 9 06 b.Tower Hamlets 25-10-94

2013–14	Southend U	11	0		
2014–15	Southend U	34	6		
2015–16	Southend U	32	9	**77**	**15**
2016–17	Huddersfield T	23	2		
2017–18	Huddersfield T	0	0		
2017–18	*Oxford U*	28	3	**28**	**3**
2017–18	*Blackburn R*	18	1	**18**	**1**
2018–19	Huddersfield T	0	0	**23**	**2**
2018–19	*Bradford C*	39	9	**39**	**9**
2019–20	Lincoln C	23	2	**23**	**2**

PETT, Tom (M) **196** **24**
H: 5 8 W: 11 00 b. 3-12-91
Internationals: England C.

2014–15	Stevenage	34	7		
2015–16	Stevenage	40	1		
2016–17	Stevenage	40	6		
2017–18	Stevenage	27	6	**141**	**20**
2017–18	Lincoln C	9	1		
2018–19	Lincoln C	44	3		
2019–20	Lincoln C	2	0	**55**	**4**

SAULT, Ben (M) **0** **0**
b. 26-9-02

2019–20	Lincoln C	0	0		

SCULLY, Anthony (M) **5** **2**

2018–19	West Ham U	0	0		
2019–20	Lincoln C	5	2	**5**	**2**

SHACKELL, Jason (D) **505** **19**
H: 6 4 W: 13 06 b.Stevenage 27-9-83

2002–03	Norwich C	2	0		
2003–04	Norwich C	6	0		
2004–05	Norwich C	11	0		
2005–06	Norwich C	17	0		
2006–07	Norwich C	43	3		
2007–08	Norwich C	39	0		
2008–09	Norwich C	15	0	**133**	**3**
2008–09	Wolverhampton W	12	0		
2009–10	Wolverhampton W	0	0	**12**	**0**
2009–10	*Doncaster R*	21	1	**21**	**1**
2010–11	Barnsley	44	3		
2011–12	Barnsley	0	0	**44**	**3**
2011–12	Derby Co	46	1		
2012–13	Burnley	44	2		
2013–14	Burnley	46	2		
2014–15	Burnley	38	0	**128**	**4**
2015–16	Derby Co	46	1		
2016–17	Derby Co	8	0		
2017–18	Derby Co	0	0	**100**	**2**
2017–18	*Millwall*	7	0	**7**	**0**
2018–19	Lincoln C	34	4		
2019–20	Lincoln C	26	2	**60**	**6**

SHEEHAN, Alan (D) **381** **24**
H: 5 11 W: 11 02 b.Athlone 14-9-86
Internationals: Republic of Ireland U21.

2004–05	Leicester C	1	0		
2005–06	Leicester C	2	0		
2006–07	Leicester C	0	0		
2006–07	*Mansfield T*	10	0	**10**	**0**
2007–08	Leicester C	20	1	**23**	**1**
2007–08	*Leeds U*	10	1		
2008–09	Leeds U	11	1		
2008–09	*Crewe Alex*	3	0	**3**	**0**
2009–10	Leeds U	0	0	**21**	**2**
2009–10	*Oldham Ath*	8	1	**8**	**1**
2009–10	*Swindon T*	22	1		
2010–11	Swindon T	21	1	**43**	**2**
2011–12	Notts Co	39	2		
2012–13	Notts Co	33	0		
2013–14	Notts Co	42	7		
2014–15	Bradford C	23	1		
2014–15	*Peterborough U*	2	0	**2**	**0**
2015–16	Bradford C	2	0	**25**	**1**
2015–16	*Notts Co*	14	2	**128**	**11**
2015–16	*Luton T*	20	1		
2016–17	Luton T	34	2		
2017–18	Luton T	42	3		
2018–19	Luton T	17	0		
2019–20	Luton T	4	0	**117**	**6**
2019–20	Lincoln C	1	0	**1**	**0**

SMITH, Grant (M) **16** **0**
b. 20-11-93

2012–13	Brighton & HA	0	0		
2013–14	Brighton & HA	0	0		

From Farnborough, Hayes & Yeading, Bognor Regis T, Boreham Wood.

2018–19	Lincoln C	16	0		
2019–20	Lincoln C	0	0	**16**	**0**

VICKERS, Josh (G) **93** **0**
H: 6 0 W: 11 05 b.Billericay 1-12-95
From Arsenal.

2015–16	Swansea C	0	0		
2016–17	Swansea C	0	0		
2016–17	*Barnet*	23	0	**23**	**0**
2017–18	Lincoln C	17	0		
2018–19	Lincoln C	18	0		
2019–20	Lincoln C	35	0	**70**	**0**

Players retained or with offer of contract
Roughan, Curtin Sean Patrick.

Scholars
A-Oyouni, Ziyad; Bucci, Gianluca Franco; Finlay, Tyler James; Flitton, Ryan Bradley; Gee, Max Thomas Samuel; Gruszczynski, Kacper Daniel; Liversidge, Tobias Alexander; Long, Samuel James; Odokonyero, Nathan Atoro; Parsons, Niall Stephen; Sault, Ben Jack; Scott, Cameo Ferrell Chino; Tear, Haydn Matthew; Tetlow, Jasper Michael Brian; Woodcock, Joshua Lewis; Woolley, Ross Haigh.

LIVERPOOL (45)

ADRIAN (G) **168** **0**
H: 6 2 W: 12 00 b.Seville 3-1-87

2008–09	Real Betis	0	0		
2009–10	Real Betis	0	0		
2010–11	Real Betis	0	0		
2011–12	Real Betis	0	0		
2012–13	Real Betis	32	0	**32**	**0**
2013–14	West Ham U	20	0		
2014–15	West Ham U	38	0		
2015–16	West Ham U	32	0		
2016–17	West Ham U	16	0		
2017–18	West Ham U	19	0		
2018–19	West Ham U	0	0	**125**	**0**
2019–20	Liverpool	11	0	**11**	**0**

ALEXANDER-ARNOLD, Trent (M) **93** **6**
b. 7-10-98
Internationals: England U16, U17, U18, U19, U21, Full caps.

2016–17	Liverpool	7	0		
2017–18	Liverpool	19	1		
2018–19	Liverpool	29	1		
2019–20	Liverpool	38	4	**93**	**6**

ALISSON, Ramses (G) **148 0**
H: 6 4 W: 14 05 b.Novo Hamburgo 2-10-92
Internationals: Brazil U17, U21, Full caps.
2013 Internacional 6 0
2014 Internacional 11 0
2015 Internacional 26 0
2016 Internacional 1 0 **44 0**
2016–17 Roma 0 0
2017–18 Roma 37 0 **37 0**
2018–19 Liverpool 38 0
2019–20 Liverpool 29 0 **67 0**

BEARNE, Jack (F) **0 0**
b.Nottingham 15-9-01
2019–20 Liverpool 0 0

BOYES, Morgan (D) **0 0**
Internationals: Wales U19.
2019–20 Liverpool 0 0

BREWSTER, Rhian (F) **20 10**
Internationals: England U16, U17, U18, U21
From Chelsea.
2016–17 Liverpool 0 0
2017–18 Liverpool 0 0
2018–19 Liverpool 0 0
2019–20 Liverpool 0 0
2019–20 *Swansea C* 20 10 **20 10**

CAIN, Jake (M) **0 0**
2019–20 Liverpool 0 0

CHIRIVELLA, Pedro (M) **49 2**
b. 23-5-97
Internationals: Spain U17.
2014–15 Valencia 0 0
2015–16 Liverpool 1 0
2016–17 Liverpool 0 0
2016–17 *Go Ahead Eagles* 17 2 **17 2**
2017–18 Liverpool 0 0
2017–18 *Willem II* 31 0 **31 0**
2018–19 Liverpool 0 0
2019–20 Liverpool 0 0 **1 0**
Transferred to Nantes, June 2020.

CHRISTIE-DAVIES, Isaac (M) **0 0**
b.Brighton 18-9-97
Internationals: England U16, U17. Wales U21.
2018–19 Liverpool 0 0
2019–20 Liverpool 0 0
2019–20 *Cercle Brugge* 0 0

CLARKSON, Leighton (M) **0 0**
2019–20 Liverpool 0 0

CLAYTON, Tom (D) **0 0**
b.Rainford 16-11-00
Internationals: Scotland U19.
2019–20 Liverpool 0 0

CLYNE, Nathaniel (D) **307 5**
H: 5 9 W: 10 07 b.Stockwell 5-4-91
Internationals: England U19, U21, Full caps.
2008–09 Crystal Palace 26 0
2009–10 Crystal Palace 22 1
2010–11 Crystal Palace 46 0
2011–12 Crystal Palace 28 0 **122 1**
2012–13 Southampton 34 1
2013–14 Southampton 25 0
2014–15 Southampton 35 2 **94 3**
2015–16 Liverpool 33 1
2016–17 Liverpool 37 0
2017–18 Liverpool 3 0
2018–19 Liverpool 4 0
2018–19 *Bournemouth* 14 0 **14 0**
2019–20 Liverpool 0 0 **77 1**

DIXON-BONNER, Elijah (M) **0 0**
b.London 1-1-01
Internationals: England U17.
2019–20 Liverpool 0 0

EJARIA, Oviemuno (M) **79 6**
H: 6 0 W: 11 11 b.Southwark 18-11-97
Internationals: England U20, U21.
From Arsenal.
2016–17 Liverpool 2 0
2017–18 Liverpool 0 0
2017–18 *Sunderland* 11 1 **11 1**
2018–19 Liverpool 0 0
2018–19 *Rangers* 14 1 **14 1**
2018–19 *Reading* 16 1
2019–20 Liverpool 0 0 **2 0**
2019–20 *Reading* 36 3 **52 4**

ELLIOTT, Harvey (M) **4 0**
b.Esbjerg 4-4-03
Internationals: England U16, U17.
2018–19 Fulham 2 0 **2 0**
2019–20 Liverpool 2 0 **2 0**

FABINHO, Henrique (M) **224 26**
H: 6 2 W: 12 04 b.Campinas 23-10-93
Internationals: Brazil Full caps.
From Fluminese.
2012–13 Rio Ave 0 0
2012–13 *Real Madrid* 1 0 **1 0**
2013–14 Rio Ave 0 0
2013–14 *Monaco* 26 0
2014–15 Rio Ave 0 0
2014–15 *Monaco* 36 1
2015–16 Monaco 34 6
2016–17 Monaco 37 9
2017–18 Monaco 34 7 **167 23**
2018–19 Liverpool 28 1
2019–20 Liverpool 28 2 **56 3**

FIRMINO, Roberto (M) **353 103**
H: 5 11 W: 12 00 b.Maceio 2-10-91
Internationals: Brazil Full caps.
2009 Figueirense 2 0
2010 Figueirense 36 8 **38 8**
2010–11 Hoffenheim 11 3
2011–12 Hoffenheim 30 7
2012–13 Hoffenheim 33 5
2013–14 Hoffenheim 33 16
2014–15 Hoffenheim 33 7 **140 38**
2015–16 Liverpool 31 10
2016–17 Liverpool 35 11
2017–18 Liverpool 37 15
2018–19 Liverpool 34 12
2019–20 Liverpool 38 9 **175 57**

GALLACHER, Tony (D) **17 0**
b.Glasgow 23-7-99
Internationals: Scotland U16, U17.
2015–16 Falkirk 0 0
2016–17 Falkirk 6 0
2017–18 Falkirk 11 0
2018–19 Falkirk 0 0 **17 0**
2018–19 Liverpool 0 0
2019–20 Liverpool 0 0

GEORGE, Shamal (G) **4 0**
b.Wirral 6-1-98
2017–18 Liverpool 0 0
2017–18 *Carlisle U* 4 0 **4 0**
2018–19 Liverpool 0 0
2018–19 *Tranmere R* 0 0
2019–20 Liverpool 0 0

GOMEZ, Joseph (D) **93 0**
H: 6 2 W: 14 00 b.Catford 23-5-97
Internationals: England U16, U17, U19, U21, Full caps.
2014–15 Charlton Ath 21 0 **21 0**
2015–16 Liverpool 5 0
2016–17 Liverpool 0 0
2017–18 Liverpool 23 0
2018–19 Liverpool 16 0
2019–20 Liverpool 28 0 **72 0**

GRABARA, Kamil (G) **44 0**
H: 6 3 W: 11 11 b.Ruda Slaska 8-1-99
Internationals: Poland U17, U18, U21.
From Ruch Chorzow.
2016–17 Liverpool 0 0
2017–18 Liverpool 0 0
2018–19 Liverpool 0 0
2018–19 *AGF Aarhus* 16 0 **16 0**
2019–20 Liverpool 0 0
2019–20 *Huddersfield T* 28 0 **28 0**

GRUJIC, Marko (M) **116 18**
b. 13-4-96
Internationals: Serbia U16, U17, U19, U20, U21, Full caps.
2012–13 Red Star Belgrade 1 0
2013–14 Red Star Belgrade 0 0
2014–15 Red Star Belgrade 9 0
2014–15 *Kolubara* 5 2 **5 2**
2015–16 Red Star Belgrade 29 6 **39 6**
2016–17 Liverpool 5 0
2017–18 Liverpool 3 0
2017–18 *Cardiff C* 13 1 **13 1**
2018–19 Liverpool 0 0
2018–19 *Hertha Berlin* 22 5
2019–20 Liverpool 0 0 **8 0**
2019–20 *Hertha Berlin* 29 4 **51 9**

HARDY, Joe (F) **0 0**
b.Wirral 26-9-98
From Manchester C, Brentford.
2019–20 Liverpool 0 0

HENDERSON, Jordan (M) **350 31**
H: 6 0 W: 10 07 b.Sunderland 17-6-90
Internationals: England U19, U20, U21, Full caps.
2008–09 Sunderland 1 0
2008–09 *Coventry C* 10 1 **10 1**
2009–10 Sunderland 33 1
2010–11 Sunderland 37 3 **71 4**
2011–12 Liverpool 37 2
2012–13 Liverpool 30 5
2013–14 Liverpool 35 4
2014–15 Liverpool 37 6
2015–16 Liverpool 17 2
2016–17 Liverpool 24 1
2017–18 Liverpool 27 1
2018–19 Liverpool 32 1
2019–20 Liverpool 30 4 **269 26**

HILL, Thomas (M) **0 0**
b.Formby 13-10-02
2019–20 Liverpool 0 0

HOEVER, Ki-Jana (D) **0 0**
b.Amsterdam 18-1-02
Internationals: Netherlands U16, U17, U18.
From Ajax.
2018–19 Liverpool 0 0
2019–20 Liverpool 0 0

JONES, Curtis (M) **6 1**
b. 30-1-01
Internationals: England U16, U17, U18, U19.
2017–18 Liverpool 0 0
2018–19 Liverpool 0 0
2019–20 Liverpool 6 1 **6 1**

KANE, Herbie (M) **45 6**
H: 5 9 W: 10 08 b.Bristol 23-11-98
Internationals: England U16, U17, U18.
2018–19 Liverpool 0 0
2018–19 *Doncaster R* 38 4 **38 4**
2019–20 Liverpool 0 0
2019–20 *Hull C* 7 2 **7 2**

KARIUS, Loris (G) **175 0**
H: 6 2 W: 11 11 b.Biberach 22-6-93
Internationals: Germany U16, U17, U18, U19, U20, U21.
2009–10 Manchester C 0 0
2010–11 Manchester C 0 0
2011–12 Manchester C 0 0
2012–13 Manchester C 0 0
2012–13 Mainz 05 1 0
2013–14 Mainz 05 23 0
2014–15 Mainz 05 33 0
2015–16 Mainz 05 34 0 **91 0**
2016–17 Liverpool 10 0
2017–18 Liverpool 19 0
2018–19 Liverpool 0 0
2018–19 *Besiktas* 30 0
2019–20 Liverpool 0 0 **29 0**
2019–20 *Besiktas* 25 0 **55 0**

KEITA, Naby (M) **183 39**
H: 5 8 W: 10 01 b.Conakry 10-2-95
Internationals: Guinea Full caps.
2013–14 Istres 23 4 **23 4**
2014–15 Red Bull Salzburg 30 5
2015–16 Red Bull Salzburg 29 12 **59 17**
2016–17 RB Leipzig 31 8
2017–18 RB Leipzig 27 6 **58 14**
2018–19 Liverpool 25 2
2019–20 Liverpool 18 2 **43 4**

KELLEHER, Caoimhin (G) **0 0**
H: 5 11 b.Cork 23-11-98
Internationals: Republic of Ireland U17, U19, U21.
2018–19 Liverpool 0 0
2019–20 Liverpool 0 0

KOURMETIO, Billy (D) **0 0**
b. 14-11-02
From Lyon, Orleans.
2019–20 Liverpool 0 0

LALLANA, Adam (M) **366 66**
H: 5 8 W: 11 06 b.St Albans 10-5-88
Internationals: England U18, U19, U21, Full caps.
2005–06 Southampton 0 0
2006–07 Southampton 1 0
2007–08 Southampton 5 1
2007–08 *Bournemouth* 3 0 **3 0**
2008–09 Southampton 40 1
2009–10 Southampton 44 15
2010–11 Southampton 36 8
2011–12 Southampton 41 11
2012–13 Southampton 30 3
2013–14 Southampton 38 9 **235 48**
2014–15 Liverpool 27 5
2015–16 Liverpool 30 4
2016–17 Liverpool 31 8
2017–18 Liverpool 12 0
2018–19 Liverpool 13 0
2019–20 Liverpool 15 1 **128 18**

LAROUCI, Yasser (M) **0 0**
b.El Oued 1-1-01
From Le Havre.

2019–20	Liverpool	0	0		

LEWIS, Adam (D) **0 0**
b.Liverpool 8-11-99
Internationals: England U16, U17, U19, U20.

2019–20	Liverpool	0	0		

LONERGAN, Andrew (G) **353 1**
H: 6 4 W: 13 02 b.Preston 19-10-83
Internationals: Republic of Ireland U16. England U20.

2000–01	Preston NE	1	0		
2001–02	Preston NE	0	0		
2002–03	Preston NE	0	0		
2002–03	*Darlington*	2	0	**2**	**0**
2003–04	Preston NE	8	0		
2004–05	Preston NE	23	1		
2005–06	Preston NE	0	0		
2005–06	*Wycombe W*	2	0	**2**	**0**
2006–07	Preston NE	13	0		
2006–07	*Swindon T*	1	0	**1**	**0**
2007–08	Preston NE	43	0		
2008–09	Preston NE	46	0		
2009–10	Preston NE	45	0		
2010–11	Preston NE	29	0	**208**	**1**
2011–12	Leeds U	35	0		
2012–13	Bolton W	5	0		
2013–14	Bolton W	17	0		
2014–15	Bolton W	29	0	**51**	**0**
2015–16	Fulham	29	0	**29**	**0**
2016–17	Wolverhampton W	11	0		
2017–18	Wolverhampton W	0	0	**11**	**0**
2017–18	Leeds U	7	0	**42**	**0**
2018–19	Middlesbrough	0	0		
2018–19	*Rochdale*	7	0	**7**	**0**
2019–20	Liverpool	0	0		

LONGSTAFF, Luis (M) **0 0**
b.Darlington 24-2-00
Internationals: England U16, U17.

2019–20	Liverpool	0	0		

LOVREN, Dejan (D) **321 11**
H: 6 2 W: 13 02 b.Karlovac 5-7-89
Internationals: Croatia U17, U18, U19, U20, U21, Full caps.

2005–06	Dinamo Zagreb	1	0		
2006–07	Dinamo Zagreb	0	0		
2006–07	*Inter Zapresic*	21	0		
2007–08	Dinamo Zagreb	0	0		
2007–08	*Inter Zapresic*	29	1	**50**	**1**
2008–09	Dinamo Zagreb	22	1		
2009–10	Dinamo Zagreb	14	0	**37**	**1**
2009–10	Lyon	8	0		
2010–11	Lyon	28	0		
2011–12	Lyon	18	1		
2012–13	Lyon	18	1	**72**	**2**
2013–14	Southampton	31	2	**31**	**2**
2014–15	Liverpool	26	0		
2015–16	Liverpool	24	0		
2016–17	Liverpool	29	2		
2017–18	Liverpool	29	2		
2018–19	Liverpool	13	1		
2019–20	Liverpool	10	0	**131**	**5**

MANE, Sadio (F) **279 117**
H: 5 9 W: 12 00 b.Sedhiou 10-4-92
Internationals: Senegal U23, Full caps.

2011–12	Metz	19	1		
2012–13	Metz	3	1	**22**	**2**
2012–13	Red Bull Salzburg	26	16		
2013–14	Red Bull Salzburg	33	13		
2014–15	Red Bull Salzburg	4	2	**63**	**31**
2014–15	Southampton	30	10		
2015–16	Southampton	37	11	**67**	**21**
2016–17	Liverpool	27	13		
2017–18	Liverpool	29	10		
2018–19	Liverpool	36	22		
2019–20	Liverpool	35	18	**127**	**63**

MATIP, Joel (M) **279 18**
H: 6 4 W: 13 01 b.Bochum 8-8-91
Internationals: Cameroon Full caps.

2009–10	Schalke 04	20	3		
2010–11	Schalke 04	26	0		
2011–12	Schalke 04	30	3		
2012–13	Schalke 04	32	0		
2013–14	Schalke 04	31	3		
2014–15	Schalke 04	21	2		
2015–16	Schalke 04	34	3	**194**	**14**
2016–17	Liverpool	29	1		
2017–18	Liverpool	25	1		
2018–19	Liverpool	22	1		
2019–20	Liverpool	9	1	**85**	**4**

MILLAR, Liam (F) **33 2**
b. 27-9-99
Internationals: Canada U20, U23, Full caps.

2018–19	Liverpool	0	0		
2018–19	*Kilmarnock*	13	1		
2019–20	Liverpool	0	0		
2019–20	*Kilmarnock*	20	1	**33**	**2**

MILNER, James (M) **544 57**
H: 5 9 W: 11 00 b.Leeds 4-1-86
Internationals: England U16, U17, U19, U20, U21, Full caps.

2002–03	Leeds U	18	2		
2003–04	Leeds U	30	3	**48**	**5**
2003–04	*Swindon T*	6	2	**6**	**2**
2004–05	Newcastle U	25	1		
2005–06	Newcastle U	3	0		
2005–06	*Aston Villa*	27	1		
2006–07	Newcastle U	35	3		
2007–08	Newcastle U	29	2		
2008–09	Newcastle U	2	0	**94**	**6**
2008–09	Aston Villa	36	3		
2009–10	Aston Villa	36	7		
2010–11	Aston Villa	1	1	**100**	**12**
2010–11	Manchester C	32	0		
2011–12	Manchester C	26	3		
2012–13	Manchester C	26	4		
2013–14	Manchester C	31	1		
2014–15	Manchester C	32	5	**147**	**13**
2015–16	Liverpool	28	5		
2016–17	Liverpool	36	7		
2017–18	Liverpool	32	0		
2018–19	Liverpool	31	5		
2019–20	Liverpool	22	2	**149**	**19**

MINAMINO, Takumi (F) **208 49**
b. 16-1-95
Internationals: Japan U17, U20, U23, Full caps.

2012	Cerezo Osaka	3	0		
2013	Cerezo Osaka	29	5		
2014	Cerezo Osaka	30	2	**62**	**7**
2014–15	Red Bull Salzburg	14	3		
2015–16	Red Bull Salzburg	32	10		
2016–17	Red Bull Salzburg	21	11		
2017–18	Red Bull Salzburg	28	7		
2018–19	Red Bull Salzburg	27	6		
2019–20	Red Bull Salzburg	14	5	**136**	**42**
2019–20	Liverpool	10	0	**10**	**0**

NORRIS, James (D) **0 0**
b.Liverpool 4-4-03
Internationals: England U16, U17.

2019–20	Liverpool	0	0		

ORIGI, Divock (F) **195 39**
H: 6 1 W: 11 11 b.Oostende 18-4-95
Internationals: Belgium U16, U17, U19, U21, Full caps.

2012–13	Lille	10	1		
2013–14	Lille	30	5		
2014–15	Lille	33	8	**73**	**14**
2015–16	Liverpool	16	5		
2016–17	Liverpool	34	7		
2017–18	Liverpool	1	0		
2017–18	*Wolfsburg*	31	6	**31**	**6**
2018–19	Liverpool	12	3		
2019–20	Liverpool	28	4	**91**	**19**

OXLADE-CHAMBERLAIN, Alex (M) **232 25**
H: 5 11 W: 11 00 b.Portsmouth 15-8-93
Internationals: England U18, U19, U21, Full caps.

2009–10	Southampton	2	0		
2010–11	Southampton	34	9	**36**	**9**
2011–12	Arsenal	16	2		
2012–13	Arsenal	25	1		
2013–14	Arsenal	14	2		
2014–15	Arsenal	23	1		
2015–16	Arsenal	22	1		
2016–17	Arsenal	29	2		
2017–18	Arsenal	3	0	**132**	**9**
2017–18	Liverpool	32	3		
2018–19	Liverpool	2	0		
2019–20	Liverpool	30	4	**64**	**7**

PHILLIPS, Nathaniel (D) **19 0**
b.Bolton 21-3-97

2019–20	Liverpool	0	0		
2019–20	*Stuttgart*	19	0	**19**	**0**

ROBERTSON, Andrew (D) **263 11**
H: 5 10 W: 10 00 b.Glasgow 11-3-94
Internationals: Scotland U21, Full caps.

2012–13	Queen's Park	34	2	**34**	**2**
2013–14	Dundee U	36	3	**36**	**3**
2014–15	Hull C	24	0		
2015–16	Hull C	42	2		
2016–17	Hull C	33	1	**99**	**3**
2017–18	Liverpool	22	1		
2018–19	Liverpool	36	0		
2019–20	Liverpool	36	2	**94**	**3**

SALAH, Mohamed (M) **285 130**
H: 5 9 W: 11 04 b.Basion 15-6-92
Internationals: Egypt U20, U23, Full caps.

2010–11	Al-Mokawloon	21	4		
2011–12	Al-Mokawloon	15	7	**36**	**11**
2012–13	Basle	29	5		
2013–14	Basle	18	4	**47**	**9**
2013–14	Chelsea	10	2		
2014–15	Chelsea	3	0		
2014–15	*Fiorentina*	16	6	**16**	**6**
2015–16	Chelsea	0	0	**13**	**2**
2015–16	*Roma*	34	14		
2016–17	Roma	31	15	**65**	**29**
2017–18	Liverpool	36	32		
2018–19	Liverpool	38	22		
2019–20	Liverpool	34	19	**108**	**73**

SHAQIRI, Xherdan (M) **274 52**
H: 5 7 W: 11 05 b.Gnjilane 10-10-91
Internationals: Switzerland U17, U18, U19, U21, Full caps.

2009–10	Basel	32	4		
2010–11	Basel	29	5		
2011–12	Basel	31	9	**92**	**18**
2012–13	Bayern Munich	26	4		
2013–14	Bayern Munich	17	6		
2014–15	Bayern Munich	9	1	**52**	**11**
2014–15	Inter Milan	15	1	**15**	**1**
2015–16	Stoke C	27	3		
2016–17	Stoke C	21	4		
2017–18	Stoke C	36	8	**84**	**15**
2018–19	Liverpool	24	6		
2019–20	Liverpool	7	1	**31**	**7**

STEWART, Layton (F) **0 0**
b.Liverpool 2-9-02
Internationals: England U18.

2019–20	Liverpool	0	0		

VAN DEN BERG, Sepp (D) **22 0**
b.Zwolle 20-12-01
Internationals: Netherlands U19.

2017–18	PEC Zwolle	7	0		
2018–19	PEC Zwolle	15	0	**22**	**0**
2019–20	Liverpool	0	0		

VAN DIJK, Virgil (D) **295 29**
H: 6 4 W: 14 07 b.Breda 8-7-91
Internationals: Netherlands U19, U21, Full caps.

2010–11	Groningen	5	2		
2011–12	Groningen	23	3		
2012–13	Groningen	34	2	**62**	**7**
2013–14	Celtic	36	5		
2014–15	Celtic	35	4		
2015–16	Celtic	5	0	**76**	**9**
2015–16	Southampton	34	3		
2016–17	Southampton	21	1		
2017–18	Southampton	12	0	**67**	**4**
2017–18	Liverpool	14	0		
2018–19	Liverpool	38	4		
2019–20	Liverpool	38	5	**90**	**9**

WIJNALDUM, Georginio (M) **399 89**
H: 5 8 W: 10 10 b.Rotterdam 11-11-90
Internationals: Netherlands U17, U19, U21, Full caps.

2006–07	Feyenoord	3	0		
2007–08	Feyenoord	10	1		
2008–09	Feyenoord	33	4		
2009–10	Feyenoord	31	4		
2010–11	Feyenoord	34	14	**111**	**23**
2011–12	PSV Eindhoven	32	9		
2012–13	PSV Eindhoven	33	14		
2013–14	PSV Eindhoven	11	4		
2014–15	PSV Eindhoven	33	14	**109**	**41**
2015–16	Newcastle U	38	11	**38**	**11**
2016–17	Liverpool	36	6		
2017–18	Liverpool	33	1		
2018–19	Liverpool	35	3		
2019–20	Liverpool	37	4	**141**	**14**

WILLIAMS, Neco (D) **6 0**
b. 13-4-01
Internationals: Wales U19.

2019–20	Liverpool	6	0	**6**	**0**

WILSON, Harry (M) **91 29**
H: 5 8 W: 11 00 b.Wrexham 22-3-97
Internationals: Wales U17, U19, U21, Full caps.

2015–16	Liverpool	0	0		
2015–16	*Crewe Alex*	7	0	**7**	**0**
2016–17	Liverpool	0	0		
2017–18	Liverpool	0	0		

2017–18 *Hull C* 13 7 **13 7**
2018–19 Liverpool 0 0
2018–19 *Derby Co* 40 15 **40 15**
2019–20 Liverpool 0 0
2019–20 *Bournemouth* 31 7 **31 7**

WINTERBOTTOM, Ben (G) **0 0**
b.Preston 16-7-01
From Blackburn R.
2019–20 Liverpool 0 0

WOODBURN, Ben (F) **24 1**
H: 5 9 W: 11 05 b.Chester 16-11-99
Internationals: Wales U16, U17, U19, Full caps.
2016–17 Liverpool 5 0
2017–18 Liverpool 1 0
2018–19 Liverpool 0 0
2018–19 *Sheffield U* 7 0 **7 0**
2019–20 Liverpool 0 0 **6 0**
2019–20 *Oxford U* 11 1 **11 1**

Players retained or with offer of contract
Awoniyi, Taiwo; Beck, Owen Michael; Cordoba, Anderson Arroyo; Coyle, Liam; Glatzel, Paul Milton; Jaros, Viteslav; O'Rourke, Fidel; Ojo, Oluwaseyi; Ritaccio, Matteo; Savage, Remi Eugene; Sharif, Abdulrahman Mohamoud; Williams, Rhys.

Scholars
Bradley, Conor; Brookwell, Niall; Corness, Dominic; Elliott, Harvey Daniel James; Kelly, Oscar George; Koumetio, Billy Dawson; Morton, Tyler Scott; Ojrzynski, Jakub; Quansah, Jarell Amorin; Rodrigues, Abel; Turner, Alex; Varesanovic, Dal; Wilson, Sean William; Winterbottom, Benjamin Harry; Woltman, Max Reuben.

LUTON T (46)

BERRY, Luke (D) **201 41**
H: 5 10 W: 11 05 b.Bassingbourn 12-7-92
2014–15 Barnsley 31 1 **31 1**
2015–16 Cambridge U 46 12
2016–17 Cambridge U 45 17
2017–18 Cambridge U 3 0 **94 29**
2017–18 Luton T 34 7
2018–19 Luton T 21 3
2019–20 Luton T 21 1 **76 11**

BRADLEY, Sonny (D) **332 19**
H: 6 0 W: 11 05 b.Hedon 14-6-92
2011–12 Hull C 2 0
2011–12 *Aldershot T* 14 0
2012–13 Hull C 0 0 **2 0**
2012–13 *Aldershot T* 42 1 **56 1**
2013–14 Portsmouth 33 2 **33 2**
2014–15 Crawley T 26 1
2015–16 Crawley T 46 1 **72 2**
2016–17 Plymouth Arg 44 7
2017–18 Plymouth Arg 40 4 **84 11**
2018–19 Luton T 45 0
2019–20 Luton T 40 3 **85 3**

BUTTERFIELD, Jacob (D) **318 28**
H: 5 10 W: 11 00 b.Bradford 10-6-90
2007–08 Barnsley 3 0
2008–09 Barnsley 3 0
2009–10 Barnsley 20 1
2010–11 Barnsley 40 2
2011–12 Barnsley 24 5 **90 8**
2012–13 Norwich C 0 0
2012–13 *Bolton W* 8 0 **8 0**
2012–13 *Crystal Palace* 9 0 **9 0**
2013–14 Norwich C 0 0
2013–14 Middlesbrough 31 3 **31 3**
2014–15 Huddersfield T 45 6
2015–16 Huddersfield T 5 1 **50 7**
2015–16 Derby Co 37 7
2016–17 Derby Co 40 1
2017–18 Derby Co 3 0
2017–18 *Sheffield W* 20 0 **20 0**
2018–19 Derby Co 0 0 **80 8**
2018–19 *Bradford C* 15 1 **15 1**
2019–20 Luton T 15 1 **15 1**

COLLINS, James S (F) **430 155**
H: 6 2 W: 13 08 b.Coventry 1-12-90
Internationals: Republic of Ireland U19, U21, Full caps.
2008–09 Aston Villa 0 0
2009–10 Aston Villa 0 0
2009–10 *Darlington* 7 2 **7 2**
2010–11 Aston Villa 0 0
2010–11 *Burton Alb* 10 4 **10 4**
2010–11 Shrewsbury T 24 8
2011–12 Shrewsbury T 42 14
2012–13 Swindon T 45 15 **45 15**
2013–14 Hibernian 36 6 **36 6**
2014–15 Shrewsbury T 45 15
2015–16 Shrewsbury T 23 5 **134 42**
2015–16 *Northampton T* 21 8 **21 8**
2016–17 Crawley T 45 20 **45 20**
2017–18 Luton T 42 19
2018–19 Luton T 44 25
2019–20 Luton T 46 14 **132 58**

CORNICK, Harry (F) **167 28**
H: 5 11 W: 13 03 b.Poole 6-3-95
2013–14 Bournemouth 0 0
2014–15 Bournemouth 0 0
2015–16 Bournemouth 0 0
2015–16 *Yeovil T* 36 7 **36 7**
2016–17 Bournemouth 0 0
2016–17 *Leyton Orient* 11 1 **11 1**
2016–17 *Gillingham* 6 0 **6 0**
2017–18 Luton T 37 5
2018–19 Luton T 32 6
2019–20 Luton T 45 9 **114 20**

CRANIE, Martin (D) **384 4**
H: 6 1 W: 12 09 b.Yeovil 23-9-86
Internationals: England U17, U18, U19, U20, U21.
2003–04 Southampton 1 0
2004–05 Southampton 3 0
2004–05 *Bournemouth* 3 0 **3 0**
2005–06 Southampton 11 0
2006–07 Southampton 1 0 **16 0**
2006–07 *Yeovil T* 12 0 **12 0**
2007–08 Portsmouth 2 0
2007–08 *QPR* 6 0 **6 0**
2008–09 Portsmouth 0 0
2008–09 *Charlton Ath* 19 0 **19 0**
2009–10 Portsmouth 0 0 **2 0**
2009–10 Coventry C 40 1
2010–11 Coventry C 36 0
2011–12 Coventry C 38 0 **114 1**
2012–13 Barnsley 36 0
2013–14 Barnsley 35 0
2014–15 Barnsley 39 1 **110 1**
2015–16 Huddersfield T 37 0
2016–17 Huddersfield T 14 0
2017–18 Huddersfield T 3 0 **54 0**
2017–18 Middlesbrough 9 0
2018–19 Middlesbrough 0 0 **9 0**
2018–19 Sheffield U 15 0 **15 0**
2019–20 Luton T 24 2 **24 2**

DANIELS, Donervon (D) **140 7**
H: 6 1 W: 14 05 b.Montserrat 24-11-93
Internationals: England U20.
2011–12 WBA 0 0
2012–13 WBA 0 0
2012–13 *Tranmere R* 13 1 **13 1**
2013–14 WBA 0 0
2013–14 *Gillingham* 3 1 **3 1**
2014–15 WBA 0 0
2014–15 *Blackpool* 19 1
2014–15 *Aberdeen* 9 0 **9 0**
2015–16 Wigan Ath 42 3
2016–17 Wigan Ath 1 0
2017–18 Wigan Ath 1 0 **44 3**
2017–18 *Rochdale* 15 0 **15 0**
2018–19 Blackpool 24 0 **43 1**
2019–20 Doncaster R 10 0 **10 0**
2019–20 Luton T 3 1 **3 1**

GALLOWAY, Brendon (M) **40 0**
H: 6 2 W: 13 10 b.Zimbabwe 17-3-96
Internationals: England U17, U18, U19, U21.
2011–12 Milton Keynes D 1 0
2012–13 Milton Keynes D 1 0
2013–14 Milton Keynes D 8 0 **10 0**
2014–15 Everton 2 0
2015–16 Everton 15 0
2016–17 Everton 0 0
2016–17 *WBA* 3 0 **3 0**
2017–18 Everton 0 0
2017–18 *Sunderland* 7 0 **7 0**
2018–19 Everton 0 0 **17 0**
2019–20 Luton T 3 0 **3 0**

HYLTON, Danny (F) **378 111**
H: 6 0 W: 11 13 b.Camden 25-2-89
2008–09 Aldershot T 29 5
2009–10 Aldershot T 21 3
2010–11 Aldershot T 33 5
2011–12 Aldershot T 44 13
2012–13 Aldershot T 27 4 **154 30**
2013–14 Rotherham U 1 0 **1 0**
2013–14 *Bury* 7 2 **7 2**
2013–14 *AFC Wimbledon* 17 3 **17 3**
2014–15 Oxford U 44 14
2015–16 Oxford U 41 12 **85 26**
2016–17 Luton T 39 21
2017–18 Luton T 39 21
2018–19 Luton T 25 8
2019–20 Luton T 11 0 **114 50**

ISTED, Harry (G) **0 0**
b. 5-3-97
From Southampton, Stoke C.
2017–18 Luton T 0 0
2018–19 Luton T 0 0
2019–20 Luton T 0 0

JERVIS, Jake (F) **261 54**
H: 6 3 W: 12 13 b.Birmingham 17-9-91
2009–10 Birmingham C 0 0
2009–10 *Hereford U* 7 2
2010–11 Birmingham C 0 0
2010–11 *Notts Co* 10 0 **10 0**
2010–11 *Hereford U* 4 0 **11 2**
2011–12 Birmingham C 0 0
2011–12 *Swindon T* 12 3 **12 3**
2011–12 *Preston NE* 5 2 **5 2**
2012–13 Birmingham C 2 0 **2 0**
2012–13 *Carlisle U* 5 3 **5 3**
2012–13 *Tranmere R* 4 1 **4 1**
2012–13 *Portsmouth* 3 1
2012–13 Elazigspor 4 1 **4 1**
2013–14 Portsmouth 15 4 **18 5**
2014–15 Ross Co 27 4 **27 4**
2015–16 Plymouth Arg 42 11
2016–17 Plymouth Arg 42 12
2017–18 Plymouth Arg 24 4 **108 27**
2017–18 Luton T 10 0
2018–19 Luton T 2 0
2018–19 *AFC Wimbledon* 23 2 **23 2**
2019–20 Luton T 0 0 **12 0**
2019–20 *Salford C* 20 4 **20 4**

JONES, Lloyd (D) **73 4**
H: 6 3 W: 11 11 b.Plymouth 7-10-95
Internationals: Wales U17, U19. England U19, U20.
2012–13 Liverpool 0 0
2013–14 Liverpool 0 0
2014–15 Liverpool 0 0
2014–15 *Cheltenham T* 6 0 **6 0**
2014–15 *Accrington S* 11 1 **11 1**
2015–16 Liverpool 0 0
2015–16 *Blackpool* 10 0 **10 0**
2016–17 Liverpool 0 0
2016–17 *Swindon T* 24 2 **24 2**
2017–18 Liverpool 0 0
2017–18 Luton T 1 0
2018–19 Luton T 1 0
2018–19 *Plymouth Arg* 9 1 **9 1**
2019–20 Luton T 4 0 **6 0**
2019–20 *Northampton T* 7 0 **7 0**

KIOSO, Peter (D) **1 0**
b.Swords 15-8-99
2019–20 Luton T 1 0 **1 0**

LEE, Elliot (F) **123 29**
H: 5 11 W: 11 05 b.Co. Durham 16-12-94
2011–12 West Ham U 0 0
2012–13 West Ham U 0 0
2013–14 West Ham U 1 0
2013–14 *Colchester U* 4 1
2014–15 West Ham U 1 0
2014–15 *Southend U* 0 0
2014–15 *Luton T* 11 3
2015–16 West Ham U 0 0 **2 0**
2015–16 *Blackpool* 4 0 **4 0**
2015–16 *Colchester U* 15 2 **19 3**
2016–17 Barnsley 6 0 **6 0**
2017–18 Luton T 32 10
2018–19 Luton T 38 12
2019–20 Luton T 11 1 **92 26**

LUALUA, Kazenga (F) **246 23**
H: 5 11 W: 12 00 b.Kinshasa 10-12-90
2007–08 Newcastle U 2 0
2008–09 Newcastle U 3 0
2008–09 *Doncaster R* 4 0 **4 0**
2009–10 Newcastle U 1 0
2009–10 *Brighton & HA* 11 0
2010–11 Newcastle U 2 0
2010–11 *Brighton & HA* 11 4
2011–12 Newcastle U 0 0 **8 0**
2011–12 Brighton & HA 27 1
2012–13 Brighton & HA 22 5
2013–14 Brighton & HA 32 1
2014–15 Brighton & HA 34 3
2015–16 Brighton & HA 18 3
2016–17 Brighton & HA 3 0
2016–17 *QPR* 11 1
2017–18 Brighton & HA 0 0 **158 17**
2017–18 *QPR* 8 0 **19 1**

2017–18 Sunderland 6 0 **6 0**
2018–19 Luton T 22 2
2019–20 Luton T 29 3 **51 5**

McMANAMAN, Callum (F) 193 18
H: 5 9 W: 11 03 b.Huyton 25-4-91
Internationals: England U20.
2008–09 Wigan Ath 1 0
2009–10 Wigan Ath 0 0
2010–11 Wigan Ath 3 0
2011–12 Wigan Ath 2 0
2011–12 *Blackpool* 14 2 **14 2**
2012–13 Wigan Ath 20 2
2013–14 Wigan Ath 30 3
2014–15 Wigan Ath 23 5
2014–15 WBA 8 0
2015–16 WBA 12 0
2016–17 WBA 0 0 **20 0**
2016–17 *Sheffield W* 11 0 **11 0**
2017–18 Sunderland 24 1 **24 1**
2018–19 Wigan Ath 22 1 **101 11**
2019–20 Luton T 23 4 **23 4**

MONCUR, George (M) 219 37
H: 5 9 W: 10 00 b.Swindon 18-8-93
Internationals: England U18.
2010–11 West Ham U 0 0
2011–12 West Ham U 0 0
2011–12 *AFC Wimbledon* 20 2 **20 2**
2012–13 West Ham U 0 0
2013–14 West Ham U 0 0
2013–14 *Partick Thistle* 2 1 **2 1**
2014–15 Colchester U 41 8
2015–16 Colchester U 45 12 **86 20**
2016–17 Peterborough U 13 2 **13 2**
2016–17 Barnsley 12 2
2017–18 Barnsley 34 2
2018–19 Barnsley 21 1 **67 5**
2018–19 Luton T 14 6
2019–20 Luton T 17 1 **31 7**

MUSONDA, Frankie (D) 3 0
H: 6 0 W: 11 03 b.Bedford 12-12-97
2015–16 Luton T 3 0
2016–17 Luton T 0 0
2017–18 Luton T 0 0
2018–19 Luton T 0 0
2019–20 Luton T 0 0 **3 0**

NEUFVILLE, Josh (M) 0 0
b.Luton
2017–18 Luton T 0 0
2018–19 Luton T 0 0
2019–20 Luton T 0 0

PANTER, Corey (D) 0 0
2018–19 Luton T 0 0
2019–20 Luton T 0 0

PEARSON, Matthew (D) 203 19
H: 6 3 W: 11 05 b.Keighley 3-8-93
Internationals: England U18, C.
2012–13 Rochdale 9 0
2013–14 Rochdale 0 0 **9 0**
From FC Halifax T.
2015–16 Accrington S 46 3
2016–17 Accrington S 43 8 **89 11**
2017–18 Barnsley 17 0 **17 0**
2018–19 Luton T 46 6
2019–20 Luton T 42 2 **88 8**

PECK, Jake (M) 0 0
2017–18 Luton T 0 0
2018–19 Luton T 0 0
2019–20 Luton T 0 0

POTTS, Danny (D) 151 8
H: 5 8 W: 11 00 b.Barking 13-4-94
Internationals: USA U20. England U18, U19, U20.
2011–12 West Ham U 3 0
2012–13 West Ham U 2 0
2012–13 *Colchester U* 5 0 **5 0**
2013–14 West Ham U 0 0
2013–14 *Portsmouth* 5 0 **5 0**
2014–15 West Ham U 0 0 **5 0**
2015–16 Luton T 14 0
2016–17 Luton T 23 0
2017–18 Luton T 42 6
2018–19 Luton T 24 1
2019–20 Luton T 33 1 **136 8**

REA, Glen (D) 146 4
H: 6 0 W: 11 07 b.Brighton 3-9-94
Internationals: Republic of Ireland U21.
2013–14 Brighton & HA 0 0
2014–15 Brighton & HA 0 0
2015–16 Brighton & HA 0 0
2015–16 *Southend U* 14 0 **14 0**
2015–16 *Luton T* 10 0
2016–17 Luton T 39 2
2017–18 Luton T 46 1
2018–19 Luton T 22 1
2019–20 Luton T 15 0 **132 4**

RUDDOCK, Pelly (M) 197 15
H: 5 9 W: 9 13 b.Hendon 17-7-93
2011–12 West Ham U 0 0
2012–13 West Ham U 0 0
2013–14 West Ham U 0 0
2014–15 Luton T 16 1
2015–16 Luton T 21 2
2016–17 Luton T 42 2
2017–18 Luton T 28 2
2018–19 Luton T 46 5
2019–20 Luton T 44 3 **197 15**

SHEA, James (G) 158 0
H: 5 11 W: 12 00 b.Islington 16-6-91
2009–10 Arsenal 0 0
2010–11 Arsenal 0 0
2011–12 Arsenal 0 0
2011–12 *Dagenham & R* 1 0 **1 0**
2012–13 Arsenal 0 0
2013–14 Arsenal 0 0
2014–15 AFC Wimbledon 38 0
2015–16 AFC Wimbledon 21 0
2016–17 AFC Wimbledon 36 0 **95 0**
2017–18 Luton T 8 0
2018–19 Luton T 41 0
2019–20 Luton T 13 0 **62 0**

SHINNIE, Andrew (M) 246 30
H: 5 11 W: 10 13 b.Aberdeen 17-7-89
Internationals: Scotland U19, U21, Full caps.
2005–06 Rangers 0 0
2006–07 Rangers 2 0
2007–08 Rangers 0 0
2008–09 Rangers 0 0
2009–10 Rangers 0 0
2010–11 Rangers 0 0 **2 0**
2011–12 Inverness CT 19 7
2012–13 Inverness CT 38 12 **57 19**
2013–14 Birmingham C 26 2
2014–15 Birmingham C 27 2
2015–16 Birmingham C 14 0
2015–16 *Rotherham U* 3 0 **3 0**
2016–17 Birmingham C 0 0 **67 4**
2016–17 *Hibernian* 27 1 **27 1**
2017–18 Luton T 28 1
2018–19 Luton T 41 4
2019–20 Luton T 21 1 **90 6**

SLUGA, Simon (G) 154 0
b. 17-3-93
2013–14 Pomorac 31 0 **31 0**
2014–15 Lokomotiva 26 0 **26 0**
2015–16 Rijeka 2 0
2016–17 Rijeka 0 0
2017–18 Rijeka 27 0
2018–19 Rijeka 35 0 **64 0**
2019–20 Luton T 33 0 **33 0**

STECH, Marek (G) 144 0
H: 6 3 W: 14 00 b.Prague 28-1-90
Internationals: Czech Republic U17, U21, Full caps.
2008–09 West Ham U 0 0
2008–09 *Wycombe W* 2 0 **2 0**
2009–10 West Ham U 0 0
2009–10 *Bournemouth* 1 0 **1 0**
2010–11 West Ham U 0 0
2011–12 West Ham U 0 0
2011–12 *Yeovil T* 5 0
2011–12 *Leyton Orient* 2 0 **2 0**
2012–13 Yeovil T 46 0
2013–14 Yeovil T 26 0 **77 0**
2014–15 Sparta Prague 17 0
2015–16 Sparta Prague 2 0
2016–17 Sparta Prague 0 0 **19 0**
2017–18 Luton T 38 0
2018–19 Luton T 5 0
2019–20 Luton T 0 0
2019–20 Luton T 0 0 **43 0**

TUNNICLIFFE, Ryan (M) 236 9
H: 6 0 W: 14 02 b.Bury 30-12-92
Internationals: England U16, U17.
2009–10 Manchester U 0 0
2010–11 Manchester U 0 0
2011–12 Manchester U 0 0
2011–12 *Peterborough U* 27 0 **27 0**
2012–13 Manchester U 0 0
2012–13 *Barnsley* 2 0 **2 0**
2013–14 Manchester U 0 0
2013–14 *Ipswich T* 27 0 **27 0**
2013–14 Fulham 3 0
2013–14 *Wigan Ath* 5 0
2014–15 Fulham 22 0
2014–15 *Blackburn R* 17 1 **17 1**
2015–16 Fulham 27 2
2016–17 Fulham 7 0 **59 2**
2016–17 *Wigan Ath* 9 1 **14 1**
2017–18 Millwall 24 1
2018–19 Millwall 26 3 **50 4**
2019–20 Luton T 40 1 **40 1**

Players retained or with offer of contract
Beckwith, Samuel Wayne; Mpanzu, Pelly Ruddock; Parker, Tiernan Christopher Luke.

Scholars
Boorn, Joshua John Batten; Halsey, Joseph Zak Jake; Horlick, Jameson Edward Alexander; Jones, Avan Chima Allan; Kalonda, Jonas; Lucas, Tra; Moloney, Matthew Thomas; Nicolson, Callum Andrew; Pettit, Casey Anthony; Stevens, Ben Charles; Wilson, Coree Jason.

MACCLESFIELD T (47)

ARCHIBALD, Theo (M) 58 5
H: 5 11 W: 9 06 b.Glasgow 5-3-98
Internationals: Scotland U16, U19, U21.
2016–17 Celtic 0 0
2016–17 *Albion R* 14 0 **14 0**
2017–18 Brentford 2 0
2018–19 Forest Green R 14 1 **14 1**
2018–19 Brentford 0 0 **2 0**
2019–20 Macclesfield T 28 4 **28 4**

AUSTIN, Connor (D) 0 0
2019–20 Macclesfield T 0 0

BLYTH, Jacob (F) 79 12
H: 6 3 W: 12 02 b.Nuneaton 14-8-92
2012–13 Leicester C 0 0
2012–13 *Burton Alb* 2 0
2012–13 *Notts Co* 4 0 **4 0**
2013–14 Leicester C 0 0
2013–14 *Northampton T* 11 3 **11 3**
2014–15 Leicester C 0 0
2014–15 *Burton Alb* 22 5 **24 5**
2015–16 Leicester C 0 0
2015–16 *Cambridge U* 5 1 **5 1**
2015–16 *Blackpool* 8 2 **8 2**
2016–17 Motherwell 8 0 **8 0**
From Barrow.
2019–20 Macclesfield T 19 1 **19 1**

CAMERON, Nathan (D) 218 13
H: 6 2 W: 12 04 b.Birmingham 21-11-91
Internationals: England U20.
2009–10 Coventry C 0 0
2010–11 Coventry C 25 0
2011–12 Coventry C 14 0
2012–13 Coventry C 9 0 **48 0**
2012–13 *Northampton T* 3 0 **3 0**
2013–14 Bury 27 4
2014–15 Bury 46 2
2015–16 Bury 28 3
2016–17 Bury 4 0
2017–18 Bury 21 2 **126 11**
2018–19 Macclesfield T 25 2
2019–20 Macclesfield T 16 0 **41 2**

CHARLES-COOK, Reice (G) 78 0
H: 6 1 W: 12 08 b.London 8-4-94
2013–14 Bury 2 0 **2 0**
2014–15 Coventry C 0 0
2015–16 Coventry C 37 0
2016–17 Coventry C 15 0 **52 0**
2017–18 Swindon T 22 0 **22 0**
2018–19 Sonderjyske 0 0
2018–19 Shrewsbury T 0 0
2019–20 Shrewsbury T 0 0
2019–20 Macclesfield T 2 0 **2 0**

CLEGG, Joshua (M) 0 0
2019–20 Macclesfield T 0 0

COBEY, Joe (F) 0 0
2019–20 Macclesfield T 0 0

FITZPATRICK, David (D) 61 3
H: 5 10 W: 11 07 b.Manchester 22-2-90
Internationals: England C.
2018–19 Macclesfield T 40 3
2019–20 Macclesfield T 21 0 **61 3**

FREGAPANE, Rocco (M) 0 0
From Manchester U.
2019–20 Macclesfield T 0 0

GNAHOUA, Arthur (F) 42 5
H: 6 2 W: 12 08 b.London 5-4-92
From Stalybridge Celtic, Macclesfield T, Kidderminster H.
2017–18 Shrewsbury T 11 1
2018–19 Shrewsbury T 1 0 **12 1**
2018–19 Carlisle U 1 0 **1 0**
2019–20 Macclesfield T 29 4 **29 4**

HAMBLIN, Harry (M) **4 0**
b. 13-10-99
2019–20 Southampton 0 0
2019–20 Macclesfield T 4 0 **4 0**

HARRIS, Jay (M) **46 2**
H: 5 7 W: 11 07 b.Liverpool 15-4-87
From Accrington S, Chester C, Wrexham.
2018–19 Tranmere R 21 1 **21 1**
2019–20 Macclesfield T 25 1 **25 1**

HOLLAND, Sean (M) **0 0**
2019–20 Macclesfield T 0 0

HORSFALL, Fraser (D) **26 0**
H: 6 3 W: 12 13 b. 12-11-96
Internationals: England C.
2015–16 Huddersfield T 0 0
2016–17 Huddersfield T 0 0
2017–18 Huddersfield T 0 0
From Kidderminster H.
2019–20 Macclesfield T 26 0 **26 0**

IRONSIDE, Joe (F) **53 7**
H: 5 11 W: 11 11 b.Middlesbrough 16-10-93
Internationals: England C.
2012–13 Sheffield U 12 0
2013–14 Sheffield U 4 0
2014–15 Sheffield U 0 0 **16 0**
2014–15 *Hartlepool U* 4 1 **4 1**
From Alfreton T, Nuneaton T, Kidderminster H.
2019–20 Macclesfield T 33 6 **33 6**

JAMES, Tyler (D) **0 0**
2019–20 Green Gully 0 0
2019–20 Macclesfield T 0 0

JUPP, Ben (G) **0 0**
2019–20 Macclesfield T 0 0

KELLEHER, Fiacre (D) **79 2**
b. 10-3-96
2016–17 Celtic 0 0
2016–17 Peterhead 0 0
2017–18 Oxford U 0 0
2018–19 Oxford U 0 0
2018–19 *Macclesfield T* 42 1
2019–20 Macclesfield T 37 1 **79 2**

KYOBE, Trevor (M) **0 0**
2019–20 Macclesfield T 0 0

LOGAN, Liam (M) **0 0**
2019–20 Macclesfield T 0 0

McCOURT, Jak (M) **122 9**
H: 5 10 W: 10 10 b.Leicester 6-7-95
2013–14 Leicester C 0 0
2013–14 *Torquay U* 11 0 **11 0**
2014–15 Leicester C 0 0
2015–16 Leicester C 0 0
2015–16 *Port Vale* 2 0 **2 0**
2015–16 Barnsley 1 0 **1 0**
2016–17 Northampton T 26 1 **26 1**
2017–18 Chesterfield 34 5 **34 5**
2018–19 Swindon T 27 1 **27 1**
2019–20 Macclesfield T 21 2 **21 2**

MEALING, Ryan (M) **0 0**
2019–20 Macclesfield T 0 0

NTAMBWE, Brice (M) **92 4**
H: 6 1 W: 12 13 b.Brussels 29-4-93
Internationals: Belgium U16, U17, U19, U20, U21.
2011–12 Birmingham C 0 0
2012–13 Mons 6 0
2013–14 Mons 19 0
2014–15 Mons 2 0 **27 0**
2014–15 Lierse 1 0
2015–16 Lierse 0 0
2016–17 Lierse 18 1
2017–18 Lierse 21 1 **40 2**
2017–18 *Oosterwijk* 9 1 **9 1**
2018–19 Partick Thistle 5 1 **5 1**
2018–19 Macclesfield T 8 0
2019–20 Macclesfield T 3 0 **11 0**

OSIPITAN, Jamie (D) **0 0**
2019–20 Macclesfield T 0 0

PRICE, Lewis (M) **0 0**
2019–20 Macclesfield T 0 0

ROSE, Michael (D) **490 37**
H: 5 11 W: 12 04 b.Salford 28-7-82
Internationals: England C.
1999–2000 Manchester U 0 0
2000–01 Manchester U 0 0
2001–02 Manchester U 0 0
From Hereford U
2004–05 Yeovil T 40 1
2005–06 Yeovil T 1 0 **41 1**
2005–06 *Cheltenham T* 3 0 **3 0**
2005–06 *Scunthorpe U* 15 0 **15 0**
2006–07 Stockport Co 25 3
2007–08 Stockport Co 28 3
2008–09 Stockport Co 27 0
2009–10 Stockport Co 24 2 **104 8**
2009–10 *Norwich C* 12 1 **12 1**
2010–11 Swindon T 35 3 **35 3**
2010–11 Colchester U 0 0
2011–12 Colchester U 14 0
2012–13 Colchester U 22 2 **36 2**
2012–13 Rochdale 14 2
2013–14 Rochdale 42 4
2014–15 Rochdale 32 1
2015–16 Rochdale 30 1 **118 8**
2016–17 Morecambe 43 7
2017–18 Morecambe 42 2 **85 9**
2018–19 Macclesfield T 40 5
2019–20 Macclesfield T 1 0 **41 5**

SEYMOUR, Connor (D) **0 0**
2019–20 Macclesfield T 0 0

STEPHENS, Ben (M) **45 4**
b. 9-8-97
From Oadby T, Kettering T, Stratford T.
2018–19 Macclesfield T 22 1
2019–20 Macclesfield T 23 3 **45 4**

TOLLITT, Ben (M) **21 1**
b. 30-11-94
2015–16 Portsmouth 12 1
2016–17 Portsmouth 0 0 **12 1**
2018–19 Tranmere R 4 0 **4 0**
2019–20 Blackpool 0 0
2019–20 Macclesfield T 5 0 **5 0**

VASSELL, Theo (D) **32 2**
b. 2-1-97
2014–15 Stoke C 0 0
2015–16 Oldham Ath 0 0
2016–17 Walsall 0 0
From Gateshead.
2018–19 Port Vale 15 0 **15 0**
2019–20 Macclesfield T 17 2 **17 2**

VINCENTI, Peter (F) **280 46**
H: 6 2 W: 11 13 b.St Peter 7-7-86
2007–08 Millwall 0 0
2010–11 Stevenage 5 1 **5 1**
2010–11 Aldershot T 23 6
2011–12 Aldershot T 42 6
2012–13 Aldershot T 39 2 **104 14**
2013–14 Rochdale 42 5
2014–15 Rochdale 37 13
2015–16 Rochdale 38 8
2016–17 Rochdale 14 1 **131 27**
2017–18 Coventry C 24 3 **24 3**
2018–19 Macclesfield T 16 1
2019–20 Macclesfield T 0 0 **16 1**

WILSON, Donovan (F) **24 1**
b.Yate 14-3-97
2014–15 Wolverhampton W 0 0
2015–16 Wolverhampton W 0 0
2016–17 Wolverhampton W 1 0
2017–18 Wolverhampton W 0 0
2017–18 *Port Vale* 8 1 **8 1**
2018–19 Wolverhampton W 0 0 **1 0**
2018–19 *Exeter C* 10 0 **10 0**
2019–20 Macclesfield T 5 0 **5 0**

MANCHESTER C (48)

ADARABIOYO, Tosin (D) **63 3**
H: 6 3 b. 24-9-97
Internationals: England U16, U17, U18, U19.
2014–15 Manchester C 0 0
2015–16 Manchester C 0 0
2016–17 Manchester C 0 0
2017–18 Manchester C 0 0
2018–19 Manchester C 0 0
2018–19 *WBA* 29 0 **29 0**
2019–20 Manchester C 0 0
2019–20 *Blackburn R* 34 3 **34 3**

AGUERO, Sergio (F) **492 277**
H: 5 8 W: 11 09 b.Buenos Aires 2-6-88
Internationals: Argentina U17, U20, U23, Full caps.
2002–03 Independiente 1 0
2003–04 Independiente 5 0
2004–05 Independiente 12 5
2005–06 Independiente 36 18 **54 23**
2006–07 Atletico Madrid 38 6
2007–08 Atletico Madrid 37 19
2008–09 Atletico Madrid 37 17
2009–10 Atletico Madrid 31 12
2010–11 Atletico Madrid 32 20 **175 74**
2011–12 Manchester C 34 23
2012–13 Manchester C 30 12
2013–14 Manchester C 23 17
2014–15 Manchester C 33 26
2015–16 Manchester C 30 24
2016–17 Manchester C 31 20
2017–18 Manchester C 25 21
2018–19 Manchester C 33 21
2019–20 Manchester C 24 16 **263 180**

AMBROSE, Thierry (F) **81 14**
H: 5 10 W: 11 00 b.Sens 28-3-97
Internationals: France U16, U17, U18, U19.
2014–15 Manchester C 0 0
2015–16 Manchester C 0 0
2016–17 Manchester C 0 0
2017–18 Manchester C 0 0
2017–18 *NAC Breda* 31 10 **31 10**
2018–19 Manchester C 0 0
2018–19 *Lens* 32 4 **32 4**
2019–20 Manchester C 0 0
2019–20 *Metz* 18 0 **18 0**

ARZANI, Daniel (M) **23 2**
H: 5 7 W: 11 07 b.Khorramabad 4-1-99
Internationals: Australia U17, U20, U23, Full caps.
2016–17 Melbourne C 6 0
2017–18 Melbourne C 16 2 **22 2**
2018–19 Manchester C 0 0
2018–19 *Celtic* 1 0
2019–20 Manchester C 0 0
2019–20 *Celtic* 0 0 **1 0**

BERNABE, Adrian (M) **0 0**
b. 26-5-01
Internationals: Spain U17.
From Espanyol, Barcelona.
2018–19 Manchester C 0 0
2019–20 Manchester C 0 0

BERNARDO SILVA, Mota (M) **207 43**
H: 5 8 W: 9 11 b.Lisbon 10-8-94
Internationals: Portugal U19, U21, Full caps.
2013–14 Benfica 1 0 **1 0**
2014–15 Monaco 32 9
2015–16 Monaco 32 7
2016–17 Monaco 37 8 **101 24**
2017–18 Manchester C 35 6
2018–19 Manchester C 36 7
2019–20 Manchester C 34 6 **105 19**

BOLTON, Luke (F) **34 0**
b.Manchester 7-10-99
Internationals: England U20.
2018–19 Manchester C 0 0
2018–19 *Wycombe W* 10 0 **10 0**
2019–20 Manchester C 0 0
2019–20 *Luton T* 24 0 **24 0**

BRAVO, Claudio (G) **421 2**
H: 6 0 W: 11 00 b.Viluco 13-4-83
Internationals: Chile U23, Full caps.
2003 Colo Colo 25 1
2004 Colo Colo 18 0
2005 Colo Colo 36 0
2006 Colo Colo 14 0 **93 1**
2006–07 Real Sociedad 29 0
2007–08 Real Sociedad 0 0
2008–09 Real Sociedad 32 0
2009–10 Real Sociedad 25 1
2010–11 Real Sociedad 38 0
2011–12 Real Sociedad 37 0
2012–13 Real Sociedad 31 0
2013–14 Real Sociedad 37 0 **229 1**
2014–15 Barcelona 37 0
2015–16 Barcelona 32 0
2016–17 Barcelona 1 0 **70 0**
2016–17 Manchester C 22 0
2017–18 Manchester C 3 0
2018–19 Manchester C 0 0
2019–20 Manchester C 4 0 **29 0**

DE BRUYNE, Kevin (M) **303 70**
H: 5 11 W: 12 00 b.Ghent 28-6-91
Internationals: Belgium U18, U19, U21, Full caps.
2008–09 Genk 2 0
2009–10 Genk 30 3
2010–11 Genk 32 5
2011–12 Genk 15 6 **79 14**
2011–12 Chelsea 0 0
2012–13 Chelsea 0 0
2012–13 *Werder Bremen* 33 10 **33 10**
2013–14 Chelsea 3 0 **3 0**
2014–15 Wolfsburg 34 10
2015–16 Wolfsburg 2 0 **36 10**

2015–16	Manchester C	25	7		
2016–17	Manchester C	36	6		
2017–18	Manchester C	37	8		
2018–19	Manchester C	19	2		
2019–20	Manchester C	35	13	**152**	**36**

DIONKOU, Alpha (D) 0 0

b. 10-10-01
Internationals: Spain U17, U20.
From Real Mallorca.

2019–20	Manchester C	0	0		

DOYLE, Tommy (M) 1 0

b. 17-10-01
Internationals: England U16, U17, U18, U19.

2019–20	Manchester C	1	0	**1**	**0**

EDERSON, de Moraes (G) 212 0

H: 6 2 W: 13 08 b.Osasco 17-8-93
Internationals: Brazil U23, Full caps.

2011–12	Ribeirao	29	0	**29**	**0**
2012–13	Rio Ave	2	0		
2013–14	Rio Ave	18	0		
2014–15	Rio Ave	17	0	**37**	**0**
2015–16	Benfica	10	0		
2016–17	Benfica	27	0	**37**	**0**
2017–18	Manchester C	36	0		
2018–19	Manchester C	38	0		
2019–20	Manchester C	35	0	**109**	**0**

FERNANDINHO, Luis (M) 479 63

H: 5 10 W: 10 09 b.Londrina 4-5-85
Internationals: Brazil Full caps.

2003	Paranaense	29	5		
2004	Paranaense	41	9		
2005	Paranaense	2	0	**72**	**14**
2005–06	Shakhtar Donetsk	22	1		
2006–07	Shakhtar Donetsk	25	1		
2007–08	Shakhtar Donetsk	29	11		
2008–09	Shakhtar Donetsk	21	5		
2009–10	Shakhtar Donetsk	24	4		
2010–11	Shakhtar Donetsk	15	3		
2011–12	Shakhtar Donetsk	24	4		
2012–13	Shakhtar Donetsk	23	2	**183**	**20**
2013–14	Manchester C	33	5		
2014–15	Manchester C	33	3		
2015–16	Manchester C	33	2		
2016–17	Manchester C	32	2		
2017–18	Manchester C	34	5		
2018–19	Manchester C	29	1		
2019–20	Manchester C	30	0	**224**	**18**

FODEN, Phil (M) 41 6

H: 5 7 W: 11 00 b. 28-5-00
Internationals: England U16, U17, U18, U19, U21.

2016–17	Manchester C	0	0		
2017–18	Manchester C	5	0		
2018–19	Manchester C	13	1		
2019–20	Manchester C	23	5	**41**	**6**

GABRIEL JESUS, Fernando (F) 149 57

b. 3-4-97
Internationals: Brazil U20, U23, Full caps.

2015	Palmeiras	20	4		
2016	Palmeiras	27	12		
2016–17	Palmeiras	0	0	**47**	**16**
2016–17	Manchester C	10	7		
2017–18	Manchester C	29	13		
2018–19	Manchester C	29	7		
2019–20	Manchester C	34	14	**102**	**41**

GARCIA, Aleix (D) 79 8

H: 5 8 W: 9 08 b.Ulldecona 28-6-97
Internationals: Spain U16, U17, U18, U19, U21.

2014–15	Villareal	1	0	**1**	**0**
2015–16	Manchester C	0	0		
2016–17	Manchester C	4	0		
2017–18	Manchester C	0	0		
2017–18	*Girona*	20	1		
2018–19	Manchester C	0	0		
2018–19	*Girona*	31	2	**51**	**3**
2019–20	Manchester C	0	0	**4**	**0**
2019–20	*Excel Mouscron*	23	5	**23**	**5**

GARCIA, Eric (D) 13 0

H: 6 0 b.Barcelona 9-1-01
Internationals: Spain U17, U19, U21.
From Barcelona.

2018–19	Manchester C	0	0		
2019–20	Manchester C	13	0	**13**	**0**

GOMES, Claudio (M) 0 0

H: 5 11 W: 11 00 b.Argenteuil 23-7-00
Internationals: France U16, U17, U18, U19, U20.

2017–18	Paris Saint-Germain	0	0		
2018–19	Manchester C	0	0		
2019–20	Manchester C	0	0		
2019–20	*PSV Eindhoven*	0	0		

GRIMSHAW, Daniel (G) 0 0

H: 6 1 W: 12 02 b.Manchester 16-1-98

2018–19	Manchester C	0	0		
2019–20	Manchester C	0	0		

GUNDOGAN, Ilkay (M) 255 31

H: 5 11 W: 11 00 b.Gelsenkirchen 24-10-90
Internationals: Germany U18, U19, U20, U21, Full caps.

2008–09	Bochum	0	0		
2008–09	Nuremburg	1	0		
2009–10	Nuremburg	22	1		
2010–11	Nuremburg	25	5	**48**	**6**
2011–12	Borussia Dortmund	28	3		
2012–13	Borussia Dortmund	28	3		
2013–14	Borussia Dortmund	1	0		
2014–15	Borussia Dortmund	23	3		
2015–16	Borussia Dortmund	25	1	**105**	**10**
2016–17	Manchester C	10	3		
2017–18	Manchester C	30	4		
2018–19	Manchester C	31	6		
2019–20	Manchester C	31	2	**102**	**15**

HARRISON, Jack (M) 142 24

b.Stoke-on-Trent 20-11-96
Internationals: England U21.

2016	New York C	21	4		
2017	New York C	34	10	**55**	**14**
2017–18	Manchester C	0	0		
2017–18	*Middlesbrough*	4	0	**4**	**0**
2018–19	Manchester C	0	0		
2018–19	*Leeds U*	37	4		
2019–20	Manchester C	0	0		
2019–20	*Leeds U*	46	6	**83**	**10**

HARWOOD-BELLIS, Taylor (D) 0 0

b.Stockport 30-1-02
Internationals: England U16, U17, U19.

2019–20	Manchester C	0	0		

ILIC, Ivan (M) 38 6

b.Nis 17-3-01
Internationals: Serbia U16, U17, U19, U21.

2016–17	Red Star Belgrade	1	0	**1**	**0**
2017–18	Manchester C	0	0		
2018–19	Manchester C	0	0		
2018–19	*Zemun*	16	3	**16**	**3**
2019–20	Manchester C	0	0		
2019–20	*NAC Breda*	21	3	**21**	**3**

ILIC, Luka (M) 52 9

H: 6 0 b.Nis 2-7-99
Internationals: Serbia U17, U18, U21.

2016–17	Red Star Belgrade	0	0		
2017–18	Manchester C	0	0		
2017–18	*Red Star Belgrade*	14	2	**14**	**2**
2018–19	Manchester C	0	0		
2018–19	*NAC Breda*	16	2		
2019–20	Manchester C	0	0		
2019–20	*NAC Breda*	22	5	**38**	**7**

JOAO CANCELO, Cavaco (D) 143 4

b.Barreiro 27-5-94
Internationals: Portugal U16, U17, U18, U19, U20, U21, Full caps.

2012–13	Benfica	0	0		
2013–14	Benfica	1	0	**1**	**0**
2014–15	Valencia	10	0		
2015–16	Valencia	28	1		
2016–17	Valencia	35	1		
2017–18	Valencia	1	0	**74**	**2**
2017–18	*Inter Milan*	26	1	**26**	**1**
2018–19	Juventus	25	1		
2019–20	Juventus	0	0	**25**	**1**
2019–20	Manchester C	17	0	**17**	**0**

LAPORTE, Aymeric (D) 253 13

H: 6 2 W: 13 05 b.Agen 27-5-94
Internationals: France U17, U18, U19, U21.

2011–12	Basconia	33	2	**33**	**2**
2012–13	Athletic Bilbao	15	0		
2013–14	Athletic Bilbao	35	2		
2014–15	Athletic Bilbao	33	0		
2015–16	Athletic Bilbao	26	3		
2016–17	Athletic Bilbao	33	2		
2017–18	Athletic Bilbao	19	0	**161**	**7**
2017–18	Manchester C	9	0		
2018–19	Manchester C	35	3		
2019–20	Manchester C	15	1	**59**	**4**

MAHREZ, Riyad (M) 276 66

H: 5 10 W: 9 10 b.Sarcelles 21-2-91
Internationals: Algeria Full caps.

2011–12	Le Havre	9	0		
2012–13	Le Havre	32	4		
2013–14	Le Havre	17	2	**58**	**6**
2013–14	Leicester C	19	3		
2014–15	Leicester C	30	4		
2015–16	Leicester C	37	17		
2016–17	Leicester C	36	6		
2017–18	Leicester C	36	12	**158**	**42**
2018–19	Manchester C	27	7		
2019–20	Manchester C	33	11	**60**	**18**

MENDY, Benjamin (D) 199 2

H: 5 11 W: 11 05 b.Longjumeau 17-7-94
Internationals: France U16, U17, U18, U19, U21, Full caps.

2011–12	Le Havre	29	0		
2012–13	Le Havre	28	0	**57**	**0**
2013–14	Marseille	24	1		
2014–15	Marseille	33	0		
2015–16	Marseille	24	1	**81**	**2**
2016–17	Monaco	25	0	**25**	**0**
2017–18	Manchester C	7	0		
2018–19	Manchester C	10	0		
2019–20	Manchester C	19	0	**36**	**0**

MURIC, Arijanet (G) 5 0

H: 6 6 W: 12 11 b.Zurich 7-11-98
Internationals: Montenegro U21. Kosovo Full caps.

2017–18	Manchester C	0	0		
2018–19	Manchester C	0	0		
2018–19	*NAC Breda*	1	0	**1**	**0**
2019–20	Manchester C	0	0		
2019–20	*Nottingham F*	4	0	**4**	**0**

NMECHA, Felix (M) 0 0

b.Hamburg 10-10-00
Internationals: England U16, U18, U19. Germany U18

2018–19	Manchester C	0	0		
2019–20	Manchester C	0	0		

NMECHA, Lukas (F) 60 4

H: 6 0 W: 12 08 b.Hamburg 14-12-98
Internationals: England U16, U17, U18, U19, U21. Germany U21.

2017–18	Manchester C	2	0		
2018–19	Manchester C	0	0		
2018–19	*Preston NE*	41	4	**41**	**4**
2019–20	Manchester C	0	0	**2**	**0**
2019–20	*Wolfsburg*	6	0	**6**	**0**
2019–20	*Middlesbrough*	11	0	**11**	**0**

OTAMENDI, Nicolas (D) 293 22

H: 5 10 W: 11 09 b.Buenos Aires 12-2-88
Internationals: Argentina Full caps.

2007–08	Velez Sarsfield	1	0		
2008–09	Velez Sarsfield	18	0		
2009–10	Velez Sarsfield	19	1		
2010–11	Velez Sarsfield	2	0	**40**	**1**
2010–11	Porto	15	5		
2011–12	Porto	20	1		
2012–13	Porto	29	1		
2013–14	Porto	13	0	**77**	**7**
2013–14	*Atletico Mineiro*	5	0	**5**	**0**
2014–15	Valencia	35	6	**35**	**6**
2015–16	Manchester C	30	1		
2016–17	Manchester C	30	1		
2017–18	Manchester C	34	4		
2018–19	Manchester C	18	0		
2019–20	Manchester C	24	2	**136**	**8**

PALMER, Cole (M) 0 0

b. 6-5-02
Internationals: England U16, U17, U18.

2019–20	Manchester C	0	0		

ROBERTS, Patrick (M) 107 16

H: 5 6 W: 10 06 b.Kingston upon Thames 5-2-97
Internationals: England U16, U17, U18, U19, U20.

2013–14	Fulham	2	0		
2014–15	Fulham	17	0	**19**	**0**
2015–16	Manchester C	1	0		
2015–16	*Celtic*	11	6		
2016–17	Manchester C	0	0		
2016–17	*Celtic*	32	9		
2017–18	Manchester C	0	0		
2017–18	*Celtic*	12	0	**55**	**15**
2018–19	Manchester C	0	0		
2018–19	*Girona*	19	0	**19**	**0**
2019–20	Manchester C	0	0	**1**	**0**
2019–20	*Norwich C*	3	0	**3**	**0**
2019–20	*Middlesbrough*	10	1	**10**	**1**

RODRI, Rodrigo Hernandez (M) 132 7

b.Madrid 22-6-96
Internationals: Spain U16, U19, U21, Full caps.

2014–15	Villareal	0	0		
2015–16	Villareal	3	0		
2016–17	Villareal	23	0		
2017–18	Villareal	37	1	**63**	**1**
2018–19	Atletico Madrid	34	3	**34**	**3**
2019–20	Manchester C	35	3	**35**	**3**

ROGERS, Morgan (M) **0 0**
b.Halesowen 26-7-02
Internationals: England U16, U17, U18.

2018–19	WBA	0	0		
2019–20	Manchester C	0	0		

SANDLER, Philippe (D) **39 0**
H: 6 2 W: 11 11 b.Amersterdam 10-2-97
Internationals: Netherlands U20.

2016–17	PEC Zwolle	7	0		
2017–18	PEC Zwolle	23	0	**30**	**0**
2018–19	Manchester C	0	0		
2019–20	Manchester C	0	0		
2019–20	*Anderlecht*	9	0	**9**	**0**

SANE, Leroy (M) **137 36**
H: 5 8 W: 9 13 b.Essen 11-1-96
Internationals: Germany U19, U21, Full caps.

2013–14	Schalke 04	1	0		
2014–15	Schalke 04	13	3		
2015–16	Schalke 04	33	8	**47**	**11**
2016–17	Manchester C	26	5		
2017–18	Manchester C	32	10		
2018–19	Manchester C	31	10		
2019–20	Manchester C	1	0	**90**	**25**

SILVA, David (F) **511 90**
H: 5 7 W: 10 07 b.Arguineguin 8-1-86
Internationals: Spain U16, U17, U19, U20, U21, Full caps.

2003–04	Mestalla	14	1	**14**	**1**
2004–05	Eibar	35	5	**35**	**5**
2005–06	Celta Vigo	34	3	**34**	**3**
2006–07	Valencia	36	5		
2007–08	Valencia	34	4		
2008–09	Valencia	19	4		
2009–10	Valencia	30	8	**119**	**21**
2010–11	Manchester C	35	4		
2011–12	Manchester C	36	6		
2012–13	Manchester C	32	4		
2013–14	Manchester C	27	7		
2014–15	Manchester C	32	12		
2015–16	Manchester C	24	2		
2016–17	Manchester C	34	4		
2017–18	Manchester C	29	9		
2018–19	Manchester C	33	6		
2019–20	Manchester C	27	6	**309**	**60**

SMITH, Matthew (M) **44 2**
b.Redditch 22-11-99
Internationals: Wales U17, U19, U21, Full caps.

2018–19	Manchester C	0	0		
2018–19	*FC Twente*	34	2	**34**	**2**
2019–20	Manchester C	0	0		
2019–20	*QPR*	8	0	**8**	**0**
2019–20	*Charlton Ath*	2	0	**2**	**0**

STERLING, Raheem (F) **259 86**
H: 5 7 W: 10 00 b.Kingston 8-12-94
Internationals: England U16, U17, U19, U21, Full caps.

2011–12	Liverpool	3	0		
2012–13	Liverpool	24	2		
2013–14	Liverpool	33	9		
2014–15	Liverpool	35	7	**95**	**18**
2015–16	Manchester C	31	6		
2016–17	Manchester C	33	7		
2017–18	Manchester C	33	18		
2018–19	Manchester C	34	17		
2019–20	Manchester C	33	20	**164**	**68**

STONES, John (D) **186 1**
H: 6 2 W: 11 00 b.Barnsley 28-5-94
Internationals: England U19, U20, U21, Full caps.

2011–12	Barnsley	2	0		
2012–13	Barnsley	22	0	**24**	**0**
2012–13	Everton	0	0		
2013–14	Everton	21	0		
2014–15	Everton	23	1		
2015–16	Everton	33	0	**77**	**1**
2016–17	Manchester C	27	0		
2017–18	Manchester C	18	0		
2018–19	Manchester C	24	0		
2019–20	Manchester C	16	0	**85**	**0**

TASENDE, Jose (D) **118 5**
H: 5 7 W: 10 10 b.Coristanco 4-1-97
Internationals: Spain U17, U21.

2014–15	Manchester C	0	0		
2015	*New York C*	14	0	**14**	**0**
2015–16	Manchester C	0	0		
2016–17	Manchester C	0	0		
2016–17	*Girona*	0	0		
2016–17	*Mallorca*	17	0	**17**	**0**
2017–18	Manchester C	0	0		
2017–18	*NAC Breda*	34	3	**34**	**3**
2018–19	PSV Einhoven	34	1	**34**	**1**
2019–20	Manchester C	6	0	**6**	**0**
2019–20	*RB Leipzig*	13	1	**13**	**1**

WALKER, Kyle (D) **349 7**
H: 5 10 W: 11 07 b.Sheffield 28-5-90
Internationals: England U19, U21, Full caps.

2008–09	Sheffield U	2	0		
2008–09	*Northampton T*	9	0	**9**	**0**
2009–10	Tottenham H	2	0		
2009–10	*Sheffield U*	26	0	**28**	**0**
2010–11	Tottenham H	1	0		
2010–11	*QPR*	20	0	**20**	**0**
2010–11	*Aston Villa*	15	1	**15**	**1**
2011–12	Tottenham H	37	2		
2012–13	Tottenham H	36	0		
2013–14	Tottenham H	26	1		
2014–15	Tottenham H	15	0		
2015–16	Tottenham H	33	1		
2016–17	Tottenham H	33	0	**183**	**4**
2017–18	Manchester C	32	0		
2018–19	Manchester C	33	1		
2019–20	Manchester C	29	1	**94**	**2**

ZINCHENKO, Alexander (M) **84 2**
H: 5 9 W: 9 08 b.Radomyshi 15-12-96
Internationals: Ukraine U16, U17, U18, U19, U21, Full caps.

2014–15	Ufa	7	0		
2015–16	Ufa	24	2	**31**	**2**
2016–17	Manchester C	0	0		
2016–17	PSV	12	0		
2017–18	PSV	0	0	**12**	**0**
2017–18	Manchester C	8	0		
2018–19	Manchester C	14	0		
2019–20	Manchester C	19	0	**41**	**0**

Players retained or with offer of contract
Agyepong, Thomas; Amankwah, Yeboah; Aminu, Mohammed; Bazunu, Gavin Okeroghene; Braaf, Jayden Jezairo; Dele-Bashiru, Oluwafisayo Faruq; Diskerud, Mikkel Morgenstar Palssonn; Doyle, Thomas; Fernandes Cantin, Paolo; Fiorini, Lewis Paul; Herrera Ravelo, Yangel Clemente; Itakura, Kou; Knight, Benjamin Leo; Latibeaudiere, Joel Owen; McDonald, Rowan Alexander; Meshino, Ryotaro; Moreno Duran, Marlos; Moulden, Louie; Ogbeta, Nathanael; Palaversa, Ante; Robinson, Samson Alfie Philip; Ross Palmer Brown, Erik; Simmonds, Keyendrah Qwamalik Tegan; Sobowale, Oluwatimilehin; Steffen, Zackary Thomas; Tedic, Slobodan; Touaizi Zoubdi, Nabil; Wright-Phillips, D'Margio Cameron.

Scholars
Bobb, Oscar; Burns, Finley Jack; Delap, Liam Rory; Edozie, Samuel Ikechukwu; Egan-Riley, Conrad Jaden; Gbadebo, Camron Israel; Hodge, Joseph Shaun; McAtee, James John; Nuamah Oduroh, Kwaku; Robertson, Alexander Sean Pablo; Slicker, Cieran Peter; Tarensi Cordon, Oscar; Trafford, James Harrington; Wilson-Esbrand, Joshua Darius Kamani.

MANCHESTER U (49)

BAILLY, Eric (D) **94 1**
H: 6 2 W: 12 02 b.Bingerville 12-4-94
Internationals: Ivory Coast Full caps.

2014–15	Espanyol	5	0	**5**	**0**
2014–15	Villareal	10	0		
2015–16	Villareal	25	0	**35**	**0**
2016–17	Manchester U	25	0		
2017–18	Manchester U	13	1		
2018–19	Manchester U	12	0		
2019–20	Manchester U	4	0	**54**	**1**

BERNARD, Di'shon (D) **0 0**
b.London 14-10-00
From Chelsea.

2019–20	Manchester U	0	0		

BISHOP, Nathan (G) **31 0**
H: 6 1 W: 11 05 b. 15-10-99
Internationals: England U20.

2016–17	Southend U	0	0		
2017–18	Southend U	1	0		
2018–19	Southend U	18	0		
2019–20	Southend U	12	0	**31**	**0**
2019–20	Manchester U	0	0		

BORTHWICK-JACKSON, Cameron (D) **55 2**
H: 6 3 W: 13 10 b.Manchester 2-2-97
Internationals: England U16, U17, U19, U20.

2015–16	Manchester U	10	0		
2016–17	Manchester U	0	0		
2016–17	*Wolverhampton W*	6	0	**6**	**0**
2017–18	Manchester U	0	0		
2017–18	*Leeds U*	1	0	**1**	**0**
2018–19	Manchester U	0	0		
2018–19	*Scunthorpe U*	29	2	**29**	**2**
2019–20	Manchester U	0	0	**10**	**0**
2019–20	*Tranmere R*	3	0	**3**	**0**
2019–20	*Oldham Ath*	6	0	**6**	**0**

BRUNO FERNANDES, Miguel (M) **239 66**
b.Maia 8-9-94
Internationals: Portugal U19, U20, U21, U23, Full caps.

2012–13	Novara	23	4	**23**	**4**
2013–14	Udinese	24	4		
2014–15	Udinese	31	3		
2015–16	Udinese	31	3	**86**	**10**
2016–17	Sampdoria	33	5	**33**	**5**
2017–18	Sporting Lisbon	33	11		
2018–19	Sporting Lisbon	33	20		
2019–20	Sporting Lisbon	17	8	**83**	**39**
2019–20	Manchester U	14	8	**14**	**8**

BUGHAIL-MELLOR, D'Mani (F) **0 0**

2019–20	Manchester U	0	0		

CASTRO, Joel (G) **44 0**
H: 6 2 W: 12 13 b. 28-6-96
Internationals: Switzerland U16, U17. Portugal U17, U18, U19, U20, U21.

2015–16	Manchester U	0	0		
2015–16	*Rochdale*	6	0	**6**	**0**
2016–17	Manchester U	1	0		
2016–17	*Belenenses*	8	0	**8**	**0**
2017–18	Manchester U	0	0		
2018–19	Manchester U	0	0		
2018–19	*Vitoria Setubal*	9	0	**9**	**0**
2018–19	*Kortrijk*	0	0		
2019–20	Manchester U	0	0	**1**	**0**
2019–20	*Hearts*	20	0	**20**	**0**

CHONG, Tahith (F) **5 0**
H: 6 1 W: 11 00 b.Willwmstad 1-12-91
Internationals: Netherlands U16, U17, U19, U20, U21.
From Feyenoord.

2018–19	Manchester U	2	0		
2019–20	Manchester U	3	0	**5**	**0**

DALOT, Diogo (D) **26 0**
H: 6 0 W: 11 11 b.Braga 18-3-99
Internationals: Portugal U16, U17, U19, U20, U21.

2016–17	Porto	0	0		
2017–18	Porto	6	0	**6**	**0**
2018–19	Manchester U	16	0		
2019–20	Manchester U	4	0	**20**	**0**

DE GEA, David (G) **370 0**
H: 6 3 W: 12 13 b.Madrid 7-11-90
Internationals: Spain U15, U17, U19, U20, U21, U23, Full caps.

2009–10	Atletico Madrid	19	0		
2010–11	Atletico Madrid	38	0	**57**	**0**
2011–12	Manchester U	29	0		
2012–13	Manchester U	28	0		
2013–14	Manchester U	37	0		
2014–15	Manchester U	37	0		
2015–16	Manchester U	34	0		
2016–17	Manchester U	35	0		
2017–18	Manchester U	37	0		
2018–19	Manchester U	38	0		
2019–20	Manchester U	38	0	**313**	**0**

FOSU-MENSAH, Timothy (D) **48 0**
H: 5 10 W: 10 10 b.Amsterdam 3-1-98
Internationals: Netherlands U16, U17, U19, U21, Full caps.

2015–16	Manchester U	8	0		
2016–17	Manchester U	4	0		
2017–18	Manchester U	0	0		
2017–18	*Crystal Palace*	21	0	**21**	**0**
2018–19	Manchester U	0	0		
2018–19	*Fulham*	12	0	**12**	**0**
2019–20	Manchester U	3	0	**15**	**0**

FRED, Frederico (M) **180 18**
H: 5 7 W: 10 10 b.Belo Horizonte 5-3-93
Internationals: Brazil U20, Full caps.

2012	Internacional	28	6		
2013	Internacional	5	1	**33**	**7**
2013–14	Shakhtar Donetsk	23	2		
2014–15	Shakhtar Donetsk	22	1		
2015–16	Shakhtar Donetsk	12	2		
2016–17	Shakhtar Donetsk	18	2		
2017–18	Shakhtar Donetsk	26	3	**101**	**10**
2018–19	Manchester U	17	1		
2019–20	Manchester U	29	0	**46**	**1**

GALBRAITH, Ethan (M) **0** **0**
Internationals: Northern Ireland U17, U19, U21, Full caps.
From Linfield.

2019–20	Manchester U	0	0		

GARNER, James (M) **2** **0**
b.Birkenhead 13-3-01
Internationals: England U17, U18, U19.

2018–19	Manchester U	1	0		
2019–20	Manchester U	1	0	**2**	**0**

GOMES, Angel (M) **5** **0**
b.Enfield 31-8-00
Internationals: England U16, U17, U18, U19, U20.

2016–17	Manchester U	1	0		
2017–18	Manchester U	0	0		
2018–19	Manchester U	2	0		
2019–20	Manchester U	2	0	**5**	**0**

GRANT, Lee (G) **468** **0**
H: 6 3 W: 13 01 b.Hemel Hempstead 27-1-83
Internationals: England U16, U17, U18, U19, U21.

2000–01	Derby Co	0	0		
2001–02	Derby Co	0	0		
2002–03	Derby Co	29	0		
2003–04	Derby Co	36	0		
2004–05	Derby Co	2	0		
2005–06	Derby Co	0	0		
2005–06	*Burnley*	1	0		
2005–06	*Oldham Ath*	16	0	**16**	**0**
2006–07	Derby Co	7	0		
2007–08	Sheffield W	44	0		
2008–09	Sheffield W	46	0		
2009–10	Sheffield W	46	0	**136**	**0**
2010–11	Burnley	25	0		
2011–12	Burnley	43	0		
2012–13	Burnley	46	0	**115**	**0**
2013–14	Derby Co	46	0		
2014–15	Derby Co	40	0		
2015–16	Derby Co	10	0		
2016–17	Derby Co	0	0	**170**	**0**
2016–17	*Stoke C*	28	0		
2017–18	Stoke C	3	0	**31**	**0**
2018–19	Manchester U	0	0		
2019–20	Manchester U	0	0		

GREENWOOD, Mason (F) **34** **10**
b. 1-10-01
Internationals: England U17, U18, U21.

2018–19	Manchester U	3	0		
2019–20	Manchester U	31	10	**34**	**10**

HAMILTON, Ethan (M) **40** **5**
b.Edinburgh 18-10-98
Internationals: Scotland U16, U19.

2017–18	Manchester U	0	0		
2018–19	Manchester U	0	0		
2018–19	*Rochdale*	14	4		
2019–20	*Rochdale*	0	0	**14**	**4**
2019–20	Manchester U	0	0		
2019–20	*Southend U*	14	0	**14**	**0**
2019–20	*Bolton W*	12	1	**12**	**1**

HENDERSON, Dean (G) **127** **0**
H: 6 3 W: 12 13 b.Whitehaven 12-3-97
Internationals: England U16, U17, U20, U21.

2015–16	Manchester U	0	0		
2016–17	Manchester U	0	0		
2016–17	*Grimsby T*	7	0	**7**	**0**
2017–18	Manchester U	0	0		
2017–18	*Shrewsbury T*	38	0	**38**	**0**
2018–19	Manchester U	0	0		
2018–19	*Sheffield U*	46	0		
2019–20	Manchester U	0	0		
2019–20	*Sheffield U*	36	0	**82**	**0**

IGHALO, Odion Jude (F) **297** **109**
H: 6 2 W: 11 00 b.Lagos 16-6-89
Internationals: Nigeria U20, Full caps.

2007	Lyn	7	3		
2008	Lyn	13	6	**20**	**9**
2008–09	Udinese	6	1		
2009–10	Udinese	0	0		
2010–11	Udinese	0	0		
2010–11	*Cesena*	3	0	**3**	**0**
2010–11	*Granada*	21	4		
2011–12	Udinese	0	0		
2011–12	*Granada*	30	6		
2012–13	Udinese	0	0		
2012–13	*Granada*	28	5		
2013–14	Udinese	0	0		
2013–14	*Granada*	16	2	**95**	**17**
2014–15	Udinese	0	0	**6**	**1**
2014–15	*Watford*	35	20		
2015–16	Watford	37	15		
2016–17	Watford	18	1	**90**	**36**
2017	Changchun Yatai	27	15		
2018	Changchun Yatai	28	21	**55**	**36**
2019	Shanghai Shenhua	17	10	**17**	**10**

On loan from Shanghai Shenhua.

2019–20	Manchester U	11	0	**11**	**0**

JAMES, Daniel (M) **66** **7**
b. 10-11-97
Internationals: Wales U17, U19, U20, U21, Full caps.

2015–16	Swansea C	0	0		
2016–17	Swansea C	0	0		
2017–18	Swansea C	0	0		
2017–18	*Shrewsbury T*	0	0		
2018–19	Swansea C	33	4	**33**	**4**
2019–20	Manchester U	33	3	**33**	**3**

JONES, Phil (D) **200** **2**
H: 5 11 W: 11 02 b.Preston 21-2-92
Internationals: England U19, U21, Full caps.

2009–10	Blackburn R	9	0		
2010–11	Blackburn R	26	0	**35**	**0**
2011–12	Manchester U	29	1		
2012–13	Manchester U	17	0		
2013–14	Manchester U	26	1		
2014–15	Manchester U	22	0		
2015–16	Manchester U	10	0		
2016–17	Manchester U	18	0		
2017–18	Manchester U	23	0		
2018–19	Manchester U	18	0		
2019–20	Manchester U	2	0	**165**	**2**

KOVAR, Matej (G) **0** **0**
b. 17-5-00
Internationals: Czech Republic U18, U19, U20.
From Slovacko.

2019–20	Manchester U	0	0		

LAIRD, Ethan (D) **0** **0**
b.Basingstoke 5-8-01
Internationals: England U17, U18, U19.

2019–20	Manchester U	0	0		

LEVITT, Dylan (M) **0** **0**
b. 17-11-00
Internationals: Wales U17, U19, U21.

2019–20	Manchester U	0	0		

LINDELOF, Victor (D) **180** **4**
H: 6 2 W: 12 11 b.Vasteras 17-7-94
Internationals: Sweden U17, U19, U21, Full caps.

2009	Vasteras	1	0		
2010	Vasteras	9	0		
2011	Vasteras	27	0		
2012	Vasteras	13	0	**50**	**0**
2012–13	Benfica	0	0		
2013–14	Benfica	1	0		
2014–15	Benfica	0	0		
2015–16	Benfica	15	1		
2016–17	Benfica	32	1	**48**	**2**
2017–18	Manchester U	17	0		
2018–19	Manchester U	30	1		
2019–20	Manchester U	35	1	**82**	**2**

LINGARD, Jesse (M) **180** **29**
H: 5 3 W: 11 11 b.Warrington 15-12-92
Internationals: England U17, U21, Full caps.

2011–12	Manchester U	0	0		
2012–13	Manchester U	0	0		
2012–13	*Leicester C*	5	0	**5**	**0**
2013–14	Manchester U	0	0		
2013–14	*Birmingham C*	13	6	**13**	**6**
2013–14	*Brighton & HA*	15	3	**15**	**3**
2014–15	Manchester U	1	0		
2014–15	*Derby Co*	14	2	**14**	**2**
2015–16	Manchester U	25	4		
2016–17	Manchester U	25	1		
2017–18	Manchester U	33	8		
2018–19	Manchester U	27	4		
2019–20	Manchester U	22	1	**133**	**18**

MAGUIRE, Harry (D) **311** **18**
H: 6 2 W: 12 06 b.Mosborough 5-3-93
Internationals: England U21, Full caps.

2010–11	Sheffield U	5	0		
2011–12	Sheffield U	44	1		
2012–13	Sheffield U	44	3		
2013–14	Sheffield U	41	5	**134**	**9**
2014–15	Hull C	3	0		
2014–15	*Wigan Ath*	16	1	**16**	**1**
2015–16	Hull C	22	0		
2016–17	Hull C	29	2	**54**	**2**
2017–18	Leicester C	38	2		
2018–19	Leicester C	31	3		
2019–20	Leicester C	0	0	**69**	**5**
2019–20	Manchester U	38	1	**38**	**1**

MARTIAL, Anthony (F) **197** **62**
H: 5 11 W: 12 08 b.Massy 5-12-95
Internationals: France U16, U17, U18, U19, U21, Full caps.

2012–13	Lyon	3	0	**3**	**0**
2013–14	Monaco	11	2		
2014–15	Monaco	35	9		
2015–16	Monaco	3	0	**49**	**11**
2015–16	Manchester U	31	11		
2016–17	Manchester U	25	4		
2017–18	Manchester U	30	9		
2018–19	Manchester U	27	10		
2019–20	Manchester U	32	17	**145**	**51**

MATA, Juan (M) **430** **94**
H: 5 7 W: 11 00 b.Ocon de Villafranca 28-4-88
Internationals: Spain U16, U17, U19, U20, U21, U23, Full caps.

2006–07	Real Madrid B	39	10	**39**	**10**
2007–08	Valencia	24	5		
2008–09	Valencia	37	11		
2009–10	Valencia	35	9		
2010–11	Valencia	33	8	**129**	**33**
2011–12	Chelsea	34	6		
2012–13	Chelsea	35	12		
2013–14	Chelsea	13	0	**82**	**18**
2013–14	Manchester U	15	6		
2014–15	Manchester U	33	9		
2015–16	Manchester U	38	6		
2016–17	Manchester U	25	6		
2017–18	Manchester U	28	3		
2018–19	Manchester U	22	3		
2019–20	Manchester U	19	0	**180**	**33**

MATIC, Nemanja (M) **374** **18**
H: 6 4 W: 13 02 b.Sabac 1-8-88
Internationals: Serbia U21, Full caps.

2005–06	Jedinstvo	7	0		
2006–07	Jedinstvo	9	0	**16**	**0**
2006–07	Kosice	13	1		
2007–08	Kosice	25	1		
2008–09	Kosice	29	2	**67**	**4**
2009–10	Chelsea	2	0		
2010–11	Chelsea	0	0		
2010–11	*Vitesse*	27	2	**27**	**2**
2011–12	Benfica	16	1		
2012–13	Benfica	26	3		
2013–14	Benfica	14	2	**56**	**6**
2013–14	Chelsea	17	0		
2014–15	Chelsea	36	1		
2015–16	Chelsea	33	2		
2016–17	Chelsea	35	1	**123**	**4**
2017–18	Manchester U	36	1		
2018–19	Manchester U	28	1		
2019–20	Manchester U	21	0	**85**	**2**

McTOMINAY, Scott (M) **58** **6**
H: 5 10 W: 10 03 b.Lancaster 8-12-96
Internationals: Scotland Full caps.

2016–17	Manchester U	2	0		
2017–18	Manchester U	13	0		
2018–19	Manchester U	16	2		
2019–20	Manchester U	27	4	**58**	**6**

MENGI, Teden (D) **0** **0**
Internationals: England U16, U17, U18.

2019–20	Manchester U	0	0		

MITCHELL, Demetri (D) **30** **0**
H: 5 9 W: 11 11 b.Manchester 11-1-97
Internationals: England U16, U17, U18, U20.

2016–17	Manchester U	1	0		
2017–18	Manchester U	0	0		
2017–18	*Hearts*	9	0		
2018–19	Manchester U	0	0		
2018–19	*Hearts*	20	0	**29**	**0**
2019–20	Manchester U	0	0	**1**	**0**

O'HARA, Kieran (G) **75** **0**
b. 22-4-96
Internationals: Republic of Ireland U21, Full caps.

2015–16	Manchester U	0	0		
2015–16	*Morecambe*	5	0		
2016–17	Morecambe	0	0	**5**	**0**
2016–17	Manchester U	0	0		
2017–18	Manchester U	0	0		
2018–19	Manchester U	0	0		
2018–19	*Macclesfield T*	37	0	**37**	**0**
2019–20	Manchester U	0	0		
2019–20	*Burton Alb*	33	0	**33**	**0**

PEREIRA, Andreas (M) **103** **8**
H: 5 10 W: 10 06 b.Duffel 1-1-96
Internationals: Belgium U16, U17. Brazil U20, U23, Full caps.

2014–15	Manchester U	1	0		
2015–16	Manchester U	4	0		

2016–17 Manchester U 0 0
2016–17 *Granada* 35 5 35 5
2017–18 Manchester U 0 0
2017–18 *Valencia* 23 1 23 1
2018–19 Manchester U 15 1
2019–20 Manchester U 25 1 45 2

POGBA, Paul (M) 235 53
H: 6 1 W: 12 08 b.Lagny-sur-Marne 15-3-93
Internationals: France U16, U17, U18, U19, U20, Full caps.
2009–10 Manchester U 0 0
2010–11 Manchester U 0 0
2011–12 Manchester U 3 0
2012–13 Juventus 27 5
2013–14 Juventus 36 7
2014–15 Juventus 26 8
2015–16 Juventus 35 8 124 28
2016–17 Manchester U 30 5
2017–18 Manchester U 27 6
2018–19 Manchester U 35 13
2019–20 Manchester U 16 1 111 25

PUIGMAL, Arnau (M) 0 0
Internationals: Spain U17, U18, U19.
From Espanyol.
2019–20 Manchester U 0 0

RAMAZANI, Largie (F) 0 0
Internationals: Belgium U17, U18, U19.
From Charlton Ath.
2019–20 Manchester U 0 0

RASHFORD, Marcus (F) 142 44
H: 5 11 W: 11 00 b.Manchester 31-10-97
Internationals: England U16, U18, U20, U21, Full caps.
2015–16 Manchester U 11 5
2016–17 Manchester U 32 5
2017–18 Manchester U 35 7
2018–19 Manchester U 33 10
2019–20 Manchester U 31 17 142 44

ROJO, Marcos (D) 177 9
H: 6 2 W: 12 06 b.La Plata 20-3-90
Internationals: Argentina Full caps.
2008–09 Estudiantes 6 1
2009–10 Estudiantes 18 0
2010–11 Estudiantes 19 2
2011–12 Spartak Moscow 8 0 8 0
2012–13 Sporting Lisbon 24 1
2013–14 Sporting Lisbon 25 4 49 5
2014–15 Manchester U 22 0
2015–16 Manchester U 16 0
2016–17 Manchester U 21 1
2017–18 Manchester U 9 0
2018–19 Manchester U 5 0
2019–20 Manchester U 3 0 76 1
2019–20 *Estudiantes* 1 0 44 3

ROMERO, Sergio (G) 176 0
H: 6 4 W: 13 01 b.Yrigoyen 22-2-87
Internationals: Argentina U20, Full caps.
2006–07 Racing Club 5 0 5 0
2007–08 AZ Alkmaar 12 0
2008–09 AZ Alkmaar 28 0
2009–10 AZ Alkmaar 27 0
2010–11 AZ Alkmaar 23 0
2011–12 AZ Alkmaar 0 0 90 0
2011–12 Sampdoria 29 0
2012–13 Sampdoria 32 0
2013–14 Sampdoria 0 0
2013–14 *Monaco* 3 0 3 0
2014–15 Sampdoria 10 0 71 0
2015–16 Manchester U 4 0
2016–17 Manchester U 2 0
2017–18 Manchester U 1 0
2018–19 Manchester U 0 0
2019–20 Manchester U 0 0 7 0

SANCHEZ, Alexis (F) 461 143
H: 5 6 W: 11 09 b.Tocopilla 19-12-88
Internationals: Chile U20, Full caps.
2005 Cobreloa 35 3
2006 Cobreloa 12 6 47 9
2006–07 Udinese 0 0
2006–07 *Colo Colo* 32 5 32 5
2007–08 *River Plate* 23 4 23 4
2008–09 Udinese 32 3
2009–10 Udinese 32 5
2010–11 Udinese 31 12 95 20
2011–12 Barcelona 25 11
2012–13 Barcelona 29 8
2013–14 Barcelona 34 19 88 38
2014–15 Arsenal 35 16
2015–16 Arsenal 30 13
2016–17 Arsenal 38 24
2017–18 Arsenal 19 7 122 60
2017–18 Manchester U 12 2
2018–19 Manchester U 20 1
2019–20 Manchester U 0 0 32 3
2019–20 *Inter Milan* 22 4 22 4

SHAW, Luke (D) 156 1
H: 6 1 W: 11 11 b.Kingston 12-7-95
Internationals: England U16, U17, U21, Full caps.
2011–12 Southampton 0 0
2012–13 Southampton 25 0
2013–14 Southampton 35 0 60 0
2014–15 Manchester U 16 0
2015–16 Manchester U 5 0
2016–17 Manchester U 11 0
2017–18 Manchester U 11 0
2018–19 Manchester U 29 1
2019–20 Manchester U 24 0 96 1

SMALLING, Chris (D) 249 15
H: 6 4 W: 14 02 b.Greenwich 22-11-89
Internationals: England U18, U20, U21, Full caps.
2008–09 Fulham 1 0
2009–10 Fulham 12 0 13 0
2010–11 Manchester U 16 0
2011–12 Manchester U 19 1
2012–13 Manchester U 15 0
2013–14 Manchester U 25 1
2014–15 Manchester U 25 4
2015–16 Manchester U 35 0
2016–17 Manchester U 18 1
2017–18 Manchester U 29 4
2018–19 Manchester U 24 1
2019–20 Manchester U 0 0 206 12
2019–20 *Roma* 30 3 30 3

TANNER, George (D) 23 0
2019–20 Manchester U 0 0
2019–20 *Morecambe* 23 0 23 0
2019–20 *Salford C* 0 0

TAYLOR, Max (D) 0 0
2019–20 Manchester U 0 0

TUANZEBE, Axel (D) 40 0
H: 6 0 W: 11 11 b.Bunia 14-11-97
Internationals: England U19, U20, U21.
2015–16 Manchester U 0 0
2016–17 Manchester U 4 0
2017–18 Manchester U 1 0
2017–18 *Aston Villa* 5 0
2018–19 Manchester U 0 0
2018–19 *Aston Villa* 25 0 30 0
2019–20 Manchester U 5 0 10 0

WAN BISSAKA, Aaron (M) 77 0
b. 26-11-97
Internationals: DR Congo U20. England U20, U21.
2016–17 Crystal Palace 0 0
2017–18 Crystal Palace 7 0
2018–19 Crystal Palace 35 0 42 0
2019–20 Manchester U 35 0 35 0

WILLIAMS, Brandon (D) 17 1
b.Manchester 3-9-00
Internationals: England U20.
2018–19 Manchester U 0 0
2019–20 Manchester U 17 1 17 1

YOUNG, Ashley (M) 447 64
H: 5 10 W: 10 03 b.Stevenage 9-7-85
Internationals: England U21, Full caps.
2002–03 Watford 0 0
2003–04 Watford 5 3
2004–05 Watford 34 0
2005–06 Watford 39 13
2006–07 Watford 20 3 98 19
2006–07 Aston Villa 13 2
2007–08 Aston Villa 37 9
2008–09 Aston Villa 36 7
2009–10 Aston Villa 37 5
2010–11 Aston Villa 34 7 157 30
2011–12 Manchester U 25 6
2012–13 Manchester U 19 0
2013–14 Manchester U 20 2
2014–15 Manchester U 26 2
2015–16 Manchester U 18 1
2016–17 Manchester U 12 0
2017–18 Manchester U 30 2
2018–19 Manchester U 30 2
2019–20 Manchester U 12 0 192 15
Transferred to Inter Milan, January 2020.

Players retained or with offer of contract
Bejger, Lukasz; Carney, Jacob Andrew; Devine, Reece; Elanga, Anthony David Junior; Emeran, Noam Fritz; Ercolani, Luca; Fish, William Thomas; Guadagno, Johan Elia; Hardley, Bjorn Bryan; Helm, Mark; Hoelgebaum Pereira, Andreas Hugo; Hoogewerf, Dillon Ifunanya Chukwu; Mastny, Ondrej; McCann, Charlie Liam; Mejbri, Hannibal; Mejia Piedrahita, Jose Mateo; Stanley, Connor Scott; Traore, Aliou Badara; Wellens, Charlie Gerard Richard; Woolston, Paul Hudson.

Scholars
Denham, Oliver James; Dodgson, Owen Joel; Gallagher-Allison, Calen; Haygarth, Maxwell James; Hockenhull, Ben; Hughes, Iestyn Tomos; Iqbal, Zidane Aamar; Mee, Dermot William; Neville, Harvey James; Savage, Charlie William Henry; Sotona, Ayodeji Oluwatunmise.

MANSFIELD T (50)

BENNING, Malvind (D) 237 11
H: 5 10 W: 12 00 b.Sandwell 2-11-93
2012–13 Walsall 10 0
2013–14 Walsall 16 2
2014–15 Walsall 20 0 46 2
2014–15 *York C* 9 0 9 0
2015–16 Mansfield T 31 4
2016–17 Mansfield T 45 1
2017–18 Mansfield T 28 1
2018–19 Mansfield T 45 3
2019–20 Mansfield T 33 0 182 9

BISHOP, Neil (M) 512 29
H: 6 1 W: 12 10 b.Stockton 7-8-81
Internationals: England C.
2007–08 Barnet 39 2
2008–09 Barnet 44 1 83 3
2009–10 Notts Co 43 1
2010–11 Notts Co 43 1
2011–12 Notts Co 41 2
2012–13 Notts Co 41 7 168 11
2013–14 Blackpool 35 1 35 1
2014–15 Scunthorpe U 35 4
2015–16 Scunthorpe U 42 1
2016–17 Scunthorpe U 42 5
2017–18 Scunthorpe U 35 1 154 11
2018–19 Mansfield T 44 3
2019–20 Mansfield T 28 0 72 3

CAMPBELL, Maison (G) 0 0
2019–20 Mansfield T 0 0

CHARSLEY, Harry (M) 10 0
H: 5 10 W: 10 01 b.Wirral 1-11-96
Internationals: Republic of Ireland U17, U19, U21.
2017–18 Everton 0 0
2017–18 *Bolton W* 1 0 1 0
2018–19 Everton 0 0
2019–20 Mansfield T 9 0 9 0

CHISHOLM, Jamie (D) 0 0
2019–20 Mansfield T 0 0

CLARKE, James (D) 12 0
b. 2-4-00
Internationals: Republic of Ireland U18.
2018–19 Burnley 0 0
2019–20 Mansfield T 12 0 12 0

CLARKE, Ollie (M) 268 16
H: 5 11 W: 11 11 b.Bristol 29-6-92
2009–10 Bristol R 0 0
2010–11 Bristol R 1 0
2011–12 Bristol R 0 0
2012–13 Bristol R 5 0
2013–14 Bristol R 32 2
2015–16 Bristol R 33 2
2016–17 Bristol R 30 4
2017–18 Bristol R 40 1
2018–19 Bristol R 40 6
2019–20 Bristol R 27 1 208 16
2019–20 Mansfield T 0 0

COOK, Andy (F) 71 20
H: 6 0 W: 11 03 b.Bishop Auckland 18-10-90
Internationals: England C.
2018–19 Walsall 43 13 43 13
2019–20 Mansfield T 23 7 23 7
2019–20 *Tranmere R* 5 0 5 0

DAVIES, Craig (F) 460 104
H: 6 2 W: 13 05 b.Burton-on-Trent 9-1-86
Internationals: Wales U17, U19, U21, Full caps.
2004–05 Oxford U 28 6
2005–06 Oxford U 20 2 48 8
2005–06 Verona 0 0

2006–07 Wolverhampton W 23 0 **23 0**
2007–08 Oldham Ath 32 10
2008–09 Oldham Ath 12 0
2008–09 *Stockport Co* 9 5 **9 5**
2008–09 Brighton & HA 16 1
2009–10 Brighton & HA 5 0 **21 1**
2009–10 *Yeovil T* 4 0 **4 0**
2009–10 *Port Vale* 24 7 **24 7**
2010–11 Chesterfield 41 23 **41 23**
2011–12 Barnsley 40 11
2012–13 Barnsley 20 8 **60 19**
2012–13 Bolton W 18 4
2013–14 Bolton W 8 0
2013–14 *Preston NE* 15 5 **15 5**
2014–15 Bolton W 27 6 **53 10**
2015–16 Wigan Ath 26 2
2016–17 Wigan Ath 14 1 **40 3**
2016–17 Scunthorpe U 19 0 **19 0**
2017–18 Oldham Ath 40 11 **84 21**
2018–19 Mansfield T 14 2
2019–20 Mansfield T 5 0 **19 2**

FIELDING, Tom (F) 0 0
From Leicester C.
2018–19 Mansfield T 0 0
2019–20 Mansfield T 0 0

GIBBENS, Lewis (D) 1 0
b. 10-11-99
2018–19 Mansfield T 1 0
2019–20 Mansfield T 0 0 **1 0**

GORDON, Kellan (M) 50 6
b.Burton 25-12-97
2017–18 Derby Co 0 0
2017–18 *Swindon T* 26 3 **26 3**
2018–19 Derby Co 0 0
2018–19 *Lincoln C* 6 2
2019–20 *Lincoln C* 0 0 **6 2**
2019–20 Mansfield T 18 1 **18 1**

GRAHAM, Jordan (F) 8 0
b.Peterborough 30-12-97
2017–18 Mansfield T 0 0
2018–19 Mansfield T 8 0
2019–20 Mansfield T 0 0 **8 0**

KHAN, Otis (M) 120 15
H: 5 9 W: 11 03 b.Ashton-under-Lyme 5-9-95
2013–14 Sheffield U 2 0
2014–15 Sheffield U 0 0
2015–16 Sheffield U 0 0 **2 0**
2015–16 Barnsley 3 0 **3 0**
2016–17 Yeovil T 29 6
2017–18 Yeovil T 38 6 **67 12**
2018–19 Mansfield T 22 2
2019–20 Mansfield T 21 1 **43 3**
2019–20 *Newport Co* 5 0 **5 0**

KNOWLES, Jimmy (F) 5 1
2018–19 Mansfield T 0 0
2019–20 Mansfield T 5 1 **5 1**

LAW, Jason (F) 0 0
2015–16 Mansfield T 0 0
2016–17 Mansfield T 0 0
2017–18 Mansfield T 0 0
2018–19 Mansfield T 0 0
2019–20 Mansfield T 0 0

LOGAN, Conrad (G) 268 0
H: 6 2 W: 14 00 b.Letterkenny 18-4-86
2003–04 Leicester C 0 0
2004–05 Leicester C 0 0
2005–06 Leicester C 0 0
2005–06 *Boston U* 13 0 **13 0**
2006–07 Leicester C 18 0
2007–08 Leicester C 0 0
2007–08 *Stockport Co* 34 0
2008–09 Leicester C 0 0
2008–09 *Luton T* 22 0 **22 0**
2008–09 *Stockport Co* 7 0 **41 0**
2009–10 Leicester C 2 0
2010–11 Leicester C 3 0
2010–11 *Bristol R* 16 0 **16 0**
2011–12 Leicester C 0 0
2011–12 *Rotherham U* 19 0 **19 0**
2012–13 Leicester C 0 0
2013–14 Leicester C 0 0
2014–15 Leicester C 0 0 **23 0**
2014–15 *Rochdale* 19 0
2015–16 Hibernian 2 0 **2 0**
2016–17 Rochdale 24 0 **43 0**
2016–17 Mansfield T 0 0
2017–18 Mansfield T 45 0
2018–19 Mansfield T 17 0
2019–20 Mansfield T 22 0 **84 0**
2019–20 *Forest Green R* 5 0 **5 0**

MACDONALD, Alex (F) 323 29
H: 5 7 W: 11 04 b.Warrington 14-4-90
Internationals: Scotland U19, U21.
2007–08 Burnley 2 0
2008–09 Burnley 3 0
2009–10 Burnley 0 0
2009–10 *Falkirk* 11 1 **11 1**
2010–11 Burnley 0 0
2010–11 *Inverness CT* 10 1 **10 1**
2011–12 Burnley 5 0
2011–12 *Plymouth Arg* 18 4
2012–13 Burnley 1 0 **11 0**
2012–13 *Plymouth Arg* 16 1 **34 5**
2012–13 *Burton Alb* 15 1
2013–14 Burton Alb 35 0
2014–15 Burton Alb 21 6 **71 7**
2014–15 Oxford U 15 3
2015–16 Oxford U 40 5
2016–17 Oxford U 22 1 **77 9**
2016–17 Mansfield T 18 1
2017–18 Mansfield T 41 3
2018–19 Mansfield T 21 1
2019–20 Mansfield T 29 1 **109 6**

MAYNARD, Nicky (F) 390 128
H: 5 11 W: 11 00 b.Winsford 11-12-86
2005–06 Crewe Alex 1 1
2006–07 Crewe Alex 31 16
2007–08 Crewe Alex 27 14 **59 31**
2008–09 Bristol C 43 11
2009–10 Bristol C 42 20
2010–11 Bristol C 13 6
2011–12 Bristol C 27 8 **125 45**
2011–12 West Ham U 14 2
2012–13 West Ham U 0 0 **14 2**
2012–13 Cardiff C 4 1
2013–14 Cardiff C 8 0
2013–14 *Wigan Ath* 16 4 **16 4**
2014–15 Cardiff C 10 1 **22 2**
2015–16 Milton Keynes D 35 7
2016–17 Milton Keynes D 31 2 **66 9**
2017–18 Aberdeen 18 0 **18 0**
2018–19 Bury 37 21 **37 21**
2019–20 Mansfield T 33 14 **33 14**

OLEJNIK, Robert (G) 357 0
H: 6 0 W: 15 06 b.Vienna 26-11-86
Internationals: Austria U21.
2004–05 Aston Villa 0 0
2005–06 Aston Villa 0 0
2006–07 Aston Villa 0 0
2006–07 *Lincoln C* 0 0
2007–08 Falkirk 13 0
2008–09 Falkirk 15 0
2009–10 Falkirk 38 0
2010–11 Falkirk 36 0 **102 0**
2011–12 Torquay U 46 0 **46 0**
2012–13 Peterborough U 46 0
2013–14 Peterborough U 42 0
2014–15 Peterborough U 0 0 **88 0**
2014–15 *Scunthorpe U* 13 0 **13 0**
2014–15 *York C* 16 0 **16 0**
2015–16 Exeter C 45 0
2016–17 Exeter C 18 0 **63 0**
2017–18 Mansfield T 1 0
2018–19 Mansfield T 17 0
2019–20 Mansfield T 11 0 **29 0**

PEARCE, Krystian (D) 362 24
H: 6 1 W: 13 05 b.Birmingham 5-1-90
Internationals: England U17, U19. Barbados Full caps.
2006–07 Birmingham C 0 0
2007–08 Birmingham C 0 0
2007–08 *Port Vale* 12 0 **12 0**
2007–08 *Notts Co* 8 1
2008–09 Birmingham C 0 0
2008–09 *Scunthorpe U* 39 0 **39 0**
2009–10 Birmingham C 0 0
2009–10 *Peterborough U* 2 0 **2 0**
2009–10 Huddersfield T 1 0 **1 0**
2010–11 Notts Co 27 1
2011–12 Notts Co 27 3
2012–13 Notts Co 2 1 **64 6**
2012–13 *Barnet* 17 1 **17 1**
2013–14 Torquay U 35 4 **35 4**
2015–16 Mansfield T 38 3
2016–17 Mansfield T 41 3
2017–18 Mansfield T 38 1
2018–19 Mansfield T 46 4
2019–20 Mansfield T 29 2 **192 13**

PRESTON, Matt (D) 123 9
b. 16-3-95
2013–14 Walsall 0 0
2014–15 Walsall 1 0
2015–16 Walsall 10 2
2016–17 Walsall 30 1
2017–18 Walsall 0 0 **41 3**
2017–18 Swindon T 21 2 **21 2**
2018–19 Mansfield T 39 3
2019–20 Mansfield T 22 1 **61 4**

RILEY, Joe (D) 156 6
H: 6 0 W: 11 02 b.Salford 13-10-91
2011–12 Bolton W 3 0
2012–13 Bolton W 0 0
2013–14 Bolton W 0 0
2014–15 Bolton W 0 0 **3 0**
2014–15 *Oxford U* 22 0 **22 0**
2014–15 Bury 17 1
2015–16 Bury 33 1 **50 2**
2016–17 Shrewsbury T 32 1
2017–18 Shrewsbury T 10 1 **42 2**
2018–19 Plymouth Arg 18 0
2019–20 Plymouth Arg 15 1 **33 1**
2019–20 Mansfield T 6 1 **6 1**

ROSE, Danny (F) 227 57
H: 5 8 W: 9 00 b.Barnsley 10-12-93
2010–11 Barnsley 1 0
2011–12 Barnsley 4 0
2012–13 Barnsley 8 1
2013–14 Barnsley 3 0
2013–14 *Bury* 6 3
2014–15 Barnsley 1 0 **17 1**
2014–15 *Bury* 35 10
2015–16 Bury 28 5 **69 18**
2016–17 Mansfield T 37 9
2017–18 Mansfield T 39 14
2018–19 Mansfield T 34 4
2019–20 Mansfield T 31 11 **141 38**

SINCLAIR, Tyrese (F) 0 0
2018–19 Mansfield T 0 0
2019–20 Radcliffe 0 0
2019–20 Mansfield T 0 0

SKETCHLEY, Kian (D) 0 0
2019–20 Mansfield T 0 0

SMITH, Alistair (M) 5 0
2018–19 Mansfield T 0 0
2019–20 Mansfield T 5 0 **5 0**

STERLING-JAMES, Omari (M) 44 2
b.Birmingham 15-9-93
Internationals: St Kitts and Nevis Full caps.
2014–15 Cheltenham T 22 1 **22 1**
From Gloucester C, Solihull Moors.
2017–18 Mansfield T 13 0
2018–19 Mansfield T 1 0
2019–20 Mansfield T 8 1 **22 1**

STONE, Aiden (G) 3 0
b. 20-7-99
2018–19 Burnley 0 0
2019–20 Mansfield T 3 0 **3 0**

SWEENEY, Ryan (D) 123 5
b.Kingston upon Thames 15-4-97
Internationals: Republic of Ireland U19, U21.
2014–15 AFC Wimbledon 3 0
2015–16 AFC Wimbledon 10 0 **13 0**
2016–17 Stoke C 0 0
2016–17 *Bristol R* 16 0
2017–18 Stoke C 0 0
2017–18 *Bristol R* 23 3 **39 3**
2018–19 Stoke C 0 0
2018–19 *Mansfield T* 38 1
2019–20 Mansfield T 33 1 **71 2**

TOMLINSON, Willem (M) 35 1
H: 5 10 W: 10 03 b.Burnley 27-1-98
2015–16 Blackburn R 0 0
2016–17 Blackburn R 1 0
2017–18 Blackburn R 4 0
2018–19 Blackburn R 0 0 **5 0**
2018–19 Mansfield T 12 0
2019–20 Mansfield T 18 1 **30 1**

WHITE, Hayden (D) 128 3
H: 6 1 W: 10 10 b.Greenwich 15-4-95
2013–14 Bolton W 2 0
2014–15 Bolton W 3 0
2014–15 *Carlisle U* 8 0 **8 0**
2014–15 *Bury* 2 0 **2 0**
2014–15 *Notts Co* 3 0 **3 0**
2015–16 Bolton W 0 0 **5 0**
2015–16 *Blackpool* 29 1 **29 1**
2016–17 Peterborough U 6 0 **6 0**
2016–17 *Mansfield T* 18 1
2017–18 Mansfield T 28 1
2018–19 Mansfield T 19 0
2019–20 Mansfield T 10 0 **75 2**

Players retained or with offer of contract
Hamilton, Christopher Nathan.

Scholars
Adams, Joshua Joseph; Armsden, Jordan David-Lee; Boyle, Jamie Matthew; Caine, Nathan Ross; Campbell, Maison Scott; Chisholm, Jamie; Cooper, Frank George; Fisher, Isaac Raymond; Hill, Ethan Thomas; King, Larell Parker; Lawson, Sha'Mar Malik; Molyneaux, Rio Charles; Saunders, Nathan Anthony; Scott, Joshua David; Sketchley, Kian James; Tomlin, Kyle William.

MIDDLESBROUGH (51)

ASSOMBALONGA, Britt (F) 276 108
H: 5 9 W: 11 13 b.Kinshasa 6-12-92
Internationals: DR Congo Full caps.
2010–11 Watford 0 0
2011–12 Watford 4 0
2012–13 Watford 0 0
2012–13 *Southend U* 43 15 **43 15**
2013–14 Watford 0 0 **4 0**
2013–14 Peterborough U 43 23 **43 23**
2014–15 Nottingham F 29 15
2015–16 Nottingham F 4 1
2016–17 Nottingham F 32 14 **65 30**
2017–18 Middlesbrough 44 15
2018–19 Middlesbrough 42 14
2019–20 Middlesbrough 35 11 **121 40**

AYALA, Daniel (M) 242 23
H: 6 3 W: 13 03 b.Sevilla 7-11-90
Internationals: Spain U21.
2007–08 Liverpool 0 0
2008–09 Liverpool 0 0
2009–10 Liverpool 5 0
2010–11 Liverpool 0 0 **5 0**
2010–11 *Hull C* 12 1 **12 1**
2010–11 *Derby Co* 17 0 **17 0**
2011–12 Norwich C 7 0
2012–13 Norwich C 0 0
2012–13 *Nottingham F* 12 1 **12 1**
2013–14 Norwich C 0 0 **7 0**
2013–14 Middlesbrough 19 3
2014–15 Middlesbrough 30 4
2015–16 Middlesbrough 35 3
2016–17 Middlesbrough 14 1
2017–18 Middlesbrough 33 7
2018–19 Middlesbrough 33 1
2019–20 Middlesbrough 25 2 **189 21**

BOLA, Marc (D) 78 2
H: 6 1 W: 12 04 b.Greenwich 9-12-97
2016–17 Arsenal 0 0
2016–17 *Notts Co* 13 0 **13 0**
2017–18 Arsenal 0 0
2017–18 *Bristol R* 18 0 **18 0**
2018–19 Blackpool 35 2
2019–20 Middlesbrough 7 0 **7 0**
2019–20 *Blackpool* 5 0 **40 2**

BROWNE, Marcus (M) 58 10
b. 18-12-97
2015–16 West Ham U 0 0
2016–17 West Ham U 0 0
2016–17 *Wigan Ath* 0 0
2017–18 West Ham U 0 0
2018–19 West Ham U 0 0
2018–19 *Oxford U* 34 6
2019–20 Middlesbrough 13 0 **13 0**
2019–20 *Oxford U* 11 4 **45 10**

BRYNN, Solomon (G) 0 0
2019–20 Middlesbrough 0 0

BURRELL, Rumarn (F) 4 0
b.Birmingham 16-12-00
2018–19 Grimsby T 4 0 **4 0**
2019–20 Middlesbrough 0 0

CLAYTON, Adam (M) 386 20
H: 5 9 W: 11 11 b.Manchester 14-1-89
Internationals: England U20.
2007–08 Manchester C 0 0
2008–09 Manchester C 0 0
2009–10 Manchester C 0 0
2009–10 *Carlisle U* 28 1 **28 1**
2010–11 Leeds U 4 0
2010–11 *Peterborough U* 7 0 **7 0**
2010–11 *Milton Keynes D* 6 1 **6 1**
2011–12 Leeds U 43 6 **47 6**
2012–13 Huddersfield T 43 4
2013–14 Huddersfield T 42 7 **85 11**
2014–15 Middlesbrough 41 0
2015–16 Middlesbrough 43 1
2016–17 Middlesbrough 34 0
2017–18 Middlesbrough 32 0
2018–19 Middlesbrough 36 0
2019–20 Middlesbrough 27 0 **213 1**

COULSON, Hayden (D) 49 1
b. 17-6-98
Internationals: England U16, U17, U18, U19.
2018–19 Middlesbrough 0 0
2018–19 *St Mirren* 6 0 **6 0**
2018–19 *Cambridge U* 14 0 **14 0**
2019–20 Middlesbrough 29 1 **29 1**

DIJKSTEEL, Anfernee (M) 57 1
b. 27-10-96
Internationals: Netherlands U20.
2016–17 Charlton Ath 0 0
2017–18 Charlton Ath 10 0
2018–19 Charlton Ath 30 1
2019–20 Charlton Ath 1 0 **41 1**
2019–20 Middlesbrough 16 0 **16 0**

FLETCHER, Ashley (F) 133 24
b.Keighley 12-10-95
Internationals: England U20.
2015–16 Manchester U 0 0
2015–16 *Barnsley* 21 5 **21 5**
2016–17 West Ham U 16 0 **16 0**
2017–18 Middlesbrough 16 1
2017–18 *Sunderland* 16 2 **16 2**
2018–19 Middlesbrough 21 5
2019–20 Middlesbrough 43 11 **80 17**

FRIEND, George (D) 365 12
H: 6 2 W: 13 01 b.Barnstaple 19-10-87
2008–09 Exeter C 4 0
2008–09 Wolverhampton W 6 0
2009–10 Wolverhampton W 1 0 **7 0**
2009–10 *Millwall* 6 0 **6 0**
2009–10 *Southend U* 6 1 **6 1**
2009–10 *Scunthorpe U* 4 0 **4 0**
2009–10 *Exeter C* 13 1 **17 1**
2010–11 Doncaster R 32 1
2011–12 Doncaster R 27 0
2012–13 Doncaster R 0 0 **59 1**
2012–13 Middlesbrough 34 0
2013–14 Middlesbrough 41 3
2014–15 Middlesbrough 42 1
2015–16 Middlesbrough 40 1
2016–17 Middlesbrough 24 0
2017–18 Middlesbrough 33 2
2018–19 Middlesbrough 38 2
2019–20 Middlesbrough 14 0 **266 9**

FRY, Dael (D) 100 0
H: 6 1 W: 11 05 b.Middlesbrough 30-8-97
Internationals: England U17, U18, U19, U20, U21.
2015–16 Middlesbrough 7 0
2016–17 Middlesbrough 0 0
2016–17 *Rotherham U* 10 0 **10 0**
2017–18 Middlesbrough 13 0
2018–19 Middlesbrough 34 0
2019–20 Middlesbrough 36 0 **90 0**

FRYER, Joe (G) 47 0
b.Chester-le-Street 14-11-95
2016–17 Middlesbrough 0 0
2016–17 *Hartlepool U* 14 0 **14 0**
2017–18 Middlesbrough 0 0
2017–18 *Stevenage* 28 0 **28 0**
2018–19 Middlesbrough 0 0
2018–19 *Carlisle U* 5 0 **5 0**
2019–20 Middlesbrough 0 0

GESTEDE, Rudy (F) 270 63
H: 6 4 W: 13 07 b.Nancy 10-10-88
Internationals: France U19. Benin Full caps.
2008–09 Metz 5 0
2009–10 *Cannes* 22 4 **22 4**
2010–11 Metz 11 3 **16 3**
2010–11 Metz B 3 1 **3 1**
2011–12 Cardiff C 25 2
2012–13 Cardiff C 27 5
2013–14 Cardiff C 3 0 **55 7**
2013–14 Blackburn R 27 13
2014–15 Blackburn R 39 20 **66 33**
2015–16 Aston Villa 32 5
2016–17 Aston Villa 18 4 **50 9**
2016–17 Middlesbrough 16 1
2017–18 Middlesbrough 19 3
2018–19 Middlesbrough 4 0
2019–20 Middlesbrough 19 2 **58 6**

HACKNEY, Hayden (M) 0 0
2019–20 Middlesbrough 0 0

HOWSON, Jonathan (M) 491 49
H: 5 11 W: 12 01 b.Morley 21-5-88
Internationals: England U21.
2006–07 Leeds U 9 1
2007–08 Leeds U 26 3
2008–09 Leeds U 40 4
2009–10 Leeds U 45 4
2010–11 Leeds U 46 10
2011–12 Leeds U 19 1 **185 23**
2011–12 Norwich C 11 1
2012–13 Norwich C 30 2
2013–14 Norwich C 27 2
2014–15 Norwich C 34 8
2015–16 Norwich C 36 3
2016–17 Norwich C 38 6 **176 22**
2017–18 Middlesbrough 43 3
2018–19 Middlesbrough 46 1
2019–20 Middlesbrough 41 0 **130 4**

JOHNSON, Marvin (F) 160 11
H: 5 10 W: 11 09 b.Birmingham 1-12-90
From Solihull Moors, Kidderminster H.
2014–15 Motherwell 11 0
2015–16 Motherwell 38 5
2016–17 Motherwell 4 1 **53 6**
2016–17 Oxford U 39 3
2017–18 Oxford U 2 0 **41 3**
2017–18 Middlesbrough 17 1
2018–19 Middlesbrough 0 0
2018–19 *Sheffield U* 11 0 **11 0**
2019–20 Middlesbrough 38 1 **55 2**

KIERNAN, Cole (F) 0 0
b. 3-1-02
2019–20 Sunderland 0 0
2019–20 Middlesbrough 0 0

KOKOLO, Williams (D) 0 0
b. 9-6-00
From Monaco.
2018–19 Sunderland 0 0
2019–20 Middlesbrough 0 0

LIDDLE, Ben (M) 7 0
b.Durham 21-9-98
2018–19 Middlesbrough 0 0
2018–19 *Forest Green R* 2 0 **2 0**
2019–20 Middlesbrough 1 0 **1 0**
2019–20 *Scunthorpe U* 4 0 **4 0**

MAHMUTOVIC, Enes (D) 44 0
H: 6 3 W: 12 08 b. 22-5-97
Internationals: Luxembourg U21, Full caps.
2014–15 Fola Esch 1 0
2015–16 Fola Esch 2 0
2016–17 Fola Esch 22 0 **25 0**
2017–18 Middlesbrough 0 0
2018–19 Middlesbrough 0 0
2018–19 *Yeovil T* 4 0 **4 0**
2019–20 Middlesbrough 0 0
2019–20 *MMV Maastricht* 15 0 **15 0**

MALLEY, Connor (M) 5 1
b.Newcastle 20-3-00
2018–19 Middlesbrough 0 0
2019–20 Middlesbrough 0 0
2019–20 *Ayr U* 5 1 **5 1**

McNAIR, Paddy (D) 106 11
H: 5 8 W: 11 05 b.Ballyclare 27-4-95
Internationals: Northern Ireland U16, U17, U19, U21, Full caps.
2011–12 Manchester U 0 0
2012–13 Manchester U 0 0
2013–14 Manchester U 0 0
2014–15 Manchester U 16 0
2015–16 Manchester U 8 0 **24 0**
2016–17 Sunderland 9 0
2017–18 Sunderland 16 5 **25 5**
2018–19 Middlesbrough 16 0
2019–20 Middlesbrough 41 6 **57 6**

MEJIAS, Tomas (G) 39 0
H: 6 5 W: 13 02 b.Madrid 30-1-89
Internationals: Spain U19, U20.
2010–11 Real Madrid 1 0
2011–12 Real Madrid 0 0
2012–13 Real Madrid 0 0
2013–14 Real Madrid 0 0 **1 0**
2013–14 *Middlesbrough* 1 0
2014–15 Middlesbrough 7 0
2015–16 Middlesbrough 0 0
2016–17 Middlesbrough 0 0
2016–17 *Rayo Vallecano* 2 0 **2 0**
2017–18 Middlesbrough 0 0
2018–19 Omonia 28 0 **28 0**
2019–20 Middlesbrough 0 0 **8 0**

MOUKOUDI, Harold (D) 67 6
b. 27-11-97
Internationals: France U16, U17, U18, U20. Cameroon Full caps.
2014–15 Le Havre 0 0
2015–16 Le Havre 0 0
2016–17 Le Havre 7 0

2017–18 Le Havre 35 4
2018–19 Le Havre 17 2 **59 6**
2019–20 Saint-Etienne 0 0
On loan from Saint-Etienne.
2019–20 Middlesbrough 8 0 **8 0**

O'NEILL, Tyrone (F) 1 0
b.Middlesbrough 12-10-99
2018–19 Middlesbrough 0 0
2019–20 Middlesbrough 1 0 **1 0**

PEARS, Aynsley (G) 24 0
b. 23-4-98
Internationals: England U19.
2017–18 Middlesbrough 0 0
2018–19 Middlesbrough 0 0
2019–20 Middlesbrough 24 0 **24 0**

SAVILLE, George (M) 231 25
H: 5 9 W: 11 07 b.Camberley 1-6-93
Internationals: Northern Ireland Full caps.
2010–11 Chelsea 0 0
2011–12 Chelsea 0 0
2012–13 Chelsea 0 0
2012–13 *Millwall* 3 0
2013–14 Chelsea 0 0
2013–14 *Brentford* 40 3 **40 3**
2014–15 Wolverhampton W 7 0
2014–15 *Bristol C* 7 1 **7 1**
2015–16 Wolverhampton W 19 5
2015–16 *Millwall* 12 0
2016–17 Wolverhampton W 24 1 **50 6**
2017–18 Millwall 44 10
2018–19 Millwall 4 0 **63 10**
2018–19 *Middlesbrough* 34 4
2019–20 Middlesbrough 37 1 **71 5**

SHOTTON, Ryan (D) 283 13
H: 6 3 W: 13 05 b.Stoke 30-9-88
2006–07 Stoke C 0 0
2007–08 Stoke C 0 0
2008–09 Stoke C 0 0
2008–09 *Tranmere R* 33 5 **33 5**
2009–10 Stoke C 0 0
2009–10 *Barnsley* 30 0 **30 0**
2010–11 Stoke C 2 0
2011–12 Stoke C 23 1
2012–13 Stoke C 23 0
2013–14 Stoke C 0 0 **48 1**
2013–14 *Wigan Ath* 9 1 **9 1**
2014–15 Derby Co 25 2
2015–16 Derby Co 6 0 **31 2**
2015–16 *Birmingham C* 9 1
2016–17 Birmingham C 43 2
2017–18 Birmingham C 1 0 **53 3**
2017–18 Middlesbrough 24 1
2018–19 Middlesbrough 34 0
2019–20 Middlesbrough 21 0 **79 1**

SPENCE, Djed (D) 22 1
H: 6 0 W: 11 03 b.London 9-8-00
From Fulham.
2018–19 Middlesbrough 0 0
2019–20 Middlesbrough 22 1 **22 1**

STOJANOVIC, Dejan (G) 113 0
b.Feldkirch 19-7-93
Internationals: Macedonia U21.
2009–10 Lustenau 1 0
2010–11 Lustenau 23 0 **24 0**
2011–12 Bologna 0 0
2012–13 Bologna 4 0
2013–14 Bologna 1 0
2014–15 Bologna 5 0
2014–15 *Crotone* 2 0 **2 0**
2015–16 Bologna 0 0 **10 0**
2016–17 St Gallen 4 0
2017–18 St Gallen 13 0
2018–19 St Gallen 34 0
2019–20 St Gallen 18 0 **69 0**
2019–20 Middlesbrough 8 0 **8 0**

STUBBS, Sam (D) 44 0
b. 20-11-98
2016–17 Wigan Ath 0 0
2017–18 Wigan Ath 0 0
2017–18 *Crewe Alex* 5 0 **5 0**
2018–19 Middlesbrough 0 0
2018–19 *Notts Co* 17 0 **17 0**
2019–20 Middlesbrough 0 0
2019–20 *Hamilton A* 19 0 **19 0**
2019–20 *ADO Den Haag* 3 0 **3 0**

TAVERNIER, Marcus (M) 69 7
b.Leeds 22-3-99
Internationals: England U19, U20.
2017–18 Middlesbrough 5 1
2017–18 *Milton Keynes D* 7 0 **7 0**
2018–19 Middlesbrough 20 3
2019–20 Middlesbrough 37 3 **62 7**

WALKER, Stephen (F) 20 1
b.Middlesbrough 11-10-00
Internationals: England U17, U18, U19.
2018–19 Middlesbrough 0 0
2018–19 *Milton Keynes D* 7 0 **7 0**
2019–20 Middlesbrough 7 0 **7 0**
2019–20 *Crewe Alex* 6 1 **6 1**

WING, Lewis (M) 88 13
b.Durham 23-5-95
From Shildon.
2017–18 Middlesbrough 0 0
2017–18 *Yeovil T* 20 3 **20 3**
2018–19 Middlesbrough 28 3
2019–20 Middlesbrough 40 7 **68 10**

WOOD-GORDON, Nathan (D) 1 0
b.Middlesbrough 31-5-02
Internationals: England U16, U17, U19.
From Stockton T.
2018–19 Middlesbrough 0 0
2019–20 Middlesbrough 1 0 **1 0**

Players retained or with offer of contract
Folarin, Samuel Oluwatimilchin; Gibson, Joseph William; Hemming, Zachary; James, Bradley David; Jones, Isaiah Benjamin Montell; Stubbs, Sam Alan; Sykes, Cain.

Scholars
Balde, Almanzar Alberto; Coburn, Joshua Guy; Collins, Sam Robert; Cornet, Isiah Jean-Louis Casimir; Dodds, Daniel; Essien, Harold Jimaimah; Flatters, Harry David; Fletcher, Isaac Andrew; Green, Harry Steven; Hannah, Jack Benjamin; Hood, Nicholas Joseph; Metcalfe, Max Cameron; Nelson, Andrew James; Reed, Lucas James; Ridley, Joseph; Robinson, Jack; Stephenson, Terry Gewelling; Swan, Oliver Jay; Waites, George Arthur Aitcheson; Willis, Pharrell Jeremiah Kieran; Wilson, Andrew.

MILLWALL (52)

ALEXANDER, George (F) 1 0
b. 22-6-01
2018–19 Millwall 1 0
2019–20 Millwall 0 0 **1 0**

BIALKOWSKI, Bartosz (G) 329 0
H: 6 3 W: 12 10 b.Braniewo 6-7-87
Internationals: Poland U20, U21, Full caps.
2004–05 Gornik Zabrze 7 0 **7 0**
2005–06 Southampton 5 0
2006–07 Southampton 8 0
2007–08 Southampton 1 0
2008–09 Southampton 0 0
2009–10 Southampton 7 0
2009–10 *Barnsley* 2 0 **2 0**
2010–11 Southampton 0 0
2011–12 Southampton 1 0 **22 0**
2012–13 Notts Co 40 0
2013–14 Notts Co 44 0 **84 0**
2014–15 Ipswich T 31 0
2015–16 Ipswich T 20 0
2016–17 Ipswich T 44 0
2017–18 Ipswich T 45 0
2018–19 Ipswich T 28 0 **168 0**
2019–20 Millwall 46 0 **46 0**

BODVARSSON, Jon Dadi (F) 302 56
H: 6 3 W: 13 05 b.Selfoss 25-5-92
Internationals: Iceland U19, U21, Full caps.
2008 Selfoss 0 0
2009 Selfoss 16 1
2010 Selfoss 21 3
2011 Selfoss 21 7
2012 Selfoss 22 7 **80 18**
2013 Viking 23 1
2014 Viking 29 5
2015 Viking 29 9 **81 15**
2015–16 Kaiserslautern 15 2 **15 2**
2016–17 Wolverhampton W 42 3 **42 3**
2017–18 Reading 33 7
2018–19 Reading 20 7 **53 14**
2019–20 Millwall 31 4 **31 4**

BRADBURY, Harvey (F) 4 0
b. 29-12-98
2016–17 Portsmouth 0 0
2017–18 Watford 0 0
2018–19 Watford 0 0
2018–19 Oxford U 1 0 **1 0**
2019–20 Millwall 0 0
2019–20 *Morecambe* 3 0 **3 0**

BRADSHAW, Tom (F) 299 77
H: 5 5 W: 11 02 b.Shrewsbury 27-7-92
Internationals: Wales U19, U21, Full caps.
2009–10 Shrewsbury T 6 3
2010–11 Shrewsbury T 26 6
2011–12 Shrewsbury T 8 1
2012–13 Shrewsbury T 21 0
2013–14 Shrewsbury T 28 7 **89 17**
2014–15 Walsall 29 17
2015–16 Walsall 41 17 **70 34**
2016–17 Barnsley 42 8
2017–18 Barnsley 39 9
2018–19 Barnsley 4 1 **85 18**
2018–19 Millwall 10 0
2019–20 Millwall 45 8 **55 8**

BROWN, James (D) 29 0
H: 6 1 W: 12 06 b. 12-1-98
2016–17 Millwall 0 0
2017–18 Millwall 0 0
2017–18 *Carlisle U* 27 0 **27 0**
2018–19 Millwall 0 0
2018–19 *Livingston* 1 0 **1 0**
2018–19 *Lincoln C* 0 0
2019–20 Millwall 1 0 **1 0**

BUREY, Tyler (F) 4 0
b. 9-1-01
2018–19 AFC Wimbledon 3 0 **3 0**
2019–20 Millwall 1 0 **1 0**

COOPER, Jake (D) 187 19
H: 6 4 W: 13 05 b.Bracknell 3-2-95
Internationals: England U18, U19, U20.
2013–14 Reading 0 0
2014–15 Reading 15 2
2015–16 Reading 24 2
2016–17 Reading 3 0 **42 4**
2016–17 *Millwall* 15 2
2017–18 Millwall 38 4
2018–19 Millwall 46 6
2019–20 Millwall 46 3 **145 15**

DEBRAH, Jesse (F) 0 0
H: 6 0 W: 11 07 b. 11-1-00
2018–19 Millwall 0 0
2019–20 Millwall 0 0

FERGUSON, Shane (D) 219 8
H: 5 9 W: 10 01 b.Limavady 12-7-91
Internationals: Northern Ireland U17, U19, U21, B, Full caps.
2008–09 Newcastle U 0 0
2009–10 Newcastle U 0 0
2010–11 Newcastle U 7 0
2011–12 Newcastle U 7 0
2012–13 Newcastle U 9 0
2012–13 *Birmingham C* 11 1
2013–14 Newcastle U 0 0
2013–14 *Birmingham C* 18 0 **29 1**
2014–15 Newcastle U 0 0
2014–15 *Rangers* 0 0
2015–16 Newcastle U 0 0 **23 0**
2015–16 Millwall 39 3
2016–17 Millwall 40 2
2017–18 Millwall 24 0
2018–19 Millwall 35 2
2019–20 Millwall 29 0 **167 7**

FIELDING, Frank (G) 324 0
H: 5 11 W: 12 00 b.Blackburn 4-4-88
Internationals: England U19, U21.
2006–07 Blackburn R 0 0
2007–08 Blackburn R 0 0
2007–08 *Wycombe W* 36 0 **36 0**
2008–09 Blackburn R 0 0
2008–09 *Northampton T* 12 0 **12 0**
2008–09 *Rochdale* 23 0
2009–10 Blackburn R 0 0
2009–10 *Rochdale* 18 0 **41 0**
2010–11 Blackburn R 0 0
2010–11 Derby Co 16 0
2011–12 Derby Co 44 0
2012–13 Derby Co 16 0 **76 0**
2013–14 Bristol C 16 0
2014–15 Bristol C 46 0
2015–16 Bristol C 21 0
2016–17 Bristol C 27 0
2017–18 Bristol C 43 0
2018–19 Bristol C 5 0 **158 0**
2019–20 Millwall 1 0 **1 0**

HUTCHINSON, Shaun (D) 279 20
H: 6 1 W: 12 04 b.Newcastle upon Tyne 23-11-90
2008–09 Motherwell 1 0
2009–10 Motherwell 5 3
2010–11 Motherwell 19 1
2011–12 Motherwell 30 1

2012–13 Motherwell 31 1
2013–14 Motherwell 35 1 **121 7**
2014–15 Fulham 25 2
2015–16 Fulham 9 0 **34 2**
2016–17 Millwall 16 2
2017–18 Millwall 46 2
2018–19 Millwall 26 1
2019–20 Millwall 36 6 **124 11**

LEONARD, Ryan (D) 299 23
H: 6 0 W: 11 01 b.Plympton 24-5-92
2009–10 Plymouth Arg 1 0
2010–11 Plymouth Arg 0 0 **1 0**
2011–12 Southend U 17 1
2012–13 Southend U 22 2
2013–14 Southend U 43 5
2014–15 Southend U 41 3
2015–16 Southend U 37 2
2016–17 Southend U 43 3
2017–18 Southend U 25 4 **228 20**
2017–18 Sheffield U 13 0
2018–19 Sheffield U 3 0 **16 0**
2018–19 Millwall 37 2
2019–20 Millwall 17 1 **54 3**

MAHONEY, Connor (M) 96 4
H: 5 9 W: 10 08 b.Blackburn 12-2-97
Internationals: England U17, U18, U20.
2013–14 Accrington S 4 0 **4 0**
2013–14 Blackburn R 0 0
2014–15 Blackburn R 0 0
2015–16 Blackburn R 2 0
2016–17 Blackburn R 14 0 **16 0**
2017–18 Bournemouth 0 0
2017–18 *Barnsley* 8 0 **8 0**
2018–19 Bournemouth 0 0
2018–19 *Birmingham C* 30 2 **30 2**
2019–20 Millwall 38 2 **38 2**

McCARTHY, Jason (D) 158 10
H: 6 1 W: 12 08 b.Southampton 7-11-95
2013–14 Southampton 0 0
2014–15 Southampton 1 0
2015–16 Southampton 0 0
2015–16 *Wycombe W* 35 2
2016–17 Southampton 0 0 **1 0**
2016–17 *Walsall* 46 5 **46 5**
2017–18 Barnsley 21 0 **21 0**
2018–19 Wycombe W 44 2
2019–20 Millwall 2 0 **2 0**
2019–20 *Wycombe W* 9 1 **88 5**

McNAMARA, Danny (D) 21 0
b. 27-12-98
Internationals: Republic of Ireland U21.
2018–19 Millwall 0 0
2019–20 Millwall 0 0
2019–20 Millwall 0 0
2019–20 *Newport Co* 21 0 **21 0**
2019–20 *St Johnstone* 0 0

MITCHELL, Billy (M) 8 0
b. 7-4-01
2018–19 Millwall 1 0
2019–20 Millwall 7 0 **8 0**

MULLER, Hayden (D) 1 0
b. 7-2-02
2019–20 Millwall 1 0 **1 0**

O'BRIEN, Aiden (F) 200 34
H: 5 8 W: 10 12 b.Islington 4-10-93
Internationals: Republic of Ireland U17, U19, U21, Full caps.
2010–11 Millwall 0 0
2011–12 Millwall 0 0
2012–13 Millwall 0 0
2012–13 *Crawley T* 9 0 **9 0**
2013–14 Millwall 0 0
2013–14 *Torquay U* 3 0 **3 0**
2014–15 Millwall 19 2
2015–16 Millwall 43 10
2016–17 Millwall 43 13
2017–18 Millwall 30 4
2018–19 Millwall 35 2
2019–20 Millwall 18 3 **188 34**

PEARCE, Alex (D) 353 20
H: 6 0 W: 11 10 b.Wallingford 9-11-88
Internationals: Scotland U19, U21, Full caps.
2006–07 Reading 0 0
2006–07 *Northampton T* 15 1 **15 1**
2007–08 Reading 0 0
2007–08 *Bournemouth* 11 0 **11 0**
2007–08 *Norwich C* 11 0 **11 0**
2008–09 Reading 16 1
2008–09 *Southampton* 9 2 **9 2**
2009–10 Reading 25 4
2010–11 Reading 21 1
2011–12 Reading 46 5
2012–13 Reading 19 0
2013–14 Reading 45 3
2014–15 Reading 40 0 **212 14**
2015–16 Derby Co 0 0
2015–16 *Bristol C* 7 0 **7 0**
2016–17 Derby Co 40 2
2017–18 Derby Co 7 1
2018–19 Derby Co 1 0 **48 3**
2018–19 *Millwall* 11 0
2019–20 Millwall 29 0 **40 0**

ROMEO, Mahlon (M) 162 2
H: 5 10 W: 11 05 b.Westminster 19-9-95
Internationals: Antigua and Barbuda Full caps.
2012–13 Gillingham 1 0
2013–14 Gillingham 0 0
2014–15 Gillingham 0 0 **1 0**
2015–16 Millwall 18 1
2016–17 Millwall 32 0
2017–18 Millwall 27 1
2018–19 Millwall 41 0
2019–20 Millwall 43 0 **161 2**

SANDFORD, Ryan (G) 0 0
b. 21-2-99
Internationals: England U16, U17, U18.
2019–20 Millwall 0 0

SKALAK, Jiri (F) 179 21
H: 5 9 W: 10 10 b.Pardubice 12-3-92
Internationals: Czech Republic U16, U17, U18, U19, U20, U21, Full caps.
2010–11 Sparta Prague 0 0
2011–12 Sparta Prague 0 0
2011–12 *MFA Ruzomberok* 27 3 **27 3**
2012–13 Sparta Prague 7 0
2012–13 *1.FC Slovacko* 9 0 **9 0**
2013–14 Sparta Prague 3 0
2013–14 *Zbrojovka Brno* 24 3 **24 3**
2014–15 Sparta Prague 0 0 **10 0**
2014–15 *Mlada Boleslav* 24 6
2015–16 Mlada Boleslav 16 6 **40 12**
2015–16 Brighton & HA 12 2
2016–17 Brighton & HA 31 0
2017–18 Brighton & HA 0 0 **43 2**
2018–19 Millwall 14 0
2019–20 Millwall 12 1 **26 1**

SMITH, Matt (F) 310 72
H: 6 6 W: 14 00 b.Birmingham 7-6-89
2011–12 Oldham Ath 28 3
2011–12 *Macclesfield T* 8 1 **8 1**
2012–13 Oldham Ath 34 6 **62 9**
2013–14 Leeds U 39 12
2014–15 Leeds U 3 0 **42 12**
2014–15 Fulham 15 5
2014–15 *Bristol C* 14 7 **14 7**
2015–16 Fulham 20 2
2016–17 Fulham 16 2 **51 9**
2016–17 QPR 16 4
2017–18 QPR 41 11
2018–19 QPR 35 6 **92 21**
2019–20 Millwall 41 13 **41 13**

THOMPSON, Ben (M) 133 8
H: 5 11 W: 12 04 b. 3-10-95
2014–15 Millwall 0 0
2015–16 Millwall 28 1
2016–17 Millwall 38 0
2017–18 Millwall 3 0
2018–19 Portsmouth 23 2 **23 2**
2018–19 Millwall 13 4
2019–20 Millwall 28 1 **110 6**

TIENSIA, Junior (D) 0 0
2019–20 Millwall 0 0

WALLACE, Jed (M) 284 52
H: 5 10 W: 10 12 b.Reading 15-12-93
Internationals: England U19.
2011–12 Portsmouth 0 0
2012–13 Portsmouth 22 6
2013–14 Portsmouth 44 7
2014–15 Portsmouth 44 14 **110 27**
2015–16 Wolverhampton W 9 0
2015–16 *Millwall* 12 1
2016–17 Wolverhampton W 9 0 **18 0**
2016–17 *Millwall* 16 3
2017–18 Millwall 43 6
2018–19 Millwall 42 5
2019–20 Millwall 43 10 **156 25**

WALLACE, Murray (D) 258 12
H: 6 2 W: 11 07 b.Glasgow 10-1-93
Internationals: Scotland U20, U21.
2011–12 Falkirk 19 2 **19 2**
2011–12 Huddersfield T 0 0
2012–13 Huddersfield T 6 1
2013–14 Huddersfield T 17 0
2014–15 Huddersfield T 26 2
2015–16 Huddersfield T 2 0 **51 3**
2015–16 *Scunthorpe U* 33 2
2016–17 Scunthorpe U 46 2
2017–18 Scunthorpe U 45 1 **124 5**
2018–19 Millwall 21 2
2019–20 Millwall 43 0 **64 2**

WILLIAMS, Shaun (M) 421 60
H: 5 9 W: 11 11 b.Dublin 19-10-86
Internationals: Republic of Ireland U21, U23, Full caps.
2007 Drogheda U 0 0
2007 *Dundalk* 19 9 **19 9**
2008 Drogheda U 4 0
2008 *Finn Harps* 14 2 **14 2**
2009 Drogheda U 1 0 **5 0**
2009 Sporting Fingal 13 7
2010 Sporting Fingal 32 5 **45 12**
2011–12 Milton Keynes D 39 8
2012–13 Milton Keynes D 44 3
2013–14 Milton Keynes D 25 8 **108 19**
2013–14 Millwall 17 1
2014–15 Millwall 38 2
2015–16 Millwall 33 2
2016–17 Millwall 44 4
2017–18 Millwall 35 2
2018–19 Millwall 31 5
2019–20 Millwall 32 2 **230 18**

Players retained or with offer of contract
Davis, Jayden Kyle Andrew; Duncan, Reuben John; Mitchell, Alexander Paul; Moss, Daniel Thomas; Olaofe, Isaac Tanitoluwaloba; Ransom, Harry William Dominique; Skeffington, Samuel; Strachan, Robert Alex; Topalloj, Besart; Wright, Joseph Dennis.

Scholars
Abdulmalik, Abdulsabur Oluwatosin; Allen, Alfie-John Terence; Barton, Jay Joseph; Bate, Oliver John; Bennett, Benjamin Joseph; Boateng, Nana Osei; Briscoe, Tyrese Owen; Ezennolim, Chibuike Udogu; Fanshawe, Leighton Nana Kofi; Gillmore, Jordan James; Miller, Ezekiel Ethan Niyah; Munting, Jacob Frederick Neil; Penney, Arthur James; Robert-Hutton, Kyle Christian.

MILTON KEYNES D (53)

AGARD, Kieran (F) 325 89
H: 5 10 W: 10 10 b.Newham 10-10-89
2006–07 Everton 0 0
2007–08 Everton 0 0
2008–09 Everton 0 0
2009–10 Everton 1 0
2010–11 Everton 0 0 **1 0**
2010–11 *Kilmarnock* 8 1 **8 1**
2010–11 *Peterborough U* 0 0
2011–12 Yeovil T 29 6 **29 6**
2012–13 Rotherham U 30 6
2013–14 Rotherham U 46 21
2014–15 Rotherham U 2 0 **78 27**
2014–15 Bristol C 39 13
2015–16 Bristol C 25 2 **64 15**
2016–17 Milton Keynes D 42 12
2017–18 Milton Keynes D 41 6
2018–19 Milton Keynes D 43 20
2019–20 Milton Keynes D 19 2 **145 40**

ASONGANYI, Dylan (F) 6 0
b. 10-12-00
2017–18 Milton Keynes D 0 0
2018–19 Milton Keynes D 3 0
2019–20 Milton Keynes D 3 0 **6 0**

BIRD, Jay (F) 0 0
2017–18 Milton Keynes D 0 0
2018–19 Milton Keynes D 0 0
2019–20 Milton Keynes D 0 0

BOATENG, Hiram (M) 136 3
H: 5 7 W: 11 00 b.Wandsworth 8-1-96
2012–13 Crystal Palace 0 0
2013–14 Crystal Palace 0 0
2013–14 *Crawley T* 1 0 **1 0**
2014–15 Crystal Palace 0 0
2015–16 Crystal Palace 1 0
2015–16 *Plymouth Arg* 24 1 **24 1**
2016–17 Crystal Palace 0 0 **1 0**
2016–17 *Bristol R* 9 0 **9 0**
2016–17 *Northampton T* 16 0 **16 0**
2017–18 Exeter C 38 1
2018–19 Exeter C 27 1 **65 2**
2019–20 Milton Keynes D 20 0 **20 0**

BOWERY, Jordan (F) **306** **47**
H: 6 1 W: 12 00 b.Nottingham 2-7-91
2008–09 Chesterfield 3 0
2009–10 Chesterfield 10 0
2010–11 Chesterfield 27 1
2011–12 Chesterfield 40 8
2012–13 Chesterfield 3 1 **83** **10**
2012–13 Aston Villa 10 0
2013–14 Aston Villa 9 0 **19** **0**
2013–14 *Doncaster R* 3 0 **3** **0**
2014–15 Rotherham U 33 5
2015–16 Rotherham U 7 0 **40** **5**
2015–16 *Bradford C* 3 0 **3** **0**
2015–16 Oxford U 17 7 **17** **7**
2016–17 Leyton Orient 17 1 **17** **1**
2016–17 *Crewe Alex* 19 2
2017–18 Crewe Alex 45 12
2018–19 Crewe Alex 44 8 **108** **22**
2019–20 Milton Keynes D 16 2 **16** **2**

BRENNAN, Finlay (D) **0** **0**
2019–20 Milton Keynes D 0 0

BRITTAIN, Callum (F) **97** **4**
H: 5 10 W: 10 10 b.Bedford 12-3-98
Internationals: England U20.
2015–16 Milton Keynes D 0 0
2016–17 Milton Keynes D 6 0
2017–18 Milton Keynes D 29 2
2018–19 Milton Keynes D 31 1
2019–20 Milton Keynes D 31 1 **97** **4**

CARGILL, Baily (D) **88** **2**
H: 6 2 W: 13 10 b.Winchester 13-10-95
Internationals: England U20.
2012–13 Bournemouth 0 0
2013–14 Bournemouth 0 0
2013–14 *Torquay U* 5 0 **5** **0**
2014–15 Bournemouth 0 0
2015–16 Bournemouth 0 0
2015–16 *Coventry C* 5 1 **5** **1**
2016–17 Bournemouth 1 0
2016–17 *Gillingham* 9 1 **9** **1**
2017–18 Bournemouth 0 0 **1** **0**
2017–18 *Fleetwood T* 11 0 **11** **0**
2017–18 *Partick Thistle* 16 0 **16** **0**
2018–19 Milton Keynes D 29 0
2019–20 Milton Keynes D 12 0 **41** **0**

FREEMAN, John (M) **0** **0**
2019–20 Milton Keynes D 0 0

GILBEY, Alex (M) **219** **20**
H: 6 0 W: 11 07 b.Dagenham 9-12-94
2011–12 Colchester U 0 0
2012–13 Colchester U 3 0
2013–14 Colchester U 36 1
2014–15 Colchester U 34 1
2015–16 Colchester U 37 5 **110** **7**
2016–17 Wigan Ath 15 2
2017–18 Wigan Ath 2 0 **17** **2**
2017–18 Milton Keynes D 23 3
2018–19 Milton Keynes D 39 3
2019–20 Milton Keynes D 30 5 **92** **11**

GLADWIN, Ben (D) **107** **13**
H: 6 3 b.Reading 8-6-92
2013–14 Swindon T 13 0
2014–15 Swindon T 34 8
2015–16 QPR 7 0
2015–16 *Swindon T* 13 2
2015–16 *Bristol C* 1 0 **1** **0**
2016–17 QPR 7 0 **14** **0**
2016–17 *Swindon T* 18 2 **78** **12**
2017–18 Blackburn R 5 0
2018–19 Blackburn R 0 0 **5** **0**
2019–20 Milton Keynes D 9 1 **9** **1**

HARLEY, Ryan (M) **286** **43**
H: 5 11 W: 11 00 b.Bristol 22-1-85
2004–05 Bristol C 2 0
2005–06 Bristol C 0 0 **2** **0**
From Weston-super-Mare.
2008–09 Exeter C 31 4
2009–10 Exeter C 44 10
2010–11 Exeter C 21 6
2010–11 Swansea C 0 0
2010–11 *Exeter C* 21 4
2011–12 Swansea C 0 0
2011–12 Brighton & HA 16 2
2012–13 Brighton & HA 2 0 **18** **2**
2012–13 *Milton Keynes D* 8 0
2013–14 Swindon T 21 1
2014–15 Swindon T 0 0 **21** **1**
2014–15 Exeter C 25 4
2015–16 Exeter C 28 4
2016–17 Exeter C 31 5
2017–18 Exeter C 19 1 **220** **38**
2018–19 Milton Keynes D 14 2
2019–20 Milton Keynes D 3 0 **25** **2**

HEALEY, Rhys (M) **96** **31**
H: 5 8 W: 10 10 b.Manchester 6-12-94
2012–13 Cardiff C 0 0
2013–14 Cardiff C 1 0
2014–15 Cardiff C 0 0
2014–15 *Colchester U* 21 4 **21** **4**
2015–16 Cardiff C 0 0
2015–16 *Dundee* 7 1 **7** **1**
2016–17 Newport Co 17 6 **17** **6**
2016–17 Cardiff C 7 1
2017–18 Cardiff C 3 0
2018–19 Milton Keynes D 18 8
2018–19 Cardiff C 3 0 **14** **1**
2019–20 Milton Keynes D 19 11 **37** **19**

HOUGHTON, Jordan (M) **164** **7**
H: 6 2 W: 12 13 b.Chertsey 9-11-95
Internationals: England U16, U17, U20.
2015–16 Chelsea 0 0
2015–16 *Gillingham* 11 1 **11** **1**
2015–16 *Plymouth Arg* 10 1 **10** **1**
2016–17 Chelsea 0 0
2016–17 *Doncaster R* 32 1
2017–18 Chelsea 0 0
2017–18 *Doncaster R* 37 0 **69** **1**
2018–19 Milton Keynes D 44 2
2019–20 Milton Keynes D 30 2 **74** **4**

KASUMU, David (M) **22** **1**
b. 5-10-99
2015–16 Milton Keynes D 0 0
2016–17 Milton Keynes D 0 0
2017–18 Milton Keynes D 1 0
2018–19 Milton Keynes D 0 0
2019–20 Milton Keynes D 21 1 **22** **1**

LEACH, Ollie (D) **0** **0**
2019–20 Milton Keynes D 0 0

LEWINGTON, Dean (D) **681** **22**
H: 5 11 W: 11 07 b.Kingston 18-5-84
2002–03 Wimbledon 1 0
2003–04 Wimbledon 28 1 **29** **1**
2004–05 Milton Keynes D 43 2
2005–06 Milton Keynes D 44 1
2006–07 Milton Keynes D 45 1
2007–08 Milton Keynes D 45 0
2008–09 Milton Keynes D 40 2
2009–10 Milton Keynes D 42 1
2010–11 Milton Keynes D 42 3
2011–12 Milton Keynes D 46 3
2012–13 Milton Keynes D 38 1
2013–14 Milton Keynes D 43 1
2014–15 Milton Keynes D 41 3
2015–16 Milton Keynes D 46 1
2016–17 Milton Keynes D 36 1
2017–18 Milton Keynes D 22 0
2018–19 Milton Keynes D 46 1
2019–20 Milton Keynes D 33 0 **652** **21**

MARTIN, Russell (M) **508** **25**
H: 6 0 W: 11 08 b.Brighton 4-1-86
Internationals: Scotland Full caps.
2004–05 Wycombe W 7 0
2005–06 Wycombe W 23 3
2006–07 Wycombe W 42 2
2007–08 Wycombe W 44 0 **116** **5**
2008–09 Peterborough U 46 1
2009–10 Peterborough U 10 0 **56** **1**
2009–10 Norwich C 26 0
2010–11 Norwich C 46 5
2011–12 Norwich C 33 2
2012–13 Norwich C 31 3
2013–14 Norwich C 31 0
2014–15 Norwich C 45 2
2015–16 Norwich C 30 3
2016–17 Norwich C 37 1
2017–18 Norwich C 5 0 **284** **16**
2017–18 *Rangers* 15 1 **15** **1**
2018–19 Walsall 8 0 **8** **0**
2018–19 Milton Keynes D 18 1
2019–20 Milton Keynes D 11 1 **29** **2**

MASON, Joe (F) **244** **55**
H: 5 9 W: 11 11 b.Plymouth 13-5-91
Internationals: Republic of Ireland U18, U19, U21.
2009–10 Plymouth Arg 19 3
2010–11 Plymouth Arg 34 7 **53** **10**
2011–12 Cardiff C 39 9
2012–13 Cardiff C 28 6
2013–14 Cardiff C 0 0
2013–14 *Bolton W* 16 6
2014–15 Cardiff C 7 1
2014–15 *Bolton W* 12 4 **28** **10**
2015–16 Cardiff C 23 6 **97** **22**
2015–16 Wolverhampton W 16 3
2016–17 Wolverhampton W 19 3
2017–18 Wolverhampton W 0 0
2017–18 *Burton Alb* 6 1 **6** **1**
2018 *Colorado Rapids* 11 3 **11** **3**
2018–19 Wolverhampton W 0 0 **35** **6**
2018–19 *Portsmouth* 1 0 **1** **0**
2019–20 Milton Keynes D 13 3 **13** **3**

McGRANDLES, Conor (M) **146** **9**
H: 6 0 W: 10 00 b.Falkirk 24-9-95
2012–13 Falkirk 26 2
2013–14 Falkirk 36 5
2014–15 Falkirk 3 0
2014–15 Norwich C 1 0
2015–16 Norwich C 0 0
2015–16 *Falkirk* 5 0 **70** **7**
2016–17 Norwich C 0 0 **1** **0**
2017–18 Milton Keynes D 19 0
2018–19 Milton Keynes D 25 1
2019–20 Milton Keynes D 31 1 **75** **2**

MOORE, Stuart (G) **28** **0**
H: 6 2 W: 11 05 b.Sandown 8-9-94
2013–14 Reading 0 0
2014–15 Reading 0 0
2015–16 Reading 0 0
2015–16 *Peterborough U* 4 0 **4** **0**
2016–17 Reading 0 0
2016–17 *Luton T* 8 0 **8** **0**
2017–18 Swindon T 10 0 **10** **0**
2018–19 Milton Keynes D 6 0
2019–20 Milton Keynes D 0 0 **6** **0**

MOORE-TAYLOR, Jordan (D) **197** **11**
H: 5 10 W: 13 01 b.Exeter 21-1-94
2012–13 Exeter C 7 0
2013–14 Exeter C 29 1
2014–15 Exeter C 26 2
2015–16 Exeter C 32 0
2016–17 Exeter C 42 5
2017–18 Exeter C 24 2 **160** **10**
2018–19 Milton Keynes D 23 1
2019–20 Milton Keynes D 14 0 **37** **1**

NICHOLLS, Lee (G) **203** **0**
H: 6 3 W: 13 05 b.Huyton 5-10-92
Internationals: England U19.
2009–10 Wigan Ath 0 0
2010–11 Wigan Ath 0 0
2010–11 *Hartlepool U* 0 0
2010–11 *Shrewsbury T* 0 0
2010–11 *Sheffield W* 0 0
2011–12 Wigan Ath 0 0
2011–12 *Accrington S* 9 0 **9** **0**
2012–13 Wigan Ath 0 0
2012–13 *Northampton T* 46 0 **46** **0**
2013–14 Wigan Ath 6 0
2014–15 Wigan Ath 1 0
2015–16 Wigan Ath 2 0 **9** **0**
2015–16 *Bristol R* 15 0 **15** **0**
2016–17 Milton Keynes D 8 0
2017–18 Milton Keynes D 41 0
2018–19 Milton Keynes D 40 0
2019–20 Milton Keynes D 35 0 **124** **0**

NOMBE, Sam (F) **27** **2**
H: 5 9 W: 11 00 b. 22-10-98
2016–17 Milton Keynes D 0 0
2017–18 Milton Keynes D 6 0
2018–19 Milton Keynes D 0 0
2019–20 Milton Keynes D 21 2 **27** **2**

PATTISON, Charlie (M) **0** **0**
b. 28-12-00
2018–19 Milton Keynes D 0 0
2019–20 Milton Keynes D 0 0

POOLE, Regan (D) **76** **0**
b.Cardiff 18-6-98
Internationals: Wales U17, U19, U20, U21.
2014–15 Newport Co 11 0
2015–16 Newport Co 4 0
2015–16 Manchester U 0 0
2016–17 Manchester U 0 0
2017–18 Manchester U 0 0
2017–18 *Northampton T* 22 0 **22** **0**
2018–19 Manchester U 0 0
2018–19 *Newport Co* 20 0 **35** **0**
2019–20 Milton Keynes D 19 0 **19** **0**

REEVES, Ben (D) **205** **33**
H: 5 10 W: 10 07 b.Verwood 19-11-91
Internationals: Northern Ireland Full caps.
2008–09 Southampton 0 0
2009–10 Southampton 0 0
2010–11 Southampton 0 0
2011–12 Southampton 2 0
2011–12 *Dagenham & R* 5 0 **5** **0**
2012–13 Southampton 3 0 **5** **0**
2012–13 *Southend U* 10 1 **10** **1**
2013–14 Milton Keynes D 28 7

2014–15 Milton Keynes D 30 7
2015–16 Milton Keynes D 18 3
2016–17 Milton Keynes D 34 7
2017–18 Charlton Ath 29 3
2018–19 Charlton Ath 29 4 **58 7**
2019–20 Milton Keynes D 17 1 **127 25**

SORINOLA, Matthew (D) 0 0
b. 19-2-01
2019–20 Milton Keynes D 0 0

WALSH, Joe (D) 220 12
H: 5 11 W: 11 00 b.Cardiff 15-5-92
Internationals: Wales U17, U19, U21.
2010–11 Swansea C 0 0
2011–12 Swansea C 0 0
2012–13 Crawley T 30 2
2013–14 Crawley T 39 5
2014–15 Crawley T 28 1 **97 8**
2014–15 *Milton Keynes D* 2 0
2015–16 Milton Keynes D 18 1
2016–17 Milton Keynes D 39 1
2017–18 Milton Keynes D 10 0
2018–19 Milton Keynes D 30 2
2019–20 Milton Keynes D 24 0 **123 4**

WILLIAMS, George B (D) 159 5
H: 5 9 W: 11 00 b.Hillingdon 14-4-93
2011–12 Milton Keynes D 2 0
From Worcester C.
2014–15 Barnsley 4 0
2015–16 Barnsley 19 1 **23 1**
2016–17 Milton Keynes D 33 2
2017–18 Milton Keynes D 43 1
2018–19 Milton Keynes D 30 0
2019–20 Milton Keynes D 28 1 **136 4**

Scholars
Bailey, Joshua William; Black, Malaki Jemain Zidane; Brennan, Finlay Michael; Carter, Thomas Charles; Crane, Max Ambrose; Davies, Jack Allan; Deall, Rio Christopher; Freeman, John David; Holmes, James Simon; Jallow, Momodou Talibeh; Leach, Oliver Henry George; Riley, Harry Thomas; Robinson, Jamie Kyle; Rose, George Brian Alan; Rowley, Tom; Sule, Jamal Oshiomah.

MORECAMBE (54)

ANDRE MENDES, Filipe Silva (G) 0 0
2019–20 Morecambe 0 0

BAKARE, Ibrahim (D) 0 0
2019–20 Morecambe 0 0

BREWITT, Tom (D) 22 1
From AFC Fylde.
2019–20 Morecambe 22 1 **22 1**

BROWNSWORD, Tyler (D) 1 0
b. 31-12-99
2017–18 Morecambe 0 0
2018–19 Morecambe 1 0
2019–20 Morecambe 0 0 **1 0**

BUXTON, Adam (D) 85 4
H: 6 1 W: 12 10 b.Liverpool 12-5-92
2010–11 Wigan Ath 0 0
2011–12 Wigan Ath 0 0
2012–13 Wigan Ath 0 0
2013–14 Wigan Ath 0 0
2013–14 *Burton Alb* 0 0
2013–14 *Accrington S* 11 0
2014–15 Accrington S 17 1
2015–16 Accrington S 28 1 **56 2**
2016–17 Portsmouth 0 0
2018–19 Tranmere R 16 1 **16 1**
2019–20 Morecambe 13 1 **13 1**

CONLAN, Luke (D) 127 0
H: 5 11 W: 11 05 b.Portaferry 31-10-94
Internationals: Northern Ireland U16, U17, U19, U21.
2011–12 Burnley 0 0
2012–13 Burnley 0 0
2013–14 Burnley 0 0
2014–15 Burnley 0 0
2015–16 Burnley 0 0
2015–16 *St Mirren* 3 0 **3 0**
2015–16 *Morecambe* 16 0
2016–17 Morecambe 21 0
2017–18 Morecambe 27 0
2018–19 Morecambe 40 0
2019–20 Morecambe 20 0 **124 0**

CRANSTON, Jordan (D) 128 4
H: 5 11 W: 13 01 b.Wednesfield 11-3-93
Internationals: Wales U19.
2012–13 Wolverhampton W 0 0
2013–14 Wolverhampton W 0 0
2014–15 Notts Co 9 0 **9 0**
2015–16 Cheltenham T 0 0
2016–17 Cheltenham T 38 0
2017–18 Cheltenham T 22 0 **60 0**
2018–19 Morecambe 35 4
2019–20 Morecambe 24 0 **59 4**

DIAGOURAGA, Toumani (M) 425 17
H: 6 2 W: 11 05 b.Paris 10-6-87
2004–05 Watford 0 0
2005–06 Watford 1 0
2005–06 *Swindon T* 8 0
2006–07 Watford 0 0
2006–07 *Rotherham U* 7 0 **7 0**
2007–08 Watford 0 0 **1 0**
2007–08 *Hereford U* 41 2
2008–09 Hereford U 45 2 **86 4**
2009–10 Peterborough U 19 0 **19 0**
2009–10 *Brentford* 20 0
2010–11 Brentford 32 1
2011–12 Brentford 35 4
2012–13 Brentford 39 1
2013–14 Brentford 19 0
2013–14 *Portsmouth* 8 0 **8 0**
2014–15 Brentford 38 0
2015–16 Brentford 27 0 **210 6**
2015–16 Leeds U 17 2
2016–17 Leeds U 1 0
2016–17 *Ipswich T* 12 0 **12 0**
2017–18 Leeds U 0 0 **18 2**
2017–18 Plymouth Arg 15 3 **15 3**
2017–18 Fleetwood T 17 1 **17 1**
2018–19 Swindon T 12 0
2019–20 Swindon T 0 0 **20 0**
2019–20 Morecambe 12 1 **12 1**

ELLISON, Kevin (M) 653 129
H: 6 0 W: 12 00 b.Liverpool 23-2-79
2000–01 Leicester C 1 0
2001–02 Leicester C 0 0 **1 0**
2001–02 Stockport Co 11 0
2002–03 Stockport Co 23 1
2003–04 Stockport Co 14 1 **48 2**
2003–04 *Lincoln C* 11 0 **11 0**
2004–05 Chester C 24 9
2004–05 Hull C 16 1
2005–06 Hull C 23 1 **39 2**
2006–07 Tranmere R 34 4 **34 4**
2007–08 Chester C 36 11
2008–09 Chester C 39 8 **99 28**
2008–09 Rotherham U 0 0
2009–10 Rotherham U 39 8
2010–11 Rotherham U 23 3 **62 11**
2010–11 *Bradford C* 7 1 **7 1**
2011–12 Morecambe 34 15
2012–13 Morecambe 40 11
2013–14 Morecambe 42 10
2014–15 Morecambe 43 11
2015–16 Morecambe 44 9
2016–17 Morecambe 45 8
2017–18 Morecambe 40 9
2018–19 Morecambe 43 7
2019–20 Morecambe 21 1 **352 81**

FLEMING, Andy (M) 269 19
H: 6 1 W: 12 00 b.Liverpool 18-2-89
Internationals: England C.
2006–07 Wrexham 2 0
2007–08 Wrexham 4 0 **6 0**
2010–11 Morecambe 30 2
2011–12 Morecambe 17 2
2012–13 Morecambe 32 5
2013–14 Morecambe 35 2
2014–15 Morecambe 35 2
2015–16 Morecambe 33 3
2016–17 Morecambe 30 2
2017–18 Morecambe 32 0
2018–19 Morecambe 19 1
2019–20 Morecambe 0 0 **263 19**

HALSTEAD, Mark (G) 61 0
H: 6 3 W: 14 00 b.Blackpool 1-9-90
2009–10 Blackpool 0 0
2010–11 Blackpool 1 0
2011–12 Blackpool 0 0
2012–13 Blackpool 2 0
2013–14 Blackpool 0 0 **3 0**
2014–15 Shrewsbury T 1 0
2015–16 Shrewsbury T 16 0
2016–17 Shrewsbury T 3 0 **20 0**
From Southport.
2018–19 Morecambe 26 0
2019–20 Morecambe 12 0 **38 0**

HOWARD, Michael (F) 1 0
b.Southport 17-10-99
2019–20 Morecambe 1 0 **1 0**

JAGNE, Lamin (M) 2 0
b. 28-10-97
2018–19 Morecambe 2 0
2019–20 Morecambe 0 0 **2 0**

KENYON, Alex (M) 221 8
H: 5 11 W: 11 12 b.Preston 17-7-92
2013–14 Morecambe 39 0
2014–15 Morecambe 37 3
2015–16 Morecambe 29 3
2016–17 Morecambe 19 0
2017–18 Morecambe 38 0
2018–19 Morecambe 32 1
2019–20 Morecambe 27 1 **221 8**

LAVELLE, Sam (D) 89 3
H: 6 0 W: 12 00 b. 3-10-96
Internationals: Scotland U18, U19.
2017–18 Morecambe 27 1
2018–19 Morecambe 31 1
2019–20 Morecambe 31 1 **89 3**

LEITCH-SMITH, AJ (F) 283 51
H: 5 11 W: 12 04 b.Crewe 6-3-90
2008–09 Crewe Alex 0 0
2009 *IBV* 18 5 **18 5**
2009–10 Crewe Alex 1 0
2010–11 Crewe Alex 16 5
2011–12 Crewe Alex 38 8
2012–13 Crewe Alex 28 4
2013–14 Crewe Alex 20 2 **103 19**
2014–15 Yeovil T 33 2 **33 2**
2015–16 Port Vale 37 10 **37 10**
2016–17 Shrewsbury T 16 1
2017–18 Shrewsbury T 0 0 **16 1**
2017–18 *Dundee* 28 6 **28 6**
2018–19 Morecambe 25 6
2019–20 Morecambe 23 2 **48 8**

LYNCH, Joe (M) 0 0
b. 11-10-99
2019–20 Morecambe 0 0

MBULU, Christian (D) 13 0
b. 6-8-96
2015–16 Millwall 0 0
2016–17 Millwall 0 0
2017–18 Millwall 0 0
2018–19 Motherwell 6 0 **6 0**
2019–20 Crewe Alex 4 0 **4 0**
2019–20 Morecambe 3 0 **3 0**

MENDES GOMES, Carlos (F) 31 2
b. 14-11-98
From Atletico Madrid, West Didsbury & Chorlton.
2018–19 Morecambe 15 0
2019–20 Morecambe 16 2 **31 2**

O'SULLIVAN, John (M) 159 10
H: 5 11 W: 13 01 b.Birmingham 18-9-93
Internationals: Republic of Ireland U19, U21.
2011–12 Blackburn R 0 0
2012–13 Blackburn R 1 0
2013–14 Blackburn R 0 0
2014–15 Blackburn R 2 0
2014–15 *Accrington S* 13 4
2014–15 *Barnsley* 8 0 **8 0**
2015–16 Blackburn R 2 0
2015–16 *Rochdale* 2 0 **2 0**
2015–16 *Bury* 19 0 **19 0**
2016–17 Blackburn R 0 0 **5 0**
2016–17 *Accrington S* 19 1 **32 5**
2016–17 Carlisle U 17 1
2017–18 Carlisle U 18 1 **35 2**
2018–19 Blackpool 13 0 **13 0**
2018–19 *Dundee* 11 0 **11 0**
2019–20 Morecambe 34 3 **34 3**

OATES, Rhys (D) 109 11
H: 6 0 W: 11 09 b.Pontefract 4-12-94
2012–13 Barnsley 0 0
2013–14 Barnsley 0 0
2014–15 Barnsley 9 0 **9 0**
2015–16 Hartlepool U 38 2
2016–17 Hartlepool U 26 3 **64 5**
2018–19 Morecambe 31 6
2019–20 Morecambe 5 0 **36 6**

OLD, Steven (D) 282 19
H: 6 3 W: 13 05 b. 17-2-86
Internationals: New Zealand U17, U20, U23, Full caps.
2005–06 Young Heart Manawatu 19 1 **19 1**
2006–07 Newcastle Jets 9 0 **9 0**
2007–08 Wellington Phoenix 12 1 **12 1**
2008 Macarthur Rams 4 1 **4 1**
2008–09 Kilmarnock 0 0
2009–10 Kilmarnock 10 0
2010–11 Kilmarnock 0 0 **10 0**

2010–11 *Cowdenbeath* 4 0 **4 0**
From Basingstoke T, Sutton U.
2013 Shijiazhuang Yongchang 28 1 **28 1**
2014 Ljungskile 22 4
2015 Ljungskile 24 2 **46 6**
2016 GAIS 21 0
2017 GAIS 12 1 **33 1**
2017–18 Morecambe 41 4
2018–19 Morecambe 39 2
2019–20 Morecambe 37 2 **117 8**

ROCHE, Barry (G) 575 1
H: 6 5 W: 14 08 b.Dublin 6-4-82
Internationals: Republic of Ireland U21.
1999–2000 Nottingham F 0 0
2000–01 Nottingham F 2 0
2001–02 Nottingham F 0 0
2002–03 Nottingham F 1 0
2003–04 Nottingham F 8 0
2004–05 Nottingham F 2 0 **13 0**
2005–06 Chesterfield 41 0
2006–07 Chesterfield 40 0
2007–08 Chesterfield 45 0 **126 0**
2008–09 Morecambe 46 0
2009–10 Morecambe 42 0
2010–11 Morecambe 42 0
2011–12 Morecambe 44 0
2012–13 Morecambe 42 0
2013–14 Morecambe 45 0
2014–15 Morecambe 14 0
2015–16 Morecambe 42 1
2016–17 Morecambe 41 0
2017–18 Morecambe 42 0
2018–19 Morecambe 20 0
2019–20 Morecambe 16 0 **436 1**

SLEW, Jordan (F) 138 11
H: 6 3 W: 12 11 b.Sheffield 7-9-92
Internationals: England U19.
2010–11 Sheffield U 7 2
2011–12 Sheffield U 4 1 **11 3**
2011–12 Blackburn R 1 0
2011–12 *Stevenage* 9 0 **9 0**
2012–13 Blackburn R 0 0
2012–13 *Oldham Ath* 3 0 **3 0**
2012–13 *Rotherham U* 7 0 **7 0**
2013–14 Blackburn R 0 0
2013–14 *Ross Co* 20 1 **20 1**
2014–15 Blackburn R 0 0 **1 0**
2014–15 *Port Vale* 9 2 **9 2**
2014–15 Cambridge U 13 1
2015–16 Cambridge U 10 0 **23 1**
2015–16 Chesterfield 7 0 **7 0**
2016–17 Plymouth Arg 32 4 **32 4**
2017–18 Rochdale 5 0 **5 0**
From Boston U.
2019–20 Morecambe 11 0 **11 0**

STOCKTON, Cole (F) 171 32
H: 6 1 W: 11 11 b.Huyton 13-3-94
2011–12 Tranmere R 1 0
2012–13 Tranmere R 31 3
2013–14 Tranmere R 21 2
2014–15 Tranmere R 22 4
2015–16 Tranmere R 0 0
2015–16 *Morecambe* 7 2
2016–17 Tranmere R 0 0
2016–17 *Morecambe* 19 5
2017–18 Hearts 12 9 **12 9**
2017–18 Carlisle U 12 1 **12 1**
2018–19 Tranmere R 16 1 **91 10**
2019–20 Morecambe 30 5 **56 12**

SUTTON, Ritchie (D) 119 2
H: 6 0 W: 11 04 b.Stoke-on-Trent 29-4-86
2005–06 Crewe Alex 0 0
From Stafford R, Northwich Vic, FC Halifax T, Nantwich T
2010–11 Port Vale 11 0 **11 0**
2013–14 Mansfield T 36 0
2014–15 Mansfield T 34 0 **70 0**
2018–19 Tranmere R 9 1 **9 1**
2018–19 Morecambe 14 0
2019–20 Morecambe 15 1 **29 1**

TUTTE, Andrew (M) 258 23
H: 5 9 W: 10 10 b.Huyton 21-9-90
Internationals: England U19, U20.
2007–08 Manchester C 0 0
2008–09 Manchester C 0 0
2009–10 Manchester C 0 0
2010–11 Manchester C 0 0
2010–11 *Rochdale* 7 0
2010–11 *Shrewsbury T* 2 0 **2 0**
2010–11 *Yeovil T* 15 2 **15 2**
2011–12 Rochdale 40 1
2012–13 Rochdale 37 7
2013–14 Rochdale 11 2 **95 10**
2013–14 Bury 19 1
2014–15 Bury 42 3
2015–16 Bury 22 4
2016–17 Bury 17 1
2017–18 Bury 16 0 **116 9**
2018–19 Morecambe 18 2
2019–20 Morecambe 12 0 **30 2**

WILDIG, Aaron (M) 234 16
H: 5 9 W: 11 02 b.Hereford 15-4-92
Internationals: Wales U16.
2009–10 Cardiff C 11 1
2010–11 Cardiff C 2 0
2010–11 *Hamilton A* 3 0 **3 0**
2011–12 Cardiff C 0 0 **13 1**
2011–12 *Shrewsbury T* 12 2
2012–13 Shrewsbury T 21 1
2013–14 Shrewsbury T 30 2
2014–15 Shrewsbury T 1 0 **64 5**
2014–15 *Morecambe* 9 1
2015–16 Morecambe 32 2
2016–17 Morecambe 28 2
2017–18 Morecambe 31 1
2018–19 Morecambe 26 1
2019–20 Morecambe 28 3 **154 10**

Scholars
Beverley, Jack Andrew; Da, Silva Mendes Andre Filipe; Djau, Codjovi Amilcar Adulai; Edgar, Lewis Jack; Edwards, Cole Daniel; Farrington, Callum Sean; Giacomini, Joshua Michael; Giwa, Adeyinka Oluwayesi; Greenwood, Jack; Lowe, Benjamin James; Ly, Bryan Calum; Mason, Ryan Thomas; Morton, Josh; O'Brien, Harry James Kenneth; Obasoto, Abimbola Emmanuel; Price, Freddie Connor Burrows; Shogbeni, Abdulmojeed Eniola; Spraggon, Louis Jake.

NEWCASTLE U (55)

AARONS, Rolando (M) 70 4
H: 5 9 W: 10 08 b.Kingston 16-11-95
Internationals: England U20.
2014–15 Newcastle U 4 1
2015–16 Newcastle U 10 1
2016–17 Newcastle U 4 0
2017–18 Newcastle U 4 0
2017–18 *Verona* 11 0 **11 0**
2018–19 Newcastle U 0 0
2018–19 *Liberec* 12 0 **12 0**
2018–19 *Sheffield W* 9 1 **9 1**
2019–20 Newcastle U 0 0 **22 2**
2019–20 *Wycombe W* 10 1 **10 1**
2019–20 *Motherwell* 6 0 **6 0**

ALLAN, Thomas (F) 0 0
b. 23-9-99
2019–20 Newcastle U 0 0

ALMIRON, Miguel (M) 182 34
H: 5 10 W: 11 00 b.Asuncion 13-11-93
Internationals: Paraguay U17, U20, Full caps.
2013 Cerro Porteno 6 1
2014 Cerro Porteno 14 0
2015 Cerro Porteno 19 5 **39 6**
2015 Lanus 10 0
2016 Lanus 25 3 **35 3**
2017 Atalanta 30 9
2018 Atalanta 32 12 **62 21**
2018–19 Newcastle U 10 0
2019–20 Newcastle U 36 4 **46 4**

ATSU, Christian (F) 194 22
H: 5 8 W: 10 09 b.Ada Foah 10-1-92
Internationals: Ghana Full caps.
2010–11 Porto 0 0
2011–12 Porto 0 0
2011–12 *Rio Ave* 27 6 **27 6**
2012–13 Porto 17 1 **17 1**
2013–14 Chelsea 0 0
2013–14 *Vitesse* 26 5 **26 5**
2014–15 Chelsea 0 0
2014–15 *Everton* 5 0 **5 0**
2015–16 Chelsea 0 0
2015–16 *Bournemouth* 0 0
2015–16 *Malaga* 12 2 **12 2**
2016–17 Chelsea 0 0
2016–17 *Newcastle U* 32 5
2017–18 Newcastle U 28 2
2018–19 Newcastle U 28 1
2019–20 Newcastle U 19 0 **107 8**

BARLASER, Daniel (M) 70 3
H: 6 0 W: 9 11 b.Gateshead 18-1-97
Internationals: Turkey U16, U17. England U18.
2015–16 Newcastle U 0 0
2016–17 Newcastle U 0 0
2017–18 Newcastle U 0 0
2017–18 *Crewe Alex* 4 0 **4 0**
2018–19 Newcastle U 0 0
2018–19 *Accrington S* 39 1 **39 1**
2019–20 Newcastle U 0 0
2019–20 *Rotherham U* 27 2 **27 2**

BENTALEB, Nabil (M) 131 12
H: 6 2 W: 10 09 b.Lille, France 24-11-94
Internationals: France U18. Algeria Full caps.
2012–13 Tottenham H 0 0
2013–14 Tottenham H 15 0
2014–15 Tottenham H 26 0
2015–16 Tottenham H 5 0
2016–17 Tottenham H 0 0 **46 0**
2016–17 *Schalke 04* 32 5
2017–18 Schalke 04 16 4
2018–19 Schalke 04 25 3
2019–20 Schalke 04 0 0 **73 12**
On loan from Schalke 04.
2019–20 Newcastle U 12 0 **12 0**

CARROLL, Andy (F) 280 71
H: 6 4 W: 11 00 b.Gateshead 6-1-89
Internationals: England U19, U21, Full caps.
2006–07 Newcastle U 4 0
2007–08 Newcastle U 4 0
2007–08 *Preston NE* 11 1 **11 1**
2008–09 Newcastle U 14 3
2009–10 Newcastle U 39 17
2010–11 Newcastle U 19 11
2010–11 Liverpool 7 2
2011–12 Liverpool 35 4
2012–13 Liverpool 2 0 **44 6**
2012–13 *West Ham U* 24 7
2013–14 West Ham U 15 2
2014–15 West Ham U 14 5
2015–16 West Ham U 27 9
2016–17 West Ham U 18 7
2017–18 West Ham U 16 3
2018–19 West Ham U 12 0 **126 33**
2019–20 Newcastle U 19 0 **99 31**

CASS, Lewis (D) 0 0
b. 27-2-00
2018–19 Newcastle U 0 0
2019–20 Newcastle U 0 0

CHARMAN, Luke (F) 0 0
b.Durham 9-12-97
2018–19 Newcastle U 0 0
2018–19 *Accrington S* 0 0
2019–20 Newcastle U 0 0

CLARK, Ciaran (D) 213 17
H: 6 2 W: 12 00 b.Harrow 26-9-89
Internationals: England U17, U18, U19, U20. Republic of Ireland Full caps.
2008–09 Aston Villa 0 0
2009–10 Aston Villa 1 0
2010–11 Aston Villa 19 3
2011–12 Aston Villa 15 1
2012–13 Aston Villa 29 1
2013–14 Aston Villa 27 0
2014–15 Aston Villa 25 1
2015–16 Aston Villa 18 1 **134 7**
2016–17 Newcastle U 34 3
2017–18 Newcastle U 20 2
2018–19 Newcastle U 11 3
2019–20 Newcastle U 14 2 **79 10**

COLBACK, Jack (M) 312 17
H: 5 9 W: 11 05 b.Killingworth 24-10-89
Internationals: England U20.
2007–08 Sunderland 0 0
2008–09 Sunderland 0 0
2009–10 Sunderland 1 0
2009–10 *Ipswich T* 37 4
2010–11 Sunderland 11 0
2010–11 *Ipswich T* 13 0 **50 4**
2011–12 Sunderland 35 1
2012–13 Sunderland 35 0
2013–14 Sunderland 33 3 **115 4**
2014–15 Newcastle U 35 4
2015–16 Newcastle U 29 1
2016–17 Newcastle U 29 0
2017–18 Newcastle U 0 0
2017–18 *Nottingham F* 16 1
2018–19 Newcastle U 0 0
2018–19 *Nottingham F* 38 3 **54 4**
2019–20 Newcastle U 0 0 **93 5**

DARLOW, Karl (G) 168 0
H: 6 1 W: 12 05 b.Northampton 8-10-90
2009–10 Nottingham F 0 0
2010–11 Nottingham F 1 0
2011–12 Nottingham F 0 0
2012–13 Nottingham F 20 0

2012–13	*Walsall*	9	0	**9**	**0**
2013–14	Nottingham F	43	0		
2014–15	Newcastle U	0	0		
2014–15	*Nottingham F*	42	0	**106**	**0**
2015–16	Newcastle U	9	0		
2016–17	Newcastle U	34	0		
2017–18	Newcastle U	10	0		
2018–19	Newcastle U	0	0		
2019–20	Newcastle U	0	0	**53**	**0**

DUBRAVKA, Martin (G) 291 0
H: 6 3 W: 13 01 b.Zilina 15-1-89
Internationals: Slovakia U19, U21, Full caps.

2008–09	Zilina	1	0		
2009–10	Zilina	26	0		
2010–11	Zilina	24	0		
2011–12	Zilina	8	0		
2012–13	Zilina	26	0		
2013–14	Zilina	13	0	**98**	**0**
2013–14	Esbjerg	15	0		
2014–15	Esbjerg	33	0		
2015–16	Esbjerg	18	0	**66**	**0**
2016–17	Slovan Liberec	28	0	**28**	**0**
2017–18	Sparta Prague	11	0	**11**	**0**
2017–18	*Newcastle U*	12	0		
2018–19	Newcastle U	38	0		
2019–20	Newcastle U	38	0	**88**	**0**

DUMMETT, Paul (D) 203 4
H: 5 10 W: 10 02 b.Newcastle 26-9-91
Internationals: Wales U21, Full caps.

2010–11	Newcastle U	0	0		
2011–12	Newcastle U	0	0		
2012–13	Newcastle U	0	0		
2012–13	*St Mirren*	30	2	**30**	**2**
2013–14	Newcastle U	18	1		
2014–15	Newcastle U	25	0		
2015–16	Newcastle U	23	1		
2016–17	Newcastle U	45	0		
2017–18	Newcastle U	20	0		
2018–19	Newcastle U	26	0		
2019–20	Newcastle U	16	0	**173**	**2**

ELLIOT, Rob (G) 162 0
H: 6 3 W: 14 10 b.Chatham 30-4-86
Internationals: Republic of Ireland U19, Full caps.

2004–05	Charlton Ath	0	0		
2004–05	*Notts Co*	4	0	**4**	**0**
2005–06	Charlton Ath	0	0		
2006–07	Charlton Ath	0	0		
2006–07	*Accrington S*	7	0	**7**	**0**
2007–08	Charlton Ath	1	0		
2008–09	Charlton Ath	23	0		
2009–10	Charlton Ath	33	0		
2010–11	Charlton Ath	35	0		
2011–12	Charlton Ath	4	0	**96**	**0**
2011–12	Newcastle U	0	0		
2012–13	Newcastle U	10	0		
2013–14	Newcastle U	2	0		
2014–15	Newcastle U	3	0		
2015–16	Newcastle U	21	0		
2016–17	Newcastle U	3	0		
2017–18	Newcastle U	16	0		
2018–19	Newcastle U	0	0		
2019–20	Newcastle U	0	0	**55**	**0**

FERNANDEZ, Federico (D) 286 8
H: 6 3 W: 13 01 b.Tres Algarrobos 21-2-89
Internationals: Argentina U20, Full caps.

2008–09	Estudiantes	14	2		
2009–10	Estudiantes	12	0		
2010–11	Estudiantes	33	1	**59**	**3**
2011–12	Napoli	16	0		
2012–13	Napoli	2	0		
2012–13	*Getafe*	14	1	**14**	**1**
2013–14	Napoli	26	0	**44**	**0**
2014–15	Swansea C	28	0		
2015–16	Swansea C	32	1		
2016–17	Swansea C	27	0		
2017–18	Swansea C	30	1		
2018–19	Swansea C	1	0	**118**	**2**
2018–19	Newcastle U	19	0		
2019–20	Newcastle U	32	2	**51**	**2**

GAYLE, Dwight (F) 237 91
H: 5 10 W: 11 07 b.Walthamstow 20-10-89

2011–12	Dagenham & R	0	0		
2012–13	Dagenham & R	18	7	**18**	**7**
2012–13	Peterborough U	29	13	**29**	**13**
2013–14	Crystal Palace	23	7		
2014–15	Crystal Palace	25	5		
2015–16	Crystal Palace	16	3	**64**	**15**
2016–17	Newcastle U	32	23		
2017–18	Newcastle U	35	6		
2018–19	Newcastle U	0	0		
2018–19	*WBA*	39	23	**39**	**23**
2019–20	Newcastle U	20	4	**87**	**33**

GIBSON, Liam (D) 22 0
H: 6 1 W: 12 08 b.Stanley 25-4-97

2015–16	Newcastle U	0	0		
2016–17	Newcastle U	0	0		
2017–18	Newcastle U	0	0		
2018–19	Newcastle U	0	0		
2018–19	Accrington S	5	0	**5**	**0**
2019–20	*Grimsby T*	17	0	**17**	**0**
2019–20	Newcastle U	0	0		

HARKER, Nathan (G) 0 0
b. 5-11-98

2018–19	Newcastle U	0	0		
2019–20	Newcastle U	0	0		

HAYDEN, Isaac (D) 131 6
H: 6 2 W: 12 06 b.Chelmsford 22-3-95
Internationals: England U16, U17, U18, U19, U20, U21.

2011–12	Arsenal	0	0		
2012–13	Arsenal	0	0		
2013–14	Arsenal	0	0		
2014–15	Arsenal	0	0		
2015–16	Arsenal	0	0		
2015–16	*Hull C*	18	1	**18**	**1**
2016–17	Newcastle U	33	2		
2017–18	Newcastle U	26	1		
2018–19	Newcastle U	25	1		
2019–20	Newcastle U	29	1	**113**	**5**

JOELINTON, de Lira (F) 139 27
b. 14-8-96
Internationals: Brazil U17.

2014	Sport Recife	7	2		
2015	Sport Recife	5	1	**12**	**3**
2015–16	Hoffenheim	1	0		
2016–17	Hoffenheim	0	0		
2016–17	Rapid Vienna	33	8		
2017–18	Hoffenheim	0	0		
2017–18	Rapid Vienna	27	7	**60**	**15**
2018–19	Hoffenheim	28	7	**29**	**7**
2019–20	Newcastle U	38	2	**38**	**2**

KI, Sung-Yeung (M) 253 24
H: 6 2 W: 11 10 b.Gwangju 24-1-89
Internationals: South Korea U17, U20, U23, Full caps.

2009–10	Celtic	10	0		
2010–11	Celtic	26	3		
2011–12	Celtic	30	6	**66**	**9**
2012–13	Swansea C	29	0		
2013–14	Swansea C	1	0		
2013–14	*Sunderland*	27	3	**27**	**3**
2014–15	Swansea C	33	8		
2015–16	Swansea C	28	2		
2016–17	Swansea C	23	0		
2017–18	Swansea C	25	2	**139**	**12**
2018–19	Newcastle U	18	0		
2019–20	Newcastle U	3	0	**21**	**0**

Transferred to Mallorca, January 2020.

KRAFTH, Emil (D) 194 4
b.Ljungby 2-8-94
Internationals: Sweden U17, U19, U21, Full caps.

2011	Osters	24	0	**24**	**0**
2012	Helsingborgs	9	0		
2013	Helsingborgs	27	1		
2014	Helsingborgs	28	1		
2015	Helsingborgs	12	1	**76**	**3**
2015–16	Bologna	4	0		
2016–17	Bologna	26	0		
2017–18	Bologna	12	0	**42**	**0**
2018–19	Amiens	35	1	**35**	**1**
2019–20	Newcastle U	17	0	**17**	**0**

LASCELLES, Jamaal (D) 215 13
H: 6 2 W: 13 01 b.Derby 11-11-93
Internationals: England U18, U19, U20, U21.

2010–11	Nottingham F	0	0		
2011–12	Nottingham F	1	0		
2011–12	*Stevenage*	7	1	**7**	**1**
2012–13	Nottingham F	2	0		
2013–14	Nottingham F	29	2		
2014–15	Newcastle U	0	0		
2014–15	*Nottingham F*	26	1	**58**	**3**
2015–16	Newcastle U	18	2		
2016–17	Newcastle U	43	3		
2017–18	Newcastle U	33	3		
2018–19	Newcastle U	32	0		
2019–20	Newcastle U	24	1	**150**	**9**

LAZAAR, Achraf (D) 137 5
H: 5 8 W: 10 08 b.Casablanca 22-1-92
Internationals: Morocco Full caps.

2011–12	Varese	0	0		
2012–13	Varese	21	0		
2013–14	Varese	17	0	**38**	**0**
2013–14	Palermo	14	0		
2014–15	Palermo	29	2		
2015–16	Palermo	30	1		
2016–17	Palermo	0	0	**73**	**3**
2016–17	Newcastle U	4	0		
2017–18	Newcastle U	0	0		
2017–18	*Benevento*	9	1	**9**	**1**
2018–19	Newcastle U	0	0		
2018–19	*Sheffield W*	4	0	**4**	**0**
2019–20	Newcastle U	0	0	**4**	**0**
2019–20	*Cosenza*	9	1	**9**	**1**

LAZARO, Valentino (F) 166 17
b.Graz 24-3-96
Internationals: Austria U16, U17, U18, U21, Full caps.

2012–13	Red Bull Salzburg	5	0		
2013–14	Red Bull Salzburg	11	2		
2013–14	*Liefering*	3	0	**3**	**0**
2014–15	Red Bull Salzburg	25	4		
2015–16	Red Bull Salzburg	17	2		
2016–17	Red Bull Salzburg	29	3		
2017–18	Red Bull Salzburg	0	0	**87**	**11**
2017–18	Hertha Berlin	26	2		
2018–19	Hertha Berlin	31	3	**57**	**5**
2019–20	Inter Milan	6	0	**6**	**0**

On loan from Inter Milan.

2019–20	Newcastle U	13	1	**13**	**1**

LEJEUNE, Florian (D) 223 15
H: 6 2 W: 12 11 b.Paris 20-5-91
Internationals: France U20.

2008–09	Agde	3	2	**3**	**2**
2009–10	Istres	14	0		
2010–11	Istres	28	3	**42**	**3**
2011–12	Villarreal	2	0		
2012–13	Villarreal	3	0	**5**	**0**
2012–13	Brest	10	0		
2013–14	Brest	11	0	**21**	**0**
2014–15	Girona	38	4		
2015–16	Manchester C	0	0		
2015–16	*Girona*	38	3	**76**	**7**
2016–17	Eibar	34	1	**34**	**1**
2017–18	Newcastle U	24	0		
2018–19	Newcastle U	12	0		
2019–20	Newcastle U	6	2	**42**	**2**

LONGSTAFF, Matthew (M) 9 2
b. 21-3-00
Internationals: England U20.

2019–20	Newcastle U	9	2	**9**	**2**

LONGSTAFF, Sean (M) 106 16
H: 5 11 W: 10 03 b.North Shields 30-10-97

2016–17	Newcastle U	0	0		
2016–17	*Kilmarnock*	16	3		
2016–17	Newcastle U	0	0		
2016–17	*Kilmarnock*	16	3	**32**	**6**
2017–18	Newcastle U	0	0		
2017–18	*Blackpool*	42	8	**42**	**8**
2018–19	Newcastle U	9	1		
2019–20	Newcastle U	23	1	**32**	**2**

MANQUILLO, Javier (D) 127 1
H: 5 11 W: 12 04 b.Madrid 5-5-94
Internationals: Spain U16, U17, U18, U19, U20, U21.

2012–13	Atletico Madrid	3	0		
2013–14	Atletico Madrid	3	0		
2014–15	Atletico Madrid	0	0		
2014–15	*Liverpool*	10	0	**10**	**0**
2015–16	Atletico Madrid	0	0		
2015–16	*Marseille*	31	0	**31**	**0**
2016–17	Atletico Madrid	0	0	**6**	**0**
2016–17	*Sunderland*	20	1	**20**	**1**
2017–18	Newcastle U	21	0		
2018–19	Newcastle U	18	0		
2019–20	Newcastle U	21	0	**60**	**0**

MURPHY, Jacob (M) 199 37
H: 5 9 W: 11 03 b.Wembley 24-2-95
Internationals: England U18, U19, U20, U21.

2013–14	Norwich C	0	0		
2013–14	*Swindon T*	6	0	**6**	**0**
2013–14	*Southend U*	7	1	**7**	**1**
2014–15	Norwich C	0	0		
2014–15	*Blackpool*	9	2	**9**	**2**
2014–15	*Scunthorpe U*	3	0	**3**	**0**
2014–15	*Colchester U*	11	4	**11**	**4**
2015–16	Norwich C	0	0		
2015–16	*Coventry C*	40	9	**40**	**9**
2016–17	Norwich C	37	9	**37**	**9**
2017–18	Newcastle U	25	1		
2018–19	Newcastle U	9	0		
2018–19	*WBA*	13	2	**13**	**2**
2019–20	Newcastle U	0	0	**34**	**1**
2019–20	*Sheffield W*	39	9	**39**	**9**

MUTO, Yoshinori (M) 152 44
H: 5 10 W: 10 12 b.Tokyo 15-7-92
Internationals: Japan Full caps.

Season	Club				
2013	FC Tokyo	1	0		
2014	FC Tokyo	33	13		
2015	FC Tokyo	17	10	**51**	**23**
2015–16	Mainz 05	20	7		
2016–17	Mainz 05	29	5		
2017–18	Mainz 05	27	8	**76**	**20**
2018–19	Newcastle U	17	1		
2019–20	Newcastle U	8	0	**25**	**1**

RITCHIE, Matt (M) 428 90
H: 5 8 W: 11 00 b.Gosport 10-9-89
Internationals: Scotland Full caps.

Season	Club				
2008–09	Portsmouth	0	0		
2008–09	*Dagenham & R*	37	11	**37**	**11**
2009–10	Portsmouth	2	0		
2009–10	*Notts Co*	16	3	**16**	**3**
2009–10	*Swindon T*	4	0		
2010–11	Portsmouth	5	0	**7**	**0**
2010–11	Swindon T	36	7		
2011–12	Swindon T	40	10		
2012–13	Swindon T	27	9	**107**	**26**
2012–13	Bournemouth	17	3		
2013–14	Bournemouth	30	9		
2014–15	Bournemouth	46	15		
2015–16	Bournemouth	37	4	**130**	**31**
2016–17	Newcastle U	42	12		
2017–18	Newcastle U	35	3		
2018–19	Newcastle U	36	2		
2019–20	Newcastle U	18	2	**131**	**19**

SAINT-MAXIMIN, Allan (F) 153 16
b.Chatenay-Malabry 12-3-97
Internationals: France U16, U17, U20, U21.

Season	Club				
2013–14	Saint-Etienne	3	0		
2014–15	Saint-Etienne	9	0		
2015–16	Saint-Etienne	0	0		
2015–16	*Hannover 96*	16	1	**16**	**1**
2016–17	Saint-Etienne	0	0	**12**	**0**
2016–17	*Bastia*	34	3	**34**	**3**
2017–18	Monaco	1	0	**1**	**0**
2017–18	Nice	30	3		
2018–19	Nice	34	6		
2019–20	Nice	0	0	**64**	**9**
2019–20	Newcastle U	26	3	**26**	**3**

SAIVET, Henri (M) 225 24
H: 5 9 W: 10 08 b.Dakar 26-10-90
Internationals: France U16, U17, U18, U21. Senegal Full caps.

Season	Club				
2007–08	Bordeaux	1	0		
2008–09	Bordeaux	1	0		
2009–10	Bordeaux	3	0		
2010–11	Bordeaux	6	0		
2010–11	*Angers*	18	3	**18**	**3**
2011–12	Bordeaux	24	1		
2012–13	Bordeaux	34	8		
2013–14	Bordeaux	33	6		
2014–15	Bordeaux	14	0		
2015–16	Bordeaux	18	2	**134**	**17**
2015–16	Newcastle U	4	0		
2016–17	Newcastle U	0	0		
2016–17	*Saint-Etienne*	27	1	**27**	**1**
2017–18	Newcastle U	1	1		
2017–18	*Sivasspor*	12	0	**12**	**0**
2018–19	Newcastle U	0	0		
2018–19	*Bursaspor*	29	2	**29**	**2**
2019–20	Newcastle U	0	0	**5**	**1**

SCHAR, Fabian (D) 174 18
H: 6 1 W: 13 05 b.Wil 20-12-91
Internationals: Switzerland U20, U21, U23, Full caps.

Season	Club				
2012–13	FC Basel	21	4		
2013–14	FC Basel	22	4		
2014–15	FC Basel	30	1	**73**	**9**
2015–16	1899 Hoffenheim	24	1		
2016–17	1899 Hoffenheim	6	0	**30**	**1**
2017–18	Deportivo La Coruna	25	2	**25**	**2**
2018–19	Newcastle U	24	4		
2019–20	Newcastle U	22	2	**46**	**6**

SCOTT, Kyle (M) 14 2
H: 5 8 W: 9 06 b.Bath 22-12-97
Internationals: England U16, Republic of Ireland U17, USA U18, U20.

Season	Club				
2017–18	Chelsea	0	0		
2018–19	Chelsea	0	0		
2018–19	*Telstar*	14	2	**14**	**2**
2019–20	Newcastle U	0	0		

SHELVEY, Jonjo (M) 307 38
H: 6 1 W: 11 02 b.Romford 27-2-92
Internationals: England U16, U17, U19, U21, Full caps.

Season	Club				
2007–08	Charlton Ath	2	0		
2008–09	Charlton Ath	16	3		
2009–10	Charlton Ath	24	4	**42**	**7**
2010–11	Liverpool	15	0		
2011–12	Liverpool	13	1		
2011–12	*Blackpool*	10	6	**10**	**6**
2012–13	Liverpool	19	1	**47**	**2**
2013–14	Swansea C	32	6		
2014–15	Swansea C	31	3		
2015–16	Swansea C	16	1	**79**	**10**
2015–16	Newcastle U	15	0		
2016–17	Newcastle U	42	5		
2017–18	Newcastle U	30	1		
2018–19	Newcastle U	16	1		
2019–20	Newcastle U	26	6	**129**	**13**

SORENSEN, Elias (F) 9 0
b. 18-9-99
Internationals: Denmark U17, U19, U21.
From HB Koge.

Season	Club				
2018–19	Newcastle U	0	0		
2018–19	*Blackpool*	1	0	**1**	**0**
2019–20	Newcastle U	0	0		
2019–20	*Carlisle U*	8	0	**8**	**0**

STERRY, Jamie (D) 29 0
H: 5 11 W: 11 00 b.Newcastle upon Tyne 21-11-95

Season	Club				
2014–15	Newcastle U	0	0		
2015–16	Newcastle U	1	0		
2016–17	Newcastle U	2	0		
2016–17	*Coventry C*	16	0	**16**	**0**
2017–18	Newcastle U	0	0		
2017–18	*Crewe Alex*	9	0		
2018–19	Newcastle U	0	0		
2018–19	*Crewe Alex*	1	0	**10**	**0**
2019–20	Newcastle U	0	0	**3**	**0**

TURNER, Jake (G) 0 0
b.Wilmslow 25-2-99
Internationals: England U18, U19.

Season	Club				
2016–17	Bolton W	0	0		
2017–18	Bolton W	0	0		
2018–19	Bolton W	0	0		
2019–20	Newcastle U	0	0		
2019–20	*Morecambe*	0	0		

WATTS, Kelland (M) 24 1
b. 3-11-99
Internationals: England U19.

Season	Club				
2018–19	Newcastle U	0	0		
2019–20	*Stevenage*	16	0	**16**	**0**
2019–20	Newcastle U	1	0	**1**	**0**
2019–20	*Mansfield T*	7	1	**7**	**1**

WILLEMS, Jetro (D) 223 13
b.Rotterdam 30-3-94
Internationals: Netherlands U17, U19, U21, Full caps.

Season	Club				
2010–11	Sparta Rotterdam	13	0		
2011–12	Sparta Rotterdam	3	0	**16**	**0**
2011–12	PSV Eindhoven	20	1		
2012–13	PSV Eindhoven	26	0		
2013–14	PSV Eindhoven	28	4		
2014–15	PSV Eindhoven	30	2		
2015–16	PSV Eindhoven	15	2		
2016–17	PSV Eindhoven	24	2	**143**	**11**
2017–18	Eintracht Frankfurt	23	0		
2018–19	Eintracht Frankfurt	22	0	**45**	**0**
2019–20	Eintracht Frankfurt	0	0		

On loan from Eintracht Frankfurt.

Season	Club				
2019–20	Newcastle U	19	2	**19**	**2**

WOODMAN, Freddie (G) 73 0
H: 6 1 W: 10 12 b.London 4-3-97
Internationals: England U16, U17, U18, U19, U20, U21.

Season	Club				
2014–15	Newcastle U	0	0		
2014–15	*Hartlepool U*	0	0		
2015–16	Newcastle U	0	0		
2015–16	*Crawley T*	11	0	**11**	**0**
2016–17	Newcastle U	0	0		
2016–17	*Kilmarnock*	14	0	**14**	**0**
2017–18	Newcastle U	0	0		
2017–18	*Aberdeen*	5	0	**5**	**0**
2018–19	Newcastle U	0	0		
2019–20	*Swansea C*	43	0	**43**	**0**

YEDLIN, DeAndre (D) 192 5
H: 5 9 W: 11 07 b.Seattle 9-7-93
Internationals: USA U20, Full caps.

Season	Club				
2013	Seattle Sounders	33	2		
2014	Seattle Sounders	29	0	**62**	**2**
2014–15	Tottenham H	1	0		
2015–16	Tottenham H	0	0	**1**	**0**
2015–16	*Sunderland*	23	0	**23**	**0**
2016–17	Newcastle U	27	1		
2017–18	Newcastle U	34	0		
2018–19	Newcastle U	29	1		
2019–20	Newcastle U	16	1	**106**	**3**

YOUNG, Jack (M) 0 0

Season	Club				
2019–20	Newcastle U	0	0		

Players retained or with offer of contract
Anderson, Elliot Junior; Bailey, Owen John Edward; Barrett, Ryan Thomas; Flaherty, Stanley; Francillette, Ludwig Georges; Langley, Daniel David; Longelo-Mbule, Rosaire; McEntee, Oisin Michael; Sangare, Mohammed; Toure, Fode Yannick; Walters, Oliver Reece; White, Joe Peter; Wilson, Adam Ayiro.

Scholars
Brannen, Lewis Paul; Brown, William George; Carlyon, Nathan Matthew; De Bolle, Lucas; Ebanks, Tai Graham; Gamblin, Lucas Ralph; Gilchrist, Josh Gordon; Harrison, Joshua; Marshall, Oliver Joshua; Midgley, Thomas Jack; Oliver, Joe Alexander; Reed, Kain; Rounsfell, George David Alan; Scott, Joshua; Stephenson, Dylan Jay; Swailes, Jude Christopher; Thomson, Regan Alexander.

NEWPORT CO (56)

ABRAHAMS, Tristan (F) 73 10
H: 5 9 W: 10 08 b.Lewisham 29-12-98

Season	Club				
2016–17	Leyton Orient	9	2	**9**	**2**
2017–18	Norwich C	0	0		
2018–19	Norwich C	0	0		
2018–19	*Exeter C*	16	1	**16**	**1**
2018–19	*Yeovil T*	15	3	**15**	**3**
2019–20	Newport Co	33	4	**33**	**4**

AMOND, Padraig (F) 446 121
H: 5 11 W: 12 05 b.Carlow 15-4-88
Internationals: Republic of Ireland U21.

Season	Club				
2006	Shamrock R	10	1		
2007	Shamrock R	6	1		
2007	*Kildare Co*	13	5	**13**	**5**
2008	Shamrock R	26	9		
2009	Shamrock R	20	4	**62**	**15**
2010	Sligo R	27	17	**27**	**17**
2010–11	Pacos	17	0	**17**	**0**
2011–12	Accrington S	42	7		
2012–13	Accrington S	36	9		
2013–14	Accrington S	0	0	**78**	**16**
2013–14	Morecambe	45	11		
2014–15	Morecambe	37	8	**82**	**19**

From Grimsby T.

Season	Club				
2016–17	Hartlepool U	46	14	**46**	**14**
2017–18	Newport Co	43	13		
2018–19	Newport Co	45	14		
2019–20	Newport Co	33	8	**121**	**35**

AZEEZ, Adebayo (F) 203 22
H: 6 0 W: 12 07 b.Orpington 8-1-94
Internationals: England U19.

Season	Club				
2012–13	Charlton Ath	0	0		
2012–13	*Wycombe W*	4	0	**4**	**0**
2012–13	*Leyton Orient*	1	0	**1**	**0**
2013–14	Charlton Ath	0	0		
2013–14	*Torquay U*	9	2	**9**	**2**
2013–14	*Dagenham & R*	15	3	**15**	**3**
2014–15	AFC Wimbledon	43	5		
2015–16	AFC Wimbledon	42	7	**85**	**12**
2016–17	Partick Thistle	38	2	**38**	**2**
2017–18	Cambridge U	13	0		
2018–19	Cambridge U	26	2	**39**	**2**
2018–19	Newport Co	12	1		
2019–20	Newport Co	0	0	**12**	**1**

BAKER, Ashley (D) 16 0
b. 30-10-96
Internationals: Wales U19, U21.

Season	Club				
2017–18	Sheffield W	1	0		
2018–19	Sheffield W	11	0		
2019–20	Sheffield W	0	0	**12**	**0**
2019–20	Newport Co	4	0	**4**	**0**

BENNETT, Scott (D) 294 23
H: 5 10 W: 12 10 b.Newquay 30-11-90

Season	Club				
2008–09	Exeter C	0	0		
2009–10	Exeter C	0	0		
2010–11	Exeter C	1	0		
2011–12	Exeter C	15	3		
2012–13	Exeter C	43	6		
2013–14	Exeter C	45	6		
2014–15	Exeter C	28	3	**132**	**18**
2015–16	Notts Co	6	0	**6**	**0**
2015–16	*Newport Co*	12	0		
2015–16	*York C*	11	0	**11**	**0**
2016–17	Newport Co	39	0		
2017–18	Newport Co	28	2		
2018–19	Newport Co	38	2		
2019–20	Newport Co	28	1	**145**	**5**

COLLINS, Lewis (M) **6 0**
b.Newport 9-5-01
Internationals: Wales U17, U19.
2017–18 Newport Co 0 0
2018–19 Newport Co 0 0
2019–20 Newport Co 6 0 **6 0**

DEMETRIOU, Mickey (D) **187 18**
b.Durrington 12-3-90
Internationals: England C.
2014–15 Shrewsbury T 42 3
2015–16 Shrewsbury T 1 0
2015–16 *Cambridge U* 15 0 **15 0**
2016–17 Shrewsbury T 0 0 **43 3**
2016–17 Newport Co 17 4
2017–18 Newport Co 46 7
2018–19 Newport Co 45 4
2019–20 Newport Co 21 0 **129 15**

DOLAN, Matthew (M) **225 15**
b.Hartlepool 11-2-93
2010–11 Middlesbrough 0 0
2011–12 Middlesbrough 0 0
2012–13 Middlesbrough 0 0
2012–13 *Yeovil T* 8 1
2013–14 Middlesbrough 0 0
2013–14 *Hartlepool U* 20 2
2013–14 *Bradford C* 11 0
2014–15 Bradford C 13 0 **24 0**
2014–15 *Hartlepool U* 2 0 **22 2**
2015–16 Yeovil T 39 3
2016–17 Yeovil T 38 4 **85 8**
2017–18 Newport Co 40 3
2018–19 Newport Co 32 2
2019–20 Newport Co 22 0 **94 5**

EKPITETA, Marvel (D) **0 0**
b.London 26-8-95
From North Greenford, AFC Hayes, Chelmsford C, Heybridge Swifts, Bishop's Stortford, East Thurrock U, Wealdstone, Hungerford T.
2019–20 Newport Co 0 0

EVANS, Ioan (M) **0 0**
2019–20 Newport Co 0 0

FOULSTON, Jay (D) **0 0**
b. 27-11-00
2017–18 Newport Co 0 0
2018–19 Newport Co 0 0
2019–20 Newport Co 0 0

FRANKS, Fraser (D) **151 10**
H: 6 0 W: 10 12 b.Hammersmith 22-11-90
Internationals: England C.
2009–10 Brentford 0 0
2011–12 AFC Wimbledon 4 0 **4 0**
2014–15 Luton T 13 0 **13 0**
2015–16 Stevenage 38 3
2016–17 Stevenage 41 3
2017–18 Stevenage 30 1 **109 7**
2018–19 Newport Co 25 3
2019–20 Newport Co 0 0 **25 3**

GEORGE, Ryan (M) **0 0**
b. 27-11-01
2019–20 Newport Co 0 0

HAYNES, Ryan (D) **136 2**
H: 5 7 W: 10 10 b.Northampton 27-9-95
2012–13 Coventry C 1 0
2013–14 Coventry C 2 0
2014–15 Coventry C 26 1
2015–16 Coventry C 9 0
2015–16 *Cambridge U* 10 0 **10 0**
2016–17 Coventry C 19 0
2017–18 Coventry C 21 0 **78 1**
2018–19 Shrewsbury T 16 0 **16 0**
2019–20 Newport Co 32 1 **32 1**

HILLIER, Ryan (F) **0 0**
2019–20 Newport Co 0 0

HOWKINS, Kyle (D) **46 1**
H: 6 5 W: 12 11 b.Walsall 4-5-96
2015–16 WBA 0 0
2016–17 WBA 0 0
2016–17 *Mansfield T* 15 0 **15 0**
2017–18 WBA 0 0
2017–18 *Cambridge U* 2 0 **2 0**
2017–18 *Port Vale* 10 0
2018–19 WBA 0 0
2018–19 *Port Vale* 3 0 **13 0**
2019–20 Newport Co 16 1 **16 1**

JEFFERIES, Dom (M) **0 0**
2019–20 Newport Co 0 0

JONES, Callum (D) **0 0**
2019–20 Newport Co 0 0

KING, Tom (G) **72 0**
H: 6 1 b.Plymouth 9-3-95
Internationals: England U17.
2011–12 Crystal Palace 0 0
2012–13 Crystal Palace 0 0
2013–14 Crystal Palace 0 0
2014–15 Millwall 0 0
2015–16 Millwall 0 0
2016–17 Millwall 11 0
2017–18 Millwall 0 0
2017–18 *Stevenage* 18 0 **18 0**
2018–19 Millwall 0 0 **11 0**
2018–19 *AFC Wimbledon* 12 0 **12 0**
2019–20 Newport Co 31 0 **31 0**

LABADIE, Joss (M) **287 38**
H: 5 7 W: 11 02 b.Croydon 31-8-90
2008–09 WBA 0 0
2008–09 *Shrewsbury T* 1 0
2009–10 WBA 0 0
2009–10 *Shrewsbury T* 13 5 **14 5**
2009–10 *Cheltenham T* 11 0 **11 0**
2009–10 *Tranmere R* 9 3
2010–11 Tranmere R 34 2
2011–12 Tranmere R 27 5 **70 10**
2012–13 Notts Co 24 2
2012–13 *Torquay U* 7 4
2013–14 Notts Co 15 1 **39 3**
2013–14 *Torquay U* 10 1 **17 5**
2014–15 Dagenham & R 24 2
2015–16 Dagenham & R 28 4 **52 6**
2016–17 Newport Co 19 3
2017–18 Newport Co 25 3
2018–19 Newport Co 13 0
2019–20 Newport Co 27 3 **84 9**

LEADBITTER, Daniel (D) **109 0**
H: 6 0 W: 11 00 b.Newcastle upon Tyne 17-10-90
2011–12 Torquay U 2 0
2012–13 Torquay U 13 0 **15 0**
From Hereford U.
2015–16 Bristol R 33 0
2016–17 Bristol R 30 0
2017–18 Bristol R 17 0
2018–19 Bristol R 11 0 **91 0**
2019–20 Newport Co 3 0 **3 0**

MATT, Jamille (F) **217 47**
H: 6 1 W: 11 11 b.Walsall 20-10-89
2012–13 Fleetwood T 14 3
2013–14 Fleetwood T 25 8
2014–15 Fleetwood T 0 0
2015–16 Fleetwood T 17 3 **56 14**
2015–16 *Stevenage* 8 1 **8 1**
2015–16 *Plymouth Arg* 11 5 **11 5**
2016–17 Blackpool 32 3
2017–18 Blackpool 0 0 **32 3**
2017–18 *Grimsby T* 34 4 **34 4**
2018–19 Newport Co 43 14
2019–20 Newport Co 33 6 **76 20**

O'BRIEN, Mark (D) **160 4**
H: 5 11 W: 12 02 b.Dublin 20-11-92
Internationals: Republic of Ireland U19.
2008–09 Derby Co 1 0
2009–10 Derby Co 0 0
2010–11 Derby Co 2 0
2011–12 Derby Co 20 0
2012–13 Derby Co 9 0
2013–14 Derby Co 0 0 **32 0**
2014–15 Motherwell 19 0 **19 0**
2015–16 Luton T 6 0 **6 0**
From Southport.
2016–17 Newport Co 20 1
2017–18 Newport Co 28 0
2018–19 Newport Co 34 2
2019–20 Newport Co 21 1 **103 4**

POLEON, Dominic (F) **211 32**
H: 6 3 W: 12 13 b.Newham 7-9-93
2012–13 Leeds U 6 2
2012–13 *Bury* 7 2 **7 2**
2012–13 *Sheffield U* 7 0 **7 0**
2013–14 Leeds U 19 1
2014–15 Leeds U 4 0 **29 3**
2014–15 Oldham Ath 35 4
2015–16 Oldham Ath 25 4 **60 8**
2016–17 AFC Wimbledon 41 8 **41 8**
2017–18 Bradford C 32 6 **32 6**
2018–19 Crawley T 30 5 **30 5**
2019–20 Newport Co 5 0 **5 0**

SHEEHAN, Josh (M) **125 12**
H: 6 0 W: 11 11 b.Pembrey 30-3-95
Internationals: Wales U19, U21.
2013–14 Swansea C 0 0
2014–15 Swansea C 0 0
2014–15 *Yeovil T* 13 0
2015–16 Swansea C 0 0
2015–16 *Yeovil T* 13 2 **26 2**
2016–17 Swansea C 0 0
2016–17 *Newport Co* 20 5
2017–18 Newport Co 13 2
2018–19 Newport Co 33 1
2019–20 Newport Co 33 2 **99 10**

STOJSAVLJEVIC, Lazar (D) **0 0**
From Woking.
2018–19 Millwall 0 0
2019–20 Newport Co 0 0
Transferred to Vojvodina, January 2020.

TOURAY, Momodou (F) **1 0**
H: 5 11 W: 10 06 b. 30-7-99
Internationals: Wales U18, U19, U21.
2016–17 Newport Co 0 0
2017–18 Newport Co 1 0
2018–19 Newport Co 0 0
2019–20 Newport Co 0 0 **1 0**

TOWNSEND, Nick (G) **24 0**
H: 5 11 W: 13 11 b.Solihull 1-11-94
2012–13 Birmingham C 0 0
2013–14 Birmingham C 0 0
2014–15 Birmingham C 0 0
2015–16 Barnsley 8 0
2016–17 Barnsley 0 0
2017–18 Barnsley 8 0 **16 0**
2018–19 Newport Co 3 0
2019–20 Newport Co 5 0 **8 0**

WATTS, Elis (D) **0 0**
2019–20 Newport Co 0 0

WHITELY, Corey (M) **10 0**
b. 11-7-91
From Waltham Forest, Enfield T, Dagenham & R, Ebbsfleet U.
2019–20 Newport Co 10 0 **10 0**

WILLMOTT, Robbie (M) **159 8**
H: 5 9 W: 12 00 b.Harlow 16-5-90
Internationals: England C.
2013–14 Newport Co 46 3
2014–15 Newport Co 16 1
From Ebbsfleet U, Chelmsford C.
2017–18 Newport Co 39 2
2018–19 Newport Co 31 2
2019–20 Newport Co 27 0 **159 8**

WOODIWISS, Joe (D) **0 0**
2019–20 Newport Co 0 0

Scholars
Bates, Luis Andrew; Benham, Dewi Sion Edwyn; Brain, Callum Johnathon; Cirotto, Louie John; Evans, Ioan Langdon; Fahiya, Ruben Ross; George, Ryan James; Graham, Connor Rhys; Jefferies, Dominic William; Jones, Callum Oliver; Lewi-Hillier, Ryan David; Livermore, Aneurin Riley; Maher, Zachary Jamie; Twamley, Lewys Morgan; Watts, Elis William; Woodiwiss, Joseph Michael; Wright, Thomas Josep.

NORTHAMPTON T (57)

ADAMS, Nicky (F) **509 39**
H: 5 10 W: 11 00 b.Bolton 16-10-86
Internationals: Wales U21.
2005–06 Bury 15 1
2006–07 Bury 19 1
2007–08 Bury 43 12
2008–09 Leicester C 12 0
2008–09 *Rochdale* 14 1
2009–10 Leicester C 18 0 **30 0**
2009–10 *Leyton Orient* 6 0 **6 0**
2010–11 Brentford 7 0 **7 0**
2010–11 Rochdale 30 0
2011–12 Rochdale 41 4 **85 5**
2012–13 Crawley T 46 8
2013–14 Crawley T 24 1 **70 9**
2013–14 Rotherham U 15 1 **15 1**
2013–14 Bury 0 0
2014–15 Bury 38 1
2015–16 Northampton T 39 3
2016–17 Carlisle U 42 3
2017–18 Carlisle U 17 0 **59 3**
2018–19 Bury 46 2 **161 17**
2019–20 Northampton T 37 1 **76 4**

ANDERSON, Paul (M) **347 33**
H: 5 9 W: 10 04 b.Leicester 23-7-88
Internationals: England U19.
2005–06 Hull C 0 0
2005–06 Liverpool 0 0
2006–07 Liverpool 0 0
2007–08 Liverpool 0 0
2007–08 *Swansea C* 31 7 **31 7**

2008–09 Liverpool 0 0
2008–09 *Nottingham F* 26 2
2009–10 Nottingham F 37 4
2010–11 Nottingham F 36 3
2011–12 Nottingham F 17 0
2012–13 Nottingham F 0 0 **116 9**
2012–13 Bristol C 29 3 **29 3**
2013–14 Ipswich T 31 5
2014–15 Ipswich T 35 1 **66 6**
2015–16 Bradford C 11 0
2016–17 Bradford C 3 0 **14 0**
2016–17 Northampton T 36 6
2016–17 Mansfield T 0 0
2017–18 Mansfield T 33 1
2018–19 Mansfield T 0 0 **33 1**
2018–19 Plymouth Arg 4 0 **4 0**
2019–20 Northampton T 18 1 **54 7**

ARNOLD, Steve (G) 60 0
H: 6 1 W: 13 02 b.Welham Green 22-8-89
Internationals: England C.
2012–13 Stevenage 30 0
2013–14 Stevenage 3 0 **33 0**
From Forest Green R, Dover Ath.
2017–18 Gillingham 0 0
2018–19 Shrewsbury T 23 0 **23 0**
2019–20 Northampton T 4 0 **4 0**

BALLINGER, Jacob (D) 0 0
2019–20 Northampton T 0 0

CHUKWUEMEKA, Caleb (F) 0 0
2019–20 Northampton T 0 0

CORNELL, David (G) 136 0
H: 5 11 W: 11 07 b.Gorseinon 28-3-91
Internationals: Wales U17, U19, U21.
2009–10 Swansea C 0 0
2010–11 Swansea C 0 0
2011–12 Swansea C 0 0
2011–12 *Hereford U* 25 0 **25 0**
2012–13 Swansea C 0 0
2013–14 Swansea C 0 0
2013–14 *St Mirren* 5 0 **5 0**
2014–15 Swansea C 0 0
2014–15 *Portsmouth* 0 0
2015–16 Oldham Ath 14 0 **14 0**
2016–17 Northampton T 6 0
2017–18 Northampton T 6 0
2018–19 Northampton T 46 0
2019–20 Northampton T 34 0 **92 0**

GOODE, Charlie (D) 117 8
b. 3-8-95
Internationals: England C.
2015–16 Scunthorpe U 10 1
2016–17 Scunthorpe U 20 0
2017–18 Scunthorpe U 13 1
2018–19 Scunthorpe U 21 3 **64 5**
2018–19 *Northampton T* 17 0
2019–20 Northampton T 36 3 **53 3**

HALL-JOHNSON, Reece (M) 45 0
H: 5 8 W: 10 08 b.Aylesbury 9-5-95
2013–14 Norwich C 0 0
2014–15 Norwich C 0 0
2015–16 Norwich C 0 0
From Maidstone U, Bishop's Stortford, Braintree T.
2017–18 Grimsby T 12 0
2018–19 Grimsby T 28 0 **40 0**
2019–20 Northampton T 5 0 **5 0**

HARDING, Michael (F) 0 0
2019–20 Northampton T 0 0

HARRIMAN, Michael (D) 237 10
H: 5 6 W: 11 10 b.Chichester 23-10-92
Internationals: Republic of Ireland U18, U19, U21.
2010–11 QPR 0 0
2011–12 QPR 1 0
2012–13 QPR 1 0
2012–13 *Wycombe W* 20 0
2013–14 QPR 0 0
2013–14 *Gillingham* 34 1 **34 1**
2014–15 QPR 0 0 **2 0**
2014–15 *Luton T* 35 1 **35 1**
2015–16 Wycombe W 45 7
2016–17 Wycombe W 38 0
2017–18 Wycombe W 18 1
2018–19 Wycombe W 24 0 **145 8**
2019–20 Northampton T 21 0 **21 0**

HOSKINS, Sam (F) 218 28
H: 5 8 W: 10 07 b.Dorchester 4-2-93
2011–12 Southampton 0 0
2011–12 *Preston NE* 0 0
2011–12 *Rotherham U* 8 2 **8 2**
2012–13 Southampton 0 0
2012–13 *Stevenage* 14 1 **14 1**
2013–14 Yeovil T 19 0
2014–15 Yeovil T 12 1 **31 1**
2015–16 Northampton T 34 6
2016–17 Northampton T 25 3
2017–18 Northampton T 27 2
2018–19 Northampton T 42 5
2019–20 Northampton T 37 8 **165 24**

HUGHES, Ryan (D) 1 0
b. 24-4-01
2018–19 Northampton T 1 0
2019–20 Northampton T 0 0 **1 0**

JOHNSTON, Ethan (F) 0 0
2019–20 Northampton T 0 0

KAJA, Egli (M) 32 0
H: 5 10 W: 12 04 b. 26-7-97
Internationals: Albania U21.
2015–16 AFC Wimbledon 2 0
2016–17 AFC Wimbledon 1 0
2017–18 AFC Wimbledon 19 0
2018–19 AFC Wimbledon 0 0 **22 0**
2018–19 *Livingston* 6 0 **6 0**
2019–20 Northampton T 4 0 **4 0**

LASHLEY, Bradley (G) 0 0
b. 12-9-00
2019–20 Northampton T 0 0

LINES, Chris (M) 461 37
H: 6 2 W: 12 00 b.Bristol 30-11-88
2005–06 Bristol R 4 0
2006–07 Bristol R 7 0
2007–08 Bristol R 27 3
2008–09 Bristol R 45 4
2009–10 Bristol R 42 10
2010–11 Bristol R 42 3
2011–12 Bristol R 1 0
2011–12 Sheffield W 41 3
2012–13 Sheffield W 6 0 **47 3**
2012–13 *Milton Keynes D* 16 0 **16 0**
2013–14 Port Vale 34 1
2014–15 Port Vale 27 2 **61 3**
2015–16 Bristol R 33 0
2016–17 Bristol R 44 3
2017–18 Bristol R 42 5
2018–19 Bristol R 19 1 **306 29**
2019–20 Northampton T 31 2 **31 2**

MARSHALL, Mark (M) 305 22
H: 5 7 W: 10 07 b.Jamaica 9-5-86
2008–09 Swindon T 12 0
2009–10 Swindon T 7 0 **19 0**
2009–10 *Hereford U* 8 0 **8 0**
2010–11 Barnet 46 6
2011–12 Barnet 25 1 **71 7**
2013–14 Coventry C 14 0 **14 0**
2014–15 Port Vale 46 7 **46 7**
2015–16 Bradford C 31 0
2016–17 Bradford C 42 6 **73 6**
2017–18 Charlton Ath 27 1
2018–19 Charlton Ath 22 1 **49 2**
2019–20 Gillingham 18 0 **18 0**
2019–20 Northampton T 7 0 **7 0**

MARTIN, Joe (M) 306 15
H: 6 0 W: 12 13 b.Dagenham 29-11-88
Internationals: England U16, U17.
2005–06 Tottenham H 0 0
2006–07 Tottenham H 0 0
2007–08 Tottenham H 0 0
2007–08 *Blackpool* 1 0
2008–09 Blackpool 15 0
2009–10 Blackpool 6 0 **22 0**
2010–11 Gillingham 17 1
2011–12 Gillingham 35 1
2012–13 Gillingham 38 2
2013–14 Gillingham 46 2
2014–15 Gillingham 25 2 **161 8**
2015–16 Millwall 29 2
2016–17 Millwall 23 1 **52 3**
2017–18 Stevenage 39 2
2018–19 Bristol R 10 1 **10 1**
2018–19 Stevenage 5 1 **44 3**
2019–20 Northampton T 17 0 **17 0**

McCORMACK, Alan (M) 444 26
H: 5 8 W: 11 00 b.Dublin 10-1-84
Internationals: Republic of Ireland U19.
2002–03 Preston NE 0 0
2003–04 Preston NE 5 0
2003–04 *Leyton Orient* 10 0 **10 0**
2004–05 Preston NE 3 0
2004–05 *Southend U* 7 2
2005–06 Preston NE 0 0
2005–06 *Motherwell* 24 2 **24 2**
2006–07 Preston NE 3 0 **11 0**
2006–07 Southend U 22 3
2007–08 Southend U 42 8
2008–09 Southend U 34 2
2009–10 Southend U 41 3 **146 18**
2010–11 Charlton Ath 24 1 **24 1**
2011–12 Swindon T 40 2
2012–13 Swindon T 40 0 **80 2**
2013–14 Brentford 43 1
2014–15 Brentford 18 1
2015–16 Brentford 27 0
2016–17 Brentford 11 0 **99 2**
2017–18 Luton T 16 1
2018–19 Luton T 19 0 **35 1**
2019–20 Northampton T 15 0 **15 0**

McWILLIAMS, Cameron (M) 0 0
2017–18 Northampton T 0 0
2018–19 Northampton T 0 0
2019–20 Northampton T 0 0

McWILLIAMS, Shaun (M) 66 1
b.Northampton 14-8-98
2014–15 Northampton T 0 0
2015–16 Northampton T 0 0
2016–17 Northampton T 5 0
2017–18 Northampton T 19 0
2018–19 Northampton T 25 0
2019–20 Northampton T 17 1 **66 1**

MORIAS, Junior (F) 94 16
H: 5 8 W: 10 10 b.Kingston 4-7-95
2012–13 Wycombe W 19 0
2013–14 Wycombe W 9 0
2014–15 Wycombe W 0 0 **28 0**
From Boreham Wood, Whitehawk, St Albans C.
2016–17 Peterborough U 20 4
2017–18 Peterborough U 25 6 **45 10**
2018–19 Northampton T 19 6
2019–20 Northampton T 2 0 **21 6**
Transferred to St Mirren, August 2019.

NEWELL, Jack (M) 0 0
2018–19 Northampton T 0 0
2019–20 Northampton T 0 0

OLIVER, Vadaine (F) 214 29
H: 6 2 W: 12 04 b.Sheffield 21-10-91
2010–11 Sheffield W 0 0
2011–12 Sheffield W 0 0
From Lincoln C.
2013–14 Crewe Alex 25 2
2014–15 Crewe Alex 9 1 **34 3**
2014–15 *Mansfield T* 30 7 **30 7**
2015–16 York C 37 7 **37 7**
2016–17 Notts Co 19 1 **19 1**
2017–18 Morecambe 34 3
2018–19 Morecambe 30 4 **64 7**
2019–20 Northampton T 30 4 **30 4**

POLLOCK, Scott (M) 16 1
b. 12-3-01
2018–19 Northampton T 5 0
2019–20 Northampton T 11 1 **16 1**

ROBERTS, Morgan (F) 5 0
b. 22-12-00
2017–18 Northampton T 1 0
2018–19 Northampton T 3 0
2019–20 Northampton T 1 0 **5 0**

SMITH, Harry (F) 81 15
H: 6 5 b. 18-5-95
From Sittingbourne, Folkestone Invicta.
2016–17 Millwall 9 1
2017–18 Millwall 0 0 **9 1**
2017–18 *Swindon T* 14 2 **14 2**
2018–19 Macclesfield T 39 8 **39 8**
2019–20 Northampton T 19 4 **19 4**

TURNBULL, Jordan (D) 198 6
H: 6 1 W: 11 05 b.Trowbridge 30-10-94
Internationals: England U19, U20.
2014–15 Southampton 0 0
2014–15 *Swindon T* 44 1
2015–16 Southampton 0 0
2015–16 *Swindon T* 42 0 **86 1**
2016–17 Coventry C 36 0
2017–18 Coventry C 0 0 **36 0**
2017–18 *Partick Thistle* 0 0
2017–18 Northampton T 14 0
2018–19 Northampton T 31 0
2019–20 Northampton T 31 5 **76 5**

WARBURTON, Matthew (F) 18 1
From Curzon Ashton, Salford C, Stockport Co.
2019–20 Northampton T 18 1 **18 1**

WATERS, Billy (M) 152 22
H: 5 9 W: 11 07 b.Epsom 15-10-94
2012–13 Crewe Alex 0 0

2013–14	Crewe Alex	9	0		
2014–15	Crewe Alex	16	2	**25**	**2**
2016–17	Cheltenham T	46	12		
2017–18	Northampton T	17	0		
2017–18	*Cambridge U*	18	2	**18**	**2**
2018–19	Northampton T	15	2		
2018–19	*Cheltenham T*	18	4	**64**	**16**
2019–20	*Newport Co*	6	0	**6**	**0**
2019–20	Northampton T	7	0	**39**	**2**

WATSON, Ryan (M) **110 7**
H: 6 1 W: 11 07 b.Crewe 7-7-93

2011–12	Wigan Ath	0	0		
2012–13	Wigan Ath	0	0		
2012–13	*Accrington S*	0	0		
2013–14	Leicester C	0	0		
2014–15	Leicester C	0	0		
2014–15	*Northampton T*	5	0		
2015–16	Leicester C	0	0		
2015–16	*Northampton T*	11	0		
2016–17	Barnet	19	1		
2017–18	Barnet	28	1	**47**	**2**
2018–19	Milton Keynes D	22	0	**22**	**0**
2019–20	Northampton T	25	5	**41**	**5**

WHALER, Sean (M) **0 0**

2017–18	Northampton T	0	0		
2018–19	Northampton T	0	0		
2019–20	Northampton T	0	0		

WILLIAMS, Andy (F) **488 115**
H: 5 11 W: 11 09 b.Hereford 14-8-86

2006–07	Hereford U	41	8		
2007–08	Bristol R	41	4		
2008–09	Bristol R	4	1		
2008–09	*Hereford U*	26	2	**67**	**10**
2009–10	Bristol R	43	3	**88**	**8**
2010–11	Yeovil T	37	6		
2011–12	Yeovil T	35	16		
2012–13	Swindon T	40	11		
2013–14	Swindon T	3	0		
2013–14	*Yeovil T*	9	0	**81**	**22**
2014–15	Swindon T	46	21	**89**	**32**
2015–16	Doncaster R	46	12		
2016–17	Doncaster R	37	11		
2017–18	Doncaster R	9	0	**92**	**23**
2018–19	Northampton T	39	12		
2019–20	Northampton T	32	8	**71**	**20**

WILLIAMS, Jay (D) **10 0**
b. 4-10-00

2018–19	Northampton T	10	0		
2019–20	Northampton T	0	0	**10**	**0**

Scholars
Bailey, Richie Dion; Ballinger, Jacob Bryan; Berry, Dylan Andrew; Chukwuemeka, Chigozier Caleb; Clark, Ewan Edward; Cross, Liam James; Dyche, Max; Flanagan, Joshua Francis; Fowler, Jordan Lee; Gilbert, Lewis George; Gordo-Douglas, Urijah Jesse; Harding, Michael Joshua Francis; Patching, Lewis John; Price, Haydn James; Scott, Thomas William; Smith, Ryan Nathan.

NORWICH C (58)

AARONS, Maximillian (D) **77 2**
b.London 4-1-00
Internationals: England U19, U21.
From Luton T.

2018–19	Norwich C	41	2		
2019–20	Norwich C	36	0	**77**	**2**

ADSHEAD, Daniel (M) **11 0**
H: 5 6 W: 10 03 b. 2-9-01
Internationals: England U18, U19.

2017–18	Rochdale	1	0		
2018–19	Rochdale	10	0	**11**	**0**
2019–20	Norwich C	0	0		

AMADOU, Ibrahim (M) **172 4**
b.Douala 6-4-93
Internationals: France U19.

2010–11	Nancy	0	0		
2011–12	Nancy	0	0		
2012–13	Nancy	1	0		
2013–14	Nancy	20	0		
2014–15	Nancy	36	2	**57**	**2**
2015–16	Lille	22	1		
2016–17	Lille	35	1		
2017–18	Lille	30	0	**87**	**2**
2018–19	Sevilla	17	0		
2019–20	Sevilla	0	0	**17**	**0**

On loan from Sevilla.

2019–20	Norwich C	11	0	**11**	**0**

BUSHIRI, Rocky (D) **50 0**
b. 30-11-99
Internationals: Belgium U19, U21.

2017–18	Oostende	8	0		
2018–19	Oostende	0	0	**8**	**0**
2018–19	*Eupen*	31	0	**31**	**0**
2019–20	Norwich C	0	0		
2019–20	*Blackpool*	4	0	**4**	**0**
2019–20	*Sint-Truiden*	7	0	**7**	**0**

BYRAM, Samuel (M) **180 9**
H: 5 11 W: 11 04 b.Thurrock 16-9-93

2012–13	Leeds U	44	3		
2013–14	Leeds U	25	0		
2014–15	Leeds U	39	3		
2015–16	Leeds U	22	3	**130**	**9**
2015–16	West Ham U	4	0		
2016–17	West Ham U	18	0		
2017–18	West Ham U	5	0		
2018–19	West Ham U	0	0	**27**	**0**
2018–19	*Nottingham F*	6	0	**6**	**0**
2019–20	Norwich C	17	0	**17**	**0**

CANTWELL, Todd (M) **71 9**
b. 27-2-98
Internationals: England U17, U21.

2017–18	Norwich C	0	0		
2017–18	*Fortuna Sittard*	10	2	**10**	**2**
2018–19	Norwich C	24	1		
2019–20	Norwich C	37	6	**61**	**7**

DRMIC, Josip (F) **190 50**
b.Lachen 8-8-92
Internationals: Switzerland U19, U21, U23, Full caps.

2009–10	FC Zurich	4	0		
2010–11	FC Zurich	7	0		
2011–12	FC Zurich	20	5		
2012–13	FC Zurich	31	13	**62**	**18**
2013–14	Nurenberg	33	17	**33**	**17**
2014–15	Bayer Leverkusen	25	6	**25**	**6**
2015–16	Borussia M'gladbach	13	1		
2015–16	*Hamburg*	6	1	**6**	**1**
2016–17	Borussia M'gladbach	12	0		
2017–18	Borussia M'gladbach	13	4		
2018–19	Borussia M'gladbach	5	2	**43**	**7**
2019–20	Norwich C	21	1	**21**	**1**

DUDA, Ondrej (M) **168 27**
b.Snina 15-12-94
Internationals: Slovakia U19, U21, Full caps.

2012–13	Kosice	13	0		
2013–14	Kosice	19	5	**32**	**5**
2013–14	Legia Warsaw	12	3		
2014–15	Legia Warsaw	27	5		
2015–16	Legia Warsaw	27	2		
2016–17	Legia Warsaw	1	0	**67**	**10**
2016–17	Hertha Berlin	3	0		
2017–18	Hertha Berlin	17	1		
2018–19	Hertha Berlin	32	11		
2019–20	Hertha Berlin	7	0	**59**	**12**

On loan from Hertha Berlin.

2019–20	Norwich C	10	0	**10**	**0**

EMI, Buendia (M) **149 18**
H: 5 7 W: 11 05 b.Mar del Plata 25-12-96
Internationals: Spain U19. Argentina U20.

2013–14	Getafe	0	0		
2014–15	Getafe	6	0		
2015–16	Getafe	17	1		
2016–17	Getafe	12	2		
2017–18	Getafe	0	0	**35**	**3**
2017–18	*Cultural Leonesa*	40	6	**40**	**6**
2018–19	Norwich C	38	8		
2019–20	Norwich C	36	1	**74**	**9**

ENIGBOKAN-BLOOMFIELD, Mason (F) **27 4**
b.Westminster 6-11-96

2014–15	Dagenham & R	1	0	**1**	**0**

From Chelmsford C, Billericay T, Grays Ath, Brentwood T, Dagenham & R.

2018–19	Norwich C	0	0		
2018–19	*Hamilton A*	5	1	**5**	**1**
2019–20	Norwich C	0	0		
2019–20	*Crawley T*	21	3	**21**	**3**

FAHRMANN, Ralf (G) **191 0**
b.Karl-Marx-Stadt 27-9-88
Internationals: Germany U16, U17, U18, U19, U20, U21.

2007–08	Schalke 04	0	0		
2008–09	Schalke 04	3	0		
2009–10	Eintracht Frankurt	3	0		
2010–11	Eintracht Frankurt	15	0	**18**	**0**
2011–12	Schalke 04	3	0		
2012–13	Schalke 04	0	0		
2013–14	Schalke 04	22	0		
2014–15	Schalke 04	25	0		
2015–16	Schalke 04	34	0		
2016–17	Schalke 04	34	0		
2017–18	Schalke 04	34	0		
2018–19	Schalke 04	17	0		
2019–20	Schalke 04	0	0	**172**	**0**

On loan from Schalke 04.

2019–20	Norwich C	1	0	**1**	**0**

FAMEWO, Akin (D) **26 0**
H: 5 11 W: 10 06 b.Lewisham 9-11-98

2016–17	Luton T	3	0		
2017–18	Luton T	3	0		
2018–19	Luton T	0	0	**6**	**0**
2018–19	*Grimsby T*	10	0	**10**	**0**
2018–19	Norwich C	0	0		
2019–20	Norwich C	1	0	**1**	**0**
2019–20	*St Mirren*	9	0	**9**	**0**

GILMOUR, Charlie (M) **24 0**
b.Brighton 11-2-99
Internationals: England U16, U17. Scotland U16, U17, U19.

2017–18	Arsenal	0	0		
2018–19	Arsenal	0	0		
2019–20	Norwich C	0	0		
2019–20	*Telstar*	24	0	**24**	**0**

GODFREY, Ben (M) **115 6**
H: 6 0 W: 11 09 b.York 15-1-98
Internationals: England U20, U21.

2014–15	York C	0	0		
2015–16	York C	12	1	**12**	**1**
2015–16	Norwich C	0	0		
2016–17	Norwich C	2	0		
2017–18	Norwich C	0	0		
2017–18	*Shrewsbury T*	40	1		
2018–19	Norwich C	31	4		
2019–20	Norwich C	30	0	**63**	**4**
2019–20	*Shrewsbury T*	0	0	**40**	**1**

HANLEY, Grant (D) **249 10**
H: 6 2 W: 12 00 b.Dumfries 20-11-91
Internationals: Scotland U19, U21, Full caps.

2008–09	Blackburn R	0	0		
2009–10	Blackburn R	1	0		
2010–11	Blackburn R	7	0		
2011–12	Blackburn R	23	1		
2012–13	Blackburn R	39	2		
2013–14	Blackburn R	38	1		
2014–15	Blackburn R	31	1		
2015–16	Blackburn R	44	2	**183**	**7**
2016–17	Newcastle U	10	1		
2017–18	Newcastle U	0	0	**10**	**1**
2017–18	Norwich C	32	1		
2018–19	Norwich C	9	1		
2019–20	Norwich C	15	0	**56**	**2**

HEISE, Philip (D) **180 9**
b. 20-6-91

2011–12	Preussen Munster	16	0		
2012–13	Preussen Munster	21	1	**37**	**1**
2013–14	Heidenheim	38	2		
2014–15	Heidenheim	30	2	**68**	**4**
2015–16	Stuttgart	5	0		
2016–17	Stuttgart	1	0	**6**	**0**
2016–17	Dynamo Dresden	17	1		
2017–18	Dynamo Dresden	26	2		
2018–19	Dynamo Dresden	15	1	**58**	**4**
2018–19	Norwich C	0	0		
2019–20	Norwich C	0	0		
2019–20	*Nurnberg*	11	0	**11**	**0**

HERNANDEZ, Onel (M) **157 15**
b.Moron 1-2-93
Internationals: Germany U18.

2010–11	Arminia Bielefeld	10	0		
2011–12	Arminia Bielefeld	18	0	**28**	**0**
2012–13	Werder Bremen	0	0		
2013–14	Werder Bremen	0	0		
2013–14	Wolfsburg	0	0		
2014–15	Wolfsburg	0	0		
2015–16	Wolfsburg	0	0		
2016–17	Eintracht Brauschweig	34	5		
2017–18	Eintracht Brauschweig	17	1	**51**	**6**
2017–18	Norwich C	12	0		
2018–19	Norwich C	40	8		
2019–20	Norwich C	26	1	**78**	**9**

IDAH, Adam (F) **12 0**
b. 11-2-01
Internationals: Republic of Ireland U16, U17, U18, U19, U21.

2019–20	Norwich C	12	0	**12**	**0**

JAIYESIMI, Diallang (M) **60 7**
b.Southwark 18-3-99
From Dulwich Hamlet.

2017–18	Norwich C	0	0		
2017–18	*Grimsby T*	30	0	**30**	**0**
2018–19	Norwich C	0	0		

2018–19	*Yeovil T*	9	2	**9**	**2**
2019–20	Norwich C	0	0		
2019–20	*Swindon T*	21	5	**21**	**5**

KLOSE, Timm (D) **251 19**
H: 6 5 W: 13 10 b.Frankfurt am Main 9-5-88
Internationals: Switzerland U21, U23, Full caps.

2009–10	Thun	29	2		
2010–11	Thun	30	3	**59**	**5**
2011–12	Nuremburg	13	0		
2012–13	Nuremburg	32	2	**45**	**2**
2013–14	Wolfsburg	10	0		
2014–15	Wolfsburg	12	1		
2015–16	Wolfsburg	8	1	**30**	**2**
2015–16	Norwich C	10	1		
2016–17	Norwich C	32	1		
2017–18	Norwich C	37	4		
2018–19	Norwich C	31	4		
2019–20	Norwich C	7	0	**117**	**10**

KRUL, Tim (G) **291 0**
H: 6 2 W: 11 08 b.Den Haag 3-4-88
Internationals: Netherlands U16, U17, U19, U20, U21, Full caps.

2005–06	Newcastle U	0	0		
2006–07	Newcastle U	0	0		
2007–08	*Falkirk*	22	0	**22**	**0**
2007–08	Newcastle U	0	0		
2008–09	Newcastle U	0	0		
2008–09	*Carlisle U*	9	0	**9**	**0**
2009–10	Newcastle U	3	0		
2010–11	Newcastle U	21	0		
2011–12	Newcastle U	38	0		
2012–13	Newcastle U	24	0		
2013–14	Newcastle U	36	0		
2014–15	Newcastle U	30	0		
2015–16	Newcastle U	8	0		
2016–17	Newcastle U	0	0		
2016–17	*Ajax*	0	0		
2016–17	*AZ Alkmaar*	18	0	**18**	**0**
2017–18	Newcastle U	0	0	**160**	**0**
2017–18	Brighton & HA	0	0		
2018–19	Norwich C	46	0		
2019–20	Norwich C	36	0	**82**	**0**

LEITNER, Moritz (M) **167 4**
H: 5 9 W: 10 03 b.Munich 8-12-92
Internationals: Austria U17. Germany U19, U20, U21.

2010–11	1860 Munich	16	0	**16**	**0**
2010–11	Borussia Dortmund	0	0		
2010–11	*Augsburg*	9	0		
2011–12	Borussia Dortmund	17	0		
2012–13	Borussia Dortmund	25	0		
2013–14	Borussia Dortmund	0	0		
2013–14	*Stuttgart*	21	1		
2014–15	Borussia Dortmund	0	0		
2014–15	*Stuttgart*	19	1	**40**	**2**
2015–16	Borussia Dortmund	8	0	**50**	**0**
2016–17	Lazio	2	0	**2**	**0**
2017–18	Augsburg	0	0	**9**	**0**
2017–18	*Norwich C*	12	0		
2018–19	Norwich C	29	2		
2019–20	Norwich C	9	0	**50**	**2**

LEWIS, Jamal (D) **92 1**
b. 25-1-98
Internationals: Northern Ireland U19, U21, Full caps.

2017–18	Norwich C	22	0		
2018–19	Norwich C	42	0		
2019–20	Norwich C	28	1	**92**	**1**

MAIR, Archie (G) **0 0**
b.Turriff 10-2-01
Internationals: Scotland U17, U19.
From Aberdeen.

2019–20	Norwich C	0	0		

MARTIN, Josh (M) **5 0**
From Arsenal.

2019–20	Norwich C	5	0	**5**	**0**

McCALLUM, Sam (D) **33 2**
b. 2-9-00

2018–19	Coventry C	7	0		
2019–20	Norwich C	0	0		
2019–20	*Coventry C*	26	2	**33**	**2**

McGOVERN, Michael (G) **292 0**
H: 6 2 W: 13 07 b.Enniskillen 12-7-84
Internationals: Northern Ireland U19, U21, Full caps.

2004–05	Celtic	0	0		
2004–05	*Stranraer*	19	0	**19**	**0**
2005–06	Celtic	0	0		
2006–07	Celtic	0	0		
2006–07	*St Johnstone*	1	0	**1**	**0**
2007–08	Celtic	0	0		
2008–09	Dundee U	0	0		
2009–10	Ross Co	35	0		
2010–11	Ross Co	36	0	**71**	**0**
2011–12	Falkirk	35	0		
2012–13	Falkirk	35	0		
2013–14	Falkirk	34	0	**104**	**0**
2014–15	Hamilton A	38	0		
2015–16	Hamilton A	37	0	**75**	**0**
2016–17	Norwich C	20	0		
2017–18	Norwich C	0	0		
2018–19	Norwich C	0	0		
2019–20	Norwich C	2	0	**22**	**0**

McLEAN, Kenny (M) **334 44**
H: 6 0 W: 11 00 b.Rutherglen 8-1-92
Internationals: Scotland U19, U21, Full caps.

2009–10	St Mirren	0	0		
2009–10	*Arbroath*	20	1	**20**	**1**
2010–11	St Mirren	19	0		
2011–12	St Mirren	28	4		
2012–13	St Mirren	29	3		
2013–14	St Mirren	30	7		
2014–15	St Mirren	25	7	**131**	**21**
2014–15	Aberdeen	13	0		
2015–16	Aberdeen	38	6		
2016–17	Aberdeen	38	4		
2017–18	Aberdeen	22	3		
2017–18	Norwich C	0	0		
2017–18	*Aberdeen*	15	5	**126**	**18**
2018–19	Norwich C	20	3		
2019–20	Norwich C	37	1	**57**	**4**

MORRIS, Carlton (F) **129 19**
H: 6 1 W: 13 05 b.Cambridge 16-12-95
Internationals: England U19.

2014–15	Norwich C	1	0		
2014–15	*Oxford U*	7	0	**7**	**0**
2014–15	*York C*	8	0	**8**	**0**
2015–16	Norwich C	0	0		
2015–16	*Hamilton A*	32	8	**32**	**8**
2016–17	Norwich C	0	0		
2016–17	*Rotherham U*	8	0		
2017–18	Norwich C	0	0		
2017–18	*Shrewsbury T*	42	6	**42**	**6**
2018–19	Norwich C	0	0		
2019–20	Norwich C	0	0	**1**	**0**
2019–20	*Rotherham U*	21	3	**29**	**3**
2019–20	*Milton Keynes D*	10	2	**10**	**2**

ODUSINA, Timi (D) **0 0**
b.Croydon 28-10-99

2018–19	Norwich C	0	0		
2019–20	Norwich C	0	0		

OXBOROUGH, Aston (G) **0 0**
H: 6 5 b.Great Yarmouth 9-5-98
Internationals: England U16.

2018–19	Norwich C	0	0		
2019–20	Norwich C	0	0		

PAYNE, Alfie (M) **0 0**
b.Norwich 7-10-99

2018–19	Norwich C	0	0		
2019–20	Norwich C	0	0		

PUKKI, Teemu (F) **327 126**
H: 5 9 W: 10 06 b.Kotka 29-3-90
Internationals: Finland U17, U19, U21, Full caps.

2006	KooTeePee	5	0		
2007	KooTeePee	24	3	**29**	**3**
2008–09	Sevilla	1	0	**1**	**0**
2010	HJK Helsinki	7	2		
2011	HJK Helsinki	18	11	**25**	**13**
2011–12	Schalke 04	19	5		
2012–13	Schalke 04	17	3		
2013–14	Schalke 04	1	0	**37**	**8**
2013–14	Celtic	25	7		
2014–15	Celtic	1	0	**26**	**7**
2014–15	Brondby	27	9		
2015–16	Brondby	33	9		
2016–17	Brondby	34	20		
2017–18	Brondby	36	17	**130**	**55**
2018–19	Norwich C	43	29		
2019–20	Norwich C	36	11	**79**	**40**

RAGGETT, Sean (D) **60 5**
H: 5 11 W: 12 04 b.Gillingham 17-4-93
Internationals: England C.
From Dover Ath.

2017–18	Lincoln C	25	2	**25**	**2**
2017–18	Norwich C	2	0		
2018–19	Norwich C	0	0		
2018–19	*Rotherham U*	7	1	**7**	**1**
2019–20	Norwich C	0	0	**2**	**0**
2019–20	*Portsmouth*	26	2	**26**	**2**

RICHARDS, Caleb (D) **34 1**
b. 8-9-98

2017–18	Blackpool	0	0		
2018–19	Norwich C	0	0		
2019	*Tampa Bay Rowdies*	34	1	**34**	**1**
2019–20	Norwich C	0	0		

RUPP, Lukas (M) **175 17**
b.Heidelberg 8-1-91

2009–10	Karlsruher	2	0		
2010–11	Karlsruher	24	3	**26**	**3**
2011–12	Borussia M'gladbach	3	0		
2012–13	Borussia M'gladbach	21	0		
2013–14	Borussia M'gladbach	10	0	**34**	**0**
2014–15	Paderborn	31	4	**31**	**4**
2015–16	Stuttgart	29	5	**29**	**5**
2016–17	Hoffenheim	14	2		
2017–18	Hoffenheim	21	3		
2018–19	Hoffenheim	1	0		
2019–20	Hoffenheim	7	0	**43**	**5**
2019–20	Norwich C	12	0	**12**	**0**

SRBENY, Dennis (F) **127 41**
b.Berlin 5-5-94

2013–14	Hansa Rostock	2	0		
2014–15	Hansa Rostock	18	1	**20**	**1**
2015–16	BFC Dynamo	22	10		
2016–17	BFC Dynamo	33	18	**55**	**28**
2017–18	Paderborn	15	9	**15**	**9**
2017–18	Norwich C	14	1		
2018–19	Norwich C	15	1		
2019–20	Norwich C	8	1	**37**	**3**

Transferred to Paderborn, January 2020.

STIEPERMANN, Marco (F) **266 30**
H: 5 11 W: 11 11 b.Dortmund 9-2-91
Internationals: Germany U16, U17, U18, U19, U20.

2008–09	Borussia Dortmund	0	0		
2009–10	Borussia Dortmund	3	1		
2010–11	Borussia Dortmund	4	0		
2011–12	Borussia Dortmund	0	0	**7**	**1**
2011–12	*Aachen*	21	2	**21**	**2**
2012–13	Energie Cottbus	27	2		
2013–14	Energie Cottbus	29	5	**56**	**7**
2014–15	Greuther Furth	31	4		
2015–16	Greuther Furth	30	5	**61**	**9**
2016–17	Bochum	31	1	**31**	**1**
2017–18	VfL Bochum	0	0		
2017–18	Norwich C	23	1		
2018–19	Norwich C	43	9		
2019–20	Norwich C	24	0	**90**	**10**

TETTEY, Alexander (M) **370 21**
H: 5 11 W: 10 09 b.Accra 4-4-86
Internationals: Norway U18, U19, U21, Full caps.

2004–05	Rosenborg	0	0		
2005–06	Rosenborg	10	1		
2006–07	Rosenborg	21	1		
2007–08	Rosenborg	25	4		
2008–09	Rosenborg	28	6		
2009–10	Rosenborg	1	0	**85**	**12**
2009–10	Rennes	24	0		
2010–11	Rennes	17	1		
2011–12	Rennes	19	1	**60**	**2**
2012–13	Norwich C	27	0		
2013–14	Norwich C	21	1		
2014–15	Norwich C	36	2		
2015–16	Norwich C	23	2		
2016–17	Norwich C	35	0		
2017–18	Norwich C	23	0		
2018–19	Norwich C	30	1		
2019–20	Norwich C	30	1	**225**	**7**

THOMAS, Jordan (D) **1 0**
From Huddersfield T.

2019–20	Norwich C	1	0	**1**	**0**

THOMPSON, Louis (M) **120 6**
H: 5 11 W: 11 10 b.Bristol 19-12-94
Internationals: Wales U19, U21.

2012–13	Swindon T	4	0		
2013–14	Swindon T	28	2		
2014–15	Norwich C	0	0		
2014–15	*Swindon T*	32	2		
2015–16	Norwich C	0	0		
2015–16	*Swindon T*	28	2	**92**	**6**
2016–17	Norwich C	3	0		
2017–18	Norwich C	0	0		
2018–19	Norwich C	6	0		
2019–20	Norwich C	0	0	**9**	**0**
2019–20	*Shrewsbury T*	10	0	**10**	**0**
2019–20	*Milton Keynes D*	9	0	**9**	**0**

THORVALDSSON, Isak (F) **4 0**
Internationals: Iceland U16, U17, U18, U19.
From Afturelding.

2019–20	Norwich C	0	0		

2019–20	*Fleetwood T*	2	0	**2**	**0**
2019–20	*St Mirren*	2	0	**2**	**0**

TRYBULL, Tom (M) 143 5
H: 5 11 W: 11 05 b.Berlin 9-3-93
Internationals: Germany U17, U18, U19, U20.

2010–11	Hansa Rostock	17	0	**17**	**0**
2011–12	Werder Bremen	15	1		
2012–13	Werder Bremen	4	0		
2013–14	Werder Bremen	2	0	**21**	**1**
2013–14	St Pauli	12	0		
2014–15	St Pauli	3	0	**15**	**0**
2015–16	Greuther Furth	0	0		
2016–17	Den Haag	23	1	**23**	**1**
2017–18	Norwich C	20	2		
2018–19	Norwich C	31	1		
2019–20	Norwich C	16	0	**67**	**3**

VRANCIC, Mario (M) 250 30
H: 6 1 W: 12 02 b.Slavonski Brod 23-5-89
Internationals: Germany U17, U19, U20. Bosnia-Herzegovina Full caps.

2006–07	Mainz 05	1	0		
2007–08	Mainz 05	5	0		
2008–09	Mainz 05	3	0		
2009–10	Mainz 05	0	0	**9**	**0**
2009–10	*Rot Weiss Ahlen*	12	0	**12**	**0**
2010–11	Borussia Dortmund	0	0		
2011–12	Borussia Dortmund	0	0		
2012–13	Paderborn	33	5		
2013–14	Paderborn	30	5		
2014–15	Paderborn	30	2	**93**	**12**
2015–16	Darmstadt	22	2		
2016–17	Darmstadt	23	4	**45**	**6**
2017–18	Norwich C	35	1		
2018–19	Norwich C	36	10		
2019–20	Norwich C	20	1	**91**	**12**

ZIMMERMANN, Christoph (D) 96 3
b.Dusseldorf 12-1-93

2011–12	Borussia M'gladbach	0	0		
2012–13	Borussia M'gladbach	0	0		
2013–14	Borussia M'gladbach	0	0		
2014–15	Borussia Dortmund	0	0		
2015–16	Borussia Dortmund	0	0		
2016–17	Borussia Dortmund	0	0		
2017–18	Norwich C	39	1		
2018–19	Norwich C	40	2		
2019–20	Norwich C	17	0	**96**	**3**

Players retained or with offer of contract
Ahadme Yahyai, Gassan; Barden, Daniel James; Buendia Stati, Emiliano; Dickson-Peters, Thomas Grant Delroy; Fitzpatrick, Aidan; Hondermarck, William Mbongo Desire; Hutchinson, Shae Armari Akpojotor; Lomas, Louis James; McAlear, Reece; McCracken, Jon Douglas; Milovanovic, Saul John; Nizet, Rob; Omobamidele, Andrew Abiola; Omotoye, Tyrese Demola Huxley; Richardson, Matthew David Oscar; Rose, Joseph Matthew; Sitti, Melvin Ayiko; Tomkinson, Jonathan Robert.

Scholars
Ahmadi, Arash; Berkeley, Anthonius James; Blair, Samuel Frederick; Brown, Zak Jazi Theo; Dronfield, Zachary Gage; Earley, Saxon Owen; Harsani Giurgi, Joshua Alexander; Jackson, Eddie Robert; Kamara, Abu Bakarr; Khumbeni, Nelson Wilfred; Pitcher, Harry James; Rowe, Jonathan David Henry; Springett, Tony Gary; Stewart, Sean Patrick; Vaughan, Ethen James; Warner, Jaden Lemar.

NOTTINGHAM F (59)

ADOMAH, Albert (F) 519 82
H: 6 1 W: 11 08 b.Lambeth 13-12-87
Internationals: Ghana Full caps.

2007–08	Barnet	22	5		
2008–09	Barnet	45	9		
2009–10	Barnet	45	5	**112**	**19**
2010–11	Bristol C	46	5		
2011–12	Bristol C	45	5		
2012–13	Bristol C	40	7	**131**	**17**
2013–14	Middlesbrough	42	12		
2014–15	Middlesbrough	43	5		
2015–16	Middlesbrough	43	6		
2016–17	Middlesbrough	2	0	**130**	**23**
2016–17	Aston Villa	38	3		
2017–18	Aston Villa	39	14		
2018–19	Aston Villa	36	4	**113**	**21**
2019–20	Nottingham F	24	2	**24**	**2**
2019–20	*Cardiff C*	9	0	**9**	**0**

AMEOBI, Sam (F) 233 19
H: 6 3 W: 10 04 b.Newcastle upon Tyne 1-5-92
Internationals: Nigeria U20. England U21.

2010–11	Newcastle U	1	0		
2011–12	Newcastle U	10	0		
2012–13	Newcastle U	8	0		
2012–13	*Middlesbrough*	9	1	**9**	**1**
2013–14	Newcastle U	10	0		
2014–15	Newcastle U	25	2		
2015–16	Newcastle U	0	0		
2015–16	*Cardiff C*	36	1	**36**	**1**
2016–17	Newcastle U	4	0	**58**	**2**
2016–17	*Bolton W*	20	2		
2017–18	Bolton W	35	4		
2018–19	Bolton W	30	4	**85**	**10**
2019–20	Nottingham F	45	5	**45**	**5**

APPIAH, Arvin (F) 6 0
b. 5-1-01
Internationals: England U16, U17, U18, U19.

2018–19	Nottingham F	6	0		
2019–20	Nottingham F	0	0	**6**	**0**

Transferred to Almeria, September 2019.

BENALOUANE, Yohan (D) 191 6
H: 6 1 W: 12 06 b.Bagnois-sur-Ceze 28-3-87
Internationals: France U21. Tunisia Full caps.

2007–08	Saint-Etienne	6	1		
2008–09	Saint-Etienne	29	1		
2009–10	Saint-Etienne	29	1		
2010–11	Saint-Etienne	1	0	**65**	**3**
2010–11	Cesena	15	0		
2011–12	Cesena	11	0		
2012–13	Cesena	0	0	**26**	**0**
2012–13	*Parma*	21	1		
2013–14	Parma	4	0	**25**	**1**
2013–14	*Atalanta*	17	0		
2014–15	Atalanta	27	1	**44**	**1**
2015–16	Leicester C	4	0		
2015–16	*Fiorentina*	0	0		
2016–17	Leicester C	11	0		
2017–18	Leicester C	1	0		
2018–19	Leicester C	0	0	**16**	**0**
2018–19	Nottingham F	14	1		
2019–20	Nottingham F	1	0	**15**	**1**

BONG, Gaetan (D) 284 3
H: 6 0 W: 11 09 b.Sakbayeme 25-4-88
Internationals: France U21. Cameroon Full caps.

2005–06	Metz	3	0		
2006–07	Metz	2	0		
2007–08	Metz	11	0		
2008–09	Metz	0	0	**16**	**0**
2008–09	*Tours*	34	0	**34**	**0**
2009–10	Valenciennes	29	2		
2010–11	Valenciennes	22	1		
2011–12	Valenciennes	28	0		
2012–13	Valenciennes	29	0		
2013–14	Valenciennes	1	0	**109**	**3**
2013–14	Olympiacos	19	0	**19**	**0**
2014–15	Wigan Ath	14	0	**14**	**0**
2015–16	Brighton & HA	16	0		
2016–17	Brighton & HA	24	0		
2017–18	Brighton & HA	25	0		
2018–19	Brighton & HA	22	0		
2019–20	Brighton & HA	4	0	**91**	**0**
2019–20	Nottingham F	1	0	**1**	**0**

BOSTOCK, John (M) 201 28
b.Lambeth 15-1-92
Internationals: England U16, U17, U19.

2007–08	Crystal Palace	4	0	**4**	**0**
2008–09	Tottenham H	0	0		
2009–10	Tottenham H	0	0		
2009–10	*Brentford*	9	2	**9**	**2**
2010–11	Tottenham H	0	0		
2010–11	*Hull C*	11	2	**11**	**2**
2011–12	Tottenham H	0	0		
2011–12	*Sheffield W*	4	0	**4**	**0**
2011–12	*Swindon T*	3	0		
2012–13	Tottenham H	0	0		
2012–13	*Swindon T*	8	0	**11**	**0**
2013	*Toronto*	7	0	**7**	**0**
2013–14	Royal Antwerp	29	1		
2014–15	Royal Antwerp	2	0	**31**	**1**
2014–15	OH Leuven	26	11		
2015–16	OH Leuven	25	7	**51**	**18**
2016–17	Lens	31	5		
2017–18	Lens	11	0	**42**	**5**
2017–18	Bursaspor	8	0	**8**	**0**
2018–19	Toulouse	16	0		
2019–20	Toulouse	0	0	**16**	**0**

On loan from Toulouse.

2019–20	Nottingham F	7	0	**7**	**0**

BRIDCUTT, Liam (M) 285 4
H: 5 9 W: 11 07 b.Reading 8-5-89
Internationals: Scotland Full caps.

2007–08	Chelsea	0	0		
2007–08	*Yeovil T*	9	0	**9**	**0**
2008–09	Chelsea	0	0		
2008–09	*Watford*	6	0	**6**	**0**
2009–10	Chelsea	0	0		
2009–10	*Stockport Co*	15	0	**15**	**0**
2010–11	Chelsea	0	0		
2010–11	Brighton & HA	37	2		
2011–12	Brighton & HA	43	0		
2012–13	Brighton & HA	41	0		
2013–14	Brighton & HA	11	0	**132**	**2**
2013–14	Sunderland	12	0		
2014–15	Sunderland	18	0		
2015–16	Sunderland	0	0	**30**	**0**
2015–16	*Leeds U*	24	0		
2016–17	Leeds U	25	0	**49**	**0**
2017–18	Nottingham F	27	1		
2018–19	Nottingham F	1	0		
2019–20	Nottingham F	0	0	**28**	**1**
2019–20	*Bolton W*	11	0	**11**	**0**
2019–20	*Lincoln C*	5	1	**5**	**1**

CASH, Matty (M) 141 14
H: 6 2 W: 10 01 b.Slough 7-8-97

2015–16	Nottingham F	0	0		
2015–16	*Dagenham & R*	12	3	**12**	**3**
2016–17	Nottingham F	28	0		
2017–18	Nottingham F	23	2		
2018–19	Nottingham F	36	6		
2019–20	Nottingham F	42	3	**129**	**11**

CHEMA, Rodriguez (D) 150 12
b.Caudete 3-3-92

2012–13	Atletico Madrid	0	0		
2013–14	Alcorcon	9	1		
2014–15	Alcorcon	23	0		
2015–16	Alcorcon	33	5	**65**	**6**
2016–17	Levante	33	3		
2017–18	Levante	25	1		
2018–19	Levante	19	2		
2019–20	Levante	0	0	**77**	**6**
2019–20	Nottingham F	8	0	**8**	**0**

Transferred to Getafe, January 2020.

CLOUGH, Zach (F) 104 26
H: 5 7 b.Manchester 8-3-95

2013–14	Bolton W	0	0		
2014–15	Bolton W	8	5		
2015–16	Bolton W	28	7		
2016–17	Bolton W	23	9		
2016–17	Nottingham F	14	4		
2017–18	Nottingham F	13	0		
2017–18	*Bolton W*	9	1	**68**	**22**
2018–19	Nottingham F	0	0		
2018–19	*Rochdale*	9	0	**9**	**0**
2019–20	Nottingham F	0	0	**27**	**4**

DARIKWA, Tendayi (M) 204 10
H: 6 2 W: 12 02 b.Nottingham 13-12-91
Internationals: Zimbabwe Full caps.

2010–11	Chesterfield	0	0		
2011–12	Chesterfield	2	0		
2012–13	Chesterfield	36	5		
2013–14	Chesterfield	41	3		
2014–15	Chesterfield	46	1	**125**	**9**
2015–16	Burnley	21	1		
2016–17	Burnley	0	0	**21**	**1**
2017–18	Nottingham F	30	0		
2018–19	Nottingham F	28	0		
2019–20	Nottingham F	0	0	**58**	**0**

DAWSON, Michael (D) 469 23
H: 6 2 W: 12 02 b.Leyburn 18-11-83
Internationals: England U21, B, Full caps.

2000–01	Nottingham F	0	0		
2001–02	Nottingham F	1	0		
2002–03	Nottingham F	38	5		
2003–04	Nottingham F	30	1		
2004–05	Nottingham F	14	1		
2004–05	Tottenham H	5	0		
2005–06	Tottenham H	32	0		
2006–07	Tottenham H	37	1		
2007–08	Tottenham H	27	1		
2008–09	Tottenham H	16	1		
2009–10	Tottenham H	29	2		
2010–11	Tottenham H	24	1		
2011–12	Tottenham H	7	0		
2012–13	Tottenham H	27	1		
2013–14	Tottenham H	32	0	**236**	**7**
2014–15	Hull C	28	1		
2015–16	Hull C	32	1		
2016–17	Hull C	22	3		
2017–18	Hull C	40	3	**122**	**8**
2018–19	Nottingham F	10	0		
2019–20	Nottingham F	18	1	**111**	**8**

EDSER, Toby (M) **0** **0**

From Charlton Ath.

2016–17	Nottingham F	0	0		
2017–18	Nottingham F	0	0		
2018–19	Nottingham F	0	0		
2018–19	*Port Vale*	0	0		
2019–20	Nottingham F	0	0		

EN-NEYAH, Yassine (M) **0** **0**

From Bohemians.

2019–20	Nottingham F	0	0		

FORNAH, Tyrese (M) **5** **0**

b. 11-9-99

2019–20	Nottingham F	0	0		
2019–20	*Casa Pia*	5	0	**5**	**0**

GOMIS, Virgil (F) **21** **0**

b. 16-4-99

2018–19	Nottingham F	0	0		
2018–19	*Notts Co*	10	0	**10**	**0**
2019–20	Nottingham F	0	0		
2019–20	*Macclesfield T*	11	0	**11**	**0**

GRABBAN, Lewis (F) **432** **142**

H: 6 0 W: 11 03 b.Croydon 12-1-88

2005–06	Crystal Palace	0	0		
2006–07	Crystal Palace	8	1		
2006–07	*Oldham Ath*	9	0	**9**	**0**
2007–08	Crystal Palace	2	0	**10**	**1**
2007–08	*Motherwell*	6	0	**6**	**0**
2007–08	Millwall	13	3		
2008–09	Millwall	31	6		
2009–10	Millwall	11	0		
2009–10	*Brentford*	7	2		
2010–11	Millwall	1	0	**56**	**9**
2010–11	Brentford	22	5	**29**	**7**
2011–12	Rotherham U	43	18	**43**	**18**
2012–13	Bournemouth	42	13		
2013–14	Bournemouth	44	22		
2014–15	Norwich C	35	12		
2015–16	Norwich C	6	1	**41**	**13**
2015–16	Bournemouth	15	0		
2016–17	Bournemouth	3	0		
2016–17	*Reading*	16	3	**16**	**3**
2017–18	Bournemouth	0	0	**104**	**35**
2017–18	*Sunderland*	19	12	**19**	**12**
2017–18	*Aston Villa*	15	8	**15**	**8**
2018–19	Nottingham F	39	16		
2019–20	Nottingham F	45	20	**84**	**36**

HEFELE, Michael (D) **174** **14**

H: 6 4 W: 13 10 b.Pfaffenhofen 1-9-90

2010–11	Unterhaching	27	0		
2011–12	Unterhaching	6	1	**33**	**1**
2012–13	Greuther Furth	1	0		
2013–14	Greuther Furth	2	0	**3**	**0**
2013–14	*Wacker Burghausen*	15	0	**15**	**0**
2014–15	Dynamo Dresden	31	3		
2015–16	Dynamo Dresden	38	7	**69**	**10**
2016–17	Huddersfield T	37	3		
2017–18	Huddersfield T	2	0	**39**	**3**
2018–19	Nottingham F	15	0		
2019–20	Nottingham F	0	0	**15**	**0**

JENKINSON, Carl (D) **116** **3**

H: 6 1 W: 12 02 b.Harlow 8-2-92

Internationals: Finland U19, U21. England U17, U21, Full caps.

2010–11	Charlton Ath	8	0	**8**	**0**
2010–11	Arsenal	0	0		
2011–12	Arsenal	9	0		
2012–13	Arsenal	14	0		
2013–14	Arsenal	14	1		
2014–15	Arsenal	0	0		
2014–15	*West Ham U*	32	0		
2015–16	Arsenal	0	0		
2015–16	*West Ham U*	20	2	**52**	**2**
2016–17	Arsenal	1	0		
2017–18	Arsenal	0	0		
2017–18	*Birmingham C*	7	0	**7**	**0**
2018–19	Arsenal	3	0		
2019–20	Arsenal	0	0	**41**	**1**
2019–20	Nottingham F	8	0	**8**	**0**

JOAO CARVALHO, Antonio (M) **83** **6**

H: 5 8 W: 10 06 b.Castanheira de Pera 9-3-97

Internationals: Portugal U16, U17, U18, U19, U20, U21.

2014–15	Benfica	0	0		
2015–16	Benfica	0	0		
2016–17	Benfica	0	0		
2016–17	*Vitoria Setubal*	15	1	**15**	**1**
2017–18	Benfica	7	0	**7**	**0**
2018–19	Nottingham F	38	4		
2019–20	Nottingham F	23	1	**61**	**5**

JOHNSON, Brennan (M) **4** **0**

b.Nottingham 23-5-01

Internationals: England U16, U17. Wales U19, U21.

2019–20	Nottingham F	4	0	**4**	**0**

LAWRENCE-GABRIEL, Jordan (D) **9** **0**

b.London 25-9-98

From Southend U.

2019–20	Nottingham F	0	0		
2019–20	*Scunthorpe U*	9	0	**9**	**0**

LOLLEY, Joe (F) **190** **32**

H: 5 10 W: 11 05 b.Redditch 25-8-92

Internationals: England C.

2013–14	Huddersfield T	6	1		
2014–15	Huddersfield T	17	2		
2015–16	Huddersfield T	32	4		
2015–16	*Scunthorpe U*	6	0	**6**	**0**
2016–17	Huddersfield T	19	1		
2017–18	Huddersfield T	6	1	**80**	**9**
2017–18	Nottingham F	16	3		
2018–19	Nottingham F	46	11		
2019–20	Nottingham F	42	9	**104**	**23**

McGUANE, Marcus (M) **14** **1**

b.Greenwich 2-2-99

Internationals: Republic of Ireland U17. England U17, U18, U19.

2017–18	Arsenal	0	0		
2018–19	Barcelona	0	0		
2019–20	Barcelona	0	0		
2019–20	*Telstar*	14	1	**14**	**1**
2019–20	Nottingham F	0	0		

MIGHTEN, Alex (F) **8** **0**

b.Nottingham 11-4-02

Internationals: England U16, U17, U18.

2019–20	Nottingham F	8	0	**8**	**0**

MILOSEVIC, Alexander (D) **178** **15**

H: 6 3 W: 12 13 b.Sundbyburg 30-1-92

Internationals: Serbia U17. Sweden U19, U21, U23, Full caps.

2010	Vasalunds IF	24	5	**24**	**5**
2011	Allsvenskan	29	0		
2012	Allsvenskan	6	1		
2013	Allsvenskan	18	5		
2014	Allsvenskan	27	3	**80**	**9**
2014–15	Besiktas	1	0		
2015–16	Besiktas	1	0		
2015–16	*Hannover 96*	10	0	**10**	**0**
2016–17	Besiktas	0	0		
2016–17	*Darmstadt 98*	18	0	**18**	**0**
2017–18	Besiktas	0	0	**2**	**0**
2017–18	Caykur Rizespor	5	0	**5**	**0**
2018	AIK	27	0	**27**	**0**
2018–19	Nottingham F	12	1		
2019–20	Nottingham F	0	0	**12**	**1**

NUNO DA COSTA, Joia (M) **115** **32**

Internationals: Cape Verde Full caps.

From Aubagne.

2015–16	Valenciennes	23	10		
2016–17	Valenciennes	22	9	**45**	**19**
2017–18	Strasbourg	26	5		
2018–19	Strasbourg	34	8		
2019–20	Strasbourg	0	0	**60**	**13**
2019–20	Nottingham F	10	0	**10**	**0**

PANTILIMON, Costel (G) **224** **0**

H: 6 5 W: 15 02 b.Bacau 1-2-87

Internationals: Romania U17, U19, U21, Full caps.

2005–06	Aerostar Bacau	9	0	**9**	**0**
2006–07	Poli Timisoara	8	0		
2007–08	Poli Timisoara	5	0	**13**	**0**
2008–09	Timisoara	31	0		
2009–10	Timisoara	21	0		
2010–11	Timisoara	28	0	**80**	**0**
2011–12	*Manchester C*	0	0		
2012–13	Manchester C	0	0		
2013–14	Manchester C	7	0	**7**	**0**
2014–15	Sunderland	28	0		
2015–16	Sunderland	17	0	**45**	**0**
2015–16	Watford	0	0		
2016–17	Watford	2	0		
2017–18	Watford	0	0	**2**	**0**
2017–18	*Deportivo La Coruna*	6	0	**6**	**0**
2017–18	*Nottingham F*	13	0		
2018–19	Nottingham F	44	0		
2019–20	Nottingham F	0	0	**57**	**0**
2019–20	*Omonia*	5	0	**5**	**0**

RICHARDSON, Jayden (D) **18** **1**

b. 4-9-00

2019–20	Nottingham F	0	0		
2019–20	*Exeter C*	18	1	**18**	**1**

SAMBA, Brice (G) **86** **0**

b.Linzolo 25-4-94

2010–11	Le Havre	0	0		
2011–12	Le Havre	0	0		
2012–13	Le Havre	0	0		
2012–13	Marseille	0	0		
2013–14	Marseille	1	0		
2014–15	Marseille	0	0		
2015–16	Marseille	0	0		
2015–16	*Nancy*	2	0	**2**	**0**
2016–17	Marseille	0	0	**1**	**0**
2017–18	Caen	4	0		
2018–19	Caen	38	0		
2019–20	Caen	1	0	**43**	**0**
2019–20	Nottingham F	40	0	**40**	**0**

SEMEDO, Alfa (M) **89** **8**

b.Bissau 30-8-97

2016–17	Benfica	0	0		
2016–17	*Vilafranquense*	29	4	**29**	**4**
2017–18	Morirense	28	2	**28**	**2**
2018–19	Benfica	5	0		
2018–19	*Espanyol*	3	0	**3**	**0**
2019–20	Benfica	0	0	**5**	**0**

On loan from Benfica.

2019–20	Nottingham F	24	2	**24**	**2**

SHELVEY, George (G) **0** **0**

b. 22-4-01

2019–20	Nottingham F	0	0		

SMITH, Jordan (G) **59** **0**

b.Nottingham 8-8-94

Internationals: Costa Rica U17, U20, Full caps.

2013–14	Nottingham F	0	0		
2014–15	Nottingham F	0	0		
2015–16	Nottingham F	0	0		
2016–17	Nottingham F	15	0		
2017–18	Nottingham F	29	0		
2018–19	Nottingham F	0	0		
2018–19	*Barnsley*	1	0	**1**	**0**
2018–19	*Mansfield T*	12	0	**12**	**0**
2019–20	Nottingham F	2	0	**46**	**0**

SOLE, Liam (M) **0** **0**

2018–19	Milton Keynes D	0	0		
2019–20	Nottingham F	0	0		

SOW, Samba (M) **246** **5**

b.Bamako 29-4-89

Internationals: Mali Full caps.

2008–09	Lens	1	0		
2009–10	Lens	31	1		
2010–11	Lens	10	0		
2011–12	Lens	23	0		
2012–13	Lens	25	0	**90**	**1**
2013–14	Kardemir Karabukspor	32	0		
2014–15	Kardemir Karabukspor	18	1	**50**	**1**
2015–16	Kayserispor	16	1		
2016–17	Kayserispor	25	2	**41**	**3**
2017–18	Dynamo Moscow	23	0		
2018–19	Dynamo Moscow	17	0	**40**	**0**
2019–20	Nottingham F	25	0	**25**	**0**

STEELE, Luke (G) **322** **0**

H: 6 2 W: 12 00 b.Peterborough 24-9-84

Internationals: England U18, U19, U20.

2001–02	Peterborough U	2	0	**2**	**0**
2001–02	Manchester U	0	0		
2002–03	Manchester U	0	0		
2003–04	Manchester U	0	0		
2004–05	Manchester U	0	0		
2004–05	*Coventry C*	32	0		
2005–06	Manchester U	0	0		
2006–07	WBA	0	0		
2006–07	*Coventry C*	5	0	**37**	**0**
2007–08	WBA	2	0	**2**	**0**
2007–08	*Barnsley*	14	0		
2008–09	Barnsley	10	0		
2009–10	Barnsley	39	0		
2010–11	Barnsley	46	0		
2011–12	Barnsley	36	0		
2012–13	Barnsley	33	0		
2013–14	Barnsley	31	0	**209**	**0**
2014–15	Panathinaikos	29	0		
2015–16	Panathinaikos	28	0		
2016–17	Panathinaikos	8	0		
2017–18	Panathinaikos	0	0	**65**	**0**
2017–18	Bristol C	5	0	**5**	**0**
2018–19	Nottingham F	2	0		
2019–20	Nottingham F	0	0	**2**	**0**
2019–20	*Millwall*	0	0		

TAYLOR, Jake (M) **18** **5**

2019–20	Nottingham F	0	0		
2019–20	*Port Vale*	18	5	**18**	**5**

TIAGO SILVA, Rafael (M) 227 23
b.Lisbon 2-6-93
Internationals: Portugal U20, U21, U23.

2012–13	Belenenses	37	4		
2013–14	Belenenses	24	1		
2014–15	Belenenses	20	1		
2015–16	Belenenses	17	2	**98**	**8**
2016–17	Feirense	27	6		
2017–18	Feirense	29	3		
2018–19	Feirense	29	3		
2019–20	Feirense	0	0	**85**	**12**
2019–20	Nottingham F	44	3	**44**	**3**

TOBIAS FIGUEIREDO, Pereira (D) 107 7
H: 6 2 W: 13 03 b.Satao 2-2-94
Internationals: Portugal U17, U18, U19, U20, U21, U23.

2012–13	Sporting Lisbon	0	0		
2013–14	Sporting Lisbon	0	0		
2013–14	*Reus*	13	1	**13**	**1**
2014–15	Sporting Lisbon	14	2		
2015–16	Sporting Lisbon	1	0		
2016–17	Sporting Lisbon	2	0		
2016–17	*Nacional*	22	1	**22**	**1**
2017–18	Sporting Lisbon	0	0		
2017–18	*Nottingham F*	12	0		
2018–19	Sporting Lisbon	0	0	**17**	**2**

On loan from Sporting Lisbon.

2018–19	Nottingham F	13	0		
2019–20	Nottingham F	30	3	**55**	**3**

WALKER, Tyler (F) 138 47
H: 5 10 W: 9 13 b. 17-10-96
Internationals: England U20.

2013–14	Nottingham F	0	0		
2014–15	Nottingham F	7	1		
2015–16	Nottingham F	14	0		
2015–16	*Burton Alb*	6	1	**6**	**1**
2016–17	Nottingham F	0	0		
2016–17	*Stevenage*	8	3	**8**	**3**
2016–17	*Port Vale*	6	2	**6**	**2**
2017–18	Nottingham F	12	3		
2017–18	*Bolton W*	5	0	**5**	**0**
2018–19	Nottingham F	0	0		
2018–19	*Mansfield T*	44	22	**44**	**22**
2019–20	*Lincoln C*	29	14	**29**	**14**
2019–20	Nottingham F	7	1	**40**	**5**

WATSON, Ben (M) 446 39
H: 5 10 W: 10 11 b.Camberwell 9-7-85
Internationals: England U21.

2002–03	Crystal Palace	5	0		
2003–04	Crystal Palace	16	1		
2004–05	Crystal Palace	21	0		
2005–06	Crystal Palace	42	4		
2006–07	Crystal Palace	25	3		
2007–08	Crystal Palace	42	5		
2008–09	Crystal Palace	18	5	**169**	**18**
2008–09	Wigan Ath	10	2		
2009–10	Wigan Ath	5	1		
2009–10	*QPR*	16	2	**16**	**2**
2009–10	*WBA*	7	1	**7**	**1**
2010–11	Wigan Ath	29	3		
2011–12	Wigan Ath	21	3		
2012–13	Wigan Ath	12	1		
2013–14	Wigan Ath	25	2		
2014–15	Wigan Ath	9	1	**111**	**13**
2014–15	Watford	20	0		
2015–16	Watford	35	2		
2016–17	Watford	4	0		
2017–18	Watford	8	0	**67**	**2**
2017–18	Nottingham F	14	0		
2018–19	Nottingham F	17	0		
2019–20	Nottingham F	45	3	**76**	**3**

WORRALL, Joe (D) 132 3
H: 6 3 b.Nottingham 10-1-97
Internationals: England U20, U21.

2015–16	Nottingham F	0	0		
2015–16	*Dagenham & R*	14	1	**14**	**1**
2016–17	Nottingham F	21	0		
2017–18	Nottingham F	31	1		
2018–19	Nottingham F	0	0		
2018–19	Rangers	22	0	**22**	**0**
2019–20	Nottingham F	46	1	**98**	**2**

WRIGHT, Jordan (G) 0 0

2015–16	Nottingham F	0	0		
2016–17	Nottingham F	0	0		
2017–18	Nottingham F	0	0		
2018–19	Nottingham F	0	0		
2019–20	Nottingham F	0	0		

YATES, Ryan (M) 96 9
b.Nottingham 21-11-97

2016–17	Nottingham F	0	0		
2016–17	*Shrewsbury T*	12	0	**12**	**0**
2017–18	Nottingham F	0	0		
2017–18	*Notts Co*	25	3	**25**	**3**
2017–18	*Scunthorpe U*	16	2	**16**	**2**
2018–19	Nottingham F	16	1		
2019–20	Nottingham F	27	3	**43**	**4**

YURI RIBEIRO, Oliveira (D) 52 1
b. 24-1-97
Internationals: Portugal U16, U17, U18, U19, U20, U21.

2014–15	Benfica	0	0		
2015–16	Benfica	0	0		
2016–17	Benfica	0	0		
2017–18	Benfica	0	0		
2017–18	*Rio Ave*	25	1	**25**	**1**
2018–19	Benfica	0	0		
2019–20	Nottingham F	27	0	**27**	**0**

Players retained or with offer of contract
Antunes, Carvalho Joao Antonio; Asare, Keith; Back, Finley Jude William; Barnes, Joshua William; Dekel, Daks Ethan; Larsson, Julian; Maia, Da Silva Tiago Rafael; Marles, Galliani Adrian; Oliveira, Ribeiro Yuri; Pereira, Figueiredo Tobias; Preston, Daniel James; Rama, Rezart; Swan, William Jonathan; Thomas-Sadler, Morgan Lee.

Scholars
Amekortu, Francky Arnord; Andrew, Elliott Nicholas; Bello, Silvio Olabode; Boland, Luke Thomas; Donnelly, Aaron Martin; Doorba-Baptist, Luca William; Gibso-Hammond, Alexander Monroe; Hammond, Oliver Jack; Jackso-Davis, Jovel Nii Odartey; Libur-Hines, Nykah JarOne; Mbakop, Fankwe William Jordan; Mutoti, Tawanda Fortune; Sanders, Samuel John; Spooner, Malique Tyrese; Statham, Michael Joseph.

OLDHAM ATH (60)

ADAMS, Kielen (F) 1 0

2018–19	Bradford C	0	0		
2019–20	Oldham Ath	1	0	**1**	**0**

AKPA AKPRO, Jean-Louis (F) 396 58
H: 6 0 W: 10 12 b.Toulouse 4-1-85

2004–05	Toulouse	13	0		
2005–06	Toulouse	14	3	**27**	**3**
2006–07	*Brest*	15	2	**15**	**2**
2007–08	FC Brussels	3	0	**3**	**0**
2008–09	Grimsby T	20	3		
2009–10	Grimsby T	36	5	**56**	**8**
2010–11	Rochdale	32	4		
2011–12	Rochdale	41	7	**73**	**11**
2012–13	Tranmere R	28	8		
2013–14	Tranmere R	25	2	**53**	**10**
2013–14	*Bury*	10	0	**10**	**0**
2014–15	Shrewsbury T	45	9		
2015–16	Shrewsbury T	38	6	**83**	**15**
2016–17	Barnet	23	1		
2016–17	*Yeovil T*	13	2	**13**	**2**
2017–18	Barnet	26	3	**49**	**4**
2018–19	Masfut	11	3	**11**	**3**
2019–20	Oldham Ath	3	0	**3**	**0**

ALLEN, Ellis (G) 0 0

2019–20	Oldham Ath	0	0		

AZANKPO, Desire (F) 125 44
Internationals: Benin Full caps.

2010–11	Generation Foot Dakar	0	0		
2011–12	Generation Foot Dakar	0	0		
2012–13	Metz	0	0		
2013–14	Metz	0	0		
2013–14	Jeunesse	11	6	**11**	**6**
2014–15	Le Puy Foot 43	19	7	**19**	**7**
2015–16	Pagny sur Moselle	18	11		
2016–17	Pagny sur Moselle	3	1	**21**	**12**
2017–18	Epinal	21	11	**21**	**11**
2018–19	Senica	25	4	**25**	**4**
2019–20	Oldham Ath	28	4	**28**	**4**

BRANGER, Johan (M) 113 30
H: 6 0 W: 12 06 b.Sens 5-7-93
Internationals: Gabon Full caps.

2011–12	Auxerre	0	0		
2012–13	Auxerre	0	0		
2013–14	Auxerre	0	0		
2014–15	US Raon-l'Etape	20	8	**20**	**8**
2015–16	FC Sens	16	4		
2016–17	FC Sens	0	0	**16**	**4**
2017–18	FC Dieppe	26	11	**26**	**11**
2018–19	Oldham Ath	35	5		
2019–20	Oldham Ath	16	2	**51**	**7**

COKE, Giles (M) 292 26
H: 6 0 W: 11 11 b.Westminster 3-6-86

2004–05	Mansfield T	9	0		
2005–06	Mansfield T	40	4		
2006–07	Mansfield T	21	1	**70**	**5**
2007–08	Northampton T	20	5		
2008–09	Northampton T	32	2	**52**	**7**
2009–10	Motherwell	32	2	**32**	**2**
2010–11	Sheffield W	27	4		
2011–12	Sheffield W	0	0		
2011–12	*Bury*	30	6	**30**	**6**
2012–13	Sheffield W	16	0		
2012–13	*Swindon T*	4	0	**4**	**0**
2013–14	Sheffield W	28	1		
2014–15	Sheffield W	13	1	**84**	**6**
2014–15	*Bolton W*	4	0	**4**	**0**
2015–16	Ipswich T	10	0		
2016–17	Ipswich T	0	0	**10**	**0**
2017–18	Chesterfield	2	0	**2**	**0**
2018–19	Oldham Ath	4	0		
2019–20	Oldham Ath	0	0	**4**	**0**

DE LA PAZ, Zeus (G) 40 0
b. 11-3-95
Internationals: Curacao U20, Full caps.

2013–14	PSV Eindhoven	0	0		
2014–15	PSV Eindhoven	0	0		

From Nuneaton T.

2017	Cincinnati Dutch Lions	14	0	**14**	**0**
2017–18	Oldham Ath	0	0		
2018–19	Oldham Ath	3	0		
2019–20	Oldham Ath	23	0	**26**	**0**

DEARNLEY, Zachary (M) 17 5
b. 28-9-98
Internationals: England U16, U18.

2017–18	Manchester U	0	0		
2016–17	Manchester U	0	0		
2018–19	Manchester U	0	0		
2018–19	*Oldham Ath*	9	1		
2019–20	Oldham Ath	8	4	**17**	**5**

DOLAN, Callum (M) 0 0

2019–20	Oldham Ath	0	0		

EAGLES, Chris (M) 364 54
H: 5 10 W: 11 07 b.Hemel Hempstead 19-11-85

2003–04	Manchester U	0	0		
2004–05	Manchester U	0	0		
2004–05	*Watford*	13	1		
2005–06	Manchester U	0	0		
2005–06	*Sheffield W*	25	3	**25**	**3**
2005–06	*Watford*	17	3	**30**	**4**
2006–07	Manchester U	2	1		
2006–07	*NEC Nijmegen*	15	1	**15**	**1**
2007–08	Manchester U	4	0	**6**	**1**
2008–09	Burnley	43	8		
2009–10	Burnley	34	2		
2010–11	Burnley	43	11	**120**	**21**
2011–12	Bolton W	34	4		
2012–13	Bolton W	43	12		
2013–14	Bolton W	16	1	**93**	**17**
2014–15	Blackpool	7	1	**7**	**1**
2014–15	Charlton Ath	15	2	**15**	**2**
2015–16	Bury	4	0	**4**	**0**
2016–17	Accrington S	6	0	**6**	**0**
2016–17	Port Vale	20	4	**20**	**4**
2017–18	Ross Co	8	0	**8**	**0**

From free agent.

2019–20	Oldham Ath	15	0	**15**	**0**

EGERT, Tomas (D) 46 1
b. 1-8-94

2014–15	Slovan Liberec	0	0		
2014–15	*Spartak Trnava*	1	0	**1**	**0**
2015–16	Slovan Liberec	0	0		
2015–16	*Slavoj Vysehrad*	21	1	**21**	**1**
2016–17	Slovan Liberec	0	0		
2016–17	*Viktoria Zizkov*	15	0	**15**	**0**
2017–18	Burton Alb	3	0	**3**	**0**
2019–20	Oldham Ath	6	0	**6**	**0**

EMMERSON, Zac (F) 2 0

2019–20	Oldham Ath	2	0	**2**	**0**

FAGE, Dylan (M) 12 0

2016–17	Auxerre	0	0		
2017–18	Auxerre	0	0		
2018–19	Auxerre	0	0		
2019–20	Oldham Ath	12	0	**12**	**0**

GASKELL, Reece (M) 1 0

2019–20	Oldham Ath	1	0	**1**	**0**

GONZALES, Florian (M) 0 0
Internationals: France U16.
From Auxerre.

2019–20	Oldham Ath	0	0		

GRUNDY, Jack (D) 0 0

2019–20	Oldham Ath	0	0		

HAYMER, Tom (D) 72 6
b. 16-11-99

2017–18	Oldham Ath	7	1		
2018–19	Oldham Ath	28	2		
2019–20	Oldham Ath	37	3	**72**	**6**

IACOVITTI, Alex (D) **57 2**

b. 2-9-97

Internationals: Scotland U17, U19, U21.

2015–16	Nottingham F	0	0		
2016–17	Nottingham F	2	0		
2016–17	*Mansfield T*	8	0	**8**	**0**
2017–18	Nottingham F	0	0		
2017–18	*Forest Green R*	14	1	**14**	**1**
2018–19	Nottingham F	0	0	**2**	**0**
2018–19	*Oldham Ath*	9	1		
2019–20	Oldham Ath	24	0	**33**	**1**

JONES, David (M) **377 27**

H: 5 11 W: 10 10 b.Southport 4-11-84

Internationals: England U21.

2003–04	Manchester U	0	0		
2004–05	Manchester U	0	0		
2005–06	Manchester U	0	0		
2005–06	*Preston NE*	24	3	**24**	**3**
2005–06	NEC Nijmegen	17	6	**17**	**6**
2006–07	Manchester U	0	0		
2006–07	Derby Co	28	6		
2007–08	Derby Co	14	1	**42**	**7**
2008–09	Wolverhampton W	34	4		
2009–10	Wolverhampton W	20	1		
2010–11	Wolverhampton W	12	1	**66**	**6**
2011–12	Wigan Ath	16	0		
2012–13	Wigan Ath	13	0	**29**	**0**
2012–13	*Blackburn R*	12	2	**12**	**2**
2013–14	Burnley	46	1		
2014–15	Burnley	36	0		
2015–16	Burnley	41	1		
2016–17	Burnley	1	0	**124**	**2**
2016–17	Sheffield W	29	0		
2017–18	Sheffield W	27	1		
2018–19	Sheffield W	1	0	**57**	**1**
2019–20	Oldham Ath	6	0	**6**	**0**

JONES, Taylor (D) **0 0**

2019–20	Oldham Ath	0	0		

KOKOS, Marvin (M) **3 1**

b. 12-10-00

2016–17	Marseille	0	0		
2017–18	Martigues	0	0		
2018–19	Ajaccio	3	1	**3**	**1**
2019–20	Oldham Ath	0	0		

MAOUCHE, Mohamed (M) **128 11**

b. 22-1-93

2010–11	Saint-Etienne	0	0		
2011–12	Servette	0	0		
2012–13	Servette	0	0		
2013–14	Servette	0	0		
2014–15	Lausanne Sport	16	1	**16**	**1**
2015–16	Tours	15	0		
2016–17	Tours	31	3		
2017–18	Tours	0	0	**46**	**3**
2017–18	Oldham Ath	1	0		
2018–19	Oldham Ath	34	4		
2019–20	Oldham Ath	31	3	**66**	**7**

McCANN, Chris (M) **397 36**

H: 6 1 W: 11 11 b.Dublin 21-7-87

Internationals: Republic of Ireland U19.

2005–06	Burnley	23	2		
2006–07	Burnley	38	5		
2007–08	Burnley	35	5		
2008–09	Burnley	44	6		
2009–10	Burnley	7	0		
2010–11	Burnley	4	1		
2011–12	Burnley	46	4		
2012–13	Burnley	41	4	**238**	**27**
2013–14	Wigan Ath	27	2		
2014–15	Wigan Ath	17	2		
2015–16	Wigan Ath	38	4	**82**	**8**
2016–17	*Coventry C*	13	1	**13**	**1**
2017	Atlanta U	24	0		
2018	Atlanta U	24	1	**48**	**0**
2019–20	Oldham Ath	16	0	**16**	**0**

McHALE, Dominic (M) **1 0**

H: 5 11 W: 11 07 b. 1-1-95

2013–14	Barnsley	0	0		
2014–15	Barnsley	0	0		

From Ramsbottom U, Northwich Vic, Achyronas Liopetriou, Salford C, Southport, Ashton U, FC United of Manchester.

2019–20	Oldham Ath	1	0	**1**	**0**

McKINNEY, Lewis (M) **2 0**

2019–20	Oldham Ath	2	0	**2**	**0**

MILLS, Zak (D) **121 2**

b. 28-5-92

From Histon, Boston U.

2016–17	Grimsby T	30	0		
2017–18	Grimsby T	28	0	**58**	**0**
2018–19	Morecambe	38	1	**38**	**1**
2019–20	Oldham Ath	25	1	**25**	**1**

MISSILOU, Christopher (M) **142 15**

H: 5 11 W: 11 00 b.Auxerre 18-7-92

Internationals: France U18. Congo Full caps.

2009–10	Auxerre	0	0		
2010–11	Auxerre	0	0		
2011–12	Auxerre	1	0		
2012–13	Auxerre	0	0	**1**	**0**
2013–14	Evry	11	1	**11**	**1**
2014–15	Stade Brestpos 29	1	0	**1**	**0**
2015–16	Montceau	12	0		
2016–17	Montceau	24	7	**36**	**7**
2017–18	Entente Sannois	6	0	**6**	**0**
2017–18	Le Puy Foot 43	15	3	**15**	**3**
2018–19	Oldham Ath	42	1		
2019–20	Oldham Ath	30	3	**72**	**4**

NEPOMUCENO, Gevaro (F) **225 18**

H: 5 9 W: 10 08 b. 10-11-92

Internationals: Curacao Full caps.

2010–11	Den Bosch	2	0		
2011–12	Den Bosch	13	1	**15**	**1**
2012–13	Fortuna Sittard	17	2		
2013–14	Fortuna Sittard	38	5	**55**	**7**
2014–15	Petrolui Ploiesti	25	1		
2015–16	Petrolui Ploiesti	22	0	**47**	**1**
2015–16	Maritimo Funchal	7	0		
2016–17	Maritimo Funchal	5	0	**12**	**0**
2016–17	*Famalicao*	13	0	**13**	**0**
2017–18	Maritimo	0	0		
2017–18	Oldham Ath	26	1		
2018–19	Oldham Ath	42	6		
2019–20	Oldham Ath	15	2	**83**	**9**

ROBINSON, Harry (M) **1 0**

b. 26-9-00

Internationals: Northern Ireland U16, U19, U21.

From Glenavon.

2018–19	Oldham Ath	1	0		
2019–20	Oldham Ath	0	0	**1**	**0**

Transferred to Motherwell, March 2020.

ROWE, Danny (F) **10 3**

H: 6 1 W: 13 02 b.Blackpool 29-1-90

2012–13	Fleetwood T	0	0		

From Lincoln C, AFC Fylde.

2019–20	Oldham Ath	10	3	**10**	**3**

SEFIL, Sonhy (D) **60 4**

b. 16-6-94

2012–13	Sedan	0	0		
2013–14	Auxerre	0	0		
2014–15	Auxerre	6	0		
2015–16	Auxerre	15	3	**21**	**3**
2016–17	Asteras Tripolis	5	0	**5**	**0**
2017–18	Lyon Duchere	30	1	**30**	**1**
2018–19	Oldham Ath	0	0		
2019–20	Oldham Ath	4	0	**4**	**0**

STOTT, Jamie (D) **16 0**

b. 22-12-97

2016–17	Oldham Ath	4	0		
2017–18	Oldham Ath	0	0		
2018–19	Oldham Ath	3	0		
2019–20	Oldham Ath	9	0	**16**	**0**

SWABY-NEAVIN, Javid (D) **1 0**

2018–19	Oldham Ath	1	0		
2019–20	Oldham Ath	0	0	**1**	**0**

SYLLA, Mohamad (M) **45 1**

b. 1-12-93

From Entente SSG.

2018–19	Oldham Ath	15	0		
2019–20	Oldham Ath	30	1	**45**	**1**

VERA, Urko (F) **240 67**

b. 14-5-87

2010–11	Lemona	18	13	**18**	**13**
2010–11	Athletic Club	5	1	**5**	**1**
2011–12	Hercules	33	11	**33**	**11**
2012–13	Ponferradina	14	2	**14**	**2**
2012–13	Alcorcon	9	1	**9**	**1**
2013–14	Eibar	31	5	**31**	**5**
2014–15	Mirandes	38	17		
2015	Jeonbuk Motors	6	0	**6**	**0**
2015–16	Osasuna	19	3	**19**	**3**
2016–17	Huesca	14	1	**14**	**1**
2016–17	Mirandes	16	5	**54**	**22**
2017–18	CFR Cluj	15	5		
2017–18	*Astra*	10	1	**10**	**1**
2018–19	CFR Cluj	2	0	**17**	**5**
2018–19	Oldham Ath	5	1		
2019–20	Oldham Ath	5	1	**10**	**2**

Transferred to Guijuelo, January 2020.

WHEATER, David (D) **409 31**

H: 6 5 W: 12 12 b.Redcar 14-2-87

Internationals: England U16, U17, U18, U19, U21.

2004–05	Middlesbrough	0	0		
2005–06	Middlesbrough	6	0		
2005–06	*Doncaster R*	7	1	**7**	**1**
2006–07	Middlesbrough	2	1		
2006–07	*Wolverhampton W*	1	0	**1**	**0**
2006–07	*Darlington*	15	2	**15**	**2**
2007–08	Middlesbrough	34	3		
2008–09	Middlesbrough	32	1		
2009–10	Middlesbrough	42	1		
2010–11	Middlesbrough	24	3	**140**	**9**
2010–11	Bolton W	7	0		
2011–12	Bolton W	24	2		
2012–13	Bolton W	4	0		
2013–14	Bolton W	23	1		
2014–15	Bolton W	17	1		
2015–16	Bolton W	28	1		
2016–17	Bolton W	43	9		
2017–18	Bolton W	33	1		
2018–19	Bolton W	33	0	**212**	**15**
2019–20	Oldham Ath	34	4	**34**	**4**

WILSON, Scott (F) **54 12**

b. 11-1-93

From Bath C, Paulton R, Western-super-Mare, Eastleigh.

2018–19	Macclesfield T	33	10	**33**	**10**
2019–20	Oldham Ath	21	2	**21**	**2**

WOODS, Gary (G) **202 0**

H: 6 1 W: 11 00 b.Kettering 1-10-90

Internationals: England U18.

2008–09	Doncaster R	1	0		
2009–10	Doncaster R	0	0		
2010–11	Doncaster R	16	0		
2011–12	Doncaster R	14	0		
2012–13	Doncaster R	42	0		
2013–14	Doncaster R	0	0	**73**	**0**
2013–14	Watford	0	0		
2014–15	Leyton Orient	17	0		
2015–16	Leyton Orient	0	0	**17**	**0**
2015–16	*Ross Co*	12	0	**12**	**0**
2016–17	Hamilton A	21	0		
2017–18	Hamilton A	32	0		
2018–19	Hamilton A	32	0	**85**	**0**
2019–20	Oldham Ath	15	0	**15**	**0**

Scholars

Allen, Ellis Frank Fabien; Chapman, MacKenzie Jon; Gaskell, Reece; Grundy, Jack William; Hackett, Andrew James; Higgins, Sean Michael; Hough, Benjamin Isaac; Jones, Taylor Jay; Leech, Charley Jon; Loforte, Tique Da Silva Ivanilson; Luamba, Junior; McKinney, Lewis Christopher Mark; Oseh, Robert Oshomoshiofu; Pickford, Ryan Paul; Speed, Callum; Sutton, William Joseph; Williams, Jack Bobby Owen; Wych, Kyle Craig.

OXFORD U (61)

AGYEI, Daniel (F) **59 11**

H: 6 0 W: 12 02 b.Dansoman 1-6-97

2014–15	AFC Wimbledon	0	0		
2015–16	Burnley	0	0		
2016–17	Burnley	3	0		
2016–17	*Coventry C*	16	4	**16**	**4**
2017–18	Burnley	0	0		
2017–18	*Walsall*	18	4	**18**	**4**
2017–18	*Blackpool*	9	0	**9**	**0**
2018–19	Burnley	0	0		
2019–20	Burnley	0	0	**3**	**0**
2019–20	Oxford U	13	3	**13**	**3**

ALLARDYCE, Sam (D) **0 0**

b. 1-9-00

From Manchester U.

2018–19	Bury	0	0		
2019–20	Oxford U	0	0		

ATKINSON, Robert (D) **0 0**

b. 13-7-98

From Eastleigh.

2019–20	Oxford U	0	0		

BERKOE, Kevin (D) **0 0**

b. 5-7-01

From Wolverhampton W.

2019–20	Oxford U	0	0		

BRANNAGAN, Cameron (M) **99 8**

H: 5 11 W: 11 03 b.Manchester 9-5-96

Internationals: England U18, U20.

2013–14	Liverpool	0	0		
2014–15	Liverpool	0	0		
2015–16	Liverpool	3	0		
2016–17	Liverpool	0	0		

2016–17 *Fleetwood T* 13 0 **13 0**
2017–18 Liverpool 0 0 **3 0**
2017–18 Oxford U 12 0
2018–19 Oxford U 41 3
2019–20 Oxford U 30 5 **83 8**

CADDEN, Chris (M) 146 8
b.Bellshill 19-9-96
Internationals: Scotland U21, Full caps.
2013–14 Motherwell 3 0
2014–15 Motherwell 3 0
2014–15 *Albion R* 10 2 **10 2**
2015–16 Motherwell 20 2
2016–17 Motherwell 36 3
2017–18 Motherwell 33 0
2018–19 Motherwell 20 1 **115 6**
2019–20 Columbus Crew 0 0
On loan from Columbus Crew.
2019–20 Oxford U 21 0 **21 0**

DICKIE, Rob (D) 125 4
H: 6 0 W: 11 09 b.Wokingham 3-3-96
Internationals: England U18, U19.
2015–16 Reading 1 0
2016–17 Reading 0 0
2016–17 *Cheltenham T* 20 2 **20 2**
2017–18 Reading 0 0 **1 0**
2017–18 *Lincoln C* 18 0 **18 0**
2017–18 Oxford U 15 1
2018–19 Oxford U 37 1
2019–20 Oxford U 34 0 **86 2**

EASTWOOD, Simon (G) 218 0
H: 6 2 W: 10 13 b.Huddersfield 26-6-89
Internationals: England U18, U19.
2005–06 Huddersfield T 0 0
2006–07 Huddersfield T 0 0
2007–08 Huddersfield T 0 0
2008–09 Huddersfield T 1 0
2009–10 Huddersfield T 0 0 **1 0**
2009–10 *Bradford C* 22 0 **22 0**
2010–11 Oxford U 0 0
From FC Halifax T.
2012–13 Portsmouth 27 0 **27 0**
2013–14 Blackburn R 7 0
2014–15 Blackburn R 6 0
2015–16 Blackburn R 0 0 **13 0**
2016–17 Oxford U 46 0
2017–18 Oxford U 46 0
2018–19 Oxford U 34 0
2019–20 Oxford U 29 0 **155 0**

FORDE, Anthony (M) 226 13
H: 5 9 W: 10 10 b.Limerick 16-11-93
Internationals: Republic of Ireland U19, U21.
2011–12 Wolverhampton W 6 0
2012–13 Wolverhampton W 12 0
2012–13 *Scunthorpe U* 8 0 **8 0**
2013–14 Wolverhampton W 3 0 **21 0**
2014–15 Walsall 37 3
2015–16 Walsall 41 4 **78 7**
2016–17 Rotherham U 32 2
2017–18 Rotherham U 41 2
2018–19 Rotherham U 28 1 **101 5**
2019–20 Oxford U 18 1 **18 1**

GOODRHAM, Tyler (M) 0 0
2019–20 Oxford U 0 0

GORRIN, Alejandro (M) 135 1
b.Tenerife 1-8-93
2011–12 Sunderland 0 0
2012–13 Sunderland 0 0
2013–14 Sunderland 0 0
2014–15 Wellington Phoenix 25 0
2015–16 Wellington Phoenix 24 0
2016–17 Wellington Phoenix 23 1 **72 1**
2017–18 Boavista 0 0
2017–18 Sepsi 12 0 **12 0**
2018–19 Motherwell 20 0 **20 0**
2019–20 Oxford U 31 0 **31 0**

HALL, Robert (F) 160 19
H: 6 2 W: 10 05 b.Aylesbury 20-10-93
Internationals: England U16, U17, U18, U19.
2010–11 West Ham U 0 0
2011–12 West Ham U 3 0
2011–12 *Oxford U* 13 5
2011–12 *Milton Keynes D* 2 0
2012–13 West Ham U 1 0 **4 0**
2012–13 *Birmingham C* 13 0 **13 0**
2012–13 *Bolton W* 1 0
2013–14 Bolton W 22 1
2014–15 Bolton W 9 0
2014–15 *Milton Keynes D* 7 3
2015–16 Bolton W 0 0 **32 1**
2015–16 *Milton Keynes D* 27 2 **36 5**
2016–17 Oxford U 26 6
2017–18 Oxford U 13 2
2018–19 Oxford U 4 0
2019–20 Oxford U 13 0 **69 13**
2019–20 *Forest Green R* 6 0 **6 0**

HANSON, Jamie (F) 83 1
H: 6 3 W: 12 06 b.Burton-upon-Trent 10-11-95
Internationals: England U20.
2012–13 Derby Co 0 0
2013–14 Derby Co 0 0
2014–15 Derby Co 2 1
2015–16 Derby Co 18 0
2016–17 Derby Co 5 0
2016–17 *Wigan Ath* 17 0 **17 0**
2017–18 Derby Co 6 0 **31 1**
2018–19 Oxford U 30 0
2019–20 Oxford U 5 0 **35 0**

HARRIS, Max (G) 0 0
b.Gloucester 14-9-99
2018–19 Oxford U 0 0
2019–20 Oxford U 0 0

HENRY, James (M) 427 78
H: 6 1 W: 11 11 b.Reading 10-6-89
Internationals: Scotland U16, U19. England U18, U19.
2006–07 Reading 0 0
2006–07 *Nottingham F* 1 0 **1 0**
2007–08 Reading 0 0
2007–08 *Bournemouth* 11 4 **11 4**
2007–08 *Norwich C* 3 0 **3 0**
2008–09 Reading 7 0
2008–09 *Millwall* 16 3
2009–10 Reading 3 0 **10 0**
2009–10 *Millwall* 9 5
2010–11 Millwall 42 5
2011–12 Millwall 39 0
2012–13 Millwall 35 5
2013–14 Millwall 5 0 **146 18**
2013–14 Wolverhampton W 32 10
2014–15 Wolverhampton W 37 5
2015–16 Wolverhampton W 39 7
2016–17 Wolverhampton W 2 0 **110 22**
2016–17 *Bolton W* 30 1 **30 1**
2017–18 Oxford U 42 10
2018–19 Oxford U 44 11
2019–20 Oxford U 30 12 **116 33**

JAMES, Owen (F) 1 0
b. 13-10-00
2017–18 Oxford U 1 0
2018–19 Oxford U 0 0
2019–20 Oxford U 0 0 **1 0**

JONES, Nico (D) 34 0
b. 3-2-02
2018–19 Oxford U 3 0
2019–20 Oxford U 31 0 **34 0**

KELLY, Liam (M) 86 7
b. 22-11-95
Internationals: Republic of Ireland U19, U21.
2014–15 Reading 0 0
2015–16 Reading 0 0
2016–17 Reading 28 1
2017–18 Reading 34 5
2018–19 Reading 20 1 **82 7**
2019–20 Feyenoord 1 0 **1 0**
On loan from Feyenoord.
2019–20 Oxford U 3 0 **3 0**

LOFTHOUSE, Kyran (F) 0 0
b.Oxford 21-10-00
2018–19 Oxford U 0 0
2019–20 Oxford U 0 0

LONG, Sam (D) 52 2
H: 5 10 W: 11 11 b.Oxford 16-1-95
2012–13 Oxford U 1 0
2013–14 Oxford U 3 0
2014–15 Oxford U 10 1
2015–16 Oxford U 1 0
2016–17 Oxford U 3 0
2017–18 Oxford U 0 0
2018–19 Oxford U 18 0
2019–20 Oxford U 16 1 **52 2**

LOPES, Fabio (F) 0 0
From Sporting Lisbon, Bicester T, Brackley T.
2018–19 Oxford U 0 0
2019–20 Oxford U 0 0

MACKIE, Jamie (F) 403 56
H: 5 8 W: 11 00 b.Dorking 22-9-85
Internationals: Scotland Full caps.
2003–04 Wimbledon 13 0 **13 0**
2004–05 Milton Keynes D 3 0 **3 0**
From Exeter C
2007–08 Plymouth Arg 13 3
2008–09 Plymouth Arg 43 5
2009–10 Plymouth Arg 42 8 **98 16**
2010–11 QPR 25 9
2011–12 QPR 31 7
2012–13 QPR 29 2
2013–14 Nottingham F 45 4 **45 4**
2014–15 Reading 32 5 **32 5**
2015–16 QPR 15 1
2016–17 QPR 18 1
2017–18 QPR 20 4 **138 24**
2018–19 Oxford U 42 5
2019–20 Oxford U 32 2 **74 7**

McCREADIE, Aaron (M) 0 0
2019–20 Oxford U 0 0

MOORE, Elliott (D) 72 8
b. 16-3-97
Internationals: England U18, U20.
2016–17 Leicester C 0 0
2017–18 Leicester C 0 0
2017–18 *OH Leuven* 24 2
2018–19 Leicester C 0 0
2018–19 *OH Leuven* 28 5 **52 7**
2019–20 Oxford U 20 1 **20 1**

MOUSINHO, John (M) 462 23
H: 6 1 W: 12 07 b.Hounslow 30-4-86
2005–06 Brentford 7 0
2006–07 Brentford 34 0
2007–08 Brentford 23 2 **64 2**
2008–09 Wycombe W 34 2
2009–10 Wycombe W 39 1 **73 3**
2010–11 Stevenage 38 7
2011–12 Stevenage 19 3
2012–13 Preston NE 24 1
2013–14 Preston NE 2 0 **26 1**
2013–14 *Gillingham* 4 1 **4 1**
2013–14 *Stevenage* 16 1 **73 11**
2014–15 Burton Alb 42 2
2015–16 Burton Alb 46 0
2016–17 Burton Alb 32 0
2017–18 Burton Alb 1 0 **121 2**
2017–18 Oxford U 40 1
2018–19 Oxford U 35 2
2019–20 Oxford U 26 0 **101 3**

NAPA, Malachi (M) 29 0
b. 26-5-99
From Reading.
2017–18 Oxford U 14 0
2018–19 Oxford U 0 0
2018–19 *Macclesfield T* 15 0 **15 0**
2019–20 Oxford U 0 0 **14 0**

RUFFELS, Joshua (M) 216 15
H: 5 10 W: 11 11 b.Oxford 23-10-93
2011–12 Coventry C 1 0
2012–13 Coventry C 0 0 **1 0**
2013–14 Oxford U 29 1
2014–15 Oxford U 33 0
2015–16 Oxford U 16 0
2016–17 Oxford U 20 2
2017–18 Oxford U 38 5
2018–19 Oxford U 44 4
2019–20 Oxford U 35 3 **215 15**

SOLE, Fabio (M) 0 0
From Reading.
2019–20 Oxford U 0 0

SPASOV, Slavi (F) 1 0
b. 31-12-01
2018–19 Oxford U 1 0
2019–20 Oxford U 0 0 **1 0**

STEPHENS, Jack (G) 2 0
b. 2-8-97
2014–15 Oxford U 0 0
2015–16 Oxford U 0 0
2016–17 Oxford U 0 0
2017–18 Oxford U 0 0
2018–19 Oxford U 2 0
2019–20 Oxford U 0 0 **2 0**

SYKES, Mark (M) 32 1
b. 4-8-97
Internationals: Northern Ireland U19, U21.
From Glenavon.
2018–19 Oxford U 9 0
2019–20 Oxford U 23 1 **32 1**

THORNE, George (M) 112 4
H: 6 2 W: 13 01 b.Chatham 4-1-93
Internationals: England U16, U17, U18, U19.
2009–10 WBA 1 0
2010–11 WBA 1 0
2011–12 WBA 3 0
2011–12 *Portsmouth* 14 0 **14 0**
2012–13 WBA 5 0
2012–13 *Peterborough U* 7 1 **7 1**
2013–14 WBA 0 0 **10 0**
2013–14 *Watford* 8 0 **8 0**
2013–14 *Derby Co* 9 1
2014–15 Derby Co 3 0
2015–16 Derby Co 34 2
2016–17 Derby Co 0 0
2017–18 Derby Co 20 0

2018–19	Derby Co	0	0		
2018–19	*Luton T*	3	0	**3**	**0**
2019–20	Derby Co	0	0	**66**	**3**
2019–20	Oxford U	4	0	**4**	**0**

ZAMOURI, Oussama (M)				**90**	**15**
b.Tidhirat 18-2-96					
2016–17	Telstar	30	3		
2017–18	Telstar	30	3	**60**	**6**
2018–19	Dordrecht	30	9		
2019–20	Dordrecht	0	0	**30**	**9**
2019–20	Oxford U	0	0		

Players retained or with offer of contract
Elechi, Chickanele Michael; Sade, Lichtenfeld Yoav.

Scholars
Chamber-Parillon, Leon Nelson; Crook, Callum James; Edwards, Jordan Stanley Blake; Evans, Max James; Ferguson, Connor Daniel Keith; Gardner, Jack David; Goodrham, Tyler Charlie; Grant, Trey Darnell; Johnson, Samuel Jack; Milton, Viktor Henry; Niemczycki, Damian; Plumley, Kie; Sole, Fabio Calogero Antonio.

PETERBOROUGH U (62)

BARKER, Kyle (M)				**0**	**0**
b. 16-12-00					
2019–20	Peterborough U	0	0		

BEEVERS, Mark (D)				**437**	**21**
H: 6 4 W: 13 00 b.Barnsley 21-11-89					
Internationals: England U19.					
2006–07	Sheffield W	2	0		
2007–08	Sheffield W	28	0		
2008–09	Sheffield W	34	0		
2009–10	Sheffield W	35	0		
2010–11	Sheffield W	28	2		
2011–12	Sheffield W	7	0		
2011–12	*Milton Keynes D*	14	1	**14**	**1**
2012–13	Sheffield W	6	0	**140**	**2**
2012–13	Millwall	35	1		
2013–14	Millwall	28	0		
2014–15	Millwall	25	2		
2015–16	Millwall	42	4	**130**	**7**
2016–17	Bolton W	45	7		
2017–18	Bolton W	44	1		
2018–19	Bolton W	32	3	**121**	**11**
2019–20	Peterborough U	32	0	**32**	**0**

BENNETT, Rhys (D)				**263**	**14**
H: 6 3 W: 12 00 b.Manchester 1-9-91					
2011–12	Bolton W	0	0		
2011–12	*Falkirk*	19	0	**19**	**0**
2012–13	Rochdale	33	2		
2013–14	Rochdale	22	0		
2014–15	Rochdale	39	2		
2015–16	Rochdale	16	2	**110**	**6**
2016–17	Mansfield T	46	2		
2017–18	Mansfield T	38	2	**84**	**4**
2018–19	Peterborough U	37	4		
2019–20	Peterborough U	13	0	**50**	**4**

BLAKE-TRACY, Frazer (D)				**14**	**0**
From Dereham T, Lowestoft, King's Lynn T.					
2019–20	Peterborough U	14	0	**14**	**0**

BOYD, George (M)				**489**	**86**
H: 5 10 W: 11 07 b.Chatham 2-10-85					
Internationals: Scotland B, Full caps.					
2006–07	Peterborough U	20	6		
2007–08	Peterborough U	46	12		
2008–09	Peterborough U	46	9		
2009–10	Peterborough U	32	9		
2009–10	*Nottingham F*	6	1	**6**	**1**
2010–11	Peterborough U	43	15		
2011–12	Peterborough U	45	7		
2012–13	Peterborough U	31	6		
2012–13	*Hull C*	13	4		
2013–14	Hull C	29	2		
2014–15	Hull C	1	0	**43**	**6**
2014–15	Burnley	35	5		
2015–16	Burnley	44	5		
2016–17	Burnley	36	2	**115**	**12**
2017–18	Sheffield W	20	2		
2018–19	Sheffield W	20	1	**40**	**3**
2019–20	Peterborough U	22	0	**285**	**64**

BURROWS, Harrison (M)				**4**	**0**
2017–18	Peterborough U	0	0		
2018–19	Peterborough U	0	0		
2019–20	Peterborough U	4	0	**4**	**0**

BUTLER, Dan (D)				**206**	**9**
b.Cowes 26-8-94					
2012–13	Portsmouth	17	0		
2013–14	Portsmouth	1	0		
2014–15	Portsmouth	30	0		
2015–16	Portsmouth	0	0	**48**	**0**
2016–17	Newport Co	40	3		
2017–18	Newport Co	44	1		
2018–19	Newport Co	45	3	**129**	**7**
2019–20	Peterborough U	29	2	**29**	**2**

CARTWRIGHT, Samuel (D)				**0**	**0**
2017–18	Peterborough U	0	0		
2018–19	Peterborough U	0	0		
2019–20	Peterborough U	0	0		

CHAPMAN, Aaron (G)				**106**	**0**
H: 6 8 W: 14 07 b.Rotherham 29-5-90					
2013–14	Chesterfield	0	0		
2014–15	Chesterfield	0	0		
2014–15	*Accrington S*	3	0		
2015–16	Chesterfield	0	0		
2015–16	*Bristol R*	5	0	**5**	**0**
2016–17	Accrington S	15	0		
2017–18	Accrington S	45	0	**63**	**0**
2018–19	Peterborough U	32	0		
2019–20	*Tranmere R*	6	0	**6**	**0**
2019–20	Peterborough U	0	0	**32**	**0**

CLARKE, Flynn (M)				**0**	**0**
2019–20	Peterborough U	0	0		

COOKE, Callum (F)				**86**	**7**
H: 5 8 W: 11 05 b.Peterlee 21-2-97					
Internationals: England U16, U17, U18.					
2016–17	Middlesbrough	0	0		
2016–17	*Crewe Alex*	18	4	**18**	**4**
2017–18	Middlesbrough	0	0		
2017–18	*Blackpool*	30	2	**30**	**2**
2018–19	Peterborough U	13	1		
2019–20	Peterborough U	0	0	**13**	**1**
2019–20	*Bradford C*	25	0	**25**	**0**

COOPER, George (M)				**183**	**21**
H: 5 9 W: 11 05 b.Warrington 2-11-96					
2014–15	Crewe Alex	22	3		
2015–16	Crewe Alex	27	1		
2016–17	Crewe Alex	46	9		
2017–18	Crewe Alex	27	1	**122**	**14**
2017–18	Peterborough U	13	2		
2018–19	Peterborough U	21	2		
2019–20	Peterborough U	0	0	**34**	**4**
2019–20	*Plymouth Arg*	27	3	**27**	**3**

COPPING, Bobby (D)				**0**	**0**
2019–20	Peterborough U	0	0		

DEMBELE, Siriki (M)				**99**	**14**
b. 7-9-96					
From Dundee U.					
2017–18	Grimsby T	36	4	**36**	**4**
2018–19	Peterborough U	38	5		
2019–20	Peterborough U	25	5	**63**	**10**

EISA, Mohamed (F)				**79**	**37**
H: 6 0 W: 11 00 b. 12-7-94					
From Dartford, Corinthian, Greenwich Bor.					
2017–18	Cheltenham T	45	23	**45**	**23**
2018–19	Bristol C	5	0	**5**	**0**
2019–20	Peterborough U	29	14	**29**	**14**

HARRIS, Luke (M)				**0**	**0**
2019–20	Peterborough U	0	0		

JADE-JONES, Ricky (M)				**11**	**0**
2019–20	Peterborough U	11	0	**11**	**0**

JONES, Archie (M)				**0**	**0**
2019–20	Peterborough U	0	0		

KANU, Idris (F)				**27**	**1**
b. 5-12-99					
From Aldershot T.					
2017–18	Peterborough U	18	0		
2018–19	Peterborough U	0	0		
2018–19	*Port Vale*	3	1	**3**	**1**
2019–20	Peterborough U	6	0	**24**	**0**

KENT, Frankie (D)				**155**	**7**
H: 6 2 W: 12 00 b.Romford 21-11-95					
2013–14	Colchester U	1	0		
2014–15	Colchester U	10	0		
2015–16	Colchester U	26	0		
2016–17	Colchester U	13	0		
2017–18	Colchester U	37	2		
2018–19	Colchester U	40	4	**127**	**6**
2019–20	Peterborough U	28	1	**28**	**1**

MADDISON, Marcus (M)				**219**	**53**
H: 5 9 W: 11 03 b.Sedgefield 26-9-93					
Internationals: England C.					
2014–15	Peterborough U	29	7		
2015–16	Peterborough U	39	11		
2016–17	Peterborough U	41	9		
2017–18	Peterborough U	41	8		
2018–19	Peterborough U	40	8		
2019–20	Peterborough U	22	9	**212**	**52**
2019–20	*Hull C*	7	1	**7**	**1**

MASON, Niall (M)				**128**	**3**
b. 10-1-97					
2015–16	Aston Villa	0	0		
2016–17	Aston Villa	0	0		
2016–17	*Doncaster R*	38	0		
2017–18	Doncaster R	40	3		
2018–19	Doncaster R	20	0	**98**	**3**
2019–20	Peterborough U	30	0	**30**	**0**

MENSAH, Benjamin (M)				**0**	**0**
2019–20	Peterborough U	0	0		

NAISMITH, Jason (D)				**209**	**8**
H: 6 1 W: 13 02 b.Paisley 25-6-94					
Internationals: Scotland U17, U18, U20, U21.					
2011–12	St Mirren	2	0		
2012–13	St Mirren	0	0		
2012–13	*Greenock Morton*	4	0	**4**	**0**
2012–13	*Cowdenbeath*	5	0	**5**	**0**
2013–14	St Mirren	27	2		
2014–15	St Mirren	38	2		
2015–16	St Mirren	5	0		
2016–17	St Mirren	21	0	**93**	**4**
2016–17	Ross Co	16	0		
2017–18	Ross Co	35	2	**51**	**2**
2018–19	Peterborough U	43	1		
2019–20	Peterborough U	0	0	**43**	**1**
2019–20	*Hibernian*	13	1	**13**	**1**

O'HARA, Mark (M)				**194**	**15**
H: 6 0 W: 11 07 b.Barrhead 12-12-95					
Internationals: Scotland U19, U21.					
2012–13	Kilmarnock	17	0		
2013–14	Kilmarnock	14	0		
2014–15	Kilmarnock	18	0		
2015–16	Kilmarnock	29	0	**78**	**0**
2016–17	Dundee	28	5		
2017–18	Dundee	32	4	**60**	**9**
2018–19	Peterborough U	22	4		
2018–19	*Lincoln C*	17	1	**17**	**1**
2019–20	Peterborough U	0	0	**22**	**4**
2019–20	*Motherwell*	17	1	**17**	**1**

O'MALLEY, Conor (G)				**23**	**0**
H: 6 3 W: 13 01 b. 1-8-94					
From St Patrick's Ath.					
2017–18	Peterborough U	9	0		
2018–19	Peterborough U	14	0		
2019–20	Peterborough U	0	0	**23**	**0**

PYM, Christy (G)				**186**	**0**
H: 6 0 W: 11 09 b.Exeter 24-4-95					
Internationals: England U20.					
2012–13	Exeter C	0	0		
2013–14	Exeter C	9	0		
2014–15	Exeter C	25	0		
2015–16	Exeter C	0	0		
2016–17	Exeter C	28	0		
2017–18	Exeter C	46	0		
2018–19	Exeter C	43	0	**151**	**0**
2019–20	Peterborough U	35	0	**35**	**0**

REED, Louis (M)				**133**	**6**
b. 25-7-97					
Internationals: England U18, U19, U20.					
2013–14	Sheffield U	1	0		
2014–15	Sheffield U	19	0		
2015–16	Sheffield U	19	0		
2016–17	Sheffield U	0	0		
2017–18	Sheffield U	0	0	**39**	**0**
2017–18	*Chesterfield*	42	4	**42**	**4**
2018–19	Peterborough U	28	1		
2019–20	Peterborough U	24	1	**52**	**2**

ROLT, Bradley (F)				**0**	**0**
2019–20	Peterborough U	0	0		

ROUDETTE-GREGORY, Khaya (M)				**0**	**0**
2019–20	Peterborough U	0	0		

RUZVIDZO, Shaun (M)				**0**	**0**
2019–20	Peterborough U	0	0		

TASDEMIR, Serhat (M)				**10**	**0**
Internationals: Azerbaijan U19.					
From AFC Fylde.					
2019–20	Peterborough U	10	0	**10**	**0**

TAYLOR, Jack (D)				**63**	**4**
H: 6 1 W: 11 00 b. 23-6-98					
Internationals: Republic of Ireland U21.					
2016–17	Barnet	14	0		
2017–18	Barnet	38	2	**52**	**2**
From Barnet.					
2019–20	Peterborough U	11	2	**11**	**2**

THOMPSON, Nathan (D)				**249**	**4**
H: 5 7 W: 11 02 b.Chester 9-11-90					
2009–10	Swindon T	0	0		
2010–11	Swindon T	3	0		
2011–12	Swindon T	5	0		

2012–13	Swindon T	26	0		
2013–14	Swindon T	41	1		
2014–15	Swindon T	35	0		
2015–16	Swindon T	23	1		
2016–17	Swindon T	34	2	**167**	**4**
2017–18	Portsmouth	36	0		
2018–19	Portsmouth	31	0	**67**	**0**
2019–20	Peterborough U	15	0	**15**	**0**

TONEY, Ivan (F) **220** **76**
H: 5 10 W: 12 00 b.Northampton 16-3-96

2012–13	Northampton T	0	0		
2013–14	Northampton T	13	3		
2014–15	Northampton T	40	8	**53**	**11**
2015–16	Newcastle U	2	0		
2015–16	*Barnsley*	15	1	**15**	**1**
2016–17	Newcastle U	0	0		
2016–17	*Shrewsbury T*	19	6	**19**	**6**
2016–17	*Scunthorpe U*	15	6		
2017–18	Newcastle U	0	0	**2**	**0**
2017–18	*Wigan Ath*	24	4	**24**	**4**
2017–18	*Scunthorpe U*	16	8	**31**	**14**
2018–19	Peterborough U	44	16		
2019–20	Peterborough U	32	24	**76**	**40**

WARD, Joe (M) **88** **7**
b. 9-4-95
Internationals: England C.

2015–16	Brighton & HA	0	0		
2016–17	Brighton & HA	0	0		
2017–18	Peterborough U	17	0		
2018–19	Peterborough U	43	4		
2019–20	Peterborough U	28	3	**88**	**7**

WOODYARD, Alex (M) **122** **3**
H: 5 9 W: 10 00 b.Gravesend 3-5-93
Internationals: England C.

2010–11	Southend U	3	0		
2011–12	Southend U	0	0		
2012–13	Southend U	5	0		
2013–14	Southend U	0	0	**8**	**0**

From Dartford, Concord Rangers, Braintree T.

2017–18	Lincoln C	46	2	**46**	**2**
2018–19	Peterborough U	43	0		
2019–20	Peterborough U	14	0	**57**	**0**
2019–20	*Tranmere R*	11	1	**11**	**1**

Scholars
Allen, Joshua Henry; Blackmore, William Oliver; Gyima-Bio, Nicky William Adjei; Harris, Luke; Horne, Taylor Brian; Jones, Archie Joseph; Keane, Shaun Kyle; Mensah, Benjamin Brakoh Boateng; O'Connell, Charlie; Peters, Connor Troy; Powell, Aaron Jay; Rolt, Bradley Jordan Ali; Roudette, Gregory Khaya Matteo; Rudman, Nathan Paul; Ruzvidzo, Shaun; Salmon, Toby Joe.

PLYMOUTH ARG (63)

AIMSON, Will (D) **94** **6**
H: 5 10 W: 11 00 b.Christchurch 1-1-94

2013–14	Hull C	0	0		
2014–15	Hull C	0	0		
2014–15	*Tranmere R*	2	0	**2**	**0**
2015–16	Hull C	0	0		
2015–16	Blackpool	15	0		
2016–17	Blackpool	18	0		
2017–18	Blackpool	17	0	**50**	**0**
2018–19	Bury	37	4	**37**	**4**
2019–20	Plymouth Arg	5	2	**5**	**2**

BAXTER, Jose (F) **195** **42**
H: 5 10 W: 11 07 b.Bootle 7-2-92
Internationals: England U16, U17.

2008–09	Everton	3	0		
2009–10	Everton	2	0		
2010–11	Everton	1	0		
2011–12	Everton	1	0		
2011–12	*Tranmere R*	14	3	**14**	**3**
2012–13	Everton	0	0		
2012–13	Crystal Palace	0	0		
2012–13	Oldham Ath	39	13		
2013–14	Oldham Ath	4	2		
2013–14	Sheffield U	35	6		
2014–15	Sheffield U	34	10		
2015–16	Sheffield U	24	4	**93**	**20**
2016–17	Everton	0	0		
2017–18	Everton	0	0	**7**	**0**
2018–19	Oldham Ath	29	4	**72**	**19**
2019–20	Plymouth Arg	9	0	**9**	**0**

Transferred to Memphis 901, February 2020.

BOYD, Jude (M) **0** **0**

2019–20	Plymouth Arg	0	0		

CANAVAN, Niall (D) **262** **22**
H: 6 3 W: 12 00 b.Guiseley 11-4-91
Internationals: Republic of Ireland U21.

2009–10	Scunthorpe U	7	1		
2010–11	Scunthorpe U	8	0		
2010–11	*Shrewsbury T*	3	0	**3**	**0**
2011–12	Scunthorpe U	12	1		
2012–13	Scunthorpe U	40	6		
2013–14	Scunthorpe U	45	4		
2014–15	Scunthorpe U	32	3		
2015–16	Scunthorpe U	10	0	**154**	**15**
2015–16	*Rochdale*	11	1		
2016–17	Rochdale	25	2		
2017–18	Rochdale	3	0	**39**	**3**
2018–19	Plymouth Arg	33	2		
2019–20	Plymouth Arg	33	2	**66**	**4**

CLEAL, Jarvis (D) **1** **0**
From WBA.

2019–20	Plymouth Arg	1	0	**1**	**0**

COOPER, Michael (G) **2** **0**
b. 8-10-99

2017–18	Plymouth Arg	1	0		
2018–19	Plymouth Arg	1	0		
2019–20	Plymouth Arg	0	0	**2**	**0**

EDWARDS, Joe (D) **292** **21**
H: 5 8 W: 11 07 b.Gloucester 31-10-90

2009–10	Bristol C	0	0		
2010–11	Bristol C	2	0		
2011–12	Bristol C	2	0		
2011–12	*Yeovil T*	4	1		
2012–13	Bristol C	0	0	**4**	**0**
2012–13	Yeovil T	35	2		
2013–14	Yeovil T	46	1		
2014–15	Yeovil T	34	0	**119**	**4**
2015–16	Colchester U	42	2	**42**	**2**
2016–17	Walsall	43	3		
2017–18	Walsall	30	7		
2018–19	Walsall	20	2	**93**	**12**
2019–20	Plymouth Arg	34	3	**34**	**3**

FLETCHER, Alex (F) **18** **1**
H: 5 10 W: 10 10 b. 9-2-99

2016–17	Plymouth Arg	0	0		
2017–18	Plymouth Arg	14	1		
2018–19	Plymouth Arg	4	0		
2019–20	Plymouth Arg	0	0	**18**	**1**

GRANT, Conor (M) **101** **6**
H: 5 9 W: 12 08 b.Fazakerley 18-4-95
Internationals: England U18.

2013–14	Everton	0	0		
2014–15	Everton	0	0		
2014–15	*Motherwell*	11	1	**11**	**1**
2015–16	Everton	0	0		
2015–16	*Doncaster R*	19	2		
2016–17	Everton	0	0		
2016–17	*Ipswich T*	6	0	**6**	**0**
2016–17	*Doncaster R*	21	1	**40**	**3**
2017–18	Everton	0	0		
2017–18	*Crewe Alex*	17	0	**17**	**0**
2018–19	Plymouth Arg	10	0		
2019–20	Plymouth Arg	17	2	**27**	**2**

GRANT, Joel (F) **349** **58**
H: 6 0 W: 12 01 b.Acton 26-8-87
Internationals: Jamaica U20, Full caps.

2005–06	Watford	7	0		
2006–07	Watford	0	0	**7**	**0**

From Aldershot T.

2008–09	Crewe Alex	28	2		
2009–10	Crewe Alex	43	9		
2010–11	Crewe Alex	25	5	**96**	**16**
2011–12	Wycombe W	30	4		
2012–13	Wycombe W	41	10	**71**	**14**
2013–14	Yeovil T	34	3		
2014–15	Yeovil T	21	3	**55**	**6**
2015–16	Exeter C	26	4		
2016–17	Exeter C	20	4	**46**	**8**
2017–18	Plymouth Arg	33	6		
2018–19	Plymouth Arg	17	4		
2019–20	Plymouth Arg	24	4	**74**	**14**

JEPHCOTT, Luke (F) **23** **7**
b.Truro 26-1-00
Internationals: Wales U19.

2018–19	Plymouth Arg	9	0		
2019–20	Plymouth Arg	14	7	**23**	**7**

LAW, Ryan (D) **0** **0**

2017–18	Plymouth Arg	0	0		
2018–19	Plymouth Arg	0	0		
2019–20	Plymouth Arg	0	0		

LOLOS, Klaidi (F) **4** **0**
Internationals: Greece U19.

2017–18	Plymouth Arg	0	0		
2018–19	Plymouth Arg	0	0		
2019–20	Plymouth Arg	4	0	**4**	**0**

MAYOR, Danny (M) **321** **33**
H: 6 0 W: 11 12 b.Leyland 18-10-90

2008–09	Preston NE	0	0		
2008–09	*Tranmere R*	3	0	**3**	**0**
2009–10	Preston NE	7	0		
2010–11	Preston NE	21	0		
2011–12	Preston NE	36	2		
2012–13	Preston NE	0	0	**64**	**2**
2012–13	Sheffield W	8	0		
2012–13	*Southend U*	5	0	**5**	**0**
2013–14	Sheffield W	0	0	**8**	**0**
2013–14	Bury	39	5		
2014–15	Bury	44	8		
2015–16	Bury	44	5		
2016–17	Bury	21	3		
2017–18	Bury	20	1		
2018–19	Bury	39	8	**207**	**30**
2019–20	Plymouth Arg	34	1	**34**	**1**

McCORMICK, Luke (G) **212** **0**
H: 6 0 W: 13 12 b.Coventry 15-8-83

2012–13	Oxford U	15	0	**15**	**0**
2013–14	Plymouth Arg	27	0		
2014–15	Plymouth Arg	46	0		
2015–16	Plymouth Arg	40	0		
2016–17	Plymouth Arg	46	0		
2017–18	Plymouth Arg	9	0		
2018–19	Swindon T	17	0		
2019–20	Swindon T	12	0	**29**	**0**
2019–20	Plymouth Arg	0	0	**168**	**0**

McFADZEAN, Callum (D) **111** **5**
b.Sheffield 16-1-94
Internationals: England U16. Scotland U21.

2010–11	Sheffield U	0	0		
2011–12	Sheffield U	0	0		
2012–13	Sheffield U	8	0		
2013–14	Sheffield U	7	0		
2013–14	*Chesterfield*	4	0	**4**	**0**
2013–14	*Burton Alb*	7	1		
2014–15	Sheffield U	0	0		
2014–15	*Burton Alb*	9	1	**16**	**2**
2015–16	Sheffield U	1	0	**16**	**0**
2015–16	*Stevenage*	6	0	**6**	**0**
2016–17	Kilmarnock	4	0	**4**	**0**

From Alfreton T, Guiseley.

2018–19	Bury	40	0	**40**	**0**
2019–20	Plymouth Arg	25	3	**25**	**3**

MOORE, Byron (M) **426** **46**
H: 6 0 W: 10 06 b.Stoke 24-8-88

2006–07	Crewe Alex	0	0		
2007–08	Crewe Alex	33	3		
2008–09	Crewe Alex	36	3		
2009–10	Crewe Alex	32	3		
2010–11	Crewe Alex	38	6		
2011–12	Crewe Alex	42	8		
2012–13	Crewe Alex	41	4		
2013–14	Crewe Alex	40	3	**262**	**30**
2014–15	Port Vale	15	1		
2015–16	Port Vale	36	3	**51**	**4**
2016–17	Bristol R	27	2		
2017–18	Bristol R	20	0	**47**	**2**
2018–19	Bury	36	5	**36**	**5**
2019–20	Plymouth Arg	30	5	**30**	**5**

MOORE, Tafari (D) **28** **0**
H: 5 8 b.London 5-7-97
Internationals: England U16, U17, U18, U19, U20.

2015–16	Arsenal	0	0		
2016–17	Arsenal	0	0		
2017–18	Arsenal	0	0		
2017–18	Arsenal	0	0		
2017–18	*Wycombe W*	13	0	**13**	**0**
2018–19	Plymouth Arg	14	0		
2019–20	Plymouth Arg	0	0	**14**	**0**
2019–20	*Colchester U*	1	0	**1**	**0**

PECK, Michael (M) **0** **0**
b.Truro 26-3-01

2018–19	Plymouth Arg	0	0		
2019–20	Plymouth Arg	0	0		

PURRINGTON, Tom (M) **0** **0**
b.Exeter 24-10-00

2018–19	Plymouth Arg	0	0		
2019–20	Plymouth Arg	0	0		

RANDELL, Adam (M) **4** **0**
b.Plymouth 1-10-00

2018–19	Plymouth Arg	0	0		
2019–20	Plymouth Arg	4	0	**4**	**0**

RUDDEN, Zak (F) **45** **14**
b. 6-2-00
Internationals: Scotland U16, U17, U19.

2018–19	Rangers	0	0		
2018–19	*Falkirk*	31	12	**31**	**12**

2019–20 Rangers 0 0
On loan from Rangers.
2019–20 Plymouth Arg 14 2 **14 2**

SARCEVIC, Antoni (M) 258 37
H: 5 10 W: 11 00 b.Manchester 13-3-92
Internationals: England C.
2009–10 Crewe Alex 0 0
2010–11 Crewe Alex 6 1
2011–12 Crewe Alex 6 0 **12 1**
From Chester.
2013–14 Fleetwood T 42 13
2014–15 Fleetwood T 37 2
2015–16 Fleetwood T 39 3 **118 18**
2016–17 Shrewsbury T 12 0 **12 0**
2016–17 Plymouth Arg 17 2
2017–18 Plymouth Arg 30 3
2018–19 Plymouth Arg 37 3
2019–20 Plymouth Arg 32 10 **116 18**

SAWYER, Gary (D) 398 7
H: 6 0 W: 11 08 b.Bideford 5-7-85
2004–05 Plymouth Arg 0 0
2005–06 Plymouth Arg 0 0
2006–07 Plymouth Arg 22 0
2007–08 Plymouth Arg 31 1
2008–09 Plymouth Arg 13 3
2009–10 Plymouth Arg 29 1
2009–10 *Bristol C* 2 0 **2 0**
2010–11 Bristol R 37 0
2011–12 Bristol R 24 0 **61 0**
2012–13 Leyton Orient 34 1
2013–14 Leyton Orient 22 0
2014–15 Leyton Orient 13 0 **69 1**
2015–16 Plymouth Arg 43 0
2016–17 Plymouth Arg 21 0
2017–18 Plymouth Arg 46 1
2018–19 Plymouth Arg 33 0
2019–20 Plymouth Arg 28 0 **266 6**

SMITH-BROWN, Ashley (D) 106 3
H: 5 10 W: 10 10 b.Manchester 31-3-96
Internationals: England U16, U17, U18, U19, U20.
2016–17 Manchester C 0 0
2016–17 *NAC Breda* 29 1
2016–17 Manchester C 0 0
2016–17 NAC Breda 29 1 **58 2**
2017–18 Manchester C 0 0
2017–18 *Hearts* 2 0 **2 0**
2017–18 *Oxford U* 9 0 **9 0**
2018–19 Plymouth Arg 31 1
2019–20 Plymouth Arg 0 0 **31 1**
2019–20 *Oldham Ath* 6 0 **6 0**

TAYLOR, Ryan (F) 365 53
H: 6 2 W: 10 10 b.Rotherham 4-5-88
2005–06 Rotherham U 1 0
2006–07 Rotherham U 10 0
2007–08 Rotherham U 35 6
2008–09 Rotherham U 33 4
2009–10 Rotherham U 19 0
2009–10 *Exeter C* 7 0 **7 0**
2010–11 Rotherham U 34 11 **132 21**
2011–12 Bristol C 7 1
2012–13 Bristol C 25 1
2013–14 Bristol C 7 0 **39 2**
2013–14 Portsmouth 18 6
2014–15 Portsmouth 37 9 **55 15**
2015–16 Oxford U 22 3
2016–17 Oxford U 21 1 **43 4**
2016–17 Plymouth Arg 18 4
2017–18 Plymouth Arg 21 5
2018–19 Plymouth Arg 33 0
2019–20 Plymouth Arg 17 2 **89 11**

TELFORD, Dominic (F) 90 12
H: 5 9 W: 11 05 b.Burnley 5-12-96
2014–15 Blackpool 14 1
2015–16 Blackpool 0 0 **14 1**
2016–17 Stoke C 0 0
2017–18 Stoke C 0 0
2017–18 *Bristol R* 19 3 **19 3**
2018–19 Bury 38 6 **38 6**
2019–20 Plymouth Arg 19 2 **19 2**

WILSON, Ruben (D) 0 0
2019–20 Plymouth Arg 0 0

WOOTTON, Scott (D) 189 4
H: 6 2 W: 13 00 b.Birkenhead 12-9-91
Internationals: England U17.
2009–10 Manchester U 0 0
2010–11 Manchester U 0 0
2010–11 *Tranmere R* 7 1 **7 1**
2011–12 Manchester U 0 0
2011–12 *Peterborough U* 11 0
2011–12 *Nottingham F* 13 0 **13 0**
2012–13 Manchester U 0 0
2012–13 *Peterborough U* 2 1 **13 1**
2013–14 Manchester U 0 0
2013–14 Leeds U 20 0
2014–15 Leeds U 23 0
2014–15 *Rotherham U* 7 0 **7 0**
2015–16 Leeds U 23 0 **66 0**
2016–17 Milton Keynes D 1 1
2017–18 Milton Keynes D 38 0 **39 1**
2018–19 Plymouth Arg 9 0
2019–20 Plymouth Arg 35 1 **44 1**

Scholars
Boyd, Jude Michael; Burdon, Isaac Lewis; Cleal, Jarvis Jai; Collum, Reuben; Coombes, Tyler Lee; Craske, Finley Thomas; Crocker, Scott Lee; Mansaray, Alimamy; Medine, Jeremiah; Miller, Charles Louis; Shirley, Rhys Bowles; Tomlinson, Oliver Joseph; Townsend, Harry Robert Peter; Wilson, Rubin James; Wotton, Alfie Samuel.

PORT VALE (64)

AMOO, David (F) 296 36
H: 5 10 W: 12 03 b.Southwark 23-4-91
2007–08 Liverpool 0 0
2008–09 Liverpool 0 0
2009–10 Liverpool 0 0
2010–11 Liverpool 0 0
2010–11 *Milton Keynes D* 3 0 **3 0**
2010–11 *Hull C* 7 1 **7 1**
2011–12 Liverpool 0 0
2011–12 *Bury* 27 4 **27 4**
2012–13 Preston NE 17 0 **17 0**
2012–13 Tranmere R 11 1
2013–14 Tranmere R 0 0 **11 1**
2013–14 Carlisle U 43 8
2014–15 Carlisle U 27 5 **70 13**
2015–16 Partick Thistle 37 5
2016–17 Partick Thistle 25 1 **62 6**
2017–18 Cambridge U 24 2
2018–19 Cambridge U 43 5 **67 7**
2019–20 Port Vale 32 4 **32 4**

ARCHER, Jordan (F) 163 0
2011–12 Tottenham H 0 0
2012–13 Tottenham H 0 0
2012–13 *Wycombe W* 27 0 **27 0**
2013–14 Tottenham H 0 0
2014–15 Tottenham H 0 0
2014–15 *Northampton T* 13 0 **13 0**
2014–15 *Millwall* 0 0
2015–16 Millwall 39 0
2016–17 Millwall 36 0
2017–18 Millwall 45 0 **120 0**
2018–19 Bury 0 0
2019–20 Port Vale 3 0 **3 0**

ATKINSON, Will (M) 359 27
H: 5 10 W: 10 07 b.Beverley 14-10-88
2006–07 Hull C 0 0
2007–08 Hull C 0 0
2007–08 *Port Vale* 4 0
2007–08 *Mansfield T* 12 0
2008–09 Hull C 0 0
2009–10 Hull C 2 1
2009–10 *Rochdale* 15 3
2010–11 Hull C 4 0
2010–11 *Rotherham U* 3 1 **3 1**
2010–11 *Rochdale* 21 2 **36 5**
2011–12 Hull C 0 0 **6 1**
2011–12 *Plymouth Arg* 22 4 **22 4**
2011–12 *Bradford C* 12 1
2012–13 Bradford C 42 1 **54 2**
2013–14 Southend U 45 2
2014–15 Southend U 36 2
2015–16 Southend U 36 2
2016–17 Southend U 37 4 **154 10**
2017–18 Mansfield T 39 2
2018–19 Mansfield T 18 1 **69 3**
2019–20 Port Vale 11 1 **15 1**

BENNETT, Richie (F) 101 21
b.Oldham 3-3-91
From Ashton U, Northwich Vic, Barrow.
2017–18 Carlisle U 38 6
2018–19 Carlisle U 21 4 **59 10**
2018–19 *Morecambe* 16 5 **16 5**
2019–20 Port Vale 26 6 **26 6**

BRISLEY, Shaun (M) 328 14
H: 6 2 W: 12 02 b.Macclesfield 6-5-90
2007–08 Macclesfield T 10 2
2008–09 Macclesfield T 38 0
2009–10 Macclesfield T 33 1
2010–11 Macclesfield T 14 0
2011–12 Macclesfield T 29 3 **124 6**
2011–12 Peterborough U 11 0
2012–13 Peterborough U 28 0
2013–14 Peterborough U 22 0
2014–15 Peterborough U 15 1
2014–15 *Scunthorpe U* 7 0 **7 0**
2015–16 Peterborough U 2 0 **78 1**
2015–16 *Northampton T* 9 1 **9 1**
2015–16 *Leyton Orient* 16 1 **16 1**
2016–17 Carlisle U 28 2 **28 2**
2017–18 Notts Co 37 2
2018–19 Notts Co 20 0 **57 2**
2019–20 Port Vale 9 1 **9 1**

BROWN, Scott (G) 443 0
H: 6 2 W: 13 01 b.Wolverhampton 26-4-85
From Welshpool T
2003–04 Bristol C 0 0
2004–05 Cheltenham T 0 0
2005–06 Cheltenham T 1 0
2006–07 Cheltenham T 11 0
2007–08 Cheltenham T 0 0
2008–09 Cheltenham T 35 0
2009–10 Cheltenham T 46 0
2010–11 Cheltenham T 46 0
2011–12 Cheltenham T 22 0
2012–13 Cheltenham T 46 0
2013–14 Cheltenham T 45 0
2014–15 Aberdeen 25 0
2015–16 Aberdeen 13 0 **38 0**
2016–17 Wycombe W 3 0
2016–17 *Cheltenham T* 21 0 **273 0**
2017–18 Wycombe W 46 0 **49 0**
2018–19 Port Vale 46 0
2019–20 Port Vale 37 0 **83 0**

BROWNE, Rhys (M) 79 5
H: 5 10 W: 12 08 b.Romford 16-11-95
Internationals: Antigua and Barbuda Full caps.
From Norwich C, Charlton Ath, Aldershot T.
2016–17 Grimsby T 5 0 **5 0**
2017–18 Yeovil T 35 4
2018–19 Yeovil T 28 1 **63 5**
2019–20 Port Vale 11 0 **11 0**

BURGESS, Scott (M) 44 5
H: 5 10 W: 11 00 b.Warrington 27-6-96
2013–14 Bury 1 0
2014–15 Bury 0 0
2015–16 Bury 3 0
2016–17 Bury 16 2
2017–18 Bury 0 0
2018–19 Bury 0 0 **20 2**
2019–20 Port Vale 24 3 **24 3**

CAMPBELL-GORDON, Ryan (D) 1 0
2018–19 Port Vale 0 0
2019–20 Port Vale 1 0 **1 0**

CONLON, Tom (M) 118 6
H: 5 8 W: 9 11 b.Stoke-on-Trent 3-2-96
2013–14 Peterborough U 1 0 **1 0**
2014–15 Stevenage 13 0
2015–16 Stevenage 32 2
2016–17 Stevenage 4 0
2017–18 Stevenage 12 0 **61 2**
2018–19 Port Vale 34 3
2019–20 Port Vale 22 1 **56 4**

CROOKES, Adam (D) 33 0
b.Lincoln 18-11-97
2017–18 Nottingham F 0 0
2018–19 Nottingham F 0 0
2018–19 *Lincoln C* 0 0
2018–19 *Port Vale* 19 0
2019–20 Port Vale 14 0 **33 0**

CULLEN, Mark (F) 200 41
H: 5 9 W: 11 11 b.Ashington 21-4-92
2009–10 Hull C 3 1
2010–11 Hull C 17 0
2010–11 *Bradford C* 4 0 **4 0**
2011–12 Hull C 4 0
2011–12 *Bury* 4 0
2012–13 Hull C 0 0
2012–13 Hull C 0 0 **24 1**
2012–13 *Bury* 10 1 **14 1**
2014–15 Luton T 42 13 **42 13**
2015–16 Blackpool 41 9
2016–17 Blackpool 27 9
2017–18 Blackpool 9 0
2018–19 Blackpool 12 3 **89 21**
2018–19 *Carlisle U* 9 0 **9 0**
2019–20 Port Vale 18 5 **18 5**

EVANS, Callum (D) 24 1
H: 5 10 W: 11 05 b.Bristol 11-10-95
From Manchester U.
2015–16 Barnsley 0 0

2016–17	Barnsley	3	0	**3**	**0**
2017–18	Forest Green R	2	0	**2**	**0**
2018–19	Macclesfield T	14	1	**14**	**1**
2019–20	Port Vale	5	0	**5**	**0**

GIBBONS, James (D) **77** **1**
H: 5 9 W: 9 11 b. 16-3-98

2016–17	Port Vale	0	0		
2017–18	Port Vale	30	0		
2018–19	Port Vale	15	0		
2019–20	Port Vale	32	1	**77**	**1**

HURST, Alex (M) **0** **0**
b. 6-10-99
From Matlock T, Bradford PA.

2019–20	Port Vale	0	0		

JOYCE, Luke (M) **465** **14**
H: 5 11 W: 12 03 b.Bolton 9-7-87

2005–06	Wigan Ath	0	0		
2005–06	Carlisle U	0	0		
2006–07	Carlisle U	16	1		
2007–08	Carlisle U	3	1		
2008–09	Carlisle U	7	0		
2009–10	Accrington S	41	1		
2010–11	Accrington S	27	1		
2011–12	Accrington S	43	2		
2012–13	Accrington S	44	0		
2013–14	Accrington S	46	1		
2014–15	Accrington S	45	3	**246**	**8**
2015–16	Carlisle U	37	0		
2016–17	Carlisle U	45	1		
2017–18	Carlisle U	38	2	**146**	**5**
2018–19	Port Vale	37	0		
2019–20	Port Vale	36	1	**73**	**1**

KENNEDY, Kieran (D) **24** **0**
H: 5 10 W: 11 00 b.Urmston 23-9-93
Internationals: England U19.

2011–12	Manchester C	0	0		
2012–13	Manchester C	0	0		
2013–14	Manchester C	0	0		
2013–14	*Leicester C*	0	0		
2014–15	Leicester C	0	0		
2015–16	Motherwell	22	0		
2016–17	Motherwell	0	0	**22**	**0**

From AFC Fylde, Macclesfield T.

2018–19	Shrewsbury T	1	0	**1**	**0**
2019–20	Port Vale	1	0	**1**	**0**

LEGGE, Leon (D) **357** **33**
H: 6 1 W: 11 02 b.Bexhill 1-7-85

2009–10	Brentford	29	2		
2010–11	Brentford	30	3		
2011–12	Brentford	28	4		
2012–13	Brentford	7	0	**94**	**9**
2012–13	Gillingham	22	2		
2013–14	Gillingham	37	2		
2014–15	Gillingham	22	4	**81**	**8**
2015–16	Cambridge U	39	3		
2016–17	Cambridge U	44	6		
2017–18	Cambridge U	27	2	**110**	**11**
2018–19	Port Vale	35	1		
2019–20	Port Vale	37	4	**72**	**5**

LLOYD, Ryan (M) **36** **0**
H: 5 10 W: 10 03 b.Newcastle-u-Lyme 1-2-94

2010–11	Port Vale	1	0		
2011–12	Port Vale	2	0		
2012–13	Port Vale	6	0		
2013–14	Port Vale	3	0		
2014–15	Port Vale	0	0		
2015–16	Port Vale	5	0		
2016–17	Port Vale	0	0		

From Darlington.

2018–19	Macclesfield T	13	0	**13**	**0**
2019–20	Port Vale	6	0	**23**	**0**

MADDISON, Johnny (G) **15** **0**
H: 6 0 W: 11 12 b.Chester le Street 4-9-94

2012–13	Crawley T	0	0		
2013–14	Crawley T	0	0		
2014–15	Crawley T	0	0		
2015–16	Leicester C	0	0		
2016–17	Yeovil T	5	0		
2017–18	Yeovil T	10	0	**15**	**0**
2019–20	Port Vale	0	0		

MONTANO, Cristian (F) **228** **26**
H: 5 11 W: 12 00 b.Cali 11-12-91

2010–11	West Ham U	0	0		
2011–12	West Ham U	0	0		
2011–12	*Notts Co*	15	4	**15**	**4**
2011–12	*Swindon T*	4	1	**4**	**1**
2011–12	*Dagenham & R*	10	3	**10**	**3**
2011–12	*Oxford U*	9	2	**9**	**2**
2012–13	Oldham Ath	30	1		
2013–14	Oldham Ath	10	2	**40**	**3**
2014–15	America de Cali	9	1	**9**	**1**
2015–16	Bristol R	27	2		
2016–17	Bristol R	25	1	**52**	**3**
2017–18	Port Vale	30	4		
2018–19	Port Vale	29	5		
2019–20	Port Vale	30	0	**89**	**9**

OYELEKE, Emmanuel (M) **45** **3**
H: 5 9 W: 11 11 b.Wandsworth 24-12-92

2011–12	Brentford	1	0		
2012–13	Brentford	0	0		
2012–13	*Northampton T*	2	0	**2**	**0**
2013–14	Brentford	0	0		
2014–15	Brentford	0	0	**1**	**0**
2014–15	Exeter C	0	0		
2015–16	Exeter C	8	0	**8**	**0**

From Aldershot T.

2018–19	Port Vale	28	3		
2019–20	Port Vale	6	0	**34**	**3**

POPE, Tom (F) **469** **124**
H: 6 3 W: 11 03 b.Stoke 27-8-85

2005–06	Crewe Alex	0	0		
2006–07	Crewe Alex	4	0		
2007–08	Crewe Alex	26	7		
2008–09	Crewe Alex	26	10	**56**	**17**
2009–10	Rotherham U	35	3		
2010–11	Rotherham U	18	1	**53**	**4**
2010–11	*Port Vale*	13	3		
2011–12	Port Vale	41	5		
2012–13	Port Vale	46	31		
2013–14	Port Vale	43	12		
2014–15	Port Vale	33	8		
2015–16	Bury	36	6		
2016–17	Bury	37	4	**73**	**10**
2016–17	Port Vale	0	0		
2017–18	Port Vale	41	17		
2018–19	Port Vale	38	11		
2019–20	Port Vale	32	6	**287**	**93**

PUGH, Danny (M) **359** **17**
H: 6 0 W: 12 10 b.Cheadle Hulme 19-10-82

2000–01	Manchester U	0	0		
2001–02	Manchester U	0	0		
2002–03	Manchester U	1	0		
2003–04	Manchester U	0	0	**1**	**0**
2004–05	Leeds U	38	5		
2005–06	Leeds U	12	0		
2006–07	Preston NE	45	4		
2007–08	Preston NE	7	0		
2007–08	Stoke C	30	0		
2008–09	Stoke C	17	0		
2009–10	Stoke C	7	1		
2010–11	Stoke C	10	0		
2010–11	*Preston NE*	5	0	**57**	**4**
2011–12	Stoke C	3	0	**67**	**1**
2011–12	Leeds U	34	2		
2012–13	Leeds U	4	0		
2012–13	*Sheffield W*	16	1	**16**	**1**
2013–14	Leeds U	20	2	**108**	**9**
2014–15	Coventry C	5	0	**5**	**0**
2015–16	Bury	39	0	**39**	**0**
2016–17	Blackpool	18	0	**18**	**0**
2016–17	Port Vale	14	0		
2017–18	Port Vale	33	2		
2018–19	Port Vale	1	0		
2019–20	Port Vale	0	0	**48**	**2**

SMITH, Nathan (D) **170** **10**
H: 6 0 W: 11 05 b.Madeley 3-4-96

2013–14	Port Vale	0	0		
2014–15	Port Vale	0	0		
2015–16	Port Vale	0	0		
2016–17	Port Vale	46	4		
2017–18	Port Vale	46	1		
2018–19	Port Vale	44	0		
2019–20	Port Vale	34	5	**170**	**10**

TRICKETT-SMITH, Dan (M) **0** **0**
Internationals: England U16.
From Sacramento Republic, Leek T.

2017–18	Port Vale	0	0		
2018–19	Port Vale	0	0		
2019–20	Port Vale	0	0		

WORRALL, David (M) **402** **32**
H: 6 0 W: 11 03 b.Manchester 12-6-90

2006–07	Bury	1	0		
2007–08	Bury	0	0		
2007–08	WBA	0	0		
2008–09	*Accrington S*	4	0	**4**	**0**
2008–09	*Shrewsbury T*	9	0	**9**	**0**
2009–10	WBA	0	0		
2009–10	Bury	40	4		
2010–11	Bury	40	2		
2011–12	Bury	41	3		
2012–13	Bury	41	2	**163**	**11**
2013–14	Rotherham U	3	1	**3**	**1**
2013–14	*Oldham Ath*	18	1	**18**	**1**
2014–15	Southend U	38	6		
2015–16	Southend U	35	3	**73**	**9**
2016–17	Millwall	33	1	**33**	**1**
2017–18	Port Vale	40	4		
2018–19	Port Vale	25	1		
2019–20	Port Vale	34	4	**99**	**9**

Scholars
Agho, Nelson Iradia; Barrett, Kenniel Devon Arnold; Bradbury, Thyler Owen; Campbell, Hayden Matthew; Chambers, Luke George; Chimenes, Maxwell Georges-Kwame; Dyer, Ammar Christopher Deacon; Gregors, Thomas Michael; Hallchurch, Alexander George Ewart; Hickson, Liam John Lewis; Lake, Louis Jaye; Lennon, Michael Edward; Robins, Reece David; Stevens, Jack Thomas; Tams, William David Francis.

PORTSMOUTH (65)

BASS, Alex (G) **16** **0**
H: 6 2 W: 11 00 b.Southampton 1-1-97

2014–15	Portsmouth	0	0		
2015–16	Portsmouth	0	0		
2016–17	Portsmouth	0	0		
2017–18	Portsmouth	1	0		
2018–19	Portsmouth	0	0		
2019–20	Portsmouth	15	0	**16**	**0**

BOLTON, James (D) **87** **3**
H: 5 11 W: 11 11 b.Stone 13-8-94
Internationals: England C.
From Macclesfield T, Halifax T, Gateshead.

2017–18	Shrewsbury T	33	1		
2018–19	Shrewsbury T	31	1	**64**	**2**
2019–20	Portsmouth	23	1	**23**	**1**

BROWN, Lee (M) **303** **20**
H: 6 0 W: 12 06 b.Bromley 10-8-90
Internationals: England C.

2008–09	QPR	0	0		
2009–10	QPR	1	0		
2010–11	QPR	0	0	**1**	**0**
2011–12	Bristol R	42	7		
2012–13	Bristol R	39	3		
2013–14	Bristol R	41	2		
2015–16	Bristol R	46	6		
2016–17	Bristol R	41	0		
2017–18	Bristol R	33	1	**242**	**19**
2018–19	Portsmouth	44	0		
2019–20	Portsmouth	16	1	**60**	**1**

BURGESS, Christian (D) **245** **12**
H: 6 5 W: 13 02 b. 7-10-91

2012–13	Middlesbrough	1	0		
2013–14	Middlesbrough	0	0	**1**	**0**
2013–14	*Hartlepool U*	41	0	**41**	**0**
2014–15	Peterborough U	30	2	**30**	**2**
2015–16	Portsmouth	37	2		
2016–17	Portsmouth	44	4		
2017–18	Portsmouth	35	0		
2018–19	Portsmouth	25	1		
2019–20	Portsmouth	32	3	**173**	**10**

CANNON, Andy (M) **121** **5**
H: 5 9 W: 11 09 b.Ashton-under-Lyne 14-3-96

2014–15	Rochdale	18	0		
2015–16	Rochdale	25	0		
2016–17	Rochdale	25	2		
2017–18	Rochdale	21	2		
2018–19	Rochdale	12	0	**101**	**4**
2018–19	Portsmouth	2	0		
2019–20	Portsmouth	18	1	**20**	**1**

CASEY, Matthew (D) **0** **0**

2017–18	Portsmouth	0	0		
2018–19	Portsmouth	0	0		
2019–20	Portsmouth	0	0		

CLOSE, Ben (M) **116** **13**
H: 5 9 W: 11 11 b.Portsmouth 8-8-96

2013–14	Portsmouth	0	0		
2014–15	Portsmouth	6	0		
2015–16	Portsmouth	7	0		
2016–17	Portsmouth	0	0		
2017–18	Portsmouth	40	2		
2018–19	Portsmouth	34	8		
2019–20	Portsmouth	29	3	**116**	**13**

CURTIS, Ronan (F) **74** **22**
H: 6 0 W: 12 02 b.Derry 29-3-96
Internationals: Republic of Ireland U21, Full caps.

2018–19	Portsmouth	41	11		
2019–20	Portsmouth	33	11	**74**	**22**

DOWNING, Paul (D) **280** **7**
H: 6 1 W: 12 06 b.Taunton 26-10-91

2009–10	WBA	0	0		

2009–10	*Hereford U*	6	0		
2010–11	WBA	0	0		
2010–11	*Hereford U*	0	0	**6**	**0**
2010–11	*Swansea C*	0	0		
2011–12	WBA	0	0		
2011–12	*Barnet*	26	0	**26**	**0**
2012–13	Walsall	31	1		
2013–14	Walsall	44	1		
2014–15	Walsall	35	1		
2015–16	Walsall	46	3	**156**	**6**
2016–17	Milton Keynes D	37	0		
2017–18	Milton Keynes D	0	0	**37**	**0**
2017–18	Blackburn R	28	1		
2018–19	Blackburn R	3	0	**31**	**1**
2018–19	*Doncaster R*	18	0	**18**	**0**
2019–20	Portsmouth	6	0	**6**	**0**

EVANS, Gary (F) 471 84
H: 6 0 W: 12 08 b.Stockport 26-4-88

2007–08	Macclesfield T	42	7		
2008–09	Macclesfield T	40	12	**82**	**19**
2009–10	Bradford C	43	11		
2010–11	Bradford C	36	3	**79**	**14**
2011–12	Rotherham U	32	7		
2012–13	Rotherham U	13	2	**45**	**9**
2012–13	Fleetwood T	16	1		
2013–14	Fleetwood T	34	6		
2014–15	Fleetwood T	43	3	**93**	**10**
2015–16	Portsmouth	40	10		
2016–17	Portsmouth	41	5		
2017–18	Portsmouth	32	2		
2018–19	Portsmouth	42	10		
2019–20	Portsmouth	17	5	**172**	**32**

FLINT, Josh (M) 0 0
b.Waterlooville 13-10-00

2018–19	Portsmouth	0	0
2019–20	Portsmouth	0	0

HACKETT-FAIRCHILD, Recco (F) 12 0
H: 6 3 W: 11 00 b. 30-6-98
From Norwich C.

2017–18	Charlton Ath	5	0		
2018–19	Charlton Ath	7	0	**12**	**0**
2019–20	Portsmouth	0	0		

HANCOTT, Joe (D) 0 0

2017–18	Portsmouth	0	0
2018–19	Portsmouth	0	0
2019–20	Portsmouth	0	0

HARNESS, Marcus (M) 128 11
H: 6 0 W: 11 00 b.Coventry 1-8-94

2013–14	Burton Alb	3	0		
2014–15	Burton Alb	18	0		
2015–16	Burton Alb	5	0		
2016–17	Burton Alb	10	0		
2017–18	Burton Alb	0	0		
2017–18	*Port Vale*	35	1	**35**	**1**
2018–19	Burton Alb	32	5	**68**	**5**
2019–20	Portsmouth	25	5	**25**	**5**

HARRISON, Ellis (F) 196 37
H: 5 11 W: 12 06 b.Newport 1-2-94
Internationals: Wales U21.

2010–11	Bristol R	1	0		
2011–12	Bristol R	0	0		
2012–13	Bristol R	13	3		
2013–14	Bristol R	25	1		
2015–16	Bristol R	30	7		
2015–16	*Hartlepool U*	2	0	**2**	**0**
2016–17	Bristol R	37	8		
2017–18	Bristol R	44	12	**150**	**31**
2018–19	Ipswich T	16	1	**16**	**1**
2019–20	Portsmouth	28	5	**28**	**5**

HAUNSTRUP, Brandon (D) 32 0
b. 26-10-96

2015–16	Portsmouth	1	0		
2016–17	Portsmouth	0	0		
2017–18	Portsmouth	16	0		
2018–19	Portsmouth	5	0		
2019–20	Portsmouth	10	0	**32**	**0**

HAWKINS, Oliver (F) 95 15
b. 8-4-92
From North Greenford U, Hillingdon Bor, Northwood, Hemel Hempstead T.

2015–16	Dagenham & R	18	1	**18**	**1**
2017–18	Portsmouth	31	7		
2018–19	Portsmouth	39	7		
2019–20	Portsmouth	7	0	**77**	**14**

LETHBRIDGE, Bradley (F) 0 0

2017–18	Portsmouth	0	0
2018–19	Portsmouth	0	0
2019–20	Portsmouth	0	0

MACGILLIVRAY, Craig (G) 86 0
H: 6 2 W: 12 04 b.Harrogate 12-1-93

2014–15	Walsall	2	0		
2015–16	Walsall	5	0		
2016–17	Walsall	5	0	**12**	**0**
2017–18	Shrewsbury T	8	0	**8**	**0**
2018–19	Portsmouth	46	0		
2019–20	Portsmouth	20	0	**66**	**0**

MALONEY, Leon (M) 0 0
b. 13-5-01

2018–19	Portsmouth	0	0
2019–20	Portsmouth	0	0

Transferred to Volendam, January 2020.

MARQUIS, John (F) 305 95
H: 6 1 W: 11 03 b.Lewisham 16-5-92

2009–10	Millwall	1	0		
2010–11	Millwall	11	4		
2011–12	Millwall	17	1		
2012–13	Millwall	10	0		
2013–14	Millwall	2	0		
2013–14	*Portsmouth*	5	1		
2013–14	*Torquay U*	5	3	**5**	**3**
2013–14	*Northampton T*	14	2		
2014–15	Millwall	1	0		
2014–15	*Cheltenham T*	13	1	**13**	**1**
2014–15	*Gillingham*	21	8	**21**	**8**
2015–16	Millwall	10	0	**52**	**5**
2015–16	*Leyton Orient*	13	0	**13**	**0**
2015–16	*Northampton T*	15	6	**29**	**8**
2016–17	Doncaster R	45	26		
2017–18	Doncaster R	45	14		
2018–19	Doncaster R	44	21	**134**	**61**
2019–20	Portsmouth	33	8	**38**	**9**

MAY, Adam (M) 24 0
b. 6-12-97

2014–15	Portsmouth	1	0		
2015–16	Portsmouth	1	0		
2016–17	Portsmouth	0	0		
2017–18	Portsmouth	13	0		
2018–19	Portsmouth	0	0		
2019–20	Portsmouth	0	0	**15**	**0**
2019–20	*Swindon T*	9	0	**9**	**0**

McCRORIE, Ross (M) 78 4
b. 18-3-98
Internationals: Scotland U16, U17, U19, U20, U21.

2015–16	Rangers	0	0		
2015–16	*Ayr U*	11	2	**11**	**2**
2016–17	Rangers	0	0		
2016–17	*Dumbarton*	9	0	**9**	**0**
2017–18	Rangers	21	2		
2018–19	Rangers	20	0		
2019–20	Rangers	0	0	**41**	**2**

On loan from Rangers.

2019–20	Portsmouth	17	0	**17**	**0**

McGEE, Luke (G) 87 0
H: 6 2 W: 12 08 b.Edgware 9-2-95
Internationals: England U17.

2014–15	Tottenham H	0	0		
2015–16	Tottenham H	0	0		
2016–17	Tottenham H	0	0		
2016–17	*Peterborough U*	39	0	**39**	**0**
2017–18	Portsmouth	44	0		
2018–19	Portsmouth	0	0		
2019–20	Portsmouth	0	0	**44**	**0**
2019–20	*Bradford C*	4	0	**4**	**0**

MNOGA, Haji (D) 0 0
b.Portsmouth 16-4-02
Internationals: England U17.

2018–19	Portsmouth	0	0
2019–20	Portsmouth	0	0

MORRIS, Bryn (M) 74 4
H: 6 0 W: 11 01 b.Hartlepool 25-4-96
Internationals: England U16, U17, U18, U19, U20.

2012–13	Middlesbrough	1	0		
2013–14	Middlesbrough	1	0		
2014–15	Middlesbrough	0	0		
2014–15	*Burton Alb*	5	0	**5**	**0**
2015–16	Middlesbrough	0	0		
2015–16	*Coventry C*	6	0	**6**	**0**
2015–16	*York C*	3	0	**3**	**0**
2015–16	*Walsall*	1	0	**1**	**0**
2016–17	Middlesbrough	0	0	**2**	**0**
2016–17	*Shrewsbury T*	13	0		
2017–18	Shrewsbury T	18	0		
2018–19	Shrewsbury T	0	0	**31**	**0**
2018–19	*Wycombe W*	19	3	**19**	**3**
2018–19	Portsmouth	7	1		
2019–20	Portsmouth	0	0	**7**	**1**

NAYLOR, Tom (D) 254 18
H: 5 11 W: 11 05 b.Sutton-in-Ashfield 28-6-91

2011–12	Derby Co	8	0		
2012–13	Derby Co	0	0		
2012–13	*Bradford C*	5	0	**5**	**0**
2013–14	Derby Co	0	0		
2013–14	*Newport Co*	33	1	**33**	**1**
2014–15	Derby Co	0	0	**8**	**0**
2014–15	*Cambridge U*	8	0	**8**	**0**
2014–15	*Burton Alb*	17	0		
2015–16	Burton Alb	41	6		
2016–17	Burton Alb	33	3		
2017–18	Burton Alb	33	3	**124**	**12**
2018–19	Portsmouth	43	4		
2019–20	Portsmouth	33	1	**76**	**5**

PITMAN, Brett (F) 490 166
H: 6 0 W: 11 00 b.Jersey 31-1-88

2005–06	Bournemouth	19	1		
2006–07	Bournemouth	29	5		
2007–08	Bournemouth	39	6		
2008–09	Bournemouth	39	17		
2009–10	Bournemouth	46	26		
2010–11	Bournemouth	2	3		
2010–11	Bristol C	39	13		
2011–12	Bristol C	35	7		
2012–13	Bristol C	3	0	**77**	**20**
2012–13	Bournemouth	26	19		
2013–14	Bournemouth	34	5		
2014–15	Bournemouth	34	13	**268**	**95**
2015–16	Ipswich T	42	10		
2016–17	Ipswich T	22	4	**64**	**14**
2017–18	Portsmouth	38	24		
2018–19	Portsmouth	32	11		
2019–20	Portsmouth	11	2	**81**	**37**

REW, Harvey (D) 0 0
b.Portsmouth 25-9-02
Internationals: Wales U17.

2019–20	Portsmouth	0	0

TEGGART, Eoin (F) 0 0
Internationals: Northern Ireland U17.
From Cliftonville.

2019–20	Portsmouth	0	0

WALKES, Anton (M) 68 4
b. 8-2-97

2016–17	Tottenham H	0	0		
2017	*Atlanta U*	21	2	**21**	**2**
2017–18	Tottenham H	0	0		
2017–18	*Portsmouth*	12	1		
2018–19	Portsmouth	24	1		
2019–20	Portsmouth	11	0	**47**	**2**

Transferred to Atlanta U, January 2020.

WHATMOUGH, Jack (D) 87 1
b.Gosport 19-8-96
Internationals: England U18, U19.

2012–13	Portsmouth	0	0		
2013–14	Portsmouth	12	0		
2014–15	Portsmouth	22	0		
2015–16	Portsmouth	2	0		
2016–17	Portsmouth	10	1		
2017–18	Portsmouth	14	0		
2018–19	Portsmouth	26	0		
2019–20	Portsmouth	1	0	**87**	**1**

WILLIAMS, Ryan (F) 175 16
H: 5 11 W: 12 00 b.Perth 28-10-93
Internationals: Australia U20, U23, Full caps.

2011–12	Portsmouth	4	0		
2011–12	Fulham	0	0		
2012–13	Fulham	0	0		
2013–14	Fulham	0	0		
2013–14	*Oxford U*	36	7	**36**	**7**
2014–15	Fulham	2	0	**2**	**0**
2014–15	*Barnsley*	5	0		
2015–16	Barnsley	5	0		
2016–17	Barnsley	16	1	**26**	**1**
2017–18	Rotherham U	42	4		
2018–19	Rotherham U	39	1	**81**	**5**
2019–20	Portsmouth	26	3	**30**	**3**

Players retained or with offer of contract
Turnbull, Duncan Edward.

Scholars
Anderson, Harry James; Bell, Charlie George; Brook, Harrison Phillip; Bruce, Thomas Douglas; Hancott, Joe Mark; Kavanagh, Harry John; Kelly, Liam James; Lee, Seokjae; Lethbridge, Bradley Stephen; Pitman, Leon Neil David; Robb, Ethan David; Stanley, Alfie Frederick James; Storey, Gerard Ciaran; Teggart, Eoin James.

PRESTON NE (66)

ARMER, Jack (D) **0 0**
b. 16-4-01
Internationals: Scotland U17.
2019–20 Preston NE 0 0

BARKHUIZEN, Tom (F) **272 57**
H: 5 9 W: 11 00 b.Blackpool 4-7-93
2011–12 Blackpool 0 0
2011–12 *Hereford U* 38 11 **38 11**
2012–13 Blackpool 0 0
2012–13 *Fleetwood T* 13 1 **13 1**
2013–14 Blackpool 14 1
2014–15 Blackpool 7 0 **21 1**
2014–15 *Morecambe* 5 0
2015–16 Morecambe 40 10
2016–17 Morecambe 14 5 **59 15**
2016–17 Preston NE 17 6
2017–18 Preston NE 46 8
2018–19 Preston NE 34 6
2019–20 Preston NE 44 9 **141 29**

BAUER, Patrick (D) **210 13**
H: 6 4 W: 13 08 b.Backnang 28-10-92
Internationals: Germany U17, U18, U20.
2010–11 Stuttgart 0 0
2011–12 Stuttgart 0 0
2012–13 Stuttgart 0 0
2013–14 Maritimo 16 0
2014–15 Maritimo 29 2 **45 2**
2015–16 Charlton Ath 19 1
2016–17 Charlton Ath 36 4
2017–18 Charlton Ath 34 3
2018–19 Charlton Ath 35 0 **124 8**
2019–20 Preston NE 41 3 **41 3**

BAXTER, Jack (M) **0 0**
b.Chorley 27-10-00
2018–19 Preston NE 0 0
2019–20 Preston NE 0 0

BAYLISS, Tom (M) **63 8**
b. 6-4-99
Internationals: England U19.
2017–18 Coventry C 24 5
2018–19 Coventry C 38 3
2019–20 Coventry C 0 0 **62 8**
2019–20 Preston NE 1 0 **1 0**

BODIN, Billy (M) **245 52**
H: 5 11 W: 11 00 b.Swindon 24-3-92
Internationals: Wales U17, U19, U21, Full caps.
2009–10 Swindon T 0 0
2010–11 Swindon T 5 0
2011–12 Swindon T 11 3 **16 3**
2011–12 *Torquay U* 17 5
2011–12 *Crewe Alex* 8 0 **8 0**
2012–13 Torquay U 43 5
2013–14 Torquay U 27 1 **87 11**
2014–15 Northampton T 4 0 **4 0**
2015–16 Bristol R 38 13
2016–17 Bristol R 36 13
2017–18 Bristol R 21 9 **95 35**
2017–18 Preston NE 17 1
2018–19 Preston NE 0 0
2019–20 Preston NE 18 2 **35 3**

BROWNE, Alan (M) **220 30**
H: 5 8 W: 11 03 b.Cork 15-4-95
Internationals: Republic of Ireland U19, U21, Full caps.
2013–14 Preston NE 8 1
2014–15 Preston NE 20 3
2015–16 Preston NE 36 3
2016–17 Preston NE 31 0
2017–18 Preston NE 44 7
2018–19 Preston NE 38 12
2019–20 Preston NE 43 4 **220 30**

BURKE, Graham (F) **82 5**
H: 5 11 W: 11 11 b.Dublin 21-9-93
Internationals: Republic of Ireland U19, U21, Full caps.
2010–11 Aston Villa 0 0
2011–12 Aston Villa 0 0
2012–13 Aston Villa 0 0
2013–14 Aston Villa 0 0
2013–14 *Shrewsbury T* 3 0 **3 0**
2014–15 Aston Villa 0 0
2014–15 *Notts Co* 7 1
2015–16 Notts Co 31 2
2016–17 Notts Co 5 0 **43 3**
From Shamrock R.
2018–19 Preston NE 12 1
2018–19 *Gillingham* 12 1 **12 1**
2019–20 Preston NE 0 0 **12 1**
2019–20 *Shamrock R* 12 0 **12 0**

CROWE, Michael (G) **0 0**
H: 6 2 W: 11 11 b.London 13-11-95
Internationals: Wales U19, U21, Full caps.
2013–14 Ipswich T 0 0
2014–15 Ipswich T 0 0
2015–16 Ipswich T 0 0
2015–16 *Stevenage* 0 0
2016–17 Ipswich T 0 0
2017–18 Ipswich T 0 0
2018–19 Preston NE 0 0
2019–20 Preston NE 0 0

DAVIES, Ben (D) **205 3**
H: 6 1 W: 11 09 b.Barrow 11-8-95
2012–13 Preston NE 3 0
2013–14 Preston NE 0 0
2013–14 *York C* 44 0 **44 0**
2014–15 Preston NE 4 0
2014–15 *Tranmere R* 3 0 **3 0**
2015–16 Preston NE 0 0
2015–16 *Newport Co* 19 0 **19 0**
2016–17 Preston NE 0 0
2016–17 *Fleetwood T* 22 1 **22 1**
2017–18 Preston NE 34 1
2018–19 Preston NE 40 1
2019–20 Preston NE 36 0 **117 2**

EARL, Joshua (D) **49 0**
b. 24-10-98
2017–18 Preston NE 19 0
2018–19 Preston NE 14 0
2019–20 Preston NE 0 0 **33 0**
2019–20 *Bolton W* 9 0 **9 0**
2019–20 *Ipswich T* 7 0 **7 0**

FISHER, Darnell (M) **171 1**
H: 5 9 W: 11 00 b.Reading 1-5-94
2012–13 Celtic 0 0
2013–14 Celtic 12 0
2014–15 Celtic 5 0
2015–16 Celtic 0 0 **17 0**
2015–16 *St Johnstone* 23 1 **23 1**
2016–17 Rotherham U 34 0 **34 0**
2017–18 Preston NE 34 0
2018–19 Preston NE 35 0
2019–20 Preston NE 28 0 **97 0**

GALLAGHER, Paul (F) **539 90**
H: 6 1 W: 11 00 b.Glasgow 9-8-84
Internationals: Scotland U21, B, Full caps.
2002–03 Blackburn R 1 0
2003–04 Blackburn R 26 3
2004–05 Blackburn R 16 2
2005–06 Blackburn R 1 0
2005–06 *Stoke C* 37 11
2006–07 Blackburn R 16 1
2007–08 Blackburn R 0 0
2007–08 *Preston NE* 19 1
2007–08 *Stoke C* 7 0 **44 11**
2008–09 Blackburn R 0 0
2008–09 *Plymouth Arg* 40 13 **40 13**
2009–10 Blackburn R 1 0 **61 6**
2009–10 Leicester C 41 7
2010–11 Leicester C 41 10
2011–12 Leicester C 28 8
2012–13 Leicester C 8 0
2012–13 Sheffield U 6 1 **6 1**
2013–14 Leicester C 0 0
2013–14 *Preston NE* 28 6
2014–15 Leicester C 0 0 **118 25**
2014–15 *Preston NE* 46 7
2015–16 Preston NE 41 5
2016–17 Preston NE 31 1
2017–18 Preston NE 32 2
2018–19 Preston NE 40 6
2019–20 Preston NE 33 6 **270 34**

GINNELLY, Josh (M) **63 5**
b.Coventry 24-3-97
2013–14 Shrewsbury T 0 0
2014–15 Shrewsbury T 3 0 **3 0**
2015–16 Burnley 0 0
2016–17 Burnley 0 0
2016–17 *Walsall* 9 0
2017–18 Burnley 0 0
2017–18 *Lincoln C* 15 2 **15 2**
2018–19 Walsall 21 2 **30 2**
2018–19 Preston NE 5 0
2019–20 Preston NE 1 0 **6 0**
2019–20 *Bristol R* 9 1 **9 1**

HARROP, Josh (M) **79 8**
H: 5 9 W: 11 00 b.Stockport 15-12-95
Internationals: England U20.
2016–17 Manchester U 1 1 **1 1**
2017–18 Preston NE 38 2
2018–19 Preston NE 8 0
2019–20 Preston NE 32 5 **78 7**

HUDSON, Matthew (G) **1 0**
H: 6 4 b.Southport 29-7-98
2014–15 Preston NE 0 0
2015–16 Preston NE 1 0
2016–17 Preston NE 0 0
2017–18 Preston NE 0 0
2018–19 Preston NE 0 0
2018–19 *Bury* 0 0
2019–20 Preston NE 0 0 **1 0**

HUGHES, Andrew (D) **209 9**
b.Cardiff 5-6-92
Internationals: Wales U18, U23.
2013–14 Newport Co 26 2
2014–15 Newport Co 16 1
2015–16 Newport Co 25 0 **67 3**
2016–17 Peterborough U 39 1
2017–18 Peterborough U 43 2 **82 3**
2018–19 Preston NE 32 3
2019–20 Preston NE 28 0 **60 3**

HUNTINGTON, Paul (D) **373 22**
H: 6 3 W: 12 08 b.Carlisle 17-9-87
Internationals: England U18.
2005–06 Newcastle U 0 0
2006–07 Newcastle U 11 1
2007–08 Newcastle U 0 0 **11 1**
2007–08 Leeds U 17 2
2008–09 Leeds U 4 0
2009–10 Leeds U 0 0 **21 2**
2009–10 Stockport Co 26 0 **26 0**
2010–11 Yeovil T 40 5
2011–12 Yeovil T 37 2 **77 7**
2012–13 Preston NE 37 3
2013–14 Preston NE 23 2
2014–15 Preston NE 32 5
2015–16 Preston NE 38 0
2016–17 Preston NE 33 1
2017–18 Preston NE 44 1
2018–19 Preston NE 22 0
2019–20 Preston NE 9 0 **238 12**

JOHNSON, Daniel (M) **226 44**
H: 5 8 W: 10 07 b.Kingston, Jamaica 8-10-92
2010–11 Aston Villa 0 0
2011–12 Aston Villa 0 0
2012–13 Aston Villa 0 0
2012–13 *Yeovil T* 5 0 **5 0**
2013–14 Aston Villa 0 0
2014–15 Aston Villa 0 0
2014–15 *Chesterfield* 11 0 **11 0**
2014–15 *Oldham Ath* 6 3 **6 3**
2014–15 Preston NE 20 8
2015–16 Preston NE 43 8
2016–17 Preston NE 40 4
2017–18 Preston NE 33 3
2018–19 Preston NE 35 6
2019–20 Preston NE 33 12 **204 41**

LEDSON, Ryan (M) **130 4**
H: 5 9 W: 10 12 b.Liverpool 19-8-97
Internationals: England U16, U17, U18, U19, U20.
2013–14 Everton 0 0
2014–15 Everton 0 0
2015–16 Everton 0 0
2015–16 *Cambridge U* 27 0 **27 0**
2016–17 Oxford U 22 1
2017–18 Oxford U 44 3 **66 4**
2018–19 Preston NE 24 0
2019–20 Preston NE 13 0 **37 0**

MAGUIRE, Sean (F) **236 78**
H: 5 9 W: 11 10 b.Luton 1-5-94
Internationals: Republic of Ireland U19, U21, Full caps.
2010–11 West Ham U 0 0
2011 *Waterford U* 8 1
2011–12 West Ham U 0 0
2012 *Waterford U* 26 13 **34 14**
2012–13 West Ham U 0 0
2013–14 West Ham U 0 0
2014 *Sligo R* 18 1 **18 1**
2014–15 West Ham U 0 0
2014–15 *Accrington S* 33 7 **33 7**
2015 Dundalk 6 0 **6 0**
2016 Cork C 30 18
2017 Cork C 21 20 **51 38**
2017–18 Preston NE 24 10
2018–19 Preston NE 26 3
2019–20 Preston NE 44 5 **94 18**

MOULT, Louis (F) **149 47**
H: 6 0 W: 13 05 b.Stoke 14-5-92
2009–10 Stoke C 1 0
2010–11 Stoke C 0 0
2010–11 *Bradford C* 11 1 **11 1**

2011–12 Stoke C 0 0
2011–12 *Accrington S* 4 0 **4 0**
2012–13 Stoke C 0 0 **1 0**
2012–13 Northampton T 13 1 **13 1**
From Nuneaton T, Wrexham.
2015–16 Motherwell 38 15
2016–17 Motherwell 31 15
2017–18 Motherwell 15 8 **84 38**
2017–18 Preston NE 10 2
2018–19 Preston NE 24 4
2019–20 Preston NE 2 1 **36 7**

NUGENT, Dave (F) 600 153
H: 5 11 W: 12 13 b.Liverpool 2-5-85
Internationals: England U20, U21, Full caps.
2001–02 Bury 5 0
2002–03 Bury 31 4
2003–04 Bury 26 3
2004–05 Bury 26 11 **88 18**
2004–05 Preston NE 18 8
2005–06 Preston NE 32 10
2006–07 Preston NE 44 15
2007–08 Portsmouth 15 0
2008–09 Portsmouth 16 3
2009–10 Portsmouth 3 0
2009–10 *Burnley* 30 6 **30 6**
2010–11 Portsmouth 44 13 **78 16**
2011–12 Leicester C 42 15
2012–13 Leicester C 42 14
2013–14 Leicester C 46 20
2014–15 Leicester C 29 5 **159 54**
2015–16 Middlesbrough 38 8
2016–17 Middlesbrough 4 0 **42 8**
2016–17 Derby Co 17 6
2017–18 Derby Co 37 9
2018–19 Derby Co 31 2 **85 17**
2019–20 Preston NE 24 1 **118 34**

O'REILLY, Adam (M) 1 0
b. 11-5-01
Internationals: Republic of Ireland U17, U19.
2017–18 Preston NE 0 0
2018–19 Preston NE 1 0
2019–20 Preston NE 0 0 **1 0**

PEARSON, Ben (M) 194 4
H: 5 5 W: 11 03 b.Oldham 4-1-95
Internationals: England U16, U17, U18, U19, U21, Full caps.
2013–14 Manchester U 0 0
2014–15 Manchester U 0 0
2014–15 *Barnsley* 22 1
2015–16 Manchester U 0 0
2015–16 *Barnsley* 23 1 **45 2**
2015–16 Preston NE 15 0
2016–17 Preston NE 31 1
2017–18 Preston NE 35 0
2018–19 Preston NE 30 0
2019–20 Preston NE 38 1 **149 2**

POTTS, Brad (M) 291 38
H: 6 2 W: 12 09 b.Carlisle 3-7-94
Internationals: England U19.
2012–13 Carlisle U 27 0
2013–14 Carlisle U 37 2
2014–15 Carlisle U 39 7 **103 9**
2015–16 Blackpool 45 6
2016–17 Blackpool 42 10 **87 16**
2017–18 Barnsley 37 3
2018–19 Barnsley 22 6 **59 9**
2018–19 Preston NE 10 2
2019–20 Preston NE 32 2 **42 4**

RAFFERTY, Joe (D) 249 4
H: 6 0 W: 11 11 b.Liverpool 6-10-93
Internationals: Republic of Ireland U18, U19.
2012–13 Rochdale 21 0
2013–14 Rochdale 31 0
2014–15 Rochdale 31 1
2015–16 Rochdale 31 1
2016–17 Rochdale 40 0
2017–18 Rochdale 33 1
2018–19 Rochdale 27 0 **214 3**
2018–19 Preston NE 6 0
2019–20 Preston NE 29 1 **35 1**

RIPLEY, Connor (G) 139 0
H: 5 11 W: 11 13 b.Middlesbrough 13-2-93
Internationals: England U19, U20.
2010–11 Middlesbrough 1 0
2011–12 Middlesbrough 1 0
2011–12 *Oxford U* 1 0 **1 0**
2012–13 Middlesbrough 0 0
2013–14 Middlesbrough 0 0
2013–14 *Bradford C* 0 0
2014 *Ostersunds* 14 0 **14 0**
2014–15 Middlesbrough 0 0
2015–16 Middlesbrough 0 0
2015–16 *Motherwell* 36 0 **36 0**
2016–17 Middlesbrough 0 0
2016–17 *Oldham Ath* 46 0 **46 0**
2017–18 Middlesbrough 0 0
2017–18 *Burton Alb* 2 0 **2 0**
2017–18 *Bury* 15 0 **15 0**
2018–19 Middlesbrough 0 0 **2 0**
2018–19 *Accrington S* 21 0 **21 0**
2018–19 Preston NE 2 0
2019–20 Preston NE 0 0 **2 0**

RUDD, Declan (G) 217 0
H: 6 3 W: 12 06 b.Diss 16-1-91
Internationals: England U16, U17, U19, U20, U21, Full caps.
2008–09 Norwich C 0 0
2009–10 Norwich C 7 0
2010–11 Norwich C 1 0
2011–12 Norwich C 2 0
2012–13 Norwich C 0 0
2012–13 *Preston NE* 14 0
2013–14 Norwich C 0 0
2013–14 *Preston NE* 46 0
2014–15 Norwich C 0 0
2015–16 Norwich C 11 0
2016–17 Norwich C 0 0 **21 0**
2016–17 *Charlton Ath* 38 0 **38 0**
2017–18 Preston NE 16 0
2018–19 Preston NE 36 0
2019–20 Preston NE 46 0 **158 0**

SIMPSON, Connor (F) 13 1
b.Guisborough 24-1-00
2016–17 Hartlepool U 2 0 **2 0**
2017–18 Preston NE 1 0
2018–19 Preston NE 0 0
2018–19 *Carlisle U* 8 1 **8 1**
2019–20 Preston NE 0 0 **1 0**
2019–20 *Accrington S* 2 0 **2 0**

SINCLAIR, Scott (F) 334 80
H: 5 10 W: 10 00 b.Bath 26-3-89
Internationals: England U17, U18, U19, U20, U21. Great Britain.
2004–05 Bristol R 2 0 **2 0**
2005–06 Chelsea 0 0
2006–07 Chelsea 2 0
2006–07 *Plymouth Arg* 15 2 **15 2**
2007–08 Chelsea 1 0
2007–08 *QPR* 9 1 **9 1**
2007–08 *Charlton Ath* 3 0 **3 0**
2007–08 *Crystal Palace* 6 2 **6 2**
2008–09 Chelsea 2 0
2008–09 *Birmingham C* 14 0 **14 0**
2009–10 Chelsea 0 0 **5 0**
2009–10 *Wigan Ath* 18 1 **18 1**
2010–11 Swansea C 43 19
2011–12 Swansea C 38 8
2012–13 Swansea C 1 1 **82 28**
2012–13 Manchester C 11 0
2013–14 Manchester C 0 0
2013–14 *WBA* 8 0 **8 0**
2014–15 Manchester C 2 0 **13 0**
2014–15 *Aston Villa* 9 1
2015–16 Aston Villa 27 2 **36 3**
2016–17 Celtic 35 21
2017–18 Celtic 35 10
2018–19 Celtic 33 9
2019–20 Celtic 2 0 **105 40**
2019–20 Preston NE 18 3 **18 3**

STOCKLEY, Jayden (F) 241 70
H: 6 2 W: 12 07 b.Poole 10-10-93
2009–10 Bournemouth 2 0
2010–11 Bournemouth 4 0
2011–12 Bournemouth 10 0
2011–12 *Accrington S* 9 3 **9 3**
2012–13 Bournemouth 0 0
2013–14 Bournemouth 0 0
2013–14 *Leyton Orient* 8 1 **8 1**
2013–14 *Torquay U* 19 1 **19 1**
2014–15 Bournemouth 0 0
2014–15 *Cambridge U* 3 2 **3 2**
2014–15 *Luton T* 13 3 **13 3**
2015–16 Bournemouth 0 0 **16 0**
2015–16 *Portsmouth* 9 2 **9 2**
2015–16 *Exeter C* 22 10
2016–17 Aberdeen 27 5 **27 5**
2017–18 Exeter C 41 19
2018–19 Exeter C 25 16 **88 45**
2018–19 Preston NE 17 4
2019–20 Preston NE 32 4 **49 8**

STOREY, Jordan (D) 51 3
H: 6 2 W: 12 00 b. 2-9-97
2016–17 Exeter C 0 0
2017–18 Exeter C 13 2 **13 2**
2018–19 Preston NE 28 1
2019–20 Preston NE 10 0 **38 1**

WALKER, Ethan (F) 1 0
b. 28-7-02
2018–19 Preston NE 1 0
2019–20 Preston NE 0 0 **1 0**

Scholars
Corcoran, James Hugh; Coulton, Lewis Thomas; Dolan, Tyrhys; Dooley, Ben Michael; Earl, Lewis Robert Ian; Hollan-Wilkinson, Jacob William; Huddart, Harry Lee Joseph; Lombard, Oliver Michael; McFayden, Lincoln Tye; McManus, Brian Frank; Nicholson, Kyi Joseph Samuel; Nolan, Joseph Edward; Potts, Louis John; Rodwel-Grant, Joseph Edward; Williams, Tyler Michael.

QPR (67)

ALFA, Ody (F) 0 0
b. 9-3-99
2019–20 QPR 0 0

BALL, Dominic (D) 129 2
H: 6 0 W: 12 06 b.Welwyn Garden City 2-8-95
Internationals: Northern Ireland U16, U17, U19, U21. England U19, U20.
2013–14 Tottenham H 0 0
2014–15 Tottenham H 0 0
2014–15 *Cambridge U* 11 0 **11 0**
2015–16 Tottenham H 0 0
2015–16 *Rangers* 21 0 **21 0**
2016–17 Rotherham U 13 0
2016–17 *Peterborough U* 6 1 **6 1**
2017–18 Rotherham U 0 0
2017–18 *Aberdeen* 16 0 **0**
2018–19 Rotherham U 0 0 **13 0**
2018–19 *Aberdeen* 31 0 **47 0**
2019–20 QPR 31 1 **31 1**

BANSAL-McNULTY, Amrit (M) 0 0
b. 16-3-00
2018–19 QPR 0 0
2019–20 QPR 0 0

BARBET, Yoann (D) 167 8
H: 6 2 W: 12 11 b.Talence 10-5-93
Internationals: France U18.
2014–15 Chamois Niortais 33 2 **33 2**
2015–16 Brentford 18 1
2016–17 Brentford 23 1
2017–18 Brentford 34 3
2018–19 Brentford 32 1 **107 6**
2019–20 QPR 27 0 **27 0**

BARNES, Dillon (G) 24 0
H: 6 4 W: 11 11 b. 8-4-96
From Bedford T.
2015–16 Colchester U 0 0
2016–17 Colchester U 0 0
2017–18 Colchester U 2 0
2018–19 Colchester U 22 0 **24 0**
2019–20 QPR 0 0

BETTACHE, Faysal (M) 3 0
b.Westminster 7-7-00
2018–19 QPR 0 0
2019–20 QPR 3 0 **3 0**

BRZOZOWSKI, Marcin (G) 0 0
b. 29-10-98
Internationals: Poland U19.
2015–16 QPR 0 0
2016–17 QPR 0 0
2017–18 QPR 0 0
2018–19 QPR 0 0
2019–20 QPR 0 0

CAMERON, Geoff (D) 347 15
H: 6 3 W: 13 02 b.Attleboro 11-7-85
Internationals: USA Full caps.
2008 Houston D 24 1
2009 Houston D 32 2
2010 Houston D 16 3
2011 Houston D 37 5
2012 Houston D 15 0 **124 11**
2012–13 Stoke C 35 0
2013–14 Stoke C 37 2
2014–15 Stoke C 27 0
2015–16 Stoke C 30 0
2016–17 Stoke C 19 0
2017–18 Stoke C 20 0
2018–19 Stoke C 0 0 **168 2**
2018–19 *QPR* 19 1
2019–20 QPR 36 1 **55 2**

CARLYLE, Nathan (D) 0 0
b.
2018–19 QPR 0 0
2019–20 QPR 0 0

CHAIR, Ilias (M) 67 11
b.Lierse 30-10-97
Internationals: Morocco U23.
2015–16 Lierse 2 0
2016–17 Lierse 0 0 **2 0**
2017–18 QPR 4 1
2018–19 QPR 4 0
2018–19 *Stevenage* 16 6 **16 6**
2019–20 QPR 41 4 **49 5**

DALLING, Deshane (F) 0 0
b.London 13-8-98
From Huddersfield T.
2018–19 QPR 0 0
2019–20 QPR 0 0

DIENG, Timothy (G) 59 0
b. 23-11-94
2010–11 Red Star Zurich 0 0
2011–12 Grasshoppers 0 0
2012–13 Grasshoppers 0 0
2012–13 *Grenchen* 3 0 **3 0**
2013–14 Grasshoppers 0 0
2014–15 Grasshoppers 0 0
2015–16 MSV Duisburg 0 0
2016–17 QPR 0 0
2017–18 QPR 0 0
2018–19 QPR 0 0
2018–19 *Stevenage* 13 0 **13 0**
2018–19 *Dundee* 16 0 **16 0**
2019–20 QPR 0 0
2019–20 *Doncaster R* 27 0 **27 0**

DUKE-McKENNA, Stephen (M) 0 0
H: 5 7 b.Liverpool 17-8-00
Internationals: Guyana Full caps.
2017–18 Everton 0 0
2018–19 Bolton W 0 0
2019–20 QPR 0 0

EZE, Eberechi (M) 124 25
H: 5 8 W: 10 08 b. 29-6-98
Internationals: England U20, U21.
From Millwall.
2016–17 QPR 0 0
2017–18 Wycombe W 20 5 **20 5**
2017–18 QPR 16 2
2018–19 QPR 42 4
2019–20 QPR 46 14 **104 20**

GUBBINS, Joseph (D) 1 0
b. 3-8-01
2019–20 QPR 1 0 **1 0**

HALL, Grant (D) 166 7
H: 5 9 W: 11 02 b.Brighton 29-10-91
2009–10 Brighton & HA 0 0
2010–11 Brighton & HA 0 0
2011–12 Brighton & HA 1 0 **1 0**
2012–13 Tottenham H 0 0
2013–14 Tottenham H 0 0
2013–14 *Swindon T* 27 0 **27 0**
2014–15 Tottenham H 0 0
2014–15 *Birmingham C* 7 0 **7 0**
2014–15 *Blackpool* 12 1 **12 1**
2015–16 QPR 39 1
2016–17 QPR 34 0
2017–18 QPR 4 0
2018–19 QPR 12 0
2019–20 QPR 30 5 **119 6**

HAMALAINEN, Niko (M) 35 0
b.Florida 3-5-97
Internationals: Finland U18, U19, U21, Full caps.
2014–15 QPR 0 0
2015–16 QPR 0 0
2015–16 *Dagenham & R* 1 0 **1 0**
2016–17 QPR 3 0
2017–18 QPR 0 0
2018–19 QPR 0 0
2018–19 *Los Angeles FC* 3 0 **3 0**
2019–20 QPR 0 0 **3 0**
2019–20 *Kilmarnock* 28 0 **28 0**

KAKAY, Osman (D) 31 0
b.Westminster 25-8-97
Internationals: Sierra Leone Full caps.
2015–16 QPR 0 0
2015–16 *Livingston* 10 0 **10 0**
2016–17 QPR 1 0
2016–17 Chesterfield 8 0
2017–18 Chesterfield 0 0 **8 0**
2017–18 QPR 2 0
2018–19 QPR 3 0
2019–20 *Partick Thistle* 0 0
2019–20 QPR 7 0 **13 0**

KANE, Todd (D) 187 11
H: 5 11 W: 11 00 b.Huntingdon 17-9-93
Internationals: England U19.
2011–12 Chelsea 0 0
2012–13 Chelsea 0 0
2012–13 *Preston NE* 3 0 **3 0**
2012–13 *Blackburn R* 14 0
2013–14 Chelsea 0 0
2013–14 *Blackburn R* 27 2 **41 2**
2014–15 Chelsea 0 0
2014–15 *Bristol C* 5 0 **5 0**
2014–15 *Nottingham F* 8 1 **8 1**
2015–16 Chelsea 0 0
2015–16 *NEC* 31 1 **31 1**
2016–17 Chelsea 0 0
2017–18 Chelsea 0 0
2017–18 *FC Groningen* 11 0 **11 0**
2017–18 *Oxford U* 17 3 **17 3**
2018–19 Chelsea 0 0
2018–19 *Hull C* 39 3 **39 3**
2019–20 QPR 32 1 **32 1**

KELLY, Liam (G) 105 0
b.Glasgow 23-1-96
Internationals: Scotland U16, U17, U19, U21.
2015–16 Rangers 0 0
2015–16 *East Fife* 16 0 **16 0**
2016–17 Rangers 0 0
2016–17 *Livingston* 34 0
2017–18 Rangers 0 0
2018–19 Livingston 36 0 **70 0**
2019–20 QPR 19 0 **19 0**

LEISTNER, Toni (D) 227 6
H: 6 3 W: 13 05 b.Dresden 19-8-90
2010–11 Dynamo Dresden 1 0
2011–12 Dynamo Dresden 3 0
2012–13 Dynamo Dresden 1 0
2012–13 *Hallescher* 13 0 **13 0**
2013–14 Dynamo Dresden 16 0 **21 0**
2014–15 Union Berlin 30 1
2015–16 Union Berlin 26 1
2016–17 Union Berlin 30 1
2017–18 Union Berlin 29 1 **115 4**
2018–19 QPR 43 2
2019–20 QPR 22 0 **65 2**
2019–20 *Cologne* 13 0 **13 0**

LUMLEY, Joe (G) 113 0
H: 6 3 W: 11 07 b.Harlow 15-2-95
2013–14 QPR 0 0
2014–15 QPR 0 0
2014–15 *Accrington S* 5 0 **5 0**
2014–15 *Morecambe* 0 0
2015–16 QPR 1 0
2015–16 *Stevenage* 0 0
2016–17 QPR 0 0
2016–17 *Bristol R* 19 0 **19 0**
2017–18 QPR 2 0
2017–18 *Blackpool* 17 0 **17 0**
2018–19 QPR 42 0
2019–20 QPR 27 0 **72 0**

MANNING, Ryan (F) 105 11
H: 5 8 W: 10 06 b.Galway 14-6-96
Internationals: Republic of Ireland U17, U19, U21.
From Galway U.
2016–17 QPR 18 1
2017–18 QPR 19 2
2018–19 QPR 9 0
2018–19 *Rotherham U* 18 4 **18 4**
2019–20 QPR 41 4 **87 7**

MASTERSON, Conor (D) 12 1
b.Dublin 8-9-98
Internationals: Republic of Ireland U16, U17, U18, U19, U21.
2015–16 Liverpool 0 0
2016–17 Liverpool 0 0
2017–18 Liverpool 0 0
2019–20 QPR 12 1 **12 1**

OTEH, Aramide (F) 48 5
b.London 10-9-98
From Tottenham H.
2017–18 QPR 6 1
2018–19 QPR 2 0
2018–19 *Walsall* 13 1 **13 1**
2019–20 *Bradford C* 18 3 **18 3**
2019–20 QPR 9 0 **17 1**

OWENS, Charlie (M) 2 0
b. 7-12-97
Internationals: Northern Ireland U19, U21.
2017–18 QPR 0 0
2018–19 QPR 0 0
2018–19 *Wycombe W* 2 0 **2 0**
2019–20 QPR 0 0

PHILLIPS, Giles (D) 11 0
2018–19 QPR 0 0
2019–20 *Wycombe W* 11 0 **11 0**

PUGH, Marc (M) 453 72
H: 5 11 W: 11 04 b.Bacup 2-4-87
2005–06 Burnley 0 0
2005–06 Bury 6 1
2006–07 Bury 35 3 **41 4**
2007–08 Shrewsbury T 37 4
2008–09 Shrewsbury T 7 0 **44 4**
2008–09 *Luton T* 4 0 **4 0**
2008–09 *Hereford U* 9 1
2009–10 Hereford U 40 13 **49 14**
2010–11 Bournemouth 41 12
2011–12 Bournemouth 42 8
2012–13 Bournemouth 40 6
2013–14 Bournemouth 42 5
2014–15 Bournemouth 42 9
2015–16 Bournemouth 26 3
2016–17 Bournemouth 21 2
2017–18 Bournemouth 20 0
2018–19 Bournemouth 0 0 **274 45**
2018–19 *Hull C* 14 3 **14 3**
2019–20 QPR 27 2 **27 2**

RAMKILDE, Marco (F) 5 0
b.Aalborg 9-5-98
Internationals: Denmark U16, U17, U18, U19.
2015–16 AaB 1 0
2016–17 AaB 3 0
2017–18 AaB 0 0
2018–19 AaB 0 0 **4 0**
2019–20 QPR 1 0 **1 0**

RANGEL, Angel (D) 403 13
H: 5 11 W: 11 09 b.Barcelona 28-10-82
2006–07 Terrassa 34 2 **34 2**
2007–08 Swansea C 43 2
2008–09 Swansea C 40 1
2009–10 Swansea C 38 0
2010–11 Swansea C 38 2
2011–12 Swansea C 34 0
2012–13 Swansea C 33 3
2013–14 Swansea C 30 0
2014–15 Swansea C 27 0
2015–16 Swansea C 23 0
2016–17 Swansea C 18 1
2017–18 Swansea C 4 0 **328 9**
2018–19 QPR 20 2
2019–20 QPR 21 0 **41 2**

SAMUEL, Bright (F) 146 12
H: 5 9 W: 11 05 b. 1-2-97
2014–15 Blackpool 6 0
2015–16 Blackpool 23 0
2016–17 Blackpool 31 4
2017–18 Blackpool 4 0 **64 4**
2017–18 QPR 18 1
2018–19 QPR 27 2
2019–20 QPR 37 5 **82 8**

SHODIPO, Olamide (M) 39 0
b.Dublin 5-7-97
Internationals: Republic of Ireland U19, U21.
2016–17 QPR 11 0
2016–17 *Port Vale* 6 0 **6 0**
2017–18 QPR 0 0
2017–18 *Colchester U* 6 0 **6 0**
2018–19 QPR 4 0
2019–20 QPR 12 0 **27 0**

SMYTH, Paul (M) 50 6
b. 10-9-97
Internationals: Northern Ireland U19, U21, Full caps.
2017–18 Linfield 0 0
2017–18 QPR 13 2
2018–19 QPR 3 0
2018–19 *Accrington S* 15 3 **15 3**
2019–20 QPR 0 0 **16 2**
2019–20 *Wycombe W* 19 1 **19 1**

WALKER, Lewis (F) 4 0
b. 10-5-98
2015–16 Derby Co 0 0
2016–17 Derby Co 0 0
2017–18 QPR 0 0
2018–19 QPR 4 0
2019–20 QPR 0 0 **4 0**

WALLACE, Lee (D) 340 24
b.Edinburgh 1-8-87
Internationals: Scotland U19, U20, U21, Full caps.
2004–05 Hearts 13 0
2005–06 Hearts 13 0
2006–07 Hearts 17 0
2007–08 Hearts 21 0
2008–09 Hearts 34 2
2009–10 Hearts 32 1
2010–11 Hearts 9 0 **139 3**
2011–12 Rangers 28 2
2012–13 Rangers 33 3
2013–14 Rangers 28 3

2014–15	Rangers	31	3		
2015–16	Rangers	36	7		
2016–17	Rangers	27	3		
2017–18	Rangers	5	0		
2018–19	Rangers	2	0	**190**	**21**
2019–20	QPR	11	0	**11**	**0**

Players retained or with offer of contract

Dickinson, Tyla Dez; Domi, Franklin; Drewe, Aaron Michael; Duncan, Dylan; Frailing, Jake Lewis John; Kefalas, Themistoklis; Kendall, Charley George; Osayi, Samuel Bright; Remy, Shiloh Samuel; Wells, Ben Michael; Williams-Lowe, Kayden Lavon; Woollard-Innocent, Kai Hamilton.

Scholars

Aoraha, Alexander; Babajide, Oluwabunmi Rilwan Ayodele; De, Silva Dillon Senan; Evangelista, Conte Raheem; Eze, Chimaechi Nwodim; Ferreira, De Paiva Alison Junio; Griffiths, Lemar Anthony; Hayes, Ryan Alexander; Jud-Boyd, Arkell Nicholas Cecil; Kargbo, Hamzad Sayeed; Mahoney, Murphy Joseph; Mahorn, Trent Reagen; McLean, Mason Ashley Francis; Mema, Armelindo; Middlehurst, Thomas Daniel; Orafu, Nathaniel Ikechukwu; Pitblado, Isaac James Millar.

READING (68)

ADAM, Charlie (M) 394 73

H: 6 1 W: 12 00 b.Dundee 10-12-85

Internationals: Scotland U21, B, Full caps.

2004–05	Rangers	1	0		
2004–05	*Ross Co*	10	2	**10**	**2**
2005–06	Rangers	1	0		
2005–06	*St Mirren*	29	5	**29**	**5**
2006–07	Rangers	32	11		
2007–08	Rangers	16	2		
2008–09	Rangers	9	0	**59**	**13**
2008–09	Blackpool	13	2		
2009–10	Blackpool	43	16		
2010–11	Blackpool	35	12	**91**	**30**
2011–12	Liverpool	28	2	**28**	**2**
2012–13	Stoke C	27	3		
2013–14	Stoke C	31	7		
2014–15	Stoke C	29	7		
2015–16	Stoke C	22	1		
2016–17	Stoke C	24	1		
2017–18	Stoke C	11	0		
2018–19	Stoke C	12	0	**156**	**19**
2019–20	Reading	21	2	**21**	**2**

ALUKO, Sone (M) 331 49

H: 5 8 W: 9 10 b.Birmingham 19-2-89

Internationals: England U16, U17, U18, U19. Nigeria U20, Full caps.

2005–06	Birmingham C	0	0		
2006–07	Birmingham C	0	0		
2007–08	Birmingham C	0	0		
2007–08	*Aberdeen*	20	3		
2008–09	Birmingham C	0	0		
2008–09	*Blackpool*	1	0	**1**	**0**
2008–09	Aberdeen	32	2		
2009–10	Aberdeen	22	3		
2010–11	Aberdeen	28	2	**102**	**10**
2011–12	Rangers	21	12	**21**	**12**
2012–13	Hull C	23	8		
2013–14	Hull C	17	1		
2014–15	Hull C	25	1		
2015–16	Hull C	25	3	**90**	**13**
2016–17	Fulham	45	8		
2017–18	Fulham	4	0	**49**	**8**
2017–18	Reading	39	3		
2018–19	Reading	19	1		
2018–19	*Beijing Renhe*	8	2	**8**	**2**
2019–20	Reading	2	0	**60**	**4**

ANDERSSON, Jokull (G) 0 0

b. 25-8-01

Internationals: Iceland U17, U19.

From Afturelding.

2019–20	Reading	0	0		

BALDOCK, Sam (F) 332 100

H: 5 7 W: 10 07 b.Buckingham 15-3-89

Internationals: England U20.

2005–06	Milton Keynes D	0	0		
2006–07	Milton Keynes D	1	0		
2007–08	Milton Keynes D	5	0		
2008–09	Milton Keynes D	40	12		
2009–10	Milton Keynes D	20	5		
2010–11	Milton Keynes D	30	12		
2011–12	Milton Keynes D	4	4	**100**	**33**
2011–12	West Ham U	23	5		
2012–13	West Ham U	0	0	**23**	**5**
2012–13	Bristol C	34	10		
2013–14	Bristol C	45	24		
2014–15	Bristol C	4	0	**83**	**34**
2014–15	Brighton & HA	20	3		
2015–16	Brighton & HA	28	4		
2016–17	Brighton & HA	31	11		
2017–18	Brighton & HA	2	0	**81**	**18**
2018–19	Reading	21	5		
2019–20	Reading	24	5	**45**	**10**

BARROW, Modou (F) 253 58

H: 5 9 W: 9 13 b.Banjul 13-10-92

Internationals: Gambia Full caps.

2010	Mjolby Al	15	6	**15**	**6**
2011	Mjolby Sodra	19	23	**19**	**23**
2012	Norrkping	7	0	**7**	**0**
2013	Varbergs	28	2	**28**	**2**
2014	Ostersunds FK	19	9	**19**	**9**
2014–15	Swansea C	11	0		
2014–15	*Nottingham F*	4	0	**4**	**0**
2015–16	Swansea C	22	1		
2015–16	*Blackburn R*	4	0	**4**	**0**
2016–17	Swansea C	18	0	**51**	**1**
2016–17	*Leeds U*	5	0	**5**	**0**
2017–18	Reading	41	10		
2018–19	Reading	35	4		
2019–20	Reading	1	0	**77**	**14**
2019–20	*Denizlispor*	24	3	**24**	**3**

Transferred to Jeonbuk Hyundai Motors, July 2020.

BLACKETT, Tyler (D) 137 0

H: 6 1 W: 11 12 b.Manchester 2-4-94

Internationals: England U16, U17, U18, U19, U21.

2012–13	Manchester U	0	0		
2013–14	Manchester U	0	0		
2013–14	*Blackpool*	5	0	**5**	**0**
2013–14	*Birmingham C*	8	0	**8**	**0**
2014–15	Manchester U	11	0		
2015–16	Manchester U	0	0	**11**	**0**
2015–16	*Celtic*	3	0	**3**	**0**
2016–17	Reading	34	0		
2017–18	Reading	25	0		
2018–19	Reading	31	0		
2019–20	Reading	20	0	**110**	**0**

BOYCE-CLARKE, Coniah (G) 0 0

b. 1-3-03

Internationals: England U16, U17.

2019–20	Reading	0	0		

BOYE, Lucas (F) 145 11

b.San Gregorio 28-2-96

2014	River Plate	17	1		
2015	River Plate	9	1		
2015	*Newell's Old Boys*	7	1		
2016	River Plate	0	0	**26**	**2**
2016	*Newell's Old Boys*	16	1	**23**	**2**
2016–17	Torino	30	1		
2017–18	Torino	11	0		
2017–18	*Celta Vigo*	13	0	**13**	**0**
2018–19	Torino	0	0		
2018–19	*AEK Athens*	23	6	**23**	**6**
2019–20	Torino	0	0	**41**	**1**

On loan from Torino.

2019–20	Reading	19	0	**19**	**0**

BURLEY, Andre (D) 0 0

2019–20	Reading	0	0		

COLEMAN, Ethan (M) 0 0

b. 28-1-00

2019–20	Reading	0	0		

DORSETT, Jeriel (D) 0 0

Internationals: England U18.

2019–20	Reading	0	0		

EAST, Ryan (M) 1 0

b. 7-8-98

2017–18	Reading	0	0		
2018–19	Reading	1	0		
2019–20	Reading	0	0	**1**	**0**

FELIPE ARARUNA, Hoffmann (M) 22 0

2016	Sao Paulo	0	0		
2017	Sao Paulo	8	0		
2018	Sao Paulo	11	0	**19**	**0**
2019–20	Reading	3	0	**3**	**0**

FROST, Tyler (M) 0 0

b. 7-7-99

2017–18	Reading	0	0		
2018–19	Reading	0	0		
2019–20	Reading	0	0		

GUNTER, Chris (D) 454 4

H: 5 11 W: 11 02 b.Newport 21-7-89

Internationals: Wales U17, U19, U21, Full caps.

2006–07	Cardiff C	15	0		
2007–08	Cardiff C	13	0	**28**	**0**
2007–08	Tottenham H	2	0		
2008–09	Tottenham H	3	0	**5**	**0**
2008–09	*Nottingham F*	8	0		
2009–10	Nottingham F	44	1		
2010–11	Nottingham F	43	0		
2011–12	Nottingham F	46	1	**141**	**2**
2012–13	Reading	20	0		
2013–14	Reading	44	0		
2014–15	Reading	38	0		
2015–16	Reading	44	0		
2016–17	Reading	46	1		
2017–18	Reading	46	1		
2018–19	Reading	22	0		
2019–20	Reading	20	0	**280**	**2**

HOLMES, Thomas (D) 12 0

b. 12-3-00

2017–18	Reading	1	0		
2018–19	Reading	0	0		
2019–20	Reading	0	0	**1**	**0**
2019–20	*KSV Roeselare*	11	0	**11**	**0**

HOUSE, Ben (F) 6 0

b. 5-7-99

Internationals: Scotland U20, U21.

2018–19	Reading	0	0		
2018–19	*Swindon T*	6	0	**6**	**0**
2019–20	Reading	0	0		

LOADER, Danny (F) 28 1

b. 28-8-00

Internationals: England U16, U17, U18, U19, U20.

From Wycombe W.

2017–18	Reading	0	0		
2018–19	Reading	21	1		
2019–20	Reading	7	0	**28**	**1**

LUCAS JOAO, Eduardo (F) 218 53

H: 6 4 W: 12 08 b.Luanda 4-9-93

Internationals: Portugal U20, U21, U23, Full caps.

2012–13	Nacional	0	0		
2012–13	*Mirandela*	27	12	**27**	**12**
2013–14	Nacional	16	0		
2014–15	Nacional	30	6	**46**	**6**
2015–16	Sheffield W	40	6		
2016–17	Sheffield W	10	0		
2016–17	*Blackburn R*	13	3	**13**	**3**
2017–18	Sheffield W	31	9		
2018–19	Sheffield W	31	10		
2019–20	Sheffield W	1	1	**113**	**26**
2019–20	Reading	19	6	**19**	**6**

MANNONE, Vito (G) 208 0

H: 6 0 W: 11 08 b.Milan 2-3-88

Internationals: Italy U21.

2005–06	Arsenal	0	0		
2006–07	Arsenal	0	0		
2006–07	*Barnsley*	2	0	**2**	**0**
2007–08	Arsenal	0	0		
2008–09	Arsenal	1	0		
2009–10	Arsenal	5	0		
2010–11	Arsenal	0	0		
2010–11	*Hull C*	10	0		
2011–12	Arsenal	0	0		
2011–12	*Hull C*	21	0	**31**	**0**
2012–13	Arsenal	9	0	**15**	**0**
2013–14	Sunderland	29	0		
2014–15	Sunderland	10	0		
2015–16	Sunderland	19	0		
2016–17	Sunderland	9	0	**67**	**0**
2017–18	Reading	41	0		
2018–19	Reading	6	0		
2019	*Minnesota U*	34	0	**34**	**0**
2019–20	Reading	0	0	**47**	**0**
2019–20	*Esbjerg*	12	0	**12**	**0**

MASIKA, Ajub (F) 152 33

b.Pumwani 10-9-92

Internationals: Kenya Full caps.

2011–12	Genk	6	0		
2012–13	Genk	11	0		
2013–14	Genk	12	0		
2014–15	Genk	1	0		
2014–15	*Lierse*	20	1		
2015–16	Genk	0	0	**30**	**0**
2015–16	*Lierse*	22	7		
2016–17	Lierse	20	6	**62**	**14**
2017	Beijing Renhe	23	8		
2018	Beijing Renhe	14	7		
2018	*Heilongjiang Lava Spring*	6	2	**6**	**2**
2019	Beijing Renhe	12	2	**49**	**17**

On loan from Beijing Renhe.

2019–20	Reading	5	0	**5**	**0**

McCLEARY, Garath (M) 353 36

H: 5 10 W: 12 06 b.Oxford 15-5-87

Internationals: Jamaica Full caps.

2007–08	Nottingham F	8	1		

2008–09	Nottingham F	39	1		
2009–10	Nottingham F	24	0		
2010–11	Nottingham F	18	2		
2011–12	Nottingham F	22	9	**111**	**13**
2011–12	Reading	0	0		
2012–13	Reading	31	3		
2013–14	Reading	42	5		
2014–15	Reading	26	1		
2015–16	Reading	34	4		
2016–17	Reading	41	9		
2017–18	Reading	18	0		
2018–19	Reading	31	0		
2019–20	Reading	19	1	**242**	**23**

McINTYRE, Tom (D) 12 0
b. 6-11-98
Internationals: Scotland U17, U20, U21.

2018–19	Reading	2	0		
2019–20	Reading	10	0	**12**	**0**

McNULTY, Marc (M) 278 92
H: 5 10 W: 11 00 b.Edinburgh 14-9-92
Internationals: Scotland Full caps.

2009–10	Livingston	9	1		
2010–11	Livingston	5	1		
2011–12	Livingston	30	11		
2012–13	Livingston	26	7		
2013–14	Livingston	35	17	**105**	**37**
2014–15	Sheffield U	31	9		
2015–16	Sheffield U	5	1		
2015–16	*Portsmouth*	27	10	**27**	**10**
2016–17	Sheffield U	4	0	**40**	**10**
2016–17	*Bradford C*	15	1	**15**	**1**
2016–17	Coventry C	0	0		
2017–18	Coventry C	42	23	**42**	**23**
2018–19	Reading	13	1		
2018–19	*Hibernian*	15	7		
2019–20	Reading	0	0	**13**	**1**
2019–20	*Sunderland*	15	2	**15**	**2**
2019–20	*Hibernian*	6	1	**21**	**8**

MEDFORD-SMITH, Ramarni (D) 0 0

2018–19	Reading	0	0		
2019–20	Reading	0	0		

MEITE, Yakou (M) 114 29
H: 6 0 W: 11 05 b.Paris 11-2-96
Internationals: Ivory Coast U17, U20, U23, Full caps.

2015–16	Paris Saint-Germain	1	0	**1**	**0**
2016–17	Reading	14	1		
2017–18	Reading	0	0		
2017–18	*Sochaux*	22	3	**22**	**3**
2018–19	Reading	37	12		
2019–20	Reading	40	13	**91**	**26**

MOORE, Liam (D) 263 7
H: 6 1 W: 13 08 b.Loughborough 31-1-93
Internationals: England U17, U20, U21.

2011–12	Leicester C	2	0		
2011–12	*Bradford C*	17	0	**17**	**0**
2012–13	Leicester C	16	0		
2012–13	*Brentford*	7	0		
2013–14	Leicester C	30	1		
2014–15	Leicester C	11	0		
2014–15	*Brentford*	3	0	**10**	**0**
2015–16	Leicester C	0	0	**59**	**1**
2015–16	*Bristol C*	10	0	**10**	**0**
2016–17	Reading	40	1		
2017–18	Reading	46	3		
2018–19	Reading	38	1		
2019–20	Reading	43	1	**167**	**6**

MORRISON, Michael (D) 443 27
H: 6 0 W: 12 00 b.Bury St Edmunds 3-3-88
Internationals: England C.

2008–09	Leicester C	35	3		
2009–10	Leicester C	31	2		
2010–11	Leicester C	11	0	**77**	**5**
2010–11	Sheffield W	12	0	**12**	**0**
2011–12	Charlton Ath	45	4		
2012–13	Charlton Ath	44	1		
2013–14	Charlton Ath	45	1		
2014–15	Charlton Ath	2	0	**136**	**6**
2014–15	Birmingham C	21	0		
2015–16	Birmingham C	46	3		
2016–17	Birmingham C	31	3		
2017–18	Birmingham C	33	1		
2018–19	Birmingham C	43	7	**174**	**14**
2019–20	Reading	44	2	**44**	**2**

NEVERS, Thierry (M) 0 0
b. 26-3-02

2019–20	Reading	0	0		

NOVAKOVICH, Andrija (F) 67 28
b. 21-9-96
Internationals: USA U17, U18, U20, Full caps.

2014–15	Reading	2	0		
2015–16	Reading	0	0		
2016–17	Reading	0	0		
2017–18	Reading	0	0		
2017–18	*Telstar*	35	19	**35**	**19**
2018–19	Reading	0	0		
2018–19	*Fortuna Sittard*	29	9	**29**	**9**
2019–20	Reading	1	0	**3**	**0**

Transferred to Frosinone, September 2019.

OBITA, Jordan (M) 190 9
H: 5 11 W: 11 08 b.Oxford 8-12-93
Internationals: England U18, U19, U21.

2010–11	Reading	0	0		
2011–12	Reading	0	0		
2011–12	*Barnet*	5	0	**5**	**0**
2011–12	*Gillingham*	6	3	**6**	**3**
2012–13	Reading	0	0		
2012–13	*Portsmouth*	8	1	**8**	**1**
2012–13	*Oldham Ath*	8	0	**8**	**0**
2013–14	Reading	34	1		
2014–15	Reading	43	0		
2015–16	Reading	26	0		
2016–17	Reading	37	2		
2017–18	Reading	2	0		
2018–19	Reading	0	0		
2019–20	Reading	21	2	**163**	**5**

ODIMAYO, Akinwale (D) 0 0
b. 28-11-99

2019–20	Reading	0	0		

OLISE, Michael (M) 23 0
b. 12-12-01
Internationals: France U18.

2018–19	Reading	4	0		
2019–20	Reading	19	0	**23**	**0**

OSHO, Gabriel (D) 7 0
b.Reading 14-8-98

2018–19	Reading	2	0		
2019–20	Reading	5	0	**7**	**0**

PELE, Judilson (M) 189 18
H: 5 10 W: 11 09 b.Agualva-Cacem 29-9-91
Internationals: Portugal U18, U19, U20, U21. Guinea-Bissau Full caps.

2008–09	Belenenses	3	0		
2009–10	Belenenses	13	0		
2010–11	Belenenses	16	0		
2010–11	Genoa	0	0		
2011–12	AC Milan	0	0		
2012–13	AC Milan	0	0		
2012–13	*Arsenal Kyiv*	5	0	**5**	**0**
2013–14	AC Milan	0	0		
2013–14	*Olhanense*	13	0	**13**	**0**
2014–15	AC Milan	0	0		
2014–15	*Belenenses*	30	6	**62**	**6**
2015–16	Benfica	0	0		
2015–16	*Pacos Ferreira*	29	4	**29**	**4**
2016–17	Benfica	0	0		
2016–17	*Feirense*	1	0	**1**	**0**
2017–18	Rio Ave	31	7	**31**	**7**
2018–19	Monaco	8	0		
2018–19	*Nottingham F*	9	0	**9**	**0**

On loan from Monaco.

2019–20	Monaco	0	0	**8**	**0**
2019–20	Reading	31	1	**31**	**1**

POPA, Adrian (F) 308 40
H: 5 7 W: 11 00 b.Horezu 24-7-88
Internationals: Romania Full caps.

2006–07	Stiinta Timisoara	3	2		
2007–08	Stiinta Timisoara	25	2		
2008–09	Stiinta Timisoara	0	0	**28**	**4**
2008–09	*Buftea*	11	2	**11**	**2**
2008–09	*Gloria Buzzau*	11	0	**11**	**0**
2009–10	Universitatea Cluj	23	3	**23**	**3**
2010–11	Concordia Chiajna	27	4		
2011–12	Concordia Chiajna	30	3		
2012–13	Concordia Chiajna	4	3	**61**	**10**
2012–13	Steau Bucharest	30	1		
2013–14	Steau Bucharest	28	7		
2014–15	Steau Bucharest	28	5		
2015–16	Steau Bucharest	32	4		
2016–17	Steau Bucharest	19	3	**137**	**20**
2016–17	Reading	8	1		
2017–18	Reading	6	0		
2017–18	*Al-Taawoun*	9	0	**9**	**0**
2018–19	Reading	1	0		
2018–19	*Ludogorets*	13	0	**13**	**0**
2019–20	Reading	0	0	**15**	**1**

PUSCAS, George (F) 156 45
b.Marghita 8-4-96
Internationals: Romania U17, U19, U21, Full caps.

2012–13	Bihor Oradea	13	2	**13**	**2**
2013–14	Inter Milan	0	0		
2014–15	Inter Milan	4	0		
2015–16	Inter Milan	0	0		
2015–16	*Bari*	17	5	**17**	**5**
2016–17	Inter Milan	0	0		
2016–17	*Benevento*	21	7		
2017–18	Inter Milan	0	0	**4**	**0**
2017–18	*Benevento*	11	1	**32**	**8**
2017–18	*Novara*	19	9	**19**	**9**
2018–19	Palermo	33	9	**33**	**9**
2019–20	Reading	38	12	**38**	**12**

RAFAEL CABRAL, Barbosa (G) 172 0
b.Sorocaba 20-5-90
Internationals: Brazil U23, Full caps.

2010	Santos	32	0		
2011	Santos	32	0		
2012	Santos	25	0		
2013	Santos	5	0	**94**	**0**
2013–14	Napoli	8	0		
2014–15	Napoli	23	0		
2015–16	Napoli	0	0		
2016–17	Napoli	1	0		
2017–18	Napoli	0	0	**32**	**0**
2018–19	Sampdoria	2	0		
2019–20	Sampdoria	0	0	**2**	**0**
2019–20	Reading	44	0	**44**	**0**

RICHARDS, Omar (D) 51 2
H: 6 1 W: 10 12 b. 15-2-98
Internationals: England U21.

2017–18	Reading	13	2		
2018–19	Reading	10	0		
2019–20	Reading	28	0	**51**	**2**

RINOMHOTA, Andy (M) 63 2
b. 21-4-97
From AFC Portchester.

2017–18	Reading	0	0		
2018–19	Reading	26	1		
2019–20	Reading	37	1	**63**	**2**

SMITH, Sam (F) 54 8
H: 5 11 W: 11 07 b. 8-3-98

2017–18	Reading	8	1		
2018–19	Reading	0	0		
2018–19	*Oxford U*	15	0	**15**	**0**
2018–19	*Shrewsbury T*	3	0	**3**	**0**
2019–20	Reading	0	0	**8**	**1**
2019–20	*Cambridge U*	28	7	**28**	**7**

SOUTHWOOD, Luke (G) 15 0
b. 6-12-97
Internationals: England U19, U20.

2019–20	Reading	0	0		
2019–20	*Hamilton A*	15	0	**15**	**0**

SWIFT, John (M) 184 28
H: 6 0 W: 11 07 b.Portsmouth 23-6-95
Internationals: England U16, U17, U18, U19, U20, U21.

2013–14	Chelsea	1	0		
2014–15	Chelsea	0	0		
2014–15	*Rotherham U*	3	0	**3**	**0**
2014–15	*Swindon T*	18	2	**18**	**2**
2015–16	Chelsea	0	0	**1**	**0**
2015–16	*Brentford*	27	7	**27**	**7**
2016–17	Reading	36	8		
2017–18	Reading	24	2		
2018–19	Reading	34	3		
2019–20	Reading	41	6	**135**	**19**

WALKER, Sam (G) 266 0
H: 6 5 W: 14 00 b.Gravesend 2-10-91

2009–10	Chelsea	0	0		
2010–11	Chelsea	0	0		
2010–11	*Barnet*	7	0	**7**	**0**
2011–12	Chelsea	0	0		
2011–12	*Northampton T*	21	0	**21**	**0**
2011–12	*Yeovil T*	20	0	**20**	**0**
2012–13	Chelsea	0	0		
2012–13	*Bristol R*	11	0	**11**	**0**
2012–13	*Colchester U*	19	0		
2013–14	Colchester U	46	0		
2014–15	Colchester U	45	0		
2015–16	Colchester U	0	0		
2016–17	Colchester U	46	0		
2017–18	Colchester U	44	0	**200**	**0**
2018–19	Reading	7	0		
2019–20	Reading	0	0	**7**	**0**

WATSON, Tennai (D) 30 0
b. 4-3-97

2015–16	Reading	0	0		
2016–17	Reading	3	0		
2017–18	Reading	0	0		
2018–19	Reading	0	0		
2018–19	*AFC Wimbledon*	24	0	**24**	**0**
2019–20	Reading	0	0	**3**	**0**
2019–20	*Coventry C*	3	0	**3**	**0**

YIADOM, Andy (M) 219 12
H: 5 11 W: 11 11 b.Camden 9-12-91
Internationals: England C. Ghana Full caps.
2011–12 Barnet 7 1
2012–13 Barnet 39 3
2015–16 Barnet 40 6 **86 10**
2016–17 Barnsley 32 0
2017–18 Barnsley 32 0 **64 0**
2018–19 Reading 45 1
2019–20 Reading 24 1 **69 2**

Players retained or with offer of contract
Ajose, Joseph Ayomikun; Azeez, Oluwafemi Javier; Bristow, Ethan David; Gomes, Osorio Claudio; Hewitt, Joshua David; Hines-Samuels, Imari-Narain Che; Holsgrove, Jordan William; Lawless, Conor Michael John; Pendlebury, Oliver Jack; Tetek, Dejan.

Scholars
Abbey, Nelson Ighodaro; Anderson, Alfie Donal; Boyc-Clarke, Coniah Chronicles; Collins, Harvey Robert; Hamilton, Jordan Jewel; Holden, James William; Leavy, Kian; Melvi-Lambert, Nahum; Obamakinwa, Emmanuel Olorunfemi; Sackey, Lynford; Talent, Aryeetey Malachi Stephen; Turkson, Yaw; Vieira, Mcgiff Augustus Manuel; Vinagre, Pedrosa Neves Pedro.

ROCHDALE (69)

ANDREW, Calvin (F) 386 36
H: 6 0 W: 12 11 b.Luton 19-12-86
2004–05 Luton T 8 0
2005–06 Luton T 1 1
2005–06 *Grimsby T* 8 1 **8 1**
2005–06 *Bristol C* 3 0 **3 0**
2006–07 Luton T 7 1
2007–08 Luton T 39 2 **55 4**
2008–09 Crystal Palace 7 0
2008–09 *Brighton & HA* 9 2 **9 2**
2009–10 Crystal Palace 27 1
2010–11 Crystal Palace 13 0
2010–11 *Millwall* 3 0 **3 0**
2010–11 *Swindon T* 10 1 **10 1**
2011–12 Crystal Palace 6 0 **53 1**
2011–12 *Leyton Orient* 10 0 **10 0**
2012–13 Port Vale 22 1
2013–14 Port Vale 0 0 **22 1**
2013–14 Mansfield T 15 1 **15 1**
2013–14 York C 8 1 **8 1**
2014–15 Rochdale 32 5
2015–16 Rochdale 30 6
2016–17 Rochdale 39 7
2017–18 Rochdale 31 3
2018–19 Rochdale 38 3
2019–20 Rochdale 20 0 **190 24**

BAAH, Kwadwo (F) 7 0
2019–20 Rochdale 7 0 **7 0**

BRADLEY, Lewis (M) 3 0
b. 29-5-01
2018–19 Rochdale 1 0
2019–20 Rochdale 2 0 **3 0**

BRIERLEY, Ethan (M) 0 0
2019–20 Rochdale 0 0

CAMPS, Callum (M) 201 25
b.Stockport 30-11-95
Internationals: Northern Ireland U18, U21.
2012–13 Rochdale 2 0
2013–14 Rochdale 0 0
2014–15 Rochdale 12 1
2015–16 Rochdale 32 5
2016–17 Rochdale 44 8
2017–18 Rochdale 42 2
2018–19 Rochdale 41 3
2019–20 Rochdale 28 6 **201 25**

CLARKSON, Louie (M) 0 0
2019–20 Rochdale 0 0

DONE, Matt (M) 450 42
H: 5 10 W: 10 04 b.Oswestry 22-6-88
2005–06 Wrexham 6 0
2006–07 Wrexham 34 1
2007–08 Wrexham 26 0 **66 1**
2008–09 Hereford U 36 0
2009–10 Hereford U 20 0 **56 0**
2010–11 Rochdale 33 5
2011–12 Barnsley 31 4
2012–13 Barnsley 13 0 **44 4**
2012–13 *Hibernian* 7 0 **7 0**
2013–14 Rochdale 38 0
2014–15 Rochdale 23 10
2014–15 Sheffield U 15 7
2015–16 Sheffield U 31 4
2016–17 Sheffield U 31 3 **77 14**
2017–18 Rochdale 46 6
2018–19 Rochdale 36 2
2019–20 Rochdale 24 0 **200 23**

DOOLEY, Stephen (M) 44 3
H: 5 11 W: 12 08 b.Portstewart 19-10-91
Internationals: Northern Ireland U17, U19.
From Coleraine, Derry C, Cork C.
2018–19 Rochdale 22 0
2019–20 Rochdale 22 3 **44 3**

DUNNE, Joe (D) 0 0
2018–19 Rochdale 0 0
2019–20 Rochdale 0 0

GILLAM, Matthew (F) 20 2
H: 5 9 W: 11 07 b. 4-10-98
2016–17 Rochdale 0 0
2017–18 Rochdale 8 1
2018–19 Rochdale 10 1
2019–20 Rochdale 2 0 **20 2**

HENDERSON, Ian (F) 547 144
H: 5 10 W: 11 06 b.Thetford 25-1-85
Internationals: England U18, U20.
2002–03 Norwich C 20 1
2003–04 Norwich C 19 4
2004–05 Norwich C 3 0
2005–06 Norwich C 24 1
2006–07 Norwich C 2 0 **68 6**
2006–07 *Rotherham U* 18 1 **18 1**
2007–08 Northampton T 23 0
2008–09 Northampton T 3 0 **26 0**
2008–09 Luton T 19 1 **19 1**
2009–10 Colchester U 13 2
2009–10 *Ankaragucu* 2 0 **2 0**
2010–11 Colchester U 36 10
2011–12 Colchester U 46 9
2012–13 Colchester U 22 3 **117 24**
2012–13 Rochdale 12 3
2013–14 Rochdale 45 11
2014–15 Rochdale 44 22
2015–16 Rochdale 39 13
2016–17 Rochdale 42 15
2017–18 Rochdale 39 13
2018–19 Rochdale 45 20
2019–20 Rochdale 31 15 **297 112**

HOPPER, Harrison (M) 1 0
b. 24-12-00
2018–19 Rochdale 0 0
2019–20 Rochdale 1 0 **1 0**

KEOHANE, Jimmy (M) 116 9
H: 5 11 W: 11 05 b.Wexford 22-1-91
Internationals: Republic of Ireland U19.
2010–11 Bristol C 0 0
2011–12 Bristol C 0 0
2011–12 Exeter C 4 0
2012–13 Exeter C 33 3
2013–14 Exeter C 20 3
2014–15 Exeter C 23 3
2015–16 Exeter C 0 0 **80 9**
From Woking, Sligo R, Cork C.
2018–19 Rochdale 8 0
2019–20 Rochdale 28 0 **36 0**

LILLIS, Josh (G) 299 0
H: 6 0 W: 12 08 b.Derby 24-6-87
2006–07 Scunthorpe U 1 0
2007–08 Scunthorpe U 3 0
2008–09 Scunthorpe U 5 0
2008–09 *Notts Co* 5 0 **5 0**
2009–10 Scunthorpe U 8 0
2009–10 *Grimsby T* 4 0 **4 0**
2009–10 *Rochdale* 1 0
2010–11 Scunthorpe U 15 0
2010–11 *Rochdale* 23 0
2011–12 Scunthorpe U 6 0 **38 0**
2012–13 Rochdale 46 0
2013–14 Rochdale 45 0
2014–15 Rochdale 16 0
2015–16 Rochdale 40 0
2016–17 Rochdale 14 0
2017–18 Rochdale 40 0
2018–19 Rochdale 27 0
2019–20 Rochdale 0 0 **252 0**

LUND, Matthew (M) 231 35
H: 6 0 W: 11 13 b.Manchester 21-11-90
Internationals: Northern Ireland U21, Full caps.
2009–10 Stoke C 0 0
2010–11 Stoke C 0 0
2010–11 *Hereford U* 2 0 **2 0**
2011–12 Stoke C 0 0
2011–12 *Oldham Ath* 3 0 **3 0**
2011–12 *Bristol R* 13 2
2012–13 Stoke C 0 0
2012–13 *Bristol R* 18 2 **31 4**
2012–13 Southend U 12 1 **12 1**
2013–14 Rochdale 40 8
2014–15 Rochdale 14 2
2015–16 Rochdale 29 1
2016–17 Rochdale 29 9
2017–18 Burton Alb 12 1 **12 1**
2017–18 *Bradford C* 10 2 **10 2**
2018–19 Scunthorpe U 22 2
2019–20 Scunthorpe U 22 4 **44 6**
2019–20 Rochdale 5 1 **117 21**

LYNCH, Jay (G) 10 0
H: 6 2 W: 13 04 b.Salford 31-3-93
2012–13 Bolton W 0 0
2013–14 Bolton W 0 0
2014–15 Accrington S 2 0 **2 0**
From Salford C, AFC Fylde.
2019–20 Rochdale 8 0 **8 0**

McLAUGHLIN, Ryan (D) 87 3
H: 5 9 W: 10 12 b.Belfast 30-9-94
Internationals: Northern Ireland U16, U17, U19, U21, Full caps.
2011–12 Liverpool 0 0
2012–13 Liverpool 0 0
2013–14 Liverpool 0 0
2013–14 *Barnsley* 9 0 **9 0**
2014–15 Liverpool 0 0
2015–16 Liverpool 0 0
2015–16 *Aberdeen* 4 0 **4 0**
2016–17 Oldham Ath 36 2
2017–18 Oldham Ath 16 1 **52 3**
2018–19 Blackpool 6 0 **6 0**
2018–19 Rochdale 13 0
2019–20 Rochdale 3 0 **16 0**

McNULTY, Jim (D) 367 7
H: 6 1 W: 12 00 b.Runcorn 13-2-85
Internationals: Scotland U17, U19.
2006–07 Macclesfield T 15 0
2007–08 Macclesfield T 19 1 **34 1**
2007–08 Stockport Co 11 0
2008–09 Stockport Co 26 1 **37 1**
2008–09 Brighton & HA 5 1
2009–10 Brighton & HA 8 0
2009–10 *Scunthorpe U* 3 0
2010–11 Brighton & HA 0 0 **13 1**
2010–11 *Scunthorpe U* 6 0 **9 0**
2011–12 Barnsley 44 2
2012–13 Barnsley 12 0
2013–14 Barnsley 0 0 **56 2**
2013–14 *Tranmere R* 12 0 **12 0**
2013–14 Bury 21 0
2014–15 Bury 25 0 **46 0**
2015–16 Rochdale 46 0
2016–17 Rochdale 35 0
2017–18 Rochdale 40 1
2018–19 Rochdale 25 1
2019–20 Rochdale 14 0 **160 2**

McSHANE, Paul (D) 350 14
H: 6 0 W: 11 05 b.Wicklow 6-1-86
Internationals: Republic of Ireland U21, Full caps.
2002–03 Manchester U 0 0
2003–04 Manchester U 0 0
2004–05 Manchester U 0 0
2004–05 *Walsall* 4 1 **4 1**
2005–06 Manchester U 0 0
2005–06 *Brighton & HA* 38 3 **38 3**
2006–07 WBA 32 2 **32 2**
2007–08 Sunderland 21 0
2008–09 Sunderland 3 0
2008–09 *Hull C* 17 1
2009–10 Sunderland 0 0 **24 0**
2009–10 Hull C 27 0
2010–11 Hull C 19 0
2010–11 *Barnsley* 10 1 **10 1**
2011–12 Hull C 1 0
2011–12 *Crystal Palace* 11 0 **11 0**
2012–13 Hull C 25 2
2013–14 Hull C 10 0
2014–15 Hull C 20 1 **119 4**
2015–16 Reading 35 0
2016–17 Reading 30 3
2017–18 Reading 26 0
2018–19 Reading 5 0 **96 3**
2019–20 Rochdale 16 0 **16 0**

MORLEY, Aaron (M) 28 3
b. 27-2-00
2016–17 Rochdale 2 0
2017–18 Rochdale 0 0
2018–19 Rochdale 3 0
2019–20 Rochdale 23 3 **28 3**

O'CONNELL, Eoghan (D) **107 4**
H: 6 1 W: 12 08 b.Cork 13-8-95
Internationals: Republic of Ireland U19, U21.
2013–14 Celtic 1 0
2014–15 Celtic 3 0
2015–16 Celtic 1 0
2015–16 *Oldham Ath* 2 0 **2 0**
2016 *Cork C* 7 1 **7 1**
2016–17 Celtic 2 0 **7 0**
2016–17 *Walsall* 17 1 **17 1**
2017–18 Bury 12 0
2018–19 Bury 31 2 **43 2**
2019–20 Rochdale 31 0 **31 0**

PHILLIPS, Toby (M) **0 0**
2019–20 Rochdale 0 0

RATHBONE, Oliver (M) **112 9**
H: 5 7 W: 10 06 b.Blackburn 10-10-96
From Manchester U.
2016–17 Rochdale 27 2
2017–18 Rochdale 33 1
2018–19 Rochdale 28 4
2019–20 Rochdale 24 2 **112 9**

RYAN, James (M) **405 38**
H: 5 8 W: 11 08 b.Maghull 6-9-88
Internationals: Republic of Ireland U21.
2006–07 Liverpool 0 0
2007–08 Liverpool 0 0
2007–08 *Shrewsbury T* 4 0 **4 0**
2008–09 Accrington S 44 10
2009–10 Accrington S 39 3
2010–11 Accrington S 46 9 **129 22**
2011–12 Scunthorpe U 24 2
2012–13 Scunthorpe U 45 2 **69 4**
2013–14 Chesterfield 39 2
2014–15 Chesterfield 44 4 **83 6**
2015–16 Fleetwood T 43 2
2016–17 Fleetwood T 16 0 **59 2**
2017–18 Blackpool 36 3
2018–19 Blackpool 1 0 **37 3**
2019–20 Rochdale 24 1 **24 1**

TAVARES, Fabio (F) **14 1**
b. 22-1-01
2018–19 Rochdale 0 0
2019–20 Rochdale 14 1 **14 1**

THOMAS, Peter (F) **0 0**
2019–20 Rochdale 0 0

WADE, Bradley (G) **0 0**
b.Gloucester 3-7-00
2018–19 Rochdale 0 0
2019–20 Rochdale 0 0

WILBRAHAM, Aaron (F) **600 130**
H: 6 3 W: 12 04 b.Knutsford 21-10-79
1997–98 Stockport Co 7 1
1998–99 Stockport Co 26 0
1999–2000 Stockport Co 26 4
2000–01 Stockport Co 36 12
2001–02 Stockport Co 21 3
2002–03 Stockport Co 15 7
2003–04 Stockport Co 41 8 **172 35**
2004–05 Hull C 19 2 **19 2**
2004–05 *Oldham Ath* 4 2 **4 2**
2005–06 Milton Keynes D 31 4
2005–06 *Bradford C* 5 1 **5 1**
2006–07 Milton Keynes D 32 7
2007–08 Milton Keynes D 35 10
2008–09 Milton Keynes D 33 16
2009–10 Milton Keynes D 35 10
2010–11 Milton Keynes D 10 2 **176 49**
2010–11 Norwich C 12 1
2011–12 Norwich C 11 1 **23 2**
2012–13 Crystal Palace 21 0
2013–14 Crystal Palace 4 0 **25 0**
2014–15 Bristol C 37 18
2015–16 Bristol C 43 8
2016–17 Bristol C 31 4 **111 30**
2017–18 Bolton W 23 2 **23 2**
2018–19 Rochdale 23 4
2019–20 Rochdale 19 3 **42 7**

WILLIAMS, M Jordan (M) **85 0**
H: 6 0 W: 12 02 b.Bangor 6-11-95
Internationals: Wales U17, U21.
2014–15 Liverpool 0 0
2014–15 *Notts Co* 8 0 **8 0**
2015–16 Liverpool 0 0
2015–16 *Swindon T* 9 0
2016–17 Liverpool 0 0
2016–17 *Swindon T* 0 0 **9 0**
2017–18 Liverpool 0 0
2017–18 *Rochdale* 12 0
2018–19 Rochdale 28 0
2019–20 Rochdale 28 0 **68 0**

Players retained or with offer of contract
Mulvey, Keaton Christopher.

Scholars
Chalton, Benjamin Barry; Chorlton, Louie Joseph; Clarkson, Louie James; Cullen, Adam James; D'Souza, Louie Isaac; Duarte, Gouveia Joao Vasco; Dunne, Joseph William; Kinsella, Morgan James; Kisimba, Musambya Hugue; Lee, Harry Mackenzie; Moreland, Morgan Jake; Nock, Luke John; Patrick, Oliver Edward; Phillips, Toby Rae; Piper, Morgan Daniel Allan; Wright, Joseph Philip.

ROTHERHAM U (70)

BILBOE, Laurence (G) **0 0**
b. 21-2-98
2016–17 Rotherham U 0 0
2017–18 Rotherham U 0 0
2018–19 Rotherham U 0 0
2019–20 Rotherham U 0 0

CLARKE, Trevor (D) **8 0**
b. 26-3-98
Internationals: Republic of Ireland U17, U19, U21.
2019–20 Rotherham U 8 0 **8 0**

CROOKS, Matt (M) **166 30**
H: 6 0 W: 11 05 b.Leeds 20-1-94
2011–12 Huddersfield T 0 0
2012–13 Huddersfield T 0 0
2013–14 Huddersfield T 0 0
2014–15 Huddersfield T 1 0 **1 0**
2014–15 *Hartlepool U* 3 0 **3 0**
2014–15 Accrington S 16 0
2015–16 Accrington S 32 6 **48 6**
2016–17 Rangers 2 0 **2 0**
2016–17 *Scunthorpe U* 12 3 **12 3**
2017–18 Northampton T 30 4
2018–19 Northampton T 21 5 **51 9**
2018–19 Rotherham U 16 3
2019–20 Rotherham U 33 9 **49 12**

GRATTON, Jacob (F) **0 0**
2019–20 Rotherham U 0 0

HASTIE, Jake (M) **81 12**
b.Law 18-3-99
Internationals: Scotland U21.
2016–17 Motherwell 3 0
2017–18 Motherwell 0 0
2017–18 *Airdrieonians* 31 2 **31 2**
2018–19 Motherwell 14 6 **17 6**
2018–19 *Alloa Ath* 19 1 **19 1**
2019–20 Rangers 0 0
On loan from Rangers.
2019–20 Rotherham U 14 3 **14 3**

IHIEKWE, Michael (D) **150 7**
H: 6 1 W: 12 02 b.Liverpool 20-11-92
Internationals: England C.
2011–12 Wolverhampton W 0 0
2012–13 Wolverhampton W 0 0
2013–14 Wolverhampton W 0 0
2013–14 *Cheltenham T* 13 0 **13 0**
2014–15 Tranmere R 38 1 **38 1**
2017–18 Rotherham U 31 1
2018–19 Rotherham U 15 2
2018–19 *Accrington S* 20 1 **20 1**
2019–20 Rotherham U 33 2 **79 5**

JONES, Billy (M) **476 25**
H: 5 11 W: 13 00 b.Shrewsbury 24-3-87
Internationals: England U16, U17, U19, U20.
2003–04 Crewe Alex 27 1
2004–05 Crewe Alex 20 0
2005–06 Crewe Alex 44 6
2006–07 Crewe Alex 41 1 **132 8**
2007–08 Preston NE 29 0
2008–09 Preston NE 44 3
2009–10 Preston NE 44 4
2010–11 Preston NE 43 6 **160 13**
2011–12 WBA 18 0
2012–13 WBA 27 1
2013–14 WBA 21 0 **66 1**
2014–15 Sunderland 14 0
2015–16 Sunderland 24 1
2016–17 Sunderland 27 1
2017–18 Sunderland 22 1 **87 3**
2018–19 Rotherham U 21 0
2019–20 Rotherham U 10 0 **31 0**

KAYODE, Joshua (F) **5 3**
2017–18 Rotherham U 0 0
2018–19 Rotherham U 0 0
2019–20 Rotherham U 0 0
2019–20 *Carlisle U* 5 3 **5 3**

LADAPO, Freddie (F) **125 38**
H: 6 0 W: 12 06 b.Romford 1-2-93
2011–12 Colchester U 0 0
2012–13 Colchester U 4 0
2013–14 Colchester U 2 0 **6 0**
From Margate.
2015–16 Crystal Palace 0 0
2016–17 Crystal Palace 0 0
2016–17 *Oldham Ath* 17 2 **17 2**
2016–17 *Shrewsbury T* 15 4 **15 4**
2017–18 Crystal Palace 1 0 **1 0**
2017–18 Southend U 10 0 **10 0**
2018–19 Plymouth Arg 45 18 **45 18**
2019–20 Rotherham U 31 14 **31 14**

LAMY, Julien (F) **21 1**
b.Paris 6-11-99
2016–17 Brest 0 0
2017–18 Plabennec 16 1 **16 1**
2018–19 WBA 0 0
2019–20 Rotherham U 3 0 **3 0**
2019–20 *AFC Wimbledon* 2 0 **2 0**

LINDSAY, Jamie (M) **137 9**
b.Motherwell 11-9-95
Internationals: Scotland U16, U17, U19.
2015–16 Celtic 0 0
2015–16 *Dumbarton* 23 0 **23 0**
2016–17 Celtic 0 0
2016–17 *Greenock Morton* 31 0 **31 0**
2017–18 Celtic 0 0
2017–18 *Ross County* 26 2
2018–19 Ross County 35 6 **61 8**
2019–20 Rotherham U 22 1 **22 1**

MACDONALD, Shaun (M) **221 11**
H: 6 1 W: 11 04 b.Swansea 17-6-88
Internationals: Wales U19, U21, Full caps.
2005–06 Swansea C 7 0
2006–07 Swansea C 8 0
2007–08 Swansea C 1 0
2008–09 Swansea C 5 0
2008–09 *Yeovil T* 4 2
2009–10 Swansea C 3 0
2009–10 *Yeovil T* 31 3
2010–11 Swansea C 0 0
2010–11 *Yeovil T* 26 4 **61 9**
2011–12 Swansea C 0 0 **24 0**
2011–12 Bournemouth 25 1
2012–13 Bournemouth 28 0
2013–14 Bournemouth 23 0
2014–15 Bournemouth 5 0
2015–16 Bournemouth 3 0 **84 1**
2016–17 Wigan Ath 39 1
2017–18 Wigan Ath 0 0
2018–19 Wigan Ath 0 0 **39 1**
2019–20 Rotherham U 13 0 **13 0**

MATTOCK, Joe (D) **361 8**
H: 5 11 W: 12 05 b.Leicester 15-5-90
Internationals: England U17, U19, U21.
2006–07 Leicester C 4 0
2007–08 Leicester C 31 0
2008–09 Leicester C 31 1
2009–10 Leicester C 0 0 **66 1**
2009–10 WBA 29 0
2010–11 WBA 0 0
2010–11 *Sheffield U* 13 0 **13 0**
2011–12 WBA 0 0 **29 0**
2011–12 *Portsmouth* 7 0 **7 0**
2011–12 *Brighton & HA* 15 1 **15 1**
2012–13 Sheffield W 7 0
2013–14 Sheffield W 23 2
2014–15 Sheffield W 27 0 **57 2**
2015–16 Rotherham U 35 1
2016–17 Rotherham U 36 0
2017–18 Rotherham U 35 1
2018–19 Rotherham U 44 1
2019–20 Rotherham U 24 1 **174 4**

OGBENE, Chiedozie (M) **45 1**
H: 5 9 W: 11 11 b. 1-5-97
From Cork C, Limerick.
2017–18 Brentford 2 0
2018–19 Brentford 4 0
2018–19 *Exeter C* 14 0 **14 0**
2019–20 Brentford 0 0 **6 0**
2019–20 Rotherham U 25 1 **25 1**

OLOSUNDE, Matthew (D) **32 0**
b. 7-3-98
Internationals: USA U17, U20, U23, Full caps.
From Manchester U.
2019–20 Rotherham U 32 0 **32 0**

PRICE, Lewis (G) **150 0**
H: 6 3 W: 13 05 b.Bournemouth 19-7-84
Internationals: Wales U19, U21, Full caps.
2002–03 Ipswich T 0 0
2003–04 Ipswich T 1 0

2004–05 Ipswich T 8 0
2004–05 *Cambridge U* 6 0 **6 0**
2005–06 Ipswich T 25 0
2006–07 Ipswich T 34 0 **68 0**
2007–08 Derby Co 6 0
2008–09 Derby Co 0 0
2008–09 *Milton Keynes D* 2 0 **2 0**
2008–09 *Luton T* 1 0 **1 0**
2009–10 Derby Co 0 0 **6 0**
2009–10 *Brentford* 13 0 **13 0**
2010–11 Crystal Palace 1 0
2011–12 Crystal Palace 5 0
2012–13 Crystal Palace 0 0
2013–14 Crystal Palace 0 0
2013–14 *Mansfield T* 5 0 **5 0**
2014–15 Crystal Palace 0 0 **6 0**
2014–15 *Crawley T* 18 0 **18 0**
2015–16 Sheffield W 5 0 **5 0**
2016–17 Rotherham U 17 0
2017–18 Rotherham U 1 0
2018–19 Rotherham U 1 0
2019–20 Rotherham U 1 0 **20 0**

PROCTOR, Jamie (F) 264 41
H: 6 2 W: 12 03 b.Preston 25-3-92
2009–10 Preston NE 1 0
2010–11 Preston NE 5 1
2010–11 *Stockport Co* 7 0 **7 0**
2011–12 Preston NE 31 3 **37 4**
2012–13 Swansea C 0 0
2012–13 *Shrewsbury T* 2 0 **2 0**
2012–13 Crawley T 18 7
2013–14 Crawley T 44 6 **62 13**
2014–15 Fleetwood T 41 8
2015–16 Fleetwood T 23 4 **64 12**
2015–16 Bradford C 18 5 **18 5**
2016–17 Bolton W 21 0 **21 0**
2016–17 *Carlisle U* 17 4 **17 4**
2017–18 Rotherham U 4 0
2018–19 Rotherham U 16 2
2019–20 Rotherham U 3 0 **23 2**
2019–20 *Scunthorpe U* 13 1 **13 1**

ROBERTSON, Clark (D) 223 9
H: 6 2 W: 12 00 b.Aberdeen 5-9-93
Internationals: Scotland U19, U21.
2009–10 Aberdeen 3 0
2010–11 Aberdeen 13 0
2011–12 Aberdeen 9 0
2012–13 Aberdeen 23 0
2013–14 Aberdeen 8 0
2014–15 Aberdeen 1 0 **57 0**
2015–16 Blackpool 38 1
2016–17 Blackpool 44 0
2017–18 Blackpool 39 3 **121 4**
2018–19 Rotherham U 28 3
2019–20 Rotherham U 17 2 **45 5**

SMITH, Michael (F) 281 67
H: 6 4 W: 11 02 b.Wallsend 17-10-91
2011–12 Charlton Ath 0 0
2011–12 *Accrington S* 6 3 **6 3**
2012–13 Charlton Ath 0 0
2012–13 *Colchester U* 8 1 **8 1**
2013–14 Charlton Ath 0 0
2013–14 *AFC Wimbledon* 23 9 **23 9**
2013–14 Swindon T 20 8
2014–15 Swindon T 40 13
2015–16 Swindon T 5 0 **65 21**
2015–16 *Barnsley* 13 0 **13 0**
2015–16 *Portsmouth* 16 4
2016–17 Portsmouth 18 3 **34 7**
2016–17 *Northampton T* 14 2
2017–18 Northampton T 0 0 **14 2**
2017–18 *Bury* 19 1 **19 1**
2017–18 Rotherham U 20 6
2018–19 Rotherham U 45 8
2019–20 Rotherham U 34 9 **99 23**

SOUTHERN-COOPER, Jake (M) 0 0
b. 1-1-00
2018–19 Rotherham U 0 0
2019–20 Rotherham U 0 0

THOMPSON, Adam (D) 224 5
H: 6 2 W: 12 10 b.Harlow 28-9-92
Internationals: Northern Ireland U17, U19, U21, Full caps.
2010–11 Watford 10 1
2011–12 Watford 0 0
2011–12 *Brentford* 20 0 **20 0**
2012–13 Watford 4 0
2012–13 *Wycombe W* 2 0 **2 0**
2012–13 *Barnet* 1 0 **1 0**
2013–14 Watford 0 0 **14 1**
2013–14 Southend U 16 0
2014–15 Southend U 28 0
2015–16 Southend U 25 2
2016–17 Southend U 40 1 **109 3**
2017–18 Bury 15 0
2017–18 *Bradford C* 9 0 **9 0**
2018–19 Bury 44 1 **59 1**
2019–20 Rotherham U 10 0 **10 0**

TILT, Curtis (D) 100 5
H: 6 4 W: 11 11 b. 4-8-91
From Halesowen T, Hednesford T, AFC Telford U, Wrexham.
2017–18 Blackpool 42 1
2018–19 Blackpool 37 4
2019–20 Blackpool 20 0 **99 5**
2019–20 Rotherham U 1 0 **1 0**

VASSELL, Kyle (F) 161 32
H: 6 0 W: 12 04 b.Milton Keynes 7-2-93
Internationals: Northern Ireland Full caps.
2013–14 Peterborough U 6 0
2014–15 Peterborough U 17 5
2014–15 *Oxford U* 6 1 **6 1**
2015–16 Peterborough U 5 0 **28 5**
2015–16 *Dagenham & R* 8 0 **8 0**
2015–16 *Shrewsbury T* 13 0 **13 0**
2016–17 Blackpool 34 11
2017–18 Blackpool 29 11 **63 22**
2018–19 Rotherham U 23 0
2019–20 Rotherham U 20 4 **43 4**

WILES, Ben (M) 53 3
b. 17-4-99
2017–18 Rotherham U 0 0
2018–19 Rotherham U 20 0
2019–20 Rotherham U 33 3 **53 3**

WOOD, Richard (D) 463 30
H: 6 3 W: 12 13 b.Ossett 5-7-85
2002–03 Sheffield W 3 1
2003–04 Sheffield W 12 0
2004–05 Sheffield W 34 1
2005–06 Sheffield W 30 1
2006–07 Sheffield W 12 0
2007–08 Sheffield W 27 2
2008–09 Sheffield W 42 0
2009–10 Sheffield W 11 2 **171 7**
2009–10 Coventry C 24 3
2010–11 Coventry C 40 1
2011–12 Coventry C 17 1
2012–13 Coventry C 36 3 **117 8**
2013–14 Charlton Ath 21 0 **21 0**
2014–15 Rotherham U 6 0
2014–15 *Crawley T* 10 3 **10 3**
2015–16 Rotherham U 13 0
2015–16 *Fleetwood T* 6 0 **6 0**
2015–16 *Chesterfield* 5 0 **5 0**
2016–17 Rotherham U 29 3
2017–18 Rotherham U 36 4
2018–19 Rotherham U 26 2
2019–20 Rotherham U 23 3 **133 12**

YATES, Jerry (M) 101 21
H: 5 9 W: 10 10 b.Doncaster 10-11-96
2014–15 Rotherham U 1 0
2015–16 Rotherham U 0 0
2016–17 Rotherham U 21 1
2017–18 Rotherham U 17 1
2018–19 *Carlisle U* 23 6 **23 6**
2018–19 Rotherham U 7 0
2019–20 Rotherham U 1 0 **47 2**
2019–20 *Swindon T* 31 13 **31 13**

Players retained or with offer of contract
Cooper, Jake; Ogunfaolu-Kayode, Joshua Akinola.

Scholars
Beeden, Harrison Clark; Ellis, Elliot David Peter; Etia, Jacques Creussier; Evans, Wilfred Peel; Farrar, Charlie Ellis; Gateshill, Robert Steven; Greaves, Jerome Dylan; Hanley, Samuel Stephen; Hodgkinson, Luke James Miller; Hull, Jake Matthew; Kenny, Ethan Morgan; Makwedza, Bolton Bernard; Millen, Josh; Salah, Haroon; Scott, George Henry Christopher; Smith, Charles Oliver; Spence, Joel James; Wenham, Travon Tremayne.

SALFORD C (71)

ANDRADE, Bruno (M) 121 14
H: 5 9 W: 11 09 b.Aveiro 2-10-93
2010–11 QPR 1 0
2011–12 QPR 1 0
2011–12 *Aldershot T* 1 0 **1 0**
2012–13 QPR 0 0
2012–13 *Wycombe W* 23 2 **23 2**
2013–14 QPR 0 0
2013–14 *Stevenage* 13 0
2014–15 QPR 0 0 **2 0**
2014–15 *Stevenage* 16 1 **29 1**
From Woking, Boreham Wood.
2018–19 Lincoln C 42 10
2019–20 Lincoln C 17 1 **59 11**
2019–20 Salford C 7 0 **7 0**

ARMSTRONG, Luke (F) 43 4
b. 2-7-96
2015–16 Cowdenbeath 6 0 **6 0**
From Blyth Spartans
2017–18 Middlesbrough 0 0
2018–19 Middlesbrough 0 0
2018–19 *Accrington S* 16 3 **16 3**
2019–20 Salford C 21 1 **21 1**

BEESLEY, Jake (F) 14 2
H: 6 1 W: 10 08 b.Sheffield 2-12-96
2013–14 Chesterfield 0 0
2014–15 Chesterfield 0 0
2015–16 Chesterfield 0 0
2016–17 Chesterfield 7 0 **7 0**
From Chesterfield.
2019–20 Salford C 7 2 **7 2**

CLARKE, Tom (D) 323 15
H: 6 0 W: 11 02 b.Sowerby Bridge 21-12-87
Internationals: England U18, U19.
2004–05 Huddersfield T 12 0
2005–06 Huddersfield T 17 1
2006–07 Huddersfield T 9 0
2007–08 Huddersfield T 3 0
2008–09 Huddersfield T 15 1
2008–09 *Bradford C* 6 0 **6 0**
2009–10 Huddersfield T 21 0
2010–11 Huddersfield T 5 1
2011–12 Huddersfield T 14 0
2011–12 *Leyton Orient* 10 0 **10 0**
2012–13 Huddersfield T 0 0 **96 3**
2013–14 Preston NE 42 4
2014–15 Preston NE 43 1
2015–16 Preston NE 35 0
2016–17 Preston NE 42 4
2017–18 Preston NE 18 2
2018–19 Preston NE 21 1
2019–20 Preston NE 10 0 **211 12**
2019–20 Salford C 0 0

CONWAY, Craig (M) 466 45
H: 5 7 W: 10 07 b.Irvine 2-5-85
Internationals: Scotland Full caps.
2002–03 Ayr U 1 0
2003–04 Ayr U 6 0
2004–05 Ayr U 23 3
2005–06 Ayr U 31 4 **61 7**
2006–07 Dundee U 30 0
2007–08 Dundee U 15 1
2008–09 Dundee U 36 5
2009–10 Dundee U 33 4
2010–11 Dundee U 22 3 **136 13**
2011–12 Cardiff C 31 3
2012–13 Cardiff C 27 2
2013–14 Cardiff C 0 0 **58 5**
2013–14 *Brighton & HA* 13 1 **13 1**
2013–14 Blackburn R 18 4
2014–15 Blackburn R 38 3
2015–16 Blackburn R 35 3
2016–17 Blackburn R 42 6
2017–18 Blackburn R 24 2
2018–19 Blackburn R 21 1 **178 19**
2019–20 Salford C 20 0 **20 0**

DIESERUVWE, Emmanuel (F) 63 4
H: 6 5 W: 11 05 b.Leeds 5-1-94
2013–14 Sheffield W 0 0
2013–14 *Fleetwood T* 4 0 **4 0**
2014–15 Sheffield W 0 0
2014–15 *Chesterfield* 9 0
2015–16 Chesterfield 16 0 **25 0**
2015–16 *Mansfield T* 10 1 **10 1**
From Kidderminster H, Salford C.
2019–20 Salford C 20 3 **20 3**
2019–20 *Oldham Ath* 4 0 **4 0**

DOYLE, Alex (M) 1 0
2019–20 Salford C 1 0 **1 0**

EASTHAM, Ashley (D) 293 13
H: 6 3 W: 12 06 b.Preston 22-3-91
2009–10 Blackpool 1 0
2009–10 *Cheltenham T* 20 0
2010–11 Blackpool 0 0
2010–11 *Cheltenham T* 9 0 **29 0**
2010–11 *Carlisle U* 0 0
2011–12 Blackpool 0 0
2011–12 *Bury* 25 2
2012–13 Blackpool 0 0 **1 0**
2012–13 *Fleetwood T* 1 0

2012–13 *Notts Co* 4 0 **4 0**
2012–13 *Bury* 19 0 **44 2**
2013–14 Rochdale 15 0
2014–15 Rochdale 41 2
2015–16 Rochdale 20 2 **76 4**
2016–17 Fleetwood T 35 2
2017–18 Fleetwood T 45 3
2018–19 Fleetwood T 45 2
2019–20 Fleetwood T 9 0 **135 7**
2019–20 Salford C 4 0 **4 0**

ELLIOTT, Tom (F) 253 39
H: 6 3 W: 12 00 b.Hunslet 9-11-90
Internationals: England U16, U18.
2006–07 Leeds U 3 0
2007–08 Leeds U 0 0
2008–09 Leeds U 0 0
2008–09 *Macclesfield T* 6 0 **6 0**
2009–10 Leeds U 0 0
2009–10 *Bury* 16 1 **16 1**
2010–11 Leeds U 0 0 **3 0**
2010–11 *Rotherham U* 6 0 **6 0**
2011–12 Hamilton A 7 0 **7 0**
2011–12 Stockport Co 42 7 **42 7**
2014–15 Cambridge U 30 8 **30 8**
2015–16 AFC Wimbledon 39 6
2016–17 AFC Wimbledon 39 9 **78 15**
2017–18 Millwall 24 4
2018–19 Millwall 33 3
2019–20 Millwall 0 0 **57 7**
2019–20 Salford C 8 1 **8 1**

EVANS, William (G) 0 0
2019–20 Salford C 0 0

GAFFNEY, Rory (M) 123 24
H: 6 0 W: 12 04 b.Tuam 23-10-89
2014–15 Cambridge U 0 0
2015–16 Cambridge U 6 2 **6 2**
2015–16 *Bristol R* 24 8
2016–17 Bristol R 34 6
2017–18 Bristol R 42 7 **100 21**
2019–20 Salford C 2 0 **2 0**
2019–20 *Walsall* 15 1 **15 1**

GIBSON, Darron (M) 151 6
H: 6 0 W: 12 04 b.Derry 25-10-87
Internationals: Republic of Ireland U21, B, Full caps.
2005–06 Manchester U 0 0
2006–07 Manchester U 0 0
2007–08 Manchester U 0 0
2007–08 *Wolverhampton W* 21 1 **21 1**
2008–09 Manchester U 3 1
2009–10 Manchester U 15 2
2010–11 Manchester U 12 0
2011–12 Manchester U 1 0 **31 3**
2011–12 Everton 11 1
2012–13 Everton 23 1
2013–14 Everton 1 0
2014–15 Everton 9 0
2015–16 Everton 7 0
2016–17 Everton 0 0 **51 2**
2016–17 Sunderland 12 0
2017–18 Sunderland 15 0 **27 0**
2018–19 Wigan Ath 18 0 **18 0**
2019–20 Salford C 3 0 **3 0**

HOGAN, Liam (D) 32 0
H: 6 0 W: 12 02 b. 8-2-89
2012–13 Fleetwood T 0 0
2013–14 Fleetwood T 16 0
2014–15 Fleetwood T 4 0 **20 0**
From Tranmere R, Gateshead.
2019–20 Salford C 12 0 **12 0**

JONES, Dan (D) 43 0
H: 6 0 W: 12 05 b.Bishop Auckland 14-12-94
Internationals: England C.
2013–14 Hartlepool U 1 0
2014–15 Hartlepool U 25 0
2015–16 Hartlepool U 11 0 **37 0**
2016–17 Grimsby T 3 0 **3 0**
From Barrow.
2019–20 Salford C 3 0 **3 0**

JONES, Joey (D) 20 0
b.Kingston upon Thames 15-4-94
Internationals: Northern Ireland U16, U17, U19, U21.
2019–20 Salford C 20 0 **20 0**

LETHEREN, Kyle (G) 105 0
H: 6 2 W: 13 00 b.Swansea 26-12-87
Internationals: Wales U21.
2010–11 Kilmarnock 0 0
2011–12 Kilmarnock 2 0
2012–13 Kilmarnock 9 0 **11 0**
2013–14 Dundee 35 0
2014–15 Dundee 15 0 **50 0**
2015–16 Blackpool 5 0
2016–17 Blackpool 0 0 **5 0**
From York C.
2017–18 Plymouth Arg 7 0
2018–19 Plymouth Arg 13 0 **20 0**
2019–20 Salford C 19 0 **19 0**

LLOYD, Danny (F) 40 10
b. 3-12-91
From Stockport Co.
2017–18 Peterborough U 31 8 **31 8**
2019–20 Salford C 9 2 **9 2**

LOWE, Jason (M) 253 3
H: 6 0 W: 12 08 b.Wigan 2-9-91
Internationals: England U20, U21.
2009–10 Blackburn R 0 0
2010–11 Blackburn R 1 0
2010–11 *Oldham Ath* 7 2 **7 2**
2011–12 Blackburn R 32 0
2012–13 Blackburn R 36 0
2013–14 Blackburn R 39 1
2014–15 Blackburn R 12 0
2015–16 Blackburn R 10 0
2016–17 Blackburn R 43 0 **173 1**
2017–18 WBA 0 0
2017–18 Birmingham C 9 0 **9 0**
2018–19 Bolton W 35 0
2019–20 Bolton W 29 0 **64 0**
2019–20 Salford C 0 0

MAYNARD, Lois (D) 22 1
b.Cheetham Hill 22-1-89
Internationals: St Kitts and Nevis Full caps.
From Yeovil T, Woking, Eastleigh.
2019–20 Salford C 22 1 **22 1**

McFARLANE, Ewan (G) 0 0
2018–19 Oldham Ath 0 0
2019–20 Oldham Ath 0 0
2019–20 Salford C 0 0

NEAL, Chris (G) 240 0
H: 6 2 W: 12 04 b.St Albans 23-10-85
2004–05 Preston NE 1 0
2005–06 Preston NE 0 0
2006–07 Preston NE 0 0
2006–07 *Shrewsbury T* 0 0
2007–08 *Morecambe* 0 0
2007–08 Preston NE 0 0
2008–09 Preston NE 0 0 **1 0**
2009–10 Shrewsbury T 7 0
2010–11 Shrewsbury T 22 0
2011–12 Shrewsbury T 35 0 **64 0**
2012–13 Port Vale 46 0
2013–14 Port Vale 31 0
2014–15 Port Vale 40 0
2015–16 Port Vale 6 0 **123 0**
2015–16 *Doncaster R* 2 0 **2 0**
2015–16 *Bury* 10 0 **10 0**
2016–17 Fleetwood T 17 0
2017–18 Fleetwood T 8 0 **25 0**
2019–20 Salford C 15 0 **15 0**

O'CONNOR, Michael (M) 420 39
H: 6 1 W: 11 08 b.Belfast 6-10-87
Internationals: Northern Ireland U21, B, Full caps.
2005–06 Crewe Alex 2 0
2006–07 Crewe Alex 29 0
2007–08 Crewe Alex 23 0
2008–09 Crewe Alex 23 3 **77 3**
2008–09 *Lincoln C* 10 1
2009–10 Scunthorpe U 32 2
2010–11 Scunthorpe U 32 8
2011–12 Scunthorpe U 33 1 **97 11**
2012–13 Rotherham U 35 6
2013–14 Rotherham U 29 2 **64 8**
2014–15 Port Vale 44 6
2015–16 Port Vale 26 4 **70 10**
2016–17 Notts Co 32 2
2017–18 Notts Co 6 0 **38 2**
2018–19 Lincoln C 39 2
2019–20 Lincoln C 17 1 **66 4**
2019–20 Salford C 8 1 **8 1**

PIERGIANNI, Carl (D) 25 0
b.Peterborough 3-5-92
2010–11 Peterborough U 1 0 **1 0**
From Stockport Co, Corby T, Boston U, South Melbourne.
2019–20 Salford C 13 0 **13 0**
2019–20 *Oldham Ath* 11 0 **11 0**

POND, Nathan (M) 185 2
H: 6 3 W: 11 00 b.Preston 5-1-85
Internationals: Montserat Full caps.
2012–13 Fleetwood T 12 0
2013–14 Fleetwood T 41 1
2014–15 Fleetwood T 27 1
2015–16 Fleetwood T 21 0
2016–17 Fleetwood T 32 0
2017–18 Fleetwood T 30 0 **163 2**
2019–20 Salford C 22 0 **22 0**

RODNEY, Devante (F) 7 2
b.Manchester 19-5-98
From Sheffield W.
2016–17 Hartlepool U 4 2 **4 2**
From Hartlepool U.
2019–20 Salford C 3 0 **3 0**

ROONEY, Adam (F) 274 149
H: 5 10 W: 12 03 b.Dublin 21-4-87
Internationals: Republic of Ireland U21.
2005–06 Stoke C 5 4
2006–07 Stoke C 10 0
2006–07 *Yeovil T* 3 0 **3 0**
2007–08 Stoke C 0 0 **15 4**
2007–08 *Chesterfield* 22 7 **22 7**
2007–08 *Bury* 16 3 **16 3**
2008–09 Inverness CT 30 5
2009–10 Inverness CT 35 24
2010–11 Inverness CT 37 15 **102 44**
2011–12 Birmingham C 18 4
2012–13 Birmingham C 0 0 **18 4**
2012–13 *Swindon T* 29 9 **29 9**
2013–14 Oldham Ath 24 4 **24 4**
2013–14 Aberdeen 13 7
2014–15 Aberdeen 37 18
2015–16 Aberdeen 27 20
2016–17 Aberdeen 38 12
2017–18 Aberdeen 36 9 **151 66**
2019–20 Salford C 32 8 **32 8**
2019–20 *Solihull Moors* 0 0

SHELTON, Mark (M) 5 1
H: 6 0 W: 11 00 b. 12-9-96
2014–15 Burton Alb 0 0
2015–16 Burton Alb 0 0
From Ilkeston, Alfreton T.
2019–20 Salford C 5 1 **5 1**

SMITH, Martin (M) 27 1
H: 5 10 W: 11 00 b.Sunderland 25-1-96
2014–15 Sunderland 0 0
2015–16 Sunderland 0 0
2015–16 *Carlisle U* 2 0 **2 0**
2016–17 Kilmarnock 10 1 **10 1**
From Coleraine.
2018–19 Swindon T 11 0 **11 0**
2019–20 Salford C 4 0 **4 0**

THOMAS-ASANTE, Brandon (F) 42 6
H: 5 11 W: 12 08 b. 29-12-98
2016–17 Milton Keynes D 6 0
2017–18 Milton Keynes D 15 0
2018–19 Milton Keynes D 1 0 **22 0**
2019–20 Salford C 20 6 **20 6**

THRELKELD, Oscar (D) 126 4
H: 6 0 W: 12 04 b.Bolton 15-12-94
2013–14 Bolton W 2 0
2014–15 Bolton W 4 0
2015–16 Bolton W 3 0 **9 0**
2015–16 *Plymouth Arg* 25 1
2016–17 Plymouth Arg 36 2
2017–18 Plymouth Arg 24 0
2018–19 Waasland-Beveren 2 0 **2 0**
On loan from Wassland-Beveren.
2018–19 Plymouth Arg 12 1 **97 4**
2019–20 Salford C 18 0 **18 0**

TOURAY, Ibou (D) 35 4
H: 5 10 W: 10 09 b.Liverpool 24-12-94
Internationals: Gambia Full caps.
2013–14 Everton 0 0
2014–15 Everton 0 0
2019–20 Salford C 35 4 **35 4**

TOWELL, Richie (D) 227 56
H: 5 8 W: 10 06 b.Dublin 17-7-91
Internationals: Republic of Ireland U17, U19, U21.
2010–11 Celtic 1 0
2011–12 Celtic 0 0
2011–12 *Hibernian* 16 0
2012–13 Celtic 0 0 **1 0**
2012–13 *Hibernian* 14 1 **30 1**
2013 Dundalk 31 7
2014 Dundalk 33 11
2015 Dundalk 32 25 **96 43**
2015–16 Brighton & HA 0 0
2016–17 Brighton & HA 1 0
2017–18 Brighton & HA 0 0
2017–18 *Rotherham U* 39 5
2018–19 Brighton & HA 0 0 **1 0**
2018–19 *Rotherham U* 34 4 **73 9**
2019–20 Salford C 26 3 **26 3**

WALKER, Tom (M) **33 1**
H: 6 0 b.Salford 12-12-95
Internationals: England C.
2014–15 Bolton W 11 1
2015–16 Bolton W 7 0
2016–17 Bolton W 0 0 **18 1**
2016–17 *Bury* 11 0 **11 0**
From Stockport Co, FC United of Manchester.
2019–20 Salford C 4 0 **4 0**

WHITEHEAD, Danny (M) **30 1**
H: 5 10 W: 10 11 b.Trafford 23-10-93
2013–14 West Ham U 0 0
2014–15 West Ham U 0 0
2014–15 Accrington S 2 0 **2 0**
From Macclesfield T.
2015–16 Wigan Ath 0 0
2016–17 Wigan Ath 0 0
2016–17 *Cheltenham T* 6 0 **6 0**
2017–18 Wigan Ath 0 0
2019–20 Salford C 12 1 **12 1**
2019–20 *Macclesfield T* 10 0 **10 0**

WILSON, James (F) **92 15**
H: 6 0 W: 12 04 b.Biddulph 1-12-95
Internationals: England U16, U19, U20, U21.
2013–14 Manchester U 1 2
2014–15 Manchester U 13 1
2015–16 Manchester U 1 0
2015–16 *Brighton & HA* 25 5 **25 5**
2016–17 Manchester U 0 0
2016–17 *Derby Co* 4 0 **4 0**
2017–18 Manchester U 0 0
2017–18 *Sheffield U* 8 1 **8 1**
2018–19 Manchester U 0 0 **15 3**
2018–19 *Aberdeen* 24 4
2019–20 Aberdeen 11 0 **35 4**
2019–20 Salford C 5 2 **5 2**

WISEMAN, Scott (D) **407 7**
H: 6 0 W: 11 06 b.Hull 9-10-85
Internationals: England U20. Gibraltar Full caps.
2003–04 Hull C 2 0
2004–05 Hull C 3 0
2004–05 *Boston U* 2 0 **2 0**
2005–06 Hull C 11 0
2006–07 Hull C 0 0 **16 0**
2006–07 *Rotherham U* 18 1 **18 1**
2006–07 *Darlington* 10 0
2007–08 Darlington 7 0 **17 0**
2008–09 Rochdale 32 0
2009–10 Rochdale 36 1
2010–11 Rochdale 37 0
2011–12 Barnsley 43 1
2012–13 Barnsley 36 0
2013–14 Barnsley 23 0 **102 1**
2013–14 Preston NE 15 0
2014–15 Preston NE 22 2 **37 2**
2015–16 Scunthorpe U 24 0
2016–17 Scunthorpe U 24 2 **48 2**
2017–18 Chesterfield 24 0 **24 0**
2017–18 *Rochdale* 13 0 **118 1**
2019–20 Salford C 25 0 **25 0**

Players retained or with offer of contract
Gardner, Daniel Keith.

Scholars
Evans, William Hayden; Ghaly, Ryan Nathan; Hill, Cameron James; Jones, Daniel Lee; Perry, Philip Edward; Rydel, Ben Daniel; Shepherd, Tomas David; Smith, Anton Benjamin Daniel; Timmis, Jaden Robert; Williams, Thomas Max.

SCUNTHORPE U (72)

BEDEAU, Jacob (D) **18 1**
H: 6 0 W: 12 04 b.Waltham Forest 24-12-99
2016–17 Bury 7 0 **7 0**
2017–18 Aston Villa 0 0
2018–19 Aston Villa 0 0
2019–20 Scunthorpe U 11 1 **11 1**

BEESTIN, Alfie (F) **37 2**
H: 5 10 W: 11 11 b.Leeds 1-10-97
2016–17 Doncaster R 3 0
2017–18 Doncaster R 26 2
2018–19 Doncaster R 5 0 **34 2**
2019–20 Scunthorpe U 3 0 **3 0**

BURGESS, Cameron (D) **135 6**
H: 6 4 W: 12 11 b.Aberdeen 21-10-95
Internationals: Scotland U18, U19. Australia U20, U23.
2014–15 Fulham 4 0
2014–15 *Ross Co* 0 0
2015–16 Fulham 0 0
2016–17 Fulham 0 0 **4 0**
2016–17 *Oldham Ath* 23 1 **23 1**
2016–17 *Bury* 18 0 **18 0**
2017–18 Scunthorpe U 25 2
2018–19 Scunthorpe U 36 1
2019–20 Scunthorpe U 0 0 **61 3**
2019–20 *Salford C* 29 2 **29 2**

BUTLER, Andy (D) **576 49**
H: 6 0 W: 13 00 b.Doncaster 4-11-83
2003–04 Scunthorpe U 35 2
2004–05 Scunthorpe U 37 10
2005–06 Scunthorpe U 16 1
2006–07 Scunthorpe U 11 1
2006–07 *Grimsby T* 4 0 **4 0**
2007–08 Scunthorpe U 36 2
2008–09 Huddersfield T 42 4
2009–10 Huddersfield T 11 0 **53 4**
2009–10 *Blackpool* 7 0 **7 0**
2010–11 Walsall 31 4
2011–12 Walsall 42 5
2012–13 Walsall 41 3
2013–14 Walsall 45 2
2014–15 Sheffield U 0 0
2014–15 *Walsall* 7 0 **166 14**
2014–15 Doncaster R 33 3
2015–16 Doncaster R 40 4
2016–17 Doncaster R 44 3
2017–18 Doncaster R 36 4
2018–19 Doncaster R 40 1 **193 15**
2019–20 Scunthorpe U 18 0 **153 16**

BUTROID, Lewis (D) **17 0**
H: 5 9 W: 10 08 b. 17-9-98
2016–17 Scunthorpe U 0 0
2017–18 Scunthorpe U 7 0
2018–19 Scunthorpe U 6 0
2019–20 Scunthorpe U 4 0 **17 0**

CLARKE, Jordan (D) **259 10**
H: 6 0 W: 11 02 b.Coventry 19-11-91
Internationals: England U19, U20.
2009–10 Coventry C 12 0
2010–11 Coventry C 21 1
2011–12 Coventry C 19 1
2012–13 Coventry C 20 0
2013–14 Coventry C 41 1
2014–15 Coventry C 11 1 **124 4**
2014–15 *Yeovil T* 5 2 **5 2**
2014–15 Scunthorpe U 24 0
2015–16 Scunthorpe U 33 2
2016–17 Scunthorpe U 23 1
2017–18 Scunthorpe U 23 0
2018–19 Scunthorpe U 15 1
2019–20 Scunthorpe U 12 0 **130 4**

COLCLOUGH, Ryan (F) **161 25**
H: 6 3 W: 13 01 b.Budapest 27-12-94
2012–13 Crewe Alex 18 1
2013–14 Crewe Alex 8 2
2014–15 Crewe Alex 7 2
2015–16 Crewe Alex 27 7 **60 12**
2015–16 Wigan Ath 10 2
2016–17 Wigan Ath 10 0
2016–17 *Milton Keynes D* 18 5 **18 5**
2017–18 Wigan Ath 26 4 **46 6**
2018–19 Scunthorpe U 17 2
2019–20 Scunthorpe U 20 0 **37 2**

COLLINS, Tom (G) **0 0**
2019–20 Scunthorpe U 0 0

CUMMINGS, Joe (D) **0 0**
2016–17 Sheffield U 0 0
2017–18 Sheffield U 0 0
2017–18 Charlton Ath 0 0
2018–19 Charlton Ath 0 0
2019–20 Scunthorpe U 0 0

DALES, Andy (M) **35 1**
b. 13-11-94
Internationals: England C.
2013–14 Derby Co 0 0
From Mickleover Sports.
2018–19 Scunthorpe U 20 1
2018–19 *Dundee* 10 0 **10 0**
2019–20 Scunthorpe U 3 0 **23 1**
2019–20 *Hamilton A* 2 0 **2 0**

DAWSON, Joey (M) **0 0**
b. 30-5-03
2019–20 Scunthorpe U 0 0

EISA, Abobaker (M) **52 8**
b. 5-1-96
From Uxbridge, Wealdstone.
2017–18 Shrewsbury T 5 1
2018–19 Shrewsbury T 4 0
2018–19 *Colchester U* 14 2 **14 2**
2019–20 Shrewsbury T 1 0 **10 1**
2019–20 Scunthorpe U 28 5 **28 5**

EL-MHANNI, Yasin (M) **6 0**
b. 26-10-95
From Farnborough, Lewes.
2016–17 Newcastle U 0 0
2017–18 Newcastle U 0 0
2018–19 Scunthorpe U 5 0
2019–20 Scunthorpe U 1 0 **6 0**

GILLIEAD, Alex (F) **166 14**
H: 6 0 W: 11 00 b.Shotley Bridge 11-2-96
Internationals: England U16, U17, U18, U20.
2014–15 Newcastle U 0 0
2015–16 Newcastle U 0 0
2015–16 *Carlisle U* 35 5 **35 5**
2016–17 Newcastle U 0 0
2016–17 *Luton T* 18 1 **18 1**
2016–17 *Bradford C* 9 0
2017–18 Newcastle U 0 0
2017–18 *Bradford C* 42 1 **51 1**
2018–19 Shrewsbury T 27 1 **27 1**
2019–20 Scunthorpe U 35 6 **35 6**

GREEN, Devarn (F) **2 0**
b. 26-8-96
2014–15 Blackburn R 0 0
2015–16 Blackburn R 0 0
From Tranmere R, Southport.
2019–20 Scunthorpe U 2 0 **2 0**

HALLAM, Jordan (M) **12 1**
b. 6-10-98
2016–17 Sheffield U 0 0
From Southport.
2018 Viking 5 0 **5 0**
2018–19 Scunthorpe U 7 1
2019–20 Scunthorpe U 0 0 **7 1**

HAMMILL, Adam (M) **382 33**
H: 5 11 W: 11 07 b.Liverpool 25-1-88
Internationals: England U19, U21.
2005–06 Liverpool 0 0
2006–07 Liverpool 0 0
2006–07 *Dunfermline Ath* 13 1 **13 1**
2007–08 Liverpool 0 0
2007–08 *Southampton* 25 0 **25 0**
2008–09 Liverpool 0 0
2008–09 *Blackpool* 22 1 **22 1**
2008–09 *Barnsley* 14 1
2009–10 Barnsley 39 4
2010–11 Barnsley 25 8
2010–11 Wolverhampton W 10 0
2011–12 Wolverhampton W 9 0
2011–12 *Middlesbrough* 10 0 **10 0**
2012–13 Wolverhampton W 4 0 **23 0**
2012–13 *Huddersfield T* 16 2
2013–14 Huddersfield T 44 4
2014–15 Huddersfield T 5 0
2014–15 *Rotherham U* 14 0 **14 0**
2015–16 Huddersfield T 1 0 **66 6**
2015–16 Barnsley 25 4
2016–17 Barnsley 37 3
2017–18 Barnsley 38 0 **178 20**
2018–19 St Mirren 13 4 **13 4**
2018–19 Scunthorpe U 15 1
2019–20 Scunthorpe U 3 0 **18 1**

HORNSHAW, George (M) **0 0**
2017–18 Scunthorpe U 0 0
2018–19 Scunthorpe U 0 0
2019–20 Scunthorpe U 0 0

HORSFIELD, James (M) **47 1**
H: 5 10 W: 11 00 b.Hazel Grove 21-9-95
2015–16 Manchester C 0 0
2015–16 *Doncaster R* 2 0 **2 0**
2016–17 Manchester C 0 0
2016–17 *NAC Breda* 16 1
2017–18 NAC Breda 7 0 **23 1**
2018–19 Scunthorpe U 11 0
2018–19 *Dundee* 11 0 **11 0**
2019–20 Scunthorpe U 0 0 **11 0**

KELSEY, Adam (G) **0 0**
2016–17 Scunthorpe U 0 0
2017–18 Scunthorpe U 0 0
2018–19 Scunthorpe U 0 0
2019–20 Scunthorpe U 0 0

McARDLE, Rory (D) **485 24**
H: 6 1 W: 11 04 b.Doncaster 1-5-87
Internationals: Northern Ireland U21, Full caps.
2005–06 Sheffield W 0 0
2005–06 *Rochdale* 19 1
2006–07 Sheffield W 1 0 **1 0**
2006–07 Rochdale 25 0
2007–08 Rochdale 43 3
2008–09 Rochdale 41 2
2009–10 Rochdale 20 0 **148 6**

2010–11	Aberdeen	28	2		
2011–12	Aberdeen	25	0	**53**	**2**
2012–13	Bradford C	40	2		
2013–14	Bradford C	41	3		
2014–15	Bradford C	43	3		
2015–16	Bradford C	35	3		
2016–17	Bradford C	24	1	**183**	**12**
2017–18	Scunthorpe U	36	1		
2018–19	Scunthorpe U	38	0		
2019–20	Scunthorpe U	26	3	**100**	**4**

McATEE, John (F) 20 3
b. 23-7-99

2016–17	Shrewsbury T	1	0		
2017–18	Shrewsbury T	0	0		
2018–19	Shrewsbury T	0	0	**1**	**0**
2019–20	Scunthorpe U	19	3	**19**	**3**

McGAHEY, Harrison (D) 171 0
b.Preston 26-9-95

2013–14	Blackpool	4	0	**4**	**0**
2014–15	Sheffield U	15	0		
2014–15	*Tranmere R*	4	0	**4**	**0**
2015–16	Sheffield U	7	0	**22**	**0**
2016–17	Rochdale	36	0		
2017–18	Rochdale	42	0		
2018–19	Rochdale	21	0	**99**	**0**
2018–19	Scunthorpe U	10	0		
2019–20	Scunthorpe U	32	0	**42**	**0**

NTLHE, Kgosietsile (D) 155 8
H: 5 9 W: 10 05 b.Pretoria 21-2-94
Internationals: South Africa U20, Full caps.

2010–11	Peterborough U	0	0		
2011–12	Peterborough U	2	0		
2012–13	Peterborough U	12	1		
2013–14	Peterborough U	27	2		
2014–15	Peterborough U	28	1		
2015–16	Peterborough U	7	0		
2016–17	Peterborough U	0	0	**76**	**4**
2016–17	Stevenage	22	0	**22**	**0**
2017–18	Rochdale	20	0		
2018–19	Rochdale	19	3	**39**	**3**
2019–20	Scunthorpe U	18	1	**18**	**1**

O'MALLEY, Mason (D) 0 0
From Huddersfield T.

2019–20	Scunthorpe U	0	0		

OLOMOLA, Olufela (F) 71 15
H: 5 7 b.London 5-9-97

2015–16	Southampton	0	0		
2016–17	Southampton	0	0		
2017–18	Southampton	0	0		
2017–18	*Yeovil T*	21	7		
2018–19	Scunthorpe U	6	0		
2018–19	*Yeovil T*	17	3	**38**	**10**
2019–20	Scunthorpe U	0	0	**6**	**0**
2019–20	*Carlisle U*	27	5	**27**	**5**

PERCH, James (D) 481 19
H: 5 11 W: 11 05 b.Mansfield 29-9-85

2002–03	Nottingham F	0	0		
2003–04	Nottingham F	0	0		
2004–05	Nottingham F	22	0		
2005–06	Nottingham F	38	3		
2006–07	Nottingham F	46	5		
2007–08	Nottingham F	30	0		
2008–09	Nottingham F	37	3		
2009–10	Nottingham F	17	1	**190**	**12**
2010–11	Newcastle U	13	0		
2011–12	Newcastle U	25	0		
2012–13	Newcastle U	27	1	**65**	**1**
2013–14	Wigan Ath	40	0		
2014–15	Wigan Ath	41	3	**81**	**3**
2015–16	QPR	35	0		
2016–17	QPR	32	0		
2017–18	QPR	7	0	**74**	**0**
2018–19	Scunthorpe U	41	2		
2019–20	Scunthorpe U	30	1	**71**	**3**

POTTS, Reon (F) 0 0
From Sheffield U.

2019–20	Scunthorpe U	0	0		

PUGH, Tom (M) 1 0
b.Doncaster 27-9-00
Internationals: Wales U21.

2018–19	Scunthorpe U	0	0		
2019–20	Scunthorpe U	1	0	**1**	**0**

ROWE, Jai (D) 1 0
From Nuneaton, Barwell.

2019–20	Scunthorpe U	1	0	**1**	**0**

SONGO'O, Yann (D) 172 6
H: 6 0 W: 12 00 b.Yaounde 17-11-91
Internationals: France U16. Cameroon U20.

2011–12	Sabadell	6	0	**6**	**0**
2013	Sporting Kansas C	0	0		
2013	*Orlando C*	12	1	**12**	**1**
2013–14	Blackburn R	0	0		
2013–14	*Ross Co*	17	3	**17**	**3**
2014–15	Blackburn R	0	0		
2016–17	Plymouth Arg	46	2		
2017–18	Plymouth Arg	33	0		
2018–19	Plymouth Arg	42	0	**121**	**2**
2019–20	Scunthorpe U	16	0	**16**	**0**

VAN VEEN, Kevin (F) 230 74
H: 6 1 W: 11 11 b.Eindhoven 1-6-91

2013–14	JVC Cuyk	29	20	**29**	**20**
2014–15	FC Oss	20	16	**20**	**16**
2014–15	Scunthorpe U	20	2		
2015–16	Scunthorpe U	20	2		
2015–16	*Cambuur Leeuwarden*	12	1	**12**	**1**
2016–17	Scunthorpe U	33	10		
2017–18	Scunthorpe U	21	5		
2017–18	Northampton T	10	0		
2018–19	Northampton T	25	7	**35**	**7**
2018–19	Scunthorpe U	13	1		
2019–20	Scunthorpe U	27	10	**134**	**30**

WARD, Jamie (M) 396 92
H: 5 5 W: 9 04 b.Birmingham 12-5-86
Internationals: Northern Ireland U18, U21, Full caps.

2003–04	Aston Villa	0	0		
2004–05	Aston Villa	0	0		
2005–06	Aston Villa	0	0		
2005–06	*Stockport Co*	9	1	**9**	**1**
2006–07	Torquay U	25	9	**25**	**9**
2006–07	Chesterfield	9	3		
2007–08	Chesterfield	35	12		
2008–09	Chesterfield	23	14	**67**	**29**
2008–09	Sheffield U	16	2		
2009–10	Sheffield U	28	7		
2010–11	Sheffield U	19	0	**63**	**9**
2010–11	Derby Co	13	5		
2011–12	Derby Co	37	4		
2012–13	Derby Co	25	12		
2013–14	Derby Co	38	7		
2014–15	Derby Co	25	6	**138**	**34**
2015–16	Nottingham F	31	2		
2016–17	Nottingham F	18	1		
2016–17	*Burton Alb*	18	4	**18**	**4**
2017–18	Nottingham F	8	0		
2017–18	*Cardiff C*	4	0	**4**	**0**
2018–19	Nottingham F	0	0	**57**	**3**
2018–19	*Charlton Ath*	9	1	**9**	**1**
2019–20	Scunthorpe U	6	2	**6**	**2**

WATSON, Rory (G) 32 0
b. 5-2-96

2014–15	Hull C	0	0		
2015–16	Hull C	0	0		
2015–16	*Scunthorpe U*	0	0		
2016–17	Scunthorpe U	0	0		
2017–18	Scunthorpe U	4	0		
2018–19	Scunthorpe U	5	0		
2019–20	Scunthorpe U	23	0	**32**	**0**

WOOTTON, Kyle (M) 90 14
H: 6 2 W: 12 04 b. 11-10-96

2014–15	Scunthorpe U	12	1		
2015–16	Scunthorpe U	20	3		
2016–17	Scunthorpe U	2	1		
2016–17	*Cheltenham T*	16	2	**16**	**2**
2017–18	Stevenage	8	1	**8**	**1**
2017–18	Scunthorpe U	1	0		
2018–19	Scunthorpe U	26	6		
2019–20	Scunthorpe U	5	0	**66**	**11**

Players retained or with offer of contract
Baker, Harry Ben; Bedeau, Jacob.

Scholars
Barks, Charles David; Chadli, Luca Charles; Crosher, Benjamin James Jack; Dawson, Joey; Gallimore, Daniel James; Gallimore, Levi; Jessop, Harry Peter; Kemp, Oliver George; Marques, Alves Silva Raynner; Shrimpton, Finley Thomas; Train, Aidan; Virgo, Patrick Henry; Wilkinson, Alexander Eric; Wilson, Cameron Harry.

SHEFFIELD U (73)

BALDOCK, George (M) 247 9
H: 5 9 W: 10 07 b.Buckingham 26-1-93

2009–10	Milton Keynes D	1	0		
2010–11	Milton Keynes D	2	0		
2011–12	Milton Keynes D	0	0		
2011–12	*Northampton T*	5	0	**5**	**0**
2012–13	Milton Keynes D	2	0		
2013–14	Milton Keynes D	38	2		
2014–15	Milton Keynes D	9	0		
2014–15	*Oxford U*	12	1		
2015–16	Milton Keynes D	15	0		
2015–16	*Oxford U*	27	2	**39**	**3**
2016–17	Milton Keynes D	37	0	**104**	**2**
2017–18	Sheffield U	34	1		
2018–19	Sheffield U	27	1		
2019–20	Sheffield U	38	2	**99**	**4**

BASHAM, Chris (M) 365 17
H: 5 11 W: 12 08 b.Hebburn 20-7-88

2007–08	Bolton W	0	0		
2007–08	*Rochdale*	13	0	**13**	**0**
2008–09	Bolton W	11	1		
2009–10	Bolton W	8	0	**19**	**1**
2010–11	Blackpool	2	0		
2011–12	Blackpool	17	2		
2012–13	Blackpool	26	1		
2013–14	Blackpool	40	2	**85**	**5**
2014–15	Sheffield U	37	0		
2015–16	Sheffield U	44	3		
2016–17	Sheffield U	43	2		
2017–18	Sheffield U	45	2		
2018–19	Sheffield U	41	4		
2019–20	Sheffield U	38	0	**248**	**11**

BERGE, Sander (M) 131 5
b.Baerum 14-2-98
Internationals: Norway U16, U17, U18, U19, U21, Full caps.

2013	Asker	1	0		
2014	Asker	7	0	**8**	**0**
2015	Valerenga	11	0		
2016	Valerenga	25	0	**36**	**0**
2016–17	Genk	9	0		
2017–18	Genk	13	0		
2018–19	Genk	28	0		
2019–20	Genk	23	4	**73**	**4**
2019–20	Sheffield U	14	1	**14**	**1**

BRYAN, Kean (M) 50 3
H: 6 1 b.Manchester 1-11-96
Internationals: England U16, U17, U19, U20.

2016–17	Manchester C	0	0		
2016–17	*Bury*	12	0	**12**	**0**
2017–18	Manchester C	0	0		
2017–18	*Oldham Ath*	32	2	**32**	**2**
2018–19	Sheffield U	0	0		
2019–20	Sheffield U	0	0		
2019–20	*Bolton W*	6	1	**6**	**1**

CLARKE, Leon (F) 458 138
H: 6 2 W: 14 02 b.Birmingham 10-2-85

2003–04	Wolverhampton W	0	0		
2003–04	*Kidderminster H*	4	0	**4**	**0**
2004–05	Wolverhampton W	28	7		
2005–06	Wolverhampton W	24	1		
2005–06	*QPR*	1	0		
2005–06	*Plymouth Arg*	5	0	**5**	**0**
2006–07	Wolverhampton W	22	5		
2006–07	Sheffield W	10	1		
2006–07	*Oldham Ath*	5	3	**5**	**3**
2007–08	Sheffield W	8	3		
2007–08	*Southend U*	16	8	**16**	**8**
2008–09	Sheffield W	29	8		
2009–10	Sheffield W	36	6	**83**	**18**
2010–11	QPR	13	0	**14**	**0**
2010–11	*Preston NE*	6	1	**6**	**1**
2011–12	Swindon T	2	0	**2**	**0**
2011–12	*Chesterfield*	14	9	**14**	**9**
2011–12	Charlton Ath	7	0		
2011–12	*Crawley T*	4	1	**4**	**1**
2012–13	Charlton Ath	0	0	**7**	**0**
2012–13	*Scunthorpe U*	15	11	**15**	**11**
2012–13	Coventry C	12	8		
2013–14	Coventry C	23	15	**35**	**23**
2013–14	Wolverhampton W	13	1		
2014–15	Wolverhampton W	16	2	**103**	**16**
2014–15	*Wigan Ath*	10	1		
2015–16	Bury	32	15	**32**	**15**
2016–17	Sheffield U	23	7		
2017–18	Sheffield U	39	19		
2018–19	Sheffield U	24	3		
2018–19	*Wigan Ath*	15	3	**25**	**4**
2019–20	Sheffield U	2	0	**88**	**29**

DEWHURST, Marcus (G) 0 0
b.Kingston upon Hull
Internationals: England U17, U18, U19.

2019–20	Sheffield U	0	0		
2019–20	*Carlisle U*	0	0		

DUFFY, Mark (M) 378 38
H: 5 9 W: 11 05 b.Liverpool 7-10-85

2008–09	Morecambe	9	1		
2009–10	Morecambe	35	4		
2010–11	Morecambe	22	0	**66**	**5**
2010–11	Scunthorpe U	22	1		
2011–12	Scunthorpe U	37	2		
2012–13	Scunthorpe U	43	5	**102**	**8**
2013–14	Doncaster R	36	2	**36**	**2**

2014–15 Birmingham C 4 0
2014–15 *Chesterfield* 3 0 **3 0**
2015–16 Birmingham C 0 0 **4 0**
2015–16 *Burton Alb* 45 8 **45 8**
2016–17 Sheffield U 39 6
2017–18 Sheffield U 36 3
2018–19 Sheffield U 36 6
2019–20 Sheffield U 0 0 **111 15**
2019–20 *Stoke C* 6 0 **6 0**
2019–20 *ADO Den Haag* 5 0 **5 0**

EASTWOOD, Jake (G) 16 0
b. 3-10-96
2017–18 Chesterfield 4 0 **4 0**
2017–18 Sheffield U 1 0
2018–19 Sheffield U 0 0
2019–20 Sheffield U 0 0 **1 0**
2019–20 *Scunthorpe U* 11 0 **11 0**

EGAN, John (D) 247 20
H: 6 1 W: 11 11 b.Cork 20-10-92
Internationals: Republic of Ireland U17, U19, U21, Full caps.
2009–10 Sunderland 0 0
2010–11 Sunderland 0 0
2011–12 Sunderland 0 0
2011–12 *Crystal Palace* 1 0 **1 0**
2011–12 *Sheffield U* 1 0
2012–13 Sunderland 0 0
2012–13 *Bradford C* 4 0 **4 0**
2013–14 Sunderland 0 0
2013–14 *Southend U* 13 1 **13 1**
2014–15 Gillingham 45 4
2015–16 Gillingham 36 6 **81 10**
2016–17 Brentford 34 4
2017–18 Brentford 33 2 **67 6**
2018–19 Sheffield U 44 1
2019–20 Sheffield U 36 2 **81 3**

FLECK, John (M) 370 23
H: 5 9 W: 11 05 b.Glasgow 24-8-91
Internationals: Scotland U17, U19, U21, Full caps.
2007–08 Rangers 1 0
2008–09 Rangers 8 1
2009–10 Rangers 15 1
2010–11 Rangers 13 0
2011–12 Rangers 4 0 **41 2**
2011–12 *Blackpool* 7 0 **7 0**
2012–13 Coventry C 35 3
2013–14 Coventry C 43 1
2014–15 Coventry C 44 0
2015–16 Coventry C 40 4 **162 8**
2016–17 Sheffield U 44 4
2017–18 Sheffield U 41 2
2018–19 Sheffield U 45 2
2019–20 Sheffield U 30 5 **160 13**

FREEMAN, Kieron (D) 201 15
H: 5 10 W: 12 05 b.Nottingham 21-3-92
Internationals: Wales U17, U19, U21, Full caps.
2010–11 Nottingham F 0 0
2011–12 Nottingham F 0 0
2011–12 *Notts Co* 19 1
2012–13 Derby Co 19 0
2013–14 Derby Co 6 0
2013–14 *Notts Co* 16 0 **35 1**
2013–14 *Sheffield U* 12 0
2014–15 Derby Co 0 0 **25 0**
2014–15 *Mansfield T* 11 0 **11 0**
2014–15 Sheffield U 19 1
2015–16 Sheffield U 19 0
2015–16 *Portsmouth* 7 0 **7 0**
2016–17 Sheffield U 41 10
2017–18 Sheffield U 10 1
2018–19 Sheffield U 20 2
2019–20 Sheffield U 2 0 **123 14**

FREEMAN, Luke (F) 344 41
H: 6 0 W: 10 00 b.Dartford 22-3-92
Internationals: England U16, U17.
2007–08 Gillingham 1 0 **1 0**
2008–09 Arsenal 0 0
2009–10 Arsenal 0 0
2010–11 Arsenal 0 0
2010–11 *Yeovil T* 13 2 **13 2**
2011–12 Arsenal 0 0
2011–12 Stevenage 26 7
2012–13 Stevenage 39 2
2013–14 Stevenage 45 6 **110 15**
2014–15 Bristol C 46 7
2015–16 Bristol C 41 1
2016–17 Bristol C 18 2 **105 10**
2016–17 QPR 16 2
2017–18 QPR 45 5
2018–19 QPR 43 7 **104 14**
2019–20 Sheffield U 11 0 **11 0**

GRAHAM, Sam (D) 15 0
b. 13-8-00
2018–19 Sheffield U 0 0
2018–19 *Oldham Ath* 7 0 **7 0**
2018–19 *Central Coast Mariners* 8 0 **8 0**
2019–20 Sheffield U 0 0

HENEGHAN, Ben (D) 109 4
b.Bolton 19-9-93
Internationals: England C.
2016–17 Motherwell 37 0
2017–18 Motherwell 4 1 **41 1**
2017–18 Sheffield U 0 0
2018–19 Sheffield U 0 0
2018–19 *Blackpool* 42 1
2019–20 Sheffield U 0 0
2019–20 *Blackpool* 26 2 **68 3**

HOLMES, Ricky (M) 272 53
H: 6 2 W: 11 11 b.Southend 19-6-87
Internationals: England C.
2010–11 Barnet 25 2
2011–12 Barnet 41 8
2012–13 Barnet 25 5 **91 15**
2013–14 Portsmouth 40 2
2014–15 Portsmouth 13 0 **53 2**
2014–15 Northampton T 21 5
2015–16 Northampton T 28 9 **49 14**
2016–17 Charlton Ath 35 13
2017–18 Charlton Ath 23 6 **58 19**
2017–18 Sheffield U 5 0
2018–19 Sheffield U 0 0
2018–19 *Oxford U* 16 3 **16 3**
2018–19 *Gillingham* 0 0
2019–20 Sheffield U 0 0 **5 0**

JAGIELKA, Phil (D) 582 32
H: 6 0 W: 13 01 b.Manchester 17-8-82
Internationals: England U20, U21, B, Full caps.
1999–2000 Sheffield U 1 0
2000–01 Sheffield U 15 0
2001–02 Sheffield U 23 3
2002–03 Sheffield U 42 0
2003–04 Sheffield U 43 3
2004–05 Sheffield U 46 0
2005–06 Sheffield U 46 8
2006–07 Sheffield U 38 4
2007–08 Everton 34 1
2008–09 Everton 34 0
2009–10 Everton 12 0
2010–11 Everton 33 1
2011–12 Everton 30 2
2012–13 Everton 36 2
2013–14 Everton 26 0
2014–15 Everton 37 4
2015–16 Everton 21 0
2016–17 Everton 27 3
2017–18 Everton 25 0
2018–19 Everton 7 1 **322 14**
2019–20 Sheffield U 6 0 **260 18**

LUNDSTRAM, John (M) 225 14
H: 5 11 W: 11 09 b.Liverpool 18-2-94
Internationals: England U17, U18, U19, U20.
2011–12 Everton 0 0
2012–13 Everton 0 0
2012–13 *Doncaster R* 14 0 **14 0**
2013–14 Everton 0 0
2013–14 *Yeovil T* 14 2 **14 2**
2013–14 *Leyton Orient* 7 0
2014–15 Everton 0 0
2014–15 *Blackpool* 17 0 **17 0**
2014–15 *Leyton Orient* 4 0 **11 0**
2014–15 *Scunthorpe U* 7 0 **7 0**
2015–16 Oxford U 37 3
2016–17 Oxford U 45 1 **82 4**
2017–18 Sheffield U 36 3
2018–19 Sheffield U 10 0
2019–20 Sheffield U 34 5 **80 8**

McBURNIE, Oliver (F) 134 40
H: 6 2 W: 10 04 b.Bradford 6-4-96
Internationals: Scotland U19, U21, Full caps.
2013–14 Bradford C 8 0
2014–15 Bradford C 7 0 **15 0**
2015–16 Swansea C 0 0
2015–16 *Newport Co* 3 3 **3 3**
2015–16 *Bristol R* 5 0 **5 0**
2016–17 Swansea C 5 0
2017–18 Swansea C 11 0
2017–18 *Barnsley* 17 9 **17 9**
2018–19 Swansea C 42 22
2019–20 Swansea C 0 0 **58 22**
2019–20 Sheffield U 36 6 **36 6**

McGOLDRICK, David (F) 411 102
H: 6 1 W: 11 10 b.Nottingham 29-11-87
Internationals: Republic of Ireland Full caps.
2003–04 Notts Co 4 0
2004–05 Notts Co 0 0
2005–06 Southampton 1 0
2005–06 *Notts Co* 6 0 **10 0**
2006–07 Southampton 9 0
2006–07 *Bournemouth* 12 6 **12 6**
2007–08 Southampton 8 0
2007–08 *Port Vale* 17 2 **17 2**
2008–09 Southampton 46 12 **64 12**
2009–10 Nottingham F 33 3
2010–11 Nottingham F 21 5
2011–12 Nottingham F 9 0
2011–12 *Sheffield W* 4 1 **4 1**
2012–13 Nottingham F 0 0 **63 8**
2012–13 *Coventry C* 22 16 **22 16**
2012–13 *Ipswich T* 13 4
2013–14 Ipswich T 31 14
2014–15 Ipswich T 26 7
2015–16 Ipswich T 24 4
2016–17 Ipswich T 30 5
2017–18 Ipswich T 22 6 **146 40**
2018–19 Sheffield U 45 15
2019–20 Sheffield U 28 2 **73 17**

MOORE, Simon (G) 155 0
H: 6 3 W: 12 02 b.Sandown 19-5-90
Internationals: Isle of Wight Full caps.
2009–10 Brentford 1 0
2010–11 Brentford 10 0
2011–12 Brentford 10 0
2012–13 Brentford 43 0 **64 0**
2013–14 Cardiff C 0 0
2013–14 *Bristol C* 11 0 **11 0**
2014–15 Cardiff C 10 0
2015–16 Cardiff C 7 0 **17 0**
2016–17 Sheffield U 43 0
2017–18 Sheffield U 18 0
2018–19 Sheffield U 0 0
2019–20 Sheffield U 2 0 **63 0**

MORRISON, Ravel (M) 80 12
H: 5 9 W: 11 02 b.Wythenshawe 2-2-93
Internationals: England U16, U17, U18, U21.
2009–10 Manchester U 0 0
2010–11 Manchester U 0 0
2011–12 Manchester U 0 0
2011–12 West Ham U 1 0
2012–13 West Ham U 0 0
2012–13 *Birmingham C* 27 3 **27 3**
2013–14 West Ham U 16 3
2013–14 *QPR* 15 6
2014–15 West Ham U 1 0 **18 3**
2014–15 *Cardiff C* 7 0 **7 0**
2015–16 Lazio 4 0
2016–17 Lazio 0 0 **4 0**
2016–17 *QPR* 5 0 **20 6**
2019–20 Sheffield U 1 0 **1 0**
2019–20 *Middlesbrough* 3 0 **3 0**

MOUSSET, Lys (M) 122 23
H: 6 0 W: 12 08 b.Montvilliers 8-2-96
Internationals: France U20, U21.
2013–14 Le Havre 5 0
2014–15 Le Havre 1 0
2015–16 Le Havre 28 14 **34 14**
2016–17 Bournemouth 11 0
2017–18 Bournemouth 23 2
2018–19 Bournemouth 24 1 **58 3**
2019–20 Sheffield U 30 6 **30 6**

NORRINGTON-DAVIES, Rhys (D) 27 1
b. 22-4-99
Internationals: Wales U19, U21.
2017–18 Sheffield U 0 0
2018–19 Sheffield U 0 0
2019–20 Sheffield U 0 0
2019–20 *Rochdale* 27 1 **27 1**

NORWOOD, Oliver (M) 350 24
H: 5 11 W: 11 13 b.Burnley 12-4-91
Internationals: England U16, U17. Northern Ireland U19, U21, B, Full caps.
2009–10 Manchester U 0 0
2010–11 Manchester U 0 0
2010–11 *Carlisle U* 6 0 **6 0**
2011–12 Manchester U 0 0
2011–12 *Scunthorpe U* 15 1 **15 1**
2011–12 *Coventry C* 18 2 **18 2**
2012–13 Huddersfield T 39 3
2013–14 Huddersfield T 40 5
2014–15 Huddersfield T 1 0 **80 8**
2014–15 Reading 38 1
2015–16 Reading 43 3 **81 4**
2016–17 Brighton & HA 33 0
2017–18 Brighton & HA 0 0 **33 0**

2017–18 *Fulham* 36 5 **36 5**
2018–19 Sheffield U 43 3
2019–20 Sheffield U 38 1 **81 4**

O'CONNELL, Jack (D) 268 13
H: 6 3 W: 13 05 b.Liverpool 29-3-94
Internationals: England U18, U19.
2012–13 Blackburn R 0 0
2012–13 *Rotherham U* 3 0 **3 0**
2012–13 *York C* 18 0 **18 0**
2013–14 Blackburn R 0 0
2013–14 *Rochdale* 38 0
2014–15 Blackburn R 0 0
2014–15 *Rochdale* 29 5 **67 5**
2014–15 Brentford 0 0
2015–16 Brentford 16 1 **16 1**
2016–17 Sheffield U 44 4
2017–18 Sheffield U 46 0
2018–19 Sheffield U 41 3
2019–20 Sheffield U 33 0 **164 7**

OSBORN, Ben (D) 225 15
H: 5 9 W: 11 11 b.Derby 5-8-94
Internationals: England U18, U19, U20.
2011–12 Nottingham F 0 0
2012–13 Nottingham F 0 0
2013–14 Nottingham F 8 0
2014–15 Nottingham F 37 3
2015–16 Nottingham F 36 3
2016–17 Nottingham F 46 4
2017–18 Nottingham F 46 4
2018–19 Nottingham F 39 1 **212 15**
2019–20 Sheffield U 13 0 **13 0**

PARKHOUSE, David (F) 4 0
b. 24-10-99
Internationals: Northern Ireland U17, U21.
From Maiden C.
2018–19 Sheffield U 0 0
2019–20 Sheffield U 0 0
2019–20 *Stevenage* 4 0 **4 0**

RETSOS, Panagiotis (D) 47 1
b.Johannesburg 9-8-98
Internationals: Greece U17, U18, U19, U21, Full caps.
2016–17 Olympiacos 18 0
2017–18 Olympiacos 2 0 **20 0**
2017–18 Bayer Leverkusen 24 1
2018–19 Bayer Leverkusen 0 0
2019–20 Bayer Leverkusen 3 0 **27 1**
On loan from Bayer Leverkusen.
2019–20 Sheffield U 0 0

ROBINSON, Callum (F) 191 39
H: 5 10 W: 11 11 b.Birmingham 2-2-95
Internationals: England U16, U17, U19, U20. Republic of Ireland Full caps.
2013–14 Aston Villa 4 0
2014–15 Aston Villa 0 0
2014–15 *Preston NE* 25 4
2015–16 Aston Villa 0 0 **4 0**
2015–16 *Bristol C* 6 0 **6 0**
2015–16 *Preston NE* 14 2
2016–17 Preston NE 42 10
2017–18 Preston NE 41 7
2018–19 Preston NE 27 12 **149 35**
2019–20 Sheffield U 16 1 **16 1**
2019–20 *WBA* 16 3 **16 3**

ROBINSON, Jack (D) 179 4
H: 5 11 W: 10 08 b.Warrington 1-9-93
Internationals: England U16, U17, U18, U19, U21.
2009–10 Liverpool 1 0
2010–11 Liverpool 2 0
2011–12 Liverpool 0 0
2012–13 Liverpool 0 0
2012–13 *Wolverhampton W* 11 0 **11 0**
2013–14 Liverpool 0 0 **3 0**
2013–14 *Blackpool* 34 0 **34 0**
2014–15 QPR 0 0
2014–15 *Huddersfield T* 30 0 **30 0**
2015–16 QPR 1 0
2016–17 QPR 7 0
2017–18 QPR 31 2 **39 2**
2018–19 Nottingham F 38 2
2019–20 Nottingham F 18 0 **56 2**
2019–20 Sheffield U 6 0 **6 0**

RODWELL, Jack (D) 190 12
H: 6 2 W: 12 08 b.Southport 11-3-91
Internationals: England U16, U17, U19, U21, Full caps.
2007–08 Everton 2 0
2008–09 Everton 19 0
2009–10 Everton 26 2
2010–11 Everton 24 0
2011–12 Everton 14 2 **85 4**
2012–13 Manchester C 11 2
2013–14 Manchester C 5 0 **16 2**
2014–15 Sunderland 23 3
2015–16 Sunderland 22 1
2016–17 Sunderland 20 0
2017–18 Sunderland 2 1 **67 5**
2018–19 Blackburn R 21 1 **21 1**
2019–20 Sheffield U 1 0 **1 0**

SHARP, Billy (F) 537 230
H: 5 9 W: 11 00 b.Sheffield 5-2-86
2004–05 Sheffield U 2 0
2004–05 *Rushden & D* 16 9 **16 9**
2005–06 Scunthorpe U 37 23
2006–07 Scunthorpe U 45 30 **82 53**
2007–08 Sheffield U 29 4
2008–09 Sheffield U 22 4
2009–10 Sheffield U 0 0
2009–10 *Doncaster R* 33 15
2010–11 Doncaster R 29 15
2011–12 Doncaster R 20 10
2011–12 Southampton 15 9
2012–13 Southampton 2 0
2012–13 *Nottingham F* 39 10 **39 10**
2013–14 Southampton 0 0 **17 9**
2013–14 *Reading* 10 2 **10 2**
2013–14 *Doncaster R* 16 4 **98 44**
2014–15 Leeds U 33 5 **33 5**
2015–16 Sheffield U 44 21
2016–17 Sheffield U 46 30
2017–18 Sheffield U 34 13
2018–19 Sheffield U 40 23
2019–20 Sheffield U 25 3 **242 98**

SLATER, Regan (M) 48 2
b. 11-9-99
2016–17 Sheffield U 0 0
2017–18 Sheffield U 1 0
2018–19 Sheffield U 0 0
2018–19 *Carlisle U* 35 2 **35 2**
2019–20 Sheffield U 0 0 **1 0**
2019–20 *Scunthorpe U* 12 0 **12 0**

SMITH, Tyler (F) 38 6
b. 4-12-98
2018–19 Sheffield U 0 0
2018–19 *Doncaster R* 14 2 **14 2**
2019–20 Sheffield U 0 0
2019–20 *Bristol R* 20 3 **20 3**
2019–20 *Rochdale* 4 1 **4 1**

STEVENS, Enda (D) 349 10
H: 6 0 W: 12 04 b.Dublin 9-7-90
Internationals: Republic of Ireland U21, Full caps.
2008 UCD 2 0 **2 0**
2009 St Patrick's Ath 30 0 **30 0**
2010 Shamrock R 18 0
2011 Shamrock R 27 0 **45 0**
2011–12 Aston Villa 0 0
2012–13 Aston Villa 7 0
2013–14 Aston Villa 0 0
2013–14 *Notts Co* 2 0 **2 0**
2013–14 *Doncaster R* 13 0
2014–15 Aston Villa 0 0 **7 0**
2014–15 *Northampton T* 4 1 **4 1**
2014–15 *Doncaster R* 28 1 **41 1**
2015–16 Portsmouth 45 0
2016–17 Portsmouth 45 1 **90 1**
2016–17 Sheffield U 0 0
2017–18 Sheffield U 45 1
2018–19 Sheffield U 45 4
2019–20 Sheffield U 38 2 **128 7**

THOMAS, Nathan (F) 179 28
H: 5 10 W: 12 08 b.Barwick 27-9-94
2013–14 Plymouth Arg 10 0
2014–15 Plymouth Arg 9 1 **19 1**
2014–15 Motherwell 2 0 **2 0**
2015–16 Mansfield T 17 1 **17 1**
2015–16 Hartlepool U 22 5
2016–17 Hartlepool U 33 9 **55 14**
2017–18 Sheffield U 1 0
2017–18 *Shrewsbury T* 11 2 **11 2**
2018–19 Sheffield U 0 0
2018–19 *Notts Co* 25 1 **25 1**
2018–19 *Carlisle U* 16 4
2019–20 Sheffield U 0 0 **1 0**
2019–20 *Carlisle U* 33 5 **49 9**

VERRIPS, Michael (G) 66 0
b.Velp 3-12-96
Internationals: Netherlands U19, U21.
2014–15 FC Twente 0 0
2015–16 FC Twente 0 0
2016–17 Sparta Rotterdam 1 0
2017–18 Sparta Rotterdam 0 0 **1 0**
2017–18 *MVV Maastricht* 38 0 **38 0**
2018–19 Mechelen 27 0
2019–20 Mechelen 0 0 **27 0**
2019–20 Sheffield U 0 0

WRIGHT, Jake (D) 287 0
H: 5 10 W: 11 07 b.Keighley 11-3-86
2005–06 Bradford C 1 0 **1 0**
From Halifax T, Crawley T
2009–10 Brighton & HA 6 0 **6 0**
2010–11 Oxford U 35 0
2011–12 Oxford U 43 0
2012–13 Oxford U 42 0
2013–14 Oxford U 31 0
2014–15 Oxford U 42 0
2015–16 Oxford U 29 0 **222 0**
2016–17 Sheffield U 30 0
2017–18 Sheffield U 17 0
2019–20 Sheffield U 0 0 **47 0**
2019–20 *Bolton W* 11 0 **11 0**

ZIVKOVIC, Richairo (F) 174 50
b.Assen 5-9-96
Internationals: Netherlands U18, U19, U20, U21.
2012–13 Groningen 4 0
2013–14 Groningen 33 11 **37 11**
2014–15 Ajax 7 1
2015–16 Ajax 0 0
2015–16 *Willem II* 16 2 **16 2**
2016–17 Ajax 0 0 **7 1**
2016–17 *Utrecht* 34 9 **34 9**
2017–18 Oostende 29 9
2018–19 Oostende 21 3 **50 12**
2019 Changun Yatai 25 15 **25 15**
On loan from Changun Yatai.
2019–20 Sheffield U 5 0 **5 0**

Players retained or with offer of contract
Amissah, Jordan; Belehouan, Seri Jean Leroy; Broadbent, George; Hall, Ashton Vincent; Mallon, Stephen Anthony; Ndiaye, Iliman Cheikh Baroy.

Scholars
Ackroyd, Sam Richard; Ayari, Hassan Ben Kamel; Boyes, Harry; Brookes, Andre Chance; Brunt, Zak Rian; Cappello, Angelo Santo; Chapman, Joshua Matthew; Cullinan, Harvey; Foulstone, Harrison Alan; Gaxha, Leonardo; Gomis, Nicksoen; Gordon, Kyron; Grant, Kamarl Antonio; Jebbison, Daniel David; Kelly, Jacob Edward; Kelly, Samuel Walter; Maguire, Francis William; Neal, Harrison; Osula, William Idamudia Daugard; Seriki, Oluwafemi Ibrahim; Skerritt, Tristan Devere; Viggars, Ryan James; Williams, Tommy John Albert.

SHEFFIELD W (74)

BANNAN, Barry (D) 331 14
H: 5 10 W: 10 08 b.Glasgow 1-12-89
Internationals: Scotland U21, Full caps.
2008–09 Aston Villa 0 0
2008–09 *Derby Co* 10 1 **10 1**
2009–10 Aston Villa 0 0
2009–10 *Blackpool* 20 1 **20 1**
2010–11 Aston Villa 12 0
2010–11 *Leeds U* 7 0 **7 0**
2011–12 Aston Villa 28 1
2012–13 Aston Villa 24 0
2013–14 Aston Villa 0 0 **64 1**
2013–14 Crystal Palace 15 1
2014–15 Crystal Palace 7 0
2014–15 *Bolton W* 16 0 **16 0**
2015–16 Crystal Palace 0 0 **22 1**
2015–16 Sheffield W 35 2
2016–17 Sheffield W 43 1
2017–18 Sheffield W 29 0
2018–19 Sheffield W 41 5
2019–20 Sheffield W 44 2 **192 10**

BATES, David (D) 84 4
b.Kirkaldy 5-10-96
Internationals: Scotland U21, Full caps.
2013–14 Raith R 0 0
2014–15 Raith R 0 0
2014–15 *East Stirlingshire* 17 1 **17 1**
2015–16 Raith R 10 0 **10 0**
2015–16 *Brechin C* 10 1 **10 1**
2016–17 Rangers 7 0
2017–18 Rangers 15 1 **22 1**
2018–19 Hamburg 25 1
2019–20 Hamburg 0 0 **25 1**
On loan from Hamburg.
2019–20 Sheffield W 0 0

BORNER, Julian (M) 208 19
b.Weimar 21-1-91
Internationals: Germany U16, U17, U18.
2009–10 Energi Cottbus 1 0

2010–11 Energi Cottbus 0 0
2011–12 Energi Cottbus 5 0
2012–13 Energi Cottbus 15 1
2013–14 Energi Cottbus 16 0 **37 1**
2014–15 Arminia Bielefeld 25 4
2015–16 Arminia Bielefeld 31 2
2016–17 Arminia Bielefeld 26 4
2017–18 Arminia Bielefeld 27 4
2018–19 Arminia Bielefeld 25 3 **134 17**
2019–20 Sheffield W 37 1 **37 1**

BORUKOV, Preslav (F) 0 0
b. 23-4-00
Internationals: Bulgaria U17.
From Levski.
2019–20 Sheffield W 0 0

BRENNAN, Ciaran (D) 0 0
b.Kilkenny 5-5-00
Internationals: Republic of Ireland U18.
From Waterford.
2019–20 Sheffield W 0 0

DA CRUZ, Alessio (F) 103 17
b.Almere 18-1-97
Internationals: Netherlands U18, U20.
2014–15 FC Twente 0 0
2015–16 FC Twente 3 0
2016–17 FC Twente 0 0 **3 0**
2016–17 *Dordrecht* 29 5 **29 5**
2017–18 Novara 19 5 **19 5**
2017–18 Parma 6 0
2018–19 Parma 3 0
2018–19 *Spezia* 14 2 **14 2**
2018–19 *Ascoli* 15 5 **15 5**
2019–20 Parma 0 0 **9 0**
On loan from Parma.
2019–20 Sheffield W 14 0 **14 0**

DAWSON, Cameron (G) 60 0
H: 6 0 W: 10 12 b.Sheffield 7-7-95
Internationals: England U18, U19.
2013–14 Sheffield W 0 0
2013–14 *Plymouth Arg* 0 0
2014–15 Sheffield W 0 0
2015–16 Sheffield W 0 0
2016–17 Wycombe W 1 0 **1 0**
2016–17 Sheffield W 4 0
2017–18 Chesterfield 2 0 **2 0**
2017–18 Sheffield W 3 0
2018–19 Sheffield W 26 0
2019–20 Sheffield W 24 0 **57 0**

FLETCHER, Steven (F) 482 134
H: 6 1 W: 12 00 b.Shrewsbury 26-3-87
Internationals: Scotland U20, U21, B, Full caps.
2003–04 Hibernian 5 0
2004–05 Hibernian 20 5
2005–06 Hibernian 34 8
2006–07 Hibernian 31 6
2007–08 Hibernian 32 13
2008–09 Hibernian 34 11 **156 43**
2009–10 Burnley 35 8 **35 8**
2010–11 Wolverhampton W 29 10
2011–12 Wolverhampton W 32 12 **61 22**
2012–13 Sunderland 28 11
2013–14 Sunderland 20 3
2014–15 Sunderland 30 5
2015–16 Sunderland 16 4 **94 23**
2015–16 *Marseille* 12 2 **12 2**
2016–17 Sheffield W 38 10
2017–18 Sheffield W 19 2
2018–19 Sheffield W 40 11
2019–20 Sheffield W 27 13 **124 36**

FORESTIERI, Fernando (F) 299 73
H: 5 8 W: 10 07 b.Rosario 16-1-90
Internationals: Italy U17, U19, U20, U21.
2006–07 Genoa 1 1 **1 1**
2007–08 Siena 17 1
2008–09 Siena 2 0 **19 1**
2008–09 Vicenza 13 5 **13 5**
2009–10 Malaga 19 1 **19 1**
2010–11 Empoli 17 3 **17 3**
2011–12 Bari 27 2 **27 2**
2012–13 Udinese 0 0
2012–13 *Watford* 28 8
2013–14 Watford 28 7
2014–15 Watford 24 5 **80 20**
2015–16 Sheffield W 36 15
2016–17 Sheffield W 35 12
2017–18 Sheffield W 10 5
2018–19 Sheffield W 25 6
2019–20 Sheffield W 17 2 **123 40**

FOX, Morgan (D) 200 5
H: 6 1 W: 12 03 b.Chelmsford 21-9-93
Internationals: Wales U21.
2012–13 Charlton Ath 0 0
2013–14 Charlton Ath 6 0
2013–14 *Notts Co* 7 1 **7 1**
2014–15 Charlton Ath 31 0
2015–16 Charlton Ath 42 1
2016–17 Charlton Ath 24 0 **103 1**
2016–17 Sheffield W 10 1
2017–18 Sheffield W 28 0
2018–19 Sheffield W 25 0
2019–20 Sheffield W 27 2 **90 3**

GRANT, Conor (M) 0 0
b. 23-7-01
Internationals: Republic of Ireland U17, U19.
From Shamrock R.
2019–20 Sheffield W 0 0

HARRIS, Kedeem (M) 153 10
H: 5 9 W: 10 08 b.Westminster 8-6-93
2009–10 Wycombe W 2 0
2010–11 Wycombe W 0 0
2011–12 Wycombe W 17 0 **19 0**
2011–12 Cardiff C 0 0
2012–13 Cardiff C 0 0
2013–14 Cardiff C 0 0
2013–14 *Brentford* 10 1 **10 1**
2014–15 Cardiff C 14 1
2015–16 Cardiff C 3 0
2015–16 *Barnsley* 11 0 **11 0**
2016–17 Cardiff C 37 4
2017–18 Cardiff C 3 0
2018–19 Cardiff C 13 1 **70 6**
2019–20 Sheffield W 43 3 **43 3**

HUGHES, Ben (D) 0 0
From Manchester C.
2019–20 Sheffield W 0 0

HUNT, Alex (M) 6 0
b.Sheffield 29-5-00
2018–19 Sheffield W 0 0
2019–20 Sheffield W 6 0 **6 0**

HUTCHINSON, Sam (M) 158 5
H: 6 0 W: 11 07 b.Windsor 3-8-89
Internationals: England U18, U19.
2006–07 Chelsea 1 0
2007–08 Chelsea 0 0
2008–09 Chelsea 0 0
2009–10 Chelsea 2 0
2010–11 Chelsea 0 0
2011–12 Chelsea 2 0
2012–13 Chelsea 0 0
2012–13 *Nottingham F* 9 1 **9 1**
2013–14 Chelsea 0 0 **5 0**
2013–14 *Vitesse* 1 0 **1 0**
2013–14 *Sheffield W* 10 1
2014–15 Sheffield W 20 0
2015–16 Sheffield W 25 0
2016–17 Sheffield W 33 2
2017–18 Sheffield W 8 0
2018–19 Sheffield W 24 0
2019–20 Sheffield W 23 1 **143 4**

IORFA, Dominic (D) 167 6
H: 6 2 W: 12 04 b.Southend-on-Sea 24-6-95
Internationals: England U18, U20, U21.
2013–14 Wolverhampton W 0 0
2013–14 *Shrewsbury T* 7 0 **7 0**
2014–15 Wolverhampton W 20 0
2015–16 Wolverhampton W 42 0
2016–17 Wolverhampton W 22 0
2017–18 Wolverhampton W 0 0
2017–18 *Ipswich T* 23 1 **23 1**
2018–19 Wolverhampton W 0 0 **84 0**
2018–19 Sheffield W 12 3
2019–20 Sheffield W 41 2 **53 5**

JONES, Paul (G) 281 0
H: 6 3 W: 13 00 b.Maidstone 28-6-86
2008–09 Exeter C 46 0
2009–10 Exeter C 26 0
2010–11 Exeter C 18 0
2010–11 *Peterborough U* 1 0
2011–12 Peterborough U 35 0 **36 0**
2012–13 Crawley T 46 0
2013–14 Crawley T 46 0
2014–15 Portsmouth 46 0
2015–16 Portsmouth 9 0 **55 0**
2015–16 *Crawley T* 8 0 **100 0**
2016–17 Norwich C 0 0
2017–18 Norwich C 0 0
2017–18 *Exeter C* 0 0 **90 0**
2018–19 Fleetwood T 0 0
2019–20 Sheffield W 0 0

KIRBY, Connor (M) 36 1
b. 10-9-98
2017–18 Sheffield W 1 0
2018–19 Sheffield W 1 0
2019–20 Sheffield W 0 0 **2 0**
2019–20 *Macclesfield T* 34 1 **34 1**

LEE, Jack (D) 0 0
b.Sunderland 19-12-98
From Sunderland.
2018–19 Sheffield W 0 0
2019–20 Sheffield W 0 0

LEE, Kieran (D) 321 25
H: 6 1 W: 12 00 b.Stalybridge 22-6-88
2006–07 Manchester U 1 0
2007–08 Manchester U 0 0 **1 0**
2007–08 *QPR* 7 0 **7 0**
2008–09 Oldham Ath 7 0
2009–10 Oldham Ath 24 1
2010–11 Oldham Ath 43 2
2011–12 Oldham Ath 43 2 **117 5**
2012–13 Sheffield W 23 0
2013–14 Sheffield W 26 1
2014–15 Sheffield W 33 6
2015–16 Sheffield W 43 5
2016–17 Sheffield W 26 5
2017–18 Sheffield W 15 3
2018–19 Sheffield W 2 0
2019–20 Sheffield W 28 0 **196 20**

LEES, Tom (D) 418 16
H: 6 1 W: 12 04 b.Warwick 28-11-90
Internationals: England U21.
2008–09 Leeds U 0 0
2009–10 Leeds U 0 0
2009–10 *Accrington S* 39 0 **39 0**
2010–11 Leeds U 0 0
2010–11 *Bury* 45 4 **45 4**
2011–12 Leeds U 42 2
2012–13 Leeds U 40 1
2013–14 Leeds U 41 0 **123 3**
2014–15 Sheffield W 44 0
2015–16 Sheffield W 34 3
2016–17 Sheffield W 35 1
2017–18 Sheffield W 29 1
2018–19 Sheffield W 42 2
2019–20 Sheffield W 27 2 **211 9**

LUONGO, Massimo (F) 266 26
H: 5 8 W: 11 10 b.Sydney 25-9-92
Internationals: Australia U20, Full caps.
2010–11 Tottenham H 0 0
2011–12 Tottenham H 0 0
2012–13 Tottenham H 0 0
2012–13 *Ipswich T* 9 0 **9 0**
2012–13 *Swindon T* 7 1
2013–14 Swindon T 44 6
2014–15 Swindon T 34 6 **85 13**
2015–16 QPR 30 0
2016–17 QPR 35 1
2017–18 QPR 39 6
2018–19 QPR 41 3
2019–20 QPR 0 0 **145 10**
2019–20 Sheffield W 27 3 **27 3**

NUHIU, Atdhe (F) 375 63
H: 6 6 W: 13 05 b.Prishtina 29-7-89
Internationals: Austria U19, U20, U21. Kosovo Full caps.
2008–09 Austria Karnten 16 2
2009–10 Austria Karnten 3 0 **19 2**
2009–10 SV Ried 27 6 **27 6**
2010–11 Rapid Vienna 28 5
2011–12 Rapid Vienna 31 8 **59 13**
2012–13 Eskisehirspor 28 2 **28 2**
2013–14 Sheffield W 38 8
2014–15 Sheffield W 43 8
2015–16 Sheffield W 41 3
2016–17 Sheffield W 20 0
2017–18 Sheffield W 28 11
2018–19 Sheffield W 34 4
2019–20 Sheffield W 38 6 **242 40**

ODUBAJO, Moses (M) 232 16
H: 5 9 W: 11 05 b.Greenwich 28-7-93
Internationals: England U20.
2011–12 Leyton Orient 3 1
2012–13 Leyton Orient 44 2
2013–14 Leyton Orient 46 10 **93 13**
2014–15 Brentford 45 3
2015–16 Hull C 42 0
2016–17 Hull C 0 0
2017–18 Hull C 0 0 **42 0**
2018–19 Brentford 30 0 **75 3**
2019–20 Sheffield W 22 0 **22 0**

PALMER, Liam (M) **269 1**
H: 6 2 W: 12 10 b.Worksop 19-9-91
Internationals: Scotland U19, U21, Full caps.

2010–11	Sheffield W	9	0		
2011–12	Sheffield W	14	1		
2012–13	Sheffield W	0	0		
2012–13	*Tranmere R*	43	0		
2013–14	*Tranmere R*	0	0	**43**	**0**
2013–14	Sheffield W	39	0		
2014–15	Sheffield W	35	0		
2015–16	Sheffield W	15	0		
2016–17	Sheffield W	21	0		
2017–18	Sheffield W	25	0		
2018–19	Sheffield W	35	0		
2019–20	Sheffield W	33	0	**226**	**1**

PELUPESSY, Joey (M) **173 3**
H: 5 8 W: 9 13 b.Nijverdal 15-5-93

2012–13	FC Twente	3	0		
2013–14	FC Twente	0	0	**3**	**0**
2014–15	Heracles	17	1		
2015–16	Heracles	34	0		
2016–17	Heracles	34	1		
2017–18	Heracles	18	0	**103**	**2**
2017–18	Sheffield W	17	1		
2018–19	Sheffield W	33	0		
2019–20	Sheffield W	17	0	**67**	**1**

PENNEY, Matt (D) **36 1**
b.Chesterfield 11-2-98

2016–17	Sheffield W	0	0		
2016–17	*Bradford C*	1	0	**1**	**0**
2017–18	Sheffield W	0	0		
2017–18	*Mansfield T*	2	0	**2**	**0**
2018–19	Sheffield W	16	0		
2019–20	Sheffield W	0	0	**16**	**0**
2019–20	*St Pauli*	17	1	**17**	**1**

PRESTON, Fraser (G) **3 0**
b. 1-10-98
Internationals: Scotland U16, U19.

2017–18	Sheffield W	0	0		
2018–19	Sheffield W	3	0		
2019–20	Sheffield W	0	0	**3**	**0**

REACH, Adam (M) **302 32**
H: 6 1 W: 11 07 b.Gateshead 3-2-93
Internationals: England U19, U20.

2010–11	Middlesbrough	1	1		
2011–12	Middlesbrough	1	0		
2012–13	Middlesbrough	16	2		
2013–14	Middlesbrough	2	0		
2013–14	*Shrewsbury T*	22	3	**22**	**3**
2013–14	*Bradford C*	18	3	**18**	**3**
2014–15	Middlesbrough	39	2		
2015–16	Middlesbrough	4	1		
2015–16	*Preston NE*	35	4	**35**	**4**
2016–17	Middlesbrough	0	0	**63**	**6**
2016–17	Sheffield W	39	3		
2017–18	Sheffield W	46	4		
2018–19	Sheffield W	42	8		
2019–20	Sheffield W	37	1	**164**	**16**

RHODES, Jordan (F) **437 188**
H: 6 1 W: 11 03 b.Oldham 5-2-90
Internationals: Scotland U21, Full caps.

2007–08	Ipswich T	8	1		
2008–09	Ipswich T	2	0	**10**	**1**
2008–09	*Rochdale*	5	2	**5**	**2**
2008–09	*Brentford*	14	7	**14**	**7**
2009–10	Huddersfield T	45	19		
2010–11	Huddersfield T	37	16		
2011–12	Huddersfield T	40	35		
2012–13	Huddersfield T	2	2	**124**	**72**
2012–13	Blackburn R	43	27		
2013–14	Blackburn R	46	25		
2014–15	Blackburn R	45	21		
2015–16	Blackburn R	25	10	**159**	**83**
2015–16	Middlesbrough	18	6		
2016–17	Middlesbrough	6	0	**24**	**6**
2016–17	*Sheffield W*	18	3		
2017–18	Sheffield W	31	5		
2018–19	Sheffield W	0	0		
2018–19	*Norwich C*	36	6	**36**	**6**
2019–20	Sheffield W	16	3	**65**	**11**

SHAW, Liam (M) **2 0**
H: 5 10 b. 12-3-01

2018–19	Sheffield W	0	0		
2019–20	Sheffield W	2	0	**2**	**0**

STOBBS, Jack (M) **10 0**
H: 5 11 W: 13 05 b.Leeds 27-2-97

2013–14	Sheffield W	1	0		
2014–15	Sheffield W	0	0		
2015–16	Sheffield W	1	0		
2016–17	Sheffield W	0	0		
2017–18	Port Vale	5	0	**5**	**0**
2017–18	Sheffield W	3	0		
2018–19	Sheffield W	0	0		
2019–20	Sheffield W	0	0	**5**	**0**

URHOGHIDE, Osaze (D) **3 0**

2017–18	AFC Wimbledon	0	0		
2018–19	AFC Wimbledon	0	0		
2019–20	Sheffield W	3	0	**3**	**0**

VAN AKEN, Joost (D) **121 4**
H: 5 10 W: 11 11 b.Haarlem 13-5-94
Internationals: Netherlands U21.

2013–14	Heerenveen	6	2		
2014–15	Heerenveen	30	0		
2015–16	Heerenveen	20	0		
2016–17	Heerenveen	26	1		
2017–18	Heerenveen	2	0	**84**	**3**
2017–18	Sheffield W	14	0		
2018–19	Sheffield W	1	0		
2019–20	Sheffield W	0	0	**15**	**0**
2019–20	*Osnabruck*	22	1	**22**	**1**

WALDOCK, Liam (M) **0 0**
b. 25-9-00

2019–20	Sheffield W	0	0		

WESTWOOD, Keiren (G) **449 0**
H: 6 1 W: 13 10 b.Manchester 23-10-84
Internationals: Republic of Ireland Full caps.

2001–02	Manchester C	0	0		
2002–03	Manchester C	0	0		
2003–04	Manchester C	0	0		
2003–04	*Oldham Ath*	0	0		
2004–05	Manchester C	0	0		
2005–06	Manchester C	0	0		
2005–06	Carlisle U	35	0		
2006–07	Carlisle U	46	0		
2007–08	Carlisle U	46	0	**127**	**0**
2008–09	Coventry C	46	0		
2009–10	Coventry C	44	0		
2010–11	Coventry C	41	0	**131**	**0**
2011–12	Sunderland	9	0		
2012–13	Sunderland	0	0		
2013–14	Sunderland	10	0	**19**	**0**
2014–15	Sheffield W	43	0		
2015–16	Sheffield W	34	0		
2016–17	Sheffield W	43	0		
2017–18	Sheffield W	18	0		
2018–19	Sheffield W	20	0		
2019–20	Sheffield W	14	0	**172**	**0**

WILDSMITH, Joe (G) **47 0**
H: 6 0 W: 10 03 b.Sheffield 28-12-95
Internationals: England U20.

2013–14	Sheffield W	0	0		
2014–15	Sheffield W	0	0		
2014–15	*Barnsley*	2	0	**2**	**0**
2015–16	Sheffield W	9	0		
2016–17	Sheffield W	1	0		
2017–18	Sheffield W	26	0		
2018–19	Sheffield W	0	0		
2019–20	Sheffield W	9	0	**45**	**0**

WINNALL, Sam (F) **228 84**
H: 5 9 W: 11 04 b.Wolverhampton 19-1-91

2009–10	Wolverhampton W	0	0		
2010–11	Wolverhampton W	0	0		
2010–11	*Burton Alb*	19	7	**19**	**7**
2011–12	Wolverhampton W	0	0		
2011–12	*Hereford U*	8	2	**8**	**2**
2011–12	*Inverness CT*	2	0	**2**	**0**
2012–13	Wolverhampton W	0	0		
2012–13	*Shrewsbury T*	4	0	**4**	**0**
2013–14	Scunthorpe U	45	23	**45**	**23**
2014–15	Barnsley	32	9		
2015–16	Barnsley	43	21		
2016–17	Barnsley	22	11	**97**	**41**
2016–17	Sheffield W	14	3		
2017–18	Sheffield W	2	1		
2017–18	*Derby Co*	17	6	**17**	**6**
2018–19	Sheffield W	7	0		
2019–20	Sheffield W	13	1	**36**	**5**

Players retained or with offer of contract
Dawodu, Joshua; Galvin, Ryan Francis Patrick; Hidalgo, Gasparini Manuel Federico; Render, Joshua Ben.

Scholars
Bonnington, Alex; Brandy, L'varn Joseph; Cox, Luke Joseph; Curtis, Charlie Luke; Dutra, Aguas Paulo Jorge; Ellery, Johnson Michael Jamie; Erat-Thompson, Declan Sebastian; Farmer, Lewis J.; Glaves, Corey Alan; Glover, Jay Michael; Hagan, Charles Junior; Hall, Luke Charles; Hare, Alexander Charles; Jackson, Luke John; Kenyon, Toby James; Oliver, Sam David; Reaney, Charlie Alexander; Trueman, William Henry Mangham; Vasalo, Elliott Phillip; Yates, Luke David Richard; Zottos, Basile.

SHREWSBURY T (75)

AGIUS, Sam (G) **0 0**
b.Walsall 9-3-02

2018–19	Shrewsbury T	0	0		
2019–20	Shrewsbury T	0	0		

BARNETT, Ryan (M) **1 0**
b. 23-9-99

2016–17	Shrewsbury T	0	0		
2017–18	Shrewsbury T	0	0		
2018–19	Shrewsbury T	1	0		
2019–20	Shrewsbury T	0	0	**1**	**0**

BECKLES, Omar (D) **140 10**
H: 6 2 W: 12 04 b.Kettering 25-10-91
Internationals: Grenada Full caps.
From Aldershot T.

2016–17	Accrington S	41	2		
2017–18	Accrington S	2	1	**43**	**3**
2017–18	Shrewsbury T	33	3		
2018–19	Shrewsbury T	36	1		
2019–20	Shrewsbury T	28	3	**97**	**7**

BURGOYNE, Harry (G) **24 0**
H: 6 4 W: 13 05 b.Ludlow 28-12-96

2015–16	Wolverhampton W	0	0		
2016–17	Barnet	2	0	**2**	**0**
2016–17	Wolverhampton W	6	0		
2017–18	Wolverhampton W	1	0		
2018–19	Wolverhampton W	0	0		
2018–19	*Falkirk*	15	0	**15**	**0**
2019–20	Wolverhampton W	0	0	**7**	**0**
2019–20	Shrewsbury T	0	0		

CATON, Charlie (F) **0 0**

2019–20	Shrewsbury T	0	0		

CUMMINGS, Jason (F) **194 69**
H: 5 10 W: 10 10 b.Edinburgh 1-8-95
Internationals: Scotland U19, U21, Full caps.

2013–14	Hibernian	16	0		
2014–15	Hibernian	33	18		
2015–16	Hibernian	33	18		
2016–17	Hibernian	32	19	**114**	**55**
2017–18	Nottingham F	14	1		
2017–18	*Rangers*	15	2	**15**	**2**
2018–19	Nottingham F	0	0		
2018–19	*Peterborough U*	22	6	**22**	**6**
2018–19	*Luton T*	5	1	**5**	**1**
2019–20	Nottingham F	0	0	**14**	**1**
2019–20	Shrewsbury T	24	4	**24**	**4**

EBANKS-LANDELL, Ethan (M) **173 15**
H: 5 6 W: 11 02 b.Oldbury 16-12-92

2009–10	Wolverhampton W	0	0		
2010–11	Wolverhampton W	0	0		
2011–12	Wolverhampton W	0	0		
2012–13	Wolverhampton W	0	0		
2012–13	*Bury*	24	0	**24**	**0**
2013–14	Wolverhampton W	7	2		
2014–15	Wolverhampton W	14	2		
2015–16	Wolverhampton W	21	1		
2016–17	Wolverhampton W	0	0		
2016–17	*Sheffield U*	34	5	**34**	**5**
2017–18	Wolverhampton W	0	0		
2017–18	*Milton Keynes D*	29	2	**29**	**2**
2018–19	Wolverhampton W	0	0	**42**	**5**
2018–19	*Rochdale*	16	2	**16**	**2**
2019–20	Shrewsbury T	28	1	**28**	**1**

EDWARDS, Dave (M) **473 61**
H: 5 11 W: 11 04 b.Shrewsbury 3-2-86
Internationals: Wales U21, Full caps.

2002–03	Shrewsbury T	1	0		
2003–04	Shrewsbury T	0	0		
2004–05	Shrewsbury T	27	5		
2005–06	Shrewsbury T	30	2		
2006–07	Shrewsbury T	45	5		
2007–08	Luton T	19	4	**19**	**4**
2007–08	Wolverhampton W	10	1		
2008–09	Wolverhampton W	44	3		
2009–10	Wolverhampton W	20	1		
2010–11	Wolverhampton W	15	1		
2011–12	Wolverhampton W	26	3		
2012–13	Wolverhampton W	24	2		
2013–14	Wolverhampton W	30	9		
2014–15	Wolverhampton W	41	6		
2015–16	Wolverhampton W	29	5		
2016–17	Wolverhampton W	44	10		
2017–18	Wolverhampton W	1	0	**284**	**41**
2017–18	Reading	32	3		
2018–19	Reading	0	0	**32**	**3**
2018–19	Shrewsbury T	6	0		
2019–20	Shrewsbury T	29	1	**138**	**13**

FANE, Ousmane (M) **80** **0**
H: 6 4 W: 12 08 b.Paris 13-12-93
From Kidderminster H.

2016–17	Oldham Ath	39	0		
2017–18	Oldham Ath	41	0		
2018–19	Oldham Ath	0	0	**80**	**0**
2019–20	Shrewsbury T	0	0		

Transferred to UiTM, February 2020.

GOLBOURNE, Scott (M) **391** **7**
H: 5 8 W: 11 08 b.Bristol 29-2-88
Internationals: England U17, U19.

2004–05	Bristol C	9	0		
2005–06	Bristol C	5	0		
2005–06	Reading	1	0		
2006–07	Reading	0	0		
2006–07	*Wycombe W*	34	1	**34**	**1**
2007–08	Reading	1	0		
2007–08	*Bournemouth*	5	0	**5**	**0**
2008–09	Reading	0	0	**2**	**0**
2008–09	*Oldham Ath*	8	0	**8**	**0**
2009–10	Exeter C	34	0		
2010–11	Exeter C	44	2		
2011–12	Exeter C	26	0	**104**	**2**
2011–12	Barnsley	12	1		
2012–13	Barnsley	31	1		
2013–14	Barnsley	4	0	**47**	**2**
2013–14	Wolverhampton W	40	1		
2014–15	Wolverhampton W	27	0		
2015–16	Wolverhampton W	20	0	**87**	**1**
2015–16	Bristol C	16	0		
2016–17	Bristol C	19	0		
2017–18	Bristol C	0	0	**49**	**0**
2017–18	*Milton Keynes D*	25	0	**25**	**0**
2018–19	Shrewsbury T	15	0		
2019–20	Shrewsbury T	15	1	**30**	**1**

GOSS, Sean (M) **47** **2**
H: 5 10 W: 11 03 b.Wegberg 1-10-95

2015–16	Manchester U	0	0		
2016–17	Manchester U	0	0		
2016–17	QPR	6	0		
2017–18	QPR	0	0		
2017–18	*Rangers*	13	2	**13**	**2**
2018–19	QPR	0	0		
2018–19	*St Johnstone*	6	0	**6**	**0**
2019–20	QPR	0	0	**6**	**0**
2019–20	Shrewsbury T	22	0	**22**	**0**

GREGORY, Cameron (G) **0** **0**

2017–18	Shrewsbury T	0	0
2018–19	Shrewsbury T	0	0
2019–20	Shrewsbury T	0	0

JOHN-LEWIS, Lemell (M) **238** **23**
H: 5 10 W: 11 10 b.Hammersmith 17-5-89

2006–07	Lincoln C	0	0		
2007–08	Lincoln C	21	3		
2008–09	Lincoln C	27	4		
2009–10	Lincoln C	24	1	**72**	**8**
2010–11	Bury	39	2		
2011–12	Bury	28	5		
2012–13	Bury	16	2	**83**	**9**
From Grimsby T.					
2015–16	Newport Co	28	3		
2016–17	Newport Co	2	0	**30**	**3**
2017–18	Shrewsbury T	34	2		
2018–19	Shrewsbury T	17	1		
2019–20	Shrewsbury T	2	0	**53**	**3**

LAURENT, Josh (M) **127** **6**
H: 6 0 W: 11 00 b.Leytonstone 6-5-95

2013–14	QPR	0	0		
2014–15	QPR	0	0		
2015–16	Brentford	0	0		
2015–16	*Newport Co*	3	0	**3**	**0**
2015–16	Hartlepool U	3	0		
2016–17	Hartlepool U	25	1	**28**	**1**
2016–17	Wigan Ath	1	0		
2017–18	Wigan Ath	0	0	**1**	**0**
2017–18	*Bury*	22	1	**22**	**1**
2018–19	Shrewsbury T	42	2		
2019–20	Shrewsbury T	31	2	**73**	**4**

LOVE, Donald (D) **63** **0**
H: 5 10 W: 11 05 b.Rochdale 2-12-94
Internationals: Scotland U17, U19, U21.

2015–16	Manchester U	1	0	**1**	**0**
2015–16	*Wigan Ath*	7	0	**7**	**0**
2016–17	Sunderland	12	0		
2017–18	Sunderland	11	0		
2018–19	Sunderland	4	0	**27**	**0**
2019–20	Shrewsbury T	28	0	**28**	**0**

MORISON, Steven (F) **417** **93**
H: 6 2 W: 13 07 b.Enfield 29-8-83
Internationals: England C. Wales Full caps.

2001–02	Northampton T	1	0		
2002–03	Northampton T	13	1		
2003–04	Northampton T	5	1		
2004–05	Northampton T	4	1	**23**	**3**
From Stevenage B.					
2008–09	Millwall	0	0		
2009–10	Millwall	43	20		
2010–11	Millwall	40	15		
2011–12	Norwich C	34	9		
2012–13	Norwich C	19	1	**53**	**10**
2012–13	Leeds U	15	3		
2013–14	Leeds U	0	0		
2013–14	*Millwall*	41	8		
2014–15	Leeds U	26	2	**41**	**5**
2015–16	Millwall	46	15		
2016–17	Millwall	38	11		
2017–18	Millwall	44	5		
2018–19	Millwall	41	1	**293**	**75**
2019–20	Shrewsbury T	7	0	**7**	**0**

MURPHY, Joe (G) **537** **0**
H: 6 2 W: 13 06 b.Dublin 21-8-81
Internationals: Republic of Ireland U21, Full caps.

1999–2000	Tranmere R	21	0		
2000–01	Tranmere R	20	0		
2001–02	Tranmere R	22	0	**63**	**0**
2002–03	WBA	2	0		
2003–04	WBA	3	0		
2004–05	WBA	0	0	**5**	**0**
2004–05	*Walsall*	25	0		
2005–06	Sunderland	0	0		
2005–06	*Walsall*	14	0	**39**	**0**
2006–07	Scunthorpe U	45	0		
2007–08	Scunthorpe U	45	0		
2008–09	Scunthorpe U	42	0		
2009–10	Scunthorpe U	40	0		
2010–11	Scunthorpe U	29	0	**201**	**0**
2011–12	Coventry C	46	0		
2012–13	Coventry C	45	0		
2013–14	Coventry C	46	0	**137**	**0**
2014–15	Huddersfield T	2	0		
2014–15	*Chesterfield*	0	0		
2015–16	Huddersfield T	7	0		
2016–17	Huddersfield T	0	0	**9**	**0**
2016–17	*Bury*	16	0		
2017–18	Bury	17	0		
2018–19	Bury	46	0	**79**	**0**
2019–20	Shrewsbury T	4	0	**4**	**0**

MWANDWE, Lifumpa (F) **0** **0**
b. 29-12-00

2017–18	Shrewsbury T	0	0
2018–19	Shrewsbury T	0	0
2019–20	Shrewsbury T	0	0

NORBURN, Oliver (M) **128** **15**
H: 6 1 W: 12 13 b.Leicester 26-10-92

2011–12	Leicester C	0	0		
2011–12	*Bristol R*	5	0		
2012–13	Bristol R	35	3		
2013–14	Bristol R	16	0	**56**	**3**
2014–15	Plymouth Arg	14	0	**14**	**0**
From Guiseley, Macclesfield T, Tranmere R.					
2018–19	Shrewsbury T	41	9		
2019–20	Shrewsbury T	17	3	**58**	**12**

PIERRE, Aaron (D) **219** **18**
H: 6 1 W: 13 12 b.Southall 17-2-93
Internationals: Grenada Full caps.

2011–12	Brentford	0	0		
2012–13	Brentford	0	0		
2013–14	Brentford	0	0		
2013–14	*Wycombe W*	8	1		
2014–15	Wycombe W	42	4		
2015–16	Wycombe W	40	2		
2016–17	Wycombe W	39	2	**129**	**9**
2017–18	Northampton T	19	0		
2018–19	Northampton T	41	6	**60**	**6**
2019–20	Shrewsbury T	30	3	**30**	**3**

ROWLAND, James (M) **0** **0**
b.Walsall 3-12-01
From WBA.

2018–19	Shrewsbury T	0	0
2019–20	Shrewsbury T	0	0

SEARS, Ryan (D) **7** **0**
b. 13-12-98

2016–17	Shrewsbury T	0	0		
2017–18	Shrewsbury T	0	0		
2018–19	Shrewsbury T	5	0		
2019–20	Shrewsbury T	2	0	**7**	**0**

TAYLOR, Kian (M) **0** **0**
H: 5 10 b.Leicester 10-1-01

2018–19	Shrewsbury T	0	0
2019–20	Shrewsbury T	0	0

UDOH, Daniel (F) **40** **4**
H: 6 0 W: 13 01 b. 30-8-96
Internationals: Nigeria U17.

2015–16	Crewe Alex	6	0		
2016–17	Crewe Alex	9	0	**15**	**0**
From AFC Telford U.					
2019–20	Shrewsbury T	25	4	**25**	**4**

VELA, Joshua (M) **171** **12**
H: 5 11 W: 11 07 b.Salford 14-12-93

2010–11	Bolton W	0	0		
2011–12	Bolton W	3	0		
2012–13	Bolton W	4	0		
2013–14	Bolton W	0	0		
2013–14	*Notts Co*	7	0	**7**	**0**
2014–15	Bolton W	29	0		
2015–16	Bolton W	31	2		
2016–17	Bolton W	46	9		
2017–18	Bolton W	30	1		
2018–19	Bolton W	17	0	**160**	**12**
2019–20	Hibernian	0	0		
2019–20	Shrewsbury T	4	0	**4**	**0**

VINCELOT, Romain (M) **371** **29**
H: 5 9 W: 11 02 b.Poitiers 29-10-85

2004–05	Chamois Niortais	3	0	**3**	**0**
2005–06	Chemois Niortais	28	1		
2006–07	Chemois Niortais	9	0		
2007–08	Chemois Niortais	6	0	**43**	**1**
2008–09	Gueugnon	20	0	**20**	**0**
2009–10	Dagenham & R	9	1		
2010–11	Dagenham & R	46	12	**55**	**13**
2011–12	Brighton & HA	15	1		
2012–13	Brighton & HA	0	0	**15**	**1**
2012–13	*Gillingham*	9	1	**9**	**1**
2012–13	Leyton Orient	15	1		
2013–14	Leyton Orient	39	0		
2014–15	Leyton Orient	27	2	**81**	**3**
2015–16	Coventry C	45	4	**45**	**4**
2016–17	Bradford C	45	2		
2017–18	Bradford C	38	4	**83**	**6**
2018–19	Crawley T	12	0	**12**	**0**
2018–19	Shrewsbury T	3	0		
2019–20	Shrewsbury T	2	0	**5**	**0**

WALKER, Brad (M) **150** **11**
H: 6 1 W: 12 08 b. 25-4-95

2012–13	Hartlepool U	0	0		
2013–14	Hartlepool U	36	3		
2014–15	Hartlepool U	28	5		
2015–16	Hartlepool U	23	1		
2016–17	Hartlepool U	20	1	**107**	**10**
2017–18	Crewe Alex	27	1		
2018–19	Crewe Alex	1	0	**28**	**1**
2019–20	Shrewsbury T	15	0	**15**	**0**

WARD, Luke (D) **0** **0**
b. 25-9-01
From Wolverhampton W.

2018–19	Shrewsbury T	0	0
2019–20	Shrewsbury T	0	0

WHALLEY, Shaun (M) **173** **24**
H: 5 9 W: 10 08 b.Whiston 7-8-87

2014–15	Luton T	18	3	**18**	**3**
2015–16	Shrewsbury T	24	6		
2016–17	Shrewsbury T	32	3		
2017–18	Shrewsbury T	44	8		
2018–19	Shrewsbury T	32	2		
2019–20	Shrewsbury T	23	2	**155**	**21**

WILLIAMS, Ro-Shaun (M) **41** **0**
b. 9-3-98
Internationals: England U17, U18, U19.

2015–16	Manchester U	0	0		
2016–17	Manchester u	0	0		
2017–18	Manchester u	0	0		
2018–19	Manchester U	0	0		
2018–19	Shrewsbury T	16	0		
2019–20	Shrewsbury T	25	0	**41**	**0**

Scholars
Agius, Samuel Thomas; Aris, Nigel Achuche Anayo; Bell, Jacob Philip; Bevan, Jaden Thomas; Burton, Luke Aaron; Caton, Charlie George; Davies, Thomas Iwan; Dixon, Charlie Graham; Duberry, Lewis Joseph; Elmore, Archie Nicholas; Grosvenor, Ryan Christopher; Hartley, Zac Darren; O'Toole, Ethan David; Redding, Lewis William; Sears, Edan Martin; Thomas, William Luke; Turner, Jamaine Noel; Walker, Daniel Richard; Ward, Luke Allan James.

SOUTHAMPTON (76)

ADAMS, Che (F) 193 49
H: 5 10 W: 10 06 b.Leicester 13-7-96
Internationals: England C, U20.

2014–15	Sheffield U	10	0		
2015–16	Sheffield U	36	11		
2016–17	Sheffield U	1	0	**47**	**11**
2016–17	Birmingham C	40	7		
2017–18	Birmingham C	30	5		
2018–19	Birmingham C	46	22	**116**	**34**
2019–20	Southampton	30	4	**30**	**4**

ARMSTRONG, Stuart (M) 284 49
H: 6 0 W: 10 10 b.Inverness 30-3-92
Internationals: Scotland U19, U21, Full caps.

2010–11	Dundee U	12	0		
2011–12	Dundee U	23	1		
2012–13	Dundee U	36	3		
2013–14	Dundee U	36	8		
2014–15	Dundee U	20	6	**127**	**18**
2014–15	Celtic	15	1		
2015–16	Celtic	25	4		
2016–17	Celtic	31	15		
2017–18	Celtic	27	3	**98**	**23**
2018–19	Southampton	29	3		
2019–20	Southampton	30	5	**59**	**8**

BARNES, Marcus (F) 8 0
b.Reading 1-12-96

2017–18	Southampton	0	0		
2017–18	*Yeovil T*	8	0	**8**	**0**
2018–19	Southampton	0	0		
2019–20	Southampton	0	0		

BEDNAREK, Jan (D) 112 3
H: 6 2 W: 12 02 b.Slupca 12-4-96
Internationals: Poland U16, U17, U18, U19, U20, U21, Full caps.

2013–14	Lech Poznan	2	0		
2014–15	Lech Poznan	2	0		
2015–16	Lech Poznan	0	0		
2015–16	*Gornik Leczna*	17	0	**17**	**0**
2016–17	Lech Poznan	27	1	**31**	**1**
2017–18	Southampton	5	1		
2018–19	Southampton	25	0		
2019–20	Southampton	34	1	**64**	**2**

BERTRAND, Ryan (D) 374 8
H: 5 10 W: 11 00 b.Southwark 5-8-89
Internationals: England U17, U18, U19, U20, U21, Full caps. Great Britain.

2006–07	Chelsea	0	0		
2006–07	*Bournemouth*	5	0	**5**	**0**
2007–08	Chelsea	0	0		
2007–08	*Oldham Ath*	21	0	**21**	**0**
2007–08	*Norwich C*	18	0		
2008–09	Chelsea	0	0		
2008–09	*Norwich C*	38	0	**56**	**0**
2009–10	Chelsea	0	0		
2009–10	*Reading*	44	1	**44**	**1**
2010–11	Chelsea	1	0		
2010–11	*Nottingham F*	19	0	**19**	**0**
2011–12	Chelsea	7	0		
2012–13	Chelsea	19	0		
2013–14	Chelsea	1	0	**28**	**0**
2013–14	*Aston Villa*	16	0	**16**	**0**
2014–15	Southampton	34	2		
2015–16	Southampton	32	1		
2016–17	Southampton	28	2		
2017–18	Southampton	35	0		
2018–19	Southampton	24	1		
2019–20	Southampton	32	1	**185**	**7**

BOUFAL, Sofiane (M) 194 24
H: 5 7 W: 11 09 b.Paris 17-9-93
Internationals: Morocco Full caps.

2012–13	Angers	2	0		
2013–14	Angers	28	0		
2014–15	Angers	16	4	**46**	**4**
2014–15	Lille	14	3		
2015–16	Lille	29	11		
2016–17	Lille	0	0	**43**	**14**
2016–17	Southampton	24	1		
2017–18	Southampton	26	2		
2018–19	Southampton	0	0		
2018–19	*Celta Vigo*	35	3	**35**	**3**
2019–20	Southampton	20	0	**70**	**3**

CARRILLO, Guido (F) 248 50
H: 6 3 W: 13 08 b.La Plata 25-5-91

2010–11	Estudiantes	5	0		
2011–12	Estudiantes	21	2		
2012–13	Estudiantes	29	4		
2013–14	Estudiantes	37	13		
2014	Estudiantes	17	5		
2015	Estudiantes	11	4	**120**	**28**
2015–16	Monaco	31	4		
2016–17	Monaco	19	7		
2017–18	Monaco	15	4	**65**	**15**
2017–18	Southampton	7	0		
2018–19	Southampton	0	0		
2018–19	*Leganes*	32	6		
2019–20	Southampton	0	0	**7**	**0**
2019–20	*Leganes*	24	1	**56**	**7**

DANSO, Kevin (D) 47 3
b.Dachau 3-9-93
Internationals: Austria U16, U17, U18, U19, U21.

2015–16	Augsburg	0	0		
2016–17	Augsburg	7	0		
2017–18	Augsburg	16	2		
2018–19	Augsburg	18	1		
2019–20	Augsburg	0	0	**41**	**3**

On loan from Augsburg.

2019–20	Southampton	6	0	**6**	**0**

DJENEPO, Moussa (F) 67 11
b.Bamako 15-1-98
Internationals: Mali U20, Full caps.

2017–18	Standard Liege	17	1		
2018–19	Standard Liege	32	8	**49**	**9**
2019–20	Southampton	18	2	**18**	**2**

FERRY, Will (M) 0 0
Internationals: Republic of Ireland U18, U19.

2016–17	Bury	0	0		
2017–18	Southampton	0	0		
2018–19	Southampton	0	0		
2019–20	Southampton	0	0		

FORSTER, Fraser (G) 323 0
H: 6 0 W: 12 00 b.Hexham 17-3-88
Internationals: England Full caps.

2007–08	Newcastle U	0	0		
2008–09	Newcastle U	0	0		
2008–09	*Stockport Co*	6	0	**6**	**0**
2009–10	Newcastle U	0	0		
2009–10	*Bristol R*	4	0	**4**	**0**
2009–10	*Norwich C*	38	0	**38**	**0**
2010–11	Newcastle U	0	0		
2010–11	*Celtic*	36	0		
2011–12	Newcastle U	0	0		
2011–12	*Celtic*	33	0		
2012–13	Celtic	34	0		
2013–14	Celtic	37	0		
2014–15	Southampton	30	0		
2015–16	Southampton	18	0		
2016–17	Southampton	38	0		
2017–18	Southampton	20	0		
2018–19	Southampton	1	0		
2019–20	Southampton	0	0	**107**	**0**
2019–20	*Celtic*	28	0	**168**	**0**

GUNN, Angus (G) 68 0
H: 6 0 W: 12 02 b.Norwich 22-1-96
Internationals: England U16, U17, U18, U19, U20, U21.

2013–14	Manchester C	0	0		
2014–15	Manchester C	0	0		
2015–16	Manchester C	0	0		
2016–17	Manchester C	0	0		
2017–18	Manchester C	0	0		
2017–18	*Norwich C*	46	0	**46**	**0**
2018–19	Southampton	12	0		
2019–20	Southampton	10	0	**22**	**0**

HESKETH, Jake (M) 54 4
H: 5 6 W: 9 13 b. 27-3-96

2014–15	Southampton	2	0		
2015–16	Southampton	0	0		
2016–17	Southampton	0	0		
2017–18	Southampton	0	0		
2018–19	Southampton	0	0		
2018–19	Southampton	0	0		
2018–19	*Burton Alb*	16	1	**16**	**1**
2018–19	*Milton Keynes D*	16	2	**16**	**2**
2019–20	Southampton	0	0	**2**	**0**
2019–20	*Lincoln C*	20	1	**20**	**1**

HOEDT, Wesley (D) 143 4
H: 6 2 W: 12 02 b.Alkmaar 6-3-94
Internationals: Netherlands U20, U20, Full caps.

2013–14	AZ Alkmaar	2	0		
2014–15	AZ Alkmaar	24	2	**26**	**2**
2015–16	Lazio	25	0		
2016–17	Lazio	23	2		
2017–18	Lazio	0	0	**48**	**2**
2017–18	Southampton	28	0		
2018–19	Southampton	13	0		
2018–19	*Celta Vigo*	10	0	**10**	**0**
2019–20	Southampton	0	0	**41**	**0**
2019–20	*Royal Antwerp*	18	0	**18**	**0**

HOJBJERG, Pierre (M) 165 6
H: 6 1 W: 12 11 b. 5-8-95
Internationals: Denmark U16, U17, U19, U21, Full caps.

2012–13	Bayern Munich	2	0		
2013–14	Bayern Munich	7	0		
2014–15	Bayern Munich	8	0		
2014–15	*Augsburg*	16	2	**16**	**2**
2015–16	Bayern Munich	7	0	**17**	**0**
2015–16	*Schalke*	23	0	**23**	**0**
2016–17	Southampton	22	0		
2017–18	Southampton	23	0		
2018–19	Southampton	31	4		
2019–20	Southampton	33	0	**109**	**4**

INGS, Danny (F) 225 77
H: 5 10 W: 11 07 b.Winchester 16-3-92
Internationals: England U21, Full caps.

2009–10	Bournemouth	0	0		
2010–11	Bournemouth	26	7		
2011–12	Bournemouth	1	0	**27**	**7**
2011–12	Burnley	15	3		
2012–13	Burnley	32	3		
2013–14	Burnley	40	21		
2014–15	Burnley	35	11	**122**	**38**
2015–16	Liverpool	6	2		
2016–17	Liverpool	0	0		
2017–18	Liverpool	8	1		
2018–19	Liverpool	0	0	**14**	**3**
2018–19	*Southampton*	24	7		
2019–20	Southampton	38	22	**62**	**29**

JANKEWITZ, Alexandre (M) 0 0
b.Vevey 25-12-01
Internationals: Switzerland U16, U17, U18, U19.
From Servette.

2019–20	Southampton	0	0		

JOHNSON, Tyreke (M) 1 0
b.Swindon 3-11-98
From Watford, Swindon T.

2018–19	Southampton	1	0		
2019–20	Southampton	0	0	**1**	**0**

JONES, Alfie (D) 44 3
b. 7-10-97

2018–19	Southampton	0	0		
2018–19	*St Mirren*	14	1	**14**	**1**
2019–20	Southampton	0	0		
2019–20	*Gillingham*	30	2	**30**	**2**

LEMINA, Mario (M) 150 7
H: 6 0 W: 12 00 b.Libreville 1-9-93
Internationals: France U20, U21. Gabon Full caps.

2012–13	Lorient	10	0		
2013–14	Lorient	4	0	**14**	**0**
2013–14	Marseille	14	0		
2014–15	Marseille	23	2		
2015–16	Marseille	4	0	**41**	**2**
2015–16	Juventus	10	2		
2016–17	Juventus	19	1	**29**	**3**
2017–18	Southampton	25	1		
2018–19	Southampton	21	1		
2019–20	Southampton	0	0	**46**	**2**
2019–20	*Galatasaray*	20	0	**20**	**0**

LEWIS, Harry (G) 0 0
b. 20-12-97
Internationals: England U18.

2015–16	Shrewsbury T	0	0		
2016–17	Shrewsbury T	0	0		
2016–17	Southampton	0	0		
2017–18	Southampton	0	0		
2018–19	Southampton	0	0		
2019–20	Southampton	0	0		

LONG, Shane (F) 445 94
H: 5 10 W: 11 02 b.Co. Tipperary 22-1-87
Internationals: Republic of Ireland B, U21, Full caps.

2005	Cork C	1	0	**1**	**0**
2005–06	Reading	11	3		
2006–07	Reading	21	2		
2007–08	Reading	29	3		
2008–09	Reading	37	9		
2009–10	Reading	31	6		
2010–11	Reading	44	21		
2011–12	Reading	1	0	**174**	**44**
2011–12	WBA	32	8		
2012–13	WBA	34	8		
2013–14	WBA	15	3	**81**	**19**
2013–14	Hull C	15	4	**15**	**4**
2014–15	Southampton	32	5		
2015–16	Southampton	28	10		
2016–17	Southampton	32	3		
2017–18	Southampton	30	2		
2018–19	Southampton	26	5		
2019–20	Southampton	26	2	**174**	**27**

McCARTHY, Alex (G) **218** **0**
H: 6 4 W: 11 12 b.Guildford 3-12-89
Internationals: England U21, Full caps.

2008–09	Reading	0	0		
2008–09	*Aldershot T*	4	0	**4**	**0**
2009–10	Reading	0	0		
2009–10	*Yeovil T*	44	0	**44**	**0**
2010–11	Reading	13	0		
2010–11	*Brentford*	3	0	**3**	**0**
2011–12	Reading	0	0		
2011–12	*Leeds U*	6	0	**6**	**0**
2011–12	*Ipswich T*	10	0	**10**	**0**
2012–13	Reading	13	0		
2013–14	Reading	44	0	**70**	**0**
2014–15	QPR	3	0	**3**	**0**
2015–16	Crystal Palace	7	0	**7**	**0**
2016–17	Southampton	0	0		
2017–18	Southampton	18	0		
2018–19	Southampton	25	0		
2019–20	Southampton	28	0	**71**	**0**

McQUEEN, Sam (M) **43** **2**
H: 5 9 W: 11 00 b.Southampton 6-2-95
Internationals: England U21.

2011–12	Southampton	0	0		
2012–13	Southampton	0	0		
2013–14	Southampton	0	0		
2014–15	Southampton	0	0		
2015–16	Southampton	0	0		
2015–16	*Southend U*	18	2	**18**	**2**
2016–17	Southampton	13	0		
2017–18	Southampton	7	0		
2018–19	Southampton	0	0		
2018–19	*Middlesbrough*	5	0	**5**	**0**
2019–20	Southampton	0	0	**20**	**0**

N'LUNDULU, Daniel (F) **0** **0**
b. 5-2-99
Internationals: England U16.

2019–20	Southampton	0	0		

O'CONNOR, Thomas (M) **28** **1**
b. 21-4-99
Internationals: Republic of Ireland U19, U21.

2019–20	Southampton	0	0		
2019–20	*Gillingham*	28	1	**28**	**1**

OBAFEMI, Michael (F) **28** **4**
H: 5 7 W: 11 03 b.Dublin 6-7-00
Internationals: Republic of Ireland U19, Full caps.
From Leyton Orient.

2017–18	Southampton	1	0		
2018–19	Southampton	6	1		
2019–20	Southampton	21	3	**28**	**4**

RAMSEY, Kayne (D) **6** **0**
b. 10-10-00
From Chelsea.

2018–19	Southampton	1	0		
2019–20	Southampton	0	0	**1**	**0**
2019–20	*Shrewsbury T*	5	0	**5**	**0**

REDMOND, Nathan (M) **312** **36**
H: 5 8 W: 11 11 b.Birmingham 6-3-94
Internationals: England U16, U17, U18, U19, U20, U21, Full caps.

2011–12	Birmingham C	24	5		
2012–13	Birmingham C	38	2	**62**	**7**
2013–14	Norwich C	34	1		
2014–15	Norwich C	43	4		
2015–16	Norwich C	35	6	**112**	**11**
2016–17	Southampton	37	7		
2017–18	Southampton	31	1		
2018–19	Southampton	38	6		
2019–20	Southampton	32	4	**138**	**18**

REED, Harrison (M) **114** **4**
H: 5 9 W: 11 09 b.Worthing 27-1-95
Internationals: England U19, U20.

2011–12	Southampton	0	0		
2012–13	Southampton	0	0		
2013–14	Southampton	4	0		
2014–15	Southampton	9	0		
2015–16	Southampton	1	0		
2016–17	Southampton	3	0		
2017–18	Southampton	0	0		
2017–18	*Norwich C*	39	1	**39**	**1**
2018–19	Southampton	0	0		
2018–19	*Blackburn R*	33	3	**33**	**3**
2019–20	Southampton	0	0	**17**	**0**
2019–20	*Fulham*	25	0	**25**	**0**

ROMEU, Oriol (M) **271** **5**
H: 6 0 W: 12 06 b.Ulldecona 24-9-91
Internationals: Spain U17, U19, U20, U21, U23.

2008–09	Barcelona B	5	0		
2009–10	Barcelona B	26	0		
2010–11	Barcelona B	18	1	**49**	**1**
2010–11	Barcelona	1	0	**1**	**0**
2011–12	Chelsea	16	0		
2012–13	Chelsea	6	0		
2013–14	Chelsea	0	0		
2013–14	*Valencia*	13	0	**13**	**0**
2014–15	Chelsea	0	0	**22**	**0**
2014–15	*Stuttgart*	27	0	**27**	**0**
2015–16	Southampton	29	1		
2016–17	Southampton	35	1		
2017–18	Southampton	34	1		
2018–19	Southampton	31	1		
2019–20	Southampton	30	0	**159**	**4**

ROSE, Jack (G) **13** **0**
H: 6 0 W: 11 11 b.Solihull 31-1-95

2014–15	WBA	0	0		
2014–15	*Accrington S*	4	0	**4**	**0**
2015–16	WBA	0	0		
2015–16	*Crawley T*	5	0	**5**	**0**
2016–17	WBA	0	0		
2017–18	Southampton	0	0		
2018–19	Southampton	0	0		
2019–20	Southampton	0	0		
2019–20	*Walsall*	4	0	**4**	**0**

SCOTT, Tommy (G) **0** **0**
b. 13-9-99

2017–18	Yeovil T	0	0		
2018–19	Yeovil T	0	0		
2019–20	Southampton	0	0		

SIMS, Josh (M) **44** **0**
b. 28-3-97
Internationals: England U17, U18, U20.
From Portsmouth.

2016–17	Southampton	7	0		
2017–18	Southampton	6	0		
2018–19	Southampton	7	0		
2018–19	*Reading*	17	0	**17**	**0**
2019–20	Southampton	0	0	**20**	**0**
2019–20	*New York Red Bulls*	7	0	**7**	**0**

SLATTERY, Callum (M) **8** **1**
b. 8-2-99
Internationals: England U16, U17, U20.

2018–19	Southampton	3	0		
2019–20	Southampton	0	0	**3**	**0**
2019–20	*De Graafschap*	5	1	**5**	**1**

SMALLBONE, William (M) **9** **0**
b. 21-2-00
Internationals: Republic of Ireland U18, U19.

2016–17	Southampton	0	0		
2017–18	Southampton	0	0		
2018–19	Southampton	0	0		
2019–20	Southampton	9	0	**9**	**0**

STEPHENS, Jack (D) **160** **5**
H: 6 1 W: 13 03 b.Torpoint 27-1-94
Internationals: England U18, U19, U20, U21.

2010–11	Plymouth Arg	5	0	**5**	**0**
2010–11	Southampton	0	0		
2011–12	Southampton	0	0		
2012–13	Southampton	0	0		
2013–14	Southampton	0	0		
2013–14	*Swindon T*	10	0		
2014–15	Southampton	0	0		
2014–15	*Swindon T*	37	1	**47**	**1**
2015–16	Southampton	0	0		
2015–16	*Middlesbrough*	1	0	**1**	**0**
2015–16	*Coventry C*	16	0	**16**	**0**
2016–17	Southampton	17	0		
2017–18	Southampton	22	2		
2018–19	Southampton	24	1		
2019–20	Southampton	28	1	**91**	**4**

TELLA, Nathan (F) **1** **0**
b. 5-7-99
From Arsenal.

2019–20	Southampton	1	0	**1**	**0**

VALERY, Yann (D) **34** **2**
H: 5 11 W: 11 00 b.Champigny-sur-Marne 22-2-99
Internationals: France U17, U18.
From Rennes.

2018–19	Southampton	23	2		
2019–20	Southampton	11	0	**34**	**2**

VESTERGAARD, Jannik (D) **227** **15**
H: 6 6 W: 15 02 b.Copenhagen 3-8-92
Internationals: Denmark U18, U19, U20, U21, Full caps.

2010–11	Hoffenheim	1	0		
2011–12	Hoffenheim	23	2		
2012–13	Hoffenheim	16	0		
2013–14	Hoffenheim	25	1		
2014–15	Hoffenheim	6	1	**71**	**4**
2014–15	Werder Bremen	15	1		
2015–16	Werder Bremen	33	2	**48**	**3**
2016–17	Borussia M'gladbach	34	4		
2017–18	Borussia M'gladbach	32	3	**66**	**7**
2018–19	Southampton	23	0		
2019–20	Southampton	19	1	**42**	**1**

VOKINS, Jake (D) **1** **0**
b.Oxford 17-3-00
Internationals: England U17, U18, U19.

2019–20	Southampton	1	0	**1**	**0**

WARD-PROWSE, James (M) **231** **22**
H: 5 8 W: 10 06 b.Portsmouth 1-11-94
Internationals: England U17, U19, U20, U21, Full caps.

2011–12	Southampton	0	0		
2012–13	Southampton	15	0		
2013–14	Southampton	34	0		
2014–15	Southampton	25	1		
2015–16	Southampton	33	2		
2016–17	Southampton	30	4		
2017–18	Southampton	30	3		
2018–19	Southampton	26	7		
2019–20	Southampton	38	5	**231**	**22**

YOSHIDA, Maya (D) **222** **11**
H: 6 2 W: 12 03 b.Nagasaki 24-8-88
Internationals: Japan U23, Full caps.

2010–11	VVV	20	0		
2011–12	VVV	32	5		
2012–13	VVV	2	0	**54**	**5**
2012–13	Southampton	32	0		
2013–14	Southampton	8	1		
2014–15	Southampton	22	1		
2015–16	Southampton	20	1		
2016–17	Southampton	23	1		
2017–18	Southampton	24	2		
2018–19	Southampton	17	0		
2019–20	Southampton	8	0	**154**	**6**
2019–20	*Sampdoria*	14	0	**14**	**0**

Players retained or with offer of contract
Bellis, Samuel Lawrence Alexander; Brennan, Sean Anthony; Bycroft, Jack Thomas; Chauke, Kgaogelo; El Younossi, Mohamed; Keogh, Seamas; Klarer, Christoph; Kpohomouh, Pascal; Latham, Kingsley Finn; Ledwidge, Kameron Malcolm; Mitchell, Ramello Dejorn; Olaigbe, Kazeem Aderemi J.; Olufunwa, Oludare Samuel Araba; Robise, Enzo; Smales Braithwaite, Benjamin; Vidal, Oriol Romeu; Watts, Caleb Cassius.

Scholars
Agbontohoma, David Osaretim; Bailey, Samuel James; Burnett, Ethan Darren; Cluett, Ryan; Davey, Teddy Jay; Defise, Lucas Nsiona K; Glean, Rio Kamil; Hall, Matthew Gary; Idowu, Roland; Morris, James William; Otseh-Taiwo, Zuriel Jonathan; Rus, Marco; Saunders, Michael; Smith, Jayden Pharell Llamar Mills; Tizzard, William James; Turner, Jack Henry; Watts, Callum Neil; Wright, Oliver Lennon George.

SOUTHEND U (77)

ACQUAH, Emile (F) **10** **1**
b. 13-7-00

2018–19	Southend U	3	0		
2019–20	Southend U	7	1	**10**	**1**

BARRATT, Sam (M) **10** **0**
b. 25-8-95
Internationals: England C.
From Bracknell T, Maidenhead U.

2018–19	Southend U	1	0		
2019–20	Southend U	9	0	**10**	**0**

BLACKMAN, Andre (D) **71** **0**
H: 5 11 W: 11 05 b.Lambeth 10-11-90

2009–10	Bristol C	0	0		

From AFC Wimbledon.

2011–12	Celtic	3	0		
2012–13	Celtic	0	0	**3**	**0**
2012–13	*Inverness CT*	2	0	**2**	**0**
2013–14	Plymouth Arg	6	0	**6**	**0**
2014–15	Blackpool	3	0	**3**	**0**
2015–16	MAS Fez	3	0	**3**	**0**
2016–17	Crawley T	32	0	**32**	**0**
2017–18	Barnet	19	0	**19**	**0**
2018–19	Gillingham	0	0		
2019–20	Southend U	3	0	**3**	**0**

BWOMONO, Elvis (D) **75** **1**
H: 5 9 W: 9 13 b. 29-11-98

2017–18	Southend U	11	0		
2018–19	Southend U	30	0		
2019–20	Southend U	34	1	**75**	**1**

CLIFFORD, Tom (D) 9 0

b. 9-2-99

2018–19	Southend U	1	0		
2019–20	Southend U	8	0	**9**	**0**

COKER, Kenny (F) 2 0

2019–20	Southend U	2	0	**2**	**0**

COX, Simon (F) 446 122

H: 5 10 W: 10 12 b.Reading 28-4-87

Internationals: Republic of Ireland Full caps.

2005–06	Reading	2	0		
2006–07	Reading	0	0		
2006–07	*Brentford*	13	0	**13**	**0**
2006–07	*Northampton T*	8	3	**8**	**3**
2007–08	Reading	0	0		
2007–08	Swindon T	36	15		
2008–09	Swindon T	45	29	**81**	**44**
2009–10	WBA	28	9		
2010–11	WBA	19	1		
2011–12	WBA	18	0		
2012–13	WBA	0	0	**65**	**10**
2012–13	Nottingham F	39	5		
2013–14	Nottingham F	34	8	**73**	**13**
2014–15	Reading	37	8		
2015–16	Reading	13	1	**52**	**9**
2015–16	*Bristol C*	4	0	**4**	**0**
2016–17	Southend U	44	16		
2017–18	Southend U	42	10		
2018–19	Southend U	45	15		
2019–20	Southend U	19	2	**150**	**43**

Transferred to Western Sydney W, January 2020.

DEMETRIOU, Jason (D) 414 32

H: 5 11 W: 10 08 b.Newham 18-11-87

Internationals: Cyprus Full caps.

2005–06	Leyton Orient	3	0		
2006–07	Leyton Orient	15	2		
2007–08	Leyton Orient	43	3		
2008–09	Leyton Orient	43	4		
2009–10	Leyton Orient	39	1	**143**	**10**
2010–11	AEK Larnaca	15	0		
2011–12	AEK Larnaca	23	1		
2012–13	AEK Larnaca	19	3	**57**	**4**
2013–14	An Famagusta	19	1		
2014–15	An Famagusta	25	0	**44**	**1**
2015–16	Walsall	43	3	**43**	**3**
2016–17	Southend U	41	1		
2017–18	Southend U	42	8		
2018–19	Southend U	24	2		
2019–20	Southend U	20	3	**127**	**14**

DIENG, Timothee (M) 195 11

H: 5 11 W: 12 00 b.Grenoble 9-4-92

2011–12	Brest	0	0		
2012–13	Brest	2	0		
2013–14	Brest	4	0	**6**	**0**
2014–15	Oldham Ath	22	0		
2015–16	Oldham Ath	38	1	**60**	**1**
2016–17	Bradford C	39	3		
2017–18	Bradford C	26	2	**65**	**5**
2018–19	Southend U	43	3		
2019–20	Southend U	21	2	**64**	**5**

EGBRI, Terrell (M) 6 1

2019–20	Southend U	6	1	**6**	**1**

GARD, Lewis (M) 4 1

b. 26-8-99

2017–18	Southend U	2	0		
2018–19	Southend U	0	0		
2019–20	Southend U	2	1	**4**	**1**

GOODSHIP, Brandon (F) 41 4

b. 1-1-86

Internationals: England C.

2013–14	Bournemouth	0	0		
2014–15	Bournemouth	0	0		
2015–16	Bournemouth	0	0		
2015–16	*Yeovil T*	10	1		
2016–17	Yeovil T	8	0	**18**	**1**

From Weymouth.

2019–20	Southend U	23	3	**23**	**3**

HOWARD, Rob (D) 0 0

b. 15-9-99

From Arsenal, Colchester U.

2018–19	Southend U	0	0		
2019–20	Southend U	0	0		

HUMPHRYS, Stephen (F) 79 18

b.Oldham 15-9-97

2016–17	Fulham	2	0		
2016–17	*Shrewsbury T*	14	2	**14**	**2**
2017–18	Fulham	0	0		
2017–18	*Rochdale*	16	2	**16**	**2**
2018–19	Fulham	0	0	**2**	**0**
2018–19	*Scunthorpe U*	16	4	**16**	**4**
2018–19	Southend U	10	5		
2019–20	Southend U	21	5	**31**	**10**

HUTCHINSON, Isaac (M) 30 1

b.Eastbourne 10-4-00

From Brighton & HA.

2018–19	Southend U	8	0		
2019–20	Southend U	22	1	**30**	**1**

HYAM, Luke (M) 159 4

H: 5 10 W: 11 05 b.Ipswich 24-10-91

2010–11	Ipswich T	10	0		
2011–12	Ipswich T	8	0		
2012–13	Ipswich T	30	1		
2013–14	Ipswich T	35	1		
2014–15	Ipswich T	16	1		
2015–16	Ipswich T	15	0		
2015–16	*Rotherham U*	5	0	**5**	**0**
2016–17	Ipswich T	0	0		
2017–18	Ipswich T	17	0	**131**	**3**
2018–19	Southend U	18	1		
2019–20	Southend U	5	0	**23**	**1**

KELMAN, Charlie (F) 28 6

b. 2-11-01

Internationals: USA U18, U20.

2018–19	Southend U	10	1		
2019–20	Southend U	18	5	**28**	**6**

KIERNAN, Rob (D) 174 5

H: 6 1 W: 11 13 b.Rickmansworth 13-1-91

Internationals: Republic of Ireland U18, U19, U21.

2008–09	Watford	0	0		
2009–10	Watford	0	0		
2009–10	*Kilmarnock*	4	0	**4**	**0**
2010–11	Watford	0	0		
2010–11	*Yeovil T*	3	0	**3**	**0**
2010–11	*Bradford C*	8	0	**8**	**0**
2010–11	*Wycombe W*	2	0	**2**	**0**
2011–12	Wigan Ath	0	0		
2011–12	*Accrington S*	3	0	**3**	**0**
2012–13	Wigan Ath	0	0		
2012–13	*Burton Alb*	6	0	**6**	**0**
2012–13	*Brentford*	8	0	**8**	**0**
2013–14	Wigan Ath	12	1		
2013–14	*Southend U*	12	0		
2014–15	Wigan Ath	17	0	**29**	**1**
2014–15	*Birmingham C*	12	1	**12**	**1**
2015–16	Rangers	33	0		
2016–17	Rangers	24	1	**57**	**1**
2017–18	Southend U	1	0		
2018–19	Southend U	10	1		
2019–20	Southend U	19	1	**42**	**2**

Transferred to Orange Co, January 2020.

KINALI, Eren (M) 6 0

2019–20	Southend U	6	0	**6**	**0**

KLASS, Michael (M) 10 0

b. 9-2-99

From QPR.

2017–18	Southend U	0	0		
2018–19	Southend U	10	0		
2019–20	Southend U	0	0	**10**	**0**

KYPRIANOU, Harry (D) 18 1

b. 16-3-97

Internationals: Cyprus U21.

2013–14	Watford	0	0		
2014–15	Watford	0	0		
2015–16	Watford	0	0		
2015–16	Southend U	0	0		
2016–17	Southend U	3	1		
2017–18	Southend U	13	0		
2018–19	Southend U	1	0		
2019–20	Southend U	1	0	**18**	**1**

LENNON, Harry (M) 68 5

H: 6 3 W: 11 11 b.Barking 16-12-94

2012–13	Charlton Ath	0	0		
2013–14	Charlton Ath	2	0		
2014–15	Charlton Ath	0	0		
2014–15	*Cambridge U*	2	0	**2**	**0**
2014–15	*Gillingham*	2	0		
2015–16	Charlton Ath	19	2		
2015–16	*Gillingham*	6	2	**8**	**2**
2016–17	Charlton Ath	2	0		
2017–18	Charlton Ath	10	0	**33**	**2**
2018–19	Southend U	9	0		
2019–20	Southend U	16	1	**25**	**1**

MANTOM, Sam (M) 246 27

H: 5 9 W: 11 00 b.Stourbridge 20-2-92

Internationals: England U17.

2010–11	WBA	0	0		
2010–11	*Tranmere R*	2	0	**2**	**0**
2010–11	*Oldham Ath*	4	0	**4**	**0**
2011–12	WBA	0	0		
2011–12	*Walsall*	13	3		
2012–13	WBA	0	0		
2012–13	Walsall	29	2		
2013–14	Walsall	43	5		
2014–15	Walsall	12	0		
2015–16	Walsall	37	8	**134**	**18**
2016–17	Scunthorpe U	26	2		
2017–18	Scunthorpe U	8	0	**34**	**2**
2017–18	*Southend U*	7	0		
2018–19	Southend U	43	5		
2019–20	Southend U	22	2	**72**	**7**

McLAUGHLIN, Stephen (M) 243 33

H: 5 9 W: 11 12 b.Derry 14-6-90

2011	Derry C	33	3		
2012	Derry C	24	10	**57**	**13**
2012–13	Nottingham F	0	0		
2013–14	Nottingham F	3	0		
2013–14	*Bristol C*	5	0	**5**	**0**
2014–15	Nottingham F	6	0	**9**	**0**
2014–15	*Notts Co*	13	0	**13**	**0**
2014–15	*Southend U*	6	1		
2015–16	Southend U	17	1		
2016–17	Southend U	34	7		
2017–18	Southend U	45	6		
2018–19	Southend U	30	1		
2019–20	Southend U	27	4	**159**	**20**

MILLIGAN, Mark (M) 345 33

b.Sydney 4-8-85

Internationals: Australia U20, U23, Full caps.

2001–02	Parramatta Eagles	2	0	**2**	**0**
2002–03	Northern Spirit	2	0		
2003–04	Northern Spirit	14	1	**16**	**1**
2004–05	Blacktown C Demons	9	5	**9**	**5**
2004–05	Sydney	3	0		
2005–06	Sydney	10	0		
2006–07	Sydney	17	1		
2007–08	Sydney	13	0	**43**	**1**
2008–09	Newcastle Jets	11	1	**11**	**1**
2009	Shanghai Shenhua	20	0	**20**	**0**
2010	JEF U	15	0		
2011	JEF U	29	1		
2011–12	*Melbourne Victory*	10	1		
2012	JEF U	9	2	**53**	**3**
2012–13	Melbourne Victory	20	8		
2013–14	Melbourne Victory	20	4		
2014–15	Melbourne Victory	18	1		
2015–16	Bani Yas	21	3		
2016–17	Bani Yas	22	2	**43**	**5**
2017–18	Melbourne Victory	14	3	**82**	**17**
2017–18	Al-Ahli Jidda	8	0	**8**	**0**
2018–19	Hibernian	28	0	**28**	**0**
2019–20	Southend U	30	0	**30**	**0**

MITCHELL-NELSON, Miles (D) 6 0

2017–18	Southend U	0	0		
2018–19	Southend U	0	0		
2019–20	Southend U	6	0	**6**	**0**

OSAOABE, Emmanuel (M) 86 7

b.Dundalk 1-10-96

2015–16	Gillingham	18	2		
2016–17	Gillingham	24	1	**42**	**3**
2017–18	Cambridge U	4	0		
2017–18	*Newport Co*	3	0	**3**	**0**
2018–19	Cambridge U	12	0	**16**	**0**
2019–20	Macclesfield T	25	4	**25**	**4**
2019–20	Southend U	0	0		

OXLEY, Mark (G) 222 1

H: 5 11 W: 11 05 b.Aston 2-6-90

Internationals: England U18.

2008–09	Hull C	0	0		
2009–10	Hull C	0	0		
2009–10	*Grimsby T*	3	0	**3**	**0**
2010–11	Hull C	0	0		
2011–12	Hull C	0	0		
2012–13	Hull C	1	0		
2012–13	*Burton Alb*	3	0	**3**	**0**
2013–14	Hull C	0	0		
2013–14	*Oldham Ath*	36	0	**36**	**0**
2014–15	Hull C	0	0	**1**	**0**
2014–15	*Hibernian*	35	1		
2015–16	Hibernian	34	0	**69**	**1**
2016–17	Southend U	20	0		
2017–18	Southend U	46	0		
2018–19	Southend U	25	0		
2019–20	Southend U	19	0	**110**	**0**

PHILLIPS, Harry (M) 2 1

2017–18	Southend U	0	0		
2018–19	Southend U	0	0		
2019–20	Southend U	2	1	**2**	**1**

RALPH, Nathan (D) 78 2

H: 5 9 W: 11 00 b.Dunmow 14-2-93

2011–12	Peterborough U	0	0		
2012–13	Yeovil T	14	1		
2013–14	Yeovil T	0	0		
2014–15	Yeovil T	21	0	**35**	**1**
2015–16	Newport Co	0	0		

From Woking.

2018–19	Dundee	26	1	**26**	**1**
2019–20	Southend U	17	0	**17**	**0**

RIDGEWELL, Liam (D) **441 24**
H: 5 10 W: 10 03 b.Bexley 21-7-84
Internationals: England U19, U20, U21.

2001–02	Aston Villa	0	0		
2002–03	Aston Villa	0	0		
2002–03	*Bournemouth*	5	0	**5**	**0**
2003–04	Aston Villa	11	0		
2004–05	Aston Villa	15	0		
2005–06	Aston Villa	32	5		
2006–07	Aston Villa	21	1	**79**	**6**
2007–08	Birmingham C	35	1		
2008–09	Birmingham C	36	1		
2009–10	Birmingham C	31	3		
2010–11	Birmingham C	36	4		
2011–12	Birmingham C	14	0	**152**	**9**
2011–12	WBA	13	1		
2012–13	WBA	30	0		
2013–14	WBA	33	1	**76**	**2**
2014	Portland Timbers	15	2		
2014–15	*Wigan Ath*	6	0	**6**	**0**
2015	Portland Timbers	37	1		
2015–16	*Brighton & HA*	5	0	**5**	**0**
2016	Portland Timbers	22	1		
2017	Portland Timbers	17	3		
2018	Portland Timbers	19	0	**110**	**7**
2018–19	Hull C	7	0	**7**	**0**
2019–20	Southend U	1	0	**1**	**0**

ROBINSON, Theo (F) **413 99**
H: 5 9 W: 10 03 b.Birmingham 22-1-89
Internationals: Jamaica Full caps.

2005–06	Watford	1	0		
2006–07	Watford	1	0		
2007–08	Watford	0	0		
2007–08	*Hereford U*	43	13	**43**	**13**
2008–09	Watford	3	0	**5**	**0**
2008–09	*Southend U*	21	7		
2009–10	Huddersfield T	37	13		
2010–11	Huddersfield T	1	0		
2010–11	Millwall	11	3		
2010–11	*Derby Co*	13	2		
2011–12	Derby Co	39	10		
2012–13	Derby Co	28	8		
2012–13	*Huddersfield T*	6	0	**44**	**13**
2013–14	Millwall	0	0	**11**	**3**
2013–14	Derby Co	0	0	**80**	**20**
2013–14	Doncaster R	31	5		
2014–15	Doncaster R	32	4	**63**	**9**
2014–15	*Scunthorpe U*	8	3	**8**	**3**
2015–16	Motherwell	10	0	**10**	**0**
2015–16	Port Vale	14	2	**14**	**2**
2016–17	Southend U	18	2		
2017–18	Southend U	25	5		
2018–19	Southend U	24	4		
2018–19	*Swindon T*	16	7	**16**	**7**
2019–20	Southend U	3	0	**91**	**18**
2019–20	*Colchester U*	28	11	**28**	**11**

RUSH, Matt (F) **7 0**

2019–20	Southend U	7	0	**7**	**0**

SEADEN, Harry (G) **1 0**
b.Southend-on-Sea 23-4-01
Internationals: England U16, U17.

2018–19	Southend U	0	0		
2019–20	Southend U	1	0	**1**	**0**

SHAUGHNESSY, Joe (D) **251 9**
b.Reading 6-7-92
Internationals: Republic of Ireland U21.

2009–10	Aberdeen	0	0		
2010–11	Aberdeen	1	0		
2011–12	Aberdeen	1	0		
2011–12	*Forfar Ath*	26	3	**26**	**3**
2012–13	Aberdeen	23	0		
2013–14	Aberdeen	26	0		
2014–15	Aberdeen	3	0	**54**	**0**
2014–15	*Falkirk*	9	0	**9**	**0**
2015–16	St Johnstone	37	1		
2016–17	St Johnstone	38	1		
2017–18	St Johnstone	38	1		
2018–19	St Johnstone	33	3	**146**	**6**
2019–20	Southend U	16	0	**16**	**0**

TAYLOR, Callum (G) **1 0**

2019–20	Southend U	1	0	**1**	**0**

TAYLOR, Richard (D) **2 0**

2018–19	Burnley	0	0		
2019–20	Southend U	2	0	**2**	**0**

WHITE, John (D) **432 7**
H: 6 0 W: 12 01 b.Maldon 26-7-86

2004–05	Colchester U	20	0		
2005–06	Colchester U	35	0		
2006–07	Colchester U	16	0		
2007–08	Colchester U	21	0		
2008–09	Colchester U	26	0		
2009–10	Colchester U	39	0		
2009–10	*Southend U*	5	0		
2010–11	Colchester U	22	0		
2011–12	Colchester U	26	0		
2012–13	Colchester U	22	0	**227**	**0**
2013–14	Southend U	41	1		
2014–15	Southend U	42	0		
2015–16	Southend U	29	1		
2016–17	Southend U	13	1		
2017–18	Southend U	31	2		
2018–19	Southend U	33	2		
2019–20	Southend U	11	0	**205**	**7**

Scholars
Acquah, Emile; Anyadike, Damaray Chukwemeka; Benton, Jon; Brogan, Samuel William Peter; Brown, Cameron Marcel; Chandler, Reiss Billy; Coker, Oliver; Dabbs, Ben Derek Harry; Davis, Tommy; Eastwood, Freddy John; Egbri, Terrell Evieoghene; Grossart, Jamie William; Knock, Samuel David; Lambourne, Thomas John Joseph; Mitchel-Nelson, Miles Nathaniel; Mpenga, Issa Ali; Quamina, Tendi; Rush, Matthew Thomas; Seaden, Harry John; Shala, Ergis; Stewart, O'Shane Christan; Taylor, Callum; Udebh-Osimeh, Idemudia Mohammed; Unwin, Robert David; Wallace, Jimmy Terence.

STEVENAGE (78)

BASTIEN, Sacha (G) **15 0**
b. 22-1-95

2013–14	Reims	0	0		
2014–15	Reims	1	0	**1**	**0**
2017–18	Bastia-Borgo	3	0	**3**	**0**
2018–19	US Granville	10	0	**10**	**0**
2019–20	Stevenage	1	0	**1**	**0**

BERMAN, Jack (G) **0 0**

2019–20	Stevenage	0	0		

BYROM, Joel (M) **246 16**
H: 6 0 W: 12 04 b.Accrington 14-9-86
Internationals: England C.

2004–05	Blackburn R	0	0		
2005–06	Blackburn R	0	0		
2006–07	Accrington S	1	0	**1**	**0**

From Clitheroe, Southport, Clitheroe, Northwich Vic.

2010–11	Stevenage	7	0		
2011–12	Stevenage	32	4		
2012–13	Preston NE	22	2		
2013–14	Preston NE	11	2	**33**	**4**
2013–14	*Oldham Ath*	4	0	**4**	**0**
2014–15	Northampton T	39	3		
2015–16	Northampton T	35	2		
2016–17	Northampton T	2	0	**76**	**5**
2016–17	Mansfield T	22	0		
2017–18	Mansfield T	19	1	**41**	**1**
2018–19	Stevenage	46	2		
2019–20	Stevenage	6	0	**91**	**6**

CARROLL, Canice (M) **46 2**
b. 26-1-99
Internationals: Republic of Ireland U17, U18, U19, U21.

2015–16	Oxford U	0	0		
2016–17	Oxford U	4	0		
2017–18	Oxford U	12	1		
2018–19	Oxford U	0	0	**16**	**1**
2018–19	Brentford	0	0		
2018–19	*Swindon T*	17	1	**17**	**1**
2019–20	Brentford	0	0		
2019–20	*Carlisle U*	9	0	**9**	**0**
2019–20	Stevenage	4	0	**4**	**0**

CARTER, Charlie (M) **29 5**
b. 25-10-96

2019–20	Stevenage	29	5	**29**	**5**

CASSIDY, Jake (F) **138 21**
H: 5 10 W: 11 02 b.Glan Conwy 9-2-93
Internationals: Wales U19, U21.

2010–11	Wolverhampton W	0	0		
2011–12	Wolverhampton W	0	0		
2011–12	*Tranmere R*	10	5		
2012–13	Wolverhampton W	6	0		
2012–13	*Tranmere R*	26	11		
2013–14	Wolverhampton W	14	0		
2013–14	*Tranmere R*	19	1		
2014–15	Wolverhampton W	0	0	**20**	**0**
2014–15	*Tranmere R*	0	0	**55**	**17**
2014–15	*Notts Co*	16	3	**16**	**3**
2014–15	*Southend U*	17	0	**17**	**0**
2015–16	Oldham Ath	21	0		
2016–17	Oldham Ath	0	0	**21**	**0**

From Guiseley, Hartlepool U, Maidenhead U.

2019–20	Stevenage	9	1	**9**	**1**

COWLEY, Jason (F) **18 2**
From Redditch Bor, Redditch, Bromsgrove Sporting, AFC Telford U.

2019–20	Stevenage	18	2	**18**	**2**

CUTHBERT, Scott (D) **410 20**
H: 6 2 W: 14 00 b.Alexandria 15-6-87
Internationals: Scotland U19, U20, U21, B.

2004–05	Celtic	0	0		
2005–06	Celtic	0	0		
2006–07	Celtic	0	0		
2006–07	*Livingston*	4	1	**4**	**1**
2007–08	Celtic	0	0		
2008–09	Celtic	0	0		
2008–09	*St Mirren*	29	0	**29**	**0**
2009–10	Swindon T	39	3		
2010–11	Swindon T	41	2	**80**	**5**
2011–12	Leyton Orient	33	1		
2012–13	Leyton Orient	18	0		
2013–14	Leyton Orient	44	4		
2014–15	Leyton Orient	38	2	**133**	**7**
2015–16	Luton T	36	0		
2016–17	Luton T	38	1		
2017–18	Luton T	23	2	**97**	**3**
2018–19	Stevenage	46	2		
2019–20	Stevenage	21	2	**67**	**4**

DABO, Diaguely (M) **164 3**
b.Saint-Leu 26-8-92

2010–11	Lorient	0	0		
2011–12	Lorient	0	0		
2012–13	Cannes	11	0	**11**	**0**
2013–14	Senart-Moissy	19	1	**19**	**1**
2014–15	Beauvais	20	0	**20**	**0**
2015–16	Dieppe	29	1	**29**	**1**
2016–17	Epinal	29	0	**29**	**0**
2017–18	Leval	23	1	**23**	**1**
2018–19	Avranches	25	0	**25**	**0**
2019–20	Stevenage	8	0	**8**	**0**

DENTON, Tyler (D) **40 0**
H: 5 8 W: 10 06 b.Dewsbury 6-9-95
Internationals: England U17.

2016–17	Leeds U	0	0		
2017–18	Leeds U	0	0		
2017–18	*Port Vale*	15	0	**15**	**0**
2018–19	Leeds U	0	0		
2018–19	*Peterborough U*	10	0	**10**	**0**
2019–20	Stevenage	15	0	**15**	**0**

DIGBY, Paul (M) **98 1**
H: 5 9 W: 10 00 b.Sheffield 2-2-95
Internationals: England U19, U20.

2011–12	Barnsley	4	0		
2012–13	Barnsley	0	0		
2013–14	Barnsley	5	0		
2014–15	Barnsley	11	0		
2015–16	Barnsley	1	0	**21**	**0**
2015–16	*Ipswich T*	4	0		
2016–17	Ipswich T	4	0	**8**	**0**
2016–17	Mansfield T	0	0		
2017–18	Mansfield T	15	0	**15**	**0**
2018–19	Forest Green R	37	1	**37**	**1**
2019–20	Stevenage	17	0	**17**	**0**

EL-ABD, Adam (D) **463 12**
H: 5 10 W: 13 05 b.Brighton 11-9-84
Internationals: Egypt Full caps.

2003–04	Brighton & HA	11	0		
2004–05	Brighton & HA	16	0		
2005–06	Brighton & HA	29	0		
2006–07	Brighton & HA	42	1		
2007–08	Brighton & HA	35	1		
2008–09	Brighton & HA	31	0		
2009–10	Brighton & HA	35	1		
2010–11	Brighton & HA	37	1		
2011–12	Brighton & HA	23	0		
2012–13	Brighton & HA	32	1		
2013–14	Brighton & HA	9	0	**300**	**5**
2013–14	Bristol C	14	0		
2014–15	Bristol C	2	0		
2014–15	*Bury*	24	1	**24**	**1**
2015–16	Bristol C	0	0	**16**	**0**
2015–16	*Swindon T*	13	0	**13**	**0**
2015–16	*Gillingham*	8	0	**8**	**0**
2016–17	Shrewsbury T	28	2	**28**	**2**
2017–18	Wycombe W	36	1		
2018–19	Wycombe W	34	3		
2019–20	Wycombe W	2	0	**72**	**4**
2019–20	Stevenage	2	0	**2**	**0**

FARMAN, Paul (G) **81 0**
H: 6 5 W: 14 07 b.North Shields 2-11-89
Internationals: England C.
From Blyth Spartans, Gateshead.
2017–18 Lincoln C 13 0 **13 0**
2018–19 Stevenage 33 0
2019–20 Stevenage 35 0 **68 0**

FERNANDEZ, Luis (D) **4 0**
2019–20 Stevenage 4 0 **4 0**

FIELDING, Jamie (D) **3 0**
2019–20 Stevenage 3 0 **3 0**

GEORGIOU, Andronicos (F) **4 0**
b.Enfield 28-10-99
2017–18 Stevenage 3 0
2018–19 Stevenage 1 0
2019–20 Stevenage 0 0 **4 0**

HUSIN, Noor (M) **47 2**
H: 5 10 W: 10 03 b.Mazar-i-Sharif 3-3-97
Internationals: Afganistan Full caps.
2015–16 Reading 0 0
2016–17 Crystal Palace 0 0
2016–17 *Accrington S* 11 1 **11 1**
2017–18 Notts Co 12 1
2018–19 Notts Co 14 0 **26 1**
2019–20 Stevenage 10 0 **10 0**

IONTTON, Arthur (M) **27 1**
b.Enfield 16-12-00
2017–18 Stevenage 2 0
2018–19 Stevenage 18 1
2019–20 Stevenage 7 0 **27 1**

JACKSON, Simeon (M) **323 72**
H: 5 10 W: 10 12 b.Kingston, Jamaica 28-3-87
Internationals: Canada U20, Full caps.
2004–05 Rushden & D 3 0
2005–06 Rushden & D 14 5
2006–07 Rushden & D 0 0
2007–08 Rushden & D 0 0 **17 5**
2007–08 Gillingham 18 4
2008–09 Gillingham 41 17
2009–10 Gillingham 42 14 **101 35**
2010–11 Norwich C 38 13
2011–12 Norwich C 22 3
2012–13 Norwich C 13 1 **73 17**
2013–14 E Braunschweig 9 0 **9 0**
2013–14 Millwall 14 2 **14 2**
2014–15 Coventry C 28 3 **28 3**
2015–16 Barnsley 9 0 **9 0**
2015–16 Blackburn R 17 2 **17 2**
2016–17 Walsall 38 7
2017–18 Walsall 8 0 **46 7**
2017–18 *Grimsby T* 5 1 **5 1**
2019–20 Kilmarnock 0 0
2019–20 Stevenage 4 0 **4 0**

KENNEDY, Ben (F) **161 28**
H: 5 10 W: 11 00 b. 12-1-97
Internationals: Northern Ireland U17, U19, U21.
2014–15 Stevenage 15 4
2015–16 Stevenage 22 2
2016–17 Stevenage 36 8
2017–18 Stevenage 35 7
2018–19 Stevenage 25 6
2018–19 *Newport Co* 10 1 **10 1**
2019–20 Stevenage 18 0 **151 27**

LEESLEY, Joe (F) **8 0**
b. 29-4-94
Internationals: England C.
On loan from Harrogate T.
2019–20 Stevenage 8 0 **8 0**

LIST, Elliott (M) **106 9**
b.Camberwell 12-5-97
From Crystal Palace.
2015–16 Gillingham 6 0
2016–17 Gillingham 15 0
2017–18 Gillingham 23 2
2018–19 Gillingham 37 5
2019–20 Gillingham 4 0 **85 7**
2019–20 Stevenage 21 2 **21 2**

NEWTON, Danny (F) **80 22**
b.Liverpool 18-3-91
From Tamworth.
2017–18 Stevenage 45 14
2018–19 Stevenage 25 6
2019–20 Stevenage 10 2 **80 22**

NUGENT, Ben (D) **185 4**
H: 6 1 W: 13 00 b.Street 28-11-93
2012–13 Cardiff C 12 1
2013–14 Cardiff C 0 0
2013–14 *Brentford* 0 0
2013–14 *Peterborough U* 11 0 **11 0**
2014–15 Cardiff C 0 0 **12 1**
2014–15 *Yeovil T* 23 1 **23 1**
2015–16 Crewe Alex 39 1
2016–17 Crewe Alex 20 0 **59 1**
2017–18 Gillingham 23 0 **23 0**
2018–19 Stevenage 34 1
2019–20 Stevenage 23 0 **57 1**

PARRETT, Dean (M) **202 19**
H: 5 10 W: 11 04 b.Hampstead 16-11-91
Internationals: England U16, U17, U19, U20.
2008–09 Tottenham H 0 0
2009–10 Tottenham H 0 0
2009–10 *Aldershot T* 4 0 **4 0**
2010–11 Tottenham H 0 0
2010–11 *Plymouth Arg* 8 1 **8 1**
2010–11 *Charlton Ath* 9 1 **9 1**
2011–12 Tottenham H 0 0
2011–12 *Yeovil T* 10 1 **10 1**
2012–13 Tottenham H 0 0
2012–13 *Swindon T* 3 0 **3 0**
2013–14 Stevenage 12 1
2014–15 Stevenage 30 4
2015–16 Stevenage 27 3
2016–17 AFC Wimbledon 32 5
2017–18 AFC Wimbledon 23 2 **55 7**
2018–19 Gillingham 27 1 **27 1**
2019–20 Stevenage 17 0 **86 8**

READING, Patrick (D) **1 0**
b. 29-5-99
Internationals: Scotland U21.
From Middlesbrough.
2019–20 Stevenage 1 0 **1 0**

REID, Alex (F) **11 2**
b. 6-9-95
2016–17 Fleetwood T 0 0
2017–18 Fleetwood T 0 0
2018–19 Stevenage 11 2
2019–20 Stevenage 0 0 **11 2**

REVELL, Alex (F) **519 101**
H: 6 3 W: 13 00 b.Cambridge 7-7-83
2000–01 Cambridge U 4 0
2001–02 Cambridge U 24 2
2002–03 Cambridge U 9 0
2003–04 Cambridge U 20 3 **57 5**
From Braintree T.
2006–07 Brighton & HA 38 7
2007–08 Brighton & HA 21 6 **59 13**
2007–08 Southend U 8 0
2008–09 Southend U 23 4
2009–10 Southend U 3 0 **34 4**
2009–10 *Swindon T* 10 2 **10 2**
2009–10 Wycombe W 15 6 **15 6**
2010–11 Leyton Orient 39 13
2011–12 Leyton Orient 5 0 **44 13**
2011–12 Rotherham U 40 10
2012–13 Rotherham U 41 6
2013–14 Rotherham U 45 8
2014–15 Rotherham U 24 4 **150 28**
2014–15 Cardiff C 16 2
2015–16 Cardiff C 10 0 **26 2**
2015–16 *Wigan Ath* 6 1 **6 1**
2015–16 Milton Keynes D 17 4 **17 4**
2016–17 Northampton T 32 8
2017–18 Northampton T 15 2 **47 10**
2017–18 Stevenage 12 6
2018–19 Stevenage 40 7
2019–20 Stevenage 2 0 **54 13**

ROLLINSON, Joel (M) **1 0**
2017–18 Reading 0 0
2018–19 Reading 0 0
2019–20 Stevenage 1 0 **1 0**

SMITH, Jack (D) **1 0**
2019–20 Stevenage 1 0 **1 0**

SMYTH, Liam (F) **4 0**
b. 6-9-01
Internationals: Northern Ireland U19.
2018–19 Stevenage 3 0
2019–20 Stevenage 1 0 **4 0**

SOARES, Tom (M) **450 39**
H: 6 0 W: 11 04 b.Reading 10-7-86
Internationals: England U20, U21.
2003–04 Crystal Palace 3 0
2004–05 Crystal Palace 22 0
2005–06 Crystal Palace 44 1
2006–07 Crystal Palace 37 3
2007–08 Crystal Palace 39 6
2008–09 Crystal Palace 4 1 **149 11**
2008–09 Stoke C 7 0
2008–09 *Charlton Ath* 11 1 **11 1**
2009–10 Stoke C 0 0
2009–10 *Sheffield W* 25 2 **25 2**
2010–11 Stoke C 0 0
2011–12 Stoke C 0 0 **7 0**
2011–12 *Hibernian* 10 2 **10 2**
2012–13 Bury 23 2
2013–14 Bury 30 6
2014–15 Bury 43 8
2015–16 Bury 42 4
2016–17 Bury 26 2 **164 22**
2016–17 AFC Wimbledon 15 0
2017–18 AFC Wimbledon 31 1
2018–19 AFC Wimbledon 23 0 **69 1**
2019–20 Stevenage 15 0 **15 0**

SONUPE, Emmanuel (M) **46 4**
b.London 21-3-96
Internationals: England U16, U18.
2014–15 Tottenham H 0 0
2014–15 *St Mirren* 4 0 **4 0**
2015–16 Tottenham H 0 0
2016–17 Northampton T 1 0 **1 0**
From Kidderminster H.
2018–19 Stevenage 32 3
2019–20 Stevenage 9 1 **41 4**

TAYLOR, Paul (F) **200 23**
H: 5 11 W: 11 02 b.Liverpool 4-11-87
2008–09 Chester C 9 0 **9 0**
2009–10 Montegnee 1 0 **1 0**
2009–10 *Charleoi* 3 0 **3 0**
2010–11 Anderlecht 0 0
2010–11 Peterborough U 1 0
2011–12 Peterborough U 44 12
2012–13 Peterborough U 3 0
2012–13 Ipswich T 3 0
2013–14 Ipswich T 18 1
2013–14 *Peterborough U* 6 0
2014–15 Ipswich T 0 0
2014–15 *Rotherham U* 17 0 **17 0**
2014–15 *Blackburn R* 5 0 **5 0**
2015–16 Ipswich T 0 0 **21 1**
2016–17 Peterborough U 39 3 **93 15**
2017–18 Bradford C 27 6 **27 6**
2018–19 Doncaster R 14 1 **14 1**
2019–20 Stevenage 10 0 **10 0**

TIMLIN, Michael (M) **404 20**
H: 5 8 W: 11 08 b.New Cross 19-3-85
Internationals: Republic of Ireland U17, U21.
2002–03 Fulham 0 0
2003–04 Fulham 0 0
2004–05 Fulham 0 0
2005–06 Fulham 0 0
2005–06 *Scunthorpe U* 1 0 **1 0**
2005–06 *Doncaster R* 3 0 **3 0**
2006–07 Fulham 0 0
2006–07 *Swindon T* 24 1
2007–08 Fulham 0 0
2007–08 *Swindon T* 10 1
2008–09 Swindon T 41 2
2009–10 Swindon T 21 0
2010–11 Swindon T 22 2
2010–11 *Southend U* 8 1
2011–12 Swindon T 1 0 **119 6**
2011–12 Southend U 39 4
2012–13 Southend U 25 0
2013–14 Southend U 36 2
2014–15 Southend U 32 3
2015–16 Southend U 21 2
2016–17 Southend U 27 1
2017–18 Southend U 34 0 **222 13**
2018–19 Stevenage 42 1
2019–20 Stevenage 17 0 **59 1**

TOWNSEND-WEST, Mackye (D) **0 0**
2019–20 Stevenage 0 0

VANCOOTEN, Terence (D) **50 0**
H: 6 1 W: 12 04 b. 29-12-97
Internationals: Guyana Full caps.
2016–17 Reading 0 0
2017–18 Stevenage 22 0
2018–19 Stevenage 12 0
2019–20 Stevenage 16 0 **50 0**

WILDIN, Luther (M) **60 2**
b. 3-12-97
Internationals: Antigua and Barbuda U20, Full caps.
2015–16 Notts Co 0 0
2016–17 Notts Co 0 0
From Nuneaton T.
2018–19 Stevenage 39 1
2019–20 Stevenage 21 1 **60 2**

Scholars
Arai, Yasin; Berman, Jack Louie; Bunyan, Jake; Dreyer, Sam Wilson; Krasniqi, Drilon; Leslie, Joe Ryan; Townsend, West MacKye Dre; Williams, Alfie Keith.

STOKE C (79)

AFOBE, Benik (F) 273 68
H: 5 10 W: 11 00 b.Leyton 12-2-93
Internationals: England U16, U17, U19, U21. DR Congo Full caps.
2009–10 Arsenal 0 0
2010–11 Arsenal 0 0
2010–11 *Huddersfield T* 28 5 **28 5**
2011–12 Arsenal 0 0
2011–12 *Reading* 3 0 **3 0**
2012–13 Arsenal 0 0
2012–13 *Bolton W* 20 2 **20 2**
2012–13 *Millwall* 5 0 **5 0**
2013–14 Arsenal 0 0
2013–14 *Sheffield W* 12 2 **12 2**
2014–15 Arsenal 0 0
2014–15 *Milton Keynes D* 22 10 **22 10**
2014–15 Wolverhampton W 21 13
2015–16 Wolverhampton W 25 9
2015–16 Bournemouth 15 4
2016–17 Bournemouth 31 6
2017–18 Bournemouth 17 0 **63 10**
2017–18 *Wolverhampton W* 16 6
2018–19 Wolverhampton W 0 0 **62 28**
2018–19 *Stoke C* 45 8
2019–20 Stoke C 1 0 **46 8**
2019–20 *Bristol C* 12 3 **12 3**

ALLEN, Joe (M) 371 29
H: 5 6 W: 9 10 b.Carmarthen 14-3-90
Internationals: Wales U17, U19, U21, Full caps. Great Britain.
2006–07 Swansea C 1 0
2007–08 Swansea C 6 0
2008–09 Swansea C 23 1
2009–10 Swansea C 21 0
2010–11 Swansea C 40 2
2011–12 Swansea C 36 4
2012–13 Swansea C 0 0 **127 7**
2012–13 Liverpool 27 0
2013–14 Liverpool 24 1
2014–15 Liverpool 21 1
2015–16 Liverpool 19 2 **91 4**
2016–17 Stoke C 36 6
2017–18 Stoke C 36 2
2018–19 Stoke C 46 6
2019–20 Stoke C 35 4 **153 18**

BATTH, Danny (D) 337 21
H: 6 3 W: 13 05 b.Brierley Hill 21-9-90
2009–10 Wolverhampton W 0 0
2009–10 *Colchester U* 17 1 **17 1**
2010–11 Wolverhampton W 0 0
2010–11 *Sheffield U* 1 0 **1 0**
2010–11 *Sheffield W* 10 0
2011–12 Wolverhampton W 0 0
2011–12 *Sheffield W* 44 2 **54 2**
2012–13 Wolverhampton W 12 1
2013–14 Wolverhampton W 46 2
2014–15 Wolverhampton W 44 4
2015–16 Wolverhampton W 38 2
2016–17 Wolverhampton W 39 4
2017–18 Wolverhampton W 16 1
2018–19 Wolverhampton W 0 0 **195 14**
2018–19 *Middlesbrough* 10 0 **10 0**
2018–19 Stoke C 17 0
2019–20 Stoke C 43 4 **60 4**

BAUER, Moritz (D) 162 0
H: 5 11 W: 11 07 b.Veltheim 25-1-92
Internationals: Switzerland U19, U21. Austria Full caps.
2011–12 Grasshopper 16 0
2012–13 Grasshopper 13 0
2013–14 Grasshopper 15 0
2014–15 Grasshopper 16 0
2015–16 Grasshopper 33 0 **93 0**
2016–17 Rubin Kazan 21 0
2017–18 Rubin Kazan 16 0 **37 0**
2017–18 Stoke C 15 0
2018–19 Stoke C 8 0
2019–20 Stoke C 0 0 **23 0**
2019–20 *Celtic* 9 0 **9 0**

BURSIK, Josef (G) 16 0
Internationals: England U17, U18, U19, U20.
From AFC Wimbledon.
2019–20 Stoke C 0 0
2019–20 *Accrington S* 16 0 **16 0**

BUTLAND, Jack (G) 262 0
H: 6 4 W: 12 00 b.Clevedon 10-3-93
Internationals: England U16, U17, U19, U20, U21, Full caps.
2009–10 Birmingham C 0 0
2010–11 Birmingham C 0 0
2011–12 Birmingham C 0 0
2011–12 *Cheltenham T* 24 0 **24 0**
2012–13 Birmingham C 46 0 **46 0**
2012–13 Stoke C 0 0
2013–14 Stoke C 3 0
2013–14 *Barnsley* 13 0 **13 0**
2013–14 *Leeds U* 16 0 **16 0**
2014–15 Stoke C 3 0
2014–15 *Derby Co* 6 0 **6 0**
2015–16 Stoke C 31 0
2016–17 Stoke C 5 0
2017–18 Stoke C 35 0
2018–19 Stoke C 45 0
2019–20 Stoke C 35 0 **157 0**

CAMPBELL, Tyrese (F) 55 14
b.Derby 16-9-97
Internationals: England U17, U20.
From Manchester C.
2017–18 Stoke C 4 0
2018–19 Stoke C 3 0
2018–19 *Shrewsbury T* 15 5 **15 5**
2019–20 Stoke C 33 9 **40 9**

CLUCAS, Sam (M) 304 43
H: 5 10 W: 11 08 b.Lincoln 25-9-90
Internationals: England C.
2009–10 Lincoln C 0 0
2010–11 Jerez Industrial 20 0 **20 0**
2011–12 Hereford U 17 0 **17 0**
From Hereford U.
2013–14 Mansfield T 38 8
2014–15 Mansfield T 5 0 **43 8**
2014–15 Chesterfield 41 9 **41 9**
2015–16 Hull C 44 6
2016–17 Hull C 37 3
2017–18 Hull C 3 0 **84 9**
2017–18 Swansea C 29 3 **29 3**
2018–19 Stoke C 26 3
2019–20 Stoke C 44 11 **70 14**

COLLINS, Nathan (D) 17 0
b. 30-4-01
Internationals: Republic of Ireland U17, U19, U21.
2018–19 Stoke C 3 0
2019–20 Stoke C 14 0 **17 0**

COUSINS, Jordan (D) 206 8
H: 5 10 W: 11 05 b.Greenwich 6-3-94
Internationals: England U16, U17, U18, U20.
2011–12 Charlton Ath 0 0
2012–13 Charlton Ath 0 0
2013–14 Charlton Ath 42 2
2014–15 Charlton Ath 44 3
2015–16 Charlton Ath 39 2 **125 7**
2016–17 QPR 18 0
2017–18 QPR 15 0
2018–19 QPR 28 1 **61 1**
2019–20 Stoke C 20 0 **20 0**

DAVIES, Adam (G) 188 0
H: 6 1 W: 11 11 b.Rinteln 17-7-92
Internationals: Wales Full caps.
2009–10 Everton 0 0
2010–11 Everton 0 0
2011–12 Everton 0 0
2012–13 Sheffield W 0 0
2013–14 Sheffield W 0 0
2014–15 Barnsley 23 0
2015–16 Barnsley 38 0
2016–17 Barnsley 46 0
2017–18 Barnsley 35 0
2018–19 Barnsley 42 0 **184 0**
2019–20 Stoke C 4 0 **4 0**

DIOUF, Mame (F) 305 86
H: 6 1 W: 12 00 b.Dakar 16-12-87
Internationals: Senegal Full caps.
2007 Molde 21 9
2008 Molde 23 7
2009 Molde 29 16 **73 32**
2009–10 Manchester U 5 1
2010–11 Manchester U 0 0
2010–11 *Blackburn R* 26 3 **26 3**
2011–12 Manchester U 0 0 **5 1**
2011–12 Hannover 96 10 6
2012–13 Hannover 96 28 12
2013–14 Hannover 96 19 8 **57 26**
2014–15 Stoke C 34 11
2015–16 Stoke C 26 5
2016–17 Stoke C 27 1
2017–18 Stoke C 35 6
2018–19 Stoke C 14 0
2019–20 Stoke C 8 1 **144 24**

EDWARDS, Thomas (D) 46 1
b. 22-1-99
Internationals: England U20.
2016–17 Stoke C 0 0
2017–18 Stoke C 6 0
2018–19 Stoke C 27 1
2019–20 Stoke C 13 0 **46 1**

ETEBO, Peter (F) 114 10
H: 5 8 W: 11 00 b.Lagos 9-11-95
Internationals: Nigeria U23, Full caps.
From Warri Wolves.
2015–16 Feirense 4 1
2016–17 Feirense 23 2
2017–18 Feirense 18 4 **45 7**
2017–18 *Las Palmas* 14 0 **14 0**
2018–19 Stoke C 34 2
2019–20 Stoke C 11 0 **45 2**
2019–20 *Getafe* 10 1 **10 1**

FEDERICI, Adam (G) 235 1
H: 6 2 W: 14 02 b.Nowra 31-1-85
Internationals: Australia U20, U23, Full caps.
2005–06 Reading 0 0
2006–07 Reading 2 0
2007–08 Reading 0 0
2008–09 Reading 15 1
2008–09 *Southend U* 10 0 **10 0**
2009–10 Reading 46 0
2010–11 Reading 34 0
2011–12 Reading 46 0
2012–13 Reading 21 0
2013–14 Reading 2 0
2014–15 Reading 43 0 **209 1**
2015–16 Bournemouth 6 0
2016–17 Bournemouth 2 0
2017–18 Bournemouth 0 0 **8 0**
2017–18 *Nottingham F* 0 0
2018–19 Stoke C 1 0
2019–20 Stoke C 7 0 **8 0**

GREGORY, Lee (F) 244 70
H: 6 2 b.Sheffield 26-8-88
2014–15 Millwall 39 9
2015–16 Millwall 41 18
2016–17 Millwall 37 17
2017–18 Millwall 43 10
2018–19 Millwall 44 10 **204 64**
2019–20 Stoke C 40 6 **40 6**

INCE, Tom (M) 341 82
H: 5 10 W: 10 06 b.Stockport 30-1-92
Internationals: England U17, U19, U21.
2009–10 Liverpool 0 0
2010–11 Liverpool 0 0
2010–11 *Notts Co* 6 2 **6 2**
2011–12 Blackpool 33 6
2012–13 Blackpool 44 18
2013–14 Blackpool 23 7 **100 31**
2013–14 *Crystal Palace* 8 1 **8 1**
2014–15 Hull C 7 0 **7 0**
2014–15 *Nottingham F* 6 0 **6 0**
2014–15 *Derby Co* 18 11
2015–16 Derby Co 42 12
2016–17 Derby Co 45 14 **105 37**
2017–18 Huddersfield T 33 2 **33 2**
2018–19 Stoke C 38 6
2019–20 Stoke C 38 3 **76 9**

LINDSAY, Liam (D) 190 11
H: 6 4 W: 12 07 b.Paisley 12-10-95
2012–13 Partick Thistle 1 0
2013–14 *Alloa Ath* 10 0 **10 0**
2013–14 Partick Thistle 1 0
2014–15 Partick Thistle 1 0
2014–15 Airdrieonians 13 1 **13 1**
2015–16 Partick Thistle 25 1
2016–17 Partick Thistle 36 6 **64 7**
2017–18 Barnsley 42 1
2018–19 Barnsley 41 1 **83 2**
2019–20 Stoke C 20 1 **20 1**

MARTINS INDI, Bruno (D) 271 9
H: 6 1 W: 11 09 b.Barreiro, Portugal 8-2-92
Internationals: Netherlands U17, U19, U21, Full caps.
2010–11 Feyenoord 15 1
2011–12 Feyenoord 29 1
2012–13 Feyenoord 32 1
2013–14 Feyenoord 26 2 **102 5**
2014–15 Porto 24 2
2015–16 Porto 23 0
2016–17 Porto 0 0 **47 2**
2016–17 *Stoke C* 35 1
2017–18 Stoke C 17 0
2018–19 Stoke C 37 1
2019–20 Stoke C 33 0 **122 2**

McCLEAN, James (M) 382 48
H: 5 11 W: 11 00 b.Derry 22-4-89
Internationals: Northern Ireland U21. Republic of Ireland Full caps.
2009 Derry C 27 1
2010 Derry C 30 10
2011 Derry C 16 7 **73 18**
2011–12 Sunderland 23 5

2012–13 Sunderland 36 2
2013–14 Sunderland 0 0 **59 7**
2013–14 Wigan Ath 37 3
2014–15 Wigan Ath 36 6 **73 9**
2015–16 WBA 35 2
2016–17 WBA 34 1
2017–18 WBA 30 1 **99 4**
2018–19 Stoke C 42 3
2019–20 Stoke C 36 7 **78 10**

McJANNAETT, Cameron (D) 0 0
b.Milton Keynes 6-9-98
From Luton T.
2019–20 Stoke C 0 0

NDIAYE, Papa Badou (M) 245 52
H: 5 10 W: 10 10 b.Dakar 27-10-90
Internationals: Senegal Full caps.
2012 Bodo/Glimt 29 3
2013 Bodo/Glimt 27 12
2014 Bodo/Glimt 30 9
2015 Bodo/Glimt 16 4 **102 28**
2015–16 Osmanlispor 33 11
2016–17 Osmanlispor 26 6 **59 17**
2017–18 Galatasaray 17 1
2017–18 Stoke C 13 2
2018–19 Stoke C 1 0
2018–19 *Galatasaray* 23 3 **40 4**
2019–20 Stoke C 13 0 **27 2**
2019–20 *Trabzonspor* 17 1 **17 1**

NGOY, Julien (F) 42 8
H: 6 1 W: 10 01 b.Antwerp 2-11-97
Internationals: Belgium U16, U17, U21.
2016–17 Stoke C 5 0
2017–18 Stoke C 1 0
2017–18 *Walsall* 13 3 **13 3**
2018–19 Stoke C 0 0
2019–20 Stoke C 1 0 **7 0**
2019–20 *Grasshopper* 22 5 **22 5**

NNA NOUKEU, Blondy (G) 0 0
b. 17-9-01
2019–20 Stoke C 0 0

OAKLEY-BOOTHE, Tashan (M) 2 0
H: 5 10 W: 11 00 b.Lambeth 14-2-00
Internationals: England U16, U17, U18.
2017–18 Tottenham H 0 0
2018–19 Tottenham H 0 0
2019–20 Tottenham H 0 0
2019–20 Stoke C 2 0 **2 0**

PORTER, Adam (M) 0 0
2019–20 Stoke C 0 0

POWELL, Nick (F) 216 56
H: 6 0 W: 10 05 b.Crewe 23-3-94
Internationals: England U16, U17, U18, U19, U21.
2010–11 Crewe Alex 17 0
2011–12 Crewe Alex 38 14 **55 14**
2012–13 Manchester U 2 1
2013–14 Manchester U 0 0
2013–14 *Wigan Ath* 31 7
2014–15 Manchester U 0 0
2014–15 *Leicester C* 3 0 **3 0**
2015–16 Manchester U 1 0 **3 1**
2015–16 *Hull C* 3 0 **3 0**
2016–17 Wigan Ath 21 6
2017–18 Wigan Ath 39 15
2018–19 Wigan Ath 32 8 **123 36**
2019–20 Stoke C 29 5 **29 5**

SHAWCROSS, Ryan (D) 400 22
H: 6 3 W: 13 13 b.Buckley 4-10-87
Internationals: England U21, Full caps.
2006–07 Manchester U 0 0
2007–08 Manchester U 0 0
2007–08 Stoke C 41 7
2008–09 Stoke C 30 3
2009–10 Stoke C 28 2
2010–11 Stoke C 36 1
2011–12 Stoke C 36 2
2012–13 Stoke C 37 1
2013–14 Stoke C 37 1
2014–15 Stoke C 32 2
2015–16 Stoke C 20 0
2016–17 Stoke C 35 1
2017–18 Stoke C 27 1
2018–19 Stoke C 36 1
2019–20 Stoke C 5 0 **400 22**

SMITH, Tommy (D) 212 4
H: 6 1 W: 13 02 b.Warrington 14-4-92
2012–13 Huddersfield T 0 0
2013–14 Huddersfield T 24 0
2014–15 Huddersfield T 41 0
2015–16 Huddersfield T 36 0
2016–17 Huddersfield T 42 4
2017–18 Huddersfield T 24 0
2018–19 Huddersfield T 15 0 **182 4**
2019–20 Stoke C 30 0 **30 0**

SORENSON, Lasse (M) 8 0
b. 21-10-99
From Esbjerg.
2017–18 Stoke C 1 0
2018–19 Stoke C 1 0
2019–20 Stoke C 6 0 **8 0**

SOUTAR, Harry (D) 60 5
H: 6 6 W: 12 08 b.Aberdeen 22-6-98
Internationals: Scotland U17, U19. Australia U23, Full caps.
2015–16 Dundee U 2 1
2016–17 Dundee U 0 0 **2 1**
2016–17 Stoke C 0 0
2017–18 Stoke C 0 0
2017–18 *Ross Co* 13 0 **13 0**
2018–19 Stoke C 0 0
2018–19 *Fleetwood T* 11 1
2019–20 Stoke C 0 0
2019–20 *Fleetwood T* 34 3 **45 4**

THOMPSON, Jordan (M) 120 6
H: 5 9 W: 10 03 b.Belfast 3-1-97
Internationals: Northern Ireland U17, U19, U21, Full caps.
2015–16 Rangers 2 0
2015–16 *Airdrieonians* 7 1 **7 1**
2016–17 Rangers 0 0
2016–17 *Raith R* 29 1 **29 1**
2017–18 Rangers 0 0 **2 0**
2017–18 *Livingston* 11 0 **11 0**
2018–19 Blackpool 38 3
2019–20 Blackpool 18 1 **56 4**
2019–20 Stoke C 15 0 **15 0**

TYMON, Josh (D) 20 0
b. 22-5-99
Internationals: England U17, U18, U19, U20.
2015–16 Hull C 0 0
2016–17 Hull C 5 0 **5 0**
2017–18 Stoke C 3 0
2017–18 *Milton Keynes D* 9 0 **9 0**
2018–19 Stoke C 1 0
2019–20 *Famalicao* 0 0
2019–20 Stoke C 2 0 **6 0**

VERLINDEN, Thibaud (M) 25 3
b. 9-7-99
Internationals: Belgium U16, U17, U19.
From Club Bruges.
2016–17 Stoke C 0 0
2017–18 Stoke C 0 0
2017–18 *St Pauli* 0 0
2018–19 Stoke C 5 0
2019–20 Stoke C 5 0 **10 0**
2019–20 *Bolton W* 15 3 **15 3**

VOKES, Sam (F) 421 94
H: 6 1 W: 13 10 b.Lymington 21-10-89
Internationals: Wales U21, Full caps.
2006–07 Bournemouth 13 4
2007–08 Bournemouth 41 12 **54 16**
2008–09 Wolverhampton W 36 6
2009–10 Wolverhampton W 5 0
2009–10 *Leeds U* 8 1 **8 1**
2010–11 Wolverhampton W 2 0
2010–11 *Bristol C* 1 0 **1 0**
2010–11 *Sheffield U* 6 1 **6 1**
2010–11 *Norwich C* 4 1 **4 1**
2011–12 Wolverhampton W 4 0
2011–12 *Burnley* 9 2
2011–12 *Brighton & HA* 14 3 **14 3**
2012–13 Wolverhampton W 0 0 **47 6**
2012–13 Burnley 46 4
2013–14 Burnley 39 20
2014–15 Burnley 15 0
2015–16 Burnley 43 15
2016–17 Burnley 37 10
2017–18 Burnley 30 4
2018–19 Burnley 20 3 **239 58**
2018–19 Stoke C 12 3
2019–20 Stoke C 36 5 **48 8**

WARD, Stephen (D) 454 27
H: 5 11 W: 12 02 b.Dublin 20-8-85
Internationals: Republic of Ireland U20, U21, B, Full caps.
2003 Bohemians 6 0
2004 Bohemians 16 2
2005 Bohemians 29 7
2006 Bohemians 21 2 **72 11**
2006–07 Wolverhampton W 18 3
2007–08 Wolverhampton W 29 0
2008–09 Wolverhampton W 42 0
2009–10 Wolverhampton W 22 0
2010–11 Wolverhampton W 34 1
2011–12 Wolverhampton W 38 3
2012–13 Wolverhampton W 39 2
2013–14 Wolverhampton W 0 0 **222 9**
2013–14 *Brighton & HA* 44 4 **44 4**
2014–15 Burnley 9 0
2015–16 Burnley 24 1
2016–17 Burnley 37 1
2017–18 Burnley 28 1
2018–19 Burnley 3 0 **101 3**
2019–20 Stoke C 15 0 **15 0**

WIMMER, Kevin (D) 166 6
H: 6 2 W: 13 05 b.Wels 15-11-92
Internationals: Austria U18, U21, Full caps.
2011–12 LASK Linkz 28 4 **28 4**
2012–13 Cologne 9 0
2013–14 Cologne 26 2
2014–15 Cologne 32 0 **67 2**
2015–16 Tottenham H 10 0
2016–17 Tottenham H 5 0
2017–18 Tottenham H 0 0 **15 0**
2017–18 Stoke C 17 0
2018–19 Stoke C 0 0
2018–19 *Hannover 96* 22 0 **22 0**
2019–20 Stoke C 0 0 **17 0**
2019–20 *Excel Mouscron* 17 0 **17 0**

WOODS, Ryan (M) 266 4
H: 5 8 W: 13 01 b.Norton Canes 13-12-93
2012–13 Shrewsbury T 2 0
2013–14 Shrewsbury T 41 1
2014–15 Shrewsbury T 43 0
2015–16 Shrewsbury T 5 0 **91 1**
2015–16 Brentford 41 2
2016–17 Brentford 42 0
2017–18 Brentford 39 1
2018–19 Brentford 0 0 **122 3**
2018–19 Stoke C 27 0
2019–20 Stoke C 8 0 **35 0**
2019–20 *Millwall* 18 0 **18 0**

Players retained or with offer of contract
Corrigan, Ryan Michael; Forrester, William Samuel; Kyeremateng, Gabriel.

Scholars
Akandji, Mohamed; Broome, Nathan Lee; Coates, Kieran David Tyler; Cooper, Paul Oyemwinmina; Doucoure, Ibrahima; Fernandes, Kevin; Godfrinne, Andre Marie Paul; Jarrett, Patrick Daniel; Jones, Edward Thomas; Jones, Reece Edward; Macari, Lewis Jon; Malone, Daniel Eric; Melbourne, Jamie; Nash, Henry George; Ndene, Julius Kimathi; Nixon, Thomas George Joseph; O'Driscoll, Varian Ethon Sean; Porter, Adam Matthew; Sanali, Soiyir; Sparrow, Thomas Lance; Taylor, Connor; Verma, Jai.

SUNDERLAND (80)

BAINBRIDGE, Jack (D) 0 0
b.Southport 21-5-98
2018–19 Sunderland 0 0
2019–20 Sunderland 0 0

BALDWIN, Jack (D) 224 12
H: 6 1 W: 11 00 b.Barking 30-6-93
2011–12 Hartlepool U 17 0
2012–13 Hartlepool U 32 2
2013–14 Hartlepool U 28 2 **77 4**
2013–14 Peterborough U 11 0
2014–15 Peterborough U 11 0
2015–16 Peterborough U 18 1
2016–17 Peterborough U 27 1
2017–18 Peterborough U 33 2 **100 4**
2018–19 Sunderland 34 3
2019–20 Sunderland 0 0 **34 3**
2019–20 *Salford C* 13 1 **13 1**

BURGE, Lee (G) 145 0
H: 5 11 W: 11 00 b.Hereford 9-1-93
2011–12 Coventry C 0 0
2012–13 Coventry C 0 0
2013–14 Coventry C 0 0
2014–15 Coventry C 18 0
2015–16 Coventry C 9 0
2016–17 Coventry C 33 0
2017–18 Coventry C 40 0
2018–19 Coventry C 40 0 **140 0**
2019–20 Sunderland 5 0 **5 0**

CONNELLY, Lee (F) 4 1
b. 18-10-99
Internationals: Scotland U16, U17.
2018–19 Sunderland 0 0
2019–20 Sunderland 0 0
2019–20 *Alloa Ath* 4 1 **4 1**

DIAMOND, Jack (F) **0 0**
b.Gateshead 12-1-00

2018–19	Sunderland	0	0		
2019–20	Sunderland	0	0		

DOBSON, George (M) **115 2**
H: 6 1 b.Harold Wood 15-11-97
From Arsenal.

2015–16	West Ham U	0	0		
2016–17	West Ham U	0	0		
2016–17	*Walsall*	21	1		
2017–18	Sparta Rotterdam	5	0	**5**	**0**
2017–18	Walsall	21	1		
2018–19	Walsall	39	0	**81**	**2**
2019–20	Sunderland	29	0	**29**	**0**

EMBLETON, Elliot (M) **32 3**
H: 5 8 W: 10 01 b. 2-4-99
Internationals: England U17, U18, U19, U20.

2016–17	Sunderland	0	0		
2017–18	Sunderland	2	0		
2018–19	Sunderland	0	0		
2018–19	*Grimsby T*	27	3	**27**	**3**
2019–20	Sunderland	3	0	**5**	**0**

FLANAGAN, Tom (D) **190 9**
H: 6 2 W: 11 05 b.Hammersmith 21-10-91
Internationals: Northern Ireland U21, Full caps.

2009–10	Milton Keynes D	1	0		
2010–11	Milton Keynes D	2	0		
2011–12	Milton Keynes D	21	3		
2012–13	Milton Keynes D	0	0		
2012–13	*Gillingham*	13	1	**13**	**1**
2012–13	*Barnet*	9	0	**9**	**0**
2013–14	Milton Keynes D	7	0		
2013–14	*Stevenage*	2	0	**2**	**0**
2014–15	Milton Keynes D	6	0	**37**	**3**
2014–15	*Plymouth Arg*	4	0	**4**	**0**
2015–16	Burton Alb	18	0		
2016–17	Burton Alb	30	0		
2017–18	Burton Alb	27	2	**75**	**2**
2018–19	Sunderland	32	2		
2019–20	Sunderland	18	1	**50**	**3**

GAMBLE, Owen (M) **0 0**

2017–18	Sunderland	0	0		
2018–19	Sunderland	0	0		
2019–20	Sunderland	0	0		

GOOCH, Lynden (M) **114 16**
H: 5 8 W: 10 12 b.Santa Cruz 24-12-95
Internationals: Republic of Ireland U18. USA U20, Full caps.

2015–16	Sunderland	0	0		
2015–16	*Doncaster R*	10	0	**10**	**0**
2016–17	Sunderland	11	0		
2017–18	Sunderland	24	1		
2018–19	Sunderland	39	5		
2019–20	Sunderland	30	10	**104**	**16**

GRIGG, Will (M) **348 110**
H: 5 11 W: 11 00 b.Solihull 3-7-91
Internationals: Northern Ireland U19, U21, Full caps.

2008–09	Walsall	1	0		
2009–10	Walsall	0	0		
2010–11	Walsall	28	4		
2011–12	Walsall	29	4		
2012–13	Walsall	41	19	**99**	**27**
2013–14	Brentford	34	5		
2014–15	Brentford	0	0	**34**	**5**
2014–15	*Milton Keynes D*	44	20	**44**	**20**
2015–16	Wigan Ath	40	25		
2016–17	Wigan Ath	33	5		
2017–18	Wigan Ath	43	19		
2018–19	Wigan Ath	17	4	**133**	**53**
2018–19	Sunderland	18	4		
2019–20	Sunderland	20	1	**38**	**5**

HACKETT, Jake (M) **0 0**
b.Durham 10-1-00

2018–19	Sunderland	0	0		
2019–20	Sunderland	0	0		

HUME, Denver (D) **41 1**
b. 11-8-96

2017–18	Sunderland	1	0		
2018–19	Sunderland	8	0		
2019–20	Sunderland	32	1	**41**	**1**

HUNTER, Jordan (M) **0 0**
b.Garstang 6-12-99
From Liverpool.

2018–19	Sunderland	0	0		
2019–20	Sunderland	0	0		

LAFFERTY, Kyle (F) **345 72**
H: 6 4 W: 11 00 b.Northern Ireland 16-9-87
Internationals: Northern Ireland U17, U19, U21, Full caps.

2005–06	Burnley	11	1		
2005–06	*Darlington*	9	3	**9**	**3**
2006–07	Burnley	35	4		
2007–08	Burnley	37	5	**83**	**10**
2008–09	Rangers	25	6		
2009–10	Rangers	28	7		
2010–11	Rangers	31	11		
2011–12	Rangers	20	7		
2012–13	Sion	25	5	**25**	**5**
2013–14	Palermo	34	11	**34**	**11**
2014–15	Norwich C	18	1		
2014–15	*Caykur Rizespor*	14	2	**14**	**2**
2015–16	Norwich C	1	0		
2015–16	*Birmingham C*	6	1	**6**	**1**
2016–17	Norwich C	12	1	**31**	**2**
2017–18	Hearts	35	12		
2018–19	Hearts	2	1		
2019–20	Rangers	19	4	**123**	**35**
2019–20	Sarpsborg 08	9	1	**9**	**1**
2019–20	Sunderland	11	2	**11**	**2**

LEADBITTER, Grant (M) **473 53**
H: 5 9 W: 11 06 b.Chester-le-Street 7-1-86
Internationals: England U16, U17, U19, U20, U21.

2002–03	Sunderland	0	0		
2003–04	Sunderland	0	0		
2004–05	Sunderland	0	0		
2005–06	Sunderland	12	0		
2005–06	*Rotherham U*	5	1	**5**	**1**
2006–07	Sunderland	44	7		
2007–08	Sunderland	31	2		
2008–09	Sunderland	23	2		
2009–10	Sunderland	1	0		
2009–10	Ipswich T	38	3		
2010–11	Ipswich T	44	5		
2011–12	Ipswich T	34	5		
2012–13	Ipswich T	0	0	**116**	**13**
2012–13	Middlesbrough	42	3		
2013–14	Middlesbrough	39	6		
2014–15	Middlesbrough	43	11		
2015–16	Middlesbrough	41	4		
2016–17	Middlesbrough	13	1		
2017–18	Middlesbrough	32	3		
2018–19	Middlesbrough	2	0	**212**	**28**
2018–19	Sunderland	15	0		
2019–20	Sunderland	14	0	**140**	**11**

LYNCH, Joel (D) **387 20**
H: 6 1 W: 12 10 b.Eastbourne 3-10-87
Internationals: England Youth. Wales Full caps.

2005–06	Brighton & HA	16	1		
2006–07	Brighton & HA	39	0		
2007–08	Brighton & HA	22	1		
2008–09	Brighton & HA	2	0	**79**	**2**
2008–09	*Nottingham F*	23	0		
2009–10	Nottingham F	10	0		
2010–11	Nottingham F	12	0		
2011–12	Nottingham F	35	3	**80**	**3**
2012–13	Huddersfield T	22	1		
2013–14	Huddersfield T	29	2		
2014–15	Huddersfield T	34	3		
2015–16	Huddersfield T	37	2	**122**	**8**
2016–17	QPR	30	3		
2017–18	QPR	25	1		
2018–19	QPR	35	3	**90**	**7**
2019–20	Sunderland	16	0	**16**	**0**

MAGUIRE, Chris (F) **414 80**
H: 5 7 W: 10 05 b.Bellshill 16-1-89
Internationals: Scotland U16, U19, U21, Full caps.

2005–06	Aberdeen	1	0		
2006–07	Aberdeen	19	1		
2007–08	Aberdeen	28	4		
2008–09	Aberdeen	31	3		
2009–10	Aberdeen	17	1		
2009–10	*Kilmarnock*	14	4	**14**	**4**
2010–11	Aberdeen	35	7	**131**	**16**
2011–12	Derby Co	7	1	**7**	**1**
2011–12	*Portsmouth*	11	3	**11**	**3**
2012–13	Sheffield W	10	1		
2013–14	Sheffield W	27	9		
2013–14	*Coventry C*	3	2	**3**	**2**
2014–15	Sheffield W	42	8	**79**	**18**
2015–16	Rotherham U	14	0	**14**	**0**
2015–16	Oxford U	21	4		
2016–17	Oxford U	42	13	**63**	**17**
2017–18	Bury	24	2	**24**	**2**
2018–19	Sunderland	33	7		
2019–20	Sunderland	35	10	**68**	**17**

McGEADY, Aiden (M) **430 74**
H: 5 10 W: 11 03 b.Glasgow 4-4-86
Internationals: Republic of Ireland Full caps.

2003–04	Celtic	4	1		
2004–05	Celtic	27	4		
2005–06	Celtic	20	4		
2006–07	Celtic	34	5		
2007–08	Celtic	36	7		
2008–09	Celtic	29	3		
2009–10	Celtic	35	7	**185**	**31**
2010–11	Spartak Moscow	11	2		
2011–12	Spartak Moscow	31	3		
2012–13	Spartak Moscow	17	5		
2013–14	Spartak Moscow	13	1	**72**	**11**
2013–14	Everton	16	0		
2014–15	Everton	16	1		
2015–16	Everton	0	0		
2015–16	*Sheffield W*	13	1	**13**	**1**
2016–17	Everton	0	0	**32**	**1**
2016–17	*Preston NE*	34	8	**34**	**8**
2017–18	Sunderland	35	7		
2018–19	Sunderland	34	11		
2019–20	Sunderland	15	4	**84**	**22**
2019–20	*Charlton Ath*	10	0	**10**	**0**

McGEOUCH, Dylan (M) **131 2**
H: 5 10 W: 10 11 b.Glasgow 15-1-93
Internationals: Scotland U16, U17, U19, U21, Full caps.

2011–12	Celtic	6	1		
2012–13	Celtic	12	1		
2013–14	Celtic	1	0	**19**	**2**
2013–14	*Coventry C*	8	0	**8**	**0**
2014–15	Hibernian	2	0		
2015–16	Hibernian	19	0		
2016–17	Hibernian	18	0		
2017–18	Hibernian	35	0	**74**	**0**
2018–19	Sunderland	22	0		
2019–20	Sunderland	8	0	**30**	**0**

Transferred to Aberdeen, January 2020.

McLAUGHLIN, Conor (D) **247 8**
H: 6 0 W: 11 02 b.Belfast 26-7-91
Internationals: Northern Ireland U21, Full caps.

2009–10	Preston NE	0	0		
2010–11	Preston NE	7	0		
2011–12	Preston NE	17	0	**24**	**0**
2011–12	*Shrewsbury T*	4	0	**4**	**0**
2012–13	Fleetwood T	19	0		
2013–14	Fleetwood T	35	0		
2014–15	Fleetwood T	39	1		
2015–16	Fleetwood T	37	2		
2016–17	Fleetwood T	42	4	**172**	**7**
2017–18	Millwall	24	1		
2018–19	Millwall	8	0	**32**	**1**
2019–20	Sunderland	15	0	**15**	**0**

McLAUGHLIN, Jon (G) **369 0**
H: 6 2 W: 13 00 b.Edinburgh 9-9-87
Internationals: Scotland Full caps.

2008–09	Bradford C	1	0		
2009–10	Bradford C	7	0		
2010–11	Bradford C	25	0		
2011–12	Bradford C	23	0		
2012–13	Bradford C	23	0		
2013–14	Bradford C	46	0	**125**	**0**
2014–15	Burton Alb	45	0		
2015–16	Burton Alb	45	0		
2016–17	Burton Alb	43	0	**133**	**0**
2017–18	Hearts	33	0	**33**	**0**
2018–19	Sunderland	46	0		
2019–20	Sunderland	32	0	**78**	**0**

MGUNGA-KIMPIOKA, Benjamin (M) **8 1**
b. 21-2-00
Internationals: Sweden U19, U21.
From IK Sirius.

2018–19	Sunderland	4	0		
2019–20	Sunderland	4	1	**8**	**1**

MUMBA, Bali (F) **5 0**
b. 8-10-01
Internationals: England U16, U17, U18, U19.

2017–18	Sunderland	1	0		
2018–19	Sunderland	4	0		
2019–20	Sunderland	0	0	**5**	**0**

NEILL, Daniel (M) **0 0**

2018–19	Sunderland	0	0		
2019–20	Sunderland	0	0		

O'NIEN, Luke (M) **174 24**
b. 21-11-94

2013–14	Watford	1	0		
2014–15	Watford	0	0	**1**	**0**
2015–16	Wycombe W	35	5		
2016–17	Wycombe W	31	3		
2017–18	Wycombe W	35	7	**101**	**15**

2018–19 Sunderland 37 5
2019–20 Sunderland 35 4 **72 9**

OZTURK, Alim (D) 165 8
H: 6 3 W: 13 05 b.Alkmaar 17-11-92
Internationals: Turkey U21.
2010–11 Cambuur 0 0
2011–12 Cambuur 5 0
2012–13 Cambuur 8 0 **13 0**
2013–14 Trabzonspor 0 0
2013–14 *1461 Trabzon* 18 2 **18 2**
2014–15 Hearts 33 4
2015–16 Hearts 24 1
2016–17 Hearts 5 0 **62 5**
2016–17 Boluspur 20 1
2017–18 Boluspur 20 0 **40 1**
2018–19 Sunderland 10 0
2019–20 Sunderland 22 0 **32 0**

PATTERSON, Anthony (G) 0 0
b. 10-5-00
2018–19 Sunderland 0 0
2019–20 Sunderland 0 0

POWER, Max (M) 302 29
H: 5 11 W: 11 13 b.Bebington 27-7-93
2010–11 Tranmere R 0 0
2011–12 Tranmere R 4 0
2012–13 Tranmere R 27 3
2013–14 Tranmere R 33 2
2014–15 Tranmere R 45 7 **109 12**
2015–16 Wigan Ath 44 6
2016–17 Wigan Ath 42 0
2017–18 Wigan Ath 40 5
2018–19 Wigan Ath 1 0 **127 11**
2018–19 Sunderland 35 4
2019–20 Sunderland 31 2 **66 6**

ROBSON, Ethan (M) 38 5
H: 5 8 W: 10 12 b. 25-10-96
2016–17 Sunderland 0 0
2017–18 Sunderland 9 0
2018–19 Sunderland 0 0
2018–19 *Dundee* 13 2 **13 2**
2019–20 Sunderland 0 0 **9 0**
2019–20 *Grimsby T* 16 3 **16 3**

SAMMUT, Ruben (M) 12 0
b.Maidstone 26-9-97
Internationals: Scotland U16, U19, U20, U21.
2018–19 Chelsea 0 0
2018–19 *Falkirk* 12 0 **12 0**
2019–20 Sunderland 0 0

SCOWEN, Josh (M) 286 16
H: 5 10 W: 11 09 b.Cheshunt 28-3-93
2010–11 Wycombe W 2 0
2011–12 Wycombe W 0 0
2012–13 Wycombe W 34 1
2013–14 Wycombe W 37 1
2014–15 Wycombe W 18 1 **91 3**
2014–15 Barnsley 21 4
2015–16 Barnsley 34 4
2016–17 Barnsley 41 2 **96 10**
2017–18 QPR 42 1
2018–19 QPR 35 2
2019–20 QPR 18 0 **95 3**
2019–20 Sunderland 4 0 **4 0**

SMITH, Tommy (D) 321 28
H: 6 2 W: 12 02 b.Macclesfield 31-3-90
Internationals: England U17, U18. New Zealand Full caps.
2007–08 Ipswich T 0 0
2008–09 Ipswich T 2 0
2009–10 Ipswich T 14 0
2009–10 *Brentford* 8 0 **8 0**
2010–11 Ipswich T 22 3
2010–11 *Colchester U* 6 0 **6 0**
2011–12 Ipswich T 26 3
2012–13 Ipswich T 38 3
2013–14 Ipswich T 45 6
2014–15 Ipswich T 42 4
2015–16 Ipswich T 45 2
2016–17 Ipswich T 10 0
2017–18 Ipswich T 3 0 **247 21**
2018 Colorado Rapids 33 4
2019 Colorado Rapids 27 3 **60 7**
2019–20 Sunderland 0 0

TAYLOR, Brandon (D) 0 0
b.Gateshead 10-5-99
2018–19 Sunderland 0 0
2019–20 Sunderland 0 0

WATMORE, Duncan (F) 80 6
H: 5 9 W: 11 05 b.Cheadle Hulme 8-3-94
Internationals: England U20, U21.
2013–14 Sunderland 0 0
2013–14 *Hibernian* 9 1 **9 1**
2014–15 Sunderland 0 0
2015–16 Sunderland 23 3
2016–17 Sunderland 14 0
2017–18 Sunderland 6 0
2018–19 Sunderland 11 1
2019–20 Sunderland 17 1 **71 5**

WILLIS, Jordan (D) 214 6
H: 5 11 W: 11 00 b.Coventry 24-8-94
Internationals: England U18, U19.
2011–12 Coventry C 3 0
2012–13 Coventry C 1 0
2013–14 Coventry C 28 0
2014–15 Coventry C 34 0
2015–16 Coventry C 4 0
2016–17 Coventry C 36 3
2017–18 Coventry C 35 0
2018–19 Coventry C 38 1 **179 4**
2019–20 Sunderland 35 2 **35 2**

WYKE, Charlie (F) 239 71
b.Middlesbrough 6-12-92
2011–12 Middlesbrough 0 0
2012–13 Middlesbrough 0 0
2012–13 *Hartlepool U* 25 2
2013–14 Middlesbrough 0 0
2013–14 *AFC Wimbledon* 17 2 **17 2**
2014–15 Middlesbrough 0 0
2014–15 *Hartlepool U* 13 4 **38 6**
2014–15 Carlisle U 17 6
2015–16 Carlisle U 34 12
2016–17 Carlisle U 26 14 **77 32**
2016–17 Bradford C 16 7
2017–18 Bradford C 40 15 **56 22**
2018–19 Sunderland 24 4
2019–20 Sunderland 27 5 **51 9**

Players retained or with offer of contract
Dunne, Cieran James.

Scholars
Almond, Patrick Joseph; Armstrong, Jack William; Baggs, Joshua William; Basey, Oliver Paul; Bruce, Ryan; Cameron, Adam Stuart; Compper, Lilyan Christian; Dicicco, McKenzie Michael; Edmundsson, Andrias; Evans, Kane; Foster, James Henry; Gooch, Ryan; Jones, Daniel Alan; Kiernan, Cole David; Krakue, Jonathan Kojo; Leonard, Ryan John; Miller, Liam Ian; Neil, Daniel; Newman, Jack Callum; Ord, Harry; Slack, Connor James; Smith, Thomas; Taylor, Ellis James; Watts, Louis Jake; Wombwell, Ryan Robert.

SWANSEA C (81)

ASORO, Joel (F) 56 6
H: 5 9 W: 11 11 b. 27-4-99
Internationals: Sweden U17, U21.
2016–17 Sunderland 1 0
2017–18 Sunderland 26 3 **27 3**
2018–19 Swansea C 14 0
2019–20 Swansea C 0 0 **14 0**
2019–20 *Groningen* 15 3 **15 3**

AYEW, Andre (F) 162 41
H: 5 9 W: 11 05 b.Seclin 17-12-89
Internationals: Ghana U20, Full caps.
2015–16 Swansea C 34 12
2016–17 West Ham U 25 6
2017–18 West Ham U 18 3 **43 9**
2017–18 Swansea C 12 0
2018–19 Swansea C 0 0
2018–19 *Fenerbahce* 29 5 **29 5**
2019–20 Swansea C 44 15 **90 27**

BAKER-RICHARDSON, Courtney (F) 19 3
H: 6 1 W: 11 07 b.Coventry 5-12-95
2013–14 Coventry C 0 0
2014–15 Coventry C 0 0
From Tamworth, Nuneaton T, Redditch U, Kettering T, Leamington.
2017–18 Swansea C 0 0
2018–19 Swansea C 17 3
2019–20 Swansea C 0 0 **17 3**
2019–20 *Accrington S* 2 0 **2 0**

BENDA, Steven (G) 24 0
H: 6 4 W: 13 01 b.Stuttgart 1-1-98
From Aalen, Heidenheim, TSV 1860.
2018–19 Swansea C 0 0
2019–20 Swansea C 0 0
2019–20 *Swindon T* 24 0 **24 0**

BIDWELL, Jake (D) 349 5
H: 6 0 W: 11 00 b.Southport 21-3-93
Internationals: England U16, U17, U18, U19.
2009–10 Everton 0 0
2010–11 Everton 0 0
2011–12 Everton 0 0
2011–12 *Brentford* 24 0
2012–13 Everton 0 0
2012–13 *Brentford* 40 0
2013–14 Brentford 38 0
2014–15 Brentford 43 0
2015–16 Brentford 45 3 **190 3**
2016–17 QPR 36 0
2017–18 QPR 46 2
2018–19 QPR 40 0 **122 2**
2019–20 Swansea C 37 0 **37 0**

BYERS, George (M) 57 4
H: 5 11 W: 11 07 b.Ilford 29-5-96
Internationals: Scotland U16, U17.
2014–15 Watford 1 0
2015–16 Watford 0 0 **1 0**
2016–17 Swansea C 0 0
2017–18 Swansea C 0 0
2018–19 Swansea C 21 2
2019–20 Swansea C 35 2 **56 4**

CABANGO, Ben (D) 21 1
b.Cardiff 30-5-00
Internationals: Wales U17, U19, U21.
2018–19 Swansea C 0 0
2019–20 Swansea C 21 1 **21 1**

CARROLL, Tommy (M) 166 3
H: 5 10 W: 10 00 b.Watford 28-5-92
Internationals: England U19, U21.
2010–11 Tottenham H 0 0
2010–11 *Leyton Orient* 12 0 **12 0**
2011–12 Tottenham H 0 0
2011–12 *Derby Co* 12 1 **12 1**
2012–13 Tottenham H 7 0
2013–14 Tottenham H 0 0
2013–14 *QPR* 26 0 **26 0**
2014–15 Tottenham H 0 0
2014–15 *Swansea C* 13 0
2015–16 Tottenham H 19 1
2016–17 Tottenham H 1 0 **27 1**
2016–17 Swansea C 17 1
2017–18 Swansea C 37 0
2018–19 Swansea C 12 0
2018–19 *Aston Villa* 2 0 **2 0**
2019–20 Swansea C 8 0 **87 1**

CELINA, Bersant (F) 136 19
H: 5 4 W: 9 06 b.Prizren 9-9-96
Internationals: Norway U16, U17. Kosovo Full caps.
2014–15 Manchester C 0 0
2015–16 Manchester C 1 0
2016–17 Manchester C 0 0
2016–17 *FC Twente* 27 5 **27 5**
2017–18 Manchester C 0 0 **1 0**
2017–18 *Ipswich T* 35 7 **35 7**
2018–19 Swansea C 38 5
2019–20 Swansea C 35 2 **73 7**

COOPER, Brandon (D) 0 0
b.Bridgend 14-1-00
Internationals: Wales U21.
2018–19 Swansea C 0 0
2019–20 Swansea C 0 0

CULLEN, Liam (F) 6 1
b.Tenby 23-4-99
Internationals: Wales U16, U17, U19, U20, U21.
2018–19 Swansea C 0 0
2019–20 Swansea C 6 1 **6 1**

DE BOER, Kees (M) 0 0
b.Volendam 13-5-00
From Ajax.
2019–20 Swansea C 0 0

DHANDA, Yan (F) 21 4
H: 5 8 W: 10 03 b.Birmingham 14-12-98
Internationals: England U16, U17.
From Liverpool.
2018–19 Swansea C 5 1
2019–20 Swansea C 16 3 **21 4**

DYER, Nathan (M) 378 31
H: 5 5 W: 9 00 b.Trowbridge 29-11-87
2005–06 Southampton 17 0
2005–06 *Burnley* 5 2 **5 2**
2006–07 Southampton 18 0
2007–08 Southampton 17 1
2008–09 Southampton 4 0 **56 1**
2008–09 *Sheffield U* 7 1 **7 1**
2008–09 *Swansea C* 17 2
2009–10 Swansea C 40 2
2010–11 Swansea C 46 2
2011–12 Swansea C 34 5
2012–13 Swansea C 37 3
2013–14 Swansea C 27 6

2014–15 Swansea C 32 3
2015–16 Swansea C 1 0
2015–16 *Leicester C* 12 1 **12 1**
2016–17 Swansea C 8 0
2017–18 Swansea C 24 0
2018–19 Swansea C 22 2
2019–20 Swansea C 10 1 **298 26**

EVANS, Cameron James (D) 0 0
Internationals: Wales U17, U19.
2019–20 Swansea C 0 0

EVANS, Jack (M) 0 0
b.Swansea 25-4-98
Internationals: Wales U19, U20, U21.
2019–20 Swansea C 0 0
2019–20 *Mansfield T* 0 0

FULTON, Jay (M) 104 6
H: 5 10 W: 10 08 b.Bolton 4-4-94
Internationals: Scotland U18, U19, U21.
2013–14 Swansea C 2 0
2014–15 Swansea C 2 0
2015–16 Swansea C 2 0
2015–16 *Oldham Ath* 11 0 **11 0**
2016–17 Swansea C 11 0
2017–18 Swansea C 2 0
2017–18 *Wigan Ath* 5 1 **5 1**
2018–19 Swansea C 33 2
2019–20 Swansea C 36 3 **88 5**

GARRICK, Jordan (F) 11 2
b. 15-7-98
2019–20 Swansea C 11 2 **11 2**

GOULD, Joshua (G) 0 0
2019–20 Swansea C 0 0

GRIMES, Matt (M) 217 10
H: 5 10 W: 11 00 b.Exeter 15-7-95
Internationals: England U20, U21.
2013–14 Exeter C 35 1
2014–15 Exeter C 23 4 **58 5**
2014–15 Swansea C 3 0
2015–16 Swansea C 1 0
2015–16 *Blackburn R* 13 0 **13 0**
2016–17 Swansea C 0 0
2016–17 *Leeds U* 7 0 **7 0**
2017–18 Swansea C 0 0
2017–18 *Northampton T* 44 4 **44 4**
2018–19 Swansea C 45 1
2019–20 Swansea C 46 0 **95 1**

JOHN, Declan (M) 100 3
H: 5 10 W: 11 10 b.Merthyr Tydfil 30-6-95
Internationals: Wales U17, U19, Full caps.
2010–11 Llanelli 1 0 **1 0**
2011–12 Afan Lido 5 0 **5 0**
2012–13 Cardiff C 0 0
2013–14 Cardiff C 20 0
2014–15 Cardiff C 6 0
2014–15 *Barnsley* 9 0 **9 0**
2015–16 Cardiff C 1 0
2015–16 *Chesterfield* 6 0 **6 0**
2016–17 Cardiff C 15 0
2017–18 Cardiff C 0 0 **42 0**
2017–18 Rangers 26 3 **26 3**
2018–19 Swansea C 10 0
2019–20 Swansea C 1 0 **11 0**
2019–20 *Sunderland* 0 0

KALULU, Aldo (F) 83 14
b.Lyon 21-1-96
Internationals: France U18.
2015–16 Lyon 10 2
2016–17 Lyon 4 1
2016–17 *Rennes* 10 0 **10 0**
2017–18 Lyon 0 0 **14 3**
2017–18 *Sochaux* 31 11 **31 11**
2018–19 Basel 17 0
2019–20 Basel 0 0 **17 0**
On loan from Basel.
2019–20 Swansea C 11 0 **11 0**

McKAY, Barrie (M) 212 25
H: 5 9 W: 11 00 b.Paisley 30-12-94
Internationals: Scotland U18, U19, U21, Full caps.
2011–12 Rangers 1 0
2012–13 Rangers 31 1
2013–14 Rangers 2 0
2013–14 *Greenock Morton* 18 3 **18 3**
2014–15 Rangers 0 0
2014–15 *Raith R* 23 1 **23 1**
2015–16 Rangers 34 6
2016–17 Rangers 35 5 **103 12**
2017–18 Nottingham F 26 5 **26 5**
2018–19 Swansea C 30 2
2019–20 Swansea C 4 0 **34 2**
2019–20 *Fleetwood T* 8 2 **8 2**

MONTERO, Jefferson (M) 280 35
H: 5 8 W: 11 00 b.Babahoyo 1-9-89
Internationals: Ecuador Full caps.
2007 Emelec 22 2
2008 Independiente de Valle 25 8
2008–09 *Dorados* 5 1 **5 1**
2009 Independiente de Valle 12 11 **37 19**
2010–11 Villareal 9 1
2010–11 *Levante* 11 0 **11 0**
2011–12 Villareal 0 0 **9 1**
2011–12 *Real Betis* 32 1 **32 1**
2012–13 Morelia 32 4
2013–14 Morelia 25 5 **57 9**
2014–15 Swansea C 30 1
2015–16 Swansea C 23 0
2016–17 Swansea C 13 0
2017–18 Swansea C 0 0
2017–18 *Getafe* 4 0 **4 0**
2017–18 *Emelec* 7 0 **29 2**
2018–19 Swansea C 12 0
2018–19 *WBA* 4 1 **4 1**
2019–20 Swansea C 0 0 **78 1**
2019–20 *Birmingham C* 14 0 **14 0**

MULDER, Erwin (G) 255 0
H: 6 4 W: 13 12 b.Zevenaar 3-3-89
Internationals: Netherlands B, U19, U20, U21.
2007–08 Feyenoord 1 0
2008–09 Feyenoord 0 0
2008–09 *Excelsior* 36 0 **36 0**
2009–10 Feyenoord 10 0
2010–11 Feyenoord 17 0
2011–12 Feyenoord 34 0
2012–13 Feyenoord 22 0
2013–14 Feyenoord 32 0
2014–15 Feyenoord 4 0 **120 0**
2015–16 Heerenveen 34 0
2016–17 Heerenveen 36 0
2017–18 Heerenveen 0 0 **70 0**
2017–18 Swansea C 0 0
2018–19 Swansea C 25 0
2019–20 Swansea C 4 0 **29 0**

NAUGHTON, Kyle (M) 350 11
H: 5 11 W: 11 07 b.Sheffield 11-11-88
Internationals: England U21.
2006–07 Sheffield U 0 0
2007–08 *Gretna* 18 0 **18 0**
2007–08 Sheffield U 0 0
2008–09 Sheffield U 40 1
2009–10 Sheffield U 0 0 **40 1**
2009–10 Tottenham H 1 0
2009–10 *Middlesbrough* 15 0 **15 0**
2010–11 Tottenham H 0 0
2010–11 *Leicester C* 34 5 **34 5**
2011–12 Tottenham H 0 0
2011–12 *Norwich C* 32 0 **32 0**
2012–13 Tottenham H 14 0
2013–14 Tottenham H 22 0
2014–15 Tottenham H 5 0 **42 0**
2014–15 Swansea C 10 0
2015–16 Swansea C 27 0
2016–17 Swansea C 31 1
2017–18 Swansea C 34 0
2018–19 Swansea C 35 1
2019–20 Swansea C 32 3 **169 5**

NORDFELDT, Kristoffer (G) 239 0
H: 6 3 W: 13 05 b.Stockholm 23-6-89
Internationals: Sweden U19, U21, Full caps.
2006 Brommapojkarna 0 0
2007 Brommapojkarna 0 0
2008 Brommapojkarna 29 0
2009 Brommapojkarna 21 0
2010 Brommapojkarna 25 0
2011 Brommapojkarna 28 0 **103 0**
2011–12 Heerenveen 6 0
2012–13 Heerenveen 33 0
2013–14 Heerenveen 35 0
2014–15 Heerenveen 38 0 **112 0**
2015–16 Swansea C 1 0
2016–17 Swansea C 1 0
2017–18 Swansea C 0 0
2018–19 Swansea C 22 0
2019–20 Swansea C 0 0 **24 0**
Transferred to Genclerbirligi, January 2020.

PETERSON, Kristoffer (M) 139 27
b.Gothenburg 28-11-94
Internationals: Sweden U17, U21, Full caps.
2011–12 Liverpool 0 0
2012–13 Liverpool 0 0
2013–14 Liverpool 0 0
2013–14 *Tranmere R* 6 0 **6 0**
2014–15 Utrecht 20 2
2015–16 Utrecht 7 0
2015–16 *Roda* 14 1 **14 1**
2016–17 Heracles 15 4
2017–18 Heracles 33 7
2018–19 Heracles 33 12 **81 23**
2019–20 Swansea C 7 0 **7 0**
2019–20 *Utrecht* 4 1 **31 3**

ROBERTS, Connor (D) 135 6
H: 5 9 W: 11 03 b.Neath 23-9-95
Internationals: Wales U19, U21, Full caps.
2014–15 Swansea C 0 0
2015–16 Swansea C 0 0
2015–16 *Yeovil T* 45 0 **45 0**
2016–17 Bristol R 2 0 **2 0**
2016–17 Swansea C 0 0
2017–18 Swansea C 4 0
2017–18 *Middlesbrough* 1 0 **1 0**
2018–19 Swansea C 45 5
2019–20 Swansea C 38 1 **87 6**

RODON, Joe (D) 60 0
b.Swansea 22-10-97
Internationals: Wales U20, U21, Full caps.
2015–16 Swansea C 0 0
2016–17 Swansea C 0 0
2017–18 Swansea C 0 0
2017–18 *Cheltenham T* 12 0 **12 0**
2018–19 Swansea C 27 0
2019–20 Swansea C 21 0 **48 0**

ROUTLEDGE, Wayne (M) 504 48
H: 5 6 W: 11 02 b.Sidcup 7-1-85
Internationals: England U20, U21.
2001–02 Crystal Palace 2 0
2002–03 Crystal Palace 26 4
2003–04 Crystal Palace 44 6
2004–05 Crystal Palace 38 0 **110 10**
2005–06 Tottenham H 3 0
2005–06 *Portsmouth* 13 0 **13 0**
2006–07 Tottenham H 0 0
2006–07 *Fulham* 24 0 **24 0**
2007–08 Tottenham H 2 0 **5 0**
2007–08 Aston Villa 1 0
2008–09 Aston Villa 1 0 **2 0**
2008–09 *Cardiff C* 9 2 **9 2**
2008–09 QPR 19 1
2009–10 QPR 25 2
2009–10 Newcastle U 17 3
2010–11 Newcastle U 17 0 **34 3**
2010–11 *QPR* 20 5 **64 8**
2011–12 Swansea C 28 1
2012–13 Swansea C 36 5
2013–14 Swansea C 35 2
2014–15 Swansea C 29 3
2015–16 Swansea C 28 2
2016–17 Swansea C 27 3
2017–18 Swansea C 15 0
2018–19 Swansea C 24 5
2019–20 Swansea C 21 4 **243 25**

RUSHESHA, Tivonge (D) 0 0
b. 24-7-02
Internationals: Wales U17.
2019–20 Swansea C 0 0

VAN DER HOORN, Mike (D) 183 15
H: 6 3 W: 12 11 b.Almere 15-10-92
Internationals: Netherlands U20, U21.
2010–11 Utrecht 1 0
2011–12 Utrecht 12 2
2012–13 Utrecht 31 4 **44 6**
2013–14 Ajax 3 0
2014–15 Ajax 15 2
2015–16 Ajax 15 1 **33 3**
2016–17 Swansea C 8 1
2017–18 Swansea C 24 1
2018–19 Swansea C 46 3
2019–20 Swansea C 28 1 **106 6**

ZABRET, Gregor (G) 0 0
H: 6 2 W: 12 11 b.Ljubljana 18-8-95
Internationals: Slovenia U16, U17, U19, U21.
2013–14 Swansea C 0 0
2014–15 Swansea C 0 0
2015–16 Swansea C 0 0
2016–17 Swansea C 0 0
2017–18 Swansea C 0 0
2018–19 Swansea C 0 0
2019–20 Swansea C 0 0
2019–20 *Oldham Ath* 0 0

Players retained or with offer of contract
Blake, Matthew; Campbell, Rio Anthony; Cooper, Oliver Joseph; Govea, Merlin Jordy Jair; Lewis, Joe Cameron; McKay, Barrie.

Scholars
A-Hamadi, Ali Ibrahim Karim Ali; Bevan, Ryan Peter; Butler, Scott James; Clancy, Charlie Mark Patrick; Clarke, Morgan James;

Davies, Thomas Craig; Edwards, Jacob Lloyd; Erickson, Benjamin James; Gibbings, Bradley William; Hutchings, Joshua; Jones, Jacob Alexander; Kenko, Djoudie Erick Ryan; Makokowe, Panashe; McKendry, Luke John; Moti, Adnaan Rahim; Motruk, Luke Ivan; Murphy, Michael James; Owen, Bailey Elis; Rickard, Jamie William; Shields, Connor Liam; Thomas, Jake; Thomas, Joshua John; Webb, Lewis Michael; Williams, Cian Owain.

SWINDON T (82)

ANDERSON, Keshi (F) 129 22
H: 5 9 W: 10 10 b.Luton 15-11-95
2014–15 Crystal Palace 0 0
2015–16 Crystal Palace 0 0
2015–16 *Doncaster R* 7 3 **7 3**
2016–17 Crystal Palace 0 0
2016–17 *Bolton W* 8 1 **8 1**
2016–17 *Northampton T* 14 3 **14 3**
2017–18 Swindon T 37 5
2018–19 Swindon T 43 4
2019–20 Swindon T 20 6 **100 15**

BANCROFT, Jacob (F) 1 0
b. 9-4-01
2018–19 Swindon T 1 0
2019–20 Swindon T 0 0 **1 0**

BAUDRY, Mathieu (D) 257 16
H: 6 2 W: 12 08 b.Le Havre 24-2-88
2007–08 Troyes 2 1
2008–09 Troyes 17 0
2009–10 Troyes 7 0 **26 1**
2010–11 Bournemouth 3 1
2011–12 Bournemouth 7 0 **10 1**
2011–12 *Dagenham & R* 11 0 **11 0**
2012–13 Leyton Orient 24 3
2013–14 Leyton Orient 39 2
2014–15 Leyton Orient 31 1
2015–16 Leyton Orient 34 2 **128 8**
2016–17 Doncaster R 31 5
2017–18 Doncaster R 22 1 **53 6**
2018–19 Milton Keynes D 5 0 **5 0**
2019–20 Swindon T 24 0 **24 0**

BROADBENT, Tom (D) 50 0
H: 6 3 W: 14 02 b. 15-2-92
From Farnborough, Petersfield T, Hayes & Yeading U.
2017–18 Bristol R 22 0
2018–19 Bristol R 7 0 **29 0**
2018–19 Swindon T 12 0
2019–20 Swindon T 9 0 **21 0**

CADDIS, Paul (D) 327 21
H: 5 7 W: 10 07 b.Irvine 19-4-88
Internationals: Scotland U19, U21, Full caps.
2007–08 Celtic 2 0
2008–09 Celtic 5 0
2008–09 *Dundee U* 11 0 **11 0**
2009–10 Celtic 10 0 **17 0**
2010–11 Swindon T 38 1
2011–12 Swindon T 39 4
2012–13 Swindon T 0 0
2012–13 *Birmingham C* 27 0
2013–14 Birmingham C 38 5
2014–15 Birmingham C 45 6
2015–16 Birmingham C 39 4
2016–17 Birmingham C 0 0 **149 15**
2016–17 Bury 13 0 **13 0**
2017–18 Blackburn R 14 0 **14 0**
2018–19 Bradford C 27 1 **27 1**
2019–20 Swindon T 19 0 **96 5**

CHESHIRE, Anthony (D) 0 0
2019–20 Swindon T 0 0

CONROY, Dion (D) 59 1
b.Redhill 11-12-95
From Chelsea.
2016–17 Swindon T 14 0
2017–18 Swindon T 7 0
2018–19 Swindon T 27 1
2019–20 Swindon T 11 0 **59 1**

CURRAN, Taylor (D) 3 0
b. 7-7-00
2018–19 Southend U 0 0
2018–19 Swindon T 1 0
2019–20 Swindon T 2 0 **3 0**

DONOHUE, Dion (M) 103 1
H: 5 11 W: 10 06 b.Bodedern 26-8-93
2015–16 Chesterfield 17 0
2016–17 Chesterfield 37 1
2017–18 Chesterfield 2 0 **56 1**
2017–18 Portsmouth 32 0
2018–19 Portsmouth 10 0 **42 0**
2019–20 Mansfield T 0 0
2019–20 Swindon T 5 0 **5 0**

DOUGHTY, Michael (M) 212 24
H: 6 1 W: 12 10 b.Westminster 20-11-92
Internationals: Wales U19, U21.
2010–11 QPR 0 0
2011–12 QPR 0 0
2011–12 *Crawley T* 16 0 **16 0**
2011–12 *Aldershot T* 5 0 **5 0**
2012–13 QPR 0 0
2012–13 *St Johnstone* 5 0 **5 0**
2013–14 QPR 0 0
2013–14 *Stevenage* 36 2 **36 2**
2014–15 QPR 3 0
2014–15 *Gillingham* 9 0 **9 0**
2015–16 QPR 5 0
2015–16 *Swindon T* 20 5
2016–17 QPR 4 0 **12 0**
2016–17 *Swindon T* 14 2
2017–18 Peterborough U 34 1 **34 1**
2018–19 Swindon T 30 13
2019–20 Swindon T 31 1 **95 21**

DOYLE, Eoin (F) 377 134
H: 6 0 W: 11 07 b.Tallaght 12-3-88
2009 Sligo 15 3
2010 Sligo 35 6
2011 Sligo 34 20 **84 29**
2011–12 Hibernian 13 1
2012–13 Hibernian 36 10 **49 11**
2013–14 Chesterfield 43 11
2014–15 Chesterfield 26 21 **69 32**
2014–15 Cardiff C 16 5
2015–16 Cardiff C 0 0 **16 5**
2015–16 *Preston NE* 28 4
2016–17 Preston NE 11 1
2016–17 *Portsmouth* 12 2 **12 2**
2017–18 Preston NE 0 0 **39 5**
2017–18 *Oldham Ath* 30 14 **30 14**
2018–19 Bradford C 44 11
2019–20 Bradford C 6 0 **50 11**
2019–20 Swindon T 28 25 **28 25**

FRYERS, Zeki (D) 87 2
H: 6 0 W: 12 00 b.Manchester 9-9-92
Internationals: England U16, U17, U19.
2011–12 Manchester U 2 0 **2 0**
2012–13 Standard Liege 7 0 **7 0**
2012–13 Tottenham H 0 0
2013–14 Tottenham H 7 0 **7 0**
2014–15 Crystal Palace 1 0
2014–15 *Rotherham U* 10 0 **10 0**
2014–15 *Ipswich T* 3 0 **3 0**
2015–16 Crystal Palace 0 0
2016–17 Crystal Palace 8 0 **9 0**
2017–18 Barnsley 22 1
2018–19 Barnsley 5 0 **27 1**
2019–20 Swindon T 22 1 **22 1**

GIAMATTEI, Massimo (M) 0 0
2019–20 Swindon T 0 0

GRAHAM, Ralph (M) 0 0
2019–20 Swindon T 0 0

GRANT, Anthony (M) 507 15
H: 5 10 W: 11 01 b.Lambeth 4-6-87
Internationals: England U16, U17, U19.
2004–05 Chelsea 1 0
2005–06 Chelsea 0 0
2005–06 *Oldham Ath* 2 0 **2 0**
2006–07 Chelsea 0 0
2006–07 *Wycombe W* 40 0 **40 0**
2007–08 Chelsea 0 0 **1 0**
2007–08 *Luton T* 4 0 **4 0**
2007–08 *Southend U* 10 0
2008–09 Southend U 35 1
2009–10 Southend U 38 0
2010–11 Southend U 43 8
2011–12 Southend U 33 1 **159 10**
2012–13 Stevenage 41 0 **41 0**
2013–14 Crewe Alex 38 2
2014–15 Crewe Alex 43 2 **81 4**
2015–16 Port Vale 38 1
2016–17 Port Vale 20 0 **58 1**
2016–17 Peterborough U 11 0
2017–18 Peterborough U 38 0 **49 0**
2018–19 Shrewsbury T 42 0
2019–20 *Shrewsbury T* 0 0 **42 0**
2019–20 Swindon T 30 0 **30 0**

HAINES, Luke (M) 0 0
2019–20 Swindon T 0 0

HENRY, Will (G) 5 0
b. 6-7-98
2015–16 Swindon T 2 0
2016–17 Swindon T 3 0
2017–18 Swindon T 0 0
2018–19 Swindon T 0 0
2019–20 Swindon T 0 0 **5 0**

HOLLAND, Toby (M) 0 0
2019–20 Swindon T 0 0

HOPE, Hallam (F) 203 40
H: 5 10 W: 12 00 b.Manchester 17-3-94
Internationals: England U16, U17, U18, U19. Barbados Full caps.
2010–11 Everton 0 0
2011–12 Everton 0 0
2012–13 Everton 0 0
2013–14 Everton 0 0
2013–14 *Northampton T* 3 1 **3 1**
2013–14 *Bury* 8 5
2014–15 Everton 0 0
2014–15 *Sheffield W* 4 0 **4 0**
2014–15 Bury 19 0
2015–16 Bury 6 0
2015–16 *Carlisle U* 21 4
2016–17 Bury 33 3 **66 8**
2017–18 Carlisle U 41 9
2018–19 Carlisle U 40 14
2019–20 Carlisle U 23 2 **125 29**
2019–20 Swindon T 5 2 **5 2**

HUNT, Robert (M) 116 2
H: 5 7 W: 10 08 b.Dagenham 7-7-95
2013–14 Brighton & HA 0 0
2014–15 Brighton & HA 0 0
2015–16 Brighton & HA 0 0
2016–17 Brighton & HA 1 0 **1 0**
2016–17 *Oldham Ath* 10 0
2017–18 Oldham Ath 33 0
2018–19 Oldham Ath 38 1 **81 1**
2019–20 Swindon T 34 1 **34 1**

IANDOLO, Ellis (M) 62 1
b. 22-8-97
From Maidstone U.
2015–16 Swindon T 12 0
2016–17 Swindon T 10 0
2017–18 Swindon T 12 1
2018–19 Swindon T 15 0
2019–20 Swindon T 13 0 **62 1**

ISGROVE, Lloyd (M) 91 2
H: 5 10 W: 11 05 b.Yeovil 12-1-93
Internationals: Wales U21, Full caps.
2011–12 Southampton 0 0
2012–13 Southampton 0 0
2013–14 Southampton 0 0
2013–14 *Peterborough U* 8 1 **8 1**
2014–15 Southampton 1 0
2014–15 *Sheffield W* 8 0 **8 0**
2015–16 Southampton 0 0
2015–16 *Barnsley* 27 0
2016–17 Southampton 0 0 **1 0**
2017–18 Barnsley 16 1
2018–19 Barnsley 2 0 **45 1**
2018–19 *Portsmouth* 0 0
2019–20 Swindon T 29 0 **29 0**

LYDEN, Jordan (M) 35 2
H: 5 10 W: 11 00 b.Perth 30-1-96
Internationals: Australia U20.
2015–16 Aston Villa 4 0
2016–17 Aston Villa 0 0
2017–18 Aston Villa 0 0
2018–19 Aston Villa 0 0 **4 0**
2018–19 *Oldham Ath* 10 1 **10 1**
2019–20 Swindon T 21 1 **21 1**

MATTHEWS, Archie (G) 0 0
2018–19 Swindon T 0 0
2019–20 Swindon T 0 0

McGILP, Cameron (M) 4 0
H: 5 11 b.Glasgow 8-2-98
2016–17 Melbourne Victory 1 0
2017–18 Melbourne Victory 0 0 **1 0**
From Melbourne Victory.
2018–19 Birmingham C 0 0
2018–19 Swindon T 1 0
2019–20 Swindon T 2 0 **3 0**

McGLASHAN, Jermaine (M) 307 26
H: 5 7 W: 10 00 b.Croydon 14-4-88
2010–11 Aldershot T 38 1
2011–12 Aldershot T 23 4 **61 5**
2011–12 Cheltenham T 16 2
2012–13 Cheltenham T 45 4
2013–14 Cheltenham T 43 6 **104 12**
2014–15 Gillingham 40 5
2015–16 Gillingham 17 0 **57 5**
2016–17 Southend U 35 3
2017–18 Southend U 26 1 **61 4**
2018–19 Swindon T 24 0
2019–20 Swindon T 0 0 **24 0**

PALMER, Matthew (M) **193 7**
H: 5 10 W: 12 06 b.Derby 1-8-93

2012–13	Burton Alb	2	0		
2013–14	Burton Alb	40	0		
2014–15	Burton Alb	33	4		
2015–16	Burton Alb	14	0		
2015–16	*Oldham Ath*	14	1	**14**	**1**
2016–17	Burton Alb	36	1		
2017–18	Burton Alb	11	1	**136**	**6**
2017–18	Rotherham U	14	0		
2018–19	Rotherham U	10	0		
2019–20	Rotherham U	0	0	**24**	**0**
2019–20	*Bradford C*	18	0	**18**	**0**
2019–20	Swindon T	1	0	**1**	**0**

PARSONS, Harry (F) **0 0**

2019–20	Swindon T	0	0

REID, Tyler (D) **11 0**
b. 2-9-97

2017–18	Swansea C	0	0		
2017–18	*Newport Co*	7	0	**7**	**0**
2018–19	Swansea C	0	0		
2019–20	Swindon T	4	0	**4**	**0**

ROMANSKI, Joe (D) **6 1**
b.Reading 3-2-00

2017–18	Swindon T	2	0		
2018–19	Swindon T	4	1		
2019–20	Swindon T	0	0	**6**	**1**

ROSE, Danny (M) **214 15**
H: 5 7 W: 10 04 b.Bristol 21-2-88
Internationals: England C.

2006–07	Manchester U	0	0		
2007–08	Manchester U	0	0		

From Oxford U, Newport Co

2012–13	Fleetwood T	0	0		
2012–13	*Aldershot T*	34	2	**34**	**2**
2013–14	Oxford U	40	4		
2014–15	Oxford U	29	2		
2015–16	Oxford U	13	0	**82**	**6**
2015–16	Northampton T	15	1	**15**	**1**
2016–17	Portsmouth	38	5		
2017–18	Portsmouth	15	0		
2018–19	Portsmouth	1	0	**54**	**5**
2018–19	Swindon T	10	0		
2019–20	Swindon T	19	1	**29**	**1**

SANOKHO, Sidy (M) **0 0**
b. 8-5-97
From Furiani-Agliani.

2019–20	Swindon T	0	0

SMITH, Sam (G) **0 0**

2019–20	Swindon T	0	0

TWINE, Scott (F) **25 1**
H: 5 9 W: 10 12 b.Swindon 14-7-99

2015–16	Swindon T	0	0		
2016–17	Swindon T	1	0		
2017–18	Swindon T	4	0		
2018–19	Swindon T	14	1		
2019–20	Swindon T	6	0	**25**	**1**

WOOLERY, Kaiyne (F) **125 14**
H: 5 10 W: 11 07 b.Hackney 11-1-95

2014–15	Bolton W	1	0		
2014–15	*Notts Co*	5	0	**5**	**0**
2015–16	Bolton W	17	2		
2016–17	Bolton W	1	0	**19**	**2**
2016–17	Wigan Ath	1	0	**1**	**0**
2017–18	Swindon T	37	4		
2018–19	Swindon T	29	6		
2019–20	Swindon T	34	2	**100**	**12**

ZAKUANI, Gaby (D) **452 15**
H: 6 1 W: 12 13 b.DR Congo 31-5-86
Internationals: DR Congo Full caps.

2002–03	Leyton Orient	1	0		
2003–04	Leyton Orient	10	2		
2004–05	Leyton Orient	33	0		
2005–06	Leyton Orient	43	1	**87**	**3**
2006–07	Fulham	0	0		
2006–07	*Stoke C*	9	0		
2007–08	Fulham	0	0		
2007–08	*Stoke C*	19	0	**28**	**0**
2008–09	Fulham	0	0		
2008–09	Peterborough U	32	1		
2009–10	Peterborough U	29	0		
2010–11	Peterborough U	30	2		
2011–12	Peterborough U	41	1		
2012–13	Peterborough U	33	1		
2013–14	Peterborough U	15	0		
2013–14	*Kalloni*	15	1	**15**	**1**
2014–15	Peterborough U	22	1		
2015–16	Peterborough U	24	3	**226**	**9**
2016–17	Northampton T	21	2	**21**	**2**
2017–18	Gillingham	40	0		
2018–19	Gillingham	29	0		
2019–20	Gillingham	0	0	**69**	**0**
2019–20	Swindon T	6	0	**6**	**0**

Scholars
Case, Oliver Loddington; Cheshire, Anthony Alexander; Francis, Christopher Lucius; Giamattei, Massimo William; Haynes, Sonny; Holland, Toby Steven; King, William Martin; Lynn, Anthony Steven; Moore, Thomas Kenneth; Parsons, Harry John; Rendell, Louis William; Smith, Samuel Luca; Storr, Kai Douglas; Suter, Thomas Raymond; Taylor, Joshua James; Wells, Rhys Jay; Whitfield, Max Thomas.

TOTTENHAM H (83)

ALDERWEIRELD, Toby (D) **314 16**
H: 6 1 W: 11 11 b.Wilrijk 2-3-89
Internationals: Belgium U26, U17, U18, U19, U21, Full caps.

2008–09	Ajax	5	0		
2009–10	Ajax	31	2		
2010–11	Ajax	26	2		
2011–12	Ajax	29	1		
2012–13	Ajax	32	2		
2013–14	Ajax	4	0	**127**	**7**
2013–14	Atletico Madrid	12	1	**12**	**1**
2014–15	Southampton	26	1	**26**	**1**
2015–16	Tottenham H	38	4		
2016–17	Tottenham H	30	1		
2017–18	Tottenham H	14	0		
2018–19	Tottenham H	34	0		
2019–20	Tottenham H	33	2	**149**	**7**

ALLI, Bamidele (M) **228 72**
H: 6 1 W: 11 12 b.Watford 11-4-96
Internationals: England U17, U18, U19, U21, Full caps.

2012–13	Milton Keynes D	0	0		
2013–14	Milton Keynes D	33	6		
2014–15	Milton Keynes D	39	16	**72**	**22**
2015–16	Tottenham H	33	10		
2016–17	Tottenham H	37	18		
2017–18	Tottenham H	36	9		
2018–19	Tottenham H	25	5		
2019–20	Tottenham H	25	8	**156**	**50**

AMOS, Luke (M) **54 4**
H: 5 10 W: 11 00 b.Hatfield 23-2-97
Internationals: England U18.

2016–17	Tottenham H	0	0		
2016–17	*Southend U*	3	0	**3**	**0**
2017–18	Tottenham H	0	0		
2017–18	*Stevenage*	16	2	**16**	**2**
2018–19	Tottenham H	1	0	**1**	**0**
2019–20	*QPR*	34	2	**34**	**2**

AURIER, Serge (D) **234 13**
H: 5 9 W: 11 11 b.Paris 24-12-92
Internationals: Ivory Coast Full caps.

2009–10	Lens	5	0		
2010–11	Lens	26	0		
2011–12	Lens	16	0	**47**	**0**
2011–12	Toulouse	10	1		
2012–13	Toulouse	28	1		
2013–14	Toulouse	34	6		
2014–15	Toulouse	0	0	**72**	**8**
2014–15	*Paris Saint-Germain*	14	0		
2015–16	Paris Saint-Germain	21	2		
2016–17	Paris Saint-Germain	22	0	**57**	**2**
2017–18	Paris Saint-Germain	0	0		
2017–18	Tottenham H	17	2		
2018–19	Tottenham H	8	0		
2019–20	Tottenham H	33	1	**58**	**3**

AUSTIN, Brandon (G) **14 0**
b.Hemel Hempstead 8-1-99
Internationals: USA U18. England U20, U21.

2019–20	Tottenham H	0	0		
2019–20	*Viborg*	14	0	**14**	**0**

BERGWIJN, Steven (M) **126 32**
b.Amsterdam 8-10-97
Internationals: Netherlands U17, U18, U19, U20, U21, Full caps.

2014–15	PSV Eindhoven	1	0		
2015–16	PSV Eindhoven	5	0		
2016–17	PSV Eindhoven	25	2		
2017–18	PSV Eindhoven	32	8		
2018–19	PSV Eindhoven	33	14		
2019–20	PSV Eindhoven	16	5	**112**	**29**
2019–20	Tottenham H	14	3	**14**	**3**

CARTER-VICKERS, Cameron (D) **92 1**
H: 6 1 W: 13 08 b.Westcliff on Sea 31-12-97
Internationals: USA U18, U20, U23, Full caps.

2015–16	Tottenham H	0	0		
2016–17	Tottenham H	0	0		
2017–18	Tottenham H	0	0		
2017–18	*Sheffield U*	17	1	**17**	**1**
2017–18	*Ipswich T*	17	0	**17**	**0**
2018–19	Tottenham H	0	0		
2018–19	*Swansea C*	30	0	**30**	**0**
2019–20	Tottenham H	0	0		
2019–20	*Stoke C*	12	0	**12**	**0**
2019–20	*Luton T*	16	0	**16**	**0**

CIRKIN, Dennis (D) **0 0**
Internationals: England U17.

2019–20	Tottenham H	0	0

CLARKE, Jack (F) **29 2**
b.York 23-11-00
Internationals: England U20.

2017–18	Leeds U	0	0		
2018–19	Leeds U	22	2		
2019–20	Tottenham H	0	0		
2019–20	*Leeds U*	1	0	**23**	**2**
2019–20	*QPR*	6	0	**6**	**0**

DAVIES, Ben (D) **199 6**
H: 5 7 W: 12 00 b.Neath 24-4-93
Internationals: Wales U19, Full caps.

2011–12	Swansea C	0	0		
2012–13	Swansea C	37	1		
2013–14	Swansea C	34	2	**71**	**3**
2014–15	Tottenham H	14	0		
2015–16	Tottenham H	17	0		
2016–17	Tottenham H	23	1		
2017–18	Tottenham H	29	2		
2018–19	Tottenham H	27	0		
2019–20	Tottenham H	18	0	**128**	**3**

DIER, Eric (D) **201 11**
H: 6 3 W: 13 08 b.Cheltenham 15-1-94
Internationals: England U18, U19, U20, U21, Full caps.

2012–13	Sporting Lisbon	14	1		
2013–14	Sporting Lisbon	13	0	**27**	**1**
2014–15	Tottenham H	28	2		
2015–16	Tottenham H	37	3		
2016–17	Tottenham H	36	2		
2017–18	Tottenham H	34	0		
2018–19	Tottenham H	20	3		
2019–20	Tottenham H	19	0	**174**	**10**

ERIKSEN, Christian (M) **339 76**
H: 5 9 W: 10 02 b.Middelfart 14-2-92
Internationals: Denmark U17, U18, U19, U21, Full caps.

2009–10	Ajax	15	0		
2010–11	Ajax	28	6		
2011–12	Ajax	33	7		
2012–13	Ajax	33	10		
2013–14	Ajax	4	2	**113**	**25**
2013–14	Tottenham H	25	7		
2014–15	Tottenham H	38	10		
2015–16	Tottenham H	35	6		
2016–17	Tottenham H	36	8		
2017–18	Tottenham H	37	10		
2018–19	Tottenham H	35	8		
2019–20	Tottenham H	20	2	**226**	**51**

Transferred to Inter Milan, January 2020.

ETETE, Kion (F) **4 0**
b. 28-11-01

2018–19	Notts Co	4	0	**4**	**0**
2019–20	Tottenham H	0	0		

EYOMA, Timothy (D) **0 0**
H: 6 1 W: 11 11 b.Hackney 29-1-00
Internationals: England U16, U17, U18, U19.

2018–19	Tottenham H	0	0
2019–20	Tottenham H	0	0
2019–20	*Lincoln C*	0	0

FERNANDES, Gedson (M) **36 0**
b.Sao Tome 9-1-99
Internationals: Portugal U16, U17, U19, U20, U21, Full caps.

2016–17	Benfica	0	0		
2017–18	Benfica	0	0		
2018–19	Benfica	22	0		
2019–20	Benfica	7	0	**29**	**0**

On loan from Benfica.

2019–20	Tottenham H	7	0	**7**	**0**

FOYTH, Juan (D) **23 1**
H: 5 10 W: 10 12 b.La Plata 12-1-98
Internationals: Argentina U20, Full caps.

2017	Estudiantes	7	0		
2017–18	Estudiantes	0	0	**7**	**0**
2017–18	Tottenham H	0	0		
2018–19	Tottenham H	12	1		
2019–20	Tottenham H	4	0	**16**	**1**

GAZZANIGA, Paulo (G) **95 0**
H: 6 5 W: 14 02 b.Santa Fe 2-1-92
Internationals: Argentina Full caps.

2011–12	Gillingham	20	0	**20**	**0**
2012–13	Southampton	9	0		
2013–14	Southampton	8	0		
2014–15	Southampton	2	0		
2015–16	Southampton	2	0		
2016–17	Southampton	0	0	**21**	**0**
2016–17	*Rayo Vallecano*	32	0	**32**	**0**
2017–18	Tottenham H	1	0		
2018–19	Tottenham H	3	0		
2019–20	Tottenham H	18	0	**22**	**0**

GEORGIOU, Anthony (M) **12 0**
H: 5 10 W: 11 07 b.Lewisham 24-2-97
Internationals: Cyprus Full caps.

2017–18	Tottenham H	0	0		
2018–19	Tottenham H	0	0		
2018–19	*Levante*	0	0		
2019–20	Tottenham H	0	0		
2019–20	*Ipswich T*	10	0	**10**	**0**
2019–20	*Bolton W*	2	0	**2**	**0**

KANE, Harry (F) **263 157**
H: 6 0 W: 10 00 b.Chingford 28-7-93
Internationals: England U17, U19, U20, U21, Full caps.

2010–11	Tottenham H	0	0		
2010–11	*Leyton Orient*	18	5	**18**	**5**
2011–12	Tottenham H	0	0		
2011–12	*Millwall*	22	7	**22**	**7**
2012–13	Tottenham H	1	0		
2012–13	*Norwich C*	3	0	**3**	**0**
2012–13	*Leicester C*	13	2	**13**	**2**
2013–14	Tottenham H	10	3		
2014–15	Tottenham H	34	21		
2015–16	Tottenham H	38	25		
2016–17	Tottenham H	30	29		
2017–18	Tottenham H	37	30		
2018–19	Tottenham H	28	17		
2019–20	Tottenham H	29	18	**207**	**143**

LAMELA, Erik (F) **249 39**
H: 6 0 W: 10 13 b.Buenos Aires 4-3-92
Internationals: Argentina U20, Full caps.

2008–09	River Plate	1	0		
2009–10	River Plate	1	0		
2010–11	River Plate	32	4	**34**	**4**
2011–12	Roma	29	4		
2012–13	Roma	32	15	**61**	**19**
2013–14	Tottenham H	9	0		
2014–15	Tottenham H	33	2		
2015–16	Tottenham H	34	5		
2016–17	Tottenham H	9	1		
2017–18	Tottenham H	25	2		
2018–19	Tottenham H	19	4		
2019–20	Tottenham H	25	2	**154**	**16**

LLORIS, Hugo (G) **478 0**
H: 6 2 W: 12 03 b.Nice 26-12-86
Internationals: France U18, U19, U20, U21, Full caps.

2005–06	Nice	5	0		
2006–07	Nice	37	0		
2007–08	Nice	30	0	**72**	**0**
2008–09	Lyon	35	0		
2009–10	Lyon	36	0		
2010–11	Lyon	37	0		
2011–12	Lyon	36	0		
2012–13	Lyon	2	0	**146**	**0**
2012–13	Tottenham H	27	0		
2013–14	Tottenham H	37	0		
2014–15	Tottenham H	35	0		
2015–16	Tottenham H	37	0		
2016–17	Tottenham H	34	0		
2017–18	Tottenham H	36	0		
2018–19	Tottenham H	33	0		
2019–20	Tottenham H	21	0	**260**	**0**

LO CELSO, Giovani (M) **134 16**
b.Rosario 9-4-96
Internationals: Argentina U23, Full caps.

2014	Rosario Central	0	0		
2015	Rosario Central	13	0		
2016	Rosario Central	14	2		
2016–17	Paris Saint-Germain	4	0		
2016–17	*Rosario Central*	9	1	**36**	**3**
2017–18	Paris Saint-Germain	33	4		
2018–19	Paris Saint-Germain	1	0	**38**	**4**
2018–19	Real Betis	32	9		
2019–20	Real Betis	0	0	**32**	**9**
2019–20	Tottenham H	28	0	**28**	**0**

LUCAS MOURA, Rodrigues (M) **300 67**
H: 5 8 W: 10 06 b.Sao Paulo 13-8-92
Internationals: Brazil U20, U23, Full caps.

2010	Sao Paulo	25	4		
2011	Sao Paulo	28	9		
2012	Sao Paulo	21	6	**74**	**19**
2012–13	Paris Saint-Germain	10	0		
2013–14	Paris Saint-Germain	36	5		
2014–15	Paris Saint-Germain	29	7		
2015–16	Paris Saint-Germain	36	9		
2016–17	Paris Saint-Germain	37	12		
2017–18	Paris Saint-Germain	5	1	**153**	**34**
2017–18	Tottenham H	6	0		
2018–19	Tottenham H	32	10		
2019–20	Tottenham H	35	4	**73**	**14**

MARSH, George (M) **26 0**
b.Penbury 5-11-98

2018–19	Tottenham H	0	0		
2019–20	Tottenham H	0	0		
2019–20	*Leyton Orient*	26	0	**26**	**0**

NDOMBELE, Tanguy (M) **120 5**
b.Longjumeau 28-12-96
Internationals: France U21, Full caps.

2016–17	Amiens	30	2		
2017–18	Amiens	3	0	**33**	**2**
2017–18	*Lyon*	32	0		
2018–19	Lyon	34	1	**66**	**1**
2019–20	Tottenham H	21	2	**21**	**2**

NKOUDOU, Georges (M) **84 39**
b. 13-2-95
Internationals: France U17, U19, U20, U21.

2013–14	Nantes	6	1		
2014–15	Nantes	28	16	**34**	**17**
2015–16	Marseilles	28	22	**28**	**22**
2016–17	Marseille	0	0		
2016–17	Tottenham H	8	0		
2017–18	Tottenham H	1	0		
2017–18	*Burnley*	8	0	**8**	**0**
2018–19	Tottenham H	1	0		
2018–19	*Monaco*	3	0	**3**	**0**
2019–20	Tottenham H	1	0	**11**	**0**

Transferred to Besiktas, August 2020.

PARROTT, Troy (F) **2 0**
Internationals: Republic of Ireland U17, U19, U21, Full caps.
From Belvedere.

2019–20	Tottenham H	2	0	**2**	**0**

ROLES, Jack (M) **23 5**
b.London 26-2-99
Internationals: Cyprus U19, U21, Full caps.

2019–20	Tottenham H	0	0		
2019–20	*Cambridge U*	23	5	**23**	**5**

ROSE, Danny (M) **218 9**
H: 5 8 W: 11 11 b.Doncaster 2-6-90
Internationals: England U17, U19, U21, Full caps. Great Britain.

2007–08	Tottenham H	0	0		
2008–09	Tottenham H	0	0		
2008–09	*Watford*	7	0	**7**	**0**
2009–10	Tottenham H	1	1		
2010–11	Tottenham H	4	0		
2010–11	*Bristol C*	17	0	**17**	**0**
2011–12	Tottenham H	11	0		
2012–13	Tottenham H	0	0		
2012–13	*Sunderland*	27	1	**27**	**1**
2013–14	Tottenham H	22	1		
2014–15	Tottenham H	28	3		
2015–16	Tottenham H	24	1		
2016–17	Tottenham H	18	2		
2017–18	Tottenham H	10	0		
2018–19	Tottenham H	26	0		
2019–20	Tottenham H	12	0	**156**	**8**
2019–20	*Newcastle U*	11	0	**11**	**0**

SANCHEZ, Davinson (D) **133 7**
H: 6 2 W: 13 01 b.Caloto 12-6-96
Internationals: Columbia U17, U20, U23, Full caps.

2013	Atletico Nacional	2	0		
2014	Atletico Nacional	1	0		
2015	Atletico Nacional	5	0		
2016	Atletico Nacional	10	0	**18**	**0**
2016–17	Ajax	32	6		
2017–18	Ajax	0	0	**32**	**6**
2017–18	Tottenham H	31	0		
2018–19	Tottenham H	23	1		
2019–20	Tottenham H	29	0	**83**	**1**

SESSEGNON, Ryan (D) **112 22**
H: 5 10 W: 11 02 b.Roehampton 18-5-00
Internationals: England U16, U17, U19, U21.

2016–17	Fulham	25	5		
2017–18	Fulham	46	15		
2018–19	Fulham	35	2		
2019–20	Fulham	0	0	**106**	**22**
2019–20	Tottenham H	6	0	**6**	**0**

SISSOKO, Moussa (M) **424 34**
H: 6 2 W: 13 00 b.Le Blanc Mesnil 16-8-89
Internationals: France U16, U17, U18, U19, U21, Full caps.

2007–08	Toulouse	29	1		
2008–09	Toulouse	35	4		
2009–10	Toulouse	37	7		
2010–11	Toulouse	35	5		
2011–12	Toulouse	35	2		
2012–13	Toulouse	19	1	**190**	**20**
2012–13	Newcastle U	12	3		
2013–14	Newcastle U	35	3		
2014–15	Newcastle U	34	4		
2015–16	Newcastle U	37	1	**118**	**11**
2016–17	Tottenham H	25	0		
2017–18	Tottenham H	33	1		
2018–19	Tottenham H	29	0		
2019–20	Tottenham H	29	2	**116**	**3**

SKINNER, Aaron (D) **0 0**

2018–19	Bury	0	0		
2019–20	Tottenham H	0	0		

SKIPP, Oliver (M) **15 0**
H: 5 9 W: 11 00 b.Hatfield 16-9-00
Internationals: England U16, U17, U18, U21.

2018–19	Tottenham H	8	0		
2019–20	Tottenham H	7	0	**15**	**0**

SON, Heung-Min (M) **295 94**
H: 6 0 W: 12 00 b.Chuncheon 8-7-92
Internationals: South Korea U17, U23, Full caps.

2010–11	Hamburg	13	3		
2011–12	Hamburg	27	5		
2012–13	Hamburg	33	12	**73**	**20**
2013–14	Bayer Leverkusen	31	10		
2014–15	Bayer Leverkusen	30	11		
2015–16	Bayer Leverkusen	1	0	**62**	**21**
2015–16	Tottenham H	28	4		
2016–17	Tottenham H	34	14		
2017–18	Tottenham H	37	12		
2018–19	Tottenham H	31	12		
2019–20	Tottenham H	30	11	**160**	**53**

STERLING, Kazaiah (F) **11 1**
H: 5 9 W: 11 03 b.Enfield 9-11-98
Internationals: England U17, U18.
From Leyton Orient.

2017–18	Tottenham H	0	0		
2018–19	Tottenham H	0	0		
2018–19	*Sunderland*	8	1	**8**	**1**
2019–20	Tottenham H	0	0		
2019–20	*Doncaster R*	3	0	**3**	**0**
2019–20	*Leyton Orient*	0	0		

TANGANGA, Japhet (D) **6 0**
Internationals: England U16, U17, U18, U19, U20.

2019–20	Tottenham H	6	0	**6**	**0**

TRACEY, Shilow (F) **7 1**
From Ebbsfleet U.

2016–17	Tottenham H	0	0		
2017–18	Tottenham H	0	0		
2018–19	Tottenham H	0	0		
2019–20	Tottenham H	0	0		
2019–20	*Macclesfield T*	7	1	**7**	**1**

VERTONGHEN, Jan (D) **399 32**
H: 6 2 W: 12 05 b.Sint-Niklaas 24-4-87
Internationals: Belgium U16, U21, Full caps.

2006–07	Ajax	3	0		
2006–07	*RKC*	12	3	**12**	**3**
2007–08	Ajax	31	2		
2008–09	Ajax	26	4		
2009–10	Ajax	32	3		
2010–11	Ajax	32	6		
2011–12	Ajax	31	8	**155**	**23**
2012–13	Tottenham H	34	4		
2013–14	Tottenham H	23	0		
2014–15	Tottenham H	32	0		
2015–16	Tottenham H	29	0		
2016–17	Tottenham H	33	0		
2017–18	Tottenham H	36	0		
2018–19	Tottenham H	22	1		
2019–20	Tottenham H	23	1	**232**	**6**

VORM, Michel (G) **273 0**
H: 6 0 W: 13 03 b.Nieuwegein 20-10-83
Internationals: Netherlands Full caps.
2005–06 Den Bosch 35 0 **35 0**
2006–07 Utrecht 33 0
2007–08 Utrecht 11 0
2008–09 Utrecht 26 0
2009–10 Utrecht 33 0
2010–11 Utrecht 33 0 **136 0**
2011–12 Swansea C 37 0
2012–13 Swansea C 26 0
2013–14 Swansea C 26 0 **89 0**
2014–15 Tottenham H 4 0
2015–16 Tottenham H 1 0
2016–17 Tottenham H 5 0
2017–18 Tottenham H 1 0
2018–19 Tottenham H 2 0
2019–20 Tottenham H 0 0 **13 0**

WALCOTT, Malachi (D) **0 0**
Internationals: England U16, U17.
2019–20 Tottenham H 0 0

WALKER-PETERS, Kyle (F) **22 0**
H: 5 8 W: 9 13 b.Edmonton 13-4-97
Internationals: England U18, U19, U20, U21.
2015–16 Tottenham H 0 0
2016–17 Tottenham H 0 0
2017–18 Tottenham H 3 0
2018–19 Tottenham H 6 0
2019–20 Tottenham H 3 0 **12 0**
2019–20 *Southampton* 10 0 **10 0**

WANYAMA, Victor (M) **264 22**
H: 6 2 W: 11 12 b.Nairobi 25-6-91
Internationals: Kenya Full caps.
2009–10 Beerschot 19 0
2010–11 Beerschot 30 2 **49 2**
2011–12 Celtic 29 4
2012–13 Celtic 32 6 **61 10**
2013–14 Southampton 23 0
2014–15 Southampton 32 3
2015–16 Southampton 30 1 **85 4**
2016–17 Tottenham H 36 4
2017–18 Tottenham H 18 1
2018–19 Tottenham H 13 1
2019–20 Tottenham H 2 0 **69 6**
2019–20 Montreal Impact 0 0
Transferred to Montreal Impact, March 2020.

WHITE, Harvey (M) **0 0**
b.Maidstone 19-9-01
Internationals: England U18.
2019–20 Tottenham H 0 0

WHITEMAN, Alfie (G) **0 0**
b. 2-10-98
Internationals: England U16, U17, U18, U19.
2016–17 Tottenham H 0 0
2017–18 Tottenham H 0 0
2018–19 Tottenham H 0 0
2019–20 Tottenham H 0 0

WINKS, Harry (M) **94 2**
H: 5 10 W: 10 03 b.Hemel Hempstead 2-2-96
Internationals: England U17, U18, U19, U20, U21, Full caps.
2013–14 Tottenham H 0 0
2014–15 Tottenham H 0 0
2015–16 Tottenham H 0 0
2016–17 Tottenham H 21 1
2017–18 Tottenham H 16 0
2018–19 Tottenham H 26 1
2019–20 Tottenham H 31 0 **94 2**

Players retained or with offer of contract
Bennett, J'Neil Lloyd; Bowden, Jamie Patrick; De Bie, Jonathan; De Santiago Alonso, Yago; Fagan-Walcott, Malachi Michael; Lyons-Foster, Brooklyn; Markanday, Dilan Kumar; Mukendi, Jeremie; Okedina, Jubril Adesope; Oluwayemi, Oluwaferanmi Joshua; Pochettino Grippaldi, Maurizio; Richards, Rodel Kurai; Shashoua, Armando; Skinner, Aaron William; Thorpe, Elliot Morgan.

Scholars
Asante, Enock Amponsah; Carrington Alberdi, Eddie; Cesay, Kallum; Cooper, Chay; Craig, Matthew George; Craig, Michael James; John, Nile Omari Mckenzie; Kurylowicz, Kacper; Kyezu, Jeremy; Lo-Tutala, Thimothee Jacques Orcel; Lusala, Dermi; Muir, Marqes; Mundle, Romaine Lee; Pedder, Rafferty; Robson, Max; Solberg, Isak Midttun; Whittaker, Tarrelle Ricardo Kabirizi.

TRANMERE R (84)

BANKS, Oliver (D) **186 21**
H: 6 3 W: 11 11 b.Rotherham 21-9-92
2010–11 Rotherham U 1 1
2011–12 Rotherham U 0 0 **1 1**
From FC United of Manchester.
2013–14 Chesterfield 25 7
2014–15 Chesterfield 24 0
2014–15 *Northampton T* 3 0 **3 0**
2015–16 Chesterfield 32 2 **81 9**
2016–17 Oldham Ath 33 2
2017–18 Oldham Ath 7 0 **40 2**
2017–18 *Swindon T* 17 3 **17 3**
2018–19 Tranmere R 33 3
2019–20 Tranmere R 11 3 **44 6**

BLACKHAM, Joe (M) **0 0**
b. 10-9-01
2019–20 Tranmere R 0 0

BURTON, Jake (F) **0 0**
b. 15-11-01
2019–20 Tranmere R 0 0

CAPRICE, Jake (M) **75 0**
H: 5 10 W: 11 07 b.Lambeth 11-11-92
2011–12 Crystal Palace 0 0
2012–13 Blackpool 0 0
2012–13 *Dagenham & R* 8 0 **8 0**
2013–14 Blackpool 0 0
2013–14 *St Mirren* 6 0 **6 0**
From Lincoln C, Woking, Leyton Orient.
2018–19 Tranmere R 41 0
2019–20 Tranmere R 20 0 **61 0**

CLARKE, Peter (D) **672 49**
H: 6 0 W: 12 00 b.Southport 3-1-82
Internationals: England U21.
1998–99 Everton 0 0
1999–2000 Everton 0 0
2000–01 Everton 1 0
2001–02 Everton 7 0
2002–03 Everton 0 0
2002–03 *Blackpool* 16 3
2002–03 *Port Vale* 13 1 **13 1**
2003–04 Everton 1 0
2003–04 *Coventry C* 5 0 **5 0**
2004–05 Everton 0 0 **9 0**
2004–05 Blackpool 38 5
2005–06 Blackpool 46 6
2006–07 Southend U 38 2
2007–08 Southend U 45 4
2008–09 Southend U 43 4 **126 10**
2009–10 Huddersfield T 46 5
2010–11 Huddersfield T 46 4
2011–12 Huddersfield T 31 0
2012–13 Huddersfield T 43 0
2013–14 Huddersfield T 26 0 **192 9**
2014–15 Blackpool 39 2 **139 16**
2015–16 Bury 45 1
2016–17 Oldham Ath 46 5
2017–18 Oldham Ath 19 2
2017–18 *Bury* 18 1 **63 2**
2018–19 Oldham Ath 42 3 **107 10**
2019–20 Fleetwood T 12 1 **12 1**
2019–20 Tranmere R 6 0 **6 0**

DANNS, Neil (M) **501 72**
H: 5 10 W: 10 12 b.Liverpool 23-11-82
Internationals: Guyana Full caps.
2000–01 Blackburn R 0 0
2001–02 Blackburn R 0 0
2002–03 Blackburn R 2 0
2003–04 Blackpool 12 2
2003–04 Blackburn R 1 0
2003–04 *Hartlepool U* 9 1 **9 1**
2004–05 Blackburn R 0 0 **3 0**
2004–05 Colchester U 32 11
2005–06 Colchester U 41 8 **73 19**
2006–07 Birmingham C 29 3
2007–08 Birmingham C 2 0 **31 3**
2007–08 Crystal Palace 4 0
2008–09 Crystal Palace 20 2
2009–10 Crystal Palace 42 8
2010–11 Crystal Palace 37 8 **103 18**
2011–12 Leicester C 29 5
2012–13 Leicester C 1 0
2012–13 *Bristol C* 9 2 **9 2**
2012–13 *Huddersfield T* 17 2 **17 2**
2013–14 Leicester C 0 0 **30 5**
2013–14 Bolton W 33 6
2014–15 Bolton W 41 1
2015–16 Bolton W 32 2 **106 9**
2016–17 Bury 18 2
2016–17 *Blackpool* 13 2 **25 4**
2017–18 Bury 25 5
2018–19 Bury 34 2 **77 9**
2019–20 Tranmere R 18 0 **18 0**

DAVIES, Scott (G) **187 0**
H: 6 0 W: 10 13 b.Blackpool 27-2-87
2007–08 Morecambe 10 0
2008–09 Morecambe 0 0
2009–10 Morecambe 1 0
2012–13 Fleetwood T 45 0
2013–14 Fleetwood T 28 0
2014–15 Fleetwood T 0 0 **73 0**
2014–15 *Morecambe* 10 0 **21 0**
2014–15 *Accrington S* 19 0 **19 0**
2018–19 Tranmere R 46 0
2019–20 Tranmere R 28 0 **74 0**

ELLIS, Mark (D) **299 21**
H: 6 2 W: 12 04 b.Kingsbridge 30-9-88
2007–08 Bolton W 0 0
2009–10 Torquay U 27 3
2010–11 Torquay U 27 2
2011–12 Torquay U 35 3 **89 8**
2012–13 Crewe Alex 44 5
2013–14 Crewe Alex 37 1 **81 6**
2014–15 Shrewsbury T 32 2
2015–16 Shrewsbury T 9 1 **41 3**
2015–16 Carlisle U 30 0
2016–17 Carlisle U 7 0
2017–18 Carlisle U 23 2 **60 2**
2018–19 Tranmere R 25 0
2019–20 Tranmere R 3 2 **28 2**

FERRIER, Morgan (F) **53 10**
H: 6 1 W: 12 08 b.London 15-11-94
Internationals: England C.
From Nottingham F, Crystal Palace, Bishop's Stortford, Hemel Hempstead T, Dagenham & R, Boreham Wood.
2018–19 Walsall 33 5 **33 5**
2019–20 Tranmere R 20 5 **20 5**

GILMOUR, Harvey (M) **26 3**
b. 15-12-98
2016–17 Sheffield U 0 0
2017–18 Sheffield U 0 0
2018–19 Tranmere R 22 3
2019–20 Tranmere R 4 0 **26 3**

GOULDBOURNE, Ethan (M) **0 0**
b. 10-10-00
2019–20 Tranmere R 0 0

HAYDEN, Kyle (D) **0 0**
2019–20 Tranmere R 0 0

JENNINGS, Connor (F) **90 12**
H: 6 0 W: 12 00 b.Manchester 21-1-91
Internationals: England C.
2011–12 Scunthorpe U 4 0
2012–13 Scunthorpe U 12 0
2013–14 Scunthorpe U 0 0 **16 0**
From Wrexham.
2018–19 Tranmere R 45 8
2019–20 Tranmere R 29 4 **74 12**

JONES, Ben (G) **0 0**
2019–20 Tranmere R 0 0

McCULLOUGH, Luke (D) **142 0**
H: 6 2 W: 12 11 b.Portadown 15-2-94
Internationals: Northern Ireland U16, U17, U19, U20, U21, Full caps.
2012–13 Manchester U 0 0
2012–13 *Cheltenham T* 1 0 **1 0**
2013–14 Doncaster R 14 0
2014–15 Doncaster R 33 0
2015–16 Doncaster R 32 0
2016–17 Doncaster R 7 0
2017–18 Doncaster R 13 0
2018–19 Doncaster R 0 0 **99 0**
2018–19 *Tranmere R* 36 0
2019–20 Tranmere R 6 0 **42 0**

MONTHE, Emmanuel (D) **87 3**
H: 6 0 W: 12 08 b. 26-1-95
2013–14 QPR 0 0
From Southport, Whitehawk, Hayes & Yeading, Havant & Waterford, Bath C.
2017–18 Forest Green R 13 0 **13 0**
2018–19 Tranmere R 43 2
2019–20 Tranmere R 31 1 **74 3**

MORRIS, Kieron (M) **191 18**
H: 5 10 W: 11 01 b.Hereford 3-6-94
2012–13 Walsall 0 0
2013–14 Walsall 2 0
2014–15 Walsall 14 2
2015–16 Walsall 33 3
2016–17 Walsall 35 5
2017–18 Walsall 42 3
2018–19 Walsall 17 2 **143 15**
2018–19 *Tranmere R* 14 1
2019–20 Tranmere R 34 2 **48 3**

MULLIN, Paul (F) **210 41**
H: 5 10 W: 11 01 b. 6-11-94

2013–14	Huddersfield T	0	0		
2014–15	Morecambe	42	8		
2015–16	Morecambe	40	9		
2016–17	Morecambe	40	8	**122**	**25**
2017–18	Swindon T	40	6	**40**	**6**
2018–19	Tranmere R	22	5		
2019–20	Tranmere R	20	3	**42**	**8**
2019–20	*Cambridge U*	6	2	**6**	**2**

MUSUAMBA, Harrison (D) **0 0**
b. 20-5-02

2019–20	Tranmere R	0	0		

NELSON, Sid (D) **113 1**
H: 6 1 b.London 1-1-96

2013–14	Millwall	0	0		
2014–15	Millwall	14	0		
2015–16	Millwall	9	0		
2016–17	Millwall	3	0		
2016–17	*Newport Co*	14	0	**14**	**0**
2017–18	Millwall	0	0		
2017–18	*Yeovil T*	12	0	**12**	**0**
2017–18	*Chesterfield*	15	1	**15**	**1**
2018–19	Millwall	0	0	**26**	**0**
2018–19	*Swindon T*	20	0	**20**	**0**
2018–19	*Tranmere R*	7	0		
2019–20	Tranmere R	19	0	**26**	**0**

NUGENT, George (M) **0 0**

2018–19	Tranmere R	0	0		
2019–20	Tranmere R	0	0		

PASSANT, Bailey (G) **0 0**

2018–19	Tranmere R	0	0		
2019–20	Tranmere R	0	0		

PAYNE, Stefan (F) **129 20**
H: 5 10 W: 11 07 b.Lambeth 10-8-91
Internationals: England C.

2009–10	Fulham	0	0		
2010–11	Gillingham	16	0		
2011–12	Gillingham	12	1	**28**	**1**
2011–12	*Aldershot T*	1	0	**1**	**0**

From Sutton U, Macclesfield T, Ebbsfleet U, AFC Hornchurch, Dover Ath.

2015–16	Barnsley	0	0		
2016–17	Barnsley	7	0		
2016–17	*Shrewsbury T*	12	2		
2017–18	Barnsley	2	0	**9**	**0**
2017–18	Shrewsbury T	38	11		
2018–19	Bristol R	20	2	**20**	**2**
2018–19	*Shrewsbury T*	6	0	**56**	**13**
2019–20	Tranmere R	15	4	**15**	**4**

PERKINS, David (D) **474 17**
H: 5 6 W: 11 06 b.Heysham 21-6-82
Internationals: England C.

2006–07	Rochdale	18	0		
2007–08	Rochdale	40	4		
2008–09	Colchester U	38	5		
2009–10	Colchester U	5	1		
2009–10	*Chesterfield*	13	1	**13**	**1**
2009–10	*Stockport Co*	22	0	**22**	**0**
2010–11	Colchester U	36	1	**79**	**7**
2011–12	Barnsley	33	1		
2012–13	Barnsley	35	1		
2013–14	Barnsley	23	0	**91**	**2**
2013–14	Blackpool	20	0		
2014–15	Blackpool	45	0	**65**	**0**
2015–16	Wigan Ath	45	0		
2016–17	Wigan Ath	27	0		
2017–18	Wigan Ath	13	1	**85**	**1**
2018–19	Rochdale	17	0	**75**	**4**
2018–19	Tranmere R	17	2		
2019–20	Tranmere R	27	0	**44**	**2**

PILLING, Luke (G) **1 0**
b. 25-7-97
Internationals: Wales U17, U21.

2013–14	Tranmere R	0	0		
2014–15	Tranmere R	0	0		
2018–19	Tranmere R	0	0		
2019–20	Tranmere R	1	0	**1**	**0**

POTTER, Darren (M) **422 17**
H: 6 0 W: 10 08 b.Liverpool 21-12-84
Internationals: Republic of Ireland Full caps.

2001–02	Liverpool	0	0		
2002–03	Liverpool	0	0		
2003–04	Liverpool	0	0		
2004–05	Liverpool	2	0		
2005–06	Liverpool	0	0		
2005–06	*Southampton*	10	0	**10**	**0**
2006–07	Liverpool	0	0	**2**	**0**
2006–07	Wolverhampton W	38	0		
2007–08	Wolverhampton W	18	0		
2008–09	Wolverhampton W	0	0	**56**	**0**
2008–09	*Sheffield W*	17	2		
2009–10	Sheffield W	46	3		
2010–11	Sheffield W	33	3	**96**	**8**
2011–12	Milton Keynes D	40	2		
2012–13	Milton Keynes D	46	4		
2013–14	Milton Keynes D	29	0		
2014–15	Milton Keynes D	40	2		
2015–16	Milton Keynes D	37	0		
2016–17	Milton Keynes D	37	1	**229**	**9**
2017–18	Rotherham U	16	0		
2018–19	Rotherham U	1	0	**17**	**0**
2019–20	Tranmere R	12	0	**12**	**0**

RAY, George (D) **152 5**
H: 5 10 W: 11 03 b.Warrington 13-10-93
Internationals: Wales U21.

2011–12	Crewe Alex	0	0		
2012–13	Crewe Alex	4	0		
2013–14	Crewe Alex	9	0		
2014–15	Crewe Alex	35	2		
2015–16	Crewe Alex	22	0		
2016–17	Crewe Alex	23	1		
2017–18	Crewe Alex	12	0		
2018–19	Crewe Alex	32	2	**137**	**5**
2019–20	Tranmere R	15	0	**15**	**0**

RIDEHALGH, Liam (D) **186 3**
H: 5 10 W: 11 05 b.Halifax 20-4-91

2009–10	Huddersfield T	0	0		
2010–11	Huddersfield T	20	0		
2011–12	Huddersfield T	0	0		
2011–12	*Swindon T*	11	0	**11**	**0**
2011–12	*Chesterfield*	20	1		
2012–13	Huddersfield T	0	0		
2012–13	*Chesterfield*	14	0	**34**	**1**
2012–13	*Rotherham U*	20	0	**20**	**0**
2013–14	Huddersfield T	0	0	**20**	**0**
2013–14	*Tranmere R*	36	1		
2014–15	Tranmere R	18	0		
2018–19	Tranmere R	18	0		
2019–20	Tranmere R	29	1	**101**	**2**

SINNOT, Lewis (D) **0 0**
b. 4-3-02

2019–20	Tranmere R	0	0		

SPELLMAN, Carl (M) **0 0**

2018–19	Tranmere R	0	0		
2019–20	Tranmere R	0	0		

TAYLOR, Corey (F) **35 2**
b.Erdington 23-9-97
Internationals: England U17.

2015–16	Aston Villa	0	0		
2016–17	Aston Villa	1	0		
2017–18	Aston Villa	0	0		
2018–19	Aston Villa	0	0	**1**	**0**
2018–19	*Walsall*	10	0	**10**	**0**
2019–20	Tranmere R	24	2	**24**	**2**

THOMPSON, Bailey (F) **0 0**
b. 7-6-01

2019–20	Tranmere R	0	0		

WALKER-RICE, Danny (F) **0 0**

2018–19	Tranmere R	0	0		
2019–20	Tranmere R	0	0		

WOODS, Calum (D) **286 11**
H: 5 11 W: 11 07 b.Liverpool 5-2-87

2006–07	Dunfermline Ath	12	0		
2007–08	Dunfermline Ath	25	0		
2008–09	Dunfermline Ath	30	5		
2009–10	Dunfermline Ath	29	2		
2010–11	Dunfermline Ath	32	3	**128**	**10**
2011–12	Huddersfield T	26	0		
2012–13	Huddersfield T	27	0		
2013–14	Huddersfield T	19	1	**72**	**1**
2014–15	Preston NE	18	0		
2015–16	Preston NE	32	0		
2016–17	Preston NE	0	0		
2017–18	Preston NE	16	0		
2018–19	Preston NE	1	0	**67**	**0**
2018–19	*Bradford C*	6	0	**6**	**0**
2019–20	Tranmere R	13	0	**13**	**0**

Scholars
Bickerstaffe, Joseph; Blackham, Joe; Burton, Jake Joshua; Corness, Nathan; Farley, Harry James; Ferguson, Cameron Duncan; Gouldbourne, Ethan; Hayde, Kyle William; Jones, Benjamin Thomas; Musuamba, Harrison; Nugent, George Thomas; Quinn, Michael Sean; Rhami, Joshua Demitrius; Shead, Louis James; Sinnott, Lewis Robert; Stratulis, Ryan William; Walton, Jacob William.

WALSALL (85)

ADEBAYO, Elijah (D) **64 15**
b.Brent 7-1-98

2017–18	Fulham	0	0		
2017–18	*Cheltenham T*	7	2	**7**	**2**
2018–19	Fulham	0	0		
2018–19	*Swindon T*	25	5	**25**	**5**
2018–19	*Stevenage*	2	0	**2**	**0**
2019–20	Walsall	30	8	**30**	**8**

BATES, Alfie (M) **13 1**

2018–19	Walsall	0	0		
2019–20	Walsall	13	1	**13**	**1**

CANDLIN, Mitchell (F) **8 0**
H: 6 0 W: 11 09 b. 8-6-00

2016–17	Walsall	5	0		
2017–18	Walsall	3	0		
2018–19	Walsall	0	0		
2018–19	*Blackburn R*	0	0		
2019–20	Walsall	0	0	**8**	**0**

CLARKE, James (D) **139 5**
H: 6 0 W: 13 03 b.Aylesbury 17-11-89
From Watford, Oxford U, Oxford C, Salisbury C, Woking.

2015–16	Bristol R	37	0		
2016–17	Bristol R	22	0		
2017–18	Bristol R	11	0		
2018–19	Bristol R	42	2	**112**	**2**
2019–20	Walsall	27	3	**27**	**3**

COCKERILL-MOLLETT, Callum (D) **10 0**
H: 5 10 W: 11 00 b. 15-1-99
Internationals: Republic of Ireland U18, U19.

2016–17	Walsall	0	0		
2017–18	Walsall	1	0		
2018–19	Walsall	0	0		
2019–20	Walsall	9	0	**10**	**0**

FACEY, Shay (D) **81 1**
H: 5 10 W: 10 00 b.Manchester 7-1-95
Internationals: England U16, U17, U19, U20.

2013–14	Manchester C	0	0		
2014–15	Manchester C	0	0		
2014–15	New York City	0	0		
2015–16	Manchester C	0	0		
2015–16	*New York City*	22	0	**22**	**0**
2015–16	*Rotherham U*	5	0	**5**	**0**
2016–17	Manchester C	0	0		
2016–17	*Heerenveen*	3	0		
2017–18	Heerenveen	0	0	**3**	**0**
2017–18	Northampton T	15	1		
2018–19	Northampton T	23	0	**38**	**1**
2019–20	Walsall	13	0	**13**	**0**

FOULKES, Joe (D) **0 0**

2019–20	Walsall	0	0		

GORDON, Josh (F) **71 16**
H: 5 10 W: 11 00 b.Stoke-on-Trent 19-1-95
From Stafford Rangers.

2017–18	Leicester C	0	0		
2018–19	Walsall	37	7		
2019–20	Walsall	34	9	**71**	**16**

GUTHRIE, Danny (M) **292 16**
H: 5 9 W: 11 06 b.Shrewsbury 18-4-87
Internationals: England U16.

2004–05	Liverpool	0	0		
2005–06	Liverpool	0	0		
2006–07	Liverpool	3	0		
2006–07	*Southampton*	10	0	**10**	**0**
2007–08	Liverpool	0	0	**3**	**0**
2007–08	*Bolton W*	25	0	**25**	**0**
2008–09	Newcastle U	24	2		
2009–10	Newcastle U	38	4		
2010–11	Newcastle U	14	0		
2011–12	Newcastle U	16	1	**92**	**7**
2012–13	Reading	21	1		
2013–14	Reading	32	4		
2014–15	Reading	9	0	**62**	**5**
2014–15	*Fulham*	6	0	**6**	**0**
2015–16	Blackburn R	16	0		
2016–17	Blackburn R	24	1	**40**	**1**
2018	Mitra Kukar	29	2	**29**	**2**
2019–20	Walsall	25	1	**25**	**1**

HARDY, James (M) **11 1**
b. 11-5-96
Internationals: England C.
From AFC Fylde.

2019–20	Walsall	11	1	**11**	**1**

JULES, Zak (D) **49 1**
b. 2-7-97
Internationals: Scotland U17, U18, U19, U20, U21.

2016–17	Reading	0	0		
2016–17	*Motherwell*	10	1	**10**	**1**
2017–18	Shrewsbury T	0	0		
2017–18	*Chesterfield*	6	0	**6**	**0**
2017–18	*Port Vale*	2	0	**2**	**0**
2018–19	Macclesfield T	14	0	**14**	**0**
2019–20	Walsall	17	0	**17**	**0**

KIERSEY, Jack (M) **2 0**
b.Manchester 26-9-98

2018–19	Everton	0	0		
2019–20	Walsall	2	0	**2**	**0**

KINSELLA, Liam (M) **100 1**
b.Colchester 23-2-96
Internationals: Republic of Ireland U19, U21.

2013–14	Walsall	0	0		
2014–15	Walsall	4	0		
2015–16	Walsall	7	1		
2016–17	Walsall	8	0		
2017–18	Walsall	19	0		
2018–19	Walsall	31	0		
2019–20	Walsall	31	0	**100**	**1**

LAVERY, Caolan (F) **160 31**
H: 5 11 W: 11 12 b.Red Deer 22-10-92
Internationals: Canada U17. Northern Ireland U19, U21.

2012–13	Sheffield W	0	0		
2012–13	*Southend U*	3	0	**3**	**0**
2013–14	Sheffield W	21	4		
2013–14	*Plymouth Arg*	8	3	**8**	**3**
2014–15	Sheffield W	13	2		
2014–15	*Chesterfield*	8	3	**8**	**3**
2015–16	Sheffield W	0	0	**34**	**6**
2015–16	*Portsmouth*	13	4	**13**	**4**
2016–17	Sheffield U	27	4		
2017–18	Sheffield U	3	0		
2017–18	*Rotherham U*	14	2	**14**	**2**
2018–19	Sheffield U	0	0	**30**	**4**
2018–19	*Bury*	23	5	**23**	**5**
2019–20	Walsall	27	4	**27**	**4**

LEAK, Tom (D) **0 0**

2019–20	Walsall	0	0		

LIDDLE, Gary (D) **540 28**
H: 6 1 W: 12 06 b.Middlesbrough 15-6-86

2003–04	Middlesbrough	0	0		
2004–05	Middlesbrough	0	0		
2005–06	Middlesbrough	0	0		
2006–07	Hartlepool U	42	3		
2007–08	Hartlepool U	41	2		
2008–09	Hartlepool U	43	0		
2009–10	Hartlepool U	40	3		
2010–11	Hartlepool U	42	6		
2011–12	Hartlepool U	39	4	**247**	**18**
2012–13	Notts Co	46	0		
2013–14	Notts Co	32	4	**78**	**4**
2014–15	Bradford C	41	1		
2015–16	Bradford C	20	2	**61**	**3**
2015–16	Chesterfield	15	0		
2016–17	Chesterfield	26	1	**41**	**1**
2016–17	Carlisle U	21	1		
2017–18	Carlisle U	41	0		
2018–19	Carlisle U	39	1	**101**	**2**
2019–20	Walsall	12	0	**12**	**0**

McDONALD, Wesley (F) **37 5**
H: 5 9 W: 12 02 b.Lambeth 4-5-97

2015–16	Birmingham C	0	0		
2016–17	Birmingham C	0	0		
2017–18	Birmingham C	0	0		
2018–19	Yeovil T	9	0	**9**	**0**
2019–20	Walsall	28	5	**28**	**5**

NOLAN, Jack (M) **4 0**
Internationals: England U17.

2018–19	Reading	0	0		
2019–20	Walsall	4	0	**4**	**0**

NORMAN, Cameron (D) **34 0**
H: 6 2 W: 11 09 b.Norwich 12-10-95
From Norwich C, Concord Rangers, Needham Market, King's Lynn T.

2018–19	Oxford U	7	0	**7**	**0**
2018–19	Walsall	9	0		
2019–20	Walsall	18	0	**27**	**0**

PEARCE, Luke (F) **0 0**

2019–20	Walsall	0	0		

PERRY, Sam (M) **0 0**

2019–20	Walsall	0	0		

ROBERTS, Kory (D) **27 0**
H: 6 0 W: 11 07 b.Birmingham 17-12-97

2016–17	Walsall	4	0		
2017–18	Walsall	21	0		
2018–19	Walsall	0	0		
2019–20	Walsall	2	0	**27**	**0**

ROBERTS, Liam (G) **99 0**
H: 6 0 W: 12 13 b.Walsall 24-11-94

2012–13	Walsall	0	0		
2013–14	Walsall	0	0		
2014–15	Walsall	0	0		
2015–16	Walsall	1	0		
2016–17	Walsall	0	0		
2017–18	Walsall	24	0		
2018–19	Walsall	42	0		
2019–20	Walsall	32	0	**99**	**0**

ROGERSON, Dominic (G) **0 0**

2019–20	Walsall	0	0		

SADLER, Matthew (D) **466 10**
H: 5 11 W: 11 08 b.Birmingham 26-2-85
Internationals: England U17, U18, U19.

2001–02	Birmingham C	0	0		
2002–03	Birmingham C	2	0		
2003–04	Birmingham C	0	0		
2003–04	*Northampton T*	7	0	**7**	**0**
2004–05	Birmingham C	0	0		
2005–06	Birmingham C	8	0		
2006–07	Birmingham C	36	0		
2007–08	Birmingham C	5	0	**51**	**0**
2007–08	Watford	15	0		
2008–09	Watford	15	0		
2009–10	Watford	0	0		
2009–10	*Stockport Co*	20	0	**20**	**0**
2010–11	Watford	0	0	**30**	**0**
2010–11	*Shrewsbury T*	46	0		
2011–12	Walsall	46	1		
2012–13	Crawley T	46	1		
2013–14	Crawley T	46	1		
2014–15	Rotherham U	0	0		
2014–15	*Crawley T*	10	0	**102**	**2**
2014–15	*Oldham Ath*	8	0	**8**	**0**
2014–15	Shrewsbury T	0	0		
2015–16	Shrewsbury T	24	2		
2016–17	Shrewsbury T	34	2		
2017–18	Shrewsbury T	42	1		
2018–19	Shrewsbury T	29	0	**175**	**5**
2019–20	Walsall	27	2	**73**	**3**

SCARR, Dan (D) **72 2**
b. 24-12-94
From Reddich U, Stourbridge.

2017–18	Birmingham C	0	0		
2017–18	*Wycombe W*	22	1	**22**	**1**
2018–19	Birmingham C	0	0		
2018–19	Walsall	17	1		
2019–20	Walsall	33	0	**50**	**1**

SINCLAIR, Stuart (M) **141 7**
H: 5 7 W: 10 08 b.Houghton Conquest 9-11-87
From Luton T, Cambridge C, Bedford T, Dunstable T, Arlesey T, Salisbury C.

2015–16	Bristol R	30	2		
2016–17	Bristol R	38	1		
2017–18	Bristol R	29	2		
2018–19	Bristol R	18	0	**115**	**5**
2019–20	Walsall	26	2	**26**	**2**

WILLIS, Joe (M) **0 0**

2019–20	Walsall	0	0		

Scholars
Allamb-John, Jayden Nathaniel Anton; Barry, Oscar Stanley; Campbell, Jayden Vincent Michael; Coogan, Danny Peter; Dallaywaters, Benjamin Kevin Campbell; Foulkes, Joseph James; Francis, Ade Lamarr; Friel, Benjamin Michael; Lynch, Jack Daniel; McSkeane, Alex Martin; Moss, Perry; Mukadam, Saif Ismail; Perry, Samuel Paul; Petrovics, Alex Arpad; Rogerson, Dominic James Philip; Sharp, Kyle David; Walker, Lewis; Walton, Jak James; Willis, Joseph; Zona, Luke.

WATFORD (86)

BACHMANN, Daniel (G) **34 0**
H: 6 3 W: 12 11 b.Vienna 9-7-94
Internationals: Austria U16, U17, U18, U19, U21.

2011–12	Stoke C	0	0		
2012–13	Stoke C	0	0		
2013–14	Stoke C	0	0		
2014–15	Stoke C	0	0		
2015–16	Stoke C	0	0		
2015–16	*Ross Co*	1	0	**1**	**0**
2015–16	*Bury*	8	0	**8**	**0**
2016–17	Stoke C	0	0		
2017–18	Watford	0	0		
2018–19	Watford	0	0		
2018–19	*Kilmarnock*	25	0	**25**	**0**
2019–20	Watford	0	0		

BALOGUN, Jamal (D) **0 0**
b. 18-1-00

2018–19	Reading	0	0		
2019–20	Watford	0	0		

BARRETT, Mason (D) **0 0**
From West Ham U.

2019–20	Watford	0	0		

BENNETTS, Jayden (M) **0 0**
b. 26-6-01

2019–20	Watford	0	0		

CAPOUE, Etienne (M) **354 23**
H: 6 2 W: 11 10 b.Niort 11-7-88
Internationals: France U18, U19, U21, Full caps.

2006–07	Toulouse	0	0		
2007–08	Toulouse	5	0		
2008–09	Toulouse	32	1		
2009–10	Toulouse	33	0		
2010–11	Toulouse	37	2		
2011–12	Toulouse	33	3		
2012–13	Toulouse	34	7	**174**	**13**
2013–14	Tottenham H	12	1		
2014–15	Tottenham H	12	0	**24**	**1**
2015–16	Watford	33	0		
2016–17	Watford	37	7		
2017–18	Watford	23	1		
2018–19	Watford	33	1		
2019–20	Watford	30	0	**156**	**9**

CATHCART, Craig (D) **319 13**
H: 6 2 W: 11 06 b.Belfast 6-2-89
Internationals: Northern Ireland U16, U17, U20, U21, Full caps.

2005–06	Manchester U	0	0		
2006–07	Manchester U	0	0		
2007–08	Manchester U	0	0		
2007–08	*Antwerp*	13	2	**13**	**2**
2008–09	Manchester U	0	0		
2008–09	*Plymouth Arg*	31	1	**31**	**1**
2009–10	Manchester U	0	0		
2009–10	*Watford*	12	0		
2010–11	Blackpool	30	1		
2011–12	Blackpool	27	0		
2012–13	Blackpool	25	1		
2013–14	Blackpool	30	1	**112**	**3**
2014–15	Watford	29	3		
2015–16	Watford	35	1		
2016–17	Watford	15	0		
2017–18	Watford	7	0		
2018–19	Watford	36	3		
2019–20	Watford	29	0	**163**	**7**

CHALOBAH, Nathaniel (D) **140 9**
H: 6 1 W: 11 11 b.Sierra Leone 12-12-94
Internationals: England U16, U17, U19, U20, U21, Full caps.

2010–11	Chelsea	0	0		
2011–12	Chelsea	0	0		
2012–13	Chelsea	0	0		
2012–13	*Watford*	38	5		
2013–14	Chelsea	0	0		
2013–14	*Nottingham F*	12	2	**12**	**2**
2013–14	*Middlesbrough*	19	1	**19**	**1**
2014–15	Chelsea	0	0		
2014–15	*Burnley*	4	0	**4**	**0**
2014–15	*Reading*	15	1	**15**	**1**
2015–16	Chelsea	0	0		
2015–16	*Napoli*	5	0	**5**	**0**
2016–17	Chelsea	10	0	**10**	**0**
2017–18	Watford	6	0		
2018–19	Watford	9	0		
2019–20	Watford	22	0	**75**	**5**

CLEVERLEY, Tom (M) **262 27**
H: 5 9 W: 10 07 b.Basingstoke 12-8-89
Internationals: England U20, U21, Full caps. Great Britain.

2007–08	Manchester U	0	0		
2008–09	Manchester U	0	0		
2008–09	*Leicester C*	15	2	**15**	**2**
2009–10	Manchester U	0	0		
2009–10	*Watford*	33	11		
2010–11	Manchester U	0	0		
2010–11	*Wigan Ath*	25	3	**25**	**3**
2011–12	Manchester U	10	0		
2012–13	Manchester U	22	2		
2013–14	Manchester U	22	1		

2014–15	Manchester U	1	0	**55**	**3**
2014–15	*Aston Villa*	31	3	**31**	**3**
2015–16	Everton	22	2		
2016–17	Everton	10	0	**32**	**2**
2016–17	*Watford*	17	0		
2017–18	Watford	23	1		
2018–19	Watford	13	1		
2019–20	Watford	18	1	**104**	**14**

DAHLBERG, Pontus (G) **39** **0**
H: 6 4 W: 13 03 b.Alvangen 21-1-99
Internationals: Sweden U17, U19, U21, Full caps.

2015	Gothenburg	0	0		
2016	Gothenburg	0	0		
2017	Gothenburg	29	0		
2018	Gothenburg	10	0	**39**	**0**
2018–19	Watford	0	0		
2019–20	Watford	0	0		
2019–20	*Emmen*	0	0		

DALBY, Sam (F) **18** **1**
b.Leytonstone 17-1-00

2016–17	Leyton Orient	16	1		
2017–18	Leyton Orient	0	0	**16**	**1**
2018–19	Leeds U	0	0		
2018–19	*Morecambe*	2	0	**2**	**0**
2019–20	Watford	0	0		

DAWSON, Craig (D) **326** **39**
H: 6 0 W: 12 04 b.Rochdale 6-5-90
Internationals: England U21. Great Britain.

2008–09	Rochdale	0	0		
2009–10	Rochdale	42	9		
2010–11	WBA	0	0		
2010–11	*Rochdale*	45	10	**87**	**19**
2011–12	WBA	8	0		
2012–13	WBA	1	0		
2012–13	*Bolton W*	16	4	**16**	**4**
2013–14	WBA	12	0		
2014–15	WBA	29	2		
2015–16	WBA	38	4		
2016–17	WBA	37	4		
2017–18	WBA	28	2		
2018–19	WBA	41	2	**194**	**14**
2019–20	Watford	29	2	**29**	**2**

DEENEY, Troy (F) **491** **152**
H: 5 11 W: 12 00 b.Solihull 29-6-88

2006–07	Walsall	1	0		
2007–08	Walsall	35	1		
2008–09	Walsall	45	12		
2009–10	Walsall	42	14	**123**	**27**
2010–11	Watford	36	3		
2011–12	Watford	43	11		
2012–13	Watford	40	19		
2013–14	Watford	44	24		
2014–15	Watford	42	21		
2015–16	Watford	38	13		
2016–17	Watford	37	10		
2017–18	Watford	29	5		
2018–19	Watford	32	9		
2019–20	Watford	27	10	**368**	**125**

DELE-BASHIRU, Ayotomiwa (M) **0** **0**
H: 6 0 W: 10 10 b. 17-9-99
Internationals: England U16, U20.

2017–18	Manchester C	0	0		
2018–19	Manchester C	0	0		
2019–20	Watford	0	0		

DEULOFEU, Gerard (F) **173** **26**
H: 5 10 W: 11 01 b.Riudarenes 13-3-94
Internationals: Spain U16, U17, U19, U20, U21, Full caps.

2010–11	Barcelona	0	0		
2011–12	Barcelona	1	0		
2012–13	Barcelona	1	0		
2013–14	Barcelona	0	0		
2013–14	*Everton*	25	3		
2014–15	Barcelona	0	0		
2014–15	*Sevilla*	17	1	**17**	**1**
2015–16	Everton	26	2		
2016–17	Everton	11	0	**62**	**5**
2016–17	*AC Milan*	17	4	**17**	**4**
2017–18	Barcelona	10	1	**12**	**1**
2017–18	*Watford*	7	1		
2018–19	Watford	30	10		
2019–20	Watford	28	4	**65**	**15**

DOUCOURE, Abdoulaye (M) **219** **29**
b.Meulan-en-Yvelines 1-1-93
Internationals: France U17, U18, U19, U20, U21.

2012–13	Rennes	4	1		
2013–14	Rennes	20	6		
2014–15	Rennes	35	3		
2015–16	Rennes	16	2	**75**	**12**
2015–16	Watford	0	0		
2015–16	*Granada*	15	0	**15**	**0**
2016–17	Watford	20	1		
2017–18	Watford	37	7		
2018–19	Watford	35	5		
2019–20	Watford	37	4	**129**	**17**

FEMENIA, Kiko (M) **237** **11**
H: 5 9 W: 9 11 b.Sanet i Negrals 2-2-91
Internationals: Spain U18, U19, U20.

2007–08	Hercules	1	0		
2008–09	Hercules	1	0		
2009–10	Hercules	35	3		
2010–11	Hercules	34	1	**71**	**4**
2011–12	Barcelona	0	0		
2012–13	Barcelona	0	0		
2013–14	Real Madrid	0	0		
2014–15	Alcorcon	17	0	**17**	**0**
2015–16	Alaves	38	5		
2016–17	Alaves	31	0	**69**	**5**
2017–18	Watford	23	1		
2018–19	Watford	29	1		
2019–20	Watford	28	0	**80**	**2**

FOLIVI, Michael (F) **22** **2**
H: 5 11 W: 12 06 b.Brent 25-2-98

2016–17	Watford	1	0		
2016–17	*Coventry C*	1	0	**1**	**0**
2017–18	Watford	0	0		
2018–19	Watford	0	0		
2018–19	*AFC Wimbledon*	10	2		
2019–20	Watford	0	0	**1**	**0**
2019–20	*AFC Wimbledon*	10	0	**20**	**2**

FOSTER, Ben (G) **427** **0**
H: 6 2 W: 12 08 b.Leamington Spa 3-4-83
Internationals: England Full caps.

2000–01	Stoke C	0	0		
2001–02	Stoke C	0	0		
2002–03	Stoke C	0	0		
2003–04	Stoke C	0	0		
2004–05	Stoke C	0	0		
2004–05	*Kidderminster H*	2	0	**2**	**0**
2004–05	*Wrexham*	17	0	**17**	**0**
2005–06	Manchester U	0	0		
2005–06	*Watford*	44	0		
2006–07	Manchester U	0	0		
2006–07	*Watford*	29	0		
2007–08	Manchester U	1	0		
2008–09	Manchester U	2	0		
2009–10	Manchester U	9	0	**12**	**0**
2010–11	Birmingham C	38	0		
2011–12	Birmingham C	0	0	**38**	**0**
2011–12	*WBA*	37	0		
2012–13	WBA	30	0		
2013–14	WBA	24	0		
2014–15	WBA	28	0		
2015–16	WBA	15	0		
2016–17	WBA	38	0		
2017–18	WBA	37	0	**209**	**0**
2018–19	Watford	38	0		
2019–20	Watford	38	0	**149**	**0**

FOULQUIER, Dimitri (D) **169** **5**
b.Sarcelles 23-3-93
Internationals: France U18, U19, U20, U21, Guadeloupe Full caps.

2010–11	Rennes	0	0		
2011–12	Rennes	2	0		
2012–13	Rennes	15	0		
2013–14	Rennes	2	0	**19**	**0**
2013–14	Granada	24	0		
2014–15	Granada	25	0		
2015–16	Granada	21	1		
2016–17	Granada	22	0		
2017–18	Strasbourg	16	0	**16**	**0**
2018–19	Watford	0	0		
2018–19	*Getafe*	22	3	**22**	**3**
2019–20	Watford	3	0	**3**	**0**
2019–20	*Granada*	17	1	**109**	**2**

GOMES, Heurelho (G) **435** **0**
H: 6 3 W: 12 13 b.Minas Gerais 15-2-81
Internationals: Brazil U23, Full caps.

2001	Cruzeiro	0	0		
2002	Cruzeiro	14	0		
2003	Cruzeiro	40	0		
2004	Cruzeiro	5	0	**59**	**0**
2004–05	PSV Eindhoven	30	0		
2005–06	PSV Eindhoven	32	0		
2006–07	PSV Eindhoven	32	0		
2007–08	PSV Eindhoven	34	0	**128**	**0**
2008–09	Tottenham H	34	0		
2009–10	Tottenham H	31	0		
2010–11	Tottenham H	30	0		
2011–12	Tottenham H	0	0		
2012–13	Tottenham H	0	0		
2012–13	*Hoffenheim*	9	0	**9**	**0**
2013–14	Tottenham H	0	0	**95**	**0**
2014–15	Watford	44	0		
2015–16	Watford	38	0		
2016–17	Watford	38	0		
2017–18	Watford	24	0		
2018–19	Watford	0	0		
2019–20	Watford	0	0	**144**	**0**

GRAY, Andre (F) **207** **64**
H: 5 10 W: 12 06 b.Shrewsbury 26-6-91
Internationals: England C.

2009–10	Shrewsbury T	4	0	**4**	**0**

From Hinckley U, Luton T.

2014–15	Brentford	45	16		
2015–16	Brentford	2	2	**47**	**18**
2015–16	Burnley	41	23		
2016–17	Burnley	32	9	**73**	**32**
2017–18	Watford	31	5		
2018–19	Watford	29	7		
2019–20	Watford	23	2	**83**	**14**

HINDS, Kaylen (F) **14** **0**
b.Brent 28-1-98
Internationals: England U16, U17, U18, U20.

2016–17	Arsenal	0	0		
2016–17	*Stevenage*	13	0	**13**	**0**
2017–18	Wolfsburg	1	0		
2018–19	Wolfsburg	0	0	**1**	**0**
2019–20	Watford	0	0		

HOLEBAS, Jose (M) **339** **37**
H: 6 0 W: 12 06 b.Aschaffenburg 27-6-84
Internationals: Greece Full caps.

2005–06	Viktoria Kahl	33	15	**33**	**15**
2006–07	1860 Munich	0	0		
2007–08	1860 Munich	19	2		
2008–09	1860 Munich	24	1		
2009–10	1860 Munich	31	4	**74**	**7**
2010–11	Olympiacos	24	1		
2011–12	Olympiacos	23	2		
2012–13	Olympiacos	28	4		
2013–14	Olympiacos	19	2	**94**	**9**
2014–15	Roma	24	1	**24**	**1**
2015–16	Watford	11	0		
2016–17	Watford	33	2		
2017–18	Watford	28	0		
2018–19	Watford	28	3		
2019–20	Watford	14	0	**114**	**5**

HUGHES, Will (M) **242** **14**
H: 6 1 W: 11 08 b.Weybridge 7-4-95
Internationals: England U17, U21.

2011–12	Derby Co	3	0		
2012–13	Derby Co	35	2		
2013–14	Derby Co	41	3		
2014–15	Derby Co	42	2		
2015–16	Derby Co	6	0		
2016–17	Derby Co	38	2	**165**	**9**
2017–18	Watford	15	2		
2018–19	Watford	32	2		
2019–20	Watford	30	1	**77**	**5**

HUNGBO, Joseph (M) **0** **0**

2018–19	Crystal Palace	0	0		
2019–20	Watford	0	0		

JAKUBIAK, Alex (F) **129** **19**
H: 5 10 W: 10 06 b.Westminster 27-8-96
Internationals: Scotland U19.

2013–14	Watford	1	0		
2014–15	Watford	0	0		
2014–15	*Oxford U*	9	1	**9**	**1**
2014–15	*Dagenham & R*	23	4	**23**	**4**
2015–16	Watford	0	0		
2016–17	Watford	0	0		
2016–17	*Fleetwood T*	3	0	**3**	**0**
2016–17	*Wycombe W*	10	1	**10**	**1**
2017–18	Watford	0	0		
2017–18	*Falkirk*	14	5	**14**	**5**
2018–19	Watford	0	0		
2018–19	*Bristol R*	38	2	**38**	**2**
2019–20	Watford	0	0	**1**	**0**
2019–20	*Gillingham*	24	6	**24**	**6**
2019–20	*St Mirren*	7	0	**7**	**0**

JANJEVA, Andi (D) **0** **0**
b. 11-10-02

2019–20	Watford	0	0		

JANMAAT, Daryl (D) **318** **20**
H: 6 1 W: 12 13 b.Leidschendam 22-7-89
Internationals: Netherlands U20, U21, Full caps.

2007–08	Den Haag	25	2	**25**	**2**
2008–09	Heerenveen	10	0		
2009–10	Heerenveen	28	0		
2010–11	Heerenveen	24	3		
2011–12	Heerenveen	22	2	**84**	**5**
2012–13	Feyenoord	32	3		
2013–14	Feyenoord	30	2	**62**	**5**
2014–15	Newcastle U	37	1		
2015–16	Newcastle U	32	2		
2016–17	Newcastle U	2	0	**71**	**3**
2016–17	Watford	27	2		
2017–18	Watford	23	3		
2018–19	Watford	18	0		
2019–20	Watford	8	0	**76**	**5**

JOAO PEDRO, de Jesus (F) **3 0**
b. 26-9-01
2019–20 Fluminense 0 0
2019–20 Watford 3 0 **3 0**

KABASELE, Christian (D) **242 20**
b.Lubumbashi 24-2-91
Internationals: Belgium U19, U20, Full caps.
2008–09 Eupen 3 0
2009–10 Eupen 1 0
2010–11 Eupen 3 0
2010–11 *Mechelen* 4 1 **4 1**
2011–12 Ludogorets 11 3 **11 3**
2012–13 Eupen 26 4
2013–14 Eupen 26 2 **59 6**
2014–15 Genk 34 2
2015–16 Genk 42 4 **76 6**
2016–17 Watford 16 2
2017–18 Watford 28 2
2018–19 Watford 21 0
2019–20 Watford 27 0 **92 4**

MARIAPPA, Adrian (D) **365 6**
H: 5 10 W: 11 12 b.Harrow 3-10-86
Internationals: Jamaica Full caps.
2005–06 Watford 3 0
2006–07 Watford 19 0
2007–08 Watford 25 0
2008–09 Watford 39 1
2009–10 Watford 46 1
2010–11 Watford 45 1
2011–12 Watford 39 1
2012–13 Reading 29 1
2013–14 Reading 0 0 **29 1**
2013–14 Crystal Palace 24 1
2014–15 Crystal Palace 12 0
2015–16 Crystal Palace 3 0 **39 1**
2016–17 Watford 7 0
2017–18 Watford 28 0
2018–19 Watford 26 0
2019–20 Watford 20 0 **297 4**

MASINA, Adam (D) **167 5**
H: 5 10 W: 10 12 b.Khouribga 2-1-94
Internationals: Italy U21.
2013–14 Bologna 0 0
2014–15 Bologna 28 1
2015–16 Bologna 33 2
2016–17 Bologna 32 1
2017–18 Bologna 34 0 **127 4**
2018–19 Watford 14 0
2019–20 Watford 26 1 **40 1**

NAVARRO, Marc (D) **37 3**
H: 6 2 W: 12 06 b.Barcelona 2-7-85
From Barcelona.
2014–15 Espanyol 0 0
2015–16 Espanyol 0 0
2016–17 Espanyol 12 2
2017–18 Espanyol 19 1 **31 3**
2018–19 Watford 2 0
2019–20 Watford 0 0 **2 0**
2019–20 *Leganes* 4 0 **4 0**

PARKES, Adam (G) **0 0**
b. 30-11-99
Internationals: England U17.
From Southampton.
2019–20 Watford 0 0

PENARANDA, Adalberto (F) **81 9**
b.El Vigia 31-5-97
Internationals: Venezuela U17, U20, Full caps.
2013–14 Dep La Guaira 18 1
2014–15 Dep La Guaira 19 3 **37 4**
2015–16 Udinese 0 0
2015–16 Watford 0 0
2015–16 *Granada* 23 5 **23 5**
2016–17 Watford 0 0
2016–17 *Malaga* 3 0
2017–18 Watford 0 0
2017–18 *Malaga* 13 0 **16 0**
2018–19 Watford 0 0
2019–20 Watford 0 0
2019–20 *Eupen* 5 0 **5 0**

PEREYRA, Roberto (M) **281 28**
H: 6 2 W: 11 11 b.Argentina 17-1-91
Internationals: Argentina U20, Full caps.
2008–09 River Plate 1 0
2009–10 River Plate 15 0
2010–11 River Plate 27 0 **43 0**
2011–12 Udinese 11 1
2012–13 Udinese 37 5
2013–14 Udinese 36 2
2014–15 Udinese 0 0 **84 8**
2014–15 *Juventus* 35 4
2015–16 Juventus 13 0 **48 4**
2016–17 Watford 13 2
2017–18 Watford 32 5
2018–19 Watford 33 6
2019–20 Watford 28 3 **106 16**

PERKINS, Teddy (D) **0 0**
2016–17 Leyton Orient 0 0
2017–18 Leyton Orient 0 0
2018–19 Burnley 0 0
2019–20 Watford 0 0

PRODL, Sebastien (D) **269 17**
H: 6 4 W: 13 05 b.Graz 21-6-87
Internationals: Austria U19, U20, Full caps.
2006–07 Sturm Graz 16 1
2007–08 Sturm Graz 27 3 **43 4**
2008–09 Werder Bremen 22 0
2009–10 Werder Bremen 9 1
2010–11 Werder Bremen 25 1
2011–12 Werder Bremen 16 2
2012–13 Werder Bremen 28 1
2013–14 Werder Bremen 27 2
2014–15 Werder Bremen 22 3 **149 10**
2015–16 Watford 21 2
2016–17 Watford 33 1
2017–18 Watford 21 0
2018–19 Watford 1 0
2019–20 Watford 1 0 **77 3**
Transferred to Udinese, February 2020.

PUSSETTO , Ignacio (M) **140 20**
b.Canada Rosquin 21-12-95
2012–13 Atletico de Rafaela 0 0
2013–14 Atletico de Rafaela 11 0
2014 Atletico de Rafaela 3 0
2015 Atletico de Rafaela 19 2
2016 Atletico de Rafaela 11 2 **44 4**
2016–17 Huracan 15 2
2017–18 Huracan 27 9 **42 11**
2018–19 Udinese 35 4
2019–20 Udinese 12 1 **47 5**
2019–20 Watford 7 0 **7 0**

QUINA, Domingos (F) **12 1**
b. 18-11-99
Internationals: Portugal U17, U18, U19, U20.
2016–17 West Ham U 0 0
2017–18 West Ham U 0 0
2018–19 Watford 8 1
2019–20 Watford 4 0 **12 1**

SARR, Ismaila (M) **118 23**
b.Saint-Louis 25-2-98
Internationals: Senegal U23, Full caps.
2016–17 Metz 31 5 **31 5**
2017–18 Rennes 24 5
2018–19 Rennes 35 8
2019–20 Rennes 0 0 **59 13**
2019–20 Watford 28 5 **28 5**

SEMA, Ken (M) **189 26**
H: 5 10 W: 11 03 b.Norrkoping 30-9-93
Internationals: Sweden U23, Full caps.
2013 IFK Norrkoping 0 0
2013 *IF Sylvia* 22 4 **22 4**
2014 Ljungskile 30 7
2015 Ljungskile 30 4 **60 11**
2016 Ostersunds 23 4
2017 Ostersunds 24 4
2018 Ostersunds 11 0 **58 8**
2018–19 Watford 17 1
2019–20 Watford 0 0 **17 1**
2019–20 *Udinese* 32 2 **32 2**

SINCLAIR, Jerome (F) **69 5**
H: 5 8 W: 12 06 b.Birmingham 20-9-96
Internationals: England U16, U17.
2012–13 Liverpool 0 0
2013–14 Liverpool 0 0
2014–15 Liverpool 2 0
2014–15 *Wigan Ath* 1 0 **1 0**
2015–16 Liverpool 0 0 **2 0**
2016–17 Watford 5 0
2016–17 *Birmingham C* 5 0 **5 0**
2017–18 Watford 4 0
2018–19 Watford 0 0
2018–19 *Sunderland* 13 1 **13 1**
2018–19 *Oxford U* 16 4 **16 4**
2019–20 Watford 0 0 **9 0**
2019–20 *VVV Venlo* 23 0 **23 0**

SPENCER-ADAMS, Bayli (D) **0 0**
b. 26-6-01
From Arsenal.
2019–20 Watford 0 0

SUCCESS, Isaac (F) **112 9**
H: 6 1 W: 11 03 b. 7-1-96
Internationals: Nigeria U17, U20, Full caps.
2014–15 Granada 19 1
2015–16 Granada 30 6 **49 7**
2016–17 Watford 19 1
2017–18 Watford 0 0
2017–18 *Malaga* 9 0 **9 0**
2018–19 Watford 30 1
2019–20 Watford 5 0 **54 2**

WELBECK, Danny (F) **232 46**
H: 6 1 W: 11 07 b.Manchester 26-11-90
Internationals: England U17, U18, U19, U21, Full caps.
2007–08 Manchester U 0 0
2008–09 Manchester U 3 1
2009–10 Manchester U 5 0
2009–10 *Preston NE* 8 2 **8 2**
2010–11 Manchester U 0 0
2010–11 *Sunderland* 26 6 **26 6**
2011–12 Manchester U 30 9
2012–13 Manchester U 27 1
2013–14 Manchester U 25 9
2014–15 Manchester U 2 0 **92 20**
2014–15 Arsenal 25 4
2015–16 Arsenal 11 4
2016–17 Arsenal 16 2
2017–18 Arsenal 28 5
2018–19 Arsenal 8 1 **88 16**
2019–20 Watford 18 2 **18 2**

WHELAN, Callum (M) **0 0**
b.Barnsley 24-9-98
2018–19 Manchester U 0 0
2019–20 Watford 0 0

WILMOT, Ben (M) **38 2**
H: 6 2 W: 12 08 b. 4-11-99
Internationals: England U19, U20, U21.
2016–17 Stevenage 0 0
2017–18 Stevenage 10 0 **10 0**
2018–19 Watford 2 0
2018–19 *Udinese* 5 0 **5 0**
2019–20 Watford 0 0 **2 0**
2019–20 *Swansea C* 21 2 **21 2**

WISE, Henry (M) **0 0**
b. 1-1-00
From Arsenal.
2019–20 Watford 0 0

retained or with offer of contract
Agyakwa, Derek Emmanuel Adjei; Alvarado Hoyos, Jamie Alberto; Barrozo Rodrigues, Matheus Aias; Becerra Maya, Juan Camillo; Crichlow, Kane Sinclair; Elitim Sepulveda, Juergen Farid; Estupinan Tenorio, Pervis Josue; Fobi, Kingsley; Forster, Harry James; Hernandez Suarez, Juan Camilo; Langston, George James Barbosa; Lo-Everton, Sonny Blu; Mbaye, Mamadou; McLean Cassidy, Ryan Michael; Phillips, Daniel Shaquille Jabari; Roberts, Myles Conrad; Santana Ferreira, Matheus Henrique; Segura Portocarrero, Jorge Andres; Sibo, Kwasi; Stuparevic, Filip; Suarez Charris, Luis Javier; Velasquez Reyes, Williams Daniel.

Scholars
Adebiyi, Emmanuel; Baptiste, Dante Astor Kareem; Broome, Jack David; Burchell, Jack Oliver; Conteh, Kamil Amadu; Harrison, Jordan Carter; Horsewood, Thomas Roger; Hoskins, James Michael; Hudson, Harry Jonathan; Hutchinson, Dominic Charles; Janjeva, Andi; Lawal, Mohammed Olabosun; MacLean, Ryan Thomas William; Matthews, James John; McKiernan, John Joshua; Sankoh, Imaad Suffian aziz; Thompson, Max; White, Harvey Batterson.

WBA (87)

AJAYI, Semi (D) **159 17**
H: 6 4 W: 13 00 b.Croydon 9-11-93
Internationals: Nigeria U20, Full caps.
2012–13 Charlton Ath 0 0
2013–14 Charlton Ath 0 0
2014–15 Arsenal 0 0
2014–15 *Cardiff C* 0 0
2015–16 Cardiff C 0 0
2015–16 *AFC Wimbledon* 5 0 **5 0**
2015–16 *Crewe Alex* 13 0 **13 0**
2016–17 Cardiff C 0 0
2016–17 *Rotherham U* 17 1
2017–18 Rotherham U 35 4
2018–19 Rotherham U 46 7 **98 12**
2019–20 WBA 43 5 **43 5**

AL HABSI, Ali (G) **321** **0**
H: 6 4 W: 12 06 b.Oman 30-12-81
Internationals: Oman Full caps.

2003	Lyn	13	0		
2004	Lyn	24	0		
2005	Lyn	25	0	**62**	**0**
2005–06	Bolton W	0	0		
2006–07	Bolton W	0	0		
2007–08	Bolton W	10	0		
2008–09	Bolton W	0	0		
2009–10	Bolton W	0	0		
2010–11	Bolton W	0	0	**10**	**0**
2010–11	*Wigan Ath*	34	0		
2011–12	Wigan Ath	38	0		
2012–13	Wigan Ath	29	0		
2013–14	Wigan Ath	24	0		
2014–15	Wigan Ath	11	0	**136**	**0**
2014–15	*Brighton & HA*	1	0	**1**	**0**
2015–16	Reading	32	0		
2016–17	Reading	46	0	**78**	**0**
2017–18	Al-Hilal	13	0		
2017–18	Al-Hilal	21	0	**34**	**0**
2019–20	WBA	0	0		

AUSTIN, Charlie (F) **323** **143**
H: 6 2 W: 13 03 b.Hungerford 5-7-89

2009–10	Swindon T	33	19		
2010–11	Swindon T	21	12	**54**	**31**
2010–11	Burnley	4	0		
2011–12	Burnley	41	16		
2012–13	Burnley	37	25	**82**	**41**
2013–14	QPR	31	17		
2014–15	QPR	35	18		
2015–16	QPR	16	10	**82**	**45**
2015–16	Southampton	7	1		
2016–17	Southampton	15	6		
2017–18	Southampton	24	7		
2018–19	Southampton	25	2		
2019–20	Southampton	0	0	**71**	**16**
2019–20	WBA	34	10	**34**	**10**

BARRY, Gareth (M) **680** **54**
H: 5 11 W: 12 06 b.Hastings 23-2-81
Internationals: England B, U21, Full caps.

1997–98	Aston Villa	2	0		
1998–99	Aston Villa	32	2		
1999–2000	Aston Villa	30	1		
2000–01	Aston Villa	30	0		
2001–02	Aston Villa	20	0		
2002–03	Aston Villa	35	3		
2003–04	Aston Villa	36	3		
2004–05	Aston Villa	34	7		
2005–06	Aston Villa	36	3		
2006–07	Aston Villa	35	8		
2007–08	Aston Villa	37	9		
2008–09	Aston Villa	38	5	**365**	**41**
2009–10	Manchester C	34	2		
2010–11	Manchester C	33	2		
2011–12	Manchester C	34	1		
2012–13	Manchester C	31	1		
2013–14	Manchester C	0	0	**132**	**6**
2013–14	*Everton*	32	3		
2014–15	Everton	33	0		
2015–16	Everton	33	0		
2016–17	Everton	33	2	**131**	**5**
2017–18	WBA	25	1		
2018–19	WBA	24	1		
2019–20	WBA	3	0	**52**	**2**

BARTLEY, Kyle (D) **208** **13**
H: 5 11 W: 11 00 b.Stockport 22-5-91
Internationals: England U16, U17.

2008–09	Arsenal	0	0		
2009–10	Arsenal	0	0		
2009–10	*Sheffield U*	14	0		
2010–11	Arsenal	0	0		
2010–11	*Sheffield U*	21	0	**35**	**0**
2010–11	*Rangers*	5	1		
2011–12	Arsenal	0	0		
2011–12	*Rangers*	19	0	**24**	**1**
2012–13	Arsenal	0	0		
2012–13	Swansea C	2	0		
2013–14	Swansea C	2	0		
2013–14	*Birmingham C*	17	3	**17**	**3**
2014–15	Swansea C	7	0		
2015–16	Swansea C	5	0		
2016–17	Swansea C	0	0		
2016–17	*Leeds U*	45	6	**45**	**6**
2017–18	Swansea C	5	0	**21**	**0**
2018–19	WBA	28	1		
2019–20	WBA	38	2	**66**	**3**

BOND, Jonathan (G) **91** **0**
H: 6 3 W: 13 03 b.Hemel Hempstead 19-5-93
Internationals: Wales U17, U19. England U20, U21.

2010–11	Watford	0	0		
2011–12	Watford	1	0		
2011–12	*Dagenham & R*	5	0	**5**	**0**
2011–12	*Bury*	6	0	**6**	**0**
2012–13	Watford	8	0		
2013–14	Watford	10	0		
2014–15	Watford	3	0	**22**	**0**
2015–16	Reading	14	0		
2016–17	Reading	0	0		
2016–17	*Gillingham*	7	0	**7**	**0**
2017–18	Reading	0	0	**14**	**0**
2017–18	*Peterborough U*	37	0	**37**	**0**
2018–19	WBA	0	0		
2019–20	WBA	0	0		

BRUNT, Chris (M) **522** **67**
H: 6 1 W: 13 04 b.Belfast 14-12-84
Internationals: Northern Ireland U19, U21, U23, Full caps.

2002–03	Middlesbrough	0	0		
2003–04	Middlesbrough	0	0		
2003–04	Sheffield W	9	2		
2004–05	Sheffield W	42	4		
2005–06	Sheffield W	44	7		
2006–07	Sheffield W	44	11		
2007–08	Sheffield W	1	0	**140**	**24**
2007–08	WBA	34	4		
2008–09	WBA	34	8		
2009–10	WBA	40	13		
2010–11	WBA	34	4		
2011–12	WBA	29	2		
2012–13	WBA	31	2		
2013–14	WBA	28	3		
2014–15	WBA	34	2		
2015–16	WBA	22	0		
2016–17	WBA	31	3		
2017–18	WBA	26	0		
2018–19	WBA	32	2		
2019–20	WBA	7	0	**382**	**43**

BURKE, Oliver (M) **117** **12**
H: 5 9 W: 11 11 b.Melton Mowbray 7-4-97
Internationals: Scotland U19, U20, Full caps.

2014–15	Nottingham F	2	0		
2014–15	*Bradford C*	2	0	**2**	**0**
2015–16	Nottingham F	18	2		
2016–17	Nottingham F	5	4	**25**	**6**
2016–17	RB Leipzig	25	1	**25**	**1**
2017–18	WBA	15	0		
2018–19	WBA	3	0		
2018–19	*Celtic*	14	4	**14**	**4**
2019–20	WBA	2	0	**20**	**0**
2019–20	*Alaves*	31	1	**31**	**1**

EDWARDS, Kyle (M) **55** **3**
H: 5 8 W: 10 01 b.Dudley 17-2-98
Internationals: England U16, U17, U20.

2015–16	WBA	0	0		
2016–17	WBA	0	0		
2017–18	WBA	0	0		
2017–18	*Exeter C*	23	0	**23**	**0**
2018–19	WBA	6	1		
2019–20	WBA	26	2	**32**	**3**

FERGUSON, Nathan (D) **21** **1**
b. 6-10-00
Internationals: England U18, U19, U20.

2017–18	WBA	0	0		
2018–19	WBA	0	0		
2019–20	WBA	21	1	**21**	**1**

FIELD, Sam (M) **48** **2**
b. 8-5-98
Internationals: England U18, U19, U20.

2015–16	WBA	1	0		
2016–17	WBA	8	0		
2017–18	WBA	10	1		
2018–19	WBA	12	1		
2019–20	WBA	0	0	**31**	**2**
2019–20	*Charlton Ath*	17	0	**17**	**0**

FITZWATER, Jack (D) **51** **4**
H: 6 2 W: 11 00 b.Solihull 23-9-97

2015–16	WBA	0	0		
2015–16	*Chesterfield*	1	0	**1**	**0**
2016–17	WBA	0	0		
2017–18	WBA	0	0		
2017–18	*Forest Green R*	14	1	**14**	**1**
2017–18	*Walsall*	15	3		
2018–19	WBA	0	0		
2018–19	*Walsall*	21	0	**36**	**3**
2019–20	WBA	0	0		

FURLONG, Darnell (D) **150** **5**
b. 31-10-95

2014–15	QPR	3	0		
2015–16	QPR	0	0		
2015–16	*Northampton T*	10	0	**10**	**0**
2015–16	*Cambridge U*	21	0	**21**	**0**
2016–17	QPR	14	0		
2016–17	*Swindon T*	24	2	**24**	**2**
2017–18	QPR	22	0		
2018–19	QPR	25	1	**64**	**1**
2019–20	WBA	31	2	**31**	**2**

GIBBS, Kieran (M) **227** **7**
H: 5 10 W: 10 02 b.Lambeth 26-9-89
Internationals: England U19, U20, U21, Full caps.

2007–08	Arsenal	0	0		
2007–08	*Norwich C*	7	0	**7**	**0**
2008–09	Arsenal	8	0		
2009–10	Arsenal	3	0		
2010–11	Arsenal	7	0		
2011–12	Arsenal	16	1		
2012–13	Arsenal	27	0		
2013–14	Arsenal	28	0		
2014–15	Arsenal	22	0		
2015–16	Arsenal	15	1		
2016–17	Arsenal	11	0		
2017–18	Arsenal	0	0	**137**	**2**
2017–18	WBA	33	0		
2018–19	WBA	36	4		
2019–20	WBA	14	1	**83**	**5**

GROSICKI, Kamil (M) **404** **72**
H: 5 11 W: 12 04 b.Szczecin 8-6-88
Internationals: Poland U19, U21, Full caps.

2005–06	Pognon Szczecin	2	0		
2006–07	Pognon Szczecin	21	2	**23**	**2**
2007–08	Legia Warsaw	11	1		
2007–08	Sion	8	2	**8**	**2**
2008–09	Legia Warsaw	0	0	**11**	**1**
2008–09	Jagiellonia	13	4		
2009–10	Jagiellonia	30	4		
2010–11	Jagiellonia	15	6	**58**	**14**
2010–11	Sivasspor	17	6		
2011–12	Sivasspor	40	7		
2012–13	Sivasspor	28	2		
2013–14	Sivasspor	5	0	**90**	**15**
2013–14	Rennes	13	0		
2014–15	Rennes	19	0		
2015–16	Rennes	33	9		
2016–17	Rennes	16	4	**81**	**13**
2016–17	Hull C	15	0		
2017–18	Hull C	37	9		
2018–19	Hull C	39	9		
2019–20	Hull C	28	6	**119**	**24**
2019–20	WBA	14	1	**14**	**1**

HARPER, Rekeem (M) **31** **1**
H: 6 0 W: 10 01 b. 8-3-00
Internationals: England U17, U19.

2016–17	WBA	0	0		
2017–18	WBA	1	0		
2017–18	*Blackburn R*	4	0	**4**	**0**
2018–19	WBA	16	1		
2019–20	WBA	10	0	**27**	**1**

HEGAZI, Ahmed (D) **173** **4**
H: 6 5 W: 11 03 b.Ismalia 25-1-91
Internationals: Egypt U20, U23, Full caps.

2009–10	Ismaily	12	0		
2010–11	Ismaily	7	0		
2011–12	Ismaily	9	0	**28**	**0**
2012–13	Fiorentina	2	0		
2013–14	Fiorentina	1	0		
2014–15	Fiorentina	0	0	**3**	**0**
2014–15	*Perugia*	10	0	**10**	**0**
2015–16	Al Ahly	29	0		
2016–17	Al Ahly	11	0	**40**	**0**
2017–18	WBA	38	2		
2018–19	WBA	38	1		
2019–20	WBA	16	1	**92**	**4**

JOHNSTONE, Samuel (G) **232** **0**
H: 6 0 W: 12 10 b.Preston 25-3-93
Internationals: England U16, U17, U19, U20.

2009–10	Manchester U	0	0		
2010–11	Manchester U	0	0		
2011–12	Manchester U	0	0		
2011–12	*Scunthorpe U*	12	0	**12**	**0**
2012–13	Manchester U	0	0		
2012–13	*Walsall*	7	0	**7**	**0**
2013–14	Manchester U	0	0		
2013–14	*Yeovil T*	1	0	**1**	**0**
2013–14	*Doncaster R*	18	0		
2014–15	Manchester U	0	0		
2014–15	*Doncaster R*	10	0	**28**	**0**
2014–15	*Preston NE*	22	0		
2015–16	Manchester U	0	0		
2015–16	*Preston NE*	4	0	**26**	**0**
2016–17	Manchester U	0	0		
2016–17	*Aston Villa*	21	0		
2017–18	Manchester U	0	0		
2017–18	*Aston Villa*	45	0	**66**	**0**
2018–19	WBA	46	0		
2019–20	WBA	46	0	**92**	**0**

KROVINOVIC, Filip (M)				**167**	**21**
b.Zagreb 29-8-95					
Internationals: Croatia U19, U21.					
2012–13	NK Zagreb	2	0		
2013–14	NK Zagreb	32	7		
2014–15	NK Zagreb	35	3		
2015–16	NK Zagreb	6	2	**75**	**12**
2015–16	Rio Ave	9	0		
2016–17	Rio Ave	26	5	**35**	**5**
2017–18	Benfica	13	1		
2018–19	Benfica	4	0		
2019–20	Benfica	0	0	**17**	**1**
On loan from Benfica.					
2019–20	WBA	40	3	**40**	**3**

LEKO, Jonathan (M)				**48**	**5**
H: 6 0 W: 11 11 b.Kinshasa 24-4-99					
Internationals: England U16, U17, U18, U19, U20.					
2015–16	WBA	5	0		
2016–17	WBA	9	0		
2017–18	*Bristol C*	11	0	**11**	**0**
2017–18	WBA	0	0		
2018–19	WBA	2	0		
2019–20	WBA	0	0	**16**	**0**
2019–20	*Charlton Ath*	21	5	**21**	**5**

LIVERMORE, Jake (M)				**343**	**18**
H: 5 9 W: 12 08 b.Enfield 14-11-89					
Internationals: England Full caps.					
2006–07	Tottenham H	0	0		
2007–08	Tottenham H	0	0		
2007–08	*Milton Keynes D*	5	0	**5**	**0**
2008–09	Tottenham H	0	0		
2008–09	*Crewe Alex*	0	0		
2009–10	Tottenham H	1	0		
2009–10	*Derby Co*	16	1	**16**	**1**
2009–10	*Peterborough U*	9	1	**9**	**1**
2010–11	Tottenham H	0	0		
2010–11	*Ipswich T*	12	0	**12**	**0**
2010–11	*Leeds U*	5	0	**5**	**0**
2011–12	Tottenham H	24	0		
2012–13	Tottenham H	11	0		
2013–14	Tottenham H	0	0	**36**	**0**
2013–14	*Hull C*	36	3		
2014–15	Hull C	35	1		
2015–16	Hull C	34	4		
2016–17	Hull C	21	1	**126**	**9**
2016–17	WBA	16	0		
2017–18	WBA	34	2		
2018–19	WBA	39	2		
2019–20	WBA	45	3	**134**	**7**

MATHEUS PEREIRA, Fellipe (M)				**103**	**19**
b. 5-5-95					
2013–14	Sporting Lisbon	0	0		
2014–15	Sporting Lisbon	0	0		
2015–16	Sporting Lisbon	8	0		
2016–17	Sporting Lisbon	7	1		
2017–18	Sporting Lisbon	0	0		
2017–18	*Chaves*	27	7	**27**	**7**
2018–19	Sporting Lisbon	0	0		
2018–19	*Nuremberg*	19	3	**19**	**3**
2019–20	Sporting Lisbon	0	0	**15**	**1**
On loan from Sporting Lisbon.					
2019–20	WBA	42	8	**42**	**8**

MORTON, Callum (F)				**9**	**5**
b. 19-1-00					
From Yeovil T.					
2019–20	WBA	0	0		
2019–20	*Northampton T*	9	5	**9**	**5**

O'SHEA, Dara (D)				**44**	**3**
b. 4-3-99					
Internationals: Republic of Ireland U18, U19, U21.					
2018–19	WBA	0	0		
2018–19	*Exeter C*	27	0	**27**	**0**
2019–20	WBA	17	3	**17**	**3**

PALMER, Alex (G)				**39**	**0**
b. 10-8-96					
Internationals: England U16.					
2014–15	WBA	0	0		
2015–16	WBA	0	0		
2016–17	WBA	0	0		
2017–18	WBA	0	0		
2018–19	WBA	0	0		
2018–19	*Oldham Ath*	1	0	**1**	**0**
2018–19	*Notts Co*	1	0	**1**	**0**
2019–20	WBA	0	0		
2019–20	*Plymouth Arg*	37	0	**37**	**0**

PELTIER, Lee (D)				**439**	**5**
H: 5 10 W: 12 00 b.Liverpool 11-12-86					
Internationals: England U18.					
2004–05	Liverpool	0	0		
2005–06	Liverpool	0	0		
2006–07	Liverpool	0	0		
2006–07	*Hull C*	7	0	**7**	**0**
2007–08	Liverpool	0	0		
2007–08	Yeovil T	34	0		
2008–09	Yeovil T	35	1	**69**	**1**
2009–10	Huddersfield T	42	0		
2010–11	Huddersfield T	38	1		
2011–12	Leicester C	40	2		
2012–13	Leicester C	0	0	**40**	**2**
2012–13	Leeds U	41	0		
2013–14	Leeds U	25	1	**66**	**1**
2013–14	*Nottingham F*	7	0	**7**	**0**
2014–15	Huddersfield T	11	0	**91**	**1**
2014–15	Cardiff C	15	0		
2015–16	Cardiff C	41	0		
2016–17	Cardiff C	28	0		
2017–18	Cardiff C	30	0		
2018–19	Cardiff C	20	0		
2019–20	Cardiff C	25	0	**159**	**0**
2019–20	WBA	0	0		

PHILLIPS, Matthew (M)				**394**	**57**
H: 6 0 W: 12 10 b.Aylesbury 13-3-91					
Internationals: England U19, U20. Scotland Full caps.					
2007–08	Wycombe W	2	0		
2008–09	Wycombe W	37	3		
2009–10	Wycombe W	36	5		
2010–11	Wycombe W	3	0	**78**	**8**
2010–11	Blackpool	27	1		
2011–12	Blackpool	33	7		
2011–12	*Sheffield U*	6	5	**6**	**5**
2012–13	Blackpool	34	4		
2013–14	Blackpool	0	0	**94**	**12**
2013–14	QPR	21	3		
2014–15	QPR	25	3		
2015–16	QPR	44	8	**90**	**14**
2016–17	WBA	27	4		
2017–18	WBA	30	2		
2018–19	WBA	30	5		
2019–20	WBA	39	7	**126**	**18**

RICHARDS, Rico (M)				**0**	**0**
b. 27-9-03					
Internationals: England U16.					
2019–20	WBA	0	0		

ROBSON-KANU, Hal (F)				**364**	**52**
H: 5 7 W: 11 08 b.Acton 21-5-89					
Internationals: England U19, U20. Wales U21, Full caps.					
2007–08	Reading	0	0		
2007–08	*Southend U*	8	3		
2008–09	Reading	0	0		
2008–09	*Southend U*	14	2	**22**	**5**
2008–09	*Swindon T*	20	4	**20**	**4**
2009–10	Reading	17	0		
2010–11	Reading	27	5		
2011–12	Reading	36	4		
2012–13	Reading	25	7		
2013–14	Reading	36	4		
2014–15	Reading	29	1		
2015–16	Reading	28	3		
2016–17	Reading	0	0	**198**	**24**
2016–17	WBA	29	3		
2017–18	WBA	21	2		
2018–19	WBA	35	4		
2019–20	WBA	39	10	**124**	**19**

SAWYERS, Romaine (M)				**313**	**23**
H: 5 9 W: 11 00 b.Birmingham 2-11-91					
Internationals: St Kitts and Nevis U23, Full caps.					
2009–10	WBA	0	0		
2010–11	WBA	0	0		
2010–11	*Port Vale*	1	0	**1**	**0**
2011–12	WBA	0	0		
2011–12	*Shrewsbury T*	7	0	**7**	**0**
2012–13	WBA	0	0		
2012–13	Walsall	4	0		
2013–14	Walsall	44	6		
2014–15	Walsall	42	4		
2015–16	Walsall	46	6	**136**	**16**
2016–17	Brentford	43	2		
2017–18	Brentford	42	4		
2018–19	Brentford	42	0	**127**	**6**
2019–20	WBA	42	1	**42**	**1**

SHOTTON, Saul (D)				**4**	**0**
H: 6 0 W: 11 11 b. 10-11-00					
2017–18	Bury	4	0		
2018–19	Bury	0	0	**4**	**0**
2019–20	WBA	0	0		

SOULE, Jamie (F)				**0**	**0**
Internationals: England U17.					
2019–20	WBA	0	0		

TOWNSEND, Conor (D)				**168**	**6**
H: 5 4 W: 9 11 b.Hessle 4-3-93					
2011–12	Hull C	0	0		
2012–13	Hull C	0	0		
2012–13	*Chesterfield*	20	1	**20**	**1**
2013–14	Hull C	0	0		
2013–14	*Carlisle U*	12	0	**12**	**0**
2014–15	Hull C	0	0		
2014–15	*Dundee U*	17	0	**17**	**0**
2014–15	*Scunthorpe U*	6	0		
2015–16	Hull C	0	0		
2015–16	Scunthorpe U	20	1		
2016–17	Scunthorpe U	24	0		
2017–18	Scunthorpe U	30	4	**80**	**5**
2018–19	WBA	12	0		
2019–20	WBA	27	0	**39**	**0**

TULLOCH, Rayhaan (F)				**0**	**0**
b.Birmingham 20-1-01					
Internationals: England U16, U17, U18.					
2017–18	WBA	0	0		
2018–19	WBA	0	0		
2019–20	WBA	0	0		

WILSON, Kane (D)				**63**	**1**
H: 5 10 W: 11 03 b. 11-3-00					
Internationals: England U16, U17.					
2016–17	WBA	0	0		
2017–18	WBA	0	0		
2017–18	*Exeter C*	19	1		
2018–19	WBA	0	0		
2018–19	*Walsall*	14	0	**14**	**0**
2018–19	*Exeter C*	17	0	**36**	**1**
2019–20	WBA	0	0		
2019–20	*Tranmere R*	13	0	**13**	**0**

ZOHORE, Kenneth (F)				**181**	**42**
H: 6 4 W: 12 06 b.Copenhagen 31-1-94					
Internationals: Denmark U17, U18, U19, U21.					
2009–10	Copenhagen	1	0		
2010–11	Copenhagen	15	1		
2011–12	Copenhagen	0	0	**16**	**1**
2011–12	Fiorentina	0	0		
2012–13	Fiorentina	0	0		
2013–14	Fiorentina	0	0		
2013–14	*Brondby*	25	5	**25**	**5**
2014–15	Fiorentina	0	0		
2014–15	*Gothenburg*	11	2	**11**	**2**
2015–16	Odense BK	16	7	**16**	**7**
2015–16	KV Kortrijk	0	0		
2015–16	*Cardiff C*	12	2		
2016–17	Cardiff C	29	12		
2017–18	Cardiff C	36	9		
2018–19	Cardiff C	19	1	**96**	**24**
2019–20	WBA	17	3	**17**	**3**

Players retained or with offer of contract
Azaz, Finn; Clayton-Phillips, Nicholas; Elsayed, Ali Elsayed Ahmed; Griffiths, Joshua James; Harmon, George; Solanke, Babatomiwa Jonathan; Windsor, Owen James.

Scholars
Andrews, Jamie; Ashton, Eoin Thomas; Ashworth, Zachary; Asomugha, Stanley; Boruc, Maksymilian Pawel; Brown, Zak; Cann, Ted; Delaney, Zak; Dwyer, Vinnie Conor; Dyce, Tyrese; Emery, Jamie Lewis; Faal, Modou Lamin; Fellows, Tom Allen; Gardne-Hickman, Taylor; Gilbert, Alexander George Henry; Grant, Ryan Liam; Hill, Carrick Matthew; Ingram, Ethan John; Iroegbunam, Timothy Emeka; King, Toby; Malcolm, Jovan Anthony; Martinez, Pablo Jacob; Neto, Teixeira Aurio Clinton; Ojebode, Yusuff Akinola Olatunji; Sharpe, Tom; Shepherd, Jacob Lewis; Smith, Lewis Cameron; Taylor, Caleb Joaquin; Taylor, Peter James; Thorndike, Finley; Wakeling, Jacob Andrew; White, Aksum; Williams, Harry; Williams, Remarl Theo Reshaun.

WEST HAM U (88)

AFOLAYAN, Oladapo (F)				**16**	**1**
H: 5 11 b. 1-1-97					
Internationals: England C.					
2018–19	West Ham U	0	0		
2018–19	*Oldham Ath*	10	0	**10**	**0**
2019–20	West Ham U	0	0		
2019–20	*Mansfield T*	6	1	**6**	**1**

AJETI, Albian (F) 115 44
b.Basle 26-2-97
Internationals: Switzerland U16, U17, U18, U20, U21, Full caps.

2013–14	Basel	2	1		
2014–15	Basel	4	1		
2015–16	Basel	5	1		
2015–16	Augsburg	1	0		
2016–17	Augsburg	0	0	**1**	**0**
2016–17	*St Gallen*	29	10		
2017–18	St Gallen	7	3	**36**	**13**
2017–18	Basel	25	14		
2018–19	Basel	32	14		
2019–20	Basel	1	0	**69**	**31**
2019–20	West Ham U	9	0	**9**	**0**

ALESE, Ajibola (D) 10 0
b.Islington 17-1-01
Internationals: England U16, U17, U18, U19.

2019–20	West Ham U	0	0		
2019–20	*Accrington S*	10	0	**10**	**0**

ANANG, Joseph (G) 0 0
b. 8-6-00
Internationals: England U20.

2019–20	West Ham U	0	0		

ANTONIO, Michael (M) 341 77
H: 6 0 W: 11 11 b.Wandsworth 28-3-90

2008–09	Reading	0	0		
2008–09	*Cheltenham T*	9	0	**9**	**0**
2009–10	Reading	1	0		
2009–10	*Southampton*	28	3	**28**	**3**
2010–11	Reading	21	1		
2011–12	Reading	6	0		
2011–12	*Colchester U*	15	4	**15**	**4**
2011–12	*Sheffield W*	14	5		
2012–13	Reading	0	0	**28**	**1**
2012–13	Sheffield W	37	8		
2013–14	Sheffield W	27	4	**78**	**17**
2014–15	Nottingham F	46	14		
2015–16	Nottingham F	4	2	**50**	**16**
2015–16	West Ham U	26	8		
2016–17	West Ham U	29	9		
2017–18	West Ham U	21	3		
2018–19	West Ham U	33	6		
2019–20	West Ham U	24	10	**133**	**36**

BALBUENA, Fabian (D) 275 16
H: 5 11 W: 11 07 b.Ciudad del Este 23-8-91
Internationals: Paraguay Full caps.

2010	Cerro Porteno	7	0		
2011	Cerro Porteno	28	4		
2012	Cerro Porteno	41	1	**76**	**5**
2013	Rubio Nu	17	1	**17**	**1**
2013	Nacional	14	0		
2014	Nacional	16	1	**30**	**1**
2014	Libertad	16	1		
2015	Libertad	26	2		
2016	Libertad	1	0	**43**	**3**
2016	Corinthians	29	0		
2017	Corinthians	32	4		
2018	Corinthians	8	0	**69**	**4**
2018–19	West Ham U	23	1		
2019–20	West Ham U	17	1	**40**	**2**

BOWEN, Jarrod (F) 137 53
b.Leominster 1-1-96

2014–15	Hull C	0	0		
2015–16	Hull C	0	0		
2016–17	Hull C	7	0		
2017–18	Hull C	42	14		
2018–19	Hull C	46	22		
2019–20	Hull C	29	16	**124**	**52**
2019–20	West Ham U	13	1	**13**	**1**

COSTA DA ROSA, Bernardo (M) 0 0

2019–20	West Ham U	0	0		

COVENTRY, Conor (M) 7 0
b. 25-3-00
Internationals: Republic of Ireland U17, U18, U21.

2018–19	West Ham U	0	0		
2019–20	West Ham U	0	0		
2019–20	*Lincoln C*	7	0	**7**	**0**

CRESSWELL, Aaron (D) 390 19
H: 5 7 W: 10 05 b.Liverpool 15-12-89
Internationals: England Full caps.

2008–09	Tranmere R	13	1		
2009–10	Tranmere R	14	0		
2010–11	Tranmere R	43	4	**70**	**5**
2011–12	Ipswich T	44	1		
2012–13	Ipswich T	46	3		
2013–14	Ipswich T	42	2	**132**	**6**
2014–15	West Ham U	38	2		
2015–16	West Ham U	37	2		
2016–17	West Ham U	26	0		
2017–18	West Ham U	36	1		
2018–19	West Ham U	20	0		
2019–20	West Ham U	31	3	**188**	**8**

CULLEN, Josh (M) 133 3
H: 5 8 W: 11 00 b.Southend-on-Sea 4-7-96
Internationals: England U16. Republic of Ireland U19, U21, Full caps.

2014–15	West Ham U	0	0		
2015–16	West Ham U	1	0		
2015–16	*Bradford C*	15	0		
2016–17	West Ham U	0	0		
2016–17	*Bradford C*	40	1	**55**	**1**
2017–18	West Ham U	2	0		
2017–18	*Bolton W*	12	0	**12**	**0**
2018–19	West Ham U	0	0		
2018–19	*Charlton Ath*	29	1		
2019–20	West Ham U	0	0	**3**	**0**
2019–20	*Charlton Ath*	34	1	**63**	**2**

DIANGANA, Grady (M) 47 8
b. 19-4-98
Internationals: England U20, U21.

2016–17	West Ham U	0	0		
2017–18	West Ham U	0	0		
2018–19	West Ham U	17	0		
2019–20	West Ham U	0	0	**17**	**0**
2019–20	*WBA*	30	8	**30**	**8**

DIOP, Issa (D) 142 9
H: 6 4 W: 13 03 b.Toulouse 9-1-97
Internationals: France U16, U17, U18, U19, U20, U21.

2015–16	Toulouse	21	1		
2016–17	Toulouse	30	2		
2017–18	Toulouse	26	2	**77**	**5**
2018–19	West Ham U	33	1		
2019–20	West Ham U	32	3	**65**	**4**

FABIANSKI, Lukasz (G) 297 0
H: 6 3 W: 13 01 b.Costrzyn nad Odra 18-4-85
Internationals: Poland U21, Full caps.

2005–06	Legia	30	0		
2006–07	Legia	23	0	**53**	**0**
2007–08	Arsenal	3	0		
2008–09	Arsenal	6	0		
2009–10	Arsenal	4	0		
2010–11	Arsenal	14	0		
2011–12	Arsenal	0	0		
2012–13	Arsenal	4	0		
2013–14	Arsenal	1	0	**32**	**0**
2014–15	Swansea C	37	0		
2015–16	Swansea C	37	0		
2016–17	Swansea C	37	0		
2017–18	Swansea C	38	0	**149**	**0**
2018–19	West Ham U	38	0		
2019–20	West Ham U	25	0	**63**	**0**

FELIPE ANDERSON, Gomes (M) 259 42
H: 5 10 W: 10 12 b.Braslìia 15-4-93
Internationals: Brazil U17, U20, U23, Full caps.

2010	Santos	5	0		
2011	Santos	18	1		
2012	Santos	35	6		
2013	Santos	3	0	**61**	**7**
2013–14	Lazio	13	0		
2014–15	Lazio	32	10		
2015–16	Lazio	35	7		
2016–17	Lazio	36	4		
2017–18	Lazio	21	4	**137**	**25**
2018–19	West Ham U	36	9		
2019–20	West Ham U	25	1	**61**	**10**

FORNALS, Pablo (M) 165 14
b.Castellon de la Plana 22-2-96
Internationals: Spain U21, Full caps.

2015–16	Malaga	27	1		
2016–17	Malaga	32	6	**59**	**7**
2017–18	Villareal	35	3		
2018–19	Villareal	35	2	**70**	**5**
2019–20	West Ham U	36	2	**36**	**2**

FREDERICKS, Ryan (M) 187 2
H: 5 8 W: 11 10 b.Potters Bar 10-10-92
Internationals: England U19.

2010–11	Tottenham H	0	0		
2011–12	Tottenham H	0	0		
2012–13	Tottenham H	0	0		
2012–13	*Brentford*	4	0	**4**	**0**
2013–14	Tottenham H	0	0		
2013–14	*Millwall*	14	1	**14**	**1**
2014–15	Tottenham H	0	0		
2014–15	*Middlesbrough*	17	0	**17**	**0**
2015–16	Bristol C	4	0	**4**	**0**
2015–16	Fulham	32	0		
2016–17	Fulham	30	0		
2017–18	Fulham	44	0	**106**	**0**
2018–19	West Ham U	15	1		
2019–20	West Ham U	27	0	**42**	**1**

GONCALO CARDOSO, Bento (D) 15 0
Internationals: Portugal U19.

2018–19	Boavista	15	0		
2019–20	Boavista	0	0	**15**	**0**
2019–20	West Ham U	0	0		

HALLER, Sebastien (F) 224 78
b.Ris-Orangis 22-6-94
Internationals: France U16, U17, U18, U19, U20, U21.

2012–13	Auxerre	17	2		
2013–14	Auxerre	25	4		
2014–15	Auxerre	8	0	**50**	**6**
2014–15	Utrecht	17	11		
2015–16	Utrecht	33	17		
2016–17	Utrecht	32	13	**82**	**41**
2017–18	Eintracht Frankfurt	31	9		
2018–19	Eintracht Frankfurt	29	15	**60**	**24**
2019–20	West Ham U	32	7	**32**	**7**

HERNANDEZ, Javier (F) 342 125
H: 5 8 W: 9 11 b.Guadalajara 1-6-88
Internationals: Mexico U20, Full caps.

2005–06	Tapatio	11	0		
2006–07	Tapatio	12	3		
2006–07	Guadalajara	7	1		
2007–08	Guadalajara	5	0		
2007–08	Tapatio	15	6		
2008–09	Tapatio	7	2	**45**	**11**
2008–09	Guadalajara	22	4		
2009–10	Guadalajara	28	21	**62**	**26**
2010–11	Manchester U	27	13		
2011–12	Manchester U	28	10		
2012–13	Manchester U	22	10		
2013–14	Manchester U	24	4		
2014–15	Manchester U	1	0		
2014–15	*Real Madrid*	23	7	**23**	**7**
2015–16	Manchester U	1	0	**103**	**37**
2015–16	Bayer Leverkusen	28	17		
2016–17	Bayer Leverkusen	26	11	**54**	**28**
2017–18	West Ham U	28	8		
2018–19	West Ham U	25	7		
2019–20	West Ham U	2	1	**55**	**16**

Transferred to Sevilla, September 2019; transferred to LA Galaxy, January 2020.

HOLLAND, Nathan (M) 12 2
b. 19-6-98
Internationals: England U16, U17, U18, U19.

2016–17	West Ham U	0	0		
2017–18	West Ham U	0	0		
2018–19	West Ham U	0	0		
2019–20	West Ham U	2	0	**2**	**0**
2019–20	*Oxford U*	10	2	**10**	**2**

HUGILL, Jordan (F) 216 51
H: 6 0 W: 10 01 b.Middlesbrough 4-6-92

2013–14	Port Vale	20	4	**20**	**4**
2014–15	Preston NE	3	0		
2014–15	*Tranmere R*	6	1	**6**	**1**
2014–15	*Hartlepool U*	8	4	**8**	**4**
2015–16	Preston NE	29	3		
2016–17	Preston NE	44	12		
2017–18	Preston NE	27	8	**103**	**23**
2017–18	West Ham U	3	0		
2018–19	West Ham U	0	0		
2018–19	*Middlesbrough*	37	6	**37**	**6**
2019–20	West Ham U	0	0	**3**	**0**
2019–20	*QPR*	39	13	**39**	**13**

JOHNSON, Ben (M) 4 0
b. 21-1-00

2017–18	West Ham U	0	0		
2018–19	West Ham U	1	0		
2019–20	West Ham U	3	0	**4**	**0**

KEMP, Daniel (M) 6 1
Internationals: England U19, U20.
From Chelsea.

2016–17	West Ham U	0	0		
2017–18	West Ham U	0	0		
2018–19	West Ham U	0	0		
2019–20	West Ham U	0	0		
2019–20	*Stevenage*	6	1	**6**	**1**

LANZINI, Manuel (M) 258 43
H: 5 7 W: 11 00 b.Ituzaingo 15-2-93
Internationals: Argentina U20, Full caps.

2010–11	River Plate	22	0		
2010–11	*Fluminense*	22	2		
2011–12	River Plate	0	0		
2011–12	*Fluminense*	6	1	**28**	**3**
2012–13	River Plate	26	8		
2013–14	River Plate	36	4	**84**	**12**
2014–15	Al-Jazira	24	8		
2015–16	Al-Jazira	0	0	**24**	**8**

2015–16 *West Ham U* 26 6
2016–17 West Ham U 35 8
2017–18 West Ham U 27 5
2018–19 West Ham U 10 1
2019–20 West Ham U 24 0 **122** **20**

LEWIS, Alfie (M) **0** **0**
2019–20 West Ham U 0 0

MARTIN, David E (G) **347** **0**
H: 6 1 W: 13 04 b.Romford 22-1-86
Internationals: England U16, U17, U18, U19.
2003–04 Wimbledon 2 0 **2** **0**
2004–05 Milton Keynes D 15 0
2005–06 Milton Keynes D 0 0
2005–06 Liverpool 0 0
2006–07 Liverpool 0 0
2006–07 *Accrington S* 10 0 **10** **0**
2007–08 Liverpool 0 0
2008–09 Liverpool 0 0
2008–09 *Leicester C* 25 0 **25** **0**
2009–10 Liverpool 0 0
2009–10 *Tranmere R* 3 0 **3** **0**
2009–10 *Leeds U* 0 0
2009–10 *Derby Co* 2 0 **2** **0**
2010–11 Milton Keynes D 43 0
2011–12 Milton Keynes D 46 0
2012–13 Milton Keynes D 31 0
2013–14 Milton Keynes D 40 0
2014–15 Milton Keynes D 39 0
2015–16 Milton Keynes D 35 0
2016–17 Milton Keynes D 40 0 **289** **0**
2017–18 Millwall 1 0
2018–19 Millwall 10 0 **11** **0**
2019–20 West Ham U 5 0 **5** **0**

MASUAKU, Arthur (D) **158** **2**
b. 7-11-93
Internationals: France U18, U19. DR Congo Full caps.
2012–13 Valenciennes 0 0
2013–14 Valenciennes 27 1 **27** **1**
2014–15 Olympiacos 27 0
2015–16 Olympiacos 24 1 **51** **1**
2016–17 West Ham U 13 0
2017–18 West Ham U 27 0
2018–19 West Ham U 23 0
2019–20 West Ham U 17 0 **80** **0**

NGAKIA, Jeremy (D) **5** **0**
2019–20 West Ham U 5 0 **5** **0**

NOBLE, Mark (M) **458** **55**
H: 5 11 W: 12 00 b.West Ham 8-5-87
Internationals: England U16, U17, U18, U19, U21.
2004–05 West Ham U 13 0
2005–06 West Ham U 5 0
2005–06 *Hull C* 5 0 **5** **0**
2006–07 West Ham U 10 2
2006–07 *Ipswich T* 13 1 **13** **1**
2007–08 West Ham U 31 3
2008–09 West Ham U 29 3
2009–10 West Ham U 27 2
2010–11 West Ham U 26 4
2011–12 West Ham U 45 8
2012–13 West Ham U 28 4
2013–14 West Ham U 38 3
2014–15 West Ham U 28 2
2015–16 West Ham U 37 7
2016–17 West Ham U 30 3
2017–18 West Ham U 29 4
2018–19 West Ham U 31 5
2019–20 West Ham U 33 4 **440** **54**

OGBONNA, Angelo (D) **345** **5**
H: 6 2 W: 13 08 b.Cassino 23-5-88
Internationals: Italy U21, Full caps.
2006–07 Torino 4 0
2007–08 Torino 0 0
2007–08 *Crotone* 22 0 **22** **0**
2008–09 Torino 19 0
2009–10 Torino 28 1
2010–11 Torino 35 0
2011–12 Torino 39 0
2012–13 Torino 22 0 **147** **1**
2013–14 Juventus 16 0
2014–15 Juventus 25 0 **41** **0**
2015–16 West Ham U 28 0
2016–17 West Ham U 20 0
2017–18 West Ham U 32 1
2018–19 West Ham U 24 1
2019–20 West Ham U 31 2 **135** **4**

RANDOLPH, Darren (G) **382** **0**
H: 6 1 W: 12 02 b.Dublin 12-5-87
Internationals: Republic of Ireland U21, B, Full caps.
2004–05 Charlton Ath 0 0
2005–06 Charlton Ath 0 0
2006–07 Charlton Ath 1 0
2006–07 *Gillingham* 3 0 **3** **0**
2007–08 Charlton Ath 1 0
2007–08 *Bury* 14 0 **14** **0**
2008–09 Charlton Ath 1 0
2008–09 *Hereford U* 13 0 **13** **0**
2009–10 Charlton Ath 11 0 **14** **0**
2010–11 Motherwell 37 0
2011–12 Motherwell 38 0
2012–13 Motherwell 36 0 **111** **0**
2013–14 Birmingham C 46 0
2014–15 Birmingham C 45 0 **91** **0**
2015–16 West Ham U 6 0
2016–17 West Ham U 22 0
2017–18 Middlesbrough 46 0
2018–19 Middlesbrough 46 0
2019–20 Middlesbrough 14 0 **106** **0**
2019–20 West Ham U 2 0 **30** **0**

REID, Winston (D) **277** **11**
H: 6 3 W: 13 10 b.North Shore 3-7-88
Internationals: Denmark U19, U20, U21. New Zealand Full caps.
2005–06 Midtjylland 9 0
2006–07 Midtjylland 11 0
2007–08 Midtjylland 9 0
2008–09 Midtjylland 25 2
2009–10 Midtjylland 29 0 **83** **2**
2010–11 West Ham U 7 0
2011–12 West Ham U 28 3
2012–13 West Ham U 36 1
2013–14 West Ham U 22 1
2014–15 West Ham U 30 1
2015–16 West Ham U 24 1
2016–17 West Ham U 30 2
2017–18 West Ham U 17 0
2018–19 West Ham U 0 0
2019–20 West Ham U 0 0 **194** **9**
Transferred to Sporting Kansas C, February 2020.

RICE, Declan (M) **99** **3**
b. 14-1-99
Internationals: Republic of Ireland U16, U17, U19, U21, Full caps.
2016–17 West Ham U 1 0
2017–18 West Ham U 26 0
2018–19 West Ham U 34 2
2019–20 West Ham U 38 1 **99** **3**

ROBERTO, Jimenez (G) **287** **0**
b.Madrid 10-2-86
Internationals: Spain U17, U18, U19, U20, U21.
2004–05 Atletico Madrid 0 0
2005–06 Atletico Madrid 1 0
2006–07 Atletico Madrid 0 0
2007–08 Atletico Madrid 0 0
2007–08 *Gimnastic* 28 0 **28** **0**
2008–09 Recreativo 0 0
2009–10 Atletico Madrid 3 0 **4** **0**
2009–10 Zaragoza 15 0
2010–11 Benfica 25 0 **25** **0**
2011–12 Zaragoza 38 0
2012–13 Zaragoza 33 0 **86** **0**
2013–14 Olympiacos 32 0
2014–15 Olympiacos 29 0
2015–16 Olympiacos 28 0 **89** **0**
2016–17 Espanyol 4 0
2017–18 Espanyol 0 0
2017–18 *Malaga* 34 0 **34** **0**
2018–19 Espanyol 0 0 **4** **0**
2019–20 West Ham U 8 0 **8** **0**
2019–20 *Alaves* 9 0 **9** **0**

SANCHEZ, Carlos (M) **360** **15**
H: 6 0 W: 12 08 b.Quidbo 6-2-86
Internationals: Colombia Full caps.
2005–06 River Plate 14 0
2006–07 River Plate 26 1 **40** **1**
2007–08 Valenciennes 34 0
2008–09 Valenciennes 37 1
2009–10 Valenciennes 28 5
2010–11 Valenciennes 28 2
2011–12 Valenciennes 21 1
2012–13 Valenciennes 27 2 **175** **11**
2013–14 Elche 30 0 **30** **0**
2014–15 Aston Villa 28 1
2015–16 Aston Villa 20 0
2016–17 Aston Villa 0 0 **48** **1**
2016–17 *Fiorentina* 31 1
2017–18 Fiorentina 9 1 **40** **2**
2017–18 *Espanyol* 14 0 **14** **0**
2018–19 West Ham U 7 0
2019–20 West Ham U 6 0 **13** **0**

SNODGRASS, Robert (M) **483** **92**
H: 6 0 W: 12 02 b.Glasgow 7-9-87
Internationals: Scotland U20, U21, Full caps.
2003–04 Livingston 0 0
2004–05 Livingston 17 2
2005–06 Livingston 27 4
2006–07 Livingston 6 0
2006–07 *Stirling Alb* 12 5 **12** **5**
2007–08 Livingston 31 9 **81** **15**
2008–09 Leeds U 42 9
2009–10 Leeds U 44 7
2010–11 Leeds U 37 6
2011–12 Leeds U 43 13 **166** **35**
2012–13 Norwich C 37 6
2013–14 Norwich C 30 6 **67** **12**
2014–15 Hull C 1 0
2015–16 Hull C 24 4
2016–17 Hull C 20 7 **45** **11**
2016–17 West Ham U 15 0
2017–18 West Ham U 0 0
2017–18 *Aston Villa* 40 7 **40** **7**
2018–19 West Ham U 33 2
2019–20 West Ham U 24 5 **72** **7**

SOUCEK, Tomas (M) **153** **34**
b. 27-2-95
Internationals: Czech Republic U19, U20, U21, Full caps.
2014–15 Slavia Prague 0 0
2014–15 *Viktoria Zizkov* 14 0 **14** **0**
2015–16 Slavia Prague 29 7
2016–17 Slavia Prague 7 0
2016–17 *Slovan Liberec* 12 0 **12** **0**
2017–18 Slavia Prague 27 3
2018–19 Slavia Prague 34 13
2019–20 Slavia Prague 17 8 **114** **31**
On loan from Slavia Prague.
2019–20 West Ham U 13 3 **13** **3**

TROTT, Nathan (G) **23** **0**
H: 6 0 W: 11 00 b. 21-11-98
Internationals: Bermuda U17. England U18, U20.
2017–18 West Ham U 0 0
2018–19 West Ham U 0 0
2019–20 West Ham U 0 0
2019–20 *AFC Wimbledon* 23 0 **23** **0**

WILSHERE, Jack (M) **182** **8**
H: 5 7 W: 11 03 b.Stevenage 1-1-92
Internationals: England U16, U17, U19, U21, Full caps.
2008–09 Arsenal 1 0
2009–10 Arsenal 1 0
2009–10 *Bolton W* 14 1 **14** **1**
2010–11 Arsenal 35 1
2011–12 Arsenal 0 0
2012–13 Arsenal 25 0
2013–14 Arsenal 24 3
2014–15 Arsenal 14 2
2015–16 Arsenal 3 0
2016–17 Arsenal 2 0
2016–17 *Bournemouth* 27 0 **27** **0**
2017–18 Arsenal 20 1 **125** **7**
2018–19 West Ham U 8 0
2019–20 West Ham U 8 0 **16** **0**

XANDE SILVA, Nascimento (F) **27** **1**
b. 16-3-97
Internationals: Portugal U16, U17, U18, U19, U20.
2014–15 Vitoria Guimaraes 1 0
2015–16 Vitoria Guimaraes 20 1
2016–17 Vitoria Guimaraes 4 0
2017–18 Vitoria Guimaraes 1 0 **26** **1**
2018–19 West Ham U 1 0
2019–20 West Ham U 0 0 **1** **0**

YARMOLENKO, Andriy (M) **278** **109**
H: 6 2 W: 12 00 b.Saint Petersburg 23-10-89
Internationals: Ukraine U19, U21, Full caps.
2007–08 Dynamo Kyiv 1 1
2008–09 Dynamo Kyiv 10 0
2009–10 Dynamo Kyiv 28 7
2010–11 Dynamo Kyiv 26 11
2011–12 Dynamo Kyiv 28 12
2012–13 Dynamo Kyiv 27 11
2013–14 Dynamo Kyiv 26 12
2014–15 Dynamo Kyiv 26 14
2015–16 Dynamo Kyiv 23 13
2016–17 Dynamo Kyiv 28 15
2017–18 Dynamo Kyiv 5 3 **228** **99**
2017–18 Borussia Dortmund 18 3 **18** **3**
2018–19 West Ham U 9 2
2019–20 West Ham U 23 5 **32** **7**

ZABALETA, Pablo (D) **449 20**
H: 5 8 W: 10 12 b.Buenos Aires 16-1-85
Internationals: Argentina U20, U23, Full caps.

2002–03	San Lorenzo	11	0		
2003–04	San Lorenzo	27	3		
2004–05	San Lorenzo	28	5	**66**	**8**
2005–06	Espanyol	27	2		
2006–07	Espanyol	21	0		
2007–08	Espanyol	32	1	**80**	**3**
2008–09	Manchester C	29	1		
2009–10	Manchester C	27	0		
2010–11	Manchester C	26	2		
2011–12	Manchester C	21	1		
2012–13	Manchester C	30	2		
2013–14	Manchester C	35	1		
2014–15	Manchester C	29	1		
2015–16	Manchester C	13	0		
2016–17	Manchester C	20	1	**230**	**9**
2017–18	West Ham U	37	0		
2018–19	West Ham U	26	0		
2019–20	West Ham U	10	0	**73**	**0**

Players retained or with offer of contract
Adarkwa, Sean Jordan; Akinola, Olatunji Oluwasehun; Diallo, Amadou; Dju, Mesaque Geremias; Hegyi, Krisztian; Longelo Mbule, Emmanuel; Odubeko, Ademipo Ibrahim.

Scholars
Adebayo, Iyiola El-Ameen; Adu, Michael Asare; Appiah-Forson, Keenan; Ashby, Harrison; Caiger, Samuel Alfie; Chesters, Daniel Peter; Corbett, Kai Michael James; Fevrier, Jayden Raymond; Giddings, Jake Patrick Moy; Greenidge, William Winston; Heal, Benjamin Atticus William; Jinadu, Daniel Oluwagbolade; Kileba, Gael Mulamba; Nebyla, Sebastian; Ngakia, Jeremy; Nsumbu, Samuel; Okotcha, Joshua; Parkes, Veron Brandon; Peake, Lennon; Roach, Joshua Michael Phillip; Sanneh, Serine; Swyer, Kamarai Joshua; Thomas, Brandon Val; Veliky, Christian.

WIGAN ATH (89)

BALOGUN, Leon (D) **126 6**
H: 6 3 W: 12 11 b.Berlin 28-6-88
Internationals: Nigeria Full caps.

2008–09	Hannover 96	1	0		
2009–10	Hannover 96	2	0	**3**	**0**
2010–11	Werder Bremen	3	0		
2011–12	Werder Bremen	0	0	**3**	**0**
2012–13	Fortuna Dusseldorf	17	0		
2013–14	Fortuna Dusseldorf	11	0	**28**	**0**
2014–15	Darmstadt 98	21	4	**21**	**4**
2015–16	Mainz 05	21	1		
2016–17	Mainz 05	17	0		
2017–18	Mainz 05	14	0	**52**	**1**
2018–19	Brighton & HA	8	1		
2019–20	Brighton & HA	0	0	**8**	**1**
2019–20	Wigan Ath	11	0	**11**	**0**

BANINGIME, Divin (F) **0 0**
b. 13-10-00

2017–18	Wigan Ath	0	0
2018–19	Wigan Ath	0	0
2019–20	Wigan Ath	0	0

BURGESS, Luke (M) **0 0**
b. 3-3-99

2017–18	Wigan Ath	0	0
2018–19	Wigan Ath	0	0
2019–20	Wigan Ath	0	0
2019–20	*Salford C*	0	0

BYRNE, Nathan (D) **290 16**
H: 5 10 W: 10 10 b.St Albans 5-6-92

2010–11	Tottenham H	0	0		
2010–11	*Brentford*	11	0	**11**	**0**
2011–12	Tottenham H	0	0		
2011–12	*Bournemouth*	9	0	**9**	**0**
2012–13	Tottenham H	0	0		
2012–13	*Crawley T*	12	1	**12**	**1**
2012–13	*Swindon T*	7	0		
2013–14	Swindon T	36	4		
2014–15	Swindon T	42	3		
2015–16	Swindon T	5	3	**90**	**10**
2015–16	Wolverhampton W	24	2		
2016–17	Wolverhampton W	0	0	**24**	**2**
2016–17	Wigan Ath	14	0		
2016–17	*Charlton Ath*	17	1	**17**	**1**
2017–18	Wigan Ath	44	0		
2018–19	Wigan Ath	30	1		
2019–20	Wigan Ath	39	1	**127**	**2**

DUNKLEY, Cheyenne (D) **185 20**
H: 6 2 W: 13 05 b.Wolverhampton 13-2-92
Internationals: England C.
From Kidderminster H.

2014–15	Oxford U	9	0		
2015–16	Oxford U	29	4		
2016–17	Oxford U	40	3	**78**	**7**
2017–18	Wigan Ath	43	7		
2018–19	Wigan Ath	38	0		
2019–20	Wigan Ath	26	6	**107**	**13**

EVANS, Lee (M) **201 13**
H: 6 1 W: 13 12 b.Newport 24-7-94
Internationals: Wales U21, Full caps.

2012–13	Wolverhampton W	0	0		
2013–14	Wolverhampton W	26	2		
2014–15	Wolverhampton W	18	1		
2015–16	Wolverhampton W	0	0		
2015–16	*Bradford C*	35	4	**35**	**4**
2016–17	Wolverhampton W	15	0		
2017–18	Wolverhampton W	0	0	**59**	**3**
2017–18	*Wigan Ath*	20	1		
2017–18	Sheffield U	19	2		
2018–19	Sheffield U	2	0	**21**	**2**
2018–19	*Wigan Ath*	34	1		
2019–20	Wigan Ath	32	2	**86**	**4**

EVANS, Owen (G) **35 0**
Internationals: Wales U19, U21.
From Hereford U.

2016–17	Wigan Ath	0	0		
2017–18	Wigan Ath	0	0		
2018–19	Wigan Ath	0	0		
2019–20	Wigan Ath	0	0		
2019–20	*Macclesfield T*	24	0	**24**	**0**
2019–20	*Cheltenham T*	11	0	**11**	**0**

FOX, Danny (D) **432 15**
H: 5 11 W: 12 06 b.Winsford 29-5-86
Internationals: England U21. Scotland Full caps.

2004–05	Everton	0	0		
2004–05	*Stranraer*	11	1	**11**	**1**
2005–06	Walsall	33	0		
2006–07	Walsall	44	3		
2007–08	Walsall	22	3	**99**	**6**
2007–08	Coventry C	18	1		
2008–09	Coventry C	39	5		
2009–10	Coventry C	0	0	**57**	**6**
2009–10	Celtic	15	0	**15**	**0**
2009–10	Burnley	14	1		
2010–11	Burnley	35	0		
2011–12	Burnley	1	0	**50**	**1**
2011–12	Southampton	41	0		
2012–13	Southampton	20	1		
2013–14	Southampton	3	0	**64**	**1**
2013–14	Nottingham F	14	0		
2014–15	Nottingham F	27	0		
2015–16	Nottingham F	10	0		
2016–17	Nottingham F	23	0		
2017–18	Nottingham F	23	0		
2018–19	Nottingham F	18	0	**115**	**0**
2018–19	Wigan Ath	10	0		
2019–20	Wigan Ath	11	0	**21**	**0**

GARNER, Joe (F) **424 118**
H: 5 10 W: 11 02 b.Blackburn 12-4-88
Internationals: England U16, U17, U19.

2004–05	Blackburn R	0	0		
2005–06	Blackburn R	0	0		
2006–07	Blackburn R	0	0		
2006–07	*Carlisle U*	18	5		
2007–08	Carlisle U	31	14		
2008–09	Nottingham F	28	7		
2009–10	Nottingham F	18	2		
2010–11	Nottingham F	0	0		
2010–11	*Huddersfield T*	16	0	**16**	**0**
2010–11	*Scunthorpe U*	18	6	**18**	**6**
2011–12	Nottingham F	2	0	**48**	**9**
2011–12	Watford	22	1		
2012–13	Watford	2	0	**24**	**1**
2012–13	*Carlisle U*	16	7	**65**	**26**
2012–13	Preston NE	14	0		
2013–14	Preston NE	35	18		
2014–15	Preston NE	37	25		
2015–16	Preston NE	41	6		
2016–17	Preston NE	2	0	**129**	**49**
2016–17	Rangers	31	7	**31**	**7**
2017–18	Ipswich T	32	10	**32**	**10**
2018–19	Wigan Ath	33	8		
2019–20	Wigan Ath	28	2	**61**	**10**

GELHARDT, Joe (F) **19 1**
b.Liverpool 4-5-02
Internationals: England U16, U17, U18.

2018–19	Wigan Ath	1	0		
2019–20	Wigan Ath	18	1	**19**	**1**

GOLDEN, Tylor (D) **0 0**
b.Ipswich 8-11-99

2017–18	Wigan Ath	0	0
2018–19	Wigan Ath	0	0
2019–20	Wigan Ath	0	0

GYOLLAI, Daniel (G) **0 0**
b.Bekescsaba 7-4-97
Internationals: Hungary U18, U19, U21.
From Stoke C.

2019–20	Wigan Ath	0	0

JACOBS, Michael (M) **351 54**
H: 5 9 W: 11 08 b.Rothwell 23-3-92

2009–10	Northampton T	0	0		
2010–11	Northampton T	41	5		
2011–12	Northampton T	46	6	**87**	**11**
2012–13	Derby Co	38	2		
2013–14	Derby Co	3	0	**41**	**2**
2013–14	Wolverhampton W	30	8		
2014–15	Wolverhampton W	12	0	**42**	**8**
2014–15	*Blackpool*	5	1	**5**	**1**
2015–16	Wigan Ath	35	10		
2016–17	Wigan Ath	43	3		
2017–18	Wigan Ath	44	12		
2018–19	Wigan Ath	22	4		
2019–20	Wigan Ath	32	3	**176**	**32**

JOLLEY, Charlie (F) **1 0**
b.Liverpool 13-1-01

2018–19	Wigan Ath	1	0		
2019–20	Wigan Ath	0	0	**1**	**0**

JONES, Jamie (G) **289 0**
H: 6 2 W: 14 05 b.Kirkby 18-2-89

2007–08	Everton	0	0		
2008–09	Leyton Orient	20	0		
2009–10	Leyton Orient	36	0		
2010–11	Leyton Orient	35	0		
2011–12	Leyton Orient	6	0		
2012–13	Leyton Orient	26	0		
2013–14	Leyton Orient	28	0	**151**	**0**
2014–15	Preston NE	17	0		
2014–15	*Coventry C*	4	0	**4**	**0**
2014–15	*Rochdale*	13	0	**13**	**0**
2015–16	Preston NE	0	0	**17**	**0**
2015–16	*Colchester U*	17	0	**17**	**0**
2015–16	Stevenage	17	0		
2016–17	Stevenage	36	0	**53**	**0**
2017–18	Wigan Ath	15	0		
2018–19	Wigan Ath	12	0		
2019–20	Wigan Ath	7	0	**34**	**0**

KIPRE, Cedric (D) **110 3**
H: 6 3 W: 12 02 b.Paris 9-12-96
Internationals: Ivory Coast U23.

2014–15	Leicester C	0	0		
2015–16	Leicester C	0	0		
2016–17	Leicester C	0	0		
2017–18	Motherwell	36	1	**36**	**1**
2018–19	Wigan Ath	38	0		
2019–20	Wigan Ath	36	2	**74**	**2**

LANG, Callum (F) **89 26**
H: 5 11 W: 11 00 b. 8-9-98

2016–17	Wigan Ath	0	0		
2017–18	Wigan Ath	0	0		
2017–18	*Morecambe*	30	10	**30**	**10**
2018–19	Wigan Ath	0	0		
2018–19	*Oldham Ath*	42	13	**42**	**13**
2019–20	Wigan Ath	1	0	**1**	**0**
2019–20	*Shrewsbury T*	16	3	**16**	**3**

LONG, Adam (D) **0 0**
b. 11-11-00

2017–18	Wigan Ath	0	0
2018–19	Wigan Ath	0	0
2019–20	Wigan Ath	0	0

LOWE, Jamal (F) **157 31**
H: 6 0 W: 12 06 b.Harrow 21-7-94
Internationals: England C.

2012–13	Barnet	8	0	**8**	**0**

From St Albans C, Hemel Hempstead T, Hampton & Richmond.

2016–17	Portsmouth	14	4		
2017–18	Portsmouth	44	6		
2018–19	Portsmouth	45	15		
2019–20	Portsmouth	0	0	**103**	**25**
2019–20	Wigan Ath	46	6	**46**	**6**

MACLEOD, Lewis (M) **105 15**
H: 5 9 W: 11 05 b.Law 16-6-94
Internationals: Scotland U16, U17, U18, U19, U21.

2012–13	Rangers	21	3		
2013–14	Rangers	18	5		
2014–15	Rangers	13	3	**52**	**11**
2014–15	Brentford	0	0		

2015–16 Brentford 1 0
2016–17 Brentford 13 0
2017–18 Brentford 10 1
2018–19 Brentford 17 3 **41 4**
2019–20 Wigan Ath 12 0 **12 0**

MARSHALL, David (G) 493 0
H: 6 3 W: 13 04 b.Glasgow 5-3-85
Internationals: Scotland Youth, U21, B, Full caps.
2003–04 Celtic 11 0
2004–05 Celtic 18 0
2005–06 Celtic 4 0
2006–07 Celtic 2 0 **35 0**
2006–07 Norwich C 2 0
2007–08 Norwich C 46 0
2008–09 Norwich C 46 0 **94 0**
2008–09 Cardiff C 0 0
2009–10 Cardiff C 43 0
2010–11 Cardiff C 11 0
2011–12 Cardiff C 45 0
2012–13 Cardiff C 46 0
2013–14 Cardiff C 37 0
2014–15 Cardiff C 38 0
2015–16 Cardiff C 40 0
2016–17 Cardiff C 4 0 **264 0**
2016–17 Hull C 16 0
2017–18 Hull C 2 0
2018–19 Hull C 43 0 **61 0**
2019–20 Wigan Ath 39 0 **39 0**

MASSEY, Gavin (F) 318 42
H: 5 11 W: 11 06 b.Watford 14-10-92
2009–10 Watford 1 0
2010–11 Watford 3 0
2011–12 Watford 3 0
2011–12 *Yeovil T* 16 3 **16 3**
2011–12 *Colchester U* 8 0
2012–13 Watford 0 0 **7 0**
2012–13 Colchester U 40 6
2013–14 Colchester U 30 3
2014–15 Colchester U 46 7
2015–16 Colchester U 42 4 **166 20**
2016–17 Leyton Orient 36 8 **36 8**
2017–18 Wigan Ath 42 6
2018–19 Wigan Ath 20 5
2019–20 Wigan Ath 31 0 **93 11**

McGUFFIE, Will (D) 0 0
b.Birkenhead 27-10-00
From Wolverhampton W.
2017–18 Wigan Ath 0 0
2018–19 Wigan Ath 0 0
2019–20 Wigan Ath 0 0

MERRIE, Christopher (M) 0 0
b.Liverpool 2-11-98
From Everton.
2017–18 Wigan Ath 0 0
2018–19 Wigan Ath 0 0
2019–20 Wigan Ath 0 0

MOORE, Kieffer (F) 179 51
H: 6 5 W: 13 01 b.Torquay 8-8-92
Internationals: England C. Wales Full caps.
From Truro C, Dorchester T.
2013–14 Yeovil T 20 4
2014–15 Yeovil T 30 3 **50 7**
2015 Viking 9 0 **9 0**
From Forest Green R, Torquay U.
2016–17 Ipswich T 11 0
2017–18 Ipswich T 0 0 **11 0**
2017–18 *Rotherham U* 22 13 **22 13**
2017–18 Barnsley 20 4
2018–19 Barnsley 31 17
2019–20 Barnsley 0 0 **51 21**
2019–20 Wigan Ath 36 10 **36 10**

MORSY, Sam (M) 339 19
H: 5 9 W: 12 06 b.Wolverhampton 10-9-91
Internationals: Egypt Full caps.
2009–10 Port Vale 1 0
2010–11 Port Vale 16 1
2011–12 Port Vale 26 1
2012–13 Port Vale 28 2 **71 4**
2013–14 Chesterfield 34 1
2014–15 Chesterfield 39 2
2015–16 Chesterfield 26 4 **99 7**
2015–16 Wigan Ath 16 1
2016–17 Barnsley 14 0 **14 0**
2016–17 Wigan Ath 15 1
2017–18 Wigan Ath 41 2
2018–19 Wigan Ath 40 1
2019–20 Wigan Ath 43 3 **155 8**

NAISMITH, Kal (F) 226 36
H: 5 7 W: 13 02 b.Glasgow 18-2-92
Internationals: Scotland U16, U17.
2013–14 Accrington S 38 10
2014–15 Accrington S 35 4 **73 14**
2015–16 Portsmouth 19 3
2015–16 *Hartlepool U* 4 0 **4 0**
2016–17 Portsmouth 37 13
2017–18 Portsmouth 26 2 **82 18**
2018–19 Wigan Ath 30 1
2019–20 Wigan Ath 37 3 **67 4**

OBI, Chuckwuemeka (D) 0 0
b. 6-6-01
2016–17 Bury 0 0
2016–17 Liverpool 0 0
2017–18 Liverpool 0 0
2018–19 Liverpool 0 0
2018–19 Wigan Ath 0 0
2019–20 Wigan Ath 0 0

PEARCE, Tom (D) 23 2
b.Ormskirk 12-4-98
Internationals: England U20, U21.
From Everton.
2017–18 Leeds U 5 1
2018–19 Leeds U 2 0 **7 1**
2018–19 *Scunthorpe U* 9 1 **9 1**
2019–20 Wigan Ath 7 0 **7 0**

PERRY, Alex (M) 0 0
b.Liverpool 4-3-98
2016–17 Bolton W 0 0
2017–18 Bolton W 0 0
2018–19 Wigan Ath 0 0
2019–20 Wigan Ath 0 0

PILKINGTON, Anthony (M) 371 72
H: 5 11 W: 12 00 b.Blackburn 3-11-87
Internationals: Republic of Ireland U21, Full caps.
2006–07 Stockport Co 24 5
2007–08 Stockport Co 29 6
2008–09 Stockport Co 24 5 **77 16**
2008–09 Huddersfield T 16 2
2009–10 Huddersfield T 43 7
2010–11 Huddersfield T 31 10 **90 19**
2011–12 Norwich C 30 8
2012–13 Norwich C 30 5
2013–14 Norwich C 15 1 **75 14**
2014–15 Cardiff C 20 1
2015–16 Cardiff C 41 9
2016–17 Cardiff C 34 7
2017–18 Cardiff C 8 3
2018–19 Cardiff C 0 0 **103 20**
2018–19 Wigan Ath 10 0
2019–20 Wigan Ath 16 3 **26 3**

ROBERTS, Gary (F) 473 83
H: 5 10 W: 11 09 b.Chester 18-3-84
Internationals: England C.
2006–07 Accrington S 14 8 **14 8**
2006–07 Ipswich T 33 2
2007–08 Ipswich T 21 1 **54 3**
2007–08 *Crewe Alex* 4 0 **4 0**
2008–09 Huddersfield T 43 9
2009–10 Huddersfield T 43 7
2010–11 Huddersfield T 37 9
2011–12 Huddersfield T 39 6 **162 31**
2012–13 Swindon T 39 4 **39 4**
2013–14 Chesterfield 40 11
2014–15 Chesterfield 34 6 **74 17**
2015–16 Portsmouth 33 7
2016–17 Portsmouth 41 10
2017–18 Portsmouth 0 0 **74 17**
2017–18 Wigan Ath 27 1
2018–19 Wigan Ath 16 2
2019–20 Wigan Ath 9 0 **52 3**

ROBINSON, Antonee (D) 94 1
H: 6 0 W: 11 07 b.Milton Keynes 8-8-97
Internationals: USA U18, Full caps.
2015–16 Everton 0 0
2016–17 Everton 0 0
2017–18 Everton 0 0
2017–18 *Bolton W* 30 0 **30 0**
2018–19 Everton 0 0
2018–19 *Wigan Ath* 26 0
2019–20 Wigan Ath 38 1 **64 1**

WEBBER, Patrick (D) 0 0
b.Worthing 20-1-99
2016–17 Ipswich T 0 0
2017–18 Ipswich T 0 0
2018–19 Ipswich T 0 0
2019–20 Wigan Ath 0 0

WEIR, Jensen (M) 1 0
b.Warrington 31-1-02
Internationals: Scotland U16, U17. England U17, U18.
2017–18 Wigan Ath 0 0
2018–19 Wigan Ath 1 0
2019–20 Wigan Ath 0 0 **1 0**

WILLIAMS, Joe (M) 102 2
H: 5 10 W: 10 06 b.Liverpool 8-12-96
Internationals: England U20.
2014–15 Everton 0 0
2015–16 Everton 0 0
2016–17 Everton 0 0
2017–18 Everton 0 0
2017–18 *Barnsley* 34 1 **34 1**
2018–19 Everton 0 0
2018–19 *Bolton W* 30 0 **30 0**
2019–20 Wigan Ath 38 1 **38 1**

WINDASS, Josh (M) 193 46
H: 5 9 W: 10 10 b.Hull 9-1-93
2013–14 Accrington S 10 0
2014–15 Accrington S 35 6
2015–16 Accrington S 30 15 **75 21**
2016–17 Rangers 21 0
2017–18 Rangers 33 13
2018–19 Rangers 1 0 **55 13**
2018–19 Wigan Ath 39 5
2019–20 Wigan Ath 15 4 **54 9**
2019–20 *Sheffield W* 9 3 **9 3**

Players retained or with offer of contract
Crankshaw, Oliver Samuel; Joseph, Kyle Alexander; Robinson, Luke James; Sanders, Jack Tom; Smith, Scott William.

Scholars
Aasgaard, Thelonious Gerard; Adeeko, Babajide Ezekiel; Broe, Oliver Jack; Brown, Millen Edward; Carragher, James Lee; Costello, Thomas Anthony; Dobie, Zach Louis; Fulton, Jason Richard; Isherwood, Louis James; Jolley, Harry Thomas; Jones, Bobby; Lloyd, Kieran David; McGee, Harry David; McGurk, Sean; McHugh, Harry; McWilliam, Joseph Norman; O'Neill, Mackenzie David; Snell, Marcus James; Tickle, Samuel Lloyd.

WOLVERHAMPTON W (90)

ASHLEY-SEAL, Benny (F) 5 0
b.Southwark 21-11-98
From Norwich C.
2018–19 Wolverhampton W 0 0
2019–20 Wolverhampton W 0 0
2019–20 *Accrington S* 5 0 **5 0**

BENNETT, Ryan (M) 371 16
H: 6 2 W: 11 00 b.Thurrock 6-3-90
Internationals: England U18, U21.
2006–07 Grimsby T 5 0
2007–08 Grimsby T 40 1
2008–09 Grimsby T 45 5
2009–10 Grimsby T 13 0 **103 6**
2009–10 Peterborough U 22 1
2010–11 Peterborough U 34 4
2011–12 Peterborough U 32 1 **88 6**
2011–12 Norwich C 8 0
2012–13 Norwich C 15 1
2013–14 Norwich C 16 1
2014–15 Norwich C 7 0
2015–16 Norwich C 22 0
2016–17 Norwich C 33 0 **101 2**
2017–18 Wolverhampton W 29 1
2018–19 Wolverhampton W 34 1
2019–20 Wolverhampton W 11 0 **74 2**
2019–20 *Leicester C* 5 0 **5 0**

BOLY, Willy (D) 220 12
H: 6 1 W: 12 11 b. 3-2-91
Internationals: France U16, U17, U19.
2010–11 Auxerre 8 1
2011–12 Auxerre 33 1
2012–13 Auxerre 25 1
2013–14 Auxerre 30 0
2014–15 Auxerre 1 0 **97 3**
2014–15 Braga 0 0
2015–16 Braga 22 2
2016–17 Braga 3 0 **25 2**
2016–17 Porto 4 0
2017–18 Porto 0 0 **4 0**
2017–18 *Wolverhampton W* 36 3
2018–19 Wolverhampton W 36 4
2019–20 Wolverhampton W 22 0 **94 7**

BRUNO JORDAO, Andre (M) 27 4
b.Marinha Grande 12-10-98
Internationals: Portugal U18, U19, U20, U21.
2015–16 Uniao de Leiria 23 4 **23 4**
2016–17 Braga 0 0
2017–18 Braga 0 0
2017–18 *Lazio* 0 0
2018–19 Braga 0 0

2018–19	*Lazio*	3	0		
2019–20	Lazio	0	0	**3**	**0**
2019–20	Wolverhampton W	1	0	**1**	**0**

BUUR, Oskar (D) **11 1**
b.Skanderborg 31-3-98
Internationals: Denmark U16, U17, U18, U19.

2014–15	AGF	8	0		
2015–16	AGF	1	0		
2016–17	AGF	1	0	**10**	**0**
2017–18	Wolverhampton W	1	1		
2018–19	Wolverhampton W	0	0		
2019–20	Wolverhampton W	0	0	**1**	**1**

CAMPANA, Leonardo (F) **0 0**
b.Guayaquil 24-7-00
Internationals: Ecuador U20, Full caps.

2016–17	Barcelona	0	0		
2017–18	Barcelona	0	0		
2018–19	Barcelona	0	0		
2019–20	Barcelona	0	0		
2019–20	Wolverhampton W	0	0		

CAMPBELL, Chem (M) **0 0**

2019–20	Wolverhampton W	0	0		

COADY, Conor (D) **283 9**
H: 6 1 W: 11 05 b.Liverpool 25-2-93
Internationals: England U16, U17, U18, U19, U20.

2010–11	Liverpool	0	0		
2011–12	Liverpool	0	0		
2012–13	Liverpool	1	0		
2013–14	Liverpool	0	0	**1**	**0**
2013–14	*Sheffield U*	39	5	**39**	**5**
2014–15	Huddersfield T	45	3	**45**	**3**
2015–16	Wolverhampton W	37	0		
2016–17	Wolverhampton W	40	0		
2017–18	Wolverhampton W	45	1		
2018–19	Wolverhampton W	38	0		
2019–20	Wolverhampton W	38	0	**198**	**1**

CRISTOVAO, Flavio (M) **0 0**

2019–20	Wolverhampton W	0	0		

CUNDLE, Luke (M) **0 0**
b.Warrington 26-4-02

2019–20	Wolverhampton W	0	0		

CUTRONE, Patrick (F) **94 19**
b.Como 3-1-98
Internationals: Italy U16, U17, U18, U19, U21, Full caps.

2016–17	AC Milan	1	0		
2017–18	AC Milan	28	10		
2018–19	AC Milan	34	3	**63**	**13**
2019–20	Wolverhampton W	12	2	**12**	**2**
2019–20	*Fiorentina*	19	4	**19**	**4**

DAI, Wai-Tsun (M) **8 0**
b. 24-7-99
From Reading.

2017–18	Bury	8	0	**8**	**0**
2018–19	Oxford U	0	0		
2019–20	Wolverhampton W	0	0		

DANIEL PODENCE, Castelo (F) **90 13**
b. 21-10-95
Internationals: Portugal U16, U18, U19, U20, U21.

2012–13	Sporting Lisbon	0	0		
2013–14	Sporting Lisbon	0	0		
2014–15	Sporting Lisbon	0	0		
2015–16	Sporting Lisbon	0	0		
2016–17	Sporting Lisbon	13	0		
2016–17	*Moreirense*	14	4	**14**	**4**
2017–18	Sporting Lisbon	12	0	**25**	**0**
2018–19	Olympiacos	27	5		
2019–20	Olympiacos	15	3	**42**	**8**
2019–20	Wolverhampton W	9	1	**9**	**1**

DENDONCKER, Leander (M) **182 15**
H: 6 2 W: 12 02 b.Passendale 15-4-95
Internationals: Belgium U16, U17, U19, U21, Full caps.

2013–14	Anderlecht	0	0		
2014–15	Anderlecht	26	2		
2015–16	Anderlecht	23	1		
2016–17	Anderlecht	40	5		
2017–18	Anderlecht	36	1	**125**	**9**

On loan from Anderlecht.

2018–19	Wolverhampton W	19	2		
2019–20	Wolverhampton W	38	4	**57**	**6**

DIALLO, Sadou (M) **9 0**
Internationals: England U19.
From Manchester C.

2018–19	Wolverhampton W	0	0		
2019–20	Wolverhampton W	0	0		
2019–20	*Accrington S*	9	0	**9**	**0**

DOHERTY, Matthew (M) **290 23**
H: 6 0 W: 12 08 b.Dublin 17-1-92
Internationals: Republic of Ireland U19, U21, Full caps.

2010–11	Wolverhampton W	0	0		
2011–12	Wolverhampton W	1	0		
2011–12	*Hibernian*	13	2	**13**	**2**
2012–13	Wolverhampton W	13	1		
2012–13	*Bury*	17	1	**17**	**1**
2013–14	Wolverhampton W	18	1		
2014–15	Wolverhampton W	33	0		
2015–16	Wolverhampton W	34	2		
2016–17	Wolverhampton W	42	4		
2017–18	Wolverhampton W	45	4		
2018–19	Wolverhampton W	38	4		
2019–20	Wolverhampton W	36	4	**260**	**20**

ENNIS, Niall (F) **30 6**
H: 5 10 W: 12 00 b.Wolverhampton 20-5-99
Internationals: England U17, U18, U19.

2017–18	Wolverhampton W	0	0		
2017–18	*Shrewsbury T*	1	0	**1**	**0**
2018–19	Wolverhampton W	0	0		
2019–20	Wolverhampton W	0	0		
2019–20	*Doncaster R*	29	6	**29**	**6**

ENOBAKHARE, Bright (F) **67 7**
H: 6 0 W: 12 06 b. 8-2-98
Internationals: Nigeria U23.

2015–16	Wolverhampton W	7	0		
2016–17	Wolverhampton W	13	0		
2017–18	Wolverhampton W	21	1		
2018–19	Wolverhampton W	0	0		
2018–19	*Kilmarnock*	6	0	**6**	**0**
2018–19	*Coventry C*	18	6	**18**	**6**
2019–20	Wolverhampton W	0	0	**41**	**1**
2019–20	*Wigan Ath*	2	0	**2**	**0**

Transferred to AEK Athens, June 2020.

GILES, Ryan (M) **20 1**
H: 5 10 W: 11 00 b.Telford 26-1-00
Internationals: England U20.

2018–19	Wolverhampton W	0	0		
2019–20	Wolverhampton W	0	0		
2019–20	*Shrewsbury T*	19	1	**19**	**1**
2019–20	*Coventry C*	1	0	**1**	**0**

GRAHAM, Jordan (M) **52 2**
H: 6 0 W: 10 10 b.Coventry 5-3-95
Internationals: England U16, U17.

2011–12	Aston Villa	0	0		
2012–13	Aston Villa	0	0		
2013–14	Aston Villa	0	0		
2013–14	*Ipswich T*	2	0		
2013–14	*Bradford C*	1	0	**1**	**0**
2014–15	Wolverhampton W	0	0		
2015–16	Wolverhampton W	11	1		
2015–16	*Oxford U*	5	0		
2016–17	Wolverhampton W	2	0		
2017–18	Wolverhampton W	1	0		
2017–18	*Fulham*	3	0	**3**	**0**
2018–19	Wolverhampton W	0	0		
2018–19	*Ipswich T*	4	0	**6**	**0**
2018–19	*Oxford U*	16	1	**21**	**1**
2019–20	Wolverhampton W	0	0	**14**	**1**
2019–20	*Gillingham*	7	0	**7**	**0**

HELDER COSTA, Wander (M) **170 23**
H: 5 10 W: 11 07 b.Luanda 12-1-94
Internationals: Portugal U16, U17, U18, U19, U20, U21, U23, Full caps.

2013–14	Benfica	0	0		
2014–15	Benfica	0	0		
2014–15	*Deportivo La Coruna*	6	0	**6**	**0**
2015–16	Benfica	0	0		
2015–16	*Monaco*	25	3	**25**	**3**
2016–17	Benfica	0	0		
2016–17	*Wolverhampton W*	35	10		
2017–18	Wolverhampton W	36	5		
2018–19	Wolverhampton W	25	1		
2019–20	Wolverhampton W	0	0	**96**	**16**
2019–20	*Leeds U*	43	4	**43**	**4**

JIMENEZ, Raul (F) **252 78**
H: 6 2 W: 12 04 b.Tepeji 5-5-91
Internationals: Mexico U23, Full caps.

2011–12	America	15	2		
2012–13	America	29	11		
2013–14	America	27	12		
2014–15	America	4	4	**75**	**29**
2014–15	Atletico Madrid	21	1	**21**	**1**
2015–16	Benfica	28	5		
2016–17	Benfica	19	7		
2017–18	Benfica	33	6		
2018–19	Benfica	0	0	**80**	**18**
2018–19	*Wolverhampton W*	38	13		
2019–20	Wolverhampton W	38	17	**76**	**30**

JOAO MOUTINHO, Felipe (M) **480 36**
H: 5 7 W: 9 08 b.Portimao 8-9-86
Internationals: Portugal U17, U18, U19, U21, B, Full caps.

2004–05	Sporting Lisbon	15	0		
2005–06	Sporting Lisbon	34	4		
2006–07	Sporting Lisbon	29	4		
2007–08	Sporting Lisbon	30	5		
2008–09	Sporting Lisbon	27	3		
2009–10	Sporting Lisbon	28	5	**163**	**21**
2010–11	Porto	27	0		
2011–12	Porto	29	3		
2012–13	Porto	27	1	**83**	**4**
2013–14	Monaco	31	1		
2014–15	Monaco	37	4		
2015–16	Monaco	26	1		
2016–17	Monaco	31	2		
2017–18	Monaco	33	1	**158**	**9**
2018–19	Wolverhampton W	38	1		
2019–20	Wolverhampton W	38	1	**76**	**2**

JOHN, Cameron (D) **18 2**
b. 24-8-99

2018–19	Wolverhampton W	0	0		
2019–20	Wolverhampton W	0	0		
2019–20	*Doncaster R*	18	2	**18**	**2**

JOHNSON, Connor (D) **11 0**
b.Kettering 10-3-98

2016–17	Wolverhampton W	0	0		
2017–18	Wolverhampton W	0	0		
2018–19	Wolverhampton W	0	0		
2018–19	*Walsall*	7	0	**7**	**0**
2019–20	Wolverhampton W	0	0		
2019–20	*Kilmarnock*	4	0	**4**	**0**

JONNY, Castro (D) **251 6**
H: 5 9 W: 11 00 b.Vigo 3-3-94
Internationals: Spain U18, U19, U20, U21, Full caps.

2011–12	Celta Vigo	0	0		
2012–13	Celta Vigo	19	0		
2013–14	Celta Vigo	26	0		
2014–15	Celta Vigo	36	0		
2015–16	Celta Vigo	36	1		
2016–17	Celta Vigo	30	0		
2017–18	Celta Vigo	36	2	**183**	**3**
2018–19	Atletico Madrid	0	0		
2018–19	*Wolverhampton W*	33	1		
2019–20	Wolverhampton W	35	2	**68**	**3**

JOTA, Diogo (F) **179 55**
H: 5 10 W: 11 00 b.Massarelos 4-12-96
Internationals: Portugal U19, U21, U23, Full caps.

2014–15	Pacos Ferreira	10	2		
2015–16	Pacos Ferreira	31	12	**41**	**14**
2016–17	Atletico Madrid	0	0		
2016–17	*Porto*	27	8	**27**	**8**
2017–18	Atletico Madrid	0	0		
2017–18	*Wolverhampton W*	44	17		
2018–19	Wolverhampton W	33	9		
2019–20	Wolverhampton W	34	7	**111**	**33**

KILMAN, Max (D) **4 0**
b.London 23-5-97
From Maidenhead U.

2018–19	Wolverhampton W	1	0		
2019–20	Wolverhampton W	3	0	**4**	**0**

LEO BONATINI, Lohner (F) **149 48**
b. 28-3-94
Internationals: Brazil U17.

2013	Cruzeiro	0	0		
2013	*Goias*	5	0		
2014	Cruzeiro	0	0		
2014	Goias	1	0	**6**	**0**
2014–15	Estoril	15	4		
2015	Cruzeiro	0	0		
2015–16	Estoril	33	17	**48**	**21**
2016–17	Al Hilal	25	12		
2017–18	Al Hilal	0	0	**25**	**12**
2017–18	*Wolverhampton W*	43	12		
2018–19	Wolverhampton W	7	0		
2018–19	*Nottingham F*	5	0	**5**	**0**
2019–20	Wolverhampton W	0	0	**50**	**12**
2019–20	*Vitoria Guimaraes*	15	3	**15**	**3**

MATHESON, Luke (D) **23 1**
b.Manchester 3-10-02
Internationals: England U17, U18.

2018–19	Rochdale	3	0		
2019–20	Wolverhampton W	0	0		
2019–20	*Rochdale*	20	1	**23**	**1**

MIR, Rafa (F) **63 16**
H: 6 1 W: 11 11 b.Murcia 18-6-97
Internationals: Spain U21.

2014–15	Valencia	0	0		

2015–16 Valencia 0 0
2016–17 Valencia 2 0
2017–18 Valencia 0 0 2 0
2017–18 Wolverhampton W 2 0
2018–19 Wolverhampton W 0 0
2018–19 *Las Palmas* 30 7 30 7
2019–20 Wolverhampton W 0 0 2 0
2019–20 *Nottingham F* 11 0 11 0
2019–20 *Huesca* 18 9 18 9

NEVES, Ruben (M) 174 15
H: 5 11 W: 12 08 b. 13-3-97
Internationals: Portugal U16, U17, U18, U21, U23, Full caps.
2014–15 Porto 24 1
2015–16 Porto 22 1
2016–17 Porto 13 1 59 3
2017–18 Wolverhampton W 42 6
2018–19 Wolverhampton W 35 4
2019–20 Wolverhampton W 38 2 115 12

NORRIS, Will (G) 86 0
H: 6 5 W: 11 09 b.Royston 12-7-93
2014–15 Cambridge U 3 0
2015–16 Cambridge U 21 0
2016–17 Cambridge U 45 0 69 0
2017–18 Wolverhampton W 1 0
2018–19 Wolverhampton W 1 0
2019–20 Wolverhampton W 0 0 2 0
2019–20 *Ipswich T* 15 0 15 0

OFOSU-AYEH, Phil (D) 204 6
H: 6 0 b.Moers 15-9-91
2009–10 SV Wilhelmshaven 4 1
2010–11 SV Wilhelmshaven 26 1 30 2
2011–12 Rot-Weiss Erfurt 27 0
2012–13 Rot-Weiss Erfurt 32 1 59 1
2013–14 Duisburg 33 1 33 1
2014–15 VfR Aalen 32 1 32 1
2015–16 Entracht Braunschweig 20 0
2016–17 Entracht Braunschweig 16 1 36 1
2017–18 Wolverhampton W 0 0
2018–19 Wolverhampton W 0 0
2018–19 *Hansa Rostock* 5 0 5 0
2019–20 Wolverhampton W 0 0
2019–20 *Wurzbuger Kickers* 9 0 9 0

OTASOWIE, Owen (M) 0 0
Internationals: USA U18.
2019–20 Wolverhampton W 0 0

PEDRO NETO, Lomba (M) 36 4
b.Viana do Castelo 9-3-00
Internationals: Portugal U17, U18, U19, U20, U21.
2016–17 Braga 2 1
2017–18 Braga 1 0
2018–19 Braga 0 0 3 1
2018–19 *Lazio* 4 0
2019–20 Lazio 0 0 4 0
2019–20 Wolverhampton W 29 3 29 3

PERRY, Taylor (M) 0 0
b. 15-8-01
2019–20 Wolverhampton W 0 0

RICHARDS, Lewis (D) 0 0
Internationals: Republic of Ireland U19.
2019–20 Wolverhampton W 0 0

RONAN, Connor (M) 72 2
H: 5 8 W: 11 00 b.Rochdale 6-3-98
Internationals: England U17. Republic of Ireland U17, U19, U21.
2015–16 Wolverhampton W 0 0
2016–17 Wolverhampton W 4 0
2017–18 Wolverhampton W 3 0
2017–18 *Portsmouth* 16 0 16 0
2018–19 Wolverhampton W 0 0
2018–19 *Walsall* 11 0 11 0
2019–20 Wolverhampton W 0 0 7 0
2019–20 *Dunajska Streda* 28 1 28 1
2019–20 *Blackpool* 10 1 10 1

RUBEN VINAGRE, Goncalo (D) 42 1
b. 9-4-99
Internationals: Portugal U16, U17, U18, U19, U20, U21.
2016–17 Monaco 0 0
2017–18 Monaco 0 0
2017–18 *Wolverhampton W* 9 1
2018–19 Wolverhampton W 17 0
2019–20 Wolverhampton W 16 0 42 1

RUDDY, John (G) 415 0
H: 6 3 W: 12 07 b.St Ives 24-10-86
Internationals: England Full caps.
2003–04 Cambridge U 1 0
2004–05 Cambridge U 38 0 39 0
2005–06 Everton 1 0
2005–06 *Walsall* 5 0 5 0
2005–06 *Rushden & D* 3 0 3 0
2005–06 *Chester C* 4 0 4 0
2006–07 Everton 0 0
2006–07 *Stockport Co* 11 0
2006–07 *Wrexham* 5 0 5 0
2006–07 *Bristol C* 1 0 1 0
2007–08 Everton 0 0
2007–08 *Stockport Co* 12 0 23 0
2008–09 Everton 0 0
2008–09 *Crewe Alex* 19 0 19 0
2009–10 Everton 0 0 1 0
2009–10 *Motherwell* 34 0 34 0
2010–11 Norwich C 45 0
2011–12 Norwich C 37 0
2012–13 Norwich C 15 0
2013–14 Norwich C 38 0
2014–15 Norwich C 46 0
2015–16 Norwich C 27 0
2016–17 Norwich C 27 0 235 0
2017–18 Wolverhampton W 45 0
2018–19 Wolverhampton W 1 0
2019–20 Wolverhampton W 0 0 46 0

RUI PATRICIO, Pedro (G) 402 0
H: 6 2 W: 13 03 b.Marrazes 15-2-88
Internationals: Portugal U16, U17, U18, U19, U20, U21, Full caps.
2006–07 Sporting Lisbon 1 0
2007–08 Sporting Lisbon 20 0
2008–09 Sporting Lisbon 26 0
2009–10 Sporting Lisbon 30 0
2010–11 Sporting Lisbon 30 0
2011–12 Sporting Lisbon 28 0
2012–13 Sporting Lisbon 30 0
2013–14 Sporting Lisbon 30 0
2014–15 Sporting Lisbon 33 0
2015–16 Sporting Lisbon 34 0
2016–17 Sporting Lisbon 31 0
2017–18 Sporting Lisbon 34 0 327 0
2018–19 Wolverhampton W 37 0
2019–20 Wolverhampton W 38 0 75 0

SAISS, Romain (M) 275 18
H: 6 3 W: 12 00 b.Bourg-de-Peage 26-3-90
Internationals: Morocco Full caps.
2010–11 Valence 13 4 13 4
2011–12 Clermont 17 1
2012–13 Clermont 31 0 48 1
2013–14 Le Havre 27 1
2014–15 Le Havre 34 2 61 3
2015–16 Angers 35 2 35 2
2016–17 Wolverhampton W 24 0
2017–18 Wolverhampton W 42 4
2018–19 Wolverhampton W 19 2
2019–20 Wolverhampton W 33 2 118 8

SAMUELS, Austin (F) 0 0
b. 20-11-00
Internationals: England U16.
2019–20 Wolverhampton W 0 0

SANDERSON, Dion (M) 10 0
b. 15-12-99
2019–20 Wolverhampton W 0 0
2019–20 *Cardiff C* 10 0 10 0

SHABANI, Meritan (M) 2 0
b.Munich 15-3-99
2017–18 Bayern Munich 1 0
2018–19 Bayern Munich 1 0 2 0
2019–20 Wolverhampton W 0 0

SONDERGAARD, Andreas (G) 0 0
b. 17-1-01
Internationals: Denmark U16, U17, U18, U19.
2019–20 Wolverhampton W 0 0

TAYLOR, Terry (M) 0 0
b. 29-6-01
Internationals: Wales U21.
From Aberdeen.
2019–20 Wolverhampton W 0 0

TRAORE, Adama (F) 139 10
H: 5 10 W: 12 00 b.L'Hospitalet de Llobregat 25-1-96
Internationals: Spain U16, U17, U19, U21.
2013–14 Barcelona 1 0
2014–15 Barcelona 0 0 1 0
2015–16 Aston Villa 10 0
2016–17 Aston Villa 1 0 11 0
2016–17 Middlesbrough 27 0
2017–18 Middlesbrough 34 5 61 5
2018–19 Wolverhampton W 29 1
2019–20 Wolverhampton W 37 4 66 5

VALLEJO , Jesus (D) 90 3
b.Zaragoza 30-11-97
Internationals: Spain U16, U17, U19, U21.
2014–15 Zaragoza 31 1
2015–16 Real Madrid 0 0
2015–16 *Zaragoza* 20 0 51 1
2016–17 Real Madrid 0 0
2016–17 *Eintracht Frankfurt* 25 1 25 1
2017–18 Real Madrid 7 0
2018–19 Real Madrid 5 1
2019–20 Real Madrid 0 0 12 1
On loan from Real Madrid.
2019–20 Wolverhampton W 2 0 2 0

WATT, Elliot (M) 12 1
b.Preston 11-3-18
Internationals: Scotland U17, U19, U21.
From Preston NE.
2018–19 Wolverhampton W 0 0
2019–20 Wolverhampton W 0 0
2019–20 *Carlisle U* 12 1 12 1

WHITE, Morgan (M) 53 0
b. 27-1-00
Internationals: England U16, U17, U18, U19, U21.
2016–17 Wolverhampton W 7 0
2017–18 Wolverhampton W 13 0
2018–19 Wolverhampton W 26 0
2019–20 Wolverhampton W 7 0 53 0

Players retained or with offer of contract
Agboola, Michael; Carty, Conor Thomas; Castro Otto, Jonatan; Corbeanu, Theodor Alexander; Csoka, Daniel; Dadashov, Renat; Estrada, Pascal Juan; Gibbs-White, Morgan Anthony; Goncalves Miranda, Roderick Jefferson; He, Zhenyu; Herc, Christian; Hesketh, Owen James; Joseph, Joseph; Kitolano, John Shuguto; Lomba Neto, Pedro; Lonwijk, Nigel Cello; Marques, Christian Fernandes; Mayounga-Ngolou, Cyriaque; Neto Hanne, Boubacar Rafael; Nya, Raphael; O'Shaughnessy, Joseph Peter David; Pardington, James; Scott, Jack David; Smith, Jackson; Wan, Nathaniel Shio Hong; Wang, Jiahao; Young, Joe Michael.

Scholars
Abbey, Jediael Yeboah; Bueno Lopez, Hugo; Bugarin Londono, Erik; Forrester, Jaden Joshua; Hodnett, Jack Mikey James; McLaughlin, Lee James; Parker, Todd William; Pinnington, Dean Stanley; Sangare, Faisu.

WYCOMBE W (91)

AKINFENWA, Adebayo (F) 620 194
H: 5 11 W: 13 07 b.Nigeria 10-5-82
2001 Atlantas 19 4
2002 Atlantas 4 1 23 5
From Barry T.
2003–04 Boston U 3 0 3 0
2003–04 Leyton Orient 1 0 1 0
2003–04 Rushden & D 0 0
2003–04 Doncaster R 9 4 9 4
2004–05 Torquay U 37 14 37 14
2005–06 Swansea C 34 9
2006–07 Swansea C 25 5
2007–08 Swansea C 0 0 59 14
2007–08 Millwall 7 0 7 0
2007–08 Northampton T 15 7
2008–09 Northampton T 33 13
2009–10 Northampton T 40 17
2010–11 Gillingham 44 11
2011–12 Northampton T 39 18
2012–13 Northampton T 41 16 168 71
2013–14 Gillingham 34 10 78 21
2014–15 AFC Wimbledon 45 13
2015–16 AFC Wimbledon 38 6 83 19
2016–17 Wycombe W 42 12
2017–18 Wycombe W 42 17
2018–19 Wycombe W 36 7
2019–20 Wycombe W 32 10 152 46

ALLSOP, Ryan (G) 194 0
H: 6 2 W: 12 06 b.Birmingham 17-6-92
Internationals: England U17.
2012–13 Leyton Orient 20 0 20 0
2012–13 Bournemouth 10 0
2013–14 Bournemouth 12 0
2014–15 Bournemouth 0 0
2014–15 *Coventry C* 24 0 24 0
2015–16 Bournemouth 1 0
2015–16 *Wycombe W* 18 0
2015–16 Portsmouth 0 0

2016–17 Bournemouth 1 0
2017–18 Bournemouth 0 0 **24 0**
2017–18 *Blackpool* 22 0 **22 0**
2017–18 *Lincoln C* 16 0 **16 0**
2018–19 Wycombe W 38 0
2019–20 Wycombe W 32 0 **88 0**

BLOOMFIELD, Matt (M) 470 38
H: 5 9 W: 11 00 b.Felixstowe 8-2-84
Internationals: England U19.
2001–02 Ipswich T 0 0
2002–03 Ipswich T 0 0
2003–04 Ipswich T 0 0
2003–04 Wycombe W 12 1
2004–05 Wycombe W 26 2
2005–06 Wycombe W 39 5
2006–07 Wycombe W 41 4
2007–08 Wycombe W 35 4
2008–09 Wycombe W 20 0
2009–10 Wycombe W 14 2
2010–11 Wycombe W 34 3
2011–12 Wycombe W 31 2
2012–13 Wycombe W 2 1
2013–14 Wycombe W 32 0
2014–15 Wycombe W 33 1
2015–16 Wycombe W 27 1
2016–17 Wycombe W 33 5
2017–18 Wycombe W 37 3
2018–19 Wycombe W 28 2
2019–20 Wycombe W 26 2 **470 38**

CHARLES, Darius (M) 285 18
H: 6 1 W: 13 05 b.Ealing 10-12-87
Internationals: England C.
2004–05 Brentford 1 0
2005–06 Brentford 2 0
2006–07 Brentford 17 1
2007–08 Brentford 17 0 **37 1**
From Ebbsfleet U.
2010–11 Stevenage 28 2
2011–12 Stevenage 28 4
2012–13 Stevenage 37 1
2013–14 Stevenage 22 4
2014–15 Stevenage 29 2 **144 13**
2015–16 Burton Alb 0 0
2015–16 *AFC Wimbledon* 9 0
2016–17 AFC Wimbledon 34 2
2017–18 AFC Wimbledon 31 0 **74 2**
2018–19 Wycombe W 5 0
2019–20 Wycombe W 25 2 **30 2**

FREEMAN, Nick (M) 94 5
b. 7-11-95
From Histon, Hemel Hempstead T, Biggleswade T.
2016–17 Wycombe W 14 0
2017–18 Wycombe W 27 3
2018–19 Wycombe W 27 0
2019–20 Wycombe W 26 2 **94 5**

GAPE, Dominic (M) 139 3
H: 5 11 W: 10 13 b.Southampton 9-9-94
2012–13 Southampton 0 0
2013–14 Southampton 0 0
2014–15 Southampton 1 0
2015–16 Southampton 0 0
2016–17 Southampton 0 0 **1 0**
2016–17 Wycombe W 32 1
2017–18 Wycombe W 35 1
2018–19 Wycombe W 43 1
2019–20 Wycombe W 28 0 **138 3**

GARDINER-SMITH, Jacob (M) 0 0
b.Cambridge 3-7-97
From St Albans C.
2019–20 Wycombe W 0 0

GRIMMER, Jack (M) 152 3
H: 6 0 W: 12 06 b.Aberdeen 25-1-94
Internationals: Scotland U16, U17, U18, U19, U21.
2009–10 Aberdeen 2 0
2010–11 Aberdeen 2 0
2011–12 Aberdeen 0 0 **4 0**
2011–12 Fulham 0 0
2012–13 Fulham 0 0
2013–14 Fulham 0 0
2013–14 *Port Vale* 13 1 **13 1**
2014–15 Fulham 13 0
2014–15 *Shrewsbury T* 6 0
2015–16 Fulham 0 0
2015–16 *Shrewsbury T* 21 1
2016–17 Fulham 0 0 **13 0**
2016–17 *Shrewsbury T* 24 0 **51 1**
2017–18 Coventry C 42 1
2018–19 Coventry C 11 0 **53 1**
2019–20 Wycombe W 18 0 **18 0**

JACOBSON, Joe (D) 459 40
H: 5 11 W: 12 06 b.Cardiff 17-11-86
Internationals: Wales U21.
2005–06 Cardiff C 1 0
2006–07 Cardiff C 0 0 **1 0**
2006–07 *Accrington S* 6 1
2006–07 *Bristol R* 11 0
2007–08 Bristol R 40 1
2008–09 Bristol R 22 0 **73 1**
2009–10 Oldham Ath 15 0
2010–11 Oldham Ath 1 0 **16 0**
2010–11 Accrington S 26 2 **32 3**
2011–12 Shrewsbury T 39 1
2012–13 Shrewsbury T 30 2
2013–14 Shrewsbury T 41 4 **110 7**
2014–15 Wycombe W 42 3
2015–16 Wycombe W 34 1
2016–17 Wycombe W 39 3
2017–18 Wycombe W 46 6
2018–19 Wycombe W 36 7
2019–20 Wycombe W 30 9 **227 29**

JOMBATI, Sido (D) 270 9
H: 6 0 W: 11 11 b.Lisbon 20-8-87
2011–12 Cheltenham T 36 2
2012–13 Cheltenham T 37 1
2013–14 Cheltenham T 43 1 **116 4**
2014–15 Wycombe W 35 0
2015–16 Wycombe W 34 1
2016–17 Wycombe W 25 2
2017–18 Wycombe W 20 1
2018–19 Wycombe W 33 1
2019–20 Wycombe W 7 0 **154 5**

KASHKET, Scott (M) 92 19
H: 5 9 W: 10 06 b.London 6-7-95
2014–15 Leyton Orient 1 0
2015–16 Leyton Orient 15 1
2016–17 Leyton Orient 0 0 **16 1**
2016–17 Wycombe W 21 10
2017–18 Wycombe W 9 1
2018–19 Wycombe W 27 3
2019–20 Wycombe W 19 4 **76 18**

MACKAIL-SMITH, Craig (F) 446 124
H: 6 3 W: 12 04 b.Watford 25-2-84
Internationals: England C. Scotland Full caps.
2006–07 Peterborough U 15 8
2007–08 Peterborough U 36 12
2008–09 Peterborough U 46 23
2009–10 Peterborough U 43 10
2010–11 Peterborough U 45 27
2011–12 Brighton & HA 45 9
2012–13 Brighton & HA 29 11
2013–14 Brighton & HA 5 0
2014–15 Brighton & HA 30 1 **109 21**
2014–15 *Peterborough U* 3 0
2015–16 Luton T 33 4
2016–17 Luton T 2 0 **35 4**
2016–17 *Peterborough U* 18 5 **206 85**
2017–18 Wycombe W 41 8
2018–19 Wycombe W 21 3
2018–19 *Notts Co* 16 3 **16 3**
2019–20 Wycombe W 0 0 **62 11**
2019–20 *Stevenage* 18 0 **18 0**

MASCOLL, Jamie (M) 4 0
From Dulwich Hamlet.
2017–18 Charlton Ath 0 0
2018–19 Charlton Ath 0 0
2019–20 Wycombe W 4 0 **4 0**

ONYEDINMA, Fred (M) 179 24
H: 6 1 b.London 24-11-96
2013–14 Millwall 4 0
2014–15 Millwall 2 0
2014–15 *Wycombe W* 25 8
2015–16 Millwall 34 4
2016–17 Millwall 42 3
2017–18 Millwall 37 1
2018–19 Millwall 1 0 **120 8**
2018–19 *Wycombe W* 21 4
2019–20 Wycombe W 13 4 **59 16**

PARKER, Josh (F) 191 31
H: 5 11 W: 12 00 b.Slough 1-12-90
Internationals: Antigua and Barbuda Full caps.
2009–10 QPR 4 0
2010–11 QPR 1 0 **5 0**
2010–11 *Northampton T* 3 0 **3 0**
2010–11 *Wycombe W* 1 0
2011–12 Oldham Ath 13 0 **13 0**
2011–12 *Dagenham & R* 8 0 **8 0**
2012–13 Oxford U 15 0 **15 0**
2013–14 Domzale 25 11 **25 11**
2014–15 Red Star Belgrade 9 2
2015–16 Red Star Belgrade 3 2 **12 4**
2015–16 *Aberdeen* 7 0 **7 0**
2016–17 Gillingham 16 2
2017–18 Gillingham 42 10
2018–19 Gillingham 21 4 **79 16**
2018–19 Charlton Ath 10 0 **10 0**
2019–20 Wycombe W 13 0 **14 0**

PATTISON, Alex (F) 46 0
b. 6-9-97
2016–17 Middlesbrough 0 0
2017–18 Middlesbrough 0 0
2018–19 Middlesbrough 0 0
2018–19 *Yeovil T* 29 0 **29 0**
2019–20 Wycombe W 17 0 **17 0**

SAMUEL, Alex (F) 117 10
H: 6 0 W: 11 11 b.Neath 20-9-95
Internationals: Wales U18.
From Aberystwyth T.
2014–15 Swansea C 0 0
2015–16 Swansea C 0 0
2015–16 *Greenock Morton* 26 2 **26 2**
2016–17 Swansea C 0 0
2016–17 *Newport Co* 18 2 **18 2**
2017–18 Stevenage 22 0 **22 0**
2018–19 Wycombe W 30 5
2019–20 Wycombe W 21 1 **51 6**

STEWART, Anthony (D) 192 9
H: 5 10 W: 12 03 b.Brixton 18-9-92
2011–12 Wycombe W 4 0
2012–13 Wycombe W 19 1
2013–14 Wycombe W 33 3
2014–15 Crewe Alex 10 0 **10 0**
2015–16 Wycombe W 27 1
2016–17 Wycombe W 31 1
2017–18 Wycombe W 17 1
2018–19 Wycombe W 17 0
2019–20 Wycombe W 34 2 **182 9**

THOMPSON, Curtis (M) 150 3
H: 5 10 W: 12 06 b.Nottingham 2-9-93
2011–12 Notts Co 0 0
2012–13 Notts Co 2 0
2013–14 Notts Co 11 0
2014–15 Notts Co 31 0
2015–16 Notts Co 26 2
2016–17 Notts Co 13 0
2017–18 Notts Co 0 0 **83 2**
2017–18 *Wycombe W* 7 0
2018–19 Wycombe W 39 1
2019–20 Wycombe W 21 0 **67 1**

WHEELER, David (M) 221 41
H: 5 11 W: 12 00 b.Brighton 4-10-90
2013–14 Exeter C 35 3
2014–15 Exeter C 45 7
2015–16 Exeter C 31 6
2016–17 Exeter C 38 17
2017–18 Exeter C 2 0 **151 33**
2017–18 QPR 9 1
2018–19 Portsmouth 11 0 **11 0**
2018–19 QPR 0 0 **9 1**
2018–19 *Milton Keynes D* 19 4 **19 4**
2019–20 Wycombe W 31 3 **31 3**

YATES, Cameron (G) 0 0
b.Edinburgh 14-2-99
From Leicester C.
2018–19 Wycombe W 0 0
2019–20 Wycombe W 0 0

ENGLISH LEAGUE PLAYERS – INDEX

NATIONAL LIST OF REFEREES FOR SEASON 2019–20

Adcock, James
Atkinson, Martin
Attwell, Stuart
Backhouse, Anthony
Bankes, Peter
Bond, Darren
Boyeson, Carl
Bramall, Tom
Breakspear, Charles
Brooks, John
Busby, John
Coggins, Antony
Coote, David
Coy, Martin
Davies, Andy
Dean, Mike
Donohue, Matthew
Doughty, Leigh
Drysdale, Darren
Duncan, Scott
Edwards, Marc
Eltringham, Geoff
England, Darren
Finnie, Will
Friend, Kevin
Gillett, Jarred
Haines, Andy
Hair, Neil
Handley, Darren
Harrington, Tony
Hicks, Craig
Hooper, Simon
Horwood, Graham
Huxtable, Brett
Ilderton, Eddie
Johnson, Kevin
Jones, Rob
Joyce, Ross
Kavanagh, Christopher
Kettle, Trevor
Kinseley, Nick
Langford, Oliver
Lewis, Rob
Linington, James
Madley, Andy
Marriner, Andre
Marsden, Paul
Martin, Stephen
Mason, Lee
Moss, Jonathan
Nield, Tom
Oldham, James
Oldham, Scott
Oliver, Michael
Pawson, Craig
Pollard, Christopher
Probert, Lee
Purkiss, Sam
Robinson, Tim
Rock, David
Salisbury, Graham
Salisbury, Michael
Sarginson, Chris
Scott, Graham
Simpson, Jeremy
Smith, Josh
Stockbridge, Seb
Stroud, Keith
Swabey, Lee
Taylor, Anthony
Tierney, Paul
Toner, Ben
Ward, Gavin
Webb, David
Whitestone, Dean
Woolmer, Andy
Wright, Peter
Yates, Ollie
Young, Alan

ASSISTANT REFEREES

Amey, Justin
Amphlett, Marvyn
Aspinall, Natalie
Atkin, Robert
Avent, David
Aylott, Andrew
Barnard, Nicholas
Bartlett, Richard
Beck, Simon
Bennett, Simon
Benton, David
Beswick, Gary
Betts, Lee
Bickle, Oliver
Blunden, Darren
Bonneywell, Dan
Bristow, Matthew
Brown, Conor
Brown, Stephen
Burt, Stuart
Butler, Stuart
Byrne, George
Byrne, Helen
Cann, Darren
Cheosiaua, Ravel
Clark, Joe
Clayton, Alan
Clayton, Simon
Cook, Dan
Cook, Daniel
Cooper, Ian
Cooper, Nicholas
Cropp, Barry
Crowhurst, Leigh
Crysell, Adam
Cunliffe, Mark
Da Costa, Anthony
Dabbs, Robert
Dallison, Andrew
Davies, Neil
Denton, Michael
Dermott, Philip
Derrien, Mark
Desborough, Mike
Dudley, Ian
Duncan, Mark
Dwyer, Mark
Eaton, Derek
Farmer, Aaron
Farrell, Conor
Finch, Stephen
Fitch-Jackson, Carl
Flynn, John
Foley, Matt
Ford, Declan
Fox, Andrew
Freeman, Lee
Fyvie, Graeme
Garratt, Andrew
George, Michael
Gill, Bhupinder
Gooch, Peter
Gordon, Barry
Graham, Paul
Gratton, Danny
Greenhalgh, Nick
Griffiths, Mark
Grunnill, Wayne
Hanley, Michael

Harty, Thomas
Hatzidakis, Constantine
Hendley, Andrew
Hilton, Gary
Hobday, Paul
Hodskinson, Paul
Holmes, Adrian
Hopton, Nick
Howick, Kevin
Howson, Akil
Hudson, Shaun
Hunt, David
Hunt, Jonathan
Husband, Christopher
Hussin, Ian
Hyde, Robert
Isherwood, Chris
Jackson, Oliver
Jones, Mark
Jones, Matthew
Kane, Graham
Karaivanov, Hristo
Kelly, Paul
Kendall, Richard
Khan, Abbas
Kidd, Christopher
Kirkup, Peter
Laver, Andrew
Leach, Daniel
Ledger, Scott
Lee, Matthew
Lennard, Harry
Lewis, Sam
Liddle, Geoffrey
Lister, Paul
Long, Simon
Lugg, Nigel
Mackey, Oliver
Mainwaring, James
Marks, Louis
Maskell, Garry
Massey-Ellis, Sian
Matthews, Adam
Mcdonough, Michael
Mcgrath, Matthew
Mellor, Gareth
Merchant, Robert
Meredith, Steven
Moore, Anthony
Morris, Kevin
Morris, Richard
Mulraine, Kevin
Newhouse, Paul
Nunn, Adam
Ogles, Samuel
Parry, Matthew
Pashley, Alix
Perry, Marc
Plane, Steven
Plowright, David
Pottage, Mark
Powell, Christopher
Rashid, Lisa
Read, Gregory
Rees, Paul
Robathan, Daniel
Ross, Alasdair
Rushton, Steven
Russell, Geoffrey
Russell, Mark
Scholes, Mark
Sharp, Neil
Shaw, Simon
Simpson, Joe
Smallwood, Billy
Smart, Edward
Smedley, Ian
Smith, Matthew
Smith, Michael
Smith, Rob
Smith, Wade
Stokes, Joseph
Street, Duncan
Taylor, Craig
Taylor, Grant
Tranter, Adrian
Treleaven, Dean
Vallance, James
Venamore, Lee
Viccars, Gareth
Wade, Christopher
Wade, Stephen
Ward, Christopher
Waters, Adrian
Webb, Michael
West, Richard
Whitaker, Ryan
Wigglesworth, Richard
Wild, Richard
Wilding, Darren
Wilkes, Matthew
Williams, Andrew
Williams, Ollie
Wilson, James
Wilson, Marc
Wood, Timothy
Woodward, Daniel
Woodward, Richard
Yates, Paul

MANAGERS – IN AND OUT 2019–20

JULY 2019

10 Darren Moore appointed manager of Doncaster R.
15 Steve Bruce resigns as manager of Sheffield W.
17 Steve Bruce appointed manager of Newcastle U.

AUGUST 2019

15 Sol Campbell leaves as manager of Macclesfield T by mutual consent.
16 Jan Siewert sacked as manager of Huddersfield T.
19 Daryl McMahon appointed manager of Macclesfield T.
22 Phil Parkinson resigns as manager of Bolton W.
31 Keith Hill appointed manager of Bolton W.

SEPTEMBER 2019

6 Garry Monk appointed manager of Sheffield W.
6 Kevin Bond resigns as manager of Southend U.
7 Javi Gracia sacked as manager of Watford.
7 Quique Sanchez Flores appointed manager of Watford.
9 Danny Cowley leaves as manager of Lincoln C and takes over as manager of Huddersfield T.
9 Dino Maamria sacked as manager of Stevenage.
19 Laurent Banide sacked as manager of Oldham Ath.
19 Dino Maamria appointed manager of Oldham Ath.

OCTOBER 2019

3 Neil Harris resigns as manager of Millwall.
8 Daniel Stendel sacked as manager of Barnsley.
8 Jack Ross sacked as manager of Sunderland.
9 Jose Gomes sacked as manager of Reading.
14 Mark Bowen appointed manager of Reading.
16 Carl Fletcher appointed manager of Leyton Orient.
17 Phil Parkinson appointed manager of Sunderland.
20 Wally Downes sacked as manager of AFC Wimbledon.
21 Gary Rowett appointed manager of Millwall.
22 Sol Campbell appointed manager of Southend U.
23 Glyn Hodges appointed manager of AFC Wimbledon.
28 Jim Bentley resigns as manager of Morecambe to become manager of National League side AFC Fylde.

NOVEMBER 2019

1 Nathan Jones sacked as manager of Stoke C.
2 Paul Tisdale sacked as manager of Milton Keynes D.
3 Russell Martin appointed manager of Milton Keynes D.
7 Derek Adams appointed manager of Morecambe.
8 Michael O'Neill appointed manager of Stoke C, but continues his role as Northern Ireland manager until the end of their Euro 2020 campaign.
11 Neil Warnock leaves as manager of Cardiff C by mutual consent.
13 Steven Pressley sacked as manager of Carlisle U.
14 Carl Fletcher sacked as manager of Leyton Orient.
15 Michael Jolley sacked as manager of Grimsby T.
16 Neil Harris appointed manager of Cardiff C.
19 Mauricio Pochettino sacked as manager of Tottenham H.
20 Jose Mourinho appointed manager of Tottenham H.
20 Gerhard Struber appointed manager of Barnsley.
26 Chris Beech appointed manager of Carlisle U.
29 Unai Emery sacked as manager of Arsenal.

DECEMBER 2019

1 Quique Sanchez Flores sacked as manager of Watford.
2 Gabriele Cioffi leaves as manager of Crawley T by mutual consent.
4 Pep Clotet appointed manager of Birmingham C after being in temporary charge.
5 Marco Silva sacked as manager of Everton.
5 John Yems appointed manager of Crawley T.
6 Nigel Pearson appointed manager of Watford.
14 John Dempster sacked as manager of Mansfield T.
15 Graham Westley appointed manager of Stevenage.
17 Graham Coughlan leaves as manager of Bristol R to take over as manager of Mansfield T.
20 Mikel Arteta appointed manager of Arsenal.
21 Carlo Ancelotti appointed manager of Everton.
23 Ben Garner appointed manager of Bristol R.
31 Ian Holloway appointed manager of Grimsby T.

JANUARY 2020

2 Daryl McMahon resigns as manager of Macclesfield T to take over as manager of National League side Dagenham & R.
7 Ross Embleton appointed manager of Leyton Orient.
16 Mark Kennedy appointed manager of Macclesfield T.
29 Colin Calderwood sacked as manager of Cambridge U.
29 Paul Hurst sacked as manager of Scunthorpe U.

FEBRUARY 2020

3 Gary Bowyer sacked as manager of Bradford C.
4 Stuart McCall appointed manager of Bradford C.
12 Simon Grayson sacked as manager of Blackpool.
16 Graham Westley resigns as manager of Stevenage.

APRIL 2020

24 Graeme Jones leaves as manager of Luton T by mutual consent.

MAY 2020

18 Nigel Clough resigns as manager of Burton Alb. Jake Buxton takes charge as Player-Manager.
28 Nathan Jones appointed manager of Luton T.

JUNE 2020

8 Pep Clotet to leave as manager of Birmingham C at the end of the season.
12 Keith Hill to leave as manager of Bolton W when his contract expires at the end of June.
23 Jonathan Woodgate sacked as manager of Middlesbrough.
23 Neil Warnock appointed manager of Middlesbrough.
30 Sol Campbell leaves as manager of Southend U by mutual consent.

JULY 2020

1 Ian Evatt appointed manager of Bolton W.
4 Lee Johnson sacked as manager of Bristol C.
6 Micky Mellon leaves as manager of Tranmere R to become manager of Dundee U.
14 John McGreal sacked as manager of Colchester U.
18 Mike Jackson appointed as manager of Tranmere R.
19 Nigel Pearson sacked as manager of Watford.
19 Danny Cowley sacked as manager of Huddersfield T.
23 Carlos Corberan appointed manager of Huddersfield T.
28 Steve Ball appointed manager of Colchester U.
31 Aitor Karanka appointed manager of Birmingham C.

AUGUST 2020

1 Eddie Howe leaves as manager of Bournemouth by mutual consent.
1 Paul Cook leaves as manager of Wigan Ath.
1 Harry Kewell appointed manager of Oldham Ath.
7 Jason Tindall appointed manager of Bournemouth.
10 Dean Holden appointed manager of Bristol C.
13 Mark Molesley appointed manager of Southend U.
15 Vladimir Ivić appointed manager of Watford.
28 Tim Flowers appointed manager of Macclesfield T.
29 Veljko Paunović appointed manager of Reading replacing Mark Bowen.

TRANSFERS 2019–20

**Transfer to be completed at the end of the season.*

JUNE 2019	*From*	*To*	*Fee in £*
18 Adams, Ebou	Ebbsfleet U	Forest Green R	Undisclosed
5 Adams, Nicky	Bury	Northampton T	Free
25 Adebayo, Elijah	Fulham	Walsall	Free
18 Adshead, Daniel	Rochdale	Norwich C	Undisclosed
11 Aina, Ola	Chelsea	Torino	Undisclosed
25 Aldred, Tom	Bury	Brisbane Roar	Free
28 Allen, Jamie	Burton Alb	Coventry C	Undisclosed
6 Alston, Blair	St Johnstone	Hamilton A	Free
25 Amadi-Holloway, Aaron	Shrewsbury T	Brisbane Roar	Undisclosed
24 Ameobi, Sammy	Bolton W	Nottingham F	Free
17 Andrew, Danny	Doncaster R	Fleetwood T	Free
28 Aneke, Chuks	Milton Keynes D	Charlton Ath	Free
5 Arnold, Steve	Shrewsbury T	Northampton T	Undisclosed
28 Babel, Ryan	Fulham	Galatasaray	Free
18 Barbet, Yoann	Brentford	QPR	Free
18 Baudry, Mathieu	Milton Keynes D	Swindon T	Free
19 Bauer, Patrick	Charlton Ath	Preston NE	Free
21 Bennett, Richie	Carlisle U	Port Vale	Free
28 Bentley, Daniel	Brentford	Bristol C	Undisclosed
26 Blackett-Taylor, Corey	Aston Villa	Tranmere R	Free
7 Bolton, James	Shrewsbury T	Portsmouth	Free
4 Bonham, Jack	Brentford	Gillingham	Free
17 Bonne, Macauley	Leyton Orient	Charlton Ath	Undisclosed
11 Bowery, Jordan	Crewe Alex	Milton Keynes D	Free
13 Brewitt, Tom	AFC Fylde	Morecambe	Free
19 Bryson, Craig	Derby Co	Aberdeen	Free
27 Camacho, Rafael	Liverpool	Sporting Lisbon	£5m
14 Campbell, Tahvon	Forest Green R	Cheltenham T	Free
11 Carey, Graham	Plymouth Arg	CSKA Sofia	Free
24 Cisse, Ousseynou	Milton Keynes D	Gillingham	Free
21 Clarke, Matt	Portsmouth	Brighton & HA	Undisclosed
18 Collins, Aaron	Morecambe	Forest Green R	Free
19 Collins, Brad	Chelsea	Barnsley	Free
29 Connell, Luca	Bolton W	Celtic	Undisclosed
21 Cook, Andy	Walsall	Mansfield T	Undisclosed
25 Cousins, Jordan	QPR	Stoke C	Free
28 Cranie, Martin	Sheffield U	Luton T	Free
26 Cullen, Mark	Blackpool	Port Vale	Free
5 Dabo, Fankaty	Chelsea	Coventry C	Free
26 Dasilva, Jay	Chelsea	Bristol C	Undisclosed
25 Davies, Adam	Barnsley	Stoke C	Free
11 Davies, Tom	Coventry C	Bristol R	Free
27 Day, Joe	Newport Co	Cardiff C	Free
20 Devitt, Jamie	Carlisle U	Blackpool	Undisclosed
8 Devlin, Nicky	Walsall	Livingston	Free
25 Doidge, Christian	Forest Green R	Hibernian	Undisclosed
14 Donaldson, Clayton	Bolton W	Bradford C	Free
21 Downing, Paul	Blackburn R	Portsmouth	Free
21 Downing, Stewart	Middlesbrough	Blackburn R	Free
21 Edmundson, George	Oldham Ath	Rangers	Undisclosed
27 Edwards, Joe	Walsall	Plymouth Arg	Free
14 Edwards, Ryan	Plymouth Arg	Blackpool	Free
3 Eisa, Mo	Bristol C	Peterborough U	Undisclosed
15 Elphick, Tommy	Aston Villa	Huddersfield T	Free
14 Ferguson, Nathan	Dulwich Hamlet	Crawley T	Undisclosed
3 Fernandes, Edimilson	West Ham U	Mainz	Undisclosed
27 Fielding, Frank	Bristol C	Millwall	Free
25 Fisher, Alex	Yeovil T	Exeter C	Free
3 Forde, Anthony	Rotherham U	Oxford U	Free
17 Fryers, Zeki	Barnsley	Swindon T	Free
26 Gambin, Luke	Luton T	Colchester U	Free
5 Gardner, Gary	Aston Villa	Birmingham C	Undisclosed
25 Gillesphey, Macaulay	Carlisle U	Brisbane Roar	Free
10 Goodship, Brandon	Weymouth	Southend	Free
10 Green, Matt	Salford C	Grimsby T	Free
25 Gregory, Lee	Millwall	Stoke C	Free
17 Hall-Johnson, Reece	Grimsby T	Northampton T	Free
18 Hanson, James	AFC Wimbledon	Grimsby T	Free
24 Hardy, James	AFC Fylde	Walsall	Free
12 Hare, Josh	Eastleigh	Bristol R	Free
21 Harrison, Ellis	Ipswich T	Portsmouth	Undisclosed
7 Hazard, Eden	Chelsea	Real Madrid	£89m

4	Hedges, Ryan	Barnsley	Aberdeen	Free
26	Hewitt, Elliott	Notts Co	Grimsby T	Free
8	Hodson, Lee	Rangers	Gillingham	Free
11	Howkins, Kyle	WBA	Newport Co	Free
24	Hunt, Rob	Oldham Ath	Swindon T	Free
25	Ingram, Matt	QPR	Hull C	Undisclosed
5	Ironside, Joe	Kidderminster H	Macclesfield T	Free
11	Ismail, Zeli	Walsall	Bradford C	Free
12	James, Daniel	Swansea C	Manchester U	£15m
19	James, Reece	Sunderland	Doncaster R	Undisclosed
26	James, Tom	Yeovil T	Hibernian	Undisclosed
5	Jota	Birmingham C	Aston Villa	Undisclosed
28	Justin, James	Luton T	Leicester C	Undisclosed
14	Kelly, Liam	Livingston	QPR	Undisclosed
3	Kennedy, Kieran	Wrexham	Port Vale	Free
22	Kent, Frankie	Colchester U	Peterborough U	Undisclosed
7	King, Tom	Millwall	Newport Co	Free
5	Knoyle, Kyle	Swindon T	Cambridge U	Free
3	Kone, Lamine	Sunderland	Strasbourg	Undisclosed
21	Koroma, Josh	Leyton Orient	Huddersfield T	Undisclosed
25	Ladapo, Freddie	Plymouth Arg	Rotherham U	£500,000
24	Lameiras, Ruben	Plymouth Arg	FC Famalicao	Free
20	Leadbitter, Daniel	Bristol R	Newport Co	Free
25	Lindsay, Liam	Barnsley	Stoke C	£2m
4	Little, Mark	Bolton W	Bristol R	Free
26	Lloyd, Ryan	Macclesfield T	Port Vale	Free
28	Lockyer, Tom	Bristol R	Charlton Ath	Free
10	Long, Christopher	Blackpool	Motherwell	Free
13	Longridge, Jackson	Dunfermline Ath	Bradford C	Undisclosed
21	Lubala, Beryly	Birmingham C	Crawley T	Free
3	MacDonald, Shaun	Wigan Ath	Rotherham U	Free
3	Marquis, John	Doncaster R	Portsmouth	Undisclosed
3	Martin, David	Millwall	West Ham U	Free
4	Mason, Joe	Wolverhampton W	Milton Keynes D	Free
28	Maxted, Jonny	Accrington S	Exeter C	Free
5	McCormack, Alan	Luton T	Northampton T	Free
5	McCourt, Jak	Swindon T	Macclesfield T	Free
11	McKirdy, Harry	Aston Villa	Carlisle U	Free
4	McManaman, Callum	Wigan Ath	Luton T	Free
21	Mills, Zak	Morecambe	Oldham Ath	Free
19	Morris, Josh	Scunthorpe U	Fleetwood T	Free
26	Morris, Kieron	Walsall	Tranmere R	Free
27	Nelson, Curtis	Oxford U	Cardiff C	Free
26	Nelson, Sid	Millwall	Tranmere R	Free
9	Newell, Joe	Rotherham U	Hibernian	Free
10	Norwood, James	Tranmere R	Ipswich T	Undisclosed
18	O'Connor, Paudie	Leeds U	Bradford C	Undisclosed
11	O'Keefe, Stuart	Cardiff C	Gillingham	Free
28	O'Shea, Jay	Bury	Brisbane Roar	Free
29	Osadebe, Emmanuel	Cambridge U	Macclesfield T	Free
17	Pask, Josh	West Ham U	Coventry C	Free
28	Payne, Stefan	Bristol R	Tranmere R	Free
3	Perez, Lucas	West Ham U	Alaves	Undisclosed
24	Pierre, Aaron	Northampton T	Shrewsbury T	Undisclosed
14	Poole, Regan	Manchester U	Milton Keynes D	Free
28	Potter, Darren	Rotherham U	Tranmere R	Free
7	Powell, Daniel	Northampton T	Crewe Alex	Free
25	Powell, Nick	Wigan Ath	Stoke C	Free
24	Ray, George	Crewe Alex	Tranmere R	Free
24	Reid, Reuben	Forest Green R	Cheltenham T	Free
3	Reid, Tyler	Swansea C	Swindon T	Free
20	Roscrow, Adam	Cardiff Metropolitan University	AFC Wimbledon	Undisclosed
25	Smith, Adam	Bristol R	Forest Green R	Free
13	Stewart, Greg	Birmingham C	Rangers	Free
14	Stojsavljevic, Lazar	Millwall	Newport Co	Free
28	Szmodics, Sammie	Colchester U	Bristol C	Undisclosed
4	Taylor, Ash	Northampton T	Aberdeen	Free
13	Thomas, Luke	Derby Co	Barnsley	Undisclosed
21	Tollitt, Ben	Tranmere R	Blackpool	Free
28	Valencia, Antonio	Manchester U	LDU Quito	Free
25	Vaughan, James	Wigan Ath	Bradford C	Free
27	Vaulks, Will	Rotherham U	Cardiff C	£2.1m
24	Vellios, Apostolos	Nottingham F	Atromitos	Undisclosed
28	Walker, Jamie	Wigan Ath	Hearts	Free
14	Wallace, Lee	Rangers	QPR	Free
28	Wan-Bissaka, Aaron	Crystal Palace	Manchester U	£50m
21	Ward, Lewis	Reading	Exeter C	Undisclosed
26	Ward, Stephen	Burnley	Stoke C	Free

28 Warren, Gary	Yeovil T	Exeter C	Free
27 Washington, Connor	Sheffield U	Hearts	Free
3 Watson, Ryan	Milton Keynes D	Northampton T	Free
24 Webster, Byron	Scunthorpe U	Carlisle U	Free
25 Whitely, Corey	Ebbsfleet U	Newport Co	Undisclosed
17 Wilkinson, Conor	Dagenham & R	Leyton Orient	Undisclosed
3 Williams, Joe	Everton	Wigan Ath	Undisclosed
26 Williams, Ryan	Rotherham U	Portsmouth	Free
13 Willock, Matty	Manchester U	Gillingham	Free
26 Woods, Calum	Bradford C	Tranmere R	Free
25 Woods, Gary	Hamilton A	Oldham Ath	Free
14 Wright, Josh	Bradford C	Leyton Orient	Free
JULY 2019			
25 Abrahams, Tristan	Norwich C	Newport Co	Free
22 Adam, Charlie	Stoke C	Reading	Free
1 Adams, Che	Birmingham C	Southampton	Undisclosed
30 Adams, Kielen	Bradford C	Oldham Ath	Free
10 Adomah, Albert	Aston Villa	Nottingham F	Free
2 Aimson, Will	Bury	Plymouth Arg	Free
20 Ajayi, Semi	Rotherham U	WBA	Undisclosed
3 Ajose, Nicky	Charlton Ath	Exeter C	Free
25 Alessandra, Lewis	Notts Co	Morecambe	Free
8 Amoo, David	Cambridge U	Port Vale	Free
15 Amos, Ben	Bolton W	Charlton Ath	Free
4 Andreu, Tony	Coventry C	St Mirren	Free
1 Angol, Lee	Shrewsbury T	Leyton Orient	Undisclosed
12 Ansarifard, Karim	Nottingham F	Al-Sailiya	Undisclosed
1 Archer, Jordan	Bury	Port Vale	Free
30 Archibald, Theo	Brentford	Macclesfield T	Free
26 Armstrong, Luke	Middlesbrough	Salford C	Undisclosed
25 Ayew, Jordan	Swansea C	Crystal Palace	£2.5m
2 Ball, Dominic	Rotherham U	QPR	Free
16 Barclay, Ben	Brighton & HA	Accrington S	Free
22 Barnes, Dillon	Colchester U	QPR	Undisclosed
25 Baxter, Jose	Oldham Ath	Plymouth Arg	Free
17 Bernard, Dom	Birmingham C	Forest Green R	Free
2 Bidwell, Jake	QPR	Swansea C	Free
29 Billing, Philip	Huddersfield T	Bournemouth	£15m
13 Bishop, Colby	Leamington	Accrington S	Undisclosed
18 Blackman, Nick	Derby Co	Maccabi Tel Aviv	Free
1 Blyth, Jacob	Barrow	Macclesfield T	Free
12 Bodvarsson, Jon Dadi	Reading	Millwall	Undisclosed
28 Bola, Marc	Blackpool	Middlesbrough	Undisclosed
4 Bowry, Dan	Charlton Ath	Cheltenham T	Free
15 Boyd, George	Sheffield W	Peterborough U	Free
24 Bradley, Alex	WBA	Lincoln C	Free
24 Braithwaite, Martin	Middlesbrough	Leganes	Undisclosed
4 Brown, Jevani	Cambridge U	Colchester U	Undisclosed
26 Browne, Marcus	West Ham U	Middlesbrough	Undisclosed
27 Browne, Rhys	Yeovil T	Port Vale	Free
6 Bulka, Marcin	Chelsea	Paris Saint-Germain	Free
3 Burge, Lee	Coventry C	Sunderland	Free
30 Butterfield, Jacob	Derby Co	Luton T	Free
16 Byram, Sam	West Ham U	Norwich C	£750,000
25 Cameron, Geoff	Stoke C	QPR	Free
2 Carter, Charlie	Chesterfield	Stevenage	Undisclosed
19 Chaplin, Conor	Coventry C	Barnsley	Undisclosed
2 Clarke, Jack	Leeds U	Tottenham H	Undisclosed (loaned back)
29 Clarke, Trevor	Shamrock R	Rotherham U	Undisclosed
3 Coutts, Paul	Sheffield U	Fleetwood T	Free
4 Cowan-Hall, Paris	Wycombe W	Colchester U	Free
29 Dallas, Andrew	Rangers	Cambridge U	Undisclosed
1 Dawson, Craig	WBA	Watford	Undisclosed
1 Dawson, Kevin	Cheltenham T	Forest Green R	Free
24 Dele-Bashiru, Tom	Manchester C	Watford	Compensation
15 Delph, Fabian	Manchester C	Everton	Undisclosed
11 Denton, Tyler	Leeds U	Stevenage	Undisclosed
2 Digby, Paul	Forest Green R	Stevenage	Undisclosed
25 Dobson, George	Walsall	Sunderland	Undisclosed
9 Donohue, Dion	Portsmouth	Mansfield T	Free
10 Eaves, Tom	Gillingham	Hull C	Free
23 Edwards, Ryan	Hearts	Burton Alb	Free
20 Evans, Callum	Macclesfield T	Port Vale	Free
2 Facey, Shay	Northampton T	Walsall	Free
25 Fer, Leroy	Swansea C	Feyenoord	Free
1 Fernandes, Michael	Farnborough T	Colchester U	Undisclosed
5 Fitzpatrick, Aidan	Partick Thistle	Norwich C	£350,000

19 Flint, Aden	Middlesbrough	Cardiff C	£4m
1 Fosu, Tariqe	Charlton Ath	Oxford U	Undisclosed
13 Francis-Angol, Zaine	AFC Fylde	Accrington S	Free
3 Freeman, Luke	QPR	Sheffield U	Undisclosed
23 Furlong, Darnell	QPR	WBA	Undisclosed
13 Gallagher, Sam	Southampton	Blackburn R	Undisclosed
3 Galloway, Brendan	Everton	Luton T	Free
13 Gerken, Dean	Ipswich T	Colchester U	Free
9 Gilliead, Alex	Shrewsbury T	Scunthorpe U	Undisclosed
1 Gilmartin, Rene	Colchester U	Bristol C	Free
3 Goode, Charlie	Scunthorpe U	Northampton T	Undisclosed
25 Gordon, Kellan	Derby Co	Mansfield T	Undisclosed
5 Grant, Jorge	Nottingham F	Lincoln C	Undisclosed
22 Grimmer, Jack	Coventry C	Wycombe W	Free
30 Gueye, Idrissa	Everton	Paris Saint-Germain	£30m
3 Halme, Aapo	Leeds U	Barnsley	Undisclosed
17 Hardie, Ryan	Rangers	Blackpool	Undisclosed
18 Harness, Marcus	Burton Alb	Portsmouth	Undisclosed
13 Harris, Kadeem	Cardiff C	Sheffield W	Free
29 Hayden, Aaron	Wolverhampton W	Carlisle U	Free
12 Haynes, Ryan	Shrewsbury T	Newport Co	Undisclosed
16 Healey, Rhys	Cardiff C	Milton Keynes D	Undisclosed
6 Henderson, Stephen	Nottingham F	Crystal Palace	Free
4 Herrera, Ander	Manchester U	Paris Saint-Germain	Free
22 Horsfall, Fraser	Kidderminster H	Macclesfield T	Free
1 Hunt, Johnny	Stevenage	Hamilton A	Free
1 Ings, Danny	Liverpool	Southampton	£20m
30 Isgrove, Lloyd	Barnsley	Swindon T	Free
1 Jaakkola, Anssi	Reading	Bristol R	Free
4 Jagielka, Phil	Everton	Sheffield U	Free
23 Janssen, Vincent	Tottenham H	Monterrey	Undisclosed
8 Jansson, Pontus	Leeds U	Brentford	Undisclosed
5 Johnson, Bradley	Derby Co	Blackburn R	Free
19 Jones, Dan	Notts Co	Cambridge U	Free
26 Jules, Zak	Macclesfield T	Walsall	Undisclosed
1 Kalas, Tomas	Chelsea	Bristol C	Undisclosed
27 Kane, Todd	Chelsea	QPR	Free
8 Kelly, Liam	Reading	Feyenoord	Undisclosed
1 Kiersey, Jack	Everton	Walsall	Free
8 Kitching, Liam	Leeds U	Forest Green R	Undisclosed
4 Knight-Percival, Nathaniel	Bradford C	Carlisle U	Free
11 Konsa, Ezri	Brentford	Aston Villa	£12m
9 Leahy, Luke	Walsall	Bristol R	Free
16 Letheren, Kyle	Plymouth Arg	Salford C	Free
26 Liddle, Gary	Carlisle U	Walsall	Free
24 Lindsay, Jamie	Ross Co	Rotherham U	Undisclosed
1 List, Elliott	Gillingham	Stevenage	Undisclosed
25 Lookman, Ademola	Everton	RB Leipzig	£22.5m
12 Love, Donald	Sunderland	Shrewsbury T	Free
25 Luiz, Douglas	Manchester C	Aston Villa	£15m
26 Lyden, Jordan	Aston Villa	Swindon T	Free
25 Lynch, Joe	Crewe Alex	Morecambe	Free
12 Macleod, Lewis	Brentford	Wigan Ath	Free
15 Maguire, Joe	Fleetwood T	Accrington S	Free
9 Mahoney, Connor	Bournemouth	Millwall	Undisclosed
25 Mandron, Mikael	Colchester U	Gillingham	Free
19 Manga, Bruno	Cardiff C	Dijon	£3m
8 Marshall, David	Hull C	Wigan Ath	Free
25 Marshall, Mark	Charlton Ath	Gillingham	Free
23 Mascoll, Jamie	Charlton Ath	Wycombe W	Free
3 Masterson, Conor	Liverpool	QPR	Free
2 Maynard, Nicky	Bury	Mansfield T	Free
1 Mayor, Danny	Bury	Plymouth Arg	Free
1 McCarron, Liam	Carlisle U	Leeds U	Undisclosed
30 McCarthy, Jason	Wycombe W	Millwall	Undisclosed
11 McDonald, Wes	Birmingham C	Walsall	Free
15 McFadzean, Callum	Bury	Plymouth Arg	Free
1 McLaughlin, Conor	Millwall	Sunderland	Free
26 McLoughlin, Sean	Cork C	Hull C	Undisclosed
1 Mikel, John Obi	Middlesbrough	Trabzonspor	Free
1 Milligan, Mark	Hibernian	Southend U	Free
8 Mings, Tyrone	Bournemouth	Aston Villa	£20m
1 Monreal, Nacho	Arsenal	Real Sociedad	Undisclosed
23 Moore, Byron	Bury	Plymouth Arg	Free
9 Moreno, Alberto	Liverpool	Villarreal	Free
19 Morrison, Michael	Birmingham C	Reading	Free
21 Mousset, Lys	Bournemouth	Sheffield U	£10m
4 Murphy, Joe	Bury	Shrewsbury T	Free

5 Narsingh, Luciano	Swansea C	Feyenoord	Free
5 Nasri, Samir	West Ham U	Anderlecht	Free
4 Ntlhe, Kgosi	Rochdale	Scunthorpe U	Free
17 Nugent, David	Derby Co	Preston NE	Free
4 O'Neill, Luke	Gillingham	AFC Wimbledon	Free
2 O'Sullivan, John	Blackpool	Morecambe	Free
24 Obiang, Pedro	West Ham U	Sassuolo	Undisclosed
11 Odubajo, Moses	Brentford	Sheffield W	Free
14 Ojo, Funso	Scunthorpe U	Aberdeen	£125,000
30 Okazaki, Shinji	Leicester C	Malaga	Free
3 Oliver, Vadaine	Morecambe	Northampton T	Free
5 Olosunde, Matthew	Manchester U	Rotherham U	Free
30 Onyedinma, Fred	Millwall	Wycombe W	Undisclosed
26 Osborn, Ben	Nottingham F	Sheffield U	Undisclosed
22 Oshilaja, Deji	AFC Wimbledon	Charlton Ath	Free
29 Oviedo, Bryan	Sunderland	FC Copenhagen	Free
15 Parrett, Dean	Gillingham	Stevenage	Free
9 Pattison, Alex	Middlesbrough	Wycombe W	Free
3 Payne, Jack	Huddersfield T	Lincoln C	Free
4 Perez, Ayoze	Newcastle U	Leicester C	£30m
8 Pieters, Erik	Stoke C	Burnley	Undisclosed
2 Pinnock, Ethan	Barnsley	Brentford	Undisclosed
5 Powell, Jack	Maidstone U	Crawley T	Free
27 Pugh, Marc	Bournemouth	QPR	Free
2 Purrington, Ben	Rotherham U	Charlton Ath	Undisclosed
9 Ralph, Nathan	Dundee	Southend U	Undisclosed
6 Raya, David	Blackburn R	Brentford	Undisclosed
26 Reilly, Callum	Gillingham	AFC Wimbledon	Free
15 Robinson, Antonee	Everton	Wigan Ath	Undisclosed
12 Robinson, Callum	Preston NE	Sheffield U	Undisclosed
9 Rodriguez, Jay	WBA	Burnley	Undisclosed
19 Rondon, Salomon	WBA	Dalian Yifang	Undisclosed
1 Rowe, Tommy	Doncaster R	Bristol C	Free
23 Ruddy, Jack	Wolverhampton W	Ross Co	Free
29 Ryan, Jimmy	Blackpool	Rochdale	Free
11 Sadler, Mat	Shrewsbury T	Walsall	Free
18 Saiz, Samu	Leeds U	Girona	Undisclosed
28 Sako, Bakary	Crystal Palace	Denizlispor	Free
27 Sawyers, Romaine	Brentford	WBA	Undisclosed
8 Seedorf, Sherwin	Wolverhampton W	Motherwell	Free
15 Sherif, Lamine Kaba	Leicester C	Accrington S	Free
2 Sibbick, Toby	AFC Wimbledon	Barnsley	Undisclosed
9 Smerdon, Noah	Gloucester C	Exeter C	Undisclosed
23 Smith, Martin	Swindon T	Salford C	Free
1 Smith, Matt	QPR	Millwall	Undisclosed
15 Smith, Tommy	Huddersfield T	Stoke C	Undisclosed
14 Songo'o, Yann	Plymouth Arg	Scunthorpe U	Free
1 Sowunmi, Omar	Yeovil T	Colchester U	Free
8 Stacey, Jack	Luton T	Bournemouth	£4m
27 Stevens, Matty	Peterborough U	Forest Green R	Undisclosed
2 Stokes, Chris	Bury	Stevenage	Free
30 Suttner, Markus	Brighton & HA	Fortuna Dusseldorf	Undisclosed
18 Tafazolli, Ryan	Peterborough U	Hull C	Free
1 Targett, Matt	Southampton	Aston Villa	Undisclosed
11 Telford, Dom	Bury	Plymouth Arg	Undisclosed
17 Trippier, Kieran	Tottenham H	Atletico Madrid	£20m
11 Tunnicliffe, Jordan	AFC Fylde	Crawley T	Free
1 Tunnicliffe, Ryan	Millwall	Luton T	Free
1 van la Parra, Rajiv	Huddersfield T	Red Star Belgrade	Undisclosed
18 Vassell, Theo	Port Vale	Macclesfield T	Free
17 Vela, Josh	Bolton W	Hibernian	Free
1 Walker, Laurie	Hemel Hempstead T	Milton Keynes D	Free
2 Weaire, Matthew	Brighton & HA	Colchester	Free
30 Wheeler, David	QPR	Wycombe W	Free
9 White, Tom	Gateshead	Blackburn R	Undisclosed
30 Whyte, Gavin	Oxford U	Cardiff C	Undisclosed
5 Wilks, Mallik	Leeds U	Barnsley	Undisclosed
13 Willis, Jordan	Coventry C	Sunderland	Free
4 Wilson, James	Manchester U	Aberdeen	Free
19 Wilson, Scott	Macclesfield T	Oldham Ath	Free
19 Zohore, Kenneth	Cardiff C	WBA	Undisclosed
AUGUST 2019			
5 Adrian	West Ham U	Liverpool	Free
10 Agyei, Dan	Burnley	Oxford U	Undisclosed
8 Austin, Charlie	Southampton	WBA	£4m
2 Baptiste, Alex	QPR	Doncaster R	Free
9 Barker, Brandon	Manchester C	Rangers	Undisclosed

2	Bayliss, Tom	Coventry C	Preston NE	Undisclosed
2	Bielik, Krystian	Arsenal	Derby Co	Undisclosed
30	Brisley, Shaun	Notts Co	Port Vale	Free
5	Cahill, Gary	Chelsea	Crystal Palace	Free
8	Carroll, Andy	West Ham U	Newcastle U	Free
29	Carruthers, Samir	Sheffield U	Cambridge U	Free
22	Cattermole, Lee	Sunderland	VVV Venlo	Free
9	Charles-Cook, Reice	Shrewsbury T	Macclesfield T	Free
12	Charles, Dion	Southport	Accrington S	Undisclosed
1	Clarke, Peter	Oldham Ath	Fleetwood T	Free
9	Damour, Loic	Cardiff C	Hearts	Free
7	Danilo	Manchester C	Juventus	£34.1m
1	Dennis, Louis	Portsmouth	Leyton Orient	Undisclosed
7	Dijksteel, Anfernee	Charlton Ath	Middlesbrough	Undisclosed
1	Dolan, Callum	Altrincham	Oldham Ath	Free
2	Doyle, Lewis	Southport	Accrington S	Free
15	Eisa, Abo	Shrewsbury T	Scunthorpe U	Undisclosed
8	Elder, Callum	Leicester C	Hull C	Undisclosed
6	Evans, Ched	Sheffield U	Fleetwood T	Undisclosed
1	Ferrier, Morgan	Walsall	Tranmere R	Undisclosed
1	Foley, Sam	Northampton T	St Mirren	Free
21	Fonte, Rui	Fulham	Braga	Undisclosed
1	Gilks, Matt	Lincoln C	Fleetwood T	Free
6	Godden, Matt	Peterborough U	Coventry C	Undisclosed
16	Goss, Sean	QPR	Shrewsbury T	Undisclosed
12	Guthrie, Jon	Walsall	Livingston	Free
1	Gyollai, Daniel	Stoke C	Wigan Ath	Free
1	Harris, Jay	Tranmere R	Macclesfield T	Free
1	Heaton, Tom	Burnley	Aston Villa	£8m
19	Hemed, Tomer	Brighton & HA	Charlton Ath	Free
2	Honeyman, George	Sunderland	Hull C	Undisclosed
3	Hurst, Alex	Bradford (Park Avenue)	Port Vale	Undisclosed
1	Husin, Noor	Notts Co	Stevenage	Free
5	Ideguchi, Yosuke	Leeds U	Gamba Osaka	Undisclosed
8	Iwobi, Alex	Arsenal	Everton	£34m
7	Jenkinson, Carl	Arsenal	Nottingham F	Undisclosed
6	Joao, Lucas	Sheffield W	Reading	Undisclosed
7	Johnston, George	Liverpool	Feyenoord	Undisclosed
8	Jones, Alfie	Milton Keynes D	Crawley T	Free
6	Jones, Paul	Fleetwood T	Sheffield W	
10	Jorgensen, Mathias	Huddersfield T	Fenerbahce	Undisclosed
6	Koscielny, Laurent	Arsenal	Bordeaux	£4.6m
6	Lavery, Caolan	Sheffield U	Walsall	Undisclosed
10	Lewis, Aaron	Swansea C	Lincoln C	Free
8	Lopes, Leonardo Da Silva	Wigan Ath	Hull C	Undisclosed
1	Lowe, Jamal	Portsmouth	Wigan Ath	Undisclosed
8	Luiz, David	Chelsea	Arsenal	£8m
8	Lukaku, Romelu	Manchester U	Internazionale	£74m
1	Lukebakio, Dodi	Watford	Hertha Berlin	Undisclosed
8	Luongo, Massimo	QPR	Sheffield W	Undisclosed
19	Lynch, Jay	AFC Fylde	Rochdale	Free
26	Lynch, Joel	QPR	Sunderland	Free
27	Macdonald, Calum	Derby Co	Blackpool	Free
8	Magennis, Josh	Bolton W	Hull C	Undisclosed
5	Maguire, Harry	Leicester C	Manchester U	£80m
5	Maupay, Neal	Brentford	Brighton & HA	Undisclosed
9	McAllister, Kyle	Derby Co	St Mirren	Undisclosed
2	McBurnie, Oli	Swansea C	Sheffield U	£17.5m
7	McCarthy, James	Everton	Crystal Palace	£3m
4	Mignolet, Simon	Liverpool	Club Brugge	£6.4m
30	Mirallas, Kevin	Everton	Antwerp	Free
1	Moore, Elliott	Leicester C	Oxford U	Undisclosed
5	Moore, Kieffer	Barnsley	Wigan Ath	Undisclosed
22	Morias, Junior	Northampton T	St Mirren	Undisclosed
8	Morison, Steve	Millwall	Shrewsbury T	Free
1	Naismith, Steven	Norwich C	Hearts	Free
1	Nuttall, Joe	Blackburn R	Blackpool	Undisclosed
2	Obika, Jonathan	Oxford U	St Mirren	Free
8	Odour, Clarke	Leeds U	Barnsley	Undisclosed
29	Ogbene, Chiedozie	Brentford	Rotherham U	Undisclosed
8	Onomah, Josh	Tottenham H	Fulham	Swap
2	Oxford, Reece	West Ham U	Augsburg	Undisclosed
16	Oztumer, Erhun	Bolton W	Charlton Ath	Free
8	Pack, Marlon	Bristol C	Cardiff C	Undisclosed
1	Palmer, Kasey	Chelsea	Bristol C	Undisclosed
1	Parker, Josh	Charlton Ath	Wycombe W	Free
2	Peacock-Farrell, Bailey	Leeds U	Burnley	£2.5m

8 Pearce, Tom	Leeds U	Wigan Ath	Undisclosed
30 Pritchard, Harry	Blackpool	Bradford C	Free
6 Puncheon, Jason	Crystal Palace	Pafos	Free
1 Reeves, Ben	Charlton Ath	Milton Keynes D	Free
5 Richards, Marc	Swindon T	Cambridge U	Free
2 Ridgewell, Liam	Hull C	Southend U	Free
5 Rollinson, Joel	Reading	Stevenage	Free
6 Roofe, Kemar	Leeds U	Anderlecht	Undisclosed
6 Rooney, Wayne	DC United	Derby Co	Undisclosed
1 Sarkic, Oliver	Leeds U	Burton Alb	Free
30 Scannell, Sean	Bradford C	Blackpool	Free
8 Sessegnon, Ryan	Fulham	Tottenham H	£25m
1 Shaughnessy, Joe	St Johnstone	Southend U	Free
2 Soares, Tom	AFC Wimbledon	Stevenage	Free
6 Souare, Pape	Crystal Palace	Troyes	Free
21 Sturridge, Daniel	Liverpool	Trabzonspor	Free
9 Taylor, Jon	Peterborough U	Doncaster R	Free
27 Thompson, Adam	Bury	Rotherham U	Free
8 Thompson, Dominic	Arsenal	Brentford	Undisclosed
16 Thompson, Nathan	Portsmouth	Peterborough U	Free
8 Tierney, Kieran	Celtic	Arsenal	£25m
8 Vassell, Isaac	Birmingham C	Cardiff C	Undisclosed
19 Vincent-Young, Kane	Colchester U	Ipswich T	Undisclosed
15 Waterfall, Luke	Shrewsbury T	Grimsby T	Free
3 Webster, Adam	Bristol C	Brighton & HA	£20m
3 Weir, James	Hull C	Bolton W	Free
7 Welbeck, Danny	Arsenal	Watford	Free
1 Wheater, David	Bolton W	Oldham Ath	Free
14 Whelan, Glenn	Aston Villa	Hearts	Free
2 Wilson, James	Lincoln C	Ipswich T	Free
5 Yearwood, Dru	Southend U	Brentford	Undisclosed
16 Young, Jordan	Swindon T	Coventry C	Free

SEPTEMBER 2019

2 Appiah, Arvin	Nottingham F	Almeria	£8m
1 Ariyibi, Gboly	Nottingham F	Panaitolikos	Undisclosed
2 Ayite, Floyd	Fulham	Genclerbirligi	Undisclosed
2 Bunney, Joe	Northampton T	Bolton W	Free
2 Crawford, Ali	Doncaster R	Bolton W	Free
2 Cummings, Jason	Nottingham F	Shrewsbury T	Undisclosed
2 Darmian, Matteo	Manchester U	Parma	Undisclosed
2 Defour, Steven	Burnley	Royal Antwerp	Free
2 Duncan, Bobby	Liverpool	Fiorentina	£1.8m
2 Edwards, Marcus	Tottenham H	Vitoria Guimaraes	Undisclosed
6 El-Abd, Adam	Wycombe W	Stevenage	Free
2 Emmanuel, Josh	Ipswich T	Bolton W	
2 Frimpong, Jeremie	Manchester C	Celtic	Undisclosed
2 Gonzalez, Lorenzo	Manchester C	Malaga	Undisclosed
2 Hernandez, Javier	West Ham U	Sevilla	Undisclosed
2 Kent, Ryan	Liverpool	Rangers	£7m
2 Llorente, Fernando	Tottenham H	Napoli	Free
2 Murphy, Daryl	Nottingham F	Bolton W	Free
2 Nwakali, Kelechi	Arsenal	Huesca	Undisclosed
2 O'Connor, Lee	Manchester U	Celtic	Undisclosed
2 O'Grady, Chris	Oldham Ath	Bolton W	Free
2 Okaka, Stefano	Watford	Udinese	Undisclosed
2 Poleon, Dominic	Crawley T	Newport Co	Free
21 Shotton, Saul	Bury	WBA	Free

DECEMBER 2019

31 Adebowale, Manny	Eastbourne Bor	Crawley T	Undisclosed
31 Baptiste, Shandon	Oxford U	Brentford	Undisclosed
31 Baston, Borja	Swansea C	Aston Villa	Free
31 Bishop, Nathan	Southend U	Manchester U	Undisclosed
31 Bowen, Jarrod	Hull C	West Ham U	£20m
31 Burgoyne, Harry	Wolverhampton W	Shrewsbury T	Undisclosed
31 Carroll, Canice	Brentford	Stevenage	Undisclosed
31 Daly, James	Crystal Palace	Bristol R	Undisclosed
31 Delaney, Ryan	Rochdale	Bolton W	Undisclosed
31 Deslandes, Sylvain	Wolverhampton W	Arges Pitesti	Undisclosed
31 Eastham, Ashley	Fleetwood T	Salford C	Undisclosed
31 Fosu, Tariqe	Oxford U	Brentford	Undisclosed
31 Garmston, Bradley	Gillingham	Grimsby T	Free
31 Garrity, Ben	Warrington T	Blackpool	Undisclosed
31 Green, Devarn	Southport	Scunthorpe U	Undisclosed
31 Grosicki, Kamil	Hull C	WBA	Undisclosed
31 Guthrie, Kurtis	Stevenage	Bradford C	Undisclosed
31 Hamblin, Harry	Southampton	Macclesfield T	Free
31 Harries, Cian	Swansea C	Bristol R	Free

31 Howe, Teddy	Reading	Blackpool	Undisclosed
31 Lamptey, Tariq	Chelsea	Brighton & HA	Undisclosed
31 Lund, Matty	Scunthorpe U	Rochdale	Undisclosed
31 Matheson, Luke	Rochdale	Wolverhampton W	£1m (loaned back)
31 McCallum, Sam	Coventry C	Norwich C	Undisclosed
31 Mellis, Jacob	Mansfield T	Bolton W	Free
31 Mola, Clinton	Chelsea	Stuttgart	Undisclosed
31 Novak, Lee	Scunthorpe U	Bradford C	Undisclosed
31 Oakley-Boothe, Tashan	Tottenham H	Stoke C	Undisclosed
31 Palmer, Matty	Rotherham U	Swindon T	Free
31 Patrick, Omari	Bradford C	Carlisle U	Undisclosed
31 Peltier, Lee	Cardiff C	WBA	Free
31 Reading, Patrick	Middlesbrough	Stevenage	Undisclosed
31 Scott, James	Motherwell	Hull C	Undisclosed
31 Stokes, Chris	Stevenage	Forest Green R	Undisclosed
31 Templeton, David	Burton Alb	Hamilton A	Free
31 Tilt, Curtis	Blackpool	Rotherham U	Undisclosed
31 Wilson, James	Aberdeen	Salford C	Undisclosed
JANUARY 2020			
24 Akinde, John	Lincoln C	Gillingham	Undisclosed
24 Alessandra, Lewis	Morecambe	Carlisle U	Free
16 Anderton, Nick	Blackpool	Carlisle U	Undisclosed
13 Andrade, Bruno	Lincoln C	Salford C	Undisclosed
16 Archer, Jordan	Oxford U	Fulham	Free
9 Atkinson, Rob	Eastleigh	Oxford U	Undisclosed
13 Baker, Ashley	Sheffield W	Newport Co	Undisclosed
22 Banks, Scott	Dundee U	Crystal Palace	Undisclosed
7 Barrett, Josh	Reading	Bristol R	Undisclosed
27 Bialkowski, Bartosz	Ipswich T	Millwall	Undisclosed
30 Bong, Gaetan	Brighton & HA	Nottingham F	Undisclosed
25 Boyce, Liam	Burton Alb	Hearts	Undisclosed
13 Branthwaite, Jarrad	Carlisle U	Everton	Undisclosed
30 Brownhill, Josh	Bristol C	Burnley	£9m
14 Cassidy, Jake	Maidenhead U	Stevenage	Undisclosed
7 Cavaleiro, Ivan	Wolverhampton W	Fulham	Undisclosed
9 Clarke, Billy	Plymouth Arg	Grimsby T	Free
1 Clarke, Peter	Fleetwood T	Tranmere R	Free
27 Cole, Devante	Wigan Ath	Doncaster R	Undisclosed
16 Cox, Simon	Southend U	Western Sydney W	Free
10 Coyle, Lewie	Leeds U	Fleetwood T	Undisclosed
24 Decordova-Reid, Bobby	Cardiff C	Fulham	Undisclosed
2 Diagouraga, Toumani	Swindon T	Morecambe	Free
17 Dickenson, Brennan	Milton Keynes D	Exeter C	Free
30 Doyle, Eoin	Bradford C	Swindon T	Undisclosed
10 Edun, Tayo	Fulham	Lincoln C	Undisclosed
9 Elliott, Tom	Millwall	Salford C	Free
28 Eriksen, Christian	Tottenham H	Internazionale	£16.9m
29 Evans, Antony	Everton	Paderborn	Undisclosed
6 Faal, Muhammadu	Enfield	Bolton W	Undisclosed
10 Gladwin, Ben	Blackburn R	Milton Keynes D	Free
6 Grant, Anthony	Shrewsbury T	Swindon T	Undisclosed
30 Guy, Callum	Blackpool	Carlisle U	Undisclosed
6 Hackett-Fairchild, Reeco	Bromley	Portsmouth	Undisclosed
30 Hinds, Akeem	Rotherham U	Lincoln C	Free
22 Hope, Hallam	Carlisle U	Swindon T	Undisclosed
23 Hopper, Tom	Southend U	Lincoln C	Undisclosed
10 Hunt, Max	Derby Co	Carlisle U	Undisclosed
25 Husband, James	Norwich C	Blackpool	Undisclosed
17 Jarvis, Dan	Stoke C	Wrexham	Free
27 Johnson, Danny	Dundee	Leyton Orient	Undisclosed
22 Kioso, Peter	Hartlepool U	Luton T	Undisclosed
20 Kodjia, Jonathan	Aston Villa	Al-Gharafa	Undisclosed
16 Madine, Gary	Cardiff C	Blackpool	Free
30 Maloney, Leon	Portsmouth	FC Volendam	Undisclosed
6 March, Josh	Leamington	Forest Green R	Undisclosed
25 Marshall, Mark	Gillingham	Northampton T	Free
24 Maxwell, Chris	Preston NE	Blackpool	Free
3 May, Alfie	Doncaster R	Cheltenham T	Undisclosed
24 Mbulu, Christian	Crewe Alex	Morecambe	Free
7 McGeouch, Dylan	Sunderland	Aberdeen	Undisclosed
10 Melbourne, Max	WBA	Lincoln C	Undisclosed
24 Mooy, Aaron	Huddersfield T	Brighton & HA	Undisclosed
30 Mottley-Henry, Dylan	Barnsley	Bradford C	Free
16 Nolan, Jack	Reading	Walsall	Undisclosed
14 Nordfeldt, Kristoffer	Swansea C	Genclerbirligi	Free
15 O'Connor, Michael	Lincoln C	Salford C	Undisclosed
30 O'Kane, Eunan	Leeds U	Luton T	Undisclosed

30 Okenabirhie, Fejiri	Shrewsbury T	Doncaster R	Undisclosed
14 Powell, Joe	West Ham U	Burton Alb	Undisclosed
15 Randolph, Darren	Middlesbrough	West Ham U	Undisclosed
25 Riley, Joe	Plymouth Arg	Mansfield T	Free
21 Robinson, Jack	Nottingham F	Sheffield U	Undisclosed
30 Rodriguez, Chema	Nottingham F	Getafe	Undisclosed
16 Rowe, Danny	AFC Fylde	Oldham Ath	Undisclosed
16 Samuelsen, Martin	West Ham U	Hull C	Undisclosed
27 Scowen, Josh	QPR	Sunderland	Undisclosed
8 Sinclair, Scott	Celtic	Preston NE	Undisclosed
10 Stearman, Richard	Sheffield U	Huddersfield T	Free
21 Suliman, Easah	Aston Villa	Vitoria Guimaraes	Undisclosed
7 Taylor, Jack	Barnet	Peterborough U	£500,000
6 Thomason, George	Longridge T	Bolton W	Undisclosed
17 Thompson, Jordan	Blackpool	Stoke C	Undisclosed
22 Thorne, George	Derby Co	Oxford U	Free
1 Thorniley, Jordan	Sheffield W	Blackpool	Undisclosed
15 Tillson, Jordan	Exeter	Ross Co	Undisclosed
17 Toffolo, Harry	Lincoln C	Huddersfield T	Undisclosed
20 Vela, Josh	Hibernian	Shrewsbury T	Free
9 Walkes, Anton	Portsmouth	Atlanta U	Undisclosed
30 Wells, Nahki	Burnley	Bristol C	£5m
24 Whelan, Glenn	Hearts	Fleetwood T	Free
27 Yacob, Claudio	Nottingham F	Nacional	Free
17 Young, Ashley	Manchester U	Internazionale	£1.28m
24 Zeegelaar, Marvin	Watford	Udinese	Undisclosed
FEBRUARY 2020			
18 Burton, Robbie	Arsenal	Dinamo Zagreb	Undisclosed
17 Cavare, Dimitri	Barnsley	FC Sion	Undisclosed
3 Scully, Anthony	West Ham U	Lincoln C	Undisclosed
MARCH 2020			
4 Wanyama, Victor	Tottenham H	Montreal Impact	Free
JUNE 2020			
29 Anderson, Keshi	Swindon T	Blackpool	Free
6 Bassey, Calvin	Leicester C	Rangers	Free*
22 Bowery, Jordan	Milton Keynes D	Mansfield T	Undisclosed
23 Burgess, Christian	Portsmouth	Royal Union Saint-Gilloise	Free*
30 Charles-Cook, Regan	Gillingham	Ross Co	Free
26 Iacovitti, Alex	Oldham Ath	Ross Co	Free
18 Matthews, Sam	Bristol R	Crawley T	Free
15 McGinley, Nathan	Forest Green R	Motherwell	Free
23 McLaughlin, Jon	Sunderland	Rangers	Free
24 O'Hara, Mark	Peterborough U	Motherwell	Undisclosed
23 Schneiderlin, Morgan	Everton	Nice	Undisclosed*
24 Soares, Cedric	Southampton	Arsenal	Undisclosed*
30 Stankovic, Jon Gorenc	Huddersfield T	Sturm Graz	Free*
29 Stech, Marek	Luton T	Mansfield T	Free
JULY 2020			
2 Arthur, Festus	Stockport Co	Hull C	Undisclosed
20 Baldwin, Jack	Sunderland	Bristol R	Free
24 Balogun, Leon	Wigan Ath	Rangers	Free
19 Barrow, Mo	Reading	Jeonbuk Hyundai Motors	Undisclosed
20 Bellingham, Jude	Birmingham C	Borussia Dortmund	Undisclosed
3 Cadden, Nicky	Greenock Morton	Forest Green R	Undisclosed
16 Cisse, Ousseynou	Gillingham	Leyton Orient	Free
17 Clarke, Billy	Grimsby T	Bradford C	Free
1 Clarke, Ollie	Bristol R	Mansfield T	Free
14 Clarke, Tom	Preston NE	Salford C	Free
21 Comley, Brandon	Colchester U	Bolton W	Free
7 Costa, Helder	Wolverhampton W	Leeds U	£16m
21 Digby, Paul	Stevenage	Cambridge U	Free
10 Doyle, Eoin	Swindon T	Bolton W	Free
21 Ehmer, Max	Gillingham	Bristol R	Free
8 Ekpiteta, Marvin	Leyton Orient	Blackpool	Free
15 Emmerson, Zak	Oldham Ath	Brighton & HA	Undisclosed
7 Evans, Jack	Blackburn R	Forest Green R	Free
17 Foderingham, Wes	Rangers	Sheffield U	Free
18 Grant, Josh	Chelsea	Bristol R	Free
22 Hamilton, CJ	Mansfield T	Blackpool	Undisclosed
22 Haunstrup, Brandon	Portsmouth	Kilmarnock	Undisclosed
1 Hornby, Fraser	Everton	Reims	Undisclosed
17 Hunter, Ash	Fleetwood T	Salford C	Undisclosed
22 Johnson, Billy	Norwich C	Stevenage	Free
8 Knockaert, Anthony	Brighton &HA	Fulham	Undisclosed
13 Lawless, Steven	Livingston	Burton Alb	Free
22 Lowe, Jason	Bolton W	Salford C	Free

10 Marshall, Ross	Maidstone	Stevenage	Free
20 Matt, Jamille	Newport Co	Forest Green R	Free
15 McGee, Luke	Portsmouth	Forest Green R	Free
5 Miller, Mickel	Hamilton A	Rotherham U	Free
16 Mills, Zak	Oldham Ath	Port Vale	Free
21 Moore-Taylor, Jordan	Milton Keynes D	Forest Green R	Free
20 Mullin, Paul	Tranmere R	Cambridge U	Free
15 O'Hare, Callum	Aston Villa	Coventry C	Free
8 Pinnock, Mitch	AFC Wimbledon	Kilmarnock	Free
17 Rawson, Farrend	Forest Green R	Mansfield T	Free
7 Rodney, Devante	Salford C	Port Vale	Free
24 Ross, Ethan	Colchester U	Lincoln C	Free
3 Sane, Leroy	Manchester C	Bayern Munich	£44.7m
15 Sarcevic, Antoni	Plymouth Arg	Bolton W	Free
9 Sarkic, Oliver	Burton Alb	Blackpool	Free
20 Shaughnessy, Joe	Southend U	St Mirren	Free
11 Sutton, Levi	Scunthorpe U	Bradford C	Free
1 Sweeney, Dan	Barnet	Forest Green R	Free
20 Taft, George	Cambridge U	Bolton W	Free
24 Vincelot, Romain	Shrewsbury T	Stevenage	Free
2 Wilks, Mallik	Barnsley	Hull C	Undisclosed
8 Wilson, Kane	WBA	Forest Green R	Free
21 Yates, Jerry	Rotherham U	Blackpool	Undisclosed
16 Young, Jake	Sheffield U	Forest Green R	Free
1 Zanzala, Offrande	Accrington S	Crewe Alex	Free

THE NEW FOREIGN LEGION 2019–20

**Transfer to be completed at the end of the season.*

JUNE 2019	*From*	*To*	*Fee in £*
21 Andersen, Mads Juel	AC Horsens	Barnsley	Undisclosed
24 Drmic, Josip	Borussia Moenchengladbach	Norwich C	Free
10 El Ghazi, Anwar	Lille	Aston Villa	Undisclosed
14 Fornals, Pablo	Villarreal	West Ham U	£24m
3 Glatzel, Robert	Heidenheim	Cardiff C	Reported £5.5m
25 Gomes, Andre	Barcelona	Everton	£22m
14 Henley, Adam	Real Salt Lake	Bradford C	Free
14 Jobello, Wesley	Ajaccio	Coventry C	Undisclosed
20 Kastaneer, Gervane	NAC Breda	Coventry C	Undisclosed
26 Radlinger, Samuel	Hannover 96	Barnsley	Undisclosed
27 Van den Berg, Sepp	PEC Zwolle	Liverpool	£1.3m
25 Ugbu, Moses	Al-Ain	Grimsby T	Free
3 Valencia, Joel	Piast Gliwice	Brentford	Undisclosed
13 Van Stappershoef, Jordi	FC Volendam	Bristol R	Free
13 Wesley	Club Brugge	Aston Villa	Undisclosed
JULY 2019			
23 Azankpo, Desire Segbe	FK Senica	Oldham Ath	Free
8 Bockhorn, Herbert	Borussia Dortmund	Huddersfield T	Undisclosed
10 Borner, Julian	Arminia Bielefeld	Sheffield W	Free
18 Crowley, Dan	Willem	Birmingham C	Undisclosed
30 Cutrone, Patrick	AC Milan	Wolverhampton W	£16m
5 Diaby, Bambo	Lokeren	Barnsley	Undisclosed
16 Engels, Bjorn	Reims	Aston Villa	Undisclosed
30 Fage, Dylan	Auxerre	Oldham Ath	Free
30 Gonzales, Florian	Auxerre	Oldham Ath	Free
11 Guthrie, Danny	Mitra Kukar	Walsall	Free
28 Guzman, Ivan	Catalans UE Olot	Birmingham C	Free
17 Haller, Sebastien	Eintracht Frankfurt	West Ham U	£45m
10 Jensen, Mathias	Celta Vigo	Brentford	Undisclosed
23 Joelinton	Hoffenheim	Newcastle U	Undisclosed
3 Kaikai, Sullay	NAC Breda	Blackpool	Free
22 Kokos, Marvin	Gazelec Ajaccio	Oldham Ath	Free
1 Kovacic, Mateo	Real Madrid	Chelsea	£40m
2 Martinelli, Gabriel	Ituano	Arsenal	Undisclosed
9 Mbenza, Isaac	Montpellier	Huddersfield T	Undisclosed
28 Medina, Agustin	UE Cornella	Birmingham C	Undisclosed
4 Mejias, Tomas	Omonia Nicosia	Middlesbrough	Free
16 Morrison, Ravel	Ostersunds	Sheffield U	Free
2 Ndombele, Tanguy	Lyon	Tottenham H	£53.8m
8 Ribeiro, Yuri	Benfica	Nottingham F	Undisclosed
4 Rodri	Atletico Madrid	Manchester C	£68.2m
25 Saliba, William	Saint-Etienne	Arsenal	£27m (loaned back)
5 Silva, Tiago	Feirense	Nottingham F	Undisclosed
19 Sluga, Simon	Rijeka	Luton T	£1.34m

26 Sunjic, Ivan	Dinamo Zagreb	Birmingham C	Undisclosed
8 Tielemans, Youri	Monaco	Leicester C	Undisclosed
24 Trezeguet	Kasimpasa	Aston Villa	£8.75m
AUGUST 2019			
8 Ajeti, Albian	FC Basel	West Ham U	£8m
7 Cancelo, Joao	Juventus	Manchester C	£60m
6 Cardosa, Goncalo	Boavista	West Ham U	Reported £2.7m
8 Chema	Levante	Nottingham F	Undisclosed
6 Dadashov, Renat	Estoril	Wolverhampton W	Undisclosed
1 Danjuma, Arnaut	Club Bruges	Bournemouth	£13.7m
9 Dervisoglu, Halil	Sparta Rotterdam	Brentford	Undisclosed
2 Gbamin, Jean-Philippe	Mainz	Everton	£25m
6 Gimenez, Alvaro	Almeria	Birmingham C	£1.4m
2 Jordao, Bruno	Lazio	Wolverhampton W	Undisclosed
4 Kean, Moise	Juventus	Everton	Undisclosed
8 Krafth, Emil	Amiens	Newcastle U	Undisclosed
5 Massengo, Han-Noah	Monaco	Bristol C	Undisclosed
5 Mbeumo, Bryan	Troyes	Brentford	Undisclosed
8 Nagy, Adam	Bologna	Bristol C	Undisclosed
1 Nakamba, Marvelous	Club Brugge	Aston Villa	Undisclosed
1 Pepe, Nicolas	Lille	Arsenal	£72m
2 Peterson, Kristoffer	Heracles	Swansea C	Undisclosed
8 Praet, Dennis	Sampdoria	Leicester C	Undisclosed
7 Puscas, George	Internazionale	Reading	Undisclosed
6 Rafael	Sampdoria	Reading	Free
2 Saint-Maximin, Allan	Nice	Newcastle U	Undisclosed
7 Samba, Brice	Caen	Nottingham F	Undisclosed
8 Sarr, Ismaila	Rennes	Watford	Undisclosed
8 Schmidt, Patrick	Admira Wacker	Barnsley	Undisclosed
8 Shabani, Meritan	Bayern Munich	Wolverhampton W	Undisclosed
1 Sow, Samba	Dinamo Moscow	Nottingham F	Undisclosed
7 Villalba, Fran	Valencia	Birmingham C	Free
8 Yapi, Romaric	Paris Saint-Germain	Brighton & HA	Undisclosed
SEPTEMBER 2019			
5 van Velzen, Gyliano	Roda JC	Crawley T	Free
NOVEMBER 2019			
6 Bela, Jeremie	Albacete	Birmingham C	Free
DECEMBER 2019			
31 Grandin, Elliot	JS Saint-Pierroise	Grimsby T	Undisclosed
JANUARY 2020			
30 Araruna, Felipe	Sao Paulo	Reading	Undisclosed
23 Barry, Louie	Barcelona	Aston Villa	£880,000
30 Berge, Sander	Genk	Sheffield U	£22m
29 Bergwijn, Steven	PSV Eindhoven	Tottenham H	£27m
21 Caprile, Elia	Chievo	Leeds U	Undisclosed
29 da Costa, Nuno	Strasbourg	Nottingham F	Undisclosed
17 Dabo, Diaguely	Epinal	Stevenage	Free
30 Fernandes, Bruno	Sporting Lisbon	Manchester U	£47m
10 Lafferty, Kyle	Sarpsborg 08	Sunderland	Free
28 Lo Celso, Giovani	Real Betis	Tottenham H	£27.2m
30 Podence, Daniel	Olympiacos	Wolverhampton W	£16.6m
14 Pussetto, Ignacio	Udinese	Watford	£7m
6 Ritzmaier, Marcel	Wolfsberg	Barnsley	Undisclosed
13 Rupp, Lukas	Hoffenheim	Norwich C	Undisclosed
20 Samatta, Mbwana	Genk	Aston Villa	£8.5m
24 Sollbauer, Michael	Wolfsberg	Barnsley	Undisclosed
16 Stojanovic, Dejan	St Gallen	Middlesbrough	Undisclosed
FEBRUARY 2020			
6 te Wierik, Mike	FC Groningen	Derby Co	Free*
8 Wilson, Donovan	Burgos	Macclesfield T	Free
APRIL 2020			
29 Gueye, Pape	Le Havre	Watford	Free*
10 Sinani, Danel	F91 Dudelange	Norwich C	Undisclosed*
JUNE 2020			
24 Mari, Pablo	Flamengo	Arsenal	Undisclosed*
18 Werner, Timo	RB Leipzig	Chelsea	Undisclosed*
JULY 2020			
6 Dacosta, Julien	Niort	Coventry C	Free
3 Hamer, Gustavo	PEC Zwolle	Coventry C	£1.5m
16 Hilssner, Marcel	SC Paderborn	Coventry C	Undisclosed
23 Meslier, Illan	Lorient	Leeds U	Undisclosed
14 Montsma, Lewis	FC Dordrecht	Lincoln C	Free
20 Sorensen, Jacob	Esbjerg	Norwich C	Undisclosed

ENGLISH LEAGUE HONOURS 1888–2020

**Won or placed on goal average (ratio), goal difference or most goals scored. ‡Not promoted after play-offs. No official competition during 1915–19 and 1939–46, regional leagues operated.*

FOOTBALL LEAGUE (1888–89 to 1891–92) – TIER 1

MAXIMUM POINTS: *a* 44; *b* 52.

1	1888–89*a*	Preston NE	40	Aston Villa	29	Wolverhampton W	28
1	1889–90*a*	Preston NE	33	Everton	31	Blackburn R	27
1	1890–91*a*	Everton	29	Preston NE	27	Notts Co	26
1	1891–92*b*	Sunderland	42	Preston NE	37	Bolton W	36

DIVISION 1 (1892–93 to 1991–92)

MAXIMUM POINTS: *c* 60; *d* 68; *e* 76; *f* 84; *g* 126; *h* 120; *k* 114.

1	1892–93*c*	Sunderland	48	Preston NE	37	Everton	36
1	1893–94*c*	Aston Villa	44	Sunderland	38	Derby Co	36
1	1894–95*c*	Sunderland	47	Everton	42	Aston Villa	39
1	1895–96*c*	Aston Villa	45	Derby Co	41	Everton	39
1	1896–97*c*	Aston Villa	47	Sheffield U*	36	Derby Co	36
1	1897–98*c*	Sheffield U	42	Sunderland	37	Wolverhampton W*	35
1	1898–99*d*	Aston Villa	45	Liverpool	43	Burnley	39
1	1899–1900*d*	Aston Villa	50	Sheffield U	48	Sunderland	41
1	1900–01*d*	Liverpool	45	Sunderland	43	Notts Co	40
1	1901–02*d*	Sunderland	44	Everton	41	Newcastle U	37
1	1902–03*d*	The Wednesday	42	Aston Villa*	41	Sunderland	41
1	1903–04*d*	The Wednesday	47	Manchester C	44	Everton	43
1	1904–05*d*	Newcastle U	48	Everton	47	Manchester C	46
1	1905–06*e*	Liverpool	51	Preston NE	47	The Wednesday	44
1	1906–07*e*	Newcastle U	51	Bristol C	48	Everton*	45
1	1907–08*e*	Manchester U	52	Aston Villa*	43	Manchester C	43
1	1908–09*e*	Newcastle U	53	Everton	46	Sunderland	44
1	1909–10*e*	Aston Villa	53	Liverpool	48	Blackburn R*	45
1	1910–11*e*	Manchester U	52	Aston Villa	51	Sunderland*	45
1	1911–12*e*	Blackburn R	49	Everton	46	Newcastle U	44
1	1912–13*e*	Sunderland	54	Aston Villa	50	Sheffield W	49
1	1913–14*e*	Blackburn R	51	Aston Villa	44	Middlesbrough*	43
1	1914–15*e*	Everton	46	Oldham Ath	45	Blackburn R*	43
1	1919–20*f*	WBA	60	Burnley	51	Chelsea	49
1	1920–21*f*	Burnley	59	Manchester C	54	Bolton W	52
1	1921–22*f*	Liverpool	57	Tottenham H	51	Burnley	49
1	1922–23*f*	Liverpool	60	Sunderland	54	Huddersfield T	53
1	1923–24*f*	Huddersfield T*	57	Cardiff C	57	Sunderland	53
1	1924–25*f*	Huddersfield T	58	WBA	56	Bolton W	55
1	1925–26*f*	Huddersfield T	57	Arsenal	52	Sunderland	48
1	1926–27*f*	Newcastle U	56	Huddersfield T	51	Sunderland	49
1	1927–28*f*	Everton	53	Huddersfield T	51	Leicester C	48
1	1928–29*f*	Sheffield W	52	Leicester C	51	Aston Villa	50
1	1929–30*f*	Sheffield W	60	Derby Co	50	Manchester C*	47
1	1930–31*f*	Arsenal	66	Aston Villa	59	Sheffield W	52
1	1931–32*f*	Everton	56	Arsenal	54	Sheffield W	50
1	1932–33*f*	Arsenal	58	Aston Villa	54	Sheffield W	51
1	1933–34*f*	Arsenal	59	Huddersfield T	56	Tottenham H	49
1	1934–35*f*	Arsenal	58	Sunderland	54	Sheffield W	49
1	1935–36*f*	Sunderland	56	Derby Co*	48	Huddersfield T	48
1	1936–37*f*	Manchester C	57	Charlton Ath	54	Arsenal	52
1	1937–38*f*	Arsenal	52	Wolverhampton W	51	Preston NE	49
1	1938–39*f*	Everton	59	Wolverhampton W	55	Charlton Ath	50
1	1946–47*f*	Liverpool	57	Manchester U*	56	Wolverhampton W	56
1	1947–48*f*	Arsenal	59	Manchester U*	52	Burnley	52
1	1948–49*f*	Portsmouth	58	Manchester U*	53	Derby Co	53
1	1949–50*f*	Portsmouth*	53	Wolverhampton W	53	Sunderland	52
1	1950–51*f*	Tottenham H	60	Manchester U	56	Blackpool	50
1	1951–52*f*	Manchester U	57	Tottenham H*	53	Arsenal	53
1	1952–53*f*	Arsenal*	54	Preston NE	54	Wolverhampton W	51
1	1953–54*f*	Wolverhampton W	57	WBA	53	Huddersfield T	51
1	1954–55*f*	Chelsea	52	Wolverhampton W*	48	Portsmouth*	48
1	1955–56*f*	Manchester U	60	Blackpool*	49	Wolverhampton W	49
1	1956–57*f*	Manchester U	64	Tottenham H*	56	Preston NE	56
1	1957–58*f*	Wolverhampton W	64	Preston NE	59	Tottenham H	51
1	1958–59*f*	Wolverhampton W	61	Manchester U	55	Arsenal*	50
1	1959–60*f*	Burnley	55	Wolverhampton W	54	Tottenham H	53
1	1960–61*f*	Tottenham H	66	Sheffield W	58	Wolverhampton W	57
1	1961–62*f*	Ipswich T	56	Burnley	53	Tottenham H	52
1	1962–63*f*	Everton	61	Tottenham H	55	Burnley	54
1	1963–64*f*	Liverpool	57	Manchester U	53	Everton	52
1	1964–65*f*	Manchester U*	61	Leeds U	61	Chelsea	56

1	1965–66*f*	Liverpool	61	Leeds U*	55	Burnley	55
1	1966–67*f*	Manchester U	60	Nottingham F*	56	Tottenham H	56
1	1967–68*f*	Manchester C	58	Manchester U	56	Liverpool	55
1	1968–69*f*	Leeds U	67	Liverpool	61	Everton	57
1	1969–70*f*	Everton	66	Leeds U	57	Chelsea	55
1	1970–71*f*	Arsenal	65	Leeds U	64	Tottenham H*	52
1	1971–72*f*	Derby Co	58	Leeds U*	57	Liverpool*	57
1	1972–73*f*	Liverpool	60	Arsenal	57	Leeds U	53
1	1973–74*f*	Leeds U	62	Liverpool	57	Derby Co	48
1	1974–75*f*	Derby Co	53	Liverpool*	51	Ipswich T	51
1	1975–76*f*	Liverpool	60	QPR	59	Manchester U	56
1	1976–77*f*	Liverpool	57	Manchester C	56	Ipswich T	52
1	1977–78*f*	Nottingham F	64	Liverpool	57	Everton	55
1	1978–79*f*	Liverpool	68	Nottingham F	60	WBA	59
1	1979–80*f*	Liverpool	60	Manchester U	58	Ipswich T	53
1	1980–81*f*	Aston Villa	60	Ipswich T	56	Arsenal	53
1	1981–82*g*	Liverpool	87	Ipswich T	83	Manchester U	78
1	1982–83*g*	Liverpool	82	Watford	71	Manchester U	70
1	1983–84*g*	Liverpool	80	Southampton	77	Nottingham F*	74
1	1984–85*g*	Everton	90	Liverpool*	77	Tottenham H	77
1	1985–86*g*	Liverpool	88	Everton	86	West Ham U	84
1	1986–87*g*	Everton	86	Liverpool	77	Tottenham H	71
1	1987–88*h*	Liverpool	90	Manchester U	81	Nottingham F	73
1	1988–89*k*	Arsenal*	76	Liverpool	76	Nottingham F	64
1	1989–90*k*	Liverpool	79	Aston Villa	70	Tottenham H	63
1	1990–91*k*	Arsenal[1]	83	Liverpool	76	Crystal Palace	69
1	1991–92*g*	Leeds U	82	Manchester U	78	Sheffield W	75

[1] *Arsenal deducted 2pts due to player misconduct in match on 20/10/1990 v Manchester U at Old Trafford.*

PREMIER LEAGUE (1992–93 to 2019–20)

MAXIMUM POINTS: *a* 126; *b* 114.

1	1992–93*a*	Manchester U	84	Aston Villa	74	Norwich C	72
1	1993–94*a*	Manchester U	92	Blackburn R	84	Newcastle U	77
1	1994–95*a*	Blackburn R	89	Manchester U	88	Nottingham F	77
1	1995–96*b*	Manchester U	82	Newcastle U	78	Liverpool	71
1	1996–97*b*	Manchester U	75	Newcastle U*	68	Arsenal*	68
1	1997–98*b*	Arsenal	78	Manchester U	77	Liverpool	65
1	1998–99*b*	Manchester U	79	Arsenal	78	Chelsea	75
1	1999–2000*b*	Manchester U	91	Arsenal	73	Leeds U	69
1	2000–01*b*	Manchester U	80	Arsenal	70	Liverpool	69
1	2001–02*b*	Arsenal	87	Liverpool	80	Manchester U	77
1	2002–03*b*	Manchester U	83	Arsenal	78	Newcastle U	69
1	2003–04*b*	Arsenal	90	Chelsea	79	Manchester U	75
1	2004–05*b*	Chelsea	95	Arsenal	83	Manchester U	77
1	2005–06*b*	Chelsea	91	Manchester U	83	Liverpool	82
1	2006–07*b*	Manchester U	89	Chelsea	83	Liverpool*	68
1	2007–08*b*	Manchester U	87	Chelsea	85	Arsenal	83
1	2008–09*b*	Manchester U	90	Liverpool	86	Chelsea	83
1	2009–10*b*	Chelsea	86	Manchester U	85	Arsenal	75
1	2010–11*b*	Manchester U	80	Chelsea*	71	Manchester C	71
1	2011–12*b*	Manchester C*	89	Manchester U	89	Arsenal	70
1	2012–13*b*	Manchester U	89	Manchester C	78	Chelsea	75
1	2013–14*b*	Manchester C	86	Liverpool	84	Chelsea	82
1	2014–15*b*	Chelsea	87	Manchester C	79	Arsenal	75
1	2015–16*b*	Leicester C	81	Arsenal	71	Tottenham H	70
1	2016–17*b*	Chelsea	93	Tottenham H	86	Manchester C	78
1	2017–18*b*	Manchester C	100	Manchester U	81	Tottenham H	77
1	2018–19*b*	Manchester C	98	Liverpool	97	Chelsea	72
1	2019–20*b*	Liverpool	99	Manchester C	81	Mancheser U*	66

DIVISION 2 (1892–93 to 1991–92) – TIER 2

MAXIMUM POINTS: *a* 44; *b* 56; *c* 60; *d* 68; *e* 76; *f* 84; *g* 126; *h* 132; *k* 138.

2	1892–93*a*	Small Heath	36	Sheffield U	35	Darwen	30
2	1893–94*b*	Liverpool	50	Small Heath	42	Notts Co	39
2	1894–95*c*	Bury	48	Notts Co	39	Newton Heath*	38
2	1895–96*c*	Liverpool*	46	Manchester C	46	Grimsby T*	42
2	1896–97*c*	Notts Co	42	Newton Heath	39	Grimsby T	38
2	1897–98*c*	Burnley	48	Newcastle U	45	Manchester C	39
2	1898–99*d*	Manchester C	52	Glossop NE	46	Leicester Fosse	45
2	1899–1900*d*	The Wednesday	54	Bolton W	52	Small Heath	46
2	1900–01*d*	Grimsby T	49	Small Heath	48	Burnley	44
2	1901–02*d*	WBA	55	Middlesbrough	51	Preston NE*	42
2	1902–03*d*	Manchester C	54	Small Heath	51	Woolwich A	48
2	1903–04*d*	Preston NE	50	Woolwich A	49	Manchester U	48
2	1904–05*d*	Liverpool	58	Bolton W	56	Manchester U	53
2	1905–06*e*	Bristol C	66	Manchester U	62	Chelsea	53
2	1906–07*e*	Nottingham F	60	Chelsea	57	Leicester Fosse	48
2	1907–08*e*	Bradford C	54	Leicester Fosse	52	Oldham Ath	50
2	1908–09*e*	Bolton W	52	Tottenham H*	51	WBA	51
2	1909–10*e*	Manchester C	54	Oldham Ath*	53	Hull C*	53
2	1910–11*e*	WBA	53	Bolton W	51	Chelsea	49

2	1911–12*e*	Derby Co*	54	Chelsea	54	Burnley	52
2	1912–13*e*	Preston NE	53	Burnley	50	Birmingham	46
2	1913–14*e*	Notts Co	53	Bradford PA*	49	Woolwich A	49
2	1914–15*e*	Derby Co	53	Preston NE	50	Barnsley	47
2	1919–20*f*	Tottenham H	70	Huddersfield T	64	Birmingham	56
2	1920–21*f*	Birmingham*	58	Cardiff C	58	Bristol C	51
2	1921–22*f*	Nottingham F	56	Stoke C*	52	Barnsley	52
2	1922–23*f*	Notts Co	53	West Ham U*	51	Leicester C	51
2	1923–24*f*	Leeds U	54	Bury*	51	Derby Co	51
2	1924–25*f*	Leicester C	59	Manchester U	57	Derby Co	55
2	1925–26*f*	Sheffield W	60	Derby Co	57	Chelsea	52
2	1926–27*f*	Middlesbrough	62	Portsmouth*	54	Manchester C	54
2	1927–28*f*	Manchester C	59	Leeds U	57	Chelsea	54
2	1928–29*f*	Middlesbrough	55	Grimsby T	53	Bradford PA*	48
2	1929–30*f*	Blackpool	58	Chelsea	55	Oldham Ath	53
2	1930–31*f*	Everton	61	WBA	54	Tottenham H	51
2	1931–32*f*	Wolverhampton W	56	Leeds U	54	Stoke C	52
2	1932–33*f*	Stoke C	56	Tottenham H	55	Fulham	50
2	1933–34*f*	Grimsby T	59	Preston NE	52	Bolton W*	51
2	1934–35*f*	Brentford	61	Bolton W*	56	West Ham U	56
2	1935–36*f*	Manchester U	56	Charlton Ath	55	Sheffield U*	52
2	1936–37*f*	Leicester C	56	Blackpool	55	Bury	52
2	1937–38*f*	Aston Villa	57	Manchester U*	53	Sheffield U	53
2	1938–39*f*	Blackburn R	55	Sheffield U	54	Sheffield W	53
2	1946–47*f*	Manchester C	62	Burnley	58	Birmingham C	55
2	1947–48*f*	Birmingham C	59	Newcastle U	56	Southampton	52
2	1948–49*f*	Fulham	57	WBA	56	Southampton	55
2	1949–50*f*	Tottenham H	61	Sheffield W*	52	Sheffield U*	52
2	1950–51*f*	Preston NE	57	Manchester C	52	Cardiff C	50
2	1951–52*f*	Sheffield W	53	Cardiff C*	51	Birmingham C	51
2	1952–53*f*	Sheffield U	60	Huddersfield T	58	Luton T	52
2	1953–54*f*	Leicester C*	56	Everton	56	Blackburn R	55
2	1954–55*f*	Birmingham C*	54	Luton T*	54	Rotherham U	54
2	1955–56*f*	Sheffield W	55	Leeds U	52	Liverpool*	48
2	1956–57*f*	Leicester C	61	Nottingham F	54	Liverpool	53
2	1957–58*f*	West Ham U	57	Blackburn R	56	Charlton Ath	55
2	1958–59*f*	Sheffield W	62	Fulham	60	Sheffield U*	53
2	1959–60*f*	Aston Villa	59	Cardiff C	58	Liverpool*	50
2	1960–61*f*	Ipswich T	59	Sheffield U	58	Liverpool	52
2	1961–62*f*	Liverpool	62	Leyton Orient	54	Sunderland	53
2	1962–63*f*	Stoke C	53	Chelsea*	52	Sunderland	52
2	1963–64*f*	Leeds U	63	Sunderland	61	Preston NE	56
2	1964–65*f*	Newcastle U	57	Northampton T	56	Bolton W	50
2	1965–66*f*	Manchester C	59	Southampton	54	Coventry C	53
2	1966–67*f*	Coventry C	59	Wolverhampton W	58	Carlisle U	52
2	1967–68*f*	Ipswich T	59	QPR*	58	Blackpool	58
2	1968–69*f*	Derby Co	63	Crystal Palace	56	Charlton Ath	50
2	1969–70*f*	Huddersfield T	60	Blackpool	53	Leicester C	51
2	1970–71*f*	Leicester C	59	Sheffield U	56	Cardiff C*	53
2	1971–72*f*	Norwich C	57	Birmingham C	56	Millwall	55
2	1972–73*f*	Burnley	62	QPR	61	Aston Villa	50
2	1973–74*f*	Middlesbrough	65	Luton T	50	Carlisle U	49
2	1974–75*f*	Manchester U	61	Aston Villa	58	Norwich C	53
2	1975–76*f*	Sunderland	56	Bristol C*	53	WBA	53
2	1976–77*f*	Wolverhampton W	57	Chelsea	55	Nottingham F	52
2	1977–78*f*	Bolton W	58	Southampton	57	Tottenham H*	56
2	1978–79*f*	Crystal Palace	57	Brighton & HA*	56	Stoke C	56
2	1979–80*f*	Leicester C	55	Sunderland	54	Birmingham C*	53
2	1980–81*f*	West Ham U	66	Notts Co	53	Swansea C*	50
2	1981–82*g*	Luton T	88	Watford	80	Norwich C	71
2	1982–83*g*	QPR	85	Wolverhampton W	75	Leicester C	70
2	1983–84*g*	Chelsea*	88	Sheffield W	88	Newcastle U	80
2	1984–85*g*	Oxford U	84	Birmingham C	82	Manchester C*	74
2	1985–86*g*	Norwich C	84	Charlton Ath	77	Wimbledon	76
2	1986–87*g*	Derby Co	84	Portsmouth	78	Oldham Ath‡	75
2	1987–88*h*	Millwall	82	Aston Villa*	78	Middlesbrough	78
2	1988–89*k*	Chelsea	99	Manchester C	82	Crystal Palace	81
2	1989–90*k*	Leeds U*	85	Sheffield U	85	Newcastle U‡	80
2	1990–91*k*	Oldham Ath	88	West Ham U	87	Sheffield W	82
2	1991–92*k*	Ipswich T	84	Middlesbrough	80	Derby Co	78

FIRST DIVISION (1992–93 to 2003–04)

MAXIMUM POINTS: 138

2	1992–93	Newcastle U	96	West Ham U*	88	Portsmouth‡	88
2	1993–94	Crystal Palace	90	Nottingham F	83	Millwall‡	74
2	1994–95	Middlesbrough	82	Reading‡	79	Bolton W	77
2	1995–96	Sunderland	83	Derby Co	79	Crystal Palace‡	75
2	1996–97	Bolton W	98	Barnsley	80	Wolverhampton W‡	76
2	1997–98	Nottingham F	94	Middlesbrough	91	Sunderland‡	90

2	1998–99	Sunderland	105	Bradford C	87	Ipswich T‡	86
2	1999–2000	Charlton Ath	91	Manchester C	89	Ipswich T	87
2	2000–01	Fulham	101	Blackburn R	91	Bolton W	87
2	2001–02	Manchester C	99	WBA	89	Wolverhampton W‡	86
2	2002–03	Portsmouth	98	Leicester C	92	Sheffield U‡	80
2	2003–04	Norwich C	94	WBA	86	Sunderland‡	79

FOOTBALL LEAGUE CHAMPIONSHIP (2004–05 to 2019–20)

MAXIMUM POINTS: 138

2	2004–05	Sunderland	94	Wigan Ath	87	Ipswich T‡	85
2	2005–06	Reading	106	Sheffield U	90	Watford	81
2	2006–07	Sunderland	88	Birmingham C	86	Derby Co	84
2	2007–08	WBA	81	Stoke C	79	Hull C	75
2	2008–09	Wolverhampton W	90	Birmingham C	83	Sheffield U‡	80
2	2009–10	Newcastle U	102	WBA	91	Nottingham F‡	79
2	2010–11	QPR	88	Norwich C	84	Swansea C*	80
2	2011–12	Reading	89	Southampton	88	West Ham U	86
2	2012–13	Cardiff C	87	Hull C	79	Watford‡	77
2	2013–14	Leicester C	102	Burnley	93	Derby Co‡	85
2	2014–15	Bournemouth	90	Watford	89	Norwich C	86
2	2015–16	Burnley	93	Middlesbrough*	89	Brighton & HA‡	89
2	2016–17	Newcastle U	94	Brighton & HA	93	Reading‡	85
2	2017–18	Wolverhampton W	99	Cardiff C	90	Fulham	88
2	2018–19	Norwich C	94	Sheffield U	89	Leeds U‡	83
2	2019–20	Leeds U	93	WBA	83	Brentford*‡	81

DIVISION 3 (1920–1921) – TIER 3

MAXIMUM POINTS: *a* 84.

3	1920–21*a*	Crystal Palace	59	Southampton	54	QPR	53

DIVISION 3—SOUTH (1921–22 to 1957–58)

MAXIMUM POINTS: *a* 84; *b* 92.

3	1921–22*a*	Southampton*	61	Plymouth Arg	61	Portsmouth	53
3	1922–23*a*	Bristol C	59	Plymouth Arg*	53	Swansea T	53
3	1923–24*a*	Portsmouth	59	Plymouth Arg	55	Millwall	54
3	1924–25*a*	Swansea T	57	Plymouth Arg	56	Bristol C	53
3	1925–26*a*	Reading	57	Plymouth Arg	56	Millwall	53
3	1926–27*a*	Bristol C	62	Plymouth Arg	60	Millwall	56
3	1927–28*a*	Millwall	65	Northampton T	55	Plymouth Arg	53
3	1928–29*a*	Charlton Ath*	54	Crystal Palace	54	Northampton T*	52
3	1929–30*a*	Plymouth Arg	68	Brentford	61	QPR	51
3	1930–31*a*	Notts Co	59	Crystal Palace	51	Brentford	50
3	1931–32*a*	Fulham	57	Reading	55	Southend U	53
3	1932–33*a*	Brentford	62	Exeter C	58	Norwich C	57
3	1933–34*a*	Norwich C	61	Coventry C*	54	Reading*	54
3	1934–35*a*	Charlton Ath	61	Reading	53	Coventry C	51
3	1935–36*a*	Coventry C	57	Luton T	56	Reading	54
3	1936–37*a*	Luton T	58	Notts Co	56	Brighton & HA	53
3	1937–38*a*	Millwall	56	Bristol C	55	QPR*	53
3	1938–39*a*	Newport Co	55	Crystal Palace	52	Brighton & HA	49
3	1946–47*a*	Cardiff C	66	QPR	57	Bristol C	51
3	1947–48*a*	QPR	61	Bournemouth	57	Walsall	51
3	1948–49*a*	Swansea T	62	Reading	55	Bournemouth	52
3	1949–50*a*	Notts Co	58	Northampton T*	51	Southend U	51
3	1950–51*b*	Nottingham F	70	Norwich C	64	Reading*	57
3	1951–52*b*	Plymouth Arg	66	Reading*	61	Norwich C	61
3	1952–53*b*	Bristol R	64	Millwall*	62	Northampton T	62
3	1953–54*b*	Ipswich T	64	Brighton & HA	61	Bristol C	56
3	1954–55*b*	Bristol C	70	Leyton Orient	61	Southampton	59
3	1955–56*b*	Leyton Orient	66	Brighton & HA	65	Ipswich T	64
3	1956–57*b*	Ipswich T*	59	Torquay U	59	Colchester U	58
3	1957–58*b*	Brighton & HA	60	Brentford*	58	Plymouth Arg	58

DIVISION 3—NORTH (1921–22 to 1957–58)

MAXIMUM POINTS: *a* 76; *b* 84; *c* 80; *d* 92.

3	1921–22*a*	Stockport Co	56	Darlington*	50	Grimsby T	50
3	1922–23*a*	Nelson	51	Bradford PA	47	Walsall	46
3	1923–24*b*	Wolverhampton W	63	Rochdale	62	Chesterfield	54
3	1924–25*b*	Darlington	58	Nelson*	53	New Brighton	53
3	1925–26*b*	Grimsby T	61	Bradford PA	60	Rochdale	59
3	1926–27*b*	Stoke C	63	Rochdale	58	Bradford PA	55
3	1927–28*b*	Bradford PA	63	Lincoln C	55	Stockport Co	54
3	1928–29*b*	Bradford C	63	Stockport Co	62	Wrexham	52
3	1929–30*b*	Port Vale	67	Stockport Co	63	Darlington*	50
3	1930–31*b*	Chesterfield	58	Lincoln C	57	Wrexham*	54
3	1931–32*c*	Lincoln C*	57	Gateshead	57	Chester	50
3	1932–33*b*	Hull C	59	Wrexham	57	Stockport Co	54
3	1933–34*b*	Barnsley	62	Chesterfield	61	Stockport Co	59

3	1934–35*b*	Doncaster R	57	Halifax T	55	Chester	54
3	1935–36*b*	Chesterfield	60	Chester*	55	Tranmere R	55
3	1936–37*b*	Stockport Co	60	Lincoln C	57	Chester	53
3	1937–38*b*	Tranmere R	56	Doncaster R	54	Hull C	53
3	1938–39*b*	Barnsley	67	Doncaster R	56	Bradford C	52
3	1946–47*b*	Doncaster R	72	Rotherham U	64	Chester	56
3	1947–48*b*	Lincoln C	60	Rotherham U	59	Wrexham	50
3	1948–49*b*	Hull C	65	Rotherham U	62	Doncaster R	50
3	1949–50*b*	Doncaster R	55	Gateshead	53	Rochdale*	51
3	1950–51*d*	Rotherham U	71	Mansfield T	64	Carlisle U	62
3	1951–52*d*	Lincoln C	69	Grimsby T	66	Stockport Co	59
3	1952–53*d*	Oldham Ath	59	Port Vale	58	Wrexham	56
3	1953–54*d*	Port Vale	69	Barnsley	58	Scunthorpe U	57
3	1954–55*d*	Barnsley	65	Accrington S	61	Scunthorpe U*	58
3	1955–56*d*	Grimsby T	68	Derby Co	63	Accrington S	59
3	1956–57*d*	Derby Co	63	Hartlepools U	59	Accrington S*	58
3	1957–58*d*	Scunthorpe U	66	Accrington S	59	Bradford C	57

DIVISION 3 (1958–59 to 1991–92)

MAXIMUM POINTS: 92; 138 FROM 1981–82.

3	1958–59	Plymouth Arg	62	Hull C	61	Brentford*	57
3	1959–60	Southampton	61	Norwich C	59	Shrewsbury T*	52
3	1960–61	Bury	68	Walsall	62	QPR	60
3	1961–62	Portsmouth	65	Grimsby T	62	Bournemouth*	59
3	1962–63	Northampton T	62	Swindon T	58	Port Vale	54
3	1963–64	Coventry C*	60	Crystal Palace	60	Watford	58
3	1964–65	Carlisle U	60	Bristol C*	59	Mansfield T	59
3	1965–66	Hull C	69	Millwall	65	QPR	57
3	1966–67	QPR	67	Middlesbrough	55	Watford	54
3	1967–68	Oxford U	57	Bury	56	Shrewsbury T	55
3	1968–69	Watford*	64	Swindon T	64	Luton T	61
3	1969–70	Orient	62	Luton T	60	Bristol R	56
3	1970–71	Preston NE	61	Fulham	60	Halifax T	56
3	1971–72	Aston Villa	70	Brighton & HA	65	Bournemouth*	62
3	1972–73	Bolton W	61	Notts Co	57	Blackburn R	55
3	1973–74	Oldham Ath	62	Bristol R*	61	York C	61
3	1974–75	Blackburn R	60	Plymouth Arg	59	Charlton Ath	55
3	1975–76	Hereford U	63	Cardiff C	57	Millwall	56
3	1976–77	Mansfield T	64	Brighton & HA	61	Crystal Palace*	59
3	1977–78	Wrexham	61	Cambridge U	58	Preston NE*	56
3	1978–79	Shrewsbury T	61	Watford*	60	Swansea C	60
3	1979–80	Grimsby T	62	Blackburn R	59	Sheffield W	58
3	1980–81	Rotherham U	61	Barnsley*	59	Charlton Ath	59
3	1981–82	Burnley*	80	Carlisle U	80	Fulham	78
3	1982–83	Portsmouth	91	Cardiff C	86	Huddersfield T	82
3	1983–84	Oxford U	95	Wimbledon	87	Sheffield U*	83
3	1984–85	Bradford C	94	Millwall	90	Hull C	87
3	1985–86	Reading	94	Plymouth Arg	87	Derby Co	84
3	1986–87	Bournemouth	97	Middlesbrough	94	Swindon T	87
3	1987–88	Sunderland	93	Brighton & HA	84	Walsall	82
3	1988–89	Wolverhampton W	92	Sheffield U*	84	Port Vale	84
3	1989–90	Bristol R	93	Bristol C	91	Notts Co	87
3	1990–91	Cambridge U	86	Southend U	85	Grimsby T*	83
3	1991–92	Brentford	82	Birmingham C	81	Huddersfield T‡	78

SECOND DIVISION (1992–93 to 2003–04)

MAXIMUM POINTS: 138

3	1992–93	Stoke C	93	Bolton W	90	Port Vale‡	89
3	1993–94	Reading	89	Port Vale	88	Plymouth Arg*‡	85
3	1994–95	Birmingham C	89	Brentford‡	85	Crewe Alex‡	83
3	1995–96	Swindon T	92	Oxford U	83	Blackpool‡	82
3	1996–97	Bury	84	Stockport Co	82	Luton T‡	78
3	1997–98	Watford	88	Bristol C	85	Grimsby T	72
3	1998–99	Fulham	101	Walsall	87	Manchester C	82
3	1999–2000	Preston NE	95	Burnley	88	Gillingham	85
3	2000–01	Millwall	93	Rotherham U	91	Reading‡	86
3	2001–02	Brighton & HA	90	Reading	84	Brentford*‡	83
3	2002–03	Wigan Ath	100	Crewe Alex	86	Bristol C*‡	83
3	2003–04	Plymouth Arg	90	QPR	83	Bristol C‡	82

FOOTBALL LEAGUE ONE (2004–05 to 2019–20)

MAXIMUM POINTS: 138

3	2004–05	Luton T	98	Hull C	86	Tranmere R‡	79
3	2005–06	Southend U	82	Colchester U	79	Brentford‡	76
3	2006–07	Scunthorpe U	91	Bristol C	85	Blackpool	83
3	2007–08	Swansea C	92	Nottingham F	82	Doncaster R*	80
3	2008–09	Leicester C	96	Peterborough U	89	Milton Keynes D‡	87
3	2009–10	Norwich C	95	Leeds U	86	Millwall	85
3	2010–11	Brighton & HA	95	Southampton	92	Huddersfield T‡	87
3	2011–12	Charlton Ath	101	Sheffield W	93	Sheffield U‡	90

3	2012–13	Doncaster R	84	Bournemouth	83	Brentford‡	79		
3	2013–14	Wolverhampton W	103	Brentford	94	Leyton Orient‡	86		
3	2014–15	Bristol C	99	Milton Keynes D	91	Preston NE	89		
3	2015–16	Wigan Ath	87	Burton Alb	85	Walsall‡	84		
3	2016–17	Sheffield U	100	Bolton W	86	Scunthorpe U*‡	82		
3	2017–18	Wigan Ath	98	Blackburn R	96	Shrewsbury T‡	87		
3	2018–19	Luton T	94	Barnsley	91	Charlton Ath*	88		
3	2019–20[2]	Coventry C	67	Rotherham U	62	Wycombe W	59		

[2] *Season curtailed due to COVID-19 pandemic. League positions decided on points-per-game basis.*

DIVISION 4 (1958–59 to 1991–92) – TIER 4

MAXIMUM POINTS: 92; 138 FROM 1981–82.

4	1958–59	Port Vale	64	Coventry C*	60	York C	60	Shrewsbury T	58
4	1959–60	Walsall	65	Notts Co*	60	Torquay U	60	Watford	57
4	1960–61	Peterborough U	66	Crystal Palace	64	Northampton T*	60	Bradford PA	60
4	1961–62[3]	Millwall	56	Colchester U	55	Wrexham	53	Carlisle U	52
4	1962–63	Brentford	62	Oldham Ath*	59	Crewe Alex	59	Mansfield T*	57
4	1963–64	Gillingham*	60	Carlisle U	60	Workington	59	Exeter C	58
4	1964–65	Brighton & HA	63	Millwall*	62	York C	62	Oxford U	61
4	1965–66	Doncaster R*	59	Darlington	59	Torquay U	58	Colchester U*	56
4	1966–67	Stockport Co	64	Southport*	59	Barrow	59	Tranmere R	58
4	1967–68	Luton T	66	Barnsley	61	Hartlepools U	60	Crewe Alex	58
4	1968–69	Doncaster R	59	Halifax T	57	Rochdale*	56	Bradford C	56
4	1969–70	Chesterfield	64	Wrexham	61	Swansea C	60	Port Vale	59
4	1970–71	Notts Co	69	Bournemouth	60	Oldham Ath	59	York C	56
4	1971–72	Grimsby T	63	Southend U	60	Brentford	59	Scunthorpe U	57
4	1972–73	Southport	62	Hereford U	58	Cambridge U	57	Aldershot*	56
4	1973–74	Peterborough U	65	Gillingham	62	Colchester U	60	Bury	59
4	1974–75	Mansfield T	68	Shrewsbury T	62	Rotherham U	59	Chester*	57
4	1975–76	Lincoln C	74	Northampton T	68	Reading	60	Tranmere R	58
4	1976–77	Cambridge U	65	Exeter C	62	Colchester U*	59	Bradford C	59
4	1977–78	Watford	71	Southend U	60	Swansea C*	56	Brentford	56
4	1978–79	Reading	65	Grimsby T*	61	Wimbledon*	61	Barnsley	61
4	1979–80	Huddersfield T	66	Walsall	64	Newport Co	61	Portsmouth*	60
4	1980–81	Southend U	67	Lincoln C	65	Doncaster R	56	Wimbledon	55
4	1981–82	Sheffield U	96	Bradford C*	91	Wigan Ath	91	Bournemouth	88
4	1982–83	Wimbledon	98	Hull C	90	Port Vale	88	Scunthorpe U	83
4	1983–84	York C	101	Doncaster R	85	Reading*	82	Bristol C	82
4	1984–85	Chesterfield	91	Blackpool	86	Darlington	85	Bury	84
4	1985–86	Swindon T	102	Chester C	84	Mansfield T	81	Port Vale	79
4	1986–87	Northampton T	99	Preston NE	90	Southend U	80	Wolverhampton W‡	79
4	1987–88	Wolverhampton W	90	Cardiff C	85	Bolton W	78	Scunthorpe U*‡	77
4	1988–89	Rotherham U	82	Tranmere R	80	Crewe Alex	78	Scunthorpe U*‡	77
4	1989–90	Exeter C	89	Grimsby T	79	Southend U	75	Stockport Co‡	74
4	1990–91	Darlington	83	Stockport Co*	82	Hartlepool U	82	Peterborough U	80
4	1991–92[4]	Burnley	83	Rotherham U*	77	Mansfield T	77	Blackpool	76

[3] *Maximum points: 88 owing to Accrington Stanley's resignation.*
[4] *Maximum points: 126 owing to Aldershot being expelled (and only 23 teams started the competition).*

THIRD DIVISION (1992–93 to 2003–04)

MAXIMUM POINTS: ***a*** **126;** ***b*** **138.**

4	1992–93*a*	Cardiff C	83	Wrexham	80	Barnet	79	York C	75
4	1993–94*a*	Shrewsbury T	79	Chester C	74	Crewe Alex	73	Wycombe W	70
4	1994–95*a*	Carlisle U	91	Walsall	83	Chesterfield	81	Bury‡	80
4	1995–96*b*	Preston NE	86	Gillingham	83	Bury	79	Plymouth Arg*	78
4	1996–97*b*	Wigan Ath*	87	Fulham	87	Carlisle U	84	Northampton T	72
4	1997–98*b*	Notts Co	99	Macclesfield T	82	Lincoln C	72	Colchester U*	74
4	1998–99*b*	Brentford	85	Cambridge U	81	Cardiff C	80	Scunthorpe U	74
4	1999–2000*b*	Swansea C	85	Rotherham U	84	Northampton T	82	Darlington‡	79
4	2000–01*b*	Brighton & HA	92	Cardiff C	82	Chesterfield[5]	80	Hartlepool U‡	77
4	2001–02*b*	Plymouth Arg	102	Luton T	97	Mansfield T	79	Cheltenham T	78
4	2002–03*b*	Rushden & D	87	Hartlepool U	85	Wrexham	84	Bournemouth	74
4	2003–04*b*	Doncaster R	92	Hull C	88	Torquay U*	81	Huddersfield T	81

[5] *Chesterfield deducted 9pts for irregularities.*

FOOTBALL LEAGUE TWO (2004–05 to 2019–20)

MAXIMUM POINTS: 138

4	2004–05	Yeovil T	83	Scunthorpe U*	80	Swansea C	80	Southend U	80
4	2005–06	Carlisle U	86	Northampton T	83	Leyton Orient	81	Grimsby T‡	78
4	2006–07	Walsall	89	Hartlepool U	88	Swindon T	85	Milton Keynes D‡	84
4	2007–08	Milton Keynes D	97	Peterborough U	92	Hereford U	88	Stockport Co	82
4	2008–09	Brentford	85	Exeter C	79	Wycombe W*	78	Bury‡	78
4	2009–10	Notts Co	93	Bournemouth	83	Rochdale	82	Morecambe*‡	73
4	2010–11	Chesterfield	86	Bury	81	Wycombe W	80	Shrewsbury T‡	79
4	2011–12	Swindon T	93	Shrewsbury T	88	Crawley T	84	Southend U‡	83
4	2012–13	Gillingham	83	Rotherham U	79	Port Vale	78	Burton Alb	76
4	2013–14	Chesterfield	84	Scunthorpe U*	81	Rochdale	81	Fleetwood T	76
4	2014–15	Burton Alb	94	Shrewsbury T	89	Bury	85	Wycombe W*‡	84
4	2015–16	Northampton T	99	Oxford U	86	Bristol R*	85	Accrington S‡	85
4	2016–17	Portsmouth*	87	Plymouth Arg	87	Doncaster R	85	Luton T‡	77
4	2017–18	Accrington S	93	Luton T	88	Wycombe W	84	Exeter C‡	80
4	2018–19	Lincoln C	85	Bury*	79	Milton Keynes D	79	Mansfield T‡	76
4	2019–20[6]	Swindon T*	69	Crewe Alex	69	Plymouth Arg	68	Cheltenham T‡	64

[6] *Season curtailed due to COVID-19 pandemic. League positions decided on points-per-game basis.*

LEAGUE TITLE WINS

DIVISION 1 (1888–89 to 1991–92) – TIER 1
Liverpool 18, Arsenal 10, Everton 9, Aston Villa 7, Manchester U 7, Sunderland 6, Newcastle U 4, Sheffield W 4 (2 as The Wednesday), Huddersfield T 3, Leeds U 3, Wolverhampton W 3, Blackburn R 2, Burnley 2, Derby Co 2, Manchester C 2, Portsmouth 2, Preston NE 2, Tottenham H 2, Chelsea 1, Ipswich T 1, Nottingham F 1, Sheffield U 1, WBA 1.

PREMIER LEAGUE (1992–93 to 2019–20) – TIER 1
Manchester U 13, Chelsea 5, Manchester C 4, Arsenal 3, Blackburn R 1, Leicester C 1, Liverpool 1.

DIVISION 2 (1892–93 TO 1991–92) – TIER 2
Leicester C 6, Manchester C 6, Sheffield W 5 (1 as The Wednesday), Birmingham C 4 (1 as Small Heath), Derby Co 4, Liverpool 4, Ipswich T 3, Leeds U 3, Middlesbrough 3, Notts Co 3, Preston NE 3, Aston Villa 2, Bolton W 2, Burnley 2, Chelsea 2, Grimsby T 2, Manchester U 2, Norwich C 2, Nottingham F 2, Stoke C 2, Tottenham H 2, WBA 2, West Ham U 2, Wolverhampton W 2, Blackburn R 1, Blackpool 1, Bradford C 1, Brentford 1, Bristol C 1, Bury 1, Coventry C 1, Crystal Palace 1, Everton 1, Fulham 1, Huddersfield T 1, Luton T 1, Millwall 1, Newcastle U 1, Oldham Ath 1, Oxford U 1, QPR 1, Sheffield U 1, Sunderland 1.

FIRST DIVISION (1992–93 to 2003–04) – TIER 2
Sunderland 1, Bolton W 1, Charlton Ath 1, Crystal Palace 1, Fulham 1, Manchester C 1, Middlesbrough 1, Newcastle U 1, Norwich C 1, Nottingham F 1, Portsmouth 1.

FOOTBALL LEAGUE CHAMPIONSHIP (2004–05 to 2019–20) – TIER 2
Newcastle U 2, Reading 2, Sunderland 2, Wolverhampton W 2, Bournemouth 1, Burnley 1, Cardiff C 1, Leeds U 1, Leicester C 1, Norwich C 1, QPR 1, WBA 1,

DIVISION 3—SOUTH (1920–21 to 1957–58) – TIER 3
Bristol C 3, Charlton Ath 2, Ipswich T 2, Millwall 2, Notts Co 2, Plymouth Arg 2, Swansea T 2, Brentford 1, Brighton & HA 1, Bristol R 1, Cardiff C 1, Coventry C 1, Crystal Palace 1, Fulham 1, Leyton Orient 1, Luton T 1, Newport Co 1, Norwich C 1, Nottingham F 1, Portsmouth 1, QPR 1, Reading 1, Southampton 1.

DIVISION 3—NORTH (1921–22 to 1957–58) – TIER 3
Barnsley 3, Doncaster R 3, Lincoln C 3, Chesterfield 2, Grimsby T 2, Hull C 2, Port Vale 2, Stockport Co 2, Bradford C 1, Bradford PA 1, Darlington 1, Derby Co 1, Nelson 1, Oldham Ath 1, Rotherham U 1, Scunthorpe U 1, Stoke C 1, Tranmere R 1, Wolverhampton W 1.

DIVISION 3 (1958–59 to 1991–92) – TIER 3
Oxford U 2, Portsmouth 2, Aston Villa 1, Blackburn R 1, Bolton W 1, Bournemouth 1, Bradford C 1, Brentford 1, Bristol R 1, Burnley 1, Bury 1, Cambridge U 1, Carlisle U 1, Coventry C 1, Grimsby T 1, Hereford U 1, Hull C 1, Mansfield T 1, Northampton T 1, Oldham Ath 1, Orient 1, Plymouth Arg 1, Preston NE 1, QPR 1, Reading 1, Rotherham U 1, Shrewsbury T 1, Southampton 1, Sunderland 1, Watford 1, Wolverhampton W 1, Wrexham 1.

SECOND DIVISION (1992–93 to 2003–04) – TIER 3
Birmingham C 1, Brighton & HA 1, Bury 1, Fulham 1, Millwall 1, Plymouth Arg 1, Preston NE 1, Reading 1, Stoke C 1, Swindon T 1, Watford 1, Wigan Ath 1.

FOOTBALL LEAGUE ONE (2004–05 to 2019–20) – TIER 3
Luton T 2, Wigan Ath 2, Brighton & HA 1, Bristol C 1, Charlton Ath 1, Coventry C 1, Doncaster R 1, Leicester C 1, Norwich C 1, Scunthorpe U 1, Sheffield U 1, Southend U 1, Swansea C 1, Wolverhampton W 1.

DIVISION 4 (1958–59 to 1991–92) – TIER 4
Chesterfield 2, Doncaster R 2, Peterborough U 2, Brentford 1, Brighton & HA 1, Burnley 1, Cambridge U 1, Darlington 1, Exeter C 1, Gillingham 1, Grimsby T 1, Huddersfield T 1, Lincoln C 1, Luton T 1, Mansfield T 1, Millwall 1, Northampton T 1, Notts Co 1, Port Vale 1, Reading 1, Rotherham U 1, Sheffield U 1, Southend U 1, Southport 1, Stockport Co 1, Swindon T 1, Walsall 1, Watford 1, Wimbledon 1, Wolverhampton W 1, York C 1.

THIRD DIVISION (1992–93 to 2003–04) – TIER 4
Brentford 1, Brighton & HA 1, Cardiff C 1, Carlisle U 1, Doncaster R 1, Notts Co 1, Plymouth Arg 1, Preston NE 1, Rushden & D 1, Shrewsbury T 1, Swansea C 1, Wigan Ath 1.

FOOTBALL LEAGUE TWO (2004–05 to 2019–20) – TIER 4
Chesterfield 2, Swindon T 2, Accrington S 1, Brentford 1, Burton Alb 1, Carlisle U 1, Gillingham 1, Lincoln C 1, Milton Keynes D 1, Northampton T 1, Notts Co 1, Portsmouth 1, Walsall 1, Yeovil T 1.

PROMOTED AFTER PLAY-OFFS

1986–87	Charlton Ath to Division 1; Swindon T to Division 2; Aldershot to Division 3
1987–88	Middlesbrough to Division 1; Walsall to Division 2; Swansea C to Division 3
1988–89	Crystal Palace to Division 1; Port Vale to Division 2; Leyton Orient to Division 3
1989–90	Sunderland to Division 1; Notts Co to Division 2; Cambridge U to Division 3
1990–91	Notts Co to Division 1; Tranmere R to Division 2; Torquay U to Division 3
1991–92	Blackburn R to Premier League; Peterborough U to First Division; Blackpool to Second Division
1992–93	Swindon T to Premier League; WBA to First Division; York C to Second Division
1993–94	Leicester C to Premier League; Burnley to First Division; Wycombe W to Second Division
1994–95	Bolton W to Premier League; Huddersfield T to First Division; Wycombe W to Second Division
1995–96	Leicester C to Premier League; Bradford C to First Division; Plymouth Arg to Second Division
1996–97	Crystal Palace to Premier League; Crewe Alex to First Division; Northampton T to Second Division
1997–98	Charlton Ath to Premier League; Grimsby T to First Division; Colchester U to Second Division
1998–99	Watford to Premier League; Manchester C to First Division; Scunthorpe U to Second Division
1999–2000	Ipswich to Premier League; Gillingham to First Division; Peterborough U to Second Division
2000–01	Bolton W to Premier league; Walsall to First Division; Blackpool to Second Division
2001–02	Birmingham C to Premier League; Stoke C to First Division; Cheltenham T to Second Division
2002–03	Wolverhampton W to Premier League; Cardiff C to First Division; Bournemouth to Second Division
2003–04	Crystal Palace to Premier League; Brighton & HA to First Division; Huddersfield T to Second Division
2004–05	West Ham U to Premier League; Sheffield W to Championship; Southend U to Football League One
2005–06	Watford to Premier League; Barnsley to Championship; Cheltenham T to Football League One
2006–07	Derby Co to Premier League; Blackpool to Championship; Bristol R to Football League One
2007–08	Hull C to Premier League; Doncaster R to Championship; Stockport Co to Football League One
2008–09	Burnley to Premier League; Scunthorpe U to Championship; Gillingham to Football League One
2009–10	Blackpool to Premier League; Millwall to Championship; Dagenham & R to Football League One
2010–11	Swansea C to Premier League; Peterborough U to Championship; Stevenage to Football League One
2011–12	West Ham U to Premier League; Huddersfield T to Championship; Crewe Alex to Football League One
2012–13	Crystal Palace to Premier League; Yeovil T to Championship; Bradford C to Football League One
2013–14	QPR to Premier League; Rotherham U to Championship; Fleetwood T to Football League One
2014–15	Norwich C to Premier League; Preston NE to Championship; Southend U to Football League One
2015–16	Hull C to Premier League; Barnsley to Championship; AFC Wimbledon to Football League One
2016–17	Huddersfield T to Premier League; Millwall to Championship; Blackpool to Football League One
2017–18	Fulham to Premier League; Rotherham U to Championship; Coventry C to Football League One
2018–19	Aston Villa to Premier League; Charlton Ath to Championship; Tranmere R to Football League One
2019–20	Fulham to Premier League; Wycombe W to Championship; Northampton T to Football League One

RELEGATED CLUBS

1891–92 League extended. Newton Heath, Sheffield W and Nottingham F admitted. *Second Division formed* including Darwen.
1892–93 In Test matches, Sheffield U and Darwen won promotion in place of Notts Co and Accrington S.
1893–94 In Tests, Liverpool and Small Heath won promotion. Newton Heath and Darwen relegated.
1894–95 After Tests, Bury promoted, Liverpool relegated.
1895–96 After Tests, Liverpool promoted, Small Heath relegated.
1896–97 After Tests, Notts Co promoted, Burnley relegated.
1897–98 Test system abolished after success of Stoke C and Burnley. League extended. Blackburn R and Newcastle U elected to First Division. *Automatic promotion and relegation introduced.*

DIVISION 1 TO DIVISION 2 (1898–99 to 1991–92)

1898–99 Bolton W and Sheffield W
1899–1900 Burnley and Glossop NE
1900–01 Preston NE and WBA
1901–02 Small Heath and Manchester C
1902–03 Grimsby T and Bolton W
1903–04 Liverpool and WBA
1904–05 League extended. Bury and Notts Co, two bottom clubs in First Division, re-elected.
1905–06 Nottingham F and Wolverhampton W
1906–07 Derby Co and Stoke C
1907–08 Bolton W and Birmingham C
1908–09 Manchester C and Leicester Fosse
1909–10 Bolton W and Chelsea
1910–11 Bristol C and Nottingham F
1911–12 Preston NE and Bury
1912–13 Notts Co and Woolwich Arsenal
1913–14 Preston NE and Derby Co
1914–15 Tottenham H and Chelsea*
1919–20 Notts Co and Sheffield W
1920–21 Derby Co and Bradford PA
1921–22 Bradford C and Manchester U
1922–23 Stoke C and Oldham Ath
1923–24 Chelsea and Middlesbrough
1924–25 Preston NE and Nottingham F
1925–26 Manchester C and Notts Co
1926–27 Leeds U and WBA
1927–28 Tottenham H and Middlesbrough
1928–29 Bury and Cardiff C
1929–30 Burnley and Everton
1930–31 Leeds U and Manchester U
1931–32 Grimsby T and West Ham U
1932–33 Bolton W and Blackpool
1933–34 Newcastle U and Sheffield U
1934–35 Leicester C and Tottenham H
1935–36 Aston Villa and Blackburn R
1936–37 Manchester U and Sheffield W
1937–38 Manchester C and WBA
1938–39 Birmingham C and Leicester C
1946–47 Brentford and Leeds U
1947–48 Blackburn R and Grimsby T
1948–49 Preston NE and Sheffield U
1949–50 Manchester C and Birmingham C
1950–51 Sheffield W and Everton
1951–52 Huddersfield T and Fulham
1952–53 Stoke C and Derby Co
1953–54 Middlesbrough and Liverpool
1954–55 Leicester C and Sheffield W
1955–56 Huddersfield T and Sheffield U
1956–57 Charlton Ath and Cardiff C
1957–58 Sheffield W and Sunderland
1958–59 Portsmouth and Aston Villa
1959–60 Luton T and Leeds U
1960–61 Preston NE and Newcastle U
1961–62 Chelsea and Cardiff C
1962–63 Manchester C and Leyton Orient
1963–64 Bolton W and Ipswich T
1964–65 Wolverhampton W and Birmingham C
1965–66 Northampton T and Blackburn R
1966–67 Aston Villa and Blackpool
1967–68 Fulham and Sheffield U
1968–69 Leicester C and QPR
1969–70 Sunderland and Sheffield W
1970–71 Burnley and Blackpool
1971–72 Huddersfield T and Nottingham F
1972–73 Crystal Palace and WBA
1973–74 Southampton, Manchester U, Norwich C
1974–75 Luton T, Chelsea, Carlisle U
1975–76 Wolverhampton W, Burnley, Sheffield U
1976–77 Sunderland, Stoke C, Tottenham H
1977–78 West Ham U, Newcastle U, Leicester C
1978–79 QPR, Birmingham C, Chelsea
1979–80 Bristol C, Derby Co, Bolton W
1980–81 Norwich C, Leicester C, Crystal Palace
1981–82 Leeds U, Wolverhampton W, Middlesbrough
1982–83 Manchester C, Swansea C, Brighton & HA
1983–84 Birmingham C, Notts Co, Wolverhampton W
1984–85 Norwich C, Sunderland, Stoke C
1985–86 Ipswich T, Birmingham C, WBA
1986–87 Leicester C, Manchester C, Aston Villa
1987–88 Chelsea**, Portsmouth, Watford, Oxford U
1988–89 Middlesbrough, West Ham U, Newcastle U
1989–90 Sheffield W, Charlton Ath, Millwall
1990–91 Sunderland and Derby Co
1991–92 Luton T, Notts Co, West Ham U

***Relegated after play-offs.*
**Subsequently re-elected to Division 1 when League was extended after the War.*

PREMIER LEAGUE TO DIVISION 1 (1992–93 to 2003–04)

1992–93 Crystal Palace, Middlesbrough, Nottingham F
1993–94 Sheffield U, Oldham Ath, Swindon T
1994–95 Crystal Palace, Norwich C, Leicester C, Ipswich T
1995–96 Manchester C, QPR, Bolton W
1996–97 Sunderland, Middlesbrough, Nottingham F
1997–98 Bolton W, Barnsley, Crystal Palace
1998–99 Charlton Ath, Blackburn R, Nottingham F
1999–2000 Wimbledon, Sheffield W, Watford
2000–01 Manchester C, Coventry C, Bradford C
2001–02 Ipswich T, Derby Co, Leicester C
2002–03 West Ham U, WBA, Sunderland
2003–04 Leicester C, Leeds U, Wolverhampton W

PREMIER LEAGUE TO CHAMPIONSHIP (2004–05 to 2019–20)

2004–05 Crystal Palace, Norwich C, Southampton
2005–06 Birmingham C, WBA, Sunderland
2006–07 Sheffield U, Charlton Ath, Watford
2007–08 Reading, Birmingham C, Derby Co
2008–09 Newcastle U, Middlesbrough, WBA
2009–10 Burnley, Hull C, Portsmouth
2010–11 Birmingham C, Blackpool, West Ham U
2011–12 Bolton W, Blackburn R, Wolverhampton W
2012–13 Wigan Ath, Reading, QPR
2013–14 Norwich C, Fulham, Cardiff C
2014–15 Hull C, Burnley, QPR
2015–16 Newcastle U, Norwich C, Aston Villa
2016–17 Hull C, Middlesbrough, Sunderland
2017–18 Swansea C, Stoke C, WBA
2018–19 Cardiff C, Fulham, Huddersfield T
2019–20 Bournemouth, Watford, Norwich C

DIVISION 2 TO DIVISION 3 (1920–21 to 1991–92)

1920–21 Stockport Co
1921–22 Bradford PA and Bristol C
1922–23 Rotherham Co and Wolverhampton W
1923–24 Nelson and Bristol C
1924–25 Crystal Palace and Coventry C
1925–26 Stoke C and Stockport Co
1926–27 Darlington and Bradford C
1927–28 Fulham and South Shields
1928–29 Port Vale and Clapton Orient
1929–30 Hull C and Notts Co
1930–31 Reading and Cardiff C
1931–32 Barnsley and Bristol C
1932–33 Chesterfield and Charlton Ath
1933–34 Millwall and Lincoln C
1934–35 Oldham Ath and Notts Co
1935–36 Port Vale and Hull C
1936–37 Doncaster R and Bradford C
1937–38 Barnsley and Stockport Co
1938–39 Norwich C and Tranmere R
1946–47 Swansea T and Newport Co
1947–48 Doncaster R and Millwall
1948–49 Nottingham F and Lincoln C
1949–50 Plymouth Arg and Bradford PA
1950–51 Grimsby T and Chesterfield
1951–52 Coventry C and QPR
1952–53 Southampton and Barnsley
1953–54 Brentford and Oldham Ath
1954–55 Ipswich T and Derby Co
1955–56 Plymouth Arg and Hull C
1956–57 Port Vale and Bury
1957–58 Doncaster R and Notts Co
1958–59 Barnsley and Grimsby T
1959–60 Bristol C and Hull C
1960–61 Lincoln C and Portsmouth
1961–62 Brighton & HA and Bristol R
1962–63 Walsall and Luton T
1963–64 Grimsby T and Scunthorpe U
1964–65 Swindon T and Swansea T
1965–66 Middlesbrough and Leyton Orient
1966–67 Northampton T and Bury
1967–68 Plymouth Arg and Rotherham U
1968–69 Fulham and Bury
1969–70 Preston NE and Aston Villa
1970–71 Blackburn R and Bolton W
1971–72 Charlton Ath and Watford
1972–73 Huddersfield T and Brighton & HA
1973–74 Crystal Palace, Preston NE, Swindon T
1974–75 Millwall, Cardiff C, Sheffield W
1975–76 Oxford U, York C, Portsmouth
1976–77 Carlisle U, Plymouth Arg, Hereford U
1977–78 Blackpool, Mansfield T, Hull C
1978–79 Sheffield U, Millwall, Blackburn R
1979–80 Fulham, Burnley, Charlton Ath
1980–81 Preston NE, Bristol C, Bristol R
1981–82 Cardiff C, Wrexham, Orient
1982–83 Rotherham U, Burnley, Bolton W
1983–84 Derby Co, Swansea C, Cambridge U
1984–85 Notts Co, Cardiff C, Wolverhampton W
1985–86 Carlisle U, Middlesbrough, Fulham
1986–87 Sunderland**, Grimsby T, Brighton & HA
1987–88 Huddersfield T, Reading, Sheffield U**
1988–89 Shrewsbury T, Birmingham C, Walsall
1989–90 Bournemouth, Bradford C, Stoke C
1990–91 WBA and Hull C
1991–92 Plymouth Arg, Brighton & HA, Port Vale

FIRST DIVISION TO SECOND DIVISION (1992–93 to 2003–04)

1992–93 Brentford, Cambridge U, Bristol R
1993–94 Birmingham C, Oxford U, Peterborough U
1994–95 Swindon T, Burnley, Bristol C, Notts Co
1995–96 Millwall, Watford, Luton T
1996–97 Grimsby T, Oldham Ath, Southend U
1997–98 Manchester C, Stoke C, Reading
1998–99 Bury, Oxford U, Bristol C
1999–2000 Walsall, Port Vale, Swindon T
2000–01 Huddersfield T, QPR, Tranmere R
2001–02 Crewe Alex, Barnsley, Stockport Co
2002–03 Sheffield W, Brighton & HA, Grimsby T
2003–04 Walsall, Bradford C, Wimbledon

FOOTBALL LEAGUE CHAMPIONSHIP TO FOOTBALL LEAGUE ONE (2004–05 to 2019–20)

2004–05 Gillingham, Nottingham F, Rotherham U
2005–06 Crewe Alex, Millwall, Brighton & HA
2006–07 Southend U, Luton T, Leeds U
2007–08 Leicester C, Scunthorpe U, Colchester U
2008–09 Norwich C, Southampton, Charlton Ath
2009–10 Sheffield W, Plymouth Arg, Peterborough U
2010–11 Preston NE, Sheffield U, Scunthorpe U
2011–12 Portsmouth, Coventry C, Doncaster R
2012–13 Peterborough U, Wolverhampton W, Bristol C
2013–14 Doncaster R, Barnsley, Yeovil T
2014–15 Millwall, Wigan Ath, Blackpool
2015–16 Charlton Ath, Milton Keynes D, Bolton W
2016–17 Blackburn R, Wigan Ath, Rotherham U
2017–18 Barnsley, Burton Alb, Sunderland
2018–19 Rotherham U, Bolton W, Ipswich T
2019–20 Charlton Ath, Wigan Ath, Hull C

DIVISION 3 TO DIVISION 4 (1958–59 to 1991–92)

1958–59 Stockport Co, Doncaster R, Notts Co, Rochdale
1959–60 York C, Mansfield T, Wrexham, Accrington S
1960–61 Tranmere R, Bradford C, Colchester U, Chesterfield
1961–62 Torquay U, Lincoln C, Brentford, Newport Co
1962–63 Bradford PA, Brighton & HA, Carlisle U, Halifax T
1963–64 Millwall, Crewe Alex, Wrexham, Notts Co
1964–65 Luton T, Port Vale, Colchester U, Barnsley
1965–66 Southend U, Exeter C, Brentford, York C
1966–67 Swansea T, Darlington, Doncaster R, Workington
1967–68 Grimsby T, Colchester U, Scunthorpe U, Peterborough U (demoted)
1968–69 Northampton T, Hartlepool, Crewe Alex, Oldham Ath
1969–70 Bournemouth, Southport, Barrow, Stockport Co
1970–71 Reading, Bury, Doncaster R, Gillingham
1971–72 Mansfield T, Barnsley, Torquay U, Bradford C
1972–73 Rotherham U, Brentford, Swansea C, Scunthorpe U
1973–74 Cambridge U, Shrewsbury T, Southport, Rochdale
1974–75 Bournemouth, Tranmere R, Watford, Huddersfield T
1975–76 Aldershot, Colchester U, Southend U, Halifax T
1976–77 Reading, Northampton T, Grimsby T, York C
1977–78 Port Vale, Bradford C, Hereford U, Portsmouth
1978–79 Peterborough U, Walsall, Tranmere R, Lincoln C
1979–80 Bury, Southend U, Mansfield T, Wimbledon
1980–81 Sheffield U, Colchester U, Blackpool, Hull C
1981–82 Wimbledon, Swindon T, Bristol C, Chester
1982–83 Reading, Wrexham, Doncaster R, Chesterfield
1983–84 Scunthorpe U, Southend U, Port Vale, Exeter C
1984–85 Burnley, Orient, Preston NE, Cambridge U
1985–86 Lincoln C, Cardiff C, Wolverhampton W, Swansea C
1986–87 Bolton W**, Carlisle U, Darlington, Newport Co
1987–88 Rotherham U**, Grimsby T, York C, Doncaster R
1988–89 Southend U, Chesterfield, Gillingham, Aldershot
1989–90 Cardiff C, Northampton T, Blackpool, Walsall
1990–91 Crewe Alex, Rotherham U, Mansfield T
1991–92 Bury, Shrewsbury T, Torquay U, Darlington

*** Relegated after play-offs.*

SECOND DIVISION TO THIRD DIVISION (1992–93 to 2003–04)

1992–93 Preston NE, Mansfield T, Wigan Ath, Chester C
1993–94 Fulham, Exeter C, Hartlepool U, Barnet
1994–95 Cambridge U, Plymouth Arg, Cardiff C, Chester C, Leyton Orient
1995–96 Carlisle U, Swansea C, Brighton & HA, Hull C
1996–97 Peterborough U, Shrewsbury T, Rotherham U, Notts Co
1997–98 Brentford, Plymouth Arg, Carlisle U, Southend U
1998–99 York C, Northampton T, Lincoln C, Macclesfield T
1999–2000 Cardiff C, Blackpool, Scunthorpe U, Chesterfield
2000–01 Bristol R, Luton T, Swansea C, Oxford U
2001–02 Bournemouth, Bury, Wrexham, Cambridge U
2002–03 Cheltenham T, Huddersfield T, Mansfield T Northampton T
2003–04 Grimsby T, Rushden & D, Notts Co, Wycombe W

FOOTBALL LEAGUE ONE TO FOOTBALL LEAGUE TWO (2004–05 to 2019–20)

2004–05 Torquay U, Wrexham, Peterborough U, Stockport Co
2005–06 Hartlepool U, Milton Keynes D, Swindon T, Walsall
2006–07 Chesterfield, Bradford C, Rotherham U, Brentford
2007–08 Bournemouth, Gillingham, Port Vale, Luton T
2008–09 Northampton T, Crewe Alex, Cheltenham T, Hereford U
2009–10 Gillingham, Wycombe W, Southend U, Stockport Co
2010–11 Dagenham & R, Bristol R, Plymouth Arg, Swindon T
2011–12 Wycombe W, Chesterfield, Exeter C, Rochdale
2012–13 Scunthorpe U, Bury, Hartlepool U, Portsmouth
2013–14 Tranmere R, Carlisle U, Shrewsbury T, Stevenage
2014–15 Notts Co, Crawley T, Leyton Orient, Yeovil T
2015–16 Doncaster R, Blackpool, Colchester U, Crewe Alex
2016–17 Port Vale, Swindon T, Coventry C, Chesterfield
2017–18 Oldham Ath, Northampton T, Milton Keynes D, Bury
2018–19 Plymouth Arg, Walsall, Scunthorpe U, Bradford C
2019–20 Tranmere R, Southend U, Bolton W

LEAGUE STATUS FROM 1986–87

RELEGATED FROM LEAGUE

1986–87 Lincoln C
1987–88 Newport Co
1988–89 Darlington
1989–90 Colchester U
1990–91 —
1991–92 —
1992–93 Halifax T
1993–94 —
1994–95 —
1995–96 —
1996–97 Hereford U
1997–98 Doncaster R
1998–99 Scarborough
1999–2000 Chester C
2000–01 Barnet
2001–02 Halifax T
2002–03 Shrewsbury T, Exeter C
2003–04 Carlisle U, York C
2004–05 Kidderminster H, Cambridge U
2005–06 Oxford U, Rushden & D
2006–07 Boston U, Torquay U
2007–08 Mansfield T, Wrexham
2008–09 Chester C, Luton T
2009–10 Grimsby T, Darlington
2010–11 Lincoln C, Stockport Co
2011–12 Hereford U, Macclesfield T
2012–13 Barnet, Aldershot T
2013–14 Bristol R, Torquay U
2014–15 Cheltenham T, Tranmere R
2015–16 Dagenham & R, York C
2016–17 Hartlepool U, Leyton Orient
2017–18 Barnet, Chesterfield
2018–19 Notts Co, Yeovil T
2019–20 Macclesfield T

PROMOTED TO LEAGUE

1986–87 Scarborough
1987–88 Lincoln C
1988–89 Maidstone U
1989–90 Darlington
1990–91 Barnet
1991–92 Colchester U
1992–93 Wycombe W
1993–94 —
1994–95 —
1995–96 —
1996–97 Macclesfield T
1997–98 Halifax T
1998–99 Cheltenham T
1999–2000 Kidderminster H
2000–01 Rushden & D
2001–02 Boston U
2002–03 Yeovil T, Doncaster R
2003–04 Chester C, Shrewsbury T
2004–05 Barnet, Carlisle U
2005–06 Accrington S, Hereford U
2006–07 Dagenham & R, Morecambe
2007–08 Aldershot T, Exeter C
2008–09 Burton Alb, Torquay U
2009–10 Stevenage B, Oxford U
2010–11 Crawley T, AFC Wimbledon
2011–12 Fleetwood T, York C
2012–13 Mansfield T, Newport Co
2013–14 Luton T, Cambridge U
2014–15 Barnet, Bristol R
2015–16 Cheltenham T, Grimsby T
2016–17 Lincoln C, Forest Green R
2017–18 Macclesfield T, Tranmere R
2018–19 Leyton Orient, Salford C
2019–20 Barrow, Harrogate T

APPLICATIONS FOR RE-ELECTION

FOURTH DIVISION

Eleven: Hartlepool U.
Seven: Crewe Alex.
Six: Barrow (lost League place to Hereford U 1972), Halifax T, Rochdale, Southport (lost League place to Wigan Ath 1978), York C.
Five: Chester C, Darlington, Lincoln C, Stockport Co, Workington (lost League place to Wimbledon 1977).
Four: Bradford PA (lost League place to Cambridge U 1970), Newport Co, Northampton T.
Three: Doncaster R, Hereford U.
Two: Bradford C, Exeter C, Oldham Ath, Scunthorpe U, Torquay U.
One: Aldershot, Colchester U, Gateshead (lost League place to Peterborough U 1960), Grimsby T, Swansea C, Tranmere R, Wrexham, Blackpool, Cambridge U, Preston NE.

Accrington S resigned and Oxford U were elected 1962.
Port Vale were forced to re-apply following expulsion in 1968.
Aldershot expelled March 1992. Maidstone U resigned August 1992.

THIRD DIVISIONS NORTH & SOUTH

Seven: Walsall.
Six: Exeter C, Halifax T, Newport Co.
Five: Accrington S, Barrow, Gillingham, New Brighton, Southport.
Four: Rochdale, Norwich C.
Three: Crystal Palace, Crewe Alex, Darlington, Hartlepool U, Merthyr T, Swindon T.
Two: Aberdare Ath, Aldershot, Ashington, Bournemouth, Brentford, Chester, Colchester U, Durham C, Millwall, Nelson, QPR, Rotherham U, Southend U, Tranmere R, Watford, Workington.
One: Bradford C, Bradford PA, Brighton & HA, Bristol R, Cardiff C, Carlisle U, Charlton Ath, Gateshead, Grimsby T, Mansfield T, Shrewsbury T, Torquay U, York C.

LEAGUE ATTENDANCES SINCE 1946–47

Season	*Matches*	*Total*	*Div. 1*	*Div. 2*	*Div. 3 (S)*	*Div. 3 (N)*
1946–47	1848	35,604,606	15,005,316	11,071,572	5,664,004	3,863,714
1947–48	1848	40,259,130	16,732,341	12,286,350	6,653,610	4,586,829
1948–49	1848	41,271,414	17,914,667	11,353,237	6,998,429	5,005,081
1949–50	1848	40,517,865	17,278,625	11,694,158	7,104,155	4,440,927
1950–51	2028	39,584,967	16,679,454	10,780,580	7,367,884	4,757,109
1951–52	2028	39,015,866	16,110,322	11,066,189	6,958,927	4,880,428
1952–53	2028	37,149,966	16,050,278	9,686,654	6,704,299	4,708,735
1953–54	2028	36,174,590	16,154,915	9,510,053	6,311,508	4,198,114
1954–55	2028	34,133,103	15,087,221	8,988,794	5,996,017	4,051,071
1955–56	2028	33,150,809	14,108,961	9,080,002	5,692,479	4,269,367
1956–57	2028	32,744,405	13,803,037	8,718,162	5,622,189	4,601,017
1957–58	2028	33,562,208	14,468,652	8,663,712	6,097,183	4,332,661
		Total	*Div. 1*	*Div. 2*	*Div. 3*	*Div. 4*
1958–59	2028	33,610,985	14,727,691	8,641,997	5,946,600	4,276,697
1959–60	2028	32,538,611	14,391,227	8,399,627	5,739,707	4,008,050
1960–61	2028	28,619,754	12,926,948	7,033,936	4,784,256	3,874,614
1961–62	2015	27,979,902	12,061,194	7,453,089	5,199,106	3,266,513
1962–63	2028	28,885,852	12,490,239	7,792,770	5,341,362	3,261,481
1963–64	2028	28,535,022	12,486,626	7,594,158	5,419,157	3,035,081
1964–65	2028	27,641,168	12,708,752	6,984,104	4,436,245	3,512,067
1965–66	2028	27,206,980	12,480,644	6,914,757	4,779,150	3,032,429
1966–67	2028	28,902,596	14,242,957	7,253,819	4,421,172	2,984,648
1967–68	2028	30,107,298	15,289,410	7,450,410	4,013,087	3,354,391
1968–69	2028	29,382,172	14,584,851	7,382,390	4,339,656	3,075,275
1969–70	2028	29,600,972	14,868,754	7,581,728	4,223,761	2,926,729
1970–71	2028	28,194,146	13,954,337	7,098,265	4,377,213	2,764,331
1971–72	2028	28,700,729	14,484,603	6,769,308	4,697,392	2,749,426
1972–73	2028	25,448,642	13,998,154	5,631,730	3,737,252	2,081,506
1973–74	2027	24,982,203	13,070,991	6,326,108	3,421,624	2,163,480
1974–75	2028	25,577,977	12,613,178	6,955,970	4,086,145	1,992,684
1975–76	2028	24,896,053	13,089,861	5,798,405	3,948,449	2,059,338
1976–77	2028	26,182,800	13,647,585	6,250,597	4,152,218	2,132,400
1977–78	2028	25,392,872	13,255,677	6,474,763	3,332,042	2,330,390
1978–79	2028	24,540,627	12,704,549	6,153,223	3,374,558	2,308,297
1979–80	2028	24,623,975	12,163,002	6,112,025	3,999,328	2,349,620
1980–81	2028	21,907,569	11,392,894	5,175,442	3,637,854	1,701,379
1981–82	2028	20,006,961	10,420,793	4,750,463	2,836,915	1,998,790
1982–83	2028	18,766,158	9,295,613	4,974,937	2,943,568	1,552,040
1983–84	2028	18,358,631	8,711,448	5,359,757	2,729,942	1,557,484
1984–85	2028	17,849,835	9,761,404	4,030,823	2,667,008	1,390,600
1985–86	2028	16,488,577	9,037,854	3,551,968	2,490,481	1,408,274
1986–87	2028	17,379,218	9,144,676	4,168,131	2,350,970	1,715,441
1987–88	2030	17,959,732	8,094,571	5,341,599	2,751,275	1,772,287
1988–89	2036	18,464,192	7,809,993	5,887,805	3,035,327	1,791,067
1989–90	2036	19,445,442	7,883,039	6,867,674	2,803,551	1,891,178
1990–91	2036	19,508,202	8,618,709	6,285,068	2,835,759	1,768,666
1991–92	2064*	20,487,273	9,989,160	5,809,787	2,993,352	1,694,974
		Total	*Premier*	*Div. 1*	*Div. 2*	*Div. 3*
1992–93	2028	20,657,327	9,759,809	5,874,017	3,483,073	1,540,428
1993–94	2028	21,683,381	10,644,551	6,487,104	2,972,702	1,579,024
1994–95	2028	21,856,020	11,213,168	6,044,293	3,037,752	1,560,807
1995–96	2036	21,844,416	10,469,107	6,566,349	2,843,652	1,965,308
1996–97	2036	22,783,163	10,804,762	6,931,539	3,195,223	1,851,639
1997–98	2036	24,692,608	11,092,106	8,330,018	3,503,264	1,767,220
1998–99	2036	25,435,542	11,620,326	7,543,369	4,169,697	2,102,150
1999–2000	2036	25,341,090	11,668,497	7,810,208	3,700,433	2,161,952
2000–01	2036	26,030,167	12,472,094	7,909,512	3,488,166	2,160,395
2001–02	2036	27,756,977	13,043,118	8,352,128	3,963,153	2,398,578
2002–03	2036	28,343,386	13,468,965	8,521,017	3,892,469	2,460,935
2003–04	2036	29,197,510	13,303,136	8,772,780	4,146,495	2,975,099
		Total	*Premier*	*Championship*	*League One*	*League Two*
2004–05	2036	29,245,870	12,878,791	9,612,761	4,270,674	2,483,644
2005–06	2036	29,089,084	12,871,643	9,719,204	4,183,011	2,315,226
2006–07	2036	29,541,949	13,058,115	10,057,813	4,135,599	2,290,422
2007–08	2036	29,914,212	13,708,875	9,397,036	4,412,023	2,396,278
2008–09	2036	29,881,966	13,527,815	9,877,552	4,171,834	2,304,765
2009–10	2036	30,057,892	12,977,251	9,909,882	5,043,099	2,127,660
2010–11	2036	29,459,105	13,406,990	9,595,236	4,150,547	2,306,332
2011–12	2036	29,454,401	13,148,465	9,784,100	4,091,897	2,429,939
2012–13	2036	29,225,443	13,653,958	9,662,232	3,485,290	2,423,963
2013–14	2036	29,629,309	13,930,810	9,168,922	4,126,701	2,402,876
2014–15	2036	30,052,575	13,746,753	9,838,940	3,884,414	2,582,468
2015–16	2036	30,207,923	13,852,291	9,705,865	3,955,385	2,694,382
2016–17	2036	31,727,248	13,612,316	11,106,918	4,385,178	2,622,836
2017–18	2036	32,656,695	14,560,349	11,313,826	4,303,525	2,478,995
2018–19	2035	32,911,714	14,515,181	11,119,775	4,811,797	2,464,961
2019–20	1572†	25,151,300	11,323,981	8,265,475	3,501,237	2,060,607

**Figures include matches played by Aldershot. †Premier League and Championship games behind closed doors from 17 June 2020. League 1 and 2 curtailed from 9 June 2020.*
Football League official total for their three divisions in 2001–02 was 14,716,162.

ENGLISH LEAGUE ATTENDANCES 2019–20

PREMIER LEAGUE ATTENDANCES

	Average Gate			*Season 2019–20*	
	2018–19	*2019–20*	*+/–%*	*Highest*	*Lowest*
Arsenal	59,899	60,279	+0.64	60,383	60,031
Aston Villa	36,027	41,661	+15.64	42,010	40,867
Bournemouth	10,532	10,510	–0.20	10,832	10,020
Brighton & HA	30,426	30,358	–0.22	30,640	29,398
Burnley	20,534	20,260	–1.34	21,924	18,227
Chelsea	40,441	40,563	+0.30	40,694	40,243
Crystal Palace	25,455	25,060	–1.55	25,486	23,497
Everton	39,043	39,150	+0.27	39,374	38,772
Leicester C	31,851	32,061	+0.66	32,211	31,613
Liverpool	52,983	53,143	+0.30	53,333	51,430
Manchester C	54,130	54,361	+0.43	54,512	53,922
Manchester U	74,498	72,726	–2.38	73,737	63,328
Newcastle U	51,121	48,251	–5.61	52,219	42,303
Norwich C	26,014	27,025	+3.89	27,110	26,781
Sheffield U	26,177	30,869	+17.92	32,024	30,079
Southampton	30,328	29,675	–2.15	31,712	26,302
Tottenham H	54,216	59,384	+9.53	61,104	56,308
Watford	20,016	20,837	+4.10	21,634	19,711
West Ham U	58,336	59,896	+2.67	59,962	59,519
Wolverhampton W	31,030	31,360	+1.06	31,746	30,522

TOTAL ATTENDANCES: 11,323,981 (288 games)
Average 39,319 (+2.94%)
HIGHEST: 73,737 Manchester U v Liverpool
LOWEST: 10,020 Bournemouth v Burnley
HIGHEST AVERAGE: 72,726 Manchester U
LOWEST AVERAGE: 10,510 Bournemouth

SKY BET ENGLISH FOOTBALL LEAGUE CHAMPIONSHIP ATTENDANCES

	Average Gate			*Season 2019–20*	
	2018–19	*2019–20*	*+/–%*	*Highest*	*Lowest*
Barnsley	12,527	14,061	+12.25	17,789	11,510
Birmingham C	22,483	20,412	–9.21	22,120	18,161
Blackburn R	14,550	13,873	–4.65	19,963	11,401
Brentford	10,257	11,699	+14.06	12,324	10,417
Bristol C	21,080	21,810	+3.46	24,022	19,742
Cardiff C	31,408	22,822	–27.34	28,529	20,884
Charlton Ath	11,827	18,017	+52.33	25,363	13,488
Derby Co	26,850	26,727	–0.46	28,454	24,697
Fulham	24,371	18,204	–25.31	19,020	16,856
Huddersfield T	23,340	21,748	–6.82	23,805	19,703
Hull C	12,165	11,553	–5.03	16,326	9,757
Leeds U	34,033	35,321	+3.78	36,514	34,006
Luton T	9,516	10,048	+5.59	10,070	10,001
Middlesbrough	23,217	19,933	–14.15	25,313	17,961
Millwall	13,636	13,734	+0.72	17,109	10,021
Nottingham F	28,144	27,724	–1.49	29,455	24,577
Preston NE	14,160	13,579	–4.10	19,165	10,093
QPR	13,866	13,721	–1.04	16,186	11,669
Reading	14,991	14,407	–3.89	16,918	10,088
Sheffield W	24,429	23,733	–2.85	28,028	21,370
Stoke C	25,200	22,828	–9.41	25,436	20,216
Swansea C	18,737	16,151	–13.80	20,270	14,162
WBA	24,148	24,053	–0.39	25,618	21,803
Wigan Ath	11,663	11,347	–2.71	23,792	8,965

TOTAL ATTENDANCES: 8,265,475 (444 games)
Average 18,616 (–7.76%)
HIGHEST: 36,514 Leeds U v Huddersfield T
LOWEST: 8,965 Wigan Ath v Reading
HIGHEST AVERAGE: 35,321 Leeds U
LOWEST AVERAGE: 10,048 Luton T

Premier League and Football League attendance averages and highest crowd figures for 2019–20 are unofficial.
Premier League and Championship games behind closed doors from 17 June 2020. League 1 and 2 curtailed from 9 June 2020.

SKY BET ENGLISH FOOTBALL LEAGUE ONE ATTENDANCES

	Average Gate			*Season 2019–20*	
	2018–19	*2019–20*	*+/–%*	*Highest*	*Lowest*
Accrington S	2,764	2,862	+3.56	5,034	1,816
AFC Wimbledon	4,297	4,383	+2.00	4,804	3,674
Blackpool	5,517	8,770	+58.97	11,359	6,816
Bolton W	14,636	11,511	–21.35	14,003	5,454
Bristol R	8,320	7,348	–11.68	9,096	6,370
Burton Alb	3,351	2,986	–10.89	4,565	1,880
Coventry C	12,363	6,677	–45.99	10,055	4,672
Doncaster R	8,098	8,252	+1.90	12,432	6,740
Fleetwood T	3,165	3,130	–1.09	4,884	2,319
Gillingham	5,050	5,148	+1.95	7,214	4,212
Ipswich T	17,765	19,549	+10.04	24,051	15,678
Lincoln C	9,006	8,986	–0.22	10,264	7,783
Milton Keynes D	8,224	9,246	+12.43	13,621	6,393
Oxford U	7,315	7,636	+4.39	10,525	5,622
Peterborough U	7,365	7,371	+0.08	10,071	3,851
Portsmouth	18,223	17,804	–2.30	18,801	16,355
Rochdale	3,550	3,632	+2.33	5,560	2,286
Rotherham U	9,880	8,906	–9.86	10,706	7,883
Shrewsbury T	6,407	6,059	–5.44	8,117	4,699
Southend U	6,932	6,192	–10.67	8,632	5,066
Sunderland	32,157	30,118	–6.34	33,821	26,538
Tranmere R	6,552	6,777	+3.43	8,568	5,026
Wycombe W	5,329	5,521	+3.60	8,523	3,286

TOTAL ATTENDANCES: 3,501,237 (400 games)
Average 8,753 (+0.41%)
HIGHEST: 33,821 Sunderland v Bolton W
LOWEST: 1,816 Accrington S v Peterborough U
HIGHEST AVERAGE: 30,118 Sunderland
LOWEST AVERAGE: 2,862 Accrington S

SKY BET ENGLISH FOOTBALL LEAGUE TWO ATTENDANCES

	Average Gate			*Season 2019–20*	
	2018–19	*2019–20*	*+/–%*	*Highest*	*Lowest*
Bradford C	16,130	14,309	–11.29	17,668	12,731
Cambridge U	4,338	4,178	–3.69	5,408	3,444
Carlisle U	4,712	4,140	–12.14	6,039	2,822
Cheltenham T	3,134	3,203	+2.19	5,788	1,222
Colchester U	3,522	3,634	+3.20	5,519	2,954
Crawley T	2,290	2,232	–2.56	2,636	1,944
Crewe Alex	3,762	4,580	+21.75	7,705	3,249
Exeter C	4,418	4,847	+9.71	7,924	3,527
Forest Green R	2,701	2,542	–5.88	4,216	1,514
Grimsby T	4,430	4,599	+3.81	7,385	2,508
Leyton Orient	5,445	5,504	+1.09	7,042	3,587
Macclesfield T	2,389	1,998	–16.37	3,467	1,389
Mansfield T	4,897	4,419	–9.78	5,848	3,567
Morecambe	2,033	2,264	+11.36	3,899	1,517
Newport Co	3,409	3,867	+13.43	5,048	3,048
Northampton T	5,100	5,101	+0.01	6,260	4,038
Oldham Ath	4,364	3,466	–20.59	5,278	2,438
Plymouth Arg	9,852	10,338	+4.93	15,062	8,446
Port Vale	4,431	4,862	+9.74	5,931	3,347
Salford C	2,489	2,997	+20.39	3,770	2,297
Scunthorpe U	4,227	3,546	–16.10	6,855	2,746
Stevenage	2,715	2,906	+7.05	4,357	2,156
Swindon T	6,390	7,788	+21.87	13,095	5,524
Walsall	4,927	4,664	–5.35	6,301	3,554

TOTAL ATTENDANCES: 2,060,607 (440 games)
Average 4,683 (+4.87%)
HIGHEST: 17,668 Bradford C v Grimsby T
LOWEST: 1,222 Cheltenham T v Plymouth Arg
HIGHEST AVERAGE: 14,309 Bradford C
LOWEST AVERAGE: 1,998 Macclesfield T

LEAGUE CUP FINALS 1961–2020

*Played as a two-leg final until 1966. All subsequent finals played at Wembley except between 2001 and 2007 (inclusive) which were played at Millennium Stadium, Cardiff. *After extra time.*

FOOTBALL LEAGUE CUP

1961	Rotherham U v Aston Villa	2-0
	Aston Villa v Rotherham U	3-0*
	Aston Villa won 3-2 on aggregate.	
1962	Rochdale v Norwich C	0-3
	Norwich C v Rochdale	1-0
	Norwich C won 4-0 on aggregate.	
1963	Birmingham C v Aston Villa	3-1
	Aston Villa v Birmingham C	0-0
	Birmingham C won 3-1 on aggregate.	
1964	Stoke C v Leicester C	1-1
	Leicester C v Stoke C	3-2
	Leicester C won 4-3 on aggregate.	
1965	Chelsea v Leicester C	3-2
	Leicester C v Chelsea	0-0
	Chelsea won 3-2 on aggregate.	
1966	West Ham U v WBA	2-1
	WBA v West Ham U	4-1
	WBA won 5-3 on aggregate.	
1967	QPR v WBA	3-2
1968	Leeds U v Arsenal	1-0
1969	Swindon T v Arsenal	3-1*
1970	Manchester C v WBA	2-1*
1971	Tottenham H v Aston Villa	2-0
1972	Stoke C v Chelsea	2-1
1973	Tottenham H v Norwich C	1-0
1974	Wolverhampton W v Manchester C	2-1
1975	Aston Villa v Norwich C	1-0
1976	Manchester C v Newcastle U	2-1
1977	Aston Villa v Everton	0-0
Replay	Aston Villa v Everton	1-1*
	(at Hillsborough)	
Replay	Aston Villa v Everton	3-2*
	(at Old Trafford)	
1978	Nottingham F v Liverpool	0-0*
Replay	Nottingham F v Liverpool	1-0
	(at Old Trafford)	
1979	Nottingham F v Southampton	3-2
1980	Wolverhampton W v Nottingham F	1-0
1981	Liverpool v West Ham U	1-1*
Replay	Liverpool v West Ham U	2-1
	(at Villa Park)	

MILK CUP

1982	Liverpool v Tottenham H	3-1*
1983	Liverpool v Manchester U	2-1*
1984	Liverpool v Everton	0-0*
Replay	Liverpool v Everton	1-0
	(at Maine Road)	
1985	Norwich C v Sunderland	1-0
1986	Oxford U v QPR	3-0

LITTLEWOODS CUP

1987	Arsenal v Liverpool	2-1
1988	Luton T v Arsenal	3-2
1989	Nottingham F v Luton T	3-1
1990	Nottingham F v Oldham Ath	1-0

RUMBELOWS LEAGUE CUP

1991	Sheffield W v Manchester U	1-0
1992	Manchester U v Nottingham F	1-0

COCA-COLA CUP

1993	Arsenal v Sheffield W	2-1
1994	Aston Villa v Manchester U	3-1
1995	Liverpool v Bolton W	2-1
1996	Aston Villa v Leeds U	3-0
1997	Leicester C v Middlesbrough	1-1*
Replay	Leicester C v Middlesbrough	1-0*
	(at Hillsborough)	
1998	Chelsea v Middlesbrough	2-0*

WORTHINGTON CUP

1999	Tottenham H v Leicester C	1-0
2000	Leicester C v Tranmere R	2-1
2001	Liverpool v Birmingham C	1-1*
	Liverpool won 5-4 on penalties.	
2002	Blackburn R v Tottenham H	2-1
2003	Liverpool v Manchester U	2-0

CARLING CUP

2004	Middlesbrough v Bolton W	2-1
2005	Chelsea v Liverpool	3-2*
2006	Manchester U v Wigan Ath	4-0
2007	Chelsea v Arsenal	2-1
2008	Tottenham H v Chelsea	2-1*
2009	Manchester U v Tottenham H	0-0*
	Manchester U won 4-1 on penalties.	
2010	Manchester U v Aston Villa	2-1
2011	Birmingham C v Arsenal	2-1
2012	Liverpool v Cardiff C	2-2*
	Liverpool won 3-2 on penalties.	

CAPITAL ONE CUP

2013	Swansea C v Bradford C	5-0
2014	Manchester C v Sunderland	3-1
2015	Chelsea v Tottenham H	2-0
2016	Manchester C v Liverpool	1-1*
	Manchester C won 3-1 on penalties.	

EFL CUP

2017	Manchester U v Southampton	3-2

CARABAO CUP

2018	Manchester C v Arsenal	3-0
2019	Manchester C v Chelsea	0-0*
	Manchester C won 4-3 on penalties.	
2020	Manchester C v Aston Villa	2-1

LEAGUE CUP WINS

Liverpool 8, Manchester C 7, Aston Villa 5, Chelsea 5, Manchester U 5, Nottingham F 4, Tottenham H 4, Leicester C 3, Arsenal 2, Birmingham C 2, Norwich C 2, Wolverhampton W 2, Blackburn R 1, Leeds U 1, Luton T 1, Middlesbrough 1, Oxford U 1, QPR 1, Sheffield W 1, Stoke C 1, Swansea C 1, Swindon T 1, WBA 1.

APPEARANCES IN FINALS

Liverpool 12, Manchester U 9, Aston Villa 9, Arsenal 8, Chelsea 8, Manchester C 8, Tottenham H 8, Nottingham F 6, Leicester C 5, Norwich C 4, Birmingham C 3, Middlesbrough 3, WBA 3, Bolton W 2, Everton 2, Leeds U 2, Luton T 2, QPR 2, Sheffield W 2, Southampton 2, Stoke C 2, Sunderland 2, West Ham U 2, Wolverhampton W 2, Blackburn R 1, Bradford C 1, Cardiff C 1, Newcastle U 1, Oldham Ath 1, Oxford U 1, Rochdale 1, Rotherham U 1, Swansea C 1, Swindon T 1, Tranmere R 1, Wigan Ath 1.

APPEARANCES IN SEMI-FINALS

Liverpool 17, Arsenal 15, Aston Villa 15, Manchester U 15, Tottenham H 15, Chelsea 14, Manchester C 12, West Ham U 9, Blackburn R 6, Leicester C 6, Nottingham F 6, Birmingham C 5, Everton 5, Leeds U 5, Middlesbrough 5, Norwich C 5, Bolton W 4, Burnley 4, Crystal Palace 4, Ipswich T 4, Sheffield W 4, Sunderland 4, WBA 4, Bristol C 3, QPR 3, Southampton 3, Stoke C 3, Swindon T 3, Wolverhampton W 3, Cardiff C 2, Coventry C 2, Derby Co 2, Luton T 2, Oxford U 2, Plymouth Arg 2, Sheffield U 2, Tranmere R 2, Watford 2, Wimbledon 2, Blackpool 1, Bradford C 1, Burton Alb 1, Bury 1, Carlisle U 1, Chester C 1, Huddersfield T 1, Hull C 1, Newcastle U 1, Oldham Ath 1, Peterborough U 1, Rochdale 1, Rotherham U 1, Shrewsbury T 1, Stockport Co 1, Swansea C 1, Walsall 1, Wigan Ath 1, Wycombe W 1.

CARABAO CUP 2019–20

■ *Denotes player sent off.*

FIRST ROUND

Tuesday, 6 August 2019

Portsmouth (2) 3 *(Harrison 30, 54, Close 39)*
Birmingham C (0) 0 9913

Portsmouth: (433) MacGillivray; Walkes, Downing (Raggett 85), Burgess, Brown (Haunstrup 77); Cannon, Naylor, Close; Harness, Harrison (Pitman 78), Curtis.
Birmingham C: (3421) Stockdale; Harding, Bajrami, Clarke-Salter; Dacres-Cogley, Gardner C, Medina, Seddon; Bellingham (Boyd-Munce 81), Lakin; Crowley (Bailey 55).
Referee: Neil Hair.

Tuesday, 13 August 2019

Accrington S (0) 1 *(Bishop 61 (pen))*
Sunderland (1) 3 *(McNulty 17, McGeady 79, Wyke 90)* 2343

Accrington S: (442) Evtimov; Johnson, Sykes, Hughes, Maguire; Clark, Barclay (Carvalho 90), Finley, McConville; Baker-Richardson (Pritchard 78), Bishop.
Sunderland: (442) Burge; O'Nien, Ozturk, Willis, McLaughlin C; Maguire (Wyke 77), Power (Dobson 86), Leadbitter, Gooch; Grigg (McGeady 69), McNulty.
Referee: Darren Drysdale.

AFC Wimbledon (1) 2 *(Wagstaff 8, O'Neill 90)*
Milton Keynes D (1) 2 *(McGrandles 16, Kasumu 50)* 2191

AFC Wimbledon: (4132) Tzanev; O'Neill, Kalambayi, Thomas, Guinness-Walker (Osew 62); Hartigan; Connolly (McDonald 62), Wagstaff, Reilly; Appiah (Folivi 73), Pigott.
Milton Keynes D: (3412) Nicholls; Poole, Martin, Cargill; Brittain, Kasumu, McGrandles, Lewington; Harley (Gilbey 64); Bowery, Agard (Asonganyi 69).
Milton Keynes D won 4-2 on penalties.
Referee: Craig Hicks.

Barnsley (0) 0
Carlisle U (1) 3 *(McKirdy 24, Bridge 58 (pen), Thomas 64)* 5208

Barnsley: (433) Collins; Williams J, Halme, Andersen, Pinillos; Wilks (Thomas 61), McGeehan, Styles (Miller 74); Chaplin (Bahre 60), Woodrow, Thiam.
Carlisle U: (433) Collin; Elliot, Webster, Knight-Percival, Iredale; Bridge, Jones M, Scougall; Thomas (Hope 76), Loft (Hayden 81), McKirdy (Olomola 65).
Referee: Ben Toner.

Blackburn R (0) 3 *(Dack 70, Rothwell 90, Downing 90)*
Oldham Ath (1) 2 *(Nepomuceno 14, Maouche 80)* 5215

Blackburn R: (4231) Leutwiler; Nyambe, Platt (Chapman 60), Grayson, Cunningham; Smallwood (Rothwell 53), Evans (Dack 63); Brereton, Buckley, Downing; Graham.
Oldham Ath: (451) Woods; Mills, Sefil, Iacovitti, Smith-Brown; Fage (Hamer 87), Sylla, Missilou, Maouche, Nepomuceno (Branger 66); Azankpo (Wilson 80).
Referee: Tom Nield.

Blackpool (1) 2 *(Turton 31, Gnanduillet 90 (pen))*
Macclesfield T (1) 2 *(Bushiri 39 (og), Gomis 65)* 3715

Blackpool: (343) Mafoumbi; Bushiri, Edwards, Anderton; Feeney, Spearing (Pritchard 76), Thompson, Turton (Nottingham 86); Hardie (Delfouneso 62), Gnanduillet, KaiKai.
Macclesfield T: (3412) Evans; O'Keeffe (Archibald 46), Kelleher, Vassell; Horsfall, Kirby, Harris, Clarke; Osadebe; Stephens (Gomis 62), Blyth (Welch-Hayes 81).
Macclesfield T won 4-2 on penalties.
Referee: Martin Coy.

Bradford C (0) 0
Preston NE (2) 4 *(Green 13, Barkhuizen 19, 53, Harrop 71)* 3456

Bradford C: (4141) Hornby; French, O'Connor A, O'Connor P, Longridge; Akpan; Scannell (Patrick 73), Devine (Colville 73), Anderson, Wood; Doyle.
Preston NE: (4141) Ripley; Browne, Clarke, Storey, Rafferty; Ledson; Barkhuizen, Potts (Walker 80), Bayliss, Green (Ginnelly 72); Stockley (Harrop 71).
Referee: Matthew Donohue.

Brentford (0) 1 *(Forss 69)*
Cambridge U (1) 1 *(Richards 3)* 5215

Brentford: (4231) Daniels; Clarke (Henry 33), Dalsgaard, Racic, Thompson; Yearwood (Jensen 55), Marcondes; Mbeumo, Valencia, Zamburek (Watkins 64); Forss.
Cambridge U: (352) Burton; Darling, John, Taft; Davies, Lambe, Lewis, Maris (Hannant 72), Dunk; Richards (Knibbs 60), Dallas (Jones 73).
Cambridge U won 5-4 on penalties.
Referee: Lee Swabey.

Bristol R (1) 3 *(Smith 38, 49, Clarke-Harris 67)*
Cheltenham T (0) 0 2909

Bristol R: (4312) Jaakkola; Hare, Kilgour, Davies, Leahy; Clarke O (Rodman 76), Ogogo, Bennett; Sercombe; Clarke-Harris (Adeboyejo 68), Smith (Nichols 71).
Cheltenham T: (352) Flinders; Raglan, Tozer, Greaves; Long, Clements, Thomas (Lloyd 65), Doyle-Hayes, Debayo (Bowry 77); Addai (Campbell 46), Varney.
Referee: Graham Salisbury.

Charlton Ath (0) 0
Forest Green R (0) 0 2693

Charlton Ath: (41212) Amos; Sarpong-Wiredu, Oshilaja, Sarr, Doughty; Forster-Caskey; Lapslie, Field (Ocran 78); Morgan; Bonne, Aneke (Quitirna 62).
Forest Green R: (343) Wollacott; Godwin-Malife, Kitching, McGinley; Bernard, Adams, Morton, Mills J; Mondal, Stevens (McCoulsky 69), Allen (Grubb 64).
Forest Green R won 5-3 on penalties.
Referee: John Busby.

Colchester U (0) 3 *(Eastman 77, Comley 90, Senior 90)*
Swindon T (0) 0 1595

Colchester U: (4231) Gerken; Jackson, Eastman, Prosser, Bramall■; Lapslie, Stevenson; Gambin (Senior 72), Brown, Nouble; Norris (Comley 84).
Swindon T: (4231) McCormick; Hunt, Ballard, Broadbent (McGlashan 82), Fryers; May (Lyden 76), Doughty; Twine (Isgrove 66), Anderson, Woolery; Yates■.
Referee: Charles Breakspear.

Coventry C (3) 4 *(Hiwula 2, 28, Godden 23, Bakayoko 88)*
Exeter C (0) 1 *(Sweeney 81)* 1155

Coventry C: (433) Wilson; Dabo, Hyam, Rose, McCallum; Westbrooke, Kelly, Shipley (Eccles 75); Jobello (Kastaneer 81), Godden (Bakayoko 63), Hiwula.
Exeter C: (442) Maxted; Sweeney, Warren, Moxey (Martin A 57), Sparkes; Jay, Collins (Chrisene 88), Tillson, Martin L; Fisher (Woodman 57), Seymour.
Referee: Scott Oldham.

Gillingham (1) 2 *(Hanlan 26 (pen), Ndjoli 90 (pen))*
Newport Co (0) 2 *(Abrahams 84, Amond 90 (pen))* 1996

Gillingham: (433) Bonham; Hodson, Ehmer, Ogilvie, Fuller; Charles-Cook (Woods 90), Byrne, Jones; Ndjoli■, Hanlan (Mandron 85), Jakubiak (Marshall 70).
Newport Co: (3412) Townsend; Howkins, O'Brien (Demetriou 90), Stojsavljevic (Amond 29); Leadbitter, Bennett (Sheehan 80), Maloney, Nurse; Dolan; Abrahams, Whitely.
Newport Co won 4-1 on penalties.
Referee: Trevor Kettle.

Grimsby T (1) 1 *(Cook 40)*
Doncaster R (0) 0 2470

Grimsby T: (433) McKeown; Hendrie, Pollock, Davis, Gibson (Hessenthaler 65); Cook, Hewitt, Ring (Green 79); Vernam, Ogbu, Wright (Cardwell 90).
Doncaster R: (4231) Dieng; Halliday, Anderson T, John, James; Blair (May 79), Whiteman (Sheaf 46); Kiwomya (Taylor J 59), Crawford, Sadlier; Ennis.
Referee: John Brooks.

Huddersfield T (0) 0

Lincoln C (0) 1 *(Anderson 55)* 6908

Huddersfield T: (433) Schofield; Bockhorn, Stankovic, Edmonds-Green, Brown J; Bacuna, Chalobah, Brown R (Mounie 77); Kachunga, Koroma (van La Parra 73), Mbenza.
Lincoln C: (4231) Smith; Lewis, Bolger, Bostwick (Eardley 61), Toffolo; Chapman, Morrell (O'Connor 48); Anderson, Payne, Andrade; Akinde (Walker 71).
Referee: Peter Wright.

Luton T (2) 3 *(Jones 8, Lee 17 (pen), Shinnie 55)*

Ipswich T (0) 1 *(Dobra 74)* 5435

Luton T: (3412) Shea; Bree, Jones, Galloway; Bolton (Neufville 46), Shinnie, Berry, LuaLua (Cranie 46); Brown (McManaman 66); Cornick, Lee.
Ipswich T: (4411) Norris; Emmanuel, Chambers, Wilson, Clements; Edwards (Rowe 61), Dozzell, Huws (Downes 66), Dobra; Judge (Jackson 77); Roberts.
Referee: Brett Huxtable.

Mansfield T (0) 2 *(Pearce 57, Sterling-James 68)*

Morecambe (1) 2 *(Old 18, 59)* 1884

Mansfield T: (3412) Logan; White, Pearce, Sweeney; Gordon, Donohue (Tomlinson 46), Smith, Benning; Khan; Cook (Rose 66), Hamilton (Sterling-James 66).
Morecambe: (3412) Halstead; Sutton (Buxton 76), Lavelle, Old; Tanner, Brewitt, Cranston, Conlan■; Alessandra (Kenyon 46); Miller, Oates (O'Sullivan 76).
Morecambe won 6-5 on penalties.
Referee: Robert Lewis.

Middlesbrough (0) 2 *(Fletcher 75, Bola 90)*

Crewe Alex (2) 2 *(Porter 42, Kirk 45)* 7897

Middlesbrough: (433) Pears; Dijksteel, Wood-Gordon, Friend, Bola; Tavernier, Clayton (McNair 46), Saville; Browne, Gestede (Fletcher 61), Walker (Assombalonga 46).
Crewe Alex: (442) Richards; Ng, Lancashire (Sass-Davies 74), Nolan, Pickering; Ainley (Green 77), Lowery (Jones 82), Wintle, Kirk; Porter, Dale.
Crewe Alex won 4-2 on penalties.
Referee: Michael Salisbury.

Nottingham F (0) 1 *(Tiago Silva 59)*

Fleetwood T (0) 0 7432

Nottingham F: (433) Samba; Jenkinson, Worrall, Tobias Figueiredo, Yuri Ribeiro; Tiago Silva, Sow (Johnson 65), Bostock; Appiah (Cash 76), Mir, Ameobi.
Fleetwood T: (433) Cairns; Coyle, Souttar, Clarke P, Andrew; Coutts, Rossiter (Wallace R 78), Biggins (McAleny 63); Burns, Madden, Hunter (Morris J 53).
Referee: Alan Young.

Oxford U (0) 1 *(Brannagan 88)*

Peterborough U (0) 0 2798

Oxford U: (451) Eastwood; Long, Dickie, Moore, Ruffels; Hall (Henry 79), Sykes, Hanson, Brannagan, Forde (Berkoe 78); Napa (Woodburn 22).
Peterborough U: (41212) Pym; Naismith (Mason 70), Kent, Beevers, Blake-Tracy; Reed (Ward 76); Knight, Boyd (Burrows 75); Tasdemir; Toney, Eisa.
Referee: Ollie Yates.

Plymouth Arg (0) 2 *(McFadzean 59, Telford 62)*

Leyton Orient (0) 0 5573

Plymouth Arg: (3142) Cooper M; Joshua Grant, Canavan, Sawyer; Edwards (Baxter 61); Riley, Grant C, Mayor (Randell 74), McFadzean; Telford, Taylor (Moore B 61).
Leyton Orient: (352) Brill; Ekpiteta, Coulson, Happe; Judd, Clay, Wright, Gorman (Brophy 69), Widdowson; Dennis (Wilkinson 68), Angol.
Referee: Antony Coggins.

Port Vale (0) 1 *(Cullen 53 (pen))*

Burton Alb (1) 2 *(Boyce 9, Fraser 62)* 2252

Port Vale: (433) Brown; Gibbons, Legge, Smith, Crookes; Worrall (Bennett 68), Joyce (Lloyd 88), Conlon; Amoo, Cullen (Pope 77), Montano.
Burton Alb: (433) O'Hara; Brayford, O'Toole, Wallace, Hutchinson (Daniel 56); Edwards, Quinn (Buxton 71), Fraser; Akins, Boyce, Sarkic (Sbarra 74).
Referee: Paul Marsden.

QPR (2) 3 *(Wells 15, Chair 26, Manning 86 (pen))*

Bristol C (2) 3 *(Diedhiou 13, Hunt 41, Walsh 59)* 5795

QPR: (532) Kelly; Kane (Mlakar 60), Ball, Leistner, Barbet, Manning; Smith, Scowen (Owens 74), Pugh (Amos 60); Chair, Wells.
Bristol C: (442) Bentley; Hunt (Baker 64), Wright, Moore, Rowe; Eliasson, Massengo, Walsh, Szmodics (Nagy 72); Semenyo (O'Dowda 63), Diedhiou.
QPR won 5-4 on penalties.
Referee: Andy Davies.

Rochdale (1) 5 *(Henderson 27 (pen), Pyke 64, Camps 66, 73, Rathbone 86)*

Bolton W (1) 2 *(Darcy 14, Politic 48)* 3362

Rochdale: (4231) Sanchez; Matheson, Magloire, McNulty, Norrington-Davies; Williams MJ, Morley (Rathbone 62); Done (Pyke 62), Camps, Dooley; Henderson (Andrew 81).
Bolton W: (442) Matthews; Brockbank, Edwards (Boon 54), Zouma, Lowe; King-Harmes, Weir, Murphy L, Politic (Hurford-Lockett 69); Brown (Brown-Sterling 78), Darcy.
Referee: Andy Haines.

Salford C (0) 0

Leeds U (1) 3 *(Nketiah 43, Berardi 50, Klich 58)* 4518

Salford C: (3142) Neal; Jones J, Pond, Piergianni; Maynard; Threlkeld (Gaffney 62), Towell, Whitehead, Touray; Beesley (Lloyd 69), Dieseruvwe (Rooney 70).
Leeds U: (4141) Casilla; Berardi, White, Davis, Alioski (Harrison 78); Phillips; Helder Costa, Shackleton, Klich, Clarke (McCalmont 70); Nketiah (Bamford 78).
Referee: Keith Stroud.

Scunthorpe U (0) 0

Derby Co (0) 1 *(Buchanan 78)* 3679

Scunthorpe U: (4411) Watson; Perch, McArdle, Butler, Ntlhe; Gilliead, Lund, Slater, Colclough (Songo'o 74); McAtee (Dawson 74); Novak (Hammill 26).
Derby Co: (433) Hamer; Lowe, Bielik, Davies, Buchanan; Bird (Evans 46), Shinnie, Knight (Whittaker 87); Bennett (Sibley 75), Marriott, Paterson.
Referee: Robert Jones.

Shrewsbury T (0) 0

Rotherham U (3) 4 *(Crooks 2, Vassell 3, Ladapo 45, Wood 84)* 2813

Shrewsbury T: (352) Murphy; Ebanks-Landell, Waterfall (Pierre 6), Beckles; Barnett, Rowland, Walker, McCormick, Golbourne (Whalley 46); Okenabirhie, Morison (Giles 78).
Rotherham U: (433) Price; Olosunde, Ihiekwe, Wood, Robertson; Wiles (Lindsay 76), Barlaser, Crooks; Morris (Smith 6), Ladapo (MacDonald 64), Vassell.
Referee: Anthony Backhouse.

Stevenage (1) 1 *(Parrett 14)*

Southend U (0) 2 *(Kelman 47, 55)* 1315

Stevenage: (442) Farman; Wildin, Vancooten, Cuthbert (Sonupe 59), Fernandez; Carter (Cowley 77), Soares, Husin, Parrett (Iontton 50); Taylor, Guthrie.
Southend U: (442) Bishop; Bwomono, Shaughnessy, Lennon (White 26), Ralph; Hutchinson, Milligan, Mantom, McLaughlin (Blackman 77); Cox, Kelman (Robinson 90).
Referee: Christopher Sarginson.

Swansea C (0) 3 *(Ayew 80, 88, Byers 83)*

Northampton T (0) 1 *(Warburton 61)* 8058

Swansea C: (4231) Nordfeldt; Naughton, Cabango, Wilmot, John; Dhanda (De Boer 90), Byers; Routledge, McKay (Garrick 72), Peterson (Ayew 62); Surridge.
Northampton T: (4231) Cornell; Williams J, Turnbull, Wharton, Bunney; McWilliams S, Watson; Warburton (Roberts 78), Waters (Lines 65), Hoskins; Williams A (Smith 65).
Referee: Kevin Johnson.

Tranmere R (0) 0

Hull C (3) 3 *(Toral 1, Milinkovic 6, Tafazolli 45)* 3421

Tranmere R: (451) Davies; Wilson, Monthe, Ray, Ridehalgh; Morris, Potter (Jennings 62), Perkins, Blackett-Taylor (Ponticelli 80), Banks; Ferrier (Mullin 62).
Hull C: (4411) Ingram; McKenzie, Pennington, Tafazolli, Fleming; Bowler, Da Silva Lopes, Honeyman, Milinkovic (Dicko 63); Toral (Batty 71); Magennis (Eaves 63).
Referee: Sebastian Stockbridge.

Walsall (0) 2 *(Lavery 54 (pen), 71)*

Crawley T (1) 3 *(Morais 21, Dallison 48, Nadesan 56)* 2451

Walsall: (352) Roberts L; Clarke, Sadler, Jules (McDonald 53); Norman, Sinclair, Bates (Hardy 53), Kinsella, Cockerill-Mollett; Adebayo, Gordon (Lavery 53).
Crawley T: (4231) Luyambula; Francomb, Tunnicliffe, Dallison, Doherty; Payne, Camara; Morais (Ferguson 69), Nadesan (Grego-Cox 59), Nathaniel-George (Allarakhia 81); Palmer.
Referee: Carl Boyeson.

WBA (1) 1 *(Austin 9)*

Millwall (1) 2 *(Bradshaw 28, O'Brien 55)* 10,704

WBA: (4231) Bond; Furlong, Ajayi, O'Shea, Townsend; Harper, Brunt; Burke, Edwards (Krovinovic 60), Diangana (Sawyers 70); Austin (Matheus Pereira 60).
Millwall: (442) Steele; McCarthy, Hutchinson, Wallace M, Ferguson; O'Brien (Romeo 64), Molumby (Williams 63), Leonard, Skalak; Bodvarsson, Bradshaw (Thompson 80).
Referee: Ross Joyce.

Wigan Ath (0) 0

Stoke C (1) 1 *(Vokes 10)* 3821

Wigan Ath: (4231) Jones; Sterling, Dunkley, Mulgrew, Naismith; Williams, Roberts; Massey (Merrie 72), Enobakhare (Weir 83), Lowe; Lang (Jolley 73).
Stoke C: (343) Federici; Collins, Carter-Vickers, Lindsay; Edwards, Cousins, Woods, McClean; Duffy (Hogan 80), Vokes (Campbell 80), Clucas (Etebo 70).
Referee: Dean Whitestone.

Wycombe W (0) 1 *(Samuel 59)*

Reading (0) 1 *(Puscas 63)* 4802

Wycombe W: (4231) Allsop; Grimmer, Stewart, Phillips, Mascoll; Gape, Pattison; Kashket (Onyedinma 71), Freeman, Parker (Wheeler 71); Samuel (Akinfenwa 71).
Reading: (532) Rafael Cabral; Rinomhota, Moore, Morrison, McIntyre, Richards; Adam (Swift 63), Pele, Ejaria (Loader 80); Boye (Baldock 46), Puscas.
Reading won 4-2 on penalties.
Referee: Darren England.

SECOND ROUND

Tuesday, 27 August 2019

Bristol R (0) 1 *(Nichols 64)*

Brighton & HA (0) 2 *(Connolly 55, Murray 90)* 5864

Bristol R: (532) Jaakkola; Hare, Davies, Craig, Kilgour, Leahy; Clarke O (Smith 69), Upson, Ogogo; Nichols (Rodman 79), Adeboyejo (Clarke-Harris 63).
Brighton & HA: (343) Button; Balogun, Webster, Bong; Alzate, Mooy, Gross, Bernardo; Jahanbakhsh, Connolly, Murray.
Referee: Matthew Donohue.

Burton Alb (2) 4 *(Boyce 34, 45, 74, Edwards 51)*

Morecambe (0) 0 1500

Burton Alb: (433) O'Hara; Brayford (Sbarra 77), O'Toole (Nartey 75), Wallace, Daniel; Edwards, Quinn, Fraser; Akins, Boyce (Templeton 82), Sarkic.
Morecambe: (4231) Halstead; Tanner, Sutton, Old, Conlan; Wildig (Jagne 85), Brewitt; Oates, Alessandra (Leitch-Smith 77), Ellison; Stockton (Miller 70).
Referee: Sebastian Stockbridge.

Cardiff C (0) 0

Luton T (1) 3 *(Hoilett 43 (og), Sheehan 63, Jervis 70)* 4111

Cardiff C: (442) Day; Coxe, Nelson, Flint, Brown; Whyte (Waite 71), Paterson, Vaulks, Hoilett; Vassell (Moore 46), Bogle (Madine 65).
Luton T: (41212) Shea; Bree (Bolton 46), Jones, Sheehan, Galloway; Mpanzu; Berry, Moncur; Brown; Lee, Jervis (McManaman 81).
Referee: Tony Harrington.

Crawley T (1) 1 *(Lubala 17)*

Norwich C (0) 0 5109

Crawley T: (4231) Luyambula; Sesay (Francomb 87), Tunnicliffe, Dallison, Doherty; Bulman, Ferguson; Grego-Cox, Camara (Morais 34), Lubala; Palmer.
Norwich C: (4231) Fahrmann; Byram (Aarons 86), Zimmermann (Emi 55), Klose (Godfrey 27), Heise; Amadou, Vrancic; Roberts, Srbeny, McLean; Idah.
Referee: John Busby.

Crewe Alex (0) 1 *(Wintle 84)*

Aston Villa (3) 6 *(Konsa 4, Hourihane 24, 45, Davis 69, Guilbert 76, Grealish 87)* 7173

Crewe Alex: (433) Richards; Ng, Lancashire, Nolan, Adebisi; Wintle, Ainley, Lowery (Jones 68); Dale, Porter (Anene 46), Kirk (Finney 66).
Aston Villa: (433) Steer; Elmohamady, Konsa, Hause, Targett (Guilbert 43); Hourihane, Nakamba, Lansbury; Jota (Grealish 68), Davis (Archer 82), El Ghazi.
Referee: Jarred Gillett.

Crystal Palace (0) 0

Colchester U (0) 0 8898

Crystal Palace: (3412) Hennessey; Woods, Kelly (Cahill 46), Dann; Townsend, McCarthy, Victor Camarasa, Riedewald; Meyer (Ayew 73); Wickham (Zaha 63), Benteke.
Colchester U: (442) Gerken; Jackson, Eastman, Prosser, Clampin; Senior (Cowan-Hall 90), Comley, Stevenson (Chilvers 77), Gambin (Brown 80); Nouble, Norris.
Colchester U won 5-4 on penalties.
Referee: Andy Woolmer.

Fulham (0) 0

Southampton (0) 1 *(Obafemi 57)* 8467

Fulham: (4222) Rodak; Christie, McDonald, Le Marchand, Bryan; Johansen (Francois 80), O'Riley; De La Torre (Davis 90), Kamara (Taylor-Crossdale 90); Onomah, Reid.
Southampton: (4222) McCarthy; Cedric, Bednarek (Yoshida 60), Danso, Hojbjerg; Romeu, Ward-Prowse; Boufal, Djenepo; Obafemi (Ings 68), Redmond (Long 76).
Referee: Rob Jones.

Leeds U (0) 2 *(Nketiah 67, Helder Costa 81)*

Stoke C (2) 2 *(Batth 39, Vokes 44)* 30,002

Leeds U: (3142) Casilla; Berardi, Phillips, Davis; McCalmont (Forshaw 46); Helder Costa, Bogusz, Shackleton (White 46), Douglas; Nketiah, Clarke (Harrison 46).
Stoke C: (532) Butland; Smith, Carter-Vickers, Batth, Martins Indi, Ward; Woods (Duffy 90), Clucas, Ince (Cousins 85); Vokes, Campbell (Etebo 70).
Stoke C won 5-4 on penalties.
Referee: Oliver Langford.

Newport Co (0) 0

West Ham U (1) 2 *(Wilshere 43, Fornals 65)* 6382

Newport Co: (4222) Townsend; McNamara, Howkins, O'Brien, Haynes; Dolan (Bennett 64), Sheehan; Willmott (Collins 81), Whitely (Maloney 64); Amond, Abrahams.
West Ham U: (4141) Roberto; Zabaleta, Balbuena, Diop, Cresswell; Sanchez; Snodgrass, Wilshere (Coventry 82), Fornals, Antonio (Felipe Anderson 8); Ajeti.
Referee: Stephen Martin.

Nottingham F (2) 3 *(Adomah 25, Lolley 35, Joao Carvalho 79)*

Derby Co (0) 0 26,971

Nottingham F: (433) Samba; Cash, Tobias Figueiredo, Worrall (Chema 83), Yuri Ribeiro; Johnson (Joao Carvalho 57), Bostock, Semedo; Lolley (Tiago Silva 68), Mir, Adomah.
Derby Co: (4231) Hamer; Holmes, Davies, Clarke, Buchanan; Shinnie (Bird 83), Evans; Whittaker (Mitchell-Lawson 70), Sibley (Marriott 58), Paterson; Bennett.
Referee: John Brooks.

Oxford U (0) 2 *(Sykes 87, Henry 90 (pen))*

Millwall (1) 2 *(Bodvarsson 29, 52)* 3693

Oxford U: (433) Eastwood; Long, Mousinho, Moore, Berkoe; Baptiste (Thorne 67), Hanson, Sykes; Hall (Woodburn 67), Mackie (Henry 77), Forde.
Millwall: (442) Steele; McCarthy, Hutchinson, Cooper, Ferguson; Mitchell, O'Brien, Williams, Molumby (Wallace M 90); Elliott (Thompson 63), Bodvarsson.
Oxford U won 4-2 on penalties.
Referee: Craig Hicks.

Plymouth Arg (1) 2 *(Taylor 22, Baxter 55)*

Reading (1) 4 *(Barrett 35, 72, Meite 87 (pen), 90)* 8365

Plymouth Arg: (3142) Cooper M; Wootton, Canavan, Joshua Grant (Sawyer 71); Edwards; Moore T, Baxter (Grant C 64), Mayor, McFadzean; Rudden, Taylor (Lolos 46).
Reading: (4411) Walker; Howe, Osho, Odimayo, Obita; Olise (Baldock 64), Rinomhota, Adam (Boye 70), Barrett (Morrison 90); Loader; Meite.
Referee: Kevin Johnson.

Preston NE (2) 2 *(Huntington 20, Harrop 26)*

Hull C (1) 2 *(Magennis 34 (pen), Bowen 90)* 6093

Preston NE: (4231) Ripley; Browne, Storey, Huntington, Ginnelly (Rafferty 79); Bayliss, Ledson; Potts, Harrop, Green (Bodin 69); Barkhuizen (Stockley 46).
Hull C: (433) Ingram; McKenzie, Pennington, Tafazolli, Fleming (Stewart 37); Toral, Batty (Eaves 78), Da Silva Lopes; Bowler (Bowen 61), Dicko, Magennis.
Preston NE won 5-4 on penalties.
Referee: David Webb.

Rochdale (2) 2 *(Morley 11, Done 31)*

Carlisle U (0) 1 *(Bridge 71 (pen))* 1974

Rochdale: (4231) Sanchez; Matheson, O'Connell, Magloire, Keohane; Ryan (Pyke 63), Morley; Dooley (Rathbone 68), Camps, Done (McLaughlin 86); Andrew.
Carlisle U: (433) Collin; Elliot, Webster, Knight-Percival, Iredale; Bridge, Jones M (Carroll 53), Scougall; Thomas, Olomola (Sorensen 64), Hope (McKirdy 53).
Referee: Peter Wright.

Sheffield U (2) 2 *(Stearman 31, Norwood 45)*

Blackburn R (0) 1 *(Gallagher 72)* 9714

Sheffield U: (352) Moore; Jagielka, Stearman, Bryan (Stevens 24); Freeman K, Besic, Norwood (Mousset 66), Morrison, Osborn; McBurnie (Freeman L 46), Sharp.
Blackburn R: (4231) Leutwiler; Nyambe, Lenihan, Williams, Cunningham; Evans, Smallwood (Travis 65); Buckley, Dack (Gallagher 60), Rothwell (Rankin-Costello 71); Armstrong.
Referee: Geoff Eltringham.

Southend U (0) 1 *(Goodship 54)*

Milton Keynes D (2) 4 *(Healey 35, Brittain 41, Boateng 82, Nombe 90)* 2433

Southend U: (433) Bishop; Demetriou (Bwomono 46), Shaughnessy, Lennon, Blackman (Ndukwu 68); Mantom, Milligan, Hamilton; Cox, Humphrys, Goodship.
Milton Keynes D: (3412) Moore; Walsh, Poole, Martin; Brittain, Gilbey, Kasumu, Lewington; Healey (Boateng 66); Bowery (Williams 81), Agard (Nombe 66).
Referee: Neil Hair.

Watford (1) 3 *(Sarr 37, Janmaat 56, Penaranda 69)*

Coventry C (0) 0 12,257

Watford: (442) Gomes; Janmaat, Mariappa, Kabasele, Foulquier; Sarr (Dele-Bashiru 72), Quina, Chalobah, Success; Pereyra (Penaranda 64), Welbeck.
Coventry C: (433) Wilson; Dabo, Rose, Hyam, Mason (McCallum 46); Eccles (Shipley 64), Kelly, O'Hare; Kastaneer (Godden 61), Bakayoko, Hiwula.
Referee: Gavin Ward.

Wednesday, 28 August 2019

Bournemouth (0) 0

Forest Green R (0) 0 9657

Bournemouth: (442) Travers; Stacey, Mepham, Simpson, Rico; Wilson H (King 60), Kilkenny (Billing 84), Surman, Ibe; Wilson C (Fraser 61), Solanke.
Forest Green R: (541) Wollacott; Bernard, Godwin-Malife, Rawson, Kitching, McGinley; Mondal (Mills J 78), Dawson, Morton, Grubb (Adams 46); Stevens (Allen 63).
Bournemouth won 3-0 on penalties.
Referee: Dean Whitestone.

Burnley (1) 1 *(Rodriguez 11)*

Sunderland (1) 3 *(Grigg 35, Flanagan 47, Dobson 50)* 7445

Burnley: (442) Hart; Bardsley (Lowton 78), Long, Gibson, Taylor; Lennon (Wood 69), Hendrick, Drinkwater, McNeil; Rodriguez, Vydra.
Sunderland: (4231) Burge; McLaughlin C, Flanagan, Baldwin, Hume; Dobson, McGeouch; O'Nien (Power 87), Embleton, Gooch; Grigg (Wyke 78).
Referee: Darren England.

Lincoln C (1) 2 *(Anderson 1, Andrade 70)*

Everton (1) 4 *(Digne 36, Sigurdsson 59 (pen), Iwobi 81, Richarlison 88)* 9971

Lincoln C: (4231) Smith; Lewis, Bolger, Shackell (Bostwick 61), Toffolo; O'Connor, Morrell (Eardley 61); Anderson, Payne (Grant 64), Andrade; Akinde.
Everton: (4231) Pickford; Sidibe, Keane, Holgate, Digne; Schneiderlin, Delph (Calvert-Lewin 74); Richarlison, Sigurdsson, Iwobi (Walcott 82); Kean (Tosun 74).
Referee: Darren Bond.

Newcastle U (0) 1 *(Muto 53)*

Leicester C (1) 1 *(Maddison 34)* 22,727

Newcastle U: (541) Darlow; Krafth (Manquillo 50), Schar, Fernandez, Clark, Willems (Dummett 78); Longstaff, Shelvey, Hayden, Ritchie (Atsu 45); Muto.
Leicester C: (4411) Schmeichel; Ricardo Pereira, Morgan (Evans 57), Soyuncu, Fuchs; Perez, Choudhury (Praet 46), Tielemans, Barnes; Maddison; Vardy.
Leicester C won 4-2 on penalties.
Referee: Tim Robinson.

QPR (0) 0

Portsmouth (0) 2 *(Marquis 77 (pen), Harness 81)* 7783

QPR: (4231) Kelly; Kane, Leistner, Barbet, Manning; Owens, Smith; Pugh (Ball 75), Chair (Wells 60), Samuel (Eze 60); Mlakar.
Portsmouth: (433) MacGillivray; Burgess, Downing, Naylor, Haunstrup; Harness, McCrorie, Close (Walkes 90); Evans (Cannon 60), Marquis, Curtis.
Referee: Ross Joyce.

Rotherham U (0) 0

Sheffield W (0) 1 *(Nuhiu 90)* 8679

Rotherham U: (433) Iversen; Olosunde, Ihiekwe, Wood, Robertson; Wiles, Barlaser (MacDonald 67), Crooks (Lindsay 61); Ladapo, Smith (Proctor 74), Vassell.
Sheffield W: (442) Dawson; Iorfa, Bates, Thorniley, Fox; Murphy (Bannan 65), Pelupessy (Forestieri 76), Luongo, Winnall (Harris 46); Rhodes, Nuhiu.
Referee: Charles Breakspear.

Swansea C (5) 6 *(Peterson 1, Byers 20, Surridge 24, 45, Garrick 31, Routledge 76)*

Cambridge U (0) 0 8763

Swansea C: (4231) Nordfeldt; Naughton (Rushesha 67), Cabango, Wilmot, John; Byers, Carroll (Evans 73); Garrick (McKay 62), Routledge, Peterson; Surridge.
Cambridge U: (352) Burton; Darling, John, Taylor G (Hannant 46); Davies, Lambe, Maris, Roles, Dunk; Knibbs (Smith 71), Dallas (Knowles 71).
Referee: Michael Salisbury.

Tuesday, 10 September 2019

Grimsby T (0) 0

Macclesfield T (0) 0 3011

Grimsby T: (433) McKeown; Hendrie, Pollock (Hewitt 90), Ohman (Cardwell 90), Gibson; Whitehouse, Hessenthaler, Robson (Wright 60); Green, Hanson, Ogbu.
Macclesfield T: (4411) Evans; Welch-Hayes, Horsfall, Kelleher (Cameron 90), Vassell; Archibald, Kirby, Harris, O'Keeffe; Osadebe (Gnahoua 70); Ironside.
Grimsby T won 5-4 on penalties.
Referee: Darren Drysdale.

THIRD ROUND

Tuesday, 24 September 2019

Arsenal (1) 5 *(Martinelli 31, 90, Holding 71, Willock 77, Nelson 84)*

Nottingham F (0) 0 53,160

Arsenal: (4231) Martinez; Chambers, Mustafi, Holding, Tierney (Bellerin 77); Torreira, Willock; Smith-Rowe (Saka 45), Ozil (Ceballos 71), Nelson; Martinelli.
Nottingham F: (4231) Muric; Cash, Tobias Figueiredo, Chema, Robinson; Johnson, Tiago Silva; Lolley (Lawrence-Gabriel 81), Joao Carvalho (Ameobi 59), Yuri Ribeiro (Mighten 78); Adomah.
Referee: Darren England.

Colchester U (0) 0

Tottenham H (0) 0 9481

Colchester U: (433) Gerken; Jackson (Cowan-Hall 50), Eastman, Prosser, Bramall; Stevenson (Norris 78), Comley, Lapslie; Senior, Nouble, Gambin (Brown 68).
Tottenham H: (3421) Gazzaniga; Dier, Sanchez, Tanganga (Son 66); Walker-Peters, Skipp (Lamela 78), Wanyama, Davies; Lucas Moura, Alli; Parrott (Eriksen 66).
Colchester U won 4-3 on penalties.
Referee: Jarred Gillett.

Crawley T (1) 1 *(Ferguson 38)*

Stoke C (1) 1 *(Vokes 23)* 4165

Crawley T: (4141) Luyambula; Sesay, Tunnicliffe, Dallison, Doherty; Bulman (Nathaniel-George 90); Grego-Cox, Camara (Allarakhia 90), Ferguson, Lubala; Palmer.
Stoke C: (343) Federici; Collins■, Batth, Lindsay (Etebo 46); Smith, Cousins, Woods, Ward; Campbell (Duffy 46), Vokes, Hogan (Carter-Vickers 64).
Crawley T won 5-3 on penalties.
Referee: Kevin Johnson.

Luton T (0) 0

Leicester C (2) 4 *(Gray 34, Justin 44, Tielemans 79, Iheanacho 86)* 8260

Luton T: (4312) Shea; Bolton, Jones, Sheehan, Potts; Berry, Mpanzu, Butterfield; Moncur (Brown 60); McManaman (LuaLua 72), Lee (Cornick 60).
Leicester C: (4141) Ward; Justin, Morgan, Evans, Fuchs; Ndidi (Choudhury 77); Gray, Praet, Tielemans, Albrighton; Perez (Iheanacho 71).
Referee: Matthew Donohue.

Portsmouth (0) 0

Southampton (2) 4 *(Ings 21, 44, Cedric 77, Redmond 86)* 18,707

Portsmouth: (4231) MacGillivray; Bolton, Hawkins (Downing 59), Burgess, Haunstrup; Naylor, Close (McCrorie 82); Williams (Evans 78), Pitman, Curtis; Marquis.
Southampton: (433) McCarthy; Cedric, Bednarek, Yoshida, Bertrand; Ward-Prowse, Romeu, Hojbjerg; Obafemi (Redmond 72), Adams, Ings (Long 83).
Referee: Kevin Friend.

Preston NE (0) 0

Manchester C (3) 3 *(Sterling 19, Gabriel Jesus 35, Ledson 42 (og))* 22,025

Preston NE: (4231) Ripley; Fisher, Storey, Davies, Rafferty; Ledson, Browne; Potts, Johnson (Bayliss 76), Harrop (Ginnelly 71); Barkhuizen (Nugent 63).
Manchester C: (433) Bravo; Joao Cancelo, Harwood-Bellis, Garcia, Angelino (Mendy 60); Foden, Gundogan, Silva (Bernabe 63); Bernardo Silva, Gabriel Jesus, Sterling (Mahrez 73).
Referee: Lee Mason.

Sheffield W (0) 0

Everton (2) 2 *(Calvert-Lewin 6, 10)* 21,485

Sheffield W: (442) Dawson; Odubajo, Iorfa, Thorniley, Fox; Reach, Pelupessy, Luongo, Murphy (Harris 59); Winnall (Rhodes 65), Nuhiu (Fletcher 70).
Everton: (4231) Pickford; Sidibe, Mina, Holgate, Digne; Davies, Delph (Schneiderlin 90); Richarlison (Walcott 67), Iwobi, Bernard (Sigurdsson 76); Calvert-Lewin.
Referee: Jeremy Simpson.

Watford (1) 2 *(Welbeck 28, Pereyra 79)*

Swansea C (1) 1 *(Surridge 34)* 8903

Watford: (4222) Gomes; Janmaat, Prodl, Kabasele, Masina; Chalobah, Doucoure (Sarr 61); Quina (Cleverley 56), Pereyra; Gray (Deulofeu 77), Welbeck.
Swansea C: (4231) Nordfeldt; Roberts, Cabango, van der Hoorn, John; Byers, Grimes; Dyer (Garrick 80), Dhanda (Routledge 66), Peterson (McKay 70); Surridge.
Referee: Darren Bond.

Wednesday, 25 September 2019

Brighton & HA (0) 1 *(Roberts 61)*

Aston Villa (2) 3 *(Jota 22, Hourihane 33, Grealish 77)* 14,982

Brighton & HA: (343) Button; Duffy (Yapi 72), Roberts, Bong; Davies A, Baluta, Jenks (Spong 82), Cochrane; Gwargis, Connolly (Longman 58), Richards.
Aston Villa: (433) Steer; Elmohamady, Konsa, Hause, Targett; McGinn (Grealish 66), Douglas Luiz, Hourihane; Jota, Davis, Trezeguet (Ramsey 80).
Referee: Graham Scott.

Burton Alb (1) 2 *(Sarkic 14, Broadhead 72)*

Bournemouth (0) 0 2505

Burton Alb: (433) O'Hara; Akins, O'Toole, Nartey, Hutchinson; Edwards, Wallace, Fraser (Sbarra 90); Broadhead (Dyer 87), Boyce, Sarkic.
Bournemouth: (4231) Travers; Francis (Wilson C 61), Mepham, Simpson, Kelly; Cook L, Surman; Kilkenny (Wilson H 46), Ibe, Fraser; Solanke (Danjuma 61).
Referee: John Busby.

Chelsea (3) 7 *(Barkley 4, Batshuayi 7, 86, Pedro 43 (pen), Zouma 56, James 82, Hudson-Odoi 89)*

Grimsby T (1) 1 *(Green 19)* 39,674

Chelsea: (4231) Caballero; James, Zouma, Guehi, Alonso (Maatsen 66); Barkley, Gilmour; Pulisic, Pedro (Anjorin 67), Hudson-Odoi; Batshuayi.
Grimsby T: (532) McKeown; Hewitt, Hendrie, Davis, Pollock, Gibson (Cook 70); Clifton (Wright 56), Whitehouse, Hessenthaler; Hanson, Green (Ogbu 64).
Referee: Keith Stroud.

Manchester U (0) 1 *(Greenwood 68)*

Rochdale (0) 1 *(Matheson 76)* 58,313

Manchester U: (4231) Romero; Wan Bissaka, Tuanzebe, Jones (Williams 46), Rojo; Fred, Pogba; Andreas Pereira, Lingard (Mata 85), Chong (James 60); Greenwood.
Rochdale: (4231) Sanchez; Matheson, Keohane, McNulty, Norrington-Davies; Morley, Williams MJ; Dooley (Wilbraham 74), Camps, Rathbone (Andrew 81); Henderson (Ryan 90).
Manchester U won 5-3 on penalties
Referee: John Brooks.

Milton Keynes D (0) 0

Liverpool (1) 2 *(Milner 41, Hoever 69)* 28,521

Milton Keynes D: (352) Moore; Williams, Poole, Walsh; Brittain, Kasumu (Houghton 61), McGrandles, Gilbey (Boateng 72), Dickenson (Martin 46); Bowery, Nombe.
Liverpool: (433) Kelleher; Hoever (van den Berg 90), Gomez, Lovren, Milner; Oxlade-Chamberlain (Kane 82), Lallana, Keita (Chirivella 63); Elliott, Brewster, Jones.
Referee: Oliver Langford.

Oxford U (0) 4 *(Moore 55, Taylor 71, Fosu 84, Baptiste 90)*

West Ham U (0) 0 10,450

Oxford U: (451) Eastwood; Long, Dickie, Moore, Ruffels; Hall (Fosu 79), Brannagan, Thorne (Sykes 23), Baptiste, Forde; Mackie (Taylor 70).
West Ham U: (4141) Roberto; Zabaleta, Balbuena, Diop, Masuaku; Sanchez; Snodgrass (Noble 74), Wilshere (Felipe Anderson 66), Fornals, Holland (Haller 57); Ajeti.
Referee: Robert Jones.

Sheffield U (0) 0

Sunderland (1) 1 *(Power 9)* 11,675

Sheffield U: (352) Moore; Jagielka, Stearman, Bryan (Fleck 70); Freeman K, Freeman L, Besic, Morrison, Osborn; Robinson C (Clarke 57), Mousset (McBurnie 57).
Sunderland: (4231) Burge; McLaughlin C, Flanagan, Lynch, De Bock; McGeouch, Power; Maguire (Dobson 90), O'Nien, Embleton (Hume 46); Wyke.
Referee: Tim Robinson.

Wolverhampton W (1) 1 *(Bruno Jordao 27)*

Reading (0) 1 *(Boye 90)* 20,702

Wolverhampton W: (343) Ruddy; Vallejo , Bennett, Kilman; Doherty, Bruno Jordao (Perry 42), Neves, Ruben Vinagre; Pedro Neto (Cundle 83), Cutrone, Gibbs-White (Shabani 74).
Reading: (541) Virginia; Howe (Puscas 66), Miazga, McIntyre (Ejaria 56), Blackett, Richards; Meite, Adam (Swift 56), Rinomhota, Boye; Barrett.
Wolverhampton W won 4-2 on penalties.
Referee: Peter Bankes.

FOURTH ROUND

Tuesday, 29 October 2019

Burton Alb (0) 1 *(Boyce 52)*

Leicester C (2) 3 *(Iheanacho 7, Tielemans 20, Maddison 89)* 6186

Burton Alb: (433) O'Hara; Brayford, O'Toole, Wallace, Hutchinson (Dyer 46); Edwards (Sbarra 88), Quinn, Fraser; Sarkic (Templeton 88), Boyce, Broadhead.
Leicester C: (4141) Ward; Justin, Morgan, Evans, Fuchs; Choudhury (Ndidi 88); Gray, Praet (Maddison 83), Tielemans, Albrighton; Iheanacho (Barnes 66).
Referee: Darren England.

Crawley T (1) 1 *(Bulman 20)*

Colchester U (1) 3 *(Norris 22, Luyambula 53 (og), Gambin 79)* 5612

Crawley T: (4411) Luyambula; Sesay (Young 67), Tunnicliffe, Dallison, Doherty; Allarakhia (Nadesan 82), Bulman, Ferguson, Lubala; Grego-Cox; Enigbokan-Bloomfield (Palmer 54).
Colchester U: (4231) Gerken; Jackson, Eastman, Prosser, Bramall; Stevenson, Comley; Senior (Lapslie 83), Adubofour-Poku (Gambin 74), Nouble; Norris (Harriott 61).
Referee: Tony Harrington.

Everton (0) 2 *(Holgate 72, Richarlison 90)*

Watford (0) 0 34,979

Everton: (4231) Pickford; Coleman, Mina (Keane 41), Holgate, Digne; Andre Gomes, Delph; Kean (Walcott 46), Iwobi, Richarlison; Calvert-Lewin (Tosun 80).
Watford: (532) Gomes; Foulquier, Mariappa, Prodl (Kabasele 65), Cathcart, Femenia; Hughes, Chalobah, Quina (Doucoure 39); Gray, Pereyra (Deulofeu 67).
Referee: Simon Hooper.

Manchester C (2) 3 *(Otamendi 20, Aguero 38, 56)*

Southampton (0) 1 *(Stephens 75)* 37,143

Manchester C: (433) Bravo; Walker (Joao Cancelo 65), Otamendi, Garcia, Angelino (Stones 79); Bernardo Silva, Doyle, Foden; Mahrez, Aguero, Gabriel Jesus (Bernabe 87).
Southampton: (532) McCarthy; Valery, Danso, Stephens, Bednarek, Hojbjerg; Ward-Prowse, Romeu (Vokins 90), Armstrong; Long (Redmond 68), Boufal (Adams 69).
Referee: Jonathan Moss.

Oxford U (1) 1 *(Hall 25)*

Sunderland (0) 1 *(McNulty 78)* 11,108

Oxford U: (433) Eastwood; Long, Dickie, Moore, Ruffels; Henry, Gorrin, Baptiste (Mousinho 90); Hall (Forde 81), Taylor (Mackie 81), Fosu.
Sunderland: (3511) McLaughlin J; Flanagan, Willis, Lynch (Grigg 56); McLaughlin C, Dobson, Leadbitter, Power, Hume (O'Nien 68); McGeady; McNulty.
Oxford U won 4-2 on penalties.
Referee: Jeremy Simpson.

Wednesday, 30 October 2019

Aston Villa (1) 2 *(El Ghazi 28, Elmohamady 57)*

Wolverhampton W (0) 1 *(Cutrone 54)* 34,962

Aston Villa: (433) Steer; Elmohamady, Konsa, Hause, Taylor; Lansbury (McGinn 81), Douglas Luiz, Hourihane; El Ghazi, Davis (Kodjia 50), Trezeguet.
Wolverhampton W: (343) Ruddy; Vallejo , Bennett, Kilman; Sanderson, Bruno Jordao (Taylor 71), Perry, Ruben Vinagre; Campbell (Ashley-Seal 68), Cutrone, Pedro Neto (Cristovao 77).
Referee: Lee Mason.

Chelsea (0) 1 *(Batshuayi 61)*

Manchester U (1) 2 *(Rashford 25 (pen), 73)* 38,645

Chelsea: (433) Caballero; James, Zouma, Guehi, Alonso; Gilmour (Mount 70), Jorginho, Kovacic; Hudson-Odoi, Batshuayi (Abraham 78), Pulisic (Pedro 70).
Manchester U: (3412) Romero; Lindelof (Martial 66), Maguire, Rojo; Wan Bissaka, McTominay, Fred, Williams; Lingard (Andreas Pereira 67); James, Rashford (Young 80).
Referee: Paul Tierney.

Liverpool (2) 5 *(Mustafi 6 (og), Milner 43 (pen), Oxlade-Chamberlain 58, Origi 62, 90)*

Arsenal (3) 5 *(Torreira 19, Martinelli 26, 36, Maitland-Niles 54, Willock 70)* 52,694

Liverpool: (433) Kelleher; Williams, Gomez, van den Berg, Milner; Oxlade-Chamberlain (Chirivella 81), Lallana, Keita (Jones 55); Elliott, Brewster, Origi.
Arsenal: (4411) Martinez; Bellerin, Mustafi, Holding, Kolasinac (Tierney 83); Maitland-Niles, Torreira (Ceballos 72), Willock, Saka; Ozil (Guendouzi 65); Martinelli.
Liverpool won 5-4 on penalties.
Referee: Andre Marriner.

QUARTER-FINALS

Tuesday, 17 December 2019

Aston Villa (4) 5 *(Hourihane 14, Boyes 17 (og), Kodjia 37, 45, Wesley 90)*

Liverpool (0) 0 30,323

Aston Villa: (433) Nyland; Elmohamady, Chester (Hause 77), Konsa, Taylor; Lansbury, Douglas Luiz, Hourihane; Jota, Kodjia (Wesley 73), Trezeguet.
Liverpool: (433) Kelleher; Hoever (Norris 82), van den Berg, Boyes, Gallacher; Christie-Davies (Clarkson 77), Chirivella, Kane; Elliott, Longstaff (Bearne 65), Hill.
Referee: Lee Mason.

Wednesday, 18 December 2019

Everton (0) 2 *(Davies 70, Baines 90)*

Leicester C (2) 2 *(Maddison 26, Evans 29)* 39,027

Everton: (442) Pickford; Coleman, Keane, Mina, Baines; Iwobi (Tosun 78), Davies, Holgate, Bernard (Kean 46); Richarlison (Gordon 84), Calvert-Lewin.
Leicester C: (4141) Schmeichel; Ricardo Pereira, Morgan, Evans, Chilwell; Ndidi; Perez (Gray 69), Praet (Choudhury 86), Maddison, Albrighton (Soyuncu 82); Vardy.
Leicester C won 4-2 on penalties.
Referee: Jonathan Moss.

Manchester U (0) 3 *(Rashford 51, Jackson 55 (og), Martial 61)*

Colchester U (0) 0 57,559

Manchester U: (4231) Romero; Young, Tuanzebe (Garner 65), Maguire, Shaw (Williams 62); Andreas Pereira, Matic; Greenwood, Mata, Rashford (Lingard 62); Martial.
Colchester U: (451) Gerken; Jackson, Eastman, Prosser, Bramall; Harriott (Adubofour-Poku 77), Pell (Stevenson 66), Comley (Gambin 73), Lapslie, Nouble; Norris.
Referee: David Coote.

Oxford U (0) 1 *(Taylor 46)*

Manchester C (1) 3 *(Joao Cancelo 22, Sterling 50, 70)* 11,817

Oxford U: (433) Archer; Long, Dickie, Moore, Ruffels; Baptiste (Mousinho 87), Gorrin, Brannagan; Agyei (Sykes 57), Taylor (Mackie 75), Fosu.

Manchester C: (433) Bravo; Joao Cancelo, Harwood-Bellis, Garcia, Zinchenko; Foden, Rodri (Gundogan 59), Bernardo Silva; Mahrez, Sterling (Bernabe 76), Angelino (Gabriel Jesus 62).
Referee: Andrew Madley.

SEMI-FINALS FIRST LEG

Tuesday, 7 January 2020

Manchester U (0) 1 *(Rashford 70)*

Manchester C (3) 3 *(Bernardo Silva 17, Mahrez 33, Andreas Pereira 38 (og))* 69,023

Manchester U: (4231) de Gea; Wan Bissaka, Lindelof, Jones, Williams; Andreas Pereira, Fred; James (Gomes 64), Lingard (Matic 46), Rashford; Greenwood (Martial 81).
Manchester C: (433) Bravo; Walker, Fernandinho, Otamendi, Mendy; De Bruyne (Gabriel Jesus 80), Rodri, Gundogan; Mahrez (Foden 86), Bernardo Silva, Sterling.
Referee: Mike Dean.

Wednesday, 8 January 2020

Leicester C (0) 1 *(Iheanacho 74)*

Aston Villa (1) 1 *(Guilbert 28)* 31,280

Leicester C: (352) Schmeichel; Soyuncu, Evans, Fuchs; Ricardo Pereira, Praet (Choudhury 46), Tielemans (Albrighton 79), Maddison, Chilwell; Perez (Iheanacho 69), Vardy.
Aston Villa: (343) Nyland; Konsa, Mings, Hause; Guilbert, Douglas Luiz, Nakamba (Lansbury 86), Taylor; Trezeguet (Hourihane 67), El Ghazi (Vassilev 74), Grealish.
Referee: Chris Kavanagh.

SEMI-FINALS SECOND LEG

Tuesday, 28 January 2020

Aston Villa (1) 2 *(Targett 12, Trezeguet 90)*

Leicester C (0) 1 *(Iheanacho 72)* 39,300

Aston Villa: (343) Nyland; Konsa, Mings, Hause; Guilbert (Elmohamady 84), Douglas Luiz, Nakamba, Targett; El Ghazi (Trezeguet 77), Samatta (Davis 67), Grealish.
Leicester C: (3421) Schmeichel; Soyuncu, Evans, Chilwell; Ricardo Pereira, Tielemans, Ndidi, Barnes (Gray 86); Perez (Vardy 56), Maddison; Iheanacho.
Aston Villa won 3-2 on aggregate.
Referee: Mike Dean.

Wednesday, 29 January 2020

Manchester C (0) 0

Manchester U (1) 1 *(Matic 35)* 51,000

Manchester C: (3241) Bravo, Walker, Otamendi, Joao Cancelo, Rodri, Gundogan, Mahrez (Silva 68), De Bruyne (Stones 90), Bernardo Silva, Sterling, Aguero (Gabriel Jesus 90).
Manchester U: (3412) de Gea; Lindelof, Maguire, Shaw (Mata 79); Wan Bissaka, Fred, Matic■, Williams; Lingard (Andreas Pereira 65); Greenwood (James 46), Martial.
Manchester C won 3-2 on aggregate.
Referee: Andre Marriner.

CARABAO CUP FINAL 2019–20

Sunday, 1 March 2020

(at Wembley Stadium, attendance 82,145)

Aston Villa (1) 1 Manchester C (2) 2

Aston Villa: (4231) Nyland; Guilbert, Engels, Mings, Targett; Douglas Luiz, Nakamba; Elmohamady (Trezeguet 70), Grealish, El Ghazi (Hourihane 70); Samatta (Davis 80).
Scorer: Samatta 41.

Manchester C: (4231) Bravo; Walker, Stones, Fernandinho, Zinchenko; Gundogan (De Bruyne 58), Rodri; Foden, Silva (Bernardo Silva 77), Sterling; Aguero (Gabriel Jesus 84).
Scorers: Aguero 20, Rodri 30.

Referee: Lee Mason.

The Manchester City squad celebrates winning the EFL Cup following their 2-1 success over Aston Villa in the final in March. (Action Images via Reuters/Matthew Childs)

LEAGUE CUP ATTENDANCES 1960–2020

Season	*Attendances*	*Games*	*Average*
1960–61	1,204,580	112	10,755
1961–62	1,030,534	104	9,909
1962–63	1,029,893	102	10,097
1963–64	945,265	104	9,089
1964–65	962,802	98	9,825
1965–66	1,205,876	106	11,376
1966–67	1,394,553	118	11,818
1967–68	1,671,326	110	15,194
1968–69	2,064,647	118	17,497
1969–70	2,299,819	122	18,851
1970–71	2,035,315	116	17,546
1971–72	2,397,154	123	19,489
1972–73	1,935,474	120	16,129
1973–74	1,722,629	132	13,050
1974–75	1,901,094	127	14,969
1975–76	1,841,735	140	13,155
1976–77	2,236,636	147	15,215
1977–78	2,038,295	148	13,772
1978–79	1,825,643	139	13,134
1979–80	2,322,866	169	13,745
1980–81	2,051,576	161	12,743
1981–82	1,880,682	161	11,681
1982–83	1,679,756	160	10,498
1983–84	1,900,491	168	11,312
1984–85	1,876,429	167	11,236
1985–86	1,579,916	163	9,693
1986–87	1,531,498	157	9,755
1987–88	1,539,253	158	9,742
1988–89	1,552,780	162	9,585
1989–90	1,836,916	168	10,934
1990–91	1,675,496	159	10,538
1991–92	1,622,337	164	9,892
1992–93	1,558,031	161	9,677
1993–94	1,744,120	163	10,700
1994–95	1,530,478	157	9,748
1995–96	1,776,060	162	10,963
1996–97	1,529,321	163	9,382
1997–98	1,484,297	153	9,701
1998–99	1,555,856	153	10,169
1999–2000	1,354,233	153	8,851
2000–01	1,501,304	154	9,749
2001–02	1,076,390	93	11,574
2002–03	1,242,478	92	13,505
2003–04	1,267,729	93	13,631
2004–05	1,313,693	93	14,216
2005–06	1,072,362	93	11,531
2006–07	1,098,403	93	11,811
2007–08	1,332,841	94	14,179
2008–09	1,329,753	93	14,298
2009–10	1,376,405	93	14,800
2010–11	1,197,917	93	12,881
2011–12	1,209,684	93	13,007
2012–13	1,210,031	93	13,011
2013–14	1,362,360	93	14,649
2014–15	1,274,413	93	13,690
2015–16	1,430,554	93	15,382
2016–17	1,462,722	93	15,728
2017–18	1,454,912	93	15,644
2018–19	1,275,575	93	13,716
2019–20	1,337,845	92	14,542

CARABAO CUP 2019–20

Round	*Aggregate*	*Games*	*Average*
One	144,992	34	4,264
Two	227,042	25	9,082
Three	333,008	16	20,813
Four	221,329	8	27,666
Quarter-finals	138,726	4	34,682
Semi-finals	190,603	4	47,651
Final	82,145	1	82,145
Total	1,337,845	92	14,542

FOOTBALL LEAGUE TROPHY FINALS 1984–2020

The 1984 final was played at Boothferry Park, Hull. All subsequent finals played at Wembley except between 2001 and 2007 (inclusive) which were played at Millennium Stadium, Cardiff.

ASSOCIATE MEMBERS' CUP
1984	Bournemouth v Hull C	2-1

FREIGHT ROVER TROPHY
1985	Wigan Ath v Brentford	3-1
1986	Bristol C v Bolton W	3-0
1987	Mansfield T v Bristol C	1-1*
	Mansfield T won 5-4 on penalties	

SHERPA VANS TROPHY
1988	Wolverhampton W v Burnley	2-0
1989	Bolton W v Torquay U	4-1

LEYLAND DAF CUP
1990	Tranmere R v Bristol R	2-1
1991	Birmingham C v Tranmere R	3-2

AUTOGLASS TROPHY
1992	Stoke C v Stockport Co	1-0
1993	Port Vale v Stockport Co	2-1
1994	Swansea C v Huddersfield T	1-1*
	Swansea C won 3-1 on penalties	

AUTO WINDSCREENS SHIELD
1995	Birmingham C v Carlisle U	1-0*
1996	Rotherham U v Shrewsbury T	2-1
1997	Carlisle U v Colchester U	0-0*
	Carlisle U won 4-3 on penalties	
1998	Grimsby T v Bournemouth	2-1
1999	Wigan Ath v Millwall	1-0
2000	Stoke C v Bristol C	2-1

LDV VANS TROPHY
2001	Port Vale v Brentford	2-1
2002	Blackpool v Cambridge U	4-1
2003	Bristol C v Carlisle U	2-0
2004	Blackpool v Southend U	2-0
2005	Wrexham v Southend U	2-0*

FOOTBALL LEAGUE TROPHY
2006	Swansea C v Carlisle U	2-1

JOHNSTONE'S PAINT TROPHY
2007	Doncaster R v Bristol R	3-2*
2008	Milton Keynes D v Grimsby T	2-0
2009	Luton T v Scunthorpe U	3-2*
2010	Southampton v Carlisle U	4-1
2011	Carlisle U v Brentford	1-0
2012	Chesterfield v Swindon T	2-0
2013	Crewe Alex v Southend U	2-0
2014	Peterborough U v Chesterfield	3-1
2015	Bristol C v Walsall	2-0
2016	Barnsley v Oxford U	3-2

EFL CHECKATRADE TROPHY
2017	Coventry C v Oxford U	2-1
2018	Lincoln C v Shrewsbury T	1-0
2019	Portsmouth v Sunderland	2-2*
	Portsmouth won 5-4 on penalties	

EFL LEASING.COM TROPHY
2020†	Portsmouth v Salford C	

**After extra time. †Due to the COVID-19 pandemic, the final due to be played on Sunday 5 April 2020 was postponed.*

FOOTBALL LEAGUE TROPHY WINS
Bristol C 3, Birmingham C 2, Blackpool 2, Carlisle U 2, Port Vale 2, Stoke C 2, Swansea C 2, Wigan Ath 2, Barnsley 1, Bolton W 1, Bournemouth 1, Chesterfield 1, Coventry C 1, Crewe Alex 1, Doncaster R 1, Grimsby T 1, Lincoln C 1, Luton T 1, Mansfield T 1, Milton Keynes D 1, Peterborough U 1, Portsmouth 1, Rotherham U 1, Southampton 1, Tranmere R 1, Wolverhampton W 1, Wrexham 1.

APPEARANCES IN FINALS
Carlisle U 6, Bristol C 5, Brentford 3, Southend U 3, Birmingham C 2, Blackpool 2, Bolton W 2, Bournemouth 2, Bristol R 2, Chesterfield 2, Grimsby T 2, Oxford U 2, Port Vale 2, Shrewsbury T 2, Stockport Co 2, Stoke C 2, Swansea C 2, Tranmere R 2, Wigan Ath 2, Barnsley 1, Burnley 1, Cambridge U 1, Colchester U 1, Coventry C 1, Crewe Alex 1, Doncaster R 1, Huddersfield T 1, Hull C 1, Lincoln C 1, Luton T 1, Mansfield T 1, Millwall 1, Milton Keynes D 1, Peterborough U 1, Portsmouth 1, Rotherham U 1, Scunthorpe U 1, Southampton 1, Sunderland 1, Swindon T 1, Torquay U 1, Walsall 1, Wolverhampton W 1, Wrexham 1.

EFL TROPHY ATTENDANCES 2019–20

Round	*Aggregate*	*Games*	*Average*
One	145,989	93	1,570
Two	17,706	16	1,107
Three	8,677	8	1,085
Quarter-finals	9.330	4	2.333
Semi-finals	18,805	2	9,403
Final			
Total	200,507	123	1,630

EFL LEASING.COM TROPHY 2019–20

▪ *Denotes player sent off.*
In the group stages drawn matches were decided on a penalty shoot-out. Two points were awarded to the team that won on penalties (DW). The team that lost on penalties were awarded one point (DL).

NORTHERN SECTION GROUP A

Tuesday, 3 September 2019

Grimsby T (0) 1 *(Cardwell 49)*

Scunthorpe U (1) 2 *(van Veen 28, 75)* 1302

Grimsby T: (442) Russell; Starbuck, Pollock, Gibson, Ring; Wright, Hewitt, Robson (Hendrie 66), Vernam (Adlard 88); Rose A (McPherson 74), Cardwell.
Scunthorpe U: (4132) Eastwood; Clarke, McArdle, McGahey, Perch▪; Songo'o; Colclough, McAtee (Slater 73), Gilliead (Eisa 73); van Veen (Hornshaw 88), Miller.
Referee: Andy Haines.

Tuesday, 24 September 2019

Scunthorpe U (0) 1 *(Colclough 88)*

Leicester C U21 (0) 1 *(Dewsbury-Hall 87)* 572

Scunthorpe U: (4411) Eastwood; Clarke, Butler, Jordan Bedeau, Ntlhe; Colclough, Slater, Sutton, Eisa (Dales 59); McAtee (Butroid 80); Miller.
Leicester C U21: (4231) Jakupovic; Clark, Johnson, Benkovic, Ughelumba; Leshabela, Dewsbury-Hall; Reghba (Thomas L 57), Wright (Shade 83), Muskwe; Hirst (Eppiah 76).
Leicester C U21 won 3-1 on penalties.
Referee: Paul Marsden.

Tuesday, 8 October 2019

Sunderland (0) 3 *(Watmore 68, McNulty 79, Grigg 86)*

Grimsby T (0) 2 *(Green 59, Ogbu 81)* 6952

Sunderland: (442) Burge; Mumba (Gooch 82), Taylor, Lynch, Hume; Watmore (Connelly 89), Dobson, Leadbitter, O'Nien; McNulty, Grigg (Kiernan 90).
Grimsby T: (442) McKeown; Hewitt, Pollock, Davis, Ring (Waterfall 84); Vernam (Cardwell 63), Cook, Whitehouse, Rose A (Hessenthaler 56); Green, Ogbu.
Referee: Stephen Martin.

Tuesday, 29 October 2019

Grimsby T (1) 1 *(Ogbu 31)*

Leicester C U21 (0) 2 *(Eppiah 68, 90)* 341

Grimsby T: (433) Russell; Hewitt, Davis, Pollock, Gibson (Ring 74); Clifton, Hessenthaler, Robson (Cook 61); Cardwell (Vernam 61), Ogbu, Rose A.
Leicester C U21: (4231) Johansson; Clark, Benkovic, Johnson, Ughelumba; Thomas G, Dewsbury-Hall; Wright, Muskwe (Arlott-John 87), Leshabela (Eppiah 46); Hirst.
Referee: Sebastian Stockbridge.

Tuesday, 5 November 2019

Sunderland (1) 1 *(Maguire 14)*

Leicester C U21 (0) 2 *(Hirst 50 (pen), Dewsbury-Hall 53)* 7649

Sunderland: (442) McLaughlin J; McLaughlin C, Ozturk (Willis 37), Flanagan, De Bock; Mbunga-Kimpioka (McGeady 69), McGeouch, Leadbitter, Watmore (Grigg 74); Maguire, McNulty.
Leicester C U21: (532) Johansson; Clark, Johnson, Benkovic, Ughelumba, Thomas L; Thomas G, Dewsbury-Hall, Wright (Leshabela 84); Muskwe (Eppiah 70), Hirst.
Referee: Ross Joyce.

Tuesday, 12 November 2019

Scunthorpe U (0) 3 *(Novak 66 (pen), 90, Eisa 88)*

Sunderland (0) 0 1002

Scunthorpe U: (442) Eastwood; Clarke, McArdle, Jacob Bedeau, Brown; Gilliead (Dales 89), Perch, Lund (Pugh 90), Eisa; McAtee (van Veen 57), Novak.
Sunderland: (433) Burge; O'Nien▪, Willis, Lynch (De Bock 46), Hume; Dobson, Leadbitter, Power; Watmore (Maguire 74), McNulty, McGeady.
Referee: Darren Handley.

North Group A	P	W	DW	DL	L	F	A	GD	Pts
Leicester C U21	3	2	1	0	0	5	3	2	8
Scunthorpe U	3	2	0	1	0	6	2	4	7
Sunderland	3	1	0	0	2	4	7	–3	3
Grimsby T	3	0	0	0	3	4	7	–3	0

NORTHERN SECTION GROUP B

Wednesday, 7 August 2019

Oldham Ath (2) 3 *(Azankpo 20, Iacovitti 29, Stott 81)*

Liverpool U21 (2) 2 *(Williams 4, Elliott 44)* 1522

Oldham Ath: (442) Zabret; Hamer, Stott, Smith-Brown, Iacovitti; Eagles (Adams 69), Fage, Sylla, Nepomuceno; Vera (Dolan 75), Azankpo (Gonzales 46).
Liverpool U21: (433) Atherton; Williams, van den Berg, Boyes, Larouci; Lewis, Chirivella, Christie-Davies (Dixon-Bonner 51); Elliott (Bearne 66), Duncan, Jones.
Referee: Paul Marsden.

Tuesday, 3 September 2019

Accrington S (0) 2 *(Carvalho 53, McConville 72)*

Fleetwood T (0) 1 *(Madden 90 (pen))* 923

Accrington S: (442) Savin; Barclay (Johnson 86), Sykes, Hughes, Maguire; Pritchard (Charles 70), Edwards, Sheriff (Finley 29), Carvalho; McConville, Bishop.
Fleetwood T: (433) Cairns; Coyle, Eastham, Clarke P, Andrew; Rossiter, Dempsey, Biggins▪; Burns (Morris J 19), Evans (Saunders 74), Hunter (Madden 70).
Referee: Darren Handley.

Wednesday, 25 September 2019

Fleetwood T (0) 1 *(Clarke P 76)*

Liverpool U21 (0) 1 *(Williams 78)* 866

Fleetwood T: (433) Gilks; Holgate (Garner 46), Eastham, Clarke P, Rydel; Sowerby (Matete 68), Sheron, Baggley; Mooney, Saunders, Hunter (Morris S 69).
Liverpool U21: (343) Winterbottom; Clayton, Kourmetio, Boyes; Williams, Dixon-Bonner, Cain, Gallacher; Larouci, Stewart, Hill.
Fleetwood T won 4-3 on penalties.
Referee: Martin Coy.

Tuesday, 8 October 2019

Oldham Ath (0) 0

Accrington S (2) 3 *(Diallo 30, Zanzala 42 (pen), Clark 86)* 1107

Oldham Ath: (442) Zabret; Hamer, Egert, Stott, Iacovitti; Fage▪, Sylla, Missilou (Smith-Brown 78), Smith (Kokos 74); Adams (Morais 46), Wilson.
Accrington S: (433) Savin; Edwards, Rodgers, Sykes, Francis-Angol; Sheriff, Barclay, Diallo (Finley 61); Clark (Sousa 88), Zanzala (Charles 71), Carvalho.
Referee: Ben Toner.

Tuesday, 29 October 2019

Accrington S (2) 5 *(Sykes 30, Baker-Richardson 45, Charles 52, Clark 61, Simpson 74)*

Liverpool U21 (1) 2 *(Dixon-Bonner 8, Stewart 77)* 1002

Accrington S: (442) Bursik; Edwards, Sykes, Alese, Opoku; Clark (Sousa 75), Conneely, Sheriff, Pritchard (Simpson 67); Baker-Richardson (Carvalho 46), Charles.
Liverpool U21: (433) Winterbottom; Gallacher, Clayton, Savage, Norris; Dixon-Bonner, Cain, Christie-Davies; Stewart, Varesanovic (Beck 81), Hill.
Referee: Andy Haines.

Wednesday, 13 November 2019

Fleetwood T (4) 5 *(Clarke P 9, Morris J 11, Sowerby 14, Burns 40, Madden 51)*

Oldham Ath (1) 2 *(Smith 25, Azankpo 78)* 535

Fleetwood T: (433) Cairns; Southam-Hales, Clarke P, Dunne, Andrew; Dempsey (Matete 70), Rossiter, Sowerby; Burns, Madden (Garner 70), Morris J (Hayes 74).
Oldham Ath: (4231) de la Paz; Mills, Hamer, Stott, Iacovitti; McCann, Sylla; Eagles (Maouche 46), Morais (Wilson 46), Smith; Emmerson (Azankpo 65).
Referee: Andy Haines.

North Group B	P	W	DW	DL	L	F	A	GD	Pts
Accrington S	3	3	0	0	0	10	3	7	9
Fleetwood T	3	1	1	0	1	7	5	2	5
Oldham Ath	3	1	0	0	2	5	10	–5	3
Liverpool U21	3	0	0	1	2	5	9	–4	1

NORTHERN SECTION GROUP C

Tuesday, 3 September 2019

Salford C (0) 2 *(Lloyd 80 (pen), Rooney 82)*

Aston Villa U21 (0) 0 916

Salford C: (4231) Letheren; Threlkeld (Wiseman 73), Jones J, Burgess C, Jones D; Shelton, Smith (Thomas-Asante 61); Walker (Dieseruvwe 73), Whitehead, Lloyd; Rooney.
Aston Villa U21: (4231) Searle; Walker, Suliman, Revan, Rowe; Birch (Guy 81), Brunt; Wright, Clarke, Tait (Philogene-Bidace 60); Archer.
Referee: Rob Lewis.

Tuesday, 8 October 2019

Tranmere R (1) 2 *(Ray 14, Jennings 78)*

Aston Villa U21 (1) 1 *(Archer 2)* 978

Tranmere R: (442) Pilling; Caprice, Ray (Ridehalgh 82), Monthe, Borthwick-Jackson; Morris, Potter, Gilmour, Blackett-Taylor (Mullin 82); Ponticelli, Jennings.
Aston Villa U21: (4231) Searle; Walker, Suliman, Revan, Rowe; Birch (Sohna 90), Brunt (Vassilev 86); Wright (Odutayo 68), Clarke, Tait; Archer.
Referee: Ollie Yates.

Tuesday, 12 November 2019

Tranmere R (0) 0

Salford C (1) 2 *(Threlkeld 2, Hogan 56)* 1196

Tranmere R: (433) Pilling; Caprice, Nelson, Ray, Borthwick-Jackson; Jennings, Potter, Maddox (Morris 75); Blackett-Taylor, Payne (Hepburn-Murphy 75), Ferrier (Walker-Rice 84).
Salford C: (352) Neal; Hughes (Lloyd 46), Hogan, Piergianni; Wiseman, Whitehead (Jervis 28), Doyle, Threlkeld (Baldwin 75), Jones D; Thomas-Asante, Dieseruvwe.
Referee: James Adcock.

North Group C	P	W	DW	DL	L	F	A	GD	Pts
Salford C	2	2	0	0	0	4	0	4	6
Tranmere R	2	1	0	0	1	2	3	–1	3
Aston Villa U21	2	0	0	0	2	1	4	–3	0
Bury*	0	0	0	0	0	0	0	0	0

Bury expelled.

NORTHERN SECTION GROUP D

Tuesday, 3 September 2019

Macclesfield T (1) 2 *(Fitzpatrick 19, Gomis 63)*

Newcastle U U21 (0) 1 *(Charman 48)* 525

Macclesfield T: (3412) Charles-Cook; Clarke, Cameron, Horsfall; O'Keeffe, Rose, Kirby, Fitzpatrick; Gnahoua (Stephens 66); Gomis (Archibald 78), Blyth (Osadebe 65).
Newcastle U U21: (4141) Turner; Sterry, Cass, McEntee, Walters; Bailey; Allan, Charman, Scott K (Young 69), Longelo (Anderson 76); Toure (White 69).
Referee: Ollie Yates.

Port Vale (0) 2 *(Amoo 63 (pen), Archer 75)*

Shrewsbury T (1) 1 *(Kennedy 27 (og))* 1008

Port Vale: (433) Brown; Gibbons, Kennedy, Smith, Crookes; Jake Taylor (Cullen 64), Evans, Lloyd; Amoo (Worrall 71), Pope (Archer 60), Montano.
Shrewsbury T: (352) Murphy; Walker, Ebanks-Landell, Love (Morison 84); Barnett, Thompson (McCormick 59), Goss, Laurent, Golbourne; Whalley, Udoh.
Referee: Leigh Doughty.

Tuesday, 24 September 2019

Macclesfield T (1) 2 *(Ironside 16, Archibald 90)*

Port Vale (1) 3 *(Burgess 34, Bennett 52, Jake Taylor 74)* 757

Macclesfield T: (3412) Charles-Cook; Horsfall, Cameron (Welch-Hayes 63), Fitzpatrick; Clarke, Rose, Ntambwe, O'Keeffe (Archibald 46); Stephens; Ironside, Blyth (Osadebe 73).
Port Vale: (4312) Brown; Gibbons, Kennedy, Brisley, Crookes; Burgess (Hurst 90), Joyce (Oyeleke 70), Jake Taylor; Lloyd; Bennett, Cullen (Archer 46).
Referee: Carl Boyeson.

Tuesday, 8 October 2019

Shrewsbury T (2) 3 *(Okenabirhie 22, Cummings 33, Edwards 87)*

Newcastle U U21 (0) 0 1408

Shrewsbury T: (352) Murphy; Williams, Walker, Love; Whalley, Goss, Edwards, Thompson (Laurent 60), Golbourne; Okenabirhie (Barnett 88), Cummings (Udoh 73).
Newcastle U U21: (442) Langley; Sterry, McEntee, Cass, Walters; Allan, Young, White (Francillette 39), Anderson (Fernandez 39); Charman (Stephenson 66), Scott K.
Referee: Peter Wright.

Tuesday, 12 November 2019

Port Vale (1) 2 *(Cullen 40, 85)*

Newcastle U U21 (0) 1 *(Anderson 50)* 571

Port Vale: (442) Maddison; Atkinson (Campbell-Gordon 64), Brisley, Kennedy, Evans; Trickett-Smith, Lloyd, Conlon (Jake Taylor 62), Browne; Archer (Burgess 65), Cullen.
Newcastle U U21: (4231) Turner; Sterry, Cass, Francillette, Walters; Young, Sangare; Allan, Scott K (Longelo 64), Anderson (Scott J 82); Charman.
Referee: Paul Marsden.

Wednesday, 13 November 2019

Shrewsbury T (1) 3 *(Thompson 28, Edwards 74, Walker 83)*

Macclesfield T (0) 1 *(Archibald 59)* 1065

Shrewsbury T: (343) Murphy; Williams, Ebanks-Landell, Golbourne; Whalley, Laurent, Walker, Giles; Thompson (Love■ 67), Okenabirhie (John-Lewis 88), Edwards.
Macclesfield T: (3412) Charles-Cook; Horsfall, Kelleher, Vassell; Welch-Hayes (Fitzpatrick 46), Harris, Kirby, Archibald; Osadebe (Rose 76); Ironside (Gnahoua 46), Stephens.
Referee: Michael Salisbury.

North Group D	P	W	DW	DL	L	F	A	GD	Pts
Port Vale	3	3	0	0	0	7	4	3	9
Shrewsbury T	3	2	0	0	1	7	3	4	6
Macclesfield T	3	1	0	0	2	5	7	–2	3
Newcastle U U21	3	0	0	0	3	2	7	–5	0

NORTHERN SECTION GROUP E

Tuesday, 27 August 2019

Mansfield T (0) 1 *(Sterling-James 87)*

Everton U21 (1) 1 *(Gordon 28)* 824

Mansfield T: (442) Stone; Benning, Preston, Gibbens, Clarke; Mellis, Sterling-James, Law (Khan 46), Smith (Sinclair 90); Hamilton, Knowles (MacDonald 46).
Everton U21: (451) Tyrer; Foulds, Feeney, Denny (Astley 86), John; Charsley, Adeniran (Simms 68 (Mampala 88)), Baningime■, Markelo, Gordon; Evans.
Everton U21 won 4-1 on penalties.
Referee: Ben Toner.

Tuesday, 3 September 2019

Crewe Alex (0) 1 *(Green 87)*

Burton Alb (3) 3 *(Quinn 13, Fraser 23, Akins 45)* 917

Crewe Alex: (433) Richards; Ng, Hunt, Nolan, Adebisi; Jones (Wintle 46), Finney (Green 46), Ainley (Pickering 46); Dale, Anene, Kirk.
Burton Alb: (433) O'Hara; Brayford (Anderson 84), O'Toole, Wallace, Hutchinson; Edwards, Quinn, Fraser (Beardsley 90); Sbarra, Akins, Templeton (Sarkic 70).
Referee: Anthony Backhouse.

Tuesday, 1 October 2019

Burton Alb (0) 0

Everton U21 (1) 2 *(Simms 6, Evans 59)* 435

Burton Alb: (433) Bywater; Akins, O'Toole, Daniel (Nartey 62), Hutchinson; Edwards, Wallace, Sbarra; Templeton (Fraser 62), Boyce, Dyer (Sarkic 62).
Everton U21: (433) Tyrer; Astley, Feeney, Gibson, Foulds; Charsley, Markelo, Adeniran; Evans (Denny 75), Simms (Dobbin 83), Gordon (Mampala 87).
Referee: Andy Haines.

Tuesday, 8 October 2019

Mansfield T (1) 1 *(Knowles 18)*

Crewe Alex (1) 1 *(Finney 45)* 800

Mansfield T: (3412) Olejnik; Preston, Shaughnessy, Sweeney; Clarke, Smith, Tomlinson (Mellis 52 (Benning 71)), Hamilton; Afolayan; Knowles (Khan 83), Cook.
Crewe Alex: (433) Richards; Johnson, Ng, Nolan, Adebisi (Pickering 84); Green (Jones 77), Wintle, Ainley; Dale (Kirk 84), Anene, Finney.
Crewe Alex won 4-3 on penalties.
Referee: James Oldham.

Tuesday, 5 November 2019

Crewe Alex (1) 2 *(Ainley 43, Dale 78)*

Everton U21 (1) 2 *(Niasse 3, 75)* 851

Crewe Alex: (4222) Richards; Ng, Mbulu (Johnson 90), Nolan (Finney 74), Pickering; Wintle, Jones; Lowery, Ainley; Dale, Anene.
Everton U21: (532) Tyrer; John (Denny 46), Astley, Feeney, Gibson, Foulds; Baningime, Onyango (Anderson 76), Markelo; Niasse, Charsley (Simms 69).
Crewe Alex won 5-4 on penalties.
Referee: Christopher Sarginson.

Tuesday, 12 November 2019

Burton Alb (1) 1 *(Templeton 35)*

Mansfield T (2) 2 *(Rose 23, Sweeney 34)* 485

Burton Alb: (433) Garratt; Akins, O'Toole (Brayford 76), Buxton (Sarkic 46), Daniel; Wallace, Quinn, Edwards; Sbarra, Templeton (Anderson 71), Fraser.
Mansfield T: (352) Olejnik; Shaughnessy, Preston, Sweeney; Clarke, Tomlinson, Smith, Mellis (Afolayan 68), Hamilton; Sterling-James (MacDonald 88), Rose (Graham 62).
Referee: Leigh Doughty.

North Group E	P	W	DW	DL	L	F	A	GD	Pts
Everton U21	3	1	1	1	0	5	3	2	6
Mansfield T	3	1	0	2	0	4	3	1	5
Crewe Alex	3	0	2	0	1	4	6	–2	4
Burton Alb	3	1	0	0	2	4	5	–1	3

NORTHERN SECTION GROUP F

Tuesday, 3 September 2019

Bolton W (1) 1 *(Politic 8)*

Bradford C (0) 1 *(O'Connor P 51)* 9062

Bolton W: (442) Alexander; Brockbank, Senior, Zouma, Boon; King-Harmes (Fitzmartin 76), Graham, Weir, Politic (White 82); Darcy, Brown (Brown-Sterling 65).
Bradford C: (3511) Hornby; French, O'Connor P, Richards-Everton; Gibson, Anderson, Devine, Pritchard (Wood 66), Longridge; Devitt (Patrick 17); Donaldson (Ismail 63).
Bradford C won 4-3 on penalties.
Referee: Martin Coy.

Wednesday, 11 September 2019

Rochdale (0) 0

Manchester C U21 (1) 2 *(Braaf 31, Bernabe 58)* 1172

Rochdale: (442) Lynch; Matheson, Morley, McNulty, Keohane (Gillam 76); Bradley, Ryan, Rathbone (Hopper 76), Phillips; Andrew (Thomas 84), Tavares.
Manchester C U21: (433) Grimshaw; Dionkou, Amankwah, Harwood-Bellis (McDonald 83), Ogbeta; Doyle, Pozo (Dele-Bashiru 89), Braaf; Knight, Touaizi (Fiorini 89), Bernabe.
Referee: Michael Salisbury.

Tuesday, 24 September 2019

Bradford C (1) 1 *(Akpan 21)*

Manchester C U21 (1) 2 *(Rogers 27, Doyle 63)* 868

Bradford C: (442) Sykes-Kenworthy; Henley, French, Richards-Everton, Longridge; Ismail (Staunton 46), Akpan, Devine, Patrick; McCartan (Sikora 66), Oteh (Morris 73).
Manchester C U21: (433) Grimshaw; Robinson, McDonald, Amankwah, Ogbeta; Doyle, Pozo, Dele-Bashiru; Braaf (Fiorini 90), Knight (Touaizi 82), Rogers (Palmer 88).
Referee: Ross Joyce.

Tuesday, 1 October 2019

Rochdale (0) 1 *(Wilbraham 56)*

Bolton W (1) 1 *(Crawford 45)* 1412

Rochdale: (442) Lynch; Matheson, Keohane, Norrington-Davies, Gillam; Bradley (Hopper 90), Morley, Ryan, Dooley (Andrew 11); Tavares, Wilbraham (Baah 82).
Bolton W: (4411) Matthews; Emmanuel, Bridcutt, Zouma, Chicksen; Verlinden, Lowe, Graham (Hobbs 73), Politic; Crawford; Buckley.
Rochdale won 5-3 on penalties.
Referee: Leigh Doughty.

Tuesday, 29 October 2019

Bolton W (1) 3 *(Crawford 4, O'Grady 66, 89)*

Manchester C U21 (1) 1 *(Zouma 13 (og))* 2616

Bolton W: (4231) Matthews; Emmanuel, Zouma, Lowe, Chicksen; Murphy L, Weir (Graham 37); Dodoo, Crawford, O'Grady; Murphy D (Politic 46).
Manchester C U21: (433) Grimshaw; Dionkou, Harwood-Bellis, Burns (McAtee 82), Wilson; Dele-Bashiru, McDonald, Fiorini (Rogers 72); Palmer, Touaizi, Ogunby (Knight 73).
Referee: Peter Wright.

Tuesday, 12 November 2019

Bradford C (1) 1 *(French 15)*

Rochdale (2) 2 *(Pyke 29, Tavares 35)* 761

Bradford C: (433) Sykes-Kenworthy; Mellor, O'Connor, French, Longridge; Cooke, Reeves (Taylor 62), Anderson; Patrick (Richards-Everton 75), Oteh (Devine 63), Ismail.
Rochdale: (433) Lynch; Gillam, Keohane, Dunne, Done; Bradley (Clarkson 80), Hopper, Ryan (Camps 69); Pyke (Baah 61), Wilbraham, Tavares.
Referee: Darren Drysdale.

North Group F	P	W	DW	DL	L	F	A	GD	Pts
Manchester C U21	3	2	0	0	1	5	4	1	6
Bolton W	3	1	0	2	0	5	3	2	5
Rochdale	3	1	1	0	1	3	4	–1	5
Bradford C	3	0	1	0	2	3	5	–2	2

NORTHERN SECTION GROUP G

Tuesday, 3 September 2019

Blackpool (2) 5 *(Heneghan 4, Nottingham 45, Hardie 51, KaiKai 89, Nuttall 90)*

Morecambe (1) 1 *(Ellison 22)* 2319

Blackpool: (3412) Mafoumbi; Nottingham, Heneghan, Anderton; Feeney (Turton 46), Virtue (Shaw 66), Guy, MacDonald; Scannell (KaiKai 78); Hardie, Nuttall.
Morecambe: (442) Halstead; Tanner, Lavelle, Sutton, Conlan (Buxton 63); Oates, Wildig (Lynch 66), Cranston, Ellison; O'Sullivan (Mendes Gomes 76), Stockton.
Referee: Marc Edwards.

Tuesday, 24 September 2019

Carlisle U (2) 2 *(Hope 35, Loft 45)*

Wolverhampton W U21 (2) 4 *(Ashley-Seal 19, 47 (pen), 64, Dai 39)* 893

Carlisle U: (541) Gray; Elliot, Jones G (Hayden 61), Mellish, Branthwaite, Iredale; Sorensen, Bridge, Carroll, Hope; Loft (McKirdy 77).
Wolverhampton W U21: (3412) Sondergaard; Nya, Cristovao, Richards; Rasmussen, Taylor (Hanne 70), Watt, Thompson; Dai (Otasowie 85); Samuels, Ashley-Seal (He 81).
Referee: Sebastian Stockbridge.

Tuesday, 1 October 2019

Morecambe (1) 2 *(Brewitt 25, Howard 81)*

Wolverhampton W U21 (2) 2 *(Watt 23, Samuels 29)* 514

Morecambe: (442) Halstead; Tanner, Lavelle, Old, Buxton; Cranston, Brewitt (Howard 74), Wildig, Ellison; Oates (O'Sullivan 78), Stockton (Mendes Gomes 86).
Wolverhampton W U21: (352) Sondergaard; Sanderson, Marques, Richards; Rasmussen (Otasowie 78), Taylor (Dai 90), Watt, Perry, Thompson; Samuels, Ashley-Seal.
Wolverhampton W U21 won 5-4 on penalties.
Referee: Ross Joyce.

Tuesday, 15 October 2019

Carlisle U (1) 2 *(Loft 45, Carroll 87)*

Blackpool (1) 1 *(Gray 25 (og))* 911

Carlisle U: (343) Gray; Branthwaite, Mellish, Hayden; Elliot, Carroll, Scougall, Iredale; Sorensen, Loft (Thomas 66), McKirdy (Bridge 21 (Sagaf 65)).
Blackpool: (442) Mafoumbi; Nottingham, Edwards, Anderton, MacDonald; Shaw (Bange 72), Spearing, Guy, Scannell; Hardie (Gnanduillet 53), Delfouneso (Turton 58).
Referee: Darren Handley.

Tuesday, 5 November 2019

Blackpool (0) 1 *(Bushiri 90)*

Wolverhampton W U21 (0) 0 1036

Blackpool: (343) Howard; Bushiri, Tilt, Edwards; Turton, Virtue, Guy, MacDonald (Feeney 67); Hardie (Gnanduillet 74), Scannell (KaiKai 79), Nuttall.
Wolverhampton W U21: (532) Sondergaard; Sanderson, Otasowie, Francis, Csoka, Richards; Taylor, Watt, Perry; Ashley-Seal, Campbell (Graham 73).
Referee: Anthony Backhouse.

Tuesday, 12 November 2019

Morecambe (0) 3 *(Tutte 61 (pen), Wildig 67, Conlan 90)*

Carlisle U (1) 1 *(Branthwaite 26)* 802

Morecambe: (433) Halstead; Tanner, Lavelle, Old, Conlan; Tutte (Kenyon 75), Brewitt, Wildig; O'Sullivan (Leitch-Smith 55), Stockton, Alessandra (Sutton 55).
Carlisle U: (352) Gray; Branthwaite, Knight-Percival (McKirdy 69), Mellish; Elliot (Jones G 84), Bridge, Carroll, Sagaf (Olomola 71), Iredale; Sorensen, Loft.
Referee: Graham Salisbury.

North Group G	P	W	DW	DL	L	F	A	GD	Pts
Blackpool	3	2	0	0	1	7	3	4	6
Wolverhampton W U21	3	1	1	0	1	6	5	1	5
Morecambe	3	1	0	1	1	6	8	–2	4
Carlisle U	3	1	0	0	2	5	8	–3	3

NORTHERN SECTION GROUP H

Tuesday, 6 August 2019

Rotherham U (0) 0

Manchester U U21 (0) 2 *(Laird 69, Ramazani 73)* 3105

Rotherham U: (433) Price; Olosunde, Southern-Cooper, Wood, Hinds; Wiles, Barlaser (Crooks 46), Lindsay (MacDonald 68); Ladapo (Smith 54), Proctor, Morris.
Manchester U U21: (4231) Kovar; Laird, O'Connor, Bernard, Williams; Garner, Levitt; Ramazani, Gomes, Chong; Bughail-Mellor.
Referee: Graham Salisbury.

Tuesday, 3 September 2019

Doncaster R (0) 3 *(John 55, Sterling 69, May 80)*

Lincoln C (1) 1 *(Akinde 43)* 2170

Doncaster R: (4231) Dieng; Halliday, Anderson T, John, James; Sheaf (Blair 62), Whiteman; Sadlier, Coppinger (Taylor J 46), May; Ennis (Sterling 62).
Lincoln C: (4231) Smith; Anderson, Bolger, Bostwick (Toffolo 46), Melbourne; Connolly, O'Connor (Payne 62); Andrade, Grant (Walker 63), Chapman; Akinde.
Referee: Scott Oldham.

Tuesday, 1 October 2019

Lincoln C (0) 0

Manchester U U21 (1) 1 *(Garner 20)* 3532

Lincoln C: (4231) Smith; Lewis, Bolger, Melbourne, Toffolo; Chapman, O'Connor (Connolly 71); Anderson (Payne 74), Hesketh (Andrade 62), Grant; Akinde.
Manchester U U21: (4231) Kovar; Puigmal, Mengi, Bernard, Devine; Levitt (Helm 74), Garner; Traore, Galbraith, Chong (Elanga 46); Ramazani.
Referee: Rob Lewis.

Tuesday, 8 October 2019

Rotherham U (1) 3 *(Wright 11 (og), Morris 67, Clarke 77)*

Doncaster R (1) 2 *(Sadlier 37, Wright 54)* 2192

Rotherham U: (433) Price; Jones, Southern-Cooper, Robertson, Mattock; Wiles, MacDonald (Lindsay 54), Barlaser (Kayode 73); Ladapo (Clarke 46), Morris, Lamy.
Doncaster R: (4231) Lawlor; Halliday (Daniels 46), Wright, Blaney, Amos; Greaves, Gomes; Kiwomya, Sadlier (May 46), Longbottom; Thomas (Taylor J 76).
Referee: Marc Edwards.

Tuesday, 29 October 2019

Doncaster R (0) 1 *(May 61)*

Manchester U U21 (0) 2 *(Galbraith 71, Greenwood 90)* 3845

Doncaster R: (4231) Lawlor; Halliday, Wright, Daniels, James; Whiteman (Sheaf 46), Gomes; Kiwomya, Ennis (Sadlier 46), May; Thomas (Watters 69).
Manchester U U21: (4231) Kovar; Laird, Mengi, Bernard, Devine; Puigmal (Helm 77), Galbraith; Ramazani (Elanga 86), Bughail-Mellor, Chong; Greenwood.
Referee: Alan Young.

Tuesday, 12 November 2019

Lincoln C (2) 3 *(Akinde 12 (pen), 14, Walker 87)*

Rotherham U (0) 0 1860

Lincoln C: (4231) Smith; Anderson, Connolly, Melbourne, Coker (Toffolo 60); Pett, Frecklington (Hesketh 58); Payne (Walker 82), Chapman, Grant; Akinde.
Rotherham U: (442) Price; Olosunde, Southern-Cooper, Thompson (Robertson 69), Hinds; Lamy (Ogbene 58), Lindsay, Barlaser, Hastie (Morris 69); Ladapo, Smith.
Referee: James Oldham.

North Group H	P	W	DW	DL	L	F	A	GD	Pts
Manchester U U21	3	3	0	0	0	5	1	4	9
Doncaster R	3	1	0	0	2	6	6	0	3
Lincoln C	3	1	0	0	2	4	4	0	3
Rotherham U	3	1	0	0	2	3	7	–4	3

SOUTHERN SECTION GROUP A

Tuesday, 3 September 2019

Gillingham (1) 2 *(O'Keefe 23, Mandron 78)*

Colchester U (1) 3 *(Cowan-Hall 8, 62, Robinson 55)* 1055

Gillingham: (41212) Walsh; Hodson, Tucker, Ogilvie, O'Connor; O'Keefe; Marshall, Cisse (Jakubiak 70); Charles-Cook (Byrne 73); Mandron, Ndjoli (Lee 70).
Colchester U: (4231) Ross; Sarpong-Wiredu, Sowunmi (Eastman 60), Kensdale, Clampin; Comley, Chilvers (James 82); Cowan-Hall (Senior 76), Brown, Adubofour-Poku; Robinson.
Referee: David Rock.

Ipswich T (0) 2 *(Roberts 47, 66)*

Tottenham H U21 (1) 1 *(Shashoua 8)* 5377

Ipswich T: (3412) Norris; Woolfenden, Wilson, Kenlock; Donacien, Huws, Nolan, Edwards; El Mizouni; Roberts (Simpson 68), Dobra.
Tottenham H U21: (433) Whiteman; Okedina, Eyoma, Lyons-Foster, Hinds; Oakley-Boothe (Patterson 70), White (Asante 86), Shashoua; Markanday, Richards, Tracey.
Referee: Craig Hicks.

Tuesday, 8 October 2019

Colchester U (1) 1 *(Norris 44)*

Tottenham H U21 (0) 1 *(Oakley-Boothe 75)* 1061

Colchester U: (4231) Ross; Sarpong-Wiredu (Jackson 76), Sowunmi, Eastman, Clampin; Chilvers, Lapslie (Comley 68); Senior, Brown, Adubofour-Poku (Robinson 80); Norris.
Tottenham H U21: (4231) de Bie; Eyoma, Walcott, Binks, Hinds; Bowden (Patterson 67), White; Oakley-Boothe, Shashoua, Tracey (Markanday 76); Richards (Etete 89).
Tottenham H U21 won 6-5 on penalties.
Referee: Alan Young.

Ipswich T (2) 4 *(Huws 8, Roberts 21, Mandron 61 (og), Keane 87)*

Gillingham (0) 0 5271

Ipswich T: (3412) Norris; Woolfenden, Nsiala, Wilson (Hughes 80); Donacien (Edwards 46), El Mizouni, Huws, Kenlock; Rowe; Keane, Roberts (Dobra 46).
Gillingham: (41212) Walsh; Hodson, Tucker, Ogilvie, Garmston; Cisse; Woods, Marshall; Pringle; Mandron (Lee 69), Charles-Cook (Jakubiak 69).
Referee: Tom Nield.

Tuesday, 12 November 2019

Colchester U (0) 1 *(Clampin 80)*

Ipswich T (0) 0 5104

Colchester U: (4231) Ross; Sarpong-Wiredu (Jackson 57), Sowunmi, Prosser, Clampin; Lapslie, Pell; Senior (Adubofour-Poku 65), Brown, Nouble (Robinson 71); Norris.
Ipswich T: (4411) Holy; Donacien, Wilson, Nsiala, Kenlock; Edwards (Chirewa 90), McGavin, Huws, Georgiou (Gibbs 87); El Mizouni (Hughes 87); Folami.
Referee: Sam Purkiss.

Gillingham (1) 2 *(Jakubiak 25, Tucker 79)*

Tottenham H U21 (0) 0 1196

Gillingham: (442) Walsh; Hodson, Tucker, Ogilvie, Garmston; Marshall, Cisse, Woods (O'Keefe 78), Charles-Cook; Ndjoli, Jakubiak.
Tottenham H U21: (4231) Whiteman; Okedina, Eyoma, Binks, Lyons-Foster (Pochettino 79); Oakley-Boothe (Patterson 46), White; Tracey, Shashoua, Bennett; Richards (Clarke 74).
Referee: Neil Hair.

South Group A	P	W	DW	DL	L	F	A	GD	Pts
Colchester U	3	2	0	1	0	5	3	2	7
Ipswich T	3	2	0	0	1	6	2	4	6
Gillingham	3	1	0	0	2	4	7	–3	3
Tottenham H U21	3	0	1	0	2	2	5	–3	2

SOUTHERN SECTION GROUP B

Tuesday, 3 September 2019

Oxford U (0) 2 *(Brannagan 77, Baptiste 85)*

Norwich C U21 (0) 1 *(Hutchinson 64)* 1084

Oxford U: (4231) Stevens; Long, Dickie, Mousinho, Berkoe; Hanson, Baptiste; Hall, Fosu (Sykes 58), Forde (Lofthouse 66); Agyei (Brannagan 66).
Norwich C U21: (4411) Johnson; Thomas, Jones, Famewo, Nizet; Martin (Jackson 90), Milovanovic, McAlear (Khumbeni 90), Hondermarck (Dickson-Peters 84); Scully; Hutchinson.
Referee: Christopher Sarginson.

Portsmouth (0) 1 *(Pitman 70)*

Crawley T (0) 0 3784

Portsmouth: (433) Bass; Bolton, Downing, Raggett, Haunstrup; Evans (Pitman 46), Naylor, Close; Maloney, Harrison, Marquis.
Crawley T: (4231) Luyambula; Francomb, Dallison (Tunnicliffe 46), Sendles-White, Young; Payne, Powell (Ferguson 54); Nathaniel-George, Nadesan, Allarakhia (Galach 80); Enigbokan-Bloomfield.
Referee: James Linington.

Saturday, 14 September 2019

Portsmouth (2) 3 *(Harrison 10, 60, Flint 44)*

Norwich C U21 (0) 1 *(Scully 67)* 2855

Portsmouth: (4231) Bass; Bolton, Hawkins, Raggett, Hancott; Cannon, Walkes; Maloney (Williams 71), Flint (Close 72), Teggart (Marquis 77); Harrison.
Norwich C U21: (4411) Mair; Thomas, Jones (Omobamidele 73), Famewo, Nizet; Fitzpatrick, Milovanovic, McAlear, Adshead; Ahadme (Scully 61); Thorvaldsson (Hondermarck 85).
Referee: Brett Huxtable.

Tuesday, 1 October 2019

Crawley T (0) 1 *(Nathaniel-George 63)*

Norwich C U21 (1) 2 *(Ahadme 19, Lomas 74)* 361

Crawley T: (4141) Luyambula; Young, Sendles-White, Dallison, Doherty; Payne; van Velzen, Boadu (Ferguson 50), Allarakhia, Nathaniel-George; Lubala (Galach 59).
Norwich C U21: (4411) Johnson; Lomas, Omobamidele, Famewo, Heise; Martin (Hondermarck 88), Adshead, Milovanovic, Nizet (Scully 70); Thorvaldsson; Ahadme.
Referee: Alan Young.

Tuesday, 8 October 2019

Oxford U (1) 2 *(Taylor 21, Dickie 90)*

Portsmouth (1) 2 *(Lethbridge 33, Walkes 85)* 1548

Oxford U: (433) Eastwood; Long, Dickie, Moore, Ruffels; Brannagan, Gorrin (Sole 86), Baptiste (Lopes 73); Hall, Taylor (Agyei 69), Sykes.
Portsmouth: (4231) Bass; Walkes, Downing, Hancott, Haunstrup; Cannon, Rew (Close 46); Williams, Flint (Evans 46), Maloney; Lethbridge (Harrison 63).
Portsmouth won 5-4 on penalties.
Referee: Will Finnie.

Tuesday, 12 November 2019

Crawley T (0) 1 *(Enigbokan-Bloomfield 50)*

Oxford U (2) 4 *(Hall 12, 57 (pen), 73 (pen), Forde 28 (pen))* 412

Crawley T: (4141) Luyambula; Francomb■, McNerney (Tunnicliffe 46), Dallison, Sesay (Young 46); Sendles-White; Nadesan (Lubala 46), Boadu, Camara, Nathaniel-George; Enigbokan-Bloomfield.
Oxford U: (433) Stevens; Forde (Long 46), Mousinho, Jones, Berkoe; Sykes, Gorrin (Goodrham 76), Baptiste; Hall, Agyei, Zamouri (Lopes 63).
Referee: Josh Smith.

South Group B	P	W	DW	DL	L	F	A	GD	Pts
Portsmouth	3	2	1	0	0	6	3	3	8
Oxford U	3	2	0	1	0	8	4	4	7
Norwich C U21	3	1	0	0	2	4	6	–2	3
Crawley T	3	0	0	0	3	2	7	–5	0

SOUTHERN SECTION GROUP C

Tuesday, 3 September 2019

AFC Wimbledon (0) 0

Brighton & HA U21 (0) 2 *(Tzanev 52 (og), Radulovic 89)* 388

AFC Wimbledon: (352) Tzanev; Kalambayi (Wood 77), Nightingale, Thomas; Stabana, McLoughlin, Hartigan, Pinnock (Rudoni 66), Osew; Folivi (Pigott 76), Roscrow.
Brighton & HA U21: (4231) Steele; Davies A (Yapi 77), Tsoungui, Freestone, Cochrane; Alzate, Crofts; Gwargis, Davies J (Radulovic 83), Richards; Longman (Cashman 77).
Referee: Lee Swabey.

Leyton Orient (1) 2 *(Happe 6, Gorman 90)*

Southend U (0) 0 1562

Leyton Orient: (4231) Sargeant; Judd (Ling 46), Happe, Ekpiteta, Ogie; Gorman, Marsh; Alabi, Maguire-Drew (Clay 84), Dennis (Angol 66); Harrold.
Southend U: (433) Oxley; Bwomono, Lennon, Shaughnessy, Blackman; Hamilton, Kiernan, Mantom; Ndukwu (Goodship 46), Acquah (Cox 52), Hutchinson■.
Referee: Chris Pollard.

Tuesday, 1 October 2019

Southend U (0) 0

Brighton & HA U21 (0) 2 *(Richards 50, O'Hora 81)* 641

Southend U: (433) Bishop; Demetriou, Shaughnessy, Kiernan, Blackman; Dieng (Acquah 61), Mantom, Hyam; Ndukwu (Humphrys 73), Goodship, McLaughlin (Egbri 61).
Brighton & HA U21: (4231) Steele; Davies A, O'Hora, Roberts, Cochrane; Baluta, Jenks; Davies J, Richards (Cashman 78), Gwargis (Radulovic 62); Longman (Yapi 86).
Referee: Trevor Kettle.

Tuesday, 8 October 2019

AFC Wimbledon (1) 3 *(Pigott 3 (pen), Folivi 49, Reilly 79)*

Leyton Orient (0) 0 642

AFC Wimbledon: (352) Trott; Kalambayi, Delaney, Thomas; Wagstaff (Stabana 60), Pinnock, Sanders, Reilly, Osew (Guinness-Walker 84); Folivi, Pigott (Forss 60).
Leyton Orient: (433) Sargeant; Judd, Happe, Ekpiteta (Sweeney 46), Ogie (Coulson 61); Gorman, Marsh, Maguire-Drew; Dennis, Alabi, Dayton (Brophy 61).
Referee: Charles Breakspear.

Wednesday, 6 November 2019

Leyton Orient (0) 1 *(Dennis 63)*

Brighton & HA U21 (1) 1 *(Cashman 33)* 709

Leyton Orient: (433) Sargeant; Judd, Ekpiteta, Turley (Happe 61), Ogie; Kyprianou, Maguire-Drew, Clay; Dennis, Alabi, Brophy (Dayton 60).
Brighton & HA U21: (442) Button; Davies A, Tsoungui, Roberts (Leonard 89), Cochrane; Richards (Yapi 85), Jenks, Baluta, Gwargis; Wilson (Vukoj 71), Cashman.
Leyton Orient won 4-2 on penalties.
Referee: Kevin Johnson.

Wednesday, 13 November 2019

Southend U (2) 3 *(Ralph 25, Hamilton 45, Hopper 80)*

AFC Wimbledon (1) 1 *(Wood 35)* 717

Southend U: (343) Bishop; Kiernan, Milligan, Taylor; Bwomono, Hamilton, Dieng, Ralph; Cox (Rush 85), Acquah (Goodship 74), McLaughlin (Hopper 74).
AFC Wimbledon: (352) McDonnell; Madelin, Kalambayi, Reilly; Stabana (Awoyejo 71), Hartigan, Assal (McNab 60), Rudoni, Guinness-Walker; Appiah (Robinson 46), Wood.
Referee: Will Finnie.

South Group C	P	W	DW	DL	L	F	A	GD	Pts
Brighton & HA U21	3	2	0	1	0	5	1	4	7
Leyton Orient	3	1	1	0	1	3	4	−1	5
AFC Wimbledon	3	1	0	0	2	4	5	−1	3
Southend U	3	1	0	0	2	3	5	−2	3

SOUTHERN SECTION GROUP D

Tuesday, 3 September 2019

Coventry C (0) 0

Walsall (0) 0 1005

Coventry C: (433) Wilson; Watson, Williams, McFadzean, McCallum; Bartlett, Eccles, O'Hare (Bapaga 74); Wakefield (Biamou 78), Bakayoko, Kastaneer (Burroughs 59).
Walsall: (442) Rose; Facey, Liddle, Jules, Pring; Holden (Norman 67), Guthrie (Hardy 61), Bates, Kinsella; Gordon (Gaffney 66), Adebayo.
Coventry C won 5-4 on penalties.
Referee: Will Finnie.

Forest Green R (1) 3 *(Stevens 29, 89, Grubb 71)*

Southampton U21 (1) 2 *(Hale 16, N'Lundulu 80)* 653

Forest Green R: (3412) Thomas; Godwin-Malife, Kitching, McGinley; Winchester (Jones D 68), Dawson (Jones I 68), Morton, Mondal; Taylor (Grubb 46); Stevens, McCoulsky.
Southampton U21: (352) Bycroft; Klarer, O'Driscoll, Kpohomouh; Ramsay, Defise, Smallbone, Turner (Chauke 55), Vokins; Hale (Mitchell 61), N'Lundulu (Agbontohoma 90).
Referee: Brett Huxtable.

Tuesday, 1 October 2019

Walsall (1) 1 *(Scarr 45)*

Southampton U21 (0) 0 732

Walsall: (352) Roberts L; Scarr, Sadler, Jules; Norman, Bates, Liddle, Kinsella, Cockerill-Mollett (McDonald 46); Gordon (Adebayo 79), Gaffney (Roberts K 90).
Southampton U21: (352) Lewis; Klarer, O'Driscoll, Ledwidge (Norton 64); Ramsay, Jankewitz, Slattery, Defise, Vokins; Hansen (Mitchell 76), N'Lundulu.
Referee: Peter Wright.

Tuesday, 8 October 2019

Forest Green R (0) 0

Coventry C (0) 0 924

Forest Green R: (3412) Wollacott; Godwin-Malife, McGinley, Adams; Shephard (Bernard 18), Grubb (Kitching 5), Morton, Mondal; Allen; Collins (Stevens 62), Covil.
Coventry C: (433) Wilson; Watson, McFadzean, Rose, McCallum; Eccles, Kelly, Westbrooke; Wakefield (Kastaneer 35), Bakayoko (Godden 69), Bapaga (O'Hare 79).
Forest Green R won 8-7 on penalties.
Referee: David Rock.

Tuesday, 5 November 2019

Coventry C (0) 3 *(Biamou 52, 55 (pen), 90)*

Southampton U21 (0) 2 *(Slattery 61 (pen), 84)* 375

Coventry C: (433) Wilson; Watson (Dabo 46), Drysdale, McFadzean, Mason; Eccles, Walsh, Shipley; Kastaneer (Young 87), Biamou, Bapaga.
Southampton U21: (433) Lewis; Ramsay, O'Driscoll, Kpohomouh, Ledwidge; Chauke (Defise 74), Slattery, Jankewitz; Hale (Hansen 62), Norton, Olaigbe.
Referee: Ben Toner.

Tuesday, 12 November 2019

Walsall (2) 6 *(Gordon 23, 33, 50 (pen), McDonald 72, Kinsella 74, Norman 90)*

Forest Green R (0) 0 621

Walsall: (442) Roberts L; Norman, Liddle, Scarr, Cockerill-Mollett; Holden, Bates (Kiersey 69), Kinsella, McDonald; Lavery (Hardy 59), Gordon (Adebayo 59).
Forest Green R: (4231) Smith; Jones I, Godwin-Malife, Mills M (Dawson 64), McGinley; Morton, Bunker (Jones D 64); Covil (Artwell 64), Taylor, Mondal; Collins■.
Referee: Tom Nield.

South Group D	P	W	DW	DL	L	F	A	GD	Pts
Walsall	3	2	0	1	0	7	0	7	7
Coventry C	3	1	1	1	0	3	2	1	6
Forest Green R	3	1	1	0	1	3	8	−5	5
Southampton U21	3	0	0	0	3	4	7	−3	0

SOUTHERN SECTION GROUP E

Tuesday, 3 September 2019

Exeter C (1) 1 *(Ajose 5)*

Cheltenham T (0) 0 786

Exeter C: (433) Maxted; Richardson, Warren, Parkes, Woodman; Taylor (Key 53), Tillson, Jay; Ajose (Chrisene 87), Fisher (Williams 62), Seymour.
Cheltenham T: (352) Lovett; Bowry, Tozer, Greaves (Raglan 78); Brennan (Long 78), Broom, Chamberlain (Addai 78), Thomas, Debayo; Lloyd, Campbell.
Referee: Darren Drysdale.

Wednesday, 4 September 2019

Newport Co (4) 4 *(Abrahams 10, Whitely 12, Collins 32, Hillier 42)*

West Ham U U21 (1) 5 *(Scully 1, 88, Powell 47 (pen), Parkes 53, Corbett 83)* 581

Newport Co: (442) Townsend; Leadbitter, Howkins, Ekpiteta, Watts; Collins (Inniss■ 59), Dolan (Evans 46), Maloney, Whitely; Abrahams (Hillier 22), Jefferies.
West Ham U U21: (4231) Anang; Greenidge (Appiah-Forson 46), Okotcha (Caiger 46), Johnson, Hannam; Costa Da Rosa, Lewis; Kemp, Powell, Parkes (Corbett 71); Scully.
Referee: John Busby.

Tuesday, 8 October 2019

Cheltenham T (1) 4 *(Smith 25, 55, 64, Lloyd 67)*

West Ham U U21 (3) 3 *(Kemp 11, 31, Costa Da Rosa 34)* 1020

Cheltenham T: (352) Lovett; Bowry, Greaves, Boyle; Long, Clements, Lloyd (Evans-Harriot 85), Ince, Hussey; Campbell (Addai 85), Smith.
West Ham U U21: (451) Anang; Caiger, Adebayo (Watson 79), Hannam (Appiah-Forson 32), Emmanuel; Kemp, Lewis, Costa Da Rosa (Parkes 89), Powell, Holland; Scully.
Referee: Christopher Sarginson.

Newport Co (0) 0

Exeter C (1) 2 *(Jay 40, 71)* 635

Newport Co: (352) Townsend; Jefferies, Ekpiteta, Inniss; Maloney (Evans 75), Whitely, Watts (George 46), Dolan, Nurse; Abrahams (Hillier 77), Poleon.
Exeter C: (3412) Maxted; Dean, Martin A, Parkes (Sweeney 59); Richardson, Atangana (Bowman 60), Tillson, Woodman; Jay; Seymour, Fisher (Chrisene 79).
Referee: Lee Swabey.

Tuesday, 12 November 2019

Cheltenham T (3) 4 *(Sheaf 17, Addai 34, Long 37, Tozer 84)*

Newport Co (5) 7 *(Maloney 8, 45, 53, Dolan 27 (pen), Abrahams 30, 43, 68)* 774

Cheltenham T: (352) Lovett; Raglan, Tozer, Boyle; Long, Sheaf (Reid 59), Ince, Clements, Hussey (Greaves 58); Lloyd, Addai.
Newport Co: (442) Townsend; Jefferies, Howkins, Woodiwiss (Bennett 90), Nurse; Whitely, Maloney, Dolan (Jones 82), Collins; Poleon, Abrahams (Hillier 76).
Referee: Andy Woolmer.

Wednesday, 13 November 2019

Exeter C (1) 3 *(Randall 9, 88, Tillson 78)*

West Ham U U21 (1) 1 *(Powell 18 (pen))* 807

Exeter C: (352) Visser; Sweeney (Richardson 46), Hartridge, Moxey (Bowman 58); Seymour (Chrisene 79), Tillson, Dean, Taylor, Sparkes; Key, Randall.
West Ham U U21: (433) Hegyi; Ashby (Caiger 71), Parker, Baptiste, Emmanuel; Lewis, Costa Da Rosa, Powell; Chesters (Corbett 79), Kemp, Holland.
Referee: Andy Davies.

South Group E	P	W	DW	DL	L	F	A	GD	Pts
Exeter C	3	3	0	0	0	6	1	5	9
Newport Co	3	1	0	0	2	11	11	0	3
West Ham U U21	3	1	0	0	2	9	11	−2	3
Cheltenham T	3	1	0	0	2	8	11	−3	3

SOUTHERN SECTION GROUP F

Tuesday, 6 August 2019

Swindon T (1) 2 *(Ballard 18, May 47)*

Chelsea U21 (2) 3 *(Anjorin 12, 16, Brown 60)* 1995

Swindon T: (451) McCormick; Reid, Ballard, Broadbent, Hunt; Isgrove (McGlashan 70), Doughty, Diagouraga, May, Iandolo (Yates 46); Anderson (Woolery 70).
Chelsea U21: (442) Cumming; Lamptey, Guehi, Mola, Maatsen; Uwakwe (Lewis 84), Gilmour, McEachran (Lavinier 22), Castillo; Anjorin (Wakely 55), Brown.
Referee: Alan Young.

Tuesday, 3 September 2019

Plymouth Arg (1) 1 *(Moore B 40)*

Bristol R (1) 1 *(Nichols 30)* 2518

Plymouth Arg: (532) Palmer; Moore T, Joshua Grant, Aimson (Wootton 46), Sawyer, Cooper G; Baxter (Boyd 81), Randell, Sarcevic; Moore B (Rudden 67), Lolos.
Bristol R: (532) van Stappershoef; Rodman, Little, Menayese, Craig, Kelly; Bennett, Upson (Ogogo 6 (Hoole 61)), Nichols (Smith 75); Adeboyejo, Hargreaves.
Plymouth Arg won 5-3 on penalties.
Referee: Keith Stroud.

Tuesday, 24 September 2019

Bristol R (0) 2 *(Adeboyejo 59, Sercombe 73)*

Chelsea U21 (1) 1 *(Brown 31)* 1144

Bristol R: (352) van Stappershoef; Menayese, Davies, Kilgour; Rodman, Bennett (Tomlinson 81), Upson, Sercombe, Kelly; Smith (Nichols 60), Adeboyejo (Moore 84).
Chelsea U21: (4231) Cumming; Lamptey (Colwill 82), Simeu, Wakely, Lavinier; Mola (Broja 90), McEachran; Ballo, Russell (Simons 78), Nunn; Brown.
Referee: Antony Coggins.

Tuesday, 8 October 2019

Swindon T (0) 0

Plymouth Arg (2) 3 *(Rudden 15, Joel Grant 36, Riley 66)* 1199

Swindon T: (4312) Benda; Reid, Curran (Broadbent 41), Zakuani, Iandolo (Hunt 54); Rose, May, Doughty; Isgrove; Woolery, Doyle (Twine 72).
Plymouth Arg: (3142) Cooper M; Wootton, Canavan, Joshua Grant; Edwards; Riley, Sarcevic (Wilson 78), Grant C (Randell 56), Sawyer; Joel Grant, Rudden (Taylor 72).
Referee: Chris Pollard.

Tuesday, 29 October 2019

Plymouth Arg (0) 0

Chelsea U21 (0) 1 *(Russell 90)* 1725

Plymouth Arg: (3142) Cooper M; Aimson (Canavan 89), Wootton, Sawyer; Randell; Riley, Cooper G (Joshua Grant 66), Sarcevic, McFadzean; Moore B, Clarke (Joel Grant 63).
Chelsea U21: (4231) Cumming; Lawrence, Wakely, Mola, Lavinier (Livramento 83); Russell, McEachran; Anjorin (Colwill 73), Ballo, Nunn (Broja 90); Brown.
Referee: John Busby.

Wednesday, 13 November 2019

Bristol R (0) 1 *(Little 73)*

Swindon T (0) 0 1083

Bristol R: (352) van Stappershoef; Kilgour, Craig, Menayese; Little, Bennett (Tomlinson 69), Upson, Clarke O, Leahy (Holmes-Dennis 56); Nichols, Clarke-Harris (Adeboyejo 69).
Swindon T: (352) McCormick; Zakuani, Curran, Broadbent; Reid, Sanokho, Diagouraga, Rose (May 6), Hunt (Iandolo 17); Twine, Parsons (Holland 70).
Referee: Ollie Yates.

South Group F	P	W	DW	DL	L	F	A	GD	Pts
Bristol R	3	2	0	1	0	4	2	2	7
Chelsea U21	3	2	0	0	1	5	4	1	6
Plymouth Arg	3	1	1	0	1	4	2	2	5
Swindon T	3	0	0	0	3	2	7	−5	0

SOUTHERN SECTION GROUP G

Tuesday, 3 September 2019

Stevenage (0) 0

Milton Keynes D (1) 3 *(McGrandles 16, Nombe 78, 84)* 789

Stevenage: (3412) Bastien; Fernandez, Soares (Mackail-Smith 10 (Kennedy 59)), Watts; Fielding, Smith, Iontton, Denton; Carter; Cowley, List (Georgiou 65).
Milton Keynes D: (442) Moore; Williams, Martin, Walsh, Lewington; Houghton, Kasumu, McGrandles, Dickenson (Cargill 64); Bowery (Boateng 65), Nombe.
Referee: Sam Purkiss.

Tuesday, 1 October 2019

Milton Keynes D (0) 1 *(Agard 50)*

Fulham U21 (0) 0 1473

Milton Keynes D: (343) Moore; Poole (Brennan 90), Martin, Moore-Taylor (McGrandles 46); Sorinola (Brittain 73), Boateng, Gilbey, Lewington; Agard, Asonganyi, Dickenson.
Fulham U21: (4231) Ashby-Hammond; Drameh, Asare, McAvoy, Mundle-Smith; Francois, Davis (Hilton 69); De La Torre, Harris (Jasper 86), Santos-Clase (Carvalho 59); Taylor-Crossdale.
Referee: Darren Drysdale.

Tuesday, 8 October 2019

Wycombe W (0) 0

Stevenage (1) 1 *(Cowley 6)* 766

Wycombe W: (433) Yates; Phillips, Jombati, Jacobson, Mascoll; Gardiner-Smith, Thompson (Gape 63), Ofoborh; Kashket (Akinfenwa 72), Parker, Aarons (Wheeler 63).
Stevenage: (352) Farman; Cuthbert, Iontton (El-Abd 50), Stokes (Nugent 68); Fielding, Carter, Timlin, Watts, Denton; Guthrie, Cowley (Taylor 76).
Referee: Josh Smith.

Tuesday, 29 October 2019

Stevenage (1) 1 *(Carter 35)*

Fulham U21 (0) 1 *(Abraham 90)* 442

Stevenage: (4231) Bastien; Husin, Iontton, Watts, Denton; Byrom, Timlin; Carter (Rollinson 55), Parrett (Cowley 46), Sonupe (Fielding 79); Mackail-Smith.
Fulham U21: (4231) Norman; Drameh, Asare, Mundle-Smith, Edun; Cisse (O'Riley 46), Davis (Hilton 46); Harris (Abraham 79), Carvalho, De La Torre; Taylor-Crossdale.
Stevenage won 4-2 on penalties.
Referee: Craig Hicks.

Tuesday, 5 November 2019

Wycombe W (0) 1 *(Aarons 50)*

Fulham U21 (1) 2 *(Harris 10, Abraham 83)* 512

Wycombe W: (433) Yates; Gardiner-Smith, Jombati, Phillips, Mascoll; Freeman, Ofoborh, Pattison; Kashket (Aarons 46), Samuel (Grimmer 65), Parker.
Fulham U21: (4141) Norman; Drameh, Asare, Mundle-Smith, Edun; O'Riley; Santos-Clase, Harris (Davis 67), Hilton, Jasper (Carvalho 75); Abraham.
Referee: Chris Pollard.

Tuesday, 12 November 2019

Milton Keynes D (1) 1 *(Dickenson 32)*

Wycombe W (0) 2 *(Ofoborh 58, Parker 90)* 1101

Milton Keynes D: (41212) Moore; Brittain, Williams, Cargill, Sorinola (Brennan 81); Houghton; Kasumu, Boateng; Asonganyi (McGrandles 63); Dickenson (Mason 72), Agard■.
Wycombe W: (433) Yates; Gardiner-Smith, Jombati, Phillips■, Mascoll (Jacobson 90); Pattison, Ofoborh, Freeman; Kashket (Smyth 46), Parker, Samuel (Wheeler 73).
Referee: David Rock.

South Group G	P	W	DW	DL	L	F	A	GD	Pts
Milton Keynes D	3	2	0	0	1	5	2	3	6
Stevenage	3	1	1	0	1	2	4	–2	5
Fulham U21	3	1	0	1	1	3	3	0	4
Wycombe W	3	1	0	0	2	3	4	–1	3

SOUTHERN SECTION GROUP H

Tuesday, 27 August 2019

Northampton T (0) 1 *(Hoskins 82)*

Arsenal U21 (0) 1 *(Olayinka 78)* 2515

Northampton T: (451) Fisher; Turnbull, Bunney, Goode, McWilliams S; Watson, Hoskins, Waters, Warburton (Williams A 84), Pollock (Lines 70); Smith (Oliver 74).
Arsenal U21: (433) Macey; Bola (Omole■ 30), Olowu, Swanson (Ogungbo 84), Clarke; Smith-Rowe, Olayinka, McEneff (Burton 73); Balogun, Coyle, Tormey.
Northampton T won 4-3 on penalties.
Referee: Rob Lewis.

Tuesday, 3 September 2019

Northampton T (0) 0

Peterborough U (2) 2 *(Kanu 21, Dembele 24)* 2234

Northampton T: (4231) Fisher; McWilliams S, Williams J, Wharton, Martin; Watson (Oliver 64), Lines; Waters, Warburton (Hoskins 51), Adams (Roberts 78); Smith.
Peterborough U: (41212) Pym; Thompson (Mason 67), Kent, Bennett, Butler; Reed; Ward, Burrows (Knight 78); Tasdemir (Toney 79); Dembele, Kanu.
Referee: Josh Smith.

Tuesday, 1 October 2019

Peterborough U (0) 1 *(Ward 66)*

Arsenal U21 (0) 0 3131

Peterborough U: (41212) Pym; Ward, Cartwright, Bennett, Butler; Barker; Woodyard, Burrows; Tasdemir (Jade-Jones 78); Dembele, Kanu.
Arsenal U21: (3412) Macey; Clarke, Mavropanos, Medley; Swanson, Smith-Rowe (Azeez 77), Burton, Bola; Cottrell (McEneff 77); Tormey, Greenwood (Butler-Oyedeji 78).
Referee: Christopher Sarginson.

Tuesday, 8 October 2019

Cambridge U (0) 0

Northampton T (1) 1 *(Smith 17)* 764

Cambridge U: (352) Burton; Darling, John, Taylor G; Davies, Lewis, Worman (Knibbs 66), Maris, Dunk; Dallas, Smith (Richards 66).
Northampton T: (4231) Fisher; Hall-Johnson, Turnbull, Wharton, Harriman; Pollock, McWilliams S (McCormack 67); Waters, Warburton (Hoskins 84), Williams A (Roberts 67); Smith.
Referee: Sam Purkiss.

Tuesday, 5 November 2019

Cambridge U (1) 1 *(Knibbs 40)*

Arsenal U21 (0) 1 *(John-Jules 59)* 914

Cambridge U: (352) Burton; Darling, John (Dunk 65), Taylor G; Davies, Lambe, Maris, O'Neil■, Jones; Knibbs (Smith 85), Dallas (Knoyle 65).
Arsenal U21: (3412) Macey; McGuinness (Coyle 74), Mavropanos, Medley; Olowu, Burton, Smith, Omole; Olayinka (Cottrell 67); John-Jules, Tormey (Greenwood 86).
Arsenal U21 won 4-3 on penalties.
Referee: Charles Breakspear.

Tuesday, 12 November 2019

Peterborough U (2) 2 *(Ward 9, Jade-Jones 30)*

Cambridge U (0) 1 *(Knibbs 79)* 3425

Peterborough U: (41212) Chapman; Ward (Mensah 46), Bennett, Cartwright (Copping 46), Blake-Tracy; Barker; Tasdemir (Jones 74), Burrows; Dembele; Jade-Jones, Kanu.
Cambridge U: (442) Burton; Davies, Darling, Taft, Dunk (Jones 69); Worman (Richards 69), Lewis, Maris, Norville-Williams; Dallas (Smith 69), Knibbs.
Referee: Chris Pollard.

South Group H	P	W	DW	DL	L	F	A	GD	Pts
Peterborough U	3	3	0	0	0	5	1	4	9
Northampton T	3	1	1	0	1	2	3	–1	5
Arsenal U21	3	0	1	1	1	2	3	–1	3
Cambridge U	3	0	0	1	2	2	4	–2	1

NORTHERN SECTION SECOND ROUND

Tuesday, 26 November 2019

Everton U21 (0) 0

Fleetwood T (1) 4 *(Andrew 2, Coutts 75, Madden 79, Burns 87)* 624

Everton U21: (4231) Tyrer; Astley, Ouzounidis, Gibson, Foulds; Baningime (Onyango 44 (Charsley 71)), Markelo; Adeniran, Evans, Gordon (Simms 76); Niasse.
Fleetwood T: (433) Crellin; Coyle, Clarke, Dunne, Andrew; Coutts, McAleny (Dempsey 62), Sowerby; Burns, Evans (Madden 77), Hunter (Morris J 62).
Referee: Michael Salisbury.

Wednesday, 27 November 2019

Blackpool (0) 1 *(Nuttall 70)*

Scunthorpe U (2) 3 *(van Veen 12, Eisa 25, 90)* 1196

Blackpool: (352) Howard; Bushiri, Edwards, Tilt; Turton, Thompson, Scannell (KaiKai 57), Guy■, MacDonald (Virtue 57); Hardie (Delfouneso 57), Nuttall.
Scunthorpe U: (442) Eastwood; Clarke, McGahey, McArdle, Ntlhe; Gilliead (Dales 90), Perch, Lund, Eisa; Novak, van Veen (McAtee 90).
Referee: Ben Toner.

Tuesday, 3 December 2019

Port Vale (0) 2 *(Browne 64, Jake Taylor 82)*

Mansfield T (0) 2 *(Hamilton 50, Sterling-James 90)* 1164

Port Vale: (433) Brown; Atkinson, Brisley (Legge 35), Smith, Evans; Burgess, Joyce, Lloyd (Jake Taylor 74); Worrall, Cullen (Archer 86), Browne.
Mansfield T: (442) Olejnik; Clarke, Shaughnessy, Sweeney, Benning; MacDonald (Knowles 86), Smith (Sterling-James 87), Bishop, Khan (Mellis 74); Cook, Hamilton.
Port Vale won 4-2 on penalties.
Referee: Marc Edwards.

Salford C (1) 3 *(Armstrong 43, 47, Towell 87)*

Wolverhampton W U21 (0) 0 505

Salford C: (442) Letheren; Threlkeld (Wiseman 81), Piergianni, Hogan, Jones D; Jervis (Dieseruvwe 80), Jones J, Towell, Lloyd; Armstrong (Touray 71), Thomas-Asante.
Wolverhampton W U21: (532) Sondergaard; Sanderson, Marques, Francis, Csoka (Kitolano 64), Richards; Taylor, Watt, Cundle (Samuels 64); Graham, Campbell.
Referee: Scott Oldham.

Shrewsbury T (1) 1 *(Golbourne 24)*

Manchester C U21 (0) 1 *(Doyle 68)* 1384

Shrewsbury T: (352) O'Leary; Williams, Beckles, Golbourne; Laurent (McCormick 79), Goss, Norburn, Walker, Giles; John-Lewis (Okenabirhie 68), Udoh (Edwards 83).
Manchester C U21: (433) Grimshaw; Dionkou (Fiorini 90), McDonald, Harwood-Bellis, Ogbeta; Doyle, Pozo, Bernabe; Poveda-Ocampo, Touaizi (Simmonds 69), Rogers (Dele-Bashiru 64).
Manchester C U21 won 6-5 on penalties.
Referee: Peter Wright.

Wednesday, 4 December 2019

Doncaster R (0) 0

Leicester C U21 (1) 3 *(Muskwe 13, 66, Hirst 89)* 1322

Doncaster R: (3412) Lawlor; Daniels, Anderson T, Blaney (Wright 46); Halliday (Bingham 46), Greaves (Gomes 64), Whiteman, Amos; Taylor J; May, Thomas.
Leicester C U21: (3412) Johansson (Davies 46); Amartey, Johnson, Ughelumba; Clark, Thomas G, Dewsbury-Hall, Thomas L; Wright (Leshabela 75); Hirst, Muskwe (Reghba 88).
Referee: Ollie Yates.

Tranmere R (2) 3 *(Hepburn-Murphy 2, Jennings 40, Blackett-Taylor 54)*

Manchester U U21 (2) 2 *(Chong 9, 31)* 632

Tranmere R: (442) Pilling; Woods (Ridehalgh 90), Nelson, Ray, Wilson; Walker-Rice, Maddox, Spellman (Danns 66), Hepburn-Murphy (Blackett-Taylor 50); Jennings, Payne.
Manchester U U21: (4231) Kovar; Laird, Mengi, Bernard, Devine (Taylor 71); Galbraith, Helm (Sotona■ 89); Gomes, Chong, Traore; Bughail-Mellor.
Referee: Ross Joyce.

Tuesday, 10 December 2019

Accrington S (1) 2 *(Zanzala 10, Bishop 85)*

Bolton W (0) 0 930

Accrington S: (442) Bursik; Edwards, Sykes, Alese, Opoku; Clark, Conneely, Finley (Sheriff 81), Pritchard (Carvalho 79); Zanzala (Bishop 46), Charles.
Bolton W: (4141) Matthews; Emmanuel, Zouma (Chicksen 46), Earl, Lowe; Senior; Darcy, Weir (Verlinden 46), Graham, Politic; O'Grady (Dodoo 69).
Referee: Sebastian Stockbridge.

SOUTHERN SECTION SECOND ROUND

Tuesday, 3 December 2019

Brighton & HA U21 (0) 0

Newport Co (0) 0 292

Brighton & HA U21: (3412) Steele; O'Hora, Baluta, Roberts (Richards 56); Yapi, Jenks, Cochrane, Gwargis; Davies J; Cashman, Radulovic (Tolaj 69).
Newport Co: (442) King; McNamara, Woodiwiss, Dolan (Haynes 84), Nurse; Whitely (Abrahams 75), Jefferies, Maloney, Collins; Poleon (Evans 84), Matt.
Newport Co won 5-4 on penalties.
Referee: Sam Purkiss.

Colchester U (0) 1 *(Stokes 61 (og))*

Stevenage (2) 2 *(Cowley 4 (pen), 31)* 959

Colchester U: (4231) Ross; Jackson (Lapslie 19), Eastman, Prosser, Bramall; Comley, Pell (Gambin 62); Senior, Adubofour-Poku, Harriott (Robinson 76); Nouble.
Stevenage: (3412) Farman; Vancooten, Digby (Carter 74), Stokes; List (Fernandez 65), Soares, Timlin, Lakin (Cuthbert 77); Sonupe; Cowley, Mackail-Smith.
Referee: Neil Hair.

Milton Keynes D (0) 2 *(Agard 61, Mason 71)*

Coventry C (0) 0 1686

Milton Keynes D: (41212) Nicholls; Williams, Walsh, Cargill, Lewington; Houghton; McGrandles (Kasumu 74), Boateng (Dickenson■ 74); Gilbey; Agard (Bowery 87), Mason.
Coventry C: (433) Wilson; Watson, Drysdale, Williams, Mason; Allen, Eccles, O'Hare (Shipley 60); Kastaneer (Jones 77), Bakayoko (Biamou 77), Hiwula.
Referee: Charles Breakspear.

Portsmouth (1) 2 *(Maloney 39, Harness 62)*

Northampton T (1) 1 *(Harriman 12)* 2413

Portsmouth: (4231) Bass; Bolton, Downing, Raggett, Walkes; Cannon (Close 85), McCrorie (Haunstrup 63); Harness, Evans, Maloney (Marquis 63); Pitman.
Northampton T: (3412) Arnold; Hall-Johnson, Wharton, Turnbull; Harriman, Pollock, Watson, Martin (Williams J 69); McWilliams (Waters 50); Warburton, Smith (Harding 69).
Referee: Will Finnie.

Walsall (0) 3 *(Lavery 52 (pen), McDonald 79, Scarr 90)*

Chelsea U21 (2) 2 *(Lamptey 3, 10)* 941

Walsall: (442) Roberts L; Facey, Clarke, Scarr, Cockerill-Mollett (Roberts K 10); Holden (Hardy 51), Guthrie (Bates 58), Kinsella, McDonald; Lavery, Gaffney.
Chelsea U21: (4231) Cumming; Lamptey (Russell 76), Guehi, Mola, Maatsen; McEachran (Wakely 46), Gilmour; Ballo, Anjorin (Broja 82), Lawrence; Brown.
Referee: Antony Coggins.

Wednesday, 4 December 2019

Bristol R (1) 1 *(Kilgour 16)*

Leyton Orient (1) 1 *(Angol 20)* 865

Bristol R: (352) van Stappershoef; Menayese, Craig, Kilgour; Rodman, Clarke O, Upson (Tomlinson 58), Sercombe, Holmes-Dennis (Kelly 76); Smith (Adeboyejo 46), Clarke-Harris.
Leyton Orient: (4141) Sargeant; Ling, Turley, Ekpiteta, Widdowson; Kyprianou; Maguire-Drew (Dayton 82), Wright, Marsh, Angol (Harrold 73); Wilkinson (Sotiriou 60).
Bristol R won 4-2 on penalties.
Referee: Josh Smith.

Exeter C (0) 0

Oxford U (0) 0 483

Exeter C: (352) Visser; Dyer, Parkes, Woodman (Sparkes 65); Richardson, Tillson, Jay, Kite, Randall; Martin L (Sweeney 65), Fisher (Seymour 62).
Oxford U: (433) Stevens; Long (Mousinho 90), Dickie, Moore, Ruffels; Sykes, Gorrin, Forde; Hall, Mackie (Hanson 68), Agyei (Lopes 84).
Exeter C won 3-0 on penalties.
Referee: Kevin Johnson.

Peterborough U (1) 1 *(Jade-Jones 32)*

Ipswich T (1) 1 *(El Mizouni 23)* 2310

Peterborough U: (3412) Chapman; Mason, Bennett, Butler; Kanu (Toney 84), Woodyard, Barker, Ward (Kent 63); Tasdemir; Jade-Jones (Eisa 84), Dembele.
Ipswich T: (433) Przybek; Cotter, Henderson, Skuse (Smith 46), Kenlock; El Mizouni, McGavin, Huws; Dobra, Norwood, Roberts.
Ipswich T won 6-5 on penalties.
Referee: Graham Salisbury.

NORTHERN SECTION THIRD ROUND

Tuesday, 7 January 2020

Fleetwood T (0) 2 *(Morris J 50, Andrew 68)*

Accrington S (1) 2 *(Pritchard 35, Sykes 90)* 548

Fleetwood T: (433) Cairns; Southam-Hales (Coyle 63), Eastham, Souttar, Andrew; Biggins, Sowerby, Matete (Dempsey 63); Morris J (Madden 76), McAleny, Saunders.
Accrington S: (4231) Bursik; Johnson (Rodgers 84), Sykes, Alese, Opoku; Barclay (Carvalho 62), Conneely; Charles, Finley, Pritchard; Zanzala (Sousa 82).
Accrington S won 5-3 on penalties.
Referee: Rob Lewis.

Salford C (1) 3 *(Burgess C 35, Armstrong 79, Jervis 84)*

Port Vale (0) 0 630

Salford C: (442) Letheren; Wiseman, Burgess C, Hughes, Touray; Jervis (Pond 87), Whitehead (Threlkeld 76), Baldwin, Lloyd; Armstrong, Rooney (Dieseruvwe 76).
Port Vale: (433) Brown; Gibbons, Brisley, Smith, Montano; Atkinson, Joyce, Conlon; Browne (Archer 66), Cullen, Bennett (Lloyd 87).
Referee: Christopher Sarginson.

Tranmere R (1) 1 *(Payne 31)*

Leicester C U21 (0) 2 *(Hirst 52, Muskwe 74)* 901

Tranmere R: (352) Pilling; Ray, Nelson (Burton 17), Spellman; Hayden, McCullough (Blackham 63), Nugent (Sinnot 81), Gilmour, Walker-Rice; Payne, Mullin.
Leicester C U21: (3412) Jakupovic; O'Connor (Reghba 46), Johnson, Ughelumba; Clark, Thomas G, Dewsbury-Hall, Thomas L; Leshabela (Daley-Campbell 90); Hirst, Muskwe.
Referee: Martin Coy.

Wednesday, 8 January 2020

Scunthorpe U (3) 3 *(van Veen 9, 28, Lund 32)*

Manchester C U21 (0) 1 *(Doyle 71 (pen))* 1270

Scunthorpe U: (4411) Watson; Clarke, McGahey, Bedeau, Brown; Gilliead (Colclough 74), Sutton, Lund, Eisa; McAtee (Hallam 73); van Veen (Miller 46).
Manchester C U21: (433) Grimshaw; Dionkou, McDonald (Rogers 83), Harwood-Bellis, Ogbeta; Doyle, Pozo (Nmecha 66), Bernabe; Knight, Simmonds (Touaizi 12), Braaf.
Referee: Leigh Doughty.

SOUTHERN SECTION THIRD ROUND

Saturday, 4 January 2020

Exeter C (1) 2 *(Ajose 45, Martin L 90)*

Ipswich T (0) 1 *(Keane 57)* 2299

Exeter C: (532) Maxted; Richardson, Dyer, Warren (Dean 46), Hartridge, Randall; Taylor, Atangana, Jay; Seymour (Bowman 69), Ajose (Martin L 76).
Ipswich T: (3412) Holy; Nsiala, Wilson, Woolfenden; Edwards (Norwood 90), Dozzell, Skuse, Kenlock; Bishop (El Mizouni 75); Sears (Jackson 63), Keane.
Referee: Josh Smith.

Tuesday, 7 January 2020

Newport Co (3) 3 *(Abrahams 4, Amond 25, Sorinola 35 (og))*

Milton Keynes D (0) 0 767

Newport Co: (41212) Townsend; Jefferies (Collins 84), Inniss, O'Brien (Howkins 75), Haynes; Bennett (Poleon 70); Sheehan, Nurse; Dolan; Abrahams, Amond.
Milton Keynes D: (41212) Moore; Poole, Williams, Cargill, Sorinola (Walsh 72); Houghton (Healey 63); Kasumu, Boateng (Gilbey 71); Reeves; Agard, Nombe.
Referee: John Busby.

Walsall (0) 1 *(Lavery 86 (pen))*

Portsmouth (1) 2 *(Marquis 23, Harrison 82)* 1082

Walsall: (352) Roberts L; Clarke, Scarr (McDonald 56), Jules; Norman, Holden, Perry, Kinsella, Pring; Gaffney (Lavery 56), Adebayo (Willis 73).
Portsmouth: (4231) MacGillivray; Mnoga (Seddon 63), Downing, Raggett, Burgess; Evans, Close; Harness, Marquis, Hackett-Fairchild (Naylor 63); Hawkins (Harrison 72).
Referee: Anthony Backhouse.

Wednesday, 8 January 2020

Bristol R (0) 0

Stevenage (1) 1 *(Mackail-Smith 17)* 1180

Bristol R: (4231) van Stappershoef; Kilgour, Menayese (Rodman 66), Craig, Kelly (Holmes-Dennis 73); Upson■, Sercombe; Mitchell-Lawson, Barrett, Bennett (Tomlinson 54); Adeboyejo.
Stevenage: (4231) Bastien; List, Digby, Nugent, Denton; Soares (Vancooten 56), Lakin; Parrett (Guthrie 61), Kennedy (Timlin 89), Leesley; Mackail-Smith.
Referee: Darren Handley.

QUARTER-FINALS

Tuesday, 21 January 2020

Exeter C (2) 3 *(Ajose 25, Jay 30, 48)*

Stevenage (0) 0 1190

Exeter C: (532) Ward; Richardson (Martin A 67), Sweeney, Parkes, Moxey, Randall; Taylor (Holmes 77), Atangana, Jay; Bowman (Seymour 54), Ajose.
Stevenage: (4141) Farman; Wildin, Digby, Nugent (Carter 62), Stokes; Dabo; List (Jackson 56), Parrett, Lakin, Leesley (Kennedy 27); Cassidy.
Referee: Antony Coggins.

Portsmouth (1) 2 *(Marquis 13, McGeehan 66)*

Scunthorpe U (0) 1 *(Eisa 62)* 5382

Portsmouth: (4231) MacGillivray; Bolton (Burgess 49), Whatmough, Raggett, Haunstrup; Close, McGeehan; Harness (Naylor 88), Evans, Williams; Marquis.
Scunthorpe U: (4411) Watson; Sutton (Miller 89), McGahey, Bedeau, Brown; Gilliead, Perch, Lund, Eisa; McAtee (Beestin 79); Novak (van Veen 78).
Referee: Kevin Johnson.

Salford C (1) 2 *(Burgess C 45, Elliott 49)*

Accrington S (1) 1 *(Finley 11)* 1401

Salford C: (442) Neal; Threlkeld, Hogan, Burgess C, Touray; Conway (Wiseman 75), Baldwin, Jones J, Jervis; Armstrong (Thomas-Asante 88), Elliott (Pond 76).
Accrington S: (41212) Bursik; Johnson, Sykes, Hughes, Alese; Conneely; Clark, Pritchard; Finley; Charles, Zanzala.
Referee: Marc Edwards.

Tuesday, 4 February 2020

Newport Co (1) 1 *(Bennett 13)*

Leicester C U21 (0) 0 1357

Newport Co: (3142) Townsend; Leadbitter, Howkins, Demetriou; Bennett; Willmott, Dolan (Labadie 75), Sheehan, Nurse; Abrahams (Green 76), Matt (Amond 80).
Leicester C U21: (541) Johansson; Daley-Campbell (Pennant 79), Johnson, O'Connor (Leshabela 46), Ughelumba, Thomas L; Eppiah, Wright, James, Reghba; Hirst.
Referee: Ben Toner.

SEMI-FINALS

Tuesday, 18 February 2020

Portsmouth (0) 3 *(Harness 86, McGeehan 90, Marquis 90)*

Exeter C (0) 2 *(Taylor 78, Burgess 89 (og))* 14,735

Portsmouth: (4231) Bass; McCrorie, Burgess, Raggett, Seddon; Naylor, Close (Hawkins 54); Harness, McGeehan, Curtis; Harrison (Marquis 24).
Exeter C: (532) Ward; Richardson, Dyer, Warren, Parkes, Randall; Kite, Taylor, Law (Collins 79); Fisher (Seymour 68), Martin L (Williams 72).
Referee: Craig Hicks.

Wednesday, 19 February 2020

Newport Co (0) 0

Salford C (0) 0 4070

Newport Co: (4132) King; Willmott (Abrahams 90), Inniss, Demetriou, Haynes (Collins 82); Bennett; Sheehan, Labadie, Dolan; Amond (Green 69), Matt.
Salford C: (442) Neal; Threlkeld, Burgess C, Pond, Touray; Towell (Conway 80), Gibson, Baldwin (Rooney 90), Jervis; Thomas-Asante, Elliott (Wilson 80).
Salford C won 6-5 on penalties.
Referee: Anthony Backhouse.

EFL LEASING.COM TROPHY FINAL 2019–20

Sunday, 5 April 2020

(at Wembley Stadium)

Portsmouth v Salford C

Due to the COVID-19 pandemic, the final was postponed.

FA CUP FINALS 1872–2020

VENUES

1872 and 1874–92	Kennington Oval	1895–1914	Crystal Palace
1873	Lillie Bridge	1915	Old Trafford, Manchester
1893	Fallowfield, Manchester	1920–22	Stamford Bridge
1894	Everton	2001–06	Millennium Stadium, Cardiff
1923–2000	Wembley Stadium (old)	2007 to date	Wembley Stadium (new)

THE FA CUP

1872	Wanderers v Royal Engineers	1-0
1873	Wanderers v Oxford University	2-0
1874	Oxford University v Royal Engineers	2-0
1875	Royal Engineers v Old Etonians	1-1*
Replay	Royal Engineers v Old Etonians	2-0
1876	Wanderers v Old Etonians	1-1*
Replay	Wanderers v Old Etonians	3-0
1877	Wanderers v Oxford University	2-1*
1878	Wanderers v Royal Engineers	3-1

Wanderers won the cup outright, but it was restored to the Football Association.

1879	Old Etonians v Clapham R	1-0
1880	Clapham R v Oxford University	1-0
1881	Old Carthusians v Old Etonians	3-0
1882	Old Etonians v Blackburn R	1-0
1883	Blackburn Olympic v Old Etonians	2-1*
1884	Blackburn R v Queen's Park, Glasgow	2-1
1885	Blackburn R v Queen's Park, Glasgow	2-0
1886	Blackburn R v WBA	0-0
Replay	Blackburn R v WBA	2-0
	(at Racecourse Ground, Derby Co)	

A special trophy was awarded to Blackburn R for third consecutive win.

1887	Aston Villa v WBA	2-0
1888	WBA v Preston NE	2-1
1889	Preston NE v Wolverhampton W	3-0
1890	Blackburn R v The Wednesday	6-1
1891	Blackburn R v Notts Co	3-1
1892	WBA v Aston Villa	3-0
1893	Wolverhampton W v Everton	1-0
1894	Notts Co v Bolton W	4-1
1895	Aston Villa v WBA	1-0

FA Cup was stolen from a shop window in Birmingham and never found.

1896	The Wednesday v Wolverhampton W	2-1
1897	Aston Villa v Everton	3-2
1898	Nottingham F v Derby Co	3-1
1899	Sheffield U v Derby Co	4-1
1900	Bury v Southampton	4-0
1901	Tottenham H v Sheffield U	2-2
Replay	Tottenham H v Sheffield U	3-1
	(at Burnden Park, Bolton W)	
1902	Sheffield U v Southampton	1-1
Replay	Sheffield U v Southampton	2-1
1903	Bury v Derby Co	6-0
1904	Manchester C v Bolton W	1-0
1905	Aston Villa v Newcastle U	2-0
1906	Everton v Newcastle U	1-0
1907	The Wednesday v Everton	2-1
1908	Wolverhampton W v Newcastle U	3-1
1909	Manchester U v Bristol C	1-0
1910	Newcastle U v Barnsley	1-1
Replay	Newcastle U v Barnsley	2-0
	(at Goodison Park, Everton)	
1911	Bradford C v Newcastle U	0-0
Replay	Bradford C v Newcastle U	1-0
	(at Old Trafford, Manchester U)	

Trophy was given to Lord Kinnaird – he made nine FA Cup Final appearances – for services to football.

1912	Barnsley v WBA	0-0
Replay	Barnsley v WBA	1-0
	(at Bramall Lane, Sheffield U)	
1913	Aston Villa v Sunderland	1-0
1914	Burnley v Liverpool	1-0
1915	Sheffield U v Chelsea	3-0
1920	Aston Villa v Huddersfield T	1-0*
1921	Tottenham H v Wolverhampton W	1-0
1922	Huddersfield T v Preston NE	1-0
1923	Bolton W v West Ham U	2-0
1924	Newcastle U v Aston Villa	2-0
1925	Sheffield U v Cardiff C	1-0
1926	Bolton W v Manchester C	1-0
1927	Cardiff C v Arsenal	1-0
1928	Blackburn R v Huddersfield T	3-1
1929	Bolton W v Portsmouth	2-0
1930	Arsenal v Huddersfield T	2-0
1931	WBA v Birmingham	2-1
1932	Newcastle U v Arsenal	2-1
1933	Everton v Manchester C	3-0
1934	Manchester C v Portsmouth	2-1
1935	Sheffield W v WBA	4-2
1936	Arsenal v Sheffield U	1-0
1937	Sunderland v Preston NE	3-1
1938	Preston NE v Huddersfield T	1-0*
1939	Portsmouth v Wolverhampton W	4-1
1946	Derby Co v Charlton Ath	4-1*
1947	Charlton Ath v Burnley	1-0*
1948	Manchester U v Blackpool	4-2
1949	Wolverhampton W v Leicester C	3-1
1950	Arsenal v Liverpool	2-0
1951	Newcastle U v Blackpool	2-0
1952	Newcastle U v Arsenal	1-0
1953	Blackpool v Bolton W	4-3
1954	WBA v Preston NE	3-2
1955	Newcastle U v Manchester C	3-1
1956	Manchester C v Birmingham C	3-1
1957	Aston Villa v Manchester U	2-1
1958	Bolton W v Manchester U	2-0
1959	Nottingham F v Luton T	2-1
1960	Wolverhampton W v Blackburn R	3-0
1961	Tottenham H v Leicester C	2-0
1962	Tottenham H v Burnley	3-1
1963	Manchester U v Leicester C	3-1
1964	West Ham U v Preston NE	3-2
1965	Liverpool v Leeds U	2-1*
1966	Everton v Sheffield W	3-2
1967	Tottenham H v Chelsea	2-1
1968	WBA v Everton	1-0*
1969	Manchester C v Leicester C	1-0
1970	Chelsea v Leeds U	2-2*
Replay	Chelsea v Leeds U	2-1
	(at Old Trafford, Manchester U)	
1971	Arsenal v Liverpool	2-1*
1972	Leeds U v Arsenal	1-0
1973	Sunderland v Leeds U	1-0
1974	Liverpool v Newcastle U	3-0
1975	West Ham U v Fulham	2-0
1976	Southampton v Manchester U	1-0
1977	Manchester U v Liverpool	2-1
1978	Ipswich T v Arsenal	1-0
1979	Arsenal v Manchester U	3-2
1980	West Ham U v Arsenal	1-0
1981	Tottenham H v Manchester C	1-1*
Replay	Tottenham H v Manchester C	3-2

1982	Tottenham H v QPR	1-1*
Replay	Tottenham H v QPR	1-0
1983	Manchester U v Brighton & HA	2-2*
Replay	Manchester U v Brighton & HA	4-0
1984	Everton v Watford	2-0
1985	Manchester U v Everton	1-0*
1986	Liverpool v Everton	3-1
1987	Coventry C v Tottenham H	3-2*
1988	Wimbledon v Liverpool	1-0
1989	Liverpool v Everton	3-2*
1990	Manchester U v Crystal Palace	3-3*
Replay	Manchester U v Crystal Palace	1-0
1991	Tottenham H v Nottingham F	2-1*
1992	Liverpool v Sunderland	2-0
1993	Arsenal v Sheffield W	1-1*
Replay	Arsenal v Sheffield W	2-1*
1994	Manchester U v Chelsea	4-0

THE FA CUP SPONSORED BY LITTLEWOODS POOLS

1995	Everton v Manchester U	1-0
1996	Manchester U v Liverpool	1-0
1997	Chelsea v Middlesbrough	2-0
1998	Arsenal v Newcastle U	2-0

THE AXA-SPONSORED FA CUP

1999	Manchester U v Newcastle U	2-0
2000	Chelsea v Aston Villa	1-0
2001	Liverpool v Arsenal	2-1
2002	Arsenal v Chelsea	2-0

THE FA CUP

2003	Arsenal v Southampton	1-0
2004	Manchester U v Millwall	3-0
2005	Arsenal v Manchester U	0-0*
	Arsenal won 5-4 on penalties.	
2006	Liverpool v West Ham U	3-3*
	Liverpool won 3-1 on penalties.	

THE FA CUP SPONSORED BY E.ON

2007	Chelsea v Manchester U	1-0*
2008	Portsmouth v Cardiff C	1-0
2009	Chelsea v Everton	2-1
2010	Chelsea v Portsmouth	1-0
2011	Manchester C v Stoke C	1-0

THE FA CUP WITH BUDWEISER

2012	Chelsea v Liverpool	2-1
2013	Wigan Ath v Manchester C	1-0
2014	Arsenal v Hull C	3-2*

THE FA CUP

2015	Arsenal v Aston Villa	4-0

THE EMIRATES FA CUP

2016	Manchester U v Crystal Palace	2-1*
2017	Arsenal v Chelsea	2-1
2018	Chelsea v Manchester U	1-0
2019	Manchester C v Watford	6-0
2020	Arsenal v Chelsea	2-1

**After extra time.*

FA CUP WINS

Arsenal 14, Manchester U 12, Chelsea 8, Tottenham H 8, Aston Villa 7, Liverpool 7, Blackburn R 6, Manchester C 6, Newcastle U 6, Everton 5, The Wanderers 5, WBA 5, Bolton W 4, Sheffield U 4, Wolverhampton W 4, Sheffield W 3, West Ham U 3, Bury 2, Nottingham F 2, Old Etonians 2, Portsmouth 2, Preston NE 2, Sunderland 2, Barnsley 1, Blackburn Olympic 1, Blackpool 1, Bradford C 1, Burnley 1, Cardiff C 1, Charlton Ath 1, Clapham R 1, Coventry C 1, Derby Co 1, Huddersfield T 1, Ipswich T 1, Leeds U 1, Notts Co 1, Old Carthusians 1, Oxford University 1, Royal Engineers 1, Southampton 1, Wigan Ath 1, Wimbledon 1.

APPEARANCES IN FINALS

Arsenal 21, Manchester U 20, Chelsea 14, Liverpool 14, Everton 13, Newcastle U 13, Aston Villa 11, Manchester C 11, WBA 10, Tottenham H 9, Blackburn R 8, Wolverhampton W 8, Bolton W 7, Preston NE 7, Old Etonians 6, Sheffield U 6, Sheffield W 6, Huddersfield T 5, Portsmouth 5, *The Wanderers 5, West Ham U 5, Derby Co 4, Leeds U 4, Leicester C 4, Oxford University 4, Royal Engineers 4, Southampton 4, Sunderland 4, Blackpool 3, Burnley 3, Cardiff C 3, Nottingham F 3, Barnsley 2, Birmingham C 2, *Bury 2, Charlton Ath 2, Clapham R 2, Crystal Palace 2, Notts Co 2, Queen's Park (Glasgow) 2, Watford 2, *Blackburn Olympic 1, *Bradford C 1, Brighton & HA 1, Bristol C 1, *Coventry C 1, Fulham 1, Hull C 1, *Ipswich T 1, Luton T 1, Middlesbrough 1, Millwall 1, *Old Carthusians 1, QPR 1, Stoke C 1, *Wigan Ath 1, *Wimbledon 1.
* *Denotes undefeated in final.*

APPEARANCES IN SEMI-FINALS

Arsenal 30, Manchester U 30, Everton 26, Chelsea 24, Liverpool 24, Aston Villa 21, Tottenham H 21, WBA 20, Blackburn R 18, Newcastle U 17, Sheffield W 16, Manchester C 15, Wolverhampton W 15, Bolton W 14, Sheffield U 14, Derby Co 13, Nottingham F 12, Southampton 12, Sunderland 12, Preston NE 10, Birmingham C 9, Burnley 8, Leeds U 8, Huddersfield T 7, Leicester C 7, Portsmouth 7, West Ham U 7, Watford 7, Fulham 6, Old Etonians 6, Oxford University 6, Millwall 5, Notts Co 5, The Wanderers 5, Cardiff C 4, Crystal Palace (professional club) 4, Luton T 4, Queen's Park (Glasgow) 4, Royal Engineers 4, Stoke C 4, Barnsley 3, Blackpool 3, Clapham R 3, Ipswich T 3, Middlesbrough 3, Norwich C 3, Old Carthusians 3, Oldham Ath 3, The Swifts 3, Blackburn Olympic 2, Brighton & HA 2, Bristol C 2, Bury 2, Charlton Ath 2, Grimsby T 2, Hull C 2, Reading 2, Swansea T 2, Swindon T 2, Wigan Ath 2, Wimbledon 2, Bradford C 1, Cambridge University 1, Chesterfield 1, Coventry C 1, Crewe Alex 1, Crystal Palace (amateur club) 1, Darwen 1, Derby Junction 1, Glasgow R 1, Marlow 1, Old Harrovians 1, Orient 1, Plymouth Arg 1, Port Vale 1, QPR 1, Shropshire W 1, Wycombe W 1, York C 1.

FA CUP ATTENDANCES 1969–2020

	1st Round	2nd Round	3rd Round	4th Round	5th Round	6th Round	Semi-finals & Final	Total	No. of matches	Average per match
1969–70	345,229	195,102	925,930	651,374	319,893	198,537	390,700	3,026,765	170	17,805
1970–71	329,687	230,942	956,683	757,852	360,687	304,937	279,644	3,220,432	162	19,879
1971–72	277,726	236,127	986,094	711,399	486,378	230,292	248,546	3,158,562	160	19,741
1972–73	259,432	169,114	938,741	735,825	357,386	241,934	226,543	2,928,975	160	18,306
1973–74	214,236	125,295	840,142	747,909	346,012	233,307	273,051	2,779,952	167	16,646
1974–75	283,956	170,466	914,994	646,434	393,323	268,361	291,369	2,968,903	172	17,261
1975–76	255,533	178,099	867,880	573,843	471,925	206,851	205,810	2,759,941	161	17,142
1976–77	379,230	192,159	942,523	631,265	373,330	205,379	258,216	2,982,102	174	17,139
1977–78	258,248	178,930	881,406	540,164	400,751	137,059	198,020	2,594,578	160	16,216
1978–79	243,773	185,343	880,345	537,748	243,683	263,213	249,897	2,604,002	166	15,687
1979–80	267,121	204,759	804,701	507,725	364,039	157,530	355,541	2,661,416	163	16,328
1980–81	246,824	194,502	832,578	534,402	320,530	288,714	339,250	2,756,800	169	16,312
1981–82	236,220	127,300	513,185	356,987	203,334	124,308	279,621	1,840,955	160	11,506
1982–83	191,312	150,046	670,503	452,688	260,069	193,845	291,162	2,209,625	154	14,348
1983–84	192,276	151,647	625,965	417,298	181,832	185,382	187,000	1,941,400	166	11,695
1984–85	174,604	137,078	616,229	320,772	269,232	148,690	242,754	1,909,359	157	12,162
1985–86	171,142	130,034	486,838	495,526	311,833	184,262	192,316	1,971,951	168	11,738
1986–87	209,290	146,761	593,520	349,342	263,550	119,396	195,533	1,877,400	165	11,378
1987–88	204,411	104,561	720,121	443,133	281,461	119,313	177,585	2,050,585	155	13,229
1988–89	212,775	121,326	690,199	421,255	206,781	176,629	167,353	1,966,318	164	12,173
1989–90	209,542	133,483	683,047	412,483	351,423	123,065	277,420	2,190,463	170	12,885
1990–91	194,195	121,450	594,592	530,279	276,112	124,826	196,434	2,038,518	162	12,583
1991–92	231,940	117,078	586,014	372,576	270,537	155,603	201,592	1,935,340	160	12,095
1992–93	241,968	174,702	612,494	377,211	198,379	149,675	293,241	2,047,670	161	12,718
1993–94	190,683	118,031	691,064	430,234	172,196	134,705	228,233	1,965,146	159	12,359
1994–95	219,511	125,629	640,017	438,596	257,650	159,787	174,059	2,015,249	161	12,517
1995–96	185,538	115,669	748,997	391,218	274,055	174,142	156,500	2,046,199	167	12,252
1996–97	209,521	122,324	651,139	402,293	199,873	67,035	191,813	1,843,998	151	12,211
1997–98	204,803	130,261	629,127	455,557	341,290	192,651	172,007	2,125,696	165	12,883
1998–99	191,954	132,341	609,486	431,613	359,398	181,005	202,150	2,107,947	155	13,599
1999–2000	181,485	127,728	514,030	374,795	182,511	105,443	214,921	1,700,913	158	10,765
2000–01	171,689	122,061	577,204	398,241	256,899	100,663	177,778	1,804,535	151	11,951
2001–02	198,369	119,781	566,284	330,434	249,190	173,757	171,278	1,809,093	148	12,224
2002–03	189,905	104,103	577,494	404,599	242,483	156,244	175,498	1,850,326	150	12,336
2003–04	162,738	117,967	624,732	347,964	292,521	156,780	167,401	1,870,103	149	12,551
2004–05	161,197	98,702	602,152	477,472	339,082	127,914	193,233	1,999,752	146	13,697
2005–06	188,876	107,456	654,570	388,339	286,225	163,449	177,723	1,966,638	160	12,291
2006–07	168,884	113,924	708,628	478,924	340,612	230,064	177,810	2,218,846	158	14,043
2007–08	175,195	99,528	704,300	356,404	276,903	142,780	256,210	2,011,320	152	13,232
2008–09	161,526	96,923	631,070	529,585	297,364	149,566	264,635	2,131,669	163	13,078
2009–10	147,078	100,476	613,113	335,426	288,604	144,918	254,806	1,884,421	151	12,480
2010–11	169,259	101,291	637,202	390,524	284,311	164,092	250,256	1,996,935	150	13,313
2011–12	155,858	92,267	640,700	391,214	250,666	194,971	262,064	1,987,740	151	13,164
2012–13	135,642	115,965	645,676	373,892	288,509	221,216	234,210	2,015,110	156	12,917
2013–14	144,709	75,903	668,242	346,706	254,084	156,630	243,350	1,889,624	149	12,682
2014–15	156,621	111,434	609,368	515,229	208,908	233,341	258,780	2,093,681	153	13,684
2015–16	134,914	94,855	755,187	397,217	235,433	227,262	253,793	2,098,661	149	14,085
2016–17	147,448	97,784	685,467	409,084	212,842	163,620	261,552	1,977,797	156	12,678
2017–18	125,978	87,075	712,036	371,650	210,328	140,641	245,730	1,893,438	149	12,708
2018–19	146,449	92,928	655,501	402,836	146,476	86,028	237,467	1,767,685	150	11,785
2019–20*	160,471	91,200	697,152	489,571	233,190			1,671,584	149	11,219

**Due to the COVID-19 pandemic, the 6th Round, Semi-finals and Final were played behind closed doors.*

THE EMIRATES FA CUP 2019–20

PRELIMINARY AND QUALIFYING ROUNDS

**After extra time.*

EXTRA PRELIMINARY ROUND

Consett v Dunston	1-1, 2-5
Newton Aycliffe v Northallerton T	0-2
Kendal T v Hemsworth MW	0-4
Shildon v Garforth T	0-0, 2-3
Whitley Bay v Hebburn T	1-7
Ashington v Albion Sports	2-0
Billingham T v Yorkshire Amateur	3-0
West Auckland T v Bridlington T	1-3
North Shields v Guisborough T	2-2, 0-1
Bishop Auckland v Thornaby	0-2
Sunderland RCA v Sunderland Ryhope CW	0-0, 2-1
Seaham Red Star v Penrith	4-2
Harrogate Railway Ath v Whickham	1-10
Nostell MW v Stockton T	2-2, 1-5
Hall Road Rangers v Goole	0-3
Knaresborough T v Newcastle Benfield	0-3
Vauxhall Motors v Winsford U	1-2
Charnock Richard v Lower Breck	2-1
Thackley v Handsworth	1-4
Longridge T v Barnoldswick T	6-1
Irlam v Ashton Ath	4-0
Skelmersdale U v Penistone Church	1-1, 5-2
Northwich Vic v Silsden	2-2, 4-3
AFC Liverpool v Burscough	2-3
Avro v Litherland Remyca	3-4
Runcorn T v Rylands	2-0
Squires Gate v West Didsbury & Chorlton	1-2
Clitheroe v 1874 Northwich	1-2
Eccleshill U v Bootle	2-1
Athersley Recreation v Padiham	0-4
City of Liverpool v Campion	3-1
Liversedge v Abbey Hey	5-1
Coventry Sphinx v Coventry U	1-1, 1-0
Lye T v Lutterworth T	0-3
Worcester C v Stone Old Alleynians	4-1
Romulus v Wolverhampton Casuals	0-0, 2-1*
(1-1 at the end of normal time)	
Lichfield C v Highgate U	3-2
Haughmond v Walsall Wood	3-2
Atherstone T v Stourport Swifts	1-3
Congleton T v Westfields	1-1, 1-4
Hanley T v Leicester Road	2-3
Boldmere St Michaels v Daventry T	3-1
Tividale v Wednesfield	2-1
Racing Club Warwick v AFC Wulfrunians	0-2
Dunkirk v Gresley	1-1
Tie awarded to Gresley – Dunkirk removed	
Sporting Khalsa v Rugby T	5-4
Heather St Johns v Wolverhampton SC	2-0
Malvern T v Whitchurch Alport	1-2
Hallam v Staveley MW	0-2
Radford v Heanor T	0-7
Winterton Rangers v Grimsby Bor	2-1
Quorn v Sherwood Colliery	1-2
Shepshed Dynamo v Maltby Main	2-4
Leicester Nirvana v Oadby T	2-1
Worksop T v Melton T	1-2
Sleaford T v AFC Mansfield	0-7
Mulbarton W v Boston T	0-0, 2-4
South Normanton Ath v Selston	5-0
Bottesford T v Long Eaton U	2-8
Barton T v Carlton T	3-2
Anstey Nomads v Kirby Muxloe	0-3
Loughborough University v Ilkeston T	3-1
Potton U v Ely C	1-2
March Town U v Norwich U	2-1
Walsham Le Willows v Peterborough Northern Star	1-2
Eynesbury R v Wellingborough T	3-3, 1-4
Desborough T v Histon	1-3
Thetford T v Rothwell Corinthians	0-1
Biggleswade v Mildenhall T	4-1
Holbeach U v Fakenham T	2-0
Bugbrooke St Michaels v Norwich CBS	1-0
Biggleswade U v Swaffham T	1-0

Harborough T v Deeping Rangers	1-2
Newmarket T v Arlesey T	2-2, 0-1
Gorleston v Pinchbeck U	1-0
Northampton ON Chenecks v Godmanchester R	2-3
Great Yarmouth T v Wellingborough Whitworths	4-2
Kirkley & Pakefield v Wroxham	2-2, 2-3
Walthamstow v Sporting Bengal U	5-0
Hackney Wick v Framlingham T	1-3
Haverhill R v Colney Heath	1-6
Crawley Green v Takeley	2-5
Hadley v Redbridge	4-2
Hoddesdon T v Brantham Ath	2-0
Woodbridge T v Coggeshall U	1-0
Barkingside v Stansted	4-1
Clapton v Stowmarket T	0-6
Hullbridge Sports v Stanway R	1-2
London Colney v Hadleigh U	2-0
Sawbridgeworth T v Halstead T	1-3
FC Clacton v St Margaretsbury	3-0
Southend Manor v Long Melford	0-0, 3-3*
Long Melford won 5-4 on penalties	
Leyton Ath v Cockfosters	0-1
Stotfold v Harpenden T	3-1
Ilford v Harwich & Parkeston	1-2
Woodford T v White Ensign	1-1, 1-3*
(1-1 at the end of normal time)	
West Essex v Whitton U	1-2
Saffron Walden T v Baldock T	1-0
Fairford T v Enfield	3-2
AFC Hayes v Wembley	1-1, 2-3
Clanfield 85 v Shortwood U	1-3
Dunstable T v Chipping Sodbury T	3-2
Slimbridge v Edgware T	1-0
Tuffley R v North Greenford U	1-1, 1-2
Royal Wootton Bassett T v Aylesbury Vale Dynamos	1-1, 0-1
Abingdon U v Brimscombe & Thrupp	1-2
London Tigers v Thame Rangers	0-2
Newport Pagnell T v Cheltenham Saracens	6-2
Leverstock Green v Ardley U	1-1, 1-3
Oxhey Jets v Flackwell Heath	0-4
Burnham v Tring Ath	2-1
Bishop's Cleeve v Easington Sports	3-0
Wantage T v Brackley T Saints	1-1, 2-1
Leighton T v Thornbury T	4-1
Shrivenham v Holmer Green	1-1, 1-1*
Shrivenham won 5-4 on penalties	
Harefield U v Lydney T	3-0
Longlevens v Malmesbury Vic	3-0
Winslow U v Roman Glass St George	2-3
AFC Croydon Ath v Virginia Water	1-0
Loxwood v Abbey Rangers	1-1, 0-2
Balham v Rushtall	1-0
Crawley Down Gatwick v Newhaven	0-2
Cray Valley (PM) v Chatham T	2-1
Erith & Belvedere v Peacehaven & Telscombe	1-1, 1-1*
Erith & Belvedere won 5-3 on penalties	
Bridon Ropes v Broadfields U	3-1
Tunbridge Wells v Pagham	1-1, 2-0
Corinthian v Little Common	1-2
Walton & Hersham v Southall	2-4
Horley T v Bearsted	2-2, 2-0
Egham T v Lancing	2-2, 4-4*
Egham T won 4-3 on penalties	
Lordswood v Steyning T	0-1
CB Hounslow U v Sheerwater	2-1
Horsham YMCA v Croydon	2-1
Saltdean U v Eastbourne U	6-1
Chertsey T v Cobham	1-1, 4-2
Tower Hamlets v Selsey	2-1
Chichester C v Erith T	3-1
Bexhill U v Eastbourne T	1-6
Hassocks v Langney W	2-0
Arundel v Banstead Ath	2-0
Redhill v K Sports	2-1
Glebe v Hollands & Blair	3-1
Colliers Wood U v Shoreham	2-3

Sheppey U v East Preston	4-1
Guildford C v Tooting Bec	3-2
Punjab U v Broadbridge Heath	0-1
Sutton Ath v Deal T	3-2
Sutton Common R v Molesey	1-1, 1-0
Spelthorne Sports v Lingfield	1-1, 4-0
Greenwich Bor v Canterbury C	2-3
Crowborough Ath v AFC Varndeanians	1-2
Welling T v AFC Uckfield T	1-4
Hanworth Villa v Fisher	3-2
Beckenham T v Raynes Park Vale	4-3
Solent University v Portland U	0-3
Shaftesbury v Knaphill	1-4
Cowes Sports v Lymington T	0-4
Fleet T v Farnham T	2-2, 2-1
Brockenhurst v AFC Stoneham	0-2
Bournemouth v Frimley Green	2-1
Windsor v Reading C	0-3
Bemerton Heath Harlequins v Andover New Street	3-3, 2-3
Sholing v Tadley Calleva	1-0
Ascot U v Badshot Lea	2-2, 1-2
Binfield v United Services Portsmouth	3-2
Romsey T v Hamble Club	1-5
Amesbury T v Christchurch	2-7
Westbury U v Fareham T	0-1
Hamworthy U v Bashley	3-0
AFC Portchester v Hythe & Dibden	2-2, 2-3
Horndean v Camberley T	5-3
Alresford T v Baffins Milton R	0-0, 1-2
Cheddar v Bradford T	2-3
Bitton v Bridport	2-1
Wellington v Cribbs	1-1, 1-5
Keynsham T v Brislington	0-1
Exmouth T v Barnstaple T	2-0
Saltash U v Clevedon T	1-2
Plymouth Parkway v Buckland Ath	1-0
Willand R v AFC St Austell	2-1
Tavistock v Hengrove Ath	3-0
Street v Odd Down	4-1
Shepton Mallet v Cadbury Heath	3-1
Bridgwater T v Hallen	1-0

PRELIMINARY ROUND

Dunston v Goole	2-2, 4-1
Newcastle Benfield v Workington	1-0
Seaham Red Star v Guisborough T	3-1
Billingham T v Ossett U	3-4
Whickham v Thornaby	1-2
Garforth T v Colne	0-4
Ashington v Marske U	1-3
Sunderland RCA v Hemsworth MW	1-0
Pickering T v Bridlington T	3-1
Brighouse T v Morpeth T	2-2, 2-3
Pontefract Collieries v Hebburn T	1-1, 4-0
Frickley Ath v Tadcaster Alb	0-1
Northallerton T v Stockton T	0-3
Widnes v Mossley	2-2, 3-2
City of Liverpool v Skelmersdale U	2-1
Sheffield v Litherland Remyca	2-1
Eccleshill U v Glossop North End	1-1, 1-3
Stalybridge Celtic v West Didsbury & Chorlton	0-0, 3-2
Ramsbottom U v Winsford U	3-3, 3-1
Charnock Richard v Longridge T	1-1, 2-0
Trafford v Burscough	2-0
Liversedge v Droylsden	1-0
Atherton Colleries v Runcorn Linnets	2-1
1874 Northwich v Handsworth	6-0
Northwich Vic v Prescot Cables	2-1
Stocksbridge Park Steels v Irlam	2-3
Padiham v Marine	1-1, 0-3
Radcliffe v Runcorn T	0-0, 1-2
Kidsgrove Ath v Newcastle T	1-1, 2-1
Mickleover Sports v Coventry Sphinx	3-0
Coleshill T v Whitchurch Alport	0-3
Tividale v Chasetown	0-5
AFC Wulfrunians v Leek T	0-1
Stourport Swifts v Boldmere St Michaels	0-0, 1-4
Bromsgrove Sporting v Leicester Road	2-1
Bedworth U v Halesowen T	1-1, 1-3
Belper T v Sporting Khalsa	1-1, 3-1*
(1-1 at the end of normal time)	
Romulus v Market Drayton T	6-0
Heather St Johns v Worcester C	1-0
Gresley v Sutton Coldfield T	1-2
Lichfield C v Haughmond	3-0
Westfields v Lutterworth T	2-3
Barton T v Grantham T	1-3
Loughborough Dynamo v Sherwood Colliery	2-2, 1-0
Melton T v Cleethorpes T	1-3
Boston T v Leicester Nirvana	0-0, 1-0
Heanor T v AFC Mansfield	0-0, 1-2
Long Eaton U v South Normanton Ath	1-1, 0-1
Maltby Main v Loughborough University	4-1
Winterton Rangers v Kirby Muxloe	0-1
Staveley MW v Lincoln U	2-1
Spalding U v Dereham T	2-4
Great Yarmouth T v Rothwell Corinthians	0-2
Peterborough Sports v Bugbrooke St Michaels	7-0
Gorleston v Kempston R	0-1
Bedford T v Deeping Rangers	0-1
Wisbech T v Ely C	2-2, 4-0
March Town U v Wellingborough T	2-1
Corby T v Holbeach U	4-0
Wroxham v Stamford	2-4
Cambridge C v Barton R	0-2
Arlesey T v Peterborough Northern Star	2-0
Biggleswade v Yaxley	4-0
Bury T v Histon	1-2
Godmanchester R v St Neots T	1-1, 1-3
Soham T Rangers v Biggleswade U	2-0
Walthamstow v Great Wakering R	2-0
Cockfosters v Coggeshall T	0-4
Harwich & Parkeston v Romford	0-2
Long Melford v Colney Heath	0-2
Hadley v Hoddesdon T	2-0
London Colney v Halstead T	5-0
Whitton U v Hertford T	2-1
AFC Sudbury v Felixstowe & Walton U	2-1
FC Romania v Ware	3-3, 1-2
Grays Ath v Heybridge Swifts	5-2
FC Clacton v Witham T	1-1, 2-3*
(2-2 at the end of normal time)	
Barking v Aveley	2-1
Stotfold v Canvey Island	0-2
Bowers & Pitsea v Barkingside	4-2
Saffron Walden T v Maldon & Tiptree	1-2
Harlow T v Brentwood T	1-1, 1-2
Tilbury v Stanway R	3-1
Wingate & Finchley v Welwyn Garden C	2-0
Cheshunt v Stowmarket T	1-0
Basildon U v Framlingham T	7-1
Waltham Abbey v Woodbridge T	4-0
Takeley v White Ensign	3-3, 3-2*
(2-2 at the end of normal time)	
Cirencester T v North Greenford U	5-0
Aylesbury Vale Dynamos v North Leigh	4-5
Shrivenham v Chalfont St Peter	0-2
Longlevens v Northwood	1-0
Wantage T v Thame Rangers	2-2, 4-2*
(2-2 at the end of normal time)	
Bishop's Cleeve v Kidlington	1-4
Dunstable T v Shortwood U	4-1
Highworth T v Ardley U	3-0
Marlow v Cinderford T	2-4
Fairford T v Hanwell T	2-3
Wembley v Berkhamsted	2-3
Didcot T v Roman Glass St George	2-1
Thame U v Leighton T	3-3, 1-2
Evesham U v Harefield U	2-1
Slimbridge v Burnham	1-1, 1-1*
Burnham won 5-4 on penalties	
Brimscombe & Thrupp v Aylesbury U	1-3
AFC Dunstable v Hayes & Yeading U	0-0, 1-2*
(1-1 at the end of normal time)	
Newport Pagnell T v Flackwell Heath	1-2
Tooting & Mitcham U v Faversham T	1-0
Sittingbourne v Uxbridge	2-0
Horsham YMCA v Egham T	2-1
Little Common v Three Bridges	2-1
Cray W v Hythe T	5-0
Sutton Ath v Ashford T (Middx)	6-0
Sutton Common R v Eastbourne T	3-0
Steyning T v Ramsgate	1-4
Herne Bay v AFC Croydon Ath	2-2, 1-0
Chertsey T v Erith & Belvedere	5-1

Sheppey U v Glebe 3-1
Whitehawk v Saltdean U 2-0
Cray Valley (PM) v Whyteleafe 0-2
Whitstable T v Newhaven 3-1
Burgess Hill T v Sevenoaks T 0-3
VCD Ath v AFC Uckfield T 3-3, 1-1*
VCD Ath won 5-4 on penalties
Bedfont Sports v Hanworth Villa 3-2
Redhill v Balham 1-4
South Park v Canterbury C 2-1
East Grinstead T v Abbey Rangers 0-1
Tower Hamlets v Horsham 1-6
Arundel v Shoreham 1-0
Beckenham T v Ashford U 0-1
Phoenix Sports v Staines T 0-6
Southall v Spelthorne Sports 1-2
Bridon Ropes v Chichester C 2-7
Chipstead v Hassocks 0-0, 3-2
Guildford C v AFC Varndeanians 1-2
Haywards Heath T v Tunbridge Wells 2-1
CB Hounslow U v Horley T 0-3
Hastings U v Broadbridge Heath 2-1
Portland U v Hamworthy U 4-3
Hythe & Dibden v Horndean 2-1
Hamble Club v Sholing 0-1
Reading C v Moneyfields 0-3
Christchurch v Badshot Lea 1-2
Fleet T v Baffins Milton R 3-0
Bournemouth v Bracknell T 0-5
Binfield v Lymington T 3-2
Thatcham T v Andover New Street 7-1
Blackfield & Langley v AFC Totton 2-1
Winchester C v AFC Stoneham 1-1, 3-1
Basingstoke T v Westfield 0-2
Knaphill v Fareham T 0-1
Plymouth Parkway v Paulton R 5-2
Yate T v Exmouth T 2-2, 0-2
Bridgwater T v Brislington 7-0
Cribbs v Bideford 0-1
Clevedon T v Bristol Manor Farm 2-5
Tavistock v Frome T 2-1
Shepton Mallet v Melksham T 1-1, 3-2
Bradford T v Larkhall Ath 3-1
Street v Willand R 1-5
Bitton v Mangotsfield U 2-3

FIRST ROUND QUALIFYING

Thornaby v Ossett U 2-2, 0-6
1874 Northwich v Pickering T 2-0
Scarborough Ath v Marske U 1-1, 2-1*
Lancaster C v Northwich Vic 0-0, 2-1
FC United of Manchester v Atherton Collieries 2-2, 1-0
Dunston v Sunderland RCA 0-0, 5-0
Liversedge v Stockton T 0-2
Newcastle Benfield v Runcorn T 2-3
Warrington T v City of Liverpool 2-2, 4-0
Charnock Richard v Irlam 0-4
Widnes v Whitby T 0-4
Tadcaster Alb v Ashton U 2-2, 4-2
Stalybridge Celtic v Marine 0-2
Trafford v Bamber Bridge 3-0
Glossop North End v Pontefract Collieries 1-3
South Shields v Colne 0-0, 0-1
Maltby Main v Ramsbottom U 1-5
Morpeth T v Hyde U 3-1
Seaham Red Star v Witton Alb 0-1
Kirby Muxloe v Boston T 0-1
Lutterworth T v Hednesford T 0-3
Halesowen T v Lichfield C 7-1
South Normanton Ath v Coalville T 0-1
Tamworth v Nuneaton Bor 3-1
Loughborough Dynamo v Heather St Johns 1-0
Barwell v AFC Mansfield 4-1
Romulus v Buxton 0-4
Banbury U v Gainsborough Trinity 2-2, 0-1
Matlock T v Basford U 2-1
Stratford T v Boldmere St Michaels 6-1
Rushall Olympic v Sheffield 3-1
Belper T v Alvechurch 1-0
Nantwich T v Grantham T 3-1
Kidsgrove Ath v Cleethorpes T 2-1
Sutton Coldfield T v Redditch U 1-1, 3-1
Stafford Rangers v Mickleover Sports 3-0
Bromsgrove Sporting v Stourbridge 0-1
Whitchurch Alport v Leek T 0-2
Chasetown v Staveley MW 1-0
Wingate & Finchley v London Colney 4-1
Soham T Rangers v Whitton U 3-0
Takeley v Potters Bar T 0-1
Deeping Rangers v AFC Sudbury 2-2, 3-2
Enfield T v AFC Rushden & Diamonds 1-0
Kings Langley v Barking 3-1
Hornchurch v Kempston R 6-0
Cheshunt v Brightlingsea Regent 1-0
Stamford v Witham T 1-0
Biggleswade v Tilbury 2-1
Basildon U v Coggeshall T 2-1
Royston T v Rothwell Corinthians 7-2
Histon v Maldon & Tiptree 0-3
Waltham Abbey v Canvey Island 2-2, 1-2
Colney Heath v Corby T 1-3
Dunstable T v Bishop's Stortford 3-5
Grays Ath v March Town U (walkover)
Tie awarded to March Town U – Grays Ath removed
Barton R v Romford 4-0
Aylesbury U v Walthamstow 0-3
St Ives T v Berkhamsted 2-1
Ware v Leiston 5-1
East Thurrock U v Peterborough Sports 1-1, 2-3
Wisbech T v Hitchin T 1-2
Bowers & Pitsea v Brentwood T 2-1
St Neots T v Biggleswade T 2-2, 0-2
Hadley v Arlesey T 3-2
Dereham T v Needham Market 1-1, 1-2
Lowestoft T v Leighton T 2-0
Whitstable T v Folkestone Invicta 0-4
Chesham U v Fleet T 4-2
Whyteleafe v Merstham 1-0
Chertsey T v Sheppey U 4-1
Chichester C v Chalfont St Peter 2-0
Hartley Wintney v Spelthorne Sports 3-0
Bracknell T v Carshalton Ath 0-2
Kingstonian v Walton Casuals 2-0
Leatherhead v Lewes 2-2, 2-2*
Lewes won 3-1 on penalties
Hanwell T v Staines T 2-3
South Park v Badshot Lea 1-3
Tooting & Mitcham U v AFC Varndeanians 3-1
Whitehawk v Abbey Rangers 0-1
Hastings U v Worthing 3-3, 2-3*
Haywards Heath T v Hayes & Yeading U 0-1
Harrow Bor v Binfield 5-0
Horley T v Balham 1-3
Cray W v Bedfont Sports 2-1
Westfield v Chipstead 0-1
Haringey Bor v Herne Bay 3-0
Corinthian Casuals v Sevenoaks T 4-0
Sutton Common R v Beaconsfield T 1-3
Ashford U v Farnborough 0-3
Ramsgate v Arundel 0-0, 4-0
Sutton Ath v Flackwell Heath 1-1, 1-3
VCD Ath v Moneyfields 1-2
Bognor Regis T v Sittingbourne 3-0
Little Common v Hendon 0-1
Horsham YMCA v Margate 1-2
Metropolitan Police v Horsham 1-1, 2-3
Weston-super-Mare v Fareham T 3-0
Cinderford T v Bideford 5-3
Didcot T v Poole T 0-1
Truro C v Wimborne T 2-1
Plymouth Parkway v Merthyr T 0-1
Bridgwater T v Bristol Manor Farm 1-3
Winchester C v Taunton T 0-3
Willand R v North Leigh 1-2
Burnham v Tiverton T 2-3
Hythe & Dibden v Kidlington 2-4
Tavistock v Shepton Mallet 3-3, 2-1
Highworth T v Exmouth T 4-2
Wantage T v Swindon Supermarine 0-3
Longlevens v Portland U 0-2
Thatcham T v Salisbury 2-3
Cirencester T v Gosport Bor 1-0
Evesham U v Dorchester T 0-2
Mangotsfield U v Blackfield & Langley 0-5
Sholing v Bradford T 3-0

SECOND ROUND QUALIFYING
Marine v Dunston 1-2
Southport v Scarborough Ath 5-2
Chester v Altrincham 1-1, 0-1
Curzon Ashton v Blyth Spartans 4-4, 0-1
Bradford (Park Avenue) v Morpeth T 2-4
Irlam v York C 0-2
Ashton U v Pontefract Collieries 1-0
Colne v Ossett U 0-0, 4-0
1874 Northwich v Whitby T 0-1
FC United of Manchester v Warrington T 1-2
Trafford v Darlington 1-3
Gateshead v Ramsbottom U 6-0
Guiseley v Stockton T 1-0
Lancaster C v Spennymoor T 0-5
Runcorn T v Farsley Celtic 1-3
Alfreton T v King's Lynn T 1-1, 1-2
Stamford v Boston U 0-4
Leamington v Chasetown 2-2, 2-1*
(1-1 at the end of normal time)
Kettering T v Sutton Coldfield T 1-1, 1-2
Belper T v Witton Alb 0-0, 1-0*
(0-0 at the end of normal time)
Loughborough Dynamo v Tamworth 0-3
AFC Telford U v Nantwich T 0-3
Rushall Olympic v Gainsborough Trinity 2-0
Halesowen T v Stratford T 4-1
Boston T v Leek T 0-4
Buxton v Corby T 5-0
Matlock T v Kidsgrove Ath 1-2
Hednesford T v Barwell 3-2
Kidderminster H v Stafford Rangers 0-0, 0-3
Coalville T v Stourbridge 1-2
Beaconsfield T v Hemel Hempstead T 1-0
Corinthian Casuals v Chelmsford C 2-0
Kingstonian v March Town U 3-0
Walthamstow v Abbey Rangers 1-1, 1-2
Balham v Royston T 3-5
Tonbridge Angels v Eastbourne Bor 1-2
Margate v Concord Rangers 3-1
Hendon v Deeping Rangers 3-2
St Ives T v Canvey Island 0-0, 2-3*
(2-2 at the end of normal time)
Maidstone U v Cheshunt 4-1
Potters Bar T v Hornchurch 2-0
Bishop's Stortford v Peterborough Sports 1-2
Dulwich Hamlet v Bognor Regis T 6-1
Flackwell Heath v Slough T 0-3
Billericay T v Basildon U 1-0
Tooting & Mitcham U v Dorking W 1-0
Hadley v Ramsgate 1-0
Lewes v Bowers & Pitsea 1-2
Cray W v Soham T Rangers 5-2
Harrow Bor v Carshalton Ath 0-1
Biggleswade v Chertsey T 1-3
Biggleswade T v Ware 1-2
Badshot Lea v Hayes & Yeading U 0-4
Lowestoft T v Needham Market 4-0
Barton R v Hitchin T 0-1
Enfield T v Braintree T 2-0
Maldon & Tiptree v Wingate & Finchley 4-2
Moneyfields v Whyteleafe 0-2
Hartley Wintney v Chichester C 0-0, 0-1
Horsham v Dartford 0-2
St Albans C v Worthing 2-2, 3-1
Kings Langley v Folkestone Invicta 4-0
Haringey Bor v Staines T 5-0
Farnborough v Wealdstone 0-5
Welling U v Chipstead 7-0
Chesham U v Hampton & Richmond Bor 1-2
Weston-super-Mare v Merthyr T 2-1
Sholing v Weymouth 0-3
Hereford v Truro C 5-2
Portland U v Salisbury 0-1
Havant & Waterlooville v Taunton T 2-1
Cirencester T v Chippenham T 2-2, 3-4*
(2-2 at the end of normal time)
Tavistock v Highworth T 4-0
Tiverton T v Bristol Manor Farm 2-4
Poole T v Hungerford T 2-1
Swindon Supermarine v Bath C 0-4
Oxford C v North Leigh 7-0
Kidlington v Gloucester C 0-5
Brackley T v Cinderford T 4-0
Blackfield & Langley v Dorchester T 1-0

THIRD ROUND QUALIFYING
Ashton U v Spennymoor T 2-6
Halesowen T v Altrincham 0-2
Hednesford T v Blyth Spartans 4-2
Nantwich T v Morpeth T 1-0
Peterborough Sports v Guiseley 1-0
Leek T v King's Lynn T 0-2
Whitby T v Gloucester C 1-1, 3-1
Kidsgrove Ath v Gateshead 0-1
Stourbridge v Stafford Rangers 2-1
Belper T v Rushall Olympic 2-1
Buxton v York C 1-2
Tamworth v Hereford 0-0, 0-0*
Tamworth won 3-1 on penalties
Dunston v Colne 2-3
Farsley Celtic v Southport 0-5
Leamington v Darlington 0-2
Sutton Coldfield T v Boston U 0-1
Brackley T v Warrington T 2-0
Oxford C v Hampton & Richmond Bor 2-0
Lowestoft T v Carshalton Ath 1-2
Dulwich Hamlet v Eastbourne Bor 3-0
Canvey Island v Bowers & Pitsea 1-1, 1-1*
Bowers & Pitsea won 5-3 on penalties
Bristol Manor Farm v Wealdstone 0-0, 0-4
Kingstonian v Weston-super-Mare 1-1, 4-1
Haringey Bor v Cray W 1-0
Welling U v Tavistock 4-1
Maldon & Tiptree v Chertsey T 6-1
Chippenham T v Slough T 3-3, 3-2
Salisbury v Margate 2-4
Abbey Rangers v Whyteleafe 0-2
Kings Langley v Corinthian Casuals 3-0
Ware v Potters Bar T 1-2
Hayes & Yeading U v Hendon 5-4
Royston T v Beaconsfield T 2-1
Tooting & Mitcham U v Poole T 0-2
Havant & Waterlooville v Hadley 3-0
Billericay T v Bath C 4-2
Blackfield & Langley v Dartford 1-4
Weymouth v St Albans C 4-1
Chichester C v Enfield T 1-0
Maidstone U v Hitchin T 2-1

FOURTH ROUND QUALIFYING
Hednesford T v Boston U 0-1
Gateshead v Colne 5-0
Barrow v Solihull Moors 0-1
Whitby T v Stourbridge 1-1, 2-3
Hartlepool U v Brackley T 1-0
Nantwich T v King's Lynn T 1-0
Chorley v Spennymoor T 2-0
Southport v Altrincham 1-3
Tamworth v Darlington 0-3
York C v Stockport Co 2-0
Notts Co v Belper T 2-1
Chesterfield v Wrexham 1-1, 0-1
FC Halifax T v Harrogate T 1-2
AFC Fylde v Peterborough Sports 6-1
Whyteleafe v Chippenham T 0-3
Haringey Bor v Yeovil T 0-3
Havant & Waterlooville v Dulwich Hamlet 1-2
Ebbsfleet U v Woking 1-1, 1-0
Welling U v Eastleigh 0-0, 2-4
Bromley v Aldershot T 4-3
Maidstone U v Kings Langley 4-1
Maidenhead U v Wealdstone 1-1, 2-0
Oxford C v Margate 2-1
Bowers & Pitsea v Chichester C 1-2
Hayes & Yeading U v Poole T 1-1, 3-2
Royston T v Maldon & Tiptree 1-3
Potters Bar T v Barnet 1-1, 1-3
Torquay U v Boreham Wood 3-2
Sutton U v Billericay T 1-1, 2-5
Weymouth v Dover Ath 1-2
Dartford v Kingstonian 2-3
Carshalton Ath v Dagenham & R 2-1

THE EMIRATES FA CUP 2019–20

COMPETITION PROPER

▪ *Denotes player sent off.*

FIRST ROUND

Friday, 8 November 2019

Dulwich Hamlet (0) 1 *(Smith C 49)*

Carlisle U (2) 4 *(Olomola 8, McKirdy 37, 86, Jones M 55)* 3336

Dulwich Hamlet: (4231) Grainger; McCoy, Orlu (Hunte 84), Smith C, Smith N; Dempsey, Vose; Yusuff (Akinyemi 66), Chapman, Monakana (Clunis 66); Mills.
Carlisle U: (343) Collin; Branthwaite, Webster, Mellish; Jones G, Bridge (Carroll 84), Jones M, Iredale; Thomas (Sagaf 57), Olomola (Loft 80), McKirdy.
Referee: James Oldham.

Saturday, 9 November 2019

Accrington S (0) 0

Crewe Alex (1) 2 *(Kirk 45, Porter 67 (pen))* 1655

Accrington S: (41212) Evtimov; Johnson (Carvalho 69), Hughes▪, Alese, Opoku (Sykes 74); Conneely; Clark, McConville (Charles 46); Finley; Bishop, Pritchard.
Crewe Alex: (433) Jaaskelainen; Ng, Hunt, Mbulu, Pickering; Green, Wintle, Lowery; Dale, Porter, Kirk.
Referee: Neil Hair.

AFC Wimbledon (1) 1 *(Pigott 43)*

Doncaster R (0) 1 *(Anderson T 63)* 2777

AFC Wimbledon: (352) Trott; O'Neill, Kalambayi, Thomas; Wagstaff, Hartigan, Pinnock, McLoughlin (Reilly 74), Osew (Guinness-Walker 79); Pigott, Appiah.
Doncaster R: (4231) Dieng; Halliday, Anderson T, Wright, Amos; Sheaf, Gomes; Sadlier (Bingham 81), Coppinger, Taylor J (May 59); Thomas.
Referee: Darren Drysdale.

Blackpool (3) 4 *(Delfouneso 9, Gnanduillet 24, Virtue 45, KaiKai 84)*

Morecambe (1) 1 *(Stockton 45)* 5371

Blackpool: (3412) Alnwick; Edwards, Heneghan, Husband; Feeney (Nuttall 79), Spearing, Virtue (Guy 61), MacDonald (Turton 61); KaiKai; Delfouneso, Gnanduillet.
Morecambe: (433) Halstead; Tanner, Lavelle, Old, Conlan; Tutte (Leitch-Smith 46), Brewitt, Wildig; O'Sullivan (Cranston 74), Stockton (Miller 67), Alessandra.
Referee: Ross Joyce.

Bolton W (0) 0

Plymouth Arg (1) 1 *(McFadzean 11)* 6992

Bolton W: (442) Matthews; Emmanuel, Zouma, Wright, Chicksen (Earl 55); Dodoo, Murphy L, Lowe, Graham (Politic 66); Murphy D (Hall 71), O'Grady.
Plymouth Arg: (352) Palmer; Wootton, Canavan, Sawyer; Joshua Grant, Sarcevic, Edwards, Mayor, McFadzean; Moore B (Telford 90), Joel Grant (Clarke 76).
Referee: Rob Lewis.

Cambridge U (0) 1 *(Smith 90)*

Exeter C (1) 1 *(Fisher 34)* 2302

Cambridge U: (352) Burton; Taylor G, Ward (Dunk 63), Taft; Knoyle, Lewis, Maris, O'Neil (Lambe 63), Jones (Knibbs 75); Richards, Smith.
Exeter C: (3412) Maxted; Sweeney, Martin A, Parkes; Williams, Atangana (Tillson 78), Collins, Woodman; Fisher (Seymour 82); Bowman (Martin L 77), Jay.
Referee: Peter Wright.

Carshalton Ath (0) 1 *(Pattison 72)*

Boston U (2) 4 *(Thanoj 33, 90, Shiels 37, Wright 90)* 1859

Carshalton Ath: (442) Perntreou; Price, Dudley (Adeniyi 65), Read, Hamilton-Downes; Samuels, Hein (Koroma 46), Pappoe (Bradford 42), Haxhiu; Korboa, Pattison.
Boston U: (442) Crookes; Duhaney, Ainge (Penny 46), Shiels, Whittle; Thanoj, Platt, Abbott, Woolford; Knowles (Rollins 78), Thewlis (Wright 84).
Referee: Tom Reeves.

Cheltenham T (0) 1 *(Addai 90)*

Swindon T (0) 1 *(Yates 90)* 3456

Cheltenham T: (532) Flinders; Long, Raglan, Tozer, Boyle, Hussey; Broom (Sheaf 66), Thomas, Ince (Doyle-Hayes 74); Smith (Addai 66), Varney.
Swindon T: (442) Benda; Hunt, Baudry, Fryers, Donohue; Doughty, Lyden, Rose, Jaiyesimi; Woolery, Yates.
Referee: Scott Oldham.

Colchester U (0) 0

Coventry C (2) 2 *(Shipley 11, McCallum 27)* 2919

Colchester U: (4231) Gerken; Jackson, Eastman, Prosser, Bramall; Comley, Stevenson; Senior (Norris 70), Adubofour-Poku (Sowunmi 46), Harriott (Gambin 55); Nouble.
Coventry C: (343) Wilson; Rose, McFadzean, Hyam; Dabo, Kelly, Walsh, McCallum; Westbrooke (Eccles 90), Bakayoko, Shipley (O'Hare 74).
Referee: Christopher Sarginson.

Crawley T (1) 4 *(Nadesan 35, Grego-Cox 82, 90, Nathaniel-George 90)*

Scunthorpe U (0) 1 *(Colclough 79)* 1706

Crawley T: (4141) Morris; Young, Tunnicliffe, Dallison, Sesay; Bulman; Grego-Cox, Camara, Ferguson, Lubala; Nadesan (Nathaniel-George 70).
Scunthorpe U: (442) Eastwood; Perch, Butler, McArdle, Brown; Gilliead, Lund, Songo'o (Novak 65), Colclough; van Veen, Proctor (Eisa 76).
Referee: Lee Swabey.

Ebbsfleet U (1) 2 *(Josh Payne 7, Ugwu 89 (pen))*

Notts Co (1) 3 *(Wootton 34, 58, Turner 90)* 1206

Ebbsfleet U: (442) Holmes; King, Lawless (Umerah 63), Ekpiteta, Cordner; Weston, Egan (Sutherland 67), Josh Payne, Blackman; Ugwu, Reid (Adeloye 81).
Notts Co: (442) Slocombe; McCrory, Turner, Rawlinson, Brindley; Booty (Bakayogo 90), Rose, Doyle, Boldewijn; Thomas (Tyson 85), Wootton.
Referee: Carl Brook.

Forest Green R (3) 4 *(Stevens 38, Aitchison 45, Mills J 45, Shephard 65)*

Billericay T (0) 0 1419

Forest Green R: (4231) Wollacott; Mills J, Kitching (McGinley 78), Rawson, Bernard; Adams, Winchester (Taylor 69); Shephard, Aitchison (Frear 64), Collins; Stevens.
Billericay T: (4231) Julian; Ramsay, Kefalas, Henry, Nunn; Deering (Reynolds 77), Loft; Potter, Paxman (Emmanuel 46), Alfa (Phillips 58); Robinson.
Referee: Graham Salisbury.

Grimsby T (1) 1 *(Waterfall 43)*

Newport Co (0) 1 *(Amond 80 (pen))* 2086

Grimsby T: (433) Russell; Waterfall, Ohman, Pollock, Gibson; Whitehouse (Clifton 83), Hessenthaler, Robson; Green (Rose A 68), Hanson, Cook (Cardwell 89).
Newport Co: (352) King; Inniss, Bennett (Poleon 77), O'Brien; Willmott, Labadie, Sheehan, Nurse (Whitely 65), Haynes; Abrahams (Amond 64), Matt.
Referee: Leigh Doughty.

Ipswich T (0) 1 *(Dozzell 79)*

Lincoln C (1) 1 *(Walker 37)* 11,598

Ipswich T: (433) Norris; Donacien, Nsiala, Wilson, Kenlock; Downes (Rowe 84), Dozzell, Huws; Dobra (Edwards 65), Keane, Georgiou (Norwood 86).
Lincoln C: (4231) Vickers; Eardley, Shackell, Connolly, Toffolo; O'Connor (Chapman 51), Morrell; Andrade (Anderson 84), Payne, Hesketh (Grant 77); Walker.
Referee: Kevin Johnson.

Maidenhead U (1) 1 *(Cassidy 25)*

Rotherham U (0) 3 *(Ihiekwe 69, Ladapo 75, Crooks 78)* 1924

Maidenhead U: (451) Dunn; Nana Ofori-Twumasi, Ellul, Massey■, Steer (Thompson-Brissett 79); Sheckelford, Comley, Upward, Smile (Whitehall 79), Kelly (Davies 59); Cassidy.
Rotherham U: (4411) Iversen; Olosunde (Hastie 62), Ihiekwe, Wood (Thompson 37), Jones; Ogbene, Wiles, Barlaser, Morris; Crooks; Smith (Ladapo 53).
Referee: Ollie Yates.

Maidstone U (1) 1 *(Wishart 19)*

Torquay U (0) 0 2330

Maidstone U: (541) Cole; Hoyte, Johnson, Elokobi, Pennell, Chesmain; Kyei (Amaluzor 90), James, Khan, Wishart; Akanbi (Edwards 78).
Torquay U: (442) Cavagnari; Wynter, Cameron, Cundy, Davis (Lewis 28); Lumbombo Kalala (Keating 80), Buse, Vincent, Whitfield; Janneh, Reid.
Referee: Joe Hull.

Mansfield T (0) 1 *(Maynard 81)*

Chorley (0) 0 2418

Mansfield T: (442) Logan; Gordon, Sweeney, Preston, Benning; MacDonald (Hamilton 64), Bishop, Tomlinson (Mellis 78), Khan; Cook (Rose 72), Maynard.
Chorley: (532) Urwin; Challoner, Ross (Newby A 84), Meppen-Walter, Baines, Blakeman; Cottrell, Smith, Nortey; Massanka (Carver 57), Vernam (Almond 63).
Referee: Savvas Yianni.

Milton Keynes D (0) 0

Port Vale (1) 1 *(Worrall 20)* 3598

Milton Keynes D: (4231) Nicholls; Brittain, Poole, Moore-Taylor, Lewington; Gilbey (Houghton 84), Kasumu (Boateng 70); Reeves, McGrandles, Dickenson (Mason 61); Bowery.
Port Vale: (433) Brown; Gibbons, Legge, Smith, Montano; Burgess (Evans 88), Joyce, Jake Taylor; Amoo, Bennett (Pope 68), Worrall.
Referee: Craig Hicks.

Nantwich T (0) 0

AFC Fylde (1) 1 *(Croasdale 44)* 1544

Nantwich T: (442) Hall; Bourne, Harrison, Langley, Devine; Lawrie (Mwasile 77), Hughes, Webb, Walsh (Schousboe 83); Malkin (McDonald 87), Cooke.
AFC Fylde: (442) Lavercombe; Burke, Byrne, Whitmore, Taylor; Kosylo (Yeates 73), Croasdale, Philliskirk, Bradley (Haughton 63); Rowe, Williams (Hornby-Forbes 84).
Referee: Ben Speedie.

Oxford C (0) 1 *(Wiltshire 80)*

Solihull Moors (3) 5 *(McCallum 10, Ball 32, 42, 46, 51)* 667

Oxford C: (4231) King; Jones (Rowe 55), Tapp, Oastler, Jefford; Fleet, Ashby; Wiltshire, McEachran (Moore-Azille 70), Owusu; Brown (Nyammey 56).
Solihull Moors: (433) Boot; Vaughan, Howe, Gudger, Reckord; Storer, Ball (Hawkridge 67), Gunning; Wright (Yussuf 55), McCallum (Blissett 71), Beesley.
Referee: Thomas Parsons.

Salford C (0) 1 *(Towell 83)*

Burton Alb (0) 1 *(Fraser 78)* 2724

Salford C: (433) Neal; Threlkeld, Pond, Burgess C, Touray; Jones J, Maynard, Towell; Conway (Whitehead 51), Rooney, Armstrong (Dieseruvwe 67).
Burton Alb: (433) O'Hara; Brayford, O'Toole, Buxton, Akins; Edwards (Sbarra 73), Quinn, Fraser; Broadhead, Boyce, Templeton (Wallace 62).
Referee: Alan Young.

Shrewsbury T (1) 1 *(Laurent 28)*

Bradford C (1) 1 *(Oteh 19)* 3764

Shrewsbury T: (343) Murphy; Ebanks-Landell, Pierre, Beckles; Love, Norburn, Goss (Edwards 71), Golbourne (Giles 81); Whalley, Cummings (Okenabirhie 57), Laurent.
Bradford C: (442) O'Donnell; Henley, Richards-Everton, O'Connor A, Wood; Connolly (O'Connor P 86), Devine, Akpan, Ismail (Anderson 57); Oteh, Vaughan (Mellor 57).
Referee: Sam Purkiss.

Stevenage (0) 1 *(List 56)*

Peterborough U (0) 1 *(Maddison 79)* 2981

Stevenage: (352) Farman; Vancooten, Cuthbert, Stokes; Sonupe, Timlin, Carter, Watts (Nugent 12), Parrett (List 16); Lakin, Guthrie (El-Abd 76).
Peterborough U: (442) Pym; Thompson (Ward 73), Kent, Beevers, Butler; Woodyard, Maddison, Reed (Mason 67), Burrows; Toney, Eisa (Dembele 67).
Referee: Nicholas Kinseley.

Stourbridge (1) 2 *(Lloyd 25, Grocott 52)*

Eastleigh (1) 2 *(Barnett 35, Rendell 86)* 1846

Stourbridge: (442) Wren; Green, Fisher (Birch 80), Williams, Brown; Tonks, Bellis (Winwood 60), Turton, Lloyd; Grocott (Landell 70), Scrivens.
Eastleigh: (433) Stryjek; Seaman (Barnes 76), Atkinson, Boyce, Hollands; Smart, Payne, Barnett (Williamson 37); Bearwish (Partington 58), Rendell, Miley.
Referee: Sam Barrott.

Sunderland (1) 1 *(McGeady 15)*

Gillingham (0) 1 *(Lee 46)* 7892

Sunderland: (4231) McLaughlin J; McLaughlin C, Lynch, Willis, De Bock; Power, Dobson; O'Nien, Maguire (Watmore 77), McGeady; Grigg (McNulty 66).
Gillingham: (4312) Bonham; Fuller, Ehmer, Ogilvie, O'Connor; O'Keefe, Jones, Byrne; Lee (Charles-Cook 90); Hanlan, Mandron.
Referee: Michael Salisbury.

Tranmere R (1) 2 *(Morris 3, 67)*

Wycombe W (1) 2 *(Jacobson 26, Samuel 55)* 3849

Tranmere R: (442) Davies; Wilson, Nelson, Monthe, Ridehalgh; Morris, Danns, Perkins, Caprice (Blackett-Taylor 68); Jennings, Hepburn-Murphy (Ferrier 68).
Wycombe W: (4231) Allsop; Jombati, Stewart, Charles, Jacobson; Thompson, Gape (Ofoborh 90); Wheeler, Bloomfield (Freeman 80), Aarons; Samuel (Akinfenwa 70).
Referee: Martin Coy.

Walsall (0) 2 *(Lavery 86, Bates 89)*

Darlington (1) 2 *(Holness 17, Wheatley 90)* 2882

Walsall: (352) Rose; Scarr■, Sadler, Jules (McDonald 22); Facey, Kinsella, Bates, Holden (Hardy 22), Pring; Gaffney (Lavery 62), Adebayo.
Darlington: (433) Connell; Hedley■, Storey, Galbraith, Watson; Hatfield, Wheatley, Holness (Bascome 78); Thompson (Donawa 68), Campbell (Laing 75), Rivers.
Referee: Adrian Quelch.

Sunday, 10 November 2019

Barnet (0) 0

Fleetwood T (1) 2 *(Evans 29, Hunter 90)* 1100

Barnet: (4231) Loach; Alexander, Sweeney, Reynolds, Johnson; Dunne (Chime 81), Taylor H; Vilhete (Akinola 81), Taylor J, Tutonda (Mason-Clark 57); Walker.
Fleetwood T: (433) Crellin; Coyle, Eastham, Souttar, Andrew; Coutts, Rossiter, Dempsey (Hunter 69); Morris J (Burns 76), Evans, McAleny (Madden 62).
Referee: John Busby.

Bristol R (0) 1 *(Leahy 78)*

Bromley (0) 1 *(Bush 83)* 3649

Bristol R: (442) Jaakkola; Little, Craig, Kilgour, Kelly; Rodman (Leahy 77), Upson, Ogogo, Sercombe; Adeboyejo (Nichols 56), Smith (Clarke-Harris 56).
Bromley: (4231) Huddart; Kizzi, Holland, Bush, Edmonds-Green (Wood 60); Bingham, Raymond; Coulson (Rees 44), Mekki (Clifton 61), Hackett-Fairchild; Cheek.
Referee: Daniel Middleton.

Chippenham T (0) 0

Northampton T (3) 3 *(Smith 22, Oliver 26, 45)* 2625

Chippenham T: (433) Puddy; Tyler, Richards, McDonald, Foulston; Rigg (Youssef 79), Haines (Gunner 56), Whelan; Chambers, Jarvis (Hopper 68), Zebroski.
Northampton T: (532) Arnold; Adams, Goode, Turnbull (Harriman 64), Wharton, Anderson; Lines, Warburton (Pollock 62), McCormack (Waters 68); Oliver, Smith.
Referee: Chris Pollard.

Dover Ath (0) 1 *(Sotiriou 84)*
Southend U (0) 0 1754
Dover Ath: (4231) Mersin; Simpson, Doe, Rooney, Taylor; Munns (Cumberbatch 89), Woods; Rigg (Sotiriou 81), Reason, Gobern (L'Ghoul 73); Effiong.
Southend U: (3412) Bishop; Shaughnessy (Kiernan 60), Dieng, Lennon; Bwomono, Hamilton, Hutchinson, Ralph; McLaughlin (Acquah 72); Hopper, Goodship (Cox 72).
Referee: David Rock.

Gateshead (0) 1 *(Agnew 53)*
Oldham Ath (1) 2 *(Morais 28, Smith 77)* 2199
Gateshead: (4231) James; Nicholson, Lees, Nelson, Barrow; Deverdics, Agnew (Preston 83); Tear, Olley, O'Donnell; Kayode.
Oldham Ath: (4231) de la Paz; Hamer, Egert (Mills 76), Stott, Iacovitti; McCann, Missilou (Maouche 12); Eagles (Sylla 60), Morais, Smith; Wilson.
Referee: Josh Smith.

Hayes & Yeading U (0) 0
Oxford U (1) 2 *(Long 29, Hall 69)* 1501
Hayes & Yeading U: (4231) Smith; Grant, Robinson, McDevitt, Williams; Cook (Della Verde 85), Donnelly (Toomey 46); Rowe (Little 46), Clark, Jalloh; Obi.
Oxford U: (433) Eastwood; Cadden, Dickie, Moore, Long; Baptiste (Sykes 75), Gorrin, Henry; Forde (Hall 69), Taylor (Agyei 90), Fosu.
Referee: Darren Handley.

Leyton Orient (0) 1 *(Dayton 67)*
Maldon & Tiptree (1) 2 *(Parish 43, Slew 65)* 3425
Leyton Orient: (4411) Sargeant; Ling (Alabi 74), Coulson, Happe, Widdowson; Maguire-Drew, Wright, Clay, Brophy; Dennis (Dayton 59 (Gorman 78)); Harrold.
Maldon & Tiptree: (433) McNamara; Awotwi (Cracknell 63), Gordon (Akins 71), Girdlestone, Kazeem; Dombaxe, Ngamvoulou, Hyde; Parish■, Hughes, Slew (Coombes 87).
Referee: Charles Breakspear.

Macclesfield T (0) 0
Kingstonian (2) 4 *(Hector 7, Theophanous 11, 69, Bennett 47)* 996
Macclesfield T: (442) Evans; Fregapane, Seymour, Mealing, Osipitan (Kyobe 29); Holland (Clegg 84), Kirby, O'Keeffe, Clarke; James (Price 84), Gomis.
Kingstonian: (442) Tolfrey; Cooper, Cook, Saraiva, Clohessy; Hector (Bamba 78), Beaney, Bennett (Thompson 84), Kavanagh; Hall (Sow 72), Theophanous.
Referee: Will Finnie.

Wrexham (0) 0
Rochdale (0) 0 3274
Wrexham: (433) Lainton; Carrington, Lawlor, Pearson, Jennings; Summerfield, Young, Wright; Rutherford, Grant, Tollitt (Harris M 46).
Rochdale: (433) Sanchez; Keohane, O'Connell, Ryan, Norrington-Davies; Williams MJ, Morley (Tavares 55), Camps; Pyke (McLaughlin 67), Henderson, Done (Andrew 84).
Referee: Trevor Kettle.

York C (0) 0
Altrincham (0) 1 *(Peers 82)* 3222
York C: (3412) Jameson; Newton, McNulty, Tait; Griffiths (Langstaff 84), Moke, Bond, Ferguson; Maguire (Durrell 77); Green (Burrow 59), Kempster.
Altrincham: (442) Thompson; Densmore, Hannigan, Jones, White; Johnston (Hampson 90), Moult, Williams (Richman 86), Ceesay (Hulme 67); Peers, Hancock.
Referee: James Bell.

Monday, 11 November 2019

Harrogate T (1) 1 *(Beck 7)*
Portsmouth (2) 2 *(Haunstrup 17, Curtis 41)* 3048
Harrogate T: (442) Belshaw; Fallowfield, Smith W, Hall, Smith G; Kiernan (Bradley 70), Falkingham, Burrell (Emmett 31), Diamond (Thomson 63); Beck, Muldoon.
Portsmouth: (4231) MacGillivray; Haunstrup, Burgess, Raggett (Downing 31), Brown; Naylor (Walkes 24), Close; Williams, Evans, Curtis; Marquis.
Referee: Anthony Backhouse.

Tuesday, 12 November 2019

Yeovil T (1) 1 *(D'Ath 3)*
Hartlepool U (2) 4 *(James 6, Holohan 20, Kabamba 59, Toure 86 (pen))* 2361
Yeovil T: (41212) Nelson; Hippolyte, Collins, Wilkinson■, Hutton; Lee; D'Ath, Worthington (Tilley 60); Smith J (Omotayo 82); Murphy, Dagnall (Duffus 60).
Hartlepool U: (433) Killip; Kitching (Richardson 90), Raynes, Kerr, Kioso; Holohan (Williams 57), Mafuta, Featherstone; James, Kabamba (Toure 71), Donaldson.
Referee: Peter Gibbons.

Bye: Chichester C.

FIRST ROUND REPLAYS

Tuesday, 19 November 2019

Bradford C (0) 0
Shrewsbury T (0) 1 *(Edwards 66)* 3888
Bradford C: (442) O'Donnell; Pritchard (Devine 77), O'Connor A, Richards-Everton, Oteh (Mellor 77); Connolly, Cooke, Henley, Wood; Vaughan, Akpan (Ismail 85).
Shrewsbury T: (442) Murphy; Ebanks-Landell, Williams, Beckles, Golbourne; Whalley (Thompson 87), Laurent, Walker (Edwards 54), Norburn; Love, Cummings (Okenabirhie 68).
Referee: Paul Marsden.

Bromley (0) 0
Bristol R (1) 1 *(Clarke-Harris 3)* 4558
Bromley: (4231) Huddart; Kizzi, Holland, Bush, Wood; Bingham, Raymond (Edmonds-Green 70); Coulson, Rees (Klass 89), Hackett-Fairchild (Mekki 88); Cheek.
Bristol R: (352) van Stappershoef; Menayese, Craig, Kilgour; Little (Rodman 59), Sercombe, Ogogo, Clarke O, Leahy; Nichols (Adeboyejo 72), Clarke-Harris.
Referee: Chris Pollard.

Burton Alb (1) 4 *(Akins 42, Templeton 64, Brayford 70, Sarkic 81)*
Salford C (0) 1 *(Touray 52)* 1479
Burton Alb: (41212) O'Hara; Brayford (Sbarra 83), O'Toole, Buxton, Wallace; Quinn; Edwards, Fraser (Daniel 79); Templeton (Dyer 75); Akins, Sarkic.
Salford C: (352) Neal; Piergianni, Hogan, Burgess C (Thomas-Asante 76); Wiseman, Towell, Threlkeld, Jones J (Maynard 61), Touray; Armstrong, Rooney (Dieseruvwe 81).
Referee: Marc Edwards.

Doncaster R (0) 2 *(Coppinger 52, Bingham 70)*
AFC Wimbledon (0) 0 3413
Doncaster R: (433) Dieng; Halliday, Anderson T, Wright, James; Sheaf, Whiteman, Gomes; Coppinger (May 77), Thomas (Bingham 67), Taylor J (Sadlier 90).
AFC Wimbledon: (352) Trott; O'Neill, Delaney, Thomas (Kalambayi 76); Wagstaff, Hartigan (Sanders 80), Pinnock, Reilly (McLoughlin 67), Osew; Pigott, Appiah.
Referee: Christopher Sarginson.

Eastleigh (0) 3 *(Rendell 50 (pen), Smart 69, Johnson 78)*
Stourbridge (0) 0 1509
Eastleigh: (532) Stryjek; Smart, Atkinson, Boyce, Johnson (Bearwish 79), Seaman; Miley, Payne, Hollands; Williamson (Beale 90), Rendell (Barnes 70).
Stourbridge: (442) Wren; Green, Williams■, Carter, Brown; Bellis (Cook 75), Tonks, Turton, Nicholls (Grocott 57); Scrivens (Birch 83), Lloyd.
Referee: Peter Gibbons.

Exeter C (0) 1 *(Fisher 70)*
Cambridge U (0) 0 2719
Exeter C: (532) Maxted; Woodman (Sparkes 64), Moxey, Martin A, Sweeney, Williams; Collins, Jay, Law (Atangana 80); Fisher, Martin L (Seymour 64).
Cambridge U: (532) Burton; Dunk, Darling, Ward, Taylor G (Dallas 76), Knoyle; Maris, O'Neil, Roles; Knibbs (Jones 83), Smith.
Referee: Sam Purkiss.

Gillingham (0) 1 *(Hanlan 105)*
Sunderland (0) 0 3561
Gillingham: (41212) Bonham; Fuller, Ehmer, Tucker, Ogilvie; Jones; Byrne, O'Keefe; Lee; Hanlan, Jakubiak (Ndjoli 59).
Sunderland: (352) Burge; Ozturk (Bainbridge 91), Taylor, De Bock; O'Nien, Maguire, Leadbitter, Power, Hume (McGeouch 106); Grigg (Connelly 113), Watmore (McGeady 64).
aet. Referee: Alan Young.

Peterborough U (1) 2 *(Eisa 11, Jade-Jones 90)*
Stevenage (0) 0 3593
Peterborough U: (41212) Pym; Mason, Kent, Beevers, Butler; Woodyard; Thompson, Burrows (Ward 64); Maddison; Toney, Eisa (Jade-Jones 69).
Stevenage: (352) Farman; Nugent, Cuthbert (Cowley 70), Fernandez (Smyth 90); Sonupe, Timlin (Mackail-Smith 70), Carter, Soares, Stokes; List, Lakin.
Referee: Ollie Yates.

Rochdale (1) 1 *(McShane 8)*
Wrexham (0) 0 1628
Rochdale: (433) Sanchez; Keohane, McShane (Ryan 45), O'Connell, Done; Williams MJ, Camps, Morley; Tavares (Wilbraham 64), Henderson, Pyke (Andrew 80).
Wrexham: (433) Lainton; Carrington, Pearson, Lawlor, Jennings; Summerfield, Young, Wright (Redmond 84); Rutherford, Grant, Tollitt (McIntosh 84).
Referee: Sebastian Stockbridge.

Swindon T (0) 0
Cheltenham T (0) 1 *(Addai 50)* 3000
Swindon T: (451) Benda; Hunt, Baudry, Fryers, Iandolo (Reid 88); Jaiyesimi (Twine 82), Rose (Sanokho 75), Doughty, Lyden, Woolery; Yates.
Cheltenham T: (352) Flinders; Greaves, Raglan, Tozer; Long (Clements 31), Thomas, Doyle-Hayes, Broom, Hussey; Smith (Reid 61), Addai (Lloyd 80).
Referee: Darren Drysdale.

Wednesday, 20 November 2019

Darlington (0) 0
Walsall (0) 1 *(Lavery 68)* 3106
Darlington: (433) Connell; Hedley, Storey, Galbraith, Liddle; Hatfield, Wheatley (Laing 80), Holness; Rivers, Thompson, Campbell.
Walsall: (442) Roberts; Norman, Clarke, Sadler, Cockerill-Mollett; Holden, Liddle (Bates 59), Kinsella, McDonald (Scarr 83); Lavery, Gordon (Gaffney 79).
Referee: Scott Oldham.

Lincoln C (0) 0
Ipswich T (0) 1 *(Judge 90)* 6781
Lincoln C: (4411) Vickers; Eardley, Bolger, Shackell, Toffolo; Anderson, Chapman, Hesketh, Grant; Andrade (Payne 35); Akinde (Walker 80).
Ipswich T: (433) Holy; Donacien, Nsiala, Wilson, Kenlock; McGavin (El Mizouni 66), Dozzell (Hughes 90), Huws; Judge, Keane, Georgiou.
Referee: Andy Haines.

Newport Co (0) 2 *(Amond 50, Labadie 90)*
Grimsby T (0) 0 2053
Newport Co: (352) Townsend; Bennett, O'Brien, Whitely (Matt 75); Inniss, Labadie, Haynes, Sheehan, Willmott; Abrahams (Poleon 90), Amond (Dolan 90).
Grimsby T: (532) McKeown; Hewitt (Whitehouse 82), Waterfall, Pollock■, Davis, Gibson; Cook, Hessenthaler, Robson; Green (Cardwell 55), Rose A (Clifton 79).
Referee: Darren Handley.

Wycombe W (1) 1 *(Stewart 45)*
Tranmere R (0) 2 *(Ferrier 55, Morris 115)* 2928
Wycombe W: (433) Allsop; Grimmer, Stewart, Phillips, Mascoll; Thompson (Pattison 65), Gape, Freeman; Smyth (Wheeler 76), Akinfenwa (Samuel 46), Kashket (Parker 101).
Tranmere R: (532) Davies; Caprice, Ray (Borthwick-Jackson 46), Nelson, Monthe, Wilson■; Potter, Jennings, Morris; Ferrier (Blackett-Taylor 85), Payne (Hepburn-Murphy 73).
aet. Referee: Graham Salisbury.

SECOND ROUND

Friday, 29 November 2019

Maldon & Tiptree (0) 0
Newport Co (0) 1 *(Amond 90)* 1876
Maldon & Tiptree: (433) McNamara; Awotwi, Gordon, Akins, Girdlestone (Kazeem 79); Ngamvoulou, Dombaxe (Kaid 90), Hyde; Parish, Hughes, Slew.
Newport Co: (3412) Townsend; O'Brien (Poleon 59), Inniss, Howkins (Nurse 69); Jefferies, Dolan, Sheehan, Haynes; Amond; Matt, Abrahams.
Referee: Sebastian Stockbridge.

Saturday, 30 November 2019

Cheltenham T (1) 1 *(Reid 3 (pen))*
Port Vale (0) 3 *(Pope 60, 63, 68)* 2725
Cheltenham T: (352) Flinders; Tozer, Boyle, Greaves; Long, Ince, Broom (Sheaf 61), Doyle-Hayes (Smith 82), Hussey; Addai, Reid (Reilly 45).
Port Vale: (433) Brown; Gibbons, Legge, Smith, Montano; Jake Taylor, Joyce, Conlon (Brisley 90); Amoo, Pope, Browne.
Referee: Ross Joyce.

Eastleigh (0) 1 *(Barnes 86)*
Crewe Alex (1) 1 *(Dale 36)* 1806
Eastleigh: (532) Stryjek; Partington, Atkinson, Boyce, Hollands, Seaman; Miley (Barnes 83), Payne, Smart (Green 77); Rendell, Barnett.
Crewe Alex: (433) Jaaskelainen; Ng, Mbulu, Nolan, Pickering; Green, Wintle, Lowery; Dale (Powell 70), Porter, Kirk (Jones 87).
Referee: John Busby.

Forest Green R (1) 2 *(Collins 11, Jones G 78 (og))*
Carlisle U (1) 2 *(Thomas 40, 76)* 1504
Forest Green R: (4312) Wollacott; Shephard, Kitching, Rawson, Bernard (Grubb 85); Adams (Dawson 69), Winchester, Mills J; Aitchison (Mondal 65); Stevens, Collins.
Carlisle U: (433) Collin; Iredale (Mellish 83), Carroll, Webster, Hayden; Jones M, Jones G, Thomas; Scougall, Olomola (McKirdy 75), Loft (Hope 59).
Referee: Trevor Kettle.

Kingstonian (0) 0
AFC Fylde (2) 2 *(Williams 9, 45)* 1460
Kingstonian: (442) Tolfrey; Clohessy, Cook, Cooper, Saraiva; Bennett, Beaney, Kavanagh (Sow 74), Hector (Bamba 65); Hall (Davies 74), Theophanous.
AFC Fylde: (442) Hornby; Burke, Byrne, Whitmore, Duxbury; Bradley (Kosylo 75), Philliskirk, Croasdale, Yeates (Craigen 85); Williams, Rowe (Montrose 65).
Referee: Lee Swabey.

Oldham Ath (0) 0
Burton Alb (1) 1 *(Boyce 23)* 2858
Oldham Ath: (541) de la Paz; Iacovitti (Wilson 86), Stott, Wheater, Hamer, Mills; Smith, Missilou (Maouche 30), McCann, Morais; Azankpo (Akpa Akpro 78).
Burton Alb: (4231) O'Hara; Daniel, Buxton, O'Toole, Akins; Wallace, Quinn; Templeton (Fraser 74), Edwards, Sbarra (Hutchinson 82); Boyce.
Referee: Andy Davies.

Portsmouth (0) 2 *(Close 56, Pitman 90)*
Altrincham (0) 1 *(Hancock 83 (pen))* 8539
Portsmouth: (4231) MacGillivray; Haunstrup, Hawkins, Burgess, Brown; Walkes, Close; Harness, Marquis (Pitman 46), Curtis (Williams 46); Harrison.
Altrincham: (442) Thompson; Densmore, Hannigan, Jones, White; Johnston (Hampson 88), Moult, Williams (Richman 84), Hulme; Hancock, Peers (Harrop 80).
Referee: Tom Nield.

Shrewsbury T (0) 2 *(Laurent 88, Walker 90)*
Mansfield T (0) 0 3678
Shrewsbury T: (343) O'Leary; Williams, Ebanks-Landell, Pierre; Love, Norburn■, Laurent, Golbourne; Edwards (Walker 86), Cummings (Goss 62), Okenabirhie (Udoh 86).
Mansfield T: (352) Logan; Sweeney, Pearce (Benning 80), Preston; Mellis, Hamilton, Smith (Sterling-James 80), Shaughnessy, Gordon; Maynard (Khan 89), Cook.
Referee: Andy Haines.

Walsall (0) 0
Oxford U (0) 1 *(Henry 84)* 3224
Walsall: (433) Roberts L; Facey, Clarke, Sadler, Cockerill-Mollett; Holden, Bates (Guthrie 55), Kinsella; Gordon, Gaffney (Scarr 55), Lavery (Adebayo 75).
Oxford U: (433) Eastwood; Cadden, Dickie, Mousinho, Ruffels; Henry, Gorrin, Forde (Moore 90); Sykes (Hall 66), Taylor (Mackie 87), Fosu.
Referee: Leigh Doughty.

Sunday, 1 December 2019

Blackpool (0) 3 *(Elokobi 47 (og), Delfouneso 50, 51)*
Maidstone U (1) 1 *(Khan 29)* 3977
Blackpool: (3412) Alnwick; Edwards, Heneghan, Husband; Feeney (Weston 89), Spearing, Virtue (Thompson 78), MacDonald (Turton 46); KaiKai; Nuttall, Delfouneso.
Maidstone U: (451) Cole; Hoyte, Elokobi, Chesmain, Johnson; Wishart, Marshall, James (Temelci 80), Khan, Allen (Amaluzor 60); Akanbi (McClure 25).
Referee: James Adcock.

Bristol R (0) 1 *(Sercombe 74)*
Plymouth Arg (0) 1 *(Sarcevic 84 (pen))* 6215
Bristol R: (3421) Jaakkola; Menayese■, Craig, Kilgour; Little, Upson (Smith 46), Ogogo, Leahy; Clarke O, Sercombe; Clarke-Harris.
Plymouth Arg: (3142) Palmer; Wootton, Canavan, Sawyer; Joshua Grant (Cooper 78); Edwards, Sarcevic, Mayor, McFadzean (Grant C 53); Moore B, Joel Grant (Telford 56).
Referee: Will Finnie.

Coventry C (0) 1 *(O'Hare 90)*
Ipswich T (0) 1 *(Keane 51)* 2878
Coventry C: (3421) Marosi; Rose, McFadzean, Hyam; Dabo, Kelly, Walsh, McCallum; Westbrooke (Bakayoko 57), Shipley (O'Hare 57); Biamou.
Ipswich T: (4231) Norris; Donacien, Woolfenden, Wilson, Garbutt; Downes, Dozzell; Judge, Nolan, Rowe (Edwards 76); Keane (Jackson 82).
Referee: Anthony Backhouse.

Crawley T (1) 1 *(Palmer 44)*
Fleetwood T (1) 2 *(Morris J 41, Madden 66)* 2000
Crawley T: (4141) Morris; Young, Tunnicliffe, Dallison, Sesay (Doherty 68); Francomb (Ferguson 78); Grego-Cox, Nadesan, Bulman, Lubala; Palmer.
Fleetwood T: (433) Crellin; Coyle, Eastham, Souttar, Andrew; Coutts, Sowerby, Dempsey; Burns (Madden 64), Evans (Garner 90), Morris J.
Referee: Matthew Donohue.

Exeter C (2) 2 *(Bowman 21, Atangana 29)*
Hartlepool U (0) 2 *(Featherstone 73, Kabamba 79)* 3638
Exeter C: (352) Maxted; Sweeney, Martin A, Moxey; Williams, Atangana, Collins, Law (Taylor 69), Sparkes; Seymour (Martin L 69), Bowman.
Hartlepool U: (442) Killip; Richardson, Raynes (Cunningham 72), Kerr, Kitching; Mafuta (Kabamba 72), Featherstone, Hawkes, Donaldson; Toure, James.
Referee: Josh Smith.

Gillingham (2) 3 *(Byrne 11, Lee 15, Hanlan 68)*
Doncaster R (0) 0 3216
Gillingham: (3412) Bonham; Tucker, Ehmer, Ogilvie; Fuller (Hodson 90), Jones, Byrne, O'Connor; Lee; Hanlan (Willock 90), Mandron (Ndjoli 90).
Doncaster R: (4231) Dieng; Halliday, Wright, John, James; Whiteman, Sheaf; Sadlier (May 64), Coppinger, Gomes (Thomas 64); Bingham (Taylor J 84).
Referee: Darren Handley.

Northampton T (2) 3 *(Wharton 3, Oliver 25, Smith 76)*
Notts Co (0) 1 *(Dennis 84)* 4489
Northampton T: (3412) Arnold; Goode, Wharton, Turnbull; Adams, McCormack (Warburton 77), Lines, Hoskins; Anderson (Watson 69); Williams A, Oliver (Smith 62).
Notts Co: (442) Slocombe; Brindley, Rawlinson, Turner, McCrory; Boldewijn, Rose, Doyle, Booty (Shields 46); Wootton (Tyson 85), Thomas (Dennis 77).
Referee: Paul Marsden.

Peterborough U (1) 3 *(Toney 7, Kent 79, Eisa 84)*
Dover Ath (0) 0 4239
Peterborough U: (41212) Pym; Thompson, Kent, Beevers, Blake-Tracy (Mason 75); Reed; Ward, Butler (Woodyard 67); Maddison (Tasdemir 82); Toney, Eisa.
Dover Ath: (41212) Worgan; Rooney, Doe, De Havilland, Taylor; Cumberbatch (Jeffrey 82); Woods, Munns; Reason (L'Ghoul 65); Modeste (Ratti 71), Rigg.
Referee: Brett Huxtable.

Rochdale (0) 0
Boston U (0) 0 2583
Rochdale: (433) Sanchez; Matheson, O'Connell, Williams MJ, Norrington-Davies; Camps, Morley (Wilbraham 32), Bradley (Rathbone 58); Pyke (Tavares 78), Henderson, Done.
Boston U: (433) Crookes; Duhaney, Shiels, Bird, Whittle; Abbott, Platt, Thanoj (Wafula 75); Thewlis (Tuton 90), Knowles (Wright 80), Rollins.
Referee: Dean Whitestone.

Tranmere R (0) 5 *(Blackett-Taylor 62, 85, Ferrier 64, 71, 75)*
Chichester C (0) 1 *(Peake 90)* 4370
Tranmere R: (442) Davies; Caprice, Nelson, Monthe, Ridehalgh; Morris, Perkins, Potter (Danns 62), Blackett-Taylor; Hepburn-Murphy (Jennings 46), Ferrier (Mullin 78).
Chichester C: (4231) Mowthorpe; Davidson, Cody (Peake 77), Heath, Hutchings; Rowlatt, Horncastle; Haitham (Axell 67), Iordache, Jones (Biggs 83); Clack.
Referee: Darren Drysdale.

Monday, 2 December 2019

Solihull Moors (2) 3 *(Osborne 6, Gudger 8, Ball 62)*
Rotherham U (0) 4 *(Ladapo 76, Ihiekwe 79, Smith 88, 90)* 2317
Solihull Moors: (433) Boot; Vaughan, Howe, Gudger, Reckord; Ball, Storer, Gunning; Osborne (Wright 89), McCallum (Blissett 75), Beesley (Jones 82).
Rotherham U: (442) Iversen; Olosunde, Ihiekwe, Thompson, Robertson; Morris (Ogbene 54), Barlaser (Crooks 66), Wiles, Clarke (Smith 26); Vassell, Ladapo.
Referee: Carl Boyeson.

SECOND ROUND REPLAYS

Tuesday, 10 December 2019

Carlisle U (1) 1 *(Hayden 41)*
Forest Green R (0) 0 1736
Carlisle U: (433) Collin; Hayden, Webster (Knight-Percival 88), Branthwaite, Jones G; Carroll, Jones M, Scougall (McKirdy 61); Thomas, Hope (Elliot 90), Loft.
Forest Green R: (4231) Smith; Shephard, Bernard (Godwin-Malife 83), Rawson, Kitching; Winchester, Adams; Mondal, Taylor (Stevens 61), Grubb (Mills M 46); Collins.
Referee: Andy Haines.

Crewe Alex (1) 3 *(Anene 39, 63, Johnson 55 (og))*
Eastleigh (0) 1 *(Barnes 90)* 2184
Crewe Alex: (433) Jaaskelainen; Ng, Hunt, Nolan, Pickering; Wintle, Finney (Green 81), Lowery; Dale (Powell 52), Porter (Anene 32), Kirk.
Eastleigh: (532) Stryjek; Seaman, Boyce, Johnson, Atkinson, Green (Smart 64); Hollands, Payne, Miley; Rendell (Bearwish 82), Barnett (Barnes 64).
Referee: Sam Purkiss.

Hartlepool U (0) 1 *(Hawkes 93)*
Exeter C (0) 0 2398
Hartlepool U: (442) Killip; Richardson, Kerr, Raynes, Kitching; Donaldson, Featherstone, Mafuta, Hawkes (Crichlow-Noble 103); James (Kabamba 59), Toure (Holohan 115).
Exeter C: (352) Maxted; Sweeney, Martin A, Parkes; Richardson (Williams 56), Collins, Taylor (Moxey 92), Law, Sparkes■; Bowman (Atangana 81), Martin L (Fisher 62).
aet. Referee: Scott Oldham.

Ipswich T (0) 1 *(Garbutt 84)*
Coventry C (2) 2 *(Shipley 18, Biamou 33)* 6515
Ipswich T: (442) Holy; Kenlock, Nsiala, Woolfenden, Cotter (Garbutt 46); Judge (Nolan 88), Huws (Keane 88), Skuse, Edwards; Norwood, Jackson.

Coventry C: (4231) Marosi; McCallum, Rose, McFadzean, Dabo; Walsh, Kelly; Shipley (Bakayoko 64), Allen (Westbrooke 82), O'Hare; Biamou (Godden 71).
Referee: Ben Toner.

Monday, 16 December 2019

Boston U (0) 1 *(Thewlis 49)*

Rochdale (1) 2 *(Crookes 4 (og), Morley 79 (pen))* 4190

Boston U: (433) Crookes; Penny, Shiels, Bird, Whittle; Wafula (Wright 83), Platt, Woolford (Walker 90); Thewlis, Knowles (Ainge 87), Rollins.
Rochdale: (433) Sanchez; Matheson, O'Connell, Norrington-Davies, Keohane; Ryan (Dooley 66), Morley, Camps; Done (Andrew 88), Henderson (Pyke 11), Wilbraham.
Referee: Ollie Yates.

Tuesday, 17 December 2019

Plymouth Arg (0) 0

Bristol R (0) 1 *(Rodman 68)* 6585

Plymouth Arg: (352) Palmer; Wootton, Joshua Grant, Sawyer; Moore B, Sarcevic, Edwards (Grant C 83), Mayor, Cooper; Telford (Clarke 83), Joel Grant (Rudden 66).
Bristol R: (352) Jaakkola; Menayese, Craig, Kilgour; Rodman, Hargreaves (Bennett 83), Upson, Sercombe, Leahy; Nichols (Adeboyejo 82), Smith (Kelly 87).
Referee: Andy Woolmer.

THIRD ROUND

Saturday, 4 January 2020

Birmingham C (1) 2 *(Crowley 4, Bela 90)*

Blackburn R (0) 1 *(Armstrong 61 (pen))* 7330

Birmingham C: (442) Camp; Colin, Clarke-Salter (Harding 69), Dean, Pedersen; Crowley, Davis, Gardner G (Sunjic 58), Montero (Bela 46); Alvaro Gimenez, Maghoma.
Blackburn R: (442) Leutwiler; Bennett (Williams 39), Adarabioyo, Lenihan, Bell; Armstrong, Johnson, Downing (Buckley 78), Rothwell; Brereton (Chapman 57), Gallagher.
Referee: Oliver Langford.

Bournemouth (1) 4 *(Billing 8, 79, Wilson C 67, Solanke 82)*

Luton T (0) 0 10,064

Bournemouth: (4411) Travers; Francis, Mepham, Simpson, Rico (Cook S 78); Wilson H, Billing, Surman, Fraser (Dobre 80); Stanislas (Wilson C 66); Solanke.
Luton T: (41212) Sluga; Pearson, Daniels, Jones, Sheehan (Bree 77); Rea; Shinnie, Butterfield (Berry 68); Moncur (Bolton 68); Lee, Cornick.
Referee: Darren England.

Brentford (1) 1 *(Marcondes 43)*

Stoke C (0) 0 7575

Brentford: (343) Daniels; Racic, Pinnock, Sorensen; Roerslev Rasmussen, Marcondes, Yearwood, Thompson (Oksanen 86); Zamburek (Hammar 80), Dervisoglu (Da Silva 81), Valencia.
Stoke C: (4231) Davies; Edwards, Collins, Lindsay, Martins Indi; Cousins (Ngoy 81), Woods; Ince (Verlinden 71), Powell, Campbell; Gregory (Vokes 63).
Referee: Keith Stroud.

Brighton & HA (0) 0

Sheffield W (0) 1 *(Reach 65)* 20,349

Brighton & HA: (352) Button; Duffy, Balogun (Connolly 46), Webster; Schelotto, Stephens, Alzate, Bissouma (Jahanbakhsh 63), Bong (Bernardo 71); Maupay, Gross.
Sheffield W: (4141) Dawson; Urhoghide, Borner, Iorfa, Fox; Lee; Reach (Lees 90), Pelupessy, Luongo, Murphy (Harris 71); Fletcher (Winnall 55).
Referee: Andre Marriner.

Bristol C (1) 1 *(Diedhiou 30)*

Shrewsbury T (0) 1 *(Goss 48)* 9730

Bristol C: (442) Maenpaa; Pereira, Kalas (Baker 74), Moore, Dasilva (O'Dowda 60); Eliasson, Nagy, Massengo, Palmer; Watkins (Weimann 60), Diedhiou.
Shrewsbury T: (352) Murphy; Williams, Ebanks-Landell, Pierre; Love, Goss, Norburn, Giles (Lang 87), Golbourne; Laurent, Udoh (Whalley 66).
Referee: John Busby.

Burnley (3) 4 *(Rodriguez 8, 52, Pieters 15, Hendrick 23)*

Peterborough U (1) 2 *(Toney 39, Jade-Jones 76)* 8043

Burnley: (442) Hart; Lowton, Tarkowski, Long, Pieters; Lennon, Hendrick, Cork (Westwood 90), Gudmundsson (Taylor 46); Wood (Vydra 74), Rodriguez.
Peterborough U: (41212) Pym; Mason, Bennett, Beevers, Butler; Reed (Barker 63); Brown, Boyd; Maddison; Eisa (Jade-Jones 58), Toney.
Referee: Robert Jones.

Cardiff C (0) 2 *(Paterson 50, Whyte 55)*

Carlisle U (2) 2 *(Bridge 12, McKirdy 45)* 5282

Cardiff C: (4231) Smithies; Coxe (Tomlin 78), Morrison, Bamba, Bennett; Vaulks, Bacuna; Murphy J, Paterson, Whyte; Ward (Glatzel 78).
Carlisle U: (433) Collin; Jones G, Webster, Hayden, Mellish; Watt, Jones M, Bridge (Scougall 56); McKirdy (Charters 90), Hope, Thomas (Loft 80).
Referee: Geoff Eltringham.

Fleetwood T (0) 1 *(McAleny 90)*

Portsmouth (0) 2 *(Bolton 66, Marquis 71)* 2145

Fleetwood T: (4231) Cairns; Coyle, Eastham (McAleny 83), Souttar, Andrew; Dempsey, Coutts (Sowerby 73); Burns, Morris J, Madden (Saunders 81); Evans.
Portsmouth: (4231) Bass; Bolton, Burgess, Raggett, Seddon (Close 81); Walkes, Naylor; Harness, Cannon, Curtis; Marquis.
Referee: Marc Edwards.

Fulham (0) 2 *(Knockaert 54, Arter 74)*

Aston Villa (0) 1 *(El Ghazi 63)* 12,980

Fulham: (433) Rodak; Christie, Hector, Mawson, Odoi; Onomah (Stansfield 82), McDonald (Arter 72), Johansen; Knockaert, Ivan Cavaleiro (De La Torre 84), Bryan.
Aston Villa: (433) Nyland; Elmohamady, Engels, Chester, Taylor; Lansbury, Nakamba (Vassilev 80), Hourihane; Jota (Trezeguet 76), Kodjia, El Ghazi (Ramsey 86).
Referee: Craig Pawson.

Leicester C (2) 2 *(Pearce 19 (og), Barnes 40)*

Wigan Ath (0) 0 30,330

Leicester C: (433) Ward; Justin, Morgan (Soyuncu 26), Benkovic (Fuchs 67), Chilwell; Albrighton, Mendy (Ndidi 77), Praet; Choudhury, Gray, Barnes.
Wigan Ath: (4231) Marshall; Sterling (Lowe 45), Dunkley, Kipre, Pearce (Robinson 81); Evans L, Morsy; Williams, Dowell, Massey; Windass (Gelhardt 64).
Referee: Simon Hooper.

Manchester C (2) 4 *(Zinchenko 19, Aguero 42, Harwood-Bellis 58, Foden 76)*

Port Vale (1) 1 *(Pope 35)* 52,433

Manchester C: (433) Bravo; Joao Cancelo, Stones, Harwood-Bellis, Angelino; Silva, Gundogan (Doyle 77), Zinchenko; Bernardo Silva (Mahrez 77), Aguero, Foden.
Port Vale: (442) Brown; Gibbons, Smith, Legge, Burgess (Conlon 61); Worrall, Joyce, Jake Taylor (Atkinson 61), Montano; Pope (Cullen 79), Amoo.
Referee: Lee Mason.

Millwall (1) 3 *(Smith 7, Mahoney 64 (pen), Bradshaw 82)*

Newport Co (0) 0 6009

Millwall: (442) Bialkowski; McCarthy (Brown 83), Pearce, Cooper, Wallace M; Mahoney, Molumby, Mitchell, Skalak (Ferguson 79); Bodvarsson, Smith (Bradshaw 59).
Newport Co: (4231) King; Bennett, O'Brien, Demetriou, Haynes (Whitely 74); Labadie (Dolan 80), Sheehan; Abrahams (Collins 80), Amond, Nurse; Matt.
Referee: Tony Harrington.

Oxford U (0) 4 *(Hall 52, Baptiste 66, Fosu 84, Taylor 87 (pen))*

Hartlepool U (1) 1 *(Kitching 9)* 6240

Oxford U: (433) Archer; Long, Dickie, Moore, Ruffels; Gorrin, Baptiste (Lopes 83), Sykes; Hall (Agyei 80), Mackie (Taylor 66), Fosu.
Hartlepool U: (4411) Beeney; Kioso, Raynes (Molyneux 83), Kerr, Richardson (Hamilton 70); Donaldson, Featherstone, Mafuta, Kitching; Holohan; Kabamba (Toure 65).
Referee: Michael Salisbury.

Preston NE (0) 2 *(Bodin 48, Harrop 84)*

Norwich C (3) 4 *(Idah 2, 38, 61 (pen), Hernandez 28)* 7616

Preston NE: (4231) Ripley; Fisher, Storey, Davies, Rafferty; Ledson, Bayliss; Bodin, Potts, Harrop; Stockley.
Norwich C: (4231) McGovern; Byram, Zimmermann, Amadou, Lewis; Trybull (Hanley 68), Leitner; Cantwell (Aarons 82), Stiepermann, Hernandez; Idah (McLean 86).
Referee: Martin Atkinson.

Reading (0) 2 *(Baldock 56, Loader 66)*

Blackpool (1) 2 *(Delfouneso 28, Gnanduillet 60)* 10,181

Reading: (442) Walker; Burley (Medford-Smith 84), Miazga, Howe, Richards; McCleary, Rinomhota, Olise, Obita; Baldock (Loader 59), Boye (Aluko 68).
Blackpool: (4231) Howard; Turton, Heneghan, Tilt, MacDonald (Husband 71); Spearing, Virtue; Delfouneso, Guy, Feeney (Ward 89); Gnanduillet.
Referee: John Brooks.

Rochdale (0) 1 *(Wilbraham 79)*

Newcastle U (1) 1 *(Almiron 17)* 8593

Rochdale: (4231) Sanchez; Magloire (Matheson 30), Williams MJ, O'Connell, Keohane; Ryan, Rathbone; Dooley (McLaughlin 69), Camps, Baah (Wilbraham 46); Henderson.
Newcastle U: (532) Dubravka; Yedlin, Krafth, Fernandez, Hayden, Atsu; Longstaff M, Longstaff S, Almiron (Ritchie 64); Joelinton, Muto (Ki 53).
Referee: David Coote.

Rotherham U (2) 2 *(Smith 20, Vassell 43)*

Hull C (1) 3 *(Eaves 16, 66, 90)* 6044

Rotherham U: (442) Iversen; Thompson■, Ihiekwe, Wood, Olosunde; Ogbene (Ladapo 78), Crooks, Barlaser, Wiles; Smith (Morris 90), Vassell (Lindsay 71).
Hull C: (433) Ingram; McKenzie, Burke, Tafazolli, Fleming (Bowen 61); Batty (Irvine 61), Kane, Da Silva Lopes; Bowler (Grosicki 61), Eaves, Lewis-Potter.
Referee: Anthony Backhouse.

Southampton (0) 2 *(Smallbone 47, Vokins 87)*

Huddersfield T (0) 0 20,091

Southampton: (442) Gunn; Danso (Cedric 75), Vestergaard, Yoshida, Vokins; Smallbone (Armstrong 71), Romeu, Ward-Prowse, Boufal (Obafemi 78); Adams, Long.
Huddersfield T: (433) Coleman; Simpson, Schindler, Stankovic, Brown J; Hogg, Chalobah, O'Brien (Koroma 83); Hadergjonaj , Campbell (Mounie 61), Bacuna (Ahearne-Grant 66).
Referee: Tim Robinson.

Watford (3) 3 *(Dele-Bashiru 12, Chalobah 14, Pereyra 34)*

Tranmere R (0) 3 *(Jennings 65, Monthe 78, Mullin 87 (pen))* 14,373

Watford: (433) Bachmann; Mariappa, Dawson, Spencer-Adams (Barrett 77), Masina; Quina (Whelan 61), Chalobah (Joao Pedro 46), Dele-Bashiru; Success, Gray, Pereyra■.
Tranmere R: (532) Chapman; Caprice, Clarke, Monthe, Nelson (Woods 46), Morris; Danns, Jennings, Perkins; Ferrier (Mullin 81), Payne (Blackett-Taylor 46).
Referee: Graham Scott.

Wolverhampton W (0) 0

Manchester U (0) 0 31,381

Wolverhampton W: (343) Ruddy; Dendoncker, Coady, Kilman; Doherty, Saiss (Joao Moutinho 71), Neves, Ruben Vinagre (Jonny 75); Traore, Ashley-Seal (Jimenez 46), Pedro Neto.
Manchester U: (4231) Romero; Young, Lindelof, Maguire, Williams; Andreas Pereira, Matic; Chong (Dalot 82), Mata (Fred 70), James (Rashford 70); Greenwood.
Referee: Paul Tierney.

Sunday, 5 January 2020

Bristol R (2) 2 *(Clarke-Harris 6 (pen), Craig 32)*

Coventry C (1) 2 *(Walsh 31, Craig 53 (og))* 7000

Bristol R: (352) van Stappershoef; Menayese, Craig, Kilgour; Rodman, Hargreaves (Adeboyejo 88), Upson, Sercombe, Leahy (Holmes-Dennis 83); Nichols (Bennett 64), Clarke-Harris.
Coventry C: (3421) Marosi; Rose, McFadzean, Hyam; Dabo, Walsh, Kelly, McCallum (Mason 84); Westbrooke (Allen 73), Shipley (O'Hare 51); Godden.
Referee: Gavin Ward.

Burton Alb (1) 2 *(Edwards 45, Fraser 90)*

Northampton T (3) 4 *(Adams 10, Watson 23, Goode 45, Hoskins 70)* 3810

Burton Alb: (4231) O'Hara; Brayford (Sarkic 74), Nartey (O'Toole 37), Buxton, Daniel; Edwards, Quinn; Templeton (Sbarra 71), Fraser, Akins; Boyce.
Northampton T: (3412) Cornell; Goode, Wharton, Turnbull; Williams A (Harriman 55), Lines, Watson, Adams; Anderson (Pollock 75); Hoskins, Oliver (Warburton 71).
Referee: Jeremy Simpson.

Charlton Ath (0) 0

WBA (1) 1 *(Zohore 32)* 6426

Charlton Ath: (442) Phillips; Oshilaja, Green (Hemed 60), Solly, Sarr; Odoh, Sarpong-Wiredu (Williams 70), Stevenson, Vennings; Davison, Henry (Morgan 60).
WBA: (442) Bond; Townsend, Hegazi, O'Shea, Fitzwater; Brunt, Harper (Shotton 90), Barry, Edwards (Tulloch 90); Zohore, Austin.
Referee: David Webb.

Chelsea (2) 2 *(Hudson-Odoi 6, Barkley 33)*

Nottingham F (0) 0 40,492

Chelsea: (433) Caballero; James, Christensen, Tomori, Emerson Palmieri; Barkley, Jorginho, Kovacic (Mount 69); Hudson-Odoi, Batshuayi, Pedro (Lamptey 76).
Nottingham F: (442) Smith; Jenkinson, Dawson, Tobias Figueiredo (Benalouane 46), Yuri Ribeiro; Adomah, Yates, Semedo (Fornah 69), Joao Carvalho; Mighten, Johnson (En-Neyah 81).
Referee: Peter Bankes.

Crewe Alex (0) 1 *(Green 48)*

Barnsley (1) 3 *(Brown 3, Chaplin 75, Thomas 90)* 5158

Crewe Alex: (433) Jaaskelainen; Ng, Wintle, Hunt, Pickering; Ainley (Finney 82), Green, Lowery; Powell, Anene, Kirk (Dale 76).
Barnsley: (4312) Collins; Williams J, Diaby, Andersen, Oduor (Williams B 78); Brown, Thomas, Mowatt; Dougall; Chaplin, Simoes (Schmidt 72).
Referee: James Linington.

Crystal Palace (0) 0

Derby Co (1) 1 *(Martin 32)* 15,507

Crystal Palace: (451) Hennessey; Kelly, Kouyate, Cahill, Riedewald (Woods 76); Pierrick (Tomkins 73), McCarthy, Milivojevic■, Meyer (McArthur 39), Ayew; Wickham.
Derby Co: (4231) Roos; Bogle, Davies, Forsyth, Malone; Huddlestone (Bird 75), Rooney; Whittaker (Holmes 72), Sibley (Waghorn 90), Lawrence; Martin.
Referee: Michael Oliver.

Gillingham (0) 0

West Ham U (0) 2 *(Zabaleta 74, Fornals 90)* 10,913

Gillingham: (41212) Bonham; Fuller (Ndjoli 86), Ehmer, Tucker, Ogilvie; Jones; O'Keefe, O'Connor (Marshall 79); Lee; Hanlan, Jakubiak (Charles-Cook 79).
West Ham U: (3142) Fabianski; Diop, Balbuena, Ogbonna; Rice; Fredericks (Zabaleta 43), Snodgrass (Fornals 70), Lanzini, Masuaku; Haller, Felipe Anderson (Sanchez 90).
Referee: Andrew Madley.

Liverpool (0) 1 *(Jones 71)*

Everton (0) 0 52,583

Liverpool: (433) Adrian; Williams, Phillips, Gomez, Milner (Larouci 9); Lallana, Chirivella, Jones; Elliott (Brewster 79), Minamino (Oxlade-Chamberlain 70), Origi.
Everton: (3421) Pickford; Coleman (Kean 63), Mina, Holgate; Sidibe, Schneiderlin, Sigurdsson (Delph 63), Digne; Walcott (Bernard 79), Richarlison; Calvert-Lewin.
Referee: Jonathan Moss.

Middlesbrough (0) 1 *(Fletcher 50)*

Tottenham H (0) 1 *(Lucas Moura 61)* 26,693

Middlesbrough: (3421) Mejias; Howson, McNair, Fry; Spence, Clayton, Saville, Coulson (Johnson 67); Roberts (Gestede 69), Tavernier; Fletcher (Nmecha 76).
Tottenham H: (352) Gazzaniga; Dier, Alderweireld, Vertonghen; Aurier, Eriksen, Winks (Lamela 56), Alli, Sessegnon (Lo Celso 56); Lucas Moura, Son.
Referee: Stuart Attwell.

QPR (3) 5 *(Hugill 21, 45, Samuel 29, Wallace 76, Scowen 90)*

Swansea C (0) 1 *(Byers 60)* 6712

QPR: (4231) Kelly; Kane, Cameron (Gubbins 90), Masterson, Wallace; Scowen, Ball; Samuel (Shodipo 69), Pugh, Chair (Dalling 80); Hugill.
Swansea C: (4231) Nordfeldt; Roberts, Cooper, Bidwell, John; Carroll, Fulton; Dyer (Borja Baston 58), McKay (Celina 57), Peterson (Byers 57); Kalulu.
Referee: Stephen Martin.

Sheffield U (1) 2 *(Robinson C 8, Clarke 60)*

AFC Fylde (0) 1 *(Williams 78)* 11,133

Sheffield U: (352) Verrips (Henderson 41); Bryan, Jagielka, Rodwell (Basham 58); Osborn, Freeman L, Besic, Morrison, Freeman K; Clarke, Robinson C (Stearman 88).
AFC Fylde: (4231) Hornby; Jameson, Whitmore, Byrne, Burke; Philliskirk, Croasdale; Williams, Haughton (Yeates 65), Bradley (Craigen 85); Rowe (Willoughby 65).
Referee: Jarred Gillett.

Monday, 6 January 2020

Arsenal (0) 1 *(Nelson 55)*

Leeds U (0) 0 58,403

Arsenal: (4231) Martinez; Papastathopoulos, Holding, Luiz, Kolasinac; Guendouzi, Xhaka; Pepe (Saka 90), Ozil (Willock 77), Nelson (Martinelli 67); Lacazette.
Leeds U: (4141) Meslier; Ayling (Stevens 78), White, Berardi, Douglas; Phillips; Harrison, Gotts (Dallas 60), Klich, Alioski (Helder Costa 61); Bamford.
Referee: Anthony Taylor.

THIRD ROUND REPLAYS

Tuesday, 14 January 2020

Blackpool (0) 0

Reading (1) 2 *(Boye 42, Obita 82)* 5213

Blackpool: (4231) Howard; Husband, Tilt, Heneghan, Turton; Spearing (Thompson 74), Virtue (Ward 61); Feeney (Nuttall 85), Guy, Delfouneso; Gnanduillet.
Reading: (442) Walker; Richards, Burley (Dorsett 87), McIntyre, Howe; Obita, Olise, Rinomhota (Adam 90), McCleary; Loader (Aluko 86), Boye.
Referee: Darren Bond.

Coventry C (1) 3 *(Biamou 4, 56, Pask 50)*

Bristol R (0) 0 2693

Coventry C: (343) Marosi; Rose, McFadzean (Shipley 85), Hyam; Pask, Walsh (Eccles 71), Kelly, Mason; Allen, Biamou, O'Hare (Jones 60).
Bristol R: (4231) van Stappershoef; Kilgour, Menayese, Craig, Holmes-Dennis (Adeboyejo 46); Upson (Clarke O 84), Sercombe; Rodman, Hargreaves (Kelly 62), Leahy; Clarke-Harris.
Referee: Anthony Backhouse.

Newcastle U (3) 4 *(O'Connell 17 (og), Longstaff M 20, Almiron 26, Joelinton 82)*

Rochdale (0) 1 *(Williams MJ 86)* 29,786

Newcastle U: (433) Darlow; Krafth, Lascelles (Allan 57), Lejeune, Ritchie (Shelvey 69); Hayden, Longstaff S, Longstaff M; Atsu, Joelinton, Almiron (Carroll 62).
Rochdale: (4231) Sanchez (Lynch 46); Matheson, Williams MJ, O'Connell, Norrington-Davies (Tavares 69); Ryan, Keohane; Dooley, Camps (Andrew 79), Henderson; Wilbraham.
Referee: Graham Scott.

Shrewsbury T (0) 1 *(Pierre 89)*

Bristol C (0) 0 7194

Shrewsbury T: (343) Murphy; Williams, Ebanks-Landell, Pierre; Love, Goss (Cummings 88), Norburn, Golbourne; Giles (Whalley 69), Udoh (Lang 69), Laurent.
Bristol C: (442) Bentley; Rowe, Baker (Moore 39), Williams, Hunt (Semenyo 90); Paterson (Palmer 66), Nagy, Brownhill, Eliasson; Weimann, Diedhiou.
Referee: David Webb.

Tottenham H (2) 2 *(Lo Celso 2, Lamela 15)*

Middlesbrough (0) 1 *(Saville 83)* 49,202

Tottenham H: (4231) Gazzaniga; Tanganga, Sanchez, Vertonghen, Sessegnon; Dier (Alli 85), Winks; Lo Celso, Eriksen, Lamela; Lucas Moura (Son 61).
Middlesbrough: (532) Mejias; Spence (Tavernier 74), Howson, McNair, Fry, Johnson; Wing, Clayton, Liddle (Saville 57); Nmecha (Gestede 78), Fletcher.
Referee: Craig Pawson.

Wednesday, 15 January 2020

Carlisle U (1) 3 *(Thomas 7, McKirdy 51, 64)*

Cardiff C (2) 4 *(Flint 18, 48, Murphy J 45, Ward 57)* 4381

Carlisle U: (433) Collin; Jones G, Webster, Mellish (Olomola 81), Iredale; Jones M (Charters 87), Watt, Scougall (Loft 67); Thomas, McKirdy, Hope.
Cardiff C: (4231) Smithies; Coxe (Bennett 70), Bamba, Flint, Richards; Vaulks, Ralls; Murphy J, Whyte (Pack 83), Ward; Paterson.
Referee: Darren Handley.

Manchester U (0) 1 *(Mata 67)*

Wolverhampton W (0) 0 67,025

Manchester U: (4231) Romero; Wan Bissaka, Lindelof, Maguire, Williams; Fred, Matic; Mata, Greenwood (Andreas Pereira 64), James (Rashford 64 (Lingard 80)); Martial.
Wolverhampton W: (343) Ruddy; Dendoncker, Coady, Saiss; Doherty, Neves, Joao Moutinho, Jonny (Ruben Vinagre 75); Pedro Neto (Gibbs-White 71), Jimenez, Traore (Rasmussen 88).
Referee: Kevin Friend.

Thursday, 23 January 2020

Tranmere R (1) 2 *(Monthe 36, Mullin 104)*

Watford (0) 1 *(Hinds 68)* 10,039

Tranmere R: (4231) Davies; Caprice, Clarke, Monthe, Ridehalgh; Danns (Gilmour 100), Perkins; Morris, Jennings, Blackett-Taylor (Woods 109); Ferrier (Mullin 64 (Payne 117)).
Watford: (442) Bachmann; Barrett, Kabasele, Spencer-Adams, Holebas; Whelan, Quina (Wise 106), Dele-Bashiru (Hinds 46), Hungbo (Bennetts 99); Joao Pedro (Dalby 81), Gray.
aet. Referee: Tony Harrington.

FOURTH ROUND

Friday, 24 January 2020

Northampton T (0) 0

Derby Co (0) 0 7798

Northampton T: (3412) Cornell; Harriman, Goode, Turnbull; Hoskins, Lines, Watson, Adams (Roberts 87); Anderson (Pollock 75); Williams A (Warburton 61), Oliver.
Derby Co: (4231) Roos; Wisdom, Davies, Forsyth, Malone; Rooney, Bird; Knight (Whittaker 82), Sibley (Bogle 75), Martin; Marriott (Waghorn 66).
Referee: Darren England.

QPR (0) 1 *(Wells 90)*

Sheffield W (1) 2 *(Fox 43, Winnall 90)* 11,871

QPR: (4141) Lumley; Kane, Leistner, Masterson, Manning; Ball; Clarke (Samuel 66), Eze, Chair (Wells 73), Pugh; Hugill.
Sheffield W: (442) Dawson; Odubajo, Lees, Borner, Fox; Harris, Pelupessy, Hutchinson (Hunt 54), Murphy (Reach 72); Winnall, Rhodes (Nuhiu 76).
Referee: Keith Stroud.

Saturday, 25 January 2020

Brentford (0) 0

Leicester C (1) 1 *(Iheanacho 4)* 12,221

Brentford: (433) Daniels; Roerslev Rasmussen, Jeanvier, Racic, Thompson (Henry 77); Yearwood, Mokotjo (Da Silva 46), Marcondes; Valencia (Mbeumo 82), Dervisoglu, Zamburek.
Leicester C: (4231) Ward; Justin, Morgan, Soyuncu, Fuchs; Choudhury, Praet; Gray (Maddison 78), Perez, Albrighton; Iheanacho (Dewsbury-Hall 68).
Referee: Chris Kavanagh.

Burnley (0) 1 *(Pieters 72)*

Norwich C (0) 2 *(Hanley 53, Drmic 57)* 8071

Burnley: (442) Hart; Lowton, Tarkowski, Long, Pieters; Lennon, Cork (Hendrick 65), Westwood, Brady (McNeil 80); Wood (Vydra 65), Rodriguez.
Norwich C: (4231) Fahrmann; Byram, Hanley, Zimmermann, Lewis; Vrancic, Trybull; Rupp, Stiepermann (Duda 81), Hernandez (McLean 84); Drmic (Pukki 89).
Referee: Michael Oliver.

Coventry C (0) 0

Birmingham C (0) 0 21,193

Coventry C: (3421) Marosi; Rose, Hyam, McFadzean; Dabo, Kelly, Walsh, McCallum; Westbrooke (Biamou 68), Shipley (O'Hare 69); Godden (Bakayoko 81).
Birmingham C: (442) Camp; Colin, Dean, Clarke-Salter, Pedersen; Bellingham (Gardner G 85), Sunjic, McEachran, Montero (Maghoma 85); Mrbati (Bela 56), Jutkiewicz.
Referee: Tim Robinson.

Hull C (0) 1 *(Grosicki 78)*

Chelsea (1) 2 *(Batshuayi 6, Tomori 64)* 24,109

Hull C: (433) Long; McKenzie, Burke, Tafazolli, Lichaj; Da Silva Lopes, Kane, Honeyman (Samuelsen 69); Bowen, Eaves (Magennis 69), Wilks (Grosicki 60).
Chelsea: (433) Caballero; Azpilicueta, Zouma, Tomori, Alonso; Barkley, Kovacic, Mount (Willian 68); Hudson-Odoi (Gilmour 68), Batshuayi, Pedro (Lamptey 90).
Referee: Craig Pawson.

Millwall (0) 0

Sheffield U (0) 2 *(Besic 62, Norwood 84)* 12,653

Millwall: (4411) Bialkowski; Wallace M, Cooper, Pearce, Brown; Ferguson (Bradshaw 71), Molumby, Mitchell, Mahoney (Wallace J 73); O'Brien; Smith (Bodvarsson 71).
Sheffield U: (352) Henderson; O'Connell, Jagielka, Basham; Osborn, Freeman L (Robinson J 80), Norwood, Besic, Freeman K; Robinson C (Clarke 67), Sharp.
Referee: Anthony Taylor.

Newcastle U (0) 0

Oxford U (0) 0 52,221

Newcastle U: (541) Darlow; Yedlin, Schar, Lascelles, Clark, Ritchie; Almiron, Longstaff S (Hayden 87), Bentaleb (Atsu 80), Saint-Maximin (Longstaff M 70); Joelinton.
Oxford U: (433) Eastwood; Long, Dickie, Moore, Ruffels; Sykes, Gorrin (Hanson 90), Baptiste; Fosu (Agyei 87), Mackie (Holland 77), Browne.
Referee: Robert Jones.

Portsmouth (2) 4 *(Close 37, Marquis 45, Curtis 62, Burgess 76)*

Barnsley (0) 2 *(Woodrow 60, Chaplin 90)* 13,286

Portsmouth: (4231) Bass; Bolton, Burgess, Raggett, Seddon; Close, Naylor; Williams (Harness 78), Cannon (Evans 90), Curtis; Marquis (Harrison 90).
Barnsley: (4312) Collins; Williams J, Sollbauer , Andersen, Oduor; Thomas (Mowatt 46), Halme (Dougall 69), Ritzmaier; Woodrow; Brown, Chaplin.
Referee: Graham Scott.

Reading (1) 1 *(Meite 8)*

Cardiff C (1) 1 *(Paterson 5)* 12,798

Reading: (4411) Walker; Howe, Miazga (Osho 66), McIntyre■, Richards; McCleary, Rinomhota, Adam, Meite; Aluko; Loader (House 74 (Burley 83)).
Cardiff C: (343) Smithies; Flint, Bamba, Bennett; Bacuna, Ralls (Pack 30), Vaulks, Murphy J (Hoilett 78); Whyte, Glatzel, Paterson.
Referee: Marc Edwards.

Southampton (0) 1 *(Boufal 87)*

Tottenham H (0) 1 *(Son 58)* 29,282

Southampton: (442) Gunn; Danso (Boufal 71), Stephens, Bednarek, Bertrand; Armstrong (Djenepo 43), Ward-Prowse, Hojbjerg, Redmond; Obafemi (Adams 74), Ings.
Tottenham H: (433) Lloris; Aurier, Alderweireld, Sanchez, Tanganga; Fernandes (Lamela 56), Winks, Alli (Dier 88); Lo Celso, Lucas Moura, Son.
Referee: Peter Bankes.

West Ham U (0) 0

WBA (1) 1 *(Townsend 9)* 58,911

West Ham U: (4222) Randolph; Zabaleta, Balbuena (Ogbonna 46), Diop, Cresswell; Sanchez (Noble 46), Rice; Fornals (Antonio 46), Lanzini; Haller, Ajeti.
WBA: (4411) Bond; O'Shea, Ajayi■, Hegazi, Townsend; Phillips (Tulloch 62), Barry, Brunt, Edwards; Krovinovic (Bartley 74); Austin (Zohore 70).
Referee: Stuart Attwell.

Sunday, 26 January 2020

Manchester C (2) 4 *(Gundogan 8 (pen), Bernardo Silva 19, Gabriel Jesus 72, 75)*

Fulham (0) 0 39,223

Manchester C: (4231) Bravo; Joao Cancelo, Otamendi (Stones 74), Garcia, Angelino; Bernardo Silva, Gundogan (Rodri 75); Mahrez (Sterling 53), Silva, Foden; Gabriel Jesus.
Fulham: (3412) Rodak; Hector, Ream■, Kongolo (Jasper 83); Christie, Johansen, Sessegnon, Bryan; Reid (Odoi 78); Ivan Cavaleiro (Cairney 67), Onomah.
Referee: Kevin Friend.

Shrewsbury T (0) 2 *(Cummings 65 (pen), 75)*

Liverpool (1) 2 *(Jones 15, Love 46 (og))* 9510

Shrewsbury T: (352) O'Leary; Williams, Ebanks-Landell, Pierre; Love, Laurent, Norburn (Edwards 26), Goss, Golbourne; Whalley (Udoh 85), Lang (Cummings 60).
Liverpool: (433) Adrian; Williams, Matip (Salah 79), Lovren, Larouci; Chirivella, Fabinho, Jones; Elliott (Oxlade-Chamberlain 71), Minamino (Firmino 85), Origi.
Referee: Andre Marriner.

Tranmere R (0) 0

Manchester U (5) 6 *(Maguire 10, Dalot 13, Lingard 16, Jones 41, Martial 45, Greenwood 56 (pen))* 13,779

Tranmere R: (4411) Davies; Caprice, Clarke, Monthe, Ridehalgh; Morris, Danns, Perkins (Gilmour 65), Blackett-Taylor (Hepburn-Murphy 74); Jennings; Ferrier (Mullin 74).
Manchester U: (3412) Romero; Lindelof, Jones, Maguire (Williams 64); Dalot, Andreas Pereira, Matic (Fred 46), Shaw; Lingard; Greenwood, Martial (Chong 46).
Referee: Lee Mason.

Monday, 27 January 2020

Bournemouth (0) 1 *(Surridge 90)*

Arsenal (2) 2 *(Saka 5, Nketiah 26)* 10,308

Bournemouth: (4411) Travers; Smith, Cook S, Ake, Simpson (Francis 76); Wilson H (Wilson C 76), Surman, Gosling, Cook L; Fraser; Solanke (Surridge 89).
Arsenal: (4231) Martinez; Bellerin, Mustafi (Holding 62), Papastathopoulos, Saka; Guendouzi, Xhaka; Pepe (Ceballos 69), Willock (Maitland-Niles 90), Martinelli; Nketiah.
Referee: Martin Atkinson.

FOURTH ROUND REPLAYS

Tuesday, 4 February 2020

Birmingham C (0) 2 *(Dean 90, Bela 120)*

Coventry C (0) 2 *(Roberts 50 (og), Biamou 114)* 11,680

Birmingham C: (442) Camp; Harding, Dean, Roberts, Pedersen; Maghoma (Gardner G 103), McEachran (Boyd-Munce 18), Sunjic, Bellingham (Jutkiewicz 69); Montero, Concannon (Bela 57).
Coventry C: (352) Marosi; Hyam, Pask, McFadzean; Dabo, Shipley (Allen 72), Kelly (Walsh 106), Westbrooke (O'Hare 72), Mason; Biamou, Bakayoko (Godden 82).
aet; Birmingham C won 4-1 on penalties.
Referee: Darren Bond.

Cardiff C (1) 3 *(Murphy J 19, 93, Glatzel 54)*

Reading (0) 3 *(Richards 69, Rinomhota 79, Meite 116)* 4832

Cardiff C: (4231) Etheridge; Bagan (Bennett 82), Flint, Bamba, Richards; Pack, Vaulks; Murphy J, Ward (Paterson 77), Whyte (Sang 91); Glatzel.
Reading: (352) Walker; Blackett (Obita 97), Morrison, Osho; Richards, Adam (McCleary 46), Swift, Pele (Rinomhota 63), Gunter; Puscas (Aluko 46), Meite.
aet; Reading won 4-1 on penalties.
Referee: Gavin Ward.

Derby Co (2) 4 *(Wisdom 28, Holmes 35, Marriott 51, Rooney 77 (pen))*

Northampton T (0) 2 *(Adams 47, Hoskins 84 (pen))* 15,860

Derby Co: (4141) Roos; Wisdom, Clarke, Davies, Malone; Shinnie; Marriott (Sibley 78), Rooney, Holmes (Knight 69), Lawrence; Martin (Waghorn 84).
Northampton T: (3412) Cornell; Harriman, Goode, Wharton; Anderson, Lines (Pollock 58), Watson, Adams (Martin 62); Hoskins; Williams A, Oliver (Warburton 46).
Referee: Richard Wild.

Liverpool (0) 1 *(Williams 75 (og))*

Shrewsbury T (0) 0 52,399

Liverpool: (433) Kelleher; Williams, Hoever, van den Berg, Lewis; Clarkson (Boyes 90), Chirivella, Cain; Elliott (Dixon-Bonner 90), Millar (Hardy 82), Jones.
Shrewsbury T: (433) O'Leary; Love, Ebanks-Landell, Williams, Golbourne; Pierre, Edwards, Laurent; Whalley (Walker 82), Lang (Udoh 57), Goss (Cummings 74).
Referee: Andrew Madley.

Oxford U (0) 2 *(Kelly 84, Holland 90)*

Newcastle U (2) 3 *(Longstaff S 15, Joelinton 30, Saint-Maximin 116)* 11,520

Oxford U: (433) Eastwood; Long, Dickie, Moore, Ruffels; Sykes, Gorrin (Agyei 72), Brannagan (Thorne 104); Browne (Kelly 62), Mackie (Taylor 58), Holland.
Newcastle U: (532) Darlow; Yedlin, Schar, Lascelles, Lejeune (Clark 97), Ritchie; Longstaff S, Longstaff M, Bentaleb (Atsu 103); Joelinton (Saint-Maximin 37), Almiron (Hayden 90).
aet. Referee: Peter Banks.

Wednesday, 5 February 2020

Tottenham H (1) 3 *(Stephens 12 (og), Lucas Moura 78, Son 87 (pen))*

Southampton (1) 2 *(Long 34, Ings 72)* 56,046

Tottenham H: (352) Lloris; Tanganga, Alderweireld, Vertonghen (Fernandes 54); Aurier, Ndombele (Alli 61), Dier, Winks, Sessegnon (Sanchez 90); Lucas Moura, Son.
Southampton: (442) Gunn; Ward-Prowse (Vestergaard 40), Stephens, Bednarek, Bertrand; Boufal (Armstrong 67), Romeu, Hojbjerg, Redmond; Long (Adams 81), Ings.
Referee: David Coote.

FIFTH ROUND

Monday, 2 March 2020

Portsmouth (0) 0

Arsenal (1) 2 *(Papastathopoulos 45, Nketiah 51)* 18,839

Portsmouth: (4231) Bass; McCrorie, Bolton, Burgess, Seddon; Close, McGeehan; Williams, Evans (Cannon 74), Harness (Curtis 67); Harrison (Marquis 67).
Arsenal: (4231) Martinez; Papastathopoulos, Luiz, Pablo Mari, Saka; Guendouzi, Torreira (Ceballos 16); Nelson (Maitland-Niles 90), Willock (Xhaka 87), Martinelli; Nketiah.
Referee: Mike Dean.

Tuesday, 3 March 2020

Chelsea (1) 2 *(Willian 13, Barkley 64)*

Liverpool (0) 0 40,103

Chelsea: (433) Arrizabalaga; Azpilicueta, Rudiger, Zouma, Alonso; Barkley, Gilmour, Kovacic (Mount 42); Willian (Jorginho 51), Giroud (James 90), Pedro.
Liverpool: (433) Adrian; Williams, Gomez, van Dijk, Robertson; Lallana (Salah 80), Fabinho, Jones (Milner 70); Mane, Minamino, Origi (Firmino 70).
Referee: Chris Kavanagh.

Reading (1) 1 *(Puscas 43 (pen))*

Sheffield U (1) 2 *(McGoldrick 2, Sharp 105)* 15,129

Reading: (451) Rafael Cabral; Yiadom, Miazga, Morrison, Obita; Meite (McCleary 106), Rinomhota (Baldock 106), Swift, Ejaria (Pele 98), Olise (Masika 98); Puscas.
Sheffield U: (352) Henderson; Basham, Egan, O'Connell; Baldock, Lundstram, Berge (Robinson J 99), Freeman L (Retsos 106), Osborn; Mousset (McBurnie 61), McGoldrick (Sharp 79).
aet.
Referee: Kevin Friend.

WBA (0) 2 *(Phillips 74, Zohore 90)*

Newcastle U (2) 3 *(Almiron 33, 45, Lazaro 47)* 21,557

WBA: (433) Bond; Furlong, O'Shea, Bartley, Gibbs; Harper, Barry (Krovinovic 57), Brunt (Tulloch 86); Phillips, Austin (Zohore 67), Edwards.
Newcastle U: (4231) Darlow; Manquillo, Lascelles, Schar, Rose; Longstaff S, Bentaleb; Lazaro (Lejeune 90), Almiron (Shelvey 71), Saint-Maximin (Gayle 80); Joelinton.
Referee: Anthony Taylor.

Wednesday, 4 March 2020

Leicester C (0) 1 *(Ricardo Pereira 82)*

Birmingham C (0) 0 27,181

Leicester C: (4141) Schmeichel; Ricardo Pereira, Evans, Soyuncu, Chilwell; Ndidi (Tielemans 60); Albrighton, Praet, Maddison (Choudhury 84), Gray (Barnes 66); Iheanacho.
Birmingham C: (442) Camp; Colin, Clarke-Salter, Dean, Pedersen; Harding (Gardner G 71), Kieftenbeld (Montero 84), Sunjic, Mrbati (Crowley 84); Jutkiewicz, Hogan.
Referee: Jonathan Moss.

Sheffield W (0) 0

Manchester C (0) 1 *(Aguero 53)* 20,995

Sheffield W: (532) Wildsmith; Murphy, Palmer, Iorfa, Borner (Lees 46), Fox; Lee (Hunt 63), Pelupessy, Bannan; Da Cruz, Forestieri (Fletcher 56).
Manchester C: (433) Bravo; Joao Cancelo, Stones, Otamendi, Mendy; Bernardo Silva, Rodri, Silva; Mahrez, Aguero (Sterling 86), Gabriel Jesus.
Referee: Michael Oliver.

Tottenham H (1) 1 *(Vertonghen 13)*

Norwich C (0) 1 *(Drmic 78)* 58,007

Tottenham H: (4231) Vorm; Aurier, Sanchez, Dier, Vertonghen; Skipp, Winks (Ndombele 81); Lucas Moura (Lamela 70), Lo Celso, Bergwijn (Fernandes 54); Alli (Parrott 96).
Norwich C: (4231) Krul; Aarons, Hanley, Godfrey, Lewis; Trybull (Tettey 89), Vrancic (McLean 67); Emi (Stiepermann 97), Rupp (Idah 72), Cantwell; Drmic.
aet; Norwich C won 3-2 on penalties.
Referee: Paul Tierney.

Thursday, 5 March 2020

Derby Co (0) 0

Manchester U (2) 3 *(Shaw 33, Ighalo 41, 70)* 31,379

Derby Co: (4231) Roos; Bogle, Evans, Forsyth, Lowe; Bird, Rooney; Knight, Sibley (Shinnie 80), Lawrence (Whittaker 44); Waghorn (Marriott 67).
Manchester U: (4231) Romero; Dalot, Bailly, Lindelof, Shaw (Williams 80); McTominay, Fred (Martial 73); Mata, Bruno Fernandes (Andreas Pereira 67), Lingard; Ighalo.
Referee: Craig Pawson.

SIXTH ROUND

Saturday, 27 June 2020

Norwich C (0) 1 *(Cantwell 75)*

Manchester U (0) 2 *(Ighalo 51, Maguire 118)* 0

Norwich C: (3421) Krul; Aarons, Godfrey, Klose■; Emi (Duda 91), Tettey, McLean, Lewis (Idah 118); Rupp (Hernandez 62), Cantwell (Trybull 90); Pukki (Drmic 71).
Manchester U: (4231) Romero; Dalot (Williams 63), Bailly (Martial 96), Maguire, Shaw; McTominay (Matic 78), Fred (Pogba 78); Mata (Greenwood 63), Bruno Fernandes, Lingard (Rashford 63); Ighalo.
aet. Referee: Jon Moss.

Sunday, 28 June 2020

Leicester C (0) 0

Chelsea (0) 1 *(Barkley 63)* 0

Leicester C: (4141) Schmeichel; Justin, Evans, Soyuncu, Chilwell; Ndidi; Perez (Albrighton 57), Praet (Choudhury 57), Tielemans, Barnes (Gray 76); Vardy.
Chelsea: (433) Caballero; James (Azpilicueta 46), Rudiger, Zouma, Emerson Palmieri; Mount (Barkley 46), Kante, Gilmour (Kovacic 46); Willian (Pedro 78), Abraham, Pulisic (Loftus-Cheek 72).
Referee: Mike Dean.

Newcastle U (0) 0

Manchester C (1) 2 *(De Bruyne 37 (pen), Sterling 68)* 0

Newcastle U: (541) Darlow; Manquillo, Schar, Lascelles, Fernandez, Rose (Lazaro 75); Almiron (Joelinton 65), Hayden (Longstaff M 79), Longstaff S, Saint-Maximin (Yedlin 74); Carroll (Gayle 64).
Manchester C: (4231) Bravo; Walker (Joao Cancelo 71), Otamendi, Laporte, Mendy; De Bruyne (Rodri 71), Gundogan; Mahrez (Foden 64), Silva (Bernardo Silva 64), Sterling; Gabriel Jesus.
Referee: Lee Mason.

Sheffield U (0) 1 *(McGoldrick 87)*

Arsenal (1) 2 *(Pepe 25 (pen), Ceballos 90)* 0

Sheffield U: (352) Henderson; Basham (Sharp 75), Egan, Robinson J; Baldock (Freeman K 62), Lundstram (Berge 35), Norwood, Fleck, Stevens; McBurnie, McGoldrick.
Arsenal: (343) Martinez; Mustafi, Luiz (Holding 54), Kolasinac; Maitland-Niles, Xhaka, Willock (Ceballos 67), Tierney; Pepe (Papastathopoulos 90), Lacazette (Nketiah 67), Saka.
Referee: Paul Tierney.

SEMI-FINALS (at Wembley Stadium)

Saturday, 18 July 2020

Arsenal (1) 2 *(Aubameyang 19, 71)*

Manchester C (0) 0 0

Arsenal: (343) Martinez; Mustafi (Holding 87), Luiz, Tierney; Bellerin, Ceballos (Kolasinac 88), Xhaka, Maitland-Niles; Pepe (Willock 72), Lacazette (Torreira 78), Aubameyang.
Manchester C: (4231) Ederson; Walker, Garcia, Laporte, Mendy; De Bruyne, Gundogan (Rodri 66); Mahrez (Foden 66), Silva (Fernandinho 87), Sterling; Gabriel Jesus.
Referee: Jon Moss.

Sunday, 19 July 2020

Manchester U (0) 1 *(Bruno Fernandes 85 (pen))*

Chelsea (1) 3 *(Giroud 45, Mount 46, Maguire 74 (og))* 0

Manchester U: (3412) de Gea; Bailly (Martial 45), Maguire, Lindelof; Wan Bissaka (Fosu-Mensah 79), Fred (Pogba 55), Matic, Williams; Bruno Fernandes; James (Greenwood 56), Rashford (Ighalo 79).
Chelsea: (343) Caballero; Azpilicueta, Zouma, Rudiger; James, Jorginho, Kovacic (Loftus-Cheek 86), Alonso; Willian (Hudson-Odoi 80), Giroud (Abraham 80), Mount (Pedro 90).
Referee: Mike Dean.

THE EMIRATES FA CUP FINAL 2019–20

Saturday, 1 August 2020

(at Wembley Stadium – behind closed doors)

Arsenal (1) 2 Chelsea (1) 1

Arsenal: (343) Martinez; Holding, Luiz (Papastathopoulos 88), Tierney (Kolasinac 90); Bellerin, Ceballos, Xhaka, Maitland-Niles; Pepe, Lacazette (Nketiah 82), Aubameyang.
Scorers: Aubameyang 28 (pen), 67.

Chelsea: (343) Caballero; Azpilicueta (Christensen 35), Zouma, Rudiger (Hudson-Odoi 78); James, Jorginho, Kovacic■, Alonso; Mount (Barkley 78), Giroud (Abraham 78), Pulisic (Pedro 49).
Scorer: Pulisic 5.

Referee: Anthony Taylor.

Pierre-Emerick Aubameyang scores Arsenal's second goal in their 2-1 victory over Chelsea in the FA Cup Final. (Adam Davy/PA Wire/PA Images)

NATIONAL LEAGUE 2019–20

Due to the COVID-19 pandemic, the National League (including National League North and South) was suspended on 16 March 2020. The suspension was to last until at least 3 April 2020. On 31 March the National League was suspended indefinitely. On 9 April all National League clubs were asked to support an ordinary resolution to end the season. On 22 April, with almost 90% of clubs responding and a clear majority in favour of the resolution, the league's board announced that the season was to be ended.

NATIONAL LEAGUE TABLE 2019–20

			Home					*Away*					*Total*							
		P	*W*	*D*	*L*	*F*	*A*	*W*	*D*	*L*	*F*	*A*	*W*	*D*	*L*	*F*	*A*	*GD*	*Pts*	*PPG*
1	Barrow	37	13	2	4	33	15	8	5	5	35	24	21	7	9	68	39	29	70	1.89
2	Harrogate T¶	37	12	4	3	32	16	7	5	6	29	28	19	9	9	61	44	17	66	1.78
3	Notts Co (R)	38	10	8	2	36	16	7	4	7	25	22	17	12	9	61	38	23	63	1.66
4	Yeovil T (R)	37	9	6	3	34	19	8	3	8	27	25	17	9	11	61	44	17	60	1.62
5	Boreham Wood	37	7	7	4	24	18	9	5	5	31	22	16	12	9	55	40	15	60	1.62
6	FC Halifax T	37	10	3	7	31	26	7	4	6	19	23	17	7	13	50	49	1	58	1.57
7	Barnet	35	7	6	3	26	19	7	6	6	26	23	14	12	9	52	42	10	54	1.54
8	Stockport Co (P)	39	9	3	7	28	28	7	7	6	23	26	16	10	13	51	54	–3	58	1.49
9	Solihull Moors	38	12	1	6	29	15	3	9	7	19	22	15	10	13	48	37	11	55	1.45
10	Woking (P)	38	8	6	5	22	22	7	4	8	28	33	15	10	13	50	55	–5	55	1.45
11	Dover Ath	38	6	6	8	30	27	9	3	6	19	22	15	9	14	49	49	0	54	1.42
12	Hartlepool U	39	8	5	6	28	23	6	8	6	28	27	14	13	12	56	50	6	55	1.41
13	Bromley	38	8	6	5	37	26	6	4	9	20	26	14	10	14	57	52	5	52	1.37
14	Torquay U (P)	36	9	2	7	27	26	5	4	9	29	35	14	6	16	56	61	–5	48	1.33
15	Sutton U	38	6	7	6	31	26	6	7	6	16	16	12	14	12	47	42	5	50	1.32
16	Eastleigh	37	6	8	3	22	18	5	5	10	21	37	11	13	13	43	55	–12	46	1.24
17	Dagenham & R	37	7	6	6	29	24	4	5	9	11	20	11	11	15	40	44	–4	44	1.19
18	Aldershot T	39	7	6	6	28	25	5	4	11	15	30	12	10	17	43	55	–12	46	1.18
19	Wrexham	37	7	7	4	23	16	4	3	12	23	33	11	10	16	46	49	–3	43	1.16
20	Chesterfield	38	6	4	9	31	34	5	7	7	24	31	11	11	16	55	65	–10	44	1.16
21	Maidenhead U	38	4	4	12	20	30	8	1	9	24	28	12	5	21	44	58	–14	41	1.08
22	Ebbsfleet U	39	4	6	9	23	33	6	6	8	24	35	10	12	17	47	68	–21	42	1.08
23	AFC Fylde	37	5	6	8	20	26	4	6	8	24	34	9	12	16	44	60	–16	39	1.05
24	Chorley (P)	38	3	5	11	13	30	1	9	9	18	35	4	14	20	31	65	–34	26	0.68

PPG = Points-per-game. ¶ Harrogate T promoted via play-offs.

NATIONAL LEAGUE PLAY-OFFS 2019–20

NATIONAL LEAGUE PLAY-OFF ELIMINATORS

Friday 17 July 2020

Boreham Wood (0) 2 *(Smith K 54, Rhead 80)*

FC Halifax T (1) 1 *(Sho-Silva 19)* 0

Boreham Wood: Smith G; Fyfield, Ricketts, Ilesanmi, Smith K, Murtagh, Champion, Rhead, Marsh (Shaibu 86), Tshimanga, Thomas.
FC Halifax T: Johnson; Clarke, Brown, Staunton, Maher, Duckworth, Williams (Earing 74), Allen, King C (King J 74), Cooper, Sho-Silva (Redshaw 63).
Referee: Paul Howard.

Saturday 18 July 2020

Yeovil T (0) 0

Barnet (0) 2 *(McCallum 53, Vilhete 86)* 0

Yeovil T: Nelson; Lee, Dickinson, Collins, Wilkinson, Skendi, Worthington (Smith 61), Hutton, Murphy (Richards 75), Hippolyte, Duffus (Dagnall 74).
Barnet: Loach; Ricardo, Taylor H, Tutonda, Dunne, Vilhete, Johnson, Adams, McCallum (Edwards 90), Walker (Pavey 86), Mason-Clark (Elito 65).
Referee: Carl Brook.

NATIONAL LEAGUE PLAY-OFF SEMI-FINALS

Saturday 25 July 2020

Harrogate T (0) 1 *(Muldoon 64)*

Boreham Wood (1) 0 0

Harrogate T: Belshaw; Hall, Smith W, Burrell, Kerry, Falkingham, Thomson (Emmett 80), Fallowfield, Muldoon (Beck 90), Diamond, Martin (Stead 63).
Boreham Wood: Ashmore; Fyfield, Ricketts, Ilesanmi, Smith K (Yussuf 78), Murtagh, Champion, Rhead, Marsh (Shaibu 71), Tshimanga, Thomas.
Referee: Simon Mather.

Saturday 25 July 2020

Notts Co (1) 2 *(Dennis 37, Roberts 59)*

Barnet (0) 0 0

Notts Co: Slocombe; Turner, Lacey, Brindley, Bagan, O'Brien J, Doyle, Rose, Dennis (Boldewijn 74), Wootton, Roberts (Thomas 86).
Barnet: Loach; Ricardo, Taylor H, Tutonda (Coulthirst 71), Dunne, Vilhete, Johnson, Adams, McCallum, Walker (Akinola 62), Mason-Clark.
Referee: Samuel Barrott.

NATIONAL LEAGUE PLAY-OFF FINAL

Wembley, Sunday 2 August 2020

Harrogate T (2) 3 *(Thomson 5, Hall 28, Diamond 71)*

Notts Co (0) 1 *(Roberts 46)* 0

Harrogate T: Belshaw; Fallowfield, Burrell, Thomson, Smith W, Falkingham, Hall, Kerry, Martin (Stead 61), Muldoon (Beck 86), Diamond.
Notts Co: Slocombe; Rose, Turner, Wootton, Doyle, O'Brien J (Thomas 46), Dennis (Boldewijn 46), Brindley (Kelly-Evans 87), Lacey, Bagan, Roberts.
Referee: James Bell.

NATIONAL LEAGUE ATTENDANCES BY CLUB 2019–20

	Aggregate 2019–20	*Average 2019–20*	*Highest Attendance 2019–20*
Notts Co	104,206	5,210	9,090 v AFC Fylde
Stockport Co	82,491	4,342	5,587 v Chesterfield
Wrexham	73,043	4,058	5,941 v Barrow
Chesterfield	69,725	3,670	5,432 v Notts Co
Hartlepool U	63,743	3,355	3,868 v Ebbsfleet U
Yeovil T	53,119	2,951	5,056 v Torquay U
Torquay U	46,780	2,599	4,165 v Yeovil T
FC Halifax T	42,826	2,141	3,460 v Stockport Co
Woking	40,561	2,135	3,922 v Aldershot T
Barrow	38,181	2,010	3,307 v Notts Co
Bromley	37,969	1,998	3,122 v Notts Co
Eastleigh	31,137	1,832	2,668 v Notts Co
Aldershot T	33,934	1,786	2,768 v Hartlepool U
Sutton U	32,724	1,722	2,189 v Yeovil T
AFC Fylde	27,932	1,470	2,764 v Stockport Co
Solihull Moors	26,664	1,403	3,212 v Notts Co
Dagenham & R	26,617	1,401	2,345 v Solihull Moors
Maidenhead U	26,773	1,339	1,778 v Aldershot T
Harrogate T	24,718	1,301	2,415 v Wrexham
Chorley	24,152	1,271	2,693 v Stockport Co
Barnet	19,430	1,214	1,666 v Yeovil T
Dover Ath	22,084	1,104	1,520 v Dagenham & R
Ebbsfleet U	18,610	979	1,293 v Notts Co
Boreham Wood	13,033	724	1,401 v Barnet

NATIONAL LEAGUE LEADING GOALSCORERS 2019–20

Player	*Team*	*League*	*FA Cup*	*FA Trophy*	*Play-Offs*	*Total*
Jamie Reid	Torquay U	18	1	2	0	21
Scott Quigley	Barrow	20	0	0	0	20
Rhys Murphy	Yeovil T	17	0	3	0	20
John Rooney	Barrow	17	0	2	0	19
Kabongo Tshimanga	Boreham Wood	18	0	0	0	18
Kyle Wooton	Notts Co	13	3	2	0	18
Simeone Akinola	Barnet	15	0	2	0	17
Harry Beautyman	Sutton U	15	1	1	0	17
Jake Hyde	Woking	16	0	0	0	16
Inih Effiong	Dover Ath	16	0	0	0	16
Courtney Duffus	Yeovil T	13	0	3	0	16
Jack Muldoon	Harrogate T	13	0	2	1	16
Kristian Dennis	Notts Co	12	1	2	1	16
Tyrone Marsh	Boreham Wood	14	1	0	0	15
Michael Cheek	Bromley	13	2	0	0	15
Paul McCallum	Solihull Moors	13	1	0	1	15
Includes 5 league goals and 1 National League play-off goal on loan to Barnet.						
Daniel Whitehall	Maidenhead U	13	0	2	0	15
Gozie Ugwu	Ebbsfleet U	12	1	1	0	14
Gime Toure	Hartlepool U	12	1	0	0	13
Liam McAlinden	FC Halifax T	12	0	0	0	12
Includes 2 league goals for Stockport Co.						
Tyrone Barnett	Eastleigh	11	1	0	0	12
Mike Fondop-Talum	Chesterfield	10	1	0	0	11
Wes Thomas	Notts Co	10	0	0	0	10

NATIONAL LEAGUE NORTH LEADING GOALSCORERS 2019–20

League goals only

Player	*Team*	
Adam Marriott	King's Lynn T	28
Lee Ndlovu	Brackley T	20
Akwasi Asante	Chester	18
Aaron Martin	Guisley	17
Glen Taylor	Spennymoor T	17
Josh March	Leamington	16
Amari Morgan-Smith	Alfreton T	15
Adam Campbell	Darlington	15
Jordan Burrow	York C	15
Josh Hancock	Altrincham	14
Jordan Hulme	Altrincham	14
Jordan Thewlis	Boston U	12
Dominic Knowles	Boston U	12
Ashleigh Chambers	Kidderminister H	12
Marcus Dinanga	AFC Telford U	11
Callum Roberts	Blyth Spartans	11
David Morgan	Southport	11

NATIONAL LEAGUE SOUTH LEADING GOALSCORERS 2019–20

League goals only

Player	*Team*	
Jonah Ayunga	Havant & Waterlooville	17
Joe Iaciofano	St Albans C	17
Darren McQueen	Dartford	16
Elliott Romain	Dartford	16
Includes 5 league goals for Eastbourne Bor		
Jake Robinson	Billericay T	14
Jason Prior	Dorking W	14
Shaun Jeffers	Chelmsford C	13
Danny Mills	Dulwich Hamlet	13
Tom Smith	Bath C	13
Ross Lafayette	Wealdstone	12
Dan Roberts	Slough T	12
Danilo Oris-Dadomo	Hampton & Richmond Bor	12
Femi Akinwande	Billericay T	12
Includes 6 league goals for Braintree T		

NATIONAL LEAGUE NORTH 2019–20

(P) *Promoted into division at end of 2018–19 season.* (R) *Relegated into division at end of 2018–19 season.*

NATIONAL LEAGUE NORTH TABLE 2019–20

			Home					*Away*					*Total*							
		P	*W*	*D*	*L*	*F*	*A*	*W*	*D*	*L*	*F*	*A*	*W*	*D*	*L*	*F*	*A*	*GD*	*Pts*	*PPG*
1	King's Lynn T (P)	32	11	3	3	34	17	8	4	3	29	22	19	7	6	63	39	24	64	2.00
2	York C	34	9	5	3	24	15	10	4	3	28	13	19	9	6	52	28	24	66	1.94
3	Boston U	32	10	3	2	23	11	7	4	6	23	21	17	7	8	46	32	14	58	1.81
4	Brackley T	34	8	8	1	33	9	8	4	5	28	16	16	12	6	61	25	36	60	1.76
5	Altrincham¶	33	11	4	1	43	16	5	5	7	19	24	16	9	8	62	40	22	57	1.73
6	Chester	32	10	3	3	36	16	5	6	5	22	22	15	9	8	58	38	20	54	1.69
7	Gateshead (R)	31	10	3	4	29	15	4	7	3	18	16	14	10	7	47	31	16	52	1.68
8	Spennymoor T	34	12	3	3	45	21	3	7	6	18	24	15	10	9	63	45	18	55	1.62
9	Guiseley	33	7	3	7	26	20	7	5	4	26	21	14	8	11	52	41	11	50	1.52
10	Darlington	33	9	3	5	25	19	5	3	8	18	31	14	6	13	43	50	–7	48	1.45
11	Farsley Celtic (P)	34	7	4	6	26	22	7	2	8	24	23	14	6	14	50	45	5	48	1.41
12	Southport	32	7	3	6	24	21	5	4	7	16	20	12	7	13	40	41	–1	43	1.34
13	Alfreton T	32	7	3	6	31	24	5	1	10	17	31	12	4	16	48	55	–7	40	1.25
14	AFC Telford U	34	6	4	7	30	29	5	5	7	21	27	11	9	14	51	56	–5	42	1.24
15	Kidderminster H	33	3	4	9	18	24	7	4	6	21	19	10	8	15	39	43	–4	38	1.15
16	Hereford	35	4	10	3	20	20	5	2	11	19	36	9	12	14	39	56	–17	39	1.11
17	Gloucester C*	30	6	3	5	21	18	3	3	10	18	39	9	6	15	39	57	–18	33	1.10
18	Leamington	32	6	6	4	19	13	3	2	11	20	38	9	8	15	39	51	–12	35	1.09
19	Kettering T (P)	31	4	6	5	19	21	3	5	8	17	25	7	11	13	36	46	–10	32	1.03
20	Curzon Ashton	33	6	3	7	20	17	2	7	8	14	25	8	10	15	34	42	–8	34	1.03
21	Blyth Spartans	33	3	3	10	16	37	3	2	12	16	41	6	5	22	32	78	–46	23	0.70
22	Bradford (Park Avenue)	33	3	2	12	15	37	2	3	11	10	43	5	5	23	25	80	–55	20	0.61

*PPG = Points-per-game. *Gloucester C transferred from National League South.*

¶ Altrincham promoted via play-offs.

NATIONAL LEAGUE NORTH PLAY-OFFS 2019–20

NATIONAL LEAGUE NORTH PLAY-OFF ELIMINATORS

Sunday 19 July 2020

Altrincham (1) 3 *(Hancock 33, Durrell 53 (pen), 60)*

Chester (0) 2 *(Glendon 63, Hughes 79)* 0

Altrincham: Thompson; White, Durrell (Mahon 67), Moult, Hannigan, Hampson, Hancock, Mullarkey, Lundstram (Richman 67), Hulme (Peers 73), Mooney (Harrop 85).
Chester: Gray; Roberts K, Livesey, Grand (Morgan 68), Taylor (Waters 74), Glendon, Johnston, Burton (Stopforth 57), Jackson, Waring (Hughes 74), Elliott (Dudley 57).
Referee: David McNamara.

Brackley T (1) 1 *(Byrne 45)*

Gateshead (1) 1 *(Southern-Cooper 45)* 0

Brackley T: Lewis; Franklin (Daire 87), Dean, Myles, Armson, Baker (Fairlamb 75), Walker, Byrne, Lowe, Murombedzi (Maye 90), Ndlovu (Smith 90).
Gateshead: James; Williamson, Nicholson, Deverdics, Agnew (Pattison 89), Olley, Forbes, Southern-Cooper, O'Donnell, Keating (Blackett 70), Preston.
Referee: Scott Simpson.
Gateshead won 6-5 on penalties.

NATIONAL LEAGUE NORTH PLAY-OFF SEMI-FINALS

Saturday 25 July 2020

York C (0) 0

Altrincham (1) 2 *(Hancock 7, Peers 76)* 0

York C: Jameson; Griffiths, Tait, McNulty (Langstaff 77), Newton, Ferguson, Buxton, McLaughlin (Maguire 53), Green (Moke 53), Kempster, Burrow.
Altrincham: Thompson; White (Richman 70), Hampson, Mullarkey, Hannigan, Moult, Mooney (Peers 64), Lundstam, Hulme, Hancock (Williams 79), Durrell (Mahon 79).
Referee: Scott Tallis.

Saturday 25 July 2020

Boston U (2) 5 *(Thewlis 34 (pen), 43 (pen), Rollins 62, Wright 70, 79)*

Gateshead (1) 3 *(O'Donnell 19, Nicolson 51 (pen), Keating 84)* 0

Boston U: Crook; Challoner, Shiels, Garner, Whittle, Thanoj (Heslop 88), Platt, Abbott, Thewlis (Nicholson 81), Wright (Knowles 88), Rollins.
Gateshead: James; Nicholson, Williamson, Southern-Cooper, Agnew (Blackett 78), Deverdics, Forbes, Hunter (Keating 70), Olley, O'Donnell, Preston.
Referee: Robert Massey-Ellis.

NATIONAL LEAGUE NORTH PLAY-OFF FINAL

Wembley, Saturday 1 August 2020

Boston U (0) 0

Altrincham (0) 1 *(Mooney 63)* 0

Boston U: Crook; Challoner, Whittle, Platt (Nicholson 84), Garner, Shiels, Thonoj, Abbott, Wright (Knowles 13), Thewlis (Mulhearn 71), Rollins.
Altrincham: Thompson; Richman, Hampson, Mullarkey, Hannigan, Moult, Mooney (Mahon 70), Lundstram, Hulme (Williams 86), Hancock, Durrell (Peers 69).
Referee: Adam Herczeg.

NATIONAL LEAGUE SOUTH 2019–20

(P) *Promoted into division at end of 2018–19 season.* (R) *Relegated into division at end of 2018–19 season.*

NATIONAL LEAGUE SOUTH TABLE 2019–20

			Home					*Away*					*Total*							
		P	*W*	*D*	*L*	*F*	*A*	*W*	*D*	*L*	*F*	*A*	*W*	*D*	*L*	*F*	*A*	*GD*	*Pts*	*PPG*
1	Wealdstone	33	15	0	2	39	12	7	4	5	30	23	22	4	7	69	35	34	70	2.12
2	Havant & Waterlooville (R)	34	8	4	5	28	20	11	6	0	36	17	19	10	5	64	37	27	67	1.97
3	Weymouth (P)¶	35	11	4	3	36	17	6	8	3	24	18	17	12	6	60	35	25	63	1.80
4	Bath C	35	10	5	2	28	15	8	4	6	22	22	18	9	8	50	37	13	63	1.80
5	Slough T	35	9	5	3	22	14	8	4	6	29	24	17	9	9	51	38	13	60	1.71
6	Dartford	34	8	6	4	33	20	8	2	6	27	26	16	8	10	60	46	14	56	1.65
7	Dorking W (P)	35	9	4	5	32	22	5	4	8	26	34	14	8	13	58	56	2	50	1.43
8	Hampton & Richmond Bor	33	6	4	7	28	25	8	1	7	23	25	14	5	14	51	50	1	47	1.42
9	Maidstone U (R)	33	7	6	4	29	19	5	3	8	19	25	12	9	12	48	44	4	45	1.36
10	Chelmsford C	34	7	8	2	36	25	4	3	10	19	31	11	11	12	55	56	–1	44	1.29
11	Hemel Hempstead T	34	8	3	6	19	17	4	5	8	17	26	12	8	14	36	43	–7	44	1.29
12	Welling U	34	8	2	7	25	22	4	4	9	13	24	12	6	16	38	46	–8	42	1.24
13	Oxford C	34	6	3	8	24	37	5	6	6	23	23	11	9	14	47	60	–13	42	1.24
14	Chippenham T	35	7	6	5	22	24	3	6	8	17	21	10	12	13	39	45	–6	42	1.20
15	Tonbridge Angels (P)	31	6	3	4	26	23	3	6	9	20	31	9	9	13	46	54	–8	36	1.16
16	Concord Rangers	32	6	4	7	28	23	4	3	8	16	25	10	7	15	44	48	–4	37	1.16
17	Billericay T	32	6	7	1	25	17	2	6	10	21	38	8	13	11	46	55	–9	37	1.16
18	Eastbourne Bor	33	6	6	5	26	27	2	8	6	12	27	8	14	11	38	54	–16	38	1.15
19	Dulwich Hamlet	35	5	4	9	29	29	4	6	7	22	21	9	10	16	51	50	1	37	1.06
20	St Albans C	35	3	6	8	17	27	6	4	8	24	27	9	10	16	41	54	–13	37	1.06
21	Braintree T (R)	35	5	4	9	21	28	5	1	11	23	39	10	5	20	44	67	–23	35	1.00
22	Hungerford T	33	4	2	10	14	24	4	2	11	24	40	8	4	21	38	64	–26	28	0.85

PPG = Points-per-game. ¶ Weymouth promoted via play-offs.

NATIONAL LEAGUE SOUTH PLAY-OFFS 2019–20

NATIONAL LEAGUE SOUTH PLAY-OFF ELIMINATOR

Sunday 19 July 2020

Bath C (0) 1 *(Brunt 80 (pen))*

Dorking (2) 2 *(McShane 6, Prior 41)* 0

Bath C: Clarke; Ball, Hartridge, Bowry, James (Smith Z 71), Smith T, Riley-Lowe (Brunt 46), Martin, Pearson (Stearn 89), Richards, Mann (Watkins 58).
Dorking: Howes; Harris, Philpott, Taylor (Richards 76), McManus, Wheeler (Gallagher D 46), Beard (Dyett 31), Buchanan (Gallagher J 76), Prior, Muitt (Briggs 57), McShane.
Referee: Sunny Sukhvir Gill.

Slough T (0) 0

Dartford (0) 3 *(Sheringham 47, 55, Wandio 85)* 0

Slough T: Turner; Hollis, Jackman, Togwell S (Kuhl 67), Harris W, Worsfold (Hodges 76), Wells, Lench (Davies 67), Togwell L (Roberts 56), Bird, Harris B.
Dartford: Sesay; Bonner, Braham-Barrett, Hill, Jebb, McQueen (Wanadio 82), Wynter, Noor Husin (Noble 79), Hyde, Sheringham, Romain (Marsh-Brown 86).
Referee: Richie Watkins.

NATIONAL LEAGUE SOUTH PLAY-OFF SEMI-FINALS

Saturday 25 July 2020

Havant & Waterlooville (1) 1 *(Ayunga 13)*

Dartford (0) 2 *(McQueen 59, 69 (pen))* 0

Havant & Waterlooville: Wornes; Read (Drury 46), Straker, Beckwith, Magri, Fogden (Tarbuck 66), Kedwell (Gomis 46), Ayunga, Deacon (Paul 46), Bailey, Taylor!.
Dartford: Sesay; Ming (Hyde 46), Braham-Barrett, Briggs (Marsh-Brown 46), Bonner, Hill, Jebb, Husin (Noble 65), Romain (Sheringham 87), McQueen (Wanadio 82), Wynter.
Referee: Tom Bishop.

Saturday 25 July 2020

Weymouth (2) 3 *(McQuoid 3 (pen), Anthony 11, Odubade 90)*

Dorking W (0) 2 *(McShane 72, Buchanan 84)* 0

Weymouth: Ward; Camp, Harfield, Ngalo (Murray 60), McCarthy, McQuoid, Anthony, Wakefield (Zubar 83), Robinson (Whelan 60), Brooks (Odubade 83), Hobson.
Dorking: Howes; Philpot, Dyet (Gallagher D 15), Harris, McManus, Prior, Muitt (Gallagher J 46), McShane, Briggs, Taylor (Buchanan 60), Wheeler (Richards 60).
Referee: Daniel Lamport.

NATIONAL LEAGUE SOUTH PLAY-OFF FINAL

Wembley, Sunday 2 August 2020

Weymouth (0) 0

Dartford (0) 0 0

Weymouth: Ward; Camp, Harfield, Ngalo (Murray 55), McCarthy, McQuoid (Thomson 56), Anthony, Wakefield (Odubade 85), Robinson (Whelan 70), Brooks, Hobson.
Dartford: Sesay; Wynter, Braham-Barrett, Hyde (Noble 87), Hill, Bonner, Jebb, Husin, Romain, McQueen, Sheringham (Marsh-Brown 71).
Weymouth won 3-0 on penalties.
Referee: Robert Whitton.

AFC FYLDE

Ground: Mill Farm Sports Village, Coronation Way, Wesham PR4 3JZ.
Tel: (01772) 682 593. *Website:* afcfylde.co.uk *Email:* info@afcfylde.co.uk *Year Formed:* 1988.
Record Attendance: 3,858 v Chorley, National League North, 26 December 2016. *Nickname:* 'The Coasters'.
Manager: Jim Bentley. *Colours:* White shirts with blue and red trim, white shorts, white socks.

AFC FYLDE – NATIONAL LEAGUE 2019–20 LEAGUE RECORD

Match No.	*Date*	*Venue*	*Opponents*	*Result*		*H/T Score*	*Lg Pos.*	*Goalscorers*	*Atten-dance*
1	Aug 3	A	Aldershot T	W	2-1	1-0	4	Byrne 29, Rowe (pen) 63	2003
2	6	H	Chorley	D	0-0	0-0	7		2443
3	10	H	Ebbsfleet U	W	1-0	1-0	4	Rowe (pen) 4	1136
4	13	A	Hartlepool U	D	2-2	0-1	6	Croasdale 2 81, 83	3222
5	17	H	Woking	L	1-4	0-2	10	Montrose 56	1172
6	24	A	FC Halifax T	L	1-4	1-2	12	Rowe 45	1913
7	26	H	Harrogate T	D	0-0	0-0	14		1317
8	31	A	Bromley	D	2-2	2-1	14	Williams 2 7, 40	1541
9	Sept 3	A	Stockport Co	L	1-2	0-2	18	Williams 60	3912
10	14	A	Yeovil T	L	2-3	0-2	21	Willoughby 2 59, 86	2395
11	21	H	Eastleigh	W	3-1	1-0	19	Bradley 34, Williams 57, Croasdale 77	1134
12	24	H	Wrexham	W	3-2	1-2	15	Rowe 29, Bradley 59, Haughton 68	1289
13	28	A	Notts Co	L	0-2	0-1	18		9090
14	Oct 1	H	Barnet	L	0-4	0-1	18		997
15	5	A	Torquay U	L	1-2	0-1	19	Williams 52	2440
16	8	H	Chesterfield	L	1-3	0-0	21	Hornby-Forbes 90	1217
17	26	A	Boreham Wood	W	2-0	1-0	19	Taylor 19, Bradley 90	501
18	29	A	Maidenhead U	D	1-1	0-0	19	Byrne 73	1010
19	Nov 2	H	Dover Ath	D	0-0	0-0	20		1185
20	16	A	Solihull Moors	L	1-3	1-3	20	Croasdale 45	1389
21	23	H	Dagenham & R	W	3-0	3-0	19	Yeates 16, Williams 44, Rowe 45	1268
22	26	A	Wrexham	W	1-0	1-0	18	Philliskirk 30	2941
23	Dec 7	A	Barnet	L	1-2	0-1	18	Rowe 60	661
24	10	H	Sutton U	D	0-0	0-0	18		1054
25	21	H	Yeovil T	D	2-2	1-0	20	Osho (og) 35, Bradley 72	1427
26	26	A	Barrow	D	1-1	0-0	19	Croasdale 85	3267
27	28	H	Stockport Co	L	1-2	1-0	20	Croasdale 6	2764
28	Jan 1	H	Barrow	L	0-1	0-0	21		2409
29	18	H	Torquay U	L	2-3	1-2	22	Walker 13, Williams 78	1504
30	25	A	Chesterfield	D	1-1	0-1	22	Haughton 76	3262
31	Feb 1	H	Boreham Wood	L	1-2	1-1	22	Williams 33	1285
32	11	A	Eastleigh	D	2-2	2-0	22	Walker 32, Proctor 45	1509
33	22	A	Dover Ath	L	1-5	1-2	23	Walker (pen) 6	1027
34	Mar 3	H	Notts Co	L	1-2	1-1	23	Williams 18	1353
35	7	H	Solihull Moors	D	0-0	0-0	23		1310
36	10	A	Dagenham & R	W	2-1	0-0	23	Walker 48, Whitmore 90	1064
37	14	H	Aldershot T	W	1-0	1-0	23	Philliskirk 20	1668
38	17	A	Sutton U	Cancelled					
39	21	A	Chorley	Cancelled					
40	24	H	Maidenhead U	Cancelled					
41	28	H	Hartlepool U	Cancelled					
42	Apr 4	A	Ebbsfleet U	Cancelled					
43	10	A	Harrogate T	Cancelled					
44	13	H	FC Halifax T	Cancelled					
45	18	A	Woking	Cancelled					
46	25	H	Bromley	Cancelled					

Final League Position: 23 (on points-per-game basis)

GOALSCORERS

League (44): Williams 9, Croasdale 6, Rowe 6 (2 pens), Bradley 4, Walker 4 (1 pen), Byrne 2, Haughton 2, Philliskirk 2, Willoughby 2, Hornby-Forbes 1, Montrose 1, Proctor 1, Taylor 1, Whitmore 1, Yeates 1, own goal 1.
FA Cup (10): Rowe 3, Williams 3, Bradley 1, Croasdale 1, Haughton 1, Kosylo 1.
FA Trophy (11): Haughton 4, Williams 3, Bradley 1, Burke 1, Byrne 1, Rowe 1.

Montgomery 13	Burke 28	Whitmore 31 + 3	Byrne 37	Duxbury 18	Bradley 19 + 11	Croasdale 36	Craigen 12 + 3	Yeates 18 + 11	Rowe 28	Willoughby 7 + 12	Haughton 15 + 13	Kosylo 11 + 12	Philliskirk 26 + 5	Jameson 12 + 7	Williams 29 + 3	Montrose 9 + 4	N'Gwatala — + 3	Lavercombe 5	Hornby-Forbes 3 + 3	Hornby 16	Taylor 11 + 2	Walker 8 + 1	Proctor 7 + 1	Miller 1 + 2	French 4 + 1	Lillis 3	Thompson — + 2	*Match No.*
1	2^{2}	3	4	5	6	7	8	9^{1}	10	11^{3}	12	13	14															1
1	2^{1}	3	4^{2}	5	6^{3}	8	7	9	10	11	13		14	12														2
1	4	5	6	7	3	8	2	10^{1}	11^{2}	12	9^{3}	13			14													3
1	5^{1}	4	3	2	14	7	6^{2}	12	11		9	13	8		10^{3}													4
1	2^{2}	3	4	5	12	6■		13	11	14	8	10	9^{3}			7^{1}												5
1		3^{1}	4	5			2	10	8	11^{2}	12	9	7		13	6^{3}	14											6
1			3	5		6	2	9^{3}	11	14	8^{2}	10^{1}		4	13	7	12											7
1		12	3	5		6	2	9^{2}	11	13	14	10^{1}	7	4	8^{3}													8
1			4	5		7	2^{2}	9^{1}	10	13	12	11	8	3	6													9
1		13	4	2	14	7	5^{1}	8^{2}	10	12	9^{3}		6	3	11													10
		4	3	6^{3}	2	7		12	9	11^{1}	13		8	5^{2}	10		14	1										11
		3^{1}	2	6	13	7			9	11^{2}	12		8	4	10			1	5									12
			4	2	6	8	13	12	11		10^{2}		7	3	9			1	5^{1}									13
		12	3	5	8	6	13		10		9^{2}		7^{1}	4	11			1	2									14
	5^{2}	4	3	2^{3}	7	8	6	10^{1}	11		14			12	9			1	13									15
	8	4	2		9	5^{3}	11	10^{2}	6^{1}		12	13		3	7				14	1								16
1	2	4	3		13	6		12	11		9^{1}	10^{2}	7		8						5							17
1	2	4	3		12	6			11		9^{1}	10	7		8						5							18
1	2	4	3		13	6^{2}		12	11		8^{1}	10	7	14	9						5^{3}							19
	2	4	3		7^{1}	6		13	10			11^{2}	8	12	9				14	1	5^{3}							20
	2	4	3	5	8^{3}	6^{1}		10	11^{2}		14	13	7		9	12				1								21
	2	4	3	5^{3}	8^{2}	6		10	11^{1}			14	7	13	9	12				1								22
	2	4	3	5	8^{2}	6		10	11^{1}		13	14	7^{3}		9	12				1								23
	8	4	3		9	5		11^{1}	6			13		12	7■	2				1	10^{2}							24
	2	4	3		7	6^{3}	12	11^{2}	10	14		9^{1}	8	13						1	5							25
	9	4	2		10^{2}	6		13	7	12	11^{1}	5	8	3^{3}						1	14							26
	2	6	5		13	7	4^{2}	10^{1}	11		12	14	8^{3}		9					1	3							27
	2	4	3		9^{3}	7			10^{1}	13	12	14■	8	5	11	6^{2}				1								28
	8	4	2		9	5				13	11^{2}		6	3^{1}	7					1	12	10						29
	5	4	3		13	7		12			8^{3}		14		10	6				1	2	9^{1}	11^{2}					30
	5	4	3		12	7					8^{1}	13	14		10	6^{2}				1	2	9^{3}	11					31
	5	4	3		13	7					9^{3}	14			10	6				1	2^{2}	8^{1}	11	12				32
	2	4	3			8		13					12		10	7^{1}				1		9	11	5	6^{2}			33
	5	2	3			8^{1}		13		7			10		6					1	4^{2}	11	9		12			34
	2	5	4			6				11			7		8	12						9^{2}	10^{1}		3	1	13	35
	4	3	2		5^{2}	7		10^{1}		14			8		9							11^{3}	12		6	1	13	36
	3	2	6		5^{2}	7		10^{3}		13			8		9							12	11^{1}	14	4	1		37
																												38
																												39
																												40
																												41
																												42
																												43
																												44
																												45
																												46

FA Cup

Fourth Qualifying	Peterborough Sports	(h)	6-1
First Round	Nantwich T	(a)	1-0
Second Round	Kingstonian	(a)	2-0
Third Round	Sheffield U	(a)	1-2

FA Trophy

First Round	Curzon Ashton	(h)	1-0
Second Round	Southport	(h)	4-1
Third Round	Dorking W	(a)	4-2
Quarter-Finals	Harrogate T	(h)	2-3

aet.

ALDERSHOT TOWN

Ground: The EBB Stadium at the Recreation Ground, High Street, Aldershot, Hampshire GU11 1TW.
Tel: (01252) 320 211. *Website:* www.theshots.co.uk *Email:* admin@theshots.co.uk *Year Formed:* 1926.
Record Attendance: 19,138 v Carlisle U, FA Cup 4th rd (replay), 28 January 1970. *Nickname:* 'The Shots'.
Manager: Danny Searle. *Colours:* Red shirts with thin blue stripes and blue sleeves, blue shorts with red trim, red socks with blue trim.

ALDERSHOT TOWN – NATIONAL LEAGUE 2019–20 LEAGUE RECORD

Match No.	*Date*	*Venue*	*Opponents*	*Result*		*H/T Score*	*Lg Pos.*	*Goalscorers*	*Attendance*
1	Aug 3	H	AFC Fylde	L	1-2	0-1	15	Shields [75]	2003
2	6	A	Woking	W	1-0	1-0	12	Berkeley-Agyepong [23]	3922
3	10	A	Solihull Moors	L	1-2	0-1	15	Chislett [87]	1109
4	13	H	Bromley	L	0-1	0-1	19		1774
5	17	H	FC Halifax T	D	1-1	1-0	19	Fowler [1]	1539
6	24	A	Torquay U	L	0-2	0-1	22		2668
7	26	H	Sutton U	D	1-1	0-0	21	Berkeley-Agyepong [90]	1662
8	31	A	Ebbsfleet U	W	2-1	1-0	19	Eyoma [43], Chislett [59]	1109
9	Sept 7	H	Barrow	L	1-2	0-1	21	Chislett [80]	1163
10	14	A	Stockport Co	W	2-1	2-0	20	Panayiotou [29], Santos [33]	4279
11	17	A	Barnet	L	0-2	0-0	20		1069
12	21	H	Wrexham	W	1-0	0-0	17	Panayiotou [90]	1673
13	24	H	Yeovil T	L	1-3	1-2	20	Hunt [19]	1684
14	28	A	Chesterfield	L	1-2	1-1	21	Chislett [11]	3657
15	Oct 5	A	Chorley	D	0-0	0-0	21		1425
16	8	H	Dover Ath	W	4-0	2-0	17	Mullings [25], Berkeley-Agyepong [32], Powell [53], Santos [58]	1255
17	12	H	Hartlepool U	L	0-3	0-1	18		2768
18	26	A	Harrogate T	L	0-1	0-0	20		1507
19	29	A	Boreham Wood	D	0-0	0-0	20		619
20	Nov 2	H	Maidenhead U	W	2-0	0-0	19	Panayiotou [63], Whittingham [90]	1602
21	16	A	Dagenham & R	L	1-6	0-4	19	Tinkler [77]	1616
22	23	H	Notts Co	W	2-1	2-1	18	Bettamer [27], Whittingham [43]	2211
23	26	A	Yeovil T	D	2-2	1-1	19	Chislett (pen) [27], Powell [56]	2545
24	30	H	Chesterfield	D	2-2	1-0	19	Chislett (pen) [45], Powell [70]	1637
25	Dec 7	A	Barrow	L	0-1	0-1	19		2024
26	21	H	Stockport Co	W	2-1	1-0	19	Tanner [16], Bettamer [65]	1891
27	28	H	Barnet	D	0-0	0-0	19		2107
28	Jan 1	H	Eastleigh	W	3-1	1-0	18	Chislett 2 [32, 59], Tanner [69]	1953
29	4	A	Wrexham	W	2-1	0-0	16	Chislett [63], Bettamer [69]	4222
30	18	H	Chorley	D	3-3	2-2	16	Tanner [16], Bettamer [30], Rance [83]	1931
31	25	A	Dover Ath	L	0-2	0-1	17		1113
32	28	A	Eastleigh	D	0-0	0-0	16		2130
33	Feb 1	H	Harrogate T	D	1-1	1-0	18	Bettamer [44]	1704
34	8	A	Hartlepool U	L	0-2	0-2	18		3442
35	22	A	Maidenhead U	W	2-1	2-0	16	Rance [8], Panayiotou [21]	1778
36	25	H	Boreham Wood	W	3-2	0-1	14	Lyons-Foster 2 [53, 68], Berkeley-Agyepong [71]	1274
37	Mar 7	H	Dagenham & R	L	0-1	0-0	17		2103
38	10	A	Notts Co	L	1-3	1-1	17	Tanner [17]	4287
39	14	A	AFC Fylde	L	0-1	0-1	16		1668
40	21	H	Woking	Cancelled					
41	28	A	Bromley	Cancelled					
42	Apr 4	H	Solihull Moors	Cancelled					
43	10	A	Sutton U	Cancelled					
44	13	H	Torquay U	Cancelled					
45	18	A	FC Halifax T	Cancelled					
46	25	H	Ebbsfleet U	Cancelled					

Final League Position: 18 (on points-per-game basis)

GOALSCORERS

League (43): Chislett 9 (2 pens), Bettamer 5, Berkeley-Agyepong 4, Panayiotou 4, Tanner 4, Powell 3, Lyons-Foster 2, Rance 2, Santos 2, Whittingham 2, Eyoma 1, Fowler 1, Hunt 1, Mullings 1, Shields 1, Tinkler 1.
FA Cup (3): Bettamer 1, Mullings 1, Tinkler 1.
FA Trophy (1): Bettamer 1.

Walker M 39	Tinkler 30	Kinsella 34	Finney 23	O'Dwyer 1 + 1	Rance 28 + 3	Santos 15 + 11	Rowe 13 + 3	Mullings 16 + 7	Shields 17 + 5	Panayiotou 18 + 11	Fowler 15 + 2	Berkeley-Agyepong 15 + 6	Chislett 31 + 6	Whittingham 9 + 15	Eyoma 7 + 6	Lyons-Foster 25 + 6	Hunt 19 + 2	Fletcher 3 + 3	Powell 20	Bettamer 17 + 2	Anderson 3	Walker L 8 + 5	Tanner 12	Taylor — + 1	Koue Niate 8	van Velzen — + 4	Drais 2 + 1	Miller — + 1	Grant 1	*Match No.*
1	2	3	4	5²	6	7¹	8	9	10	11³	12	13	14																	1
1	2	5	3		6		7	11	10	12	4	9²	8¹	13																2
1	2	5	3		6		7²	11	10¹	12	4	9³	8	13	14															3
1	2	5	3		6	7²		11	12	10¹	4		9	13	8															4
1	2	5	3		7	9³		11	10	13	4		12	8¹	6²	14														5
1	2	3	10¹	12	4	5³		6	7		11		14	8²	9	13														6
1	2	3				13		5	6¹	7	10	12²	11	8	9	4														7
1	2	3			6			10	11		5		9	7	8	4														8
1	2	3			4	13		6¹	7		10		11	8²	9³	5	12	14												9
1	3	4				7		13	9	10	12		8¹	14		5²	2	11³	6											10
1	2	3				5²		14	6	7³			8	12	13	4	9	10¹	11											11
1		2				8		13	9¹	10	3		7		12	5	4	11²	6											12
1		2				4³		13	5²	6	8	12	9		7¹	3	10	14	11											13
1	2	4				6		9		10		8¹	7			11	3	12	5											14
1	2	3			13	5²		14	10³	11¹		9	8			4	6		7	12										15
1	2	3			12	5		6²	14			9¹	8³		13	4	10		11	7										16
1	2	3			12	6		10²	14			8¹	7³		13	4	5		9	11										17
1	2	3	7		4			6	13				9²	12		5	10		11	8¹										18
1	2	3	7		4			6		13		9²	12			5	10		11	8¹										19
1	3	5			8²	9		10¹		12		14	6	13		4	2		7	11³										20
1	2		4		6	8³	12	11		9¹		14	10²			5	3		7	13										21
1	2³	3	7		4			14	5²			13	9	6		12	10		11	8¹										22
1		2	4		6	12			10³	13			8	7²		14	5		9	11¹	3									23
1	2	3	8		4	12	6²		7¹				10³				13		11	9	5	14								24
1	2	6	4		7	13		12		10³				9	14		3²		8		5	11¹								25
1	2	3	5		4	12				13			7¹	14			9		11	6³		8²	10							26
1	3	4			7				13				8	12		5	2		6	9		10²	11¹							27
1	2	3			6	14	13			12			7			4	5		8²	9		10¹	11³							28
1	2	3			4	14	12			8²			7	13		5	9		11³	6			10¹							29
1	2▮	3	11		4	12	9			8²			7³			5				6		13	10¹	14						30
1		2	4		5	12	6		9²	13			8	7		3▮				10		11¹								31
1	2	5	4		6	7¹	8			13		10²	9	12						11					3					32
1	2	5	4¹		6		7					9²	8	13		12				10		14	11³		3					33
1	2	3			6	14	7			13		9	8²			5				10¹		12	11³		4					34
1		2²	6		3		4			5	7	8				12						10¹	11		9	13				35
1			6		2		4			5	7	8²	12	13		3						10¹	11		9					36
1			4		7²		8¹			9³	2	6	14			5						10	11		3	12	13			37
1			6				3			4	7	9³	8	14		2							11¹		10	13	5²	12		38
1			2							11	4	8	7²	12		5						13	10		3	14	6³		9¹	39
																														40
																														41
																														42
																														43
																														44
																														45
																														46

FA Cup
Fourth Qualifying Bromley (a) 3-4

FA Trophy
First Round Torquay U (a) 1-5

BARNET

Ground: The Hive Stadium, Camrose Avenue, Edgware, London HA8 6AG. *Tel:* (020) 8381 3800.
Website: www.barnetfc.com *Email:* tellus@barnetfc.com *Year Formed:* 1888.
Record Attendance: 11,026 v Wycombe Wanderers, FA Amateur Cup 4th rd, 1951–52. *Nickname:* 'The Bees'.
Manager: Peter Beadle. *Colours:* Amber shirts with black trim, black shorts, amber socks.

BARNET – NATIONAL LEAGUE 2019–20 LEAGUE RECORD

Match No.	*Date*		*Venue*	*Opponents*	*Result*		*H/T Score*	*Lg Pos.*	*Goalscorers*	*Attendance*
1	Aug	3	H	Yeovil T	W	1-0	0-0	8	Akinola (pen) [61]	1666
2		6	A	Sutton U	D	1-1	1-0	7	Akinola (pen) [38]	1761
3		10	A	Notts Co	W	2-1	1-1	3	Reynolds [28], Akinola [75]	4096
4		13	H	Dover Ath	L	0-1	0-0	10		1143
5		17	H	Chesterfield	D	2-2	1-1	9	Taylor, J [4], Akinola (pen) [63]	1119
6		24	A	Wrexham	D	1-1	1-1	10	Sparkes [8]	4533
7		26	H	Torquay U	D	2-2	0-2	10	Mason-Clarke [49], Taylor, J [89]	1621
8		31	A	Eastleigh	W	2-1	1-0	8	Taylor, J [16], Coulthirst [90]	1922
9	Sept	14	H	Maidenhead U	W	1-0	0-0	9	Walker [66]	1086
10		17	H	Aldershot T	W	2-0	0-0	5	Mason-Clarke [47], Fonguck [56]	1069
11		21	A	FC Halifax T	L	2-4	2-2	6	Akinola [17], Adams [19]	1941
12		24	A	Ebbsfleet U	L	0-3	0-2	8		805
13		28	H	Solihull Moors	D	0-0	0-0	9		1052
14	Oct	1	A	AFC Fylde	W	4-0	1-0	5	Santos [10], Akinola [51], Walker [56], Vilhete [66]	997
15		5	A	Dagenham & R	D	1-1	1-1	6	Walker [43]	1556
16		8	H	Bromley	L	1-2	1-1	9	Walker [10]	1083
17		12	H	Woking	D	2-2	0-1	10	Vilhete [58], Mason-Clarke [90]	1651
18		26	A	Hartlepool U	L	0-2	0-2	12		3089
19		29	A	Harrogate T	L	1-2	1-2	15	Tutonda [36]	1121
20	Nov	2	H	Chorley	W	2-1	0-1	10	Taylor, J (pen) [62], Vilhete [79]	1040
21		16	H	Stockport Co	L	1-2	0-0	15	Mason-Clarke [70]	1536
22		23	A	Barrow	L	1-2	0-2	16	Taylor, J [85]	2120
23		26	H	Ebbsfleet U	W	5-2	2-1	15	Taylor, J [27], Akinola 3 (1 pen) [43, 57, 72 (p)], Walker [67]	776
24	Dec	7	H	AFC Fylde	W	2-1	1-0	10	Taylor, J [37], Akinola [90]	661
25		21	A	Maidenhead U	W	4-1	2-1	10	Akinola 2 (1 pen) [35 (p), 90], Tutonda [42], Alexander [47]	1625
26		28	A	Aldershot T	D	0-0	0-0	12		2107
27	Jan	1	A	Boreham Wood	D	0-0	0-0	11		1401
28		4	H	FC Halifax T	D	1-1	0-1	11	Taylor, J [58]	1333
29		25	A	Bromley	W	2-1	1-1	13	Walker [26], Akinola [54]	2035
30	Feb	1	H	Hartlepool U	W	2-1	0-0	11	McCallum [64], Akinola [80]	1321
31		11	A	Solihull Moors	L	0-1	0-1	13		501
32		22	A	Chorley	W	1-0	1-0	12	McCallum [2]	925
33	Mar	3	H	Boreham Wood	D	2-2	1-0	13	Reynolds [11], McCallum [79]	1273
34		7	A	Stockport Co	D	1-1	1-1	13	Akinola (pen) [8]	5011
35		10	A	Woking	W	3-1	1-0	10	McCallum [25], Walker 2 [76, 90]	1486
36		14	A	Yeovil T	Cancelled					
37		17	H	Barrow	Cancelled					
38		21	H	Sutton U	Cancelled					
39		24	H	Harrogate T	Cancelled					
40		28	A	Dover Ath	Cancelled					
41	Apr	4	H	Notts Co	Cancelled					
42		7	H	Dagenham & R	Cancelled					
43		10	A	Torquay U	Cancelled					
44		13	H	Wrexham	Cancelled					
45		18	A	Chesterfield	Cancelled					
46		25	H	Eastleigh	Cancelled					

Final League Position: 7 (on points-per-game basis)

GOALSCORERS

League (52): Akinola 15 (6 pens), Taylor, J 8 (1 pen), Walker 8, Mason-Clarke 4, McCallum 4, Vilhete 3, Reynolds 2, Tutonda 2, Adams 1, Alexander 1, Coulthirst 1, Fonguck 1, Santos 1, Sparkes 1.
FA Cup (4): Walker 2, Mason-Clark 1, Taylor, J 1 (1 pen).
FA Trophy (9): Walker 5, Akinola 2, Alexander 1, Sparkes 1.
National League Play-Offs (2): McCallum 1, Vilhete 1.

Loach 35	Alexander 34	Santos 20 + 1	Reynolds 30	Tutonda 21 + 3	Taylor H 26	Taylor J 23 + 1	Dunne 22 + 3	Elito 10 + 5	Sparkes 9 + 8	Akinola 30 + 2	Coulthirst 1 + 6	Mason-Clarke 13 + 13	Johnson 17 + 2	Boucaud 4 + 3	Barham 2 + 2	Rowan 2 + 1	Adams 11 + 5	Walker 19 + 7	Hernandez 3	Fonguck 15 + 4	Vasiliou — + 5	Pavey 4 + 4	Vilhete 12 + 9	Sweeney 18	Chime — + 1	Edwards — + 1	McCallum 4 + 1	*Match No.*
1	2	3	4	5	6	7	8	9^{1}	10	11^{2}	12	13																1
1	2		6	3	4	5	7	8	10^{1}	11	12	9																2
1	2	3	4	5	6	7	8	9^{3}	12	11^{2}	14	10^{1}	13															3
1	2	4	3	5^{3}	6	8	7	11^{1}	14	10	13	9^{2}		12														4
1	2		3		4	8	6	9	5	11		10		7^{1}	12													5
1	2	4			5	8^{1}	7	13	11	9^{2}	10	12		14		3^{3}	6											6
1	2	3			5	9	13		6	10^{1}	14	12		8^{3}		4^{2}	7	11										7
1	2	4	3		5^{2}	9			6	10	13	8		12			7^{1}	11										8
1	2	4	3			5				10		9^{2}			14	13	7	11^{1}	6	8^{3}	12							9
1	2	4	3			5			7	8		11^{2}					6	10^{1}		9	13	12						10
1	2	5	3			6				10^{3}		9^{1}					7	14	4	8^{2}	13	11	12					11
1	3	5	4			6				10		9						12	2	7^{2}	13	11	8^{1}					12
1	2	4	3		8	5				7								12		9		6^{1}	10	11				13
1	2	4	3	14	7	5				6		11^{2}						9^{3}		13		12	8^{1}	10				14
1	2	4	3	14	7	5				6^{1}		11^{2}						9^{3}		12		13	8	10				15
1	2	4	3	10	6					14		13					12	9^{3}		7^{2}		5	8	11^{1}				16
1	2	6	3	5^{2}	4			14		10^{3}		12					9^{1}	11				13	8	7				17
1	2	3^{1}		10	5	4■	13	8^{2}				12	14	6^{3}				9					7	11				18
1	4		6	2	3		7	9^{1}		11			5					12					8	10				19
1	2		4	10		12	5	8^{1}				13	3	6^{3}				9		14			7	11^{2}				20
1	2		4	10^{1}	7		6	8				11	3					9						5	12			21
1	4		6		3	2	7^{1}	8		13		10^{2}	5					11^{3}		14			12	9				22
1			3	6	5	4	7			10^{2}			2				13	11^{1}		8^{3}	14		12	9				23
1	2		4	11^{2}	8	6	5		12	7			3				14	10^{3}		9^{1}			13					24
1	2		7	6	5	4	8			10^{3}			3				12	11^{2}		9^{1}			13			14		25
1	5		7	4^{1}	2	3	8		13	10		12	6					11^{3}		9^{2}			14					26
1	2		4	10	8	6	5			7		12	3		11^{2}					9^{1}			13					27
1	2^{2}		4	10^{3}	8	6	5		14	7		13	3		11^{1}					9			12					28
1	2		4	5			6	13	14	11^{2}			3				7	10^{1}		9^{3}			12	8				29
1	2		4	10			5		13	7^{1}			3				6	9^{2}					8	11			12	30
1	2	12	4	10^{3}			5	13	14	7			3				6^{2}	9					8^{1}	11				31
1	2	5	4	10			6	12		7^{1}			3					13					9^{2}	11			8	32
1	2	6	4^{2}		5		12		8	10		13	3				7^{1}							9			11	33
1	3	5		14	2		6		7^{1}	10^{3}		12	4					13		8^{2}				9			11	34
1	2	4		10	8		5			6^{1}		13	3				14	12		9^{2}				11			7^{3}	35
																												36
																												37
																												38
																												39
																												40
																												41
																												42
																												43
																												44
																												45
																												46

FA Cup

Fourth Qualifying	Potters Bar T	(a)	1-1
Replay	Potters Bar T	(h)	3-1
First Round	Fleetwood T	(h)	0-2

National League Play-Offs

Eliminator	Yeovil T	(a)	2-0
Semi-Finals	Notts Co	(a)	0-2

FA Trophy

First Round	Weymouth	(h)	2-1
Second Round	Farsley Celtic	(a)	1-1
Replay	Farsley Celtic	(h)	2-0
Third Round	Barrow	(h)	3-0
Quarter-Finals	Halesowen T	(h)	1-2

aet.

BARROW

Ground: The Progression Solicitors Stadium, Wilkie Road, Barrow-in-Furness, Cumbria LA14 5UW.
Tel: (01229) 666 010. *Website:* www.barrowafc.com *Email:* office@barrowafc.com *Year Formed:* 1901.
Record Attendance: 16,854 v Swansea T, FA Cup 3rd rd, 9 January 1954. *Nickname:* 'The Bluebirds'.
Manager: David Dunn. *Colours:* Blue shirts with white trim, blue shorts with white trim, white socks with blue trim.

BARROW – NATIONAL LEAGUE 2019–20 LEAGUE RECORD

Match No.	Date		Venue	Opponents	Result		H/T Score	Lg Pos.	Goalscorers	Attendance
1	Aug	3	A	Wrexham	L	1-2	1-0	15	Granite 13	5941
2		6	H	Harrogate T	L	0-3	0-1	22		1602
3		10	H	Eastleigh	W	2-0	0-0	16	Stryjek (og) 51, Quigley 90	1060
4		13	A	Stockport Co	L	2-3	1-0	20	Quigley 3, Rooney 67	4183
5		17	H	Yeovil T	W	1-0	0-0	14	Quigley 46	1218
6		24	A	Chesterfield	D	2-2	2-1	15	Barry 18, Quigley 24	3812
7		26	H	FC Halifax T	L	1-2	1-0	19	Hardcastle 2	1451
8		31	A	Woking	L	2-3	1-0	21	Dyson 26, Kay 74	1787
9	Sept	3	H	Hartlepool U	L	0-1	0-0	21		1257
10		7	A	Aldershot T	W	2-1	1-0	19	Rooney 45, Kay 69	1163
11		14	H	Solihull Moors	W	3-0	2-0	14	Rooney 2 7, 45, Quigley 46	1152
12		21	A	Ebbsfleet U	W	3-0	1-0	10	Rooney 8, Quigley 2 46, 70	878
13		24	A	Chorley	W	3-1	2-1	7	Rooney 2 (2 pens) 29, 67, Dyson 45	1272
14		28	H	Maidenhead U	W	2-0	1-0	7	Rooney (pen) 36, Quigley 57	1401
15	Oct	5	A	Bromley	W	2-1	1-0	5	Angus 36, Quigley 53	2043
16		8	H	Boreham Wood	W	3-1	2-1	4	Quigley 2 13, 82, Angus 18	1758
17		26	A	Torquay U	L	2-4	1-2	5	Angus 10, Brown 56	2280
18		29	A	Dagenham & R	W	2-0	2-0	5	Angus 13, Quigley 25	1122
19	Nov	2	H	Sutton U	W	1-0	0-0	4	Kay 51	1827
20		16	A	Notts Co	W	3-0	2-0	1	Angus 10, Rooney 13, Hindle 87	5287
21		23	H	Barnet	W	2-1	2-0	1	Kay 27, Rooney 30	2120
22		26	H	Chorley	D	2-2	2-2	1	Kay 22, Rooney 30	2324
23		30	A	Maidenhead U	W	4-0	1-0	1	Quigley 12, Angus 54, Brough 64, Dyson 87	1239
24	Dec	7	H	Aldershot T	W	1-0	1-0	1	Angus 22	2024
25		26	H	AFC Fylde	D	1-1	0-0	1	Quigley 66	3267
26		28	A	Hartlepool U	D	2-2	0-0	1	Hardcastle 46, Angus 68	3790
27	Jan	1	A	AFC Fylde	W	1-0	0-0	1	Quigley 51	2409
28		4	H	Ebbsfleet U	W	7-0	3-0	1	White 15, Rooney 3 26, 83, 89, Quigley 2 44, 76, Dyson 70	2303
29		18	H	Bromley	W	2-0	1-0	1	Angus 34, Rooney 73	3155
30		25	A	Boreham Wood	D	1-1	1-0	1	Kay 34	1099
31		28	A	Solihull Moors	D	0-0	0-0	1		892
32	Feb	1	H	Torquay U	W	2-1	0-0	1	Rooney 71, Quigley 75	2586
33		4	A	Dover Ath	L	1-2	0-1	1	Rooney (pen) 81	972
34		18	H	Dover Ath	W	1-0	0-0	1	Angus 73	2016
35		22	A	Sutton U	D	2-2	2-1	1	Quigley 2 28, 39	1871
36		29	H	Dagenham & R	W	2-1	2-1	1	White 6, Brough 28	2353
37	Mar	7	H	Notts Co	L	0-2	0-0	1		3307
38		14	H	Wrexham	Cancelled					
39		17	A	Barnet	Cancelled					
40		28	H	Stockport Co	Cancelled					
41	Apr	1	A	Harrogate T	Cancelled					
42		4	A	Eastleigh	Cancelled					
43		10	A	FC Halifax T	Cancelled					
44		13	H	Chesterfield	Cancelled					
45		18	A	Yeovil T	Cancelled					
46		25	H	Woking	Cancelled					

Final League Position: 1 (on points-per-game basis)

GOALSCORERS

League (68): Quigley 20, Rooney 17 (4 pens), Angus 10, Kay 6, Dyson 4, Brough 2, Hardcastle 2, White 2, Barry 1, Brown 1, Granite 1, Hindle 1, own goal 1.
FA Cup (0).
FA Trophy (11): Angus 2, Hindle 2 (1 pen), Rooney 2 (1 pen), Barry 1, Hardcastle 1, Harrison 1, Kay 1, Penfold 1.

Dixon 37	Brough 31	Taylor 26 + 6	Granite 7	Hird 33	Rooney 37	Quigley 34 + 1	Hardcastle 23 + 13	Kay 32 + 3	Angus 34 + 2	Barry 30	Harrison 5 + 24	Greaves 3 + 6	Hindle 3 + 19	Dyson 13 + 15	Brown 10 + 7	Waddington — + 2	Platt 29	Penfold — + 3	White 16 + 2	Jones 4	Soule — + 2	*Match No.*
1	2	3	4	5	6	7^{1}	8^{2}	9^{3}	10	11	12	13	14									1
1	5	6	3	4	8	12	7^{1}	11	9	2	10^{2}	13										2
1	5	6	3	2	7^{1}	11	13	8	9	4	10^{2}			12								3
1	5^{1}	6	3	4	8	11	13	7^{3}	9	2	10^{2}			14	12							4
1		5		3	7	10	6		8^{2}	2		9^{1}	12	11	4	13						5
1		5		3	7	10^{2}	6	12	8^{3}	2	14	9	13	11^{1}	4							6
1	2	3^{3}	4	5	6	7	8^{1}	12	9^{2}	11		13	14	10								7
1		5		3	8	10^{2}	6	13	9	2	12	7		11^{1}	4							8
1	4	5		3	8^{1}		7^{3}	9^{2}	13	2	10	12		11		14	6					9
1	2	3		4	5		13	6	8^{1}	11	10		12	9^{2}			7					10
1	2	7		4	6	10^{1}	12	8	9^{2}	5	14		13	11^{3}			3					11
1	4	8		5	6	11^{3}	12	7	10^{1}	3	14		13	9^{2}			2					12
1	2			4	7	11^{3}	8	6	10^{1}	5	13	14	12	9^{2}			3					13
1	2	3		4	5	6^{1}	12	7	9^{2}	11	14		13	10^{3}			8					14
1	2	8		4	7	11^{1}	9^{2}	6	10^{3}	5	13		12	14			3					15
1	2	3		4	5	6^{1}	12	7	9^{3}	11	13		14	10^{2}			8					16
1	2	8		4	7▪	11	12	6^{1}	10^{2}	5			9^{3}		13		3	14				17
1	3	8	5		7	11	12	6	10^{3}				9^{1}	13	2		4^{2}	14				18
1	3	4	5		7	8^{1}		9			12	13	6^{3}	11^{2}	2		10	14				19
1	4				7	11^{1}	9	6	10^{2}	3	13		14	12	2		5		8^{3}			20
1		12		5	6	11^{3}	7	8	10^{2}	3	13		14		4		2		9^{1}			21
1	2	6^{2}		5	7	10^{1}	8	9	11^{3}	4	13		14				3		12			22
1	2	12		4	7	11	9^{3}	6	10^{2}	3	13			14			5		8^{1}			23
1	2			4	7	11^{2}	9^{1}	6	10^{3}	3	14		13	12			5		8			24
1	2	14		3	4^{3}	5	6^{2}	7▪	10^{1}	11				13	12		8		9			25
1	2^{3}			3	9	11^{1}	8		10^{2}	6	13		14	12	5		4		7			26
1		7		2	8	11^{2}	13	9	12	5	14			10^{1}	4		3		6^{3}			27
1		5		2	6	10	7	8^{2}	11^{1}	4^{3}	14		13	12			3		9			28
1	5	6		3	7^{1}	11^{2}	13	8	10^{3}	2	14			12			4		9			29
1	5	7		3	9	10^{1}	8^{3}	6	11^{2}	4	14			13			2		12			30
1	4	7		3	9	10^{3}	14	6	11^{1}				12	13	5		2		8^{2}			31
1	2	13		3	4	5	6^{2}	7^{3}	10^{1}	11	12				14		8		9			32
1	4	3			9	10	8^{1}	6^{2}	11	5^{3}	14		13	12			2		7			33
1	4	12		5	6	11^{3}	7^{2}	8	10^{1}		13						3		9	2	14	34
1	5	8		3	9	10	12	6^{2}	11^{3}						13		4		7^{1}	2	14	35
1	4	13		5	6	11	7	8^{1}	10						12		2		9^{2}	3		36
1	2			3	4	5▪	6	7^{2}	10^{3}		12			14	13		8^{1}		9	11		37
																						38
																						39
																						40
																						41
																						42
																						43
																						44
																						45
																						46

FA Cup

Fourth Qualifying	Solihull Moors	(h)	0-1

FA Trophy

First Round	Atherton Collieries	(a)	2-2
Replay	Atherton Collieries	(h)	2-0
Second Round	FC United of Manchester	(h)	7-0
Third Round	Barnet	(a)	0-3

BOREHAM WOOD

Ground: Meadow Park, Broughinge Road, Borehamwood, Hertfordshire WD6 5AL. *Tel:* (02089) 535 097.
Website: borehamwoodfootballclub.co.uk *Email:* see website. *Year Formed:* 1948.
Record Attendance: 4,030 v Arsenal, Friendly, 13 July 2001. *Nickname:* 'The Wood' *Manager:* Luke Garrard.
Colours: White shirts, white shorts, white socks.

BOREHAM WOOD – NATIONAL LEAGUE 2019–20 LEAGUE RECORD

Match No.	*Date*		*Venue*	*Opponents*	*Result*		*H/T Score*	*Lg Pos.*	*Goalscorers*	*Attendance*
1	Aug	3	A	Torquay U	L	1-2	0-0	15	Marsh [90]	3138
2		6	H	Wrexham	D	2-2	0-1	18	Murtagh 2 [83, 90]	845
3		10	H	Chesterfield	D	2-2	1-2	20	Tshimanga (pen) [15], McDonnell [53]	715
4		13	A	Dagenham & R	W	3-0	1-0	12	Tshimanga 2 (1 pen) [18, 86 (p)], Shaibu [88]	1179
5		17	H	Sutton U	L	0-1	0-0	16		407
6		24	A	Bromley	L	0-1	0-1	18		1443
7		26	H	Ebbsfleet U	L	1-2	0-2	20	Marsh [76]	533
8		31	A	Chorley	W	3-1	2-0	17	Marsh [31], Stephens [38], Challoner (og) [47]	1035
9	Sept	3	A	Eastleigh	L	0-2	0-1	19		1641
10		7	H	Dover Ath	W	3-1	2-1	15	Tshimanga 2 [2, 18], Marsh [62]	493
11		14	A	Harrogate T	D	0-0	0-0	16		942
12		21	H	Stockport Co	W	4-0	3-0	12	Tshimanga 2 [19, 41], Thomas [27], Marsh [89]	744
13		24	H	Notts Co	L	1-2	0-1	18	Marsh (pen) [84]	756
14		28	A	Woking	W	2-1	1-1	12	Tshimanga 2 [39, 48]	2219
15	Oct	5	H	Solihull Moors	W	1-0	0-0	11	Marsh [90]	540
16		8	A	Barrow	L	1-3	1-2	14	Marsh [31]	1758
17		12	A	FC Halifax T	W	2-0	1-0	11	Champion [44], McDonnell [75]	2244
18		26	H	AFC Fylde	L	0-2	0-1	14		501
19		29	H	Aldershot T	D	0-0	0-0	13		619
20	Nov	2	A	Yeovil T	D	1-1	0-1	15	Tshimanga [90]	2879
21		16	H	Maidenhead U	W	2-1	0-0	13	Tshimanga [72], Shaibu [87]	624
22		23	A	Hartlepool U	D	2-2	1-0	12	Thomas (pen) [27], Tshimanga [50]	3377
23		26	A	Notts Co	D	2-2	1-2	14	Shaibu [15], Thomas (pen) [90]	3256
24		30	H	Woking	W	1-0	1-0	9	Marsh [15]	682
25	Dec	7	A	Dover Ath	W	2-0	1-0	9	Thomas (pen) [33], Shaibu [59]	728
26		21	H	Harrogate T	W	2-1	1-1	6	Marsh [14], Tshimanga [90]	501
27		28	H	Eastleigh	D	2-2	1-1	8	Mingoia [9], Fyfield [46]	601
28	Jan	1	H	Barnet	D	0-0	0-0	8		1401
29		4	A	Stockport Co	W	3-1	3-0	7	Marsh 2 [2, 22], Tshimanga [44]	4074
30		18	A	Solihull Moors	W	2-0	1-0	5	Thomas [32], Smith, K [67]	882
31		25	H	Barrow	D	1-1	0-1	5	Marsh [67]	1099
32	Feb	1	A	AFC Fylde	W	2-1	1-1	5	Tshimanga [19], Fyfield [73]	1285
33		22	H	Yeovil T	W	1-0	0-0	3	Tshimanga [73]	1040
34		25	A	Aldershot T	L	2-3	1-0	3	Smith, K [13], May [86]	1274
35		29	H	Hartlepool U	D	1-1	1-0	4	Tshimanga [1]	932
36	Mar	3	A	Barnet	D	2-2	0-1	5	Smith, K [61], Marsh [73]	1273
37		7	A	Maidenhead U	W	1-0	1-0	4	Tshimanga [22]	1296
38		14	H	Torquay U	Cancelled					
39		17	H	FC Halifax T	Cancelled					
40		21	A	Wrexham	Cancelled					
41		28	H	Dagenham & R	Cancelled					
42	Apr	4	A	Chesterfield	Cancelled					
43		10	A	Ebbsfleet U	Cancelled					
44		13	H	Bromley	Cancelled					
45		18	A	Sutton U	Cancelled					
46		25	H	Chorley	Cancelled					

Final League Position: 5 (on points-per-game basis)

GOALSCORERS

League (55): Tshimanga 18 (2 pens), Marsh 14 (1 pen), Thomas 5 (3 pens), Shaibu 4, Smith, K 3, Fyfield 2, McDonnell 2, Murtagh 2, Champion 1, May 1, Mingoia 1, Stephens 1, own goal 1.
FA Cup (2): Marsh 1, own goal 1.
FA Trophy (0).
National League Play-Offs (2): Rhead 1, Smith K 1.

Gregory 14	Ilesanmi 35	Champion 33 + 1	Stephens 28 + 2	Mingoia 16 + 6	McDonnell 14 + 3	Tshimanga 37	Murtagh 31	Fyfield 24 + 1	Thomas 29 + 3	Smith K 32	Shaibu 10 + 20	Marsh 32 + 4	Ricketts 29 + 3	Thompson 6 + 2	Woodards 8 + 3	Shakes 2 + 17	Wickham — + 1	Ashmore 23	Yussuf — + 3	Rhead 3 + 2	May 1 + 1	Smith G — + 1	Match No.
1	2	3	4	5	6^{3}	7^{1}	8	9■	10^{2}	11	12	13	14										1
1	2^{1}	6	3	7	8	10^{3}	9		13	5	12	11^{2}		4	14								2
1	2	6	3	7	9	10	8			4	12	11^{1}		5									3
1	3	4	5	6	7^{3}	8	9^{2}			11	13	10^{1}	12		2	14							4
1	3	4	5	6	7	8	9^{3}		13	11	12	10^{1}	14		2^{2}								5
1		4	5	6^{1}	7	8		9	12	10	11^{3}	13	3		2^{2}	14							6
1	3■	5^{2}	6		7^{3}	8^{1}	9		10	11	12	14	4	13	2								7
1			3		7^{2}	11^{3}	6		8	9	13	10	5	4	2^{1}	12	14						8
1	2^{3}	13■	3		12	10	6		7	9	14	11^{1}	5^{2}	4		8							9
1	5		2			10^{1}	7	3	8^{2}	9	13	11	6	4		12							10
1	5	2	3			10	7	4	8	9	12	11^{1}	6										11
1	5	2	3	12		10^{2}	7	4	8^{1}	9^{3}	14	11	6			13							12
1	9	2	3	12	14	11^{2}	7	4	8		13	10	6^{1}			5^{3}							13
1	4	5	2	7^{2}		10^{1}	8	3	9		13	11	6■			12							14
	9	2	3	5	7^{1}	11	6	4	8			10				12		1					15
	3		4	13	5	6^{3}	7^{2}	9	10		12	8		11^{1}	2	14		1					16
	3	4		5^{2}	6	7^{3}	8	10	11		14	9		12	2^{1}	13		1					17
	9	2^{1}	3	12		11	7	4	8^{2}	5	13	10	6					1					18
	9	2	3			11^{1}	7	4	8	5	12	10	6					1					19
	2	7	3			11	8		9	5	12	10	6		4^{1}			1					20
	4	2	3			11^{1}	7		8	5	9	10	6			12		1					21
	2	5	3			11	7		8	4	9^{1}	10	6			12		1					22
	4	2	3	12	13	11	7		8	5	9^{2}	10	6^{1}					1					23
	4	2	3^{1}		7	11		12	8	5	9^{2}	10	6			13		1					24
	4	2	3			11	7		8	5	9^{1}	10	6			12		1					25
	8	2	3	13		11	7	4^{3}		5	9^{2}	10^{1}	6		14	12		1					26
	8	2	3	9		11	7	4		5	10^{1}		6			12		1					27
	8	2	3^{2}	9^{1}		11	7	4		5	10	13	6		12			1					28
	3	5				11	7	2	8^{1}	4	9	10	6			12		1					29
	4	2		9		11	7	3	8	5		10^{1}	6					1	12				30
	4	2		9^{1}		11	7	3	8	5		10	6					1	12				31
	4	2		9^{1}		11	7	3	8	5		10	6			12		1					32
	4	2	13	9^{2}	7^{1}	11		3	8	5		10	6					1		12			33
	4	2		9^{2}	7^{1}	11		3	8	5^{3}		10	6					1	14	12	13		34
	3	7				11^{1}		2	8	4	12	9	5					1		10	6		35
	4	6	3			11		2	8	5		9	7					1		10			36
	4	2	12			11^{1}	7	3	8	5^{3}	13	9^{2}	6					1■		10		14	37
																							38
																							39
																							40
																							41
																							42
																							43
																							44
																							45
																							46

FA Cup

Fourth Qualifying	Torquay U	(a)	2-3

National League Play-Offs

Eliminator	Halifax T	(h)	2-1
Semi-Finals	Harrogate T	(a)	0-1

FA Trophy

First Round	Royston T	(a)	0-2

BROMLEY

Ground: Westminster Waste Stadium, Bromley, Kent BR2 9EF. *Tel:* (02084) 605 291. *Website:* bromleyfc.tv
Email: info@bromleyfc.co.uk *Year Formed:* 1892. *Record Attendance:* 10,798 v Nigeria, Friendly, 24 September 1949.
Nickname: 'The Ravens', 'The Lillywhites'. *Manager:* Neil Smith. *Colours:* White shirts with black and gold trim, white shorts with black trim, white socks with black and gold trim.

BROMLEY – NATIONAL LEAGUE 2019–20 LEAGUE RECORD

Match No.	Date	Venue	Opponents	Result		H/T Score	Lg Pos.	Goalscorers	Attendance
1	Aug 3	A	Chorley	D	0-0	0-0	13		1469
2	6	H	Ebbsfleet U	W	3-1	2-0	5	Cheek [19], Bingham 2 [30, 73]	1719
3	10	H	Torquay U	D	3-3	2-1	7	Holland [1], Kizzi [45], Raymond [70]	1398
4	13	A	Aldershot T	W	1-0	1-0	5	Holland [28]	1774
5	17	A	Hartlepool U	W	3-2	2-2	3	Cheek [9], Hackett-Fairchild 2 [27, 75]	3171
6	24	H	Boreham Wood	W	1-0	1-0	2	Cheek [45]	1443
7	26	A	Maidenhead U	W	2-1	0-0	2	Hackett-Fairchild 2 [77, 89]	1511
8	31	H	AFC Fylde	D	2-2	1-2	3	Bingham [16], Raymond (pen) [63]	1541
9	Sept 4	A	Dagenham & R	D	1-1	0-1	3	Hackett-Fairchild [90]	1526
10	7	H	Chesterfield	W	2-1	1-0	3	Cheek 2 [26, 73]	2110
11	14	A	Eastleigh	D	1-1	0-0	2	Coulson [63]	1752
12	21	H	Notts Co	W	2-1	1-1	1	Doughty [2], McCoulsky [73]	3122
13	24	H	Woking	W	1-0	1-0	1	Cheek [38]	2358
14	28	A	Yeovil T	L	1-3	1-1	1	Cheek [22]	3960
15	Oct 5	H	Barrow	L	1-2	0-1	2	Cheek [86]	2043
16	8	A	Barnet	W	2-1	1-1	2	Bush [25], Kizzi [57]	1083
17	12	A	Solihull Moors	L	1-2	0-1	2	Doughty [90]	2120
18	26	H	FC Halifax T	W	5-0	0-0	1	Mekki [53], Hackett-Fairchild [59], Bush [65], Rees [73], Kizzi [90]	2215
19	29	H	Stockport Co	D	2-2	2-2	1	Hackett-Fairchild [18], Minihan (og) [37]	2205
20	Nov 2	A	Wrexham	L	0-1	0-0	1		3469
21	16	H	Harrogate T	D	3-3	1-3	2	Hackett-Fairchild [45], Bush 2 [48, 73]	2177
22	23	A	Sutton U	W	2-0	1-0	2	Williamson [14], Cheek [79]	1762
23	26	A	Woking	L	1-2	1-1	3	Coulson [15]	1769
24	30	H	Yeovil T	D	1-1	0-0	2	Raymond (pen) [65]	2261
25	Dec 7	A	Chesterfield	W	2-1	0-1	2	Williamson [77], Evans (og) [82]	3270
26	21	H	Eastleigh	L	2-3	1-2	3	Cheek [20], Coker [90]	1651
27	26	A	Dover Ath	L	0-3	0-2	3		1210
28	28	H	Dagenham & R	W	3-0	1-0	3	Cheek [43], Coulson [83], Rees [89]	2312
29	Jan 1	H	Dover Ath	W	3-0	1-0	3	Raymond (pen) [45], Rees [49], Cheek [88]	2011
30	4	A	Notts Co	L	1-2	0-1	4	Cheek [50]	5192
31	18	A	Barrow	L	0-2	0-1	4		3155
32	25	H	Barnet	L	1-2	1-1	4	Rees [42]	2035
33	Feb 1	A	FC Halifax T	L	1-2	1-2	7	Kizzi [45]	2026
34	8	H	Solihull Moors	D	2-2	0-0	6	Raymond [79], Whitely [90]	1716
35	15	A	Stockport Co	L	0-1	0-0	8		4611
36	22	H	Wrexham	L	0-2	0-1	9		1743
37	29	H	Sutton U	L	0-1	0-1	12		1909
38	Mar 7	A	Harrogate T	D	1-1	0-0	12	Bradley (og) [86]	1339
39	14	A	Chorley	Cancelled					
40	21	A	Ebbsfleet U	Cancelled					
41	28	H	Aldershot T	Cancelled					
42	Apr 4	A	Torquay U	Cancelled					
43	10	H	Maidenhead U	Cancelled					
44	13	A	Boreham Wood	Cancelled					
45	18	H	Hartlepool U	Cancelled					
46	25	A	AFC Fylde	Cancelled					

Final League Position: 13 (on points-per-game basis)

GOALSCORERS

League (57): Cheek 13, Hackett-Fairchild 8, Raymond 5 (3 pens), Bush 4, Kizzi 4, Rees 4, Bingham 3, Coulson 3, Doughty 2, Holland 2, Williamson 2, Coker 1, McCoulsky 1, Mekki 1, Whitely 1, own goals 3.
FA Cup (5): Cheek 2, Bush 1, Holland 1, Kizzi 1.
FA Trophy (0).

Cousins 18	Kizzi 36	Bush 33 + 1	Holland 24 + 3	Wood 33	Higgs 4 + 7	Raymond 30 + 5	Bingham 30 + 1	Hackett-Fairchild 20 + 3	Coulson 36 + 2	Cheek 37	Porter 4 + 1	Clifton 2 + 22	Klass 5 + 12	Mekki 10 + 8	Okoye 9 + 3	Rees 23 + 7	Doughty 6 + 2	Henry — + 3	McCoulsky — + 4	Huddart 20	Edmonds-Green 4 + 3	Williamson 14 + 3	Tanner — + 2	Dunne — + 1	Winfield 12 + 1	Coker — + 5	Chambers 2 + 1	Whitely 6 + 2	Rowe — + 2	*Match No.*
1	2	3	4	5	6^3	7	8	9	10^1	11^2	12	13	14																	1
1	2	3	5	6		7	8	10	4^2	11^3	9^1	12	13	14																2
1	2	4	6	5	13	7	8	10^1	3^3	11	9^2	12		14																3
1	2	4	5	6	12	7	8		3^3	11	9^1	14		10^2	13															4
1	2	3	4	5		6^1	7	9	10^3	11	8^2	14			13	12														5
1	2	3	4^1	5		6	7	8	10^2	11			14	12	13	9^3														6
1	2	3		5		6	7	8	12	11			9^2	10^1	4	13														7
1	2	9		3		6	8	10	5^2	7		13		12	4	11^1														8
1	2	3		6		7^2	8	9	5^1	11		12	14	13	4	10^3														9
1	2	3	14	5		6	7	8^1	10	11^2			13		4	9^3	12													10
1	2	3	12	5		6	7	8	10^2			11^1			4	13	9^3	14												11
1	2	3		6		7	8	10	5^1	11^3		14	13		4		9^2		12											12
1	2	3		6			7	9	5^2	11		13			4	10	8^1		12											13
1^1	2	3	12	6			7	11	5^2	10		13			4	8	9^3		14											14
			3	5		8	7	9^1	2	11		10^2	14	13	4		6^3		12	1										15
	2	4	3	5		7	6	8	9	11^2		13	12				10^1			1										16
	2	4	3	5		8^2	7	9	10^3	11			6^1	14		13	12			1										17
	2	4	3	5				8	10	11^1		13	7	9^2		6^3		14		1	12									18
	2	8	4	3		13		10	5	6		14	9^1	7^2		11^3				1	12									19
	4	3	5	6		8^3	7	10^2	2	11		14	9^1	12						1	13									20
	2	3	6	7		5		9	12	11				8^1		10				1	4									21
	2	4	3			12	8		6	11			13	9^2		7				1	5^3	10^1	14							22
	2	4	6			12	7		3^3	9			13	8^1		11^2				1	5	10	14							23
		4■	5	6		7	8^3		2	9^1			13			11		14		1	3	10^2		12						24
	4	2	5	6^1		7	8		3	10						9				1		11			12					25
	2		5	6^1		7	8		4	11				9^2		13				1		10			3	12				26
	2		4	5	14	6^1	7		10^3	11				8^2		12				1		9			3	13				27
	2	9		3	14	6	8	12	5	7^2						11^1				1		10^3			4	13				28
	2	9		3	12	6	8	13	5^2	7^1						11				1		10			4^3	14				29
	2	3■	5	6		7^2	8	12	4^3	11			14			9^1				1		10				13				30
	8		2	5	14	6^1			9	11^2		13				7^3				1		10			3		4	12		31
	2	3		6	12	7^1			5	9		14				11				1		10^2			4		13	8^3		32
	2	12	5■		3	7			6	8^3		14				10				1		13			4		11^1	9^2		33
1	3	4		6	8	7			2	11		13				9^1						10^2			5			12		34
1	2	3		5	7^3	6	12		10	11^2		14				9^1						13			4			8		35
1	3	4		6		7^3	8		2	11^1		14				13						10^2			5			9	12	36
1	2^2	5	3			13	7^3		10	11		14				6						9^1			4			8	12	37
	2	4	6			14	7^1		5	11		13		8^3		10				1		12			3^2			9		38
																														39
																														40
																														41
																														42
																														43
																														44
																														45
																														46

FA Cup

Fourth Qualifying	Aldershot	(h)	4-3
First Round	Bristol R	(a)	1-1
Replay	Bristol R	(h)	0-1

FA Trophy

First Round	Dorking W	(a)	0-3

CHESTERFIELD

Ground: Technique Stadium, 1866 Sheffield Road, Whittington Moor, Chesterfield, Derbyshire S41 8NZ.
Tel: (01246) 269 300. *Website:* www.chesterfield-fc.co.uk *Email:* reception@chesterfield-fc.co.uk *Year Formed:* 1866.
Record Attendance: 30,968 v Newcastle U, Division 2, 7 April 1939 (at Saltergate); 10,089 v Rotherham U, FL 2, 18 March 2011 (at b2net Stadium (now called the Technique Stadium)). *Nickname:* 'The Blues', 'The Spireites'.
Caretaker Manager: John Pemberton. *Colours:* Blue shirts with white trim, white shorts with blue trim, blue socks.

CHESTERFIELD – NATIONAL LEAGUE 2019–20 LEAGUE RECORD

Match No.	Date	Venue	Opponents	Result		H/T Score	Lg Pos.	Goalscorers	Attendance
1	Aug 3	H	Dover Ath	L	1-2	0-0	15	Boden 72	4332
2	6	A	Maidenhead U	D	1-1	0-0	19	Yarney 77	1471
3	10	A	Boreham Wood	D	2-2	2-1	21	Boden 26, Smith, J 44	715
4	13	H	Woking	L	1-2	0-0	23	Boden 86	3927
5	17	A	Barnet	D	2-2	1-1	22	Fondop-Talum 2 2, 48	1119
6	24	H	Barrow	D	2-2	1-2	21	Boden (pen) 45, Fondop-Talum 80	3812
7	26	A	Stockport Co	L	0-2	0-0	22		5587
8	31	H	Dagenham & R	D	1-1	0-1	22	Fondop-Talum 68	3708
9	Sept 3	H	FC Halifax T	L	2-3	0-2	22	Fondop-Talum 49, Rowley 89	3844
10	7	A	Bromley	L	1-2	0-1	24	Mandeville 72	2110
11	14	H	Torquay U	W	1-0	1-0	22	Boden 12	3706
12	21	A	Sutton U	L	0-4	0-2	23		1649
13	24	A	Hartlepool U	D	1-1	1-1	23	Denton 37	2953
14	28	H	Aldershot T	W	2-1	1-1	22	Boden 39, Mandeville 55	3657
15	Oct 5	H	Eastleigh	L	1-2	1-1	22	Denton 15	3632
16	8	A	AFC Fylde	W	3-1	0-0	22	Weston 55, Fondop-Talum 2 66, 81	1217
17	15	A	Wrexham	W	1-0	1-0	18	Chambers (og) 32	3479
18	26	H	Notts Co	W	1-0	1-0	18	Nepomuceno 27	5432
19	Nov 2	A	Ebbsfleet U	D	2-2	1-1	18	Boden 12, Hollis 56	1025
20	16	H	Chorley	L	2-3	0-2	18	Weston 68, Boden 82	4090
21	23	A	Harrogate T	L	1-3	1-1	20	Fondop-Talum 10	1710
22	26	H	Hartlepool U	L	1-5	1-2	21	Kioso (og) 45	3420
23	30	A	Aldershot T	D	2-2	0-1	21	Boden 50, Denton 90	1637
24	Dec 7	H	Bromley	L	1-2	1-0	23	Fondop-Talum 15	3270
25	10	H	Yeovil T	L	1-2	0-2	23	Weston 61	3161
26	21	A	Torquay U	W	3-0	1-0	22	McKay 1, Weston 54, Hollis 68	2288
27	26	H	Solihull Moors	D	2-2	2-1	22	Fondop-Talum 1, McKay 17	3203
28	28	A	FC Halifax T	L	0-1	0-0	22		2420
29	Jan 1	A	Solihull Moors	L	0-3	0-1	22		1200
30	4	H	Sutton U	W	1-0	0-0	22	Smith, J 50	3283
31	18	A	Eastleigh	W	2-0	0-0	21	Denton 54, Smith, J 80	2073
32	25	H	AFC Fylde	D	1-1	1-0	21	Smith, J 32	3262
33	Feb 1	A	Notts Co	L	0-3	0-0	21		6347
34	8	H	Wrexham	W	3-2	1-1	21	Denton 25, Mandeville 72, Weston 90	3728
35	22	H	Ebbsfleet U	W	4-0	0-0	21	Tyson 3 60, 77, 83, Weston 90	3346
36	Mar 3	H	Harrogate T	L	3-4	2-2	21	Denton 26, Mandeville 29, Boden 82	2912
37	7	A	Chorley	W	2-1	1-0	20	Denton 40, Cropper 64	1256
38	14	A	Dover Ath	D	1-1	0-0	19	Denton (pen) 80	1214
39	21	H	Maidenhead U	Cancelled					
40	24	A	Yeovil T	Cancelled					
41	28	A	Woking	Cancelled					
42	Apr 4	H	Boreham Wood	Cancelled					
43	10	H	Stockport Co	Cancelled					
44	13	A	Barrow	Cancelled					
45	18	H	Barnet	Cancelled					
46	25	A	Dagenham & R	Cancelled					

Final League Position: 20 (on points-per-game basis)

GOALSCORERS

League (55): Boden 10 (1 pen), Fondop-Talum 10, Denton 8 (1 pen), Weston 6, Mandeville 4, Smith, J 4, Tyson 3, Hollis 2, McKay 2, Cropper 1, Nepomuceno 1, Rowley 1, Yarney 1, own goals 2.
FA Cup (1): Fondop-Talum 1.
FA Trophy (0).

Jalal 29	Buchanan 24 + 1	Yarney 26 + 3	Evans 37 + 1	Rowley 18 + 5	Weston 29 + 3	Weir 9 + 10	Smith J 24 + 5	McKay 5 + 9	Mandeville 18 + 13	Boden 27 + 7	Wakefield 1 + 2	Hollis 31	Wedgbury 13	Maguire 14 + 1	Sheridan 15 + 3	Gerrard 10	McGlashan 6 + 8	Fondop-Talum 20 + 9	Coddington 9 + 1	Denton 17 + 8	Nepomuceno 15	Spyrou 1 + 4	Shaw Liam 3 + 1	Tootle 3	Sharman 2 + 1	Cropper 8	Tyson 4 + 2	Hutchinson — + 2	Fitzsimons — + 1	*Match No.*
1	2	3	4	5	6	7^1	8	9	10	11	12																			1
1	5^3	2	4	9		12	6^1	13	11	10		3	7^2	8	14															2
1	5	2	4	9^2	13	12	6		11	10		3	7^1	8■																3
1	2	3	4	6	14	7^3	9^2	12	10	11		5	8^1		13															4
1	6	2^1	3		7	12	13		11	10^3		5^2			14	4	8	9												5
1	2	13	3	14		5^1	12		4	8		9			10^2	6^3	7	11												6
1	5	2	3	8		13	7	14	12	11^2				6^3		4	9^1	10												7
		2^1	3	5		6^2	9		12	8		10		4		7	13	11	1											8
		13	2	8	12		7	14	9	10^3		4^2		3		5	6^1	11	1											9
		2	3	12	8		7	13	9	11^2				5		4	6^1	10	1											10
		2	3	6	7	12	8		9^3	10^2		5		4			14	13	1	11^1										11
		2	3	9	7	8^2	6^3	14	12	11^1		4						10	1	13	5									12
1		2	3	6	9				13	12	8^1	4	7					10^2		11	5									13
1		2	3	4	5				6	8^2	14	11	9^1					13		10^3	7	12								14
1		2	3	4^3	5				6	8^2		11	9^1				13	14		10	7	12								15
1		2	3	6^2	7		9		13			4	8		5		14	12		11^1		10^3								16
1		2	5	7	6					12		4	8		3			11^1		10	9									17
1		2	3	7	6		8			9^1		4			5			12		10^2	11	13								18
1^1	3^3		2	6		7	8			9^2		4			5		14	10	12		11	13								19
1	6^2		3	9	7	2^3	8		12	11		4		13	5			14		10^1										20
1	2		3		7^1		13		10^2	12				4	5		9	11			6		8							21
			2	5			7		12	11			8^2	3	4		14	13^3	1	10^1	9		6							22
	7^3		3		8				13	11				5	6	4	14		1	12	10		9^1	2^2						23
			4		8					10^2		6		2^1	7	5		9	1	12	11		13	3						24
	12		3		8					10^3		5		6	7	4	14	11	1	13	9^2			2^1						25
1	7		12	13	8	2^3		9^1				4		6	5	3		10^2		14	11									26
1	8	2	3	12	6		13	9^1				4		7^2	5			10			11									27
1	10	6^1	3		7		12	9	13	11		4			2			8^3		14	5^2									28
1	2^3	3^2	4	13	7	12		8^1	10	11		5			6			9		14										29
1	2		3		8	7^2	5	14	9^3	11^1		4	6					10■		13					12					30
1	6	12	4		9		8	14	13	10^1		5	7^2							11					3^3	2				31
1	6	3	4		9	14	8		12	10^3		5	7^1							11						2^2	13			32
1	6	3	4		9	14	8	13	12	10^2		5	7^3							11						2^1				33
1	6	3	4		8		7		12	13		5						10		11^2						2	9^1			34
1	6	3	4		8	13	7		9^1	14		5						10^2		11^3						2	12			35
1	6	3^2	4		8		7		9^1	14		5						12		11						2	10^3	13		36
1^1	6	3	4		8	13	7		9^2	14		5								11^3						2	10		12	37
1	6	3	4		8		7		9									12		11					5	2^2	10^1	13		38
																														39
																														40
																														41
																														42
																														43
																														44
																														45
																														46

FA Cup

Fourth Qualifying	Wrexham	(h)	1-1
Replay	Wrexham	(a)	0-1

FA Trophy

First Round	Notts Co	(h)	0-1

CHORLEY

Ground: The Chorley Group Victoria Park Stadium, Duke Street, Chorley, Lancashire PR7 3DU.
Tel: (01257) 230 007. *Website:* www.chorleyfc.com *Email:* See website. *Year Formed:* 1883.
Record Attendance: 15,153 v Preston NE, FA Cup 2nd rd, 6 December 1986 (at Ewood Park); 9,679 v Darwen, FA Cup 4th qualifying rd, 15 November 1932 (at Victoria Park). *Nickname:* 'The Magpies'. *Manager:* Jamie Vermiglio.
Colours: Black and white striped shirts, black shorts with white trim, black socks with white trim.

CHORLEY – NATIONAL LEAGUE 2019–20 LEAGUE RECORD

Match No.	*Date*	*Venue*	*Opponents*	*Result*	*H/T Score*	*Lg Pos.*	*Goalscorers*	*Attendance*
1	Aug 3	H	Bromley	D 0-0	0-0	13		1469
2	6	A	AFC Fylde	D 0-0	0-0	17		2443
3	10	A	Sutton U	D 2-2	2-1	14	Meppen-Walter [7], Holroyd [10]	1436
4	13	H	Solihull Moors	L 1-6	0-2	21	Newby, A [53]	1020
5	17	A	Maidenhead U	L 1-4	1-2	23	Carver [25]	1172
6	24	H	Hartlepool U	D 0-0	0-0	23		1395
7	26	A	Notts Co	L 1-5	1-1	24	Baines [9]	5082
8	31	H	Boreham Wood	L 1-3	0-2	24	Holroyd (pen) [77]	1035
9	Sept 3	A	Harrogate T	L 0-2	0-1	24		792
10	7	H	Stockport Co	W 3-0	2-0	22	Holroyd 2 [6, 27], Newby, E [90]	2693
11	14	A	Dover Ath	D 1-1	0-1	23	Holroyd [67]	1011
12	21	H	Woking	D 1-1	1-1	22	Holroyd [8]	1346
13	24	H	Barrow	L 1-3	1-2	24	Challoner [25]	1272
14	28	A	Dagenham & R	D 0-0	0-0	24		1212
15	Oct 5	H	Aldershot T	D 0-0	0-0	23		1425
16	8	A	FC Halifax T	D 0-0	0-0	23		2117
17	12	A	Eastleigh	D 0-0	0-0	23		2053
18	26	H	Yeovil T	L 1-2	0-1	24	Massanka [71]	1279
19	29	H	Ebbsfleet U	L 0-4	0-2	24		921
20	Nov 2	A	Barnet	L 1-2	1-0	24	Carver [31]	1040
21	16	A	Chesterfield	W 3-2	2-0	24	Vernam 2 (1 pen) [15, 74 (p)], Meppen-Walter [19]	4090
22	23	H	Torquay U	W 1-0	1-0	24	Carver [24]	1281
23	26	A	Barrow	D 2-2	2-2	23	Vernam [9], Carver [16]	2324
24	30	H	Dagenham & R	W 1-0	0-0	22	Newby, A [63]	1262
25	Dec 7	A	Stockport Co	L 2-4	1-2	24	Newby, A [7], Massanka [90]	4510
26	21	H	Dover Ath	D 1-1	0-0	23	Newby, A [72]	1054
27	26	A	Wrexham	L 1-3	0-2	24	Massanka [90]	4784
28	28	H	Harrogate T	L 0-2	0-1	24		1077
29	Jan 1	H	Wrexham	L 0-2	0-0	24		1684
30	4	A	Woking	L 0-1	0-0	24		1748
31	18	A	Aldershot T	D 3-3	2-2	24	Newby, A 2 (1 pen) [9, 90 (p)], Cardwell [25]	1931
32	25	H	FC Halifax T	L 0-1	0-0	24		1263
33	Feb 1	A	Yeovil T	D 1-1	1-0	24	Hall [45]	2729
34	15	A	Ebbsfleet U	L 0-1	0-0	24		712
35	22	H	Barnet	L 0-1	0-1	24		925
36	29	A	Torquay U	L 0-2	0-1	24		2126
37	Mar 3	H	Eastleigh	L 1-2	1-0	24	Hall [2]	495
38	7	H	Chesterfield	L 1-2	0-1	24	Hall [76]	1256
39	14	A	Bromley	Cancelled				
40	21	H	AFC Fylde	Cancelled				
41	28	A	Solihull Moors	Cancelled				
42	Apr 4	H	Sutton U	Cancelled				
43	10	H	Notts Co	Cancelled				
44	13	A	Hartlepool U	Cancelled				
45	18	H	Maidenhead U	Cancelled				
46	25	A	Boreham Wood	Cancelled				

Final League Position: 24 (on points-per-game basis)

GOALSCORERS

League (31): Holroyd 6 (1 pen), Newby, A 6 (1 pen), Carver 4, Hall 3, Massanka 3, Vernam 3 (1 pen), Meppen-Walter 2, Baines 1, Cardwell 1, Challoner 1, Newby, E 1.
FA Cup (2): Holroyd 1 (1 pen), Newby, A 1.
FA Trophy (4): Holroyd 2 (1 pen), Carver 1, O'Keefe 1.

Anyon 4	Challoner 33 + 1	Teague 21	Leather 10	Blakeman 26 + 5	Newby A 31 + 6	O'Keefe 16 + 12	Baines 28 + 5	Newby E 16 + 12	Holroyd 16 + 11	Carver 27 + 4	Massanka 10 + 14	Meppen-Walter 35	Ross 21 + 5	Dodds 4 + 13	Cottrell 23 + 6	Crellin 9	Nortey 19 + 5	Urwin 25	Almond — + 3	Smith 17	Vernam 4	Cardwell 1	Duxbury 8	Kay 4	Adams — + 1	Hall 6	Kiwomya 4 + 1	Match No.
1	2	3	4	5	6	7	8	9	10^{1}	11	12																	1
1	2	4		3	6^{3}	7	10	9	11^{2}	8	13	5^{1}	12	14														2
1	2	5		3	9^{2}	7	4	8^{3}	11^{1}	10	12	6		13	14													3
1	2	4		3	10	7	6^{3}		13	9	11^{2}	5	12	14	8^{1}													4
	2	4	5^{1}	3^{3}	7	8	13	10	14	9	12	6			11^{2}	1												5
	2	4	5	3	9	7^{3}	12	14	13	10	11^{2}	6^{1}			8	1												6
	12	3^{3}	4	2	5^{2}	6■	11	8	13	7^{1}	14		9		10	1												7
	2	4	5	3	6		10	8^{2}	12	7	11^{1}			13	9	1												8
	2		4	3^{3}	9^{1}	7	6	12	10^{2}	14	11	5		13	8	1												9
	2	3^{2}	4		6^{3}	7	10	14	11^{1}	8		5	12	13	9	1												10
	2	3	4	12	6^{1}	7	10^{2}	14	11^{3}	8	13	5			9	1												11
	2	3	4^{3}	12	9	7^{2}	6	14	11^{1}	10		5		13	8	1												12
	2	3	4^{1}	12	10	7^{2}	5^{3}	14	9	11		6			8	1	13											13
	2	4^{3}		3	14		9	6		13	11^{2}	5	12	8^{1}	7		10	1										14
	2	4^{1}		3^{3}	13		8	6^{2}	11	14	10	5	12		7		9	1										15
	2			3	12	13	9		14	5^{2}	11^{3}	4	6	8^{1}	7		10	1										16
	2			3	13	14	6		11^{1}	9^{3}	12	4	5	10^{2}	8		7	1										17
	2			3^{1}	5		8	13	11		10	4	6		7		9^{2}	1	12									18
	2	4^{2}		3^{3}		14	12		11^{1}		10	5	6	8	7		9	1	13									19
	2				12	13	9	5^{1}		4^{3}	11	3	6		7^{2}		10	1	14	8								20
	5			6^{3}	9^{2}	13	3			10		7	4	14	12		2	1		8	11^{1}							21
	5			6	9^{2}	12	2			10^{1}	13	7	4		14		3	1		8	11^{3}							22
	2			3	9^{1}	13	6			10^{3}	12	4	5		14		7	1		8^{2}	11							23
		3		2	9^{1}	13	6		14	10		4	7		12		5^{2}	1		8	11^{3}							24
	2	4^{1}		3^{2}	6		12	13	11^{3}	7	14	5	8				10	1		9								25
	2			3	5	12	9		11^{1}	6^{3}	14	4	7	13			10^{2}	1		8								26
	2			3	10	7^{2}	5^{3}	12	11	9^{1}	14	4	6				13	1		8								27
	2	3		5^{3}	9		6	12	11^{2}	10	13	4		14			7^{1}	1		8								28
	2	4^{1}		3	10			7	12	11	13	5	6		8^{2}			1		9								29
	4			5^{2}	10	14	3^{3}	7	13	11		6	2		8^{1}		12	1		9								30
	2	3^{2}			5			14	13	6		4			8		9	1				7^{1}	10	11	12^{3}			31
	2	3			11	12		8	13			4^{1}			9		5	1					6	7		10^{2}		32
	5				11	7^{1}	12					6	4		8			1		9			2	3		10■		33
	2				4	5^{3}		13		6		3	7		8^{2}		14	1		9			10	11^{1}			12	34
	2				9^{3}	7		8		12		4	3		13		14	1		6^{2}			5			10	11^{1}	35
				2^{1}	12	14	5	9				3	4	13			6	1		8			7			10^{2}	11^{3}	36
				12	3		8	5				2	6	13			9	1		7			10			11^{2}	4^{1}	37
				12	3^{2}		8	5				2^{1}	6	13			9	1		7			10			11	4	38
																												39
																												40
																												41
																												42
																												43
																												44
																												45
																												46

FA Cup

Fourth Qualifying	Spennymoor T	(h)	2-0
First Round	Mansfield T	(a)	0-1

FA Trophy

First Round	Matlock T	(a)	2-2
Replay	Matlock T	(h)	2-2

(aet; Matlock T won 4-3 on penalties)

DAGENHAM & REDBRIDGE

Ground: Chigwell Construction Stadium, Victoria Road, Dagenham, Essex RM10 7XL.
Tel: (020) 8592 1549. *Website:* www.daggers.co.uk *Email:* info@daggers.co.uk *Year Formed:* 1992.
Record Attendance: 5,949 v Ipswich T, FA Cup 3rd rd, 5 January 2002. *Nickname:* 'The Daggers'.
Manager: Daryl McMahon. *Colours:* White shirts, red shorts, blue socks.

DAGENHAM & REDBRIDGE – NATIONAL LEAGUE 2019–20 LEAGUE RECORD

Match No.	Date		Venue	Opponents	Result		H/T Score	Lg Pos.	Goalscorers	Attendance
1	Aug	3	H	Woking	L	0-2	0-1	23		1549
2		6	A	Dover Ath	W	2-1	1-1	15	Balanta 26, Brundle (pen) 54	1520
3		10	A	FC Halifax T	L	0-1	0-1	17		1895
4		13	H	Boreham Wood	L	0-3	0-1	22		1179
5		17	H	Harrogate T	W	4-2	2-2	15	Balanta 2 60, 85, Kandi 14, Brundle 29	1043
6		24	A	Eastleigh	D	1-1	1-0	16	Luque 15	1631
7		26	H	Yeovil T	W	3-2	0-0	11	Quigley 2 64, 90, Onariase 81	1453
8		31	A	Chesterfield	D	1-1	1-0	11	Luque 35	3708
9	Sept	4	H	Bromley	D	1-1	1-0	12	Balanta 2	1526
10		7	A	Maidenhead U	W	1-0	0-0	10	Dobson (pen) 47	1551
11		14	H	Hartlepool U	W	3-1	1-0	5	Quigley 2 24, 82, Balanta 69	1392
12		21	A	Torquay U	D	0-0	0-0	7		2524
13		24	A	Sutton U	W	2-0	2-0	6	Grant 43, Dobson 45	1513
14		28	H	Chorley	D	0-0	0-0	5		1212
15	Oct	5	H	Barnet	D	1-1	1-1	7	Balanta 40	1556
16		8	A	Notts Co	L	0-2	0-1	10		3670
17		26	H	Wrexham	W	2-1	1-0	10	Balanta 45, Kandi 57	1254
18		29	H	Barrow	L	0-2	0-2	10		1122
19	Nov	2	A	Solihull Moors	L	1-2	1-1	14	Grant 20	1214
20		9	A	Stockport Co	L	0-1	0-0	15		3771
21		16	H	Aldershot T	W	6-1	4-0	12	House 2 6, 15, Onariase 17, Luque 25, Wright, W 69, Quigley 76	1616
22		23	A	AFC Fylde	L	0-3	0-3	13		1268
23		26	H	Sutton U	L	1-2	0-0	16	Brundle 52	1070
24		30	A	Chorley	L	0-1	0-0	16		1262
25	Dec	7	H	Maidenhead U	L	1-2	0-1	17	McQueen 64	1083
26		21	A	Hartlepool U	L	0-1	0-0	18		3259
27		26	H	Ebbsfleet U	D	1-1	0-0	17	Kandi 86	1402
28		28	A	Bromley	L	0-3	0-1	18		2312
29	Jan	1	A	Ebbsfleet U	D	1-1	0-1	20	Wright, W 85	1015
30		4	H	Torquay U	D	0-0	0-0	19		1542
31		25	H	Notts Co	W	2-0	0-0	20	Reid 2 61, 80	1697
32	Feb	1	A	Wrexham	D	0-0	0-0	20		4024
33		8	H	Stockport Co	D	1-1	0-0	20	Kandi 90	1512
34		22	H	Solihull Moors	W	2-0	2-0	19	Brundle 10, Balanta 43	2345
35		29	A	Barrow	L	1-2	1-2	19	Reid 10	2353
36	Mar	7	A	Aldershot T	W	1-0	0-0	18	Brundle 86	2103
37		10	H	AFC Fylde	L	1-2	0-0	18	Brundle 80	1064
38		14	A	Woking	Cancelled					
39		21	H	Dover Ath	Cancelled					
40		28	A	Boreham Wood	Cancelled					
41	Apr	4	H	FC Halifax T	Cancelled					
42		7	A	Barnet	Cancelled					
43		10	A	Yeovil T	Cancelled					
44		13	H	Eastleigh	Cancelled					
45		18	A	Harrogate T	Cancelled					
46		25	H	Chesterfield	Cancelled					

Final League Position: 17 (on points-per-game basis)

GOALSCORERS

League (40): Balanta 8, Brundle 6 (1 pen), Quigley 5, Kandi 4, Luque 3, Reid 3, Dobson 2 (1 pen), Grant 2, House 2, Onariase 2, Wright, W 2, McQueen 1.
FA Cup (1): Grant 1.
FA Trophy (5): Brundle 2, Luque 2, Quigley 1.

Justham 37	Eleftheriou 18 + 1	Onariase 27 + 1	Clark 33	Croll 29 + 1	Brundle 27	Odametey 3 + 3	McQueen 18 + 5	Balanta 21 + 1	Graham 10 + 11	Quigley 21 + 9	Luque 23 + 5	Dobson 12 + 10	Grant 6 + 20	Robinson 32 + 1	Wright W 21 + 6	Phipps 6 + 3	Kandi 15 + 8	Wood 3 + 1	Gordon 12 + 2	Stevenson 10	Deering 8 + 1	House 8 + 1	Wright D — + 2	Zakuani 1	Reid 5 + 1	Weston 1 + 3	Match No.
1	2	3	4	5	6	7^{2}	8^{1}	9	10^{3}	11	12	13	14														1
1	2		3	4	6			9^{1}	5	11	10^{3}	8^{2}	13	7	12	14											2
1	2^{3}		3	4	6		14	9	5	11	10^{2}	8^{1}	13	7	12												3
1	2		3	4	6			9	5	11^{2}	10^{1}	8^{3}	14	7	12		13										4
1			4	5	7		2	11^{3}		14	9^{2}		12		3	8	10	6^{1}	13								5
1			3	4	6		8	9^{1}	13	12	10^{2}		11	14	2	7			5^{3}								6
1	2^{1}	3	4	5	7		9	10	6^{2}	11	12	13		8													7
1		2	3	4	6		5	10^{3}		11^{2}	9	14	13		12	7			8^{1}								8
1		3	4	5	6			10	12	11	9^{1}	8^{2}		7	2	13											9
1		4	3	5				9		11^{1}	10	8	12	6	2	7											10
1		3	4	5			12	10^{2}	13	11	9^{3}	8^{1}	14	7	2	6											11
1		3	4	5		13		10	12	11^{2}	9^{1}	8	14	7	2	6^{3}											12
1		3	4	5		12	6	10^{3}	9^{2}	13	14	8	11^{1}	7	2												13
1		3	5^{1}	4▮		14	6	7		9	10^{3}	11^{2}	13	8	2				12								14
1	13	3				6	2	9	10^{1}	11		8^{2}	12	7	4				5								15
1		3		4		6	8^{2}	9	10^{1}	11^{3}	13	14	12	7	2				5								16
1		3		4	6		13	9^{3}	12	14	10	8		7	2		11^{1}	5^{2}									17
1		3		4	6				10	12	9	8^{2}	13	7	2		11	5^{1}									18
1		3	4		6		8^{1}		9	12	13	14	10^{3}	7	2		11^{2}			5							19
1	2	3	4		6		8		13	11	9^{2}	14	10^{1}	7			12			5^{3}							20
1	2	3^{2}	4		6					13	10		14	7	12		9			5	8^{1}	11^{3}					21
1	2		4		6^{3}				12	11	9^{1}	13	10	7	3		8^{2}	14		5							22
1	2^{2}		4		6		7			11	9	13	12	8	3		10^{1}			5							23
1	2		4		6		9^{2}			11^{1}	10	13	12	7	3		8			5							24
1			3	4	6		8^{2}			11^{1}	10	13	12	7	2		9			5							25
1	2^{1}	3	4	7^{3}	6		8		12	11	10^{2}		13				9			5			14				26
1		3	4	5	6▮		13		12	11^{2}	8^{1}			7	2		9					10					27
1	2^{2}	3	4	5			9		12	13			11	7	8		10			6^{1}							28
1		3	4^{1}	6			7			13	9^{3}		12	8	2		10			5^{2}		11	14				29
1		3	6	7			2^{2}			11^{1}	9		12	8	4		10		5		13						30
1	5	12	6	3	7		14		13					8			10		2^{3}		9^{2}			4^{1}	11		31
1	2	3	4	5	8									7			12		6		9	10^{1}			11		32
1	2	3	4	5	8			12						7			14		6^{1}		9	10			11^{2}	13^{3}	33
1	2	3	4	5	8			10^{1}						7		13	12		6		9	11^{2}					34
1	2^{2}	3	4	12	7			9						6^{1}			14		5		8	10			11^{3}	13	35
1	3^{3}	4	5	6	2			10						8^{2}			13		7		9	12			11^{1}	14	36
1		3	4	5	8			10						7^{2}	14		12		6		9	11^{3}			13	2^{1}	37
																											38
																											39
																											40
																											41
																											42
																											43
																											44
																											45
																											46

FA Cup

Fourth Qualifying	Carshalton Ath	(a)	1-2

FA Trophy

First Round	Sutton U	(a)	1-1
Replay	Sutton U	(h)	3-2
aet.			
Second Round	Notts Co	(a)	1-2

DOVER ATHLETIC

Ground: Crabble Athletic Ground, Lewisham Road, Dover, Kent CT17 0JB. *Tel:* (01304) 822 373.
Website: doverathletic.com *Email:* enquiries@doverathletic.com *Year Formed:* 1894 as Dover FC, reformed as Dover Ath 1983. *Record Attendance:* 7,000 v Folkestone, 13 October 1951 (Dover FC); 5,645 v Crystal Palace, FA Cup 3rd rd, 4 January 2015 (Dover Ath). *Nickname:* 'The Whites'. *Manager:* Andy Hessenthaler.
Colours: White shirts with black trim, black shorts with white trim, black socks.

DOVER ATHLETIC – NATIONAL LEAGUE 2019–20 LEAGUE RECORD

Match No.	Date	Venue	Opponents	Result	H/T Score	Lg Pos.	Goalscorers	Attendance
1	Aug 3	A	Chesterfield	W 2-1	0-0	4	Pavey 2 [77, 85]	4332
2	6	H	Dagenham & R	L 1-2	1-1	11	Pavey [37]	1520
3	10	H	Wrexham	W 2-1	0-1	6	Modeste [72], Pearson (og) [90]	1187
4	13	A	Barnet	W 1-0	0-0	4	Effiong [90]	1143
5	17	H	Torquay U	L 1-2	0-0	7	Effiong (pen) [88]	1217
6	24	A	Sutton U	W 2-1	1-1	6	Modeste [10], Effiong [50]	1552
7	26	H	Woking	L 1-2	1-1	6	Modeste [31]	1358
8	31	A	Harrogate T	W 2-0	0-0	5	Effiong 2 [68, 89]	900
9	Sept 3	H	Ebbsfleet U	D 1-1	0-1	6	De Havilland [53]	1247
10	7	A	Boreham Wood	L 1-3	1-2	7	Effiong [21]	493
11	14	H	Chorley	D 1-1	1-0	7	Modeste [20]	1011
12	21	A	Hartlepool U	W 2-0	1-0	5	Effiong (pen) [37], Rigg [84]	3329
13	24	A	Maidenhead U	W 2-1	1-0	5	Cumberbatch [18], L'Ghoul [76]	1015
14	28	H	FC Halifax T	L 0-2	0-1	6		1020
15	Oct 5	H	Notts Co	D 2-2	1-1	8	Taylor [35], Lokko [57]	1463
16	8	A	Aldershot T	L 0-4	0-2	11		1255
17	26	H	Stockport Co	L 0-1	0-1	16		1154
18	29	H	Eastleigh	W 3-1	2-0	11	Gobern [17], Effiong 2 (1 pen) [30, 72 (p)]	726
19	Nov 2	A	AFC Fylde	D 0-0	0-0	12		1185
20	16	A	Yeovil T	W 1-0	0-0	10	Doe [62]	2986
21	23	H	Solihull Moors	D 1-1	1-1	9	Effiong [6]	1027
22	26	H	Maidenhead U	L 3-4	2-3	12	Sotiriou 2 [5, 14], Rooney [66]	687
23	Dec 7	H	Boreham Wood	L 0-2	0-1	15		728
24	21	A	Chorley	D 1-1	0-0	15	Lokko [90]	1054
25	26	H	Bromley	W 3-0	2-0	12	Modeste [25], De Havilland [29], Effiong [75]	1210
26	28	A	Ebbsfleet U	W 1-0	1-0	11	Woods [14]	1222
27	Jan 1	A	Bromley	L 0-3	0-1	13		2011
28	11	H	Hartlepool U	D 1-1	0-1	13	L'Ghoul [90]	1023
29	18	A	Notts Co	D 0-0	0-0	12		5157
30	25	H	Aldershot T	W 2-0	1-0	12	Lokko [15], Ogie [51]	1113
31	28	A	FC Halifax T	L 2-4	1-2	12	Binnom-Williams (og) [21], Woods [50]	1726
32	Feb 1	A	Stockport Co	W 2-0	0-0	9	Effiong 2 [49, 80]	4506
33	4	H	Barrow	W 2-1	1-0	8	De Havilland [18], Woods [88]	972
34	18	A	Barrow	L 0-1	0-0	9		2016
35	22	H	AFC Fylde	W 5-1	2-1	6	Poleon [36], Effiong 3 (1 pen) [45 (p), 74, 78], Taylor [89]	1027
36	29	A	Solihull Moors	L 0-3	0-1	8		773
37	Mar 7	H	Yeovil T	L 0-1	0-0	11		1180
38	14	H	Chesterfield	D 1-1	0-0	12	L'Ghoul [89]	1214
39	17	A	Eastleigh	Cancelled				
40	21	A	Dagenham & R	Cancelled				
41	28	H	Barnet	Cancelled				
42	Apr 4	A	Wrexham	Cancelled				
43	10	A	Woking	Cancelled				
44	13	H	Sutton U	Cancelled				
45	18	A	Torquay U	Cancelled				
46	25	H	Harrogate T	Cancelled				

Final League Position: 11 (on points-per-game basis)

GOALSCORERS

League (49): Effiong 16 (4 pens), Modeste 5, De Havilland 3, L'Ghoul 3, Lokko 3, Pavey 3, Woods 3, Sotiriou 2, Taylor 2, Cumberbatch 1, Doe 1, Gobern 1, Ogie 1, Poleon 1, Rigg 1, Rooney 1, own goals 2.
FA Cup (3): Jeffrey 1, Reason 1, Sotiriou 1.
FA Trophy (2): Lokko 1, Reason 1.

Worgan 24	Passley 29	Doe 14 + 1	Lokko 27	Taylor 24 + 5	Woods 33	Gobern 22 + 2	Munns 27 + 2	Modeste 20 + 8	Rigg 22 + 8	Effiong 34 + 2	Pavey 6 + 4	Reason 26 + 4	L'Ghoul 11 + 18	De Havilland 29	Simpson 19 + 1	Cumberbatch 10 + 5	Hinchiri 3 + 2	Rooney 10 + 8	Jeffrey 3 + 11	Mersin 10	Ratti — + 3	Sotiriou 1 + 1	Yusuff — + 11	Ogie 7 + 1	Maynard-Brewer 4	Poleon 3 + 3	*Match No.*
1	2	3	4	5	6	7	8^{3}	9^{1}	10	11^{2}	12	13	14														1
1	2	3	4	5	6	8	7^{1}	13	14	10^{3}	11	9^{2}	12														2
1	2		4		7	8^{2}	6^{3}	13	9^{1}	10	11		12	3	5	14											3
1	2		4	3	6			7^{2}	10	13	8^{1}		12	5		9	11										4
1			4	5^{1}		6	7	12		10	11	8^{3}	13	3	2	14	9^{2}										5
1	2		3		7	13		10	9^{2}	11	14	6^{1}	12	5	4	8^{3}											6
1	2		4		8	5	9	11^{1}	13	12	10^{3}	14	6^{2}	3		7[illegible]											7
1	2		3		6	5	8		10	11		9	7	4													8
1	2		4		6	5	7		11	10	12	8	9^{1}	3													9
1	2	13	3		7^{1}	5^{2}	8			11	10	9	12	4			6^{3}	14									10
1	2	3			7	6	8^{1}	10	14	11^{3}	13	9	12	4	5^{2}												11
1	2^{1}	4		12	6			11	9^{2}	10		8		3	5	7		13									12
1		3		5	7			11^{1}	10	9		8^{2}	12	4	2	6	13										13
1		3		5^{2}	7			11^{3}	10	9		8	12	4	2	6^{1}		14	13								14
1	2	4	5	6			7	12	11^{3}	10		8	9^{1}	3^{2}		13			14								15
1	2	4	5	3	7		12			8		6^{3}	13		11^{1}	9^{2}	14		10								16
	5		3^{2}	9			7^{1}	11^{3}	13	10		8		2		6		4	12	1	14						17
	2^{3}	3		12	7	6^{1}	8		11^{2}	10		9			5	14		4	13	1							18
	2	3			6	7	8^{1}		10	11		9			5			4	12	1							19
		3		5	6	7	8^{2}		11	10			9^{1}		2			4	12	1	13						20
		3		5	7	8	6^{3}	14	10^{1}	11		9^{2}	13		2			4		1		12					21
		3		5	7	8^{2}	6^{3}	12		11^{1}		9	14		2			4	13	1		10					22
1	5	3	4	9	7			10	11^{1}			8^{2}	13			6^{3}		2	12		14						23
1	2		4	14	7			10^{2}		11		8^{3}	12	3	5			6	9^{1}				13				24
1	2		3	5	6	7^{2}	10^{3}	9	14	11			8^{1}	4				12	13								25
	2		4	5	6		7^{1}	11^{2}	14	10		8	9^{3}	3					13	1			12				26
	2		4	3	7	14	10^{1}	11		8		6^{2}	9^{3}	5					12	1			13				27
1	2		3	5	6	7	10^{3}	9^{1}	12	11			13	4					8^{2}				14				28
1	2		3	6^{3}	7	8		10^{2}	9	11^{1}		13		4				14					12	5			29
	2		3	6^{3}	7	8	14		10	11^{1}		9^{2}	12	4						1			13	5			30
	2		4	8^{2}	7	6			10^{1}	11		9		3				12		1			13	5			31
	2		4	12	8	7^{1}	6^{2}		11	10		9^{3}		3	5	14									1	13	32
	2^{1}		4	6	7		9	12	10^{2}	11		8^{3}		3	5									14	1	13	33
			5^{2}	6	8		10	13	11^{3}	9		7^{1}		3	2			12						4	1	14	34
				13	3		6	7^{2}	14	4			5^{3}	2	11			8					12	9	1	10^{1}	35
1				8^{1}	6		7	9		11			10	3	2			4					12	5			36
1	2		4	3		10	8	9^{2}		6		13	7^{3}	5	12								14			11^{1}	37
1	2		4^{3}			8	7	9^{2}	10				13	3		6^{1}		12					14	5		11	38
																											39
																											40
																											41
																											42
																											43
																											44
																											45
																											46

FA Cup

Fourth Qualifying	Weymouth	(a)	2-1
First Round	Southend U	(h)	1-0
Second Round	Peterborough U	(a)	0-3

FA Trophy

First Round	King's Lynn T	(a)	2-2

(aet; King's Lynn T won 4-2 on penalties)

EASTLEIGH

Ground: The Silverlake Stadium, Ten Acres, Stoneham Lane, Eastleigh, Hampshire SO50 9HT. *Tel:* (02380) 613 361.
Website: eastleighfc.com *Email:* admin@eastleighfc.com *Year Formed:* 1946.
Record Attendance: 5,250 v Bolton W, FA Cup 3rd rd, 9 January 2016. *Nickname:* 'Spitfires'.
Manager: Ben Strevens. *Colours:* Blue shirts with white trim, blue shorts with white trim, blue socks with white trim.

EASTLEIGH – NATIONAL LEAGUE 2019–20 LEAGUE RECORD

Match No.	Date	Venue	Opponents	Result		H/T Score	Lg Pos.	Goalscorers	Attendance
1	Aug 3	H	Notts Co	W	1-0	1-0	8	Johnson 13	2668
2	6	A	Yeovil T	L	0-1	0-1	13		2813
3	10	A	Barrow	L	0-2	0-0	18		1060
4	13	H	Sutton U	D	1-1	1-1	16	Atkinson 12	1750
5	17	A	Stockport Co	L	0-2	0-0	21		3869
6	24	H	Dagenham & R	D	1-1	0-1	20	Barnett 47	1631
7	26	A	Solihull Moors	W	2-1	1-0	17	Hollands 2 18, 50	1779
8	31	H	Barnet	L	1-2	0-1	20	McKnight 69	1922
9	Sept 3	H	Boreham Wood	W	2-0	1-0	14	Williamson 6, Hollands 54	1641
10	7	A	Ebbsfleet U	D	1-1	0-1	13	Barnett 62	865
11	14	H	Bromley	D	1-1	0-0	15	Miley 85	1752
12	21	A	AFC Fylde	L	1-3	0-1	20	Hollands 48	1134
13	24	A	Torquay U	W	3-2	0-1	16	Hollands 51, Barnes 78, Bearwish 90	2005
14	28	H	Hartlepool U	D	1-1	0-1	15	Hollands 71	1838
15	Oct 5	A	Chesterfield	W	2-1	1-1	14	Barnett 45, Barnes 55	3632
16	8	H	Maidenhead U	W	2-1	1-1	13	Hollands 26, Barnett 64	1548
17	12	H	Chorley	D	0-0	0-0	13		2053
18	26	A	Woking	D	1-1	0-0	13	Rendell 90	1910
19	29	A	Dover Ath	L	1-3	0-2	16	Barnett 61	726
20	Nov 2	H	Harrogate T	W	4-2	2-1	11	Rendell 3 (1 pen) 37 (p), 41, 70, Bearwish 57	1592
21	23	A	FC Halifax T	D	1-1	0-1	15	Johnson 55	1817
22	26	H	Torquay U	W	3-2	3-0	11	Rendell (pen) 25, Hollands 28, Andrews (og) 35	1888
23	Dec 3	H	Wrexham	L	0-2	0-2	14		1542
24	7	H	Ebbsfleet U	D	1-1	1-1	13	Rendell 39	1715
25	21	A	Bromley	W	3-2	2-1	12	Winfield (og) 32, Barnett 45, Boyce 52	1651
26	28	A	Boreham Wood	D	2-2	1-1	13	Hollands 45, Barnett 90	601
27	Jan 1	A	Aldershot T	L	1-3	0-1	14	Barnett 67	1953
28	7	A	Hartlepool U	L	1-2	0-0	16	Smart 52	2478
29	18	H	Chesterfield	L	0-2	0-0	17		2073
30	25	A	Maidenhead U	L	0-2	0-2	19		1176
31	28	H	Aldershot T	D	0-0	0-0	18		2130
32	Feb 1	H	Woking	W	2-0	2-0	16	Payne 11, Barnett 19	1885
33	11	H	AFC Fylde	D	2-2	0-2	16	Hollands 52, Alabi (pen) 76	1509
34	22	A	Harrogate T	L	0-3	0-2	18		1249
35	Mar 3	A	Chorley	W	2-1	0-1	17	Barnett 2 60, 90	495
36	7	A	Wrexham	D	0-0	0-0	16		3436
37	14	A	Notts Co	L	0-4	0-1	16		4942
38	17	H	Dover Ath	Cancelled					
39	21	H	Yeovil T	Cancelled					
40	28	A	Sutton U	Cancelled					
41	31	H	FC Halifax T	Cancelled					
42	Apr 4	H	Barrow	Cancelled					
43	10	H	Solihull Moors	Cancelled					
44	13	A	Dagenham & R	Cancelled					
45	18	H	Stockport Co	Cancelled					
46	25	A	Barnet	Cancelled					

Final League Position: 16 (on points-per-game basis)

GOALSCORERS

League (43): Barnett 11, Hollands 10, Rendell 6 (2 pens), Barnes 2, Bearwish 2, Johnson 2, Alabi 1 (1 pen), Atkinson 1, Boyce 1, McKnight 1, Miley 1, Payne 1, Smart 1, Williamson 1, own goals 2.
FA Cup (11): Rendell 4 (3 pens), Barnes 2, Barnett 1, Bearwish 1, Johnson 1, Smart 1, Williamson 1.
FA Trophy (8): Barnes 1, Beale 1, Bearwish 1, McKnight 1, Miley 1, Rendell 1, Seaman 1, Smart 1.

Stryjek 37	Partington 35	Johnson 10	Wynter 10 + 1	Boyce 34	Green 23 + 2	Hollands 37	Miley 33 + 2	Payne 37	Barnett 28 + 6	Williamson 14 + 6	Rendell 15 + 19	McKnight 10 + 7	Smart 18 + 11	Atkinson 23 + 1	Bearwish 4 + 15	Baughan — + 1	Seaman 13 + 5	Barnes 8 + 6	Godwin-Malife 4	Alabi 4 + 3	Scrimshaw 3 + 6	Baldwin 4	Grubb 3	Match No.
1	2	3	4	5	6	7	8	9	10^2	11^1	12	13												1
1	2	3	4	5^2	6	7^3	8	9	10^1	11	12	13	14											2
1	3	5^1	2	6	4	9^2	8	7^3		10	11	12	14	13										3
1	2		8	5	3	11	9^3	6	13	10	7^1	14	12	4^2										4
1	2		8	4	3	11	9	6	12	10^2	7^3	5^1	13		14									5
1	2			4	5	7	8^2	6	10	11^3	13	12	9^1	3		14								6
1	2	3		5		7	6	8	10^2	11^1	12	9	13	4										7
1	2	3		4	5	7		8	10^2	11^1	12	6	9■		13									8
1	5	3		4	6	7		8	10^1	11^2	13	9					2	12						9
1	3	4		5	6	7	13	8	10	11^1	14	9^2					2^3	12						10
1	5			4	6	7	14	8	10^3	11	12	9^2		3			2^1	13						11
1	2			5	6	7	3	8		11	13	9^2		4			12	10^1						12
1	2			4	5	7	8^3	6		10^2		12	9	3	13		14	11^1						13
1	3				5	7	9	8	12	11^1	14		2	4	13		6^3	10^2						14
1	5			4	6	7	8	9	10^1	12	13		2^3	3			14	11^2						15
1	5			4	6	7	8	9	10^1	12	13		2	3				11^2						16
1	2			5	3	9	8^1	6	10	12	14		7^2	4			13	11^3						17
1	5			4		7	6	8	11	13	9	12		3^1	10^2		2							18
1	3^2			4		7	5	8	10	12	11	6^1	9		13		2							19
1				4		7	6	8	10^1	12	11		2	3	9		5							20
1	6	4		3		7	9	8	12		10		2^1	5			13	11^2						21
1	2	4^2				9	8	6	13		10		7	3	12		5	11^1						22
1				3	13	8	7^2	5	10		9		6	2	11^1		4	12						23
1	3■			6	4^1	7	9^2	8	11^3		10		13	5	14		2	12						24
1	2	4^1		5		9	8	7	11^2		10		12	3	13		6							25
1	3			5		8	6^1	7	10		11	9^2		4	13		2	12						26
1	2		13	4^2		9	8	6	11		10		7^1	3	12		5							27
1	3		2			11	10	5	7		6	4	8		9									28
1	2		5	4	6^3	8	9^2	7	11^1		14		12						3	10	13			29
1	6		5	4		8^3	9	7	11^2		14		13	3					2^1	10	12			30
1	2		4	3		7	6	8	12		9^2		13	5	14					11^3	10^1			31
1	2		5	4	12	8	6	7	10^1		14			3^2					9	13	11^3			32
1	2			4	3	9	8	5	6				7		12				11^2	13	10^1			33
1	2			4	3^1	8	9	7^3	11				12	6	14					10^2	13	5		34
1	2			4	5	7	8	6	10		14		9^2							13	12	3^3	11^1	35
1	2			5	3	9	8	6	11^2		13		7^3		14						12	4	10^1	36
1	2			4	5	7^3	8	6	10^2		13		9^1		14						12	3	11	37
																								38
																								39
																								40
																								41
																								42
																								43
																								44
																								45
																								46

FA Cup

Fourth Qualifying	Welling U	(a)	0-0
Replay	Welling U	(h)	4-2
First Round	Stourbridge	(a)	2-2
Replay	Stourbridge	(h)	3-0
Second Round	Crewe Alex	(h)	1-1
Replay	Crewe Alex	(a)	1-3

FA Trophy

First Round	Yate T	(h)	6-1
Second Round	Matlock T	(h)	2-1
Third Round	Harrogate T	(a)	0-2

EBBSFLEET UNITED

Ground: The Kuflink Stadium, Stonebridge Road, Northfleet, Kent DA11 9GN.
Tel: (01474) 533 796. *Website:* ebbsfleetunited.co.uk *Email:* info@eufc.co.uk *Year Formed:* 1946 (as Gravesend and Northfleet), 2007 (renamed Ebbsfleet United).
Record Attendance: 12,032 v Sunderland, FA Cup 4th rd, 12 February 1963. *Nickname:* 'The Fleet'.
Manager: Dennis Kutrieb. *Colours:* Red shirts with white trim, red shorts with white trim, red socks with white trim.

EBBSFLEET UNITED – NATIONAL LEAGUE 2019–20 LEAGUE RECORD

Match No.	Date	Venue	Opponents	Result	H/T Score	Lg Pos.	Goalscorers	Attendance
1	Aug 3	H	FC Halifax T	L 1-4	1-1	24	Goddard [39]	1091
2	6	A	Bromley	L 1-3	0-2	24	Thomas [89]	1719
3	10	A	AFC Fylde	L 0-1	0-1	24		1136
4	13	H	Yeovil T	L 1-3	0-1	24	Thomas [78]	1057
5	17	A	Solihull Moors	L 1-2	1-1	24	Weston [9]	955
6	24	H	Notts Co	D 2-2	1-1	24	Umerah [45], O'Brien, J (og) [61]	1293
7	26	A	Boreham Wood	W 2-1	2-0	23	Ball [13], Ugwu [16]	533
8	31	H	Aldershot T	L 1-2	0-1	23	Ugwu [82]	1109
9	Sept 3	A	Dover Ath	D 1-1	1-0	23	Obileye [13]	1247
10	7	H	Eastleigh	D 1-1	1-0	23	Reid [37]	865
11	14	A	Woking	D 2-2	0-1	24	Reid [84], Weston [90]	1942
12	21	H	Barrow	L 0-3	0-1	24		878
13	24	H	Barnet	W 3-0	2-0	22	Weston [33], Reid [36], Obileye [71]	805
14	28	A	Wrexham	L 0-1	0-0	23		3627
15	Oct 5	A	Harrogate T	L 0-2	0-1	24		742
16	8	H	Torquay U	L 2-4	1-2	24	Umerah 2 [35, 81]	908
17	12	H	Maidenhead U	L 1-2	1-1	24	Umerah [19]	1003
18	26	A	Sutton U	W 3-2	1-1	23	Butler (og) [10], Josh Payne [61], Ugwu (pen) [90]	1566
19	29	A	Chorley	W 4-0	2-0	23	Ekpiteta [5], Ugwu 2 [43, 60], Morgan [86]	921
20	Nov 2	H	Chesterfield	D 2-2	1-1	22	Ugwu 2 (1 pen) [17, 51 (p)]	1025
21	16	H	Hartlepool U	D 2-2	0-2	23	Weston 2 [72, 81]	1086
22	23	A	Stockport Co	D 1-1	1-0	23	Adeloye [34]	4167
23	26	A	Barnet	L 2-5	1-2	24	Obileye [37], Ugwu [56]	776
24	30	H	Wrexham	W 2-1	1-1	23	Jennings (og) [10], Weston [74]	1036
25	Dec 7	A	Eastleigh	D 1-1	1-1	22	Weston [5]	1715
26	26	A	Dagenham & R	D 1-1	0-0	23	Reid [62]	1402
27	28	H	Dover Ath	L 0-1	0-1	23		1222
28	Jan 1	H	Dagenham & R	D 1-1	1-0	23	Reid [6]	1015
29	4	A	Barrow	L 0-7	0-3	23		2303
30	18	H	Harrogate T	L 0-2	0-1	23		822
31	25	A	Torquay U	D 0-0	0-0	23		2300
32	28	H	Woking	W 2-1	0-0	23	Adeloye 2 [70, 89]	674
33	Feb 1	H	Sutton U	D 1-1	1-0	23	Ekpiteta [7]	979
34	15	H	Chorley	W 1-0	0-0	22	King [57]	712
35	22	A	Chesterfield	L 0-4	0-0	22		3346
36	25	A	Maidenhead U	W 3-1	3-1	22	Umerah [17], Ugwu 2 [30, 32]	973
37	29	H	Stockport Co	L 0-1	0-0	22		1030
38	Mar 7	A	Hartlepool U	W 1-0	0-0	22	Ugwu (pen) [78]	3868
39	14	A	FC Halifax T	W 1-0	1-0	21	Ugwu [16]	2154
40	21	H	Bromley	Cancelled				
41	28	A	Yeovil T	Cancelled				
42	Apr 4	H	AFC Fylde	Cancelled				
43	10	H	Boreham Wood	Cancelled				
44	13	A	Notts Co	Cancelled				
45	18	H	Solihull Moors	Cancelled				
46	25	A	Aldershot T	Cancelled				

Final League Position: 22 (on points-per-game basis)

GOALSCORERS

League (47): Ugwu 12 (3 pens), Weston 7, Reid 5, Umerah 5, Adeloye 3, Obileye 3, Ekpiteta 2, Thomas 2, Ball 1, Goddard 1, King 1, Morgan 1, Josh Payne 1, own goals 3.
FA Cup (4): Reid 2, Josh Payne 1, Ugwu 1 (1 pen).
FA Trophy (3): Obileye 1 (1 pen), Reid 1, Ugwu 1.

Ashmore 5	King 34	Thomas 8 + 1	Lawless 6 + 5	Obileye 22 + 5	Wilson 28	Ball 14	Ugwu 31 + 7	Goddard 18 + 3	Weston 26 + 1	Grimes 27 + 5	Umerah 22 + 8	Shields 1 + 5	Egan 6 + 13	Thomas-Asante — + 3	N'Gala 3 + 1	Holmes 21 + 1	Sutherland 26 + 4	Reid 18 + 3	Biabi — + 5	Cordner 19 + 1	Achuba — + 1	Payne Josh 22	Adeloye 4 + 18	Blackman 11 + 3	Ekpiteta 20	Morgan 5	Palmer 6	Gregory 7	McGlashan 8 + 2	Mekki 7 + 1	Timlin 4	*Match No.*
1	2■	3	4^{2}	5	6^{1}	7	8	9	10^{3}	11	12	13	14																			1
1		2	5^{1}	3	6	7	11	8	9	4		10	12																			2
1	5	2	7^{1}	3	8^{3}	9	10	6	12	4	11^{2}			13	14																	3
1	6	2		4	5^{1}	8	11	9	7	3	10^{2}	12		13																		4
1	5	3		6		8	11	9^{1}	7	4	10^{2}	13		12	2																	5
	6	4	7^{2}		2	9	12	10	8	5	11^{1}	14			3^{3}	1	13															6
	2	12	13	3	4	5	6^{3}	7^{2}	8	10	9^{1}	14				1	11															7
	4		6^{1}		5	8	11	9	7	3	10^{3}				2^{2}	1	13	12	14													8
	2	5		3^{1}	6	7	12		9	13	10^{2}					1	8	11		4												9
	5	2		4	6	8	13		7		10^{1}					1	9	11^{2}	12	3												10
	5		13	2	4	7^{2}	12	8^{3}	6		10		14			1	9^{1}	11		3												11
	9			2^{3}	8^{2}	5	10		6	4	13		12			1	7	11^{1}	14	3												12
	5			3	6^{2}	8			7^{3}	2	10		12			1	9^{1}	11	13	4	14											13
	8^{2}			4	5	6^{1}	12		7	2	10^{3}		13			1	9	11	14	3												14
	4			13	5		10		6	3			7^{2}			1	8^{1}	11		2		9	12									15
	3^{2}				5		9		6	4	11					1	8	10^{1}		2		7	12	13								16
	5			12	2		11		7		10^{1}					1	14			4		9	13	3^{2}	6^{3}	8						17
	2		12				4		5	14			13			1^{2}	6^{3}	9		7		10		3^{1}	8	11						18
	2^{2}			14			4		5	12	13						6	9^{1}		7		10		3^{3}	8	11	1					19
							10		7	3	13		12				8^{2}	11^{1}		4		6		2	5	9	1					20
	2			13	3^{3}		4^{2}		5	7	6■						8^{1}	14				10	12		9	11	1					21
	2			3			4		5	6^{3}			14				7	9^{1}		13		10	11	12	8^{2}		1					22
	7			5^{2}			10		6				13				9^{1}	11		3		8	12	4	2		1					23
	3		6				10		7				9^{1}			1	13	12		4		8	11^{2}	5	2							24
	5						10^{1}		6	3	12		7			1	8	11^{2}		4		9	13		2							25
	3				2		10^{1}	13	9	5	14		8^{2}			1	6	11^{3}		4		7	12									26
	3			6			11	12	9^{3}		13					1	8^{1}	10^{2}		4		7	14	2	5							27
	6			4			10	9^{1}					12			1	7^{2}	11		5		8	13	3	2							28
	6■						10^{1}	7		3	12						8	11^{2}		4		9	13	2	5		1					29
				2	3		12	4^{1}		6	5^{3}		7^{2}				8					10■	13		9			1	11	14		30
	4			6	2		11	8		5	10^{1}		13										12		3			1	9^{2}	7		31
				4	6		11	7^{1}		3	10						8						12		2			1	9	5		32
				2	3		4	13		6	5^{2}						7						9	12	8			1	10^{1}	11		33
	2			3^{2}	4		6^{1}	7^{3}		14							8					10	13	5	9			1	12	11		34
	3			4^{2}	5^{1}		14	8		12							7					9	11	6	2^{3}			1	13	10		35
	2				3		4			6	5^{3}		14			12	7^{1}					9	13					1^{2}	10	11	8	36
	4		13		2		10	6^{1}		3	11					1						8^{2}	12						7	9	5	37
	2			12	3		4			6	5^{2}		7			1						10^{1}	13		9				11		8	38
	4		13		2^{1}		10	7		3	11^{2}					1						9	12		5				8		6	39
																																40
																																41
																																42
																																43
																																44
																																45
																																46

FA Cup

Fourth Qualifying	Woking	(h)	1-1
Replay	Woking	(a)	1-0
First Round	Notts Co	(h)	2-3

FA Trophy

First Round	Enfield T	(a)	2-0
Second Round	King's Lynn T	(h)	1-0
Third Round	Royston T	(a)	0-2

aet.

FC HALIFAX TOWN

Ground: The MBi Shay Stadium, Halifax HX1 2YT. *Tel:* (01422) 341 222.
Website: fchalifaxtown.com *Email:* tonyallan@fchalifaxtown.com *Year Formed:* 1911 (Reformed 2008).
Record Attendance: 36,855 v Tottenham H, FA Cup 5th rd, 15 February 1953. *Nickname:* 'The Shaymen'.
Manager: Pete Wild. *Colours:* Blue shirts with yellow trim, blue shorts with yellow trim, blue socks with yellow trim.

FC HALIFAX TOWN – NATIONAL LEAGUE 2019–20 LEAGUE RECORD

Match No.	Date	Venue	Opponents	Result	H/T Score	Lg Pos.	Goalscorers	Attendance
1	Aug 3	A	Ebbsfleet U	W 4-1	1-1	1	King, C [11], Maher [70], Earing [72], Clarke [90]	1091
2	6	H	Hartlepool U	W 2-0	0-0	1	Staunton [54], Sho-Silva [68]	2632
3	10	H	Dagenham & R	W 1-0	1-0	1	McAlinden [15]	1895
4	13	A	Wrexham	L 0-1	0-0	2		5517
5	17	A	Aldershot T	D 1-1	0-1	4	Binnom-Williams [82]	1539
6	24	H	AFC Fylde	W 4-1	2-1	4	McAlinden [10], Sho-Silva [35], King, C [53], Binnom-Williams [76]	1913
7	26	A	Barrow	W 2-1	0-1	3	Nolan [50], McAlinden (pen) [64]	1451
8	31	H	Solihull Moors	W 2-1	1-0	2	McAlinden 2 [15, 49]	2053
9	Sept 3	A	Chesterfield	W 3-2	2-0	1	Allen [8], Clarke [33], King, C [46]	3844
10	7	H	Yeovil T	L 0-2	0-1	2		2341
11	14	A	Notts Co	L 0-1	0-0	3		5188
12	21	H	Barnet	W 4-2	2-2	2	Sho-Silva 2 [12, 90], McAlinden [15], Nolan [70]	1941
13	24	H	Harrogate T	L 0-1	0-0	2		1918
14	28	A	Dover Ath	W 2-0	1-0	2	King, C 2 [11, 90]	1020
15	Oct 5	A	Maidenhead U	W 1-0	1-0	1	McAlinden [2]	1249
16	8	H	Chorley	D 0-0	0-0	1		2117
17	12	H	Boreham Wood	L 0-2	0-1	1		2244
18	26	A	Bromley	L 0-5	0-0	3		2215
19	29	A	Sutton U	W 1-0	0-0	2	Duckworth [53]	1326
20	Nov 2	H	Torquay U	L 2-4	0-2	3	McAlinden [80], Duckworth [90]	2065
21	16	A	Woking	D 0-0	0-0	4		2242
22	23	H	Eastleigh	D 1-1	1-0	4	Sho-Silva [1]	1817
23	26	A	Harrogate T	D 2-2	1-0	5	McAlinden (pen) [11], King, C [77]	1185
24	Dec 7	A	Yeovil T	L 0-2	0-1	7		2975
25	21	H	Notts Co	L 2-4	1-0	8	McCoulsky [45], Allen [57]	2491
26	26	A	Stockport Co	L 1-5	0-2	10	McAlinden [65]	5536
27	28	H	Chesterfield	W 1-0	0-0	10	Redshaw (pen) [66]	2420
28	Jan 1	H	Stockport Co	D 0-0	0-0	9		3460
29	4	A	Barnet	D 1-1	1-0	10	Redshaw [24]	1333
30	18	H	Maidenhead U	W 5-2	1-1	7	Cooper [31], Redshaw [62], Rodney [68], Allen [83], Duckworth [89]	1981
31	25	A	Chorley	W 1-0	0-0	6	King, C [60]	1263
32	28	H	Dover Ath	W 4-2	2-1	4	Rodney 2 [14, 78], Binnom-Williams [45], De Havilland (og) [66]	1726
33	Feb 1	H	Bromley	W 2-1	2-1	3	Maher [32], Rodney [42]	2026
34	22	A	Torquay U	L 0-1	0-0	4		2053
35	Mar 3	H	Sutton U	W 1-0	0-0	3	Rodney (pen) [88]	1637
36	7	H	Woking	L 0-2	0-2	5		1995
37	14	H	Ebbsfleet U	L 0-1	0-1	6		2154
38	17	A	Boreham Wood	Cancelled				
39	21	A	Hartlepool U	Cancelled				
40	28	H	Wrexham	Cancelled				
41	31	A	Eastleigh	Cancelled				
42	Apr 4	A	Dagenham & R	Cancelled				
43	10	H	Barrow	Cancelled				
44	13	A	FC Halifax T	Cancelled				
45	18	H	Aldershot T	Cancelled				
46	25	A	Solihull Moors	Cancelled				

Final League Position: 6 (on points-per-game basis)

GOALSCORERS

League (50): McAlinden 10 (2 pens), King, C 7, Rodney 5 (1 pen), Sho-Silva 5, Allen 3, Binnom-Williams 3, Duckworth 3, Redshaw 3 (1 pen), Clarke 2, Maher 2, Nolan 2, Cooper 1, Earing 1, McCoulsky 1, Staunton 1, own goal 1.
FA Cup (1): Maher 1.
FA Trophy (6): Redshaw 2, Maher 1, Sho-Silva 1, Staunton 1, Williams 1.
National League Play-Offs (1): Sho-Silva 1.

Johnson 37	Duckworth 27 + 3	Binnom-Williams 25	Clarke 33	Brown 21	King C 24 + 7	Sho-Silva 26 + 9	Staunton 37	Williams 20 + 5	King J 21 + 11	Maher 19 + 4	Allen 20 + 12	Earing 3 + 7	Odelusi — + 2	Nolan 21 + 6	McAlinden 20 + 7	MacDonald 4 + 5	Cooper 25 + 2	Southwell 1 + 6	Hanson 5	Redshaw 9 + 5	McCoulsky 1 + 4	Rodney 8	*Match No.*
1	2	3	4	5	6	7^{3}	8	9^{2}	10^{1}	11	12	13	14										1
1	2	3	4	5	6^{1}	7^{3}	8	9^{2}	10	11	12			13	14								2
1	2	3	4	5	7^{3}	8	9		12	11^{1}	6	14		13	10^{2}								3
1	7	9	2	3	4	5^{2}	10		11^{1}		6		13	8	12								4
1	2	3	4	5	8	12	9		11^{1}		7	13		6^{2}	10								5
1	2	3	4	5	8^{3}	9^{2}	10		12		7^{1}	13		6	11	14							6
1	2	3	4	5	8^{1}	9	10		12		7^{2}			6	11	13							7
1	2	3	4	5^{1}		9	10		8		7	12		6	11								8
1	2	3	4		8^{1}	9^{2}	6		12		10	7		5	11	13							9
1	2	3	4		8^{2}	9	10	13	11^{1}		6	7^{3}		5	12	14							10
1	2	4	5		7^{1}	10	6	13	12		9			3	11^{2}		8						11
1	2	3	4		12	11	6	8^{2}	7					5	10^{1}		9	13					12
1	2	3	4		12	6	7	10^{1}	9^{2}					5	8		11	13					13
1	2	3	4		9	6^{2}	7	10^{1}	12			14		5	8^{3}		11	13					14
1	2	3	4		6^{3}	7^{1}	8	10^{2}	13		12			5	9		11	14					15
1	2	3	4		12	14	8	10^{3}	6^{1}		13			5^{2}	9		11	7					16
1	2	3	4		7^{2}	8	9		12	13	6^{1}			5^{3}	10		11	14					17
1	2	3■	4			7	8		12	11^{1}	6			5	9^{2}		10	13					18
1	2		3			10	5		8^{2}	14	13	12		4	11^{1}	7^{3}	9		6				19
1	2		3			6	7			14	12	5^{2}		4^{3}	8	10^{1}	11		9	13			20
1	4	5	6■	7	8^{1}	11	2	10	13	3						9^{2}	12						21
1	2	3		4	5^{2}	6	7		13	11	12				8	9^{1}	10						22
1	2	3		4	12	10	6	13	7^{2}	14	9			5	11^{3}		8^{1}						23
1	5			2		11	3	12	10^{3}		8			7^{2}	9^{1}		6		4	13	14		24
1	5		3	4	12	11	6	10^{2}		7	8				13		14		2^{1}		9^{3}		25
1	5			4	9^{3}	11^{2}	3	13		2	8			7^{1}	10		6			12	14		26
1			2	3	5^{1}	13	6	8	7	11	4^{2}				12		9			10			27
1			2	3	6^{2}		5	8	7	4	11^{1}				12		9			10	13		28
1			2	3	5^{1}	12	6	8	7	11	4^{2}				13		9			10^{3}	14		29
1	12		2	3	4	14	5	7	6^{1}	10	13						8			9^{3}		11^{2}	30
1	13	4	5		6^{2}	14	2	8	7	3	12						9			10^{3}		11^{1}	31
1	14	2	3		4		5	7	6^{3}	10	12			13			8^{2}			9^{1}		11	32
1	2	3	4		9^{1}	14	10	11		6	8			12			5^{2}			13		7^{3}	33
1			2	3	4^{1}	5	6	8		10	13						9		7	12		11^{2}	34
1			2	3	13	4^{2}	5^{3}	7	6	10	12			14			8			9^{1}		11	35
1			2	3	12	14	5^{1}	7	6	10	4			13			8^{3}			9^{2}		11	36
1		2	3			12	5	7	6^{1}	9				4^{2}		13	8			10		11	37
																							38
																							39
																							40
																							41
																							42
																							43
																							44
																							45
																							46

FA Cup

Fourth Qualifying	Harrogate T	(h)	1-2

National League Play-Offs

Eliminator	Boreham Wood	(a)	1-2

FA Trophy

First Round	Wrexham	(h)	4-0
Second Round	Torquay U	(a)	2-1
Third Round	Halesowen T	(h)	0-1

HARROGATE TOWN

Ground: CNG Stadium, Wetherby Road, Harrogate HG2 7SA. *Tel:* (01423) 210 600.
Website: harrogatetownafc.com *Email:* enquiries@harrogatetownafc.com *Year Formed:* 1914.
Record Attendance: 4,280 v Harrogate Railway, Whitworth Cup Final, May 1950.
Nickname: 'Town', 'Sulphurites'. *Manager:* Simon Weaver.
Colours: Yellow shirts with black trim, black shorts, yellow socks with black trim.

HARROGATE TOWN – NATIONAL LEAGUE 2019–20 LEAGUE RECORD

Match No.	*Date*	*Venue*	*Opponents*	*Result*	*H/T Score*	*Lg Pos.*	*Goalscorers*	*Attendance*
1	Aug 3	H	Solihull Moors	D 2-2	0-1	11	Beck [55], Leesley [57]	1045
2	6	A	Barrow	W 3-0	1-0	2	Smith, W 2 [34, 56], Hall [86]	1602
3	10	A	Woking	L 0-1	0-1	9		1470
4	13	H	Notts Co	L 0-2	0-1	14		1863
5	17	A	Dagenham & R	L 2-4	2-2	18	Balanta (og) [7], Kiernan [24]	1043
6	24	H	Stockport Co	W 2-1	0-0	14	Beck [53], Bradley [90]	1326
7	26	A	AFC Fylde	D 0-0	0-0	15		1317
8	31	H	Dover Ath	L 0-2	0-0	18		900
9	Sept 3	H	Chorley	W 2-0	1-0	12	Kiernan [4], Muldoon [47]	792
10	7	A	Torquay U	L 2-4	1-0	17	Stead 2 (1 pen) [33 (p), 58]	2527
11	14	H	Boreham Wood	D 0-0	0-0	18		942
12	21	A	Maidenhead U	D 1-1	1-1	18	Jones [9]	1127
13	24	A	FC Halifax T	W 1-0	0-0	14	Beck [87]	1918
14	28	H	Sutton U	W 2-0	1-0	11	Thomson [35], Muldoon (pen) [90]	769
15	Oct 5	H	Ebbsfleet U	W 2-0	1-0	10	Kiernan 2 [40, 59]	742
16	8	A	Wrexham	D 1-1	0-1	12	Fallowfield [80]	3435
17	12	A	Yeovil T	W 2-1	0-0	8	Kiernan [71], Muldoon [78]	3237
18	26	H	Aldershot T	W 1-0	0-0	4	Emmett [90]	1507
19	29	H	Barnet	W 2-1	2-1	4	Muldoon [15], Smith, G [19]	1121
20	Nov 2	A	Eastleigh	L 2-4	1-2	6	Kiernan [9], Muldoon [69]	1592
21	16	A	Bromley	D 3-3	3-1	7	Emmett [13], Kiernan [37], Muldoon (pen) [41]	2177
22	23	H	Chesterfield	W 3-1	1-1	6	Falkingham [37], Fallowfield [65], Muldoon [71]	1710
23	26	H	FC Halifax T	D 2-2	0-1	7	Thomson [54], Staunton (og) [90]	1185
24	30	A	Sutton U	L 1-3	0-1	7	Falkingham [68]	1490
25	Dec 7	H	Torquay U	W 2-1	1-0	6	Bradley [10], Stead [55]	1348
26	21	A	Boreham Wood	L 1-2	1-1	7	Bradley [39]	501
27	26	H	Hartlepool U	W 4-1	0-0	4	Kerry [54], Muldoon 2 (1 pen) [58 (p), 90], Falkingham [68]	2383
28	28	A	Chorley	W 2-0	1-0	4	Muldoon [27], Stead [67]	1077
29	Jan 1	A	Hartlepool U	W 1-0	0-0	4	Stead [57]	3481
30	4	H	Maidenhead U	W 1-0	0-0	3	Hall [60]	1281
31	18	A	Ebbsfleet U	W 2-0	1-0	2	Hall [39], Muldoon [63]	822
32	25	H	Wrexham	L 0-2	0-1	2		2415
33	Feb 1	A	Aldershot T	D 1-1	0-1	2	Kerry [70]	1704
34	11	H	Yeovil T	W 3-0	1-0	2	Thomson 2 [43, 73], Diamond [52]	801
35	22	H	Eastleigh	W 3-0	2-0	2	Falkingham [20], Diamond [43], Muldoon [68]	1249
36	Mar 3	A	Chesterfield	W 4-3	2-2	2	Stead 2 [9, 60], Thomson [34], Muldoon [90]	2912
37	7	H	Bromley	D 1-1	0-0	2	Diamond [47]	1339
38	13	A	Solihull Moors	Cancelled				
39	24	A	Barnet	Cancelled				
40	Apr 1	H	Barrow	Cancelled				
41	4	H	Woking	Cancelled				
42	7	A	Notts Co	Cancelled				
43	10	H	AFC Fylde	Cancelled				
44	13	A	Stockport Co	Cancelled				
45	18	H	Dagenham & R	Cancelled				
46	25	A	Dover Ath	Cancelled				

Final League Position: 2 (on points-per-game basis)

GOALSCORERS

League (61): Muldoon 13 (3 pens), Kiernan 7, Stead 7 (1 pen), Thomson 5, Falkingham 4, Beck 3, Bradley 3, Diamond 3, Hall 3, Emmett 2, Fallowfield 2, Kerry 2, Smith, W 2, Jones 1, Leesley 1, Smith, G 1, own goals 2.
FA Cup (3): Beck 3.
FA Trophy (10): Kerry 2, Muldoon 2, Bradley 1, Diamond 1, Emmett 1, Hall 1, Kiernan 1, own goal 1.
National League Play-Offs (4): Diamond 1, Hall 1, Muldoon 1, Thomson 1.

Belshaw 37	Smith G 18 + 3	Falkingham 32	Burrell 34	Emmett 15 + 12	Beck 19 + 6	Leesley 5 + 1	Kiernan 25 + 8	Muldoon 36 + 1	Hall 33	Smith W 36	Fallowfield 24 + 2	Kerry 15 + 1	Stead 16 + 11	Brown 4 + 4	Jones 2 + 4	Thomson 10 + 12	Bradley 20 + 3	Diamond 20 + 7	Taylor — + 1	Hancox 5	Harratt — + 4	Kougoun 1	*Match No.*
1	2	3	4	5^{3}	6	7	8	9^{2}	10	11^{1}	12	13	14										1
1	2	3	4	13	5	6^{2}	7	9^{1}	10	11		8	12										2
1	2	5	6	12	9	10	7	11^{1}	3	4		8^{2}	13										3
1	2	5	6	12	9^{3}	10	7^{1}	11	3	4■			14	8^{2}	13								4
1	2^{1}	5	6	7	9	11^{2}	8	10	3		4				13	12							5
1	12	6	2^{1}	7	9^{2}		11	10	4	3	5		13				8						6
1		6	2	7	9^{1}		11	10	4	3	5		12	13			8^{2}						7
1		4	3	7	9^{3}	12	11	10^{2}	6	5	2		13	8^{1}	14								8
1	3	7^{1}	4	12	13		9	11^{2}	6	5	2		10^{3}	8				14					9
1	2		6	7^{2}	12		8^{1}	11	3	4	5		10■	9	13								10
1	2		6	7	12		9	11^{1}	3	4	5				8^{2}		10	13					11
1	2		6		13		8	12	3	4	5		11^{1}		7^{3}	14	9	10^{2}					12
1	3		4		6		7^{1}	9	10	11	2			13		5	8^{2}	12					13
1	3		4	14	6		7^{3}	9	10	11	2			13		5^{1}	8^{2}	12					14
1	2	7	6		10		8^{1}	11	4	3	5						9	12					15
1	2	6	7	13	10		8^{2}	11	3	4	5						9^{1}	12					16
1	4	6	7	14	9		5^{2}	10^{3}	2	3	8		12			13		11^{1}					17
1	3	4	5	12	6		7^{2}	9^{3}		10	2		14			13	8	11^{1}					18
1	2	4	5	14	11		6^{3}	9^{1}		3	8		13■			12	7	10^{2}					19
1	3^{2}	4	5	12	6		7^{3}	9		10	2					13	8^{1}	11	14				20
1	4	6		7^{2}	9		8	10	3	2	5					12	13	11^{1}					21
1		7	8		9		6^{1}	10	2	3	4					12		11		5			22
1		5	6■		9		12	10	2	3	4		13			7^{2}		11^{1}		8			23
1		3		5			12	7	8	9	2		6			4		10^{1}		11			24
1		6		12			9^{2}	11^{1}	3	2		7	10			8	5	13		4			25
1		6	2	13			10^{1}	9	4	3		7^{2}		12		11	8			5			26
1		7	6	4				10	2	3		8	9			12	5	11^{1}					27
1		2	3	6^{1}				9	4	5		8	10			12	7	11					28
1		4	5	6^{1}	12		13	10	3	2		8	9^{2}				7	11					29
1	12	4	5	6^{3}	13		14	9	2	3^{2}		8	10^{1}				7	11					30
1		5	4	7^{1}			14	10^{2}	3	9		6	8			12	2	11^{3}			13		31
1		4	5	6^{2}			13	10^{1}	2	3		8	9				7	11			12		32
1		4	5				6	10	2	3	12	8	9			13	7^{1}	11^{2}					33
1	14	3	4				12	8^{1}	9	10^{3}	2	7	6^{2}			5		11			13		34
1		4	6				12	10^{3}	2	3	5	8	11			7^{1}	14	9^{2}			13		35
1		5	6					10	2	3	4	8	9			7		11					36
1		5	6					10		2	4	8^{1}	9			7	12	11				3	37
																							38
																							39
																							40
																							41
																							42
																							43
																							44
																							45
																							46

FA Cup

Fourth Qualifying	FC Halifax T	(a)	2-1
First Round	Portsmouth	(h)	1-2

National League Play-Offs

Semi-Finals	Boreham Wood	(h)	1-0
Final	Notts Co	Wembley	3-1

FA Trophy

First Round	Hartlepool U	(h)	3-2
Second Round	Darlington	(a)	2-0
Third Round	Eastleigh	(h)	2-0
Quarter-Finals	AFC Fylde	(a)	3-2
aet.			
Semi-Finals 1st leg	Notts Co	(a)	P-P
Semi-Finals 2nd leg	Notts Co	(h)	P-P

HARTLEPOOL UNITED

Ground: The Northern Gas and Power Stadium, Clarence Road, Hartlepool TS24 8BZ. *Tel:* (01429) 272 584.
Website: www.hartlepoolunited.co.uk *Email:* enquires@hartlepoolunited.co.uk
Year Formed: 1908. *Record Attendance:* 17,426 v Manchester U, FA Cup 3rd rd, 5 January 1957.
Nickname: 'The Pool', 'Monkey Hangers'. *Manager:* Dave Challinor.
Colours: Blue shirts with white trim, blue shorts with white trim, blue socks with white trim.

HARTLEPOOL UNITED – NATIONAL LEAGUE 2019–20 LEAGUE RECORD

Match No.	Date		Venue	Opponents	Result		H/T Score	Lg Pos.	Goalscorers	Attendance
1	Aug	3	H	Sutton U	L	1-3	1-2	22	Toure [45]	3812
2		6	A	FC Halifax T	L	0-2	0-0	22		2632
3		10	A	Maidenhead U	W	1-0	0-0	19	Muir [53]	1330
4		13	H	AFC Fylde	D	2-2	1-0	17	Toure 2 [3, 59]	3222
5		17	H	Bromley	L	2-3	2-2	20	Holohan [13], Mafuta [39]	3171
6		24	A	Chorley	D	0-0	0-0	19		1395
7		26	H	Wrexham	W	4-2	1-1	16	Toure 2 [43, 60], Noble 2 (1 pen) [48 (p), 52]	3462
8		31	A	Torquay U	W	2-1	1-0	9	Kennedy [16], Kioso [80]	2683
9	Sept	3	A	Barrow	W	1-0	0-0	8	Donaldson [71]	1257
10		7	H	Woking	D	1-1	1-0	9	Noble (pen) [45]	3429
11		14	A	Dagenham & R	L	1-3	0-1	11	Donaldson [80]	1392
12		21	H	Dover Ath	L	0-2	0-1	14		3329
13		24	H	Chesterfield	D	1-1	1-1	17	Kioso [9]	2953
14		28	A	Eastleigh	D	1-1	1-0	16	Toure [11]	1838
15	Oct	5	H	Yeovil T	W	2-1	0-0	15	Toure [47], Kennedy [90]	3273
16		9	A	Stockport Co	L	1-2	0-2	16	Kabamba [86]	3465
17		12	A	Aldershot T	W	3-0	1-0	15	Hawkes [4], Holohan [80], Kabamba [90]	2768
18		26	H	Barnet	W	2-0	2-0	11	Kabamba 2 [6, 27]	3089
19	Nov	2	A	Notts Co	D	2-2	2-1	13	Holohan [8], James [42]	5258
20		5	H	Solihull Moors	L	0-1	0-0	13		2703
21		16	A	Ebbsfleet U	D	2-2	2-0	14	Holohan 2 [32, 42]	1086
22		23	H	Boreham Wood	D	2-2	0-1	14	Featherstone [70], Toure (pen) [84]	3377
23		26	A	Chesterfield	W	5-1	2-1	10	Mafuta 2 [23, 56], James [27], Toure 2 [48, 68]	3420
24	Dec	7	A	Woking	L	1-2	1-0	14	Toure (pen) [25]	2127
25		21	H	Dagenham & R	W	1-0	0-0	13	Kitching [78]	3259
26		26	A	Harrogate T	L	1-4	0-0	14	Kabamba [76]	2383
27		28	H	Barrow	D	2-2	0-0	15	Holohan [55], Donaldson [76]	3790
28	Jan	1	H	Harrogate T	L	0-1	0-0	16		3481
29		7	H	Eastleigh	W	2-1	0-0	13	Holohan [51], Shelton [67]	2478
30		11	A	Dover Ath	D	1-1	1-0	12	Lokko (og) [22]	1023
31		18	A	Yeovil T	D	2-2	1-2	11	Kioso [27], Mafuta [71]	2716
32		25	H	Stockport Co	W	2-0	1-0	11	Keena [32], Shelton [52]	3766
33	Feb	1	A	Barnet	L	1-2	0-0	13	Sweeney (og) [75]	1321
34		8	H	Aldershot T	W	2-0	2-0	10	Molyneux [6], Shelton [20]	3442
35		22	H	Notts Co	W	2-0	0-0	11	Featherstone 2 [47, 58]	3839
36		29	A	Boreham Wood	D	1-1	0-1	11	Toure [46]	932
37	Mar	3	A	Solihull Moors	W	1-0	0-0	8	Keena [86]	896
38		7	H	Ebbsfleet U	L	0-1	0-0	10		3868
39		14	A	Sutton U	D	1-1	0-1	9	Holohan [52]	2126
40		21	H	FC Halifax T	Cancelled					
41		28	A	AFC Fylde	Cancelled					
42	Apr	4	H	Maidenhead U	Cancelled					
43		10	A	Wrexham	Cancelled					
44		13	H	Chorley	Cancelled					
45		18	A	Bromley	Cancelled					
46		25	H	Torquay U	Cancelled					

Final League Position: 12 (on points-per-game basis)

GOALSCORERS

League (56): Toure 12 (2 pens), Holohan 8, Kabamba 5, Mafuta 4, Donaldson 3, Featherstone 3, Kioso 3, Noble 3 (2 pens), Shelton 3, James 2, Keena 2, Kennedy 2, Hawkes 1, Kitching 1, Molyneux 1, Muir 1, own goals 2.
FA Cup (9): Kabamba 2, Donaldson 1, Featherstone 1, Hawkes 1, Holohan 1, James 1, Kitching 1, Toure 1 (1 pen).
FA Trophy (2): Donaldson 1, Hamilton 1.

Killip 33	Richardson 9 + 1	Kerr 22 + 1	Raynes 28	Crichlow-Noble 2	Mafuta 29 + 4	Kennedy 10 + 8	Noble 10 + 2	Toure 29 + 5	James 13 + 7	Kabamba 16 + 9	Featherstone 29 + 6	Kitching 35 + 3	Holohan 18 + 11	Kioso 27 + 1	Williams — + 3	Donaldson 33 + 1	Muir 3 + 6	Cunningham 8 + 2	Anderson 3 + 1	Bale — + 1	Hawkes 7 + 11	Hamilton 1 + 5	Liddle 15	Shelton 13 + 1	Beeney 6	Molyneux 6 + 4	Keena 4 + 4	Southam-Hales 7	Odusina 8	Harker 5 + 2	Match No.
1	2^1	3	4	5^3	6	7	8	9^2	10	11	12	13	14																		1
1		3	4	5^1	6	8^3	9	12	11	10	7^2		13	2	14																2
1		3	4		6^1	14	8	10		11^3	7	5	13	2		9^2	12														3
1		3	4		7	12	9^2	10	13		8	6	14			2^1	11	5^3													4
1		3	4		6	14	13	10	12		7^2	5^1	8	2		9^3	11														5
1		2	3		7			10^2	14	13	8	5	9	12		6	11^3		4^1												6
1		3	4		7	8^2	9^1	10^3	11		12	6		2				5		13	14										7
1		3	4		7	8	9^1	10	11^2		13	6		2		12		5													8
1		3	4		7	8	9	11^1		12		6		2		10		5													9
1		3	4		7	8^1	9^2	11			12	6	13	2		10		5													10
1		3^1	4		7	8^2	9	11		12		6		2		10		5			13										11
1	7^2		3		6		8^1	10	12	11	13■	5		2		9■		4													12
1	4		3		7	8	12	11	13	10		5	6^1	2							9^2										13
1	3		4		7	8		10^1	12	11^2		6	9	2			13	5													14
1	5	3	4		7	8		11^1	9^2	13	12	6		2		10															15
1	4^3	2	3		7			11	10^2	13	6	8	14	5^1		9					12										16
1		4	3		7	14		11^3	12	10	6	5	13	2		8^1					9^2										17
1		3	4		6	13		12	11^3	10	8	5	7^1	2		9^2					14										18
1		3	4		7	13			10^1	11	6	5	8^3	2	14	9^2	12														19
1		3	4		7^3				9	11^1	6	5	8	2	12	10^2	14				13										20
1		3	4		6	13		12	10	11^1	7	5	8^2	2		9															21
1		4	3^2		7^3			13	10	11	6	8	9^1	2		5		12			14										22
1	12	4	3		6			10^3	11^1	13	7	8		2		5	14				9^2										23
1	2	3	4		6^1			11	10	13	7	5				9					8^2	12									24
1			4		7^1			11		12	6	5		2		10					9^2	13	3	8							25
1			4^3		6^2			11		12	7^1	5	13	2		10					8	9	3	14							26
1	5^2	4						10		11^1	6	12	8	2		9						13	3	7							27
	5		3^2					10^3		11	6	12	7	2		9						13	4	8^1	1	14					28
		12^2	4^1		7					11	6	5	9	2		10			13				3	8	1						29
					6					11^1	7	5	9^2	2		10		13	4			12	3	8	1						30
					7	13					6^1	5	10	2		8	14		4^3				3	9	1	12	11^2				31
					12			10^2			6	5	8			9							3	7	1	13	11^1	2	4		32
								10			6^2	5	7■			9					14		3	8^3	1	13	11^1	2	4	12	33
1					12			11			5	4				9					14		2	7^2		8^3	13	6	3	10^1	34
1					12			11^3			6	3	14			8							2	7		9^1	13	5	4	10^2	35
1								11			5	4	13			7					12		2	6		8^1		9	3	10^2	36
1								10^3			6	5	14			8					12		3	7^1		9	13	2	4	11^2	37
1								10			5	4	7^2			8					13		2	6^1		9	11		3	12	38
1					14			12			6	5	7			8^3					9		4			10^1	13	2	3	11^2	39
																															40
																															41
																															42
																															43
																															44
																															45
																															46

FA Cup

Fourth Qualifying	Brackley T	(h)	1-0
First Round	Yeovil T	(a)	4-1
Second Round	Exeter C	(a)	2-2
Replay	Exeter C	(h)	1-0
aet.			
Third Round	Oxford U	(a)	1-4

FA Trophy

First Round	Harrogate T	(a)	2-3

MAIDENHEAD UNITED

Ground: York Road, Maidenhead, Berkshire SL6 1SF. *Tel:* (01628) 636 314.
Website: pitchero.com/clubs/maidenheadunited *Email:* social@maidenheadunitedfc.org *Year Formed:* 1870.
Record Attendance: 7,920 v Southall, FA Amateur Cup quarter-final, 7 March 1936. *Nickname:* 'The Magpies'.
Manager: Alan Devonshire. *Colours:* Black and white striped shirts with red trim, black shorts with red trim, white socks with red trim.

MAIDENHEAD UNITED – NATIONAL LEAGUE 2019–20 LEAGUE RECORD

Match No.	*Date*		*Venue*	*Opponents*	*Result*		*H/T Score*	*Lg Pos.*	*Goalscorers*	*Attendance*
1	Aug	3	A	Stockport Co	W	1-0	0-0	8	Cassidy ^{79}	4626
2		6	H	Chesterfield	D	1-1	0-0	7	Clerima ^{60}	1471
3		10	H	Hartlepool U	L	0-1	0-0	11		1330
4		13	A	Torquay U	W	2-0	1-0	8	Kelly ^{31}, Fenelon ^{90}	2946
5		17	H	Chorley	W	4-1	2-1	4	Kelly ^{24}, Cassidy (pen) ^{35}, Whitehall 2 $^{90, 90}$	1172
6		24	A	Yeovil T	W	2-1	0-0	5	Smile ^{56}, Whitehall ^{85}	2179
7		26	H	Bromley	L	1-2	0-0	5	Smile ^{65}	1511
8		31	A	Sutton U	W	3-0	0-0	4	Fenelon ^{61}, Cassidy ^{79}, Whitehall (pen) ^{90}	1554
9	Sept	3	A	Wrexham	D	2-2	1-1	4	Young (og) ^{22}, Smile ^{67}	3667
10		7	H	Dagenham & R	L	0-1	0-0	4		1551
11		14	A	Barnet	L	0-1	0-0	6		1086
12		21	H	Harrogate T	D	1-1	1-1	8	Fenelon ^{21}	1127
13		24	H	Dover Ath	L	1-2	0-1	9	Whitehall ^{61}	1015
14		28	A	Barrow	L	0-2	0-1	14		1401
15	Oct	5	H	FC Halifax T	L	0-1	0-1	16		1249
16		8	A	Eastleigh	L	1-2	1-1	16	Whitehall ^{28}	1548
17		12	A	Ebbsfleet U	W	2-1	1-1	16	Whitehall ^{21}, Upward ^{76}	1003
18		26	H	Solihull Moors	W	1-0	0-0	15	Clerima ^{90}	1152
19		29	H	AFC Fylde	D	1-1	0-0	14	Kelly ^{48}	1010
20	Nov	2	A	Aldershot T	L	0-2	0-0	16		1602
21		16	A	Boreham Wood	L	1-2	0-0	17	Sekajja (pen) ^{81}	624
22		23	H	Woking	L	2-3	0-2	17	Whitehall 2 $^{60, 85}$	1307
23		26	A	Dover Ath	W	4-3	3-2	17	Cassidy 2 $^{11, 44}$, Upward ^{36}, Ellul ^{53}	687
24		30	H	Barrow	L	0-4	0-1	17		1239
25	Dec	7	A	Dagenham & R	W	2-1	1-0	16	Clerima 2 $^{28, 71}$	1083
26		21	H	Barnet	L	1-4	1-2	16	Kelly ^{27}	1625
27		26	A	Notts Co	L	0-3	0-3	18		5128
28		28	H	Wrexham	W	2-0	1-0	17	Whitehall 2 $^{23, 53}$	1472
29	Jan	1	H	Notts Co	D	0-0	0-0	17		1657
30		4	A	Harrogate T	L	0-1	0-0	18		1281
31		18	A	FC Halifax T	L	2-5	1-1	19	Upward ^{45}, Mensah ^{90}	1981
32		25	H	Eastleigh	W	2-0	2-0	18	Whitehall 2 (1 pen) $^{7 (p), 33}$	1176
33	Feb	1	A	Solihull Moors	W	2-0	0-0	17	Akintunde ^{66}, Alfa ^{85}	797
34		22	H	Aldershot T	L	1-2	0-2	20	Clerima ^{66}	1778
35		25	H	Ebbsfleet U	L	1-3	1-3	20	Mundle-Smith ^{9}	973
36		29	A	Woking	L	0-2	0-0	20		2019
37	Mar	7	H	Boreham Wood	L	0-1	0-1	21		1296
38		14	H	Stockport Co	L	1-2	1-0	22	Alfa ^{27}	1662
39		21	A	Chesterfield	Cancelled					
40		24	A	AFC Fylde	Cancelled					
41		28	H	Torquay U	Cancelled					
42	Apr	4	A	Hartlepool U	Cancelled					
43		10	A	Bromley	Cancelled					
44		13	H	Yeovil T	Cancelled					
45		18	A	Chorley	Cancelled					
46		25	H	Sutton U	Cancelled					

Final League Position: 21 (on points-per-game basis)

GOALSCORERS

League (44): Whitehall 13 (2 pens), Cassidy 5 (1 pen), Clerima 5, Kelly 4, Fenelon 3, Smile 3, Upward 3, Alfa 2, Akintunde 1, Ellul 1, Mensah 1, Mundle-Smith 1, Sekajja 1 (1 pen), own goal 1.
FA Cup (4): Kelly 2, Cassidy 1, Lafayette 1.
FA Trophy (7): Fenelon 2, Whitehall 2, Ellul 1, Kelly 1, Smile 1.

Ashby-Hammond 22	Clerima 23 + 1	Steer 23 + 3	Ellul 32	Nana Ofori-Twumasi 30 + 1	Massey 35	Comley 24 + 2	Upward 34 + 1	Smile 31 + 3	Cassidy 25 + 3	Akintunde 15 + 12	Mensah 8 + 17	Davies Aron 14 + 6	Whitehall 22 + 14	Kelly 22 + 7	Fenelon 8 + 11	Sheckelford 23 + 4	Landers — + 2	Keetch — + 3	Grant 2 + 1	Dunn 16	Thompson-Brissett — + 2	Sekajja 1 + 3	Alfa 3 + 5	Mundle-Smith 4 + 1	Asonganyi 1	Acquah — + 1	Match No.
1	2	3	4	5	6	7^3	8	9^1	10	11^2	12	13	14														1
1	2^1	3	4	7	10	5	8	9	6			13	11^2	12													2
1	2	3	4	7	10		8	9	6^2	13	12	5^1	11^3	14													3
1	2		3	8	10		9	11^3	5		7^1	4	13	6^2	12	14											4
1			2	7	10	12	9	11^2	4		6^3	3	14	5^1	13	8											5
1			2	7	10	12	9	11^2	4		6^1	3^3	13	5	14	8											6
1		2	3	7	10	5^1	9	11		8^2	14		6	13	4^3	12											7
1		2	5	4	3	6	7	8^1	9	12	10^3		13		11^2		14										8
1		2	4	3	5	6	7	8^2	10	11^3	12	14	13		9^1												9
1		2	3	4	6		8	7	10	12	13	5^1	11^3		9^2			14									10
1		2	3	4	6		7^2	8	10	11^3	13	5	12		9^1		14										11
1	12	4	5^2	2	3	6	7^1	8	11	13	10^3	14			9												12
1	2			7	4		8	5	10	9^3	11	3^1	12			13		14	6^2								13
1		2	3	8	10	5^1	9	11^2	6	14	7^3	4	13	12													14
		2	3	8	10	4	9	11	5	12	6^1		7^2			13				1							15
		12	2		10	4	9	11		8^1	13	14	6	5^3		7			3^2	1							16
	2	3	4	5	6		8	9^3	12	13	14		11	10^2		7^1				1							17
	2		3	7	10	4	9	11^1	5				12	6		8				1							18
	2^1			7	10	3	9	11	4		13	12	6	5^2		8				1							19
			2	4	3	8	6^3	7^1	9		12		11	10^2		5				1	13	14					20
		2	3▮	8^1			10	11	5		12	4	7^2	6^3		9				1	14	13					21
	2	3				5	7	8^1	9	14	13	4	12	10^3		6				1		11^2					22
	2	3	4▮				7	8	9	11^1		5^2		10		6			13	1		12					23
	2	5			4		7	8	9	11^1	13	6	12	10^2		3				1							24
	2	3		14	10	4	9	11^1	5	13	12		7^2	6^3		8				1							25
	2	3	6		5	7	8^2	9^1	11		14		12	10^3	13	4				1							26
	2	3	4	9	11	6		13	7			5^1	12	8^2	14	10^3				1							27
	2	14	3	5	6	8	7		13	11^3			10^1	12	9^2	4				1							28
	4	5	6	2	3	8	7		12	11			10^1	9						1							29
	2	3▮	6	4	5	8	7^1		9	11^3	14		10^2	12▮	13					1							30
1			2	5	10		8	11		7^1	13	3^3	4		12	6		14					9^2				31
1	2	13	3	6	10		9	11^1		8^2			5	4^3	14	7							12				32
1			2	6	10	3	9			8^2			5	4^1	13	7							12	11			33
1	2		3^1	7	10	4^2	12	14		9^3			6	5		8							13	11			34
1	2				4	8	6	7^1		12			11	10	9^2	3							13	5			35
1	2	3^2	6		5	7	8	9^1					10	11^3	13	4							12	14			36
1	2^2	3	4	8	11	5^3		12		13			7	6^1	14	9							10				37
1	8		4	6^3	2			7		14			9	12		5							11^1	3	10^2	13	38
																											39
																											40
																											41
																											42
																											43
																											44
																											45
																											46

FA Cup

Fourth Qualifying	Wealdstone	(h)	1-1
Replay	Wealdstone	(a)	2-0
First Round	Rotherham U	(h)	1-3

FA Trophy

First Round	Hemel Hemstead T	(h)	4-2
Second Round	Halesowen T	(a)	2-2
Replay	Halesowen T	(h)	1-3

NOTTS COUNTY

Ground: Meadow Lane Stadium, Meadow Lane, Nottingham NG2 3HJ. *Tel:* (0115) 952 9000.
Website: www.nottscountyfc.co.uk *Email:* office@nottscountyfc.co.uk *Year Formed:* 1862.
Record Attendance: 47,310 v York C, FA Cup 6th rd, 12 March 1955. *Nickname:* 'The Magpies'.
Manager: Neal Ardley. *Colours:* Black and white striped shirts, black shorts, white socks.

NOTTS COUNTY – NATIONAL LEAGUE 2019–20 LEAGUE RECORD

Match No.	*Date*	*Venue*	*Opponents*	*Result*	*H/T Score*	*Lg Pos.*	*Goalscorers*	*Attendance*
1	Aug 3	A	Eastleigh	L 0-1	0-1	19		2668
2	6	H	Stockport Co	D 1-1	1-0	20	O'Brien, J [36]	5820
3	10	H	Barnet	L 1-2	1-1	23	Boldewijn [9]	4096
4	13	A	Harrogate T	W 2-0	1-0	15	Dennis (pen) [45], Boldewijn [88]	1863
5	18	H	Wrexham	D 1-1	0-0	17	Dennis [69]	6263
6	24	A	Ebbsfleet U	D 2-2	1-1	17	Turner [11], Booty [48]	1293
7	26	H	Chorley	W 5-1	1-1	12	Tyson [30], Boldewijn [49], Dennis [53], Thomas 2 [65, 71]	5082
8	31	A	Yeovil T	L 1-3	0-1	15	Dennis (pen) [90]	2424
9	Sept 3	H	Solihull Moors	D 0-0	0-0	15		4152
10	7	A	Sutton U	D 1-1	0-1	14	Wootton [52]	2059
11	14	H	FC Halifax T	W 1-0	0-0	13	Wootton [57]	5188
12	21	A	Bromley	L 1-2	1-1	16	Wootton [35]	3122
13	24	A	Boreham Wood	W 2-1	1-0	11	Gregory (og) [41], Osborne [66]	756
14	28	H	AFC Fylde	W 2-0	1-0	8	Thomas [19], McCrory [80]	9090
15	Oct 5	A	Dover Ath	D 2-2	1-1	12	Rose (pen) [41], Dennis [90]	1463
16	8	H	Dagenham & R	W 2-0	1-0	7	Booty [24], Dennis [87]	3670
17	12	H	Torquay U	W 2-0	1-0	5	Brindley [8], Dennis [48]	5265
18	26	A	Chesterfield	L 0-1	0-1	8		5432
19	29	A	Woking	W 4-0	2-0	7	Boldewijn 2 [7, 73], Thomas 2 [18, 60]	2175
20	Nov 2	H	Hartlepool U	D 2-2	1-2	7	Thomas 2 [44, 61]	5258
21	16	H	Barrow	L 0-3	0-2	9		5287
22	23	A	Aldershot T	L 1-2	1-2	11	Wootton [36]	2211
23	26	H	Boreham Wood	D 2-2	2-1	9	Wootton 2 [30, 41]	3256
24	Dec 7	H	Sutton U	D 1-1	1-0	12	Thomas [14]	5652
25	21	A	FC Halifax T	W 4-2	0-1	11	Wootton 2 [48, 90], Rose 2 (1 pen) [60, 81 (p)]	2491
26	26	H	Maidenhead U	W 3-0	3-0	9	Wootton [21], Osborne [29], Dennis [43]	5128
27	28	A	Solihull Moors	W 1-0	0-0	6	Thomas [72]	3212
28	Jan 1	A	Maidenhead U	D 0-0	0-0	7		1657
29	4	H	Bromley	W 2-1	1-0	5	Thomas [4], Rawlinson [70]	5192
30	18	H	Dover Ath	D 0-0	0-0	6		5157
31	25	A	Dagenham & R	L 0-2	0-0	7		1697
32	Feb 1	H	Chesterfield	W 3-0	0-0	6	Boldewijn [51], Wootton 2 [59, 76]	6347
33	15	H	Woking	D 1-1	0-0	6	Dennis [70]	5074
34	22	A	Hartlepool U	L 0-2	0-0	7		3839
35	Mar 3	A	AFC Fylde	W 2-1	1-1	6	Boldewijn [13], Long [76]	1353
36	7	A	Barrow	W 2-0	0-0	6	Crawford [67], Roberts [72]	3307
37	10	H	Aldershot T	W 3-1	1-1	3	Roberts [35], Dennis 2 [59, 67]	4287
38	14	H	Eastleigh	W 4-0	1-0	3	Wootton 2 [15, 62], Dennis [54], Roberts [70]	4942
39	17	A	Torquay U	Cancelled				
40	24	A	Stockport Co	Cancelled				
41	Apr 4	A	Barnet	Cancelled				
42	7	H	Harrogate T	Cancelled				
43	10	A	Chorley	Cancelled				
44	13	H	Ebbsfleet U	Cancelled				
45	18	A	Wrexham	Cancelled				
46	25	H	Yeovil T	Cancelled				

Final League Position: 3 (on points-per-game basis)

GOALSCORERS

League (61): Wootton 13, Dennis 12 (2 pens), Thomas 10, Boldewijn 7, Roberts 3, Rose 3 (2 pens), Booty 2, Osborne 2, Brindley 1, Crawford 1, Long 1, McCrory 1, O'Brien, J 1, Rawlinson 1, Turner 1, Tyson 1, own goal 1.
FA Cup (6): Wootton 3, Boldewijn 1, Dennis 1, Turner 1.
FA Trophy (10): Dennis 2, Wootton 2, Crawford 1, Doyle 1, O'Brien, J 1, Osborne 1, Rawlinson 1, Wilson 1.
National League Play-Offs (1): Roberts 1.

Slocombe 29	McCrory 25	Rose 36	O'Brien J 12 + 5	Doyle 27 + 2	Tyson 6 + 7	Boldewijn 36 + 1	Oxlade-Chamberlain 1	Kelly-Evans 16 + 2	Bakayogo 14	Bird 3 + 8	Hemmings 1 + 1	Turner 19 + 2	Tootle — + 2	Rawlinson 31 + 3	Graham 7 + 3	Dunn 1 + 2	Dennis 16 + 14	Campbell — + 1	Booty 13 + 7	Osborne 8 + 4	Thomas 22 + 10	Wootton 29 + 2	Shields 7 + 7	Brindley 24	Fitzsimons 3	Lacey 11	Crawford 2 + 6	Roberts 7 + 1	McDonnell 6	Long 3 + 1	Wilson 1 + 2	Bagan 2	Match No.
1	2■	3	4	5■	6	7	8^1	9^3	10	11^2	12	13	14																				1
1		2	3		4^2	5		8	9	11^1	7	13		6	10	12																	2
1		8	9^1		10	11		4^3	5			2^2	13	3	6	7	12	14															3
1		6			9^2	10		4	5			2		3	14	13	8^3		7	11^1	12												4
1	2	3	13	6	12	8						4		9	11		7^2		10^1	14	5^3												5
1	2	3	12	6	13	8						4		9^2	11		7^1		10		5												6
1	2	3	5	6	8^3	9		10^1	11^2			4			13		7		14		12												7
1	2		4	6		8		10				3		13	11^2		7		9^1		5	12											8
1	5	7	8	6		10^1		3				4			2		12				9	11											9
1	6	7		8		10		4				2		3^2	14		9^1		5^3		13	11	12										10
1	5	6	7	8■		9						2^2		12	3				13		11^1	10		4									11
1	5	6	7^1			10			3^2	13				2			9^3		8	14	12	11		4									12
1	5	6				9^2			3	13				2					7	11^1	8	10	12	4									13
1	6	7				9^1			4	14				3			13		5	11^2	8^3	10	12	2									14
1		2				5			9			3		6			13		8	11^2	4^1	7	12	10									15
1		2		12		5			9^2	14		3		6			13		8		4^3	7	11^1	10									16
1		6		7		11		12	4^1			5		2			10^2		13		14	8	9^3	3									17
1	5	6		7	14	9			3^1			4					8^3		13		12	10	11^2	2									18
1	2	3		6		7						4		8					10		5^1	9	12	11									19
1	2	3		6		7						4		8			13		12		5^2	9	11^1	10									20
1	2	3		6		7^1						4		8			13		10		5^2	9	12	11									21
1	2	3^3		6	14	7^2						4		8			13		10		5^1	9	12	11									22
1	2	3		6	12	7						4		8■					13		5^1	9	11^2	10									23
1	2	3		6		7						4		8			13		12		5^1	9	11^2	10									24
	5	6^1		7		8		12						3			13				11	10	9^2	2^3	1	4	14						25
1	2	3^3		4		6^2		9		14				7			5			10	13	8^1				11	12						26
1		6		8	11^1	13		2	4	14				5						12	9^2	10				3	7^3						27
1	5	6		7	12	9		3						2			8^2			11^1	13	10				4							28
1	5	6		7		9				12				2			13			11^1	8^2	10		3		4							29
1	2	3		5	13	6								7			12			10^1	4^2	8		9		11							30
		6	13	8■		9			3					5			10^1				12	11		2	1	4		7^2					31
		6	7^2			10		3		14				2			12				9^1	11		4	1	5	13	8^3					32
		2	3			5		8		9				6			4					7		10				11	1				33
		6^3	12	7		10		3						2			11^1			14		9		5			13	8^2	1	4			34
		6	12	8		10^2		3						2			14				9^1	11		4				7^3	1	5	13		35
	2		3	5										6							4^3	12		7		9	8	13	1	14	11^2	10^1	36
	2	3^1	4	13		6		8						12			5					7				9	14	11^3	1	10^2			37
		2^1		3		5								6			4^3				13	7		8		9	12	11^2	1		14	10	38
																																	39
																																	40
																																	41
																																	42
																																	43
																																	44
																																	45
																																	46

FA Cup

Fourth Qualifying	Belper T		(h)	2-1
First Round	Ebbsfleet U		(a)	3-2
Second Round	Northampton T		(a)	1-3

National League Play-Offs

Semi-Finals	Barnet		(h)	2-0
Final	Harrogate T	Wembley		1-3

FA Trophy

First Round	Chesterfield	(a)	1-0
Second Round	Dagenham & R	(h)	2-1
Third Round	Yeovil T	(a)	2-1
Quarter-Finals	Aveley	(h)	5-0
Semi-Finals 1st leg	Harrogate T	(h)	P-P
Semi-Finals 2nd leg	Harrogate T	(a)	P-P

SOLIHULL MOORS

Ground: The Automated Technology Group Stadium, Damson Parkway, Solihull, West Midlands B92 9EJ.
Tel: (0121) 705 6770. *Website:* www.solihullmoorsfc.co.uk *Email:* info@solihullmoorsfc.co.uk *Year Formed:* 2007.
Record Attendance: 3,681 v Leyton Orient, National League, 22 April 2019. *Nickname:* 'Moors'.
Manager: Jimmy Shan. *Colours:* Blue shirts with yellow trim, blue shorts with yellow trim, blue socks with yellow trim.

SOLIHULL MOORS – NATIONAL LEAGUE 2019–20 LEAGUE RECORD

Match No.	Date		Venue	Opponents	Result		H/T Score	Lg Pos.	Goalscorers	Attendance
1	Aug	3	A	Harrogate T	D	2-2	1-0	11	Blissett [35], McCallum [66]	1045
2		6	H	Torquay U	W	3-0	3-0	2	Osborne 2 [6, 43], Hawkridge (pen) [9]	1613
3		10	H	Aldershot T	W	2-1	1-0	2	McCallum (pen) [40], Stenson [76]	1109
4		13	A	Chorley	W	6-1	2-0	1	McCallum 2 (1 pen) [14, 65 (p)], Blissett 3 [41, 52, 58], Wright [83]	1020
5		17	H	Ebbsfleet U	W	2-1	1-1	1	Osborne [35], King (og) [80]	955
6		24	A	Woking	L	0-2	0-2	3		1997
7		26	H	Eastleigh	L	1-2	0-1	4	Hancox [69]	1779
8		31	A	FC Halifax T	L	1-2	0-1	7	Nicholls [56]	2053
9	Sept	3	A	Notts Co	D	0-0	0-0	7		4152
10		14	A	Barrow	L	0-3	0-2	12		1152
11		21	H	Yeovil T	L	0-1	0-0	15		1525
12		24	H	Stockport Co	W	2-0	0-0	10	Howe [52], Reckord [62]	1339
13		28	A	Barnet	D	0-0	0-0	13		1052
14	Oct	1	H	Wrexham	W	3-1	2-0	9	Osborne 2 [11, 70], Reckord [25]	1425
15		5	A	Boreham Wood	L	0-1	0-0	12		540
16		8	H	Sutton U	W	2-0	1-0	7	Beesley [20], Wright (pen) [73]	3043
17		12	H	Bromley	W	2-1	1-0	6	Gunning [41], Wright [53]	2120
18		26	A	Maidenhead U	L	0-1	0-0	9		1152
19	Nov	2	H	Dagenham & R	W	2-1	1-1	9	Ball [2], McCallum [59]	1214
20		5	A	Hartlepool U	W	1-0	0-0	6	Beesley [59]	2703
21		16	H	AFC Fylde	W	3-1	3-1	3	Wright [14], McCallum (pen) [19], Howe [25]	1389
22		23	A	Dover Ath	D	1-1	1-1	3	Osborne [28]	1027
23		26	A	Stockport Co	W	4-1	0-1	2	McCallum 2 [52, 67], Ball [58], Osborne [81]	3142
24	Dec	7	A	Wrexham	L	0-2	0-2	5		3113
25		26	A	Chesterfield	D	2-2	1-2	5	Ball [44], Wright [90]	3203
26		28	H	Notts Co	L	0-1	0-0	7		3212
27	Jan	1	H	Chesterfield	W	3-0	1-0	6	Beesley 2 [29, 70], McCallum [79]	1200
28		4	A	Yeovil T	D	0-0	0-0	6		2907
29		18	H	Boreham Wood	L	0-2	0-1	9		882
30		25	A	Sutton U	D	0-0	0-0	9		1618
31		28	H	Barrow	D	0-0	0-0	8		892
32	Feb	1	H	Maidenhead U	L	0-2	0-0	8		797
33		8	A	Bromley	D	2-2	0-0	9	Bush (og) [68], Carline [77]	1716
34		11	H	Barnet	W	1-0	1-0	6	Hawkridge (pen) [19]	501
35		22	A	Dagenham & R	L	0-2	0-2	8		2345
36		29	H	Dover Ath	W	3-0	1-0	6	Simpson (og) [36], Howe 2 [70, 82]	773
37	Mar	3	H	Hartlepool U	L	0-1	0-0	7		896
38		7	A	AFC Fylde	D	0-0	0-0	7		1310
39		13	H	Harrogate T	Cancelled					
40		21	A	Torquay U	Cancelled					
41		28	H	Chorley	Cancelled					
42	Apr	4	A	Aldershot T	Cancelled					
43		10	A	Eastleigh	Cancelled					
44		13	H	Woking	Cancelled					
45		18	A	Ebbsfleet U	Cancelled					
46		25	H	FC Halifax T	Cancelled					

Final League Position: 9 (on points-per-game basis)

GOALSCORERS

League (48): McCallum 9 (3 pens), Osborne 7, Wright 5 (1 pen), Beesley 4, Blissett 4, Howe 4, Ball 3, Hawkridge 2 (2 pens), Reckord 2, Carline 1, Gunning 1, Hancox 1, Nicholls 1, Stenson 1, own goals 3.
FA Cup (9): Ball 5, Daly 1, Gudger 1, McCallum 1, Osborne 1.
FA Trophy (2): Beesley 1, Jones 1.
Tunnock's Caramel Wafer Scottish League Challenge Cup (4): Carter 1, Howe 1, Stenson 1, Yussuf 1.

Boot 38	Reckord 27 + 5	Storer 34 + 1	Daly 16	Gudger 34	Osborne 24 + 1	McCallum 19 + 2	Hawkridge 19 + 12	Blissett 14 + 5	Vaughan 24 + 2	Howe 38	Carter 9 + 9	Wright 17 + 14	Stenson 2 + 5	Hancox 8 + 11	Carline 8 + 4	Williams 15 + 2	Nicholls 2 + 3	Neufville — + 10	Yussuf 3 + 6	Gunning 15	Ball 18 + 5	Beesley 22 + 1	Jones — + 3	Drysdale 3	Cowley 4 + 2	Maxwell — + 2	Bajrami 4	Clayton-Phillips 1 + 3	*Match No.*
1	2	3	4	5	6^2	7^1	8	9^3	10	11	12	13	14																1
1	2^3	7	3	4	8^1	10^2	9	11	5	6	12	14		13															2
1	2	3	4	5	6^2	7	8^1	9^3	10	11	12		13	14															3
1	2^3	7	4	5	8	10^1	9	11^2	3	6		12	13	14															4
1		2	3	4	5	6	8^2	9^1	10	11	13	12		7^3	14														5
1	3^1	4	5	6	7^3	9	13	12		11	8	10^2		14		2													6
1	2^1	3	4	5			7	8	9	11	6		10^2	12			13												7
1	6	7^1	3^3	4	8		10	11	5	2	14		13	9^2			12												8
1	4	5		6	7		9^2	10		2	8		12	13		3	11^1												9
1	3	6		4	7^1		9		14	5	8		11^3	13		2■	10^2	12											10
1	2^3	3	4	5	6		7^2		9^1	10	12	8					14	13	11										11
1	5	3	4	6	7^3	12	13		9	2		10^1						14	11^2	8									12
1	2	3	4	5	6^1	7^2	13		10^3	11		9						14	12	8									13
1	2	3	4	5	6^3	7^2	13		10	11		9^1						14	12	8									14
1	2	3	4	5^1	6				9^2	10		8				12		14	11^3	7	13								15
1	2	3^1	4	5	6				9	10		8^3						14	13	7	12	11^2							16
1	2	8	3	4	9^2		14		6	7		10^1						13		5^3	12	11							17
1	2	3	4	5	6^1	14	12		9	10		8^3								7^2	13	11							18
1	2	3		4		5^2	12		8	9		7							13	6	10^1	11							19
1	2	3		4		5^3	13		8	9		7^1						14	12	6^2	10	11							20
1	2			3	4	5^3	13	12	8	9		7^2						14		6^1	10	11							21
1	2	12		3	4	5		13	8	9		7^1								6	10	11^2							22
1	2	6		3	7^2	9	14	10^3	4	5									13		8	11^1	12						23
1	2^1	3		4	5	6		13	8	9		12				14				7^2	10	11^3							24
1	2	3		4	5^3	6	13	7^1	8	9		14									10	11^2	12						25
1	3^2	8		5	6^3	9^1	12			4		10			14	2					7	11	13						26
1	14	6		4	8^1	9		10^3		2		12			7	5				3	13	11^2							27
1	14	7		3	13	10^3			5^2	6		12			8	2				4	9^1	11							28
1	13	3		4■		5			12	9		8^3		14	6^2	2				7^1	10	11							29
1		6					7		4^1	5				12	8	2					9	11		3	10				30
1	3^3	4					6			9	14	12		13	7	2					10^1	11		5	8^2				31
1	3	4^2					6			9	14	12		13	7	2					10	11		5^3	8^1				32
1		5		3			8	9^3		2	6^2	10		7	12	4						11^1			14	13			33
1				3			6^2	7		9	4	8^3		5	14	2					10	11^1			12	13			34
1				2			5^2	7^3		10	3	12		4	6						11	14			8^1		9	13	35
1	12	3		4			7			9	5	14		6^1		2					10^3	11^2					8	13	36
1	13	3		4			6^3			8	12	14		5^1		2					9	10					7	11^2	37
1		6					9	13		2	7	12		8^2	4	5					10^1	11^3					3	14	38
																													39
																													40
																													41
																													42
																													43
																													44
																													45
																													46

FA Cup

Fourth Qualifying	Barrow	(a)	1-0
First Round	Oxford C	(a)	5-1
Second Round	Rotherham U	(h)	3-4

FA Trophy

First Round	Darlington	(h)	2-2
Replay	Darlington	(a)	0-1

Tunnock's Caramel Wafer Scottish League Challenge Cup

Third Round	Kelty Hearts	(a)	1-1
(Solihull Moors won 4-3 on penalties)			
Fourth Round	Rangers U21	(h)	3-3
(Rangers U21 won 4-3 on penalties)			

STOCKPORT COUNTY

Ground: Edgeley Park, Hardcastle Road, Edgeley, Stockport, Cheshire SK3 9DD. *Tel:* (0161) 286 8888.
Website: www.stockportcounty.com *Email:* mark.lockyear@stockportcounty.com *Year Formed:* 1883.
Record Attendance: 27,833 v Liverpool, FA Cup 5th rd, 11 February 1950. *Nickname:* 'County' or 'The Hatters'.
Manager: Jim Gannon. *Colours:* Blue shirts with yellow trim, blue shorts, white socks.

STOCKPORT COUNTY – NATIONAL LEAGUE 2019–20 LEAGUE RECORD

Match No.	*Date*	*Venue*	*Opponents*	*Result*	*H/T Score*	*Lg Pos.*	*Goalscorers*	*Attendance*
1	Aug 3	H	Maidenhead U	L 0-1	0-0	19		4626
2	6	A	Notts Co	D 1-1	0-1	20	Osborne ^{71}	5820
3	10	A	Yeovil T	D 1-1	0-1	22	Thomas ^{87}	2602
4	13	H	Barrow	W 3-2	0-1	13	Mulhern ^{48}, Keane ^{52}, Thomas ^{70}	4183
5	17	H	Eastleigh	W 2-0	0-0	8	Thomas ^{59}, Osborne ^{83}	3869
6	24	A	Harrogate T	L 1-2	0-0	11	Bell ^{69}	1326
7	26	H	Chesterfield	W 2-0	0-0	7	Osborne ^{46}, Bell ^{79}	5587
8	31	A	Wrexham	W 2-1	2-0	6	Palmer ^{19}, Minihan ^{39}	5777
9	Sept 3	H	AFC Fylde	W 2-1	2-0	5	Jackson, B ^{19}, Craigen (og) ^{21}	3912
10	7	A	Chorley	L 0-3	0-2	5		2693
11	14	H	Aldershot T	L 1-2	0-2	7	Piggott ^{75}	4279
12	21	A	Boreham Wood	L 0-4	0-3	9		744
13	24	A	Solihull Moors	L 0-2	0-0	12		1339
14	28	H	Torquay U	L 0-4	0-4	17		4275
15	Oct 5	A	Sutton U	D 0-0	0-0	17		1808
16	9	H	Hartlepool U	W 2-1	2-0	15	Palmer ^{5}, Walker, T ^{21}	3465
17	26	A	Dover Ath	W 1-0	1-0	17	Mulhern ^{31}	1154
18	29	A	Bromley	D 2-2	2-2	17	Osborne ^{24}, Walker, T ^{34}	2205
19	Nov 2	H	Woking	L 1-3	0-1	17	Mulhern ^{86}	3888
20	9	H	Dagenham & R	W 1-0	0-0	13	Bell ^{90}	3771
21	16	A	Barnet	W 2-1	0-0	11	Osborne ^{75}, Mulhern ^{90}	1536
22	23	H	Ebbsfleet U	D 1-1	0-1	10	Walker, S ^{90}	4167
23	26	H	Solihull Moors	L 1-4	1-0	13	Turnbull ^{45}	3142
24	30	A	Torquay U	W 5-1	0-0	8	Walker, T ^{47}, Bell ^{50}, Osborne ^{62}, Rodney ^{86}, Mulhern ^{90}	2659
25	Dec 7	H	Chorley	W 4-2	2-1	8	Bell 2 $^{27, 66}$, Arthur ^{45}, Walker, T ^{80}	4510
26	21	A	Aldershot T	L 1-2	0-1	9	Rodney ^{57}	1891
27	26	H	FC Halifax T	W 5-1	2-0	7	Arthur ^{24}, Osborne 3 $^{42, 52, 73}$, Brown (og) ^{61}	5536
28	28	A	AFC Fylde	W 2-1	0-1	5	Walker, T ^{53}, Cowan ^{61}	2764
29	Jan 1	A	FC Halifax T	D 0-0	0-0	5		3460
30	4	H	Boreham Wood	L 1-3	0-3	8	Rodney ^{51}	4074
31	18	H	Sutton U	D 0-0	0-0	8		5079
32	25	A	Hartlepool U	L 0-2	0-1	10		3766
33	Feb 1	H	Dover Ath	L 0-2	0-0	12		4506
34	8	A	Dagenham & R	D 1-1	0-0	11	McAlinden ^{89}	1512
35	15	H	Bromley	W 1-0	0-0	10	Hogan ^{53}	4611
36	22	A	Woking	D 1-1	1-1	10	Lloyd ^{6}	2189
37	29	A	Ebbsfleet U	W 1-0	0-0	7	Palmer ^{87}	1030
38	Mar 7	H	Barnet	D 1-1	1-1	9	Palmer ^{45}	5011
39	14	A	Maidenhead U	W 2-1	0-1	7	Palmer ^{57}, McAlinden ^{76}	1662
40	24	H	Notts Co	Cancelled				
41	28	A	Barrow	Cancelled				
42	Apr 4	H	Yeovil T	Cancelled				
43	10	A	Chesterfield	Cancelled				
44	13	H	Harrogate T	Cancelled				
45	18	A	Eastleigh	Cancelled				
46	25	H	Wrexham	Cancelled				

Final League Position: 8 (on points-per-game basis)

GOALSCORERS

League (51): Osborne 9, Bell 6, Mulhern 5, Palmer 5, Walker, T 5, Rodney 3, Thomas 3, Arthur 2, McAlinden 2, Cowan 1, Hogan 1, Jackson, B 1, Keane 1, Lloyd 1, Minihan 1, Piggott 1, Turnbull 1, Walker, S 1, own goals 2.
FA Cup (0).
FA Trophy (5): Thomas 2, Minihan 1, Palmer 1, Walker, T 1.

Hinchliffe 38	Minihan 31 + 4	Palmer 36	Keane 34 + 1	Cowan 27 + 4	Thomas 31 + 6	Turnbull 28 + 2	Dimaio 8 + 10	Walker S 24 + 4	Kirby 4 + 4	Mulhern 15 + 13	Osborne 31 + 7	Bell 16 + 21	Jackson B 10 + 14	Arthur 23 + 8	Curran — + 2	Downing — + 1	Piggott 1 + 1	Leesley 8 + 2	Ormson 1	Hammill 2 + 2	Walker T 14 + 1	Garratt 11	Rodney 9 + 3	Clarke 4	McAlinden 5 + 4	Archer 3	Lloyd 8	Maynard 1	Hogan 5	Bennett 1	*Match No.*
1	2	3	4	5	6³	7	8²	9	10¹	11	12	13	14																		1
1	2	5	6	3	7¹	4		8	11²	9	10	12	13																		2
1	5¹	2	3	4	12	7	14	8³	13	11	9	10²	6																		3
1	2	3	4	5	6	7	8³		12	11²	9	13	10¹	14																	4
1	2	3	5	4	10¹	7	8²		14	11³	9	12	6	13																	5
1	2	3	4	5	6³	7	8²	12	14	11¹	9	13	10																		6
1	2	3	4	5	6	7	13	8²	9	11¹	10³	12		14																	7
1	2	3	4	5	8	6²		7	10¹	14	9	11³		13	12																8
1	2	3	4	5	10		12	8		13	9³	11¹	7²	6		14															9
1	2¹	3	4	5	6	7	14	9			8²	12	10³		13		11														10
1	2¹	3	4	5	8	6³	14	7			9	11	12				13	10²													11
	12		5	3	2³	7	13	9		14	8¹	10	6²	4				11	1												12
1	2		4	5	10	7	9¹	6■		11²	12	13	14	3				8³													13
1	2		4	5	8	6	13			11¹	7	14	12	3				10³		9²											14
1	2	5	4	3	7	6		8		11¹	10	12						13		9²											15
1	2	3	4	12	10¹	7		8		13	14	9²		6				5			11³										16
1	2	3	14		9	6¹		7		11²	12	13		4							8	5	10³								17
1	2	3	7	14	6			9		11²	8¹	13	12	4							10³	5									18
1	2	3			8³	6		7		12	9		14	4						13	10²	5¹	11								19
1	2	3	4		5¹		14			6³	7	12	13	8							10	9²	11								20
1	2	3	6		14			7		12	8	11²	13	4							9³	5	10¹								21
1	2	3	8		14			12		10	6	13	11	4							7²	5³	9¹								22
1		3		2	6	7³		9		13	8²	11¹		4				5		14	12		10								23
1	2	3	6		8³			7		14	9	11¹	12	4							10²	5	13								24
1	2	4	5		12	3				13	6	7¹		8				14			10³	9	11²								25
1	2³	3	9		13	7		14		11¹	8²	12		4							6	5	10								26
1	2	3	6	14	8	7		13		12	9²	11³		4							10¹	5									27
1	13	4	5	3	12	14		6			7¹	10		2				9			8³		11²								28
1		3	4	2	6¹	7				13	8	11		5				10			9²		12								29
1	2¹	3	9	13	6³	7				14	8	11		4							10	5²	12								30
1		3	7	2	6²	9				13	8¹	14	12	4										5	10	11³					31
1	13	3	7	2	6	9¹					8	12		4										5²	14	11³	10				32
1		3	6	2	7	8■					12	13	14	4										5	10¹	9²	11³				33
1	12	3	7	2	6		8²					11³	14	4										5¹	13		10	9			34
1	2	3	6	5	8²		12	7			9³	13		14											11		10¹		4		35
1	2	3	6	5¹	8²			7			9	12	13	14											11³		10		4		36
1	8	3	6	2		12	14	7³			9¹	13	5												11²		10		4		37
1	5	2		6		7	4³	8			13	10¹	9²	14											12		11		3		38
1	2	3		5	8	6	9³	7			12			14											13		10¹		4	11²	39
																															40
																															41
																															42
																															43
																															44
																															45
																															46

FA Cup

Fourth Qualifying	York C	(a)	0-2

FA Trophy

First Round	Blyth Spartans	(h)	4-2
Second Round	Dorking W	(a)	1-1
Replay	Dorking W	(h)	0-4

SUTTON UNITED

Ground: The Borough Sports Ground, Gander Green Lane, Sutton, Surrey SM1 2EY. *Tel:* (0208) 644 4440.
Website: www.suttonunited.net *Email:* info@suttonunited.net *Year Formed:* 1898.
Record Attendance: 14,000 v Leeds U, FA Cup 4th rd, 24 January 1970. *Nickname:* 'The U's'.
Manager: Matt Gray. *Colours:* Amber shirts with chocolate trim, amber shorts with chocolate trim, amber socks with chocolate trim.

SUTTON UNITED – NATIONAL LEAGUE 2019–20 LEAGUE RECORD

Match No.	*Date*		*Venue*	*Opponents*	*Result*		*H/T Score*	*Lg Pos.*	*Goalscorers*	*Attendance*
1	Aug	3	A	Hartlepool U	W	3-1	2-1	2	Beautyman 2 [7, 23], Randall [90]	3812
2		6	H	Barnet	D	1-1	0-1	4	Beautyman [57]	1761
3		10	H	Chorley	D	2-2	1-2	7	Jarvis [14], Milsom [54]	1436
4		13	A	Eastleigh	D	1-1	1-1	11	Collins [14]	1750
5		17	A	Boreham Wood	W	1-0	0-0	6	Wright [82]	407
6		24	H	Dover Ath	L	1-2	1-1	8	Collins [45]	1552
7		26	A	Aldershot T	D	1-1	0-0	9	Collins (pen) [83]	1662
8		31	H	Maidenhead U	L	0-3	0-0	13		1554
9	Sept	3	A	Yeovil T	L	0-1	0-0	17		2279
10		7	H	Notts Co	D	1-1	1-0	16	Beautyman [11]	2059
11		14	A	Wrexham	D	1-1	0-0	17	Beautyman [63]	3824
12		21	H	Chesterfield	W	4-0	2-0	13	Jarvis 2 [23, 77], Wright [34], Beautyman [90]	1649
13		24	H	Dagenham & R	L	0-2	0-2	19		1513
14		28	A	Harrogate T	L	0-2	0-1	19		769
15	Oct	5	H	Stockport Co	D	0-0	0-0	18		1808
16		8	A	Solihull Moors	L	0-2	0-1	19		3043
17		26	H	Ebbsfleet U	L	2-3	1-1	21	Ajiboye [24], Bugiel [75]	1566
18		29	H	FC Halifax T	L	0-1	0-0	21		1326
19	Nov	2	A	Barrow	L	0-1	0-0	23		1827
20		16	A	Torquay U	W	2-1	1-1	21	Ajiboye [12], Beautyman [69]	2770
21		23	H	Bromley	L	0-2	0-1	22		1762
22		26	A	Dagenham & R	W	2-1	0-0	20	Eastmond [65], Wright [68]	1070
23		30	H	Harrogate T	W	3-1	1-0	20	Beautyman [29], Wright 2 [72, 87]	1490
24	Dec	7	A	Notts Co	D	1-1	0-1	21	Beautyman [76]	5652
25		10	A	AFC Fylde	D	0-0	0-0	19		1054
26		21	H	Wrexham	W	3-1	2-0	17	Bugiel 3 (1 pen) [12, 36, 66 (p)]	1637
27		26	A	Woking	W	2-0	2-0	16	Bugiel 2 [1, 29]	2257
28		28	H	Yeovil T	W	3-2	2-2	16	Beautyman [24], Goodliffe [42], Ajiboye [63]	2189
29	Jan	1	H	Woking	W	6-2	5-0	12	Beautyman 2 (1 pen) [8, 43 (p)], Goodliffe [17], Wright [27], Ajiboye [30], Dundas [90]	1965
30		4	A	Chesterfield	L	0-1	0-0	12		3283
31		18	A	Stockport Co	D	0-0	0-0	15		5079
32		25	H	Solihull Moors	D	0-0	0-0	15		1618
33	Feb	1	A	Ebbsfleet U	D	1-1	0-1	14	Beautyman [50]	979
34		22	H	Barrow	D	2-2	1-2	15	Beautyman 2 (1 pen) [45, 66 (p)]	1871
35		29	A	Bromley	W	1-0	1-0	15	Bugiel [16]	1909
36	Mar	3	A	FC Halifax T	L	0-1	0-0	15		1637
37		7	H	Torquay U	W	2-0	2-0	14	Milsom [19], Randall [37]	1842
38		14	H	Hartlepool U	D	1-1	1-0	14	Olaofe [3]	2126
39		17	H	AFC Fylde	Cancelled					
40		21	A	Barnet	Cancelled					
41		28	H	Eastleigh	Cancelled					
42	Apr	4	A	Chorley	Cancelled					
43		10	H	Aldershot T	Cancelled					
44		13	A	Dover Ath	Cancelled					
45		18	H	Boreham Wood	Cancelled					
46		25	A	Maidenhead U	Cancelled					

Final League Position: 15 (on points-per-game basis)

GOALSCORERS

League (47): Beautyman 15 (2 pens), Bugiel 7 (1 pen), Wright 6, Ajiboye 4, Collins 3 (1 pen), Jarvis 3, Goodliffe 2, Milsom 2, Randall 2, Dundas 1, Eastmond 1, Olaofe 1.
FA Cup (3): Beautyman 1, Bugiel 1, Wright 1.
FA Trophy (3): Bugiel 2, Beautyman 1 (1 pen).

Butler 19	Bennett 8	Barden 35	Goodliffe 35	Collins 16 + 1	Bolarinwa 13 + 4	Davis 26 + 1	Beautyman 34	Randall 17 + 6	Milsom 24 + 4	Jarvis 16 + 9	Ajiboye 29 + 8	Bugiel 24 + 6	Matsuzaka 5 + 4	Dundas — + 27	Kearney — + 3	Wright 18 + 10	Eastmond 21 + 3	Tuson-Firth 2 + 2	Wyatt 18 + 1	Reid 14 + 7	Tzanev 19	John 17	Kealy 1 + 2	Olaofe 4 + 1	Rowe 3	Brown W — + 1	*Match No.*
1	2	3	4^{3}	5	6^{2}	7	8	9	10	11^{1}	12	13	14														1
1	2	3	4	5	13	6^{2}	7	9	10	11^{3}	8^{1}	14		12													2
1	2	3	4	5	6^{2}		8	9	10	11^{3}	13	7^{1}		12	14												3
1	2	3	4	5	6		8	9^{3}	10	11^{2}	12	7^{1}	14			13											4
1	2	3	4	5	6	7			11		10^{3}	8^{2}		12		13	9^{1}	14									5
1	2^{2}		4	3	5	7	6		11	13	10	9^{1}				12	8^{3}	14									6
1			2	12	3	4	5		9	11	7^{3}		10^{2}	14		13	6	8^{1}									7
1	2		3	4^{1}	5	6^{3}	7		10	11^{2}	9	12■		14	13		8										8
1		2	3	4		5	6			11^{3}	8^{2}			13	14	12	7	9^{1}	10								9
1		2	3	4	13	5	6		9	10	8^{1}			12		11^{2}	7										10
1		2	3^{1}	4	5	6^{2}	7		10	11^{3}	9	13	14				8■		12								11
1		2	4	3	7		6	8^{2}	5	11^{1}	10	12		14		9^{3}				13							12
1		2	4	3	7		6	12	5	11^{2}	10^{3}			13		9^{1}	8			14							13
1		2	3	4	5^{1}		6	9^{2}	10	11	8^{3}			14		12	7			13							14
1		3^{3}	2	4^{1}		12	11	8^{2}	5	9	7		13			10	6			14							15
1	2^{1}	3^{3}	4		6	7	8		9	11^{2}	12		5	14		13				10							16
1		2	3^{3}			4	6	8^{1}	10	13	7	5	11	14		9^{2}				12							17
1		5^{2}	2			10	4	14	7	12	6^{1}	9	3			11^{3}	13			8							18
1		2^{1}	3			4	6	8^{3}	9	12	13	5^{2}	10			14	7			11							19
		5	2			6	7	13			9^{1}	11^{2}				12	8		3	10	1	4					20
		3^{1}		4		5	7	13		14	9	6^{2}				12	8		10	11^{3}	1	2					21
		4		5^{3}		6	7			14	9	10^{2}		12		11^{1}	8		3	13	1	2					22
		3	4			5^{1}	7				12	6^{2}		13		9	8		10	11	1	2					23
		3	4				6	12	13		8	5^{3}		14		9	7^{2}		10	11^{1}	1	2					24
		3	4			5	7	6		11^{3}	8^{1}	12		14		9^{2}			10	13	1	2					25
		5	3			6			14	13	7^{3}	10^{2}		12		11^{1}	8		4	9	1	2					26
		5	3			6		8		14	12	10^{2}		13		11^{3}	7		4	9^{1}	1	2					27
		4	3			5	6	12	9	10^{2}	8			13		11^{1}	7				1	2					28
		5	3		14		6	9^{3}	12		8^{2}	10^{1}		13		11	7		4		1	2					29
		8	3			9	4		5			10		12		11	7■			6^{1}	1	2					30
		5	4			6	7			12	8	11^{1}				10			3	9	1	2					31
		5	3			6	7				8	10				11			4	9	1	2					32
		2	3		13	5	7				8^{2}	6^{1}		12		9^{3}			10	11	1	4	14				33
		5	2			6^{1}	7	9	12		8	10^{3}		13					4		1	3	14	11^{2}			34
		2	3				5	8	10		7^{1}	4		12					9		1			11^{2}	6	13	35
		2	3		4			7^{2}	10		13	5^{3}		14					9	11	1		8^{1}	12	6		36
		2					5^{1}	7	10		8	4^{2}		13			12		9		1	3		11	6		37
		2	3				6	8	10		7	5^{2}		13			12		9		1	4		11^{1}			38
																											39
																											40
																											41
																											42
																											43
																											44
																											45
																											46

FA Cup

Fourth Qualifying	Billericay T	(h)	1-1
Replay	Billericay T	(a)	2-5

FA Trophy

First Round	Dagenham & R	(h)	1-1
Replay *aet.*	Dagenham & R	(a)	2-3

TORQUAY UNITED

Ground: Plainmoor, Marnham Road, Torquay, Devon TQ1 3PS. *Tel:* (01803) 328 666.
Website: www.torquayunited.com *Email:* reception@torquayunited.com *Year Formed:* 1899.
Record Attendance: 21,908 v Huddersfield T, FA Cup 4th rd, 29 January 1955. *Nickname:* 'The Gulls'.
Manager: Gary Johnson. *Colours:* Yellow shirts with blue trim, blue shorts, white socks.

TORQUAY UNITED – NATIONAL LEAGUE 2019–20 LEAGUE RECORD

Match No.	*Date*	*Venue*	*Opponents*	*Result*		*H/T Score*	*Lg Pos.*	*Goalscorers*	*Attendance*
1	Aug 3	H	Boreham Wood	W	2-1	0-0	4	Edwards 61, Reid 63	3138
2	6	A	Solihull Moors	L	0-3	0-3	16		1613
3	10	A	Bromley	D	3-3	1-2	13	Reid (pen) 35, Lemonheigh-Evans 63, Andrews 69	1398
4	13	H	Maidenhead U	L	0-2	0-1	18		2946
5	17	A	Dover Ath	W	2-1	0-0	13	Hall 50, Reid 52	1217
6	24	H	Aldershot T	W	2-0	1-0	7	Reid 45, Edwards 51	2668
7	26	A	Barnet	D	2-2	2-0	8	Koue Niate 5, Little 30	1621
8	31	H	Hartlepool U	L	1-2	0-1	10	Reid 51	2683
9	Sept 3	A	Woking	D	1-1	0-0	11	Whitfield 79	2599
10	7	H	Harrogate T	W	4-2	0-1	8	Andrews 51, Lumbombo Kalala 70, Reid 2 73, 80	2527
11	14	A	Chesterfield	L	0-1	0-1	10		3706
12	21	H	Dagenham & R	D	0-0	0-0	11		2524
13	24	H	Eastleigh	L	2-3	1-0	13	Whitfield 35, Andrews 55	2005
14	28	A	Stockport Co	W	4-0	4-0	10	Reid 2 (1 pen) 18 (p), 44, Arthur (og) 25, Keane (og) 42	4275
15	Oct 5	H	AFC Fylde	W	2-1	1-0	9	Lumbombo Kalala 8, Buse 90	2440
16	8	A	Ebbsfleet U	W	4-2	2-1	6	Andrews 8, Reid 24, Buse 47, Davis 54	908
17	12	A	Notts Co	L	0-2	0-1	9		5265
18	26	H	Barrow	W	4-2	2-1	7	Reid 2 (1 pen) 31, 43 (p), Little 2 51, 75	2280
19	29	H	Wrexham	W	1-0	0-0	6	Davis 56	2313
20	Nov 2	A	FC Halifax T	W	4-2	2-0	5	Cameron 8, Reid 2 (1 pen) 17 (p), 64, Lumbombo Kalala 90	2065
21	16	H	Sutton U	L	1-2	1-1	6	Wynter 32	2770
22	23	A	Chorley	L	0-1	0-1	8		1281
23	26	A	Eastleigh	L	2-3	0-3	8	Andrews 48, Keating 46	1888
24	30	H	Stockport Co	L	1-5	0-0	10	Whitfield 75	2659
25	Dec 7	A	Harrogate T	L	1-2	0-1	11	Reid (pen) 68	1348
26	21	H	Chesterfield	L	0-3	0-1	14		2288
27	26	A	Yeovil T	L	2-6	1-3	15	Hall 29, Whitfield 90	5056
28	28	H	Woking	W	4-1	2-1	14	Hall 25, Reid 37, Whitfield 71, Keating 90	2895
29	Jan 1	H	Yeovil T	L	0-2	0-1	15		4165
30	4	A	Dagenham & R	D	0-0	0-0	14		1542
31	18	A	AFC Fylde	W	3-2	2-1	13	Hall 15, Reid 29, Whitfield 60	1504
32	25	H	Ebbsfleet U	D	0-0	0-0	14		2300
33	Feb 1	A	Barrow	L	1-2	0-0	15	Cameron 63	2586
34	22	H	FC Halifax T	W	1-0	0-0	14	Azeez 68	2053
35	29	H	Chorley	W	2-0	1-0	14	Cundy 45, Reid 80	2126
36	Mar 7	A	Sutton U	L	0-2	0-2	15		1842
37	14	A	Boreham Wood	Cancelled					
38	17	H	Notts Co	Cancelled					
39	21	H	Solihull Moors	Cancelled					
40	24	A	Wrexham	Cancelled					
41	28	A	Maidenhead U	Cancelled					
42	Apr 4	H	Bromley	Cancelled					
43	10	H	Barnet	Cancelled					
44	13	A	Torquay U	Cancelled					
45	18	H	Dover Ath	Cancelled					
46	25	A	Hartlepool U	Cancelled					

Final League Position: 14 (on points-per-game basis)

GOALSCORERS

League (56): Reid 18 (5 pens), Whitfield 6, Andrews 5, Hall 4, Little 3, Lumbombo Kalala 3, Buse 2, Cameron 2, Davis 2, Edwards 2, Keating 2, Azeez 1, Cundy 1, Koue Niate 1, Lemonheigh-Evans 1, Wynter 1, own goals 2.
FA Cup (3): Andrews 1, Reid 1, Whitfield 1.
FA Trophy (6): Janneh 2, Reid 2 (1 pen), Keating 1, Lemonheigh-Evans 1.

MacDonald 11	Wynter 27 + 2	Cameron 34	Koue Niate 13 + 2	Hall 19	Duku 4 + 11	Little 12 + 5	Andrews 23 + 9	Vincent 16 + 3	Reid 32	Lumbombo Kalala 18 + 14	Lemonheigh-Evans 20 + 2	Edwards 2 + 5	Keating 6 + 13	Lewis 16 + 9	Covolan 25	Davis 16	Touray — + 1	Whitfield 27 + 1	Cundy 25	Dickson 1 + 1	Buse 15 + 2	Koszela — + 2	Janneh 7 + 1	Medford-Smith 4	Bansal-McNulty 2	Lewington 1 + 7	James 2 + 2	Nemane 6 + 3	Longridge 6	Warren 3	Azeez 3	Match No.
1	2	3	4	5	6[1]	7	8[3]	9	10	11[2]	12	13	14																			1
1	2	3	4	6	12	7	14		11	13	10	8[2]	9[3]	5[1]																		2
1	2	3	4	7		8[1]	9[3]	5[2]	11	6	10	12	14	13																		3
1	2	3	4[3]	5[1]	12	6	7[2]	8	10	11	9		14	13																		4
	2	3	4	6▪		7	9		11[1]	8[3]	10[2]	12	13		1	5	14															5
	2	4	3		14	7	8[1]	13	10	9[3]	11	6[2]	12		1	5																6
	2	4	5	6	14	7	8[2]	13	10	11[3]	9		12		1	3[1]																7
	2[2]	3	4	7	12	8	9[3]	13	11	6[1]	10			14	1	5																8
	2	3		6	9	7[1]	13	8[2]	11	14	10[3]			4	1	5		12														9
	2	4			9[1]		10[3]	7	11	12				3[2]	1	6		8	5	13	14											10
	2	3			10[1]			7	11	8					1	6		9	5	4[2]	12	13										11
	2	3					13	7	11	9[1]			12	4[2]	1	6		10	5		8											12
	2	4			13		6[2]	7	9	12			5		1	3		11[1]	10		8											13
	2	4			13		10[1]	6	11	9[2]			12	14	1	5		7[3]	3		8											14
	2	3				12	10	6[2]	11	8[1]				13	1	5		9	4		7											15
	2	4			12	13	5	6	8[1]	9[2]					1	3		11	10		7											16
	3	4			13	12	11[1]	5[2]	10	8					1	7		9	2		6											17
	2	4				5	6[3]	7[2]	9	13		12		14	1	3		11[1]	10		8											18
1	2	4					5[3]	6[1]	8	9[2]		13		14		3		11	10		7		12									19
	2	4	14				5	6[3]	8	12				13	1	3		11[1]	9		7		10[2]									20
	5	6	2[3]		13			8[2]	10	12					1			7[1]	4		9	14	11	3								21
1	4	5			13		11			8[2]			12	6[1]				9	3		7		10	2								22
	2	3	4[2]				10			13			9	12	1			8	5		7		11	6[1]								23
1	2	3		5[3]					10[1]	13	12							9	6		7		11	4	8[2]	14						24
	2	3	13				7		9	5[2]	8		12	4	1			11	10[1]						6[3]	14						25
1	2	3	4							12	7		14	5				11			6[3]		8▪			13	9[2]	10[1]				26
1	2	3		5			9[2]			13[3]	10		14					8	4		6[1]					11	7	12				27
		2	3	6[1]			12		8		7		5	4	1			11[3]	9							13	14	10[2]				28
		2	3▪	6[1]			12		11		10		9	4[2]	1			8	5							14	13	7[3]				29
		4		6			8		10		9		7	2	1			5	3				11									30
				3		12	13		5[3]	6[1]	4		14	2	1			11	9									10[2]	7	8		31
				6[1]		12	13		11	7[3]	10			2	1			9	5							14		8[2]	3	4		32
		2		4		5[2]	13		7	12	6[1]			3	1			11[3]								14		10	8	9		33
	14	2		4		6[1]	12		8	13	7			3	1			11[3]	10										9		5[2]	34
1		2		7			9		10		8[1]			3				6	5									12	4		11	35
1	12	2		4[1]			6		8	13	7			3				11	10									14	9[2]		5[3]	36
																																37
																																38
																																39
																																40
																																41
																																42
																																43
																																44
																																45
																																46

FA Cup

Fourth Qualifying	Boreham Wood	(h)	3-2
First Round	Maidstone U	(a)	0-1

FA Trophy

First Round	Aldershot T	(h)	5-1
Second Round	FC Halifax T	(h)	1-2

WOKING

Ground: The Laithwaite Community Stadium, Kingfield, Woking, Surrey GU22 9AA. *Tel:* (01483) 722 470.
Website: wokingfc.co.uk *Email:* admin@wokingfc.co.uk *Year Formed:* 1889.
Record Attendance: 7,020 v Finchley, FA Amateur Cup 4th rd, 1957–58. *Nickname:* 'The Cardinals'.
Manager: Alan Dowson. *Colours:* Red and white halved shirts, black shorts, white socks.

WOKING – NATIONAL LEAGUE 2019–20 LEAGUE RECORD

Match No.	*Date*		*Venue*	*Opponents*	*Result*		*H/T Score*	*Lg Pos.*	*Goalscorers*	*Attendance*
1	Aug	3	A	Dagenham & R	W	2-0	1-0	3	Ferdinand [7], Diarra [53]	1549
2		6	H	Aldershot T	L	0-1	0-1	10		3922
3		10	H	Harrogate T	W	1-0	1-0	5	Donnellan [19]	1470
4		13	A	Chesterfield	W	2-1	0-0	3	Meite [52], Tarpey [60]	3927
5		17	A	AFC Fylde	W	4-1	2-0	2	Tarpey [17], Ferdinand [39], Hyde 2 (1 pen) [83, 86 (p)]	1172
6		24	H	Solihull Moors	W	2-0	2-0	1	Hyde [12], Parry [16]	1997
7		26	A	Dover Ath	W	2-1	1-1	1	Hyde [42], Edser [88]	1358
8		31	H	Barrow	W	3-2	0-1	1	Johnson [51], Hyde 2 (1 pen) [67 (p), 78]	1787
9	Sept	3	H	Torquay U	D	1-1	0-0	2	Tarpey [53]	2599
10		7	A	Hartlepool U	D	1-1	0-1	1	Hodges [79]	3429
11		14	H	Ebbsfleet U	D	2-2	1-0	1	Johnson [8], Hyde [77]	1942
12		21	A	Chorley	D	1-1	1-1	3	Tarpey [22]	1346
13		24	A	Bromley	L	0-1	0-1	3		2358
14		28	H	Boreham Wood	L	1-2	1-1	4	Ferdinand [11]	2219
15	Oct	5	H	Wrexham	D	1-1	0-0	4	Ferdinand [76]	2061
16		8	A	Yeovil T	L	1-3	0-3	5	Meite [67]	3397
17		12	A	Barnet	D	2-2	1-0	7	Gerring [15], Shelton [53]	1651
18		26	H	Eastleigh	D	1-1	0-0	6	Loza [90]	1910
19		29	H	Notts Co	L	0-4	0-2	8		2175
20	Nov	2	A	Stockport Co	W	3-1	1-0	8	Hyde 2 [22, 76], Tarpey [69]	3888
21		16	H	FC Halifax T	D	0-0	0-0	8		2242
22		23	A	Maidenhead U	W	3-2	2-0	7	Diarra [10], Loza [44], Hyde [75]	1307
23		26	H	Bromley	W	2-1	1-1	4	Tarpey [43], Hyde [74]	1769
24		30	A	Boreham Wood	L	0-1	0-1	5		682
25	Dec	7	H	Hartlepool U	W	2-1	0-1	4	Hyde [66], Tarpey [78]	2127
26		26	H	Sutton U	L	0-2	0-2	6		2257
27		28	A	Torquay U	L	1-4	1-2	9	Hyde [12]	2895
28	Jan	1	A	Sutton U	L	2-6	0-5	10	Meite 2 [73, 87]	1965
29		4	H	Chorley	W	1-0	0-0	9	Tarpey [51]	1748
30		18	A	Wrexham	L	0-3	0-1	10		3671
31		25	H	Yeovil T	W	1-0	1-0	8	Donnellan [21]	2642
32		28	A	Ebbsfleet U	L	1-2	0-0	9	Hyde (pen) [53]	674
33	Feb	1	A	Eastleigh	L	0-2	0-2	10		1885
34		15	A	Notts Co	D	1-1	0-0	11	Kretzschmar [50]	5074
35		22	H	Stockport Co	D	1-1	1-1	13	Wall [11]	2189
36		29	H	Maidenhead U	W	2-0	0-0	9	Jarvis [62], Hyde [83]	2019
37	Mar	7	A	FC Halifax T	W	2-0	2-0	8	Kretzschmar (pen) [15], Hyde [44]	1995
38		10	H	Barnet	L	1-3	0-1	9	Cook [85]	1486
39		14	H	Dagenham & R	Cancelled					
40		21	A	Aldershot T	Cancelled					
41		28	H	Chesterfield	Cancelled					
42	Apr	4	A	Harrogate T	Cancelled					
43		10	H	Dover Ath	Cancelled					
44		13	A	Solihull Moors	Cancelled					
45		18	H	AFC Fylde	Cancelled					
46		25	A	Barrow	Cancelled					

Final League Position: 10 (on points-per-game basis)

GOALSCORERS

League (50): Hyde 16 (3 pens), Tarpey 8, Ferdinand 4, Meite 4, Diarra 2, Donnellan 2, Johnson 2, Kretzschmar 2 (1 pen), Loza 2, Cook 1, Edser 1, Gerring 1, Hodges 1, Jarvis 1, Parry 1, Shelton 1, Wall 1.
FA Cup (1): Kretzchmar 1 (1 pen).
FA Trophy (1): Kretzschmar 1 (1 pen).

Ross 36	Cook 33 + 1	Parry 17 + 2	Gerring 32	Diarra 31 + 1	Casey 35	Ferdinand 32 + 2	Donnellan 25 + 5	Kretzschmar 13 + 11	Hyde 28 + 4	Tarpey 34 + 2	Meite 5 + 10	Poku 18 + 8	Johnson 9 + 3	Collier 7 + 7	Edser 11 + 2	Hodges 1 + 16	Loza 22 + 2	Tiehi — + 1	Shelton 3	Rea 7	Gray 2 + 3	Howes 2	Wareham — + 3	Neufville 3 + 5	Wall 4 + 3	Harris 3	Dempsey 5	Jarvis — + 2	Match No.
1	2	3	4	5	6	7	8	9^{1}	10^{2}	11^{3}	12	13	14																1
1	2	3	4	5	6	7	8^{2}	9^{1}	10^{3}	11	12	14	13																2
1	5	2	3	4^{1}	9	7	8		14	10^{3}	11^{2}	6	13	12															3
1	2	3	4		5	7	6		12	10^{3}	11^{2}	14	9		8^{1}	13													4
1	2	3	4		5	6	7		12	10^{2}	11^{1}	14	9		8^{3}	13													5
1	2	3	4		5	6	8^{1}		9	10^{2}	13	12	11	14	7^{3}														6
1	2	3	4		5	6	7^{2}		10^{1}	9^{3}	12	14	11		8	13													7
1	2	4	3^{2}	12	5	7	6		11^{3}	10	14	13	9		8^{1}														8
1	2		3	4	5		6^{1}		11^{2}	10	13	7	9	12	8														9
1	2		3	4	5	6			10	9		7	11		8^{1}	12													10
1	2	12	4^{1}	5	3	6			11	10		7	8^{2}	13	9^{3}	14													11
1	2	14	3■	4	5	6			10^{3}	9		7	11^{2}		8^{1}	12	13												12
1	2	4		5	3	7	6^{3}	8^{1}				10^{2}		9	14	13	11	12											13
1	2	4		5	3	6			10	9		7^{1}			8	12	11												14
1	2	4		6	3	8	5	14	9^{3}	10^{2}	13				7^{1}	12	11												15
1	2	4	5^{3}	7	3	8	6	13		11	12	9^{2}				14	10^{1}												16
1	14	3	4		2	5	12	6^{2}		11	10			7	13		9^{3}		8^{1}										17
1			3	4	2	13		7^{2}	6	5^{1}	14			8		12	10		9	11^{3}									18
1	2		4	5	3	7	12		8	6							10		9	11^{1}									19
1	2		4	5	3	7	9		8	6							10			11									20
1	5		7	4	6	8	3^{1}	12	9	11						13	10			2^{2}									21
1	2		4	5	3		7	12	10	9^{2}		8^{1}					11			6	13								22
1	2		5	4	3		6	13	11	10		8^{1}		12			9^{2}			7									23
1	2		4	5	3		9	8^{1}	7	6						12	10■			11^{2}	13								24
1	2		4		3	6	11^{1}	8	7	5^{2}		10		9		12					13								25
1	2		4	5	3	7	6^{2}	13	10	9		8^{1}				12	11												26
	2		3	4		12		7	6	5		9■		8^{2}		13	10				11^{1}	1							27
	2	3^{1}	4	5		7	6	12			10			8		9^{3}	13				11^{2}	1	14						28
1	2		3	4		6	5	12	11^{2}	10^{1}	13	8		7			9												29
1	2		4	5	3	7	10^{1}		8^{2}	6^{3}		9		14			11■							12	13				30
1		3		4	2	6	5	13	9	11^{1}		7^{3}		14										10	12	8^{2}			31
1		3		4	2	6	5	12	10	13		7												9	11^{1}	8^{2}			32
1		3		4	2	5	8	13	6^{3}	14		7^{1}					11							10	12	9^{2}			33
1	2		4	5	3	7	13	8		6^{2}							10							12	11^{1}		9		34
1	2		4	5	3	7		8		6^{2}		13					10							12	11		9^{1}		35
1	2		4	5	3	6	14	7^{1}	12	11^{2}							9								10^{3}		8	13	36
1	2		4	5	3	7	14	9	8^{2}	6^{3}							11^{1}						13	12			10		37
1	2		4	5	3	7		9^{1}	8	6^{3}							11						14	13			10^{2}	12	38
																													39
																													40
																													41
																													42
																													43
																													44
																													45
																													46

FA Cup

Fourth Qualifying	Ebbsfleet U	(a)	1-1
Replay	Ebbsfleet U	(h)	0-1

FA Trophy

First Round	Kingstonian	(a)	1-3

WREXHAM

Ground: Racecourse Ground, Mold Road, Wrexham, Wales LL11 2AH. *Tel:* (01978) 891 864.
Website: wrexhamafc.co.uk *Email:* info@wrexhamfc.tv *Year Formed:* 1872.
Record Attendance: 34,445 v Manchester U, FA Cup 4th rd, 26 January 1957. *Nickname:* 'Red Dragons'.
Manager: Dean Keates. *Colours:* Red shirts with white trim, white shorts with red trim, white socks with red trim.

WREXHAM – NATIONAL LEAGUE 2019–20 LEAGUE RECORD

Match No.	*Date*	*Venue*	*Opponents*	*Result*		*H/T Score*	*Lg Pos.*	*Goalscorers*	*Attendance*
1	Aug 3	H	Barrow	W	2-1	0-1	4	Hooper [47], Grant [61]	5941
2	6	A	Boreham Wood	D	2-2	1-0	6	Harris, M [13], Grant [69]	845
3	10	A	Dover Ath	L	1-2	1-0	10	Harris, M [36]	1187
4	13	H	FC Halifax T	W	1-0	0-0	9	Harris, M [78]	5517
5	18	A	Notts Co	D	1-1	0-0	9	Redmond [74]	6263
6	24	H	Barnet	D	1-1	1-1	9	Hooper [2]	4533
7	26	A	Hartlepool U	L	2-4	1-1	13	Wright [38], Grant (pen) [56]	3462
8	31	H	Stockport Co	L	1-2	0-2	16	McIntosh [84]	5777
9	Sept 3	H	Maidenhead U	D	2-2	1-1	16	Young [63], Oswell [39]	3667
10	14	H	Sutton U	D	1-1	0-0	19	Grant (pen) [88]	3824
11	21	A	Aldershot T	L	0-1	0-0	21		1673
12	24	A	AFC Fylde	L	2-3	2-1	21	Lawlor [8], Oswell [45]	1289
13	28	H	Ebbsfleet U	W	1-0	0-0	20	Rutherford [74]	3627
14	Oct 1	A	Solihull Moors	L	1-3	0-2	20	Grant [63]	1425
15	5	A	Woking	D	1-1	0-0	20	Jennings [48]	2061
16	8	H	Harrogate T	D	1-1	1-0	20	Grant [6]	3435
17	15	H	Chesterfield	L	0-1	0-1	21		3479
18	26	A	Dagenham & R	L	1-2	0-1	22	Young [51]	1254
19	29	A	Torquay U	L	0-1	0-0	22		2313
20	Nov 2	H	Bromley	W	1-0	0-0	21	Young [77]	3469
21	23	H	Yeovil T	D	3-3	2-2	21	Wright [23], Rutherford [45], Grant [47]	3583
22	26	H	AFC Fylde	L	0-1	0-1	22		2941
23	30	A	Ebbsfleet U	L	1-2	1-1	24	Kennedy [30]	1036
24	Dec 3	A	Eastleigh	W	2-0	2-0	21	Patrick 2 [16, 41]	1542
25	7	H	Solihull Moors	W	2-0	2-0	20	Patrick [21], Jennings [45]	3113
26	21	A	Sutton U	L	1-3	0-2	21	Jennings [90]	1637
27	26	H	Chorley	W	3-1	2-0	21	Hooper 2 [6, 10], Patrick [88]	4784
28	28	A	Maidenhead U	L	0-2	0-1	21		1472
29	Jan 1	A	Chorley	W	2-0	0-0	19	Redmond [72], Patrick [80]	1684
30	4	H	Aldershot T	L	1-2	0-0	20	Hooper [90]	4222
31	18	H	Woking	W	3-0	1-0	18	Summerfield 2 (1 pen) [14, 78 (p)], Jarvis [47]	3671
32	25	A	Harrogate T	W	2-0	1-0	16	Jennings [11], Hooper [74]	2415
33	Feb 1	H	Dagenham & R	D	0-0	0-0	19		4024
34	8	A	Chesterfield	L	2-3	1-1	19	Evans (og) [21], Ponticelli [68]	3728
35	22	A	Bromley	W	2-0	1-0	17	Keillor-Dunn [11], Ponticelli [89]	1743
36	29	A	Yeovil T	L	0-3	0-1	17		3040
37	Mar 7	H	Eastleigh	D	0-0	0-0	19		3436
38	14	A	Barrow	Cancelled					
39	21	H	Boreham Wood	Cancelled					
40	24	H	Torquay U	Cancelled					
41	28	A	FC Halifax T	Cancelled					
42	Apr 4	H	Dover Ath	Cancelled					
43	10	H	Hartlepool U	Cancelled					
44	13	A	Barnet	Cancelled					
45	18	H	Notts Co	Cancelled					
46	25	A	Stockport Co	Cancelled					

Final League Position: 19 (on points-per-game basis)

GOALSCORERS

League (46): Grant 7 (2 pens), Hooper 6, Patrick 5, Jennings 4, Harris, M 3, Young 3, Oswell 2, Ponticelli 2, Redmond 2, Rutherford 2, Summerfield 2 (1 pen), Wright 2, Jarvis 1, Keillor-Dunn 1, Kennedy 1, Lawlor 1, McIntosh 1, own goal 1.
FA Cup (2): Grant 1, Hooper 1.
FA Trophy (0).
Tunnock's Caramel Wafer Scottish League Challenge Cup (5): McIntosh 2 (1 pen), Bickerstaff 1, Redmond 1, Tollitt 1.

Dibble 16	Jennings 30	Pearson 31	Lawlor 31	Summerfield 26 + 4	Young 36 + 1	Redmond 15 + 5	Grant 25 + 2	Carrington 21 + 3	Harris M 12 + 12	Hooper 16 + 3	Rutherford 19 + 14	McIntosh 1 + 7	Oswell 9 + 11	Chambers 11 + 1	Barnum-Bobb 10	Wright 12 + 3	Tollitt 5 + 7	Barton 6 + 1	Lainton 21	Horsfield 3	Reid 4 + 2	Kennedy 15 + 1	Patrick 7 + 3	Jarvis 6	Keillor-Dunn 3 + 3	Ponticelli 4 + 1	Thompson 5	Harris J 4 + 1	Garratt 3	Barker — + 1	*Match No.*
1	2	3	4	5	6	7^1	8	9	10^3	11^2	12	13	14																		1
1	2	3	4	5	6	7^1	9	8	10	11	12																				2
1	2	3	4	5	6	7^2	8■	9	10^1	11^3	13		14	12																	3
1	3	4	5■	6	7	8^1		12	9	10^3	13	11^2	14		2																4
1	3	4		5	6^2	7^1			10	11	8	13		9	2	12															5
1	3	4		5^1	6	7^2			10	11	8^3	13		9	2		12	14													6
1		3	5■		14	6^2	10	7	13	9^1		12			2	8	11^3	4													7
1		3		4	5	6^2	7	9	11			12	8^1	10	2		13														8
1	2	3		5^1	6	13	10	7			12	14	11	4		8^2	9^3														9
1	2	3		4^1	5	13	7	8	11		14		12	10		9^2	6^3														10
1	2	5		13	8		9	6	11^2		14		10	3		7^1	12	4^3													11
1	3	4	5^3	6	7	8^1	13		11^2		14	12	9	10	2																12
1	4^3	3	5	8	9	6^1	13	7	10^2	14	12		11		2																13
1	3	4	5	6	7		8	10	13	12	11		9^2		2^1																14
1	4		5	6	8		11	7^1	12		9		10	2				3													15
1	3	4	6	7	8		10				9		11		2		12	5^1													16
	5		3	6^3	8		11		12		9^2		10^1	4	2	14	13	7	1												17
	2		3	14	4	13	5		12	11^3	6^2			10		9		7^1	1	8											18
	2		3	4^2	5	14	6		11^3		7^1		12	10		9	13		1	8											19
	2	3	4	5	6		11	13	12		7					9	10^1		1	8^2											20
		2	3	4	5		7	8			9					11	6^1		1		10^2	12	13								21
	2	3	4	5^1	6	14	10	7	12		8^2					9^3	13		1				11								22
	2	3	5	6	8		10		12		9^1					7			1			4	11								23
	2	3	5		6		10^1	7	12		8		13			9			1			4	11^2								24
	2	3	4		5		6	7			8		12			11			1			9	10^1								25
	2	3	5	12	6	7^3	10^2	8	14	13	9								1			4	11^1								26
	6	5	4	7	9	8^2	10			11^1	12								1		2	3	13								27
	2	3	6^2	7	8	9^3	10	14		11	12								1		4^1	5	13								28
	2		3		5	6	9	7	14	11^3	8^1		13						1		12	4	10^2								29
	2		3	12	4	5	6^2	7	13	11									1		10^1	8	9								30
	2	3	4	5	6			7^1		11^2	8		14						1		13	9		10^3	12						31
	2	3	4	5	6			7		11^2	8								1			9		10^1	12	13					32
	2^2	3	4	5	6					11	7								1			8		10^1	13		9	12			33
		5^1	7	8	9					11	12								1			3				10	2	6	4		34
		5	6		7						13		14			12			1			3^2		9	10^1	11^3	2	8	4		35
		2^2	3		4								12						1			7		10^1	11	5	8	9	6	13	36
		4	5		6			7			12								1			3		10^1	9	11	2	8			37
																															38
																															39
																															40
																															41
																															42
																															43
																															44
																															45
																															46

FA Cup

Fourth Qualifying	Chesterfield	(a)	1-1
Replay	Chesterfield	(h)	1-0
First Round	Rochdale	(h)	0-0
Replay	Rochdale	(a)	0-1

FA Trophy

First Round	FC Halifax T	(a)	0-4

Tunnock's Caramel Wafer Scottish League Challenge Cup

Third Round	Ayr U	(h)	1-1
(Wrexham won 6-5 on penalties)			
Fourth Round	St Mirren U21	(h)	4-1
Quarter-Finals	Rangers U21	(a)	0-2

YEOVIL TOWN

Ground: Huish Park, Lufton Way, Yeovil, Somerset BA22 8YF. *Tel:* (01935) 423 662. *Website:* www.ytfc.net *Email:* info@ytfc.net *Year Formed:* 1895. *Record Attendance:* 16,318 v Sunderland, FA Cup 4th rd, 29 January 1949 (at Huish); 9,527 v Leeds U, FL 1, 25 April 2008 (at Huish Park). *Nickname:* 'The Glovers'. *Manager:* Darren Sarll. *Colours:* Green and white hooped shirts, white shorts with green trim, white socks with green trim.

YEOVIL TOWN – NATIONAL LEAGUE 2019–20 LEAGUE RECORD

Match No.	Date	Venue	Opponents	Result	H/T Score	Lg Pos.	Goalscorers	Attendance
1	Aug 3	A	Barnet	L 0-1	0-0	19		1666
2	6	H	Eastleigh	W 1-0	1-0	13	Duffus [2]	2813
3	10	H	Stockport Co	D 1-1	1-0	11	Duffus [21]	2602
4	13	A	Ebbsfleet U	W 3-1	1-0	7	Murphy [27], Hutton [47], Whelan [81]	1057
5	17	A	Barrow	L 0-1	0-0	12		1218
6	24	H	Maidenhead U	L 1-2	0-0	13	Duffus [86]	2179
7	26	A	Dagenham & R	L 2-3	0-0	18	Murphy [46], Worthington [82]	1453
8	31	H	Notts Co	W 3-1	1-0	12	Duffus [40], Wilkinson [81], Hippolyte [84]	2424
9	Sept 3	H	Sutton U	W 1-0	0-0	9	Bradbury [68]	2279
10	7	A	FC Halifax T	W 2-0	1-0	6	Omotayo 2 [4, 66]	2341
11	14	H	AFC Fylde	W 3-2	2-0	4	Murphy [5], Hippolyte [14], Smith, J [78]	2395
12	21	A	Solihull Moors	W 1-0	0-0	4	Wilkinson [57]	1525
13	24	A	Aldershot T	W 3-1	2-1	4	Hippolyte [8], Smith, J [38], Murphy [59]	1684
14	28	H	Bromley	W 3-1	1-1	3	Smith, J [45], Okoye (og) [72], Lee [77]	3960
15	Oct 5	A	Hartlepool U	L 1-2	0-0	3	Murphy [90]	3273
16	8	H	Woking	W 3-1	3-0	3	Murphy 2 [12, 41], Smith, J [45]	3397
17	12	H	Harrogate T	L 1-2	0-0	3	Murphy [90]	3237
18	26	A	Chorley	W 2-1	1-0	2	Worthington [8], Murphy [86]	1279
19	Nov 2	H	Boreham Wood	D 1-1	1-0	2	Smith, J [7]	2879
20	16	H	Dover Ath	L 0-1	0-0	5		2986
21	23	A	Wrexham	D 3-3	2-2	5	Murphy 3 [4, 39, 67]	3583
22	26	H	Aldershot T	D 2-2	1-1	6	Skendi [38], Murphy (pen) [72]	2545
23	30	A	Bromley	D 1-1	0-0	4	Murphy [90]	2261
24	Dec 7	H	FC Halifax T	W 2-0	1-0	3	Duffus 2 [34, 90]	2975
25	10	A	Chesterfield	W 2-1	2-0	2	Hippolyte [2], Murphy (pen) [24]	3161
26	21	A	AFC Fylde	D 2-2	0-1	2	Duffus 2 [79, 80]	1427
27	26	H	Torquay U	W 6-2	3-1	2	Hippolyte [3], Skendi [7], Duffus 3 [15, 60, 87], Dagnall [72]	5056
28	28	A	Sutton U	L 2-3	2-2	2	Murphy [26], Skendi [38]	2189
29	Jan 1	A	Torquay U	W 2-0	1-0	2	Duffus [16], Murphy [90]	4165
30	4	H	Solihull Moors	D 0-0	0-0	2		2907
31	18	H	Hartlepool U	D 2-2	2-1	3	Worthington [23], Lee [42]	2716
32	25	A	Woking	L 0-1	0-1	3		2642
33	Feb 1	H	Chorley	D 1-1	0-1	4	Richards, M [88]	2729
34	11	A	Harrogate T	L 0-3	0-1	4		801
35	22	A	Boreham Wood	L 0-1	0-0	5		1040
36	29	H	Wrexham	W 3-0	1-0	3	Duffus [42], Wilkinson [55], Skendi [90]	3040
37	Mar 7	A	Dover Ath	W 1-0	0-0	3	Richards, M [47]	1180
38	14	H	Barnet	Cancelled				
39	21	A	Eastleigh	Cancelled				
40	24	H	Chesterfield	Cancelled				
41	28	H	Ebbsfleet U	Cancelled				
42	Apr 4	A	Stockport Co	Cancelled				
43	10	H	Dagenham & R	Cancelled				
44	13	A	Maidenhead U	Cancelled				
45	18	H	Barrow	Cancelled				
46	25	A	Notts Co	Cancelled				

Final League Position: 4 (on points-per-game basis)

GOALSCORERS

League (61): Murphy 17 (2 pens), Duffus 13, Hippolyte 5, Smith, J 5, Skendi 4, Wilkinson 3, Worthington 3, Lee 2, Omotayo 2, Richards, M 2, Bradbury 1, Dagnall 1, Hutton 1, Whelan 1, own goal 1.
FA Cup (4): Dagnall 2, D'Ath 1, Wilkinson 1.
FA Trophy (8): Duffus 3, Murphy 3, Bradbury 1, Dagnall 1.
National League Play-Offs (0).

Nelson 22 + 1	Alcock 14 + 3	Collins 26 + 1	Bradbury 16 + 3	Hutton 23 + 4	Worthington 23 + 8	D'Ath 21 + 4	Hippolyte 29 + 2	Skendi 26 + 10	Whelan 6 + 2	Murphy 28 + 2	Seager — + 2	Shako — + 1	Duffus 25 + 6	Ojo — + 1	McCoy — + 5	Dickinson 26 + 1	Lee 30 + 2	Rogers 1 + 2	Wilkinson 25 + 1	Brzozowski 2	Omotayo 10 + 4	O'Brien 6	Tilley 6 + 13	Smith J 17 + 3	Smith A 5	Dagnall 6 + 14	Williams 2 + 1	Osho 5 + 1	Cann 2	Richards M 4 + 3	Cooper 1 + 2	Match No.
1	2	3	4	5^{2}	6	7	8^{1}	9	10	11	12	13																				1
1	2	3	5	4	6	7^{1}		8	9	11			10	12																		2
1	2	3	9	11	4	5		8	10^{1}	6			7		12																	3
1	2	3^{2}	4	12	5	6^{1}	7	8	9	10^{3}			11			13	14															4
1	2		9	11^{1}	4^{2}	5^{3}	6	8	10		12		7		14	3	13															5
1	2		9		4	5^{3}	6^{2}	8	10^{1}	12			7			3	11	13	14													6
	2^{3}		10	12	5	6^{1}	14	9	13	7			8			3	11^{2}		4	1												7
			9	10	4^{3}	5^{1}	7	14	13				8			2	11^{2}	12	3	1	6											8
	13		9	10^{3}	4		6^{2}	14					7			2	11	8^{1}	3		5	1	12									9
	13		9	10^{1}	4		6	8					7^{2}		14	2	11^{3}		3		5	1	12									10
		3^{1}	14	9	5		8	13		6^{3}						2	10		4		7	1	11^{2}	12								11
	2	4			7	14	10^{2}	13		8						3	11^{1}		6		9	1	12	5^{3}								12
	2	4			7^{1}	12	10	11		8^{3}					14	3			6		9		13	5^{2}	1							13
	2	4			7^{3}	12	10	14		8^{2}						3	11		5		9		13	6^{1}	1							14
		2		5		8^{1}	7^{2}	13		11					14	4	6		3		10^{3}		12	9	1							15
		3		5	7	12		14		9			10^{2}			2	8		4				11^{1}	6^{3}	1	13						16
		3	4	5^{3}	8^{2}		7	13		10			11^{1}				6		2		12			9	1	14						17
1		2	10	11	4^{2}	5	7	9		6			8^{1}								13		12	3^{3}		14						18
1		4		3	14	6^{2}	7	8		11			12				9		2				13	5^{1}		10^{3}						19
1		2	4	3	6^{3}	7	8			10^{2}			13				9				11		12	5^{1}		14						20
1		2	8	9^{2}		5	7	12		6			14				10		4^{1}				11	3^{3}		13						21
1		2	3	4		6^{2}	7	8		11			13				9						10^{1}	5		12						22
1		2■	4	3^{3}	12	7	5	8		10			11^{2}				9				13			6^{1}		14						23
1					12	3	6	7					5^{1}			2	8				4■					11	9	10				24
1			14		12	3^{2}	5	7		4^{3}			6			2	8						13			11^{1}	9	10				25
1		13			14	7^{1}	8^{2}	2		9			10			5	6^{3}		4				12			11		3				26
1		3^{3}		12		7	9^{2}	8		10^{1}			11			5	6		4				14			13		2				27
1				2		7	9^{3}	8		10			11			5	6^{2}		4				14			13	12	3^{1}				28
1	2^{2}	4			13		7^{3}	8		12			10^{1}			5	6		3				9			11■		14				29
1	2	3			14	8^{1}	12	9		10			11			5	6^{3}		4		13		7^{2}									30
		3		2	7		8	9		10■			12			5	6^{1}		4					13					1	11^{2}		31
		3		2^{1}	14		7^{2}	9		10			11^{3}			5	6		4					8		13			1	12		32
	5^{1}	3			8^{3}		7	13		10			12			2	6		4			1		9^{2}		14				11		33
1	13			2^{2}			7■	8		11			10^{3}			5	6		3					9^{1}		12				14	4	34
1	2^{1}	3		13	8^{3}			7		10^{2}			11			5	6		4					12		9				14		35
12		3		2	8			7					10			5	6^{1}		4			1^{2}		9		13				11^{3}	14	36
1		3	14	2	7^{3}			8					11			5	6		4					9^{1}		12				10^{2}	13	37
																																38
																																39
																																40
																																41
																																42
																																43
																																44
																																45
																																46

FA Cup

Fourth Qualifying	Haringey Bor	(a)	3-0
First Round	Hartlepool U	(h)	1-4

National League Play-Offs

Eliminator	Barnet	(h)	0-2

FA Trophy

First Round	Welling U	(h)	3-1
Second Round	Hampton & Richmond Bor	(h)	4-0
Third Round	Notts Co	(h)	1-2

SCOTTISH LEAGUE TABLES 2019–20

(P) *Promoted into division at end of 2018–19 season.* (R) *Relegated into division at end of 2018–19 season.*

Due to COVID-19 pandemic the SPFL abandoned the season with League positions awarded on a points-per-game basis for the SPFL Ladbrokes Championship, SPFL Ladbrokes League One and SPFL Ladbrokes League Two on 15 April 2020 without relegation from SPFL Ladbrokes League Two. The SPFL Ladbrokes Premiership was abandoned with League positions awarded on a points-per-game basis on 18 May 2020.

SPFL LADBROKES PREMIERSHIP 2019–20

			Home					Away					Total							
		P	*W*	*D*	*L*	*F*	*A*	*W*	*D*	*L*	*F*	*A*	*W*	*D*	*L*	*F*	*A*	*GD*	*Pts*	*PPG*
1	Celtic	30	14	0	1	50	7	12	2	1	39	12	26	2	2	89	19	70	80	2.67
2	Rangers	29	11	1	2	33	7	10	3	2	31	12	21	4	4	64	19	45	67	2.31
3	Motherwell	30	7	1	7	23	23	7	3	5	18	15	14	4	12	41	38	3	46	1.53
4	Aberdeen	30	7	3	5	23	19	5	6	4	17	17	12	9	9	40	36	4	45	1.50
5	Livingston	30	8	4	2	19	8	2	5	9	22	31	10	9	11	41	39	2	39	1.30
6	St Johnstone	29	5	6	5	19	26	3	6	4	9	20	8	12	9	28	46	–18	36	1.24
7	Hibernian	30	5	7	3	26	22	4	3	8	16	27	9	10	11	42	49	–7	37	1.23
8	Kilmarnock	30	6	5	4	20	15	3	1	11	11	26	9	6	15	31	41	–10	33	1.10
9	St Mirren	30	5	6	4	13	13	2	2	11	11	28	7	8	15	24	41	–17	29	0.97
10	Ross Co (P)	30	5	3	6	17	23	2	5	9	12	37	7	8	15	29	60	–31	29	0.97
11	Hamilton A	30	4	3	9	16	26	2	6	6	14	24	6	9	15	30	50	–20	27	0.90
12	Hearts	30	2	7	6	19	23	2	4	9	12	29	4	11	15	31	52	–21	23	0.77

SPFL LADBROKES CHAMPIONSHIP 2019–20

			Home					Away					Total							
		P	*W*	*D*	*L*	*F*	*A*	*W*	*D*	*L*	*F*	*A*	*W*	*D*	*L*	*F*	*A*	*GD*	*Pts*	*PPG*
1	Dundee U	28	10	3	1	35	10	8	2	4	17	12	18	5	5	52	22	30	59	2.11
2	Inverness CT	27	8	2	3	24	14	6	1	7	15	18	14	3	10	39	32	7	45	1.67
3	Dundee (R)	27	7	2	4	17	14	4	6	4	15	17	11	8	8	32	31	1	41	1.52
4	Ayr U	27	6	3	5	18	14	6	1	6	20	21	12	4	11	38	35	3	40	1.48
5	Arbroath (P)	26	6	4	3	14	10	4	2	7	10	16	10	6	10	24	26	–2	36	1.38
6	Dunfermline Ath	28	7	3	5	25	17	3	4	6	16	19	10	7	11	41	36	5	37	1.32
7	Greenock Morton	28	6	5	3	27	22	4	1	9	18	30	10	6	12	45	52	–7	36	1.29
8	Alloa Ath	28	4	4	6	12	19	3	6	5	21	24	7	10	11	33	43	–10	31	1.11
9	Queen of the South	28	4	2	8	17	20	3	5	6	11	20	7	7	14	28	40	–12	28	1.00
10	Partick Thistle	27	2	4	7	13	22	4	4	6	19	25	6	8	13	32	47	–15	26	0.96

SPFL LADBROKES LEAGUE ONE 2019–20

			Home					Away					Total							
		P	*W*	*D*	*L*	*F*	*A*	*W*	*D*	*L*	*F*	*A*	*W*	*D*	*L*	*F*	*A*	*GD*	*Pts*	*PPG*
1	Raith R	28	9	4	1	29	14	6	4	4	20	19	15	8	5	49	33	16	53	1.89
2	Falkirk (R)	28	10	2	2	35	5	4	8	2	19	13	14	10	4	54	18	36	52	1.86
3	Airdrieonians	28	7	4	4	20	13	7	2	4	18	14	14	6	8	38	27	11	48	1.71
4	Montrose	28	9	0	5	29	19	6	2	6	19	19	15	2	11	48	38	10	47	1.68
5	East Fife	28	6	6	2	27	19	6	3	5	17	17	12	9	7	44	36	8	45	1.61
6	Dumbarton	28	6	3	5	16	14	5	2	7	19	30	11	5	12	35	44	–9	38	1.36
7	Clyde (P)	28	7	4	3	27	18	2	3	9	8	25	9	7	12	35	43	–8	34	1.21
8	Peterhead (P)	27	5	4	5	16	14	2	1	10	14	30	7	5	15	30	44	–14	26	0.96
9	Forfar Ath	28	4	3	7	17	22	2	3	9	9	25	6	6	16	26	47	–21	24	0.86
10	Stranraer	27	2	4	6	13	20	0	6	9	15	37	2	10	15	28	57	–29	16	0.59

SPFL LADBROKES LEAGUE TWO 2019–20

			Home					Away					Total							
		P	*W*	*D*	*L*	*F*	*A*	*W*	*D*	*L*	*F*	*A*	*W*	*D*	*L*	*F*	*A*	*GD*	*Pts*	*PPG*
1	Cove Rangers	28	14	0	0	37	7	8	2	4	39	27	22	2	4	76	34	42	68	2.43
2	Edinburgh C	27	10	2	2	28	9	7	2	4	21	19	17	4	6	49	28	21	55	2.04
3	Elgin C	28	7	2	5	30	19	5	5	4	18	15	12	7	9	48	34	14	43	1.54
4	Cowdenbeath	27	10	2	2	23	15	2	3	8	14	20	12	5	10	37	35	2	41	1.52
5	Queen's Park	28	6	5	3	21	17	5	2	7	16	18	11	7	10	37	35	2	40	1.43
6	Stirling Alb	28	3	3	7	13	21	7	3	5	21	14	10	6	12	34	35	–1	36	1.29
7	Annan Ath	27	6	4	4	24	22	3	0	10	9	32	9	4	14	33	54	–21	31	1.15
8	Stenhousemuir (R)	28	3	4	8	16	29	4	4	5	16	19	7	8	13	32	48	–16	29	1.04
9	Albion R	26	5	2	5	23	23	1	4	9	14	28	6	6	14	37	51	–14	24	0.92
10	Brechin C (R)	27	2	3	8	12	25	2	2	10	19	35	4	5	18	31	60	–29	17	0.63

PPG = Points-per-game.

SCOTTISH LEAGUE ATTENDANCES 2019–20

SPFL LADBROKES PREMIERSHIP ATTENDANCES

	Average Gate			*Season 2019–20*	
	2018–19	*2019–20*	*+/–%*	*Highest*	*Lowest*
Aberdeen	14,925	13,836	–7.29	16,410	12,325
Celtic	57,778	57,944	+0.29	59,131	54,584
Hamilton A	2,829	2,565	–9.34	5,300	1,075
Hearts	17,564	16,751	–4.63	19,313	14,681
Hibernian	17,741	16,729	–5.70	20,197	14,486
Kilmarnock	6,895	5,856	–15.06	9,196	4,083
Livingston	3,664	3,542	–3.33	8,640	1,076
Motherwell	5,448	5,575	+2.32	8,822	3,191
Rangers	49,564	49,238	–0.66	50,012	47,583
Ross Co	3,850	4,664	+21.16	6,575	3,301
St Johnstone	3,891	4,091	+5.14	8,743	2,231
St Mirren	5,352	5,376	+0.47	7,332	4,240

SPFL LADBROKES CHAMPIONSHIP ATTENDANCES

	Average Gate			*Season 2019–20*	
	2018–19	*2019–20*	*+/–%*	*Highest*	*Lowest*
Alloa Ath	1,179	1,125	–4.51	1,827	661
Arbroath	951	1,462	+53.81	4,052	801
Ayr U	2,157	1,778	–17.59	3,167	777
Dundee	6,025	5,277	–12.41	11,233	4,228
Dundee U	5,079	8,496	+67.30	14,108	6,929
Dunfermline Ath	5,009	4,152	–17.11	6,480	3,397
Greenock Morton	1,943	1,607	–17.28	2,742	1,120
Inverness CT	2,548	2,117	–16.92	2,902	1,760
Partick Thistle	3,043	2,699	–11.31	4,101	1,714
Queen of the South	1,656	1,396	–15.65	2,041	1,094

SPFL LADBROKES LEAGUE ONE ATTENDANCES

	Average Gate			*Season 2019–20*	
	2018–19	*2019–20*	*+/–%*	*Highest*	*Lowest*
Airdrieonians	764	1,038	+35.93	2,530	600
Clyde	638	947	+48.44	2,048	507
Dumbarton	618	663	+7.31	982	364
East Fife	698	824	+18.05	1,998	425
Falkirk	4,743	3,713	–21.71	4,060	3,289
Forfar Ath	665	645	–3.07	998	370
Montrose	789	664	–15.92	1,095	423
Peterhead	668	687	+2.80	1,513	443
Raith R	1,556	1,839	+18.20	3,235	975
Stranraer	339	350	+3.24	549	190

SPFL LADBROKES LEAGUE TWO ATTENDANCES

	Average Gate			*Season 2019–20*	
	2018–19	*2019–20*	*+/–%*	*Highest*	*Lowest*
Albion R	286	301	+5.10	484	209
Annan Ath	398	347	–12.86	459	211
Brechin C	581	426	–26.72	705	338
Cove R	N/A	765	N/A	1,264	391
Cowdenbeath	355	350	–1.24	448	221
Edinburgh C	401	324	–19.17	494	194
Elgin C	623	636	+2.09	1,002	453
Queen's Park	611	583	–4.64	837	449
Stenhousemuir	571	554	–3.01	824	336
Stirling Alb	588	563	–4.18	741	423

ABERDEEN

Year Formed: 1903. *Ground & Address:* Pittodrie Stadium, Pittodrie St, Aberdeen AB24 5QH. *Telephone:* 01224 650400. *Fax:* 01224 644173. *E-mail:* feedback@afc.co.uk *Website:* www.afc.co.uk
Ground Capacity: 20,866 (all seated). *Size of Pitch:* 105m × 66m.
Chairman: Dave Cormack.
Manager: Derek McInnes. *Assistant Manager:* Tony Docherty. *Reserve Team Manager:* Paul Sheerin.
Club Nicknames: 'The Dons'; 'The Reds'; 'The Dandies'.
Record Attendance: 45,061 v Hearts, Scottish Cup 4th rd, 13 March 1954.
Record Transfer Fee received: £1,750,000 for Eoin Jess to Coventry C (February 1996).
Record Transfer Fee paid: £1,000,000 for Paul Bernard from Oldham Ath (September 1995).
Record Victory: 13-0 v Peterhead, Scottish Cup 3rd rd, 10 February 1923.
Record Defeat: 0-9 v Celtic, Premier League, 6 November 2010.
Most Capped Player: Alex McLeish, 77 (Scotland).
Most League Appearances: 556: Willie Miller, 1973-90.
Most League Goals in Season (Individual): 38: Benny Yorston, Division I, 1929-30.
Most Goals Overall (Individual): 199: Joe Harper, 1969-72; 1976-81.

ABERDEEN – SPFL LADBROKES PREMIERSHIP 2019–20 LEAGUE RECORD

Match No.	*Date*	*Venue*	*Opponents*	*Result*		*H/T Score*	*Lg Pos.*	*Goalscorers*	*Attendance*
1	Aug 4	H	Hearts	W	3-2	1-0	3	Cosgrove 2 (1 pen) 13, 80 (p), Hedges 85	16,410
2	11	A	St Mirren	L	0-1	0-1	4		6199
3	24	A	Kilmarnock	D	0-0	0-0	5		5250
4	31	H	Ross Co	W	3-0	2-0	4	Leigh 34, Cosgrove (pen) 37, Hedges 50	13,006
5	Sept 14	H	St Johnstone	D	1-1	1-1	4	Hedges 28	13,272
6	21	A	Livingston	W	2-0	1-0	3	Considine 29, Cosgrove (pen) 90	2803
7	28	A	Rangers	L	0-5	0-2	4		49,992
8	Oct 5	H	Hibernian	D	1-1	0-0	4	Cosgrove 86	13,880
9	19	A	Motherwell	W	3-0	1-0	4	Cosgrove 15, McGinn 53, Zak Vyner 60	5640
10	27	H	Celtic	L	0-4	0-4	5		15,079
11	30	A	Hamilton A	W	1-0	1-0	4	Ferguson 14	1687
12	Nov 2	H	Kilmarnock	W	3-0	2-0	4	Main 11, Cosgrove 27, McKenna 81	13,131
13	9	A	Ross Co	W	3-1	1-1	3	McGinn 10, Hedges 52, Considine 70	6510
14	24	A	St Johnstone	D	1-1	1-0	3	Cosgrove 21	3917
15	30	H	St Mirren	W	2-1	1-1	3	Cosgrove 6, McGinn 56	12,829
16	Dec 4	H	Rangers	D	2-2	1-2	3	Gallagher, J 39, Considine 48	14,790
17	7	A	Hibernian	L	0-3	0-0	4		16,767
18	14	H	Hamilton A	W	1-0	0-0	3	Cosgrove 53	12,325
19	21	A	Celtic	L	1-2	1-1	4	Cosgrove 35	59,131
20	26	H	Livingston	W	2-1	1-0	4	McLennan 13, Anderson 81	14,518
21	29	A	Hearts	D	1-1	0-0	4	McGinn 68	17,788
22	Jan 22	H	Motherwell	L	0-1	0-1	4		12,365
23	26	A	St Mirren	D	0-0	0-0	4		5302
24	Feb 1	A	Rangers	D	0-0	0-0	4		50,012
25	5	H	St Johnstone	L	0-1	0-1	4		12,552
26	11	A	Hamilton A	W	3-1	3-0	3	Main 15, McGinn 23, McLennan 45	1218
27	16	H	Celtic	L	1-2	1-1	3	Taylor 27	14,135
28	22	H	Ross Co	L	1-2	1-1	4	Main 28	14,860
29	Mar 4	A	Kilmarnock	D	2-2	1-2	4	McGinn 38, McLennan 50	4217
30	7	H	Hibernian	W	3-1	0-1	4	Jackson (og) 64, Considine 66, Main 82	14,388
31	13	A	Motherwell	Cancelled					
32	21	A	Livingston	Cancelled					
33	Apr 3	H	Hearts	Cancelled					
34	Fixtures 34–38 decided after 33 game league split.								
35									
36									
37									
38									

Final League Position: 4 (on points-per-game basis)

Honours

League Champions: Division I 1954-55; Premier Division 1979-80, 1983-84, 1984-85.
Runners-up: Premiership 2014-15, 2015-16, 2016-17, 2017-18; Division I 1910-11, 1936-37, 1955-56, 1970-71, 1971-72; Premier Division 1977-78, 1980-81, 1981-82, 1988-89, 1989-90, 1990-91, 1992-93, 1993-94.
Scottish Cup Winners: 1947, 1970, 1982, 1983, 1984, 1986, 1990; *Runners-up:* 1937, 1953, 1954, 1959, 1967, 1978, 1993, 2000, 2017.
League Cup Winners: 1955-56, 1976-77, 1985-86, 1989-90, 1995-96, 2013-14; *Runners-up:* 1946-47, 1978-79, 1979-80, 1987-88, 1988-89, 1992-93, 1999-2000, 2016-17, 2018-19.
Drybrough Cup Winners: 1971, 1980.

European: *European Cup:* 12 matches (1980-81, 1984-85, 1985-86); *Cup Winners' Cup:* 39 matches (1967-68, 1970-71, 1978-79, 1982-83 winners, 1983-84 semi-finals, 1986-87, 1990-91, 1993-94); *UEFA Cup:* 56 matches (*Fairs Cup:* 1968-69. *UEFA Cup:* 1971-72, 1972-73, 1973-74, 1977-78, 1979-80, 1981-82, 1987-88, 1988-89, 1989-90, 1991-92, 1994-95, 1996-97, 2000-01, 2002-03, 2007-08). *Europa League:* 32 matches (2009-10, 2014-15, 2015-16, 2016-17, 2017-18, 2018-19, 2019-20).

Club colours: All: Red with white trim.

Goalscorers: *League (40):* Cosgrove 11 (3 pens), McGinn 6, Considine 4, Hedges 4, Main 4, McLennan 3, Anderson 1, Ferguson 1, Gallagher, J 1, Leigh 1, McKenna 1, Taylor 1, Zak Vyner 1, own goal 1.
William Hill Scottish Cup (7): Cosgrove 3 (3 pens), Considine 1, Ferguson 1, Kennedy 1, own goal 1.
Betfred Scottish League Cup (4): Cosgrove 3 (2 pens), Considine 1.
Tunnock's Caramel Wafer Scottish League Challenge Cup (0).
UEFA Europa League (10): Cosgrove 6 (2 pens), Ferguson 1, Leigh 1, McGinn 1, Wright 1.

Lewis J 30	Logan S 23 + 3	Considine A 25 + 2	McKenna S 24	Leigh G 18	Ojo F 16	Ferguson L 28	Wilson J 7 + 4	Gallagher J 11 + 11	Wright S 2 + 1	Cosgrove S 22 + 3	Hedges R 14 + 8	McGinn N 22 + 6	Anderson B 1 + 10	Vyner Zak 15 + 1	McLennan C 9 + 9	Main C 12 + 6	Bryson C 5 + 3	Devlin M 11 + 3	Campbell D 6 + 9	Ross E 1 + 1	Gleeson S — + 1	Taylor A 14	McGeouch D 6 + 1	Kennedy M 7 + 1	Hernandez R 1 + 1	Match No.
1	2	3	4	5	6	7	8^{2}	9^{1}	10^{3}	11	12	13	14													1
1		3	4	5^{3}	6	8	14	12	9^{2}		7	13		2	10^{1}	11										2
1	2	3	4^{1}	5	7	8	9^{3}	11		10		14		12	13		6^{2}									3
1		4		5	6	7		14	12	11	8^{3}	10^{2}	13	2			9^{1}	3								4
1		4		5	6^{1}	7	14	12		11	10	8^{2}		2	13		9^{3}	3								5
1	14	4		5		7		6		13	10^{2}	8		2^{3}	12	11^{1}		3	9							6
1	2			5		7		12		10^{2}	11	9^{3}		4	8^{1}	14		3	6	13						7
1	2	3	4	5		8■		12		11	9	13				10■			7^{2}	6^{1}						8
1	2	5	4	6^{3}			10^{1}	9		11		7^{2}		8	12			3	13		14					9
1	2	5	4	7			12	8^{3}		11		10^{1}		6	9^{2}		13	3	14							10
1	2	4	3	5		7				11	8^{2}	10		6	13		9^{1}		12							11
1	2	14	4	5		7		12		11^{2}	8^{3}	10^{1}		6	13	9		3								12
1	2	5	4	7		6				11^{2}	10^{1}	8	14			12	9^{3}	3	13							13
1	2	5	4	8^{1}		7		13		10	9^{3}	6	14			11^{2}	12	3								14
1	12	3	4	5		6		9		11	8^{3}	10^{1}		2	13	14			7^{2}							15
1	5	4^{1}	3	9		6	11^{2}	8		10	12			7	13							2				16
1	5^{2}	4	3	9		6	11^{3}	8		10	12			7^{1}		13			14			2				17
1	2	12	4	5^{2}	7^{3}	6	9	13		11	8^{1}	10							14			3				18
1	2	5	4		8^{1}	7	9^{2}	13		10■		11^{3}		6	12	14						3				19
1	5		4		7^{1}	6		12			9^{2}	10	13	2	8^{3}	11			14			3				20
1	2		4		6^{3}	7	13	10			14	12	9	5^{2}		11^{1}			8			3				21
1	2^{1}	5	4		7^{3}	9		8		11	12	10	14			13						3^{2}	6			22
1	2	5	4		6	9				11	12	8^{2}	13									3	7^{1}	10		23
1	2	5	4		6	9		12		11		10^{2}						13	14			3	7^{1}	8^{3}		24
1		5	4			6		8^{1}		11	9	13	14					12				3^{2}	7	10	2^{3}	25
1	13	4	3		7	8				14		5^{1}			11^{3}	10		2	12				6^{2}	9		26
1	2	5	4		7^{1}	6				13		9			8	11	12					3		10^{2}		27
1	2	5	4			7				11^{1}	13	9^{2}			6^{3}	10			8■			3	14	12		28
1	2	5			8	7					13	10^{1}	12		6^{2}	11		4				3		9		29
1	2^{3}	4			7	6						10^{1}	12		5^{2}	11		13				3	8	9	14	30
																										31
																										32
																										33
																										34
																										35
																										36
																										37
																										38

AIRDRIEONIANS

Year Formed: 2002. *Ground & Address:* The Penny Cars Stadium, New Broomfield, Craigneuk Avenue, Airdrie ML6 8QZ. *Telephone:* (Stadium) 01236 622000. *Fax:* 01236 622001.
E-mail: enquiries@airdriefc.com *Website:* www.airdriefc.com
Ground Capacity: 10,101 (all seated). *Size of Pitch:* 105m × 67m.
Chairman: Martin Ferguson. *Director of Football:* Stuart Millar.
Manager: Ian Murray. *First Team Coach:* Bryan Prunty.
Club Nickname: 'The Diamonds'.
Record Attendance: 9,044 v Rangers, League 1, 23 August 2013.
Record Victory: 11-0 v Gala Fairydean, Scottish Cup 3rd rd, 19 November 2011.
Record Defeat: 0-7 v Partick Thistle, First Division, 20 October 2012.
Most League Appearances: 222: Paul Lovering, 2004-12.
Most League Goals in Season (Individual): 23: Andy Ryan, 2016-17.
Most Goals Overall (Individual): 43: Bryan Prunty, 2005-08, 2015-16.

AIRDRIEONIANS – SPFL LADBROKES LEAGUE ONE 2019–20 LEAGUE RECORD

Match No.	*Date*	*Venue*	*Opponents*	*Result*	*H/T Score*	*Lg Pos.*	*Goalscorers*	*Attendance*
1	Aug 3	H	Forfar Ath	L 0-2	0-0	10		780
2	10	A	Montrose	W 1-0	0-0	4	Smith [71]	685
3	17	H	Clyde	W 3-1	0-1	4	Roberts [47], Carrick [80], Gallagher, C [90]	1054
4	24	A	East Fife	L 1-4	0-2	4	Gallagher, C [90]	620
5	31	H	Falkirk	D 0-0	0-0	7		1888
6	Sept 14	A	Dumbarton	W 1-0	1-0	4	McKay [44]	813
7	21	H	Raith R	L 0-1	0-0	5		1132
8	28	H	Stranraer	D 2-2	0-2	5	Smith [66], McKay [90]	600
9	Oct 5	A	Peterhead	W 2-1	1-1	4	Gallagher, C [4], Carrick (pen) [75]	619
10	19	H	Montrose	L 1-3	1-2	5	Smith [3]	642
11	26	A	Forfar Ath	W 4-1	0-1	4	Carrick [52], Gallagher, C [53], Smith [80], Roy [89]	487
12	Nov 2	H	Dumbarton	W 3-1	3-1	4	Gallagher, C [1], Carrick 2 [35, 39]	727
13	9	A	Falkirk	W 2-1	1-0	3	McKay [32], Gallagher, C [90]	4000
14	16	A	Stranraer	W 2-0	0-0	1	Gallagher, C [54], Carrick [89]	387
15	30	H	East Fife	W 4-0	3-0	1	Gallagher, C [9], Carrick 2 (1 pen) [39 (p), 41], Roy [83]	910
16	Dec 7	A	Raith R	L 0-1	0-1	2		1823
17	14	H	Peterhead	W 2-1	2-1	2	Gallagher, C [5], Carrick (pen) [42]	646
18	21	A	Clyde	L 1-3	1-2	3	Carrick [41]	1094
19	28	H	Falkirk	D 1-1	1-1	2	Carrick (pen) [39]	2530
20	Jan 4	H	Forfar Ath	W 1-0	0-0	2	Wedderburn [73]	833
21	11	A	East Fife	D 2-2	2-1	3	Gallagher, C 2 [12, 28]	783
22	25	H	Stranraer	D 0-0	0-0	3		749
23	Feb 1	H	Raith R	L 0-1	0-1	3		1296
24	8	A	Dumbarton	D 0-0	0-0	3		594
25	15	H	Clyde	W 2-0	2-0	3	Ryan [3], McKay [30]	913
26	22	A	Peterhead	W 2-0	0-0	3	Ryan (pen) [46], Thomson [83]	557
27	29	A	Montrose	L 0-1	0-1	3		766
28	Mar 7	H	East Fife	W 1-0	1-0	3	Carrick [16]	867
29	14	A	Forfar Ath	Cancelled				
30	21	H	Dumbarton	Cancelled				
31	28	A	Raith R	Cancelled				
32	Apr 4	A	Falkirk	Cancelled				
33	11	H	Montrose	Cancelled				
34	18	A	Stranraer	Cancelled				
35	25	H	Peterhead	Cancelled				
36	May 2	A	Clyde	Cancelled				

Final League Position: 3 (on points-per-game basis)

Honours
League Champions: Second Division 2003-04.
Runners-up: Second Division 2007-08.
League Challenge Cup Winners: 2008-09; *Runners-up:* 2003-04.

Club colours: Shirt: White with red diamond. Shorts: White with red trim. Socks: White with red trim.

Goalscorers: *League (38):* Carrick 12 (4 pens), Gallagher, C 11, McKay 4, Smith 4, Roy 2, Ryan 2 (1 pen), Roberts 1, Thomson 1, Wedderburn 1.
William Hill Scottish Cup (4): Crighton 2, MacDonald 1, Roberts 1.
Betfred Scottish League Cup (7): Roy 3 (1 pen), Eckersley 1, Gallagher, C 1, Smith 1, Wedderburn 1.
Tunnock's Caramel Wafer Scottish League Challenge Cup (4): Gallagher, C 2, Carrick 1, Smith 1.

Hutton D 18 + 1	Fordyce C 28	Kerr J 11 + 1	Crighton S 25 + 1	Eckersley A 6 + 2	Millar K 21 + 5	Wedderburn N 13 + 7	Gallagher C 21 + 4	Cowan J 1 + 1	Roy A 5 + 15	Smith C 27	Thomson C 7 + 11	O'Reilly Ewan 1 + 1	Carrick D 17 + 7	McKay P 26	Roberts K 14 + 7	Hawkshaw D 2 + 7	MacDonald K 23 + 1	McCann L 20 + 1	Reilly C 2 + 4	Wilson R 3 + 1	Pyott P — + 1	Ryan A 6 + 1	Gallacher S 7	Murray I 4 + 1	*Match No.*
1	2	3^{3}	4	5	6	7	8	9^{2}	10^{1}	11	12	13	14												1
1	2		4	5	14	7^{3}			11^{2}	10	9^{1}	8	13	3	6	12									2
1	4		3	5^{1}	14	7	13		10^{3}	11	8		9^{2}	2	6		12								3
1	3		4		7^{3}	6^{2}	12		14	11	8		9^{1}	5	10		2	13							4
1	2	4	3		8		10^{1}		14	11^{3}	6^{2}		13	7		12	9	5							5
1	2	4	3^{2}	13	6	12	11			9	14		10^{3}	7			5	8^{1}							6
1^{3}	2	4	3	9	6		10			11	13		14	8			5^{1}		7^{2}	12					7
	4^{3}		3	5		7	11		10	6	8^{2}		14	2	12	13			9^{1}	1					8
1	2	4^{3}	3	9	13	7	10		14	11^{1}			12	6	8^{2}		5								9
	3	4	2			7	11^{2}			10			12	5^{1}	13	8	6	9		1					10
	4		3		12	7^{2}	10	14	13	9			11^{1}	6	8^{3}		2	5		1					11
1	4		3		7	14	10^{1}		13	9			11	2^{2}	6^{3}		5	8	12						12
1	4		3		7		11		12	9			10^{1}	2	6^{2}		5	8	13						13
1	4		3		7	13	10^{3}		12	9			11^{2}	2	6^{1}		5	8	14						14
1	4		3	14	9		11^{3}		12	6			10	7	8^{1}	13	2	5^{2}							15
1	4■		3		9^{3}		10		13	6			11	7	8^{1}	12	2^{2}	5	14						16
1	4		3		9	14	10^{3}			6^{2}	13		11	7	12	8^{1}	2	5							17
1	4		3		9		11^{2}		8	6	12		10	7	13		2^{3}	5^{1}			14				18
1	4	14	3^{2}		7		11^{1}		13	8	12		10	6	9^{3}		2	5							19
1	4		3		7	13	11^{1}			8	14		10	6	9^{3}	12	2^{2}	5							20
1	4		3		6^{1}		11^{2}		14	8^{3}	13		10	7	9		2	5				12			21
	4	2^{1}	3		7	13	11		14	6^{2}	12		8^{3}	5				9				10	1		22
	4		3		8^{1}	12	14		13	6			11	2^{3}	9^{2}		7	5				10	1		23
	4		3		8	7	11^{1}		13	6					12		2	5				10^{2}	1	9	24
	4	3			9	7	14			8	13			6^{1}	12		2	5				11^{2}	1	10^{3}	25
	3	4			9	6				8^{2}	12			7		13	2	5				11	1	10^{1}	26
14	3	4	12		9^{3}	7			13		10			6			2	5^{1}				11	1^{2}	8	27
	2	3	4		14	8	10			11^{1}	5^{2}		7	6^{3}	13		9						1	12	28
																									29
																									30
																									31
																									32
																									33
																									34
																									35
																									36

ALBION ROVERS

Year Formed: 1882. *Ground & Address:* Reigart Stadium, Main St, Coatbridge ML5 3RB. *Telephone/Fax:* 01236 606334.
E-mail: secretary@albionroversfc.com *Website:* albionroversfc.co.uk
Ground capacity: 1,572 (seated: 489). *Size of Pitch:* 101m × 66m.
Chairman (Interim): Ian Benton.
Manager: Brian Reid. *Assistant Manager:* Scott MacKenzie.
Club Nickname: 'The Wee Rovers'.
Previous Grounds: Cowheath Park, Meadow Park, Whifflet.
Record Attendance: 27,381 v Rangers, Scottish Cup 2nd rd, 8 February 1936.
Record Transfer Fee received: £40,000 from Motherwell for Bruce Cleland (1979).
Record Transfer Fee paid: £7,000 for Gerry McTeague to Stirling Alb, September 1989.
Record Victory: 12-0 v Airdriehill, Scottish Cup 1st rd, 3 September 1887.
Record Defeat: 1-11 v Partick Thistle, League Cup 2nd rd, 11 August 1993.
Most Capped Player: Jock White, 1 (2), Scotland.
Most League Appearances: 399: Murdy Walls, 1921-36.
Most League Goals in Season (Individual): 41: Jim Renwick, Division II, 1932-33.
Most Goals Overall (Individual): 105: Bunty Weir, 1928-31.

ALBION ROVERS – SPFL LADBROKES LEAGUE TWO 2019–20 LEAGUE RECORD

Match No.	Date	Venue	Opponents	Result		H/T Score	Lg Pos.	Goalscorers	Attendance
1	Aug 3	A	Stenhousemuir	W	3-2	1-0	3	Fotheringham 33, East 46, Byrne (pen) 84	423
2	10	H	Cove R	D	4-4	1-3	3	Byrne 2, East 57, Wilson 73, Osadolor 83	347
3	17	A	Annan Ath	L	2-3	1-3	6	Wilson 12, East (pen) 65	449
4	24	H	Brechin C	L	0-1	0-1	7		323
5	31	H	Stirling Alb	W	2-1	0-1	6	Byrne (pen) 48, Osadolor 61	355
6	Sept 14	A	Queen's Park	D	1-1	1-0	5	East 23	546
7	21	H	Edinburgh C	L	1-3	0-2	6	Byrne 54	276
8	28	A	Cowdenbeath	L	0-1	0-1	7		364
9	Oct 5	H	Elgin C	L	1-3	0-2	8	Osadolor 90	275
10	29	A	Cove R	L	0-3	0-1	8		633
11	Nov 2	A	Stirling Alb	L	0-3	0-0	9		603
12	9	H	Stenhousemuir	W	2-1	2-1	8	East 25, Morena 38	209
13	16	A	Edinburgh C	L	2-3	1-0	9	Roberts 38, Scally 58	386
14	Dec 7	H	Queen's Park	W	2-0	2-0	9	Byrne 2 13, 18	273
15	14	A	Elgin C	D	2-2	1-0	9	Scally 42, East 74	458
16	21	H	Annan Ath	W	4-2	2-0	7	Byrne 2 (1 pen) 4 (p), 65, Scally 31, See 61	210
17	28	A	Brechin C	D	0-0	0-0	8		459
18	Jan 4	H	Stirling Alb	L	0-3	0-3	8		484
19	25	A	Queen's Park	D	2-2	2-0	8	Byrne 8, See 29	594
20	Feb 1	H	Cove R	D	2-2	0-1	9	East 82, Roberts 86	292
21	8	H	Brechin C	W	4-1	2-1	8	Byrne 2 38, 45, Scally 51, Roberts 59	282
22	15	A	Stenhousemuir	L	0-1	0-1	9		756
23	22	A	Annan Ath	L	1-2	0-2	9	See 48	322
24	29	H	Elgin C	L	1-2	1-2	9	Scally 3	283
25	Mar 3	A	Cowdenbeath	L	1-2	1-1	9	Wilson 28	221
26	7	A	Edinburgh C	L	0-3	0-1	9		229
27	14	H	Queen's Park	Cancelled					
28	17	H	Edinburgh C	Cancelled					
29	21	A	Cove Rangers	Cancelled					
30	24	H	Cowdenbeath	Cancelled					
31	28	A	Stirling Alb	Cancelled					
32	Apr 4	H	Annan Ath	Cancelled					
33	11	A	Brechin C	Cancelled					
34	18	H	Cowdenbeath	Cancelled					
35	25	A	Elgin C	Cancelled					
36	May 2	H	Stenhousemuir	Cancelled					

Final League Position: 9 (on points-per-game basis)

Honours
League Champions: Division II 1933-34; Second Division 1988-89; League Two 2014-15.
Runners-up: Division II 1913-14, 1937-38, 1947-48; Third Division 2010-11.
Promoted via play-offs: 2010-11 (to Second Division).
Scottish Cup Runners-up: 1920.

Club colours: Shirt: Yellow with red trim. Shorts: Red. Socks: Red with yellow tops.

Goalscorers: *League (37):* Byrne 11 (3 pens), East 7 (1 pen), Scally 5, Osadolor 3, Roberts 3, See 3, Wilson 3, Fotheringham 1, Morena 1.
William Hill Scottish Cup (7): Breen 2, See 2, Osadolor 1, Roberts 1, own goal 1.
Betfred Scottish League Cup (3): East 1, Paterson 1, Stewart 1.
Tunnock's Caramel Wafer Scottish League Challenge Cup (1): Osadolor 1.

Smith C 2	Lynas A 19 + 1	Wilson L 7 + 3	Fagan S 11	Clarke R 25	Roberts S 24 + 1	Morena G 18 + 1	Fotheringham G 3	Stewart J 6 + 1	East E 17 + 9	Byrne D 25 + 1	Osadolor S 7 + 8	Paterson N 4 + 5	Graham W 15 + 5	Scally D 14 + 9	Goodfellow R 22	Wharton B 17 + 2	Phillips G 10 + 3	Breen J 3 + 6	Home C 1 + 4	See O 10 + 8	Krones J 14	Potts D 2	McDonald D — + 1	Doherty K — + 2	McAllister N 8	Hunter L 1	Breadner C 1 + 2	El-Zubaidi A (Trialist) — + 1	*Match No.*
1	2	3	4	5	6	7^{1}	8^{3}	9	10^{2}	11	12	13	14																1
1	2	4	3	5	6	7	8^{3}	9	10^{1}	11^{2}	13		12	14															2
	2	4^{2}	3	5	6	7^{1}	8	9	14	11^{3}	10		13		1	12													3
		3	2	5	6	7^{3}		9^{1}	10	12	11		8^{2}	13	1	4	14												4
	2^{2}	14	3■	5^{3}	6	7^{1}			10	9	11		8	12	1	4		13											5
	2	12		5	9				11	6^{1}	10^{3}		7	14	1	4	8		3^{2}	13									6
	2	3		5	9				11^{2}	6	10^{3}		7^{1}	12	1	4	8	13		14									7
	2		3	5	9	8^{3}			10^{1}	6	13		7	12	1		11^{2}	14			4								8
	2		3	5	9^{3}			6^{1}	11^{2}	10	13		7		1		8	12		14	4								9
	2^{1}		4	5	6	8^{3}		13	9^{2}	11	10		7	14			3			12		1							10
			5	3	6			7^{3}	12	9^{2}	10^{1}		8	13			2			11	4	1	14						11
			2	5	6	7^{1}			10	11^{2}	12			9^{3}	1	3	8			13	4			14					12
	2		3^{2}	5	9				10	11			13	6^{1}	1	7	8		12		4								13
	2			5	9	7			10^{2}	11	12		8^{1}	6^{3}	1	3	13	14			4								14
	2			5	9	7^{2}			10	11^{3}				6	1	3	8^{1}	13	12	14	4								15
	2			5		7			9	11	12			6^{3}	1	3	14	8^{2}	13	10^{1}	4								16
	2			5	13	7^{2}			9	11^{1}	14			6	1	3		8	12	10^{3}	4								17
	2				9^{2}				11	10^{1}		7^{3}	13	6	1	3	5	8		12	4			14					18
	2■			5	9	12			13	11		7	6^{1}	8	1	4				10^{2}					3				19
				5	9	7^{2}			12	11		13	8	6	1	3				10^{1}	4				2				20
				5	9	8			12	11		13	7^{2}	6^{1}	1	3				10	4				2				21
				2	9^{2}	8^{1}			12	10		13	7	6	1	4				11	3				5				22
	13	12		5	9	7^{2}			14	11			8	6	1	3				10	4^{1}				2^{3}				23
	2	4		5	9				11^{1}	10		12	7^{2}	6	1					14					3	8^{3}	13		24
	2	4^{3}		5	6	7^{1}			14	10		8		9^{2}	1	12				11					3		13		25
	2			5	9^{3}	7			14	10		8		13	1	3				11^{1}					4■		6^{2}	12	26
																													27
																													28
																													29
																													30
																													31
																													32
																													33
																													34
																													35
																													36

ALLOA ATHLETIC

Year Formed: 1878. *Ground & Address:* Indodrill Stadium, Recreation Park, Clackmannan Rd, Alloa FK10 1RY. *Telephone:* 01259 722695. *Fax:* 01259 210886. *E-mail:* fcadmin@alloaathletic.co.uk *Website:* www.alloaathletic.co.uk
Ground Capacity: 3,100 (seated: 919). *Size of Pitch:* 102m × 69m.
Chairman: Mike Mulraney. *Secretary:* Ewen Cameron.
Manager: Peter Grant. *Assistant Manager:* Paddy Connolly.
Club Nicknames: 'The Wasps'; 'The Hornets'.
Previous Grounds: West End Public Park: Gabberston Park; Bellevue Park.
Record Attendance: 15,467 v Celtic, Scottish Cup 5th rd, 5 February 1955.
Record Transfer Fee received: £100,000 for Martin Cameron to Bristol R (July 2000).
Record Transfer Fee paid: £26,000 for Ross Hamilton from Stenhousemuir (July 2000).
Record Victory: 9-0 v Selkirk, Scottish Cup 1st rd, 28 November 2005.
Record Defeat: 0-10 v Dundee, Division II, 8 March 1947; v Third Lanark, League Cup, 8 August 1953.
Most Capped Player: Jock Hepburn, 1, Scotland.
Most League Appearances: 239: Peter Smith 1960-69.
Most League Goals in Season (Individual): 49: 'Wee' Willie Crilley, Division II, 1921-22.
Most Goals Overall (Individual): 91: Willie Irvine, 1996-2001.

ALLOA ATHLETIC – SPFL LADBROKES CHAMPIONSHIP 2019–20 LEAGUE RECORD

Match No.	*Date*	*Venue*	*Opponents*	*Result*		*H/T Score*	*Lg Pos.*	*Goalscorers*	*Attendance*
1	Aug 3	H	Partick Thistle	D	1-1	1-0	5	Hetherington 34	1672
2	10	A	Greenock Morton	L	1-4	1-1	10	Cawley 22	1646
3	24	H	Arbroath	L	0-1	0-1	10		661
4	31	A	Queen of the South	W	1-0	0-0	7	Trouten 58	1294
5	Sept 14	A	Dundee	L	1-2	1-2	8	Dick 10	4453
6	21	H	Ayr U	L	1-4	0-4	9	O'Hara 61	902
7	28	A	Dunfermline Ath	D	1-1	0-0	10	Brown 50	3496
8	Oct 4	H	Dundee U	W	1-0	1-0	7	O'Hara 18	1717
9	19	A	Inverness CT	D	2-2	1-0	9	Buchanan 5, Trouten 89	2036
10	26	H	Queen of the South	D	2-2	0-2	9	Trouten 64, O'Hara 65	875
11	29	H	Dundee	L	0-3	0-2	9		1218
12	Nov 2	A	Arbroath	L	1-2	1-2	9	Trouten 35	921
13	9	H	Dunfermline Ath	W	2-1	1-1	8	Trouten (pen) 17, Cawley 72	1602
14	26	A	Partick Thistle	D	1-1	1-1	9	Trouten 15	1714
15	30	H	Inverness CT	L	0-2	0-2	9		721
16	Dec 7	A	Dundee U	L	1-2	1-1	10	Reynolds (og) 12	7615
17	14	A	Ayr U	L	1-2	0-2	10	O'Hara 67	1117
18	21	H	Greenock Morton	L	0-2	0-0	10		727
19	28	A	Dunfermline Ath	W	3-1	2-1	10	Brown 21, O'Hara 25, Flannigan (pen) 66	4257
20	Jan 4	H	Partick Thistle	D	1-1	0-0	10	Brown 62	1827
21	21	H	Arbroath	W	2-0	2-0	10	O'Hara 2 24, 27	765
22	25	A	Queen of the South	W	3-2	2-0	9	O'Hara 2 8, 81, Thomson 14	1169
23	Feb 1	A	Inverness CT	D	1-1	1-0	9	Flannigan (pen) 30	1914
24	14	H	Dundee U	D	0-0	0-0	9		1442
25	22	A	Greenock Morton	D	4-4	2-4	8	Trouten 20, Cawley 22, O'Hara 85, Deas 90	1214
26	29	H	Ayr U	L	0-2	0-1	8		915
27	Mar 3	A	Dundee	D	0-0	0-0	8		4356
28	7	H	Inverness CT	W	2-0	2-0	8	Connelly 12, Trouten 28	712
29	14	A	Partick Thistle	Cancelled					
30	21	A	Dundee U	Cancelled					
31	28	H	Dunfermline Ath	Cancelled					
32	Apr 4	H	Dundee	Cancelled					
33	11	A	Ayr U	Cancelled					
34	18	H	Queen of the South	Cancelled					
35	25	H	Greenock Morton	Cancelled					
36	May 2	A	Arbroath	Cancelled					

Final League Position: 8 (on points-per-game basis)

Honours
League Champions: Division II 1921-22; Third Division 1997-98, 2011-12.
Runners-up: Division II 1938-39; Second Division 1976-77, 1981-82, 1984-85, 1988-89, 1999-2000, 2001-02, 2009-10, 2012-13; League One 2016-17.
Promoted via play-offs: 2012-13 (to First Division); 2017-18 (to Championship).
League Challenge Cup Winners: 1999-2000; *Runners-up:* 2001-02, 2014-15.

Club colours: Shirt: Gold and black hoops. Shorts: Black. Socks: Black with gold hoops.

Goalscorers: *League (33):* O'Hara 10, Trouten 8 (1 pen), Brown 3, Cawley 3, Flannigan 2 (2 pens), Buchanan 1, Connelly 1, Deas 1, Dick 1, Hetherington 1, Thomson 1, own goal 1.
William Hill Scottish Cup (5): O'Hara 3, Cawley 1, Taggart 1.
Betfred Scottish League Cup (8): Buchanan 3, Trouten 3, Cawley 1, O'Hara 1.
Tunnock's Caramel Wafer Scottish League Challenge Cup (2): Thomson 1, Trouten 1.

Parry N 6	Robertson J 21 + 3	Graham A 17	Taggart S 28	Dick L 18	Cawley K 26	Trouten A 19 + 3	Flannigan I 25	Hetherington S 25	Buchanan L 9 + 14	O'Hara K 27	Thomson R 12 + 11	Stirling A — + 2	Deas R 24	Brown A 9 + 5	Malcolm B 10	MacDonald J 18	O'Donnel C 1 + 2	Connelly L 1 + 3	Wilson A — + 1	Stirling B 6 + 1	Wright K 4	Banks S 2 + 2	*Match No.*
1	2	3	4	5	6	7^1	8	9	10^2	11	12	13											1
1	13	3■	2	5	6^2	7^1	8	9	10^3	11	14		4	12									2
1	2		4	5	6^2	7	9	8■	11^1	10	12	13	3										3
1	12	3	2	5	6	9^2	7		14	11^3	10^1		4	13	8								4
		3	2	5	7^1	10	8	9	12	6	11		4			1							5
	13	3	2	5	7		9	8	10^2	6	11		4^1	12		1							6
	6	4	2		9	10	7	8	12	11^1			3	5		1							7
	5	3	2		6	10	8■	7	12	11			4	9^1		1							8
	5	3	2		6	8		7	10^1	11	12		4	9		1							9
	5	3	2		6^1	10	8	7	12	11			4	9		1							10
	5	3	2			10	8	7	11	6			4	9^1		1	12						11
	5	3	2			10	7	8	13	11	12		4	6^2	9^1	1							12
	5	3	2		6	11	8			10	12		4	9^1	7	1							13
	7	3	2	5	8^2	9	6		13	10	11^1		4			1	12						14
	6	3	2	5■	7	10	8	9		11			4			1							15
	6	4	2		8^1	10	9	7^2	13	11	12		3		5	1							16
	7	3	2		6	10		8	13	11^2	14		4	12	5^3	1	9^1						17
	8	3	2	5	6		9	7	10		11		4			1							18
	3		2	5	7		9	8	11^1	10	12		4	6		1							19
	2		3		6		7	8	10^1	11	12		4	9	5	1							20
	2		3	5	6		7	8	12	11	10^1		4		9^2	1		13					21
	5		2	3	7		8	6	14	10	11^3		4		9^1	1^2			12	13			22
	8		2	3	7	12	9	6		10	11^1		4							5	1		23
			6	5	9	13	8	7		10	11^1		4		2^2			12		3	1		24
			3	5	6	9	7	8	13	11	10^1		4							2^2	1	12	25
			3	4^1	6	9	7	8		10	11				5^2			13		2	1	12	26
1	3		2	4	7	12	6	8	13	10	11^1									5		9^2	27
1	2^1		4	5	6	10		8	12	11	13			14				9^2		3		7^3	28
																							29
																							30
																							31
																							32
																							33
																							34
																							35
																							36

ANNAN ATHLETIC

Year Formed: 1942. *Ground & Address:* Galabank, North Street, Annan DG12 5DQ. *Telephone:* 01461 204108.
E-mail: annanathletic.enquiries@btconnect.com *Website:* www.annanathleticfc.com
Ground capacity: 2,517 (seated: 500). *Size of Pitch:* 100m × 62m.
Chairman: Philip Jones. *Vice-Chairman:* Russell Brown.
Secretary: Alan Irving.
Player/Manager: Peter Murphy.
Assistant Manager: Darren Barr.
Club Nicknames: 'Galabankies'; 'Black and Golds'.
Previous Ground: Mafeking Park.
Record attendance: 2,517, v Rangers, Third Division, 15 September 2012.
Record Victory: 6-0 v Elgin C, Third Division, 7 March 2009.
Record Defeat: 1-8 v Inverness CT, Scottish Cup 3rd rd, 24 January 1998.
Most League Appearances: 285: Peter Watson, 2008-18.
Most League Goals in Season (Individual): 22: Peter Weatherson, 2014-15.
Most Goals Overall (Individual): 56: Peter Weatherson, 2013-17.

ANNAN ATHLETIC – SPFL LADBROKES LEAGUE TWO 2019–20 LEAGUE RECORD

Match No.	*Date*	*Venue*	*Opponents*	*Result*	*H/T Score*	*Lg Pos.*	*Goalscorers*	*Attendance*
1	Aug 3	A	Brechin C	W 1-0	0-0	4	Swinglehurst [64]	338
2	10	H	Elgin C	D 1-1	0-0	4	Douglas [81]	376
3	17	H	Albion R	W 3-2	3-1	3	Swinglehurst [20], Nade [28], Lynas (og) [36]	449
4	24	A	Cowdenbeath	L 1-3	0-1	4	Nade [51]	286
5	31	H	Stenhousemuir	D 1-1	1-1	5	Nade [31]	362
6	Sept 14	A	Edinburgh C	L 0-4	0-1	6		253
7	21	H	Stirling Alb	D 0-0	0-0	5		398
8	28	A	Cove R	L 0-3	0-1	6		642
9	Oct 5	A	Queen's Park	W 2-1	2-0	5	McLean [18], Muir [22]	449
10	Nov 2	A	Elgin C	L 0-4	0-3	7		483
11	9	H	Cowdenbeath	W 1-0	0-0	6	Wilkie [51]	307
12	12	H	Brechin C	W 5-2	3-2	4	Flanagan [6], McLean 2 (1 pen) [12, 28 (p)], Walker [46], McLear [75]	253
13	16	A	Stirling Alb	L 0-2	0-1	4		512
14	30	H	Cove R	W 6-1	3-1	4	Flanagan [27], Watson, B [29], Muir 3 (2 pens) [33 (p), 56 (p), 88], Joseph [78]	459
15	Dec 7	A	Stenhousemuir	W 2-1	1-1	4	Douglas [30], Wilkie [90]	422
16	14	H	Edinburgh C	L 0-2	0-0	4		287
17	21	A	Albion R	L 2-4	0-2	4	Ballantyne [68], Nade [81]	210
18	28	H	Queen's Park	W 3-2	2-1	4	Muir 2 [9, 39], Flanagan [53]	449
19	Jan 4	A	Cowdenbeath	L 1-3	0-3	4	Sonkur [69]	312
20	11	H	Elgin C	L 0-4	0-1	4		211
21	18	H	Stirling Alb	L 2-3	0-1	4	Wooding-Holt [64], Muir [90]	402
22	25	A	Cove R	L 0-2	0-1	5		735
23	Feb 1	H	Stenhousemuir	L 0-3	0-3	7		284
24	8	A	Edinburgh C	L 0-3	0-1	7		203
25	22	H	Albion R	W 2-1	2-0	7	Joseph [18], Flanagan [24]	322
26	29	A	Queen's Park	L 0-2	0-2	7		734
27	Mar 7	H	Cowdenbeath	D 0-0	0-0	7		299
28	14	A	Stirling Alb	Cancelled				
29	18	A	Brechin C	Cancelled				
30	21	H	Edinburgh C	Cancelled				
31	28	H	Brechin C	Cancelled				
32	Apr 4	A	Albion R	Cancelled				
33	11	H	Cove Rangers	Cancelled				
34	18	A	Elgin C	Cancelled				
35	25	A	Stenhousemuir	Cancelled				
36	May 2	H	Queen's Park	Cancelled				

Final League Position: 7 (on points-per-game basis)

Honours
League Two Runners-up: 2013-14.
League Challenge Cup: Semi-finals: 2009-10, 2011-12.

Club colours: Shirt: Gold with black trim. Shorts: Black. Socks: Gold.

Goalscorers: *League (33):* Muir 7 (2 pens), Flanagan 4, Nade 4, McLean 3 (1 pen), Douglas 2, Joseph 2, Swinglehurst 2, Wilkie 2, Ballantyne 1, McLear 1, Sonkur 1, Walker 1, Watson, B 1, Wooding-Holt 1, own goal 1.
William Hill Scottish Cup (7): Muir 3 (2 pens), Flanagan 2, McLean 2 (1 pen).
Betfred Scottish League Cup (3): Douglas 1, McLear 1, Wooding-Holt 1.
Tunnock's Caramel Wafer Scottish League Challenge Cup (1): Currie 1.

Taylor Aaran 6	Douglas M 20	Bradley K 22 + 1	Swinglehurst S 19	Ballantyne J 21 + 5	McLean S 21 + 3	Griffiths E 2 + 4	Wilkie K 24 + 1	McLear L 11 + 8	Joseph N 11 + 3	Muir T 22 + 2	Sonkur A 11 + 3	Nade C 13 + 10	Barr D 14 + 2	Currie R 1 + 7	Watson B 15 + 5	Walker J 6 + 3	Smith C (Trialist) 3	Emerson H — + 3	Smith C 10	Flanagan N 15	Wooding-Holt J 4 + 3	Avci L 4	Hewitt M 5	Watson P 5	Docherty M 5	Scullion C (Trialist) — + 1	Mitchell A 4	Clark C 3	*Match No.*
1	2	3^{1}	4	14	6	7^{2}	8	9	10^{3}	11	12	13																	1
1	2		4	5	6		8	9^{1}		10	3	11	7	12															2
1	2	7	4	5	6	13	8^{1}	9		10		11^{2}	3		12														3
1	2	3	4	5^{2}	6	7^{1}	8	9		10		11				13													4
1	2	3^{2}	4	5	6		8	9^{3}		10^{1}	14	11	7	13	12														5
1	3		4^{2}	5	6	12	8	9^{1}		13		11	7		14	10^{3}													6
	3	2		13	9		7	10		11^{2}			4	14	8	5^{3}	1	12											7
	2	5			6		7	12	13	11^{1}	4	10^{2}	3			9	1	14											8
	2	7		9	6	12	8	13		10	4	11^{2}	3^{1}				1												9
	2	7	4■	5	6^{1}		8			10^{3}	3	12		13	14				1	9									10
	2	7		5	6^{1}		8		14	10^{2}	3	13	4		12				1	9									11
	3■	2		5^{2}	6	14	8	13			4	11	7^{3}		10^{1}	12			1	9									12
		2	4	14	6		8^{3}			12	3	10	7		11^{2}	5^{1}			1	9									13
	3	2	4	5	6		8^{3}	12	7	10				14	11^{2}				1	9^{1}	13								14
	3	2	4	5			7	14	8	10^{3}		13	12		11^{2}				1	9									15
	3	2	4■	5^{3}	6		8		7^{2}	11	12	13		14	10^{1}				1	9									16
	3	2		5	6		8		7^{2}	11	4^{1}	12	13		10				1	9									17
	3	2		5	6		8	12	7	10^{2}		13	4	14	11^{3}				1	9^{1}									18
	3	2		5^{1}	12		7	13		10	4	11■	8		6^{2}				1	9									19
	2^{3}	5	4	13	7		6^{2}	9^{1}	12				3	11	10					8	14	1							20
	2	7	4	5	6		8		9^{2}	10			3^{1}		11			13			12	1							21
		2	4	5	9		8		6		3	10			11						7	1							22
		7	4	5	6^{1}		8			10		11										1	2	3	9	12			23
			4					12		11	3	9^{1}								8	6		2	7	10		1	5	24
			4		14		12^{3}	10^{1}	9	11^{2}		13								6	7		2	3	8		1	5	25
		12	4	5	13			11	9^{3}	10		14								6^{2}	7		2	3	8^{1}		1		26
		7	4				6	10	9	11^{1}		12											2	3	8		1	5	27
																													28
																													29
																													30
																													31
																													32
																													33
																													34
																													35
																													36

ARBROATH

Year Formed: 1878. *Ground & Address:* Gayfield Park, Arbroath DD11 1QB. *Telephone:* 01241 872157. *Fax:* 01241 431125. *E-mail:* arbroathfc@outlook.com *Website:* www.arbroathfc.co.uk
Ground Capacity: 6,600 (seated: 861). *Size of Pitch:* 105m × 65m.
Chairman: Mike Caird. *Secretary:* Dr Gary Callon.
Manager: Dick Campbell. *Assistant Manager:* Ian Campbell.
Club Nickname: 'The Red Lichties'.
Previous Ground: Lesser Gayfield.
Record Attendance: 13,510 v Rangers, Scottish Cup 3rd rd, 23 February 1952.
Record Transfer Fee received: £120,000 for Paul Tosh to Dundee (August 1993).
Record Transfer Fee paid: £20,000 for Douglas Robb from Montrose (1981).
Record Victory: 36-0 v Bon Accord, Scottish Cup 1st rd, 12 September 1885.
Record Defeat: 0-8 v Kilmarnock, Division II, 3 January 1949; 1-9 v Celtic, League Cup 3rd rd, 25 August 1993.
Most Capped Player: Ned Doig, 2 (5), Scotland.
Most League Appearances: 445: Tom Cargill, 1966-81.
Most League Goals in Season (Individual): 45: Dave Easson, Division II, 1958-59.
Most Goals Overall (Individual): 120: Jimmy Jack, 1966-71.

ARBROATH – SPFL LADBROKES CHAMPIONSHIP 2019–20 LEAGUE RECORD

Match No.	*Date*	*Venue*	*Opponents*	*Result*		*H/T Score*	*Lg Pos.*	*Goalscorers*	*Attendance*
1	Aug 3	H	Queen of the South	D	0-0	0-0	7		1100
2	10	A	Inverness CT	L	1-2	1-1	9	Linn [26]	2298
3	24	A	Alloa Ath	W	1-0	1-0	5	Linn [17]	661
4	31	H	Dunfermline Ath	W	1-0	0-0	4	Donnelly [50]	1624
5	Sept 13	H	Partick Thistle	D	1-1	1-0	3	Thomson [14]	1214
6	21	A	Dundee U	L	1-2	0-0	5	Donnelly [52]	7877
7	28	H	Ayr U	L	0-3	0-3	6		1105
8	Oct 5	A	Dundee	L	0-2	0-1	7		5045
9	19	H	Greenock Morton	W	1-0	0-0	6	Linn [74]	1009
10	26	A	Partick Thistle	W	3-1	1-0	5	Donnelly [37], McKenna (pen) [74], Hamilton [77]	2793
11	29	A	Dunfermline Ath	L	0-2	0-0	5		3488
12	Nov 2	H	Alloa Ath	W	2-1	2-1	5	Linn [16], Donnelly [27]	921
13	9	H	Inverness CT	W	3-0	1-0	5	Stewart [28], Linn (pen) [54], Kader [86]	1173
14	16	A	Greenock Morton	L	0-1	0-1	5		1185
15	Dec 7	H	Dundee	D	1-1	1-0	6	Linn [37]	2170
16	10	A	Ayr U	D	1-1	0-1	5	McKenna (pen) [48]	777
17	14	H	Dundee U	L	0-1	0-1	6		4052
18	21	A	Queen of the South	L	0-2	0-1	7		1094
19	28	A	Inverness CT	W	1-0	0-0	7	Donnelly [47]	2287
20	Jan 4	H	Greenock Morton	L	1-2	1-2	7	Stewart [23]	1273
21	21	A	Alloa Ath	L	0-2	0-2	7		765
22	25	H	Partick Thistle	W	2-1	2-0	6	McKenna [6], Wighton [34]	1418
23	Feb 1	A	Dundee U	W	1-0	1-0	5	Wighton [26]	8056
24	15	H	Queen of the South	W	2-0	2-0	4	Gold [6], Hilson [35]	801
25	Mar 4	H	Dunfermline Ath	D	0-0	0-0	6		1146
26	7	A	Greenock Morton	D	1-1	0-0	6	Wighton [49]	1472
27	14	H	Inverness CT	Cancelled					
28	17	H	Ayr U	Cancelled					
29	21	A	Queen of the South	Cancelled					
30	24	A	Dundee	Cancelled					
31	27	H	Dundee U	Cancelled					
32	Apr 4	A	Partick Thistle	Cancelled					
33	11	A	Dunfermline Ath	Cancelled					
34	18	H	Dundee	Cancelled					
35	25	A	Ayr U	Cancelled					
36	May 2	H	Alloa Ath	Cancelled					

Final League Position: 5 (on points-per-game basis)

Honours
League Champions: League One 2018-19. Third Division 2010-11; League Two 2016-17.
Runners-up: Division II 1934-35, 1958-59, 1967-68, 1971-72; Second Division 2000-01; Third Division 1997-98, 2006-07.
Promoted via play-offs: 2007-08 (to Second Division).
Scottish Cup: Semi-finals 1947, Quarter-finals 1993.

Club colours: Shirt: Maroon with white trim. Shorts: Maroon. Socks: Maroon.

Goalscorers: *League (24):* Linn 6 (1 pen), Donnelly 5, McKenna 3 (2 pens), Wighton 3, Stewart 2, Gold 1, Hamilton 1, Hilson 1, Kader 1, Thomson 1.
William Hill Scottish Cup (4): McKenna 2 (1 pen), Linn 1, Stewart 1.
Betfred Scottish League Cup (10): Gold 2, Spence 2, Doris 1, Hamilton 1, Kader 1, Linn 1, McKenna 1, Thomson 1.
Tunnock's Caramel Wafer Scottish League Challenge Cup (0).

Jamieson D 7	Thomson J 17 + 1	Little R 26	Wilson R 1	Hamilton C 26	Stewart S 15 + 2	Murphy J 10 + 7	Whatley M 22 + 1	Linn B 21 + 2	Doris S 3 + 9	Spence G 5 + 6	McKenna M 15 + 7	Gold D 17 + 3	Kader O 4 + 15	O'Brien T 25	Donnelly L 14 + 7	Campbell J 2 + 7	Virtanen M 18 + 2	Stirling B 4 + 2	Gaston D 19	Swankie G 3 + 3	Hilson D 6	Chalmers L — + 1	Wighton C 5	Craigen J 1 + 3	*Match No.*
1	2	3	4	5	6^{3}	7^{2}	8	9^{1}	10	11	12	13	14												1
1	2	3		5	6^{2}	7^{3}	8	9	10^{1}	11	12	13		4	14										2
1	2	3		5		7	8	10	13	11^{2}	9^{3}	6^{1}	14	4		12									3
1	2	3		5		9	7	10^{1}		11^{2}	6	8^{3}	14	4	12	13									4
1	2	4		5		9	7	10^{3}	12	11^{2}	6	8^{1}		3	14	13									5
1	2	3		5		8	7^{1}	9	12		6	10^{3}		4	11^{2}	13	14								6
1	2	3		5		6^{2}	7^{1}	11			9		14	4	10	8^{3}	12	13							7
	2	3		5		12		10^{3}	11	14	6^{2}	8^{1}	13	4			7	9	1						8
	2	4		5	6^{2}		7	10	14		12	9^{3}		3	11^{1}	13	8		1						9
	2	3		5	6^{2}		7	10^{1}			12	8^{3}	14	4	11	13	9		1						10
	2^{2}	3		5		10		9	13	12	6			4	11^{3}	7	8^{1}	14	1						11
		3		5	6^{1}		8	10^{2}		12	14	9	13	4	11^{3}		7	2	1						12
		3		5	6^{2}		8	11^{1}	12		14	9	13	4	10^{3}		7	2	1						13
		3		5	6^{2}	7	8	10^{3}	12		14	9	13	4	11^{1}			2	1						14
		3		5	9^{1}	14	8^{3}	11^{2}			10	2	6	4	12	13	7		1						15
		3		5	9	14	7	11^{3}	13		10^{1}	2^{2}	6	4	12		8		1						16
		3		5	2	12	8^{1}	9^{3}		13	11		6^{2}	4	10		7		1	14					17
		3		5	2	12	8	9^{3}	14	13	11		6^{2}	4	10^{1}		7		1						18
		3		5	6	14	2	9^{2}		13	10	8^{1}	12	4	11^{3}		7		1						19
	13	4		5	6		2^{2}	9^{1}			10	8^{3}	14	3	11		7		1	12					20
	2	4		5	9^{3}	8^{1}		6^{2}			11		12	3	13		7		1		10	14			21
	2	3		5			7				10	12	13	4	11^{1}		8		1	14	6^{2}		9^{3}		22
	2	3		5	13		9					6^{3}	14	4			7		1	8^{2}	10^{1}		11	12	23
	2	3		5	13	14	8^{1}					7^{3}		4			9		1	6^{2}	10		11	12	24
	2	3		5			9^{3}	12				7^{1}		4	14		8		1	6^{2}	10		11	13	25
	2	3		5	6		13	14					12	4	10^{2}		8		1		9^{3}		11	7^{1}	26
																									27
																									28
																									29
																									30
																									31
																									32
																									33
																									34
																									35
																									36

AYR UNITED

Year Formed: 1910. *Ground & Address:* Somerset Park, Tryfield Place, Ayr KA8 9NB. *Telephone:* 01292 263435. *Fax:* 01292 281314. *E-mail:* info@ayrunitedfc.co.uk *Website:* ayrunitedfc.co.uk
Ground Capacity: 10,185 (seated: 1,597). *Size of Pitch:* 101m × 66m.
Chairman: Lachlan Cameron.
Vice Chairman: David Smith.
Manager: Mark Kerr. *Assistant Manager:* Michael McArdle.
Club Nickname: 'The Honest Men'.
Record Attendance: 25,225 v Rangers, Division I, 13 September 1969.
Record Transfer Fee received: £300,000 for Steve Nicol to Liverpool (October 1981).
Record Transfer Fee paid: £90,000 for Mark Campbell from Stranraer (March 1999).
Record Victory: 11-1 v Dumbarton, League Cup, 13 August 1952.
Record Defeat: 0-9 in Division I v Rangers (1929); v Hearts (1931); B Division v Third Lanark (1954).
Most Capped Player: Jim Nisbet, 3, Scotland.
Most League Appearances: 459: John Murphy, 1963-78.
Most League League and Cup Goals in Season (Individual): 66: Jimmy Smith, 1927-28.
Most League and Cup Goals Overall (Individual): 213: Peter Price, 1955-61.

AYR UNITED – SPFL LADBROKES CHAMPIONSHIP 2019–20 LEAGUE RECORD

Match No.	Date	Venue	Opponents	Result	H/T Score	Lg Pos.	Goalscorers	Attendance
1	Aug 3	H	Greenock Morton	W 4-2	1-0	2	Moffat 9, McCowan 55, Forrest 64, McGuffie 90	1935
2	10	A	Dundee	L 0-1	0-0	4		5520
3	24	H	Queen of the South	W 1-0	1-0	3	Kelly 26	2005
4	31	A	Partick Thistle	W 3-2	1-2	2	McCowan 24, Doolan 72, Kelly 78	3060
5	Sept 14	H	Dundee U	W 2-0	1-0	2	Harvie 9, Forrest (pen) 75	3167
6	21	A	Alloa Ath	W 4-1	4-0	2	Forrest 2 (1 pen) 10 (p), 31, Roscoe 13, McCowan 20	902
7	28	A	Arbroath	W 3-0	3-0	2	Forrest 2 12, 20, Kelly 27	1105
8	Oct 5	H	Inverness CT	L 0-2	0-1	2		1912
9	19	A	Dunfermline Ath	L 2-3	1-1	2	Ashcroft (og) 43, Forrest 57	3905
10	25	H	Dundee	L 1-2	1-2	2	McCowan 38	1627
11	29	A	Greenock Morton	W 3-2	0-0	2	Moore 50, McCowan 55, McGuffie 78	1431
12	Nov 2	H	Partick Thistle	W 4-1	2-0	2	Moore 2 11, 48, Moffat 18, Forrest 52	2558
13	9	A	Queen of the South	L 1-3	1-1	2	Moffat 38	1850
14	Dec 3	H	Dunfermline Ath	L 0-1	0-0	3		1361
15	7	A	Inverness CT	L 0-2	0-1	4		1833
16	10	H	Arbroath	D 1-1	1-0	4	Kelly 22	777
17	14	H	Alloa Ath	W 2-1	2-0	3	Docherty 2 6, 12	1117
18	21	A	Dundee U	L 0-4	0-1	3		7744
19	28	H	Queen of the South	L 1-2	0-1	4	Muirhead (pen) 77	2062
20	Jan 4	A	Dunfermline Ath	W 1-0	1-0	3	Moore 38	3915
21	25	H	Inverness CT	W 1-0	0-0	3	Kelly 61	1602
22	31	A	Partick Thistle	D 1-1	0-1	3	Forrest (pen) 52	2416
23	Feb 25	H	Greenock Morton	L 1-2	1-1	4	Malley 22	1336
24	29	A	Alloa Ath	W 2-0	1-0	3	Drinan 9, Forrest 82	915
25	Mar 3	H	Dundee U	D 0-0	0-0	3		1674
26	7	H	Dundee	D 0-0	0-0	3		1758
27	10	A	Dundee	L 0-2	0-1	4		4670
28	13	A	Queen of the South	Cancelled				
29	17	A	Arbroath	Cancelled				
30	20	H	Partick Thistle	Cancelled				
31	28	A	Inverness CT	Cancelled				
32	Apr 4	H	Dunfermline Ath	Cancelled				
33	11	H	Alloa Ath	Cancelled				
34	17	A	Greenock Morton	Cancelled				
35	25	H	Arbroath	Cancelled				
36	May 2	A	Dundee U	Cancelled				

Final League Position: 4 (on points-per-game basis)

Honours
League Champions: Division II 1911-12, 1912-13, 1927-28, 1936-37, 1958-59, 1965-66; Second Division 1987-88, 1996-97; League One 2017-18.
Runners-up: Division II 1910-11, 1955-56, 1968-69; Second Division 2008-09; League One 2015-16.
Promoted via play-offs: 2008-09 (to First Division); 2010-11 (to First Division); 2015-16 (to Championship).
Scottish Cup: Semi-finals 2002.
League Cup: Runners-up: 2001-02.
League Challenge Cup Runners-up: 1990-91, 1991-92.

Club colours: Shirt: White with black trim. Shorts: Black. Socks: White.

Goalscorers: *League (38):* Forrest 10 (3 pens), Kelly 5, McCowan 5, Moore 4, Moffat 3, Docherty 2, McGuffie 2, Doolan 1, Drinan 1, Harvie 1, Malley 1, Muirhead 1 (1 pen), Roscoe 1, own goal 1.
William Hill Scottish Cup (2): Bell 1, Drinan 1.
Betfred Scottish League Cup (12): McCowan 3, Moffat 3, Doolan 2, Geggan 1, Kelly 1, McGuffie 1, Murdoch 1.
Tunnock's Caramel Wafer Scottish League Challenge Cup (1): Roscoe 1.

Doohan R 27	Geggan A 14 + 3	Bell S 16	Roscoe S 18 + 2	Harvie D 27	Murdoch A 4	Docherty R 21 + 1	Kelly S 27	McCowan L 19 + 5	Moffat M 21 + 6	Forrest A 25	McGuffie C — + 12	Adams J 3 + 1	Doolan K 1 + 10	Muirhead A 21 + 2	Kerr M 12 + 4	Houston J 18 + 5	McKenzie M — + 10	Moore C 10 + 1	Drinan A 7	Tiffoney S 1 + 5	Gillespie G 1 + 3	Malley C 4 + 1	*Match No.*
1	2	3	4	5	6	7	8^{3}	9^{1}	10^{2}	11	12	13	14										1
1	2	3	14	5	6	7^{1}	8	9	10^{2}	11	13	4^{3}	12										2
1	2	3		5	6	7	8	9^{1}	10^{2}	11	12	4^{3}	13	14									3
1	2^{2}	3		5	6^{1}	7	8	9^{3}	13	11	14	4	10		12								4
1	2		4	5		7	8	9^{1}	10	11				3	6	12							5
1	2		4	5		9	7	6^{2}	11^{3}	10^{1}			12	3	8	13	14						6
1	2		4	5		6	8	9^{1}	10^{3}	11			13	3	7^{2}	12	14						7
1	6^{1}		4	5		7	8	9	10	11			12	3		2							8
1	2		4	5		6	8	9^{1}	10	11			13	3	7^{2}	12							9
1	6^{2}		4	5		7	8	9^{1}	10	11^{3}	13		14	3		2		12					10
1			4	5		7	8	6^{1}	10^{3}	9	12		13	3		2	14	11^{2}					11
1	14		4	5		7	8	6	10^{1}	9^{3}	12		13	3		2		11^{2}					12
1			4	5		8	9	7■	11	6^{1}				3		2	12	10					13
1	6		4	5		7	8		9^{1}	11^{2}	13			3		2	12	10					14
1	6^{3}		4	5		7	8		9^{1}	11^{2}	13			3	14	2	12	10					15
1		3	4	9		7	8^{1}	13	10^{2}					2	6	5	12	11					16
1	12	4		5		7	8	9^{1}	13	11				3	6^{2}	2	14	10^{3}					17
1	13	4		5		7^{3}	9	6^{2}	14	10	12			3	8■	2		11^{1}					18
1	8	4		5		12	7	9^{1}	11^{2}	6^{3}	14			3		2	13	10					19
1	2^{2}	4		5		6	8	9^{1}	14	11	13			3	7	12		10^{3}					20
1		4	12	5		6	8		9^{1}	11^{2}				3	7	2	13		10				21
1		4		5		6^{2}	8	13	9^{1}	11				3	7^{3}	2			10	12	14		22
1		4	3	2			8	12	11	9^{1}					13	5			10	14	7^{3}	6^{2}	23
1		3	4	5			8	7	13	10				14	6^{2}	2			11^{1}	12		9^{3}	24
1		3	4	5			9	10^{1}	12	8^{2}				7	6^{3}	2			11	14		13	25
1		4	3	5			8	14	9^{2}	11^{3}				6		2			10	12	13	7^{1}	26
1		4	3	5			8	14	9					6^{3}	13	2			10	11^{1}	12	7^{2}	27
																							28
																							29
																							30
																							31
																							32
																							33
																							34
																							35
																							36

BRECHIN CITY

Year Formed: 1906. *Ground & Address:* Glebe Park, Trinity Rd, Brechin, Angus DD9 6BJ. *Telephone:* 01356 622856. *Fax:* 01382 206331. *E-mail:* secretary@brechincityfc.com *Website:* www.brechincity.com
Ground Capacity: 4,123 (seated: 1,528). *Size of Pitch:* 101m × 61m.
Chairman: Ken Ferguson. *Vice-Chairman:* Martin Smith. *Secretary:* Grant Hood.
Manager: Mark Wilson. *Assistant Manager:* Stevie Campbell.
Club Nicknames: 'The City'; 'The Hedgemen'.
Previous Ground: Nursery Park.
Record Attendance: 8,122 v Aberdeen, Scottish Cup 3rd rd, 3 February 1973.
Record Transfer Fee received: £100,000 for Scott Thomson to Aberdeen (1991) and Chris Templeman to Morton (2004).
Record Transfer Fee paid: £16,000 for Sandy Ross from Berwick Rangers (1991).
Record Victory: 12-1 v Thornhill, Scottish Cup 1st rd, 28 January 1926.
Record Defeat: 0-10 v Airdrieonians, Albion R and Cowdenbeath, all in Division II, 1937-38.
Most League Appearances: 459: David Watt, 1975-89.
Most League Goals in Season (Individual): 26: Ronald McIntosh, Division II, 1959-60.
Most Goals Overall (Individual): 131: Ian Campbell, 1977-85.

BRECHIN CITY – SPFL LADBROKES LEAGUE TWO 2019–20 LEAGUE RECORD

Match No.	Date	Venue	Opponents	Result		H/T Score	Lg Pos.	Goalscorers	Attendance
1	Aug 3	H	Annan Ath	L	0-1	0-0	7		338
2	10	A	Edinburgh C	L	1-2	0-1	9	McManus [57]	246
3	17	H	Queen's Park	L	0-3	0-2	10		412
4	24	A	Albion R	W	1-0	1-0	9	McManus [36]	323
5	31	A	Cowdenbeath	L	1-2	1-2	9	McCord [2]	394
6	Sept 14	H	Cove R	L	2-4	2-4	10	Watt [3], Ngoy [22]	460
7	21	A	Stenhousemuir	L	0-1	0-0	10		435
8	28	H	Elgin C	W	2-1	0-0	9	McManus [47], Inglis [90]	349
9	Oct 5	H	Stirling Alb	D	1-1	0-0	9	McManus [47]	451
10	Nov 2	H	Edinburgh C	L	2-3	0-1	10	Ngoy 2 [84, 90]	353
11	9	A	Queen's Park	L	2-5	1-4	10	McManus (pen) [22], Watt [84]	572
12	12	A	Annan Ath	L	2-5	2-3	10	Crawford 2 [2, 26]	253
13	16	A	Cove R	L	0-3	0-0	10		862
14	30	H	Stenhousemuir	L	1-2	0-1	10	McCord [50]	401
15	Dec 7	A	Stirling Alb	W	4-2	2-2	10	Inglis [31], McManus 2 (1 pen) [40 (p), 56], McMinn [74]	521
16	14	H	Cowdenbeath	W	2-1	2-0	10	Hamilton 2 [16, 35]	368
17	21	A	Elgin C	L	1-3	0-1	10	Knox (pen) [85]	659
18	28	H	Albion R	D	0-0	0-0	10		459
19	Jan 4	H	Cove R	L	1-5	0-1	10	McCord [53]	705
20	11	A	Stenhousemuir	D	2-2	1-0	10	Hamilton 2 [35, 84]	629
21	25	A	Cowdenbeath	L	2-3	0-2	10	Allan [60], Hill [61]	382
22	Feb 1	H	Elgin C	L	1-2	1-0	10	Scott [29]	412
23	8	A	Albion R	L	1-4	1-2	10	Inglis (pen) [22]	282
24	22	A	Edinburgh C	D	0-0	0-0	10		230
25	26	H	Queen's Park	D	0-0	0-0	10		394
26	29	H	Stirling Alb	L	0-2	0-0	10		433
27	Mar 7	A	Cove R	L	2-3	0-1	10	Scott 2 (1 pen) [62, 90 (p)]	578
28	14	A	Elgin C	Cancelled					
29	18	H	Annan Ath	Cancelled					
30	21	H	Cowdenbeath	Cancelled					
31	28	A	Annan Ath	Cancelled					
32	Apr 4	H	Stenhousemuir	Cancelled					
33	11	H	Albion R	Cancelled					
34	18	A	Queen's Park	Cancelled					
35	25	A	Stirling Alb	Cancelled					
36	May 2	H	Edinburgh C	Cancelled					

Final League Position: 10 (on points-per-game basis)

Honours
League Champions: Second Division 1982-83, 1989-90, 2004-05; Third Division 2001-02; C Division 1953-54.
Runners-up: Second Division 1992-93, 2002-03; Third Division 1995-96.
Promoted via play-offs: 2016-17 (to Championship).
Scottish Cup: Quarter-finals 2011.
League Cup: Semi-finals 1957.
League Challenge Cup Runners-up: 2002-03.

Club colours: Shirt: Red with white trim. Shorts: Red with white trim. Socks: Red.

Goalscorers: *League (31):* McManus 7 (2 pens), Hamilton 4, Inglis 3 (1 pen), McCord 3, Ngoy 3, Scott 3 (1 pen), Crawford 2, Watt 2, Allan 1, Hill 1, Knox 1 (1 pen), McMinn 1.
William Hill Scottish Cup (2): McManus 1, own goal 1.
Betfred Scottish League Cup (1): Reekie 1.
Tunnock's Caramel Wafer Scottish League Challenge Cup (4): Reekie 3, Page 1.

Sinclair R 6	Duncanson L 6 + 6	Hill D 24	Reekie S 20 + 1	McLaughlin C 14	Hamilton O 20 + 6	McIntosh S 18 + 1	McCord R 24 + 1	Knox M 10 + 7	McManus P 19 + 5	Crawford R 4 + 11	Inglis K 18 + 5	Ngoy E 4 + 9	Watt L 6 + 5	Reid J — + 4	Page J 24	Brown R 18	O'Neil P 1 + 1	McLeod Kay F — + 1	McMinn L 20	Allan P 18 + 1	Jackson A 6 + 1	Laverty A 1 + 1	Scott M 6	McCabe R 4 + 1	Petkov A 4	Strachan L 2	Match No.
1	2	3	4	5	6	7	8	9^{2}	10	11^{1}	12	13															1
1	2^{3}	3^{2}	4	5	6^{1}	7	8	9	10	11	14		12	13													2
1		4	2	5	9		7	11^{2}	10	12			6^{1}	13	3	8											3
1^{2}	14	3	2	5	6^{1}		9		11		10^{3}		7	13	4	8	12										4
		4	2	5	6^{1}		11	13		12	9^{3}	10	3^{2}		8	7	1	14									5
	14	4	3	5	6^{1}		8	9	10^{2}	13	12	11^{3}	7			2			1								6
		3	2	5	12■		9	6^{1}	10	13	8	11^{2}			4	7			1								7
		4	2	5			9	10^{1}	11		8	12	13		3	7			1	6^{2}							8
		4	2	5^{1}	13		9	10^{2}	11		8	14	12		3	7^{3}			1	6							9
		4	2	8^{1}	12	5	10^{2}		11		9^{3}	13		14	3	7			1	6							10
		4^{1}	6	2	13	5	7	12	11			10^{3}	14		3	8^{2}			1	9							11
1			3	5■	10	2	12	6		11^{2}	9	13			4	8^{1}				7							12
1		4	2		6^{1}	5	8	10^{2}	11	12	7	13			3					9							13
		4	2		6	5	8		11	13	10^{1}	12			3	7^{2}			1	9							14
		3	2		6	5	9	12	11^{2}	13	10^{1}				4	7			1	8							15
		4■	2		6	5	10		11^{1}	12	9^{2}		13		3	7			1	8							16
	2^{2}				6^{3}	5	10	13	11^{1}	12	9	14	7		4	3			1	8							17
	2				9	5	10	12	11^{2}	8	6^{1}	13	7■		4	3			1								18
	13	3	2		8	5	9	10^{1}	11	12					4	6			1	7^{2}							19
		3	2		8	5	9^{2}	12	13		10^{1}				4	6			1	7	11						20
	2	3			6^{2}	5^{3}	7	14	11	12	9^{1}				4				1	8	10	13					21
	2^{2}	3		5	6	13	8		14						4				1	7	11^{3}	9^{1}	10	12			22
	14	4	2	9^{1}	12	5^{3}			13		8				3	7			1	6	10^{2}		11				23
	13	3	2^{2}		12	5			10^{1}		9				4				1	7			11	8	6		24
		2			5	9	7		12		13				4				1	8	10^{2}		11	6^{1}	3		25
		2	12		5		7		14		13				4^{2}				1	8^{1}	11^{3}		10	6	3	9	26
	13	5			7	2^{1}	9				10^{2}				4				1	12	14		11	8	3	6^{3}	27
																											28
																											29
																											30
																											31
																											32
																											33
																											34
																											35
																											36

CELTIC

Year Formed: 1888. *Ground & Address:* Celtic Park, Glasgow G40 3RE. *Telephone:* 0871 226 1888. *Fax:* 0141 551 8106.
E-mail: customerservices@celticfc.co.uk *Website:* www.celticfc.net
Ground Capacity: 60,832 (all seated). *Size of Pitch:* 105m × 68m.
Chairman: Ian Bankier. *Chief Executive:* Peter Lawwell.
Manager: Neil Lennon. *Assistant Manager:* John Kennedy. *First-Team Coach:* Damien Duff.
Club Nicknames: 'The Bhoys'; 'The Hoops'; 'The Celts'.
Record Attendance: 92,000 v Rangers, Division I, 1 January 1938.
Record Transfer Fee received: £25,000,000 for Kieran Tierney to Arsenal (August 2019).
Record Transfer Fee paid: £9,000,000 for Odsonne Édouard from Paris Saint-Germain (June 2018).
Record Victory: 11-0 Dundee, Division I, 26 October 1895. *Record Defeat:* 0-8 v Motherwell, Division I, 30 April 1937.
Most Capped Player: Pat Bonner, 80, Republic of Ireland. *Most League Appearances:* 486: Billy McNeill, 1957-75.
Most League Goals in Season (Individual): 50: James McGrory, Division I, 1935-36.
Most League Goals Overall (Individual): 397: James McGrory, 1922-39.

Honours

League Champions: (51 times) Division I 1892-93, 1893-94, 1895-96, 1897-98, 1904-05, 1905-06, 1906-07, 1907-08, 1908-09, 1909-10, 1913-14, 1914-15, 1915-16, 1916-17, 1918-19, 1921-22, 1925-26, 1935-36, 1937-38, 1953-54, 1965-66, 1966-67, 1967-68, 1968-69, 1969-70, 1970-71, 1971-72, 1972-73, 1973-74; Premier Division 1976-77, 1978-79, 1980-81, 1981-82, 1985-86, 1987-88, 1997-98, 2000-01, 2001-02, 2003-04, 2005-06, 2006-07, 2007-08, 2011-12, 2012-13; Premiership 2013-14, 2014-15, 2015-16, 2016-17, 2017-18, 2018-19, 2019-20. *Runners-up:* 31 times.
Scottish Cup Winners: (39 times) 1892, 1899, 1900, 1904, 1907, 1908, 1911, 1912, 1914, 1923, 1925, 1927, 1931, 1933, 1937, 1951, 1954, 1965, 1967, 1969, 1971, 1972, 1974, 1975, 1977, 1980, 1985, 1988, 1989, 1995, 2001, 2004, 2005, 2007, 2011, 2013, 2017, 2018, 2019. *Runners-up:* 18 times.
League Cup Winners: (19 times) 1956-57, 1957-58, 1965-66, 1966-67, 1967-68, 1968-69, 1969-70, 1974-75, 1982-83, 1997-98, 1999-2000, 2000-01, 2005-06, 2008-09, 2014-15, 2016-17, 2017-18, 2018-19, 2019-20. *Runners-up:* 15 times.

CELTIC – SPFL LADBROKES PREMIERSHIP 2019–20 LEAGUE RECORD

Match No.	*Date*	*Venue*	*Opponents*	*Result*		*H/T Score*	*Lg Pos.*	*Goalscorers*	*Attendance*
1	Aug 3	H	St Johnstone	W	7-0	3-0	1	Johnston [9], Christie 3 [26, 30, 67], Ntcham [72], Edouard [80], Griffiths [86]	58,877
2	10	A	Motherwell	W	5-2	2-1	1	Ajer [14], Griffiths [41], Forrest [66], Edouard [76], Christie (pen) [86]	8822
3	25	H	Hearts	W	3-1	1-0	1	Berra (og) [29], McGregor [54], Halkett (og) [60]	58,763
4	Sept 1	A	Rangers	W	2-0	1-0	1	Edouard [32], Hayes [90]	49,873
5	14	A	Hamilton A	W	1-0	1-0	1	Forrest [4]	5300
6	22	H	Kilmarnock	W	3-1	1-1	1	Edouard 2 [44, 53], Christie [57]	57,137
7	28	A	Hibernian	D	1-1	1-1	1	Christie [24]	18,339
8	Oct 6	A	Livingston	L	0-2	0-0	2		8196
9	19	H	Ross Co	W	6-0	1-0	1	Elyounoussi 2 [4, 72], Edouard 2 [47, 50], McGregor [49], Forrest [55]	58,560
10	27	A	Aberdeen	W	4-0	4-0	1	Edouard [10], Frimpong [15], Forrest [37], Elyounoussi [44]	15,079
11	30	H	St Mirren	W	2-0	0-0	1	Elyounoussi [49], Forrest [54]	56,127
12	Nov 10	H	Motherwell	W	2-0	1-0	1	Edouard [19], Tait (og) [54]	57,137
13	23	H	Livingston	W	4-0	1-0	1	Edouard [19], Brown [57], Forrest 2 [64, 90]	58,247
14	Dec 1	A	Ross Co	W	4-1	2-1	1	Christie 2 [11, 38], Rogic [67], Johnston [73]	6512
15	4	H	Hamilton A	W	2-1	1-0	1	Christie [13], Brown [90]	54,584
16	15	H	Hibernian	W	2-0	1-0	1	Frimpong [39], Edouard [66]	57,598
17	18	A	Hearts	W	2-0	2-0	1	Christie [28], Ntcham [40]	17,297
18	21	H	Aberdeen	W	2-1	1-1	1	Jullien [7], Edouard [66]	59,131
19	26	A	St Mirren	W	2-1	2-0	1	McGregor [22], Forrest [32]	6797
20	29	H	Rangers	L	1-2	1-1	1	Edouard [41]	58,902
21	Jan 22	A	Kilmarnock	W	3-1	1-0	1	Edouard [25], Griffiths [51], Jullien [73]	8307
22	25	H	Ross Co	W	3-0	1-0	1	McGregor (pen) [37], Edouard 2 [65, 68]	58,785
23	29	A	St Johnstone	W	3-0	3-0	1	Ntcham [6], Forrest [20], Griffiths [26]	8743
24	Feb 2	A	Hamilton A	W	4-1	1-1	1	Edouard 2 [35, 81], Jullien [78], Forrest [90]	4708
25	5	A	Motherwell	W	4-0	1-0	1	Edouard 2 [9, 80], Griffiths [51], McGregor [75]	8534
26	12	H	Hearts	W	5-0	1-0	1	Ntcham [30], Jullien [46], McGregor [53], Christie [67], Simunovic [80]	57,431
27	16	A	Aberdeen	W	2-1	1-1	1	McGregor [10], Ajer [81]	14,135
28	23	H	Kilmarnock	W	3-1	2-1	1	Ajer [28], Edouard [33], Griffiths [62]	58,883
29	Mar 4	A	Livingston	D	2-2	1-1	1	McGregor [16], Rogic [90]	8640
30	7	H	St Mirren	W	5-0	2-0	1	Griffiths 3 [18, 44, 74], Edouard [54], McGregor (pen) [90]	58,998
31	15	A	Rangers	Cancelled					
32	21	H	St Johnstone	Cancelled					
33	Apr 5	A	Hibernian	Cancelled					
34	Fixtures 34–38 decided after 33 game league split.								
35									
36									
37									
38									

Final League Position: 1 (on points-per-game basis)

European: *European Cup/Champions League:* 212 matches (1966-67 winners, 1967-68, 1968-69, 1969-70 runners-up, 1970-71, 1971-72, 1972-73, 1973-74 semi-finals, 1974-75, 1977-78, 1979-80, 1981-82, 1982-83, 1986-87, 1988-89, 1998-99, 2001-02, 2002-03, 2003-04, 2004-05, 2005-06, 2006-07, 2007-08, 2008-09, 2009-10, 2010-11, 2012-13, 2013-14, 2014-15, 2015-16, 2016-17, 2017-18, 2018-19, 2019-20). *Cup Winners' Cup:* 38 matches (1963-64 semi-finals, 1965-66 semi-finals, 1975-76, 1980-81, 1984-85, 1985-86, 1989-90, 1995-96). *UEFA Cup:* 75 matches (*Fairs Cup:* 1962-63, 1964-65. *UEFA Cup:* 1976-77, 1983-84, 1987-88, 1991-92, 1992-93, 1993-94, 1996-97, 1997-98, 1998-99, 1999-2000, 2000-01, 2001-02, 2002-03 runners-up, 2003-04 quarter-finals). *Europa League:* 52 matches (2009-10, 2010-11, 2011-12, 2014-15, 2015-16, 2017-18, 2018-19, 2019-20).

Club colours: Shirt: Green and white hoops. Shorts: White. Socks: Green with white hoops.

Goalscorers: *League (89):* Edouard 22, Christie 11 (1 pen), Forrest 10, Griffiths 9, McGregor 9 (2 pens), Elyounoussi 4, Jullien 4, Ntcham 4, Ajer 3, Brown 2, Frimpong 2, Johnston 2, Rogic 2, Hayes 1, Simunovic 1, own goals 3.
William Hill Scottish Cup (6): Bayo 1, Brown 1, Christie 1, Griffiths 1, McGregor 1, Ntcham 1.
Betfred Scottish League Cup (13): Brown 2, Elyounoussi 2, Ntcham 2, Bayo 1, Forrest 1, Johnston 1, Jullien 1, McGregor 1, Rogic 1, Sinclair 1.
Tunnock's Caramel Wafer Scottish League Challenge Cup (3): Aitchison 1, Okoflex 1, Robertson 1.
Champions League (16): Christie 4 (1 pen), Edouard 2, Forrest 2, McGregor 2, Ajer 1, Griffiths 1, Johnston 1, Shved 1, Sinclair 1, own goal 1.
UEFA Europa League (18): Edouard 4 (1 pen), Christie 3 (1 pen), Forrest 3, Johnston 2, Jullien 2, Morgan 2, Elyounoussi 1, Ntcham 1.

Bain S 2	Elhamed H 3 + 2	Bitton N 9 + 6	Ajer K 28	Bolingoli Mbombo B 14	Brown S 29	McGregor C 30	Forrest J 28	Christie R 17 + 7	Johnston M 4 + 7	Edouard O 25 + 2	Ralston A — + 2	Ntcham J 17 + 6	Griffiths L 10 + 11	Jullien C 28	Morgan L 3 + 2	Sinclair S — + 2	Forster F 28	Bayo V 1 + 7	Bauer M 6 + 3	Hayes J 5 + 9	Elyounoussi M 7 + 3	Rogic T 6 + 10	Frimpong J 12 + 2	Shved M — + 1	Taylor G 11 + 1	Simunovic J 6	Dembele K — + 1	Klimala P — + 2	Welsh S 1	Match No.
1	2^{3}	3	4	5	6	7	8	9^{1}	10^{2}	11	12	13	14																	1
1		3	2	5	6	9	8^{3}	13		12		7^{1}	11^{2}	4	10	14														2
		4	2^{3}	5	6	7	8	10	12		14	9^{2}	13	3			1	11^{1}												3
	2	4^{3}		5	6	7	8^{2}	9	10^{1}	11		12		3			1		13	14										4
	2		3	5	6	7	8	9^{3}		11^{1}				4			1	13		14	10^{2}	12								5
	13		4	5	6	7	8	10		11		9^{3}		3^{1}			1		2^{2}	12		14								6
			4	5	6	7	8^{3}	10		11^{2}		9^{1}		3		14	1	13	2	12										7
			4	5^{2}	6^{3}	7	8^{1}	9■		11		14		3			1	12	2	13	10									8
		13	4	5	6	7^{3}	8^{1}			11^{2}				3			1	12			10	9	2	14						9
		12	4	5	6	7	8			11^{2}				3^{1}			1	13		14	10^{3}	9	2							10
			4		6^{2}	7	8	9		11^{1}		12		3	13		1		2	14	10				5^{3}					11
			4		6	7	8^{2}	12		11		9		3	13		1			5	10^{1}		2							12
			3		6	7	8	10		11^{3}		14	13	4			1			5^{1}		9^{2}	2		12					13
		14	4		6	7^{3}	10	8	12				13	3	11^{2}		1					9^{1}	2		5					14
		3	4		6	7	10^{3}	8	12			9^{1}	13		11^{2}		1		2				14		5					15
		4	2	5	6	7	10^{1}			11^{2}		9	12	3			1					13	8							16
		12	4		6	9	10^{2}	8		11^{1}		7	13	3			1			5			2							17
			4	5	6	7	10^{1}	8	12	11^{3}		9^{2}	13	3			1					14	2							18
			4	5	7	6	10^{2}	8	12	11^{1}		9	13	3			1						2							19
		13	4	5	6	7	8^{2}	9^{3}	10^{1}	11		12	14	3			1						2							20
			4		7	8			12	10^{3}		6	11^{1}	3			1	14	13	9			5^{2}			2				21
					6	7	8		10^{2}	12		9^{1}	11^{3}	4			1		2	5		13				3	14			22
			4		7	8	5		13	11^{2}		6	10^{1}	3			1		12						9	2^{3}		14		23
			4		7	8	5	12		11		6^{2}	10	3			1			13		14			9^{3}				2^{1}	24
			4		6	7	5	12		11^{1}		8^{3}	10^{2}	3			1					14			9	2		13		25
			2		6	7	5^{1}	12		11		9^{3}	10^{2}	4			1				13	14			8	3				26
		3	2		7	6	5	13		11		8^{1}	10^{2}	4			1			12		14			9^{3}					27
		14	4			7		8		11^{3}			10^{1}	3			1	12			13	6^{2}	5		9	2				28
		2	4		7	8	5	6^{1}		11			14	3			1				10^{2}	13	12		9^{3}					29
	14	2	4^{3}		6	7	5	12		10^{1}			11	3			1				13	9^{2}			8					30
																														31
																														32
																														33
																														34
																														35
																														36
																														37
																														38

CLYDE

Year Formed: 1877. *Ground & Address:* Broadwood Stadium, Cumbernauld, G68 9NE. *Telephone:* 01236 451511. *Fax:* 01236 733490. *E-mail:* info@clydefc.co.uk *Website:* www.clydefc.co.uk
Ground Capacity: 8,086 (all seated). *Size of Pitch:* 100m × 68m.
Chairman: John Taylor. *Vice Chairman:* Gordon Thomson.
Manager: Danny Lennon. *Assistant Manager:* Allan Moore.
Club Nickname: 'The Bully Wee'.
Previous Grounds: Barrowfield Park 1877-98; Shawfield Stadium 1898-1986; Firhill Stadium 1986-91; Douglas Park 1991-94.
Record Attendance: 52,000 v Rangers, Division I, 21 November 1908.
Record Transfer Fee received: £200,000 from Blackburn R for Gordon Greer (May 2001).
Record Transfer Fee paid: £14,000 for Harry Hood from Sunderland (1966).
Record Victory: 11-1 v Cowdenbeath, Division II, 6 October 1951.
Record Defeat: 0-11 v Dumbarton, Scottish Cup 4th rd, 22 November, 1879; v Rangers, Scottish Cup 4th rd, 13 November 1880.
Most Capped Player: Tommy Ring, 12, Scotland.
Most League Appearances: 420: Brian Ahern, 1971-81; 1987-88.
Most League Goals in Season (Individual): 32: Bill Boyd, 1932-33.
Most Goals Overall (Individual): 124: Tommy Ring, 1950-60.

CLYDE – SPFL LADBROKES LEAGUE ONE 2019–20 LEAGUE RECORD

Match No.	*Date*	*Venue*	*Opponents*	*Result*		*H/T Score*	*Lg Pos.*	*Goalscorers*	*Attendance*
1	Aug 3	H	East Fife	D	1-1	1-0	5	Goodwillie (pen) [10]	836
2	10	A	Raith R	L	2-5	0-2	9	Goodwillie [78], Love [89]	1707
3	17	A	Airdrieonians	L	1-3	1-0	10	Goodwillie [2]	1054
4	24	H	Falkirk	W	1-0	1-0	9	Lamont [34]	2048
5	31	A	Forfar Ath	D	0-0	0-0	8		650
6	Sept 14	H	Stranraer	W	6-1	3-0	6	Goodwillie 5 (3 pens) [30 (p), 33 (p), 43, 55 (p), 86], Darren Smith [81]	753
7	21	A	Peterhead	D	1-1	1-1	7	Goodwillie [17]	682
8	28	A	Dumbarton	W	2-1	0-1	4	McStay [61], Johnston [75]	851
9	Oct 5	H	Montrose	L	0-2	0-2	6		721
10	19	H	Raith R	D	2-2	0-2	6	Goodwillie 2 [54, 68]	1202
11	26	A	Falkirk	W	1-0	0-0	6	Darren Smith [81]	4021
12	Nov 2	A	Stranraer	L	0-3	0-2	6		418
13	9	H	Peterhead	L	1-2	0-2	7	Rumsby [78]	649
14	26	A	East Fife	D	0-0	0-0	7		425
15	30	H	Dumbarton	L	1-2	1-1	7	Johnston [7]	721
16	Dec 7	H	Forfar Ath	D	0-0	0-0	8		510
17	14	A	Montrose	L	0-4	0-1	8		583
18	21	H	Airdrieonians	W	3-1	2-1	7	Petkov [7], Goodwillie 2 [21, 90]	1094
19	28	A	Peterhead	L	0-2	0-1	8		585
20	Jan 4	H	Stranraer	D	3-3	0-2	8	Goodwillie 3 (1 pen) [53, 59 (p), 84]	823
21	25	H	East Fife	W	2-1	0-0	7	Goodwillie [62], Lang [88]	954
22	Feb 1	A	Forfar Ath	L	1-2	0-1	8	Cuddihy [52]	566
23	15	A	Airdrieonians	L	0-2	0-2	8		913
24	22	A	Raith R	L	0-1	0-0	8		1527
25	25	A	Dumbarton	L	0-1	0-0	8		468
26	29	H	Falkirk	W	3-2	2-1	7	Lamont [3], Goodwillie 2 (1 pen) [43 (p), 53]	1784
27	Mar 3	H	Montrose	W	2-1	1-0	7	Love [12], Grant [51]	507
28	7	H	Dumbarton	W	2-0	0-0	7	Goodwillie [49], Rankin [90]	658
29	14	A	Stranraer	Cancelled					
30	21	H	Peterhead	Cancelled					
31	28	A	East Fife	Cancelled					
32	Apr 4	H	Forfar Ath	Cancelled					
33	11	A	Falkirk	Cancelled					
34	18	H	Raith R	Cancelled					
35	25	A	Montrose	Cancelled					
36	May 2	H	Airdrieonians	Cancelled					

Final League Position: 7 (on points-per-game basis)

Honours
League Champions: Division II 1904-05, 1951-52, 1956-57, 1961-62, 1972-73; Second Division 1977-78, 1981-82, 1992-93, 1999-2000.
Runners-up: Division II 1903-04, 1905-06, 1925-26, 1963-64; First Division 2002-03, 2003-04; League Two 2018-19.
Promoted via play-offs: 2018-19 (to League Two).
Scottish Cup Winners: 1939, 1955, 1958; *Runners-up:* 1910, 1912, 1949.
League Cup: Semi-finals 1956, 1957, 1968.
League Challenge Cup Runners-up: 2006-07.

Club colours: Shirt: White with red trim. Shorts: Black. Socks: Black.

Goalscorers: *League (35):* Goodwillie 20 (6 pens), Johnston 2, Lamont 2, Love 2, Darren Smith 2, Cuddihy 1, Grant 1, Lang 1, McStay 1, Petkov 1, Rankin 1, Rumsby 1.
William Hill Scottish Cup (3): Goodwillie 1 (1 pen), Love 1, Darren Smith 1.
Betfred Scottish League Cup (6): Goodwillie 2 (1 pen), Darren Smith 1, Syvertsen 1, Wallace 1, own goal 1.
Tunnock's Caramel Wafer Scottish League Challenge Cup (9): Goodwillie 2 (1 pen), McNiff 2, Johnston 1, Love 1, McStay 1, own goals 2.

Mitchell D 28	Cuddihy B 20 + 2	Rumsby S 23 + 1	Petkov A 10 + 4	McNiff M 26	McStay C 20 + 3	Grant R 28	Smith Darren 9 + 13	Johnston C 16 + 8	Wallace T 8 + 9	Goodwillie D 25	Howie C 16 + 2	Lamont M 23 + 5	Duffie K 3 + 4	Love A 17 + 5	Lyon R 9 + 3	Allison L 1 + 3	McMullin M 3	McNiven L — + 1	Wylde G 3 + 4	Lang T 7	Rankin J 1 + 6	Livingstone A 6	Cunningham R 6	Match No.
1	2^{1}	3	4	5	6	7	8	9	10	11^{2}	12	13												1
1		3	4	5	10	7	9^{1}	6^{3}	8	11		12	2^{2}	13	14									2
1	2^{1}	3	4	5	13	6		8^{2}	7	11	14	9^{3}		12	10									3
1		4	3	5	7^{2}	8	12	14	13	11	2	10^{1}		9^{3}	6									4
1		4		5	7	8	6^{1}	12	13	11	3	10		9^{2}	2									5
1	2	4		5	6^{3}	7	13	8	12	11	3	9^{1}	14	10^{2}										6
1	2	4	14	5	6	7	12	8^{1}	13	11■	3	9^{2}		10^{3}										7
1	2	4	12	5	6	7	11	8^{1}	13		3	9^{2}	14	10^{3}										8
1	2^{2}	4		5	6	7	11	8	13		3	9^{3}	14	10^{1}	12									9
1	2	4	7^{1}	5	10^{3}	8	9^{2}	14		11	3	12		13	6									10
1	7^{3}	3		5	12	8	13	6^{1}		11	4	10		9^{2}	2	14								11
1	13	4		5	7^{2}	8	12	6	9^{3}	11	3	10^{1}			2	14								12
1	2	4		3	8	7	12	11^{2}	14	10^{3}		9	13		6	5^{1}								13
1	2	3	12	5	7	6		13	8^{3}	11	4	10^{1}				14	9^{2}							14
1	2	4	12	5	7^{1}	8	13	6	14	11	3^{2}	10					9^{3}							15
1	6	4	3	5	8	7	11^{1}	9				10^{2}	2	12				13						16
1	6	4	3		8	7^{2}	10^{3}	9		11		12	2	13	14		5^{1}							17
1	10	4	3	5		8	12	6	7	11		2		9^{1}										18
1	6	4	3	5		8	10		7	11		2		9										19
1	2■	4	3	5		8	12	6^{1}	7	11		10		9^{2}					13					20
1		3		5		6	12	7^{1}	13	11	2	8		10^{2}					9^{3}	4	14			21
1	7	3^{3}		5		6	12	13		11	2	8		10^{2}					9^{1}	4	14			22
1	2	3			12	6	14			11	4	13			7^{2}				10^{3}		9	5	8^{1}	23
1				7	8^{2}	4				10	2	11		9^{1}					13	3	12	5	6	24
1	12			7	8	4		13		11	2^{1}	10		6^{2}					14	3		5^{3}	9	25
1	2	14		7	8	4				11		10^{1}		9^{3}					13	3	12	5	6^{2}	26
1	2			4	8	6	13	14		11		9^{2}		7^{3}						3	12	5	10^{1}	27
1				4	8	6		13		11		9^{2}		7^{1}	2					3	12	5	10	28
																								29
																								30
																								31
																								32
																								33
																								34
																								35
																								36

COVE RANGERS

Year Formed: 1922. *Ground & Address:* Balmoral Stadium, Wellington Circle, Altens, Aberdeen AB12 3JG. *Telephone:* 01224 392 111. *Fax:* 01224 392 858. *E-mail:* dlittle@coverangersfc.com *Website:* www.coverangersfc.com
Ground Capacity: 2322 (356 seated). *Size of Pitch:* 105yd × 68yd.
Chairman: Keith Moorhouse. *Vice Chairman:* Graeme Reid. *Secretary:* Duncan Little.
Manager: Paul Hartley. *Assistant Manager:* Gordon Young.
Club Nickname: 'Wee Rangers', 'Toonsers'.
Previous Grounds: Allan Park.
Record Attendance: 2,100 v Deveronvale, 2009, Highland League.
Record Transfer Fee received: Scott Paterson, £25,000 from Liverpool March 1992.
Record Transfer Fee paid: £14,000 for Harry Hood from Sunderland (1966).
Record Victory: 7-1 v Stirling Albion, League Two, 10 March 2020.
Record Defeat: 0-7 v Ross County, League Cup Group rd, 30 July 2016.
Most League Appearances: 28: Stuart McKenzie and Connor Scully 2019-20.
Most League Goals in Season (Individual): 24: Mitch Megginson, 2019-20.
Most Goals Overall (Individual): 24: Mitch Megginson, 2019-20.

COVE RANGERS – SPFL LADBROKES LEAGUE TWO 2019–20 LEAGUE RECORD

Match No.	*Date*	*Venue*	*Opponents*	*Result*		*H/T Score*	*Lg Pos.*	*Goalscorers*	*Attendance*
1	Aug 3	H	Edinburgh C	W	5-0	3-0	1	Megginson 2 [31, 37], Milne, H 2 [41, 68], Brown [87]	995
2	10	A	Albion R	D	4-4	3-1	1	Milne, H [17], Masson [38], Glass [41], Megginson [86]	347
3	17	H	Cowdenbeath	W	3-2	1-0	1	Masson [17], Glass 2 [60, 90]	880
4	24	A	Stirling Alb	W	2-1	1-0	1	Fyvie [27], Smith [52]	605
5	31	H	Queen's Park	W	3-0	1-0	1	Higgins [21], Smith [68], Fyvie [84]	661
6	Sept 14	A	Brechin C	W	4-2	4-2	1	Masson [10], Megginson [21], Glass [30], Fyvie [36]	460
7	21	A	Elgin C	W	2-0	1-0	1	Megginson [3], Antoniazzi [86]	1002
8	28	H	Annan Ath	W	3-0	1-0	1	Higgins [30], Antoniazzi [63], Aird [82]	642
9	Oct 5	A	Stenhousemuir	L	2-3	1-3	1	Masson [3], Scott [88]	552
10	29	H	Albion R	W	3-0	1-0	1	Megginson 2 [25, 79], Ross [75]	633
11	Nov 2	A	Cowdenbeath	W	3-1	2-1	1	Megginson [30], Aird 2 [36, 78]	425
12	9	H	Stirling Alb	W	1-0	0-0	1	Megginson (pen) [88]	825
13	16	H	Brechin C	W	3-0	0-0	1	Megginson [78], Glass [83], Ross [90]	862
14	30	A	Annan Ath	L	1-6	1-3	1	Masson [8]	459
15	Dec 7	A	Edinburgh C	L	1-2	1-2	1	Scott [34]	439
16	14	H	Stenhousemuir	W	2-1	0-0	1	Scott [53], Robertson [87]	391
17	21	A	Queen's Park	W	3-1	2-0	1	Megginson 2 [25, 90], Masson [27]	478
18	28	H	Elgin C	W	2-0	1-0	1	Glass [31], Megginson [87]	1264
19	Jan 4	A	Brechin C	W	5-1	1-0	1	Masson 2 [31, 65], Megginson 2 [74, 82], Fyvie [86]	705
20	18	H	Cowdenbeath	W	3-1	2-0	1	Megginson (pen) [35], McAllister (pen) [45], Masson [53]	707
21	25	H	Annan Ath	W	2-0	1-0	1	Megginson [23], Masson [85]	735
22	Feb 1	A	Albion R	D	2-2	1-0	1	Megginson [7], Masson [65]	292
23	8	A	Elgin C	L	0-3	0-2	1		849
24	15	H	Edinburgh C	W	2-1	0-0	1	Higgins [55], McAllister [88]	909
25	22	H	Queen's Park	W	2-0	2-0	1	Masson [3], Davidson (og) [41]	627
26	29	A	Stenhousemuir	W	3-0	2-0	1	Megginson 2 (1 pen) [33, 50 (p)], McAllister [42]	596
27	Mar 7	H	Brechin C	W	3-2	1-0	1	Megginson 2 (1 pen) [13 (p), 48], Masson [54]	578
28	10	A	Stirling Alb	W	7-1	5-0	1	Megginson 2 [9, 38], Fyvie [17], Milne, H [21], Masson 2 [31, 61], Brown [82]	423
29	14	A	Cowdenbeath	Cancelled					
30	21	H	Albion R	Cancelled					
31	28	A	Edinburgh C	Cancelled					
32	Apr 4	H	Elgin C	Cancelled					
33	11	A	Annan Ath	Cancelled					
34	18	H	Stenhousemuir	Cancelled					
35	25	A	Queen's Park	Cancelled					
36	May 2	H	Stirling Alb	Cancelled					

Final League Position: 1 (on points-per-game basis)

Honours
League Champions: League Two 2019-20.
Scottish Highland League Champions: 2000-01, 2007-08, 2008-09, 2012-13, 2015-16, 2017-18, 2018-19.
Promoted via play-offs: 2018-19.

Club colours: Shirts: Blue with white trim. Shorts: Blue. Socks: White.

Goalscorers: *League (76):* Megginson 24 (4 pens), Masson 15, Glass 6, Fyvie 5, Milne, H 4, Aird 3, Higgins 3, McAllister 3 (1 pen), Scott 3, Antoniazzi 2, Brown 2, Ross 2, Smith 2, Robertson 1, own goal 1.
William Hill Scottish Cup (0).
Betfred Scottish League Cup (6): Masson 2 (1 pen), Megginson 2, Antoniazzi 1, Glass 1.
Tunnock's Caramel Wafer Scottish League Challenge Cup (6): Brown 1, Megginson 1, Park 1, Robertson 1, Scott 1, Scully 1.

McKenzie S 28	Yule B 26 + 1	Ross S 26 + 1	Higgins D 19 + 1	Milne H 25	Redman J 2 + 5	Glass D 16	Scully C 28	Masson J 27	Antoniazzi C 5 + 3	Megginson M 25	Robertson J 2 + 15	Park D — + 2	Brown J — + 9	Scott M 6 + 11	Strachan R 17	Fyvie F 24	Smith M 3 + 5	Aird F 7 + 2	Redford A 1	Leighton T 3 + 4	Mulligan J 4 + 4	McAllister R 8	Watson B 6 + 1	Meekison A — + 3	*Match No.*
1	2	3	4	5	6	7^2	8	9	10^3	11^1	12	13	14												1
1	2	3	4	5	6^1	7	8	9	10^2	11		13		12											2
1	2		3	5		8	7	11	9^1	10^2	13				4	6	12								3
1	2	12	3	5	13	9^2	6	10^3		11	14				4	7	8^1								4
1	2	4	3	5		9^2	6	10	12	11				13		7	8^1								5
1	7	2	3	5		9^3	6	10^1	13	11				14	4^2	8	12								6
1	2	3	4	5	12	9^3	6	10	13	11^2				14		8	7^1								7
1	2	4	3	5		9^3	6	10^2	8^1	11	13					7	14	12							8
1	2^2	4	3	5		9	7^3	10	8^1	11				13		6	14	12							9
1	2	3	4	5		9^2	6	10^3		11			13	12		8	14	7^1							10
1	2	3	4	5		9	6	10		11^1				12		8		7							11
1	2	3	4	5		9	6^2	10		11	12			13		8		7^1							12
1	2	3	4	5	14	8	6^3	10^1		11	13			12		9		7^2							13
1	2	3	4^1	5^2	12	8■	6	9			11		13	10				7							14
1	2	3					6	10		11	12			8	4	9		7	5^1						15
1	2	3			14		8	9		10	13		12	11	4	7^2		6^1		5^3					16
1	2	3^2				6	8	9		10	12		13	11^1	4	7				5					17
1	2	3		5^2		6^3	8	9		10	13		14	11^1	4	7				12					18
1	2	3		5			6	10		11	8^2		13	9^1	4	7^3				14	12				19
1	2	3		5			7	9		10	13			12	4	8					6^1	11^2			20
1	2	3		5			7	9		11				13	4	8				12	6^2	10^1			21
1	8	3		5			7	9		10	13				4					2	6^2	11^1	12		22
1	2	3	13	5			7	9			12				4	8^2					10^1	11	6		23
1	5	2	4	8			7	11			13				3^2	6				12		10	9^1		24
1		2	4	8			7	11		9	13				3	6					12	10^1	5^2		25
1	6^1	2	3	5			8			10			12		4	7					14	11^3	9^2	13	26
1	12	2	3	5			7	9^2		10					4	8						11^1	6	13	27
1	8	2	4	5			7	10^2		11^3			14		3	6					13		9^1	12	28
																									29
																									30
																									31
																									32
																									33
																									34
																									35
																									36

COWDENBEATH

Year Formed: 1882. *Ground & Address:* Central Park, Cowdenbeath KY4 9QQ. *Telephone:* 01383 610166. *Fax:* 01383 512132.
E-mail: office@cowdenbeathfc.com *Website:* www.cowdenbeathfc.com
Ground Capacity: 4,370 (seated: 1,431). *Size of Pitch:* 95m × 60m.
Chairman: Donald Findlay QC. *Finance Director and Secretary:* David Allan.
Club Nicknames: 'The Blue Brazil'; 'Cowden'; 'The Miners'.
Manager: Gary Bollan. *Assistant Manager:* Craig Easton. *First-Team Coach:* Ian Flaherty.
Previous Ground: North End Park.
Record Attendance: 25,586 v Rangers, League Cup quarter-final, 21 September 1949.
Record Transfer Fee received: £30,000 for Nicky Henderson to Falkirk (March 1994).
Record Victory: 12-0 v Johnstone, Scottish Cup 1st rd, 21 January 1928.
Record Defeat: 1-11 v Clyde, Division II, 6 October 1951; 0-10 v Hearts, Championship, 28 February 2015.
Most Capped Player: Jim Paterson, 3, Scotland.
Most League and Cup Appearances: 491, Ray Allan 1972-75, 1979-89.
Most League Goals in Season (Individual): 54, Rab Walls, Division II, 1938-39.
Most Goals Overall (Individual): 127, Willie Devlin, 1922-26, 1929-30.

COWDENBEATH – SPFL LADBROKES LEAGUE TWO 2019–20 LEAGUE RECORD

Match No.	*Date*		*Venue*	*Opponents*	*Result*		*H/T Score*	*Lg Pos.*	*Goalscorers*	*Attendance*
1	Aug	3	A	Elgin C	L	0-3	0-1	9		612
2		10	H	Stirling Alb	W	1-0	0-0	6	Kris Renton 49	401
3		17	A	Cove R	L	2-3	0-1	8	Mullen (pen) 67, Cox 78	880
4		24	H	Annan Ath	W	3-1	1-0	5	Buchanan 39, Smith, C 70, Mullen 85	286
5		31	H	Brechin C	W	2-1	2-1	3	Thomas 6, Mullen (pen) 42	394
6	Sept	14	A	Stenhousemuir	W	3-0	1-0	3	Barr 20, Cox 67, Thomas 73	605
7		21	A	Queen's Park	W	3-0	0-0	3	Mullen (pen) 54, Barr 77, Allan 90	514
8		28	H	Albion R	W	1-0	1-0	3	Mullen (pen) 37	364
9	Oct	5	H	Edinburgh C	W	1-0	1-0	2	Cox 44	422
10		29	A	Stirling Alb	D	0-0	0-0	3		451
11	Nov	2	H	Cove R	L	1-3	1-2	3	Cox 15	425
12		9	A	Annan Ath	L	0-1	0-0	3		307
13		16	H	Queen's Park	W	1-0	1-0	3	Buchanan 20	448
14	Dec	7	H	Elgin C	D	0-0	0-0	3		307
15		14	A	Brechin C	L	1-2	0-2	3	Buchanan 90	368
16		21	H	Stenhousemuir	W	3-1	2-1	3	Herd 6, Swan 33, Allan 82	312
17		28	A	Edinburgh C	L	0-2	0-0	3		494
18	Jan	4	H	Annan Ath	W	3-1	3-0	3	Smith, C 17, Cox 30, Herd 45	312
19		18	A	Cove R	L	1-3	0-2	3	Cox 57	707
20		25	H	Brechin C	W	3-2	2-0	3	Allan 6, Thomas 27, Barr 75	382
21	Feb	1	A	Queen's Park	L	0-1	0-1	3		616
22		8	A	Stenhousemuir	D	2-2	2-1	3	Allan 28, Taylor 32	620
23		15	H	Stirling Alb	L	1-4	1-3	3	Mullen 32	328
24		29	H	Edinburgh C	D	1-1	1-0	5	Kris Renton 38	302
25	Mar	3	H	Albion R	W	2-1	1-1	3	Barr 40, Kris Renton 67	221
26		7	A	Annan Ath	D	0-0	0-0	3		299
27		10	A	Elgin C	L	2-3	1-0	4	Allan 7, Sheerin 66	512
28		14	H	Cove Rangers	Cancelled					
29		21	A	Brechin C	Cancelled					
30		24	A	Albion R	Cancelled					
31		28	H	Stenhousemuir	Cancelled					
32	Apr	4	A	Stirling Alb	Cancelled					
33		11	H	Queen's Park	Cancelled					
34		18	A	Albion R	Cancelled					
35		25	A	Edinburgh C	Cancelled					
36	May	2	H	Elgin C	Cancelled					

Final League Position: 4 (on points-per-game basis)

Honours
League Champions: Division II 1913-14, 1914-15, 1938-39; Second Division 2011-12; Third Division 2005-06.
Runners-up: Division II 1921-22, 1923-24, 1969-70; Second Division 1991-92; Third Division 2000-01, 2008-09.
Promoted via play-offs: 2009-10 (to First Division).
Scottish Cup: Quarter-finals 1931.
League Cup: Semi-finals 1959, 1970.

Club colours: Shirt: Royal blue with white trim. Shorts: White. Socks: Black with red tops.

Goalscorers: *League (37):* Cox 6, Mullen 6 (4 pens), Allan 5, Barr 4, Buchanan 3, Kris Renton 3, Thomas 3, Herd 2, Smith, C 2, Sheerin 1, Swan 1, Taylor 1.
William Hill Scottish Cup (1): Cox 1.
Betfred Scottish League Cup (2): Buchanan 1, Taylor 1.
Tunnock's Caramel Wafer Scottish League Challenge Cup (1): Barr 1.

Dabrowski M 12	Pyper J 8 + 2	Todd J 26	Barr C 26 + 1	Valentine E 1 + 4	Buchanan R 25 + 1	Herd M 7 + 4	Miller K 23	Taylor G 14 + 7	Cox D 20 + 2	Renton Kris 21 + 1	Swan H 14 + 3	Allan J 11 + 11	Thomas A 16 + 5	Mullen F 19	Hamilton C 19 + 1	Smith C 15	Sneddon K 1 + 2	Morrison P 4	Rae J (Trialist) 2	Rae J 9	Morrison G 4	Sheerin J — + 1	Match No.
1	2	3	4	5[1]	6	7■	8	9[2]	10	11	12	13											1
1	2	4	3		7		6	12	10	11	5	9[1]	8										2
1		5	4		6		7	12	9	11[1]			8	2	3	10							3
1		3	4		9	12[3]	8[1]	13	10[2]	11			7	2	5	6	14						4
1		4	2		6		7	10[1]		11	12		8	5	3	9							5
1	13	4	2		6		8[3]	12	10[1]	11		14	7	5	3	9[2]							6
	13	4	3		7		8[1]	11[2]	6	10		12	9	2	5			1					7
		2	3		5		6		10	8			7	9	4	11		1					8
		2	3		5		6		10	8		12	7	9	4	11[1]		1					9
1		3	7		8		9		6[1]	11	5	13	12		4	10	2[2]						10
1		3	4		8		6	13	7	11	2	12	9[1]		5	10[2]							11
1	2	4	3		7		8	6[1]		11	5	12	9			10							12
1	5	2	3		6	12		7[1]	9■	10	8				4	11							13
1	2	3	4		6	7		9[1]		11	5	12			8	10							14
1	2	3	4	13	9	8[2]		12		11■	5[3]	6	14		7	10[1]							15
		3	4	13		8[1]	9	10[3]			6	11[2]	12	2	5	7	14		1				16
		4	2		12	8[1]	7	6	13		9	10		5	3	11[2]		1					17
	4	3	12		9	8	7		10		5	11[1]		2		6			1				18
	4[3]		3	14	9	8[1]	7	6	10■		5[2]	11	13	2	12					1			19
		4	2		6		8		10			11	9	5	3					1	7		20
		3[2]	5	12	9	13	7		11	14		10[3]	6[1]	2	4					1	8		21
		4	3		7			9	6	11		10		5	2					1	8		22
		4	3		6		8	9[3]	12	11	13	10[1]	14	5	2■					1	7[2]		23
		3	4		6		7	9[1]	10	11	5	12	8	2						1			24
		4	3		8		7	9[1]	6	11	5	12	10	2						1			25
		3	4		6		7	9[1]	10	11	5	12	8	2						1			26
		3■	4		7	14	8	12	6	11[3]		10[1]	9[2]	2	5					1		13	27
																							28
																							29
																							30
																							31
																							32
																							33
																							34
																							35
																							36

DUMBARTON

Year Formed: 1872. *Ground:* C&G Systems Stadium, Castle Road, Dumbarton G82 1JJ. *Telephone/Fax:* 01389 762569.
E-mail: office@dumbartonfc.com *Website:* www.dumbartonfootballclub.com
Ground Capacity: total: 2,025 (all seated). *Size of Pitch:* 98m × 67m.
Chairman: John Steele. *Vice-Chairman:* Colin Hosie.
Manager: Jim Duffy. *Assistant Manager:* Barry Smith.
Club Nicknames: 'The Sons'; 'Sons of the Rock'.
Previous Grounds: Broadmeadow; Ropework Lane; Townend Ground; Boghead Park; Cliftonhill Stadium.
Record Attendance: 18,000 v Raith R, Scottish Cup, 2 March 1957.
Record Transfer Fee received: £300,000 for Neill Collins to Sunderland (July 2004).
Record Transfer Fee paid: £50,000 for Charlie Gibson from Stirling Alb (1989).
Record Victory: 13-1 v Kirkintilloch Central, Scottish Cup 1st rd, 1 September 1888.
Record Defeat: 1-11 v Albion R, Division II, 30 January 1926: v Ayr U, League Cup, 13 August 1952.
Most Capped Player: James McAulay, 9, Scotland.
Most League Appearances: 298: Andy Jardine, 1957-67.
Most Goals in Season (Individual): 38: Kenny Wilson, Division II, 1971-72. *(League and Cup):* 46 Hughie Gallacher, 1955-56.
Most Goals Overall (Individual): 202: Hughie Gallacher, 1954-62

DUMBARTON – SPFL LADBROKES LEAGUE ONE 2019–20 LEAGUE RECORD

Match No.	Date	Venue	Opponents	Result	H/T Score	Lg Pos.	Goalscorers	Attendance
1	Aug 3	H	Raith R	L 0-1	0-0	9		870
2	10	A	Falkirk	L 0-6	0-5	10		4060
3	17	A	Peterhead	W 3-2	1-2	6	Langan 42, Crossan 68, Layne 79	688
4	24	H	Stranraer	W 3-1	1-1	5	Layne 2 25, 76, Tumilty 63	583
5	31	A	Montrose	W 2-1	2-0	2	Layne 2 21, 34	480
6	Sept 14	H	Airdrieonians	L 0-1	0-1	5		813
7	21	A	East Fife	D 2-2	1-0	6	McGeever 37, Layne (pen) 48	719
8	28	H	Clyde	L 1-2	1-0	7	Crossan 42	851
9	Oct 5	H	Forfar Ath	W 3-1	3-0	5	Neill 11, Frizzell 2 28, 34	532
10	19	A	Stranraer	D 0-0	0-0	4		289
11	26	H	Peterhead	W 1-0	0-0	5	McGeever 54	600
12	Nov 2	A	Airdrieonians	L 1-3	1-3	5	Tumilty 16	727
13	9	H	East Fife	L 2-4	2-2	6	McGeever 33, Watson, C (og) 38	702
14	16	H	Falkirk	D 1-1	1-0	6	Layne 29	982
15	30	A	Clyde	W 2-1	1-1	5	McKee 17, Layne 48	721
16	Dec 7	H	Montrose	L 0-2	0-1	6		459
17	14	A	Forfar Ath	W 4-3	2-3	6	McKee 22, Crossan 44, Tumilty 58, McCallum (og) 73	431
18	21	A	Raith R	W 2-0	2-0	5	Crossan 28, McGeever 40	1504
19	28	H	Stranraer	D 1-1	0-0	6	Tierney 85	656
20	Jan 4	A	Falkirk	L 0-3	0-1	6		3807
21	25	A	Peterhead	L 0-1	0-0	6		531
22	Feb 1	A	East Fife	L 2-4	1-2	6	Neill 45, Jones 59	536
23	8	H	Airdrieonians	D 0-0	0-0	6		594
24	15	A	Montrose	L 1-2	0-1	6	Crossan 90	423
25	25	H	Clyde	W 1-0	0-0	6	Neill 67	468
26	29	H	Raith R	W 1-0	0-0	6	Carswell 90	804
27	Mar 3	H	Forfar Ath	W 2-0	1-0	6	Forbes 33, Quitongo, J 69	364
28	7	A	Clyde	L 0-2	0-0	6		658
29	14	H	Falkirk	Cancelled				
30	21	A	Airdrieonians	Cancelled				
31	28	A	Stranraer	Cancelled				
32	Apr 4	H	Peterhead	Cancelled				
33	11	A	Raith R	Cancelled				
34	18	H	East Fife	Cancelled				
35	25	A	Forfar Ath	Cancelled				
36	May 2	H	Montrose	Cancelled				

Final League Position: 6 (on points-per-game basis)

Honours
League Champions: Division I 1890-91 (shared with Rangers), 1891-92; Division II 1910-11, 1971-72; Second Division 1991-92; Third Division 2008-09.
Runners-up: First Division 1983-84; Division II 1907-08; Second Division 1994-95; Third Division 2001-02.
Promoted via play-offs: 2011-12 (Second Division).
Scottish Cup Winners: 1883; *Runners-up:* 1881, 1882, 1887, 1891, 1897.
League Challenge Cup: Runners-up: 2017-18.

Club colours: Shirt: Yellow and black vertical stripes. Shorts: Black. Socks: Yellow with black tops.

Goalscorers: *League (35):* Layne 8 (1 pen), Crossan 5, McGeever 4, Neill 3, Tumilty 3, Frizzell 2, McKee 2, Carswell 1, Forbes 1, Jones 1, Langan 1, Quitongo, J 1, Tierney 1, own goals 2.
William Hill Scottish Cup (3): Frizzell 1, Layne 1, McGeever 1.
Betfred Scottish League Cup (3): Crossan 1, Neill 1, Tierney 1.
Tunnock's Caramel Wafer Scottish League Challenge Cup (0).

Brennan C 28	Crawford L 5 + 3	McGeever R 26	Neill M 28	Quitongo R 25	Hutton K 20 + 1	Carswell S 24 + 1	McKee J 24	Crossan P 20 + 5	McCluskey S 18 + 7	Tierney R 4 + 10	Layne I 15 + 6	Scullion C 5 + 6	Langan R 15 + 7	McMillan J 1 + 5	Zata M — + 3	Tumilty R 17	Shiels M 3 + 5	Frizzell A 9	Wardrop S 7	Wilson C 1 + 2	Forbes R 6 + 1	Jones R 4 + 3	Quitongo J 3 + 3	Match No.
1	2	3	4	5	6¹	7	8	9³	10	11²	12	13	14											1
1	5³	3	4	9	6	7	8	10¹	11		12	13		2²	14									2
1	2³	3	4	5	6		7	9		14	10¹	11²	8	12	13									3
1		3	4	5	6	12	7	10		14	11¹	9²	8³	13		2								4
1		3	4	5	7	8	9	11¹	12	13	10²		6³	14		2								5
1		3	4	5	7	8		11²	9		10	13	6¹			2	12							6
1	13	4	3	5	8	7	6²	14	10³		11		9¹			2	12							7
1		3²	4	5³		6	7	10¹	9	13	11	14	8			2	12							8
1			4	5	3	7	8	9	12		10¹		6			2		11						9
1			4	5	3	7	8	9³	12	13	10¹		6²			2	14	11						10
1		8	4	5	7	3	6	11²	13	14	10¹		12			2		9³						11
1		3	4		7	8	6	12	10	13	11¹					2	5	9²						12
1		3	4		7	8	6³	10	9¹		12	13	14			2	5²	11						13
1		3	4	5³	7	8	6¹	10²	14		9		12	13		2		11						14
1		3	4	5²	8	7	6	13	10¹		11³		12	14		2		9						15
1		3	4	5	8		7	9²	10¹		11		12			2	13	6						16
1		3	4	5	7		6	12		13	11³	14	9			2	10²	8¹						17
1		3	4	5	7	9	6	11²	13	12		10¹	8			2								18
1		3	4	5	7	8	6		12	11		10	9¹			2								19
1	13	3	4	5	7	8			6	11		10²	9¹		12	2								20
1	13	3	4	5		7	11	9	6	10²			8¹						2	12				21
1		3	4	5	7	8	11		9										2		6¹	10	12	22
1		3	4	5		8		12	9				7						2		6	11	10¹	23
1		3	4	5		7		8	6	13									2	11¹	9	10²	12	24
1	2	3	4	5		6	9	7¹	11		12		14								8³	13	10²	25
1		3	4	5		7	9	11	6		12		8²						2		13	10¹		26
1		3	4	5		7	6	10³	8		12								2	14	9²	13	11¹	27
1	5	3	4		14	7³	6	10	8²		11¹								2		9	13	12	28
																								29
																								30
																								31
																								32
																								33
																								34
																								35
																								36

DUNDEE

Year Formed: 1893. *Ground & Address:* Kilmac Stadium at Dens Park, Sandeman St, Dundee DD3 7JY. *Telephone:* 01382 889966. *Fax:* 01382 832284. *E-mail:* reception@dundeefc.co.uk *Website:* www.dundeefc.co.uk
Ground Capacity: 11,850 (all seated). *Size of Pitch:* 101m × 66m.
Chairmain: Tim Keyes. *Managing Director:* John Nelms. *Technical Director:* Gordon Strachan.
Manager: James McPake. *First Team Coach:* Dave Mackay.
Club Nicknames: 'The Dark Blues'; 'The Dee'.
Previous Ground: Carolina Port 1893-98.
Record Attendance: 43,024 v Rangers, Scottish Cup 2nd rd, 7 February 1953.
Record Transfer Fee received: £1,500,000 for Robert Douglas to Celtic (October 2000).
Record Transfer Fee paid: £600,000 for Fabian Caballero from Sol de América (Paraguay) (July 2000).
Record Victory: 10-0 Division II v Alloa Ath, 9 March 1947 and v Dunfermline Ath, 22 March 1947.
Record Defeat: 0-11 v Celtic, Division I, 26 October 1895.
Most Capped Player: Alex Hamilton, 24, Scotland.
Most League Appearances: 400: Barry Smith, 1995-2006.
Most League Goals in Season (Individual): 32: Alan Gilzean, 1963-64.
Most Goals Overall (Individual): 169: Alan Gilzean 1960-61.

DUNDEE – SPFL LADBROKES CHAMPIONSHIP 2019–20 LEAGUE RECORD

Match No.	Date	Venue	Opponents	Result		H/T Score	Lg Pos.	Goalscorers	Attendance
1	Aug 2	A	Dunfermline Ath	D	2-2	1-2	1	Johnson 2 (2 pens) 45, 75	5227
2	10	H	Ayr U	W	1-0	0-0	2	Nelson 74	5520
3	24	H	Inverness CT	D	0-0	0-0	4		5016
4	30	A	Dundee U	L	2-6	1-4	5	Hemmings 22, Nelson 70	14,108
5	Sept 14	H	Alloa Ath	W	2-1	2-1	5	Johnson 2, McGhee 39	4453
6	21	A	Greenock Morton	L	0-1	0-1	6		1901
7	27	A	Queen of the South	D	1-1	1-1	5	McGhee 11	1249
8	Oct 5	H	Arbroath	W	2-0	1-0	4	McDaid 2 38, 59	5045
9	19	H	Partick Thistle	L	1-3	1-0	5	McGowan, P 25	5010
10	25	A	Ayr U	W	2-1	2-1	4	McDaid 16, McGowan, P 32	1627
11	29	A	Alloa Ath	W	3-0	2-0	4	Hemmings 2 15, 39, Mackie 75	1218
12	Nov 1	H	Greenock Morton	W	2-1	0-0	3	Hemmings 63, Ness 80	4228
13	8	H	Dundee U	L	0-2	0-0	3		11,233
14	23	A	Inverness CT	L	0-1	0-1	4		2184
15	30	H	Queen of the South	L	1-2	0-1	4	Johnson 90	4517
16	Dec 7	A	Arbroath	D	1-1	0-1	5	Hemmings 61	2170
17	14	H	Dunfermline Ath	W	4-3	3-1	5	Devine (og) 15, Hemmings 25, McGowan, P 34, Johnson 46	4699
18	21	A	Partick Thistle	W	1-0	1-0	4	McGowan, P 31	2957
19	27	A	Dundee U	D	1-1	0-1	3	Dorrans 50	14,007
20	Jan 4	H	Inverness CT	L	0-2	0-2	4		5040
21	24	A	Dunfermline Ath	L	0-2	0-2	4		3722
22	Feb 1	A	Greenock Morton	D	1-1	1-1	6	Hemmings 12	1643
23	8	H	Partick Thistle	W	2-0	2-0	4	Hemmings 2 23, 34	4816
24	22	A	Queen of the South	W	1-0	0-0	3	Forster 72	1126
25	Mar 3	H	Alloa Ath	D	0-0	0-0	4		4356
26	7	A	Ayr U	D	0-0	0-0	4		1758
27	10	H	Ayr U	W	2-0	1-0	3	Hemmings 11, Crankshaw 90	4670
28	14	H	Dunfermline Ath	Cancelled					
29	21	A	Inverness CT	Cancelled					
30	24	H	Arbroath	Cancelled					
31	28	H	Queen of the South	Cancelled					
32	Apr 4	A	Alloa Ath	Cancelled					
33	11	H	Greenock Morton	Cancelled					
34	18	A	Arbroath	Cancelled					
35	24	H	Dundee U	Cancelled					
36	May 2	A	Partick Thistle	Cancelled					

Final League Position: 3 (on points-per-game basis)

Honours
League Champions: Division I 1961-62; First Division 1978-79, 1991-92, 1997-98; Championship 2013-14; Division II 1946-47, 1947-48.
Runners-up: Division I 1902-03, 1906-07, 1908-09, 1948-49; First Division 1980-81, 2007-08, 2009-10, 2011-12.
Scottish Cup Winners: 1910; *Runners-up:* 1925, 1952, 1964, 2003.
League Cup Winners: 1951-52, 1952-53, 1973-74; *Runners-up:* 1967-68, 1980-81, 1995-96.
League Challenge Cup Winners: 1990-91, 2009-10; *Runners-up:* 1994-95.

European: *European Cup:* 8 matches (1962-63 semi-finals). *Cup Winners' Cup:* 2 matches: (1964-65).
UEFA Cup: 22 matches: (*Fairs Cup:* 1967-68 semi-finals. *UEFA Cup:* 1971-72, 1973-74, 1974-75, 2003-04).

Club colours: All: Navy blue.

Goalscorers: *League (32):* Hemmings 10, Johnson 5 (2 pens), McGowan, P 4, McDaid 3, McGhee 2, Nelson 2, Crankshaw 1, Dorrans 1, Forster 1, Mackie 1, Ness 1, own goal 1.
William Hill Scottish Cup (0).
Betfred Scottish League Cup (5): Johnson 2 (1 pen), Nelson 2 (1 pen), Curran C 1.
Tunnock's Caramel Wafer Scottish League Challenge Cup (1): Kerr 1.

Hamilton J 16	McGhee J 24	Forster J 23	Meekings J 13 + 2	Kerr C 20 + 2	Robertson F 11 + 5	Byrne S 19 + 3	Marshall J 17	McGowan P 22 + 2	Johnson D 11 + 8	Nelson A 9 + 10	Todd J 3 + 10	McDaid D 23 + 1	Ness J 4 + 4	Hemmings K 23 + 2	McPake J 3 + 4	Dorrans G 21 + 1	Mackie S 9 + 3	Hazard C 11	Moore C — + 1	Cunningham M — + 1	Callachan R 3	Cameron L 1	Crankshaw O 1 + 5	Berra C 6	Elliot C 4 + 2	Field T — + 1	*Match No.*
1	2	3	4^{1}	5	6	7	8	9	10	11^{2}	12	13															1
1	3	4		2	7	14	5	9^{2}	11^{3}	13	12	8	6	10^{1}													2
1	4	3		2	8^{2}	6	5	7^{1}	11^{3}	14	12	9		10	13												3
1	4^{1}	3	14	2		6	5	12	11^{2}	13	8^{3}	9	7	10													4
1	4	3		2	8	7	5	10^{1}	11^{2}	14	12	9		13	6^{3}												5
1	4	3		2	8	7^{1}	5	10	11^{3}	12		6		14	9^{2}	13											6
1	4	3		2	8	12	5		13	11^{1}		9		10	6^{2}	7											7
1	2	3	4		13	7^{1}	8^{3}	9	14		12	11		10^{2}		6	5										8
1	5	4	3		12	7^{3}	2	9^{2}			13	10		11	14	6	8^{1}										9
	4	3		2		8	5	9^{3}	13	11^{1}	14	6		10^{2}		7	12	1									10
	3	4		2		6	5	9^{2}		10^{1}		8	14	11	13	7^{3}	12	1									11
	3	4		2		6	5^{2}	9^{1}	13	10^{3}		8	14	11		7	12	1									12
	4	3		2		6		9^{1}	12	10^{2}		8		11	13	7	5	1									13
	2^{2}	3	4	14		6^{3}		9^{1}	12		13	11	8	10		7	5	1									14
1	4	3		2	7^{2}				12		6	10	8^{1}	11		9	5		13								15
1	4	3		2	13	7^{1}		12	11		6^{2}	9		10		8	5										16
1	4^{2}	3	13	2	8	12	5	9	10^{3}	14		6^{1}		11		7											17
1	3		4	2	6		5	9^{1}	10^{3}	12	14		13	11^{2}		7	8										18
1	3		4	2	9		5	7	11^{1}	12				10		6	8										19
1	4		3	2	7		5	9	10^{1}		12			11		6	8^{2}			13							20
1	4		3	2			5	10^{2}	12			6		11		8					7	9^{1}	13				21
	5	3		2		9						10		11		6		1			8		7^{1}	4	12		22
		3	4		12	8^{3}		10		13		9		11^{1}		7		1			6^{2}		14	2	5		23
		2	3	13		5		8^{1}		10^{2}		6		11		7		1					12	4	9		24
	9^{1}	3	4			6		10		11		5				7		1					12	2	8		25
	7^{3}	3	2	5^{2}		6		10		12		9^{1}		11		8		1						4	13	14	26
		3	4		13	6		9^{2}		11^{3}		5	14	10^{1}		7		1					12	2	8		27
																											28
																											29
																											30
																											31
																											32
																											33
																											34
																											35
																											36

DUNDEE UNITED

Year Formed: 1909 (1923). *Ground & Address:* Tannadice Park, Tannadice St, Dundee DD3 7JW. *Telephone:* 01382 833166. *Fax:* 01382 889398. *E-mail:* admin@dundeeunited.co.uk *Website:* www.dundeeunitedfc.co.uk
Ground Capacity: 14,223 (all seated). *Size of Pitch:* 100m × 66m.
Chairman: Mark Ogren. *Chief Executive:* Jamie Kirk.
Manager: Micky Mellon. *Assistant Manager:* Stephen Frail.
Club Nicknames: 'The Terrors'; 'The Arabs'.
Previous Name: Dundee Hibernian (up to 1923).
Record Attendance: 28,000 v Barcelona, Fairs Cup, 16 November 1966.
Record Transfer Fee received: £4,000,000 for Duncan Ferguson from Rangers (July 1993).
Record Transfer Fee paid: £750,000 for Steven Pressley from Coventry C (July 1995).
Record Victory: 14-0 v Nithsdale Wanderers, Scottish Cup 1st rd, 17 January 1931.
Record Defeat: 1-12 v Motherwell, Division II, 23 January 1954.
Most Capped Player: Maurice Malpas, 55, Scotland.
Most League Appearances: 618: Maurice Malpas, 1980-2000.
Most Appearances in European Matches: 76: Dave Narey (record for Scottish player at the time).
Most League Goals in Season (Individual): 40: John Coyle, Division II, 1955-56.
Most Goals Overall (Individual): 199: Peter McKay, 1947-54.

DUNDEE UNITED – SPFL LADBROKES CHAMPIONSHIP 2019–20 LEAGUE RECORD

Match No.	*Date*	*Venue*	*Opponents*	*Result*	*H/T Score*	*Lg Pos.*	*Goalscorers*	*Attendance*
1	Aug 3	H	Inverness CT	W 4-1	2-1	1	Shankland 4 [7, 31, 53, 86]	7023
2	9	A	Partick Thistle	W 2-1	0-1	1	Shankland [55], Pawlett [73]	3218
3	24	A	Dunfermline Ath	W 2-0	2-0	1	Shankland 2 [10, 30]	6480
4	30	H	Dundee	W 6-2	4-1	1	Butcher 2 [14, 40], Appere [33], Shankland (pen) [36], Harkes [46], Smith, C [83]	14,108
5	Sept 14	A	Ayr U	L 0-2	0-1	1		3167
6	21	H	Arbroath	W 2-1	0-0	1	Shankland 2 [88, 90]	7877
7	28	H	Greenock Morton	W 6-0	3-0	1	Shankland 3 [1, 5, 56], McMullan 2 [41, 80], Chalmers [84]	7404
8	Oct 4	A	Alloa Ath	L 0-1	0-1	1		1717
9	19	A	Queen of the South	L 0-4	0-2	1		1909
10	26	H	Dunfermline Ath	W 2-0	2-0	1	Shankland [9], Clark [27]	7682
11	29	H	Partick Thistle	W 1-0	0-0	1	Shankland [62]	6929
12	Nov 2	A	Inverness CT	W 3-0	1-0	1	Rooney (og) [20], Clark [72], Shankland (pen) [76]	2902
13	8	A	Dundee	W 2-0	0-0	1	Clark (pen) [56], Shankland [64]	11,233
14	16	H	Queen of the South	W 3-0	2-0	1	McMullan [22], Clark [45], Stanton [49]	7675
15	Dec 7	H	Alloa Ath	W 2-1	1-1	1	Clark [45], Appere [55]	7615
16	10	A	Greenock Morton	W 2-1	2-1	1	Appere [5], Shankland [31]	1120
17	14	A	Arbroath	W 1-0	1-0	1	Stanton [6]	4052
18	21	H	Ayr U	W 4-0	1-0	1	Stanton [42], Shankland (pen) [57], Clark [61], Harkes [87]	7744
19	27	H	Dundee	D 1-1	1-0	1	Clark [5]	14,007
20	Jan 4	A	Queen of the South	W 1-0	0-0	1	Connolly [48]	2041
21	11	A	Partick Thistle	W 4-1	2-0	1	Shankland 3 [38, 60, 65], Sporle [45]	4101
22	25	H	Greenock Morton	D 1-1	0-1	1	Shankland [90]	7644
23	Feb 1	H	Arbroath	L 0-1	0-1	1		8056
24	14	A	Alloa Ath	D 0-0	0-0	1		1442
25	21	H	Inverness CT	W 2-1	1-1	1	Appere [12], Shankland [59]	7583
26	29	A	Dunfermline Ath	L 0-2	0-1	1		6261
27	Mar 3	A	Ayr U	D 0-0	0-0	1		1674
28	7	H	Partick Thistle	D 1-1	1-0	1	Powers [19]	7603
29	14	A	Greenock Morton	Cancelled				
30	21	H	Alloa Ath	Cancelled				
31	27	A	Arbroath	Cancelled				
32	Apr 3	H	Queen of the South	Cancelled				
33	10	A	Inverness CT	Cancelled				
34	18	H	Dunfermline Ath	Cancelled				
35	24	A	Dundee	Cancelled				
36	May 2	H	Ayr U	Cancelled				

Final League Position: 1 (on points-per-game basis)

Honours: *League Champions:* Premier Division 1982-83; Championship 2019-20; Division II 1924-25, 1928-29.
Runners-up: Division II 1930-31, 1959-60; First Division 1995-96; Championship 2018-19.
Scottish Cup Winners: 1994, 2010; *Runners-up:* 1974, 1981, 1985, 1987, 1988, 1991, 2005, 2014.
League Cup Winners: 1979-80, 1980-81; *Runners-up:* 1981-82, 1984-85, 1997-98, 2007-08, 2014-15.
League Challenge Cup Winners, 2016-17; *Runners-up:* 1995-96.

European: *European Cup:* 8 matches (1983-84, semi-finals). *Cup Winners' Cup:* 10 matches (1974-75, 1988-89, 1994-95). *UEFA Cup:* 86 matches (*Fairs Cup:* 1966-67, 1969-70, 1970-71. *UEFA Cup:* 1975-76, 1977-78, 1978-79, 1979-80, 1980-81, 1981-82, 1982-83, 1984-85, 1985-86, 1986-87 runners-up, 1987-88, 1989-90, 1990-91, 1993-94, 1997-98, 2005-06). *Europa League:* 6 matches (2010-2011, 2011-12, 2012-13).

Club colours: Shirt: Tangerine with black trim. Shorts: Black. Socks: Black with tangerine tops.

Goalscorers: *League (52):* Shankland 24 (3 pens), Clark 7 (1 pen), Appere 4, McMullan 3, Stanton 3, Butcher 2, Harkes 2, Chalmers 1, Connolly 1, Pawlett 1, Powers 1, Smith, C 1, Sporle 1, own goal 1.
William Hill Scottish Cup (4): Shankland 2, Appere 1, Sporle 1.
Betfred Scottish League Cup (6): Shankland 2, Appere 1, Butcher 1, Sporle 1, Watson 1.
Tunnock's Caramel Wafer Scottish League Challenge Cup (0).

Siegrist B 28	Smith L 28	Connolly M 12 + 5	Reynolds M 24 + 2	Robson J 22 + 1	McMullan P 18 + 4	Stanton S 13 + 4	Butcher C 22	Appere L 20 + 6	Shankland L 26	Clark N 15 + 3	Smith C 1 + 9	Harkes I 20 + 6	Banks S — + 1	Pawlett P 13 + 4	King A 1 + 8	Sow O 2 + 1	Brown T 5	Sporle A 5 + 6	Chalmers L — + 3	Watson P 18 + 1	Mochrie C — + 4	Glass D 2 + 3	Powers D 8	Bingham R 5	*Match No.*
1	2	3	4	5	6	7^{1}	8	9	10^{3}	11^{2}	12	13	14												1
1	2	3	4	5	8	6^{1}	7	10	11	9^{2}		13		12											2
1	2		4	5	6	8^{2}	3	11	10^{3}	9^{1}		7		12	13	14									3
1	2	3^{1}	4	5	6	8	7	11	10^{3}	14	13	12		9^{2}											4
1	2		4	5	6	8^{2}	7	10	11	13	14	12		9^{1}			3^{3}								5
1	2		4	5	12	6	3	8^{2}	11		10^{3}	7		9^{1}				13	14						6
1	5		4		8	12	6^{3}	14	11^{1}			7		9^{2}			3	10	13	2					7
1	5		4		6	8^{1}		12	10		14	7^{2}		11	13		3	9^{3}		2					8
1	5		4		9	8	6	10	11	12		7^{1}					3			2					9
1	2		4	5	6		8^{1}	12	11	10^{2}	14	7		9^{3}	13		3								10
1	2		4	5	6	13	3	12	11	10^{3}		8		9^{1}	7^{2}					14					11
1	2	14	4	5	6^{2}	12	7	9	11^{1}	10^{3}	13	8								3					12
1	2	14	4	5	6^{3}	12	8	9	11^{2}	10^{1}	13	7								3					13
1	2		4	5	8^{1}	7^{2}	6	10		11^{3}	12	9							13	3	14				14
1	2		4	5	8^{2}	7	6	10		11^{1}		9			13			12		3					15
1	2	13	4	5		8^{1}	6	10	11	9^{2}		7			12					3					16
1	2	13	4	5	12	7^{2}	6	10	11	8^{1}		9								3					17
1	2	13	4^{2}	5	8^{1}	10	6^{3}	12	11	9		7			14					3					18
1	2		4	5	6		8	9	10	11^{1}		7						12		3					19
1	2	3^{3}	13	5			7^{1}	6	11	10	14				12			9		4		8^{2}			20
1	5	3	4					11	10	9^{3}				12	14			8		2^{2}	13	6^{1}	7		21
1	2	4	3	5				6	11			8		9^{2}		10^{1}		12			13		7		22
1	2	3	4^{2}	5			8		10			13		6		11^{1}		9			14	12^{3}	7		23
1	2	4		5			9		10			8^{1}		6				12		3			7	11	24
1	2	4	14	5	13		7	6	11			12		9^{2}						3			8^{1}	10^{3}	25
1	2	4		5	12			9	11			6^{2}		8^{1}				14		3		13	7	10^{3}	26
1	2	3	5	13	6^{1}			9	11			8		12						4			7	10^{2}	27
1	2	3	5		6			12	11			8		9^{2}						4		13	7	10^{1}	28
																									29
																									30
																									31
																									32
																									33
																									34
																									35
																									36

DUNFERMLINE ATHLETIC

Year Formed: 1885. *Ground & Address:* East End Park, Halbeath Road, Dunfermline KY12 7RB.
Telephone: 01383 724295. *Fax:* 01383 745 959. *E-mail:* enquiries@dafc.co.uk
Website: www.dafc.co.uk
Ground Capacity: 11,380 (all seated). *Size of Pitch:* 105m × 65m.
Chairman: Ross McArthur. *Vice-Chairman:* Billy Braisby.
Head Coach: Stevie Crawford. *First Team Coach:* Jason Dair.
Club Nickname: 'The Pars'.
Record Attendance: 27,816 v Celtic, Division I, 30 April 1968.
Record Transfer Fee received: £650,000 for Jackie McNamara to Celtic (October 1995).
Record Transfer Fee paid: £540,000 for Istvan Kozma from Bordeaux (September 1989).
Record Victory: 11-2 v Stenhousemuir, Division II, 27 September 1930.
Record Defeat: 1-13 v St. Bernard's, Scottish Cup 1st rd, 15 September 1883.
Most Capped Player: Colin Miller 16 (61), Canada.
Most League Appearances: 497: Norrie McCathie, 1981-96.
Most League Goals in Season (Individual): 53: Bobby Skinner, Division II, 1925-26.
Most Goals Overall (Individual): 212: Charles Dickson, 1954-64.

DUNFERMLINE ATHLETIC – SPFL LADBROKES CHAMPIONSHIP 2019–20 LEAGUE RECORD

Match No.	*Date*	*Venue*	*Opponents*	*Result*		*H/T Score*	*Lg Pos.*	*Goalscorers*	*Attendance*
1	Aug 2	H	Dundee	D	2-2	2-1	1	Dow [13], Nisbet [35]	5227
2	10	A	Queen of the South	D	1-1	1-0	6	Turner [8]	1562
3	24	H	Dundee U	L	0-2	0-2	8		6480
4	31	A	Arbroath	L	0-1	0-0	9		1624
5	Sept 14	H	Inverness CT	L	0-1	0-0	10		3446
6	21	A	Partick Thistle	W	3-0	2-0	7	Nisbet [23], Dow [31], Turner [49]	2820
7	28	H	Alloa Ath	D	1-1	0-0	7	Turner [57]	3496
8	Oct 5	A	Greenock Morton	D	1-1	0-0	9	Ryan [87]	1690
9	19	H	Ayr U	W	3-2	1-1	7	Kiltie [28], Ashcroft [63], Ryan [84]	3905
10	26	A	Dundee U	L	0-2	0-2	8		7682
11	29	H	Arbroath	W	2-0	0-0	6	Nisbet 2 [59, 78]	3488
12	Nov 2	H	Queen of the South	W	2-0	0-0	6	Dow [57], Nisbet [82]	3621
13	9	A	Alloa Ath	L	1-2	1-1	6	Nisbet (pen) [33]	1602
14	30	H	Partick Thistle	W	5-1	4-0	6	Nisbet 4 (2 pens) [4 (p), 22 (p), 31, 49], Martin, L [10]	3948
15	Dec 3	A	Ayr U	W	1-0	0-0	4	Nisbet [68]	1361
16	7	H	Greenock Morton	W	3-1	1-0	3	Nisbet 2 (1 pen) [21 (p), 84], Kiltie [52]	3515
17	14	A	Dundee	L	3-4	1-3	4	Dow [16], Nisbet [69], Martin, L [72]	4699
18	21	A	Inverness CT	L	0-2	0-1	5		2116
19	28	H	Alloa Ath	L	1-3	1-2	5	Nisbet [20]	4257
20	Jan 4	H	Ayr U	L	0-1	0-1	5		3915
21	11	A	Greenock Morton	L	2-3	1-1	5	Murray [23], Nisbet [90]	1470
22	24	H	Dundee	W	2-0	2-0	5	Dow [28], Nisbet [40]	3722
23	Feb 1	A	Queen of the South	W	3-2	2-1	4	McGill [14], Devine [45], Ashcroft [82]	1302
24	25	H	Inverness CT	L	1-2	0-1	7	Thomas [70]	3397
25	29	H	Dundee U	W	2-0	1-0	6	Nisbet [26], Afolabi [60]	6261
26	Mar 4	A	Arbroath	D	0-0	0-0	5		1146
27	7	H	Queen of the South	D	1-1	0-1	5	Afolabi (pen) [46]	3597
28	10	A	Partick Thistle	D	1-1	0-0	5	Murray [72]	2078
29	14	A	Dundee	Cancelled					
30	21	H	Greenock Morton	Cancelled					
31	28	A	Alloa Ath	Cancelled					
32	Apr 4	A	Ayr U	Cancelled					
33	11	H	Arbroath	Cancelled					
34	18	A	Dundee U	Cancelled					
35	25	H	Partick Thistle	Cancelled					
36	May 2	A	Inverness CT	Cancelled					

Final League Position: 6 (on points-per-game basis)

Honours
League Champions: First Division 1988-89, 1995-96, 2010-11; Division II 1925-26; Second Division 1985-86; League One 2015-16.
Runners-up: First Division 1986-87, 1993-94, 1994-95, 1999-2000; Division II 1912-13, 1933-34, 1954-55, 1957-58, 1972-73; Second Division 1978-79; League One 2013-14.
Scottish Cup Winners: 1961, 1968; *Runners-up:* 1965, 2004, 2007.
League Cup Runners-up: 1949-50, 1991-92, 2005-06.
League Challenge Cup Runners-up: 2007-08.

European: *Cup Winners' Cup:* 14 matches (1961-62, 1968-69 semi-finals). *UEFA Cup:* 32 matches (*Fairs Cup:* 1962-63, 1964-65, 1965-66, 1966-67, 1969-70. *UEFA Cup:* 2004-05, 2007-08).

Club colours: Shirt: Black and white stripes. Shorts: Black. Socks: Black.

Goalscorers: *League (41):* Nisbet 18 (4 pens), Dow 5, Turner 3, Afolabi 2 (1 pen), Ashcroft 2, Kiltie 2, Martin, L 2, Murray 2, Ryan 2, Devine 1, McGill 1, Thomas 1.
William Hill Scottish Cup (0).
Betfred Scottish League Cup (14): Nisbet 5, Beadling 3, Turner 2, Coley 1, Comrie 1, Dow 1, Ryan 1.
Tunnock's Caramel Wafer Scottish League Challenge Cup (1): Kiltie 1.

Scully R 12	Comrie A 27	Ashcroft L 25	Murray E 10	Martin L 24 + 2	Dow R 22	Paton P 23 + 1	Beadling T 11 + 10	Coley J 3 + 4	Nisbet K 23 + 2	McCann L 6 + 8	Todd Matthew — + 5	Edwards J 11 + 4	Ryan A 7 + 6	Turner K 23 + 3	Morrison S 1 + 3	Devine D 15 + 2	Cochrane H 7 + 5	McGill G 6 + 7	Gill C 10	Kiltie G 15	Thomson J 3 + 8	McDonald A — + 2	Ross E 4 + 4	Thomas D 8	Fon Williams O 6	Afolabi J 6	*Match No.*
1	2	3	4	5	6²	7	8	9¹	10	11³	12	13	14														1
1	2	3	4²	5	6	7	8	12	11	13			9¹	10³	14												2
1	2	3		5	6	7	8²	9³	11	13	14		10¹	12	4												3
1	2	3		5		8	7¹	9³	10	11²			14	6		4	12	13									4
	2	4		3		7	8	13	10	11²		5³		6¹		14	12		1	9							5
	2	4		3	8¹	6	13		9	12		5		7			14	11²	1	10³							6
	2	3		4	6²		12	13	10	11¹		5		8			7		1	9							7
	2	3		4	6		10		11			5	12	8	13		7¹		1	9²							8
	2	3		4	6	7	14	12	11²			5	13	8³			10¹		1	9							9
	2	3		4¹	6	7			13			5	10	9³		12	8²	14	1	11							10
1	2	3		4	6³	7	12		11²			5	10¹	8			13	14		9							11
1	2	3		4	6	7	12		10			5	11¹	8						9							12
1	2	3		4	6	8	13		10	12		5³	11¹	7²				14		9							13
	2	4		5	6¹	7³	8		10²				11			3	12	13	1	9	14						14
	2	4²		5	6		8		10¹			12	13	9		3	7		1	11							15
	2			3	6		7¹		11			5		10²	13	4	8		1	9	12						16
1	2	3		5	6	12	8¹		10	14				9²		4	7³			11■	13						17
1	2	3		5	6	8	7³		10	11¹			14	12		4					9²	13					18
1	2	3		4	6	7			11	13	14	5¹		8²						10	9³	12					19
1	2	4		5	9³	7			10	13	14			8¹		3				11	12		6²				20
1	2	3	8²	5	6	7³	14		11					13		4		10¹					12	9			21
	2	3	5		6¹	7			10					8		4		11²	1		13		12	9			22
	2	3	5		6	7	13		12					8		4		11²						9	1	10¹	23
	2	3¹	5	14	6³	7			11					8		4		13					12	9	1	10²	24
	2¹	3	5	12		7	14		11³					8		4					13		6²	9	1	10	25
		3¹	5	2		7				12		14		8		4		10²			6³		13	9	1	11	26
	2		5	3		7				10¹	12			8		4		14			13		9³	6	1	11²	27
	2		5	3		7	12					13		8³		4		11¹			14		9²	6	1	10	28
																											29
																											30
																											31
																											32
																											33
																											34
																											35
																											36

EAST FIFE

Year Formed: 1903. *Ground & Address:* Locality Hub Bayview Stadium, Harbour View, Methil, Fife KY8 3RW. *Telephone:* 01333 426323. *Fax:* 01333 426376. *E-mail:* office@eastfifefc.info. *Website:* www.eastfifefc.info
Ground Capacity: 1,992. *Size of Pitch:* 105m × 65m.
Chairman: Jim Stevenson. *Vice-Chairman:* David Marshall.
Manager: Darren Young. *Assistant Manager:* Tony McMinn.
Club Nickname: 'The Fifers'.
Previous Ground: Bayview Park.
Record Attendance: 22,515 v Raith Rovers, Division I, 2 January 1950 (Bayview Park); 4,700 v Rangers, League One, 26 October 2013 (Bayview Stadium).
Record Transfer Fee received: £150,000 for Paul Hunter from Hull C (March 1990).
Record Transfer Fee paid: £70,000 for John Sludden from Kilmarnock (July 1991).
Record Victory: 13-2 v Edinburgh C, Division II, 11 December 1937.
Record Defeat: 0-9 v Hearts, Division I, 5 October 1957.
Most Capped Player: George Aitken, 5 (8), Scotland.
Most League Appearances: 517: David Clarke, 1968-86.
Most League Goals in Season (Individual): 41: Jock Wood, Division II; 1926-27 and Henry Morris, Division II, 1947-48.
Most Goals Overall (Individual): 225: Phil Weir, 1922-35.

EAST FIFE – SPFL LADBROKES LEAGUE ONE 2019–20 LEAGUE RECORD

Match No.	*Date*	*Venue*	*Opponents*	*Result*	*H/T Score*	*Lg Pos.*	*Goalscorers*	*Attendance*
1	Aug 3	A	Clyde	D 1-1	0-1	5	Dowds [59]	836
2	10	H	Peterhead	D 1-1	1-1	5	Wallace [45]	570
3	24	H	Airdrieonians	W 4-1	2-0	6	Davidson, R [7], Watt [23], Dunsmore [56], Agnew [71]	620
4	31	H	Raith R	W 4-2	1-1	4	Dowds [19], Higgins [57], Wallace [65], Agnew [90]	1792
5	Sept 7	A	Forfar Ath	W 2-1	0-1	1	Agnew [61], Dowds [63]	619
6	14	A	Montrose	W 3-1	1-0	1	Dunsmore 2 [41, 68], Wallace [84]	561
7	21	H	Dumbarton	D 2-2	0-1	2	Murdoch [58], Agnew (pen) [73]	719
8	28	A	Falkirk	D 0-0	0-0	2		3933
9	Oct 5	H	Stranraer	D 1-1	1-0	2	Wallace [17]	526
10	19	H	Forfar Ath	W 1-0	1-0	2	Boyd [8]	667
11	26	A	Raith R	D 1-1	1-1	2	Boyd [25]	2907
12	Nov 2	H	Montrose	L 0-1	0-1	3		704
13	9	A	Dumbarton	W 4-2	2-2	2	Denholm [8], Watt 2 [30, 65], Boyd [54]	702
14	26	H	Clyde	D 0-0	0-0	3		425
15	30	A	Airdrieonians	L 0-4	0-3	4		910
16	Dec 7	H	Falkirk	D 0-0	0-0	4		1182
17	14	A	Stranraer	W 2-0	0-0	3	Davidson, R [64], Agnew [90]	274
18	21	A	Peterhead	W 2-1	1-0	2	Denholm [21], Agnew [78]	599
19	28	H	Raith R	L 3-5	1-3	4	Agnew [28], Dowds [61], Wallace [71]	1998
20	Jan 4	A	Montrose	L 0-1	0-1	5		833
21	11	H	Airdrieonians	D 2-2	1-2	4	Dunsmore [8], Watson, C [89]	783
22	25	A	Clyde	L 1-2	0-0	4	Dunsmore [51]	954
23	Feb 1	H	Dumbarton	W 4-2	2-1	4	McGeever (og) [4], Higgins [27], Murdoch [70], Agnew [79]	536
24	15	H	Peterhead	W 1-0	1-0	4	Dowds [22]	520
25	18	A	Falkirk	L 0-2	0-0	4		3376
26	22	H	Stranraer	W 4-2	2-0	4	Dowds [18], Agnew (pen) [45], Denholm [50], Wallace [59]	491
27	29	A	Forfar Ath	W 1-0	1-0	4	Denholm [1]	644
28	Mar 7	A	Airdrieonians	L 0-1	0-1	4		867
29	14	H	Montrose	Cancelled				
30	21	A	Raith R	Cancelled				
31	28	H	Clyde	Cancelled				
32	Apr 4	A	Stranraer	Cancelled				
33	11	H	Forfar Ath	Cancelled				
34	18	A	Dumbarton	Cancelled				
35	25	H	Falkirk	Cancelled				
36	May 2	A	Peterhead	Cancelled				

Final League Position: 5 (on points-per-game basis)

Honours
League Champions: Division II 1947-48; Third Division 2007-08; League Two 2015-16.
Runners-up: Division II 1929-30, 1970-71; Second Division 1983-84, 1995-96; Third Division 2002-03.
Scottish Cup Winners: 1938; *Runners-up:* 1927, 1950.
League Cup Winners: 1947-48, 1949-50, 1953-54.

Club colours: Shirt: Gold and black stripes. Shorts: White. Socks: Black.

Goalscorers: *League (44):* Agnew 9 (2 pens), Dowds 6, Wallace 6, Dunsmore 5, Denholm 4, Boyd 3, Watt 3, Davidson, R 2, Higgins 2, Murdoch 2, Watson, C, 1, own goal 1.
William Hill Scottish Cup (3): Dowds 1, Watson, C 1, Watt 1.
Betfred Scottish League Cup (5): Agnew 2 (1 pen), Duggan 1, Dunsmore 1, Watt 1.
Tunnock's Caramel Wafer Scottish League Challenge Cup (0).

Hart J 13	Murdoch S 28	Dunlop R 18	Higgins C 28	Slattery P 21 + 3	Watt L 17 + 5	Davidson R 27	Agnew S 28	Dunsmore A 23 + 4	Wallace R 22	Duggan C 3 + 4	Dowds A 21 + 7	Hunter L 3 + 6	Church D 7 + 5	Denholm D 12 + 11	Watson C 10 + 8	Allen J — + 1	Boyd S 5 + 4	Healy J — + 1	Long B 15	Baker L 2 + 4	Smith K 1 + 4	Morrison C 4 + 2	*Match No.*
1	2	3	4	5	6^{2}	7	8	9	10	11^{1}	12	13											1
1	2	3	4	5^{1}	9^{2}	7	8	6	11		10		12	13									2
1	2	3	4	5	9	7^{3}	8	6^{2}	10	13	11^{1}	14		12									3
1	2	3	4	5	9	7	8	6^{2}	10^{3}		11^{1}	14		13	12								4
1	2	3	4	5	6^{1}	8	7	9^{3}	11		10^{2}		14	13	12								5
1	2	3	4	5^{2}	9^{1}	8	7	6	11		10^{3}		13	12		14							6
1	2	3	4	5^{1}	9^{2}	7	8	6^{3}	10		11		12	14			13						7
1	2	3	4	5	9	7	8	6			10			12			11^{1}						8
1	2	3	4	5	9^{2}	7	8	6^{3}	11		10^{1}	13		14	12								9
1	2	3	4		9	7	8	6^{2}	10		12		5		13		11^{1}						10
1	2	3	4	13	9^{2}	7	8	6			10		5	12			11^{1}						11
1	2^{2}	3	4		12	7	8	6^{1}			10		5	9	13		11						12
1	3		4	5	8^{3}	6	7			12	11^{1}	13		10	2		9^{2}	14					13
	3		4	5	9	6	7	8		11^{2}	12			10^{1}	2		13		1				14
	3		4	5^{3}	10	7	8	6		11^{2}	13		14	9^{1}	2		12		1				15
	4		3	9		6	8	5	10^{1}	12	11	7			2				1				16
	2		3	9		6	8	5	10		11	7^{1}		12	4				1				17
	2		4		12	7	8	5^{3}	11	13	10^{1}	14	9	6^{2}	3				1				18
	3		4	12	9^{1}		8	6	11		10	7^{2}	5		2				1	13			19
	3		4		9^{3}	8	7	6	10		11^{1}		5^{2}	13	2		12		1	14			20
	3		4	12		7	8	6	11		13		5^{3}	9^{2}	2				1	10^{1}	14		21
	2		4	5	13	7	8	6	10		12			9^{1}	3				1	11^{2}			22
	2	3	4	5		7	8	6^{3}	11		10^{1}			9^{2}	14				1	13		12	23
	2	3	4	5	13	7	8	6^{2}	11		10^{3}			9^{1}					1		14	12	24
	2	3	4	5	8	7	9	13	11		12								1		10^{1}	6^{2}	25
	2	3	4	5		7	8	14	10^{2}		11^{3}			9^{1}	13				1	12		6	26
	2	3	4	5		7	8	13	10^{1}		11			9^{2}	14				1		12	6^{3}	27
	2	3	4	5^{3}	12	7■	8	13	10		11			9^{2}					1		14	6^{1}	28
																							29
																							30
																							31
																							32
																							33
																							34
																							35
																							36

EDINBURGH CITY

Year formed: 1928 (disbanded 1955, reformed from Postal United in 1986).
Ground & Address: Ainslie Park Stadium, 94 Pilton Drive, Edinburgh EH5 2HF (for 3 seasons from 2017-18 whilst Meadowbank Stadium is redeveloped). *Telephone:* 0845 463 1932.
E-mail: admin@edinburghcityfc.com *Website:* edinburghcityfc.com
Ground Capacity: 3,127 (seated 504). *Size of Pitch:* 96m × 66m
Chairman: Jim Brown. *Director of Football:* Jim Jefferies.
Manager: James McDonaugh. *Coach:* Colin Jack.
Previous name: Postal United.
Club Nickname: 'The Citizens'.
Previous Grounds: City Park 1928-55; Fernieside 1986-95; Meadowbank Stadium 1996-2017.
Record victory: 5-0 v King's Park, Division II (1935-36); 6-1 and 7-2 v Brechin City, Division II (1937-38).
Record defeat: 1-11 v Rangers, Scottish Cup, 19 January 1929.
Most League Appearances: 112: Marc Laird, 2016-20.
Most League Goals in Season (Individual): 30: Blair Henderson, League Two, 2018-19.
Most Goals Overall (Individual): 45: Blair Henderson, 2018-20.

EDINBURGH CITY – SPFL LADBROKES LEAGUE TWO 2019–20 LEAGUE RECORD

Match No.	*Date*	*Venue*	*Opponents*	*Result*	*H/T Score*	*Lg Pos.*	*Goalscorers*	*Attendance*
1	Aug 3	A	Cove R	L 0-5	0-3	10		995
2	10	H	Brechin C	W 2-1	1-0	7	Harris 22, Shepherd 90	246
3	17	H	Stirling Alb	W 1-0	0-0	4	McIntyre 48	359
4	24	A	Stenhousemuir	W 3-1	0-1	2	Henderson, B 56, Laird 69, Shepherd 78	387
5	31	A	Elgin C	D 3-3	2-0	2	Thomson 2 (2 pens) 31, 87, Bronsky (og) 43	453
6	Sept 14	H	Annan Ath	W 4-0	1-0	2	Harris 25, Laird 49, Kane 55, Smith, A 89	253
7	21	A	Albion R	W 3-1	2-0	2	Harris 2, Handling 7, Smith, A 81	276
8	28	H	Queen's Park	W 2-1	0-0	2	Shepherd 57, Harris 62	352
9	Oct 5	A	Cowdenbeath	L 0-1	0-1	3		422
10	29	H	Stenhousemuir	W 4-0	2-0	2	Shepherd 8, Balatoni 11, Wilson 57, Handling 62	194
11	Nov 2	A	Brechin C	W 3-2	1-0	2	Laird 25, Handling 2 (1 pen) 85, 90 (p)	353
12	9	H	Elgin C	D 1-1	0-1	2	Smith, A 84	378
13	16	H	Albion R	W 3-2	0-1	2	Handling (pen) 48, Court 78, Henderson, B (pen) 90	386
14	30	A	Queen's Park	L 1-2	0-1	2	Smith, A 90	594
15	Dec 7	H	Cove R	W 2-1	2-1	2	Henderson, L 2 9, 30	439
16	14	A	Annan Ath	W 2-0	0-0	2	Henderson, L 51, Handling 79	287
17	21	A	Stirling Alb	W 1-0	0-0	2	Smith, A 90	741
18	28	H	Cowdenbeath	W 2-0	0-0	2	Henderson, L 61, Court 88	494
19	Jan 4	A	Elgin C	W 1-0	1-0	2	Shepherd 27	675
20	11	H	Queen's Park	L 1-2	1-0	2	Henderson, L 17	442
21	25	A	Stenhousemuir	W 2-1	0-1	2	Handling 54, Shepherd 78	502
22	Feb 1	H	Stirling Alb	L 0-1	0-0	2		336
23	8	H	Annan Ath	W 3-0	1-0	2	Handling 2 (1 pen) 17 (p), 65, Henderson, L 90	203
24	15	A	Cove R	L 1-2	0-0	2	Shepherd 48	909
25	22	H	Brechin C	D 0-0	0-0	2		230
26	29	A	Cowdenbeath	D 1-1	0-1	2	Laird 80	302
27	Mar 7	H	Albion R	W 3-0	1-0	2	Henderson, B (pen) 14, Handling 65, Harris 67	229
28	14	H	Stenhousemuir	Cancelled				
29	17	A	Albion R	Cancelled				
30	21	A	Annan Ath	Cancelled				
31	28	H	Cove Rangers	Cancelled				
32	Apr 4	A	Queen's Park	Cancelled				
33	11	H	Elgin C	Cancelled				
34	18	A	Stirling Alb	Cancelled				
35	25	H	Cowdenbeath	Cancelled				
36	May 2	A	Brechin C	Cancelled				

Final League Position: 2 (on points-per-game basis)

Honours
League Champions: Scottish Lowland League Champions: 2014-15, 2015-16. *Runners-up:* League Two 2019-20.
Promoted via play-offs: 2015-16 (to League Two).
League Challenge Cup: Semi-finals 2018-19.

Club colours: Shirt: White. Shorts: Black. Socks: White.

Goalscorers: *League (49):* Handling 10 (3 pens), Shepherd 7, Henderson, L 6, Harris 5, Smith, A 5, Laird 4, Henderson, B 3 (2 pens), Court 2, Thomson 2 (2 pens), Balatoni 1, Kane 1, McIntyre 1, Wilson 1, own goal 1.
William Hill Scottish Cup (7): Handling 2 (1 pen), Henderson, B 2, Court 1, Harris 1, McIntyre 1.
Betfred Scottish League Cup (2): Handling 1, Henderson, B 1 (1 pen).
Tunnock's Caramel Wafer Scottish League Challenge Cup (1): Henderson, B 1.

Antell C 5	Crane C 21 + 3	Balatoni C 26	Henderson L 20	McIntyre R 12 + 2	Harris A 22 + 2	Laird M 25	Sinclair J 10 + 3	Kane C 12 + 8	Handling D 24 + 1	Henderson B 10 + 6	Shepherd S 20 + 6	Court J 6 + 15	Adamson R 1 + 1	Watson A 3 + 1	Brown L 17 + 4	Smith A 5 + 11	Thomson C 20 + 1	Beveridge D — + 1	McAdams A 10	Brown A 1	Dunn J — + 1	Newman S — + 2	Wilson A 8 + 2	Stewart K 3 + 5	Rae J (Trialist) 3	Martin A 3	Savoury G 5 + 1	Holmes G — + 5	Mason K 5	Match No.
1■	2	3	4■	5	6^{1}	7	8^{2}	9	10	11^{3}	12	13	14																	1
	5	3		4	9	8		2	12	14	13	11	1	6^{2}	7^{3}	10^{1}														2
1	5	3	4	9	10^{3}	8		14	6^{2}	11^{1}	12	13			7		2													3
1	5	3	4	9^{2}	11^{3}	8		14		10	12			6^{1}	7	13	2													4
1^{3}	5	3	4	9	10	8^{1}					11	14		6^{2}	7	13	2	12												5
	5	3		9	10	8	12	4	6^{1}		11^{2}	13			7^{3}	14	2		1											6
	5	3		9	10^{3}	8	13	4	6		11^{2}					12	2		1	7^{1}	14									7
	5	3		9	10	8	13	4	6^{2}		11^{3}	14			7^{1}	12	2		1											8
	5	3		9	10		8^{3}	4	6		11^{2}	12		13	7^{1}		2■		1			14								9
		4	5	9	10^{3}	8^{1}	7	3^{2}	6		11	14			13	12			1				2							10
	13	4	5	9	10	8	7^{1}	3	6		11^{3}				14	12			1				2^{2}							11
	14	3	5^{1}	9^{3}	10	8	7^{2}	4	6	13	11					12			1					2						12
	5	3		13	9^{2}	8		4	11	12	10	14			7	6^{3}			1					2^{1}						13
	5	4			9	7		2	6	10	13	11^{1}			8^{3}	12	14		1				3^{2}							14
	5	3	4		9^{2}	8			6	10^{1}	11^{3}	12			7	14	2		1					13						15
	5^{3}	3	4		9^{1}	8			6	10	11^{2}	14			7	12	2							13	1					16
	2	4	3					14	6	9	11^{2}	12			7	10^{1}	5						13	8^{3}	1					17
		4	5		9^{2}	8		14	6		10^{3}	13			7	11^{1}	2						3	12	1					18
		3	5		9^{2}	8		13	6		11	14			7^{1}	10^{3}	2						4	12		1				19
	13	3	5		9^{2}	8^{3}			6		10	11			7^{1}		2					14	4	12		1				20
	7	3	5		9^{1}	8	6^{3}	12	11		10^{2}	13			14		2						4			1				21
1	7	3^{2}	5		9	8^{3}	6^{1}		11	14	10						2						4				12	13		22
	5		4	14		7^{2}	8	3	6	10		11^{1}			13		2										9^{3}	12	1	23
	5^{3}	3	4			7	8^{2}	13	6	14	10	11^{1}					2										9	12	1	24
	5	3	4		12	7	8^{2}		6	13	10	11^{1}					2										9^{3}	14	1	25
	6	3	8		13	4		12	7	10	11^{1}	14			5^{2}		2										9^{3}		1	26
	5^{1}	3	4		9^{2}	8^{3}			6	11	13				7		2						14				10	12	1	27
																														28
																														29
																														30
																														31
																														32
																														33
																														34
																														35
																														36

ELGIN CITY

Year Formed: 1893. *Ground and Address:* Borough Briggs, Borough Briggs Road, Elgin IV30 1AP.
Telephone: 01343 551114. *Fax:* 01343 547921. *E-mail:* elgincityfc@btconnect.com *Website:* www.elgincity.net
Ground Capacity: 3,927 (seated: 478). *Size of pitch:* 102m × 68m.
Chairman: Graham Tatters.
Manager: Gavin Price. *Assistant Manager:* Keith Gibson.
Previous name: Elgin City United 1900-03.
Club Nicknames: 'City'; 'The Black & Whites'.
Previous Grounds: Association Park 1893-95; Milnfield Park 1895-1909; Station Park 1909-19; Cooper Park 1919-21.
Record Attendance: 12,608 v Arbroath, Scottish Cup, 17 February 1968.
Record Transfer Fee received: £32,000 for Michael Teasdale to Dundee (January 1994).
Record Transfer Fee paid: £10,000 for Russell McBride from Fraserburgh (July 2001).
Record Victory: 18-1 v Brora Rangers, North of Scotland Cup, 6 February 1960.
Record Defeat: 1-14 v Hearts, Scottish Cup, 4 February 1939.
Most League Appearances: 306: Mark Nicholson, 2007-17.
Most League Goals in Season (Individual): 21: Craig Gunn, 2015-16.
Most Goals Overall (Individual): 128: Craig Gunn, 2009-17.

ELGIN CITY – SPFL LADBROKES LEAGUE TWO 2019–20 LEAGUE RECORD

Match No.	Date	Venue	Opponents	Result	H/T Score	Lg Pos.	Goalscorers	Attendance
1	Aug 3	H	Cowdenbeath	W 3-0	1-0	2	Sutherland 2 43, 48, Spark 51	612
2	10	A	Annan Ath	D 1-1	0-0	2	Sutherland 76	376
3	17	H	Stenhousemuir	L 0-1	0-0	5		738
4	24	A	Queen's Park	D 0-0	0-0	6		577
5	31	H	Edinburgh C	D 3-3	0-2	7	Sutherland 2 55, 73, Hester 62	453
6	Sept 14	A	Stirling Alb	L 0-1	0-1	7		482
7	21	H	Cove R	L 0-2	0-1	8		1002
8	28	A	Brechin C	L 1-2	0-0	8	Sutherland 58	349
9	Oct 5	A	Albion R	W 3-1	2-0	6	MacEwan 34, Sutherland 39, Clarke (og) 85	275
10	26	H	Queen's Park	W 3-1	3-1	4	Cameron 23, Sutherland 2 30, 39	658
11	Nov 2	H	Annan Ath	W 4-0	3-0	4	Cameron 4, Omar 2 5, 85, Sutherland (pen) 24	483
12	9	A	Edinburgh C	D 1-1	1-0	4	Hester 44	378
13	30	H	Stirling Alb	L 1-2	0-1	6	Bronsky 73	564
14	Dec 3	A	Stenhousemuir	D 2-2	2-1	6	Hester 29, MacEwan 31	336
15	7	A	Cowdenbeath	D 0-0	0-0	5		307
16	14	H	Albion R	D 2-2	0-1	5	Sutherland (pen) 47, MacEwan 71	458
17	21	H	Brechin C	W 3-1	1-0	5	Hester 24, Sutherland (pen) 60, Mackay 90	659
18	28	A	Cove R	L 0-2	0-1	5		1264
19	Jan 4	H	Edinburgh C	L 0-1	0-1	6		675
20	11	A	Annan Ath	W 4-0	1-0	5	Hester 2 42, 71, Sutherland 67, Omar 81	211
21	18	H	Stenhousemuir	L 2-3	0-2	6	Mackay 78, Bronsky 80	573
22	25	A	Stirling Alb	W 2-1	1-0	4	Sutherland 40, Hester 50	584
23	Feb 1	A	Brechin C	W 2-1	0-1	4	Sutherland 83, Osadolor 86	412
24	8	H	Cove R	W 3-0	2-0	4	Hester 2, Bronsky 23, MacEwan 46	849
25	15	A	Queen's Park	L 0-2	0-1	5		582
26	29	A	Albion R	W 2-1	2-1	4	Omar 2, Hester 6	283
27	Mar 7	H	Stirling Alb	W 3-1	3-1	4	Osadolor 21, Hester 29, MacPhee (pen) 43	666
28	10	H	Cowdenbeath	W 3-2	0-1	3	MacPhee 48, Sutherland 56, Cameron 68	512
29	14	H	Brechin C	Cancelled				
30	21	A	Stenhousemuir	Cancelled				
31	28	H	Queen's Park	Cancelled				
32	Apr 4	A	Cove Rangers	Cancelled				
33	11	A	Edinburgh C	Cancelled				
34	18	H	Annan Ath	Cancelled				
35	25	H	Albion R	Cancelled				
36	May 2	A	Cowdenbeath	Cancelled				

Final League Position: 3 (on points-per-game basis)

Honours
League Runners-up: League Two 2015-16.
Scottish Cup: Quarter-finals 1968.
Highland League Champions: winners 15 times.

Club colours: Shirt: Black and white stripes. Shorts: Black. Socks: Black.

Goalscorers: *League (48):* Sutherland 16 (3 pens), Hester 10, MacEwan 4, Omar 4, Bronsky 3, Cameron 3, Mackay 2, MacPhee 2 (1 pen), Osadolor 2, Spark 1, own goal 1.
William Hill Scottish Cup (4): Cameron 1, Hester 1, MacEwan 1, Sutherland 1.
Betfred Scottish League Cup (7): Sutherland 4, Bronsky 1, Dingwall 1, Hester 1.
Tunnock's Caramel Wafer Scottish League Challenge Cup (15): Hester 7, Sutherland 5 (1 pen), Cooper 1, Mackay 1, Omar 1.

McHale T 28	Wilson D 10 + 2	Bronsky S 27	McGowan J 1 + 2	Spark E 21	Cooper M 25 + 3	MacEwan R 23 + 3	Dingwall R 21 + 6	O'Keefe C 11 + 6	Hester K 27	Sutherland S 25 + 1	Willis K — + 4	Loveland O — + 2	Scott L — + 1	McDonald A 12	Mackay D 17 + 7	Sopel A — + 7	Cameron B 22	Omar R 15 + 7	Aitken M 1 + 10	McHardy D 4 + 6	Thompson J — + 1	Harper C 4	Osadolor S 1 + 7	Graham R 7 + 1	MacPhee A 6	*Match No.*
1	2	3	4	5	6	7	8^2	9^1	10^3	11	12	13	14													1
1	2	3	12	5^3	6	7	8		10^1	11	13			4	9^2	14										2
1	2^2	3	14	5	6^3	7	8		10	11	12			4	9^1	13										3
1	2	4		5	12	7	6		10	11^1	13			3			8	9^2								4
1	2^1	3		5	13	7^2	8		10	11				4			6	9	12							5
1	2	4		5	6^2	13	7^1		10^3	11				3		14	8	9	12							6
1	2	3		5	6^2	9	8		10^1	11				4	13		7		12							7
1	2	3		5	4	6^1	8		10	11					9^2	13	7		12							8
1		4		5	2	6^2	8		11^3	10				3^1	9		7		12	13	14					9
1		3		5	2	13	4^3		10^2	11				8	6^1		7	9	12	14						10
1		3		5	2	12	8^1		10^3	11				4	9^2	14	7	6		13						11
1		4		5	2		8	13	10^2	11				3	9^1		7	6		12						12
1		4		2	5	9^1	7	6^3	11^2	10				3	12		8	13	14							13
1		4		5	2	6	7		10^3	11					9^2	14	8	12	13	3^1						14
1		4		5	2	6	8	14	10^2	11				3	9^1		7^3	12	13							15
1		3		5	2	6	8	12		11					9^1			7	10	4						16
1	13	3^2		5	2	7	8	9^3	11^1	10					12			6	14	4						17
1	2			5^3	3	7	8^1	9^2	11	10		14			12	13		6		4						18
1	2^1	4			3	8	14	9^3	10	11					13		7	6^2		12		5				19
1		4			3	2	8^3	9^1	10^2	11					13		7	6		14		5	12			20
1		4			3	2	8^2	9	10	11					14		7	6^1				5^3	13	12		21
1		4			3	7	12	13	10^2	11					6^1		8	9^3				5	14	2		22
1		4			2	7	14	12	10^3	11					6^1		8	9^2					13	3	5	23
1		3			2	8	13	9^1	10	11^3					6^2		7	12					14	4	5	24
1		3		5^3	2	8	14	9^2	11						6^1		7	13					12	4	10	25
1	12	3		2	6		7	13	10^1						9		8	11						4	5^2	26
1		3		2^2	12	8		9^1	10	14					6		7	13					11^3	4	5	27
1		3			2	8	14	9^2	10^3	11					6^1		7	12					13	4	5	28
																										29
																										30
																										31
																										32
																										33
																										34
																										35
																										36

FALKIRK

Year Formed: 1876. *Ground & Address:* The Falkirk Stadium, 4 Stadium Way, Falkirk FK2 9EE. *Telephone:* 01324 624121. *Fax:* 01324 612418. *Email:* post@falkirkfc.co.uk *Website:* www.falkirkfc.co.uk
Ground Capacity: 8,750 (all seated). *Size of Pitch:* 105m × 68m.
Chairman: Gary Deans.
Head Coaches: Lee Miller and David McCracken.
Club Nickname: 'The Bairns'.
Previous Grounds: Randyford 1876-81; Blinkbonny Grounds 1881-83; Brockville Park 1883-2003.
Record Attendance: 23,100 v Celtic, Scottish Cup 3rd rd, 21 February 1953.
Record Transfer Fee received: £945,000 for Conor McGrandles to Norwich C (August 2014).
Record Transfer Fee paid: £225,000 to Chelsea for Kevin McAllister (August 1991).
Record Victory: 11-1 v Tillicoultry, Scottish Cup 1st rd, 7 Sep 1889.
Record Defeat: 1-11 v Airdrieonians, Division I, 28 April 1951.
Most Capped Player: Alex Parker, 14 (15), Scotland.
Most League Appearances: 451: Tom Ferguson, 1919-32.
Most League Goals in Season (Individual): 43: Evelyn Morrison, Division I, 1928-29.
Most Goals Overall (Individual): 154: Kenneth Dawson, 1934-51.

FALKIRK – SPFL LADBROKES LEAGUE ONE 2019–20 LEAGUE RECORD

Match No.	Date	Venue	Opponents	Result	H/T Score	Lg Pos.	Goalscorers	Attendance
1	Aug 3	A	Peterhead	D 0-0	0-0	7		1513
2	10	H	Dumbarton	W 6-0	5-0	3	Sammon 2 [7, 53], McManus 3 [11, 34, 42], Telfer [38]	4060
3	17	H	Montrose	W 2-1	1-1	1	Sammon 2 [31, 56]	3736
4	24	A	Clyde	L 0-1	0-1	2		2048
5	31	A	Airdrieonians	D 0-0	0-0	3		1888
6	Sept 14	H	Forfar Ath	W 3-0	2-0	3	Doyle [14], Longridge 2 [18, 86]	3663
7	21	A	Stranraer	W 3-0	1-0	3	McMillan [24], Telfer [67], Gomis [81]	549
8	28	H	East Fife	D 0-0	0-0	3		3933
9	Oct 5	A	Raith R	D 2-2	2-0	3	Longridge [3], Sammon [17]	2756
10	19	H	Peterhead	W 4-0	2-0	3	Sammon [13], McMillan [36], Longridge [59], McManus [64]	3289
11	26	H	Clyde	L 0-1	0-0	3		4021
12	Nov 2	A	Forfar Ath	W 2-0	1-0	1	Durnan [33], Travis (og) [86]	998
13	9	H	Airdrieonians	L 1-2	0-1	4	McManus [71]	4000
14	16	A	Dumbarton	D 1-1	0-1	4	McManus (pen) [90]	982
15	30	H	Stranraer	W 3-0	2-0	3	McManus [18], Doyle [40], Durnan [72]	3488
16	Dec 7	A	East Fife	D 0-0	0-0	3		1182
17	14	H	Raith R	D 1-1	0-1	4	McManus [58]	4024
18	21	A	Montrose	W 3-2	1-0	4	McMillan [39], McManus [52], Connolly [90]	1095
19	28	A	Airdrieonians	D 1-1	1-1	3	McMillan [34]	2530
20	Jan 4	H	Dumbarton	W 3-0	1-0	3	Telfer [38], McManus 2 [63, 85]	3807
21	11	A	Peterhead	W 3-1	2-1	2	McManus 3 (1 pen) [9, 24, 62 (p)]	886
22	25	H	Forfar Ath	W 6-0	1-0	2	Stanger (og) [45], Hall 2 [72, 87], Connolly 2 [83, 89], Dixon [90]	3522
23	Feb 1	A	Stranraer	D 1-1	1-0	2	Connolly [31]	546
24	18	H	East Fife	W 2-0	0-0	2	Doyle [72], McManus [77]	3376
25	22	H	Montrose	W 1-0	1-0	2	McManus (pen) [40]	3561
26	29	A	Clyde	L 2-3	1-2	2	Telfer (pen) [45], Longridge [90]	1784
27	Mar 3	A	Raith R	D 1-1	0-0	2	McManus [69]	3235
28	7	H	Peterhead	W 3-0	2-0	2	Miller, L [9], McManus 2 (1 pen) [25 (p), 61]	3507
29	14	A	Dumbarton	Cancelled				
30	21	H	Stranraer	Cancelled				
31	28	A	Forfar Ath	Cancelled				
32	Apr 4	H	Airdrieonians	Cancelled				
33	11	H	Clyde	Cancelled				
34	18	A	Montrose	Cancelled				
35	25	A	East Fife	Cancelled				
36	May 2	H	Raith R	Cancelled				

Final League Position: 2 (on points-per-game basis)

Honours
League Champions: Division II 1935-36, 1969-70, 1974-75; First Division 1990-91, 1993-94, 2002-03, 2004-05; Second Division 1979-80;
Runners-up: Division I 1907-08, 1909-10; First Division 1985-86, 1988-89, 1997-98, 1998-99; Division II 1904-05, 1951-52, 1960-61; Championship: 2015-16, 2016-17; League One 2019-20.
Scottish Cup Winners: 1913, 1957; *Runners-up:* 1997, 2009, 2015.
League Cup Runners-up: 1947-48.
League Challenge Cup Winners: 1993-94, 1997-98, 2004-05, 2011-12.

European: *Europa League:* 2 matches (2009-10).

Club colours: All: Navy blue with white trim.

Goalscorers: *League (54):* McManus 19 (4 pens), Sammon 6, Longridge 5, Connolly 4, McMillan 4, Telfer 4 (1 pen), Doyle 3, Durnan 2, Hall 2, Dixon 1, Gomis 1, Miller, L 1, own goals 2.
William Hill Scottish Cup (6): Sammon 3, McManus 2, Dixon 1.
Betfred Scottish League Cup (6): McManus 3, Johnstone 1, Leitch 1, Sammon 1.
Tunnock's Caramel Wafer Scottish League Challenge Cup (1): Longridge 1.

Bell C 11	Doyle M 28	Buchanan G 25	Durnan M 21 + 1	Dixon P 28	Telfer C 15 + 5	Gomis M 20 + 2	McShane I 9 + 5	Tidser M 9	McManus D 26	Sammon C 17 + 10	Toshney L 7 + 1	Connolly A 17 + 8	Johnstone D — + 7	Longridge L 18 + 6	Moore L — + 2	MacLean R — + 7	Mutch R 17 + 1	McMillan D 12 + 7	Miller G 15 + 1	Leitch R — + 3	De Vita R 3 + 4	Hall B 6	Todd J 3 + 1	Miller L 1 + 3	*Match No.*
1	2	3	4^{2}	5	6^{3}	7	8	9^{1}	10	11	12	13	14												1
1	2	3		5	6		7^{3}	8	10^{2}	11	4	9^{1}	14	12	13										2
1	2	4		5	6	13	7^{2}	8	10	11	3	9^{1}		12											3
1	2^{3}	4		5	6	7		8^{2}	10	11	3	13	14	9^{1}		12									4
1^{1}	2	4	3	5		6	7^{3}	8	9	10		11^{2}		13		14	12								5
1	2	4	3	5	8^{3}	7	12		10^{1}	11^{2}		9	14	6				13							6
1	2	4	3	5	8^{1}	7	12		10^{3}	13		9	14	6				11^{2}							7
1	2	7	3	5	9	8			11^{1}	13		6	12	4				10^{2}							8
1	2	4	3	5	8^{1}	6^{2}	12	7^{3}		11		13		9				10	14						9
1	2	4	3	5	8	6			11	10^{1}		12		7^{2}	13			9							10
1	2	4	3	5	8	7■			9	11		12		6^{1}				10							11
	2	3	4	5			7	8	11	10^{1}		9^{2}		6		13	1	12							12
	2	3	4	5		7	6	8^{1}	10	13		12		9			1	11^{2}							13
	2	3	4	5	6^{2}	7			11	14		8^{1}		9^{3}		12	1	13	10						14
	5	3	4	9	12	8^{1}	14		11	10^{2}	2		13	6^{3}			1		7						15
	5	3	4	9	12	8^{1}			11	10^{2}	2			6^{3}			1	13	7	14					16
	5	3	2	9	8■	12■	6^{3}		10^{2}	13				7		14	1	11^{1}	4						17
	5	3		9			6^{1}	8	10	14	4	12		7^{3}		13	1	11^{2}	2						18
	5	3	2	9			6		10	14	4^{2}	12		8^{1}		13^{3}	1	11	7						19
	5	3	2	9	8^{3}	4			10	12		6^{2}					1	11^{1}	7	14	13				20
	5	2	3	4	9^{3}	6^{2}			11^{1}	10		8					1	13	7	14	12				21
	2		4	5					10	11^{1}		9		13			1	12	7		6^{2}	3	8		22
	2	3	4	5	14	8^{2}			11	12		6^{1}		13			1	10^{3}	7				9		23
	2	3		5	13	8^{2}			11	10^{1}		9		6^{3}			1		7			4	12	14	24
	2	3	12	5		8^{2}	14		10■	11		9^{3}					1		7		13	4	6^{1}		25
	2	3		5^{2}	6	8^{1}				10		9		14			1	11^{3}	7		12	4		13	26
	2		3	5		7^{1}			11			10		8			1		6		9	4		12	27
	2		3	5	12				11^{2}	13		9		6			1	14	7		8^{3}	4		10^{1}	28
																									29
																									30
																									31
																									32
																									33
																									34
																									35
																									36

FORFAR ATHLETIC

Year Formed: 1885. *Ground & Address:* Station Park, Carseview Road, Forfar DD8 3BT. *Telephone:* 01307 463576. *Fax:* 01307 466956. *E-mail:* david.mcgregor@forfarathletic.co.uk *Website:* www.forfarathletic.co.uk
Ground Capacity: 6,777 (seated: 739). *Size of Pitch:* 103m × 64m.
Chairman: Ross Graham. *Secretary:* David McGregor.
Manager: Stuart Malcolm. *Assistant Manager:* Barry Sellars.
Club Nicknames: 'The Loons'; 'The Sky Blues'.
Record Attendance: 10,780 v Rangers, Scottish Cup 2nd rd, 2 February 1970.
Record Transfer Fee received: £65,000 for David Bingham to Dunfermline Ath (September 1995).
Record Transfer Fee paid: £50,000 for Ian McPhee from Airdrieonians (1991).
Record Victory: 14-1 v Lindertis, Scottish Cup 1st rd, 1 September 1888.
Record Defeat: 2-12 v King's Park, Division II, 2 January 1930.
Most League Appearances: 463: Ian McPhee, 1978-88 and 1991-98.
Most League Goals in Season (Individual): 46: Dave Kilgour, Division II, 1929-30.
Most Goals Overall: 125: John Clark, 1978-91.

FORFAR ATHLETIC – SPFL LADBROKES LEAGUE ONE 2019–20 LEAGUE RECORD

Match No.	Date	Venue	Opponents	Result	H/T Score	Lg Pos.	Goalscorers	Attendance
1	Aug 3	A	Airdrieonians	W 2-0	0-0	1	Andrew Jackson 53, Tapping 55	780
2	10	H	Stranraer	W 1-0	0-0	2	Hilson (pen) 76	523
3	24	A	Peterhead	L 0-1	0-0	3		676
4	31	H	Clyde	D 0-0	0-0	6		650
5	Sept 7	H	East Fife	L 1-2	1-0	6	Forbes 42	619
6	14	A	Falkirk	L 0-3	0-2	8		3663
7	21	H	Montrose	W 2-0	1-0	4	Docherty 45, Bain 89	670
8	28	H	Raith R	L 1-2	1-0	6	McLean 45	847
9	Oct 5	A	Dumbarton	L 1-3	0-3	7	Kirkpatrick 48	532
10	19	A	East Fife	L 0-1	0-1	7		667
11	26	H	Airdrieonians	L 1-4	1-0	8	Hilson 34	487
12	Nov 2	H	Falkirk	L 0-2	0-1	10		998
13	9	A	Montrose	L 0-3	0-1	10		753
14	26	A	Raith R	D 0-0	0-0	9		975
15	30	H	Peterhead	W 2-1	1-0	9	Forbes 21, MacKintosh 69	449
16	Dec 7	A	Clyde	D 0-0	0-0	9		510
17	14	H	Dumbarton	L 3-4	3-2	9	Travis 2 2, 29, Hilson (pen) 45	431
18	21	A	Stranraer	W 4-2	2-0	9	Docherty 16, Hilson 34, Forbes 59, Burns 81	212
19	28	H	Montrose	L 2-3	2-1	9	Forbes 14, MacKintosh 33	943
20	Jan 4	A	Airdrieonians	L 0-1	0-0	9		833
21	11	H	Raith R	D 1-1	1-0	9	Forbes 9	832
22	25	A	Falkirk	L 0-6	0-1	9		3522
23	Feb 1	H	Clyde	W 2-1	1-0	9	Kirkpatrick 2 19, 55	566
24	15	H	Stranraer	D 1-1	1-0	9	Whyte 14	370
25	25	A	Peterhead	D 1-1	0-0	9	Doris 82	443
26	29	H	East Fife	L 0-1	0-1	9		644
27	Mar 3	A	Dumbarton	L 0-2	0-1	9		364
28	7	A	Raith R	L 1-2	0-1	9	Coupe 90	1551
29	14	H	Airdrieonians	Cancelled				
30	21	A	Montrose	Cancelled				
31	28	H	Falkirk	Cancelled				
32	Apr 4	A	Clyde	Cancelled				
33	11	A	East Fife	Cancelled				
34	18	H	Peterhead	Cancelled				
35	25	H	Dumbarton	Cancelled				
36	May 2	A	Stranraer	Cancelled				

Final League Position: 9 (on points-per-game basis)

Honours
League Champions: Second Division 1983-84; Third Division 1994-95; C Division 1948-49.
Runners-up: League One 2018-19; Third Division 1996-97, 2009-10; League Two 2016-17.
Promoted via play-offs: 2009-10 (to Second Division); 2016-17 (to League One).
Scottish Cup: Semi-finals 1982.
League Cup: Semi-finals 1977-78.
League Challenge Cup: Semi-finals 2004-05.

Club colours: Shirt: Sky blue. Shorts: White. Socks: Sky blue.

Goalscorers: *League (26):* Forbes 5, Hilson 4 (2 pens), Kirkpatrick 3, Docherty 2, MacKintosh 2, Travis 2, Bain 1, Burns 1, Coupe 1, Doris 1, Andrew Jackson 1, McLean 1, Tapping 1, Whyte 1.
William Hill Scottish Cup (1): Tapping 1.
Betfred Scottish League Cup (10): Hilson 3 (2 pens), Travis 3, Forbes 1, Andrew Jackson 1, Kirkpatrick 1, Tapping 1.
Tunnock's Caramel Wafer Scottish League Challenge Cup (1): MacKintosh 1.

McCallum M 28	Meechan R 28	Whyte D 27	Docherty M 20 + 1	Burns S 7 + 1	Forbes R 18 + 2	Tapping C 23 + 3	Irvine G 25	Kirkpatrick J 16 + 6	Hilson D 16 + 1	Jackson Andrew 6 + 6	Coupe C 7 + 17	Robertson S 8 + 9	Aitken M — + 7	Travis M 16	Currie R 1 + 6	Bain J 18 + 2	MacKintosh M 11 + 4	McLean R 2 + 3	MacPhee A 4 + 2	Stanger G 3 + 1	Doris S 7	Shanley R — + 1	Leitch R 4 + 2	Barr B 5 + 1	Coll B 5	McKenzie Marc — + 1	McKenzie Mark 3	Match No.
1	2	3	4	5	6	7^2	8	9^1	10	11^3	12	13	14															1
1	2	3	4	5	6	8	7	9^2	10^1	11^3	12	14	13															2
1	2		4	5	6^3	8	7	9^2	10	11^1	13	12	14	3														3
1	2	4	5			9^2	7	6^3	10	11^1	14	8		3	12	13												4
1	2	4	14	5	6	7	8^3	9^1	10	13	12			3	11^2													5
1	2	3	4		9^3	6	8^1	14	11^2	12	10				13	5	7											6
1	2	3	8		9	7	5	10^1		11^2	13			4	12^3	6	14											7
1	2	3	8		9^3	7	5	13			10			4		6^2	14	11^1	12									8
1	2	3	5	14	6	9^3	8^1	10			12			4			7	11^2	13									9
1	2	3	7	9^3	8	14		10			11^2			4	12	6^1		13	5									10
1	2	3	5		8^3	6	7^1	11^2	10		12			4	13			14	9									11
1	2	3	9^2			8^1		14	10		11^3	7		4	13	6	12		5									12
1	2	3	8		13	10		12	11		9^1	7		4		6^2			5									13
1	2	3	8		12	9^2	7	10^1	11		13			4		5	6											14
1	2	3	9^2		8^1	10	7		11		12	13		4		5	6											15
1	2	3	9		8^1	10	7		11	13	12			4		5	6^2											16
1	2	3	7		9	10	6		11	13		12		4^2		5	8^1											17
1	4	3	9	10^3	8^2		2		11^1	12	13	7				5	6	14										18
1	4	3	7^1	10^3	9^2	13	2		11	12	14	6				5	8											19
1	3	4			10	8	2	13	12	11^2	9^3	7	14			5	6^1											20
1	2	4	7^2		9	10	6	8^1	11		12	13				5				3								21
1	2	4	7		9^2		6	8				13				5	10^1			3	11	12						22
1	2	3				9^3	6	8				14	12	4		5	13				11^2		7^1	10				23
1	2	4				7^3	6	9			13	14		3^1						12	11		8^2	10	5			24
1	2	3				12	7	11				8^2				14				4^3	10		6^1	9	5	13		25
1	3	4				8	7	6^2			12		14			2					11		13	9^1	5^3		10	26
1	3	4				8	7	14			9^1					2	6^2				10		13	12	5		11^3	27
1	3	4				8	2				13	7	12								10^2		6^1	9	5		11	28
																												29
																												30
																												31
																												32
																												33
																												34
																												35
																												36

GREENOCK MORTON

Year Formed: 1874. *Ground & Address:* Cappielow Park, Sinclair St, Greenock PA15 2TU. *Telephone:* 01475 723571. *Fax:* 01475 781084. *E-mail:* admin@gmfc.net *Website:* www.gmfc.net
Ground Capacity: 11,612 (seated: 6,062). *Size of Pitch:* 100m × 65m.
Chairman: Crawford Rae. *Chief Executive:* Dave MacKinnon.
Manager: David Hopkin. *Assistant Manager:* Anton McElhone.
Club Nickname: 'The Ton'.
Previous Grounds: Grant Street 1874; Garvel Park 1875; Cappielow Park 1879; Ladyburn Park 1882; Cappielow Park 1883.
Record Attendance: 23,500 v Celtic, 29 April 1922.
Record Transfer Fee received: £500,000 for Derek Lilley to Leeds U (March 1997).
Record Transfer Fee paid: £250,000 for Janne Lindberg and Marko Rajamäki from MyPa, Finland (November 1994).
Record Victory: 11-0 v Carfin Shamrock, Scottish Cup 4th rd, 13 November 1886.
Record Defeat: 1-10 v Port Glasgow Ath, Division II, 5 May, 1894 and v St Bernards, Division II, 14 October 1933.
Most Capped Player: Jimmy Cowan, 25, Scotland.
Most League Appearances: 534: Derek Collins, 1987-98, 2001-05.
Most League Goals in Season (Individual): 58: Allan McGraw, Division II, 1963-64.
Most Goals Overall (Individual): 136: Andy Ritchie, 1976-83.

GREENOCK MORTON – SPFL LADBROKES CHAMPIONSHIP 2019–20 LEAGUE RECORD

Match No.	*Date*	*Venue*	*Opponents*	*Result*		*H/T Score*	*Lg Pos.*	*Goalscorers*	*Attendance*
1	Aug 3	A	Ayr U	L	2-4	0-1	9	Tumilty 73, Cadden 79	1935
2	10	H	Alloa Ath	W	4-1	1-1	3	McHugh 3 5, 61, 74, Lyon 53	1646
3	23	H	Partick Thistle	W	3-2	0-2	2	Cadden 72, Sutton 77, McLean 80	2197
4	30	A	Inverness CT	L	0-5	0-1	4		2136
5	Sept 14	A	Queen of the South	L	0-1	0-1	6		1302
6	21	H	Dundee	W	1-0	1-0	4	Grant 45	1901
7	28	A	Dundee U	L	0-6	0-3	5		7404
8	Oct 5	H	Dunfermline Ath	D	1-1	0-0	5	McAlister 90	1690
9	19	A	Arbroath	L	0-1	0-0	8		1009
10	26	H	Inverness CT	W	2-1	1-1	7	McHugh 2 6, 81	1408
11	29	H	Ayr U	L	2-3	0-0	8	Baird 47, McHugh 61	1431
12	Nov 1	A	Dundee	L	1-2	0-0	8	Salkeld 64	4228
13	9	A	Partick Thistle	L	1-2	0-0	9	Baird 61	2751
14	16	H	Arbroath	W	1-0	1-0	8	Lyon 3	1185
15	Dec 7	A	Dunfermline Ath	L	1-3	0-1	8	Lyon 62	3515
16	10	H	Dundee U	L	1-2	1-2	8	Smith, L (og) 25	1120
17	21	A	Alloa Ath	W	2-0	0-0	8	Cadden 64, Baird 67	727
18	28	H	Partick Thistle	L	1-2	1-1	9	Jacobs (pen) 30	2742
19	Jan 4	A	Arbroath	W	2-1	2-1	9	Sutton 12, Colville 20	1273
20	11	H	Dunfermline Ath	W	3-2	1-1	8	Jacobs 2 42, 84, McAlister 49	1470
21	25	A	Dundee U	D	1-1	1-0	7	Orsi 17	7644
22	Feb 1	H	Dundee	D	1-1	1-1	7	McAlister 26	1643
23	8	H	Queen of the South	D	2-2	0-1	7	McHugh (pen) 59, Nesbitt 76	1380
24	22	H	Alloa Ath	D	4-4	4-2	7	Jacobs 15, Colville 40, Tumilty 44, McHugh 45	1214
25	25	A	Ayr U	W	2-1	1-1	6	Orsi 29, Cadden 72	1336
26	29	A	Queen of the South	W	4-0	2-0	5	Tumilty 25, Nesbitt 44, Cadden 77, McGuffie 88	1116
27	Mar 3	A	Inverness CT	L	2-3	0-1	5	Nesbitt 61, Lyon 76	1772
28	7	H	Arbroath	D	1-1	0-0	7	McGinty 90	1472
29	14	H	Dundee U	Cancelled					
30	21	A	Dunfermline Ath	Cancelled					
31	28	A	Partick Thistle	Cancelled					
32	Apr 4	H	Inverness CT	Cancelled					
33	11	A	Dundee	Cancelled					
34	17	H	Ayr U	Cancelled					
35	25	A	Alloa Ath	Cancelled					
36	May 2	H	Queen of the South	Cancelled					

Final League Position: 7 (on points-per-game basis)

Honours
League Champions: First Division 1977-78, 1983-84, 1986-87; Division II 1949-50, 1963-64, 1966-67; Second Division 1994-95, 2006-07; League One 2014–15; Third Division 2002-03.
Runners-up: Division 1 1916-17; First Division 2012-13; Second Division 2005-06;. Division II 1899-1900, 1928-29, 1936-37.
Scottish Cup Winners: 1922; *Runners-up:* 1948.
League Cup Runners-up: 1963-64.
League Challenge Cup Runners-up: 1992-93.

European: *UEFA Cup:* 2 matches (*Fairs Cup:* 1968-69).

Club colours: Shirt: Blue and white hoops. Shorts: White with blue trim. Socks: White with blue tops.

Goalscorers: *League (45):* McHugh 8 (1 pen), Cadden 5, Jacobs 4 (1 pen), Lyon 4, Baird 3, McAlister 3, Nesbitt 3, Tumilty 3, Colville 2, Orsi 2, Sutton 2, Grant 1, McGinty 1, McGuffie 1, McLean 1, Salkeld 1, own goal 1.
William Hill Scottish Cup (4): Cadden 2, Lyon 1, McHugh 1 (1 pen).
Betfred Scottish League Cup (17): Cadden 3 (1 pen), McHugh 3, Nesbitt 2, Sutton 2, Grant 1, Jacobs 1, Muirhead 1, Strapp 1, own goals 3.
Tunnock's Caramel Wafer Scottish League Challenge Cup (1): Sutton 1.

Ramsbottom S 8	McLean B 8 + 3	Grant P 15 + 1	van Schaik H 1	Tumilty R 9 + 2	Jacobs K 24	Nesbitt A 15 + 5	McAlister J 27 + 1	Cadden N 21 + 1	Muirhead R 8 + 5	Sutton J 10 + 9	Blues C 6 + 7	McHugh B 14 + 6	Salkeld C 5 + 8	Strapp L 22 + 1	Millar C 12 + 7	Lyon R 12 + 6	Orsi K 6 + 6	Rogers D 20	Colville L 15 + 4	Welsh S 15	Baird J 24	King B — + 6	Livingstone A 4	McGinty S 7	Doolan K — + 1	McGuffie C — + 4	*Match No.*
1	2	3^{2}	4	5	6	7^{3}	8	9	10^{1}	11	12	13	14														1
1	4			13	2	9^{3}	3	11			6^{1}	10^{2}	14	5	7	8	12										2
	3	4^{1}			7	10	2	9		13	8^{3}	11		5	12	6^{2}		1	14								3
	4				7	10^{1}	3	9^{2}	14	13		11	12	5	8			1	6^{3}	2							4
	14				8		3	10		12		11^{3}	13	5^{1}	9^{2}	6		1	7	2	4						5
	14	4					8	10		11	12		13	5	7^{3}	6^{2}		1	9^{1}	2	3						6
		4					8	9		11^{2}	12	10		5	7^{3}	6^{1}		1	13	2	3	14					7
1		4			5	11	7			14	8^{3}	10	13		6^{1}	12			9^{2}	2	3						8
1		3			8	6^{1}	9	10^{3}		11	7^{2}	14		5		13				2	4	12					9
1		4			6		7		13			11	8^{3}	5	12	9			10^{2}	2^{1}	3	14					10
1		4			7	13	6^{1}		10^{3}	14		11	8^{2}	5		9				2	3	12					11
1		3			6	14	8^{2}		7	12		10^{3}	11	5	9^{1}	13				2	4						12
1		4			6^{3}	13	7			14		11	10^{1}	5	8^{2}	9				2	3	12					13
	3^{3}	4			7		6			14		11^{1}	10^{2}	9	12	8		1		5	2	13					14
		4			5	12	7	8^{1}	10			11	14		6^{3}	13		1		3^{2}	2		9				15
		4			6	7	9^{1}	12		11^{2}		13^{3}	14			8		1	10	2	3		5				16
		3			5	9	6^{3}	11		10^{1}					12	7^{2}	14	1	13	4	2		8				17
		4^{1}			6	7	9	10	13	11^{3}				12		8		1	14	2	3		5^{2}				18
	3	14			5		7	9^{3}	10	11^{1}	12			4	6^{2}		13	1	8		2						19
	4			12	2		8^{3}	6	11	10^{2}	14			5	7^{1}		13	1	9		3						20
	4			2	6		9	10^{1}	11			12		5	13		7^{2}	1	8		3						21
				2	6▮	13	8	10^{3}	14	11^{1}				5	12		7^{2}	1	9		3			4			22
				2		7	8	10			13	11^{2}		5^{1}	6^{3}		12	1	9		3			4	14		23
				2	6	7	8^{2}	10^{3}				11^{1}		5	13		12	1	9		3			4		14	24
				5	6	8^{2}	13	10			7^{3}	12		2			11^{1}	1	9		4			3		14	25
				2	6^{2}	8^{1}	7	10	14		12			5			11^{3}	1	9		4			3		13	26
	14			2		8^{1}	6	10			7			5		12	11^{2}	1	9^{3}		4			3		13	27
				2^{1}	8	6	7	9	10^{3}	14		13		5		12	11^{2}	1			3			4			28
																											29
																											30
																											31
																											32
																											33
																											34
																											35
																											36

HAMILTON ACADEMICAL

Year Formed: 1874. *Ground:* Hope Stadium, New Douglas Park, Cadzow Avenue, Hamilton ML3 0FT. *Telephone:* 01698 368652. *Fax:* 01698 285422. *E-mail:* office@acciesfc.co.uk *Website:* www.hamiltonacciesfc.co.uk
Ground Capacity: 6,078 (all seated). *Size of Pitch:* 105m × 68m.
Chairman: Allan Maitland. *Vice-Chairman:* Les Gray.
Head Coach: Brian Rice. *First-Team Coach:* Guillaume Beuzelin.
Club Nickname: 'The Accies'.
Previous Grounds: Bent Farm; South Avenue; South Haugh; Douglas Park; Cliftonhill Stadium; Firhill Stadium.
Record Attendance: 28,690 v Hearts, Scottish Cup 3rd rd, 3 March 1937 (at Douglas Park); 5,895 v Rangers, 28 February 2009 (at New Douglas Park).
Record Transfer Fee received: £1,200,000 (rising to £3,200,000) for James McCarthy to Wigan Ath (July 2009).
Record Transfer Fee paid: £180,000 for Tomas Cerny from Sigma Olomouc (July 2009).
Record Victory: 10-2 v Greenock Morton, Scottish Championship, 3 May 2014.
Record Defeat: 1-11 v Hibernian, Division I, 6 November 1965.
Most Capped Player: Colin Miller, 29 (61), Canada, 1988-94.
Most League Appearances: 452: Rikki Ferguson, 1974-88.
Most League Goals in Season (Individual): 35: David Wilson, Division I; 1936-37.
Most Goals Overall (Individual): 246: David Wilson, 1928-39.

HAMILTON ACADEMICAL – SPFL LADBROKES PREMIERSHIP 2019–20 LEAGUE RECORD

Match No.	Date	Venue	Opponents	Result	H/T Score	Lg Pos.	Goalscorers	Attendance
1	Aug 3	A	Ross Co	L 0-3	0-2	7		4071
2	10	H	Kilmarnock	W 2-0	1-0	6	Smith, L 20, Oakley 49	2766
3	24	H	Motherwell	L 1-3	1-2	9	Cunningham (pen) 24	2927
4	31	A	Hearts	D 2-2	0-1	7	Oakley 2 50, 73	15,347
5	Sept 14	H	Celtic	L 0-1	0-1	8		5300
6	21	A	St Mirren	D 0-0	0-0	8		4807
7	28	H	Livingston	W 2-1	1-1	8	Alston 45, Cunningham (pen) 84	1075
8	Oct 6	A	Rangers	L 0-5	0-2	8		48,838
9	19	H	Hibernian	D 1-1	0-1	8	Cunningham (pen) 59	2680
10	26	A	St Johnstone	L 2-3	1-1	8	Miller 25, Davies (pen) 84	2231
11	30	H	Aberdeen	L 0-1	0-1	10		1687
12	Nov 2	H	Ross Co	D 2-2	0-1	8	Smith, L 52, Oakley 64	1268
13	9	A	Kilmarnock	D 2-2	2-1	10	Miller 2, Davies 25	5045
14	24	H	Rangers	L 1-3	1-2	11	Smith, L 14	5100
15	30	A	Livingston	D 0-0	0-0	9		1076
16	Dec 4	A	Celtic	L 1-2	0-1	10	Ogboe 90	54,584
17	7	H	St Mirren	L 0-1	0-0	11		1962
18	14	A	Aberdeen	L 0-1	0-0	12		12,325
19	21	H	Hearts	W 2-1	0-0	11	Miller 64, Collar 72	2654
20	26	H	St Johnstone	L 0-1	0-0	11		1536
21	29	A	Motherwell	W 2-1	0-1	11	McGowan 68, Moyo 77	6048
22	Jan 22	A	Hibernian	L 1-2	1-0	11	Gogic 18	15,674
23	25	H	Livingston	L 2-4	1-2	11	Want 14, Woods 57	1487
24	Feb 2	H	Celtic	L 1-4	1-1	12	Ogboe 27	4708
25	5	A	St Mirren	D 1-1	1-0	11	Templeton 25	4537
26	11	H	Aberdeen	L 1-3	0-3	11	Ogboe 84	1218
27	15	A	Hearts	D 2-2	2-0	11	Ogboe 2 (1 pen) 5, 16 (p)	16,437
28	22	H	Motherwell	D 0-0	0-0	11		2531
29	Mar 4	A	Rangers	W 1-0	0-0	11	Moyo 56	48,167
30	7	H	Kilmarnock	W 1-0	0-0	10	Ogboe (pen) 90	2145
31	14	A	Ross Co	Cancelled				
32	21	H	Hibernian	Cancelled				
33	Apr 4	A	St Johnstone	Cancelled				
34	Fixtures 34–38 decided after 33 game league split.							
35								
36								
37								
38								

Final League Position: 11 (on points-per-game basis)

Honours
League Champions: Division II 1903-04; First Division 1985-86, 1987-88, 2007-08; Third Division 2000-01.
Runners-up: Division II 1952-53, 1964-65; Second Division 1996-97, 2003-04; Championship 2013-14.
Promoted via play-offs: 2013-14 (to Premiership).
Scottish Cup Runners-up: 1911, 1935. *League Cup:* Semi-finalists three times.
League Challenge Cup Winners: 1991-92, 1992-93; *Runners-up:* 2005-06, 2011-12.

Club colours: Shirt: Red and white hoops. Shorts: White. Socks: White.

Goalscorers: *League (30):* Ogboe 6 (2 pens), Oakley 4, Cunningham 3 (3 pens), Miller 3, Smith, L 3, Davies 2 (1 pen), Moyo 2, Alston 1, Collar 1, Gogic 1, McGowan 1, Templeton 1, Want 1, Woods 1.
William Hill Scottish Cup (6): Dales 1, Martin 1, McMann 1, Miller 1, Smith, L 1, Winter 1.
Betfred Scottish League Cup (8): Cunningham 4 (2 pens), Alston 1, McMann 1, Ogboe 1, Smith, L 1.
Tunnock's Caramel Wafer Scottish League Challenge Cup (4): Winter 2 (1 pen), Breen 1, Slaven 1.

Fon Williams O 15	McGowan A 22	Gogic A 29	McKenna C 2+1	McMann S 27	Alston B 14+5	MacKinnon D 3+3	Hunt J 10+6	Cunningham R 6+3	Ogboe M 16+7	Oakley G 17+4	Fjortoft M 5+2	Moyo D 8+12	Smith L 17+6	Stubbs S 19	Easton B 17+1	Miller M 16+5	Hamilton J 11+1	Stanger G 1	Collar W 14+2	Hughes R 5+3	Want S 9+2	Beck A 2+4	Davies S 5+8	Martin S 18+2	Southwood L 15	Dales A 1+1	Woods S 3	Winter A —+3	Templeton D 3+3	Mimnaugh R —+1	*Match No.*
1	2	3	4[2]	5	6	7	8	9[3]	10	11[1]	12	13	14																		1
1	2	6		5	9	7	14	10[2]	13	11[1]			8[3]	3	4▪	12															2
1	2	7				8		10[2]	13	11[1]			6	3		12	4▪	5	9												3
1	2[3]	7			9	13			11	10[2]	3	12	6	4	5				8[1]	14											4
1		8	14	2	7				12	11[1]	5[2]		9	3	4				10		6[3]	13									5
1	2	7		5	9				11[2]	10▪		13	6[1]	3	4				8[3]	12		14									6
1	2	7		5	9			13	10[2]			14	6[3]	3	4	12				8			11[1]								7
1		8	2	6	9					11	3[2]		12	4	5		13			7		10[1]									8
1		7		5	8			12	10[1]	13			9[2]	3	4	11[3]				6			14	2							9
1	2	7		5		12				11[3]		13		3	4	10				6		9[1]	14	8[2]							10
1		7		5				10[2]		11		12	9[1]	3		8	4			6			13	2							11
1		7		5			14	10[2]		11			9[3]	4		8[1]	3			13	2		12	6▪							12
1		6		5		12	8			11[2]	14	13	9[3]	4▪		7	3				2		10[1]								13
	5	7		9			2	13	11[2]	12			8[1]		3	6	4						10		1						14
	5	7		9			2		11[1]	10[2]		12	8	4	3	6								13	1						15
	2	7		5					12	13		11[1]	9[3]	4	3	6			8[2]			14		10	1						16
	5	7▪		9			2[1]		11[2]	12		14	8	3	4	6							10[3]	13	1						17
	5			9			2	7[3]	13	11[1]		14		3		10	4		6			12		8[2]	1						18
	2	6		5			14			10[3]			12	3	13	9	4		7[1]				11[2]	8	1						19
	2	7		5	13		14			10[2]		11[3]		3	4	9			6[1]				12	8	1						20
	2	8		5	12		13		14	11[2]		10[3]		3	4	9			6					7[1]	1						21
1		6		2	9[2]				12	11[1]	3		13		4	10			5				14	7		8[3]					22
1		7		5	12				11[1]		3		9[3]			10			8[2]		4			6		14	2	13			23
	2	6		5	9				11[2]			10[1]					3▪		7[3]		12		14	8	1		4		13		24
	2	6		5	14		8		10[2]			12	13		4	11[3]					3			7	1				9[1]		25
	2	6		5	7		8		11			14			4[3]				13		12			9	1		3[2]		10[1]		26
	2[1]	6		5	12		8		11[2]			10[3]					4▪		7		3		14	9	1				13		27
	5	3			8[1]		2		11			10[2]	12						6[3]		4			7	1			13	9	14	28
	2	6		5	8		14		10			11[2]	9[3]			12	4				3			7[1]	1			13			29
	2	6		5	8[1]				10			11[3]	9			12▪	3[2]		13		4			7	1				14		30
																															31
																															32
																															33
																															34
																															35
																															36
																															37
																															38

HEART OF MIDLOTHIAN

Year Formed: 1874. *Ground & Address:* Tynecastle Stadium, McLeod Street, Edinburgh EH11 2NL. *Telephone:* 0333 043 1874. *Fax:* 0131 200 7222. *E-mail:* supporterservices@homplc.co.uk *Website:* www.heartsfc.co.uk
Ground Capacity: 20,099. *Size of Pitch:* 100m × 64m.
Chairman: Ann Budge. *Chief Executive:* Andrew McKinlay
Manager: Robbie Neilson. *Assistant Managers:* Gordon Forrest, Lee McCulloch.
Club Nicknames: 'Hearts'; 'Jambos'; 'Jam Tarts'.
Previous Grounds: The Meadows 1874; Powderhall 1878; Old Tynecastle 1881; Tynecastle Park 1886.
Record Attendance: 53,396 v Rangers, Scottish Cup 3rd rd, 13 February 1932 (57,857 v Barcelona, 28 July 2007 at Murrayfield).
Record Transfer Fee received: £9,000,000 for Craig Gordon to Sunderland (August 2008).
Record Transfer Fee paid: £850,000 for Mirsad Beslija from Genk (January 2006).
Record Victory: 15-0 v King's Park, Scottish Cup 2nd rd, 13 February 1937 (21-0 v Anchor, EFA Cup, 30 October 1880).
Record Defeat: 1-8 v Vale of Leven, Scottish Cup 3rd rd, 1883; 0-7 v Celtic, Scottish Cup 4th rd, 1 December 2013.
Most Capped Player: Steven Pressley, 32, Scotland.
Most League Appearances: 515: Gary Mackay, 1980-97.
Most League Goals in Season (Individual): 44: Barney Battles, 1930-31.
Most Goals Overall (Individual): 214: John Robertson, 1983-98.

HEART OF MIDLOTHIAN – SPFL LADBROKES PREMIERSHIP 2019–20 LEAGUE RECORD

Match No.	Date	Venue	Opponents	Result	H/T Score	Lg Pos.	Goalscorers	Attendance
1	Aug 4	A	Aberdeen	L 2-3	0-1	8	Naismith 68, Walker 76	16,410
2	10	H	Ross Co	D 0-0	0-0	8		15,652
3	25	A	Celtic	L 1-3	0-1	11	Washington 81	58,763
4	31	H	Hamilton A	D 2-2	1-0	11	Clare 20, Berra 58	15,347
5	Sept 14	H	Motherwell	L 2-3	0-1	12	Ikpeazu 61, Meshino 86	15,862
6	22	A	Hibernian	W 2-1	0-0	8	Ikpeazu 70, Hickey 84	19,828
7	28	A	St Mirren	D 0-0	0-0	9		5901
8	Oct 5	H	Kilmarnock	L 0-1	0-1	9		16,711
9	20	H	Rangers	D 1-1	1-1	10	Meshino 6	17,573
10	26	A	Livingston	D 0-0	0-0	9		3854
11	30	A	St Johnstone	L 0-1	0-0	11		3104
12	Nov 9	H	St Mirren	W 5-2	3-2	9	Naismith 6, McLoughlin (og) 30, Bozanic 42, Walker 46, Mulraney 77	16,165
13	23	A	Kilmarnock	L 0-3	0-3	9		6278
14	Dec 1	A	Rangers	L 0-5	0-2	10		49,811
15	4	H	Livingston	D 1-1	0-1	9	MacLean 88	14,681
16	7	A	Motherwell	L 0-1	0-1	10		4745
17	14	H	St Johnstone	L 0-1	0-0	11		16,347
18	18	H	Celtic	L 0-2	0-2	11		17,297
19	21	A	Hamilton A	L 1-2	0-0	12	Bozanic 82	2654
20	26	H	Hibernian	L 0-2	0-2	12		19,313
21	29	H	Aberdeen	D 1-1	0-0	12	Meshino 49	17,788
22	Jan 22	A	Ross Co	D 0-0	0-0	12		4301
23	26	H	Rangers	W 2-1	0-0	12	Naismith 57, Boyce 83	18,539
24	Feb 1	A	St Johnstone	D 3-3	2-1	11	Boyce 26, Naismith 31, Clare 90	6002
25	5	H	Kilmarnock	L 2-3	0-2	12	Clare (pen) 79, Halkett 89	16,211
26	12	A	Celtic	L 0-5	0-1	12		57,431
27	15	H	Hamilton A	D 2-2	0-2	12	Walker 48, Halkett 87	16,437
28	Mar 3	A	Hibernian	W 3-1	0-0	11	Clare (pen) 53, Bozanic 65, Washington 80	20,197
29	7	H	Motherwell	D 1-1	0-1	12	Washington 49	17,339
30	11	A	St Mirren	L 0-1	0-0	12		5662
31	15	A	Livingston	Cancelled				
32	21	H	Ross Co	Cancelled				
33	Apr 3	A	Aberdeen	Cancelled				
34	Fixtures 34–38 decided after 33 game league split.							
35								
36								
37								
38								

Final League Position: 12 (on points-per-game basis)

Honours
League Champions: Division I 1894-95, 1896-97, 1957-58, 1959-60; First Division 1979-80; Championship 2014-15.
Runners-up: Division I 1893-94, 1898-99, 1903-04, 1905-06, 1914-15, 1937-38, 1953-54, 1956-57, 1958-59, 1964-65; Premier Division 1985-86, 1987-88, 1991-92, 2005-06; First Division 1977-78, 1982-83.
Scottish Cup Winners: 1891, 1896, 1901, 1906, 1956, 1998, 2006, 2012; *Runners-up:* 1903, 1907, 1968, 1976, 1986, 1996, 2019.
League Cup Winners: 1954-55, 1958-59, 1959-60, 1962-63; *Runners-up:* 1961-62, 1996-97, 2012-13.

European: *European Cup:* 8 matches (1958-59, 1960-61, 2006-07). *Cup Winners' Cup:* 10 matches (1976-77, 1996-97, 1998-99). *UEFA Cup:* 46 matches (*Fairs Cup:* 1961-62, 1963-64, 1965-66. *UEFA Cup:* 1984-85, 1986-87, 1988-89, 1990-91, 1992-93, 1993-94, 2000-01, 2003-04, 2004-05, 2006-07). *Europa League:* 12 matches (2010-11, 2011-12, 2012-13, 2016-17).

Club colours: Shirt: Maroon. Shorts: White with maroon trim. Socks: Maroon.

Goalscorers: *League (31):* Clare 4 (2 pens), Naismith 4, Bozanic 3, Meshino 3, Walker 3, Washington 3, Boyce 2, Halkett 2, Ikpeazu 2, Berra 1, Hickey 1, MacLean 1, Mulraney 1, own goal 1.
William Hill Scottish Cup (7): Clare 2 (1 pen), Bozanic 1, Halkett 1, Henderson 1, Irving 1, Naismith 1.
Betfred Scottish League Cup (10): Halkett 4, Irving 1, MacLean 1, McDonald 1, Smith 1, Walker 1, Washington 1 (1 pen).
Tunnock's Caramel Wafer Scottish League Challenge Cup (8): Keena 3, Baur 1, Henderson 1, Petkov 1, Watson 1, Zanatta 1.

Zlamal Z 8	Smith M 23	Souttar J 7	Berra C 18 + 1	Halkett C 24	Hickey A 22	Walker J 10 + 5	Clare S 24 + 2	Irving A 14 + 4	Mulraney J 12 + 5	Ikpeazu U 15 + 8	Dikamona C 8 + 3	Washington C 7 + 8	Naismith S 14 + 3	White A 12 + 2	Damour L 13 + 5	Henderson E 5 + 6	Bozanic O 13 + 5	Joel Pereira D 20	Whelan G 13 + 2	Brandon J 6 + 3	Doyle C 2	Meshino R 9 + 10	MacLean S 8 + 3	Morrison C 2 + 2	Keena A 1 + 4	Wighton C 1 + 1	Garuccio B 2 + 2	Avdijaj D 1 + 2	Moore L 6 + 1	Sibbick T 2	Boyce L 6 + 2	Langer M 1 + 1	McDonald A 1	*Match No.*
1	2	3^2	4	5	6▮	7	8	9^1	10^3	11	12	13	14																					1
1	2		4	3		6	7		12	11^3		10	9^2	5	8^1	13	14																	2
	2^3		4	3	5		9	8	11^1	13		10		14	7^2			1	6	12														3
			4	3	2		9	7^3	8			11	14	5^1		10^2			6	13	1	12												4
			4	3	5		6	8^3	9	11		14			12				7	2^1	1	13	10^2											5
	4^1		3	2	5		9^2	13	8	11	14				7^3			1	6			10		12										6
	3		12	2^2	4			13	8	11				14	6^3			1	7			10^1	9	5										7
	2		3		5		11	7^3	9^1		4				6^2		12	1	8			10	13		14									8
	3		4		2		9	14	10^3	11				5^1			7	1	6	12		8^2	13											9
	3		4		5		6	8		11	12						7	1		2^2		10^1	9^3	13	14									10
	3		4		2	12	9^2			11				5	7^3		8	1	13			14	10	6^1										11
	3		4		5	9^1		7	12	10^2	2		11	8^3	13		6	1				14												12
	2		4		5^2	8	13		12	9^3	3^1		11	10			7	1	6			14												13
			4	3	5	9^3			14	11^1			10	6^2	12		7	1	8	2		13												14
1	2		4	3		8^2	9		10	13			11^1		6^3				7	5		14	12											15
	2		4	3		8^3	6		11▮	12								1	7	5		9^2	10^1		14	13								16
1	5		3	4	2	6^2	9^3			13					14		7		8			12	11		10^1									17
	7		4	3	5		12		9^1						6	14	8^3	1	13	2^2			10			11								18
	4			3	5		2		12	10			8^2	9^3	6^1	14	13	1	7				11											19
	7		4	3	5		2		11^1	10				8^3	6^2	12	13	1				9			14									20
	6			4	5		2▮	7		11^1	3	13			12	8	9^3	1				10^2					14							21
		3		4		14		7		13	5^1	10	11			12	8^3	1									2	6^2	9					22
		4		3			2	7		14		13	9	5^3		10	12	1											8^2	6^1	11			23
		3		4			2	7		12		13	9	5		10^3		1				8^1						14		6^2	11			24
		4		3		14	2	7		12		13	9	5		10^3		1											8^2		11	6^1		25
	6^1	4		3		10	2^3	7				12	9					1									5		14		11	13▮	8^2	26
1	7	4		3	5^3	6	2^1	8		11^2		13	9														14	12			10			27
1	5			4	2	13	7				3	10^1	12		8	14	9												6^2		11^3			28
1	2			3	5	12	6^2				4	11	10		7		8^3					14							9^1		13			29
1	2			3	5		9^3	13			4	11	10		7^1		8^2					14							6		12			30
																																		31
																																		32
																																		33
																																		34
																																		35
																																		36
																																		37
																																		38

HIBERNIAN

Year Formed: 1875. *Ground & Address:* Easter Road Stadium, 12 Albion Place, Edinburgh EH7 5QG. *Telephone:* 0131 661 2159. *Fax:* 0131 659 6488. *E-mail:* club@hibernianfc.co.uk *Website:* www.hibernianfc.co.uk
Ground Capacity: 20,421 (all seated). *Size of Pitch:* 105m × 68m.
Chairman: Ronald Gordon. *Chief Executive:* Leean Dempster.
Manager: Jack Ross. *Assistant Head Coach:* John Potter.
Club Nickname: 'Hibs'; 'Hibees'.
Previous Grounds: Meadows 1875-78; Powderhall 1878-79; Mayfield 1879-80; First Easter Road 1880-92; Second Easter Road 1892.
Record Attendance: 65,860 v Hearts, Division I, 2 January 1950.
Record Transfer Fee received: £4,400,000 for Scott Brown from Celtic (2007).
Record Transfer Fee paid: £700,000 for Ulises de la Cruz to LDU Quito (2001).
Record Victory: 15-1 v Pebbles Rovers, Scottish Cup 2nd rd, 11 February 1961.
Record Defeat: 0-10 v Rangers, Division I, 24 December 1898.
Most Capped Player: Lawrie Reilly, 38, Scotland.
Most League Appearances: 446: Arthur Duncan, 1969-84.
Most League Goals in Season (Individual): 42: Joe Baker, 1959-60.
Most Goals Overall (Individual): 233: Lawrie Reilly, 1945-58.

HIBERNIAN – SPFL LADBROKES PREMIERSHIP 2019–20 LEAGUE RECORD

Match No.	Date	Venue	Opponents	Result	H/T Score	Lg Pos.	Goalscorers	Attendance
1	Aug 3	H	St Mirren	W 1-0	0-0	3	Allan, S 85	16,631
2	11	A	Rangers	L 1-6	1-2	7	Horgan 40	49,718
3	24	H	St Johnstone	D 2-2	1-0	7	Jackson 25, Kamberi 69	15,315
4	31	A	Motherwell	L 0-3	0-1	9		5964
5	Sept 14	A	Kilmarnock	L 0-2	0-0	9		5458
6	22	H	Hearts	L 1-2	0-0	11	Mallan 47	19,828
7	28	H	Celtic	D 1-1	1-1	11	Ajer (og) 7	18,339
8	Oct 5	A	Aberdeen	D 1-1	0-0	10	Porteous 48	13,880
9	19	A	Hamilton A	D 1-1	1-0	10	Mallan 22	2680
10	26	H	Ross Co	D 2-2	0-0	11	Horgan 50, Allan, S 56	15,452
11	30	H	Livingston	D 2-2	0-2	9	Allan, S (pen) 62, Boyle 90	14,662
12	Nov 9	A	St Johnstone	W 4-1	2-0	8	Doidge 3 2, 17, 58, Allan, S 48	3931
13	23	H	Motherwell	W 3-1	2-1	6	Doidge 21, Kamberi 25, Horgan 86	15,984
14	26	A	St Mirren	W 2-1	1-0	6	Doidge 28, Mallan (pen) 82	5377
15	30	H	Kilmarnock	D 2-2	1-0	6	Doidge 19, Naismith 47	16,180
16	Dec 4	A	Ross Co	L 1-2	1-0	6	Doidge 34	4196
17	7	H	Aberdeen	W 3-0	0-0	6	Boyle 2 52, 68, Kamberi 74	16,767
18	15	A	Celtic	L 0-2	0-1	6		57,598
19	20	H	Rangers	L 0-3	0-2	6		19,540
20	26	A	Hearts	W 2-0	2-0	5	Boyle 2 6, 31	19,313
21	29	A	Livingston	L 0-2	0-0	6		4902
22	Jan 22	H	Hamilton A	W 2-1	0-1	6	Doidge 64, Hanlon 86	15,674
23	25	A	Motherwell	D 0-0	0-0	6		5767
24	Feb 1	H	St Mirren	D 2-2	2-2	6	Allan, S 25, Doidge 43	16,325
25	5	A	Rangers	L 1-2	1-1	6	Hanlon 35	49,427
26	12	H	Ross Co	W 3-0	2-0	6	McNulty 7, Doidge 41, Jackson 83	14,486
27	16	A	Kilmarnock	W 2-1	2-1	6	Docherty 28, Jackson 45	5370
28	22	H	Livingston	D 1-1	0-0	6	Doidge 50	15,553
29	Mar 3	H	Hearts	L 1-3	0-0	6	Hallberg 89	20,197
30	7	A	Aberdeen	L 1-3	1-0	6	Doidge 39	14,388
31	14	H	St Johnstone	Cancelled				
32	21	A	Hamilton A	Cancelled				
33	Apr 5	H	Celtic	Cancelled				
34	Fixtures 34–38 decided after 33 game league split.							
35								
36								
37								
38								

Final League Position: 7 (on points-per-game basis)

Honours
League Champions: Division I 1902-03, 1947-48, 1950-51, 1951-52; First Division 1980-81, 1998-99; Championship 2016-17; Division II 1893-94, 1894-95, 1932-33.
Runners-up: Division I 1896-97, 1946-47, 1949-50, 1952-53, 1973-74, 1974-75; Championship 2014-15.
Scottish Cup Winners: 1887, 1902, 2016; *Runners-up:* 1896, 1914, 1923, 1924, 1947, 1958, 1972, 1979, 2001, 2012, 2013.
League Cup Winners: 1972-73, 1991-92, 2006-07; *Runners-up:* 1950-51, 1968-69, 1974-75, 1985-86, 1993-94, 2003-04, 2015-16.
Drybrough Cup Winners: 1972-73, 1973-74.

European: *European Cup:* 6 matches (1955-56 semi-finals). *Cup Winners' Cup:* 6 matches (1972-73). *UEFA Cup:* 64 matches (*Fairs Cup:* 1960-61 semi-finals, 1961-62, 1962-63, 1965-66, 1967-68, 1968-69, 1970-71. *UEFA Cup:* 1973-74, 1974-75, 1975-76, 1976-77, 1978-79, 1989-90, 1992-93, 2001-02, 2005-06. *Europa League:* 10 matches 2010-11, 2013-14, 2018-19).

Club colours: Shirt: Green with white sleeves. Shorts: White. Socks: Green.

Goalscorers: *League (42):* Doidge 12, Allan, S 5 (1 pen), Boyle 5, Horgan 3, Jackson 3, Kamberi 3, Mallan 3 (1 pen), Hanlon 2, Docherty 1, Hallberg 1, McNulty 1, Naismith 1, Porteous 1, own goal 1.
William Hill Scottish Cup (15): Doidge 4, McNulty 3, Allan, S 2 (1 pen), Docherty 2, Boyle 1, Gullan 1, Jackson 1, Omeonga 1.
Betfred Scottish League Cup (15): Kamberi 5, Allan, S 3 (2 pens), Doidge 2, Hallberg 1, James 1, Murray 1, Newell 1, Vela 1.
Tunnock's Caramel Wafer Scottish League Challenge Cup (3): Gullan 1, Porteous 1, Shaw 1 (1 pen).

Marciano O 19	Whittaker S 5 + 2	Jackson A 12 + 2	Hanlon P 30	James T 6	Vela J 9 + 1	Mallan S 14 + 6	Horgan D 12 + 16	Allan S 28 + 2	Newell J 13 + 6	Kamberi F 16 + 4	Mackie S 1 + 1	Slivka V 12 + 4	Doidge C 25 + 3	McGregor D 4 + 2	Murray F — + 7	Gray D 3 + 1	Stevenson L 26 + 1	Middleton G 4 + 2	Shaw O — + 4	Naismith J 13	Porteous R 14	Hallberg M 18 + 2	Maxwell C 11 + 1	Boyle M 15 + 5	Omeonga S 4 + 4	Gullan J 1 + 4	McGinn P 6 + 1	Docherty G 5 + 1	McNulty M 4 + 2	*Match No.*
1	2	3	4	5^{3}	6^{1}	7	8^{2}	9	10	11	12	13	14																	1
1	2		4		7	6	8^{2}	9^{3}	10^{1}	14	5■		11	3	12	13														2
1	12	3	4		7	8	14	6^{1}		10		13	11^{2}			2^{3}	5	9												3
1	2	4	3		13	8	6	10		11		7^{1}					5	9^{2}	12											4
1			4		7	8	9^{1}	10	13	11			12				5			2	3	6^{2}								5
			4		6	7	10^{2}	9		11			13				5	12		2	3	8^{1}	1							6
	12	3^{2}	4	2	7	8	13	9	14				11				5	10^{3}				6^{1}	1							7
			4	2	7	8	10^{3}	9	14	13			11^{1}				5	12			3	6^{2}	1							8
			4	2	6^{3}	9	8^{1}	12	10^{2}	14			11		13		5				3	7	1							9
		14	4		6	8	12	9^{2}	10^{3}	11					13		5			2	3	7^{1}	1							10
			4	2		6	8	9		12			11				5	10^{1}			3	7^{2}	1	13						11
			4			13	14	7^{3}	6^{2}	11		8	10^{1}				5			2	3	9	1	12						12
			4			14	13	9^{3}	8^{2}	11^{1}		7	10				5			2	3	6	1	12						13
			4			14	13	9^{3}	8^{2}	11^{1}		7	10				5			2	3	6	1	12						14
			4			12	14	9^{2}	8^{1}	11^{3}		7	10				5			2	3	6	1	13						15
			4			12	14	9		10^{3}		6^{2}	11				5		13	2	3	7^{1}	1	8						16
1		13	4			8		9		11^{2}		12	10				5		14	2	3	6^{1}		7^{3}						17
1^{2}			4			9	13	8^{3}		11			10^{1}		14		5			2	3	7	12	6						18
1			4			8^{2}	13	9^{3}		11^{1}		12	10	14			5			2	3■	6		7						19
1			4			12	10^{2}	9^{1}	13			7	11	3			5			2		6		8						20
1			4				10^{3}	9^{2}	14			7	11	3	12		5		13	2		6^{1}		8						21
1		3	4				14	9^{1}	12	10		6^{2}	11			2	5					7^{3}		8	13					22
1		3	4	2			6^{2}	12	8	9^{1}			10				5							11	7	13				23
1			4				10^{1}	9	7^{2}				11	3		2^{3}	5							8	6		12	13	14	24
1	6	3^{3}	4				13	9^{2}	10^{1}				11	12			5							8	7		2		14	25
1		3	4					9^{3}	8			6^{1}	11		12									5	13	14	2	7	10^{2}	26
1		3	4				14	9^{2}	8^{1}			6^{3}	10				12							5	13		2	7	11	27
1		3	4				14	9^{3}				6^{1}	10		12		8^{2}							5		13	2	7	11	28
1		3	4				12	9^{1}					10				8					14		5	6	13	2	7^{3}	11^{2}	29
1	6■	3	4				14	9^{3}					10				8^{1}					12		5	13	11^{2}	2	7		30
																														31
																														32
																														33
																														34
																														35
																														36
																														37
																														38

INVERNESS CALEDONIAN THISTLE

Year Formed: 1994. *Ground & Address:* Caledonian Stadium, Stadium Road, Inverness IV1 1FF. *Telephone:* 01463 222880. *Fax:* 01463 227479. *E-mail:* info@ictfc.co.uk *Website:* ictfc.com
Ground Capacity: 7,780 (all seated). *Size of Pitch:* 105m × 68m.
Chairman: Ross Morrison. *Chief Executive:* Scot Gardiner.
Manager: John Robertson. *Assistant Manager:* Scott Kellacher.
Club Nicknames: 'Caley Thistle'; 'Caley Jags'; 'ICT'.
Record Attendance: 7,753 v Rangers, SPL, 20 January 2008.
Record Transfer Fee received: £400,000 for Marius Niculae to Dinamo Bucharest (July 2008).
Record Transfer Fee paid: £65,000 for John Rankin from Ross Co (July 2006).
Record Victory: 8-1 v Annan Ath, Scottish Cup 3rd rd, 24 January 1998; 7-0 v Ayr U, First Division, 24 April 2010; 7-0 v Arbroath, League Cup Northern Section Group C, 30 July 2016.
Record Defeats: 0-6 v Airdrieonians, First Division, 21 Sep 2000; 0-6 v Celtic, League Cup 3rd rd, 22 Sep 2010; 0-6 v Celtic, Scottish Premiership, 27 April 2014; 0-6 v Celtic, Scottish Cup 5th rd, 11 February 2017.
Most Capped Player: Richard Hastings, 38 (59), Canada.
Most League Appearances: 490: Ross Tokely, 1995-2012.
Most League Goals in Season: 27: Iain Stewart, 1996-97; Denis Wyness, 2002-03.
Most Goals Overall (Individual): 118: Denis Wyness, 2000-03, 2005-08.

INVERNESS CALEDONIAN TH – SPFL LADBROKES CHAMPIONSHIP 2019–20 LEAGUE RECORD

Match No.	Date	Venue	Opponents	Result		H/T Score	Lg Pos.	Goalscorers	Attendance
1	Aug 3	A	Dundee U	L	1-4	1-2	10	Walsh 29	7023
2	10	H	Arbroath	W	2-1	1-1	5	Doran 44, Storey 82	2298
3	24	A	Dundee	D	0-0	0-0	6		5016
4	30	H	Greenock Morton	W	5-0	1-0	2	Keatings 2 43, 46, White 67, Donaldson 77, Todorov 80	2136
5	Sept 14	A	Dunfermline Ath	W	1-0	0-0	3	Welsh (pen) 87	3446
6	21	H	Queen of the South	W	2-0	2-0	3	Welsh 15, Walsh 19	1760
7	28	H	Partick Thistle	L	1-3	1-1	3	White 21	2469
8	Oct 5	A	Ayr U	W	2-0	1-0	3	Vincent 31, Rooney 64	1912
9	19	H	Alloa Ath	D	2-2	0-1	3	Tremarco 61, White 85	2036
10	26	A	Greenock Morton	L	1-2	1-1	3	Curry 27	1408
11	29	A	Queen of the South	W	2-0	1-0	3	Doran 30, Todorov 90	1221
12	Nov 2	H	Dundee U	L	0-3	0-1	4		2902
13	9	A	Arbroath	L	0-3	0-1	4		1173
14	23	H	Dundee	W	1-0	1-0	3	Doran 16	2184
15	30	A	Alloa Ath	W	2-0	2-0	2	Taggart (og) 38, Doran 45	721
16	Dec 7	H	Ayr U	W	2-0	1-0	2	White 20, Storey 63	1833
17	14	A	Partick Thistle	L	1-3	0-0	2	Keatings 57	2144
18	21	H	Dunfermline Ath	W	2-0	1-0	2	Rooney 33, McCart 80	2116
19	28	H	Arbroath	L	0-1	0-0	2		2287
20	Jan 4	A	Dundee	W	2-0	2-0	2	Doran 17, Keatings 24	5040
21	25	A	Ayr U	L	0-1	0-0	2		1602
22	Feb 1	H	Alloa Ath	D	1-1	0-1	2	White 59	1914
23	21	A	Dundee U	L	1-2	1-1	2	White 32	7583
24	25	A	Dunfermline Ath	W	2-1	1-0	2	Doran 23, Walsh 77	3397
25	Mar 3	H	Greenock Morton	W	3-2	1-0	2	White 18, Rooney 67, Todorov 90	1772
26	7	A	Alloa Ath	L	0-2	0-2	2		712
27	10	H	Queen of the South	W	3-1	1-0	2	Vincent 30, Keatings 57, Storey 79	1811
28	14	A	Arbroath	Cancelled					
29	17	H	Partick Thistle	Cancelled					
30	21	H	Dundee	Cancelled					
31	28	H	Ayr U	Cancelled					
32	Apr 4	A	Greenock Morton	Cancelled					
33	10	H	Dundee U	Cancelled					
34	18	A	Partick Thistle	Cancelled					
35	25	A	Queen of the South	Cancelled					
36	May 2	H	Dunfermline Ath	Cancelled					

Final League Position: 2 (on points-per-game basis)

Honours
League Champions: First Division 2003-04, 2009-10; Third Division 1996-97.
Runners-up: Championship 2019-20; Second Division 1998-99.
Scottish Cup Winners: 2015; Semi-finals 2003, 2004, 2019.
League Cup Runners-up: 2013-14.
League Challenge Cup Winners: 2003-04, 2017-18; *Runners-up:* 1999-2000, 2009-10.

European: *Europa League:* 4 matches (2015-16).

Club colours: Shirt: Blue and red vertical stripes. Shorts: Blue. Socks: Blue with red trim.

Goalscorers: *League (39):* White 7, Doran 6, Keatings 5, Rooney 3, Storey 3, Todorov 3, Walsh 3, Vincent 2, Welsh 2 (1 pen), Curry 1, Donaldson 1, McCart 1, Tremarco 1, own goal 1.
William Hill Scottish Cup (6): Doran 1, Todorov 1, Trafford 1, Tremarco 1, Welsh 1, White 1.
Betfred Scottish League Cup (7): Todorov 2, White 2, Donaldson 1, Doran 1, Keatings 1.
Tunnock's Caramel Wafer Scottish League Challenge Cup (8): Storey 2, Curry 1, Doran 1, Keatings 1, Machado 1, Todorov 1, Trafford 1.

Ridgers M 27	McKay B 8 + 1	Donaldson C 20	McCart J 19	Tremarco C 25	Doran A 22 + 4	Carson D 20 + 7	Trafford C 17 + 3	Walsh T 11 + 6	Keatings J 16 + 5	White J 22 + 4	Vincent J 15 + 4	Todorov N 4 + 18	Storey M 22 + 5	Rooney S 24 + 1	MacGregor R 6 + 8	Welsh S 3 + 2	Machado M — + 1	Curry M 3 + 6	McHattie K 9 + 3	Harper C 1 + 1	Toshney L 3	Match No.
1	2^{3}	3	4	5	6	7	8	9	10^{1}	11^{2}	12	13	14									1
1		3	4	5	9^{1}	7		6	10	11^{2}	8	13	12	2								2
1		3	4	5	9	7		6^{3}	10^{2}	12	8	14	11^{1}	2	13							3
1		3	4	5	9^{1}	8		6	10^{3}	11^{2}	7	13	12	2	14							4
1		3	4	5	9	7^{3}		6^{1}		10^{2}	8	13	11	2	14	12						5
1		3	4	5	9	13		6		11	7	12	10^{2}	2		8^{1}						6
1		3	4	5	9^{3}	12				11	7	13	10^{2}	2	6^{1}	8	14					7
1		3	4	5	10	13	12			11^{2}	6	14	8	2	9^{3}	7^{1}						8
1		3	4	5	9^{3}	13	8^{2}		14	11	7		6	2	10^{1}			12				9
1		3	4	5		6		13	10	11^{3}	7	12	8^{1}	2	14			9^{2}				10
1		3	4	5	6^{2}	7	8	13			14	11	12	2	10^{1}			9^{3}				11
1		3	4	5	9^{1}	7	8	13	10	11	14		12	2^{2}				6^{3}				12
1	2	3	4	5	14	8	7	6^{2}	10^{1}	12		11^{3}	9					13				13
1	2^{3}	3	4	5^{2}	6	7	8		14	11^{1}		12	10	13					9			14
1		3	4^{3}	5	6	8	7		11^{1}	10			9^{2}	2	13			12	14			15
1		3	4	5^{2}	9	7	8		10^{1}	11^{3}		14	6	2	13				12			16
1		3	4	5^{3}	10^{1}	6	7		9	11^{2}		12	8	2				13		14		17
1		3	4		9^{3}	7	8		10^{1}	11^{2}	12	14	6	2				13	5			18
1		3	4		9^{2}	7	8		10^{1}	11^{3}		14	6	2	12			13	5			19
1	12	4		5	11	13	8^{3}		9	14	7	10^{2}	6^{1}	2					3			20
1	3			5	9	12	7^{3}	13	10^{1}	11	8	14	6^{2}	2					4			21
1	3			5	9	14	8^{1}	10^{3}		11	7^{2}		6	2	13	12			4			22
1	3			5	13	7^{3}	12	10^{1}	9	11	6	14	8^{2}	2					4			23
1	3			5	10^{2}	6	14	13	12	11	7		8^{1}	2	9^{3}						4	24
1				5	12	7	8	6	14	11^{2}		13	9^{3}	2	10^{1}				4		3	25
1	3			5^{2}	10	6	7	9	13	11		14	8^{3}	2					12		4^{1}	26
1				4	13	7	9	12	10^{3}	14	8	11	6^{2}	2					3	5^{1}		27
																						28
																						29
																						30
																						31
																						32
																						33
																						34
																						35
																						36

KILMARNOCK

Year Formed: 1869. *Ground & Address:* The BBSP Stadium, Rugby Park, Kilmarnock KA1 2DP. *Telephone:* 01563 545300. *Fax:* 01563 522181. *E-mail:* info@kilmarnockfc.co.uk *Website:* www.kilmarnockfc.co.uk
Ground Capacity: 18,128 (all seated). *Size of Pitch:* 102m × 67m.
Director: Billy Bowie.
Manager: Alex Dyer. *Assistant Manager:* Andy Millen.
Club Nickname: 'Killie'.
Previous Grounds: Rugby Park (Dundonald Road); The Grange; Holm Quarry; Rugby Park 1899.
Record Attendance: 35,995 v Rangers, Scottish Cup Quarter-final, 10 March 1962.
Record Transfer Fee received: £2,200,000 for Greg Taylor to Celtic (August 2019).
Record Transfer Fee paid: £340,000 for Paul Wright from St Johnstone (1995).
Record Victory: 11-1 v Paisley Academical, Scottish Cup 1st rd, 18 January 1930.
Record Defeat: 1-9 v Celtic, Division I, 13 August 1938.
Most Capped Player: Joe Nibloe, 11, Scotland.
Most League Appearances: 481: Alan Robertson, 1972-88.
Most League Goals in Season (Individual): 34: Harry 'Peerie' Cunningham 1927-28; Andy Kerr 1960-61.
Most Goals Overall (Individual): 148: Willy Culley, 1912-23.

KILMARNOCK – SPFL LADBROKES PREMIERSHIP 2019–20 LEAGUE RECORD

Match No.	*Date*	*Venue*	*Opponents*	*Result*	*H/T Score*	*Lg Pos.*	*Goalscorers*	*Attendance*
1	Aug 4	H	Rangers	L 1-2	0-1	9	O'Donnell [83]	9196
2	10	A	Hamilton A	L 0-2	0-1	12		2766
3	24	H	Aberdeen	D 0-0	0-0	12		5250
4	31	A	St Johnstone	W 1-0	1-0	6	O'Donnell [40]	3427
5	Sept 14	H	Hibernian	W 2-0	0-0	6	Millar [56], El Makrini [79]	5458
6	22	A	Celtic	L 1-3	1-1	7	Brophy [33]	57,137
7	28	H	Ross Co	D 0-0	0-0	7		4906
8	Oct 5	A	Hearts	W 1-0	1-0	6	Mulraney (og) [42]	16,711
9	19	H	Livingston	W 2-1	1-0	5	Dicker [39], McKenzie [56]	4828
10	26	H	St Mirren	W 1-0	0-0	3	Dicker [78]	6389
11	30	A	Motherwell	L 1-2	1-1	5	Thomas [31]	4676
12	Nov 2	A	Aberdeen	L 0-3	0-2	5		13,131
13	9	H	Hamilton A	D 2-2	1-2	5	El Makrini [45], Brophy [48]	5045
14	23	H	Hearts	W 3-0	3-0	5	Burke 2 [9, 16], Brophy [14]	6278
15	30	A	Hibernian	D 2-2	0-1	5	Bruce [66], Del Fabro [90]	16,180
16	Dec 4	H	St Johnstone	D 0-0	0-0	5		4083
17	7	A	Livingston	L 0-3	0-0	5		1531
18	14	A	Ross Co	L 0-1	0-0	5		3688
19	21	H	Motherwell	L 0-1	0-0	5		5688
20	26	A	Rangers	L 0-1	0-0	6		49,885
21	29	A	St Mirren	L 0-1	0-1	7		6363
22	Jan 22	H	Celtic	L 1-3	0-1	7	Kabamba [66]	8307
23	25	A	St Johnstone	L 1-2	1-1	7	Burke (pen) [22]	2609
24	Feb 1	H	Ross Co	W 3-1	0-1	7	Brophy 2 (1 pen) [54, 57 (p)], Kabamba [82]	4733
25	5	A	Hearts	W 3-2	2-0	7	Findlay [24], Burke [38], Brophy [50]	16,211
26	12	H	Rangers	W 2-1	0-1	7	O'Donnell [77], Brophy [89]	8096
27	16	H	Hibernian	L 1-2	1-2	7	Burke [30]	5370
28	23	A	Celtic	L 1-3	1-2	7	Brophy (pen) [6]	58,883
29	Mar 4	H	Aberdeen	D 2-2	2-1	7	Brophy (pen) [17], Kiltie [23]	4217
30	7	A	Hamilton A	L 0-1	0-0	8		2145
31	14	H	St Mirren	Cancelled				
32	21	A	Motherwell	Cancelled				
33	Apr 4	H	Livingston	Cancelled				
34	Fixtures 34–38 decided after 33 game league split.							
35								
36								
37								
38								

Final League Position: 8 (on points-per-game basis)

Honours
League Champions: Division I 1964-65;. Division II 1897-98, 1898-99.
Runners-up: Division I 1959-60, 1960-61, 1962-63, 1963-64; First Division 1975-76, 1978-79, 1981-82, 1992-93; Division II 1953-54, 1973-74; Second Division 1989-90.
Scottish Cup Winners: 1920, 1929, 1997; *Runners-up:* 1898, 1932, 1938, 1957, 1960.
League Cup Winners: 2011-12; *Runners-up:* 1952-53, 1960-61, 1962-63, 2000-01, 2006-07.

European: *European Cup:* 4 matches (1965-66). *Cup Winners' Cup:* 4 matches (1997-98). *UEFA Cup:* 32 matches (*Fairs Cup:* 1964-65, 1966-67 semi-finals, 1969-70, 1970-71. *UEFA Cup:* 1998-99, 1999-2000, 2001-02).

Club colours: Shirt: Blue with white stripes. Shorts: White. Socks: Blue.

Goalscorers: *League (31):* Brophy 9 (3 pens), Burke 5 (1 pen), O'Donnell 3, Dicker 2, El Makrini 2, Kabamba 2, Bruce 1, Del Fabro 1, Findlay 1, Kiltie 1, McKenzie 1, Millar 1, Thomas 1, own goal 1.
William Hill Scottish Cup (9): Findlay 2, Kabamba 2, Brophy 1, Bruce 1, El Makrini 1, Johnson 1, Kiltie 1.
Betfred Scottish League Cup (1): Thomas 1.
Tunnock's Caramel Wafer Scottish League Challenge Cup (0).
UEFA Europa League (2): Brophy 1 (1 pen), Findlay 1.

Branescu L 26	O'Donnell S 28	Broadfoot K 6 + 3	Findlay S 18	Taylor G 2	Power A 28	Dicker G 30	El Makrini M 19 + 2	Burke C 20 + 6	Brophy E 24 + 4	McKenzie R 24 + 3	Kiltie G 2 + 8	Bruce A 11 + 5	Millar L 14 + 6	Cameron I — + 1	Thomas D 3 + 17	Hamalainen N 27 + 1	Del Fabro D 21 + 1	Millen R 2 + 2	Wilson I 3 + 1	Sow O 2 + 6	St Clair H — + 2	Johnson C 3 + 1	Jackson S 1 + 3	Hendrie S 1 + 1	Koprivec J 4 + 1	Bunn H 2 + 1	Kabamba N 9	Taylor A — + 1	Connel K — + 1	*Match No.*
1	2	3	4	5	6	7	8^{2}	9	10	11^{1}	12	13																		1
1	2	3^{3}	4	5	7	8		6	10^{2}	9	13		11^{1}	12	14															2
1	2	3^{2}	4		6	7	8	9	10^{3}	13		12	11^{1}		14	5														3
1	2				8	7	6		10^{3}	9^{1}		3	11^{2}		12	5	4	13	14											4
1	2		4		6	7	8		10^{2}	9			11^{1}		13	5	3			12										5
1	2		4		8	7	9		10^{1}	6^{3}			11^{2}		14	5	3			13	12									6
1	2		4		6	7	8			9		3	11^{1}		12	5				10										7
1	2		3		8	6	9	7^{2}	11^{3}	13		14	10^{1}		12	5	4													8
1	2		4		6	7	8^{2}	9	10^{3}	11^{1}		14	12		13	5	3													9
1	2		4^{1}		6	7	8	13	10	9		12	11^{2}		14	5	3^{3}													10
1	2				7	6	9	14	12	8^{1}		4■	13		10^{3}	5						3	11^{2}							11
1	2				4	3		10^{2}	11	6			8^{3}		9^{1}	5			7		13		14	12						12
1	2				6	7	10	13	11	8^{2}		4^{1}	14		9^{3}	5	3						12							13
1	2				6	7	8	9^{1}	10^{3}	11^{2}		4	13		14	5	3			12										14
1	2				6	7	8^{1}	9		11^{2}		4	13		14	5	3			10^{3}			12							15
1	2				6	7	8^{2}	9	10^{3}	14		4	11^{1}		13	5	3			12										16
1	2				6	7	8^{2}	14	10	9^{1}		4	11^{3}		13	5	3			12										17
1	2				7	6	12	8	11	9^{2}			10^{1}		13	5	4					3								18
1	2				6	7	8^{2}	10	11	9^{1}			12		13	5	3					4								19
1					7	8	9^{2}	13	12	11		4	10^{3}		14	5	3	2^{1}	6											20
1						8	14	6^{2}	11	9^{3}		3	10		13	5	4	2^{1}	7	12										21
	2		4		6	7	9^{3}	8	12		14	3^{2}				5	13								1	10^{1}	11			22
	2		3		7	6		8	12		9					5	4								1	10^{1}	11			23
1	2	14	4		7	8		6^{3}	10^{1}	9^{2}	12					5	3									13	11			24
1■	2	12	3^{1}		7	8		6	10^{2}	9^{3}	13					5	4								14		11			25
	2		4		7	8		6^{1}	10^{2}	9						5	3	12				13			1		11			26
	2	13	3		7^{1}	8		6	11	9^{2}	12					5	4								1		10			27
1	5	4	3		8■	6	7^{3}	12	10^{2}		13					9	2^{1}										11	14		28
1	2	3	4			8		6	10	7	9					5											11			29
1	2	3	4		7	8		6	11^{1}	9^{3}	13					12								5^{2}			10		14	30
																														31
																														32
																														33
																														34
																														35
																														36
																														37
																														38

LIVINGSTON

Year Formed: 1974. *Ground:* Tony Macaroni Arena, Almondvale Stadium, Alderstone Road, Livingston EH54 7DN.
Telephone: 01506 417000. *Fax:* 01506 429948.
E-mail: lfcreception@livingstonfc.co.uk *Website:* livingstonfc.co.uk
Ground Capacity: 9,865 (all seated). *Size of Pitch:* 98m × 69m.
Chairman: Robert Wilson. *Chief Executive:* John Ward.
Manager: Gary Holt. *Assistant Manager:* David Martindale.
Club Nickname: 'Livi Lions'.
Previous Ground: Meadowbank Stadium (as Meadowbank Thistle).
Record Attendance: 10,024 v Celtic, Premier League, 18 August 2001.
Record Transfer Fee received: £2,000,000 for Lyndon Dykes to QPR (August 2020).
Record Transfer Fee paid: £120,000 for Wes Hoolahan from Shelbourne (December 2005).
Record Victory: 8-0 v Stranraer, League Cup, 1st rd, 31 July 2012.
Record Defeat: 0-8 v Hamilton A. Division II, 14 December 1974.
Most League Appearances: 446: Walter Boyd, 1979-89.
Most League Goals in Season (Individual): 22: Leigh Griffiths, 2008-09; Iain Russell, 2010-11; Liam Buchanan, 2016-17.
Most Goals Overall (Individual): 64: David Roseburgh, 1986-93.

LIVINGSTON – SPFL LADBROKES PREMIERSHIP 2019–20 LEAGUE RECORD

Match No.	*Date*	*Venue*	*Opponents*	*Result*		*H/T Score*	*Lg Pos.*	*Goalscorers*	*Attendance*
1	Aug 3	H	Motherwell	D	0-0	0-0	4		2633
2	10	A	St Johnstone	D	2-2	2-0	7	Pitman [13], Lawless [39]	2349
3	24	A	Ross Co	W	4-1	3-1	3	Guthrie [3], Lawless [14], Dykes [26], Stobbs [52]	4237
4	31	H	St Mirren	W	2-1	1-0	3	Lithgow [26], Dykes [58]	2346
5	Sept 14	A	Rangers	L	1-3	0-0	5	Lawless (pen) [47]	48,793
6	21	H	Aberdeen	L	0-2	0-1	6		2803
7	28	A	Hamilton A	L	1-2	1-1	6	Lithgow [15]	1075
8	Oct 6	H	Celtic	W	2-0	0-0	6	Robinson [47], Dykes [73]	8196
9	19	A	Kilmarnock	L	1-2	0-1	7	Del Fabro (og) [84]	4828
10	26	H	Hearts	D	0-0	0-0	7		3854
11	30	A	Hibernian	D	2-2	2-0	6	Lawless [38], Sibbald [41]	14,662
12	Nov 2	A	Motherwell	L	1-2	0-0	7	Lawless (pen) [60]	4423
13	10	H	Rangers	L	0-2	0-1	7		8071
14	23	A	Celtic	L	0-4	0-1	8		58,247
15	30	H	Hamilton A	D	0-0	0-0	7		1076
16	Dec 4	A	Hearts	D	1-1	1-0	8	Bartley [35]	14,681
17	7	H	Kilmarnock	W	3-0	0-0	7	Guthrie [54], Dykes [65], Lawless [81]	1531
18	14	A	St Mirren	D	3-3	2-1	8	Souda 2 [13, 56], Guthrie [45]	4344
19	21	H	Ross Co	W	4-0	2-0	6	Lamie [31], Dykes 3 [41, 50, 73]	1201
20	26	A	Aberdeen	L	1-2	0-1	7	Dykes [86]	14,518
21	29	H	Hibernian	W	2-0	0-0	5	Hanlon (og) [62], Guthrie [77]	4902
22	Jan 22	H	St Johnstone	W	1-0	0-0	5	Pitman [56]	1140
23	25	A	Hamilton A	W	4-2	2-1	5	Sibbald [15], Taylor-Sinclair [32], Lawless (pen) [62], Pitman [65]	1487
24	Feb 1	H	Motherwell	W	1-0	0-0	5	Taylor-Sinclair [68]	1932
25	5	A	Ross Co	L	0-2	0-1	5		3301
26	12	H	St Mirren	W	2-1	1-0	5	Lawless (pen) [34], Dykes [46]	1263
27	16	A	Rangers	L	0-1	0-0	5		48,302
28	22	A	Hibernian	D	1-1	0-0	5	Taylor-Sinclair [56]	15,553
29	Mar 4	H	Celtic	D	2-2	1-1	5	Guthrie [24], Robinson [46]	8640
30	7	A	St Johnstone	L	0-1	0-0	5		3008
31	15	H	Hearts	Cancelled					
32	21	H	Aberdeen	Cancelled					
33	Apr 4	A	Kilmarnock	Cancelled					
34	Fixtures 34–38 decided after 33 game league split.								
35									
36									
37									
38									

Final League Position: 5 (on points-per-game basis)

Honours
League Champions: First Division 2000-01; Second Division 1986-87, 1998-99, 2010-11; League One 2016-17; Third Division 1995-96, 2009-10.
Runners-up: Second Division 1982-83; First Division 1987-88; Championship 2017-18.
Promoted via play-offs: 2017-18 (to Premiership).
Scottish Cup: Semi-finals 2001, 2004.
League Cup Winners: 2003-04. Semi-finals 1984-85.
League Challenge Cup Winners: 2014-15; *Runners-up:* 2000-01.

European: *UEFA Cup:* 4 matches (2002-03).

Club colours: All: Amber with black trim.

Goalscorers: *League (41):* Dykes 9, Lawless 8 (4 pens), Guthrie 5, Pitman 3, Taylor-Sinclair 3, Lithgow 2, Robinson 2, Sibbald 2, Souda 2, Bartley 1, Lamie 1, Stobbs 1, own goals 2.
William Hill Scottish Cup (3): Lawless 2 (2 pens), Dykes 1.
Betfred Scottish League Cup (12): Lamie 3, Dykes 2, Sibbald 2, Souda 2, Lawless 1 (1 pen), Lithgow 1, Pitman 1.
Tunnock's Caramel Wafer Scottish League Challenge Cup (1): Henderson 1 (1 pen).

Stewart R 7	Devlin N 11	Lithgow A 9 + 3	Lamie R 19 + 3	McMillan J 19 + 2	Bartley M 27 + 1	Jacobs K 14 + 10	Souda A 11 + 6	Pitman S 23	Lawless S 29 + 1	Dykes L 25	Sibbald C 14 + 5	Pepe C — + 2	Miller L — + 3	Crawford Robert 13 + 7	Tiffoney S 1 + 7	Guthrie J 28	Robinson S 13 + 9	Stobbs J 1 + 3	Erskine C 3 + 7	Savane I — + 1	Lawson S 13 + 6	Sarkic M 14	Odofin H 3 + 4	Taylor-Sinclair A 12 + 2	McCrorie R 8	Brown C 9	Menga D — + 3	Schofield R 1	Ambrose E 3	Match No.
1	2	3	4	5^{2}	6	7	8^{3}	9	10	11^{1}	12	13	14																	1
1	2	3	4	5^{2}	6	7	8^{3}	9	10^{1}	11	12			13	14															2
1	2	4	5		6	7^{2}		8	9	11				13		3	10^{1}	12^{3}	14											3
1	2	3		5^{3}	6		10^{1}		8	11				7	13	4		14	9^{2}	12										4
1	2		3^{3}	5	8	7^{2}	13		6	11■		14		9		4	12		10^{1}											5
1	2		3	5	6^{1}	9			8					7	14	4	11^{3}	12	10^{2}		13									6
1	5	4	2		6		11^{2}		9		13			7	12	3	10^{1}	8^{3}			14									7
	2		4	5	6	7			9^{1}	10^{2}			14	8		3	11^{3}				12	1	13							8
	2	13	3	5	6	8	14		7^{2}	11			12	9^{1}		4	10^{3}					1								9
	2^{1}	3	12	5^{2}	6	9	10■		8					7	14	4	11^{3}					1	13							10
		3	12	5	6	14		9	8^{3}		10^{1}			7	13	4	11^{2}					1	2							11
		3	5		6	10^{1}		9	12		13			7	11^{2}	4					8	1	2							12
			4	5	6	14	12	9	8	11				7^{3}		3					10^{2}	1	2^{1}	13						13
			4	5^{2}	6	12		9	8^{1}	11				7^{3}	14	3					10	1	13	2						14
			3	12	6^{2}	2		9	10	11				7^{1}		4	13		14		8^{3}	1		5						15
			3		6	2^{2}		9	10^{3}	11	7^{1}					4	8		13		12	1	14	5						16
		12	4		6	14	10^{1}	9	8^{2}	11	7^{3}					3	13				2	1		5						17
		12	4		8	13	10^{2}	9	6	11	7^{3}					3	14				2	1		5^{1}						18
		3	5		6	12	10^{3}	9	8	11^{1}	7^{2}					4	14		13		2	1								19
			4		7		10^{1}	9	8	11	6^{2}					3	12		13		2	1		5						20
			3	5	6	7	14	9	11^{2}	10^{1}	8^{3}			12		4			13		2	1								21
			12	5^{2}	6	7		9	8^{3}	11				14		4	10		13		2^{1}				1	3				22
				2	6	14	10^{1}	9	8^{3}	11^{2}	7			13		4	12							5	1	3				23
				2	6			9	8	11	7					4	10							5	1	3				24
				2^{1}	6			9	8	11	7^{3}			13		4	10^{2}				14			5	1	3	12			25
				2^{1}	6^{2}	12		9	8	11	7					4	10^{3}				14			5	1	3	13			26
			2	13		7	5^{1}	10	9^{3}	11	14			8^{2}		4					6					3	12	1		27
				6^{1}		12	13	7	10^{3}	11^{2}	8					3	14				5			9	1	4			2	28
					12		14	7	10^{1}	11^{3}	8			13		3	6^{2}				5			9	1	4			2	29
	5			9^{2}	7	13		6	10^{3}	11	8^{1}					3	12							14	1	4			2	30
																														31
																														32
																														33
																														34
																														35
																														36
																														37
																														38

MONTROSE

Year Formed: 1879. *Ground & Address:* Links Park, Wellington St, Montrose DD10 8QD. *Telephone:* 01674 673200. *Fax:* 01674 677311. *E-mail:* office@montrosefc.co.uk *Website:* www.montrosefc.co.uk
Ground Capacity: total: 4,936, (seated: 1,338). *Size of Pitch:* 100m × 64m.
Chairman: John Crawford. *Secretary:* Brian Petrie.
Manager: Stewart Petrie. *Assistant Manager:* Ross Campbell.
Club Nickname: 'The Gable Endies'.
Record Attendance: 8,983 v Dundee, Scottish Cup 3rd rd, 17 March 1973.
Record Transfer Fee received: £50,000 for Gary Murray to Hibernian (December 1980).
Record Transfer Fee paid: £17,500 for Jim Smith from Airdrieonians (February 1992).
Record Victory: 12-0 v Vale of Leithen, Scottish Cup 2nd rd, 4 January 1975.
Record Defeat: 0-13 v Aberdeen, 17 March 1951.
Most Capped Player: Alexander Keillor, 2 (6), Scotland.
Most League Appearances: 432: David Larter, 1987-98.
Most League Goals in Season (Individual): 28: Brian Third, Division II, 1972-73.
Most Goals Overall (Individual): 126: Bobby Livingstone, 1967-79.

MONTROSE – SPFL LADBROKES LEAGUE ONE 2019–20 LEAGUE RECORD

Match No.	Date	Venue	Opponents	Result	H/T Score	Lg Pos.	Goalscorers	Attendance
1	Aug 3	A	Stranraer	D 2-2	0-1	3	Masson 76, Callaghan 78	343
2	10	H	Airdrieonians	L 0-1	0-0	7		685
3	17	A	Falkirk	L 1-2	1-1	9	Skelly 17	3736
4	24	A	Raith R	L 0-3	0-0	10		1437
5	31	H	Dumbarton	L 1-2	0-2	10	Lyons 75	480
6	Sept 14	H	East Fife	L 1-3	0-1	10	Lyons 53	561
7	21	A	Forfar Ath	L 0-2	0-1	10		670
8	28	H	Peterhead	W 4-3	3-1	10	MacBeath 13, Webster 2 28, 67, Watson 44	497
9	Oct 5	A	Clyde	W 2-0	2-0	9	Webster (pen) 41, MacBeath 44	721
10	19	A	Airdrieonians	W 3-1	2-1	8	Lyons 2 16, 90, Webster 31	642
11	26	H	Stranraer	W 2-1	1-0	7	Dillon 17, Cammy Ballantyne 84	611
12	Nov 2	A	East Fife	W 1-0	1-0	7	Webster 37	704
13	9	H	Forfar Ath	W 3-0	1-0	5	Lyons 33, Whyte (og) 47, Struthers 81	753
14	16	A	Peterhead	D 0-0	0-0	5		717
15	30	H	Raith R	L 0-1	0-0	6		780
16	Dec 7	A	Dumbarton	W 2-0	1-0	5	Steeves 35, McGeever (og) 76	459
17	14	H	Clyde	W 4-0	1-0	5	Steeves 38, Lyons 66, Rennie 2 85, 89	583
18	21	H	Falkirk	L 2-3	0-1	6	Masson 67, Webster (pen) 85	1095
19	28	A	Forfar Ath	W 3-2	1-2	5	Campbell, R 13, Webster 65, Steeves 90	943
20	Jan 4	H	East Fife	W 1-0	1-0	4	Milne 35	833
21	25	A	Raith R	L 3-4	0-3	5	Johnston 55, Niang 58, Quinn 76	1717
22	Feb 1	H	Peterhead	W 4-3	3-1	5	Cameron Ballantyne 2, Lyons 2 15, 27, Allan 60	698
23	15	H	Dumbarton	W 2-1	1-0	5	Lyons 16, Webster 54	423
24	22	A	Falkirk	L 0-1	0-1	5		3561
25	29	H	Airdrieonians	W 1-0	1-0	5	Webster (pen) 25	766
26	Mar 3	A	Clyde	L 1-2	0-1	5	Lyons 53	507
27	7	H	Stranraer	W 4-1	1-0	5	Watson 40, Johnston 2 74, 90, Callaghan 90	528
28	10	A	Stranraer	W 1-0	0-0	4	McLean 72	190
29	14	A	East Fife	Cancelled				
30	21	H	Forfar Ath	Cancelled				
31	28	A	Peterhead	Cancelled				
32	Apr 4	H	Raith R	Cancelled				
33	11	A	Airdrieonians	Cancelled				
34	18	H	Falkirk	Cancelled				
35	25	H	Clyde	Cancelled				
36	May 2	A	Dumbarton	Cancelled				

Final League Position: 4 (on points-per-game basis)

Honours
League Champions: Second Division 1984-85; League Two 2017-18.
Runners-up: Second Division 1990-91; Third Division 1994-95.
Scottish Cup: Quarter-finals 1973, 1976.
League Cup: Semi-finals 1975-76.
League Challenge Cup: Semi-finals 1992-93, 1996-97.

Club colours: Shirt: Blue with white sleeves. Shorts: Blue. Socks: White.

Goalscorers: *League (48):* Lyons 10, Webster 9 (3 pens), Johnston 3, Steeves 3, Callaghan 2, MacBeath 2, Masson 2, Rennie 2, Watson 2, Allan 1, Cameron Ballantyne 1, Cammy Ballantyne 1, Campbell, R 1, Dillon 1, McLean 1, Milne 1, Niang 1, Quinn 1, Skelly 1, Struthers 1, own goals 2.
William Hill Scottish Cup (1): Campbell, R 1.
Betfred Scottish League Cup (4): Allan 1, Campbell, R 1, Masson 1, Skelly 1 (1 pen).
Tunnock's Caramel Wafer Scottish League Challenge Cup (2): Lyons 1, Milne 1.

Fleming A 10	Waddell K 6+1	Allan M 25+2	Dillon S 26	Webster G 25+2	Masson T 17+4	Cregg P 5	Milne L 10+8	Steeves A 26	Campbell R 2+8	Callaghan L 14+3	Lyons B 22+4	Watson P 14+5	McLean R 4+5	Ballantyne Cammy 26	Skelly J 3+1	Campbell I 3+2	Rennie M 8+3	Lennox A 18	Ballantyne Cameron 15+6	Johnston C 7+11	MacBeath J 6+4	Niang M 9+5	Struthers S 3+6	Quinn A 3+2	Hawke L 1+2	Match No.
1	2	3^{2}	4	5	6	7^{3}	8	9	10^{1}	11	12	13	14													1
1	3	12	4■	9^{3}	6	7^{2}	11	5	13	8	14			2	10^{1}											2
1	3	12	4	6		8	9	5^{3}			10	7^{2}	14	2	11^{1}	13										3
1	4	8^{3}	3	6		7	9		14		12		13	2	11^{2}	5	10^{1}									4
	3		4	12		7	6		14	8^{1}	9		11^{2}	2	13	5	10^{3}	1								5
	4	9	3	7	8■		14	6			10	12				5^{2}	11^{1}	1	2^{3}	13						6
	13	4	3					5	14	8	9	7^{2}		2			10^{1}	1	6	12	11^{3}					7
		4	3	9				5		8	10^{3}	7^{2}		2		14	12	1	6	13	11^{1}					8
		4	3	9				5		8	10^{1}	7^{3}		2			13■	1	6	14	11^{2}	12				9
		4	3	7	14			5		6	10	8^{3}		2				1	9^{1}	12	11^{2}	13				10
		3	4	6	14			5		8^{1}	11^{3}	7		2				1	9^{2}		10	12	13			11
		3	4	9	13			5		7^{3}	11	8^{1}		2				1	14	12	10^{2}	6				12
		4	3	6	7			5		8^{3}	10^{2}			2			11^{1}	1	13		14	9	12			13
		4	3	6^{1}	7			5		8^{2}	10	14		2			11^{3}	1			13	9	12			14
		4	3	7	6		12	5			10			2				1	9^{3}	11^{2}	13	8^{1}	14			15
		3	4	7^{2}	8		12	5			10	13		2				1	9^{1}	11^{3}	14	6				16
		3	4	7	8		14	5			10	12		2			13	1	9^{2}			6^{3}	11^{1}			17
		3	4	6	7		14	5	12		13	9^{3}		2			10	1				8^{2}	11^{1}			18
		3	4	6	7		10^{2}	5	11^{3}		8^{1}	9		2				1	12	13			14			19
		3	4	9	6		8	5	13		11^{3}	7^{2}		2			10^{1}	1	12	14						20
		4	3	7^{1}	6			5	14			9^{2}		2				1	8	11		12	10^{3}	13		21
		3	4	9^{2}	6^{3}		12	5			11			2				1	8	10^{1}		7		14	13	22
1		3	4	11^{1}	6		13	5		7^{3}	9		12	2					8	10^{2}			14			23
1		4^{1}	3	7^{3}	6		12	9		14	10		13	5					8^{2}	11				2		24
1		3	4	9			6	5		14	11	7^{1}	10^{2}	2					8^{3}	13		12				25
1		3	4	12	13		6	5		9	11			2					8^{1}	14		7^{3}			10^{2}	26
1		3		9	6		8^{3}	5		14	11^{2}	7	10^{1}	2					12	13				4		27
1		3		6^{3}	8			5	13	9^{1}		7	11	2					12	10^{2}				4	14	28
																										29
																										30
																										31
																										32
																										33
																										34
																										35
																										36

MOTHERWELL

Year Formed: 1886. *Ground & Address:* Fir Park Stadium, Motherwell ML1 2QN. *Telephone:* 01698 333333. *Fax:* 01698 338001.
E-mail: mfcenquiries@motherwellfc.co.uk *Website:* www.motherwellfc.co.uk
Ground Capacity: 13,742 (all seated). *Size of Pitch:* 105m × 65m.
Chairman: James McMahon. *Chief Executive:* Alan Burrows.
Manager: Stephen Robinson. *Assistant Manager:* Keith Lasley.
Club Nicknames: 'The Well'; 'The Steelmen'.
Previous Grounds: The Meadows; Dalziel Park.
Record Attendance: 35,632 v Rangers, Scottish Cup 4th rd replay, 12 March 1952.
Record Transfer Fee received: £3,000,000 (rising to £3,250,000) for David Turnbull to Celtic (August 2020).
Record Transfer Fee paid: £500,000 for John Spencer from Everton (January 1999).
Record Victory: 12-1 v Dundee U, Division II, 23 January 1954.
Record Defeat: 0-8 v Aberdeen, Premier Division, 26 March 1979.
Most Capped Player: Stephen Craigan, 54, Northern Ireland.
Most League Appearances: 626: Bobby Ferrier, 1918-37.
Most League Goals in Season (Individual): 52: Willie McFadyen, Division I, 1931-32.
Most Goals Overall (Individual): 283: Hugh Ferguson, 1916-25.

MOTHERWELL – SPFL LADBROKES PREMIERSHIP 2019–20 LEAGUE RECORD

Match No.	*Date*	*Venue*	*Opponents*	*Result*		*H/T Score*	*Lg Pos.*	*Goalscorers*	*Attendance*
1	Aug 3	A	Livingston	D	0-0	0-0	4		2633
2	10	H	Celtic	L	2-5	1-2	9	Donnelly 2 12, 90	8822
3	24	A	Hamilton A	W	3-1	2-1	6	Gogic (og) 17, Donnelly (pen) 21, Long 51	2927
4	31	H	Hibernian	W	3-0	1-0	5	Seedorf 22, Donnelly (pen) 80, Hylton 86	5964
5	Sept 14	A	Hearts	W	3-2	1-0	3	Gallagher 20, Seedorf 52, Hylton 66	15,862
6	21	H	Ross Co	L	1-2	0-0	4	Campbell 61	4620
7	28	A	St Johnstone	W	1-0	1-0	3	Cole 42	2972
8	Oct 5	H	St Mirren	W	2-0	1-0	3	Scott 39, Long 86	5101
9	19	H	Aberdeen	L	0-3	0-1	3		5640
10	27	A	Rangers	L	1-2	1-1	4	Cole 21	49,629
11	30	H	Kilmarnock	W	2-1	1-1	3	Donnelly 14, Cole 54	4676
12	Nov 2	H	Livingston	W	2-1	0-0	3	Long 47, Campbell 83	4423
13	10	A	Celtic	L	0-2	0-1	4		57,137
14	23	A	Hibernian	L	1-3	1-2	4	Polworth 9	15,984
15	30	H	St Johnstone	W	4-0	1-0	4	Cole 29, Hartley 49, Carroll 72, Manzinga 89	4092
16	Dec 4	A	St Mirren	W	3-0	2-0	4	Scott 2 28, 33, Campbell 67	4240
17	7	H	Hearts	W	1-0	1-0	3	Long 40	4745
18	15	H	Rangers	L	0-2	0-1	4		8359
19	21	A	Kilmarnock	W	1-0	0-0	3	Carroll 67	5688
20	26	A	Ross Co	W	2-1	0-1	3	Maciver 81, Gallagher 90	4181
21	29	H	Hamilton A	L	1-2	1-0	3	Long 5	6048
22	Jan 22	A	Aberdeen	W	1-0	1-0	3	Donnelly 45	12,365
23	25	H	Hibernian	D	0-0	0-0	3		5767
24	Feb 1	A	Livingston	L	0-1	0-0	3		1932
25	5	H	Celtic	L	0-4	0-1	3		8534
26	12	A	St Johnstone	L	1-2	1-1	4	Long 32	2655
27	22	A	Hamilton A	D	0-0	0-0	3		2531
28	25	H	St Mirren	L	1-2	1-0	3	Donnelly (pen) 12	3636
29	Mar 4	H	Ross Co	W	4-1	2-1	3	O'Hara 17, Campbell 2 25, 75, Watt 90	3191
30	7	A	Hearts	D	1-1	1-0	3	Long 21	17,339
31	13	H	Aberdeen	Cancelled					
32	21	H	Kilmarnock	Cancelled					
33	Apr 4	A	Rangers	Cancelled					
34	Fixtures 34–38 decided after 33 game league split.								
35									
36									
37									
38									

Final League Position: 3 (on points-per-game basis)

Honours
League Champions: Division I 1931-32;. First Division 1981-82, 1984-85; Division II 1953-54, 1968-69.
Runners-up: Premier Division 1994-95, 2012-13; Premiership 2013-14; Division I 1926-27, 1929-30, 1932-33, 1933-34; Division II 1894-95, 1902-03.
Scottish Cup: 1952, 1991; *Runners-up:* 1931, 1933, 1939, 1951, 2011, 2018.
League Cup Winners: 1950-51; *Runners-up:* 1954-55, 2004-05, 2017-18.

European: *Champions League:* 2 matches (2012-13). *Cup Winners' Cup:* 2 matches (1991-92). *UEFA Cup:* 8 matches (1994-95, 1995-96, 2008-09). *Europa League:* 18 matches (2009-10, 2010-11, 2012-13, 2013-14, 2014-15).

Club colours: Shirt: Amber with maroon band. Shorts: White. Socks: Amber and maroon bands.

Goalscorers: *League (41):* Donnelly 7 (3 pens), Long 7, Campbell 5, Cole 4, Scott 3, Carroll 2, Gallagher 2, Hylton 2, Seedorf 2, Hartley 1, Maciver 1, Manzinga 1, O'Hara 1, Polworth 1, Watt 1, own goal 1.
William Hill Scottish Cup (8): Long 3, Aarons 1, Campbell 1, O'Hara 1, Polworth 1, Watt 1.
Betfred Scottish League Cup (14): Donnelly 4 (1 pen), Scott 3, Hylton 2, Hartley 1, Ilic 1, Long 1, Polworth 1, Seedorf 1.
Tunnock's Caramel Wafer Scottish League Challenge Cup (1): Semple 1.

Gillespie M 30	Tait R 12 + 2	Gallagher D 30	Dunne C 3	Carroll J 21	Campbell A 30	Donnelly L 22	Polworth L 28 + 2	Hylton J 18 + 10	Ilic C 3 + 5	Scott J 15 + 7	Seedorf S 9 + 13	Long C 21 + 4	Cole D 12 + 7	Grimshaw L 25	Hartley P 23 + 2	Maguire B 4 + 3	O'Hara M 9 + 8	Mugabi B 6 + 4	Manzinga C — + 6	Maciver R 1 + 6	Ndjoli M — + 1	Aarons R 6	Watt T 2 + 2	Turnbull D — + 2	*Match No.*
1	2	3	4	5	6	7	8	9^{2}	10^{3}	11^{1}	12	13	14												1
1	5	3	4		7	8	6	11^{3}	12	14	9^{1}	10^{2}	13	2											2
1		2	4		6	8	7^{2}	12		11^{3}	9^{1}	10	13	5	3	14									3
1		3		5	7	8	6	13		11^{3}	9^{2}	10^{1}	12	2	4	14									4
1		4		5	7	6	8	12		9^{3}	11^{2}	13	10^{1}	2	3		14								5
1	14	3		5▮	7	6	8^{3}	12		10^{1}	11^{2}		9	2	4		13								6
1	5	4			7	8▮	6	12	13	11^{2}	9^{1}	14	10^{3}	2	3										7
1	2	3			6		8	12	14	10^{3}	11^{1}	13	9^{2}	7	4	5									8
1	5	3			8		7	13		11^{1}	9	10	14	2	4^{3}	6^{2}		12							9
1	12	3		9^{3}	6	7	8	13			14	11^{2}	10	2	4			5^{1}							10
1		3		5	7	6	8	9^{2}		13	12	10	11^{1}	2	4										11
1		3		5	7	6	8	11^{3}		12	13	10^{1}	9^{2}	2	4			14							12
1	4^{3}	3		9	8		6	13		14	12	11^{1}	10^{2}	2		7		5							13
1		3		5	7^{1}		8	9^{2}		14	12	10	11	2	4	6^{3}	13								14
1		3		5	7	6	8^{1}	11^{2}		12		10^{3}	9	2	4		14		13						15
1		3		5	7^{2}	6	8	11^{1}		10	13		9^{3}	2			12	4	14						16
1		3		5	7	6	8^{1}	11		9^{3}		10^{2}	12	2	13		14	4							17
1		3		5	6	7	8^{3}	11^{2}		12	13	10	9	2			14	4^{1}							18
1		3		5	6	7^{2}	12	11^{3}		9	13	10^{1}	14	2	4		8								19
1	2	3		5	6^{1}		7	11		10	9				4		8			12					20
1		3		5	7		8^{2}	11^{1}		9^{3}	12	10		2	13		6	4		14					21
1		3		5	8	6	9		12^{3}	10^{1}		11^{2}		2	4		7	14		13					22
1		3		5	7	6	8		9^{1}	11^{2}	12			2	4				13	10^{3}	14				23
1	2	3		5	6	8	7^{1}	11^{2}	9^{3}			10			4		14	13	12						24
1		3		5	7	6	8	11^{1}			12	10^{3}		2	4				14	13		9^{2}			25
1		3		5	6	7	14	11^{2}				10^{3}		2	4		8		13▮			9^{1}	12		26
1	5	3			7	6	8	13				10▮			4		2			12		9^{1}	11^{2}		27
1	2	3			7^{1}	6	8	11^{3}			14				4		9^{2}			12		5	10	13	28
1	5	3			6		8	11	13			10^{2}		2	4		7					9^{1}	12		29
1	5	3			6^{2}		8^{1}	11				10		2	4	12	7					9		13	30
																									31
																									32
																									33
																									34
																									35
																									36
																									37
																									38

PARTICK THISTLE

Year Formed: 1876. *Ground & Address:* Energy Check Stadium at Firhill, 80 Firhill Rd, Glasgow G20 7AL. *Telephone:* 0141 579 1971. *Fax:* 0141 945 1525. *E-mail:* mail@ptfc.co.uk *Website:* ptfc.co.uk
Ground Capacity: 10,102 (all seated). *Size of Pitch:* 105m × 68m.
Chairman: Jacqui Low. *Chief Executive:* Gerry Britton.
Manager: Ian McCall. *Assistant Managers:* Alan Archibald and Neil Scally.
Club Nickname: 'The Jags'.
Previous Grounds: Overnewton Park; Jordanvale Park; Muirpark; Inchview; Meadowside Park.
Record Attendance: 49,838 v Rangers, Division I, 18 February 1922. *Ground Record:* 54,728, Scotland v Ireland, 25 February 1928.
Record Transfer Fee received: £350,000 for Liam Lindsay to Barnsley (June 2017); £350,000 for Aidan Fitzpatrick to Norwich C (July 2019).
Record Transfer Fee paid: £85,000 for Andy Murdoch from Celtic (February 1991).
Record Victory: 16-0 v Royal Albert, Scottish Cup 1st rd, 17 January 1931.
Record Defeat: 0-10 v Queen's Park, Scottish Cup 5th rd, 3 December 1881.
Most Capped Player: Alan Rough, 51 (53), Scotland.
Most League Appearances: 410: Alan Rough, 1969-82.
Most League Goals in Season (Individual): 41: Alex Hair, Division I, 1926-27.
Most Goals Overall (Individual): 229: Willie Sharp, 1939-57.

PARTICK THISTLE – SPFL LADBROKES CHAMPIONSHIP 2019–20 LEAGUE RECORD

Match No.	Date	Venue	Opponents	Result	H/T Score	Lg Pos.	Goalscorers	Attendance
1	Aug 3	A	Alloa Ath	D 1-1	0-1	5	Cardle 60	1672
2	9	H	Dundee U	L 1-2	1-0	8	Saunders 23	3218
3	23	A	Greenock Morton	L 2-3	2-0	9	Miller 25, De Vita 28	2197
4	31	H	Ayr U	L 2-3	2-1	10	Bannigan (pen) 14, Gordon 43	3060
5	Sept 13	A	Arbroath	D 1-1	0-1	9	Miller 65	1214
6	21	H	Dunfermline Ath	L 0-3	0-2	10		2820
7	28	A	Inverness CT	W 3-1	1-1	9	Zanatta 10, Miller 46, Palmer 82	2469
8	Oct 5	H	Queen of the South	L 0-1	0-0	10		2910
9	19	A	Dundee	W 3-1	0-1	10	Miller 85, Gordon 88, Mansell 90	5010
10	26	H	Arbroath	L 1-3	0-1	10	Bannigan (pen) 59	2793
11	29	A	Dundee U	L 0-1	0-0	10		6929
12	Nov 2	A	Ayr U	L 1-4	0-2	10	Cardle 79	2558
13	9	H	Greenock Morton	W 2-1	0-0	10	Gordon 2 59, 66	2751
14	26	H	Alloa Ath	D 1-1	1-1	10	Zanatta 38	1714
15	30	A	Dunfermline Ath	L 1-5	0-4	10	Cole 74	3948
16	Dec 7	A	Queen of the South	W 2-1	0-1	9	Cardle 70, Cole 85	1314
17	14	H	Inverness CT	W 3-1	0-0	8	Jones 48, Saunders 64, Zanatta 90	2144
18	21	H	Dundee	L 0-1	0-1	9		2957
19	28	A	Greenock Morton	W 2-1	1-1	8	Jones 5, O'Ware 61	2742
20	Jan 4	A	Alloa Ath	D 1-1	0-0	8	Bannigan (pen) 74	1827
21	11	H	Dundee U	L 1-4	0-2	9	Miller 87	4101
22	25	A	Arbroath	L 1-2	0-2	10	Graham 90	1418
23	31	H	Ayr U	D 1-1	1-0	10	Graham 33	2416
24	Feb 8	A	Dundee	L 0-2	0-2	10		4816
25	Mar 3	H	Queen of the South	D 0-0	0-0	10		2122
26	7	A	Dundee U	D 1-1	0-1	10	Bannigan (pen) 52	7603
27	10	H	Dunfermline Ath	D 1-1	0-0	10	Graham 90	2078
28	14	H	Alloa Ath	Cancelled				
29	17	A	Inverness CT	Cancelled				
30	20	A	Ayr U	Cancelled				
31	28	H	Greenock Morton	Cancelled				
32	Apr 4	H	Arbroath	Cancelled				
33	11	A	Queen of the South	Cancelled				
34	18	H	Inverness CT	Cancelled				
35	25	A	Dunfermline Ath	Cancelled				
36	May 2	H	Dundee	Cancelled				

Final League Position: 10 (on points-per-game basis)

Honours
League Champions: First Division 1975-76, 2001-02, 2012-13; Division II 1896-97, 1899-1900, 1970-71; Second Division 2000-01.
Runners-up: First Division 1991-92, 2008-09; Division II 1901-02.
Promoted via play-offs: 2005-06 (to First Division).
Scottish Cup Winners: 1921; *Runners-up:* 1930.
League Cup Winners: 1971-72; *Runners-up:* 1953-54, 1956-57, 1958-59.
League Challenge Cup Runners-up: 2012-13.

European: *Fairs Cup:* 4 matches (1963-64). *UEFA Cup:* 2 matches (1972-73). *Intertoto Cup:* 4 matches (1995-96).

Club colours: Shirt: Yellow with red stripes. Shorts: Black. Socks: Red and yellow hoops.

Goalscorers: *League (32):* Miller 5, Bannigan 4 (4 pens), Gordon 4, Cardle 3, Graham 3, Zanatta 3, Cole 2, Jones 2, Saunders 2, De Vita 1, Mansell 1, O'Ware 1, Palmer 1.
William Hill Scottish Cup (2): Bannigan 1 (1 pen), Cole 1.
Betfred Scottish League Cup (11): Gordon 3, Miller 3, Penrice 1, Robson 1, Saunders 1, Williamson 1, own goal 1.
Tunnock's Caramel Wafer Scottish League Challenge Cup (9): Miller 2, Cardle 1, Cole 1, De Vita 1, Harkins 1, Mansell 1, Penrice 1, Slater 1.

Sneddon J 6	Saunders S 15+1	O'Ware T 20	McGinty S 17+2	Williamson R 15	Gordon S 9+7	Bannigan S 25	Penrice J 24+2	Cardle J 19+3	Mansell L 2+11	Robson T 11+5	Miller K 20+1	Jones A 10+2	De Vita R 3+6	Palmer C 10+3	Fox S 21	Hall B 2	Zanatta D 13+10	Kakay O 11	Cole R 16+3	Harkins G —+9	Slater C 3+3	Austin M —+1	O'Connor L 4	MacKinnon D 2	Graham B 6	Barjonas J 2+3	Brownlie D 5	Rudden Z 3+1	Mayo L 3	*Match No.*
1	2^3	3	4	5	6	7	8	9^2	10^1	11	12	13	14																	1
1	3		4	2	12	6	5	8	13	10^3	9	11^2	14	7^1																2
	3		4	2	12	7^3	5	14	10^2	13	11	9	6^1	8	1															3
1			4	2	6▮	8▮		13	14	5^3	9	11^1	12	7		3	10^2													4
		3	4				5	9^1	13	8^2	10		12	7	1		11	2	6											5
		3	4		9^3	7	5	8^2	12	14	11		13		1		10^1	2	6											6
	3^3	6	4	2	12	9	13	7		5^2	11			8^1	1		10		14											7
		3	4	2	6^1	7	13	8		5^3	11		14	9^2	1		10		12											8
	3	8^3	4	5	12	7	2	6	13		11		10^1		1			9^2		14										9
		3	4	2	7	8	5			9^1	11		10^2		1		12	6^3		14	13									10
	3		4	2	7	9	5	10^2	12		11^1			6	1		8			13										11
	4		3	2	9^1	8	5	6	12		11^3			7	1		10^2			14	13									12
		3	4		12	7▮	9		14		11^3			8	1	2	10^2	5	6^1		13									13
1		3	4				5	11			10			6			9	2	7		8									14
1	3^3	4▮	12			7	5	9^2		13	10			14			11^1	2	8		6									15
1	3		4			7	5	6		9^1	11	10^2					12	2	8	13										16
	4	3		2		8	5	6^3			10^1	11^2		14	1		12	9	7	13										17
	4^3	3		2		8	5	6		14	11	10^2			1		12	9^1	7	13										18
	4	3		2		8	5	9^3			10	11^2		14	1		12	6	7^1	13										19
	3		4	2		7	5	9	14		10^3	11^1			1		12		8	13	6^2									20
	4	3	14	2^3		8	5	6^1		12	10	11^2			1		9		7			13								21
	2	3	4^2			6	9	12				11^3			1		14		7				5	8^1	10	13				22
		4				7	5	8							1		10^2		9				2	6^1	11	12	3	13		23
	12	4			13	7	5	8^3				14			1		10		9				2^2		11	6^1	3			24
		3			13	8	7^2			9					1		14		12				5		10	6^3	2	11^1	4	25
		3			6^3	8	7		14	9					1		12		5						11^2	13	2	10^1	4	26
		3			5	7	8^2		13	9					1		12		6						10		2	11^1	4	27
																														28
																														29
																														30
																														31
																														32
																														33
																														34
																														35
																														36

PETERHEAD

Year Formed: 1891. *Ground and Address:* Balmoor Stadium, Balmoor Terrace, Peterhead AB42 1EQ.
Telephone: 01779 478256. *Fax:* 01779 490682. *E-mail:* office@peterheadfc.co.uk *Website:* www.peterheadfc.org
Ground Capacity: 3,150 (seated: 1,000). *Size of Pitch:* 101m × 64m.
Chairman: Rodger Morrison.
Manager: Jim McInally. *Assistant Manager:* David Nicholls.
Club Nickname: 'Blue Toon'.
Previous Ground: Recreation Park.
Record Attendance: 8,643 v Raith R, Scottish Cup 4th rd replay, 25 February 1987 (Recreation Park); 4,855 v Rangers, Third Division, 19 January 2013 (at Balmoor).
Record Victory: 9-0 v Colville Park, Scottish Cup 2nd rd, 14 October 2017.
Record Defeat: 0-13 v Aberdeen, Scottish Cup 3rd rd, 10 February 1923.
Most League Appearances: 275: Martin Bavidge, 2003-13.
Most League Goals in Season (Individual): 32: Rory McAllister, 2013-14.
Most Goals Overall (Individual): 194: Rory McAllister, 2008, 2011-19.

PETERHEAD – SPFL LADBROKES LEAGUE ONE 2019–20 LEAGUE RECORD

Match No.	Date	Venue	Opponents	Result	H/T Score	Lg Pos.	Goalscorers	Attendance
1	Aug 3	H	Falkirk	D 0-0	0-0	7		1513
2	10	A	East Fife	D 1-1	1-1	6	Lyle 34	570
3	17	H	Dumbarton	L 2-3	2-1	8	Fraser 3, Brown, J 36	688
4	24	H	Forfar Ath	W 1-0	0-0	7	Leitch 47	676
5	31	A	Stranraer	W 2-1	2-0	5	Brown, S 2 19, 34	265
6	Sept 14	A	Raith R	L 0-4	0-2	7		1436
7	21	H	Clyde	D 1-1	1-1	8	Lyle 5	682
8	28	A	Montrose	L 3-4	1-3	8	Brown, S 20, Dunlop 49, Stevenson 52	497
9	Oct 5	H	Airdrieonians	L 1-2	1-1	8	Ferguson 26	619
10	19	A	Falkirk	L 0-4	0-2	9		3289
11	26	A	Dumbarton	L 0-1	0-0	9		600
12	Nov 2	H	Raith R	W 2-0	1-0	8	Leitch 35, Fraser 74	610
13	9	A	Clyde	W 2-1	2-0	8	McAllister 2 22, 30	649
14	16	H	Montrose	D 0-0	0-0	8		717
15	30	A	Forfar Ath	L 1-2	0-1	8	McAllister (pen) 68	449
16	Dec 7	H	Stranraer	W 3-0	1-0	7	Conroy 2 34, 51, Brown, S 88	505
17	14	A	Airdrieonians	L 1-2	1-2	7	Brown, S 45	646
18	21	H	East Fife	L 1-2	0-1	8	Brown, S 84	599
19	28	H	Clyde	W 2-0	1-0	7	Lyle 30, Brown, S 86	585
20	Jan 4	A	Raith R	L 1-2	1-2	7	Lyle 11	1807
21	11	H	Falkirk	L 1-3	1-2	7	Durnan (og) 26	886
22	25	H	Dumbarton	W 1-0	0-0	8	Armour 82	531
23	Feb 1	A	Montrose	L 3-4	1-3	7	Cook 44, Lyle 68, Brown, S 80	698
24	15	A	East Fife	L 0-1	0-1	7		520
25	22	H	Airdrieonians	L 0-2	0-0	7		557
26	25	H	Forfar Ath	D 1-1	0-0	7	Boyd 49	443
27	Mar 7	A	Falkirk	L 0-3	0-2	8		3507
28	14	H	Raith R	Cancelled				
29	17	A	Stranraer	Cancelled				
30	21	A	Clyde	Cancelled				
31	28	H	Montrose	Cancelled				
32	Apr 4	A	Dumbarton	Cancelled				
33	11	H	Stranraer	Cancelled				
34	18	A	Forfar Ath	Cancelled				
35	25	A	Airdrieonians	Cancelled				
36	May 2	H	East Fife	Cancelled				

Final League Position: 8 (on points-per-game basis)

Honours
League Champions: League Two 2013-14, 2018-19.
Runners up: Third Division 2004-05, 2012-13; League Two 2017-18.
Scottish Cup: Quarter-finals 2001.
League Challenge Cup: Runners up: 2015-16.

Club colours: Shirt: Royal blue with white trim. Shorts: Royal blue with white trim. Socks: Light blue.

Goalscorers: *League (30):* Brown, S 8, Lyle 5, McAllister 3 (1 pen), Conroy 2, Fraser 2, Leitch 2, Armour 1, Boyd 1, Brown, J 1, Cook 1, Dunlop 1, Ferguson 1, Stevenson 1, own goal 1.
William Hill Scottish Cup (0).
Betfred Scottish League Cup (3): Armour 1, Lyle 1, McAllister 1 (1 pen).
Tunnock's Caramel Wafer Scottish League Challenge Cup (0).

Fleming G 27	Brown J 23 + 3	Eadie C 11 + 2	Dunlop M 9 + 1	Boyle P 25	Ferry S 17	Brown S 27	Smith A 10 + 13	Fraser G 17 + 7	Leitch J 23	Lyle D 16 + 8	Stevenson J 16 + 6	Armour B 7 + 11	Norris A — + 3	Hooper S 16 + 1	Willox R — + 1	McAllister R 14 + 4	Gibson W — + 1	Conroy R 16 + 6	Ferguson D 12 + 6	McCarthy A 1 + 2	Cook A 4 + 1	Boyd S 3 + 3	Bollan L 3	*Match No.*
1	2	3	4	5	6	7	8^2	9^3	10	11^1	12	13	14											1
1	2	3	4^1	5		8		7^3	9	10	6^2	11	13	12	14									2
1	2	3	4	5	7^3	6	8^1	9	10	11^2						12	13	14						3
1	2	3	4	5	6	7	8	9^3	10^2			13	14			11^1		12						4
1	2	3	4	5	6	7^2	8	9^1	10^3			14				11■		12	13					5
1	2	3	4	5	6	8	10^2	9^3	7^1	12		11						14	13					6
1	14		4^1	5	6	7	13	8^3		9	2	12				11		10^2	3					7
1	2		3	5	7^3	6	13	9^2		10^1	8	14				11		12	4					8
1	3		14	5^1		7	11^3	8		12	6^2	13		4		10		9	2					9
1	4			5		7	12	8	10^1	13	14	6		3		11		9^3	2^2					10
1	3			5		7	12	9^1	8	11	2^2	6^3		4		10		13	14					11
1	3			5	6	7		8	10	11^3	2^1	14		4		12		9^2	13					12
1	4			5	7	8	12	6^1	10	13	2			3		11^3		9^2	14					13
1	3			5	6	7^2	13	12	10	9^1	2			4		11		8						14
1		3		5		8	11^1	7^2	9	13	12	14		4		10		6	2^3					15
1	3^2			5	6	7	8^1		10	14	12	13		4		11		9^3	2					16
1	3			5	6	7^3	8^2	12	10	13	14			4		11		9^1	2					17
1	3			5	6	7	13	12	10		8^2	14		4		11^1		9^3	2					18
1	3	14		5	6■	7	12	9^3		11^1	10^2	8		4		13			2					19
1	3	12		5^1		9	14		8^3	11	10	6		4		13		7	2^2					20
1	14	3	4^1			7	13		6	9^2	10	8^3		5		11			2■	12				21
1	3			5		6		14	7	9^2	2	13		4				8^1		12	10^3	11		22
1	3			5		6	12	13	7	9	2^1			4					14	8^3	10	11^2		23
1	14	4		5		6	13	7^1	8	11^2				3				9^3	2		10	12		24
1	2	3^2		5	6	7	11	8^3	10	14	13							9^1				12	4	25
1	3				6	7	12	13	8	9^2	2							5			10^1	11	4	26
1	3	2		5	8	9		13	10^2	11^3	7							6^1			12	14	4	27
																								28
																								29
																								30
																								31
																								32
																								33
																								34
																								35
																								36

QUEEN OF THE SOUTH

Year Formed: 1919. *Ground & Address:* Palmerston Park, Dumfries DG2 9BA. *Telephone:* 01387 254853.
Fax: 01387 240470. *E-mail:* admin@qosfc.com *Website:* www.qosfc.com
Ground Capacity: 8,690 (seated: 3,377) *Size of Pitch:* 102m × 66m.
Chairman: Billy Hewitson. *Vice-Chairman:* Craig Paterson.
Manager: Allan Johnston. *Assistant Manager:* Sandy Clark.
Club Nickname: 'The Doonhamers'.
Record Attendance: 26,552 v Hearts, Scottish Cup 3rd rd, 23 February 1952.
Record Transfer Fee received: £250,000 for Andy Thomson to Southend U (July 1994).
Record Transfer Fee paid: £30,000 for Jim Butter from Alloa Ath (1995).
Record Victory: 11-1 v Stranraer, Scottish Cup 1st rd, 16 January 1932.
Record Defeat: 2-10 v Dundee, Division I, 1 December 1962.
Most Capped Player: Billy Houliston, 3, Scotland.
Most League Appearances: 731: Allan Ball, 1963-82.
Most League Goals in Season (Individual): 37: Jimmy Gray, Division II, 1927-28.
Most Goals in Season: 43: Stephen Dobbie, 2018-19.
Most Goals Overall (Individual): 251: Jim Patterson, 1949-63.

QUEEN OF THE SOUTH – SPFL LADBROKES CHAMPIONSHIP 2019–20 LEAGUE RECORD

Match No.	*Date*	*Venue*	*Opponents*	*Result*	*H/T Score*	*Lg Pos.*	*Goalscorers*	*Attendance*
1	Aug 3	A	Arbroath	D 0-0	0-0	7		1100
2	10	H	Dunfermline Ath	D 1-1	0-1	7	Oliver [62]	1562
3	24	A	Ayr U	L 0-1	0-1	7		2005
4	31	H	Alloa Ath	L 0-1	0-0	8		1294
5	Sept 14	H	Greenock Morton	W 1-0	1-0	7	El Bakhtaoui [16]	1302
6	21	A	Inverness CT	L 0-2	0-2	8		1760
7	27	H	Dundee	D 1-1	1-1	7	Hamilton [6]	1249
8	Oct 5	A	Partick Thistle	W 1-0	0-0	6	Brownlie [60]	2910
9	19	H	Dundee U	W 4-0	2-0	4	Dobbie 2 [18, 70], Holt [28], Paton [77]	1909
10	26	A	Alloa Ath	D 2-2	2-0	6	Dobbie [35], Hamilton [36]	875
11	29	H	Inverness CT	L 0-2	0-1	7		1221
12	Nov 2	A	Dunfermline Ath	L 0-2	0-0	7		3621
13	9	H	Ayr U	W 3-1	1-1	7	Holt [18], Murray [67], Oliver [74]	1850
14	16	A	Dundee U	L 0-3	0-2	7		7675
15	30	A	Dundee	W 2-1	1-0	7	Dobbie 2 [29, 90]	4517
16	Dec 7	H	Partick Thistle	L 1-2	1-0	7	Murray [20]	1314
17	21	H	Arbroath	W 2-0	1-0	6	Pybus [33], Little (og) [87]	1094
18	28	A	Ayr U	W 2-1	1-0	6	Semple [4], Dobbie (pen) [58]	2062
19	Jan 4	H	Dundee U	L 0-1	0-0	6		2041
20	25	H	Alloa Ath	L 2-3	0-2	8	Hamilton [52], Dobbie [58]	1169
21	Feb 1	H	Dunfermline Ath	L 2-3	1-2	8	Oliver [10], Dobbie (pen) [59]	1302
22	8	A	Greenock Morton	D 2-2	1-0	8	Petravicius [18], Hamilton [73]	1380
23	15	A	Arbroath	L 0-2	0-2	8		801
24	22	H	Dundee	L 0-1	0-0	9		1126
25	29	H	Greenock Morton	L 0-4	0-2	9		1116
26	Mar 3	A	Partick Thistle	D 0-0	0-0	9		2122
27	7	A	Dunfermline Ath	D 1-1	1-0	9	Oliver [3]	3597
28	10	A	Inverness CT	L 1-3	0-1	9	Semple [72]	1811
29	13	H	Ayr U	Cancelled				
30	21	H	Arbroath	Cancelled				
31	28	A	Dundee	Cancelled				
32	Apr 3	A	Dundee U	Cancelled				
33	11	H	Partick Thistle	Cancelled				
34	18	A	Alloa Ath	Cancelled				
35	25	H	Inverness CT	Cancelled				
36	May 2	A	Greenock Morton	Cancelled				

Final League Position: 9 (on points-per-game basis)

Honours
League Champions: Division II 1950-51; Second Division 2001-02, 2012-13.
Runners-up: Division II 1932-33, 1961-62, 1974-75; Second Division 1980-81, 1985-86; Division Three 1924-25.
Scottish Cup Runners-up: 2007-08.
League Cup: semi-finals 1950-51, 1960-61.
League Challenge Cup Winners: 2002-03, 2012-13; *Runners-up:* 1997-98, 2010-11.

European: *UEFA Cup:* 2 matches (2008-09).

Club colours: Shirt: Royal blue with white trim. Shorts: White. Socks: Royal blue.

Goalscorers: *League (28):* Dobbie 8 (2 pens), Hamilton 4, Oliver 4, Holt 2, Murray 2, Semple 2, Brownlie 1, El Bakhtaoui 1, Paton 1, Petravicius 1, Pybus 1, own goal 1.
William Hill Scottish Cup (1): Murray 1.
Betfred Scottish League Cup (10): Dobbie 2, Murray 2, Kilday 1, Mercer 1, Oliver 1, Paton 1, Semple 1, own goal 1.
Tunnock's Caramel Wafer Scottish League Challenge Cup (2): Dobbie 1 (1 pen), Murray 1.

McCrorie R 19	Mercer S 23	Semple C 9 + 2	Brownlie D 18	Holt K 27	Pybus D 26	Kidd L 15 + 5	Paton M 12 + 10	Oliver G 13 + 7	Murray C 15 + 4	Hamilton J 11 + 11	McCarthy A — + 4	Kilday L 25	El Bakhtaoui F 15	Dobbie S 25	Lyon D 16 + 5	Irving R — + 3	Osman A 9 + 2	Stewart R 9	Devine D 5	Wilson I 8	Ledger M 5	Petravicius D 3 + 4	Match No.
1	2	3	4	5	6	7^{1}	8	9	10	11	12												1
1	2	3^{1}	4	5	6	12	9^{2}	8	10	13		7	11										2
1	2		3	5	7	6^{3}		9^{1}	8	13		4	11	10^{2}	12	14							3
1	2		3	5	7^{1}	12	6^{2}		8	13		4	11	10	9								4
1	2		3	5	7	8	12	9^{1}	6^{2}	13		4	11	10^{3}	14								5
1	2		3	5	7^{2}	8	12	9^{3}	6^{1}	13	14	4	11	10									6
1	2^{1}		3	5	7	8	6			10		4	9	11	12								7
1	2		4	5	6^{1}	8	7^{3}		12	10^{2}		3	9	11	14		13						8
1	2		3	5	6^{2}	7	8^{1}	12	14	10^{3}		4	9	11			13						9
1	2		4	5	7	6	8	12		10^{1}		3	9	11									10
1	2		3	5	6		7^{2}	13	12	10^{1}		4	9	11			8						11
1	2	4		5	7	9			12	11		3	10^{1}	8	13		6^{2}						12
1	2		3	5	7^{1}	8		12	6	10^{3}	13	4		11^{2}	9	14							13
1	2	12^{3}	4	5	7	8	14	10	6^{2}		13	3^{1}		11	9								14
1	2		3	5	7		12		6^{1}			4	11	10	8		9						15
1	2		3	5		12	8^{1}	11	10	13		4	9		6^{2}		7						16
1	2		3	5	7				6			4	10	11	9		8						17
1	2	3^{1}		5	6		12	13	8			4	10	11^{2}	9		7						18
1	2	13	3	5			7^{2}		9	10^{1}		4		11	6	12	8						19
	2^{2}		3	5	7		12	10^{1}	9	13				11	6		8	1	4				20
				5	6	7	8	11		10				9	2			1	3	4			21
				5	8		12	10^{2}		13		4		11	6			1	3	7	2	9^{1}	22
				5	8^{3}	13	14		10^{2}	12		4		11	6			1	3	7	2^{1}	9	23
	5	4		9	6	12		13		14		2		10			7^{3}	1	3^{1}	8		11^{2}	24
	2^{2}	4		5	7		9^{1}	13		10		3		11	6			1		8		12	25
		4		5	9	7		10				3		11^{1}	6			1		8	2	12	26
		4		9	7	5^{1}	12	10				3		11	6			1		8	2^{2}	13	27
	9	4			7^{2}	5^{3}	13	10		14		3		11^{1}	6			1		8	2	12	28
																							29
																							30
																							31
																							32
																							33
																							34
																							35
																							36

QUEEN'S PARK

Year Formed: 1867. *Ground & Address:* Hampden Park, Mount Florida, Glasgow G42 9BA. *Telephone:* 0141 632 1275. *Fax:* 0141 636 1612. *E-mail:* secretary@queensparkfc.co.uk *Website:* queensparkfc.co.uk
Ground Capacity: 51,866 (all seated). *Size of Pitch:* 105m × 68m.
President: Gerry Crawley. *Treasurer:* David Gordon.
Head Coach: Ray McKinnon. *Assistant Head Coach:* Laurie Ellis.
Club Nickname: 'The Spiders'.
Previous Grounds: 1st Hampden (Recreation Ground); (Titwood Park was used as an interim measure between 1st & 2nd Hampdens); 2nd Hampden (Cathkin); 3rd Hampden.
Record Attendance: 95,772 v Rangers, Scottish Cup 1st rd, 18 January 1930.
Record for Ground: 149,547 Scotland v England, 1937.
Record Transfer Fees: Not applicable due to amateur status from 1867-2019.
Record Victory: 16-0 v St. Peter's, Scottish Cup 1st rd, 12 Sep 1885.
Record Defeat: 0-9 v Motherwell, Division I, 26 April 1930.
Most Capped Player: Walter Arnott, 14, Scotland.
Most League Appearances: 532: Ross Caven, 1982-2002.
Most League Goals in Season (Individual): 30: William Martin, Division I, 1937-38.
Most Goals Overall (Individual): 163: James B. McAlpine, 1919-33.

QUEEN'S PARK – SPFL LADBROKES LEAGUE TWO 2019–20 LEAGUE RECORD

Match No.	*Date*	*Venue*	*Opponents*	*Result*		*H/T Score*	*Lg Pos.*	*Goalscorers*	*Attendance*
1	Aug 3	A	Stirling Alb	W	1-0	0-0	4	Galt 76	701
2	10	H	Stenhousemuir	D	1-1	0-0	4	Kouider-Aisser (pen) 90	565
3	17	A	Brechin C	W	3-0	2-0	2	Moore 10, Galt 19, Block 82	412
4	24	H	Elgin C	D	0-0	0-0	3		577
5	31	A	Cove R	L	0-3	0-1	4		661
6	Sept 14	H	Albion R	D	1-1	0-1	4	Kouider-Aisser 90	546
7	21	H	Cowdenbeath	L	0-3	0-0	4		514
8	28	A	Edinburgh C	L	1-2	0-0	4	Block 77	352
9	Oct 5	H	Annan Ath	L	1-2	0-2	7	Galt 84	449
10	26	A	Elgin C	L	1-3	1-3	7	Kouider-Aisser 26	658
11	Nov 2	A	Stenhousemuir	W	3-0	1-0	5	Kouider-Aisser 31, McGorry 49, Galt 71	646
12	9	H	Brechin C	W	5-2	4-1	5	Kouider-Aisser 2 11, 53, McGorry 15, Lidohren (pen) 25, Summers 35	572
13	16	A	Cowdenbeath	L	0-1	0-1	6		448
14	30	H	Edinburgh C	W	2-1	1-0	5	Purdue 13, Kouider-Aisser 84	594
15	Dec 7	A	Albion R	L	0-2	0-2	6		273
16	14	H	Stirling Alb	D	1-1	0-1	6	Finnie 80	501
17	21	H	Cove R	L	1-3	0-2	6	Kouider-Aisser 50	478
18	28	A	Annan Ath	L	2-3	1-2	7	Moore 35, Kouider-Aisser 78	449
19	Jan 4	H	Stenhousemuir	W	2-1	2-0	7	Moore 26, Mortimer 40	837
20	11	A	Edinburgh C	W	2-1	0-1	6	Mortimer 52, Kouider-Aisser 56	442
21	25	H	Albion R	D	2-2	0-2	7	Galt 50, Kouider-Aisser (pen) 64	594
22	Feb 1	H	Cowdenbeath	W	1-0	1-0	6	Slater 9	616
23	8	A	Stirling Alb	W	3-1	0-1	5	Moore 2 72, 90, Grant, P 85	642
24	15	H	Elgin C	W	2-0	1-0	4	Kouider-Aisser 5, Galt 77	582
25	22	A	Cove R	L	0-2	0-2	4		627
26	26	A	Brechin C	D	0-0	0-0	4		394
27	29	H	Annan Ath	W	2-0	2-0	3	MacLean 19, Kouider-Aisser (pen) 27	734
28	Mar 7	A	Stenhousemuir	D	0-0	0-0	5		581
29	14	A	Albion R	Cancelled					
30	21	H	Stirling Alb	Cancelled					
31	28	A	Elgin C	Cancelled					
32	Apr 4	H	Edinburgh C	Cancelled					
33	11	A	Cowdenbeath	Cancelled					
34	18	H	Brechin C	Cancelled					
35	25	H	Cove Rangers	Cancelled					
36	May 2	A	Annan Ath	Cancelled					

Final League Position: 5 (on points-per-game basis)

Honours
League Champions: Division II 1922-23; B Division 1955-56; Second Division 1980-81; Third Division 1999-2000.
Runners-up: Third Division 2011-12; League Two 2014-15.
Promoted via play-offs: 2006-07 (to Second Division); 2015-16 (to League One).
Scottish Cup Winners: 1874, 1875, 1876, 1880, 1881, 1882, 1884, 1886, 1890, 1893; *Runners-up:* 1892, 1900.
FA Cup Runners-up: 1884, 1885.
FA Charity Shield: 1899 (shared with Aston Villa).

Club colours: Shirt: Black and white thin hoops. Shorts: White. Socks: Black.

Goalscorers: *League (37):* Kouider-Aisser 13 (3 pens), Galt 6, Moore 5, Block 2, McGorry 2, Mortimer 2, Finnie 1, Grant, P 1, Lidohren 1 (1 pen), MacLean 1, Purdue 1, Slater 1, Summers 1.
William Hill Scottish Cup (4): Kouider-Aisser 2, Agyeman 1, Galt 1.
Betfred Scottish League Cup (4): Kouider-Aisser 1, Purdue 1, Summers 1, own goal 1.
Tunnock's Caramel Wafer Scottish League Challenge Cup (2): Kouider-Aisser 1, Martin 1.

Muir W 26	Jamieson N 22	Magee L 5	Little C 18	Mortimer W 14 + 1	Lidohren J 21 + 4	Block T 14 + 1	Summers C 18 + 2	Galt D 26	Kouider-Aisser S 27 + 1	Purdue J 6 + 8	Agyeman A 2 + 12	Thomson R 1 + 6	Moore K 12 + 11	Clark C 10 + 1	Grant J 3 + 1	Gibson S 4 + 1	McGorry C 7 + 4	Foy C 6 + 1	Main L 8 + 2	Rae J (Trialist) 2	Finnie R 12 + 2	Grant P 8	MacLean R 5 + 2	Davidson J 7 + 1	Morrison S 7	Doig J 7	Slater C 4 + 1	King A 6	*Match No.*
1	2	3	4	5	6	7	8	9	10	11^{1}	12																		1
1	2^{1}	3	4	5	7	6	8^{2}	11	10	9^{3}		12	13	14															2
1	2	3	4	5^{3}	7	6	8	11	10^{2}	14		13	9^{1}		12														3
1	2	3^{3}	4	5	7^{1}	6	8	11	10		12	13	9^{2}			14													4
1	2	3^{1}	4	5	7^{3}	6	8	11	10	9^{2}	14	12					13												5
1	2		4		8	7		10^{2}	13		11	12	14	9	5	3^{3}	6^{1}												6
1	2		4^{2}			6	12	11	10	9		7	13	8^{1}	5	3													7
1	2		4	5	7	6		11^{2}	10	13	12		9	8		3^{1}													8
1	4		3		7	8	5	10	11	6^{1}	12		9		2^{2}		13												9
1	4			12	7	2	5	9	11		8		10^{1}			6^{2}	3	13											10
1	2		4	5	9		8	11^{1}	10				12	3			7		6										11
	4		2	8	11		5	9	10^{1}	13	14	12		3			6^{3}		7^{2}	1									12
	4		2^{3}	5^{2}	9	13	8	7	10				14	3			11^{1}		6	1	12▪								13
1	2		4	5	9	6	8		10	11^{1}			12	3					7										14
1			4^{1}	5^{3}	9	7^{2}	8	11	10		14		12	3				2	6		13								15
1	4				11	7^{3}	5	9	10	12	13			3^{2}			14	2	6^{1}		8								16
1	2		4		9	6^{2}	8	11	10				13	3			12		7^{1}		5								17
1	2		4^{1}		9		8	11	10	12			7				6	3			5								18
1			2	8	9		5		10	12	13		11^{1}				7	3	6^{2}		4								19
1	2^{2}		4	5	6		8	11	10		13		9^{1}					3	12		7								20
1				5^{2}	6		8	11^{1}	10	13	14		9^{3}					3			2	4	7	12					21
1	4						13	9	10^{2}	12											8	3	11	6	2	5	7^{1}		22
1	4							6	11		13		12								5	3	10^{2}	8	9^{1}	2		7	23
1	3				13			10	11				8^{1}								2	4	12	7	6	5		9^{2}	24
1	3				2^{1}			10	11				8									4		7	6	5	12	9	25
1					13			10	11				8^{1}								2	4	12	6	7	5^{2}	3	9	26
1					13			10	11				12						14		2	4	8^{1}	7	3	5	6^{3}	9^{2}	27
1					13			8	11				12								5	3	10^{2}	6	4	2	9▪	7^{1}	28
																													29
																													30
																													31
																													32
																													33
																													34
																													35
																													36

RAITH ROVERS

Year Formed: 1883. *Ground & Address:* Stark's Park, Pratt St, Kirkcaldy KY1 1SA. *Telephone:* 01592 263514. *Fax:* 01592 642833. *E-mail:* info@raithrovers.net *Website:* www.raithrovers.net
Ground Capacity: 8,473 (all seated). *Size of Pitch:* 103m × 64m.
Chairman: John Sim. *Vice Chairmen:* Steven MacDonald and David Sinton.
Manager: John McGlynn. *Assistant Manager:* Paul Smith.
Club Nickname: 'Rovers'.
Previous Grounds: Robbie's Park.
Record Attendance: 31,306 v Hearts, Scottish Cup 2nd rd, 7 February 1953.
Record Transfer Fee received: £900,000 for Steve McAnespie to Bolton W (September 1995).
Record Transfer Fee paid: £225,000 for Paul Harvey from Airdrieonians (July 1996).
Record Victory: 10-1 v Coldstream, Scottish Cup 2nd rd, 13 February 1954.
Record Defeat: 2-11 v Morton, Division II, 18 March 1936.
Most Capped Player: David Morris, 6, Scotland.
Most League Appearances: 430: Willie McNaught, 1946-51.
Most League Goals in Season (Individual): 38: Norman Haywood, Division II, 1937-38.
Most Goals Overall (Individual): 154: Gordon Dalziel (League), 1987-94.

RAITH ROVERS – SPFL LADBROKES LEAGUE ONE 2019–20 LEAGUE RECORD

Match No.	Date	Venue	Opponents	Result	H/T Score	Lg Pos.	Goalscorers	Attendance
1	Aug 3	A	Dumbarton	W 1-0	0-0	2	Anderson, G [79]	870
2	10	H	Clyde	W 5-2	2-0	1	Hendry (pen) [13], Bowie [23], Anderson, G [49], Vitoria [63], Smith [79]	1707
3	17	A	Stranraer	L 2-3	0-1	2	Miller [48], Spencer [70]	404
4	24	H	Montrose	W 3-0	0-0	1	Bowie [80], Gullan [84], Melingui [90]	1437
5	31	A	East Fife	L 2-4	1-1	1	Allan [10], Gullan [84]	1792
6	Sept 14	H	Peterhead	W 4-0	2-0	2	Anderson, G [7], Miller 2 [29, 67], Vaughan [52]	1436
7	21	A	Airdrieonians	W 1-0	0-0	1	Anderson, G [55]	1132
8	28	A	Forfar Ath	W 2-1	0-1	1	Vaughan [51], MacDonald, K [90]	847
9	Oct 5	H	Falkirk	D 2-2	0-2	1	Miller [60], Armstrong [78]	2756
10	19	A	Clyde	D 2-2	2-0	1	Bowie [11], Gullan [29]	1202
11	26	H	East Fife	D 1-1	1-1	1	Spencer [35]	2907
12	Nov 2	A	Peterhead	L 0-2	0-1	2		610
13	9	H	Stranraer	W 3-1	1-0	1	Gullan 2 [45, 60], Baird [49]	1364
14	26	H	Forfar Ath	D 0-0	0-0	2		975
15	30	A	Montrose	W 1-0	0-0	2	Spencer [68]	780
16	Dec 7	H	Airdrieonians	W 1-0	1-0	1	Matthews [42]	1823
17	14	A	Falkirk	D 1-1	1-0	1	Gullan [37]	4024
18	21	H	Dumbarton	L 0-2	0-2	1		1504
19	28	A	East Fife	W 5-3	3-1	1	Gullan 2 [8, 90], MacDonald, K 2 [21, 37], Tait [54]	1998
20	Jan 4	H	Peterhead	W 2-1	2-1	1	Tait [9], Gullan [24]	1807
21	11	A	Forfar Ath	D 1-1	0-1	1	Baird [72]	832
22	25	H	Montrose	W 4-3	3-0	1	Matthews [8], Bowie 2 [25, 42], Tait [66]	1717
23	Feb 1	A	Airdrieonians	W 1-0	1-0	1	Matthews [4]	1296
24	8	A	Stranraer	D 1-1	1-0	1	Baird [36]	327
25	22	H	Clyde	W 1-0	0-0	1	MacLean [78]	1527
26	29	A	Dumbarton	L 0-1	0-0	1		804
27	Mar 3	H	Falkirk	D 1-1	0-0	1	MacLean [47]	3235
28	7	H	Forfar Ath	W 2-1	1-0	1	Armstrong [9], Baird [76]	1551
29	14	A	Peterhead	Cancelled				
30	21	H	East Fife	Cancelled				
31	28	H	Airdrieonians	Cancelled				
32	Apr 4	A	Montrose	Cancelled				
33	11	H	Dumbarton	Cancelled				
34	18	A	Clyde	Cancelled				
35	25	H	Stranraer	Cancelled				
36	May 2	A	Falkirk	Cancelled				

Final League Position: 1 (on points-per-game basis)

Honours
League Champions: First Division 1992-93, 1994-95; League One 2019-20; Second Division 2002-03, 2008-09; Division II 1907-08, 1909-10 (shared with Leith Ath), 1937-38, 1948-49.
Runners-up: Division II 1908-09, 1926-27, 1966-67;. Second Division 1975-76, 1977-78, 1986-87; League One 2017-18.
Scottish Cup Runners-up: 1913.
League Cup Winners: 1994-95; *Runners-up:* 1948-49.
League Challenge Cup Winners: 2013-14.

European: *UEFA Cup:* 6 matches (1995-96).

Club colours: Shirt: Navy with light blue trim. Shorts: Navy. Socks: Navy with white tops.

Goalscorers: *League (49):* Gullan 9, Bowie 5, Anderson, G 4, Baird 4, Miller 4, MacDonald, K 3, Matthews 3, Spencer 3, Tait 3, Armstrong 2, MacLean 2, Vaughan 2, Allan 1, Hendry 1 (1 pen), Melingui 1, Smith 1, Vitoria 1.
William Hill Scottish Cup (2): Baird 1, Bowie 1.
Betfred Scottish League Cup (4): Allan 2, Bowie 1, Miller 1.
Tunnock's Caramel Wafer Scottish League Challenge Cup (13): Allan 3, Bowie 3, Hendry 3 (2 pens), Armstrong 1, Benedictus 1, Matthews 1, McKay 1.

McGurn D 10 + 1	Miller M 19	Davidson I 22	Benedictus K 26 + 1	MacDonald K 28	Bowie K 19 + 6	Matthews R 18 + 2	Hendry R 22	Spencer B 23 + 4	Allan L 10 + 3	Anderson G 14 + 7	Smith J — + 6	Vitoria J — + 7	Tait D 9 + 4	Melingui B — + 2	Gullan J 14 + 4	McKay D 10 + 4	Munro R 13 + 1	Anderson S 8	Vaughan L 2	Baird J 13 + 6	Armstrong D 6 + 8	Dingwall T 7 + 9	Watson J 5 + 2	Thomson R 5	MacLean S 5 + 1	*Match No.*
1	2	3	4	5	6	7	8	9	10^{1}	11^{2}	12	13														1
1	2	3	4	5	10^{2}	6^{1}	7	8	11	9^{3}	13	12	14													2
1	2	3	4	5	11^{2}	6	7	8	10	9^{1}	12			13												3
1	2	3	4	5	10^{1}	6	8	7	11^{3}	9^{2}				13	12	14										4
1	2	3	4	5	11^{1}	6^{2}	7	8	10	12					9	13										5
	5	2	4	8			6^{3}	7	11	10^{1}			14		12	13	1	3	9^{2}							6
12	5	2	4	8	13		6	7	10	11^{1}		14			9^{3}		1^{2}	3								7
1	5	2	4	8	14		6	7	9^{2}	11^{3}					12			3	10^{1}	13						8
1	6	5	4^{2}	9			7	8	10^{3}	11					12	2^{1}		3		14	13					9
1	2	3	12	5	10		6	7							9^{2}			4■		11	8^{1}	13				10
1	2	3	4	5	11	7		8			13				10					12	6^{1}	9^{2}				11
1	2	3■	4	5	11^{1}	7		8		13	14				10^{2}					12	6^{3}	9				12
	5^{1}		4	9^{2}	11^{3}	6		7		14					8	2	1	3		10	12		13			13
			4	5	6^{3}	7			11^{2}	13			8^{1}		9	2	1	3		10	12	14				14
		6	4	5		7		9		12			8^{1}		10	2	1	3^{2}		11^{3}	14	13				15
		3■	4	5	11^{3}	7■		8	13	10		14			9^{2}	2	1					6^{1}	12			16
			4■	5	11		8	7	14	9^{1}					10^{2}	3	1			13	12	6^{3}	2			17
				4	9^{1}		7	6	12	8	14	13			11	3	1			10^{3}		5^{2}	2			18
			3	4	13		7	8		6^{1}		14	9^{3}		10	5	1			11^{2}		12	2			19
			4	5	12	13	8	9		6^{3}			7^{2}		10	3■	1			11^{1}		14	2			20
		3	4	5	13	12	8	9^{1}		6^{3}		14	7		10		1			11^{2}			2			21
	2	3^{1}	4	5	10^{2}	7	8	12		13			9			14	1			11		6^{3}				22
	2	3	4	5	8^{1}	7	6	14					10^{3}							9^{2}	12	13		1	11	23
	2	3	4	5	8^{2}	7	6	13					10^{1}							9^{3}	12	14		1	11	24
		3	4	5	9^{2}	8	7	12					6^{1}			2				10^{3}	13	14		1	11	25
	2	3	4	5	14	6	7	8		13										10^{3}	11^{2}	9^{1}		1	12	26
	2	3	4	5	10	7	8	9^{1}					13				12				6			1^{2}	11	27
	2	3	4	5	10^{3}	7	8	9^{2}					14				1			13	6^{1}	12			11	28
																										29
																										30
																										31
																										32
																										33
																										34
																										35
																										36

RANGERS

Year Formed: 1873. *Ground & Address:* Ibrox Stadium, 150 Edmiston Drive, Glasgow G51 2XD.
Telephone: 0871 702 1972. *Fax:* 0870 600 1978. *Website:* rangers.co.uk
Ground Capacity: 51,082 (all seated). *Size of Pitch:* 105m × 68m.
Chairman (Interim): Douglas Park. *Deputy Chairman:* John Bennett.
Manager: Steven Gerrard. *Assistant Manager:* Gary McAllister.
Club Nickname: 'The Gers'; 'The Teddy Bears'.
Previous Grounds: Flesher's Haugh, Burnbank, Kinning Park, Old Ibrox.
Record Attendance: 118,567 v Celtic, Division I, 2 January 1939.
Record Transfer Fee received: £9,000,000 for Alan Hutton to Tottenham H (January 2008).
Record Transfer Fee paid: £12,000,000 for Tore Andre Flo from Chelsea (November 2000).
Record Victory: 13-0 v Possilpark, Scottish Cup 1st rd, 6 October 1877; v Uddingston, Scottish Cup 3rd rd, 10 November 1877; v Kelvinside Athletic, Scottish Cup 2nd rd, 28 September 1889.
Record Defeat: 1-7 v Celtic, League Cup Final, 19 October 1957.
Most Capped Player: Ally McCoist, 60, Scotland. *Most League Appearances:* 496: John Greig, 1962-78.
Most League Goals in Season (Individual): 44: Sam English, Division I, 1931-32.
Most Goals Overall (Individual): 355: Ally McCoist; 1985-98.

Honours

League Champions: (54 times) Division I 1890-91 (shared with Dumbarton), 1898-99, 1899-1900, 1900-01, 1901-02, 1910-11, 1911-12, 1912-13, 1917-18, 1919-20, 1920-21, 1922-23, 1923-24, 1924-25, 1926-27, 1927-28, 1928-29, 1929-30, 1930-31, 1932-33, 1933-34, 1934-35, 1936-37, 1938-39, 1946-47, 1948-49, 1949-50, 1952-53, 1955-56, 1956-57, 1958-59, 1960-61, 1962-63, 1963-64, 1974-75. Premier Division: 1975-76, 1977-78, 1986-87, 1988-89, 1989-90, 1990-91, 1991-92, 1992-93, 1993-94, 1994-95, 1995-96, 1996-97, 1998-99, 1999-2000, 2002-03, 2004-05, 2008-09, 2009-10, 2010-11. *Runners-up, tier 1:* 32 times. Championship 2015-16. League One 2013-14. Third Division 2012-13.
Scottish Cup Winners: (33 times) 1894, 1897, 1898, 1903, 1928, 1930, 1932, 1934, 1935, 1936, 1948, 1949, 1950, 1953, 1960, 1962, 1963, 1964, 1966, 1973, 1976, 1978, 1979, 1981, 1992, 1993, 1996, 1999, 2000, 2002, 2003, 2008, 2009; *Runners-up:* 18 times.

RANGERS – SPFL LADBROKES PREMIERSHIP 2019–20 LEAGUE RECORD

Match No.	*Date*	*Venue*	*Opponents*	*Result*	*H/T Score*	*Lg Pos.*	*Goalscorers*	*Atten-dance*
1	Aug 4	A	Kilmarnock	W 2-1	1-0	4	Arfield ^{16}, Goldson ^{90}	9196
2	11	H	Hibernian	W 6-1	2-1	2	Defoe 3 $^{9, 15, 74}$, Morelos 2 $^{77, 89}$, Ojo ^{90}	49,718
3	25	A	St Mirren	W 1-0	0-0	2	Barisic ^{59}	7332
4	Sept 1	H	Celtic	L 0-2	0-1	2		49,873
5	14	H	Livingston	W 3-1	0-0	2	Tavernier ^{55}, Morelos ^{71}, Barker ^{79}	48,793
6	22	A	St Johnstone	W 4-0	0-0	2	Morelos ^{47}, Goldson ^{61}, Defoe 2 $^{88, 90}$	6251
7	28	H	Aberdeen	W 5-0	2-0	2	Tavernier 2 (2 pens) $^{20, 71}$, Stewart ^{40}, Morelos ^{50}, Defoe ^{80}	49,992
8	Oct 6	H	Hamilton A	W 5-0	2-0	1	Defoe 3 $^{7, 63, 71}$, Goldson ^{34}, Barisic ^{61}	48,838
9	20	A	Hearts	D 1-1	1-1	2	Morelos ^{39}	17,573
10	27	H	Motherwell	W 2-1	1-1	2	Defoe ^{45}, Helander ^{80}	49,629
11	30	A	Ross Co	W 4-0	3-0	2	Morelos 2 $^{20, 71}$, Jack 2 $^{29, 37}$	6575
12	Nov 10	A	Livingston	W 2-0	1-0	2	Aribo ^{33}, Morelos ^{52}	8071
13	24	A	Hamilton A	W 3-1	2-1	2	Jack ^{7}, Kent 2 $^{43, 90}$	5100
14	Dec 1	H	Hearts	W 5-0	2-0	2	Morelos ^{11}, Kent ^{37}, Berra (og) ^{64}, Stewart 2 $^{80, 85}$	49,811
15	4	A	Aberdeen	D 2-2	2-1	2	Arfield ^{18}, Jack ^{30}	14,790
16	15	A	Motherwell	W 2-0	1-0	2	Katic ^{27}, Morelos ^{69}	8359
17	20	A	Hibernian	W 3-0	2-0	2	Kent ^{4}, Aribo ^{9}, Defoe ^{53}	19,540
18	26	H	Kilmarnock	W 1-0	0-0	2	Morelos ^{65}	49,885
19	29	A	Celtic	W 2-1	1-1	2	Kent ^{36}, Katic ^{56}	58,902
20	Jan 22	H	St Mirren	W 1-0	1-0	2	Defoe ^{34}	49,297
21	26	A	Hearts	L 1-2	0-0	2	Kent ^{47}	18,539
22	29	H	Ross Co	W 2-0	1-0	2	Defoe ^{41}, Arfield ^{47}	47,583
23	Feb 1	H	Aberdeen	D 0-0	0-0	2		50,012
24	5	H	Hibernian	W 2-1	1-1	2	Edmundson ^{45}, Hagi ^{84}	49,427
25	12	A	Kilmarnock	L 1-2	1-0	2	Arfield ^{32}	8096
26	16	H	Livingston	W 1-0	0-0	2	Arfield ^{59}	48,302
27	23	A	St Johnstone	D 2-2	0-1	2	Kamberi ^{50}, Aribo ^{71}	8286
28	Mar 4	H	Hamilton A	L 0-1	0-0	2		48,167
29	8	A	Ross Co	W 1-0	0-0	2	Kent ^{77}	6400
30	15	H	Celtic	Cancelled				
31	22	A	St Mirren	Cancelled				
32	Apr 4	H	Motherwell	Cancelled				
33	TBC	H	St Johnstone	Cancelled				
34	Fixtures 34–38 decided after 33 game league split.							
35								
36								
37								
38								

Final League Position: 2 (on points-per-game basis)

League Cup Winners: (27 times) 1946-47, 1948-49, 1960-61, 1961-62, 1963-64, 1964-65, 1970-71, 1975-76, 1977-78, 1978-79, 1981-82, 1983-84, 1984-85, 1986-87, 1987-88, 1988-89, 1990-91, 1992-93, 1993-94, 1996-97, 1998-99, 2001-02, 2002-03, 2004-05, 2007-08, 2009-10, 2010-11; *Runners-up:* 8 times.
League Challenge Cup Winners: 2015-16; *Runners-up:* 2013-14.

European: *European Cup:* 161 matches (1956-57, 1957-58, 1959-60 semi-finals, 1961-62, 1963-64, 1964-65, 1975-76, 1976-77, 1978-79, 1987-88, 1989-90, 1990-91, 1991-92, 1992-93 final pool, 1993-94, 1994-95, 1995-96; 1996-97, 1997-98, 1999-2000, 2000-01, 2001-02, 2003-04, 2004-05, 2005-06, 2007-08, 2008-09, 2009-10, 2010-11, 2011-12).

Cup Winners' Cup: 54 matches (1960-61 runners-up, 1962-63, 1966-67 runners-up, 1969-70, 1971-72 winners, 1973-74, 1977-78, 1979-80, 1981-82, 1983-84).

UEFA Cup: 88 matches (*Fairs Cup:* 1967-68, 1968-69 semi-finals, 1970-71. *UEFA Cup:* 1982-83, 1984-85, 1985-86, 1986-87, 1988-89, 1997-98, 1998-99, 1999-2000, 2000-01, 2001-02, 2002-03, 2004-05, 2006-07, 2007-08 runners-up). *Europa League:* 18 matches (2010-11, 2011-12, 2017-18, 2019-20).

Club colours: Shirt: Royal blue with red and white trim. Shorts: White with blue trim. Socks: Black with red tops.

Goalscorers: *League (64):* Defoe 13, Morelos 12, Kent 7, Arfield 5, Jack 4, Aribo 3, Goldson 3, Stewart 3, Tavernier 3 (2 pens), Barisic 2, Katic 2, Barker 1, Edmundson 1, Hagi 1, Helander 1, Kamberi 1, Ojo 1, own goal 1.

William Hill Scottish Cup (6): Arfield 3, Aribo 1, Defoe 1 (1 pen), Morelos 1.

Betfred Scottish League Cup (7): Morelos 2, Aribo 1, Defoe 1, Helander 1, Kamara 1, own goal 1.
Tunnock's Caramel Wafer Scottish League Challenge Cup (11): Barjonas 3, Grezda 2, McPake 2, Mebude 2 (1 pen), Atakayi 1, Young-Coombes 1.
UEFA Europa League (33): Morelos 14 (1 pen), Aribo 4, Ojo 4, Defoe 2, Hagi 2, Arfield 1, Davis 1, Edmundson 1, Goldson 1, Jack 1, Katic 1, Kent 1.

Foderingham W 2	Tavernier J 24	Goldson C 29	Katic N 17 + 2	Barisic B 22	Davis S 20 + 4	Jack R 19	Aribo J 25 + 2	Ojo S 9 + 10	Arfield S 22 + 4	Morelos A 18 + 8	Jones J 2 + 5	Stewart G 3 + 13	Edmundson G 4 + 3	McGregor A 27	Flanagan J 5	Defoe J 11 + 9	Halliday A 4 + 2	Helander F 8	Kamara G 18 + 1	King A — + 2	Kent R 18 + 3	Barker B 2 + 4	Polster M 3 + 3	Murphy J — + 2	Hagi I 6 + 1	Kamberi F 1 + 5	*Match No.*
1	2	3	4	5	6^3	7	8	9^1	10^2	11	12	13	14														1
	2	3	4		7	6	8	9		12	11^3	13		1	5^1	10^2	14										2
	2	3		5	12	7	6		9^3	13	11^1			1		10^2		4	8	14							3
	2	3	4		7	6	11^1	12	9	13	14■			1	5	10^3			8^2								4
	2	3	4		6		8^3	9	7	10^2				1		14	5			13	11^1	12					5
	2	4		5	7	6	9	10^2	12	11^3		14		1		13		3				8^1					6
	2	3	4	5	7^1	6		9^3	11	10^2		8	14	1		12						13					7
	2	3		5	7^2			8^1	9^3	14		10	4	1		11			6				12	13			8
	2	3	4	5	7		8	11^2	9^1	10^3		13		1		14			6		12						9
	2	3		5	7		8^3	13	6	14		11^1		1		10		4			12	9^2					10
1	2	4		5^3		7^1	6	9	11	10^2						14	12	3	8					13			11
	2	3		5		7	8^2	12	9	10^1		14		1		13		4	6		11^3						12
	2	3		5	13	7	6^2	12	9^3	14				1		10^1		4	8		11						13
	2	3		5	7		8	12	9	10^2		14		1		13		4	6^3		11^1						14
	2	3	13		8	7	10	12	6^2	11				1	5			4			9^1						15
	2	3	4	5		7	9^3		6^1	10■		14		1		13			8		11^2		12				16
	2	3	4	5		7^3	9^1	12	6			14		1		10			8		11^2	13					17
	2	3	4	5	14	7	9		6^2	12		13		1		10^3			8		11^1						18
	2	3	4	5	7^2	6	9		12	10■			13	1					8^1		11						19
		3	4	5	7	6	9^1	13	12					1	2	10			8^2		11						20
		3	4	5	7	6^3	9	14	13					1	2^2	10			8^1		11		12				21
		3	4	5	7^3		12	9	6	13	14			1		10^1			8		11^2		2				22
		3	4	5	7		9	12	6^3	10				1					8^1		11		2^2		13	14	23
	2	3		5	7		9^2		6	10	13	12	4	1					14		11^1				8^3		24
	2	3	4			7	9^2		6	11		12		1			5				10				8^1	13	25
	2	3	4		7	6	14		8	10^3		13		1			5				11^1				9^2	12	26
	2	3	4		13	8	7		6	10^1		14		1			5^2				11				9^3	12	27
	2^3	3		5	6		8			10			4	1		13			7^2		12	14			9	11^1	28
		3	14	5	7		8			11^3	13		4	1					6^2		10		2		9^1	12	29
																											30
																											31
																											32
																											33
																											34
																											35
																											36
																											37
																											38

ROSS COUNTY

Year Formed: 1929. *Ground & Address:* The Global Energy Stadium, Victoria Park, Dingwall IV15 9QZ. *Telephone:* 01349 860860. *Fax:* 01349 866277. *E-mail:* info@rosscountyfootballclub.co.uk
Website: www.rosscountyfootballclub.co.uk
Ground Capacity: 6,700 (all seated). *Size of Ground:* 105 × 68m.
Chairman: Roy MacGregor. *Club Secretary:* Fiona MacBean.
Manager: Stuart Kettlewell. *Assistant Manager:* Richard Brittain.
Club Nickname: 'The Staggies'.
Record Attendance: 6,110 v Celtic, Premier League, 18 August 2012.
Record Transfer Fee received: £500,000 for Liam Boyce to Burton Albion (June 2017).
Record Transfer Fee paid: £100,000 for Ross Draper from Inverness CT (August 2017).
Record Victory: 11-0 v St Cuthbert Wanderers, Scottish Cup 1st rd, 11 December 1993.
Record Defeat: 0-7 v Kilmarnock, Scottish Cup 3rd rd, 17 February 1962.
Most League Appearances: 308: Michael Gardyne, 2006-07, 2008-12, 2014-19.
Most League Goals in Season: 24: Andrew Barrowman, 2007-08.
Most League Goals (Overall): 48: Liam Boyce, 2014-17.

ROSS COUNTY – SPFL LADBROKES PREMIERSHIP 2019–20 LEAGUE RECORD

Match No.	*Date*	*Venue*	*Opponents*	*Result*	*H/T Score*	*Lg Pos.*	*Goalscorers*	*Attendance*
1	Aug 3	H	Hamilton A	W 3-0	2-0	2	Chalmers 30, McKay 36, Ross C Stewart 57	4071
2	10	A	Hearts	D 0-0	0-0	2		15,652
3	24	H	Livingston	L 1-4	1-3	4	Ross C Stewart 44	4237
4	31	A	Aberdeen	L 0-3	0-2	8		13,006
5	Sept 14	H	St Mirren	W 2-1	0-0	7	Ross C Stewart 62, Fraser, M 90	3637
6	21	A	Motherwell	W 2-1	0-0	5	Graham 75, Ross C Stewart 88	4620
7	28	A	Kilmarnock	D 0-0	0-0	5		4906
8	Oct 5	H	St Johnstone	D 2-2	1-1	5	Chalmers 10, Spittal 68	4124
9	19	A	Celtic	L 0-6	0-1	6		58,560
10	26	A	Hibernian	D 2-2	0-0	6	Graham 74, Chalmers 90	15,452
11	30	H	Rangers	L 0-4	0-3	7		6575
12	Nov 2	A	Hamilton A	D 2-2	1-0	6	McKay 1, Graham 88	1268
13	9	H	Aberdeen	L 1-3	1-1	6	Mullin (pen) 5	6510
14	23	A	St Mirren	L 1-2	1-1	7	Graham 24	4708
15	Dec 1	H	Celtic	L 1-4	1-2	8	Ross C Stewart 24	6512
16	4	H	Hibernian	W 2-1	0-1	7	Ross C Stewart 2 65, 75	4196
17	14	H	Kilmarnock	W 1-0	0-0	7	Erwin 90	3688
18	21	A	Livingston	L 0-4	0-2	8		1201
19	26	H	Motherwell	L 1-2	1-0	8	Spittal 24	4181
20	29	A	St Johnstone	D 1-1	0-0	8	Vigurs 73	2658
21	Jan 22	H	Hearts	D 0-0	0-0	8		4301
22	25	A	Celtic	L 0-3	0-1	9		58,785
23	29	A	Rangers	L 0-2	0-1	9		47,583
24	Feb 1	A	Kilmarnock	L 1-3	1-0	9	Vigurs 25	4733
25	5	H	Livingston	W 2-0	1-0	9	McKay 2 3, 59	3301
26	12	A	Hibernian	L 0-3	0-2	9		14,486
27	15	H	St Johnstone	D 1-1	0-1	9	McKay 90	3569
28	22	A	Aberdeen	W 2-1	1-1	9	McKay 2 43, 88	14,860
29	Mar 4	A	Motherwell	L 1-4	1-2	9	Fontaine 3	3191
30	8	H	Rangers	L 0-1	0-0	9		6400
31	14	H	Hamilton A	Cancelled				
32	21	A	Hearts	Cancelled				
33	Apr 4	H	St Mirren	Cancelled				
34	Fixtures 34–38 decided after 33 game league split.							
35								
36								
37								
38								

Final League Position: 10 (on points-per-game basis)

Honours
League Champions: First Division 2011-12; Championship 2018-19; Second Division 2007-08; Third Division 1998-99.
Scottish Cup Runners-up: 2010.
League Cup Winners: 2015-16.
League Challenge Cup Winners: 2006-07, 2010-11, 2018-19; *Runners-up:* 2004-05, 2008-09.

Club colours: Shirt: Navy blue with red and white trim. Shorts: Navy blue. Socks: Navy blue with red tops.

Goalscorers: *League (29):* McKay 7, Ross C Stewart 7, Graham 4, Chalmers 3, Spittal 2, Vigurs 2, Erwin 1, Fontaine 1, Fraser, M 1, Mullin 1 (1 pen).
William Hill Scottish Cup (0).
Betfred Scottish League Cup (14): McKay 4, Ross C Stewart 4, Graham 2, Spittal 2, Mullin 1, Paton 1.
Tunnock's Caramel Wafer Scottish League Challenge Cup (5): Gallagher 2, Keillor-Dunn 2, Murray 1.

Laidlaw R 17	Fraser M 25 + 1	Morris C 17	Fontaine L 22	Kelly S 18	Mullin J 21 + 6	Chalmers J 6 + 8	Vigurs I 16	Gardyne M 13 + 1	McKay B 22 + 5	Stewart Ross C 19 + 2	Graham B 5 + 13	Spittal B 10 + 10	Paton H 11 + 8	Draper R 8 + 3	Watson K 14 + 3	Grivosti T 5 + 1	Foster R 20 + 1	Power S — + 1	Henderson E 6 + 3	Spence L 10 + 5	Erwin L 11 + 6	Baxter N 13	Donaldson C 7	Tillson J 5 + 2	Shaw O 2 + 5	Cowie D 7 + 2	*Match No.*
1	2	3	4	5	6^3	7	8	9^2	10^1	11	12	13	14														1
1	2	3	4	5	6		8^2	9	11^1	10	13	12		7													2
1	2	3	4^3	5	6	7^2	8^1		10	11		9	14		12	13											3
1	2	4			6^1		7	9	10^3	11^2	13	12			3	8	5	14									4
1	2		4		14	12	8^1	6	10^3	11	13		9		3		5		7^2								5
1	2		3			13		6	11	10	14	12	8^1		4	9^3	5		7^2								6
1	2				14	7		11	10^2	9	13	6^3	12		3	4	5		8^1								7
1	2		4		13	8		6	10^2	11	12	7^3		14	3	9^1	5										8
1	3		4		10^3	7		8^2		11	12	9^1	14	6	2		5			13							9
1	2		4	5	13	14		6	11		12			7	3		9^3		10^1	8^2							10
1	2		4	5		9^1		14	13	11	10^3			8	12	3^2	6			7							11
1	2		4		13			8	9^2	10	12			6	3		5		14	7^1	11^3						12
1	2	3	4	5	7	14		9	13	12	11^3								8	6^1	10^2						13
	2	4	3	5	9	13			11	6^2	10^1	12							8	7^3	14	1					14
		3	4	5	6					10	12		8		2		9			7	11^1	1					15
	13	3	4	5	6			9^1	14	11	10^3		8				2^2			7	12	1					16
		3	4	5	6			9^1	12	11	10^3		7				2		14	8^2	13	1					17
	4	3		5	6^2	12			10^3	11		13	7^1				2		14	8	9	1					18
		3	4	5	6	13			11^2	10	12	9^1	7				2			8■		1					19
		4^3	3	5	7	14	9		10^2	11^1	12■	6	8		13		2					1					20
	5			2	9		7		11^1			6^3	12		4					14	10	1	3	8^2	13		21
	5^1			2	10^3		7					6	13		4		12			14	11	1	3	9		8^2	22
	2			5	6		8^2		11^1			10		13	3					12	14	1	4	7		9^3	23
	2				9		7		13			12	14		3		5				11	1	4	6^2	10^1	8^3	24
	5	3	4	9			8		10^3				6^1	7							11^2	1	2	14	12	13	25
	5		4	9	13		8		10				6^2	7^3	2						11^1	1	3		14	12	26
1	2	3			5		8		10			14	12	7^1			9				13		4		11^2	6^3	27
1	2	4	3		5		8		11^1			12	6^2	14			9				10^3				13	7	28
1	2	3	4		6		8		10	13		9^1					5				11^3			12	14	7^2	29
1	2	3	4		6		9^1		11	10		12					5			13	14			7^2		8^3	30
																											31
																											32
																											33
																											34
																											35
																											36
																											37
																											38

ST JOHNSTONE

Year Formed: 1884. *Ground & Address:* McDiarmid Park, Crieff Road, Perth PH1 2SJ. *Telephone:* 01738 459090. *Fax:* 01738 625 771. *E-mail:* enquiries@perthsaints.co.uk *Website:* perthstjohnstonefc.co.uk
Ground Capacity: 10,673 (all seated). *Size of Pitch:* 105m × 68m.
Chairman: Steve Brown. *Vice-Chairman:* Charlie Fraser.
Manager: Callum Davidson. *Assistant Manager:* Alec Cleland.
Club Nickname: 'Saints'.
Previous Grounds: Recreation Grounds; Muirton Park.
Record Attendance: 29,972 v Dundee, Scottish Cup 2nd rd, 10 February 1951 (Muirton Park): 10,545 v Dundee, Premier Division, 23 May 1999 (McDiarmid Park).
Record Transfer Fee received: £1,750,000 for Callum Davidson to Blackburn R (March 1998).
Record Transfer Fee paid: £400,000 for Billy Dodds from Dundee (January 1994).
Record Victory: 9-0 v Albion R, League Cup, 9 March 1946.
Record Defeat: 1-10 v Third Lanark, Scottish Cup 1st rd, 24 January 1903.
Most Capped Player: Nick Dasovic, 26, Canada.
Most League Appearances: 362: Steven Anderson, 2004-19.
Most League Goals in Season (Individual): 36: Jimmy Benson, Division II, 1931-32.
Most Goals Overall (Individual): 140: John Brogan, 1977-83.

ST JOHNSTONE – SPFL LADBROKES PREMIERSHIP 2019–20 LEAGUE RECORD

Match No.	*Date*	*Venue*	*Opponents*	*Result*		*H/T Score*	*Lg Pos.*	*Goalscorers*	*Attendance*
1	Aug 3	A	Celtic	L	0-7	0-3	8		58,877
2	10	H	Livingston	D	2-2	0-2	10	Kennedy [55], Hendry [82]	2349
3	24	A	Hibernian	D	2-2	0-1	10	O'Halloran [68], Kerr [90]	15,315
4	31	H	Kilmarnock	L	0-1	0-1	12		3427
5	Sept 14	A	Aberdeen	D	1-1	1-1	11	O'Halloran [43]	13,272
6	22	H	Rangers	L	0-4	0-0	12		6251
7	28	H	Motherwell	L	0-1	0-1	12		2972
8	Oct 5	A	Ross Co	D	2-2	1-1	12	May [34], Kennedy [51]	4124
9	19	A	St Mirren	L	0-2	0-1	12		4791
10	26	H	Hamilton A	W	3-2	1-1	12	Wotherspoon 2 [36, 60], Hendry [89]	2231
11	30	H	Hearts	W	1-0	0-0	8	Berra (og) [58]	3104
12	Nov 9	H	Hibernian	L	1-4	0-2	11	May [90]	3931
13	24	H	Aberdeen	D	1-1	0-1	12	Kennedy [71]	3917
14	30	A	Motherwell	L	0-4	0-1	12		4092
15	Dec 4	A	Kilmarnock	D	0-0	0-0	11		4083
16	14	A	Hearts	W	1-0	0-0	10	Hendry [74]	16,347
17	21	H	St Mirren	D	0-0	0-0	10		3318
18	26	A	Hamilton A	W	1-0	0-0	9	McCann [80]	1536
19	29	H	Ross Co	D	1-1	0-0	9	Hendry [84]	2658
20	Jan 22	A	Livingston	L	0-1	0-0	9		1140
21	25	H	Kilmarnock	W	2-1	1-1	8	McCann [7], Wotherspoon [83]	2609
22	29	H	Celtic	L	0-3	0-3	8		8743
23	Feb 1	H	Hearts	D	3-3	1-2	8	May 2 (1 pen) [17, 62 (p)], McCann [52]	6002
24	5	A	Aberdeen	W	1-0	1-0	8	McCann [6]	12,552
25	12	H	Motherwell	W	2-1	1-1	8	Hendry [27], Kane [90]	2655
26	15	A	Ross Co	D	1-1	1-0	8	May [33]	3569
27	23	H	Rangers	D	2-2	1-0	8	Hendry [8], May [80]	8286
28	Mar 4	A	St Mirren	D	0-0	0-0	8		4287
29	7	H	Livingston	W	1-0	0-0	7	Hendry [84]	3008
30	14	A	St Johnstone	Cancelled					
31	21	A	Celtic	Cancelled					
32	Apr 4	H	Hamilton A	Cancelled					
33	TBC	A	Rangers	Cancelled					
34	Fixtures 34–38 decided after 33 game league split.								
35									
36									
37									
38									

Final League Position: 6 (on points-per-game basis)

Honours
League Champions: First Division 1982-83, 1989-90, 1996-97, 2008-09; Division II 1923-24, 1959-60, 1962-63.
Runners-up: Division II 1931-32; First Division 2005-06, 2006-07; Second Division 1987-88.
Scottish Cup Winners: 2014.
League Cup Runners-up: 1969-70, 1998-99.
League Challenge Cup Winners: 2007-08; *Runners-up:* 1996-97.

European: *UEFA Cup:* 10 matches (1971-72, 1999-2000). *Europa League:* 14 matches (2012-13, 2013-14, 2014-15, 2015-16, 2017-18).

Club colours: Shirt: Blue with white trim. Shorts: White with blue trim. Socks: Blue and white hoops.

Goalscorers: *League (28):* Hendry 7, May 6 (1 pen), McCann 4, Kennedy 3, Wotherspoon 3, O'Halloran 2, Kane 1, Kerr 1, own goal 1.
William Hill Scottish Cup (5): Booth 1, Davidson 1, Hendry 1, May 1, own goal 1.
Betfred Scottish League Cup (6): Kennedy 2, Tanser 2 (2 pens), Hendry 1, Kane 1.
Tunnock's Caramel Wafer Scottish League Challenge Cup (1): Northcott 1.

Clark Z 29	Foster R 2	Duffy W 11	Vihmann M 2 + 2	Kerr J 29	Tanser S 19 + 2	Davidson M 17	Craig L 9 + 6	Callachan R 1 + 1	O'Halloran M 14 + 10	Kennedy M 16 + 2	McCann A 26 + 3	Hendry C 5 + 15	Swanson D 3 + 4	Kane C 11 + 12	Gordon L 16	May S 20 + 4	Wright D 16 + 6	Ralston A 21 + 1	Holt J 15 + 2	Wotherspoon D 15 + 6	Booth C 12 + 1	McCart J 7 + 1	Butcher M 3 + 3	Match No.
1	2	3	4	5	6	7	8	9^{2}	10	11^{1}	12	13												1
1	2		4	3	5	7	13		10	6	8^{1}	12	9^{2}	11										2
1		2		3	5	9	8^{1}		10	6	7	12	13	11^{2}	4									3
1		2^{3}		3	5	7	8^{2}		11	6^{1}	9		14	10	4	12	13							4
1				3	5	7			11^{2}	6^{1}	9	13			4	10^{3}	12	2	8	14				5
1				3	5	7		13	10	6^{2}	8^{3}			14	4	11	12	2		9^{1}				6
1				3	5	7			10^{3}	12	9^{1}		13	14	4	11	6^{2}	2	8					7
1		4	13	3	5	6			14	8^{2}	7		9^{3}	12		11		2^{1}		10				8
1		3		4	5	6			12	8	14	13	10^{3}			11	9^{2}	2	7^{1}					9
1		4		3	5	6	14			9^{1}	7	13		12		11^{3}	8^{2}	2		10				10
1		4		3	5	6	13			9^{2}	7	14		12		11^{3}	8	2		10^{1}				11
1		3		4	5	7			13	11^{1}	8	12				10	6^{2}	2	14	9^{3}				12
1		3		4	5	8▮				10^{1}	9	13▮		12		11^{3}	6	2	7^{2}	14				13
1		3^{3}	14	4	5				13	6	7			11		10^{1}	12	2	8	9^{2}				14
1				4			7		11^{1}	13	6			10	3		9^{2}	2	8	12	5			15
1				3		7	13		10	8^{2}	6	12			4	11^{1}		5	9^{3}	14	2			16
1				4		7			10	9^{2}	12	11^{1}			3	13	6	2	8^{3}	14	5			17
1				4	14	7			6^{2}		8	13		11^{3}	3	10^{1}	12	2		9	5			18
1				4		8			14	10	9	12		11^{2}	3	13	6^{3}	2	7^{1}		5			19
1				4	14		7^{2}		11		6	13		12	3	10^{1}	9	2^{3}	8		5			20
1				3	9						6	13		10^{2}	2	11	5^{1}	12	7	8	4			21
1		5		3	9		12		10		6	11^{3}		14	2				7^{1}	8	4^{2}	13		22
1				3	9^{2}		8		12		7			10	2^{1}	11^{3}		5		6	13	4	14	23
1				3			9		6^{2}		10			13		11^{1}	12	2	8	7	5	4		24
1				3			6^{2}				9	11^{3}		13		14	7	2	8^{1}	10	5	4	12	25
1				2	9				12		6	14		11^{3}	3	10^{1}	5		13	7		4	8^{2}	26
1				3			14		13		8	11^{1}		12		10^{2}	6	2^{3}		9	5	4	7	27
1				3			8▮		12		7		13	10^{1}		11^{2}	6	2		9^{3}	5	4	14	28
1				2	9				12		6	10^{1}		14	3	11^{3}	5		8^{2}	13		4	7	29
																								30
																								31
																								32
																								33
																								34
																								35
																								36
																								37
																								38

ST MIRREN

Year Formed: 1877. *Ground & Address:* The Simple Digital Arena, St Mirren Park, Greenhill Road, Paisley PA3 1RU. *Telephone:* 0141 889 2558. *Fax:* 0141 848 6444. *E-mail:* info@stmirren.com *Website:* www.stmirren.com
Ground Capacity: 7,937 (all seated). *Size of Pitch:* 105m × 68m.
Chairman: Gordon Scott. *Chief Executive:* Tony Fitzpatrick.
Manager: Jim Goodwin. *Assistant Manager:* Lee Sharp.
Club Nickname: 'The Buddies'.
Previous Grounds: Shortroods 1877-79, Thistle Park Greenhill 1879-83, Westmarch 1883-94, Love Street 1894-2009.
Record Attendance: 47,438 v Celtic, League Cup, 20 August 1949.
Record Transfer Fee received: £850,000 for Ian Ferguson to Rangers (February 1988).
Record Transfer Fee paid: £400,000 for Thomas Stickroth from Bayer Uerdingen (March 1990).
Record Victory: 15-0 v Glasgow University, Scottish Cup 1st rd, 30 January 1960.
Record Defeat: 0-9 v Rangers, Division I, 4 December 1897.
Most Capped Player: Godmundur Torfason, 29, Iceland.
Most League Appearances: 403: Hugh Murray, 1997-2012.
Most League Goals in Season (Individual): 45: Dunky Walker, Division I, 1921-22.
Most League Goals Overall (Individual): 222: David McCrae, 1923-34.

ST MIRREN – SPFL LADBROKES PREMIERSHIP 2019–20 LEAGUE RECORD

Match No.	*Date*	*Venue*	*Opponents*	*Result*		*H/T Score*	*Lg Pos.*	*Goalscorers*	*Attendance*
1	Aug 3	A	Hibernian	L	0-1	0-0	6		16,631
2	11	H	Aberdeen	W	1-0	1-0	5	Durmus [13]	6199
3	25	H	Rangers	L	0-1	0-0	8		7332
4	31	A	Livingston	L	1-2	0-1	10	Magennis [64]	2346
5	Sept 14	A	Ross Co	L	1-2	0-0	10	Andreu [72]	3637
6	21	H	Hamilton A	D	0-0	0-0	9		4807
7	28	H	Hearts	D	0-0	0-0	10		5901
8	Oct 5	A	Motherwell	L	0-2	0-1	11		5101
9	19	H	St Johnstone	W	2-0	1-0	9	Obika [37], Mullen [61]	4791
10	26	A	Kilmarnock	L	0-1	0-0	10		6389
11	30	A	Celtic	L	0-2	0-0	12		56,127
12	Nov 9	A	Hearts	L	2-5	2-3	12	Obika [21], Mullen [33]	16,165
13	23	H	Ross Co	W	2-1	1-1	10	McLoughlin [43], Foley [88]	4708
14	26	H	Hibernian	L	1-2	0-1	10	Morias [90]	5377
15	30	A	Aberdeen	L	1-2	1-1	11	Obika [23]	12,829
16	Dec 4	H	Motherwell	L	0-3	0-2	12		4240
17	7	A	Hamilton A	W	1-0	0-0	9	MacPherson [52]	1962
18	14	H	Livingston	D	3-3	1-2	9	Morias [33], Obika 2 [61, 73]	4344
19	21	A	St Johnstone	D	0-0	0-0	9		3318
20	26	H	Celtic	L	1-2	0-2	10	MacPherson [89]	6797
21	29	H	Kilmarnock	W	1-0	1-0	10	Durmus [17]	6363
22	Jan 22	A	Rangers	L	0-1	0-1	10		49,297
23	26	H	Aberdeen	D	0-0	0-0	10		5302
24	Feb 1	A	Hibernian	D	2-2	2-2	10	McCarthy [14], Andreu [18]	16,325
25	5	H	Hamilton A	D	1-1	0-1	10	Durmus [72]	4537
26	12	A	Livingston	L	1-2	0-1	10	Obika [50]	1263
27	25	A	Motherwell	W	2-1	0-1	10	Obika [50], Durmus [87]	3636
28	Mar 4	H	St Johnstone	D	0-0	0-0	10		4287
29	7	A	Celtic	L	0-5	0-2	11		58,998
30	11	H	Hearts	W	1-0	0-0	9	Obika [48]	5662
31	14	A	Kilmarnock	Cancelled					
32	22	H	Rangers	Cancelled					
33	Apr 4	A	Ross Co	Cancelled					
34	Fixtures 34–38 decided after 33 game league split.								
35									
36									
37									
38									

Final League Position: 9 (on points-per-game basis)

Honours
League Champions: First Division 1976-77, 1999-2000, 2005-06; Division II 1967-68; Championship 2017-18.
Runners-up: First Division 2004-05; Division II 1935-36.
Scottish Cup Winners: 1926, 1959, 1987; *Runners-up:* 1908, 1934, 1962.
League Cup Winners: 2012-13; *Runners-up:* 1955-56, 2009-10.
League Challenge Cup Winners: 2005-06; *Runners-up:* 2016-17.
B&Q Cup Runners-up: 1993-94. *Anglo-Scottish Cup:* 1979-80.

European: *Cup Winners' Cup:* 4 matches (1987-88). *UEFA Cup:* 10 matches (1980-81, 1983-84, 1985-86).

Club colours: Shirt: Black and white stripes. Shorts: Black. Socks: Black with white tops.

Goalscorers: *League (24):* Obika 8, Durmus 4, Andreu 2, MacPherson 2, Morias 2, Mullen 2, Foley 1, Magennis 1, McCarthy 1, McLoughlin 1.
William Hill Scottish Cup (8): Obika 4, Foley 1, Jakubiak 1, Mullen 1, own goal 1.
Betfred Scottish League Cup (3): Cooke 1, Djorkaeff 1 (1 pen), Mullen 1.
Tunnock's Caramel Wafer Scottish League Challenge Cup (4): Breadner 1, Henderson 1, Jack 1, MacPherson 1.

Hladky V 30	MacPherson C 15 + 1	McLoughlin S 21	MacKenzie G 9 + 1	McGinn P 21 + 1	Flynn R 22	Foley S 27	Magennis K 22	Andreu T 16 + 12	Durmus I 21 + 7	Mullen D 7 + 10	Obika J 26 + 4	Breadner C — + 2	Djorkaeff O — + 2	Waters C 27	McAllister K 4 + 11	Morias J 14 + 12	Broadfoot K 7 + 1	McGinn S 7 + 2	Cooke C — + 6	Glover S 1	McCarthy C 9	Famewo A 9	Jakubiak A 4 + 3	McGrath J 4 + 3	Hodson L 5 + 2	Wallace R 2 + 1	Chabbi S — + 2	*Match No.*
1	2	3	4	5	6	7	8	9^3	10^2	11^1	12	13	14															1
1		4	3	2	7	6	8	9^3	10^1	13	11^2	14		5	12													2
1		4	3	2	6	7	8	9^1	10^2	14	11^3			5	12	13												3
1		4	3	2	7^1	6	8	9^3	13	14	11			5	10^2	12												4
1		3	4^3	2	7	9	6	13	14		11^2			5	10^1	8	12											5
1		4		2	6	7	8	9^3	10^2	13	14			5	12	11^1	3											6
1		4		2	6	7	8	9^2	10^3	13	12			5	14	11^1	3											7
1		3		2	7^1	8	6	12	9^3	11^2	10		14	5		13	4											8
1		4		2		8	6	9^1	13	11^2	10			5		12	3	7										9
1	2	4		5		7	8^1	9^2	13	10	11					12	3	6										10
1		4		2	7^3	9	6^2	12	10^1	13	11			5		14	3	8										11
1		4	13	2		7	8	10^3	12	9	11			5		14	3^1	6^2										12
1		4	3	2	7	6	8^1	12	10^3	9^2	11			5	13			14										13
1		4	3	2	9^1	7	6		10^3	12	11^2			5	13	14		8										14
1		4	3	2	7	9^3	8^2	10^1	12		11			5	13	14		6										15
1	12	4	3^2	2	7		10^1	9		8	11^3			5	14	13		6										16
1	7	4		3^1	2		8^2	14	10		11			5	6^3	9		13	12									17
1	8	4			2		6	12	9	14	10			5	7^3	11^2			13	3^1								18
1	8	4		3	2	7	6	12	9^2		11			5		10^1			13									19
1	6	4		3	2	8	7	12	9^2		11			5		10^1			13									20
1	8	4		5	2	3	6	7^1	9		10					11			12									21
1	8^1			4	2	9	10^2	13	12	14	11			6		7^3					3	5						22
1	6			13	2	7		9^1	10^2		11			5		8			12		4	3						23
1	6				2	7		9^1	10^2		11			5		8^3					4	3	12	13	14			24
1	7				2^1	6		9	10		13			5		11^2					3	4	14	8^3	12			25
1	8					7			9^1	14	11			5	12	6^2					3	4	10^3	13	2			26
1	6					7		12	8		10^3			5		14					3	4	11^2	9^1	2	13		27
1						8		12	9^2		10			5		13					3	4	11^1	6	2	7^3	14	28
1	8					4		7			10^3			6	14	11^1					3	5	12	9^2	2		13	29
1	6^3					8		13	11^1		10			5	14						3^2	4	9	12	2	7		30
																												31
																												32
																												33
																												34
																												35
																												36
																												37
																												38

STENHOUSEMUIR

Year Formed: 1884. *Ground & Address:* Ochilview Park, Gladstone Rd, Stenhousemuir FK5 4QL. *Telephone:* 01324 562992. *Fax:* 01324 562980. *E-mail:* info@stenhousemuirfc.com *Website:* www.stenhousemuirfc.com
Ground Capacity: 3,776 (seated: 626). *Size of Pitch:* 101m × 66m.
Chairman: Iain McMenemy. *Vice-Chairman:* David Reid. *Chief Executive:* Jamie Swinney.
Manager: Davie Irons. *Assistant Manager:* Kevin McGoldrick.
Club Nickname: 'The Warriors'.
Previous Grounds: Tryst Ground 1884-86; Goschen Park 1886-90.
Record Attendance: 12,500 v East Fife, Scottish Cup quarter-final, 11 March 1950.
Record Transfer Fee received: £70,000 for Euan Donaldson to St Johnstone (May 1995).
Record Transfer Fee paid: £20,000 to Livingston for Ian Little (June 1995); £20,000 to East Fife for Paul Hunter (September 1995).
Record Victory: 9-2 v Dundee U, Division II, 16 April 1937.
Record Defeat: 2-11 v Dunfermline Ath, Division II, 27 September 1930.
Most League Appearances: 434: Jimmy Richardson, 1957-73.
Most League Goals in Season (Individual): 32: Robert Taylor, Division II, 1925-26.

STENHOUSEMUIR – SPFL LADBROKES LEAGUE TWO 2019–20 LEAGUE RECORD

Match No.	Date	Venue	Opponents	Result	H/T Score	Lg Pos.	Goalscorers	Attendance
1	Aug 3	H	Albion R	L 2-3	0-1	6	Hopkirk 50, Cook 78	423
2	10	A	Queen's Park	D 1-1	0-0	8	Hopkirk 47	565
3	17	A	Elgin C	W 1-0	0-0	7	Munro, A 68	738
4	24	H	Edinburgh C	L 1-3	1-0	8	McGuigan 7	387
5	31	A	Annan Ath	D 1-1	1-1	8	McGuigan 29	362
6	Sept 14	H	Cowdenbeath	L 0-3	0-1	8		605
7	21	H	Brechin C	W 1-0	0-0	7	Hopkirk 68	435
8	28	A	Stirling Alb	D 1-1	1-0	5	Halleran 32	602
9	Oct 5	H	Cove R	W 3-2	3-1	4	Marsh 9, Hopkirk 22, McGuigan (pen) 45	552
10	29	A	Edinburgh C	L 0-4	0-2	6		194
11	Nov 2	H	Queen's Park	L 0-3	0-1	6		646
12	9	A	Albion R	L 1-2	1-2	7	McGuigan 34	209
13	30	A	Brechin C	W 2-1	1-0	8	Cook 17, Dykes 70	401
14	Dec 3	H	Elgin C	D 2-2	1-2	8	Biabi (pen) 33, Munro, A 90	336
15	7	H	Annan Ath	L 1-2	1-1	8	Hopkirk 24	422
16	14	A	Cove R	L 1-2	0-0	8	Tiffoney 63	391
17	21	A	Cowdenbeath	L 1-3	1-2	9	McBride 17	312
18	28	H	Stirling Alb	L 0-2	0-1	9		824
19	Jan 4	A	Queen's Park	L 1-2	0-2	9	Cook 47	837
20	11	H	Brechin C	D 2-2	0-1	9	Munro, A 63, Hopkirk 80	629
21	18	A	Elgin C	W 3-2	2-0	8	Spence 2 1, 90, McGuigan 37	573
22	25	H	Edinburgh C	L 1-2	1-0	9	Hopkirk 12	502
23	Feb 1	A	Annan Ath	W 3-0	3-0	8	Blair 28, Biabi 33, Moore 42	284
24	8	H	Cowdenbeath	D 2-2	1-2	9	Spence 7, Hopkirk 57	620
25	15	H	Albion R	W 1-0	1-0	7	Biabi 20	756
26	29	H	Cove R	L 0-3	0-2	8		596
27	Mar 3	A	Stirling Alb	D 0-0	0-0	8		457
28	7	H	Queen's Park	D 0-0	0-0	8		581
29	14	A	Edinburgh C	Cancelled				
30	21	H	Elgin C	Cancelled				
31	28	A	Cowdenbeath	Cancelled				
32	Apr 4	A	Brechin C	Cancelled				
33	11	H	Stirling Alb	Cancelled				
34	18	A	Cove Rangers	Cancelled				
35	25	H	Annan Ath	Cancelled				
36	May 2	A	Albion R	Cancelled				

Final League Position: 8 (on points-per-game basis)

Honours
League Runners-up: Third Division 1998-99.
Promoted via play-offs: 2008-09 (to Second Division); 2017-18 (to League One).
Scottish Cup: Semi-finals 1902-03. Quarter-finals 1948-49, 1949-50, 1994-95.
League Cup: Quarter-finals 1947-48, 1960-61, 1975-76.
League Challenge Cup Winners: 1995-96.

Club colours: Shirt: Maroon with white trim. Shorts: White. Socks: Maroon.

Goalscorers: *League (32):* Hopkirk 8, McGuigan 5 (1 pen), Biabi 3 (1 pen), Cook 3, Munro, A 3, Spence 3, Blair 1, Dykes 1, Halleran 1, Marsh 1, McBride 1, Moore 1, Tiffoney 1.
William Hill Scottish Cup (0).
Betfred Scottish League Cup (4): McGuigan 2, Munro, A 1, own goal 1.
Tunnock's Caramel Wafer Scottish League Challenge Cup (7): Hopkirk 2, Watters 2, Anderson 1, McGuigan 1, McLaughlin 1.

Smith G 27	McLaughlin S 28	Munro A 23	Marsh D 14	McIlduff A 2	Scullion L 5+6	Dykes D 10+2	McKernon J 5+1	Cook A 19	Hopkirk D 24+2	McGuigan M 18+7	Munro M 6+2	Watters R —+7	Anderson K 3+10	Gibbons K 2+1	O'Neil C 9+4	Halleran T 7+2	Gibson W 8	McBride C 6+8	Armstrong J 15	Tiffoney J 16	Blair R 14	Biabi B 10+4	Terry D 1	Marley K —+1	McBrearty C 4+4	Wilson R 9	Spence G 9	Moore C 8	Massougahou A —+1	Burns S 4	Harkins G 2+1	*Match No.*
1	2	3	4	5^1	6^3	7	8^2	9	10	11	12	13	14																			1
1	2	4	3	5^3	6^2	7^1	13	9	10	11	8			12	14																	2
1	2	4	3		5^2	6	8	9		10		13	11^1	7^3	12	14																3
1	2	3	4		6^1	7	5	9	13	10		14	11^2	8^3	12																	4
1	2	3	4				7	8	11	10			12		5	6^1	9															5
1	2	3	4		14	13	7	8^2	12	11			10^3		5	6^1	9															6
1	5	4	3		12			9^1	11^2	10	8		13		2	7	6															7
1	5	3	4		12	13		9^1	11	10^2	6^3		14		2	8	7															8
1	5	3	4		12			9	10	11^2	6^1		13		2	8	7															9
1	5	3	4		12			9■	11^1	10^2	6		14		2	8^3	7	13														10
1	5	3			7	9			11	12	6^1				2^2	13	8	10	4													11
1	9^1	2	3		14			6	11	10			12		5^2	7^3	8	13	4													12
1	5	4	2			7		9	10^1	12								13	3	6	8	11^2										13
1	2	4	3^1			7		9	11	13								12	5^2	6	8	10										14
1	6	4				8^1		5	7	12								10	3	2	9	11										15
1	9	4				7		5	6■	12			13					10^1	3	2	8	11^2										16
	5		3			8		9		10			13		2^2			11	4	6	7		1^1	12								17
1	2	3						9	6	11		13	12					7^1	5	4	8	10^2										18
1	7	4						2	11	10		12			13			9^2	3	5	6^1				8							19
1	5	4						9^1	6	11^2								13		2	8	12			7	3	10					20
1	5	4							6	11^2								13		2	8	12			7^1	3	10	9				21
1	5	4■							6	11^2								12		2	8	13			7^3	3	10^1	9	14			22
1	7								6^3			14						12	4	2	8^2	11^1			13	3	10	9		5		23
1	7								6			12							4	2		10^1				3	11	9		5	8	24
1	7								9	14									3	5	8^2	11^1			13	4	10^3	6		2	12	25
1	7								9	14	12								3	5		11^3			13	4	10	6		2^2	8■^{1}	26
1	7	3							9	10^2									5	2	6^1	12			13	4	11	8				27
1	7	3							11										2	5	6	10				4	9	8				28
																																29
																																30
																																31
																																32
																																33
																																34
																																35
																																36

STIRLING ALBION

Year Formed: 1945. *Ground & Address:* Forthbank Stadium, Springkerse, Stirling FK7 7UJ. *Telephone:* 01786 450399. *Fax:* 01786 448592. *E-mail:* office@stirlingalbionfc.co.uk *Website:* www.stirlingalbionfc.co.uk
Ground Capacity: 3,808 (seated: 2,508). *Size of Pitch:* 101m × 68m.
Chairman and Operations Director: Stuart Brown.
Manager: Kevin Rutkiewicz.
Club Nickname: 'The Binos'.
Previous Ground: Annfield 1945-92.
Record Attendance: 26,400 v Celtic, Scottish Cup 4th rd, 14 March 1959 (Annfield); 3,808 v Aberdeen, Scottish Cup 4th rd, 15 February 1996 (Forthbank).
Record Transfer Fee received: £90,000 for Stephen Nicholas to Motherwell (March 1999).
Record Transfer Fee paid: £25,000 for Craig Taggart from Falkirk (August 1994).
Record Victory: 20-0 v Selkirk, Scottish Cup 1st rd, 8 December 1984.
Record Defeat: 0-9 v Dundee U, Division I, 30 December 1967; 0-9 v Ross Co, Scottish Cup 5th rd, 6 February 2010.
Most League Appearances: 504: Matt McPhee, 1967-81.
Most League Goals in Season (Individual): 27: Joe Hughes, Division II, 1969-70.
Most Goals Overall (Individual): 129: Billy Steele, 1971-83.

STIRLING ALBION – SPFL LADBROKES LEAGUE TWO 2019–20 LEAGUE RECORD

Match No.	*Date*	*Venue*	*Opponents*	*Result*		*H/T Score*	*Lg Pos.*	*Goalscorers*	*Attendance*
1	Aug 3	H	Queen's Park	L	0-1	0-0	7		701
2	10	A	Cowdenbeath	L	0-1	0-0	10		401
3	17	A	Edinburgh C	L	0-1	0-0	9		359
4	24	H	Cove R	L	1-2	0-1	10	Peters 84	605
5	31	A	Albion R	L	1-2	1-0	10	Peters 17	355
6	Sept 14	H	Elgin C	W	1-0	1-0	9	Peters 10	482
7	21	A	Annan Ath	D	0-0	0-0	9		398
8	28	H	Stenhousemuir	D	1-1	0-1	10	Heaver 87	602
9	Oct 5	A	Brechin C	D	1-1	0-0	10	McLean 68	451
10	29	H	Cowdenbeath	D	0-0	0-0	9		451
11	Nov 2	H	Albion R	W	3-0	0-0	8	Duffy 59, McGregor 69, Heaver 82	603
12	9	A	Cove R	L	0-1	0-0	9		825
13	16	H	Annan Ath	W	2-0	1-0	7	Jardine 38, Duffy 68	512
14	30	A	Elgin C	W	2-1	1-0	7	Bikey 33, Peters 90	564
15	Dec 7	H	Brechin C	L	2-4	2-2	7	Heaver 7, Mackin 36	521
16	14	A	Queen's Park	D	1-1	1-0	7	Mackin 35	501
17	21	H	Edinburgh C	L	0-1	0-0	8		741
18	28	A	Stenhousemuir	W	2-0	1-0	6	Mackin 4, Wilson 90	824
19	Jan 4	A	Albion R	W	3-0	3-0	5	Duffy 3 (1 pen) 6 (p), 33, 40	484
20	18	A	Annan Ath	W	3-2	1-0	5	Duffy 2 (1 pen) 21, 54 (p), Docherty 57	402
21	25	H	Elgin C	L	1-2	0-1	6	McGregor 59	584
22	Feb 1	A	Edinburgh C	W	1-0	0-0	5	McGregor 69	336
23	8	H	Queen's Park	L	1-3	1-0	6	Bikey 25	642
24	15	A	Cowdenbeath	W	4-1	3-1	6	Bikey 12, Duffy 2 18, 37, Wright 60	328
25	29	A	Brechin C	W	2-0	0-0	6	Bikey 54, Creaney 84	433
26	Mar 3	H	Stenhousemuir	D	0-0	0-0	6		457
27	7	A	Elgin C	L	1-3	1-3	6	Wilson 27	666
28	10	H	Cove R	L	1-7	0-5	6	Duffy 80	423
29	14	H	Annan Ath	Cancelled					
30	21	A	Queen's Park	Cancelled					
31	28	H	Albion R	Cancelled					
32	Apr 4	H	Cowdenbeath	Cancelled					
33	11	A	Stenhousemuir	Cancelled					
34	18	H	Edinburgh C	Cancelled					
35	25	H	Brechin C	Cancelled					
36	May 2	A	Cove Rangers	Cancelled					

Final League Position: 6 (on points-per-game basis)

Honours
League Champions: Division II 1952-53, 1957-58, 1960-61, 1964-65; Second Division 1976-77, 1990-91, 1995-96, 2009-10; Division C 1946-47.
Runners-up: Division II 1948-49, 1950-51; Second Division 2006-07; Third Division 2003-04.
Promoted via play-offs: 2006-07 (to First Division); 2013-14 (to League One).
League Cup: Semi-finals 1961-62.
League Challenge Cup: Semi-finals 1995-96, 1999-2000.

Club colours: Shirt: Red with white sleeves. Shorts: Red with white trim. Socks: Red and white hoops.

Goalscorers: *League (34):* Duffy 10 (2 pens), Bikey 4, Peters 4, Heaver 3, Mackin 3, McGregor 3, Wilson 2, Creaney 1, Docherty 1, Jardine 1, McLean 1, Wright 1.
William Hill Scottish Cup (2): Heaver 2.
Betfred Scottish League Cup (3): Wilson 2, Mackin 1.
Tunnock's Caramel Wafer Scottish League Challenge Cup (2): Duffy 1, Peters 1.

Currie B 16	McLean P 26 + 1	McGeachie R 25	Banner K 12 + 4	Lowdon J 4 + 1	Nicoll K 16 + 3	Thomson C 12 + 5	Jardine D 20 + 3	Wilson D 22 + 2	Willis P 12 + 5	Mackin D 14 + 7	Hawke L 3 + 3	Truesdale C 4 + 5	Duffy D 19 + 4	Docherty D 13 + 6	Peters J 5 + 5	Bikey D 12 + 7	McGregor J 23	Creaney J 18	Wright M 9 + 5	Heaver S 9 + 5	Binnie C 3 + 1	Hogarth N 9	Scott F — + 2	Hughes R 2 + 3	Match No.
1	2	3■	4	5	6^{1}	7	8	9	10	11	12														1
1	3		4■	5	7	6^{1}	9	8	13	10^{2}	11	2	12												2
1	4^{2}	3		5	7		6	12	9	14	13	2^{1}	10	8	11^{3}										3
1	2	3^{2}	4	5	7	13	6^{3}	12	9			14	10	8^{1}	11										4
1	3■		4	13	7■	5	9	8^{1}	6^{2}			2	11	12	10^{3}	14									5
1		4	2			10	6	7		12		13	11^{2}	14	8^{1}	9^{3}	3	5							6
1	3	2			14	8	6	7^{1}		10^{3}	12		9^{2}			11	4	5	13						7
1	3	2			7	13	6	8^{1}			10		9^{2}			11	4	5		12					8
1	4	2			8	7	6	9	13		11^{2}		12				3	5		10^{1}					9
1	4	2			7	9	6	8	12	14			11^{1}				3	5^{2}	13	10^{3}					10
1	3	5			7^{1}	2	9	8^{3}	10	14			6^{2}	12			4		13	11					11
1	3	2			7	13	9	8^{2}	10	14			6	12			4	5^{3}		11^{1}					12
1	4	2	8			13	6		9^{3}			14	11■			7^{2}	3	5	12	10^{1}					13
1	4	5	12			2	8	7	9^{3}	10^{2}				13	14	6^{1}	3			11					14
1	3	2				5	7	8^{3}	9	11				13	12	6^{1}	4		14	10^{2}					15
1^{3}	3	5			7	13	8		9	10					14	6^{1}	4	2■		11^{2}	12				16
	3	5	14		7^{3}	2	9			11			13	8	10^{2}	12	4			6^{1}	1				17
	4	2	14		7		12	8		10^{1}			11^{2}	6^{3}	13		3	5	9		1				18
	4	2	12				8	7		10		14	11^{1}	9		13	3^{3}	5	6^{2}		1				19
	3	2			7		12	9		10			11^{3}	8^{2}		13	4	5	6^{1}			1	14		20
	4	2					8	7		10^{2}			11^{1}	9		13	3	5	6^{3}	12		1	14		21
	4	2	8					7		10^{3}		14	11^{1}	9		12	3	5	6^{2}			1		13	22
	4	5	6					8	14				11	7^{2}		10^{3}	3	2	9^{1}	13		1		12	23
	4	5	7					8^{2}	13				9^{1}	6	14	11	3	2^{3}	10			1		12	24
	2	9	3		13			7		12			10^{2}	6		8^{1}	4	5	11^{3}	14		1			25
	4	2			7		12	8	9^{1}	10						11	3	5				1		6	26
	3	5	4		12			7^{2}		13			10^{3}	8		11	2^{1}	9	6	14		1			27
	12		4		8■	5	6		9^{3}	10^{1}		2^{2}	13	7		14	3					1		11	28
																									29
																									30
																									31
																									32
																									33
																									34
																									35
																									36

STRANRAER

Year Formed: 1870. *Ground & Address:* Stair Park, London Rd, Stranraer DG9 8BS. *Telephone and Fax:* 01776 703271.
E-mail: secretary@stranraerfc.org *Website:* www.stranraerfc.org
Ground Capacity: 4,178 (seated: 1,830). *Size of Pitch:* 103m × 64m.
Chairman: Iain Dougan. *Vice Chairman:* Shaun Niven.
Manager: Stephen Farrell. *Assistant Manager:* Frank McKeown.
Club Nicknames: 'The Blues'; 'The Clayholers'.
Record Attendance: 6,500 v Rangers, Scottish Cup 1st rd, 24 January 1948.
Record Transfer Fee received: £90,000 for Mark Campbell to Ayr U (1999).
Record Transfer Fee paid: £35,000 for Michael Moore from St Johnstone (March 2005).
Record Victory: 9-0 v St Cuthbert Wanderers, Scottish Cup 2nd rd, 23 October 2010; 9-0 v Wigtown & Bladnoch, Scottish Cup 2nd rd, 22 October 2011.
Record Defeat: 1-11 v Queen of the South, Scottish Cup 1st rd, 16 January 1932.
Most League Appearances: 301: Keith Knox, 1986-90; 1999-2001.
Most League Goals in Season (Individual): 27: Derek Frye, 1977-78.
Most Goals Overall (Individual): 136: Jim Campbell, 1965-75.

STRANRAER – SPFL LADBROKES LEAGUE ONE 2019–20 LEAGUE RECORD

Match No.	Date	Venue	Opponents	Result		H/T Score	Lg Pos.	Goalscorers	Attendance
1	Aug 3	H	Montrose	D	2-2	1-0	3	Hilton 22, Pignatiello 80	343
2	10	A	Forfar Ath	L	0-1	0-0	7		523
3	17	H	Raith R	W	3-2	1-0	5	McManus 16, Dangana 83, Elliott 85	404
4	24	A	Dumbarton	L	1-3	1-1	8	Murphy 20	583
5	31	H	Peterhead	L	1-2	0-2	9	Dangana 85	265
6	Sept 14	A	Clyde	L	1-6	0-3	9	Hilton 66	753
7	21	H	Falkirk	L	0-3	0-1	9		549
8	28	A	Airdrieonians	D	2-2	2-0	9	Allan 8, Hilton 31	600
9	Oct 5	A	East Fife	D	1-1	0-1	10	Jones 83	526
10	19	H	Dumbarton	D	0-0	0-0	10		289
11	26	A	Montrose	L	1-2	0-1	10	Hilton 71	611
12	Nov 2	H	Clyde	W	3-0	2-0	9	Cummins 6, Robertson 39, Stewart (pen) 90	418
13	9	A	Raith R	L	1-3	0-1	9	Stewart 75	1364
14	16	H	Airdrieonians	L	0-2	0-0	10		387
15	30	A	Falkirk	L	0-3	0-2	10		3488
16	Dec 7	A	Peterhead	L	0-3	0-1	10		505
17	14	H	East Fife	L	0-2	0-0	10		274
18	21	H	Forfar Ath	L	2-4	0-2	10	Jones 2 57, 83	212
19	28	A	Dumbarton	D	1-1	0-0	10	Hilton 88	656
20	Jan 4	A	Clyde	D	3-3	2-0	10	Elliott 2 32, 82, Allan 42	823
21	25	A	Airdrieonians	D	0-0	0-0	10		749
22	Feb 1	H	Falkirk	D	1-1	0-1	10	Thomson 52	546
23	8	H	Raith R	D	1-1	0-1	10	Stevenson (pen) 54	327
24	15	A	Forfar Ath	D	1-1	0-1	10	Stevenson 56	370
25	22	A	East Fife	L	2-4	0-2	10	Robertson 78, Vitoria 78	491
26	Mar 7	A	Montrose	L	1-4	0-1	10	Fleming (og) 65	528
27	10	H	Montrose	L	0-1	0-0	10		190
28	14	H	Clyde	Cancelled					
29	17	H	Peterhead	Cancelled					
30	21	A	Falkirk	Cancelled					
31	28	H	Dumbarton	Cancelled					
32	Apr 4	H	East Fife	Cancelled					
33	11	A	Peterhead	Cancelled					
34	18	H	Airdrieonians	Cancelled					
35	25	A	Raith R	Cancelled					
36	May 2	H	Forfar Ath	Cancelled					

Final League Position: 10 (on points-per-game basis)

Honours
League Champions: Second Division 1993-94, 1997-98; Third Division 2003-04.
Runners-up: Second Division 2004-05; Third Division 2007-08; League One 2014-15.
Promoted via play-offs: 2011-12 (to Second Division).
Scottish Cup: Quarter-finals 2003.
League Cup: Quarter-finals 1968-69.
League Challenge Cup Winners: 1996-97. Semi-finals: 2000-01, 2014-15.

Club colours: Shirt: Blue with light blue trim. Shorts: White with blue trim. Socks: Blue with red tops.

Goalscorers: *League (28):* Hilton 5, Elliott 3, Jones 3, Allan 2, Dangana 2, Robertson 2, Stevenson 2 (1 pen), Stewart 2 (1 pen), Cummins 1, McManus 1, Murphy 1, Pignatiello 1, Thomson 1, Vitoria 1, own goal 1.
William Hill Scottish Cup (1): Hilton 1 (1 pen).
Betfred Scottish League Cup (9): Cummins 2, Elliott 2, Stewart 2 (2 pens), Allan 1, Hilton 1, McManus 1.
Tunnock's Caramel Wafer Scottish League Challenge Cup (0).

Currie M 24	Smith D 3+2	Hamilton L 14	Hamill J 19+2	Cummins A 25	Allan J 25	McManus C 27	Hilton J 18+6	Thomson R 19+1	Stewart M 5+6	Dangana D 7+10	Pignatiello C 16+4	Jones R 4+8	Murphy L 6+8	Robertson S 25	Smith I 2+7	Burgess D 3	Elliott C 19+5	Stirling A 19+1	McIntyre L 3	Agnew R —+1	Dunn L —+1	Stevenson R 8	Johnstone D 3+2	Vitoria J 3+2	Fyfe D —+2	Match No.
1	2	3	4	5	6^{3}	7	8	9	10^{1}	11^{2}	12	13	14													1
1	8	4^{2}	3	2		6	9^{3}	7		11^{1}	10	12	13	5	14											2
	13	5	4	3	6	8				11	9^{2}		7	2^{1}	12	1	10									3
		2	3^{2}	4	9	7	14	6	12	11^{3}			8^{1}	5	13	1	10									4
		3	4	5	6	8	7^{3}	9	10^{2}	13		12		2	14	1	11^{1}									5
1	2^{3}		3	4■	5	8	12	7	11^{1}				14	6	9^{2}		10	13								6
1			2		5	4	6	8	10^{3}	13	14	12	7^{2}	3			11^{1}	9								7
1			2	4	5	7	9^{2}	6	14	13■	12		10^{3}	3			11^{1}	8								8
1			2	3	5	6	9	7^{3}		13	12	14	10^{1}	4			11^{2}	8								9
1		3		4	5	6	9^{3}	7^{2}		13	8		12	2	14		11^{1}	10								10
1		3		4	5^{1}	6	9	7^{3}	13	14	8	12		2			11^{2}	10								11
1		4^{1}	12	3	5	7	6	11^{2}	14	10^{3}	8			2			13	9								12
1		3		4	5	8	6	10^{3}	12	11^{1}	7^{2}		13	2			14	9								13
1		4	2		5	8	6^{1}		10	14	7^{2}		13	3	12		11^{3}	9								14
1		4	7	3	9	6	10^{1}		13		5		12	2			11^{2}	8								15
1		4	7^{1}	3^{3}		6	10			14	5	13	9	2	11^{2}		12	8								16
1		5		3	6	8	7^{2}			12	2	11^{3}	14	4^{1}	13		10	9								17
1	12	5^{2}		3	6	8	7^{1}			13	2	11		4			10	9								18
1				4	5	7	6			11^{2}	2^{1}	10					9	8	3	12	13					19
1			14	3	5	7	6	13			2	10		4			9^{1}	8^{3}				11^{2}	12			20
1			7	4	5	6	12	8^{1}			2	14		3			11					10^{3}	9^{2}	13		21
1			8	4	5	7	12	11			2			3			6^{1}					10		9		22
1			7	4	5	8	12	6			2			3				9				10	11^{1}			23
1			7	4	5	8	12	6^{2}						3			13	9	2			10	11^{1}			24
1			7	4	5	8	10^{1}	6						3			13	9	2^{2}			11		12		25
1			2	4	5	7		9						3			10	6^{1}				8		11	12	26
1			2	4	5	7		8^{2}						3			6	10				11	12	9^{1}	13	27
																										28
																										29
																										30
																										31
																										32
																										33
																										34
																										35
																										36

SCOTTISH LEAGUE HONOURS 1890–2020

*=Until 1921–22 season teams were equal if level on points, unless a play-off took place. §Not promoted after play-offs. *Won or placed on goal average (ratio), goal difference or most goals scored (goal average from 1921–22 until 1971–72 when it was replaced by goal difference). No official competition during 1939–46; regional leagues operated.*

DIVISION 1 (1890–91 to 1974–75) – TIER 1

Tier	Season	Max Pts	First	Pts	Second	Pts	Third	Pts
1	1890–91	36	Dumbarton=	29	Rangers=	29	Celtic	21
	Dumbarton and Rangers held title jointly after indecisive play-off ended 2-2. Celtic deducted 4 points for fielding an ineligible player.							
1	1891–92	44	Dumbarton	37	Celtic	35	Hearts	34
1	1892–93	36	Celtic	29	Rangers	28	St Mirren	20
1	1893–94	36	Celtic	29	Hearts	26	St Bernard's	23
1	1894–95	36	Hearts	31	Celtic	26	Rangers	22
1	1895–96	36	Celtic	30	Rangers	26	Hibernian	24
1	1896–97	36	Hearts	28	Hibernian	26	Rangers	25
1	1897–98	36	Celtic	33	Rangers	29	Hibernian	22
1	1898–99	36	Rangers	36	Hearts	26	Celtic	24
1	1899–1900	36	Rangers	32	Celtic	25	Hibernian	24
1	1900–01	40	Rangers	35	Celtic	29	Hibernian	25
1	1901–02	36	Rangers	28	Celtic	26	Hearts	22
1	1902–03	44	Hibernian	37	Dundee	31	Rangers	29
1	1903–04	52	Third Lanark	43	Hearts	39	Celtic / Rangers=	38
1	1904–05	52	Celtic=	41	Rangers=	41	Third Lanark	35
	Celtic won title after beating Rangers 2-1 in play-off.							
1	1905–06	60	Celtic	49	Hearts	43	Airdrieonians	38
1	1906–07	68	Celtic	55	Dundee	48	Rangers	45
1	1907–08	68	Celtic	55	Falkirk	51	Rangers	50
1	1908–09	68	Celtic	51	Dundee	50	Clyde	48
1	1909–10	68	Celtic	54	Falkirk	52	Rangers	46
1	1910–11	68	Rangers	52	Aberdeen	48	Falkirk	44
1	1911–12	68	Rangers	51	Celtic	45	Clyde	42
1	1912–13	68	Rangers	53	Celtic	49	Hearts / Airdrieonians=	41
1	1913–14	76	Celtic	65	Rangers	59	Hearts / Morton=	54
1	1914–15	76	Celtic	65	Hearts	61	Rangers	50
1	1915–16	76	Celtic	67	Rangers	56	Morton	51
1	1916–17	76	Celtic	64	Morton	54	Rangers	53
1	1917–18	68	Rangers	56	Celtic	55	Kilmarnock / Morton=	43
1	1918–19	68	Celtic	58	Rangers	57	Morton	47
1	1919–20	84	Rangers	71	Celtic	68	Motherwell	57
1	1920–21	84	Rangers	76	Celtic	66	Hearts	50
1	1921–22	84	Celtic	67	Rangers	66	Raith R	51
1	1922–23	76	Rangers	55	Airdrieonians	50	Celtic	46
1	1923–24	76	Rangers	59	Airdrieonians	50	Celtic	46
1	1924–25	76	Rangers	60	Airdrieonians	57	Hibernian	52
1	1925–26	76	Celtic	58	Airdrieonians*	50	Hearts	50
1	1926–27	76	Rangers	56	Motherwell	51	Celtic	49
1	1927–28	76	Rangers	60	Celtic*	55	Motherwell	55
1	1928–29	76	Rangers	67	Celtic	51	Motherwell	50
1	1929–30	76	Rangers	60	Motherwell	55	Aberdeen	53
1	1930–31	76	Rangers	60	Celtic	58	Motherwell	56
1	1931–32	76	Motherwell	66	Rangers	61	Celtic	48
1	1932–33	76	Rangers	62	Motherwell	59	Hearts	50
1	1933–34	76	Rangers	66	Motherwell	62	Celtic	47
1	1934–35	76	Rangers	55	Celtic	52	Hearts	50
1	1935–36	76	Celtic	66	Rangers*	61	Aberdeen	61
1	1936–37	76	Rangers	61	Aberdeen	54	Celtic	52
1	1937–38	76	Celtic	61	Hearts	58	Rangers	49
1	1938–39	76	Rangers	59	Celtic	48	Aberdeen	46
1	1946–47	60	Rangers	46	Hibernian	44	Aberdeen	39
1	1947–48	60	Hibernian	48	Rangers	46	Partick Thistle	36
1	1948–49	60	Rangers	46	Dundee	45	Hibernian	39
1	1949–50	60	Rangers	50	Hibernian	49	Hearts	43
1	1950–51	60	Hibernian	48	Rangers*	38	Dundee	38
1	1951–52	60	Hibernian	45	Rangers	41	East Fife	37
1	1952–53	60	Rangers*	43	Hibernian	43	East Fife	39
1	1953–54	60	Celtic	43	Hearts	38	Partick Thistle	35
1	1954–55	60	Aberdeen	49	Celtic	46	Rangers	41
1	1955–56	68	Rangers	52	Aberdeen	46	Hearts*	45
1	1956–57	68	Rangers	55	Hearts	53	Kilmarnock	42
1	1957–58	68	Hearts	62	Rangers	49	Celtic	46
1	1958–59	68	Rangers	50	Hearts	48	Motherwell	44
1	1959–60	68	Hearts	54	Kilmarnock	50	Rangers*	42
1	1960–61	68	Rangers	51	Kilmarnock	50	Third Lanark	42
1	1961–62	68	Dundee	54	Rangers	51	Celtic	46
1	1962–63	68	Rangers	57	Kilmarnock	48	Partick Thistle	46
1	1963–64	68	Rangers	55	Kilmarnock	49	Celtic*	47
1	1964–65	68	Kilmarnock*	50	Hearts	50	Dunfermline Ath	49
1	1965–66	68	Celtic	57	Rangers	55	Kilmarnock	45
1	1966–67	68	Celtic	58	Rangers	55	Clyde	46
1	1967–68	68	Celtic	63	Rangers	61	Hibernian	45

1	1968–69	68	Celtic	54	Rangers	49	Dunfermline Ath	45
1	1969–70	68	Celtic	57	Rangers	45	Hibernian	44
1	1970–71	68	Celtic	56	Aberdeen	54	St Johnstone	44
1	1971–72	68	Celtic	60	Aberdeen	50	Rangers	44
1	1972–73	68	Celtic	57	Rangers	56	Hibernian	45
1	1973–74	68	Celtic	53	Hibernian	49	Rangers	48
1	1974–75	68	Rangers	56	Hibernian	49	Celtic*	45

PREMIER DIVISION (1975–76 to 1997–98)

1	1975–76	72	Rangers	54	Celtic	48	Hibernian	43
1	1976–77	72	Celtic	55	Rangers	46	Aberdeen	43
1	1977–78	72	Rangers	55	Aberdeen	53	Dundee U	40
1	1978–79	72	Celtic	48	Rangers	45	Dundee U	44
1	1979–80	72	Aberdeen	48	Celtic	47	St Mirren	42
1	1980–81	72	Celtic	56	Aberdeen	49	Rangers*	44
1	1981–82	72	Celtic	55	Aberdeen	53	Rangers	43
1	1982–83	72	Dundee U	56	Celtic*	55	Aberdeen	55
1	1983–84	72	Aberdeen	57	Celtic	50	Dundee U	47
1	1984–85	72	Aberdeen	59	Celtic	52	Dundee U	47
1	1985–86	72	Celtic*	50	Hearts	50	Dundee U	47
1	1986–87	88	Rangers	69	Celtic	63	Dundee U	60
1	1987–88	88	Celtic	72	Hearts	62	Rangers	60
1	1988–89	72	Rangers	56	Aberdeen	50	Celtic	46
1	1989–90	72	Rangers	51	Aberdeen*	44	Hearts	44
1	1990–91	72	Rangers	55	Aberdeen	53	Celtic*	41
1	1991–92	88	Rangers	72	Hearts	63	Celtic	62
1	1992–93	88	Rangers	73	Aberdeen	64	Celtic	60
1	1993–94	88	Rangers	58	Aberdeen	55	Motherwell	54
1	1994–95	108	Rangers	69	Motherwell	54	Hibernian	53
1	1995–96	108	Rangers	87	Celtic	83	Aberdeen*	55
1	1996–97	108	Rangers	80	Celtic	75	Dundee U	60
1	1997–98	108	Celtic	74	Rangers	72	Hearts	67

PREMIER LEAGUE (1998–99 to 2012–13)

1	1998–99	108	Rangers	77	Celtic	71	St Johnstone	57
1	1999–2000	108	Rangers	90	Celtic	69	Hearts	54
1	2000–01	114	Celtic	97	Rangers	82	Hibernian	66
1	2001–02	114	Celtic	103	Rangers	85	Livingston	58
1	2002–03	114	Rangers*	97	Celtic	97	Hearts	63
1	2003–04	114	Celtic	98	Rangers	81	Hearts	68
1	2004–05	114	Rangers	93	Celtic	92	Hibernian*	61
1	2005–06	114	Celtic	91	Hearts	74	Rangers	73
1	2006–07	114	Celtic	84	Rangers	72	Aberdeen	65
1	2007–08	114	Celtic	89	Rangers	86	Motherwell	60
1	2008–09	114	Rangers	86	Celtic	82	Hearts	59
1	2009–10	114	Rangers	87	Celtic	81	Dundee U	63
1	2010–11	114	Rangers	93	Celtic	92	Hearts	63
1	2011–12	114	Celtic	93	Rangers	73	Motherwell	62

Rangers deducted 10 points for entering administration.

1	2012–13	114	Celtic	79	Motherwell	63	St Johnstone	56

SPFL SCOTTISH PREMIERSHIP (2013–14 to 2019–20)

1	2013–14	114	Celtic	99	Motherwell	70	Aberdeen	68
1	2014–15	114	Celtic	92	Aberdeen	75	Inverness CT	65
1	2015–16	114	Celtic	86	Aberdeen	71	Hearts	65
1	2016–17	114	Celtic	106	Aberdeen	76	Rangers	67
1	2017–18	114	Celtic	82	Aberdeen	73	Rangers	70
1	2018–19	114	Celtic	87	Rangers	78	Kilmarnock*	67
1	2019–20	114	Celtic	80	Rangers	67	Motherwell	46

The 2019–20 season was curtailed due to the COVID-19 pandemic and positions awarded on a points-per-game basis.

DIVISION 2 (1893–93 to 1974–75) – TIER 2

Tier	*Season*	*Max Pts*	*First*	*Pts*	*Second*	*Pts*	*Third*	*Pts*
2	1893–94	36	Hibernian	29	Cowlairs	27	Clyde	24
2	1894–95	36	Hibernian	30	Motherwell	22	Port Glasgow Ath	20
2	1895–96	36	Abercorn	27	Leith Ath	23	Renton / Kilmarnock=	21
2	1896–97	36	Partick Thistle	31	Leith Ath	27	Airdrieonians / Kilmarnock=	21
2	1897–98	36	Kilmarnock	29	Port Glasgow Ath	25	Morton	22
2	1898–99	36	Kilmarnock	32	Leith Ath	27	Port Glasgow Ath	25
2	1899–1900	36	Partick Thistle	29	Morton	28	Port Glasgow Ath	20
2	1900–01	36	St Bernard's	26	Airdrieonians	23	Abercorn	21
2	1901–02	44	Port Glasgow Ath	32	Partick Thistle	30	Motherwell	26
2	1902–03	44	Airdrieonians	35	Motherwell	28	Ayr U / Leith Ath=	27
2	1903–04	44	Hamilton A	37	Clyde	29	Ayr U	28
2	1904–05	44	Clyde	32	Falkirk	28	Hamilton A	27
2	1905–06	44	Leith Ath	34	Clyde	31	Albion R	27
2	1906–07	44	St Bernard's	32	Vale of Leven=	27	Arthurlie=	27
2	1907–08	44	Raith R	30	Dumbarton=	27	Ayr U=	27

Dumbarton deducted 2 points for registration irregularities.

2	1908–09	44	Abercorn	31	Raith R=	28	Vale of Leven=	28
2	1909–10	44	Leith Ath=	33	Raith R=	33	St Bernard's	27

Leith Ath and Raith R held title jointly, no play-off game played.

2	1910–11	44	Dumbarton	31	Ayr U	27	Albion R	25

2	1911–12	44	Ayr U	35	Abercorn	30	Dumbarton	27
2	1912–13	52	Ayr U	34	Dunfermline Ath	33	East Stirlingshire	32
2	1913–14	44	Cowdenbeath	31	Albion R	27	Dunfermline Ath / Dundee U=	26
2	1914–15	52	Cowdenbeath=	37	St Bernard's=	37	Leith Ath=	37

Cowdenbeath won title after a round robin tournament between the three tied clubs.

2	1921–22	76	Alloa Ath	60	Cowdenbeath	47	Armadale	45
2	1922–23	76	Queen's Park	57	Clydebank	50	St Johnstone	48

Clydebank and St Johnstone both deducted 2 points for fielding an ineligible player.

2	1923–24	76	St Johnstone	56	Cowdenbeath	55	Bathgate	44
2	1924–25	76	Dundee U	50	Clydebank	48	Clyde	47
2	1925–26	76	Dunfermline Ath	59	Clyde	53	Ayr U	52
2	1926–27	76	Bo'ness	56	Raith R	49	Clydebank	45
2	1927–28	76	Ayr U	54	Third Lanark	45	King's Park	44
2	1928–29	72	Dundee U	51	Morton	50	Arbroath	47
2	1929–30	76	Leith Ath*	57	East Fife	57	Albion R	54
2	1930–31	76	Third Lanark	61	Dundee U	50	Dunfermline Ath	47
2	1931–32	76	East Stirlingshire*	55	St Johnstone	55	Raith R*	46
2	1932–33	68	Hibernian	54	Queen of the South	49	Dunfermline Ath	47

Armadale and Bo'ness were expelled for failing to meet match guarantees. Their records were expunged.

2	1933–34	68	Albion R	45	Dunfermline Ath*	44	Arbroath	44
2	1934–35	68	Third Lanark	52	Arbroath	50	St Bernard's	47
2	1935–36	68	Falkirk	59	St Mirren	52	Morton	48
2	1936–37	68	Ayr U	54	Morton	51	St Bernard's	48
2	1937–38	68	Raith R	59	Albion R	48	Airdrieonians	47
2	1938–39	68	Cowdenbeath	60	Alloa Ath*	48	East Fife	48
2	1946–47	52	Dundee	45	Airdrieonians	42	East Fife	31
2	1947–48	60	East Fife	53	Albion R	42	Hamilton A	40
2	1948–49	60	Raith R*	42	Stirling Alb	42	Airdrieonians*	41
2	1949–50	60	Morton	47	Airdrieonians	44	Dunfermline Ath*	36
2	1950–51	60	Queen of the South*	45	Stirling Alb	45	Ayr U*	36
2	1951–52	60	Clyde	44	Falkirk	43	Ayr U	39
2	1952–53	60	Stirling Alb	44	Hamilton A	43	Queen's Park	37
2	1953–54	60	Motherwell	45	Kilmarnock	42	Third Lanark*	36
2	1954–55	60	Airdrieonians	46	Dunfermline Ath	42	Hamilton A	39
2	1955–56	72	Queen's Park	54	Ayr U	51	St Johnstone	49
2	1956–57	72	Clyde	64	Third Lanark	51	Cowdenbeath	45
2	1957–58	72	Stirling Alb	55	Dunfermline Ath	53	Arbroath	47
2	1958–59	72	Ayr U	60	Arbroath	51	Stenhousemuir	46
2	1959–60	72	St Johnstone	53	Dundee U	50	Queen of the South	49
2	1960–61	72	Stirling Alb	55	Falkirk	54	Stenhousemuir	50
2	1961–62	72	Clyde	54	Queen of the South	53	Morton	44
2	1962–63	72	St Johnstone	55	East Stirlingshire	49	Morton	48
2	1963–64	72	Morton	67	Clyde	53	Arbroath	46
2	1964–65	72	Stirling Alb	59	Hamilton A	50	Queen of the South	45
2	1965–66	72	Ayr U	53	Airdrieonians	50	Queen of the South	47
2	1966–67	76	Morton	69	Raith R	58	Arbroath	57
2	1967–68	72	St Mirren	62	Arbroath	53	East Fife	49
2	1968–69	72	Motherwell	64	Ayr U	53	East Fife*	48
2	1969–70	72	Falkirk	56	Cowdenbeath	55	Queen of the South	50
2	1970–71	72	Partick Thistle	56	East Fife	51	Arbroath	46
2	1971–72	72	Dumbarton*	52	Arbroath	52	Stirling Alb*	50
2	1972–73	72	Clyde	56	Dumfermline Ath	52	Raith R*	47
2	1973–74	72	Airdrieonians	60	Kilmarnock	58	Hamilton A	55
2	1974–75	76	Falkirk	54	Queen of the South*	53	Montrose	53

Elected to First Division: 1894 Clyde; 1895 Hibernian; 1896 Abercorn; 1897 Partick Thistle; 1899 Kilmarnock; 1900 Morton and Partick Thistle; 1902 Port Glasgow and Partick Thistle; 1903 Airdrieonians and Motherwell; 1905 Falkirk and Aberdeen; 1906 Clyde and Hamilton A; 1910 Raith R; 1913 Ayr U and Dumbarton.

FIRST DIVISION (1975–76 to 2012–13)

2	1975–76	52	Partick Thistle	41	Kilmarnock	35	Montrose	30
2	1976–77	78	St Mirren	62	Clydebank	58	Dundee	51
2	1977–78	78	Morton*	58	Hearts	58	Dundee	57
2	1978–79	78	Dundee	55	Kilmarnock*	54	Clydebank	54
2	1979–80	78	Hearts	53	Airdrieonians	51	Ayr U*	44
2	1980–81	78	Hibernian	57	Dundee	52	St Johnstone	51
2	1981–82	78	Motherwell	61	Kilmarnock	51	Hearts	50
2	1982–83	78	St Johnstone	55	Hearts	54	Clydebank	50
2	1983–84	78	Morton	54	Dumbarton	51	Partick Thistle	46
2	1984–85	78	Motherwell	50	Clydebank	48	Falkirk	45
2	1985–86	78	Hamilton A	56	Falkirk	45	Kilmarnock*	44
2	1986–87	88	Morton	57	Dunfermline Ath	56	Dumbarton	53
2	1987–88	88	Hamilton A	56	Meadowbank Thistle	52	Clydebank	49
2	1988–89	78	Dunfermline Ath	54	Falkirk	52	Clydebank	48
2	1989–90	78	St Johnstone	58	Airdrieonians	54	Clydebank	44
2	1990–91	78	Falkirk	54	Airdrieonians	53	Dundee	52
2	1991–92	88	Dundee	58	Partick Thistle*	57	Hamilton A	57
2	1992–93	88	Raith R	65	Kilmarnock	54	Dunfermline Ath	52
2	1993–94	88	Falkirk	66	Dunfermline Ath	65	Airdrieonians	54
2	1994–95	108	Raith R	69	Dunfermline Ath*	68	Dundee	68
2	1995–96	108	Dunfermline Ath	71	Dundee U*	67	Greenock Morton	67
2	1996–97	108	St Johnstone	80	Airdrieonians	60	Dundee*	58
2	1997–98	108	Dundee	70	Falkirk	65	Raith R*	60
2	1998–99	108	Hibernian	89	Falkirk	66	Ayr U	62
2	1999–2000	108	St Mirren	76	Dunfermline Ath	71	Falkirk	68

2	2000–01	108	Livingston	76	Ayr U	69	Falkirk	56
2	2001–02	108	Partick Thistle	66	Airdrieonians	56	Ayr U*	52
2	2002–03	108	Falkirk	81	Clyde	72	St Johnstone	67
2	2003–04	108	Inverness CT	70	Clyde	69	St Johnstone	57
2	2004–05	108	Falkirk	75	St Mirren*	60	Clyde	60
2	2005–06	108	St Mirren	76	St Johnstone	66	Hamilton A	59
2	2006–07	108	Gretna	66	St Johnstone	65	Dundee*	53
2	2007–08	108	Hamilton A	76	Dundee	69	St Johnstone	58
2	2008–09	108	St Johnstone	65	Partick Thistle	55	Dunfermline Ath	51
2	2009–10	108	Inverness CT	73	Dundee	61	Dunfermline Ath	58
2	2010–11	108	Dunfermline Ath	70	Raith R	60	Falkirk	58
2	2011–12	108	Ross Co	79	Dundee	55	Falkirk	52
2	2012–13	108	Partick Thistle	78	Greenock Morton	67	Falkirk	53

SPFL SCOTTISH CHAMPIONSHIP (2013–14 to 2019–20)

2	2013–14	108	Dundee	69	Hamilton A	67	Falkirk§	66
2	2014–15	108	Hearts	91	Hibernian§	70	Rangers§	67
2	2015–16	108	Rangers	81	Falkirk*§	70	Hibernian§	70
2	2016–17	108	Hibernian	71	Falkirk§	60	Dundee U§	57
2	2017–18	108	St Mirren	74	Livingston	62	Dundee U§	61
2	2018–19	108	Ross Co	71	Dundee U§	65	Inverness CT§	56
2	2019–20	108	Dundee U	59	Inverness CT	45	Dundee	41

The 2019–20 season was curtailed due to the COVID-19 pandemic and positions awarded on a points-per-game basis.

SECOND DIVISION (1975–76 to 2012–13) – TIER 3

Tier	*Season*	*Max Pts*	*First*	*Pts*	*Second*	*Pts*	*Third*	*Pts*
3	1975–76	52	Clydebank*	40	Raith R	40	Alloa Ath	35
3	1976–77	78	Stirling Alb	55	Alloa Ath	51	Dunfermline Ath	50
3	1977–78	78	Clyde*	53	Raith R	53	Dunfermline Ath*	48
3	1978–79	78	Berwick Rangers	54	Dunfermline Ath	52	Falkirk	50
3	1979–80	78	Falkirk	50	East Stirlingshire	49	Forfar Ath	46
3	1980–81	78	Queen's Park	50	Queen of the South	46	Cowdenbeath	45
3	1981–82	78	Clyde	59	Alloa Ath*	50	Arbroath	50
3	1982–83	78	Brechin C	55	Meadowbank Thistle	54	Arbroath	49
3	1983–84	78	Forfar Ath	63	East Fife	47	Berwick Rangers	43
3	1984–85	78	Montrose	53	Alloa Ath	50	Dunfermline Ath	49
3	1985–86	78	Dunfermline Ath	57	Queen of the South	55	Meadowbank Thistle	49
3	1986–87	78	Meadowbank Thistle	55	Raith R*	52	Stirling Alb*	52
3	1987–88	78	Ayr U	61	St Johnstone	59	Queen's Park	51
3	1988–89	78	Albion R	50	Alloa Ath	45	Brechin C	43
3	1989–90	78	Brechin C	49	Kilmarnock	48	Stirling Alb	47
3	1990–91	78	Stirling Alb	54	Montrose	46	Cowdenbeath	45
3	1991–92	78	Dumbarton	52	Cowdenbeath	51	Alloa Ath	50
3	1992–93	78	Clyde	54	Brechin C*	53	Stranraer	53
3	1993–94	78	Stranraer	56	Berwick Rangers	48	Stenhousemuir*	47
3	1994–95	108	Greenock Morton	64	Dumbarton	60	Stirling Alb	58
3	1995–96	108	Stirling Alb	81	East Fife	67	Berwick Rangers	60
3	1996–97	108	Ayr U	77	Hamilton A	74	Livingston	64
3	1997–98	108	Stranraer	61	Clydebank	60	Livingston	59
3	1998–99	108	Livingston	77	Inverness CT	72	Clyde	53
3	1999–2000	108	Clyde	65	Alloa Ath	64	Ross Co	62
3	2000–01	108	Partick Thistle	75	Arbroath	58	Berwick Rangers*	54
3	2001–02	108	Queen of the South	67	Alloa Ath	59	Forfar Ath	53
3	2002–03	108	Raith R	59	Brechin C	55	Airdrie U	54
3	2003–04	108	Airdrie U	70	Hamilton A	62	Dumbarton	60
3	2004–05	108	Brechin C	72	Stranraer	63	Greenock Morton	62
3	2005–06	108	Gretna	88	Greenock Morton§	70	Peterhead*§	57
3	2006–07	108	Greenock Morton	77	Stirling Alb	69	Raith R§	62
3	2007–08	108	Ross Co	73	Airdrie U	66	Raith R§	60
3	2008–09	108	Raith R	76	Ayr U	74	Brechin C§	62
3	2009–10	108	Stirling Alb*	65	Alloa Ath§	65	Cowdenbeath	59
3	2010–11	108	Livingston	82	Ayr U*	59	Forfar Ath§	59
3	2011–12	108	Cowdenbeath	71	Arbroath§	63	Dumbarton	58
3	2012–13	108	Queen of the South	92	Alloa Ath	67	Brechin C	61

SPFL SCOTTISH LEAGUE ONE (2013–14 to 2019–20)

3	2013–14	108	Rangers	102	Dunfermline Ath§	63	Stranraer§	51
3	2014–15	108	Greenock Morton	69	Stranraer§	67	Forfar Ath	66
3	2015–16	108	Dunfermline Ath	79	Ayr U	61	Peterhead§	59
3	2016–17	108	Livingston	81	Alloa Ath§	62	Airdrieonians§	52
3	2017–18	108	Ayr U	76	Raith R§	75	Alloa Ath	60
3	2018–19	108	Arbroath	70	Forfar Ath§	63	Raith R§	60
3	2019–20	108	Raith R	53	Falkirk	52	Airdrieonians	48

The 2019–20 season was curtailed due to the COVID-19 pandemic and positions awarded on a points-per-game basis.

THIRD DIVISION (1994–95 to 2012–13) – TIER 4

Tier	*Season*	*Max Pts*	*First*	*Pts*	*Second*	*Pts*	*Third*	*Pts*
4	1994–95	108	Forfar Ath	80	Montrose	67	Ross Co	60
4	1995–96	108	Livingston	72	Brechin C	63	Inverness CT	57
4	1996–97	108	Inverness CT	76	Forfar Ath*	67	Ross Co	67
4	1997–98	108	Alloa Ath	76	Arbroath	68	Ross Co	67
4	1998–99	108	Ross Co	77	Stenhousemuir	64	Brechin C	59
4	1999–2000	108	Queen's Park	69	Berwick Rangers	66	Forfar Ath	61
4	2000–01	108	Hamilton A*	76	Cowdenbeath	76	Brechin C	72

4	2001–02	108	Brechin C	73	Dumbarton	61	Albion R	59
4	2002–03	108	Greenock Morton	72	East Fife	71	Albion R	70
4	2003–04	108	Stranraer	79	Stirling Alb	77	Gretna	68
4	2004–05	108	Gretna	98	Peterhead	78	Cowdenbeath	51
4	2005–06	108	Cowdenbeath*	76	Berwick Rangers§	76	Stenhousemuir§	73
4	2006–07	108	Berwick Rangers	75	Arbroath§	70	Queen's Park	68
4	2007–08	108	East Fife	88	Stranraer	65	Montrose§	59
4	2008–09	108	Dumbarton	67	Cowdenbeath	63	East Stirlingshire§	61
4	2009–10	108	Livingston	78	Forfar Ath	63	East Stirlingshire§	61
4	2010–11	108	Arbroath	66	Albion R	61	Queen's Park*§	59
4	2011–12	108	Alloa Ath	77	Queen's Park§	63	Stranraer	58
4	2012–13	108	Rangers	83	Peterhead§	59	Queen's Park§	56

SPFL SCOTTISH LEAGUE TWO (2013–14 to 2019–20)

4	2013–14	108	Peterhead	76	Annan Ath§	63	Stirling Alb	57
4	2014–15	108	Albion R	71	Queen's Park§	61	Arbroath§	56
4	2015–16	108	East Fife	62	Elgin C§	59	Clyde§	56
4	2016–17	108	Abroath	66	Forfar Ath	64	Annan Ath§	58
4	2017–18	108	Montrose	77	Peterhead§	76	Stirling Alb§	55
4	2018–19	108	Peterhead	79	Clyde	74	Edinburgh C§	67
4	2019–20	108	Cove Rangers	68	Edinburgh C	55	Elgin C	43

The 2019–20 season was curtailed due to the COVID-19 pandemic and positions awarded on a points-per-game basis.

RELEGATED CLUBS

RELEGATED FROM DIVISION I (1921–22 to 1973–74)

1921–22 *Dumbarton, Queen's Park, Clydebank
1922–23 Albion R, Alloa Ath
1923–24 Clyde, Clydebank
1924–25 Ayr U, Third Lanark
1925–26 Raith R, Clydebank
1926–27 Morton, Dundee U
1927–28 Bo'ness, Dunfermline Ath
1928–29 Third Lanark, Raith R
1929–30 Dundee U, St Johnstone
1930–31 Hibernian, East Fife
1931–32 Dundee U, Leith Ath
1932–33 Morton, East Stirlingshire
1933–34 Third Lanark, Cowdenbeath
1934–35 St Mirren, Falkirk
1935–36 Airdrieonians, Ayr U
1936–37 Dunfermline Ath, Albion R
1937–38 Dundee, Morton
1938–39 Queen's Park, Raith R
1946–47 Kilmarnock, Hamilton A
1947–48 Airdrieonians, Queen's Park
1948–49 Morton, Albion R
1949–50 Queen of the South, Stirling Alb
1950–51 Clyde, Falkirk
1951–52 Morton, Stirling Alb
1952–53 Motherwell, Third Lanark
1953–54 Airdrieonians, Hamilton A
1954–55 *No clubs relegated as league extended to 18 teams*
1955–56 Clyde, Stirling Alb
1956–57 Dunfermline Ath, Ayr U
1957–58 East Fife, Queen's Park
1958–59 Falkirk, Queen of the South
1959–60 Stirling Alb, Arbroath
1960–61 Clyde, Ayr U
1961–62 St Johnstone, Stirling Alb
1962–63 Clyde, Raith R
1963–64 Queen of the South, East Stirlingshire
1964–65 Airdrieonians, Third Lanark
1965–66 Morton, Hamilton A
1966–67 St Mirren, Ayr U
1967–68 Motherwell, Stirling Alb
1968–69 Falkirk, Arbroath
1969–70 Raith R, Partick Thistle
1970–71 St Mirren, Cowdenbeath
1971–72 Clyde, Dunfermline Ath
1972–73 Kilmarnock, Airdrieonians
1973–74 East Fife, Falkirk

**Season 1921–22 – only 1 club promoted, 3 clubs relegated.*

RELEGATED FROM PREMIER DIVISION (1974–75 to 1997–98)

1974–75 *No relegation due to League reorganisation*
1975–76 Dundee, St Johnstone
1976–77 Hearts, Kilmarnock
1977–78 Ayr U, Clydebank
1978–79 Hearts, Motherwell
1979–80 Dundee, Hibernian
1980–81 Kilmarnock, Hearts
1981–82 Partick Thistle, Airdrieonians
1982–83 Morton, Kilmarnock
1983–84 St Johnstone, Motherwell
1984–85 Dumbarton, Morton
1985–86 *No relegation due to League reorganisation*
1986–87 Clydebank, Hamilton A
1987–88 Falkirk, Dunfermline Ath, Morton
1988–89 Hamilton A
1989–90 Dundee
1990–91 *No clubs relegated*
1991–92 St Mirren, Dunfermline Ath
1992–93 Falkirk, Airdrieonians
1993–94 St Johnstone, Raith R, Dundee
1994–95 Dundee U
1995–96 Partick Thistle, Falkirk
1996–97 Raith R
1997–98 Hibernian

RELEGATED FROM PREMIER LEAGUE (1998–99 to 2012–13)

1998–99 Dunfermline Ath
1999–2000 *No relegation due to League reorganisation*
2000–01 St Mirren
2001–02 St Johnstone
2002–03 *No clubs relegated*
2003–04 Partick Thistle
2005–06 Livingston
2006–07 Dunfermline Ath
2007–08 Gretna
2008–09 Inverness CT
2009–10 Falkirk
2010–11 Hamilton A
2011–12 Dunfermline Ath, Rangers (demoted to Third Division)
2012–13 Dundee

RELEGATED FROM SPFL SCOTTISH PREMIERSHIP (2013–14 to 2019–20)

2013–14 Hibernian, Hearts
2014–15 St Mirren
2015–16 Dundee U
2016–17 Inverness CT
2017–18 Ross Co, Partick Thistle
2018–19 Dundee
2019–20 Hearts

RELEGATED FROM FIRST DIVISION (1975–76 to 2012–13)

1975–76 Dunfermline Ath, Clyde
1976–77 Raith R, Falkirk
1977–78 Alloa Ath, East Fife
1978–79 Montrose, Queen of the South
1979–80 Arbroath, Clyde
1980–81 Stirling Alb, Berwick Rangers
1981–82 East Stirlingshire, Queen of the South
1982–83 Dunfermline Ath, Queen's Park
1983–84 Raith R, Alloa Ath
1984–85 Meadowbank Thistle, St Johnstone
1985–86 Ayr U, Alloa Ath
1986–87 Brechin C, Montrose
1987–88 East Fife, Dumbarton
1988–89 Kilmarnock, Queen of the South
1989–90 Albion R, Alloa Ath
1990–91 Clyde, Brechin C
1991–92 Montrose, Forfar Ath
1992–93 Meadowbank Thistle, Cowdenbeath
1993–94 Dumbarton, Stirling Alb, Clyde, Morton, Brechin C
1994–95 Ayr U, Stranraer
1995–96 Hamilton A, Dumbarton
1996–97 Clydebank, East Fife
1997–98 Partick Thistle, Stirling Alb
1998–99 Hamilton A, Stranraer
1999–2000 Clydebank
2000–01 Greenock Morton, Alloa Ath
2001–02 Raith R
2002–03 Alloa Ath, Arbroath
2003–04 Ayr U, Brechin C
2004–05 Partick Thistle, Raith R
2005–06 Stranraer, Brechin C
2006–07 Airdrie U, Ross Co
2007–08 Stirling Alb
2008–09 Livingstone *(for breaching rules)*, Clyde
2009–10 Airdrie U, Ayr U
2010–11 Cowdenbeath, Stirling Alb
2011–12 Ayr U, Queen of the South
2012–13 Dunfermline Ath, Airdrie U

RELEGATED FROM SPFL SCOTTISH CHAMPIONSHIP (2013–14 to 2019–20)

2013–14 Greenock Morton
2014–15 Cowdenbeath
2015–16 Livingston, Alloa Ath
2016–17 Raith R, Ayr U
2017–18 Brechin C, Dumbarton
2018–19 Falkirk
2019–20 Partick Thistle

RELEGATED FROM SECOND DIVISION (1993–94 to 2012–13)

1993–94 Alloa Ath, Forfar Ath, East Stirlingshire, Montrose, Queen's Park, Arbroath, Albion R, Cowdenbeath
1994–95 Meadowbank Thistle, Brechin C
1995–96 Forfar Ath, Montrose
1996–97 Dumbarton, Berwick Rangers
1997–98 Stenhousemuir, Brechin C
1998–99 East Fife, Forfar Ath
1999–2000 Hamilton A *(after being deducted 15 points)*
2000–01 Queen's Park, Stirling Alb
2001–02 Greenock Morton
2002–03 Stranraer, Cowdenbeath
2003–04 East Fife, Stenhousemuir
2004–05 Arbroath, Berwick Rangers
2005–06 Dumbarton
2006–07 Stranraer, Forfar Ath
2007–08 Cowdenbeath, Berwick Rangers
2008–09 Queen's Park, Stranraer
2009–10 Arbroath, Clyde
2010–11 Alloa Ath, Peterhead
2011–12 Stirling Alb
2012–13 Albion R

RELEGATED FROM SPFL SCOTTISH LEAGUE ONE (2013–14 to 2019–20)

2013–14 East Fife, Arbroath
2014–15 Stirling Alb
2015–16 Cowdenbeath, Forfar Ath
2016–17 Peterhead, Stenhousmuir
2017–18 Albion R, Queen's Park
2018–19 Stenhousemuir, Brechin C
2019–20 Stranraer

RELEGATED FROM SPFL SCOTTISH LEAGUE TWO (2015–16 to 2019–20)

2015–16 East Stirlingshire
2016–17 None
2017–18 None
2018–19 Berwick Rangers
2019–20 None

SCOTTISH LEAGUE CHAMPIONSHIP WINS

Rangers 54, Celtic 51, Aberdeen 4, Hearts 4, Hibernian 4, Dumbarton 2, Dundee 1, Dundee U 1, Kilmarnock 1, Motherwell 1, Third Lanark 1.

The totals for Rangers and Dumbarton each include the shared championship of 1890–91.

Since the formation of the Scottish Football League in 1890, there have been periodic reorganisations of the leagues to allow for expansion, improve competition and commercial aspects of the game. The table below lists the league names by tier and chronology. This table can be used to assist when studying the records.

Tier	Division	
1	Scottish League Division I	1890–1939
	Scottish League Division A	1946–1956
	Scottish League Division I	1956–1975
	Premier Division	1975–1998
	Scottish Premier League	1998–2013
	SPFL Premiership	2013–
2	Scottish League Division II	1893–1939
	Scottish League Division B	1946–1956
	Scottish League Division II	1956–1975
	First Division	1975–2013
	SPFL Championship	2013–
3	Scottish League Division III	1923–1926
	Scottish League Division C	1946–1949
	Second Division	1975–2013
	SPFL League One	2013–
4	Third Division	1994–2013
	SPFL League Two	2013–

In 2013–14 the SPFL introduced play-offs to determine a second promotion/relegation place for the Premiership, Championship and League One.

The team finishing second bottom of the Premiership plays two legs against the team from the Championship that won the eliminator games played between the teams finishing second, third and fourth.

For both the Championship and League One, the team finishing second bottom joins the teams from second, third and fourth places of the lower league in a play-off series of two-legged semi-finals and finals.

In 2014–15 a play-off was introduced for promotion/relegation from League Two. The team finishing bottom of League Two plays two legs against the victors of the eliminator games between the winners of the Highland and Lowland leagues.

SCOTTISH LEAGUE CUP FINALS 1946–2020

SCOTTISH LEAGUE CUP

1946–47	Rangers v Aberdeen	4-0
1947–48	East Fife v Falkirk	0-0*
Replay	East Fife v Falkirk	4-1
1948–49	Rangers v Raith R	2-0
1949–50	East Fife v Dunfermline Ath	3-0
1950–51	Motherwell v Hibernian	3-0
1951–52	Dundee v Rangers	3-2
1952–53	Dundee v Kilmarnock	2-0
1953–54	East Fife v Partick Thistle	3-2
1954–55	Hearts v Motherwell	4-2
1955–56	Aberdeen v St Mirren	2-1
1956–57	Celtic v Partick Thistle	0-0*
Replay	Celtic v Partick Thistle	3-0
1957–58	Celtic v Rangers	7-1
1958–59	Hearts v Partick Thistle	5-1
1959–60	Hearts v Third Lanark	2-1
1960–61	Rangers v Kilmarnock	2-0
1961–62	Rangers v Hearts	1-1*
Replay	Rangers v Hearts	3-1
1962–63	Hearts v Kilmarnock	1-0
1963–64	Rangers v Morton	5-0
1964–65	Rangers v Celtic	2-1
1965–66	Celtic v Rangers	2-1
1966–67	Celtic v Rangers	1-0
1967–68	Celtic v Dundee	5-3
1968–69	Celtic v Hibernian	6-2
1969–70	Celtic v St Johnstone	1-0
1970–71	Rangers v Celtic	1-0
1971–72	Partick Thistle v Celtic	4-1
1972–73	Hibernian v Celtic	2-1
1973–74	Dundee v Celtic	1-0
1974–75	Celtic v Hibernian	6-3
1975–76	Rangers v Celtic	1-0
1976–77	Aberdeen v Celtic	2-1*
1977–78	Rangers v Celtic	2-1*
1978–79	Rangers v Aberdeen	2-1

BELL'S LEAGUE CUP

1979–80	Dundee U v Aberdeen	0-0*
Replay	Dundee U v Aberdeen	3-0
1980–81	Dundee U v Dundee	3-0

SCOTTISH LEAGUE CUP

1981–82	Rangers v Dundee U	2-1
1982–83	Celtic v Rangers	2-1
1983–84	Rangers v Celtic	3-2*

SKOL CUP

1984–85	Rangers v Dundee U	1-0
1985–86	Aberdeen v Hibernian	3-0
1986–87	Rangers v Celtic	2-1
1987–88	Rangers v Aberdeen	3-3*
	Rangers won 5-3 on penalties.	
1988–89	Rangers v Aberdeen	3-2
1989–90	Aberdeen v Rangers	2-1*
1990–91	Rangers v Celtic	2-1*
1991–92	Hibernian v Dunfermline Ath	2-0
1992–93	Rangers v Aberdeen	2-1*

SCOTTISH LEAGUE CUP

1993–94	Rangers v Hibernian	2-1

COCA-COLA CUP

1994–95	Raith R v Celtic	2-2*
	Raith R won 6-5 on penalties.	
1995–96	Aberdeen v Dundee	2-0
1996–97	Rangers v Hearts	4-3
1997–98	Celtic v Dundee U	3-0

SCOTTISH LEAGUE CUP

1998–99	Rangers v St Johnstone	2-1

CIS INSURANCE CUP

1999–2000	Celtic v Aberdeen	2-0
2000–01	Celtic v Kilmarnock	3-0
2001–02	Rangers v Ayr U	4-0
2002–03	Rangers v Celtic	2-1
2003–04	Livingston v Hibernian	2-0
2004–05	Rangers v Motherwell	5-1
2005–06	Celtic v Dunfermline Ath	3-0
2006–07	Hibernian v Kilmarnock	5-1
2007–08	Rangers v Dundee U	2-2*
	Rangers won 3-2 on penalties.	

CO-OPERATIVE INSURANCE CUP

2008–09	Celtic v Rangers	2-0*
2009–10	Rangers v St Mirren	1-0
2010–11	Rangers v Celtic	2-1*

SCOTTISH COMMUNITIES LEAGUE CUP

2011–12	Kilmarnock v Celtic	1-0
2012–13	St Mirren v Hearts	3-2
2013–14	Aberdeen v Inverness CT	0-0*
	Aberdeen won 4-2 on penalties.	

SCOTTISH LEAGUE CUP PRESENTED BY QTS

2014–15	Celtic v Dundee U	2-0
2015–16	Ross Co v Hibernian	2-1

BETFRED SCOTTISH LEAGUE CUP

2016–17	Celtic v Aberdeen	3-0
2017–18	Celtic v Motherwell	2-0
2018–19	Celtic v Aberdeen	1-0
2019–20	Celtic v Rangers	1-0

**After extra time.*

SCOTTISH LEAGUE CUP WINS

Rangers 27, Celtic 19, Aberdeen 6, Hearts 4, Dundee 3, East Fife 3, Hibernian 3, Dundee U 2, Kilmarnock 1, Livingston 1, Motherwell 1, Partick Thistle 1, Raith R 1, Ross Co 1, St Mirren 1.

APPEARANCES IN FINALS

Rangers 35, Celtic 34, Aberdeen 15, Hibernian 10, Dundee U 7, Hearts 7, Dundee 6, Kilmarnock 6, Motherwell 4, Partick Thistle 4, Dunfermline Ath 3, East Fife 3, St Mirren 3, Raith R 2, St Johnstone 2, Ayr U 1, Falkirk 1, Inverness CT 1, Livingston 1, Morton 1, Ross Co 1, Third Lanark 1.

BETFRED SCOTTISH LEAGUE CUP 2019–20

▪ *Denotes player sent off.*
PW = Drawn match won on penalties (2 pts).
PL = Drawn match lost on penalties (1 pt).
* *Qualified for Second Round as best runners-up.*

NORTHERN SECTION

FIRST ROUND – GROUP A

Friday, 12 July 2019

Hearts (1) 1 *(Irving 44)*

Dundee U (1) 1 *(Shankland 9)* 9091

Hearts: (442) Zlamal; Smith, Souttar, Berra, Hickey; Walker (McDonald 80), Clare, Irving▪, Mulraney (Zanatta 75); Washington, Ikpeazu (Bozanic 84).
Dundee U: (4411) Siegrist; Smith L, Connolly, Reynolds, Sporle (Butcher 46); McMullan, Stanton (Banks 73), Bouhenna, Robson; Clark; Shankland (Appere 63).
Hearts won 5-3 on penalties.

Saturday, 13 July 2019

Cowdenbeath (2) 2 *(Buchanan 17, Taylor 27)*

East Fife (0) 0 469

Cowdenbeath: (4132) Dabrowski; Pyper, Todd, Barr, Mullen; Miller; Cox (Allan 82), Thomas, Buchanan; Taylor, Kris Renton (Herd 89).
East Fife: (442) Long; Watson C, Dunlop, Slattery, Higgins; Denholm (Smith 75), Murdoch, Hunter (Agnew 63), Watt (Dowds 63); Wallace, Duggan.

Tuesday, 16 July 2019

Cowdenbeath (0) 0

Hearts (2) 2 *(Halkett 8, McDonald 22)* 2311

Cowdenbeath: (442) Dabrowski; Pyper, Todd, Barr, Mullen; Buchanan, Miller, Thomas (Herd 84), Taylor (Allan 80); Cox, Kris Renton.
Hearts: (442) Zlamal; Smith, Berra, Halkett, Burns; McDonald, Clare, Bozanic, Zanatta (Walker 85); MacLean (Keena 76), Washington (Ikpeazu 61).

Stenhousemuir (0) 1 *(Munro A 70)*

Dundee U (0) 2 *(Watson 51, Butcher 54)* 1156

Stenhousemuir: (442) Marley; Hopkirk, Munro A, McKernon, McIlduff; McLaughlin, Halleran, Munro M, Cook (Daramola 84); McGuigan (Anderson 67), Scullion (Luke 84).
Dundee U: (4231) Siegrist; Watson, Connolly, Harkes (Stanton 53), Robson; Reynolds, Butcher (King 63); McMullan (Smith C 67), Appere, Chalmers; Shankland.

Friday, 19 July 2019

Dundee U (1) 3 *(Sporle 26, Shankland 59, Appere 86)*

Cowdenbeath (0) 0 2526

Dundee U: (442) Mehmet; Smith L, Connolly, Reynolds, Sporle; McMullan (Chalmers 76), Stanton, Butcher, Banks (Appere 81); Clark (Harkes 77), Shankland.
Cowdenbeath: (442) Dabrowski; Herd (Allan 46), Todd, Pyper, Mullen; Buchanan, Thomas, Miller, Taylor; Cox, Kris Renton.

Saturday, 20 July 2019

East Fife (0) 2 *(Agnew 56, 86 (pen))*

Stenhousemuir (0) 0 308

East Fife: (442) Hart; Dunsmore, Dunlop, Higgins, Slattery; Denholm (Watt 83), Murdoch, Hunter (Smith 76), Agnew; Dowds (Davidson R 77), Duggan.
Stenhousemuir: (352) Smith; Munro A, Marsh, McKernon; O'Neil, Halleran (Munro M 63), Hopkirk, Anderson (Cook 57), McIlduff; McGuigan (Watters 77), Scullion.

Tuesday, 23 July 2019

Dundee U (0) 0

East Fife (1) 2 *(Dunsmore 38, Watt 51)* 2778

Dundee U: (442) Siegrist; Smith L, Watson, Reynolds, Sporle (Robson 54); McMullan, Stanton, Butcher, Banks (Appere 58); Shankland, Clark (Mochrie 71).
East Fife: (442) Hart; Murdoch, Dunlop, Watson C, Slattery; Dunsmore, Agnew, Davidson R, Watt (Denholm 72); Wallace (Duggan 65), Dowds (Hunter 80).

Wednesday, 24 July 2019

Hearts (0) 2 *(Halkett 82, 87)*

Stenhousemuir (0) 1 *(McGuigan 77)* 7299

Hearts: (442) Zlamal; Smith, Souttar, Halkett, Hickey; McDonald (Mulraney 57), Clare, Bozanic, Walker; MacLean (Ikpeazu 57), Washington (Keena 60).
Stenhousemuir: (442) Smith; McLaughlin, Munro A, Marsh, McIlduff; Scullion (Anderson 90), McKernon (Watters 83), Munro M (Halleran 63), Cook; McGuigan, Hopkirk.

Saturday, 27 July 2019

East Fife (0) 1 *(Duggan 54)*

Hearts (1) 1 *(Walker 15)* 1998

East Fife: (442) Long; Murdoch, Dunlop, Higgins, Slattery; Watt (Dowds 80), Agnew, Hunter (Davidson R 63), Dunsmore; Wallace, Duggan.
Hearts: (4411) Zlamal; Smith, Halkett, Berra, Hickey; Zanatta (Keena 63), Clare, Irving (Bozanic 68), Mulraney; Walker; Ikpeazu (MacLean 80).
East Fife won 7-6 on penalties.

Stenhousemuir (1) 2 *(McGuigan 33, Todd 85 (og))*

Cowdenbeath (0) 0 262

Stenhousemuir: (442) Smith; McLaughlin, Munro A, Marsh, McIlduff; Luke (Scullion 65), Dykes, Munro M, Cook; Hopkirk, McGuigan (Anderson 90).
Cowdenbeath: (442) Dabrowski; Pyper, Todd, Barr, Valentine (Mullen 83); Buchanan, Thomas, Miller (Swan 84), Taylor; Allan, Cox.

Group A Table	P	W	PW	PL	L	F	A	GD	Pts
Hearts	4	2	1	1	0	6	3	3	9
East Fife*	4	2	1	0	1	5	3	2	8
Dundee U	4	2	0	1	1	6	4	2	7
Stenhousemuir	4	1	0	0	3	4	6	–2	3
Cowdenbeath	4	1	0	0	3	2	7	–5	3

FIRST ROUND – GROUP B

Saturday, 13 July 2019

Forfar Ath (2) 3 *(Travis 20, Kirkpatrick 45, Andrew Jackson 65)*

Brechin C (0) 0 462

Forfar Ath: (433) McCallum; Meechan, Travis, Whyte, Burns; Forbes (Coupe 66), Irvine (Robertson 70), Docherty; Hilson, Andrew Jackson (Aitken 80), Kirkpatrick.
Brechin C: (451) McMinn; McIntosh, Smith, Reekie, Duncanson; Reid, Brown, Inglis, McCord, Knox; McManus.

Ross Co (2) 4 *(Mullin 7, Ross C Stewart 13, 46, McKay 85)*

Montrose (0) 1 *(Allan 51)* 1159

Ross Co: (442) Laidlaw; Fraser M, Watson, Fontaine, Kelly S; Mullin (Power 78), Lindsay, Chalmers (Vigurs 69), Spittal; Ross C Stewart (McKay 60), Graham.
Montrose: (442) Lennox; Cammy Ballantyne, Allan, Dillon, Steeves; Webster, Callaghan, Cregg (Masson 56), Lyons (Rennie 69); Milne, Skelly (McLean 55).

Tuesday, 16 July 2019

Brechin C (0) 0

Ross Co (2) 4 *(Ross C Stewart 33, 44, McKay 49, Spittal 75)* 272

Brechin C: (451) O'Neil; McIntosh, Reekie, Hill, McLaughlin; Hamilton (Reid 62), Brown (Inglis 61), McCord, Watt (Duncanson 72), Knox; McManus.
Ross Co: (442) Laidlaw; Fraser M (Watson 76), Morris, Grivosti, Chalmers; Mullin (Spittal 62), Vigurs, Paton, Power; Ross C Stewart (Graham 61), McKay.

Montrose (0) 1 *(Masson 72)*

St Johnstone (0) 0 866

Montrose: (451) Fleming; Cammy Ballantyne, Allan, Dillon, Steeves; Milne, Masson, Cregg, Watson (Callaghan 71), Rennie (Lyons 57); McLean (Skelly 71).
St Johnstone: (433) Parish; Foster, Duffy, Kerr, Tanser; Callachan (McMillan 75), Davidson, McCann; Swanson (McClean 68), Hendry, O'Halloran.

Saturday, 20 July 2019

Montrose (1) 1 *(Skelly 9 (pen))*

Forfar Ath (1) 4 *(Hilson 25 (pen), 45 (pen), Travis 56, 71)* 611

Montrose: (433) Lennox (Fleming 18); Cammy Ballantyne, Waddell (Lyons 54), Dillon, Steeves; Masson, Cregg, Callaghan; Webster, Rennie, Skelly (Campbell R 65).
Forfar Ath: (451) McCallum; Bain (Meechan 76), Docherty, Travis, Burns; Coupe (Forbes 65), Robertson (Andrew Jackson 72), Irvine, Tapping, Kirkpatrick; Hilson.

Sunday, 21 July 2019

St Johnstone (1) 1 *(Tanser 8 (pen))*

Ross Co (2) 2 *(McKay 30, 45)* 1648

St Johnstone: (442) Clark; Foster, Anderson, Kerr, Tanser; Wotherspoon (Kennedy 46), Davidson, Craig, Swanson (Hendry 68); O'Halloran, Kane (McMillan 78).
Ross Co: (433) Laidlaw; Watson, Grivosti (Fraser M 85), Fontaine, Kelly S; Mullin, Vigurs, Chalmers; Ross C Stewart, McKay (Graham 76), Spittal (Gardyne 69).

Wednesday, 24 July 2019

Ross Co (1) 2 *(Graham 15, 76)*

Forfar Ath (0) 0 1002

Ross Co: (4411) Laidlaw; Fraser M, Morris, Fontaine, Kelly S; Gardyne, Paton (Chalmers 72), Vigurs, Spittal (Power 62); McKay (Ross C Stewart 62); Graham.
Forfar Ath: (4411) McCallum; Meechan, Docherty, Whyte, Bain; Coupe, Robertson (Aitken 72), MacKintosh (Irvine 53), Forbes (Kirkpatrick 74); Tapping; Andrew Jackson.

St Johnstone (2) 4 *(Tanser 6 (pen), Kane 33, Hendry 74, Kennedy 76)*

Brechin C (0) 0 1497

St Johnstone: (442) Clark; Foster, Kerr, Duffy, Tanser; Swanson, Davidson, McClean (McCann 78), Kennedy; Kane (Hendry 60), O'Halloran (Northcott 68).
Brechin C: (451) McMinn; McIntosh, Reekie, Hill, McLaughlin; Reid, Brown, McCord (Duncanson 64), Inglis, Knox; McManus (Crawford 46).

Saturday, 27 July 2019

Brechin C (0) 1 *(Reekie 73)*

Montrose (0) 1 *(Campbell R 57)* 405

Brechin C: (442) Sinclair; Duncanson, Reekie, Hill, McLaughlin; Reid (Crawford 71), McIntosh, Brown (Inglis 65), Knox; McManus (Ngoy 87), Hamilton.
Montrose: (352) Lennox; Waddell, Allan (Lyons 46), Dillon; Webster, Masson, Cregg, Milne, Steeves; Campbell R (McLean 74), Skelly (Rennie 65).
Montrose won 4-2 on penalties.

Forfar Ath (1) 2 *(Tapping 2, Forbes 53)*

St Johnstone (0) 1 *(Kennedy 65)* 1009

Forfar Ath: (442) McCallum; Meechan, Whyte, Travis, Burns; Forbes (Coupe 74), Irvine (Robertson 85), Tapping, Kirkpatrick; Hilson, Andrew Jackson (Aitken 88).
St Johnstone: (433) Parish; Duffy, Kerr, Vihmann, Tanser (Callachan 46); McCann, McClean (McMillan 58), Craig; Swanson (Northcott 72), Hendry, Kennedy.

Group B Table	*P*	*W*	*PW*	*PL*	*L*	*F*	*A*	*GD*	*Pts*
Ross Co	4	4	0	0	0	12	2	10	12
Forfar Ath*	4	3	0	0	1	9	4	5	9
Montrose	4	1	1	0	2	4	9	–5	5
St Johnstone	4	1	0	0	3	6	5	1	3
Brechin C	4	0	0	1	3	1	12	–11	1

FIRST ROUND – GROUP C

Saturday, 13 July 2019

Arbroath (1) 2 *(Kader 44, Doris 90)*

Elgin C (1) 1 *(Sutherland 29)* 485

Arbroath: (442) Jamieson; Thomson, Little, O'Brien, Hamilton; Kader, Whatley (Gold 70), Swankie, Linn; Doris, Spence (McKenna 70).
Elgin C: (442) McHale; Wilson, McDonald, Bronsky, Spark; Cooper, Omar, Dingwall, McHardy (MacEwan 79); Hester (Willis 88), Sutherland.

Stirling Alb (0) 1 *(Wilson 70)*

Hibernian (1) 1 *(Allan S 44 (pen))* 2184

Stirling Alb: (4411) Currie; McLean (Truesdale 58), McGregor, McGeachie, Lowdon; Jardine, Wilson, Docherty, Thomson; Willis (Peters 86); Hawke (Mackin 65).
Hibernian: (433) Maxwell; Whittaker, Hanlon, Jackson, James; Campbell, Allan S, Horgan; Doidge, Newell (Murray 72), Mallan.
Hibernian won 5-4 on penalties.

Tuesday, 16 July 2019

Alloa Ath (0) 3 *(Trouten 54, Buchanan 57, Cawley 75)*

Elgin C (1) 3 *(Dingwall 30, Sutherland 55, Bronsky 88)* 316

Alloa Ath: (442) Parry; Robertson, Graham, Taggart, Dick; Cawley, Hetherington, Flannigan, Brown (Stirling 69); Trouten, Buchanan (O'Hara 69).
Elgin C: (442) McHale; Wilson, McGowan, Bronsky, Spark; Cooper, Dingwall, MacEwan, Omar (Sopel 80); Willis (O'Keefe 62), Sutherland.
Elgin C won 6-5 on penalties.

Wednesday, 17 July 2019

Stirling Alb (0) 1 *(Mackin 47)*

Arbroath (2) 6 *(Gold 1, 57, McKenna 28, Hamilton 82, Spence 87, 90)* 474

Stirling Alb: (433) Binnie; Truesdale, Banner (McGregor 46), McGeachie, Lowdon; Jardine (Heaver 67), Wilson, Docherty; Thomson, Mackin, Scott (Peters 78).
Arbroath: (442) Gaston; Thomson (Murphy 37), Wilson, O'Brien, Hamilton; McKenna, Whatley, Gold, Linn; Doris (Spence 46), Swankie (Kader 63).

Saturday, 20 July 2019

Elgin C (2) 3 *(Sutherland 7, 80, Hester 13)*

Stirling Alb (0) 0 507

Elgin C: (442) McHale; Wilson, Bronsky, McDonald (McGowan 85), Spark; Cooper, MacEwan, Dingwall, O'Keefe (Willis 74); Sutherland, Hester (Loveland 82).
Stirling Alb: (442) Currie; McLean, McGregor, Rodger, Lowdon; Wright, Docherty, Wilson (Jardine 50), Heaver (Mackin 65); Willis, Peters (Hawke 56).

Hibernian (0) 2 *(Doidge 68, James 84)*

Alloa Ath (0) 0 5470

Hibernian: (442) Marciano; Whittaker, McGregor, Hanlon, James; Boyle (Shaw 85), Mallan, Campbell (Murray 46), Horgan; Doidge, Kamberi (Allan S 46).
Alloa Ath: (442) Parry (Henry 72); Robertson, Graham, Taggart, Dick; Cawley, Hetherington, Flannigan, Brown; O'Hara, Trouten (Buchanan 63).

Tuesday, 23 July 2019

Alloa Ath (0) 2 *(O'Hara 69, Buchanan 86)*

Stirling Alb (0) 1 *(Wilson 51)* 412

Alloa Ath: (442) Henry; Robertson, Graham, Taggart, Dick; Cawley, Hetherington, Flannigan, Stirling (Trouten 58); Buchanan, O'Hara.
Stirling Alb: (451) Binnie; McLean, McGeachie, McGregor (Banner 40), Lowdon; Thomson (Mackin 83), Docherty, Jardine, Wilson (Nicoll 77), Willis; Hawke.

Hibernian (2) 3 *(Kamberi 3, Allan S 44 (pen), Murray 87)*

Arbroath (0) 0 4769

Hibernian: (4141) Maxwell; James, Jackson, Hanlon, Mackie; Vela (Murray 59); Boyle (Horgan 78), Mallan, Allan S, Newell (Shaw 78); Kamberi.
Arbroath: (442) Jamieson; Thomson, Wilson, O'Brien, Hamilton; McKenna, Whatley (Kader 60), Gold, Linn (Stewart 46); Doris (Spence 60), Murphy.

Friday, 26 July 2019

Elgin C (0) 0

Hibernian (1) 2 *(Newell 10, Kamberi 62)* 2106

Elgin C: (442) McHale; Wilson (Willis 78), Bronsky, McDonald, Spark; Cooper, MacEwan (O'Keefe 60), Dingwall, Omar (Loveland 88); Sutherland, Hester.
Hibernian: (442) Marciano; Whittaker, McGregor, Jackson, Mackie; Horgan (Boyle 66), Mallan, Vela, Newell; Kamberi (Shaw 83), Doidge (Allan S 76).

Saturday, 27 July 2019

Arbroath (1) 2 *(Linn 18, Thomson 74)*

Alloa Ath (1) 3 *(Buchanan 18, Trouten 51, 78)* 590

Arbroath: (442) Gaston; Thomson, Little, O'Brien, Hamilton; Kader (Stewart 28), Swankie, Gold, Linn; Doris (Donnelly 67), Spence (McKenna 67).
Alloa Ath: (442) Henry; Robertson, Graham, Taggart, Dick; Cawley, Brown, Flannigan, Trouten; Buchanan (Thomson 63), O'Hara (Stirling 75).

Group C Table	P	W	PW	PL	L	F	A	GD	Pts
Hibernian	4	3	1	0	0	8	1	7	11
Alloa Ath	4	2	0	1	1	8	8	0	7
Arbroath	4	2	0	0	2	10	8	2	6
Elgin C	4	1	1	0	2	7	7	0	5
Stirling Alb	4	0	0	1	3	3	12	–9	1

FIRST ROUND – GROUP D

Saturday, 13 July 2019

Peterhead (2) 2 *(Lyle 20, McAllister 39 (pen))*

Cove Rangers (1) 1 *(Masson 14 (pen))* 744

Peterhead: (4231) Fleming; Eadie, Brown J, Hooper (Stevenson 19), Boyle; Ferry, Brown S; Lyle, Smith, Leitch (Gibson 80); McAllister (Armour 67).
Cove Rangers: (4411) McKenzie; Yule, Ross, Kelly, Milne H; Park (Macleod 80), Scully, Brown, Masson; Burnett; Megginson (Milne C 17).

Raith R (0) 0

Dundee (2) 3 *(Nelson 14, 29 (pen), Curran C 75)* 2584

Raith R: (442) Munro; McKay, Davidson, Mendy, MacDonald K; Spencer, Hendry (Tait 83), Matthews, Vitoria (Miller 72); Allan, Bowie (Anderson G 72).
Dundee: (4411) Hamilton; Kerr, Meekings, McGhee, Marshall; Todd (Robertson 68), Byrne, Ness, McDaid (Curran C 73); McGowan P; Nelson (Cameron 80).

Tuesday, 16 July 2019

Peterhead (0) 0

Inverness CT (0) 0 606

Peterhead: (4231) Fleming; Eadie, Brown J, Dunlop, Boyle; Ferry, Brown S (Leitch 88); Stevenson, Gibson, Fraser (McAllister 64); Smith (Armour 79).
Inverness CT: (343) Ridgers; McKay (Vincent 46), Donaldson, McCart; Curry (Macgregor 79), Trafford, Carson, Tremarco; Keatings (Todorov 67), White, Walsh.
Peterhead won 11-10 on penalties.

Wednesday, 17 July 2019

Cove Rangers (0) 0

Dundee (0) 0 1410

Cove Rangers: (442) McKenzie; Kelly, Ross, Higgins, Milne H; Park, Yule, Scully, Masson; Scott, Brown (Meres 73 (Burnett 84)).
Dundee: (4231) Hamilton; Kerr, Forster, McGhee, Marshall; Byrne, Ness (Mulligan 71); Curran C (Todd 56), McGowan P, Robertson (McDaid 56); Nelson.
Dundee won 3-2 on penalties.

Saturday, 20 July 2019

Dundee (0) 0

Peterhead (0) 0 2322

Dundee: (4411) Hamilton; Kerr, Forster, Meekings, Marshall; Mulligan (Curran C 63), Byrne (Cunningham 76), Robertson, McDaid; McGowan P; Nelson.
Peterhead: (352) Fleming; Eadie, Brown J, Boyle; Stevenson, Ferry, Brown S, Leitch, Fraser (Gibson 67); Lyle (Armour 73), McAllister (Smith 33).
Dundee won 4-2 on penalties.

Inverness CT (1) 4 *(White 6, Donaldson 56, Doran 58, Todorov 90)*

Raith R (0) 1 *(Allan 50)* 1054

Inverness CT: (442) Ridgers; Carson, Donaldson, McCart, Tremarco; Walsh, Doran (Curry 83), Vincent, Trafford; White (Todorov 78), Keatings (Macgregor 72).
Raith R: (442) Munro; Miller, Benedictus, Mendy, MacDonald K; McKay, Hendry (Tait 89), Davidson, Anderson G (Bowie 78); Allan (Vitoria 82), Matthews.

Tuesday, 23 July 2019

Inverness CT (1) 3 *(White 38, Keatings 55, Todorov 71)*

Cove Rangers (1) 2 *(Megginson 45, 46)* 1042

Inverness CT: (4411) Ridgers; McKay, Donaldson, McCart, Tremarco; Doran (Curry 64), Carson, Vincent, Walsh; Keatings (Macgregor 69); White (Todorov 63).
Cove Rangers: (442) McKenzie; Yule, Redford, Higgins, Milne H; Park (Burnett 80), Glass, Scully (Brown 81), Masson; Scott, Megginson■.

Raith R (2) 3 *(Bowie 4, Miller 21, Allan 80)*

Peterhead (0) 1 *(Armour 88)* 788

Raith R: (442) Munro; Miller, Davidson (Mendy 78), Benedictus, MacDonald K; Matthews (Watson 81), Hendry, Spencer, Vitoria (Anderson G 66); Bowie, Allan.
Peterhead: (442) Fleming; Eadie, Brown J, Dunlop, Boyle; Stevenson (Fraser 52), Brown S (Willox 83), Leitch, Gibson; Lyle (Armour 71), Smith.

Saturday, 27 July 2019

Cove Rangers (1) 3 *(Masson 45, Antoniazzi 52, Glass 73)*

Raith R (0) 0 791

Cove Rangers: (4411) McKenzie; Yule, Ross (Redford 46), Strachan, Milne H; Park, Higgins, Glass, Masson (Burnett 69); Antoniazzi; Scott (Brown 65).
Raith R: (4411) McGurn; Watson, Davidson (Mendy 63), Benedictus, MacDonald K; Spencer (Vitoria 58), Matthews, Hendry, Anderson G; Bowie; Allan.

Sunday, 28 July 2019

Dundee (1) 1 *(Johnson 33)*

Inverness CT (0) 0 2066

Dundee: (442) Hamilton; Kerr, Forster, Meekings, McGhee; Byrne, McGowan P (McDaid 79), Robertson, Marshall; Nelson (Mulligan 90), Johnson (Todd 67).
Inverness CT: (4411) Ridgers; McKay, Donaldson, McCart, Tremarco; Doran (Curry 78), Trafford (Carson 56), Vincent, Walsh; Keatings; White (Todorov 78).

Group D Table	P	W	PW	PL	L	F	A	GD	Pts
Dundee	4	2	2	0	0	4	0	4	10
Inverness CT	4	2	0	1	1	7	4	3	7
Peterhead	4	1	1	1	1	3	4	–1	6
Cove Rangers	4	1	0	1	2	6	5	1	4
Raith R	4	1	0	0	3	4	11	–7	3

SOUTHERN SECTION

FIRST ROUND – GROUP E

Saturday, 13 July 2019

Annan Ath (0) 0

Dumbarton (0) 1 *(Tierney 63)* 264

Annan Ath: (442) Taylor; Douglas, Sonkur, Swinglehurst (Currie 72), Ballantyne; McLean, Griffiths, Wooding-Holt, Wilkie (Joseph 61); Muir, Nade (McLear 46).
Dumbarton: (4312) Pettigrew; Crawford, Neill, Carswell, Quitongo R; Hutton, Zata (Langan 79), McMillan; McCluskey; Crossan (McGeever 84), Tierney.

Queen of the South (0) 0

Motherwell (0) 3 *(Donnelly 71 (pen), Seedorf 90, Hylton 90)* 1956

Queen of the South: (433) McCrorie; Mercer, Kilday, Brownlie, Holt; Pybus, Hamilton (Irving 87), McCarthy; Kidd, Dobbie, Murray.
Motherwell: (433) Gillespie; Tait, Gallagher, Dunne, Carroll; Donnelly, Campbell, Semple; Ilic (Seedorf 54), Long (Scott 4), Cole (Hylton 59).

Tuesday, 16 July 2019

Greenock Morton (5) 6 *(Neill 15 (og), Grant 17, Jacobs 23, Strapp 31, Sutton 45, McHugh 69)*

Dumbarton (0) 1 *(Neill 63)* 1228

Greenock Morton: (442) Ramsbottom; McAlister, McLean, Grant, Strapp (McHugh 59); Salkeld, Jacobs, Lyon, Cadden; Sutton (Muirhead 66), Nesbitt (McGrattan 76).
Dumbarton: (4411) Brennan; Crawford, Neill, McGeever, Quitongo R; Langan (Zata 75), Carswell, Hutton, Crossan (McMillan 67); McCluskey; Tierney.

Queen of the South (3) 3 *(Murray 23, Mercer 26, Dobbie 42)*

Annan Ath (1) 3 *(Douglas 34, McLear 54, Wooding-Holt 81)* 1115

Queen of the South: (4231) McCrorie; Mercer (Pybus 54), Kilday, Brownlie, Holt; Kidd, McCarthy; Murray, Oliver, Paton (Hamilton 74); Dobbie.
Annan Ath: (442) Taylor; Douglas, Sonkur, Swinglehurst, Ballantyne; McLean, Bradley, Wooding-Holt, Wilkie (Joseph 60); Muir, McLear (Nade 72).
Queen of the South won 5-4 on penalties.

Friday, 19 July 2019

Motherwell (1) 4 *(Scott 22, 66, Hylton 76, Donnelly 82)*

Greenock Morton (0) 0 3167

Motherwell: (433) Gillespie; Tait, Gallagher, Dunne, Carroll (Grimshaw 69); Polworth (Maguire 77), Campbell, Donnelly; Seedorf (Ilic 63), Scott, Hylton.
Greenock Morton: (433) Ramsbottom; McAlister, McLean (Salkeld 53), Grant, Strapp; Lyon, Nesbitt, Jacobs; Millar, Sutton (McHugh 75), Cadden (Muirhead 65).

Saturday, 20 July 2019

Dumbarton (1) 1 *(Crossan 8)*

Queen of the South (4) 4 *(Paton 10, Oliver 13, Dobbie 17, Murray 22)* 580

Dumbarton: (4411) Brennan; McMillan, Neill, McGeever, Quitongo R; McKee, Carswell (Langan 78), Hutton, Crossan (Zata 75); McCluskey; Tierney (Crawford 46).
Queen of the South: (4231) McCrorie; Pybus, Kilday, Brownlie (Gourlay 79), Holt; Kidd, McCarthy (Irving 61); Murray, Oliver, Paton; Dobbie (Hamilton 55).

Tuesday, 23 July 2019

Annan Ath (0) 0

Greenock Morton (3) 5 *(Nesbitt 7, 83, Cadden 33, 43, Muirhead 90)* 478

Annan Ath: (4312) Avci; Douglas, Sonkur, Swinglehurst (Barr 85), Ballantyne; McLean, Bradley, Wooding-Holt; Joseph (Nade 46); Muir, Wilkie (Currie 69).
Greenock Morton: (433) Ramsbottom; Tumilty, Grant, McAlister, Strapp; Jacobs, Nesbitt (McGrattan 84), Lyon; McHugh, Sutton (Muirhead 67), Cadden (Salkeld 71).

Dumbarton (0) 0

Motherwell (1) 2 *(Ilic 42, Hartley 76)* 1394

Dumbarton: (352) Pettigrew; McGeever (Langan 86), Carswell, Neill; Crawford, McKee, Hutton, Zata (Scullion 81), Quitongo R; Crossan (Layne 84), McCluskey.
Motherwell: (433) Gillespie; Grimshaw, Gallagher, Hartley, Tait; Maguire, Campbell, Polworth (Semple 80); Ilic (Seedorf 62), Scott (Long 50), Hylton.

Saturday, 27 July 2019

Greenock Morton (2) 3 *(Sutton 31, Cadden 45 (pen), McHugh 56)*

Queen of the South (1) 3 *(Kilday 4, McAlister 62 (og), Semple 78)* 1388

Greenock Morton: (4231) Ramsbottom; Tumilty, McAlister, Grant, Strapp (van Schaik 58); Lyon (Salkeld 74), Jacobs; McHugh (Blues 67), Nesbitt, Cadden; Sutton.
Queen of the South: (4411) McCrorie; Mercer, Semple, Kilday, Holt; Paton, Kidd, Pybus, Murray; Oliver; Hamilton (McCarthy 65).
Greenock Morton won 4-3 on penalties.

Motherwell (2) 4 *(Donnelly 20, 89, Polworth 44, Scott 90)*

Annan Ath (0) 0 2763

Motherwell: (343) Gillespie; Donnelly, Hartley, Dunne; Grimshaw, Semple, Polworth (Sloth 46), Carroll; Ilic, Long (Scott 70), Seedorf (Hylton 66).
Annan Ath: (442) Avci; Douglas, Swinglehurst, Bradley, Ballantyne; McLean, Wooding-Holt (Griffiths 54), Wilkie, Joseph (McLear 78); Muir, Nade.

Group E Table	P	W	PW	PL	L	F	A	GD	Pts
Motherwell	4	4	0	0	0	13	0	13	12
Greenock Morton*	4	2	1	0	1	14	8	6	8
Queen of the South	4	1	1	1	1	10	10	0	6
Dumbarton	4	1	0	0	3	3	12	–9	3
Annan Ath	4	0	0	1	3	3	13	–10	1

FIRST ROUND – GROUP F

Saturday, 13 July 2019

Hamilton A (0) 0

Queen's Park (0) 0 756

Hamilton A: (352) Fon Williams; McKenna, Gogic, Easton (Miller 69); McMann, Hughes, MacKinnon, Alston, Hunt (McGowan 55); Davies (Ogboe 64), Oakley.
Queen's Park: (343) Muir; Jamieson, Magee, Little; Mortimer (Grant J 85), McGorry, Block, Clark; Purdue (Agyeman 77), Kouider-Aisser (Moore 64), Galt.
Queen's Park won 6-5 on penalties.

Partick Thistle (0) 1 *(Crighton 66 (og))*

Airdrieonians (0) 0 2241

Partick Thistle: (3412) Sneddon; Saunders, O'Ware, McGinty; Williamson, Gordon (Palmer 46), Bannigan, Penrice; Cardle (Robson 83); Miller, Mansell (Golasso 69).
Airdrieonians: (442) Hutton; Fordyce, Crighton, Kerr, Eckersley; Thomson (Hawkshaw 81), Millar, Wedderburn, Gallagher C (Roberts 73); Carrick, Roy (O'Reilly 67).

Tuesday, 16 July 2019

Queen's Park (0) 1 *(Kouider-Aisser 56)*

Partick Thistle (2) 2 *(Miller 6, Robson 36)* 944

Queen's Park: (343) Muir; Jamieson, Magee, Little; Grant J, McGorry, Block, Clark; Purdue (Agyeman 69), Moore (Kouider-Aisser 52), Galt.
Partick Thistle: (352) Sneddon; Saunders, O'Ware, McGinty; Williamson, Gordon (Penrice 79), Palmer, Bannigan, Robson; Cardle (Mansell 63), Miller (Jones 81).

Wednesday, 17 July 2019

Clyde (0) 1 *(Syvertsen 57)*

Hamilton A (1) 3 *(McMann 31, Alston 50, Smith L 76)* 504

Clyde: (4231) Mitchell; Duffie, Rumsby, Howie, McNiff; Cuddihy (Goodwillie 81), Grant; Johnston, Wallace (McStay 74), Syvertsen; Darren Smith (Lamont 68).
Hamilton A: (352) Fon Williams; McKenna, Gogic, Easton; McGowan, Alston, Smith L, Hughes (MacKinnon 66), McMann; Miller (Fjortoft 81), Ogboe (Oakley 64).

Saturday, 20 July 2019

Hamilton A (1) 2 *(Cunningham 17, 54)*

Partick Thistle (1) 2 *(Williamson 16, Gordon 73)* 1693

Hamilton A: (352) Fon Williams; McKenna, Gogic, Easton (Want 46); McGowan, Alston, Hughes (MacKinnon 30), Cunningham, McMann; Ogboe (Oakley 64), Smith L.
Partick Thistle: (343) Fox; O'Ware, McGinty, Penrice; Williamson, Palmer (Mansell 60), Bannigan, Robson (De Vita 69); Gordon, Miller, Cardle (Jones 85).
Hamilton A won 6-5 on penalties.

Sunday, 21 July 2019

Clyde (0) 2 *(Goodwillie 75 (pen), 85)*

Airdrieonians (2) 3 *(Roy 34 (pen), 59, Eckersley 39)* 858

Clyde: (4231) Mitchell; Cuddihy, Rumsby, Howie, McNiff; McStay (Wallace 60), Grant; Johnston, Lamont, Darren Smith (Goodwillie 61); Syvertsen (Lyon 70).
Airdrieonians: (433) Hutton; Fordyce, Crighton, Kerr, Eckersley; Cowan (Millar 78), O'Reilly (Russell 64), Wedderburn; Thomson, Smith, Roy (Carrick 72).

Wednesday, 24 July 2019

Airdrieonians (0) 2 *(Wedderburn 54, Gallagher C 82)*

Queen's Park (1) 2 *(Summers 6, Purdue 74)* 645

Airdrieonians: (4231) Hutton; Fordyce, Kerr, Crighton (Gallagher C 80), Eckersley; Wedderburn, Millar; Smith, Hawkshaw (Carrick 73), Thomson (O'Reilly 64); Roy.
Queen's Park: (352) Muir; Jamieson (Moore 78), Clark, Little; Mortimer (Grant J 66), Purdue, McGorry (Main 13), Galt, Summers; Kouider-Aisser, Agyeman.
Airdrieonians won 12-11 on penalties.

Partick Thistle (1) 3 *(Gordon 12, 60, Miller 49)*

Clyde (1) 2 *(Wallace 25, Bannigan 65 (og))* 2403

Partick Thistle: (433) Fox; Williamson, Saunders, McGinty, Robson; Palmer (Miller 46), Bannigan, De Vita (Wilson 87); Gordon, Mansell (Jones 67), Cardle.
Clyde: (4411) Mitchell; Cuddihy (Lamont 76), Rumsby, Howie, McNiff; Johnston, Grant, Wallace, Duffie; Syvertsen (Lyon 63); Goodwillie (Darren Smith 63).

Saturday, 27 July 2019

Airdrieonians (2) 2 *(Smith 10, Roy 24)*

Hamilton A (0) 3 *(Cunningham 48 (pen), 60 (pen), Ogboe 89)* 814

Airdrieonians: (433) Hutton; Fordyce, Crighton, Kerr, Eckersley; Cowan (Roberts 55), Wedderburn (Carrick 80), Millar; Smith, Gallagher C (Thomson 73), Roy.
Hamilton A: (442) Fon Williams; McGowan, Want, McKenna, McMann; Smith L (Oakley 78), MacKinnon, Mimnaugh (Gogic 90), Alston; Cunningham (Fjortoft 90), Ogboe.

Sunday, 28 July 2019

Queen's Park (0) 1 *(Howie 86 (og))*

Clyde (1) 1 *(Darren Smith 23)* 414

Queen's Park: (343) Muir; Magee, Clark, Little; Grant J, Lidohren, Block (Main 68), Summers; Moore (Kouider-Aisser 57), Agyeman, Purdue (Martin 65).
Clyde: (4231) Mitchell; Cuddihy, Rumsby, Howie, McNiff; McStay, Wallace; Lyon, Lamont, Darren Smith (Fitzpatrick 80); Syvertsen (Goodwillie 64).
Queen's Park won 5-4 on penalties.

Group F Table	P	W	PW	PL	L	F	A	GD	Pts
Partick Thistle	4	3	0	1	0	8	5	3	10
Hamilton A*	4	2	1	1	0	8	5	3	9
Airdrieonians	4	1	1	0	2	7	8	–1	5
Queen's Park	3	0	1	1	1	3	4	–1	3
Clyde	3	0	0	0	3	5	9	–4	0

FIRST ROUND – GROUP G

Saturday, 13 July 2019

Berwick Rangers (0) 0

Ayr U (5) 7 *(Moffat 21, 36, McCowan 26, 70, Doolan 35, 86, McGuffie 42)* 603

Berwick Rangers: (4231) Brennan; Lumsden, Cook, Waugh, Forster; Smith E, Smith A; Wright (Rose 46), Barr, Windram (Purves 83); Healy (Jack 84).
Ayr U: (4411) Doohan; Geggan (Ferguson 61), Muirhead, Roscoe, Harvie; McCowan, Kerr, Kelly, McGuffie (Forrest 71); Moffat (Ross 67); Doolan.

Falkirk (0) 1 *(Sammon 90)*

Livingston (1) 1 *(Dykes 36)* 2121

Falkirk: (442) Bell; Doyle, Durnan, Buchanan, Dixon; Connolly (Johnstone 69), McShane, Tidser, MacLean (Toshney 80); Sammon, Telfer.
Livingston: (4231) Sarkic; McMillan, Pepe, Lithgow, Lamie; Jacobs, Bartley; Robinson (Tiffoney 72), Pitman, Lawless (Souda 77); Dykes (Miller L 83).
Livingston won 4-3 on penalties.

Tuesday, 16 July 2019

Falkirk (1) 1 *(McManus 9)*

Stranraer (0) 0 1838

Falkirk: (442) Mutch; Doyle, Durnan, Buchanan, Dixon; Connolly (MacLean 67 (McShane 82)), Tidser, Gomis, Telfer; Johnstone (Sammon 60), McManus.
Stranraer: (352) Currie; Cummins, Hamilton, Hamill; Robertson, Thomson, McManus, Smith D (Elliott 64), Allan; Pignatiello (Hilton 75), Stewart (Dangana 67).

Livingston (1) 2 *(Souda 25, Lamie 83)*

Ayr U (0) 1 *(Murdoch 51)* 1097

Livingston: (4231) Stewart; Devlin, Lithgow, Pepe, Lamie; Crawford, Bartley (Jacobs 72); Lawless (Erskine 79), Pitman, Souda (Tiffoney 65); Dykes.
Ayr U: (442) Doohan; Ferguson, Bell, Roscoe (Muirhead 46), Harvie; Murdoch, Kelly, Docherty, McCowan; Moffat, Doolan (Forrest 46).

Saturday, 20 July 2019

Ayr U (1) 2 *(McCowan 26, Geggan 75)*

Falkirk (1) 1 *(McManus 42)* 1605

Ayr U: (442) Doohan; Geggan, Muirhead, Bell, Harvie; Murdoch, Kerr (Ross 73), Kelly, Forrest (McGuffie 46); Moffat (Doolan 46), McCowan.
Falkirk: (433) Bell; Doyle, Buchanan, Durnan■, Dixon; Gomis (Leitch 72), Tidser (Johnstone 83), McShane; Connolly (Toshney 49), McManus, Telfer.

Stranraer (4) 6 *(Elliott 19, Allan 38, McManus 41, Stewart 45 (pen), 75 (pen), Hilton 63)*

Berwick Rangers (0) 0 247

Stranraer: (532) Burgess; Smith D (Pignatiello 67), Robertson, Cummins, Hamilton, Allan; McManus, Hilton, Thomson (Smith I 73); Stewart, Elliott (Dangana 56).
Berwick Rangers: (442) Brennan; Lumsden, Chalmers, Waugh, Gray; Wright, Forster, Barr, Windram (Jack 78); Healy, Rose (Purves 69).

Tuesday, 23 July 2019

Berwick Rangers (0) 0

Falkirk (1) 3 *(McManus 13, Leitch 51, Johnstone 76)* 509

Berwick Rangers: (442) Brennan; Lumsden, Cook, Waugh, Gray; Wright, Forster (Chalmers 59), Barr (Jack 68), Windram (Purves 72); Healy, Rose.
Falkirk: (442) Mutch; Doyle, Toshney, Buchanan, Dixon; Leitch (Tidser 67), McShane (Telfer 67), Gomis, Connolly; McManus, Johnstone.

Stranraer (0) 1 *(Elliott 57)*

Livingston (2) 2 *(Lawless 42 (pen), Souda 45)* 402

Stranraer: (541) Currie; Robertson, Cummins, Hamill, Hamilton, Allan; Elliott, McManus, Thomson, Hilton (Smith I 80); Stewart (Dangana 69).
Livingston: (4231) Stewart; Devlin, Lithgow, McMillan, Lamie; Jacobs (Crawford 73), Bartley; Lawless (Erskine 76), Pitman, Souda (Tiffoney 81); Dykes.

Saturday, 27 July 2019

Ayr U (2) 2 *(Moffat 2, Kelly 44)*

Stranraer (1) 2 *(Cummins 42, 86)* 1430

Ayr U: (442) Doohan; Ferguson, Bell, Roscoe, Harvie; McCowan (Forrest 78), Docherty, Murdoch, Kelly (Kerr 69); Doolan (McGuffie 56), Moffat.
Stranraer: (343) Burgess; Hamilton (Smith I 82), Hamill, Cummins; Smith D (Robertson 72), McManus, Thomson, Allan; Hilton, Elliott, Pignatiello (Dangana 64).
Stranraer won 6-5 on penalties.

Livingston (3) 5 *(Lamie 2, 81, Sibbald 16, 84, Lithgow 24)*

Berwick Rangers (0) 0 692

Livingston: (4231) Sarkic; Devlin, Lithgow, Pepe, Lamie; Crawford, Bartley (Lawson 46); Souda (Lawless 63), Pitman, Sibbald; Dykes (Miller L 63).
Berwick Rangers: (442) Brennan; Brian, Cook, Gray (Lumsden 46), Waugh; Jack, Barr, Forster, Windram (Purves 70); Healy (Chalmers 63), Rose.

Group G Table	P	W	PW	PL	L	F	A	GD	Pts
Livingston	4	3	1	0	0	10	3	7	11
Ayr U	4	2	0	1	1	12	5	7	7
Falkirk	4	2	0	1	1	6	3	3	7
Stranraer	4	1	1	0	2	9	5	4	5
Berwick Rangers	4	0	0	0	4	0	21	–21	0

FIRST ROUND – GROUP H

Saturday, 13 July 2019

East Kilbride (0) 0

Albion R (1) 1 *(Stewart 25)* 230

East Kilbride: (352) Martin; Reid, Cairns, Brownlie; Stevenson (Sinnamon 60), Holmes, Woods (Winter 73), Brady, Bell (Coll 58); Kavanagh, Paton.
Albion R: (442) Goodfellow; Lynas, Krones, Wharton, Clarke; Roberts, Fotheringham (Phillips 53), Morena, Stewart (Paterson 80); East, Byrne (Osadolor 80).

Sunday, 14 July 2019

St Mirren (0) 2 *(Cooke 63, Mullen 65)*

Dunfermline Ath (3) 3 *(Dow 18, Ryan 24, Beadling 40)* 2067

St Mirren: (41212) Hladky; McGinn P, Baird, MacKenzie, Erhahon; McGinn S (Djorkaeff 79); Magennis, Flynn; Andreu; Mullen, Cooke.
Dunfermline Ath: (4132) Scully; Comrie, Morrison, Ashcroft, Martin L; Paton; Dow (McCann 89), Beadling, Coley; Nisbet (McGill 62), Ryan (Turner 70).

Wednesday, 17 July 2019

Dunfermline Ath (5) 6 *(Turner 2, 53, Nisbet 19, 25, 45, Comrie 40)*

Albion R (0) 0 1693

Dunfermline Ath: (442) Scully; Comrie, Ashcroft, Morrison, Martin L; Dow (Allan 59), Paton (McGill 59), Beadling, McCann; Nisbet (Edwards 66), Turner.
Albion R: (442) Goodfellow (Smith 46); Lynas, Wharton, Krones (Fagan 46), Clarke; Roberts, Morena, Paterson, Phillips; East (Osadolor 60), Byrne.

St Mirren (0) 1 *(Djorkaeff 88 (pen))*

Edinburgh C (0) 0 1235

St Mirren: (4411) Hladky; MacPherson, Baird, MacKenzie, McGinn P; Magennis (Erhahon 62), McGinn S, Flynn, Djorkaeff; Andreu (Mullen 65); Cooke (Breadner 90).
Edinburgh C: (352) Antell; McIntyre, Balatoni, Henderson L; Thomson, Laird, Sinclair (Smith A 74), Walker, Crane; Shepherd (Handling 75), Harris.

Saturday, 20 July 2019

East Kilbride (0) 0

St Mirren (0) 0 644

East Kilbride: (442) Martin; Sinnamon, Reid, Brownlie, Coll; Winter (Carmichael 57), Holmes (Stevenson 71), Cairns, Woods; Paton (Kavanagh 64), Brady.
St Mirren: (4411) Hladky; MacPherson, Baird, McGinn P, Erhahon; Magennis (Cooke 70), McGinn S (Kellermann 61), Flynn, Djorkaeff; Andreu; Mullen.
East Kilbride won 6-5 on penalties.

Edinburgh C (0) 1 *(Handling 87)*

Dunfermline Ath (0) 0 1035

Edinburgh C: (442) Antell; Thomson, Balatoni, Henderson L, Crane; Smith A (Handling 63), Watson (Walker 75), Laird, McIntyre; Harris, Court (Shepherd 68).
Dunfermline Ath: (442) Scully; Comrie, Ashcroft, Morrison, Martin L; Dow, Paton, Beadling (McGill 88), Coley (McCann 73); Nisbet, Ryan (Turner 56).

Tuesday, 23 July 2019

Albion R (0) 0

St Mirren (0) 0 512

Albion R: (442) Smith; Lynas, Fagan (Wharton 78), Wilson, Clarke; Roberts, Fotheringham, Morena, Stewart (Phillips 76); Osadolor, East.
St Mirren: (442) Hladky; MacPherson (McAllister 7), Baird, McGinn P, Erhahon; Magennis, Andreu, Flynn, Djorkaeff (Breadner 80); Mullen, Cooke.
St Mirren won 4-3 on penalties.

Edinburgh C (0) 0

East Kilbride (0) 1 *(Brady 71)* 208

Edinburgh C: (4231) Antell; Kane, Balatoni, Henderson L, Crane; Sinclair, Walker; Watson (Harris 58), Handling (Court 58), Smith A (Henderson B 77); Shepherd.
East Kilbride: (442) Martin; Stevenson, Reid, Brownlie, Coll; Weir (Sinnamon 60), Holmes (Brady 70), Cairns, Kavanagh (Woods 65); Paton, Carmichael.

Saturday, 27 July 2019

Albion R (1) 2 *(East 8, Paterson 54)*

Edinburgh C (0) 1 *(Henderson B 62 (pen))* 157

Albion R: (442) Smith; Lynas, Fagan, Wilson, Clarke; Roberts, Fotheringham (Wharton 84), Morena (Paterson 37), Stewart; Byrne (Scally 79), East.
Edinburgh C: (4231) Antell; Thomson, Balatoni, Henderson L, Crane; Harris, Laird; Sinclair (Henderson B 57), Court (Handling 57), McIntyre; Shepherd (Smith A 72).

Dunfermline Ath (3) 4 *(Nisbet 3, 50, Coley 7, Beadling 16)*

East Kilbride (0) 0 1607

Dunfermline Ath: (442) Scully; Comrie, Murray, Ashcroft, Martin L; Dow (McCann 67), Paton (Allan 74), Beadling, Coley; Nisbet (Ryan 63), Turner.
East Kilbride: (442) Martin; Reid (Stevenson 73), Cairns, Brownlie, Sinnamon; Winter (Kavanagh 63), Brady, Holmes, Woods; Paton, Carmichael (Malcolm 67).

Group H Table	*P*	*W*	*PW*	*PL*	*L*	*F*	*A*	*GD*	*Pts*
Dunfermline Ath	4	3	0	0	1	13	3	10	9
Albion R	4	2	0	1	1	3	7	−4	7
St Mirren	4	1	1	1	1	3	3	0	6
East Kilbride	4	1	1	0	2	1	5	−4	5
Edinburgh C	4	1	0	0	3	2	4	−2	3

SECOND ROUND

Friday, 16 August 2019

Motherwell (0) 1 *(Long 60)*

Hearts (2) 2 *(Smith 40, Washington 45 (pen))* 5597

Motherwell: (433) Gillespie; Grimshaw, Gallagher, Dunne, Tait; Polworth, Campbell (Ilic 78), Donnelly; Seedorf, Scott (Long 46), Hylton (Cole 46).
Hearts: (433) Joel Pereira; Smith, Halkett, Berra, Hickey; Clare (Bozanic 88), Damour, Irving; Walker (MacLean 38), Washington, Mulraney (White 84).

Saturday, 17 August 2019

Celtic (0) 2 *(Johnston 55, Forrest 114)*

Dunfermline Ath (0) 1 *(Beadling 77)* 27,318

Celtic: (442) Gordon; Elhamed, Jullien, Ajer (Ntcham 76), Bolingoli-Mbombo (Hayes 91); Johnston (Morgan 115), Bitton, McGregor, Christie; Griffiths (Forrest 56), Edouard.
Dunfermline Ath: (451) Scully; Comrie, Ashcroft, Morrison, Martin L; Dow (Todd 112), Paton, Turner (Coley 65), Beadling, Edwards (Ryan 75); Nisbet (McGill 85).
aet.

Forfar Ath (0) 1 *(Hilson 63)*

Livingston (1) 2 *(Dykes 34, Pitman 53)* 884

Forfar Ath: (442) McCallum; Meechan, Travis, Docherty, Burns (Bain 70); Forbes (Aitken 82), Tapping, Irvine, Kirkpatrick (Coupe 70); Andrew Jackson, Hilson.
Livingston: (433) Sarkic; Devlin, Guthrie, Lithgow, Lamie (Savane 84); Bartley, Crawford, Pitman; Lawless (Erskine 74), Souda (Robinson 46), Dykes.

Hibernian (2) 5 *(Allan S 20, Vela 32, Kamberi 55, 104, Doidge 120)*

Greenock Morton (2) 3 *(McHugh 39, Stevenson 45 (og), Whittaker 90 (og))* 6557

Hibernian: (4411) Maxwell; Gray (Whittaker 74), McGregor (Jackson 14), Hanlon, Stevenson; Middleton (Murray 79), Slivka, Vela, Horgan (Doidge 92); Allan S; Kamberi.
Greenock Morton: (442) Rogers; Jacobs (Orsi 117), McAlister, McLean, Strapp; Blues (Tumilty 76), Millar (Sutton 80), Lyon, Nesbitt (Salkeld 84); McHugh, Cadden.
aet.

Kilmarnock (0) 1 *(Thomas 113)*

Hamilton A (0) 0 3762

Kilmarnock: (4411) Branescu; O'Donnell, Broadfoot, Findlay, Taylor; Burke (Thomas 105), Power, El Makrini (Dicker 91), McKenzie (Millar 61); Cameron (Kiltie 98); Brophy.
Hamilton A: (4231) Fon Williams; McGowan, Stubbs, Hamilton, McMann; MacKinnon, Gogic (Hughes 100); Smith L, Collar (Mimnaugh 76), Cunningham (Miller 60); Oakley (Ogboe 87).
aet.

Partick Thistle (0) 3 *(Miller 80, Penrice 96, Saunders 114)*
Ross Co (0) 2 *(Spittal 60, Paton 105)* 2053
Partick Thistle: (433) Fox; Williamson, Saunders, McGinty, Penrice; Gordon (Palmer 85), Bannigan, De Vita (Robson 70); Cardle (Mansell 70), Miller, Jones (O'Ware 101).
Ross Co: (442) Laidlaw; Fraser M, Watson, Fontaine, Kelly S; Spittal (Mullin 64), Draper (Vigurs 52), Chalmers (Paton 91), Gardyne; McKay, Ross C Stewart (Erwin 75).
aet.

Sunday, 18 August 2019

Dundee (1) 1 *(Johnson 43 (pen))*
Aberdeen (0) 2 *(Considine 90, Cosgrove 103)* 5740
Dundee: (451) Hamilton; Kerr, Forster, McGhee, Marshall; Byrne, Robertson (Moore 98), Ness (McGowan P 74), Todd (Meekings 86), McDaid; Johnson (Nelson 62).
Aberdeen: (442) Lewis; Logan, Considine, McKenna, Leigh; Hedges (Wilson 65), Ojo, Bryson (Campbell 62), McGinn (McLennan 57); Gallagher (Vyner 119), Cosgrove.
aet.

East Fife (0) 0
Rangers (1) 3 *(Defoe 26, Dunlop 56 (og), Aribo 84)* 1991
East Fife: (442) Hart; Murdoch, Dunlop, Higgins, Slattery; Dunsmore, Davidson R (Watson C 81), Agnew, Watt (Denholm 81); Wallace, Dowds (Duggan 68).
Rangers: (433) Foderingham; Polster, Helander, Edmundson, Halliday; Aribo, Docherty (King 60), Kamara; Stewart (Barker 59), Defoe, Jones (Hastie 79).

QUARTER-FINALS

Wednesday, 25 September 2019

Celtic (1) 5 *(Bayo 15, Rogic 46, Ntcham 56, 63, Sinclair 76)*
Partick Thistle (0) 0 25,008
Celtic: (4231) Gordon; Frimpong (Hendry 79), Elhamed, Ajer, Hayes; Ntcham, McGregor (Brown 62); Elyounoussi (Sinclair 66), Rogic, Morgan; Bayo.
Partick Thistle: (4411) Fox; Williamson, O'Ware, McGinty, Penrice; Cardle (De Vita 59), Palmer, Bannigan, Robson; Gordon (Cole 74); Miller (Mansell 64).

Hearts (1) 2 *(MacLean 22, Halkett 90)*
Aberdeen (2) 2 *(Cosgrove 12 (pen), 31 (pen))* 12,866
Hearts: (442) Joel Pereira; Smith, Halkett, Berra, Hickey; Mulraney, Whelan, Damour (Keena 75), Meshino (Morrison 80 (Irving 114)); MacLean (Clare 69), Ikpeazu.
Aberdeen: (4231) Lewis; Logan, Considine, Devlin (Anderson 119), Leigh; Campbell (Vyner 78), Ferguson; Wilson (Gallagher 52), McLennan (McGinn 64), Hedges; Cosgrove.
aet; Hearts won 3-0 on penalties.

Kilmarnock (0) 0
Hibernian (0) 0 4780
Kilmarnock: (433) Branescu; O'Donnell, Del Fabro, Findlay, Hamalainen; Power, Dicker, El Makrini (Thomas 94); Burke (McKenzie 86), Brophy (Sow 89), St Clair (Millar 64).
Hibernian: (4231) Maxwell; James, Porteous■, Hanlon, Stevenson; Hallberg (Newell 84), Vela; Horgan (Shaw 70), Mallan, Middleton (Allan S 70); Doidge (Jackson 120).
aet; Hibernian won 5-4 on penalties.

Livingston (0) 0
Rangers (1) 1 *(Kamara 5)* 8160
Livingston: (4231) Sarkic; Devlin, Guthrie, Lamie, McMillan (Pepe 84); Bartley (Lawson 78), Crawford; Lawless, Jacobs, Souda (Robinson 73); Dykes.
Rangers: (433) McGregor; Tavernier, Goldson, Helander, Barisic; Kamara (King 72), Jack, Aribo (Davis 22); Ojo, Morelos, Arfield.

SEMI-FINALS

Saturday, 2 November 2019

Hibernian (1) 2 *(Hallberg 36, Kamberi 58)*
Celtic (3) 5 *(Elyounoussi 17, 44, McGregor 21, Brown 56, 90)* 46,782
Hibernian: (451) Maxwell; James, Hanlon, Jackson, Stevenson; Horgan (Slivka 68), Mallan, Vela (Kamberi 46), Allan S, Hallberg; Doidge (Boyle 76).
Celtic: (4231) Forster; Frimpong, Jullien, Ajer, Bolingoli-Mbombo (Hayes 46); Brown, McGregor; Forrest (Elhamed 67), Rogic (Christie 79), Elyounoussi; Edouard.

Sunday, 3 November 2019

Rangers (1) 3 *(Helander 45, Morelos 47, 62)*
Hearts (0) 0 49,310
Rangers: (433) McGregor; Tavernier, Goldson, Helander, Barisic; Davis, Jack (Arfield 77), Kamara; Kent (Aribo 66), Morelos, Ojo (Defoe 82).
Hearts: (4231) Joel Pereira; Hickey, Smith (Naismith 53), Berra, White; Whelan (Irving 27), Bozanic; Clare, Meshino, Wighton; MacLean (Ikpeazu 40).

BETFRED SCOTTISH LEAGUE CUP FINAL 2019–20

Sunday, 8 December 2019

(at Hampden Park, attendance 51,117)

Celtic (0) 1 **Rangers (0) 0**

Celtic: (4231) Forster; Frimpong■, Jullien, Ajer, Hayes; Brown, McGregor; Forrest (Bitton 66), Christie, Elyounoussi (Johnston 46); Morgan (Edouard 59).
Scorer: Jullien 60

Rangers: (433) McGregor; Tavernier, Goldson, Helander (Katic 84), Barisic; Kamara (Defoe 71), Jack, Aribo (Barker 74); Arfield, Morelos, Kent.

Referee: Willie Collum.

TUNNOCK'S CARAMEL WAFER SCOTTISH LEAGUE CHALLENGE CUP 2019–20

■ *Denotes player sent off.*

FIRST ROUND – NORTH

Tuesday, 6 August 2019

Albion R (1) 1 *(Osadolor 34)*
Hearts U21 (2) 4 *(Petkov 24, Keena 29, 78, Henderson 75)* 207

Brora Rangers (1) 6 *(Nicolson 11, Davidson 46, Wagenaar 64, Gillespie 71, MacLeod 75, Williamson 90)*
Aberdeen U21 (0) 0 150

Fraserburgh (1) 2 *(Beagrie 24, Barbour S 90)*
Ross Co U21 (1) 3 *(Murray 25, Gallagher 54, Keillor-Dunn 67)* 225

Hibernian U21 (2) 3 *(Porteous 4, Gullan 33, Shaw 79 (pen))*
Elgin C (3) 4 *(Hester 8, 39, Sutherland 36, Cooper 90)* 424

Livingston U21 (0) 1 *(Henderson 90 (pen))*
Formartine U (2) 3 *(McGowan 9, Gethins 19, Wood 84)* 120

St Johnstone U21 (1) 1 *(Northcott 2)*
Cove R (1) 4 *(Brown 27, Park 79, Megginson 81, Scott 88)* 175

FIRST ROUND – SOUTH

Tuesday, 6 August 2019

Berwick Rangers (0) 1 *(Purves 71)*
Rangers U21 (2) 2 *(Mebude 24 (pen), McPake 31)* 303

Kelty Hearts (2) 4 *(Carstairs 25, Austin 36, Mutch 49, Linton 81)*
Kilmarnock U21 (0) 0 509

Queen's Park (1) 2 *(Kouider-Aisser 39, Martin 72)*
Celtic U21 (2) 2 *(Aitchison 16, Okoflex 29)* 321
(Celtic U21 won 4-3 on penalties.)

St Mirren U21 (1) 1 *(Breadner 32)*
East Kilbride (0) 0 245

Wednesday, 7 August 2019

Hamilton A U21 (1) 4 *(Breen 37, Winter 69 (pen), 77, Slaven 81)*
BSC Glasgow (0) 0 164

Motherwell U21 (1) 1 *(Semple 18)*
Spartans (0) 0 170

SECOND ROUND – NORTH

Tuesday, 13 August 2019

Brechin C (3) 4 *(Reekie 20, 44, 90, Page 36)*
Elgin C (3) 5 *(Sutherland 1, Hester 3, 39, 65, Mackay 64)* 217

Brechin C: (442) Sinclair; McIntosh (Duncanson 35), Page, Reekie, McLaughlin; Reid, McCord, Watt, Knox; Crawford (McManus 70), Ngoy.
Elgin C: (442) McHale; Wilson, Bronsky, McDonald, Spark (McGowan 74); Willis (Cooper 46), MacEwan, Dingwall, Mackay; Hester (Sopel 82), Sutherland.

Brora Rangers (0) 1 *(MacLeod 47)*
Cove Rangers (0) 2 *(Scully 72, Robertson 81)* 300

Brora Rangers: (442) Malin; MacDonald N, Nicolson, Williamson, MacDonald A; Maclean, Gillespie (Wagenaar 71), Gavin Morrison, Brindle (Docherty 82); MacLeod (Mackay 55), MacRae.
Cove Rangers: (442) McKenzie; Kelly, Strachan, Higgins, Redford; Park (Glass 64), Scully, Scott (Yule 64), Masson; Brown (Robertson 64), Megginson.

East Fife (0) 0
Stirling Alb (1) 2 *(Duffy 37, Peters 67)* 419

East Fife: (442) Hart; Watson C, Dunlop, Higgins, Slattery; Denholm (Dunsmore 74), Hunter, McConville, Watt; Smith (Wallace 57), Cosgrove (Dowds 57).
Stirling Alb: (442) Binnie; Truesdale, McLean, Banner, Lowdon; Willis (Scott 90), Nicoll, Docherty, Jardine; Peters (Hawke 84), Duffy (Wright 79).

Hearts U21 (0) 3 *(Baur 71, Keena 80, Zanatta 82)*
Cowdenbeath (0) 1 *(Barr 87)* 326

Hearts U21: (352) Stone; Petkov, Hamilton, Baur; Logan, Ritchie (Smith 85), Cochrane, McDonald, Burns; Zanatta, Keena (Currie 85).
Cowdenbeath: (4411) Dabrowski; Mullen, Pyper, Todd, Valentine; Buchanan, Thomas, Miller (Barr 78), Swan (Sheerin 41); Cox■; Kris Renton.

Montrose (1) 2 *(Milne 38, Lyons 71)*
Forfar Ath (1) 1 *(MacKintosh 36)* 531

Montrose: (433) Lennox; Cammy Ballantyne, Allan, Campbell I, Steeves; Milne, Cregg, Watson (Callaghan 65); Lyons, McLean (Campbell R 73), Skelly (Webster 65).
Forfar Ath: (4231) McCallum; Bain, Whyte (Docherty 10), Travis, Burns; Robertson, MacKintosh (Tapping 63); Forbes, Kirkpatrick, Coupe; Aitken (Hilson 63).

Peterhead (0) 0
Formartine U (0) 0 551

Peterhead: (4411) Fleming; Brown J, Eadie, Hooper (Brown S 36), Norris; Stevenson, Fraser, Willox (Leitch 67), Smith; Armour (Conroy 60); McAllister.
Formartine U: (442) Main; Mackintosh, Clark, McKeown, Lawrence (Smith 74); Leyden (Wood 71), Anderson S, Strachan, Lisle; Gethins, McGowan (Rodger 88).
Formartine U won 7-6 on penalties.

Ross Co U21 (0) 2 *(Keillor-Dunn 55, Gallagher 83)*
Raith R (2) 3 *(Allan 32, 35, Matthews 89)* 241

Ross Co U21: (4411) Dixon-Hodge; Kelly T, Murray, Hughes, Reid; Keillor-Dunn, Fraser R, Gallagher, MacDonald (Wright 58); Paton; Wallace.
Raith R: (4411) McGurn; Miller, Watson, Benedictus (Davidson 64), McKay; Tait (Spencer 66), Matthews, Hendry, Smith (MacDonald K 69); Anderson G; Allan.

SECOND ROUND – SOUTH

Tuesday, 13 August 2019

Annan Ath (1) 1 *(Currie 20)*
Kelty Hearts (0) 1 *(Ashe 69)* 307

Annan Ath: (442) Taylor; Douglas, Sonkur, Griffiths, Ballantyne (McLear 63); McLean, Bradley, Wilkie, Wooding-Holt; Muir, Currie (Nade 74).
Kelty Hearts: (442) MacKenzie; Philp, Carstairs■, Ashe, Cennerazzo; Mutch (Husband 25), Reilly, McKirdy, Dodd (Campbell 90); Ritchie (Linton 28), Russell.
Kelty Hearts won 6-5 on penalties.

Clyde (1) 4 *(Goodwillie 6, Love 59, McNiff 72, Devine 84 (og))*
Motherwell U21 (0) 0 372

Clyde: (4411) Mitchell; Cuddihy (Johnston 63), McNiff, Howie (Rumsby 73), Allison; Lyon, Grant, Fitzpatrick (Darren Smith 26), Love; Lamont; Goodwillie.
Motherwell U21: (433) Morrison; Brown, Devine, Hussain, Carroll; Robertson, Kettings, McDonald; Maciver, Starrs, Cook (Williamson 61).

Dumbarton (0) 0
St Mirren U21 (1) 1 *(Jack 30)* 279

Dumbarton: (352) Pettigrew; McMillan (Hutton 37), McGeever, Neill; Crawford, McKee (Crossan 66), Zata, Carswell (Quitongo R 34), Scullion; Layne, Tierney.

St Mirren U21: (343) Lyness; McAllister, McBrearty, Glover; Grant, Kellermann, Erhahon, Breadner; Gray (Jamieson 72), Jack, Reilly.

Falkirk (1) 1 *(Longridge 10)*

Celtic U21 (1) 1 *(Robertson 11)* 1706

Falkirk: (4411) Mutch; Miller G, Buchanan, Doyle, Moore (Telfer 80); Leitch (Connolly 80), McShane, Gomis (Sammon 86), MacLean; Longridge; Johnstone.
Celtic U21: (4231) Mullen; Ralston, Deas, Welsh, Church; Connell, Robertson; Miller, Henderson, Okoflex (Burt 75); Aitchison.
Falkirk won 6-5 on penalties.

Hamilton A U21 (0) 0

Airdrieonians (1) 1 *(Carrick 14)* 323

Hamilton A U21: (4231) Southwood; Meikle, Hamilton, Stanger, McCann; Collar (Forrest 70), Mimnaugh; Munro, Winter, Reilly; Slaven.
Airdrieonians: (4312) Hutton; McKay, Kerr, Fordyce, MacDonald; Thomson (Roberts 62), Millar, Cowan; Hawkshaw (Smith 75); Gallagher C (Roy 88), Carrick.

Stenhousemuir (1) 2 *(Watters 33, 74)*

Edinburgh C (0) 1 *(Henderson B 72)* 178

Stenhousemuir: (442) Marley; O'Neil, McKernon, Marsh, McLaughlin; Scullion, Gibbons (Dykes 75), Halleran, Cook; Watters (Hopkirk 90), Anderson (McGuigan 88).
Edinburgh C: (451) Adamson; Kane, Balatoni, McIntyre, Crane; Watson, Brown, Laird, Harris, Smith A (Shepherd 58 (Handling 62)); Court (Henderson B 58).

Stranraer (0) 0

Rangers U21 (0) 2 *(McPake 58, Barjonas 82)* 524

Stranraer: (343) Burgess; Robertson, Hamill, Cummins; Pignatiello, McManus, Smith I (Mitchell 69), Smith D; Hilton, Thomson (Agnew 81), Murphy.
Rangers U21: (442) Wright; Houston, Finlayson, Breen, Patterson; Grezda (Lowry 84), Barjonas, Thomson, Kennedy (Maxwell 78); Mebude, McPake.

THIRD ROUND

Friday, 6 September 2019

Waterford (1) 3 *(Chvedukas 27, Phelan 79, Madika 84)*

Hearts U21 (0) 1 *(Watson 72)* 300

Waterford: (433) Martin; O'Keeffe, Slevin, Murphy, Power; Chvedukas, Holland, Lunney (Phelan 46); Fitzgerald (Madika 62), Whelan, Galvin (Beresford 80).
Hearts U21: (442) Mason; Logan, Hamilton, Watson, Baur; Sandison (Henderson 46), Ritchie (McGill 85), Cochrane, Morrison; Keena, Smith.

Saturday, 7 September 2019

Airdrieonians (1) 3 *(Gallagher C 19, 72, Smith 77)*

Bohemians (1) 2 *(Allardice 45, Wade-Slater 74)* 730

Airdrieonians: (433) Gallacher S; MacDonald, Fordyce, Crighton, Kerr; Thomson (Hawkshaw 83), McKay, Millar; Gallagher C, Carrick (Eckersley 79), Roy (Smith 65).
Bohemians: (4231) Kelly; Lyons, Barker, Barry, Kirk; Allardice, McCourt (Tierney 73); Wade-Slater (Devoy 86), Ward, Graydon; Swan (Wright 78).

Clyde (0) 3 *(McStay 62, Goodwillie 76 (pen), McNiff 78)*

Queen of the South (1) 2 *(Murray 4, Dobbie 47 (pen))* 667

Clyde: (442) Mitchell; Lyon (Wallace 84), Rumsby, Howie, McNiff; Love (Cuddihy 71), Grant, McStay, Darren Smith (Johnston 46); Goodwillie, Lamont.
Queen of the South: (4411) Leighfield; Mercer, Kilday, Brownlie, Holt; Paton (Hamilton 82), Pybus, Lyon, Murray; El Bakhtaoui; Dobbie.

Connah's Quay Nomads (0) 1 *(Bakare 75)*

Cove R (0) 0 327

Connah's Quay Nomads: (433) Brass; Farquharson, Horan, Disney (Owens 66), Roberts; Owen J (Wignall 57), Holmes, Morris; Bakare, Wilde, Woolfe (Insall 57).
Cove R: (4231) McKenzie; Yule, Ross, Higgins, Milne H; Scully, Strachan; Smith (Scott 81), Glass, Masson; Megginson.

Dundee U (0) 0

Arbroath (0) 0 2568

Dundee U: (442) Mehmet; Smith L, Watson, Sporle, Robson; Smith C (McMullan 70), King, Harkes, Pawlett (Stanton 82); Clark, Appere (Shankland 70).
Arbroath: (442) Gaston; Thomson, Little, Stirling, O'Brien; McKenna, Gold (Murphy 68), Whatley, Kader (Linn 68); Donnelly, Doris (Spence 73).
Arbroath won 4-3 on penalties.

Dunfermline Ath (1) 1 *(Kiltie 29)*

Alloa Ath (1) 2 *(Thomson 40, Trouten 53)* 1448

Dunfermline Ath: (4321) Gill; Comrie, Lang (Edwards 61), Ashcroft, Martin L; Beadling, Paton, Matthew Todd (Nisbet 60); Turner, Kiltie; McGill (Ryan 59).
Alloa Ath: (442) Parry (Henry 31); Robertson, Graham, Taggart, Dick; Cawley, Flannigan, Hetherington, Trouten; O'Hara (Malcolm 76), Thomson (Buchanan 57).

Formartine U (0) 0

Glenavon (1) 3 *(Daniels 13, Marshall 70, McCloskey 83)* 470

Formartine U: (433) Main; Mackintosh, McKeown, Clark, Lawrence; Rodger, Anderson S, Strachan; Lisle, Wood, McGowan (Gethins 65).
Glenavon: (442) Tuffey; Harmon, Doyle, Singleton, Burns; Hall (Beggs 84), Marshall, Garrett, Daniels; Mitchell (Hamilton 81), O'Mahony (McCloskey 72).

Inverness CT (2) 3 *(Todorov 25, Doran 31, Storey 57)*

Greenock Morton (0) 1 *(Sutton 78)* 1021

Inverness CT: (442) Mackay; Rooney, Donaldson, McHattie, Harper; Macgregor, Welsh, Trafford, Doran (Machado 65); Storey (Hyde 90), Todorov (White 80).
Greenock Morton: (352) Ramsbottom; McLean, Grant, Baird; Colville, Orsi, Livingstone (Easdale 89), Salkeld (Sutton 66), Blues; Lyon (Jacobs 62), Muirhead.

Kelty Hearts (1) 1 *(Russell 38)*

Solihull Moors (0) 1 *(Sealey-Harris 72)* 1146

Kelty Hearts: (4411) MacKenzie; Philp, Cennerazzo, Ashe, Linton; Dodd, Reilly, Husband (Bragg 79), McKirdy; Russell; Austin.
Solihull Moors: (433) Boot; Williams, Howe, Gudger, Reckord; Osborne (Vaughan 87), Storer, Carter; Sealey-Harris (Nicholls 77), Blissett (Hawkridge 70), Hancox.
Solihull Moors won 4-2 on penalties.

Montrose (0) 0

Partick Thistle (1) 2 *(Cardle 2, Miller 53)* 831

Montrose: (433) Lennox; Cammy Ballantyne, Dillon, Waddell, Campbell I; Webster (Masson 71), Allan, Milne; Skelly (Johnston 56), Campbell R (Rennie 71), Lyons.
Partick Thistle: (433) Fox; Williamson, O'Ware, McGinty, Penrice; Cole (Hall 77), Niang (Watson 86), Robson (Mansell 80); Cardle, De Vita, Miller.

Raith R (1) 2 *(Hendry 17 (pen), 50 (pen))*

Falkirk (0) 0 1771

Raith R: (442) Munro; Miller, Davidson (Anderson S 53), Benedictus, MacDonald K; Tait (Vaughan 72), Hendry, Spencer, Anderson G; Bowie (McKay 76), Allan.
Falkirk: (433) Mutch; Miller G, Durnan, Buchanan, Dixon; Telfer, McShane, Longridge; Leitch (McManus 56), Johnstone (Sammon 71), Moore (Connolly 56).

St Mirren U21 (0) 1 *(MacPherson 80)*

Stirling Alb (0) 0 450

St Mirren U21: (4231) Lyness; Grant, McBrearty, Glover, Walker (McMaster 76); MacPherson, Gray; Breadner, Jack (McCaw 88), Reilly (Henderson 72); Jamieson.
Stirling Alb: (4231) Binnie; Truesdale, McLean, Banner, Creaney (Mackin 80); Docherty, Jardine; Heaver (Scott 62), Peters, Bikey (Thomson 76); Wright.

Stenhousemuir (0) 1 *(Anderson 48)*

The New Saints (0) 1 *(Brobbel 86)* 335

Stenhousemuir: (451) Smith; O'Neil, Marsh, Munro A, McLaughlin; Scullion (Hopkirk 71), Halleran, McKernon, Gibson, McIlduff (Gibbons 88); Anderson (Watters 81).
The New Saints: (4312) Harrison; Lewis (Spender 72), Davies, Harrington, Marriott; Brobbel, Redmond, Cieslewicz; Edwards; Byrne (Whitehouse 59), Draper (Ebbe 67).
Stenhousemuir won 3-1 on penalties.

Wrexham (0) 1 *(Bickerstaff 70)*

Ayr U (0) 1 *(Roscoe 86)* 1697

Wrexham: (4231) Szczepaniak; Barnum-Bobb, Tharme (Thorn 87), Lawlor, Bickerstaff; Barton, Cleworth; Rutherford, Redmond (Jones 80), Tollitt; McIntosh (Williams 72).
Ayr U: (442) Hare-Reid; Geggan, Bell, Roscoe, Muirhead (Ecrepont 15); McCowan, Kerr, Docherty, Forrest; Doolan (McKenzie 72), Moffat.
Wrexham won 6-5 on penalties.

Sunday, 8 September 2019

Dundee (1) 1 *(Kerr 18)*

Elgin C (0) 2 *(Omar 56, Sutherland 58)* 1619

Dundee: (442) Ferrie■; Kerr, McGhee, Meekings, Mackie (Sharp 60); Todd, Byrne (Anderson 76), Ness (Nelson 46), McDaid; McGowan P, Hemmings.
Elgin C: (442) McHale; Wilson, Bronsky, McDonald, Spark; Cameron, Cooper, Dingwall, Omar (Sopel 83); Hester (MacEwan 70), Sutherland.

Wednesday, 18 September 2019

Ballymena U (0) 0

Rangers U21 (0) 1 *(Atakayi 87)* 895

Ballymena U: (352) Williamson; Ervin, Addis, Harpur; Kane (Millar 29), Burns, Lavery, Kelly (Carville 80), Balmer; Mayse, McGinty (Friel 74).
Rangers U21: (433) Wright; Patterson, Finlayson, Breen, Maxwell (Atakayi 46); Grezda (Young-Coombes 84), Docherty, Mayo; Barjonas, Mebude, Kennedy.

FOURTH ROUND

Friday, 11 October 2019

Stenhousemuir (1) 3 *(McLaughlin 30, Hopkirk 61, McGuigan 90)*

Waterford (1) 2 *(Fitzgerald 24, O'Connor 74)* 559

Stenhousemuir: (442) Smith; O'Neil, Munro A, Marsh, McLaughlin; McBride (Anderson 63), Gibson, Halleran (Watters 81), Cook; McGuigan, Hopkirk.
Waterford: (451) Martin; Power, Feely, Slevin, Kavanagh; Fitzgerald (Figueira 70), Poynton, Galvin, Holland, O'Halloran (O'Connor 70); Walsh (Lunney 70).

Saturday, 12 October 2019

Airdrieonians (0) 0

Elgin C (0) 2 *(Hester 88, Sutherland 90 (pen))* 615

Airdrieonians: (433) Hutton; MacDonald (Moore 90), Fordyce, Crighton, Eckersley; Roberts, McKay (Wedderburn 71), Hawkshaw; Carrick, Smith, Roy (Gallagher C 62).
Elgin C: (442) McHale; Wilson, Bronsky, McDonald, Spark; Cooper (MacEwan 79), Cameron, Dingwall, Mackay (Omar 67); Hester (McHardy 90), Sutherland.

Arbroath (0) 0

Clyde (1) 2 *(Johnston 9, Little 68 (og))* 806

Arbroath: (442) Gaston; Stirling, Little, O'Brien, Hamilton; McKenna (Linn 65), Whatley, Murphy (Gold 71), Kader; Doris, Spence (Donnelly 65).
Clyde: (442) Mitchell; Cuddihy, Howie, Rumsby, McNiff; Johnston (Wallace 66), Grant, McStay, Lyon (Duffie 77); Goodwillie, Darren Smith (Love 80).

Inverness CT (1) 3 *(Curry 42, Trafford 64, Machado 88)*

Alloa Ath (0) 0 973

Inverness CT: (442) Mackay; Rooney, Donaldson, McHattie, Harper; Curry (White 75), Carson, Trafford (Vincent 78), Doran; Storey, MacGregor (Machado 85).
Alloa Ath: (442) MacDonald; Robertson, Graham, Taggart, Gilhooley; Cawley, Trouten, Flannigan, Brown (O'Donnel 86); O'Hara (Thomson 65), Buchanan.

Partick Thistle (1) 2 *(De Vita 34, Penrice 77)*

Connah's Quay Nomads (0) 0 1380

Partick Thistle: (352) Fox; Saunders, O'Ware, McGinty; Williamson, Kakay, Bannigan, Cardle (Robson 70), Penrice; Miller, De Vita (Slater 84).
Connah's Quay Nomads: (442) Brass; Disney (Dool 80), Farquharson, Horan, Roberts (Owens 84); Poole, Morris, Owen J (Insall 58), Holmes; Bakare, Wilde.

Raith R (2) 3 *(Bowie 15, Armstrong 32, Allan 90)*

Glenavon (1) 1 *(Marshall 24)* 1301

Raith R: (4231) Munro; Miller, Anderson S, Davidson, MacDonald K; Spencer, Hendry; Armstrong (Tait 82), Anderson G (Dingwall 60), Bowie; Baird (Allan 68).
Glenavon: (541) Tuffey; Harmon (McCloskey 77), Larmour, Doyle (Hall 77), Singleton, Burns; Wearen, Marshall, Garrett (Hamilton 86), Beggs; Mitchell.

Wrexham (0) 4 *(Redmond 46, McIntosh 55 (pen), 73, Tollitt 89)*

St Mirren U21 (0) 1 *(Henderson 68)* 1468

Wrexham: (41212) Lainton; Tharme, Chambers, Cleworth, Thorn; Jones; Wright, Redmond; Tollitt (Huxley 90); Bickerstaff (Robinson-Murray 78), McIntosh.
St Mirren U21: (4231) Lyness; Grant (Jamieson 59), McAllister, Glover, Erhahon; McBrearty, MacPherson; Henderson, Gray, Breadner (Reilly 82); Jack (McCaw 86).

Tuesday, 29 October 2019

Solihull Moors (2) 3 *(Howe 8, Yussuf 36, Carter 60)*

Rangers U21 (1) 3 *(Barjonas 11, Grezda 69, 84)* 1598

Solihull Moors: (433) Boot; Neufville, Williams, Howe, Hancox; Carter, Hawkridge, Ball (Bigirimana 56); Yussuf (Reckord 83), McCallum, Blissett (Beesley 55).
Rangers U21: (451) Budinauckas; Patterson, Finlayson, Breen, Maxwell; Grezda, Barjonas, Williamson (Atakayi 46), Dickson (Young-Coombes 80), Kennedy; Mebude.
Rangers U21 won 4-3 on penalties.

QUARTER-FINALS

Friday, 15 November 2019

Raith R (2) 3 *(Bowie 6, 25, McKay 56)*

Elgin C (1) 2 *(Hester 35, Sutherland 84)* 1108

Raith R: (352) Munro; Davidson, Anderson S, Benedictus; McKay, Armstrong (Anderson G 79), Matthews, Spencer, MacDonald K; Baird (Allan 70), Bowie (Dingwall 79).
Elgin C: (442) McHale; Cooper (McHardy 75), McDonald, Bronsky, Spark; Omar■, Cameron, Dingwall, Mackay (O'Keefe 57); Hester (MacEwan 69), Sutherland.

Saturday, 16 November 2019

Inverness CT (0) 0

Clyde (0) 0 1066

Inverness CT: (4411) Ridgers; McKay, Donaldson, McCart, Tremarco; Storey, Vincent, Trafford (Carson 81), Doran; Curry (Keatings 63); White (Todorov 70).
Clyde: (4411) Mitchell; Duffie, Howie, Rumsby, McNiff; Lyon (McMullin 83), McStay, Cuddihy, Grant; Wallace; Darren Smith (Lamont 72).
Inverness CT won 4-2 on penalties.

Rangers U21 (1) 2 *(Barjonas 35, Young-Coombes 71)*

Wrexham (0) 0 5426

Rangers U21: (433) Wright; Patterson (Young-Coombes 31), Edmundson, Breen, Flanagan; Mayo, Barjonas, Maxwell; Dickson (Butterworth 87), Atakayi (Lyall 76), Kennedy.
Wrexham: (433) Dibble; Barnum-Bobb, Tharme, Chambers, Thorn; Robinson-Murray (Bickerstaff 60), Cleworth, Redmond; Jones (Huxley 80), Oswell, McIntosh.

Stenhousemuir (0) 1 *(Hopkirk 68)*
Partick Thistle (1) 4 *(Cole 34, Harkins 70, Slater 79, Miller 86)* 1244

Stenhousemuir: (4141) Smith; Marsh, Armstrong, Munro A, McLaughlin; Gibson (McBride 81); Tiffoney, Dykes (Halleran 81), McGuigan (Anderson 63), Cook; Hopkirk.
Partick Thistle: (442) Fox; Williamson, O'Ware, Hall, Penrice; Cardle, Cole, Slater, De Vita (Robson 53); Miller, Mansell (Harkins 62).

SEMI-FINALS

Friday, 14 February 2020

Partick Thistle (0) 1 *(Mansell 83)*
Raith R (1) 2 *(Benedictus 31, Hendry 74)* 2196

Partick Thistle: (442) Fox; O'Connor, Saunders, O'Ware, Penrice; Cardle (Robson 89), Cole (Austin 70), Bannigan, Gordon; Graham, Jones (Mansell 59).
Raith R: (433) Thomson; McKay, Davidson, Benedictus, MacDonald K; Tait (Spencer 64), Hendry, Matthews; Bowie (Armstrong 75), MacLean, Baird (Dingwall 76).

Sunday, 16 February 2020

Inverness CT (1) 2 *(Keatings 44, Storey 73)*
Rangers U21 (1) 1 *(Mebude 6)* 1741

Inverness CT: (4411) Ridgers; Rooney, Toshney, McHattie, Tremarco; Storey, Carson, Trafford (Keatings■ 29), Walsh (Doran 79); Vincent; White (Todorov 74).
Rangers U21: (433) Firth; Patterson, Palmer (McCausland 83), Breen, Shiels (Maxwell 87); Hastie (Young-Coombes 75), Finlayson, McPake; Dickson, Mebude, Kennedy.

TUNNOCK'S CARAMEL WAFER SCOTTISH LEAGUE CHALLENGE CUP FINAL 2019–20

Sunday, 8 March 2020

(at McDiamid Park)

Due to the COVID-19 pandemic, the final was postponed.

LEAGUE CHALLENGE FINALS 1990–2020

B&Q CENTENARY CUP

1990–91	Dundee v Ayr U	3-2*

B&Q CUP

1991–92	Hamilton A v Ayr U	1-0
1992–93	Hamilton A v Morton	3-2
1993–94	Falkirk v St Mirren	3-0
1994–95	Airdrieonians v Dundee	3-2*

SCOTTISH LEAGUE CHALLENGE CUP

1995–96	Stenhousemuir v Dundee U	0-0*
	Stenhousemuir won 5-4 on penalties.	
1996–97	Stranraer v St Johnstone	1-0
1997–98	Falkirk v Queen of the South	1-0
1998–99	*No competition.*	
	Suspended due to lack of sponsorship.	

BELL'S CHALLENGE CUP

1999–2000	Alloa Ath v Inverness CT	4-4*
	Alloa Ath won 5-4 on penalties.	
2000–01	Airdrieonians v Livingston	2-2*
	Airdrieonians won 3-2 on penalties.	
2001–02	Airdrieonians v Alloa Ath	2-1

BELL'S CUP

2002–03	Queen of the South v Brechin C	2-0
2003–04	Inverness CT v Airdrie U	2-0
2004–05	Falkirk v Ross Co	2-1
2005–06	St Mirren v Hamilton A	2-1

SCOTTISH LEAGUE CHALLENGE CUP

2006–07	Ross Co v Clyde	1-1*
	Ross Co won 5-4 on penalties.	
2007–08	St Johnstone v Dunfermline Ath	3-2

ALBA CHALLENGE CUP

2008–09	Airdrie U v Ross Co	2-2*
	Airdrie U won 3-2 on penalties.	
2009–10	Dundee v Inverness CT	3-2
2010–11	Ross Co v Queen of the South	2-0

RAMSDENS CUP

2011–12	Falkirk v Hamilton A	1-0
2012–13	Queen of the South v Partick Thistle	1-1*
	Queen of the South won 6-5 on penalties.	
2013–14	Raith R v Rangers	1-0*

PETROFAC TRAINING SCOTTISH LEAGUE CHALLENGE CUP

2014–15	Livingston v Alloa Athletic	4-0
2015–16	Rangers v Peterhead	4-0

IRN-BRU SCOTTISH LEAGUE CHALLENGE CUP

2016–17	Dundee U v St Mirren	2-1
2017–18	Inverness CT v Dumbarton	1-0
2018–19	Ross Co v Connah's Quay Nomads	3-1

TUNNOCK'S CARAMEL WAFER SCOTTISH LEAGUE CHALLENGE CUP

2019–20†	Raith R v Inverness CT	P-P

**After extra time. †Due to the COVID-19 pandemic, the final due to be played on Sunday 8 March 2020 was postponed.*

SCOTTISH CUP FINALS 1874–2020

SCOTTISH FA CUP

1874	Queen's Park v Clydesdale	2-0
1875	Queen's Park v Renton	3-0
1876	Queen's Park v Third Lanark	1-1
Replay	Queen's Park v Third Lanark	2-0
1877	Vale of Leven v Rangers	1-1
Replay	Vale of Leven v Rangers	1-1
2nd Replay	Vale of Leven v Rangers	3-2
1878	Vale of Leven v Third Lanark	1-0
1879	Vale of Leven v Rangers	1-1
	Vale of Leven awarded cup, Rangers failing to appear for replay.	
1880	Queen's Park v Thornliebank	3-0
1881	Queen's Park v Dumbarton	2-1
Replay	Queen's Park v Dumbarton	3-1
	After Dumbarton protested the first game.	
1882	Queen's Park v Dumbarton	2-2
Replay	Queen's Park v Dumbarton	4-1
1883	Dumbarton v Vale of Leven	2-2
Replay	Dumbarton v Vale of Leven	2-1
1884	Queen's Park v Vale of Leven	
	Queen's Park awarded cup, Vale of Leven failing to appear.	
1885	Renton v Vale of Leven	0-0
Replay	Renton v Vale of Leven	3-1
1886	Queen's Park v Renton	3-1
1887	Hibernian v Dumbarton	2-1
1888	Renton v Cambuslang	6-1
1889	Third Lanark v Celtic	3-0
Replay	Third Lanark v Celtic	2-1
	Replay by order of Scottish FA because of playing conditions in first match.	
1890	Queen's Park v Vale of Leven	1-1
Replay	Queen's Park v Vale of Leven	2-1
1891	Hearts v Dumbarton	1-0
1892	Celtic v Queen's Park	1-0
Replay	Celtic v Queen's Park	5-1
	After mutually protested first match.	
1893	Queen's Park v Celtic	0-1
Replay	Queen's Park v Celtic	2-1
	Replay by order of Scottish FA because of playing conditions in first match.	
1894	Rangers v Celtic	3-1
1895	St Bernard's v Renton	2-1
1896	Hearts v Hibernian	3-1
1897	Rangers v Dumbarton	5-1
1898	Rangers v Kilmarnock	2-0
1899	Celtic v Rangers	2-0
1900	Celtic v Queen's Park	4-3
1901	Hearts v Celtic	4-3
1902	Hibernian v Celtic	1-0
1903	Rangers v Hearts	1-1
Replay	Rangers v Hearts	0-0
2nd Replay	Rangers v Hearts	2-0
1904	Celtic v Rangers	3-2
1905	Third Lanark v Rangers	0-0
Replay	Third Lanark v Rangers	3-1
1906	Hearts v Third Lanark	1-0
1907	Celtic v Hearts	3-0
1908	Celtic v St Mirren	5-1
1909	Celtic v Rangers	2-2
Replay	Celtic v Rangers	1-1
	Owing to riot, the cup was withheld.	
1910	Dundee v Clyde	2-2
Replay	Dundee v Clyde	0-0*
2nd Replay	Dundee v Clyde	2-1
1911	Celtic v Hamilton A	0-0
Replay	Celtic v Hamilton A	2-0
1912	Celtic v Clyde	2-0
1913	Falkirk v Raith R	2-0
1914	Celtic v Hibernian	0-0
Replay	Celtic v Hibernian	4-1
1920	Kilmarnock v Albion R	3-2
1921	Partick Thistle v Rangers	1-0
1922	Morton v Rangers	1-0
1923	Celtic v Hibernian	1-0
1924	Airdrieonians v Hibernian	2-0
1925	Celtic v Dundee	2-1
1926	St Mirren v Celtic	2-0
1927	Celtic v East Fife	3-1
1928	Rangers v Celtic	4-0
1929	Kilmarnock v Rangers	2-0
1930	Rangers v Partick Thistle	0-0
Replay	Rangers v Partick Thistle	2-1
1931	Celtic v Motherwell	2-2
Replay	Celtic v Motherwell	4-2
1932	Rangers v Kilmarnock	1-1
Replay	Rangers v Kilmarnock	3-0
1933	Celtic v Motherwell	1-0
1934	Rangers v St Mirren	5-0
1935	Rangers v Hamilton A	2-1
1936	Rangers v Third Lanark	1-0
1937	Celtic v Aberdeen	2-1
1938	East Fife v Kilmarnock	1-1
Replay	East Fife v Kilmarnock	4-2*
1939	Clyde v Motherwell	4-0
1947	Aberdeen v Hibernian	2-1
1948	Rangers v Morton	1-1*
Replay	Rangers v Morton	1-0*
1949	Rangers v Clyde	4-1
1950	Rangers v East Fife	3-0
1951	Celtic v Motherwell	1-0
1952	Motherwell v Dundee	4-0
1953	Rangers v Aberdeen	1-1
Replay	Rangers v Aberdeen	1-0
1954	Celtic v Aberdeen	2-1
1955	Clyde v Celtic	1-1
Replay	Clyde v Celtic	1-0
1956	Hearts v Celtic	3-1
1957	Falkirk v Kilmarnock	1-1
Replay	Falkirk v Kilmarnock	2-1*
1958	Clyde v Hibernian	1-0
1959	St Mirren v Aberdeen	3-1
1960	Rangers v Kilmarnock	2-0
1961	Dunfermline Ath v Celtic	0-0
Replay	Dunfermline Ath v Celtic	2-0
1962	Rangers v St Mirren	2-0
1963	Rangers v Celtic	1-1
Replay	Rangers v Celtic	3-0
1964	Rangers v Dundee	3-1
1965	Celtic v Dunfermline Ath	3-2
1966	Rangers v Celtic	0-0
Replay	Rangers v Celtic	1-0
1967	Celtic v Aberdeen	2-0
1968	Dunfermline Ath v Hearts	3-1
1969	Celtic v Rangers	4-0
1970	Aberdeen v Celtic	3-1
1971	Celtic v Rangers	1-1
Replay	Celtic v Rangers	2-1
1972	Celtic v Hibernian	6-1
1973	Rangers v Celtic	3-2
1974	Celtic v Dundee U	3-0
1975	Celtic v Airdrieonians	3-1
1976	Rangers v Hearts	3-1
1977	Celtic v Rangers	1-0
1978	Rangers v Aberdeen	2-1
1979	Rangers v Hibernian	0-0
Replay	Rangers v Hibernian	0-0*
2nd Replay	Rangers v Hibernian	3-2*
1980	Celtic v Rangers	1-0*
1981	Rangers v Dundee U	0-0*
Replay	Rangers v Dundee U	4-1
1982	Aberdeen v Rangers	4-1*
1983	Aberdeen v Rangers	1-0*
1984	Aberdeen v Celtic	2-1*
1985	Celtic v Dundee U	2-1
1986	Aberdeen v Hearts	3-0
1987	St Mirren v Dundee U	1-0*
1988	Celtic v Dundee U	2-1
1989	Celtic v Rangers	1-0

TENNENTS SCOTTISH CUP

1990	Aberdeen v Celtic	0-0*
	Aberdeen won 9-8 on penalties.	
1991	Motherwell v Dundee U	4-3*
1992	Rangers v Airdrieonians	2-1
1993	Rangers v Aberdeen	2-1
1994	Dundee U v Rangers	1-0
1995	Celtic v Airdrieonians	1-0
1996	Rangers v Hearts	5-1
1997	Kilmarnock v Falkirk	1-0
1998	Hearts v Rangers	2-1
1999	Rangers v Celtic	1-0
2000	Rangers v Aberdeen	4-0
2001	Celtic v Hibernian	3-0
2002	Rangers v Celtic	3-2
2003	Rangers v Dundee	1-0
2004	Celtic v Dunfermline Ath	3-1
2005	Celtic v Dundee U	1-0
2006	Hearts v Gretna	1-1*
	Hearts won 4-2 on penalties.	
2007	Celtic v Dunfermline Ath	1-0

SCOTTISH FA CUP

2008	Rangers v Queen of the South	3-2

HOMECOMING SCOTTISH CUP

2009	Rangers v Falkirk	1-0

ACTIVE NATION SCOTTISH CUP

2010	Dundee U v Ross Co	3-0

SCOTTISH FA CUP

2011	Celtic v Motherwell	3-0

WILLIAM HILL SCOTTISH CUP

2012	Hearts v Hibernian	5-1
2013	Celtic v Hibernian	3-0
2014	St Johnstone v Dundee U	2-0
2015	Inverness CT v Falkirk	2-1
2016	Hibernian v Rangers	3-2
2017	Celtic v Aberdeen	2-1
2018	Celtic v Motherwell	2-0
2019	Celtic v Hearts	2-1
2020	*Still to be played.*	

**After extra time.*

SCOTTISH CUP WINS

Celtic 39, Rangers 33, Queen's Park 10, Hearts 8, Aberdeen 7, Clyde 3, Hibernian 3, Kilmarnock 3, St Mirren 3, Vale of Leven 3, Dundee U 2, Dunfermline Ath 2, Falkirk 2, Motherwell 2, Renton 2, Third Lanark 2, Airdrieonians 1, Dumbarton 1, Dundee 1, East Fife 1, Inverness CT 1, Morton 1, Partick Thistle 1, St Bernard's 1, St Johnstone 1.

APPEARANCES IN FINAL

Celtic 58, Rangers 52, Aberdeen 16, Hearts 15, Hibernian 14, Queen's Park 12, Dundee U 10, Kilmarnock 8, Motherwell 8, Vale of Leven 7, Clyde 6, Dumbarton 6, St Mirren 6, Third Lanark 6, Dundee 5, Dunfermline Ath 5, Falkirk 5, Renton 5, Airdrieonians 4, East Fife 3, Hamilton A 2, Morton 2, Partick Thistle 2, Albion R 1, Cambuslang 1, Clydesdale 1, Gretna 1, Inverness CT 1, Queen of the South 1, Raith R 1, Ross Co 1, St Bernard's 1, St Johnstone 1, Thornliebank 1.

WILLIAM HILL SCOTTISH FA CUP 2019–20

■ *Denotes player sent off.*

FIRST PRELIMINARY ROUND

Banks O'Dee v Glasgow Uni	5-0
Broxburn Ath v Tynecastle	2-0
Camelon Juniors v Newton Stewart	4-0
Coldstream v Jeanfield Swifts	1-9
Dundonald Bluebell v Auchinleck Talbot	2-2
Easthouses Lily v Penicuik Ath	1-6
Hawick Royal Albert v Threave R	1-6
Hill Of Beath Hawthorn v Blackburn U	2-0
Linlithgow Rose v Preston Ath	2-1
Lochee U v Burntisland Shipyard	7-0
St Cuthbert W v Girvan	1-7
Lothian Hutchison v Wigtown & Bladnoch	5-0
Colville Park v Whitehill Welfare	0-4

Golspie Sutherland received a bye to second preliminary round

FIRST PRELIMINARY ROUND REPLAY

Auchinleck Talbot v Dundonald Bluebell	6-1

SECOND PRELIMINARY ROUND

Banks O'Dee v Golspie Sutherland	2-0
Camelon Juniors v Auchinleck Talbot	0-2
Girvan v Broxburn Ath	0-1
Lochee U v Lothian Hutchison	5-2
Threave R v Hill Of Beath Hawthorn	0-2
Whitehill Welfare v Penicuik Ath	0-1
Jeanfield Swifts v Linlithgow Rose	2-5

FIRST ROUND

Kelty Hearts v Auchinleck Talbot	0-3
Broxburn Ath v East Stirling	3-2
Buckie Thistle v Civil Service Strollers	4-1
Caledonian Braves v Rothes	3-4
Cumbernauld Colts v Penicuik Ath	1-5
Dalbeattie Star v Gala Fairydean	1-3
Edinburgh Uni v Lochee U	1-3
Forres Mechanics v Banks O'Dee	1-4
Fort William v Vale Of Leithen	5-0
Fraserburgh v Bonnyrigg Rose	0-1
Gretna 2008 v Hill Of Beath Hawthorn	1-0
Inverurie Loco Works v Wick Academy	3-2
Keith v Stirling Uni	2-3
Linlithgow Rose v Huntly	1-0
Nairn County v Clachnacuddin	0-0
Spartans v Deveronvale	1-1
Strathspey Thistle v Lossiemouth	2-1
Turriff U v Formartine U	1-5

FIRST ROUND REPLAYS

Clachnacuddin v Nairn County	2-1
Deveronvale v Spartans	1-2

SECOND ROUND

Bonnyrigg Rose v Buckie Thistle	2-0
Edinburgh C v Banks O'Dee	3-1
Albion R v Fort William	1-1
Annan Ath v Brechin C	2-2
Auchinleck Talbot v Cove Rangers	1-0
Clachnacuddin v Brora Rangers	0-7
Cowdenbeath v Broxburn Ath	1-1
East Kilbride v Gretna 2008	3-1
Elgin C v Berwick Rangers	3-1
Formartine U v Gala Fairydean	2-2
Lochee U v BSC Glasgow	1-1
Rothes v Inverurie Loco Works	1-3
Spartans v Queen's Park	0-2
Stirling Alb v Strathspey Thistle	2-0
Stirling Uni v Linlithgow Rose	0-2
Penicuik Ath v Stenhousemuir	3-0

SECOND ROUND REPLAYS

Brechin C v Annan Ath	0-2
Broxburn Ath v Cowdenbeath	3-0
Fort William v Albion R	0-5
Gala Fairydean v Formartine U	1-2
BSC Glasgow v Lochee U	2-1

THIRD ROUND

Friday, 22 November 2019

Linlithgow Rose (1) 1 *(Coyne 20)*

Falkirk (2) 4 *(Sammon 8, 30, McManus 78, Dixon 86)* 1720

Linlithgow Rose: (4231) McKinven; Thom (Collumbine 63), McGowan, Scullion, McKinlay (Strickland 80); Gray, MacLennan; Ronald, Slaven (Danny Smith 83), Allum; Coyne.

Falkirk: (352) Mutch; Durnan, Buchanan, Toshney; Doyle, Longridge (MacLean 89), Miller G, Gomis (Tidser 73), Dixon; McManus (Johnstone 89), Sammon.

Referee: Grant Irvine.

Saturday, 23 November 2019

Albion R (0) 1 *(Crighton 51 (og))*

Airdrieonians (1) 4 *(Roberts 13, Crighton 60, 83, MacDonald 87)* 1127

Albion R: (442) Goodfellow; Lynas, Krones, Wharton, Clarke; Scally, Phillips (See 82), Morena, Roberts; Byrne, East (Osadolor 66).

Airdrieonians: (442) Hutton; MacDonald, Crighton, Fordyce, McCann; Smith, McKay, Roberts (Reilly 86), Millar; Carrick, Roy (Hawkshaw 75).

Referee: Kevin Graham.

Auchinleck Talbot (1) 1 *(Hyslop 11)*

Arbroath (0) 1 *(McKenna 84 (pen))* 921

Auchinleck Talbot: (4411) Leishman; Lyle, McPherson, McCracken, Pope; Boylan (Glasgow 66), Healy (McDowall 87), Wilson S, Samson (Shankland 67); Hyslop; Wilson G.

Arbroath: (442) Gaston; Gold, O'Brien, Little, Hamilton; Spence (Campbell 63), Whatley, Murphy (Stewart 46), Linn (Kader 81); McKenna, Donnelly.

Referee: David Lowe.

Bonnyrigg Rose (2) 2 *(Moyes 18, Brown 45)*

Montrose (1) 1 *(Campbell R 43)* 2017

Bonnyrigg Rose: (352) Weir; Young■, Moyes, Martyniuk; Brett, Horne, Stewart (Baur 85), Currie, Brown; Hunter (McGachie 75), Gray R (Gray S 70).

Montrose: (433) Fleming; Cammy Ballantyne, Waddell (Dillon 46), Campbell I, Steeves; Masson, Watson (Rennie 76), Callaghan (Niang 59); Webster, Campbell R, Lyons.

Referee: John McKendrick.

Dumbarton (1) 3 *(Frizzell 9, McGeever 72, Layne 78)*

Forfar Ath (1) 1 *(Tapping 20)* 424

Dumbarton: (4411) Brennan; McMillan, McGeever, Neill, Shiels; Frizzell, Hutton, Carswell, Crossan (Langan 80); McCluskey; Layne (Tierney 84).

Forfar Ath: (4411) McCallum; Meechan, Whyte, Travis, Bain; MacKintosh, Irvine, Robertson (Docherty 62), Tapping (Andrew Jackson 86); Kirkpatrick (Forbes 68); Hilson.

Referee: Chris Fordyce.

East Fife (2) 3 *(Dowds 16, Watt 44, Watson C 53)*

BSC Glasgow (1) 4 *(Orr 5, 90, Collins 57, Hughes 76 (pen))* 484

East Fife: (442) Hart; Watson C, Murdoch, Higgins, Slattery; Watt, Davidson R, Agnew, Denholm (Dunsmore 78); Dowds, Boyd (Duggan 60).

BSC Glasgow: (442) Marshall R; McCormack, Smith R, McMillan, Mills; Hamilton (Northcott 73), Hughes, McNab (Grehan 57), Andersen; Orr, Collins.

Referee: Matthew MacDermid.

Edinburgh C (3) 4 *(Henderson B 21, 24, Court 28, Harris 49)*

Annan Ath (0) 3 *(Flanagan 48, 80, Muir 69 (pen))* 176

Edinburgh C: (442) McAdams; Wilson, Balatoni, Kane, Crane; Handling (Smith A 84), Brown, Laird, Harris (Henderson L 76); Henderson B, Court (Shepherd 70).

Annan Ath: (442) Smith; Douglas, Barr (Joseph 63), Swinglehurst, Ballantyne; Flanagan, Bradley (Sonkur 30), Wilkie, McLean; Muir, Watson B (Nade 75).
Referee: Duncan Williams.

Elgin C (1) 1 *(MacEwan 26)*

Alloa Ath (0) 3 *(Taggart 48, Cawley 58, O'Hara 63)* 668

Elgin C: (442) McHale; Cooper, Bronsky, McDonald, Spark; MacEwan (McHardy 68), Cameron, Dingwall, O'Keefe (Wilson 84); Sutherland, Hester.
Alloa Ath: (442) MacDonald; Taggart, Deas, Graham, Dick (Gilhooley 56); Cawley, Robertson, Thomson (Buchanan 66), Flannigan; Trouten, O'Hara (O'Donnel 79).
Referee: Scott Lambie.

Formartine U (0) 0

East Kilbride (1) 4 *(Paton 20, 74, Brady 48, Holmes 58)*

Formartine U: (4141) Main; Crawford, Kelly, McKeown, Smith; Anderson S; Norris (McGowan 61), Rodger, Mackintosh (Lawrence 71), Lisle (Park 54); Wood.
East Kilbride: (442) McGinley; Stanger, Brownlie, Fisher, Coll; Winter, Holmes, Cairns, Woods; Paton, Brady (Carmichael 60).
Referee: Graham Grainger.

Greenock Morton (1) 1 *(McHugh 44 (pen))*

Brora Rangers (1) 1 *(Gillespie 29 (pen))* 925

Greenock Morton: (41212) Rogers; Jacobs, Welsh, Grant, Strapp; Millar (Cadden 70); King (Sutton 79), McAlister; Lyon; Salkeld (Nesbitt 58), McHugh.
Brora Rangers: (442) Malin; John Pickles, Williamson, Nicolson, MacDonald A; Kelly, Maclean (Wagenaar 83), Greg Morrison, Gavin Morrison (Brindle 60); MacRae (Wallace 75), Gillespie.
Referee: Craig Napier.

Inverurie Loco Works (0) 0

Broxburn Ath (0) 1 *(Miller 84)* 1129

Inverurie Loco Works: (442) Reid A; Souter, Watson, Broadhurst, Mitchell; Dingwall, Hunter, Burnett (Michie 87), Stott (McLean 79); Gauld (Angus 73), Smith.
Broxburn Ath: (451) Wallace; Beesley (Nimmo 73), Gavin, Townsley, Donaldson; Grant, Linton, Scott, Kelly, Locke (Binnie 89); Miller.
Referee: Callum Scott.

Partick Thistle (1) 1 *(Cole 1)*

Penicuik Ath (0) 0 3165

Partick Thistle: (352) Fox; Saunders, O'Ware, Hall (Kakay 46); Williamson, Palmer, Cole, Slater, Penrice; Harkins (Miller 46), Zanatta (Robson 84).
Penicuik Ath: (532) Watt; Stevenson, Forbes, Young, Page, Ponton (Kateleza 68); Watson, Connelly, Jones; Tansey (Baptie 78), McCrory-Irving (Stewart 68).
Referee: Mike Roncone.

Queen of the South (0) 1 *(Murray 90)*

Queen's Park (2) 2 *(Kouider-Aisser 15, 30)* 1066

Queen of the South: (442) McCrorie; Mercer, Brownlie, McCarthy (Paton 34), Holt; Lyon, Pybus, Kidd, Murray; Oliver, Dobbie.
Queen's Park: (442) Muir; Little, Clark, Jamieson, Summers; Block, Main, Mortimer, Galt; Kouider-Aisser, Lidohren.
Referee: David Dickinson.

Raith R (1) 1 *(Bowie 3)*

Peterhead (0) 0 1306

Raith R: (3412) Munro; Davidson, Anderson S, Benedictus; McKay, Matthews, Spencer, MacDonald K; Armstrong (Dingwall 71); Bowie (Allan 46), Baird (Anderson G 57).
Peterhead: (442) Fleming; Ferguson, Brown J, Hooper, Boyle; Conroy, Ferry (Eadie 90), Leitch, Smith (Fraser 74); McAllister, Armour (Lyle 74).
Referee: Steven Reid.

Stirling Alb (0) 0

Clyde (1) 2 *(Darren Smith 45, Goodwillie 90 (pen))* 820

Stirling Alb: (442) Currie; Creaney, McLean, McGregor, McGeachie; Willis, Jardine, Nicoll, Bikey (Thomson 83); Heaver (Wright 83), Mackin (Hawke 88).
Clyde: (442) Mitchell; McNiff, Rumsby, Howie, Duffie (Lamont 43); Darren Smith (Petkov 68), Grant, McStay, Cuddihy; Wallace (McMullin 84), Goodwillie.
Referee: Lloyd Wilson.

Stranraer (0) 1 *(Hilton 61 (pen))*

Dunfermline Ath (0) 0 431

Stranraer: (532) Currie; Pignatiello (Murphy 88), Robertson, Cummins, Hamilton, Allan; Hamill, McManus, Stirling; Hilton (Dangana 82), Elliott (Jones 90).
Dunfermline Ath: (442) Scully (Gill 23); Comrie, Devine, Martin L, Edwards; Dow (Beadling 75), Paton, Turner, McCann (Thomson 56); Ryan, Nisbet.
Referee: Alan Newlands.

THIRD ROUND REPLAYS

Wednesday, 27 November 2019

Arbroath (1) 3 *(McKenna 26, Linn 54, Stewart 64)*

Auchinleck Talbot (0) 0 1022

Arbroath: (442) Jamieson; Gold (Campbell 66), Little, O'Brien, Hamilton; Kader, Whatley, Virtanen, Linn (Stewart 61); McKenna, Donnelly (Spence 72).
Auchinleck Talbot: (4411) Leishman; Lyle, McPherson, McCracken, Pope; Glasgow (Shankland 71), White, Wilson S, Hyslop; Boylan (McDowall 61); Wilson G (Samson 61).
Referee: David Lowe.

Tuesday, 3 December 2019

Brora Rangers (0) 1 *(Williamson 65)*

Greenock Morton (1) 3 *(Lyon 18, Cadden 49, 53)* 497

Brora Rangers: (4411) Malin; Kelly, Williamson, Nicolson (Brindle 59), MacDonald A; John Pickles, Gillespie, Gavin Morrison (Wagenaar 46), Maclean; Wallace; MacRae (Mackay 85).
Greenock Morton: (352) Rogers; Welsh, Grant, Strapp; Colville, McAlister, Cadden (Nesbitt 77), Jacobs, Lyon; Muirhead (Salkeld 86), McHugh (Sutton 77).
Referee: Craig Napier.

FOURTH ROUND

Friday, 17 January 2020

Rangers (1) 2 *(Arfield 44, Defoe 66 (pen))*

Stranraer (0) 0 38,560

Rangers: (433) Foderingham; Patterson, Katic, Edmundson, Halliday; Arfield, Jack, Davis; Aribo (Kennedy 81), Defoe (Ojo 67), Jones (Barker 64).
Stranraer: (541) Currie; Pignatiello, Robertson, McManus, Cummins, Allan; Stirling (Hilton 70), Thomson (Jones 81), Hamill, Elliott (McIntyre 86); Stevenson.
Referee: John Beaton.

Saturday, 18 January 2020

Aberdeen (0) 1 *(Cosgrove 86 (pen))*

Dumbarton (0) 0 10,010

Aberdeen: (4231) Lewis; Logan, Taylor, McKenna, Considine; Anderson (Gallagher 90), Ojo; McLennan (Hedges 67), McGeouch (Campbell 78), McGinn; Cosgrove.
Dumbarton: (442) Brennan; Crawford, McGeever, Neill, Quitongo R; McCluskey, Hutton, Wilson (Zata 74), Langan (Tierney 89); Crossan (Scullion 90), McKee.
Referee: Gavin Duncan.

Alloa Ath (1) 2 *(O'Hara 18, 75)*

Inverness CT (1) 3 *(Doran 8, White 61, Trafford 86)* 590

Alloa Ath: (442) MacDonald; Robertson, Taggart, Deas, Dick; Cawley, Hetherington, Brown (Thomson 65), Flannigan; Buchanan (Connelly 62), O'Hara.
Inverness CT: (442) Ridgers; Rooney, McKay, McHattie, Tremarco; Vincent, Trafford (Carson 90), Doran, Storey (Walsh 57); Keatings (Macgregor 83), White.
Referee: William Collum.

Arbroath (0) 0

Falkirk (0) 0 1733

Arbroath: (442) Gaston; Thomson, Little, O'Brien, Hamilton; Stewart, Whatley, Virtanen, Linn (Swankie 76); McKenna, Donnelly (Chalmers 76).
Falkirk: (3412) Mutch; Buchanan, Durnan, Dixon; Doyle, Gomis, McShane, Connolly; Telfer (De Vita 77); McManus, Sammon (McMillan 85).
Referee: Greg Aitken.

Ayr U (1) 1 *(Bell 37)*

Ross Co (0) 0 1538

Ayr U: (433) Doohan; Houston, Muirhead, Bell, Harvie; Kerr, Docherty, Kelly; Moffat (Roscoe 62), Drinan (Doolan 86), Forrest (McCowan 83).
Ross Co: (451) Baxter; Foster, Donaldson, Fontaine, Kelly S; Mullin, Tillson (Henderson 74), Vigurs, Paton (Graham 57), Spittal (McKay 56); Erwin.
Referee: Andrew Dallas.

Bonnyrigg Rose (0) 0

Clyde (0) 1 *(Love 80)* 2213

Bonnyrigg Rose: (352) Weir; Horne, Moyes, Martyniuk (Docherty 85); Brett, Gray S (Gray R 79), Stewart, Currie, Brown; McGachie, Hunter (Turner 79).
Clyde: (442) Mitchell; Lang, Howie (Wallace 69), Rumsby, McNiff; Cuddihy, Lamont, Grant, Wylde (Love 71); Goodwillie, Darren Smith (McMullin 90).
Referee: Peter Stuart.

Dundee (0) 0

Motherwell (2) 3 *(Long 22, 30, 75)* 2407

Dundee: (4411) Hamilton; Kerr, Meekings, McGhee, Marshall; McGowan P (Cameron 76), Byrne (Johnson 66), Ness (Callachan 46), McDaid; Dorrans; Hemmings.
Motherwell: (433) Gillespie; Tait, Gallagher, Hartley, Carroll; O'Hara, Campbell, Polworth (Donnelly 64); Scott (Ndjoli 76), Long, Hylton (Seedorf 31).
Referee: Steven McLean.

East Kilbride (0) 1 *(Malcolm 79 (pen))*

BSC Glasgow (3) 3 *(Collins 1, McCormack 17, Grehan 39)* 671

East Kilbride: (442) McGinley; Coll, Proctor (Brady 46), Brownlie, Reid; Woods (McGrath 62), Holmes, Cairns, Paton (Stevenson 46); Malcolm, Healy.
BSC Glasgow: (442) Marshall R; Mills, McMillan, Smith R (McNab 64), McCormack; Collins, Hughes, Andersen, Hamilton (McKay 75); Grehan, Orr.
Referee: Calum Scott.

Hamilton A (3) 5 *(Dales 22, McMann 26, Martin 44, Winter 80, Miller 84)*

Edinburgh C (0) 0 1040

Hamilton A: (4231) Fon Williams; McGowan (Collar 33), Fjortoft, Easton, McMann (Hunt 46); Gogic, Martin; Dales (Winter 61), Alston, Miller; Oakley.
Edinburgh C: (442) Martin; Thomson, Balatoni, Wilson, Henderson L; Handling, Brown, Crane, Harris (Sinclair 81); Kane, Shepherd (Court 77).
Referee: Euan Anderson.

Hearts (1) 5 *(Irving 7, Clare 54, Naismith 58, Henderson 71, Halkett 90)*

Airdrieonians (0) 0 14,777

Hearts: (442) Joel Pereira; Clare, Halkett, Souttar, Hickey (Garuccio 27); Moore, Smith (Bozanic 41), Irving, Henderson; Washington, Naismith (Walker 77).
Airdrieonians: (343) Hutton; McKay, Crighton, Fordyce; MacDonald (Wedderburn 63), Millar, Kerr, McCann; Smith, Gallagher C (Roy 74), Carrick (Thomson 67).
Referee: Don Robertson.

Kilmarnock (3) 6 *(Bruce 9, Findlay 26, 44, Kiltie 62, Kabamba 89, Johnson 90)*

Queen's Park (0) 0 4198

Kilmarnock: (433) Koprivec; O'Donnell, Bruce (Johnson 56), Findlay (Kabamba 66), Hamalainen; Power, Dicker, El Makrini; Burke, Kiltie, Bunn (Connel 76).
Queen's Park: (532) Muir; Mortimer (Agyeman 64), Finnie, Foy, Little, Summers; Lidohren, Galt, Main (Grant J 79); Moore (McGuire 82), Kouider-Aisser.
Referee: Colin Steven.

Livingston (0) 3 *(Lawless 77 (pen), 90 (pen), Dykes 78)*

Raith R (1) 1 *(Baird 22)* 1725

Livingston: (4231) Schofield; Lawson, Lamie (Robinson 73), Guthrie, Brown; Bartley, Sibbald (Erskine 64); Lawless, Pitman, Souda (McMillan 80); Dykes.
Raith R: (3421) Munro; McKay, Davidson, Benedictus; Miller, Matthews, Hendry, MacDonald K; Tait (Vitoria 88), Dingwall (Bowie 79); Baird (Anderson G 76).
Referee: Alan Newlands.

Partick Thistle (0) 1 *(Bannigan 90 (pen))*

Celtic (1) 2 *(Griffiths 12, McGregor 78)* 9542

Partick Thistle: (4411) Fox; Saunders, O'Ware, McGinty, Penrice; Cole, Bannigan, MacKinnon (Slater 59), Robson; Miller (Harkins 81); Rudden (Zanatta 69).
Celtic: (41212) Forster; Frimpong, Jullien, Bitton (Simunovic 8), Taylor; Brown; Ntcham, McGregor; Rogic (Arzani 85); Griffiths (Klimala 79), Edouard.
Referee: Alan Muir.

St Johnstone (1) 3 *(Booth 4, Davidson 57, May 74)*

Greenock Morton (0) 0 2397

St Johnstone: (442) Clark; Ralston (Duffy 77), Gordon, Kerr, Booth; Wright, Davidson, McCann, Wotherspoon (Tanser 82); Kane, May (Hendry 82).
Greenock Morton: (3511) Rogers; Welsh (Sutton 66), Baird, McLean; Tumilty, Jacobs, McAlister, Cadden, Strapp; Colville (Millar 72); Muirhead (Lyon 80).
Referee: Nick Walsh.

St Mirren (0) 3 *(Obika 55, 90, Mullen 89)*

Broxburn Ath (0) 0 4327

St Mirren: (4231) Hladky; Flynn, McCarthy (Andreu 67), Famewo, Waters; Magennis, Foley; Morias, MacPherson (McGrath 60), Durmus (Mullen 60); Obika.
Broxburn Ath: (4411) Wallace; Grant, Gavin, Townsley, Donaldson; Kelly (Miller 58), Linton, Scott, Nimmo (Ross 68); Locke (Richards 79); Gibson.
Referee: David Munro.

Sunday, 19 January 2020

Dundee U (1) 2 *(Shankland 45, Appere 74)*

Hibernian (1) 2 *(Doidge 8, Boyle 47)* 9400

Dundee U: (4231) Siegrist; Smith L, Watson, Connolly, Robson; Butcher, Harkes (Glass 82); McMullan, Powers, Pawlett (Appere 63); Shankland.
Hibernian: (4231) Marciano; Naismith (Gray 46), Porteous (McGregor 52), Hanlon, Stevenson; Whittaker, Hallberg; Boyle, Allan S, Kamberi; Doidge.
Referee: Kevin Clancy.

FOURTH ROUND REPLAYS

Tuesday, 28 January 2020

Falkirk (0) 2 *(McManus 47, Sammon 66)*

Arbroath (0) 0 2704

Falkirk: (442) Mutch; Doyle, Buchanan, Durnan, Dixon; Connolly (De Vita 83), Miller G, Gomis, Telfer (Todd 74); McManus, Sammon (McMillan 70).
Arbroath: (451) Gaston; Thomson, Little, O'Brien, Hamilton; Stewart, Virtanen (Gold 59), McKenna (Chalmers 70), Whatley, Linn (Kader 70); Donnelly.
Referee: Euan Anderson.

Hibernian (1) 4 *(Allan S 40 (pen), Doidge 60, 73, 90)*

Dundee U (1) 2 *(Shankland 10, Sporle 67)* 10,451

Hibernian: (4231) Marciano; James, Jackson, Hanlon, Stevenson; Whittaker (Hallberg 81), Newell; Boyle, Allan S (Kamberi 72), Horgan (Murray 72); Doidge.
Dundee U: (451) Siegrist; Smith L, Connolly, Reynolds, Robson; Pawlett (Sow 76), Powers, Butcher, Harkes (Sporle 66), Appere (Glass 83); Shankland.
Referee: Kevin Clancy.

FIFTH ROUND

Saturday, 8 February 2020

Aberdeen (0) 0

Kilmarnock (0) 0 9430

Aberdeen: (4231) Lewis; Logan (Main 60), Devlin, McKenna, Considine; Ferguson, Ojo; Kennedy (McLennan 90), Campbell, McGinn; Cosgrove (Anderson 86).
Kilmarnock: (352) Branescu; Broadfoot, Johnson, Del Fabro; O'Donnell, Power, Dicker, McKenzie, Hamalainen; Brophy (Millen 90), Kabamba.
Referee: Nick Walsh.

Ayr U (1) 1 *(Drinan 4)*

St Johnstone (2) 2 *(Muirhead 18 (og), Hendry 27)* 2625

Ayr U: (433) Doohan; Houston, Muirhead■, Bell, Harvie; Gillespie, Kerr (Tiffoney 54), Kelly; McCowan (Roscoe 28), Drinan, Forrest (Moffat 68).
St Johnstone: (442) Clark; Ralston, Kerr, McCart, Booth; Wright, Wotherspoon, Craig, McCann; Hendry (Kane 78), May (Jones 85).
Referee: Steven McLean.

Falkirk (0) 0

Hearts (0) 1 *(Clare 50 (pen))* 5976

Falkirk: (442) Mutch; Doyle, Durnan, Buchanan, Dixon; Todd, Miller G, Gomis (Longridge 73), Connolly (Telfer 76); McManus, Sammon (McMillan 75).
Hearts: (3412) Joel Pereira; Smith, Dikamona, Halkett; Clare (Henderson 73), Langer, Irving, Garuccio; Naismith (Walker 62); Washington (McDonald 82), Boyce.
Referee: John Beaton.

Hamilton A (1) 1 *(Smith L 38)*

Rangers (1) 4 *(Arfield 25, 90, Aribo 68, Morelos 85)* 4050

Hamilton A: (442) Southwood; McGowan, Hamilton, Easton, McMann; Collar, Smith L, Gogic, Dales (Miller 37 (Alston 46)); Davies (Ogboe 36), Winter.
Rangers: (433) McGregor; Tavernier, Goldson, Edmundson, Barisic (Halliday 69); Arfield, Kamara, Hagi (Davis 73); Aribo, Morelos, Kent (Stewart 82).
Referee: Alan Muir.

Inverness CT (0) 1 *(Welsh 61)*

Livingston (0) 0 1512

Inverness CT: (4231) Ridgers; Rooney, McKay, McHattie, Tremarco; Carson, Welsh; Storey (Todorov 90), Trafford, Walsh (Vincent 83); White.
Livingston: (4231) Schofield; Lawson, Brown, Guthrie, Lamie; Bartley, Jacobs (Sibbald 77); Lawless (Menga 66), Pitman, Souda (Robinson 73); Dykes.
Referee: Don Robertson.

St Mirren (0) 1 *(Jakubiak 74)*

Motherwell (1) 1 *(O'Hara 21)* 4323

St Mirren: (4231) Hladky; Hodson (Morias 81), McCarthy, Famewo, Waters; MacPherson, Foley; Jakubiak, McGrath (McAllister 69), Durmus; Obika (Andreu 77).
Motherwell: (433) Gillespie; Grimshaw, Gallagher, Hartley, Carroll; O'Hara (Watt 80), Donnelly, Polworth; Aarons (Campbell 73), Long, Hylton.
Referee: Andrew Dallas.

Sunday, 9 February 2020

BSC Glasgow (1) 1 *(Smith R 38)*

Hibernian (2) 4 *(McNulty 11, 30, 69, Docherty 85)* 2120

BSC Glasgow: (442) Marshall R; McCormack, Smith R, McMillan, Mills; McNab (McKay 80), Andersen, Hughes, Collins; Grehan (Hamilton 89), Orr.
Hibernian: (352) Marciano; McGinn, Hanlon, Stevenson; Whittaker, Boyle (Gullan 80), Docherty, Omeonga (Hallberg 71), Horgan (Murray 60); Doidge, McNulty.
Referee: Alan Newlands.

Clyde (0) 0

Celtic (2) 3 *(Ntcham 16, Brown 40, Bayo 90)* 7536

Clyde: (4141) Mitchell; Howie, Rumsby, Lang, Livingstone; Grant; Cuddihy (Johnston 85), McStay (Cunningham 69), Rankin, Lamont (Love 79); Goodwillie.
Celtic: (4231) Bain; Bauer, Jullien, Ajer, Bolingoli-Mbombo; Ntcham, Brown; Forrest (Hayes 71), Christie, Elyounoussi (Shved 85); Klimala (Bayo 75).
Referee: Bobby Madden.

FIFTH ROUND REPLAYS

Tuesday, 18 February 2020

Motherwell (1) 4 *(Polworth 27, Watt 57, Aarons 73, Campbell 74)*

St Mirren (4) 4 *(Obika 14, 31, Hartley 33 (og), Foley 43)* 4534

Motherwell: (433) Gillespie; Grimshaw (Hylton 62), Mugabi (O'Hara 45), Hartley (Tait 46), Carroll; Donnelly, Campbell, Polworth; Aarons, Watt, Maciver (Manzinga 102).
St Mirren: (442) Hladky; Hodson, McCarthy, Famewo, Waters; Durmus (Andreu 97), MacPherson, Foley (McAllister 103), McGrath; Obika, Jakubiak (Morias 63).
aet; St Mirren won 3-2 on penalties.
Referee: Gavin Duncan.

Wednesday, 19 February 2020

Kilmarnock (1) 3 *(El Makrini 43, Brophy 98, Kabamba 116)*

Aberdeen (0) 4 *(Considine 88, Kennedy 91, Cosgrove 119 (pen), Johnson 120 (og))* 5658

Kilmarnock: (442) Branescu; O'Donnell, Broadfoot, Findlay, Hamalainen; Burke (Millen 87), Power, Dicker, El Makrini (Kiltie 91); Brophy (Johnson 118), Kabamba.
Aberdeen: (3421) Lewis; Taylor (Devlin 102), McKenna, Considine; McGeouch (Logan 46), Bryson (Campbell 46), Ferguson, Kennedy; McGinn, McLennan (Cosgrove 46); Main.
aet.
Referee: Nick Walsh.

QUARTER-FINALS

Friday, 28 February 2020

Hibernian (1) 5 *(Jackson 38, Allan S 58, Docherty 71, Omeonga 81, Gullan 84)*

Inverness CT (0) 2 *(Tremarco 73, Todorov 88)* 9937

Hibernian: (3412) Marciano; McGinn, Jackson, Hanlon; Boyle (Horgan 84), Whittaker (Omeonga 69), Docherty, Stevenson; Allan S; Doidge, McNulty (Gullan 80).
Inverness CT: (4231) Ridgers; Rooney, McKay■, McHattie, Tremarco; Carson, Trafford; Walsh, Keatings (Harper 78), Doran (Todorov 75); White (Storey 63).
Referee: Nick Walsh.

Saturday, 29 February 2020

Hearts (0) 1 *(Bozanic 58)*

Rangers (0) 0 11,428

Hearts: (4411) Zlamal; Clare, Halkett, Souttar (Dikamona 16), Hickey; Moore (Walker 89), Smith, Damour, Bozanic; Naismith; Washington (Boyce 90).
Rangers: (433) McGregor; Tavernier, Goldson, Edmundson, Barisic; Jack (Hagi 63), Davis, Arfield (Ojo 33); Aribo, Stewart (Defoe 67), Kent.
Referee: Steven McLean.

St Mirren (0) 0

Aberdeen (1) 2 *(Ferguson 7, Cosgrove 90 (pen))* 4479

St Mirren: (442) Hladky; Hodson, McCarthy, Famewo, Waters; McGrath, MacPherson (Chabbi 72), Foley, Durmus (Andreu 83); Obika, Jakubiak (McAllister 46).
Aberdeen: (433) Lewis; Logan, Taylor, McKenna (Devlin 52), Considine; Ferguson, Ojo, Campbell (Cosgrove 74); McGinn, Main (Bryson 87), Kennedy.
Referee: Don Robertson.

Sunday, 1 March 2020

St Johnstone (0) 0

Celtic (0) 1 *(Christie 81)* 8181

St Johnstone: (352) Clark; Kerr, Gordon, McCart; Wright, McCann, Butcher, Wotherspoon (O'Halloran 83), Tanser; May, Hendry (Kane 76).
Celtic: (352) Forster; Bitton, Jullien, Ajer; Forrest, Christie, Brown, McGregor, Taylor (Hayes 76); Griffiths (Rogic 65), Edouard (Bayo 87).
Referee: Bobby Madden.

Saturday, 30 October 2020

Celtic

Aberdeen

Saturday, 30 October 2020

Hearts

Hibernian

The quarter-finals and semi-finals postponed due to the COVID-19 pandemic.

WILLIAM HILL SCOTTISH CUP FINAL 2019–20

Date to be confirmed

(at Hampden Park)

Due to the COVID-19 pandemic, the final due to be played on Saturday 9 May 2020 was postponed.

The Scottish FA hope the game will be played when crowds are allowed into stadiums.

Oliver Bozanic scores the only goal of the game as Hearts defeat Rangers in their Scottish Cup quarter-final at Tynecastle in February. (Luke Nickerson/Rangers FC/PA Images)

WOMEN'S FOOTBALL 2019–20

FA WOMEN'S SUPER LEAGUE TABLE 2019–20

On 13 March 2020 the Women's Super League and FA Women's Championship were suspended until 3 April at the earliest. On 26 March 2020 the women's game below Super League and Championship level were ended immediately with no promotion or relegation. All fixtures expunged. League tables shown were as of 13 March 2020.

			Home					Away					Total							
		P	W	D	L	F	A	W	D	L	F	A	W	D	L	F	A	GD	Pts	PPG
1	Chelsea	15	8	0	0	25	4	4	3	0	22	7	12	3	0	47	11	36	39	2.60
2	Manchester C	16	8	1	0	24	5	5	0	2	15	4	13	1	2	39	9	30	40	2.50
3	Arsenal	15	6	0	1	22	6	6	0	2	18	7	12	0	3	40	13	27	36	2.40
4	Manchester U	14	5	0	2	14	3	2	2	3	10	9	7	2	5	24	12	12	23	1.64
5	Reading	14	4	2	2	13	12	2	1	3	8	12	6	3	5	21	24	–3	21	1.50
6	Everton	14	4	0	3	13	9	2	1	4	8	12	6	1	7	21	21	0	19	1.36
7	Tottenham H	15	3	1	3	7	12	3	1	4	8	12	6	2	7	15	24	–9	20	1.33
8	West Ham U	14	4	0	3	13	13	1	1	5	6	21	5	1	8	19	34	–15	16	1.14
9	Brighton & HA	16	3	3	3	10	12	0	1	6	1	18	3	4	9	11	30	–19	13	0.81
10	Bristol C	14	0	1	5	1	14	2	2	4	8	24	2	3	9	9	38	–29	9	0.64
11	Birmingham C	13	1	1	4	3	11	1	0	6	2	12	2	1	10	5	23	–18	7	0.54
12	Liverpool	14	0	3	3	5	8	1	0	7	3	12	1	3	10	8	20	–12	6	0.43

PPG = Points-per-game.
On 5 June 2020, the WSL decided to award places on a points-per-game basis.

FA WOMEN'S SUPER LEAGUE LEADING GOALSCORERS 2019–20

Player	*Team*	*Goals*
Vivianne Miedema	Arsenal	16
Bethany England	Chelsea	14
Pauline Bremer	Manchester C	10
Chloe Kelly	Everton	9
Lauren James	Manchester U	6
Ji So-Yun	Chelsea	6
Ellen White	Manchester C	6
Daniëlle van de Donk	Arsenal	5
Rachel Furness	Liverpool	5
Lauren Hemp	Manchester C	5
Adriana Leon	West Ham U	5
Kim Little	Arsenal	5
Jordan Nobbs	Arsenal	5
Guro Reiten	Chelsea	5
Ebony Salmon	Bristol C	5
Aileen Whelan	Brighton & HA	5
Fara Williams	Reading	5
Katie Zelem	Manchester U	5

FA WOMEN'S CHAMPIONSHIP TABLE 2019–20

			Home					Away					Total							
		P	W	D	L	F	A	W	D	L	F	A	W	D	L	F	A	GD	Pts	PPG
1	Aston Villa	14	7	1	0	20	6	6	0	0	19	5	13	1	0	39	11	28	40	2.86
2	Sheffield U	14	5	1	1	23	7	6	0	1	23	9	11	1	2	46	16	30	34	2.43
3	Durham	14	5	1	1	12	4	5	1	1	21	6	10	2	2	33	10	23	32	2.29
4	London C Lionesses	15	3	1	4	13	17	5	1	1	12	7	8	2	5	25	24	1	26	1.73
5	London Bees	12	2	1	3	8	10	2	2	2	8	9	4	3	5	16	19	–3	15	1.25
6	Leicester C	15	2	2	4	12	19	2	1	4	10	16	4	3	8	22	35	–13	15	1.00
7	Blackburn R	12	1	1	4	7	10	2	0	4	6	15	3	1	8	13	25	–12	10	0.83
8	Lewes	12	1	2	2	7	7	1	1	5	3	11	2	3	7	10	18	–8	9	0.75
9	Crystal Palace	14	0	2	5	5	21	2	2	3	10	12	2	4	8	15	33	–18	10	0.71
10	Coventry U	14	1	0	5	9	17	1	3	4	10	18	2	3	9	19	35	–16	9	0.64
11	Charlton Ath	12	0	3	3	3	10	0	4	2	6	11	0	7	5	9	21	–12	7	0.58

PPG = Points-per-game.
On 5 June 2020, the WSL decided to award places on a points-per-game basis. Charlton Ath not relegated after the seasons. Tier three and below were cancelled and null and void.

FA WOMEN'S CHAMPIONSHIP LEADING GOALSCORERS 2019–20

Player	*Team*	*Goals*
Katie Wilkinson	Sheffield U	14
Melissa Johnson	Aston Villa	12
Jade Pennock	Sheffield U	11
Shania Hayles	Aston Villa	8
Olivia Fergusson	Sheffield U	7
Beth Hepple	Durham	7
Molly Sharpe	Durham	7
Natasha Flint	Blackburn R	6
Emma Follis	Aston Villa	6
Paige Bailey-Gayle	Leicester C	5
Ashleigh Goddard	Crystal Palace	5
Amber Hughes	Coventry U	5
Shannon O'Brien	Coventry U	5
Aimee Palmer	Sheffield U	5
Lauren Pickett	London Bees	5
Lisa Robertson	Durham	5

WOMEN'S CONTINENTAL TYRES LEAGUE CUP 2019–20

GROUP STAGE

GROUP A TABLE

	P	W	WP	LP	L	F	A	GD	Pts
Sheffield U	5	3	0	1	1	14	8	6	10
Aston Villa	5	3	0	1	1	12	8	4	10
Liverpool	5	3	0	0	2	16	7	9	9
Durham	5	3	0	0	2	11	8	3	9
Coventry U	5	0	3	0	2	6	14	–8	6
Blackburn R	5	0	0	1	4	5	19	–14	1

GROUP B TABLE

	P	W	WP	LP	L	F	A	GD	Pts
Arsenal	5	4	0	1	0	25	0	25	13
Brighton & HA	5	3	1	0	1	13	4	9	11
Bristol C	5	3	0	1	1	11	11	0	10
London Bees	5	1	1	0	3	3	17	–14	5
Charlton Ath	5	1	0	1	3	3	12	–9	4
London C Lionesses	5	0	1	0	4	3	14	–11	2

GROUP CTABLE

	P	W	WP	LP	L	F	A	GD	Pts
Manchester U	4	4	0	0	0	19	2	17	12
Manchester C	4	3	0	0	1	11	4	7	9
Birmingham C	4	2	0	0	2	8	6	2	6
Everton	4	1	0	0	3	5	8	–3	3
Leicester C	4	0	0	0	4	2	25	–23	0

GROUP D TABLE

	P	W	WP	LP	L	F	A	GD	Pts
Chelsea	5	4	0	1	0	13	3	10	13
Reading	5	3	1	0	1	14	4	10	11
West Ham U	5	3	0	1	1	13	5	8	10
Tottenham H	5	2	1	0	2	12	11	1	8
Crystal Palace	5	1	0	0	4	3	21	–18	3
Lewes	5	0	0	0	5	6	17	–11	0

Drawn games were decided by a penalty shoot-out.
WP = match won on penalties (2 pts);
LP = match lost on penalties (1 pt).

KNOCK-OUT ROUNDS

QUARTER-FINALS

Chelsea v Aston Villa	3-1
Arsenal v Reading	1-0
Sheffield U v Manchester C	0-4
Manchester U v Brighton & HA	2-1

SEMI-FINALS

Arsenal v Manchester C	2-1
Manchester U v Chelsea	0-1

WOMEN'S CONTINENTAL TYRES LEAGUE CUP FINAL 2019–20

City Ground, Nottingham,
Saturday 29 February 2020

Chelsea (1) 2 *(England 8, 90)*

Arsenal (1) 1 *(Williamson 85)* 6743

Chelsea: Berger; Mjedle, Bright, Eriksson, Andersson, Ingle, Ji (Thorisdottir 75), Reiten, England, Kerr (Spence 90), Cuthbert.
Arsenal: Zinsberger; Quinn, Evans, Schnaderbeck, McCabe, Williamson, Roord, Van de Donk, Nobbs, Miedema, Foord.
Referee: Helen Conley.

Chelsea players and staff celebrate with the FA Women's Super League trophy.
(Harriet Lander – Chelsea FC/Chelsea FC via Getty Images)

FA WOMEN'S NATIONAL LEAGUE 2019–20

FA WOMEN'S NATIONAL LEAGUE NORTHERN PREMIER DIVISION 2019–20

			Home					Away					Total						
		P	W	D	L	F	A	W	D	L	F	A	W	D	L	F	A	GD	Pts
1	Sunderland	14	6	0	0	29	5	7	1	0	24	5	13	1	0	53	10	43	40
2	Derby Co	15	5	0	2	21	4	4	2	2	25	13	9	2	4	46	17	29	29
3	Nottingham F	13	5	0	2	18	13	4	1	1	9	6	9	1	3	27	19	8	28
4	Stoke C	14	4	1	2	14	6	4	0	3	18	11	8	1	5	32	17	15	25
5	Burnley	11	3	1	1	8	3	4	0	2	11	10	7	1	3	19	13	6	22
6	Huddersfield T	12	3	2	2	19	15	2	1	2	16	7	5	3	4	35	22	13	18
7	WBA	11	4	1	3	25	15	1	1	1	6	5	5	2	4	31	20	11	17
8	Middlesbrough	15	2	1	4	11	18	2	1	5	16	34	4	2	9	27	52	–25	14
9	AFC Fylde	14	1	2	3	8	10	2	2	4	7	14	3	4	7	15	24	–9	13
10	Loughborough Foxes	15	3	1	5	15	22	1	0	5	9	20	4	1	10	24	42	–18	13
11	Hull C	14	1	0	5	10	26	1	0	7	13	38	2	0	12	23	64	–41	6
12	Sheffield	10	0	0	4	3	21	1	0	5	4	18	1	0	9	7	39	–32	3

FA WOMEN'S NATIONAL LEAGUE SOUTHERN PREMIER DIVISION 2019–20

			Home					Away					Total						
		P	W	D	L	F	A	W	D	L	F	A	W	D	L	F	A	GD	Pts
1	Crawley Wasps	14	6	1	1	18	7	6	0	0	18	2	12	1	1	36	9	27	37
2	Watford	11	3	1	1	17	7	6	0	0	23	7	9	1	1	40	14	26	28
3	Oxford U	14	6	0	2	26	9	3	0	3	18	11	9	0	5	44	20	24	27
4	Plymouth Arg	14	4	0	2	19	9	5	0	3	23	9	9	0	5	42	18	24	27
5	Yeovil T	13	5	1	1	24	5	3	1	2	22	12	8	2	3	46	17	29	26
6	Cardiff C	13	4	0	3	11	6	4	1	1	12	3	8	1	4	23	9	14	25
7	Portsmouth	9	1	0	2	9	6	4	0	2	19	9	5	0	4	28	15	13	15
8	Milton Keynes D	14	1	1	4	4	17	3	0	5	14	13	4	1	9	18	30	–12	13
9	Gillingham	11	1	1	4	6	16	2	1	2	6	11	3	2	6	12	27	–15	11
10	Keynsham T	12	1	0	6	6	24	1	1	3	3	15	2	1	9	9	39	–30	7
11	Hounslow	14	0	1	5	1	33	0	2	6	3	40	0	3	11	4	73	–69	3
12	Chichester C	13	0	1	6	4	24	0	1	5	2	13	0	2	11	6	37	–31	2

FA WOMEN'S NATIONAL LEAGUE DIVISION ONE NORTH 2019–20

			Home					Away					Total						
		P	W	D	L	F	A	W	D	L	F	A	W	D	L	F	A	GD	Pts
1	Barnsley	14	5	2	0	17	8	7	0	0	22	6	12	2	0	39	14	25	38
2	Leeds U	17	7	1	1	18	5	5	1	2	19	11	12	2	3	37	16	21	38
3	Brighouse T	12	6	1	0	18	5	2	3	0	7	5	8	4	0	25	10	15	28
4	Liverpool Feds	15	4	2	3	16	12	4	0	2	13	4	8	2	5	29	16	13	26
5	Durham Cestria	14	2	1	2	15	8	4	3	2	18	9	6	4	4	33	17	16	22
6	Newcastle U	15	4	1	4	14	13	2	1	3	5	10	6	2	7	19	23	–4	20
7	Chester-le-Street	14	3	1	4	13	17	2	2	2	13	12	5	3	6	26	29	–3	18
8	Norton & Stockton	13	3	1	3	13	17	0	3	3	12	16	3	4	6	25	33	–8	13
9	Chorley	14	2	2	3	7	7	1	0	6	6	12	3	2	9	13	19	–6	11
10	Bolton W	15	3	1	1	8	5	0	1	9	8	28	3	2	10	16	33	–17	11
11	Stockport Co	15	1	1	5	14	23	2	1	5	11	18	3	2	10	25	41	–16	10
12	Bradford C	14	1	1	4	6	17	1	0	7	3	28	2	1	11	9	45	–36	7

FA WOMEN'S NATIONAL LEAGUE DIVISION ONE MIDLANDS 2019–20

			Home					Away					Total						
		P	W	D	L	F	A	W	D	L	F	A	W	D	L	F	A	GD	Pts
1	Wolverhampton W	15	7	0	0	44	4	7	0	1	39	6	14	0	1	83	10	73	42
2	Birmingham C	16	4	2	1	32	12	6	1	2	20	11	10	3	3	52	23	29	33
3	Bedworth U	16	4	2	2	22	21	5	1	2	28	13	9	3	4	50	34	16	30
4	The New Saints	16	7	1	1	30	16	2	2	3	16	17	9	3	4	46	33	13	30
5	Lincoln C	14	5	0	2	22	11	3	0	4	22	14	8	0	6	44	25	19	24
6	Long Eaton U	15	5	1	1	12	4	2	0	6	13	19	7	1	7	25	23	2	22
7	Leicester U	13	4	0	2	15	14	2	1	4	13	27	6	1	6	28	41	–13	19
8	Leafield Ath	14	3	1	3	19	16	2	0	5	11	19	5	1	8	30	35	–5	16
9	Sporting Khalsa	15	4	0	5	19	22	1	1	4	11	14	5	1	9	30	36	–6	16
10	Doncaster Belles	16	4	0	5	15	19	1	1	5	9	20	5	1	10	24	39	–15	16
11	Solihull Moors	14	3	0	5	13	21	0	0	6	5	32	3	0	11	18	53	–35	9
12	Burton Alb	12	0	0	4	5	32	0	0	8	5	56	0	0	12	10	88	–78	0

FA WOMEN'S NATIONAL LEAGUE DIVISION ONE SOUTH EAST 2019–20

			Home					Away					Total						
		P	*W*	*D*	*L*	*F*	*A*	*W*	*D*	*L*	*F*	*A*	*W*	*D*	*L*	*F*	*A*	*GD*	*Pts*
1	Ipswich T	14	7	1	1	29	8	4	0	1	24	3	11	1	2	53	11	42	34
2	AFC Wimbledon	14	7	1	0	18	6	3	2	1	12	6	10	3	1	30	12	18	33
3	AFC Basildon	14	5	1	1	24	14	4	1	2	20	17	9	2	3	44	31	13	29
4	Billericay T	12	6	1	0	27	6	3	0	2	12	6	9	1	2	39	12	27	28
5	Leyton Orient	12	4	0	0	16	3	4	1	3	11	11	8	1	3	27	14	13	25
6	Enfield T	13	3	2	2	19	11	4	1	1	13	6	7	3	3	32	17	15	24
7	Actonians	12	3	0	2	8	6	2	1	4	12	19	5	1	6	20	25	–5	16
8	Cambridge U	15	3	0	3	9	8	1	2	6	7	23	4	2	9	16	31	–15	14
9	Norwich C	16	1	2	5	19	38	2	0	6	15	31	3	2	11	34	69	–35	11
10	Stevenage	15	2	0	5	15	25	1	1	6	17	31	3	1	11	32	56	–24	10
11	Cambridge C	13	1	2	3	8	14	1	1	5	8	19	2	3	8	16	33	–17	9
12	Kent	14	1	0	7	9	21	0	0	6	9	29	1	0	13	18	50	–32	3

FA WOMEN'S PREMIER LEAGUE DIVISION ONE SOUTH WEST 2019–20

			Home					Away					Total						
		P	*W*	*D*	*L*	*F*	*A*	*W*	*D*	*L*	*F*	*A*	*W*	*D*	*L*	*F*	*A*	*GD*	*Pts*
1	Southampton Women's FC	11	6	1	0	34	3	4	0	0	19	2	10	1	0	53	5	48	31
2	Southampton FC Women	12	5	0	1	17	6	4	2	0	22	7	9	2	1	39	13	26	29
3	Exeter C	12	4	0	2	16	18	4	1	1	22	9	8	1	3	38	27	11	25
4	Cheltenham T	11	5	0	0	10	3	4	1	1	9	7	9	1	1	19	10	9	25
5	Chesham U	12	4	2	1	22	13	2	0	3	17	18	6	2	4	39	31	8	20
6	Larkhall Ath	8	3	1	0	12	3	2	0	2	7	12	5	1	2	19	15	4	16
7	Buckland Ath	12	1	1	2	9	11	2	1	5	13	15	3	2	7	22	26	–4	11
8	Brislington	11	1	1	3	11	18	1	1	4	11	17	2	2	7	22	35	–13	8
9	Maidenhead U	12	2	0	5	6	19	0	0	5	2	23	2	0	10	8	42	–34	6
10	Poole T	11	1	0	4	6	18	0	0	6	5	19	1	0	10	11	37	–26	3
11	Swindon T	12	1	0	5	8	22	0	0	6	7	22	1	0	11	15	44	–29	3

FA WOMEN'S NATIONAL LEAGUE CUP 2019–20

**After extra time.*

DETERMINING ROUND NORTHERN SECTION

Bedworth U v Stockport Co 4-3*
Birmingham & West Midlands v Bolton W 8-0
Brighouse T v Loughborough Foxes 2-1
Burton Alb v Derby Co 1-8
Chorley v Leafield Ath 10-2
Doncaster R Belles v Sheffield FC 1-4
Durham Cestria v Middlesbrough 2-1
Huddersfield T v Nottingham F 4-3
Leeds U v Burnley 0-3
Lincoln C v Stoke C 2-2*
Stoke C won 4-3 on penalties
Liverpool Feds v Bradford C 1-0
Long Eaton U v Chester-le-Street 7-2
Norton & Stockton Ancients v Hull C 6-2
Solihull Moors v Fylde 0-8
Sunderland v Newcastle U 3-2
The New Saints v Leicester U 6-3
WBA v Barnsley 2-4
Wolverhampton W v Sporting Khalsa 4-2

DETERMINING ROUND SOUTHERN SECTION

Billericay T v Cheltenham T 3-1
Chesham U v Brislington 8-0
Chichester C v Cambridge C 1-3
Enfield T v Norwich C 2-0
Exeter C v Plymouth Argyle 4-3
Kent Football U v AFC Basildon 0-2
Keynsham T v Buckland Ath 2-1
Leyton Orient v Cambridge U 4-3*
Maidenhead U v Cardiff C Ladies 1-5
Oxford U v Crawley Wasps 0-1
Portsmouth v Watford 2-0*
Southampton FC Women v Ipswich T 6-0
Southampton Women's FC v Poole T 2-0
Stevenage v Yeovil T 0-7
Swindon T v Milton Keynes D 0-4
Actonians v AFC Wimbledon 2-0
Hounslow v Gillingham (walkover)

PRELIMINARY ROUND NORTHERN SECTION

Norton & Stockton Ancients v Bedworth U 4-2
Sunderland v Burnley 2-0

PRELIMINARY ROUND SOUTHERN SECTION

Portsmouth v Gillingham 3-2*
Chesham U (walkover) v Keynsham T

FIRST ROUND NORTHERN SECTION

Barnsley v Sunderland 0-1
Birmingham & West Midlands v Stoke C 1-2
Fylde v Wolverhampton W 2-3*
Huddersfield T v Sheffield FC 7-2
Brighouse T v Norton & Stockton Ancients 1-0
Derby Co v The New Saints 10-1
Chorley v Durham Cestria 4-3
Long Eaton U v Liverpool Feds 2-4

FIRST ROUND SOUTHERN SECTION

Cardiff C Ladies v Milton Keynes D 0-0*
Milton Keynes D won 3-1 on penalties
Enfield T v Yeovil T 2-2*
Yeovil T won 4-2 on penalties
Southampton Women's FC v AFC Basildon 2-3
Billericay T v Cambridge C 4-0
Crawley Wasps v Actonians 1-0
Larkhall Ath v Southampton FC Women 1-3
Leyton Orient v Portsmouth 1-6
Chesham U v Exeter C 4-0

SECOND ROUND NORTHERN SECTION

Brighouse T v Derby Co 1-1*
Derby Co won 3-0 on penalties
Stoke C v Wolverhampton W 3-2
Chorley v Sunderland 0-4
Huddersfield T v Liverpool Feds 4-2

SECOND ROUND SOUTHERN SECTION

AFC Basildon v Milton Keynes D 3-3*
Milton Keynes D won 3-0 on penalties
Yeovil T v Southampton FC Women 1-2*
Chesham U v Billericay T 1-0
Crawley Wasps v Portsmouth 1-2

QUARTER-FINALS NORTHERN SECTION

Huddersfield T v Stoke C 1-3
Sunderland v Derby Co 4-0

QUARTER-FINALS SOUTHERN SECTION

Chesham U v Milton Keynes D 0-2
Portsmouth v Southampton FC Women 0-2

SEMI-FINALS

Milton Keynes D v Stoke C 0-2
Sunderland v Southampton FC Women 1-0

FA WOMEN'S NATIONAL LEAGUE CUP FINAL 2019–20

Sunderland v Stoke C P-P
Due to the COVID-19 pandemic, the final was postponed.

THE SSE WOMEN'S FA CUP 2019–20

**After extra time.*

EXTRA PRELIMINARY ROUND

Washington v Redcar T 0-13
Wakefield Trinity v Farsley Celtic 0-3
Mossley Hill (walkover) v Burnley Belvedere
Notts Co v Cleethorpes T 11-1
Port Vale v Lye T 9-0
Corby T v Bungay T 1-2
New London Lionesses v Comets 5-4
Bishop's Stortford v Hartham U 1-5
Ashford T (Middlesex) v Denham U 4-1
Burgess Hill T v Eastbourne U 3-2

PRELIMINARY ROUND

Penrith v Bishop Auckland 2-4
Boro Rangers v South Shields 1-3
Carlisle U v Hartlepool U 1-11
Redcar T v Lumley 5-0
Blyth T v Workington Reds 2-1
Alnwick T v Sunderland West End 3-5
Wetherby Ath v Harrogate T 0-10
Ossett U v Rotherham U 5-1
Ripon C v Yorkshire Amateur 0-4
Bridlington R v Bradford Park Avenue 4-2
Hepworth U v Pride Park 5-1
Farsley Celtic v Thackley 3-0
Oughtibridge War Memorial v Sheffield W 2-1
Blackburn Community Sports Club v West Kirby 6-1
Northwich Vixens v Bury 13-2
Curzon Ashton v Mossley Hill 2-2*
Mossley Hill won 4-2 on penalties
Tameside U v Fleetwood T Wrens 1-5
Manchester Stingers v Merseyrail 0-6
FC United of Manchester v Tranmere R 5-0
Accrington Girls & Ladies v Altrincham 1-3
Didsbury v West Didsbury & Chorlton 4-2
Accrington Stanley Community Trust v Morecambe 1-8
Wythenshawe Amateurs v Crewe Alex 0-8
Boston U v Loughborough Students (walkover)
AFC Leicester v Grimsby Bor 1-3
Rise Park v Notts Co 3-2*
(2-2 at the end of normal time)
Coalville T v Hykeham T 1-11
Worksop T v Mansfield T 0-9
Dronfield T v Leicester C 1-2
Lutterworth Ath v Chesterfield 0-12
Sherwood v Arnold Eagles 0-7
Oadby & Wigston v Lincoln Moorlands Railway 5-1
Arnold T v Woodlands 1-4
Kidderminster H v Leek T 3-4
Port Vale v Knowle 8-1
Droitwich Spa (walkover) v Sedgley & Gornal U
Solihull Sporting v Rugby T 7-1
Crusaders v Sandwell 5-2
Tamworth v Shrewsbury T 2-3
Kingfisher v Cookley Sports 2-4
Kidsgrove Ath v Solihull U 3-5
Coundon Court v Sutton Coldfield T 2-3
Wyrley v Shifnal T 2-4
Stockingford AA Pavilion v Stourbridge 2-1
Coventry Sphinx v AFC Telford U 2-1*
(1-1 at the end of normal time)
Wroxham v Kettering T 6-2
Haverhill R v King's Lynn T 1-3
St Ives T v Histon 0-1
AFC Sudbury v Harlow T 0-8
Riverside v Bungay T 0-15
Peterborough U v Thrapston T 14-0
Fulbourn Institute Bluebirds v Wymondham T 0-5
Netherton U v Newmarket T 1-3
Clapton Community v Margate 6-3
Aylesford v Dulwich Hamlet 2-1*
(1-1 at the end of normal time)
Fulham v New London Lionesses 3-1
Dartford v Hackney 5-0
Whyteleafe (walkover) v Millwall Lionesses
Victoire v Herne Bay 4-3*
(3-3 at the end of normal time)
Meridian v Regents Park Rangers 1-3
Sutton U v Islington Bor 0-1
Phoenix Sports v Haringey Bor 5-1
Long Lane v Ashford 0-11
Watford Development v Hemel Hempstead T 4-2
Hitchin Belles v Bowers & Pitsea 1-6
Royston T v Wodson Park 4-1
Bedford v Colney Heath 1-3
Houghton Ath v AFC Dunstable 0-1
Hartham U v St Albans 0-5
Luton T v Leigh Ramblers 7-0
Abbey Rangers v Hampton & Richmond Bor 4-3*
(3-3 at the end of normal time)
QPR Girls Development v Wargrave 11-0
Banbury U v Walton Casuals 1-2
Abingdon U v Brentford 7-0
Ascot U v Abingdon T 2-3
Ashford T (Middlesex) v Oxford C 5-2
Wantage T v Wycombe W 0-14
Steyning T v Newhaven 1-5
Oakwood v AFC Littlehampton 6-1
Pagham v Worthing 2-3
Godalming T v Eastbourne T 1-2
Milford & Witley v Tunbridge Wells Foresters 1-5
Burgess Hill T v Saltdean U 2-4*
(2-2 at the end of normal time)
Mole Valley v Bexhill U 7-0
New Milton T v Newbury 3-1
Shanklin v Alton 1-0
Bournemouth Sports v Winchester C Flyers 1-3*
(1-1 at the end of normal time)
Eastleigh v Moneyfields 1-2
Bournemouth v Feniton 6-0
Almondsbury v Longlevens 2-0
Weston-super-Mare v Middlezoy R 1-4
AEK Boco v Ilminster T 0-4
Sherborne T v Keynsham T Development 10-0
Royal Wootton Bassett T v Chipping Sodbury T 7-0
Swindon Spitfires v Portishead T 1-7
Bideford v St Agnes 5-2
Marine Academy Plymouth v AFC St Austell 1-0*
(0-0 at the end of normal time)
Torquay U v RNAS Culdrose 3-0

FIRST ROUND QUALIFYING

Harrogate T v Fleetwood T Wrens 5-0
Redcar T v Bishop Auckland 2-0
Yorkshire Amateur v Hartlepool U 0-5
FC United of Manchester v Morecambe 4-1
Altrincham v Didsbury 4-2
Hepworth U v Blackburn Community Sports Club 1-8
Farsley Celtic v Merseyrail 2-1
Bridlington R v Ossett U 0-7
Sunderland West End v Mossley Hill 4-4*
Mossley Hill won 5-4 on penalties
Blyth T v South Shields 0-1
Droitwich Spa v Shifnal T 0-3
Stockingford AA Pavilion v Coventry Sphinx 1-5
Shrewsbury T v Leek T 1-3
Sutton Coldfield T v Solihull Sporting 5-0
Arnold Eagles v Northwich Vixens 2-3
Oadby & Wigston v Crewe Alex 2-3
Chesterfield v Cookley Sports 2-0
Peterborough U v Oughtibridge War Memorial 3-0
Woodlands v Hykeham T 2-1
Rise Park v Grimsby Bor 3-2
Leicester C v Port Vale 3-2*
(2-2 at the end of normal time)
Solihull U v Loughborough Students 2-1
Mansfield T v Crusaders 4-2
Harlow T v King's Lynn T 3-1
Watford Development v Newmarket T 0-2
Histon v St Albans 0-4

Colney Heath v Royston T	2-5
AFC Dunstable v Bowers & Pitsea	2-2*
Bowers & Pitsea won 3-2 on penalties	
Luton T v Bungay T	6-0
Wroxham v Wymondham T	3-2
Victoire v Islington Bor	0-4
Clapton Community v Oakwood	2-3
Fulham v Mole Valley	5-1
Ashford v Eastbourne T	4-1
Dartford v Newhaven	4-0
Regents Park Rangers v Wycombe W	0-3
QPR Girls Development v Abbey Rangers	8-0
Whyteleafe v Worthing	0-1
Abingdon U v Aylesford	2-1
Tunbridge Wells Foresters v Phoenix Sports	1-4
Abingdon T v Walton Casuals	4-3
Ashford T (Middlesex) v Saltdean U	0-1
Shanklin v Sherborne T	0-12
Bournemouth v New Milton T	10-0
Royal Wootton Bassett T v Torquay U	8-0
Marine Academy Plymouth v Almondsbury	1-0
Portishead T v Middlezoy R	3-1*
(1-1 at the end of normal time)	
Winchester C Flyers v Bideford	9-2
Ilminster T v Moneyfields	1-4

SECOND ROUND QUALIFYING

Hartlepool U v Blackburn Community Sports Club	4-3
Bolton W v Newcastle U	1-2
Redcar T v Norton & Stockton Ancients	1-3
Harrogate T v Chorley	0-2
FC United of Manchester v Brighouse T	1-5
Barnsley v Bradford C	5-1
Chester-le-Street T v Doncaster R Belles	4-2
Leeds U v South Shields	4-1
Mossley Hill v Stockport Co	1-3
Durham Cestria v Ossett U	5-1
Farsley Celtic v Liverpool Marshalls Feds	A-A, 1-4
First match abandoned	
Burton Alb v Leicester U	0-3
Woodlands v Rise Park	2-1*
(1-1 at the end of normal time)	
Mansfield T v Birmingham & West Midlands	0-6
Leek T v Leicester C	6-0
Wolverhampton W v Shifnal T	10-0
Lincoln C v Solihull Moors	7-0
Chesterfield v Bedworth U	1-3
Altrincham v Northwich Vixens	1-5
Leafield Ath v Sporting Khalsa	2-5
Sutton Coldfield T v Solihull U	3-2
Coventry Sphinx v Crewe Alex	0-5
The New Saints v Long Eaton U	6-1
Stevenage v Peterborough U	1-2
Newmarket T v Luton T	0-4
Harlow T v Wroxham	4-3*
(2-2 at the end of normal time)	
Norwich C v Cambridge U	3-2
Cambridge C v St Albans	4-3*
(3-3 at the end of normal time)	
Ipswich T v Royston T	7-0
Wycombe W v Worthing	3-1
Kent Football U v Actonians	1-3
Dartford v Billericay T	0-7
Ashford v AFC Wimbledon	0-7
QPR Girls Development v Oakwood	9-1
Enfield T v Islington Bor	4-0
Maidenhead U v Bowers & Pitsea	1-2
Fulham v Saltdean U	1-1*
Fulham won 3-0 on penalties	
Abingdon T v Chesham U	0-4
AFC Basildon v Phoenix Sports	8-2
Abingdon U v Leyton Orient	1-4
Exeter C v Sherborne T	7-1
Portishead T v Royal Wootton Bassett T	1-0
Winchester C Flyers v Poole T	2-3
Marine Academy Plymouth v Southampton Women's FC	0-2
Southampton FC Women v Buckland Ath	8-0
Moneyfields v Larkhall Ath	2-2*
Moneyfields won 4-2 on penalties	
Cheltenham T v Brislington	5-0
Swindon T v Bournemouth	2-3

THIRD ROUND QUALIFYING

Northwich Vixens v Liverpool Marshalls Feds	2-7
Leeds U v Barnsley	0-3
Chester-le-Street T v Newcastle U	3-1
Hartlepool U v Chorley	0-8
Norton & Stockton Ancients v Durham Cestria	2-6
Stockport Co v Brighouse T	2-2*
Brighouse T won 4-2 on penalties	
Peterborough U v The New Saints	2-3
Sporting Khalsa v Lincoln C	1-3
Bedworth U v Woodlands	2-4
Leicester U v Leek T	0-1
Birmingham & West Midlands v Crewe Alex	1-2
Sutton Coldfield T v Wolverhampton W	1-5
Harlow T v Billericay T	1-2
Cambridge C v AFC Basildon	3-7
Ipswich T v Norwich C	6-1
Bowers & Pitsea v Luton T	0-3
Actonians v Fulham	3-1
QPR Girls Development v Leyton Orient	1-2
Enfield T v AFC Wimbledon	1-2
Chesham U v Wycombe W	3-0
Portishead T v Moneyfields	1-1*
Portishead T won 3-1 on penalties	
Southampton Women's FC v Bournemouth	3-1
Southampton FC Women v Poole T	11-0
Cheltenham T v Exeter C	4-3

FIRST ROUND

Crewe Alex v Barnsley	1-2*
(1-1 at the end of normal time)	
Liverpool Marshalls Feds v Brighouse T	0-4
Durham Cestria v Chester-le-Street T	1-3
The New Saints v Chorley	0-4
Leek T v Lincoln C	1-2*
(1-1 at the end of normal time)	
Wolverhampton W v Luton T	4-1
Woodlands v Billericay T	0-13
Ipswich T v AFC Basildon	5-0
Cheltenham T v Leyton Orient	0-1
Actonians v AFC Wimbledon	2-1
Chesham U v Southampton FC Women	0-1
Southampton Women's FC v Portishead T	4-0

SECOND ROUND

Chorley v Brighouse T	1-2*
(1-1 at the end of normal time)	
Derby Co v Nottingham F	2-3
Barnsley v Sheffield	4-0
Sunderland v Middlesbrough	4-3
Stoke C v Huddersfield T	1-1*
Huddersfield T won 4-3 on penalties	
Wolverhampton W v Fylde	0-1
Chester-le-Street T v Loughborough Foxes	0-4
Burnley v Hull C	2-1
WBA v Lincoln C	2-0
Hounslow v Cardiff C	0-6
Keynsham T v Watford	0-3
Yeovil T v Southampton FC Women	1-1*
Southampton FC Women won 5-4 on penalties	
Portsmouth v Leyton Orient	6-1
Southampton Women's FC v Milton Keynes D	1-1*
Southampton Women's FC won 3-2 on penalties	
Oxford U v Plymouth Arg	3-4*
(2-2 at the end of normal time)	
Chichester C v Ipswich T	0-6
Billericay T v Gillingham	2-1
Actonians v Crawley Wasps	3-1

THIRD ROUND

Fylde v Sunderland	1-4
Burnley v Nottingham F	2-1
Loughborough Foxes v Huddersfield T	2-3
Brighouse T v Barnsley	0-1

Ipswich T v Portsmouth	1-0
Watford v Plymouth Arg	5-0
Cardiff C v Southampton FC Women	1-2
Southampton Women's FC v WBA	3-1
Billericay T v Actonians	3-2

FOURTH ROUND

West Ham U v Arsenal	0-2
Manchester U v Manchester C	2-3
Lewes v Billericay T	1-1*
Lewes won 5-4 on penalties	
Charlton Ath v Chelsea	0-4
Everton v London Bees	1-0
Burnley v Leicester C	1-3
Sheffield U v Birmingham C	0-3
London C Lionesses v Reading	0-5
Bristol C v Durham	1-0*
(0-0 at the end of normal time)	
Tottenham H v Barnsley	5-0
Huddersfield T v Ipswich T	1-4
Southampton FC Women v Coventry U	1-4
Southampton Women's FC v Crystal Palace	A-A, 0-4
First match abandoned after 78 minutes due to a waterlogged pitch, 0-3	
Sunderland v Watford	2-0
Liverpool v Blackburn R	8-1
Aston Villa v Brighton & HA	2-3

FIFTH ROUND

Bristol C v Everton	0-5
Coventry U v Tottenham H	0-5
Leicester C v Reading	2-1*
(1-1 at the end of normal time)	
Crystal Palace v Brighton & HA	0-3
Manchester C v Ipswich T	10-0
Arsenal v Lewes	2-0
Sunderland v Birmingham C	0-1
Chelsea v Liverpool	1-0

QUARTER-FINALS

Arsenal v Tottenham H
Brighton & HA v Birmingham C
Everton v Chelsea
Leicester C v Manchester C

The quarter-finals, semi-finals and final postponed due to the COVID-19 pandemic.

The FA has received approval to conclude the last three rounds of the 2019–20 Women's FA Cup Final in the early part of the 2020–21 season. The final is due to be played at Wembley on Saturday 31 October.

UEFA WOMEN'S CHAMPIONS LEAGUE 2019–20

■*Denotes player sent off.*

QUALIFYING STAGE

GROUP 1 (BOSNIA-HERZEGOVINA)

ASA Tel Aviv v Breidablik	1-4
Sarajevo v Dragon 2014	5-0
Breidablik v Dragon 2014	11-0
Sarajevo v ASA Tel Aviv	1-0
Dragon 2014 v ASA Tel Aviv	0-7
Breidablik v Sarajevo	3-1

Group 1 Table	P	W	D	L	F	A	GD	Pts
Breidablik	3	3	0	0	18	2	16	9
Sarajevo	3	2	0	1	7	3	4	6
ASA Tel Aviv	3	1	0	2	8	5	3	3
Dragon 2014	3	0	0	3	0	23	–23	0

GROUP 2 (MONTENEGRO)

Olimpia Cluj v KFF Mitrovica	1-2
Breznica Pljevlja v NSA Sofia	4-4
NSA Sofia v KFF Mitrovica	0-2
Olimpia Cluj v Breznica Pljevlja	2-3
KFF Mitrovica v Breznica Pljevlja	1-0
NSA Sofia v Olimpia Cluj	2-3

Group 2 Table	P	W	D	L	F	A	GD	Pts
KFF Mitrovica	3	3	0	0	5	1	4	9
Breznica Pljevlja	3	1	1	1	7	7	0	4
Olimpia Cluj	3	1	0	2	6	7	–1	3
NSA Sofia	3	0	1	2	6	9	–3	1

GROUP 3 (SLOVENIA)

Hibernian v Tbilisi Nike	3-0
Cardiff Met v Pomurje	1-0
Hibernian v Cardiff Met	2-1
Pomurje v Tbilisi Nike	4-0
Tbilisi Nike v Cardiff Met	1-5
Pomurje v Hibernian	1-2

Group 3 Table	P	W	D	L	F	A	GD	Pts
Hibernian	3	3	0	0	7	2	5	9
Cardiff Met	3	2	0	1	7	3	4	6
Pomurje	3	1	0	2	5	3	2	3
Tbilisi Nike	3	0	0	3	1	12	–11	0

GROUP 4 (UKRAINE)

FC Minsk v Bettembourg	12-0
Split v Kharkiv	2-3
FC Minsk v Split	2-1
Kharkiv v Bettembourg	6-0
Bettembourg v Split	2-7
Kharkiv v FC Minsk	0-2

Group 4 Table	P	W	D	L	F	A	GD	Pts
FC Minsk	3	3	0	0	16	1	15	9
WFC Kharkiv	3	2	0	1	9	4	5	6
Split	3	1	0	2	10	7	3	3
Bettembourg	3	0	0	3	2	25	–23	0

GROUP 5 (SLOVAKIA)

Spartak Subotica v Anenii Noi	12-0
Slovan Bratislava v Ferencvaros	1-3
Ferencvaros v Anenii Noi	2-0
Spartak Subotica v Slovan Bratislava	7-0
Anenii Noi v Slovan Bratislava	0-1
Ferencvaros v Spartak Subotica	2-2

Group 5 Table	P	W	D	L	F	A	GD	Pts
Spartak Subotica	3	2	1	0	21	2	19	7
Ferencvaros	3	2	1	0	7	3	4	7
Slovan Bratislava	3	1	0	2	2	10	–8	3
Anenii Noi	3	0	0	3	0	15	–15	0

GROUP 6 (ESTONIA)

BIIK-Kazygurt v EB/Streymur/Skala	9-0
Flora v PK-35 Vantaa	2-3
PK-35 Vantaa v EB/Streymur/Skala	5-0
BIIK-Kazygurt v Flora	2-0
EB/Streymur/Skala v Flora	0-2
PK-35 Vantaa v BIIK-Kazygurt	1-4

Group 6 Table	P	W	D	L	F	A	GD	Pts
BIIK-Kazygurt	3	3	0	0	15	1	14	9
PK-35 Vantaa	3	2	0	1	9	6	3	6
Flora	3	1	0	2	4	5	–1	3
EB/Streymur/Skala	3	0	0	3	0	16	–16	0

GROUP 7 (LATVIA)

Braga v Sturm Graz	2-0
Apollon v Rigas FS	10-0
Sturm Graz v Rigas FS	4-0
Apollon v Braga	0-1
Rigas FS v Braga	0-8
Sturm Graz v Apollon	2-7

Group 7 Table	P	W	D	L	F	A	GD	Pts
Braga	3	3	0	0	11	0	11	9
Apollon	3	2	0	1	17	3	14	6
Sturm Graz	3	1	0	2	6	9	–3	3
Rigas FS	3	0	0	3	0	22	–22	0

GROUP 8 (BELGIUM)

LSK Kvinner v Linfield	4-0
Anderlecht v PAOK	5-0
LSK Kvinner v Anderlecht	2-3
PAOK v Linfield	2-3
Linfield v Anderlecht	1-3
PAOK v LSK Kvinner	0-1

Group 8 Table	P	W	D	L	F	A	GD	Pts
Anderlecht	3	3	0	0	11	3	8	9
LSK Kvinner	3	2	0	1	7	3	4	6
Linfield	3	1	0	2	4	9	–5	3
PAOK	3	0	0	3	2	9	–7	0

GROUP 9 (NETHERLANDS)

Besiktas v Gornik Leczna	1-1
FC Twente v Alashkert	8-0
Gornik Leczna v Alashkert	13-0
FC Twente v Besiktas	2-2
Alashkert v Besiktas	0-3
Gornik Leczna v FC Twente	0-2

Group 9 Table	P	W	D	L	F	A	GD	Pts
FC Twente	3	2	1	0	12	2	10	7
Besiktas	3	1	2	0	6	3	3	5
Gornik Leczna	3	1	1	1	14	3	11	4
Alashkert	3	0	0	3	0	24	–24	0

GROUP 10 (LITHUANIA)

Wexford Youths v Vllaznia	1-3
Universitetas Gintra v Birkirkara	1-0
Vllaznia v Birkirkara	1-0
Universitetas Gintra v Wexford Youths	1-2
Birkirkara v Wexford Youths	2-7
Vllaznia v Universitetas Gintra	1-1

Group 10 Table	P	W	D	L	F	A	GD	Pts
Vllaznia	3	2	1	0	5	2	3	7
Wexford Youths	3	2	0	1	10	6	4	6
Universitetas Gintra	3	1	1	1	3	3	0	4
Birkirkara	3	0	0	3	2	9	–7	0

KNOCKOUT STAGE

ROUND OF 32 – 1ST LEG

Ryazan-VDV v Lyon	0-9
FC Minsk v Zurich	1-0
Mitrovica v VfL Wolfsburg	0-10
Chertanovo v Glasgow C	0-1
Vllaznia v Fortuna	0-1
Gothenburg v Bayern Munich	1-2
Pitea v Brondby	0-1
St Polten v FC Twente	2-4
Juventus v Barcelona	0-2
Hibernian v Slavia Prague	1-4
Breidablik v Sparta Prague	3-2
Fiorentina v Arsenal	0-4
Anderlecht v BIIK-Kazygurt	1-1
Spartak Subotica v Atletico Madrid	2-3
Lugano v Manchester C	1-7
Braga v Paris Saint-Germain	0-7

ROUND OF 32 – 2ND LEG

		(agg)
BIIK-Kazygurt v Anderlecht	2-0	3-1
Lyon v Ryazan-VDV	7-0	16-0
Wolfsburg v Mitrovica	5-0	15-0
Fortuna v Vllaznia	2-0	3-0
Barcelona v Juventus	2-1	4-1
Twente v St Polten	1-2	5-4
Bayern Munich v Gothenburg	0-1	2-2
Bayern Munich won on away goals		
Slavia Prague v Hibernian	5-1	9-2
Manchester C v Lugano	4-0	11-1
Brondby v Pitea	1-1	2-1
Sparta Prague v Breidablik	0-1	2-4
Zurich v FC Minsk	1-3	1-4
Atletico Madrid v Spartak Subotica	1-1	4-3
Arsenal v Fiorentina	2-0	6-0
Glasgow C v Chertanovo	4-1	5-1
Paris Saint-Germain v Braga	0-0	7-0

ROUND OF 16 – 1ST LEG

BIIK-Kazygurt v Bayern Munich	0-5
Brondby v Glasgow C	0-2
VfL Wolfsburg v FC Twente	6-0
Slavia Prague v Arsenal	2-5
Fortuna v Lyon	0-4
Manchester C v Atletico Madrid	1-1
Breidablik v Paris Saint-Germain	0-4
Barcelona v FC Minsk	5-0

ROUND OF 16 – 2ND LEG

		(agg)
FC Minsk v Barcelona	1-3	1-8
Lyon v Fortuna	7-0	11-0
FC Twente v VfL Wolfsburg	0-1	0-7
Bayern Munich v BIIK-Kazygurt	2-0	7-0
Atletico Madrid v Manchester C	2-1	3-2
Paris Saint-Germain v Breidablik	3-1	7-1
Arsenal v Slavia Prague	8-0	13-2
Glasgow C v Brondby	0-2	2-2
Glasgow City won on 3-1 on penalties		

QUARTER-FINALS

Atletico Madrid v Barcelona	0-1
Lyon v Bayern Munich	2-1
Glasgow C v Wolfsburg	1-9
Arsenal v Paris Saint-Germain	1-2

SEMI-FINALS

Paris Saint-Germain v Lyon	0-1
Wolfsburg v Barcelona	1-0

UEFA WOMEN'S CHAMPIONS LEAGUE FINAL 2019–20

San Sebastian, 30 August 2020

Lyon (2) 3 *(Le Sommer 26, Kumagai 45, Gunnarsdottir 89)*

Wolfsburg (0) 1 *(Popp 59)*

Lyon: Bouhaddi; Bronze, Buchanan, Renard, Karchaoui, Gunnarsdottir, Kumagai, Cascarino D (van der Sanden 87), Marozsan (Taylor 87), Majri (Malard 90), Le Sommer (Greenwood 90).
Wolfsburg: Abt; Blasse (Bremer 78), Goessling, Doorsoun-Khajeh (Hendrich 39), Janssen, Huth (Wolter 62), Syrstad Engen, Popp, Rolfo, Harder, Pajor (Oberdorf 61).
Referee: Esther Staubli (Switzerland).

UEFA WOMEN'S EURO 2021 QUALIFYING

QUALIFYING

All matches scheduled to be played between April 2020 and June 2020 have been postponed until further notice by UEFA due to the COVID-19 pandemic. For matches scheduled to be played from September 2020, actual dates are to be confirmed.

GROUP A

Estonia v Netherlands 0-7
Kosovo v Turkey 2-0
Slovenia v Russia 0-1
Slovenia v Kosovo 5-0
Russia v Estonia 4-0
Netherlands v Turkey 3-0
Turkey v Estonia 0-0
Slovenia v Netherlands 2-4
Turkey v Slovenia 1-6
Estonia v Kosovo 1-2
Netherlands v Russia 2-0
Turkey v Netherlands 0-8
Netherlands v Slovenia 4-1
Kosovo v Russia 0-5
Kosovo v Slovenia 0-3
Russia v Turkey P-P
Slovenia v Estonia P-P
Kosovo v Netherlands P-P
Russia v Slovenia P-P
Turkey v Kosovo P-P
Netherlands v Estonia P-P
Estonia v Russia P-P
Estonia v Turkey P-P
Russia v Kosovo P-P
Russia v Netherlands TBC
Slovenia v Turkey TBC
Kosovo v Estonia TBC
Netherlands v Kosovo TBC
Estonia v Slovenia TBC
Turkey v Russia TBC

Group A Table	P	W	D	L	F	A	GD	Pts
Netherlands	6	6	0	0	28	3	25	18
Russia	4	3	0	1	10	2	8	9
Slovenia	6	3	0	3	17	10	7	9
Kosovo	5	2	0	3	4	14	–10	6
Estonia	4	0	1	3	1	13	–12	1
Turkey	5	0	1	4	1	19	–18	1

GROUP B

Israel v Italy 2-3
Denmark v Malta 8-0
Bosnia-Herzegovina v Georgia 7-1
Georgia v Italy 0-1
Bosnia-Herzegovina v Malta 2-0
Israel v Denmark 0-3
Denmark v Bosnia-Herzegovina 2-0
Malta v Italy 0-2
Italy v Bosnia-Herzegovina 2-0
Georgia v Denmark 0-2
Malta v Israel 1-1
Italy v Georgia 6-0
Italy v Malta 5-0
Israel v Bosnia-Herzegovina 1-3
Denmark v Georgia 14-0
Bosnia-Herzegovina v Israel 1-0
Malta v Georgia 2-1
Israel v Georgia 4-0
Malta v Bosnia-Herzegovina 2-3
Bosnia-Herzegovina v Denmark P-P
Italy v Israel P-P
Georgia v Israel P-P
Bosnia-Herzegovina v Italy P-P
Malta v Denmark P-P
Georgia v Malta P-P
Denmark v Israel P-P
Italy v Denmark P-P
Georgia v Bosnia-Herzegovina TBC
Denmark v Italy TBC
Israel v Malta TBC

Group B Table	P	W	D	L	F	A	GD	Pts
Italy	6	6	0	0	19	2	17	18
Denmark	5	5	0	0	29	0	29	15
Bosnia-Herzegovina	7	5	0	2	16	8	8	15
Israel	6	1	1	4	8	11	–3	4
Malta	7	1	1	5	5	22	–17	4
Georgia	7	0	0	7	2	36	–34	0

GROUP C

Faroe Islands v Wales 0-6
Northern Ireland v Norway 0-6
Belarus v Faroe Islands 6-0
Wales v Northern Ireland 2-2
Belarus v Norway 1-7
Belarus v Wales 0-1
Faroe Islands v Norway 0-13
Norway v Northern Ireland 6-0
Northern Ireland v Wales 0-0
Wales v Faroe Islands P-P
Belarus v Northern Ireland P-P
Wales v Norway P-P
Norway v Faroe Islands P-P
Northern Ireland v Belarus P-P
Northern Ireland v Faroe Islands P-P
Wales v Belarus P-P
Faroe Islands v Northern Ireland TBC
Norway v Belarus TBC
Faroe Islands v Belarus TBC
Norway v Wales TBC

Group C Table	P	W	D	L	F	A	GD	Pts
Norway	4	4	0	0	32	1	31	12
Wales	4	2	2	0	9	2	7	8
Belarus	3	1	0	2	7	8	–1	3
Northern Ireland	4	0	2	2	2	14	–12	2
Faroe Islands	3	0	0	3	0	25	–25	0

GROUP D

Moldova v Czech Republic 0-7
Spain v Azerbaijan 4-0
Czech Republic v Spain 1-5
Azerbaijan v Czech Republic 0-4
Moldova v Azerbaijan 3-1
Poland v Spain 0-0
Poland v Moldova 5-0
Azerbaijan v Poland 0-5
Spain v Moldova P-P
Poland v Azerbaijan P-P
Spain v Czech Republic P-P
Moldova v Poland P-P
Czech Republic v Azerbaijan P-P
Spain v Poland P-P
Czech Republic v Moldova P-P
Azerbaijan v Moldova TBC
Czech Republic v Poland TBC
Moldova v Spain TBC
Azerbaijan v Spain TBC
Poland v Czech Republic TBC

Group D Table	P	W	D	L	F	A	GD	Pts
Poland	3	2	1	0	10	0	10	7
Spain	3	2	1	0	9	1	8	7
Czech Republic	3	2	0	1	12	5	7	6
Moldova	3	1	0	2	3	13	–10	3
Azerbaijan	4	0	0	4	1	16	–15	0

GROUP E

Scotland v Cyprus 8-0
Albania v Finland 0-3
Albania v Portugal 0-1
Finland v Albania 8-1
Finland v Cyprus 4-0
Albania v Scotland 0-5
Portugal v Finland 1-1
Cyprus v Albania 0-2
Cyprus v Scotland P-P
Finland v Portugal P-P
Cyprus v Finland P-P
Scotland v Portugal P-P
Cyprus v Portugal P-P
Scotland v Albania P-P

Portugal v Cyprus	P-P
Finland v Scotland	P-P
Portugal v Scotland	TBC
Albania v Cyprus	TBC
Portugal v Albania	TBC
Scotland v Finland	TBC

Group E Table	P	W	D	L	F	A	GD	Pts
Finland	4	3	1	0	16	2	14	10
Scotland	2	2	0	0	13	0	13	6
Portugal	2	1	1	0	2	1	1	4
Albania	5	1	0	4	3	17	−14	3
Cyprus	3	0	0	3	0	14	−14	0

GROUP F

Iceland v Hungary	4-1
Iceland v Slovakia	1-0
Latvia v Sweden	1-4
Latvia v Slovakia	1-2
Hungary v Sweden	0-5
Sweden v Slovakia	7-0
Latvia v Iceland	0-6
Slovakia v Hungary	0-0
Hungary v Latvia	4-0
Hungary v Iceland	P-P
Slovakia v Latvia	P-P
Slovakia v Iceland	P-P
Sweden v Hungary	P-P
Iceland v Latvia	P-P
Slovakia v Sweden	P-P
Iceland v Sweden	P-P
Latvia v Hungary	P-P
Sweden v Latvia	TBC
Hungary v Slovakia	TBC
Sweden v Iceland	TBC

Group F Table	P	W	D	L	F	A	GD	Pts
Sweden	3	3	0	0	16	1	15	9
Iceland	3	3	0	0	11	1	10	9
Hungary	4	1	1	2	5	9	−4	4
Slovakia	4	1	1	2	2	9	−7	4
Latvia	4	0	0	4	2	16	−14	0

GROUP G

Kazakhstan v Serbia	0-3
Austria v North Macedonia	3-0
North Macedonia v Kazakhstan	4-1
North Macedonia v Serbia	0-6
Kazakhstan v France	0-3
Serbia v Austria	0-1
North Macedonia v Austria	0-3
France v Serbia	6-0
Austria v Kazakhstan	9-0
Serbia v North Macedonia	8-1
France v North Macedonia	P-P
Serbia v Kazakhstan	P-P
Austria v France	P-P
Kazakhstan v North Macedonia	P-P
France v Austria	P-P
Austria v Serbia	P-P
France v Kazakhstan	P-P
Serbia v France	TBC
Kazakhstan v Austria	TBC
North Macedonia v France	TBC

Group G Table	P	W	D	L	F	A	GD	Pts
Austria	4	4	0	0	16	0	16	12
Serbia	5	3	0	2	17	8	9	9
France	2	2	0	0	9	0	9	6
North Macedonia	5	1	0	4	5	21	−16	3
Kazakhstan	4	0	0	4	1	19	−18	0

GROUP H

Lithuania v Croatia	1-2
Switzerland v Lithuania	4-0
Belgium v Croatia	6-1
Lithuania v Switzerland	0-3
Romania v Belgium	0-1
Switzerland v Croatia	2-0
Romania v Lithuania	3-0
Croatia v Belgium	1-4
Switzerland v Romania	6-0
Belgium v Lithuania	6-0
Croatia v Lithuania	P-P
Croatia v Romania	P-P
Belgium v Switzerland	P-P
Lithuania v Romania	P-P
Romania v Switzerland	P-P
Lithuania v Belgium	P-P
Croatia v Switzerland	TBC
Belgium v Romania	TBC
Romania v Croatia	TBC
Switzerland v Belgium	TBC

Group H Table	P	W	D	L	F	A	GD	Pts
Belgium	4	4	0	0	17	2	15	12
Switzerland	4	4	0	0	15	0	15	12
Romania	3	1	0	2	3	7	−4	3
Croatia	4	1	0	3	4	13	−9	3
Lithuania	5	0	0	5	1	18	−17	0

GROUP I

Germany v Montenegro	10-0
Ukraine v Germany	0-8
Republic of Ireland v Montenegro	2-0
Germany v Ukraine	8-0
Greece v Germany	0-5
Republic of Ireland v Ukraine	3-2
Montenegro v Greece	0-4
Greece v Republic of Ireland	1-1
Republic of Ireland v Greece	1-0
Montenegro v Republic of Ireland	0-3
Montenegro v Ukraine	P-P
Germany v Republic of Ireland	P-P
Ukraine v Greece	P-P
Montenegro v Germany	P-P
Greece v Montenegro	P-P
Ukraine v Republic of Ireland	P-P
Greece v Ukraine	P-P
Germany v Greece	TBC
Republic of Ireland v Germany	TBC
Ukraine v Montenegro	TBC

Group I Table	P	W	D	L	F	A	GD	Pts
Republic of Ireland	5	4	1	0	10	3	7	13
Germany	4	4	0	0	31	0	31	12
Greece	4	1	1	2	5	7	−2	4
Ukraine	3	0	0	3	2	19	−17	0
Montenegro	4	0	0	4	0	19	−19	0

ENGLAND WOMEN'S INTERNATIONALS 2019–20

▪ *Denotes player sent off.*

FRIENDLIES

Leuven, Thursday 29 August 2019

Belgium (2) 3 *(Telford 38 (og), van Kerkhoven 45, 55)*

England (2) 3 *(Taylor 22, Mead 26, Parris 75 (pen))*

England: Telford (Earps 63); Daly, Houghton, McManus, Stokes, Walsh (Williamson 87), Parris (Staniforth 75), Bronze, Stanway (Williams 56), Mead, Taylor (England 75).

Bergen, Tuesday 3 September 2019

Norway (0) 2 *(Maanum 53, Hansen 89)*

England (1) 1 *(Stanway 10)*

England: Telford (Roebuck 78); Daly (Williamson 77), Houghton, Bright, Stokes, Walsh, Parris (Mead 83), Bronze, Stanway (Williams 89), Duggan, Taylor (England 77).

Middlesbrough, Saturday 5 October 2019

England (0) 1 *(England 80)*

Brazil (0) 2 *(Debinha 49, 67)* 29,238

England: Earps; Bronze, Houghton, Williamson, Greenwood, Scott, Walsh, Parris (Staniforth 74), Nobbs (Daly 58), Mead, Taylor (England 74).

Setubal, Tuesday 8 October 2019

Portugal (0) 0

England (0) 1 *(Mead 72)*

England: Roebuck; Daly (Taylor 65), Houghton, Williamson, Greenwood, Bronze, Walsh, Parris, Staniforth (Lawley 80), Mead (Hemp 86), England (Nobbs 65).

Wembley, Saturday 9 November 2019

England (1) 1 *(White 44)*

Germany (1) 2 *(Pop-p 9, Buhl 90)* 77,768

England: Earps; Bronze, Houghton, Williamson, Greenwood, Scott, Walsh, Nobbs (Stanway 77), Parris (Hemp 73), White (Taylor 73), Mead (Daly 73).

Ceske Budejovice, Tuesday 12 November 2019

Czech Republic (1) 2 *(Szewieczkova 15, 27)*

England (2) 3 *(England 17, Mead 20, Williamson 86)*

England: Telford; Bronze, Bright, Williamson, Stokes, Walsh, Parris (Hemp 64), Scott, Staniforth (Nobbs 76), Mead, England (Daly 77).

SHEBELIEVES CUP 2020

Orlando, Thursday 5 March 2020

USA (0) 2 *(Press 53, Lloyd 55)*

England (0) 0 16,531

England: Telford; Williamson, Bright (Duggan 71), Houghton, Greenwood, Stanway, Scott (Nobbs 65) Walsh, Parris (Kelly 89), White (England), Hemp.

New Jersey, Sunday 8 March 2020

Japan (0) 0

England (0) 1 *(White 84)* 14,758

England: Roebuck; Daly, Houghton, Bright, Stokes, Walsh (Williamson 60), Kelly (Parris 60), Nobbs (Scott), Stanway (Staniforth 69), Hemp (Duggan 60), England (White 69).

Frisco, Texas, Sunday 11 March 2020

England (0) 0

Spain (0) 1 *(Putellas 83)* 10,507

England: Telford; Daly, McManus, Bright (Houghton 45), Greenwood, Scott (Walsh 87), Williamson, Parris, Nobbs (Stanway 62), Duggan (Russo 70), White (Kelly 70).

ENGLAND WOMEN'S INTERNATIONAL MATCHES 1972–2020

Note: In the results that follow, WC = World Cup; EC = European (UEFA) Championships; M = Mundialito; CC = Cyprus Cup; AC = Algarve Cup. * = After extra time. Games were organised by the Women's Football Association from 1971 to 1992 and the Football Association from 1993 to date. **Bold type** indicates matches played in season 2019–20.

v ARGENTINA
WC2007 17 Sept Chengdu 6-1
WC2019 14 June Le Havre 1-0

v AUSTRALIA
2003 3 Sept Burnley 1-0
CC2015 6 Mar Nicosia 3-0
2015 27 Oct Yongchuan 1-0
2018 9 Oct London 1-1

v AUSTRIA
WC2005 1 Sept Amstetten 4-1
WC2006 20 Apr Gillingham 4-0
WC2010 25 Mar Shepherd's Bush 3-0
WC2010 21 Aug Krems 4-0
2017 10 Apr Milton Keynes 3-0
2018 8 Nov Vienna 3-0

v BELARUS
EC2007 27 Oct Walsall 4-0
EC2008 8 May Minsk 6-1
WC2013 21 Sept Bournemouth 6-0
WC2014 14 June Minsk 3-0

v BELGIUM
1978 31 Oct Southampton 3-0
1980 1 May Ostende 1-2
M1984 20 Aug Jesolo 1-1
M1984 25 Aug Caorle 2-1
1989 14 May Epinal 2-0
EC1990 17 Mar Ypres 3-0
EC1990 7 Apr Sheffield 1-0
EC1993 6 Nov Koksijde 3-0
EC1994 13 Mar Nottingham 6-0
EC2016 8 Apr Rotherham 1-1
EC2016 20 Sept Leuven 2-0
2019 29 Aug Leuven 3-3

v BOSNIA-HERZEGOVINA
EC2015 29 Nov Bristol 1-0
EC2016 12 Apr Zenica 1-0
WC2017 24 Nov Walsall 4-0
WC2018 10 Apr Zenica 2-0

v BRAZIL
2018 6 Oct Nottingham 1-0
2019 27 Feb Philadelphia 2-1
2019 5 Oct Middlesbrough 1-2

v CAMEROON
WC2019 23 June Valenciennes 3-0

v CANADA
WC1995 6 June Helsingborg 3-2
2003 19 May Montreal 0-4
2003 22 May Ottawa 0-4
CC2009 12 Mar Nicosia 3-1
CC2010 27 Feb Nicosia 0-1
CC2011 7 Mar Nicosia 0-2
CC2013 13 Mar Nicosia 1-0
2013 7 Apr Rotherham 1-0
CC2014 10 Mar Nicosia 2-0
CC2015 11 Mar Larnaca 1-0
2015 29 May Hamilton 0-1
WC2015 27 June Vancouver 2-1
2019 5 Apr Manchester 0-1

v CHINA PR
AC2005 15 Mar Guia 0-0*
2007 26 Jan Guangzhou 0-2
2015 9 Apr Manchester 2-1
2015 23 Oct Yongchuan 1-2

v COLOMBIA
WC2015 17 June Montreal 2-1

v CROATIA
EC1995 19 Nov Charlton 5-0
EC1996 18 Apr Osijek 2-0
EC2012 31 Mar Vrbovec 6-0
EC2012 19 Sept Walsall 3-0

v CZECH REPUBLIC
2005 26 May Walsall 4-1
EC2008 20 Mar Doncaster 0-0
EC2008 28 Sept Prague 5-1
2019 12 Nov Ceske Budejovice 3-2

v DENMARK
1979 19 May Hvidovre 1-3
1979 13 Sept Hull 2-2
1981 9 Sept Tokyo 0-1
EC1984 8 Apr Crewe 2-1
EC1984 28 Apr Hjorring 1-0
M1985 19 Aug Caorle 0-1
EC1987 8 Nov Blackburn 2-1
EC1988 8 May Herning 0-2
1991 28 June Nordby 0-0
1991 30 June Nordby 3-3
1999 22 Aug Odense 1-0
2001 23 Aug Northampton 0-3
2004 19 Feb Portsmouth 2-0
EC2005 8 June Blackburn 1-2
2009 22 July Swindon 1-0
2017 1 July Copenhagen 2-1
2019 25 May Walsall 2-0

v ESTONIA
2015 21 Sept Tallinn 8-0
EC2016 15 Sept Nottingham 5-0

v FINLAND
1979 19 July Sorrento 3-1
EC1987 25 Oct Kirkkonummi 2-1
EC1988 4 Sept Millwall 1-1
EC1989 1 Oct Brentford 0-0
EC1990 29 Sept Tampere 0-0
2000 28 Sept Leyton 2-1
EC2005 5 June Manchester 3-2
2009 9 Feb Larnaca 2-2
2009 11 Feb Larnaca 4-1
EC2009 3 Sept Turku 3-2
CC2012 28 Feb Nicosia 3-1
CC2014 7 Mar Larnaca 3-0
CC2015 4 Mar Larnaca 3-1

v FRANCE
1973 22 Apr Brion 3-0
1974 7 Nov Wimbledon 2-0
1977 26 Feb Longjumeau 0-0
M1988 22 July Riva del Garda 1-1
1998 15 Feb Alencon 2-3
1999 15 Sept Yeovil 0-1
2000 16 Aug Marseilles 0-1
WC2002 17 Oct Crystal Palace 0-1
WC2002 16 Nov St Etienne 0-1
WC2006 26 Mar Blackburn 0-0
WC2006 30 Sept Rennes 1-1
CC2009 7 Mar Paralimni 2-2
WC2011 9 July Leverkusen 1-1*
CC2012 4 Mar Paralimni 0-3
2012 20 Oct Paris 2-2
EC2013 18 July Linkoping 0-3
CC2014 12 Mar Nicosia 0-2
WC2015 9 June Moncton 0-1
2016 9 Mar Boca Raton 0-0
2016 21 Oct Doncaster 0-0
2017 1 Mar Pennsylvania 1-2
2017 30 July Deventer 1-0
2017 20 Oct Valenciennes 0-1
2018 1 Mar Columbus 4-1

v GERMANY
EC1990 25 Nov High Wycombe 1-4
EC1990 16 Dec Bochum 0-2
EC1994 11 Dec Watford 1-4
EC1995 23 Feb Bochum 1-2
WC1995 13 June Vasteras 0-3
1997 27 Feb Preston 4-6
WC1997 25 Sept Dessau 0-3

WC1998	8 Mar	Millwall	0-1
EC2001	30 June	Jena	0-3
WC2001	27 Sept	Kassel	1-3
WC2002	19 May	Crystal Palace	0-1
2003	11 Sept	Darmstadt	0-4
2006	25 Oct	Aalen	1-5
2007	30 Jan	Guangzhou	0-0
WC2007	14 Sept	Shanghai	0-0
2008	17 July	Unterhaching	0-3
EC2009	10 Sept	Helsinki	2-6
2014	23 Nov	Wembley	0-3
WC2015	4 July	Vancouver	1-0*
2015	26 Nov	Duisburg	0-0
2016	6 Mar	Nashville	1-2
2017	7 Mar	Washington	0-1
2018	4 Mar	New Jersey	2-2
2019	**9 Nov**	**Wembley**	**1-2**

v HUNGARY

WC2005	27 Oct	Tapolca	13-0
WC2006	11 May	Southampton	2-0

v ICELAND

EC1992	17 May	Yeovil	4-0
EC1992	19 July	Kopavogur	2-1
EC1994	8 Oct	Reykjavik	2-1
EC1994	30 Oct	Brighton	2-1
WC2002	16 Sept	Reykjavik	2-2
WC2002	22 Sept	Birmingham	1-0
2004	14 May	Peterborough	1-0
2006	9 Mar	Norwich	1-0
2007	17 May	Southend	4-0
2009	16 July	Colchester	0-2

v ITALY

1976	2 June	Rome	0-2
1976	4 June	Cesena	1-2
1977	15 Nov	Wimbledon	1-0
1979	25 July	Naples	1-3
1982	11 June	Pescara	0-2
M1984	24 Aug	Jesolo	1-1
M1985	20 Aug	Caorle	1-1
M1985	25 Aug	Caorle	3-2
EC1987	13 June	Drammen	1-2
M1988	30 July	Arco di Trento	2-1
1989	1 Nov	High Wycombe	1-1
1990	18 Aug	Wembley	1-4
EC1992	17 Oct	Solofra	2-3
EC1992	7 Nov	Rotherham	0-3
1995	25 Jan	Florence	1-1
EC1995	1 Nov	Sunderland	1-1
EC1996	16 Mar	Cosenza	1-2
1997	23 Apr	Turin	0-2
1998	21 Apr	West Bromwich	1-2
1999	26 May	Bologna	1-4
2003	25 Feb	Viareggio	0-1
2005	17 Feb	Milton Keynes	4-1
EC2009	25 Aug	Lahti	1-2
CC2010	3 Mar	Nicosia	3-2
CC2011	2 Mar	Larnaca	2-0
CC2012	6 Mar	Paralimni	1-3
CC2013	6 Mar	Nicosia	4-2
EC2014	5 Mar	Larnaca	2-0
2017	7 Apr	Port Vale	1-1

v JAPAN

1981	6 Sept	Kobe	4-0
WC2007	11 Sept	Shanghai	2-2
WC2011	5 July	Augsburg	2-0
2013	26 June	Burton	1-1
WC2015	1 July	Edmonton	1-2
2019	5 Mar	Tampa	3-0
WC2019	19 June	Nice	2-0
2020	**8 Mar**	**New Jersey**	**1-0**

v KAZAKHSTAN

WC2017	28 Nov	Colchester	5-0
WC2018	4 Sept	Pavlodar	6-0

v KOREA REPUBLIC

2010	19 Oct	Suwon	0-0
CC2011	9 Mar	Larnaca	2-0

v MALTA

WC2009	25 Oct	Blackpool	8-0
WC2010	20 May	Ta'Qali	6-0

v MEXICO

AC2005	13 Mar	Lagos	5-0
WC2011	27 June	Wolfsburg	1-1
WC2015	13 June	Moncton	2-1

v MONTENEGRO

WC2014	5 Apr	Brighton	9-0
WC2014	17 Sept	Petrovac	10-0

v NETHERLANDS

1973	9 Nov	Reading	1-0
1974	31 May	Groningen	0-3
1976	2 May	Blackpool	2-0
1978	30 Sept	Vlissingen	1-3
1989	13 May	Epinal	0-0
WC1997	30 Oct	West Ham	1-0
WC1998	23 May	Waalwijk	1-2
WC2001	4 Nov	Grimsby	0-0
WC2002	23 Mar	Den Haag	4-1
2004	18 Sept	Heerhugowaard	2-1
2004	22 Sept	Tuitjenhoorn	1-0
WC2005	17 Nov	Zwolle	1-0
WC2006	31 Aug	Charlton	4-0
2007	14 Mar	Swindon	0-1
EC2009	6 Sept	Tampere	2-1*
EC2011	27 Oct	Zwolle	0-0
EC2012	17 June	Salford	1-0
CC2015	9 Mar	Nicosia	1-1
2016	29 Nov	Tilburg	1-0
2017	3 Aug	Enschede	0-3

v NEW ZEALAND

2010	21 Oct	Suwon	0-0
WC2011	1 July	Dresden	2-1
CC2013	11 Mar	Larnaca	3-1
2019	1 June	Brighton	0-1

v NIGERIA

WC1995	10 June	Karlstad	3-2
2002	23 July	Norwich	0-1
2004	22 Apr	Reading	0-3

v NORTHERN IRELAND

1973	7 Sept	Bath	5-1
EC1982	19 Sept	Crewe	7-1
EC1983	14 May	Belfast	4-0
EC1985	25 May	Antrim	8-1
EC1986	16 Mar	Blackburn	10-0
1987	11 Apr	Leeds	6-0
AC2005	9 Mar	Paderne	4-0
EC2007	13 May	Gillingham	4-0
EC2008	6 Mar	Lurgan	2-0

v NORWAY

1981	25 Oct	Cambridge	0-3
EC1988	21 Aug	Klep-pe	0-2
EC1988	18 Sept	Blackburn	1-3
EC1990	27 May	Klep-pe	0-2
EC1990	2 Sept	Old Trafford	0-0
WC1995	8 June	Karlstad	3-2
1997	8 June	Lillestrom	0-4
WC1998	14 May	Oldham	1-2
WC1998	15 Aug	Lillestrom	0-2
EC2000	7 Mar	Norwich	0-3
EC2000	4 June	Moss	0-8
AC2002	1 Mar	Albufeira	1-3
2005	6 May	Barnsley	1-0
2008	14 Feb	Larnaca	2-1
2009	23 Apr	Shrewsbury	3-0
2014	17 Jan	La Manga	1-1
WC2015	22 June	Ottawa	2-1
2017	22 Jan	La Manga	0-1
WC2019	27 June	Le Havre	3-0
2019	**3 Sept**	**Bergen**	**1-2**

v PORTUGAL

EC1996	11 Feb	Benavente	5-0
EC1996	19 May	Brentford	3-0
EC2000	20 Feb	Barnsley	2-0
EC2000	22 Apr	Sacavem	2-2
WC2001	24 Nov	Gafanha da Nazare	1-1
WC2002	24 Feb	Portsmouth	3-0
AC2005	11 Mar	Faro	4-0
2017	27 July	Tilburg	2-1
2019	**8 Oct**	**Setubal**	**1-0**

v REPUBLIC OF IRELAND

1978	2 May	Exeter	6-1
1981	2 May	Dublin	5-0
EC1982	7 Nov	Dublin	1-0
EC1983	11 Sept	Reading	6-0
EC1985	22 Sept	Cork	6-0
EC1986	27 Apr	Reading	4-0
1987	29 Mar	Dublin	1-0

v ROMANIA

EC1998	12 Sept	Campina	4-1
EC1998	11 Oct	High Wycombe	2-1

v RUSSIA

EC2001	24 June	Jena	1-1
2003	21 Oct	Moscow	2-2
2004	19 Aug	Bristol	1-2
2007	8 Mar	Milton Keynes	6-0
EC2009	28 Aug	Helsinki	3-2
EC2013	15 July	Linkoping	1-1
WC2017	19 Sept	Tranmere	6-0
WC2018	8 June	Moscow	3-1

v SCOTLAND

1972	18 Nov	Greenock	3-2
1973	23 June	Nuneaton	8-0
1976	23 May	Enfield	5-1
1977	29 May	Dundee	1-2
EC1982	3 Oct	Dumbarton	4-0
EC1983	22 May	Leeds	2-0
EC1985	17 Mar	Preston	4-0
EC1986	12 Oct	Kirkcaldy	3-1
1989	30 Apr	Kirkcaldy	3-0
1990	6 May	Paisley	4-0
1990	12 May	Wembley	4-0
1991	20 Apr	High Wycombe	5-0
EC1992	17 Apr	Walsall	1-0
EC1992	23 Aug	Perth	2-0
1997	9 Mar	Sheffield	6-0
1997	23 Aug	Livingston	4-0
2001	27 May	Bolton	1-0
AC2002	7 Mar	Quarteira	4-1
2003	13 Nov	Preston	5-0
2005	21 Apr	Tranmere	2-1
2007	11 Mar	High Wycombe	1-0
CC2009	10 Mar	Larnaca	3-0
CC2011	4 Mar	Nicosia	0-2
CC2013	8 Mar	Larnaca	4-4
EC2017	19 July	Utrecht	6-0
WC2019	9 June	Nice	2-1

v SERBIA

EC2011	17 Sept	Belgrade	2-2
EC2011	23 Nov	Doncaster	2-0
EC2016	4 June	Wycombe	7-0
EC2016	7 June	Stara Pazova	7-0

v SLOVENIA

EC1993	25 Sept	Ljubljana	10-0
EC1994	17 Apr	Brentford	10-0
EC2011	22 Sept	Swindon	4-0
EC2012	21 June	Velenje	4-0

v SOUTH AFRICA

CC2009	5 Mar	Larnaca	6-0
CC2010	24 Feb	Larnaca	1-0

v SPAIN

EC1993	19 Dec	Osuna	0-0
EC1994	20 Feb	Bradford	0-0
EC1996	8 Sept	Montilla	1-2
EC1996	29 Sept	Tranmere	1-1
2001	22 Mar	Luton	4-2
EC2007	25 Nov	Shrewsbury	1-0
EC2008	2 Oct	Zamora	2-2
WC2010	1 Apr	Millwall	1-0
WC2010	19 June	Aranda de Duero	2-2
EC2013	12 July	Linkoping	2-3
2016	25 Oct	Guadalajara	2-1
EC2017	23 July	Breda	2-0
2019	9 Apr	Swindon	2-1
2020	**11 Mar**	**Frisco (TX)**	**0-1**

v SWEDEN

1975	15 June	Gothenburg	0-2
1975	7 Sept	Wimbledon	1-3
1979	27 July	Scafati	0-0*
1980	17 Sept	Leicester	1-1
1982	26 May	Kinna	1-1
1983	30 Oct	Charlton	2-2
EC1984	12 May	Gothenburg	0-1
EC1984	27 May	Luton	1-0
EC1987	11 June	Moss	2-3*
1989	23 May	Wembley	0-2
1995	13 May	Halmstad	0-4
1998	26 July	Dagenham	0-1
EC2001	27 June	Jena	0-4
2002	25 Jan	La Manga	0-5
AC2002	5 Mar	Lagos	3-6
EC2005	11 June	Blackburn	0-1
2006	7 Feb	Larnaca	0-0
2006	9 Feb	Achna	1-1
2008	12 Feb	Larnaca	0-2
EC2009	31 Aug	Turku	1-1
2011	17 May	Oxford	2-0
2013	4 July	Ljungskile	1-4
2014	3 Aug	Hartlepool	4-0
2017	24 Jan	La Manga	0-0
2018	11 Nov	Rotherham	0-2
WC2019	6 July	Nice	1-2

v SWITZERLAND

1975	19 Apr	Basel	3-1
1977	28 Apr	Hull	9-1
1979	23 July	Sorrento	2-0
EC1999	16 Oct	Zofingen	3-0
EC2000	13 May	Bristol	1-0
CC2010	1 Mar	Nicosia	2-2
WC2010	12 Sept	Shrewsbury	2-0
WC2010	16 Sept	Wohlen	3-2
CC2012	1 Mar	Larnaca	1-0
2017	10 June	Biel	4-0

v TURKEY

WC2009	26 Nov	Izmir	3-0
WC2010	29 July	Walsall	3-0
WC2013	26 Sept	Portsmouth	8-0
WC2013	31 Oct	Adana	4-0

v UKRAINE

EC2000	30 Oct	Kiev	2-1
EC2000	28 Nov	Leyton	2-0
WC2014	8 May	Shrewsbury	4-0
WC2014	19 June	Lviv	2-1

v USA

M1985	23 Aug	Caorle	3-1
M1988	27 July	Riva del Garda	2-0
1990	9 Aug	Blaine	0-3
1991	25 May	Hirson	1-3
1997	9 May	San Jose	0-5
1997	11 May	Portland	0-6
AC2002	3 Mar	Ferreiras	0-2
2003	17 May	Birmingham (Alabama)	0-6
2007	28 Jan	Guangzhou	1-1
WC2007	22 Sept	Tianjin	0-3
2011	2 Apr	Leyton	2-1
2015	13 Feb	Milton Keynes	0-1
2016	4 Mar	Tampa	0-1
2017	4 Mar	New Jersey	1-0
2018	8 Mar	Orlando	0-1
2019	2 Mar	Nashville	2-2
WC2019	2 July	Lyon	1-2
2020	**5 Mar**	**Orlando**	**0-2**

v USSR

1990	11 Aug	Blaine	1-1
1991	20 July	Dmitrov	2-1
1991	21 July	Kashira	2-0
1991	7 Sept	Southampton	2-0
1991	8 Sept	Brighton	1-3

v WALES

1974	17 Mar	Slough	5-0
1976	22 May	Bedford	4-0
1976	17 Oct	Ebbw Vale	2-1
1977	18 Sept	Warminster	5-0
1980	1 June	Warminster	6-1
1985	17 Aug	Ramsey (Isle of Man)	6-0
WC2013	26 Oct	Millwall	2-0
WC2014	21 Aug	Cardiff	4-0
WC2018	6 Apr	Southampton	0-0
WC2018	31 Aug	Newport	3-0

v WEST GERMANY

M1984	22 Aug	Jesolo	0-2
1990	5 Aug	Blaine	1-3

OTHER MATCHES

v ITALY B

1984	27 Aug	Monfalcone	3-1
M1988	20 July	Riva del Garda	3-0

v USA B

1990	7 Aug	Blaine	1-0

WELSH FOOTBALL 2019–20

Due to COVID-19 pandemic the Welsh FA confirmed the cancellation of the Welsh Leagues on 19 May 2020 with League positions awarded on a points-per-game basis.

JD CYMRU PREMIER LEAGUE 2019–20

			Home					*Away*					*Total*							
		P	*W*	*D*	*L*	*F*	*A*	*W*	*D*	*L*	*F*	*A*	*W*	*D*	*L*	*F*	*A*	*GD*	*Pts*	*PPG*
1	Connah's Quay Nomads	26	10	3	0	29	10	6	5	2	18	9	16	8	2	47	19	28	56	2.15
2	The New Saints	26	9	1	3	23	13	7	3	3	46	14	16	4	6	69	27	42	52	2.00
3	Bala T	26	7	3	3	25	11	8	1	4	28	12	15	4	7	53	23	30	49	1.88
4	Barry Town U	25	5	4	4	21	16	7	2	3	14	13	12	6	7	35	29	6	42	1.68
5	Caernarfon T	26	8	2	3	24	13	3	3	7	12	25	11	5	10	36	38	–2	38	1.46
6	Newtown	25	4	5	3	11	10	6	0	7	14	20	10	5	10	25	30	–5	35	1.40
7	Cardiff Metropolitan Univ	25	6	3	4	14	12	3	5	4	16	17	9	8	8	30	29	1	35	1.40
8	Cefn Druids	25	5	2	5	20	23	5	3	5	17	16	10	5	10	37	39	–2	35	1.40
9	Aberystwyth T	26	3	2	8	18	35	4	4	5	18	20	7	6	13	36	55	–19	27	1.04
10	Penybont	25	2	4	7	15	24	3	2	7	14	24	5	6	14	29	48	–19	21	0.84
11	Carmarthen T	25	2	3	8	14	26	2	3	7	14	23	4	6	15	28	49	–21	18	0.72
12	Airbus UK Broughton	26	2	2	8	12	34	2	3	9	16	33	4	5	17	28	67	–39	17	0.65

Top 6 teams split after 22 games.

PREVIOUS WELSH LEAGUE WINNERS

1993 Cwmbran Town
1994 Bangor City
1995 Bangor City
1996 Barry Town
1997 Barry Town
1998 Barry Town
1999 Barry Town
2000 TNS
2001 Barry Town
2002 Barry Town
2003 Barry Town
2004 Rhyl
2005 TNS
2006 TNS
2007 TNS
2008 Llanelli
2009 Rhyl
2010 The New Saints
2011 Bangor C
2012 The New Saints
2013 The New Saints
2014 The New Saints
2015 The New Saints
2016 The New Saints
2017 The New Saints
2018 The New Saints
2019 The New Saints
2020 Connah's Quay Nomads

JD CYMRU NORTH LEAGUE 2019–20

			Home					*Away*					*Total*							
		P	*W*	*D*	*L*	*F*	*A*	*W*	*D*	*L*	*F*	*A*	*W*	*D*	*L*	*F*	*A*	*GD*	*Pts*	*PPG*
1	Prestatyn T	26	12	1	0	41	6	10	1	2	43	13	22	2	2	84	19	65	68	2.62
2	Flint T*	24	9	0	3	38	14	7	4	1	23	10	16	4	4	61	24	37	52	2.17
3	Colwyn Bay	25	7	4	3	27	17	8	1	2	20	13	15	5	5	47	30	17	50	2.00
4	Guilsfield	22	7	3	2	29	19	7	1	2	18	8	14	4	4	47	27	20	46	2.09
5	Bangor C	23	7	2	3	20	14	4	5	2	9	12	11	7	5	29	26	3	40	1.74
6	Llanrhaeadr Ym Mochnant	23	4	1	6	15	18	7	2	3	27	20	11	3	9	42	38	4	36	1.57
7	Conwy Borough	24	3	5	4	21	24	7	1	4	24	21	10	6	8	45	45	0	36	1.50
8	Penrhyncoch	25	8	1	3	20	13	3	2	8	11	23	11	3	11	31	36	–5	36	1.44
9	Rhyl	25	6	1	6	28	20	5	1	6	17	18	11	2	12	45	38	7	35	1.40
10	Llandudno	23	5	1	7	20	20	3	3	4	15	18	8	4	11	35	38	–3	28	1.22
11	Gresford Ath	24	4	2	5	17	16	4	3	6	20	22	8	5	11	37	38	–1	29	1.21
12	Buckley T	21	4	1	4	11	20	3	2	7	14	25	7	3	11	25	45	–20	24	1.14
13	Ruthin T	25	4	3	4	19	16	3	4	7	13	24	7	7	11	32	40	–8	28	1.12
14	Llangefni T	26	2	4	8	10	23	3	3	6	13	26	5	7	14	23	49	–26	22	0.85
15	Porthmadog	24	2	3	7	11	16	2	3	7	17	31	4	6	14	28	47	–19	18	0.75
16	Corwen	23	1	3	7	13	27	2	2	8	13	28	3	5	15	26	55	–29	14	0.61
17	Llanfair U	23	0	3	8	13	27	2	0	10	13	41	2	3	18	26	68	–42	9	0.39

**Flint T promoted; Prestatyn T failed to gain a Tier 1 licence.*

JD CYMRU SOUTH LEAGUE 2019–20

			Home					*Away*					*Total*							
		P	*W*	*D*	*L*	*F*	*A*	*W*	*D*	*L*	*F*	*A*	*W*	*D*	*L*	*F*	*A*	*GD*	*Pts*	*PPG*
1	Swansea University	25	8	2	2	27	18	9	3	1	29	13	17	5	3	56	31	25	56	2.24
2	Haverfordwest Co*	25	8	2	3	37	19	9	2	1	21	7	17	4	4	58	26	32	55	2.20
3	Briton Ferry Llansawel	24	8	1	4	35	23	7	1	3	30	13	15	2	7	65	36	29	47	1.96
4	STM Sports†	22	7	2	3	28	18	5	1	4	23	16	12	3	7	51	34	17	39	1.77
5	Cambrian & Clydach Vale	23	6	5	2	22	13	5	2	3	19	18	11	7	5	41	31	10	40	1.74
6	Llanelli T	26	7	4	3	22	17	5	0	7	25	34	12	4	10	47	51	–4	40	1.54
7	Ammanford	25	7	0	6	25	26	5	1	6	19	21	12	1	12	44	47	–3	37	1.48
8	Goytre U	25	7	1	5	26	21	3	5	4	14	20	10	6	9	40	41	–1	36	1.44
9	Pontypridd T	25	5	6	3	35	20	4	2	5	17	21	9	8	8	52	41	11	35	1.40
10	Afan Lido	25	6	3	4	26	18	4	1	7	21	29	10	4	11	47	47	0	34	1.36
11	Llantwit Major	24	2	2	6	12	18	5	4	5	22	21	7	6	11	34	39	–5	27	1.13
12	Undy Ath	21	5	0	4	15	14	2	2	8	14	24	7	2	12	29	38	–9	23	1.10
13	Cwmbran Celtic	22	3	1	4	13	12	3	3	8	16	32	6	4	12	29	44	–15	22	1.00
14	Taff's Well	25	5	0	7	22	26	1	3	9	18	38	6	3	16	40	64	–24	21	0.84
15	Cwmamman U	22	4	0	7	13	25	1	2	8	9	30	5	2	15	22	55	–33	17	0.77
16	Caerau (Ely)	21	0	4	6	10	21	1	1	9	12	31	1	5	15	22	52	–30	8	0.38

**Haverfordwest Co promoted; Swansea University failed to gain a Tier 1 licence.*
†STM Sports relegated for failing to gain a Tier 2 licence.

JD WELSH FA CUP 2019–20

**After extra time.*

QUALIFYING ROUND 1

Abermule v Barmouth & Dyffryn U 0-1
Trethomas Bluebirds v AFC Whitchurch 2-0
CPD Llannefydd v Gwalchmai 7-2
Borth U v Machynlleth 6-2
Wattsville v Clwb Cymric 2-3
Treforest v Vale U 1-2
Glan Conwy v Pentraeth 8-2
Churchstoke v Waterloo R 1-6
West End v Baglan Dragons 0-1
Ely Rangers v Risca U 3-4
Llandyrnog U v Lex XI 4-2
Kerry v Dolgellau Ath Amateur 1-4
Fairwater v Aberystwyth Exiles 8-2
Llanfairfechan v Kinmel Bay 5-3
Llansantffraid Village v Four Crosses 0-2
FC Cwmaman v Penrhiwceiber Rangers 3-2
Gaerwen v Llanrwst U 2-3
Penmaenmawr Phoenix v Mochdre Sports 0-2
Montgomery T v Hay St Mary's 3-1
Lucas Cwmbran v Ton & Gelli Boys Club 4-2
Mynydd Isa Spartans v Llanuwchllyn 5-1
Penparcau v Tywyn Bryncrug 2-1
Merthyr Saints v Quar Park Rangers 4-0
Nefyn U v Llandudno Amateurs 6-4
Rhayader T v Bow Street 2-1*
Newport C v Chepstow T 2-3
Panteg v Cardiff Draconians 0-7
Penycae v Caerwys 6-0
Amlwch T v Holyhead T 3-5
Newport Civil Service v Caerphilly Ath 5-2
Pencoed Ath Boys & Girls Club v Trebanog 4-2*
Rhosllanerchrugog v Plas Madoc 2-12
Bangor 1876 v Llandudno Ath 4-1
Newport Corinthians v Canton Liberal 6-4
Penlan Social v Aberdare T 3-0
Rhydymwyn v Hawarden Rangers* 3-2
Brickfield Rangers v New Brighton Villa 2-7
Penydarren Boys & Girls v Treharris Western Ath 4-1
Abertillery Bluebirds v Dinas Powys 4-0
Bro Goronwy v Blaenau Ffestiniog Amateurs 4-5
Pontyclun v Trefelin BGC 0-1
AFC Porth v CRC Olympic 0-2
Castell Alun Colts v Llangollen T 4-0
Sully Sports v Caerleon 2-3
Blaenrhondda v Ynyshir Albs 0-2
Cefn Mawr Rangers v CPD Sychdyn 5-4
Cwmbran T v Tredegar T 1-2
Pill YMCA v Cardiff Corinthians 1-3
Coedpoeth U v Rhostyllen 3-2*
Treowen Stars v AFC Llwydcoed 3-5
Cefn Cribwr v Ynysgerwn 3-1
Aberffraw v Llandudno Junction 3-1
Cwmbach Royal Stars v Newcastle Emlyn 2-1

QUALIFYING ROUND 2

Borth U v Aberaeron 2-4*
Newport Civil Service v Monmouth T 2-6
Cefn Mawr Rangers v FC Queens Park 1-4
Aberbargoed Buds v Caldicot T 1-0
Abertillery Bluebirds v Lucas Cwmbran 3-1
Aberffraw v Glan Conwy 2-1
Trethomas Bluebirds v Croesyceiliog 2-4
AFC Llwydcoed v Cefn Cribwr 1-2
CPD Llannefydd v Llanrwst U 2-0
Vale U v Ton Pentre 1-5
Denbigh T v Mynydd Isa Spartans 2-3
Ynyshir Albs v Merthyr Saints 3-1
Builth Wells v Bridgend Street 1-0
Greenfield v Plas Madoc 4-3
Barmouth & Dyffryn U v Llanidloes T 0-1*
Cardiff Draconians v
  Pencoed Ath Boys & Girls Club 3-0
Holyhead Hotspurs v Holyhead T 3-1
Chepstow T v Clwb Cymric 4-1
Holywell T v New Brighton Villa 8-2
Caersws v Dolgellau Ath Amateur 5-3
CRC Olympic v Cardiff Corinthians 2-3
Llay Welfare v Penycae 2-3*
Four Crosses v Rhayader T 3-1
Fairwater v Garden Village 0-4
Llandrindod Wells v Carno 5-2
FC Cwmaman v Baglan Dragons 5-1
Mochdre Sports v Blaenau Ffestiniog Amateurs 2-4
Montgomery T v Berriew 2-1
Goytre v Caerleon 1-1*
  Caerleon won 6-5 on penalties
Mold Alexandra v Castell Alun Colts 8-0
Radnor Valley v Penparcau 2-4
Waterloo R v Welshpool T 5-4
Mynydd Llandegai v Nefyn U 4-7
Bangor 1876 v Penrhyndeudraeth 6-2
Newport Corinthians v Abergavenny T 0-2
Dyffryn Nantlle Vale v Bodedern 2-1
Brymbo v Rhos Aelwyd 4-2
Penlan Social v Cwmbach Royal Stars 2-1
Prestatyn Sports v Llandudno Alb 4-2
Cefn Alb v Chirk AAA 4-5
Penydarren Boys & Girls v Pontardawe T 2-3
Saltney T v Rhydymwyn 1-3
St Asaph C v Llanberis 1-3
Coedpoeth U v Llandyrnog U 4-2
Trefelin BGC v Port Talbot T 3-0
Llanrug U v Llanfairfechan 5-0
Risca U v Tredegar T 1-2

ROUND 1

Aberffraw v Llanrug U 0-1
Llanfair U v Mynydd Isa Spartans 5-3
Porthmadog v Llanberis 7-0
Llanelli T v Cwmamman U 2-1
Chepstow T v Taffs Well 3-2
Waterloo R v Mold Alexandra 1-8
Penrhyncoch v Cardiff Corinthians 2-1*
Bangor 1876 v Penycae 3-3*
  Bangor 1876 won 3-2 on penalties
Swansea Univ v Caerleon 4-1
Chirk AAA v CPD Llannefydd 0-3
Abertillery Bluebirds v Penparcau 3-1
Briton Ferry Llansawel v Undy Ath 2-2*
  Undy Ath won 4-3 on penalties
Blaenau Ffestiniog Amateurs v Buckley T 0-2
Llantwit Major v Llandrindod Wells 0-1
Nefyn U v Bangor C 0-2
Greenfield v Caersws 3-1
Croesyceiliog v Abergavenny T 2-1
Flint Town U v Four Crosses 9-0
Trefelin BGC v Llanidloes T 2-2*
  Llanidloes T won 4-3 on penalties
Corwen v Colwyn Bay 2-3
Garden Village v Goytre Utd 1-3
Dyffryn Nantlle Vale v Rhydymwyn 2-0
Guilsfield v Brymbo 2-1
Cefn Cribwr v Tredegar T 2-1*
Rhyl v Llangefni T 2-0
Coedpoeth U v Gresford Ath 0-5
Pontypridd T v Caerau (Ely) 3-1
Holyhead Hotspurs v Montgomery T 4-2
Holywell T v Llandudno 2-3
Conwy Bor v Ruthin T 1-2
Cwmbran Celtic v Pontardawe T 2-3*
Llanrhaeadr Ym Mochnant v Prestatyn T 1-4
FC Cwmaman v STM Sports 2-6
Prestatyn Sports v FC Queens Park 2-3
Ammanford v Cardiff Draconians 4-1
Afan Lido v Monmouth T 3-1
Builth Wells v Ton Pentre 2-3
Aberbargoed Buds v Aberaeron 3-1
Haverfordwest Co v Penlan Social 5-3
Cambrian & Clydach Vale v Ynyshir Albs 7-3

ROUND 2

Pontardawe T v Croesyceiliog 6-1
Chepstow T v STM Sports 0-5
Undy Ath v Swansea Univ 5-6
Bangor C v Prestatyn T 0-3
Bangor 1876 v Ruthin T 0-2
Llandudno v Llanfair U 4-1
Holyhead Hotspurs v Buckley T 0-3
Rhyl v FC Queens Park 3-0
Afan Lido v Aberbargoed Buds 2-1
Ammanford v Ton Pentre 3-1
Goytre Utd v Cefn Cribwr 6-4
Haverfordwest Co v Cambrian & Clydach Vale 1-2
Llanelli T v Penrhyncoch 0-1
Pontypridd T v Llandrindod Wells 1-0

Porthmadog v Gresford Ath	4-1
Dyffryn Nantlle Vale v Colwyn Bay	0-1
Mold Alexandra v Llanrug U	8-1
CPD Llannefydd v Guilsfield	1-5
Greenfield v Flint Town U	1-3
Abertillery Bluebirds v Llanidloes T	4-3

ROUND 3

Penybont v Porthmadog	6-1
Afan Lido v Llandudno	5-1
Abertillery Bluebirds v Connah's Quay Nomads	0-3
Swansea Univ v Cambrian & Clydach Vale	3-0
The New Saints v Mold Alexandra	9-0
Barry Town U v Newtown	0-1
Cardiff Metropolitan Univ v Pontypridd T	1-0
Aberystwyth T v Ruthin T	2-1
Cefn Druids v Guilsfield	2-0
Penrhyncoch v Prestatyn T	1-2
Goytre Utd v Caernarfon T	0-4
Flint Town U v Bala T	2-0
Pontardawe T v Buckley T	3-1
Rhyl v STM Sports	2-0
Carmarthen T v Ammanford	0-4
Colwyn Bay v Airbus UK Broughton	1-0

ROUND 4

The New Saints v Aberystwyth T	4-0
Newtown v Rhyl	4-1
Swansea Univ v Prestatyn T	0-1
Connah's Quay Nomads v Afan Lido	8-0
Cefn Druids v Pontardawe T	2-0
Ammanford v Caernarfon T	0-4
Flint Town U v Colwyn Bay	3-2
Penybont v Cardiff Metropolitan Univ	1-2

QUARTER-FINALS

Flint Town U v Prestatyn T	0-1
Connah's Quay Nomads v Cardiff Metropolitan Univ	1-2
The New Saints v Newtown	6-1
Caernarfon T v Cefn Druids	4-0

SEMI-FINALS

Caernarfon T v Cardiff Metropolitan Univ
Prestatyn T v The New Saints

Due to COVID-19 pandemic the Welsh FA confirmed the cancellation of all FAW Cup competitions on 30 July 2020. No title holders will be declared for 2019–20.

PREVIOUS WELSH CUP WINNERS

1878 Wrexham
1879 Newtown White Stars
1880 Druids
1881 Druids
1882 Druids
1883 Wrexham
1884 Oswestry White Stars
1885 Druids
1886 Druids
1887 Chirk
1888 Chirk
1889 Bangor
1890 Chirk
1891 Shrewsbury T
1892 Chirk
1893 Wrexham
1894 Chirk
1895 Newtown
1896 Bangor
1897 Wrexham
1898 Druids
1899 Druids
1900 Aberystwyth T
1901 Oswestry U
1902 Wellington T
1903 Wrexham
1904 Druids
1905 Wrexham
1906 Wellington T
1907 Oswestry U
1908 Chester
1909 Wrexham
1910 Wrexham
1911 Wrexham
1912 Cardiff C
1913 Swansea T
1914 Wrexham
1915 Wrexham
1920 Cardiff C
1921 Wrexham
1922 Cardiff C
1923 Cardiff C
1924 Wrexham
1925 Wrexham
1926 Ebbw Vale
1927 Cardiff C
1928 Cardiff C
1929 Connah's Quay
1930 Cardiff C
1931 Wrexham
1932 Swansea T
1933 Chester
1934 Bristol C
1935 Tranmere R
1936 Crewe Alex
1937 Crewe Alex
1938 Shrewsbury T
1939 South Liverpool
1940 Wellington T
1947 Chester
1948 Lovell's Ath
1949 Merthyr Tydfil
1950 Swansea T
1951 Merthyr Tydfil
1952 Rhyl
1953 Rhyl
1954 Flint Town U
1955 Barry T
1956 Cardiff C
1957 Wrexham
1958 Wrexham
1959 Cardiff C
1960 Wrexham
1961 Swansea T
1962 Bangor C
1963 Borough U
1964 Cardiff C
1965 Cardiff C
1966 Swansea T
1967 Cardiff C
1968 Cardiff C
1969 Cardiff C
1970 Cardiff C
1971 Cardiff C
1972 Wrexham
1973 Cardiff C
1974 Cardiff C
1975 Wrexham
1976 Cardiff C
1977 Shrewsbury T
1978 Wrexham
1979 Shrewsbury T
1980 Newport Co
1981 Swansea C
1982 Swansea C
1983 Swansea C
1984 Shrewsbury T
1985 Shrewsbury T
1986 Wrexham
1987 Merthyr Tydfil
1988 Cardiff C
1989 Swansea C
1990 Hereford U
1991 Swansea C
1992 Cardiff C
1993 Cardiff C
1994 Barry T
1995 Wrexham
1996 TNS
1997 Barry T
1998 Bangor C
1999 Inter Cable-Tel
2000 Bangor C
2001 Barry T
2002 Barry T
2003 Barry T
2004 Rhyl
2005 TNS
2006 Rhyl
2007 Carmarthen T
2008 Bangor C
2009 Bangor C
2010 Bangor C
2011 Llanelli
2012 The New Saints
2013 Prestatyn T
2014 The New Saints
2015 The New Saints
2016 The New Saints
2017 Bala T
2018 Connah's Quay Nomads
2019 The New Saints
2020 Not completed

NATHANIEL MG WELSH LEAGUE CUP 2019–20

**After extra time.*

ROUND 1 – NORTH

Buckley T v Rhyl	0-2
Ruthin T v Guilsfield	0-3
Prestatyn T v Llanrhaeadr Ym Mochnant	4-2
Gresford Ath v Colwyn Bay	1-0
Conwy Bor v Bangor C	0-1
Llanfair U v Llangefni T	3-1
Berriew v Corwen	0-2

ROUND 1 – SOUTH

Afan Lido v Cwmbran Celtic	0-1
Pontypridd T v STM Sports	2-3
Undy Ath v Cwmamman U	2-2*
Cwmamman U won 5-4 on penalties	
Swansea Univ v Llantwit Major	0-1
Goytre U v Caerau (Ely)	3-0
Ammanford v Penrhyncoch	2-1
Briton Ferry Llansawel v Taffs Well	3-1

ROUND 2 – NORTH

Corwen v Caernarfon T	0-2
Bala T v Gresford Ath	7-0
Rhyl v Connah's Quay Nomads	0-2
Airbus UK Broughton v Llanfair U	4-0
Cefn Druids v Prestatyn T	1-2
Bangor C v The New Saints	1-1*
Bangor C won 4-2 on penalties	
Flint Town U v Portmadog	5-1
Guilsfield v Llandudno	1-0

ROUND 2 – SOUTH

Cambrian & Clydach Vale B&GC v Aberystwyth T	3-4
Haverfordwest Co v Barry Town U	1-1*
Haverfordwest Co won 5-4 on penalties	
Newtown v Ammanford	2-0
Carmarthen T v Cwmamman U	4-1
Llanwit Major v Cardiff Metropolitan Univ	1-2
Pen-y-Bont v Goytre U	4-1
Briton Ferry Llansawel v Llanelli T	1-1*
Briton Ferry Llansawel won 4-1 on penalties	
STM Sports v Cwmbran Celtic	4-0

ROUND 3

Briton Ferry Llansawel v Carmarthen T	0-2
STM Sports v Haverfordwest Co	
STM Sports won 7-6 on penalties	1-1*
Guilsfield v Connah's Quay Nomads	1-1*
Connah's Quay Nomads won 5-3 on penalties	
Cardiff Metropolitan Univ v Aberystwyth T	0-1
Caernarfon T v Prestatyn T	1-4
Flint Town U v Airbus UK Broughton	2-1
Newtown v Pen-y-Bont	2-1
Bala T v Bangor C	1-1*
Bangor C won 7-6 on penalties	

QUARTER-FINALS

Newtown v STM Sports	2-2*
STM Sports won 4-3 on penalties	
Carmarthen T v Aberystwyth T	0-3
Connah's Quay Nomads v Flint Town U	4-1
Prestatyn T v Bala T	1-2

SEMI-FINALS

Connah's Quay Nomads v Bala T	2-0
STM Sports v Aberystwyth T	2-1

NATHANIEL MG WELSH LEAGUE CUP FINAL 2019–20

Latham Park, Newtown, Saturday 1 February 2020

Connah's Quay Nomads (2) 3 *(Wilde 30, 41, Insall 47)*

STM Sports (0) 0 667

Connah's Quay Nomads: Brass; Horan, Holmes, Owens, Farquharson (Disney 82), Harrison, Owen J (Curran 58), Morris, Wilde, Bakare, Insall (Dool 69).

STM Sports: Bateman (Frick 69); Boyer, Yohanes, Mackenzie, Biggs, Hajgato, Rutherford, Jones (Cawley 83), Evans (Worsley 66), Graham, Ahmun.

Referee: B. Markham-Jones.

THE FAW TROPHY 2019–20

**After extra time.*

ROUND 3

Llanuwchllyn v Llanrug U	1-5
CPD Llannefydd v Nefyn U	2-3*
Cefn Cribwr v Cardiff Draconians	1-2
Llandudno Alb v Mynydd Isa Spartans	3-2
Ynystawe Ath v Newport Saints	3-1
Baglan Dragons v Pill YMCA	4-1
Penrhiwceiber Rangers v Cardiff Corinthians	2-1
Holyhead Hotspurs v Penrhyndeudraeth	8-1
Berriew v Penparcau	3-2
Carno v Bow Street	3-2*
Mold Alexandra v New Brighton Villa	4-1
Llanrwst U v Bangor 1876	4-1
Lex XI v Menai Bridge Tigers	3-1
Llay Welfare v Llandudno Ath	9-1
Clydach Wasps v FC Cwmaman	4-3
Gaerwen v Brickfield Rangers	4-2*
Rhostyllen v Rhos Aelwyd	2-4
Brymbo v Holywell T	4-2
Canton Liberal v Maltsters Sports	10-0
Trebanog v Risca U	3-4
Bodedern v Llanberis	4-2
Greenfield v Cefn Mawr Rangers	0-2
Caersws v Radnor Valley	4-5*
Aberdare T v Penydarren Boys & Girls	0-4
Welshpool T v Four Crosses	6-1
Ely Rangers v Pontardawe T	2-3
Port Talbot T v Abertillery Bluebirds	1-0
Denbigh T v FC Queens Park	2-1
Cwmbran T v West End Rangers	2-0
Blaenrhondda v Pencoed Ath Boys & Girls Club	2-0
Dyffryn Nantlle Vale v Coedpoeth U	1-0
Llandudno Junction v Barmouth & Dyffryn U	0-4

ROUND 4

Canton Liberal v Pontardawe T	5-2
Clydach Wasps v Risca U	1-3
Cwmbran T v Baglan Dragons	1-5
Port Talbot v Blaenrhondda	4-1
Llanrug U v Brymbo	0-1
Ynystawe Ath v Penydarren Boys & Girls	1-2
Rhos Aelwyd v Gaerwen	4-2*
Radnor Valley v Mold Alexandra	4-3
Llay Welfare v Llanrwst U	1-3
Lex XI v Berriew	0-7
Cefn Mawr Rangers v Welshpool T	1-4
Dyffryn Nantlle Vale v Barmouth & Dyffryn U	5-0
Bodedern v Holyhead Hotspurs	0-2
Penrhiwceiber Rangers v Cardiff Draconians	6-3
Carno v Llandudno Alb	2-5
Nefyn U v Denbigh T	1-5

ROUND 5

Llanrwst U v Holyhead Hotspurs	4-5
Berriew v Llandudno Alb	1-1
Llandudno Alb won 4-2 on penalties	
Canton Liberal v Penydarren Boys & Girls	3-4
Denbigh T v Rhos Aelwyd	2-1
Dyffryn Nantlle Vale v Brymbo	1-3
Radnor Valley v Welshpool T	2-4
Baglan Dragons v Penrhiwceiber Rangers	3-1
Port Talbot v Risca U	1-1*
Risca U won 4-1 on penalties	

QUARTER-FINALS

Llandudno Alb v Risca U	2-0
Welshpool T v Holyhead Hotspurs	0-3
Baglan Dragons v Denbigh T	4-0
Brymbo v Penydarren Boys & Girls	1-2

SEMI-FINALS

Llandudno Alb v Holyhead Hotspurs	1-1*
Llandudno Alb won 4-3 on penalties	
Baglan Dragons v Penydarren Boys & Girls	1-3

FINAL

Penydarren Boys & Girls v Llandudno Alb

Due to COVID-19 pandemic the Welsh FA confirmed the cancellation of all FAW Cup competitions on 30 July 2020. No title holders will be declared for 2019–20.

NORTHERN IRISH FOOTBALL 2019–20

Due to COVID-19 pandemic the Northern Irish Football League abandoned the season on 23 June 2020. On 26 June 2020 League positions awarded on a points-per-game basis for all leagues.

NIFL DANSKE BANK PREMIERSHIP 2019–20

			Home					*Away*					*Total*							
		P	*W*	*D*	*L*	*F*	*A*	*W*	*D*	*L*	*F*	*A*	*W*	*D*	*L*	*F*	*A*	*GD*	*Pts*	*PPG*
1	Linfield	31	12	2	1	44	9	10	1	5	27	15	22	3	6	71	24	47	69	2.23
2	Coleraine	31	9	5	1	29	10	10	3	3	35	14	19	8	4	64	24	40	65	2.10
3	Crusaders	31	10	3	3	35	13	7	5	3	31	17	17	8	6	66	30	36	59	1.90
4	Cliftonville	31	9	2	4	23	11	9	3	4	25	11	18	5	8	48	22	26	59	1.90
5	Glentoran	31	10	3	3	34	13	7	4	4	26	20	17	7	7	60	33	27	58	1.87
6	Larne	31	7	6	3	32	15	9	2	4	27	14	16	8	7	59	29	30	56	1.81
7	Glenavon	31	7	5	3	27	20	3	0	13	19	51	10	5	16	46	71	–25	35	1.13
8	Carrick Rangers	31	5	0	11	17	25	5	2	8	17	22	10	2	19	34	47	–13	32	1.03
9	Dungannon Swifts	31	6	3	7	23	33	2	3	10	13	43	8	6	17	36	76	–40	30	0.97
10	Ballymena U	31	4	3	9	20	30	3	3	9	14	24	7	6	18	34	54	–20	27	0.87
11	Warrenpoint T	31	3	1	11	15	40	2	2	12	11	45	5	3	23	26	85	–59	18	0.58
12	Institute	31	1	2	12	8	41	1	7	8	15	31	2	9	20	23	72	–49	15	0.48

LEADING GOALSCORERS (League goals only)

Joe Gormley	Cliftonville	18
Robbie McDaid	Glentoran	15
Andrew Waterworth	Linfield	13
David McDaid	Larne	12
Jamie McGonigle	Crusaders	12
Hrvoje Plum	Glentoran	12
Conor McMenamin	Cliftonville	11
Joel Cooper	Linfield	11
Jonathan McMurray	Larne	11
Jordan Owens	Crusaders	11
Paul Heatley	Crusaders	10
Shayne Lavery	Linfield	10
Paul O'Neill	Glentoran	10
Alan O'Sullivan	Warrenpoint T	10
James McLaughlin	Coleraine	10
Martin Donnelly	Larne	9
Ben Doherty	Coleraine	9
Joe McCready	Ballymena U	9
Includes 8 league goals for Institute.		
Kirk Millar	Linfield	8
Cathair Friel	Ballymena U	8
Philip Lowry	Crusaders	8

IRISH LEAGUE CHAMPIONSHIP WINNERS

1891 Linfield
1892 Linfield
1893 Linfield
1894 Glentoran
1895 Linfield
1896 Distillery
1897 Glentoran
1898 Linfield
1899 Distillery
1900 Belfast Celtic
1901 Distillery
1902 Linfield
1903 Distillery
1904 Linfield
1905 Glentoran
1906 Cliftonville/ Distillery (shared)
1907 Linfield
1908 Linfield
1909 Linfield
1910 Cliftonville
1911 Linfield
1912 Glentoran
1913 Glentoran
1914 Linfield
1915 Belfast Celtic
1920 Belfast Celtic
1921 Glentoran
1922 Linfield
1923 Linfield
1924 Queen's Island
1925 Glentoran
1926 Belfast Celtic
1927 Belfast Celtic
1928 Belfast Celtic
1929 Belfast Celtic
1930 Linfield
1931 Glentoran
1932 Linfield
1933 Belfast Celtic
1934 Linfield
1935 Linfield
1936 Belfast Celtic
1937 Belfast Celtic
1938 Belfast Celtic
1939 Belfast Celtic
1940 Belfast Celtic
1948 Belfast Celtic
1949 Linfield
1950 Linfield
1951 Glentoran
1952 Glenavon
1953 Glentoran
1954 Linfield
1955 Linfield
1956 Linfield
1957 Glentoran
1958 Ards
1959 Linfield
1960 Glenavon
1961 Linfield
1962 Linfield
1963 Distillery
1964 Glentoran
1965 Derry City
1966 Linfield
1967 Glentoran
1968 Glentoran
1969 Linfield
1970 Glentoran
1971 Linfield
1972 Glentoran
1973 Crusaders
1974 Coleraine
1975 Linfield
1976 Crusaders
1977 Glentoran
1978 Linfield
1979 Linfield
1980 Linfield
1981 Glentoran
1982 Linfield
1983 Linfield
1984 Linfield
1985 Linfield
1986 Linfield
1987 Linfield
1988 Glentoran
1989 Linfield
1990 Portadown
1991 Portadown
1992 Glentoran
1993 Linfield
1994 Linfield
1995 Crusaders
1996 Portadown
1997 Crusaders
1998 Cliftonville
1999 Glentoran
2000 Linfield
2001 Linfield
2002 Portadown
2003 Glentoran
2004 Linfield
2005 Glentoran
2006 Linfield
2007 Linfield
2008 Linfield
2009 Glentoran
2010 Linfield
2011 Linfield
2012 Linfield
2013 Cliftonville
2014 Cliftonville
2015 Crusaders
2016 Crusaders
2017 Linfield
2018 Crusaders
2019 Linfield
2020 Linfield

NIFL BLUEFIN SPORT CHAMPIONSHIP 2019–20

			Home					Away					Total							
		P	*W*	*D*	*L*	*F*	*A*	*W*	*D*	*L*	*F*	*A*	*W*	*D*	*L*	*F*	*A*	*GD*	*Pts*	*PPG*
1	Portadown	31	11	2	2	40	10	9	4	3	32	20	20	6	5	72	30	42	66	2.13
2	Ballinamallard U	30	10	2	4	42	19	9	1	4	29	15	19	3	8	71	34	37	60	2.00
3	Loughgall	31	7	2	6	24	19	11	2	3	40	27	18	4	9	64	45	19	58	1.87
4	Ards	31	8	3	5	32	24	8	3	4	36	20	16	6	9	68	44	24	54	1.74
5	Newry C	30	7	2	7	32	23	8	4	2	23	9	15	6	9	55	32	23	51	1.70
6	Dundela	31	7	5	4	27	25	6	2	7	16	24	13	7	11	43	49	−6	46	1.48
7	Ballyclare Comrades	30	6	4	6	30	17	5	3	6	23	32	11	7	12	53	49	4	40	1.33
8	H&W Welders	31	5	3	7	25	25	5	2	9	27	38	10	5	16	52	63	−11	35	1.13
9	Queen's University	31	8	1	7	38	32	3	0	12	21	37	11	1	19	59	69	−10	34	1.10
10	Dergview	30	7	1	6	23	21	1	4	11	15	33	8	5	17	38	54	−16	29	0.97
11	Knockbreda	30	2	3	9	17	42	5	1	10	19	42	7	4	19	36	84	−48	25	0.83
12	PSNI	30	3	0	11	18	46	4	2	10	22	52	7	2	21	40	98	−58	23	0.77

Loughgall fielded an uneligible player v Ards on 21/9/19 (fixture was 0-0 awarded as 0-3 win to Ards) and v Knockbreda on 28/9 (fixture was won 2-1 by Loughgall awarded as 3-0 win to Knockbreda).

NIFL CHAMPIONSHIP WINNERS

1996 Coleraine
1997 Ballymena United
1998 Newry Town
1999 Distillery
2000 Omagh Town
2001 Ards
2002 Lisburn Distillery
2003 Dungannon Swifts
2004 Loughgall
2005 Armagh City
2006 Crusaders
2007 Institute
2008 Loughgall
2009 Portadown
2010 Loughgall
2011 Carrick Rangers
2012 Ballinamallard U
2013 Ards
2014 Institute
2015 Carrick Rangers
2016 Ards
2017 Warrenpoint T
2018 Institute
2019 Larne
2020 Portadown

NIFL BLUEFIN SPORT PREMIER INTERMEDIATE LEAGUE 2019–20

			Home					Away					Total							
		P	*W*	*D*	*L*	*F*	*A*	*W*	*D*	*L*	*F*	*A*	*W*	*D*	*L*	*F*	*A*	*GD*	*Pts*	*PPG*
1	Annagh U	14	5	2	0	16	7	5	1	1	16	7	10	3	1	32	14	18	33	2.36
2	Portstewart	14	6	1	0	17	5	2	5	0	11	8	8	6	0	28	13	15	30	2.14
3	Dollingstown	13	5	0	2	16	7	3	1	2	15	8	8	1	4	31	15	16	25	1.92
4	Bangor	12	4	2	1	21	13	2	0	3	9	8	6	2	4	30	21	9	20	1.67
5	Newington Youth	11	0	1	2	1	5	5	2	1	15	13	5	3	3	16	18	−2	18	1.64
6	Banbridge T	12	1	2	2	5	4	2	2	3	11	16	3	4	5	16	20	−4	13	1.08
7	Armagh C	14	2	3	2	10	12	1	2	4	5	14	3	5	6	15	26	−11	14	1.00
8	Lisburn Distillery	13	1	2	3	6	13	2	2	3	7	12	3	4	6	13	25	−12	13	1.00
9	Moyola Park	12	2	1	4	14	14	1	0	4	7	14	3	1	8	21	28	−7	10	0.83
10	Limavady U	13	2	3	3	14	16	0	0	5	7	16	2	3	8	21	32	−11	9	0.69
11	Tobermore U	12	2	0	4	10	11	0	2	4	4	14	2	2	8	14	25	−11	8	0.67

IFA DEVELOPMENT LEAGUES 2019–20

PREMIERSHIP DEVELOPMENT LEAGUE (U20)

	P	*W*	*D*	*L*	*F*	*A*	*GD*	*Pts*	*PPG*
Cliftonville Olympic	25	23	1	1	93	27	66	70	2.80
Linfield Swifts	28	21	0	7	93	33	60	63	2.25
Crusaders	30	21	3	6	78	36	42	66	2.20
Dungannon Swifts	26	15	3	8	61	52	9	48	1.85
Glentoran	26	13	2	11	63	49	14	41	1.58
Carrick Rangers	25	10	5	10	50	50	0	35	1.40
Coleraine	26	11	2	13	61	62	−1	35	1.35
Glenavon	29	13	0	16	68	69	−1	39	1.34
Larne Olympic	28	8	3	17	36	84	−48	27	0.96
Institute	30	7	3	20	33	76	−43	24	0.80
Ballymena U	28	6	4	18	44	76	−32	22	0.79
Warrenpoint T	27	2	2	23	15	81	−66	8	0.30

CHAMPIONSHIP DEVELOPMENT LEAGUE (U20)

	P	*W*	*D*	*L*	*F*	*A*	*GD*	*Pts*	*PPG*
Ballinamallard U	18	13	2	3	79	35	44	41	2.28
Loughgall	16	11	1	4	54	24	30	34	2.13
Dundela	18	12	1	5	71	29	42	37	2.06
Ards	20	12	3	5	57	32	25	39	1.95
Portadown	21	11	5	5	68	36	32	38	1.81
Knockbreda	21	10	4	7	46	51	−5	34	1.62
Limavady Youth	19	8	4	7	43	54	−11	28	1.47
Newry C	17	7	2	8	46	43	3	23	1.35
Bangor	22	8	5	9	61	52	9	29	1.32
PSNI Olympic	15	5	3	7	32	39	−7	18	1.20
Ballyclare Comrades	21	7	2	12	42	68	−26	23	1.10
Portstewart	20	6	3	11	46	66	−20	21	1.05
Moyola Park Olympic	21	5	2	14	29	62	−33	17	0.81
Lisburn Distillery	21	3	7	11	27	61	−34	16	0.76
Newington	18	3	2	13	27	76	−49	11	0.61
H&W Welders	0	0	0	0	0	0	0	0	0.00

ACADEMY LEAGUE (U18)

	P	*W*	*D*	*L*	*F*	*A*	*GD*	*Pts*	*PPG*
Dungannon Swifts	20	14	4	2	54	18	36	46	2.30
Cliftonville Strollers	19	12	4	3	42	22	20	40	2.11
Crusaders	21	12	7	2	58	25	33	43	2.05
Ards	20	11	3	6	49	35	14	36	1.80
Linfield Rangers	18	9	2	7	33	34	−1	29	1.61
Newry C	20	10	2	8	36	37	−1	32	1.60
Institute	19	7	6	6	30	26	4	27	1.42
Carrick Rangers	20	8	3	9	31	42	−11	27	1.35
Glentoran Colts	16	6	3	7	33	32	1	21	1.31
Coleraine	21	5	8	8	34	45	−11	23	1.10
Ballymena U	19	4	8	7	43	43	0	20	1.05
Glenavon	20	5	1	14	21	49	−28	16	0.80
Warrenpoint T	20	2	5	13	21	42	−21	11	0.55
Ballinamallard U	21	3	2	16	30	65	−35	11	0.52

ACADEMY LEAGUE (U16)

	P	*W*	*D*	*L*	*F*	*A*	*GD*	*Pts*	*PPG*
Coleraine	19	16	2	1	62	13	49	50	2.63
Glenavon	18	12	2	4	49	19	30	38	2.11
Crusaders	20	12	4	4	57	25	32	40	2.00
Dungannon Swifts	18	9	3	6	48	26	22	30	1.67
Glentoran Youth	16	8	2	6	37	31	6	26	1.63
Newry C	16	8	1	7	33	26	7	25	1.56
Cliftonville	18	8	3	7	39	36	3	27	1.50
Linfield	19	7	5	7	42	30	12	26	1.37
Ballinamallard U	17	7	2	8	32	32	0	23	1.35
Warrenpoint T	14	4	2	8	21	41	−20	14	1.00
Ballymena U	18	3	2	13	13	54	−41	11	0.61
Institute	16	3	0	13	9	50	−41	9	0.56
Carrick Rangers	19	2	2	15	13	72	−59	8	0.42
Ards	0	0	0	0	0	0	0	0	0.00

SADLER'S PEAKY BLINDER IRISH FA CUP 2019–20

**After extra time.*

FIRST ROUND

Albert Foundry v Bloomfield	3-1
Annagh U v Derriaghy CC	4-1
Ballynahinch Olympic v Bangor	2-3
Banbridge T v Dungiven	2-1
Barn U v Oxford Sunnyside	0-3
Belfast Celtic v Dromore Amateurs	9-1
Bryansburn Rangers v Crumlin U	1-3
Chimney Corner v Laurelvale	5-1
Comber Rec v Bangor Amateurs	2-0
Cookstown RBL v Glebe Rangers	2-3
Craigavon C v Seapatrick	5-0
Crumlin Star v Kilmore Rec	8-0
Downshire YM v Rectory Rangers	2-0
Dromara Village v Coagh U	3-6
Fivemiletown U v Ardstraw	2-3
Grove U v Newcastle	2-4
Holywood v Newbuildings U	1-4
Iveagh U v Lurgan T	1-3
Limavady U v Ballynure OB	3-0
Maiden C v Bourneview Mill	3-2
Malachians v Moneyslane	1-2
Moyola Park v Colin Valley	11-0
Rosario YC v Killyleagh YC	0-1
Rosemount Rec v Dunmurry Rec	2-3
Saintfield U v Banbridge Rangers	0-2
Sirocco Works v Seagoe	2-2*
Seagoe won 4-3 on penalties	
St James' Swifts v Abbey Villa	4-1
St Oliver Plunkett v Ballymacash Rangers	2-2*
Ballymacash Rangers won 3-2 on penalties	
Suffolk v St Luke's	3-0
Trojans v Desertmartin	3-1
Tullyvallen v Dunloy	2-2*
Dunloy won 4-3 on penalties	
Wakehurst v Ards Rangers	3-1
Woodvale v Windmill Stars	5-1
East Belfast v St Mary's	3-1
Mossley v Markethill Swifts	4-1
Cookstown Youth v Newington	0-5
Armagh C v 1st Bangor	7-0
Crewe U (walkover) v Donegal Celtic	
Hanover (walkover) v Lurgan Celtic	
Newtowne (walkover) v Drumaness Mills	
Richhill (walkover) v Ballywalter Rec	
Strabane Ath (walkover) v Ballynahinch U	

First round byes
18th Newtownabbey OB, Aquinas, Ballymoney U, Brantwood, Dollingstown, Dunmurry YM, Greenisland, Immaculata, Islandmagee, Larne Tech OB, Lisburn Distillery, Lisburn Rangers, Lower Maze, Oxford United Stars, Portstewart, Rathfriland Rangers, Shankill U, Shorts, Tandragee R, Tobermore U, Tullycarnet, Valley Rangers

SECOND ROUND

Glebe Rangers v Chimney Corner	1-1
Chimney Corner won 4-3 on penalties	
Aquinas v Craigavon C	2-1
Ardstraw v Wakehurst	4-1
Armagh C v Dunloy	2-1*
Ballymacash Rangers v Dunmurry YM	2-1
Ballymoney U v East Belfast	2-3
Banbridge Rangers v Bangor	0-3
Brantwood v Moyola Park	4-3*
Comber Rec v Coagh U	2-4
Crewe U v Crumlin U	3-4
Dollingstown v Lower Maze	5-0
Dunmurry Rec v Newbuildings U	3-2
Greenisland v Albert Foundry	2-0
Islandmagee v Shorts	5-2
Killyleagh YC v Downshire YM	1-0
Limavady U v Immaculata	2-0
Lisburn Distillery v Strabane Ath	3-2
Lurgan T v St James' Swifts	0-4
Maiden C v Tullycarnet	1-3
Moneyslane v Mossley	9-0
Newcastle v Banbridge T	0-5
Newtowne v Newington	0-2
Portstewart v Belfast Celtic	0-1
Rathfriland Rangers v Seagoe	4-2
Richhill v Valley Rangers	0-3
Shankill U v Lisburn Rangers	1-4
Suffolk v Larne Tech OB	1-4
Tandragee R v 18th Newtownabbey OB	5-7*
Tobermore U v Oxford Sunnyside	7-1
Woodvale v Annagh U	1-7
Crumlin Star (walkover) v Trojans	
Hanover (walkover) v Oxford United Stars	

THIRD ROUND

18th Newtownabbey OB v Coagh U	2-3
Ardstraw v Islandmagee	1-2
Banbridge T v Dunmurry Rec	2-1
Belfast Celtic v Annagh U	3-1
Brantwood v Crumlin U	4-3*
Brantwood won 4-3 on penalties	
Chimney Corner v Valley Rangers	0-3
Crumlin Star v Greenisland	1-0
Dollingstown v Lisburn Distillery	2-1
Hanover v Killyleagh YC	3-2
Limavady U v Aquinas	3-0
Moneyslane v Bangor	1-5
Newington v East Belfast	0-3
Rathfriland Rangers v Lisburn Rangers	3-0
St James' Swifts v Ballymacash Rangers	0-4
Tobermore U v Larne Tech OB	1-3
Tullycarnet v Armagh C	4-3

FOURTH ROUND

Banbridge T v Ballymacash Rangers	3-2
Belfast Celtic v Larne Tech OB	2-1
Brantwood v Rathfriland Rangers	2-5
Coagh U v Crumlin Star	0-1
Dollingstown v Tullycarnet	6-0
East Belfast v Islandmagee	7-1
Limavady U v Bangor	1-3
Valley Rangers v Hanover	1-5

FIFTH ROUND

Banbridge T v East Belfast	2-2*
Bambridge T won 5-4 on penalties	
Knockbreda v Dergview	3-2*
Queen's University v Linfield	2-1
Ards v Carrick Rangers	1-3
Ballinamallard U v Dollingstown	1-0
Ballyclare Comrades v H&W Welders	2-1
Ballymena U v Crumlin Star	2-0
Cliftonville v Hanover	6-0
Crusaders v Dundela	3-0
Glenavon v Coleraine	0-2
Glentoran v Portadown	2-2*
Glentoran won 5-4 on penalties	
Institute v Dungannon Swifts	2-3
Larne v Belfast Celtic	8-0
Loughgall v Rathfriland Rangers	1-2
Newry C v Bangor	3-1
Warrenpoint T v PSNI	3-1

SIXTH ROUND

Knockbreda v Ballinamallard U	2-5
Queen's University v Glentoran	2-3
Ballyclare Comrades v Larne	0-1*
Carrick Rangers v Crusaders	1-5
Cliftonville v Rathfriland Rangers	3-1
Coleraine v Banbridge T	3-0
Dungannon Swifts v Newry C	4-2*
Warrenpoint T v Ballymena U	1-2

QUARTER-FINALS

Larne v Coleraine	2-3
Ballinamallard U v Ballymena U	0-2
Dungannon Swifts v Cliftonville	1-2
Glentoran v Crusaders	2-1

SEMI-FINALS

Ballymena U v Coleraine	1-1*
Ballymena U won 3-1 on penalties	
Cliftonville v Glentoran	1-1*
Glentoran won 7-6 on penalties	

SADLER'S PEAKY BLINDER FA CUP FINAL 2019–20

Windsor Park, Belfast, Friday 31 July 2020

Ballymena U (1) 1 *(Friel 48)*

Glentoran (1) 2 *(O'Neill 22, McDaid 115)* 500

Ballymena U: Glendenning; Addis (Burns 116), Whiteside, Friel (Kane K 106), McCullough, McGrory (Kane T 37 (Balmer)), Winchester (Knowles 60), Ervin, Lecky, Millar, Kelly.

Glentoran: Morris; Van Overbeek (Smyth 89), Cowan, McClean, Kane, Crowe (O'Connor 67), Gallagher, Nasseri, O'Neill (Frazer 81), McDaid, Donnelly (Peers 117).

aet. Referee: Tim Marshall.

IRISH CUP FINALS (from 1946–47)

1946–47 Belfast Celtic 1, Glentoran 0
1947–48 Linfield 3, Coleraine 0
1948–49 Derry City 3, Glentoran 1
1949–50 Linfield 2, Distillery 1
1950–51 Glentoran 3, Ballymena U 1
1951–52 Ards 1, Glentoran 0
1952–53 Linfield 5, Coleraine 0
1953–54 Derry City 1, Glentoran 0
1954–55 Dundela 3, Glenavon 0
1955–56 Distillery 1, Glentoran 0
1956–57 Glenavon 2, Derry City 0
1957–58 Ballymena U 2, Linfield 0
1958–59 Glenavon 2, Ballymena U 0
1959–60 Linfield 5, Ards 1
1960–61 Glenavon 5, Linfield 1
1961–62 Linfield 4, Portadown 0
1962–63 Linfield 2, Distillery 1
1963–64 Derry City 2, Glentoran 0
1964–65 Coleraine 2, Glenavon 1
1965–66 Glentoran 2, Linfield 0
1966–67 Crusaders 3, Glentoran 1
1967–68 Crusaders 2, Linfield 0
1968–69 Ards 4, Distillery 2
1969–70 Linfield 2, Ballymena U 1
1970–71 Distillery 3, Derry City
1971–72 Coleraine 2, Portadown 1
1972–73 Glentoran 3, Linfield 2
1973–74 Ards 2, Ballymena U 1
1974–75 Coleraine 1:0:1, Linfield 1:0:0
1975–76 Carrick Rangers 2, Linfield 1
1976–77 Coleraine 4, Linfield 1
1977–78 Linfield 3, Ballymena U 1
1978–79 Cliftonville 3, Portadown 2
1979–80 Linfield 2, Crusaders 0
1980–81 Ballymena U 1, Glenavon 0
1981–82 Linfield 2, Coleraine 1
1982–83 Glentoran 1:2, Linfield 1:1
1983–84 Ballymena U 4, Carrick Rangers 1
1984–85 Glentoran 1:1, Linfield 1:0
1985–86 Glentoran 2, Coleraine 1
1986–87 Glentoran 1, Larne 0
1987–88 Glentoran 1, Glenavon 0
1988–89 Ballymena U 1, Larne 0
1989–90 Glentoran 3, Portadown 0
1990–91 Portadown 2, Glenavon 1
1991–92 Glenavon 2, Linfield 1
1992–93 Bangor 1:1:1, Ards 1:1:0
1993–94 Linfield 2, Bangor 0
1994–95 Linfield 3, Carrick Rangers 1
1995–96 Glentoran 1, Glenavon 0
1996–97 Glenavon 1, Cliftonville 0
1997–98 Glentoran 1, Glenavon 0
1998–99 *Portadown awarded trophy after Cliftonville were eliminated for using an ineligible player in semi-final.*
1999–2000 Glentoran 1, Portadown 0
2000–01 Glentoran 1, Linfield 0
2001–02 Linfield 2, Portadown 1
2002–03 Coleraine 1, Glentoran 0
2003–04 Glentoran 1, Coleraine 0
2004–05 Portadown 5, Larne 1
2005–06 Linfield 2, Glentoran 1
2006–07 Linfield 2, Dungannon Swifts 2 *(aet; Linfield won 3-2 on penalties).*
2007–08 Linfield 2, Coleraine 1
2008–09 Crusaders 1, Cliftonville 0
2009–10 Linfield 2, Portadown 1
2010–11 Linfield 2, Crusaders 1
2011–12 Linfield 4, Crusaders 1
2012–13 Glentoran 3, Cliftonville 1
2013–14 Glenavon 2, Ballymena U 1
2014–15 Glentoran 1, Portadown 0
2015–16 Glenavon 2, Linfield 0
2016–17 Linfield 3, Coleraine 0
2017–18 Coleraine 3, Cliftonville 1
2018–19 Crusaders 3, Ballinamallard U 0
2019–20 Glentoran 2, Ballymena U 1

BETMCLEAN NORTHERN IRELAND LEAGUE CUP 2019–20

**After extra time.*

FIRST ROUND

Armagh C v H&W Welders	0-6
Ballyclare Comrades v Knockbreda	7-1
Loughgall v Banbridge T	2-1
PSNI v Queen's University	3-1

SECOND ROUND

Ballymena U v Newington	3-0
Bangor v Carrick Rangers	5-3*
Coleraine v Annagh U	4-0
Crusaders (walkover) v Lurgan Celtic	
Dundela v Tobermore U	6-0
Dungannon Swifts v Dergview	2-0
Glenavon v Portstewart	4-1
Glentoran v Ballyclare Comrades	5-1
Larne v Lisburn Distillery	3-0
Limavady U v Ards	4-2
Loughgall v Newry C	0-1
Moyola Park v Cliftonville	1-3
Portadown v Dollingstown	1-2
Warrenpoint T v H&W Welders	2-4
Institute v PSNI	3-2
Ballinamallard U v Linfield	4-5*

THIRD ROUND

Ballymena U v Dollingstown	6-0
Cliftonville v Bangor	3-2
Coleraine v Glentoran	2-1
Dungannon Swifts v Linfield	0-4
Institute v H&W Welders	3-0
Larne v Dundela	1-3
Limavady U v Crusaders	1-4
Glenavon v Newry C	2-3

QUARTER-FINALS

Ballymena U v Crusaders	1-2*
Dundela v Coleraine	1-5
Linfield v Cliftonville	1-0
Newry C v Institute	0-1

SEMI-FINALS

Crusaders v Institute	2-0
Linfield v Coleraine	0-3

BETMCLEAN NORTHERN IRELAND LEAGUE CUP FINAL 2019–20

Windsor Park, Belfast, Saturday 15 February 2020

Coleraine (1) 2 *(Lowry 37 (pen), McLaughlin 52)*

Crusaders (1) 1 *(McGonigle 10)* 4688

Coleraine: Johns; Kane, Mullan (Allen 55), Canning, Lowry, McLaughlin (Fitzpatrick 83), Carson, O'Donnell, Parkhill, Glackin, Traynor (Jarvis 24).

Crusaders: O'Neill; Burns, Lowry, McGonigle, Caddell (Hale 76), Forsythe (Cushley 71), O'Rourke, Owens, Brown, Heatley (McGinley 63), Dummigan.

Referee: Ian McNabb.

ROLL OF HONOUR SEASON 2019–20

Competition	*Winner*	*Runner-up*
NIFL Danske Bank Premiership	Linfield	Coleraine
Sadler's Peaky Blinder Irish FA Cup	Glentoran	Ballymena U
NIFL Championship	Portadown	Ballinamallard U
NIFL Premier Intermediate	Annagh U	Portstewart
BetMcLean Northern Ireland League Cup	Coleraine	Crusaders
County Antrim Shield	Cliftonville	Ballymena U
Steel & Sons Cup	Linfield Swifts	Newington
Co Antrim Junior Shield	Ahoghill Thistle	Harryville Homers
Irish Junior Cup	Willowbank	Enniskillen Rangers
Mid Ulster Cup (Senior)	Loughgall	Glenavon
Harry Cavan Youth Cup	Cliftonvill Strollers	Institute
North West Senior Cup	Ballinamallard U	Dergview
Intermediate Cup	Dollingstown	Newington

NORTHERN IRELAND FOOTBALL WRITERS ASSOCIATION PLAYER AND MANAGER OF THE MONTH AWARDS 2019–20

NIFWA PREMIERSHIP PLAYER OF THE MONTH 2019–20

Month	*Player*	*Team*
August	Shane Lavery	Linfield
September	Mark Stafford	Linfield
October	Ben Doherty	Coleraine
November	Jamie McGonigle	Crusaders
December	Conor McMenamin	Cliftonville
January	Billy Joe Burns	Crusaders
February	Andrew Waterworth	Linfield

NIFWA MANAGER OF THE MONTH 2019–20

Month	*Manager*	*Team*
August	David Healy	Linfield
September	David Healy	Linfield
October	Oran Kennedy	Coleraine
November	Mick McDermott	Glentoran
December	Mick McDermott	Glentoran
January	Stephen Baxter	Crusaders
February	Oran Kennedy	Coleraine

CHAMPIONSHIP PLAYER OF THE MONTH 2019–20

Month	*Player*	*Team*
August	Nathaniel Ferris	Loughgall
September	Lee Bonis	Portadown
October	Adam Foley	Newry C
November	Ryan Campbell	Ballinamallard U
December	Luke Wilson	Portadown
January	Matthew Ferguson	H&W Welders
February	Eamon McAllister	Ards

EUROPEAN CUP FINALS

EUROPEAN CUP FINALS 1956–1992

Year	Winners v Runners-up		Venue	Attendance	Referee
1956	Real Madrid v Reims	4-3	Paris	38,239	A. Ellis (England)
1957	Real Madrid v Fiorentina	2-0	Madrid	124,000	L. Horn (Netherlands)
1958	Real Madrid v AC Milan	3-2*	Brussels	67,000	A. Alsteen (Belgium)
1959	Real Madrid v Reims	2-0	Stuttgart	72,000	A. Dutsch (West Germany)
1960	Real Madrid v Eintracht Frankfurt	7-3	Glasgow	127,621	J. Mowat (Scotland)
1961	Benfica v Barcelona	3-2	Berne	26,732	G. Dienst (Switzerland)
1962	Benfica v Real Madrid	5-3	Amsterdam	61,257	L. Horn (Netherlands)
1963	AC Milan v Benfica	2-1	Wembley	45,715	A. Holland (England)
1964	Internazionale v Real Madrid	3-1	Vienna	71,333	J. Stoll (Austria)
1965	Internazionale v Benfica	1-0	Milan	89,000	G. Dienst (Switzerland)
1966	Real Madrid v Partizan Belgrade	2-1	Brussels	46,745	R. Kreitlein (West Germany)
1967	Celtic v Internazionale	2-1	Lisbon	45,000	K. Tschenscher (West Germany)
1968	Manchester U v Benfica	4-1*	Wembley	92,225	C. Lo Bello (Italy)
1969	AC Milan v Ajax	4-1	Madrid	31,782	J. Ortiz de Mendibil (Spain)
1970	Feyenoord v Celtic	2-1*	Milan	53,187	C. Lo Bello (Italy)
1971	Ajax v Panathinaikos	2-0	Wembley	90,000	J. Taylor (England)
1972	Ajax v Internazionale	2-0	Rotterdam	61,354	R. Helies (France)
1973	Ajax v Juventus	1-0	Belgrade	89,484	M. Guglovic (Yugoslavia)
1974	Bayern Munich v Atletico Madrid	1-1	Brussels	48,722	V. Loraux (Belgium)
Replay	Bayern Munich v Atletico Madrid	4-0	Brussels	23,325	A. Delcourt (Belgium)
1975	Bayern Munich v Leeds U	2-0	Paris	48,374	M. Kitabdjian (France)
1976	Bayern Munich v Saint-Etienne	1-0	Glasgow	54,864	K. Palotai (Hungary)
1977	Liverpool v Moenchengladbach	3-1	Rome	52,078	R. Wurtz (France)
1978	Liverpool v Club Brugge	1-0	Wembley	92,500	C. Corver (Netherlands)
1979	Nottingham F v Malmo	1-0	Munich	57,500	E. Linemayr (Austria)
1980	Nottingham F v Hamburg	1-0	Madrid	51,000	A. Garrido (Portugal)
1981	Liverpool v Real Madrid	1-0	Paris	48,360	K. Palotai (Hungary)
1982	Aston Villa v Bayern Munich	1-0	Rotterdam	46,000	G. Konrath (France)
1983	Hamburg v Juventus	1-0	Athens	73,500	N. Rainea (Romania)
1984	Liverpool v Roma *(Liverpool won 4-2 on penalties)*	1-1*	Rome	69,693	E. Fredriksson (Sweden)
1985	Juventus v Liverpool	1-0	Brussels	58,000	A. Daina (Switzerland)
1986	Steaua Bucharest v Barcelona *(Steaua won 2-0 on penalties)*	0-0*	Seville	70,000	M. Vautrot (France)
1987	FC Porto v Bayern Munich	2-1	Vienna	57,500	A. Ponnet (Belgium)
1988	PSV Eindhoven v Benfica *(PSV won 6-5 on penalties)*	0-0*	Stuttgart	68,000	L. Agnolin (Italy)
1989	AC Milan v Steaua Bucharest	4-0	Barcelona	97,000	K.-H. Tritschler (West Germany)
1990	AC Milan v Benfica	1-0	Vienna	57,500	H. Kohl (Austria)
1991	Crvena Zvezda v Olympique Marseille *(Crvena Zvezda won 5-3 on penalties)*	0-0*	Bari	56,000	T. Lanese (Italy)
1992	Barcelona v Sampdoria	1-0*	Wembley	70,827	A. Schmidhuber (Germany)

UEFA CHAMPIONS LEAGUE FINALS 1993–2020

Year	Winners v Runners-up		Venue	Attendance	Referee
1993	Marseille† v AC Milan	1-0	Munich	64,400	K. Rothlisberger (Switzerland)
1994	AC Milan v Barcelona	4-0	Athens	70,000	P. Don (England)
1995	Ajax v AC Milan	1-0	Vienna	49,730	I. Craciunescu (Romania)
1996	Juventus v Ajax *(Juventus won 4-2 on penalties)*	1-1*	Rome	70,000	M. D. Vega (Spain)
1997	Borussia Dortmund v Juventus	3-1	Munich	59,000	S. Puhl (Hungary)
1998	Real Madrid v Juventus	1-0	Amsterdam	48,500	H. Krug (Germany)
1999	Manchester U v Bayern Munich	2-1	Barcelona	90,245	P. Collina (Italy)
2000	Real Madrid v Valencia	3-0	Paris	80,000	S. Braschi (Italy)
2001	Bayern Munich v Valencia *(Bayern Munich won 5-4 on penalties)*	1-1*	Milan	79,000	D. Jol (Netherlands)
2002	Real Madrid v Leverkusen	2-1	Glasgow	50,499	U. Meier (Switzerland)
2003	AC Milan v Juventus *(AC Milan won 3-2 on penalties)*	0-0*	Manchester	62,315	M. Merk (Germany)
2004	FC Porto v Monaco	3-0	Gelsenkirchen	53,053	K. M. Nielsen (Denmark)
2005	Liverpool v AC Milan *(Liverpool won 3-2 on penalties)*	3-3*	Istanbul	65,000	M. M. González (Spain)
2006	Barcelona v Arsenal	2-1	Paris	79,610	T. Hauge (Norway)
2007	AC Milan v Liverpool	2-1	Athens	74,000	H. Fandel (Germany)
2008	Manchester U v Chelsea *(Manchester U won 6-5 on penalties)*	1-1*	Moscow	67,310	L. Michel (Slovakia)
2009	Barcelona v Manchester U	2-0	Rome	62,467	M. Busacca (Switzerland)
2010	Internazionale v Bayern Munich	2-0	Madrid	73,490	H. Webb (England)
2011	Barcelona v Manchester U	3-1	Wembley	87,695	V. Kassai (Hungary)
2012	Chelsea v Bayern Munich *(Chelsea won 4-3 on penalties)*	1-1*	Munich	62,500	P. Proença (Portugal)
2013	Bayern Munich v Borussia Dortmund	2-1	Wembley	86,298	N. Rizzoli (Italy)
2014	Real Madrid v Atletico Madrid	4-1*	Lisbon	60,000	B. Kuipers (Netherlands)
2015	Barcelona v Juventus	3-1	Berlin	70,442	C. Cakir (Turkey)
2016	Real Madrid v Atletico Madrid *(Real Madrid won 5-3 on penalties)*	1-1*	Milan	71,942	M. Clattenburg (England)
2017	Real Madrid v Juventus	4-1	Cardiff	65,842	F. Brych (Germany)
2018	Real Madrid v Liverpool	3-1	Kiev	61,561	M. Mazic (Serbia)
2019	Liverpool v Tottenham H	2-0	Madrid	63,272	D. Skomina (Slovenia)
2020	Bayern Munich v Paris Saint-Germain	1-0	Lisbon	0	D. Orsato (Italy)

†*Subsequently stripped of title.* **After extra time.*

UEFA CHAMPIONS LEAGUE 2019–20

■ *Denotes player sent off.*

PRELIMINARY ROUND

Tuesday, 25 June 2019

Feronikeli (1) 1 *(Hoti 3)*

Lincoln Red Imps (0) 0 3000

Feronikeli: (442) Troshupa; Hoxha, Prekazi, Lladrovci, Islami; Fazliu (Malaj 87), Dabiqaj, Bojku (Thaqi 82), Hoti (Zeka 74); Rexha, Carioca.
Lincoln Red Imps: (433) Soler; Perez (Toscano 56), Chipolina R, Lopes, Chipolina J; Molina, Montesinos, Gil; Gato (Aranda 79), Aguilar (Hernandez 74), Cabrera.

Tre Penne (0) 0

FC Santa Coloma (0) 1 *(Camochu 76)* 35

Tre Penne: (433) Migani; Cesarini (Sempirni 46), Colonna, Derjai (Giacomoni 79), Palazzi; Gai, Innocenti F (Innocenti R 58), Chiaruzzi; Cibelli, Angelini, Ceccaroli.
FC Santa Coloma: (4231) Casals; San Nicolas (Pi 81), Ramos, Miranda, Cistero; Santos (Medina 87), Rebes; Andre Azevedo (Sosa 68), Alaez, Buron; Camochu.

Friday, 28 June 2019

Feronikeli (0) 2 *(Zeka 58, Rexha 87)*

FC Santa Coloma (0) 1 *(Sosa 52)* 1900

Feronikeli: (442) Troshupa; Lladrovci, Prekazi, Islami, Carioca (Topalli 67); Hoxha■, Dabiqaj, Rexha, Bojku (Potoku 90); Fazliu, Zeka (Malaj 79).
FC Santa Coloma: (442) Casals; San Nicolas, Rebes (Pi 59), Ramos, Miranda; Sosa (Andre Azevedo 82), Santos, Buron, Cistero; Medina, Camochu (Alaez 64).

FIRST QUALIFYING ROUND FIRST LEG

Tuesday, 9 July 2019

Ararat-Armenia (2) 2 *(Avetisyan 3 (pen), 45)*

AIK Solna (1) 1 *(Ogbuke Obasi 39)* 1497

Ararat-Armenia: (4231) Abakumov; Pashov, Meneses, Guzj, Achenteh; Alphonse, Malakyan (Antonov 46); Narsingh, Avetisyan (Ambartsumyan 70), Sanogo; Kobyalko (Ogana 70).
AIK Solna: (352) Linner; Granli, Dimitriadis, Mets; Lundstrom■, Hussein (Larsson 46), Adu, Elyounoussi, Saletros (Lindkvist 84); Goitom, Ogbuke Obasi (Sigthorsson 65).

Astana (0) 1 *(Postnikov 68)*

CFR Cluj (0) 0 18,587

Astana: (4141) Eric; Rukavina, Postnikov, Simunovic, Beysebekov; Logvinenko; Tomasov (Janga 58), Maevskiy, Sigurjonsson, Murtazayev (Mubele 84); Rotariu.
CFR Cluj: (433) Arlauskis; Susic, Vinicius, Burca, Camora; Bordeianu (Luis Aurelio 90), Hoban (Rondon 75), Culio; Deac, Omrani, Paun (Mailat 65).

F91 Dudelange (2) 2 *(Bettaieb 26, Stolz 45)*

Valletta (0) 2 *(Packer 64, Borg J 70)* 1152

F91 Dudelange: (352) Kips; Stumpf, Schnell, Delgado; Bouchouari, Stolz, Garos (Morren 76), Bougrine (Sinani 65), Pokar; Barbosa, Bettaieb (Pomponi 84).
Valletta: (433) Bonello; Fontanella, Borg J, Santiago (Pulis 52), Tulimieri (Dimech 62); Packer (Monticelli 83), Borg S, Muscat■; Zerafa, Nwoko, Pena.

HJK Helsinki (2) 3 *(Lappalainen 21, 66, O'Shaughnessy 42)*

HB Torshavn (0) 0 4719

HJK Helsinki: (433) Rudakov; Alho, Obilor■, O'Shaughnessy, Rafinha; Vaananen (Toivomaki 34), Dahlstrom, Kairinen; Riski, Mensah (Vertainen 78), Lappalainen (Pelvas 89).
HB Torshavn: (442) Gestsson; Davidsen, Wardum (Johansen 82), Andersen, Egilsson; Justinussen, Askham, Jensen, Samuelsen; Soylu (Hlodversson 82), Olsen (Pingel 46).

Nomme Kalju (0) 0

Shkendija (0) 1 *(Ibraimi A 81 (pen))* 1640

Nomme Kalju: (4231) Londak; Markovych, Avilov, Ugge, Kulinits; Subbotin, Mbu Alidor; Paur, Kirss (Volkov 57), Mashichev (Klein 76); Liliu.
Shkendija: (4231) Zahov; Murati, Bejtulai, Musliu, Mici; Alimi, Husmani; Ibraimi A (Imeri 90), Totre (Zejnulai 85), Radeski; Ibraimi B (Nafiu 77).

Sarajevo (1) 1 *(Oremus 29)*

Celtic (1) 3 *(Johnston 35, Edouard 51, Sinclair 85)* 24,723

Sarajevo: (4231) Kovacevic; Hebibovic, Serbecic, Lazic, Hodzic (Dokanovic 87); Velkoski, Sabanovic (Tatar 66); Oremus, Rahmanovic (Sisic 78), Milanovic; Ahmetovic.
Celtic: (4231) Bain; Ajer, Bitton, Simunovic, Johnston (Morgan 65); Forrest (Sinclair 78), Christie; McGregor, Bolingoli-Mbombo (Hayes 57), Brown; Edouard.

Suduva (0) 0

Red Star Belgrade (0) 0 3200

Suduva: (532) Kardum; Svrljuga, Kerla, Jankauskas A, Zivanovic, Slavickas; Matulevicius (Golubickas 58), Cadjenovic, Verbickas (Jankauskas E 90); Topcagic, Tadic (Gotal 46).
Red Star Belgrade: (4231) Borjan; Gobeljic, Babic, Milunovic, Rodic; Jovancic, Jovicic (Canas 69); Ben (Vukanovic 86), Marin, Ivanic; Boakye (Pavkov 71).

The New Saints (0) 2 *(Draper 49, Edwards 77)*

Feronikeli (0) 2 *(Zeka 89, Fazliu 90 (pen))* 1140

The New Saints: (352) Harrison; Spender, Marriott (Harrington 56), Davies; Routledge, Brobbel (Nembhard 66), Draper (Byrne 76), Redmond, Cieslewicz; Mullan, Edwards.
Feronikeli: (4231) Troshupa; Dabiqaj, Lladrovci, Zeka, Fazliu (Thaqi 90); Carioca (Topalli 68), Potoku; Bojku (Malaj 68), Islami, Rexha; Prekazi.

Wednesday, 10 July 2019

BATE Borisov (0) 1 *(Dragun 64)*

Piast Gliwice (1) 1 *(Parzyszek 36)* 11,529

BATE Borisov: (433) Chichkan; Rios, Volkov, Filipenko (Simovic 11), Filipovic; Baha, Yablonskiy, Dragun■; Moukam (Milic 66), Dubajic (Skavysh 57), Stasevich.
Piast Gliwice: (433) Plach; Pietrowski, Czerwinski, Korun, Kirkeskov; Valencia (Badia 90), Dziczek (Sokolowski 61), Hateley; Konczkowski, Parzyszek (Aquino 85), Felix.

Dundalk (0) 0

Riga FC (0) 0 3100

Dundalk: (442) Rogers; Gannon, Hoare, Cleary, Jarvis; Mountney (Benson 58), Shields (Boyle 46), McEleney, McGrath (Kelly D 80); Duffy, Hoban.
Riga FC: (433) Ozols; Petersons, Cernomordijs, Prenga, Rugins; Visnakovs, Saric, Laizans; Bopesu, Debelko, Rodrigues (Rakels 78).

Ferencvaros (1) 2 *(Nguen 6, Zubkov 65)*

Ludogorets Razgrad (1) 1 *(Swierczok 31)* 18,115

Ferencvaros: (4231) Dibusz; Lovrencsics, Blazic, Dvali, Heister; Ihnatenko, Kharatin (Siger 77); Zubkov, Skvarka, Nguen (Varga 83); Priskin (Lanzafame 66).
Ludogorets Razgrad: (433) Iliev; Ikoko, Terziev, Moti, Nedyalkov; Biton (Marcelinho 66), Goralski (Badji 78), Dyakov; Lukoki (Jorginho 83), Swierczok, Tchibota.

Linfield (0) 0

Rosenborg (1) 2 *(Jensen 22, Soderlund 69)* 2710

Linfield: (442) Deane; Casement, Callacher, Stafford, Clarke; Millar (Lavery 67), Hery, Mulgrew, Quinn; Waterworth, Stewart (Fallon 89).
Rosenborg: (433) Hansen; Hedenstadt, Reginiussen, Hovland, Meling; Jensen, Lundemo, Konradsen (Trondsen 72); Akintola (de Lanlay 61), Soderlund, Asen (Helland 70).

Partizani Tirana (0) 0

Qarabag (0) 0 2120

Partizani Tirana: (433) Hoxha; Ibrahimi, Bitri, Belica, Hakaj (Trashi 79); Mala, Telushi, William (Broja 68); Asani, Cinari, Mensah (Brown 58).
Qarabag: (433) Vagner; Huseynov A, Mammadov, Sadygov, Medvedev; Ozobic (Garayev 85), Michel, Almeyda; Quintana (Romero 62), Emreli (Abdullayev 73), Zoubir.

Sheriff (0) 0

Saburtalo (1) 3 *(Rolovic 30, Kokhreidze 67, Kakubava 71)* 5706

Sheriff: (442) Mikulic; Palic (Balima 46), Posmac, Jach, Cristiano; Latifi, Kendysh, Jurado (Anton 46), Hordiyenko; Boban, Palcic (Tambe 70).
Saburtalo: (442) Migineishvili; Mali, Margvelashvili, Lakvekheliani, Rekhviashvili; Diasamidze, Goncalves (Shindagoridze 70), Altunashvili, Gorgiashvili (Kakubava 61); Rolovic, Kokhreidze (Gabedava 77).

Slovan Bratislava (0) 1 *(Sporar 82)*

Sutjeska (0) 1 *(Kojasevic 90)* 11,250

Slovan Bratislava: (433) Greif; Apau, Bajric, Bozhikov, Sukhotsky; Drazic, Ljubicic, Rafael Ratao (Holman 64); Cavric (de Kamps 64), Sporar, Moha (Daniel 77).
Sutjeska: (4231) Giljen; Ciger, Nedic, Sofranac, Bulatovic; Jankovic, Erakovic; Kojasevic, Cetkovic, Vucic (Osmajic 82); Markovic (Bozovic 88).

Valur (0) 0

Maribor (1) 3 *(Pericic 43, Hotic 60, Kronaveter 86 (pen))* 1201

Valur: (433) Halldorsson; Hedlund, Sigurbjornsson, Sigurdsson H, Eiriksson; Finsen, Sigurdsson K, Petry (Ingvarsson 78); Adolphsson (Ingason 83), Pedersen, Larusson (Bartalsstovu 76).
Maribor: (433) Piric; Milec, Ivkovic, Pericic, Viler; Cretu, Kronaveter (Mesanovic 89), Vrhovec; Hotic (Kramaric 83), Tavares (Vancas 76), Kotnik.

FIRST QUALIFYING ROUND SECOND LEG

Tuesday, 16 July 2019

Feronikeli (0) 0

The New Saints (0) 1 *(Ebbe 67)* 7800

Feronikeli: (4231) Smakiqi; Islami, Prekazi, Lladrovci, Hoxha; Bojku (Malaj 83), Dabiqaj; Zeka (Topalli 64), Fazliu, Hoti (Carioca 72); Rexha.
The New Saints: (541) Harrison; Draper (Nembhard 80), Brobbel, Routledge, Davies, Spender; Edwards, Mullan, Cieslewicz (Ebbe 66), Redmond; Harrington.

HB Torshavn (1) 2 *(Pingel 17, Andersen 56)*

HJK Helsinki (0) 2 *(Riski 60, 77)* 620

HB Torshavn: (442) Gestsson; Davidsen, Askham, Andersen, Egilsson; Petersen, Johansen, Jensen, Samuelsen; Pingel, Soylu (Hlodversson 77).
HJK Helsinki: (4231) Rudakov; Alho, O'Shaughnessy, Toivomaki, Rafinha; Vaananen, Kairinen (Dahlstrom 81); Kouassivi-Benissan (Riski 46), Vertainen, Zeneli (Lappalainen 46); Mensah.

Red Star Belgrade (2) 2 *(Boakye 4, Marin 29)*

Suduva (0) 1 *(Topcagic 90)* 23,751

Red Star Belgrade: (4231) Borjan; Gobeljic, Babic, Milunovic, Rodic; Jovancic, Jovicic; Ben, Marin (Pavkov 88), Ivanic (Vukanovic 82); Boakye (Stojkovic 62).
Suduva: (532) Kardum; Svrljuga, Kerla, Jankauskas A, Zivanovic, Slavickas (Hladik 63); Golubickas, Cadjenovic, Verbickas (Ricketts 76); Gotal (Tadic 51), Topcagic.

Saburtalo (0) 1 *(Rolovic 58)*

Sheriff (3) 3 *(Latifi 3, Margvelashvili 8 (og), Tambe 11)* 7560

Saburtalo: (442) Migineishvili; Mali, Margvelashvili, Lakvekheliani, Rekhviashvili; Diasamidze, Goncalves (Shindagoridze 80), Altunashvili (Tera 70), Gorgiashvili; Rolovic (Gabedava 77), Kokhreidze.
Sheriff: (433) Mikulic; Palic■, N'Diaye, Muzek, Cristiano; Kendysh, Anton (Jach 82), Hordiyenko (Palcic 69); Latifi, Tambe, Boban (Leandro Ribeiro 69).

Shkendija (0) 1 *(Ibraimi A 62 (pen))*

Nomme Kalju (1) 2 *(Ugge 6, Liliu 90)* 2546

Shkendija: (4231) Zahov; Murati, Bejtulai, Musliu, Mici; Alimi, Husmani (Nafiu 46); Ibraimi A, Totre, Radeski; Ibraimi B (Junior 63).
Nomme Kalju: (442) Londak; Markovych, Avilov, Ugge, Kulinits; Paur (Tjapkin 87), Subbotin, Mbu Alidor, Mashichev (Volkov 60); Liliu, Klein.
Nomme Kalju won on away goals.

Valletta (1) 1 *(Fontanella 35)*

F91 Dudelange (0) 1 *(Pokar 59)* 1512

Valletta: (4141) Bonello; Borg S (Gill 90), Borg J, Pena, Camilleri; Packer; Zerafa, Pulis, Nwoko (Dimech 69), Tulimieri (Monticelli 79); Fontanella.
F91 Dudelange: (352) Kips; Schnell, Delgado, Bouchouari; Kirch, Bougrine (Natami 86), Garos, Pokar, Sinani; Stolz, Lavie (Barbosa 76).
Valletta won on away goals.

Wednesday, 17 July 2019

AIK Solna (0) 3 *(Goitom 47, 52, Larsson 62 (pen))*

Ararat-Armenia (0) 1 *(Kobyalko 77)* 11,382

AIK Solna: (352) Linner; Granli, Karlsson (Lindkvist 46), Mets; Rashidi, Larsson, Adu, Elyounoussi, Saletros; Ogbuke Obasi (Sigthorsson 72), Goitom (Dimitriadis 90).
Ararat-Armenia: (4231) Abakumov; Pashov, Guzj, Meneses, Junior; Alphonse, Antonov (Achenteh 86); Narsingh, Avetisyan (Ambartsumyan 68), Sanogo (Lima 60); Kobyalko.

Celtic (1) 2 *(Christie 26, McGregor 75)*

Sarajevo (0) 1 *(Tatar 62)* 60,000

Celtic: (4321) Bain; Ajer, Bitton, Simunovic, Morgan (Sinclair 86); Forrest, Brown, Christie (Henderson 89); McGregor, Bolingoli-Mbombo; Edouard (Griffiths 78).
Sarajevo: (433) Kovacevic; Hebibovic, Serbecic, Lazic, Hodzic; Rahmanovic (Guzina 82), Oremus, Velkoski; Tatar (Dokanovic 71), Ahmetovic, Milanovic (Sisic 59).

CFR Cluj (2) 3 *(Omrani 10, 73, Postnikov 26 (og))*

Astana (1) 1 *(Murtazayev 4)* 8092

CFR Cluj: (433) Arlauskis; Susic, Vinicius, Burca, Camora; Djokovic, Bordeianu, Culio; Deac (Hoban 86), Rondon (Costache 66), Omrani (Pereira 85).
Astana: (4141) Eric; Rukavina, Postnikov, Simunovic, Beysebekov (Anicic 81); Logvinenko; Tomasov (Mokin 62), Maevskiy, Sigurjonsson (Janga 82), Murtazayev; Rotariu.

Ludogorets Razgrad (1) 2 *(Terziev 24, Heister 69 (og))*

Ferencvaros (2) 3 *(Kharatin 17, Skvarka 21, Nguen 48)* 9000

Ludogorets Razgrad: (4231) Renan; Ikoko (Cicinho 64), Terziev, Moti■, Nedyalkov; Goralski, Dyakov; Jorginho, Marcelinho (Biton 64), Tchibota; Swierczok (Keseru 46).
Ferencvaros: (4231) Dibusz; Lovrencsics, Blazic, Dvali, Heister; Ihnatenko (Siger 57), Kharatin; Zubkov, Skvarka, Nguen (Varga 61); Priskin (Lanzafame 73).

Maribor (2) 2 *(Kronaveter 11, Tavares 32)*

Valur (0) 0 6716

Maribor: (4321) Piric; Milec, Ivkovic, Pericic, Viler; Cretu, Vrhovec (Kramaric 73), Hotic; Kronaveter (Vancas 58), Kotnik (Mesanovic 57); Tavares.
Valur: (433) Halldorsson; Saevarsson, Omarsson, Sigurbjornsson, Jonsson; Ingvarsson, Sigurdsson K (Hedlund 77), Sigurdsson H (Petry 19); Bartalsstovu, Pedersen, Adolphsson (Ingason 62).

Piast Gliwice (1) 1 *(Czerwinski 21)*

BATE Borisov (0) 2 *(Moukam 82, Volkov 87)* 9312

Piast Gliwice: (4321) Plach; Pietrowski, Czerwinski, Korun, Kirkeskov; Konczkowski (Badia 83), Dziczek, Hateley; Valencia, Felix (Aquino 87); Parzyszek.
BATE Borisov: (433) Chichkan; Rios, Volkov, Simovic, Filipovic; Baha, Yablonskiy, Berezkin (Moukam 75); Skavysh, Tuominem (Milic 57), Stasevich.

Qarabag (0) 2 *(Ozobic 51, Quintana 90)*
Partizani Tirana (0) 0 5932
Qarabag: (4141) Vagner; Medvedev, Mammadov, Sadygov, Ailton; Michel; Ozobic (Slachev 73), Almeyda, Romero (Quintana 90), Amirguliyev (Emreli 78); Zoubir.
Partizani Tirana: (433) Hoxha; Hakaj (Brown 83), Bitri, Ibrahimi, Belica; Mala, Telushi, William; Asani, Solomon (Ekuban 76), Cinari (Trashi 61).

Riga FC (0) 0
Dundalk (0) 0 6050
Riga FC: (352) Ozols; Saric, Prenga■, Cernomordijs; Petersons, Laizans (Panic 81), Rugins, Rodrigues (Felipe Brisola 50), Visnakovs (Gabovs 106); Bopesu (Rakels 52), Debelko.
Dundalk: (4141) Rogers; Gannon, Hoare, Boyle, Massey; Shields (Jarvis 99); McGrath, Benson (Kelly D 81), McEleney (Kelly G 111), Mountney (Murray 64); Hoban.
aet; Dundalk won 5-4 on penalties.

Rosenborg (1) 4 *(Konradsen 20, 51, Akintola 69, Helland 85)*
Linfield (0) 0 11,904
Rosenborg: (433) Hansen; Hedenstadt (Trondsen 46), Reginiussen, Hovland, Meling; Asen, Lundemo, Konradsen (Ceide 71); Helland, Soderlund (Akintola 58), de Lanlay.
Linfield: (442) Deane; Casement, Larkin, Callacher, Clarke; Stewart (Millar 74), Mulgrew (Fallon 59), Hery, Quinn; Kearns, Lavery (Waterworth 58).

Sutjeska (0) 1 *(Sofranac 90)*
Slovan Bratislava (0) 1 *(Sporar 49)* 4764
Sutjeska: (4231) Giljen; Ciger, Nedic, Sofranac, Bulatovic; Jankovic (Bubanja 115), Erakovic; Kojasevic, Cetkovic (Nikolic 74), Vucic (Vlaisavljevic 69); Markovic (Osmajic 86).
Slovan Bratislava: (451) Greif; Medvedev, Bajric, Bozhikov, Sukhotsky; Daniel (Cavric 46), Holman (Abena 71), Ljubicic (Rafael Ratao 106), Moha, de Kamps (Drazic 86); Sporar.
aet; Sutjeska won 3-2 on penalties.

SECOND QUALIFYING ROUND FIRST LEG

Tuesday, 23 July 2019

PSV Eindhoven (1) 3 *(Bruma 14, Malen 90, Lammers 90)*
FC Basel (1) 2 *(Ajeti 45, Alderete 79)* 31,000
PSV Eindhoven: (442) Zoet; Viergever, Luckassen, Dumfries, Bruma (Gakpo 77); Gutierrez, Sadilek, Rosario, Bergwijn; Lozano (Lammers 82), Malen.
FC Basel: (442) Omlin; Widmer, Balanta (Pululu 90), Alderete, Comert; Stocker (Okafor 65), Zuffi, Frei, Xhaka; van Wolfswinkel, Ajeti (Ademi 89).

Saburtalo (0) 0
Dinamo Zagreb (0) 2 *(Orsic 67, Petkovic 78)* 15,165
Saburtalo: (442) Migineishvili; Mali, Margvelashvili, Rekhviashvili, Lakvekheliani; Goncalves, Diasamidze (Tsnobiladze 82), Altunashvili (Gabedava 70), Tera (Kakubava 57); Rolovic, Kokhreidze.
Dinamo Zagreb: (442) Livakovic; Ivo Pinto (Situm 50), Leskovic, Peric, Leovac; Kadzior, Ademi, Gojak, Hajrovic; Gavranovic (Petkovic 68 (Sunjic 87)), Orsic.

Sutjeska (0) 0
APOEL (1) 1 *(De Vincenti 42 (pen))* 5500
Sutjeska: (442) Giljen; Bulatovic, Sofranac, Ciger, Cetkovic (Osmajic 40); Kojasevic, Jankovic, Vucic (Vlaisavljevic 79), Nedic; Erakovic, Markovic (Nikolic 66).
APOEL: (442) Belec; Lafrance, Vouros, Ioannou, Mihajlovic; Gentsoglou, Jakolis (Savic 59), De Vincenti (Matic 90), Lucas Souza; Al-Taamari, Hallenius (Pavlovic 60).

The New Saints (0) 0
FC Copenhagen (1) 2 *(Sotiriou 18, Skov 60 (pen))* 1230
The New Saints: (451) Harrison; Edwards, Harrington, Davies, Spender; Mullan, Routledge, Redmond, Brobbel, Cieslewicz (Nembhard 75); Ebbe (Draper 56).
FC Copenhagen: (442) Grytebust; Bartolec, Nelsson, Papagiannopoulos, Bengtsson; Skov, Jensen (Zeca 35), Stage, Holse; N'Doye (Wind 46), Sotiriou (Fischer 62).

Viktoria Plzen (0) 0
Olympiacos (0) 0 10,632
Viktoria Plzen: (4231) Hruska; Havel, Pernica, Brabec (Hejda 72), Hlousek; Kalvach, Hrosovsky; Kayamba, Cermak (Mihalik 83), Kopic; Krmencik (Chory 69).
Olympiacos: (4231) Sa; Elabdellaoui, Semedo, Papadopoulos (Ba 22), Tsimikas; Bouchalakis, Guilherme; Daniel Podence, Valbuena (Camara 57), Masouras (Randelovic 81); Guerrero.

Wednesday, 24 July 2019

BATE Borisov (1) 2 *(Stasevich 5 (pen), Skavysh 51)*
Rosenborg (1) 1 *(Konradsen 25)* 12,696
BATE Borisov: (433) Chichkan; Rios, Volkov, Simovic, Filipovic; Baha, Yablonskiy, Dragun; Milic (Moukam 78), Skavysh (Tuominem 85), Stasevich.
Rosenborg: (433) Hansen; Hedenstadt, Reginiussen, Hovland, Meling; Jensen, Lundemo, Konradsen; Akintola (Adegbenro 64), Soderlund, de Lanlay (Helland 77).

Celtic (3) 5 *(Ajer 36, Christie 44 (pen), 65, Griffiths 45, McGregor 77)*
Nomme Kalju (0) 0 41,872
Celtic: (4312) Bain; Ajer, Bitton, Simunovic, Bolingoli-Mbombo (Johnston 37); Forrest, Brown, McGregor; Christie (Ntcham 71); Edouard, Griffiths (Morgan 59).
Nomme Kalju: (442) Londak; Markovych, Avilov, Ugge, Kulinits; Puri, Mbu Alidor, Subbotin, Paur (Volkov 75); Klein (Mata 46), Liliu (Mashichev 84).

CFR Cluj (1) 1 *(Omrani 22)*
Maccabi Tel Aviv (0) 0 11,150
CFR Cluj: (433) Arlauskis; Susic, Vinicius, Burca, Camora; Culio, Bordeianu, Djokovic (Sylla 79); Deac (Pereira 90), Rondon (Paun 72), Omrani.
Maccabi Tel Aviv: (442) Gianniotis; Kandil, Piven, Jair Amador, Davidadze; Cohen (Micha 55), Peretz, Glazer, Rikan; Ofoedu (Blackman 67), Shechter (Atar 83).

Dundalk (0) 1 *(Hoban 78)*
Qarabag (1) 1 *(Emreli 4)* 3100
Dundalk: (433) Rogers; Gannon, Hoare, Boyle, Massey; Shields, Benson (Murray 28), McGrath; Duffy, Hoban (Kelly G 83), McEleney (Mountney 69).
Qarabag: (433) Vagner; Medvedev (Huseynov A 53), Mammadov, Sadygov, Ailton; Garayev, Slachev, Almeyda; Romero (Abdullayev 87), Emreli, Zoubir.

Ferencvaros (2) 3 *(Dvali 19, Lanzafame 36 (pen), 59)*
Valletta (0) 1 *(Yuri 85)* 18,603
Ferencvaros: (4231) Dibusz; Lovrencsics, Blazic, Dvali, Civic; Kharatin, Ihnatenko; Zubkov, Skvarka (Siger 82), Nguen (Bole 66); Lanzafame (Signevich 66).
Valletta: (4141) Bonello; Zerafa, Borg J, Borg S■, Pena; Pulis (Dimech 57); Muscat, Packer (Yuri 70), Tulimieri, Nwoko (Piciollo 82); Fontanella.

Maribor (2) 2 *(Kronaveter 6, Ivkovic 38)*
AIK Solna (1) 1 *(Goitom 28)* 7816
Maribor: (4231) Piric; Milec, Ivkovic, Pericic, Viler; Cretu, Vrhovec; Hotic, Kronaveter, Kotnik (Vancas 80); Tavares (Mesanovic 88).
AIK Solna: (352) Linner; Granli, Karlsson, Mets; Lundstrom, Larsson, Adu, Elyounoussi, Saletros (Lindkvist 79); Sigthorsson (Ogbuke Obasi 62), Goitom.

Red Star Belgrade (1) 2 *(Boakye 27, Pavkov 90)*
HJK Helsinki (0) 0 36,289
Red Star Belgrade: (4231) Borjan; Stojkovic, Babic, Milunovic, Rodic; Jovancic, Jovicic; Ben (Vukanovic 85), Marin, Ivanic (Jevtovic 63); Boakye (Pavkov 72).
HJK Helsinki: (3511) Rudakov; Toivomaki, Rafinha, Obilor; Mensah (Vayrynen 90), Dahlstrom, Parra, Kairinen, Alho; Tarasov (Kouassivi-Benissan 81); Riski.

SECOND QUALIFYING ROUND SECOND LEG

Tuesday, 30 July 2019

APOEL (2) 3 *(Pavlovic 13, 25, 66)*

Sutjeska (0) 0 8297

APOEL: (433) Belec; Mihajlovic, Vouros, Savic (Merkis 76), Ioannou; De Vincenti, Gentsoglou (Alef 78), Matic; Jakolis, Pavlovic (Bezjak 71), Al-Taamari.
Sutjeska: (4231) Giljen; Ciger, Nedic, Sofranac, Bulatovic; Jankovic, Bubanja; Kojasevic, Marusic (Cetkovic 60), Osmajic (Vlaisavljevic 72); Bozovic (Nikolic 67).

Dinamo Zagreb (0) 3 *(Orsic 77, Petkovic 88, Olmo 90)*

Saburtalo (0) 0

Dinamo Zagreb: (433) Livakovic; Ivo Pinto, Leskovic, Peric, Leovac; Kadzior (Olmo 74), Ademi, Gojak; Hajrovic (Majer 84), Gavranovic (Petkovic 63), Orsic.
Saburtalo: (433) Kupatadze; Mali (Tabatadze 59), Margvelashvili, Rekhviashvili, Kakubava; Chabradze (Jinjolava 69), Tsnobiladze, Altunashvili; Gabedava, Rolovic, Gorgiashvili (Diasamidze 61).
Behind closed doors.

FC Basel (1) 2 *(Comert 8, van Wolfswinkel 68)*

PSV Eindhoven (1) 1 *(Bruma 23)* 29,216

FC Basel: (4231) Omlin; Widmer, Comert, Alderete, Xhaka (Petretta 81); Balanta, Frei; van Wolfswinkel, Zuffi, Stocker; Ajeti.
PSV Eindhoven: (4312) Zoet; Dumfries, Luckassen, Viergever, Sadilek; Gutierrez, Bergwijn, Rosario; Lozano (Gakpo 76); Malen, Bruma.
FC Basel won on away goals.

Maccabi Tel Aviv (1) 2 *(Blackman 15, Cohen 48)*

CFR Cluj (2) 2 *(Culio 19 (pen), Rondon 42)* 11,947

Maccabi Tel Aviv: (433) Gianniotis; Kandil (Geraldes 59), Piven, Jair Amador, Davidadze; Peretz, Rikan (Cohen 46), Glazer; Blackman (Atar 72), Shechter, Micha.
CFR Cluj: (433) Arlauskis; Susic, Vinicius, Burca, Camora; Bordeianu, Culio, Djokovic; Deac (Paun 52), Omrani (Muresan 86), Rondon (Tucudean 82).

Nomme Kalju (0) 0

Celtic (1) 2 *(Kulinits 10 (og), Shved 90)* 4014

Nomme Kalju: (4231) Londak; Markovych, Avilov, Ugge, Kulinits; Subbotin (Mashichev 79), Tjapkin; Paur (Ivanjusin 83), Liliu (Mata 38), Puri; Klein.
Celtic: (4231) Gordon; Jullien, Bitton (Shved 70), Simunovic, Bolingoli-Mbombo; Ralston, Brown; Ntcham (Christie 84), Johnston (Sinclair 61), Morgan; Griffiths.

Olympiacos (0) 4 *(Guilherme 51, Guerrero 70, Brabec 73 (og), Semedo 82)*

Viktoria Plzen (0) 0 30,123

Olympiacos: (4231) Sa; Elabdellaoui, Meriah, Semedo, Tsimikas; Guilherme, Bouchalakis; Masouras, Valbuena (Camara 66), Daniel Podence (Randelovic 85); Guerrero (El Arabi 80).
Viktoria Plzen: (4231) Hruska; Reznik, Pernica, Brabec, Hlousek; Kalvach (Janosek 79), Hrosovsky; Kayamba (Kovarik 56), Mihalik (Chory 74), Kopic; Krmencik.

Valletta (1) 1 *(Fontanella 27 (pen))*

Ferencvaros (0) 1 *(Nguen 60)* 1108

Valletta: (433) Bonello; Pena, Borg J, Camilleri, Zerafa; Dimech (Nwoko 74), Muscat (Monticelli 80), Tulimieri; Yuri, Fontanella, Piciollo (Tonna 90).
Ferencvaros: (4231) Dibusz; Lovrencsics, Blazic, Dvali, Civic; Ihnatenko (Siger 33), Kharatin; Zubkov, Skvarka, Nguen (Varga 85); Lanzafame (Signevich 74).

Wednesday, 31 July 2019

AIK Solna (1) 3 *(Karlsson 4, Larsson 61, Elyounoussi 93)*

Maribor (0) 2 *(Kotnik 48, Cretu 117)* 19,179

AIK Solna: (442) Linner; Karlsson, Lundstrom (Rashidi 76), Mets, Granli (Dimitriadis 106); Larsson (Hussein 102), Adu, Saletros, Elyounoussi; Goitom, Ogbuke Obasi (Sigthorsson 32).
Maribor: (442) Piric; Viler, Milec, Ivkovic, Pericic; Kronaveter (Pihler 118), Vrhovec (Kramaric 106), Cretu, Hotic; Kotnik (Vancas 91), Tavares (Mesanovic 86).
aet; Maribor won on away goals.

FC Copenhagen (0) 1 *(Zeca 52)*

The New Saints (0) 0 12,523

FC Copenhagen: (442) Johnsson; Bartolec, Papagiannopoulos, Nelsson, Bengtsson (Varela 78); Daramy, Zeca (Daghim 59), Stage, Thomsen; Wind (Holse 59), Sotiriou.
The New Saints: (4231) Harrison; Spender, Harrington, Marriott (Hudson 78), Redmond; Routledge, Edwards; Mullan, Brobbel, Cieslewicz (Lewis 59); Ebbe (Draper 66).

HJK Helsinki (0) 2 *(Dahlstrom 46, Riski 90)*

Red Star Belgrade (0) 1 *(Jovancic 56)* 9107

HJK Helsinki: (442) Rudakov; Rafinha (Victor Luiz 66), Alho, O'Shaughnessy, Obilor; Parra (Vaananen 77), Riski, Kairinen, Dahlstrom; Mensah, Tarasov (Vayrynen 46).
Red Star Belgrade: (442) Borjan; Milunovic, Rodic, Stojkovic, Babic; Marin, Canas (Degenek 88), Jovancic, Jevtovic (Ivanic 74); Boakye (Pavkov 55), Ben.

Qarabag (1) 3 *(Romero 12, 87, Ailton 76)*

Dundalk (0) 0 5832

Qarabag: (4231) Vagner; Medvedev (Huseynov A 82), Mammadov, Sadygov, Ailton; Almeyda, Michel (Slachev 73); Romero, Ozobic (Quintana 25), Zoubir; Emreli.
Dundalk: (352) Rogers; Hoare (Murray 56), Cleary, Boyle; Gannon, McGrath, Shields, McEleney (Mountney 65), Massey; Duffy (Kelly D 79), Hoban.

Rosenborg (0) 2 *(Helland 73 (pen), Soderlund 85)*

BATE Borisov (0) 0 14,875

Rosenborg: (442) Hansen; Reginiussen, Hovland, Hedenstadt, Meling; Jensen, Konradsen, Trondsen, Soderlund; Adegbenro (de Lanlay 78), Akintola (Helland 70).
BATE Borisov: (442) Chichkan; Filipenko, Rios (Jonassen 62), Stasevich, Baha; Dragun (Dubajic 87), Simovic, Tuominem (Moukam 76), Yablonskiy; Volkov, Skavysh.

THIRD QUALIFYING ROUND FIRST LEG

Tuesday, 6 August 2019

APOEL (0) 1 *(Merkis 90)*

Qarabag (0) 2 *(Emreli 54, Gueye 69)* 9481

APOEL: (343) Belec; Vouros, Ioannou, Merkis; Jakolis (Vidigal 64), Mihajlovic, Gentsoglou (Hallenius 86), Matic (Alef 65); Al-Taamari, De Vincenti, Pavlovic.
Qarabag: (433) Vagner; Medvedev, Mammadov, Sadygov, Ailton; Slachev, Michel, Almeyda (Garayev 86); Romero (Abdullayev 85), Emreli (Gueye 68), Zoubir.

Club Brugge (1) 1 *(Vanaken 37 (pen))*

Dynamo Kyiv (0) 0 27,018

Club Brugge: (433) Mignolet; Mata, Mitrovic, Deli, Sobol; Vormer, Rits, Vanaken; Tau, Okereke, Bonaventure (Schrijvers 63).
Dynamo Kyiv: (4231) Boyko; Kedziora, Burda, Kadar, Mykolenko; Sydorchuk, Buyalsky; Karavaev (Tsygankov 46), Harmash, Verbic (De Pena 64); Biesiedin (Rodrigues 46).

Dinamo Zagreb (1) 1 *(Olmo 7)*

Ferencvaros (0) 1 *(Siger 59)* 14,283

Dinamo Zagreb: (433) Livakovic; Stojanovic, Leskovic, Peric, Leovac; Gojak (Moro 69), Ademi, Olmo; Hajrovic (Majer 69), Petkovic (Gavranovic 76), Orsic.
Ferencvaros: (433) Dibusz; Lovrencsics, Dvali, Blazic, Heister; Kharatin, Skvarka (Ihnatenko 89), Siger; Nguen (Civic 83), Signevich (Lanzafame 78), Zubkov.

PAOK (2) 2 *(Akpom 32, Leo Matos 39)*

Ajax (1) 2 *(Ziyech 10, Huntelaar 57)* 23,418

PAOK: (442) Paschalakis; Leo Matos, Crespo, Varela, Giannoulis; Leo Jaba (Stoch 79), Esiti, El Kaddouri, Biseswar (Douglas 73); Pelkas (Limnios 64), Akpom.
Ajax: (433) Onana; Veltman, Schuurs, Martinez, Tagliafico; Mazraoui (Marin 82), van de Beek, Blind; Ziyech (Neres 82), Dolberg (Huntelaar 32), Tadic.

Red Star Belgrade (1) 1 *(Pavkov 44)*

FC Copenhagen (0) 1 *(Wind 84 (pen))* 40,812

Red Star Belgrade: (4231) Borjan; Gobeljic, Degenek, Milunovic, Rodic (Jander 65); Canas, Jovancic; Ivanic, Marin, Vukanovic (Ben 76); Pavkov (Boakye 46).
FC Copenhagen: (442) Grytebust; Varela, Papagiannopoulos, Nelsson, Oviedo (Bengtsson 72); Holse (Bartolec 88), Zeca, Stage, Fischer (Mas 64); Wind, N'Doye.

Wednesday, 7 August 2019

CFR Cluj (1) 1 *(Rondon 28)*

Celtic (1) 1 *(Forrest 37)* 13,055

CFR Cluj: (442) Arlauskis; Susic, Vinicius, Burca, Camora; Deac, Luis Aurelio, Bordeianu, Djokovic; Rondon (Tucudean 75), Omrani (Paun 66).
Celtic: (4312) Bain; Ajer, Elhamed (Bitton 87), Simunovic (Jullien 74), Bolingoli-Mbombo; Forrest, Brown, McGregor; Christie; Edouard, Morgan (Ntcham 66).

FC Basel (0) 1 *(Zuffi 87)*

LASK (0) 2 *(Trauner 51, Klauss 82)* 20,470

FC Basel: (4231) Omlin; Widmer, Comert, Alderete, Riveros; Balanta (Bua 76), Frei; van Wolfswinkel, Zuffi, Stocker (Ademi 65); Pululu (Okafor 75).
LASK: (343) Schlager; Ramsebner (Pogatetz 16), Trauner, Wiesinger; Ranftl, Holland, Michorl, Renner; Goiginger (Frieser 63), Klauss (Raguz 83), Tetteh.

Istanbul Basaksehir (0) 0

Olympiacos (0) 1 *(Masouras 53)* 4301

Istanbul Basaksehir: (442) Gunok; Junior Caicara, Chedjou, Miguel Vieira, Clichy; Visca, Tekdemir (Azubuike 63), Kahveci■, Robinho; Crivelli (Ba 81), Gulbrandsen (Elia 69).
Olympiacos: (4231) Sa; Elabdellaoui, Meriah, Semedo, Tsimikas; Bouchalakis, Guilherme; Daniel Podence, Valbuena (Camara 73), Masouras (Bruno 83); Guerrero (El Arabi 89).

Krasnodar (0) 0

Porto (0) 1 *(Sergio Oliveira 89)* 34,874

Krasnodar: (433) Safonov; Petrov, Martynovich, Spajic, Ramirez; Vilhena, Kambolov (Fjoluson 72), Cabella; Wanderson, Berg, Namli (Suleymanov 66).
Porto: (442) Marchesin; Manafa, Marcano, Pepe, Alex Telles; Baro (Diaz 55), Danilo Pereira, Sergio Oliveira, Corona (Otavio 85); Marega, Tiquinho Soares (Ze Luis 74).

Maribor (0) 1 *(Tavares 71)*

Rosenborg (0) 3 *(Soderlund 50, 64, Jensen 72)* 10,316

Maribor: (4231) Piric; Milec, Ivkovic, Pericic, Viler; Pihler, Vrhovec; Hotic (Vancas 64), Kronaveter, Kotnik (Kramaric 85); Tavares.
Rosenborg: (442) Hansen; Hedenstadt, Reginiussen (Valsvik 14), Hovland, Meling; Jensen, Lundemo, Asen (Trondsen 80), Akintola; Soderlund (Helland 68), Adegbenro.

THIRD QUALIFYING ROUND SECOND LEG

Tuesday, 13 August 2019

Ajax (1) 3 *(Tadic 43 (pen), 88, Tagliafico 79)*

PAOK (1) 2 *(Biseswar 23, 90)* 53,942

Ajax: (433) Onana; Mazraoui, Veltman, Martinez, Tagliafico; Marin (Dest 46), van de Beek (de Wit 89), Blind; Ziyech, Tadic, Neres (Huntelaar 78).
PAOK: (343) Paschalakis; Varela, Crespo, Giannoulis; Leo Jaba (Limnios 71), El Kaddouri, Esiti (Misic 82), Biseswar; Pelkas (Swiderski 63), Akpom, Leo Matos.

Celtic (0) 3 *(Forrest 51, Edouard 61, Christie 76)*

CFR Cluj (1) 4 *(Deac 27, Omrani 74, 80, Tucudean 90)* 50,964

Celtic: (343) Bain; Elhamed, Ajer, Simunovic; Forrest, Brown (Bayo 88), Ntcham (Griffiths 83), McGregor; Christie, Edouard, Johnston (Morgan 75).
CFR Cluj: (442) Arlauskis; Susic, Vinicius, Burca, Camora; Bordeianu, Luis Aurelio (Paun 78), Djokovic, Deac; Omrani (Muresan 84), Rondon (Tucudean 46).

Dynamo Kyiv (1) 3 *(Buyalsky 6, Shepelev 50, Mechele 90 (og))*

Club Brugge (1) 3 *(Deli 38, Vormer 88, Openda 90)* 42,152

Dynamo Kyiv: (433) Boyko; Kedziora, Burda■, Kadar, Mykolenko; Buyalsky, Shepelev (Sol 83), Andrievsky (De Pena 46); Verbic (Biesiedin 68), Rodrigues, Tsygankov.
Club Brugge: (433) Mignolet; Mata, Mechele, Deli, Sobol; Vormer, Rits, Vanaken; Tau■, Okereke (Openda 81), Bonaventure (Diatta 52).

FC Copenhagen (1) 1 *(N'Doye 45)*

Red Star Belgrade (1) 1 *(Boakye 17)* 29,872

FC Copenhagen: (442) Grytebust; Varela (Bartolec 81), Papagiannopoulos, Nelsson, Bengtsson; Holse (Mas■ 74), Zeca, Stage (Jensen 60 (Sotiriou 120)), Fischer; Wind, N'Doye.
Red Star Belgrade: (4231) Borjan; Gobeljic, Milunovic■, Degenek, Rodic (Jander 46); Canas (Pankov 58), Jovancic; Ivanic, Marin, Vukanovic (Jevtovic 91); Boakye (Simic 81).
aet; Red Star Belgrade won 7-6 on penalties.

Ferencvaros (0) 0

Dinamo Zagreb (1) 4 *(Ademi 17, Petkovic 47, Olmo 55, Gojak 79)* 20,321

Ferencvaros: (4231) Dibusz; Lovrencsics, Blazic, Dvali, Civic■; Siger, Kharatin; Skvarka (Heister 71), Zubkov, Nguen (Varga 65); Signevich (Boli 84).
Dinamo Zagreb: (4231) Livakovic; Stojanovic, Dilaver, Peric, Leovac; Moro, Ademi (Gojak 69); Hajrovic (Majer 77), Olmo (Situm 84), Orsic; Petkovic.

LASK (0) 3 *(Ranftl 59, Goiginger 89, Raguz 90)*

FC Basel (0) 1 *(Ademi 80)* 12,966

LASK: (343) Schlager; Wiesinger, Trauner, Pogatetz; Ranftl, Michorl, Holland, Renner; Goiginger (Sabitzer 90), Klauss (Raguz 87), Tetteh (Frieser 76).
FC Basel: (433) Omlin; Widmer, Comert, Alderete, Petretta; Balanta, Frei, Zuffi (Bua 55); Stocker, Ademi, Okafor (Campo 64).

Olympiacos (0) 2 *(Semedo 55, Valbuena 78)*

Istanbul Basaksehir (0) 0 28,521

Olympiacos: (4231) Sa; Elabdellaoui, Meriah, Semedo, Tsimikas; Bouchalakis, Guilherme (Koutris 89); Masouras, Valbuena (Camara 82), Daniel Podence (Randelovic 68); Guerrero.
Istanbul Basaksehir: (442) Gunok; Junior Caicara, Miguel Vieira, Ponck, Clichy; Visca, Attamah (Ba 59), Azubuike, Elia; Crivelli (Gulbrandsen 75), Robinho (Turan 46).

Porto (0) 2 *(Ze Luis 57, Diaz 76)*

Krasnodar (3) 3 *(Vilhena 3, Suleymanov 13, 34)* 48,520

Porto: (442) Marchesin; Saravia (Ze Luis 37), Pepe, Marcano, Alex Telles; Nakajima, Sergio Oliveira (Uribe 49), Danilo Pereira, Diaz; Marega, Corona (Aboubakar 86).
Krasnodar: (433) Safonov; Petrov, Martynovich, Spajic, Ramirez; Cabella (Stotskiy 80), Kambolov, Vilhena; Suleymanov (Fjoluson 65), Berg (Ignatyev 73), Wanderson.
Krasnodar won on away goals.

Qarabag (0) 0

APOEL (1) 2 *(De Vincenti 34 (pen), Matic 68)* 31,531

Qarabag: (4141) Vagner; Medvedev, Mammadov, Sadygov, Ailton (Abdullayev 87); Michel; Romero, Slachev (Quintana 73), Almeyda■, Zoubir (Gueye 80); Emreli.
APOEL: (343) Belec; Merkis, Lafrance, Ioannou; Al-Taamari, Gentsoglou, Matic, Mihajlovic; Bezjak (Jakolis 82), Pavlovic (Lucas Souza 73), De Vincenti (Hallenius 61).

Rosenborg (0) 3 *(Soderlund 53, Konradsen 61, 81)*

Maribor (1) 1 *(Vancas 45)* 18,564

Rosenborg: (433) Hansen; Hedenstadt, Reginiussen, Hovland, Meling; Jensen (Trondsen 87), Lundemo, Konradsen (Ceide 90); Akintola, Soderlund, Adegbenro (Asen 78).
Maribor: (4231) Piric; Milec, Ivkovic, Pericic, Viler; Cretu, Vrhovec; Hotic (Kramaric 82), Kronaveter (Kotnik 69), Vancas; Tavares (Zahovic 69).

PLAY-OFF ROUND FIRST LEG

Tuesday, 20 August 2019

APOEL (0) 0

Ajax (0) 0 14,549

APOEL: (3511) Belec; Merkis, Ioannou, Joaozinho (Vidigal 82); Bezjak (Jakolis 69), Lucas Souza, Gentsoglou, Matic, Mihajlovic; Al-Taamari; Pavlovic (Hallenius 68).
Ajax: (433) Onana; Mazraoui■, Veltman, Martinez, Tagliafico; Marin (Dest 62), van de Beek, Blind; Ziyech, Tadic, Neres (Huntelaar 72).

CFR Cluj (0) 0

Slavia Prague (1) 1 *(Masopust 28)* 15,196

CFR Cluj: (433) Arlauskis; Susic, Cestor, Burca, Camora; Luis Aurelio (Paun 72), Bordeianu (Hoban 87), Djokovic; Deac, Tucudean (Rondon 46), Omrani.
Slavia Prague: (4231) Kolar; Coufal, Hovorka, Kudela, Boril; Soucek, Traore (Kral 64); Masopust (Holes 84), Stanciu, Olayinka; van Buren (Skoda 68).

LASK (0) 0

Club Brugge (1) 1 *(Vanaken 10 (pen))* 12,637

LASK: (343) Schlager; Wiesinger, Trauner, Pogatetz; Ranftl, Holland, Michorl, Renner (Raguz 67); Goiginger (Otubanjo 83), Klauss, Tetteh (Frieser 53).
Club Brugge: (433) Mignolet; Mata, Mitrovic, Deli, Sobol (Ricca 66); Vormer, Rits, Vanaken; Bonaventure, Okereke (Diatta 89), Openda (Rezaei 74).

Wednesday, 21 August 2019

Dinamo Zagreb (2) 2 *(Petkovic 9 (pen), Orsic 28)*

Rosenborg (0) 0 23,859

Dinamo Zagreb: (4411) Livakovic; Stojanovic, Dilaver, Peric, Leovac; Hajrovic (Gojak 64), Ademi, Moro, Orsic (Atiemwen 84); Olmo; Petkovic (Gavranovic 87).
Rosenborg: (433) Hansen; Hedenstadt, Reginiussen, Hovland, Meling; Jensen, Lundemo, Konradsen; Akintola (Helland 84), Soderlund, Adegbenro.

Olympiacos (1) 4 *(Guerrero 30, Randelovic 78, 85, Daniel Podence 89)*

Krasnodar (0) 0 29,132

Olympiacos: (4231) Sa; Elabdellaoui, Meriah, Semedo, Tsimikas; Bouchalakis, Guilherme; Masouras (Randelovic 75), Valbuena (Camara 87), Daniel Podence (Torosidis 90); Guerrero.
Krasnodar: (433) Safonov; Petrov, Spajic, Fjoluson, Ramirez; Cabella (Olsson 25), Kambolov, Vilhena; Wanderson, Berg (Ignatyev 69), Namli (Suleymanov 59).

Young Boys (1) 2 *(Assale 7, Hoarau 75 (pen))*

Red Star Belgrade (1) 2 *(Degenek 18, Garcia 46)* 26,375

Young Boys: (4231) von Ballmoos; Lotomba, Lustenberger, Zesiger, Garcia (Janko 67); Martins Pereira, Sierro (Fassnacht 57); Assale, Aebischer (Hoarau 73), Ngamaleu; Nsame.
Red Star Belgrade: (4231) Borjan; Gobeljic, Pankov, Degenek, Rodic; Canas, Ivanic; Garcia (Jander 55), Marin, Vukanovic (Petrovic 85); Boakye (Tomane 77).

PLAY-OFF ROUND SECOND LEG

Tuesday, 27 August 2019

Krasnodar (1) 1 *(Utkin 11)*

Olympiacos (1) 2 *(El Arabi 12, 48)* 34,627

Krasnodar: (433) Kritsyuk; Petrov (Skopintcev 56), Spajic, Fjoluson, Stotskiy; Olsson, Vilhena, Utkin (Ignatyev 67); Suleymanov (Namli 32), Berg, Wanderson.
Olympiacos: (4231) Jose Sa; Elabdellaoui, Semedo (Cisse 65), Meriah, Tsimikas; Bouchalakis, Guilherme; Masouras, Valbuena, Daniel Podence (Camara 83); El Arabi (Soudani 73).

Red Star Belgrade (0) 1 *(Vukanovic 59)*

Young Boys (0) 1 *(Ben 82 (og))* 47,487

Red Star Belgrade: (4231) Borjan; Gobeljic, Milunovic, Degenek, Rodic; Jovancic, Canas; Garcia (Ben 69), Marin, Vukanovic (Ivanic 82); Boakye (Tomane■ 60).
Young Boys: (343) von Ballmoos; Sorensen, Lustenberger, Zesiger (Fassnacht 52); Janko, Sierro (Sulejmani 65), Aebischer, Lotomba; Assale (Hoarau 65), Nsame, Ngamaleu.
Red Star Belgrade won on away goals.

Rosenborg (1) 1 *(Akintola 11)*

Dinamo Zagreb (0) 1 *(Gojak 71)* 18,173

Rosenborg: (433) Hansen; Hedenstadt (Ceide 84), Reginiussen, Hovland, Meling; Jensen, Lundemo (Trondsen 74), Konradsen; Akintola (de Lanlay 74), Soderlund, Adegbenro.
Dinamo Zagreb: (4411) Livakovic; Stojanovic, Dilaver, Peric, Leovac; Hajrovic (Gojak 66), Ademi, Moro, Orsic (Atiemwen 81); Olmo (Gavranovic 90); Petkovic.

Wednesday, 28 August 2019

Ajax (1) 2 *(Alvarez 43, Tadic 80)*

APOEL (0) 0 51,645

Ajax: (433) Onana; Dest, Veltman, Blind, Tagliafico; Alvarez (Marin 89), Ziyech (de Wit 87), Martinez; Neres, Huntelaar, Tadic.
APOEL: (541) Belec; Jakolis (De Vincenti 64), Merkis, Ioannou, Joaozinho, Mihajlovic; Al-Taamari (Vidigal 72), Matic (Hallenius 78), Lucas Souza, Bezjak; Pavlovic.

Club Brugge (0) 2 *(Vanaken 70, Bonaventure 89)*

LASK (0) 1 *(Klauss 74 (pen))* 25,319

Club Brugge: (433) Mignolet; Mata, Mitrovic, Deli, Ricca; Vormer, Rits, Vanaken; Diatta, Openda (Tau 46), Okereke (Bonaventure 88).
LASK: (343) Schlager; Pogatetz, Trauner■, Wiesinger; Ranftl, Michorl, Holland (Otubanjo 90), Renner; Frieser (Tetteh 62), Klauss, Goiginger (Raguz 72).

Slavia Prague (0) 1 *(Boril 66)*

CFR Cluj (0) 0 18,562

Slavia Prague: (4411) Kolar; Coufal, Kudela, Hovorka, Boril; Masopust (Traore 84), Soucek, Kral, Olayinka; Stanciu (Frydrych 90); Skoda (Helal 79).
CFR Cluj: (433) Arlauskis; Susic, Burca, Muresan, Camora; Luis Aurelio (Paun 64), Bordeianu, Djokovic; Deac (Hoban 70), Rondon (Tucudean 69), Omrani.

GROUP STAGE

GROUP A

Wednesday, 18 September 2019

Club Brugge (0) 0

Galatasaray (0) 0 26,616

Club Brugge: (3142) Mignolet; Mata, Mitrovic, Deli; Rits (Balanta 86); Diatta, Vormer, Vanaken, Ricca; Okereke (Openda 60), Bonaventure (Diagne 73).
Galatasaray: (433) Muslera; Mariano (Ozbayrakli 90), Luyindama, Marcao, Nagatomo; Lemina (Mor 60), Nzonzi, Seri (Donk 90); Feghouli, Falcao, Babel.

Paris Saint-Germain (2) 3 *(Di Maria 14, 33, Meunier 90)*

Real Madrid (0) 0 46,361

Paris Saint-Germain: (433) Navas; Meunier, Thiago Silva, Kimpembe, Bernat; Gueye, Marquinhos (Ander Herrera 70), Verratti; Sarabia (Diallo 89), Icardi (Choupo-Moting 60), Di Maria.
Real Madrid: (433) Courtois; Carvajal, Varane, Eder Militao, Mendy; Rodriguez (Jovic 70), Casemiro, Kroos; Bale (Vinicius Junior 79), Benzema, Hazard (Lucas 70).

Tuesday, 1 October 2019

Galatasaray (0) 0

Paris Saint-Germain (0) 1 *(Icardi 52)* 46,532

Galatasaray: (3412) Muslera; Luyindama, Donk, Marcao; Mariano, Nzonzi, Seri, Nagatomo (Bayram 77); Belhanda (Feghouli 62); Babel (Andone 64), Falcao.
Paris Saint-Germain: (433) Navas; Meunier, Thiago Silva, Kimpembe, Bernat; Gueye, Marquinhos, Verratti; Sarabia (Choupo-Moting 71), Icardi (Mbappe-Lottin 61), Di Maria (Ander Herrera 83).

Real Madrid (0) 2 *(Sergio Ramos 55, Casemiro 85)*

Club Brugge (2) 2 *(Bonaventure 9, 39)* 65,112

Real Madrid: (433) Courtois (Areola 46); Carvajal, Varane, Sergio Ramos, Nacho (Marcelo 46); Modric, Casemiro, Kroos; Lucas (Vinicius Junior 67), Benzema, Hazard.
Club Brugge: (3142) Mignolet; Mata, Mechele, Deli; Rits; Diatta, Vormer■, Vanaken, Sobol; Bonaventure (Openda 71 (Cools 87)), Tau (Schrijvers 90).

Tuesday, 22 October 2019

Club Brugge (0) 0

Paris Saint-Germain (1) 5 *(Icardi 7, 63, Mbappe-Lottin 61, 79, 83)* 26,946

Club Brugge: (3142) Mignolet; Mata, Mechele, Deli; Rits; Diatta, De Ketelaere (Okereke 57), Vanaken, Sobol (Balanta 80); Bonaventure (Openda 76), Tau.
Paris Saint-Germain: (433) Navas; Meunier, Thiago Silva, Kimpembe, Bernat; Ander Herrera (Diallo 72), Marquinhos, Verratti; Di Maria, Icardi (Paredes 65), Choupo-Moting (Mbappe-Lottin 52).

Galatasaray (0) 0

Real Madrid (1) 1 *(Kroos 18)* 48,886

Galatasaray: (3412) Muslera; Luyindama, Donk (Feghouli 46), Marcao; Mariano, Nzonzi, Seri (Mor 77), Nagatomo; Belhanda (Bayram 67); Andone, Babel.
Real Madrid: (433) Courtois; Carvajal, Varane, Sergio Ramos, Marcelo; Valverde (Rodriguez 79), Casemiro, Kroos; Rodrygo (Jovic 82), Benzema, Hazard (Vinicius Junior 79).

Wednesday, 6 November 2019

Paris Saint-Germain (1) 1 *(Icardi 21)*

Club Brugge (0) 0 47,418

Paris Saint-Germain: (433) Navas; Dagba, Thiago Silva, Kimpembe, Bernat; Gueye, Marquinhos, Verratti (Sarabia 90); Di Maria, Icardi (Cavani 72), Mbappe-Lottin (Draxler 83).
Club Brugge: (4141) Mignolet; Kossounou, Mechele, Deli, Ricca; Balanta; Bonaventure, Rits (De Ketelaere 86), Vanaken, Diatta (Schrijvers 77); Okereke (Diagne 67).

Real Madrid (4) 6 *(Rodrygo 4, 7, 90, Sergio Ramos 14 (pen), Benzema 45, 81)*

Galatasaray (0) 0 65,492

Real Madrid: (433) Courtois; Carvajal, Varane, Sergio Ramos, Marcelo (Mendy 42); Valverde, Casemiro (Modric 60), Kroos; Rodrygo, Benzema, Hazard (Isco 68).
Galatasaray: (433) Muslera; Mariano, Luyindama, Marcao, Nagatomo (Buyuk 88); Seri, Nzonzi (Bayram 46), Lemina; Feghouli, Andone (Donk 46), Babel.

Tuesday, 26 November 2019

Galatasaray (1) 1 *(Buyuk 11)*

Club Brugge (0) 1 *(Diatta 90)* 34,500

Galatasaray: (433) Muslera; Mariano, Donk, Marcao, Nagatomo; Belhanda (Mor 87), Lemina, Seri (Yardimci 90); Feghouli, Buyuk, Bayram (Inan 80).
Club Brugge: (4141) Mignolet; Mata■, Mechele, Deli, Ricca; Balanta; Bonaventure (Schrijvers 58), Rits (De Ketelaere 46), Vanaken, Diatta■; Openda (Okereke 77).

Real Madrid (1) 2 *(Benzema 17, 79)*

Paris Saint-Germain (0) 2 *(Mbappe-Lottin 81, Sarabia 83)* 75,534

Real Madrid: (4312) Courtois; Carvajal, Varane, Sergio Ramos, Marcelo; Valverde (Modric 76), Casemiro, Kroos; Isco (Rodrygo 82); Benzema, Hazard (Bale 68).
Paris Saint-Germain: (433) Navas; Meunier, Thiago Silva, Kimpembe, Bernat; Gueye (Neymar 46), Marquinhos, Verratti; Mbappe-Lottin, Icardi (Sarabia 75), Di Maria (Draxler 75).

Wednesday, 11 December 2019

Club Brugge (0) 1 *(Vanaken 55)*

Real Madrid (0) 3 *(Rodrygo 53, Vinicius Junior 64, Modric 90)* 27,306

Club Brugge: (3142) Mignolet; Kossounou, Mechele, Deli; Balanta; Vlietinck (De Ketelaere 70), Vormer, Vanaken, Sobol; Bonaventure, Tau (Schrijvers 59).
Real Madrid: (4231) Areola; Odriozola, Varane, Eder Militao, Mendy; Casemiro, Modric; Rodrygo, Isco (Valverde 84), Vinicius Junior (Diaz 73); Jovic (Benzema 77).

Paris Saint-Germain (2) 5 *(Icardi 32, Sarabia 35, Neymar 46, Mbappe-Lottin 63, Cavani 84 (pen))*

Galatasaray (0) 0 46,509

Paris Saint-Germain: (4222) Sergio Rico; Kurzawa, Marquinhos, Diallo, Bernat (Kehrer 75); Kouassi (Verratti 75), Paredes; Sarabia, Neymar; Icardi (Cavani 68), Mbappe-Lottin.
Galatasaray: (541) Muslera; Mariano, Donk, Nzonzi (Ozbayrakli 72), Marcao, Nagatomo; Belhanda, Lemina, Seri (Inan 41), Bayram; Mor (Falcao 62).

Group A Table	*P*	*W*	*D*	*L*	*F*	*A*	*GD*	*Pts*
Paris Saint-Germain	6	5	1	0	17	2	15	16
Real Madrid	6	3	2	1	14	8	6	11
Club Brugge	6	0	3	3	4	12	–8	3
Galatasaray	6	0	2	4	1	14	–13	2

GROUP B

Wednesday, 18 September 2019

Bayern Munich (1) 3 *(Coman 34, Lewandowski 80, Muller 90)*

Red Star Belgrade (0) 0 70,000

Bayern Munich: (4231) Neuer; Kimmich, Sule, Pavard, Lucas; Tolisso (Javi Martinez 65), Thiago; Coman, Coutinho (Muller 83), Perisic (Gnabry 66); Lewandowski.
Red Star Belgrade: (4231) Borjan; Gobeljic, Milunovic, Degenek, Jander; Jovancic (Vulic 62), Canas; Garcia (Vukanovic 83), Marin, van La Parra; Pavkov (Boakye 70).

Olympiacos (1) 2 *(Daniel Podence 44, Valbuena 54 (pen))*

Tottenham H (2) 2 *(Kane 26 (pen), Lucas Moura 30)* 31,001

Olympiacos: (4231) Jose Sa; Elabdellaoui, Semedo, Meriah, Tsimikas; Guilherme, Bouchalakis; Masouras (Randjelovic 78), Valbuena (Benzia 69), Daniel Podence; Guerrero (El Arabi 89).
Tottenham H: (4231) Lloris; Sanchez, Alderweireld, Vertonghen, Davies; Winks, Ndombele (Sissoko 62); Lucas Moura (Lamela 76), Eriksen, Alli (Son 73); Kane.

Tuesday, 1 October 2019

Red Star Belgrade (0) 3 *(Vulic 62, Milunovic 87, Boakye 90)*

Olympiacos (1) 1 *(Semedo 37)* 42,291

Red Star Belgrade: (4231) Borjan; Gobeljic, Milunovic, Degenek, Rodic; Jovancic (Vulic 55), Canas (Petrovic 73); Garcia, Marin, van La Parra (Boakye 61); Tomane.
Olympiacos: (4231) Jose Sa; Torosidis, Semedo, Meriah, Tsimikas; Bouchalakis, Camara (El Arabi 89); Masouras (Elabdellaoui 79), Benzia■, Lovera (Daniel Podence 61); Guerrero.

Tottenham H (1) 2 *(Son 12, Kane 61 (pen))*

Bayern Munich (2) 7 *(Kimmich 15, Lewandowski 45, 87, Gnabry 53, 55, 83, 88)* 60,127

Tottenham H: (41212) Lloris; Aurier, Alderweireld, Vertonghen, Rose; Winks (Lamela 81); Ndombele (Eriksen 64), Sissoko; Alli (Lucas Moura 71); Son, Kane.
Bayern Munich: (4231) Neuer; Pavard, Sule, Boateng (Javi Martinez 72), Alaba (Thiago 46); Kimmich, Tolisso; Coman (Perisic 71), Coutinho, Gnabry; Lewandowski.

Tuesday, 22 October 2019

Olympiacos (1) 2 *(El Arabi 23, Guilherme 79)*

Bayern Munich (1) 3 *(Lewandowski 34, 62, Tolisso 75)* 31,670

Olympiacos: (4141) Jose Sa; Elabdellaoui, Semedo, Meriah, Tsimikas; Guilherme; Daniel Podence, Bouchalakis (Lovera 69), Camara (Randjelovic 88), Masouras (Guerrero 78); El Arabi.
Bayern Munich: (4231) Neuer; Kimmich, Pavard, Lucas (Boateng 59), Alaba; Thiago, Javi Martinez (Tolisso 46); Muller (Perisic 86), Coutinho, Gnabry; Lewandowski.

Tottenham H (3) 5 *(Kane 9, 72, Son 16, 44, Lamela 57)*

Red Star Belgrade (0) 0 51,743

Tottenham H: (4231) Gazzaniga; Aurier, Sanchez, Vertonghen (Foyth 73), Davies; Sissoko, Ndombele; Lamela, Alli (Lo Celso 79), Son (Dier 68); Kane.
Red Star Belgrade: (4231) Borjan; Gobeljic, Milunovic, Degenek, Rodic; Canas (Petrovic 62), Vulic; Garcia, Marin, van La Parra (Vukanovic 82); Tomane (Pavkov 62).

Wednesday, 6 November 2019

Bayern Munich (0) 2 *(Lewandowski 69, Perisic 89)*

Olympiacos (0) 0 63,646

Bayern Munich: (4231) Neuer; Pavard, Javi Martinez, Alaba, Davies; Goretzka (Tolisso 82), Kimmich; Coman (Coutinho 90), Muller, Gnabry (Perisic 88); Lewandowski.
Olympiacos: (433) Jose Sa; Elabdellaoui, Semedo, Meriah, Tsimikas; Guilherme, Camara, Bouchalakis (Valbuena 71); Randjelovic (Masouras 61), Guerrero, Daniel Podence (El Arabi 80).

Red Star Belgrade (0) 0

Tottenham H (1) 4 *(Lo Celso 34, Son 57, 61, Eriksen 85)* 42,381

Red Star Belgrade: (4231) Borjan; Gobeljic (Jander 46), Milunovic, Degenek, Rodic; Petrovic, Jovancic (Canas 62); Garcia (Boakye 68), Marin, van La Parra; Pavkov.
Tottenham H: (4231) Gazzaniga; Foyth, Sanchez, Dier, Rose; Sissoko, Ndombele; Lo Celso (Skipp 86), Alli (Eriksen 62), Son (Sessegnon 75); Kane.

Tuesday, 26 November 2019

Red Star Belgrade (0) 0

Bayern Munich (1) 6 *(Goretzka 14, Lewandowski 53 (pen), 60, 64, 67, Tolisso 89)* 44,118

Red Star Belgrade: (4411) Borjan; Gobeljic, Milunovic, Degenek, Rodic; Garcia (Pankov 69), Canas (Vulic 61), Petrovic (Ivanic 76), Vukanovic; Marin; Boakye.
Bayern Munich: (433) Neuer; Pavard, Javi Martinez (Kimmich 68), Boateng, Davies; Tolisso, Thiago, Goretzka; Coman, Lewandowski (Muller 77), Coutinho (Perisic 60).

Tottenham H (1) 4 *(Alli 45, Kane 50, 77, Aurier 73)*

Olympiacos (2) 2 *(El Arabi 6, Semedo 19)* 57,024

Tottenham H: (4231) Gazzaniga; Aurier, Sanchez, Alderweireld, Rose; Winks, Dier (Eriksen 29); Lucas Moura (Sissoko 61), Alli (Ndombele 83), Son; Kane.
Olympiacos: (433) Jose Sa; Elabdellaoui, Semedo, Meriah, Tsimikas; Camara, Guilherme, Bouchalakis (Valbuena 74); Daniel Podence (Randjelovic 79), El Arabi (Guerrero 85), Masouras.

Wednesday, 11 December 2019

Bayern Munich (2) 3 *(Coman 14, Muller 45, Coutinho 64)*

Tottenham H (1) 1 *(Sessegnon 20)* 68,353

Bayern Munich: (433) Neuer; Pavard, Boateng, Javi Martinez (Goretzka 87), Davies; Thiago, Kimmich, Coutinho; Gnabry, Perisic (Zirkzee 86), Coman (Muller 27).
Tottenham H: (4231) Gazzaniga; Walker-Peters, Foyth, Alderweireld, Rose; Sissoko, Dier (Wanyama 81); Lo Celso (Skipp 65), Eriksen, Sessegnon; Lucas Moura (Son 65).

Olympiacos (0) 1 *(El Arabi 87 (pen))*

Red Star Belgrade (0) 0 31,896

Olympiacos: (433) Jose Sa; Elabdellaoui, Semedo, Meriah, Tsimikas; Guilherme, Camara (Guerrero 61), Bouchalakis; Daniel Podence, El Arabi (Benzia 90), Masouras (Lovera 71).
Red Star Belgrade: (4231) Borjan; Gobeljic, Milunovic, Degenek, Rodic (Jander 82); Ivanic, Petrovic; Garcia, Marin, Vukanovic (Boakye 65); Tomane (van La Parra 58).

Group B Table	*P*	*W*	*D*	*L*	*F*	*A*	*GD*	*Pts*
Bayern Munich	6	6	0	0	24	5	19	18
Tottenham H	6	3	1	2	18	14	4	10
Olympiacos	6	1	1	4	8	14	−6	4
Red Star Belgrade	6	1	0	5	3	20	−17	3

GROUP C

Wednesday, 18 September 2019

Dinamo Zagreb (3) 4 *(Leovac 10, Orsic 31, 42, 68)*

Atalanta (0) 0 28,863

Dinamo Zagreb: (343) Livakovic; Theophile-Catherine, Dilaver, Peric; Stojanovic, Moro (Gojak 73), Ademi, Leovac; Orsic (Ivanusec 76), Petkovic (Gavranovic 83), Olmo.
Atalanta: (3421) Gollini; Toloi, Djimsiti, Masiello (Malinovsky 46); Hateboer, de Roon, Freuler (Pasalic 46), Gosens; Ilicic (Barrow 88), Gomez; Zapata.

Shakhtar Donetsk (0) 0

Manchester C (2) 3 *(Mahrez 24, Gundogan 38, Gabriel Jesus 76)* 36,675

Shakhtar Donetsk: (4231) Pyatov; Bolbat, Kryvtsov, Matviyenko, Ismaily; Alan Patrick (Marcos Antonio 74), Stepanenko; Solomon (Konoplyanka 46), Marlos, Taison; Moraes (Dentinho 77).
Manchester C: (4231) Ederson; Walker (Joao Cancelo 81), Otamendi, Fernandinho, Zinchenko; Rodri (Mendy 83), Gundogan; Mahrez, De Bruyne (Bernardo Silva 77), Sterling; Gabriel Jesus.

Tuesday, 1 October 2019

Atalanta (1) 1 *(Zapata 28)*

Shakhtar Donetsk (1) 2 *(Moraes 41, Solomon 90)* 26,022

Atalanta: (3412) Gollini; Toloi, Palomino, Masiello (Muriel 68); Hateboer (Gosens 57), de Roon, Pasalic, Castagne; Gomez; Ilicic (Malinovsky 57), Zapata.
Shakhtar Donetsk: (4141) Pyatov; Bolbat (Dodo 90), Kryvtsov, Matviyenko, Ismaily; Stepanenko; Marlos (Konoplyanka 86), Kovalenko, Alan Patrick (Solomon 69), Taison; Moraes.

Manchester C (0) 2 *(Sterling 66, Foden 90)*

Dinamo Zagreb (0) 0 49,046

Manchester C: (433) Ederson; Joao Cancelo, Fernandinho, Otamendi, Mendy; Gundogan, Rodri, Silva (Foden 90); Mahrez, Aguero (Gabriel Jesus 89), Bernardo Silva (Sterling 56).
Dinamo Zagreb: (532) Livakovic; Stojanovic, Theophile-Catherine (Gavranovic 76), Dilaver, Peric, Leovac; Ademi, Moro, Olmo; Orsic (Gojak 62), Petkovic (Atiemwen 84).

Tuesday, 22 October 2019

Manchester C (2) 5 *(Aguero 34, 38 (pen), Sterling 58, 64, 69)*

Atalanta (1) 1 *(Malinovsky 28 (pen))* 49,306

Manchester C: (4231) Ederson; Walker, Rodri (Stones 41), Fernandinho, Mendy (Joao Cancelo 71); De Bruyne (Otamendi 67), Gundogan; Mahrez, Foden■, Sterling; Aguero.
Atalanta: (3412) Gollini; Toloi, Djimsiti, Masiello (Pasalic 46); Castagne, de Roon, Freuler, Gosens; Malinovsky; Ilicic (Hateboer 72), Gomez (Muriel 46).

Shakhtar Donetsk (1) 2 *(Konoplyanka 16, Dodo 75)*

Dinamo Zagreb (1) 2 *(Olmo 25, Orsic 60 (pen))* 21,526

Shakhtar Donetsk: (4231) Pyatov; Bolbat (Dodo 66), Kryvtsov, Matviyenko, Ismaily; Stepanenko, Alan Patrick; Marlos (Kovalenko 84), Taison, Konoplyanka (Solomon 66); Moraes.
Dinamo Zagreb: (541) Livakovic; Stojanovic, Theophile-Catherine, Dilaver, Peric, Leovac; Olmo, Ademi (Gojak 68), Moro, Orsic (Ivanusec 90); Gavranovic (Petkovic 62).

Wednesday, 6 November 2019

Atalanta (0) 1 *(Pasalic 49)*

Manchester C (1) 1 *(Sterling 7)* 32,147

Atalanta: (3412) Gollini; Toloi, Palomino, Djimsiti; Hateboer, de Roon, Freuler (Malinovsky 84), Castagne (Muriel 90); Gomez; Ilicic, Pasalic.
Manchester C: (433) Ederson (Bravo■ 46); Joao Cancelo, Otamendi, Fernandinho, Mendy; De Bruyne, Gundogan, Bernardo Silva; Mahrez (Walker 88), Gabriel Jesus (Aguero 73), Sterling.

Dinamo Zagreb (1) 3 *(Petkovic 25, Ivanusec 83, Ademi 89)*

Shakhtar Donetsk (1) 3 *(Alan Patrick 13, Moraes 90, Tete 90 (pen))* 28,316

Dinamo Zagreb: (352) Livakovic; Theophile-Catherine, Dilaver, Peric; Stojanovic (Ivanusec 72), Olmo, Moro■, Ademi, Leovac; Petkovic (Kadzior 90), Orsic (Gjira 77).
Shakhtar Donetsk: (4231) Pyatov; Dodo, Kryvtsov, Matviyenko (Dentinho 86), Ismaily; Alan Patrick (Tete 84), Stepanenko (Marcos Antonio 90); Marlos■, Kovalenko, Taison; Moraes.

Tuesday, 26 November 2019

Atalanta (1) 2 *(Muriel 27 (pen), Gomez 47)*

Dinamo Zagreb (0) 0 28,365

Atalanta: (3421) Gollini; Toloi, Kjaer, Palomino; Hateboer (Castagne 65), de Roon, Freuler, Gosens; Gomez (Malinovsky 90), Pasalic; Muriel (Ilicic 61).
Dinamo Zagreb: (352) Livakovic; Theophile-Catherine, Dilaver, Peric; Stojanovic (Gjira 75), Olmo (Situm 90), Ademi, Ivanusec (Gojak 67), Leovac; Petkovic, Orsic.

Manchester C (0) 1 *(Gundogan 56)*

Shakhtar Donetsk (0) 1 *(Solomon 69)* 52,020

Manchester C: (433) Ederson; Joao Cancelo, Otamendi, Fernandinho, Angelino; De Bruyne (Silva 70), Rodri (Foden 76), Gundogan; Bernardo Silva, Gabriel Jesus, Sterling.
Shakhtar Donetsk: (4141) Pyatov; Dodo, Kryvtsov, Matviyenko, Ismaily; Stepanenko; Tete, Kovalenko (Marcos Antonio 81), Alan Patrick, Konoplyanka (Solomon 65); Moraes (Sikan 90).

Wednesday, 11 December 2019

Dinamo Zagreb (1) 1 *(Olmo 10)*

Manchester C (1) 4 *(Gabriel Jesus 34, 50, 54, Foden 84)* 29,385

Dinamo Zagreb: (4411) Livakovic; Stojanovic, Ademi, Dilaver, Moubandje; Kadzior (Gjira 59), Moro, Gojak (Majer 81), Orsic (Hajrovic 81); Olmo; Petkovic.
Manchester C: (433) Bravo; Joao Cancelo, Otamendi (Harwood-Bellis 82), Garcia, Mendy; Gundogan, Rodri (Sterling 73), Foden; Mahrez, Gabriel Jesus (Zinchenko 66), Bernardo Silva.

Shakhtar Donetsk (0) 0

Atalanta (0) 3 *(Castagne 66, Pasalic 80, Gosens 90)* 26,536

Shakhtar Donetsk: (4141) Pyatov; Dodo■, Kryvtsov, Matviyenko, Ismaily; Stepanenko; Tete (Marlos 59), Kovalenko (Solomon 71), Alan Patrick, Taison; Moraes.
Atalanta: (3412) Gollini; Djimsiti, Palomino, Masiello (Malinovsky 61); Castagne, de Roon, Freuler, Gosens; Pasalic; Muriel (Ibanez 71), Gomez (Hateboer 90).

Group C Table	P	W	D	L	F	A	GD	Pts
Manchester C	6	4	2	0	16	4	12	14
Atalanta	6	2	1	3	8	12	–4	7
Shakhtar Donetsk	6	1	3	2	8	13	–5	6
Dinamo Zagreb	6	1	2	3	10	13	–3	5

GROUP D

Wednesday, 18 September 2019

Atletico Madrid (0) 2 *(Savic 70, Herrera 90)*

Juventus (0) 2 *(Cuadrado 48, Matuidi 65)* 66,283

Atletico Madrid: (442) Oblak; Trippier, Savic, Gimenez, Renan Lodi (Vitolo 76); Koke, Thomas (Herrera 76), Saul, Lemar (Correa 60); Joao Felix, Costa.
Juventus: (433) Szczesny; Danilo, Bonucci, de Ligt, Alex Sandro; Khedira (Bentancur 69), Pjanic (Ramsey 87), Matuidi; Cuadrado, Higuain (Dybala 80), Ronaldo.

Bayer Leverkusen (1) 1 *(Howedes 25 (og))*

Lokomotiv Moscow (2) 2 *(Krychowiak 16, Barinov 37)* 26,592

Bayer Leverkusen: (4231) Hradecky; Bender L, Tah, Bender S, Wendell; Aranguiz, Baumgartlinger (Amiri 71); Bellarabi, Havertz, Bailey (Alario 46); Volland.
Lokomotiv Moscow: (451) Guilherme; Ignatiev, Howedes, Corluka, Rybus; Zhemaletdinov, Barinov, Murilo, Krychowiak, Joao Mario (Idowu 90); Smolov.

Tuesday, 1 October 2019

Juventus (1) 3 *(Higuain 17, Bernardeschi 61, Ronaldo 88)*

Bayer Leverkusen (0) 0 34,525

Juventus: (4312) Szczesny; Cuadrado, Bonucci, de Ligt, Alex Sandro; Khedira (Bentancur 74), Pjanic, Matuidi; Bernardeschi (Ramsey 78); Higuain (Dybala 83), Ronaldo.
Bayer Leverkusen: (442) Hradecky; Weiser, Tah, Bender S, Wendell; Havertz, Aranguiz (Sinkgraven 80), Baumgartlinger, Demirbay (Amiri 46); Volland, Alario (Paulinho 68).

Lokomotiv Moscow (0) 0

Atletico Madrid (0) 2 *(Joao Felix 48, Thomas 58)* 27,051

Lokomotiv Moscow: (4141) Guilherme; Ignatiev (Eder 80), Howedes, Corluka, Rybus; Murilo; Zhemaletdinov (Idowu 33), Barinov, Krychowiak, Joao Mario; Smolov (Kolomeytsev 83).
Atletico Madrid: (442) Oblak; Arias, Gimenez, Felipe, Renan Lodi; Joao Felix (Hermoso 84), Thomas, Koke (Correa 87), Saul; Costa (Lemar 77), Morata.

Tuesday, 22 October 2019

Atletico Madrid (0) 1 *(Morata 78)*

Bayer Leverkusen (0) 0 56,776

Atletico Madrid: (41212) Oblak; Trippier, Gimenez (Hermoso 15), Felipe, Renan Lodi; Thomas; Herrera, Koke (Morata 70); Saul; Correa (Lemar 62), Costa.
Bayer Leverkusen: (4231) Hradecky; Weiser, Tah, Bender S (Dragovic 90), Bender L; Demirbay (Alario 84), Baumgartlinger; Bellarabi, Havertz (Paulinho 76), Amiri; Volland.

Juventus (0) 2 *(Dybala 77, 79)*

Lokomotiv Moscow (1) 1 *(Aleksey Miranchuk 30)* 38,547

Juventus: (4312) Szczesny; Cuadrado, Bonucci, de Ligt, Alex Sandro; Khedira (Higuain 48), Pjanic, Matuidi (Rabiot 65); Bentancur; Dybala (Bernardeschi 81), Ronaldo.
Lokomotiv Moscow: (532) Guilherme; Ignatiev, Murilo, Corluka, Howedes, Idowu; Krychowiak (Kolomeytsev 83), Barinov, Joao Mario; Aleksey Miranchuk, Eder.

Wednesday, 6 November 2019

Bayer Leverkusen (1) 2 *(Thomas 41 (og), Volland 55)*

Atletico Madrid (0) 1 *(Morata 90)* 28,160

Bayer Leverkusen: (4231) Hradecky; Weiser, Tah, Bender S, Wendell (Retsos 81); Aranguiz (Baumgartlinger 65), Demirbay; Bellarabi, Havertz (Dragovic 88), Amiri■; Volland.
Atletico Madrid: (41212) Oblak; Arias, Felipe, Hermoso, Renan Lodi (Lemar 52); Thomas; Koke, Saul; Correa (Herrera 70); Morata, Costa (Vitolo 61).

Lokomotiv Moscow (1) 1 *(Aleksey Miranchuk 12)*

Juventus (1) 2 *(Ramsey 3, Douglas Costa 90)* 26,881

Lokomotiv Moscow: (4411) Guilherme; Ignatiev, Howedes, Corluka, Rybus; Zhemaletdinov (Murilo 81), Barinov, Krychowiak, Joao Mario (Kolomeytsev 85); Aleksey Miranchuk; Eder.
Juventus: (4312) Szczesny; Danilo, Bonucci, Rugani, Alex Sandro; Khedira (Douglas Costa 70), Pjanic, Rabiot; Ramsey (Bentancur 64); Higuain, Ronaldo (Dybala 82).

Tuesday, 26 November 2019

Juventus (1) 1 *(Dybala 45)*

Atletico Madrid (0) 0 40,486

Juventus: (41212) Szczesny; Danilo, Bonucci, de Ligt, De Sciglio; Pjanic; Bentancur (Khedira 86), Matuidi; Ramsey (Bernardeschi 63); Dybala (Higuain 76), Ronaldo.
Atletico Madrid: (442) Oblak; Trippier, Felipe, Hermoso, Renan Lodi (Lemar 64); Saul, Herrera (Correa 60), Thomas, Koke; Morata, Vitolo (Joao Felix 54).

Lokomotiv Moscow (0) 0
Bayer Leverkusen (1) 2 *(Zhemaletdinov 11 (og), Bender S 54)* 25,757
Lokomotiv Moscow: (4411) Guilherme; Ignatiev, Howedes, Corluka, Rybus; Zhemaletdinov (Kulikov 65), Barinov, Krychowiak, Anton Miranchuk; Aleksey Miranchuk; Eder (Smolov 77).
Bayer Leverkusen: (4231) Hradecky; Retsos, Tah, Bender S, Wendell; Aranguiz, Demirbay (Bender L 90); Bellarabi (Alario 77), Diaby, Bailey (Baumgartlinger 46); Volland.

Wednesday, 11 December 2019
Atletico Madrid (1) 2 *(Joao Felix 17 (pen), Felipe 54)*
Lokomotiv Moscow (0) 0 58,426
Atletico Madrid: (442) Oblak; Trippier, Felipe, Hermoso, Renan Lodi; Correa (Herrera 68), Thomas, Koke (Lemar 73), Saul; Morata, Joao Felix (Llorente 81).
Lokomotiv Moscow: (541) Kochenkov; Idowu, Howedes, Kvirkvelia, Corluka (Magkeev 69), Rybus; Aleksey Miranchuk, Murilo, Krychowiak, Zhemaletdinov; Eder (Smolov 75).

Bayer Leverkusen (0) 0
Juventus (0) 2 *(Ronaldo 75, Higuain 90)* 29,542
Bayer Leverkusen: (442) Hradecky; Bender L, Dragovic, Bender S, Sinkgraven; Bellarabi (Bailey 66), Demirbay (Baumgartlinger 66), Aranguiz, Diaby; Havertz, Alario (Volland 82).
Juventus: (4312) Buffon; Danilo, Demiral, Rugani, De Sciglio; Cuadrado (Muratore 90), Pjanic, Rabiot (Matuidi 85); Bernardeschi (Dybala 66); Higuain, Ronaldo.

Group D Table	P	W	D	L	F	A	GD	Pts
Juventus	6	5	1	0	12	4	8	16
Atletico Madrid	6	3	1	2	8	5	3	10
Bayer Leverkusen	6	2	0	4	5	9	–4	6
Lokomotiv Moscow	6	1	0	5	4	11	–7	3

GROUP E

Tuesday, 17 September 2019
Napoli (0) 2 *(Mertens 82 (pen), Llorente 90)*
Liverpool (0) 0 38,878
Napoli: (442) Meret; Di Lorenzo, Manolas, Koulibaly, Rui; Callejon, Allan (Elmas 75), Fabian, Insigne (Zielinski 66); Mertens, Lozano (Llorente 69).
Liverpool: (433) Adrian; Alexander-Arnold, Matip, van Dijk, Robertson; Henderson (Shaqiri 87), Fabinho, Milner (Wijnaldum 66); Salah, Firmino, Mane.

Red Bull Salzburg (5) 6 *(Haland 2, 34, 45, Hwang 36, Szoboszlai 45, Ulmer 66)*
Genk (1) 2 *(Lucumi 40, Samatta 52)* 29,520
Red Bull Salzburg: (4222) Stankovic; Nissen (Farkas 83), Ramalho, Wober, Ulmer; Bernede, Junuzovic; Minamino, Szoboszlai (Okugawa 62); Hwang, Haland (Daka 72).
Genk: (4411) Coucke; Maehle, Dewaest, Lucumi, Uronen; Ito (Bongonda 46), Berge, Hrosovsky, Ndongala (Hagi 72); Heynen (Onuachu 85); Samatta.

Wednesday, 2 October 2019
Genk (0) 0
Napoli (0) 0 19,962
Genk: (4231) Coucke; Maehle, Cuesta, Lucumi, Uronen; Berge, Hrosovsky; Ito, Hagi (Heynen 90), Bongonda (Paintsil 89); Samatta.
Napoli: (442) Meret; Di Lorenzo, Manolas, Koulibaly, Rui (Malcuit 33); Callejon, Allan, Elmas (Mertens 58), Fabian; Lozano, Milik (Llorente 72).

Liverpool (3) 4 *(Mane 9, Robertson 25, Salah 36, 69)*
Red Bull Salzburg (1) 3 *(Hwang 39, Minamino 56, Haland 60)* 52,243
Liverpool: (433) Adrian; Alexander-Arnold, Gomez, van Dijk, Robertson; Henderson (Milner 62), Fabinho, Wijnaldum (Origi 64); Salah (Keita 90), Firmino, Mane.
Red Bull Salzburg: (442) Stankovic; Nissen, Onguene, Wober, Ulmer; Minamino, Mwepu, Junuzovic (Ashimeru 78), Szoboszlai (Okugawa 71); Daka (Haland 56), Hwang.

Wednesday, 23 October 2019
Genk (0) 1 *(Odey 88)*
Liverpool (1) 4 *(Oxlade-Chamberlain 2, 57, Mane 77, Salah 87)* 19,626
Genk: (4411) Coucke; Maehle, Cuesta, Lucumi, Uronen; Ito (Hagi 87), Heynen, Berge, Bongonda (Ndongala 66); Samatta; Onuachu (Odey 81).
Liverpool: (433) Alisson; Milner, Lovren, van Dijk, Robertson (Gomez 63); Oxlade-Chamberlain (Wijnaldum 74), Fabinho, Keita; Salah, Firmino (Origi 80), Mane.

Red Bull Salzburg (1) 2 *(Haland 40 (pen), 72)*
Napoli (1) 3 *(Mertens 17, 64, Insigne 73)* 29,520
Red Bull Salzburg: (4231) Stankovic (Coronel 33); Nissen, Ramalho, Wober, Ulmer; Junuzovic, Mwepu (Koita 89); Daka (Ashimeru 68), Minamino, Hwang; Haland.
Napoli: (442) Meret; Malcuit, Koulibaly, Luperto, Di Lorenzo; Callejon (Elmas 80), Allan, Fabian, Zielinski; Mertens (Llorente 76), Lozano (Insigne 65).

Tuesday, 5 November 2019
Liverpool (1) 2 *(Wijnaldum 14, Oxlade-Chamberlain 53)*
Genk (1) 1 *(Samatta 40)* 52,611
Liverpool: (433) Alisson; Alexander-Arnold, Gomez, van Dijk, Milner; Wijnaldum, Fabinho, Keita (Robertson 74); Salah, Oxlade-Chamberlain (Mane 75), Origi (Firmino 89).
Genk: (352) Coucke; Cuesta, Dewaest, Lucumi; Maehle, Hrosovsky (Bongonda 85), Berge, Heynen, De Norre (Onuachu 85); Ito (Ndongala 68), Samatta.

Napoli (1) 1 *(Lozano 44)*
Red Bull Salzburg (1) 1 *(Haland 11 (pen))* 32,862
Napoli: (442) Meret; Di Lorenzo, Maksimovic, Koulibaly, Rui (Luperto 46); Callejon, Fabian, Zielinski, Insigne; Mertens (Milik 73), Lozano (Llorente 86).
Red Bull Salzburg: (532) Coronel; Nissen, Pongracic (Mwepu 46), Onguene, Wober, Ulmer; Minamino (Ashimeru 61), Junuzovic, Szoboszlai; Haland (Daka 75), Hwang.

Wednesday, 27 November 2019
Genk (0) 1 *(Samatta 85)*
Red Bull Salzburg (2) 4 *(Daka 43, Minamino 45, Hwang 69, Haland 87)* 17,284
Genk: (4141) Coucke; Maehle, Dewaest, Lucumi, De Norre; Cuesta; Ito (Hagi 79), Hrosovsky (Onuachu 59), Berge, Paintsil (Bongonda 65); Samatta.
Red Bull Salzburg: (41212) Coronel; Nissen, Onguene, Wober, Ulmer; Junuzovic; Mwepu, Szoboszlai (Okugawa 80); Minamino (Vallci 89); Daka (Haland 62), Hwang.

Liverpool (0) 1 *(Lovren 65)*
Napoli (1) 1 *(Mertens 21)* 52,128
Liverpool: (433) Alisson; Gomez (Oxlade-Chamberlain 57), Lovren, van Dijk, Robertson; Henderson, Fabinho (Wijnaldum 19), Milner (Alexander-Arnold 78); Salah, Firmino, Mane.
Napoli: (442) Meret; Maksimovic, Manolas, Koulibaly, Rui; Di Lorenzo, Allan, Fabian, Zielinski (Younes 85); Mertens (Elmas 81), Lozano (Llorente 72).

Tuesday, 10 December 2019
Napoli (3) 4 *(Milik 3, 26, 38 (pen), Mertens 74 (pen))*
Genk (0) 0 22,265
Napoli: (442) Meret; Di Lorenzo, Manolas, Koulibaly, Rui; Callejon (Llorente 79), Allan, Fabian, Zielinski (Gaetano 72); Mertens, Milik (Lozano 78).
Genk: (442) Vandevoordt; Maehle, Dewaest, Lucumi, De Norre (Borges 82); Ito (Hagi 72), Hrosovsky, Berge, Paintsil; Samatta (Bongonda 63), Onuachu.

Red Bull Salzburg (0) 0
Liverpool (0) 2 *(Keita 57, Salah 58)* 29,520
Red Bull Salzburg: (41212) Stankovic; Nissen, Onguene, Wober, Ulmer; Junuzovic (Daka 68); Mwepu, Szoboszlai (Ashimeru 90); Minamino; Hwang, Haland (Okugawa 75).

Liverpool: (433) Alisson; Alexander-Arnold, Lovren (Gomez 53), van Dijk, Robertson; Keita (Origi 87), Henderson, Wijnaldum; Salah, Firmino (Milner 75), Mane.

Group E Table	P	W	D	L	F	A	GD	Pts
Liverpool	6	4	1	1	13	8	5	13
Napoli	6	3	3	0	11	4	7	12
Red Bull Salzburg	6	2	1	3	16	13	3	7
Genk	6	0	1	5	5	20	–15	1

GROUP F

Tuesday, 17 September 2019

Borussia Dortmund (0) 0

Barcelona (0) 0 66,099

Borussia Dortmund: (4231) Burki; Hakimi, Akanji, Hummels, Guerreiro; Witsel, Delaney; Hazard (Brandt 73), Reus, Sancho; Alcacer (Bruun Larsen 87).
Barcelona: (433) ter Stegen; Nelson Semedo, Pique, Lenglet, Jordi Alba (Sergi Roberto 40); Arthur, Busquets (Rakitic 60), de Jong; Fati (Messi 59), Suarez, Griezmann.

Internazionale (0) 1 *(Barella 90)*

Slavia Prague (0) 1 *(Olayinka 63)* 50,128

Internazionale: (352) Handanovic; D'Ambrosio, de Vrij, Skriniar; Candreva (Lazaro 49), Gagliardini, Brozovic (Barella 71), Sensi, Asamoah; Lukaku, Martinez (Politano 72).
Slavia Prague: (41212) Kolar; Coufal, Kudela, Hovorka, Boril; Soucek; Traore (Zeleny 60), Husbauer; Stanciu; Masopust (Helal 79), Olayinka (Provod 85).

Wednesday, 2 October 2019

Barcelona (0) 2 *(Suarez 58, 84)*

Internazionale (1) 1 *(Martinez 2)* 86,141

Barcelona: (433) ter Stegen; Sergi Roberto, Pique, Lenglet, Nelson Semedo; de Jong, Busquets (Vidal 53), Arthur; Messi, Suarez, Griezmann (Dembele 66).
Internazionale: (3142) Handanovic; Godin, de Vrij, Skriniar; Brozovic; Candreva (D'Ambrosio 71), Barella, Sensi (Politano 79), Asamoah; Sanchez (Gagliardini 66), Martinez.

Slavia Prague (0) 0

Borussia Dortmund (1) 2 *(Hakimi 35, 89)* 19,370

Slavia Prague: (4231) Kolar; Coufal, Kudela, Hovorka, Boril; Sevcik, Soucek; Masopust (Zeleny 76), Stanciu (Skoda 83), Olayinka; Tecl (van Buren 59).
Borussia Dortmund: (4231) Burki; Piszczek, Akanji, Hummels, Guerreiro; Delaney, Witsel; Sancho (Hazard 74), Brandt (Gotze 90), Hakimi (Zagadou 90); Reus.

Wednesday, 23 October 2019

Internazionale (1) 2 *(Martinez 22, Candreva 89)*

Borussia Dortmund (0) 0 65,673

Internazionale: (3142) Handanovic; Godin, de Vrij, Skriniar; Brozovic; Candreva, Gagliardini, Barella, Asamoah (Biraghi 80); Lukaku (Esposito 62), Martinez (Valero 90).
Borussia Dortmund: (343) Burki; Akanji (Bruun Larsen 74), Weigl, Hummels; Hakimi, Witsel, Delaney (Dahoud 65), Schulz; Sancho, Brandt, Hazard (Guerreiro 84).

Slavia Prague (0) 1 *(Boril 50)*

Barcelona (1) 2 *(Messi 3, Olayinka 57 (og))* 19,170

Slavia Prague: (4312) Kolar; Coufal, Kudela, Hovorka, Boril; Sevcik, Soucek, Zeleny (Tecl 46); Stanciu (Husbauer 77); Masopust (van Buren 76), Olayinka.
Barcelona: (433) ter Stegen; Nelson Semedo, Pique, Lenglet, Jordi Alba; de Jong, Busquets (Vidal 78), Arthur (Rakitic 84); Messi, Suarez, Griezmann (Dembele 69).

Tuesday, 5 November 2019

Barcelona (0) 0

Slavia Prague (0) 0 67,023

Barcelona: (4231) ter Stegen; Nelson Semedo, Pique, Lenglet, Jordi Alba (Sergi Roberto 46); de Jong, Busquets (Rakitic 68); Dembele (Fati 65), Vidal, Griezmann; Messi.
Slavia Prague: (4141) Kolar; Coufal, Kudela, Frydrych, Boril; Soucek; Sevcik, Traore (Tecl 57), Stanciu (Husbauer 63), Olayinka; Masopust (Provod 82).

Borussia Dortmund (0) 3 *(Hakimi 51, 77, Brandt 64)*

Internazionale (2) 2 *(Martinez 5, Vecino 40)* 66,099

Borussia Dortmund: (4231) Burki; Hakimi, Akanji, Hummels, Schulz; Witsel, Weigl; Sancho (Piszczek 82), Brandt, Hazard (Guerreiro 88); Gotze (Alcacer 64).
Internazionale: (3142) Handanovic; Godin, de Vrij, Skriniar; Brozovic; Candreva, Vecino (Sensi 68), Barella, Biraghi (Lazaro 66); Lukaku (Politano 73), Martinez.

Wednesday, 27 November 2019

Barcelona (2) 3 *(Suarez 29, Messi 33, Griezmann 67)*

Borussia Dortmund (0) 1 *(Sancho 77)* 90,071

Barcelona: (433) ter Stegen; Sergi Roberto, Umtiti, Lenglet, Firpo; Rakitic (Vidal 78), Busquets, de Jong; Messi, Suarez (Wague 90), Dembele (Griezmann 26).
Borussia Dortmund: (442) Burki; Piszczek (Zagadou 76), Akanji, Hummels, Guerreiro; Hakimi, Witsel, Weigl (Gotze 85), Schulz (Sancho 46); Brandt, Reus.

Slavia Prague (1) 1 *(Soucek 37 (pen))*

Internazionale (1) 3 *(Martinez 19, 88, Lukaku 81)* 19,370

Slavia Prague: (4132) Kolar; Coufal, Kudela, Frydrych (Takacs 83), Boril; Soucek; Sevcik, Stanciu (Traore 58), Husbauer (Zeleny 70); Masopust, Olayinka.
Internazionale: (352) Handanovic; Godin, de Vrij, Skriniar; Candreva, Vecino (Esposito 80), Valero (Gagliardini 76), Brozovic, Biraghi (Lazaro 76); Lukaku, Martinez.

Tuesday, 10 December 2019

Borussia Dortmund (1) 2 *(Sancho 10, Brandt 61)*

Slavia Prague (1) 1 *(Soucek 43)* 65,079

Borussia Dortmund: (3421) Burki; Akanji, Hummels, Zagadou; Hakimi (Balerdi 83), Weigl■, Brandt, Guerreiro; Hazard (Piszczek 83), Sancho (Dahoud 87); Reus.
Slavia Prague: (4231) Kolar; Coufal, Takacs (Husbauer 83), Kudela, Boril; Sevcik, Soucek; Masopust (Traore 72), Stanciu, Olayinka; Skoda (Helal 65).

Internazionale (1) 1 *(Lukaku 44)*

Barcelona (1) 2 *(Perez 23, Fati 86)* 71,818

Internazionale: (352) Handanovic; Godin, de Vrij, Skriniar; D'Ambrosio (Politano 75), Vecino, Brozovic, Valero (Esposito 77), Biraghi (Lazaro 69); Lukaku, Martinez.
Barcelona: (3142) Neto; Todibo, Umtiti, Lenglet; Rakitic (de Jong 63); Wague, Vidal, Alena, Firpo; Perez (Fati 85), Griezmann (Suarez 62).

Group F Table	P	W	D	L	F	A	GD	Pts
Barcelona	6	4	2	0	9	4	5	14
Borussia Dortmund	6	3	1	2	8	8	0	10
Internazionale	6	2	1	3	10	9	1	7
Slavia Prague	6	0	2	4	4	10	–6	2

GROUP G

Tuesday, 17 September 2019

Benfica (0) 1 *(Seferovic 84)*

RB Leipzig (0) 2 *(Werner 69, 78)* 46,460

Benfica: (442) Vlachodimos; Tavares, Dias, Ferro, Grimaldo; Pizzi (Rafa Silva 76), Fejsa, Taarabt, Cervi (Seferovic 76); De Tomas, Jota (David Tavares 67).
RB Leipzig: (442) Gulacsi; Mukiele, Konate, Orban, Halstenberg (Klostermann 83); Sabitzer, Laimer (Haidara 39), Demme, Forsberg (Nkunku 88); Poulsen, Werner.

Lyon (0) 1 *(Depay 51 (pen))*

Zenit St Petersburg (1) 1 *(Azmoun 41)* 47,201

Lyon: (433) Lopes; Dubois, Marcelo, Denayer, Kone; Thiago Mendes, Tousart, Reine-Adelaide (Terrier 85); Traore (Cornet 77), Dembele, Depay.
Zenit St Petersburg: (3412) Lunev; Osorio, Ivanovic, Rakitskiy; Karavaev (Shatov 78), Barrios, Douglas Santos, Zhirkov (Kuzyaev 64); Driussi; Azmoun (Ozdoev 47), Dzyuba.

Wednesday, 2 October 2019

RB Leipzig (0) 0

Lyon (1) 2 *(Depay 11, Terrier 65)* 40,194

RB Leipzig: (3412) Gulacsi; Konate (Mukiele 23), Upamecano (Nkunku 66), Orban; Klostermann, Laimer, Haidara (Forsberg 58), Halstenberg; Sabitzer; Poulsen, Werner.
Lyon: (352) Lopes; Marcelo, Andersen, Marcal; Dubois, Thiago Mendes, Aouar (Jean Lucas 87), Tousart, Kone; Terrier (Traore 69), Depay (Dembele 79).

Zenit St Petersburg (1) 3 *(Dzyuba 21, Dias 70 (og), Azmoun 78)*

Benfica (0) 1 *(De Tomas 85)* 51,683

Zenit St Petersburg: (442) Lunev; Smolnikov (Osorio 63), Ivanovic, Rakitskiy, Douglas Santos; Shatov (Karavaev 68), Ozdoev, Barrios, Driussi; Azmoun (Erokhin 81), Dzyuba.
Benfica: (4231) Vlachodimos; Tavares, Dias, Jardel, Grimaldo; Fejsa (Caio 60), Pires; Pizzi (Vinicius 60), Taarabt, Rafa Silva; Seferovic (De Tomas 81).

Wednesday, 23 October 2019

Benfica (1) 2 *(Rafa Silva 4, Pizzi 85)*

Lyon (0) 1 *(Depay 70)* 53,035

Benfica: (442) Vlachodimos; Tavares, Dias, Ferro, Grimaldo; Fernandes, Pires, Florentino, Cervi (De Tomas 78); Rafa Silva (Pizzi 20), Seferovic (Vinicius 59).
Lyon: (442) Lopes; Dubois, Marcelo, Denayer, Kone; Cornet (Traore 66), Tousart, Aouar (Reine-Adelaide 88), Terrier (Thiago Mendes 56); Dembele, Depay.

RB Leipzig (0) 2 *(Laimer 49, Sabitzer 59)*

Zenit St Petersburg (1) 1 *(Rakitskiy 25)* 41,058

RB Leipzig: (442) Gulacsi; Mukiele, Upamecano, Orban, Klostermann; Sabitzer, Laimer (Demme 86), Kampl, Forsberg; Werner (Matheus Cunha 46), Lookman (Poulsen 69).
Zenit St Petersburg: (442) Kerzhakov; Karavaev, Ivanovic, Rakitskiy, Douglas Santos; Shatov (Osorio 65), Ozdoev, Barrios, Driussi (Mak 82); Dzyuba, Azmoun (Kuzyaev 75).

Tuesday, 5 November 2019

Lyon (2) 3 *(Andersen 4, Depay 33, Traore 89)*

Benfica (0) 1 *(Seferovic 76)* 51,077

Lyon: (4231) Lopes; Dubois, Andersen, Denayer, Kone; Thiago Mendes, Tousart; Reine-Adelaide (Traore 73), Depay (Cornet 46), Aouar (Marcelo 90); Dembele.
Benfica: (442) Vlachodimos; Tavares, Dias, Ferro (Jardel 16), Grimaldo; Fernandes (Seferovic 46), Florentino, Pires, Cervi (Pizzi 73); Chiquinho, Vinicius.

Zenit St Petersburg (0) 0

RB Leipzig (1) 2 *(Demme 45, Sabitzer 63)* 50,452

Zenit St Petersburg: (532) Kerzhakov; Smolnikov (Karavaev 46), Osorio, Ivanovic (Driussi 70), Rakitskiy, Douglas Santos; Erokhin (Kuzyaev 85), Barrios, Ozdoev; Dzyuba, Azmoun.
RB Leipzig: (4231) Gulacsi; Mukiele, Klostermann, Upamecano, Halstenberg (Kampl 46); Laimer, Demme; Sabitzer, Poulsen, Forsberg (Haidara 76); Nkunku (Werner 61).

Wednesday, 27 November 2019

RB Leipzig (0) 2 *(Forsberg 90 (pen), 90)*

Benfica (1) 2 *(Pizzi 20, Vinicius 59)* 38,339

RB Leipzig: (352) Gulacsi (Mvogo 64); Klostermann, Ampadu (Mukiele 56), Upamecano; Sabitzer, Laimer, Demme, Forsberg, Saracchi (Schick 70); Nkunku, Werner.
Benfica: (442) Vlachodimos; Andre Almeida, Dias, Ferro, Grimaldo; Pizzi (Caio 90), Pires, Taarabt, Cervi (Jota 90); Vinicius (De Tomas 82), Chiquinho.

Zenit St Petersburg (1) 2 *(Dzyuba 42, Ozdoev 84)*

Lyon (0) 0 51,183

Zenit St Petersburg: (442) Kerzhakov; Karavaev, Ivanovic, Rakitskiy, Douglas Santos; Kuzyaev (Sutormin 90), Barrios, Ozdoev, Driussi (Zhirkov 81); Azmoun (Erokhin 83), Dzyuba.
Lyon: (4141) Lopes; Dubois, Marcelo, Andersen (Gouiri 83), Marcal (Kone 58); Denayer; Traore, Tousart, Reine-Adelaide, Cornet (Cherki 75); Dembele.

Tuesday, 10 December 2019

Benfica (0) 3 *(Cervi 47, Pizzi 58 (pen), Azmoun 79 (og))*

Zenit St Petersburg (0) 0 40,232

Benfica: (4411) Vlachodimos; Tavares, Ferro, Dias, Grimaldo; Pizzi, Pires (Samaris 81), Taarabt, Cervi (Seferovic 81); Chiquinho; Vinicius (Caio 89).
Zenit St Petersburg: (442) Kerzhakov; Karavaev, Osorio, Ivanovic, Douglas Santos■; Erokhin (Sutormin 65), Barrios, Ozdoev (Smolnikov 60), Shatov (Mak 90); Azmoun, Dzyuba.

Lyon (0) 2 *(Aouar 50, Depay 82)*

RB Leipzig (2) 2 *(Forsberg 9 (pen), Werner 33 (pen))* 53,288

Lyon: (4231) Lopes; Tete, Andersen, Denayer, Da Silva (Marcal 73); Thiago Mendes, Tousart (Reine-Adelaide 64); Terrier (Marcelo 87), Depay, Aouar; Dembele.
RB Leipzig: (4222) Gulacsi; Mukiele, Upamecano (Ampadu 55), Klostermann, Saracchi; Haidara, Demme; Nkunku (Laimer 75), Forsberg; Poulsen, Werner (Matheus Cunha 55).

Group G Table	P	W	D	L	F	A	GD	Pts
RB Leipzig	6	3	2	1	10	8	2	11
Lyon	6	2	2	2	9	8	1	8
Benfica	6	2	1	3	10	11	–1	7
Zenit St Petersburg	6	2	1	3	7	9	–2	7

GROUP H

Tuesday, 17 September 2019

Ajax (1) 3 *(Promes 18, Alvarez 50, Tagliafico 62)*

Lille (0) 0 51,441

Ajax: (4231) Onana; Dest, Veltman, Blind, Tagliafico; Alvarez, Martinez (Ekkelenkamp 88); Ziyech (Lang 77), Promes, Neres (Huntelaar 83); Tadic.
Lille: (442) Maignan; Celik, Fonte, Gabriel, Bradaric; Sanches (Luiz Araujo 63), Andre, Soumare (Xeka 77), Bamba; Osimhen, Ikone (Yazici 63).

Chelsea (0) 0

Valencia (0) 1 *(Rodrigo 74)* 39,469

Chelsea: (3421) Arrizabalaga; Zouma (Giroud 73), Christensen, Tomori; Azpilicueta, Jorginho, Kovacic (Barkley 80), Alonso; Willian, Mount (Pedro 16); Abraham.
Valencia: (442) Cillessen; Wass, Garay, Gabriel, Gaya; Coquelin, Kondogbia, Parejo, Cheryshev (Diakhaby 90); Rodrigo (Lee 90), Gameiro (Gomez 70).

Wednesday, 2 October 2019

Lille (1) 1 *(Osimhen 33)*

Chelsea (1) 2 *(Abraham 22, Willian 77)* 48,523

Lille: (4231) Maignan; Celik, Fonte, Gabriel, Mandava; Andre (Sanches 69), Soumare; Luiz Araujo (Xeka 75), Ikone (Yazici 62), Bamba; Osimhen.
Chelsea: (3421) Arrizabalaga; Azpilicueta, Zouma, Tomori; James (Hudson-Odoi 67), Kante, Jorginho, Alonso; Willian (Pedro 85), Mount (Kovacic 87); Abraham.

Valencia (0) 0

Ajax (2) 3 *(Ziyech 8, Promes 34, van de Beek 67)* 44,659

Valencia: (442) Cillessen; Wass, Garay, Gabriel, Jaume C; Torres (Cheryshev 76), Coquelin (Correia 70), Parejo, Goncalo Guedes; Rodrigo, Gomez (Lee 57).
Ajax: (4231) Onana; Dest, Veltman, Blind, Tagliafico; Alvarez, Martinez; Ziyech (Huntelaar 85), van de Beek (De Jong 88), Promes (Neres 81); Tadic.

Wednesday, 23 October 2019

Ajax (0) 0

Chelsea (0) 1 *(Batshuayi 86)* 52,482

Ajax: (4231) Onana; Dest, Veltman (Huntelaar 89), Blind, Tagliafico; Alvarez (De Jong 89), Martinez; Ziyech, van de Beek, Promes (Neres 74); Tadic.
Chelsea: (433) Arrizabalaga; Azpilicueta, Zouma, Tomori, Alonso; Kovacic, Jorginho, Mount; Willian (Pulisic 66), Abraham (Batshuayi 71), Hudson-Odoi (James 90).

Lille (0) 1 *(Ikone 90)*

Valencia (0) 1 *(Cheryshev 63)* 47,488

Lille: (343) Maignan; Djalo (Bamba 87), Fonte, Gabriel; Celik, Andre, Soumare, Bradaric; Yazici (Remy 71), Osimhen, Luiz Araujo (Ikone 65).
Valencia: (442) Cillessen; Wass, Gabriel, Diakhaby■, Jaume C; Coquelin, Parejo, Kondogbia (Carlos Soler 46), Cheryshev (Garay 87); Gomez, Gameiro (Lee 65).

Tuesday, 5 November 2019

Chelsea (1) 4 *(Jorginho 4 (pen), 71 (pen), Azpilicueta 63, James 74)*

Ajax (3) 4 *(Abraham 2 (og), Promes 20, Arrizabalaga 35 (og), van de Beek 55)* 39,132

Chelsea: (433) Arrizabalaga; Azpilicueta, Zouma, Tomori, Alonso (James 46); Kovacic (Batshuayi 87), Jorginho, Mount (Hudson-Odoi 60); Willian, Abraham, Pulisic.
Ajax: (4231) Onana; Mazraoui, Veltman■, Blind■, Tagliafico; van de Beek, Martinez; Neres (Schuurs 72), Ziyech (Alvarez 72), Promes; Tadic.

Valencia (0) 4 *(Parejo 66 (pen), Soumaoro 82 (og), Kondogbia 84, Torres 90)*

Lille (1) 1 *(Osimhen 25)* 38,252

Valencia: (442) Cillessen; Wass, Garay, Gabriel, Gaya; Lee (Vallejo 54), Parejo, Kondogbia, Cheryshev (Torres 30); Rodrigo (Gameiro 90), Gomez.
Lille: (343) Maignan; Soumaoro (Bamba 89), Fonte, Gabriel; Celik, Andre (Luiz Araujo 80), Soumare, Bradaric; Remy, Osimhen, Yazici (Sanches 74).

Wednesday, 27 November 2019

Lille (0) 0

Ajax (1) 2 *(Ziyech 2, Promes 59)* 48,612

Lille: (4231) Maignan; Celik, Djalo, Gabriel, Mandava; Andre (Sanches 77), Soumare; Yazici (Remy 82), Ikone, Bamba (Luiz Araujo 72); Osimhen.
Ajax: (4231) Onana; Dest, Schuurs, Martinez, Tagliafico; van de Beek, Mazraoui (Alvarez 46); Labyad (Lang 45), Ziyech (De Jong 85), Promes; Tadic.

Valencia (1) 2 *(Carlos Soler 40, Wass 82)*

Chelsea (1) 2 *(Kovacic 41, Pulisic 50)* 43,486

Valencia: (442) Cillessen; Jaume C (Gameiro 67), Garay, Gabriel, Gaya; Torres (Coquelin 74), Parejo, Wass, Carlos Soler (Lee 78); Rodrigo, Gomez.
Chelsea: (433) Arrizabalaga; James, Christensen, Zouma, Azpilicueta; Kante, Jorginho (Emerson Palmieri 72), Kovacic; Willian (Mount 80), Abraham (Batshuayi 46), Pulisic.

Tuesday, 10 December 2019

Ajax (0) 0

Valencia (1) 1 *(Rodrigo 24)* 51,931

Ajax: (4231) Onana; Mazraoui, Veltman, Blind, Tagliafico (De Jong 89); Alvarez (Dest 46), Martinez; Ziyech, van de Beek, Lang (Huntelaar 70); Tadic.
Valencia: (442) Jaume D; Wass, Gabriel■, Diakhaby, Gaya; Torres (Mangala 90), Coquelin, Parejo, Carlos Soler; Gameiro (Vallejo 54), Rodrigo.

Chelsea (2) 2 *(Abraham 19, Azpilicueta 35)*

Lille (0) 1 *(Remy 78)* 40,016

Chelsea: (433) Arrizabalaga; Azpilicueta, Rudiger, Zouma, Emerson Palmieri; Kante, Jorginho, Kovacic (Mount 82); Willian, Abraham (Batshuayi 72), Pulisic (Hudson-Odoi 62).
Lille: (4231) Maignan (Leo 72); Celik, Djalo, Gabriel, Pied; Xeka, Soumare; Luiz Araujo (Sanches 82), Yazici, Thiago Maia (Bamba 66); Remy.

Group H Table	*P*	*W*	*D*	*L*	*F*	*A*	*GD*	*Pts*
Valencia	6	3	2	1	9	7	2	11
Chelsea	6	3	2	1	11	9	2	11
Ajax	6	3	1	2	12	6	6	10
Lille	6	0	1	5	4	14	–10	1

KNOCK-OUT STAGE

ROUND OF 16 FIRST LEG

Tuesday, 18 February 2020

Atletico Madrid (1) 1 *(Saul 4)*

Liverpool (0) 0 67,443

Atletico Madrid: (442) Oblak; Vrsaljko, Savic, Felipe, Renan Lodi; Koke, Thomas, Saul, Lemar (Llorente 46); Morata (Vitolo 70), Correa (Costa 77).
Liverpool: (433) Alisson; Alexander-Arnold, Gomez, van Dijk, Robertson; Henderson (Milner 80), Fabinho, Wijnaldum; Salah (Oxlade-Chamberlain 72), Firmino, Mane (Origi 46).

Borussia Dortmund (0) 2 *(Haland 69, 77)*

Paris Saint-Germain (0) 1 *(Neymar 75)* 66,099

Borussia Dortmund: (343) Burki; Piszczek, Hummels, Zagadou; Hakimi, Can, Witsel, Guerreiro; Sancho (Schmelzer 90), Haland, Hazard (Reyna 67).
Paris Saint-Germain: (3421) Navas; Marquinhos, Thiago Silva, Kimpembe; Meunier, Gueye, Verratti, Kurzawa; Di Maria (Sarabia 76), Neymar; Mbappe-Lottin.

Wednesday, 19 February 2020

Atalanta (2) 4 *(Hateboer 16, 62, Ilicic 42, Freuler 57)*

Valencia (0) 1 *(Cheryshev 66)* 44,236

Atalanta: (3412) Gollini; Toloi, Caldara (Zapata 75), Palomino; Hateboer, de Roon, Freuler, Gosens; Pasalic (Tameze 90); Ilicic, Gomez (Malinovsky 81).
Valencia: (442) Jaume D; Wass, Diakhaby, Mangala, Gaya; Torres, Parejo, Kondogbia, Carlos Soler; Gomez (Gameiro 73), Goncalo Guedes (Cheryshev 64).

Tottenham H (0) 0

RB Leipzig (0) 1 *(Werner 58 (pen))* 60,095

Tottenham H: (442) Lloris; Aurier, Sanchez, Alderweireld, Davies; Fernandes (Ndombele 64), Lo Celso, Winks, Bergwijn; Lucas Moura, Alli (Lamela 64).
RB Leipzig: (3421) Gulacsi; Klostermann, Ampadu, Halstenberg; Mukiele, Laimer (Forsberg 83), Sabitzer, Angelino; Nkunku (Haidara 74), Werner; Schick (Poulsen 77).

Tuesday, 25 February 2020

Chelsea (0) 0

Bayern Munich (0) 3 *(Gnabry 51, 54, Lewandowski 76)* 36,761

Chelsea: (3421) Caballero; Azpilicueta (Pedro 73), Christensen, Rudiger; James, Jorginho, Kovacic, Alonso■; Mount, Barkley (Willian 61); Giroud (Abraham 61).
Bayern Munich: (4231) Neuer; Pavard, Boateng, Alaba, Davies; Kimmich, Thiago (Goretzka 90); Coman (Coutinho 66), Muller, Gnabry (Tolisso 85); Lewandowski.

Napoli (1) 1 *(Mertens 30)*

Barcelona (0) 1 *(Griezmann 57)* 44,388

Napoli: (4141) Ospina; Di Lorenzo, Manolas, Maksimovic, Rui; Demme (Allan 80); Callejon (Politano 74), Fabian, Zielinski, Insigne; Mertens (Milik 54).
Barcelona: (433) ter Stegen; Nelson Semedo, Pique (Lenglet 90), Umtiti, Firpo; Rakitic (Arthur 56), Busquets, de Jong; Vidal■, Messi, Griezmann (Fati 87).

Wednesday, 26 February 2020

Lyon (1) 1 *(Tousart 31)*

Juventus (0) 0 57,335

Lyon: (343) Lopes; Denayer, Marcelo, Marcal; Dubois (Tete 78), Tousart, Bruno Guimaraes, Cornet (Andersen 81); Toko Ekambi (Terrier 66), Dembele, Aouar.
Juventus: (433) Szczesny; Danilo, de Ligt, Bonucci, Alex Sandro; Bentancur, Pjanic (Ramsey 62), Rabiot (Bernardeschi 78); Cuadrado (Higuain 70), Dybala, Ronaldo.

Real Madrid (0) 1 *(Isco 60)*

Manchester C (0) 2 *(Gabriel Jesus 78, De Bruyne 83 (pen))* 75,615

Real Madrid: (433) Courtois; Carvajal, Varane, Sergio Ramos■, Mendy; Modric (Lucas 84), Casemiro, Valverde; Isco (Jovic 84), Benzema, Vinicius Junior (Bale 75).
Manchester C: (4411) Ederson; Walker, Otamendi, Laporte (Fernandinho 33), Mendy; Mahrez, Gundogan, Rodri, Gabriel Jesus; De Bruyne; Bernardo Silva (Sterling 73).

ROUND OF 16 SECOND LEG

Tuesday, 10 March 2020

RB Leipzig (2) 3 *(Sabitzer 10, 21, Forsberg 87)*

Tottenham H (0) 0 42,146

RB Leipzig: (343) Gulacsi; Klostermann, Upamecano, Halstenberg; Mukiele (Adams 56), Laimer, Sabitzer (Forsberg 87), Angelino; Nkunku (Haidara 59), Schick, Werner.
Tottenham H: (3421) Lloris; Tanganga, Dier, Alderweireld; Aurier (Walcott 90), Winks, Lo Celso (Fernandes 80), Sessegnon; Lamela, Lucas Moura; Alli.

Valencia (1) 3 *(Gameiro 21, 51, Torres 67)*

Atalanta (2) 4 *(Ilicic 3 (pen), 43 (pen), 71, 82)* 0

Valencia: (442) Cillessen; Wass, Coquelin (Cheryshev 74), Diakhaby (Goncalo Guedes 46), Gaya; Torres, Parejo, Kondogbia, Carlos Soler; Gameiro, Rodrigo (Florenzi 79).
Atalanta: (3412) Sportiello; Djimsiti, Caldara, Palomino; Hateboer, de Roon (Zapata 45), Freuler, Gosens; Pasalic (Tameze 83); Ilicic, Gomez (Malinovsky 78).
Behind closed doors due to the COVID-19 pandemic.

Wednesday, 11 March 2020

Liverpool (1) 2 *(Wijnaldum 43, Firmino 94)*

Atletico Madrid (0) 3 *(Llorente 97, 105, Morata 120)* 52,267

Liverpool: (433) Adrian; Alexander-Arnold, Gomez, van Dijk, Robertson; Oxlade-Chamberlain (Milner 82), Henderson (Fabinho 106), Wijnaldum (Origi 106); Salah, Firmino (Minamino 113), Mane.
Atletico Madrid: (442) Oblak; Trippier (Vrsaljko 91), Savic, Felipe, Renan Lodi; Correa (Gimenez 106), Koke, Thomas, Saul; Costa (Llorente 56), Joao Felix (Morata 103).
aet.

Paris Saint-Germain (2) 2 *(Neymar 28, Bernat 45)*

Borussia Dortmund (0) 0 0

Paris Saint-Germain: (4222) Navas; Kehrer, Marquinhos, Kimpembe, Bernat; Gueye, Paredes (Kouassi 90); Di Maria (Kurzawa 79), Neymar; Cavani, Sarabia (Mbappe-Lottin 64).
Borussia Dortmund: (343) Burki; Piszczek, Hummels, Zagadou; Hakimi (Gotze 87), Can■, Witsel (Reyna 71), Guerreiro; Hazard (Brandt 69), Haland, Sancho.
Behind closed doors due to the COVID-19 pandemic.

Friday, 7 August 2020

Juventus (1) 2 *(Ronaldo 43 (pen), 60)*

Lyon (1) 1 *(Depay 12 (pen))* 0

Juventus: (442) Szczesny; Cuadrado (Danilo 70), de Ligt, Bonucci, Alex Sandro; Bernardeschi (Dybala 71 (Olivieri 84)), Bentancur, Pjanic (Ramsey 60), Rabiot; Higuain, Ronaldo.
Lyon: (352) Lopes; Denayer (Andersen 61), Marcelo, Marcal; Dubois (Tete 90), Caqueret, Bruno Guimaraes, Aouar (Thiago Mendes 90), Cornet; Depay (Dembele 67), Toko Ekambi (Reine-Adelaide 67).
Lyon won on away goals.
Behind closed doors due to the COVID-19 pandemic.

Manchester C (1) 2 *(Sterling 9, Gabriel Jesus 68)*

Real Madrid (1) 1 *(Benzema 28)* 0

Manchester C: (433) Ederson; Walker, Fernandinho, Laporte, Joao Cancelo; De Bruyne, Rodri (Otamendi 89), Gundogan; Sterling (Silva 81), Foden (Bernardo Silva 67), Gabriel Jesus.
Real Madrid: (433) Courtois; Carvajal (Lucas 83), Varane, Eder Militao, Mendy; Modric (Valverde 83), Casemiro, Kroos; Rodrygo (Asensio 61), Benzema, Hazard (Jovic 83).
Behind closed doors due to the COVID-19 pandemic.

Saturday, 8 August 2020

Barcelona (3) 3 *(Lenglet 10, Messi 23, Suarez 45 (pen))*

Napoli (1) 1 *(Insigne 45 (pen))* 0

Barcelona: (433) ter Stegen; Nelson Semedo, Pique, Lenglet, Jordi Alba; Sergi Roberto, Rakitic, de Jong; Messi, Suarez (Firpo 90), Griezmann (Monchu 84).
Napoli: (433) Ospina; Di Lorenzo, Manolas, Koulibaly, Rui; Fabian (Elmas 79), Demme (Lobotka 46), Zielinski (Lozano 70); Callejon (Politano 70), Mertens, Insigne (Milik 79).

Bayern Munich (2) 4 *(Lewandowski 10 (pen), 83, Perisic 24, Tolisso 76)*

Chelsea (1) 1 *(Abraham 44)* 0

Bayern Munich: (4231) Neuer; Kimmich (Odriozola 71), Boateng (Sule 63), Alaba, Davies; Goretzka, Thiago (Tolisso 70); Gnabry (Javi Martinez 81), Muller, Perisic (Coutinho 64); Lewandowski.
Chelsea: (442) Caballero; James, Christensen, Zouma, Emerson Palmieri; Hudson-Odoi, Kante, Kovacic, Mount; Barkley, Abraham (Giroud 81).
Behind closed doors due to the COVID-19 pandemic.

QUARTER-FINALS (in Lisbon)

Wednesday, 12 August 2020

Atalanta (1) 1 *(Pasalic 26)*

Paris Saint-Germain (0) 2 *(Marquinhos 90, Choupo-Moting 90)* 0

Atalanta: (3412) Sportiello; Toloi, Caldara, Djimsiti (Palomino 60); Hateboer, de Roon, Freuler, Gosens (Castagne 82); Gomez (Malinovsky 59); Pasalic (Muriel 70), Zapata (Da Riva 82).
Paris Saint-Germain: (433) Navas (Sergio Rico 79); Kehrer, Thiago Silva, Kimpembe, Bernat; Ander Herrera (Draxler 72), Marquinhos, Gueye (Paredes 72); Icardi (Choupo-Moting 79), Neymar, Sarabia (Mbappe-Lottin 60).
Behind closed doors due to the COVID-19 pandemic.

Thursday, 13 August 2020

RB Leipzig (0) 2 *(Olmo 50, Adams 88)*

Atletico Madrid (0) 1 *(Joao Felix 71 (pen))* 0

RB Leipzig: (3331) Gulacsi; Klostermann, Upamecano, Halstenberg; Laimer (Adams 72), Kampl, Angelino; Sabitzer (Mukiele 90), Olmo (Schick 83), Nkunku (Haidara 83); Poulsen.
Atletico Madrid: (442) Oblak; Trippier, Savic, Gimenez, Renan Lodi ; Koke (Felipe 90), Herrera (Joao Felix 58), Saul, Carrasco; Llorente, Costa (Morata 72).
Behind closed doors due to the COVID-19 pandemic.

Friday, 14 August 2020

Barcelona (1) 2 *(Alaba 7 (og), Suarez 57)*

Bayern Munich (4) 8 *(Muller 4, 31, Perisic 21, Gnabry 27, Kimmich 63, Lewandowski 82, Coutinho 85, 89)* 0

Barcelona: (442) ter Stegen; Nelson Semedo, Pique, Lenglet, Jordi Alba; Sergi Roberto (Griezmann 46), Busquets (Fati 70), de Jong, Vidal; Messi, Suarez.
Bayern Munich: (4231) Neuer; Kimmich, Boateng (Sule 76), Alaba, Davies (Lucas 84); Thiago, Goretzka (Tolisso 84); Gnabry (Coutinho 75), Muller, Perisic (Coman 67); Lewandowski.
Behind closed doors due to the COVID-19 pandemic.

Saturday, 15 August 2020

Manchester C (0) 1 *(De Bruyne 69)*

Lyon (1) 3 *(Cornet 24, Dembele 79, 87)* 0

Manchester C: (3142) Ederson; Fernandinho (Mahrez 56), Garcia, Laporte; Rodri (Silva 84); Walker, De Bruyne, Gundogan, Joao Cancelo; Gabriel Jesus, Sterling.
Lyon: (352) Lopes; Denayer, Marcelo, Marcal; Dubois (Tete 74), Caqueret, Bruno Guimaraes (Thiago Mendes 70), Aouar, Cornet; Depay (Dembele 75), Toko Ekambi (Reine-Adelaide 87).
Behind closed doors due to the COVID-19 pandemic.

SEMI-FINALS (in Lisbon)

Tuesday, 18 August 2020

RB Leipzig (0) 0

Paris Saint-Germain (2) 3 *(Marquinhos 13, Di Maria 42, Bernat 56)* 0

RB Leipzig: (4141) Gulacsi; Mukiele, Upamecano, Klostermann (Orban 82), Angelino; Kampl (Adams 64); Laimer (Halstenberg 62), Sabitzer, Olmo (Schick 46), Nkunku (Forsberg 46); Poulsen.
Paris Saint-Germain: (433) Sergio Rico; Kehrer, Thiago Silva, Kimpembe, Bernat; Ander Herrera (Verratti 83), Marquinhos, Paredes (Draxler 83); Di Maria (Sarabia 87), Neymar, Mbappe-Lottin (Choupo-Moting 86).
Behind closed doors due to the COVID-19 pandemic.

Wednesday, 19 August 2020

Lyon (0) 0

Bayern Munich (2) 3 *(Gnabry 18, 33, Lewandowski 88)* 0

Lyon: (352) Lopes; Denayer, Marcelo, Marcal (Cherki 73); Dubois (Tete 67), Caqueret, Bruno Guimaraes (Thiago Mendes 46), Aouar, Cornet; Toko Ekambi (Reine-Adelaide 67), Depay (Dembele 58).
Bayern Munich: (4231) Neuer; Kimmich, Boateng (Sule 46), Alaba, Davies; Thiago (Tolisso 82), Goretzka (Pavard 82); Gnabry (Coutinho 75), Muller, Perisic (Coman 63); Lewandowski.
Behind closed doors due to the COVID-19 pandemic.

CHAMPIONS LEAGUE FINAL 2019–20

Sunday, 23 August 2020

(in Lisbon – behind closed doors)

Bayern Munich (0) 1 *(Coman 59)* **Paris Saint-Germain (0) 0**

Bayern Munich: (433) Neuer; Kimmich, Boateng (Sule 25), Alaba, Davies; Goretzka, Thiago (Tolisso 86), Muller; Gnabry (Coutinho 68), Lewandowski, Coman (Perisic 68).

Paris Saint-Germain: (433) Navas; Kehrer, Thiago Silva, Kimpembe, Bernat (Kurzawa 80); Marquinhos, Ander Herrera (Draxler 72), Paredes (Verratti 65); Di Maria (Choupo-Moting 80), Mbappe-Lottin, Neymar.

Referee: Daniele Orsato.

Bayern Munich's Kingsley Coman scores against PSG in the Champions League final in Lisbon. The German club's 1-0 victory gave them their sixth success in the tournament. (Peter Schatz/DPA/PA Images)

UEFA CHAMPIONS LEAGUE 2020–21

PARTICIPATING CLUBS
The list below is provisional and is subject to pending legal proceedings and final confirmation from UEFA.

PRELIMINARY ROUND
Linfield (NIR)
Drita (KOS)
Inter Club d'Escaldes (AND)
Tre Fiori (SMR)

FIRST QUALIFYING ROUND
Celtic (SCO)
Astana (KAZ)
Ludogorets Razgrad (BUL)
Red Star Belgrade (SRB)
Qarabag (AZE)
Legia Warsaw (POL)
Maccabi Tel Aviv (ISR)
Molde (NOR)
Sheriff Tiraspol (MDA)
CFR Cluj (ROU)
Ferencvaros (HUN)
Dundalk (IRL)
Slovan Bratislava (SVK)
Suduva (LTU)
Omonia (CYP)
Sarajevo (BIH)
Dinamo Tbilisi (GEO)
Fola Esch (LUX)
Djurgaardens (SWE)
Buducnost Podgorica (MNE)
Flora (EST)
Dinamo Brest (BLR)
Riga FC (LVA)
Connah's Quay Nomads (WAL)
KI Klaksvik (FRO)
Europa (GIB)
Celje (SVN)
Ararat-Armenia (ARM)
KuPS Kuopio (FIN)
KR Reykjavik (ICE)
Tirana (ALB)
Sileks (MKD)
Floriana (MLT)
Plus the preliminary round winner.

SECOND QUALIFYING ROUND – CHAMPIONS PATH
Dinamo Zagreb (CRO)
Young Boys (SUI)
Midtjylland (DEN)

SECOND QUALIFYING ROUND – LEAGUE PATH
Besiktas (TUR)
Viktoria Plzen (CZE)
Rapid Vienna (AUT)
PAOK (GRE)
AZ Alkmaar (NED)
Lokomotiva (CRO)
Plus 17 winners from the First Qualifying Round.

THIRD QUALIFYING ROUND – CHAMPIONS PATH
Olympiacos (GRE)
Slavia Prague (CZE)

THIRD QUALIFYING ROUND – LEAGUE PATH
Benfica (POR)
Dynamo Kyiv (UKR)
Gent (BEL)
Krasnodar (RUS)
Rennes (FRA)
Plus 13 winners from the Second Qualifying Round.

PLAY-OFF ROUND – CHAMPIONS PATH
Ajax (NED)
Red Bull Salzburg (AUT)
Plus 10 winners from the Third Qualifying Round.

GROUP STAGE
Champions League title holders
Europa League title holders
Real Madrid (ESP)
Liverpool (ENG)
Juventus (ITA)
Bayern Munich (GER)
Paris Saint-Germain (FRA)
Zenit St Petersburg (RUS)
Atletico Madrid (ESP)
Barcelona (ESP)
Manchester C (ENG)
Manchester U (ENG)
Sevilla (ESP)
Chelsea (ENG)
Shakhtar Donetsk (UKR)
Borussia Dortmund (GER)
Porto (POR)
RB Leipzig (GER)
Lazio (ITA)
Internazionale (ITA)
Atalanta (ITA)
Lokomotiv Moscow (RUS)
Marseille (FRA)
Club Brugge (BEL)
Borussia Monchengladbach (GER)
Istanbul Basaksehir (TUR)
Plus 6 winners from the Play-Off Round.

EUROPEAN CUP-WINNERS' CUP FINALS 1961–99

Year	Winners v Runners-up		Venue	Attendance	Referee
1961	1st Leg Fiorentina v Rangers	2-0	Glasgow	80,000	C. E. Steiner (Austria)
	2nd Leg Fiorentina v Rangers	2-1	Florence	50,000	V. Hernadi (Hungary)
1962	Atletico Madrid v Fiorentina	1-1	Glasgow	27,389	T. Wharton (Scotland)
Replay	Atletico Madrid v Fiorentina	3-0	Stuttgart	38,000	K. Tschenscher (West Germany)
1963	Tottenham Hotspur v Atletico Madrid	5-1	Rotterdam	49,000	A. van Leuwen (Netherlands)
1964	Sporting Lisbon v MTK Budapest	3-3*	Brussels	3,208	L. van Nuffel (Belgium)
Replay	Sporting Lisbon v MTK Budapest	1-0	Antwerp	13,924	G. Versyp (Belgium)
1965	West Ham U v Munich 1860	2-0	Wembley	7,974	I. Zsolt (Hungary)
1966	Borussia Dortmund v Liverpool	2-1*	Glasgow	41,657	P. Schwinte (France)
1967	Bayern Munich v Rangers	1-0*	Nuremberg	69,480	C. Lo Bello (Italy)
1968	AC Milan v Hamburg	2-0	Rotterdam	53,000	J. Ortiz de Mendibil (Spain)
1969	Slovan Bratislava v Barcelona	3-2	Basel	19,000	L. van Ravens (Netherlands)
1970	Manchester C v Gornik Zabrze	2-1	Vienna	7,968	P. Schiller (Austria)
1971	Chelsea v Real Madrid	1-1*	Athens	45,000	R. Scheurer (Switzerland)
Replay	Chelsea v Real Madrid	2-1*	Athens	19,917	R. Scheurer (Switzerland)
1972	Rangers v Dynamo Moscow	3-2	Barcelona	24,701	J. Ortiz de Mendibil (Spain)
1973	AC Milan v Leeds U	1-0	Salonika	40,154	C. Mihas (Greece)
1974	Magdeburg v AC Milan	2-0	Rotterdam	4,641	A. van Gemert (Netherlands)
1975	Dynamo Kyiv v Ferencvaros	3-0	Basle	13,000	R. Davidson (Scotland)
1976	Anderlecht v West Ham U	4-2	Brussels	51,296	R. Wurtz (France)
1977	Hamburg v Anderlecht	2-0	Amsterdam	66,000	P. Partridge (England)
1978	Anderlecht v Austria/WAC	4-0	Paris	48,679	H. Adlinger (West Germany)
1979	Barcelona v Fortuna Dusseldorf	4-3*	Basel	58,000	K. Palotai (Hungary)
1980	Valencia v Arsenal *(Valencia won 5-4 on penalties)*	0-0*	Brussels	40,000	V. Christov (Czechoslovakia)
1981	Dinamo Tbilisi v Carl Zeiss Jena	2-1	Dusseldorf	4,750	R. Lattanzi (Italy)
1982	Barcelona v Standard Liege	2-1	Barcelona	80,000	W. Eschweiler (West Germany)
1983	Aberdeen v Real Madrid	2-1*	Gothenburg	17,804	G. Menegali (Italy)
1984	Juventus v Porto	2-1	Basel	55,000	A. Prokop (Egypt)
1985	Everton v Rapid Vienna	3-1	Rotterdam	38,500	P. Casarin (Italy)
1986	Dynamo Kyiv v Atletico Madrid	3-0	Lyon	50,000	F. Wohrer (Austria)
1987	Ajax v Lokomotiv Leipzig	1-0	Athens	35,107	L. Agnolin (Italy)
1988	Mechelen v Ajax	1-0	Strasbourg	39,446	D. Pauly (West Germany)
1989	Barcelona v Sampdoria	2-0	Berne	42,707	G. Courtney (England)
1990	Sampdoria v Anderlecht	2-0*	Gothenburg	20,103	B. Galler (Switzerland)
1991	Manchester U v Barcelona	2-1	Rotterdam	43,500	B. Karlsson (Sweden)
1992	Werder Bremen v Monaco	2-0	Lisbon	16,000	P. D'Elia (Italy)
1993	Parma v Antwerp	3-1	Wembley	37,393	K.-J. Assenmacher (Germany)
1994	Arsenal v Parma	1-0	Copenhagen	33,765	V. Krondl (Czech Republic)
1995	Real Zaragoza v Arsenal	2-1	Paris	42,424	P. Ceccarini (Italy)
1996	Paris Saint-Germain v Rapid Vienna	1-0	Brussels	37,000	P. Pairetto (Italy)
1997	Barcelona v Paris Saint-Germain	1-0	Rotterdam	52,000	M. Merk (Germany)
1998	Chelsea v VfB Stuttgart	1-0	Stockholm	30,216	S. Braschi (Italy)
1999	Lazio v Mallorca	2-1	Birmingham	33,021	G. Benko (Austria)

INTER-CITIES FAIRS CUP FINALS 1958–71

Year	1st Leg		Attendance	2nd Leg	Attendance	Agg	Winner
1958	London XI v Barcelona	2-2	45,466	0-6	70,000	2-8	Barcelona
1960	Birmingham C v Barcelona	0-0	40,524	1-4	70,000	1-4	Barcelona
1961	Birmingham C v Roma	2-2	21,005	0-2	60,000	2-4	Roma
1962	Valencia v Barcelona	6-2	65,000	1-1	60,000	7-3	Valencia
1963	Dinamo Zagreb v Valencia	1-2	40,000	0-2	55,000	1-4	Valencia
1964	Real Zaragoza v Valencia	2-1	50,000	(in Barcelona, one match only)			Real Zaragoza
1965	Ferencvaros v Juventus	1-0	25,000	(in Turin, one match only)			Ferencvaros
1966	Barcelona v Real Zaragoza	0-1	70,000	4-2*	70,000	4-3	Barcelona
1967	Dinamo Zagreb v Leeds U	2-0	40,000	0-0	35,604	2-0	Dynamo Zagreb
1968	Leeds U v Ferencvaros	1-0	25,368	0-0	70,000	1-0	Leeds U
1969	Newcastle U v Ujpest Dozsa	3-0	60,000	3-2	37,000	6-2	Newcastle U
1970	Anderlecht v Arsenal	3-1	37,000	0-3	51,612	3-4	Arsenal
1971	Juventus v Leeds U	0-0	*(abandoned 51 minutes)*		42,000		
	Juventus v Leeds U *Leeds U won on away goals rule.*	2-2	42,000	1-1	42,483	3-3	Leeds U

Trophy Play-Off – *between first and last winners to decide who would have possession of the original trophy*

1971 Barcelona v Leeds U 2-1 50,000 (in Barcelona, one match only)

*After extra time.

UEFA CUP FINALS 1972–97

Year	1st Leg		Attendance	2nd Leg	Attendance	Agg	Winner
1972	Wolverhampton W v Tottenham H	1-2	38,562	1-1	54,303	2-3	Tottenham H
1973	Liverpool v Moenchengladbach	0-0	*(abandoned after 27 minutes)*		44,967		
	Liverpool v Moenchengladbach	3-0	41,169	0-2	35,000	3-2	Liverpool
1974	Tottenham H v Feyenoord	2-2	46,281	0-2	59,317	2-4	Feyenoord
1975	Moenchengladbach v FC Twente	0-0	42,368	5-1	21,767	5-1	Moenchengladbach
1976	Liverpool v Club Brugge	3-2	49,981	1-1	29,423	4-3	Liverpool
1977	Juventus v Athletic Bilbao	1-0	66,000	1-2	39,700	2-2	Juventus
	Juventus won on away goals rule.						
1978	Bastia v PSV Eindhoven	0-0	8,006	0-3	28,000	0-3	PSV Eindhoven
1979	RS Belgrade v Moenchengladbach	1-1	65,000	0-1	45,000	1-2	Moenchengladbach
1980	Moenchengladbach v E. Frankfurt	3-2	25,000	0-1	59,000	3-3	E. Frankfurt
	Eintracht Frankfurt won on away goals rule.						
1981	Ipswich T v AZ 67 Alkmaar	3-0	27,532	2-4	22,291	5-4	Ipswich T
1982	IFK Gothenburg v Hamburg	1-0	42,548	3-0	57,312	4-0	IFK Gothenburg
1983	Anderlecht v Benfica	1-0	55,000	1-1	70,000	2-1	Anderlecht
1984	Anderlecht v Tottenham H	1-1	33,000	1-1*	46,258	2-2	Tottenham H
	Tottenham H won 4-3 on penalties.						
1985	Videoton v Real Madrid	0-3	30,000	1-0	80,000	1-3	Real Madrid
1986	Real Madrid v Cologne	5-1	60,000	0-2	22,000	5-3	Real Madrid
1987	IFK Gothenburg v Dundee U	1-0	48,614	1-1	20,900	2-1	IFK Gothenburg
1988	Espanol v Bayer Leverkusen	3-0	31,180	0-3*	21,600	3-3	Bayer Leverkusen
	Bayer Leverkusen won 3-2 on penalties.						
1989	Napoli v VfB Stuttgart	2-1	81,093	3-3	64,000	5-4	Napoli
1990	Juventus v Fiorentina	3-1	47,519	0-0	30,999	3-1	Juventus
1991	Internazionale v Roma	2-0	68,887	0-1	70,901	2-1	Internazionale
1992	Torino v Ajax	2-2	65,377	0-0	40,000	2-2	Ajax
	Ajax won on away goals rule.						
1993	Borussia Dortmund v Juventus	1-3	37,000	0-3	62,781	1-6	Juventus
1994	Salzburg v Internazionale	0-1	43,000	0-1	80,345	0-2	Internazionale
1995	Parma v Juventus	1-0	22,057	1-1	80,000	2-1	Parma
1996	Bayern Munich v Bordeaux	2-0	63,000	3-1	30,000	5-1	Bayern Munich
1997	Schalke 04 v Internazionale	1-0	57,000	0-1*	81,675	1-1	Schalke 04
	Schalke 04 won 4-1 on penalties.						

UEFA CUP FINALS 1998–2009

Year	Winners v Runners-up		Venue	Attendance	Referee
1998	Internazionale v Lazio	3-0	Paris	44,412	A. L. Nieto (Spain)
1999	Parma v Olympique Marseille	3-0	Moscow	61,000	H. Dallas (Scotland)
2000	Galatasaray v Arsenal	0-0*	Copenhagen	38,919	A. L. Nieto (Spain)
	Galatasaray won 4-1 on penalties.				
2001	Liverpool v Alaves	5-4*	Dortmund	48,050	G. Veissiere (France)
	Liverpool won on sudden death 'golden goal'.				
2002	Feyenoord v Borussia Dortmund	3-2	Rotterdam	45,611	V. M. M. Pereira (Portugal)
2003	FC Porto v Celtic	3-2*	Seville	52,140	L. Michel (Slovakia)
2004	Valencia v Olympique Marseille	2-0	Gothenburg	39,000	P. Collina (Italy)
2005	CSKA Moscow v Sporting Lisbon	3-1	Lisbon	47,085	G. Poll (England)
2006	Sevilla v Middlesbrough	4-0	Eindhoven	32,100	H. Fandel (Germany)
2007	Sevilla v Espanyol	2-2*	Glasgow	47,602	M. Busacca (Switzerland)
	Sevilla won 3-1 on penalties.				
2008	Zenit St Petersburg v Rangers	2-0	Manchester	43,878	P. Fröjdfeldt (Sweden)
2009	Shakhtar Donetsk v Werder Bremen	2-1*	Istanbul	37,357	L. M. Chantalejo (Spain)

UEFA EUROPA LEAGUE FINALS 2010–20

Year	Winners v Runners-up		Venue	Attendance	Referee
2010	Atletico Madrid v Fulham	2-1*	Hamburg	49,000	N. Rizzoli (Italy)
2011	FC Porto v Braga	1-0	Dublin	45,391	V. Carballo (Spain)
2012	Atletico Madrid v Athletic Bilbao	3-0	Bucharest	52,347	W. Stark (Germany)
2013	Chelsea v Benfica	2-1	Amsterdam	46,163	B. Kuipers (Netherlands)
2014	Sevilla v Benfica	0-0*	Turin	33,120	F. Brych (Germany)
	Sevilla won 4-2 on penalties.				
2015	Sevilla v Dnipro Dnipropetrovsk	3-2	Warsaw	45,000	M. Atkinson (England)
2016	Sevilla v Liverpool	3-1	Basel	34,429	J. Eriksson (Sweden)
2017	Manchester U v Ajax	2-0	Stockholm	46,961	D. Skomina (Slovenia)
2018	Atletico Madrid v Marseille	3-0	Lyon	55,768	B. Kuipers (Netherlands)
2019	Chelsea v Arsenal	4-1	Baku	51,370	G. Rocchi (Italy)
2020	Sevilla v Internazionale	3-2	Cologne	0	D. Makkelie (Netherlands)

**After extra time.*

UEFA EUROPA LEAGUE 2019–20

▪ *Denotes player sent off.*

PRELIMINARY ROUND FIRST LEG

Ballymena U v NSI Runavik	2-0
Barry Town U v Cliftonville	0-0
KI Klaksvik v Tre Fiori	5-1
La Fiorita v Engordany	0-1
Pristina v St Joseph's	1-1
Progres Niederkorn v Cardiff Met Uni	1-0
UE Sant Julia v Europa	3-2

Thursday, 27 June 2019

Ballymena U (0) 2 *(Millar 49, Winchester 56)*

NSI Runavik (0) 0 2270

Ballymena U: (352) Ross Glendinning; Whiteside, Ervin, Balmer; Kane, Millar, Carville, Winchester (Harpur 86), McCullough; Cathair Friel (Mayse 79), Lecky.
NSI Runavik: (343) Thomsen; Langgaard (Hansen 68), Hojgaard, Davidsen; Hentze, Nervseen, Justinussen, Jogvansson-Hansen; Egilsson (Benjaminsen 70), Olsen O, Knudsen.

Barry Town U (0) 0

Cliftonville (0) 0 2106

Barry Town U: (433) Lewis; Cummings, Press, Cooper, Hugh; Green, Cotterill (Fry 82), Patten (Greening 72); Compton (Fahiya 72), McLaggon, Hood.
Cliftonville: (352) Brush; McDermott (Maguire 90), Breen, Gorman; Curran C, Bagnall, Harkin, Doherty (Gormley 79), Ives; McMenamin (Curran R 83), Donnelly R.

Progres Niederkorn (0) 1 *(de Almeida 62)*

Cardiff Met Uni (0) 0 1984

Progres Niederkorn: (4141) Flauss; Skenderovic, Vogel, de Almeida, Muratovic; Bah (Shala 60); Thill, Laterza (Borges 78), Hall, Karayer; Matias Marques.
Cardiff Met Uni: (433) Fuller; Rees, Lewis, Woolridge, Edwards; Baker, Corsby (Morgan 63), McCarthy; Evans W (Parker 85), Evans E, Spencer (Lam 75).

PRELIMINARY ROUND SECOND LEG

St Joseph's v Pristina	2-0
Cardiff Met Uni v Progres Niederkorn	2-1
(Progres Niederkorn won on away goals)	
Cliftonville v Barry Town U	4-0
Engordany v La Fiorita	2-1
Europa v UE Sant Julia	4-0
NSI Runavik v Ballymena U	0-0
Tre Fiori v KI Klaksvik	0-4

Thursday, 4 July 2019

Cardiff Met Uni (1) 2 *(Lam 2, Rees 67 (pen))*

Progres Niederkorn (0) 1 *(de Almeida 73)* 1316

Cardiff Met Uni: (433) Fuller; Rees, Lewis, Woolridge, Edwards; Baker, Corsby (Phillips 77), McCarthy; Evans E (Davies 56), Evans W, Lam (Parker 61).
Progres Niederkorn: (4141) Flauss; Matias Marques (Bastos 70), Skenderovic, Hall, Karayer; Vogel; Laterza, Muratovic (Ferino 88), Thill, de Almeida; Bah (Correia Santos 85).
(Progres Niederkorn won on away goals)

Cliftonville (2) 4 *(McMenamin 25, Gormley 44, McDermott 82, Donnelly R 84)*

Barry Town U (0) 0 1946

Cliftonville: (352) Brush; McDermott, Breen, Gorman; McMenamin (Wilson 85), Curran C, Bagnall, Doherty, Ives; Donnelly R (Maguire 86), Gormley (Harney 85).
Barry Town U: (433) Lewis; Morgan, Cooper, Press, Hugh; Greening, Patten (Fry 73), Cotterill (Compton 64); Green, McLaggon, Hood (Snaith 79).

NSI Runavik (0) 0

Ballymena U (0) 0 553

NSI Runavik: (352) Thomsen; Jogvansson-Hansen, Hojgaard, Davidsen; Knudsen, Mortensen J (Dalbud 64), Nervseen, Justinussen, Hentze (Olsen O 84); Benjaminsen (Egilsson 74), Olsen K.
Ballymena U: (352) Ross Glendinning; Ervin, Whiteside, Balmer; Kane (Andrew Burns 84), Millar, Carville, Winchester (Harpur 90), McCullough; Lecky, Cathair Friel.

FIRST QUALIFYING ROUND FIRST LEG

CSKA Sofia v OFK Titograd	4-0
Gzira United v Hajduk Split	0-2
St Joseph's v Rangers	0-4
Jeunesse Esch v Tobol	0-0
Aberdeen v RoPS Rovaniemi	2-1
AEK Larnaca v Petrocub-Hincesti	1-0
Akademija Pandev v Zrinjski Mostar	0-3
Alashkert v Makedonija GjP	3-1
Balzan v Domzale	3-4
Brann v Shamrock R	2-2
Breidablik v Vaduz	0-0
Brondby v Inter Turku	4-1
Budapest Honved v Zalgiris Vilnius	3-1
Cliftonville v Haugesund	0-1
Connah's Quay Nomads v Kilmarnock	1-2
Cork C v Progres Niederkorn	0-2
Crusaders v B36 Torshavn	2-0
Cukaricki v Banants	3-0
DAC Dunajska Streda v Cracovia	1-1
Debrecen v Kukesi	3-0
Dinamo Tbilisi v UE Engordany	6-0
Europa v Legia Warsaw	0-0
FCSB v Milsami Orhei	2-0
FK Liepaja v Dinamo Minsk	1-1
Flora v Radnicki Nis	2-0
Fola Esch v Chikhura Sachkhere	1-2
Kauno Zalgiris v Apollon Limassol	0-2
KuPS Kuopio v Vitebsk	2-0
Laci v Hapoel Be'er Sheva	1-1
Maccabi Haifa v Mura	2-0
Malmo v Ballymena U	7-0
Molde v KR Reykjavik	7-1
Narva Trans v Buducnost Podgorica	0-2
Olimpija Ljubljana v Rigas FS	2-3
Ordabasy v Torpedo Kutaisi	1-0
Pyunik v Shkupi	3-3
Radnik Bijeljina v Spartak Trnava	2-0
Riteriai v KI Klaksvik	1-1
Ruzomberok v Levski Sofia	0-2
Sabail v Universitatea Craiova	2-3
Shakhtyor Soligorsk v Hibernians	1-0
Siroki Brijeg v Kairat	1-2
Speranta Nisporeni v Neftchi	0-3
St Patrick's Ath v IFK Norrkoping	0-2
Stjarnan v FCI Levadia	2-1
Ventspils v Teuta	3-0
Zeta v Fehervar	1-5

Tuesday, 9 July 2019

St Joseph's (0) 0

Rangers (0) 4 *(Jack 50, Ojo 56, Goldson 68, Morelos 77)* 2050

St Joseph's: (433) Matteo; Lobato, Villar, Guerrero, Torres; Pecci (Hernandez 70), Cornejo, Martinez (Garro 76); Pena, Ferrer (Casciaro 69), Boro.
Rangers: (433) McGregor; Tavernier, Goldson, Katic, Barisic; Jack (Aribo 62), Davis, Kamara; Ojo, Defoe (Morelos 63), Jones (Stewart 71).

Thursday, 11 July 2019

Aberdeen (1) 2 *(McGinn 36, Cosgrove 48)*

RoPS Rovaniemi (0) 1 *(Jokelainen 90)* 14,377

Aberdeen: (433) Lewis; Logan, Devlin, McKenna, Considine; Wright (McLennan 74), Ferguson, Gallagher; McGinn (Wilson 82), Cosgrove, Hedges (Campbell 61).
RoPS Rovaniemi: (4231) Reguero; Hyvarinen, Sissoko, Katz, Taiwo; Llamas (Jantti 76), Sihvonen; Rahimi, Lingman, Muinonen (Kada 57); Kokko (Jokelainen 65).

Brann (2) 2 *(Teniste 12, Berisha 36 (pen))*

Shamrock R (1) 2 *(Lopes 34, 90)* 4560

Brann: (433) Opdal; Teniste, Acosta, Rismark, Kristiansen; Haugen, Ordagic (Jenssen 74), Lokberg (Strand 68); Koomson (Bamba 82), Berisha, Sorensen.
Shamrock R: (451) Mannus; O'Brien, Lopes, Grace, Clarke (Watts 66); Boyle, Finn (McEneff 77), Bolger, Byrne, Kavanagh; Greene (Cummins 65).

Cliftonville (0) 0

Haugesund (1) 1 *(Grindheim 42)* 1342

Cliftonville: (352) Brush; McDermott, Breen, Gorman (Maguire 85); McMenamin, Curran C (Curran R 67), Bagnall, Doherty, Ives; Gormley, Donnelly R.
Haugesund: (433) Sandvik; Desler, Bergqvist, Hansen, Sandberg; Grindheim (Krygard 46), Tronstad, Leite; Samuelsen (Knudsen 82), Kone (Velde 33), Kallevag■.

Connah's Quay Nomads (0) 1 *(Taylor 75 (og))*

Kilmarnock (0) 2 *(Brophy 82 (pen), Findlay 90)* 1410

Connah's Quay Nomads: (4141) Brass; Disney, Roberts, Horan, Harrison; Bakare; Morris, Wilde, Poole, Holmes; Owen.
Kilmarnock: (433) MacDonald; O'Donnell, Taylor, Broadfoot, Power; McKenzie (El Makrini 64), Dicker, Brophy; Findlay, Thomas (Kiltie 78), Burke.

Cork C (0) 0

Progres Niederkorn (2) 2 *(Muratovic 11, de Almeida 21 (pen))* 3137

Cork C: (352) McNulty; Buckley (Boylan 61), Casey, Coustrain (Crowley 80); Horgan (O'Sullivan 24), Hurley, McCarthy, McCormack, McLoughlin; Morrissey, Sheppard.
Progres Niederkorn: (442) de Almeida; Flauss, Hall, Karayer, Laterza; Muratovic (Mmaee 71), Silaj, Skenderovic, Tekiela (Matias Marques 90); Thill (Ferino 88), Vogel.

Crusaders (1) 2 *(Hegarty 33, Lowry 79)*

B36 Torshavn (0) 0 1112

Crusaders: (4411) O'Neill; Burns, Beverland, Hegarty, Ruddy; Forsythe (Thompson 90), Caddell (Rory Hale 63), Lowry, Heatley (Cushley 78); Clarke; Owens.
B36 Torshavn: (4231) Jorgensen; Naes, Eriksen, Jacobsen M, Mellemgaard; Jacobsen E, Nielsen; Frederiksberg, Przybylski (Agnarsson 90), Heinesen (Radosavlevic 60); Cieslewicz (Jakobsen 90).

Malmo (3) 7 *(Rosenberg 31, 33, 48, Rakip 44, 74, Brorsson 46, Molins 54)*

Ballymena U (0) 0 8667

Malmo: (442) Dahlin; Berget (Larsson 59), Brorsson, Nielsen, Safari; Rakip, Lewicki, Bachirou (Innocent 69), Rieks; Rosenberg (Antonsson 59), Molins.
Ballymena U: (352) Ross Glendinning; Balmer, Whiteside, Ervin; McGrory, Millar, Kane, Carville (Andrew Burns 51), McCullough; Winchester (McGinty 75), Lecky (Cathair Friel 72).

St Patrick's Ath (0) 0

IFK Norrkoping (0) 2 *(Thern 55, Larsen 85)* 2389

St Patrick's Ath: (442) Clarke B; Kelly, Desmond, Toner, Bermingham; Madden, Clifford (Walker 83), Lennon, Coleman (McCabe 64); Drennan, Shaw (Clarke D 64).
IFK Norrkoping: (343) Pettersson; Dagerstal, Larsen, Lauritsen; Gerson, Fransson, Thorarinsson (Haksabanovic 75), Skrabb (Binaku 86); Larsson, Nyman (Holmberg 69), Thern.

FIRST QUALIFYING ROUND SECOND LEG

Banants v Cukaricki 0-5
KI Klaksvik v Riteriai 0-0
(KI Klaksvik won on away goals.)
OFK Titograd v CSKA Sofia 0-0
Chikhura Sachkhere v Fola Esch 2-1
Apollon Limassol v Kauno Zalgiris 4-0
B36 Torshavn v Crusaders 2-3
Ballymena U v Malmo 0-4
Buducnost Podgorica v Narva Trans 4-1
Cracovia v DAC Dunajska Streda 2-2
(aet; DAC Dunajska Streda won on away goals.)
Dinamo Minsk v FK Liepaja 1-2
Domzale v Balzan 1-0
FCI Levadia v Stjarnan 3-2
(aet; Stjarnan won on away goals.)
Fehervar v Zeta 0-0
Hajduk Split v Gzira U 1-3
(Gzira U won on away goals.)
Hapoel Be'er Sheva v Laci 1-0
Haugesund v Cliftonville 5-1
Hibernians v Shakhtyor Soligorsk 0-1
IFK Norrkoping v St Patrick's Ath 2-1
Inter Turku v Brondby 2-0
Kairat v Siroki Brijeg 2-1
Kilmarnock v Connah's Quay Nomads 0-2
KR Reykjavik v Molde 0-0
Kukesi v Debrecen 1-1
Legia Warsaw v Europa 3-0
Levski Sofia v Ruzomberok 2-0
Makedonija GjP v Alashkert 0-3
Milsami Orhei v FCSB 1-2
Mura v Maccabi Haifa 2-3
Neftchi v Speranta Nisporeni 6-0
Petrocub-Hincesti v AEK Larnaca 0-1
Progres Niederkorn v Cork C 1-2
Radnicki Nis v Flora 2-2
Rangers v St Joseph's 6-0
Rigas FS v Olimpija Ljubljana 0-2
RoPS Rovaniemi v Aberdeen 1-2
Shamrock R v Brann 2-1
Shkupi v Pyunik 1-2
Spartak Trnava v Radnik Bijeljina 2-0
(aet; Spartak Trnava won 3-2 on penalties.)
Teuta v Ventspils 1-0
Tobol v Jeunesse Esch 1-1
(Jeunesse Esch won on away goals.)
Torpedo Kutaisi v Ordabasy 0-2
UE Engordany v Dinamo Tbilisi 0-1
Universitatea Craiova v Sabail 3-2
Vaduz v Breidablik 2-1
Vitebsk v KuPS Kuopio 1-1
Zalgiris Vilnius v Budapest Honved 1-1
Zrinjski Mostar v Akademija Pandev 3-0

Thursday, 18 July 2019

B36 Torshavn (1) 2 *(Samuelsen H 37, Cieslewicz 51)*

Crusaders (2) 3 *(Forsythe 3, Heatley 28, 68)* 1422

B36 Torshavn: (4231) Jorgensen; Naes (Samuelsen G 83), Eriksen, Petersen, Jacobsen E (Przybylski 62); Nielsen, Jacobsen M; Frederiksberg, Radosavlevic, Samuelsen H (Agnarsson 71); Cieslewicz.
Crusaders: (433) O'Neill; Burns, Hegarty, Beverland, Ruddy; Forsythe (Thompson 86), Caddell (Rory Hale 65), Lowry; Clarke, Owens (Cushley 83), Heatley.

Ballymena U (0) 0

Malmo (1) 4 *(Safari 27, Molins 52, Rakip 68, Gall 79)* 1736

Ballymena U: (352) Ross Glendinning; Balmer, Addis (Kelly 75), Andrew Burns; McGrory, Millar, McGinty, Harpur (Lavery 70), McCullough; Lecky (Cathair Friel 71), Mayse.
Malmo: (442) Melicharek; Nielsen, Brorsson, Safari, Lewicki (Rieks 68); Berget, Rakip (Christiansen 74), Innocent, Gall; Antonsson, Molins (Prica 61).

Haugesund (3) 5 *(Velde 5, 68, Samuelsen 36, Kone 45, Leite 52)*

Cliftonville (1) 1 *(McMenamin 17)* 2633

Haugesund: (433) Sandvik; Desler, Bergqvist, Hansen, Sandberg; Tronstad, Ikedi, Leite; Samuelsen (Ndayisenga 72), Kone (Krygard 61), Velde.
Cliftonville: (352) Brush; McDermott, Breen, Gorman; McMenamin, Curran C, Bagnall (Curran R 61), Doherty (Wilson 80), Ives; Gormley (Maguire 70), Donnelly R.

IFK Norrkoping (1) 2 *(Larsson 36, Holmberg 85)*

St Patrick's Ath (0) 1 *(Clifford 72)* 5925

IFK Norrkoping: (352) Pettersson; Dagerstal, Larsen, Lauritsen; Gerson, Fransson (Blomqvist 88), Thorarinsson, Thern, Skrabb (Binaku 63); Larsson, Nyman (Holmberg 73).
St Patrick's Ath: (352) Clarke B; Desmond, Kelly■, Toner; Madden, Coleman (Markey 64), Lennon (McCabe 73), Clifford, Bermingham; Drennan, Shaw (Clarke D 52).

Kilmarnock (0) 0

Connah's Quay Nomads (0) 2 *(Morris 50, Wilde 80)* 8306

Kilmarnock: (433) MacDonald; O'Donnell, Broadfoot, Findlay■, Taylor; Power, Dicker, El Makrini (Thomas 87); Burke (Cameron 82), Brophy, McKenzie.
Connah's Quay Nomads: (451) Brass; Disney, Holmes, Horan, Roberts (Farquharson 83); Wignall■, Poole, Owen, Morris, Bakare (Insall 70); Wilde.

Progres Niederkorn (0) 1 *(Bah 68)*
Cork C (1) 2 *(Buckley 3, McCarthy 47)* 1927
Progres Niederkorn: (4141) Flauss; Matias Marques, Skenderovic, Hall, Karayer; Vogel; Muratovic (Bah 66), Silaj, Thill (Ferino 90), de Almeida; Tekiela (Shala 85).
Cork C: (433) McNulty; Horgan, McCarthy, McLoughlin, Hurley (O'Connor K 90); Morrissey, McCormack, Buckley; O'Connor D (Griffin 82), Sheppard, Coustrain (Casey 88).

Rangers (2) 6 *(Aribo 3, Morelos 45, 57 (pen), 66, Defoe 77, 86)*
St Joseph's (0) 0 45,718
Rangers: (433) Foderingham; Polster, Goldson, Edmundson, Halliday; Aribo, Docherty (McPake 67), Kamara; Hastie (Arfield 58), Morelos (Defoe 67), Stewart.
St Joseph's: (433) Robba; Serra, Villar, Guerrero, Torres; Martinez (Reyes 72), Hernandez, Boro; Pena, Ferrer (Garro 79), Cornejo (Green 69).

RoPS Rovaniemi (1) 1 *(Kada 2)*
Aberdeen (1) 2 *(Cosgrove 27 (pen), Ferguson 90)* 2000
RoPS Rovaniemi: (4231) Reguero; Hyvarinen, Katz, Sissoko, Taiwo; Sihvonen, Muinonen (Jantti 81); Kada, Lingman, Agnaldo (Rahimi 68); Kokko (Jokelainen 66).
Aberdeen: (433) Lewis; Logan, Taylor, McKenna, Considine; Hedges, Campbell, Ferguson; Gallagher, Cosgrove (Main 66), McGinn (Wright 87).

Shamrock R (0) 2 *(Byrne 76, O'Neill 87)*
Brann (0) 1 *(Bamba 57)* 5135
Shamrock R: (352) Mannus; O'Brien, Lopes, Grace; Boyle, Watts (McEneff 63), Byrne, Bolger, Kavanagh; Finn (O'Neil 80), Cummins (Carr 75).
Brann: (433) Opdal; Teniste (Karadas 84), Acosta, Rismark, Kristiansen; Haugen, Ordagic, Strand (Jenssen 84); Sorensen, Berisha, Koomson (Bamba 46).

SECOND QUALIFYING ROUND FIRST LEG

Ararat-Armenia v Lincoln Red Imps	2-0
FC Santa Coloma v Astana	0-0
HB Torshavn v Linfield	2-2
Shkendija v F91 Dudelange	1-2
Tre Penne v Suduva	0-5
Slovan Bratislava v Feronikeli	2-1
AEK Larnaca v Levski Sofia	3-0
Alashkert v FCSB	0-3
Aris v AEL Limassol	0-0
Arsenal Tula v Neftchi	0-1
AZ Alkmaar v Hacken	0-0
Budapest Honved v Universitatea Craiova	0-0
Buducnost Podgorica v Zorya Luhansk	1-3
Chikhura Sachkhere v Aberdeen	1-1
Connah's Quay Nomads v Partizan Belgrade	0-1
CSKA Sofia v Osijek	1-0
DAC Dunajska Streda v Atromitos	1-2
Domzale v Malmo	2-2
Espanyol v Stjarnan	4-0
Fehervar v Vaduz	1-0
Flora v Eintracht Frankfurt	1-2
Gabala v Dinamo Tbilisi	0-2
Gent v Viitorul Constanta	6-3
Hapoel Be'er Sheva v Kairat	2-0
Haugesund v Sturm Graz	2-0
IFK Norrkoping v FK Liepaja	2-0
Jeunesse Esch v Vitoria de Guimaraes	0-1
Lechia Gdansk v Brondby	2-1
Legia Warsaw v KuPS Kuopio	1-0
Lokomotiv Plovdiv v Spartak Trnava	2-0
Lucerne v KI Klaksvik	1-0
Mlada Boleslav v Ordabasy	1-1
Molde v Cukaricki	0-0
Partizani Tirana v Sheriff	0-1
Piast Gliwice v Riga FC	3-2
Pyunik v Jablonec	2-1
Rangers v Progres Niederkorn	2-0
Shakhtyor Soligorsk v Esbjerg	2-0
Shamrock R v Apollon Limassol	2-1
Strasbourg v Maccabi Haifa	3-1
Torino v Debrecen	3-0
Utrecht v Zrinjski Mostar	1-1
Valur v Ludogorets Razgrad	1-1
Ventspils v Gzira United	4-0
Wolverhampton W v Crusaders	2-0
Yeni Malatyaspor v Olimpija Ljubljana	2-2

Tuesday, 23 July 2019

HB Torshavn (1) 2 *(Justinussen 37 (pen), Petersen 89)*
Linfield (1) 2 *(Waterworth 2, 88 (pen))* 751
HB Torshavn: (442) Gestsson; Davidsen, Askham, Andersen, Egilsson; Justinussen (Petersen 78), Jensen, Hlodversson (Johansen 85), Samuelsen; Pingel (Soylu 70), Olsen.
Linfield: (442) Ferguson; Casement, Stafford, Callacher, Clarke; Stewart (Millar 77), Hery, Mulgrew, Quinn (Cooper 83); Waterworth, Kearns (Lavery 81).

Thursday, 25 July 2019

Chikhura Sachkhere (1) 1 *(Koripadze 41 (pen))*
Aberdeen (0) 1 *(Cosgrove 68 (pen))* 3218
Chikhura Sachkhere: (433) Hamzic; Koripadze, Maisashvili, Mamasakhlisi, Chikvaidze; Chiteishvili (Chikhladze 74), Kashia, Sardalishvili; Dekanoidze, Ergemlidze, Lekvtadze (Pantsulaia 76).
Aberdeen: (433) Lewis; Logan, Taylor (Bryson 18), McKenna, Considine; Ojo, Ferguson, Hedges; Gallagher (Wilson 82), Cosgrove, McGinn.

Connah's Quay Nomads (0) 0
Partizan Belgrade (0) 1 *(Scekic 62)* 829
Connah's Quay Nomads: (451) Brass; Disney, Horan, Holmes, Roberts; Poole, Owen, Wilde, Morris, Woolfe (Bakare 58); Insall (Farquharson 73).
Partizan Belgrade: (433) Stojkovic; Soumah, Ivanovic (Stevanovic 73), Scekic, Pavlovic S; Zdjelar, Urosevic, Tosic; Ostojic, Sadiq (Ozegovic 46), Miletic.

Rangers (1) 2 *(Aribo 20, Ojo 54)*
Progres Niederkorn (0) 0 43,629
Rangers: (442) McGregor; Arfield (Jones 66), Aribo, Davis, Edmundson; Goldson, Halliday, Jack, Morelos (Defoe 75); Ojo (Stewart 81), Tavernier.
Progres Niederkorn: (442) Flauss; de Almeida, Ferino, Hall, Karayer; Laterza■, Muratovic (Mmaee 46), Silaj, Skenderovic (Matias Marques 33); Tekiela (Francoise 80), Vogel.

Shamrock R (1) 2 *(Grace 14, Lopes 58)*
Apollon Limassol (1) 1 *(Papoulis 5)* 5396
Shamrock R: (541) Mannus; O'Brien, Lopes, Grace, Bolger, Kavanagh; Boyle, Finn (O'Neil 77), Byrne, McEneff (Watts 85); Carr (Greene 64).
Apollon Limassol: (4231) Mall; Joao Pedro, Yuste, Szalai, Bessat; Markovic, Sachetti■; Gianniotas, Pittas (Gakpe 61), Papoulis (Aguirre 72); Zelaya (Pereyra 81).

Wolverhampton W (1) 2 *(Jota 37, Ruben Vinagre 90)*
Crusaders (0) 0 29,708
Wolverhampton W: (352) Rui Patricio; Bennett, Coady, Boly; Traore, Dendoncker, Neves (Jimenez 58), Joao Moutinho, Jonny (Ruben Vinagre 64); Gibbs-White (Saiss 85), Jota.
Crusaders: (442) O'Neill; Ward, Lowry, Burns, Hegarty; Forsythe, Clarke (Owens 61), Heatley, O'Rourke; Rory Hale (Cushley 82), Caddell (Thompson 67).

SECOND QUALIFYING ROUND SECOND LEG

F91 Dudelange v Shkendija	1-1
Feronikeli v Slovan Bratislava	0-2
Lincoln Red Imps v Ararat-Armenia	1-2
Suduva v Tre Penne	5-0
Cukaricki v Molde	1-3
Aberdeen v Chikhura Sachkhere	5-0
AEL Limassol v Aris	0-1
Apollon Limassol v Shamrock R *(aet.)*	3-1
Astana v FC Santa Coloma	4-1
Atromitos v DAC Dunajska Streda	3-2
Brondby v Lechia Gdansk *(aet.)*	4-1
Crusaders v Wolverhampton W	1-4
Debrecen v Torino	1-4
Dinamo Tbilisi v Gabala	3-0
Eintracht Frankfurt v Flora	2-1

Esbjerg v Shakhtyor Soligorsk 0-0
FCSB v Alashkert 2-3
FK Liepaja v IFK Norrkoping 0-1
Gzira United v Ventspils 2-2
Hacken v AZ Alkmaar 0-3
Jablonec v Pyunik 0-0
Kairat v Hapoel Be'er Sheva 1-1
KI Klaksvik v Lucerne 0-1
KuPS Kuopio v Legia Warsaw 0-0
Levski Sofia v AEK Larnaca 0-4
Linfield v HB Torshavn 1-0
Ludogorets Razgrad v Valur 4-0
Maccabi Haifa v Strasbourg 2-1
Malmo v Domzale 3-2
Neftchi v Arsenal Tula 3-0
Olimpija Ljubljana v Yeni Malatyaspor 0-1
Ordabasy v Mlada Boleslav 2-3
Osijek v CSKA Sofia 1-0
(aet; CSKA Sofia won 4-3 on penalties.)
Partizan Belgrade v Connah's Quay Nomads 3-0
Progres Niederkorn v Rangers 0-0
Riga FC v Piast Gliwice 2-1
(Riga FC won on away goals.)
Sheriff v Partizani Tirana 1-1
Spartak Trnava v Lokomotiv Plovdiv 3-1
(aet; Lokomotiv Plovdiv won on away goals.)
Stjarnan v Espanyol 1-3
Sturm Graz v Haugesund 2-1
Universitatea Craiova v Budapest Honved 0-0
(aet; Universitatea Craiova won 3-1 on penalties.)
Vaduz v Fehervar 2-0
(aet.)
Viitorul Constanta v Gent 2-1
Vitoria de Guimaraes v Jeunesse Esch 4-0
Zorya Luhansk v Buducnost Podgorica 1-0
Zrinjski Mostar v Utrecht 2-1
(aet.)

Thursday, 1 August 2019

Aberdeen (2) 5 *(Cosgrove 9, 20, 80, Leigh 58, Wright 65)*

Chikhura Sachkhere (0) 0 15,167

Aberdeen: (433) Lewis; Logan, Considine, McKenna, Leigh (Campbell 67); Gallagher, Ojo, Ferguson; Hedges, Cosgrove (Anderson 82), McGinn (Wright 62).
Chikhura Sachkhere: (433) Hamzic; Koripadze, Maisashvili, Mamasakhlisi, Chikvaidze; Chiteishvili (Markozashvili 52), Kashia, Sardalishvili; Lekvtadze, Ergemlidze (Chikhladze 72), Dekanoidze (Pantsulaia 52).

Apollon Limassol (1) 3 *(Zelaya 18, Markovic 64, Sardinero 102)*

Shamrock R (0) 1 *(Greene 69)* 2987

Apollon Limassol: (4231) Mall; Joao Pedro, Yuste, Tamba M'Pinda (Szalai 58), Aguirre; Markovic, Kyriakou (Pereyra 105); Gianniotas (Pittas 90), Papoulis■, Gakpe (Sardinero 77); Zelaya.
Shamrock R: (352) Mannus; O'Brien (Watts 83), Lopes, Grace■; Boyle, Byrne, McEneff (O'Neil 75), Bolger (Oluwa 105), Kavanagh; Finn (Carr 86), Greene.
aet.

Crusaders (1) 1 *(Bennett 13 (og))*

Wolverhampton W (3) 4 *(Jimenez 15, 45, Bennett 38, Forsythe 77 (og))* 2700

Crusaders: (4132) O'Neill; Lowry, Clarke (Caddell 78), Burns, Hegarty; Ward; Heatley, Owens (Cushley 80), O'Rourke; Forsythe, Rory Hale (Thompson 83).
Wolverhampton W: (532) Rui Patricio; Traore, Bennett, Coady, Boly, Jonny; Dendoncker, Neves (Saiss 68), Joao Moutinho; Jimenez (Gibbs-White 55), Jota (Ruben Vinagre 67).

Linfield (1) 1 *(Waterworth 20 (pen))*

HB Torshavn (0) 0

Linfield: (442) Ferguson; Casement, Stafford, Callacher, Quinn; Stewart (Millar 75), Hery, Mulgrew, Cooper; Waterworth, Kearns (Lavery 71).
HB Torshavn: (442) Mork; Davidsen, Askham, Andersen, Egilsson; Justinussen, Jensen, Hlodversson (Soylu 61), Samuelsen; Joensen (Petersen 75), Pingel (Olsen 61).
Behind closed doors.

Partizan Belgrade (0) 3 *(Tosic 54, Ozegovic 70, Stevanovic 73)*

Connah's Quay Nomads (0) 0 8200

Partizan Belgrade: (442) Stojkovic; Miletic, Ostojic, Pavlovic S, Brezancic (Urosevic 73); Ivanovic (Stevanovic 46), Scekic, Zdjelar, Tosic (Ozegovic 63); Soumah, Sadiq.
Connah's Quay Nomads: (4141) Brass; Disney, Horan, Holmes, Roberts; Harrison (Wignall 63); Insall (Bakare 81), Morris, Owen, Poole; Wilde (Farquharson 74).

Progres Niederkorn (0) 0

Rangers (0) 0 3867

Progres Niederkorn: (4141) Flauss; Matias Marques, Ferino, Hall, Karayer; Vogel; Mmaee (Bah 70), Silaj, Thill (Shala 64), de Almeida; Francoise (Tekiela 84).
Rangers: (451) McGregor; Tavernier, Goldson, Katic, Barisic (Halliday 46); Ojo, Jack, Kamara, Aribo, Arfield (Docherty 76); Defoe (Morelos 76).

THIRD QUALIFYING ROUND FIRST LEG

Ararat-Armenia v Saburtalo 1-2
Riga FC v HJK Helsinki 1-1
Sutjeska v Linfield 1-2
Slovan Bratislava v Dundalk 1-0
AEK Larnaca v Gent 1-1
Antwerp v Viktoria Plzen 1-0
Astana v Valletta 5-1
Austria Vienna v Apollon Limassol 1-2
Brondby v Braga 2-4
CSKA Sofia v Zorya Luhansk 1-1
F91 Dudelange v Nomme Kalju 3-1
FC Midtjylland v Rangers 2-4
FCSB v Mlada Boleslav 0-0
Feyenoord v Dinamo Tbilisi 4-0
Haugesund v PSV Eindhoven 0-1
IFK Norrkoping v Hapoel Be'er Sheva 1-1
Legia Warsaw v Atromitos 0-0
Lokomotiv Plovdiv v Strasbourg 0-1
Lucerne v Espanyol 0-3
Ludogorets Razgrad v The New Saints 5-0
Maccabi Tel Aviv v Suduva 1-2
Malmo v Zrinjski Mostar 3-0
Mariupol v AZ Alkmaar 0-0
Molde v Aris 3-0
Neftchi v Bnei Yehuda 2-2
Partizan Belgrade v Yeni Malatyaspor 3-1
Pyunik v Wolverhampton W 0-4
Rijeka v Aberdeen 2-0
Sarajevo v BATE Borisov 1-2
Sheriff v AIK Solna 1-2
Sparta Prague v Trabzonspor 2-2
Thun v Spartak Moscow 2-3
Torino v Shakhtyor Soligorsk 5-0
Universitatea Craiova v AEK Athens 0-2
Vaduz v Eintracht Frankfurt 0-5
Ventspils v Vitoria de Guimaraes 0-3

Tuesday, 6 August 2019

Sutjeska (1) 1 *(Kojasevic 11)*

Linfield (1) 2 *(Millar 38, 65)* 3850

Sutjeska: (4231) Giljen; Ciger, Sofranac, Nedic, Bulatovic; Erakovic (Bubanja 68), Jankovic; Kojasevic, Cetkovic, Marko Vucic (Vlaisavljevic 83); Bozovic (Nikolic 46).
Linfield: (4231) Ferguson; Casement, McGivern, Stafford, Clarke; Fallon (Mitchell 84), Mulgrew; Millar (Stewart 87), Hery (Kearns 90), Quinn; Lavery.

Wednesday, 7 August 2019

Slovan Bratislava (0) 1 *(Holman 86)*

Dundalk (0) 0 9980

Slovan Bratislava: (4231) Greif; Jurij Medvedev, Abena, Bozhikov, De Marco; Ljubicic, de Kamps; Rafael Ratao (Drazic 67), Holman, Moha (Daniel 77); Sporar (Cavric 80).
Dundalk: (4312) Rogers; Gannon, Cleary, Boyle, Massey; Mountney, Shields, McGrath; Murray (McEleney 70); Duffy (Kelly D 88), Hoban (Dummigan 87).

Thursday, 8 August 2019

FC Midtjylland (0) 2 *(Onyeka 58, Kaba 63)*

Rangers (1) 4 *(Morelos 43, Aribo 52, Katic 56, Arfield 70)* 9322

FC Midtjylland: (352) Hansen; Scholz, Sviatchenko, Nicolaisen (Mabil 73); Cajuste, Onyeka, Sparv (Junior Brumado 58), Evander, Andersson; Kaba, Wikheim (Anderson 58).
Rangers: (442) McGregor; Tavernier, Goldson, Katic, Flanagan; Aribo, Kamara, Jack, Arfield (Docherty 82); Morelos, Jones (Ojo 82).

Ludogorets Razgrad (3) 5 *(Harrington 10 (og), Tchibota 28, Lukoki 43, Keseru 65, Moti 76)*

The New Saints (0) 0 4120

Ludogorets Razgrad: (433) Iliev; Ikoko, Moti, Forster, Nedyalkov; Abel (Badji 61), Biton (Swierczok 77), Goralski; Lukoki, Keseru, Tchibota (Wanderson 70).
The New Saints: (4231) Harrison; Spender (Lewis 69), Harrington, Davies (Hudson 46), Marriott; Routledge, Edwards; Mullan, Brobbel, Redmond; Ebbe (Draper 61).

Pyunik (0) 0

Wolverhampton W (2) 4 *(Doherty 29, Jimenez 42, 46, Neves 90 (pen))* 13,050

Pyunik: (4231) Dragojevic; Stankov, Zhestokov, Marku, Manucharyan A; Mkrtchyan, Simonyan; Efimov (Burzanovic 55), Mahmudov (Alfred 62), Shevchuk; Miranyan.
Wolverhampton W: (352) Rui Patricio; Bennett, Coady, Boly; Doherty (Cutrone 63), Dendoncker, Saiss, Joao Moutinho, Ruben Vinagre; Jimenez (Neves 71), Jota (Jonny 63).

Rijeka (0) 2 *(Colak 62, Muric 87)*

Aberdeen (0) 0 6452

Rijeka: (433) Prskalo; Kvrzic, Zuparic, Puncec, Tomecak (Raspopovic 75); Halilovic, Lepinjica, Capan (Iglesias 85); Acosty (Muric 64), Colak, Loncar.
Aberdeen: (433) Lewis; Logan, Considine, McKenna, Leigh; Ferguson, Ojo, Gallagher (Campbell 76); Hedges (Main 86), Cosgrove, McGinn (Wright 76).

THIRD QUALIFYING ROUND SECOND LEG

Dundalk v Slovan Bratislava	1-3
Linfield v Sutjeska	3-2
Nomme Kalju v F91 Dudelange	0-1
Atromitos v Legia Warsaw	0-2
Saburtalo v Ararat-Armenia	0-2
Vitoria de Guimaraes v Ventspils	6-0
Aberdeen v Rijeka	0-2
AEK Athens v Universitatea Craiova	1-1
AIK Solna v Sheriff	1-1
Apollon Limassol v Austria Vienna	3-1
Aris v Molde	3-1
(aet.)	
AZ Alkmaar v Mariupol	4-0
BATE Borisov v Sarajevo	0-0
Bnei Yehuda v Neftchi	2-1
Braga v Brondby	3-1
Dinamo Tbilisi v Feyenoord	1-1
Eintracht Frankfurt v Vaduz	1-0
Espanyol v Lucerne	3-0
Gent v AEK Larnaca	3-0
Hapoel Be'er Sheva v IFK Norrkoping	3-1
HJK Helsinki v Riga FC	2-2
(Riga FC won on away goals.)	
Mlada Boleslav v FCSB	0-1
PSV Eindhoven v Haugesund	0-0
Rangers v FC Midtjylland	3-1
Shakhtyor Soligorsk v Torino	1-1
Spartak Moscow v Thun	2-1
Strasbourg v Lokomotiv Plovdiv	1-0
Suduva v Maccabi Tel Aviv	2-1
The New Saints v Ludogorets Razgrad	0-4
Trabzonspor v Sparta Prague	2-1
Valletta v Astana	0-4
Viktoria Plzen v Antwerp	2-1
(aet; Antwerp won on away goals.)	
Wolverhampton W v Pyunik	4-0
Yeni Malatyaspor v Partizan Belgrade	1-0
Zorya Luhansk v CSKA Sofia	1-0
Zrinjski Mostar v Malmo	1-0

Tuesday, 13 August 2019

Dundalk (0) 1 *(Duffy 70)*

Slovan Bratislava (2) 3 *(Rafael Ratao 12, Cavric 33, Daniel 90)* 4199

Dundalk: (442) Rogers; Gannon, Boyle, Cleary (Hoare 46), Massey; Mountney, Shields, Murray (McEleney 46), McGrath (Kelly G 79); Hoban, Duffy.
Slovan Bratislava: (4231) Greif; Jurij Medvedev (Apau 65), Abena, Bozhikov, De Marco; Ljubicic, de Kamps; Cavric (Daniel 61), Holman, Rafael Ratao (Sukhotsky 85); Sporar.

Linfield (2) 3 *(Stafford 7, Lavery 18, Clarke 76)*

Sutjeska (1) 2 *(Bozovic 15, 61)* 3639

Linfield: (4231) Ferguson; Casement, Stafford, McGivern, Clarke; Mulgrew, Fallon; Millar (Cooper 67), Hery, Quinn (Stewart 76); Lavery (Waterworth 79).
Sutjeska: (4231) Giljen; Ciger, Sofranac■, Nedic, Bulatovic; Erakovic (Nikolic 85), Petrovikj; Kojasevic, Cetkovic, Vlaisavljevic (Marko Vucic 63); Bozovic (Markovic 73).

Thursday, 15 August 2019

Aberdeen (0) 0

Rijeka (2) 2 *(Loncar 10, Colak 32)* 15,246

Aberdeen: (433) Lewis; Logan, McKenna, Considine, Leigh; Hedges (Wilson 75), Ojo■, Ferguson; Gallagher, Cosgrove (Main 53), McGinn (Campbell 35).
Rijeka: (433) Prskalo; Kvrzic, Zuparic, Puncec, Raspopovic; Halilovic (Iglesias 83), Lepinjica, Capan; Acosty (Vuk 82), Colak, Loncar (Muric 75).

Rangers (2) 3 *(Morelos 14, 49, Ojo 39)*

FC Midtjylland (0) 1 *(Evander 72)* 47,184

Rangers: (433) McGregor; Tavernier, Goldson, Katic, Flanagan; Kamara, Davis, Jack (Docherty 69); Ojo (Jones 69), Morelos (Defoe 81), Arfield.
FC Midtjylland: (352) Hansen; Sviatchenko, Scholz, Nicolaisen; Cajuste (Mabil 46), Onyeka, Evander, Anderson (Sparv 69), Andersson; Wikheim, Kaba (Dovbyk 82).

The New Saints (0) 0

Ludogorets Razgrad (2) 4 *(Swierczok 36, 77, Lukoki 42, Biton 90)* 712

The New Saints: (433) Harrison; Lewis, Hudson, Davies, Marriott; Harrington, Edwards, Redmond; Mullan (Whitehouse 74), Ebbe (Byrne 68), Brobbel (Cieslewicz 78).
Ludogorets Razgrad: (433) Renan; Manolev, Grigore, Forster, Cicinho; Goralski (Biton 68), Dyakov, Badji; Lukoki (Tchibota 75), Swierczok (Keseru 81), Wanderson.

Wolverhampton W (0) 4 *(Pedro Neto 54, Gibbs-White 58, Ruben Vinagre 64, Jota 87)*

Pyunik (0) 0 29,391

Wolverhampton W: (442) Ruddy; Traore, Vallejo, Coady, Kilman; Ruben Vinagre, Gibbs-White, Saiss, Joao Moutinho (Dendoncker 52); Cutrone (Jimenez 72), Pedro Neto (Jota 72).
Pyunik: (451) Dragojevic; Stankov, Zhestokov, Belov, Manucharyan A; Efimov (Galimov 46), Vardanyan, Mkrtchyan, Simonyan (Yedigaryan 71), Shevchuk (Mahmudov 75); Miranyan.

PLAY-OFF ROUND FIRST LEG

AEK Athens v Trabzonspor	1-3
Ararat-Armenia v F91 Dudelange	2-1
Astana v BATE Borisov	3-0
AZ Alkmaar v Antwerp	1-1
Braga v Spartak Moscow	1-0
Celtic v AIK Solna	2-0
Espanyol v Zorya Luhansk	3-1
FC Copenhagen v Riga FC	3-1
FCSB v Vitoria de Guimaraes	0-0
Feyenoord v Hapoel Be'er Sheva	3-0
Gent v Rijeka	2-1
Legia Warsaw v Rangers	0-0
Linfield v Qarabag	3-2
Ludogorets Razgrad v Maribor	0-0

Malmo v Bnei Yehuda 3-0
Partizan Belgrade v Molde 2-1
PSV Eindhoven v Apollon Limassol 3-0
Slovan Bratislava v PAOK 1-0
Strasbourg v Eintracht Frankfurt 1-0
Suduva v Ferencvaros 0-0
Torino v Wolverhampton W 2-3

Thursday, 22 August 2019

Celtic (0) 2 *(Forrest 48, Edouard 73)*

AIK Solna (0) 0 40,885

Celtic: (433) Gordon; Ajer, Jullien, Simunovic, Bolingoli-Mbombo; Forrest (Ntcham 82), Brown, McGregor; Christie, Edouard (Bayo 84), Johnston (Morgan 82).
AIK Solna: (352) Linner; Granli, Karlsson, Mets; Lundstrom (Rashidi 86), Larsson, Adu, Bahoui (Saletros 70), Lindkvist; Goitom, Sigthorsson (Ogbuke Obasi 72).

Legia Warsaw (0) 0

Rangers (0) 0 26,665

Legia Warsaw: (4231) Majecki; Stolarski, Lewczuk, Jedrzejczyk, Luis Rocha; Andre Martins, Cafu (Antolic 71); Vesovic (Nagy 84), Gvilia, Luquinhas; Kulenovic.
Rangers: (442) McGregor; Tavernier, Goldson, Katic, Flanagan; Aribo, Davis, Jack, Arfield (Kamara 87); Ojo, Morelos (Defoe 87).

Linfield (2) 3 *(Stafford 40, Lavery 45, 75)*

Qarabag (1) 2 *(Rherras 15, Gueye 90 (pen))* 4633

Linfield: (4231) Ferguson; Casement, Stafford, Callacher, Clarke; Mulgrew, Mitchell; Cooper (Millar 90), Hery, Quinn; Lavery (Waterworth 80).
Qarabag: (433) Vagner; Rherras, Medvedev, Sadygov, Huseynov A; Garayev, Quintana (Gueye 67), Michel; Zoubir, Emreli, Romero.

Torino (0) 2 *(De Silvestri 62, Belotti 90 (pen))*

Wolverhampton W (1) 3 *(Izzo 43 (og), Jota 60, Jimenez 72)* 24,091

Torino: (343) Sirigu; Izzo, N'Koulou, Bremer; De Silvestri, Meite (Rincon 64), Baselli, Ansaldi (Aina 71); Zaza, Belotti, Berenguer (Lukic 59).
Wolverhampton W: (532) Rui Patricio; Traore (Jonny 64), Vallejo, Coady, Boly, Ruben Vinagre; Dendoncker, Saiss, Joao Moutinho; Jimenez (Cutrone 76), Jota (Pedro Neto 69).

PLAY-OFF ROUND SECOND LEG

AIK Solna v Celtic 1-4
Antwerp v AZ Alkmaar 1-4
(aet.)
Apollon Limassol v PSV Eindhoven 0-4
BATE Borisov v Astana 2-0
Bnei Yehuda v Malmo 0-1
Eintracht Frankfurt v Strasbourg 3-0
F91 Dudelange v Ararat-Armenia 2-1
(aet; F91 Dudelange won 5-4 on penalties.)
Ferencvaros v Suduva 4-2
Hapoel Be'er Sheva v Feyenoord 0-3
Maribor v Ludogorets Razgrad 2-2
(Ludogorets Razgrad won on away goals.)
Molde v Partizan Belgrade 1-1
PAOK v Slovan Bratislava 3-2
(Slovan Bratislava won on away goals.)
Qarabag v Linfield 2-1
(Qarabag won on away goals.)
Rangers v Legia Warsaw 1-0
Riga FC v FC Copenhagen 1-0
Rijeka v Gent 1-1
Spartak Moscow v Braga 1-2
Trabzonspor v AEK Athens 0-2
(Trabzonspor won on away goals.)
Vitoria de Guimaraes v FCSB 1-0
Wolverhampton W v Torino 2-1
Zorya Luhansk v Espanyol 2-2

Thursday, 29 August 2019

AIK Solna (1) 1 *(Larsson 33 (pen))*

Celtic (2) 4 *(Forrest 17, Johnston 34, Jullien 87, Morgan 90)* 28,410

AIK Solna: (352) Linner; Granli, Karlsson, Mets; Lundstrom (Rashidi 79), Larsson, Adu, Bahoui (Hussein 62), Saletros; Ogbuke Obasi, Sigthorsson (Goitom 62).
Celtic: (4231) Gordon; Ajer (Ralston 15), Jullien, Bitton, Bolingoli-Mbombo; McGregor, Brown; Forrest, Edouard (Bayo 76), Christie; Johnston (Morgan 70).

Qarabag (1) 2 *(Romero 6, Zoubir 88)*

Linfield (0) 1 *(Lavery 90)* 18,349

Qarabag: (4231) Vagner; Medvedev, Mammadov, Sadygov, Ailton; Michel (Quintana 90), Almeyda; Emreli, Romero, Zoubir (Abdullayev 90); Gueye (Garayev 85).
Linfield: (4231) Ferguson; Casement, Stafford, Callacher, Clarke; Mulgrew, Fallon (Waterworth 78); Cooper (Stewart 81), Hery, Quinn (Millar 78); Lavery.
Qarabag won on away goals.

Rangers (0) 1 *(Morelos 90)*

Legia Warsaw (0) 0 45,463

Rangers: (433) McGregor; Barisic (Flanagan 64), Katic, Goldson, Tavernier; Arfield (Jones 72), Jack, Davis; Aribo, Morelos, Ojo (Kamara 90).
Legia Warsaw: (4231) Majecki; Stolarski (Nagy 73), Lewczuk, Jedrzejczyk, Luis Rocha; Andre Martins, Cafu; Vesovic, Gvilia, Luquinhas; Kulenovic (Niezgoda 56).

Wolverhampton W (1) 2 *(Jimenez 31, Dendoncker 59)*

Torino (0) 1 *(Belotti 58)* 29,222

Wolverhampton W: (352) Rui Patricio; Vallejo, Coady, Boly; Traore, Dendoncker, Saiss, Joao Moutinho (Neves 90), Jonny; Jimenez (Pedro Neto 90), Jota (Cutrone 81).
Torino: (352) Sirigu; Izzo, Bremer, Bonifazi; De Silvestri, Baselli, Rincon (Meite 72), Lukic, Aina (Berenguer 70); Zaza (Millico 82), Belotti.

GROUP STAGE

GROUP A

Thursday, 19 September 2019

APOEL (0) 3 *(Pavlovic 54, 58, De Vincenti 56 (pen))*

F91 Dudelange (1) 4 *(Sinani 36, 82, Bernier 51, Stolz 71)* 9313

APOEL: (532) Belec; Jakolis (Al-Taamari 46), Mihajlovic, Merkis, Ioannou, Bezjak; Lucas Souza (Joaozinho 46), Matic, Gentsoglou; De Vincenti (Efrem 76), Pavlovic.
F91 Dudelange: (4231) Joubert; Bouchouari, Schnell, Garos, Kirch (Lesquoy 63); Morren, Pokar; Stolz (Cools 90), Sinani, Bernier; Mendy (Lavie 67).

Qarabag (0) 0

Sevilla (0) 3 *(Hernandez 62, Munir 78, Torres 85)* 30,826

Qarabag: (4141) Begovic; Huseynov A, Huseynov B, Medvedev, Ailton; Garayev (Ibrahimli 85); Romero (Quintana 77), Michel, Almeyda, Zoubir; Gueye (Abdullayev 67).
Sevilla: (433) Vaclik; Pozo, Kounde, Diego Carlos, Escudero; Jordan (Lopes 58), Gudelj, Torres (Dabbur 86); Vazquez, Hernandez (Banega 72), Munir.

Thursday, 3 October 2019

F91 Dudelange (0) 1 *(Bernier 90)*

Qarabag (3) 4 *(Zoubir 11, Michel 30, Almeyda 37 (pen), Quintana 69)* 3005

F91 Dudelange: (442) Joubert; Bouchouari, Schnell, Garos■, Lesquoy; Klapp (Lavie 56), Bougrine, Pokar (Cools 72), Bernier; Sinani, Mendy (Morren 67).
Qarabag: (4141) Begovic; Medvedev, Huseynov B, Sadygov, Ailton; Garayev (Slavchev 60); Quintana (Abdullayev 81), Michel (Gueye 72), Almeyda, Zoubir; Emreli.

Sevilla (1) 1 *(Hernandez 17)*

APOEL (0) 0 30,008

Sevilla: (433) Bounou; Pozo, Kounde, Sergi Gomez, Escudero; Vazquez, Gudelj, Jordan; Lopes (Banega 72), Hernandez (Dabbur 79), Munir (Gil Salvatierra 61).

APOEL: (541) Belec; Mihajlovic, Merkis, Savic, Ioannou, Jakolis; Al-Taamari (Aloneftis 83), Lucas Souza, Gentsoglou (Efrem 80), Matic; Pavlovic (Hallenius 66).

Thursday, 24 October 2019

Qarabag (1) 2 *(Quintana 13, Ailton 58)*

APOEL (2) 2 *(Medvedev 29 (og), Hallenius 45)* 30,824

Qarabag: (433) Begovic; Medvedev, Huseynov B, Sadygov, Ailton; Michel, Garayev, Almeyda; Quintana, Gueye (Emreli 46), Zoubir.
APOEL: (532) Belec; Mihajlovic, Vouros, Merkis, Savic, Ioannou (Jakolis 67); Lucas Souza, Gentsoglou, Matic; Pavlovic (Alef 85), Hallenius (Bezjak 76).

Sevilla (0) 3 *(Vazquez 48, 75, Munir 78)*

F91 Dudelange (0) 0 26,165

Sevilla: (442) Bounou; Pozo, Kounde, Sergi Gomez (Diego Carlos 70), Escudero; Lopes (Gil Salvatierra 60), Gudelj, Vazquez, Torres; de Jong (Munir 52), Dabbur.
F91 Dudelange: (433) Joubert; Bouchouari, Schnell, Cools, Lesquoy; Stolz (Bettaieb 79), Morren, Bougrine (Natami 81); Lavie, Sinani, Bernier (Klapp 76).

Thursday, 7 November 2019

APOEL (0) 2 *(Lucas Souza 59, Ioannou 88)*

Qarabag (1) 1 *(Medvedev 10)* 2848

APOEL: (532) Belec; Mihajlovic, Vouros, Savic, Ioannou, Joaozinho (Al-Taamari 46); Matic, Lucas Souza, Gentsoglou (Bezjak 59); Pavlovic, Hallenius (Efrem 75).
Qarabag: (4141) Begovic; Medvedev, Huseynov B, Sadygov, Ailton; Garayev; Quintana (Gueye 16 (Romero 76)), Almeyda, Michel (Huseynov A 83), Zoubir; Abdullayev.

F91 Dudelange (0) 2 *(Sinani 69, 80)*

Sevilla (4) 5 *(Dabbur 17, 36, Munir 27, 33, 66)* 2848

F91 Dudelange: (4231) Joubert; Bouchouari, Garos, Cools, Kirch; Morren, Bougrine (Schnell 46); Klapp (Barbosa 46), Stolz (Lavie 86), Bernier; Sinani.
Sevilla: (4231) Bounou; Pozo, Gudelj, Sergi Gomez, Escudero; Jordan (Fernando 61), Torres (Vazquez 51); Munir, Lopes, Nolito (de Jong 51); Dabbur.

Thursday, 28 November 2019

F91 Dudelange (0) 0

APOEL (2) 2 *(Matic 12 (pen), Merkis 43)* 2912

F91 Dudelange: (343) Joubert; Cools, Schnell, Garos; Bouchouari (Bettaieb 61), Morren, Bougrine (Lavie 54), Lesquoy; Sinani■, Stolz (Pokar 77), Bernier.
APOEL: (532) Belec; Mihajlovic, Vouros■, Merkis, Savic, Ioannou (Jakolis 66); Gentsoglou (Alef 46), Lucas Souza, Matic; Al-Taamari, Hallenius (De Vincenti 84).

Sevilla (0) 2 *(Gil Salvatierra 61, Dabbur 90)*

Qarabag (0) 0 19,803

Sevilla: (4231) Bounou; Pozo, Carrico, Sergi Gomez, Escudero; Gudelj, Torres (Mena 68); Munir, Lopes (Gil Salvatierra 54), Dabbur; Hernandez (Vazquez 62).
Qarabag: (541) Begovic; Huseynov A (Abdullayev 69), Medvedev, Mammadov, Huseynov B, Ailton; Michel (Quintana 84), Garayev, Almeyda, Zoubir; Romero (Emreli 70).

Thursday, 12 December 2019

APOEL (0) 1 *(Savic 61)*

Sevilla (0) 0 5608

APOEL: (451) Belec; Mihajlovic, Merkis, Savic, Ioannou; Al-Taamari (Efrem 90), Lucas Souza, Alef, Matic, Jakolis (Makris 79); Pavlovic (De Vincenti 70).
Sevilla: (4231) Bounou; Pozo, Genaro, Sergi Gomez, Escudero; Jordan (Torres 46), Gudelj; Ocampos, Lopes, Gil Salvatierra (Mena 68); Hernandez (Dabbur 46).

Qarabag (0) 1 *(Gueye 90)*

F91 Dudelange (0) 1 *(Bougrine 63)* 5823

Qarabag: (4141) Mahammadaliyev; Medvedev, Huseynov B, Sadygov, Ailton; Garayev■; Quintana (Romero 64), Ibrahimli (Almeyda 50), Michel, Zoubir; Emreli (Gueye 75).

F91 Dudelange: (3412) Joubert; Cools, Schnell, Garos; Bouchouari, Morren, Bougrine (Pokar 84), Lesquoy; Stolz; Bettaieb (Mendy 86), Bernier (Klapp 78).

Group A Table	P	W	D	L	F	A	GD	Pts
Sevilla	6	5	0	1	14	3	11	15
APOEL	6	3	1	2	10	8	2	10
Qarabag	6	1	2	3	8	11	–3	5
F91 Dudelange	6	1	1	4	8	18	–10	4

GROUP B

Thursday, 19 September 2019

Dynamo Kyiv (0) 1 *(Buyalsky 84)*

Malmo (0) 0 17,159

Dynamo Kyiv: (433) Boyko; Kedziora, Shabanov, Kadar, Mykolenko; Buyalsky, Sydorchuk, Shepelev; Tsygankov (Karavayev 90), Rodrigues (Biesiedin 73), Verbic.
Malmo: (352) Dahlin; Nielsen, Bengtsson, Safari; Beijmo (Larsson 57), Lewicki, Bachirou, Christiansen (Antonsson 73), Rieks; Rosenberg, Traustason (Gall 86).

FC Copenhagen (0) 1 *(Santos 50)*

Lugano (0) 0 18,240

FC Copenhagen: (442) Johnsson; Varela, Nelsson, Papagiannopoulos, Bengtsson; Jensen (Mas 79), Stage, Zeca, Fischer (Oviedo 79); Santos (Daramy 77), Sotiriou.
Lugano: (451) Baumann; Yao (Holender 70), Kecskes, Maric, Daprela; Lavanchy, Custodio, Sabbatini, Vecsei (Dal Monte 82), Carlinhos; Bottani (Aratore 49).

Thursday, 3 October 2019

Lugano (0) 0

Dynamo Kyiv (0) 0 1281

Lugano: (433) Baumann; Yao, Maric, Daprela, Lavanchy; Lovric (Custodio 71), Sabbatini, Vecsei; Carlinhos, Gerndt (Holender 78), Aratore (Dal Monte 64).
Dynamo Kyiv: (433) Bushchan; Kedziora, Shabanov, Kadar, Mykolenko; Buyalsky, Sydorchuk, Shepelev (Harmash 84); Tsygankov, Rodrigues (Biesiedin 70), Verbic (De Pena 88).

Malmo (0) 1 *(Rosenberg 55)*

FC Copenhagen (1) 1 *(Nielsen 45 (og))* 19,884

Malmo: (532) Dahlin; Berget, Nielsen, Bengtsson, Safari, Rieks (Larsson 46); Christiansen (Traustason 58), Lewicki, Bachirou; Antonsson (Molins 78), Rosenberg.
FC Copenhagen: (442) Johnsson; Varela, Nelsson, Bjelland, Bengtsson; Jensen (Bartolec 85), Stage, Zeca, Fischer (Holse 70); Santos (Daramy 86), Sotiriou.

Thursday, 24 October 2019

Dynamo Kyiv (0) 1 *(Shabanov 53)*

FC Copenhagen (1) 1 *(Sotiriou 2)* 21,202

Dynamo Kyiv: (4411) Bushchan; Kedziora, Popov, Shabanov, Mykolenko; Tsygankov, Sydorchuk, Shepelev, De Pena (Harmash 80); Verbic; Biesiedin.
FC Copenhagen: (442) Johnsson; Bartolec, Papagiannopoulos, Nelsson, Oviedo; Stage, Zeca, Jensen (Varela 87), Fischer (Thomsen 75); Santos (Bendtner 89), Sotiriou.

Malmo (2) 2 *(Berget 13 (pen), Molins 32)*

Lugano (0) 1 *(Gerndt 50)* 16,789

Malmo: (352) Dahlin; Lewicki, Nielsen, Knudsen (Safari 85); Larsson, Bachirou, Innocent (Bengtsson 68), Traustason, Rieks; Molins (Rosenberg 77), Berget.
Lugano: (433) Baumann; Yao (Aratore 60), Maric, Daprela, Obexer (Holender 79); Custodio, Sabbatini, Lovric; Carlinhos, Bottani (Rodriguez 81), Gerndt.

Thursday, 7 November 2019

FC Copenhagen (1) 1 *(Stage 4)*

Dynamo Kyiv (0) 1 *(Verbic 70)* 23,166

FC Copenhagen: (442) Johnsson; Varela, Papagiannopoulos, Nelsson, Bengtsson (Bartolec 69); Stage, Jensen (Daramy 55), Zeca, Fischer (Thomsen 82); Sotiriou, Santos.
Dynamo Kyiv: (433) Bushchan; Kedziora, Popov, Shabanov, Mykolenko; Tsygankov, Sydorchuk, Shepelev; Karavayev, Biesiedin, Verbic (De Pena 89).

Lugano (0) 0

Malmo (0) 0 1875

Lugano: (4231) Baumann; Yao, Maric, Daprela, Lavanchy; Custodio, Vecsei; Carlinhos, Bottani (Gerndt 57), Aratore; Holender (Lovric 81).
Malmo: (532) Dahlin; Beijmo (Molins 64), Nielsen, Bengtsson, Safari (Knudsen 69), Rieks; Lewicki (Innocent 30), Bachirou, Traustason; Berget, Rosenberg.

Thursday, 28 November 2019

Lugano (0) 0

FC Copenhagen (1) 1 *(Thomsen 26)* 1281

Lugano: (451) Baumann; Lavanchy, Kecskes, Daprela, Obexer; Carlinhos (Dal Monte 62), Lovric, Custodio, Guidotti (Covilo 76), Aratore (Sasere 70); Bottani.
FC Copenhagen: (352) Johnsson; Papagiannopoulos, Nelsson, Bjelland; Bartolec, Mas (Jensen 74), Zeca, Thomsen (Mudrazija 79), Bengtsson; Santos (Varela 86), Sotiriou.

Malmo (1) 4 *(Bengtsson 2, Rosenberg 48, 90, Rakip 57)*

Dynamo Kyiv (2) 3 *(Mykolenko 18, Tsygankov 39, Verbic 77)* 19,224

Malmo: (532) Dahlin; Larsson (Molins 79), Nielsen, Bengtsson, Safari (Knudsen 90), Rieks; Bachirou, Innocent (Rakip 46), Traustason; Berget, Rosenberg.
Dynamo Kyiv: (4231) Bushchan; Kedziora, Shabanov, Kadar, Mykolenko; Sydorchuk■, Shepelev (Shaparenko 71); Tsygankov, Buyalsky (Harmash 89), Verbic (Karavayev 82); Biesiedin.

Thursday, 12 December 2019

Dynamo Kyiv (0) 1 *(Tsygankov 90)*

Lugano (1) 1 *(Aratore 45)* 15,774

Dynamo Kyiv: (4411) Bushchan; Kedziora (Tsitaishvili 64), Popov, Kadar, Mykolenko; Karavayev, Shepelev, Buyalsky, De Pena (Harmash 77); Tsygankov; Biesiedin (Sol 81).
Lugano: (451) Da Costa; Yao, Sulmoni, Daprela, Obexer; Dal Monte (Maric 64), Lovric (Crnigoj 84), Custodio, Guidotti (Vecsei 55), Aratore; Holender.

FC Copenhagen (0) 0

Malmo (0) 1 *(Papagiannopoulos 77 (og))* 32,941

FC Copenhagen: (442) Johnsson; Varela (Bartolec 84), Papagiannopoulos, Bjelland, Bengtsson; Mudrazija (Holse 46), Jensen, Thomsen (Santos 80), Fischer; N'Doye, Sotiriou.
Malmo: (541) Dahlin; Larsson, Nielsen, Bengtsson, Safari (Knudsen 60), Rieks; Rakip (Molins 68), Christiansen (Lewicki 80), Innocent, Traustason; Rosenberg.

Group B Table	P	W	D	L	F	A	GD	Pts
Malmo	6	3	2	1	8	6	2	11
FC Copenhagen	6	2	3	1	5	4	1	9
Dynamo Kyiv	6	1	4	1	7	7	0	7
Lugano	6	0	3	3	2	5	–3	3

GROUP C

Thursday, 19 September 2019

FC Basel (2) 5 *(Bua 9, 40, Zuffi 52, Vilhena 54 (og), Okafor 79)*

Krasnodar (0) 0 14,127

FC Basel: (4231) Omlin; Widmer, Comert, Alderete, Petretta; Xhaka, Frei; Stocker (Okafor 58), Zuffi (Campo 79), Bua; Arthur Cabral (Riveros 66).
Krasnodar: (433) Safonov; Petrov, Martynovich, Spajic, Ramirez; Vilhena, Kambolov (Utkin 46), Olsson (Namli 60); Suleymanov, Ignatyev (Berg 67), Wanderson.

Getafe (1) 1 *(Angel 18)*

Trabzonspor (0) 0 5786

Getafe: (442) Chichizola; Nyom, Djene, Bruno, Raul Garcia; Portillo, Fajr, Timor (Arambarri 90), Kenedy (Cucurella 77); Angel, Gallego (Mata 68).
Trabzonspor: (4141) Cakir; Joao Pereira, Hosseini S, Campi, Novak; Mikel; Avdijaj (Sturridge 46), Erdogan (Parmak 59), Sosa, Nwakaeme T (Uzum 83); Sorloth.

Thursday, 3 October 2019

Krasnodar (0) 1 *(Ari 69)*

Getafe (1) 2 *(Angel 35, 61)* 20,035

Krasnodar: (433) Safonov; Petrov, Martynovich, Spajic, Ramirez; Olsson (Utkin 74), Fjoluson (Ari 46), Vilhena; Suleymanov, Berg, Namli (Fernandes 70).
Getafe: (442) Chichizola; Nyom, Bruno, Cabrera, Raul Garcia; Portillo (Jason 72), Fajr, Timor■, Kenedy (Cucurella 76); Angel (Maksimovic 84), Gallego.

Trabzonspor (1) 2 *(Parmak 26, Sosa 78)*

FC Basel (1) 2 *(Widmer 20, Okafor 80)* 23,867

Trabzonspor: (4141) Cakir; Turkmen, Hosseini S, Campi, Novak; Mikel; Sorloth (Sosa 65), Erdogan, Parmak, Avdijaj (Nwakaeme T 46); Sturridge (Corekci 81).
FC Basel: (4231) Omlin; Widmer, Comert, Alderete, Petretta; Xhaka, Frei; Stocker, Zuffi (Okafor 65), Bua; Ademi (Arthur Cabral 70).

Thursday, 24 October 2019

Getafe (0) 0

FC Basel (1) 1 *(Frei 18)* 6213

Getafe: (442) Chichizola; Nyom, Djene, Bruno (Cabrera 14), Raul Garcia; Portillo (Jason 57), Maksimovic, Fajr, Kenedy; Jorge Molina (Cucurella 71), Angel.
FC Basel: (4231) Nikolic; Widmer, Comert, Alderete, Petretta; Xhaka, Zuffi; Stocker (Pululu 90), Frei, Bua■; Ademi (Arthur Cabral 69).

Trabzonspor (0) 0

Krasnodar (0) 2 *(Berg 49, Vilhena 90)* 26,405

Trabzonspor: (4141) Cakir; Joao Pereira, Fernandes, Campi (Canbaz 83), Novak; Sosa; Sari, Corekci (Erdogan 68), Parmak (Avdijaj 72), Nwakaeme T; Sorloth.
Krasnodar: (433) Safonov; Petrov, Martynovich, Spajic, Ramirez; Vilhena, Kambolov (Fjoluson 76), Olsson; Suleymanov, Berg (Ari 71), Stotskiy (Fernandes 62).

Thursday, 7 November 2019

FC Basel (1) 2 *(Arthur Cabral 8, Frei 60)*

Getafe (1) 1 *(Mata 45 (pen))* 26,298

FC Basel: (4231) Omlin; Widmer, Comert, Alderete, Riveros; Xhaka (Campo 64), Zuffi; Zhegrova (Pululu 88), Frei, Petretta; Arthur Cabral (Ademi 73).
Getafe: (442) Chichizola; Maksimovic, Bruno, Olivera, Raul Garcia; Portillo, Fajr (Angel 79), Timor (Nyom 68), Duro (Kenedy 68); Mata, Gallego.

Krasnodar (2) 3 *(Asan 27 (og), Fernandes 35, Ignatyev 90)*

Trabzonspor (0) 1 *(Nwakaeme T 90)* 21,669

Krasnodar: (433) Kritsyuk; Petrov, Martynovich, Spajic, Ramirez; Olsson (Kambolov 77), Vilhena, Fernandes (Utkin 63); Suleymanov, Ari (Ignatyev 66), Stotskiy.
Trabzonspor: (4141) Kardesler; Asan, Fernandes, Campi, Omur; Hosseini S; Corekci (Sari 87), Canbaz, Erdogan, Avdijaj (Nwakaeme T 65); Akpinar (Sorloth 72).

Thursday, 28 November 2019

Krasnodar (0) 1 *(Ari 72 (pen))*

FC Basel (0) 0 22,826

Krasnodar: (433) Kritsyuk; Petrov, Martynovich, Spajic, Ramirez; Olsson (Utkin 73), Gazinsky (Kambolov 83), Vilhena; Suleymanov (Namli 57), Ari■, Wanderson.
FC Basel: (4231) Omlin; Widmer, Bergstrom, Alderete, Riveros; Comert, Frei; Stocker (Pululu 86), Campo, Okafor (Bua 85); Ademi (Arthur Cabral 68).

Trabzonspor (0) 0

Getafe (0) 1 *(Mata 50)* 22,826

Trabzonspor: (4141) Kardesler; Asan, Hosseini S (Campi 70), Fernandes, Omur; Erdogan; Avdijaj (Aydin 59), Parmak, Baykus (Corekci 89), Uzum; Akpinar.
Getafe: (442) Chichizola; Nyom, Djene, Bruno, Olivera; Portillo, Arambarri, Fajr, Kenedy (Cucurella 86); Jorge Molina (Angel 62), Mata (Timor 73).

Thursday, 12 December 2019

FC Basel (1) 2 *(Widmer 21, Stocker 72)*

Trabzonspor (0) 0 17,921

FC Basel: (4231) Omlin; Widmer, Comert, Alderete, Petretta; Xhaka, Zuffi (Campo 78); Stocker, Frei, Pululu (Okafor 65); Arthur Cabral (Ademi 71).
Trabzonspor: (4141) Kardesler; Asan, Hosseini S (Campi 71), Fernandes, Omur; Erdogan; Avdijaj, Parmak, Onazi (Akpinar 51), Uzum; Ekuban (Baykus 78).

Getafe (0) 3 *(Cabrera 76, Jorge Molina 78, Kenedy 86)*

Krasnodar (0) 0 9389

Getafe: (442) Soria; Damian, Djene, Cabrera, Nyom; Jason (Kenedy 68), Arambarri (Timor 82), Maksimovic, Cucurella; Angel (Jorge Molina 73), Mata.
Krasnodar: (442) Kritsyuk; Petrov, Martynovich■, Spajic, Ramirez (Skopintcev 75); Suleymanov (Namli 62), Vilhena, Gazinsky, Wanderson; Ignatyev (Utkin 69), Berg.

Group C Table	P	W	D	L	F	A	GD	Pts
FC Basel	6	4	1	1	12	4	8	13
Getafe	6	4	0	2	8	4	4	12
Krasnodar	6	3	0	3	7	11	–4	9
Trabzonspor	6	0	1	5	3	11	–8	1

GROUP D

Thursday, 19 September 2019

LASK (1) 1 *(Holland 45)*

Rosenborg (0) 0 12,179

LASK: (343) Schlager; Wostry, Wiesinger, Filipovic; Ranftl, Holland, Michorl, Renner (Potzmann 57); Goiginger (Raguz 80), Klauss, Tetteh (Frieser 40).
Rosenborg: (433) Hansen; Hedenstadt, Reginiussen, Hovland, Meling; Jensen, Lundemo (Trondsen 73), Konradsen (Asen 87); Soderlund, Johnsen B (Ceide 73), Adegbenro.

PSV Eindhoven (2) 3 *(Malen 19, Coates 25 (og), Baumgartl 48)*

Sporting Lisbon (1) 2 *(Bruno Fernandes 38 (pen), Mendes 82)* 30,000

PSV Eindhoven: (4231) Zoet; Dumfries, Baumgartl, Viergever, Boscagli; Rosario, Hendrix; Bruma (Doan 78), Ihattaren (Gakpo 64), Bergwijn; Malen (Sadilek 84).
Sporting Lisbon: (41212) Ribeiro; Rosier, Coates, Neto, Acuna; Doumbia; Wendel (Camacho 90), Luis (Mendes 80); Bruno Fernandes; Bolasie, Vietto (Cabral 64).

Thursday, 3 October 2019

Rosenborg (0) 1 *(Adegbenro 70)*

PSV Eindhoven (3) 4 *(Rosario 14, Meling 37 (og), Malen 41, 78)* 10,296

Rosenborg: (433) Hansen; Meling, Hovland, Valsvik, Trondsen (Tagseth 79); Asen, Lundemo (Konradsen 62), Jensen; Babajide, Johnsen B (Soderlund 59), Adegbenro.
PSV Eindhoven: (433) Ruiter; Dumfries, Baumgartl, Viergever, Sadilek; Rosario, Hendrix (Gutierrez 72), Ihattaren (Mitroglou 80); Doan (Bruma 82), Malen, Bergwijn.

Sporting Lisbon (0) 2 *(Luiz Phellype 58, Bruno Fernandes 63)*

LASK (1) 1 *(Raguz 16)* 31,225

Sporting Lisbon: (41212) Ribeiro; Neto (Vietto 46), Coates, Mathieu, Acuna (Borja 73); Doumbia; Luis, Wendel (Eduardo Henrique 58); Bruno Fernandes; Luiz Phellype, Bolasie.
LASK: (343) Schlager; Wiesinger, Trauner, Filipovic; Ranftl, Michorl, Holland, Potzmann (Renner 72); Goiginger, Raguz (Klauss 55), Frieser (Sabitzer 80).

Thursday, 24 October 2019

PSV Eindhoven (0) 0

LASK (0) 0 35,000

PSV Eindhoven: (433) Zoet; Dumfries, Schwaab, Viergever, Sadilek; Doan (Bruma 74), Rosario, Gutierrez; Ihattaren (Thomas 84), Bergwijn, Gakpo (Mitroglou 84).
LASK: (343) Schlager; Wiesinger, Trauner, Filipovic; Ranftl, Holland, Michorl, Potzmann; Goiginger, Raguz (Klauss 71), Frieser (Tetteh 59).

Sporting Lisbon (0) 1 *(Bolasie 70)*

Rosenborg (0) 0 27,671

Sporting Lisbon: (433) Ribeiro; Rosier, Coates, Mathieu, Acuna; Bruno Fernandes, Doumbia, Wendel (Eduardo Henrique 88); Bolasie, Luiz Phellype (Mendes 64), Vietto (Borja 85).
Rosenborg: (433) Hansen; Hedenstadt, Reginiussen, Hovland, Meling; Jensen, Lundemo, Asen (Helland 81); Babajide (Konradsen 76), Soderlund, Adegbenro (Johnsen B 81).

Thursday, 7 November 2019

LASK (0) 4 *(Ranftl 56, Frieser 60, Klauss 77, 82)*

PSV Eindhoven (1) 1 *(Schwaab 5 (pen))* 14,000

LASK: (343) Schlager; Wiesinger, Trauner, Filipovic; Ranftl (Renner 81), Holland, Michorl, Potzmann; Goiginger, Raguz (Tetteh 69), Frieser (Klauss 61).
PSV Eindhoven: (433) Zoet; Dumfries, Schwaab, Viergever, Sadilek; Doan (Catic 64), Rosario, Gutierrez; Ihattaren, Gakpo, Bruma.

Rosenborg (0) 0

Sporting Lisbon (2) 2 *(Coates 16, Bruno Fernandes 38)* 11,018

Rosenborg: (433) Hansen; Hedenstadt, Reginiussen, Hovland, Meling; Jensen, Lundemo, Trondsen (Helland 78); Asen, Soderlund, Adegbenro (Johnsen B 77).
Sporting Lisbon: (3412) Ribeiro; Neto, Coates, Tiago Ilori; Rosier, Doumbia (Rodrigo Fernandes 86), Eduardo Henrique, Borja; Bruno Fernandes (Mendes 90); Bolasie (Camacho 73), Vietto.

Thursday, 28 November 2019

Rosenborg (1) 1 *(Johnsen B 45)*

LASK (1) 2 *(Goiginger 20, Frieser 54)* 5000

Rosenborg: (433) Hansen; Hedenstadt, Hovland, Valsvik, Meling; Jensen, Lundemo (Johnsen M 77), Trondsen; Babajide, Johnsen B (Botheim 67), Adegbenro (Asen 67).
LASK: (343) Schlager; Wiesinger, Trauner, Filipovic; Ranftl, Holland, Michorl, Potzmann; Goiginger (Renner 88), Klauss (Raguz 71), Frieser (Tetteh 71).

Sporting Lisbon (3) 4 *(Luiz Phellype 9, Bruno Fernandes 15, 64 (pen), Mathieu 42)*

PSV Eindhoven (0) 0 30,146

Sporting Lisbon: (433) Maximiano; Rosier, Tiago Ilori, Mathieu (Neto 73), Acuna; Bruno Fernandes, Doumbia, Wendel (Camacho 80); Bolasie, Luiz Phellype (Jese 67), Vietto.
PSV Eindhoven: (4231) Unnerstall; Dumfries, Baumgartl, Viergever, Sadilek; Rosario (Pereiro 46), Hendrix; Bruma (Gakpo 46), Malen, Ihattaren; Bergwijn (Thomas 79).

Thursday, 12 December 2019

LASK (2) 3 *(Trauner 23, Klauss 38 (pen), Raguz 90)*

Sporting Lisbon (0) 0 14,000

LASK: (343) Schlager; Wiesinger, Trauner, Filipovic (Pogatetz 88); Ranftl, Holland, Michorl, Potzmann; Goiginger, Klauss (Raguz 71), Frieser (Tetteh 64).
Sporting Lisbon: (433) Ribeiro■; Rosier, Coates, Tiago Ilori, Borja; Luis (Luiz Phellype 71), Rodrigo Fernandes (Maximiano 37), Eduardo Henrique; Jese (Doumbia 46), Mendes, Camacho.

PSV Eindhoven (0) 1 *(Ihattaren 63)*

Rosenborg (1) 1 *(Helland 22)* 24,000

PSV Eindhoven: (433) Unnerstall; Dumfries, Schwaab, Viergever, Boscagli; Ihattaren (Pereiro 70), Gutierrez, Thomas (Rosario 61); Gakpo, Bergwijn (Malen 46), Bruma.
Rosenborg: (433) Ostbo; Hedenstadt, Reginiussen, Hovland, Meling; Jensen, Trondsen, Tagseth (Lundemo 46); Helland (Botheim 75), Soderlund, Adegbenro (Ceide 81).

Group D Table	P	W	D	L	F	A	GD	Pts
LASK	6	4	1	1	11	4	7	13
Sporting Lisbon	6	4	0	2	11	7	4	12
PSV Eindhoven	6	2	2	2	9	12	–3	8
Rosenborg	6	0	1	5	3	11	–8	1

GROUP E

Thursday, 19 September 2019

CFR Cluj (1) 2 *(Deac 41 (pen), Omrani 75)*

Lazio (1) 1 *(Bastos 25)* 9222

CFR Cluj: (532) Arlauskis; Peteleu, Burca, Boli, Cestor, Camora; Bordeianu, Djokovic, Paun (Culio 84); Traore (Omrani 46), Deac (Golofca 90).
Lazio: (352) Strakosha; Vavro, Acerbi, Bastos (Adekanye 80); Lazzari, Milinkovic-Savic, Lucas, Berisha (Cataldi 67), Jony (Lulic 80); Correa, Caicedo.

Rennes (1) 1 *(Niang 37 (pen))*

Celtic (0) 1 *(Christie 59 (pen))* 27,026

Rennes: (4141) Mendy; Traore, Da Silva, Gnagnon, Morel; Martin (Camavinga 72); Raphinha, Bourigeaud, Grenier (Siebatcheu 88), Tait (Del Castillo 72); Niang.
Celtic: (4231) Forster; Elhamed, Jullien, Ajer, Bolingoli-Mbombo (Hayes 69); Brown, McGregor; Forrest, Christie, Elyounoussi (Ntcham 57); Edouard (Bayo■ 84).

Thursday, 3 October 2019

Celtic (1) 2 *(Edouard 20, Elyounoussi 59)*

CFR Cluj (0) 0 56,172

Celtic: (4231) Forster; Elhamed, Jullien, Ajer, Bolingoli-Mbombo; Brown, McGregor; Forrest (Hayes 86), Christie (Ntcham 90), Elyounoussi; Edouard.
CFR Cluj: (433) Arlauskis; Susic, Burca, Boli, Camora; Luis Aurelio (Culio 57), Bordeianu, Djokovic (Golofca 81); Omrani, Rondon (Paun 70), Deac.

Lazio (0) 2 *(Milinkovic-Savic 63, Immobile 75)*

Rennes (0) 1 *(Morel 55)* 13,072

Lazio: (352) Strakosha; Vavro, Acerbi, Bastos; Lazzari, Parolo, Cataldi (Milinkovic-Savic 53), Berisha (Luis Alberto 53), Lulic (Jony 82); Caicedo, Immobile.
Rennes: (532) Mendy; Traore, Da Silva, Gnagnon, Morel, Doumbia (Hunou 82); Camavinga (Bourigeaud 71), Martin, Grenier; Tait (Raphinha 76), Niang.

Thursday, 24 October 2019

Celtic (0) 2 *(Christie 67, Jullien 89)*

Lazio (1) 1 *(Lazzari 40)* 56,172

Celtic: (4231) Forster; Elhamed (Bitton 83), Jullien, Ajer, Bolingoli-Mbombo (Hayes 85); Brown, McGregor; Forrest, Christie, Elyounoussi (Rogic 66); Edouard.
Lazio: (352) Strakosha; Bastos, Vavro, Acerbi; Lazzari, Parolo, Lucas, Milinkovic-Savic, Jony (Lulic 69); Correa (Immobile 73), Caicedo (Cataldi 85).

Rennes (0) 0

CFR Cluj (1) 1 *(Deac 9)* 27,330

Rennes: (4231) Mendy■; Traore, Gnagnon, Morel, Maouassa (Lea Siliki 75); Bourigeaud, Camavinga■; Raphinha (Siebatcheu 80), Del Castillo (Bonet 8), Niang; Hunou.
CFR Cluj: (4141) Arlauskis; Susic■, Burca, Boli, Camora; Bordeianu (Hoban 66); Deac, Djokovic (Paun 70), Culio, Omrani; Traore (Cestor 84).

Thursday, 7 November 2019

CFR Cluj (0) 1 *(Rondon 87)*

Rennes (0) 0 11,067

CFR Cluj: (433) Arlauskis; Peteleu (Hoban 74), Burca, Boli, Camora; Djokovic, Bordeianu, Culio; Deac (Paun 89), Traore (Rondon■ 71), Omrani.
Rennes: (442) Salin; Traore, Da Silva, Gnagnon, Maouassa; Raphinha, Bourigeaud (Guitane 84), Grenier, Niang; Del Castillo (Siebatcheu 66), Hunou (Gboho 66).

Lazio (1) 1 *(Immobile 7)*

Celtic (1) 2 *(Forrest 38, Ntcham 90)* 26,155

Lazio: (352) Strakosha; Felipe, Vavro (Berisha 82), Acerbi; Lazzari, Parolo, Lucas (Luis Alberto 58), Milinkovic-Savic, Jony (Lulic 58); Caicedo, Immobile.
Celtic: (532) Forster; Forrest (Bauer 89), Elhamed (Bitton 83), Jullien, Ajer, Hayes; Christie (Ntcham 77), Brown, McGregor; Edouard, Elyounoussi.

Thursday, 28 November 2019

Celtic (2) 3 *(Morgan 21, Christie 45, Johnston 74)*

Rennes (0) 1 *(Hunou 89)* 56,172

Celtic: (4231) Forster; Bauer, Jullien, Ajer, Taylor; Brown (Bitton 76), McGregor; Christie (Griffiths 79), Ntcham, Forrest (Johnston 67); Morgan.
Rennes: (442) Mendy; Boey, Nyamsi, Gnagnon, Maouassa; Del Castillo (Hunou 74), Bourigeaud, Lea Siliki, Tait (Gboho 80); Guitane (Da Cunha 65), Siebatcheu.

Lazio (1) 1 *(Correa 24)*

CFR Cluj (0) 0 7604

Lazio: (352) Proto; Bastos, Vavro, Acerbi; Lazzari, Parolo, Cataldi, Luis Alberto (Patric Gil 80), Jony (Lulic 75); Adekanye (Caicedo 65), Correa.
CFR Cluj: (532) Arlauskis; Peteleu (Susic 73), Burca, Boli, Cestor, Camora; Culio, Bordeianu (Deac 62), Djokovic; Paun (Traore 65), Omrani.

Thursday, 12 December 2019

CFR Cluj (0) 2 *(Burca 48, Djokovic 70)*

Celtic (0) 0 12,890

CFR Cluj: (4141) Arlauskis; Susic, Burca, Cestor, Camora; Bordeianu; Deac (Hoban 85), Djokovic (Luis Aurelio 83), Culio, Omrani (Golofca 74); Traore.
Celtic: (4231) Gordon; Bauer, Jullien (Ajer 46), Bitton, Bolingoli-Mbombo; Ntcham, Robertson; Morgan (Bayo 67), Johnston (Dembele 72), Sinclair; Griffiths.

Rennes (1) 2 *(Gnagnon 30, 87)*

Lazio (0) 0 25,082

Rennes: (4231) Salin; Boey, Nyamsi, Gnagnon, Doumbia; Grenier, Lea Siliki (Camavinga 74); Da Cunha (Del Castillo 77), Gboho, Tait; Siebatcheu (Niang 70).
Lazio: (352) Proto; Bastos, Vavro (Falbo 74), Acerbi; Lazzari, Parolo, Cataldi, Luis Alberto (Berisha 59), Jony; Caicedo, Immobile (Adekanye 68).

Group E Table	*P*	*W*	*D*	*L*	*F*	*A*	*GD*	*Pts*
Celtic	6	4	1	1	10	6	4	13
CFR Cluj	6	4	0	2	6	4	2	12
Lazio	6	2	0	4	6	9	–3	6
Rennes	6	1	1	4	5	8	–3	4

GROUP F

Thursday, 19 September 2019

Eintracht Frankfurt (0) 0

Arsenal (1) 3 *(Willock 38, Saka 85, Aubameyang 87)* 47,000

Eintracht Frankfurt: (3412) Trapp; Abraham, Hasebe, Hinteregger; Da Costa (Chandler 74), Kohr■, Sow, Kostic; Kamada; Dost (Paciencia 66), Andre Silva.
Arsenal: (4231) Martinez; Chambers, Mustafi, Luiz, Kolasinac (Maitland-Niles 80); Torreira, Xhaka; Smith-Rowe (Pepe 60), Willock (Ceballos 72), Saka; Aubameyang.

Standard Liege (0) 2 *(Hanin 66 (og), M'Poku 90)*

Vitoria de Guimaraes (0) 0 13,477

Standard Liege: (433) Milinkovic-Savic; Vojvoda, Bokadi, Laifis, Gavory; Bastien, Cimirot, M'Poku; Carcela-Gonzalez (Boljevic 85), Emond (Avenatti 68), Limbombe (Vanheusden 81).
Vitoria de Guimaraes: (451) Miguel Silva; Sacko, Tapsoba, Bondarenko, Hanin; Rochinha, Poha, Agu (Pepe 70), Evangelista (Andre Pereira 77), Davidson; Leo Bonatini (Duarte 57).

Thursday, 3 October 2019

Arsenal (3) 4 *(Martinelli 13, 16, Willock 22, Ceballos 57)*

Standard Liege (0) 0 58,725

Arsenal: (4231) Martinez; Bellerin, Mustafi, Holding, Tierney; Torreira, Ceballos; Maitland-Niles (Pepe 66), Willock (Guendouzi 74), Nelson (Aubameyang 79); Martinelli.
Standard Liege: (4411) Milinkovic-Savic; Vojvoda, Vanheusden, Laifis, Gavory; Boljevic (Carcela-Gonzalez 58), Bastien, Cimirot, M'Poku; Lestienne (Amallah 80); Emond (Avenatti 73).

Vitoria de Guimaraes (0) 0

Eintracht Frankfurt (1) 1 *(Ndicka 36)* 27,000

Vitoria de Guimaraes: (433) Miguel Silva; Sacko (Rochinha 65), Tapsoba, Pedro Henrique, Hanin; Poha, Agu, Evangelista; Edwards, Leo Bonatini (Duarte 65), Davidson (Andre Pereira 78).
Eintracht Frankfurt: (3142) Ronnow; Toure, Hinteregger, Ndicka; Fernandes; Durm (Da Costa 78), Sow, Rode (Kamada 60), Kostic; Paciencia (Dost 68), Andre Silva.

Thursday, 24 October 2019

Arsenal (1) 3 *(Martinelli 32, Pepe 80, 90)*

Vitoria de Guimaraes (2) 2 *(Edwards 8, Duarte 36)* 60,195

Arsenal: (4231) Martinez; Bellerin, Mustafi, Holding, Tierney; Torreira, Willock (Ceballos 46); Maitland-Niles (Guendouzi 46), Smith-Rowe, Martinelli; Lacazette (Pepe 75).
Vitoria de Guimaraes: (451) Miguel Silva; Garcia, Frederico Venancio, Tapsoba, Hanin; Edwards (Andre Pereira 71), Almeida (Pepe 64), Agu, Poha, Davidson (Rochinha 87); Duarte.

Eintracht Frankfurt (1) 2 *(Abraham 28, Hinteregger 73)*

Standard Liege (0) 1 *(Amallah 82)* 47,000

Eintracht Frankfurt: (3421) Ronnow; Abraham, Hasebe, Hinteregger; Da Costa, Sow, Rode, Kostic (Chandler 83); Gacinovic (Kohr 75), Kamada (Fernandes 88); Paciencia.
Standard Liege: (4231) Milinkovic-Savic; Fai (M'Poku 85), Laifis, Lavalee, Gavory; Bastien, Cimirot; Carcela-Gonzalez (Oulare 75), Amallah, Boljevic; Cop (Lestienne 72).

Wednesday, 6 November 2019

Vitoria de Guimaraes (0) 1 *(Duarte 90)*

Arsenal (0) 1 *(Mustafi 80)* 17,822

Vitoria de Guimaraes: (4141) Douglas Jesus; Garcia, Frederico Venancio, Tapsoba, Rafa Soares; Agu; Edwards, Evangelista (Leo Bonatini 82), Pepe (Poha 61), Davidson (Rochinha 68); Duarte.
Arsenal: (343) Martinez; Mustafi, Papastathopoulos, Holding; Maitland-Niles, Willock (Torreira 78), Ceballos (Guendouzi 54), Tierney; Pepe, Martinelli, Saka (Lacazette 65).

Thursday, 7 November 2019

Standard Liege (0) 2 *(Vanheusden 56, Lestienne 90)*

Eintracht Frankfurt (0) 1 *(Kostic 65)* 18,526

Standard Liege: (451) Bodart; Fai, Vanheusden, Laifis, Gavory; Emond, Bastien, Amallah (M'Poku 73), Cimirot, Cop (Oulare 81); Carcela-Gonzalez (Lestienne 81).
Eintracht Frankfurt: (352) Ronnow; Abraham, Hasebe, Hinteregger; Da Costa (Chandler 89), Fernandes, Rode, Sow, Kostic; Paciencia (Dost 73), Andre Silva (Kamada 62).

Thursday, 28 November 2019

Arsenal (1) 1 *(Aubameyang 45)*

Eintracht Frankfurt (0) 2 *(Kamada 55, 64)* 49,419

Arsenal: (4231) Martinez; Chambers, Mustafi (Torreira 76), Papastathopoulos, Tierney; Luiz (Guendouzi 31), Xhaka; Martinelli (Ozil 60), Willock, Saka; Aubameyang.
Eintracht Frankfurt: (3412) Ronnow; Abraham, Hasebe, Hinteregger; Da Costa, Sow, Fernandes (Kohr 46), Kostic; Kamada; Andre Silva (Gacinovic 46), Paciencia.

Vitoria de Guimaraes (1) 1 *(Andre Pereira 45)*

Standard Liege (1) 1 *(Lestienne 39 (pen))* 11,221

Vitoria de Guimaraes: (4141) Douglas Jesus; Sacko, Tapsoba, Pedro Henrique, Hanin; Agu; Edwards (Rochinha 76), Poha, Evangelista, Andre Pereira (Leo Bonatini 86); Duarte (Davidson 45).
Standard Liege: (451) Bodart; Vojvoda, Vanheusden, Laifis, Gavory; Carcela-Gonzalez, Bastien, Cimirot, M'Poku (Cop 82), Lestienne (Amallah 71); Emond (Oulare 69).

Thursday, 12 December 2019

Eintracht Frankfurt (2) 2 *(Da Costa 31, Kamada 38)*

Vitoria de Guimaraes (1) 3 *(Rochinha 8, Al Musrati 85, Edwards 87)* 47,000

Eintracht Frankfurt: (3412) Ronnow; Abraham, Hasebe, Hinteregger; Da Costa, Rode (Fernandes 78), Sow, Kostic; Kamada; Paciencia, Andre Silva (Gacinovic 73).
Vitoria de Guimaraes: (4141) Miguel Silva; Garcia, Frederico Venancio, Pedro Henrique, Hanin; Al Musrati; Rochinha (Edwards 70), Poha (Duarte 82), Pepe, Davidson; Andre Pereira (Leo Bonatini 66).

Standard Liege (0) 2 *(Bastien 47, Amallah 69)*

Arsenal (0) 2 *(Lacazette 78, Saka 81)* 21,797

Standard Liege: (451) Bodart; Fai, Vanheusden, Laifis, Gavory; Carcela-Gonzalez, Bastien, M'Poku, Cimirot, Amallah (Lestienne 85); Emond (Avenatti 46).
Arsenal: (343) Martinez; Mavropanos, Luiz, Papastathopoulos (Martinelli 69); Maitland-Niles (Chambers 78), Guendouzi, Willock, Saka; Smith-Rowe (Aubameyang 85), Lacazette, Nelson.

Group F Table	*P*	*W*	*D*	*L*	*F*	*A*	*GD*	*Pts*
Arsenal	6	3	2	1	14	7	7	11
Eintracht Frankfurt	6	3	0	3	8	10	–2	9
Standard Liege	6	2	2	2	8	10	–2	8
Vitoria de Guimaraes	6	1	2	3	7	10	–3	5

GROUP G

Thursday, 19 September 2019

Porto (2) 2 *(Tiquinho Soares 7, 29)*

Young Boys (1) 1 *(Nsame 15 (pen))* 32,929

Porto: (433) Marchesin; Corona, Pepe, Marcano, Alex Telles; Otavio, Danilo Pereira, Uribe; Marega (Manafa 70), Tiquinho Soares (Silva 81), Diaz (Baro 66).
Young Boys: (3421) Ballmoos; Burgy, Sorensen, Zesiger; Janko, Sierro (Aebischer 69), Lustenberger, Garcia; Fassnacht (Gaudino 73), Assale; Nsame (Hoarau 61).

Rangers (1) 1 *(Ojo 23)*

Feyenoord (0) 0 46,858

Rangers: (433) McGregor; Tavernier, Goldson, Helander, Barisic; Jack, Davis, Kamara (Aribo 82); Arfield (King 90), Morelos, Ojo (Barker 74).
Feyenoord: (4231) Vermeer; Karsdorp, Botteghin, Ie, Haps; Tapia, Fer; Berghuis, Kokcu (Narsingh 65), Larsson (Jorgensen 78); Sinisterra (Toornstra 86).

Thursday, 3 October 2019

Feyenoord (0) 2 *(Toornstra 49, Karsdorp 80)*

Porto (0) 0 41,000

Feyenoord: (433) Vermeer; Karsdorp (Geertruida 85), Botteghin, Ie, Haps; Toornstra, Tapia, Fer; Berghuis, Sinisterra (Narsingh 83), Larsson (Senesi 83).
Porto: (442) Marchesin; Manafa, Pepe, Marcano, Alex Telles; Otavio, Uribe, Danilo Pereira (Silva 81), Nakajima (Diaz 53); Marega, Ze Luis (Tiquinho Soares 62).

Young Boys (0) 2 *(Assale 50, Fassnacht 90)*

Rangers (1) 1 *(Morelos 44)* 26,348

Young Boys: (442) Ballmoos; Janko, Sorensen, Zesiger, Garcia; Fassnacht, Aebischer, Lustenberger, Gaudino (Ngamaleu 73); Assale (Lotomba 67), Nsame.
Rangers: (4141) McGregor; Tavernier, Goldson, Helander, Barisic; Davis; Arfield, Jack (Stewart 65), Kamara, Ojo; Morelos.

Thursday, 24 October 2019

Porto (1) 1 *(Diaz 36)*

Rangers (1) 1 *(Morelos 44)* 31,307

Porto: (442) Marchesin; Corona, Pepe, Marcano, Alex Telles; Otavio (Costa 60), Uribe, Danilo Pereira, Diaz (Nakajima 63); Marega, Ze Luis (Tiquinho Soares 76).
Rangers: (433) McGregor; Tavernier, Goldson, Helander, Barisic; Jack (Arfield 83), Davis, Kamara; Barker (Ojo 84), Morelos, Kent (Aribo 76).

Young Boys (2) 2 *(Assale 14 (pen), Nsame 28 (pen))*

Feyenoord (0) 0 27,641

Young Boys: (442) Ballmoos; Janko, Sorensen, Zesiger, Lotomba; Fassnacht (Garcia 86), Aebischer, Lustenberger (Gaudino 42), Ngamaleu; Nsame, Assale (Burgy 66).
Feyenoord: (433) Vermeer; Geertruida, Ie (Botteghin 37), Senesi, Malacia (Haps 82); Toornstra, Fer, Kokcu (Narsingh 74); Berghuis, Sinisterra, Larsson.

Thursday, 7 November 2019

Feyenoord (1) 1 *(Berghuis 18 (pen))*

Young Boys (0) 1 *(Spielmann 71)* 45,022

Feyenoord: (433) Vermeer; Karsdorp, Ie (Senesi 73), Van Der Heijden, Haps; Toornstra, Tapia, Kokcu; Berghuis, Jorgensen, Sinisterra (Larsson 73).
Young Boys: (433) Ballmoos; Lotomba (Janko 68), Sorensen, Zesiger, Garcia; Fassnacht, Lustenberger, Aebischer; Assale (Mambimbi 87), Nsame, Ngamaleu (Spielmann 68).

Rangers (0) 2 *(Morelos 69, Davis 73)*

Porto (0) 0 49,645

Rangers: (433) McGregor; Tavernier, Goldson, Helander, Barisic; Jack, Davis, Kamara; Barker (Arfield 65), Morelos (Defoe 85), Kent (Aribo 83).
Porto: (532) Marchesin; Manafa, Mbemba, Pepe (Diaz 49), Marcano, Alex Telles; Otavio (Silva 74), Danilo Pereira, Uribe; Corona, Tiquinho Soares (Ze Luis 64).

Thursday, 28 November 2019

Feyenoord (1) 2 *(Toornstra 33, Sinisterra 68)*

Rangers (0) 2 *(Morelos 52, 65)* 47,500

Feyenoord: (433) Marsman; Geertruida, Botteghin, Senesi, Malacia; Toornstra (Ayoub 85), Fer, Kokcu; Berghuis, Sinisterra, Larsson (Narsingh 69).
Rangers: (433) McGregor; Tavernier, Goldson, Helander, Barisic; Jack, Davis, Kamara; Ojo (Arfield 77), Morelos, Kent.

Young Boys (1) 1 *(Fassnacht 6)*

Porto (0) 2 *(Aboubakar 75, 79)* 31,120

Young Boys: (442) Ballmoos; Janko (Hoarau 81), Sorensen, Zesiger, Garcia; Fassnacht, Lustenberger (Lotomba 70), Aebischer, Ngamaleu; Assale (Martins Pereira 57), Nsame.
Porto: (442) Marchesin; Mbemba (Manafa 46), Pepe, Marcano, Alex Telles; Otavio, N'Diaye (Diaz 74), Danilo Pereira, Corona (Diogo Leite 84); Marega, Aboubakar.

Thursday, 12 December 2019

Porto (3) 3 *(Diaz 14, Malacia 15 (og), Tiquinho Soares 33)*

Feyenoord (2) 2 *(Botteghin 19, Larsson 22)* 28,507

Porto: (442) Marchesin; Corona, Pepe, Marcano, Alex Telles; Otavio, Danilo Pereira, Uribe, Diaz (Sergio Oliveira 74); Marega (Mbemba 84), Tiquinho Soares (Ze Luis 75).
Feyenoord: (433) Marsman; Geertruida, Botteghin, Senesi, Malacia; Toornstra (Ayoub 72), Fer, Kokcu (Tapia 75); Berghuis, Sinisterra (Narsingh 72), Larsson.

Rangers (1) 1 *(Morelos 30)*

Young Boys (0) 1 *(Barisic 89 (og))* 49,015

Rangers: (433) McGregor; Tavernier, Goldson, Katic, Barisic; Arfield, Jack■, Kamara; Aribo, Morelos, Kent (Ojo 78).
Young Boys: (442) Ballmoos; Janko, Burgy, Sorensen, Garcia; Fassnacht, Aebischer, Martins Pereira (Mambimbi 73), Ngamaleu (Spielmann 61); Assale, Nsame (Hoarau 61).

Group G Table	P	W	D	L	F	A	GD	Pts
Porto	6	3	1	2	8	9	–1	10
Rangers	6	2	3	1	8	6	2	9
Young Boys	6	2	2	2	8	7	1	8
Feyenoord	6	1	2	3	7	9	–2	5

GROUP H

Thursday, 19 September 2019

Espanyol (0) 1 *(Vargas 60)*

Ferencvaros (1) 1 *(Javi Lopez 10 (og))* 18,125

Espanyol: (442) Diego Lopez; Javi Lopez, Naldo, Bernardo, Didac (Pedrosa 67); Melendo (Calleri 56), Roca, Lozano, Granero; Wu, Vargas (Campuzano 74).
Ferencvaros: (433) Dibusz; Botka (Lovrencsics 66), Blazic, Dvali, Heister; Siger, Kharatin, Ignatenko (Frimpong 85); Zubkov, Isael (Signevich 65), Nguen.

Ludogorets Razgrad (0) 5 *(Wanderson 47, Lukoki 50, Keseru 52, 68, 73 (pen))*

CSKA Moscow (1) 1 *(Diveev 11)* 8423

Ludogorets Razgrad: (433) Renan; Cicinho, Grigore, Forster, Nedyalkov; Abel, Badji, Marcelinho (Goralski 74); Lukoki (Jorginho 84), Keseru (Biton 86), Wanderson.
CSKA Moscow: (3142) Akinfeev; Diveev, Karpov, Magnusson; Bistrovic; Fernandes, Oblyakov, Vlasic, Kuchaev (Santos 71); Nishimura (Akhmetov 54), Bijol (Chalov 53).

Thursday, 3 October 2019

CSKA Moscow (0) 0

Espanyol (0) 2 *(Wu 64, Campuzano 90)* 22,288

CSKA Moscow: (3142) Akinfeev; Sarlija, Diveev (Gogoua 46), Magnusson; Akhmetov (Bijol 76); Fernandes, Vlasic, Bistrovic, Kuchaev (Oblyakov 67); Chalov, Sigurdsson.
Espanyol: (433) Diego Lopez; Corchia, David Lopez, Calero, Pedrosa; Victor Sanchez, Roca, Granero (Lozano 90); Wu (Piatti 76), Calleri (Campuzano 22), Vargas.

Ferencvaros (0) 0

Ludogorets Razgrad (2) 3 *(Lukoki 1, Forster 40, 64)* 16,163

Ferencvaros: (4231) Dibusz; Lovrencsics, Blazic, Frimpong, Heister; Siger (Signevich 73), Kharatin; Zubkov (Varga 80), Isael, Nguen; Boli (Skvarka 73).
Ludogorets Razgrad: (4231) Iliev; Cicinho (Ikoko 69), Grigore■, Forster, Nedyalkov; Abel, Badji; Lukoki (Goralski 57), Marcelinho (Moti 46), Wanderson; Keseru.

Thursday, 24 October 2019

CSKA Moscow (0) 0

Ferencvaros (0) 1 *(Varga 86)* 18,518

CSKA Moscow: (3142) Akinfeev; Karpov, Diveev, Magnusson; Akhmetov (Santos 75); Fernandes, Vlasic, Oblyakov, Kuchaev (Bistrovic 61); Chalov, Sigurdsson (Bijol 80).
Ferencvaros: (433) Dibusz; Lovrencsics, Blazic, Botka, Civic; Siger, Kharatin, Ignatenko; Zubkov (Dvali 89), Boli (Isael 72), Nguen (Varga 84).

Ludogorets Razgrad (0) 0

Espanyol (1) 1 *(Campuzano 13)* 10,334

Ludogorets Razgrad: (4231) Iliev; Cicinho, Moti, Forster, Nedyalkov; Abel (Biton 67), Badji; Lukoki (Swierczok 59), Marcelinho, Wanderson; Tchibota.
Espanyol: (343) Diego Lopez; Lluis Lopez, Bernardo, Didac; Corchia, Granero, Iturraspe, Javi Lopez■; Melendo (Roca 69), Campuzano (Ferreyra 78), Wu (Vargas 61).

Thursday, 7 November 2019

Espanyol (3) 6 *(Melendo 4, Lluis Lopez 19, Vargas 36 (pen), Campuzano 52, Pedrosa 73, Ferreyra 76)*

Ludogorets Razgrad (0) 0 13,963

Espanyol: (343) Diego Lopez; Lluis Lopez, Bernardo (Pedrosa 46), Calero; Corchia, Granero, Lozano, Didac; Melendo (Wu 72), Campuzano (Ferreyra 65), Vargas.
Ludogorets Razgrad: (433) Iliev; Cicinho, Terziev, Forster■, Nedyalkov; Goralski■, Badji, Marcelinho (Ikoko 21); Lukoki, Keseru (Abel 39), Wanderson (Dyakov 77).

Ferencvaros (0) 0

CSKA Moscow (0) 0 18,153

Ferencvaros: (4222) Dibusz; Lovrencsics, Blazic, Botka, Civic; Kharatin, Ignatenko; Zubkov, Skvarka (Varga 84); Boli (Isael 82), Nguen (Frimpong 90).

CSKA Moscow: (3421) Akinfeev; Karpov, Diveev, Magnusson (Nababkin■ 81); Fernandes, Akhmetov (Bistrovic 59), Bijol (Kuchaev 63), Oblyakov; Vlasic, Sigurdsson; Chalov.

Thursday, 28 November 2019

CSKA Moscow (0) 1 *(Chalov 75)*

Ludogorets Razgrad (0) 1 *(Keseru 66)* 12,948

CSKA Moscow: (3142) Akinfeev; Karpov (Bijol 76), Diveev, Magnusson; Bistrovic; Fernandes, Oblyakov, Vlasic, Kuchaev (Dzagoev 54); Chalov, Sigurdsson (Akhmetov 64).
Ludogorets Razgrad: (4231) Iliev; Cicinho, Terziev, Grigore, Nedyalkov; Abel, Badji; Lukoki, Marcelinho (Dyakov 76), Wanderson (Tchibota 81); Keseru (Swierczok 87).

Ferencvaros (1) 2 *(Siger 23, Skvarka 90 (pen))*

Espanyol (1) 2 *(Melendo 31, Darder 90)* 19,111

Ferencvaros: (4231) Dibusz; Lovrencsics, Blazic, Frimpong, Civic■; Siger (Skvarka 86), Kharatin; Isael, Nguen, Varga (Zubkov 61); Boli (Signevich 83).
Espanyol: (352) Diego Lopez; Lluis Lopez, Calero, Didac; Corchia, Lozano, Iturraspe, Granero (Moha 69), Pipa; Melendo (Calleri 81), Campuzano (Darder 88).

Thursday, 12 December 2019

Espanyol (0) 0

CSKA Moscow (0) 1 *(Vlasic 84)* 10,615

Espanyol: (352) Andres; Lluis Lopez, Naldo (Calleri 86), Javi Lopez; Pipa, Lozano, Iturraspe, Piatti (Granero 72), Pedrosa; Campuzano (Wu 46), Ferreyra.
CSKA Moscow: (3142) Pomazun; Karpov, Diveev, Magnusson; Bistrovic; Fernandes, Akhmetov (Schennikov 81), Vlasic (Bijol 86), Oblyakov; Kuchaev (Sigurdsson 78), Chalov.

Ludogorets Razgrad (1) 1 *(Lukoki 24)*

Ferencvaros (0) 1 *(Signevich 90)* 5528

Ludogorets Razgrad: (4231) Iliev; Cicinho, Terziev, Grigore, Nedyalkov; Abel, Badji; Lukoki (Tchibota 77), Marcelinho, Wanderson (Dyakov 85); Keseru (Ikoko 90).
Ferencvaros: (4231) Dibusz; Botka, Blazic, Frimpong, Heister; Kharatin (Ignatenko 84), Siger (Skvarka 79); Zubkov, Nguen, Isael; Boli (Signevich 84).

Group H Table	P	W	D	L	F	A	GD	Pts
Espanyol	6	3	2	1	12	4	8	11
Ludogorets Razgrad	6	2	2	2	10	10	0	8
Ferencvaros	6	1	4	1	5	7	−2	7
CSKA Moscow	6	1	2	3	3	9	−6	5

GROUP I

Thursday, 19 September 2019

Gent (2) 3 *(David 2, 43, Perrin 64 (og))*

Saint-Etienne (1) 2 *(Khazri 38, Kaminski 74 (og))* 14,928

Gent: (442) Kaminski; Lustig, Plastun, Ngadeu-Ngadjui, Asare; Odjidja-Ofoe, Owusu, David (Kvilitaia 90), Kums (Dejaegere 90); Yaremchuk (Bronn 81), Depoitre.
Saint-Etienne: (532) Ruffier; Debuchy, Moukoudi (Beric 72), Perrin, Kolodziejczak, Trauco; Cabaye (Bouanga 65), M'Vila, Youssouf; Hamouma (Nordin 72), Khazri.

VfL Wolfsburg (2) 3 *(Arnold 20, Mehmedi 24, Brekalo 67)*

Oleksandriya (0) 1 *(Banada 66)* 10,112

VfL Wolfsburg: (343) Pervan; Knoche, Guilavogui, Tisserand (Bruma 70); Mbabu, Gerhardt, Arnold, Roussillon; Mehmedi (Steffen 86), Weghorst, Brekalo (Nmecha 76).
Oleksandriya: (433) Pankiv; Pashaev, Dubra, Bukhal, Miroshinichenko; Banada, Dovgiy (Kovalets 46), Grechyshkin; Luchkevych (Protasov 81), Sitalo, Tretiakov (Shastal 65).

Thursday, 3 October 2019

Oleksandriya (0) 1 *(Sitalo 60)*

Gent (1) 1 *(Depoitre 6)* 7588

Oleksandriya: (433) Pankiv; Pashaev, Dubra, Bukhal, Miroshinichenko; Banada, Grechyshkin, Kovalets (Dovgiy 75); Luchkevych (Bezborodko 86), Sitalo (Shastal 80), Tretiakov.
Gent: (442) Kaminski; Lustig, Plastun, Ngadeu-Ngadjui, Asare; Kums, David, Owusu, Odjidja-Ofoe; Depoitre (Kvilitaia 85), Yaremchuk (Kubo 89).

Saint-Etienne (1) 1 *(Kolodziejczak 13)*

VfL Wolfsburg (1) 1 *(William 15)* 27,000

Saint-Etienne: (4231) Moulin; Debuchy (Moukoudi 60), Salibia, Perrin, Kolodziejczak; Youssouf, M'Vila; Hamouma, Khazri (Abi 86), Nordin; Beric (Bouanga 65).
VfL Wolfsburg: (343) Pervan; Knoche, Bruma, Tisserand; William, Guilavogui, Arnold, Roussillon (Steffen 83); Klaus, Weghorst (Nmecha 60), Brekalo (Victor 72).

Thursday, 24 October 2019

Gent (1) 2 *(Yaremchuk 41, 90)*

VfL Wolfsburg (2) 2 *(Weghorst 3, Victor 24)* 14,000

Gent: (4312) Kaminski; Lustig, Plastun, Ngadeu-Ngadjui, Asare; Kums (Diarra 87), Owusu (Bezus 60), Odjidja-Ofoe; David; Yaremchuk, Depoitre (Kvilitaia 73).
VfL Wolfsburg: (343) Pervan; Knoche, Bruma, Tisserand; William (Mbabu 46), Guilavogui, Arnold, Steffen (Roussillon 79); Victor, Weghorst, Brekalo (Nmecha 66).

Saint-Etienne (1) 1 *(Silva 8)*

Oleksandriya (1) 1 *(Silva 14 (og))* 28,573

Saint-Etienne: (433) Ruffier; Debuchy, Salibia, Kolodziejczak, Silva; Youssouf, M'Vila, Aholou (Boudebouz 46); Nordin (Abi 63), Beric (Bouanga 74), Hamouma.
Oleksandriya: (4141) Pankiv; Pashaev, Dubra, Bukhal, Miroshinichenko; Grechyshkin; Luchkevych (Shastal 80), Banada, Kovalets (Dovgiy 83), Tretiakov (Babohlo 90); Sitalo.

Thursday, 7 November 2019

Oleksandriya (0) 2 *(Bezborodko 84, Zaderaka 90)*

Saint-Etienne (1) 2 *(Khazri 24 (pen), Camara 72)* 6361

Oleksandriya: (433) Pankiv; Pashaev, Dubra, Bukhal, Miroshinichenko; Banada, Grechyshkin, Kovalets; Luchkevych (Zaderaka 78), Shastal (Bezborodko 46), Tretiakov (Stetskov 84).
Saint-Etienne: (433) Ruffier; Debuchy, Fofana, Perrin, Kolodziejczak; Youssouf, Aholou, Bouanga; Nordin (Boudebouz 87), Beric (Camara 55), Khazri (Silva 72).

VfL Wolfsburg (1) 1 *(Victor 20)*

Gent (0) 3 *(Yaremchuk 50, Depoitre 65, Ngadeu-Ngadjui 76)* 12,000

VfL Wolfsburg: (343) Pervan; Knoche (Klaus 82), Bruma, Tisserand; William, Guilavogui, Arnold (Nmecha 70), Steffen; Victor, Weghorst, Brekalo (Malli 66).
Gent: (41212) Kaminski; Lustig, Plastun, Ngadeu-Ngadjui, Asare; Owusu; Odjidja-Ofoe, Kums; David; Depoitre (Kvilitaia 90), Yaremchuk (Castro-Montes 81).

Thursday, 28 November 2019

Oleksandriya (0) 0

VfL Wolfsburg (1) 1 *(Weghorst 45 (pen))* 8000

Oleksandriya: (433) Pankiv; Pashaev, Babohlo, Dubra, Miroshinichenko; Banada, Zaporozhan, Grechyshkin; Luchkevych (Zaderaka 86), Kovalets (Bezborodko 39), Shastal (Tretiakov 55).
VfL Wolfsburg: (3421) Casteels; Tisserand, Bruma, Brooks; William (Mbabu 90), Guilavogui, Arnold, Roussillon; Victor (Steffen 61), Mehmedi (Klaus 80); Weghorst.

Saint-Etienne (0) 0

Gent (0) 0 25,315

Saint-Etienne: (3421) Ruffier; Fofana, Perrin, Kolodziejczak; Honorat, Camara, M'Vila (Beric 80), Bouanga; Boudebouz, Aholou (Nordin 64); Diony (Youssouf 73).
Gent: (4132) Kaminski; Lustig, Plastun, Ngadeu-Ngadjui■, Mohammadi; Owusu; Odjidja-Ofoe, David (Dejaegere 80), Kums; Depoitre (Castro-Montes 78), Yaremchuk (Kvilitaia 71).

Thursday, 12 December 2019

Gent (2) 2 *(Depoitre 7, 16)*

Oleksandriya (0) 1 *(Miroshinichenko 54)* 13,156

Gent: (4312) Kaminski; Castro-Montes, Plastun, Lustig, Asare; Odjidja-Ofoe, Owusu, Kums; Bezus (Diarra 80); Depoitre (Kvilitaia 90), Yaremchuk (Chakvetadze 73).
Oleksandriya: (4141) Pankiv; Pashaev, Babohlo, Dubra, Miroshinichenko; Zaporozhan (Dovgiy 46); Luchkevych, Grechyshkin, Kovalets, Tretiakov (Zaderaka 79); Bezborodko (Teixeira 86).

VfL Wolfsburg (0) 1 *(Paulo Otavio 52)*

Saint-Etienne (0) 0 10,802

VfL Wolfsburg: (433) Pervan; Mbabu, Knoche, Tisserand, Paulo Otavio (Roussillon 79); Gerhardt, Rexhbecaj, Schlager (Malli 64); Steffen, Ginczek (Nmecha 64), Brekalo.
Saint-Etienne: (433) Moulin; Palencia, Moukoudi, M'Vila, Kolodziejczak; Youssouf, Aholou (Honorat 46), Diousse (Silva 77); Nordin, Beric, Hamouma (Benkhedim 55).

Group I Table	P	W	D	L	F	A	GD	Pts
Gent	6	3	3	0	11	7	4	12
VfL Wolfsburg	6	3	2	1	9	7	2	11
Saint-Etienne	6	0	4	2	6	8	–2	4
Olexandriya	6	0	3	3	6	10	–4	3

GROUP J

Thursday, 19 September 2019

Borussia Moenchengladbach (0) 0

Wolfsberg (3) 4 *(Weissman 13, Leitgeb 31, 68, Ritzmaier 41)* 40,000

Borussia Moenchengladbach: (4312) Sommer; Lainer, Ginter, Elvedi, Bensebaini; Kramer, Zakaria, Neuhaus (Embolo 46); Benes; Thuram (Raffael 71), Plea (Herrmann 72).
Wolfsberg: (4312) Kofler; Novak, Sollbauer, Rnic, Schmitz; Schmid, Leitgeb, Ritzmaier (Wernitznig 86); Liendl; Weissman (Schmidt 84), Niangbo (Schmerbock 90).

Roma (1) 4 *(Junior Caicara 42 (og), Dzeko 58, Zaniolo 71, Kluivert 90)*

Istanbul Basaksehir (0) 0 21,348

Roma: (4231) Pau Lopez; Spinazzola, Fazio, Juan Jesus, Kolarov; Cristante (Veretout 72), Diawara; Zaniolo, Pastore (Pellegrini 64), Kluivert; Dzeko (Kalinic 74).
Istanbul Basaksehir: (433) Gunok; Junior Caicara, Ponck, Topal, Clichy; Aleksic (Azubuike 69), Tekdemir, Kahveci; Visca, Gulbrandsen (Ba 77), Turan (Crivelli 64).

Thursday, 3 October 2019

Istanbul Basaksehir (0) 1 *(Visca 55)*

Borussia Moenchengladbach (0) 1 *(Herrmann 90)* 6000

Istanbul Basaksehir: (433) Gunok; Junior Caicara, Ponck, Skrtel, Clichy; Aleksic (Azubuike 46), Tekdemir, Kahveci (Topal 89); Visca, Crivelli (Elia 78), Gulbrandsen.
Borussia Moenchengladbach: (4312) Sommer; Lainer, Ginter, Elvedi, Wendt (Bensebaini 76); Kramer (Herrmann 64), Zakaria, Neuhaus; Embolo; Thuram, Plea (Raffael 46).

Wolfsberg (0) 1 *(Liendl 51)*

Roma (1) 1 *(Spinazzola 27)* 11,169

Wolfsberg: (4312) Kofler; Novak, Sollbauer, Rnic, Schmitz; Ritzmaier (Wernitznig 90), Leitgeb, Schmid; Liendl (Schmerbock 88); Weissman (Schmidt 81), Niangbo.
Roma: (4231) Mirante; Santon, Mancini, Fazio, Spinazzola (Kolarov 80); Cristante (Veretout 82), Diawara; Kluivert, Pastore (Antonucci 77), Zaniolo; Kalinic.

Thursday, 24 October 2019

Istanbul Basaksehir (0) 1 *(Kahveci 78)*

Wolfsberg (0) 0 5000

Istanbul Basaksehir: (4141) Gunok; Junior Caicara, Ponck, Skrtel, Clichy; Topal; Visca (Ucar 90), Kahveci, Tekdemir (Azubuike 46), Gulbrandsen (Robinho 64); Crivelli.
Wolfsberg: (4312) Kofler; Novak, Sollbauer, Rnic, Schmitz (Schmerbock 90); Schmid, Leitgeb, Ritzmaier; Liendl; Weissman, Niangbo (Schmidt 76).

Roma (1) 1 *(Zaniolo 32)*

Borussia Moenchengladbach (0) 1 *(Stindl 90 (pen))* 29,037

Roma: (4141) Pau Lopez; Spinazzola, Smalling, Fazio, Kolarov; Mancini; Zaniolo (Antonucci 77), Pastore (Perotti 62), Veretout, Kluivert (Florenzi 84); Dzeko.
Borussia Moenchengladbach: (4231) Sommer; Lainer, Jantschke, Elvedi, Bensebaini; Kramer (Benes 76), Zakaria; Herrmann (Hofmann 62), Neuhaus, Thuram; Embolo (Stindl 76).

Thursday, 7 November 2019

Borussia Moenchengladbach (1) 2 *(Fazio 35 (og), Thuram 90)*

Roma (0) 1 *(Fazio 64)* 44,570

Borussia Moenchengladbach: (352) Sommer; Jantschke (Hofmann 28), Ginter, Elvedi; Lainer, Benes, Zakaria, Neuhaus (Plea 73), Wendt (Bensebaini 85); Stindl, Thuram.
Roma: (4231) Pau Lopez; Santon, Smalling, Fazio, Kolarov; Veretout, Mancini (Diawara 59); Zaniolo (Under 76), Pastore (Perotti 80), Kluivert; Dzeko.

Wolfsberg (0) 0

Istanbul Basaksehir (0) 3 *(Visca 73 (pen), Crivelli 84, 87)* 5682

Wolfsberg: (4312) Kofler; Novak, Sollbauer, Rnic■, Schmitz; Schmid, Leitgeb (Gollner 87), Ritzmaier; Liendl; Weissman, Niangbo (Schmidt 81).
Istanbul Basaksehir: (4141) Gunok; Junior Caicara, Ponck, Skrtel, Clichy; Topal; Visca, Azubuike (Elia 89), Ozcan (Turan 80), Gulbrandsen (Behich 88); Crivelli.

Thursday, 28 November 2019

Istanbul Basaksehir (0) 0

Roma (3) 3 *(Veretout 30 (pen), Kluivert 40, Dzeko 45)* 12,879

Istanbul Basaksehir: (4141) Gunok; Ponck, Skrtel (Ozcan 52), Epureanu (Robinho 46), Clichy; Topal; Visca, Azubuike, Kahveci, Gulbrandsen (Behich 16); Crivelli.
Roma: (4231) Pau Lopez; Santon, Mancini, Smalling, Kolarov (Spinazzola 53); Diawara, Veretout; Zaniolo, Pellegrini (Under 71), Kluivert; Dzeko (Mkhitaryan 72).

Wolfsberg (0) 0

Borussia Moenchengladbach (0) 1 *(Stindl 60)* 12,073

Wolfsberg: (4312) Kofler; Novak, Sollbauer, Gollner, Schmitz; Schmid (Wernitznig 75), Leitgeb, Ritzmaier; Liendl; Weissman, Niangbo (Schmerbock 85).
Borussia Moenchengladbach: (3412) Sommer; Zakaria, Strobl, Bensebaini; Lainer, Benes, Hofmann, Wendt; Stindl (Embolo 74); Thuram (Raffael 89), Plea (Herrmann 77).

Thursday, 12 December 2019

Borussia Moenchengladbach (1) 1 *(Thuram 33)*

Istanbul Basaksehir (1) 2 *(Kahveci 44, Crivelli 90)* 40,046

Borussia Moenchengladbach: (442) Sommer; Lainer, Ginter, Elvedi, Wendt; Herrmann, Kramer (Bensebaini 90), Zakaria, Neuhaus (Stindl 78); Embolo (Plea 78), Thuram.
Istanbul Basaksehir: (4141) Gunok; Junior Caicara, Ponck, Epureanu, Clichy; Topal (Ozcan 88); Visca, Aleksic (Ba 67), Kahveci (Azubuike 90), Elia; Crivelli.

Roma (2) 2 *(Perotti 7 (pen), Dzeko 19)*

Wolfsberg (1) 2 *(Florenzi 10 (og), Weissman 63)* 21,672

Roma: (4231) Mirante (Pau Lopez 62); Florenzi, Mancini, Fazio, Spinazzola; Veretout, Diawara; Under (Pellegrini 66), Mkhitaryan, Perotti (Zaniolo 67); Dzeko.
Wolfsberg: (4312) Kofler; Novak, Sollbauer, Rnic, Schmitz; Schmid, Sprangler, Wernitznig (Schofl 76); Liendl; Weissman (Hodzic 90), Niangbo (Steiger 90).

Group J Table	P	W	D	L	F	A	GD	Pts
Istanbul Basaksehir	6	3	1	2	7	9	–2	10
Roma	6	2	3	1	12	6	6	9
Borussia Moenchengladbach	6	2	2	2	6	9	–3	8
Wolfsberg	6	1	2	3	7	8	–1	5

GROUP K

Thursday, 19 September 2019

Slovan Bratislava (1) 4 *(Sporar 14, 58, Rharsalla 90, Ljubicic 90)*

Besiktas (2) 2 *(Ljajic 29 (pen), Bozhikov 45 (og))* 5273

Slovan Bratislava: (433) Greif; Medvedev, Abena, Bozhikov, Vernon De Marco; Ibrahim (Bajric 89), de Kamps (Ljubicic 82), Holman; Drazic (Daniel 76), Sporar, Rharsalla.
Besiktas: (4141) Karius; Douglas, Vida, Victor Ruiz (Hutchinson 74), Pedro Rebocho; Elneny; Diaby (Lens 79), Tokoz, Ljajic, Nkoudou (Yalcin 82); Nayir.

Wolverhampton W (0) 0

Braga (0) 1 *(Ricardo Horta 71)* 28,314

Wolverhampton W: (352) Rui Patricio; Bennett, Coady, Boly; Doherty (Traore 80), Dendoncker (Jota 76), Neves, Gibbs-White (Joao Moutinho 67), Jonny; Jimenez, Cutrone.
Braga: (451) Matheus Magalhaes; Ricardo Esgaio, Bruno Viana, Pablo Santos, Nuno Sequeira; Galeno (Trincao 84), Fransergio, Joao Palhinha, Andre Horta (Joao Novais 86), Ricardo Horta (Murilo Souza 88); Paulinho.

Thursday, 3 October 2019

Besiktas (0) 0

Wolverhampton W (0) 1 *(Boly 90)* 22,670

Besiktas: (433) Karius; Douglas, Vida, Uysal, Pedro Rebocho; Tokoz (Ozyakup 79), Elneny, Ljajic; Lens (Gonul 84), Yalcin (Nayir 27), Erkin.
Wolverhampton W: (343) Rui Patricio; Boly, Coady, Saiss; Doherty, Neves, Joao Moutinho, Jonny; Gibbs-White (Dendoncker 62), Jimenez (Cutrone 79), Pedro Neto (Traore 46).

Braga (1) 2 *(Bruno Viana 31, Galeno 63)*

Slovan Bratislava (1) 2 *(Sporar 45, Bruno Viana 87 (og))* 9077

Braga: (442) Eduardo; Ricardo Esgaio, Bruno Viana, Pablo Santos, Nuno Sequeira; Ricardo Horta (Trincao 71), Fransergio (Rui Fonte 88), Joao Palhinha, Andre Horta (Joao Novais 70); Galeno, Paulinho.
Slovan Bratislava: (532) Greif; Medvedev, Bajric, Abena, Vernon De Marco, Sukhotsky (Daniel 80); Holman (Drazic 68), Ibrahim, de Kamps (Ljubicic 68); Sporar, Rharsalla.

Thursday, 24 October 2019

Besiktas (0) 1 *(Nayir 71)*

Braga (1) 2 *(Ricardo Horta 38, Wilson Eduardo 80)* 20,956

Besiktas: (4231) Karius; Uysal (Nayir 67), Vida, Roco, Pedro Rebocho; Ozyakup (Yilmaz 61), Elneny; Boyd (Secgin 84), Ljajic, Erkin; Yalcin.
Braga: (4141) Matheus Magalhaes; Ricardo Esgaio, Bruno Viana, Pablo Santos, Nuno Sequeira; Joao Palhinha; Galeno, Joao Novais (Agbo 75), Andre Horta (Wilson Eduardo 75), Ricardo Horta; Paulinho (Rui Fonte 83).

Slovan Bratislava (1) 1 *(Sporar 11)*

Wolverhampton W (0) 2 *(Saiss 58, Jimenez 63 (pen))* 20,333

Slovan Bratislava: (4231) Greif; Medvedev, Abena, Bozhikov, Vernon De Marco; de Kamps, Ibrahim (Cavric 81); Daniel (Rafael Ratao 66), Holman (Ljubicic 57), Rharsalla; Sporar.
Wolverhampton W: (352) Rui Patricio; Boly, Coady, Kilman; Doherty, Gibbs-White (Jota■ 59), Saiss (Dendoncker 76), Joao Moutinho, Ruben Vinagre; Jimenez, Cutrone (Traore 46).

Thursday, 7 November 2019

Braga (2) 3 *(Paulinho 14, 37, Wilson Eduardo 81)*

Besiktas (1) 1 *(Boyd 29)* 8833

Braga: (442) Eduardo; Ricardo Esgaio, Bruno Viana, Wallace Santos, Nuno Sequeira; Galeno, Joao Palhinha, Fransergio, Andre Horta (Trincao 77); Paulinho (Rui Fonte 67), Ricardo Horta (Wilson Eduardo 60).
Besiktas: (442) Karius; Uysal, Vida, Roco, Erkin (Pedro Rebocho 63); Lens■, Ozyakup, Yilmaz (Elneny 72), Boyd; Yalcin (Secgin 88), Nayir.

Wolverhampton W (0) 1 *(Jimenez 90)*

Slovan Bratislava (0) 0 29,789

Wolverhampton W: (343) Rui Patricio; Dendoncker, Coady, Kilman; Doherty, Neves, Joao Moutinho, Ruben Vinagre (Jonny 90); Traore (Bennett 90), Jimenez, Pedro Neto (Cutrone 69).
Slovan Bratislava: (541) Greif; Medvedev, Bajric (Ljubicic 89), Abena, Bozhikov, Vernon De Marco; Drazic, de Kamps, Ibrahim (Daniel 90), Rafael Ratao (Sukhotsky 70); Sporar.

Thursday, 28 November 2019

Besiktas (0) 2 *(Roco 75, Ljajic 90 (pen))*

Slovan Bratislava (1) 1 *(Daniel 35)* 11,526

Besiktas: (4231) Karius; Uysal, Vida, Roco, Pedro Rebocho (Ljajic 46); Ozyakup (Yalcin 76), Elneny; Boyd (Nkoudou 46), Diaby, Erkin; Nayir.
Slovan Bratislava: (4231) Greif; Bajric, Abena, Bozhikov, Vernon De Marco; Ibrahim, de Kamps; Daniel (Rafael Ratao 86), Holman (Ljubicic 83), Rharsalla (Drazic 76); Sporar.

Braga (1) 3 *(Andre Horta 6, Paulinho 64, Fransergio 79)*

Wolverhampton W (3) 3 *(Jimenez 13, Doherty 34, Traore 35)* 12,058

Braga: (442) Eduardo; Ricardo Esgaio, Bruno Viana, Wallace Santos (Wilson Eduardo 58), Nuno Sequeira; Fransergio, Joao Palhinha, Andre Horta, Ricardo Horta (Rui Fonte 73); Galeno, Paulinho (Pablo Santos 87).
Wolverhampton W: (343) Rui Patricio; Dendoncker, Coady, Saiss; Doherty, Neves, Joao Moutinho, Jonny; Traore (Ruben Vinagre 75), Jimenez (Pedro Neto 70), Jota (Cutrone 80).

Thursday, 12 December 2019

Slovan Bratislava (1) 2 *(Sporar 42, Rharsalla 70)*

Braga (1) 4 *(Rui Fonte 44, Trincao 72, Bozhikov 75 (og), Paulinho 90)* 10,856

Slovan Bratislava: (4231) Greif; Medvedev, Abena, Bozhikov, Vernon De Marco; Ljubicic, Nono (Bajric 76); Daniel, Drazic (Rafael Ratao 78), Rharsalla; Sporar.
Braga: (4141) Tiago Sa; Ricardo Esgaio, Bruno Viana, Pablo Santos, Caju (Diogo Viana 59); Agbo; Trincao (Galeno 83), Fransergio, Joao Novais, Ricardo Horta; Rui Fonte (Paulinho 82).

Wolverhampton W (0) 4 *(Jota 57, 63, 68, Dendoncker 67)*

Besiktas (0) 0 27,866

Wolverhampton W: (352) Ruddy; Bennett, Coady, Kilman; Rasmussen, Dendoncker (Otasowie 73), Neves (Jota 56), Joao Moutinho (Perry 70), Ruben Vinagre; Cutrone, Pedro Neto.
Besiktas: (4231) Yuvakuran; Kalafat (Roco 76), Uysal, Kaya, Pedro Rebocho; Ozyakup, Secgin; Lens (Diaby 81), Yalcin (Elneny 64), Boyd; Nayir.

Group K Table	*P*	*W*	*D*	*L*	*F*	*A*	*GD*	*Pts*
Braga	6	4	2	0	15	9	6	14
Wolverhampton W	6	4	1	1	11	5	6	13
Slovan Bratislava	6	1	1	4	10	13	–3	4
Besiktas	6	1	0	5	6	15	–9	3

GROUP L

Thursday, 19 September 2019

Manchester U (0) 1 *(Greenwood 73)*

Astana (0) 0 50,783

Manchester U: (4231) Romero; Dalot, Tuanzebe, Jones, Rojo (Young 78); Fred, Matic; Greenwood, Gomes (Mata 68), Chong (Lingard 68); Rashford.
Astana: (4141) Eric; Rukavina, Postnikov, Tomasevic, Shomko; Maewski; Tomasov, Sigurjonsson, Simunovic (Logvinenko 46), Rotariu (Mubele 82); Murtazaev (Janga 46).

Partizan Belgrade (1) 2 *(Natcho 42 (pen), 61)*

AZ Alkmaar (1) 2 *(Stengs 12, Boadu 66)* 22,564

Partizan Belgrade: (4231) Stojkovic; Miletic, Ostojic, Pavlovic S, Urosevic; Scekic (Soumah 80), Zdjelar; Tosic (Markovic 63), Natcho, Asano; Umar (Gigic 88).
AZ Alkmaar: (4231) Bizot; Svensson■, Vlaar, Wuytens (Chatzidiakos 54), Wijndal; Midtsjoe, Koopmeiners; Stengs (Clasie 84), de Wit, Idrissi (Sugawara 31); Boadu.

Thursday, 3 October 2019

Astana (0) 1 *(Sigurjonsson 85)*

Partizan Belgrade (1) 2 *(Umar 28, 73)* 20,137

Astana: (4411) Eric; Rukavina, Simunovic, Tomasevic (Postnikov 15), Shomko; Rotariu, Sigurjonsson, Maewski, Beysebekov (Janga 79); Pertsukh; Khizhnichenko (Murtazaev 46).
Partizan Belgrade: (4231) Stojkovic; Miletic, Ostojic, Pavlovic S, Urosevic; Natcho, Zdjelar; Tosic (Markovic 77), Soumah (Scekic 66), Asano (Brezancic 79); Umar.

AZ Alkmaar (0) 0

Manchester U (0) 0 13,863

AZ Alkmaar: (4231) Bizot; Sugawara, Vlaar, Wuytens, Wijndal; Midtsjoe, Koopmeiners; Stengs, de Wit (Chatzidiakos 87), Idrissi; Boadu.
Manchester U: (4231) de Gea; Dalot, Lindelof, Rojo, Williams; Fred, Matic; Greenwood (Lingard 77), Mata (McTominay 83), Gomes; James (Rashford 63).

Thursday, 24 October 2019

AZ Alkmaar (2) 6 *(Koopmeiners 39 (pen), 83 (pen), Boadu 43, Stengs 77, Sugawara 85, Idrissi 90)*

Astana (0) 0 8123

AZ Alkmaar: (433) Bizot; Svensson, Vlaar (Chatzidiakos 69), Wuytens (Clasie 80), Wijndal; Midtsjoe, de Wit (Sugawara 71), Koopmeiners; Stengs, Boadu, Idrissi.
Astana: (433) Eric (Mokin 26); Beysebekov (Rukavina 43), Simunovic, Logvinenko (Postnikov 69), Shomko; Zhalmukan, Maewski, Pertsukh; Rotariu, Janga, Muzhikov.

Partizan Belgrade (0) 0

Manchester U (1) 1 *(Martial 43 (pen))* 25,627

Partizan Belgrade: (4231) Stojkovic; Miletic, Ostojic, Pavlovic S, Urosevic; Zdjelar, Natcho; Tosic (Stevanovic 75), Soumah (Pavlovic L 83), Asano (Ivanovic 90); Umar.
Manchester U: (3421) Romero; Jones, Maguire, Rojo; Wan Bissaka (James 60), Garner (Andreas Pereira 82), McTominay, Williams; Lingard, Mata; Martial (Rashford 60).

Thursday, 7 November 2019

Astana (0) 0

AZ Alkmaar (1) 5 *(Boadu 29, 77, Midtsjoe 52, Idrissi 57, Chatzidiakos 75)* 11,584

Astana: (442) Eric; Rukavina, Postnikov, Logvinenko, Shomko; Beysebekov (Muzhikov 74), Pertsukh, Maewski, Rotariu (Murtazaev 71); Tomasov, Khizhnichenko.
AZ Alkmaar: (433) Bizot; Svensson (Sugawara 61), Chatzidiakos, Wuytens, Wijndal; Midtsjoe (Clasie 67), de Wit, Koopmeiners; Stengs (Aboukhlal 77), Boadu, Idrissi.

Manchester U (2) 3 *(Greenwood 21, Martial 33, Rashford 49)*

Partizan Belgrade (0) 0 62,955

Manchester U: (4231) Romero; Wan Bissaka, Maguire, Rojo, Young; McTominay (Lingard 75), Fred (Garner 63); Greenwood, Mata, Rashford (Andreas Pereira 67); Martial.
Partizan Belgrade: (4231) Stojkovic; Miletic, Ostojic, Pavlovic S, Urosevic; Scekic, Zdjelar; Soumah, Natcho (Tosic 60), Asano (Stevanovic 70); Umar (Ivanovic 86).

Thursday, 28 November 2019

Astana (0) 2 *(Shomko 55, Bernard 62 (og))*

Manchester U (1) 1 *(Lingard 10)* 28,949

Astana: (442) Eric; Rukavina, Postnikov, Logvinenko, Shomko; Rotariu, Maewski, Sigurjonsson, Beysebekov; Khizhnichenko (Pertsukh 85), Murtazaev (Janga 90).
Manchester U: (4231) Grant; Laird, Tuanzebe, Bernard, Shaw; Levitt, Garner (Ramazani 84); Chong (Bughail-Mellor 65), Lingard, Gomes (Galbraith 89); Greenwood.

AZ Alkmaar (0) 2 *(Druijf 87, 90)*

Partizan Belgrade (2) 2 *(Asano 16, Soumah 27)* 9092

AZ Alkmaar: (433) Bizot; Svensson, Chatzidiakos (Druijf 54), Wuytens (Sugawara 60), Wijndal; Midtsjoe, de Wit (Clasie 71), Koopmeiners; Stengs, Boadu■, Idrissi.
Partizan Belgrade: (4411) Stojkovic; Miletic, Ostojic, Pavlovic S, Urosevic; Tosic (Brezancic 69), Natcho (Vujacic 90), Zdjelar, Asano; Soumah (Scekic 75); Umar.

Thursday, 12 December 2019

Manchester U (0) 4 *(Young 53, Greenwood 58, 64, Mata 62 (pen))*

AZ Alkmaar (0) 0 65,773

Manchester U: (4231) Romero; Young (Laird 68), Tuanzebe, Maguire (Jones 68), Williams; Garner, Matic; Greenwood, Mata, Andreas Pereira; Martial (Chong 59).
AZ Alkmaar: (433) Bizot; Svensson, Clasie, Wuytens, Wijndal; Midtsjoe, Koopmeiners, de Wit (Druijf 63); Sugawara (Vlaar 68), Stengs, Idrissi (Ouwejan 77).

Partizan Belgrade (3) 4 *(Soumah 4, Umar 22, 76, Asano 26)*

Astana (0) 1 *(Rotariu 79)* 8075

Partizan Belgrade: (4231) Stojkovic (Kljajic 70); Lutovac, Ostojic, Pavlovic S, Urosevic; Scekic, Zdjelar; Tosic, Soumah (Pavlovic L 64), Asano; Umar (Stevanovic 83).
Astana: (442) Eric; Rukavina, Postnikov, Logvinenko, Shomko; Rotariu, Sigurjonsson (Janga 85), Maewski, Beysebekov; Khizhnichenko, Murtazaev (Pertsukh 47).

Group L Table	P	W	D	L	F	A	GD	Pts
Manchester U	6	4	1	1	10	2	8	13
AZ Alkmaar	6	2	3	1	15	8	7	9
Partizan Belgrade	6	2	2	2	10	10	0	8
Astana	6	1	0	5	4	19	–15	3

KNOCK-OUT STAGE

ROUND OF 32 FIRST LEG

Thursday, 20 February 2020

APOEL (0) 0

FC Basel (1) 3 *(Petretta 16, Stocker 53, Arthur Cabral 66)* 8191

APOEL: (4411) Belec; Vouros, Merkis, Ioannou (Wheeler 80), Mihajlovic; Al-Taamari, Jensen, Alef, Matic; De Vincenti (Jakolis 71); Pavlovic (Hallenius 56).
FC Basel: (4231) Omlin; Widmer, Comert, Alderete, Riveros; Xhaka, Frei (Bunjaku 85); Stocker, Campo, Petretta (Pululu 80); Arthur Cabral (Ademi 74).

AZ Alkmaar (0) 1 *(Koopmeiners 86 (pen))*

LASK (1) 1 *(Raguz 26)* 12,526

AZ Alkmaar: (4141) Bizot; Svensson, Leeuwin, Koopmeiners, Wijndal; Clasie; de Wit, Evjen (Sugawara 73), Stengs, Idrissi (Druijf 81); Boadu.
LASK: (3421) Schlager; Wiesinger, Trauner, Filipovic; Ranftl, Holland, Michorl, Renner (Potzmann 56); Goiginger, Frieser (Balic 76); Raguz (Klauss 56).

Bayer Leverkusen (1) 2 *(Alario 29, Havertz 57 (pen))*

Porto (0) 1 *(Diaz 73)* 26,838

Bayer Leverkusen: (4141) Hradecky; Bender L, Bender S, Tapsoba, Sinkgraven; Aranguiz (Baumgartlinger 72); Havertz, Demirbay, Amiri, Volland (Paulinho 90); Alario (Bailey 80).
Porto: (442) Marchesin; Manafa (Nakajima 61), Mbemba, Marcano, Alex Telles; Corona, Sergio Oliveira, Uribe, Diaz (Danilo Pereira 77); Marega, Tiquinho Soares (Ze Luis 63).

CFR Cluj (0) 1 *(Deac 59 (pen))*

Sevilla (0) 1 *(En-Nesyri 82)* 14,820

CFR Cluj: (442) Arlauskis; Manea, Paulo Vinicius, Burca, Camora; Paun (Hoban 74), Bordeianu, Djokovic, Deac; Traore (Rondon 83), Omrani (Golofca 86).
Sevilla: (433) Vaclik; Jesus Navas (En-Nesyri 73), Kounde, Diego Carlos, Escudero; Fernando, Gudelj, Jordan; Suso (Vazquez 90), de Jong, Ocampos (Lopes 78).

Club Brugge (1) 1 *(Bonaventure 15)*

Manchester U (1) 1 *(Martial 36)* 27,000

Club Brugge: (3412) Mignolet; Mata, Mechele, Deli; Kossounou, Rits, Balanta (Vormer 47), De Cuyper (Schrijvers 73); Tau (De Ketelaere 62); Bonaventure, Vanaken.
Manchester U: (3421) Romero; Lindelof, Maguire, Shaw; Dalot (Bruno Fernandes 81), Andreas Pereira (Fred 71), Matic, Williams; Mata, Lingard; Martial (Ighalo 67).

Eintracht Frankfurt (2) 4 *(Kamada 12, 43, 53, Kostic 56)*

Red Bull Salzburg (0) 1 *(Hwang 85 (pen))* 47,000

Eintracht Frankfurt: (4141) Trapp; Toure, Ilsanker (Durm 86), Abraham, Ndicka; Hasebe; Kamada (Da Costa 81), Sow, Rode, Kostic; Andre Silva (Paciencia 75).
Red Bull Salzburg: (41212) Stankovic; Farkas, Onguene, Wober, Ulmer; Junuzovic; Mwepu, Szoboszlai (Camara 71); Okugawa (Adeyemi 46); Daka (Koita 46), Hwang.

FC Copenhagen (0) 1 *(N'Doye 52)*

Celtic (1) 1 *(Edouard 14)* 34,346

FC Copenhagen: (442) Johnsson; Varela, Nelsson, Sigurdsson (Papagiannopoulos 86), Oviedo (Bengtsson 73); Mas, Stage, Zeca, Jensen; N'Doye, Santos (Kaufmann 73).
Celtic: (433) Forster; Frimpong (Simunovic 84), Jullien, Ajer, Hayes; Ntcham (Elyounoussi 60), Brown (Bitton 73), McGregor; Christie, Edouard, Forrest.

Getafe (1) 2 *(Deyverson 37, Kenedy 90)*

Ajax (0) 0 14,039

Getafe: (442) Soria; Damian, Djene, Etxeita, Olivera; Nyom, Arambarri, Maksimovic, Cucurella (Kenedy 88); Deyverson (Angel 57), Mata (Jorge Molina 72).
Ajax: (4231) Bruno Varela; Dest, Alvarez (Schuurs 67), Blind, Tagliafico; van de Beek, Martinez; Tadic, Ziyech, Babel; Traore (Huntelaar 67).

Ludogorets Razgrad (0) 0

Internazionale (0) 2 *(Eriksen 71, Lukaku 90 (pen))* 10,024

Ludogorets Razgrad: (4411) Iliev; Cicinho, Terziev, Grigore, Nedyalkov; Cauly (Biton 90), Dyakov (Badji 67), Abel, Wanderson; Marcelinho; Swierczok (Tchibota 76).
Internazionale: (352) Padelli; D'Ambrosio, Ranocchia, Godin; Moses (Barella 72), Vecino, Valero, Eriksen, Biraghi (Young 81); Sanchez, Martinez (Lukaku 64).

Olympiacos (0) 0

Arsenal (0) 1 *(Lacazette 81)* 31,456

Olympiacos: (433) Jose Sa; Elabdellaoui, Semedo, Ba, Tsimikas; Bouchalakis (Fortounis 65), Guilherme, Camara; Masouras (Lovera 75), El Arabi, Valbuena.
Arsenal: (4231) Leno; Papastathopoulos (Maitland-Niles 90), Mustafi, Luiz, Saka; Guendouzi, Xhaka; Aubameyang, Willock (Pepe 75), Martinelli (Ceballos 58); Lacazette.

Rangers (0) 3 *(Hagi 67, 82, Aribo 75)*

Braga (1) 2 *(Fransergio 11, Ruiz 59)* 49,378

Rangers: (433) McGregor; Tavernier, Goldson, Katic, Barisic (Stewart 73); Arfield, Davis, Kamara (Aribo 54); Hagi, Morelos, Kent (Kamberi 68).
Braga: (352) Matheus Magalhaes; Wallace Santos (Galeno 12), Bruno Viana, Raul Silva; Ricardo Esgaio, Trincao, Fransergio, Joao Palhinha (Joao Novais 83), Nuno Sequeira; Ruiz (Ricardo Horta 70), Paulinho.

Roma (1) 1 *(Perez 13)*

Gent (0) 0 28,248

Roma: (4231) Pau Lopez; Spinazzola (Santon 69), Smalling, Fazio, Kolarov; Cristante, Veretout; Perez, Pellegrini (Mkhitaryan 79), Perotti (Kluivert 82); Dzeko.
Gent: (4312) Kaminski; Lustig, Plastun, Ngadeu-Ngadjui, Mohammadi; Kums (Marreh 90), Owusu, Odjidja-Ofoe; Bezus (Chakvetadze 74); Depoitre, David.

Shakhtar Donetsk (0) 2 *(Alan Patrick 56, Kovalenko 72)*

Benfica (0) 1 *(Pizzi 66 (pen))* 24,429

Shakhtar Donetsk: (4231) Pyatov; Bolbat, Kryvtsov, Matviyenko, Ismaily; Alan Patrick (Marcos Antonio 80), Stepanenko; Marlos (Konoplyanka 83), Kovalenko, Taison (Tete 90); Moraes.
Benfica: (442) Vlachodimos; Tavares, Dias, Ferro, Grimaldo; Chiquinho (Rafa Silva 79), Florentino, Taarabt, Cervi; Pizzi (Samaris 90), Seferovic (Vinicius 69).

Sporting Lisbon (2) 3 *(Coates 3, Sporar 44, Vietto 51)*

Istanbul Basaksehir (0) 1 *(Visca 77 (pen))* 27,392

Sporting Lisbon: (4231) Maximiano; Ristovski, Coates, Neto, Acuna; Battaglia, Wendel; Bolasie (Plata 89), Vietto, Cabral (Doumbia 81); Sporar (Mendes 71).
Istanbul Basaksehir: (442) Gunok; Junior Caicara, Ponck, Skrtel (Elia 70), Clichy; Visca, Tekdemir, Kahveci (Aleksic 81), Gulbrandsen (Ozcan 46); Ba, Crivelli.

VfL Wolfsburg (0) 2 *(Brekalo 49, Thelin 62 (og))*

Malmo (0) 1 *(Thelin 47 (pen))* 13,801

VfL Wolfsburg: (433) Casteels; Mbabu, Knoche, Brooks, Roussillon (Paulo Otavio 46); Gerhardt, Schlager (Steffen 71), Arnold; Mehmedi, Weghorst, Brekalo (Ginczek 90).
Malmo: (4411) Dahlin; Larsson, Ahmedhodzic, Bengtsson, Safari; Traustason (Rieks 22 (Berget 58)), Christiansen, Bachirou, Antonsson; Nalic; Thelin.

Wolverhampton W (1) 4 *(Jota 15, 67, 81, Neves 52)*

Espanyol (0) 0 30,435

Wolverhampton W: (343) Rui Patricio; Boly, Coady, Saiss; Doherty, Joao Moutinho, Neves, Jonny; Traore (Dendoncker 61), Jimenez (Pedro Neto 75), Jota (Daniel Podence 83).
Espanyol: (442) Andres; Gomez (Darder 75), Naldo, Calero, Didac; Wu, Victor Sanchez, Iturraspe (David Lopez 61), Vargas; Melendo (Calleri 62), Ferreyra.

ROUND OF 32 SECOND LEG

Wednesday, 26 February 2020

Braga (0) 0

Rangers (0) 1 *(Kent 61)* 18,113

Braga: (3421) Matheus Magalhaes; Bruno Viana, Carmo (Ruiz 64), Raul Silva (Galeno 53); Ricardo Esgaio, Fransergio, Joao Palhinha (Joao Novais 46), Nuno Sequeira; Trincao, Ricardo Horta; Paulinho.
Rangers: (433) McGregor; Tavernier, Goldson, Edmundson, Barisic; Jack, Davis, Arfield; Hagi (Aribo 72), Kamberi (Ojo 78), Kent.

Thursday, 27 February 2020

Ajax (1) 2 *(Danilo 10, Olivera 63 (og))*

Getafe (1) 1 *(Mata 5)* 51,487

Ajax: (433) Onana; Dest, Schuurs, Martinez, Blind; Gravenberch (Huntelaar 75), van de Beek, Eiting; Danilo (Promes 46), Tadic, Babel.
Getafe: (442) Soria; Damian, Djene, Etxeita, Olivera; Nyom, Arambarri, Maksimovic, Cucurella (Kenedy 90); Mata (Timor 90), Deyverson (Jorge Molina 70).

Arsenal (0) 1 *(Aubameyang 113)*

Olympiacos (0) 2 *(Cisse 53, El Arabi 119)* 60,242

Arsenal: (4231) Leno; Bellerin (Willock 84), Mustafi (Papastathopoulos 103), Luiz, Saka; Ceballos (Torreira 72), Xhaka; Pepe, Ozil, Aubameyang; Lacazette (Martinelli 106).
Olympiacos: (433) Jose Sa; Elabdellaoui, Ba, Cisse, Tsimikas (Lovera 114); Bouchalakis, Camara, Guilherme (Papadopoulos 117); Randjelovic (Masouras 77), El Arabi, Valbuena (Bruno Gaspar 86).
aet; Olympiacos won on away goals.

Benfica (2) 3 *(Pizzi 9, Dias 36, Rafa Silva 47)*

Shakhtar Donetsk (1) 3 *(Dias 12 (og), Stepanenko 49, Alan Patrick 71)* 48,302

Benfica: (442) Vlachodimos; Tavares, Dias, Ferro, Grimaldo; Pizzi (Jota 79), Weigl, Taarabt, Rafa Silva; Chiquinho (Seferovic 67), Dyego Sousa (Vinicius 79).
Shakhtar Donetsk: (4231) Pyatov; Dodo, Kryvtsov, Matviyenko, Ismaily; Marcos Antonio, Stepanenko; Marlos (Tete 62), Alan Patrick (Khocholava 90), Taison (Konoplyanka 86); Moraes.

Celtic (0) 1 *(Edouard 83 (pen))*

FC Copenhagen (0) 3 *(Santos 51, Mas 85, N'Doye 88)* 56,172

Celtic: (4231) Forster; Ajer, Jullien, Simunovic, Taylor; Brown, McGregor; Forrest, Rogic, Elyounoussi (Griffiths 70); Edouard.
FC Copenhagen: (442) Johnsson; Varela, Nelsson, Sigurdsson, Bengtsson; Mas (Bjelland 86), Stage, Zeca, Jensen; Kaufmann (Santos 45 (Daramy 88)), N'Doye.

Espanyol (1) 3 *(Calleri 15, 57 (pen), 90)*

Wolverhampton W (1) 2 *(Traore 22, Doherty 79)* 14,525

Espanyol: (4231) Andres; Gomez, Naldo, Calero, Pedrosa; Victor Sanchez (Lozano 61), David Lopez; Vargas, Darder (Wu 67), Melendo (Pipa 75); Calleri.
Wolverhampton W: (352) Rui Patricio; Boly, Coady, Kilman; Doherty, Gibbs-White (Pedro Neto 64), Dendoncker, Joao Moutinho, Ruben Vinagre (Saiss 58); Traore (Bruno Jordao 78), Daniel Podence.

FC Basel (1) 1 *(Frei 38 (pen))*

APOEL (0) 0 14,428

FC Basel: (4231) Nikolic; Isufi, Comert, Bergstrom, Riveros; Frei (Ramires 70), Xhaka; Stocker, Campo, Petretta (Zhegrova 46); Ademi (Arthur Cabral 32).
APOEL: (433) Waterman; Vouros, Merkis, Savic, Ioannou; Mihajlovic, Jensen, Matic; Jakolis (De Vincenti 46), Al-Taamari (Pavlovic 70), Aloneftis (Efrem 62).

Gent (1) 1 *(David 25)*

Roma (1) 1 *(Kluivert 29)* 17,557

Gent: (4312) Kaminski; Castro-Montes, Plastun (Niangbo 80), Ngadeu-Ngadjui, Mohammadi; Kums, Owusu, Odjidja-Ofoe; Bezus (Chakvetadze 66); Depoitre (Kvilitaia 66), David.
Roma: (4231) Pau Lopez; Spinazzola (Santon 67), Mancini, Smalling, Kolarov; Veretout (Fazio 78), Cristante; Perez (Villar 83), Mkhitaryan, Kluivert; Dzeko.

Internazionale (2) 2 *(Biraghi 31, Lukaku 45)*

Ludogorets Razgrad (1) 1 *(Cauly 26)*

Internazionale: (352) Padelli; D'Ambrosio (Bastoni 76), Ranocchia, Godin; Moses, Barella (Brozovic 46), Valero, Eriksen, Biraghi; Lukaku (Esposito 62), Sanchez.
Ludogorets Razgrad: (442) Iliev; Cicinho, Terziev, Grigore, Nedyalkov; Cauly, Badji, Dyakov, Wanderson (Tchibota 70); Keseru (Swierczok 64), Marcelinho (Biton 83).
Behind closed doors due to the COVID-19 pandemic.

Istanbul Basaksehir (2) 4 *(Skrtel 31, Aleksic 45, Visca 90, 119 (pen))*

Sporting Lisbon (0) 1 *(Vietto 68)* 5892

Istanbul Basaksehir: (433) Gunok; Junior Caicara, Skrtel, Epureanu, Clichy; Kahveci (Robinho 89), Azubuike (Ozcan 77), Aleksic; Visca (Ponck 120), Ba, Elia (Gulbrandsen 85).
Sporting Lisbon: (4231) Maximiano; Ristovski, Coates, Tiago Ilori, Acuna; Battaglia, Wendel (Eduardo Henrique 90); Bolasie (Plata 60), Vietto, Cabral (Doumbia 73); Sporar (Mendes 108).
aet.

LASK (1) 2 *(Raguz 44 (pen), 50)*

AZ Alkmaar (0) 0 14,000

LASK: (343) Schlager; Wiesinger■, Trauner, Filipovic; Ranftl, Holland, Michorl, Renner; Goiginger (Ramsebner 89), Raguz (Klauss 69), Frieser (Balic 61).
AZ Alkmaar: (4411) Bizot; Svensson (Evjen 76), Leeuwin (Druijf 63), Koopmeiners, Wijndal; de Wit, Midtsjoe, Clasie, Idrissi; Stengs; Boadu.

Malmo (0) 0

VfL Wolfsburg (1) 3 *(Brekalo 41, Gerhardt 65, Victor 69)* 20,500

Malmo: (4411) Dahlin; Lewicki, Ahmedhodzic, Bengtsson (Nielsen 76), Safari; Antonsson, Christiansen, Bachirou, Rieks; Nalic (Berget 56); Thelin.
VfL Wolfsburg: (433) Casteels; Steffen, Knoche, Brooks, Paulo Otavio; Arnold, Schlager (Victor 59), Gerhardt; Mehmedi, Weghorst (Ginczek 70), Brekalo (Klaus 79).

Manchester U (3) 5 *(Bruno Fernandes 27 (pen), Ighalo 34, McTominay 41, Fred 82, 90)*

Club Brugge (0) 0 70,397

Manchester U: (4231) Romero; Wan Bissaka, Bailly, Maguire, Shaw; Fred, McTominay (Greenwood 72); Mata, Bruno Fernandes (Lingard 65), James (Chong 46); Ighalo.
Club Brugge: (343) Mignolet; Mata (Mitrovic 62), Mechele, Deli■; Kossounou, Rits (De Ketelaere 79), Ricca, De Cuyper; Tau (Diatta 61), Okereke, Vanaken.

Porto (0) 1 *(Marega 65)*

Bayer Leverkusen (1) 3 *(Alario 10, Demirbay 50, Havertz 57)* 30,292

Porto: (442) Marchesin; Corona, Mbemba, Marcano, Alex Telles; Otavio, Uribe (Pepe 46), Sergio Oliveira, Diaz (Nakajima 29); Marega, Ze Luis (Tiquinho Soares■ 64).
Bayer Leverkusen: (3421) Hradecky; Tah, Bender S (Dragovic 67), Tapsoba; Bender L (Weiser 46), Amiri, Demirbay, Sinkgraven; Havertz, Diaby (Bailey 83); Alario.

Sevilla (0) 0

CFR Cluj (0) 0 31,338

Sevilla: (433) Bounou; Jesus Navas (En-Nesyri 76), Kounde, Diego Carlos, Reguilon; Jordan (Banega 57), Gudelj, Fernando; Suso (Nolito 67), de Jong, Ocampos.
CFR Cluj: (4231) Arlauskis; Manea, Paulo Vinicius, Burca (Boli 27), Camora; Bordeianu■, Djokovic (Rondon 78); Deac, Paun, Omrani (Golofca 84); Traore.
Sevilla won on away goals.

Friday, 28 February 2020

Red Bull Salzburg (1) 2 *(Ulmer 10, Onguene 71)*

Eintracht Frankfurt (1) 2 *(Andre Silva 30, 83)* 29,000

Red Bull Salzburg: (41212) Stankovic; Vallci, Ramalho, Onguene, Ulmer; Camara; Mwepu (Berisha 76), Szoboszlai (Bernede 86); Koita (Okafor 66); Daka, Hwang.
Eintracht Frankfurt: (4141) Trapp; Toure, Abraham, Hinteregger, Ndicka; Ilsanker; Kamada (Da Costa 73), Sow, Rode, Kostic (Chandler 88); Andre Silva (Paciencia 88).

ROUND OF 16 FIRST LEG

Thursday, 12 March 2020

Eintracht Frankfurt (0) 0

FC Basel (1) 3 *(Campo 27, Bua 73, Frei 85)* 0

Eintracht Frankfurt: (4141) Trapp; Toure, Abraham, Hinteregger, Ndicka; Hasebe (Ilsanker 74); Kamada (Gacinovic 78), Sow (Paciencia 46), Rode, Kostic; Andre Silva.
FC Basel: (4231) Omlin; Widmer, Comert, Alderete, Riveros; Xhaka, Frei; Stocker (Zhegrova 90), Campo (Van Der Werff 78), Petretta (Bua 68); Arthur Cabral.
Behind closed doors due the COVID-19 pandemic.

Istanbul Basaksehir (0) 1 *(Visca 88 (pen))*

FC Copenhagen (0) 0 12,205

Istanbul Basaksehir: (433) Gunok; Junior Caicara, Skrtel, Epureanu, Clichy; Aleksic, Tekdemir (Gulbrandsen 85), Kahveci; Visca (Azubuike 90), Ba, Crivelli (Robinho 74).
FC Copenhagen: (442) Johnsson; Varela, Nelsson, Bjelland, Bengtsson; Mas (Bartolec 89), Zeca, Jensen, Stage; Daramy (Kaufmann 62), Santos (Fischer 82).

LASK (0) 0

Manchester U (1) 5 *(Ighalo 28, James 58, Mata 82, Greenwood 90, Andreas Pereira 90)* 0

LASK: (343) Schlager; Ramsebner, Trauner, Ranftl; Reiter, Holland (Haudum 76), Michorl, Renner; Tetteh (Raguz 61), Klauss, Frieser (Balic 71).
Manchester U: (4231) Romero; Williams, Bailly, Maguire, Shaw; McTominay, Fred; Mata, Bruno Fernandes (Andreas Pereira 78), James (Chong 71); Ighalo (Greenwood 85).
Behind closed doors due to the COVID-19 pandemic.

Olympiacos (0) 1 *(El Arabi 54)*

Wolverhampton W (0) 1 *(Pedro Neto 67)* 0

Olympiacos: (433) Jose Sa; Elabdellaoui, Semedo■, Ba, Tsimikas; Guilherme, Bouchalakis, Camara; Valbuena (Bruno Gaspar 84), El Arabi (Fortounis 74), Masouras (Cisse 34).
Wolverhampton W: (343) Rui Patricio; Boly, Coady, Saiss; Doherty (Pedro Neto 46), Neves, Joao Moutinho (Dendoncker 85), Ruben Vinagre (Daniel Podence 79); Traore, Jimenez, Jota.
Behind closed doors due to the COVID-19 pandemic.

Rangers (0) 1 *(Edmundson 75)*

Bayer Leverkusen (1) 3 *(Havertz 37 (pen), Aranguiz 67, Bailey 88)* 47,494

Rangers: (433) McGregor; Tavernier (Polster 85), Goldson, Edmundson, Barisic; Arfield, Davis, Kamara (Hagi 68); Aribo (Kamberi 53), Morelos, Kent.
Bayer Leverkusen: (343) Hradecky; Tah, Dragovic, Tapsoba (Paulinho 68); Weiser, Aranguiz, Demirbay (Baumgartlinger 81), Wendell; Bellarabi (Bailey 62), Havertz, Diaby.

VfL Wolfsburg (0) 1 *(Brooks 48)*

Shakhtar Donetsk (1) 2 *(Moraes 16, Marcos Antonio 73)* 0

VfL Wolfsburg: (433) Casteels; Steffen, Knoche, Brooks, Paulo Otavio; Gerhardt, Arnold, Schlager (Victor 73); Mehmedi (Ginczek 80), Weghorst, Brekalo.
Shakhtar Donetsk: (4141) Pyatov; Dodo, Kryvtsov, Matviyenko, Ismaily (Khocholava 68); Marcos Antonio; Tete, Kovalenko (Maycon 66), Alan Patrick, Taison (Konoplyanka 88); Moraes.
Behind closed doors due to the COVID-19 pandemic.

Wednesday, 5 August 2020
(Single leg format; played in Germany)

Internazionale (1) 2 *(Lukaku 33, Eriksen 83)*

Getafe (0) 0 0

Internazionale: (352) Handanovic; Godin, de Vrij, Bastoni; D'Ambrosio (Biraghi 84), Barella, Brozovic (Eriksen 82), Gagliardini, Young; Lukaku, Martinez (Sanchez 70).
Getafe: (4411) Soria; Damian, Djene, Etxeita, Olivera (Portillo 88); Nyom (Jason 69), Timor, Arambarri (Duro 88), Cucurella; Maksimovic (Angel 56); Mata (Jorge Molina 69).
Behind closed doors due to the COVID-19 pandemic.

Thursday, 6 August 2020
(Single leg format; played in Germany)

Sevilla (2) 2 *(Reguilon 21, En-Nesyri 44)*

Roma (0) 0

Sevilla: (433) Bounou; Jesus Navas, Kounde, Diego Carlos, Reguilon; Jordan, Fernando, Banega; Suso (Munir 68), En-Nesyri (de Jong 90), Ocampos (Vazquez 90).
Roma: (3421) Pau Lopez; Mancini■, Ibanez, Kolarov (Villar 78); Bruno Peres, Diawara (Perez 57), Cristante, Spinazzola; Zaniolo (Pellegrini 57), Mkhitaryan; Dzeko.
Behind closed doors due to the COVID-19 pandemic.

ROUND OF 16 SECOND LEG

Wednesday, 5 August 2020

FC Copenhagen (1) 3 *(Wind 4, 53 (pen), Jensen 61)*

Istanbul Basaksehir (0) 0 0

FC Copenhagen: (4231) Johnsson; Varela, Nelsson, Bjelland, Boilesen (Bengtsson 69); Mudrazija (Stage 53), Zeca; Mas (Oviedo 84), Wind, Jensen (Bartolec 84); Kaufmann (Daramy 53).
Istanbul Basaksehir: (4141) Gunok; Junior Caicara, Skrtel, Epureanu, Clichy; Topal (Aleksic 54); Visca, Tekdemir (Elia 54), Kahveci (Ozcan 71), Crivelli (Gulbrandsen 79); Ba.
Behind closed doors due to the COVID-19 pandemic.

Manchester U (0) 2 *(Lingard 57, Martial 88)*

LASK (0) 1 *(Wiesinger 55)* 0

Manchester U: (4231) Romero; Fosu-Mensah (Mengi 84), Bailly, Maguire, Williams (Chong 72); McTominay, Fred (Andreas Pereira 64); Mata, Lingard (Pogba 63), James (Martial 84); Ighalo.
LASK: (343) Schlager; Wiesinger (Sabitzer 73), Trauner, Andrade (Filipovic 80); Ranftl, Holland, Michorl, Renner; Frieser, Raguz, Balic (Reiter 66).
Behind closed doors due to the COVID-19 pandemic.

Shakhtar Donetsk (0) 3 *(Moraes 89, 90, Solomon 90)*

VfL Wolfsburg (0) 0 0

Shakhtar Donetsk: (4231) Pyatov; Dodo, Kryvtsov, Khocholava■, Matviyenko; Marcos Antonio (Kovalenko 74), Stepanenko; Marlos (Solomon 77), Alan Patrick, Taison (Konoplyanka 86); Moraes.
VfL Wolfsburg: (4411) Casteels; Tisserand, Pongracic, Brooks■, Roussillon (Klaus 83); Victor, Schlager, Arnold, Brekalo (Guilavogui 75); Ginczek (Marmoush 62); Weghorst.
Behind closed doors due to the COVID-19 pandemic.

Thursday, 6 August 2020

Bayer Leverkusen (0) 1 *(Diaby 51)*

Rangers (0) 0 0

Bayer Leverkusen: (4231) Hradecky; Bender L (Dragovic 68), Bender S (Tah 77), Tapsoba, Sinkgraven; Aranguiz, Palacios (Stanilewicz 87); Havertz, Wirtz (Baumgartlinger 68), Diaby (Bailey 68); Volland.
Rangers: (4321) McGregor; Tavernier (Patterson 77), Goldson, Helander, Barisic; Jack, Davis (Arfield 66), Aribo; Barker (Hagi 60), Kent (Jones 66); Morelos (Stewart 77).
Behind closed doors due to the COVID-19 pandemic.

FC Basel (0) 1 *(Frei 88)*

Eintracht Frankfurt (0) 0 0

FC Basel: (4231) Nikolic; Widmer, Comert, Alderete, Petretta; Xhaka (Marchand 87), Frei; Stocker (van Wolfswinkel 66), Campo, Pululu (Van Der Werff 67); Arthur Cabral (Ademi 80).
Eintracht Frankfurt: (3412) Trapp; Abraham, Hinteregger, Ndicka (Hasebe 46); Da Costa (Chandler 67), Kohr, Rode (Ilsanker 67), Kostic; Kamada; Dost, Andre Silva (Paciencia 46).
Behind closed doors due to the COVID-19 pandemic.

Wolverhampton W (1) 1 *(Jimenez 8 (pen))*

Olympiacos (0) 0 0

Wolverhampton W: (343) Rui Patricio; Boly, Coady, Saiss; Doherty, Neves, Joao Moutinho, Jonny (Ruben Vinagre 17); Traore (Jota 57), Jimenez, Daniel Podence (Dendoncker 71).
Olympiacos: (433) Allain; Elabdellaoui, Ba, Cisse, Tsimikas; Bouchalakis (Fortounis 46), Guilherme (Cafu 82), Camara (Kouka 65); Valbuena, El Arabi, Masouras (Randjelovic 46).
Behind closed doors due to the COVID-19 pandemic.

QUARTER-FINALS (in Germany)

Monday, 10 August 2020

Internazionale (2) 2 *(Barella 15, Lukaku 21)*

Bayer Leverkusen (1) 1 *(Havertz 24)* 0

Internazionale: (352) Handanovic; Godin, de Vrij, Bastoni (Skriniar 84); D'Ambrosio (Moses 59), Barella, Brozovic, Gagliardini (Eriksen 59), Young; Lukaku, Martinez (Sanchez 64).
Bayer Leverkusen: (4231) Hradecky; Bender L (Bellarabi 85), Tah, Tapsoba, Sinkgraven (Wendell 68); Baumgartlinger (Amiri 68), Palacios (Bailey 59); Havertz, Demirbay, Diaby; Volland (Alario 85).
Behind closed doors due to the COVID-19 pandemic.

Manchester U (0) 1 *(Bruno Fernandes 95 (pen))*

FC Copenhagen (0) 0 0

Manchester U: (4231) Romero; Wan Bissaka, Bailly (Lindelof 71), Maguire, Williams; Pogba, Fred (Matic 70); Greenwood (Mata 91), Bruno Fernandes, Rashford (Lingard 113); Martial (McTominay 120).
FC Copenhagen: (442) Johnsson; Varela (Bartolec 105), Nelsson, Bjelland, Boilesen (Bengtsson 15); Mas (Oviedo 57), Stage (Mudrazija 105), Zeca, Jensen (Boving Vick 111); Daramy (Kaufmann 57), Wind.
aet.
Behind closed doors due to the COVID-19 pandemic.

Tuesday, 11 August 2020

Shakhtar Donetsk (2) 4 *(Moraes 2, Taison 22, Alan Patrick 75 (pen), Dodo 88)*

FC Basel (0) 1 *(van Wolfswinkel 90)* 0

Shakhtar Donetsk: (4231) Pyatov; Dodo, Kryvtsov, Bondar, Matviyenko; Marcos Antonio (Maycon 85), Stepanenko; Marlos (Solomon 72), Alan Patrick (Kovalenko 78), Taison (Tete 85); Moraes (Fernando 85).
FC Basel: (4141) Nikolic; Widmer, Van Der Werff (Ramires 73), Alderete, Petretta; Xhaka (Marchand 60); Stocker (van Wolfswinkel 73), Frei, Campo, Pululu; Arthur Cabral (Ademi 73).
Behind closed doors due to the COVID-19 pandemic.

Wolverhampton W (0) 0

Sevilla (0) 1 *(Ocampos 88)* 0

Wolverhampton W: (532) Rui Patricio; Doherty, Boly, Coady, Saiss, Ruben Vinagre; Dendoncker, Neves, Joao Moutinho (Pedro Neto 71); Traore (Jota 79), Jimenez.
Sevilla: (433) Bounou; Jesus Navas, Kounde, Diego Carlos, Reguilon; Banega, Fernando, Jordan (Vazquez 85); Suso (Munir 89), En-Nesyri (de Jong 85), Ocampos.
Behind closed doors due to the COVID-19 pandemic.

SEMI-FINALS (in Germany)

Sunday, 16 August 2020

Sevilla (1) 2 *(Suso 26, de Jong 78)*

Manchester U (1) 1 *(Bruno Fernandes 9 (pen))* 0

Sevilla: (433) Bounou; Jesus Navas, Kounde, Diego Carlos, Reguilon; Jordan (Gudelj 87), Fernando, Banega; Suso (Vazquez 75), En-Nesyri (de Jong 56), Ocampos (Munir 56).
Manchester U: (4231) de Gea; Wan Bissaka (James 87), Lindelof, Maguire, Williams (Fosu-Mensah 87); Pogba, Fred; Greenwood (Ighalo 90), Bruno Fernandes, Rashford (Mata 87); Martial.
Behind closed doors due to the COVID-19 pandemic.

Monday, 17 August 2020

Internazionale (1) 5 *(Martinez 19, 74, D'Ambrosio 64, Lukaku 78, 83)*

Shakhtar Donetsk (0) 0 0

Internazionale: (352) Handanovic; Godin, de Vrij, Bastoni; D'Ambrosio (Moses 81), Barella, Brozovic (Sensi 85), Gagliardini, Young (Biraghi 66); Lukaku (Esposito 85), Martinez (Eriksen 81).
Shakhtar Donetsk: (4231) Pyatov; Dodo, Kryvtsov, Khocholava, Matviyenko; Marcos Antonio, Stepanenko; Marlos (Konoplyanka 75), Alan Patrick (Solomon 59), Taison; Moraes.

EUROPA LEAGUE FINAL 2019–20

Friday, 21 August 2020

(in Cologne – behind closed doors)

Sevilla (2) 3 *(de Jong 12, 33, Lukaku 74 (og))* **Internazionale (2) 2** *(Lukaku 5 (pen), Godin 35)*

Sevilla: (433) Bounou; Jesus Navas, Kounde, Diego Carlos (Gudelj 86), Reguilon; Jordan, Fernando, Banega; Suso (Vazquez 78), de Jong (En-Nesyri 85), Ocampos (Munir 71).

Internazionale: (352) Handanovic; Godin (Candreva 90), de Vrij, Bastoni; D'Ambrosio (Moses 78), Barella, Brozovic, Gagliardini (Eriksen 78), Young; Lukaku, Martinez (Sanchez 78).

Referee: Danny Makkelie.

Luuk de Jong scores Sevilla's first goal in their entertaining 3-2 defeat of Internazionale in the Europa League Final. The Spanish side have now won the UEFA Cup/Europa League a record six times.
(pressinphoto/SIPA USA/PA Images)

UEFA EUROPA LEAGUE 2020–21

PARTICIPATING CLUBS
The list below is provisional and is subject to pending legal proceedings and final confirmation from UEFA.

PRELIMINARY ROUND
Lincoln Red Imps (GIB)
FC Santa Coloma (AND)
B36 Torshavn (FRO)
La Fiorita (SMR)
Tre Penne (SMR)
NSI Runavlk (FRO)
HB Torshavn (FRO)
UE Engordany (AND)
St Joseph's (GIB)
Prishtina (KOS)
Zeta (MNE)
Coleraine (NIR)
Barry Town U (WAL)
Glentoran (NIR)
Iskra Danilovgrad (MNE)
Gjilani (KOS)

FIRST QUALIFYING ROUND
APOEL (CYP)
Malmo (SWE)
Partizan Belgrade (SRB)
FCSB (ROU)
Maribor (SVN)
Hapoel Be'er Sheva (ISR)
Rosenborg (NOR)
Apollon Limassol (CYP)
Fehervar (HUN)
Shkendija (MKD)
The New Saints (WAL)
Dinamo Minsk (BLR)
Lech Poznan (POL)
Aberdeen (SCO)
Zrinjski Mostar (BIH)
Alashkert (ARM)
Kairat (KAZ)
Zalgiris Vilnius (LTU)
AGF Aarhus (DEN)
Motherwell (SCO)
Vaduz (LIE)
Kukesi (ALB)
Valletta (MLT)
Ventspils (LVA)
Olimpija (SVN)
Servette (SUI)
TSC Backa Topola (SRB)
Universitatea Craiova (ROU)
Nomme Kalju (EST)
Shakhtyor Soligorsk (BLR)
Hammarby (SWE)
Hafnarfjordur FH (ICE)
Bodo/Glimt (NOR)
Progres Niederkorn (LUX)
Riteriai (LTU)
CSKA Sofia (BUL)
Sutjeska Niksic (MNE)
Honved (HUN)
Maccabi Haifa (ISR)
Beitar Jerusalem (ISR)
Ordabasy (KAZ)
Neftci (AZE)
Shamrock R (IRL)
Kesla (AZE)
Sumqayit (AZE)
Lokomotiv Plovdiv (BUL)
Slavia Sofia (BUL)
Botosani (ROU)
Piast Gliwice (POL)
Cracovia (POL)
FCI Levadia (EST)
Hibernians (MLT)
DAC Dunajska Streda (SVK)
Ruzomberok (SVK)
Zilina (SVK)
Zeljeznicar (BIH)
Laci (ALB)
Mura (SVN)
Puskas Akademia (HUN)
Saburtalo Tbilisi (GEO)
Shkupi (MKD)
Petrocub Hincesti (MDA)
Differdange 03 (LUX)
Union Titus Petange (LUX)
Kauno Zalgiris (LTU)
Rigas FS (LVA)
Shirak (ARM)
Valmiera (LVA)
Noah (ARM)
Teuta (ALB)
Renova (MKD)
Borac Banja Luka (BIH)
Sfintul Gheorghe (MDA)
Dinamo-Auto (MDA)
Derry C (IRL)
Bohemians (IRL)
Inter Turku (FIN)
Ilves (FIN)
Honka (FIN)
Breidablik (ICE)
Bala T (WAL)
Dinamo Batumi (GEO)
Sirens (MLT)
Locomotivi Tbilisi (GEO)
Víkingur Reykjavík (ICE)
Paide Linnameeskond (EST)
Plus 8 winning teams from the UEFA Europa League Preliminary Round.

SECOND QUALIFYING ROUND – CHAMPIONS PATH
17 losing teams of 2020–21 UEFA Champions League First Qualifying Round
3 losing teams of 2020–21 UEFA Champions League Preliminary Round

SECOND QUALIFYING ROUND – MAIN PATH
Tottenham H (ENG)
Basel (SUI)
FC Copenhagen (DEN)
VfL Wolfsburg (GER)
BATE Borisov (BLR)
Galatasaray (TUR)
Standard Liege (BEL)
Granada (ESP)
AC Milan (ITA)
Rangers (SCO)
Reims (FRA)
Rio Ave (POR)
Dynamo Moscow (RUS)
Slovan Liberec (CZE)
Hajduk Split (CRO)
Willem II Tilburg (NED)
Kolos Kovalivka (UKR)
Jablonec (CZE)
Hartberg (AUT)
Anorthosis Famagusta (CYP)
Aris (GRE)
OFI Crete (GRE)
Vojvodina (SRB)
Osijek (CRO)
IFK Gothenburg (SWE)
Viking Stavanger (NOR)
Kaisar (KAZ)
Plus 47 winning teams from the UEFA Europa League First Qualifying Round.

THIRD QUALIFYING ROUND – CHAMPIONS PATH
10 losing teams from UEFA Champions League Second Qualifying Round (champions route).
10 winning teams from UEFA Europa League Second Qualifying Round (champions route).

THIRD QUALIFYING ROUND – MAIN PATH
Sporting Lisbon (POR)
PSV Eindhoven (NED)
Sparta Prague (CZE)
AEK Athens (GRE)
LASK (AUT)
Rostov (RUS)
Rijeka (CRO)
Charleroi (BEL)
Desna Chernihiv (UKR)
Alanyaspor (TUR)
SonderjyskE (DEN)
St Gallen (SUI)
Plus 3 losing teams from UEFA Champions League Second Qualifying Round (league path).
Plus 37 winning teams from the UEFA Europa League Second Qualifying Round (main route).

PLAY-OFF ROUND – CHAMPIONS PATH
10 winning teams from UEFA Europa League Third Qualifying round (Champions path).
6 losing teams from UEFA Champions League Third Qualifying round (champions path).

PLAY-OFF ROUND – MAIN PATH
26 winning teams from UEFA Europa League Third Qualifying round (main path).

GROUP STAGE
Arsenal (ENG)
Roma (ITA)
Napoli (ITA)
Bayer Leverkusen (GER)
Villarreal (ESP)
CSKA Moscow (RUS)
Braga (POR)
Leicester C (ENG)
Real Sociedad (ESP)
Feyenoord (NED)
TSG 1899 Hoffenheim (GER)
Zorya Luhansk (UKR)
Lille (FRA)
Nice (FRA)
Antwerp (BEL)
Sivasspor (TUR)
Wolfsberger (AUT)
Plus 4 losing teams from the UEFA Champions League Play-Offs (champions path).
Plus 2 losing teams from the UEFA Champions League Play-Offs (league path).
Plus 4 losing teams from UEFA Champions League Third Qualifying Round (league path).
Plus 8 winning teams from the UEFA Europa League Play-Offs (champions path).
Plus 13 winning teams from the UEFA Europa League Play-Offs (main path).

BRITISH AND IRISH CLUBS IN EUROPE

SUMMARY OF APPEARANCES

EUROPEAN CUP AND CHAMPIONS LEAGUE 1955–2020

(Winners in brackets) (SE = seasons entered).

ENGLAND	*SE*	*P*	*W*	*D*	*L*	*F*	*A*
Manchester U (3)	28	279	154	66	59	506	264
Liverpool (6)	24	217	121	47	49	408	196
Arsenal	21	201	101	43	57	332	218
Chelsea (1)	16	168	83	48	37	286	158
Manchester C	10	81	40	16	25	159	105
Tottenham H	6	55	25	10	20	108	83
Leeds U	4	40	22	6	12	76	41
Nottingham F (2)	3	20	12	4	4	32	14
Newcastle U	3	24	11	3	10	33	33
Everton	3	10	2	5	3	14	10
Aston Villa (1)	2	15	9	3	3	24	10
Derby Co	2	12	6	2	4	18	12
Wolverhampton W	2	8	2	2	4	12	16
Leicester C	1	10	5	2	3	11	10
Ipswich T	1	4	3	0	1	16	5
Burnley	1	4	2	0	2	8	8
Blackburn R	1	6	1	1	4	5	8
SCOTLAND							
Celtic (1)	34	212	100	36	76	324	250
Rangers	30	161	62	40	59	232	218
Aberdeen	3	12	5	4	3	14	12
Hearts	3	8	2	1	5	8	16
Dundee U	1	8	5	1	2	14	5
Dundee	1	8	5	0	3	20	14
Hibernian	1	6	3	1	2	9	5
Kilmarnock	1	4	1	2	1	4	7
Motherwell	1	2	0	0	2	0	5
WALES							
The New Saints	13	36	9	5	22	36	63
Barry Town U	6	14	4	1	9	11	38
Rhyl	2	4	0	0	4	1	19
Cwmbran T	1	2	1	0	1	4	4
Llanelli	1	2	1	0	1	1	4
Bangor C	1	2	0	0	2	0	13
NORTHERN IRELAND							
Linfield	29	69	7	23	39	56	124
Glentoran	12	28	3	7	18	20	59
Crusaders	6	14	1	2	11	7	52
Portadown	3	6	0	1	5	3	24
Cliftonville	3	6	0	1	5	1	20
Glenavon	1	2	0	1	1	0	3
Lisburn Distillery	1	2	0	1	1	3	8
Ards	1	2	0	0	2	3	10
Coleraine	1	2	0	0	2	1	11
REPUBLIC OF IRELAND							
Dundalk	11	32	4	12	16	24	57
Shamrock R	9	20	1	6	13	9	33
Shelbourne	6	20	4	8	8	21	31
Bohemians	6	18	4	4	10	13	29
Waterford U	6	14	3	0	11	15	47
Derry C	4	9	1	1	7	9	26
St Patrick's Ath	4	8	0	3	5	2	23
Cork C	3	10	2	1	7	7	16
Dublin C	3	6	1	0	5	3	25
Athlone T	2	4	0	2	2	7	14
Sligo R	2	4	0	0	4	0	9
Limerick	2	4	0	0	4	4	16
Drogheda U	1	4	2	1	1	6	5
Cork Hibernians	1	2	0	0	2	1	7
Cork Celtic	1	2	0	0	2	1	7

UEFA CUP AND EUROPA LEAGUE 1971–2020

ENGLAND	*SE*	*P*	*W*	*D*	*L*	*F*	*A*
Tottenham H (2)	15	140	78	36	26	278	121
Liverpool (3)	14	124	66	34	24	186	94
Aston Villa	13	56	24	14	18	77	60
Ipswich T (1)	10	52	30	10	12	98	53
Manchester U (1)	10	55	26	16	13	82	43
Arsenal	9	62	35	10	17	121	66
Everton	9	52	27	8	17	87	64
Newcastle U	8	72	42	17	13	123	60
Manchester C	8	52	28	13	11	84	51
Leeds U	8	46	20	10	16	66	48
Southampton	7	22	6	9	7	23	20
Blackburn R	6	22	7	8	7	27	26
Wolverhampton W	5	37	25	5	7	79	37
Chelsea (2)	5	32	22	5	5	64	30
West Ham U	4	16	6	3	7	19	16
Fulham	3	39	21	10	8	64	31
Nottingham F	3	20	10	5	5	18	16
Stoke C	3	16	8	4	4	21	16
WBA	3	12	5	2	5	15	13
Middlesbrough	2	25	13	4	8	36	24
QPR	2	12	8	1	3	39	18
Bolton W	2	18	6	10	2	18	14
Derby Co	2	10	5	2	3	32	17
Leicester C	2	4	0	1	3	3	8
Birmingham C	1	8	4	2	2	11	8
Burnley	1	6	2	3	1	7	6
Norwich C	1	6	2	2	2	6	4
Portsmouth	1	6	2	2	2	11	10
Sheffield W	1	4	2	1	1	13	7
Hull C	1	4	2	1	1	4	3
Watford	1	6	2	1	3	10	12
Wigan Ath	1	6	1	2	3	6	7
Millwall	1	2	0	1	1	2	4
SCOTLAND							
Celtic	22	121	51	28	42	184	138
Aberdeen	22	84	27	27	30	108	108
Rangers	19	110	47	35	28	150	105
Dundee U	19	82	33	25	24	134	89
Hearts	14	50	21	10	19	61	62
Hibernian	13	40	15	11	14	57	63
Motherwell	8	26	8	2	16	33	34
St Johnstone	7	24	7	7	10	25	30
Dundee	4	14	6	0	8	24	24
Kilmarnock	4	14	5	2	7	9	17
St Mirren	3	10	2	3	5	9	12
Dunfermline Ath	2	4	0	2	2	4	6
Raith R	1	6	2	1	3	10	8
Livingston	1	4	1	2	1	7	9
Falkirk	1	2	1	0	1	1	2
Inverness CT	1	2	0	1	1	0	1
Gretna	1	2	0	1	1	3	7
Queen of the South	1	2	0	0	2	2	4
Partick Thistle	1	2	0	0	2	0	4
WALES							
Bangor C	10	22	2	2	18	10	61
The New Saints	10	24	2	3	19	16	65
Llanelli	5	12	3	3	6	12	24
Bala T	5	10	3	0	7	7	19
Connah's Quay Nomads	4	12	3	1	8	7	17
Cardiff Met Univ	4	8	2	0	6	3	20
Barry Town U	3	10	2	3	5	10	20
Rhyl	3	8	2	1	5	9	12
Newtown	3	8	2	1	5	6	21
Air UK Broughton	3	6	0	4	2	6	9
Cwmbran T	3	6	0	0	6	0	21
Carmarthen T	2	6	1	0	5	8	21
Cefn Druids	2	4	0	2	2	1	7
Swansea C	1	12	4	4	4	17	10
Prestatyn T	1	4	1	0	3	3	11
Afan Lido	1	2	0	1	1	1	2
Haverfordwest Co	1	2	0	0	2	1	4
Neath	1	2	0	0	2	1	6
Port Talbot T	1	2	0	0	2	1	7
Llandudno T	1	2	0	0	2	1	7
Aberystwith T	1	2	0	0	2	0	9
NORTHERN IRELAND							
Glentoran	18	40	3	8	29	22	97
Linfield	13	40	13	9	18	49	72

Portadown	11	28	3	7	18	16	62
Crusaders	11	26	6	4	16	27	62
Glenavon	9	20	2	2	16	10	49
Coleraine	9	18	1	5	12	9	46
Cliftonville	7	20	4	4	12	15	37
Ballymena U	3	8	2	1	5	4	20
Dungannon Swifts	1	2	1	0	1	1	4
Ards	1	2	1	0	1	4	8
Bangor	1	2	0	0	2	0	6
Lisburn Distillery	1	2	0	0	2	1	11
REPUBLIC OF IRELAND							
Bohemians	14	30	3	9	18	16	56
St Patrick's Ath	11	40	10	7	23	35	61
Cork C	11	32	7	7	18	23	46
Shamrock R	10	36	9	6	21	34	64
Dundalk	9	28	7	4	17	21	52
Derry C	9	26	7	5	14	30	45
Shelbourne	6	12	0	2	10	8	28
Drogheda U	4	12	3	4	5	10	24
Sligo R	4	10	2	4	4	11	13
Longford T	3	6	1	1	4	6	12
Finn Harps	3	6	0	0	6	3	33
Athlone T	1	4	1	2	1	4	5
University College Dublin	1	4	1	0	3	3	8
Limerick	1	2	0	1	1	1	4
Sporting Fingal	1	2	0	0	2	4	6
Galway U	1	2	0	0	2	2	8
Bray W	1	2	0	0	2	0	8

EUROPEAN CUP WINNERS' CUP 1960–1999

ENGLAND	*SE*	*P*	*W*	*D*	*L*	*F*	*A*
Tottenham H (1)	6	33	20	5	8	65	34
Chelsea (2)	5	39	23	10	6	81	28
Liverpool	5	29	16	5	8	57	29
Manchester U (1)	5	31	16	9	6	55	35
West Ham U (1)	4	30	15	6	9	58	42
Arsenal (1)	3	27	15	10	2	48	20
Everton (1)	3	17	11	4	2	25	9
Manchester C (1)	2	18	11	2	5	32	13
Ipswich T	1	6	3	2	1	6	3
Leeds U	1	9	5	3	1	13	3
Leicester C	1	4	2	1	1	8	5
Newcastle U	1	2	1	0	1	2	2
Southampton	1	6	4	0	2	16	8
Sunderland	1	4	3	0	1	5	3
WBA	1	6	2	2	2	8	5
Wolverhampton W	1	4	1	1	2	6	5
SCOTLAND							
Rangers (1)	10	54	27	11	16	100	62
Aberdeen (1)	8	39	22	5	12	79	37
Celtic	8	38	21	4	13	75	37
Dundee U	3	10	3	3	4	9	10
Hearts	3	10	3	3	4	16	14
Dunfermline Ath	2	14	7	2	5	34	14
Airdrieonians	1	2	0	0	2	1	3
Dundee	1	2	0	1	1	3	4
Hibernian	1	6	3	1	2	19	10
Kilmarnock	1	4	1	2	1	5	6
Motherwell	1	2	1	0	1	3	3
St Mirren	1	4	1	2	1	1	2
WALES							
Cardiff C	14	49	16	14	19	67	61
Wrexham	8	28	10	8	10	34	35
Swansea C	7	18	3	4	11	32	37
Bangor C	3	9	1	2	6	5	12
Barry T	1	2	0	0	2	0	7
Borough U	1	4	1	1	2	2	4
Cwmbran T	1	2	0	0	2	2	12
Merthyr Tydfil	1	2	1	0	1	2	3
Newport Co	1	6	2	3	1	12	3
The New Saints (Llansantfraid)	1	2	0	1	1	1	6
NORTHERN IRELAND							
Glentoran	9	22	3	7	12	18	46
Glenavon	5	10	1	3	6	11	25
Ballymena U	4	8	0	0	8	1	25
Coleraine	4	8	0	1	7	7	34
Crusaders	3	6	0	2	4	5	18
Derry C	3	6	1	1	4	1	11
Linfield	3	6	2	0	4	6	11
Ards	2	4	0	1	3	2	17
Bangor	2	4	0	1	3	2	8
Carrick Rangers	1	4	1	0	3	7	12
Cliftonville	1	2	0	0	2	0	8
Distillery	1	2	0	0	2	1	7
Portadown	1	2	1	0	1	4	7
REPUBLIC OF IRELAND							
Shamrock R	6	16	5	2	9	19	27
Shelbourne	4	10	1	1	8	9	20
Bohemians	3	8	2	2	4	6	13
Dundalk	3	8	2	1	5	7	14
Limerick U	3	6	0	1	5	2	11
Waterford U	3	8	1	1	6	6	14
Cork C	2	4	1	0	3	2	9
Cork Hibernians	2	6	2	1	3	7	8
Galway U	2	4	0	0	4	2	11
Sligo R	2	6	1	1	4	5	11
Bray W	1	2	0	1	1	1	3
Cork Celtic	1	2	0	1	1	1	3
Finn Harps	1	2	0	1	1	2	4
Home Farm	1	2	0	1	1	1	7
St Patrick's Ath	1	2	0	0	2	1	8
University College Dublin	1	2	0	1	1	0	1

INTER-CITIES FAIRS CUP 1955–1970

ENGLAND	*SE*	*P*	*W*	*D*	*L*	*F*	*A*
Leeds U (2)	5	53	28	17	8	92	40
Birmingham C	4	25	14	6	5	51	38
Liverpool	4	22	12	4	6	46	15
Arsenal (1)	3	24	12	5	7	46	19
Chelsea	3	20	10	5	5	33	24
Everton	3	12	7	2	3	22	15
Newcastle U (1)	3	24	13	6	5	37	21
Nottingham F	2	6	3	0	3	8	9
Sheffield W	2	10	5	0	5	25	18
Burnley	1	8	4	3	1	16	5
Coventry C	1	4	3	0	1	9	8
London XI	1	8	4	1	3	14	13
Manchester U	1	11	6	3	2	29	10
Southampton	1	6	2	3	1	11	6
WBA	1	4	1	1	2	7	9
SCOTLAND							
Hibernian	7	36	18	5	13	66	60
Dunfermline Ath	5	28	16	3	9	49	31
Kilmarnock	4	20	8	3	9	34	32
Dundee U	3	10	5	1	4	11	12
Hearts	3	12	4	4	4	20	20
Rangers	3	18	8	4	6	27	17
Celtic	2	6	1	3	2	9	10
Aberdeen	1	4	2	1	1	4	4
Dundee	1	8	5	1	2	14	6
Morton	1	2	0	0	2	3	9
Partick Thistle	1	4	3	0	1	10	7
NORTHERN IRELAND							
Glentoran	4	8	1	1	6	7	22
Coleraine	2	8	2	1	5	15	23
Linfield	2	4	1	0	3	3	11
REPUBLIC OF IRELAND							
Drumcondra	2	6	2	0	4	8	19
Dundalk	2	6	1	1	4	4	25
Shamrock R	2	4	0	2	2	4	6
Cork Hibernians	1	2	0	0	2	1	6
Shelbourne	1	5	1	2	2	3	4
St Patrick's Ath	1	2	0	0	2	4	9

FIFA CLUB WORLD CUP 2019

Formerly known as the FIFA Club World Championship, this tournament is played annually between the champion clubs from all 6 continental confederations, although since 2007 the champions of Oceania must play a qualifying play-off against the champion club of the host country.

(Finals in Qatar)

▪*Denotes player sent off.*

FIRST ROUND

Doha, Wedneday, 11 December 2019

Al-Saad (1) 3 *(Bounedjah 26, Hassan 100, Pedro 114)*

Hienghene Sport (0) 1 *(Roine 46)* 7047

Al-Saad: Al Sheeb; Khoukhi, Hassan, Pedro, Al Hajri (Salman 118), Gabi, Tae-Hee (Assadalla 105), Woo-Young, Al Ansari (All Heidos 25), Bounedjah, Afif (Hashim Ali 116).
Hienghene Sport: Nyikeine; Kayara R (Hyanem 112), Bearune, Dinet, Gony, Sansot, Athale, Pedro Luis (Kayara M 55), Kai B (Kai A 80), Dahite, Roine (Matsumoto 70).
aet.
Referee: Mustapha Ghorbal (Algeria).

SECOND ROUND

Doha, Saturday, 14 December 2019

Al-Hilal (0) 1 *(Gomis 73)*

Esperance de Tunis (0) 0 7726

Al-Hilal: Al Maiouf; Al Shahrani, Hyun-Soo, Al Burayk (Al Hafith 87), Albulayhi, Carlos Eduardo, Cuellar (Gomis 65), Carrillo, Al Dawsari, Kanoo▪, Khribin (Otayf 78).
Esperance de Tunis: Ben Cherifia; Derbali, Yacoubi, Bedrane, Chetti, Coulibaly, Bonsu (Khenissi 81), Benguit (Fadaa 76), Badri, Elhouni (Bensaha 87), Ouattara.
Referee: Roberto Tobar (Chile).

Doha, Saturday, 14 December 2019

Monterrey (2) 3 *(Vangioni 23, Funes Mori 45, Rodriguez 77)*

Al-Saad (0) 2 *(Bounedjah 66, Hassan 89)* 4878

Monterrey: Barovero; Vangioni, Sanchez, Medina, Montes (Basanta 86), Pizarro (Layun 80), Gallardo, Gonzalez J, Pabon (Meza 73), Funes Mori, Rodriguez.
Al-Saad: Al Sheeb (Barsham 85); Khoukhi, Hassan, Pedro, Al Hajri (Woo-Young 71), Gabi, Tae-Hee, Salman, All Heidos, Bounedjah, Afif.
Referee: Ovidiu Hategan (Romania).

MATCH FOR FIFTH PLACE

Doha, Tuesday, 17 December 2019

Al-Saad (1) 2 *(Bounedjah 32 (pen), Al Heidos 49 (pen))*

Esperance de Tunis (4) 6 *(Elhouni 6, 42, 74, Badri 13, 25 (pen), Derbali 87)* 15,037

Al-Saad: Barsham; Ismaeil (Pedro 46), Khoukhi, Hassan▪, Gabi (Al Hajiri), Assadalla, Woo-Young, Salman, Al Heidos, Bounedjah, Afif (Hashim Ali 79).
Esperance de Tunis: Ben Cherifia; Derbali, Chemmam, Bedrane, Chetti, Coulibaly, Bonsu (Fadaa 82), Ben Romdhane (Benguit 57), Badri, Elhouni, Ouattara (Khenissi).
Referee: Abdelkader Zitouni (Tahiti).

SEMI-FINALS

Doha, Tuesday, 17 December 2019

Flamengo (0) 3 *(De Arrascaeta 49, Bruno Henrique 78, Albulayhi 82 (og))*

Al-Hilal (1) 1 *(Al Dawsari 18)* 21,588

Flamengo: Diego Alves; Rafinha, Filipe Luis, Pablo Mari, Rodrigo Caio, Everton Ribeiro, Willian Arao, De Arrascaeta (Piris Da Motta 90), Gerson (Diego 74), Gabriel Barbosa, Bruno Henrique (Vitinho 89).
Al-Hilal: Al Maiouf; Al Shahrani, Hyun-Soo, Al Burayk, Albulayhi, Carlos Eduardo, Cuellar, Carrillo▪, Al Dawsari (Al Abid 82) Gomis (Otayf 90), Giovinco (Khribin 71).
Referee: Ismail Elfath (USA).

Doha, Wednesday, 18 December 2019

Monterrey (1) 1 *(Funes Mori 14)*

Liverpool (1) 2 *(Keita 12, Firmino 90)* 45,416

Monterrey: Barovero; Vangioni, Sanchez, Medina, Montes (Layun 79), Ortiz, Pizarro (Gonzalez J 90), Gallardo, Pabon (Meza 82), Funes Mori, Rodriguez.
Liverpool: Alisson; Robertson, Gomez, Milner (Alexander-Arnold 74), Lallana, Henderson, Shaqiri (Mane 68), Oxlade-Chamberlain, Keita, Salah, Origi (Firmino 85).
Referee: Roberto Tobar (Chile).

MATCH FOR THIRD PLACE

Doha, Saturday, 21 December 2019

Monterrey (0) 2 *(Gonzalez A 55, Meza 60)*

Al-Hilal (1) 2 *(Carlos Eduardo 35, Gomis 65)* 19,318

Monterrey: Cardenas; Basanta, Layun, Gutierrez, Vasquez, Urretaviscaya, Gonzalez A (Medina 85), Meza, Gonzalez J, Mejia (Pizarro 72), Zaldivar (Funes Mori 68).
Al-Hilal: Al Maiouf; Al Shahrani, Hyun-Soo, Al Burayk, Albulayhi, Carlos Eduardo, Cuellar (Bahebri 63), Al Dawsari, Otayf (Kanoo 74), Giovinco, Khribin (Gomis 60).
Monterrey won 4-3 on penalties.
Referee: Ovidiu Hategan (Romania).

FIFA WORLD CLUB CUP FINAL 2019

Doha, Saturday, 21 December 2019

Liverpool (0) 1 *(Firmino 99)*

Flamengo (0) 0 45,416

Liverpool: Alisson; van Dijk, Robertson, Gomez, Alexander-Arnold, Henderson, Oxlade-Chamberlain (Lallana 75), Keita (Milner 100), Firmino (Origi 105), Salah (Shaqiri 120), Mane.
Flamengo: Diego Alves; Rafinha, Filipe Luis, Pablo Mari, Rodrigo Caio, Everton Ribeiro (Diego 82), Willian Arao (Berrio 120), De Arrascaeta (Vitinho 90), Gerson (Lincoln 102), Gabriel Barbosa, Bruno Henrique.
aet.
Referee: Abdulrahman Al-Jassim (Qatar).

PREVIOUS FINALS

2000 Corinthians beat Vasco da Gama 4-3 on penalties after 0-0 draw
2001–04 Not contested
2005 Sao Paulo beat Liverpool 1-0
2006 Internacional beat Barcelona 1-0
2007 AC Milan beat Boca Juniors 4-2
2008 Manchester U beat Liga De Quito 1-0
2009 Barcelona beat Estudiantes 2-1
2010 Internazionale beat TP Mazembe Englebert 3-0
2011 Barcelona beat Santos 4-0
2012 Corinthians beat Chelsea 1-0
2013 Bayern Munich beat Raja Casablanca 2-0
2014 Real Madrid beat San Lorenzo 2-0
2015 Barcelona beat River Plate 3-0
2016 Real Madrid beat Kashima Antlers 4-2 (*aet.*)
2017 Real Madrid beat Gremio 1-0
2018 Real Madrid beat Al-Ain 4-1
2019 Liverpool beat Flamengo 1-0 (*aet.*)

WORLD CLUB CHAMPIONSHIP

Played annually up to 1974 and intermittently since then between the winners of the European Cup and the winners of the South American Champions Cup – known as the Copa Libertadores. In 1980 the winners were decided by one match arranged in Tokyo in February 1981 which remained the venue until 2004, when the match was superseded by the FIFA Club World Championship. AC Milan replaced Marseille who had been stripped of their European Cup title in 1993.

1960 Real Madrid beat Penarol 0-0, 5-1
1961 Penarol beat Benfica 0-1, 5-0, 2-1
1962 Santos beat Benfica 3-2, 5-2
1963 Santos beat AC Milan 2-4, 4-2, 1-0
1964 Inter-Milan beat Independiente 0-1, 2-0, 1-0
1965 Inter-Milan beat Independiente 3-0, 0-0
1966 Penarol beat Real Madrid 2-0, 2-0
1967 Racing Club beat Celtic 0-1, 2-1, 1-0
1968 Estudiantes beat Manchester United 1-0, 1-1
1969 AC Milan beat Estudiantes 3-0, 1-2
1970 Feyenoord beat Estudiantes 2-2, 1-0
1971 Nacional beat Panathinaikos* 1-1, 2-1
1972 Ajax beat Independiente 1-1, 3-0
1973 Independiente beat Juventus* 1-0
1974 Atlético Madrid* beat Independiente 0-1, 2-0
1975 Independiente and Bayern Munich could not agree dates; no matches.
1976 Bayern Munich beat Cruzeiro 2-0, 0-0
1977 Boca Juniors beat Borussia Moenchengladbach* 2-2, 3-0
1978 Not contested
1979 Olimpia beat Malmö* 1-0, 2-1
1980 Nacional beat Nottingham Forest 1-0
1981 Flamengo beat Liverpool 3-0
1982 Penarol beat Aston Villa 2-0
1983 Gremio Porto Alegre beat Hamburg 2-1
1984 Independiente beat Liverpool 1-0
1985 Juventus beat Argentinos Juniors 4-2 on penalties after 2-2 draw
1986 River Plate beat Steaua Bucharest 1-0
1987 FC Porto beat Penarol 2-1 after extra time
1988 Nacional (Uru) beat PSV Eindhoven 7-6 on penalties after 1-1 draw
1989 AC Milan beat Atletico Nacional (Col) 1-0 after extra time
1990 AC Milan beat Olimpia 3-0
1991 Crvena Zvezda beat Colo Colo 3-0
1992 Sao Paulo beat Barcelona 2-1
1993 Sao Paulo beat AC Milan 3-2
1994 Velez Sarsfield beat AC Milan 2-0
1995 Ajax beat Gremio Porto Alegre 4-3 on penalties after 0-0 draw
1996 Juventus beat River Plate 1-0
1997 Borussia Dortmund beat Cruzeiro 2-0
1998 Real Madrid beat Vasco da Gama 2-1
1999 Manchester U beat Palmeiras 1-0
2000 Boca Juniors beat Real Madrid 2-1
2001 Bayern Munich beat Boca Juniors 1-0 after extra time
2002 Real Madrid beat Olimpia 2-0
2003 Boca Juniors beat AC Milan 3-1 on penalties after 1-1 draw
2004 Porto beat Once Caldas 8-7 on penalties after 0-0 draw

**European Cup runners-up; winners declined to take part.*

EUROPEAN SUPER CUP 2019

Played annually between the winners of the European Champions' Cup and the European Cup-Winners' Cup (UEFA Cup from 2000; UEFA Europa League from 2010). AC Milan replaced Marseille in 1993–94.

Istanbul, Wednesday 14 August 2019, attendance 38,434

Liverpool (0) 2 *(Mane 48, 95)*

Chelsea (1) 2 *(Giroud 36, Jorginho 101 (pen))*

Liverpool: Adrian; Gomez, Matip, van Dijk, Robertson (Alexander-Arnold 90), Henderson, Fabinho, Milner (Wijnaldum 64), Salah, Mane (Origi 103), Oxlade-Chamberlain (Firminho 46).

Chelsea: Kepa; Azpilicueta, Christensen (Tomori 85), Zouma, Emerson, Kante, Jorginho, Kovacic (Barkley 101), Pedro, Giroud (Abraham 74), Pulisic (Mount 74).
aet; Liverpool won 5-4 on penalties.

Referee: Stephanie Frappart (France).

PREVIOUS MATCHES

1972 Ajax beat Rangers 3-1, 3-2
1973 Ajax beat AC Milan 0-1, 6-0
1974 Not contested
1975 Dynamo Kyiv beat Bayern Munich 1-0, 2-0
1976 Anderlecht beat Bayern Munich 4-1, 1-2
1977 Liverpool beat Hamburg 1-1, 6-0
1978 Anderlecht beat Liverpool 3-1, 1-2
1979 Nottingham F beat Barcelona 1-0, 1-1
1980 Valencia beat Nottingham F 1-0, 1-2
1981 Not contested
1982 Aston Villa beat Barcelona 0-1, 3-0
1983 Aberdeen beat Hamburg 0-0, 2-0
1984 Juventus beat Liverpool 2-0
1985 Juventus v Everton not contested due to UEFA ban on English clubs
1986 Steaua Bucharest beat Dynamo Kyiv 1-0
1987 FC Porto beat Ajax 1-0, 1-0
1988 KV Mechelen beat PSV Eindhoven 3-0, 0-1
1989 AC Milan beat Barcelona 1-1, 1-0
1990 AC Milan beat Sampdoria 1-1, 2-0
1991 Manchester U beat Crvena Zvezda 1-0
1992 Barcelona beat Werder Bremen 1-1, 2-1
1993 Parma beat AC Milan 0-1, 2-0
1994 AC Milan beat Arsenal 0-0, 2-0
1995 Ajax beat Zaragoza 1-1, 4-0
1996 Juventus beat Paris Saint-Germain 6-1, 3-1
1997 Barcelona beat Borussia Dortmund 2-0, 1-1
1998 Chelsea beat Real Madrid 1-0
1999 Lazio beat Manchester U 1-0
2000 Galatasaray beat Real Madrid 2-1
2001 Liverpool beat Bayern Munich 3-2
2002 Real Madrid beat Feyenoord 3-1
2003 AC Milan beat Porto 1-0
2004 Valencia beat Porto 2-1
2005 Liverpool beat CSKA Moscow 3-1
2006 Sevilla beat Barcelona 3-0
2007 AC Milan beat Sevilla 3-1
2008 Zenit beat Manchester U 2-1
2009 Barcelona beat Shakhtar Donetsk 1-0
2010 Atletico Madrid beat Internazionale 2-0
2011 Barcelona beat Porto 2-0
2012 Atletico Madrid beat Chelsea 4-1
2013 Bayern Munch beat Chelsea 5-4 on penalties after 2-2 draw
2014 Real Madrid beat Sevilla 2-0
2015 Barcelona beat Sevilla 5-4
2016 Real Madrid beat Sevilla 3-2
2017 Real Madrid beat Manchester U 2-1
2018 Atletico Madrid beat Real Madrid 4-2 after extra time
2019 Liverpool beat Chelsea 5-4 on penalties after 2-2 draw.

INTERNATIONAL DIRECTORY

The directory provides the latest available information on international and club football in the 211 national associations in the six Confederations of FIFA, the world governing body. This includes addresses, foundation dates and team colours. FIFA-recognised internationals played in season 2019–20 (i.e. *8 July 2019 to 5 July 2020*) are listed as well as league and cup champions at club level. In Europe, the latest league tables, cup winners and top scorers for the 55 UEFA nations are given, together with all-time league and cup honours. (Key to table symbols used: (C) league champions; [1] Champions League qualifier; [2] Europa League qualifier; * team relegated; *+ team relegated after play-offs; + team not relegated after play-offs.)

The four home nations, England, Scotland, Northern Ireland and Wales, are dealt with elsewhere in the Yearbook; but basic details appear in this directory. Gozo is included here for its close links with Maltese football. Northern Cyprus is not a member of FIFA or UEFA and is the subject of an international territorial dispute. Kosovo was granted full membership of both FIFA and UEFA in May 2016 and entered World Cup 2018 qualification in September 2016, followed by participation in the 2019–20 UEFA Nations League and Euro 2020 qualifying. FYR Macedonia's results are now credited to North Macedonia, its new name from February 2019. Swaziland was renamed Eswatini in April 2018.

International match venues are indicated as follows: home (h), away (a), neutral (n); in multi-nation tournaments the host nation is deemed to be playing at home and all others are on neutral territory; where a nation is unable to play a qualifier at home the neutral venue is stated in a note.

There are currently 12 associate members and others who have affiliation to their confederations. The associate members are: AFC: Northern Mariana Islands; CAF: Reunion, Zanzibar; CONCACAF: Bonaire, French Guiana, Guadeloupe, Martinique, Saint-Martin, Sint Maarten; OFC: Kiribati, Niue, Tuvalu. Matches between full members and associate members are indicated with †.

N.B. Final league rankings for clubs tied on points are decided on goal difference unless otherwise stated.

EUROPE (UEFA)

ALBANIA

Football Association of Albania, Rruga e Elbasanit, 1000 Tirana.

Founded: 1930. *FIFA:* 1932; *UEFA:* 1954. *National Colours:* Red shirts with white trim, black shorts, red socks.

International matches 2019–20

France (a) 1-4, Iceland (h) 4-2, Turkey (a) 0-1, Moldova (a) 4-0, Andorra (h) 2-2, France (h) 0-2.

League Championship wins (1930–37; 1945–2020)

KF Tirana 25 (formerly SK Tirana; includes 17 Nentori 8); Dinamo Tirana 18; Partizani Tirana 16; Vllaznia Shkoder 9; Skenderbeu Korce 8; Elbasani 2 (incl. Labinoti 1); Flamurtari Vlore 1; Teuta 1; Kukesi 1.

Cup wins (1948–2020)

KF Tirana 16 (formerly SK Tirana; includes 17 Nentori 8); Partizani Tirana 15; Dinamo Tirana 13; Vllaznia 6; Flamurtari Vlore 4; Teuta 4; Elbasani 2 (incl. Labinoti 1); Besa 2; Laci 2; Kukesi 2; Apolonia Fier 1; Skenderbeu Korce 1.

Albanian Kategoria Superiore 2019–20

	P	*W*	*D*	*L*	*F*	*A*	*GD*	*Pts*
KF Tirana (C)[1]	36	21	7	8	67	35	32	70
Kukesi[2]	36	19	9	8	59	31	28	66
Laci[2]	36	19	7	10	61	34	27	64
Skenderbeu	36	17	7	12	42	43	–1	58
Teuta[2]	36	15	12	9	41	34	7	57
Partizani Tirana	36	15	8	13	51	40	11	53
Bylis	36	12	15	9	46	38	8	51
Vllaznia+	36	12	10	14	36	41	–5	46
Flamurtari*	36	2	9	25	32	72	–40	15
Luftetari*	36	2	8	26	19	86	–67	14

Top scorer: Nwabueze (Laci) 24.
Cup Final: Teuta 2, KF Tirana 0.

ANDORRA

Federacio Andorrana de Futbol, Avda Carlemany 67, 3er Pis, Apartado postal 65, Escaldes-Engordany.

Founded: 1994. *FIFA:* 1996; *UEFA:* 1996. *National Colours:* All red.

International matches 2019–20

Turkey (a) 0-1, France (a) 0-3, Moldova (h) 1-0, Iceland (a) 0-2, Albania (h) 2-2, Turkey (h) 0-2.

League Championship wins (1996–2020)

FC Santa Coloma 13; Principat 3; Encamp 2; Sant Julia 2; Ranger's 2; Lusitanos 2; Constel-lacio Esportiva 1; Inter Club d'Escaldes 1.

Cup wins (1991, 1994–2020)

FC Santa Coloma 10*; Principat 6*; Sant Julia 5; UE Santa Coloma 3; Constel-lacio Esportiva 1; Lusitanos 1; UE Engordany 1; Inter Club d'Escaldes 1.
**Includes one unofficial title.*

Andorran Primera Divisio Qualifying Table 2019–20

	P	*W*	*D*	*L*	*F*	*A*	*GD*	*Pts*
Inter Club d'Escaldes	21	14	5	2	37	13	24	47
FC Santa Coloma	21	13	5	3	43	11	32	44
Sant Julia	21	11	3	7	26	23	3	36
UE Engordany	21	10	5	6	33	26	7	35
UE Santa Coloma	21	9	5	7	25	23	2	32
Atletic Club d'Escaldes	21	6	5	10	23	27	–4	23
Ordino	21	2	3	16	15	52	–37	9
CE Carroi	21	2	3	16	11	38	–27	9

Championship Round 2019–20

	P	*W*	*D*	*L*	*F*	*A*	*GD*	*Pts*
Inter Club d'Escaldes (C)[1]	24	15	7	2	41	14	27	52
FC Santa Coloma[2]	24	15	6	3	48	12	36	51
UE Engordany[2]	24	11	6	7	35	29	6	39
Sant Julia	24	11	3	10	27	30	–3	36

Relegation Round 2019–20

	P	W	D	L	F	A	GD	Pts
UE Santa Coloma	24	11	6	7	34	26	8	39
Atletic Club d'Escaldes	24	8	6	10	32	29	3	30
CE Carroi+	24	3	3	16	42	46	–28	12
Ordino Encamp*	24	2	3	15	64	53	–49	9

Top scorer: Soldevila (Inter Club d'Escaldes) 16.
Cup Final: Inter Club d'Escaldes 2, FC Santa Coloma 0.

ARMENIA

Football Federation of Armenia, Khanjyan Street 27, 0010 Yerevan.

Founded: 1992. *FIFA:* 1992; *UEFA:* 1993. *National Colours:* Red shirts with white trim, red shorts, red socks.

International matches 2019–20

Italy (h) 1-3, Bosnia-Herzegovina (h) 4-2, Liechtenstein (a) 1-1, Finland (a) 0-3, Greece (h) 0-1, Italy (a) 1-9.

League Championship wins (1992–2020)

Pyunik 14 (incl. Homenetmen 1*); Shirak 4*; Alashkert 3; Araks 2 (incl. Tsement 1); Ararat-Armenia 2; Ararat Yerevan 1; FK Yerevan 1; Ulisses 1; Banants (now Urartu) 1.
**Includes one unofficial shared title.*

Cup wins (1992–2020)

Pyunik (incl. Homenetmen 1) 8; Mika 6; Ararat Yerevan 5; Banants (now Urartu) 3; Tsement 2; Shirak 2; Gandzasar Kapan 1; Alashkert 1; Noah 1.
See also Russia section for Armenian club honours in Soviet era 1936–91.

Armenian Premier League Qualifying Table 2019–20

	P	*W*	*D*	*L*	*F*	*A*	*GD*	*Pts*
Ararat-Armenia	18	11	3	4	33	15	18	34
Lori	18	9	5	4	27	19	8	32
Alashkert	18	9	4	5	33	20	13	31
Ararat Yerevan	18	9	4	5	25	18	7	31
Noah	18	9	3	6	25	19	6	30
Shirak	18	8	4	6	25	18	7	28

Pyunik	18	7	2	9	35	36	–1	23
Urartu	18	6	5	7	22	24	–2	23
Gandzasar Kapan	18	4	6	8	20	25	–5	18
FC Yerevan*	18	0	0	18	11	62	–51	0

**FC Yerevan withdrew after 15 rounds for financial reasons. Three remaining matches recorded as 0-3 defeats.*

Championship Round 2019–20

	P	*W*	*D*	*L*	*F*	*A*	*GD*	*Pts*
Ararat-Armenia (C)[1]	28	15	7	6	45	23	22	49
Noah[2]	28	14	6	8	37	27	10	48
Alashkert[2]	28	14	5	9	51	31	20	47
Shirak[2]	28	13	7	8	40	30	10	46
Lori	27	10	10	7	35	33	2	40
Ararat Yerevan	27	9	6	12	31	36	–5	33

**Match between Lori and Ararat Yerevan not played due to COVID-19 outbreak at Lori.*

Relegation Round 2019–20

	P	W	D	L	F	A	GD	Pts
Urartu	22	8	6	8	26	27	–1	30
Pyunik	22	8	2	12	39	42	–3	26
Gandzasar Kapan	22	6	7	9	25	29	–4	25

FC Yerevan withdrew; no relegation to second tier.
Top scorer: Kone (Shirak) 23.
Cup Final: Noah 5, Ararat-Armenia 5.
aet; Noah won 7-6 on penalties.

AUSTRIA

Oesterreichischer Fussball-Bund, Ernst-Happel Stadion, Sektor A/F, Meiereistrasse 7, Wien 1021.
Founded: 1904. *FIFA:* 1905; *UEFA:* 1954. *National Colours:* Red shirts, white shorts, red socks.

International matches 2019–20
Latvia (h) 6-0, Poland (a) 0-0, Israel (h) 3-1, Slovenia (a) 1-0, North Macedonia (h) 2-1, Latvia (a) 0-1.

League Championship wins (1912–2020)
Rapid Vienna 32; Austria Vienna (formerly Amateure) 24; Red Bull Salzburg 14 (incl. Austria Salzburg 3); Wacker Innsbruck 10 (incl. Swarovski Tirol 2, Tirol Innsbruck 3); Admira Vienna (now Admira Wacker Modling) 9 (incl. Wacker Vienna 1); First Vienna 6; Wiener Sportklub 3; Sturm Graz 3; WAF 1; WAC 1; Floridsdorfer 1; Hakoah 1; LASK Linz 1; Voest Linz 1; GAK Graz 1.

Cup wins (1919–2020)
Austria Vienna (formerly Amateure) 27; Rapid Vienna 14; Wacker Innsbruck 7 (incl. Swarovski Tirol 1); Red Bull Salzburg 7; Admira Vienna (now Admira Wacker Modling) 6 (incl. Wacker Vienna 1); Sturm Graz 5; GAK Graz 4; First Vienna 3; WAC 2; Ried 2; WAF 1; Wiener Sportklub 1; LASK Linz 1; Kremser 1; Stockerau 1; Karnten 1; Horn 1; Pasching 1.

Austrian Bundesliga Qualifying Table 2019–20

	P	*W*	*D*	*L*	*F*	*A*	*GD*	*Pts*
Red Bull Salzburg	22	14	6	2	74	26	48	48
LASK (–12)	22	17	3	2	50	20	30	42
Rapid Vienna	22	11	7	4	47	26	21	40
Wolfsberg	22	11	5	6	50	27	23	38
Sturm Graz	22	9	5	8	37	28	9	32
Hartberg	22	8	5	9	36	50	–14	29
Austria Vienna	22	5	10	7	33	36	–3	25
Rheindorf Altach	22	7	3	12	34	44	–10	24
Admira Wacker Modling	22	4	7	11	22	43	–21	19
WSG Swarovski Tirol	22	5	4	13	26	50	–24	19
Mattersburg	22	5	3	14	26	52	–26	18
St Polten	22	3	8	11	21	54	–33	17

NB: Points earned in Qualifying phase are halved and rounded down at start of Championship and Relegation Play-off phase.

Championship Round 2019–20

	P	*W*	*D*	*L*	*F*	*A*	*GD*	*Pts*
Red Bull Salzburg (C)[1]	32	22	8	2	110	34	76	50
Rapid Vienna[1]	32	17	7	8	64	43	21	38
Wolfsberg[2]	32	15	9	8	69	43	26	35
LASK†[2] (–4)	32	20	4	8	67	37	30	33
Hartberg[2]	32	12	6	14	52	74	–22	24
Sturm Graz	32	10	5	17	46	50	–14	19

†LASK deducted 12pts in regular season (halved to 6 in play-off round) for violating COVID-19 regulations, later reduced to 4 on appeal.

Relegation Round 2019–20

	P	*W*	*D*	*L*	*F*	*A*	*GD*	*Pts*
Austria Vienna	32	12	11	9	49	47	2	34
Rheindorf Altach	32	10	8	14	45	53	–8	26
St Polten	32	8	10	14	39	65	–26	25
Mattersburg*	32	8	6	18	39	64	–25	21
Admira Wacker Modling	32	6	10	16	29	57	–28	18
WSG Swarovski Tirol	32	6	8	18	34	66	–32	16

**Mattersburg withdrew post-season for financial reasons; WSG Swarovski Tirol reprieved from relegation.*

Europa League Play-off
Semi-final
Austria Vienna 1, Rheindorf Altach 0
Final
Austria Vienna 2, 0, Hartberg 3, 0
Top scorer: Weissman (Wolfsberg) 30.
Cup Final: Red Bull Salzburg 5, Austria Lustenau 0.

AZERBAIJAN

Association of Football Federations of Azerbaijan, 2208 Nobel prospekti, 1025 Baku.
Founded: 1992. *FIFA:* 1994; *UEFA:* 1994. *National Colours:* All red.

International matches 2019–20
Wales (a) 1-2, Croatia (h) 1-1, Bahrain (a) 3-2, Hungary (a) 0-1, Wales (h) 0-2, Slovakia (a) 0-2.

League Championship wins (1992–2020)
Neftchi 8; Qarabag 8; Kapaz 3; Shamkir 3*; FK Baku 2; Inter Baku (now Keshla) 2; Turan 1; Khazar Lankaran 1.
**Includes one unofficial title.*

Cup wins (1992–2020)*
Neftchi 7†; Qarabag 6; Kapaz 4; FK Baku 3; Khazar Lankaran 3; Inshatchi 1; Shafa 1; Keshla (formerly Inter Baku) 1; Gabala 1.
**No winner in 2019–20. †Includes one unofficial title.*

Azerbaijani Premyer Liqası 2019–20

	P	*W*	*D*	*L*	*F*	*A*	*GD*	*Pts*
Qarabag (C)[1]	20	13	6	1	34	7	27	45
Neftchi[2]	20	10	7	3	33	14	19	37
Keshla[2]	20	8	6	6	27	21	6	30
Sumqayit[2]	20	6	5	9	24	32	–8	23
Zira	20	6	5	9	25	37	–12	23
Sabah	20	5	6	9	19	27	–8	21
Sabail	20	5	5	10	16	30	–14	20
Gabala	20	5	4	11	25	35	–10	19

League curtailed after 20 rounds due to COVID-19 pandemic. Qarabag declared champions. No relegation to second tier.
Top scorers (joint): Babaei (Sumqayit), Emreli (Qarabag), Dabo, Joseph-Monrose (both Neftchi) 7.
Cup Final: Competition abandoned due to COVID-19 pandemic.

BELARUS

Belarus Football Federation, Prospekt Pobeditelei 20/3, 220020 Minsk.
Founded: 1989. *FIFA:* 1992; *UEFA:* 1993. *National Colours:* All red with white trim.

International matches 2019–20
Estonia (a) 2-1, Wales (a) 0-1, Estonia (h) 0-0, Netherlands (h) 1-2, Germany (a) 0-4, Montenegro (a) 0-2, Uzbekistan (n) 1-0, Bulgaria (a) 1-0.

League Championship wins (1992–2019)
BATE Borisov 15; Dinamo Minsk 7; Slavia Mozyr (incl. MPKC 1) 2; Dnepr Mogilev 1; Belshina Bobruisk 1; Gomel 1; Shakhtyor Soligorsk 1; Dinamo Brest 1.

Cup wins (1992–2020)
BATE Borisov 4; Dinamo Minsk 3; Belshina Bobruisk 3; Shakhtyor Soligorsk 3; Dinamo Brest 3; Slavia Mozyr (incl. MPKC 1) 2; Gomel 2; MTZ-RIPA 2; Naftan Novopolotsk 2; Neman Grodno 1; Dinamo 93 Minsk 1; Lokomotiv 96 1; FC Minsk 1; Torpedo-BelAZ Zhodino 1.
See also Russia section for Belarusian club honours in Soviet era 1936–91.

Belarusian Vysheyshaya Liga 2019

	P	*W*	*D*	*L*	*F*	*A*	*GD*	*Pts*
Dinamo Brest (C)[1]	30	23	6	1	70	22	48	75
BATE Borisov[2]	30	22	4	4	61	21	40	70
Shakhtyor Soligorsk[2]	30	20	5	5	59	21	38	65
Dinamo Minsk[2]	30	15	5	10	43	39	4	50
Isloch Minsk Raion	30	13	8	9	42	36	6	47
Torpedo-BelAZ Zhodino	30	13	6	11	41	36	5	45
Gorodeya	30	12	8	10	31	29	2	44
Slavia Mozyr	30	10	7	13	35	40	–5	37
FC Minsk‡	30	9	9	12	36	44	–8	36
Neman Grodno‡	30	10	6	14	28	37	–9	36

Slutsk	30	9	7	14	29	46	–17	34
Energetik-BGU Minsk	30	8	9	13	52	66	–14	33
Vitebsk	30	8	7	15	24	39	–15	31
Dynapro Mogilev*+†	30	8	6	16	32	42	–10	30
Gomel*	30	7	8	15	44	50	–6	29
Torpedo Minsk*§	30	1	3	26	4	63	–59	6

‡Ranking decided on head-to-head points.
†Dynapro Mogilev disbanded on relegation. §Torpedo Minsk withdrew mid-season; all subsequent matches recorded as 0-3 defeats.
Top scorer: Shkurin (Energetik-BGU Minsk) 19.
Cup Final: BATE Borisov 1, Dinamo Brest 0 *aet.*

BELGIUM

Union Royale Belge des Societes de Football-Association, 145 Avenue Houba de Strooper, B-1020 Bruxelles.
Founded: 1895. *FIFA:* 1904; *UEFA:* 1954. *National Colours:* All red.

International matches 2019–20

San Marino (a) 4-0, Scotland (a) 4-0, San Marino (h) 9-0, Kazakhstan (a) 2-0, Russia (a) 4-1, Cyprus (h) 6-1.

League Championship wins (1896–2020)

Anderlecht 34; Club Brugge 16; Union St Gilloise 11; Standard Liege 10; Beerschot VAC (became Germinal) 7; RC Brussels 6; RFC Liege 5; Daring Brussels 5; Antwerp 4; Lierse 4; Mechelen 4; Genk 4; Cercle Brugge 3; Beveren 2; RWD Molenbeek 1; Gent 1.

Cup wins (1912–14; 1927; 1935; 1954–2020)

Club Brugge 11; Anderlecht 9; Standard Liege 8; Genk 4; Antwerp 3; Gent 3; Union Saint-Gilloise 2; Cercle Brugge 2; Lierse 2; Beerschot VAC (became Germinal) 2; Beveren 2; Waterschei (became Racing Genk) 2; Mechelen 2; Beerschot Antwerpen Club (incl. Germinal Ekeren) 2; Zulte Waregem 2; Lokeren 2; Racing 1; Daring 1; Tournai 1; KFC Waregem 1; RFC Liege 1; Westerlo 1; La Louviere 1.

Belgian First Division A Final Table 2019–20

	P	W	D	L	F	A	GD	Pts
Club Brugge (C)[1]	29	21	7	1	58	14	44	70
Gent[1]	29	16	7	6	59	34	25	55
Sporting Charleroi[2]	29	15	9	5	49	23	26	54
Antwerp[2]	29	15	8	6	49	32	17	53
Standard Liege[2]	29	14	7	8	47	32	15	49
Mechelen‡	29	13	5	11	46	43	3	44
Genk‡	29	13	5	11	45	42	3	44
Anderlecht	29	11	10	8	45	29	16	43
Zulte-Waregem†	29	10	6	13	41	49	–8	36
Excel Mouscron†	29	9	9	11	38	40	–2	36
Kortrijk	29	9	6	14	40	44	–4	33
Sint-Truiden	29	9	6	14	33	50	–17	33
Eupen	29	8	6	15	28	51	–23	30
Cercle Brugge	29	7	2	20	27	54	–27	23
Oostende	29	6	4	19	29	58	–29	22
Waasland-Beveren	29	5	5	19	21	60	–39	20

‡Ranking decided on goals scored. †Ranking decided on matches won.
League curtailed due to COVID-19 pandemic. Club Brugge declared champions. First Division B to expand to 18 teams in 2020–21 so no relegation to second tier.
Top scorers (joint): David (Gent), Mbokani (Antwerp) 18.
Cup Final: Antwerp 1, Club Brugge 0.

BOSNIA-HERZEGOVINA

Football Federation of Bosnia & Herzegovina, Ferhadija 30, 71000 Sarajevo.
Founded: 1992. *FIFA:* 1996; *UEFA:* 1998. *National Colours:* Blue shirts, blue shorts, blue socks with white tops.

International matches 2019–20

Liechtenstein (h) 5-0, Armenia (a) 2-4, Finland (h) 4-1, Greece (a) 1-2, Italy (h) 0-3, Liechtenstein (a) 3-0.

League Championship wins (1998–2020)

Zeljeznicar 6; Zrinjski Mostar 6; Sarajevo 5; Siroki Brijeg 2; Brotnjo 1; Leotar 1; Modrica 1; Borac Banja Luka 1.

Cup wins (1998; 2000–20)*

Sarajevo 6; Zeljeznicar 6; Siroki Brijeg 3; Modrica 1; Orasje 1; Zrinjski Mostar 1; Slavija 1; Borac Banja Luka 1; Olimpic Sarajevo 1; Radnik Bijeljina 1.
See also Serbia section for Bosnian-Herzogovinian club honours in Yugoslav Republic era 1947–91.
**No winner in 2019–20.*

Bosnia-Herzegovinia Premijer Liga 2019–20

	P	W	D	L	F	A	GD	Pts
FK Sarajevo (C)[1]	22	13	6	3	38	19	19	45
Zeljeznicar[2]	22	12	6	4	43	21	22	42
Zrinjski Mostar[2]	22	11	5	6	30	12	18	38
Borac Banja Luka[2]	22	10	6	6	29	23	6	36
Tuzla City	22	10	5	7	27	29	–2	35
Radnik Bijeljina	22	10	4	8	34	21	13	34
Siroki Brijeg	22	8	8	6	31	26	5	32
Velez Mostar	22	9	5	8	25	23	2	32
Sloboda Tuzla	22	4	9	9	21	35	–14	21
Mladost Doboj Kakanj	22	4	6	12	21	35	–14	18
Celik Zenica* (–3)	22	5	5	12	17	33	–16	17
Zvijezda 09*	22	1	5	16	12	51	–39	8

Following relegation Celik Zenica were banned from league for financial irregularities.
Top scorer: Ahmetovic (Sarajevo) 13.
Cup Final: Competition abandoned due to COVID-19 pandemic.

BULGARIA

Bulgarian Football Union, 26 Tzar Ivan Assen II Str., 1124 Sofia.
Founded: 1923. *FIFA:* 1992; *UEFA:* 1954. *National Colours:* White shirts, green shorts, red socks.

International matches 2019–20

England (a) 0-4, Republic of Ireland (a) 1-3, Montenegro (a) 0-0, England (h) 0-6, Paraguay (h) 0-1, Czech Republic (h) 1-0, Belarus (h) 0-1.

League Championship wins (1925–2020)

CSKA Sofia 31; Levski Sofia 26; Ludogorets Razgrad 9; Slavia Sofia 7; Lokomotiv Sofia 4; Litex Lovech 4; Vladislav Varna (now Cherno More Varna) 3; Botev Plovdiv (includes Trakija) 2; Athletic Slava 1923 1; Sokol Varna (now Spartak Varna) 1; Sportklub Sofia (now Septemvri Sofia) 1; Ticha Varna (now Cherno More Varna) 1; Spartak Plovdiv 1; Beroe Stara Zagora 1; Etar 1; Lokomotiv Plovdiv 1.

Cup wins (1946–2020)

Levski Sofia (incl. Vitosha 1) 24; CSKA Sofia (incl. Sredets 3) 20; Slavia Sofia 8; Lokomotiv Sofia 4; Litex Lovech 4; Botev Plovdiv (includes Trakija) 3; Beroe Stara Zagora 2; Ludogorets Razgrad 2; Lokomotiv Plovdiv 2; Spartak Plovdiv 1; Septemvri Sofia 1; Spartak Sofia 1; Marek Dupnitsa 1; Sliven 1; Cherno More Varna 1.

Bulgarian First League Qualifying Table 2019–20

	P	W	D	L	F	A	GD	Pts
Ludogorets Razgrad	26	18	8	0	46	12	34	62
Lokomotiv Plovdiv	26	14	8	4	49	23	26	50
CSKA Sofia	26	14	8	4	41	17	24	50
Levski Sofia	26	14	7	5	43	19	24	49
Slavia Sofia	26	13	6	7	36	28	8	45
Beroe	26	14	1	11	44	34	10	43
Cherno More	26	10	10	6	32	24	8	40
Arda	26	7	10	9	27	33	–6	31
Botev Plovdiv	26	8	6	12	26	30	–4	30
Etar	26	6	9	11	31	45	–14	27
Tsarsko Selo	26	7	4	15	24	42	–18	25
Botev Vratsa	26	5	7	14	21	46	–25	22
Dunav Ruse 2010	26	4	7	15	21	49	–28	19
Vitosha Bistritsa	26	1	3	22	15	54	–39	6

Championship Round 2019–20

	P	W	D	L	F	A	GD	Pts
Ludogorets Razgrad (C)[1]	31	21	9	1	59	18	41	72
CSKA Sofia[2]	31	16	11	4	52	22	30	59
Slavia Sofia†[2]	31	16	7	8	42	32	10	55
Levski Sofia	31	15	8	8	50	30	20	53
Lokomotiv Plovdiv[2]	31	15	8	8	53	35	18	53
Beroe	31	16	1	14	50	43	7	49

†Qualified for Europa League play-off final.

Relegation Round 2019–20

Group A

	P	W	D	L	F	A	GD	Pts
Cherno More	29	12	11	6	39	27	12	47
Etar	29	7	10	12	34	48	–14	31
Tsarsko Selo+	29	9	4	16	27	46	–19	31
Vitosha Bistritsa*	29	1	3	25	15	57	–42	6

Group B

	P	W	D	L	F	A	GD	Pts
Botev Plovdiv	29	10	6	13	32	34	–2	36
Arda	29	8	11	10	28	35	–7	35
Botev Vratsa+	29	6	8	15	26	50	–24	26
Dunav Ruse 2010*	29	5	7	17	25	55	–30	22

Europa League Play-offs
Quarter-finals
Cherno More 1, Arda 0
Botev Plovdiv 1, Etar 0
Semi-final
Cherno More 0, Botev Plovdiv 1
Final
Slavia Sofia 2, Botev Plovdiv 1
Top scorer: Kamburov (Beroe) 18.
Cup Final: CSKA Sofia 0, Lokomotiv Plovdiv 0.
aet; Lokomotiv Plovdiv won 5-3 on penalties.

CHANNEL ISLANDS

Guernsey

League Championship wins (1894–2020)*
Northerners 32; Guernsey Rangers 17; Vale Recreation 15; St Martin's 14; Sylvans 10; Belgrave Wanderers 8; 2nd Bn Manchesters 3; Guernsey Rovers 2; 2nd Bn Royal Irish Regt 2; 2nd Bn Wiltshires 2; 10th Comp W Div Royal Artillery 1; 2nd Bn Leicesters 1; 2nd Bn PA Somerset Light Infantry 1; 2nd Middlesex Regt 1; Athletics 1; Band Comp 2nd Bn Royal Fusiliers 1; G&H Comp Royal Fusiliers 1; Grange 1; Yorkshire Regt (Green Howards).
**No winner in 2019–20 due to COVID-19 pandemic.*

Guernsey Priaulx League 2019–20

	P	*W*	*D*	*L*	*F*	*A*	*GD*	*Pts*
Northerners	14	12	1	1	38	18	20	37
St Martin's	14	8	4	2	35	21	14	28
Alderney	15	9	0	6	38	21	17	27
Manzur	16	7	3	6	37	32	5	24
Guernsey Rovers	16	6	3	7	29	35	–6	21
Sylvans	13	6	2	5	47	27	20	20
Belgrave Wanderers	13	5	3	5	32	32	0	18
Vale Recreation	15	4	0	11	32	36	–4	12
Guernsey Rangers	16	1	0	15	16	82	–66	3

Competition annulled due to COVID-19 pandemic. Title not awarded.

Jersey

League Championship wins (1904–2020)
Jersey Wanderers 21; First Tower United 19; St Paul's 20; Jersey Scottish 11; Beeches Old Boys 5; Magpies 4; 2nd Bn King's Own Regt 3; Oaklands 3; St Peter 3; 1st Batt Devon Regt 2; 1st Bn East Surrey Regt 2; Georgetown 2; Mechanics 2; YMCA 2; 2nd Bn East Surrey Regt 1; 20th Comp Royal Garrison Artillery 1; National Rovers 1; Sporting Academics 1; Trinity 1.

Jersey Football Combination 2019–20

	P	*W*	*D*	*L*	*F*	*A*	*GD*	*Pts*
Jersey Wanderers (C)	13	11	1	1	36	11	25	34
St Ouen	14	10	2	2	32	16	16	32
St Paul's	12	8	3	1	38	15	23	27
St Clement	10	5	1	4	26	18	8	16
Grouville	11	4	3	4	21	23	–2	15
St Peter	13	5	1	7	26	33	–7	16
Rozel Rovers	13	4	4	5	21	29	–8	16
St Brelade	13	4	1	8	26	36	–10	13
Sporting Academics	15	3	3	9	23	38	–15	12
St Lawrence	14	0	1	13	14	44	–30	1

Rankings decided on points-per-match basis.
Competition curtailed due to COVID-19 pandemic. Jersey Wanderers declared champions.

Upton Park Trophy 2020 (For Guernsey & Jersey League Champions)
Not contested due to COVID-19 pandemic.

Upton Park Trophy wins (1907–2020)*
Northerners 17 (incl. 1 shared); First Tower United 12; St Paul's 12; Jersey Wanderers 11 (incl. 1 shared); St Martin's 11; Jersey Scottish 6; Guernsey Rangers 5; Vale Recreation 4; Belgrave Wanderers 4; Beeches Old Boys 3; Old St Paul's 3; Magpies 3; Sylvans 3; St Peter 2; Jersey Mechanics 1; Jersey YMCA 1; National Rovers 1; Sporting Academics 1; Trinity 1.
**No winner in 2019–20.*

CROATIA

Croatian Football Federation, Vukovarska 269A, 10000 Zagreb.
Founded: 1912. *FIFA:* 1992; *UEFA:* 1993. *National Colours:* Red and white check shirts, white shorts, blue socks.

International matches 2019–20
Slovakia (a) 4-0, Azerbaijan (a) 1-1, Hungary (h) 3-0, Wales (a) 1-1, Slovakia (h) 3-1, Georgia (h) 2-1.

League Championship wins (1992–2020)
Dinamo Zagreb (incl. Croatia Zagreb 3) 21; Hajduk Split 6; NK Zagreb 1; Rijeka 1.

Cup wins (1992–2020)
Dinamo Zagreb (incl. Croatia Zagreb 4) 15; Hajduk Split 6; Rijeka 6; Inter Zapresic 1; Osijek 1.
See also Serbia section for Croatian club honours in Yugoslav Republic era 1947–92.

Croatian Prva HNL 2019–20

	P	*W*	*D*	*L*	*F*	*A*	*GD*	*Pts*
Dinamo Zagreb (C)[1]	36	25	5	6	62	20	42	80
Lokomotiva Zagreb[1]	36	19	8	9	57	38	19	65
Rijeka[2]	36	19	7	10	58	42	16	64
Osijek[2]	36	17	11	8	47	29	18	62
Hajduk Split[2]	36	18	6	12	60	41	19	60
Gorica	36	12	13	11	44	48	–4	49
Slaven Koprivnica	36	10	9	17	34	51	–17	39
Varazdin	36	9	9	18	29	50	–21	36
Istra 1961+	36	5	10	21	27	59	–32	25
Inter Zapresic*	36	3	8	25	32	72	–40	17

Top scorers (joint): Caktas (Hajduk Split), Colak (Rijeka), Maric (Osijek) 20.
Cup Final: Rijeka 1, Lokomotiva Zagreb 0.

CYPRUS

Cyprus Football Association, 10 Achaion Street, 2413 Engomi, PO Box 25071, 1306 Nicosia.
Founded: 1934. *FIFA:* 1948; *UEFA:* 1962. *National Colours:* All blue with white trim.

International matches 2019–20
Kazakhstan (h) 1-1, San Marino (a) 4-0, Kazakhstan (a) 2-1, Russia (h) 0-5, Scotland (h) 1-2, Belgium (a) 1-6.

League Championship wins (1935–2020)*
APOEL Nicosia 28; Omonia Nicosia 20; Anorthosis 13; AEL Limassol 6; EPA Larnaca 3; Olympiakos Nicosia 3; Apollon Limassol 3; Pezoporikos Larnaca 2; Trust 1; Cetinkaya 1.
**No winner in 2019–20.*

Cup wins (1935–2020)*
APOEL Nicosia 21; Omonia Nicosia 14; Anorthosis 10; Apollon Limassol 9; AEL Limassol 7; EPA Larnaca 5; Trust 3; Cetinkaya 2; AEK Larnaca 2; Pezoporikos Larnaca 1; Olympiakos Nicosia 1; Nea Salamis Famagusta 1; APOP Kinyras 1.
**No winner in 2019–20.*

Cypriot First Division Qualifying Table 2019–20

	P	*W*	*D*	*L*	*F*	*A*	*GD*	*Pts*
Omonia‡	22	12	7	3	31	13	18	43
Anorthosis Famagusta‡	22	13	4	5	42	21	21	43
APOEL	22	11	6	5	35	15	20	39
Apollon	22	12	2	8	38	29	9	38
AEK Larnaca	22	9	8	5	36	26	10	35
AEL Limassol	22	8	7	7	27	26	1	31
Paphos	22	8	6	8	26	26	0	30
Nea Salamis Famagusta	22	7	4	11	25	36	–11	25
Olympiakos	22	5	9	8	27	34	–7	24
Paralimni	22	5	7	10	28	42	–14	22
Ethnikos Achna	22	5	5	12	29	44	–15	20
Doxa Katokopia	22	2	5	15	13	45	–32	11

Championship Round 2019–20

	P	*W*	*D*	*L*	*F*	*A*	*GD*	*Pts*
Omonia‡[1]	23	13	7	3	34	13	21	46
Anorthosis Famagusta‡[2]	23	14	4	5	45	21	24	46
APOEL[2]	23	11	7	5	36	16	20	40
Apollon[2]	23	12	3	8	39	30	9	39
AEK Larnaca	23	9	8	6	36	29	7	35
AEL Limassol	23	8	7	8	27	29	–2	31

‡Ranking decided on head-to-head points.

Relegation Round 2019–20

	P	*W*	*D*	*L*	*F*	*A*	*GD*	*Pts*
Paphos	23	8	6	9	26	28	–2	30
Nea Salamis Famagusta	23	7	5	11	27	38	–11	26
Olympiakos	23	5	10	8	28	35	–7	25
Paralimni	23	5	8	10	29	43	–14	23
Ethnikos Achna	23	5	5	12	31	46	–15	21
Doxa Katokopia	23	3	5	15	15	45	–30	14

League curtailed due to COVID-19 pandemic. Title not awarded; no relegation to second tier as league will expand to 14 teams in 2020–21 season.
Top scorer: Trichkovski (AEK Larnaca) 20.
Cup Final: Competition abandoned due to COVID-19 pandemic.

CZECH REPUBLIC

Fotbalova Asociace Ceske Republiky, Diskarska 2431/4, PO Box 11, Praha 6 16017.

Founded: 1901. *FIFA:* 1907; *UEFA:* 1954. *National Colours:* All red.

International matches 2019–20

Montenegro (h) 3-0*, Kosovo (a) 1-2, Montenegro (a) 3-0, England (h) 2-1, Northern Ireland (h) 2-3, Kosovo (h) 2-1, Bulgaria (a) 0-1.

**Played 10.06.2019, venue incorrect in last edition.*

League Championship wins – Czechoslovakia (1925–93)

Sparta Prague 21; Slavia Prague 13; Dukla Prague (prev. UDA, now Marila Pribram) 11; Slovan Bratislava (formerly NV Bratislava) 8; Spartak Trnava 5; Banik Ostrava 3; Viktoria Zizkov 1; Inter Bratislava 1; Spartak Hradec Kralove 1; Zbrojovka Brno 1; Bohemians 1; Vitkovice 1.

Cup wins – Czechoslovakia (1961–93)

Dukla Prague 8; Sparta Prague 8; Slovan Bratislava 5; Spartak Trnava 4; Banik Ostrava 3; Lokomotiva Kosice 2; TJ Gottwaldov 1; DAC 1904 Dunajska Streda 1; 1.FC Kosice 1.

League Championship wins – Czech Republic (1994–2020)

Sparta Prague 12; Slavia Prague 6; Viktoria Plzen 5; Slovan Liberec 3; Banik Ostrava 1.

Cup wins – Czech Republic (1994–2020)

Sparta Prague 7; Slavia Prague 5; Viktoria Zizkov 2; Jablonec 2; Slovan Liberec 2; Teplice 2; Mlada Boleslav 2; Hradec Kralove (formerly Spartak) 1; Banik Ostrava 1; Viktoria Plzen 1; Sigma Olomouc 1; Fastav Zlin 1.

Czech First League Qualifying Table 2019–20

	P	W	D	L	F	A	GD	Pts
Slavia Prague	30	22	6	2	58	10	48	72
Viktoria Plzen	30	20	6	4	60	22	38	66
Sparta Pragu	30	14	8	8	55	35	20	50
Jablonec	30	14	7	9	46	41	5	49
Slovan Liberec	30	14	5	11	50	38	12	47
Banik Ostrava	30	12	9	9	42	34	8	45
Ceske Budejovice†	30	13	4	13	46	45	1	43
Bohemians 1905†‡	30	12	6	12	38	41	–3	42
Slovacko†‡	30	11	9	10	35	35	0	42
Mlada Boleslav†	30	11	7	12	48	52	–4	40
Sigma Olomouc	30	8	12	10	36	37	–1	36
Teplice	30	7	10	13	29	49	–20	31
Zlin	30	7	6	17	25	47	–22	27
Karvina	30	5	11	14	23	39	–16	26
Opava	30	5	8	17	16	47	–31	23
Pribram	30	5	6	19	19	54	–35	21

†Qualified for Europa League play-offs.

Championship Round 2019–20

	P	W	D	L	F	A	GD	Pts
Slavia Prague (C)[1]	35	26	7	2	69	12	57	85
Viktoria Plzen[1]	35	23	7	5	68	24	44	76
Sparta Prague[2]	35	17	9	9	66	40	26	60
Jablonec‡[2]	35	14	9	12	48	52	–4	51
Slovan Liberec‡§[2]	35	15	6	14	55	51	4	51
Banik Ostrava	35	12	11	12	47	43	4	47

‡Ranking decided on head-to-head points. §Qualified for Europa League play-off final.

Relegation Round 2019–20

	P	W	D	L	F	A	GD	Pts
Sigma Olomouc	33	9	13	11	39	40	–1	40
Teplice	33	9	11	13	37	51	–14	38
Zlin	33	9	6	18	30	52	–22	33
Karvina	33	5	12	16	25	46	–21	27
Opava	33	5	10	18	17	50	–33	25
Pribram	33	6	7	20	21	55	–34	25

Final two rounds of matches not played due to positive COVID-19 tests at two clubs. No relegation to second tier as league expanding to 18 teams in 2020–21.

Europa League Play-offs

First Round

Mlada Boleslav 2, 2, Ceske Budejovice 1, 0 (agg. 4-1)
Slovacko 1, 1, Bohemians 1905 2, 2 (agg. 2-4)

Second Round

Mlada Boleslav 3, 1, Bohemians 1905 0, 2 (agg. 4-2)

Final

Slovan Liberec 2, Mlada Boleslav 0

Top scorers (joint): Kozak (Sparta Prague), Musa (Slavia Prague incl. 7 for Slovan Liberec) 14.

Cup Final: Slovan Liberec 1, Sparta Prague 2.

DENMARK

Dansk Boldspil-Union, Idraettens Hus, DBU Alle 1, DK-2605, Brondby.

Founded: 1889. *FIFA:* 1904; *UEFA:* 1954. *National Colours:* Red shirts, white shorts, red socks.

International matches 2019–20

Gibraltar (a) 6-0, Georgia (a) 0-0, Switzerland (h) 1-0, Luxembourg (h) 4-0, Gibraltar (h) 6-0, Republic of Ireland (a) 1-1.

League Championship wins (1913–2020)

KB Copenhagen 15; FC Copenhagen 13; Brondby 10; B 93 Copenhagen 9; AB (Akademisk) 9; B 1903 Copenhagen 7; Frem 6; AGF Aarhus 5; Vejle 5; Esbjerg 5; AaB Aalborg 4; Hvidovre 3; OB Odense 3; FC Midtjylland 3; Koge 2; B 1909 Odense 2; Lyngby 2; Silkeborg 1; Herfolge 1; FC Nordsjaelland 1.

Cup wins (1955–2020)

AGF Aarhus 9; FC Copenhagen 8; Vejle 6; Brondby 7; OB Odense 5; Esbjerg 3; AaB Aalborg 3; Randers Freja 3; Lyngby 3; Frem 2; B 1909 Odense 2; B 1903 Copenhagen 2; Nordsjaelland 2; B 1913 Odense 1; KB Copenhagen 1; Vanlose 1; Hvidovre 1; B 93 Copenhagen 1; AB (Akademisk) 1; Viborg 1; Silkeborg 1; Randers 1; FC Midtjylland 1; SonderjyskE 1.

Danish Superliga Qualifying Table 2019–20

	P	W	D	L	F	A	GD	Pts
FC Midtjylland	26	21	2	3	42	14	28	65
FC Copenhagen	26	18	2	6	47	29	18	56
AGF Aarhus	26	14	5	7	42	28	14	47
Brondby	26	13	3	10	47	37	10	42
Nordsjaelland	26	12	5	9	48	35	13	41
AaB Aalborg	26	11	5	10	44	33	11	38
Randers	26	10	5	11	39	35	4	35
AC Horsens	26	10	4	12	25	44	–19	34
OB Odense	26	9	6	11	34	30	4	33
Lyngby	26	9	5	12	31	45	–14	32
SonderjyskE	26	6	9	11	31	44	–13	27
Hobro	26	3	14	9	25	35	–10	23
Esbjerg	26	4	6	16	22	44	–22	18
Silkeborg	26	3	7	16	31	55	–24	16

Championship Round 2019–20

	P	W	D	L	F	A	GD	Pts
FC Midtjylland (C)[1]	36	26	4	6	61	29	32	82
FC Copenhagen[2]	36	21	5	10	58	42	16	68
AGF Aarhus‡[2]	36	19	7	10	58	41	17	64
Brondby	36	16	8	12	56	42	14	56
AaB Aalborg	36	16	6	14	54	44	10	54
Nordsjaelland	36	13	8	15	59	54	5	47

‡Qualified for Europa League play-off final.

Relegation Round 2019–20

Group 1

	P	W	D	L	F	A	GD	Pts
OB Odense†	32	12	7	13	43	42	1	43
SonderjyskE[2]	32	9	11	12	37	49	–12	38
Lyngby+	32	9	7	16	34	54	–20	34
Silkeborg*	32	6	8	18	43	59	–16	26

Group 2

	P	W	D	L	F	A	GD	Pts
AC Horsens†	32	13	7	12	36	50	–14	46
Randers†	32	13	6	13	51	45	6	45
Hobro*+	32	5	15	12	35	48	–13	30
Esbjerg*	32	5	7	20	32	58	–26	22

†Qualified for Europa League play-offs.

Europa League Play-offs

Quarter-final

Randers 2, 0, OB Odense 1, 2 (agg. 2-3)

Semi-final

OB Odense 3, 1, AC Horsens 1, 1 (agg. 4-2)

Europa League Play-off final

AGF Aarhus 2, OB Odense 1

Top scorer: Schwarz (Midtjylland incl. 12 for Silkeborg) 18.

Cup Final: SonderjyskE 2, AaB Aalborg 0.

ENGLAND

The Football Association, Wembley Stadium, PO Box 1966, London SW1P 9EQ.

Founded: 1863. *FIFA:* 1905; *UEFA:* 1954. *National Colours:* White shirts with light blue trim, white shorts, red socks.

ESTONIA

Eesti Jalgpalli Liit, A. Le Coq Arena, Asula 4c, 11312 Tallinn.
Founded: 1921. *FIFA:* 1923; *UEFA:* 1992. *National Colours:* Blue shirts, black shorts, white socks.

International matches 2019–20

Belarus (h) 1-2, Netherlands (h) 0-4, Belarus (a) 0-0, Germany (h) 0-3, Ukraine (a) 0-1, Netherlands (a) 0-5.

League Championship wins (1921–40; 1992–2019)

Flora 12; Sport 9; FCI Levadia (formerly Levadia Maardu) 9; Estonia 5; Sillamae Kalev 2; Tallinna JK 2; Norma 2; Lantana (formerly Nikol) 2; Nomme Kalju 2; Olimpia Tartu 1; TVMK Tallinn 1; FCI Tallinn 1.

Cup wins (1993–2020)

FCI Levadia (incl. Levadia Maardu 2) 9; Flora 8; Tallinna Sadam 2; Narva Trans 2; TVMK Tallinn 2; Lantana (formerly Nikol) 1; Norma 1; Levadia Tallinn (pre-2004) 1; Nomme Kalju 1; FCI Tallinn 1.

Estonian Meistriliiga 2019

	P	W	D	L	F	A	GD	Pts
Flora (C)[1]	36	29	3	4	110	21	89	90
FCI Levadia[2]	36	24	6	6	98	32	66	78
Nomme Kalju[2]	36	22	11	3	79	34	45	77
Paide Linnameeskond[2]	36	23	5	8	78	30	48	74
Tartu Tammeka	36	14	7	15	57	62	–5	49
Narva Trans	36	13	9	14	57	49	8	48
Viljandi Tulevik	36	7	7	22	35	75	–40	28
Tallinna Kalev	36	6	6	24	29	89	–60	24
Kuressaare+	36	6	5	25	24	87	–63	23
Maardu Linnameeskond*	36	4	5	27	30	118	–88	17

Top scorer: Sorga (Flora) 31.
Cup Final: Flora 2, Narva Trans 1.

FAROE ISLANDS

Fotboltssamband Foroya, Gundadalur, PO Box 3028, 110 Torshavn.
Founded: 1979. *FIFA:* 1988; *UEFA:* 1990. *National Colours:* White shirts with blue trim, white shorts, white socks.

International matches 2019–20

Sweden (h) 0-4, Spain (a) 0-4, Romania (h) 0-3, Malta (h) 1-0, Norway (a) 0-4, Sweden (a) 0-3.

League Championship wins (1942–2019)

HB Torshavn 23; KI Klaksvik 18; B36 Torshavn 11; TB Tvoroyri (includes FC Suduroy and Royn) 7; GI Gota 6; B68 Toftir 3; EB/Streymur 2; Vikingur 2; SI Sorvagur 1; IF Fuglafjordur 1; B71 Sandur 1; VB Vagur 1; NSI Runavik 1.

Cup wins (1955–2019)

HB Torshavn 27; B36 Torshavn 6; KI Klaksvik 6; GI Gota 6; TB Tvoroyri (includes FC Suduroy and Royn) 5; Vikingur 5; EB/Streymur 4; NSI Runavik 3; VB Vagur 1; B71 Sandur 1.

Faroese Premier League 2019

	P	W	D	L	F	A	GD	Pts
KI Klaksvik (C)[1]	27	21	3	3	62	19	43	66
B36 Torshavn[2]	27	20	3	4	53	23	30	63
NSI Runavik[2]	27	18	3	6	65	31	34	57
HB Torshavn[2]	27	15	6	6	62	28	34	51
Vikingur	27	16	3	8	51	35	16	51
Skala	27	12	1	14	38	32	6	37
Argja Boltfelag	27	6	3	18	32	66	–34	21
TB Tvoroyri	27	5	4	18	20	57	–37	19
EB/Streymur	27	5	3	19	25	63	–38	18
IF Fuglafjordur	27	1	3	23	27	81	–54	6

No relegation as top three in second tier were all reserve teams.
Top scorer: Olsen (NSI Runavik) 26.
Cup Final: HB Torshavn 3, Vikingur 1.

FINLAND

Suomen Palloliitto Finlands Bollfoerbund, Urheilukatu 5, PO Box 191, 00251 Helsinki.
Founded: 1907. *FIFA:* 1908; *UEFA:* 1954. *National Colours:* White shirts with blue trim, white shorts, white socks.

International matches 2019–20

Greece (h) 1-0, Italy (h) 1-2, Bosnia-Herzegovina (a) 1-4, Armenia (h) 3-0, Liechtenstein (h) 3-0, Greece (a) 1-2.

League Championship wins (1908–2019)

HJK Helsinki 29; HPS Helsinki 9; FC Haka Valkeakoski 9; TPS Turku 8; HIFK Helsinki 7; KuPS Kuopio 6; Kuusysi Lahti 5; KIF Helsinki 4; AIFK Turku 3; VIFK Vaasa 3; Reipas Lahti 3; Tampere United 3; VPS Vaasa 2; KTP Kotka 2; OPS Oulu 2; Jazz Pori 2; Unitas Helsinki 1; PUS Helsinki 1; Sudet Viipuri 1; HT Helsinki 1; Ilves-Kissat 1; Pyrkiva Turku 1; KPV Kokkola 1; Ilves Tampere 1; TPV Tampere 1; MyPa Anjalankoski (renamed MYPA-47) 1; Inter Turku 1; SJK Seinajoki 1; IFK Mariehamn 1.

Cup wins (1955–2019)

HJK Helsinki 13; FC Haka Valkeakoski 12; Reipas Lahti 7; KTP Kotka 4; Ilves Tampere 3; TPS Turku 3; MyPa Anjalankoski (renamed MYPA-47) 3; KuPS Kuopio 2; Mikkeli 2; Kuusysi Lahti 2; RoPS Rovaniemi 2; Inter Turku 2; Pallo-Pojat 1; Drott (renamed Jaro) 1; HPS Helsinki 1; AIFK Turku 1; Jokerit (formerly PK-35) 1; Atlantis 1; Tampere United 1; FC Honka 1; IFK Mariehamn 1; SJK Seinajoki 1.

Finnish Veikkausliiga Qualifying Table 2019

	P	W	D	L	F	A	GD	Pts
Inter Turku	22	13	3	6	39	25	14	42
KuPS Kuopio	22	11	7	4	39	23	16	40
Ilves Tampere	22	11	7	4	29	18	11	40
HJK Helsinki	22	8	10	4	28	22	6	34
FC Honka	22	10	4	8	31	27	4	34
IFK Mariehamn	22	9	4	9	29	23	6	31
SJK Seinajoki	22	7	7	8	17	23	–6	28
FC Lahti	22	7	7	8	21	29	–8	28
HIFK Helsinki	22	6	8	8	25	29	–4	26
RoPS Rovaniemi	22	6	6	10	19	25	–6	24
KPV Kokkola	22	4	4	14	19	39	–20	16
VPS Vaasa	22	2	9	11	22	35	–13	15

Championship Round 2019

	P	W	D	L	F	A	GD	Pts
KuPS Kuopio (C)[1]	27	15	8	4	46	24	22	53
Inter Turku[2]	27	15	3	9	42	29	13	48
FC Honka‡[2]	27	14	5	8	41	29	12	47
Ilves Tampere[2]	27	13	8	6	34	25	9	47
HJK Helsinki†	27	9	10	8	33	29	4	37
IFK Mariehamn†	27	9	5	13	31	34	–3	32

Relegation Round 2019

	P	W	D	L	F	A	GD	Pts
HIFK Helsinki†	27	10	9	8	37	34	3	39
FC Lahti†	27	9	9	9	29	36	–7	36
SJK Seinajoki	27	7	9	11	18	29	–11	30
RoPS Rovaniemi	27	8	6	13	23	35	–12	30
KPV Kokkola*+	27	7	4	16	32	47	–15	25
VPS Vaasa*	27	3	10	14	30	45	–15	19

†Qualified for Europa League play-offs. ‡Qualified for Europa League play-off final.

Europa League Play-offs

Round 1
HJK Helsinki 2, FC Lahti 2 (aet, 4-2p)
IFK Mariehamn 0, HIFK Helsinki 0 (aet, 4-2p)
Round 2
HJK Helsinki 1, IFK Mariehamn 2 (aet)
Europa League Play-off final
IFK Mariehamn 1, 0, FC Honka 2, 1 (agg. 1-3)
Top scorer: Valencic (Inter Turku) 16.
Cup Final: Final match still to be played.

FRANCE

Federation Francaise de Football, 87 Boulevard de Grenelle, 75738 Paris Cedex 15.
Founded: 1919. *FIFA:* 1904; *UEFA:* 1954. *National Colours:* Blue shirts, white shorts, red socks.

International matches 2019–20

Albania (h) 4-1, Andorra (h) 3-0, Iceland (a) 1-0, Turkey (h) 1-1, Moldova (h) 2-1, Albania (a) 0-2.

League Championship wins (1933–2020)

Saint-Etienne 10; Olympique Marseille 9; Paris Saint-Germain 9; AS Monaco 8; Nantes 8; Olympique Lyonnais 7; Stade de Reims 6; Bordeaux 6; Lille OSC (includes Olympique Lillois) 4; OGC Nice 4; FC Sete 2; Sochaux 2; Racing Club Paris 1; Roubaix-Tourcoing 1; Strasbourg 1; Auxerre 1; Lens 1; Montpellier 1.

Cup wins (1918–2020)

Paris Saint-Germain 13; Olympique Marseille 10; Lille OSC 6; Saint-Etienne 6; Red Star 5; Racing Club Paris 5; AS Monaco 5; Olympique Lyonnais 5; Bordeaux 4; Auxerre 4; Strasbourg 3; OGC Nice 3; Stade Rennais 3; Nantes 3; CAS Genereaux 2; Montpellier 2; FC Sete 2; Sochaux 2; Stade de Reims 2; Sedan 2; Metz 2; Guingamp 2; Olympique de Pantin 1; CA Paris 1; Club Français 1; AS Cannes 1; Excelsior Roubaix 1; EF Nancy-Lorraine 1; Toulouse 1; Le Havre 1; AS Nancy 1; Bastia 1; Lorient 1.

French Ligue 1 2019–20

	P	W	D	L	F	A	GD	Pts
Paris Saint-Germain (C)[1]	27	22	2	3	75	24	51	68
Marseille[1]	28	16	8	4	41	29	12	56
Rennes[1]	28	15	5	8	38	24	14	50
Lille[2]	28	15	4	9	35	27	8	49
Nice[2]	28	11	8	9	41	38	3	41
Reims[2]	28	10	11	7	26	21	5	41
Lyon	28	11	7	10	42	27	15	40
Montpellier	28	11	7	10	35	34	1	40
AS Monaco	28	11	7	10	44	44	0	40
Strasbourg	27	11	5	11	32	32	0	38
Angers	28	11	6	11	28	33	–5	39
Bordeaux	28	9	10	9	40	34	6	37
Nantes	28	11	4	13	28	31	–3	37
Brest	28	8	10	10	34	37	–3	34
Metz	28	8	10	10	27	35	–8	34
Dijon	28	7	9	12	27	37	–10	30
Saint-Etienne	28	8	6	14	29	45	–16	30
Nimes	28	7	6	15	29	44	–15	27
Amiens*	28	4	11	13	31	50	–19	23
Toulouse*	28	3	4	21	22	58	–36	13

Competition abandoned due to COVID-19 pandemic. Final standings based on points-per-match average; tied averages decided on head-to-head results (if both matches between the clubs were played). Only two teams relegated to second tier.

Top scorers (joint): Ben Yedder (AS Monaco), Mbappe (Paris Saint-Germain) 18.

Cup Final: Paris Saint-Germain 1, Saint-Etienne 0.

GEORGIA

Georgian Football Federation, 76A Chavchavadze Avenue, 0179 Tbilisi.

Founded: 1990. *FIFA:* 1992; *UEFA:* 1992. *National Colours:* All white with red trim.

International matches 2019–20

Korea Republic (n) 2-2, Denmark (h) 0-0, Republic of Ireland (h) 0-0, Gibraltar (a) 3-2, Switzerland (a) 0-1, Croatia (a) 1-2.

League Championship wins (1990–2019)

Dinamo Tbilisi 17; Torpedo Kutaisi 4; WIT Georgia 2; Olimpi Rustavi (now FC Rustavi) 2; Zestafoni 2; Sioni Bolnisi 1; Dila Gori 1; Samtredia 1; Saburtalo 1.

Cup wins (1990–2019)

Dinamo Tbilisi 13; Torpedo Kutaisi 4; Lokomotivi Tbilisi 3; Ameri Tbilisi 2; Guria Lanchkhuti 1; Dinamo Batumi 1; Zestafoni 1; WIT Georgia 1; Gagra 1; Dila Gori 1; Chikhura Sachkhere 1; Saburtalo 1.

See also Russia section for Georgian club honours in Soviet era 1936–91.

Georgian Erovnuli Liga 2019

	P	W	D	L	F	A	GD	Pts
Dinamo Tbilisi (C)[1]	36	23	6	7	70	31	39	75
Dinamo Batumi‡[2]	36	21	7	8	57	31	26	70
Saburtalo‡[2]	36	21	7	8	67	36	31	70
Lokomotivi Tbilisi[2]	36	17	4	15	44	46	–2	55
Chikhura Sachkhere	36	12	11	13	48	44	4	47
Torpedo Kutaisi	36	12	8	16	53	54	–1	44
Dila Gori	36	11	10	15	40	44	–4	43
Rustavi§*+	36	9	11	16	40	56	–16	38
Sioni Bolnisi§*+	36	10	8	18	38	80	–42	38
WIT Georgia*	36	4	8	24	15	50	–35	20

‡Ranking decided on head-to-head points. §Ranking decided on head-to-head away goals scored.

Top scorer: Kutalia (Dinamo Tbilisi) 20.

Cup Final: Saburtalo 3, Lokomotivi Tbilisi 1.

GERMANY

Deutscher Fussball-Bund, Hermann-Neuberger-Haus, Otto-Fleck-Schneise 6, 60528 Frankfurt Am Main.

Founded: 1900. *FIFA:* 1904; *UEFA:* 1954. *National Colours:* White shirts with red and black trim, white shorts, white socks with red tops.

International matches 2019–20

Netherlands (h) 2-4, Northern Ireland (a) 2-0, Argentina (h) 2-2, Estonia (a) 3-0, Belarus (h) 4-0, Northern Ireland (h) 6-1.

League Championship wins (1903–2020)

Bayern Munich 29; 1.FC Nuremberg 9; Borussia Dortmund 8; Schalke 04 7; Hamburger SV 6; VfB Stuttgart 5; Borussia Moenchengladbach 5; 1.FC Kaiserslautern 4; Werder Bremen 4; 1.FC Lokomotive Leipzig 3; SpVgg Greuther Furth 3; 1.FC Cologne 3; Viktoria Berlin 2; Hertha Berlin 2; Hannover 96 2; Dresden SC 2; Union Berlin 1; Freiburger FC 1; Phoenix Karlsruhe 1; Karlsruher FV 1; Holstein Kiel 1; Fortuna Dusseldorf 1; Rapid Vienna 1; VfR Mannheim 1; Rot-Weiss Essen 1; Eintracht Frankfurt 1; Munich 1860 1; Eintracht Braunschweig 1; VfL Wolfsburg 1.

Cup wins (1935–2020)

Bayern Munich 20; Werder Bremen 6; Schalke 04 5; Eintracht Frankfurt 5; 1.FC Nuremberg 4; Borussia Dortmund 4; 1.FC Cologne 4; VfB Stuttgart 3; Borussia Moenchengladbach 3; Hamburger SV 3; Dresden SC 2; Munich 1860 2; Karlsruhe SC 2; Fortuna Dusseldorf 2; 1.FC Kaiserslautern 2; 1.FC Lokomotive Leipzig 1; Rapid Vienna 1; First Vienna 1; Rot-Weiss Essen 1; SW Essen 1; Kickers Offenbach 1; Bayer Uerdingen 1; Hannover 96 1; Bayer Leverkusen 1; VfLWolfsburg 1.

German Bundesliga 2019–20

	P	W	D	L	F	A	GD	Pts
Bayern Munich (C)[1]	34	26	4	4	100	32	68	82
Borussia Dortmund[1]	34	21	6	7	84	41	43	69
RB Leipzig[1]	34	18	12	4	81	37	44	66
Borussia M'gladbach[1]	34	20	5	9	66	40	26	65
Bayer Leverkusen[2]	34	19	6	9	61	44	17	63
TSG 1899 Hoffenheim[2]	34	15	7	12	53	53	0	52
Wolfsburg[2]	34	13	10	11	48	46	2	49
Freiburg	34	13	9	12	48	47	1	48
Eintracht Frankfurt	34	13	6	15	59	60	–1	45
Hertha Berlin	34	11	8	15	48	59	–11	41
Union Berlin	34	12	5	17	41	58	–17	41
Schalke 04	34	9	12	13	38	58	–20	39
Mainz 05	34	11	4	19	44	65	–21	37
Cologne	34	10	6	18	51	69	–18	36
Augsburg	34	9	9	16	45	63	–18	36
Werder Bremen+	34	8	7	19	42	69	–27	31
Fortuna Dusseldorf*	34	6	12	16	36	67	–31	30
Paderborn*	34	4	8	22	37	74	–37	20

Top scorer: Lewandowski (Bayern Munich) 34.

Cup Final: Bayern Munich 4, Bayer Leverkusen 2.

GIBRALTAR

Gibraltar Football Association, Bayside Sports Complex, PO Box 513, Gibraltar GX11 1AA.

Founded: 1895. *UEFA:* 2013. *National Colours:* Red shirts with white trim, red shorts, red socks.

International matches 2019–20

Georgia (a) 0-3*, Denmark (h) 0-6, Switzerland (a) 0-4, Kosovo (a) 0-1, Georgia (h) 2-3, Denmark (a) 0-6, Switzerland (h) 1-6.

**Played 7.06.2019, result omitted from last edition.*

League Championship wins (1896–2020)*

Lincoln Red Imps 24 (incl. Newcastle United 5; 1 title shared); Prince of Wales 19; Glacis United 17 (incl. 1 shared); Britannia (now Britannia XI) 14; Gibraltar United 11; Europa 7; Manchester United (now Manchester 62) 7; St Theresa's 3; Chief Construction 2; Jubilee 2; Exiles 2; South United 2; Gibraltar FC 2; Albion 1; Athletic 1; Royal Sovereign 1; Commander of the Yard 1; St Joseph's 1.

**No winner in 2019–20.*

Cup wins (1895–2020)*

Lincoln Red Imps (incl. Newcastle United 4) 17; St Joseph's 9; Europa 8; Glacis United 5; Britannia (now Britannia XI) 3; Gibraltar United 3; Manchester United (now Manchester 62) 3; Gibraltar FC 1; HMS Hood 1; 2nd Bn The King's Regt 1; AARA 1; RAF New Camp 1; 4th Bn Royal Scots 1; Prince of Wales 1; Manchester United Reserves 1; 2nd Bn Royal Green Jackets 1; RAF Gibraltar 1; St Theresa's 1.

**No winner in 2019–20.*

Gibraltarian Premier Division Qualifying Table 2019–20

	P	W	D	L	F	A	GD	Pts
Europa	11	10	1	0	58	8	50	31
St Joseph's	11	9	2	0	43	5	38	29
Lincoln Red Imps	11	9	0	2	48	9	39	27
Lynx	11	7	2	2	28	11	17	23
Magpies	11	6	0	5	22	21	1	18
Lions Gibraltar	11	4	3	4	22	25	–3	15
Mons Calpe	11	4	2	5	24	27	–3	14
Manchester 62	11	3	1	7	10	29	–19	10
Boca Juniors	11	2	3	6	16	29	–13	9
Europa Point	11	2	2	7	12	25	–13	8
Glacis United	11	2	0	9	15	47	–32	6
College 1975	11	0	0	11	5	67	–62	0

Championship Round 2019–20

	P	W	D	L	F	A	GD	Pts
Europa[1]	17	16	1	0	85	9	76	49
St Joseph's[2]	17	14	2	1	58	15	43	44
Lincoln Red Imps[2]	17	13	0	4	68	15	53	39
Lynx	17	9	2	6	37	30	7	29
Magpies	17	7	0	10	29	41	–12	21
Lions Gibraltar	17	4	3	10	30	55	–25	15

Lower Table Round 2019–20

	P	W	D	L	F	A	GD	Pts
Mons Calpe	18	10	3	5	49	29	20	33
Europa Point	18	7	4	7	35	38	–3	25
Manchester 62	18	6	1	11	21	49	–28	19
Boca Juniors	17	4	4	9	30	45	–15	16
Glacis United	17	3	1	13	21	56	–35	10
College 1975	18	0	1	17	18	99	–81	1

League curtailed due to COVID-19 pandemic. Title not awarded; no relegation to second tier.
Top scorer: Juanfri (St Joseph's) 24.
Cup Final: Competition abandoned due to COVID-19 pandemic.

GOZO

Gozo Football Association, GFA Headquarters, Mgarr Road, Xewkija, XWK 9014, Malta. (Not a member of FIFA or UEFA.)
Founded: 1936.

League Championship wins (1938–2020)
Victoria Hotspurs 13; Nadur Youngsters 12; Sannat Lions 10; Xewkija Tigers 8; Ghajnsielem 7; Xaghra United 6 (incl. Xaghra Blue Stars 1, Xaghra Young Stars 1); Salesian Youths (renamed Oratory Youths) 6; Victoria Athletics 4; Victoria Stars 1; Victoria City 1; Calypcians 1; Victoria United (renamed Victoria Wanderers) 1; Kercem Ajax 1; Zebbug Rovers 1.

Cup wins (1972–2020)*
Xewkija Tigers 11; Sannat Lions 9; Nadur Youngsters 8; Ghajnsielem 6; Xaghra United 4; Victoria Hotspurs 2; Kercem Ajax 2; Calypsians 1; Calypsians Bosco Youths 1; Qala St Joseph 1; Victoria Wanderers 1.
**No winner in 2019–20.*

Gozitan L-Ewwel Divizjoni 2019–20

	P	W	D	L	F	A	GD	Pts
Nadur Youngsters (C)	15	14	0	1	48	6	42	42
Xewkija Tigers	15	11	1	3	46	19	27	34
Victoria Hotspurs	15	9	1	5	40	18	22	28
Ghajnsielem	15	8	1	6	31	26	5	25
Kercem Ajax	15	6	1	8	20	31	–11	19
Xaghra United	15	3	2	10	17	45	–28	11
Victoria Wanderers	15	3	1	11	10	27	–17	10
Gharb Rangers*	15	2	1	12	16	56	–40	7

Competition curtailed due to COVID-19 pandemic. Nadur Youngsters declared champions. No mandatory relegation, but Gharb Rangers opted to play in second tier.
Top scorer: Nedeljkovic (Ghajnsielem) 20.
Cup Final: Competition abandoned due to COVID-19 pandemic.

GREECE

Hellenic Football Federation, Parko Goudi, PO Box 14161, 11510 Athens.
Founded: 1926. *FIFA:* 1927; *UEFA:* 1954. *National Colours:* All white.

International matches 2019–20
Finland (a) 0-1, Liechtenstein (h) 1-1, Italy (a) 0-2, Bosnia-Herzegovina (h) 2-1, Armenia (a) 1-0, Finland (h) 2-1.

League Championship wins (1927–2020)
Olympiacos 45; Panathinaikos 20; AEK Athens 12; Aris Salonika 3; PAOK 3; Larissa 1.

Cup wins (1932–2019)
Olympiacos 27; Panathinaikos 18; AEK Athens 15; PAOK 7; Panionios 2; Larissa 2; Ethnikos 1; Aris Salonika 1; Iraklis 1; Kastoria 1; OFI Crete 1.

Greek Super League Qualifying Table 2019–20

	P	W	D	L	F	A	GD	Pts
Olympiacos	26	20	6	0	53	9	44	66
PAOK	26	18	5	3	50	23	27	59
AEK Athens	26	15	6	5	42	22	20	51
Panathinaikos	26	12	8	6	35	23	12	44
OFI Crete	26	10	4	12	35	35	0	34
Aris	26	8	10	8	38	32	6	34
Atromitos	26	9	5	12	31	36	–5	32
Larissa	26	7	9	10	28	33	–5	30
Asteras Tripolis	26	8	6	12	33	37	–4	30
Lamia	26	5	12	9	19	33	–14	27
Volos	26	7	6	13	23	42	–19	27
Xanthi	26	8	6	12	21	32	–11	18
Panaitolikos	26	3	8	15	20	42	–22	17
Panionios (–6)	26	4	5	17	16	45	–29	11

Championship Round 2019–20

	P	W	D	L	F	A	GD	Pts
Olympiacos (C)[1]	36	28	7	1	74	16	58	91
PAOK[1]	36	21	10	5	58	29	29	73
AEK Athens[2]	36	20	9	7	59	32	27	69
Panathinaikos†	36	15	13	8	43	32	11	58
Aris[2]	36	10	12	14	48	51	–3	42
OFI[2]	36	10	6	20	43	56	–13	36

†Panathinaikos banned from European competition for 2020–21.

Relegation Round 2019–20

	P	W	D	L	F	A	GD	Pts
Asteras Tripolis	33	11	10	12	44	42	2	43
Atromitos	33	11	9	13	41	43	–2	42
Larissa	33	8	12	13	32	42	–10	36
Lamia	33	6	17	10	23	36	–13	35
Volos	33	8	7	18	27	54	–27	31
Panaitolikos	33	6	11	16	30	48	–18	29
Xanthi*+	33	9	9	15	25	38	–13	24
Panionios* (–6)	33	7	8	18	20	48	–28	23

Panionios deducted 6pts for breach of licensing rule.
Top scorer: El-Arabi (Olympiacos) 20.
Cup Final: Final match still to be played.

HUNGARY

Magyar Labdarugo Szovetseg, Kanai ut 2. D, 1112 Budapest.
Founded: 1901. *FIFA:* 1907; *UEFA:* 1954. *National Colours:* Red shirts, white shorts, green socks.

International matches 2019–20
Montenegro (a) 1-2, Slovakia (h) 1-2, Croatia (a) 0-3, Azerbaijan (h) 1-0, Uruguay (h) 1-2, Wales (a) 0-2.

League Championship wins (1901–2020)
Ferencvaros 31; MTK Budapest 23; Ujpest 20; Budapest Honved 14 (incl. Kispest Honved); Debrecen 7; Vasas 6; Csepel 4; Gyor 4; Videoton (renamed Fehervar) 3; Budapesti TC 2; Nagyvarad 1; Vac 1; Dunaferr (renamed Dunaujvaros) 1; Zalaegerszeg 1.

Cup wins (1910–2020)
Ferencvaros 23; MTK Budapest 12; Ujpest 10; Budapest Honved 8 (inc. Kispest Honved); Debrecen 6; Vasas 4; Gyor 4; Diosgyor 2; Fehervar (incl. Videoton 1, Vidi 1) 2; Bocskai 1; III Keruleti TUE 1; Soroksar 1; Szolnoki MAV 1; Siofoki Banyasz 1; Bekescsaba 1; Pecsi 1; Sopron 1; Kecskemet 1.
Cup not regularly held until 1964.

Hungarian Nemzeti Bajnoksag I 2019–20

	P	W	D	L	F	A	GD	Pts
Ferencvaros (C)[1]	33	23	7	3	58	24	34	76
Fehervar[2]	33	18	9	6	56	29	27	63
Puskas Akademia[2]	33	14	12	7	52	41	11	54
Mezokovesd	33	14	8	11	42	31	11	50
Budapest Honved[2]	33	12	8	13	36	44	–8	44
Ujpest‡	33	12	7	14	45	45	0	43
Zalaegerszeg‡	33	11	10	12	51	44	7	43
Kisvarda	33	12	6	15	42	43	–1	42
Diosgyor‡	33	12	5	16	40	52	–12	41
Paks‡	33	11	8	14	46	53	–7	41
Debrecen*	33	11	6	16	48	57	–9	39
Kaposvari Rakoczi*	33	4	2	27	27	80	–53	14

‡Ranking decided on matches won.
Top scorer: Rado (Zalaegerszeg) 13.
Cup Final: Budapest Honved 2, Mezokovesd 1.

ICELAND

Knattspyrnusamband Islands, Laugardal, 104 Reykjavik.
Founded: 1947. *FIFA:* 1947; *UEFA:* 1954. *National Colours:* All blue.

International matches 2019–20
Moldova (h) 3-0, Albania (a) 2-4, France (h) 0-1, Andorra (h) 2-0, Turkey (a) 0-0, Moldova (a) 2-1, Canada (n) 1-0, El Salvador (n) 1-0.

League Championship wins (1912–2019)
KR Reykjavik 27; Valur 22; Fram 18; IA Akranes 18; FH Hafnarfjordur 8; Vikingur 5; IBK Keflavik 4; IBV Vestmannaeyjar 3; KA Akureyri 1; Breidablik 1 ; Stjarnan 1.

Cup wins (1960–2019)
KR Reykjavik 14; Valur 11; IA Akranes 9; Fram 8; IBV Vestmannaeyjar 5; IBK Keflavik 4; Vikingur 2; Fylkir 2; FH Hafnarfjordur 2; IBA Akureyri 1; Breidablik 1; Stjarnan 1.

Icelandic Urvalsdeild karla 2019

	P	W	D	L	F	A	GD	Pts
KR Reykjavik (C)[1]	22	16	4	2	44	23	21	52
Breidablik[2]	22	11	5	8	45	31	14	38
FH Hafnarfjordur[2]	22	11	4	7	40	36	4	37
Stjarnan	22	9	8	5	40	34	6	35
KA	22	9	4	9	34	34	0	31
Valur	22	8	5	9	38	34	4	29
Vikingur[2]	22	7	7	8	37	35	2	28
Fylkir	22	8	4	10	38	44	–6	28
HK Kopavogur	22	7	6	9	29	29	0	27
IA Akranes	22	7	6	9	27	32	–5	27
Grindavik*	22	3	11	8	17	28	–11	20
IBV Vestmannaeyjar*	22	2	4	16	23	52	–29	10

Top scorer: Martin (IBV Vestmannaeyjar incl. 2 for Valur) 14.
Cup Final: Vikingur 1, FH Hafnarfjordur 0.

ISRAEL

Israel Football Association, Ramat Gan Stadium, 299 Aba Hilell Street, PO Box 3591, Ramat Gan 52134.
Founded: 1928. *FIFA:* 1929; *UEFA:* 1994. *National Colours:* Blue shirts with white trim, blue shorts, blue socks.

International matches 2019–20
North Macedonia (h) 1-1, Slovenia (a) 2-3, Austria (a) 1-3, Latvia (h) 3-1, Poland (h) 1-2, North Macedonia (a) 0-1.

League Championship wins (1932–2020)
Maccabi Tel Aviv 23; Hapoel Tel Aviv 14 (incl. 1 shared); Maccabi Haifa 12; Hapoel Petah Tikva 6; Beitar Jerusalem 6; Maccabi Netanya 5; Hapoel Be'er Sheva 5; Hakoah Amidar Ramat Gan 2; British Police 1; Beitar Tel Aviv 1 (shared); Hapoel Ramat Gan 1; Hapoel Kfar Saba 1; Bnei Yehuda 1; Hapoel Haifa 1; Ironi Kiryat Shmona 1.

Cup wins (1928–2020)
Maccabi Tel Aviv 23; Hapoel Tel Aviv 15; Beitar Jerusalem 7; Maccabi Haifa 6; Hapoel Haifa 4; Bnei Yehuda 4; Hapoel Kfar Saba 3; Maccabi Petah Tikva 2; Beitar Tel Aviv 2; Hapoel Petah Tikva 2; Hakoah Amidar Ramat Gan 2; Hapoel Ramat Gan 2; Hapoel Be'er Sheva 2; Maccabi Hashmonai Jerusalem 1; British Police 1; Hapoel Jerusalem 1; Maccabi Netanya 1; Hapoel Yehud 1; Hapoel Lod 1; Bnei Sakhnin 1; Ironi Kiryat Shmona 1.

Israeli Premier League Qualifying Table 2019–20

	P	W	D	L	F	A	GD	Pts
Maccabi Tel Aviv	26	19	7	0	48	7	41	64
Maccabi Haifa	26	18	4	4	58	20	38	58
Beitar Jerusalem	26	15	4	7	42	25	17	49
Hapoel Be'er Sheva	26	13	5	8	33	23	10	44
Hapoel Tel Aviv	26	11	5	10	24	36	–12	38
Hapoel Haifa	26	10	7	9	26	30	–4	37
Bnei Yehuda	26	9	7	10	23	26	–3	34
Hapoel Hadera	26	9	7	10	24	28	–4	34
Maccabi Netanya	26	8	7	11	23	32	–9	31
Ashdod	26	6	10	10	30	33	–3	28
Hapoel Kfar Saba	26	7	5	14	22	35	–13	26
Ironi Kiryat Shmona	26	6	4	16	24	35	–11	22
Sektzia Nes Tziona	26	5	6	15	17	40	–23	21
Hapoel Ra'anana	26	2	10	14	20	44	–24	16

Championship Round 2019–20

	P	W	D	L	F	A	GD	Pts
Maccabi Tel Aviv (C)[1]	36	26	9	1	63	10	53	87
Maccabi Haifa[2]	36	22	7	7	73	32	41	73
Beitar Jerusalem[2]	36	16	11	9	51	35	16	59
Hapoel Be'er Sheva[2]	36	15	10	11	44	33	11	55
Hapoel Tel Aviv	36	14	6	16	31	55	–24	48
Hapoel Haifa	36	12	11	13	39	46	–7	47

Relegation Round 2019–20

	P	W	D	L	F	A	GD	Pts
Bnei Yehuda	33	13	10	10	40	30	10	49
Ashdod	33	10	11	12	48	47	1	41
Hapoel Hadera	33	10	10	13	33	42	–9	40
Maccabi Netanya	33	11	7	15	35	46	–11	40
Hapoel Kfar Saba	33	10	8	15	28	38	–10	38
Ironi Kiryat Shmona	33	9	5	19	30	43	–13	32
Sektzia Nes Tziona*	33	8	8	17	23	46	–23	32
Hapoel Ra'anana*	33	2	11	20	27	62	–35	17

Top scorer: Rukavytsya (Maccabi Haifa) 22.
Cup Final: Hapoel Be'er Sheva 2, Maccabi Petah Tikva 0.

ITALY

Federazione Italiana Giuoco Calcio, Via Gregorio Allegri 14, 00198 Roma.
Founded: 1898. *FIFA:* 1905; *UEFA:* 1954. *National Colours:* Blue shirts, white shorts, blue socks with white tops.

International matches 2019–20
Armenia (a) 3-1, Finland (a) 2-1, Greece (h) 2-0, Liechtenstein (a) 5-0, Bosnia-Herzegovina (a) 3-0, Armenia (h) 9-1.

League Championship wins (1898–2020)
Juventus 36 (excludes two titles revoked); AC Milan 18; Internazionale 18 (includes one title awarded); Genoa 9; Pro Vercelli 7; Bologna 7; Torino 7 (excludes one title revoked); Roma 3; Fiorentina 2; Lazio 2; Napoli 2; Casale 1; Novese 1; Cagliari 1; Hellas Verona 1; Sampdoria 1.

Cup wins (1928–2020)
Juventus 13; Roma 9; Internazionale 7; Lazio 7; Fiorentina 6; Napoli 6; Torino 5; AC Milan 5; Sampdoria 4; Parma 3; Bologna 2; Vado 1; Genoa 1; Venezia 1; Atalanta 1; Vicenza 1.

Italian Serie A 2019–20

	P	W	D	L	F	A	GD	Pts
Juventus (C)[1]	38	26	5	7	76	43	33	83
Internazionale[1]	38	24	10	4	81	36	45	82
Atalanta‡[1]	38	23	9	6	98	48	50	78
Lazio‡[1]	38	24	6	8	79	42	37	78
Roma[2]	38	21	7	10	77	51	26	70
AC Milan[2]	38	19	9	10	63	46	17	66
Napoli[2]	38	18	8	12	61	50	11	62
Sassuolo	38	14	9	15	69	63	6	51
Hellas Verona‡	38	12	13	13	47	51	–4	49
Fiorentina‡	38	12	13	13	51	48	3	49
Parma‡	38	14	7	17	56	57	–1	49
Bologna	38	12	11	15	52	65	–13	47
Udinese‡	38	12	9	17	37	51	–14	45
Cagliari‡	38	11	12	15	52	56	–4	45
Sampdoria	38	12	6	20	48	65	–17	42
Torino	38	11	7	20	46	68	–22	40
Genoa	38	10	9	19	47	73	–26	39
Lecce*	38	9	8	21	52	85	–33	35
Brescia*	38	6	7	25	35	79	–44	25
SPAL 2013*	38	5	5	28	27	77	–50	20

‡Ranking decided on head-to-head points.
Top scorer: Immobile (Lazio) 36.
Cup Final: Napoli 0, Juventus 0.
Napoli won 4-2 on penalties.

KAZAKHSTAN

Football Federation of Kazakhstan, 29 Syganak Street, 9th floor, 010000 Astana.
Founded: 1914. *FIFA:* 1994; *UEFA:* 2002. *National Colours:* All yellow.

International matches 2019–20
Cyprus (a) 1-1, Russia (a) 0-1, Cyprus (h) 1-2, Belgium (h) 0-2, San Marino (a) 3-1, Scotland (a) 1-3.

League Championship wins (1992–2019)
Astana 6; Irtysh Pavlodar (includes Ansat) 5; Aktobe 5; Yelimay (renamed Spartak Semey) 3; FC Astana-64 (includes Zhenis) 3; Kairat 2; Shakhter Karagandy 2; Taraz 1; Tobol 1.

Cup wins (1992–2019)
Kairat 9; FC Astana-64 (incl. Zhenis) 3; Astana (incl. Lokomotiv) 3; Kaisar 2; Dostyk 1; Vostok 1; Yelimay (renamed Spartak Semey) 1; Irtysh Pavlodar 1; Taraz 1; Almaty 1; Tobol 1; Aktobe 1; Atyrau 1; Ordabasy 1; Shakhter Karagandy 1.

Kazakh Premer Ligasy 2019

	P	W	D	L	F	A	GD	Pts
Astana (C)[1]	33	22	3	8	67	28	39	69
Kairat[2]	33	22	2	9	65	32	33	68
Ordabasy[2]	33	19	8	6	52	24	28	65
Tobol	33	19	6	8	45	27	18	63
Zhetysu	33	16	8	9	45	25	20	56
Kaisar[2]	33	12	6	15	37	43	–6	42
Okhzetpes	33	11	7	15	44	49	–5	40
Irtysh Pavlodar	33	11	4	18	30	45	–15	37
Shakhter Karagandy	33	9	8	16	40	47	–7	35
Taraz+	33	7	8	18	28	60	–32	29
Atyrau*	33	6	8	19	25	58	–33	26
Aktobe* (–12)	33	7	6	20	35	75	–40	15

Aktobe deducted 12pts for unpaid wages.
Top scorers (joint): Eseola (Kairat), Tomasov (Astana) 19.
Cup Final: Kaisar 2, Atyrau 1.

KOSOVO

Football Federation of Kosovo, Rruga Agim Ramadani 45, Prishtina, Kosovo 10000. *Founded:* 1946. *FIFA:* 2016; *UEFA:* 2016. *National Colours:* All blue.

International matches 2019–20

Czech Republic (h) 2-1, England (a) 3-5, Gibraltar (h) 1-0, Montenegro (h) 2-0, Czech Republic (a) 1-2, England (h) 0-4.

League Championship wins (1945–97; 1999–2020)

Prishtina 14; Vellaznimi 9; KF Trepca 7; Liria 5; Buduqnosti 4; Rudari 3; Red Star 3; Drita 3; Besa Peje 3; Feronikeli 3; Jedinstvo 2; Kosova Prishtina 2; Slloga 2; Obiliqi 2; Fushe-Kosova 2; Proletari 1; KXEK Kosova 1; Rudniku 1; KNI Ramiz Sadiku 1; Dukagjini 1; Besiana 1; Hysi 1; Vushtrria 1; Trepca'89 1.

Cup wins (1992–2020)

Prishtina 7; Besa Peje 3; Feronikeli 3; Flamurtari 2; Liria 2; KF Trepca 1; KF 2 Korriku 1; Gjilani 1; Drita 1; Besiana 1; KEK-u 1; Kosova Prishtina 1; Vellaznimi 1; Hysi 1; Trepca'89 1.

Kosovar Superliga 2019–20

	P	*W*	*D*	*L*	*F*	*A*	*GD*	*Pts*
Drita (C)[1]	33	21	5	7	57	23	34	68
Gjilani[2]	33	21	5	7	61	27	34	68
Ballkani	33	19	10	4	59	25	34	67
Prishtina[2]	33	18	8	7	59	25	34	62
Feronikeli	33	14	5	14	50	40	10	47
Llapi	33	13	6	14	51	62	–11	45
Trepça'89	33	12	8	13	55	55	0	44
Drenica Skenderaj	33	12	8	13	39	40	–1	44
Flamurtari*	33	12	7	14	42	56	–14	43
Ferizaj*	33	9	2	22	34	70	–36	29
Vushtrria*	33	5	6	22	34	76	–42	21
Dukagjini*	33	5	4	24	27	69	–42	19

Four clubs relegated as Superliga to reduce to 10 clubs in 2020–21.
Top scorer: Baftiu (Ballkani) 19.
Cup Final: Prishtina 1, Ballkani 0.

LATVIA

Latvijas Futbola Federacija, Olympic Sports Centre, Grostonas Street 6B, 1013 Riga.
Founded: 1921. *FIFA:* 1922; *UEFA:* 1992. *National Colours:* All carmine red.

International matches 2019–20

Austria (a) 0-6, North Macedonia (h) 0-2, Poland (h) 0-3, Israel (a) 1-3, Slovenia (a) 0-1, Austria (h) 1-0.

League Championship wins (1922–2019)

Skonto Riga 15; ASK Riga (incl. AVN 2) 11; Sarkanais Metalurgs Liepaja 9; RFK Riga 8; Olympija Liepaya 7; VEF Riga 6; Ventspils 6; Energija Riga (incl. ESR Riga 2) 4; Elektrons Riga (incl. Alfa 1) 4; Torpedo Riga 3; Keisermezhs Riga 2; Khimikis Daugavpils 2; RAF Yelgava 2; Daugava Liepaja 2; Liepajas Metalurgs 2; JPFS/Spartaks Jurmala 2; Riga FC 2; Dinamo Riga 1; Zhmilyeva Team 1; Darba Rezervi 1; RER Riga 1; Starts Brotseni 1; Venta Ventspils 1; Jumieks Riga 1; Gauja Valmiera 1; Daugava Daugavpils 1; FK Liepaja 1.

Cup wins (1937–2019)

Skonto Riga 8; ASK Riga 7 (includes AVN 3); Elektrons Riga 7; Ventspils 7; Sarkanais Metalurgs Liepaja 4; Jelgava 4; VEF Riga 3; Tseltnieks Riga 3; RAF Yelgava 3; RFK Riga 2; Daugava Liepaja 2; Starts Brotseni 2; Selmash Liepaya 2; Yurnieks Riga 2; Khimikis Daugavpils 2; Rigas Vilki 1; Dinamo Liepaya 1; Dinamo Riga 1; RER Riga 1; Voulkan Kouldiga 1; Baltika Liepaja 1; Venta Ventspils 1; Pilots Riga 1; Lielupe Yurmala 1; Energija Riga (formerly ESR Riga) 1; Torpedo Riga 1; Daugava SKIF Riga 1; Tseltnieks Daugavpils 1; Olympija Riga 1; FK Riga 1; Liepajas Metalurgs 1; Daugava Daugavpils 1; FK Liepaja 1; Riga FC 1; Rigas FS 1.

Latvian Virsliga 2019

	P	*W*	*D*	*L*	*F*	*A*	*GD*	*Pts*
Riga FC (C)[1]	32	20	6	6	59	21	38	66
Rigas FS[2]	32	17	8	7	55	32	23	59
Ventspils[2]	32	12	11	9	47	43	4	47
Valmiera[2]	32	12	10	10	37	34	3	46
Spartaks Jurmala	32	13	5	14	49	64	–15	44
FK Liepaja	32	11	6	15	41	43	–2	39
Jelgava	32	9	11	12	34	37	–3	38
Daugava Daugavpils	32	8	7	17	27	50	–23	31
Metta/LU+	32	6	8	18	35	60	–25	26

Top scorer: Lemajic (Rigas FS incl. 5 for Riga FC) 15.
Cup Final: Rigas FS 3, Jelgava 2.

LIECHTENSTEIN

Liechtensteiner Fussballverband, Landstrasse 149, 9494 Schaan.
Founded: 1934. *FIFA:* 1974; *UEFA:* 1974. *National Colours:* Blue shirts, red shorts, blue socks.

International matches 2019–20

Bosnia-Herzegovina (a) 0-5, Greece (a) 1-1, Armenia (h) 1-1, Italy (h) 0-5, Finland (a) 0-3, Bosnia-Herzegovina (h) 0-3.
Liechtenstein has no national league. Teams compete in Swiss regional leagues.

Cup wins (1937–2020)*

Vaduz 47; FC Balzers 11; FC Triesen 8; USV Eschen/Mauren 5; FC Schaan 3.
**No winner in 2019–20.*
Cup Final: Competition abandoned due to COVID-19 pandemic.

LITHUANIA

Lietuvos Futbolo Federacija, Stadiono g. 2, 02106 Vilnius.
Founded: 1922. *FIFA:* 1923; *UEFA:* 1992. *National Colours:* Yellow shirts, green shorts, yellow socks.

International matches 2019–20

Ukraine (h) 0-3, Portugal (h) 1-5, Ukraine (a) 0-2, Serbia (h) 1-2, Portugal (a) 0-6, New Zealand (h) 1-0.

League Championship wins (1990–2019)

FBK Kaunas 8 (incl. Zalgiris Kaunas 1); Zalgiris Vilnius 7; Ekranas 7; Suduva 3; Inkaras Kaunas 2; Kareda 2; Sirijus Klaipeda 1; Mazeikiai 1.

Cup wins (1990–2019)

Zalgiris Vilnius 12; Ekranas 4; FBK Kaunas 4; Suduva 3; Kareda 2; Atlantas 2; Sirijus Klaipeda 1; Lietuvos Makabi Vilnius (renamed Neris Vilnius) 1; Inkaras Kaunas 1; Stumbras 1.

Lithuanian A Lyga Qualifying Table 2019

	P	*W*	*D*	*L*	*F*	*A*	*GD*	*Pts*
Suduva	28	25	0	3	74	15	59	75
Zalgiris Vilnius	28	21	2	5	67	22	45	65
Riteriai	28	13	7	8	44	29	15	46
Kauno Zalgiris	28	13	5	10	48	39	9	44
Panevezys	28	8	7	13	41	53	–12	31
Atlantas†	28	7	5	16	26	53	–27	26
Palanga*+†	28	5	1	21	29	70	–41	19
Stumbras*‡	28	4	3	21	12	60	–48	15

†*Atlantas and Palanga disqualified post-season for match-fixing. Six clubs will contest league in 2020.*
‡*Stumbras had licence withdrawn mid-season; all subsequent matches recorded as 0-3 defeats.*

Championship Round 2019

	P	*W*	*D*	*L*	*F*	*A*	*GD*	*Pts*
Suduva (C)[1]	33	29	0	4	95	24	71	87
Zalgiris Vilnius[2]	33	24	2	7	79	29	50	74
Riteriai[2]	33	16	7	10	57	36	21	55
Kauno Zalgiris[2]	33	16	5	12	54	45	9	53
Panevezys	33	10	7	16	49	63	–14	37
Atlantas	33	7	5	21	30	78	–48	26

Top scorer: Kis (Zalgiris Vilnius) 27.
Cup Final: Suduva 4, Banga Gargzdai 0.

LUXEMBOURG

Federation Luxembourgeoise de Football, BP 5 Rue de Limpach, 3932 Mondercange.
Founded: 1908. *FIFA:* 1910; *UEFA:* 1954. *National Colours:* White shirts with blue trim, white shorts, white socks.

International matches 2019–20

Northern Ireland (a) 0-1, Serbia (h) 1-3, Portugal (a) 0-3, Denmark (a) 0-4, Serbia (a) 2-3, Portugal (h) 0-2.

League Championship wins (1910–2020)*

Jeunesse Esch 28; F91 Dudelange 15; Spora Luxembourg 11; Stade Dudelange 10; Fola Esch 7; Red Boys Differdange 6; Union Luxembourg 6; Avenir Beggen 6; US Hollerich-Bonnevoie 5; Progres NiederKorn 3; Aris Bonnevoie 3; Sporting Club 2; Racing Club 1; National Schifflange 1; Grevenmacher 1.
**No winner in 2019–20.*

Cup wins (1922–2020)*

Red Boys Differdange 15; Jeunesse Esch 13; Union Luxembourg 10; Spora Luxembourg 8; F91 Dudelange 8; Avenir Beggen 7; Progres Niederkorn 4; Stade Dudelange 4; Grevenmacher 4; Differdange 03 4; Fola Esch 3; Alliance Dudelange 2; US Rumelange 2; Racing Club 1; US

Dudelange 1; SC Tetange 1; National Schifflange 1; Aris Bonnevoie 1; Jeunesse Hautcharage 1; Swift Hesperange 1; Etzella Ettelbruck 1; CS Petange 1; Racing 1.
**No winner in 2019–20.*

Luxembourg Nationaldivisioun 2019–20

	P	*W*	*D*	*L*	*F*	*A*	*GD*	*Pts*
Fola Esch	17	12	3	2	41	17	24	39
Progres Niederkorn	17	11	4	2	43	17	26	37
Differdange 03	17	11	2	4	36	25	11	35
UT Petange	17	10	3	4	34	23	11	33
F91 Dudelange	17	8	2	7	38	24	14	26
UNA Strassen	17	7	5	5	30	26	4	26
Racing	17	6	7	4	32	27	5	25
Jeunesse Esch	17	5	4	8	24	34	–10	19
Victoria Rosport	17	5	3	9	23	35	–12	18
Etzella Ettelbruck	17	5	2	10	22	34	–12	17
Hostert	17	5	1	11	17	37	–20	16
Mondorf-les-Bains	17	3	6	8	22	28	–6	15
Rodange 91	17	4	3	10	21	37	–16	15
Muhlenbach Blue Boys	17	3	3	11	20	39	–19	12

League curtailed due to COVID-19 pandemic. Title not awarded; no relegation to second tier. Nationaldivisioun to expand to 16 teams in 2020–21.
Top scorer: Sinani (F91 Dudelange) 14.
Cup Final: Competition abandoned due to COVID-19 pandemic.

MALTA

Malta Football Association, Millennium Stand, Floor 2, National Stadium, Ta'Qali ATD4000.
Founded: 1900. *FIFA:* 1959; *UEFA:* 1960. *National Colours:* Red shirts, white shorts, red socks.

International matches 2019–20

Norway (a) 0-2, Romania (a) 0-1, Sweden (h) 0-4, Faroe Islands (a) 0-1, Spain (a) 0-7, Norway (h) 1-2.

League Championship wins (1910–2020)

Floriana 26; Sliema Wanderers 26; Valletta 25; Hibernians 12; Hamrun Spartans 7; Birkirkara 4; Rabat Ajax 2; St George's 1; KOMR 1; Marsaxlokk 1.

Cup wins (1935–2020)*

Sliema Wanderers 21; Floriana 20; Valletta 14; Hibernians 10; Hamrun Spartans 6; Birkirkara 5; Melita 1; Gzira United 1; Zurrieq 1; Rabat Ajax 1; Balzan 1.
**No winner in 2019–20.*

Maltese Premier League 2019–20

	P	*W*	*D*	*L*	*F*	*A*	*GD*	*Pts*
Floriana (C)[1]	20	12	5	3	38	15	23	41
Valletta[2]	20	11	5	4	32	22	10	38
Hibernians[2]	20	11	4	5	34	20	14	37
Sirens[2]	20	10	5	5	30	26	4	35
Birkirkara	20	9	6	5	30	20	10	33
Gzira United	20	9	5	6	35	19	16	32
Balzan	20	8	4	8	33	29	4	28
Mosta	20	9	1	10	29	35	–6	28
Hamrun Spartans	20	6	7	7	24	25	–1	25
Sliema Wanderers	20	7	3	10	24	22	2	24
Gudja United	20	6	6	8	24	30	–6	24
St Lucia	20	6	5	9	24	33	–9	23
Senglea Athletic	20	3	7	10	21	39	–18	16
Tarxien Rainbows	20	1	1	18	18	61	–43	4

Competition curtailed due to COVID-19 pandemic. Floriana declared champions. No relegation as Maltese Premier League to expand to 16 teams in 2020–21.
Top scorer: Keqi (Floriana) 14.
Cup Final: Competition abandoned due to COVID-19 pandemic.

MOLDOVA

Federatia Moldoveneasca de Fotbal, Str. Tricolorului 39, 2012 Chisinau.
Founded: 1990. *FIFA:* 1994; *UEFA:* 1993. *National Colours:* All blue.

International matches 2019–20

Kazakhstan (n) 0-1*, Iceland (a) 0-3, Turkey (h) 0-4, Andorra (a) 0-1, Albania (h) 0-4, France (a) 1-2, Iceland (h) 1-2.
**Played 21.02.2019, result incorrect in last edition.*

League Championship wins (1992–2019)

Sheriff 18; Zimbru Chisinau 8; Constructorul 1; Dacia Chisinau 1; Milsami Orhei 1.

Cup wins (1992–2020)

Sheriff 10; Zimbru Chisinau 6; Tiligul-Tiras 3; Tiraspol 3 (incl. Constructorul 2); Milsami Orhei 2; Comrat 1; Nistru Otaci 1; Iskra-Stal 1; Zaria Balti 1; Petrocub-Hincesti 1.

Moldovan Divizia Nationala 2019

	P	*W*	*D*	*L*	*F*	*A*	*GD*	*Pts*
Sheriff (C)[1]	28	22	4	2	60	9	51	70
Sfintul Gheorghe[2]	28	16	5	7	40	28	12	53
Petrocub-Hincesti[2]	28	14	8	6	34	21	13	50
Dinamo-Auto[2]	28	12	5	11	38	37	1	41
Milsami Orhei	28	10	9	9	30	28	2	39
Speranta Nisporeni	28	8	11	9	29	34	–5	35
Zimbru Chisinau	28	3	7	18	16	43	–27	16
Codru Lozova+	28	0	5	23	8	55	–47	5

Divizia Nationala to expand to 10 teams in 2020–21.
Top scorer: Kendysh (Sheriff) 13.
Cup Final: Petrocub-Hincesti 0, Sfintul Gheorghe 0.
aet; Petrocub-Hincesti won 5-3 on penalties.

MONTENEGRO

Fudbalski Savez Crne Gore, Ulica 19. Decembar 13, PO Box 275, 81000 Podgorica.
Founded: 1931 *FIFA:* 2007; *UEFA:* 2007. *National Colours:* All red with gold trim.

International matches 2019–20

Hungary (h) 2-1, Czech Republic (h) 0-3, Bulgaria (h) 0-0, Kosovo (a) 0-2, England (a) 0-7, Belarus (h) 2-0.

League Championship wins (2006–20)

Buducnost Podgorica 4; Sutjeska 4; Mogren 2; Rudar Pljevlja 2; Zeta 1; Mladost Podgorica 1 (renamed OFK Titograd).

Cup wins (2006–20)*

Rudar Pljevlja 4; Buducnost Podgorica 2; Mladost Podgorica (renamed OFK Titograd) 2; Mogren 1; Petrovac 1; Celik 1; Lovcen 1: Sutjeska 1.
**No winner in 2019–20.*

Montenegrin Prva CFL 2019–20

	P	*W*	*D*	*L*	*F*	*A*	*GD*	*Pts*
Buducnost Podgorica (C)[1]	31	23	4	4	63	26	37	73
Sutjeska[2]	31	15	10	6	57	31	26	55
Iskra[2]	31	15	8	8	43	33	10	53
Zeta[2]	31	9	14	8	29	30	–1	41
Podgorica	31	8	16	7	34	27	7	40
Petrovac	31	9	10	12	30	46	–16	37
Rudar	31	10	5	16	38	57	–19	35
OFK Titograd+	31	7	10	14	29	38	–9	31
Kom*+	31	6	11	14	36	45	–9	29
Grbalj*	31	4	10	17	23	49	–26	22

Top scorer: Cetkovic (Sutjeska) 10.
Cup Final: Competition abandoned due to COVID-19 pandemic.

NETHERLANDS

Koninklijke Nederlandse Voetbalbond, Woudenbergseweg 56–58, Postbus 515, 3700 AM Zeist.
Founded: 1889. *FIFA:* 1904; *UEFA:* 1954. *National Colours:* Orange shirts, white shorts, orange socks.

International matches 2019–20

Germany (a) 4-2, Estonia (a) 4-0, Northern Ireland (h) 3-1, Belarus (a) 2-1, Northern Ireland (a) 0-0, Estonia (h) 5-0.

League Championship wins (1889–2020)*

Ajax 34; PSV Eindhoven 24; Feyenoord 15; HVV The Hague 10; Sparta Rotterdam 6; RAP Amsterdam 5; Go Ahead Eagles Deventer 4; HFC Haarlem 3; HBS Craeyenhout 3; Willem II Tilburg 3; RCH Heemstede 2; Heracles 2; ADO Den Haag 2; AZ 67 Alkmaar 2; VV Concordia 1; Quick Den Haag 1; Be Quick Groningen 1; NAC Breda 1; SC Enschede 1; Volewijckers Amsterdam 1; HFC Haarlem 1; BVV Den Bosch 1; Schiedam 1; Limburgia 1; EVV Eindhoven 1; SVV Rapid JC Den Heerlen (renamed Roda JC Kerkrade) 1; VV DOS (renamed FC Utrecht) 1; DWS Amsterdam 1; FC Twente 1.
**No winner in 2019–20.*

Cup wins (1899–2020)*

Ajax 19; Feyenoord 13; PSV Eindhoven 9; Quick The Hague 4; AZ 67 Alkmaar 4; HFC Haarlem 3; Sparta Rotterdam 3; FC Twente 3; FC Utrecht 3; Haarlem 2; VOC 2; HBS Craeyenhout 2; DFC 2; RCH Haarlem 2; Wageningen 2; Willem II Tilburg 2; Fortuna 54 2; FC Den Haag (includes ADO) 2; Roda JC 2; RAP Amsterdam 1; Velocitas Breda 1; HVV Den Haag 1; Concordia Delft 1; CVV 1; Schoten 1; ZFC Zaandam 1; Longa 1; VUC 1; Velocitas Groningen 1; Roermond 1; FC Eindhoven 1; VSV 1; Quick 1888 Nijmegen 1; VVV Groningen 1; NAC Breda 1; Heerenveen 1; PEC Zwolle 1; FC Groningen 1; Vitesse 1.
**No winner in 2019–20.*

Dutch Eredivisie 2019–20

	P	W	D	L	F	A	GD	Pts
Ajax	25	18	2	5	68	23	45	56
AZ Alkmaar	25	18	2	5	54	17	37	56
Feyenoord	25	14	8	3	50	35	15	50
PSV Eindhoven	26	14	7	5	54	28	26	49
Willem II Tilburg	26	13	5	8	37	34	3	44
Utrecht	25	12	5	8	50	34	16	41
Vitesse	26	12	5	9	45	35	10	41
Heracles Almelo	26	10	6	10	40	34	6	36
FC Groningen	26	10	5	11	27	26	1	35
Heerenveen	26	8	9	9	41	41	0	33
Sparta Rotterdam	26	9	6	11	41	45	–4	33
Emmen	26	9	5	12	32	45	–13	32
VVV-Venlo	26	8	4	14	24	51	–27	28
FC Twente	26	7	6	13	34	46	–12	27
PEC Zwolle	26	7	5	14	37	55	–18	26
Fortuna Sittard	26	6	8	12	29	52	–23	26
ADO Den Haag	26	4	7	15	25	54	–29	19
RKC Waalwijk	26	4	3	19	27	60	–33	15

Competition abandoned due to COVID-19 pandemic. No champion declared; no relegation to second tier.
Top scorers (joint): Berghuis (Feyenoord), Dessers (Heracles Almelo) 15.
Cup Final: Competition abandoned due to COVID-19 pandemic.

NORTH MACEDONIA

Football Federation of North Macedonia, 8-ma Udarna Brigada 31-A, PO Box 84, 1000 Skopje.
Founded: 1948. *FIFA:* 1994; *UEFA:* 1994. *National Colours:* All red.

International matches 2019–20

Israel (a) 1-1, Latvia (a) 2-0, Slovenia (h) 2-1, Poland (a) 0-2, Austria (a) 1-2, Israel (h) 1-0.

League Championship wins (1992–2020)

Vardar 11*; Rabotnicki 4; Sileks 3; Sloga Jugomagnat 3; Shkendija 3; Pobeda 2; Makedonija GjP 1; Renova 1.
**Vardar also won 1 League Championship (1986–87) in Yugoslav Republic era, later controversially annulled.*

Cup wins (1992–2020)*

Vardar 5†; Rabotnicki 4; Sloga Jugomagnat 3; Sileks 2; Pelister 2; Teteks 2; Shkendija 2; Pobeda 1; Cementarnica 55 1; Bashkimi 1; Makedonija GjP 1; Metalurg 1; Renova 1; Akademija Pandev 1.
**No winner in 2019–20. †Vardar also won 1 Cup (1961) in Yugoslav Republic era.*

North Macedonian Prva Liga Table 2019–20

	P	W	D	L	F	A	GD	Pts
Vardar (C)[1]	23	13	7	3	33	14	19	46
Sileks[1]	23	10	6	7	24	21	3	36
Shkendija[2]	23	10	5	8	38	20	18	35
Renova[2]	23	9	4	10	25	33	–8	31
Shkupi[2]	23	7	8	8	28	28	0	29
Makedonija GjP	23	7	8	8	24	28	–4	29
Akademija Pandev	23	7	7	9	20	20	0	28
Rabotnicki	23	8	4	11	21	29	–8	28
Borec	23	7	6	10	20	31	–11	27
Struga	23	6	7	10	19	28	–9	25

Competition curtailed due to COVID-19 pandemic. Vardar declared champions. No relegation as Prva Liga to expand to 12 teams in 2020–21.
Top scorer: Avramovski (Vardar) 10.
Cup Final: Competition abandoned due to COVID-19 pandemic.

NORTHERN CYPRUS

Cyprus Turkish Football Federation, 7 Memduh Asaf Street, 107 Koskluciftlik, Lefkosa. (Not a member of FIFA or UEFA.)
Founded: 1955; *National Colours:* Red shirts with white trim, red shorts, red socks.

League Championship wins (1956–63; 1969–74; 1976–2020)

Cetinkaya 14; Magusa Turk Gucu 10; Yenicami Agdelen 9; Gonyeli 9; Dogan Turk Birligi 7; Baf Ulku Yurdu 4; Kucuk Kaymakli 4; Akincilar 1; Binatli 1.

Cup wins (1956–2020)

Cetinkaya 17; Yenicami Agdelen 8; Gonyeli 8; Kucuk Kaymakli 7; Magusa Turk Gucu 6; Turk Ocagi Limasol 5; Lefke 2; Dogan Turk Birligi 2; Genclik Gucu 1; Yalova 1; Binatli 1; Cihangir 1.

Northern Cyprus Super Lig 2019–20

	P	W	D	L	F	A	GD	Pts
Magusa Turk Gucu (C)	30	24	4	2	104	31	73	76
Merit Alsancak Yesilova	30	18	5	7	82	49	33	59
Dogan Turk Birligi	30	17	6	7	60	41	19	57
Turk Ocagi Limasol	30	14	10	6	55	40	15	52
Yenicami Agdelen	30	15	6	9	86	60	26	51
Baf Ulku Yurdu	30	13	5	12	47	53	-6	44
Cihangir	30	13	4	13	66	57	9	43
Gocmenkoy	30	12	6	12	47	54	-7	42
Lefke	30	11	6	13	48	57	-9	39
Kucuk Kaymakli (–1)	30	11	5	14	54	63	-9	37
Gonyeli+	30	11	3	16	61	72	-11	36
Hamitkoy+	30	9	7	14	50	68	-18	34
Binatli+	30	9	7	14	50	62	-12	34
Duzkaya*+	30	7	5	18	41	77	-36	26
Cetinkaya*	30	6	7	17	36	56	-20	25
Genclik Gucu*	30	4	6	20	34	81	-47	18

Top scorer: Ebuka Okoye (Yenicami Agdelen) 39.
Cup Final: Yenicami Agdelen 3, Magusa Turk Gucu 1.

NORTHERN IRELAND

Irish Football Association, Donegall Avenue, Belfast BT12 6LU.
Founded: 1880. *FIFA:* 1911; *UEFA:* 1954. *National Colours:* Green shirts, white shorts, green socks.

NORWAY

Norges Fotballforbund, Ullevaal Stadion, Serviceboks 1, 0840 Oslo.
Founded: 1902. *FIFA:* 1908; *UEFA:* 1954. *National Colours:* Red shirts, white shorts, red socks.

International matches 2019–20

Malta (h) 2-0, Sweden (a) 1-1, Spain (h) 1-1, Romania (a) 1-1, Faroe Islands (h) 4-0, Malta (a) 2-1.

League Championship wins (1938–2019)

Rosenborg 25; Fredrikstad 9; Viking Stavanger 8; Lillestrom 5; Valerenga 5; Molde 4; Larvik Turn 3; Brann 3; Lyn Oslo 2; Stromsgodset 2; IK Start 2; Freidig 1; Fram 1; Skeid 1; Moss 1; Stabaek 1.

Cup wins (1902–2019)

Odd Grenland 12; Rosenborg 12; Fredrikstad 11; Lyn Oslo 8; Skeid 8; Sarpsborg 6; Brann 6; Viking Stavanger 6; Lillestrom 6; Stromsgodset 5; Orn-Horten 4; Valerenga 4; Molde 4; Frigg 3; Mjondalen 3; Mercantile 2; Bodo/Glimt 2; Tromso 2; Aalesund 2; Grane Nordstrand 1; Kvik Halden 1; Sparta 1; Gjovik/Lyn 1; Moss 1; Bryne 1; Stabaek 1; Hodd 1.
(Known as the Norwegian Championship for HM The King's Trophy.)

Norwegian Eliteserien 2019

	P	W	D	L	F	A	GD	Pts
Molde (C)[1]	30	21	5	4	72	31	41	68
Bodo/Glimt[2]	30	15	9	6	64	44	20	54
Rosenborg[2]	30	14	10	6	53	41	12	52
Odd	30	15	7	8	45	40	5	52
Viking Stavanger[2]	30	13	8	9	55	42	13	47
Kristiansund	30	11	8	11	41	41	0	41
Haugesund	30	9	13	8	44	37	7	40
Stabaek	30	10	10	10	38	36	2	40
Brann	30	10	10	10	32	37	–5	40
Valerenga	30	8	10	12	39	44	–5	34
Stromsgodset	30	8	8	14	41	54	–13	32
Sarpsborg 08	30	5	15	10	30	40	–10	30
Mjondalen	30	6	12	12	38	52	–14	30
Lillestrom*	30	7	9	14	32	47	–15	30
Tromso*	30	8	6	16	39	58	–19	30
Ranheim*	30	7	6	17	36	55	–19	27

Top scorer: Borven (Odd) 21.
Cup Final: Viking Stavanger 1, Haugesund 0.

POLAND

Polski Zwiazek Pilki Noznej, ul. Bitwy Warszawskiej 1920r. 7, 02-366 Warszawa.
Founded: 1919. *FIFA:* 1923; *UEFA:* 1954. *National Colours:* White shirts with red vertical band, red shorts, white socks.

International matches 2019–20

Slovenia (a) 0-2, Austria (h) 0-0, Latvia (a) 3-0, North Macedonia (h) 2-0, Israel (a) 2-1, Slovenia (h) 3-2.

League Championship wins (1921–2020)

Ruch Chorzow 14; Legia Warsaw 14; Gornik Zabrze 14; Wisla Krakow 13; Lech Poznan 7; Cracovia 5; Pogon Lwow 4; Widzew Lodz 4; Warta Poznan 2; Polonia Warsaw 2; Polonia Bytom 2; LKS Lodz 2; Stal Mielec 2;

Slask Wroclaw 2; Zaglebie Lubin 2; Garbarnia Krakow 1; Szombierki Bytom 1; Piast Gliwice 1.

Cup wins (1926; 1951–2020)

Legia Warsaw 19; Gornik Zabrze 6; Lech Poznan 5; Wisla Krakow 4; Zaglebie Sosnowiec 4; Ruch Chorzow 3; GKS Katowice 3; Amica Wronki 3; Polonia Warsaw 2; Slask Wroclaw 2; Arka Gdynia 2; Lechia Gdansk 2; Dyskobolia Grodzisk 2; Gwardia Warsaw 1; LKS Lodz 1; Stal Rzeszow 1; Widzew Lodz 1; Miedz Legnica 1; Wisla Plock 1; Jagiellonia Bialystok 1; Zawisza Bydgoszcz 1; Cracovia 1.

Polish Ekstraklasa Qualifying Table 2019–20

	P	*W*	*D*	*L*	*F*	*A*	*GD*	*Pts*
Legia Warsaw	30	19	3	8	63	30	33	60
Piast Gliwice	30	16	5	9	36	26	10	53
Slask Wroclaw‡	30	13	10	7	42	33	9	49
Lech Poznan‡	30	13	10	7	55	29	26	49
Cracovia	30	14	4	12	39	29	10	46
Pogon Szczecin	30	12	9	9	29	31	–2	45
Jagiellonia Bialystok	30	12	8	10	41	39	2	44
Lechia Gdansk	30	11	10	9	40	42	–2	43
Gornik Zabrze§	30	10	11	9	39	38	1	41
Rakow Czestochowa§	30	12	5	13	38	43	–5	41
Zaglebie Lubin‡	30	10	8	12	49	46	3	38
Wisla Plock‡	30	10	8	12	37	50	–13	38
Wisla Krakow	30	10	5	15	37	47	–10	35
Korona Kielce	30	8	6	16	21	37	–16	30
Arka Gdynia	30	7	8	15	28	47	–19	29
LKS Lodz	30	5	6	19	26	53	–27	21

‡Ranking decided on head-to-head points. §Ranking decided on head-to-head away goals.

Championship Round 2019–20

	P	*W*	*D*	*L*	*F*	*A*	*GD*	*Pts*
Legia Warsaw (C)[1]	37	21	6	10	70	35	35	69
Lech Poznan[2]	37	18	12	7	70	35	35	66
Piast Gliwice[2]	37	18	7	12	41	32	9	61
Lechia Gdansk	37	15	11	11	48	50	–2	56
Slask Wroclaw‡	37	14	12	11	51	46	5	54
Pogon Szczecin‡	37	14	12	11	37	39	–2	54
Cracovia [2]	37	16	5	16	49	40	9	53
Jagiellonia Bialystok	37	14	10	13	48	51	–3	52

‡Ranking decided on head-to-head points in regular season.

Relegation Round 2019–20

	P	*W*	*D*	*L*	*F*	*A*	*GD*	*Pts*
Gornik Zabrze	37	14	11	12	51	47	4	53
Rakow Czestochowa	37	16	5	16	51	56	–5	53
Zaglebie Lubin	37	15	8	14	61	53	8	53
Wisla Plock	37	14	9	14	45	54	–9	51
Wisla Krakow	37	13	6	18	44	56	–12	45
Arka Gdynia*	37	10	10	17	39	57	–18	40
Korona Kielce*	37	9	8	20	29	48	–19	35
LKS Lodz*	37	6	6	25	33	68	–35	24

†Ranking decided on head-to-head points and away goals in regular season.

Top scorer: Gytkjaer (Lech Poznan) 24.

Cup Final: Cracovia 3, Lechia Gdansk 2 *aet.*

PORTUGAL

Federacao Portuguesa de Futebol, Rua Alexandre Herculano No. 58, Apartado postal 24013, Lisboa 1250-012.

Founded: 1914. *FIFA:* 1923; *UEFA:* 1954. *National Colours:* Carmine shirts with , red shorts, red and green socks.

International matches 2019–20

Serbia (a) 4-2, Lithuania (a) 5-1, Luxembourg (h) 3-0, Ukraine (a) 1-2, Lithuania (h) 6-0, Luxembourg (a) 2-0.

League Championship wins (1935–2020)

Benfica 37; Porto 29; Sporting Lisbon 18; Belenenses 1; Boavista 1.

Cup wins (1939–2020)

Benfica 26; Sporting Lisbon 17; Porto 17; Boavista 5; Belenenses 3; Vitoria de Setubal 3; Academica de Coimbra 2; Braga 2; Leixoes 1; Estrela da Amadora 1; Beira-Mar 1; Vitoria de Guimaraes 1; Desportivo das Aves 1.

Portuguese Primeira Liga 2019–20

	P	*W*	*D*	*L*	*F*	*A*	*GD*	*Pts*
Porto (C)[1]	34	26	4	4	74	22	52	82
Benfica[1]	34	24	5	5	71	26	45	77
Braga[2]	34	18	6	10	61	40	21	60
Sporting Lisbon[2]	34	18	6	10	49	34	15	60
Rio Ave[2]	34	15	10	9	48	36	12	55
Famalicao	34	14	12	8	53	51	2	54
Vitoria de Guimaraes	34	13	11	10	53	38	15	50
Moreirense‡	34	10	13	11	42	44	–2	43
Santa Clara‡	34	11	10	13	36	41	–5	43
Gil Vicente‡	34	11	10	13	40	44	–4	43
Maritimo‡	34	9	12	13	34	42	–8	39
Boavista‡	34	10	9	15	28	39	–11	39
Pacos de Ferreira‡	34	11	6	17	36	52	–16	39
Tondela	34	9	9	16	30	44	–14	36
Belenenses	34	9	8	17	27	54	–27	35
Vitoria de Setubal*	34	7	13	14	27	43	–16	34
Portimonense	34	7	12	15	30	45	–15	33
Desportivo das Aves*	34	5	2	27	24	68	–44	17

‡Ranking decided on head-to-head points.

Vitoria de Setubal and Desportivo das Aves demoted to third tier for licensing infractions; Portimonense reprieved from relegation.

Top scorers (joint): Carlos Vinicius, Pizzi (both Benfica), Taremi (Porto) 18.

Cup Final: Porto 2, Benfica 1.

REPUBLIC OF IRELAND

Football Association of Ireland (Cumann Peile na hEireann), National Sports Campus, Abbotstown, Dublin 15.

Founded: 1921. *FIFA:* 1923; *UEFA:* 1954. *National Colours:* Green shirts, green shorts, green socks with white tops.

League Championship wins (1922–2019)

Shamrock R 17; Dundalk 14; Shelbourne 13; Bohemians 11; St Patrick's Ath 8; Waterford U 6; Cork U 5; Drumcondra 5; Sligo R 3; Cork C 3; St James's Gate 2; Cork Ath 2; Limerick 2; Athlone T 2; Derry C 2; Dolphin 1; Cork Hibernians 1; Cork Celtic 1; Drogheda U 1.

Cup wins (1922–2019)

Shamrock R 25; Dundalk 11; Bohemians 7; Shelbourne 7; Drumcondra 5; Sligo R 5; Derry C 5; Cork C 4; St Patrick's Ath 3; St James's Gate 2; Cork (incl. Fordsons 1) 2; Waterford U 2; Cork U 2; Cork Ath 2; Limerick 2; Cork Hibernians 2; Bray W 2; Longford T 2; Alton U 1; Athlone T 1; Transport 1; Finn Harps 1; Home Farm 1; UC Dublin 1; Galway U 1; Drogheda U 1; Sporting Fingal 1.

League of Ireland Premier Division 2019

	P	*W*	*D*	*L*	*F*	*A*	*GD*	*Pts*
Dundalk (C)[1]	36	27	5	4	73	18	55	86
Shamrock R[2]	36	23	6	7	62	21	41	75
Bohemians[2]	36	17	9	10	47	28	19	60
Derry C[2]	36	15	12	9	56	34	22	57
St Patrick's Ath	36	14	10	12	29	35	–6	52
Waterford	36	12	7	17	46	53	–7	43
Sligo R	36	10	12	14	38	47	–9	42
Cork C	36	9	10	17	29	49	–20	37
Finn Harps+	36	7	7	22	26	64	–38	28
UC Dublin*	36	5	4	27	25	82	–57	19

Top scorer: Ogedi-Izokwe (Derry C) 14.

Cup Final: Dundalk 1, Shamrock R 1.

aet; Shamrock R won 4-2 on penalties.

ROMANIA

Federatia Romana de Fotbal, House of Football, Str. Sergent Serbanica Vasile 12, 22186 Bucuresti.

Founded: 1909. *FIFA:* 1923; *UEFA:* 1954. *National Colours:* All yellow.

International matches 2019–20

Spain (h) 1-2, Malta (h) 1-0, Faroe Islands (a) 3-0, Norway (h) 1-1, Sweden (h) 0-2, Spain (a) 0-5.

League Championship wins (1910–2020)

Steaua Bucharest (renamed FCSB)* 26; Dinamo Bucharest 18; Venus Bucharest 8; Chinezul Timisoara 6; UTA Arad 6; CFR Cluj 6; Petrolul Ploiesti 4; Ripensia Timisoara 4; Universitatea Craiova 4; Rapid Bucharest 3; Olimpia Bucharest 2; United Ploiesti 2 (incl. Prahova Ploiesti 1); Colentina Bucharest 2; Arges Pitesti 2; Romano-Americana Bucharest 1; Coltea Brasov 1; Metalul Resita (renamed CSM Resita) 1; Unirea Tricolor 1; CA Oradea 1; Unirea Urziceni 1; Otelul Galati 1; Astra Giurgiu 1; Viitorul Constanta 1.

Cup wins (1934–2020)

Steaua Bucharest (renamed FCSB)* 23; Rapid Bucharest 13; Dinamo Bucharest 13; Universitatea Craiova 6; CFR Cluj 4; Petrolul Ploiesti 3; Ripensia Timisoara 2; UTA Arad 2; Politehnica Timisoara 2; CFR Turnu Severin 1;

Metalul Resita (renamed CSM Resita) 1; Universitatea Cluj (includes Stiinta) 1; Progresul Oradea (formerly ICO) 1; Progresul Bucharest 1; Ariesul Turda 1; Chimia Ramnicu Vilcea 1; Jiul Petrosani 1; FCU Craiova 1948 1; Gloria Bistrita 1; Astra Giurgiu 1; Voluntari 1; Viitorul Constanta 1.
**Club involved in protracted legal dispute about right to name, brand and historical honours; UEFA currently recognises FCSB as essentially the same entity as Steaua Bucharest.*

Romanian Liga 1 Qualifying Table 2019–20

	P	*W*	*D*	*L*	*F*	*A*	*GD*	*Pts*
CFR Cluj	26	15	7	4	51	16	35	52
Universitatea Craiova	26	14	4	8	41	28	13	46
Botosani	26	12	9	5	36	30	6	45
FCSB	26	13	5	8	37	29	8	44
Gaz Metan Medias	26	12	7	7	34	30	4	43
Astra Giurgiu	26	13	6	7	38	29	9	42
Viitorul Constanta	26	11	7	8	44	29	15	40
Dinamo Bucharest	26	10	4	12	37	41	–4	34
Sepsi Sfantu Gheorghe	26	7	12	7	30	26	4	33
Chindia Targoviste‡	26	6	7	13	29	47	–18	25
Hermannstadt‡	26	5	10	11	26	44	–18	25
Politehnica Iasi‡	26	5	7	14	26	40	–14	22
Academica Clinceni‡	26	4	10	12	30	47	–17	22
Voluntari	26	5	5	16	22	45	–23	20

‡Ranking decided on head-to-head points.
NB: Points earned in Qualifying phase are halved and rounded up at start of Championship and Relegation Play-off phase.

Championship Round 2019–20

	P	*W*	*D*	*L*	*F*	*A*	*GD*	*Pts*
CFR Cluj (C)[1]	10	7	2	1	17	7	10	49
Universitatea Craiova[2]	9	7	0	2	17	14	3	44
Astra Giurgiu†	8	3	3	2	12	8	4	33
Botosani[2]	10	2	3	5	10	12	–2	32
FCSB[2]	9	2	3	4	13	14	–1	31
Gaz Metan Medias	10	0	3	7	5	19	–14	25

†Astra Giurgiu failed to obtain UEFA licence and were excluded from Europa League 2090–21.

Relegation Round 2019–20

	P	*W*	*D*	*L*	*F*	*A*	*GD*	*Pts*
Viitorul Constanta	14	6	5	3	25	17	8	43
Hermannstadt	12	6	4	2	18	14	4	35
Sepsi Sfantu Gheorghe	13	4	5	4	19	17	2	34
Academica Clinceni	14	7	0	7	14	21	–7	32
Voluntari	14	6	3	5	16	12	4	31
Politehnica Iasi	14	5	4	5	17	17	0	30
Dinamo Bucharest	9	2	2	5	8	11	–3	25
Chindia Targoviste+	12	3	1	8	9	17	–8	23

Competition curtailed due to COVID-19 pandemic. CFR Cluj declared champions. No automatic relegation; bottom club only required to play relegation/promotion play-off as Liga 1 to expand to 16 teams in 2020–21.
Top scorer: Ianca (Viitorul Constanta) 18.
Cup Final: FCSB 1, Sepsi Sfantu Gheorghe 0.

RUSSIA

Russian Football Union, Ulitsa Narodnaya 7, 115 172 Moscow.
Founded: 1912. *FIFA:* 1912; *UEFA:* 1954. *National Colours:* All brick red.

International matches 2019–20
Scotland (a) 2-1, Kazakhstan (h) 1-0, Scotland (h) 4-0, Cyprus (a) 5-0, Belgium (h) 1-4, San Marino (a) 5-0.

USSR League Championship wins (1936–91)
Dynamo Kyiv 13; Spartak Moscow 12; Dynamo Moscow 11; CSKA Moscow 7; Torpedo Moscow 3; Dinamo Tbilisi 2; Dnepr Dnepropetrovsk 2; Zorya Voroshilovgrad 1; Ararat Yerevan 1; Dynamo Minsk 1; Zenit Leningrad 1.

Russian League Championship wins (1992–2020)
Spartak Moscow 10; CSKA Moscow 6; Zenit St Petersburg 6; Lokomotiv Moscow 3; Rubin Kazan 2; Spartak Vladikavkaz (formerly Alania) 1.

USSR Cup wins (1936–91)
Spartak Moscow 10; Dynamo Kyiv 9; Dynamo Moscow 6; Torpedo Moscow 6; CSKA Moscow 5; Shakhtar Donetsk 4; Lokomotiv Moscow 2; Ararat Yerevan 2; Dinamo Tbilisi 2; Zenit Leningrad 1; Karpaty Lvov 1; SKA Rostov-on-Don 1; Metalist Kharkov 1; Dnepr Dnepropetrovsk 1.

Russian Cup wins (1992–2020)
Lokomotiv Moscow 8; CSKA Moscow 7; Zenit St Petersburg 4; Spartak Moscow 3; Torpedo Moscow 1; Dynamo Moscow 1; Terek Grozny (renamed Akhmat Grozny) 1; Rubin Kazan 1; Rostov 1; Tosno 1.

Russian Premier Liga 2019–20

	P	*W*	*D*	*L*	*F*	*A*	*GD*	*Pts*
Zenit St Petersburg (C)[1]	30	22	6	2	65	18	47	72
Lokomotiv Moscow[1]	30	16	9	5	41	29	12	57
Krasnodar[1]	30	14	10	6	49	30	19	52
CSKA Moscow[2]	30	14	8	8	43	29	14	50
Rostov[2]	30	12	9	9	45	50	–5	45
Dynamo Moscow[2]	30	11	8	11	27	30	–3	41
Spartak Moscow	30	11	6	13	35	33	2	39
Arsenal Tula‡	30	11	5	14	37	41	–4	38
Ufa‡	30	8	14	8	22	24	–2	38
Rubin Kazan‡	30	8	11	11	18	28	–10	35
Ural Yekaterinburg‡	30	9	8	13	36	53	–17	35
Sochi	30	8	9	13	40	39	1	33
Akhmat Grozny§	30	7	10	13	27	46	–19	31
Tambov§	30	9	4	17	37	41	–4	31
Krylya Sovetov§*	30	8	7	15	33	40	–7	31
Orenburg*	30	7	6	17	28	52	–24	27

‡Ranking decided on head-to-head points. §Ranking decided on head-to-head points and goal difference.
Top scorers (joint): Azmoun, Dzyuba (both Zenit St Petersburg) 17.
Cup Final: Zenit St Petersburg 1, Khimki 0.

SAN MARINO

Federazione Sammarinese Giuoco Calcio, Strada di Montecchio 17, 47890 San Marino.
Founded: 1931. *FIFA:* 1988; *UEFA:* 1988. *National Colours:* Cobalt blue shirts with white trim, white shorts, cobalt blue socks.

International matches 2019–20
Belgium (h) 0-4, Cyprus (h) 0-4, Belgium (a) 0-9, Scotland (a) 0-6, Kazakhstan (h) 1-3, Russia (h) 0-5.

League Championship wins (1986–2020)
Tre Fiori 8; La Fiorita 5; Domagnano 4; Folgore Falciano 4; Tre Penne 4; Faetano 3; Murata 3; Montevito 1; Libertas 1; Cosmos 1; Pennarossa 1.

Cup wins (1937–2020)*
Libertas 11; Domagnano 8; Tre Fiori 7; Tre Penne 6; Juvenes 5; La Fiorita 5; Cosmos 4; Faetano 3; Murata 3; Dogana 2; Pennarossa 2; Juvenes/Dogana 2; Folgore Falciano 1.
**No winner in 2019–20.*

Campionato Sammarinese 2019–20

First Phase Group A

	P	*W*	*D*	*L*	*F*	*A*	*GD*	*Pts*
La Fiorita	7	5	2	0	10	3	7	17
Tre Fiori	7	4	2	1	15	7	8	14
Murata	7	4	1	2	11	8	3	13
Folgore Falciano	7	3	3	1	15	6	9	12
Pennarossa	7	4	0	3	11	11	0	12
Domagnano	7	2	1	4	8	13	–5	7
Faetano	7	1	1	5	6	11	–5	4
Juvenes/Dogana	7	0	0	7	5	22	–17	0

First Phase Group B

	P	*W*	*D*	*L*	*F*	*A*	*GD*	*Pts*
Tre Penne	6	6	0	0	20	5	15	18
Libertas	6	5	0	1	16	6	10	15
Cailungo	6	4	0	2	7	7	0	12
Virtus	6	2	1	3	10	11	–1	7
San Giovanni	6	2	0	4	6	13	–7	6
Fiorentino	6	1	1	4	8	13	–5	4
Cosmos	6	0	0	6	4	16	–12	0

Top four in each group qualify for Group 1 in Second Phase; remainder to Group 2.

Second Phase Group 1

	P	*W*	*D*	*L*	*F*	*A*	*GD*	*Pts*
Tre Fiori (C)[1]	8	6	2	0	23	11	12	20
Folgore Falciano	8	4	4	0	14	3	11	16
Tre Penne[2]	8	4	3	1	13	8	5	15
La Fiorita[2]	8	4	2	2	13	8	5	14
Murata	8	2	1	5	10	17	–7	7
Virtus	8	2	1	5	14	18	–4	7
Libertas	8	1	2	5	5	17	–12	5
Cailungo	8	1	1	6	9	19	–10	4

Second Phase Group 2

	P	*W*	*D*	*L*	*F*	*A*	*GD*	*Pts*
Faetano	7	6	1	0	17	6	11	19
Pennarossa	7	4	2	1	22	12	10	14
Domagnano	7	4	1	2	12	6	6	13

Cosmos	6	2	2	2	10	12	–2	8
Fiorentino	7	1	2	4	9	21	–12	5
San Giovanni	7	0	3	4	6	12	–6	3
Juvenes/Dogana	7	0	3	4	4	11	–7	3

Competition curtailed due to COVID-19 pandemic. Tre Fiori declared champions. UEFA ruled Folgore Falciano ineligible to compete in Europa League in 2020–21 and were replaced by La Fiorita.
Top scorer: Fedeli (Murata) 16.
Cup Final: Competition abandoned due to COVID-19 pandemic.

SCOTLAND

Scottish Football Association, Hampden Park, Glasgow G42 9AY.
Founded: 1873. *FIFA:* 1910; *UEFA:* 1954. *National Colours:* Dark blue shirts, dark blue shorts, red socks.

SERBIA

Football Association of Serbia, Terazije 35, PO Box 263, 11000 Beograd.
Founded: 1919. *FIFA:* 1921; *UEFA:* 1954. *National Colours:* Red shirts, blue shorts, white socks.

International matches 2019–20
Ukraine (a) 0-5*, Portugal (h) 2-4, Luxembourg (a) 3-1, Paraguay (h) 1-0, Lithuania (a) 2-1, Luxembourg (h) 3-2, Ukraine (h) 2-2.
**Played 07.06.2019, venue incorrect in last edition.*

Yugoslav League Championship wins (1923–40; 1946–91)
Red Star Belgrade (Crvena Zvezda) 19; Partizan Belgrade 11*; Hajduk Split 9; Gradjanski Zagreb 5; BSK Belgrade (renamed OFK) 5; Dinamo Zagreb 4; Jugoslavija Belgrade 2; Concordia Zagreb 2; Vojvodina Novi Sad 2; FC Sarajevo 2; HASK Zagreb 1; Zeljeznicar 1.
**Total includes 1 League Championship (1986–87) originally awarded to Macedonian club Vardar.*

Serbian League Championship wins (1992–2020)
Partizan Belgrade 16; Red Star Belgrade (Crvena Zvezda) 12; Obilic 1.

Yugoslav Cup wins (1923–41; 1947–91)
Red Star Belgrade (Crvena Zvezda) 12; Hajduk Split 9; Dinamo Zagreb 7; Partizan Belgrade 6; OFK Belgrade (incl. BSK 3) 5; Rijeka 2; Velez Mostar 2; HASK Zagreb 1; Jugoslavija Belgrade 1; Vardar Skopje 1; Borac Banjaluka 1.

Serbian and Serbia-Montenegro Cup wins (1991–2020)
Red Star Belgrade (Crvena Zvezda) 12; Partizan Belgrade 11; Vojvodina 2; Sartid 1; Zeleznik 1; Jagodina 1; Cukaricki 1.

Serbian SuperLiga Qualifying Table 2019–20

	P	*W*	*D*	*L*	*F*	*A*	*GD*	*Pts*
Red Star Belgrade (C)[1]	30	25	3	2	68	18	50	78
Partizan Belgrade[2]	30	20	4	6	69	25	44	64
Vojvodina[2]	30	19	5	6	47	27	20	62
TSC Backa Topola[2]	30	17	8	5	59	34	25	59
Radnicki Nis	30	16	4	10	51	37	14	52
Cukaricki	30	15	6	9	42	36	6	51
Spartak Subotica	30	14	4	12	46	48	–2	46
Vozdovac	30	13	6	11	45	41	4	45
Mladost Lucani	30	13	4	13	31	40	–9	43
Napredak	30	9	6	15	33	41	–8	33
Radnik Surdulica	30	8	7	15	34	50	–16	31
Proleter Novi Sad	30	7	9	14	30	42	–12	30
Javor Ivanjica	30	6	10	14	43	62	–19	28
Indija	30	7	4	19	26	48	–22	25
Rad Beograd	30	4	3	23	23	63	–40	15
Macva Sabac	30	2	7	21	18	53	–35	13

Competition curtailed due to COVID-19 pandemic. Championship and relegation rounds scrapped and Red Star Belgrade declared champions. No relegation to second tier.
Top scorers (joint): Lukic, Siladi (both TSC Backa Topola), Petkovic (Javor Ivanjica) 16.
Cup Final: Vojvodina 2, Partizan Belgrade 2.
aet; Vojvodina won 4-2 on penalties.

SLOVAKIA

Slovensky Futbalovy Zvaz, Trnavska cesta 100, 821 01 Bratislava.
Founded: 1938. *FIFA:* 1994; *UEFA:* 1993. *National Colours:* White shirts with blue trim, white shorts, white socks.

International matches 2019–20
Croatia (h) 0-4, Hungary (a) 2-1, Wales (h) 1-1, Paraguay (h) 1-1, Croatia (a) 1-3, Azerbaijan (h) 2-0.

League Championship wins (1938–44; 1993–2020)
Slovan Bratislava (incl. 4 as SK Bratislava) 14; Zilina 7; Kosice 2; Inter Bratislava 2; Artmedia Petrzalka 2; Trencin 2; Sparta Povazska Bystrica 1; OAP Bratislava 1; Ruzomberok 1; Spartak Trnava 1.
See also Czech Republic section for Slovak club honours in Czechoslovak era 1925–93.

Cup wins (1961; 1969–93; 1993–2020)
Slovan Bratislava 16; Spartak Trnava 6; Inter Bratislava 6; VSS Kosice 5; Lokomotiva Kosice 3; Trencin 3; Zilina 2; Dukla Banska Bystrica 2; Artmedia Petrzalka 2; DAC Dunajska Streda 1; Tatran Presov 1; Chemlon Humenne 1; Koba Senec 1; Matador Puchov 1; Ruzomberok 1; ViOn Zlate Moravce 1.

Slovak Super Liga Qualifying Table 2019–20

	P	*W*	*D*	*L*	*F*	*A*	*GD*	*Pts*
Slovan Bratislava	22	17	4	1	46	11	35	55
Zilina	22	13	6	3	38	17	21	45
DAC Dunajska Streda	22	11	5	6	31	25	6	38
Zemplin Michalovce‡	22	8	6	8	28	32	–4	30
Spartak Trnava‡	22	9	3	10	25	26	–1	30
Ruzomberok	22	6	10	6	25	27	–2	28
Trencin	22	7	6	9	39	35	4	27
Zlate Moravce	22	6	8	8	22	28	–6	26
Senica	22	6	6	10	24	33	–9	24
Sere	22	5	7	10	23	34	–11	22
Nitra	22	5	4	13	17	31	–14	19
Pohronie	22	3	7	12	19	38	–19	16

‡Ranking decided on head-to-head points.

Championship Round 2019–20

	P	*W*	*D*	*L*	*F*	*A*	*GD*	*Pts*
Slovan Bratislava (C)[1]	27	21	5	1	57	14	43	68
Zilina[2]	27	15	6	6	48	25	23	51
DAC Dunajska Streda[2]	27	15	5	7	42	28	14	50
Spartak Trnava†	27	10	5	12	30	32	–2	35
Ruzomberok†[2]	27	7	11	9	28	33	–5	32
Zemplin Michalovce†	27	8	8	11	31	49	–18	32

Relegation Round 2019–20

	P	*W*	*D*	*L*	*F*	*A*	*GD*	*Pts*
Trencin†	27	11	6	10	52	43	9	39
Zlate Moravce	27	8	9	10	27	33	–6	33
Sere	27	6	9	12	29	41	–12	27
Senica	27	6	8	13	26	40	–14	26
Pohronie	27	6	8	13	25	44	–19	26
Nitra+	27	7	4	16	23	36	–13	25

†Qualified for Europa League play-offs.
Competition curtailed due to COVID-19 pandemic. Slovan Bratislava declared champions. No automatic relegation; bottom club only required to play relegation/promotion play-off.

Europa League Play-offs
Semi-finals
Ruzomberok 1, Zemplin Michalovce 0
Spartak Trnava 3, Trencin 0
Final
Spartak Trnava 0, Ruzomberok 2
Top scorer: Sporar (Slovan Bratislava) 12.
Cup Final: Slovan Bratislava 1, Ruzomberok 0.

SLOVENIA

Nogometna Zveza Slovenije, Brnciceva 41g, PP 3986, 1001 Ljubljana.
Founded: 1920. *FIFA:* 1992; *UEFA:* 1992. *National Colours:* White shirts with blue trim, white shorts, white socks.

International matches 2019–20
Poland (h) 2-0, Israel (h) 3-2, North Macedonia (a) 1-2, Austria (h) 0-1, Latvia (h) 1-0, Poland (a) 2-3.

League Championship wins (1991–2020)
Maribor 15; Olimpija (pre-2005) 4; Gorica 4; Domzale 2; Olimpija Ljubljana (post-2005) 2; Koper 1; Celje 1.

Cup wins (1991–2020)
Maribor 9; Olimpija (pre-2005) 4; Gorica 3; Koper 3; Interblock 2; Domzale 2; Olimpija Ljubljana (post-2005) 2; Mura (pre-2005) 1; Rudar Velenje 1; Celje 1; Mura (post-2012) 1.

Slovenian PrvaLiga 2019–20

	P	*W*	*D*	*L*	*F*	*A*	*GD*	*Pts*
Celje (C)[1]	36	19	12	5	74	36	38	69
Maribor[2]	36	20	7	9	66	39	27	67

Olimpija Ljubljana[2]	36	20	7	9	73	44	29	67
Mura[2]	36	14	14	8	54	42	12	56
Aluminij	36	16	7	13	58	48	10	55
Bravo	36	13	10	13	50	53	–3	49
Tabor Sezana	36	13	7	16	45	51	–6	46
Domzale	36	12	7	17	52	64	–12	43
Triglav*+	36	9	5	22	44	87	–43	32
Rudar Velenje*	36	0	12	24	28	80	–52	12

Top scorer: Vukusic (Olimpija Ljubljana) 26.
Cup Final: Mura 2, Nafta 1903 0.

SPAIN

Real Federacion Espanola de Futbol, Calle Ramon y Cajal s/n, Apartado postale 385, 28230 Las Rozas, Madrid.
Founded: 1913. *FIFA:* 1913; *UEFA:* 1954. *National Colours:* All red with yellow trim.

International matches 2019–20
Faroe Islands (h) 4-0, Norway (a) 1-1, Sweden (a) 1-1, Malta (h) 7-0, Romania (h) 5-0.

League Championship wins (1929–36; 1940–2020)
Real Madrid 34; Barcelona 26; Atletico Madrid 10; Athletic Bilbao 8; Valencia 6; Real Sociedad 2; Real Betis 1; Sevilla 1; Deportivo La Coruna 1.

Cup wins (1903–2020)*
Barcelona 30; Athletic Bilbao (includes Vizcaya Bilbao 1) 23; Real Madrid 19; Atletico Madrid 10; Valencia 8; Real Zaragoza 6; Sevilla 5; Espanyol 4; Real Union de Irun 3; Real Sociedad (includes Ciclista) 2; Real Betis 2; Deportivo La Coruna 2; Racing de Irun 1; Arenas 1; Mallorca 1.
**No winner in 2019–20.*

Spanish La Liga 2019–20

	P	*W*	*D*	*L*	*F*	*A*	*GD*	*Pts*
Real Madrid (C)[1]	38	26	9	3	70	25	45	87
Barcelona[1]	38	25	7	6	86	38	48	82
Atletico Madrid[1]	38	18	16	4	51	27	24	70
Sevilla[1]	38	19	13	6	54	34	20	70
Villarreal[2]	38	18	6	14	63	49	14	60
Real Sociedad[2]	38	16	8	14	56	48	8	56
Granada[2]	38	16	8	14	52	45	7	56
Getafe	38	14	12	12	43	37	6	54
Valencia	38	14	11	13	46	53	–7	53
Osasuna	38	13	13	12	46	54	–8	52
Athletic Bilbao	38	13	12	13	41	38	3	51
Levante	38	14	7	17	47	53	–6	49
Real Valladolid	38	9	15	14	32	43	–11	42
Eibar	38	11	9	18	39	56	–17	42
Real Betis	38	10	11	17	48	60	–12	41
Alaves	38	10	9	19	34	59	–25	39
Celta Vigo	38	7	16	15	37	49	–12	37
Leganes*	38	8	12	18	30	51	–21	36
Mallorca*	38	9	6	23	40	65	–25	33
Espanyol*	38	5	10	23	27	58	–31	25

Top scorer: Messi (Barcelona) 25.
Cup Final: Competition suspended due to COVID-19 pandemic.

SWEDEN

Svenska Fotbollfoerbundet, Evenemangsgatan 31, PO Box 1216, SE-171 23 Solna.
Founded: 1904. *FIFA:* 1904; *UEFA:* 1954. *National Colours:* Yellow shirts with blue trim, blue shorts, yellow socks.

International matches 2019–20
Spain (a) 0-3*, Faroe Islands (a) 4-0, Norway (h) 1-1, Malta (a) 4-0, Spain (h) 1-1, Romania (a) 2-0, Faroe Islands (h) 3-0.
**Played 10.06.2019, venue incorrect in last edition.*

League Championship wins (1896–2019)
Malmo 20; IFK Gothenburg 18; IFK Norrkoping 13; Orgryte 12; AIK Solna 12; Djurgaarden 12; IF Elfsborg 6; Helsingborg 5; GAIS Gothenburg 4; Oster Vaxjo 4; Halmstad 4; Atvidaberg 2; Gothenburg IF 1; IFK Eskilstuna 1; Fassbergs 1; IF Gavic Brynas 1; IK Sleipner 1; Hammarby 1; Kalmar 1.
(Played in cup format from 1896–1925.)

Cup wins (1941–2020)
Malmo 14; AIK Solna 8; IFK Gothenburg 8; IFK Norrkoping 6; Helsingborg 5; Djurgaarden 5; Kalmar 3; IF Elfsborg 3; Atvidaberg 2; Hacken 2; GAIS Gothenburg 1; IF Raa 1; Landskrona 1; Oster Vaxjo 1; Degerfors 1; Halmstad 1; Orgryte 1; Ostersund 1.

Allsvenskan 2019

	P	*W*	*D*	*L*	*F*	*A*	*GD*	*Pts*
Djurgaarden (C)[1]	30	20	6	4	53	19	34	66
Malmo[2]	30	19	8	3	56	16	40	65
Hammarby[2]	30	20	5	5	75	38	37	65
AIK Solna	30	19	5	6	47	24	23	62
IFK Norrkoping	30	16	9	5	54	26	28	57
Hacken	30	14	7	9	44	29	15	49
IFK Gothenburg[2]	30	13	9	8	46	31	15	48
Elfsborg	30	11	10	9	44	45	–1	43
Orebro	30	9	6	15	40	56	–16	33
Helsinborg	30	8	6	16	29	49	–20	30
Sirius	30	8	5	17	34	51	–17	29
Ostersund	30	5	10	15	27	52	–25	25
Falkenberg	30	6	7	17	25	62	–37	25
Kalmar *+	30	4	11	15	22	47	–25	23
GIF Sundsvall*	30	4	8	18	31	50	–19	20
Eskilstuna*	30	4	8	18	23	55	–32	20

Top scorer: Turay (Djurgaarden) 15.
Cup Final: IFK Gothenburg 2, Malmo 1 *aet.*

SWITZERLAND

Schweizerisher Fussballverband, Worbstrasse 48, Postfach 3000, Bern 15.
Founded: 1895. *FIFA:* 1904; *UEFA:* 1954. *National Colours:* Red shirts, white shorts, red socks.

International matches 2019–20
Republic of Ireland (a) 1-1, Gibraltar (h) 4-0, Denmark (a) 0-1, Republic of Ireland (h) 2-0, Georgia (h) 1-0, Gibraltar (a) 6-1.

League Championship wins (1897–2020)
Grasshoppers 27; FC Basel 20; Servette 17; Young Boys 14; FC Zurich 12; Lausanne-Sport 7; Winterthur 3; Aarau 3; Lugano 3; La Chaux-de-Fonds 3; St Gallen 2; Neuchatel Xamax 2; Sion 2; Anglo-American Club 1; Brühl 1; Cantonal-Neuchatel 1; Etoile La Chaux-de-Fonds 1; Biel-Bienne 1; Bellinzona 1; Lucerne 1.

Cup wins (1926–2020)
Grasshoppers 19; FC Basel 13; Sion 13; FC Zurich 10; Lausanne-Sport 9; Servette 7; Young Boys 7; La Chaux-de-Fonds 6; Lugano 3; Lucerne 2; Urania Geneva 1; Young Fellows Zurich (renamed Young Fellows Juventus) 1; FC Grenchen 1; St Gallen 1; Aarau 1; Wil 1.

Swiss Super League 2019–20

	P	*W*	*D*	*L*	*F*	*A*	*GD*	*Pts*
Young Boys (C)[1]	36	23	7	6	80	41	39	76
St Gallen[2]	36	21	5	10	79	56	23	68
FC Basel[2]	36	18	8	10	74	38	36	62
Servette[2]	36	12	13	11	57	48	9	49
Lugano	36	11	14	11	46	46	0	47
Luzern	36	13	7	16	42	50	–8	46
Zurich	36	12	7	17	45	72	–27	43
Sion	36	10	9	17	40	55	–15	39
Thun*+	36	10	8	18	45	67	–22	38
Neuchatel Xamax*	36	5	12	19	33	68	–35	27

Top scorer: Nsame (Young Boys) 32.
Cup Final: Young Boys 2, FC Basel 1.

TURKEY

Turkiye Futbol Federasyonu, Hasan Dogan Milli Takimlar, Kamp ve Egitim Tesisleri, Riva, Beykoz, Istanbul.
Founded: 1923. *FIFA:* 1923; *UEFA:* 1962. *National Colours:* All red.

International matches 2019–20
Andorra (h) 1-0, Moldova (a) 4-0, Albania (h) 1-0, France (a) 1-1, Iceland (h) 0-0, Andorra (a) 2-0.

League Championship wins (1959–2020)
Galatasaray 22; Fenerbahce 19; Besiktas 13; Trabzonspor 6; Bursaspor 1; Istanbul Basaksehir 1.

Cup wins (1963–2020)
Galatasaray 18; Besiktas 9; Trabzonspor 9; Fenerbahce 6; Altay Izmir 2; Goztepe Izmir 2; Ankaragucu 2; Genclerbirligi 2; Kocaelispor 2; Eskisehirspor 1; Bursaspor 1; Sakaryaspor 1; Kayseri 1; Konyaspor 1; Akhisar Belediyespor 1.

Turkish Super Lig 2019–20

	P	*W*	*D*	*L*	*F*	*A*	*GD*	*Pts*
Istanbul Basaksehir (C)[1]	34	20	9	5	65	34	31	69
Trabzonspor†	34	18	11	5	76	42	34	65
Besiktas[1]	34	19	5	10	59	40	19	62
Sivasspor[2]	34	17	9	8	55	38	17	60
Alanyaspor[2]	34	16	9	9	61	37	24	57
Galatasaray[2]	34	15	11	8	55	37	18	56

Fenerbahce	34	15	8	11	58	46	12	53
Gaziantep	34	11	13	10	49	50	–1	46
Antalyaspor	34	11	12	11	41	52	–11	45
Kasimpasa	34	12	7	15	53	58	–5	43
Goztepe	34	11	9	14	44	49	–5	42
Genclerbirligi‡	34	9	9	16	39	56	–17	36
Konyaspor‡	34	8	12	14	36	52	–16	36
Denizlispor‡	34	9	8	17	31	48	–17	35
Rizespor‡	34	10	5	19	38	57	–19	35
Yeni Malatyaspor§	34	8	8	18	44	51	–7	32
Kayserispor§	34	8	8	18	40	72	–32	32
Ankaragucu§	34	7	11	16	31	56	–25	32

†*Trabzonspor banned from European competition for 2020–21.*
‡*Ranking decided on head-to-head points.*
§*Ranking decided on head-to-head points, goal difference and goals scored. No relegation to second tier due to COVID-19 pandemic.*
Top scorer: Sorloth (Trabzonspor) 24.
Cup Final: Trabzonspor 2, Alanyaspor 0.

UKRAINE

Football Federation of Ukraine, Provulok Laboratornyi 7-A, PO Box 55, 01133 Kyiv.
Founded: 1991. *FIFA:* 1992; *UEFA:* 1992. *National Colours:* All yellow with blue trim.

International matches 2019–20
Lithuania (a) 3-0, Nigeria (h) 2-2, Lithuania (h) 2-0, Portugal (h) 2-1, Estonia (h) 1-0, Serbia (a) 2-2.

League Championship wins (1992–2020)
Dynamo Kyiv 15; Shakhtar Donetsk 13; Tavriya Simferopol 1.

Cup wins (1992–2020)
Shakhtar Donetsk 13; Dynamo Kyiv 12; Chornomorets Odesa 2; Vorskla Poltava 1; Tavriya Simferopol 1.
See also Russia section for Ukrainian club honours in Soviet era 1936–91.

Ukrainian Premier League Qualifying Table 2019–20

	P	*W*	*D*	*L*	*F*	*A*	*GD*	*Pts*
Shakhtar Donetsk	22	19	2	1	59	14	45	59
Dynamo Kyiv	22	14	3	5	44	17	27	45
Zorya Luhansk	22	13	4	5	39	18	21	43
Desna Chernihiv	22	13	3	6	36	15	21	42
Oleksandria	22	11	4	7	30	23	7	37
Kolos Kovalivka	22	8	2	12	25	39	–14	26
SC Dnipro-1	22	7	4	11	26	34	–8	25
Mariupol	22	6	7	9	21	35	–14	25
FC Lviv	22	5	5	12	16	35	–19	20
Vorskla Poltava	22	6	2	14	15	38	–23	20
Olimpik Donetsk	22	5	3	14	17	37	–20	18
Karpaty Lviv	22	2	7	13	17	40	–23	13

Championship Round 2019–20

	P	*W*	*D*	*L*	*F*	*A*	*GD*	*Pts*
Shakhtar Donetsk (C)[1]	32	26	4	2	80	26	54	82
Dynamo Kyiv[1]	32	18	5	9	65	35	30	59
Zorya Luhansk[2]	32	17	7	8	50	29	21	58
Desna Chernihiv[2]	32	17	5	10	59	33	26	56
Oleksandria†	32	14	7	11	49	47	2	49
Kolos Kovalivka†[2]	32	10	2	20	33	59	–26	32

Relegation Round 2019–20

	P	*W*	*D*	*L*	*F*	*A*	*GD*	*Pts*
SC Dnipro-1†	30	15	4	13	42	42	0	43
Mariupol†	30	12	9	11	34	46	–12	39
Olimpik Donetsk	30	10	6	16	32	47	–15	30
Vorskla Poltava	30	9	7	16	23	48	–25	28
FC Lviv	32	5	9	18	25	57	–32	24
Karpaty Lviv	24	2	9	13	19	42	–23	15

†*Qualified for Europa League play-offs.*
After a COVID-19 outbreak at the club Karpaty Lviv defaulted in two matches, which were awarded as 0-3 defeats, and demoted to the third tier. No relegation as the Premier League is to expand to 14 clubs in 2020–21.

Europa League Play-off
Semi-finals
Kolos Kovalivka 4, SC Dnipro-1
Oleksandria 1, Mariupol 2
Final
Kolos Kovalivka 1, Mariupol 0 *aet*
Top scorer: Junior Moraes (Shakhtar Donetsk) 20.
Cup Final: Dynamo Kyiv 1, Vorskla Poltava 1.
aet; Dynamo Kyiv won 8-7 on penalties.

WALES

Football Association of Wales, 11/12 Neptune Court, Vanguard Way, Cardiff CF24 5PJ.
Founded: 1876. *FIFA:* 1910; *UEFA:* 1954. *National Colours:* All red with green trim.

SOUTH AMERICA (CONMEBOL)

ARGENTINA

Asociacion del Futbol Argentina, Viamonte 1366/76, Buenos Aires 1053.
Founded: 1893. *FIFA:* 1912; *CONMEBOL:* 1916. *National Colours:* Light blue and white striped shirts, black shorts, white socks.
International matches 2019–20
Chile (n) 0-0, Mexico (n) 4-0, Germany (a) 2-2, Ecuador (a) 6-1, Brazil (n) 1-0, Uruguay (n) 2-2.
League champions 2019–20: Boca Juniors. *Cup winners 2019:* River Plate; *2020:* Competition suspended.

BOLIVIA

Federacion Boliviana de Futbol, Avenida Libertador Bolivar 1168, Casilla 484, Cochabamba.
Founded: 1925. *FIFA:* 1926; *CONMEBOL:* 1926. *National Colours:* Green shirts, green shorts, red socks.
International matches 2019–20
Ecuador (a) 0-3, Venezuela (a) 1-4, Haiti (h) 3-1.
League champions 2019: Bolivar (Apertura); Wilstermann (Clausura). *2020:* Apertura: Competition suspended. *Cup winners:* No competition.

BRAZIL

Confederacao Brasileira de Futebol, Avenida Luis Carlos Prestes 130, Barra da Tijuca, Rio de Janeiro 22775-055.
Founded: 1914. *FIFA:* 1923; *CONMEBOL:* 1916. *National Colours:* Yellow shirts with green collar and cuffs, blue shorts, white socks.
International matches 2019–20
Colombia (n) 2-2, Peru (n) 0-1, Senegal (n) 1-1, Nigeria (n) 1-1, Argentina (n) 0-1, Korea Republic (n) 3-0.
League champions 2019: Flamengo; *2020:* Competition still being played. *Cup winners 2019:* Athletico Paranaense; *2020:* Competition still being played.

CHILE

Federacion de Futbol de Chile, Avenida Quilin 5635, Comuna Penalolen, Casilla 3733, Santiago de Chile.
Founded: 1895. *FIFA:* 1913; *CONMEBOL:* 1916. *National Colours:* Red shirts, blue shorts, blue socks.
International matches 2019–20
Argentina (n) 0-0, Honduras (a) 1-2, Colombia (n) 0-0, Guinea (n) 3-2.
League champions 2019: Universidad Catolica; *2020:* Competition still being played. *Cup winners 2019:* Colo-Colo; *2019–20:* Competition still being played.

COLOMBIA

Federacion Colombiana de Futbol, Avenida 32 No. 16–22, Bogota.
Founded: 1924. *FIFA:* 1936; *CONMEBOL:* 1936. *National Colours:* Yellow shirts with blue trim, black shorts, red socks with yellow trim.
International matches 2019–20
Brazil (n) 2-2, Venezuela (n) 0-0, Chile (n) 0-0, Algeria (n) 3-0, Peru (n) 1-0, Ecuador (n) 1-0.
League champions 2019: Junior (Apertura); America de Cali (Finalizacion). *2020:* Apertura: Competition still being played. *Cup winners 2019:* Independiente Medellin; *2020:* Competition suspended.

ECUADOR

Federacion Ecuatoriana del Futbol, Avenida Las Aguas y Calle Alianza, PO Box 09-01-7447, Guayaquil 593.
Founded: 1925. *FIFA:* 1927; *CONMEBOL:* 1927. *National Colours:* Yellow shirts, black shorts, white socks.
International matches 2019–20
Peru (n) 1-0, Bolivia (h) 3-0, Argentina (h) 1-6, Trinidad & Tobago (h) 3-0, Colombia (n) 0-1.
League champions 2019: Delfin; *2020:* Competition still being played. *Cup winners 2019:* LDU Quito; *2020:* Competition postponed.

PARAGUAY

Asociacion Paraguaya de Futbol, Calle Mayor Martinez 1393, Asuncion.
Founded: 1906. *FIFA:* 1925; *CONMEBOL:* 1921. *National Colours:* Red and white striped shirts, blue shorts, white socks with red trim.
International matches 2019–20
Japan (a) 0-2, Jordan (a) 4-2, Serbia (a) 0-1, Slovakia (a) 1-1, Bulgaria (a) 1-0, Saudi Arabia (a) 0-0.
League champions 2019: Olimpia (Apertura); Olimpia (Clausura). *Cup winners 2019:* Libertad; *2020:* Competition postponed.

PERU

Federacion Peruana de Futbol, Avenida Aviacion 2085, San Luis, Lima 30.

Founded: 1922. *FIFA:* 1924; *CONMEBOL:* 1925. *National Colours:* White shirts with red sash, white shorts, white socks.
International matches 2019–20
Ecuador (n) 0-1, Brazil (n) 1-0, Uruguay (a) 0-1, Uruguay (h) 1-1, Colombia (n) 0-1.
League champions 2019: Deportivo Binacional; *2020:* Competition still being played. *Cup winners 2019:* Atletico Grau; *2020:* Competition abandoned.

URUGUAY

Asociacion Uruguaya de Futbol, Guayabo 1531, Montevideo 11200.
Founded: 1900. *FIFA:* 1923; *CONMEBOL:* 1916. *National Colours:* Sky blue shirts, black shorts, black socks with sky blue tops.
International matches 2019–20
Costa Rica (a) 2-1, USA (a) 1-1, Peru (h) 1-0, Peru (a) 1-1, Hungary (a) 2-1, Argentina (n) 2-2.
League champions 2019: Nacional; *2020:* Competition still being played. *Cup winners:* No competition.

VENEZUELA

Federacion Venezolana de Futbol, Avenida Santos Erminy 1ra Calle las Delicias, Torre Mega II, P.H.B. Sabana Grande, 1050 Caracas.
Founded: 1926. *FIFA:* 1952; *CONMEBOL:* 1952. *National Colours:* All burgundy.
International matches 2019–20
Colombia (n) 0-0, Bolivia (h) 4-1, Trinidad & Tobago (h) 2-0, Japan (a) 4-1.
League champions 2019: Caracas; *2020:* Competition abandoned. *Cup winners 2019:* Zamora; *2020:* Competition postponed.

ASIA (AFC)

AFGHANISTAN

Afghanistan Football Federation, PO Box 128, Kabul.
Founded: 1933. *FIFA:* 1948; *AFC:* 1954. *National Colours:* Red shirts, black shorts with green trim, red socks.
International matches 2019–20
Qatar (a) 0-6, Bangladesh (h) 1-0*, Oman (a) 0-3, India (h) 1-1*, Qatar (h) 0-1*.
**Match played in Tajikistan.*
League champions 2019: Toofan Harirod; *2020:* Competition postponed. *Cup winners:* No competition.

AUSTRALIA

Football Federation Australia Ltd, Locked Bag A4071, Sydney South, NSW 1235.
Founded: 1961. *FIFA:* 1963; *AFC:* 2006. *National Colours:* All gold.
International matches 2019–20
Kuwait (a) 3-0, Nepal (h) 5-0, Chinese Taipei (a) 7-1, Jordan (a) 1-0.
League champions 2019–20: Sydney FC. *Grand Final winners 2020:* Sydney FC. *Cup winners 2019:* Adelaide United; *2020:* Competition abandoned.

BAHRAIN

Bahrain Football Association, PO Box 5464, Building 315, Road 2407, Block 934, East Riffa.
Founded: 1957. *FIFA:* 1968; *AFC:* 1969. *National Colours:* All red with gold trim.
International matches 2019–20
Jordan (n) 1-0, Saudi Arabia (n) 0-0, Kuwait (n) 1-0, Iraq (a) 1-0, Iraq (h) 1-1, Cambodia (a) 1-0, Azerbaijan (h) 2-3, Iran (h) 1-0, Hong Kong (a) 0-0, Iraq (h) 0-0*, Oman (n) 0-0, Saudi Arabia (n) 0-2, Kuwait (n) 4-2, Iraq (n) 2-2 (5-3p) Saudi Arabia (n) 1-0.
**Match played in Jordan.*
League champions 2018–19: Al-Riffa; *2019–20:* Competition suspended. *Cup winners 2018–19:* Al-Riffa; *2019–20:* Competition suspended, final to play.

BANGLADESH

Bangladesh Football Federation, BFF House, Motijheel Commercial Area, Dhaka 1000.
Founded: 1972. *FIFA:* 1976; *AFC:* 1974. *National Colours:* Green shirts with red trim, white shorts, green socks.
International matches 2019–20
Afghanistan (a) 0-1*, Bhutan (h) 2-0, Qatar (h) 0-2, India (h) 1-1, Oman (a) 1-4, Palestine (h) 0-2, Sri Lanka (h) 3-0, Burundi (h) 0-3.
**Match played in Tajikistan.*
League champions 2018–19: Bashundhara Kings; *2019–20:* Competition abandoned. *Cup winners 2019–20:* Bashundhara Kings.

BHUTAN

Bhutan Football Federation, PO Box 365, Changiiji, Thimphu 11001.
Founded: 1983. *FIFA:* 2000; *AFC:* 2000. *National Colours:* Orange shirts with yellow trim, orange shorts, orange socks.
International matches 2019–20
Bangladesh (a) 0-2.
League champions 2019: Paro. *2020:* Competition suspended. *Cup winners:* No competition.

BRUNEI

National Football Association of Brunei Darussalam, NFABD House, Jalan Pusat Persidangan, Bandar Seri Begawan BB4313.
Founded: 1959. *FIFA:* 1972; *AFC:* 1969. *National Colours:* Yellow shirts with black trim, yellow shorts with black trim, yellow socks.
International matches 2019–20
None played.
League champions 2018–19: MS ABDB; *2020:* Competition suspended. *Cup winners 2019:* Kota Rangers; *2020:* Competition suspended.

CAMBODIA

Football Federation of Cambodia, National Football Centre, Road Kabsrov Sangkat Samrongkrom, Khan Dangkor, Phnom Penh 2327 PPT3.
Founded: 1933. *FIFA:* 1954; *AFC:* 1954. *National Colours:* All blue with red trim.
International matches 2019–20
Hong Kong (h) 1-1, Bahrain (h) 0-1, Iran (a) 0-14, Iraq (h) 0-4, Mongolia (h) 1-1, Hong Kong (a) 0-2.
League champions 2019: Preah Khan Reach Svay Rieng; *2019–20:* Competition suspended. *Cup winners 2019:* Boeung Ket; *2020:* Competition still being played.

CHINA PR

Football Association of the People's Republic of China, Building A, Dongjiudasha Mansion, Xizhaosi Street, Dongcheng, Beijing 100061.
Founded: 1924. *FIFA:* 1931, rejoined 1980; *AFC:* 1974. *National Colours:* Red shirts with yellow trim, white shorts, red socks with yellow trim.
International matches 2019–20
Maldives (a) 5-0, Guam (h) 7-0, Philippines (a) 0-0, Syria (a) 1-2*, Japan (n) 1-2, Korea Republic (a) 0-1, Hong Kong (n) 2-0.
**Match played in UAE.*
League champions 2019: Guangzhou Evergrande; *2020:* Competition still being played. *Cup winners 2019:* Shanghai Shenhua; *2020:* Competition suspended.

CHINESE TAIPEI

Chinese Taipei Football Association, Room 210, 2F, 55 Chang Chi Street, Tatung, Taipei 10363.
Founded: 1936. *FIFA:* 1954; *AFC:* 1954. *National Colours:* All blue with red and white trim.
International matches 2019–20
Jordan (h) 1-2, Nepal (h) 0-2, Australia (h) 1-7, Kuwait (a) 0-9, Jordan (a) 0-5.
League champions 2019: Tatung; *2020:* Competition still being played. *Cup winners:* No competition.

GUAM

Guam Football Association, PO Box 20008, Barrigada, Guam 96921.
Founded: 1975. *FIFA:* 1996; *AFC:* 1996. *National Colours:* All dark blue with white trim.
International matches 2019–20
Maldives (h) 0-1, Philippines (h) 1-4, China PR (a) 0-7, Syria (a) 0-4*, Maldives (a) 1-3.
**Match played in UAE.*
League champions 2018–19: Rovers; *2019–20:* Competition suspended. *Cup winners 2019:* Bank of Guam Strykers; *2020:* Competition suspended, final to play.

HONG KONG

Hong Kong Football Association Ltd, 55 Fat Kwong Street, Ho Man Tin, Kowloon, Hong Kong.
Founded: 1914. *FIFA:* 1954; *AFC:* 1954. *National Colours:* Red shirts, red shorts, white socks with red trim.
International matches 2019–20
Cambodia (a) 1-1, Iran (h) 0-2, Iraq (a) 0-2, Bahrain (h) 0-0, Cambodia (h) 2-0, Korea Republic (a) 0-2, Japan (n) 0-5, China PR (n) 0-2.
League champions 2018–19: Tai Po; *2019–20:* Competition suspended. *Cup winners 2018–19:* Kitchee; *2019–20:* Competition suspended, final to play.

INDIA

All India Football Federation, Football House, Sector 19, Phase 1 Dwarka, New Delhi 110075.
Founded: 1937. *FIFA:* 1948; *AFC:* 1954. *National Colours:* Blue shirts with orange trim, blue shorts, blue socks.
International matches 2019–20
Korea DPR (h) 2-5, Syria (h) 1-1, Oman (h) 1-2, Qatar (a) 0-0, Bangladesh (h) 1-1, Afghanistan (a) 1-1*, Oman (a) 0-1.
**Match played in Tajikistan.*
League champions 2018–19: I-League: Chennai City, Super League: Bengaluru; *2019–20:* I-League: Competition suspended, Super League: ATK. *Cup winners 2019:* FC Goa; *2020:* Competition suspended.

INDONESIA

Football Association of Indonesia, Gelora Bung Karno Pintu X–XI, PO Box 2305, Senayan, Jakarta 10023.
Founded: 1930. *FIFA:* 1952; *AFC:* 1954. *National Colours:* All red.
International matches 2019–20
Malaysia (h) 2-3, Thailand (h) 0-3, UAE (a) 0-5, Vietnam (h) 1-3, Malaysia (a) 0-2.
League champions 2019: Bali United; *2019–20:* Competition suspended. *Cup winners 2018–19:* PSM Makassar; *2020:* Competition suspended.

IRAN

Football Federation IR Iran, No. 4 Third St., Seoul Avenue, Tehran 19958-73591.
Founded: 1920. *FIFA:* 1948; *AFC:* 1954. *National Colours:* All white with red trim.
International matches 2019–20
Hong Kong (a) 2-0, Cambodia (h) 14-0, Bahrain (a) 0-1, Iraq (a) 1-2*.
**Match played in Jordan.*
League champions 2019–20: Persepolis. *Cup winners 2019–20:* Tractor.

IRAQ

Iraq Football Association, Al-Shaab Stadium, PO Box 484, Baghdad.
Founded: 1948. *FIFA:* 1950; *AFC:* 1970. *National Colours:* White shirts with green trim, white shorts, white socks.
International matches 2019–20
Lebanon (h) 1-0, Palestine (h) 2-1, Syria (h) 0-0, Yemen (h) 2-1, Bahrain (h) 0-1, Bahrain (a) 1-1, Uzbekistan (n) 0-0, Hong Kong (h) 2-0, Cambodia (a) 4-0, Iran (h) 2-1*, Bahrain (h) 0-0*, Qatar (a) 2-1, UAE (n) 2-0, Yemen (n) 0-0, Bahrain (n) 2-2 (3-5p).
**Match played in Jordan.*
League champions 2018–19: Al-Shorta; *2019–20:* Competition abandoned. *Cup winners 2017–18:* No competition; *2018–19:* Al-Zawraa; *2019–20:* Competition abandoned.

JAPAN

Japan Football Association, JFA House, Football Ave., Bunkyo-ku, Tokyo 113-8311.
Founded: 1921. *FIFA:* 1929, rejoined 1950; *AFC:* 1954. *National Colours:* Blue shirts, black shorts, blue socks.
International matches 2019–20
Paraguay (h) 2-0, Myanmar (a) 2-0, Mongolia (h) 6-0, Tajikistan (a) 3-0, Kyrgyz Republic (a) 2-0, Venezuela (h) 1-4, China PR (n) 2-1, Hong Kong (n) 5-0, Korea Republic (a) 0-1.
League champions 2019: Yokohama F. Marinos; *2020:* Competition still being played. *Cup winners 2019:* Vissel Kobe; *2020:* Competition postponed.

JORDAN

Jordan Football Association, PO Box 962024, Al-Hussein Youth City, Amman 11196.
Founded: 1949. *FIFA:* 1956; *AFC:* 1970. *National Colours:* All white with red trim.
International matches 2019–20
Bahrain (n) 0-1, Kuwait (n) 1-1, Saudi Arabia (n) 3-0, Malaysia (a) 1-0, Chinese Taipei (a) 2-1, Paraguay (h) 2-4, Singapore (h) 0-0, Kuwait (h) 0-0, Nepal (h) 3-0, Australia (h) 0-1, Chinese Taipei (h) 5-0.
League champions 2018–19: Al-Faisaly; *2020:* Competition suspended. *Cup winners 2018–19:* Al-Faisaly; *2019–20:* Competition suspended.

KOREA DPR

DPR Korea Football Association, Kumsongdong, Kwangbok Street, Mangyongdae, PO Box 818, Pyongyang.
Founded: 1945. *FIFA:* 1958; *AFC:* 1974. *National Colours:* All red with white trim.
International matches 2019–20
Tajikistan (n) 1-0, Tajikistan (n) 1-0, Lebanon (h) 2-0, Sri Lanka (a) 1-0, Korea Republic (h) 0-0, Turkmenistan (a) 1-3, Lebanon (a) 0-0.
League champions 2018–19: April 25; *2019–20:* Competition suspended. *Cup winners 2019:* Ryomyong (result incorrect in last edition).

KOREA REPUBLIC

Korea Football Association, KFA House 21, Gyeonghuigung-gil 46, Jongno-Gu, Seoul 110-062.
Founded: 1933, 1948. *FIFA:* 1948; *AFC:* 1954. *National Colours:* Red shirts, black shorts, red socks.
International matches 2019–20
Georgia (n) 2-2, Turkmenistan (a) 2-0, Sri Lanka (n) 8-0, Korea DPR (a) 0-0, Lebanon (a) 0-0, Brazil (n) 0-3, Hong Kong (h) 2-0, China PR (h) 1-0, Japan (h) 1-0,
League champions 2019: Jeonbuk Hyundai Motors; *2020:* Competition still being played. *Cup winners 2019:* Suwon Bluewings; *2020:* Competition still being played.

KUWAIT

Kuwait Football Association, Block 5, Street 101, Building 141A, Jabriya, PO Box Hawalli 4020, Kuwait 32071.
Founded: 1952. *FIFA:* 1964; *AFC:* 1964. *National Colours:* All blue with white trim.
International matches 2019–20
Saudi Arabia (n) 2-1, Jordan (n) 1-1, Bahrain (n) 0-1, Nepal (h) 7-0, Australia (h) 0-3, Jordan (n) 0-0, Turkmenistan (h) 1-1, Chinese Taipei (h) 9-0, Nepal (a) 1-0, Saudi Arabia (n) 3-1, Oman (n) 1-2, Bahrain (n) 2-4.
League champions 2019–20: Al-Kuwait. *Cup winners 2019:* Al-Kuwait; *2020:* Competition still being played.

KYRGYZ REPUBLIC

Football Federation of Kyrgyz Republic, Mederova Street 1 'B', PO Box 1484, Bishkek 720082.
Founded: 1992. *FIFA:* 1994; *AFC:* 1994. *National Colours:* All red.
International matches 2019–20
Tajikistan (a) 0-1, Myanmar (h) 7-0, Mongolia (a) 2-1, Uzbekistan (a) 1-3, Japan (h) 0-2, Tajikistan (h) 1-1.
League champions 2019: Dordoi Bishkek; *2020:* Competition still being played. *Cup winners 2019:* Neftchi Kochkor-Ata.

LAOS

Lao Football Federation, FIFA Training Centre, Ban Houayhong, Chanthabuly, PO Box 1800, Vientiane 856-21.
Founded: 1951. *FIFA:* 1952; *AFC:* 1968. *National Colours:* All red.
International matches 2019–20
None played.
League champions 2019: Lao Toyota; *2020:* Competition still being played. *Cup winners 2019:* Lao Toyota.

LEBANON

Association Libanaise de Football, Verdun Street, Bristol Radwan Centre, PO Box 4732, Beirut.
Founded: 1933. *FIFA:* 1936; *AFC:* 1964. *National Colours:* All red with white trim.
International matches 2019–20
Iraq (a) 0-1, Syria (n) 2-1, Palestine (n) 0-0, Yemen (n) 1-2, Korea DPR (a) 0-2, Oman (a) 0-1, Turkmenistan (h) 2-1, Sri Lanka (a) 3-0, Korea Republic (h) 0-0, Korea DPR (h) 0-0.
League champions 2018–19: Al-Ahed; *2019–20:* Competition abandoned. *Cup winners 2018–19:* Al-Ahed; *2019–20:* Competition abandoned.

MACAO

Associacao de Futebol de Macao, Avenida Wai Leong, Taipa University of Science and Technology, Football Field Block 1, Taipa.
Founded: 1939. *FIFA:* 1978; *AFC:* 1978. *National Colours:* All green with white trim.
International matches 2019–20
None played.
League champions 2019: Chao Pak Kei. *2020:* Competition suspended. *Cup winners 2019:* Cheng Fung.

MALAYSIA

Football Association of Malaysia, 3rd Floor, Wisma FAM, Jalan SS5A/9, Kelana Jaya, Petaling Jaya 47301, Selangor Darul Ehsan.
Founded: 1933. *FIFA:* 1954; *AFC:* 1954. *National Colours:* Yellow shirts, black shorts, yellow socks with black trim.
International matches 2019–20
Jordan (h) 0-1, Indonesia (a) 3-2, UAE (h) 1-2, Sri Lanka (h) 6-0, Vietnam (a) 0-1, Tajikistan (h) 1-0, Thailand (h) 2-1, Indonesia (h) 2-0.

League champions 2019: Johor Darul Ta'zim; *2020:* Competition still being played. *Cup winners 2019:* Kedah; *2020:* Competition abandoned.

MALDIVES

Football Association of Maldives, FAM House, Ujaalahingun, Male 20388.
Founded: 1982. *FIFA:* 1986; *AFC:* 1984. *National Colours:* Red shirts white trim, white shorts, red socks with white tops.
International matches 2019–20
Guam (a) 1-0, China PR (h) 0-5, Syria (a) 1-2*, Philippines (h) 1-2, Guam (h) 3-1.
**Match played in UAE.*
League champions 2019–20: Maziya; *2019–20:* Competition postponed. *Cup winners 2018, 2019:* No competition; *2020:* Competition abandoned.

MONGOLIA

Mongolian Football Federation, PO Box 259, 15th Khoroo, Khan-Uul, Ulaanbaatar 210646.
Founded: 1959. *FIFA:* 1998; *AFC:* 1998. *National Colours:* Blue shirts with white sleeves, blue shorts, blue socks.
International matches 2019–20
Myanmar (h) 1-0, Tajikistan (h) 0-1, Japan (a) 0-6, Kyrgyz Republic (h) 1-2, Cambodia (a) 1-1, Myanmar (a) 0-1.
League champions 2019: Ulaanbaatar City; *2020:* Competition still being played. *Cup winners 2019:* Erchim.

MYANMAR

Myanmar Football Federation, National Football Training Centre, Waizayanta Road, Thuwunna, Thingankyun Township, Yangon 11070.
Founded: 1947. *FIFA:* 1948; *AFC:* 1954. *National Colours:* All red.
International matches 2019–20
Mongolia (a) 0-1, Japan (h) 0-2, Kyrgyz Republic (a) 0-7, Nepal (h) 3-0, Tajikistan (h) 4-3, Mongolia (h) 1-0.
League champions 2019: Shan United; *2020:* Competition still being played. *Cup winners 2019:* Yangon United; *2020:* Competition still being played.

NEPAL

All Nepal Football Association, ANFA House, Satdobato, Lalitpur-17, PO Box 12582, Kathmandu.
Founded: 1951. *FIFA:* 1972; *AFC:* 1954. *National Colours:* All red with white trim.
International matches 2019–20
Tajikistan (n) 0-2*, Kuwait (a) 0-7, Chinese Taipei (a) 2-0, Australia (a) 0-5, Jordan (a) 0-3, Myanmar (a) 0-3, Kuwait (h) 0-1.
**Played 02.10.2018, result incorrect in last edition.*
League champions 2019–20: Machhindra. *Cup winners 2018:* Three Star Club; *2019:* Dauphins Family Club.

OMAN

Oman Football Association, Seeb Sports Stadium, PO Box 3462, 112 Ruwi, Muscat.
Founded: 1978. *FIFA:* 1980; *AFC:* 1980. *National Colours:* All yellow with black trim.
International matches 2019–20
India (a) 2-1, Lebanon (h) 1-0, Afghanistan (h) 3-0, Qatar (a) 1-2, Bangladesh (h) 4-1, India (h) 1-0, Bahrain (n) 0-0, Kuwait (n) 2-1, Saudi Arabia (n) 1-3.
League champions 2018–19: Dhofar; *2019–20:* Competition suspended. *Cup winners 2018–19:* Sur; *2019–20:* Competition suspended.

PAKISTAN

Pakistan Football Federation, PFF Football House, Ferozepur Road, Lahore 54600, Punjab.
Founded: 1947. *FIFA:* 1948; *AFC:* 1954. *National Colours:* All white with green trim.
International matches 2019–20
None played.
League champions 2018–19: Khan Research Laboratories; *2019–20:* Competition suspended. *Cup winners 2019:* Pakistan Army.

PALESTINE

Palestinian Football Association, Nr. Faisal Al-Husseini Stadium, PO Box 4373, Jerusalem-al-Ram.
Founded: 1928. *FIFA:* 1998; *AFC:* 1998. *National Colours:* All red with white trim.
International matches 2019–20
Kyrgyz Republic (a) 2-2*, Yemen (n) 1-0, Iraq (a) 1-2, Lebanon (n) 0-0, Syria (n) 4-3, Uzbekistan (h) 2-0, Singapore (a) 1-2, Saudi Arabia (h) 0-0, Yemen (a) 0-1‡, Uzbekistan (a) 0-2, Bangladesh (a) 2-0, Sri Lanka (n) 2-0, Seychelles (n) 1-0, Burundi (n) 3-1.
**Played 11.06.2019, result incorrect in last edition. ‡ Match played in Bahrain.*
League champions 2018–19: West Bank: Hilal Al-Quds, Gaza Strip: Khadamat Rafah; *2019–20:* Competitions suspended. *Cup winners 2018–19:* West Bank: Markaz Balata, Gaza Strip: Khadamat Rafah; Palestine Cup: Final annulled.

PHILIPPINES

Philippine Football Federation, 27 Danny Floro–corner Capt. Henry Javier Streets, Oranbo, Pasig City 1600.
Founded: 1907. *FIFA:* 1930; *AFC:* 1954. *National Colours:* All white with grey trim.
International matches 2019–20
Syria (h) 2-5, Guam (a) 4-1, China PR (h) 0-0, Maldives (a) 2-1, Syria (a) 0-1*.
**Match played in UAE.*
League champions 2019: Ceres-Negros; *2020:* Competition postponed. *Cup winners 2019:* Ceres-Negros; *2020:* Competition abandoned.

QATAR

Qatar Football Association, 28th Floor, Al Bidda Tower, Corniche Street, West Bay, PO Box 5333, Doha.
Founded: 1960. *FIFA:* 1972; *AFC:* 1974. *National Colours:* All burgundy.
International matches 2019–20
Afghanistan (h) 6-0, India (h) 0-0, Bangladesh (a) 2-0, Oman (h) 2-1, Singapore (h) 2-0, Afghanistan (a) 1-0*, Iraq (h) 1-2, Yemen (h) 6-0, UAE (h) 4-2, Saudi Arabia (h) 0-1.
**Match played in Tajikistan.*
League champions 2019–20: Al-Duhail. *Cup winners 2019:* Al-Duhail; *2019–20:* Competition suspended.

SAUDI ARABIA

Saudi Arabian Football Federation, Al Mather Quarter, Prince Faisal Bin Fahad Street, PO Box 5844, Riyadh 11432.
Founded: 1956. *FIFA:* 1956; *AFC:* 1972. *National Colours:* White shirts with green trim, white shorts, white socks.
International matches 2019–20
Kuwait (n) 1-2, Bahrain (n) 0-0, Jordan (n) 0-3, Mali (h) 1-1, Yemen (a) 2-2*, Singapore (h) 3-0, Palestine (a) 0-0, Uzbekistan (a) 3-2, Paraguay (h) 0-0, Kuwait (n) 1-3, Bahrain (n) 2-0, Oman (n) 3-1, Qatar (a) 1-0, Bahrain (n) 0-1.
**Match played in Bahrain.*
League champions 2019–20: Al-Hilal. *Cup winners 2019:* Al-Taawoun; *2019–20:* Competition suspended.

SINGAPORE

Football Association of Singapore, Jalan Besar Stadium, 100 Tyrwhitt Road, Singapore 207542.
Founded: 1892. *FIFA:* 1956; *AFC:* 1954. *National Colours:* All red.
International matches 2019–20
Yemen (h) 2-2, Palestine (h) 2-1, Jordan (a) 0-0, Saudi Arabia (a) 0-3, Uzbekistan (h) 1-3, Qatar (a) 0-2, Yemen (a) 2-1*.
**Match played in Bahrain.*
League champions 2019: DPMM; *2020:* Competition abandoned. *Cup winners 2019:* Tampines Rovers.

SRI LANKA

Football Federation of Sri Lanka, 100/9 Independence Avenue, Colombo 07.
Founded: 1939. *FIFA:* 1952; *AFC:* 1954. *National Colours:* All yellow with red trim.
International matches 2019–20
UAE (n) 1-5, Turkmenistan (h) 0-2, Korea DPR (h) 0-1, Malaysia (a) 0-6, Korea Republic (a) 0-8, Lebanon (h) 0-3, Turkmenistan (a) 0-2, Palestine (n) 0-2, Bangladesh (a) 0-3.
League champions 2018–19: Defenders (formerly Army); *2019–20:* Competition abandoned. *Cup winners 2019–20:* Police.

SYRIA

Syrian Arab Federation for Football, Al Faihaa Sports Complex, PO Box 421, Damascus.
Founded: 1936. *FIFA:* 1937; *AFC:* 1970. *National Colours:* All red with white trim.
International matches 2019–20
India (a) 1-1, Lebanon (n) 1-2, Yemen (n) 1-1, Iraq (n) 0-0, Palestine (n) 3-4, Philippines (a) 5-2, Maldives (h) 2-1*, Guam (h) 4-0*, China PR (h) 2-1*, Philippines (h) 1-0*.
**Match played in UAE.*
League champions 2019–20: Teshrin. *Cup winners 2019–20:* Al-Wahda.

TAJIKISTAN

Tajikistan Football Federation, 14/3 Ayni Street, Dushanbe 734 025.
Founded: 1936. *FIFA:* 1994; *AFC:* 1994. *National Colours:* All red with green trim.
International matches 2019–20
India (a) 4-2*, Korea DPR (n) 0-1, Korea DPR (n) 0-1, Kyrgyz Republic (h) 1-0, Mongolia (a) 1-0, Japan (h) 0-3, Malaysia (a) 0-1, Myanmar (a) 3-4, Kyrgyz Republic (a) 1-1.
**Played 07.07.2019, result incorrect in last edition.*
League champions 2019: Istiklol; *2020:* Competition still being played. *Cup winners 2019:* Istiklol; *2020:* Competition still being played.

THAILAND

Football Association of Thailand, National Stadium, Gate 3, Rama 1 Road, Patumwan, Bangkok 10330.
Founded: 1916. *FIFA:* 1925; *AFC:* 1954. *National Colours:* All black with red trim.
International matches 2019–20
Vietnam (h) 0-0, Indonesia (a) 3-0, Congo (h) 1-1, UAE (h) 2-1, Malaysia (a) 1-2, Vietnam (a) 0-0.
League champions 2019: Chiangrai United; *2020–21:* Competition postponed. *Cup winners 2019:* Port.

TIMOR-LESTE

Federacao Futebol de Timor-Leste, Campo Democracia, Avenida Bairo Formosa, Dili.
Founded: 2002. *FIFA:* 2005; *AFC:* 2005. *National Colours:* Red shirts with black trim, white shorts, black and red socks.
International matches 2019–20
None played.
League champions 2019: Lalenok United. *Cup winners 2019:* Lalenok United.

TURKMENISTAN

Football Federation of Turkmenistan, Stadium Kopetdag, 245 A. Niyazov Street, Ashgabat 744 001.
Founded: 1992. *FIFA:* 1994; *AFC:* 1994. *National Colours:* All green.
International matches 2019–20
Sri Lanka (a) 2-0, Korea Republic (h) 0-2, Lebanon (a) 1-2, Kuwait (a) 1-1, Korea DPR (h) 3-1, Sri Lanka (h) 2-0.
League champions 2019: Altyn Asyr; *2020:* Competition suspended. *Cup winners 2019:* Altyn Asyr; *2020:* Competition postponed.

UNITED ARAB EMIRATES (UAE)

United Arab Emirates Football Association, Zayed Sports City, PO Box 916, Abu Dhabi.
Founded: 1971. *FIFA:* 1974; *AFC:* 1974. *National Colours:* All white with red trim.
International matches
Dominican Republic (n) 4-0, Sri Lanka (n) 5-1, Malaysia (a) 2-1, Indonesia (h) 5-0, Thailand (a) 1-2, Vietnam (a) 0-1, Yemen (n) 3-0, Iraq (n) 0-2, Qatar (a) 2-4.
League champions 2018–19: Sharjah; *2019–20:* Competition abandoned. *Cup winners 2018–19:* Shabab Al-Ahli; *2019–20:* Competition abandoned.

UZBEKISTAN

Uzbekistan Football Federation, Massiv Almazar Furkat Street 15/1, Tashkent 700 003.
Founded: 1946. *FIFA:* 1994; *AFC:* 1994. *National Colours:* All white with blue trim.
International matches 2019–20
Palestine (a) 0-2, Iraq (n) 0-0, Yemen (h) 5-0, Singapore (a) 3-1, Kyrgyz Republic (h) 3-1, Saudi Arabia (h) 2-3, Palestine (h) 2-0, Belarus (n) 0-1.
League champions 2019: Pakhtakor; *2020:* Competition still being played. *Cup winners 2019:* Pakhtakor; *2020:* Competition still being played.

VIETNAM

Vietnam Football Federation, Le Quang Dao Street, Phu Do Ward, Nam Tu Liem District, Hanoi 844.
Founded: 1960 (NV). *FIFA:* 1952 (SV), 1964 (NV); *AFC:* 1954 (SV), 1978 (SRV). *National Colours:* All red.
International matches 2019–20
Thailand (a) 0-0, Malaysia (h) 1-0, Indonesia (a) 3-1, UAE (h) 1-0, Thailand (h) 0-0.
League champions 2019: Ha Noi; *2020:* Competition still being played. *Cup winners 2019:* Ha Noi; *2020:* Competition still being played.

YEMEN

Yemen Football Association, Quarter of Sport Al Jeraf (Ali Mohsen Al-Muraisi Stadium), PO Box 908, Al-Thawra City, Sana'a.
Founded: 1940 (SY), 1962 (NY). *FIFA:* 1967 (SY), 1980 (NY); *AFC:* 1972 (SY), 1980 (NY). *National Colours:* Red shirts, white shorts, black socks.
International matches 2019–20
Palestine (n) 0-1, Syria (n) 1-1, Lebanon (n) 2-1, Iraq (a) 1-2, Singapore (a) 2-2, Saudi Arabia (h) 2-2*, Uzbekistan (a) 0-5, Palestine (h) 1-0*, Singapore (h) 1-2*, UAE (n) 0-3, Qatar (a) 0-6, Iraq (n) 0-0.
**Match played in Bahrain.*
No club competitions since January 2015 due to civil war.

NORTH AND CENTRAL AMERICA AND CARIBBEAN (CONCACAF)

ANGUILLA

Anguilla Football Association, 2 Queen Elizabeth Avenue, PO Box 1318, The Valley, AI-2640.
Founded: 1990. *FIFA:* 1996; *CONCACAF:* 1996. *National Colours:* Orange shirts with black trim, orange shorts with black trim, white socks.
International matches 2019–20
Guatemala (a) 0-10, Guatemala (h) 0-5, Puerto Rico (h) 2-3, Trinidad & Tobago (a) 0-15, Puerto Rico (a) 0-3.
League champions 2019: Competition abandoned; *2020:* Roaring Lions. *Cup winners:* No competition.

ANTIGUA & BARBUDA

Antigua & Barbuda Football Association, Ground Floor, Sydney Walling Stand, Antigua Recreation Ground, PO Box 773, St John's.
Founded: 1928. *FIFA:* 1970; *CONCACAF:* 1972. *National Colours:* All yellow with black trim.
International matches 2019–20
Curacao (h) 2-1*, St Kitts & Nevis (a) 0-3, St Kitts & Nevis (a) 3-4, Jamaica (a) 0-6, Aruba (h) 2-1, Guyana (h) 2-1, Guyana (a) 1-5, Jamaica (h) 0-2, Aruba (a) 3-2‡, Guatemala (a) 0-8.
**Played 23.03.2019, result incorrect in last edition. ‡Match played in Curacao.*
League champions 2018–19: Liberta; *2019–20:* Competition suspended. *Cup winners:* No competition.

ARUBA

Arubaanse Voetbal Bond, Technical Centre Angel Botta, Shaba 24, PO Box 376, Noord.
Founded: 1932. *FIFA:* 1988; *CONCACAF:* 1986. *National Colours:* Yellow shirts with sky blue sleeves, yellow shorts, yellow socks.
International matches 2019–20
St Lucia (a) 2-3*, Guyana (h) 0-1‡, Antigua & Barbuda (a) 1-2‡, Jamaica (a) 0-2, Jamaica (a) 0-6‡, Guyana (a) 2-4, Antigua & Barbuda (a) 2-3‡.
**Played 22.03.2019 in Antigua & Barbuda, result incorrect in last edition. ‡Match played in Curacao.*
League champions 2018–19: Racing Club Aruba; *2019–20:* Competition suspended. *Cup winners 2020:* Racing Club Aruba.

BAHAMAS

Bahamas Football Association, Rosetta Street, PO Box N-8434, Nassau, NP.
Founded: 1967. *FIFA:* 1968; *CONCACAF:* 1981. *National Colours:* Yellow shirts, black shorts, yellow socks.
International matches 2019–20
Bonaire† (h) 2-1, British Virgin Islands (a) 4-0*, British Virgin Islands (h) 3-0, Bonaire† (a) 1-1‡.
**Match played in St Kitts & Nevis. ‡Match played in Curacao.*
League champions 2018–19: Dynamos; *2019–20:* Competition suspended. *Cup winners 2017–18:* Western Warriors; not contested since.

BARBADOS

Barbados Football Association, Bottom Floor, ABC Marble Complex, PO Box 1362, Fontabelle, St Michael.
Founded: 1910. *FIFA:* 1968; *CONCACAF:* 1967. *National Colours:* Gold shirts with royal blue sleeves, gold shorts, gold socks.
International matches 2019–20
Saint-Martin† (h) 4-0, Cayman Islands (a) 2-3, US Virgin Islands (h) 1-0, US Virgin Islands (a) 4-0, Saint-Martin† (n) 0-1*, Cayman Islands (h) 3-0, Canada (n) 1-4, Canada (n) 1-4.
**Match played in Anguilla.*
League champions 2018–19: Barbados Defence Force; *2019–20:* Competition suspended. *Cup winners 2019:* Weymouth Wales.

BELIZE

Football Federation of Belize, 26 Hummingbird Highway, Belmopan, PO Box 1742, Belize City.
Founded: 1980. *FIFA:* 1986; *CONCACAF:* 1986. *National Colours:* Blue shirts with white trim, blue shorts, blue socks.
International matches 2019–20
St Vincent/Grenadines (h) 1-1, St Vincent/Grenadines (h) 1-0, French Guiana† (a) 0-3*, Grenada (h) 1-2, St Kitts & Nevis (h) 0-4, St Kitts & Nevis (a) 1-0, French Guiana† (h) 2-0, Grenada (a) 2-3.
**Match awarded 3-0 to French Guiana; Belize failed to fulfil fixture.*
League champions 2018–19: Belmopan Bandits (Opening); San Pedro Pirates (Closing); *2019–20:* Verdes (Opening); Closing season competition suspended. *Cup winners:* No competition.

BERMUDA

Bermuda Football Association, 48 Cedar Avenue, PO Box HM 745, Hamilton HM11.
Founded: 1928. *FIFA:* 1962; *CONCACAF:* 1967. *National Colours:* All red.
International matches 2019–20
Panama (h) 1-4, Panama (a) 2-0, Mexico (h) 1-5, Guatemala (h) 0-0, Mexico (a) 1-2, Jamaica (a) 0-2.
League champions 2019–20: North Village Rams. *Cup winners 2018–19:* Robin Hood; *2019–20:* Competition abandoned.

BRITISH VIRGIN ISLANDS

British Virgin Islands Football Association, Botanic Station, PO Box 4269, Road Town, Tortola VG 1110.
Founded: 1974. *FIFA:* 1996; *CONCACAF:* 1996. *National Colours:* Green shirts with gold and white trim, green shorts, gold socks.
International matches 2019–20
Bonaire† (a) 2-4*, Bahamas (h) 0-4‡, Bonaire† (h) 3-4‡, Bahamas (a) 0-3.
**Match played in Curacao. ‡Match played in St Kitts & Nevis.*
League champions 2018: One Love United; *2018–19:* No competition; *2019–20:* Competition still being played. *Cup winners:* No competition.

CANADA

Canadian Soccer Association, Place Soccer Canada, 237 Metcalfe Street, Ottawa, Ontario K2P 1R2.
Founded: 1912. *FIFA:* 1912; *CONCACAF:* 1961. *National Colours:* All red.
International matches 2019–20
Cuba (h) 6-0, Cuba (a) 1-0*, USA (h) 2-0, USA (a) 1-4, Barbados (n) 4-1, Barbados (n) 4-1, Iceland (n) 0-1.
**Match played in Cayman Islands.*
League champions 2019: Cavalry (Spring); Cavalry (Fall); Forge (Playoff). *Cup winners 2019:* Montreal Impact; *2020:* Competition still being played. (N.B. Canadian teams also compete in MLS and USL.)

CAYMAN ISLANDS

Cayman Islands Football Association, PO Box 178, Poindexter Road, Prospect, George Town, Grand Cayman KY1-1104.
Founded: 1966. *FIFA:* 1992; *CONCACAF:* 1990. *National Colours:* Red shirts with white sleeves, red shorts, red socks with white tops.
International matches 2019–20
US Virgin Islands (a) 2-0, Barbados (n) 3-2, Saint-Martin† (h) 0-3*, Saint-Martin† (h) 1-0, US Virgin Islands (h) 1-0, Barbados (a) 0-3.
**Match played in Anguilla.*
League champions 2019–20: Bodden Town. *Cup winners 2017–18:* Academy; *2018–19:* Elite; *2019–20:* No competition.

COSTA RICA

Federacion Costarricense de Futbol, 600 mts sur del Cruce de la Panasonic, San Rafael de Alajuela, Radial a Santa Ana, San Jose 670-1000.
Founded: 1921. *FIFA:* 1927; *CONCACAF:* 1961. *National Colours:* Red shirts, blue shorts, white socks.
International matches 2019–20
Uruguay (h) 1-2, Haiti (a) 1-1*, Curacao (h) 0-0, Curacao (a) 2-1, Haiti (h) 1-1, USA (a) 0-1.
**Match played in Bahamas.*
League champions 2019–20: Herediano (Apertura); Saprissa (Clausura). *Cup winners:* No competition.

CUBA

Asociacion de Futbol de Cuba, Estadio Pedro Marrero Escuela Nacional de Futbol – Mario Lopez, Avenida 41 no. 44 y 46, La Habana.
Founded: 1924. *FIFA:* 1932; *CONCACAF:* 1961. *National Colours:* All red.
International matches 2019–20
Canada (a) 0-6, Canada (h) 0-1*, USA (a) 0-7, Nicaragua (a) 0-0, Nicaragua (a) 1-0, USA (h) 0-4*.
**Match played in Cayman Islands.*
League champions 2019–20: Pinar del Rio (Apertura); Clausura season competition abandoned. *Cup winners:* No competition.

CURACAO

Curacao Football Federation, Bonamweg 49, PO Box 341, Willemstad.
Founded: 1921 (Netherlands Antilles), 2010. *FIFA:* 1932, 2010; *CONCACAF:* 1961, 2010. *National Colours:* All white.
International matches 2019–20
Haiti (h) 1-0, Haiti (a) 1-1, Costa Rica (a) 0-0, Costa Rica (h) 1-2.
League champions 2018–19: SV Vesta; *2019–20:* Competition still being played. *Cup winners:* No competition.

DOMINICA

Dominica Football Association, Patrick John Football House, Bath Estate, PO Box 1080, Roseau.
Founded: 1970. *FIFA:* 1994; *CONCACAF:* 1994. *National Colours:* All emerald green.
International matches 2019–20
Suriname (h) 1-2, St Vincent/Grenadines (a) 0-1, St Lucia (a) 1-3, St Lucia (a) 4-1, Nicaragua (a) 1-3, Nicaragua (h) 0-4, Suriname (a) 0-4, St Vincent/Grenadines (h) 1-0.
League champions 2018–19: Sagicor South Eas; *2020:* Competition still being played. *Cup winners:* No competition.

DOMINICAN REPUBLIC

Federacion Dominicana de Futbol, Centro Olimpico Juan Pablo Duarte, Apartado Postal 1953, Santo Domingo.
Founded: 1953. *FIFA:* 1958; *CONCACAF:* 1964. *National Colours:* All blue.
International matches 2019–20
UAE (n) 0-4, Montserrat (a) 1-2, El Salvador (h) 1-0, St Lucia (h) 3-0, Montserrat (h) 0-0, St Lucia (a) 0-1, El Salvador (a) 0-2.
League champions 2019: Atletico Pantoja (Apertura); Cibao (Clausura); Atletico Pantoja (Play-off). *Cup winners:* No competition.

EL SALVADOR

Federacion Salvadorena de Futbol, Avenida Jose Matias Delgado, Frente al Centro Espanol Colonia Escalon, Zona 10, San Salvador 1029.
Founded: 1935. *FIFA:* 1938; *CONCACAF:* 1961. *National Colours:* All blue.
International matches 2019–20
St Lucia (h) 3-0, Dominican Republic (a) 0-1, Montserrat (a) 2-0, St Lucia (a) 2-0, Montserrat (h) 1-0, Dominican Republic (h) 2-0, Iceland (n) 0-1.
League champions 2019–20: Alianza (Apertura); Once Deportivo (Clausura); Play-off abandoned. *Cup winner: 2018–19:* Santa Tecla; *2019–20:* Competition postponed.

GRENADA

Grenada Football Association, National Stadium, PO Box 326, St George's.
Founded: 1924. *FIFA:* 1978; *CONCACAF:* 1969. *National Colours:* All green.
International matches 2019–20
Cuba (h) 0-2*, Saint-Martin† (h) 5-2‡, Puerto Rico (a) 2-0, St Kitts & Nevis (h) 2-1, Belize (a) 2-1, French Guiana† (a) 0-0, French Guiana† (h) 1-0, St Kitts & Nevis (a) 0-0, Belize (h) 3-2.
**Played 13.10.2018, result incorrect in last edition.*
‡ Played 16.11.2018, result incorrect in last edition.
League champions 2018–19: Paradise; *2019–20:* Competition abandoned. *Cup winners 2018:* Not contested; *2019:* Hard Rock.

GUATEMALA

Federacion Nacional de Futbol de Guatemala, 2a Calle 15-57, Zona 15, Boulevard Vista Hermosa, Guatemala City 01015.
Founded: 1919. *FIFA:* 1946; *CONCACAF:* 1961. *National Colours:* White shirts with blue sash, white shorts, white socks.
International matches 2019–20
Anguilla (h) 10-0, Puerto Rico (a) 5-0, Anguilla (a) 5-0,

Bermuda (a) 0-0, Puerto Rico (h) 5-0, Antigua & Barbuda (h) 8-0.
League champions 2019–20: Municipal (Apertura); Clausura season competition abandoned. *Cup winners 2011–17:* Not contested; *2018–19:* Coban Imperial.

GUYANA

Guyana Football Federation, Lot 17, Dadanawa Street Section 'K', Campbellville, PO Box 10727, Georgetown.
Founded: 1902. *FIFA:* 1970; *CONCACAF:* 1961. *National Colours:* All yellow with black, green and red trim.
International matches 2019–20
Aruba (a) 1-0*, Jamaica (h) 0-4, Antigua & Barbuda (a) 1-2, Antigua & Barbuda (h) 5-1, Aruba (h) 4-2, Jamaica (a) 1-1.
**Match played in Curacao.*
League champions 2019: Fruta Conquerors; *2020:* Competition postponed. *Cup winners:* Not contested since 2015.

HAITI

Federation Haitienne de Football, Stade Sylvio Cator, Rue Oswald Durand, Port-au-Prince.
Founded: 1904. *FIFA:* 1933; *CONCACAF:* 1961. *National Colours:* Blue shirts with red trim, blue shorts, blue socks with red tops.
International matches 2019–20
Mexico (n) 0-1*, Curacao (a) 0-1, Curacao (h) 1-1, Costa Rica (h) 1-1‡, Bolivia (a) 1-3, Costa Rica (a) 1-1.
**Played 03.07.2019, venue incorrect in last edition.*
‡ Match played in Bahamas.
League champions 2019: Arcahaie (Ouverture); Cloture season abandoned due to civil unrest. *2020:* Ouverture season abandoned; Cloture season cancelled due to autumn/spring transition. *Cup winners:* No competition.

HONDURAS

Federacion Nacional Autonoma de Futbol de Honduras, Colonia Florencia Norte, Edificio Plaza America Ave. Roble, 1 y 2 Nivle, PO Box 827, Tegucigalpa 504.
Founded: 1935. *FIFA:* 1946; *CONCACAF:* 1961. *National Colours:* All white.
International matches 2019–20
Puerto Rico (h) 4-0, Chile (h) 2-1, Trinidad & Tobago (a) 2-0, Martinique† (h) 1-0, Martinique† (a) 1-1, Trinidad & Tobago (h) 4-0.
League champions 2019–20: Olimpia (Apertura); Clausura season competition abandoned. *Cup winners 2018:* Platense; *2019:* Not contested due to scheduling issues.

JAMAICA

Jamaica Football Federation Ltd, 20 St Lucia Crescent, Kingston 5.
Founded: 1910. *FIFA:* 1962; *CONCACAF:* 1963. *National Colours:* Gold shirts, black shorts, gold socks.
International matches 2019–20
Antigua & Barbuda (h) 6-0, Guyana (a) 4-0, Aruba (h) 2-0, Aruba (a) 6-0*, Antigua & Barbuda (a) 2-0, Guyana (h) 1-1, Bermuda (h) 2-0.
**Match played in Curacao.*
League champions 2018–19: Portmore United; *2019–20:* Competition abandoned. *Cup winners:* Not contested since 2014.

MEXICO

Federacion Mexicana de Futbol Asociacion, A.C., Colima No. 373, Colonia Roma, Delegacion Cuauhtemoc, Mexico DF 06700.
Founded: 1927. *FIFA:* 1929; *CONCACAF:* 1961. *National Colours:* All black with white trim.
International matches 2019–20
USA (a) 3-0, Argentina (n) 0-4, Trinidad & Tobago (h) 2-0, Bermuda (a) 5-1, Panama (h) 3-1, Panama (a) 3-0, Bermuda (h) 2-1.
League champions 2019–20: Monterrey (Apertura); Clausura season competition suspended. *Cup winners 2018–19:* Cruz Azul (Apertura); America (Clausura); *2019–20:* Competition still being played.

MONTSERRAT

Montserrat Football Association Inc., PO Box 505, Blakes, Montserrat.
Founded: 1994. *FIFA:* 1996; *CONCACAF:* 1996. *National Colours:* White shirts with green hoops, white shorts, white socks.
International matches 2019–20
Dominican Republic (h) 2-1, St Lucia (h) 1-1, El Salvador (h) 0-2, Dominican Republic (a) 0-0, El Salvador (a) 0-1, St Lucia (a) 1-0.
League champions: Not contested since 2016. *Cup winners:* No competition.

NICARAGUA

Federacion Nicaraguense de Futbol, Porton Principal del Hospital Bautista 1 Cuadra Abajo, 1 Cuadra al Sur y 1/2 Cuadra Abajo, Apartado Postal 976, Managua.
Founded: 1931. *FIFA:* 1950; *CONCACAF:* 1961. *National Colours:* All blue with white trim.
International matches 2019–20
St Vincent/Grenadines (h) 1-1, Suriname (a) 0-6, Dominica (h) 3-1, Dominica (a) 4-0, Cuba (h) 0-0, Cuba (h) 0-1, St Vincent/Grenadines (a) 0-1, Suriname (h) 1-2.
League champions 2019–20: Real Esteli (Apertura); Real Esteli (Clausura). *Cup winners 2019:* Managua.

PANAMA

Federacion Panamena de Futbol, Ciudad Deportiva Irving Saladino, Corregimiento de Juan Diaz, Apartado Postal 0827-00391, Zona 8, Panama City.
Founded: 1937. *FIFA:* 1938; *CONCACAF:* 1961. *National Colours:* All red.
International matches 2019–20
Bermuda (a) 4-1, Bermuda (h) 0-2, Mexico (a) 1-3, Mexico (h) 0-3.
League champions 2019: Tauro (transitional Apertura); *2020:* Apertura season competition abandoned. *Cup winners:* No competition.

PUERTO RICO

Federacion Puertorriquena de Futbol, PO Box 367567, San Juan 00936.
Founded: 1940. *FIFA:* 1960; *CONCACAF:* 1961. *National Colours:* Red and white striped shirts with blue trim, blue shorts, red socks.
International matches 2019–20
Honduras (a) 0-4, Guatemala (h) 0-5, Anguilla (a) 3-2, Guatemala (a) 0-5, Anguilla (h) 3-0.
League champions 2018–19: Metropolitan FA; *2019–20:* Competition abandoned. *Cup winners 2019:* Bayamon.

ST KITTS & NEVIS

St Kitts & Nevis Football Association, PO Box 465, Lozack Road, Basseterre.
Founded: 1932. *FIFA:* 1992; *CONCACAF:* 1992. *National Colours:* All red.
International matches 2019–20
Antigua & Barbuda (h) 3-0, Antigua & Barbuda (h) 4-3, Grenada (a) 1-2, French Guiana† (h) 2-2, Belize (a) 4-0, Belize (h) 0-1, Grenada (h) 0-0, French Guiana† (a) 1-3.
League champions 2018–19: Competition abandoned after legal proceedings; *2019–20:* Competition suspended. *Cup winners 2019:* Newtown United; *2020:* Competition suspended.

ST LUCIA

St Lucia National Football Association, Barnard Hill, PO Box 255, Castries.
Founded: 1979. *FIFA:* 1988; *CONCACAF:* 1986. *National Colours:* Sky blue shirts with yellow stripes, sky blue shorts, sky blue socks.
International matches 2019–20
El Salvador (a) 0-3, Montserrat (a) 1-1, Dominica (h) 3-1, Dominica (h) 1-4, Dominican Republic (a) 0-3, El Salvador (h) 0-2, Dominican Republic (h) 1-0, Montserrat (h) 0-1.
League champions 2019: Platinum. *Cup winners 2014–17:* Not known; *2018:* Marchand; *2019:* Gros Islet.

ST VINCENT & THE GRENADINES

St Vincent & the Grenadines Football Federation, PO Box 1278, Nichols Building (2nd Floor), Bentinck Square, Victoria Park, Kingstown.
Founded: 1979. *FIFA:* 1988; *CONCACAF:* 1986. *National Colours:* Yellow shirts, blue shorts, blue socks.
International matches 2019–20
Trinidad & Tobago (h) 1-0, Belize (a) 1-1, Belize (a) 0-1, Nicaragua (a) 1-1, Dominica (h) 1-0, Suriname (h) 2-2, Suriname (a) 1-0, Nicaragua (h) 1-0, Dominica (a) 0-1.
League champions 2019–20: Hope International. *Cup winners:* No competition.

SURINAME

Surinaamse Voetbal Bond, Letitia Vriesdelaan 7, PO Box 1223, Paramaribo.
Founded: 1920. *FIFA:* 1929; *CONCACAF:* 1961. *National Colours:* White shirts, white shorts, white socks with green tops.
International matches 2019–20
Dominica (a) 2-1, Nicaragua (h) 6-0, St Vincent/Grenadines (a) 2-2, St Vincent/Grenadines (h) 0-1, Dominica (h) 4-0, Nicaragua (a) 2-1.
League champions 2018–19: Inter Moengotapoe; *2019–20:* Competition abandoned. *Cup winners 2019:* Inter Moengotapoe; *2020:* Competition suspended.

TRINIDAD & TOBAGO

Trinidad & Tobago Football Association, 24–26 Dundonald Street, PO Box 400, Port of Spain.
Founded: 1908. *FIFA:* 1964; *CONCACAF:* 1962. *National Colours:* Red shirts with black trim, black shorts with red trim, red socks.
International matches 2019–20
St Vincent/Grenadines (a) 0-1, Martinique† (a) 1-1, Martinique† (h) 2-2, Mexico (a) 0-2, Honduras (h) 0-2, Venezuela (a) 0-2, Anguilla (h) 15-0, Ecuador (a) 0-3, Honduras (a) 0-4.
League champions 2018: W Connection; *2019–20:* Defence Force. *Cup winners:* Not contested since 2017.

TURKS & CAICOS ISLANDS

Turks & Caicos Islands Football Association, TCIFA National Academy, Venetian Road, PO Box 626, Providenciales.
Founded: 1996. *FIFA:* 1998; *CONCACAF:* 1996. *National Colours:* All black with white trim.
International matches 2019–20
Guadeloupe† (h) 0-3, Sint Maarten† (a) 5-2*, Sint Maarten† (h) 3-2, Guadeloupe† (a) 0-10.
**Match played in Curacao.*
League champions 2019–20: SWA Sharks (Apertura); Clausura season competition suspended. *Cup winners: 2019:* Academy Jaguars.

UNITED STATES OF AMERICA (USA)

US Soccer Federation, US Soccer House, 1801 S. Prairie Avenue, Chicago, IL 60616.
Founded: 1913. *FIFA:* 1914; *CONCACAF:* 1961. *National Colours:* White shirts with red and blue trim, white shorts, white socks.
International matches 2019–20
Mexico (h) 0-3, Uruguay (h) 1-1, Cuba (h) 7-0, Canada (a) 0-2, Canada (h) 4-1, Cuba (a) 4-0*, Costa Rica (h) 1-0.
**Match played in Cayman Islands.*
League champions 2019: Seattle Sounders. *2019:* Competition still being played. *Cup winners 2019:* Atlanta United; *2020:* Competition abandoned. (N.B. Teams from USA and Canada compete in MLS and USL.)

US VIRGIN ISLANDS

USVI Soccer Federation Inc., 498D Strawberry, PO Box 2346, Christiansted, St Croix 00851.
Founded: 1987. *FIFA:* 1998; *CONCACAF:* 1987. *National Colours:* All royal blue with gold trim.
International matches 2019–20
Cayman Islands (h) 0-2, Saint-Martin† (a) 2-1*, Barbados (a) 0-1, Barbados (h) 0-4, Cayman Islands (a) 0-1, Saint-Martin† (h) 1-2.
**Match played in Anguilla.*
League champions 2018–19: Helenites; *2019–20:* Competition suspended. *Cup winners:* No competition.

OCEANIA (OFC)

AMERICAN SAMOA

Football Federation American Samoa, PO Box 982 413, Pago Pago AS 96799.
Founded: 1984. *FIFA:* 1998; *OFC:* 1998. *National Colours:* All blue with white trim.
International matches 2019–20
Solomon Islands (n) 0-13, Tahiti (n) 0-1.
League champions 2019: Pago Youth. *Cup winners:* Not contested since 2014.

COOK ISLANDS

Cook Islands Football Association, Matavera Main Road, PO Box 29, Avarua, Rarotonga.
Founded: 1971. *FIFA:* 1994; *OFC:* 1994. *National Colours:* All green shirts with white trim.
International matches 2019–20
None played.
League champions 2019: Tupapa Maraerenga; *2020:* Competition still being played. *Cup winners 2019:* Tupapa Maraerenga.

FIJI

Fiji Football Association, PO Box 2514, Government Buildings, Suva.
Founded: 1938. *FIFA:* 1964; *OFC:* 1966. *National Colours:* White shirts, black shorts, white socks.
International matches 2019–20
Tuvalu† (n) 10-1, Solomon Islands (n) 4-4, Papua New Guinea (n) 1-1 (4-2p).
League champions 2019: Ba; *2020:* Competition still being played. *Cup winners 2018*: Rewa (result incorrect in last edition); *2019:* Nadi.

NEW CALEDONIA

Federation Caledonienne de Football, 7 bis, Rue Suffren Quartien latin, BP 560, Noumea 99845.
Founded: 1928. *FIFA:* 2004; *OFC:* 2004. *National Colours:* All red with white trim.
International matches 2019–20
Tahiti (n) 3-0, Tuvalu† (n) 11-0, New Zealand (n) 1-2.
League champions 2019: Hienghene Sport; *2020–21:* Competition still being played. *Cup winners 2019:* Hienghene Sport; *2020:* Competition still being played.

NEW ZEALAND

New Zealand Football, PO Box 301-043, Albany, Auckland.
Founded: 1891. *FIFA:* 1948; *OFC:* 1966. *National Colours:* All white.
International matches 2019–20
Tonga (n) 13-0*, Papua New Guinea (n) 2-0, New Caledonia (n) 2-1, Republic of Ireland (a) 1-3, Lithuania (a) 0-1.
**Played 8.07.2019, result omitted from last edition.*
League champions 2019–20: Auckland City. *Cup winners 2019:* Napier City Rovers.

PAPUA NEW GUINEA

Papua New Guinea Football Association, PO Box 957, Lae 411, Morobe Province.
Founded: 1962. *FIFA:* 1966; *OFC:* 1966. *National Colours:* All red with white trim.
International matches 2019–20
New Zealand (n) 0-2, Tonga (n) 8-0, Fiji (n) 1-1 (2-4p).
League champions 2019: Lae City (formerly Toti City); *2019–20:* Competition still being played. *Cup winners:* Not contested since 2006.

SAMOA

Football Federation Samoa, PO Box 1682, Tuanimato, Apia.
Founded: 1968. *FIFA:* 1986; *OFC:* 1986. *National Colours:* Blue shirts, white shorts, blue socks.
International matches 2019–20
Tonga (h) 2-0*, Vanuatu (h) 0-11.
**Played 12.07.2019, venue incorrect in last edition.*
League champions 2019: Lupe ole Soaga; *2020:* Competition still being played. *Cup winners:* Not contested since 2014.

SOLOMON ISLANDS

Solomon Islands Football Federation, Allan Boso Complex, Panatina Academy, PO Box 584, Honiara.
Founded: 1978. *FIFA:* 1988; *OFC:* 1988. *National Colours:* Gold shirts, blue shorts, white socks.
International matches 2019–20
American Samoa (n) 13-0, Fiji (n) 4-4.
League champions 2019–20: Solomon Warriors. *Cup winners:* No competition.

TAHITI

Federation Tahitienne de Football, Rue Gerald Coppenrath, Complexe de Fautaua, PO Box 50358, Pirae 98716.
Founded: 1989. *FIFA:* 1990; *OFC:* 1990. *National Colours:* All red.
International matches 2019–20
New Caledonia (n) 0-3, American Samoa (n) 8-1.
League champions 2019–20: AS Pirae. *Cup winners 2018–19:* AS Venus; *2019–20:* Competition abandoned.

TONGA

Tonga Football Association, Loto-Tonga Soka Centre, Valungafulu Road, Atele, PO Box 852, Nuku'alofa.
Founded: 1965. *FIFA:* 1994; *OFC:* 1994. *National Colours:* All red.
International matches 2019–20
New Zealand (n) 0-13*, Vanuatu (n) 0-14, Papua New Guinea (n) 0-8.
**Played 8.07.2019, result omitted from last edition.*
League champions 2019: Veitongo. *Cup winners:* Not contested since 2003.

VANUATU

Vanuatu Football Federation, VFF House, Lini Highway, PO Box 266, Port Vila.
Founded: 1934. *FIFA:* 1988; *OFC:* 1988. *National Colours:* Gold shirts with black trim, black shorts, gold socks with black tops.
International matches 2019–20
Tonga (n) 14-0, Samoa (a) 11-0.
League champions 2018–19: Tafea; *Grand Final winners:* Galaxy; *2019–20:* Competition suspended. *Cup winners:* No competition.

AFRICA (CAF)

ALGERIA

Federation Algerienne De Football, Chemin Ahmed Ouaked, BP 39, Dely-Ibrahim, Algiers 16000.
Founded: 1962. *FIFA:* 1963; *CAF:* 1964. *National Colours:* All white.
International matches 2019–20
Senegal (n) 1-0, Benin (h) 1-0, Morocco (h) 0-0, DR Congo (h) 1-1, Colombia (n) 3-0, Morocco (a) 0-3, Zambia (h) 5-0, Botswana (a) 1-0.
League champions 2019–20: CR Belouizdad. *Cup winners 2018–19:* CR Belouizdad; *2019–20:* Competition suspended.

ANGOLA

Federacao Angolana de Futetbol, Senado de Compl. da Cidadela Desportiva, BP 3449, Luanda.
Founded: 1979. *FIFA:* 1980; *CAF:* 1980. *National Colours:* Red shirts with yellow trim, black shorts, red socks.
International matches 2019–20
Eswatini (a) 1-1, Eswatini (h) 1-1 (4-5p), Gambia (a) 1-0, Gambia (h) 2-1, Gambia (h) 1-3, Gabon (a) 1-2.
League champions 2018–19: Primeiro de Agosto; *2019–20:* Competition abandoned. *Cup winners 2019:* Primeiro de Agosto; *2020:* Competition abandoned.

BENIN

Federation Beninoise de Football, Rue du boulevard Djassain, BP 112, 3-eme Arrondissement de Porto-Novo 01.
Founded: 1962. *FIFA:* 1962; *CAF:* 1962. *National Colours:* All yellow with red and green trim.
International matches 2019–20
Togo (h) 0-0, Togo (a) 0-1, Ivory Coast (n) 2-1, Algeria (a) 0-1, Zambia (h) 2-2, Nigeria (a) 1-2, Sierra Leone (h) 1-0.
League champions 2018–19: Buffles du Borgou; *2019–20:* Competition abandoned. *Cup winners 2019:* ESAE.

BOTSWANA

Botswana Football Association, PO Box 1396, Gaborone.
Founded: 1970. *FIFA:* 1978; *CAF:* 1976. *National Colours:* Blue shirts with black sleeves, blue shorts, blue socks with black trim.
International matches 2019–20
Zambia (h) 0-0, Zambia (a) 2-3, Malawi (h) 0-0, Malawi (a) 0-1, Liberia (h) 0-0, Egypt (a) 0-1, Zimbabwe (a) 0-0, Algeria (h) 0-1.
League champions 2019–20: Jwaneng Galaxy. *Cup winners 2019:* Orapa United; *2020:* Competition abandoned.

BURKINA FASO

Federation Burkinabe de Foot-Ball, Centre Technique National Ouaga 2000, BP 57, Ouagadougou 01.
Founded: 1960. *FIFA:* 1964; *CAF:* 1964. *National Colours:* Green shirts with red sleeves, green shorts, green socks.
International matches 2019–20
DR Congo (n) 0-0*, Morocco (a) 1-1, Ghana (a) 1-0, Gabon (n) 0-1, Ghana (h) 0-0, Uganda (h) 0-0, South Sudan (a) 2-1‡.
* *Played 09.06.2019, result incorrect in last edition.*
‡ *Match played in Sudan.*
League champions 2018–19: Rahimo; *2019–20:* Competition abandoned. *Cup winners 2019:* Rahimo; *2020:* Competition abandoned.

BURUNDI

Federation de Football du Burundi, Avenue Muyinga, BP 3426, Bujumbura.
Founded: 1948. *FIFA:* 1972; *CAF:* 1972. *National Colours:* Red shirts, white shorts, green socks.
International matches 2019–20
South Sudan (h) 2-0, South Sudan (a) 2-1*, Tanzania (h) 1-1, Tanzania (a) 1-1 (0-3p), Uganda (h) 0-3, Uganda (a) 0-3, Central African Republic (a) 0-2, Morocco (h) 0-3, Uganda (a) 1-2, Eritrea (n) 0-1, Djibouti (n) 1-2, Somalia (n) 0-1, Mauritius (n) 4-1, Seychelles (n) 3-1, Bangladesh (a) 3-0, Palestine (n) 1-3.
**Match played in Uganda.*
League champions 2019–20: Le Messager. *Cup winners 2020:* Musongati.

CAMEROON

Federation Camerounaise de Football, Avenue du 27 aout 1940, Tsinga-Yaounde, BP 1116, Yaounde.
Founded: 1959. *FIFA:* 1962; *CAF:* 1963. *National Colours:* Green shirts, red shorts, yellow socks.
International matches 2019–20
Tunisia (h) 0-0, Cape Verde Islands (h) 0-0, Rwanda (a) 1-0.
League champions 2019–20: PWD Bamenda. *Cup winners 2019:* Stade Renard de Melong; *2020:* Competition suspended.

CAPE VERDE ISLANDS

Federacao Caboverdiana de Futebol, Praia Cabo Verde, FCF CX, PO Box 234, Praia.
Founded: 1982. *FIFA:* 1986; *CAF:* 2000. *National Colours:* All blue with white trim.
International matches 2019–20
Mauritania (h) 0-0, Mauritania (a) 1-2, Togo (n) 2-1, Cameroon (a) 0-0, Mozambique (h) 2-2.
League champions 2019: CS Mindelense; *2020:* Competition postponed. *Cup winners 2019:* Santo Crucifixo; *2020:* Competition abandoned.

CENTRAL AFRICAN REPUBLIC

Federation Centrafricaine de Football, Avenue des Martyrs, BP 344, Bangui.
Founded: 1961. *FIFA:* 1964; *CAF:* 1965. *National Colours:* All white with blue trim.
International matches 2019–20
DR Congo (h) 0-2, DR Congo (a) 1-4, Burundi (h) 2-0, Mauritania (a) 0-2.
League champions 2019: Tempete Mocaf; *2019–20:* Competition abandoned. *Cup winners: 2018*: Not known; *2019*: Stade Centrafricain.

CHAD

Federation Tchadienne de Football, BP 886, N'Djamena.
Founded: 1962. *FIFA:* 1964; *CAF:* 1964. *National Colours:* Blue shirts, yellow shorts, red socks.
International matches 2019–20
Equatorial Guinea (h) 3-3, Equatorial Guinea (a) 1-2, Sudan (h) 1-3, Sudan (a) 0-0, Liberia (a) 0-1, Liberia (h) 1-0 (5-4p), Namibia (a) 1-2, Mali (h) 0-2.
League champions 2019: TP Elect-Sport; *2020:* Competition suspended. *Cup winners:* Not contested since 2015.

COMOROS

Federation Comorienne de Football, Route d'Itsandra, BP 798, Moroni.
Founded: 1979. *FIFA:* 2005; *CAF:* 2003. *National Colours:* Green shirts with white trim, green shorts, green socks.
International matches 2019–20
Namibia (h) 0-2, Namibia (a) 0-0, Togo (h) 1-1, Togo (a) 0-2, Guinea (n) 1-0, Togo (a) 1-0, Egypt (h) 0-0.
League champions 2019: Fomboni; *2020:* Competition suspended. *Cup winners 2019:* Yakele Sport; *2020:* Competition suspended.

CONGO

Federation Congolaise de Football, 80 Rue Eugene Etienne, Centre Ville, BP Box 11, Brazzaville 00 242.
Founded: 1962. *FIFA:* 1964; *CAF:* 1965. *National Colours:* All red with white trim.
International matches 2019–20
Equatorial Guinea (a) 2-2, Thailand (a) 1-1, Equatorial Guinea (h) 1-0, Senegal (h) 0-2, Guinea-Bissau (h) 3-0, Rwanda (h) 0-0.
League champions 2019–20: AS Otoho. *Cup winners 2019:* Etoile du Congo; *2020:* Competition suspended.

DR CONGO

Federation Congolaise de Football-Association, 31 Avenue de la Justice Kinshasa-Gombe, BP 1284, Kinshasa 1.
Founded: 1919. *FIFA:* 1964; *CAF:* 1964. *National Colours:* Blue shirts with red sleeves, red shorts, blue socks.
International matches 2019–20
Rwanda (h) 2-3, Central African Republic (a) 2-0, Algeria (a) 1-1, Ivory Coast (n) 1-3, Central African Republic (h) 4-1, Gabon (h) 0-0, Gambia (a) 2-2.
League champions 2019–20: TP Mazembe. *Cup winners 2019:* AS Maniema Union; *2020:* Competition suspended.

DJIBOUTI

Federation Djiboutienne de Football, Centre Technique National, BP 2694, Ville de Djibouti.
Founded: 1979. *FIFA:* 1994; *CAF:* 1994. *National Colours:* All sky blue.
International matches 2019–20
Ethiopia (h) 0-1, Ethiopia (a) 3-4, Eswatini (h) 2-1, Eswatini (a) 0-0, Gambia (h) 1-1, Gambia (a) 1-1 (2-3p),

Somalia (n) 0-0, Burundi (n) 2-1, Eritrea (n) 0-3, Uganda (a) 1-4.
League champions 2019–20: Garde Republicain/SIAF. *Cup winners 2019:* Arta/Solar7; *2020:* Competition still being played.

EGYPT

Egyptian Football Association, 5 Gabalaya Street, Gezira El Borg Post Office, Cairo.
Founded: 1921. *FIFA:* 1923; *CAF:* 1957. *National Colours:* Red shirts, white shorts, black socks.
International matches 2019–20
Botswana (h) 1-0, Liberia (h) 1-0, Kenya (h) 1-1, Comoros (a) 0-0.
League champions 2018–19: Al-Ahly; *2019–20:* Competition still being played. *Cup winners 2018–19:* Zamalek; *2019–20:* Competition suspended.

EQUATORIAL GUINEA

Federacion Ecuatoguineana de Futbol, Avenida de Hassan II, Apartado de correo 1017, Malabo.
Founded: 1957. *FIFA:* 1986; *CAF:* 1986. *National Colours:* All red with white trim.
International matches 2019–20
Liberia (h) 1-1, Chad (a) 3-3, Chad (h) 2-1, South Sudan (a) 1-1*, South Sudan (h) 1-0, Congo (h) 2-2, Togo (n) 1-1, Congo (a) 0-1, Tanzania (a) 1-2, Tunisia (h) 0-1.
**Match played in Sudan.*
League champions 2018–19: Cano Sport; *2019–20:* Competition abandoned. *Cup winners 2019:* Not contested.

ERITREA

Eritrean National Football Federation, Sematat Avenue 29–31, PO Box 3665, Asmara.
Founded: 1996. *FIFA:* 1998; *CAF:* 1998. *National Colours:* White shirts with red trim, white shorts with red trim, blue socks.
International matches 2019–20
Namibia (h) 1-2, Namibia (a) 0-2, Burundi (n) 1-0, Uganda (a) 0-2, Djibouti (n) 3-0, Somalia (n) 0-0, Kenya (n) 4-1, Uganda (a) 0-3, Sudan (h) 0-1.
League champions 2015–18: Not contested; *2019:* Red Sea; *2020:* Competition suspended.

ESWATINI (SWAZILAND)

Eswatini Football Association, Sigwaca House, Plot 582, Sheffield Road, PO Box 641, Mbabane H100.
Founded: 1968. *FIFA:* 1978; *CAF:* 1976. *National Colours:* Blue shirts with yellow trim, blue shorts, yellow socks.
International matches 2019–20
Angola (h) 1-1, Angola (a) 1-1 (5-4p), Djibouti (a) 1-2, Djibouti (h) 0-0, Zambia (h) 0-1, Zambia (a) 2-2, Guinea-Bissau (a) 0-3, Senegal (h) 1-4.
League champions 2019–20: Young Buffaloes. *Cup winners 2019:* Young Buffaloes; *2020:* Competition suspended.

ETHIOPIA

Ethiopia Football Federation, Addis Ababa Stadium, PO Box 1080, Addis Ababa.
Founded: 1943. *FIFA:* 1952; *CAF:* 1957. *National Colours:* Green shirts with yellow trim, green shorts with yellow trim, red socks.
International matches 2019–20
Djibouti (a) 1-0, Djibouti (h) 4-3, Lesotho (h) 0-0, Lesotho (a) 1-1, Rwanda (h) 0-1, Uganda (h) 0-1, Rwanda (a) 1-1, Madagascar (a) 0-1, Ivory Coast (h) 2-1.
League champions 2018–19: Mekelle 70 Enderta; *2019–20:* Competition abandoned. *Cup winners 2019:* Fasil Kenema; *2020:* Competition suspended.

GABON

Federation Gabonaise de Football, BP 181, Libreville.
Founded: 1962. *FIFA:* 1966; *CAF:* 1967. *National Colours:* Yellow shirts, blue shorts with yellow trim, blue socks with yellow tops.
International matches 2019–20
Burkina Faso (n) 1-0, Morocco (a) 3-2, DR Congo (a) 0-0, Angola (h) 2-1.
League champions 2019: Cercle Mberie Sportif; *2020:* Competition abandoned. *Cup winners:* Not contested since 2016.

GAMBIA

Gambia Football Association, Kafining Layout, Bakau, PO Box 523, Banjul.
Founded: 1952. *FIFA:* 1968; *CAF:* 1966. *National Colours:* Red shirts with green and blue trim, red shorts, red socks.
International matches 2019–20
Angola (h) 0-1, Angola (a) 1-2, Djibouti (a) 1-1, Djibouti (h) 1-1 (3-2p), Angola (a) 3-1, DR Congo (h) 2-2.
League champions 2018–19: Brikama United; *2019–20:* Competition abandoned. *Cup winners 2019:* Real Banjul; *2020:* Competition suspended.

GHANA

Ghana Football Association, General Secretariat, South East Ridge, PO Box AN 19338, Accra. *(GFA dissolved June 2018.)*
Founded: 1957. *FIFA:* 1958; *CAF:* 1958. *National Colours:* Red shirts with yellow sleeves, red shorts, red socks.
International matches 2019–20
Burkina Faso (h) 0-1, Burkina Faso (a) 0-0, South Africa (h) 2-0, Sao Tome & Principe (a) 1-0.
League champions 2019 (Special competition): Asante Kotoko; *2019–20:* Competition abandoned. *Cup winners:* Not contested since 2017.

GUINEA

Federation Guinéenne de Football, Annexe 1 du Palais du Peuple, PO Box 3645, Conakry.
Founded: 1960. *FIFA:* 1962; *CAF:* 1963. *National Colours:* Red shirts, yellow shorts, green socks.
International matches 2019–20
Senegal (a) 0-1, Comoros (n) 0-1, Chile (n) 2-3, Senegal (h) 1-0 (3-1p), Mali (a) 2-2, Namibia (h) 2-0.
League champions 2018–19: Horoya; *2019–20:* Competition abandoned. *Cup winners 2019:* Horoya; *2020:* Competition suspended.

GUINEA-BISSAU

Federacao de Futebol da Guiné-Bissau, Alto Bandim (Nova Sede), BP 375, Bissau 1035.
Founded: 1974. *FIFA:* 1986; *CAF:* 1986. *National Colours:* All red with green trim.
International matches 2019–20
Mali (h) 0-4, Mali (a) 0-3, Sao Tome & Principe (a) 1-0, Sao Tome & Principe (a) 2-1, Eswatini (h) 3-0, Congo (a) 0-3.
League champions 2018–19: Uniao Desportiva Internacional de Bissau; *2019–20:* Competition suspended. *Cup winners 2019:* Sporting Guiné-Bissau; *2020:* Competition suspended.

IVORY COAST

Federation Ivoirienne de Football, Treichville Avenue 1, 01, BP 1202, Abidjan 01.
Founded: 1960. *FIFA:* 1964; *CAF:* 1960. *National Colours:* All orange.
International matches 2019–20
Benin (n) 1-2, Tunisia (n) 2-1, Niger (a) 0-2, DR Congo (n) 3-1, Niger (h) 1-0, Niger (h) 1-0, Ethiopia (a) 1-2.
League champions 2019–20: Racing Club Abidjan. *Cup winners 2019:* FC San Pedro; *2020:* Competition abandoned.

KENYA

Football Kenya Federation, Nyayo Sports Complex, Kasarani, PO Box 12705, 00400 Nairobi.
Founded: 1960 (KFF); 2011 (FKF). *FIFA:* 1960 (2012); *CAF:* 1968 (2012). *National Colours:* All red.
International matches 2019–20
Tanzania (a) 0-0, Tanzania (h) 0-0 (1-4p), Uganda (h) 1 1, Mozambique (h) 0-1, Egypt (a) 1-1, Togo (h) 1-1, Tanzania (n) 1-0, Sudan (n) 2-1, Zanzibar† (n) 1-0, Eritrea (n) 1-4, Tanzania (n) 2-1.
League champion 2019–20: Gor Mahia. *Cup winners 2019:* Bandari; *2020:* Competition suspended.

LESOTHO

Lesotho Football Association, Bambatha Tsita Sports Arena, Old Polo Ground, PO Box 1879, Maseru 100.
Founded: 1932. *FIFA:* 1964; *CAF:* 1964. *National Colours:* Green shirts with blue and white trim, green shorts, green socks.
International matches 2019–20
South Africa (h) 3-2, South Africa (a) 3-0, Ethiopia (a) 0-0, Ethiopia (h) 1-1, Zimbabwe (a) 1-3, Malawi (h) 1-1, Zimbabwe (h) 0-0, Sierra Leone (a) 1-1, Nigeria (h) 2-4.
League champion 2019–20: Bantu. *Cup winners 2018:* Lioli; *2019:* Matlama.

LIBERIA

Liberia Football Association, Professional Building, Benson Street, PO Box 10-1066, Monrovia 1000.
Founded: 1936. *FIFA:* 1964; *CAF:* 1960. *National Colours:* Blue shirts with white trim, white shorts, red socks.

International matches 2019–20
Equatorial Guinea (a) 1-1, Senegal (h) 1-0, Senegal (a) 0-3, Sierra Leone (h) 3-1, Sierra Leone (a) 0-1, Botswana (a) 0-0, Chad (h) 1-0, Chad (a) 0-1 (4-5p), Egypt (a) 0-1.
League champions 2019: LPRC Oilers; *2019–20:* Competition abandoned. *Cup winners 2019:* LISCR; *2019–20:* Competition suspended.

LIBYA

Libyan Football Federation, General Sports Federation Building, Sports City, Goriji, PO Box 5137, Tripoli.
Founded: 1962. *FIFA:* 1964; *CAF:* 1965. *National Colours:* Red shirts, black shorts, black socks.
International matches 2019–20
Niger (n) 2-0, Tunisia (a) 0-1, Morocco (a) 1-1, Mauritania (a) 0-0, Tunisia (h) 1-2*, Tunisia (a) 1-4, Tanzania (a) 2-1‡.
**Match played in Morocco. ‡Match played in Tunisia.*
League champions 2017–18: Al-Nasr; *2018–19:* Competition abandoned; *2019–20:* Not contested. *Cup winners: 2018:* Al-Ittihad; *2019*: Not contested.

MADAGASCAR

Federation Malagasy de Football, 29 Rue de Russie Isoraka, PO Box 4409, Antananarivo 101.
Founded: 1961. *FIFA:* 1964; *CAF:* 1963. *National Colours:* All green with white trim.
International matches 2019–20
Mozambique (h) 1-0, Mozambique (a) 2-3, Namibia (h) 1-0, Namibia (a) 0-2, Ethiopia (h) 1-0, Niger (a) 6-2.
League champions 2019: Fosa Juniors; *2019–20:* Competition abandoned. *Cup winners 2019:* Fosa Juniors; *2020:* Competition abandoned.

MALAWI

Football Association of Malawi, Chiwembe Technical Centre, Off Chiwembe Road, PO Box 51657, Limbe.
Founded: 1966. *FIFA:* 1968; *CAF:* 1968. *National Colours:* All red.
International matches 2019–20
Botswana (a) 0-0, Botswana (h) 1-0, Lesotho (a) 1-1, South Sudan (h) 1-0, Uganda (a) 0-2.
League champions 2019: Nyasa Big Bullets; *2020:* Competition suspended. *Cup winners:* Not contested since 2015.

MALI

Federation Malienne de Football, Avenue du Mali, Hamdallaye ACI 2000, BP 1020, Bamako 0000.
Founded: 1960. *FIFA:* 1964; *CAF:* 1963. *National Colours:* All yellow with green and red trim.
International matches 2019–20
Guinea-Bissau (a) 4-0, Guinea-Bissau (h) 3-0, Saudi Arabia (a) 1-1, Mauritania (a) 0-0, South Africa (a) 1-2, Mauritania (h) 2-0, Guinea (h) 2-2, Chad (a) 2-0.
League champions 2018: Not contested; *2019–20:* Competition still being played. *Cup winners 2018:* Stade Malien; *2019*: Not contested; *2020:* Competition suspended.

MAURITANIA

Federation de Foot-Ball de la Rep. Islamique de Mauritanie, Route de l'Espoire, BP 566, Nouakchott.
Founded: 1961. *FIFA:* 1970; *CAF:* 1968. *National Colours:* Green shirts, yellow shorts, red socks.
International matches 2019–20
Cape Verde Islands (a) 0-0, Cape Verde Islands (h) 2-1, Tunisia (a) 0-1, Mali (h) 0-0, Libya (h) 0-0, Mali (a) 0-2, Morocco (a) 0-0, Central African Republic (h) 2-0.
League champions 2018–19: FC Nouadhibou; *2019–20:* Competition still being played. *Cup winners 2019:* ASC SNIM; *2020:* Competition still being played.

MAURITIUS

Mauritius Football Association, Sepp Blatter House, Trianon.
Founded: 1952. *FIFA:* 1964; *CAF:* 1963. *National Colours:* All white with red trim.
International matches 2019–20
Zimbabwe (h) 0-4, Zimbabwe (a) 1-3, Mozambique (h) 0-1, Mozambique (a) 0-2, Sao Tome & Principe (h) 1-3, Sao Tome & Principe (a) 1-2, Burundi (n) 1-4, Seychelles (n) 2-2.
League champions 2018–19: Pamplemousses; *2019–20:* Competition abandoned. *Cup winners 2019:* Roche-Bois Bolton City; *2020:* Competition suspended.

MOROCCO

Federation Royale Marocaine de Football, 51 bis, Avenue Ibn Sina, Agdal BP 51, Rabat 10 000.
Founded: 1955. *FIFA:* 1960; *CAF:* 1959. *National Colours:* Red shirts with white trim, green shorts, red socks with white tops.
International matches 2019–20
Burkina Faso (h) 1-1, Niger (h) 1-0, Algeria (a) 0-0, Libya (h) 1-1, Gabon (h) 2-3, Algeria (h) 3-0, Mauritania (h) 0-0, Burundi (a) 3-0.
League champions 2018–19: WAC Casablanca; *2019–20:* Competition still being played. *Cup winners 2019:* TAS Casablanca; *2020:* Competition suspended.

MOZAMBIQUE

Federacao Mocambicana de Futebol, Avenida Samora Machel 11, Caixa Postal 1467, Maputo.
Founded: 1976. *FIFA:* 1980; *CAF:* 1980. *National Colours:* Red shirts, black shorts, red socks with black tops.
International matches 2019–20
Madagascar (a) 0-1, Madagascar (h) 3-2, Mauritius (a) 1-0, Mauritius (h) 2-0, Kenya (a) 1-0, Rwanda (h) 2-0, Cape Verde Islands (a) 2-2.
League champions 2019: Costa do Sol; *2020:* Competition postponed. *Cup winners 2019:* Uniao Desportiva do Songo; *2020:* Competition postponed.

NAMIBIA

Namibia Football Association, Richard Kamuhuka Str., Soccer House, Katutura, PO Box 1345, Windhoek 9000.
Founded: 1990. *FIFA:* 1992; *CAF:* 1992. *National Colours:* All blue.
International matches 2019–20
Comoros (a) 2-0, Comoros (h) 0-0, Eritrea (a) 2-1, Eritrea (h) 2-0, Madagascar (a) 0-1, Madagascar (h) 2-0, Zambia (h) 0-2, Chad (h) 2-1, Guinea (a) 0-2.
League champions 2018–19: Black Africa; *2019–20:* Competition suspended. *Cup winners 2018:* African Stars; *2019*: Not contested.

NIGER

Federation Nigerienne de Football, Avenue Francois Mitterand, BP 10299, Niamey.
Founded: 1961. *FIFA:* 1964; *CAF:* 1964. *National Colours:* Orange shirts, white shorts, green socks.
International matches 2019–20
Libya (n) 0-2, Morocco (n) 0-1, Ivory Coast (h) 2-0, Ivory Coast (a) 0-1, Ivory Coast (a) 0-1, Madagascar (h) 2-6.
League champions 2018–19: AS SONIDEP; *2019–20:* Competition abandoned. *Cup winners 2019:* AS SONIDEP; *2020:* Competition abandoned.

NIGERIA

Nigeria Football Federation, Plot 2033, Olusegun Obasanjo Way, Zone 7, Wuse Abuja, PO Box 5101 Garki, Abuja.
Founded: 1945. *FIFA:* 1960; *CAF:* 1960. *National Colours:* Green shirts with white trim, white shorts, green socks.
International matches 2019–20
Tunisia (n) 1-0, Ukraine (a) 2-2, Togo (a) 1-4, Brazil (n) 1-1, Togo (h) 2-0, Benin (h) 2-1, Lesotho (a) 4-2
League champions 2018: Competition abandoned; Lobi Stars declared champions; *2019:* Enyimba; *2019–20:* Competition abandoned. *Cup winners 2019:* Kano Pillars; *2020:* Competition suspended.

RWANDA

Federation Rwandaise de Football Association, BP 2000, Kigali.
Founded: 1972. *FIFA:* 1978; *CAF:* 1976. *National Colours:* Yellow shirts with green trim, yellow shorts, green socks with yellow tops.
International matches 2019–20
Seychelles (a) 3-0, Seychelles (h) 7-0, DR Congo (a) 3-2, Ethiopia (a) 1-0, Tanzania (h) 0-0, Ethiopia (h) 1-1, Mozambique (a) 0-2, Cameroon (h) 0-1, Congo (h) 0-0.
League champions 2019–20: APR. *Cup winners 2019:* AS Kigali; *2020:* Not contested.

SAO TOME & PRINCIPE

Federacao Santomense de Futebol, Rua Ex-Joao de Deus No. QXXIII-426/26, BP 440, Sao Tome.
Founded: 1975. *FIFA:* 1986; *CAF:* 1986. *National Colours:* All yellow.
International matches 2019–20
Guinea-Bissau (h) 0-1, Guinea-Bissau (a) 1-2, Mauritius (a) 3-1, Mauritius (h) 2-1, Sudan (a) 0-4, Ghana (h) 0-1.
League champions 2019: Agrosport. *Cup winners 2019:* FC Porto Real; *2020:* Competition postponed.

SENEGAL

Federation Senegalaise de Football, VDN Ouest-Foire en face du Cicesi, BP 13021, Dakar.
Founded: 1960. *FIFA:* 1964; *CAF:* 1964. *National Colours:* All white with green trim.
International matches 2019–20
Algeria (n) 0-1, Liberia (a) 0-1, Liberia (h) 3-0, Guinea (h) 1-0, Brazil (n) 1-1, Guinea (a) 0-1 (1-3p), Congo (h) 2-0, Eswatini (a) 4-1.
League champions 2018–19: Generation Foot; *2019–20:* Competition abandoned. *Cup winners 2019:* Teungueth; *2020:* Competition abandoned.

SEYCHELLES

Seychelles Football Federation, Maison Football, Roche Caiman, PO Box 843, Mahé.
Founded: 1979. *FIFA:* 1986; *CAF:* 1986. *National Colours:* All red with white trim.
International matches 2019–20
Rwanda (h) 0-3, Rwanda (a) 0-7, South Sudan (a) 1-2*, South Sudan (h) 0-1, Burundi (n) 1-3, Mauritius (n) 2-2, Palestine (n) 0-1.
**Match played in Sudan.*
League champion 2019: No competition (transitional season); *2019–20:* Foresters. *Cup winners 2018–19:* Saint Louis Suns United; *2020:* Foresters.

SIERRA LEONE

Sierra Leone Football Association, 21 Battery Street, Kingtom, PO Box 672, Freetown.
Founded: 1960. *FIFA:* 1960; *CAF:* 1960. *National Colours:* All blue. *(FIFA membership suspended in October 2018 due to alleged government interference.)*
International matches 2019–20
Liberia (a) 1-3, Liberia (h) 1-0, Lesotho (h) 1-1, Benin (a) 0-1.
League champions 2019: East End Lions; *2020:* Competition abandoned. *Cup winners:* Not contested since 2016.

SOMALIA

Somali Football Federation, Mogadishu BN 03040 (DHL only).
Founded: 1951. *FIFA:* 1962; *CAF:* 1968. *National Colours:* All sky blue with white trim.
International matches 2019–20
Uganda (h) 1-3*, Uganda (a) 1-4, Zimbabwe (h) 1-0*, Zimbabwe (a) 1-3, Djibouti (n) 0-0, Uganda (a) 0-2, Burundi (n) 1-0, Eritrea (n) 0-0.
**Match played in Djibouti.*
League champions 2019–20: Mogadishu City Club. *Cup winners 2019:* Horseed; *2020:* Competition postponed.

SOUTH AFRICA

South African Football Association, 76 Nasrec Road, Nasrec, Johannesburg 2000.
Founded: 1991. *FIFA:* 1992; *CAF:* 1992. *National Colours:* Yellow shirts with green trim, green shorts, yellow socks.
International matches 2019–20
Lesotho (a) 2-3, Lesotho (h) 0-3, Mali (h) 2-1, Ghana (a) 0-2, Sudan (h) 1-0.
League champions 2018–19: Mamelodi Sundowns; *2019–20:* Competition still being played. *Cup winners 2018–19:* TS Galaxy; *2019–20:* Competition still being played.

SOUTH SUDAN

South Sudan Football Association, Juba National Stadium, Hai Himra, Talata, Juba.
Founded: 2011. *FIFA:* 2012; *CAF:* 2012. *National Colours:* White shirts with blue and red sash, white shorts, white socks.
International matches 2019–20
Burundi (a) 0-2, Burundi (h) 1-2*, Equatorial Guinea (h) 1-1‡, Equatorial Guinea (a) 0-1, Seychelles (h) 2-1‡, Seychelles (a) 1-0, Malawi (a) 0-1, Burkina Faso (h) 1-2‡.
**Match played in Uganda. ‡Match played in Sudan.*
League champions 2019: Atlabara; *2020:* Competition abandoned. *Cup winners 2020:* Al-Rabita.

SUDAN

Sudan Football Association, Baladia Street, PO Box 437, 11111 Khartoum.
Founded: 1936. *FIFA:* 1948; *CAF:* 1957. *National Colours:* All red with white trim.
International matches 2019–20
Chad (a) 3-1, Chad (h) 0-0, Tanzania (a) 1-0, Tanzania (h) 1-2, Sao Tome & Principe (h) 4-0, South Africa (a) 0 1, Zanzibar† (n) 1-1, Kenya (n) 1-2, Tanzania (n) 0-0, Eritrea (a) 1-0.
League champions 2018–19: Al-Merrikh; *2019–20:* Competition suspended. *Cup winners 2018:* Al-Merrikh; *2019:* Not contested.

TANZANIA

Tanzania Football Federation, Karume Memorial Stadium, Uhuru/Shauri Moyo Road, PO Box 1574, Ilala/Dar Es Salaam.
Founded: 1930. *FIFA:* 1964; *CAF:* 1964. *National Colours:* Blue shirts, white shorts, blue socks.
International matches 2019–20
Kenya (h) 0-0, Kenya (a) 0-0 (4-1p), Burundi (a) 1-1, Burundi (h) 1-1 (3-0p), Sudan (h) 0-1, Rwanda (a) 0-0, Sudan (a) 2-1, Equatorial Guinea (h) 2-1, Libya (a) 1-2*, Kenya (n) 0-1, Zanzibar† (n) 1-0, Sudan (n) 0-0, Uganda (a) 0-1, Kenya (n) 1-2.
**Match played in Tunisia.*
League champions 2019–20: Simba. *Cup winners 2019–20:* Simba.

TOGO

Federation Togolaise de Football, Route de Kegoue, BP 05, Lome.
Founded: 1960. *FIFA:* 1964; *CAF:* 1964. *National Colours:* All yellow.
International matches 2019–20
Benin (a) 0-0, Benin (h) 1-0, Comoros (a) 1-1, Comoros (h) 2-0, Nigeria (h) 4-1, Cape Verde Islands (n) 1-2, Equatorial Guinea (n) 1-1, Nigeria (a) 0-2, Comoros (h) 0-1, Kenya (a) 1-1.
League champions 2019–20: ASKO de Kara. *Cup winners 2018:* Gomido; *2019:* Not contested.

TUNISIA

Federation Tunisienne de Football, Stade Annexe d'El Menzah, Cite Olympique, El Menzah 1003.
Founded: 1957. *FIFA:* 1960; *CAF:* 1960. *National Colours:* All white with red trim.
International matches 2019–20
Nigeria (n) 0-1, Mauritania (h) 1-0, Ivory Coast (n) 1-2, Libya (h) 1-0, Cameroon (h) 0-0, Libya (a) 2-1*, Libya (h) 4-1, Equatorial Guinea (a) 1-0.
**Match played in Morocco.*
League champions 2019–20: Esperance de Tunis. *Cup winners 2018–19:* CS Sfaxien; *2019–20:* Competition still being played.

UGANDA

Federation of Uganda Football Associations, FUFA House, Plot No. 879, Wakaliga Road, Mengo, PO Box 22518, Kampala.
Founded: 1924. *FIFA:* 1960; *CAF:* 1960. *National Colours:* Red shirts with yellow and black trim, white shorts, red socks.
International matches 2019–20
Somalia (a) 3-1*, Somalia (h) 4-1, Kenya (a) 1-1, Burundi (a) 3-0, Ethiopia (a) 1-0, Burundi (h) 3-0, Burkina Faso (a) 0-0, Malawi (h) 2-0, Burundi (h) 2-1, Somalia (h) 2-0, Eritrea (h) 2-0, Djibouti (h) 4-1, Tanzania (h) 1-0, Eritrea (h) 3-0.
**Match played in Djibouti.*
League champions 2019–20: Vipers. *Cup winners 2018–19:* Proline; *2019–20:* Competition suspended.

ZAMBIA

Football Association of Zambia, Football House, Alick Nkhata Road, Long Acres, PO Box 34751, Lusaka.
Founded: 1929. *FIFA:* 1964; *CAF:* 1964. *National Colours:* All green.
International matches 2019–20
Botswana (a) 0-0, Botswana (h) 3-2, Eswatini (a) 1-0, Benin (a) 2-2, Eswatini (h) 2-2, Namibia (a) 2-0, Algeria (a) 0-5, Zimbabwe (h) 1-2.
League champions 2019–20: Nkana. *Cup winners:* Not contested since 2007.

ZIMBABWE

Zimbabwe Football Association, ZIFA House, 53 Livingston Avenue, PO Box CY 114, Causeway, Harare.
Founded: 1965. *FIFA:* 1965; *CAF:* 1980. *National Colours:* All gold with white trim.
International matches 2019–20
Mauritius (a) 4-0, Mauritius (h) 3-1, Somalia (a) 0-1*, Somalia (h) 3-1, Lesotho (h) 3-1, Lesotho (a) 0-0, Botswana (h) 0-0, Zambia (a) 2-1.
**Match played in Djibouti.*
League champions 2019: FC Platinum; *2020:* Competition postponed. *Cup winners 2019:* Highlanders; *2020:* Competition postponed.

EURO 2020 QUALIFYING

■ *Denotes player sent off.*

GROUP A

Friday, 22 March 2019

Bulgaria (0) 1 *(Nedelev 82 (pen))*

Montenegro (0) 1 *(Mugosa 50)* 5652

Bulgaria: (4231) Mihailov; Popov S, Bozhikov, Bodurov, Zanev; Kostadinov, Chochev (Slavchev 69); Ivanov (Kostov 51), Nedelev, Delev (Minchev 82); Popov I.
Montenegro: (4231) Petkovic; Marusic, Simic, Tomasevic, Stojkovic; Ivanic, Vukcevic; Jankovic (Boljevic 64), Mugosa (Kosovic 89), Vesovic (Jovovic 78); Beciraj.

England (2) 5 *(Sterling 24, 62, 68, Kane 45 (pen), Kalas 84 (og))*

Czech Republic (0) 0 82,575

England: (433) Pickford; Walker, Keane, Maguire, Chilwell; Alli (Rice 63), Dier (Barkley 17), Henderson; Sancho, Kane, Sterling (Hudson-Odoi 70).
Czech Republic: (4231) Pavlenka; Kaderabek, Celustka, Kalas, Novak; Soucek, Pavelka; Gebre Selassie, Darida (Masopust 67), Jankto (Vydra 46); Schick (Skoda 82).

Monday, 25 March 2019

Kosovo (0) 1 *(Zeneli 61)*

Bulgaria (1) 1 *(Bozhikov 39)* 12,580

Kosovo: (4231) Muric; Vojvoda, Rrahmani, Aliti, Kololli (Paqarada 78); Kryeziu, Shala (Zhegrova 59); Rashica, Celina (Halimi 58), Zeneli; Muriqi.
Bulgaria: (442) Mihailov; Popov S, Bodurov, Bozhikov, Nedyalkov; Malinov (Minchev 75), Kostadinov (Antov 79), Nedelev, Slavchev; Popov I, Delev (Zanev 68).

Montenegro (1) 1 *(Vesovic 17)*

England (2) 5 *(Keane 30, Barkley 39, 59, Kane 71, Sterling 81)* 8329

Montenegro: (442) Petkovic; Stojkovic, Savic, Simic (Jovetic 74), Tomasevic; Marusic, Ivanic, Vukcevic, Vesovic (Boljevic 70); Beciraj (Jankovic 61), Mugosa.
England: (433) Pickford; Walker, Maguire, Keane, Rose; Barkley (Ward-Prowse 82), Rice, Alli (Henderson 64); Sterling, Kane (Wilson 82), Hudson-Odoi.

Friday, 7 June 2019

Czech Republic (1) 2 *(Schick 19, 50)*

Bulgaria (1) 1 *(Isa 3)* 13,482

Czech Republic: (4231) Vaclik; Kaderabek, Celustka, Suchy, Novak; Pavelka, Soucek; Masopust (Kopic 65), Kral, Jankto (Krejci 83); Schick (Dolezal 79).
Bulgaria: (442) Mihailov; Popov S, Dimitrov K, Bozhikov, Nedyalkov; Minchev (Despodov 46), Malinov (Karabelyov 63), Sarmov, Nedelev (Chunchukov 82); Isa, Popov I.

Montenegro (0) 1 *(Mugosa 69)*

Kosovo (1) 1 *(Rashica 25)*

Montenegro: (4231) Mijatovic; Marusic, Vujacic, Simic, Tomasevic (Boljevic 71); Scekic (Bakic 59), Kosovic; Jankovic (Jovovic 85), Mugosa, Vesovic; Beciraj.
Kosovo: (4231) Muric; Vojvoda, Rrahmani, Aliti, Paqarada (Kololli 69); Halimi, Voca; Rashica, Celina (Rashani 78), Zeneli (Zhegrova 39); Muriqi.
Behind closed doors.

Monday, 10 June 2019

Bulgaria (1) 2 *(Popov I 43, Dimitrov K 55)*

Kosovo (1) 3 *(Rashica 14, Muriqi 64, Rashani 90)* 4994

Bulgaria: (442) Mihailov; Popov S, Bozhikov (Dimitrov K 46), Goranov, Nedyalkov; Ivanov, Kostadinov, Nedelev (Iliev 69), Despodov; Popov I, Isa (Chunchukov 79).
Kosovo: (4231) Muric; Vojvoda (Hadergjonaj 62), Rrahmani, Aliti, Kololli; Halimi, Voca (Raskaj 62); Zhegrova (Rashani 76), Celina, Rashica; Muriqi.

Czech Republic (1) 3 *(Jankto 19, Kopitovic 49 (og), Schick 82 (pen))*

Montenegro (0) 0 11,565

Czech Republic: (4231) Vaclik; Kaderabek, Celustka, Suchy, Novak; Soucek, Pavelka; Masopust (Kopic 39), Kral, Jankto (Krejci 74); Schick (Kozak 88).
Montenegro: (4231) Mijatovic; Marusic (Jankovic 60), Vujacic, Kopitovic, Radunovic; Kosovic, Vukcevic (Savicevic 67); Vesovic, Bakic, Jovovic; Mugosa (Beciraj 85).

Saturday, 7 September 2019

England (1) 4 *(Kane 24, 49 (pen), 73 (pen), Sterling 55)*

Bulgaria (0) 0 82,605

England: (433) Pickford; Trippier, Keane, Maguire, Rose; Henderson (Mount 67), Rice, Barkley; Sterling (Sancho 71), Kane (Oxlade-Chamberlain 77), Rashford.
Bulgaria: (541) Iliev; Popov S, Bodurov (Dimitrov K 65), Sarmov, Bozhikov, Nedyalkov; Ivanov (Mladenov 82), Popov I, Malinov, Wanderson; Marcelinho (Despodov 67).

Kosovo (1) 2 *(Muriqi 20, Vojvoda 66)*

Czech Republic (1) 1 *(Schick 16)* 12,678

Kosovo: (4231) Muric; Vojvoda, Rrahmani, Aliti, Hadergjonaj; Voca, Halimi (Raskaj 87); Zhegrova (Muslija 56), Celina, Rashani (Berisha 51); Muriqi.
Czech Republic: (4231) Vaclik; Kaderabek, Celustka, Suchy, Boril; Darida, Soucek; Masopust (Dolezal 80), Kral (Husbauer 72), Jankto; Schick (Krmencik 61).

Tuesday, 10 September 2019

England (5) 5 *(Sterling 8, Kane 19, Vojvoda 38 (og), Sancho 44, 45)*

Kosovo (1) 3 *(Berisha 1, 49, Muriqi 55 (pen))* 30,155

England: (433) Pickford; Alexander-Arnold, Keane, Maguire, Chilwell; Henderson, Rice, Barkley (Mount 83); Sancho (Rashford 85), Kane, Sterling.
Kosovo: (4231) Muric; Vojvoda, Rrahmani, Aliti, Hadergjonaj; Voca (Raskaj 59), Halimi; Muslija (Paqarada 46), Celina, Berisha (Hasani 85); Muriqi.

Montenegro (0) 0

Czech Republic (0) 3 *(Soucek 54, Masopust 57, Darida 90 (pen))* 5951

Montenegro: (4231) Petkovic; Marusic, Lagator, Tomasevic, Lisi (Beciraj 73); Hocko, Vukcevic (Bakic 68); Boljevic, Kosovic (Savicevic 73), Vesovic; Mugosa.
Czech Republic: (4231) Vaclik; Coufal, Celustka, Suchy (Brabec 46), Boril; Darida, Soucek; Masopust (Kopic 77), Kral, Jankto; Schick (Krmencik 90).

Friday, 11 October 2019

Czech Republic (1) 2 *(Brabec 9, Ondrasek 85)*

England (1) 1 *(Kane 5 (pen))* 20,559

Czech Republic: (4231) Vaclik; Coufal, Celustka, Brabec, Boril; Soucek, Kral; Masopust (Zmrhal 90), Darida, Jankto (Kopic 83); Schick (Ondrasek 65).
England: (4231) Pickford; Trippier, Keane, Maguire, Rose; Henderson, Rice (Abraham 88); Sancho (Rashford 73), Mount (Barkley 72), Sterling; Kane.

Montenegro (0) 0

Bulgaria (0) 0 2743

Montenegro: (4231) Petkovic; Marusic, Savic (Kosovic 39), Simic, Sekulic; Lagator, Vukcevic; Boljevic, Jovovic (Jankovic 67), Haksabanovic (Mirkovic 82); Beciraj.
Bulgaria: (4141) Iliev; Pashov, Dimitrov K, Zanev, Nedyalkov; Popov S (Kostadinov 63); Ivanov, Marcelinho (Isa 70), Malinov, Wanderson (Karagaren 77); Kraev.

Monday, 14 October 2019

Bulgaria (0) 0

England (4) 6 *(Rashford 7, Barkley 20, 32, Sterling 45, 69, Kane 85)* 17,481

Bulgaria: (541) Iliev; Pashov, Terziev, Sarmov (Kraev 46), Hadzhiev, Zanev; Despodov, Popov I, Kostadinov, Wanderson (Malinov 76); Isa (Ivanov 68).
England: (433) Pickford; Trippier, Maguire, Mings, Chilwell; Henderson, Winks, Barkley (Mount 73); Sterling (Sancho 73), Kane, Rashford (Wilson 76).

Kosovo (2) 2 *(Rrahmani 10, Muriqi 34)*

Montenegro (0) 0 12,600

Kosovo: (4231) Muric; Vojvoda (Zhegrova 89), Rrahmani, Aliti, Kololli; Shala (Raskaj 82), Berisha; Hadergjonaj, Celina (Hasani 90), Rashica; Muriqi.
Montenegro: (442) Petkovic (Mijatovic 15); Marusic, Lagator, Simic, Bulatovic; Boljevic, Vukcevic, Scekic, Jovovic (Jankovic 74); Mugosa, Kosovic (Beciraj 46).

Thursday, 14 November 2019

Czech Republic (0) 2 *(Kral 71, Celustka 79)*

Kosovo (0) 1 *(Nuhiu 50)* 10,986

Czech Republic: (4231) Vaclik; Coufal, Celustka, Brabec, Boril; Kral, Soucek; Masopust (Sevcik 76), Darida, Jankto (Kaderabek 90); Krmencik (Ondrasek 61).
Kosovo: (4231) Muric; Vojvoda, Rrahmani, Aliti, Kololli; Raskaj (Halimi 46), Berisha; Hadergjonaj (Zhegrova 77), Celina (Rashani 85), Rashica; Nuhiu.

England (5) 7 *(Oxlade-Chamberlain 11, Kane 18, 24, 37, Rashford 30, Sofranac 66 (og), Abraham 84)*

Montenegro (0) 0 77,277

England: (433) Pickford; Alexander-Arnold, Stones, Maguire, Chilwell; Oxlade-Chamberlain (Maddison 56), Winks, Mount (Gomez 70); Sancho, Kane (Abraham 57), Rashford.
Montenegro: (4321) Mijatovic; Vesovic, Sofranac, Simic, Radunovic (Raspopovic 46); Hocko, Lagator, Vukcevic; Jovovic (Jankovic 65), Haksabanovic (Boljevic 74); Beciraj.

Sunday, 17 November 2019

Bulgaria (0) 1 *(Bozhikov 56)*

Czech Republic (0) 0

Bulgaria: (4231) Georgiev; Popov S, Terziev, Bozhikov, Zanev; Kostadinov, Malinov (Tsvetkov 89); Despodov (Kraev 69), Popov I, Wanderson (Nedelev 72); Marcelinho.
Czech Republic: (4231) Kolar; Kaderabek, Celustka, Kudela, Boril; Soucek, Kral (Husbauer 71); Sevcik (Masopust 65), Darida, Jankto; Ondrasek (Dolezal 80).
Behind closed doors.

Kosovo (0) 0

England (1) 4 *(Winks 32, Kane 79, Rashford 83, Mount 90)* 12,326

Kosovo: (4141) Muric; Vojvoda, Rrahmani, Aliti, Kololli; Dresevic; Hadergjonaj (Zhegrova 73), Celina, Berisha (Halimi 65), Rashica; Nuhiu (Rashani 82).
England: (433) Pope; Alexander-Arnold (Tomori 84), Maguire, Mings, Chilwell; Oxlade-Chamberlain (Mount 72), Rice, Winks; Sterling, Kane, Hudson-Odoi (Rashford 59).

Group A Table	*P*	*W*	*D*	*L*	*F*	*A*	*GD*	*Pts*
England	8	7	0	1	37	6	31	21
Czech Republic	8	5	0	3	13	11	2	15
Kosovo	8	3	2	3	13	16	−3	11
Bulgaria	8	1	3	4	6	17	−11	6
Montenegro	8	0	3	5	3	22	−19	3

GROUP B

Friday, 22 March 2019

Luxembourg (1) 2 *(Barreiro 45, Rodrigues 55)*

Lithuania (1) 1 *(Cernych 14)* 3353

Luxembourg: (3412) Moris; Chanot, Gerson, Carlson; Jans, Barreiro (Sinani 67), Martins Pereira, Da Mota Alves (Bensi 59); Thill O; Rodrigues, Thill V (Turpel 78).
Lithuania: (4231) Setkus; Baravykas, Klimavicius, Jankauskas, Slavickas; Slivka, Kuklys; Petravicius (Valskis 61), Novikovas (Zulpa 56), Mikoliunas (Marazas 76); Cernych.

Portugal (0) 0

Ukraine (0) 0 58,355

Portugal: (433) Rui Patricio; Joao Cancelo, Pepe, Dias, Guerreiro; Neves (Rafa Silva 62), William Carvalho, Joao Moutinho (Joao Mario 87); Bernardo Silva, Andre Silva (Dyego Sousa 73), Ronaldo.
Ukraine: (4141) Pyatov; Karavayev, Kryvtsov, Matviyenko, Mykolenko; Stepanenko; Marlos (Tsygankov 66), Malinovsky, Zinchenko, Konoplyanka (Buyalsky 87); Yaremchuk (Moraes 76).

Monday, 25 March 2019

Luxembourg (1) 1 *(Turpel 34)*

Ukraine (1) 2 *(Tsygankov 40, Rodrigues 90 (og))* 4653

Luxembourg: (442) Moris; Jans, Chanot, Malget, Carlson; Rodrigues, Barreiro, Martins Pereira, Thill O (Mutsch 90); Turpel, Thill V (Bensi 74).
Ukraine: (4141) Pyatov; Butko (Karavayev 79 (Buyalsky 87)), Burda, Matviyenko, Mykolenko; Zinchenko; Tsygankov, Malinovsky, Moraes, Konoplyanka; Bezus (Yaremchuk 64).

Portugal (1) 1 *(Danilo Pereira 42)*

Serbia (1) 1 *(Tadic 7 (pen))* 50,342

Portugal: (433) Rui Patricio; Joao Cancelo, Pepe, Dias, Guerreiro; William Carvalho, Danilo Pereira, Rafa Silva (Goncalo Guedes 84); Ronaldo (Pizzi 31), Dyego Sousa (Andre Silva 57), Bernardo Silva.
Serbia: (4231) Dmitrovic; Rukavina, Milenkovic, Spajic, Mladenovic; Gacinovic (Radonjic 21), Maksimovic; Lazovic (Zivkovic 69), Tadic, Ljajic (Milinkovic-Savic 87); Mitrovic A.

Friday, 7 June 2019

Lithuania (0) 1 *(Novikovas 74)*

Luxembourg (1) 1 *(Rodrigues 21)* 3263

Lithuania: (4231) Bartkus; Mikoliunas■, Klimavicius, Palionis, Andriuskevicius; Slivka, Vorobjovas■; Cernych (Kazlauskas 89), Golubickas (Simkus 52), Novikovas; Valskis (Laukzemis 55).
Luxembourg: (442) Moris; Jans, Selimovic, Gerson, Carlson (Malget 61); Thill O (Sinani 80), Martins Pereira, Barreiro, Thill V; Rodrigues, Turpel (Bensi 67).

Ukraine (2) 5 *(Tsygankov 27, 28, Konoplyanka 46, 75, Yaremchuk 59)*

Serbia (0) 0 34,700

Ukraine: (4231) Pyatov; Karavayev, Kryvtsov, Matviyenko, Mykolenko; Malinovsky, Stepanenko (Shepelev 72); Tsygankov, Zinchenko, Konoplyanka (Kovalenko 76); Yaremchuk (Kravets 67).
Serbia: (352) Dmitrovic; Milenkovic, Spajic, Kolarov; Gacinovic, Ljajic (Fejsa 60), Tadic, Maksimovic, Kostic; Jovic (Lazovic 71), Prijovic (Mitrovic A 53).

Monday, 10 June 2019

Serbia (3) 4 *(Mitrovic A 20, 34, Jovic 35, Ljajic 90)*

Lithuania (0) 1 *(Novikovas 71 (pen))* 52

Serbia: (4231) Dmitrovic; Rukavina, Spajic, Milenkovic, Kolarov; Maksimovic, Lukic; Jovic (Katai 87), Tadic (Ljajic 81), Kostic (Zivkovic 71); Mitrovic A.
Lithuania: (343) Bartkus; Klimavicius, Jankauskas (Chvedukas 46), Palionis; Baravykas, Simkus, Slivka, Andriuskevicius; Cernych (Petravicius 68), Laukzemis (Valskis 77), Novikovas.
Behind closed doors.

Ukraine (1) 1 *(Yaremchuk 6)*

Luxembourg (0) 0 34,700

Ukraine: (4231) Pyatov; Karavayev, Kryvtsov, Matviyenko, Mykolenko; Stepanenko, Malinovsky; Tsygankov (Sobol 87), Zinchenko, Konoplyanka (Kovalenko 79); Yaremchuk.
Luxembourg: (3412) Moris; Chanot, Martins Pereira, Gerson; Jans, Thill O (Turpel 77), Barreiro, Da Graca; Thill V; Rodrigues, Da Mota Alves (Bensi 52).

Saturday, 7 September 2019

Lithuania (0) 0

Ukraine (2) 3 *(Zinchenko 7, Marlos 27, Malinovsky 61)* 5067

Lithuania: (4141) Zubas; Vorobjovas, Palionis, Girdvainis, Mikoliunas; Simkus; Golubickas (Slivka 52), Matulevicius G (Kuklys 63), Zulpa, Verbickas; Cernych (Laukzemis 68).
Ukraine: (433) Pyatov; Bolbat, Kryvtsov, Matviyenko, Mykolenko; Malinovsky (Bezus 80), Stepanenko, Zinchenko; Yarmolenko (Tsygankov 60), Yaremchuk (Moraes 65), Marlos.

Serbia (0) 2 *(Milenkovic 68, Mitrovic A 85)*

Portugal (1) 4 *(William Carvalho 42, Goncalo Guedes 58, Ronaldo 80, Bernardo Silva 86)* 39,839

Serbia: (4231) Dmitrovic; Nikola Maksimovic, Milenkovic, Nastasic, Kolarov; Matic, Milivojevic (Jovic 87); Lazovic (Ljajic 59), Tadic, Kostic (Katai 83); Mitrovic A.
Portugal: (4141) Rui Patricio; Nelson Semedo (Joao Cancelo 65), Fonte, Dias, Guerreiro; Danilo Pereira; Bernardo Silva, William Carvalho, Bruno Fernandes (Joao Moutinho 85), Goncalo Guedes (Joao Felix 70); Ronaldo.

Tuesday, 10 September 2019

Lithuania (1) 1 *(Andriuskevicius 28)*

Portugal (1) 5 *(Ronaldo 7 (pen), 61, 65, 76, William Carvalho 90)* 5067

Lithuania: (4141) Setkus; Mikoliunas, Palionis, Girdvainis, Andriuskevicius; Simkus; Slivka, Vorobjovas, Kuklys (Zulpa 69), Verbickas (Kazlauskas 77); Laukzemis (Petravicius 66).
Portugal: (433) Rui Patricio; Joao Cancelo, Fonte, Dias, Guerreiro; Bruno Fernandes (Rafa Silva 56), Neves, William Carvalho; Bernardo Silva (Pizzi 89), Ronaldo (Goncalo Guedes 79), Joao Felix.

Luxembourg (0) 1 *(Turpel 66)*

Serbia (1) 3 *(Mitrovic A 36, 78, Radonjic 55)* 6373

Luxembourg: (451) Moris; Jans, Chanot, Gerson, Carlson; Thill V (Joachim 86), Sinani (Da Mota Alves 62), Barreiro, Thill O, Rodrigues; Deville (Turpel 61).
Serbia: (4231) Dmitrovic; Rukavina, Spajic, Nikola Maksimovic, Kolarov; Lukic (Gacinovic 61), Milivojevic; Ljajic, Milinkovic-Savic (Matic 79), Katai (Radonjic 46); Mitrovic A.

Friday, 11 October 2019

Portugal (1) 3 *(Bernardo Silva 16, Ronaldo 65, Goncalo Guedes 89)*

Luxembourg (0) 0 47,305

Portugal: (433) Rui Patricio; Nelson Semedo, Pepe, Dias, Guerreiro; Bruno Fernandes, Danilo Pereira, Joao Moutinho (Neves 90); Bernardo Silva (Goncalo Guedes 77), Ronaldo, Joao Felix (Joao Mario 88).
Luxembourg: (451) Moris; Jans, Chanot, Gerson, Carlson; Thill V (Bensi 88), Bohnert (Sinani 46), Barreiro, Thill O, Rodrigues; Turpel (Da Mota Alves 59).

Ukraine (1) 2 *(Malinovsky 29, 58)*

Lithuania (0) 0 32,500

Ukraine: (4141) Pyatov; Bolbat, Kryvtsov, Matviyenko, Sobol; Stepanenko (Sydorchuk 73); Yarmolenko (Tsygankov 65), Zinchenko, Malinovsky, Marlos (Konoplyanka 59); Moraes.
Lithuania: (433) Cerniauskas; Mikoliunas, Klimavicius, Girdvainis, Andriuskevicius (Simkus 62); Vorobjovas, Zulpa, Verbickas; Novikovas, Laukzemis (Matulevicius D 77), Golubickas (Lasickas 73).

Monday, 14 October 2019

Lithuania (0) 1 *(Kazlauskas 79)*

Serbia (0) 2 *(Mitrovic A 48, 53)* 2787

Lithuania: (4141) Cerniauskas; Baravykas, Klimavicius, Girdvainis, Mikoliunas; Simkus; Lasickas, Vorobjovas, Golubickas (Kazlauskas 73), Verbickas (Zulpa 56); Matulevicius D (Laukzemis 64).
Serbia: (4231) Dmitrovic; Miletic, Milenkovic, Kolarov, Mladenovic; Milivojevic (Lukic 72), Nemanja Maksimovic; Radonjic, Ljajic (Gudelj 85), Kostic (Gacinovic 46); Mitrovic A.

Ukraine (2) 2 *(Yaremchuk 6, Yarmolenko 27)*

Portugal (0) 1 *(Ronaldo 72 (pen))* 65,883

Ukraine: (433) Pyatov; Karavayev, Kryvtsov, Matviyenko, Mykolenko (Plastun 90); Malinovsky, Stepanenko■, Zinchenko; Yarmolenko, Marlos (Konoplyanka 63), Yaremchuk (Kovalenko 73).
Portugal: (4141) Rui Patricio; Nelson Semedo, Pepe, Dias, Guerreiro; Danilo Pereira; Bernardo Silva, Joao Moutinho (Bruno Fernandes 56), Joao Mario (Bruma 68), Goncalo Guedes (Joao Felix 46); Ronaldo.

Thursday, 14 November 2019

Portugal (2) 6 *(Ronaldo 7 (pen), 22, 65, Pizzi 52, Paciencia 56, Bernardo Silva 63)*

Lithuania (0) 0 18,534

Portugal: (4231) Rui Patricio; Ricardo Pereira, Fonte, Dias, Rui; Neves, Bruno Fernandes (Joao Moutinho 72); Pizzi, Bernardo Silva (Bruma 66), Ronaldo (Jota 83); Paciencia.
Lithuania: (433) Setkus; Mikoliunas, Palionis, Girdvainis, Andriuskevicius; Slivka, Simkus, Kuklys (Matulevicius D 57); Novikovas, Cernych (Kazlauskas 81), Golubickas (Lasickas 72).

Serbia (2) 3 *(Mitrovic A 11, 43, Radonjic 70)*

Luxembourg (0) 2 *(Rodrigues 54, Turpel 75)* 1560

Serbia: (4231) Dmitrovic; Milenkovic, Nikola Maksimovic, Kolarov, Mladenovic; Milivojevic, Nemanja Maksimovic; Tadic (Lukic 90), Milinkovic-Savic (Radonjic 62), Ljajic (Djuricic 79); Mitrovic A.
Luxembourg: (4141) Moris; Jans, Chanot, Hall, Carlson; Gerson; Thill V (Sinani 79), Philipps (Skenderovic 46), Thill O (Turpel 62), Rodrigues; Deville.

Sunday, 17 November 2019

Luxembourg (0) 0

Portugal (1) 2 *(Bruno Fernandes 39, Ronaldo 86)* 8000

Luxembourg: (4231) Moris; Jans, Chanot, Gerson, Carlson; Skenderovic, Barreiro (Sinani 74); Turpel (Thill O 59), Thill V (Joachim 82), Rodrigues; Deville.
Portugal: (4141) Rui Patricio; Ricardo Pereira, Fonte, Dias, Guerreiro; Danilo Pereira; Pizzi (Joao Moutinho 62), Bruno Fernandes (Neves 90), Bernardo Silva, Ronaldo; Andre Silva (Jota 71).

Serbia (1) 2 *(Tadic 9 (pen), Mitrovic A 56)*

Ukraine (1) 2 *(Yaremchuk 32, Biesiedin 90)* 4457

Serbia: (4231) Rajkovic; Milenkovic, Nikola Maksimovic, Kolarov, Rodic; Nemanja Maksimovic (Milivojevic 76), Gudelj; Radonjic (Milinkovic-Savic 82), Tadic, Ljajic (Gacinovic 69); Mitrovic A.
Ukraine: (4141) Pyatov; Karavayev, Kryvtsov, Matviyenko, Mykolenko; Sydorchuk; Tsygankov (Biesiedin 77), Kovalenko (Shepelev 77), Malinovsky (Shakhov 88), Yaremchuk; Yarmolenko.

Group B Table	P	W	D	L	F	A	GD	Pts
Ukraine	8	6	2	0	17	4	13	20
Portugal	8	5	2	1	22	6	16	17
Serbia	8	4	2	2	17	17	0	14
Luxembourg	8	1	1	6	7	16	–9	4
Lithuania	8	0	1	7	5	25	–20	1

GROUP C

Thursday, 21 March 2019

Netherlands (2) 4 *(Depay 1, Wijnaldum 21, Depay 55 (pen), van Dijk 86)*

Belarus (0) 0 38,604

Netherlands: (433) Cillessen; Dumfries (Tete 68), de Ligt, van Dijk, Blind; Wijnaldum, de Roon (Propper 46), de Jong F; Bergwijn, Depay, Babel (Promes 59).
Belarus: (4411) Gorbunov; Shitov, Martynovich, Sivakov, Polyakov; Kovalev (Savitskiy 78), Maewski, Dragun (Laptev 86), Stasevich; Putsila; Signevich (Saroka 62).

Northern Ireland (0) 2 *(McGinn 56, Davis 75 (pen))*

Estonia (0) 0 18,176

Northern Ireland: (433) Peacock-Farrell; Dallas, Cathcart, Evans J, Lewis; McNair, Davis, Saville; McGinn (McLaughlin C 84), Lafferty (Magennis 76), Jones (Ferguson 81).
Estonia: (541) Lepmets; Kams, Baranov, Tamm, Vihmann, Pikk; Artjom Dmitrijev (Sappinen 84), Mets, Kait, Ojamaa (Vassiljev 68); Anier (Zenjov 76).

Sunday, 24 March 2019

Netherlands (0) 2 *(de Ligt 48, Depay 63)*

Germany (2) 3 *(Sane 15, Gnabry 34, Schulz 90)* 51,694

Netherlands: (433) Cillessen; Dumfries, de Ligt, van Dijk, Blind; Wijnaldum, de Roon (de Jong L 90), de Jong F; Promes, Depay, Babel (Bergwijn 46).
Germany: (3412) Neuer; Sule, Ginter, Rudiger; Kehrer, Kroos, Kimmich, Schulz; Goretzka (Gundogan 70); Gnabry (Reus 88), Sane.

Northern Ireland (1) 2 *(Evans J 30, Magennis 87)*

Belarus (1) 1 *(Stasevich 33)* 18,188

Northern Ireland: (433) Peacock-Farrell; Dallas, Cathcart, Evans J, Lewis; McNair, Davis, Saville; McGinn (Magennis 68), Lafferty (Boyce 79), Jones (Ferguson 85).
Belarus: (433) Klimovich; Shitov (Polyakov 73), Sivakov, Martynovich, Valadzko; Maewski, Hleb (Putsila 66), Dragun; Savitskiy (Nekhaychik 85), Laptev, Stasevich.

Saturday, 8 June 2019

Belarus (0) 0

Germany (1) 2 *(Sane 13, Reus 62)* 12,510

Belarus: (4231) Gutor; Shitov, Naumov, Martynovich, Palyakow; Gromyko (Korzun 56), Dragun; Kovalev (Gordeichuk 69), Maewski, Valadzko; Laptev (Skavysh 64).
Germany: (4411) Neuer; Tah, Ginter, Sule, Schulz; Gnabry (Draxler 71), Klostermann, Gundogan (Goretzka 81), Sane; Kimmich; Reus (Brandt 76).

Estonia (1) 1 *(Vassiljev 25)*

Northern Ireland (0) 2 *(Washington 77, Magennis 80)* 8378

Estonia: (4141) Lepmets; Sinyavskiy, Mets, Vihmann, Pikk; Artjom Dmitrijev; Teniste (Kams 85), Vassiljev, Kait (Tamm 84), Sappinen (Sorga 61); Zenjov.
Northern Ireland: (433) Peacock-Farrell; Smith (Jones 64), Cathcart, Evans J, Lewis; McNair, Davis, Saville (Magennis 69); Whyte, Boyce (Washington 46), Dallas.

Tuesday, 11 June 2019

Belarus (0) 0

Northern Ireland (0) 1 *(McNair 86)* 5250

Belarus: (532) Gutor; Shitov (Veretilo 71), Naumov, Martynovich, Palyakow, Nekhaychik; Korzun (Kislyak 46), Maewski, Stasevich; Kovalev, Shikavka (Laptev 58).
Northern Ireland: (451) Peacock-Farrell; Smith, Cathcart, Evans J, Lewis; Magennis (Dallas 56), McNair, Davis, Evans C (Saville 69), Jones; Washington (Lafferty 72).

Germany (5) 8 *(Reus 10, 37, Gnabry 17, 62, Goretzka 20, Gundogan 26 (pen), Werner 79, Sane 88)*

Estonia (0) 0 26,050

Germany: (451) Neuer; Kehrer, Ginter, Sule, Schulz (Halstenberg 46); Reus (Werner 65), Gundogan (Draxler 53), Kimmich, Goretzka, Sane; Gnabry.
Estonia: (541) Lepmets; Kams, Mets, Tamm, Vihmann, Pikk; Teniste, Vassiljev (Kreida 82), Artjom Dmitrijev (Kait 59), Puri; Zenjov (Ojamaa 71).

Friday, 6 September 2019

Estonia (0) 1 *(Sorga 54)*

Belarus (0) 2 *(Naumov 48, Skavysh 90)* 7314

Estonia: (433) Lepmets; Teniste, Tamm, Klavan, Pikk; Kait, Mets, Vassiljev (Artjom Dmitrijev 77); Zenjov, Sorga (Sappinen 83), Ojamaa (Sinyavskiy 86).
Belarus: (442) Gutor; Matsveychyk, Politevich, Naumov, Polyakov; Kovalev (Skavysh 77), Yablonskiy, Maewski, Stasevich; Signevich (Bakhar 64), Dragun.

Germany (1) 2 *(Gnabry 9, Kroos 73 (pen))*

Netherlands (0) 4 *(de Jong F 59, Tah 66 (og), Malen 79, Wijnaldum 90)* 51,299

Germany: (3421) Neuer; Ginter (Brandt 84), Sule, Tah; Klostermann, Kimmich, Kroos, Schulz; Werner (Havertz 61), Reus (Gundogan 61); Gnabry.
Netherlands: (3142) Cillessen; de Ligt, van Dijk, Blind; de Jong F; Dumfries (Propper 58), de Roon (Malen 58), Wijnaldum, Promes; Babel (Ake 81), Depay.

Monday, 9 September 2019

Estonia (0) 0

Netherlands (1) 4 *(Babel 17, 47, Depay 76, Wijnaldum 87)* 11,006

Estonia: (4141) Lepmets; Teniste, Tamm, Klavan, Kallaste; Mets; Zenjov (Liivak 60), Kait, Ainsalu (Artjom Dmitrijev 87), Ojamaa (Sappinen 85); Sorga.
Netherlands: (4231) Cillessen; Veltman, de Ligt, van Dijk, Blind; Propper, de Jong F (de Jong L 71); Malen (Berghuis 63), Wijnaldum, Babel (Strootman 84); Depay.

Northern Ireland (0) 0

Germany (0) 2 *(Halstenberg 48, Gnabry 90)* 18,326

Northern Ireland: (433) Peacock-Farrell; Dallas, Cathcart, Evans J, Lewis; McNair, Davis, Saville (Magennis 70); Evans C, Washington (Lavery 83), McGinn (Whyte 59).
Germany: (4231) Neuer; Klostermann, Ginter (Tah 40), Sule, Halstenberg; Kimmich, Kroos; Gnabry, Reus (Can 85), Brandt; Werner (Havertz 68).

Thursday, 10 October 2019

Belarus (0) 0

Estonia (0) 0 11,300

Belarus: (4231) Gutor; Matsveychyk, Martynovich, Politevich, Polyakov; Yablonskiy (Lisakovich 83), Maewski; Savitskiy (Bakhar 59), Dragun, Stasevich; Skavysh (Laptev 64).
Estonia: (4231) Lepmets; Teniste, Baranov, Mets, Kallaste; Kreida, Kait; Zenjov (Liivak 59), Vassiljev, Ojamaa (Miller 89); Sorga (Sappinen 80).

Netherlands (0) 3 *(Depay 80, 90, de Jong L 90)*

Northern Ireland (0) 1 *(Magennis 75)* 41,348

Netherlands: (433) Cillessen; Dumfries (de Jong L 78), de Ligt, van Dijk, Blind; Wijnaldum, de Roon (van de Beek 66), de Jong F; Bergwijn, Depay, Babel (Malen 66).
Northern Ireland: (4141) Peacock-Farrell; Smith, Cathcart, Evans J, Ferguson; Evans C (Flanagan 87); Dallas, McNair, Davis, Saville (Thompson 83); Lafferty (Magennis 66).

Sunday, 13 October 2019

Belarus (0) 1 *(Dragun 53)*

Netherlands (2) 2 *(Wijnaldum 32, 41)* 21,639

Belarus: (4411) Gutor; Veretilo, Martynovich, Naumov, Polyakov; Kovalev (Skavysh 60), Yablonskiy, Dragun, Bakhar (Ebong 70); Stasevich; Laptev (Shevchenko 83).
Netherlands: (433) Cillessen; Veltman, de Ligt, van Dijk, Blind; van de Beek (de Roon 67), Wijnaldum, de Jong F; Bergwijn (Babel 89), Malen, Promes (de Jong L 67).

Estonia (0) 0

Germany (0) 3 *(Gundogan 51, 57, Werner 71)* 12,062

Estonia: (4141) Lepmets; Baranov, Tamm, Mets, Pikk; Antonov; Kams, Ainsalu, Vassiljev (Kait 61), Liivak (Ojamaa 77); Sappinen (Zenjov 56).
Germany: (4231) Neuer; Klostermann, Can■, Sule, Halstenberg; Gundogan, Kimmich; Havertz, Reus (Serdar 77), Brandt (Amiri 86); Waldschmidt (Werner 66).

Saturday, 16 November 2019

Germany (1) 4 *(Ginter 41, Goretzka 49, Kroos 55, 83)*

Belarus (0) 0 33,164

Germany: (433) Neuer; Klostermann, Ginter, Koch, Schulz; Gundogan, Kimmich, Kroos; Goretzka, Gnabry (Waldschmidt 84 (Rudy 90)), Werner (Brandt 68).
Belarus: (442) Gutor; Matsveychyk, Martynovich, Naumov, Polyakov; Kovalev (Skavysh 78), Maewski, Dragun, Nekhaychik (Bessmertny 84); Stasevich, Laptev (Lisakovich 68).

Northern Ireland (0) 0

Netherlands (0) 0 18,404

Northern Ireland: (4231) Peacock-Farrell; Dallas, Cathcart, Evans J, Lewis (Thompson 81); Evans C (McGinn 70), Davis; Whyte, McNair, Saville (Smith 58); Magennis.
Netherlands: (4231) Cillessen; Veltman, de Ligt, van Dijk, Blind; de Roon (Propper 36), de Jong F; Berghuis (de Jong L 65), van de Beek, Promes; Babel (Ake 90).

Tuesday, 19 November 2019

Germany (2) 6 *(Gnabry 19, 47, 60, Goretzka 43, 73, Brandt 90)*

Northern Ireland (1) 1 *(Smith 7)* 42,855

Germany: (4231) ter Stegen; Klostermann (Stark 65), Can, Tah, Hector; Kimmich, Kroos; Goretzka (Serdar 73), Gundogan, Brandt; Gnabry (Amiri 80).
Northern Ireland: (4141) Peacock-Farrell; Smith, Cathcart, Flanagan, Ferguson; Davis; Evans C (McLaughlin C 65), McNair (Boyce 77), Thompson, Saville; Magennis (Lavery 83).

Netherlands (2) 5 *(Wijnaldum 6, 66, 78, Ake 18, Boadu 87)*

Estonia (0) 0 50,386

Netherlands: (4231) Cillessen; Promes, de Ligt, Ake, van Aanholt; Propper, de Jong F (Strootman 75); Stengs, Wijnaldum, Depay (Boadu 46); de Jong L (Weghorst 63).
Estonia: (4411) Lepmets; Teniste (Baranov 61), Tamm, Mets, Kallaste; Zenjov (Liivak 76), Antonov, Ainsalu, Ojamaa (Kait 83); Vassiljev; Sorga.

Group C Table	*P*	*W*	*D*	*L*	*F*	*A*	*GD*	*Pts*
Germany	8	7	0	1	30	7	23	21
Netherlands	8	6	1	1	24	7	17	19
Northern Ireland	8	4	1	3	9	13	–4	13
Belarus	8	1	1	6	4	16	–12	4
Estonia	8	0	1	7	2	26	–24	1

GROUP D

Saturday, 23 March 2019

Georgia (0) 0

Switzerland (0) 2 *(Zuber 57, Zakaria 80)* 49,207

Georgia: (4141) Loria; Kakabadze, Khocholava, Kashia, Tabidze (Kverkvelia 61); Kvekveskiri; Qazaishvili, Kankava, Gvilia, Ananidze (Katcharava 83); Kvilitaia (Lobjanidze S 73).
Switzerland: (4411) Sommer; Lichtsteiner, Schar, Akanji, Rodriguez; Embolo (Steffen 84), Zakaria, Xhaka, Freuler (Sow 89); Zuber; Gavranovic (Ajeti 60).

Gibraltar (0) 0

Republic of Ireland (0) 1 *(Hendrick 49)* 2000

Gibraltar: (442) Goldwin; Sergeant, Annesley (Priestley 64), Chipolina R, Chipolina J; Anthony Hernandez (Pons 77), Bardon, Walker, Olivero; De Barr, Casciaro L.
Republic of Ireland: (442) Randolph; Coleman, Duffy, Keogh, Stevens; McClean, Hendrick, Doherty (Brady 56), Hourihane; McGoldrick, Maguire (Arter 72).

Tuesday, 26 March 2019

Republic of Ireland (1) 1 *(Hourihane 36)*

Georgia (0) 0 40,317

Republic of Ireland: (433) Randolph; Coleman, Duffy, Keogh, Stevens; Hourihane, Hendrick, Whelan; Brady (O'Brien 74), McGoldrick (Doherty 81), McClean.
Georgia: (451) Loria; Kakabadze (Okriashvili 85), Khocholava (Kharabadze 65), Kverkvelia, Kashia; Kiteishvili, Kvekveskiri, Kankava, Gvilia, Arveladze (Qazaishvili 72); Kvilitaia.

Switzerland (1) 3 *(Freuler 19, Xhaka 66, Embolo 76)*

Denmark (0) 3 *(Jorgensen M 84, Gytkjaer 88, Dalsgaard 90)* 18,352

Switzerland: (433) Sommer; Mbabu, Elvedi, Akanji, Rodriguez (Benito 46); Zakaria, Xhaka (Sow 79), Freuler; Embolo, Ajeti (Mehmedi 71), Zuber.
Denmark: (433) Schmeichel; Dalsgaard, Kjaer, Jorgensen M, Larsen; Schone (Hojbjerg 70), Eriksen, Delaney; Poulsen, Jorgensen N (Gytkjaer 70), Braithwaite.

Friday, 7 June 2019

Denmark (0) 1 *(Hojbjerg 76)*

Republic of Ireland (0) 1 *(Duffy 85)* 34,610

Denmark: (4312) Schmeichel; Dalsgaard, Christensen A, Kjaer, Larsen; Poulsen, Delaney, Schone (Hojbjerg 72); Eriksen; Jorgensen N, Braithwaite (Dolberg 64).
Republic of Ireland: (451) Randolph; Coleman, Duffy, Keogh, Stevens; Brady (Judge 66), Hourihane (Hogan 82), Whelan, Hendrick, McClean; McGoldrick (Robinson 87).

Georgia (1) 3 *(Gvilia 30, Papunashvili 59, Arveladze 76 (pen))*

Gibraltar (0) 0 18,631

Georgia: (4231) Loria; Kakabadze, Kashia, Grigalava, Kharabadze; Kvekveskiri, Kankava (Mchedlidze 78); Merebashvili (Kiteishvili 72), Gvilia, Kvaratskhelia (Papunashvili 47); Arveladze.
Gibraltar: (532) Goldwin; Sergeant, Chipolina J, Chipolina R, Annesley (Barnett 86), Olivero; De Barr, Bardon (Coombes 77), Anthony Hernandez; Walker, Casciaro L (Pons 65).

Monday, 10 June 2019

Denmark (2) 5 *(Dolberg 13, 63, Eriksen 30 (pen), Poulsen 73, Braithwaite 90)*

Georgia (1) 1 *(Lobjanidze S 25)* 15,387

Denmark: (433) Schmeichel; Ankersen, Kjaer (Jorgensen M 36), Christensen A, Larsen; Hojbjerg, Eriksen, Delaney; Poulsen (Braithwaite 75), Skov (Wass 62), Dolberg.
Georgia: (4231) Loria; Kakabadze, Kashia, Grigalava, Navalovski; Kankava, Kvekveskiri; Parunashvili (Papunashvili 58), Kiteishvili (Lobjanidze E 75), Gvilia; Lobjanidze S.

Republic of Ireland (1) 2 *(Chipolina J 29 (og), Brady 90)*

Gibraltar (0) 0 36,281

Republic of Ireland: (442) Randolph; Coleman, Duffy, Keogh, Stevens; Robinson (Brady 73), Hourihane, Hendrick, McClean; Hogan (Maguire 66), McGoldrick.
Gibraltar: (532) Goldwin; Sergeant, Chipolina J, Chipolina R, Annesley, Olivero; De Barr, Andrew Hernandez (Jolley 75), Pons (Britto 64); Walker, Casciaro L (Bardon 10).

Thursday, 5 September 2019

Gibraltar (0) 0

Denmark (2) 6 *(Skov 6, Eriksen 34 (pen), 50 (pen), Delaney 69, Gytkjaer 73, 78)* 2076

Gibraltar: (451) Coleing; Sergeant (Jolley 83), Chipolina R, Chipolina J, Olivero; Anthony Hernandez, Walker, Annesley (Barnett 46), Andrew Hernandez, Britto (Pons 46); De Barr.
Denmark: (433) Schmeichel; Wass, Kjaer (Jorgensen 63), Christensen A, Larsen; Eriksen, Hojbjerg, Delaney (Schone 77); Skov, Gytkjaer, Poulsen (Braithwaite 64).

Republic of Ireland (0) 1 *(McGoldrick 85)*

Switzerland (0) 1 *(Schar 74)* 44,111

Republic of Ireland: (4231) Randolph; Coleman, Duffy, Keogh, Stevens; Whelan, Hourihane (Hogan 82); Robinson (Judge 58), Hendrick, McClean; McGoldrick (Browne 90).
Switzerland: (532) Sommer; Mbabu (Fernandes 90), Elvedi, Schar, Akanji, Rodriguez; Zakaria, Xhaka, Freuler (Mehmedi 90); Embolo (Ajeti 86), Seferovic.

Sunday, 8 September 2019

Georgia (0) 0

Denmark (0) 0 21,456

Georgia: (4231) Loria; Kakabadze, Kashia, Grigalava, Tabidze; Kiteishvili, Aburjania (Gvilia 86); Okriashvili, Ananidze, Qazaishvili; Kvilitaia (Daushvili 90).
Denmark: (4231) Schmeichel; Dalsgaard, Kjaer, Christensen A, Larsen; Hojbjerg (Schone 73), Delaney; Poulsen, Eriksen, Braithwaite; Dolberg (Gytkjaer 67).

Switzerland (3) 4 *(Zakaria 37, Mehmedi 43, Rodriguez 45, Gavranovic 87)*

Gibraltar (0) 0 8318

Switzerland: (352) Sommer; Elvedi, Schar, Rodriguez; Mehmedi, Zakaria, Xhaka (Vargas 74), Fernandes, Benito (Steffen 65); Embolo (Gavranovic 55), Ajeti.
Gibraltar: (451) Coleing (Goldwin 25); Sergeant, Chipolina R, Chipolina J, Olivero; Anthony Hernandez, Walker, Annesley, Andrew Hernandez (Coombes 58), Britto (Pons 67); De Barr.

Saturday, 12 October 2019

Denmark (0) 1 *(Poulsen 84)*

Switzerland (0) 0 35,964

Denmark: (4231) Schmeichel; Dalsgaard, Kjaer, Christensen A (Jorgensen M 87), Larsen (Ankersen 80); Schone (Hojbjerg 65), Delaney; Poulsen, Eriksen, Braithwaite; Cornelius.
Switzerland: (343) Sommer; Elvedi, Schar, Akanji; Lichtsteiner (Mbabu 68), Zakaria, Xhaka, Rodriguez (Drmic 88); Embolo, Seferovic, Mehmedi (Freuler 83).

Georgia (0) 0

Republic of Ireland (0) 0 24,385

Georgia: (4231) Loria; Kakabadze, Kashia, Grigalava, Tabidze; Kiteishvili (Aburjania 90), Kankava; Okriashvili (Lobjanidze E 79), Ananidze, Qazaishvili; Kvilitaia (Shengelia 73).
Republic of Ireland: (4231) Randolph; Coleman, Duffy, Egan, Doherty; Whelan, Hourihane (Williams 90); Robinson (Browne 73), Hendrick, McClean; Collins (Connolly 79).

Tuesday, 15 October 2019

Gibraltar (0) 2 *(Casciaro L 66, Chipolina R 74)*

Georgia (2) 3 *(Kharaishvili 10, Kankava 21, Kvilitaia 84)* 1455

Gibraltar: (4231) Goldwin; Sergeant, Chipolina R, Chipolina J (Barnett 82), Olivero; Mouelhi, Badr (Andrew Hernandez 81); Casciaro L, Walker (Pons 90), Britto; De Barr.
Georgia: (4231) Loria; Kakabadze, Khocholava, Grigalava, Navalovski (Kvirkvelia 90); Kankava, Ananidze; Shengelia, Qazaishvili, Kharaishvili (Kiteishvili 61); Lobjanidze E (Kvilitaia 68).

Switzerland (1) 2 *(Seferovic 16, Duffy 90 (og))*

Republic of Ireland (0) 0 24,766

Switzerland: (343) Sommer; Elvedi, Schar, Akanji; Lichtsteiner (Freuler 70), Xhaka, Zakaria, Rodriguez; Embolo (Steffen 88), Seferovic, Mehmedi (Fernandes 28).
Republic of Ireland: (3142) Randolph; Egan, Duffy, Stevens; Whelan; Coleman■, Hendrick, Browne, McClean; Connolly (Hogan 69), Collins (O'Dowda 46).

Friday, 15 November 2019

Denmark (1) 6 *(Skov 12, 64, Gytkjaer 47, Braithwaite 51, Eriksen 85, 90)*

Gibraltar (0) 0 24,033

Denmark: (4231) Schmeichel; Wass, Kjaer, Jorgensen M, Larsen (Christensen A 78); Schone (Hojbjerg 54), Delaney; Skov, Eriksen, Braithwaite (Dolberg 55); Gytkjaer.
Gibraltar: (451) Goldwin; Sergeant, Chipolina R, Chipolina J, Olivero; Casciaro L, Walker, Mouelhi (Barnett 66), Badr (Andrew Hernandez 66), Britto; De Barr (Styche 72).

Switzerland (0) 1 *(Itten 77)*

Georgia (0) 0 16,400

Switzerland: (541) Sommer; Lichtsteiner, Elvedi, Akanji, Rodriguez, Steffen; Fernandes (Sow 84), Zakaria, Xhaka, Vargas (Fassnacht 78); Ajeti (Itten 71).
Georgia: (4231) Loria; Kakabadze, Kashia, Grigalava, Khocholava; Kankava, Kiteishvili (Papunashvili 85); Shengelia, Qazaishvili, Davitashvili (Gvilia 85); Kvilitaia (Lobjanidze E 83).

Monday, 18 November 2019

Gibraltar (0) 1 *(Styche 74)*

Switzerland (1) 6 *(Itten 10, 84, Vargas 50, Fassnacht 57, Benito 75, Xhaka 86)* 2079

Gibraltar: (532) Coleing; Sergeant, Mouelhi, Chipolina R, Chipolina J, Britto; Casciaro L (Styche 62), Barnett, Badr (Pons 85); De Barr (Coombes 62), Walker.
Switzerland: (343) Sommer; Elvedi, Akanji (Comert 65), Rodriguez; Lang, Zakaria (Sow 60), Xhaka, Benito; Fassnacht, Itten, Vargas (Aebischer 85).

Republic of Ireland (0) 1 *(Doherty 85)*

Denmark (0) 1 *(Braithwaite 73)* 50,000

Republic of Ireland: (4231) Randolph; Doherty, Duffy, Egan (Clark 46), Stevens; Whelan (Maguire 81), Hourihane (Robinson 68); Browne, Hendrick, McClean; McGoldrick.
Denmark: (4222) Schmeichel; Dalsgaard, Kjaer, Jorgensen M, Larsen; Delaney (Hojbjerg 13), Schone (Christensen A 84); Poulsen, Braithwaite; Eriksen, Cornelius (Dolberg 33).

Group D Table	*P*	*W*	*D*	*L*	*F*	*A*	*GD*	*Pts*
Switzerland	8	5	2	1	19	6	13	17
Denmark	8	4	4	0	23	6	17	16
Republic of Ireland	8	3	4	1	7	5	2	13
Georgia	8	2	2	4	7	11	–4	8
Gibraltar	8	0	0	8	3	31	–28	0

GROUP E

Thursday, 21 March 2019

Croatia (1) 2 *(Barisic 43, Kramaric 79)*

Azerbaijan (1) 1 *(Sheydayev 19)* 23,146

Croatia: (4231) Kalinic L; Brekalo, Caleta-Car, Vida, Barisic; Modric (Badelj 90), Kovacic (Vlasic 73); Rakitic, Kramaric, Petkovic (Rebic 69); Perisic.
Azerbaijan: (4141) Agayev S; Medvedev, Mammadov R, Huseynov B, Rahimov; Garayev (Dadasov 88); Madatov, Eddy, Richard (Makhmudov 72), Nazarov (Abdullayev 58); Sheydayev.

Slovakia (1) 2 *(Duda 42, Rusnak 85)*

Hungary (0) 0 14,235

Slovakia: (4231) Dubravka; Pekarik, Vavro, Skriniar, Hancko; Kucka, Lobotka; Hamsik, Duda (Safranko 87), Rusnak (Mihalik 90); Mak (Stoch 79).
Hungary: (4231) Gulacsi; Orban, Lang (Holender 81), Kadar, Korhut; Lovrencsics, Nagy A; Kalmar (Dzsudzsak 61), Kleinheisler (Szoboszlai 54), Kovacs; Szalai.

Sunday, 24 March 2019

Hungary (1) 2 *(Szalai 34, Patkai 76)*

Croatia (1) 1 *(Rebic 13)* 19,400

Hungary: (4231) Gulacsi; Lovrencsics, Barath, Orban, Kadar; Nagy A, Patkai; Dzsudzsak (Bese 84), Szoboszlai (Kalmar 65), Nagy D (Varga R 40); Szalai.
Croatia: (4231) Kalinic L; Jedvaj (Petkovic 77), Lovren, Vida, Barisic (Leovac 29); Modric, Brozovic; Rebic (Brekalo 67), Rakitic, Perisic; Kramaric.

Wales (1) 1 *(James 5)*

Slovakia (0) 0 31,617

Wales: (4231) Hennessey; Roberts C, Mepham, Lawrence J, Davies B; Allen, Smith; Wilson (Vaulks 86), Brooks (Roberts T 60), James (Williams A 72); Bale.
Slovakia: (433) Dubravka; Pekarik (Safranko 90), Vavro, Skriniar, Hancko; Kucka, Lobotka, Hamsik; Rusnak, Duda (Duris 65), Mak (Stoch 69).

Saturday, 8 June 2019

Azerbaijan (0) 1 *(Madatov 69)*

Hungary (1) 3 *(Orban 18, 53, Holman 71)* 10,450

Azerbaijan: (433) Agayev S; Medvedev, Huseynov B, Mammadov R, Krivotsyuk; Richard, Garayev, Nazarov (Dadasov 86); Madatov (Abdullayev 74), Dadashov (Ramazanov 59), Sheydayev.
Hungary: (4231) Gulacsi; Lovrencsics, Orban, Barath, Korhut; Nagy A, Kleinheisler (Patkai 72); Dzsudzsak (Nemeth 86), Szoboszlai (Holman 57), Nagy D; Szalai.

Croatia (1) 2 *(Lawrence J 17 (og), Perisic 48)*

Wales (0) 1 *(Brooks 77)* 17,061

Croatia: (4231) Livakovic; Jedvaj, Lovren, Vida, Barisic; Modric, Brozovic; Brekalo (Pasalic 66), Kovacic (Badelj 76), Perisic (Skoric 90); Kramaric.
Wales: (4411) Hennessey; Roberts C, Mepham, Lawrence J, Davies B; Wilson, Allen, Smith (Brooks 65), James (Matondo 80); Vaulks (Ampadu 66); Bale.

Tuesday, 11 June 2019

Azerbaijan (1) 1 *(Sheydayev 29)*

Slovakia (3) 5 *(Lobotka 8, Kucka 27, Hamsik 30, 57, Hancko 85)* 8200

Azerbaijan: (433) Agayev S; Medvedev, Huseynov B, Krivotsyuk, Rahimov; Richard, Garayev, Eyubov (Makhmudov 79); Abdullayev (Dadashov 89), Sheydayev, Ramazanov (Madatov 61).
Slovakia: (433) Dubravka; Pekarik, Vavro, Skriniar, Hancko; Kucka, Lobotka (Gregus 84), Hamsik (Haraslin 86); Rusnak, Bozenik (Duda 71), Mak.

Hungary (0) 1 *(Patkai 80)*

Wales (0) 0 18,350

Hungary: (4231) Gulacsi; Lovrencsics, Barath, Orban, Korhut; Nagy A, Patkai; Dzsudzsak (Kleinheisler 69), Szoboszlai (Bese 83), Holender (Varga R 58); Szalai.
Wales: (4231) Hennessey; Gunter, Williams A, Lawrence J, Davies B; Allen, Ampadu (Smith 54); Lawrence T (Vokes 79), Brooks (Wilson 73), James; Bale.

Friday, 6 September 2019

Slovakia (0) 0

Croatia (1) 4 *(Vlasic 45, Perisic 46, Petkovic 72, Lovren 89)* 18,098

Slovakia: (433) Dubravka; Valjent, Vavro, Skriniar, Hancko; Kucka (Haraslin 63), Lobotka, Hamsik; Rusnak (Bozenik 46), Duda, Mak (Duris 79).
Croatia: (4231) Livakovic; Bartolec, Lovren, Vida, Barisic; Modric, Brozovic; Perisic, Vlasic (Badelj 82), Rebic (Brekalo 70); Petkovic (Pasalic 83).

Wales (1) 2 *(Pashaev 26 (og), Bale 84)*

Azerbaijan (0) 1 *(Emreli 58)* 28,385

Wales: (4231) Hennessey; Roberts C, Mepham, Rodon, Taylor (Davies B 80); Allen, Ampadu (Vokes 75); Bale, Wilson (Williams J 63), James; Lawrence T.
Azerbaijan: (4231) Agayev S; Pashaev, Medvedev, Mustafazade, Krivotsyuk; Garayev, Richard (Eyubov 69); Emreli, Nazarov (Ramazanov 86), Rahimov (Khalilzade 73); Sheydayev.

Monday, 9 September 2019

Azerbaijan (0) 1 *(Khalilzade 72)*

Croatia (1) 1 *(Modric 11 (pen))* 9150

Azerbaijan: (4231) Balayev; Pashaev (Khalilzade 46), Medvedev, Mustafazade, Krivotsyuk; Garayev, Huseynov C (Mahmudov 60); Emreli, Nazarov (Eyubov 90), Rahimov; Sheydayev.
Croatia: (4231) Livakovic; Bartolec (Brekalo 76), Lovren, Vida, Barisic; Modric, Brozovic; Perisic, Vlasic, Rebic (Orsic 86); Petkovic.

Hungary (0) 1 *(Szoboszlai 50)*

Slovakia (1) 2 *(Mak 40, Bozenik 56)* 21,700

Hungary: (442) Gulacsi; Lovrencsics (Bese 30), Barath■, Orban, Kadar; Dzsudzsak, Kleinheisler (Holender 85), Nagy A (Patkai 65), Sallai; Szalai, Szoboszlai.
Slovakia: (433) Dubravka; Satka, Vavro, Skriniar, Hancko; Kucka (Gregus 85), Lobotka, Hamsik; Rusnak, Bozenik (Duris 77), Mak (Haraslin 86).

Thursday, 10 October 2019

Croatia (3) 3 *(Modric 5, Petkovic 24, 42)*

Hungary (0) 0 32,110

Croatia: (433) Livakovic; Jedvaj, Lovren, Vida, Barisic; Modric (Kovacic 67), Brozovic, Rakitic (Vlasic 74); Perisic (Brekalo 61), Petkovic, Rebic.
Hungary: (451) Gulacsi; Lovrencsics, Orban, Kadar (Lang 46), Korhut; Dzsudzsak (Nagy D 60), Kleinheisler■, Vida, Holman, Sallai (Varga R 76); Szalai.

Slovakia (0) 1 *(Kucka 53)*

Wales (1) 1 *(Moore 25)* 18,071

Slovakia: (433) Dubravka; Pekarik, Gyomber■, Skriniar, Hancko; Kucka, Lobotka, Hamsik; Rusnak, Bozenik (Safranko 86), Mak (Haraslin 79).
Wales: (4231) Hennessey; Roberts C, Lockyer, Rodon, Davies B; Allen, Ampadu (Morrell 58); Bale, Williams J (Wilson 66), James; Moore.

Sunday, 13 October 2019

Hungary (1) 1 *(Korhut 10)*

Azerbaijan (0) 0 11,300

Hungary: (4231) Gulacsi; Lovrencsics, Barath, Orban, Korhut; Kovacs (Siger 86), Vida; Dzsudzsak (Nagy D 71), Szoboszlai (Holman 76), Sallai; Szalai.
Azerbaijan: (433) Balayev; Pashaev, Mustafazade, Huseynov B, Rahimov; Eddy, Garayev, Richard (Abdullayev 58); Ramazanov (Dadashov 85), Sheydayev, Khalilzade (Huseynov C 66).

Wales (1) 1 *(Bale 45)*

Croatia (1) 1 *(Vlasic 9)* 31,745

Wales: (4141) Hennessey; Roberts C, Lockyer, Rodon, Davies B; Ampadu (Morrell 50); Bale, Allen, Williams J (Wilson 68), James; Moore (Roberts T 86).
Croatia: (4231) Livakovic; Jedvaj, Lovren, Vida, Barisic; Modric (Badelj 90), Kovacic (Rakitic 46); Perisic, Vlasic, Brekalo; Petkovic (Rebic 64).

Saturday, 16 November 2019

Azerbaijan (0) 0

Wales (2) 2 *(Moore 10, Wilson 34)* 8622

Azerbaijan: (451) Balayev; Pashaev, Mustafazade, Huseynov B, Krivotsyuk (Khalilzade 46); Abdullayev (Ramazanov 64), Nazarov (Huseynov C 82), Garayev, Richard, Rahimov; Sheydayev.
Wales: (4231) Hennessey; Roberts C, Lockyer, Mepham, Davies B; Ampadu (Vaulks 87), Morrell; Bale (Ramsey 60), Wilson, James (Matondo 82); Moore.

Croatia (0) 3 *(Vlasic 56, Petkovic 60, Perisic 74)*

Slovakia (1) 1 *(Bozenik 32)* 8212

Croatia: (4231) Livakovic; Jedvaj, Caleta-Car, Peric, Barisic; Modric, Brozovic; Rebic (Brekalo 54), Vlasic (Kovacic 75), Perisic (Orsic 82); Petkovic.
Slovakia: (433) Dubravka; Pekarik, Vavro, Skriniar, Hancko; Kucka (Hrosovsky 79), Lobotka, Hamsik; Rusnak (Haraslin 63), Bozenik (Duris 72), Mak■.

Tuesday, 19 November 2019

Slovakia (1) 2 *(Bozenik 19, Hamsik 86)*

Azerbaijan (0) 0 7825

Slovakia: (433) Dubravka; Pekarik, Gyomber, Skriniar, Hancko; Kucka (Duda 85), Lobotka, Hamsik; Bero, Bozenik (Mraz 77), Haraslin (Duris 71).
Azerbaijan: (4231) Balayev; Huseynov A, Mustafazade, Huseynov B, Krivotsyuk (Khalilzade 73); Garayev, Eddy (Camalov 46); Isgenderli, Huseynov C (Dadashov 79), Rahimov; Sheydayev.

Wales (1) 2 *(Ramsey 15, 47)*

Hungary (0) 0 31,762

Wales: (4231) Hennessey; Roberts C, Lockyer, Mepham, Davies B; Allen, Morrell (Ampadu 50); Bale (Wilson 88), Ramsey, James; Moore.
Hungary: (4231) Gulacsi; Lovrencsics, Barath, Lang, Nagy Z; Patkai, Nagy A (Kovacs 60); Dzsudzsak (Varga R 72), Szoboszlai, Sallai (Holender 83); Szalai.

Group E Table	*P*	*W*	*D*	*L*	*F*	*A*	*GD*	*Pts*
Croatia	8	5	2	1	17	7	10	17
Wales	8	4	2	2	10	6	4	14
Slovakia	8	4	1	3	13	11	2	13
Hungary	8	4	0	4	8	11	–3	12
Azerbaijan	8	0	1	7	5	18	–13	1

GROUP F

Saturday, 23 March 2019

Malta (1) 2 *(Nwoko 13, Borg 77 (pen))*

Faroe Islands (0) 1 *(Thomsen 90)* 7531

Malta: (433) Bonello; Borg S, Caruana J, Agius■, Mbong; Muscat R (Mintoff 84), Guillaumier, Fenech P; Corbalan (Muscat Z 63), Nwoko, Mifsud (Zerafa 71).
Faroe Islands: (4411) Nielsen G; Rolantsson, Gregersen, Faero, Davidsen V; Vatnhamar S (Bartalsstovu 68), Baldvinsson (Frederiksberg 79), Hansson, Joensen R (Olsen K 72); Hendriksson; Thomsen.

Spain (1) 2 *(Rodrigo 16, Sergio Ramos 71 (pen))*
Norway (0) 1 *(King 65 (pen))* 39,752
Spain: (433) de Gea; Jesus Navas, Sergio Ramos, Martinez, Jordi Alba; Parejo (Rodri 77), Busquets, Ceballos (Canales 74); Rodrigo, Morata (Mata 89), Asensio.
Norway: (442) Jarstein; Elabdellaoui, Nordtveit, Ajer, Aleesami; Odegaard (Elyounoussi M 56), Henriksen, Selnaes, Johansen (Kamara 77); King, Elyounoussi T (Johnsen 55).

Sweden (2) 2 *(Quaison 33, Claesson 40)*
Romania (0) 1 *(Keseru 58)* 30,115
Sweden: (442) Olsen; Lustig (Krafth 24), Helander, Granqvist, Augustinsson; Forsberg (Svensson 67), Seb Larsson, Olsson K, Claesson; Quaison (Isak 88), Berg.
Romania: (4231) Tatarusanu; Manea, Sapunaru, Grigore, Bancu; Marin, Baluta T (Ivan 78); Mitrita (Keseru 46), Stanciu, Chipciu; Puscas (Hagi 64).

Tuesday, 26 March 2019

Malta (0) 0
Spain (1) 2 *(Morata 31, 73)* 16,542
Malta: (541) Bonello; Mbong (Muscat R 65), Muscat Z, Caruana J (Micallef 85), Borg S, Zerafa; Mintoff (Mifsud 69), Fenech P, Guillaumier, Corbalan; Nwoko.
Spain: (433) Arrizabalaga; Sergi Roberto, Sergio Ramos, Hermoso, Gaya; Canales, Rodri, Saul (Jesus Navas 65); Asensio, Morata (Rodrigo 78), Bernat (Muniain 56).

Norway (1) 3 *(Johnsen 41, King 59, Kamara 90)*
Sweden (0) 3 *(Claesson 70, Nordtveit 86 (og), Quaison 90)* 23,459
Norway: (442) Jarstein; Elabdellaoui, Nordtveit, Ajer, Aleesami; Odegaard, Selnaes, Henriksen, Elyounoussi M (Kamara 72); Johnsen (Sorloth 88), King.
Sweden: (442) Olsen; Krafth, Helander, Granqvist, Augustinsson; Seb Larsson (Isak 62), Ekdal (Svensson 66), Olsson K (Andersson 90), Claesson; Quaison, Berg.

Romania (3) 4 *(Deac 26, Keseru 29, 33, Puscas 63)*
Faroe Islands (1) 1 *(Davidsen V 40 (pen))* 10,502
Romania: (442) Tatarusanu; Benzar (Hagi 46), Grigore, Moti, Bancu; Deac, Stanciu (Man 77), Marin, Chipciu; Puscas, Keseru (Cicaldau 69).
Faroe Islands: (4411) Nielsen G; Rolantsson, Gregersen, Faero, Davidsen V; Bartalsstovu (Frederiksberg 66), Hendriksson, Vatnsdal (Baldvinsson 29), Joensen R; Hansson (Vatnhamar S 77); Olsen K.

Friday, 7 June 2019

Faroe Islands (1) 1 *(Olsen K 30)*
Spain (3) 4 *(Sergio Ramos 6, Jesus Navas 19, Gestsson 34 (og), Gaya 71)* 3226
Faroe Islands: (433) Gestsson; Rolantsson, Faero, Gregersen, Davidsen V; Hansson, Vatnsdal (Baldvinsson 74), Hendriksson; Vatnhamar S, Olsen K (Johannesen 68), Frederiksberg (Olsen M 86).
Spain: (433) Arrizabalaga; Jesus Navas, Hermoso, Sergio Ramos (Llorente 46), Gaya; Sergi Roberto, Rodri, Cazorla; Aspas (Asensio 56), Morata, Isco (Fabian 74).

Norway (0) 2 *(Elyounoussi T 56, Odegaard 70)*
Romania (0) 2 *(Keseru 77, 90)* 17,664
Norway: (442) Grytebust; Elabdellaoui, Nordtveit, Ajer, Aleesami; Odegaard, Selnaes, Berge, Henriksen; Elyounoussi T (Kamara 84), King.
Romania: (4231) Tatarusanu; Chipciu, Sapunaru, Grigore, Tosca; Anton, Stanciu (Maxim 72); Deac, Keseru, Grozav (Hagi 60); Puscas (Tucudean 60).

Sweden (1) 3 *(Quaison 2, Claesson 50, Isak 81)*
Malta (0) 0 26,421
Sweden: (4411) Olsen; Lustig, Jansson, Helander, Augustinsson; Forsberg, Olsson K, Ekdal (Larsson 76), Claesson; Quaison (Guidetti 84); Berg (Isak 68).
Malta: (4312) Bonello; Muscat Z, Borg S (Apap 80), Agius, Mbong; Corbalan, Muscat R, Gambin; Grech (Fenech P 64); Effiong, Montebello (Nwoko 71).

Monday, 10 June 2019

Faroe Islands (0) 0
Norway (0) 2 *(Johnsen 49, 83)* 3083
Faroe Islands: (433) Gestsson; Rolantsson, Gregersen, Faero, Davidsen V; Hansson, Baldvinsson, Hendriksson; Vatnhamar S (Frederiksberg 68), Olsen K (Johannesen 88), Joensen R (Vatnsdal 85).
Norway: (442) Hansen; Elabdellaoui, Nordtveit, Ajer, Aleesami; Odegaard, Berge, Selnaes (Midtsjoe 80), Henriksen (Johansen 71); Johnsen, Elyounoussi T (Kamara 58).

Malta (0) 0
Romania (3) 4 *(Puscas 8, 29, Chipciu 34, Man 90)* 6471
Malta: (442) Bonello; Muscat Z, Agius, Borg S, Zerafa; Muscat R, Fenech P (Grech 59), Mbong, Corbalan (Montebello 84); Effiong, Gambin (Mifsud 68).
Romania: (442) Tatarusanu; Chipciu■, Cristea, Nedelcearu (Sapunaru 35), Bancu; Hagi, Marin, Baluta T, Maxim (Rotariu 74); Puscas, Keseru (Man 64).

Spain (0) 3 *(Sergio Ramos 64 (pen), Morata 85 (pen), Oyarzabal 87)*
Sweden (0) 0 72,205
Spain: (433) Arrizabalaga; Carvajal, Sergio Ramos, Martinez (Llorente 88), Jordi Alba; Parejo, Busquets, Fabian; Asensio (Morata 65), Rodrigo (Oyarzabal 71), Isco.
Sweden: (442) Olsen; Lustig, Helander, Augustinsson, Jansson; Seb Larsson (Isak 82), Ekdal (Olsson K 86), Forsberg, Claesson (Johansson 27); Quaison, Berg.

Thursday, 5 September 2019

Faroe Islands (0) 0
Sweden (4) 4 *(Isak 12, 15, Lindelof 23, Quaison 41)* 3083
Faroe Islands: (4231) Nielsen G; Askham, Gregersen, Baldvinsson, Davidsen V; Joensen R (Vatnsdal 46), Olsen B (Olsen M 76); Vatnhamar S, Hansson, Frederiksberg (Bjartalid 63); Edmundsson.
Sweden: (442) Olsen; Lustig (Krafth 46), Lindelof, Granqvist, Bengtsson; Seb Larsson (Durmaz 73), Olsson K, Ekdal (Svensson 63), Quaison; Isak, Berg.

Norway (2) 2 *(Berge 33, King 45 (pen))*
Malta (0) 0 11,269
Norway: (442) Jarstein; Elabdellaoui, Nordtveit, Hovland, Aleesami; Odegaard, Selnaes, Berge, Johansen (Normann 76); Haland (Elyounoussi T 66), King (Johnsen 58).
Malta: (343) Bonello; Borg S, Agius, Muscat Z (Apap 20); Corbalan, Vella, Fenech P (Farrugia 64), Mbong; Grech (Effiong 77), Nwoko, Muscat R.

Romania (0) 1 *(Andone 59)*
Spain (1) 2 *(Sergio Ramos 29 (pen), Alcacer 47)* 50,024
Romania: (532) Tatarusanu; Benzar, Nedelcearu, Chiriches, Grigore, Tosca; Deac (Maxim 72), Marin, Stanciu (Hagi 63); Puscas, Keseru (Andone 56).
Spain: (433) Arrizabalaga; Jesus Navas, Llorente■, Sergio Ramos, Jordi Alba; Fabian, Busquets, Saul; Rodrigo (Oyarzabal 71), Alcacer (Hermoso 85), Ceballos (Sarabia 77).

Sunday, 8 September 2019

Romania (0) 1 *(Puscas 47)*
Malta (0) 0 13,376
Romania: (442) Tatarusanu; Chipciu, Rus, Chiriches, Stefan; Cicaldau, Marin (Stanciu 59), Bordeianu, Hagi (Grozav 72); Andone, Puscas (Keseru 77).
Malta: (352) Bonello; Borg S, Agius, Muscat Z; Corbalan, Vella (Grech 86), Muscat R, Gambin (Zerafa 81), Mbong; Nwoko (Effiong 72), Farrugia.

Spain (1) 4 *(Rodrigo 13, 50, Alcacer 89, 90)*
Faroe Islands (0) 0 23,644
Spain: (433) de Gea; Carvajal, Sergio Ramos (Nunez 84), Hermoso, Gaya; Thiago, Rodri, Parejo; Suso (Sarabia 68), Rodrigo, Oyarzabal (Alcacer 61).
Faroe Islands: (541) Nielsen G; Vatnhamar S, Vatnsdal, Gregersen, Baldvinsson (Eriksen 55), Davidsen V; Edmundsson (Bartalsstovu 66), Olsen B, Hansson, Bjartalid; Olsen K (Egilsson 87).

Sweden (0) 1 *(Forsberg 60)*

Norway (1) 1 *(Johansen 45)* 38,372

Sweden: (442) Olsen; Lustig, Lindelof, Granqvist, Bengtsson; Seb Larsson, Olsson K, Ekdal (Svensson 84), Forsberg; Quaison (Andersson 77), Isak (Berg 77).
Norway: (4411) Jarstein; Elabdellaoui, Nordtveit, Reginiussen, Aleesami; Johansen (Haland 76), Henriksen (Elyounoussi T 64), Berge, Selnaes; Odegaard; King.

Saturday, 12 October 2019

Faroe Islands (0) 0

Romania (0) 3 *(Puscas 74, Mitrita 83, Keseru 90)* 2381

Faroe Islands: (541) Nielsen G; Sorensen, Vatnsdal, Gregersen, Baldvinsson (Nielsen E 78), Davidsen V; Vatnhamar S, Olsen B (Eriksen 71), Hansson, Bjartalid; Olsen K (Edmundsson 75).
Romania: (442) Tatarusanu; Benzar, Nedelcearu, Chiriches (Rus 38), Bancu; Hagi, Anton, Stanciu, Coman (Mitrita 69); Puscas, Andone (Keseru 65).

Malta (0) 0

Sweden (1) 4 *(Danielson 11, Seb Larsson 58 (pen), 71 (pen), Agius 66 (og))* 10,702

Malta: (343) Bonello; Shaw, Agius, Muscat Z (Caruana J 66); Mbong, Muscat R (Fenech P 68), Vella, Zerafa; Gambin, Nwoko, Effiong (Mifsud 76).
Sweden: (442) Olsen; Lustig, Danielson, Granqvist, Bengtsson; Seb Larsson, Olsson K, Ekdal (Svensson 64), Forsberg; Berg (Andersson 79), Quaison (Isak 71).

Norway (0) 1 *(King 90 (pen))*

Spain (0) 1 *(Saul 47)* 25,200

Norway: (4411) Jarstein; Elabdellaoui, Nordtveit (Hovland 30), Ajer, Aleesami; Johansen (Sorloth 63), Henriksen (Johnsen 83), Berge, Selnaes; Odegaard; King.
Spain: (433) Arrizabalaga; Jesus Navas, Albiol, Sergio Ramos, Bernat (Martinez 88); Fabian, Busquets, Saul; Rodrigo, Oyarzabal (Rodri 78), Ceballos (Cazorla 64).

Tuesday, 15 October 2019

Faroe Islands (0) 1 *(Baldvinsson 71)*

Malta (0) 0 2677

Faroe Islands: (343) Nielsen G; Vatnsdal, Gregersen, Baldvinsson; Danielsen, Olsen B, Hansson, Davidsen V (Frederiksberg 85); Vatnhamar S, Edmundsson (Egilsson 90), Bjartalid (Olsen K 65).
Malta: (451) Bonello; Muscat Z, Agius, Borg S, Mbong; Muscat R (Zerafa 80), Grech, Vella, Mifsud (Effiong 71), Fenech P (Gambin 71); Nwoko.

Romania (0) 1 *(Mitrita 62)*

Norway (0) 1 *(Sorloth 90)* 29,854

Romania: (4231) Tatarusanu; Benzar, Rus, Nedelcearu, Bancu; Marin, Anton (Bordeianu 84); Deac, Stanciu, Mitrita (Nistor 79); Puscas (Andone 63).
Norway: (442) Jarstein; Elabdellaoui, Hovland, Ajer, Aleesami; Johansen (Sorloth 46), Berge, Henriksen (Normann 81), Selnaes (Johnsen 67); King, Odegaard.

Sweden (0) 1 *(Berg 50)*

Spain (0) 1 *(Rodrigo 90)* 49,712

Sweden: (442) Olsen; Lustig, Lindelof, Granqvist, Bengtsson; Seb Larsson, Olsson K, Ekdal (Svensson 83), Forsberg; Quaison (Isak 77), Berg (Andersson 90).
Spain: (41212) de Gea (Arrizabalaga 60); Carvajal (Jesus Navas 81), Albiol, Martinez, Bernat; Rodri; Fabian, Thiago (Rodrigo 66); Ceballos; Gerard, Oyarzabal.

Friday, 15 November 2019

Norway (2) 4 *(Reginiussen 4, Fossum 8, Sorloth 62, 65)*

Faroe Islands (0) 0 10,400

Norway: (442) Jarstein; Elabdellaoui, Reginiussen, Ajer, Aleesami; Fossum, Berge (Ulvestad 84), Henriksen (Daehli 71), Selnaes; Sorloth, King (Elyounoussi T 78).
Faroe Islands: (343) Nielsen G; Faero, Gregersen, Vatnsdal; Sorensen, Olsen B, Baldvinsson, Jonsson; Vatnhamar S (Bartalsstovu 78), Edmundsson (Olsen K 71), Bjartalid (Frederiksberg 71).

Romania (0) 0

Sweden (2) 2 *(Berg 18, Quaison 34)* 49,678

Romania: (442) Tatarusanu; Mogos, Rus, Nedelcearu, Bancu; Deac (Hagi 46), Baluta T, Stanciu (Alibec 73), Mitrita; Puscas, Keseru (Coman 57).
Sweden: (442) Olsen; Lustig, Lindelof, Granqvist, Bengtsson; Seb Larsson (Svensson 69), Olsson K, Ekdal, Forsberg; Berg (Isak 78), Quaison.

Spain (2) 7 *(Morata 23, Cazorla 41, Torres 62, Sarabia 63, Olmo 69, Gerard 71, Jesus Navas 85)*

Malta (0) 0 19,773

Spain: (433) Pau Lopez; Jesus Navas, Albiol, Sergio Ramos (Torres 61), Bernat; Thiago, Rodri, Cazorla (Alcacer 53); Gerard, Morata (Olmo 66), Sarabia.
Malta: (541) Bonello; Corbalan (Micallef 33), Caruana J, Agius, Muscat Z, Pisani (Grech 76); Paiber, Vella, Muscat R (Caruana T 63), Mbong; Nwoko.

Monday, 18 November 2019

Malta (1) 1 *(Fenech P 40)*

Norway (1) 2 *(King 7, Sorloth 62)* 2708

Malta: (3421) Bonello; Borg S (Apap 75), Agius, Muscat Z; Mbong, Fenech P, Vella (Effiong 61), Zerafa; Muscat R (Muscat N 70), Nwoko; Mifsud.
Norway: (442) Nyland; Svensson (Elyounoussi T 65), Reginiussen, Ajer, Meling; Daehli (Elabdellaoui 46), Berge, Henriksen, Fossum; King (Ulvestad 89), Sorloth.

Spain (4) 5 *(Fabian 8, Gerard 33, 43, Rus 45 (og), Oyarzabal 90)*

Romania (0) 0 36,198

Spain: (433) Arrizabalaga; Carvajal, Sergio Ramos (Albiol 63), Martinez, Gaya; Fabian, Busquets, Saul; Gerard (Oyarzabal 57), Morata, Cazorla (Alcacer 68).
Romania: (4231) Tatarusanu; Benzar, Rus, Nedelcearu, Tosca; Baluta, Marin (Cicaldau 65); Hagi (Nistor 73), Stanciu, Coman (Mitrita 56); Puscas.

Sweden (1) 3 *(Andersson 29, Svanberg 72, Guidetti 80)*

Faroe Islands (0) 0 19,737

Sweden: (442) Nordfeldt; Danielson, Jansson, Helander, Gagliolo; Sema (Kulusevski 65), Svanberg, Olsson K, Tankovic; Andersson (Guidetti 65), Isak.
Faroe Islands: (343) Nielsen G; Vatnsdal, Gregersen, Baldvinsson; Sorensen, Olsen B, Vatnhamar S, Davidsen V; Edmundsson (Frederiksberg 89), Olsen K (Johannesen 74), Bjartalid (Bartalsstovu 46).

Group F Table	*P*	*W*	*D*	*L*	*F*	*A*	*GD*	*Pts*
Spain	10	8	2	0	31	5	26	26
Sweden	10	6	3	1	23	9	14	21
Norway	10	4	5	1	19	11	8	17
Romania	10	4	2	4	17	15	2	14
Faroe Islands	10	1	0	9	4	30	–26	3
Malta	10	1	0	9	3	27	–24	3

GROUP G

Thursday, 21 March 2019

Austria (0) 0

Poland (0) 1 *(Piatek 68)* 40,400

Austria: (4231) Lindner; Lainer, Dragovic, Hinteregger, Wober; Grillitsch (Onisiwo 84), Baumgartlinger; Lazaro (Janko 81), Sabitzer, Alaba; Arnautovic.
Poland: (442) Szczesny; Kedziora, Glik, Bednarek, Bereszynski; Grosicki (Pazdan 90), Krychowiak, Klich, Zielinski (Piatek 59); Lewandowski, Milik (Frankowski 46).

Israel (0) 1 *(Zahavi 55)*

Slovenia (0) 1 *(Sporar 48)* 12,430

Israel: (532) Harush; Dasa, Taha, Yeini, Ben Haroush, Tawatha (Cohen Y 77); Kayal (Solomon 62), Peretz, Natcho (Cohen A 79); Zahavi, Dabbur.
Slovenia: (433) Oblak; Stojanovic, Struna, Mevlja, Jokic; Zajc (Crnigoj 62), Krhin, Kurtic; Ilicic, Sporar (Bohar 84), Verbic (Bijol 89).

North Macedonia (2) 3 *(Alioski 11, Elmas 29, 90)*

Latvia (0) 1 *(Velkovski 87 (og))* 7043

North Macedonia: (442) Dimitrievski; Ristovski, Musliu, Velkovski, Alioski; Trajkovski (Markoski 83), Bardhi, Nikolov, Hasani (Elmas 23); Nestorovski, Pandev (Ristevski 71).
Latvia: (442) Vanins (Steinbors 33); Gabovs, Dubra, Oss, Maksimenko; Tarasovs, Isajevs, Ciganiks■, Rakels; Karasausks (Tobers 68), Sabala (Uldrikis 80).

Sunday, 24 March 2019

Israel (2) 4 *(Zahavi 34, 45, 55, Dabbur 66)*

Austria (1) 2 *(Arnautovic 8, 75)* 16,180

Israel: (532) Harush; Dasa, Dgani, Yeini, Taha (Habashi 77), Ben Haroush; Kayal (Cohen A 72), Peretz, Natcho; Dabbur (Hemed 80), Zahavi.
Austria: (4231) Lindner; Ulmer, Dragovic, Hinteregger, Wober (Janko 60); Schlager (Onisiwo 60), Baumgartlinger; Lazaro, Sabitzer, Zulj (Kainz 85); Arnautovic.

Poland (0) 2 *(Lewandowski 76, Glik 84)*

Latvia (0) 0 51,112

Poland: (442) Szczesny; Kedziora, Glik, Pazdan, Reca; Grosicki (Frankowski 83), Krychowiak, Klich (Blaszczykowski 62), Zielinski; Lewandowski, Piatek (Milik 87).
Latvia: (442) Steinbors; Dubra, Oss, Maksimenko, Laizans; Rakels, Isajevs, Karasausks (Tobers 86), Ikaunieks J; Gutkovskis (Uldrikis 70), Savalnieks (Gabovs 80).

Slovenia (1) 1 *(Zajc 34)*

North Macedonia (0) 1 *(Bardhi 47)* 9872

Slovenia: (433) Oblak; Stojanovic, Struna, Mevlja, Jokic; Zajc (Zahovic 90), Krhin, Kurtic; Ilicic, Sporar (Beric 71), Verbic (Crnigoj 83).
North Macedonia: (442) Dimitrievski; Bejtulai, Velkoski, Musliu, Alioski (Ristevski 90); Ristovski, Bardhi, Nikolov, Elmas; Pandev (Trajkovski 76), Nestorovski (Markoski 88).

Friday, 7 June 2019

Austria (0) 1 *(Burgstaller 74)*

Slovenia (0) 0 19,200

Austria: (4141) Lindner; Lainer, Dragovic, Hinteregger, Ulmer; Laimer (Ilsanker 82); Lazaro, Sabitzer (Burgstaller 71), Schlager, Alaba (Kainz 90); Arnautovic.
Slovenia: (433) Oblak; Stojanovic, Mevlja, Struna, Jokic; Kurtic, Bijol (Popovic 63), Zajc (Bohar 69); Ilicic, Sporar, Crnigoj (Beric 78).

Latvia (0) 0

Israel (1) 3 *(Zahavi 10, 60, 81)* 5508

Latvia: (4231) Steinbors; Savalnieks, Dubra, Oss, Maksimenko; Tobers, Laizans (Rugins 79); Rakels, Karasausks (Kamess 67), Ikaunieks (Ciganiks 57); Gutkovskis.
Israel: (532) Harush; Dasa, Taha, Bitton, Yeini, Ben Haroush (Cohen A 81); Peretz, Natcho, Kayal (Glazer 73); Saba (Sahar 66), Zahavi.

North Macedonia (0) 0

Poland (0) 1 *(Piatek 46)* 25,000

North Macedonia: (352) Dimitrievski; Bejtulai, Velkovski, Musliu■; Ristovski (Ademi 76), Bardhi, Nikolov (Trajkovski 62), Elmas, Alioski; Pandev (Hasani 84), Nestorovski.
Poland: (4231) Fabianski; Kedziora, Bednarek, Glik, Bereszynski; Klich (Goralski 90), Krychowiak; Frankowski (Piatek 46), Zielinski, Grosicki (Rybus 69); Lewandowski.

Monday, 10 June 2019

Latvia (0) 0

Slovenia (4) 5 *(Crnigoj 24, 27, Ilicic 29 (pen), 44, Zajc 47)* 4011

Latvia: (532) Steinbors; Solovjovs, Dubra, Maksimenko (Jagodinskis 16), Oss, Savalnieks; Kamess, Tobers (Rugins 69), Laizans; Rakels (Ontuzans 78), Gutkovskis.
Slovenia: (433) Oblak; Stojanovic, Struna, Mevlja, Jokic; Zajc (Bijol 63), Popovic (Zahovic 77), Kurtic; Crnigoj (Majer 83), Beric, Ilicic.

North Macedonia (1) 1 *(Hinteregger 18 (og))*

Austria (1) 4 *(Lazaro 39, Arnautovic 62 (pen), 82, Bejtulai 87 (og))* 10,501

North Macedonia: (442) Dimitrievski; Ristovski, Bejtulai, Velkovski, Alioski; Nikolov (Hasani 67), Bardhi, Ademi, Elmas (Ristevski 55); Pandev, Nestorovski (Radeski 56).
Austria: (433) Lindner; Lainer, Dragovic (Posch 46), Hinteregger, Ulmer; Laimer, Ilsanker, Schlager; Lazaro, Arnautovic (Burgstaller 88), Sabitzer (Schaub 90).

Poland (1) 4 *(Piatek 35, Lewandowski 56 (pen), Grosicki 59, Kadzior 84)*

Israel (0) 0 57,229

Poland: (442) Fabianski; Kedziora, Bednarek, Glik, Bereszynski; Zielinski, Klich (Goralski 75), Krychowiak, Grosicki (Kadzior 77); Piatek (Milik 73), Lewandowski.
Israel: (4411) Harush; Dasa, Taha, Yeini, Ben Haroush; Bitton (Elhamed 82), Natcho, Kayal (Cohen Y 57), Peretz; Solomon (Saba 72); Zahavi.

Thursday, 5 September 2019

Israel (0) 1 *(Zahavi 55)*

North Macedonia (0) 1 *(Ademi 64)* 15,200

Israel: (532) Marciano; Dasa, Taha, Dgani, Elhamed, Ben Haroush (Kayal 60); Peretz, Natcho, Solomon; Zahavi, Dabbur (Hemed 75).
North Macedonia: (3142) Dimitrievski; Musliu, Velkovski, Ristevski; Nikolov (Trajkovski 75); Bejtulai, Ademi, Bardhi (Spirovski 83), Alioski; Nestorovski (Pandev 69), Elmas.

Friday, 6 September 2019

Austria (2) 6 *(Arnautovic 7, 53 (pen), Sabitzer 13, Steinbors 76 (og), Laimer 80, Gregoritsch 84)*

Latvia (0) 0 16,300

Austria: (4231) Stankovic; Lainer, Dragovic (Grillitsch 82), Hinteregger, Ulmer; Baumgartlinger (Ilsanker 75), Laimer; Lazaro (Gregoritsch 69), Sabitzer, Alaba; Arnautovic.
Latvia: (442) Steinbors; Petersons, Cernomordijs, Dubra, Maksimenko; Ciganiks (Savalnieks 67), Tobers (Rugins 77), Bogdaskins, Kamess; Laizans (Uldrikis 82), Gutkovskis.

Slovenia (1) 2 *(Struna 35, Sporar 65)*

Poland (0) 0 15,231

Slovenia: (4411) Oblak; Stojanovic, Struna, Mevlja, Balkovec; Bezjak, Krhin, Kurtic, Verbic (Crnigoj 62 (Beric 90)); Sporar (Popovic 85); Ilicic.
Poland: (442) Fabianski; Kedziora, Bednarek, Pazdan, Bereszynski; Zielinski, Klich (Bielik 70), Krychowiak, Grosicki (Blaszczykowski 70); Piatek (Kownacki 76), Lewandowski.

Monday, 9 September 2019

Latvia (0) 0

North Macedonia (2) 2 *(Pandev 14, Bardhi 17)* 2724

Latvia: (442) Vanins; Petersons, Cernomordijs, Maksimenko, Rugins; Ikaunieks J, Laizans, Kigurs (Punculs 76), Kamess (Sabala 84); Uldrikis (Savalnieks 46), Gutkovskis.
North Macedonia: (4231) Dimitrievski; Bejtulai, Velkovski, Musliu, Alioski; Ademi, Bardhi; Trajkovski (Nestorovski 65), Pandev (Nikolov 75), Elmas (Radeski 88); Trickovski.

Poland (0) 0

Austria (0) 0 56,788

Poland: (4231) Fabianski; Kedziora, Glik, Bednarek, Bereszynski; Bielik, Krychowiak; Kownacki (Blaszczykowski 58 (Klich 77)), Zielinski, Grosicki (Szymanski 70); Lewandowski.
Austria: (4231) Stankovic; Lainer, Posch, Dragovic, Ulmer; Baumgartlinger, Laimer (Gregoritsch 89); Lazaro (Ilsanker 77), Sabitzer, Alaba; Arnautovic.

Slovenia (1) 3 *(Verbic 43, 90, Bezjak 66)*

Israel (0) 2 *(Natcho 50, Zahavi 62)* 10,669

Slovenia: (4411) Oblak; Stojanovic, Struna (Blazic 54), Mevlja, Jokic (Balkovec 46); Bezjak, Kurtic, Krhin (Popovic 81), Verbic; Ilicic; Sporar.
Israel: (541) Marciano; Dasa, Taha, Dgani, Elhamed, Ben Haroush (Kayal 46); Weissman (Dabbur 61), Natcho, Peretz (Glazer 77), Solomon; Zahavi.

Thursday, 10 October 2019

Austria (1) 3 *(Lazaro 41, Hinteregger 56, Sabitzer 88)*

Israel (1) 1 *(Zahavi 34)* 26,200

Austria: (4231) Stankovic; Posch (Trimmel 63), Dragovic, Hinteregger, Ulmer; Baumgartlinger, Ilsanker; Lazaro, Sabitzer, Laimer (Schaub 59); Arnautovic (Gregoritsch 82).
Israel: (343) Marciano; Taha (Cohen 76), Tibi, Elhamed; Dasa, Bitton, Natcho, Tawatha (Ben Haroush 54); Solomon, Dabbur (Weissman 70), Zahavi.

Latvia (0) 0

Poland (2) 3 *(Lewandowski 9, 13, 76)* 7107

Latvia: (532) Vanins; Rugins, Oss, Dubra, Jagodinskis, Maksimenko; Kigurs (Ciganiks 86), Laizans (Tobers 72), Ikaunieks J; Gutkovskis, Rakels (Karasausks 72).
Poland: (4231) Szczesny; Kedziora, Glik, Bednarek, Rybus (Reca 80); Klich (Piatek 60), Krychowiak; Szymanski, Zielinski, Grosicki (Frankowski 77); Lewandowski.

North Macedonia (0) 2 *(Elmas 50, 68)*

Slovenia (0) 1 *(Ilicic 90 (pen))* 16,500

North Macedonia: (3412) Dimitrievski; Ristovski (Zajkov 82), Musliu, Ristevski; Nikolov, Spirovski, Ademi (Tosevski 78), Alioski; Elmas; Pandev (Trickovski 66), Nestorovski.
Slovenia: (4411) Oblak; Stojanovic, Struna, Mevlja, Balkovec; Bezjak (Beric 79), Krhin (Popovic 48), Kurtic, Verbic (Zajc 65); Ilicic; Sporar.

Sunday, 13 October 2019

Poland (0) 2 *(Frankowski 74, Milik 80)*

North Macedonia (0) 0 52,894

Poland: (4231) Szczesny; Bereszynski, Glik, Bednarek, Reca; Goralski, Krychowiak; Szymanski (Milik 68), Zielinski (Piatek 90), Grosicki (Frankowski 73); Lewandowski.
North Macedonia: (3412) Dimitrievski; Ristovski (Radeski 82), Musliu, Ristevski; Bejtulai, Nikolov (Stoilov 88), Spirovski, Alioski; Elmas; Pandev, Nestorovski (Trajkovski 73).

Slovenia (0) 0

Austria (1) 1 *(Posch 21)* 15,108

Slovenia: (442) Oblak; Stojanovic, Struna, Mevlja, Balkovec; Bezjak (Zajc 61), Krhin (Popovic■ 79), Kurtic, Verbic (Beric 69); Ilicic, Sporar.
Austria: (4231) Stankovic; Posch, Dragovic, Hinteregger, Ulmer; Ilsanker, Baumgartlinger; Lazaro (Trimmel 88), Sabitzer (Kainz 90), Laimer; Gregoritsch (Onisiwo 83).

Tuesday, 15 October 2019

Israel (3) 3 *(Dabbur 16, 42, Zahavi 26)*

Latvia (1) 1 *(Kamess 40)* 9150

Israel: (343) Marciano; Taha, Bitton, Elhamed; Dasa, Natcho, Glazer, Tawatha (Menachem 78); Saba (Elmkies 76), Zahavi, Dabbur (Weissman 84).
Latvia: (541) Steinbors; Savalnieks, Cernomordijs, Oss, Jagodinskis, Jurkovskis; Ikaunieks J (Ontuzans 86), Tarasovs, Kigurs (Laizans 68), Kamess (Ikaunieks D 78); Gutkovskis.

Saturday, 16 November 2019

Austria (1) 2 *(Alaba 7, Lainer 48)*

North Macedonia (0) 1 *(Stojanovski 90)* 41,100

Austria: (4231) Schlager; Lainer, Dragovic, Hinteregger, Ulmer; Baumgartlinger, Laimer (Ilsanker 90); Lazaro (Trimmel 79), Sabitzer, Alaba (Gregoritsch 90); Arnautovic.
North Macedonia: (3421) Dimitrievski; Ristovski, Mladenovski (Zajkov 46), Velkovski; Tosevski (Avramovski 62), Spirovski, Bardhi, Ristevski; Kostadinov, Elmas; Trajkovski (Stojanovski 13).

Israel (0) 1 *(Dabbur 88)*

Poland (1) 2 *(Krychowiak 4, Piatek 54)* 16,700

Israel: (532) Marciano; Dasa, Taha (Haziza 43), Tibi, Bitton, Ben Haroush (Menachem 65); Natcho, Glazer, Kayal (Elmkies 79); Dabbur, Zahavi.
Poland: (4231) Szczesny; Kedziora, Glik, Bednarek, Reca; Bielik, Krychowiak (Furman 84); Frankowski, Zielinski, Szymanski (Lewandowski 63); Piatek (Klich 70).

Slovenia (0) 1 *(Tarasovs 53 (og))*

Latvia (0) 0 11,224

Slovenia: (442) Oblak; Stojanovic, Struna, Mevlja, Jokic; Ilicic, Krhin (Bijol 74), Kurtic, Verbic (Bezjak 90); Vuckic (Zajc 62), Sporar.
Latvia: (433) Steinbors; Savalnieks, Dubra, Maksimenko, Jurkovskis; Tarasovs, Oss, Ikaunieks D (Uldrikis 72); Fjodorovs, Gutkovskis (Laizans 85), Kamess (Punculs 88).

Tuesday, 19 November 2019

Latvia (0) 1 *(Oss 65)*

Austria (0) 0 2781

Latvia: (442) Steinbors; Savalnieks, Dubra, Maksimenko, Jurkovskis; Fjodorovs, Grjaznovs (Cernomordijs 90), Oss, Kamess; Ikaunieks D (Tarasovs 89), Uldrikis (Gutkovskis 70).
Austria: (4231) Pervan; Trimmel, Posch, Dragovic, Wober; Baumgartlinger (Onisiwo 46), Ilsanker (Ranftl 77); Goiginger (Hinterseer 69), Grillitsch, Schaub; Gregoritsch.

North Macedonia (1) 1 *(Nikolov 45)*

Israel (0) 0 5573

North Macedonia: (4231) Dimitrievski; Ristovski, Musliu, Velkovski (Zajkov 72), Ristevski; Nikolov, Bardhi; Kostadinov, Pandev (Avramovski 79), Elmas; Stojanovski (Nestorovski 61).
Israel: (433) Harush; Dasa (Dgani 41), Tibi, Bitton, Menachem; Natcho, Glazer, Elmkies (Haziza 59); Saba (Weissman 68), Zahavi, Dabbur.

Poland (1) 3 *(Szymanski 3, Lewandowski 54, Goralski 81)*

Slovenia (1) 2 *(Matavz 14, Ilicic 61)* 53,946

Poland: (4231) Szczesny; Piszczek (Kedziora 45), Glik (Jedrzejczyk 7), Bednarek, Reca; Goralski, Krychowiak; Szymanski (Jozwiak 86), Zielinski, Grosicki; Lewandowski.
Slovenia: (4141) Oblak; Stojanovic, Blazic, Mevlja, Balkovec; Krhin; Ilicic, Bijol (Zajc 72), Kurtic■, Verbic (Rep 86); Matavz (Vuckic 89).

Group G Table	*P*	*W*	*D*	*L*	*F*	*A*	*GD*	*Pts*
Poland	10	8	1	1	18	5	13	25
Austria	10	6	1	3	19	9	10	19
North Macedonia	10	4	2	4	12	13	−1	14
Slovenia	10	4	2	4	16	11	5	14
Israel	10	3	2	5	16	18	−2	11
Latvia	10	1	0	9	3	28	−25	3

GROUP H

Friday, 22 March 2019

Albania (0) 0

Turkey (1) 2 *(Yilmaz 21, Calhanoglu 55)* 11,730

Albania: (3412) Berisha; Veseli, Ismajli, Gjimshiti; Hysaj, Abrashi, Xhaka, Balliu (Sadiku 58); Memushaj; Balaj (Grezda 58), Uzuni.
Turkey: (343) Gunok; Ali Kaldirim, Gonul (Celik 46), Demiral; Tekdemir, Ayhan, Belozoglu (Tokoz 65), Yokuslu; Calhanoglu, Tosun, Yilmaz (Turuc 88).

Andorra (0) 0

Iceland (1) 2 *(Bjarnason B 22, Kjartansson 80)* 1854

Andorra: (442) Gomes; Jesus Rubio (Sanchez J 87), Llovera, Lima, San Nicolas; Martinez A (Alaez 71), Rebes, Vales, Cervos; Martinez C (Clemente 81), Vieira.
Iceland: (4411) Halldorsson; Saevarsson, Arnason, Sigurdsson R, Skulason A; Gudmundsson J (Traustason 83), Gunnarsson (Sigurdarson 63), Bjarnason B, Sigurdsson A; Sigurdsson G; Finnbogason A (Kjartansson 70).

Moldova (0) 1 *(Ambros 89)*

France (3) 4 *(Griezmann 24, Varane 27, Giroud 36, Mbappe-Lottin 87)* 10,042

Moldova: (4231) Koselev; Jardan, Posmac, Carp, Reabciuk; Cebotaru, Ionita; Antoniuc (Ambros 73), Cociuc (Rozgoniuc 46), Ginsari; Nicolaescu (Damascan 59).
France: (451) Lloris; Pavard, Varane, Umtiti, Kurzawa; Mbappe-Lottin, Griezmann (Thauvin 73), Pogba, Kante, Matuidi (Lemar 73); Giroud (Fekir 81).

Monday, 25 March 2019

Andorra (0) 0

Albania (1) 3 *(Sadiku 21, Balaj 87, Abrashi 90)* 1373

Andorra: (442) Gomes; Jesus Rubio, Llovera, Lima, San Nicolas; Rodriguez, Rebes, Vales (Pujol 84), Sanchez J (Cervos 67); Martinez C (Alaez 73), Ferre.
Albania: (442) Berisha; Aliji, Gjimshiti, Ismajli, Hysaj; Grezda (Balaj 70), Kace, Basha (Memushaj 87), Xhaka (Abrashi 67); Uzuni, Sadiku.

France (1) 4 *(Umtiti 12, Giroud 68, Mbappe-Lottin 78, Griezmann 84)*

Iceland (0) 0 64,538

France: (4231) Lloris; Pavard, Varane, Umtiti, Kurzawa (Kimpembe 85); Pogba, Kante (Lemar 80); Mbappe-Lottin, Griezmann, Matuidi; Giroud (Sissoko 89).
Iceland: (532) Halldorsson; Saevarsson (Skulason A 84), Ingason, Arnason, Sigurdsson R, Magnusson; Sigurjonsson (Traustason 57), Gunnarsson, Bjarnason B; Sigurdsson G, Gudmundsson A (Finnbogason A 62).

Turkey (2) 4 *(Ali Kaldirim 24, Tosun 26, 54, Ayhan 70)*

Moldova (0) 0 29,456

Turkey: (433) Gunok; Celik, Demiral, Ayhan, Ali Kaldirim; Tokoz (Belozoglu 84), Tekdemir, Turuc (Karaca 78); Tosun, Yilmaz, Calhanoglu (Yazici 66).
Moldova: (4321) Koselev; Jardan, Rozgoniuc, Posmac, Reabciuk; Ionita, Carp (Turcan 46), Cebotaru; Graur, Ginsari (Antoniuc 73); Ambros (Nicolaescu 57).

Saturday, 8 June 2019

Iceland (1) 1 *(Gudmundsson J 22)*

Albania (0) 0 8968

Iceland: (4411) Halldorsson; Hermannsson, Arnason, Sigurdsson R, Skulason A; Gudmundsson J (Traustason 56), Gunnarsson, Bjarnason B, Sigurjonsson (Sigurdsson A 81); Sigurdsson G; Kjartansson (Sigthorsson 63).
Albania: (433) Berisha; Hysaj, Dermaku, Ismajli, Veseli; Abrashi, Xhaka (Ndoj 71), Basha (Kace 67); Cikalleshi (Sadiku 79), Balaj, Lenjani.

Moldova (1) 1 *(Armas 8)*

Andorra (0) 0 6712

Moldova: (4231) Koselev; Jardan, Efros, Armas, Reabciuk; Ionita■, Carp; Antoniuc (Cociuc 64), Suvorov (Cebotaru 50), Ginsari; Damascan (Boiciuc 81).
Andorra: (442) Gomes; Jesus Rubio (Martinez A 72), Llovera, Lima, San Nicolas; Clemente, Rebes (Moreno 69), Vales, Cervos; Vieira, Alaez (Sanchez A 82).

Turkey (2) 2 *(Ayhan 30, Under 40)*

France (0) 0 36,783

Turkey: (4231) Gunok; Celik, Ayhan, Demiral, Ali Kaldirim; Tekdemir, Tokoz (Omur 90); Under (Yazici 84), Kahveci (Tufan 79), Karaman; Yilmaz.
France: (433) Lloris; Pavard, Varane, Umtiti, Digne (Mendy 46); Sissoko, Matuidi (Coman 46), Pogba; Mbappe-Lottin, Giroud (Ben Yedder 72), Griezmann.

Tuesday, 11 June 2019

Albania (0) 2 *(Cikalleshi 66, Ramadani 90)*

Moldova (0) 0 5004

Albania: (433) Berisha; Hysaj, Ismajli, Mavraj, Veseli; Kace (Qose 84), Ramadani, Lenjani (Roshi 59); Abrashi, Uzuni, Sadiku (Cikalleshi 58).
Moldova: (3421) Koselev; Jardan (Graur 76), Efros, Armas; Antoniuc, Cebotaru, Carp, Reabciuk; Suvorov (Cociuc 74), Ginsari; Damascan (Boiciuc 70).

Andorra (0) 0

France (3) 4 *(Mbappe-Lottin 11, Ben Yedder 30, Thauvin 45, Zouma 60)* 3187

Andorra: (442) Gomes; Jesus Rubio, Llovera, Lima, San Nicolas; Martinez A (Jordi Rubio 58), Rebes, Vales, Cervos (Rodriguez 80); Alaez (Sanchez J 84), Vieira.
France: (4411) Lloris; Dubois, Zouma, Lenglet, Mendy; Ben Yedder (Giroud 72), Ndombele (Sissoko 64), Pogba, Mbappe-Lottin; Griezmann; Thauvin (Lemar 81).

Iceland (2) 2 *(Sigurdsson R 21, 32)*

Turkey (1) 1 *(Tokoz 40)* 9680

Iceland: (4411) Halldorsson; Hermannsson, Arnason, Sigurdsson R, Skulason A (Magnusson 69); Gudmundsson J (Traustason 79), Hallfredsson, Gunnarsson, Bjarnason B; Sigurdsson G; Bodvarsson (Sigthorsson 63).
Turkey: (4231) Gunok; Celik, Demiral, Ayhan, Ali Kaldirim; Tokoz (Yalcin 85), Tufan; Calhanoglu, Kahveci (Omur 63), Karaman (Yazici 46); Yilmaz.

Saturday, 7 September 2019

France (2) 4 *(Coman 8, 68, Giroud 27, Ikone 85)*

Albania (0) 1 *(Cikalleshi 90 (pen))* 77,655

France: (4411) Lloris; Pavard, Varane, Lenglet, Lucas (Digne 80); Coman (Ikone 77), Tolisso, Matuidi, Lemar (Fekir 84); Griezmann; Giroud.
Albania: (532) Strakosha; Hysaj, Ismajli, Mavraj, Djimsiti, Roshi; Bare, Ramadani (Gjasula 53), Abrashi (Xhaka 73); Uzuni, Balaj (Cikalleshi 61).

Iceland (1) 3 *(Sigthorsson 31, Bjarnason B 55, Bodvarsson 77)*

Moldova (0) 0 5004

Iceland: (442) Halldorsson; Hermannsson, Arnason, Sigurdsson R, Skulason A; Traustason, Gunnarsson, Sigurdsson G, Bjarnason B (Sigurjonsson 78); Bodvarsson (Kjartansson 84), Sigthorsson (Hallfredsson 63).
Moldova: (433) Koselev; Graur, Mudrac, Armas, Reabciuk; Cebotaru, Ionita, Carp (Turcan 67); Ginsari (Sandu 80), Cemirtan (Cojocaru 65), Suvorov.

Turkey (0) 1 *(Tufan 89)*

Andorra (0) 0 42,600

Turkey: (4141) Gunok; Celik, Demiral, Soyuncu, Meras (Tufan 61); Emre; Yazici, Kahveci, Calhanoglu (Kilinc 80), Yalcin (Karaman 46); Tosun.
Andorra: (442) Gomes; San Nicolas, Llovera, Lima, Cervos; Clemente (Alaez 79), Rebes, Vales, Rodriguez (Garcia M 63); Martinez C, Vieira (Garcia E 87).

Tuesday, 10 September 2019

Albania (1) 4 *(Dermaku 32, Hysaj 52, Roshi 79, Cikalleshi 82)*

Iceland (0) 2 *(Sigurdsson G 47, Sigthorsson 58)* 8652

Albania: (4312) Strakosha; Hysaj (Abrashi 73), Djimsiti (Veseli 66), Dermaku, Lenjani (Roshi 62); Gjasula, Ismajli, Bare; Memushaj; Cikalleshi, Manaj.
Iceland: (4411) Halldorsson; Hermannsson, Arnason, Sigurdsson R, Skulason A; Sigurjonsson, Gunnarsson, Hallfredsson (Sigthorsson 56), Bjarnason B (Magnusson 71); Sigurdsson G; Bodvarsson (Kjartansson 85).

France (1) 3 *(Coman 18, Lenglet 52, Ben Yedder 90)*

Andorra (0) 0 55,383

France: (4411) Lloris; Dubois, Varane, Lenglet, Digne; Ikone (Lemar 63), Sissoko, Tolisso, Coman (Fekir 85); Griezmann; Giroud (Ben Yedder 72).
Andorra: (442) Gomes; Jesus Rubio, Llovera, Lima, San Nicolas; Clemente (Jordi Rubio 80), Vales, Rebes, Cervos; Vieira (Moreno 86), Martinez C (Alaez 69).

Moldova (0) 0

Turkey (1) 4 *(Tosun 37, 79, Turuc 57, Yazici 88)* 8281

Moldova: (4411) Koselev; Graur, Efros, Mudrac, Reabciuk; Cebotaru, Turcan, Ionita (Ghecev 81), Sandu; Suvorov (Razgoniuc 75); Ginsari (Cemirtan 68).
Turkey: (442) Gunok; Celik, Ayhan, Demiral, Meras; Turuc, Tufan, Tokoz (Parmak 87), Kahveci (Yazici 80); Tosun, Karaman (Calhanoglu 70).

Friday, 11 October 2019

Andorra (0) 1 *(Vales 63)*

Moldova (0) 0 947

Andorra: (4411) Gomes; Jesus Rubio, Llovera, Lima, San Nicolas; Clemente (Rebes 73), Vales, Pujol (Rodriguez 83), Cervos; Vieira; Martinez C (Alaez 61).
Moldova: (433) Koselev; Graur, Posmac, Prepelita, Reabciuk; Mihaliov (Dedov 72), Cebotaru, Ionita; Suvorov, Boicuic, Ginsari■.

Iceland (0) 0

France (0) 1 *(Giroud 66 (pen))* 9719

Iceland: (442) Halldorsson; Palsson, Arnason, Sigurdsson R, Skulason A; Gudmundsson (Bodvarsson 16), Sigurjonsson (Finnbogason A 73), Bjarnason B, Traustason (Sigurdsson A 81); Sigurdsson G, Sigthorsson.
France: (433) Mandanda; Pavard, Varane, Lenglet, Digne; Sissoko, Tolisso, Matuidi; Coman (Ikone 88), Giroud (Ben Yedder 78), Griezmann.

Turkey (0) 1 *(Tosun 90)*

Albania (0) 0 41,438

Turkey: (433) Gunok; Celik, Ayhan (Soyuncu 46), Demiral, Meras; Tufan (Yazici 80), Tekdemir, Emre (Kahveci 66); Tosun, Yilmaz, Calhanoglu.
Albania: (3142) Strakosha; Ismajli, Dermaku, Djimsiti; Gjasula; Veseli, Bare, Memushaj (Abrashi 72), Lenjani (Roshi 57); Cikalleshi (Balaj 83), Manaj.

Monday, 14 October 2019

France (0) 1 *(Giroud 76)*

Turkey (0) 1 *(Ayhan 81)* 72,154

France: (4231) Mandanda; Pavard, Varane, Lenglet, Lucas; Tolisso, Matuidi (Lemar 76); Sissoko, Griezmann, Coman (Ikone 87); Ben Yedder (Giroud 72).
Turkey: (4141) Gunok; Celik (Ayhan 53), Demiral, Soyuncu, Meras; Yokuslu (Calhanoglu 46); Tufan (Tosun 81), Tekdemir, Kahveci, Karaman; Yilmaz.

Iceland (1) 2 *(Sigurdsson A 38, Sigthorsson 65)*

Andorra (0) 0 7169

Iceland: (442) Halldorsson; Palsson, Sigurdsson R (Ingason 68), Fjoluson, Skulason A; Sigurdsson A, Sigurdsson G, Bjarnason B (Hallfredsson 70), Traustason; Finnbogason A (Bodvarsson 64), Sigthorsson.
Andorra: (442) Gomes; San Nicolas, Lima, Llovera, Cervos; Rodriguez, Rebes, Vales, Martinez A (Garcia M 80); Alaez (Gomez 87), Vieira (Fernandez 60).

Moldova (0) 0

Albania (3) 4 *(Cikalleshi 22, Bare 34, Trashi 40, Manaj 90)* 4367

Moldova: (541) Koselev; Graur, Prepelita, Posmac, Mudrac (Razgoniuc 31), Reabciuk; Suvorov (Boicuic 60), Anton, Cebotaru, Ionita; Sidorenco (Sandu 80).
Albania: (433) Strakosha; Veseli, Ismajli (Kumbulla 89), Dermaku, Djimsiti; Abrashi, Gjasula, Trashi; Bare (Selahi 89), Manaj, Cikalleshi (Roshi 76).

Thursday, 14 November 2019

Albania (1) 2 *(Balaj 6, Manaj 55)*

Andorra (1) 2 *(Martinez C 18, 48)* 4260

Albania: (3142) Berisha; Ismajli, Djimsiti, Veseli; Ramadani (Sulejmanov 73); Roshi, Memushaj, Ndoj (Bare 60), Trashi (Hysaj 46); Balaj, Manaj.
Andorra: (442) Gomes; Jesus Rubio (Rodriguez 71), Garcia E, Llovera, San Nicolas; Clemente, Vales, Moreno, Cervos; Martinez C (Fernandez 79), Alaez (Martinez A 89).

France (1) 2 *(Varane 35, Giroud 79 (pen))*

Moldova (1) 1 *(Rata 9)* 64,367

France: (4231) Mandanda; Pavard, Varane, Lenglet, Digne; Kante, Tolisso; Mbappe-Lottin, Griezmann, Coman (Lemar 88); Giroud.
Moldova: (532) Koselev; Jardan (Graur 68), Craciun, Posmac, Armas, Platica; Carp, Cociuc, Ionita; Ginsari (Milinceanu 74), Rata (Patras 81).

Turkey (0) 0

Iceland (0) 0 48,329

Turkey: (433) Gunok; Celik (Bayram 90), Demiral, Soyuncu, Meras; Tekdemir, Yokuslu, Tufan; Under (Yazici 81), Yilmaz, Calhanoglu (Ayhan 87).
Iceland: (442) Halldorsson; Palsson, Arnason, Sigurdsson R, Skulason A (Anderson 85); Bodvarsson, Sigurdsson G, Bjarnason B, Traustason (Magnusson 63); Sigthorsson, Finnbogason A (Sigurdsson A 24).

Sunday, 17 November 2019

Albania (0) 0

France (2) 2 *(Tolisso 8, Griezmann 31)* 19,228

Albania: (532) Berisha; Hysaj (Trashi 82), Veseli, Dermaku, Djimsiti, Lenjani (Roshi 46); Bare, Gjasula, Qose (Memushaj 46); Balaj, Manaj.
France: (3412) Mandanda; Varane, Lenglet, Kimpembe; Dubois (Pavard 88), Sissoko, Tolisso, Mendy (Digne 75); Griezmann; Giroud, Ben Yedder (Fekir 85).

Andorra (0) 0

Turkey (2) 2 *(Unal 17, 21 (pen))* 2357

Andorra: (442) Gomes (Pol 87); San Nicolas, Lima, Llovera, Cervos; Martinez A, Vales, Rebes, Clemente (Jordi Rubio 85); Alaez (Rodriguez 71), Martinez C.
Turkey: (352) Cakir; Kabak, Ayhan, Demiral (Cetin 80); Sangare, Yazici, Tufan, Calhanoglu (Ozcan 60), Bayram; Kutucu (Kilinc 85), Unal.

Moldova (0) 1 *(Milinceanu 56)*

Iceland (1) 2 *(Bjarnason B 17, Sigurdsson G 65)* 6742

Moldova: (4411) Koselev; Rata, Craciun, Armas, Focsa; Carp (Cojocari 90), Ionita, Cociuc, Platica; Ginsari (Graur 83); Milinceanu (Damascan 60).
Iceland: (442) Halldorsson; Palsson, Ingason, Sigurdsson R, Skulason A; Sigurdsson A, Sigurdsson G, Bjarnason B (Magnusson 87), Anderson (Fridjonsson 55); Bodvarsson, Sigthorsson (Kjartansson 29).

Group H Table	P	W	D	L	F	A	GD	Pts
France	10	8	1	1	25	6	19	25
Turkey	10	7	2	1	18	3	15	23
Iceland	10	6	1	3	14	11	3	19
Albania	10	4	1	5	16	14	2	13
Andorra	10	1	1	8	3	20	−17	4
Moldova	10	1	0	9	4	26	−22	3

GROUP I

Thursday, 21 March 2019

Belgium (2) 3 *(Tielemans 14, Hazard E 45 (pen), 88)*

Russia (1) 1 *(Cheryshev 16)* 34,245

Belgium: (343) Courtois; Alderweireld, Boyata, Vertonghen; Castagne, Tielemans, Dendoncker, Hazard T (Chadli 84); Mertens, Batshuayi, Hazard E.
Russia: (541) Marinato; Fernandes, Nababkin, Dzhikija, Kudryashov, Zhirkov; Akhmetov, Golovin■, Kuzyaev (Anton Miranchuk 25), Cheryshev (Chalov 65); Dzyuba (Smolov 77).

Cyprus (4) 5 *(Sotiriou 19 (pen), 23 (pen), Kousoulos 26, Efrem 31, Laifis 56)*

San Marino (0) 0 3175

Cyprus: (442) Panagi; Demetriou J (Merkis 65), Kousoulos, Laifis, Ioannou N; Efrem, Papoulis (Spoljaric 53), Artymatas, Georgiou; Mitidis, Sotiriou (Makris 27).
San Marino: (532) Benedettini; Manuel Battistini, Cevoli, Simoncini, Palazzi, Rinaldi (Hirsch 46); Giardi (Lunadei 74), Golinucci E, Mularoni; Berardi F, Nanni (Vitaioli M 46).

Kazakhstan (2) 3 *(Pertsukh 6, Vorogovskiy 10, Zainutdinov 51)*

Scotland (0) 0 27,641

Kazakhstan: (532) Nepogodov; Vorogovskiy, Maliy, Postnikov, Yerlanov (Akhmetov 81), Suyumbayev; Pertsukh, Kuat, Merkel; Zainutdinov (Muzhikov 84), Murtazaev (Turysbek 68).
Scotland: (433) Bain; Palmer, Bates, McKenna, Shinnie; Armstrong, McGinn (McTominay 69), McGregor C; Forrest (McNulty 81), McBurnie (Russell 61), Burke.

Sunday, 24 March 2019

Cyprus (0) 0

Belgium (2) 2 *(Hazard E 10, Batshuayi 18)* 8728

Cyprus: (442) Pardo; Kousoulos, Junior (Georgiou 46), Merkis, Laifis; Papoulis, Margaca, Artymatas, Ioannou N; Antoniou (Makris 81), Efrem (Spoljaric 75).
Belgium: (343) Courtois; Alderweireld, Vermaelen, Vertonghen; Castagne, Tielemans, Dendoncker, Hazard T (Carrasco 68); Mertens (Januzaj 56), Batshuayi (Praet 89), Hazard E.

Kazakhstan (0) 0

Russia (2) 4 *(Cheryshev 19, 45, Dzyuba 52, Beysebekov 63 (og))* 29,582

Kazakhstan: (532) Nepogodov; Beysebekov, Akhmetov, Maliy, Logvinenko (Vorogovskiy 33), Suyumbayev; Merkel, Kuat, Pertsukh (Zhukov 85); Zainutdinov, Murtazaev (Turysbek 59).
Russia: (451) Marinato; Fernandes, Semenov, Dzhikija, Kudryashov; Ionov (Ignatiev 61), Akhmetov (Aleksey Miranchuk 72), Gazinsky, Ozdoev, Cheryshev; Dzyuba (Chalov 82).

San Marino (0) 0

Scotland (1) 2 *(McLean 4, Russell 74)* 4077

San Marino: (433) Benedettini; Manuel Battistini, Simoncini (Lunadei 86), Cevoli, Palazzi; Mularoni, Golinucci E, Golinucci A; Berardi F, Vitaioli M (Nanni 60), Hirsch (Grandoni 77).
Scotland: (442) Bain; O'Donnell, Bates, McKenna, Robertson; McLean, Armstrong (Forrest 71), McGregor C (McTominay 57), Paterson (McNulty 37); Fraser, Russell.

Saturday, 8 June 2019

Belgium (2) 3 *(Mertens 11, Castagne 14, Lukaku 50)*

Kazakhstan (0) 0 37,155

Belgium: (343) Courtois; Alderweireld, Kompany (Vermaelen 78), Vertonghen; Castagne, Witsel, De Bruyne (Tielemans 67), Hazard T; Mertens, Lukaku (Batshuayi 72), Hazard E.
Kazakhstan: (451) Nepogodov; Marochkin, Maliy, Erlanov, Beysebekov; Zhukov, Kuat (Tagybergen 78), Fedin (Aimbetov 66), Pertsukh, Vorogovskiy; Zhanglyshbay (Islamkhan 46).

Russia (4) 9 *(Cevoli 26 (og), Dzyuba 31 (pen), 73, 76, 88, Kudryashov 36, Anton Miranchuk 41, Smolov 77, 83)*

San Marino (0) 0 42,241

Russia: (433) Marinato; Fernandes, Semenov, Dzhikija, Kudryashov; Zobnin (Barinov 72), Ozdoev, Anton Miranchuk (Smolov 60); Golovin, Dzyuba, Aleksey Miranchuk (Ionov 60).
San Marino: (4231) Benedettini; Manuel Battistini, Cevoli, Vitaioli F, Grandoni; Golinucci E, Golinucci A (Lunadei 64); Palazzi (Censoni 50), Rinaldi (Tomassini 56), Mularoni; Vitaioli M.

Scotland (0) 2 *(Robertson 61, Burke 89)*

Cyprus (0) 1 *(Kousoulos 87)* 31,277

Scotland: (433) Marshall; O'Donnell, Mulgrew, McKenna, Robertson; McGinn (McTominay 79), McLean, McGregor C (Armstrong 87); Forrest, Brophy (Burke 73), Fraser.
Cyprus: (433) Pardo; Kousoulos, Ioannou N, Laifis, Margaca; Spoljaric (Kosti 70), Artymatas, Makris (Pittas 80); Efrem, Sotiriou, Ioannou M (Georgiou 66).

Tuesday, 11 June 2019

Belgium (1) 3 *(Lukaku 45, 57, De Bruyne 90)*

Scotland (0) 0 32,482

Belgium: (343) Courtois; Alderweireld, Kompany (Vermaelen 90), Vertonghen; Meunier, Tielemans (Mertens 78), Witsel, Hazard T (Carrasco 90); De Bruyne, Lukaku, Hazard E.
Scotland: (4231) Marshall; O'Donnell, Mulgrew, McKenna, Taylor; McTominay, McLean; Russell (Forrest 67), Armstrong (Fraser 32), McGregor C; Burke.

Kazakhstan (1) 4 *(Kuat 45, Fedin 61, Suyumbayev 65, Islamkhan 79)*

San Marino (0) 0 18,652

Kazakhstan: (532) Nepogodov; Vorogovskiy, Erlanov, Maliy, Shomko, Suyumbayev; Tagybergen, Kuat (Pertsukh 84), Islamkhan; Aimbetov (Fedin 58), Turysbek (Zhanglyshbay 69).
San Marino: (4312) Benedettini; Cesarini (Manuel Battistini 76), Vitaioli F, Brolli, Grandoni; Lunadei, Censoni, Mularoni; Michael Battistini (Golinucci E 46); Nanni, Vitaioli M (Berardi M 83).

Russia (1) 1 *(Ionov 38)*

Cyprus (0) 0 42,228

Russia: (433) Marinato; Fernandes, Dzhikija, Semenov, Kudryashov; Ozdoev, Zobnin (Barinov 78), Golovin; Anton Miranchuk (Aleksey Miranchuk 64), Dzyuba, Ionov (Akhmetov 90).
Cyprus: (433) Pardo; Makris (Spoljaric 81), Kousoulos, Laifis, Ioannou N; Artymatas, Kosti, Margaca; Georgiou (Efrem 45), Sotiriou, Avraam (Pittas 71).

Friday, 6 September 2019

Cyprus (1) 1 *(Sotiriou 39)*

Kazakhstan (1) 1 *(Shchetkin 2)* 5639

Cyprus: (442) Kontomis; Mintikkis, Merkis, Laifis, Ioannou N; Papoulis (Pittas 90), Kyriakou, Kousoulos, Kastanos (Georgiou 58); Sotiriou, Efrem (Kosti 73).
Kazakhstan: (541) Nepogodov; Vorogovskiy, Erlanov, Maliy, Marochkin, Suyumbayev; Kuat, Pertsukh, Tagybergen (Zhukov 82), Islamkhan (Fedin 65); Shchetkin (Aimbetov 87).

San Marino (0) 0

Belgium (1) 4 *(Batshuayi 43 (pen), 90, Mertens 57, Chadli 63)* 2523

San Marino: (532) Benedettini; Manuel Battistini, Brolli, Simoncini D, Palazzi, Grandoni; Mularoni, Golinucci E (Golinucci A 66), Giardi (Gasperoni 67); Berardi F (Vitaioli M 74), Nanni.
Belgium: (343) Courtois; Alderweireld, Denayer, Vertonghen; Meunier, De Bruyne (Praet 76), Tielemans, Carrasco; Januzaj (Chadli 56), Batshuayi, Origi (Mertens 55).

Scotland (1) 1 *(McGinn 10)*

Russia (1) 2 *(Dzyuba 40, O'Donnell 59 (og))* 32,432

Scotland: (433) Marshall; O'Donnell, Mulgrew, Cooper, Robertson; McGinn (Christie 62), McGregor C, McTominay (Phillips 78); Forrest (McLean 62), McBurnie, Fraser.
Russia: (4231) Guilherme; Fernandes, Semenov, Dzhikija, Kudryashov; Ozdoev, Zobnin (Barinov 66); Ionov (Erokhin 80), Golovin (Akhmetov 89), Zhirkov; Dzyuba.

Monday, 9 September 2019

Russia (0) 1 *(Fernandes 89)*

Kazakhstan (0) 0 31,818

Russia: (433) Guilherme; Fernandes, Semenov, Dzhikija, Zhirkov; Anton Miranchuk (Ionov 58), Ozdoev, Akhmetov (Zobnin 63); Golovin, Dzyuba, Cheryshev (Kudryashov 55).
Kazakhstan: (3421) Nepogodov; Erlanov, Maliy, Marochkin; Beysebekov, Abiken, Pertsukh, Shomko; Fedin (Muzhikov 77), Zhukov (Islamkhan 62); Shchetkin (Aimbetov 90).

San Marino (0) 0

Cyprus (2) 4 *(Kousoulos 2, 73, Papoulis 38, Artymatas 75)* 622

San Marino: (442) Benedettini; D'Addario, Vitaioli F, Simoncini D, Grandoni; Lunadei, Gasperoni (Hirsch 61), Golinucci A, Tomassini (Nanni 62); Berardi F, Vitaioli M (Cevoli 61).
Cyprus: (442) Kontomis; Artymatas, Kyriakou, Laifis, Ioannou N; Papoulis (Georgiou 46), Kousoulos, Spoljaric (Ioannou M 62), Kosti; Sotiriou, Pittas (Kastanos 74).

Scotland (0) 0

Belgium (3) 4 *(Lukaku 9, Vermaelen 24, Alderweireld 32, De Bruyne 82)* 25,524

Scotland: (442) Marshall; O'Donnell, Mulgrew, Cooper, Robertson; Snodgrass, McLean, McTominay, McGregor C (Armstrong 68); Christie (McGinn 86), Phillips (Russell 77).
Belgium: (3421) Courtois; Alderweireld, Vermaelen, Vertonghen; Meunier (Raman 90), Dendoncker, Tielemans (Verschaeren 86), Chadli (Carrasco 78); De Bruyne, Mertens; Lukaku.

Thursday, 10 October 2019

Belgium (6) 9 *(Lukaku 28, 41, Chadli 31, Brolli 35 (og), Alderweireld 43, Tielemans 45, Benteke 79, Verschaeren 84 (pen), Castagne 90)*

San Marino (0) 0 34,504

Belgium: (343) Courtois; Alderweireld, Vermaelen, Vertonghen; Castagne, Vanaken, Tielemans, Chadli; Mertens (Verschaeren 63), Lukaku (Benteke 76), Hazard E (Carrasco 63).
San Marino: (532) Benedettini; Manuel Battistini, Brolli, Simoncini D, Palazzi, Grandoni (Lunadei 78); Mularoni, Golinucci E, Giardi (Hirsch 46); Nanni, Berardi F (Golinucci A 46).

Kazakhstan (1) 1 *(Erlanov 34)*

Cyprus (0) 2 *(Sotiriou 73, Ioannou N 84)* 11,769

Kazakhstan: (343) Nepogodov; Erlanov, Maliy, Marochkin; Vorogovskiy, Pertsukh, Abiken (Fedin 80), Suyumbayev; Kuat (Tagybergen 90), Zhanglyshbay (Khizhnichenko 61), Islamkhan.
Cyprus: (442) Kontomis; Mintikkis (Papageorghiou 46), Merkis (Spoljaric 62), Laifis, Ioannou N; Kousoulos, Artymatas, Kyriakou, Kosti; Papoulis (Margaca 88), Sotiriou.

Russia (0) 4 *(Dzyuba 57, 70, Ozdoev 60, Golovin 84)*

Scotland (0) 0 65,703

Russia: (4231) Guilherme; Fernandes, Semenov, Dzhikija, Kudryashov; Ozdoev, Barinov; Ionov (Akhmetov 79), Golovin, Zhirkov (Cheryshev 66); Dzyuba (Komlichenko 87).
Scotland: (4231) Marshall; Palmer, Devlin, Mulgrew, Robertson; McGregor C, Fleck (Armstrong 82); Fraser (Christie 68), McGinn, Snodgrass; Burke (Shankland 46).

Sunday, 13 October 2019

Cyprus (0) 0

Russia (2) 5 *(Cheryshev 9, 90, Ozdoev 22, Dzyuba 79, Golovin 89)* 9439

Cyprus: (3511) Kontomis (Urko Pardo 40); Kyriakou, Merkis, Laifis■; Kousoulos, Ioannou M, Artymatas, Spoljaric (Papoulis 79), Ioannou N; Kosti; Papageorghiou (Margaca 36).
Russia: (433) Guilherme; Petrov (Karavaev 38), Semenov, Dzhikija, Kudryashov; Ozdoev, Akhmetov (Kuzyaev 61), Golovin; Ionov (Bakaev 78), Dzyuba, Cheryshev.

Kazakhstan (0) 0

Belgium (1) 2 *(Batshuayi 21, Meunier 53)* 26,801

Kazakhstan: (343) Nepogodov; Marochkin, Maliy, Kerimzhanov; Beysebekov, Zhukov (Zhanglyshbay 84), Abiken, Shomko; Fedin (Pertsukh 71), Islamkhan, Suyumbayev (Vorogovskiy 61).
Belgium: (343) Courtois; Alderweireld, Vermaelen (Mechele 90), Vertonghen; Meunier, Praet, Witsel, Hazard T; Mertens (Carrasco 78), Batshuayi (Benteke 78), Hazard E.

Scotland (3) 6 *(McGinn 12, 27, 45, Shankland 65, Findlay 67, Armstrong 86)*

San Marino (0) 0 20,699

Scotland: (4231) McLaughlin; Palmer, Devlin, Findlay, Robertson; McTominay, McGregor C (Russell 70); Christie, McGinn (Armstrong 70), Forrest; Shankland.
San Marino: (4231) Simoncini A; Manuel Battistini, Censoni, Brolli, D'Addario (Grandoni 46); Mularoni, Golinucci A; Gasperoni, Berardi (Ceccaroli 80), Giardi (Hirsch 46); Nanni.

Saturday, 16 November 2019

Cyprus (0) 1 *(Efrem 47)*

Scotland (1) 2 *(Christie 12, McGinn 53)* 7595

Cyprus: (541) Urko Pardo; Demetriou J, Karo (Kastanos 42), Merkis, Kousoulos, Ioannou N; Papoulis, Kyriakou (Theodorou 77), Kosti, Efrem (Spoljaric 74); Sotiriou.
Scotland: (4411) Marshall; Palmer, Gallagher, McKenna, Taylor; Christie (Devlin 90), Jack, McGregor C, Forrest (Burke 72); McGinn; Naismith (McBurnie 62).

Russia (0) 1 *(Dzhikija 79)*

Belgium (3) 4 *(Hazard T 19, Hazard E 33, 40, Lukaku 72)* 53,317

Russia: (4231) Guilherme; Fernandes, Semenov, Dzhikija, Petrov; Ozdoev, Zobnin (Kuzyaev 62); Ionov, Aleksey Miranchuk, Zhirkov (Bakaev 50); Dzyuba (Komlichenko 80).
Belgium: (3421) Courtois; Alderweireld, Boyata, Vermaelen (Denayer 67); Castagne, De Bruyne, Witsel, Hazard T; Mertens (Tielemans 52), Hazard E; Lukaku (Batshuayi 77).

San Marino (0) 1 *(Berardi F 76)*

Kazakhstan (3) 3 *(Zaynutdinov 6, Suyumbayev 22, Shchetkin 26)* 643

San Marino: (442) Benedettini; Manuel Battistini, Brolli, Simoncini D, Grandoni (Ceccaroli 80); Mularoni, Golinucci E, Golinucci A (Lunadei 60), Palazzi; Nanni (Hirsch 64), Berardi F.
Kazakhstan: (3421) Nepogodov; Marochkin, Maliy, Shomko; Vorogovskiy (Miroshnichenko 18), Kuat, Tagybergen (Fedin 66), Suyumbayev; Zaynutdinov, Islamkhan; Shchetkin (Aimbetov 73).

Tuesday, 19 November 2019

Belgium (4) 6 *(Benteke 16, 67, De Bruyne 35, 41, Carrasco 44, Christoforou 51 (og))*

Cyprus (1) 1 *(Ioannou N 14)* 40,568

Belgium: (343) Mignolet; Alderweireld, Denayer, Cobbaut; Hazard T, Vanaken, Tielemans, Carrasco; De Bruyne (Praet 68), Benteke (Origi 80), Hazard E (Verschaeren 64).
Cyprus: (532) Michael; Kyriakou, Christoforou, Merkis, Ioannou N (Kousoulos 67), Wheeler; Spoljaric (Efrem 79), Artymatas, Kastanos; Kosti (Papoulis 81), Sotiriou.

San Marino (0) 0

Russia (2) 5 *(Kuzyaev 3, Petrov 19, Aleksey Miranchuk 49, Ionov 56, Komlichenko 78)* 1604

San Marino: (41212) Simoncini A; D'Addario (Tomassini 64), Vitaioli F, Simoncini D, Palazzi; Censoni; Lunadei, Giardi; Gasperoni (Manuel Battistini 46); Berardi F, Bernardi (Hirsch 61).
Russia: (4231) Shunin; Petrov, Belyaev, Dzhikija, Kudryashov; Ozdoev (Zobnin 59), Kuzyaev; Ionov (Golovin 59), Aleksey Miranchuk (Komlichenko 65), Bakaev; Dzyuba.

Scotland (0) 3 *(McGinn 48, 90, Naismith 64)*

Kazakhstan (1) 1 *(Zaynutdinov 34)* 19,515

Scotland: (4231) Marshall; Palmer, Gallagher, McKenna, Taylor; Jack, McGregor C; Christie (Fleck 83), McGinn (Armstrong 90), Forrest; Naismith (Burke 78).
Kazakhstan: (3421) Nepogodov; Marochkin, Maliy, Logvinenko; Suyumbayev, Pertsukh (Kuat 74), Abiken, Shomko; Zaynutdinov, Islamkhan (Fedin 75); Shchetkin (Aimbetov 83).

Group I Table	P	W	D	L	F	A	GD	Pts
Belgium	10	10	0	0	40	3	37	30
Russia	10	8	0	2	33	8	25	24
Scotland	10	5	0	5	16	19	–3	15
Cyprus	10	3	1	6	15	20	–5	10
Kazakhstan	10	3	1	6	13	17	–4	10
San Marino	10	0	0	10	1	51	–50	0

GROUP J

Saturday, 23 March 2019

Bosnia-Herzegovina (1) 2 *(Krunic 33, Milosevic 80)*

Armenia (0) 1 *(Mkhitaryan 90 (pen))* 10,000

Bosnia-Herzegovina: (433) Sehic; Todorovic D, Bicakcic, Zukanovic, Civic; Pjanic, Besic, Krunic (Gojak 82); Visca, Dzeko (Koljic 87), Zakaric (Milosevic 64).
Armenia: (4231) Airapetyan; Hovhannisyan K, Haroyan, Calisir, Daghbashyan; Grigoryan, Mkrtchyan; Adamyan (Babayan 67), Mkhitaryan, Ghazaryan (Ozbiliz 81); Karapetyan (Briasco 67).

Italy (1) 2 *(Barella 7, Kean 74)*

Finland (0) 0 24,000

Italy: (433) Donnarumma; Piccini, Bonucci, Chiellini, Biraghi (Spinazzola 90); Barella, Jorginho, Verratti (Zaniolo 85); Kean, Immobile (Quagliarella 79), Bernardeschi.
Finland: (532) Hradecky; Granlund (Soiri 90), Toivio, Vaisanen S, Arajuuri, Pirinen; Lod, Sparv, Kamara; Hamalainen (Lappalainen 70), Pukki (Karjalainen 83).

Liechtenstein (0) 0

Greece (1) 2 *(Fortounis 45, Donis 80)* 2711

Liechtenstein: (451) Buchel B; Wolfinger, Kaufmann, Rechsteiner, Goppel; Hasler (Frick N 86), Martin Buchel (Sele A 67), Wieser, Polverino, Salanovic; Gubser (Yildiz 76).
Greece: (433) Vlachodimos; Bakakis, Siovas, Kourbelis, Koutris; Zeca, Fortounis (Koulouris 83), Samaris; Masouras, Mitroglou (Donis 23), Bakasetas (Kolovos 71).

Tuesday, 26 March 2019

Armenia (0) 0

Finland (1) 2 *(Jensen 14, Soiri 78)* 12,900

Armenia: (4231) Airapetyan; Hovhannisyan K, Haroyan, Calisir, Daghbashyan; Mkhitaryan, Grigoryan; Ozbiliz (Barseghyan 67), Ghazaryan, Babayan (Avetisyan 74); Briasco (Karapetyan 59).
Finland: (532) Hradecky; Jensen (Schuller 69), Toivio, Granlund, Arajuuri, Pirinen; Lod (Taylor 87), Sparv, Kamara; Hamalainen (Soiri 57), Pukki.

Bosnia-Herzegovina (2) 2 *(Visca 10, Pjanic 15)*

Greece (0) 2 *(Fortounis 64 (pen), Kolovos 85)* 10,500

Bosnia-Herzegovina: (433) Sehic; Bicakcic, Sunjic, Zukanovic, Kolasinac; Pjanic■, Besic, Cimirot (Krunic 90); Visca, Dzeko (Gojak 89), Duljevic (Milosevic 80).
Greece: (433) Vlachodimos; Bakakis (Koulouris 79), Papastathopoulos, Siovas, Koutris; Kourbelis (Kolovos 66), Zeca, Bouchalakis (Masouras 46); Fortounis, Donis, Samaris.

Italy (4) 6 *(Sensi 17, Verratti 32, Quagliarella 35 (pen), 45 (pen), Kean 70, Pavoletti 77)*

Liechtenstein (0) 0 19,834

Italy: (433) Sirigu; Mancini, Bonucci (Izzo 79), Romagnoli, Spinazzola; Sensi, Jorginho (Zaniolo 57), Verratti; Politano, Quagliarella (Pavoletti 72), Kean.
Liechtenstein: (442) Buchel B; Wolfinger, Kaufmann■, Hofer, Goppel; Sele A (Malin 46), Polverino, Wieser, Kuhne (Meier 68); Hasler, Salanovic (Martin Buchel 82).

Saturday, 8 June 2019

Armenia (2) 3 *(Ghazaryan 2, Karapetyan 18, Barseghyan 90)*

Liechtenstein (0) 0 9200

Armenia: (433) Airapetyan; Hambardzumyan, Haroyan, Voskanyan, Hovhannisyan K; Mkrtchyan (Grigoryan 76), Mkhitaryan, Avetisyan (Hovsepyan 78); Barseghyan, Karapetyan (Babayan 72), Ghazaryan.
Liechtenstein: (442) Hobi; Wolfinger (Brandle 85), Malin, Hofer, Goppel; Hasler, Sele A (Meier 81), Polverino, Salanovic; Frick Y (Kuhne 46), Marcel Buchel.

Finland (0) 2 *(Pukki 56, 68)*

Bosnia-Herzegovina (0) 0 16,103

Finland: (442) Hradecky; Granlund (Raitala 37), Toivio, Arajuuri, Uronen; Skrabb (Schuller 84), Sparv, Kamara, Forsell (Lappalainen 63); Pukki, Lod.
Bosnia-Herzegovina: (433) Sehic; Bicakcic, Sunjic, Zukanovic, Civic; Besic (Gojak 79), Cimirot, Saric; Visca, Dzeko, Duljevic (Bajic 69).

Greece (0) 0

Italy (3) 3 *(Barella 23, Insigne 30, Bonucci 33)* 19,828

Greece: (3412) Barkas; Papastathopoulos, Manolas, Siovas; Kourbelis (Siopis 46), Samaris (Bakasetas 77), Zeca, Fortounis; Stafylidis; Kolovos (Mavrias 46), Masouras.
Italy: (433) Sirigu; Florenzi, Bonucci, Chiellini, Emerson Palmieri (De Sciglio 68); Barella, Jorginho, Verratti (Pellegrini 81); Chiesa, Belotti (Bernardeschi 84), Insigne.

Tuesday, 11 June 2019

Greece (0) 2 *(Zeca 54, Fortounis 87)*

Armenia (2) 3 *(Karapetyan 8, Ghazaryan 33, Barseghyan 74)* 7011

Greece: (433) Vlachodimos; Mavrias (Kotsiras 17), Papastathopoulos, Siovas, Koutris; Zeca, Fortounis, Samaris (Siopis 75); Masouras, Koulouris, Pelkas (Kolovos 68).
Armenia: (433) Airapetyan; Hambardzumyan, Haroyan, Ishkhanyan, Hovhannisyan K; Mkrtchyan (Hovsepyan 56), Mkhitaryan, Grigoryan; Barseghyan, Karapetyan (Babayan 71), Ghazaryan (Avetisyan 83).

Italy (0) 2 *(Insigne 49, Verratti 86)*

Bosnia-Herzegovina (1) 1 *(Dzeko 32)* 29,100

Italy: (433) Sirigu; Mancini (De Sciglio 66), Bonucci, Chiellini, Emerson Palmieri; Barella, Jorginho, Verratti; Bernardeschi (Belotti 81), Quagliarella (Chiesa 46), Insigne.
Bosnia-Herzegovina: (433) Sehic; Todorovic D, Bicakcic, Zukanovic, Civic (Nastic 70); Besic, Pjanic, Saric; Visca, Dzeko, Gojak (Cimirot 80).

Liechtenstein (0) 0

Finland (1) 2 *(Pukki 37, Kallman 57)* 2160

Liechtenstein: (4141) Hobi; Wolfinger (Brandle 77), Kaufmann, Hofer, Rechsteiner; Wieser (Polverino 46); Sele A, Hasler, Marcel Buchel (Martin Buchel 54), Kuhne; Salanovic.
Finland: (442) Hradecky; Raitala (Vaisanen L 87), Toivio, Arajuuri, Uronen; Lod, Sparv (Schuller 61), Kamara, Lappalainen (Soiri 74); Kallman, Pukki.

Thursday, 5 September 2019

Armenia (1) 1 *(Karapetyan 11)*

Italy (1) 3 *(Belotti 28, Pellegrini 77, Hayrapetyan 80 (og))* 13,680

Armenia: (4231) Hayrapetyan; Hambardzumyan, Haroyan, Calisir, Hovhannisyan K; Grigoryan (Hovsepyan 57), Mkrtchyan; Barseghyan (Adamyan 57), Mkhitaryan, Ghazaryan (Babayan 82); Karapetyan■.
Italy: (433) Donnarumma; Florenzi, Bonucci, Romagnoli, Emerson Palmieri; Barella (Sensi 69), Jorginho, Verratti; Chiesa (Pellegrini 61), Belotti, Bernardeschi (Lasagna 83).

Bosnia-Herzegovina (1) 5 *(Gojak 11, 89, Malin 80 (og), Dzeko 85, Visca 87)*

Liechtenstein (0) 0 3825

Bosnia-Herzegovina: (433) Sehic; Todorovic D, Sunjic (Mihojevic 25), Zukanovic, Kolasinac; Krunic, Pjanic (Loncar 83), Gojak; Visca, Dzeko, Milosevic (Duljevic 55).
Liechtenstein: (4141) Buchel B; Rechsteiner, Malin, Kaufmann, Goppel; Martin Buchel; Meier (Wolfinger 64), Wieser (Brandle 85), Hasler, Salanovic; Gubser (Sele A 74).

Finland (0) 1 *(Pukki 52 (pen))*

Greece (0) 0 16,163

Finland: (442) Hradecky; Raitala, Toivio, Arajuuri, Uronen; Lod, Sparv, Kamara, Soiri (Schuller 90); Tuominen (Jensen 87), Pukki (Karjalainen 85).
Greece: (4231) Barkas; Torosidis (Bakakis 70), Manolas, Papastathopoulos, Stafylidis; Kourmpelis, Bouchalakis; Kolovos (Pelkas 60), Vrousai, Masouras; Koulouris (Pavlidis 76).

Sunday, 8 September 2019

Armenia (1) 4 *(Mkhitaryan 3, 66, Hambardzumyan 77, Loncar 90 (og))*

Bosnia-Herzegovina (1) 2 *(Dzeko 13, Gojak 70)* 12,457

Armenia: (4231) Hayrapetyan; Hambardzumyan, Haroyan, Ishkhanyan, Hovhannisyan K (Hovhannisyan A 83); Hovsepyan (Vardanyan 77), Mkrtchyan (Grigoryan 75); Barseghyan, Mkhitaryan, Adamyan; Ghazaryan.
Bosnia-Herzegovina: (4321) Sehic; Todorovic D (Bajic 85), Bicakcic, Zukanovic, Kolasinac; Besic (Loncar 80), Pjanic, Cimirot; Visca (Duljevic 64), Gojak; Dzeko.

Finland (0) 1 *(Pukki 72 (pen))*

Italy (0) 2 *(Immobile 59, Jorginho 79 (pen))* 16,292

Finland: (541) Hradecky; Granlund (Soiri 82), Toivio, Arajuuri, Vaisanen S, Uronen; Lod, Kamara, Schuller (Kauko 87), Lappalainen (Tuominen 75); Pukki.
Italy: (433) Donnarumma; Izzo, Bonucci, Acerbi, Emerson Palmieri (Florenzi 8); Barella, Jorginho, Sensi; Chiesa (Bernardeschi 72), Immobile (Belotti 76), Pellegrini.

Greece (1) 1 *(Masouras 33)*

Liechtenstein (0) 1 *(Salanovic 85)* 3445

Greece: (4231) Barkas; Bakakis, Manolas, Papastathopoulos, Tsimikas; Samaris, Bouchalakis (Zeca 62); Fetfatzidis (Pavlidis 68), Vrousai, Masouras (Giannoulis 86); Koulouris.
Liechtenstein: (4141) Buchel B; Rechsteiner (Hofer 82), Malin, Kaufmann, Goppel; Martin Buchel; Meier (Brandle 64), Hasler, Wieser, Salanovic; Gubser (Yildiz 56).

Saturday, 12 October 2019

Bosnia-Herzegovina (2) 4 *(Hajrovic 29, Pjanic 37 (pen), 58, Hodzic 73)*

Finland (0) 1 *(Pohjanpalo 79)* 8193

Bosnia-Herzegovina: (433) Sehic; Kvrzic, Kovacevic, Bicakcic, Kolasinac; Cimirot, Pjanic (Krunic 76), Saric (Jajalo 71); Visca (Hajrovic 18), Hodzic, Gojak.
Finland: (4411) Hradecky; Raitala, Toivio, Arajuuri (Vaisanen S 30), Uronen; Lod, Kamara, Sparv (Kauko 71), Soiri (Pohjanpalo 46); Tuominen; Pukki.

Italy (0) 2 *(Jorginho 63 (pen), Bernardeschi 78)*

Greece (0) 0 56,274

Italy: (433) Donnarumma; D'Ambrosio, Bonucci, Acerbi, Spinazzola; Barella (Zaniolo 87), Jorginho, Verratti; Chiesa (Bernardeschi 39), Immobile (Belotti 79), Insigne.
Greece: (4231) Paschalakis; Bakakis, Chatzidiakos, Siovas, Stafylidis; Kourmpelis, Bouchalakis (Giannoulis 75); Limnios, Zeca, Koulouris (Donis 67); Bakasetas (Mandalos 79).

Liechtenstein (0) 1 *(Frick Y 72)*

Armenia (1) 1 *(Barseghyan 19)* 2285

Liechtenstein: (3412) Buchel B; Malin, Kaufmann, Goppel; Rechsteiner, Martin Buchel, Polverino (Sele A 83), Meier (Yildiz 70); Hasler; Salanovic, Gubser (Frick Y 67).
Armenia: (433) Hayrapetyan; Hambardzumyan, Haroyan, Ishkhanyan, Hovhannisyan A; Pizzelli (Malakyan G 60), Hovsepyan (Miranyan 83), Ghazaryan (Ozbiliz 88); Barseghyan, Karapetyan, Adamyan.

Tuesday, 15 October 2019

Finland (1) 3 *(Jensen 31, Pukki 61, 88)*

Armenia (0) 0 7231

Finland: (442) Hradecky; Raitala, Toivio, Vaisanen S, Uronen; Lod, Kauko, Kamara (Schuller 87), Lappalainen (Soiri 61); Pukki, Jensen (Pohjanpalo 53).
Armenia: (4231) Hayrapetyan; Hambardzumyan, Haroyan, Ishkhanyan, Hovhannisyan A; Hovsepyan, Grigoryan (Malakyan G 72); Barseghyan (Ozbiliz 65), Ghazaryan (Babayan 77), Adamyan; Karapetyan.

Greece (1) 2 *(Pavlidis 30, Kovacevic 88 (og))*

Bosnia-Herzegovina (1) 1 *(Gojak 35)* 4512

Greece: (4231) Paschalakis; Bakakis, Chatzidiakos, Stafylidis, Giannoulis; Kourmpelis, Galanopoulos; Limnios (Fetfatzidis 84), Bakasetas, Mandalos (Masouras 60); Pavlidis (Koulouris 70).
Bosnia-Herzegovina: (433) Sehic; Kvrzic, Kovacevic, Bicakcic, Kolasinac; Cimirot (Jajalo 46), Pjanic, Saric (Duljevic 63); Hajrovic, Hodzic (Bajic 71), Gojak.

Liechtenstein (0) 0

Italy (1) 5 *(Bernardeschi 2, Belotti 70, 90, Romagnoli 77, El Shaarawy 82)* 5087

Liechtenstein: (4141) Buchel B; Rechsteiner, Kaufmann, Hofer, Goppel; Martin Buchel; Yildiz (Wolfinger 83), Polverino (Frick N 56), Hasler, Salanovic; Gubser (Frick Y 63).
Italy: (433) Sirigu; Di Lorenzo, Mancini, Romagnoli, Biraghi (Bonucci 88); Zaniolo (El Shaarawy 63), Cristante, Verratti; Bernardeschi (Tonali 74), Belotti, Grifo.

Friday, 15 November 2019

Armenia (0) 0

Greece (1) 1 *(Limnios 34)* 6450

Armenia: (541) Hayrapetyan; Hambardzumyan, Voskanyan (Avetisyan 83), Calisir, Ishkhanyan, Hovhannisyan K; Barseghyan, Grigoryan, Hovsepyan (Yedigaryan 78), Vardanyan (Sarkisov 59); Karapetyan.
Greece: (4231) Vlachodimos; Bakakis, Chatzidiakos, Stafylidis, Giannoulis; Kourmpelis, Galanopoulos; Limnios, Bakasetas (Donis 81), Mandalos (Masouras 66); Pavlidis (Koulouris 74).

Bosnia-Herzegovina (0) 0

Italy (2) 3 *(Acerbi 21, Insigne 37, Belotti 52)* 8355

Bosnia-Herzegovina: (433) Sehic; Kvrzic, Kovacevic, Bicakcic, Kolasinac; Besic (Saric 61), Pjanic (Jajalo 77), Cimirot; Visca (Hodzic 61), Dzeko, Krunic.
Italy: (433) Donnarumma (Gollini 88); Florenzi, Bonucci, Acerbi, Emerson Palmieri; Barella, Jorginho, Tonali; Bernardeschi (El Shaarawy 75), Belotti, Insigne (Castrovilli 86).

Finland (1) 3 *(Tuominen 21, Pukki 64 (pen), 75)*

Liechtenstein (0) 0 9804

Finland: (442) Hradecky; Raitala, Toivio, Arajuuri, Pirinen; Lod, Sparv (Kauko 71), Kamara, Soiri (Skrabb 78); Pukki (Karjalainen 84), Tuominen.
Liechtenstein: (4141) Buchel B; Brandle, Malin, Rechsteiner, Goppel; Martin Buchel; Meier (Sele A 90), Hasler, Polverino (Gubser 73), Salanovic; Frick Y (Kardesoglu 84).

Monday, 18 November 2019

Greece (0) 2 *(Mandalos 47, Galanopoulos 70)*

Finland (1) 1 *(Pukki 27)* 5453

Greece: (442) Vlachodimos; Bakakis, Chatzidiakos, Stafylidis, Giannoulis; Limnios, Kourmpelis, Galanopoulos (Bouchalakis 73), Mandalos (Masouras 90); Pavlidis (Koulouris 64), Bakasetas.
Finland: (4411) Joronen; Toivio (Lam 59), Vaisanen L, Vaisanen S, Raitala; Lod, Kamara, Schuller (Jensen 77), Skrabb (Soiri 78); Kauko; Pukki.

Italy (4) 9 *(Immobile 8, Zaniolo 9, 64, Barella 29, Immobile 33, Romagnoli 72, Jorginho 75 (pen), Orsolini 77, Chiesa 81)*

Armenia (0) 1 *(Babayan 79)* 27,752

Italy: (433) Sirigu (Meret 77); Di Lorenzo, Bonucci (Izzo 69), Romagnoli, Biraghi; Tonali, Jorginho, Barella (Orsolini 46); Zaniolo, Immobile, Chiesa.
Armenia: (541) Hayrapetyan; Hambardzumyan, Haroyan, Calisir, Ishkhanyan (Sarkisov 69), Hovhannisyan K; Barseghyan, Grigoryan (Simonyan 60), Yedigaryan (Avetisyan 82), Babayan; Karapetyan.

Liechtenstein (0) 0

Bosnia-Herzegovina (0) 3 *(Civic 57, Hodzic 64, 72)* 2993

Liechtenstein: (451) Buchel B; Brandle, Malin, Rechsteiner, Goppel; Wolfinger, Polverino (Frommelt 67), Martin Buchel, Hasler, Salanovic (Yildiz 46); Frick Y (Gubser 82).
Bosnia-Herzegovina: (433) Piric; Memisevic, Mihojevic (Dzeko 70), Bicakcic, Civic; Hajradinovic (Besic 64), Jajalo, Saric; Hajrovic, Hodzic, Duljevic (Hotic 46).

Group J Table	P	W	D	L	F	A	GD	Pts
Italy	10	10	0	0	37	4	33	30
Finland	10	6	0	4	16	10	6	18
Greece	10	4	2	4	12	14	−2	14
Bosnia-Herzegovina	10	4	1	5	20	17	3	13
Armenia	10	3	1	6	14	25	−11	10
Liechtenstein	10	0	2	8	2	31	−29	2

EURO 2020 PLAY-OFFS

The draw for the play-offs for EURO 2020 consisted of the 16 UEFA Nations League group winners or highest placed country if the winner had already qualified. Two semi-finals per path.
**Winner of this semi-final will play at home in the path final.*

SEMI-FINALS DRAW

PATH A
Iceland v Romania
Bulgaria v Hungary*

PATH B
Bosnia-Herzegovina v Northern Ireland*
Slovakia v Republic of Ireland

PATH C
Scotland v Israel
Norway v Serbia*

PATH D
Georgia v Belarus*
North Macedonia v Kosovo

Due to the COVID-19 pandemic in Europe, the EURO 2020 play-off matches were postponed until further notice.

EURO 2020 FINALS

GROUP STAGE DRAW

GROUP A

Turkey v Italy	Rome
Wales v Switzerland	Baku
Turkey v Wales	Baku
Italy v Switzerland	Rome
Switzerland v Turkey	Baku
Italy v Wales	Rome

GROUP B

Denmark v Finland	Copenhagen
Belgium v Russia	St Petersburg
Finland v Russia	St Petersburg
Denmark v Belgium	Copenhagen
Russia v Denmark	Copenhagen
Finland v Belgium	St Petersburg

GROUP C

If Romania win Play-off Path A, they will enter Group C. Otherwise, the winner of Play-off Path D will enter Group C.

Austria v Play-off winner D or A	Bucharest
Netherlands v Ukraine	Amsterdam
Ukraine v Play-off winner D or A	Bucharest
Netherlands v Austria	Amsterdam
Play-off winner D or A v Netherlands	Amsterdam
Ukraine v Austria	Bucharest

GROUP D

England v Croatia	Wembley
Play-off winner C v Czech Republic	Hampden
Croatia v Czech Republic	Hampden
England v Play-off winner C	Wembley
Croatia v Play-off winner C	Hampden
Czech Republic v England	Wembley

GROUP E

Poland v Play-off winner B	Dublin
Spain v Sweden	Bilbao
Sweden v Play-off winner B	Dublin
Spain v Poland	Bilbao
Play-off winner B v Spain	Bilbao
Sweden v Poland	Dublin

GROUP F

If Romania win Play-off Path A, the winner of Play-off Path D will enter Group F. Otherwise, the winner of Play-off Path A will enter Group F.

Play-off winner A or D v Portugal	Budapest
France v Germany	Munich
Play-off winner A or D v France	Budapest
Portugal v Germany	Munich
Portugal v France	Budapest
Germany v Play-off winner A or D	Munich

Due to the COVID-19 pandemic in Europe, EURO 2020 was postponed by one year until 2021. The tournament will take place from 11 June 2021 to 11 July 2021. Other competitions will be rescheduled accordingly.

EUROPEAN FOOTBALL CHAMPIONSHIP 1960–2020

Year	Winners v Runners-up		Venue	Attendance	Referee
1960	USSR v Yugoslavia	2-1*	Paris	17,966	A. E. Ellis (England)
	Winning Coach: Gavriil Kachalin				
1964	Spain v USSR	2-1	Madrid	79,115	A. E. Ellis (England)
	Winning Coach: Jose Villalonga				
1968	Italy v Yugoslavia	1-1	Rome	68,817	G. Dienst (Switzerland)
Replay	Italy v Yugoslavia	2-0	Rome	32,866	J. M. O. de Mendibil (Spain)
	Winning Coach: Ferruccio Valcareggi				
1972	West Germany v USSR	3-0	Brussels	43,066	F. Marschall (Austria)
	Winning Coach: Helmut Schon				
1976	Czechoslovakia v West Germany	2-2	Belgrade	30,790	S. Gonella (Italy)
	Czechoslovakia won 5-3 on penalties.				
	Winning Coach: Vaclav Jezek				
1980	West Germany v Belgium	2-1	Rome	47,860	N. Rainea (Romania)
	Winning Coach: Jupp Derwall				
1984	France v Spain	2-0	Paris	47,368	V. Christov (Slovakia)
	Winning Coach: Michel Hidalgo				
1988	Netherlands v USSR	2-0	Munich	62,770	M. Vautrot (France)
	Winning Coach: Rinus Michels				
1992	Denmark v Germany	2-0	Gothenburg	37,800	B. Galler (Switzerland)
	Winning Coach: Richard Moller Nielsen				
1996	Germany v Czech Republic	2-1*	Wembley	73,611	P. Pairetto (Italy)
	Germany won on sudden death 'golden goal'.				
	Winning Coach: Berti Vogts				
2000	France v Italy	2-1*	Rotterdam	48,200	A. Frisk (Sweden)
	France won on sudden death 'golden goal'.				
	Winning Coach: Roger Lemerre				
2004	Greece v Portugal	1-0	Lisbon	62,865	M. Merk (Germany)
	Winning Coach: Otto Rehhagel				
2008	Spain v Germany	1-0	Vienna	51,428	R. Rosetti (Italy)
	Winning Coach: Luis Aragones				
2012	Spain v Italy	4-0	Kiev	63,170	P. Proenca (Portugal)
	Winning Coach: Vicente del Bosque				
2016	Portugal v France	1-0*	Paris	75,868	M. Clattenburg (England)
	Winning Coach: Fernando Santos				
2020	Postponed until 2021 due to COVID-19 pandemic.				

*(*After extra time)*

OLYMPIC FOOTBALL PAST MEDALLISTS 1896–2016

* No official tournament. ** No official tournament but gold medal later awarded by IOC.

1896 Athens*
1 Denmark
2 Greece

1900 Paris*
1 Great Britain
2 France

1904 St Louis**
1 Canada
2 USA

1908 London
1 Great Britain
2 Denmark
3 Netherlands

1912 Stockholm
1 England
2 Denmark
3 Netherlands

1920 Antwerp
1 Belgium
2 Spain
3 Netherlands

1924 Paris
1 Uruguay
2 Switzerland
3 Sweden

1928 Amsterdam
1 Uruguay
2 Argentina
3 Italy

1932 Los Angeles
No tournament

1936 Berlin
1 Italy
2 Austria
3 Norway

1948 London
1 Sweden
2 Yugoslavia
3 Denmark

1952 Helsinki
1 Hungary
2 Yugoslavia
3 Sweden

1956 Melbourne
1 USSR
2 Yugoslavia
3 Bulgaria

1960 Rome
1 Yugoslavia
2 Denmark
3 Hungary

1964 Tokyo
1 Hungary
2 Czechoslovakia
3 East Germany

1968 Mexico City
1 Hungary
2 Bulgaria
3 Japan

1972 Munich
1 Poland
2 Hungary
3 E Germany/USSR

1976 Montreal
1 East Germany
2 Poland
3 USSR

1980 Moscow
1 Czechoslovakia
2 East Germany
3 USSR

1984 Los Angeles
1 France
2 Brazil
3 Yugoslavia

1988 Seoul
1 USSR
2 Brazil
3 West Germany

1992 Barcelona
1 Spain
2 Poland
3 Ghana

1996 Atlanta
1 Nigeria
2 Argentina
3 Brazil

2000 Sydney
1 Cameroon
2 Spain
3 Chile

2004 Athens
1 Argentina
2 Paraguay
3 Italy

2008 Beijing
1 Argentina
2 Nigeria
3 Brazil

2012 London
1 Mexico
2 Brazil
3 South Korea

2016 Rio
1 Brazil
2 Germany
3 Nigeria

2020 Tokyo
Postponed until 2021.

THE WORLD CUP 1930–2018

Year	Winners v Runners-up		Venue	Attendance	Referee
1930	Uruguay v Argentina *Winning Coach:* Alberto Suppici	4-2	Montevideo	68,346	J. Langenus (Belgium)
1934	Italy v Czechoslovakia *Winning Coach:* Vittorio Pozzo	2-1*	Rome	55,000	I. Eklind (Sweden)
1938	Italy v Hungary *Winning Coach:* Vittorio Pozzo	4-2	Paris	45,000	G. Capdeville (France)
1950	Uruguay v Brazil *Winning Coach:* Juan Lopez	2-1	Rio de Janeiro	173,850	G. Reader (England)
1954	West Germany v Hungary *Winning Coach:* Sepp Herberger	3-2	Berne	62,500	W. Ling (England)
1958	Brazil v Sweden *Winning Coach:* Vicente Feola	5-2	Stockholm	49,737	M. Guigue (France)
1962	Brazil v Czechoslovakia *Winning Coach:* Aymore Moreira	3-1	Santiago	68,679	N. Latychev (USSR)
1966	England v West Germany *Winning Coach:* Alf Ramsey	4-2*	Wembley	96,924	G. Dienst (Sweden)
1970	Brazil v Italy *Winning Coach:* Mario Zagallo	4-1	Mexico City	107,412	R. Glockner (East Germany)
1974	West Germany v Netherlands *Winning Coach:* Helmut Schon	2-1	Munich	78,200	J. Taylor (England)
1978	Argentina v Netherlands *Winning Coach:* Cesar Luis Menotti	3-1*	Buenos Aires	71,483	S. Gonella (Italy)
1982	Italy v West Germany *Winning Coach:* Enzo Bearzot	3-1	Madrid	90,000	A. C. Coelho (Brazil)
1986	Argentina v West Germany *Winning Coach:* Carlos Bilardo	3-2	Mexico City	114,600	R. A. Filho (Brazil)
1990	West Germany v Argentina *Winning Coach:* Franz Beckenbauer	1-0	Rome	73,603	E. C. Mendez (Mexico)
1994	Brazil v Italy *Brazil won 3-2 on penalties.* *Winning Coach:* Carlos Alberto Parreira	0-0*	Los Angeles	94,194	S. Puhl (Hungary)
1998	France v Brazil *Winning Coach:* Aime Jacquet	3-0	Paris	80,000	S. Belqola (Morocco)
2002	Brazil v Germany *Winning Coach:* Luiz Felipe Scolari	2-0	Yokohama	69,029	P. Collina (Italy)
2006	Italy v France *Italy won 5-3 on penalties.* *Winning Coach:* Marcello Lippi	1-1*	Berlin	69,000	H. Elizondo (Argentina)
2010	Spain v Netherlands *Winning Coach:* Vicente del Bosque	1-0	Johannesburg	84,490	H. Webb (England)
2014	Germany v Argentina *Winning Coach:* Joachim Low	1-0*	Rio de Janeiro	74,738	N. Rizzoli (Italy)
2018	France v Croatia *Winning Coach:* Didier Deschamps	4-2	Moscow	78,011	N. Pitana (Argentina)

*(*After extra time)*

GOALSCORING AND ATTENDANCES IN WORLD CUP FINAL ROUNDS

Year	*Venue*	*Games*	*Goals (av)*	*Attendance (av)*
1930	Uruguay	18	70 (3.9)	590,549 (32,808)
1934	Italy	17	70 (4.1)	363,000 (21,352)
1938	France	18	84 (4.7)	375,700 (20,872)
1950	Brazil	22	88 (4.0)	1,045,246 (47,511)
1954	Switzerland	26	140 (5.4)	768,607 (29,562)
1958	Sweden	35	126 (3.6)	819,810 (23,423)
1962	Chile	32	89 (2.8)	893,172 (27,912)
1966	England	32	89 (2.8)	1,563,135 (48,848)
1970	Mexico	32	95 (3.0)	1,603,975 (50,124)
1974	West Germany	38	97 (2.6)	1,865,753 (49,098)
1978	Argentina	38	102 (2.7)	1,545,791 (40,678)
1982	Spain	52	146 (2.8)	2,109,723 (40,571)
1986	Mexico	52	132 (2.5)	2,394,031 (46,039)
1990	Italy	52	115 (2.2)	2,516,215 (48,388)
1994	USA	52	141 (2.7)	3,587,538 (68,991)
1998	France	64	171 (2.7)	2,785,100 (43,517)
2002	Japan/S. Korea	64	161 (2.5)	2,705,197 (42,268)
2006	Germany	64	147 (2.3)	3,359,439 (52,491)
2010	South Africa	64	145 (2.3)	3,178,856 (49,669)
2014	Brazil	64	171 (2.7)	3,367,727 (52,621)
2018	Russia	64	169 (2.6)	3,031,768 (47,371)
Total		900	2548 (2.8)	40,470,332 (44,967)

LEADING GOALSCORERS

Year	*Player*	*Goals*
1930	Guillermo Stabile (Argentina)	8
1934	Oldrich Nejedly (Czechoslovakia)	5
1938	Leonidas da Silva (Brazil)	7
1950	Ademir (Brazil)	8
1954	Sandor Kocsis (Hungary)	11
1958	Just Fontaine (France)	13
1962	Valentin Ivanov (USSR), Leonel Sanchez (Chile), Garrincha (Brazil), Vava (Brazil), Florian Albert (Hungary), Drazen Jerkovic (Yugoslavia)	4
1966	Eusebio (Portugal)	9
1970	Gerd Muller (West Germany)	10
1974	Grzegorz Lato (Poland)	7
1978	Mario Kempes (Argentina)	6
1982	Paolo Rossi (Italy)	6
1986	Gary Lineker (England)	6
1990	Salvatore Schillaci (Italy)	6
1994	Oleg Salenko (Russia) Hristo Stoichkov (Bulgaria)	6
1998	Davor Suker (Croatia)	6
2002	Ronaldo (Brazil)	8
2006	Miroslav Klose (Germany)	5
2010	Thomas Muller (Germany), David Villa (Spain), Wesley Sneijder (Netherlands), Diego Forlan (Uruguay)	5
2014	James Rodriguez (Colombia)	6
2018	Harry Kane (England)	6

BRITISH AND IRISH INTERNATIONAL RESULTS 1872–2020

Note: In the results that follow, WC = World Cup, EC = European Championship, NL = Nations League UI = Umbro International Trophy. TF = Tournoi de France. NC = Nations Cup. Northern Ireland played as Ireland before 1921. *After extra time.

Bold type indicates matches played in season 2019–20.

ENGLAND v SCOTLAND

Played: 114; England won 48, Scotland won 41, Drawn 25. Goals: England 203, Scotland 174.

			E	*S*
1872	30 Nov	Glasgow	0	0
1873	8 Mar	Kennington Oval	4	2
1874	7 Mar	Glasgow	1	2
1875	6 Mar	Kennington Oval	2	2
1876	4 Mar	Glasgow	0	3
1877	3 Mar	Kennington Oval	1	3
1878	2 Mar	Glasgow	2	7
1879	5 Apr	Kennington Oval	5	4
1880	13 Mar	Glasgow	4	5
1881	12 Mar	Kennington Oval	1	6
1882	11 Mar	Glasgow	1	5
1883	10 Mar	Sheffield	2	3
1884	15 Mar	Glasgow	0	1
1885	21 Mar	Kennington Oval	1	1
1886	31 Mar	Glasgow	1	1
1887	19 Mar	Blackburn	2	3
1888	17 Mar	Glasgow	5	0
1889	13 Apr	Kennington Oval	2	3
1890	5 Apr	Glasgow	1	1
1891	6 Apr	Blackburn	2	1
1892	2 Apr	Glasgow	4	1
1893	1 Apr	Richmond	5	2
1894	7 Apr	Glasgow	2	2
1895	6 Apr	Everton	3	0
1896	4 Apr	Glasgow	1	2
1897	3 Apr	Crystal Palace	1	2
1898	2 Apr	Glasgow	3	1
1899	8 Apr	Aston Villa	2	1
1900	7 Apr	Glasgow	1	4
1901	30 Mar	Crystal Palace	2	2
1902	3 Mar	Aston Villa	2	2
1903	4 Apr	Sheffield	1	2
1904	9 Apr	Glasgow	1	0
1905	1 Apr	Crystal Palace	1	0
1906	7 Apr	Glasgow	1	2
1907	6 Apr	Newcastle	1	1
1908	4 Apr	Glasgow	1	1
1909	3 Apr	Crystal Palace	2	0
1910	2 Apr	Glasgow	0	2
1911	1 Apr	Everton	1	1
1912	23 Mar	Glasgow	1	1
1913	5 Apr	Chelsea	1	0
1914	14 Apr	Glasgow	1	3
1920	10 Apr	Sheffield	5	4
1921	9 Apr	Glasgow	0	3
1922	8 Apr	Aston Villa	0	1
1923	14 Apr	Glasgow	2	2
1924	12 Apr	Wembley	1	1
1925	4 Apr	Glasgow	0	2
1926	17 Apr	Manchester	0	1
1927	2 Apr	Glasgow	2	1
1928	31 Mar	Wembley	1	5
1929	13 Apr	Glasgow	0	1
1930	5 Apr	Wembley	5	2
1931	28 Mar	Glasgow	0	2
1932	9 Apr	Wembley	3	0
1933	1 Apr	Glasgow	1	2
1934	14 Apr	Wembley	3	0
1935	6 Apr	Glasgow	0	2
1936	4 Apr	Wembley	1	1
1937	17 Apr	Glasgow	1	3
1938	9 Apr	Wembley	0	1
1939	15 Apr	Glasgow	2	1
1947	12 Apr	Wembley	1	1
1948	10 Apr	Glasgow	2	0
1949	9 Apr	Wembley	1	3
WC1950	15 Apr	Glasgow	1	0
1951	14 Apr	Wembley	2	3
1952	5 Apr	Glasgow	2	1
1953	18 Apr	Wembley	2	2
WC1954	3 Apr	Glasgow	4	2
1955	2 Apr	Wembley	7	2
1956	14 Apr	Glasgow	1	1
1957	6 Apr	Wembley	2	1
1958	19 Apr	Glasgow	4	0
1959	11 Apr	Wembley	1	0
1960	9 Apr	Glasgow	1	1
1961	15 Apr	Wembley	9	3
1962	14 Apr	Glasgow	0	2
1963	6 Apr	Wembley	1	2
1964	11 Apr	Glasgow	0	1
1965	10 Apr	Wembley	2	2
1966	2 Apr	Glasgow	4	3
EC1967	15 Apr	Wembley	2	3
EC1968	24 Jan	Glasgow	1	1
1969	10 May	Wembley	4	1
1970	25 Apr	Glasgow	0	0
1971	22 May	Wembley	3	1
1972	27 May	Glasgow	1	0
1973	14 Feb	Glasgow	5	0
1973	19 May	Wembley	1	0
1974	18 May	Glasgow	0	2
1975	24 May	Wembley	5	1
1976	15 May	Glasgow	1	2
1977	4 June	Wembley	1	2
1978	20 May	Glasgow	1	0
1979	26 May	Wembley	3	1
1980	24 May	Glasgow	2	0
1981	23 May	Wembley	0	1
1982	29 May	Glasgow	1	0
1983	1 June	Wembley	2	0
1984	26 May	Glasgow	1	1
1985	25 May	Glasgow	0	1
1986	23 Apr	Wembley	2	1
1987	23 May	Glasgow	0	0
1988	21 May	Wembley	1	0
1989	27 May	Glasgow	2	0
EC1996	15 June	Wembley	2	0
EC1999	13 Nov	Glasgow	2	0
EC1999	17 Nov	Wembley	0	1
2013	14 Aug	Wembley	3	2
2014	18 Nov	Glasgow	3	1
WC2016	11 Nov	Wembley	3	0
WC2017	10 June	Glasgow	2	2

ENGLAND v WALES

Played: 102; England won 67, Wales won 14, Drawn 21. Goals: England 247, Wales 91.

			E	W
1879	18 Jan	Kennington Oval	2	1
1880	15 Mar	Wrexham	3	2
1881	26 Feb	Blackburn	0	1
1882	13 Mar	Wrexham	3	5
1883	3 Feb	Kennington Oval	5	0
1884	17 Mar	Wrexham	4	0
1885	14 Mar	Blackburn	1	1
1886	29 Mar	Wrexham	3	1
1887	26 Feb	Kennington Oval	4	0
1888	4 Feb	Crewe	5	1
1889	23 Feb	Stoke	4	1
1890	15 Mar	Wrexham	3	1
1891	7 May	Sunderland	4	1
1892	5 Mar	Wrexham	2	0
1893	13 Mar	Stoke	6	0
1894	12 Mar	Wrexham	5	1
1895	18 Mar	Queen's Club, Kensington	1	1
1896	16 Mar	Cardiff	9	1
1897	29 Mar	Sheffield	4	0
1898	28 Mar	Wrexham	3	0
1899	20 Mar	Bristol	4	0
1900	26 Mar	Cardiff	1	1
1901	18 Mar	Newcastle	6	0
1902	3 Mar	Wrexham	0	0
1903	2 Mar	Portsmouth	2	1
1904	29 Feb	Wrexham	2	2
1905	27 Mar	Liverpool	3	1
1906	19 Mar	Cardiff	1	0
1907	18 Mar	Fulham	1	1
1908	16 Mar	Wrexham	7	1
1909	15 Mar	Nottingham	2	0
1910	14 Mar	Cardiff	1	0
1911	13 Mar	Millwall	3	0
1912	11 Mar	Wrexham	2	0
1913	17 Mar	Bristol	4	3
1914	16 Mar	Cardiff	2	0
1920	15 Mar	Highbury	1	2
1921	14 Mar	Cardiff	0	0
1922	13 Mar	Liverpool	1	0
1923	5 Mar	Cardiff	2	2
1924	3 Mar	Blackburn	1	2
1925	28 Feb	Swansea	2	1
1926	1 Mar	Crystal Palace	1	3
1927	12 Feb	Wrexham	3	3
1927	28 Nov	Burnley	1	2
1928	17 Nov	Swansea	3	2
1929	20 Nov	Chelsea	6	0
1930	22 Nov	Wrexham	4	0
1931	18 Nov	Liverpool	3	1
1932	16 Nov	Wrexham	0	0
1933	15 Nov	Newcastle	1	2
1934	29 Sept	Cardiff	4	0
1936	5 Feb	Wolverhampton	1	2
1936	17 Oct	Cardiff	1	2
1937	17 Nov	Middlesbrough	2	1
1938	22 Oct	Cardiff	2	4
1946	13 Nov	Manchester	3	0
1947	18 Oct	Cardiff	3	0
1948	10 Nov	Aston Villa	1	0
WC1949	15 Oct	Cardiff	4	1
1950	15 Nov	Sunderland	4	2
1951	20 Oct	Cardiff	1	1
1952	12 Nov	Wembley	5	2
WC1953	10 Oct	Cardiff	4	1
1954	10 Nov	Wembley	3	2
1955	27 Oct	Cardiff	1	2
1956	14 Nov	Wembley	3	1
1957	19 Oct	Cardiff	4	0
1958	26 Nov	Aston Villa	2	2
1959	17 Oct	Cardiff	1	1
1960	23 Nov	Wembley	5	1
1961	14 Oct	Cardiff	1	1
1962	21 Oct	Wembley	4	0
1963	12 Oct	Cardiff	4	0
1964	18 Nov	Wembley	2	1
1965	2 Oct	Cardiff	0	0
EC1966	16 Nov	Wembley	5	1
EC1967	21 Oct	Cardiff	3	0
1969	7 May	Wembley	2	1
1970	18 Apr	Cardiff	1	1
1971	19 May	Wembley	0	0
1972	20 May	Cardiff	3	0
WC1972	15 Nov	Cardiff	1	0
WC1973	24 Jan	Wembley	1	1
1973	15 May	Wembley	3	0
1974	11 May	Cardiff	2	0
1975	21 May	Wembley	2	2
1976	24 Mar	Wrexham	2	1
1976	8 May	Cardiff	1	0
1977	31 May	Wembley	0	1
1978	3 May	Cardiff	3	1
1979	23 May	Wembley	0	0
1980	17 May	Wrexham	1	4
1981	20 May	Wembley	0	0
1982	27 Apr	Cardiff	1	0
1983	23 Feb	Wembley	2	1
1984	2 May	Wrexham	0	1
WC2004	9 Oct	Old Trafford	2	0
WC2005	3 Sept	Cardiff	1	0
EC2011	26 Mar	Cardiff	2	0
EC2011	6 Sept	Wembley	1	0
EC2016	16 June	Lens	2	1

ENGLAND v NORTHERN IRELAND

Played: 98; England won 75, Northern Ireland won 7, Drawn 16. Goals: England 323, Northern Ireland 81.

			E	NI
1882	18 Feb	Belfast	13	0
1883	24 Feb	Liverpool	7	0
1884	23 Feb	Belfast	8	1
1885	28 Feb	Manchester	4	0
1886	13 Mar	Belfast	6	1
1887	5 Feb	Sheffield	7	0
1888	31 Mar	Belfast	5	1
1889	2 Mar	Everton	6	1
1890	15 Mar	Belfast	9	1
1891	7 Mar	Wolverhampton	6	1
1892	5 Mar	Belfast	2	0
1893	25 Feb	Birmingham	6	1
1894	3 Mar	Belfast	2	2
1895	9 Mar	Derby	9	0
1896	7 Mar	Belfast	2	0
1897	20 Feb	Nottingham	6	0
1898	5 Mar	Belfast	3	2
1899	18 Feb	Sunderland	13	2
1900	17 Mar	Dublin	2	0
1901	9 Mar	Southampton	3	0
1902	22 Mar	Belfast	1	0
1903	14 Feb	Wolverhampton	4	0
1904	12 Mar	Belfast	3	1
1905	25 Feb	Middlesbrough	1	1
1906	17 Feb	Belfast	5	0
1907	16 Feb	Everton	1	0
1908	15 Feb	Belfast	3	1
1909	13 Feb	Bradford	4	0
1910	12 Feb	Belfast	1	1
1911	11 Feb	Derby	2	1
1912	10 Feb	Dublin	6	1
1913	15 Feb	Belfast	1	2
1914	14 Feb	Middlesbrough	0	3
1919	25 Oct	Belfast	1	1

Year	Date	Venue	*E*	*NI*
1920	23 Oct	Sunderland	2	0
1921	22 Oct	Belfast	1	1
1922	21 Oct	West Bromwich	2	0
1923	20 Oct	Belfast	1	2
1924	22 Oct	Everton	3	1
1925	24 Oct	Belfast	0	0
1926	20 Oct	Liverpool	3	3
1927	22 Oct	Belfast	0	2
1928	22 Oct	Everton	2	1
1929	19 Oct	Belfast	3	0
1930	20 Oct	Sheffield	5	1
1931	17 Oct	Belfast	6	2
1932	17 Oct	Blackpool	1	0
1933	14 Oct	Belfast	3	0
1935	6 Feb	Everton	2	1
1935	19 Oct	Belfast	3	1
1936	18 Nov	Stoke	3	1
1937	23 Oct	Belfast	5	1
1938	16 Nov	Manchester	7	0
1946	28 Sept	Belfast	7	2
1947	5 Nov	Everton	2	2
1948	9 Oct	Belfast	6	2
wc1949	16 Nov	Manchester	9	2
1950	7 Oct	Belfast	4	1
1951	14 Nov	Aston Villa	2	0
1952	4 Oct	Belfast	2	2
wc1953	11 Nov	Everton	3	1
1954	2 Oct	Belfast	2	0
1955	2 Nov	Wembley	3	0
1956	10 Oct	Belfast	1	1
1957	6 Nov	Wembley	2	3
1958	4 Oct	Belfast	3	3
1959	18 Nov	Wembley	2	1
1960	8 Oct	Belfast	5	2
1961	22 Nov	Wembley	1	1
1962	20 Oct	Belfast	3	1
1963	20 Nov	Wembley	8	3
1964	3 Oct	Belfast	4	3
1965	10 Nov	Wembley	2	1
EC1966	20 Oct	Belfast	2	0
EC1967	22 Nov	Wembley	2	0
1969	3 May	Belfast	3	1
1970	21 Apr	Wembley	3	1
1971	15 May	Belfast	1	0
1972	23 May	Wembley	0	1
1973	12 May	Everton	2	1
1974	15 May	Wembley	1	0
1975	17 May	Belfast	0	0
1976	11 May	Wembley	4	0
1977	28 May	Belfast	2	1
1978	16 May	Wembley	1	0
EC1979	7 Feb	Wembley	4	0
1979	19 May	Belfast	2	0
EC1979	17 Oct	Belfast	5	1
1980	20 May	Wembley	1	1
1982	23 Feb	Wembley	4	0
1983	28 May	Belfast	0	0
1984	24 Apr	Wembley	1	0
wc1985	27 Feb	Belfast	1	0
wc1985	13 Nov	Wembley	0	0
EC1986	15 Oct	Wembley	3	0
EC1987	1 Apr	Belfast	2	0
wc2005	26 Mar	Old Trafford	4	0
wc2005	7 Sept	Belfast	0	1

SCOTLAND v WALES

Played: 107; Scotland won 61, Wales won 23, Drawn 23. Goals: Scotland 243, Wales 124.

Year	Date	Venue	*S*	*W*
1876	25 Mar	Glasgow	4	0
1877	5 Mar	Wrexham	2	0
1878	23 Mar	Glasgow	9	0
1879	7 Apr	Wrexham	3	0
1880	3 Apr	Glasgow	5	1
1881	14 Mar	Wrexham	5	1
1882	25 Mar	Glasgow	5	0
1883	12 Mar	Wrexham	3	0
1884	29 Mar	Glasgow	4	1
1885	23 Mar	Wrexham	8	1
1886	10 Apr	Glasgow	4	1
1887	21 Mar	Wrexham	2	0
1888	10 Mar	Easter Road	5	1
1889	15 Apr	Wrexham	0	0
1890	22 Mar	Paisley	5	0
1891	21 Mar	Wrexham	4	3
1892	26 Mar	Tynecastle	6	1
1893	18 Mar	Wrexham	8	0
1894	24 Mar	Kilmarnock	5	2
1895	23 Mar	Wrexham	2	2
1896	21 Mar	Dundee	4	0
1897	20 Mar	Wrexham	2	2
1898	19 Mar	Motherwell	5	2
1899	18 Mar	Wrexham	6	0
1900	3 Feb	Aberdeen	5	2
1901	2 Mar	Wrexham	1	1
1902	15 Mar	Greenock	5	1
1903	9 Mar	Cardiff	1	0
1904	12 Mar	Dundee	1	1
1905	6 Mar	Wrexham	1	3
1906	3 Mar	Tynecastle	0	2
1907	4 Mar	Wrexham	0	1
1908	7 Mar	Dundee	2	1
1909	1 Mar	Wrexham	2	3
1910	5 Mar	Kilmarnock	1	0
1911	6 Mar	Cardiff	2	2
1912	2 Mar	Tynecastle	1	0
1913	3 Mar	Wrexham	0	0
1914	28 Feb	Glasgow	0	0
1920	26 Feb	Cardiff	1	1
1921	12 Feb	Aberdeen	2	1
1922	4 Feb	Wrexham	1	2
1923	17 Mar	Paisley	2	0
1924	16 Feb	Cardiff	0	2
1925	14 Feb	Tynecastle	3	1
1925	31 Oct	Cardiff	3	0
1926	30 Oct	Glasgow	3	0
1927	29 Oct	Wrexham	2	2
1928	27 Oct	Glasgow	4	2
1929	26 Oct	Cardiff	4	2
1930	25 Oct	Glasgow	1	1
1931	31 Oct	Wrexham	3	2
1932	26 Oct	Tynecastle	2	5
1933	4 Oct	Cardiff	2	3
1934	21 Nov	Aberdeen	3	2
1935	5 Oct	Cardiff	1	1
1936	2 Dec	Dundee	1	2
1937	30 Oct	Cardiff	1	2
1938	9 Nov	Tynecastle	3	2
1946	19 Oct	Wrexham	1	3
1947	12 Nov	Glasgow	1	2
1948	23 Oct	Cardiff	3	1
wc1949	9 Nov	Glasgow	2	0
1950	21 Oct	Cardiff	3	1
1951	14 Nov	Glasgow	0	1
1952	18 Oct	Cardiff	2	1
wc1953	4 Nov	Glasgow	3	3
1954	16 Oct	Cardiff	1	0
1955	9 Nov	Glasgow	2	0
1956	20 Oct	Cardiff	2	2
1957	13 Nov	Glasgow	1	1
1958	18 Oct	Cardiff	3	0
1959	4 Nov	Glasgow	1	1
1960	20 Oct	Cardiff	0	2
1961	8 Nov	Glasgow	2	0
1962	20 Oct	Cardiff	3	2
1963	20 Nov	Glasgow	2	1
1964	3 Oct	Cardiff	2	3

			S	W
EC1965	24 Nov	Glasgow	4	1
EC1966	22 Oct	Cardiff	1	1
1967	22 Nov	Glasgow	3	2
1969	3 May	Wrexham	5	3
1970	22 Apr	Glasgow	0	0
1971	15 May	Cardiff	0	0
1972	24 May	Glasgow	1	0
1973	12 May	Wrexham	2	0
1974	14 May	Glasgow	2	0
1975	17 May	Cardiff	2	2
1976	6 May	Glasgow	3	1
WC1976	17 Nov	Glasgow	1	0
1977	28 May	Wrexham	0	0
WC1977	12 Oct	Liverpool	2	0
1978	17 May	Glasgow	1	1
1979	19 May	Cardiff	0	3
1980	21 May	Glasgow	1	0
1981	16 May	Swansea	0	2
1982	24 May	Glasgow	1	0
1983	28 May	Cardiff	2	0
1984	28 Feb	Glasgow	2	1
WC1985	27 Mar	Glasgow	0	1
WC1985	10 Sept	Cardiff	1	1
1997	27 May	Kilmarnock	0	1
2004	18 Feb	Cardiff	0	4
2009	14 Nov	Cardiff	0	3
NC2011	25 May	Dublin	3	1
WC2012	12 Oct	Cardiff	1	2
WC2013	22 Mar	Glasgow	1	2

SCOTLAND v NORTHERN IRELAND

Played: 96; Scotland won 64, Northern Ireland won 15, Drawn 17. Goals: Scotland 261, Northern Ireland 81.

			S	NI
1884	26 Jan	Belfast	5	0
1885	14 Mar	Glasgow	8	2
1886	20 Mar	Belfast	7	2
1887	19 Feb	Glasgow	4	1
1888	24 Mar	Belfast	10	2
1889	9 Mar	Glasgow	7	0
1890	29 Mar	Belfast	4	1
1891	28 Mar	Glasgow	2	1
1892	19 Mar	Belfast	3	2
1893	25 Mar	Glasgow	6	1
1894	31 Mar	Belfast	2	1
1895	30 Mar	Glasgow	3	1
1896	28 Mar	Belfast	3	3
1897	27 Mar	Glasgow	5	1
1898	26 Mar	Belfast	3	0
1899	25 Mar	Glasgow	9	1
1900	3 Mar	Belfast	3	0
1901	23 Feb	Glasgow	11	0
1902	1 Mar	Belfast	5	1
1902	9 Aug	Belfast	3	0
1903	21 Mar	Glasgow	0	2
1904	26 Mar	Dublin	1	1
1905	18 Mar	Glasgow	4	0
1906	17 Mar	Dublin	1	0
1907	16 Mar	Glasgow	3	0
1908	14 Mar	Dublin	5	0
1909	15 Mar	Glasgow	5	0
1910	19 Mar	Belfast	0	1
1911	18 Mar	Glasgow	2	0
1912	16 Mar	Belfast	4	1
1913	15 Mar	Dublin	2	1
1914	14 Mar	Belfast	1	1
1920	13 Mar	Glasgow	3	0
1921	26 Feb	Belfast	2	0
1922	4 Mar	Glasgow	2	1
1923	3 Mar	Belfast	1	0
1924	1 Mar	Glasgow	2	0
1925	28 Feb	Belfast	3	0
1926	27 Feb	Glasgow	4	0
1927	26 Feb	Belfast	2	0
1928	25 Feb	Glasgow	0	1
1929	23 Feb	Belfast	7	3
1930	22 Feb	Glasgow	3	1
1931	21 Feb	Belfast	0	0
1931	19 Sept	Glasgow	3	1
1932	12 Sept	Belfast	4	0
1933	16 Sept	Glasgow	1	2
1934	20 Oct	Belfast	1	2
1935	13 Nov	Tynecastle	2	1
1936	31 Oct	Belfast	3	1
1937	10 Nov	Aberdeen	1	1
1938	8 Oct	Belfast	2	0
1946	27 Nov	Glasgow	0	0
1947	4 Oct	Belfast	0	2
1948	17 Nov	Glasgow	3	2
WC1949	1 Oct	Belfast	8	2
1950	1 Nov	Glasgow	6	1
1951	6 Oct	Belfast	3	0
1952	5 Nov	Glasgow	1	1
WC1953	3 Oct	Belfast	3	1
1954	3 Nov	Glasgow	2	2
1955	8 Oct	Belfast	1	2
1956	7 Nov	Glasgow	1	0
1957	5 Oct	Belfast	1	1
1958	5 Nov	Glasgow	2	2
1959	3 Oct	Belfast	4	0
1960	9 Nov	Glasgow	5	2
1961	7 Oct	Belfast	6	1
1962	7 Nov	Glasgow	5	1
1963	12 Oct	Belfast	1	2
1964	25 Nov	Glasgow	3	2
1965	2 Oct	Belfast	2	3
1966	16 Nov	Glasgow	2	1
1967	21 Oct	Belfast	0	1
1969	6 May	Glasgow	1	1
1970	18 Apr	Belfast	1	0
1971	18 May	Glasgow	0	1
1972	20 May	Glasgow	2	0
1973	16 May	Glasgow	1	2
1974	11 May	Glasgow	0	1
1975	20 May	Glasgow	3	0
1976	8 May	Glasgow	3	0
1977	1 June	Glasgow	3	0
1978	13 May	Glasgow	1	1
1979	22 May	Glasgow	1	0
1980	17 May	Belfast	0	1
WC1981	25 Mar	Glasgow	1	1
1981	19 May	Glasgow	2	0
WC1981	14 Oct	Belfast	0	0
1982	28 Apr	Belfast	1	1
1983	24 May	Glasgow	0	0
1983	13 Dec	Belfast	0	2
1992	19 Feb	Glasgow	1	0
2008	20 Aug	Glasgow	0	0
NC2011	9 Feb	Dublin	3	0
2015	25 Mar	Glasgow	1	0

WALES v NORTHERN IRELAND

Played: 96; Wales won 45, Northern Ireland won 27, Drawn 24. Goals: Wales 191, Northern Ireland 132.

			W	*NI*
1882	25 Feb	Wrexham	7	1
1883	17 Mar	Belfast	1	1
1884	9 Feb	Wrexham	6	0
1885	11 Apr	Belfast	8	2
1886	27 Feb	Wrexham	5	0
1887	12 Mar	Belfast	1	4
1888	3 Mar	Wrexham	11	0
1889	27 Apr	Belfast	3	1
1890	8 Feb	Shrewsbury	5	2
1891	7 Feb	Belfast	2	7
1892	27 Feb	Bangor	1	1
1893	8 Apr	Belfast	3	4
1894	24 Feb	Swansea	4	1
1895	16 Mar	Belfast	2	2
1896	29 Feb	Wrexham	6	1
1897	6 Mar	Belfast	3	4
1898	19 Feb	Llandudno	0	1
1899	4 Mar	Belfast	0	1
1900	24 Feb	Llandudno	2	0
1901	23 Mar	Belfast	1	0
1902	22 Mar	Cardiff	0	3
1903	28 Mar	Belfast	0	2
1904	21 Mar	Bangor	0	1
1905	18 Apr	Belfast	2	2
1906	2 Apr	Wrexham	4	4
1907	23 Feb	Belfast	3	2
1908	11 Apr	Aberdare	0	1
1909	20 Mar	Belfast	3	2
1910	11 Apr	Wrexham	4	1
1911	28 Jan	Belfast	2	1
1912	13 Apr	Cardiff	2	3
1913	18 Jan	Belfast	1	0
1914	19 Jan	Wrexham	1	2
1920	14 Feb	Belfast	2	2
1921	9 Apr	Swansea	2	1
1922	4 Apr	Belfast	1	1
1923	14 Apr	Wrexham	0	3
1924	15 Mar	Belfast	1	0
1925	18 Apr	Wrexham	0	0
1926	13 Feb	Belfast	0	3
1927	9 Apr	Cardiff	2	2
1928	4 Feb	Belfast	2	1
1929	2 Feb	Wrexham	2	2
1930	1 Feb	Belfast	0	7
1931	22 Apr	Wrexham	3	2
1931	5 Dec	Belfast	0	4
1932	7 Dec	Wrexham	4	1
1933	4 Nov	Belfast	1	1
1935	27 Mar	Wrexham	3	1
1936	11 Mar	Belfast	2	3
1937	17 Mar	Wrexham	4	1
1938	16 Mar	Belfast	0	1
1939	15 Mar	Wrexham	3	1
1947	16 Apr	Belfast	1	2
1948	10 Mar	Wrexham	2	0
1949	9 Mar	Belfast	2	0
WC1950	8 Mar	Wrexham	0	0
1951	7 Mar	Belfast	2	1
1952	19 Mar	Swansea	3	0
1953	15 Apr	Belfast	3	2
WC1954	31 Mar	Wrexham	1	2
1955	20 Apr	Belfast	3	2
1956	11 Apr	Cardiff	1	1
1957	10 Apr	Belfast	0	0
1958	16 Apr	Cardiff	1	1
1959	22 Apr	Belfast	1	4
1960	6 Apr	Wrexham	3	2
1961	12 Apr	Belfast	5	1
1962	11 Apr	Cardiff	4	0
1963	3 Apr	Belfast	4	1
1964	15 Apr	Swansea	2	3
1965	31 Mar	Belfast	5	0
1966	30 Mar	Cardiff	1	4
EC1967	12 Apr	Belfast	0	0
EC1968	28 Feb	Wrexham	2	0
1969	10 May	Belfast	0	0
1970	25 Apr	Swansea	1	0
1971	22 May	Belfast	0	1
1972	27 May	Wrexham	0	0
1973	19 May	Everton	0	1
1974	18 May	Wrexham	1	0
1975	23 May	Belfast	0	1
1976	14 May	Swansea	1	0
1977	3 June	Belfast	1	1
1978	19 May	Wrexham	1	0
1979	25 May	Belfast	1	1
1980	23 May	Cardiff	0	1
1982	27 May	Wrexham	3	0
1983	31 May	Belfast	1	0
1984	22 May	Swansea	1	1
WC2004	8 Sept	Cardiff	2	2
WC2005	8 Oct	Belfast	3	2
2007	6 Feb	Belfast	0	0
NC2011	27 May	Dublin	2	0
2016	24 Mar	Cardiff	1	1
EC2016	25 June	Paris	1	0

OTHER BRITISH INTERNATIONAL RESULTS 1908–2020
ENGLAND

v ALBANIA			*E*	*A*
WC1989	8 Mar	Tirana	2	0
WC1989	26 Apr	Wembley	5	0
WC2001	28 Mar	Tirana	3	1
WC2001	5 Sept	Newcastle	2	0

v ALGERIA			*E*	*A*
WC2010	18 June	Cape Town	0	0

v ANDORRA			*E*	*A*
EC2006	2 Sept	Old Trafford	5	0
EC2007	28 Mar	Barcelona	3	0
WC2008	6 Sept	Barcelona	2	0
WC2009	10 June	Wembley	6	0

v ARGENTINA			*E*	*A*
1951	9 May	Wembley	2	1
1953	17 May	Buenos Aires	0	0
(*abandoned after 21 mins*)				
WC1962	2 June	Rancagua	3	1
1964	6 June	Rio de Janeiro	0	1
WC1966	23 July	Wembley	1	0
1974	22 May	Wembley	2	2
1977	12 June	Buenos Aires	1	1
1980	13 May	Wembley	3	1
WC1986	22 June	Mexico City	1	2
1991	25 May	Wembley	2	2
WC1998	30 June	St Etienne	2	2
2000	23 Feb	Wembley	0	0
WC2002	7 June	Sapporo	1	0
2005	12 Nov	Geneva	3	2

v AUSTRALIA			*E*	*A*
1980	31 May	Sydney	2	1
1983	11 June	Sydney	0	0
1983	15 June	Brisbane	1	0
1983	18 June	Melbourne	1	1
1991	1 June	Sydney	1	0
2003	12 Feb	West Ham	1	3
2016	27 May	Sunderland	2	1

v AUSTRIA			*E*	*A*
1908	6 June	Vienna	6	1
1908	8 June	Vienna	11	1
1909	1 June	Vienna	8	1
1930	14 May	Vienna	0	0
1932	7 Dec	Chelsea	4	3
1936	6 May	Vienna	1	2
1951	28 Nov	Wembley	2	2
1952	25 May	Vienna	3	2
WC1958	15 June	Boras	2	2
1961	27 May	Vienna	1	3
1962	4 Apr	Wembley	3	1
1965	20 Oct	Wembley	2	3
1967	27 May	Vienna	1	0
1973	26 Sept	Wembley	7	0
1979	13 June	Vienna	3	4
WC2004	4 Sept	Vienna	2	2
WC2005	8 Oct	Old Trafford	1	0
2007	16 Nov	Vienna	1	0

v AZERBAIJAN			*E*	*A*
WC2004	13 Oct	Baku	1	0
WC2005	30 Mar	Newcastle	2	0

v BELARUS			*E*	*B*
WC2008	15 Oct	Minsk	3	1
WC2009	14 Oct	Wembley	3	0

v BELGIUM			*E*	*B*
1921	21 May	Brussels	2	0
1923	19 Mar	Highbury	6	1
1923	1 Nov	Antwerp	2	2
1924	8 Dec	West Bromwich	4	0
1926	24 May	Antwerp	5	3
1927	11 May	Brussels	9	1
1928	19 May	Antwerp	3	1
1929	11 May	Brussels	5	1
1931	16 May	Brussels	4	1
1936	9 May	Brussels	2	3
1947	21 Sept	Brussels	5	2
1950	18 May	Brussels	4	1
1952	26 Nov	Wembley	5	0
WC1954	17 June	Basle	4	4*
1964	21 Oct	Wembley	2	2
1970	25 Feb	Brussels	3	1
EC1980	12 June	Turin	1	1
WC1990	27 June	Bologna	1	0*
1998	29 May	Casablanca	0	0
1999	10 Oct	Sunderland	2	1
2012	2 June	Wembley	1	0
WC2018	28 June	Kaliningrad	0	1
WC2018	14 July	St Petersburg	0	2

v BOHEMIA			*E*	*B*
1908	13 June	Prague	4	0

v BRAZIL			*E*	*B*
1956	9 May	Wembley	4	2
WC1958	11 June	Gothenburg	0	0
1959	13 May	Rio de Janeiro	0	2
WC1962	10 June	Vina del Mar	1	3
1963	8 May	Wembley	1	1
1964	30 May	Rio de Janeiro	1	5
1969	12 June	Rio de Janeiro	1	2
WC1970	7 June	Guadalajara	0	1
1976	23 May	Los Angeles	0	1
1977	8 June	Rio de Janeiro	0	0
1978	19 Apr	Wembley	1	1
1981	12 May	Wembley	0	1
1984	10 June	Rio de Janeiro	2	0
1987	19 May	Wembley	1	1
1990	28 Mar	Wembley	1	0
1992	17 May	Wembley	1	1
1993	13 June	Washington	1	1
UI1995	11 June	Wembley	1	3
TF1997	10 June	Paris	0	1
2000	27 May	Wembley	1	1
WC2002	21 June	Shizuoka	1	2
2007	1 June	Wembley	1	1
2009	14 Nov	Doha	0	1
2013	6 Feb	Wembley	2	1
2013	2 June	Rio de Janeiro	2	2
2017	14 Nov	Wembley	0	0

v BULGARIA			*E*	*B*
WC1962	7 June	Rancagua	0	0
1968	11 Dec	Wembley	1	1
1974	1 June	Sofia	1	0
EC1979	6 June	Sofia	3	0
EC1979	22 Nov	Wembley	2	0
1996	27 Mar	Wembley	1	0
EC1998	10 Oct	Wembley	0	0
EC1999	9 June	Sofia	1	1
EC2010	3 Sept	Wembley	4	0
EC2011	2 Sept	Sofia	3	0
EC2019	**7 Sept**	**Wembley**	**4**	**0**
EC2019	**14 Oct**	**Sofia**	**6**	**0**

v CAMEROON			*E*	*C*
WC1990	1 July	Naples	3	2*
1991	6 Feb	Wembley	2	0
1997	15 Nov	Wembley	2	0
2002	26 May	Kobe	2	2

v CANADA			*E*	*C*
1986	24 May	Burnaby	1	0

v CHILE			*E*	*C*
WC1950	25 June	Rio de Janeiro	2	0
1953	24 May	Santiago	2	1
1984	17 June	Santiago	0	0
1989	23 May	Wembley	0	0
1998	11 Feb	Wembley	0	2
2013	15 Nov	Wembley	0	2

v CHINA PR			*E*	*CPR*
1996	23 May	Beijing	3	0

v CIS			*E*	*C*
1992	29 Apr	Moscow	2	2

v COLOMBIA			*E*	*C*
1970	20 May	Bogota	4	0
1988	24 May	Wembley	1	1
1995	6 Sept	Wembley	0	0
WC1998	26 June	Lens	2	0
2005	31 May	New Jersey	3	2
WC2018	3 July	Moscow	1	1

v COSTA RICA			*E*	*C*
WC2014	26 June	Belo Horizonte	0	0
2018	7 June	Leeds	2	0

v CROATIA			*E*	*C*
1996	24 Apr	Wembley	0	0
2003	20 Aug	Ipswich	3	1
EC2004	21 June	Lisbon	4	2
EC2006	11 Oct	Zagreb	0	2
EC2007	21 Nov	Wembley	2	3
WC2008	10 Sept	Zagreb	4	1
WC2009	9 Sept	Wembley	5	1
WC2018	11 July	Moscow	1	2
NL2018	12 Oct	Rijeka	0	0
NL2018	18 Nov	Wembley	2	1

v CYPRUS			*E*	*C*
EC1975	16 Apr	Wembley	5	0
EC1975	11 May	Limassol	1	0

v CZECHOSLOVAKIA			*E*	*C*
1934	16 May	Prague	1	2
1937	1 Dec	Tottenham	5	4
1963	29 May	Bratislava	4	2
1966	2 Nov	Wembley	0	0
WC1970	11 June	Guadalajara	1	0
1973	27 May	Prague	1	1
EC1974	30 Oct	Wembley	3	0
EC1975	30 Oct	Bratislava	1	2
1978	29 Nov	Wembley	1	0
WC1982	20 June	Bilbao	2	0
1990	25 Apr	Wembley	4	2
1992	25 Mar	Prague	2	2

v CZECH REPUBLIC			*E*	*C*
1998	18 Nov	Wembley	2	0
2008	20 Aug	Wembley	2	2
EC2019	22 Mar	Wembley	5	0
EC2019	**11 Oct**	**Prague**	**1**	**2**

v DENMARK			*E*	*D*
1948	26 Sept	Copenhagen	0	0
1955	2 Oct	Copenhagen	5	1
WC1956	5 Dec	Wolverhampton	5	2
WC1957	15 May	Copenhagen	4	1
1966	3 July	Copenhagen	2	0
EC1978	20 Sept	Copenhagen	4	3
EC1979	12 Sept	Wembley	1	0
EC1982	22 Sept	Copenhagen	2	2
EC1983	21 Sept	Wembley	0	1
1988	14 Sept	Wembley	1	0
1989	7 June	Copenhagen	1	1
1990	15 May	Wembley	1	0
EC1992	11 June	Malmo	0	0
1994	9 Mar	Wembley	1	0
WC2002	15 June	Niigata	3	0
2003	16 Nov	Old Trafford	2	3
2005	17 Aug	Copenhagen	1	4
2011	9 Feb	Copenhagen	2	1
2014	5 Mar	Wembley	1	0

v ECUADOR			*E*	*Ec*
1970	24 May	Quito	2	0
WC2006	25 June	Stuttgart	1	0
2014	4 June	Miami	2	2

v EGYPT			*E*	*Eg*
1986	29 Jan	Cairo	4	0
WC1990	21 June	Cagliari	1	0
2010	3 Mar	Wembley	3	1

v ESTONIA			*E*	*Es*
EC2007	6 June	Tallinn	3	0
EC2007	13 Oct	Wembley	3	0
EC2014	12 Oct	Tallinn	1	0
EC2015	9 Oct	Wembley	2	0

v FIFA			*E*	*FIFA*
1938	26 Oct	Highbury	3	0
1953	21 Oct	Wembley	4	4
1963	23 Oct	Wembley	2	1

v FINLAND			*E*	*F*
1937	20 May	Helsinki	8	0
1956	20 May	Helsinki	5	1
1966	26 June	Helsinki	3	0
WC1976	13 June	Helsinki	4	1
WC1976	13 Oct	Wembley	2	1
1982	3 June	Helsinki	4	1
WC1984	17 Oct	Wembley	5	0
WC1985	22 May	Helsinki	1	1
1992	3 June	Helsinki	2	1
WC2000	11 Oct	Helsinki	0	0
WC2001	24 Mar	Liverpool	2	1

v FRANCE			*E*	*F*
1923	10 May	Paris	4	1
1924	17 May	Paris	3	1
1925	21 May	Paris	3	2
1927	26 May	Paris	6	0
1928	17 May	Paris	5	1
1929	9 May	Paris	4	1
1931	14 May	Paris	2	5
1933	6 Dec	Tottenham	4	1
1938	26 May	Paris	4	2
1947	3 May	Highbury	3	0
1949	22 May	Paris	3	1
1951	3 Oct	Highbury	2	2
1955	15 May	Paris	0	1
1957	27 Nov	Wembley	4	0
EC1962	3 Oct	Sheffield	1	1
EC1963	27 Feb	Paris	2	5
WC1966	20 July	Wembley	2	0
1969	12 Mar	Wembley	5	0
WC1982	16 June	Bilbao	3	1
1984	29 Feb	Paris	0	2
1992	19 Feb	Wembley	2	0
EC1992	14 June	Malmo	0	0
TF1997	7 June	Montpellier	1	0
1999	10 Feb	Wembley	0	2
2000	2 Sept	Paris	1	1
EC2004	13 June	Lisbon	1	2
2008	26 Mar	Paris	0	1
2010	17 Nov	Wembley	1	2
EC2012	11 June	Donetsk	1	1
2015	17 Nov	Wembley	2	0
2017	13 June	Paris	2	3

v GEORGIA			*E*	*G*
WC1996	9 Nov	Tbilisi	2	0
WC1997	30 Apr	Wembley	2	0

v GERMANY			*E*	*G*
1930	10 May	Berlin	3	3
1935	4 Dec	Tottenham	3	0
1938	14 May	Berlin	6	3
1991	11 Sept	Wembley	0	1
1993	19 June	Detroit	1	2
EC1996	26 June	Wembley	1	1*
EC2000	17 June	Charleroi	1	0
WC2000	7 Oct	Wembley	0	1
WC2001	1 Sept	Munich	5	1
2007	22 Aug	Wembley	1	2
2008	19 Nov	Berlin	2	1
WC2010	27 June	Bloemfontein	1	4
2013	19 Nov	Wembley	0	1
2016	26 Mar	Berlin	3	2
2017	22 Mar	Dortmund	0	1
2017	10 Nov	Wembley	0	0

v EAST GERMANY			*E*	*EG*
1963	2 June	Leipzig	2	1
1970	25 Nov	Wembley	3	1
1974	29 May	Leipzig	1	1
1984	12 Sept	Wembley	1	0

v WEST GERMANY			*E*	*WG*
1954	1 Dec	Wembley	3	1
1956	26 May	Berlin	3	1

			E	*WG*
1965	12 May	Nuremberg	1	0
1966	23 Feb	Wembley	1	0
WC1966	30 July	Wembley	4	2*
1968	1 June	Hanover	0	1
WC1970	14 June	Leon	2	3*
EC1972	29 Apr	Wembley	1	3
EC1972	13 May	Berlin	0	0
1975	12 Mar	Wembley	2	0
1978	22 Feb	Munich	1	2
WC1982	29 June	Madrid	0	0
1982	13 Oct	Wembley	1	2
1985	12 June	Mexico City	3	0
1987	9 Sept	Dusseldorf	1	3
WC1990	4 July	Turin	1	1*

v GHANA

			E	*G*
2011	29 Mar	Wembley	1	1

v GREECE

			E	*G*
EC1971	21 Apr	Wembley	3	0
EC1971	1 Dec	Piraeus	2	0
EC1982	17 Nov	Salonika	3	0
EC1983	30 Mar	Wembley	0	0
1989	8 Feb	Athens	2	1
1994	17 May	Wembley	5	0
WC2001	6 June	Athens	2	0
WC2001	6 Oct	Old Trafford	2	2
2006	16 Aug	Old Trafford	4	0

v HONDURAS

			E	*H*
2014	7 June	Miami	0	0

v HUNGARY

			E	*H*
1908	10 June	Budapest	7	0
1909	29 May	Budapest	4	2
1909	31 May	Budapest	8	2
1934	10 May	Budapest	1	2
1936	2 Dec	Highbury	6	2
1953	25 Nov	Wembley	3	6
1954	23 May	Budapest	1	7
1960	22 May	Budapest	0	2
WC1962	31 May	Rancagua	1	2
1965	5 May	Wembley	1	0
1978	24 May	Wembley	4	1
WC1981	6 June	Budapest	3	1
WC1982	18 Nov	Wembley	1	0
EC1983	27 Apr	Wembley	2	0
EC1983	12 Oct	Budapest	3	0
1988	27 Apr	Budapest	0	0
1990	12 Sept	Wembley	1	0
1992	12 May	Budapest	1	0
1996	18 May	Wembley	3	0
1999	28 Apr	Budapest	1	1
2006	30 May	Old Trafford	3	1
2010	11 Aug	Wembley	2	1

v ICELAND

			E	*I*
1982	2 June	Reykjavik	1	1
2004	5 June	City of Manchester	6	1
EC2016	27 June	Nice	1	2

v ISRAEL

			E	*I*
1986	26 Feb	Ramat Gan	2	1
1988	17 Feb	Tel Aviv	0	0
EC2007	24 Mar	Tel Aviv	0	0
EC2007	8 Sept	Wembley	3	0

v ITALY

			E	*I*
1933	13 May	Rome	1	1
1934	14 Nov	Highbury	3	2
1939	13 May	Milan	2	2
1948	16 May	Turin	4	0
1949	30 Nov	Tottenham	2	0
1952	18 May	Florence	1	1
1959	6 May	Wembley	2	2
1961	24 May	Rome	3	2
1973	14 June	Turin	0	2
1973	14 Nov	Wembley	0	1
1976	28 May	New York	3	2
WC1976	17 Nov	Rome	0	2
WC1977	16 Nov	Wembley	2	0
EC1980	15 June	Turin	0	1

			E	*I*
1985	6 June	Mexico City	1	2
1989	15 Nov	Wembley	0	0
WC1990	7 July	Bari	1	2
WC1997	12 Feb	Wembley	0	1
TF1997	4 June	Nantes	2	0
WC1997	11 Oct	Rome	0	0
2000	15 Nov	Turin	0	1
2002	27 Mar	Leeds	1	2
EC2012	24 June	Kiev	0	0
2012	15 Aug	Berne	2	1
WC2014	14 June	Manaus	1	2
2015	31 Mar	Turin	1	1
2018	27 Mar	Wembley	1	1

v JAMAICA

			E	*J*
2006	3 June	Old Trafford	6	0

v JAPAN

			E	*J*
UI1995	3 June	Wembley	2	1
2004	1 June	City of Manchester	1	1
2010	30 May	Graz	2	1

v KAZAKHSTAN

			E	*K*
WC2008	11 Oct	Wembley	5	1
WC2009	6 June	Almaty	4	0

v KOREA REPUBLIC

			E	*KR*
2002	21 May	Seoguipo	1	1

v KOSOVO

			E	*K*
EC2019	**10 Sept**	**Southampton**	**5**	**3**
EC2019	**17 Nov**	**Pristina**	**4**	**0**

v KUWAIT

			E	*K*
WC1982	25 June	Bilbao	1	0

v LIECHTENSTEIN

			E	*L*
EC2003	29 Mar	Vaduz	2	0
EC2003	10 Sept	Old Trafford	2	0

v LITHUANIA

			E	*L*
EC2015	27 Mar	Wembley	4	0
EC2015	12 Oct	Vilnius	3	0
WC2017	26 Mar	Wembley	2	0
WC2017	8 Oct	Vilnius	1	0

v LUXEMBOURG

			E	*L*
1927	21 May	Esch-sur-Alzette	5	2
WC1960	19 Oct	Luxembourg	9	0
WC1961	28 Sept	Highbury	4	1
WC1977	30 Mar	Wembley	5	0
WC1977	12 Oct	Luxembourg	2	0
EC1982	15 Dec	Wembley	9	0
EC1983	16 Nov	Luxembourg	4	0
EC1998	14 Oct	Luxembourg	3	0
EC1999	4 Sept	Wembley	6	0
EC2006	7 Oct	Old Trafford	0	0

v MALAYSIA

			E	*M*
1991	12 June	Kuala Lumpur	4	2

v MALTA

			E	*M*
EC1971	3 Feb	Valletta	1	0
EC1971	12 May	Wembley	5	0
2000	3 June	Valletta	2	1
WC2016	8 Oct	Wembley	2	0
WC2017	1 Sept	Ta'Qali	4	0

v MEXICO

			E	*M*
1959	24 May	Mexico City	1	2
1961	10 May	Wembley	8	0
WC1966	16 July	Wembley	2	0
1969	1 June	Mexico City	0	0
1985	9 June	Mexico City	0	1
1986	17 May	Los Angeles	3	0
1997	29 Mar	Wembley	2	0
2001	25 May	Derby	4	0
2010	24 May	Wembley	3	1

v MOLDOVA

			E	*M*
WC1996	1 Sept	Chisinau	3	0
WC1997	10 Sept	Wembley	4	0
WC2012	7 Sept	Chisinau	5	0
WC2013	6 Sept	Wembley	4	0

v MONTENEGRO

			E	*M*
EC1989	8 Mar	Tirana	2	0
2010	12 Oct	Wembley	0	0
EC2011	7 Oct	Podgorica	2	2
WC2013	26 Mar	Podgorica	1	1
WC2013	11 Oct	Wembley	4	1
EC2019	25 Mar	Podgorica	5	1
EC2019	**14 Nov**	**Wembley**	**7**	**0**

v MOROCCO

			E	*M*
WC1986	6 June	Monterrey	0	0
1998	27 May	Casablanca	1	0

v NETHERLANDS

			E	*N*
1935	18 May	Amsterdam	1	0
1946	27 Nov	Huddersfield	8	2
1964	9 Dec	Amsterdam	1	1
1969	5 Nov	Amsterdam	1	0
1970	14 June	Wembley	0	0
1977	9 Feb	Wembley	0	2
1982	25 May	Wembley	2	0
1988	23 Mar	Wembley	2	2
EC1988	15 June	Dusseldorf	1	3
WC1990	16 June	Cagliari	0	0
2005	9 Feb	Villa Park	0	0
WC1993	28 Apr	Wembley	2	2
WC1993	13 Oct	Rotterdam	0	2
EC1996	18 June	Wembley	4	1
2001	15 Aug	Tottenham	0	2
2002	13 Feb	Amsterdam	1	1
2006	15 Nov	Amsterdam	1	1
2009	12 Aug	Amsterdam	2	2
2012	29 Feb	Wembley	2	3
2016	29 Mar	Wembley	1	2
2018	23 Mar	Amsterdam	1	0
NL2019	6 June	Guimaraes	1	3

v NEW ZEALAND

			E	*NZ*
1991	3 June	Auckland	1	0
1991	8 June	Wellington	2	0

v NIGERIA

			E	*N*
1994	16 Nov	Wembley	1	0
WC2002	12 June	Osaka	0	0
2018	2 June	Wembley	2	1

v NORTH MACEDONIA

			E	*M*
EC2002	16 Oct	Southampton	2	2
EC2003	6 Sept	Skopje	2	1
EC2006	6 Sept	Skopje	1	0

v NORWAY

			E	*N*
1937	14 May	Oslo	6	0
1938	9 Nov	Newcastle	4	0
1949	18 May	Oslo	4	1
1966	29 June	Oslo	6	1
WC1980	10 Sept	Wembley	4	0
WC1981	9 Sept	Oslo	1	2
WC1992	14 Oct	Wembley	1	1
WC1993	2 June	Oslo	0	2
1994	22 May	Wembley	0	0
1995	11 Oct	Oslo	0	0
2012	26 May	Oslo	1	0
2014	3 Sept	Wembley	1	0

v PANAMA

			E	*P*
WC2018	24 June	Nizhny Novgorod	6	1

v PARAGUAY

			E	*P*
WC1986	18 June	Mexico City	3	0
2002	17 Apr	Liverpool	4	0
WC2006	10 June	Frankfurt	1	0

v PERU

			E	*P*
1959	17 May	Lima	1	4
1962	20 May	Lima	4	0
2014	30 May	Wembley	3	0

v POLAND

			E	*P*
1966	5 Jan	Everton	1	1
1966	5 July	Chorzow	1	0
WC1973	6 June	Chorzow	0	2
WC1973	17 Oct	Wembley	1	1
WC1986	11 June	Monterrey	3	0
WC1989	3 June	Wembley	3	0
WC1989	11 Oct	Katowice	0	0
EC1990	17 Oct	Wembley	2	0
EC1991	13 Nov	Poznan	1	1
WC1993	29 May	Katowice	1	1
WC1993	8 Sept	Wembley	3	0
WC1996	9 Oct	Wembley	2	1
WC1997	31 May	Katowice	2	0
EC1999	27 Mar	Wembley	3	1
EC1999	8 Sept	Warsaw	0	0
WC2004	8 Sept	Katowice	2	1
WC2005	12 Oct	Old Trafford	2	1
WC2012	17 Oct	Warsaw	1	1
WC2013	15 Oct	Wembley	2	0

v PORTUGAL

			E	*P*
1947	25 May	Lisbon	10	0
1950	14 May	Lisbon	5	3
1951	19 May	Everton	5	2
1955	22 May	Oporto	1	3
1958	7 May	Wembley	2	1
WC1961	21 May	Lisbon	1	1
WC1961	25 Oct	Wembley	2	0
1964	17 May	Lisbon	4	3
1964	4 June	São Paulo	1	1
WC1966	26 July	Wembley	2	1
1969	10 Dec	Wembley	1	0
1974	3 Apr	Lisbon	0	0
EC1974	20 Nov	Wembley	0	0
EC1975	19 Nov	Lisbon	1	1
WC1986	3 June	Monterrey	0	1
1995	12 Dec	Wembley	1	1
1998	22 Apr	Wembley	3	0
EC2000	12 June	Eindhoven	2	3
2002	7 Sept	Villa Park	1	1
2004	18 Feb	Faro	1	1
EC2004	24 June	Lisbon	2	2*
WC2006	1 July	Gelsenkirchen	0	0
2016	2 June	Wembley	1	0

v REPUBLIC OF IRELAND

			E	*RI*
1946	30 Sept	Dublin	1	0
1949	21 Sept	Everton	0	2
WC1957	8 May	Wembley	5	1
WC1957	19 May	Dublin	1	1
1964	24 May	Dublin	3	1
1976	8 Sept	Wembley	1	1
EC1978	25 Oct	Dublin	1	1
EC1980	6 Feb	Wembley	2	0
1985	26 Mar	Wembley	2	1
EC1988	12 June	Stuttgart	0	1
WC1990	11 June	Cagliari	1	1
EC1990	14 Nov	Dublin	1	1
EC1991	27 Mar	Wembley	1	1
1995	15 Feb	Dublin	0	1
(abandoned after 27 mins)				
2013	29 May	Wembley	1	1
2015	7 June	Dublin	0	0

v ROMANIA

			E	*R*
1939	24 May	Bucharest	2	0
1968	6 Nov	Bucharest	0	0
1969	15 Jan	Wembley	1	1
WC1970	2 June	Guadalajara	1	0
WC1980	15 Oct	Bucharest	1	2
WC1981	29 April	Wembley	0	0
WC1985	1 May	Bucharest	0	0
WC1985	11 Sept	Wembley	1	1
1994	12 Oct	Wembley	1	1
WC1998	22 June	Toulouse	1	2
EC2000	20 June	Charleroi	2	3

v RUSSIA

			E	*R*
EC2007	12 Sept	Wembley	3	0
EC2007	17 Oct	Moscow	1	2
EC2016	11 June	Marseille	1	1

v SAN MARINO

			E	*SM*
WC1992	17 Feb	Wembley	6	0
WC1993	17 Nov	Bologna	7	1
WC2012	12 Oct	Wembley	5	0
WC2013	22 Mar	Serravalle	8	0
EC2014	9 Oct	Wembley	5	0
EC2015	5 Sept	Serravalle	6	0

		v SAUDI ARABIA	*E*	*SA*
1988	16 Nov	Riyadh	1	1
1998	23 May	Wembley	0	0

		v SERBIA-MONTENEGRO	*E*	*SM*
2003	3 June	Leicester	2	1

		v SLOVAKIA	*E*	*S*
EC2002	12 Oct	Bratislava	2	1
EC2003	11 June	Middlesbrough	2	1
2009	28 Mar	Wembley	4	0
EC2016	20 June	Lille	0	0
WC2016	4 Sept	Trnava	1	0
WC2017	4 Sept	Wembley	2	1

		v SLOVENIA	*E*	*S*
2009	5 Sept	Wembley	2	1
WC2010	23 June	Port Elizabeth	1	0
EC2014	15 Nov	Wembley	3	1
EC2015	14 June	Ljubljana	3	2
WC2016	11 Oct	Ljubljana	0	0
WC2017	5 Oct	Wembley	1	0

		v SOUTH AFRICA	*E*	*SA*
1997	24 May	Old Trafford	2	1
2003	22 May	Durban	2	1

		v SPAIN	*E*	*S*
1929	15 May	Madrid	3	4
1931	9 Dec	Highbury	7	1
WC1950	2 July	Rio de Janeiro	0	1
1955	18 May	Madrid	1	1
1955	30 Nov	Wembley	4	1
1960	15 May	Madrid	0	3
1960	26 Oct	Wembley	4	2
1965	8 Dec	Madrid	2	0
1967	24 May	Wembley	2	0
EC1968	3 Apr	Wembley	1	0
EC1968	8 May	Madrid	2	1
1980	26 Mar	Barcelona	2	0
EC1980	18 June	Naples	2	1
1981	25 Mar	Wembley	1	2
WC1982	5 July	Madrid	0	0
1987	18 Feb	Madrid	4	2
1992	9 Sept	Santander	0	1
EC 1996	22 June	Wembley	0	0
2001	28 Feb	Villa Park	3	0
2004	17 Nov	Madrid	0	1
2007	7 Feb	Old Trafford	0	1
2009	11 Feb	Seville	0	2
2011	12 Nov	Wembley	1	0
2015	13 Nov	Alicante	0	2
2016	15 Nov	Wembley	2	2
NL2018	8 Sept	Wembley	1	2
NL2018	15 Oct	Seville	3	2

		v SWEDEN	*E*	*S*
1923	21 May	Stockholm	4	2
1923	24 May	Stockholm	3	1
1937	17 May	Stockholm	4	0
1947	19 Nov	Highbury	4	2
1949	13 May	Stockholm	1	3
1956	16 May	Stockholm	0	0
1959	28 Oct	Wembley	2	3
1965	16 May	Gothenburg	2	1
1968	22 May	Wembley	3	1
1979	10 June	Stockholm	0	0
1986	10 Sept	Stockholm	0	1
WC1988	19 Oct	Wembley	0	0
WC1989	6 Sept	Stockholm	0	0
EC1992	17 June	Stockholm	1	2
UI1995	8 June	Leeds	3	3
EC1998	5 Sept	Stockholm	1	2
EC1999	5 June	Wembley	0	0
2001	10 Nov	Old Trafford	1	1
WC2002	2 June	Saitama	1	1
2004	31 Mar	Gothenburg	0	1
WC2006	20 June	Cologne	2	2
2011	15 Nov	Wembley	1	0
EC2012	15 June	Kiev	3	2
2012	14 Nov	Stockholm	2	4
WC2018	7 July	Samara	2	0

		v SWITZERLAND	*E*	*S*
1933	20 May	Berne	4	0
1938	21 May	Zurich	1	2
1947	18 May	Zurich	0	1
1948	2 Dec	Highbury	6	0
1952	28 May	Zurich	3	0
WC1954	20 June	Berne	2	0
1962	9 May	Wembley	3	1
1963	5 June	Basle	8	1
EC1971	13 Oct	Basle	3	2
EC1971	10 Nov	Wembley	1	1
1975	3 Sept	Basle	2	1
1977	7 Sept	Wembley	0	0
WC1980	19 Nov	Wembley	2	1
WC1981	30 May	Basle	1	2
1988	28 May	Lausanne	1	0
1995	15 Nov	Wembley	3	1
EC1996	8 June	Wembley	1	1
1998	25 Mar	Berne	1	1
EC2004	17 June	Coimbra	3	0
2008	6 Feb	Wembley	2	1
EC1989	8 Mar	Tirana	2	0
EC2010	7 Sept	Basle	3	1
EC2011	4 June	Wembley	2	2
EC2014	8 Sept	Basle	2	0
EC2015	8 Sept	Wembley	2	0
2018	11 Sept	Leicester	1	0
NL2019	9 June	Guimaraes	0	0

		v TRINIDAD & TOBAGO	*E*	*TT*
WC2006	15 June	Nuremberg	2	0
2008	2 June	Port of Spain	3	0

		v TUNISIA	*E*	*T*
1990	2 June	Tunis	1	1
WC1998	15 June	Marseilles	2	0
WC2018	18 June	Volgograd	2	1

		v TURKEY	*E*	*T*
WC1984	14 Nov	Istanbul	8	0
WC1985	16 Oct	Wembley	5	0
EC1987	29 Apr	Izmir	0	0
EC1987	14 Oct	Wembley	8	0
EC1991	1 May	Izmir	1	0
EC1991	16 Oct	Wembley	1	0
WC1992	18 Nov	Wembley	4	0
WC1993	31 Mar	Izmir	2	0
EC2003	2 Apr	Sunderland	2	0
EC2003	11 Oct	Istanbul	0	0
2016	22 May	Etihad Stadium	2	1

		v UKRAINE	*E*	*U*
2000	31 May	Wembley	2	0
2004	18 Aug	Newcastle	3	0
WC2009	1 Apr	Wembley	2	1
WC2009	10 Oct	Dnepr	0	1
EC2012	19 June	Donetsk	1	0
WC2012	11 Sept	Wembley	1	1
WC2013	10 Sept	Kiev	0	0

		v URUGUAY	*E*	*U*
1953	31 May	Montevideo	1	2
WC1954	26 June	Basle	2	4
1964	6 May	Wembley	2	1
WC1966	11 July	Wembley	0	0
1969	8 June	Montevideo	2	1
1977	15 June	Montevideo	0	0
1984	13 June	Montevideo	0	2
1990	22 May	Wembley	1	2
1995	29 Mar	Wembley	0	0
2006	1 Mar	Liverpool	2	1
WC2014	19 June	Sao Paulo	1	2

		v USA	*E*	*USA*
WC1950	29 June	Belo Horizonte	0	1
1953	8 June	New York	6	3
1959	28 May	Los Angeles	8	1
1964	27 May	New York	10	0
1985	16 June	Los Angeles	5	0
1993	9 June	Foxboro	0	2
1994	7 Sept	Wembley	2	0
2005	28 May	Chicago	2	1

			E	*USA*
2008	28 May	Wembley	2	0
wc2010	12 June	Rustenburg	1	1
2018	15 Nov	Wembley	3	0

v USSR			*E*	*USSR*
1958	18 May	Moscow	1	1
wc1958	8 June	Gothenburg	2	2
wc1958	17 June	Gothenburg	0	1
1958	22 Oct	Wembley	5	0
1967	6 Dec	Wembley	2	2
EC1968	8 June	Rome	2	0
1973	10 June	Moscow	2	1
1984	2 June	Wembley	0	2
1986	26 Mar	Tbilisi	1	0
EC1988	18 June	Frankfurt	1	3
1991	21 May	Wembley	3	1

v YUGOSLAVIA			*E*	*Y*
1939	18 May	Belgrade	1	2
1950	22 Nov	Highbury	2	2
1954	16 May	Belgrade	0	1
1956	28 Nov	Wembley	3	0
1958	11 May	Belgrade	0	5
1960	11 May	Wembley	3	3
1965	9 May	Belgrade	1	1
1966	4 May	Wembley	2	0
EC1968	5 June	Florence	0	1
1972	11 Oct	Wembley	1	1
1974	5 June	Belgrade	2	2
EC1986	12 Nov	Wembley	2	0
EC1987	11 Nov	Belgrade	4	1
1989	13 Dec	Wembley	2	1

SCOTLAND

v ALBANIA			*S*	*A*
NL2018	10 Sept	Glasgow	2	0
NL2018	17 Nov	Shkoder	4	0

v ARGENTINA			*S*	*A*
1977	18 June	Buenos Aires	1	1
1979	2 June	Glasgow	1	3
1990	28 Mar	Glasgow	1	0
2008	19 Nov	Glasgow	0	1

v AUSTRALIA			*S*	*A*
wc1985	20 Nov	Glasgow	2	0
wc1985	4 Dec	Melbourne	0	0
1996	27 Mar	Glasgow	1	0
2000	15 Nov	Glasgow	0	2
2012	15 Aug	Easter Road	3	1

v AUSTRIA			*S*	*A*
1931	16 May	Vienna	0	5
1933	29 Nov	Glasgow	2	2
1937	9 May	Vienna	1	1
1950	13 Dec	Glasgow	0	1
1951	27 May	Vienna	0	4
wc1954	16 June	Zurich	0	1
1955	19 May	Vienna	4	1
1956	2 May	Glasgow	1	1
1960	29 May	Vienna	1	4
1963	8 May	Glasgow	4	1
(*abandoned after 79 mins*)				
wc1968	6 Nov	Glasgow	2	1
wc1969	5 Nov	Vienna	0	2
EC1978	20 Sept	Vienna	2	3
EC1979	17 Oct	Glasgow	1	1
1994	20 Apr	Vienna	2	1
wc1996	31 Aug	Vienna	0	0
wc1997	2 Apr	Celtic Park	2	0
2003	30 Apr	Glasgow	0	2
2005	17 Aug	Graz	2	2
2007	30 May	Vienna	1	0

v BELARUS			*S*	*B*
wc1997	8 June	Minsk	1	0
wc1997	7 Sept	Aberdeen	4	1
wc2005	8 June	Minsk	0	0
wc2005	8 Oct	Glasgow	0	1

v BELGIUM			*S*	*B*
1946	23 Jan	Glasgow	2	2
1947	18 May	Brussels	1	2
1948	28 Apr	Glasgow	2	0
1951	20 May	Brussels	5	0
EC1971	3 Feb	Liege	0	3
EC1971	10 Nov	Aberdeen	1	0
1974	1 June	Brussels	1	2
EC1979	21 Nov	Brussels	0	2
EC1979	19 Dec	Glasgow	1	3
EC1982	15 Dec	Brussels	2	3
EC1983	12 Oct	Glasgow	1	1
EC1987	1 Apr	Brussels	1	4
EC1987	14 Oct	Glasgow	2	0
wc2001	24 Mar	Glasgow	2	2

			S	*B*
wc2001	5 Sept	Brussels	0	2
wc2012	16 Oct	Brussels	0	2
wc2013	6 Sept	Glasgow	0	2
2018	7 Sept	Glasgow	0	4
EC2019	11 June	Brussels	0	3
EC2019	**9 Sept**	**Glasgow**	**0**	**4**

v BOSNIA-HERZEGOVINA			*S*	*BH*
EC1999	4 Sept	Sarajevo	2	1
EC1999	5 Oct	Ibrox	1	0

v BRAZIL			*S*	*B*
1966	25 June	Glasgow	1	1
1972	5 July	Rio de Janeiro	0	1
1973	30 June	Glasgow	0	1
wc1974	18 June	Frankfurt	0	0
1977	23 June	Rio de Janeiro	0	2
wc1982	18 June	Seville	1	4
1987	26 May	Glasgow	0	2
wc1990	20 June	Turin	0	1
wc1998	10 June	St Denis	1	2
2011	27 Mar	Emirates	0	2

v BULGARIA			*S*	*B*
1978	22 Feb	Glasgow	2	1
EC1986	10 Sept	Glasgow	0	0
EC1987	11 Nov	Sofia	1	0
EC1990	14 Nov	Sofia	1	1
EC1991	27 Mar	Glasgow	1	1
2006	11 May	Kobe	5	1

v CANADA			*S*	*C*
1983	12 June	Vancouver	2	0
1983	16 June	Edmonton	3	0
1983	20 June	Toronto	2	0
1992	21 May	Toronto	3	1
2002	15 Oct	Easter Road	3	1
2017	22 Mar	Easter Road	1	1

v CHILE			*S*	*C*
1977	15 June	Santiago	4	2
1989	30 May	Glasgow	2	0

v CIS			*S*	*C*
EC1992	18 June	Norrkoping	3	0

v COLOMBIA			*S*	*C*
1988	17 May	Glasgow	0	0
1996	29 May	Miami	0	1
1998	23 May	New York	2	2

v COSTA RICA			*S*	*CR*
wc1990	11 June	Genoa	0	1
2018	23 Mar	Glasgow	0	1

v CROATIA			*S*	*C*
wc2000	11 Oct	Zagreb	1	1
wc2001	1 Sept	Glasgow	0	0
2008	26 Mar	Glasgow	1	1
wc2013	7 June	Zagreb	1	0
wc2013	15 Oct	Glasgow	2	0

v CYPRUS			*S*	*C*
WC1968	11 Dec	Nicosia	5	0
WC1969	17 May	Glasgow	8	0
WC1989	8 Feb	Limassol	3	2
WC1989	26 Apr	Glasgow	2	1
2011	11 Nov	Larnaca	2	1
EC2019	8 June	Glasgow	2	1
EC2019	**16 Nov**	**Nicosia**	**2**	**1**

v CZECHOSLOVAKIA			*S*	*C*
1937	15 May	Prague	3	1
1937	8 Dec	Glasgow	5	0
WC1961	14 May	Bratislava	0	4
WC1961	26 Sept	Glasgow	3	2
WC1961	29 Nov	Brussels	2	4*
1972	2 July	Porto Alegre	0	0
WC1973	26 Sept	Glasgow	2	1
WC1973	17 Oct	Bratislava	0	1
WC1976	13 Oct	Prague	0	2
WC1977	21 Sept	Glasgow	3	1

v CZECH REPUBLIC			*S*	*C*
EC1999	31 Mar	Glasgow	1	2
EC1999	9 June	Prague	2	3
2008	30 May	Prague	1	3
2010	3 Mar	Glasgow	1	0
EC2010	8 Oct	Prague	0	1
EC2011	3 Sept	Glasgow	2	2
2016	24 Mar	Prague	1	0

v DENMARK			*S*	*D*
1951	12 May	Glasgow	3	1
1952	25 May	Copenhagen	2	1
1968	16 Oct	Copenhagen	1	0
EC1970	11 Nov	Glasgow	1	0
EC1971	9 June	Copenhagen	0	1
WC1972	18 Oct	Copenhagen	4	1
WC1972	15 Nov	Glasgow	2	0
EC1975	3 Sept	Copenhagen	1	0
EC1975	29 Oct	Glasgow	3	1
WC1986	4 June	Nezahualcoyotl	0	1
1996	24 Apr	Copenhagen	0	2
1998	25 Mar	Ibrox	0	1
2002	21 Aug	Glasgow	0	1
2004	28 Apr	Copenhagen	0	1
2011	10 Aug	Glasgow	2	1
2016	29 Mar	Glasgow	1	0

v ECUADOR			*S*	*E*
1995	24 May	Toyama	2	1

v EGYPT			*S*	*E*
1990	16 May	Aberdeen	1	3

v ESTONIA			*S*	*E*
WC1993	19 May	Tallinn	3	0
WC1993	2 June	Aberdeen	3	1
WC1997	11 Feb	Monaco	0	0
WC1997	29 Mar	Kilmarnock	2	0
EC1998	10 Oct	Tynecastle	3	2
EC1999	8 Sept	Tallinn	0	0
2004	27 May	Tallinn	1	0
2013	6 Feb	Aberdeen	1	0

v FAROE ISLANDS			*S*	*F*
EC1994	12 Oct	Glasgow	5	1
EC1995	7 June	Toftir	2	0
EC1998	14 Oct	Aberdeen	2	1
EC1999	5 June	Toftir	1	1
EC2002	7 Sept	Toftir	2	2
EC2003	6 Sept	Glasgow	3	1
EC2006	2 Sept	Celtic Park	6	0
EC2007	6 June	Toftir	2	0
2010	16 Nov	Aberdeen	3	0

v FINLAND			*S*	*F*
1954	25 May	Helsinki	2	1
WC1964	21 Oct	Glasgow	3	1
WC1965	27 May	Helsinki	2	1
1976	8 Sept	Glasgow	6	0
1992	25 Mar	Glasgow	1	1
EC1994	7 Sept	Helsinki	2	0
EC1995	6 Sept	Glasgow	1	0
1998	22 Apr	Easter Road	1	1

v FRANCE			*S*	*F*
1930	18 May	Paris	2	0
1932	8 May	Paris	3	1
1948	23 May	Paris	0	3
1949	27 Apr	Glasgow	2	0
1950	27 May	Paris	1	0
1951	16 May	Glasgow	1	0
WC1958	15 June	Orebro	1	2
1984	1 June	Marseilles	0	2
WC1989	8 Mar	Glasgow	2	0
WC1989	11 Oct	Paris	0	3
1997	12 Nov	St Etienne	1	2
2000	29 Mar	Glasgow	0	2
2002	27 Mar	Paris	0	5
EC2006	7 Oct	Glasgow	1	0
EC2007	12 Sept	Paris	1	0
2016	4 June	Metz	0	3

v GEORGIA			*S*	*G*
EC2007	24 Mar	Glasgow	2	1
EC2007	17 Oct	Tbilisi	0	2
EC2014	11 Oct	Ibrox	1	0
EC2015	4 Sept	Tblisi	0	1

v GERMANY			*S*	*G*
1929	1 June	Berlin	1	1
1936	14 Oct	Glasgow	2	0
EC1992	15 June	Norrkoping	0	2
1993	24 Mar	Glasgow	0	1
1999	28 Apr	Bremen	1	0
EC2003	7 June	Glasgow	1	1
EC2003	10 Sept	Dortmund	1	2
EC2014	7 Sept	Dortmund	1	2
EC2015	7 Sept	Glasgow	2	3

v EAST GERMANY			*S*	*EG*
1974	30 Oct	Glasgow	3	0
1977	7 Sept	East Berlin	0	1
EC1982	13 Oct	Glasgow	2	0
EC1983	16 Nov	Halle	1	2
1985	16 Oct	Glasgow	0	0
1990	25 Apr	Glasgow	0	1

v WEST GERMANY			*S*	*WG*
1957	22 May	Stuttgart	3	1
1959	6 May	Glasgow	3	2
1964	12 May	Hanover	2	2
WC1969	16 Apr	Glasgow	1	1
WC1969	22 Oct	Hamburg	2	3
1973	14 Nov	Glasgow	1	1
1974	27 Mar	Frankfurt	1	2
WC1986	8 June	Queretaro	1	2

v GIBRALTAR			*S*	*G*
EC2015	29 Mar	Hampden	6	1
EC2015	11 Oct	Faro	6	0

v GREECE			*S*	*G*
EC1994	18 Dec	Athens	0	1
EC1995	16 Aug	Glasgow	1	0

v HONG KONG XI			*S*	*HK*
†2002	23 May	Hong Kong	4	0

†match not recognised by FIFA

v HUNGARY			*S*	*H*
1938	7 Dec	Ibrox	3	1
1954	8 Dec	Glasgow	2	4
1955	29 May	Budapest	1	3
1958	7 May	Glasgow	1	1
1960	5 June	Budapest	3	3
1980	31 May	Budapest	1	3
1987	9 Sept	Glasgow	2	0
2004	18 Aug	Glasgow	0	3
2018	27 Mar	Budapest	1	0

v ICELAND			*S*	*I*
WC1984	17 Oct	Glasgow	3	0
WC1985	28 May	Reykjavik	1	0
EC2002	12 Oct	Reykjavik	2	0
EC2003	29 Mar	Glasgow	2	1
WC2008	10 Sept	Reykjavik	2	1
WC2009	1 Apr	Glasgow	2	1

v IRAN			*S*	*I*
WC1978	7 June	Cordoba	1	1

v ISRAEL			*S*	*I*
WC1981	25 Feb	Tel Aviv	1	0
WC1981	28 Apr	Glasgow	3	1
1986	28 Jan	Tel Aviv	1	0
NL2018	11 Oct	Haifa	1	2
NL2018	20 Nov	Glasgow	3	2

v ITALY			*S*	*I*
1931	20 May	Rome	0	3
WC1965	9 Nov	Glasgow	1	0
WC1965	7 Dec	Naples	0	3
1988	22 Dec	Perugia	0	2
WC1992	18 Nov	Ibrox	0	0
WC1993	13 Oct	Rome	1	3
WC2005	26 Mar	Milan	0	2
WC2005	3 Sept	Glasgow	1	1
EC2007	28 Mar	Bari	0	2
EC2007	17 Nov	Glasgow	1	2
2016	29 May	Ta'Qali	0	1

v JAPAN			*S*	*J*
1995	21 May	Hiroshima	0	0
2006	13 May	Saitama	0	0
2009	10 Oct	Yokohama	0	2

v KAZAKHSTAN			*S*	*K*
EC2019	21 Mar	Astana	0	3
EC2019	**19 Nov**	**Glasgow**	**3**	**1**

v KOREA REPUBLIC			*S*	*KR*
2002	16 May	Busan	1	4

v LATVIA			*S*	*L*
WC1996	5 Oct	Riga	2	0
WC1997	11 Oct	Celtic Park	2	0
WC2000	2 Sept	Riga	1	0
WC2001	6 Oct	Glasgow	2	1

v LIECHTENSTEIN			*S*	*L*
EC2010	7 Sept	Glasgow	2	1
EC2011	8 Oct	Vaduz	1	0

v LITHUANIA			*S*	*L*
EC1998	5 Sept	Vilnius	0	0
EC1999	9 Oct	Glasgow	3	0
EC2003	2 Apr	Kaunas	0	1
EC2003	11 Oct	Glasgow	1	0
EC2006	6 Sept	Kaunas	2	1
EC2007	8 Sept	Glasgow	3	1
EC2010	3 Sept	Kaunas	0	0
EC2011	6 Sept	Glasgow	1	0
WC2016	8 Oct	Hampden	1	1
WC2017	1 Sept	Vilnius	3	0

v LUXEMBOURG			*S*	*L*
1947	24 May	Luxembourg	6	0
EC1986	12 Nov	Glasgow	3	0
EC1987	2 Dec	Esch	0	0
2012	14 Nov	Luxembourg	2	1

v MALTA			*S*	*M*
1988	22 Mar	Valletta	1	1
1990	28 May	Valletta	2	1
WC1993	17 Feb	Ibrox	3	0
WC1993	17 Nov	Valletta	2	0
1997	1 June	Valletta	3	2
WC2016	4 Sept	Ta'Qali	5	1
WC2017	4 Sept	Glasgow	2	0

v MEXICO			*S*	*M*
2018	3 June	Mexico City	0	1

v MOLDOVA			*S*	*M*
WC2004	13 Oct	Chisinau	1	1
WC2005	4 June	Glasgow	2	0

v MOROCCO			*S*	*M*
WC1998	23 June	St Etienne	0	3

v NETHERLANDS			*S*	*N*
1929	4 June	Amsterdam	2	0
1938	21 May	Amsterdam	3	1
1959	27 May	Amsterdam	2	1
1966	11 May	Glasgow	0	3
1968	30 May	Amsterdam	0	0
1971	1 Dec	Amsterdam	1	2
WC1978	11 June	Mendoza	3	2
1982	23 Mar	Glasgow	2	1
1986	29 Apr	Eindhoven	0	0
EC1992	12 June	Gothenburg	0	1
1994	23 Mar	Glasgow	0	1
1994	27 May	Utrecht	1	3
EC1996	10 June	Villa Park	0	0
2000	26 Apr	Arnhem	0	0
EC2003	15 Nov	Glasgow	1	0
EC2003	19 Nov	Amsterdam	0	6
WC2009	28 Mar	Amsterdam	0	3
WC2009	9 Sept	Glasgow	0	1
2017	9 Nov	Aberdeen	0	1

v NEW ZEALAND			*S*	*NZ*
WC1982	15 June	Malaga	5	2
2003	27 May	Tynecastle	1	1

v NIGERIA			*S*	*N*
2002	17 Apr	Aberdeen	1	2
2014	28 May	Craven Cottage	2	2

v NORTH MACEDONIA			*S*	*M*
WC2008	6 Sept	Skopje	0	1
WC2009	5 Sept	Glasgow	2	0
WC2012	11 Sept	Glasgow	1	1
WC2013	10 Sept	Skopje	2	1

v NORWAY			*S*	*N*
1929	26 May	Oslo	7	3
1954	5 May	Glasgow	1	0
1954	19 May	Oslo	1	1
1963	4 June	Bergen	3	4
1963	7 Nov	Glasgow	6	1
1974	6 June	Oslo	2	1
EC1978	25 Oct	Glasgow	3	2
EC1979	7 June	Oslo	4	0
WC1988	14 Sept	Oslo	2	1
WC1989	15 Nov	Glasgow	1	1
1992	3 June	Oslo	0	0
WC1998	16 June	Bordeaux	1	1
2003	20 Aug	Oslo	0	0
WC2004	9 Oct	Glasgow	0	1
WC2005	7 Sept	Oslo	2	1
WC2008	11 Oct	Glasgow	0	0
WC2009	12 Aug	Oslo	0	4
2013	19 Nov	Molde	1	0

v PARAGUAY			*S*	*P*
WC1958	11 June	Norrkoping	2	3

v PERU			*S*	*P*
1972	26 Apr	Glasgow	2	0
WC1978	3 June	Cordoba	1	3
1979	12 Sept	Glasgow	1	1
2018	30 May	Lima	0	2

v POLAND			*S*	*P*
1958	1 June	Warsaw	2	1
1960	4 May	Glasgow	2	3
WC1965	23 May	Chorzow	1	1
WC1965	13 Oct	Glasgow	1	2
1980	28 May	Poznan	0	1
1990	19 May	Glasgow	1	1
2001	25 Apr	Bydgoszcz	1	1
2014	5 Mar	Warsaw	1	0
EC2014	14 Oct	Warsaw	2	2
EC2015	8 Oct	Glasgow	2	2

v PORTUGAL			*S*	*P*
1950	21 May	Lisbon	2	2
1955	4 May	Glasgow	3	0
1959	3 June	Lisbon	0	1
1966	18 June	Glasgow	0	1
EC1971	21 Apr	Lisbon	0	2
EC1971	13 Oct	Glasgow	2	1
1975	13 May	Glasgow	1	0
EC1978	29 Nov	Lisbon	0	1
EC1980	26 Mar	Glasgow	4	1
WC1980	15 Oct	Glasgow	0	0

			S	*P*
wc1981	18 Nov	Lisbon	1	2
wc1992	14 Oct	Ibrox	0	0
wc1993	28 Apr	Lisbon	0	5
2002	20 Nov	Braga	0	2
2018	14 Oct	Glasgow	1	3

v QATAR

			S	*Q*
2015	5 June	Easter Road	1	0

v REPUBLIC OF IRELAND

			S	*RI*
wc1961	3 May	Glasgow	4	1
wc1961	7 May	Dublin	3	0
1963	9 June	Dublin	0	1
1969	21 Sept	Dublin	1	1
EC1986	15 Oct	Dublin	0	0
EC1987	18 Feb	Glasgow	0	1
2000	30 May	Dublin	2	1
2003	12 Feb	Glasgow	0	2
NC2011	29 May	Dublin	0	1
EC2014	14 Nov	Hampden	1	0
EC2015	13 June	Dublin	1	1

v ROMANIA

			S	*R*
EC1975	1 June	Bucharest	1	1
EC1975	17 Dec	Glasgow	1	1
1986	26 Mar	Glasgow	3	0
EC1990	12 Sept	Glasgow	2	1
EC1991	16 Oct	Bucharest	0	1
2004	31 Mar	Glasgow	1	2

v RUSSIA

			S	*R*
EC1994	16 Nov	Glasgow	1	1
EC1995	29 Mar	Moscow	0	0
EC2019	**6 Sept**	**Glasgow**	**1**	**2**
EC2019	**10 Oct**	**Moscow**	**0**	**4**

v SAN MARINO

			S	*SM*
EC1991	1 May	Serravalle	2	0
EC1991	13 Nov	Glasgow	4	0
EC1995	26 Apr	Serravalle	2	0
EC1995	15 Nov	Glasgow	5	0
wc2000	7 Oct	Serravalle	2	0
wc2001	28 Mar	Glasgow	4	0
EC2019	24 Mar	Serravalle	2	0
EC2019	**13 Oct**	**Glasgow**	**6**	**0**

v SAUDI ARABIA

			S	*SA*
1988	17 Feb	Riyadh	2	2

v SERBIA

			S	*Se*
wc2012	8 Sept	Glasgow	0	0
wc2013	26 Mar	Novi Sad	0	2

v SLOVAKIA

			S	*Sl*
wc2016	11 Oct	Trnava	0	3
wc2017	5 Oct	Glasgow	1	0

v SLOVENIA

			S	*Sl*
wc2004	8 Sept	Glasgow	0	0
wc2005	12 Oct	Celje	3	0
2012	29 Feb	Koper	1	1
wc2017	26 Mar	Hampden	1	0
wc2017	8 Oct	Ljubljana	2	2

v SOUTH AFRICA

			S	*SA*
2002	20 May	Hong Kong	0	2
2007	22 Aug	Aberdeen	1	0

v SPAIN

			S	*Sp*
wc1957	8 May	Glasgow	4	2
wc1957	26 May	Madrid	1	4
1963	13 June	Madrid	6	2
1965	8 May	Glasgow	0	0
EC1974	20 Nov	Glasgow	1	2
EC1975	5 Feb	Valencia	1	1
1982	24 Feb	Valencia	0	3
wc1984	14 Nov	Glasgow	3	1
wc1985	27 Feb	Seville	0	1
1988	27 Apr	Madrid	0	0
2004	3 Sept	Valencia	1	1

Match abandoned after 60 minutes; floodlight failure.

			S	*Sp*
EC2010	12 Oct	Glasgow	2	3
EC2011	11 Oct	Alicante	1	3

v SWEDEN

			S	*Sw*
1952	30 May	Stockholm	1	3
1953	6 May	Glasgow	1	2
1975	16 Apr	Gothenburg	1	1
1977	27 Apr	Glasgow	3	1
wc1980	10 Sept	Stockholm	1	0
wc1981	9 Sept	Glasgow	2	0
wc1990	16 June	Genoa	2	1
1995	11 Oct	Stockholm	0	2
wc1996	10 Nov	Ibrox	1	0
wc1997	30 Apr	Gothenburg	1	2
2004	17 Nov	Easter Road	1	4
2010	11 Aug	Stockholm	0	3

v SWITZERLAND

			S	*Sw*
1931	24 May	Geneva	3	2
1946	15 May	Glasgow	3	1
1948	17 May	Berne	1	2
1950	26 Apr	Glasgow	3	1
wc1957	19 May	Basle	2	1
wc1957	6 Nov	Glasgow	3	2
1973	22 June	Berne	0	1
1976	7 Apr	Glasgow	1	0
EC1982	17 Nov	Berne	0	2
EC1983	30 May	Glasgow	2	2
EC1990	17 Oct	Glasgow	2	1
EC1991	11 Sept	Berne	2	2
wc1992	9 Sept	Berne	1	3
wc1993	8 Sept	Aberdeen	1	1
wc1996	18 June	Villa Park	1	0
2006	1 Mar	Glasgow	1	3

v TRINIDAD & TOBAGO

			S	*TT*
2004	30 May	Easter Road	4	1

v TURKEY

			S	*T*
1960	8 June	Ankara	2	4

v UKRAINE

			S	*U*
EC2006	11 Oct	Kiev	0	2
EC2007	13 Oct	Glasgow	3	1

v URUGUAY

			S	*U*
wc1954	19 June	Basle	0	7
1962	2 May	Glasgow	2	3
1983	21 Sept	Glasgow	2	0
wc1986	13 June	Nezahualcoyotl	0	0

v USA

			S	*USA*
1952	30 Apr	Glasgow	6	0
1992	17 May	Denver	1	0
1996	26 May	New Britain	1	2
1998	30 May	Washington	0	0
2005	12 Nov	Glasgow	1	1
2012	26 May	Jacksonville	1	5
2013	15 Nov	Glasgow	0	0

v USSR

			S	*USSR*
1967	10 May	Glasgow	0	2
1971	14 June	Moscow	0	1
wc1982	22 June	Malaga	2	2
1991	6 Feb	Ibrox	0	1

v YUGOSLAVIA

			S	*Y*
1955	15 May	Belgrade	2	2
1956	21 Nov	Glasgow	2	0
wc1958	8 June	Vasteras	1	1
1972	29 June	Belo Horizonte	2	2
wc1974	22 June	Frankfurt	1	1
1984	12 Sept	Glasgow	6	1
wc1988	19 Oct	Glasgow	1	1
wc1989	6 Sept	Zagreb	1	3

v ZAIRE

			S	*Z*
wc1974	14 June	Dortmund	2	0

WALES

v ALBANIA			*W*	*A*
EC1994	7 Sept	Cardiff	2	0
EC1995	15 Nov	Tirana	1	1
2018	20 Nov	Elbasan	0	1

v ANDORRA			*W*	*A*
EC2014	9 Sept	La Vella	2	1
EC2015	13 Oct	Cardiff	2	0

v ARGENTINA			*W*	*A*
1992	3 June	Tokyo	0	1
2002	13 Feb	Cardiff	1	1

v ARMENIA			*W*	*A*
WC2001	24 Mar	Erevan	2	2
WC2001	1 Sept	Cardiff	0	0

v AUSTRALIA			*W*	*A*
2011	10 Aug	Cardiff	1	2

v AUSTRIA			*W*	*A*
1954	9 May	Vienna	0	2
1955	23 Nov	Wrexham	1	2
EC1974	4 Sept	Vienna	1	2
1975	19 Nov	Wrexham	1	0
1992	29 Apr	Vienna	1	1
EC2005	26 Mar	Cardiff	0	2
EC2005	30 Mar	Vienna	0	1
2013	6 Feb	Swansea	2	1
WC2016	6 Oct	Vienna	2	2
WC2017	2 Sept	Cardiff	1	0

v AZERBAIJAN			*W*	*A*
EC2002	20 Nov	Baku	2	0
EC2003	29 Mar	Cardiff	4	0
WC2004	4 Sept	Baku	1	1
WC2005	12 Oct	Cardiff	2	0
WC2008	6 Sept	Cardiff	1	0
WC2009	6 June	Baku	1	0
EC2019	**6 Sept**	**Cardiff**	**2**	**1**
EC2019	**16 Nov**	**Baku**	**2**	**0**

v BELARUS			*W*	*B*
EC1998	14 Oct	Cardiff	3	2
EC1999	4 Sept	Minsk	2	1
WC2000	2 Sept	Minsk	1	2
WC2001	6 Oct	Cardiff	1	0
2019	**9 Sept**	**Cardiff**	**1**	**0**

v BELGIUM			*W*	*B*
1949	22 May	Liege	1	3
1949	23 Nov	Cardiff	5	1
EC1990	17 Oct	Cardiff	3	1
EC1991	27 Mar	Brussels	1	1
WC1992	18 Nov	Brussels	0	2
WC1993	31 Mar	Cardiff	2	0
WC1997	29 Mar	Cardiff	1	2
WC1997	11 Oct	Brussels	2	3
WC2012	7 Sept	Cardiff	0	2
WC2013	15 Oct	Brussels	1	1
EC2014	16 Nov	Brussels	0	0
EC2015	12 June	Cardiff	1	0
EC2016	1 July	Lille	3	1

v BOSNIA-HERZEGOVINA			*W*	*BH*
2003	12 Feb	Cardiff	2	2
2012	15 Aug	Llanelli	0	2
EC2014	10 Oct	Cardiff	0	0
EC2015	10 Oct	Zenica	0	2

v BRAZIL			*W*	*B*
WC1958	19 June	Gothenburg	0	1
1962	12 May	Rio de Janeiro	1	3
1962	16 May	São Paulo	1	3
1966	14 May	Rio de Janeiro	1	3
1966	18 May	Belo Horizonte	0	1
1983	12 June	Cardiff	1	1
1991	11 Sept	Cardiff	1	0
1997	12 Nov	Brasilia	0	3
2000	23 May	Cardiff	0	3
2006	5 Sept	Cardiff	0	2

v BULGARIA			*W*	*B*
EC1983	27 Apr	Wrexham	1	0
EC1983	16 Nov	Sofia	0	1
EC1994	14 Dec	Cardiff	0	3
EC1995	29 Mar	Sofia	1	3
2006	15 Aug	Swansea	0	0
2007	22 Aug	Burgas	1	0
EC2010	8 Oct	Cardiff	0	1
EC2011	12 Oct	Sofia	1	0

v CANADA			*W*	*C*
1986	10 May	Toronto	0	2
1986	20 May	Vancouver	3	0
2004	30 May	Wrexham	1	0

v CHILE			*W*	*C*
1966	22 May	Santiago	0	2
2014	4 June	Valparaiso	0	2

v CHINA			*W*	*C*
2018	22 Mar	Nanning	6	0

v COSTA RICA			*W*	*CR*
1990	20 May	Cardiff	1	0
2012	29 Feb	Cardiff	0	1

v CROATIA			*W*	*C*
2002	21 Aug	Varazdin	1	1
2010	23 May	Osijek	0	2
WC2012	16 Oct	Osijek	0	2
WC2013	26 Mar	Swansea	1	2
EC2019	8 June	Osijek	1	2
EC2019	**13 Oct**	**Cardiff**	**1**	**1**

v CYPRUS			*W*	*C*
WC1992	14 Oct	Limassol	1	0
WC1993	13 Oct	Cardiff	2	0
2005	16 Nov	Limassol	0	1
EC2006	11 Oct	Cardiff	3	1
EC2007	13 Oct	Nicosia	1	3
EC2014	13 Oct	Cardiff	2	1
EC2015	3 Sept	Nicosia	1	0

v CZECHOSLOVAKIA			*W*	*C*
WC1957	1 May	Cardiff	1	0
WC1957	26 May	Prague	0	2
EC1971	21 Apr	Swansea	1	3
EC1971	27 Oct	Prague	0	1
WC1977	30 Mar	Wrexham	3	0
WC1977	16 Nov	Prague	0	1
WC1980	19 Nov	Cardiff	1	0
WC1981	9 Sept	Prague	0	2
EC1987	29 Apr	Wrexham	1	1
EC1987	11 Nov	Prague	0	2
WC1993	28 Apr	Ostrava†	1	1
WC1993	8 Sept	Cardiff†	2	2

†*Czechoslovakia played as RCS (Republic of Czechs and Slovaks).*

v DENMARK				
WC1964	21 Oct	Copenhagen	0	1
WC1965	1 Dec	Wrexham	4	2
EC1987	9 Sept	Cardiff	1	0
EC1987	14 Oct	Copenhagen	0	1
1990	11 Sept	Copenhagen	0	1
EC1998	10 Oct	Copenhagen	2	1
EC1999	9 June	Liverpool	0	2
2008	19 Nov	Brondby	1	0
2018	9 Sept	Aarhus	0	2
NL2018	16 Nov	Cardiff	1	2

v ESTONIA			*W*	*E*
1994	23 May	Tallinn	2	1
2009	29 May	Llanelli	1	0

v FAROE ISLANDS			*W*	*F*
WC1992	9 Sept	Cardiff	6	0
WC1993	6 June	Toftir	3	0

v FINLAND			*W*	*F*
EC1971	26 May	Helsinki	1	0
EC1971	13 Oct	Swansea	3	0
EC1987	10 Sept	Helsinki	1	1

			W	*F*
EC1987	1 Apr	Wrexham	4	0
WC1988	19 Oct	Swansea	2	2
WC1989	6 Sept	Helsinki	0	1
2000	29 Mar	Cardiff	1	2
EC2002	7 Sept	Helsinki	2	0
EC2003	10 Sept	Cardiff	1	1
WC2009	28 Mar	Cardiff	0	2
WC2009	10 Oct	Helsinki	1	2
2013	16 Nov	Cardiff	1	1

v FRANCE			*W*	*F*
1933	25 May	Paris	1	1
1939	20 May	Paris	1	2
1953	14 May	Paris	1	6
1982	2 June	Toulouse	1	0
2017	10 Nov	Paris	0	2

v GEORGIA			*W*	*G*
EC1994	16 Nov	Tbilisi	0	5
EC1995	7 June	Cardiff	0	1
2008	20 Aug	Swansea	1	2
WC2016	9 Oct	Cardiff	1	1
WC2017	6 Oct	Tbilisi	1	0

v GERMANY			*W*	*G*
EC1995	26 Apr	Dusseldorf	1	1
EC1995	11 Oct	Cardiff	1	2
2002	14 May	Cardiff	1	0
EC2007	8 Sept	Cardiff	0	2
EC2007	21 Nov	Frankfurt	0	0
WC2008	15 Oct	Moenchengladbach	0	1
WC2009	1 Apr	Cardiff	0	2

v EAST GERMANY			*W*	*EG*
WC1957	19 May	Leipzig	1	2
WC1957	25 Sept	Cardiff	4	1
WC1969	16 Apr	Dresden	1	2
WC1969	22 Oct	Cardiff	1	3

v WEST GERMANY			*W*	*WG*
1968	8 May	Cardiff	1	1
1969	26 Mar	Frankfurt	1	1
1976	6 Oct	Cardiff	0	2
1977	14 Dec	Dortmund	1	1
EC1979	2 May	Wrexham	0	2
EC1979	17 Oct	Cologne	1	5
WC1989	31 May	Cardiff	0	0
WC1989	15 Nov	Cologne	1	2
EC1991	5 June	Cardiff	1	0
EC1991	16 Oct	Nuremberg	1	4

v GREECE			*W*	*G*
WC1964	9 Dec	Athens	0	2
WC1965	17 Mar	Cardiff	4	1

v HUNGARY			*W*	*H*
WC1958	8 June	Sanviken	1	1
WC1958	17 June	Stockholm	2	1
1961	28 May	Budapest	2	3
EC1962	7 Nov	Budapest	1	3
EC1963	20 Mar	Cardiff	1	1
EC1974	30 Oct	Cardiff	2	0
EC1975	16 Apr	Budapest	2	1
1985	16 Oct	Cardiff	0	3
2004	31 Mar	Budapest	2	1
2005	9 Feb	Cardiff	2	0
EC2019	11 June	Budapest	0	1
EC2019	**19 Nov**	**Cardiff**	**2**	**0**

v ICELAND			*W*	*I*
WC1980	2 June	Reykjavik	4	0
WC1981	14 Oct	Swansea	2	2
WC1984	12 Sept	Reykjavik	0	1
WC1984	14 Nov	Cardiff	2	1
1991	1 May	Cardiff	1	0
2008	28 May	Reykjavik	1	0
2014	5 Mar	Cardiff	3	1

v IRAN			*W*	*I*
1978	18 Apr	Tehran	1	0

v ISRAEL			*W*	*I*
WC1958	15 Jan	Tel Aviv	2	0
WC1958	5 Feb	Cardiff	2	0
1984	10 June	Tel Aviv	0	0
1989	8 Feb	Tel Aviv	3	3
EC2015	28 Mar	Haifa	3	0
EC2015	6 Sept	Cardiff	0	0

v ITALY			*W*	*I*
1965	1 May	Florence	1	4
WC1968	23 Oct	Cardiff	0	1
WC1969	4 Nov	Rome	1	4
1988	4 June	Brescia	1	0
1996	24 Jan	Terni	0	3
EC1998	5 Sept	Liverpool	0	2
EC1999	5 June	Bologna	0	4
EC2002	16 Oct	Cardiff	2	1
EC2003	6 Sept	Milan	0	4

v JAMAICA			*W*	*J*
1998	25 Mar	Cardiff	0	0

v JAPAN			*W*	*J*
1992	7 June	Matsuyama	1	0

v KUWAIT			*W*	*K*
1977	6 Sept	Wrexham	0	0
1977	20 Sept	Kuwait	0	0

v LATVIA			*W*	*L*
2004	18 Aug	Riga	2	0

v LIECHTENSTEIN			*W*	*L*
2006	14 Nov	Swansea	4	0
WC2008	11 Oct	Cardiff	2	0
WC2009	14 Oct	Vaduz	2	0

v LUXEMBOURG			*W*	*L*
EC1974	20 Nov	Swansea	5	0
EC1975	1 May	Luxembourg	3	1
EC1990	14 Nov	Luxembourg	1	0
EC1991	13 Nov	Cardiff	1	0
2008	26 Mar	Luxembourg	2	0
2010	11 Aug	Llanelli	5	1

v MALTA			*W*	*M*
EC1978	25 Oct	Wrexham	7	0
EC1979	2 June	Valletta	2	0
1988	1 June	Valletta	3	2
1998	3 June	Valletta	3	0

v MEXICO			*W*	*M*
WC1958	11 June	Stockholm	1	1
1962	22 May	Mexico City	1	2
2012	27 May	New Jersey	0	2
2018	29 May	Pasadena	0	0

v MOLDOVA			*W*	*M*
EC1994	12 Oct	Kishinev	2	3
EC1995	6 Sept	Cardiff	1	0
WC2016	5 Sept	Cardiff	4	0
WC2017	5 Sept	Chisinau	2	0

v MONTENEGRO			*W*	*M*
2009	12 Aug	Podgorica	1	2
EC2010	3 Sept	Podgorica	0	1
EC2011	2 Sept	Cardiff	2	1

v NETHERLANDS			*W*	*N*
WC1988	14 Sept	Amsterdam	0	1
WC1989	11 Oct	Wrexham	1	2
1992	30 May	Utrecht	0	4
WC1996	5 Oct	Cardiff	1	3
WC1996	9 Nov	Eindhoven	1	7
2008	1 June	Rotterdam	0	2
2014	4 June	Amsterdam	0	2
2015	13 Nov	Cardiff	2	3

v NEW ZEALAND			*W*	*NZ*
2007	26 May	Wrexham	2	2

v NORTH MACEDONIA			*W*	*M*
WC2013	6 Sept	Skopje	1	2
WC2013	11 Oct	Cardiff	1	0

v NORWAY			*W*	*N*
EC1982	22 Sept	Swansea	1	0
EC1983	21 Sept	Oslo	0	0
1984	6 June	Trondheim	0	1
1985	26 Feb	Wrexham	1	1
1985	5 June	Bergen	2	4
1994	9 Mar	Cardiff	1	3
WC2000	7 Oct	Cardiff	1	1
WC2001	5 Sept	Oslo	2	3
2004	27 May	Oslo	0	0
2008	6 Feb	Wrexham	3	0
2011	12 Nov	Cardiff	4	1

v PANAMA			*W*	*P*
2017	14 Nov	Cardiff	1	1

v PARAGUAY			*W*	*P*
2006	1 Mar	Cardiff	0	0

v POLAND			*W*	*P*
WC1973	28 Mar	Cardiff	2	0
WC1973	26 Sept	Katowice	0	3
1991	29 May	Radom	0	0
WC2000	11 Oct	Warsaw	0	0
WC2001	2 June	Cardiff	1	2
WC2004	13 Oct	Cardiff	2	3
WC2005	7 Sept	Warsaw	0	1
2009	11 Feb	Vila Real	0	1

v PORTUGAL			*W*	*P*
1949	15 May	Lisbon	2	3
1951	12 May	Cardiff	2	1
2000	2 June	Chaves	0	3
EC2016	6 July	Lille	0	2

v QATAR			*W*	*Q*
2000	23 Feb	Doha	1	0

v REPUBLIC OF IRELAND			*W*	*RI*
1960	28 Sept	Dublin	3	2
1979	11 Sept	Swansea	2	1
1981	24 Feb	Dublin	3	1
1986	26 Mar	Dublin	1	0
1990	28 Mar	Dublin	0	1
1991	6 Feb	Wrexham	0	3
1992	19 Feb	Dublin	1	0
1993	17 Feb	Dublin	1	2
1997	11 Feb	Cardiff	0	0
EC2007	24 Mar	Dublin	0	1
EC2007	17 Nov	Cardiff	2	2
NC2011	8 Feb	Dublin	0	3
2013	14 Aug	Cardiff	0	0
WC2017	24 Mar	Dublin	0	0
WC2017	9 Oct	Cardiff	0	1
NL2018	6 Sept	Cardiff	4	1
NL2018	16 Oct	Dublin	1	0

v ROMANIA			*W*	*R*
EC1970	11 Nov	Cardiff	0	0
EC1971	24 Nov	Bucharest	0	2
1983	12 Oct	Wrexham	5	0
WC1992	20 May	Bucharest	1	5
WC1993	17 Nov	Cardiff	1	2

v RUSSIA			*W*	*R*
EC2003	15 Nov	Moscow	0	0
EC2003	19 Nov	Cardiff	0	1
WC2008	10 Sept	Moscow	1	2
WC2009	9 Sept	Cardiff	1	3
EC2016	20 June	Toulouse	3	0

v SAN MARINO			*W*	*SM*
WC1996	2 June	Serravalle	5	0
WC1996	31 Aug	Cardiff	6	0
EC2007	28 Mar	Cardiff	3	0
EC2007	17 Oct	Serravalle	2	1

v SAUDI ARABIA			*W*	*SA*
1986	25 Feb	Dahran	2	1

v SERBIA			*W*	*S*
WC2012	11 Sept	Novi Sad	1	6
WC2013	10 Sept	Cardiff	0	3
WC2016	12 Nov	Cardiff	1	1
WC2017	11 June	Belgrade	1	1

v SERBIA-MONTENEGRO			*W*	*SM*
EC2003	20 Aug	Belgrade	0	1
EC2003	11 Oct	Cardiff	2	3

v SLOVAKIA			*W*	*S*
EC2006	7 Oct	Cardiff	1	5
EC2007	12 Sept	Trnava	5	2
EC2016	11 June	Bordeaux	2	1
EC2019	24 Mar	Cardiff	1	0
EC2019	**10 Oct**	**Trnava**	**1**	**1**

v SLOVENIA			*W*	*Sl*
2005	17 Aug	Swansea	0	0

v SPAIN			*W*	*S*
WC1961	19 Apr	Cardiff	1	2
WC1961	18 May	Madrid	1	1
1982	24 Mar	Valencia	1	1
WC1984	17 Oct	Seville	0	3
WC1985	30 Apr	Wrexham	3	0
2018	11 Oct	Cardiff	1	4

v SWEDEN			*W*	*S*
WC1958	15 June	Stockholm	0	0
1988	27 Apr	Stockholm	1	4
1989	26 Apr	Wrexham	0	2
1990	25 Apr	Stockholm	2	4
1994	20 Apr	Wrexham	0	2
2010	3 Mar	Swansea	0	1
2016	5 June	Stockholm	0	3

v SWITZERLAND			*W*	*S*
1949	26 May	Berne	0	4
1951	16 May	Wrexham	3	2
1996	24 Apr	Lugano	0	2
EC1999	31 Mar	Zurich	0	2
EC1999	9 Oct	Wrexham	0	2
EC2010	12 Oct	Basle	1	4
EC2011	8 Oct	Swansea	2	0

v TRINIDAD & TOBAGO			*W*	*TT*
2006	27 May	Graz	2	1
2019	20 Mar	Wrexham	1	0

v TUNISIA			*W*	*T*
1998	6 June	Tunis	0	4

v TURKEY			*W*	*T*
EC1978	29 Nov	Wrexham	1	0
EC1979	21 Nov	Izmir	0	1
WC1980	15 Oct	Cardiff	4	0
WC1981	25 Mar	Ankara	1	0
WC1996	14 Dec	Cardiff	0	0
WC1997	20 Aug	Istanbul	4	6

v UKRAINE			*W*	*U*
WC2001	28 Mar	Cardiff	1	1
WC2001	6 June	Kiev	1	1
2016	28 Mar	Kiev	0	1

v REST OF UNITED KINGDOM			*W*	*RUK*
1951	5 Dec	Cardiff	3	2
1969	28 July	Cardiff	0	1

v URUGUAY			*W*	*U*
1986	21 Apr	Wrexham	0	0
2018	26 Mar	Nanning	0	1

v USA			*W*	*USA*
2003	27 May	San Jose	0	2

v USSR			*W*	*USSR*
WC1965	30 May	Moscow	1	2
WC1965	27 Oct	Cardiff	2	1
WC1981	30 May	Wrexham	0	0
WC1981	18 Nov	Tbilisi	0	3
1987	18 Feb	Swansea	0	0

v YUGOSLAVIA			*W*	*Y*
1953	21 May	Belgrade	2	5
1954	22 Nov	Cardiff	1	3
EC1976	24 Apr	Zagreb	0	2
EC1976	22 May	Cardiff	1	1
EC1982	15 Dec	Titograd	4	4
EC1983	14 Dec	Cardiff	1	1
1988	23 Mar	Swansea	1	2

NORTHERN IRELAND

		v ALBANIA	*NI*	*A*
wc1965	7 May	Belfast	4	1
wc1965	24 Nov	Tirana	1	1
EC1982	15 Dec	Tirana	0	0
EC1983	27 Apr	Belfast	1	0
wc1992	9 Sept	Belfast	3	0
wc1993	17 Feb	Tirana	2	1
wc1996	14 Dec	Belfast	2	0
wc1997	10 Sept	Zurich	0	1
2010	3 Mar	Tirana	0	1

		v ALGERIA	*NI*	*A*
wc1986	3 June	Guadalajara	1	1

		v ARGENTINA	*NI*	*A*
wc1958	11 June	Halmstad	1	3

		v ARMENIA	*NI*	*A*
wc1996	5 Oct	Belfast	1	1
wc1997	30 Apr	Erevan	0	0
EC2003	29 Mar	Erevan	0	1
EC2003	10 Sept	Belfast	0	1

		v AUSTRALIA	*NI*	*A*
1980	11 June	Sydney	2	1
1980	15 June	Melbourne	1	1
1980	18 June	Adelaide	2	1

		v AUSTRIA	*NI*	*A*
wc1982	1 July	Madrid	2	2
EC1982	13 Oct	Vienna	0	2
EC1983	21 Sept	Belfast	3	1
EC1990	14 Nov	Vienna	0	0
EC1991	16 Oct	Belfast	2	1
EC1994	12 Oct	Vienna	2	1
EC1995	15 Nov	Belfast	5	3
wc2004	13 Oct	Belfast	3	3
wc2005	12 Oct	Vienna	0	2
NL2018	12 Oct	Vienna	0	1
NL2018	18 Nov	Belfast	1	2

		v AZERBAIJAN	*NI*	*A*
wc2004	9 Oct	Baku	0	0
wc2005	3 Sept	Belfast	2	0
wc2012	14 Nov	Belfast	1	1
wc2013	11 Oct	Baku	0	2
wc2016	11 Nov	Belfast	4	0
wc2017	10 June	Baku	1	0

		v BARBADOS	*NI*	*B*
2004	30 May	Waterford	1	1

		v BELARUS	*NI*	*B*
2016	27 May	Belfast	3	0
EC2019	24 Mar	Belfast	2	1
EC2019	11 June	Barysaw	1	0

		v BELGIUM	*NI*	*B*
wc1976	10 Nov	Liege	0	2
wc1977	16 Nov	Belfast	3	0
1997	11 Feb	Belfast	3	0

		v BOSNIA-HERZEGOVINA	*NI*	*B*
NL2018	8 Sept	Belfast	1	2
NL2018	15 Oct	Sarajevo	0	2

		v BRAZIL	*NI*	*B*
wc1986	12 June	Guadalajara	0	3

		v BULGARIA	*NI*	*B*
wc1972	18 Oct	Sofia	0	3
wc1973	26 Sept	Sheffield	0	0
EC1978	29 Nov	Sofia	2	0
EC1979	2 May	Belfast	2	0
wc2001	28 Mar	Sofia	3	4
wc2001	2 June	Belfast	0	1
2008	6 Feb	Belfast	0	1

		v CANADA	*NI*	*C*
1995	22 May	Edmonton	0	2
1999	27 Apr	Belfast	1	1
2005	9 Feb	Belfast	0	1

		v CHILE	*NI*	*C*
1989	26 May	Belfast	0	1
1995	25 May	Edmonton	1	2
2010	30 May	Chillan	0	1
2014	4 June	Valparaiso	0	2

		v COLOMBIA	*NI*	*C*
1994	4 June	Boston	0	2

		v COSTA RICA	*NI*	*CR*
2018	3 June	San Jose	0	3

		v CROATIA	*NI*	*C*
2016	15 Nov	Belfast	0	3

		v CYPRUS	*NI*	*C*
EC1971	3 Feb	Nicosia	3	0
EC1971	21 Apr	Belfast	5	0
wc1973	14 Feb	Nicosia	0	1
wc1973	8 May	London	3	0
2002	21 Aug	Belfast	0	0
2014	5 Mar	Nicosia	0	0

		v CZECHOSLOVAKIA	*NI*	*C*
wc1958	8 June	Halmstad	1	0
wc1958	17 June	Malmo	2	1*

**After extra time*

		v CZECH REPUBLIC	*NI*	*C*
wc2001	24 Mar	Belfast	0	1
wc2001	6 June	Teplice	1	3
wc2008	10 Sept	Belfast	0	0
wc2009	14 Oct	Prague	0	0
wc2016	4 Sept	Prague	0	0
wc2017	4 Sept	Belfast	2	0
2019	**14 Oct**	**Prague**	**3**	**2**

		v DENMARK	*NI*	*D*
EC1978	25 Oct	Belfast	2	1
EC1979	6 June	Copenhagen	0	4
1986	26 Mar	Belfast	1	1
EC1990	17 Oct	Belfast	1	1
EC1991	13 Nov	Odense	1	2
wc1992	18 Nov	Belfast	0	1
wc1993	13 Oct	Copenhagen	0	1
wc2000	7 Oct	Belfast	1	1
wc2001	1 Sept	Copenhagen	1	1
EC2006	7 Oct	Copenhagen	0	0
EC2007	17 Nov	Belfast	2	1

		v ESTONIA	*NI*	*E*
2004	31 Mar	Tallinn	1	0
2006	1 Mar	Belfast	1	0
EC2011	6 Sept	Tallinn	1	4
EC2011	7 Oct	Belfast	1	2
EC2019	21 Mar	Belfast	2	0
EC2019	8 June	Tallinn	2	1

		v FAROE ISLANDS	*NI*	*F*
EC1991	1 May	Belfast	1	1
EC1991	11 Sept	Landskrona	5	0
EC2010	12 Oct	Toftir	1	1
EC2011	10 Aug	Belfast	4	0
EC2014	11 Oct	Belfast	2	0
EC2015	4 Sept	Torshavn	3	1

		v FINLAND	*NI*	*F*
wc1984	27 May	Pori	0	1
wc1984	14 Nov	Belfast	2	1
EC1998	10 Oct	Belfast	1	0
EC1998	9 Oct	Helsinki	1	4
2003	12 Feb	Belfast	0	1
2006	16 Aug	Helsinki	2	1
2012	15 Aug	Belfast	3	3
EC2015	29 Mar	Belfast	2	1
EC2015	11 Oct	Helsinki	1	1

		v FRANCE	*NI*	*F*
1928	21 Feb	Paris	0	4
1951	12 May	Belfast	2	2
1952	11 Nov	Paris	1	3
wc1958	19 June	Norrkoping	0	4
1982	24 Mar	Paris	0	4
wc1982	4 July	Madrid	1	4

			NI	*F*
1986	26 Feb	Paris	0	0
1988	27 Apr	Belfast	0	0
1999	18 Aug	Belfast	0	1

	v GEORGIA		*NI*	*G*
2008	26 Mar	Belfast	4	1

	v GERMANY		*NI*	*G*
1992	2 June	Bremen	1	1
1996	29 May	Belfast	1	1
WC1996	9 Nov	Nuremberg	1	1
WC1997	20 Aug	Belfast	1	3
EC1999	27 Mar	Belfast	0	3
EC1999	8 Sept	Dortmund	0	4
2005	4 June	Belfast	1	4
EC2016	21 June	Paris	0	1
WC2016	11 Oct	Hanover	0	2
WC2017	5 Oct	Belfast	1	3
EC2019	**9 Sept**	**Belfast**	**0**	**2**
EC2019	**19 Nov**	**Frankfurt**	**1**	**6**

	v WEST GERMANY		*NI*	*WG*
WC1958	15 June	Malmo	2	2
WC1960	26 Oct	Belfast	3	4
WC1961	10 May	Hamburg	1	2
1966	7 May	Belfast	0	2
1977	27 Apr	Cologne	0	5
EC1982	17 Nov	Belfast	1	0
EC1983	16 Nov	Hamburg	1	0

	v GREECE		*NI*	*G*
WC1961	3 May	Athens	1	2
WC1961	17 Oct	Belfast	2	0
1988	17 Feb	Athens	2	3
EC2003	2 Apr	Belfast	0	2
EC2003	11 Oct	Athens	0	1
EC2014	14 Oct	Piraeus	2	0
EC2015	8 Oct	Belfast	3	1

	v HONDURAS		*NI*	*H*
WC1982	21 June	Zaragoza	1	1

	v HUNGARY		*NI*	*H*
WC1988	19 Oct	Budapest	0	1
WC1989	6 Sept	Belfast	1	2
2000	26 Apr	Belfast	0	1
2008	19 Nov	Belfast	0	2
EC2014	7 Sept	Budapest	2	1
EC2015	7 Sept	Belfast	1	1

	v ICELAND		*NI*	*I*
WC1977	11 June	Reykjavik	0	1
WC1977	21 Sept	Belfast	2	0
WC2000	11 Oct	Reykjavik	0	1
WC2001	5 Sept	Belfast	3	0
EC2006	2 Sept	Belfast	0	3
EC2007	12 Sept	Reykjavik	1	2

	v ISRAEL		*NI*	*I*
1968	10 Sept	Jaffa	3	2
1976	3 Mar	Tel Aviv	1	1
WC1980	26 Mar	Tel Aviv	0	0
WC1981	18 Nov	Belfast	1	0
1984	16 Oct	Belfast	3	0
1987	18 Feb	Tel Aviv	1	1
2009	12 Aug	Belfast	1	1
WC2013	26 Mar	Belfast	0	2
WC2013	15 Oct	Tel Aviv	1	1
2018	11 Sept	Belfast	3	0

	v ITALY		*NI*	*I*
WC1957	25 Apr	Rome	0	1
1957	4 Dec	Belfast	2	2
WC1958	15 Jan	Belfast	2	1
1961	25 Apr	Bologna	2	3
1997	22 Jan	Palermo	0	2
2003	3 June	Campobasso	0	2
2009	6 June	Pisa	0	3
EC2010	8 Oct	Belfast	0	0
EC2011	11 Oct	Pescara	0	3

	v KOREA REPUBLIC		*NI*	*KR*
2018	24 Mar	Belfast	2	1

	v LATVIA		*NI*	*L*
WC1993	2 June	Riga	2	1
WC1993	8 Sept	Belfast	2	0
EC1995	26 Apr	Riga	1	0
EC1995	7 June	Belfast	1	2
EC2006	11 Oct	Belfast	1	0
EC2007	8 Sept	Riga	0	1
2015	13 Nov	Belfast	1	0

	v LIECHTENSTEIN		*NI*	*L*
EC1994	20 Apr	Belfast	4	1
EC1995	11 Oct	Eschen	4	0
2002	27 Mar	Vaduz	0	0
EC2007	24 Mar	Vaduz	4	1
EC2007	22 Aug	Belfast	3	1

	v LITHUANIA		*NI*	*L*
WC1992	28 Apr	Belfast	2	2
WC1993	25 May	Vilnius	1	0

	v LUXEMBOURG		*NI*	*L*
2000	23 Feb	Luxembourg	3	1
WC2012	11 Sept	Belfast	1	1
WC2013	10 Sept	Luxembourg	2	3
2019	**5 Sept**	**Belfast**	**1**	**0**

	v MALTA		*NI*	*M*
WC1988	21 May	Belfast	3	0
WC1989	26 Apr	Valletta	2	0
2000	28 Mar	Valletta	3	0
WC2000	2 Sept	Belfast	1	0
WC2001	6 Oct	Valletta	1	0
2005	17 Aug	Ta'Qali	1	1
2013	6 Feb	Ta'Qali	0	0

	v MEXICO		*NI*	*M*
1966	22 June	Belfast	4	1
1994	11 June	Miami	0	3

	v MOLDOVA		*NI*	*M*
EC1998	18 Nov	Belfast	2	2
EC1999	31 Mar	Chisinau	0	0

	v MONTENEGRO		*NI*	*M*
2010	11 Aug	Podgorica	0	2

	v MOROCCO		*NI*	*M*
1986	23 Apr	Belfast	2	1
2010	17 Nov	Belfast	1	1

	v NETHERLANDS		*NI*	*N*
1962	9 May	Rotterdam	0	4
WC1965	17 Mar	Belfast	2	1
WC1965	7 Apr	Rotterdam	0	0
WC1976	13 Oct	Rotterdam	2	2
WC1977	12 Oct	Belfast	0	1
2012	2 June	Amsterdam	0	6
EC2019	**10 Oct**	**Rotterdam**	**1**	**3**
EC2019	**16 Nov**	**Belfast**	**0**	**0**

	v NEW ZEALAND		*NI*	*N*
2017	2 June	Belfast	1	0

	v NORWAY		*NI*	*N*
1922	25 May	Bergen	1	2
EC1974	4 Sept	Oslo	1	2
EC1975	29 Oct	Belfast	3	0
1990	27 Mar	Belfast	2	3
1996	27 Mar	Belfast	0	2
2001	28 Feb	Belfast	0	4
2004	18 Feb	Belfast	1	4
2012	29 Feb	Belfast	0	3
WC2017	26 Mar	Belfast	2	0
WC2017	8 Oct	Oslo	0	1

	v PANAMA		*NI*	*P*
2018	30 May	Panama City	0	0

	v POLAND		*NI*	*P*
EC1962	10 Oct	Katowice	2	0
EC1962	28 Nov	Belfast	2	0
1988	23 Mar	Belfast	1	1
1991	5 Feb	Belfast	3	1
2002	13 Feb	Limassol	1	4
EC2004	4 Sept	Belfast	0	3
EC2005	30 Mar	Warsaw	0	1

			NI	P
wc2009	28 Mar	Belfast	3	2
wc2009	5 Sept	Chorzow	1	1
EC2016	12 June	Nice	0	1

v PORTUGAL			NI	P
wc1957	16 Jan	Lisbon	1	1
wc1957	1 May	Belfast	3	0
wc1973	28 Mar	Coventry	1	1
wc1973	14 Nov	Lisbon	1	1
wc1980	19 Nov	Lisbon	0	1
wc1981	29 Apr	Belfast	1	0
EC1994	7 Sept	Belfast	1	2
EC1995	3 Sept	Lisbon	1	1
wc1997	29 Mar	Belfast	0	0
wc1997	11 Oct	Lisbon	0	1
2005	15 Nov	Belfast	1	1
wc2012	16 Oct	Porto	1	1
wc2013	6 Sept	Belfast	2	4

v QATAR			NI	Q
2015	31 May	Crewe	1	1

v REPUBLIC OF IRELAND			NI	RI
EC1978	20 Sept	Dublin	0	0
EC1979	21 Nov	Belfast	1	0
wc1988	14 Sept	Belfast	0	0
wc1989	11 Oct	Dublin	0	3
wc1993	31 Mar	Dublin	0	3
wc1993	17 Nov	Belfast	1	1
EC1994	16 Nov	Belfast	0	4
EC1995	29 Mar	Dublin	1	1
1999	29 May	Dublin	1	0
NC2011	24 May	Dublin	0	5
2018	15 Nov	Dublin	0	0

v ROMANIA			NI	R
wc1984	12 Sept	Belfast	3	2
wc1985	16 Oct	Bucharest	1	0
1994	23 Mar	Belfast	2	0
2006	27 May	Chicago	0	2
EC2014	14 Nov	Bucharest	0	2
EC2015	13 June	Belfast	0	0

v RUSSIA			NI	R
wc2012	7 Sept	Moscow	0	2
wc2013	14 Aug	Belfast	1	0

v SAN MARINO			NI	SM
wc2008	15 Oct	Belfast	4	0
wc2009	11 Feb	Serravalle	3	0
wc2016	8 Oct	Belfast	4	0
wc2017	1 Sept	Serravalle	3	0

v ST KITTS & NEVIS			NI	SK
2004	2 June	Basseterre	2	0

v SERBIA			NI	S
2009	14 Nov	Belfast	0	1
EC2011	25 Mar	Belgrade	1	2
EC2011	2 Sept	Belfast	0	1

v SERBIA-MONTENEGRO			NI	SM
2004	28 Apr	Belfast	1	1

v SLOVAKIA			NI	S
1998	25 Mar	Belfast	1	0
wc2008	6 Sept	Bratislava	1	2
wc2009	9 Sept	Belfast	0	2
2016	4 June	Trnava	0	0

v SLOVENIA			NI	S
wc2008	11 Oct	Maribor	0	2
wc2009	1 Apr	Belfast	1	0
EC2010	3 Sept	Maribor	1	0
EC2011	29 Mar	Belfast	0	0
2016	28 Mar	Belfast	1	0

v SOUTH AFRICA			NI	SA
1924	24 Sept	Belfast	1	2

v SPAIN			NI	S
1958	15 Oct	Madrid	2	6
1963	30 May	Bilbao	1	1
1963	30 Oct	Belfast	0	1
EC1970	11 Nov	Seville	0	3
EC1972	16 Feb	Hull	1	1
wc1982	25 June	Valencia	1	0
1985	27 Mar	Palma	0	0
wc1986	7 June	Guadalajara	1	2
wc1988	21 Dec	Seville	0	4
wc1989	8 Feb	Belfast	0	2
wc1992	14 Oct	Belfast	0	0
wc1993	28 Apr	Seville	1	3
1998	2 June	Santander	1	4
2002	17 Apr	Belfast	0	5
EC2002	12 Oct	Albacete	0	3
EC2003	11 June	Belfast	0	0
EC2006	6 Sept	Belfast	3	2
EC2007	21 Nov	Las Palmas	0	1

v SWEDEN			NI	S
EC1974	30 Oct	Solna	2	0
EC1975	3 Sept	Belfast	1	2
wc1980	15 Oct	Belfast	3	0
wc1981	3 June	Solna	0	1
1996	24 Apr	Belfast	1	2
EC2007	28 Mar	Belfast	2	1
EC2007	17 Oct	Stockholm	1	1

v SWITZERLAND			NI	S
wc1964	14 Oct	Belfast	1	0
wc1964	14 Nov	Lausanne	1	2
1998	22 Apr	Belfast	1	0
2004	18 Aug	Zurich	0	0
wc2017	9 Nov	Belfast	0	1
wc2017	12 Nov	Basel	0	0

v THAILAND			NI	T
1997	21 May	Bangkok	0	0

v TRINIDAD & TOBAGO			NI	TT
2004	6 June	Bacolet	3	0

v TURKEY			NI	T
wc1968	23 Oct	Belfast	4	1
wc1968	11 Dec	Istanbul	3	0
2013	15 Nov	Adana	0	1
EC1983	30 Mar	Belfast	2	1
EC1983	12 Oct	Ankara	0	1
wc1985	1 May	Belfast	2	0
wc1985	11 Sept	Izmir	0	0
EC1986	12 Nov	Izmir	0	0
EC1987	11 Nov	Belfast	1	0
EC1998	5 Sept	Istanbul	0	3
EC1999	4 Sept	Belfast	0	3
2010	26 May	New Britain	0	2
2013	15 Nov	Adana	0	1

v UKRAINE			NI	U
wc1996	31 Aug	Belfast	0	1
wc1997	2 Apr	Kiev	1	2
EC2002	16 Oct	Belfast	0	0
EC2003	6 Sept	Donetsk	0	0
EC2016	16 June	Lyon	2	0

v URUGUAY			NI	U
1964	29 Apr	Belfast	3	0
1990	18 May	Belfast	1	0
2006	21 May	New Jersey	0	1
2014	30 May	Montevideo	0	1

v USSR			NI	USSR
wc1969	19 Sept	Belfast	0	0
wc1969	22 Oct	Moscow	0	2
EC1971	22 Sept	Moscow	0	1
EC1971	13 Oct	Belfast	1	1

v YUGOSLAVIA			NI	Y
EC1975	16 Mar	Belfast	1	0
EC1975	19 Nov	Belgrade	0	1
wc1982	17 June	Zaragoza	0	0
EC1987	29 Apr	Belfast	1	2
EC1987	14 Oct	Sarajevo	0	3
EC1990	12 Sept	Belfast	0	2
EC1991	27 Mar	Belgrade	1	4
2000	16 Aug	Belfast	1	2

REPUBLIC OF IRELAND

v ALBANIA			*RI*	*A*
wc1992	26 May	Dublin	2	0
wc1993	26 May	Tirana	2	1
EC2003	2 Apr	Tirana	0	0
EC2003	7 June	Dublin	2	1

v ALGERIA			*RI*	*A*
1982	28 Apr	Algiers	0	2
2010	28 May	Dublin	3	0

v ANDORRA			*RI*	*A*
wc2001	28 Mar	Barcelona	3	0
wc2001	25 Apr	Dublin	3	1
EC2010	7 Sept	Dublin	3	1
EC2011	7 Oct	Andorra La Vella	2	0

v ARGENTINA			*RI*	*A*
1951	13 May	Dublin	0	1
†1979	29 May	Dublin	0	0
1980	16 May	Dublin	0	1
1998	22 Apr	Dublin	0	2
2010	11 Aug	Dublin	0	1

†*Not considered a full international.*

v ARMENIA			*RI*	*A*
EC2010	3 Sept	Erevan	1	0
EC2011	11 Oct	Dublin	2	1

v AUSTRALIA			*RI*	*A*
2003	19 Aug	Dublin	2	1
2009	12 Aug	Limerick	0	3

v AUSTRIA			*RI*	*A*
1952	7 May	Vienna	0	6
1953	25 Mar	Dublin	4	0
1958	14 Mar	Vienna	1	3
wc2013	10 Sept	Vienna	0	1
1962	8 Apr	Dublin	2	3
EC1963	25 Sept	Vienna	0	0
EC1963	13 Oct	Dublin	3	2
1966	22 May	Vienna	0	1
1968	10 Nov	Dublin	2	2
EC1971	30 May	Dublin	1	4
EC1971	10 Oct	Linz	0	6
EC1995	11 June	Dublin	1	3
EC1995	6 Sept	Vienna	1	3
wc2013	26 Mar	Dublin	2	2
wc2013	10 Sept	Vienna	0	1
wc2016	12 Nov	Vienna	1	0
wc2017	11 June	Dublin	1	1

v BELARUS			*RI*	*B*
2016	31 May	Cork	1	2

v BELGIUM			*RI*	*B*
1928	12 Feb	Liege	4	2
1929	30 Apr	Dublin	4	0
1930	11 May	Brussels	3	1
wc1934	25 Feb	Dublin	4	4
1949	24 Apr	Dublin	0	2
1950	10 May	Brussels	1	5
1965	24 Mar	Dublin	0	2
1966	25 May	Liege	3	2
wc1980	15 Oct	Dublin	1	1
wc1981	25 Mar	Brussels	0	1
EC1986	10 Sept	Brussels	2	2
EC1987	29 Apr	Dublin	0	0
wc1997	29 Oct	Dublin	1	1
wc1997	16 Nov	Brussels	1	2
EC2016	18 June	Bordeaux	0	3

v BOLIVIA			*RI*	*B*
1994	24 May	Dublin	1	0
1996	15 June	New Jersey	3	0
2007	26 May	Boston	1	1

v BOSNIA-HERZEGOVINA			*RI*	*BH*
2012	26 May	Dublin	1	0
EC2015	13 Nov	Zenica	1	1
EC2015	16 Nov	Dublin	2	0

v BRAZIL			*RI*	*B*
1974	5 May	Rio de Janeiro	1	2
1982	27 May	Uberlandia	0	7
1987	23 May	Dublin	1	0
2004	18 Feb	Dublin	0	0
2008	6 Feb	Dublin	0	1
2010	2 Mar	Emirates	0	2

v BULGARIA			*RI*	*B*
wc1977	1 June	Sofia	1	2
wc1977	12 Oct	Dublin	0	0
EC1979	19 May	Sofia	0	1
EC1979	17 Oct	Dublin	3	0
wc1987	1 Apr	Sofia	1	2
wc1987	14 Oct	Dublin	2	0
2004	18 Aug	Dublin	1	1
wc2009	28 Mar	Dublin	1	1
wc2009	6 June	Sofia	1	1
2019	**10 Sept**	**Dublin**	**3**	**1**

v CAMEROON			*RI*	*C*
wc2002	1 June	Niigata	1	1

v CANADA			*RI*	*C*
2003	18 Nov	Dublin	3	0

v CHILE			*RI*	*C*
1960	30 Mar	Dublin	2	0
1972	21 June	Recife	1	2
1974	12 May	Santiago	2	1
1982	22 May	Santiago	0	1
1991	22 May	Dublin	1	1
2006	24 May	Dublin	0	1

v CHINA PR			*RI*	*CPR*
1984	3 June	Sapporo	1	0
2005	29 Mar	Dublin	1	0

v COLOMBIA			*RI*	*C*
2008	29 May	Fulham	1	0

v COSTA RICA			*RI*	*C*
2014	6 June	Philadelphia	1	1

v CROATIA			*RI*	*C*
1996	2 June	Dublin	2	2
EC1998	5 Sept	Dublin	2	0
EC1999	4 Sept	Zagreb	0	1
2001	15 Aug	Dublin	2	2
2004	16 Nov	Dublin	1	0
2011	10 Aug	Dublin	0	0
EC2012	10 June	Poznan	1	3

v CYPRUS			*RI*	*C*
wc1980	26 Mar	Nicosia	3	2
wc1980	19 Nov	Dublin	6	0
wc2001	24 Mar	Nicosia	4	0
wc2001	6 Oct	Dublin	4	0
wc2004	4 Sept	Dublin	3	0
wc2005	8 Oct	Nicosia	1	0
EC2006	7 Oct	Nicosia	2	5
EC2007	17 Oct	Dublin	1	1
2008	15 Oct	Dublin	1	0
wc2009	5 Sept	Nicosia	2	1

v CZECHOSLOVAKIA			*RI*	*C*
1938	18 May	Prague	2	2
EC1959	5 Apr	Dublin	2	0
EC1959	10 May	Bratislava	0	4
wc1961	8 Oct	Dublin	1	3
wc1961	29 Oct	Prague	1	7
EC1967	21 May	Dublin	0	2
EC1967	22 Nov	Prague	2	1
wc1969	4 May	Dublin	1	2
wc1969	7 Oct	Prague	0	3
1979	26 Sept	Prague	1	4
1981	29 Apr	Dublin	3	1
1986	27 May	Reykjavik	1	0

v CZECH REPUBLIC			*RI*	*C*
1994	5 June	Dublin	1	3
1996	24 Apr	Prague	0	2
1998	25 Mar	Olomouc	1	2
2000	23 Feb	Dublin	3	2

			RI	*C*
2004	31 Mar	Dublin	2	1
EC2006	11 Oct	Dublin	1	1
EC2007	12 Sept	Prague	0	1
2012	29 Feb	Dublin	1	1

v DENMARK

			RI	*D*
WC1956	3 Oct	Dublin	2	1
WC1957	2 Oct	Copenhagen	2	0
WC1968	4 Dec	Dublin	1	1
(*abandoned after 51 mins*)				
WC1969	27 May	Copenhagen	0	2
WC1969	15 Oct	Dublin	1	1
EC1978	24 May	Copenhagen	3	3
EC1979	2 May	Dublin	2	0
WC1984	14 Nov	Copenhagen	0	3
WC1985	13 Nov	Dublin	1	4
WC1992	14 Oct	Copenhagen	0	0
WC1993	28 Apr	Dublin	1	1
2002	27 Mar	Dublin	3	0
2007	22 Aug	Copenhagen	4	0
WC2017	11 Nov	Copenhagen	0	0
WC2017	14 Nov	Dublin	1	5
NL2018	13 Oct	Dublin	0	0
NL2018	19 Nov	Aarhus	0	0
EC2019	7 June	Copenhagen	1	1
EC2019	**18 Nov**	**Dublin**	**1**	**1**

v ECUADOR

			RI	*E*
1972	19 June	Natal	3	2
2007	23 May	New Jersey	1	1

v EGYPT

			RI	*E*
WC1990	17 June	Palermo	0	0

v ENGLAND

			RI	*E*
1946	30 Sept	Dublin	0	1
1949	21 Sept	Everton	2	0
WC1957	8 May	Wembley	1	5
WC1957	19 May	Dublin	1	1
1964	24 May	Dublin	1	3
1976	8 Sept	Wembley	1	1
EC1978	25 Oct	Dublin	1	1
EC1980	6 Feb	Wembley	0	2
1985	26 Mar	Wembley	1	2
EC1988	12 June	Stuttgart	1	0
WC1990	11 June	Cagliari	1	1
EC1990	14 Nov	Dublin	1	1
EC1991	27 Mar	Wembley	1	1
1995	15 Feb	Dublin	1	0
(*abandoned after 27 mins*)				
2013	29 May	Wembley	1	1
2015	7 June	Dublin	0	0

v ESTONIA

			RI	*E*
WC2000	11 Oct	Dublin	2	0
WC2001	6 June	Tallinn	2	0
EC2011	11 Nov	Tallinn	4	0
EC2011	15 Nov	Dublin	1	1

v FAROE ISLANDS

			RI	*F*
EC2004	13 Oct	Dublin	2	0
EC2005	8 June	Toftir	2	0
WC2012	16 Oct	Torshavn	4	1
WC2013	7 June	Dublin	3	0

v FINLAND

			RI	*F*
WC1949	8 Sept	Dublin	3	0
WC1949	9 Oct	Helsinki	1	1
1990	16 May	Dublin	1	1
2000	15 Nov	Dublin	3	0
2002	21 Aug	Helsinki	3	0

v FRANCE

			RI	*F*
1937	23 May	Paris	2	0
1952	16 Nov	Dublin	1	1
WC1953	4 Oct	Dublin	3	5
WC1953	25 Nov	Paris	0	1
WC1972	15 Nov	Dublin	2	1
WC1973	19 May	Paris	1	1
WC1976	17 Nov	Paris	0	2
WC1977	30 Mar	Dublin	1	0
WC1980	28 Oct	Paris	0	2
WC1981	14 Oct	Dublin	3	2
1989	7 Feb	Dublin	0	0
WC2004	9 Oct	Paris	0	0
WC2005	7 Sept	Dublin	0	1
WC2009	14 Nov	Dublin	0	1
WC2009	18 Nov	Paris	1	1
EC2016	26 June	Lyon	1	2
2018	28 May	Paris	0	2

v GEORGIA

			RI	*G*
EC2003	29 Mar	Tbilisi	2	1
EC2003	11 June	Dublin	2	0
WC2008	6 Sept	Mainz	2	1
WC2009	11 Feb	Dublin	2	1
2013	2 June	Dublin	3	0
EC2014	7 Sept	Tbilisi	2	1
EC2015	7 Sept	Dublin	1	0
WC2016	6 Oct	Dublin	1	0
WC2017	2 Sept	Tbilisi	1	1
EC2019	26 Mar	Dublin	1	0
EC2019	**12 Oct**	**Tbilisi**	**0**	**0**

v GERMANY

			RI	*G*
1935	8 May	Dortmund	1	3
1936	17 Oct	Dublin	5	2
1939	23 May	Bremen	1	1
1994	29 May	Hanover	2	0
WC2002	5 June	Ibaraki	1	1
EC2006	2 Sept	Stuttgart	0	1
EC2007	13 Oct	Dublin	0	0
WC2012	12 Oct	Dublin	1	6
WC2013	11 Oct	Cologne	0	3
EC2014	14 Oct	Gelsenkirchen	1	1
EC2015	8 Oct	Dublin	1	0

v WEST GERMANY

			RI	*WG*
1951	17 Oct	Dublin	3	2
1952	4 May	Cologne	0	3
1955	28 May	Hamburg	1	2
1956	25 Nov	Dublin	3	0
1960	11 May	Dusseldorf	1	0
1966	4 May	Dublin	0	4
1970	9 May	Berlin	1	2
1975	1 Mar	Dublin	1	0†
1979	22 May	Dublin	1	3
1981	21 May	Bremen	0	3†
1989	6 Sept	Dublin	1	1

†*v West Germany 'B'*

v GIBRALTAR

			RI	*G*
EC2014	11 Oct	Dublin	7	0
EC2015	4 Sept	Faro	4	0
EC2019	23 Mar	Gibraltar	1	0
EC2019	10 June	Dublin	2	0

v GREECE

			RI	*G*
2000	26 Apr	Dublin	0	1
2002	20 Nov	Athens	0	0
2012	14 Nov	Dublin	0	1

v HUNGARY

			RI	*H*
1934	15 Dec	Dublin	2	4
1936	3 May	Budapest	3	3
1936	6 Dec	Dublin	2	3
1939	19 Mar	Cork	2	2
1939	18 May	Budapest	2	2
WC1969	8 June	Dublin	1	2
WC1969	5 Nov	Budapest	0	4
WC1989	8 Mar	Budapest	0	0
WC1989	4 June	Dublin	2	0
1991	11 Sept	Gyor	2	1
2012	4 June	Budapest	0	0

v ICELAND

			RI	*I*
EC1962	12 Aug	Dublin	4	2
EC1962	2 Sept	Reykjavik	1	1
EC1982	13 Oct	Dublin	2	0
EC1983	21 Sept	Reykjavik	3	0
1986	25 May	Reykjavik	2	1
WC1996	10 Nov	Dublin	0	0
WC1997	6 Sept	Reykjavik	4	2
2017	28 Mar	Dublin	0	1

		v IRAN	*RI*	*I*
1972	18 June	Recife	2	1
wc2001	10 Nov	Dublin	2	0
wc2001	15 Nov	Tehran	0	1

		v ISRAEL	*RI*	*I*
1984	4 Apr	Tel Aviv	0	3
1985	27 May	Tel Aviv	0	0
1987	10 Nov	Dublin	5	0
EC2005	26 Mar	Tel Aviv	1	1
EC2005	4 June	Dublin	2	2

		v ITALY	*RI*	*I*
1926	21 Mar	Turin	0	3
1927	23 Apr	Dublin	1	2
EC1970	8 Dec	Rome	0	3
EC1971	10 May	Dublin	1	2
1985	5 Feb	Dublin	1	2
wc1990	30 June	Rome	0	1
1992	4 June	Foxboro	0	2
wc1994	18 June	New York	1	0
2005	17 Aug	Dublin	1	2
wc2009	1 Apr	Bari	1	1
wc2009	10 Oct	Dublin	2	2
2011	7 June	Liege	2	0
EC2012	18 June	Poznan	0	2
2014	31 May	Craven Cottage	0	0
EC2016	22 June	Lille	1	0

		v JAMAICA	*RI*	*J*
2004	2 June	Charlton	1	0

		v KAZAKHSTAN	*RI*	*K*
wc2012	7 Sept	Astana	2	1
wc2013	15 Oct	Dublin	3	1

		v LATVIA	*RI*	*L*
wc1992	9 Sept	Dublin	4	0
wc1993	2 June	Riga	2	1
EC1994	7 Sept	Riga	3	0
EC1995	11 Oct	Dublin	2	1
2013	15 Nov	Dublin	3	0

		v LIECHTENSTEIN	*RI*	*L*
EC1994	12 Oct	Dublin	4	0
EC1995	3 June	Eschen	0	0
wc1996	31 Aug	Eschen	5	0
wc1997	21 May	Dublin	5	0

		v LITHUANIA	*RI*	*L*
wc1993	16 June	Vilnius	1	0
wc1993	8 Sept	Dublin	2	0
wc1997	20 Aug	Dublin	0	0
wc1997	10 Sept	Vilnius	2	1

		v LUXEMBOURG	*RI*	*L*
1936	9 May	Luxembourg	5	1
wc1953	28 Oct	Dublin	4	0
wc1954	7 Mar	Luxembourg	1	0
EC1987	28 May	Luxembourg	2	0
EC1987	9 Sept	Dublin	2	1

		v MALTA	*RI*	*M*
EC1983	30 Mar	Valletta	1	0
EC1983	16 Nov	Dublin	8	0
wc1989	28 May	Dublin	2	0
wc1989	15 Nov	Valletta	2	0
1990	2 June	Valletta	3	0
EC1998	14 Oct	Dublin	5	0
EC1999	8 Sept	Valletta	3	2

		v MEXICO	*RI*	*M*
1984	8 Aug	Dublin	0	0
wc1994	24 June	Orlando	1	2
1996	13 June	New Jersey	2	2
1998	23 May	Dublin	0	0
2000	4 June	Chicago	2	2
2017	2 June	New Jersey	1	3

		v MOLDOVA	*RI*	*M*
wc2016	9 Oct	Chisinau	3	1
wc2017	6 Oct	Dublin	2	0

		v MONTENEGRO	*RI*	*M*
wc2008	10 Sept	Podgorica	0	0
wc2009	14 Oct	Dublin	0	0

		v MOROCCO	*RI*	*M*
1990	12 Sept	Dublin	1	0

		v NETHERLANDS	*RI*	*N*
1932	8 May	Amsterdam	2	0
1934	8 Apr	Amsterdam	2	5
1935	8 Dec	Dublin	3	5
1955	1 May	Dublin	1	0
1956	10 May	Rotterdam	4	1
wc1980	10 Sept	Dublin	2	1
wc1981	9 Sept	Rotterdam	2	2
EC1982	22 Sept	Rotterdam	1	2
EC1983	12 Oct	Dublin	2	3
EC1988	18 June	Gelsenkirchen	0	1
wc1990	21 June	Palermo	1	1
1994	20 Apr	Tilburg	1	0
wc1994	4 July	Orlando	0	2
EC1995	13 Dec	Liverpool	0	2
1996	4 June	Rotterdam	1	3
wc2000	2 Sept	Amsterdam	2	2
wc2001	1 Sept	Dublin	1	0
2004	5 June	Amsterdam	1	0
2006	16 Aug	Dublin	0	4
2016	27 May	Dublin	1	1

		v NEW ZEALAND	*RI*	*N*
2019	**14 Nov**	**Dublin**	**3**	**1**

		v NIGERIA	*RI*	*N*
2002	16 May	Dublin	1	2
2004	29 May	Charlton	0	3
2009	29 May	Fulham	1	1

		v NORTHERN IRELAND	*RI*	*NI*
EC1978	20 Sept	Dublin	0	0
EC1979	21 Nov	Belfast	0	1
wc1988	14 Sept	Belfast	0	0
wc1989	11 Oct	Dublin	3	0
wc1993	31 Mar	Dublin	3	0
wc1993	17 Nov	Belfast	1	1
EC1994	16 Nov	Belfast	4	0
EC1995	29 Mar	Dublin	1	1
1999	29 May	Dublin	0	1
NC2011	24 May	Dublin	5	0
2018	15 Nov	Dublin	0	0

		v NORTH MACEDONIA	*RI*	*M*
wc1996	9 Oct	Dublin	3	0
wc1997	2 Apr	Skopje	2	3
EC1999	9 June	Dublin	1	0
EC1999	9 Oct	Skopje	1	1
EC2011	26 Mar	Dublin	2	1
EC2011	4 June	Podgorica	2	0

		v NORWAY	*RI*	*N*
wc1937	10 Oct	Oslo	2	3
wc1937	7 Nov	Dublin	3	3
1950	26 Nov	Dublin	2	2
1951	30 May	Oslo	3	2
1954	8 Nov	Dublin	2	1
1955	25 May	Oslo	3	1
1960	6 Nov	Dublin	3	1
1964	13 May	Oslo	4	1
1973	6 June	Oslo	1	1
1976	24 Mar	Dublin	3	0
1978	21 May	Oslo	0	0
wc1984	17 Oct	Oslo	0	1
wc1985	1 May	Dublin	0	0
1988	1 June	Oslo	0	0
wc1994	28 June	New York	0	0
2003	30 Apr	Dublin	1	0
2008	20 Aug	Oslo	1	1
2010	17 Nov	Dublin	1	2

		v OMAN	*RI*	*O*
2012	11 Sept	London	4	1
2014	3 Sept	Dublin	2	0
2016	31 Aug	Dublin	4	0

		v PARAGUAY	*RI*	*P*
1999	10 Feb	Dublin	2	0
2010	25 May	Dublin	2	1

		v POLAND	*RI*	*P*
1938	22 May	Warsaw	0	6
1938	13 Nov	Dublin	3	2
1958	11 May	Katowice	2	2
1958	5 Oct	Dublin	2	2
1964	10 May	Kracow	1	3

			RI	P
1964	25 Oct	Dublin	3	2
1968	15 May	Dublin	2	2
1968	30 Oct	Katowice	0	1
1970	6 May	Dublin	1	2
1970	23 Sept	Dublin	0	2
1973	16 May	Wroclaw	0	2
1973	21 Oct	Dublin	1	0
1976	26 May	Poznan	2	0
1977	24 Apr	Dublin	0	0
1978	12 Apr	Lodz	0	3
1981	23 May	Bydgoszcz	0	3
1984	23 May	Dublin	0	0
1986	12 Nov	Warsaw	0	1
1988	22 May	Dublin	3	1
EC1991	1 May	Dublin	0	0
EC1991	16 Oct	Poznan	3	3
2004	28 Apr	Bydgoszcz	0	0
2013	19 Nov	Poznan	0	0
2008	19 Nov	Dublin	2	3
2013	6 Feb	Dublin	2	0
2013	19 Nov	Poznan	0	0
EC2015	29 Mar	Dublin	1	1
EC2015	11 Oct	Warsaw	1	2
2018	11 Sept	Wroclaw	1	1

v PORTUGAL

			RI	P
1946	16 June	Lisbon	1	3
1947	4 May	Dublin	0	2
1948	23 May	Lisbon	0	2
1949	22 May	Dublin	1	0
1972	25 June	Recife	1	2
1992	7 June	Boston	2	0
EC1995	26 Apr	Dublin	1	0
EC1995	15 Nov	Lisbon	0	3
1996	29 May	Dublin	0	1
WC2000	7 Oct	Lisbon	1	1
WC2001	2 June	Dublin	1	1
2005	9 Feb	Dublin	1	0
2014	10 June	New Jersey	1	5

v ROMANIA

			RI	R
1988	23 Mar	Dublin	2	0
WC1990	25 June	Genoa	0	0*
WC1997	30 Apr	Bucharest	0	1
WC1997	11 Oct	Dublin	1	1
2004	27 May	Dublin	1	0

v RUSSIA

			RI	R
1994	23 Mar	Dublin	0	0
1996	27 Mar	Dublin	0	2
2002	13 Feb	Dublin	2	0
EC2002	7 Sept	Moscow	2	4
EC2003	6 Sept	Dublin	1	1
EC2010	8 Oct	Dublin	2	3
EC2011	6 Sept	Moscow	0	0

v SAN MARINO

			RI	SM
EC2006	15 Nov	Dublin	5	0
EC2007	7 Feb	Serravalle	2	1

v SAUDI ARABIA

			RI	SA
WC2002	11 June	Yokohama	3	0

v SCOTLAND

			RI	S
WC1961	3 May	Glasgow	1	4
WC1961	7 May	Dublin	0	3
1963	9 June	Dublin	1	0
1969	21 Sept	Dublin	1	1
EC1986	15 Oct	Dublin	0	0
EC1987	18 Feb	Glasgow	1	0
2000	30 May	Dublin	1	2
2003	12 Feb	Glasgow	2	0
NC2011	29 May	Dublin	1	0
EC2014	14 Nov	Glasgow	0	1
EC2015	13 June	Dublin	1	1

v SERBIA

			RI	S
2008	24 May	Dublin	1	1
2012	15 Aug	Belgrade	0	0
2014	5 Mar	Dublin	1	2
WC2016	5 Sept	Belgrade	2	2
WC2017	5 Sept	Dublin	0	1

v SLOVAKIA

			RI	S
EC2007	28 Mar	Dublin	1	0
EC2007	8 Sept	Bratislava	2	2
EC2010	12 Oct	Zilina	1	1
EC2011	2 Sept	Dublin	0	0
2016	29 Mar	Dublin	2	2

v SOUTH AFRICA

			RI	SA
2000	11 June	New Jersey	2	1
2009	8 Sept	Limerick	1	0

v SPAIN

			RI	S
1931	26 Apr	Barcelona	1	1
1931	13 Dec	Dublin	0	5
1946	23 June	Madrid	1	0
1947	2 Mar	Dublin	3	2
1948	30 May	Barcelona	1	2
1949	12 June	Dublin	1	4
1952	1 June	Madrid	0	6
1955	27 Nov	Dublin	2	2
EC1964	11 Mar	Seville	1	5
EC1964	8 Apr	Dublin	0	2
WC1965	5 May	Dublin	1	0
WC1965	27 Oct	Seville	1	4
WC1965	10 Nov	Paris	0	1
EC1966	23 Oct	Dublin	0	0
EC1966	7 Dec	Valencia	0	2
1977	9 Feb	Dublin	0	1
EC1982	17 Nov	Dublin	3	3
EC1983	27 Apr	Zaragoza	0	2
1985	26 May	Cork	0	0
WC1988	16 Nov	Seville	0	2
WC1989	26 Apr	Dublin	1	0
WC1992	18 Nov	Seville	0	0
WC1993	13 Oct	Dublin	1	3
WC2002	16 June	Suwon	1	1
EC2012	14 June	Gdansk	0	4
2013	11 June	New York	0	2

v SWEDEN

			RI	S
WC1949	2 June	Stockholm	1	3
WC1949	13 Nov	Dublin	1	3
1959	1 Nov	Dublin	3	2
1960	18 May	Malmo	1	4
EC1970	14 Oct	Dublin	1	1
EC1970	28 Oct	Malmo	0	1
1999	28 Apr	Dublin	2	0
2006	1 Mar	Dublin	3	0
WC2013	22 Mar	Stockholm	0	0
WC2013	6 Sept	Dublin	1	2
EC2016	13 June	Paris	1	1

v SWITZERLAND

			RI	S
1935	5 May	Basle	0	1
1936	17 Mar	Dublin	1	0
1937	17 May	Berne	1	0
1938	18 Sept	Dublin	4	0
1948	5 Dec	Dublin	0	1
EC1975	11 May	Dublin	2	1
EC1975	21 May	Berne	0	1
1980	30 Apr	Dublin	2	0
WC1985	2 June	Dublin	3	0
WC1985	11 Sept	Berne	0	0
1992	25 Mar	Dublin	2	1
EC2002	16 Oct	Dublin	1	2
EC2003	11 Oct	Basle	0	2
WC2004	8 Sept	Basle	1	1
WC2005	12 Oct	Dublin	0	0
2016	25 Mar	Dublin	1	0
EC2019	**5 Sept**	**Dublin**	**1**	**1**
EC2019	**15 Oct**	**Geneva**	**0**	**2**

v TRINIDAD & TOBAGO

			RI	TT
1982	30 May	Port of Spain	1	2

v TUNISIA

			RI	T
1988	19 Oct	Dublin	4	0

v TURKEY

			RI	T
EC1966	16 Nov	Dublin	2	1
EC1967	22 Feb	Ankara	1	2
EC1974	20 Nov	Izmir	1	1
EC1975	29 Oct	Dublin	4	0
2014	25 May	Dublin	1	2
1976	13 Oct	Ankara	3	3
1978	5 Apr	Dublin	4	2

			RI	T
1990	26 May	Izmir	0	0
EC1990	17 Oct	Dublin	5	0
EC1991	13 Nov	Istanbul	3	1
EC2000	13 Nov	Dublin	1	1
EC2000	17 Nov	Bursa	0	0
2003	9 Sept	Dublin	2	2
2014	25 May	Dublin	1	2
2018	23 Mar	Antalya	0	1

v URUGUAY			RI	U
1974	8 May	Montevideo	0	2
1986	23 Apr	Dublin	1	1
2011	29 Mar	Dublin	2	3
2017	4 June	Dublin	3	1

v USA			RI	USA
1979	29 Oct	Dublin	3	2
1991	1 June	Boston	1	1
1992	29 Apr	Dublin	4	1
1992	30 May	Washington	1	3
1996	9 June	Boston	1	2
2000	6 June	Boston	1	1
2002	17 Apr	Dublin	2	1
2014	18 Nov	Dublin	4	1
2018	2 June	Dublin	2	1

v USSR			RI	USSR
WC1972	18 Oct	Dublin	1	2
WC1973	13 May	Moscow	0	1
EC1974	30 Oct	Dublin	3	0
EC1975	18 May	Kiev	1	2
WC1984	12 Sept	Dublin	1	0
WC1985	16 Oct	Moscow	0	2
EC1988	15 June	Hanover	1	1
1990	25 Apr	Dublin	1	0

v WALES			RI	W
1960	28 Sept	Dublin	2	3
1979	11 Sept	Swansea	1	2
1981	24 Feb	Dublin	1	3
1986	26 Mar	Dublin	0	1
1990	28 Mar	Dublin	1	0
1991	6 Feb	Wrexham	3	0
1992	19 Feb	Dublin	0	1
1993	17 Feb	Dublin	2	1
1997	11 Feb	Cardiff	0	0
EC2007	24 Mar	Dublin	1	0
EC2007	17 Nov	Cardiff	2	2
NC2011	8 Feb	Dublin	3	0
2013	14 Aug	Cardiff	0	0
WC2017	24 Mar	Dublin	0	0
WC2017	9 Oct	Cardiff	1	0
NL2018	6 Sept	Cardiff	1	4
NL2018	16 Oct	Dublin	0	1

v YUGOSLAVIA			RI	Y
1955	19 Sept	Dublin	1	4
1988	27 Apr	Dublin	2	0
EC1998	18 Nov	Belgrade	0	1
EC1999	1 Sept	Dublin	2	1

BRITISH AND IRISH INTERNATIONAL MANAGERS

England

Walter Winterbottom 1946–1962 (after period as coach); Alf Ramsey 1963–1974; Joe Mercer (caretaker) 1974; Don Revie 1974–1977; Ron Greenwood 1977–1982; Bobby Robson 1982–1990; Graham Taylor 1990–1993; Terry Venables (coach) 1994–1996; Glenn Hoddle 1996–1999; Kevin Keegan 1999–2000; Sven-Goran Eriksson 2001–2006; Steve McClaren 2006–2007; Fabio Capello 2008–2012; Roy Hodgson 2012–2016; Sam Allardyce 2016 for one match; Gareth Southgate from November 2016.

Northern Ireland

Peter Doherty 1951–1952; Bertie Peacock 1962–1967; Billy Bingham 1967–1971; Terry Neill 1971–1975; Dave Clements (player-manager) 1975–1976; Danny Blanchflower 1976–1979; Billy Bingham 1980–1994; Bryan Hamilton 1994–1998; Lawrie McMenemy 1998–1999; Sammy McIlroy 2000–2003; Lawrie Sanchez 2004–2007; Nigel Worthington 2007–2011; Michael O'Neill 2011–2020; Ian Baraclough from June 2020.

Scotland (since 1967)

Bobby Brown 1967–1971; Tommy Docherty 1971–1972; Willie Ormond 1973–1977; Ally MacLeod 1977–1978; Jock Stein 1978–1985; Alex Ferguson (caretaker) 1985–1986 Andy Roxburgh (coach) 1986–1993; Craig Brown 1993–2001; Berti Vogts 2002–2004; Walter Smith 2004–2007; Alex McLeish 2007; George Burley 2008–2009; Craig Levein 2009–2012; Gordon Strachan 2013–2017; Alex McLeish 2018–19; Steve Clarke from May 2019.

Wales (since 1974)

Mike Smith 1974–1979; Mike England 1980–1988; David Williams (caretaker) 1988; Terry Yorath 1988–1993; John Toshack 1994 for one match; Mike Smith 1994–1995; Bobby Gould 1995–1999; Mark Hughes 1999–2004; John Toshack 2004–2010; Gary Speed 2010–2011; Chris Coleman 2012–2017; Ryan Giggs from January 2018.

Republic of Ireland

Liam Tuohy 1971–1972; Johnny Giles 1973–1980 (after period as player-manager); Eoin Hand 1980–1985; Jack Charlton 1986–1996; Mick McCarthy 1996–2002; Brian Kerr 2003–2006; Steve Staunton 2006–2007; Giovanni Trapattoni 2008–2013; Martin O'Neill 2013–2018; Mick McCarthy 2018–2020; Stephen Kenny from April 2020.

OTHER BRITISH AND IRISH INTERNATIONAL MATCHES 2019–20

FRIENDLIES

■ *Denotes player sent off.*

WALES

Cardiff, Monday, 9 September 2019

Wales (1) 1 *(James 17)*

Belarus (0) 0 7666

Wales: (4231) Ward; Roberts, Mepham (Lockyer 76), Rodon, Davies B (Gunter 90); Morrell, Allen; James (Bale 50), Wilson (Vaulks 88), Williams J; Moore (Vokes 75).
Belarus: (4231) Plotnikov; Zolotov, Volkov, Politevich, Polyakov; Yablonskiy (Maewski 46), Baha (Dragun 70); Kovalev (Ebong 46), Bakhar (Klimovich 84), Skavysh (Pechenin 76); Signevich (Stasevich 70).
Referee: William Collum.

NORTHERN IRELAND

Belfast, Thursday, 5 September 2019

Northern Ireland (1) 1 *(Malget 37 (og))*

Luxembourg (0) 0 14,108

Northern Ireland: (433) Peacock-Farrell (McGovern 67); McLaughlin, Flanagan, Brown, Ferguson; Evans C (Donnelly 67), Thompson (Davis 88), Saville (McCalmont 59); Whyte (Galbraith 88), Magennis, Lafferty (Lavery 59).
Luxembourg: (442) Moris (Schon 46); Jans, Gerson, Carlson, Malget (Hall 46); Sinani (Da Mota Alves 74), Thill O (Bohnert 85), Barreiro (Philipps 73), Thill V; Rodrigues, Deville (Turpel 60).
Referee: Bryn Markham-Jones.

Prague, Monday, 14 October 2019

Czech Republic (0) 2 *(Darida 67, Kral 68)*

Northern Ireland (3) 3 *(McNair 9, 40, Evans J 23)* 9,139

Czech Republic: (4231) Pavlenka; Reznik, Simic (Celustka 46), Kudela, Krejci (Masopust 75); Husbauer (Schick 66), Kalvach (Darida 46); Zmrhal (Boril 46), Kral, Kopic; Krmencik (Ondrasek 46).
Northern Ireland: (352) McGovern; Cathcart, Evans J, Flanagan; McLaughlin C, McNair, Davis (Evans C 64), Thompson (Saville 65), Dallas; Boyce (Magennis 71), Whyte (McGinn 87).
Referee: Ivan Kruzliak.

REPUBLIC OF IRELAND

Dublin, Tuesday, 10 September 2019

Republic of Ireland (0) 3 *(Browne 56, Long K 83, Collins 86)*

Bulgaria (0) 1 *(Popov I 67 (pen))*

Republic of Ireland: (433) Travers (O'Hara 75); Christie, Egan, Long K, Hourihane (McClean 68); Browne, Judge (Byrne 59), Cullen; O'Dowda (Stevens 76), Hogan (Collins 60), Curtis (Hendrick 83).
Bulgaria: (4141) Ivanov; Goranov, Nedyalkov (Bozhikov 59), Dimitrov K (Panayotov 80), Pashov; Slavchev; Mladenov (Despodov 68), Milanov (Popov I 46), Malinov (Terziev 80), Dimitrov N (Wanderson 59); Kraev.
Referee: Tobias Welz.

Dublin, Thursday, 14 November 2019

Republic of Ireland (1) 3 *(Williams 45, Maguire 52, Robinson 75)*

New Zealand (1) 1 *(McCowatt 30)*

Republic of Ireland: (4312) O'Hara (Travers 65); O'Connor L, Long K, Clark, Williams (O'Dowda 56); Browne (Hourihane 66), Cullen, Brady; Byrne (Judge 63); Maguire (Collins 73), Parrott (Robinson 63).
New Zealand: (433) Marinovic; Roux (Payne 90), Reid (Tuiloma 46), Boxall (Smith 74), Cacace; Singh, Bell, Thomas (McGlinchey 74); Just, Wood (De Jong 76), McCowatt (Collier 85).
Referee: Rob Jenkins.

BRITISH AND IRISH INTERNATIONAL APPEARANCES 1872–2020

This is a list of full international appearances by Englishmen, Irishmen, Scotsmen and Welshmen in matches against the Home Countries and against foreign nations. It does not include unofficial matches against Commonwealth and Empire countries. The year indicated refers to the player's international debut season; i.e. 2020 is the 2019–20 season. **Bold** type indicates players who have made an international appearance in season 2019–20.

As at July 2020.

ENGLAND

Abbott, W. 1902 (Everton) 1
Abraham, K. O. T. (Tammy) 2018 (Chelsea) 4
A'Court, A. 1958 (Liverpool) 5
Adams, T. A. 1987 (Arsenal) 66
Adcock, H. 1929 (Leicester C) 5
Agbonlahor, G. 2009 (Aston Villa) 3
Alcock, C. W. 1875 (Wanderers) 1
Alderson, J. T. 1923 (Crystal Palace) 1
Aldridge, A. 1888 (WBA, Walsall Town Swifts) 2
Alexander-Arnold, T. J. 2018 (Liverpool) 9
Allen, A. 1888 (Aston Villa) 1
Allen, A. 1960 (Stoke C) 3
Allen, C. 1984 (QPR, Tottenham H) 5
Allen, H. 1888 (Wolverhampton W) 5
Allen, J. P. 1934 (Portsmouth) 2
Allen, R. 1952 (WBA) 5
Alli, B. J. (Dele) 2016 (Tottenham H) 37
Alsford, W. J. 1935 (Tottenham H) 1
Amos, A. 1885 (Old Carthusians) 2
Anderson, R. D. 1879 (Old Etonians) 1
Anderson, S. 1962 (Sunderland) 2
Anderson, V. A. 1979 (Nottingham F, Arsenal, Manchester U) 30
Anderton, D. R. 1994 (Tottenham H) 30
Angus, J. 1961 (Burnley) 1
Armfield, J. C. 1959 (Blackpool) 43
Armitage, G. H. 1926 (Charlton Ath) 1
Armstrong, D. 1980 (Middlesbrough, Southampton) 3
Armstrong, K. 1955 (Chelsea) 1
Arnold, J. 1933 (Fulham) 1
Arthur, J. W. H. 1885 (Blackburn R) 7
Ashcroft, J. 1906 (Woolwich Arsenal) 3
Ashmore, G. S. 1926 (WBA) 1
Ashton, C. T. 1926 (Corinthians) 1
Ashton, D. 2008 (West Ham U) 1
Ashurst, W. 1923 (Notts Co) 5
Astall, G. 1956 (Birmingham C) 2
Astle, J. 1969 (WBA) 5
Aston, J. 1949 (Manchester U) 17
Athersmith, W. C. 1892 (Aston Villa) 12
Atyeo, P. J. W. 1956 (Bristol C) 6
Austin, S. W. 1926 (Manchester C) 1

Bach, P. 1899 (Sunderland) 1
Bache, J. W. 1903 (Aston Villa) 7
Baddeley, T. 1903 (Wolverhampton W) 5
Bagshaw, J. J. 1920 (Derby Co) 1
Bailey, G. R. 1985 (Manchester U) 2
Bailey, H. P. 1908 (Leicester Fosse) 5
Bailey, M. A. 1964 (Charlton Ath) 2
Bailey, N. C. 1878 (Clapham R) 19
Baily, E. F. 1950 (Tottenham H) 9
Bain, J. 1877 (Oxford University) 1
Baines, L. J. 2010 (Everton) 30
Baker, A. 1928 (Arsenal) 1
Baker, B. H. 1921 (Everton, Chelsea) 2
Baker, J. H. 1960 (Hibernian, Arsenal) 8
Ball, A. J. 1965 (Blackpool, Everton, Arsenal) 72
Ball, J. 1928 (Bury) 1
Ball, M. J. 2001 (Everton) 1
Balmer, W. 1905 (Everton) 1
Bamber, J. 1921 (Liverpool) 1
Bambridge, A. L. 1881 (Swifts) 3
Bambridge, E. C. 1879 (Swifts) 18
Bambridge, E. H. 1876 (Swifts) 1
Banks, G. 1963 (Leicester C, Stoke C) 73
Banks, H. E. 1901 (Millwall) 1
Banks, T. 1958 (Bolton W) 6
Bannister, W. 1901 (Burnley, Bolton W) 2
Barclay, R. 1932 (Sheffield U) 3
Bardsley, D. J. 1993 (QPR) 2
Barham, M. 1983 (Norwich C) 2
Barkas, S. 1936 (Manchester C) 5
Barker, J. 1935 (Derby Co) 11
Barker, R. 1872 (Herts Rangers) 1
Barker, R. R. 1895 (Casuals) 1
Barkley, R. 2013 (Everton, Chelsea) 33
Barlow, R. J. 1955 (WBA) 1
Barmby, N. J. 1995 (Tottenham H, Middlesbrough, Everton, Liverpool) 23
Barnes, J. 1983 (Watford, Liverpool) 79
Barnes, P. S. 1978 (Manchester C, WBA, Leeds U) 22
Barnet, H. H. 1882 (Royal Engineers) 1
Barrass, M. W. 1952 (Bolton W) 3
Barrett, A. F. 1930 (Fulham) 1
Barrett, E. D. 1991 (Oldham Ath, Aston Villa) 3
Barrett, J. W. 1929 (West Ham U) 1
Barry, G. 2000 (Aston Villa, Manchester C) 53
Barry, L. 1928 (Leicester C) 5
Barson, F. 1920 (Aston Villa) 1
Barton, J. 1890 (Blackburn R) 1
Barton, J. 2007 (Manchester C) 1
Barton, P. H. 1921 (Birmingham) 7
Barton, W. D. 1995 (Wimbledon, Newcastle U) 3
Bassett, W. I. 1888 (WBA) 16
Bastard, S. R. 1880 (Upton Park) 1
Bastin, C. S. 1932 (Arsenal) 21
Batty, D. 1991 (Leeds U, Blackburn R, Newcastle U, Leeds U) 42
Baugh, R. 1886 (Stafford Road, Wolverhampton W) 2
Bayliss, A. E. J. M. 1891 (WBA) 1
Baynham, R. L. 1956 (Luton T) 3
Beardsley, P. A. 1986 (Newcastle U, Liverpool, Newcastle U) 59
Beasant, D. J. 1990 (Chelsea) 2
Beasley, A. 1939 (Huddersfield T) 1
Beats, W. E. 1901 (Wolverhampton W) 2
Beattie, J. S. 2003 (Southampton) 5
Beattie, T. K. 1975 (Ipswich T) 9
Beckham, D. R. J. 1997 (Manchester U, Real Madrid, LA Galaxy) 115
Becton, F. 1895 (Preston NE, Liverpool) 2
Bedford, H. 1923 (Blackpool) 2
Bell, C. 1968 (Manchester C) 48
Bennett, W. 1901 (Sheffield U) 2
Benson, R. W. 1913 (Sheffield U) 1
Bent, D. A. 2006 (Charlton Ath, Tottenham H, Sunderland, Aston Villa) 13
Bentley, D. M. 2008 (Blackburn R, Tottenham H) 7
Bentley, R. T. F. 1949 (Chelsea) 12
Beresford, J. 1934 (Aston Villa) 1
Berry, A. 1909 (Oxford University) 1
Berry, J. J. 1953 (Manchester U) 4
Bertrand, R. 2013 (Chelsea, Southampton) 19
Bestall, J. G. 1935 (Grimsby T) 1
Betmead, H. A. 1937 (Grimsby T) 1
Betts, M. P. 1877 (Old Harrovians) 1
Betts, W. 1889 (Sheffield W) 1
Beverley, J. 1884 (Blackburn R) 3
Birkett, R. H. 1879 (Clapham R) 1
Birkett, R. J. E. 1936 (Middlesbrough) 1
Birley, F. H. 1874 (Oxford University, Wanderers) 2
Birtles, G. 1980 (Nottingham F) 3
Bishop, S. M. 1927 (Leicester C) 4
Blackburn, F. 1901 (Blackburn R) 3
Blackburn, G. F. 1924 (Aston Villa) 1

Blenkinsop, E. 1928 (Sheffield W) 26
Bliss, H. 1921 (Tottenham H) 1
Blissett, L. L. 1983 (Watford, AC Milan) 14
Blockley, J. P. 1973 (Arsenal) 1
Bloomer, S. 1895 (Derby Co, Middlesbrough) 23
Blunstone, F. 1955 (Chelsea) 5
Bond, R. 1905 (Preston NE, Bradford C) 8
Bonetti, P. P. 1966 (Chelsea) 7
Bonsor, A. G. 1873 (Wanderers) 2
Booth, F. 1905 (Manchester C) 1
Booth, T. 1898 (Blackburn R, Everton) 2
Bothroyd, J. 2011 (Cardiff C) 1
Bould, S. A. 1994 (Arsenal) 2
Bowden, E. R. 1935 (Arsenal) 6
Bower, A. G. 1924 (Corinthians) 5
Bowers, J. W. 1934 (Derby Co) 3
Bowles, S. 1974 (QPR) 5
Bowser, S. 1920 (WBA) 1
Bowyer, L. D. 2003 (Leeds U) 1
Boyer, P. J. 1976 (Norwich C) 1
Boyes, W. 1935 (WBA, Everton) 3
Boyle, T. W. 1913 (Burnley) 1
Brabrook, P. 1958 (Chelsea) 3
Bracewell, P. W. 1985 (Everton) 3
Bradford, G. R. W. 1956 (Bristol R) 1
Bradford, J. 1924 (Birmingham) 12
Bradley, W. 1959 (Manchester U) 3
Bradshaw, F. 1908 (Sheffield W) 1
Bradshaw, T. H. 1897 (Liverpool) 1
Bradshaw, W. 1910 (Blackburn R) 4
Brann, G. 1886 (Swifts) 3
Brawn, W. F. 1904 (Aston Villa) 2
Bray, J. 1935 (Manchester C) 6
Brayshaw, E. 1887 (Sheffield W) 1
Bridge W. M. 2002 (Southampton, Chelsea, Manchester C) 36
Bridges, B. J. 1965 (Chelsea) 4
Bridgett, A. 1905 (Sunderland) 11
Brindle, T. 1880 (Darwen) 2
Brittleton, J. T. 1912 (Sheffield W) 5
Britton, C. S. 1935 (Everton) 9
Broadbent, P. F. 1958 (Wolverhampton W) 7
Broadis, I. A. 1952 (Manchester C, Newcastle U) 14
Brockbank, J. 1872 (Cambridge University) 1
Brodie, J. B. 1889 (Wolverhampton W) 3
Bromilow, T. G. 1921 (Liverpool) 5
Bromley-Davenport, W. E. 1884 (Oxford University) 2
Brook, E. F. 1930 (Manchester C) 18
Brooking, T. D. 1974 (West Ham U) 47
Brooks, J. 1957 (Tottenham H) 3
Broome, F. H. 1938 (Aston Villa) 7
Brown, A. 1882 (Aston Villa) 3
Brown, A. 1971 (WBA) 1
Brown, A. S. 1904 (Sheffield U) 2
Brown, G. 1927 (Huddersfield T, Aston Villa) 9
Brown, J. 1881 (Blackburn R) 5
Brown, J. H. 1927 (Sheffield W) 6
Brown, K. 1960 (West Ham U) 1
Brown, W. 1924 (West Ham U) 1
Brown, W. M. 1999 (Manchester U) 23
Bruton, J. 1928 (Burnley) 3
Bryant, W. I. 1925 (Clapton) 1
Buchan, C. M. 1913 (Sunderland) 6
Buchanan, W. S. 1876 (Clapham R) 1
Buckley, F. C. 1914 (Derby Co) 1
Bull, S. G. 1989 (Wolverhampton W) 13
Bullock, F. E. 1921 (Huddersfield T) 1
Bullock, N. 1923 (Bury) 3
Burgess, H. 1904 (Manchester C) 4
Burgess, H. 1931 (Sheffield W) 4
Burnup, C. J. 1896 (Cambridge University) 1
Burrows, H. 1934 (Sheffield W) 3
Burton, F. E. 1889 (Nottingham F) 1
Bury, L. 1877 (Cambridge University, Old Etonians) 2
Butcher, T. 1980 (Ipswich T, Rangers) 77
Butland, J. 2013 (Birmingham C, Stoke C) 9
Butler, J. D. 1925 (Arsenal) 1
Butler, W. 1924 (Bolton W) 1
Butt, N. 1997 (Manchester U, Newcastle U) 39
Byrne, G. 1963 (Liverpool) 2
Byrne, J. J. 1962 (Crystal Palace, West Ham U) 11
Byrne, R. W. 1954 (Manchester U) 33

Cahill, G. J. 2011 (Bolton W, Chelsea) 61
Callaghan, I. R. 1966 (Liverpool) 4
Calvey, J. 1902 (Nottingham F) 1
Campbell, A. F. 1929 (Blackburn R, Huddersfield T) 8
Campbell, F. L. 2012 (Sunderland) 1
Campbell, S. 1996 (Tottenham H, Arsenal, Portsmouth) 73
Camsell, G. H. 1929 (Middlesbrough) 9
Capes, A. J. 1903 (Stoke) 1
Carr, J. 1905 (Newcastle U) 2
Carr, J. 1920 (Middlesbrough) 2
Carr, W. H. 1875 (Owlerton, Sheffield) 1
Carragher, J. L. 1999 (Liverpool) 38
Carrick, M. 2001 (West Ham U, Tottenham H, Manchester U) 34
Carroll, A. T. 2011 (Newcastle U, Liverpool) 9
Carson, S. P. 2008 (Liverpool, WBA) 4
Carter, H. S. 1934 (Sunderland, Derby Co) 13
Carter, J. H. 1926 (WBA) 3
Catlin, A. E. 1937 (Sheffield W) 5
Caulker, S. A. 2013 (Tottenham H) 1
Chadwick, A. 1900 (Southampton) 2
Chadwick, E. 1891 (Everton) 7
Chalobah, N. N. 2019 (Watford) 1
Chamberlain, M. 1983 (Stoke C) 8
Chambers, H. 1921 (Liverpool) 8
Chambers, C. 2015 (Arsenal) 3
Channon, M. R. 1973 (Southampton, Manchester C) 46
Charles, G. A. 1991 (Nottingham F) 2
Charlton, J. 1965 (Leeds U) 35
Charlton, R. 1958 (Manchester U) 106
Charnley, R. O. 1963 (Blackpool) 1
Charsley, C. C. 1893 (Small Heath) 1
Chedgzoy, S. 1920 (Everton) 8
Chenery, C. J. 1872 (Crystal Palace) 3
Cherry, T. J. 1976 (Leeds U) 27
Chilwell, B. J. 2019 (Leicester C) 11
Chilton, A. 1951 (Manchester U) 2
Chippendale, H. 1894 (Blackburn R) 1
Chivers, M. 1971 (Tottenham H) 24
Christian, E. 1879 (Old Etonians) 1
Clamp, E. 1958 (Wolverhampton W) 4
Clapton, D. R. 1959 (Arsenal) 1
Clare, T. 1889 (Stoke) 4
Clarke, A. J. 1970 (Leeds U) 19
Clarke, H. A. 1954 (Tottenham H) 1
Clay, T. 1920 (Tottenham H) 4
Clayton, R. 1956 (Blackburn R) 35
Clegg, J. C. 1872 (Sheffield W) 1
Clegg, W. E. 1873 (Sheffield W, Sheffield Alb) 2
Clemence, R. N. 1973 (Liverpool, Tottenham H) 61
Clement, D. T. 1976 (QPR) 5
Cleverley, T. W. 2013 (Manchester U) 13
Clough, B. H. 1960 (Middlesbrough) 2
Clough, N. H. 1989 (Nottingham F) 14
Clyne, N. E. 2015 (Southampton, Liverpool) 14
Coates, R. 1970 (Burnley, Tottenham H) 4
Cobbold, W. N. 1883 (Cambridge University, Old Carthusians) 9
Cock, J. G. 1920 (Huddersfield T, Chelsea) 2
Cockburn, H. 1947 (Manchester U) 13
Cohen, G. R. 1964 (Fulham) 37
Cole, A. 2001 (Arsenal, Chelsea) 107
Cole, A. A. 1995 (Manchester U) 15
Cole, C. 2009 (West Ham U) 7
Cole, J. J. 2001 (West Ham U, Chelsea) 56
Colclough, H. 1914 (Crystal Palace) 1
Coleman, E. H. 1921 (Dulwich Hamlet) 1
Coleman, J. 1907 (Woolwich Arsenal) 1
Collymore, S. V. 1995 (Nottingham F, Aston Villa) 3
Common, A. 1904 (Sheffield U, Middlesbrough) 3
Compton, L. H. 1951 (Arsenal) 2
Conlin, J. 1906 (Bradford C) 1
Connelly, J. M. 1960 (Burnley, Manchester U) 20
Cook, L. J. 2018 (Bournemouth) 1
Cook, T. E. R. 1925 (Brighton) 1
Cooper, C. T. 1995 (Nottingham F) 2
Cooper, N. C. 1893 (Cambridge University) 1

Cooper, T. 1928 (Derby Co) 15
Cooper, T. 1969 (Leeds U) 20
Coppell, S. J. 1978 (Manchester U) 42
Copping, W. 1933 (Leeds U, Arsenal, Leeds U) 20
Corbett, B. O. 1901 (Corinthians) 1
Corbett, R. 1903 (Old Malvernians) 1
Corbett, W. S. 1908 (Birmingham) 3
Cork, J. F. P. 2018 (Burnley) 1
Corrigan, J. T. 1976 (Manchester C) 9
Cottee, A. R. 1987 (West Ham U, Everton) 7
Cotterill, G. H. 1891 (Cambridge University, Old Brightonians) 4
Cottle, J. R. 1909 (Bristol C) 1
Cowan, S. 1926 (Manchester C) 3
Cowans, G. S. 1983 (Aston Villa, Bari, Aston Villa) 10
Cowell, A. 1910 (Blackburn R) 1
Cox, J. 1901 (Liverpool) 3
Cox, J. D. 1892 (Derby Co) 1
Crabtree, J. W. 1894 (Burnley, Aston Villa) 14
Crawford, J. F. 1931 (Chelsea) 1
Crawford, R. 1962 (Ipswich T) 2
Crawshaw, T. H. 1895 (Sheffield W) 10
Crayston, W. J. 1936 (Arsenal) 8
Creek, F. N. S. 1923 (Corinthians) 1
Cresswell, A. W. 2017 (West Ham U) 3
Cresswell, W. 1921 (South Shields, Sunderland, Everton) 7
Crompton, R. 1902 (Blackburn R) 41
Crooks, S. D. 1930 (Derby Co) 26
Crouch, P. J. 2005 (Southampton, Liverpool, Portsmouth, Tottenham H) 42
Crowe, C. 1963 (Wolverhampton W) 1
Cuggy, F. 1913 (Sunderland) 2
Cullis, S. 1938 (Wolverhampton W) 12
Cunliffe, A. 1933 (Blackburn R) 2
Cunliffe, D. 1900 (Portsmouth) 1
Cunliffe, J. N. 1936 (Everton) 1
Cunningham, L. 1979 (WBA, Real Madrid) 6
Curle, K. 1992 (Manchester C) 3
Currey, E. S. 1890 (Oxford University) 2
Currie, A. W. 1972 (Sheffield U, Leeds U) 17
Cursham, A. W. 1876 (Notts Co) 6
Cursham, H. A. 1880 (Notts Co) 8

Daft, H. B. 1889 (Notts Co) 5
Daley, A. M. 1992 (Aston Villa) 7
Danks, T. 1885 (Nottingham F) 1
Davenport, P. 1985 (Nottingham F) 1
Davenport, J. K. 1885 (Bolton W) 2
Davies, K. C. 2011 (Bolton W) 1
Davis, G. 1904 (Derby Co) 2
Davis, H. 1903 (Sheffield W) 3
Davison, J. E. 1922 (Sheffield W) 1
Dawson, J. 1922 (Burnley) 2
Dawson, M. R. 2011 (Tottenham H) 4
Day, S. H. 1906 (Old Malvernians) 3
Dean, W. R. 1927 (Everton) 16
Deane, B. C. 1991 (Sheffield U) 3
Deeley, N. V. 1959 (Wolverhampton W) 2
Defoe, J. C. 2004 (Tottenham H, Portsmouth, Tottenham H, Sunderland) 57
Delph, F. 2015 (Aston Villa, Manchester C) 20
Devey, J. H. G. 1892 (Aston Villa) 2
Devonshire, A. 1980 (West Ham U) 8
Dewhurst, F. 1886 (Preston NE) 9
Dewhurst, G. P. 1895 (Liverpool Ramblers) 1
Dickinson, J. W. 1949 (Portsmouth) 48
Dier, E. J. E. 2016 (Tottenham H) 40
Dimmock, J. H. 1921 (Tottenham H) 3
Ditchburn, E. G. 1949 (Tottenham H) 6
Dix, R. W. 1939 (Derby Co) 1
Dixon, J. A. 1885 (Notts Co) 1
Dixon, K. M. 1985 (Chelsea) 8
Dixon, L. M. 1990 (Arsenal) 22
Dobson, A. T. C. 1882 (Notts Co) 4
Dobson, C. F. 1886 (Notts Co) 1
Dobson, J. M. 1974 (Burnley, Everton) 5
Doggart, A. G. 1924 (Corinthians) 1
Dorigo, A. R. 1990 (Chelsea, Leeds U) 15
Dorrell, A. R. 1925 (Aston Villa) 4
Douglas, B. 1958 (Blackburn R) 36
Downing, S. 2005 (Middlesbrough, Aston Villa, Liverpool, West Ham U) 35
Downs, R. W. 1921 (Everton) 1
Doyle, M. 1976 (Manchester C) 5
Drake, E. J. 1935 (Arsenal) 5
Drinkwater, D. N. 2016 (Leicester C) 3
Dublin, D. 1998 (Coventry C, Aston Villa) 4
Ducat, A. 1910 (Woolwich Arsenal, Aston Villa) 6
Dunn, A. T. B. 1883 (Cambridge University, Old Etonians) 4
Dunn, D. J. I. 2003 (Blackburn R) 1
Dunk, L. C. 2019 (Brighton & HA) 1
Duxbury, M. 1984 (Manchester U) 10
Dyer, K. C. 2000 (Newcastle U, West Ham U) 33

Earle, S. G. J. 1924 (Clapton, West Ham U) 2
Eastham, G. 1963 (Arsenal) 19
Eastham, G. R. 1935 (Bolton W) 1
Eckersley, W. 1950 (Blackburn R) 17
Edwards, D. 1955 (Manchester U) 18
Edwards, J. H. 1874 (Shropshire Wanderers) 1
Edwards, W. 1926 (Leeds U) 16
Ehiogu, U. 1996 (Aston Villa, Middlesbrough) 4
Ellerington, W. 1949 (Southampton) 2
Elliott, G. W. 1913 (Middlesbrough) 3
Elliott, W. H. 1952 (Burnley) 5
Evans, R. E. 1911 (Sheffield U) 4
Ewer, F. H. 1924 (Casuals) 2

Fairclough, P. 1878 (Old Foresters) 1
Fairhurst, D. 1934 (Newcastle U) 1
Fantham, J. 1962 (Sheffield W) 1
Fashanu, J. 1989 (Wimbledon) 2
Felton, W. 1925 (Sheffield W) 1
Fenton, M. 1938 (Middlesbrough) 1
Fenwick, T. W. 1984 (QPR, Tottenham H) 20
Ferdinand, L. 1993 (QPR, Newcastle U, Tottenham H) 17
Ferdinand, R. G. 1998 (West Ham U, Leeds U, Manchester U) 81
Field, E. 1876 (Clapham R) 2
Finney, T. 1947 (Preston NE) 76
Flanagan, J. P. 2014 (Liverpool) 1
Fleming, H. J. 1909 (Swindon T) 11
Fletcher, A. 1889 (Wolverhampton W) 2
Flowers, R. 1955 (Wolverhampton W) 49
Flowers, T. D. 1993 (Southampton, Blackburn R) 11
Forman, Frank 1898 (Nottingham F 9
Forman, F. R. 1899 (Nottingham F) 3
Forrest, J. H. 1884 (Blackburn R) 11
Forster, F. G. 2013 (Celtic, Southampton) 6
Fort, J. 1921 (Millwall) 1
Foster, B. 2007 (Manchester U, Birmingham C, WBA) 8
Foster, R. E. 1900 (Oxford University, Corinthians) 5
Foster, S. 1982 (Brighton & HA) 3
Foulke, W. J. 1897 (Sheffield U) 1
Foulkes, W. A. 1955 (Manchester U) 1
Fowler, R. B. 1996 (Liverpool, Leeds U) 26
Fox, F. S. 1925 (Millwall) 1
Francis, G. C. J. 1975 (QPR) 12
Francis, T. 1977 (Birmingham C, Nottingham F, Manchester C, Sampdoria) 52
Franklin, C. F. 1947 (Stoke C) 27
Freeman, B. C. 1909 (Everton, Burnley) 5
Froggatt, J. 1950 (Portsmouth) 13
Froggatt, R. 1953 (Sheffield W) 4
Fry, C. B. 1901 (Corinthians) 1
Furness, W. I. 1933 (Leeds U) 1

Galley, T. 1937 (Wolverhampton W) 2
Gardner, A. 2004 (Tottenham H) 1
Gardner, T. 1934 (Aston Villa) 2
Garfield, B. 1898 (WBA) 1
Garraty, W. 1903 (Aston Villa) 1
Garrett, T. 1952 (Blackpool) 3
Gascoigne, P. J. 1989 (Tottenham H, Lazio, Rangers, Middlesbrough) 57
Gates, E. 1981 (Ipswich T) 2
Gay, L. H. 1893 (Cambridge University, Old Brightonians) 3
Geary, F. 1890 (Everton) 2
Geaves, R. L. 1875 (Clapham R) 1

Gee, C. W. 1932 (Everton) 3
Geldard, A. 1933 (Everton) 4
George, C. 1977 (Derby Co) 1
George, W. 1902 (Aston Villa) 3
Gerrard, S. G. 2000 (Liverpool) 114
Gibbins, W. V. T. 1924 (Clapton) 2
Gibbs, K. J. R. 2011 (Arsenal) 10
Gidman, J. 1977 (Aston Villa) 1
Gillard, I. T. 1975 (QPR) 3
Gilliat, W. E. 1893 (Old Carthusians) 1
Goddard, P. 1982 (West Ham U) 1
Gomez, J. D. 2018 (Liverpool) 8
Goodall, F. R. 1926 (Huddersfield T) 25
Goodall, J. 1888 (Preston NE, Derby Co) 14
Goodhart, H. C. 1883 (Old Etonians) 3
Goodwyn, A. G. 1873 (Royal Engineers) 1
Goodyer, A. C. 1879 (Nottingham F) 1
Gosling, R. C. 1892 (Old Etonians) 5
Gosnell, A. A. 1906 (Newcastle U) 1
Gough, H. C. 1921 (Sheffield U) 1
Goulden, L. A. 1937 (West Ham U) 14
Graham, L. 1925 (Millwall) 2
Graham, T. 1931 (Nottingham F) 2
Grainger, C. 1956 (Sheffield U, Sunderland) 7
Gray, A. A. 1992 (Crystal Palace) 1
Gray, M. 1999 (Sunderland) 3
Greaves, J. 1959 (Chelsea, Tottenham H) 57
Green, F. T. 1876 (Wanderers) 1
Green, G. H. 1925 (Sheffield U) 8
Green, R. P. 2005 (Norwich C, West Ham U) 12
Greenhalgh, E. H. 1872 (Notts Co) 2
Greenhoff, B. 1976 (Manchester U, Leeds U) 18
Greenwood, D. H. 1882 (Blackburn R) 2
Gregory, J. 1983 (QPR) 6
Grimsdell, A. 1920 (Tottenham H) 6
Grosvenor, A. T. 1934 (Birmingham) 3
Gunn, W. 1884 (Notts Co) 2
Guppy, S. 2000 (Leicester C) 1
Gurney, R. 1935 (Sunderland) 1

Hacking, J. 1929 (Oldham Ath) 3
Hadley, H. 1903 (WBA) 1
Hagan, J. 1949 (Sheffield U) 1
Haines, J. T. W. 1949 (WBA) 1
Hall, A. E. 1910 (Aston Villa) 1
Hall, G. W. 1934 (Tottenham H) 10
Hall, J. 1956 (Birmingham C) 17
Halse, H. J. 1909 (Manchester U) 1
Hammond, H. E. D. 1889 (Oxford University) 1
Hampson, J. 1931 (Blackpool) 3
Hampton, H. 1913 (Aston Villa) 4
Hancocks, J. 1949 (Wolverhampton W) 3
Hapgood, E. 1933 (Arsenal) 30
Hardinge, H. T. W. 1910 (Sheffield U) 1
Hardman, H. P. 1905 (Everton) 4
Hardwick, G. F. M. 1947 (Middlesbrough) 13
Hardy, H. 1925 (Stockport Co) 1
Hardy, S. 1907 (Liverpool, Aston Villa) 21
Harford, M. G. 1988 (Luton T) 2
Hargreaves, F. W. 1880 (Blackburn R) 3
Hargreaves, J. 1881 (Blackburn R) 2
Hargreaves, O. 2002 (Bayern Munich, Manchester U) 42
Harper, E. C. 1926 (Blackburn R) 1
Harris, G. 1966 (Burnley) 1
Harris, P. P. 1950 (Portsmouth) 2
Harris, S. S. 1904 (Cambridge University, Old Westminsters) 6
Harrison, A. H. 1893 (Old Westminsters) 2
Harrison, G. 1921 (Everton) 2
Harrow, J. H. 1923 (Chelsea) 2
Hart, C. J. J. 2008 (Manchester C) 75
Hart, E. 1929 (Leeds U) 8
Hartley, F. 1923 (Oxford C) 1
Harvey, A. 1881 (Wednesbury Strollers) 1
Harvey, J. C. 1971 (Everton) 1
Hassall, H. W. 1951 (Huddersfield T, Bolton W) 5
Hateley, M. 1984 (Portsmouth, AC Milan, Monaco, Rangers) 32
Hawkes, R. M. 1907 (Luton T) 5
Haworth, G. 1887 (Accrington) 5
Hawtrey, J. P. 1881 (Old Etonians) 2
Haygarth, E. B. 1875 (Swifts) 1
Haynes, J. N. 1955 (Fulham) 56
Healless, H. 1925 (Blackburn R) 2
Heaton, T. 2016 (Burnley) 3
Hector, K. J. 1974 (Derby Co) 2
Hedley, G. A. 1901 (Sheffield U) 1
Hegan, K. E. 1923 (Corinthians) 4
Hellawell, M. S. 1963 (Birmingham C) 2
Henderson, J. B. 2011 (Sunderland, Liverpool) 55
Hendrie, L. A. 1999 (Aston Villa) 1
Henfrey, A. G. 1891 (Cambridge University, Corinthians) 5
Henry, R. P. 1963 (Tottenham H) 1
Heron, F. 1876 (Wanderers) 1
Heron, G. H. H. 1873 (Uxbridge, Wanderers) 5
Heskey, E. W. I. 1999 (Leicester C, Liverpool, Birmingham C, Wigan Ath, Aston Villa) 62
Hibbert, W. 1910 (Bury) 1
Hibbs, H. E. 1930 (Birmingham) 25
Hill, F. 1963 (Bolton W) 2
Hill, G. A. 1976 (Manchester U) 6
Hill, J. H. 1925 (Burnley, Newcastle U) 11
Hill, R. 1983 (Luton T) 3
Hill, R. H. 1926 (Millwall) 1
Hillman, J. 1899 (Burnley) 1
Hills, A. F. 1879 (Old Harrovians) 1
Hilsdon, G. R. 1907 (Chelsea) 8
Hinchcliffe, A. G. 1997 (Everton, Sheffield W) 7
Hine, E. W. 1929 (Leicester C) 6
Hinton, A. T. 1963 (Wolverhampton W, Nottingham F) 3
Hirst, D. E. 1991 (Sheffield W) 3
Hitchens, G. A. 1961 (Aston Villa, Internazionale) 7
Hobbis, H. H. F. 1936 (Charlton Ath) 2
Hoddle, G. 1980 (Tottenham H, Monaco) 53
Hodge, S. B. 1986 (Aston Villa, Tottenham H, Nottingham F) 24
Hodgetts, D. 1888 (Aston Villa) 6
Hodgkinson, A. 1957 (Sheffield U) 5
Hodgson, G. 1931 (Liverpool) 3
Hodkinson, J. 1913 (Blackburn R) 3
Hogg, W. 1902 (Sunderland) 3
Holdcroft, G. H. 1937 (Preston NE) 2
Holden, A. D. 1959 (Bolton W) 5
Holden, G. H. 1881 (Wednesbury OA) 4
Holden-White, C. 1888 (Corinthians) 2
Holford, T. 1903 (Stoke) 1
Holley, G. H. 1909 (Sunderland) 10
Holliday, E. 1960 (Middlesbrough) 3
Hollins, J. W. 1967 (Chelsea) 1
Holmes, R. 1888 (Preston NE) 7
Holt, J. 1890 (Everton, Reading) 10
Hopkinson, E. 1958 (Bolton W) 14
Hossack, A. H. 1892 (Corinthians) 2
Houghton, W. E. 1931 (Aston Villa) 7
Houlker, A. E. 1902 (Blackburn R, Portsmouth, Southampton) 5
Howarth, R. H. 1887 (Preston NE, Everton) 5
Howe, D. 1958 (WBA) 23
Howe, J. R. 1948 (Derby Co) 3
Howell, L. S. 1873 (Wanderers) 1
Howell, R. 1895 (Sheffield U, Liverpool) 2
Howey, S. N. 1995 (Newcastle U) 4
Huddlestone, T. A. 2010 (Tottenham H) 4
Hudson, A. A. 1975 (Stoke C) 2
Hudson, J. 1883 (Sheffield) 1
Hudson-Odoi C. J. 2019 (Chelsea) 3
Hudspeth, F. C. 1926 (Newcastle U) 1
Hufton, A. E. 1924 (West Ham U) 6
Hughes, E. W. 1970 (Liverpool, Wolverhampton W) 62
Hughes, L. 1950 (Liverpool) 3
Hulme, J. H. A. 1927 (Arsenal) 9
Humphreys, P. 1903 (Notts Co) 1
Hunt, G. S. 1933 (Tottenham H) 3
Hunt, Rev. K. R. G. 1911 (Leyton) 2
Hunt, R. 1962 (Liverpool) 34
Hunt, S. 1984 (WBA) 2
Hunter, J. 1878 (Sheffield Heeley) 7
Hunter, N. 1966 (Leeds U) 28
Hurst, G. C. 1966 (West Ham U) 49

Ince, P. E. C. 1993 (Manchester U, Internazionale, Liverpool, Middlesbrough) 53
Ings, D. 2016 (Liverpool) 1
Iremonger, J. 1901 (Nottingham F) 2

Jack, D. N. B. 1924 (Bolton W, Arsenal) 9
Jackson, E. 1891 (Oxford University) 1
Jagielka, P. N. 2008 (Everton) 40
James. D. B. 1997 (Liverpool, Aston Villa, West Ham U, Manchester C, Portsmouth) 53
Jarrett, B. G. 1876 (Cambridge University) 3
Jarvis, M. T. 2011 (Wolverhampton W) 1
Jefferis, F. 1912 (Everton) 2
Jeffers, F. 2003 (Arsenal) 1
Jenas, J. A. 2003 (Newcastle U, Tottenham H) 21
Jenkinson, C. D. 2013 (Arsenal) 1
Jezzard, B. A. G. 1954 (Fulham) 2
Johnson, A. 2005 (Crystal Palace, Everton) 8
Johnson, A. 2010 (Manchester C) 12
Johnson, D. E. 1975 (Ipswich T, Liverpool) 8
Johnson, E. 1880 (Saltley College, Stoke) 2
Johnson, G. M. C. 2004 (Chelsea, Portsmouth, Liverpool) 54
Johnson, J. A. 1937 (Stoke C) 5
Johnson, S. A. M. 2001 (Derby Co) 1
Johnson, T. C. F. 1926 (Manchester C, Everton) 5
Johnson, W. H. 1900 (Sheffield U) 6
Johnston, H. 1947 (Blackpool) 10
Jones, A. 1882 (Walsall Swifts, Great Lever) 3
Jones, H. 1923 (Nottingham F) 1
Jones, H. 1927 (Blackburn R) 6
Jones, M. D. 1965 (Sheffield U, Leeds U) 3
Jones, P. A. 2012 (Manchester U) 27
Jones, R. 1992 (Liverpool) 8
Jones, W. 1901 (Bristol C) 1
Jones, W. H. 1950 (Liverpool) 2
Joy, B. 1936 (Casuals) 1

Kail, E. I. L. 1929 (Dulwich Hamlet) 3
Kane, H. E. 2015 (Tottenham H) 45
Kay, A. H. 1963 (Everton) 1
Kean, F. W. 1923 (Sheffield W, Bolton W) 9
Keane, M. V. 2017 (Burnley, Everton) 10
Keegan, J. K. 1973 (Liverpool, Hamburg, Southampton) 63
Keen, E. R. L. 1933 (Derby Co) 4
Kelly, M. R. 2012 (Liverpool) 1
Kelly, R. 1920 (Burnley, Sunderland, Huddersfield T) 14
Kennedy, A. 1984 (Liverpool) 2
Kennedy, R. 1976 (Liverpool) 17
Kenyon-Slaney, W. S. 1873 (Wanderers) 1
Keown, M. R. 1992 (Everton, Arsenal) 43
Kevan, D. T. 1957 (WBA) 14
Kidd, B. 1970 (Manchester U) 2
King, L. B. 2002 (Tottenham H) 21
King, R. S. 1882 (Oxford University) 1
Kingsford, R. K. 1874 (Wanderers) 1
Kingsley, M. 1901 (Newcastle U) 1
Kinsey, G. 1892 (Wolverhampton W, Derby Co) 4
Kirchen, A. J. 1937 (Arsenal) 3
Kirkland, C. E. 2007 (Liverpool) 1
Kirton, W. J. 1922 (Aston Villa) 1
Knight, A. E. 1920 (Portsmouth) 1
Knight, Z. 2005 (Fulham) 2
Knowles, C. 1968 (Tottenham H) 4
Konchesky, P. M. 2003 (Charlton Ath, West Ham U) 2

Labone, B. L. 1963 (Everton) 26
Lallana, A. D. 2013 (Southampton, Liverpool) 34
Lambert, R. L. 2013 (Southampton, Liverpool) 11
Lampard, F. J. 2000 (West Ham U, Chelsea) 106
Lampard, F. R. G. 1973 (West Ham U) 2
Langley, E. J. 1958 (Fulham) 3
Langton, R. 1947 (Blackburn R, Preston NE, Bolton W) 11
Latchford, R. D. 1978 (Everton) 12
Latheron, E. G. 1913 (Blackburn R) 2
Lawler, C. 1971 (Liverpool) 4
Lawton, T. 1939 (Everton, Chelsea, Notts Co) 23
Leach, T. 1931 (Sheffield W) 2
Leake, A. 1904 (Aston Villa) 5
Lee, E. A. 1904 (Southampton) 1
Lee, F. H. 1969 (Manchester C) 27
Lee, J. 1951 (Derby Co) 1
Lee, R. M. 1995 (Newcastle U) 21
Lee, S. 1983 (Liverpool) 14
Leighton, J. E. 1886 (Nottingham F) 1
Lennon, A. J. 2006 (Tottenham H) 21
Lescott, J. P. 2008 (Everton, Manchester C) 26
Le Saux, G. P. 1994 (Blackburn R, Chelsea) 36
Le Tissier, M. P. 1994 (Southampton) 8
Lilley, H. E. 1892 (Sheffield U) 1
Linacre, H. J. 1905 (Nottingham F) 2
Lindley, T. 1886 (Cambridge University, Nottingham F) 13
Lindsay, A. 1974 (Liverpool) 4
Lindsay, W. 1877 (Wanderers) 1
Lineker, G. 1984 (Leicester C, Everton, Barcelona, Tottenham H) 80
Lingard, J. E. 2017 (Manchester U) 24
Lintott, E. H. 1908 (QPR, Bradford C) 7
Lipsham, H. B. 1902 (Sheffield U) 1
Little, B. 1975 (Aston Villa) 1
Livermore, J. C. 2013 (Tottenham H, WBA) 7
Lloyd, L. V. 1971 (Liverpool, Nottingham F) 4
Lockett, A. 1903 (Stoke) 1
Lodge, L. V. 1894 (Cambridge University, Corinthians) 5
Lofthouse, J. M. 1885 (Blackburn R, Accrington, Blackburn R) 7
Lofthouse, N. 1951 (Bolton W) 33
Loftus-Cheek, R. I. 2018 (Chelsea) 10
Longworth, E. 1920 (Liverpool) 5
Lowder, A. 1889 (Wolverhampton W) 1
Lowe, E. 1947 (Aston Villa) 3
Lucas, T. 1922 (Liverpool) 3
Luntley, E. 1880 (Nottingham F) 2
Lyttelton, Hon. A. 1877 (Cambridge University) 1
Lyttelton, Hon. E. 1878 (Cambridge University) 1

Mabbutt, G. 1983 (Tottenham H) 16
Macaulay, R. H. 1881 (Cambridge University) 1
Macrae, S. 1883 (Notts Co) 5
Maddison, F. B. 1872 (Oxford University) 1
Maddison, J. D. 2020 (Leicester C) 1
Madeley, P. E. 1971 (Leeds U) 24
Magee, T. P. 1923 (WBA) 5
Maguire, J. H. 2018 (Leicester C, Manchester U) 26
Makepeace, H. 1906 (Everton) 4
Male, C. G. 1935 (Arsenal) 19
Mannion, W. J. 1947 (Middlesbrough) 26
Mariner, P. 1977 (Ipswich T, Arsenal) 35
Marsden, J. T. 1891 (Darwen) 1
Marsden, W. 1930 (Sheffield W) 3
Marsh, R. W. 1972 (QPR, Manchester C) 9
Marshall, T. 1880 (Darwen) 2
Martin, A. 1981 (West Ham U) 17
Martin, H. 1914 (Sunderland) 1
Martyn, A. N. 1992 (Crystal Palace, Leeds U) 23
Marwood, B. 1989 (Arsenal) 1
Maskrey, H. M. 1908 (Derby Co) 1
Mason, C. 1887 (Wolverhampton W) 3
Mason, R. G. 2015 (Tottenham H) 1
Matthews, R. D. 1956 (Coventry C) 5
Matthews, S. 1935 (Stoke C, Blackpool) 54
Matthews, V. 1928 (Sheffield U) 2
Maynard, W. J. 1872 (1st Surrey Rifles) 2
McCall, J. 1913 (Preston NE) 5
McCann, G. P. 2001 (Sunderland) 1
McCarthy, A. S. 2019 (Southampton) 1
McDermott, T. 1978 (Liverpool) 25
McDonald, C. A. 1958 (Burnley) 8
Macdonald, M. 1972 (Newcastle U) 14
McFarland, R. L. 1971 (Derby Co) 28
McGarry, W. H. 1954 (Huddersfield T) 4
McGuinness, W. 1959 (Manchester U) 2
McInroy, A. 1927 (Sunderland) 1
McMahon, S. 1988 (Liverpool) 17
McManaman, S. 1995 (Liverpool, Real Madrid) 37
McNab, R. 1969 (Arsenal) 4
McNeal, R. 1914 (WBA) 2
McNeil, M. 1961 (Middlesbrough) 9
Meadows, J. 1955 (Manchester C) 1

Medley, L. D. 1951 (Tottenham H) 6
Meehan, T. 1924 (Chelsea) 1
Melia, J. 1963 (Liverpool) 2
Mercer, D. W. 1923 (Sheffield U) 2
Mercer, J. 1939 (Everton) 5
Merrick, G. H. 1952 (Birmingham C) 23
Merson, P. C. 1992 (Arsenal, Middlesbrough, Aston Villa) 21
Metcalfe, V. 1951 (Huddersfield T) 2
Mew, J. W. 1921 (Manchester U) 1
Middleditch, B. 1897 (Corinthians) 1
Milburn, J. E. T. 1949 (Newcastle U) 13
Miller, B. G. 1961 (Burnley) 1
Miller, H. S. 1923 (Charlton Ath) 1
Mills, D. J. 2001 (Leeds U) 19
Mills, G. R. 1938 (Chelsea) 3
Mills, M. D. 1973 (Ipswich T) 42
Milne, G. 1963 (Liverpool) 14
Milner, J. P. 2010 (Aston Villa, Manchester C, Liverpool) 61
Milton, C. A. 1952 (Arsenal) 1
Milward, A. 1891 (Everton) 4
Mings, T. D. 2020 (Aston Villa) 2
Mitchell, C. 1880 (Upton Park) 5
Mitchell, J. F. 1925 (Manchester C) 1
Moffat, H. 1913 (Oldham Ath) 1
Molyneux, G. 1902 (Southampton) 4
Moon, W. R. 1888 (Old Westminsters) 7
Moore, H. T. 1883 (Notts Co) 2
Moore, J. 1923 (Derby Co) 1
Moore, R. F. 1962 (West Ham U) 108
Moore, W. G. B. 1923 (West Ham U) 1
Mordue, J. 1912 (Sunderland) 2
Morice, C. J. 1872 (Barnes) 1
Morley, A. 1982 (Aston Villa) 6
Morley, H. 1910 (Notts Co) 1
Morren, T. 1898 (Sheffield U) 1
Morris, F. 1920 (WBA) 2
Morris, J. 1949 (Derby Co) 3
Morris, W. W. 1939 (Wolverhampton W) 3
Morse, H. 1879 (Notts Co) 1
Mort, T. 1924 (Aston Villa) 3
Morten, A. 1873 (Crystal Palace) 1
Mortensen, S. H. 1947 (Blackpool) 25
Morton, J. R. 1938 (West Ham U) 1
Mosforth, W. 1877 (Sheffield W, Sheffield Alb, Sheffield W) 9
Moss, F. 1922 (Aston Villa) 5
Moss, F. 1934 (Arsenal) 4
Mosscrop, E. 1914 (Burnley) 2
Mount, M. T. 2020 (Chelsea) 6
Mozley, B. 1950 (Derby Co) 3
Mullen, J. 1947 (Wolverhampton W) 12
Mullery, A. P. 1965 (Tottenham H) 35
Murphy, D. B. 2002 (Liverpool) 9

Neal, P. G. 1976 (Liverpool) 50
Needham, E. 1894 (Sheffield U) 16
Neville, G. A. 1995 (Manchester U) 85
Neville, P. J. 1996 (Manchester U, Everton) 59
Newton, K. R. 1966 (Blackburn R, Everton) 27
Nicholls, J. 1954 (WBA) 2
Nicholson, W. E. 1951 (Tottenham H) 1
Nish, D. J. 1973 (Derby Co) 5
Norman, M. 1962 (Tottenham H) 23
Nugent, D. J. 2007 (Preston NE) 1
Nuttall, H. 1928 (Bolton W) 3

Oakley, W. J. 1895 (Oxford University, Corinthians) 16
O'Dowd, J. P. 1932 (Chelsea) 3
O'Grady, M. 1963 (Huddersfield T, Leeds U) 2
Ogilvie, R. A. M. M. 1874 (Clapham R) 1
Oliver, L. F. 1929 (Fulham) 1
Olney, B. A. 1928 (Aston Villa) 2
Osborne, F. R. 1923 (Fulham, Tottenham H) 4
Osborne, R. 1928 (Leicester C) 1
Osgood, P. L. 1970 (Chelsea) 4
Osman, L. 2013 (Everton) 2
Osman, R. 1980 (Ipswich T) 11
Ottaway, C. J. 1872 (Oxford University) 2
Owen, J. R. B. 1874 (Sheffield) 1
Owen, M. J. 1998 (Liverpool, Real Madrid, Newcastle U) 89
Owen, S. W. 1954 (Luton T) 3
Oxlade-Chamberlain, A. M. D. 2012 (Arsenal, Liverpool) 35

Page, L. A. 1927 (Burnley) 7
Paine, T. L. 1963 (Southampton) 19
Pallister, G. A. 1988 (Middlesbrough, Manchester U) 22
Palmer, C. L. 1992 (Sheffield W) 18
Pantling, H. H. 1924 (Sheffield U) 1
Paravicini, P. J. de 1883 (Cambridge University) 3
Parker, P. A. 1989 (QPR, Manchester U) 19
Parker, S. M. 2004 (Charlton Ath, Chelsea, Newcastle U, West Ham U, Tottenham H) 18
Parker, T. R. 1925 (Southampton) 1
Parkes, P. B. 1974 (QPR) 1
Parkinson, J. 1910 (Liverpool) 2
Parlour, R. 1999 (Arsenal) 10
Parr, P. C. 1882 (Oxford University) 1
Parry, E. H. 1879 (Old Carthusians) 3
Parry, R. A. 1960 (Bolton W) 2
Patchitt, B. C. A. 1923 (Corinthians) 2
Pawson, F. W. 1883 (Cambridge University, Swifts) 2
Payne, J. 1937 (Luton T) 1
Peacock, A. 1962 (Middlesbrough, Leeds U) 6
Peacock, J. 1929 (Middlesbrough) 3
Pearce, S. 1987 (Nottingham F, West Ham U) 78
Pearson, H. F. 1932 (WBA) 1
Pearson, J. H. 1892 (Crewe Alex) 1
Pearson, J. S. 1976 (Manchester U) 15
Pearson, S. C. 1948 (Manchester U) 8
Pease, W. H. 1927 (Middlesbrough) 1
Pegg, D. 1957 (Manchester U) 1
Pejic, M. 1974 (Stoke C) 4
Pelly, F. R. 1893 (Old Foresters) 3
Pennington, J. 1907 (WBA) 25
Pentland, F. B. 1909 (Middlesbrough) 5
Perry, C. 1890 (WBA) 3
Perry, T. 1898 (WBA) 1
Perry, W. 1956 (Blackpool) 3
Perryman, S. 1982 (Tottenham H) 1
Peters, M. 1966 (West Ham U, Tottenham H) 67
Phelan, M. C. 1990 (Manchester U) 1
Phillips, K. 1999 (Sunderland) 8
Phillips, L. H. 1952 (Portsmouth) 3
Pickering, F. 1964 (Everton) 3
Pickering, J. 1933 (Sheffield U) 1
Pickering, N. 1983 (Sunderland) 1
Pickford, J. L. 2018 (Everton) 24
Pike, T. M. 1886 (Cambridge University) 1
Pilkington, B. 1955 (Burnley) 1
Plant, J. 1900 (Bury) 1
Platt, D. 1990 (Aston Villa, Bari, Juventus, Sampdoria, Arsenal) 62
Plum, S. L. 1923 (Charlton Ath) 1
Pointer, R. 1962 (Burnley) 3
Pope, N. D. 2018 (Burnley) 2
Porteous, T. S. 1891 (Sunderland) 1
Powell, C. G. 2001 (Charlton Ath) 5
Priest, A. E. 1900 (Sheffield U) 1
Prinsep, J. F. M. 1879 (Clapham R) 1
Puddefoot, S. C. 1926 (Blackburn R) 2
Pye, J. 1950 (Wolverhampton W) 1
Pym, R. H. 1925 (Bolton W) 3

Quantrill, A. 1920 (Derby Co) 4
Quixall, A. 1954 (Sheffield W) 5

Radford, J. 1969 (Arsenal) 2
Raikes, G. B. 1895 (Oxford University) 4
Ramsey, A. E. 1949 (Southampton, Tottenham H) 32
Rashford, M. 2016 (Manchester U) 38
Rawlings, A. 1921 (Preston NE) 1
Rawlings, W. E. 1922 (Southampton) 2
Rawlinson, J. F. P. 1882 (Cambridge University) 1
Rawson, H. E. 1875 (Royal Engineers) 1
Rawson, W. S. 1875 (Oxford University) 2
Read, A. 1921 (Tufnell Park) 1
Reader, J. 1894 (WBA) 1
Reaney, P. 1969 (Leeds U) 3

Redknapp, J. F. 1996 (Liverpool) 17
Redmond, N. D. J. 2017 (Southampton) 1
Reeves, K. P. 1980 (Norwich C, Manchester C) 2
Regis, C. 1982 (WBA, Coventry C) 5
Reid, P. 1985 (Everton) 13
Revie, D. G. 1955 (Manchester C) 6
Reynolds, J. 1892 (WBA, Aston Villa) 8
Rice, D. 2019 (West Ham U) 7
Richards, C. H. 1898 (Nottingham F) 1
Richards, G. H. 1909 (Derby Co) 1
Richards, J. P. 1973 (Wolverhampton W) 1
Richards, M. 2007 (Manchester C) 13
Richardson, J. R. 1933 (Newcastle U) 2
Richardson, K. 1994 (Aston Villa) 1
Richardson, K. E. 2005 (Manchester U) 8
Richardson, W. G. 1935 (WBA) 1
Rickaby, S. 1954 (WBA) 1
Ricketts, M. B. 2002 (Bolton W) 1
Rigby, A. 1927 (Blackburn R) 5
Rimmer, E. J. 1930 (Sheffield W) 4
Rimmer, J. J. 1976 (Arsenal) 1
Ripley, S. E. 1994 (Blackburn R) 2
Rix, G. 1981 (Arsenal) 17
Robb, G. 1954 (Tottenham H) 1
Roberts, C. 1905 (Manchester U) 3
Roberts, F. 1925 (Manchester C) 4
Roberts, G. 1983 (Tottenham H) 6
Roberts, H. 1931 (Arsenal) 1
Roberts, H. 1931 (Millwall) 1
Roberts, R. 1887 (WBA) 3
Roberts, W. T. 1924 (Preston NE) 2
Robinson, J. 1937 (Sheffield W) 4
Robinson, J. W. 1897 (Derby Co, New Brighton Tower, Southampton) 11
Robinson, P. W. 2003 (Leeds U, Tottenham H, Blackburn R) 41
Robson, B. 1980 (WBA, Manchester U) 90
Robson, R. 1958 (WBA) 20
Rocastle, D. 1989 (Arsenal) 14
Rodriguez, J. E. 2013 (Southampton) 1
Rodwell, J. 2012 (Everton) 3
Rooney, W. M. 2003 (Everton, Manchester U, D.C. United) 120
Rose, D. L. 2016 (Tottenham H) 29
Rose, W. C. 1884 (Swifts, Preston NE, Wolverhampton W) 5
Rostron, T. 1881 (Darwen) 2
Rowe, A. 1934 (Tottenham H) 1
Rowley, J. F. 1949 (Manchester U) 6
Rowley, W. 1889 (Stoke) 2
Royle, J. 1971 (Everton, Manchester C) 6
Ruddlesdin, H. 1904 (Sheffield W) 3
Ruddock, N. 1995 (Liverpool) 1
Ruddy, J. T. G. 2013 (Norwich C) 1
Ruffell, J. W. 1926 (West Ham U) 6
Russell, B. B. 1883 (Royal Engineers) 1
Rutherford, J. 1904 (Newcastle U) 11

Sadler, D. 1968 (Manchester U) 4
Sagar, C. 1900 (Bury) 2
Sagar, E. 1936 (Everton) 4
Salako, J. A. 1991 (Crystal Palace) 5
Sancho, J. M. 2019 (Borussia Dortmund) 11
Sandford, E. A. 1933 (WBA) 1
Sandilands, R. R. 1892 (Old Westminsters) 5
Sands, J. 1880 (Nottingham F) 1
Sansom, K. G. 1979 (Crystal Palace, Arsenal) 86
Saunders, F. E. 1888 (Swifts) 1
Savage, A. H. 1876 (Crystal Palace) 1
Sayer, J. 1887 (Stoke) 1
Scales, J. R. 1995 (Liverpool) 3
Scattergood, E. 1913 (Derby Co) 1
Schofield, J. 1892 (Stoke) 3
Scholes, P. 1997 (Manchester U) 66
Scott, L. 1947 (Arsenal) 17
Scott, W. R. 1937 (Brentford) 1
Seaman, D. A. 1989 (QPR, Arsenal) 75
Seddon, J. 1923 (Bolton W) 6
Seed, J. M. 1921 (Tottenham H) 5
Settle, J. 1899 (Bury, Everton) 6
Sewell, J. 1952 (Sheffield W) 6
Sewell, W. R. 1924 (Blackburn R) 1
Shackleton, L. F. 1949 (Sunderland) 5
Sharp, J. 1903 (Everton) 2
Sharpe, L. S. 1991 (Manchester U) 8
Shaw, G. E. 1932 (WBA) 1
Shaw, G. L. 1959 (Sheffield U) 5
Shaw, L. P. H. 2014 (Southampton, Manchester U) 8
Shawcross, R. J. 2013 (Stoke C) 1
Shea, D. 1914 (Blackburn R) 2
Shearer, A. 1992 (Southampton, Blackburn R, Newcastle U) 63
Shellito, K. J. 1963 (Chelsea) 1
Shelton A. 1889 (Notts Co) 6
Shelton, C. 1888 (Notts Rangers) 1
Shelvey, J. 2013 (Liverpool, Swansea C) 6
Shepherd, A. 1906 (Bolton W, Newcastle U) 2
Sheringham, E. P. 1993 (Tottenham H, Manchester U, Tottenham H) 51
Sherwood, T. A. 1999 (Tottenham H) 3
Shilton, P. L. 1971 (Leicester C, Stoke C, Nottingham F, Southampton, Derby Co) 125
Shimwell, E. 1949 (Blackpool) 1
Shorey, N. 2007 (Reading) 2
Shutt, G. 1886 (Stoke) 1
Silcock, J. 1921 (Manchester U) 3
Sillett, R. P. 1955 (Chelsea) 3
Simms, E. 1922 (Luton T) 1
Simpson, J. 1911 (Blackburn R) 8
Sinclair, T. 2002 (West Ham U, Manchester C) 12
Sinton, A. 1992 (QPR, Sheffield W) 12
Slater, W. J. 1955 (Wolverhampton W) 12
Smalley, T. 1937 (Wolverhampton W) 1
Smalling, C. L. 2012 (Manchester U) 31
Smart, T. 1921 (Aston Villa) 5
Smith, A. 1891 (Nottingham F) 3
Smith, A. 2001 (Leeds U, Manchester U, Newcastle U) 19
Smith, A. K. 1872 (Oxford University) 1
Smith, A. M. 1989 (Arsenal) 13
Smith, B. 1921 (Tottenham H) 2
Smith, C. E. 1876 (Crystal Palace) 1
Smith, G. O. 1893 (Oxford University, Old Carthusians, Corinthians) 20
Smith, H. 1905 (Reading) 4
Smith, J. 1920 (WBA) 2
Smith, Joe 1913 (Bolton W) 5
Smith, J. C. R. 1939 (Millwall) 2
Smith, J. W. 1932 (Portsmouth) 3
Smith, Leslie 1939 (Brentford) 1
Smith, Lionel 1951 (Arsenal) 6
Smith, R. A. 1961 (Tottenham H) 15
Smith, S. 1895 (Aston Villa) 1
Smith, S. C. 1936 (Leicester C) 1
Smith, T. 1960 (Birmingham C) 2
Smith, T. 1971 (Liverpool) 1
Smith, W. H. 1922 (Huddersfield T) 3
Solanke, D. A. 2018 (Liverpool) 1
Sorby, T. H. 1879 (Thursday Wanderers, Sheffield) 1
Southgate, G. 1996 (Aston Villa, Middlesbrough) 57
Southworth, J. 1889 (Blackburn R) 3
Sparks, F. J. 1879 (Herts Rangers, Clapham R) 3
Spence, J. W. 1926 (Manchester U) 2
Spence, R. 1936 (Chelsea) 2
Spencer, C. W. 1924 (Newcastle U) 2
Spencer, H. 1897 (Aston Villa) 6
Spiksley, F. 1893 (Sheffield W) 7
Spilsbury, B. W. 1885 (Cambridge University) 3
Spink, N. 1983 (Aston Villa) 1
Spouncer, W. A. 1900 (Nottingham F) 1
Springett, R. D. G. 1960 (Sheffield W) 33
Sproston, B. 1937 (Leeds U, Tottenham H, Manchester C) 11
Squire, R. T. 1886 (Cambridge University) 3
Stanbrough, M. H. 1895 (Old Carthusians) 1
Staniforth, R. 1954 (Huddersfield T) 8
Starling, R. W. 1933 (Sheffield W, Aston Villa) 2
Statham, D. J. 1983 (WBA) 3
Steele, F. C. 1937 (Stoke C) 6
Stein, B. 1984 (Luton T) 1
Stephenson, C. 1924 (Huddersfield T) 1
Stephenson, G. T. 1928 (Derby Co, Sheffield W) 3
Stephenson, J. E. 1938 (Leeds U) 2

Stepney, A. C. 1968 (Manchester U) 1
Sterland, M. 1989 (Sheffield W) 1
Sterling, R. S. 2013 (Liverpool, Manchester C) 56
Steven, T. M. 1985 (Everton, Rangers, Marseille) 36
Stevens, G. A. 1985 (Tottenham H) 7
Stevens, M. G. 1985 (Everton, Rangers) 46
Stewart, J. 1907 (Sheffield W, Newcastle U) 3
Stewart, P. A. 1992 (Tottenham H) 3
Stiles, N. P. 1965 (Manchester U) 28
Stoker, J. 1933 (Birmingham) 3
Stone, S. B. 1996 (Nottingham F) 9
Stones, J. 2014 (Everton, Manchester C) 39
Storer, H. 1924 (Derby Co) 2
Storey, P. E. 1971 (Arsenal) 19
Storey-Moore, I. 1970 (Nottingham F) 1
Strange, A. H. 1930 (Sheffield W) 20
Stratford, A. H. 1874 (Wanderers) 1
Streten, B. 1950 (Luton T) 1
Sturgess, A. 1911 (Sheffield U) 2
Sturridge, D. A. 2012 (Chelsea, Liverpool) 26
Summerbee, M. G. 1968 (Manchester C) 8
Sunderland, A. 1980 (Arsenal) 1
Sutcliffe, J. W. 1893 (Bolton W, Millwall) 5
Sutton, C. R. 1998 (Blackburn R) 1
Swan, P. 1960 (Sheffield W) 19
Swepstone, H. A. 1880 (Pilgrims) 6
Swift, F. V. 1947 (Manchester C) 19

Tait, G. 1881 (Birmingham Excelsior) 1
Talbot, B. 1977 (Ipswich T, Arsenal) 6
Tambling, R. V. 1963 (Chelsea) 3
Tarkowski, J. A. 2018 (Burnley) 2
Tate, J. T. 1931 (Aston Villa) 3
Taylor, E. 1954 (Blackpool) 1
Taylor, E. H. 1923 (Huddersfield T) 8
Taylor, J. G. 1951 (Fulham) 2
Taylor, P. H. 1948 (Liverpool) 3
Taylor, P. J. 1976 (Crystal Palace) 4
Taylor, T. 1953 (Manchester U) 19
Temple, D. W. 1965 (Everton) 1
Terry, J. G. 2003 (Chelsea) 78
Thickett, H. 1899 (Sheffield U) 2
Thomas, D. 1975 (QPR) 8
Thomas, D. 1983 (Coventry C) 2
Thomas, G. R. 1991 (Crystal Palace) 9
Thomas, M. L. 1989 (Arsenal) 2
Thompson, A. 2004 (Celtic) 1
Thompson, P. 1964 (Liverpool) 16
Thompson, P. B. 1976 (Liverpool) 42
Thompson T. 1952 (Aston Villa, Preston NE) 2
Thomson, R. A. 1964 (Wolverhampton W) 8
Thornewell, G. 1923 (Derby Co) 4
Thornley, I. 1907 (Manchester C) 1
Tilson, S. F. 1934 (Manchester C) 4
Titmuss, F. 1922 (Southampton) 2
Todd, C. 1972 (Derby Co) 27
Tomori, O. O. (Fikayo) 2020 (Chelsea) 1
Toone, G. 1892 (Notts Co) 2
Topham, A. G. 1894 (Casuals) 1
Topham, R. 1893 (Wolverhampton W, Casuals) 2
Towers, M. A. 1976 (Sunderland) 3
Townley, W. J. 1889 (Blackburn R) 2
Townrow, J. E. 1925 (Clapton Orient) 2
Townsend, A. D. 2013 (Tottenham H, Newcastle U, Crystal Palace) 13
Tremelling, D. R. 1928 (Birmingham) 1
Tresadern, J. 1923 (West Ham U) 2
Trippier, K. J. 2017 (Tottenham H) 19
Tueart, D. 1975 (Manchester C) 6
Tunstall, F. E. 1923 (Sheffield U) 7
Turnbull, R. J. 1920 (Bradford) 1
Turner, A. 1900 (Southampton) 2
Turner, H. 1931 (Huddersfield T) 2
Turner, J. A. 1893 (Bolton W, Stoke, Derby Co) 3
Tweedy, G. J. 1937 (Grimsby T) 1

Ufton, D. G. 1954 (Charlton Ath) 1
Underwood, A. 1891 (Stoke C) 2
Unsworth, D. G. 1995 (Everton) 1
Upson, M. J. 2003 (Birmingham C, West Ham U) 21
Urwin, T. 1923 (Middlesbrough, Newcastle U) 4
Utley, G. 1913 (Barnsley) 1

Vardy, J. R. 2015 (Leicester C) 26
Vassell, D. 2002 (Aston Villa) 22
Vaughton, O. H. 1882 (Aston Villa) 5
Veitch, C. C. M. 1906 (Newcastle U) 6
Veitch, J. G. 1894 (Old Westminsters) 1
Venables, T. F. 1965 (Chelsea) 2
Venison, B. 1995 (Newcastle U) 2
Vidal, R. W. S. 1873 (Oxford University) 1
Viljoen, C. 1975 (Ipswich T) 2
Viollet, D. S. 1960 (Manchester U) 2
Von Donop 1873 (Royal Engineers) 2

Wace, H. 1878 (Wanderers) 3
Waddle, C. R. 1985 (Newcastle U, Tottenham H, Marseille) 62
Wadsworth, S. J. 1922 (Huddersfield T) 9
Wainscoat, W. R. 1929 (Leeds U) 1
Waiters, A. K. 1964 (Blackpool) 5
Walcott, T. J. 2006 (Arsenal) 47
Walden, F. I. 1914 (Tottenham H) 2
Walker, D. S. 1989 (Nottingham F, Sampdoria, Sheffield W) 59
Walker, I. M. 1996 (Tottenham H, Leicester C) 4
Walker, K. A. 2012 (Tottenham H, Manchester C) 48
Walker, W. H. 1921 (Aston Villa) 18
Wall, G. 1907 (Manchester U) 7
Wallace, C. W. 1913 (Aston Villa) 3
Wallace, D. L. 1986 (Southampton) 1
Walsh, P. A. 1983 (Luton T) 5
Walters, A. M. 1885 (Cambridge University, Old Carthusians) 9
Walters, K. M. 1991 (Rangers) 1
Walters, P. M. 1885 (Oxford University, Old Carthusians) 13
Walton, N. 1890 (Blackburn R) 1
Ward, J. T. 1885 (Blackburn Olympic) 1
Ward, P. 1980 (Brighton & HA) 1
Ward, T. V. 1948 (Derby Co) 2
Ward-Prowse, J. M. E. 2017 (Southampton) 2
Waring, T. 1931 (Aston Villa) 5
Warner, C. 1878 (Upton Park) 1
Warnock, S. 2008 (Blackburn R, Aston Villa) 2
Warren, B. 1906 (Derby Co, Chelsea) 22
Waterfield, G. S. 1927 (Burnley) 1
Watson, D. 1984 (Norwich C, Everton) 12
Watson, D. V. 1974 (Sunderland, Manchester C, Werder Bremen, Southampton, Stoke C) 65
Watson, V. M. 1923 (West Ham U) 5
Watson, W. 1913 (Burnley) 3
Watson, W. 1950 (Sunderland) 4
Weaver, S. 1932 (Newcastle U) 3
Webb, G. W. 1911 (West Ham U) 2
Webb, N. J. 1988 (Nottingham F, Manchester U) 26
Webster, M. 1930 (Middlesbrough) 3
Wedlock, W. J. 1907 (Bristol C) 26
Weir, D. 1889 (Bolton W) 2
Welbeck, D. N. T. M. 2011 (Manchester U, Arsenal) 42
Welch, R. de C. 1872 (Wanderers, Harrow Chequers) 2
Weller, K. 1974 (Leicester C) 4
Welsh, D. 1938 (Charlton Ath) 3
West, G. 1969 (Everton) 3
Westwood, R. W. 1935 (Bolton W) 6
Whateley, O. 1883 (Aston Villa) 2
Wheeler, J. E. 1955 (Bolton W) 1
Wheldon, G. F. 1897 (Aston Villa) 4
White, D. 1993 (Manchester C) 1
White, T. A. 1933 (Everton) 1
Whitehead, J. 1893 (Accrington, Blackburn R) 2
Whitfeld, H. 1879 (Old Etonians) 1
Whitham, M. 1892 (Sheffield U) 1
Whitworth, S. 1975 (Leicester C) 7
Whymark, T. J. 1978 (Ipswich T) 1
Widdowson, S. W. 1880 (Nottingham F) 1
Wignall, F. 1965 (Nottingham F) 2
Wilcox, J. M. 1996 (Blackburn R, Leeds U) 3
Wilkes, A. 1901 (Aston Villa) 5
Wilkins, R. C. 1976 (Chelsea, Manchester U, AC Milan) 84
Wilkinson, B. 1904 (Sheffield U) 1

Wilkinson, L. R. 1891 (Oxford University) 1
Williams, B. F. 1949 (Wolverhampton W) 24
Williams, O. 1923 (Clapton Orient) 2
Williams, S. 1983 (Southampton) 6
Williams, W. 1897 (WBA) 6
Williamson, E. C. 1923 (Arsenal) 2
Williamson, R. G. 1905 (Middlesbrough) 7
Willingham, C. K. 1937 (Huddersfield T) 12
Willis, A. 1952 (Tottenham H) 1
Wilshaw, D. J. 1954 (Wolverhampton W) 12
Wilshere, J. A. 2011 (Arsenal) 34
Wilson, C. 2019 (Bournemouth) 4
Wilson, C. P. 1884 (Hendon) 2
Wilson, C. W. 1879 (Oxford University) 2
Wilson, G. 1921 (Sheffield W) 12
Wilson, G. P. 1900 (Corinthians) 2
Wilson, R. 1960 (Huddersfield T, Everton) 63
Wilson, T. 1928 (Huddersfield T) 1
Winks, H. B. 2018 (Tottenham H) 6
Winckworth, W. N. 1892 (Old Westminsters) 2
Windridge, J. E. 1908 (Chelsea) 8
Wingfield-Stratford, C. V. 1877 (Royal Engineers) 1
Winterburn, N. 1990 (Arsenal) 2
Wise, D. F. 1991 (Chelsea) 21
Withe, P. 1981 (Aston Villa) 11
Wollaston, C. H. R. 1874 (Wanderers) 4
Wolstenholme, S. 1904 (Everton, Blackburn R) 3
Wood, H. 1890 (Wolverhampton W) 3
Wood, R. E. 1955 (Manchester U) 3
Woodcock, A. S. 1978 (Nottingham F, Cologne, Arsenal) 42
Woodgate, J. S. 1999 (Leeds U, Newcastle U, Real Madrid, Tottenham H) 8
Woodger, G. 1911 (Oldham Ath) 1
Woodhall, G. 1888 (WBA) 2
Woodley, V. R. 1937 (Chelsea) 19
Woods, C. C. E. 1985 (Norwich C, Rangers, Sheffield W) 43
Woodward, V. J. 1903 (Tottenham H, Chelsea) 23
Woosnam, M. 1922 (Manchester C) 1
Worrall, F. 1935 (Portsmouth) 2
Worthington, F. S. 1974 (Leicester C) 8
Wreford-Brown, C. 1889 (Oxford University, Old Carthusians) 4
Wright, E. G. D. 1906 (Cambridge University) 1
Wright, I. E. 1991 (Crystal Palace, Arsenal, West Ham U) 33
Wright, J. D. 1939 (Newcastle U) 1
Wright, M. 1984 (Southampton, Derby Co, Liverpool) 45
Wright, R. I. 2000 (Ipswich T, Arsenal) 2
Wright, T. J. 1968 (Everton) 11
Wright, W. A. 1947 (Wolverhampton W) 105
Wright-Phillips, S. C. 2005 (Manchester C, Chelsea, Manchester C) 36
Wylie, J. G. 1878 (Wanderers) 1

Yates, J. 1889 (Burnley) 1
York, R. E. 1922 (Aston Villa) 2
Young, A. 1933 (Huddersfield T) 9
Young, A. S. 2008 (Aston Villa, Manchester U) 39
Young, G. M. 1965 (Sheffield W) 1
Young, L. P. 2005 (Charlton Ath) 7

Zaha, D. W. A. 2013 (Manchester U) 2
Zamora, R. L. 2011 (Fulham) 2

NORTHERN IRELAND

Addis, D. J. 1922 (Cliftonville) 1
Aherne, T. 1947 (Belfast Celtic, Luton T) 4
Alexander, T. E. 1895 (Cliftonville) 1
Allan, C. 1936 (Cliftonville) 1
Allen, J. 1887 (Limavady) 1
Anderson, J. 1925 (Distillery) 1
Anderson, T. 1973 (Manchester U, Swindon T, Peterborough U) 22
Anderson, W. 1898 (Linfield, Cliftonville) 4
Andrews, W. 1908 (Glentoran, Grimsby T) 3
Armstrong, G. J. 1977 (Tottenham H, Watford, Real Mallorca, WBA, Chesterfield) 63

Baird, C. P. 2003 (Southampton, Fulham, Reading, Burnley, WBA, Derby Co) 79
Baird, G. 1896 (Distillery) 3
Baird, H. C. 1939 (Huddersfield T) 1
Balfe, J. 1909 (Shelbourne) 2
Bambrick, J. 1929 (Linfield, Chelsea) 11
Banks, S. J. 1937 (Cliftonville) 1
Barr, H. H. 1962 (Linfield, Coventry C) 3
Barron, J. H. 1894 (Cliftonville) 7
Barry, J. 1888 (Cliftonville) 3
Barry, J. 1900 (Bohemians) 1
Barton, A. J. 2011 (Preston NE) 1
Baxter, R. A. 1887 (Distillery) 1
Baxter, S. N. 1887 (Cliftonville) 1
Bennett, L. V. 1889 (Dublin University) 1
Best, G. 1964 (Manchester U, Fulham) 37
Bingham, W. L. 1951 (Sunderland, Luton T, Everton, Port Vale) 56
Black, K. T. 1988 (Luton T, Nottingham F) 30
Black, T. 1901 (Glentoran) 1
Blair, H. 1928 (Portadown, Swansea T) 4
Blair, J. 1907 (Cliftonville) 5
Blair, R. V. 1975 (Oldham Ath) 5
Blanchflower, J. 1954 (Manchester U) 12
Blanchflower, R. D. 1950 (Barnsley, Aston Villa, Tottenham H) 56
Blayney, A. 2006 (Doncaster R, Linfield) 5
Bookman, L. J. O. 1914 (Bradford C, Luton T) 4
Bothwell, A. W. 1926 (Ards) 5
Bowler, G. C. 1950 (Hull C) 3
Boyce, L. 2011 (Werder Bremen, Ross Co, Burton Alb) 21
Boyle, P. 1901 (Sheffield U) 5
Braithwaite, R. M. 1962 (Linfield, Middlesbrough) 10
Braniff, K. R. 2010 (Portadown) 2
Breen, T. 1935 (Belfast Celtic, Manchester U) 9
Brennan, B. 1912 (Bohemians) 1
Brennan, R. A. 1949 (Luton T, Birmingham C, Fulham) 5
Briggs, W. R. 1962 (Manchester U, Swansea T) 2
Brisby, D. 1891 (Distillery) 1
Brolly, T. H. 1937 (Millwall) 4
Brookes, E. A. 1920 (Shelbourne) 1
Brotherston, N. 1980 (Blackburn R) 27
Brown, C. M. 2020 (Cardiff C) 1
Brown, J. 1921 (Glenavon, Tranmere R) 3
Brown, J. 1935 (Wolverhampton W, Coventry C, Birmingham C) 10
Brown, N. M. 1887 (Limavady) 1
Brown, W. G. 1926 (Glenavon) 1
Browne, F. 1887 (Cliftonville) 5
Browne, R. J. 1936 (Leeds U) 6
Bruce, A. 1925 (Belfast Celtic) 1
Bruce, A. S. 2013 (Hull C) 2
Bruce, W. 1961 (Glentoran) 2
Brunt, C. 2005 (Sheffield W, WBA) 65
Bryan, M. A. 2010 (Watford) 2
Buckle, H. R. 1903 (Cliftonville, Sunderland, Bristol R) 3
Buckle, J. 1882 (Cliftonville) 1
Burnett, J. 1894 (Distillery, Glentoran) 5
Burnison, J. 1901 (Distillery) 2
Burnison, S. 1908 (Distillery, Bradford, Distillery) 8
Burns, J. 1923 (Glenavon) 1
Burns, W. 1925 (Glentoran) 1
Butler, M. P. 1939 (Blackpool) 1

Camp, L. M. J. 2011 (Nottingham F) 9
Campbell, A. C. 1963 (Crusaders) 2
Campbell, D. A. 1986 (Nottingham F, Charlton Ath) 10
Campbell, James 1897 (Cliftonville) 14
Campbell, John 1896 (Cliftonville) 1
Campbell, J. P. 1951 (Fulham) 2
Campbell, R. M. 1982 (Bradford C) 2
Campbell, W. G. 1968 (Dundee) 6
Capaldi, A. C. 2004 (Plymouth Arg, Cardiff C) 22
Carey, J. J. 1947 (Manchester U) 7
Carroll, E. 1925 (Glenavon) 1

Carroll, R. E. 1997 (Wigan Ath, Manchester U, West Ham U, Olympiacos, Notts Co, Linfield) 45
Carson, J. G. 2011 (Ipswich T) 4
Carson, S. 2009 (Coleraine) 1
Carson, T. 2018 (Motherwell) 5
Casement, C. 2009 (Ipswich T) 1
Casey, T. 1955 (Newcastle U, Portsmouth) 12
Caskey, W. 1979 (Derby Co, Tulsa Roughnecks) 8
Cassidy, T. 1971 (Newcastle U, Burnley) 24
Cathcart, C. G. 2011 (Blackpool, Watford) 50
Caughey, M. 1986 (Linfield) 2
Chambers, R. J. 1921 (Distillery, Bury, Nottingham F) 12
Chatton, H. A. 1925 (Partick Thistle) 3
Christian, J. 1889 (Linfield) 1
Clarke, C. J. 1986 (Bournemouth, Southampton, QPR, Portsmouth) 38
Clarke, R. 1901 (Belfast Celtic) 2
Cleary, J. 1982 (Glentoran) 5
Clements, D. 1965 (Coventry C, Sheffield W, Everton, New York Cosmos) 48
Clingan, S. G. 2006 (Nottingham F, Norwich C, Coventry C, Kilmarnock) 39
Clugston, J. 1888 (Cliftonville) 14
Clyde, M. G. 2005 (Wolverhampton W) 3
Coates, C. 2009 (Crusaders) 6
Cochrane, D. 1939 (Leeds U) 12
Cochrane, G. 1903 (Cliftonville) 1
Cochrane, G. T. 1976 (Coleraine, Burnley, Middlesbrough, Gillingham) 26
Cochrane, M. 1898 (Distillery, Leicester Fosse) 8
Collins, F. 1922 (Celtic) 1
Collins, R. 1922 (Cliftonville) 1
Condy, J. 1882 (Distillery) 3
Connell, T. E. 1978 (Coleraine) 1
Connor, J. 1901 (Glentoran, Belfast Celtic) 13
Connor, M. J. 1903 (Brentford, Fulham) 3
Cook, W. 1933 (Celtic, Everton) 15
Cooke, S. 1889 (Belfast YMCA, Cliftonville) 3
Coote, A. 1999 (Norwich C) 6
Coulter, J. 1934 (Belfast Celtic, Everton, Grimsby T, Chelmsford C) 11
Cowan, J. 1970 (Newcastle U) 1
Cowan, T. S. 1925 (Queen's Island) 1
Coyle, F. 1956 (Coleraine, Nottingham F) 4
Coyle, L. 1989 (Derry C) 1
Coyle, R. I. 1973 (Sheffield W) 5
Craig, A. B. 1908 (Rangers, Morton) 9
Craig, D. J. 1967 (Newcastle U) 25
Craigan, S. J. 2003 (Partick Thistle, Motherwell) 54
Crawford, A. 1889 (Distillery, Cliftonville) 7
Croft, T. 1922 (Queen's Island) 3
Crone, R. 1889 (Distillery) 4
Crone, W. 1882 (Distillery) 12
Crooks, W. J. 1922 (Manchester U) 1
Crossan, E. 1950 (Blackburn R) 3
Crossan, J. A. 1960 (Sparta-Rotterdam, Sunderland, Manchester C, Middlesbrough) 24
Crothers, C. 1907 (Distillery) 1
Cumming, L. 1929 (Huddersfield T, Oldham Ath) 3
Cunningham, W. 1892 (Ulster) 4
Cunningham, W. E. 1951 (St Mirren, Leicester C, Dunfermline Ath) 30
Curran, S. 1926 (Belfast Celtic) 4
Curran, J. J. 1922 (Glenavon, Pontypridd, Glenavon) 5
Cush, W. W. 1951 (Glenavon, Leeds U, Portadown) 26

Dallas, S. A. 2011 (Crusaders, Brentford, Leeds U) 44
Dalrymple, J. 1922 (Distillery) 1
Dalton, W. 1888 (YMCA, Linfield) 11
D'Arcy, S. D. 1952 (Chelsea, Brentford) 5
Darling, J. 1897 (Linfield) 22
Davey, H. H. 1926 (Reading, Portsmouth) 5
Davis, S. 2005 (Aston Villa, Fulham, Rangers, Southampton, Rangers) 117
Davis, T. L. 1937 (Oldham Ath) 1
Davison, A. J. 1996 (Bolton W, Bradford C, Grimsby T) 3
Davison, J. R. 1882 (Cliftonville) 8
Dennison, R. 1988 (Wolverhampton W) 18
Devine, A. O. 1886 (Limavady) 4
Devine, J. 1990 (Glentoran) 1
Dickson, D. 1970 (Coleraine) 4
Dickson, T. A. 1957 (Linfield) 1
Dickson, W. 1951 (Chelsea, Arsenal) 12
Diffin, W. J. 1931 (Belfast Celtic) 1
Dill, A. H. 1882 (Knock, Down Ath, Cliftonville) 9
Doherty, I. 1901 (Belfast Celtic) 1
Doherty, J. 1928 (Portadown) 1
Doherty, J. 1933 (Cliftonville) 2
Doherty, L. 1985 (Linfield) 2
Doherty, M. 1938 (Derry C) 1
Doherty, P. D. 1935 (Blackpool, Manchester C, Derby Co, Huddersfield T, Doncaster R) 16
Doherty, T. E. 2003 (Bristol C) 9
Donaghey, B. 1903 (Belfast Celtic) 1
Donaghy, M. M. 1980 (Luton T, Manchester U, Chelsea) 91
Donnelly, L. 1913 (Distillery) 1
Donnelly, L. F. P. 2014 (Fulham, Motherwell) 2
Donnelly, M. 2009 (Crusaders) 1
Doran, J. F. 1921 (Brighton) 3
Dougan, A. D. 1958 (Portsmouth, Blackburn R, Aston Villa, Leicester C, Wolverhampton W) 43
Douglas, J. P. 1947 (Belfast Celtic) 1
Dowd, H. O. 1974 (Glenavon, Sheffield W) 3
Dowie, I. 1990 (Luton T, West Ham U, Southampton, C Palace, West Ham U, QPR) 59
Duff, M. J. 2002 (Cheltenham T, Burnley) 24
Duggan, H. A. 1930 (Leeds U) 8
Dunlop, G. 1985 (Linfield) 4
Dunne, J. 1928 (Sheffield U) 7

Eames, W. L. E. 1885 (Dublin University) 3
Eglington, T. J. 1947 (Everton) 6
Elder, A. R. 1960 (Burnley, Stoke C) 40
Elleman, A. R. 1889 (Cliftonville) 2
Elliott, S. 2001 (Motherwell, Hull C) 39
Elwood, J. H. 1929 (Bradford) 2
Emerson, W. 1920 (Glentoran, Burnley) 11
English, S. 1933 (Rangers) 2
Enright, J. 1912 (Leeds C) 1
Evans, C. J. 2009 (Manchester U, Hull C, Blackburn R) 59
Evans, J. G. 2007 (Manchester U, WBA, Leicester C) 84

Falloon, E. 1931 (Aberdeen) 2
Farquharson, T. G. 1923 (Cardiff C) 7
Farrell, P. 1901 (Distillery) 2
Farrell, P. 1938 (Hibernian) 1
Farrell, P. D. 1947 (Everton) 7
Feeney, J. M. 1947 (Linfield, Swansea T) 2
Feeney, W. 1976 (Glentoran) 1
Feeney, W. J. 2002 (Bournemouth, Luton T, Cardiff C, Oldham Ath, Plymouth Arg) 46
Ferguson, G. 1999 (Linfield) 5
Ferguson, S. K. 2009 (Newcastle U, Millwall) 42
Ferguson, W. 1966 (Linfield) 2
Ferris, J. 1920 (Belfast Celtic, Chelsea, Belfast Celtic) 6
Ferris, R. O. 1950 (Birmingham C) 3
Fettis, A. W. 1992 (Hull C, Nottingham F, Blackburn R) 25
Finney, T. 1975 (Sunderland, Cambridge U) 14
Fitzpatrick, J. C. 1896 (Bohemians) 2
Flack, H. 1929 (Burnley) 1
Flanagan, T. M. 2017 (Burton Alb) 5
Fleming, J. G. 1987 (Nottingham F, Manchester C, Barnsley) 31
Forbes, G. 1888 (Limavady, Distillery) 3
Forde, J. T. 1959 (Ards) 4
Foreman, T. A. 1899 (Cliftonville) 1
Forsythe, J. 1888 (YMCA) 2
Fox, W. T. 1887 (Ulster) 2
Frame, T. 1925 (Linfield) 1
Fulton, R. P. 1928 (Larne, Belfast Celtic) 21

Gaffikin, G. 1890 (Linfield Ath) 15
Galbraith, E. S. W. (Manchester U) 1
Galbraith, W. 1890 (Distillery) 1
Gallagher, P. 1920 (Celtic, Falkirk) 11
Gallogly, C. 1951 (Huddersfield T) 2
Gara, A. 1902 (Preston NE) 3
Gardiner, A. 1930 (Cliftonville) 5
Garrett, J. 1925 (Distillery) 1
Garrett, R. 2009 (Linfield) 5
Gaston, R. 1969 (Oxford U) 1

Gaukrodger, G. 1895 (Linfield) 1
Gault, M. 2008 (Linfield) 1
Gaussen, A. D. 1884 (Moyola Park, Magherafelt) 6
Geary, J. 1931 (Glentoran) 2
Gibb, J. T. 1884 (Wellington Park, Cliftonville) 10
Gibb, T. J. 1936 (Cliftonville) 1
Gibson W. K. 1894 (Cliftonville) 14
Gillespie, K. R. 1995 (Manchester U, Newcastle U, Blackburn R, Leicester C, Sheffield U) 86
Gillespie, S. 1886 (Hertford) 6
Gillespie, W. 1889 (West Down) 1
Gillespie, W. 1913 (Sheffield U) 25
Goodall, A. L. 1899 (Derby Co, Glossop) 10
Goodbody, M. F. 1889 (Dublin University) 2
Gordon, H. 1895 (Linfield) 3
Gordon R. W. 1891 (Linfield) 7
Gordon, T. 1894 (Linfield) 2
Gorman, R. J. 2010 (Wolverhampton W) 9
Gorman, W. C. 1947 (Brentford) 4
Gough, J. 1925 (Queen's Island) 1
Gowdy, J. 1920 (Glentoran, Queen's Island, Falkirk) 6
Gowdy, W. A. 1932 (Hull C, Sheffield W, Linfield, Hibernian) 6
Graham, W. G. L. 1951 (Doncaster R) 14
Gray, P. 1993 (Luton T, Sunderland, Nancy, Luton T, Burnley, Oxford U) 26
Greer, W. 1909 (QPR) 3
Gregg, H. 1954 (Doncaster R, Manchester U) 25
Griffin, D. J. 1996 (St Johnstone, Dundee U, Stockport Co) 29
Grigg, W. D. 2012 (Walsall, Brentford, Milton Keynes D, Wigan Ath) 13

Hall, G. 1897 (Distillery) 1
Halligan, W. 1911 (Derby Co, Wolverhampton W) 2
Hamill, M. 1912 (Manchester U, Belfast Celtic, Manchester C) 7
Hamill, R. 1999 (Glentoran) 1
Hamilton, B. 1969 (Linfield, Ipswich T, Everton, Millwall, Swindon T) 50
Hamilton, G. 2003 (Portadown) 5
Hamilton, J. 1882 (Knock) 2
Hamilton, R. 1928 (Rangers) 5
Hamilton, W. D. 1885 (Dublin Association) 1
Hamilton, W. J. 1885 (Dublin Association) 1
Hamilton, W. J. 1908 (Distillery) 1
Hamilton, W. R. 1978 (QPR, Burnley, Oxford U) 41
Hampton, H. 1911 (Bradford C) 9
Hanna, J. 1912 (Nottingham F) 2
Hanna, J. D. 1899 (Royal Artillery, Portsmouth) 1
Hannon, D. J. 1908 (Bohemians) 6
Harkin, J. T. 1968 (Southport, Shrewsbury T) 5
Harland, A. I. 1922 (Linfield) 2
Harris, J. 1921 (Cliftonville, Glenavon) 2
Harris, V. 1906 (Shelbourne, Everton) 20
Harvey, M. 1961 (Sunderland) 34
Hastings, J. 1882 (Knock, Ulster) 7
Hatton, S. 1963 (Linfield) 2
Hayes, W. E. 1938 (Huddersfield T) 4
Hazard, C. 2018 (Celtic) 1
Healy, D. J. 2000 (Manchester U, Preston NE, Leeds U, Fulham, Sunderland, Rangers, Bury) 95
Healy, P. J. 1982 (Coleraine, Glentoran) 4
Hegan, D. 1970 (WBA, Wolverhampton W) 7
Henderson, J. 1885 (Ulster) 3
Hewison, G. 1885 (Moyola Park) 2
Hill, C. F. 1990 (Sheffield U, Leicester C, Trelleborg, Northampton T) 27
Hill, M. J. 1959 (Norwich C, Everton) 7
Hinton, E. 1947 (Fulham, Millwall) 7
Hodson, L. J. S. 2011 (Watford, Milton Keynes D, Rangers) 24
Holmes, S. P. 2002 (Wrexham) 1
Hopkins, J. 1926 (Brighton) 1
Horlock, K. 1995 (Swindon T, Manchester C) 32
Houston, J. 1912 (Linfield, Everton) 6
Houston, W. 1933 (Linfield) 1
Houston, W. J. 1885 (Moyola Park) 2
Hughes, A. W. 1998 (Newcastle U, Aston Villa, Fulham, QPR, Brighton & HA, Melbourne C, Kerala Blasters, Hearts) 112
Hughes, J. 2006 (Lincoln C) 2
Hughes, M. A. 2006 (Oldham Ath) 2
Hughes, M. E. 1992 (Manchester C, Strasbourg, West Ham U, Wimbledon, Crystal Palace) 71
Hughes, P. A. 1987 (Bury) 3
Hughes, W. 1951 (Bolton W) 1
Humphries, W. M. 1962 (Ards, Coventry C, Swansea T) 14
Hunter, A. 1905 (Distillery, Belfast Celtic) 8
Hunter, A. 1970 (Blackburn R, Ipswich T) 53
Hunter, B. V. 1995 (Wrexham, Reading) 15
Hunter, R. J. 1884 (Cliftonville) 3
Hunter, V. 1962 (Coleraine) 2

Ingham, M. G. 2005 (Sunderland, Wrexham) 3
Irvine, R. J. 1962 (Linfield, Stoke C) 8
Irvine, R. W. 1922 (Everton, Portsmouth, Connah's Quay, Derry C) 15
Irvine, W. J. 1963 (Burnley, Preston NE, Brighton & HA) 23
Irving, S. J. 1923 (Dundee, Cardiff C, Chelsea) 18

Jackson, T. A. 1969 (Everton, Nottingham F, Manchester U) 35
Jamison, J. 1976 (Glentoran) 1
Jenkins, I. 1997 (Chester C, Dundee U) 6
Jennings, P. A. 1964 (Watford, Tottenham H, Arsenal, Tottenham H) 119
Johnson, D. M. 1999 (Blackburn R, Birmingham C) 56
Johnston, H. 1927 (Portadown) 1
Johnston, R. S. 1882 (Distillery) 5
Johnston, R. S. 1905 (Distillery) 1
Johnston, S. 1890 (Linfield) 4
Johnston, W. 1885 (Oldpark) 2
Johnston, W. C. 1962 (Glenavon, Oldham Ath) 2
Jones, J. 1930 (Linfield, Hibernian, Glenavon) 23
Jones, J. 1956 (Glenavon) 3
Jones, J. L. 2018 (Kilmarnock) 9
Jones, S. 1934 (Distillery, Blackpool) 2
Jones, S. G. 2003 (Crewe Alex, Burnley) 29
Jordan, T. 1895 (Linfield) 2

Kavanagh, P. J. 1930 (Celtic) 1
Keane, T. R. 1949 (Swansea T) 1
Kearns, A. 1900 (Distillery) 6
Kee, P. V. 1990 (Oxford U, Ards) 9
Keith, R. M. 1958 (Newcastle U) 23
Kelly, H. R. 1950 (Fulham, Southampton) 4
Kelly, J. 1896 (Glentoran) 1
Kelly, J. 1932 (Derry C) 11
Kelly, P. J. 1921 (Manchester C) 1
Kelly, P. M. 1950 (Barnsley) 1
Kennedy, A. L. 1923 (Arsenal) 2
Kennedy, P. H. 1999 (Watford, Wigan Ath) 20
Kernaghan, N. 1936 (Belfast Celtic) 3
Kirk, A. R. 2000 (Hearts, Boston U, Northampton T, Dunfermline Ath) 11
Kirkwood, H. 1904 (Cliftonville) 1
Kirwan, J. 1900 (Tottenham H, Chelsea, Clyde) 17

Lacey, W. 1909 (Everton, Liverpool, New Brighton) 23
Lafferty, D. P. 2012 (Burnley) 13
Lafferty, K. 2006 (Burnley, Rangers, Sion, Palermo, Norwich C, Hearts, Rangers) 75
Lavery, S. F. 2018 (Everton, Linfield) 4
Lawrie, J. 2009 (Port Vale) 3
Lawther, R. 1888 (Glentoran) 2
Lawther, W. I. 1960 (Sunderland, Blackburn R) 4
Leatham, J. 1939 (Belfast Celtic) 1
Ledwidge, J. J. 1906 (Shelbourne) 2
Lemon, J. 1886 (Glentoran, Belfast YMCA) 3
Lennon, N. F. 1994 (Crewe Alex, Leicester C, Celtic) 40
Leslie, W. 1887 (YMCA) 1
Lewis, J. 1899 (Glentoran, Distillery) 4
Lewis, J. P. 2018 (Norwich C) 12
Little, A. 2009 (Rangers) 9
Lockhart, H. 1884 (Rossall School) 1
Lockhart, N. H. 1947 (Linfield, Coventry C, Aston Villa) 8
Lomas, S. M. 1994 (Manchester C, West Ham U) 45
Loyal, J. 1891 (Clarence) 1
Lund, M. C. 2017 (Rochdale) 3

Lutton, R. J. 1970 (Wolverhampton W, West Ham U) 6
Lynas, R. 1925 (Cliftonville) 1
Lyner, D. R. 1920 (Glentoran, Manchester U, Kilmarnock) 6
Lytle, J. 1898 (Glentoran) 1

Madden, O. 1938 (Norwich C) 1
Magee, G. 1885 (Wellington Park) 3
Magennis, J. B. D. 2010 (Cardiff C, Aberdeen, St Mirren, Kilmarnock, Charlton Ath, Bolton W, Hull C) 50
Magill, E. J. 1962 (Arsenal, Brighton & HA) 26
Magilton, J. 1991 (Oxford U, Southampton, Sheffield W, Ipswich T) 52
Maginnis, H. 1900 (Linfield) 8
Mahood, J. 1926 (Belfast Celtic, Ballymena) 9
Mannus, A. 2004 (Linfield, St Johnstone) 9
Manderson, R. 1920 (Rangers) 5
Mansfield, J. 1901 (Dublin Freebooters) 1
Martin, C. 1882 (Cliftonville) 3
Martin, C. 1925 (Bo'ness) 1
Martin, C. J. 1947 (Glentoran, Leeds U, Aston Villa) 6
Martin, D. K. 1934 (Belfast Celtic, Wolverhampton W, Nottingham F) 10
Mathieson, A. 1921 (Luton T) 2
Maxwell, J. 1902 (Linfield, Glentoran, Belfast Celtic) 7
McAdams, W. J. 1954 (Manchester C, Bolton W, Leeds U) 15
McAlery, J. M. 1882 (Cliftonville) 2
McAlinden, J. 1938 (Belfast Celtic, Portsmouth, Southend U) 4
McAllen, J. 1898 (Linfield) 9
McAlpine, S. 1901 (Cliftonville) 1
McArdle, R. A. 2010 (Rochdale, Aberdeen, Bradford C) 7
McArthur, A. 1886 (Distillery) 1
McAuley, G. 2005 (Lincoln C, Leicester C, Ipswich T, WBA, Rangers) 80
McAuley, J. L. 1911 (Huddersfield T) 6
McAuley, P. 1900 (Belfast Celtic) 1
McBride, S. D. 1991 (Glenavon) 4
McCabe, J. J. 1949 (Leeds U) 6
McCabe, W. 1891 (Ulster) 1
McCalmont, A. J. 2020 (Leeds U) 1
McCambridge, J. 1930 (Ballymena, Cardiff C) 4
McCandless, J. 1912 (Bradford) 5
McCandless, W. 1920 (Linfield, Rangers) 9
McCann, G. S. 2002 (West Ham U, Cheltenham T, Barnsley, Scunthorpe U, Peterborough U) 39
McCann, P. 1910 (Belfast Celtic, Glentoran) 7
McCartan, S. V. 2017 (Accrington S, Bradford C) 2
McCarthy, J. D. 1996 (Port Vale, Birmingham C) 18
McCartney, A. 1903 (Ulster, Linfield, Everton, Belfast Celtic, Glentoran) 15
McCartney, G. 2002 (Sunderland, West Ham U, Sunderland) 34
McCashin, J. W. 1896 (Cliftonville) 5
McCavana, W. T. 1955 (Coleraine) 3
McCaw, J. H. 1927 (Linfield) 6
McClatchey, J. 1886 (Distillery) 3
McClatchey, T. 1895 (Distillery) 1
McCleary, J. W. 1955 (Cliftonville) 1
McCleery, W. 1922 (Cliftonville, Linfield) 10
McClelland, J. 1980 (Mansfield T, Rangers, Watford, Leeds U) 53
McClelland, J. T. 1961 (Arsenal, Fulham) 6
McCluggage, A. 1922 (Cliftonville, Bradford, Burnley) 13
McClure, G. 1907 (Cliftonville, Distillery) 4
McConnell, E. 1904 (Cliftonville, Glentoran, Sunderland, Sheffield W) 12
McConnell, P. 1928 (Doncaster R, Southport) 2
McConnell, W. G. 1912 (Bohemians) 6
McConnell, W. H. 1925 (Reading) 8
McCourt, F. J. 1952 (Manchester C) 6
McCourt, P. J. 2002 (Rochdale, Celtic, Barnsley, Brighton & HA, Luton T) 18
McCoy, R. K. 1987 (Coleraine) 1
McCoy, S. 1896 (Distillery) 1
McCracken, E. 1928 (Barking) 1
McCracken, R. 1921 (Crystal Palace) 4
McCracken, R. 1922 (Linfield) 1
McCracken, W. R. 1902 (Distillery, Newcastle U, Hull C) 16
McCreery, D. 1976 (Manchester U, QPR, Tulsa Roughnecks, Newcastle U, Hearts) 67
McCrory, S. 1958 (Southend U) 1
McCullough, K. 1935 (Belfast Celtic, Manchester C) 5
McCullough, L. 2014 (Doncaster R) 6
McCullough, W. J. 1961 (Arsenal, Millwall) 10
McCurdy, C. 1980 (Linfield) 1
McDonald, A. 1986 (QPR) 52
McDonald, R. 1930 (Rangers) 2
McDonnell, J. 1911 (Bohemians) 4
McElhinney, G. M. A. 1984 (Bolton W) 6
McEvilly, L. R. 2002 (Rochdale) 1
McFaul, W. S. 1967 (Linfield, Newcastle U) 6
McGarry, J. K. 1951 (Cliftonville) 3
McGaughey, M. 1985 (Linfield) 1
McGibbon, P. C. G. 1995 (Manchester U, Wigan Ath) 7
McGinn, N. 2009 (Celtic, Aberdeen, Gwangju, Aberdeen) 59
McGivern, R. 2009 (Manchester C, Hibernian, Port Vale, Shrewsbury) 24
McGovern, M. 2010 (Ross Co, Hamilton A, Norwich C) 31
McGrath, R. C. 1974 (Tottenham H, Manchester U) 21
McGregor, S. 1921 (Glentoran) 1
McGrillen, J. 1924 (Clyde, Belfast Celtic) 2
McGuire, E. 1907 (Distillery) 1
McGuire, J. 1928 (Linfield) 1
McIlroy, H. 1906 (Cliftonville) 1
McIlroy, J. 1952 (Burnley, Stoke C) 55
McIlroy, S. B. 1972 (Manchester U, Stoke C, Manchester C) 88
McIlvenny, P. 1924 (Distillery) 1
McIlvenny, R. 1890 (Distillery, Ulster) 2
McKay, W. R. 2013 (Inverness CT, Wigan Ath) 11
McKeag, W. 1968 (Glentoran) 2
McKeague, T. 1925 (Glentoran) 1
McKee, F. W. 1906 (Cliftonville, Belfast Celtic) 5
McKelvey, H. 1901 (Glentoran) 2
McKenna, J. 1950 (Huddersfield T) 7
McKenzie, H. 1922 (Distillery) 2
McKenzie, R. 1967 (Airdrieonians) 1
McKeown, N. 1892 (Linfield) 7
McKie, H. 1895 (Cliftonville) 3
Mackie, J. A. 1923 (Arsenal, Portsmouth) 3
McKinney, D. 1921 (Hull C, Bradford C) 2
McKinney, V. J. 1966 (Falkirk) 1
McKnight, A. D. 1988 (Celtic, West Ham U) 10
McKnight, J. 1912 (Preston NE, Glentoran) 2
McLaughlin, C. G. 2012 (Preston NE, Fleetwood T, Millwall, Sunderland) 38
McLaughlin, J. C. 1962 (Shrewsbury T, Swansea T) 12
McLaughlin, R. 2014 (Liverpool, Oldham Ath) 5
McLean, B. S. 2006 (Rangers) 1
McLean, T. 1885 (Limavady) 1
McMahon, G. J. 1995 (Tottenham H, Stoke C) 17
McMahon, J. 1934 (Bohemians) 1
McMaster, G. 1897 (Glentoran) 3
McMichael, A. 1950 (Newcastle U) 40
McMillan, G. 1903 (Distillery) 2
McMillan, S. T. 1963 (Manchester U) 2
McMillen, W. S. 1934 (Manchester U, Chesterfield) 7
McMordie, A. S. 1969 (Middlesbrough) 21
McMorran, E. J. 1947 (Belfast Celtic, Barnsley, Doncaster R) 15
McMullan, D. 1926 (Liverpool) 3
McNair, P. J. C. 2015 (Manchester U, Sunderland, Middlesbrough) 34
McNally, B. A. 1986 (Shrewsbury T) 5
McNinch, J. 1931 (Ballymena) 3
McPake, J. 2012 (Coventry C) 1
McParland, P. J. 1954 (Aston Villa, Wolverhampton W) 34
McQuoid, J. J. B. 2011 (Millwall) 5
McShane, J. 1899 (Cliftonville) 4
McVeigh, P. M. 1999 (Tottenham H, Norwich C) 20
McVicker, J. 1888 (Linfield, Glentoran) 2
McWha, W. B. R. 1882 (Knock, Cliftonville) 7
Meek, H. L. 1925 (Glentoran) 1
Mehaffy, J. A. C. 1922 (Queen's Island) 1
Meldon, P. A. 1899 (Dublin Freebooters) 2

Mercer, H. V. A. 1908 (Linfield) 1
Mercer, J. T. 1898 (Distillery, Linfield, Distillery, Derby Co) 12
Millar, W. 1932 (Barrow) 2
Miller, J. 1929 (Middlesbrough) 3
Milligan, D. 1939 (Chesterfield) 1
Milne, R. G. 1894 (Linfield) 28
Mitchell, E. J. 1933 (Cliftonville, Glentoran) 2
Mitchell, W. 1932 (Distillery, Chelsea) 15
Molyneux, T. B. 1883 (Ligoniel, Cliftonville) 11
Montgomery, F. J. 1955 (Coleraine) 1
Moore, C. 1949 (Glentoran) 1
Moore, P. 1933 (Aberdeen) 1
Moore, R. 1891 (Linfield Ath) 3
Moore, R. L. 1887 (Ulster) 2
Moore, W. 1923 (Falkirk) 1
Moorhead, F. W. 1885 (Dublin University) 1
Moorhead, G. 1923 (Linfield) 4
Moran, J. 1912 (Leeds C) 1
Moreland, V. 1979 (Derby Co) 6
Morgan, G. F. 1922 (Linfield, Nottingham F) 8
Morgan, S. 1972 (Port Vale, Aston Villa, Brighton & HA, Sparta Rotterdam) 18
Morrison, R. 1891 (Linfield Ath) 2
Morrison, T. 1895 (Glentoran, Burnley) 7
Morrogh, D. 1896 (Bohemians) 1
Morrow, S. J. 1990 (Arsenal, QPR) 39
Morrow, W. J. 1883 (Moyola Park) 3
Muir, R. 1885 (Oldpark) 2
Mulgrew, J. 2010 (Linfield) 2
Mulholland, T. S. 1906 (Belfast Celtic) 2
Mullan, G. 1983 (Glentoran) 4
Mulligan, J. 1921 (Manchester C) 1
Mulryne, P. P. 1997 (Manchester U, Norwich C, Cardiff C) 27
Murdock, C. J. 2000 (Preston NE, Hibernian, Crewe Alex, Rotherham U) 34
Murphy, J. 1910 (Bradford C) 3
Murphy, N. 1905 (QPR) 3
Murray, J. M. 1910 (Motherwell, Sheffield W) 3

Napier, R. J. 1966 (Bolton W) 1
Neill, W. J. T. 1961 (Arsenal, Hull C) 59
Nelis, P. 1923 (Nottingham F) 1
Nelson, S. 1970 (Arsenal, Brighton & HA) 51
Nicholl, C. J. 1975 (Aston Villa, Southampton, Grimsby T) 51
Nicholl, H. 1902 (Belfast Celtic) 3
Nicholl, J. M. 1976 (Manchester U, Toronto Blizzard, Sunderland, Toronto Blizzard, Rangers, Toronto Blizzard, WBA) 73
Nicholson, J. J. 1961 (Manchester U, Huddersfield T) 41
Nixon, R. 1914 (Linfield) 1
Nolan, I. R. 1997 (Sheffield W, Bradford C, Wigan Ath) 18
Nolan-Whelan, J. V. 1901 (Dublin Freebooters) 5
Norwood, O. J. 2011 (Manchester U, Huddersfield T, Reading, Brighton & HA) 57

O'Boyle, G. 1994 (Dunfermline Ath, St Johnstone) 13
O'Brien, M. T. 1921 (QPR, Leicester C, Hull C, Derby Co) 10
O'Connell, P. 1912 (Sheffield W, Hull C) 5
O'Connor, M. J. 2008 (Crewe Alex, Scunthorpe U, Rotherham U) 11
O'Doherty, A. 1970 (Coleraine) 2
O'Driscoll, J. F. 1949 (Swansea T) 3
O'Hagan, C. 1905 (Tottenham H, Aberdeen) 11
O'Hagan, W. 1920 (St Mirren) 2
O'Hehir, J. C. 1910 (Bohemians) 1
O'Kane, W. J. 1970 (Nottingham F) 20
O'Mahoney, M. T. 1939 (Bristol R) 1
O'Neill, C. 1989 (Motherwell) 3
O'Neill, J. 1962 (Sunderland) 1
O'Neill, J. P. 1980 (Leicester C) 39
O'Neill, M. A. M. 1988 (Newcastle U, Dundee U, Hibernian, Coventry C) 31
O'Neill, M. H. M. 1972 (Distillery, Nottingham F, Norwich C, Manchester C, Norwich C, Notts Co) 64
O'Reilly, H. 1901 (Dublin Freebooters) 3
Owens, J. 2011 (Crusaders) 1

Parke, J. 1964 (Linfield, Hibernian, Sunderland) 14
Paterson, M. A. 2008 (Scunthorpe U, Burnley, Huddersfield T) 22
Paton, P. R. 2014 (Dundee U) 4
Patterson, D. J. 1994 (Crystal Palace, Luton T, Dundee U) 17
Patterson, R. 2010 (Coleraine, Plymouth Arg) 5
Peacock, R. 1952 (Celtic, Coleraine) 31
Peacock-Farrell, B. 2018 (Leeds U, Burnley) 14
Peden, J. 1887 (Linfield, Distillery) 24
Penney, S. 1985 (Brighton & HA) 17
Percy, J. C. 1889 (Belfast YMCA) 1
Platt, J. A. 1976 (Middlesbrough, Ballymena U, Coleraine) 23
Pollock, W. 1928 (Belfast Celtic) 1
Ponsonby, J. 1895 (Distillery) 9
Potts, R. M. C. 1883 (Cliftonville) 2
Priestley, T. J. M. 1933 (Coleraine, Chelsea) 2
Pyper, Jas. 1897 (Cliftonville) 7
Pyper, John 1897 (Cliftonville) 9
Pyper, M. 1932 (Linfield) 1

Quinn, J. M. 1985 (Blackburn R, Swindon T, Leicester C, Bradford C, West Ham U, Bournemouth, Reading) 46
Quinn, S. J. 1996 (Blackpool, WBA, Willem II, Sheffield W, Peterborough U, Northampton T) 50

Rafferty, P. 1980 (Linfield) 1
Ramsey, P. C. 1984 (Leicester C) 14
Rankine, J. 1883 (Alexander) 2
Rattray, D. 1882 (Avoniel) 3
Rea, R. 1901 (Glentoran) 1
Reeves, B. N. 2015 (Milton Keynes D) 2
Redmond, R. 1884 (Cliftonville) 1
Reid, G. H. 1923 (Cardiff C) 1
Reid, J. 1883 (Ulster) 6
Reid, S. E. 1934 (Derby Co) 3
Reid, W. 1931 (Hearts) 1
Reilly, M. M. 1900 (Portsmouth) 2
Renneville, W. T. J. 1910 (Leyton, Aston Villa) 4
Reynolds, J. 1890 (Distillery, Ulster) 5
Reynolds, R. 1905 (Bohemians) 1
Rice, P. J. 1969 (Arsenal) 49
Roberts, F. C. 1931 (Glentoran) 1
Robinson, P. 1920 (Distillery, Blackburn R) 2
Robinson, S. 1997 (Bournemouth, Luton T) 7
Rogan, A. 1988 (Celtic, Sunderland, Millwall) 18
Rollo, D. 1912 (Linfield, Blackburn R) 16
Roper, E. O. 1886 (Dublin University) 1
Rosbotham, A. 1887 (Cliftonville) 7
Ross, W. E. 1969 (Newcastle U) 1
Rowland, K. 1994 (West Ham U, QPR) 19
Rowley, R. W. M. 1929 (Southampton, Tottenham H) 6
Rushe, F. 1925 (Distillery) 1
Russell, A. 1947 (Linfield) 1
Russell, S. R. 1930 (Bradford C, Derry C) 3
Ryan, R. A. 1950 (WBA) 1

Sanchez, L. P. 1987 (Wimbledon) 3
Saville, G. A. 2018 (Millwall, Middlesbrough) 21
Scott, E. 1920 (Liverpool, Belfast Celtic) 31
Scott, J. 1958 (Grimsby) 2
Scott, J. E. 1901 (Cliftonville) 1
Scott, L. J. 1895 (Dublin University) 2
Scott, P. W. 1975 (Everton, York C, Aldershot) 10
Scott, T. 1894 (Cliftonville) 13
Scott, W. 1903 (Linfield, Everton, Leeds C) 25
Scraggs, M. J. 1921 (Glentoran) 2
Seymour, H. C. 1914 (Bohemians) 1
Seymour, J. 1907 (Cliftonville) 2
Shanks, T. 1903 (Woolwich Arsenal, Brentford) 3
Sharkey, P. G. 1976 (Ipswich T) 1
Sheehan, Dr G. 1899 (Bohemians) 3
Sheridan, J. 1903 (Everton, Stoke C) 6
Sherrard, J. 1885 (Limavady) 3
Sherrard, W. C. 1895 (Cliftonville) 3
Sherry, J. J. 1906 (Bohemians) 2
Shields, R. J. 1957 (Southampton) 1
Shiels, D. 2006 (Hibernian, Doncaster R, Kilmarnock) 14
Silo, M. 1888 (Belfast YMCA) 1
Simpson, W. J. 1951 (Rangers) 12

Sinclair, J. 1882 (Knock) 2
Slemin, J. C. 1909 (Bohemians) 1
Sloan, A. S. 1925 (London Caledonians) 1
Sloan, D. 1969 (Oxford U) 2
Sloan, H. A. de B. 1903 (Bohemians) 8
Sloan, J. W. 1947 (Arsenal) 1
Sloan, T. 1926 (Cardiff C, Linfield) 11
Sloan, T. 1979 (Manchester U) 3
Small, J. M. 1887 (Clarence, Cliftonville) 4
Smith, A. W. 2003 (Glentoran, Preston NE) 18
Smith, E. E. 1921 (Cardiff C) 4
Smith, J. E. 1901 (Distillery) 2
Smith, M. 2016 (Peterborough U, Hearts) 9
Smyth, P. 2018 (QPR) 2
Smyth, R. H. 1886 (Dublin University) 1
Smyth, S. 1948 (Wolverhampton W, Stoke C) 9
Smyth, W. 1949 (Distillery) 4
Snape, A. 1920 (Airdrieonians) 1
Sonner, D. J. 1998 (Ipswich T, Sheffield W, Birmingham C, Nottingham F, Peterborough U) 13
Spence, D. W. 1975 (Bury, Blackpool, Southend U) 29
Spencer, S. 1890 (Distillery) 6
Spiller, E. A. 1883 (Cliftonville) 5
Sproule, I. 2006 (Hibernian, Bristol C) 11
Stanfield, O. M. 1887 (Distillery) 30
Steele, A. 1926 (Charlton Ath, Fulham) 4
Steele, J. 2013 (New York Red Bulls) 3
Stevenson, A. E. 1934 (Rangers, Everton) 17
Stewart, A. 1967 (Glentoran, Derby Co) 7
Stewart, D. C. 1978 (Hull C) 1
Stewart, I. 1982 (QPR, Newcastle U) 31
Stewart, R. K. 1890 (St Columb's Court, Cliftonville) 11
Stewart, T. C. 1961 (Linfield) 1
Swan, S. 1899 (Linfield) 1

Taggart, G. P. 1990 (Barnsley, Bolton W, Leicester C) 51
Taggart, J. 1899 (Walsall) 1
Taylor, M. S. 1999 (Fulham, Birmingham C, unattached) 88
Thompson, A. L. 2011 (Watford) 2
Thompson, F. W. 1910 (Cliftonville, Linfield, Bradford C, Clyde) 12
Thompson, J. 1897 (Distillery) 1
Thompson, J. A. 2018 (Rangers, Blackpool) 7
Thompson, P. 2006 (Linfield, Stockport Co) 8
Thompson, R. 1928 (Queen's Island) 1
Thompson, W. 1889 (Belfast Ath) 1
Thunder, P. J. 1911 (Bohemians) 1
Todd, S. J. 1966 (Burnley, Sheffield W) 11
Toner, C. 2003 (Leyton Orient) 2
Toner, J. 1922 (Arsenal, St Johnstone) 8
Torrans, R. 1893 (Linfield) 1
Torrans, S. 1889 (Linfield) 26
Trainor, D. 1967 (Crusaders) 1
Tuffey, J. 2009 (Partick Thistle, Inverness CT) 8
Tully, C. P. 1949 (Celtic) 10
Turner, A. 1896 (Cliftonville) 1
Turner, E. 1896 (Cliftonville) 1
Turner, W. 1886 (Cliftonville) 3
Twomey, J. F. 1938 (Leeds U) 2

Uprichard, W. N. M. C. 1952 (Swindon T, Portsmouth) 18

Vassell, K. T. 2019 (Rotherham U) 2
Vernon, J. 1947 (Belfast Celtic, WBA) 17

Waddell, T. M. R. 1906 (Cliftonville) 1
Walker, J. 1955 (Doncaster R) 1
Walker, T. 1911 (Bury) 1
Walsh, D. J. 1947 (WBA) 9
Walsh, W. 1948 (Manchester C) 5
Ward, J. J. 2012 (Derby Co, Nottingham F) 35
Waring, J. 1899 (Cliftonville) 1
Warren, P. 1913 (Shelbourne) 2
Washington, C. J. 2016 (QPR, Sheffield U, Hearts) 21
Watson, J. 1883 (Ulster) 9
Watson, P. 1971 (Distillery) 1
Watson, T. 1926 (Cardiff C) 1
Wattie, J. 1899 (Distillery) 1
Webb, C. G. 1909 (Brighton & HA) 3
Webb, S. M. 2006 (Ross Co) 4
Weir, E. 1939 (Clyde) 1
Welsh, E. 1966 (Carlisle U) 4
Whiteside, N. 1982 (Manchester U, Everton) 38
Whiteside, T. 1891 (Distillery) 1
Whitfield, E. R. 1886 (Dublin University) 1
Whitley, Jeff 1997 (Manchester C, Sunderland, Cardiff C) 20
Whitley, Jim 1998 (Manchester C) 3
Whyte, G. 2019 (Oxford U, Cardiff C) 9
Williams, J. R. 1886 (Ulster) 2
Williams, M. S. 1999 (Chesterfield, Watford, Wimbledon, Stoke C, Wimbledon, Milton Keynes D) 36
Williams, P. A. 1991 (WBA) 1
Williamson, J. 1890 (Cliftonville) 3
Willighan, T. 1933 (Burnley) 2
Willis, G. 1906 (Linfield) 4
Wilson, D. J. 1987 (Brighton & HA, Luton T, Sheffield W) 24
Wilson, H. 1925 (Linfield) 2
Wilson, K. J. 1987 (Ipswich T, Chelsea, Notts Co, Walsall) 42
Wilson, M. 1884 (Distillery) 3
Wilson, R. 1888 (Cliftonville) 1
Wilson, S. J. 1962 (Glenavon, Falkirk, Dundee) 12
Wilton, J. M. 1888 (St Columb's Court, Cliftonville, St Columb's Court) 7
Winchester, C. 2011 (Oldham Ath) 1
Wood, T. J. 1996 (Walsall) 1
Worthington, N. 1984 (Sheffield W, Leeds U, Stoke C) 66
Wright, J. 1906 (Cliftonville) 6
Wright, T. J. 1989 (Newcastle U, Nottingham F, Manchester C) 31

Young, S. 1907 (Linfield, Airdrieonians, Linfield) 9

SCOTLAND

Adam, C. G. 2007 (Rangers, Blackpool, Liverpool, Stoke C) 26
Adams, J. 1889 (Hearts) 3
Agnew, W. B. 1907 (Kilmarnock) 3
Aird, J. 1954 (Burnley) 4
Aitken, A. 1901 (Newcastle U, Middlesbrough, Leicester Fosse) 14
Aitken, G. G. 1949 (East Fife, Sunderland) 8
Aitken, R. 1886 (Dumbarton) 2
Aitken, R. 1980 (Celtic, Newcastle U, St Mirren) 57
Aitkenhead, W. A. C. 1912 (Blackburn R) 1
Albiston, A. 1982 (Manchester U) 14
Alexander, D. 1894 (East Stirlingshire) 2
Alexander, G. 2002 (Preston NE, Burnley) 40
Alexander, N. 2006 (Cardiff C) 3
Allan, D. S. 1885 (Queen's Park) 3
Allan, G. 1897 (Liverpool) 1
Allan, H. 1902 (Hearts) 1
Allan, J. 1887 (Queen's Park) 2
Allan, T. 1974 (Dundee) 2
Ancell, R. F. D. 1937 (Newcastle U) 2
Anderson, A. 1933 (Hearts) 23
Anderson, F. 1874 (Clydesdale) 1
Anderson, G. 1901 (Kilmarnock) 1
Anderson, H. A. 1914 (Raith R) 1
Anderson, J. 1954 (Leicester C) 1
Anderson, K. 1896 (Queen's Park) 3
Anderson, R. 2003 (Aberdeen, Sunderland) 11
Anderson, W. 1882 (Queen's Park) 6
Andrews, P. 1875 (Eastern) 1
Anya, I. 2013 (Watford, Derby Co) 29
Archer, J. G. 2018 (Millwall) 1
Archibald, A. 1921 (Rangers) 8
Archibald, S. 1980 (Aberdeen, Tottenham H, Barcelona) 27
Armstrong, M. W. 1936 (Aberdeen) 3
Armstrong, S. 2017 (Celtic, Southampton) 19
Arnott, W. 1883 (Queen's Park) 14
Auld, J. R. 1887 (Third Lanark) 3
Auld, R. 1959 (Celtic) 3

Bain, S. 2018 (Celtic) 3
Baird, A. 1892 (Queen's Park) 2
Baird, D. 1890 (Hearts) 3
Baird, H. 1956 (Airdrieonians) 1
Baird, J. C. 1876 (Vale of Leven) 3
Baird, S. 1957 (Rangers) 7
Baird, W. U. 1897 (St Bernard) 1
Bannan, B. 2011 (Aston Villa, Crystal Palace, Sheffield W) 27
Bannon, E. J. 1980 (Dundee U) 11
Barbour, A. 1885 (Renton) 1
Bardsley, P. A. 2011 (Sunderland) 13
Barker, J. B. 1893 (Rangers) 2
Barr, D. 2009 (Falkirk) 1
Barrett, F. 1894 (Dundee) 2
Bates, D. 2019 (Hamburg) 4
Battles, B. 1901 (Celtic) 3
Battles, B. jun. 1931 (Hearts) 1
Bauld, W. 1950 (Hearts) 3
Baxter, J. C. 1961 (Rangers, Sunderland) 34
Baxter, R. D. 1939 (Middlesbrough) 3
Beattie, A. 1937 (Preston NE) 7
Beattie, C. 2006 (Celtic, WBA) 7
Beattie, R. 1939 (Preston NE) 1
Begbie, I. 1890 (Hearts) 4
Bell, A. 1912 (Manchester U) 1
Bell, C. 2011 (Kilmarnock) 1
Bell, J. 1890 (Dumbarton, Everton, Celtic) 10
Bell, M. 1901 (Hearts) 1
Bell, W. J. 1966 (Leeds U) 2
Bennett, A. 1904 (Celtic, Rangers) 11
Bennie, R. 1925 (Airdrieonians) 3
Bernard, P. R. J. 1995 (Oldham Ath) 2
Berra, C. D. 2008 (Hearts, Wolverhampton W, Ipswich T) 41
Berry, D. 1894 (Queen's Park) 3
Berry, W. H. 1888 (Queen's Park) 4
Bett, J. 1982 (Rangers, Lokeren, Aberdeen) 25
Beveridge, W. W. 1879 (Glasgow University) 3
Black, A. 1938 (Hearts) 3
Black, D. 1889 (Hurlford) 1
Black, E. 1988 (Metz) 2
Black, I. 2013 (Rangers) 1
Black, I. H. 1948 (Southampton) 1
Blackburn, J. E. 1873 (Royal Engineers) 1
Blacklaw, A. S. 1963 (Burnley) 3
Blackley, J. 1974 (Hibernian) 7
Blair, D. 1929 (Clyde, Aston Villa) 8
Blair, J. 1920 (Sheffield W, Cardiff C) 8
Blair, J. 1934 (Motherwell) 1
Blair, J. A. 1947 (Blackpool) 1
Blair, W. 1896 (Third Lanark) 1
Blessington, J. 1894 (Celtic) 4
Blyth, J. A. 1978 (Coventry C) 2
Bone, J. 1972 (Norwich C) 2
Booth, S. 1993 (Aberdeen, Borussia Dortmund, Twente) 21
Bowie, J. 1920 (Rangers) 2
Bowie, W. 1891 (Linthouse) 1
Bowman, D. 1992 (Dundee U) 6
Bowman, G. A. 1892 (Montrose) 1
Boyd, G. I. 2013 (Peterborough U, Hull C) 2
Boyd, J. M. 1934 (Newcastle U) 1
Boyd, K. 2006 (Rangers, Middlesbrough) 18
Boyd, R. 1889 (Mossend Swifts) 2
Boyd, T. 1991 (Motherwell, Chelsea, Celtic) 72
Boyd, W. G. 1931 (Clyde) 2
Bradshaw, T. 1928 (Bury) 1
Brand, R. 1961 (Rangers) 8
Brandon, T. 1896 (Blackburn R) 1
Brazil, A. 1980 (Ipswich T, Tottenham H) 13
Breckenridge, T. 1888 (Hearts) 1
Bremner, D. 1976 (Hibernian) 1
Bremner, W. J. 1965 (Leeds U) 54
Brennan, F. 1947 (Newcastle U) 7
Breslin, B. 1897 (Hibernian) 1
Brewster, G. 1921 (Everton) 1
Bridcutt, L. 2013 (Brighton & HA, Sunderland) 2
Broadfoot, K. 2009 (Rangers) 4
Brogan, J. 1971 (Celtic) 4
Brophy, E. 2019 (Kilmarnock) 1
Brown, A. 1890 (St Mirren) 2
Brown, A. 1904 (Middlesbrough) 1
Brown, A. D. 1950 (East Fife, Blackpool) 14
Brown, G. C. P. 1931 (Rangers) 19
Brown, H. 1947 (Partick Thistle) 3
Brown, J. B. 1939 (Clyde) 1
Brown, J. G. 1975 (Sheffield U) 1
Brown, R. 1884 (Dumbarton) 2
Brown, R. 1890 (Cambuslang) 1
Brown, R. 1947 (Rangers) 3
Brown, R. jun. 1885 (Dumbarton) 1
Brown, S. 2006 (Hibernian, Celtic) 55
Brown, W. D. F. 1958 (Dundee, Tottenham H) 28
Browning, J. 1914 (Celtic) 1
Brownlie, J. 1909 (Third Lanark) 16
Brownlie, J. 1971 (Hibernian) 7
Bruce, D. 1890 (Vale of Leven) 1
Bruce, R. F. 1934 (Middlesbrough) 1
Bryson, C. 2011 (Kilmarnock, Derby Co) 3
Buchan, M. M. 1972 (Aberdeen, Manchester U) 34
Buchanan, J. 1889 (Cambuslang) 1
Buchanan, J. 1929 (Rangers) 2
Buchanan, P. S. 1938 (Chelsea) 1
Buchanan, R. 1891 (Abercorn) 1
Buckley, P. 1954 (Aberdeen) 3
Buick, A. 1902 (Hearts) 2
Burchill, M. J. 2000 (Celtic) 6
Burke, C. 2006 (Rangers, Birmingham C) 7
Burke, O. J. 2016 (Nottingham F, RB Leipzig, WBA) 11
Burley, C. W. 1995 (Chelsea, Celtic, Derby Co) 46
Burley, G. E. 1979 (Ipswich T) 11
Burns, F. 1970 (Manchester U) 1
Burns, K. 1974 (Birmingham C, Nottingham F) 20
Burns, T. 1981 (Celtic) 8
Busby, M. W. 1934 (Manchester C) 1

Cadden, C. 2018 (Motherwell) 2
Caddis, P. M. 2016 (Birmingham C) 1
Cairney, T. 2017 (Fulham) 2
Cairns, T. 1920 (Rangers) 8
Calderhead, D. 1889 (Q of S Wanderers) 1
Calderwood, C. 1995 (Tottenham H) 36
Calderwood, R. 1885 (Cartvale) 3
Caldow, E. 1957 (Rangers) 40
Caldwell, G. 2002 (Newcastle U, Hibernian, Celtic, Wigan Ath) 55
Caldwell, S. 2001 (Newcastle U, Sunderland, Burnley,Wigan Ath) 12
Callaghan, P. 1900 (Hibernian) 1
Callaghan, W. 1970 (Dunfermline Ath) 2
Cameron, C. 1999 (Hearts, Wolverhampton W) 28
Cameron, J. 1886 (Rangers) 1
Cameron, J. 1896 (Queen's Park) 1
Cameron, J. 1904 (St Mirren, Chelsea) 2
Campbell, C. 1874 (Queen's Park) 13
Campbell, H. 1889 (Renton) 1
Campbell, Jas 1913 (Sheffield W) 1
Campbell, J. 1880 (South Western) 1
Campbell, J. 1891 (Kilmarnock) 2
Campbell, John 1893 (Celtic) 12
Campbell, John 1899 (Rangers) 4
Campbell, K. 1920 (Liverpool, Partick Thistle) 8
Campbell, P. 1878 (Rangers) 2
Campbell, P. 1898 (Morton) 1
Campbell, R. 1947 (Falkirk, Chelsea) 5
Campbell, W. 1947 (Morton) 5
Canero, P. 2004 (Leicester C) 1
Carabine, J. 1938 (Third Lanark) 3
Carr, W. M. 1970 (Coventry C) 6
Cassidy, J. 1921 (Celtic) 4
Chalmers, S. 1965 (Celtic) 5
Chalmers, W. 1885 (Rangers) 1
Chalmers, W. S. 1929 (Queen's Park) 1
Chambers, T. 1894 (Hearts) 1
Chaplin, G. D. 1908 (Dundee) 1
Cheyne, A. G. 1929 (Aberdeen) 5
Christie, A. J. 1898 (Queen's Park) 3
Christie, R. 2018 (Celtic) 11
Christie, R. M. 1884 (Queen's Park) 1
Clark, J. 1966 (Celtic) 4
Clark, R. B. 1968 (Aberdeen) 17

Clarke, S. 1988 (Chelsea) 6
Clarkson, D. 2008 (Motherwell) 2
Cleland, J. 1891 (Royal Albert) 1
Clements, R. 1891 (Leith Ath) 1
Clunas, W. L. 1924 (Sunderland) 2
Collier, W. 1922 (Raith R) 1
Collins, J. 1988 (Hibernian, Celtic, Monaco, Everton) 58
Collins, R. Y. 1951 (Celtic, Everton, Leeds U) 31
Collins, T. 1909 (Hearts) 1
Colman, D. 1911 (Aberdeen) 4
Colquhoun, E. P. 1972 (Sheffield U) 9
Colquhoun, J. 1988 (Hearts) 2
Combe, J. R. 1948 (Hibernian) 3
Commons, K. 2009 (Derby Co, Celtic) 12
Conn, A. 1956 (Hearts) 1
Conn, A. 1975 (Tottenham H) 2
Connachan, E. D. 1962 (Dunfermline Ath) 2
Connelly, G. 1974 (Celtic) 2
Connolly, J. 1973 (Everton) 1
Connor, J. 1886 (Airdrieonians) 1
Connor, J. 1930 (Sunderland) 4
Connor, R. 1986 (Dundee, Aberdeen) 4
Conway, C. 2010 (Dundee U, Cardiff C) 7
Cook, W. L. 1934 (Bolton W) 3
Cooke, C. 1966 (Dundee, Chelsea) 16
Cooper, D. 1980 (Rangers, Motherwell) 22
Cooper, L. D. I. 2020 (Leeds U) 2
Cormack, P. B. 1966 (Hibernian, Nottingham F) 9
Cowan, J. 1896 (Aston Villa) 3
Cowan, J. 1948 (Morton) 25
Cowan, W, D. 1924 (Newcastle U) 1
Cowie, D. 1953 (Dundee) 20
Cowie, D. M. 2010 (Watford, Cardiff C) 10
Cox, C. J. 1948 (Hearts) 1
Cox, S. 1949 (Rangers) 24
Craig, A. 1929 (Motherwell) 3
Craig, J. 1977 (Celtic) 1
Craig, J. P. 1968 (Celtic) 1
Craig, T. 1927 (Rangers) 8
Craig, T. B. 1976 (Newcastle U) 1
Crainey, S. D. 2002 (Celtic, Southampton, Blackpool) 12
Crapnell, J. 1929 (Airdrieonians) 9
Crawford, D. 1894 (St Mirren, Rangers) 3
Crawford, J. 1932 (Queen's Park) 5
Crawford, S. 1995 (Raith R, Dunfermline Ath, Plymouth Arg) 25
Crerand, P. T. 1961 (Celtic, Manchester U) 16
Cringan, W. 1920 (Celtic) 5
Crosbie, J. A. 1920 (Ayr U, Birmingham) 2
Croal, J. A. 1913 (Falkirk) 3
Cropley, A. J. 1972 (Hibernian) 2
Cross, J. H. 1903 (Third Lanark) 1
Cruickshank, J. 1964 (Hearts) 6
Crum, J. 1936 (Celtic) 2
Cullen, M. J. 1956 (Luton T) 1
Cumming, D. S. 1938 (Middlesbrough) 1
Cumming, J. 1955 (Hearts) 9
Cummings, G. 1935 (Partick Thistle, Aston Villa) 9
Cummings, J. 2018 (Nottingham F) 2
Cummings, W. 2002 (Chelsea) 1
Cunningham, A. N. 1920 (Rangers) 12
Cunningham, W. C. 1954 (Preston NE) 8
Curran, H. P. 1970 (Wolverhampton W) 5

Dailly, C. 1997 (Derby Co, Blackburn R, West Ham U, Rangers) 67
Dalglish, K. 1972 (Celtic, Liverpool) 102
Davidson, C. I. 1999 (Blackburn R, Leicester C, Preston NE) 19
Davidson, D. 1878 (Queen's Park) 5
Davidson, J. A. 1954 (Partick Thistle) 8
Davidson, M. 2013 (St Johnstone) 1
Davidson, S. 1921 (Middlesbrough) 1
Dawson, A. 1980 (Rangers) 5
Dawson, J. 1935 (Rangers) 14
Deans, J. 1975 (Celtic) 2
Delaney, J. 1936 (Celtic, Manchester U) 13
Devine, A. 1910 (Falkirk) 1
Devlin, M. J. 2020 (Aberdeen) 3
Devlin, P. J. 2003 (Birmingham C) 10
Dewar, G. 1888 (Dumbarton) 2
Dewar, N. 1932 (Third Lanark) 3
Dick, J. 1959 (West Ham U) 1
Dickie, M. 1897 (Rangers) 3
Dickov, P. 2001 (Manchester C, Leicester C, Blackburn R) 10
Dickson, W. 1888 (Dundee Strathmore) 1
Dickson, W. 1970 (Kilmarnock) 5
Divers, J. 1895 (Celtic) 1
Divers, J. 1939 (Celtic) 1
Dixon, P. A. 2013 (Hudderfield T) 3
Dobie, R. S. 2002 (WBA) 6
Docherty, T. H. 1952 (Preston NE, Arsenal) 25
Dodds, D. 1984 (Dundee U) 2
Dodds, J. 1914 (Celtic) 3
Dodds, W. 1997 (Aberdeen, Dundee U, Rangers) 26
Doig, J. E. 1887 (Arbroath, Sunderland) 5
Donachie, W. 1972 (Manchester C) 35
Donaldson, A. 1914 (Bolton W) 6
Donnachie, J. 1913 (Oldham Ath) 3
Donnelly, S. 1997 (Celtic) 10
Dorrans, G. 2010 (WBA, Norwich C) 12
Dougal, J. 1939 (Preston NE) 1
Dougall, C. 1947 (Birmingham C) 1
Dougan, R. 1950 (Hearts) 1
Douglas, A. 1911 (Chelsea) 1
Douglas, B. 2018 (Wolverhampton W) 1
Douglas, J. 1880 (Renfrew) 1
Douglas, R. 2002 (Celtic, Leicester C) 19
Dowds, P. 1892 (Celtic) 1
Downie, R. 1892 (Third Lanark) 1
Doyle, D. 1892 (Celtic) 8
Doyle, J. 1976 (Ayr U) 1
Drummond, J. 1892 (Falkirk, Rangers) 14
Dunbar, M. 1886 (Cartvale) 1
Duncan, A. 1975 (Hibernian) 6
Duncan, D. 1933 (Derby Co) 14
Duncan, D. M. 1948 (East Fife) 3
Duncan, J. 1878 (Alexandra Ath) 2
Duncan, J. 1926 (Leicester C) 1
Duncanson, J. 1947 (Rangers) 1
Dunlop, J. 1890 (St Mirren) 1
Dunlop, W. 1906 (Liverpool) 1
Dunn, J. 1925 (Hibernian, Everton) 6
Durie, G. S. 1988 (Chelsea, Tottenham H, Rangers) 43
Durrant, I. 1988 (Rangers, Kilmarnock) 20
Dykes, J. 1938 (Hearts) 2

Easson, J. F. 1931 (Portsmouth) 3
Elliott, M. S. 1998 (Leicester C) 18
Ellis, J. 1892 (Mossend Swifts) 1
Evans, A. 1982 (Aston Villa) 4
Evans, R. 1949 (Celtic, Chelsea) 48
Ewart, J. 1921 (Bradford C) 1
Ewing, T. 1958 (Partick Thistle) 2

Farm, G. N. 1953 (Blackpool) 10
Ferguson, B. 1999 (Rangers, Blackburn R, Rangers) 45
Ferguson, D. 1988 (Rangers) 2
Ferguson, D. 1992 (Dundee U, Everton) 7
Ferguson, I. 1989 (Rangers) 9
Ferguson, J. 1874 (Vale of Leven) 6
Ferguson, R. 1966 (Kilmarnock) 7
Fernie, W. 1954 (Celtic) 12
Findlay, R. 1898 (Kilmarnock) 1
Findlay, S. J. 2020 (Kilmarnock) 1
Fitchie, T. T. 1905 (Woolwich Arsenal, Queen's Park) 4
Flavell, R. 1947 (Airdrieonians) 2
Fleck, J. A. 2020 (Sheffield U) 2
Fleck, R. 1990 (Norwich C) 4
Fleming, C. 1954 (East Fife) 1
Fleming, J. W. 1929 (Rangers) 3
Fleming, R. 1886 (Morton) 1
Fletcher, D. B. 2004 (Manchester U, WBA, Stoke C) 80
Fletcher, S. K. 2008 (Hibernian, Burnley, Wolverhampton W, Sunderland, Sheffield W) 33
Forbes, A. R. 1947 (Sheffield U, Arsenal) 14
Forbes, J. 1884 (Vale of Leven) 5
Ford, D. 1974 (Hearts) 3
Forrest, J. 1958 (Motherwell) 1
Forrest, J. 1966 (Rangers, Aberdeen) 5
Forrest, J. 2011 (Celtic) 34

Forsyth, A. 1972 (Partick Thistle, Manchester U) 10
Forsyth, C. 2014 (Derby Co) 4
Forsyth, R. C. 1964 (Kilmarnock) 4
Forsyth, T. 1971 (Motherwell, Rangers) 22
Fox, D. J. 2010 (Burnley, Southampton) 4
Foyers, R. 1893 (St Bernards) 2
Fraser, D. M. 1968 (WBA) 2
Fraser, J. 1891 (Moffat) 1
Fraser, J. 1907 (Dundee) 1
Fraser, M. J. E. 1880 (Queen's Park) 5
Fraser, R. 2017 (Bournemouth) 11
Fraser, W. 1955 (Sunderland) 2
Freedman, D. A. 2002 (Crystal Palace) 2
Fulton, W. 1884 (Abercorn) 1
Fyfe, J. H. 1895 (Third Lanark) 1

Gabriel, J. 1961 (Everton) 2
Gallacher, H. K. 1924 (Airdrieonians, Newcastle U, Chelsea, Derby Co) 20
Gallacher, K. W. 1988 (Dundee U, Coventry C, Blackburn R, Newcastle U) 53
Gallacher, P. 1935 (Sunderland) 1
Gallacher, P. 2002 (Dundee U) 8
Gallagher, D. P. 2020 (Motherwell) 2
Gallagher, P. 2004 (Blackburn R) 1
Galloway, M. 1992 (Celtic) 1
Galt, J. H. 1908 (Rangers) 2
Gardiner, I. 1958 (Motherwell) 1
Gardner, D. R. 1897 (Third Lanark) 1
Gardner, R. 1872 (Queen's Park, Clydesdale) 5
Gemmell, T. 1955 (St Mirren) 2
Gemmell, T. 1966 (Celtic) 18
Gemmill, A. 1971 (Derby Co, Nottingham F, Birmingham C) 43
Gemmill, S. 1995 (Nottingham F, Everton) 26
Gibb, W. 1873 (Clydesdale) 1
Gibson, D. W. 1963 (Leicester C) 7
Gibson, J. D. 1926 (Partick Thistle, Aston Villa) 8
Gibson, N. 1895 (Rangers, Partick Thistle) 14
Gilchrist, J. E. 1922 (Celtic) 1
Gilhooley, M. 1922 (Hull C) 1
Gilks, M. 2013 (Blackpool) 3
Gillespie, G. 1880 (Rangers, Queen's Park) 7
Gillespie, G. T. 1988 (Liverpool) 13
Gillespie, Jas 1898 (Third Lanark) 1
Gillespie, John 1896 (Queen's Park) 1
Gillespie, R. 1927 (Queen's Park) 4
Gillick, T. 1937 (Everton) 5
Gilmour, J. 1931 (Dundee) 1
Gilzean, A. J. 1964 (Dundee, Tottenham H) 22
Glass, S. 1999 (Newcastle U) 1
Glavin, R. 1977 (Celtic) 1
Glen, A. 1956 (Aberdeen) 2
Glen, R. 1895 (Renton, Hibernian) 3
Goodwillie, D. 2011 (Dundee U, Blackburn R) 3
Goram, A. L. 1986 (Oldham Ath, Hibernian, Rangers) 43
Gordon, C. A. 2004 (Hearts, Sunderland, Celtic) 54
Gordon, J. E. 1912 (Rangers) 10
Gossland, J. 1884 (Rangers) 1
Goudie, J. 1884 (Abercorn) 1
Gough, C. R. 1983 (Dundee U, Tottenham H, Rangers) 61
Gould, J. 2000 (Celtic) 2
Gourlay, J. 1886 (Cambuslang) 2
Govan, J. 1948 (Hibernian) 6
Gow, D. R. 1888 (Rangers) 1
Gow, J. J. 1885 (Queen's Park) 1
Gow, J. R. 1888 (Rangers) 1
Graham, A. 1978 (Leeds U) 11
Graham, G. 1972 (Arsenal, Manchester U) 12
Graham, J. 1884 (Annbank) 1
Graham, J. A. 1921 (Arsenal) 1
Grant, J. 1959 (Hibernian) 2
Grant, P. 1989 (Celtic) 2
Gray, A. 1903 (Hibernian) 1
Gray, A. D. 2003 (Bradford C) 2
Gray, A. M. 1976 (Aston Villa, Wolverhampton W, Everton) 20
Gray, D. 1929 (Rangers) 10
Gray, E. 1969 (Leeds U) 12
Gray, F. T. 1976 (Leeds U, Nottingham F, Leeds U) 32
Gray, W. 1886 (Pollokshields Ath) 1
Green, A. 1971 (Blackpool, Newcastle U) 6
Greer, G. 2013 (Brighton & HA) 11
Greig, J. 1964 (Rangers) 44
Griffiths, L. 2013 (Hibernian, Celtic) 19
Groves, W. 1888 (Hibernian, Celtic) 3
Gulliland, W. 1891 (Queen's Park) 4
Gunn, B. 1990 (Norwich C) 6

Haddock, H. 1955 (Clyde) 6
Haddow, D. 1894 (Rangers) 1
Haffey, F. 1960 (Celtic) 2
Hamilton, A. 1885 (Queen's Park) 4
Hamilton, A. W. 1962 (Dundee) 24
Hamilton, G. 1906 (Port Glasgow Ath) 1
Hamilton, G. 1947 (Aberdeen) 5
Hamilton, J. 1892 (Queen's Park) 3
Hamilton, J. 1924 (St Mirren) 1
Hamilton, R. C. 1899 (Rangers, Dundee) 11
Hamilton, T. 1891 (Hurlford) 1
Hamilton, T. 1932 (Rangers) 1
Hamilton, W. M. 1965 (Hibernian) 1
Hammell, S. 2005 (Motherwell) 1
Hanley, G. C. 2011 (Blackburn R, Newcastle U, Norwich C) 29
Hannah, A. B. 1888 (Renton) 1
Hannah, J. 1889 (Third Lanark) 1
Hansen, A. D. 1979 (Liverpool) 26
Hansen, J. 1972 (Partick Thistle) 2
Harkness, J. D. 1927 (Queen's Park, Hearts) 12
Harper, J. M. 1973 (Aberdeen, Hibernian, Aberdeen) 4
Harper, W. 1923 (Hibernian, Arsenal) 11
Harris, J. 1921 (Partick Thistle) 2
Harris, N. 1924 (Newcastle U) 1
Harrower, W. 1882 (Queen's Park) 3
Hartford, R. A. 1972 (WBA, Manchester C, Everton, Manchester C) 50
Hartley, P. J. 2005 (Hearts, Celtic, Bristol C) 25
Harvey, D. 1973 (Leeds U) 16
Hastings, A. C. 1936 (Sunderland) 2
Haughney, M. 1954 (Celtic) 1
Hay, D. 1970 (Celtic) 27
Hay, J. 1905 (Celtic, Newcastle U) 11
Hegarty, P. 1979 (Dundee U) 8
Heggie, C. 1886 (Rangers) 1
Henderson, G. H. 1904 (Rangers) 1
Henderson, J. G. 1953 (Portsmouth, Arsenal) 7
Henderson, W. 1963 (Rangers) 29
Hendry, E. C. J. 1993 (Blackburn R, Rangers, Coventry C, Bolton W) 51
Hendry, J. 2018 (Celtic) 3
Hepburn, J. 1891 (Alloa Ath) 1
Hepburn, R. 1932 (Ayr U) 1
Herd, A. C. 1935 (Hearts) 1
Herd, D. G. 1959 (Arsenal) 5
Herd, G. 1958 (Clyde) 5
Herriot, J. 1969 (Birmingham C) 8
Hewie, J. D. 1956 (Charlton Ath) 19
Higgins, A. 1885 (Kilmarnock) 1
Higgins, A. 1910 (Newcastle U) 4
Highet, T. C. 1875 (Queen's Park) 4
Hill, D. 1881 (Rangers) 3
Hill, D. A. 1906 (Third Lanark) 1
Hill, F. R. 1930 (Aberdeen) 3
Hill, J. 1891 (Hearts) 2
Hogg, G. 1896 (Hearts) 2
Hogg, J. 1922 (Ayr U) 1
Hogg, R. M. 1937 (Celtic) 1
Holm, A. H. 1882 (Queen's Park) 3
Holt, D. D. 1963 (Hearts) 5
Holt, G. J. 2001 (Kilmarnock, Norwich C) 10
Holton, J. A. 1973 (Manchester U) 15
Hope, R. 1968 (WBA) 2
Hopkin, D. 1997 (Crystal Palace, Leeds U) 7
Houliston, W. 1949 (Queen of the South) 3
Houston, S. M. 1976 (Manchester U) 1
Howden, W. 1905 (Partick Thistle) 1
Howe, R. 1929 (Hamilton A) 2
Howie, H. 1949 (Hibernian) 1
Howie, J. 1905 (Newcastle U) 3
Howieson, J. 1927 (St Mirren) 1
Hughes, J. 1965 (Celtic) 8

Hughes, R. D. 2004 (Portsmouth) 5
Hughes, S. R. 2010 (Norwich C) 1
Hughes, W. 1975 (Sunderland) 1
Humphries, W. 1952 (Motherwell) 1
Hunter, A. 1972 (Kilmarnock, Celtic) 4
Hunter, J. 1909 (Dundee) 1
Hunter, J. 1874 (Third Lanark, Eastern, Third Lanark) 4
Hunter, W. 1960 (Motherwell) 3
Hunter, R. 1890 (St Mirren) 1
Husband, J. 1947 (Partick Thistle) 1
Hutchison, D. 1999 (Everton, Sunderland, West Ham U) 26
Hutchison, T. 1974 (Coventry C) 17
Hutton, A. 2007 (Rangers, Tottenham H, Aston Villa) 50
Hutton, J. 1887 (St Bernards) 1
Hutton, J. 1923 (Aberdeen, Blackburn R) 10
Hyslop, T. 1896 (Stoke, Rangers) 2

Imlach, J. J. S. 1958 (Nottingham F) 4
Imrie, W. N. 1929 (St Johnstone) 2
Inglis, J. 1883 (Rangers) 2
Inglis, J. 1884 (Kilmarnock Ath) 1
Irons, J. H. 1900 (Queen's Park) 1
Irvine, B. 1991 (Aberdeen) 9
Iwelumo, C. R. 2009 (Wolverhampton W, Burnley) 4

Jack, R. 2018 (Rangers) 4
Jackson, A. 1886 (Cambuslang) 2
Jackson, A. 1925 (Aberdeen, Huddersfield T) 17
Jackson, C. 1975 (Rangers) 8
Jackson, D. 1995 (Hibernian, Celtic) 28
Jackson, J. 1931 (Partick Thistle, Chelsea) 8
Jackson, T. A. 1904 (St Mirren) 6
James, A. W. 1926 (Preston NE, Arsenal) 8
Jardine, A. 1971 (Rangers) 38
Jarvie, A. 1971 (Airdrieonians) 3
Jenkinson, T. 1887 (Hearts) 1
Jess, E. 1993 (Aberdeen, Coventry C, Aberdeen) 18
Johnston, A. 1999 (Sunderland, Rangers, Middlesbrough) 18
Johnston, L. H. 1948 (Clyde) 2
Johnston, M. 1984 (Watford, Celtic, Nantes, Rangers) 38
Johnston, R. 1938 (Sunderland) 1
Johnston, W. 1966 (Rangers, WBA) 22
Johnstone, D. 1973 (Rangers) 14
Johnstone, J. 1888 (Abercorn) 1
Johnstone, J. 1965 (Celtic) 23
Johnstone, Jas 1894 (Kilmarnock) 1
Johnstone, J. A. 1930 (Hearts) 3
Johnstone, R. 1951 (Hibernian, Manchester C) 17
Johnstone, W. 1887 (Third Lanark) 3
Jordan, J. 1973 (Leeds U, Manchester U, AC Milan) 52

Kay, J. L. 1880 (Queen's Park) 6
Keillor, A. 1891 (Montrose, Dundee) 6
Keir, L. 1885 (Dumbarton) 5
Kelly, H. T. 1952 (Blackpool) 1
Kelly, J. 1888 (Renton, Celtic) 8
Kelly, J. C. 1949 (Barnsley) 2
Kelly, L. M. 2013 (Kilmarnock) 1
Kelso, R. 1885 (Renton, Dundee) 7
Kelso, T. 1914 (Dundee) 1
Kennaway, J. 1934 (Celtic) 1
Kennedy, A. 1875 (Eastern, Third Lanark) 6
Kennedy, J. 1897 (Hibernian) 1
Kennedy, J. 1964 (Celtic) 6
Kennedy, J. 2004 (Celtic) 1
Kennedy, S. 1905 (Partick Thistle) 1
Kennedy, S. 1975 (Rangers) 5
Kennedy, S. 1978 (Aberdeen) 8
Kenneth, G. 2011 (Dundee U) 2
Ker, G. 1880 (Queen's Park) 5
Ker, W. 1872 (Queen's Park) 2
Kerr, A. 1955 (Partick Thistle) 2
Kerr, B. 2003 (Newcastle U) 3
Kerr, P. 1924 (Hibernian) 1
Key, G. 1902 (Hearts) 1
Key, W. 1907 (Queen's Park) 1
King, A. 1896 (Hearts, Celtic) 6
King, J. 1933 (Hamilton A) 2
King, W. S. 1929 (Queen's Park) 1
Kingsley, S. 2016 (Swansea C) 1
Kinloch, J. D. 1922 (Partick Thistle) 1
Kinnaird, A. F. 1873 (Wanderers) 1
Kinnear, D. 1938 (Rangers) 1
Kyle, K. 2002 (Sunderland, Kilmarnock) 10

Lambert, P. 1995 (Motherwell, Borussia Dortmund, Celtic) 40
Lambie, J. A. 1886 (Queen's Park) 3
Lambie, W. A. 1892 (Queen's Park) 9
Lamont, W. 1885 (Pilgrims) 1
Lang, A. 1880 (Dumbarton) 1
Lang, J. J. 1876 (Clydesdale, Third Lanark) 2
Latta, A. 1888 (Dumbarton) 2
Law, D. 1959 (Huddersfield T, Manchester C, Torino, Manchester U, Manchester C) 55
Law, G. 1910 (Rangers) 3
Law, T. 1928 (Chelsea) 2
Lawrence, J. 1911 (Newcastle U) 1
Lawrence, T. 1963 (Liverpool) 3
Lawson, D. 1923 (St Mirren) 1
Leckie, R. 1872 (Queen's Park) 1
Leggat, G. 1956 (Aberdeen, Fulham) 18
Leighton, J. 1983 (Aberdeen, Manchester U, Hibernian, Aberdeen) 91
Lennie, W. 1908 (Aberdeen) 2
Lennox, R. 1967 (Celtic) 10
Leslie, L. G. 1961 (Airdrieonians) 5
Levein, C. 1990 (Hearts) 16
Liddell, W. 1947 (Liverpool) 28
Liddle, D. 1931 (East Fife) 3
Lindsay, D. 1903 (St Mirren) 1
Lindsay, J. 1880 (Dumbarton) 8
Lindsay, J. 1888 (Renton) 3
Linwood, A. B. 1950 (Clyde) 1
Little, R. J. 1953 (Rangers) 1
Livingstone, G. T. 1906 (Manchester C, Rangers) 2
Lochhead, A. 1889 (Third Lanark) 1
Logan, J. 1891 (Ayr) 1
Logan, T. 1913 (Falkirk) 1
Logie, J. T. 1953 (Arsenal) 1
Loney, W. 1910 (Celtic) 2
Long, H. 1947 (Clyde) 1
Longair, W. 1894 (Dundee) 1
Lorimer, P. 1970 (Leeds U) 21
Love, A. 1931 (Aberdeen) 3
Low, A. 1934 (Falkirk) 1
Low, J. 1891 (Cambuslang) 1
Low, T. P. 1897 (Rangers) 1
Low, W. L. 1911 (Newcastle U) 5
Lowe, J. 1887 (St Bernards) 1
Lundie, J. 1886 (Hibernian) 1
Lyall, J. 1905 (Sheffield W) 1

Macari, L. 1972 (Celtic, Manchester U) 24
Mackail-Smith, C. 2011 (Peterborough U, Brighton & HA) 7
Mackay-Steven, G. 2013 (Dundee U, Aberdeen) 2
Mackie, J. C. 2011 (QPR) 9
Madden, J. 1893 (Celtic) 2
Maguire, C. 2011 (Aberdeen) 2
Main, F. R. 1938 (Rangers) 1
Main, J. 1909 (Hibernian) 1
Maley, W. 1893 (Celtic) 2
Maloney, S. R. 2006 (Celtic, Aston Villa, Celtic, Wigan Ath, Chicago Fire, Hull C) 47
Malpas, M. 1984 (Dundee U) 55
Marshall, D. J. 2005 (Celtic, Cardiff C, Hull C, Wigan Ath) 34
Marshall, G. 1992 (Celtic) 1
Marshall, H. 1899 (Celtic) 2
Marshall, J. 1885 (Third Lanark) 4
Marshall, J. 1921 (Middlesbrough, Llanelly) 7
Marshall, J. 1932 (Rangers) 3
Marshall, R. W. 1892 (Rangers) 2
Martin, B. 1995 (Motherwell) 2
Martin, C. H. 2014 (Derby Co) 17
Martin, F. 1954 (Aberdeen) 6
Martin, N. 1965 (Hibernian, Sunderland) 3
Martin, R. K. A. 2011 (Norwich C) 29
Martis, J. 1961 (Motherwell) 1
Mason, J. 1949 (Third Lanark) 7

Massie, A. 1932 (Hearts, Aston Villa) 18
Masson, D. S. 1976 (QPR, Derby Co) 17
Mathers, D. 1954 (Partick Thistle) 1
Matteo, D. 2001 (Leeds U) 6
Maxwell, W. S. 1898 (Stoke C) 1
May, J. 1906 (Rangers) 5
May, S. 2015 (Sheffield W) 1
McAllister, J. R. 2004 (Livingston) 1
McAdam, J. 1880 (Third Lanark) 1
McAllister, B. 1997 (Wimbledon) 3
McAllister, G. 1990 (Leicester C, Leeds U, Coventry C) 57
McArthur, D. 1895 (Celtic) 3
McArthur, J. 2011 (Wigan Ath, Crystal Palace) 32
McAtee, A. 1913 (Celtic) 1
McAulay, J. 1884 (Arthurlie) 1
McAulay, J. D. 1882 (Dumbarton) 9
McAulay, R. 1932 (Rangers) 2
Macauley, A. R. 1947 (Brentford, Arsenal) 7
McAvennie, F. 1986 (West Ham U, Celtic) 5
McBain, E. 1894 (St Mirren) 1
McBain, N. 1922 (Manchester U, Everton) 3
McBride, J. 1967 (Celtic) 2
McBride, P. 1904 (Preston NE) 6
McBurnie, O. R. 2018 (Swansea C, Sheffield U) 9
McCall, A. 1888 (Renton) 1
McCall, A. S. M. 1990 (Everton, Rangers) 40
McCall, J. 1886 (Renton) 5
McCalliog, J. 1967 (Sheffield W, Wolverhampton W) 5
McCallum, N. 1888 (Renton) 1
McCann, N. 1999 (Hearts, Rangers, Southampton) 26
McCann, R. J. 1959 (Motherwell) 5
McCartney, W. 1902 (Hibernian) 1
McClair, B. 1987 (Celtic, Manchester U) 30
McClory, A. 1927 (Motherwell) 3
McCloy, P. 1924 (Ayr U) 2
McCloy, P. 1973 (Rangers) 4
McCoist, A. 1986 (Rangers, Kilmarnock) 61
McColl, I. M. 1950 (Rangers) 14
McColl, R. S. 1896 (Queen's Park, Newcastle U, Queen's Park) 13
McColl, W. 1895 (Renton) 1
McCombie, A. 1903 (Sunderland, Newcastle U) 4
McCorkindale, J. 1891 (Partick Thistle) 1
McCormack, R. 2008 (Motherwell, Cardiff C, Leeds U, Fulham) 13
McCormick, R. 1886 (Abercorn) 1
McCrae, D. 1929 (St Mirren) 2
McCreadie, A. 1893 (Rangers) 2
McCreadie, E. G. 1965 (Chelsea) 23
McCulloch, D. 1935 (Hearts, Brentford, Derby Co) 7
McCulloch, L. 2005 (Wigan Ath, Rangers) 18
MacDonald, A. 1976 (Rangers) 1
McDonald, J. 1886 (Edinburgh University) 1
McDonald, J. 1956 (Sunderland) 2
McDonald, K. D. 2018 (Fulham) 5
MacDougall, E. J. 1975 (Norwich C) 7
McDougall, J. 1877 (Vale of Leven) 5
McDougall, J. 1926 (Airdrieonians) 1
McDougall, J. 1931 (Liverpool) 2
McEveley, J. 2008 (Derby Co) 3
McFadden, J. 2002 (Motherwell, Everton, Birmingham C) 48
McFadyen, W. 1934 (Motherwell) 2
Macfarlane, A. 1904 (Dundee) 5
Macfarlane, W. 1947 (Hearts) 1
McFarlane, R. 1896 (Greenock Morton) 1
McGarr, E. 1970 (Aberdeen) 2
McGarvey, F. P. 1979 (Liverpool, Celtic) 7
McGeoch, A. 1876 (Dumbreck) 4
McGeouch, D. 2018 (Hibernian) 2
McGhee, J. 1886 (Hibernian) 1
McGhee, M. 1983 (Aberdeen) 4
McGinlay, J. 1994 (Bolton W) 13
McGinn, J. 2016 (Hibernian, Aston Villa) 21
McGonagle, W. 1933 (Celtic) 6
McGrain, D. 1973 (Celtic) 62
McGregor, A. J. 2007 (Rangers, Besiktas, Hull C, Rangers) 42
McGregor, C. W. 2018 (Celtic) 19
McGregor, J. C. 1877 (Vale of Leven) 4
McGrory, J. 1928 (Celtic) 7
McGrory, J. E. 1965 (Kilmarnock) 3
McGuire, W. 1881 (Beith) 2
McGurk, F. 1934 (Birmingham) 1
McHardy, H. 1885 (Rangers) 1
McInally, A. 1989 (Aston Villa, Bayern Munich) 8
McInally, J. 1987 (Dundee U) 10
McInally, T. B. 1926 (Celtic) 2
McInnes, D. 2003 (WBA) 2
McInnes, T. 1889 (Cowlairs) 1
McIntosh, W. 1905 (Third Lanark) 1
McIntyre, A. 1878 (Vale of Leven) 2
McIntyre, H. 1880 (Rangers) 1
McIntyre, J. 1884 (Rangers) 1
MacKay, D. 1959 (Celtic) 14
Mackay, D. C. 1957 (Hearts, Tottenham H) 22
Mackay, G. 1988 (Hearts) 4
Mackay, M. 2004 (Norwich C) 5
McKay, B. 2016 (Rangers) 1
McKay, J. 1924 (Blackburn R) 1
McKay, R. 1928 (Newcastle U) 1
McKean, R. 1976 (Rangers) 1
McKenna, S. 2018 (Aberdeen) 14
McKenzie, D. 1938 (Brentford) 1
Mackenzie, J. A. 1954 (Partick Thistle) 9
McKeown, M. 1889 (Celtic) 2
McKie, J. 1898 (East Stirling) 1
McKillop, T. R. 1938 (Rangers) 1
McKimmie, S. 1989 (Aberdeen) 40
McKinlay, D. 1922 (Liverpool) 2
McKinlay, T. 1996 (Celtic) 22
McKinlay, W. 1994 (Dundee U, Blackburn R) 29
McKinnon, A. 1874 (Queen's Park) 1
McKinnon, R. 1966 (Rangers) 28
McKinnon, R. 1994 (Motherwell) 3
MacKinnon, W. 1883 (Dumbarton) 4
MacKinnon, W. W. 1872 (Queen's Park) 9
McLaren, A. 1929 (St Johnstone) 5
McLaren, A. 1947 (Preston NE) 4
McLaren, A. 1992 (Hearts, Rangers) 24
McLaren, A. 2001 (Kilmarnock) 1
McLaren, J. 1888 (Hibernian, Celtic) 3
McLaughlin, J. P. 2018 (Hearts, Sunderland) 2
McLean, A. 1926 (Celtic) 4
McLean, D. 1896 (St Bernards) 2
McLean, D. 1912 (Sheffield W) 1
McLean, G. 1968 (Dundee) 1
McLean, K. 2016 (Aberdeen, Norwich C) 10
McLean, T. 1969 (Kilmarnock) 6
McLeish, A. 1980 (Aberdeen) 77
McLeod, D. 1905 (Celtic) 4
McLeod, J. 1888 (Dumbarton) 5
MacLeod, J. M. 1961 (Hibernian) 4
MacLeod, M. 1985 (Celtic, Borussia Dortmund, Hibernian) 20
McLeod, W. 1886 (Cowlairs) 1
McLintock, A. 1875 (Vale of Leven) 3
McLintock, F. 1963 (Leicester C, Arsenal) 9
McLuckie, J. S. 1934 (Manchester C) 1
McMahon, A. 1892 (Celtic) 6
McManus, S. 2007 (Celtic, Middlesbrough) 26
McMenemy, J. 1905 (Celtic) 12
McMenemy, J. 1934 (Motherwell) 1
McMillan, I. L. 1952 (Airdrieonians, Rangers) 6
McMillan, J. 1897 (St Bernards) 1
McMillan, T. 1887 (Dumbarton) 1
McMullan, J. 1920 (Partick Thistle, Manchester C) 16
McNab, A. 1921 (Morton) 2
McNab, A. 1937 (Sunderland, WBA) 2
McNab, C. D. 1931 (Dundee) 6
McNab, J. S. 1923 (Liverpool) 1
McNair, A. 1906 (Celtic) 15
McNamara, J. 1997 (Celtic, Wolverhampton W) 33
McNamee, D. 2004 (Livingston) 4
McNaught, W. 1951 (Raith R) 5
McNaughton, K. 2002 (Aberdeen, Cardiff C) 4
McNeill, W. 1961 (Celtic) 29
McNiel, H. 1874 (Queen's Park) 10
McNiel, M. 1876 (Rangers) 2
McNulty, M. 2019 (Reading) 2
McPhail, J. 1950 (Celtic) 5

McPhail, R. 1927 (Airdrieonians, Rangers) 17
McPherson, D. 1892 (Kilmarnock) 1
McPherson, D. 1989 (Hearts, Rangers) 27
McPherson, J. 1875 (Clydesdale) 1
McPherson, J. 1879 (Vale of Leven) 8
McPherson, J. 1888 (Kilmarnock, Cowlairs, Rangers) 9
McPherson, J. 1891 (Hearts) 1
McPherson, R. 1882 (Arthurlie) 1
McQueen, G. 1974 (Leeds U, Manchester U) 30
McQueen, M. 1890 (Leith Ath) 2
McRorie, D. M. 1931 (Morton) 1
McSpadyen, A. 1939 (Partick Thistle) 2
McStay, P. 1984 (Celtic) 76
McStay, W. 1921 (Celtic) 13
McSwegan, G. 2000 (Hearts) 2
McTavish, J. 1910 (Falkirk) 1
McTominay, S. F. 2018 (Manchester U) 12
McWattie, G. C. 1901 (Queen's Park) 2
McWilliam, P. 1905 (Newcastle U) 8
Meechan, P. 1896 (Celtic) 1
Meiklejohn, D. D. 1922 (Rangers) 15
Menzies, A. 1906 (Hearts) 1
Mercer, R. 1912 (Hearts) 2
Middleton, R. 1930 (Cowdenbeath) 1
Millar, J. 1897 (Rangers) 3
Millar, J. 1963 (Rangers) 2
Miller, A. 1939 (Hearts) 1
Miller, C. 2001 (Dundee U) 1
Miller, J. 1931 (St Mirren) 5
Miller, K. 2001 (Rangers, Wolverhampton W, Celtic, Derby Co, Rangers, Bursaspor, Cardiff C, Vancouver Whitecaps) 69
Miller, L. 2006 (Dundee U, Aberdeen) 3
Miller, P. 1882 (Dumbarton) 3
Miller, T. 1920 (Liverpool, Manchester U) 3
Miller, W. 1876 (Third Lanark) 1
Miller, W. 1947 (Celtic) 6
Miller, W. 1975 (Aberdeen) 65
Mills, W. 1936 (Aberdeen) 3
Milne, J. V. 1938 (Middlesbrough) 2
Mitchell, D. 1890 (Rangers) 5
Mitchell, J. 1908 (Kilmarnock) 3
Mitchell, R. C. 1951 (Newcastle U) 2
Mochan, N. 1954 (Celtic) 3
Moir, W. 1950 (Bolton W) 1
Moncur, R. 1968 (Newcastle U) 16
Morgan, H. 1898 (St Mirren, Liverpool) 2
Morgan, L. 2018 (St Mirren) 2
Morgan, W. 1968 (Burnley, Manchester U) 21
Morris, D. 1923 (Raith R) 6
Morris, H. 1950 (East Fife) 1
Morrison, J. C. 2008 (WBA) 46
Morrison, T. 1927 (St Mirren) 1
Morton, A. L. 1920 (Queen's Park, Rangers) 31
Morton, H. A. 1929 (Kilmarnock) 2
Mudie, J. K. 1957 (Blackpool) 17
Muir, W. 1907 (Dundee) 1
Muirhead, T. A. 1922 (Rangers) 8
Mulgrew, C. P. 2012 (Celtic, Blackburn R) 44
Mulhall, G. 1960 (Aberdeen, Sunderland) 3
Munro, A. D. 1937 (Hearts, Blackpool) 3
Munro, F. M. 1971 (Wolverhampton W) 9
Munro, I. 1979 (St Mirren) 7
Munro, N. 1888 (Abercorn) 2
Murdoch, J. 1931 (Motherwell) 1
Murdoch, R. 1966 (Celtic) 12
Murphy, F. 1938 (Celtic) 1
Murphy, J. 2018 (Rangers) 2
Murray, I. 2003 (Hibernian, Rangers) 6
Murray, J. 1895 (Renton) 1
Murray, J. 1958 (Hearts) 5
Murray, J. W. 1890 (Vale of Leven) 1
Murray, P. 1896 (Hibernian) 2
Murray, S. 1972 (Aberdeen) 1
Murty, G. S. 2004 (Reading) 4
Mutch, G. 1938 (Preston NE) 1

Naismith, S. J. 2007 (Kilmarnock, Rangers, Everton, Norwich C, Hearts) 51
Napier, C. E. 1932 (Celtic, Derby Co) 5
Narey, D. 1977 (Dundee U) 35
Naysmith, G. A. 2000 (Hearts, Everton, Sheffield U) 46
Neil, R. G. 1896 (Hibernian, Rangers) 2
Neill, R. W. 1876 (Queen's Park) 5
Neilson, R. 2007 (Hearts) 1
Nellies, P. 1913 (Hearts) 2
Nelson, J. 1925 (Cardiff C) 4
Nevin, P. K. F. 1986 (Chelsea, Everton, Tranmere R) 28
Niblo, T. D. 1904 (Aston Villa) 1
Nibloe, J. 1929 (Kilmarnock) 11
Nicholas, C. 1983 (Celtic, Arsenal, Aberdeen) 20
Nicholson, B. 2001 (Dunfermline Ath) 3
Nicol, S. 1985 (Liverpool) 27
Nisbet, J. 1929 (Ayr U) 3
Niven, J. B. 1885 (Moffat) 1

O'Connor, G. 2002 (Hibernian, Lokomotiv Moscow, Birmingham C) 16
O'Donnell, F. 1937 (Preston NE, Blackpool) 6
O'Donnell, P. 1994 (Motherwell) 1
O'Donnell, S. G. 2018 (Kilmarnock) 11
Ogilvie, D. H. 1934 (Motherwell) 1
O'Hare, J. 1970 (Derby Co) 13
O'Neil, B. 1996 (Celtic, Wolfsburg, Derby Co, Preston NE) 7
O'Neil, J. 2001 (Hibernian) 1
Ormond, W. E. 1954 (Hibernian) 6
O'Rourke, F. 1907 (Airdrieonians) 1
Orr, J. 1892 (Kilmarnock) 1
Orr, R. 1902 (Newcastle U) 2
Orr, T. 1952 (Morton) 2
Orr, W. 1900 (Celtic) 3
Orrock, R. 1913 (Falkirk) 1
Oswald, J. 1889 (Third Lanark, St Bernards, Rangers) 3

Palmer, L. J. 2019 (Sheffield W) 5
Parker, A. H. 1955 (Falkirk, Everton) 15
Parlane, D. 1973 (Rangers) 12
Parlane, R. 1878 (Vale of Leven) 3
Paterson, C. T. O. 2016 (Hearts, Cardiff C) 12
Paterson, G. D. 1939 (Celtic) 1
Paterson, J. 1920 (Leicester C) 1
Paterson, J. 1931 (Cowdenbeath) 3
Paton, A. 1952 (Motherwell) 2
Paton, D. 1896 (St Bernards) 1
Paton, M. 1883 (Dumbarton) 5
Paton, R. 1879 (Vale of Leven) 2
Patrick, J. 1897 (St Mirren) 2
Paul, H. McD. 1909 (Queen's Park) 3
Paul, W. 1888 (Partick Thistle) 3
Paul, W. 1891 (Dykebar) 1
Pearson, S. P. 2004 (Motherwell, Celtic, Derby Co) 10
Pearson, T. 1947 (Newcastle U) 2
Penman, A. 1966 (Dundee) 1
Pettigrew, W. 1976 (Motherwell) 5
Phillips, J. 1877 (Queen's Park) 3
Phillips, M. 2012 (Blackpool, QPR, WBA) 16
Plenderleith, J. B. 1961 (Manchester C) 1
Porteous, W. 1903 (Hearts) 1
Pressley, S. J. 2000 (Hearts) 32
Pringle, C. 1921 (St Mirren) 1
Provan, D. 1964 (Rangers) 5
Provan, D. 1980 (Celtic) 10
Pursell, P. 1914 (Queen's Park) 1

Quashie, N. F. 2004 (Portsmouth, Southampton, WBA) 14
Quinn, J. 1905 (Celtic) 11
Quinn, P. 1961 (Motherwell) 4

Rae, G. 2001 (Dundee, Rangers, Cardiff C) 14
Rae, J. 1889 (Third Lanark) 2
Raeside, J. S. 1906 (Third Lanark) 1
Raisbeck, A. G. 1900 (Liverpool) 8
Rankin, G. 1890 (Vale of Leven) 2
Rankin, R. 1929 (St Mirren) 3
Redpath, W. 1949 (Motherwell) 9
Reid, J. G. 1914 (Airdrieonians) 3
Reid, R. 1938 (Brentford) 2
Reid, W. 1911 (Rangers) 9
Reilly, L. 1949 (Hibernian) 38
Rennie, H. G. 1900 (Hearts, Hibernian) 13
Renny-Tailyour, H. W. 1873 (Royal Engineers) 1

Rhind, A. 1872 (Queen's Park) 1
Rhodes, J. L. 2012 (Huddersfield T, Blackburn R, Sheffield W) 14
Richmond, A. 1906 (Queen's Park) 1
Richmond, J. T. 1877 (Clydesdale, Queen's Park) 3
Ring, T. 1953 (Clyde) 12
Rioch, B. D. 1975 (Derby Co, Everton, Derby Co) 24
Riordan, D. G. 2006 (Hibernian) 3
Ritchie, A. 1891 (East Stirlingshire) 1
Ritchie, H. 1923 (Hibernian) 2
Ritchie, J. 1897 (Queen's Park) 1
Ritchie, M. T. 2015 (Bournemouth, Newcastle U) 16
Ritchie, P. S. 1999 (Hearts, Bolton W, Walsall) 7
Ritchie, W. 1962 (Rangers) 1
Robb, D. T. 1971 (Aberdeen) 5
Robb, W. 1926 (Rangers, Hibernian) 2
Robertson, A. 1955 (Clyde) 5
Robertson, A. 2014 (Dundee U, Hull C, Liverpool) 34
Robertson, D. 1992 (Rangers) 3
Robertson, G. 1910 (Motherwell, Sheffield W) 4
Robertson, G. 1938 (Kilmarnock) 1
Robertson, H. 1962 (Dundee) 1
Robertson, J. 1931 (Dundee) 2
Robertson, J. 1991 (Hearts) 16
Robertson, J. N. 1978 (Nottingham F, Derby Co) 28
Robertson, J. G. 1965 (Tottenham H) 1
Robertson, J. T. 1898 (Everton, Southampton, Rangers) 16
Robertson, P. 1903 (Dundee) 1
Robertson, S. 2009 (Dundee U) 2
Robertson, T. 1889 (Queen's Park) 4
Robertson, T. 1898 (Hearts) 1
Robertson, W. 1887 (Dumbarton) 2
Robinson, R. 1974 (Dundee) 4
Robson, B. G. G. 2008 (Dundee U, Celtic, Middlesbrough) 17
Ross, M. 2002 (Rangers) 13
Rough, A. 1976 (Partick Thistle, Hibernian) 53
Rougvie, D. 1984 (Aberdeen) 1
Rowan, A. 1880 (Caledonian, Queen's Park) 2
Russell, D. 1895 (Hearts, Celtic) 6
Russell, J. 1890 (Cambuslang) 1
Russell, J. S. S. 2015 (Derby Co, Kansas City) 14
Russell, W. F. 1924 (Airdrieonians) 2
Rutherford, E. 1948 (Rangers) 1

St John, I. 1959 (Motherwell, Liverpool) 21
Saunders, S. 2011 (Motherwell) 1
Sawers, W. 1895 (Dundee) 1
Scarff, P. 1931 (Celtic) 1
Schaedler, E. 1974 (Hibernian) 1
Scott, A. S. 1957 (Rangers, Everton) 16
Scott, J. 1966 (Hibernian) 1
Scott, J. 1971 (Dundee) 2
Scott, M. 1898 (Airdrieonians) 1
Scott, R. 1894 (Airdrieonians) 1
Scoular, J. 1951 (Portsmouth) 9
Sellar, W. 1885 (Battlefield, Queen's Park) 9
Semple, W. 1886 (Cambuslang) 1
Severin, S. D. 2002 (Hearts, Aberdeen) 15
Shankland, L. 2020 (Dundee U) 2
Shankly, W. 1938 (Preston NE) 5
Sharp, G. M. 1985 (Everton) 12
Sharp, J. 1904 (Dundee, Woolwich Arsenal, Fulham) 5
Shaw, D. 1947 (Hibernian) 8
Shaw, F. W. 1884 (Pollokshields Ath) 2
Shaw, J. 1947 (Rangers) 4
Shearer, D. 1994 (Aberdeen) 7
Shearer, R. 1961 (Rangers) 4
Shinnie, A. M. 2013 (Inverness CT) 1
Shinnie, G. 2018 (Aberdeen) 6
Sillars, D. C. 1891 (Queen's Park) 5
Simpson, J. 1895 (Third Lanark) 3
Simpson, J. 1935 (Rangers) 14
Simpson, N. 1983 (Aberdeen) 5
Simpson, R. C. 1967 (Celtic) 5
Sinclair, G. L. 1910 (Hearts) 3
Sinclair, J. W. E. 1966 (Leicester C) 1
Skene, L. H. 1904 (Queen's Park) 1
Sloan, T. 1904 (Third Lanark) 1
Smellie, R. 1887 (Queen's Park) 6
Smith, A. 1898 (Rangers) 20
Smith, D. 1966 (Aberdeen, Rangers) 2
Smith, G. 1947 (Hibernian) 18
Smith, H. G. 1988 (Hearts) 3
Smith, J. 1924 (Ayr U) 1
Smith, J. 1935 (Rangers) 2
Smith, J. 1968 (Aberdeen, Newcastle U) 4
Smith, J. 2003 (Celtic) 2
Smith, J. E. 1959 (Celtic) 2
Smith, Jas 1872 (Queen's Park) 1
Smith, John 1877 (Mauchline, Edinburgh University, Queen's Park) 10
Smith, N. 1897 (Rangers) 12
Smith, R. 1872 (Queen's Park) 2
Smith, T. M. 1934 (Kilmarnock, Preston NE) 2
Snodgrass, R. 2011 (Leeds U, Norwich C, Hull C, West Ham U) 28
Somers, P. 1905 (Celtic) 4
Somers, W. S. 1879 (Third Lanark, Queen's Park) 3
Somerville, G. 1886 (Queen's Park) 1
Souness, G. J. 1975 (Middlesbrough, Liverpool, Sampdoria) 54
Souttar, J. 2019 (Hearts) 3
Speedie, D. R. 1985 (Chelsea, Coventry C) 10
Speedie, F. 1903 (Rangers) 3
Speirs, J. H. 1908 (Rangers) 1
Spencer, J. 1995 (Chelsea, QPR) 14
Stanton, P. 1966 (Hibernian) 16
Stark, J. 1909 (Rangers) 2
Steel, W. 1947 (Morton, Derby Co, Dundee) 30
Steele, D. M. 1923 (Huddersfield) 3
Stein, C. 1969 (Rangers, Coventry C) 21
Stephen, J. F. 1947 (Bradford) 2
Stevenson, G. 1928 (Motherwell) 12
Stevenson, L. 2018 (Hibernian) 1
Stewart, A. 1888 (Queen's Park) 2
Stewart, A. 1894 (Third Lanark) 1
Stewart, D. 1888 (Dumbarton) 1
Stewart, D. 1893 (Queen's Park) 3
Stewart, D. S. 1978 (Leeds U) 1
Stewart, G. 1906 (Hibernian, Manchester C) 4
Stewart, J. 1977 (Kilmarnock, Middlesbrough) 2
Stewart, M. J. 2002 (Manchester U, Hearts) 4
Stewart, R. 1981 (West Ham U) 10
Stewart, W. G. 1898 (Queen's Park) 2
Stockdale, R. K. 2002 (Middlesbrough) 5
Storrier, D. 1899 (Celtic) 3
Strachan, G. D. 1980 (Aberdeen, Manchester U, Leeds U) 50
Sturrock, P. 1981 (Dundee U) 20
Sullivan, N. 1997 (Wimbledon, Tottenham H) 28
Summers, W. 1926 (St Mirren) 1
Symon, J. S. 1939 (Rangers) 1

Tait, T. S. 1911 (Sunderland) 1
Taylor, G. J. 2019 (Kilmarnock, Celtic) 3
Taylor, J. 1872 (Queen's Park) 6
Taylor, J. D. 1892 (Dumbarton, St Mirren) 4
Taylor, W. 1892 (Hearts) 1
Teale, G. 2006 (Wigan Ath, Derby Co) 13
Telfer, P. N. 2000 (Coventry C) 1
Telfer, W. 1933 (Motherwell) 2
Telfer, W. D. 1954 (St Mirren) 1
Templeton, R. 1902 (Aston Villa, Newcastle U, Woolwich Arsenal, Kilmarnock) 11
Thompson, S. 2002 (Dundee U, Rangers) 16
Thomson, A. 1886 (Arthurlie) 1
Thomson, A. 1889 (Third Lanark) 1
Thomson, A. 1909 (Airdrieonians) 1
Thomson, A. 1926 (Celtic) 3
Thomson, C. 1904 (Hearts, Sunderland) 21
Thomson, C. 1937 (Sunderland) 1
Thomson, D. 1920 (Dundee) 1
Thomson, J. 1930 (Celtic) 4
Thomson, J. J. 1872 (Queen's Park) 3
Thomson, J. R. 1933 (Everton) 1
Thomson, K. 2009 (Rangers, Middlesbrough) 3
Thomson, R. 1932 (Celtic) 1
Thomson, R. W. 1927 (Falkirk) 1
Thomson, S. 1884 (Rangers) 2
Thomson, W. 1892 (Dumbarton) 4
Thomson, W. 1896 (Dundee) 1

Thomson, W. 1980 (St Mirren) 7
Thornton, W. 1947 (Rangers) 7
Tierney, K. 2016 (Celtic) 12
Toner, W. 1959 (Kilmarnock) 2
Townsley, T. 1926 (Falkirk) 1
Troup, A. 1920 (Dundee, Everton) 5
Turnbull, E. 1948 (Hibernian) 8
Turner, T. 1884 (Arthurlie) 1
Turner, W. 1885 (Pollokshields Ath) 2

Ure, J. F. 1962 (Dundee, Arsenal) 11
Urquhart, D. 1934 (Hibernian) 1

Vallance, T. 1877 (Rangers) 7
Venters, A. 1934 (Cowdenbeath, Rangers) 3

Waddell, T. S. 1891 (Queen's Park) 6
Waddell, W. 1947 (Rangers) 17
Wales, H. M. 1933 (Motherwell) 1
Walker, A. 1988 (Celtic) 3
Walker, F. 1922 (Third Lanark) 1
Walker, G. 1930 (St Mirren) 4
Walker, J. 1895 (Hearts, Rangers) 5
Walker, J. 1911 (Swindon T) 9
Walker, J. N. 1993 (Hearts, Partick Thistle) 2
Walker, R. 1900 (Hearts) 29
Walker, T. 1935 (Hearts) 20
Walker, W. 1909 (Clyde) 2
Wallace, I. A. 1978 (Coventry C) 3
Wallace, L. 2010 (Hearts, Rangers) 10
Wallace, R. 2010 (Preston NE) 1
Wallace, W. S. B. 1965 (Hearts, Celtic) 7
Wardhaugh, J. 1955 (Hearts) 2
Wark, J. 1979 (Ipswich T, Liverpool) 28
Watson, A. 1881 (Queen's Park) 3
Watson, J. 1903 (Sunderland, Middlesbrough) 6
Watson, J. 1948 (Motherwell, Huddersfield T) 2
Watson, J. A. K. 1878 (Rangers) 1
Watson, P. R. 1934 (Blackpool) 1
Watson, R. 1971 (Motherwell) 1
Watson, W. 1898 (Falkirk) 1
Watt, A. P. 2016 (Charlton Ath) 1
Watt, F. 1889 (Kilbirnie) 4
Watt, W. W. 1887 (Queen's Park) 1
Waugh, W. 1938 (Hearts) 1
Webster, A. 2003 (Hearts, Dundee U, Hearts) 28
Weir, A. 1959 (Motherwell) 6
Weir, D. G. 1997 (Hearts, Everton, Rangers) 69
Weir, J. 1887 (Third Lanark) 1
Weir, J. B. 1872 (Queen's Park) 4
Weir, P. 1980 (St Mirren, Aberdeen) 6
White, John 1922 (Albion R, Hearts) 2
White, J. A. 1959 (Falkirk, Tottenham H) 22
White, W. 1907 (Bolton W) 2
Whitelaw, A. 1887 (Vale of Leven) 2
Whittaker, S. G. 2010 (Rangers, Norwich C) 31
Whyte, D. 1988 (Celtic, Middlesbrough, Aberdeen) 12
Wilkie, L. 2002 (Dundee) 11
Williams, G. 2002 (Nottingham F) 5
Wilson, A. 1907 (Sheffield W) 6
Wilson, A. 1954 (Portsmouth) 1
Wilson, A. N. 1920 (Dunfermline, Middlesbrough) 12
Wilson, D. 1900 (Queen's Park) 1
Wilson, D. 1913 (Oldham Ath) 1
Wilson, D. 1961 (Rangers) 22
Wilson, D. 2011 (Liverpool) 5
Wilson, G. W. 1904 (Hearts, Everton, Newcastle U) 6
Wilson, Hugh 1890 (Newmilns, Sunderland, Third Lanark) 4
Wilson, I. A. 1987 (Leicester C, Everton) 5
Wilson, J. 1888 (Vale of Leven) 4
Wilson, M. 2011 (Celtic) 1
Wilson, P. 1926 (Celtic) 4
Wilson, P. 1975 (Celtic) 1
Wilson, R. P. 1972 (Arsenal) 2
Winters, R. 1999 (Aberdeen) 1
Wiseman, W. 1927 (Queen's Park) 2
Wood, G. 1979 (Everton, Arsenal) 4
Woodburn, W. A. 1947 (Rangers) 24
Wotherspoon, D. N. 1872 (Queen's Park) 2
Wright, K. 1992 (Hibernian) 1
Wright, S. 1993 (Aberdeen) 2
Wright, T. 1953 (Sunderland) 3
Wylie, T. G. 1890 (Rangers) 1

Yeats, R. 1965 (Liverpool) 2
Yorston, B. C. 1931 (Aberdeen) 1
Yorston, H. 1955 (Aberdeen) 1
Young, A. 1905 (Everton) 2
Young, A. 1960 (Hearts, Everton) 8
Young, G. L. 1947 (Rangers) 53
Young, J. 1906 (Celtic) 1
Younger, T. 1955 (Hibernian, Liverpool) 24

WALES

Adams, H. 1882 (Berwyn R, Druids) 4
Aizlewood, M. 1986 (Charlton Ath, Leeds U, Bradford C, Bristol C, Cardiff C) 39
Allchurch, I. J. 1951 (Swansea T, Newcastle U, Cardiff C, Swansea T) 68
Allchurch, L. 1955 (Swansea T, Sheffield U) 11
Allen, B. W. 1951 (Coventry C) 2
Allen, J. M. 2009 (Swansea C, Liverpool, Stoke C) 56
Allen, M. 1986 (Watford, Norwich C, Millwall, Newcastle U) 14
Ampadu, E. K. C. R. 2018 (Chelsea) 13
Arridge, S. 1892 (Bootle, Everton, New Brighton Tower) 8
Astley, D. J. 1931 (Charlton Ath, Aston Villa, Derby Co, Blackpool) 13
Atherton, R. W. 1899 (Hibernian, Middlesbrough) 9

Bailiff, W. E. 1913 (Llanelly) 4
Baker, C. W. 1958 (Cardiff C) 7
Baker, W. G. 1948 (Cardiff C) 1
Bale, G. F. 2006 (Southampton, Tottenham H, Real Madrid) 83
Bamford, T. 1931 (Wrexham) 5
Barnard, D. S. 1998 (Barnsley, Grimsby T) 22
Barnes, W. 1948 (Arsenal) 22
Bartley, T. 1898 (Glossop NE) 1
Bastock, A. M. 1892 (Shrewsbury T) 1
Beadles, G. H. 1925 (Cardiff C) 2
Bell, W. S. 1881 (Shrewsbury Engineers, Crewe Alex) 5
Bellamy, C. D. 1998 (Norwich C, Coventry C, Newcastle U, Blackburn R, Liverpool, West Ham U, Manchester C, Liverpool, Cardiff C) 78
Bennion, S. R. 1926 (Manchester U) 10
Berry, G. F. 1979 (Wolverhampton W, Stoke C) 5
Blackmore, C. G. 1985 (Manchester U, Middlesbrough) 39
Blake, D. J. 2011 (Cardiff C, Crystal Palace) 14
Blake, N. A. 1994 (Sheffield U, Bolton W, Blackburn R, Wolverhampton W) 29
Blew, H. 1899 (Wrexham) 22
Boden, T. 1880 (Wrexham) 1
Bodin, B. P. 2018 (Preston NE) 1
Bodin, P. J. 1990 (Swindon T, Crystal Palace, Swindon T) 23
Boulter, L. M. 1939 (Brentford) 1
Bowdler, H. E. 1893 (Shrewsbury T) 1
Bowdler, J. C. H. 1890 (Shrewsbury T, Wolverhampton W, Shrewsbury T) 4
Bowen, D. L. 1955 (Arsenal) 19
Bowen, E. 1880 (Druids) 2
Bowen, J. P. 1994 (Swansea C, Birmingham C) 2
Bowen, M. R. 1986 (Tottenham H, Norwich C, West Ham U) 41
Bowsher, S. J. 1929 (Burnley) 1
Boyle, T. 1981 (Crystal Palace) 2
Bradley, M. S. 2010 (Walsall) 1
Bradshaw, T. W. C. 2016 (Walsall, Barnsley) 3
Britten, T. J. 1878 (Parkgrove, Presteigne) 2
Brooks, D. R. 2018 (Sheffield U, Bournemouth) 12
Brookes, S. J. 1900 (Llandudno) 2
Brown, A. I. 1926 (Aberdare Ath) 1
Brown, J. R. 2006 (Gillingham, Blackburn R, Aberdeen) 3
Browning, M. T. 1996 (Bristol R, Huddersfield T) 5

Bryan, T. 1886 (Oswestry) 2
Buckland, T. 1899 (Bangor) 1
Burgess, W. A. R. 1947 (Tottenham H) 32
Burke, T. 1883 (Wrexham, Newton Heath) 8
Burnett, T. B. 1877 (Ruabon) 1
Burton, A. D. 1963 (Norwich C, Newcastle U) 9
Butler, J. 1893 (Chirk) 3
Butler, W. T. 1900 (Druids) 2

Cartwright, L. 1974 (Coventry C, Wrexham) 7
Carty, T. See McCarthy (Wrexham).
Challen, J. B. 1887 (Corinthians, Wellingborough GS) 4
Chapman, T. 1894 (Newtown, Manchester C, Grimsby T) 7
Charles, J. M. 1981 (Swansea C, QPR, Oxford U) 19
Charles, M. 1955 (Swansea T, Arsenal, Cardiff C) 31
Charles, W. J. 1950 (Leeds U, Juventus, Leeds U, Cardiff C) 38
Chester, J. G. 2014 (Hull C, WBA, Aston Villa) 35
Church, S. R. 2009 (Reading, Charlton Ath) 38
Clarke, R. J. 1949 (Manchester C) 22
Coleman, C. 1992 (Crystal Palace, Blackburn R, Fulham) 32
Collier, D. J. 1921 (Grimsby T) 1
Collins, D. L. 2005 (Sunderland, Stoke C) 12
Collins, J. M. 2004 (Cardiff C, West Ham U, Aston Villa, West Ham U) 51
Collins, W. S. 1931 (Llanelly) 1
Collison, J. D. 2008 (West Ham U) 16
Conde, C. 1884 (Chirk) 3
Cook, F. C. 1925 (Newport Co, Portsmouth) 8
Cornforth, J. M. 1995 (Swansea C) 2
Cotterill, D. R. G. B. 2006 (Bristol C, Wigan Ath, Sheffield U, Swansea C, Doncaster R, Birmingham C) 24
Coyne, D. 1996 (Tranmere R, Grimsby T, Leicester C, Burnley, Tranmere R) 16
Crofts, A. L. 2016 ((Gillingham, Brighton & HA, Norwich C, Scunthorpe U) 29
Crompton, W. 1931 (Wrexham) 3
Cross, E. A. 1876 (Wrexham) 2
Crosse, K. 1879 (Druids) 3
Crossley, M. G. 1997 (Nottingham F, Middlesbrough, Fulham) 8
Crowe, V. H. 1959 (Aston Villa) 16
Cumner, R. H. 1939 (Arsenal) 3
Curtis, A. T. 1976 (Swansea C, Leeds U, Swansea C, Southampton, Cardiff C) 35
Curtis, E. R. 1928 (Cardiff C, Birmingham) 3

Daniel, R. W. 1951 (Arsenal, Sunderland) 21
Darvell, S. 1897 (Oxford University) 2
Davies, A. 1876 (Wrexham) 2
Davies, A. 1904 (Druids, Middlesbrough) 2
Davies, A. 1983 (Manchester U, Newcastle U, Swansea C, Bradford C) 13
Davies, A. 2019 (Barnsley) 1
Davies, A. O. 1885 (Barmouth, Swifts, Wrexham, Crewe Alex) 9
Davies, A. R. 2006 (Yeovil T) 1
Davies, A. T. 1891 (Shrewsbury T) 1
Davies, B. T. 2013 (Swansea C, Tottenham H) 52
Davies, C. 1972 (Charlton Ath) 1
Davies, C. M. 2006 (Oxford U, Verona, Oldham Ath, Barnsley) 7
Davies, D. 1904 (Bolton W) 3
Davies, D. C. 1899 (Brecon, Hereford) 2
Davies, D. W. 1912 (Treharris, Oldham Ath) 2
Davies, E. Lloyd 1904 (Stoke, Northampton T) 16
Davies, E. R. 1953 (Newcastle U) 6
Davies, G. 1980 (Fulham, Manchester C) 16
Davies, Rev. H. 1928 (Wrexham) 1
Davies, Idwal 1923 (Liverpool Marine) 1
Davies, J. E. 1885 (Oswestry) 1
Davies, Jas 1878 (Wrexham) 1
Davies, John 1879 (Wrexham) 1
Davies, Jos 1888 (Newton Heath, Wolverhampton W) 7
Davies, Jos 1889 (Everton, Chirk, Ardwick, Sheffield U, Manchester C, Millwall, Reading) 11
Davies, J. P. 1883 (Druids) 2
Davies, Ll. 1907 (Wrexham, Everton, Wrexham) 13
Davies, L. S. 1922 (Cardiff C) 23
Davies, O. 1890 (Wrexham) 1
Davies, R. 1883 (Wrexham) 3
Davies, R. 1885 (Druids) 1
Davies, R. O. 1892 (Wrexham) 2
Davies, R. T. 1964 (Norwich C, Southampton, Portsmouth) 29
Davies, R. W. 1964 (Bolton W, Newcastle U, Manchester C, Manchester U, Blackpool) 34
Davies, S. 2001 (Tottenham H, Everton, Fulham) 58
Davies, S. I. 1996 (Manchester U) 1
Davies, Stanley 1920 (Preston NE, Everton, WBA, Rotherham U) 18
Davies, T. 1886 (Oswestry) 1
Davies, T. 1903 (Druids) 4
Davies, W. 1884 (Wrexham) 1
Davies, W. 1924 (Swansea T, Cardiff C, Notts Co) 17
Davies, William 1903 (Wrexham, Blackburn R) 11
Davies, W. C. 1908 (Crystal Palace, WBA, Crystal Palace) 4
Davies, W. D. 1975 (Everton, Wrexham, Swansea C) 52
Davies, W. H. 1876 (Oswestry) 4
Davis, G. 1978 (Wrexham) 3
Davis, W. O. 1913 (Millwall Ath) 5
Day, A. 1934 (Tottenham H) 1
Deacy, N. 1977 (PSV Eindhoven, Beringen) 12
Dearson, D. J. 1939 (Birmingham) 3
Delaney, M. A. 2000 (Aston Villa) 36
Derrett, S. C. 1969 (Cardiff C) 4
Dewey, F. T. 1931 (Cardiff Corinthians) 2
Dibble, A. 1986 (Luton T, Manchester C) 3
Dorman, A. 2010 (St Mirren, Crystal Palace) 3
Doughty, J. 1886 (Druids, Newton Heath) 8
Doughty, R. 1888 (Newton Heath) 2
Duffy, R. M. 2006 (Portsmouth) 13
Dummett, P. 2014 (Newcastle U) 5
Durban, A. 1966 (Derby Co) 27
Dwyer, P. J. 1978 (Cardiff C) 10

Eardley, N. 2008 (Oldham Ath, Blackpool) 16
Earnshaw, R. 2002 (Cardiff C, WBA, Norwich C, Derby Co, Nottingham F, Cardiff C) 59
Easter, J. M. 2007 (Wycombe W, Plymouth Arg, Milton Keynes D, Crystal Palace, Millwall) 12
Eastwood, F. 2008 (Wolverhampton W, Coventry C) 11
Edwards, C. 1878 (Wrexham) 1
Edwards, C. N. H. 1996 (Swansea C) 1
Edwards, D. A. 2008 (Luton T, Wolverhampton W, Reading) 43
Edwards, G. 1947 (Birmingham C, Cardiff C) 12
Edwards, H. 1878 (Wrexham Civil Service, Wrexham) 8
Edwards, J. H. 1876 (Wanderers) 1
Edwards, J. H. 1895 (Oswestry) 3
Edwards, J. H. 1898 (Aberystwyth) 1
Edwards, L. T. 1957 (Charlton Ath) 2
Edwards, R. I. 1978 (Chester, Wrexham) 4
Edwards, R. O. 2003 (Aston Villa, Wolverhampton W) 15
Edwards, R. W. 1998 (Bristol C) 4
Edwards, T. 1932 (Linfield) 1
Egan, W. 1892 (Chirk) 1
Ellis, B. 1932 (Motherwell) 6
Ellis, E. 1931 (Nunhead, Oswestry) 3
Emanuel, W. J. 1973 (Bristol C) 2
England, H. M. 1962 (Blackburn R, Tottenham H) 44
Evans, B. C. 1972 (Swansea C, Hereford U) 7
Evans, C. M. 2008 (Manchester C, Sheffield U) 13
Evans, D. G. 1926 (Reading, Huddersfield T) 4
Evans, H. P. 1922 (Cardiff C) 6
Evans, I. 1976 (Crystal Palace) 13
Evans, J. 1893 (Oswestry) 3
Evans, J. 1912 (Cardiff C) 8
Evans, J. H. 1922 (Southend U) 4
Evans, L. 2018 (Wolverhampton W, Sheffield U, Wigan Ath) 4
Evans, Len 1927 (Aberdare Ath, Cardiff C, Birmingham) 4
Evans, M. 1884 (Oswestry) 1
Evans, P. S. 2002 (Brentford, Bradford C) 2
Evans, R. 1902 (Clapton) 1
Evans, R. E. 1906 (Wrexham, Aston Villa, Sheffield U) 10
Evans, R. O. 1902 (Wrexham, Blackburn R, Coventry C) 10

Evans, R. S. 1964 (Swansea T) 1
Evans, S. J. 2007 (Wrexham) 7
Evans, T. J. 1927 (Clapton Orient, Newcastle U) 4
Evans, W. 1933 (Tottenham H) 6
Evans, W. A. W. 1876 (Oxford University) 2
Evans, W. G. 1890 (Bootle, Aston Villa) 3
Evelyn, E. C. 1887 (Crusaders) 1
Eyton-Jones, J. A. 1883 (Wrexham) 4

Farmer, G. 1885 (Oswestry) 2
Felgate, D. 1984 (Lincoln C) 1
Finnigan, R. J. 1930 (Wrexham) 1
Fletcher, C. N. 2004 (Bournemouth, West Ham U, Crystal Palace) 36
Flynn, B. 1975 (Burnley, Leeds U, Burnley) 66
Fon Williams, O. 2016 (Inverness CT) 1
Ford, T. 1947 (Swansea T, Aston Villa, Sunderland, Cardiff C) 38
Foulkes, H. E. 1932 (WBA) 1
Foulkes, W. I. 1952 (Newcastle U) 11
Foulkes, W. T. 1884 (Oswestry) 2
Fowler, J. 1925 (Swansea T) 6
Freeman, K. S. 2019 (Sheffield U) 1
Freestone, R. 2000 (Swansea C) 1

Gabbidon, D. L. 2002 (Cardiff C, West Ham U, QPR, Crystal Palace) 49
Garner, G. 2006 (Leyton Orient) 1
Garner, J. 1896 (Aberystwyth) 1
Giggs, R. J. 1992 (Manchester U) 64
Giles, D. C. 1980 (Swansea C, Crystal Palace) 12
Gillam, S. G. 1889 (Wrexham, Shrewsbury, Clapton) 5
Glascodine, G. 1879 (Wrexham) 1
Glover, E. M. 1932 (Grimsby T) 7
Godding, G. 1923 (Wrexham) 2
Godfrey, B. C. 1964 (Preston NE) 3
Goodwin, U. 1881 (Ruthin) 1
Goss, J. 1991 (Norwich C) 9
Gough, R. T. 1883 (Oswestry White Star) 1
Gray, A. 1924 (Oldham Ath, Manchester C, Manchester Central, Tranmere R, Chester) 24
Green, A. W. 1901 (Aston Villa, Notts Co, Nottingham F) 8
Green, C. R. 1965 (Birmingham C) 15
Green, G. H. 1938 (Charlton Ath) 4
Green, R. M. 1998 (Wolverhampton W) 2
Grey, Dr W. 1876 (Druids) 2
Griffiths, A. T. 1971 (Wrexham) 17
Griffiths, F. J. 1900 (Blackpool) 2
Griffiths, G. 1887 (Chirk) 1
Griffiths, J. H. 1953 (Swansea T) 1
Griffiths, L. 1902 (Wrexham) 1
Griffiths, M. W. 1947 (Leicester C) 11
Griffiths, P. 1884 (Chirk) 6
Griffiths, P. H. 1932 (Everton) 1
Griffiths, T. P. 1927 (Everton, Bolton W, Middlesbrough, Aston Villa) 21
Gunter, C. R. 2007 (Cardiff C, Tottenham H, Nottingham F, Reading) 96

Hall, G. D. 1988 (Chelsea) 9
Hallam, J. 1889 (Oswestry) 1
Hanford, H. 1934 (Swansea T, Sheffield W) 7
Harrington, A. C. 1956 (Cardiff C) 11
Harris, C. S. 1976 (Leeds U) 24
Harris, W. C. 1954 (Middlesbrough) 6
Harrison, W. C. 1899 (Wrexham) 5
Hartson, J. 1995 (Arsenal, West Ham U, Wimbledon, Coventry C, Celtic) 51
Haworth, S. O. 1997 (Cardiff C, Coventry C) 5
Hayes, A. 1890 (Wrexham) 2
Hedges, R. P. 2018 (Barnsley, Aberdeen) 3
Henley, A. D. 2016 (Blackburn R) 2
Hennessey, W. R. 2007 (Wolverhampton W, Crystal Palace) 89
Hennessey, W. T. 1962 (Birmingham C, Nottingham F, Derby Co) 39
Hersee, A. M. 1886 (Bangor) 2
Hersee, R. 1886 (Llandudno) 1
Hewitt, R. 1958 (Cardiff C) 5
Hewitt, T. J. 1911 (Wrexham, Chelsea, South Liverpool) 8

Heywood, D. 1879 (Druids) 1
Hibbott, H. 1880 (Newtown Excelsior, Newtown) 3
Higham, G. G. 1878 (Oswestry) 2
Hill, M. R. 1972 (Ipswich T) 2
Hockey, T. 1972 (Sheffield U, Norwich C, Aston Villa) 9
Hoddinott, T. F. 1921 (Watford) 2
Hodges, G. 1984 (Wimbledon, Newcastle U, Watford, Sheffield U) 18
Hodgkinson, A. V. 1908 (Southampton) 1
Holden, A. 1984 (Chester C) 1
Hole, B. G. 1963 (Cardiff C, Blackburn R, Aston Villa, Swansea C) 30
Hole, W. J. 1921 (Swansea T) 9
Hollins, D. M. 1962 (Newcastle U) 11
Hopkins, I. J. 1935 (Brentford) 12
Hopkins, J. 1983 (Fulham, Crystal Palace) 16
Hopkins, M. 1956 (Tottenham H) 34
Horne, B. 1988 (Portsmouth, Southampton, Everton, Birmingham C) 59
Howell, E. G. 1888 (Builth) 3
Howells, R. G. 1954 (Cardiff C) 2
Hugh, A. R. 1930 (Newport Co) 1
Hughes, A. 1894 (Rhos) 2
Hughes, A. 1907 (Chirk) 1
Hughes, C. M. 1992 (Luton T, Wimbledon) 8
Hughes, E. 1899 (Everton, Tottenham H) 14
Hughes, E. 1906 (Wrexham, Nottingham F, Wrexham, Manchester C) 16
Hughes, F. W. 1882 (Northwich Victoria) 6
Hughes, I. 1951 (Luton T) 4
Hughes, J. 1877 (Cambridge University, Aberystwyth) 2
Hughes, J. 1905 (Liverpool) 3
Hughes, J. I. 1935 (Blackburn R) 1
Hughes, L. M. 1984 (Manchester U, Barcelona, Manchester U, Chelsea, Southampton) 72
Hughes, P. W. 1887 (Bangor) 3
Hughes, W. 1891 (Bootle) 3
Hughes, W. A. 1949 (Blackburn R) 5
Hughes, W. M. 1938 (Birmingham) 10
Humphreys, J. V. 1947 (Everton) 1
Humphreys, R. 1888 (Druids) 1
Hunter, A. H. 1887 (FA of Wales Secretary) 1
Huws, E. W. 2014 (Manchester C, Wigan Ath, Cardiff C) 11

Isgrove, L. J. 2016 (Southampton) 1

Jackett, K. 1983 (Watford) 31
Jackson, W. 1899 (St Helens Rec) 1
James, D. O. 2019 (Swansea C, Manchester U) 10
James, E. 1893 (Chirk) 8
James, E. G. 1966 (Blackpool) 9
James, L. 1972 (Burnley, Derby Co, QPR, Burnley, Swansea C, Sunderland) 54
James, R. M. 1979 (Swansea C, Stoke C, QPR, Leicester C, Swansea C) 47
James, W. 1931 (West Ham U) 2
Jarrett, R. H. 1889 (Ruthin) 2
Jarvis, A. L. 1967 (Hull C) 3
Jenkins, E. 1925 (Lovell's Ath) 1
Jenkins, J. 1924 (Brighton & HA) 8
Jenkins, R. W. 1902 (Rhyl) 1
Jenkins, S. R. 1996 (Swansea C, Huddersfield T) 16
Jenkyns, C. A. L. 1892 (Small Heath, Woolwich Arsenal, Newton Heath, Walsall) 8
Jennings, W. 1914 (Bolton W) 11
John, D. C. 2013 (Cardiff C, Rangers, Swansea C) 7
John, R. F. 1923 (Arsenal) 15
John, W. R. 1931 (Walsall, Stoke C, Preston NE, Sheffield U, Swansea T) 14
Johnson, A. J. 1999 (Nottingham F, WBA) 15
Johnson, M. G. 1964 (Swansea T) 1
Jones, A. 1987 (Port Vale, Charlton Ath) 6
Jones, A. F. 1877 (Oxford University) 1
Jones, A. T. 1905 (Nottingham F, Notts Co) 2
Jones, Bryn 1935 (Wolverhampton W, Arsenal) 17
Jones, B. S. 1963 (Swansea T, Plymouth Arg, Cardiff C) 15
Jones, Charlie 1926 (Nottingham F, Arsenal) 8
Jones, Cliff 1954 (Swansea T, Tottenham H, Fulham) 59
Jones, C. W. 1935 (Birmingham) 2
Jones, D. 1888 (Chirk, Bolton W, Manchester C) 14

Jones, D. E. 1976 (Norwich C) 8
Jones, D. O. 1934 (Leicester C) 7
Jones, Evan 1910 (Chelsea, Oldham Ath, Bolton W) 7
Jones, F. R. 1885 (Bangor) 3
Jones, F. W. 1893 (Small Heath) 1
Jones, G. P. 1907 (Wrexham) 2
Jones, H. 1902 (Aberaman) 1
Jones, Humphrey 1885 (Bangor, Queen's Park, East Stirlingshire, Queen's Park) 14
Jones, Ivor 1920 (Swansea T, WBA) 10
Jones, Jeffrey 1908 (Llandrindod Wells) 3
Jones, J. 1876 (Druids) 1
Jones, J. 1883 (Berwyn Rangers) 3
Jones, J. 1925 (Wrexham) 1
Jones, J. L. 1895 (Sheffield U, Tottenham H) 21
Jones, J. Love 1906 (Stoke, Middlesbrough) 2
Jones, J. O. 1901 (Bangor) 2
Jones, J. P. 1976 (Liverpool, Wrexham, Chelsea, Huddersfield T) 72
Jones, J. T. 1912 (Stoke, Crystal Palace) 15
Jones, K. 1950 (Aston Villa) 1
Jones, Leslie J. 1933 (Cardiff C, Coventry C, Arsenal 11
Jones, M. A. 2007 (Wrexham) 2
Jones, M. G. 2000 (Leeds U, Leicester C) 13
Jones, P. L. 1997 (Liverpool, Tranmere R) 2
Jones, P. S. 1997 (Stockport Co, Southampton, Wolverhampton W, QPR) 50
Jones, P. W. 1971 (Bristol R) 1
Jones, R. 1887 (Bangor, Crewe Alex) 3
Jones, R. 1898 (Leicester Fosse) 1
Jones, R. 1899 (Druids) 1
Jones, R. 1900 (Bangor) 2
Jones, R. 1906 (Millwall) 2
Jones, R. A. 1884 (Druids) 4
Jones, R. A. 1994 (Sheffield W) 1
Jones, R. S. 1894 (Everton) 1
Jones, S. 1887 (Wrexham, Chester) 2
Jones, S. 1893 (Wrexham, Burton Swifts, Druids) 6
Jones, T. 1926 (Manchester U) 4
Jones, T. D. 1908 (Aberdare) 1
Jones, T. G. 1938 (Everton) 17
Jones, T. J. 1932 (Sheffield W) 2
Jones, V. P. 1995 (Wimbledon) 9
Jones, W. E. A. 1947 (Swansea T, Tottenham H) 4
Jones, W. J. 1901 (Aberdare, West Ham U) 4
Jones, W. Lot 1905 (Manchester C, Southend U) 20
Jones, W. P. 1889 (Druids, Wynnstay) 4
Jones, W. R. 1897 (Aberystwyth) 1

Keenor, F. C. 1920 (Cardiff C, Crewe Alex) 32
Kelly, F. C. 1899 (Wrexham, Druids) 3
Kelsey, A. J. 1954 (Arsenal) 41
Kenrick, S. L. 1876 (Druids, Oswestry, Shropshire Wanderers) 5
Ketley, C. F. 1882 (Druids) 1
King, A. P. 2009 (Leicester C) 50
King, J. 1955 (Swansea T) 1
Kinsey, N. 1951 (Norwich C, Birmingham C) 7
Knill, A. R. 1989 (Swansea C) 1
Koumas, J. 2001 (Tranmere R, WBA, Wigan Ath) 34
Krzywicki, R. L. 1970 (WBA, Huddersfield T) 8

Lambert, R. 1947 (Liverpool) 5
Latham, G. 1905 (Liverpool, Southport Central, Cardiff C) 10
Law, B. J. 1990 (QPR) 1
Lawrence, E. 1930 (Clapton Orient, Notts Co) 2
Lawrence, J. A. 2019 (Anderlecht) 5
Lawrence, S. 1932 (Swansea T) 8
Lawrence, T. M. 2016 (Leicester C, Derby Co) 20
Lea, A. 1889 (Wrexham) 4
Lea, C. 1965 (Ipswich T) 2
Leary, P. 1889 (Bangor) 1
Ledley, J. C. 2006 (Cardiff C, Celtic, Crystal Palace, Derby Co) 77
Leek, K. 1961 (Leicester C, Newcastle U, Birmingham C, Northampton T) 13
Legg, A. 1996 (Birmingham C, Cardiff C) 6
Lever, A. R. 1953 (Leicester C) 1
Lewis, B. 1891 (Chester, Wrexham, Middlesbrough, Wrexham) 10
Lewis, D. 1927 (Arsenal) 3
Lewis, D. 1983 (Swansea C) 1
Lewis, D. J. 1933 (Swansea T) 2
Lewis, D. M. 1890 (Bangor) 2
Lewis, J. 1906 (Bristol R) 1
Lewis, J. 1926 (Cardiff C) 1
Lewis, T. 1881 (Wrexham) 2
Lewis, W. 1885 (Bangor, Crewe Alex, Chester, Manchester C, Chester) 27
Lewis, W. L. 1927 (Swansea T, Huddersfield T) 6
Llewellyn, C. M. 1998 (Norwich C, Wrexham) 6
Lloyd, B. W. 1976 (Wrexham) 3
Lloyd, J. W. 1879 (Wrexham, Newtown) 2
Lloyd, R. A. 1891 (Ruthin) 2
Lockley, A. 1898 (Chirk) 1
Lockyer, T. A. 2018 (Bristol R, Charlton Ath) 10
Lovell, S. 1982 (Crystal Palace, Millwall) 6
Lowndes, S. R. 1983 (Newport Co, Millwall, Barnsley) 10
Lowrie, G. 1948 (Coventry C, Newcastle U) 4
Lucas, P. M. 1962 (Leyton Orient) 4
Lucas, W. H. 1949 (Swansea T) 7
Lumberg, A. 1929 (Wrexham, Wolverhampton W) 4
Lynch, J. J. 2013 (Hudderfield T) 1

MacDonald, S. B. 2011 (Swansea C, Bournemouth) 4
Maguire, G. T. 1990 (Portsmouth) 7
Mahoney, J. F. 1968 (Stoke C, Middlesbrough, Swansea C) 51
Mardon, P. J. 1996 (WBA) 1
Margetson, M. W. 2004 (Cardiff C) 1
Marriott, A. 1996 (Wrexham) 5
Martin, T. J. 1930 (Newport Co) 1
Marustik, C. 1982 (Swansea C) 6
Mates, J. 1891 (Chirk) 3
Matondo, R. 2019 (Manchester C, Schalke 04) 4
Matthews, A. J. 2011 (Cardiff C, Celtic, Sunderland) 14
Matthews, R. W. 1921 (Liverpool, Bristol C, Bradford) 3
Matthews, W. 1905 (Chester) 2
Matthias, J. S. 1896 (Brymbo, Shrewsbury T, Wolverhampton W) 5
Matthias, T. J. 1914 (Wrexham) 12
Mays, A. W. 1929 (Wrexham) 1
McCarthy, T. P. 1889 (Wrexham) 1
McMillan, R. 1881 (Shrewsbury Engineers) 2
Medwin, T. C. 1953 (Swansea T, Tottenham H) 30
Melville, A. K. 1990 (Swansea C, Oxford U, Sunderland, Fulham, West Ham U) 65
Mepham, C. J. 2018 (Brentford, Bournemouth) 10
Meredith, S. 1900 (Chirk, Stoke, Leyton) 8
Meredith, W. H. 1895 (Manchester C, Manchester U) 48
Mielczarek, R. 1971 (Rotherham U) 1
Millership, H. 1920 (Rotherham Co) 6
Millington, A. H. 1963 (WBA, Crystal Palace, Peterborough U, Swansea C) 21
Mills, T. J. 1934 (Clapton Orient, Leicester C) 4
Mills-Roberts, R. H. 1885 (St Thomas' Hospital, Preston NE, Llanberis) 8
Moore, G. 1960 (Cardiff C, Chelsea, Manchester U, Northampton T, Charlton Ath) 21
Moore, K. R. F. 2020 (Wigan Ath) 5
Morgan, C. 2007 (Milton Keynes D, Peterborough U, Preston NE) 23
Morgan, J. R. 1877 (Cambridge University, Derby School Staff) 10
Morgan, J. T. 1905 (Wrexham) 1
Morgan-Owen, H. 1902 (Oxford University, Corinthians) 4
Morgan-Owen, M. M. 1897 (Oxford University, Corinthians) 13
Morison, S. W. 2011 (Millwall, Norwich C) 20
Morley, E. J. 1925 (Swansea T, Clapton Orient) 4
Morrell, J. J. 2020 (Bristol C) 5
Morris, A. G. 1896 (Aberystwyth, Swindon T, Nottingham F) 21
Morris, C. 1900 (Chirk, Derby Co, Huddersfield T) 27
Morris, E. 1893 (Chirk) 3
Morris, H. 1894 (Sheffield U, Manchester C, Grimsby T) 3
Morris, J. 1887 (Oswestry) 1
Morris, J. 1898 (Chirk) 1
Morris, R. 1900 (Chirk, Shrewsbury T) 6

Morris, R. 1902 (Newtown, Druids, Liverpool, Leeds C, Grimsby T, Plymouth Arg) 11
Morris, S. 1937 (Birmingham) 5
Morris, W. 1947 (Burnley) 5
Moulsdale, J. R. B. 1925 (Corinthians) 1
Murphy, J. P. 1933 (WBA) 15
Myhill, G. O. 2008 (Hull C, WBA) 19

Nardiello, D. 1978 (Coventry C) 2
Nardiello, D. A. 2007 (Barnsley, QPR) 3
Neal, J. E. 1931 (Colwyn Bay) 2
Neilson, A. B. 1992 (Newcastle U, Southampton) 5
Newnes, J. 1926 (Nelson) 1
Newton, L. F. 1912 (Cardiff Corinthians) 1
Nicholas, D. S. 1923 (Stoke, Swansea T) 3
Nicholas, P. 1979 (Crystal Palace, Arsenal, Crystal Palace, Luton T, Aberdeen, Chelsea, Watford) 73
Nicholls, J. 1924 (Newport Co, Cardiff C) 4
Niedzwiecki, E. A. 1985 (Chelsea) 2
Nock, W. 1897 (Newtown) 1
Nogan, L. M. 1992 (Watford, Reading) 2
Norman, A. J. 1986 (Hull C) 5
Nurse, M. T. G. 1960 (Swansea T, Middlesbrough) 12
Nyatanga, L. J. 2006 (Derby Co, Bristol C) 34

O'Callaghan, E. 1929 (Tottenham H) 11
Oliver, A. 1905 (Bangor, Blackburn R) 2
Oster, J. M. 1998 (Everton, Sunderland) 13
O'Sullivan, P. A. 1973 (Brighton & HA) 3
Owen, D. 1879 (Oswestry) 1
Owen, E. 1884 (Ruthin Grammar School) 3
Owen, G. 1888 (Chirk, Newton Heath, Chirk) 4
Owen, J. 1892 (Newton Heath) 1
Owen, T. 1879 (Oswestry) 1
Owen, Trevor 1899 (Crewe Alex) 2
Owen, W. 1884 (Chirk) 16
Owen, W. P. 1880 (Ruthin) 12
Owens, J. 1902 (Wrexham) 1

Page, M. E. 1971 (Birmingham C) 28
Page, R. J. 1997 (Watford, Sheffield U, Cardiff C, Coventry C) 41
Palmer, D. 1957 (Swansea T) 3
Parris, J. E. 1932 (Bradford) 1
Parry, B. J. 1951 (Swansea T) 1
Parry, C. 1891 (Everton, Newtown) 13
Parry, E. 1922 (Liverpool) 5
Parry, M. 1901 (Liverpool) 16
Parry, P. I. 2004 (Cardiff C) 12
Parry, T. D. 1900 (Oswestry) 7
Parry, W. 1895 (Newtown) 1
Partridge, D. W. 2005 (Motherwell, Bristol C) 7
Pascoe, C. 1984 (Swansea C, Sunderland) 10
Paul, R. 1949 (Swansea T, Manchester C) 33
Peake, E. 1908 (Aberystwyth, Liverpool) 11
Peers, E. J. 1914 (Wolverhampton W, Port Vale) 12
Pembridge, M. A. 1992 (Luton T, Derby Co, Sheffield W, Benfica, Everton, Fulham) 54
Perry, E. 1938 (Doncaster R) 3
Perry, J. 1994 (Cardiff C) 1
Phennah, E. 1878 (Civil Service) 1
Phillips, C. 1931 (Wolverhampton W, Aston Villa) 13
Phillips, D. 1984 (Plymouth Arg, Manchester C, Coventry C, Norwich C, Nottingham F) 62
Phillips, L. 1971 (Cardiff C, Aston Villa, Swansea C, Charlton Ath) 58
Phillips, T. J. S. 1973 (Chelsea) 4
Phoenix, H. 1882 (Wrexham) 1
Pipe, D. R. 2003 (Coventry C) 1
Poland, G. 1939 (Wrexham) 2
Pontin, K. 1980 (Cardiff C) 2
Powell, A. 1947 (Leeds U, Everton, Birmingham C) 8
Powell, D. 1968 (Wrexham, Sheffield U) 11
Powell, I. V. 1947 (QPR, Aston Villa) 8
Powell, J. 1878 (Druids, Bolton W, Newton Heath) 15
Powell, Seth 1885 (Oswestry, WBA) 7
Price, H. 1907 (Aston Villa, Burton U, Wrexham) 5
Price, J. 1877 (Wrexham) 12
Price, L. P. 2006 (Ipswich T, Derby Co, Crystal Palace) 11
Price, P. 1980 (Luton T, Tottenham H) 25
Pring, K. D. 1966 (Rotherham U) 3
Pritchard, H. K. 1985 (Bristol C) 1
Pryce-Jones, A. W. 1895 (Newtown) 1
Pryce-Jones, W. E. 1887 (Cambridge University) 5
Pugh, A. 1889 (Rhostyllen) 1
Pugh, D. H. 1896 (Wrexham, Lincoln C) 7
Pugsley, J. 1930 (Charlton Ath) 1
Pullen, W. J. 1926 (Plymouth Arg) 1

Ramsey, A. J. 2009 (Arsenal, Juventus) 60
Rankmore, F. E. J. 1966 (Peterborough U) 1
Ratcliffe, K. 1981 (Everton, Cardiff C) 59
Rea, J. C. 1894 (Aberystwyth) 9
Ready, K. 1997 (QPR) 5
Reece, G. I. 1966 (Sheffield U, Cardiff C) 29
Reed, W. G. 1955 (Ipswich T) 2
Rees, A. 1984 (Birmingham C) 1
Rees, J. M. 1992 (Luton T) 1
Rees, R. R. 1965 (Coventry C, WBA, Nottingham F) 39
Rees, W. 1949 (Cardiff C, Tottenham H) 4
Ribeiro, C. M. 2010 (Bristol C) 2
Richards, A. 1932 (Barnsley) 1
Richards, A. D. J. (Jazz) 2012 (Swansea C, Cardiff C) 14
Richards, D. 1931 (Wolverhampton W, Brentford, Birmingham) 21
Richards, G. 1899 (Druids, Oswestry, Shrewsbury T) 6
Richards, R. W. 1920 (Wolverhampton W, West Ham U, Mold) 9
Richards, S. V. 1947 (Cardiff C) 1
Richards, W. E. 1933 (Fulham) 1
Ricketts, S. D. 2005 (Swansea C, Hull C, Bolton W, Wolverhampton W) 52
Roach, J. 1885 (Oswestry) 1
Robbins, W. W. 1931 (Cardiff C, WBA) 11
Roberts, A. M. 1993 (QPR) 2
Roberts, C. R. J. 2018 (Swansea C) 16
Roberts, D. F. 1973 (Oxford U, Hull C) 17
Roberts, G. W. 2000 (Tranmere R) 9
Roberts, I. W. 1990 (Watford, Huddersfield T, Leicester C, Norwich C) 15
Roberts, Jas 1913 (Wrexham) 2
Roberts, J. 1879 (Corwen, Berwyn R) 7
Roberts, J. 1881 (Ruthin) 2
Roberts, J. 1906 (Bradford C) 2
Roberts, J. G. 1971 (Arsenal, Birmingham C) 22
Roberts, J. H. 1949 (Bolton W) 1
Roberts, N. W. 2000 (Wrexham, Wigan Ath) 4
Roberts, P. S. 1974 (Portsmouth) 4
Roberts, R. 1884 (Druids, Bolton W, Preston NE) 9
Roberts, R. 1886 (Wrexham) 3
Roberts, R. 1891 (Rhos, Crewe Alex) 2
Roberts, R. L. 1890 (Chester) 1
Roberts, S. W. 2005 (Wrexham) 1
Roberts, T. D. 2019 (Leeds U) 6
Roberts, W. 1879 (Llangollen, Berwyn R) 6
Roberts, W. 1883 (Rhyl) 1
Roberts, W. 1886 (Wrexham) 4
Roberts, W. H. 1882 (Ruthin, Rhyl) 6
Robinson, C. P. 2000 (Wolverhampton W, Portsmouth, Sunderland, Norwich C, Toronto Lynx) 52
Robinson, J. R. C. 1996 (Charlton Ath) 30
Robson-Kanu, T. H. 2010 (Reading, WBA) 44
Rodon, J. P. 2020 (Swansea C) 4
Rodrigues, P. J. 1965 (Cardiff C, Leicester C, Sheffield W) 40
Rogers, J. P. 1896 (Wrexham) 3
Rogers, W. 1931 (Wrexham) 2
Roose, L. R. 1900 (Aberystwyth, London Welsh, Stoke, Everton, Stoke, Sunderland) 24
Rouse, R. V. 1959 (Crystal Palace) 1
Rowlands, A. C. 1914 (Tranmere R) 1
Rowley, T. 1959 (Tranmere R) 1
Rush, I. 1980 (Liverpool, Juventus, Liverpool) 73
Russell, M. R. 1912 (Merthyr T, Plymouth Arg) 23

Sabine, H. W. 1887 (Oswestry) 1
Saunders, D. 1986 (Brighton & HA, Oxford U, Derby Co, Liverpool, Aston Villa, Galatasaray, Nottingham F, Sheffield U, Benfica, Bradford C) 75
Savage, R. W. 1996 (Crewe Alex, Leicester C, Birmingham C) 39
Savin, G. 1878 (Oswestry) 1

Sayer, P. A. 1977 (Cardiff C) 7
Scrine, F. H. 1950 (Swansea T) 2
Sear, C. R. 1963 (Manchester C) 1
Shaw, E. G. 1882 (Oswestry) 3
Sherwood, A. T. 1947 (Cardiff C, Newport Co) 41
Shone, W. W. 1879 (Oswestry) 1
Shortt, W. W. 1947 (Plymouth Arg) 12
Showers, D. 1975 (Cardiff C) 2
Sidlow, C. 1947 (Liverpool) 7
Sisson, H. 1885 (Wrexham Olympic) 3
Slatter, N. 1983 (Bristol R, Oxford U) 22
Smallman, D. P. 1974 (Wrexham, Everton) 7
Smith, M. 2018 (Manchester C) 7
Southall, N. 1982 (Everton) 92
Speed, G. A. 1990 (Leeds U, Everton, Newcastle U, Bolton W) 85
Sprake, G. 1964 (Leeds U, Birmingham C) 37
Stansfield, F. 1949 (Cardiff C) 1
Stevenson, B. 1978 (Leeds U, Birmingham C) 15
Stevenson, N. 1982 (Swansea C) 4
Stitfall, R. F. 1953 (Cardiff C) 2
Stock, B. B. 2010 (Doncaster R) 3
Sullivan, D. 1953 (Cardiff C) 17
Symons, C. J. 1992 (Portsmouth, Manchester C, Fulham, Crystal Palace) 37

Tapscott, D. R. 1954 (Arsenal, Cardiff C) 14
Taylor, G. K. 1996 (Crystal Palace, Sheffield U, Burnley, Nottingham F) 15
Taylor, J. 1898 (Wrexham) 1
Taylor, J. W. T. 2015 (Reading) 1
Taylor, N. J. 2010 (Wrexham, Swansea C, Aston Villa) 43
Taylor, O. D. S. 1893 (Newtown) 4
Thatcher, B. D. 2004 (Leicester C, Manchester C) 7
Thomas, C. 1899 (Druids) 2
Thomas, D. A. 1957 (Swansea T) 2
Thomas, D. S. 1948 (Fulham) 4
Thomas, E. 1925 (Cardiff Corinthians) 1
Thomas, G. 1885 (Wrexham) 2
Thomas, G. S. 2018 (Leicester C) 3
Thomas, H. 1927 (Manchester U) 1
Thomas, Martin R. 1987 (Newcastle U) 1
Thomas, Mickey 1977 (Wrexham, Manchester U, Everton, Brighton & HA, Stoke C, Chelsea, WBA) 51
Thomas, R. J. 1967 (Swindon T, Derby Co, Cardiff C) 50
Thomas, T. 1898 (Bangor) 2
Thomas, W. R. 1931 (Newport Co) 2
Thomson, D. 1876 (Druids) 1
Thomson, G. F. 1876 (Druids) 2
Toshack, J. B. 1969 (Cardiff C, Liverpool, Swansea C) 40
Townsend, W. 1887 (Newtown) 2
Trainer, H. 1895 (Wrexham) 3
Trainer, J. 1887 (Bolton W, Preston NE) 20
Trollope, P. J. 1997 (Derby Co, Fulham, Coventry C, Northampton T) 9
Tudur-Jones, O. 2008 (Swansea C, Norwich C, Hibernian) 7
Turner, H. G. 1937 (Charlton Ath) 8
Turner, J. 1892 (Wrexham) 1
Turner, R. E. 1891 (Wrexham) 2
Turner, W. H. 1887 (Wrexham) 5

Van Den Hauwe, P. W. R. 1985 (Everton) 13
Vaughan, D. O. 2003 (Crewe Alex, Real Sociedad, Blackpool, Sunderland, Nottingham F) 42
Vaughan, Jas 1893 (Druids) 4
Vaughan, John 1879 (Oswestry, Druids, Bolton W) 11
Vaughan, J. O. 1885 (Rhyl) 4
Vaughan, N. 1983 (Newport Co, Cardiff C) 10
Vaughan, T. 1885 (Rhyl) 1
Vaulks, W. R. 2019 (Rotherham U, Cardiff C) 5
Vearncombe, G. 1958 (Cardiff C) 2
Vernon, T. R. 1957 (Blackburn R, Everton, Stoke C) 32
Villars, A. K. 1974 (Cardiff C) 3
Vizard, E. T. 1911 (Bolton W) 22
Vokes, S. M. 2008 (Bournemouth, Wolverhampton W, Burnley, Stoke C) 64

Walley, J. T. 1971 (Watford) 1
Walsh, I. P. 1980 (Crystal Palace, Swansea C) 18
Ward, D. 1959 (Bristol R, Cardiff C) 2
Ward, D. 2000 (Notts Co, Nottingham F) 5
Ward, D. 2016 (Liverpool, Leicester C) 7
Warner, J. 1937 (Swansea T, Manchester U) 2
Warren, F. W. 1929 (Cardiff C, Middlesbrough, Hearts) 6
Watkins, A. E. 1898 (Leicester Fosse, Aston Villa, Millwall) 5
Watkins, M. J. 2018 (Norwich C) 2
Watkins, W. M. 1902 (Stoke, Aston Villa, Sunderland, Stoke) 10
Webster, C. 1957 (Manchester U) 4
Weston, R. D. 2000 (Arsenal, Cardiff C) 7
Whatley, W. J. 1939 (Tottenham H) 2
White, P. F. 1896 (London Welsh) 1
Wilcock, A. R. 1890 (Oswestry) 1
Wilding, J. 1885 (Wrexham Olympians, Bootle, Wrexham) 9
Williams, A. 1994 (Reading, Wolverhampton W, Reading) 13
Williams, A. E. 2008 (Stockport Co, Swansea C, Everton) 86
Williams, A. L. 1931 (Wrexham) 1
Williams, A. P. 1998 (Southampton) 2
Williams, B. 1930 (Bristol C) 1
Williams, B. D. 1928 (Swansea T, Everton) 10
Williams, D. G. 1988 (Derby Co, Ipswich T) 13
Williams, D. M. 1986 (Norwich C) 5
Williams, D. R. 1921 (Merthyr T, Sheffield W, Manchester U) 8
Williams, E. 1893 (Crewe Alex) 2
Williams, E. 1901 (Druids) 5
Williams, G. 1893 (Chirk) 6
Williams, G. C. 2014 (Fulham) 7
Williams, G. E. 1960 (WBA) 26
Williams, G. G. 1961 (Swansea T) 5
Williams, G. J. 2006 (West Ham U, Ipswich T) 2
Williams, G. J. J. 1951 (Cardiff C) 1
Williams, G. O. 1907 (Wrexham) 1
Williams, H. J. 1965 (Swansea T) 3
Williams, H. T. 1949 (Newport Co, Leeds U) 4
Williams, J. H. 1884 (Oswestry) 1
Williams, J. J. 1939 (Wrexham) 1
Williams, J. P. 2013 (Crystal Palace, Charlton Ath) 21
Williams, J. T. 1925 (Middlesbrough) 1
Williams, J. W. 1912 (Crystal Palace) 2
Williams, R. 1935 (Newcastle U) 2
Williams, R. P. 1886 (Caernarvon) 1
Williams, S. G. 1954 (WBA, Southampton) 43
Williams, W. 1876 (Druids, Oswestry, Druids) 11
Williams, W. 1925 (Northampton T) 1
Wilson, H. 2013 (Liverpool) 17
Wilson, J. S. 2013 (Bristol C) 1
Witcomb, D. F. 1947 (WBA, Sheffield W) 3
Woodburn, B. 2018 (Liverpool) 10
Woosnam, A. P. 1959 (Leyton Orient, West Ham U, Aston Villa) 17
Woosnam, G. 1879 (Newtown Excelsior) 1
Worthington, T. 1894 (Newtown) 1
Wynn, G. A. 1909 (Wrexham, Manchester C) 11
Wynn, W. 1903 (Chirk) 1

Yorath, T. C. 1970 (Leeds U, Coventry C, Tottenham H, Vancouver Whitecaps) 59
Young, E. 1990 (Wimbledon, Crystal Palace, Wolverhampton W) 21

REPUBLIC OF IRELAND

Aherne, T. 1946 (Belfast Celtic, Luton T) 16
Aldridge, J. W. 1986 (Oxford U, Liverpool, Real Sociedad, Tranmere R) 69
Ambrose, P. 1955 (Shamrock R) 5
Anderson, J. 1980 (Preston NE, Newcastle U) 16
Andrews, K. J. 2009 (Blackburn R, WBA) 35
Andrews, P. 1936 (Bohemians) 1
Arrigan, T. 1938 (Waterford) 1
Arter, H. N. 2015 (Bournemouth) 16

Babb, P. A. 1994 (Coventry C, Liverpool, Sunderland) 35
Bailham, E. 1964 (Shamrock R) 1
Barber, E. 1966 (Shelbourne, Birmingham C) 2
Barrett, G. 2003 (Arsenal, Coventry C) 6
Barry, P. 1928 (Fordsons) 2
Beglin, J. 1984 (Liverpool) 15
Bennett, A. J. 2007 (Reading) 2
Bermingham, J. 1929 (Bohemians) 1
Bermingham, P. 1935 (St James' Gate) 1
Best, L. J. B. 2009 (Coventry C, Newcastle U) 7
Bonner, P. 1981 (Celtic) 80
Boyle, A. 2017 (Preston NE) 1
Braddish, S. 1978 (Dundalk) 2
Bradshaw, P. 1939 (St James' Gate) 5
Brady, F. 1926 (Fordsons) 2
Brady, R. 2013 (Hull C, Norwich C, Burnley) 46
Brady, T. R. 1964 (QPR) 6
Brady, W. L. 1975 (Arsenal, Juventus, Sampdoria, Internazionale, Ascoli, West Ham U) 72
Branagan, K. G. 1997 (Bolton W) 1
Breen, G. 1996 (Birmingham C, Coventry C, West Ham U, Sunderland) 63
Breen, T. 1937 (Manchester U, Shamrock R) 5
Brennan, F. 1965 (Drumcondra) 1
Brennan, S. A. 1965 (Manchester U, Waterford) 19
Brown, J. 1937 (Coventry C) 2
Browne, A. J. 2017 (Preston NE) 9
Browne, W. 1964 (Bohemians) 3
Bruce, A. S. 2007 (Ipswich T) 2
Buckley, L. 1984 (Shamrock R, Waregem) 2
Burke, F. 1952 (Cork Ath) 1
Burke, G. D. 2018 (Shamrock R, Preston NE) 3
Burke, J. 1929 (Shamrock R) 1
Burke, J. 1934 (Cork) 1
Butler, P. J. 2000 (Sunderland) 1
Butler, T. 2003 (Sunderland) 2
Byrne, A. B. 1970 (Southampton) 14
Byrne, D. 1929 (Shelbourne, Shamrock R, Coleraine) 3
Byrne, J. 1928 (Bray Unknowns) 1
Byrne, J. 1985 (QPR, Le Havre, Brighton & HA, Sunderland, Millwall) 23
Byrne, J. 2004 (Shelbourne) 2
Byrne, J. 2020 (Shamrock R) 2
Byrne, P. 1931 (Dolphin, Shelbourne, Drumcondra) 3
Byrne, P. 1984 (Shamrock R) 8
Byrne, S. 1931 (Bohemians) 1

Campbell, A. 1985 (Santander) 3
Campbell, N. 1971 (St Patrick's Ath, Fortuna Cologne) 11
Cannon, H. 1926 (Bohemians) 2
Cantwell, N. 1954 (West Ham U, Manchester U) 36
Carey, B. P. 1992 (Manchester U, Leicester C) 3
Carey, J. J. 1938 (Manchester U) 29
Carolan, J. 1960 (Manchester U) 2
Carr, S. 1999 (Tottenham H, Newcastle U) 44
Carroll, B. 1949 (Shelbourne) 2
Carroll, T. R. 1968 (Ipswich T, Birmingham C) 17
Carsley, L. K. 1998 (Derby Co, Blackburn R, Coventry C, Everton) 39
Cascarino, A. G. 1986 (Gillingham, Millwall, Aston Villa, Celtic, Chelsea, Marseille, Nancy) 88
Chandler, J. 1980 (Leeds U) 2
Chatton, H. A. 1931 (Shelbourne, Dumbarton, Cork) 3
Christie, C. S. F. 2015 (Derby Co, Middlesbrough, Fulham) 24
Clark, C. 2011 (Aston Villa, Newcastle U) 34
Clarke, C. R. 2004 (Stoke C) 2
Clarke, J. 1978 (Drogheda U) 1
Clarke, K. 1948 (Drumcondra) 2
Clarke, M. 1950 (Shamrock R) 1
Clinton, T. J. 1951 (Everton) 3
Coad, P. 1947 (Shamrock R) 11
Coffey, T. 1950 (Drumcondra) 1
Coleman, S. 2011 (Everton) 56
Colfer, M. D. 1950 (Shelbourne) 2
Colgan, N. 2002 (Hibernian, Barnsley) 9
Collins, F. 1927 (Jacobs) 1
Collins, J. S. 2020 (Luton T) 4
Conmy, O. M. 1965 (Peterborough U) 5
Connolly, A. A. 2020 (Brighton & HA) 2
Connolly, D. J. 1996 (Watford, Feyenoord, Wolverhampton W, Excelsior, Feyenoord, Wimbledon, West Ham U, Wigan Ath) 41
Connolly, H. 1937 (Cork) 1
Connolly, J. 1926 (Fordsons) 1
Conroy, G. A. 1970 (Stoke C) 27
Conway, J. P. 1967 (Fulham, Manchester C) 20
Corr, P. J. 1949 (Everton) 4
Courtney, E. 1946 (Cork U) 1
Cox, S. R. 2011 (WBA, Nottingham F) 30
Coyle, O. C. 1994 (Bolton W) 1
Coyne, T. 1992 (Celtic, Tranmere R, Motherwell) 22
Crowe, G. 2003 (Bohemians) 2
Cullen, J. J. 2020 (West Ham U) 2
Cummins, G. P. 1954 (Luton T) 19
Cuneen, T. 1951 (Limerick) 1
Cunningham, G. R. 2010 (Manchester C, Bristol C) 4
Cunningham, K. 1996 (Wimbledon, Birmingham C) 72
Curtis, D. P. 1957 (Shelbourne, Bristol C, Ipswich T, Exeter C) 17
Curtis, R. 2019 (Portsmouth) 3
Cusack, S. 1953 (Limerick) 1

Daish, L. S. 1992 (Cambridge U, Coventry C) 5
Daly, G. A. 1973 (Manchester U, Derby Co, Coventry C, Birmingham C, Shrewsbury T) 48
Daly, J. 1932 (Shamrock R) 2
Daly, M. 1978 (Wolverhampton W) 2
Daly, P. 1950 (Shamrock R) 1
Davis, T. L. 1937 (Oldham Ath, Tranmere R) 4
Deacy, E. 1982 (Aston Villa) 4
Delaney, D. F. 2008 (QPR, Ipswich T, Crystal Palace) 9
Delap, R. J. 1998 (Derby Co, Southampton) 11
De Mange, K. J. P. P. 1987 (Liverpool, Hull C) 2
Dempsey, J. T. 1967 (Fulham, Chelsea) 19
Dennehy, J. 1972 (Cork Hibernians, Nottingham F, Walsall) 11
Desmond, P. 1950 (Middlesbrough) 4
Devine, J. 1980 (Arsenal, Norwich C) 13
Doherty, G. M. T. 2000 (Luton T, Tottenham H, Norwich C) 34
Doherty, M. J. 2018 (Woverhampton W) 9
Donnelly, J. 1935 (Dundalk) 10
Donnelly, T. 1938 (Drumcondra, Shamrock R) 2
Donovan, D. C. 1955 (Everton) 5
Donovan, T. 1980 (Aston Villa) 2
Douglas, J. 2004 (Blackburn R, Leeds U) 8
Dowdall, C. 1928 (Fordsons, Barnsley, Cork) 3
Doyle, C. 1959 (Shelbourne) 1
Doyle, C. A. 2007 (Birmingham C, Bradford C) 4
Doyle, D. 1926 (Shamrock R) 1
Doyle, K. E. 2006 (Reading, Wolverhampton W, Colorado Rapids) 63
Doyle, L. 1932 (Dolphin) 1
Doyle, M. P. 2004 (Coventry C) 1
Duff, D. A. 1998 (Blackburn R, Chelsea, Newcastle U, Fulham) 100
Duffy, B. 1950 (Shamrock R) 1
Duffy, S. P. M. 2014 (Everton, Blackburn R, Brighton & HA) 33
Duggan, H. A. 1927 (Leeds U, Newport Co) 5
Dunne, A. P. 1962 (Manchester U, Bolton W) 33
Dunne, J. 1930 (Sheffield U, Arsenal, Southampton, Shamrock R) 15
Dunne, J. C. 1971 (Fulham) 1
Dunne, L. 1935 (Manchester C) 2
Dunne, P. A. J. 1965 (Manchester U) 5
Dunne, R. P. 2000 (Everton, Manchester C, Aston Villa, QPR) 80
Dunne, S. 1953 (Luton T) 15

Dunne, T. 1956 (St Patrick's Ath) 3
Dunning, P. 1971 (Shelbourne) 2
Dunphy, E. M. 1966 (York C, Millwall) 23
Dwyer, N. M. 1960 (West Ham U, Swansea T) 14

Eccles, P. 1986 (Shamrock R) 1
Egan, J. 2017 (Brentford, Sheffield U) 8
Egan, R. 1929 (Dundalk) 1
Eglington, T. J. 1946 (Shamrock R, Everton) 24
Elliot, R. 2014 (Newcastle U) 4
Elliott, S. W. 2005 (Sunderland) 9
Ellis, P. 1935 (Bohemians) 7
Evans, M. J. 1998 (Southampton) 1

Fagan, E. 1973 (Shamrock R) 1
Fagan, F. 1955 (Manchester C, Derby Co) 8
Fagan, J. 1926 (Shamrock R) 1
Fahey, K. D. 2010 (Birmingham C) 16
Fairclough, M. 1982 (Dundalk) 2
Fallon, S. 1951 (Celtic) 8
Fallon, W. J. 1935 (Notts Co, Sheffield W) 9
Farquharson, T. G. 1929 (Cardiff C) 4
Farrell, P. 1937 (Hibernian) 2
Farrell, P. D. 1946 (Shamrock R, Everton) 28
Farrelly, G. 1996 (Aston Villa, Everton, Bolton W) 6
Feenan, J. J. 1937 (Sunderland) 2
Finnan, S. 2000 (Fulham, Liverpool, Espanyol) 53
Finucane, A. 1967 (Limerick) 11
Fitzgerald, F. J. 1955 (Waterford) 2
Fitzgerald, P. J. 1961 (Leeds U, Chester) 5
Fitzpatrick, K. 1970 (Limerick) 1
Fitzsimons, A. G. 1950 (Middlesbrough, Lincoln C) 26
Fleming, C. 1996 (Middlesbrough) 10
Flood, J. J. 1926 (Shamrock R) 5
Fogarty, A. 1960 (Sunderland, Hartlepools U) 11
Folan, C. C. 2009 (Hull C) 7
Foley, D. J. 2000 (Watford) 6
Foley, J. 1934 (Cork, Celtic) 7
Foley, K. P. 2009 (Wolverhampton W) 8
Foley, M. 1926 (Shelbourne) 1
Foley, T. C. 1964 (Northampton T) 9
Forde, D. 2011 (Millwall) 24
Foy, T. 1938 (Shamrock R) 2
Fullam, J. 1961 (Preston NE, Shamrock R) 11
Fullam, R. 1926 (Shamrock R) 2

Gallagher, C. 1967 (Celtic) 2
Gallagher, M. 1954 (Hibernian) 1
Gallagher, P. 1932 (Falkirk) 1
Galvin, A. 1983 (Tottenham H, Sheffield W, Swindon T) 29
Gamble, J. 2007 (Cork C) 2
Gannon, E. 1949 (Notts Co, Sheffield W, Shelbourne) 14
Gannon, M. 1972 (Shelbourne) 1
Gaskins, P. 1934 (Shamrock R, St James' Gate) 7
Gavin, J. T. 1950 (Norwich C, Tottenham H, Norwich C) 7
Geoghegan, M. 1937 (St James' Gate) 2
Gibbons, A. 1952 (St Patrick's Ath) 4
Gibson, D. T. D. 2008 (Manchester U, Everton) 27
Gilbert, R. 1966 (Shamrock R) 1
Giles, C. 1951 (Doncaster R) 1
Giles, M. J. 1960 (Manchester U, Leeds U, WBA, Shamrock R) 59
Given, S. J. J. 1996 (Blackburn R, Newcastle U, Manchester C, Aston Villa, Stoke C) 134
Givens, D. J. 1969 (Manchester U, Luton T, QPR, Birmingham C, Neuchatel X) 56
Gleeson, S. M. 2007 (Wolverhampton W, Birmingham C) 4
Glen, W. 1927 (Shamrock R) 8
Glynn, D. 1952 (Drumcondra) 2
Godwin, T. F. 1949 (Shamrock R, Leicester C, Bournemouth) 13
Golding, J. 1928 (Shamrock R) 2
Goodman, J. 1997 (Wimbledon) 4
Goodwin, J. 2003 (Stockport Co) 1
Gorman, W. C. 1936 (Bury, Brentford) 13
Grace, J. 1926 (Drumcondra) 1
Grealish, A. 1976 (Orient, Luton T, Brighton & HA, WBA) 45
Green, P. J. 2010 (Derby Co, Leeds U) 20
Gregg, E. 1978 (Bohemians) 8
Griffith, R. 1935 (Walsall) 1
Grimes, A. A. 1978 (Manchester U, Coventry C, Luton T) 18

Hale, A. 1962 (Aston Villa, Doncaster R, Waterford) 14
Hamilton, T. 1959 (Shamrock R) 2
Hand, E. K. 1969 (Portsmouth) 20
Harrington, W. 1936 (Cork) 5
Harte, I. P. 1996 (Leeds U, Levante) 64
Hartnett, J. B. 1949 (Middlesbrough) 2
Haverty, J. 1956 (Arsenal, Blackburn R, Millwall, Celtic, Bristol R, Shelbourne) 32
Hayes, A. W. P. 1979 (Southampton) 1
Hayes, J. 2016 (Aberdeen) 4
Hayes, W. E. 1947 (Huddersfield T) 2
Hayes, W. J. 1949 (Limerick) 1
Healey, R. 1977 (Cardiff C) 2
Healy, C. 2002 (Celtic, Sunderland) 13
Heighway, S. D. 1971 (Liverpool, Minnesota K) 34
Henderson, B. 1948 (Drumcondra) 2
Henderson, W. C. P. 2006 (Brighton & HA, Preston NE) 6
Hendrick, J. P. 2013 (Derby Co, Burnley) 54
Hennessy, J. 1965 (Shelbourne, St Patrick's Ath) 5
Herrick, J. 1972 (Cork Hibernians, Shamrock R) 3
Higgins, J. 1951 (Birmingham C) 1
Hogan, S. A. 2018 (Aston Villa) 8
Holland, M. R. 2000 (Ipswich T, Charlton Ath) 49
Holmes, J. 1971 (Coventry C, Tottenham H, Vancouver Whitecaps) 30
Hoolahan, W. 2008 (Blackpool, Norwich C) 43
Horgan, D. J. 2017 (Preston NE, Hibernian) 6
Horlacher, A. F. 1930 (Bohemians) 7
Houghton, R. J. 1986 (Oxford U, Liverpool, Aston Villa, Crystal Palace, Reading) 73
Hourihane, C. 2017 (Aston Villa) 17
Howlett, G. 1984 (Brighton & HA) 1
Hoy, M. 1938 (Dundalk) 6
Hughton, C. 1980 (Tottenham H, West Ham U) 53
Hunt, N. 2009 (Reading) 3
Hunt, S. P. 2007 (Reading, Hull C, Wolverhampton W) 39
Hurley, C. J. 1957 (Millwall, Sunderland, Bolton W) 40
Hutchinson, F. 1935 (Drumcondra) 2

Ireland S .J. 2006 (Manchester C) 6
Irwin, D. J. 1991 (Manchester U) 56

Jordan, D. 1937 (Wolverhampton W) 2
Jordan, W. 1934 (Bohemians) 2
Judge, A. C. 2016 (Brentford, Ipswich T) 9

Kavanagh, G. A. 1998 (Stoke C, Cardiff C, Wigan Ath) 16
Kavanagh, P. J. 1931 (Celtic) 2
Keane, R. D. 1998 (Wolverhampton W, Coventry C, Internazionale, Leeds U, Tottenham H, Liverpool, Tottenham H, LA Galaxy) 146
Keane, R. M. 1991 (Nottingham F, Manchester U) 67
Keane, T. R. 1949 (Swansea T) 4
Kearin, M. 1972 (Shamrock R) 1
Kearns, F. T. 1954 (West Ham U) 1
Kearns, M. 1971 (Oxford U, Walsall, Wolverhampton W) 18
Kelly, A. T. 1993 (Sheffield U, Blackburn R) 34
Kelly, D. T. 1988 (Walsall, West Ham U, Leicester C, Newcastle U, Wolverhampton W, Sunderland, Tranmere R) 26
Kelly, G. 1994 (Leeds U) 52
Kelly, J. 1932 (Derry C) 4
Kelly, J. A. 1957 (Drumcondra, Preston NE) 47
Kelly, J. P. V. 1961 (Wolverhampton W) 5
Kelly, M. J. 1988 (Portsmouth) 4
Kelly, N. 1954 (Nottingham F) 1
Kelly, S. M. 2006 (Tottenham H, Birmingham C, Fulham, Reading) 38
Kendrick, J. 1927 (Everton, Dolphin) 4
Kenna, J. J. 1995 (Blackburn R) 27
Kennedy, M. F. 1986 (Portsmouth) 2

Kennedy, M. J. 1996 (Liverpool, Wimbledon, Manchester C, Wolverhampton W) 34
Kennedy, W. 1932 (St James' Gate) 3
Kenny, P. 2004 (Sheffield U) 7
Keogh, A. D. 2007 (Wolverhampton W, Millwall) 30
Keogh, J. 1966 (Shamrock R) 1
Keogh, R. J. 2013 (Derby Co) 26
Keogh, S. 1959 (Shamrock R) 1
Kernaghan, A. N. 1993 (Middlesbrough, Manchester C) 22
Kiely, D. L. 2000 (Charlton Ath, WBA) 11
Kiernan, F. W. 1951 (Shamrock R, Southampton) 5
Kilbane, K. D. 1998 (WBA, Sunderland, Everton, Wigan Ath, Hull C) 110
Kinnear, J. P. 1967 (Tottenham H, Brighton & HA) 26
Kinsella, J. 1928 (Shelbourne) 1
Kinsella, M. A. 1998 (Charlton Ath, Aston Villa, WBA) 48
Kinsella, O. 1932 (Shamrock R) 2
Kirkland, A. 1927 (Shamrock R) 1

Lacey, W. 1927 (Shelbourne) 3
Langan, D. 1978 (Derby Co, Birmingham C, Oxford U) 26
Lapira, J. 2007 (Notre Dame) 1
Lawler, J. F. 1953 (Fulham) 8
Lawlor, J. C. 1949 (Drumcondra, Doncaster R) 3
Lawlor, M. 1971 (Shamrock R) 5
Lawrence, L. 2009 (Stoke C, Portsmouth) 15
Lawrenson, M. 1977 (Preston NE, Brighton & HA, Liverpool) 39
Lee, A. D. 2003 (Rotherham U, Cardiff C, Ipswich T) 10
Leech, M. 1969 (Shamrock R) 8
Lenihan, D. P. 2018 (Blackburn R) 2
Lennon, C. 1935 (St James' Gate) 3
Lennox, G. 1931 (Dolphin) 2
Long, K. F. 2017 (Burnley) 13
Long, S. P. 2007 (Reading, WBA, Hull C, Southampton) 82
Lowry, D. 1962 (St Patrick's Ath) 1
Lunn, R. 1939 (Dundalk) 2
Lynch, J. 1934 (Cork Bohemians) 1

Macken, A. 1977 (Derby Co) 1
Macken J. P. 2005 (Manchester C) 1
Mackey, G. 1957 (Shamrock R) 3
Madden, O. 1936 (Cork) 1
Madden, P. 2013 (Scunthorpe U) 1
Maguire, J. 1929 (Shamrock R) 1
Maguire, S. P. 2018 (Preston NE) 8
Mahon, A. J. 2000 (Tranmere R) 2
Malone, G. 1949 (Shelbourne) 1
Mancini, T. J. 1974 (QPR, Arsenal) 5
Martin, C. 1927 (Bo'ness) 1
Martin, C. J. 1946 (Glentoran, Leeds U, Aston Villa) 30
Martin, M. P. 1972 (Bohemians, Manchester U, WBA, Newcastle U) 52
Maybury, A. 1998 (Leeds U, Hearts, Leicester C) 10
McAlinden, J. 1946 (Portsmouth) 2
McAteer, J. W. 1994 (Bolton W, Liverpool, Blackburn R, Sunderland) 52
McCann, J. 1957 (Shamrock R) 1
McCarthy, J. 1926 (Bohemians) 3
McCarthy, J. 2010 (Wigan Ath, Everton) 41
McCarthy, M. 1932 (Shamrock R) 1
McCarthy, M. 1984 (Manchester C, Celtic, Lyon, Millwall) 57
McClean, J. J. 2012 (Sunderland, Wigan Ath, WBA, Stoke C) 72
McConville, T. 1972 (Dundalk, Waterford) 6
McDonagh, Jacko 1984 (Shamrock R) 3
McDonagh, J. 1981 (Everton, Bolton W, Notts Co, Wichita Wings) 25
McEvoy, M. A. 1961 (Blackburn R) 17
McGeady, A. J. 2004 (Celtic, Spartak Moscow, Everton, Sunderland) 93
McGee, P. 1978 (QPR, Preston NE) 15
McGoldrick, D. J. 2015 (Ipswich T, Sheffield U) 12
McGoldrick, E. J. 1992 (Crystal Palace, Arsenal) 15
McGowan, D. 1949 (West Ham U) 3
McGowan, J. 1947 (Cork U) 1
McGrath, M. 1958 (Blackburn R, Bradford) 22
McGrath, P. 1985 (Manchester U, Aston Villa, Derby Co) 83
McGuire, W. 1936 (Bohemians) 1
McKenzie, G. 1938 (Southend U) 9
McLoughlin, A. F. 1990 (Swindon T, Southampton, Portsmouth) 42
McLoughlin, F. 1930 (Fordsons, Cork) 2
McMillan, W. 1946 (Belfast Celtic) 2
McNally, J. B. 1959 (Luton T) 3
McPhail, S. 2000 (Leeds U) 10
McShane, P. D. 2007 (WBA, Sunderland, Hull C, Reading) 33
Meagan, M. K. 1961 (Everton, Huddersfield T, Drogheda) 17
Meehan, P. 1934 (Drumcondra) 1
Meyler, D. J. 2013 (Sunderland, Hull C, Reading) 26
Miller, L. W. P. 2004 (Celtic, Manchester U, Sunderland, Hibernian) 21
Milligan, M. J. 1992 (Oldham Ath) 1
Monahan, P. 1935 (Sligo R) 2
Mooney, J. 1965 (Shamrock R) 2
Moore, A. 1996 (Middlesbrough) 8
Moore, P. 1931 (Shamrock R, Aberdeen, Shamrock R) 9
Moran, K. 1980 (Manchester U, Sporting Gijon, Blackburn R) 71
Moroney, T. 1948 (West Ham U, Evergreen U) 12
Morris, C. B. 1988 (Celtic, Middlesbrough) 35
Morrison, C. H. 2002 (Crystal Palace, Birmingham C, Crystal Palace) 36
Moulson, C. 1936 (Lincoln C, Notts Co) 5
Moulson, G. B. 1948 (Lincoln C) 3
Muckian, C. 1978 (Drogheda U) 1
Muldoon, T. 1927 (Aston Villa) 1
Mulligan, P. M. 1969 (Shamrock R, Chelsea, Crystal Palace, WBA, Shamrock R) 50
Munroe, L. 1954 (Shamrock R) 1
Murphy, A. 1956 (Clyde) 1
Murphy, B. 1986 (Bohemians) 1
Murphy, D. 2007 (Sunderland, Ipswich T, Newcastle U, Sheffield W) 32
Murphy, J. 1980 (Crystal Palace) 3
Murphy, J. 2004 (WBA, Scunthorpe U) 2
Murphy, P. M. 2007 (Carlisle U) 1
Murray, T. 1950 (Dundalk) 1

Newman, W. 1969 (Shelbourne) 1
Nolan. E. W. 2009 (Preston NE) 3
Nolan, R. 1957 (Shamrock R) 10

Obafemi, M. O. 2019 (Southampton) 1
O'Brien, A. 2007 (Newcastle U) 5
O'Brien, A. A. 2019 (Millwall) 5
O'Brien, A. J. 2001 (Newcastle U, Portsmouth) 26
O'Brien, F. 1980 (Philadelphia F) 3
O'Brien J. M. 2006 (Bolton W, West Ham U) 5
O'Brien, L. 1986 (Shamrock R, Manchester U, Newcastle U, Tranmere R) 16
O'Brien, M. T. 1927 (Derby Co, Walsall, Norwich C, Watford) 4
O'Brien, R. 1976 (Notts Co) 5
O'Byrne, L. B. 1949 (Shamrock R) 1
O'Callaghan, B. R. 1979 (Stoke C) 6
O'Callaghan, K. 1981 (Ipswich T, Portsmouth) 21
O'Cearuill, J. 2007 (Arsenal) 2
O'Connell, A. 1967 (Dundalk, Bohemians) 2
O'Connor, L. P. 2020 (Celtic) 1
O'Connor, T. 1950 (Shamrock R) 4
O'Connor, T. 1968 (Fulham, Dundalk, Bohemians) 7
O'Dea, D. 2010 (Celtic, Toronto, Metalurh Donetsk) 20
O'Dowda, C. J. R. 2016 (Oxford U, Bristol C) 18
O'Driscoll, J. F. 1949 (Swansea T) 3
O'Driscoll, S. 1982 (Fulham) 3
O'Farrell, F. 1952 (West Ham U, Preston NE) 9
O'Flanagan, K. P. 1938 (Bohemians, Arsenal) 10
O'Flanagan, M. 1947 (Bohemians) 1
O'Halloran, S. E. 2007 (Aston Villa) 2
O'Hanlon, K. G. 1988 (Rotherham U) 1
O'Hara, K. M. 2020 (Manchester U) 2
O'Kane, E. C. 2016 (Bournemouth, Leeds U) 7

O'Kane, P. 1935 (Bohemians) 3
O'Keefe, E. 1981 (Everton, Port Vale) 5
O'Keefe, T. 1934 (Cork, Waterford) 3
O'Leary, D. 1977 (Arsenal) 68
O'Leary, P. 1980 (Shamrock R) 7
O'Mahoney, M. T. 1938 (Bristol R) 6
O'Neill, F. S. 1962 (Shamrock R) 20
O'Neill, J. 1952 (Everton) 17
O'Neill, J. 1961 (Preston NE) 1
O'Neill, K. P. 1996 (Norwich C, Middlesbrough) 13
O'Neill, W. 1936 (Dundalk) 11
O'Regan, K. 1984 (Brighton & HA) 4
O'Reilly, J. 1932 (Brideville, Aberdeen, Brideville, St James' Gate) 20
O'Reilly, J. 1946 (Cork U) 2
O'Shea, J. F. 2002 (Manchester U, Sunderland) 118

Parrot, T. D. 2020 (Tottenham H) 1
Pearce, A. J. 2013 (Reading, Derby Co) 9
Peyton, G. 1977 (Fulham, Bournemouth, Everton) 33
Peyton, N. 1957 (Shamrock R, Leeds U) 6
Phelan, T. 1992 (Wimbledon, Manchester C, Chelsea, Everton, Fulham) 42
Pilkington, A. N. J. 2013 (Norwich C, Cardiff C) 9
Potter, D. M. 2007 (Wolverhampton W) 5

Quinn, A. 2003 (Sheffield W, Sheffield U) 8
Quinn, B. S. 2000 (Coventry C) 4
Quinn, N. J. 1986 (Arsenal, Manchester C, Sunderland) 91
Quinn, S. 2013 (Hull C, Reading) 18

Randolph, D. E. 2013 (Motherwell, West Ham U, Middlesbrough) 42
Reid, A. M. 2004 (Nottingham F, Tottenham H, Charlton Ath, Sunderland, Nottingham F) 29
Reid, C. 1931 (Brideville) 1
Reid, S. J. 2002 (Millwall, Blackburn R) 23
Rice, D. 2018 (West Ham U) 3
Richardson, D. J. 1972 (Shamrock R, Gillingham) 3
Rigby, A. 1935 (St James' Gate) 3
Ringstead, A. 1951 (Sheffield U) 20
Robinson, C. J. 2019 (Preston NE, Sheffield U) 12
Robinson, J. 1928 (Bohemians, Dolphin) 2
Robinson, M. 1981 (Brighton & HA, Liverpool, QPR) 24
Roche, P. J. 1972 (Shelbourne, Manchester U) 8
Rogers, E. 1968 (Blackburn R, Charlton Ath) 19
Rowlands, M. C. 2004 (QPR) 5
Ryan, G. 1978 (Derby Co, Brighton & HA) 18
Ryan, R. A. 1950 (WBA, Derby Co) 16

Sadlier, R. T. 2002 (Millwall) 1
Sammon, C. 2013 (Derby Co) 9
Savage, D. P. T. 1996 (Millwall) 5
Saward, P. 1954 (Millwall, Aston Villa, Huddersfield T) 18
Scannell, T. 1954 (Southend U) 1
Scully, P. J. 1989 (Arsenal) 1
Sheedy, K. 1984 (Everton, Newcastle U) 46
Sheridan, C. 2010 (Celtic, CSKA Sofia) 3
Sheridan, J. J. 1988 (Leeds U, Sheffield W) 34
Slaven, B. 1990 (Middlesbrough) 7
Sloan, J. W. 1946 (Arsenal) 2
Smyth, M. 1969 (Shamrock R) 1
Squires, J. 1934 (Shelbourne) 1
Stapleton, F. 1977 (Arsenal, Manchester U, Ajax, Le Havre, Blackburn R) 71
Staunton, S. 1989 (Liverpool, Aston Villa, Liverpool, Aston Villa) 102
St Ledger-Hall, S. P. 2009 (Preston NE, Leicester C) 37
Stevens, E. J. 2018 (Sheffield U) 14
Stevenson, A. E. 1932 (Dolphin, Everton) 7
Stokes, A. 2007 (Sunderland, Celtic) 9
Strahan, F. 1964 (Shelbourne) 5
Sullivan, J. 1928 (Fordsons) 1
Swan, M. M. G. 1960 (Drumcondra) 1
Synnott, N. 1978 (Shamrock R) 3

Taylor, T. 1959 (Waterford) 1
Thomas, P. 1974 (Waterford) 2
Thompson, J. 2004 (Nottingham F) 1
Townsend, A. D. 1989 (Norwich C, Chelsea, Aston Villa, Middlesbrough) 70
Travers, M. 2020 (Bournemouth) 2
Traynor, T. J. 1954 (Southampton) 8
Treacy, K. 2011 (Preston NE, Burnley) 6
Treacy, R. C. P. 1966 (WBA, Charlton Ath, Swindon T, Preston NE, WBA, Shamrock R) 42
Tuohy, L. 1956 (Shamrock R, Newcastle U, Shamrock R) 8
Turner, C. J. 1936 (Southend U, West Ham U) 10
Turner, P. 1963 (Celtic) 2

Vernon, J. 1946 (Belfast Celtic) 2

Waddock, G. 1980 (QPR, Millwall) 21
Walsh, D. J. 1946 (Linfield, WBA, Aston Villa) 20
Walsh, J. 1982 (Limerick) 1
Walsh, M. 1976 (Blackpool, Everton, QPR, Porto) 21
Walsh, M. 1982 (Everton) 4
Walsh, W. 1947 (Manchester C) 9
Walters, J. R. 2011 (Stoke C, Burnley) 54
Ward, S. R. 2011 (Wolverhampton W, Burnley) 50
Waters, J. 1977 (Grimsby T) 2
Watters, F. 1926 (Shelbourne) 1
Weir, E. 1939 (Clyde) 3
Westwood, K. 2009 (Coventry C, Sunderland, Sheffield W) 21
Whelan, G. D. 2008 (Stoke C, Aston Villa, Hearts) 91
Whelan, R. 1964 (St Patrick's Ath) 2
Whelan, R. 1981 (Liverpool, Southend U) 53
Whelan, W. 1956 (Manchester U) 4
White, J. J. 1928 (Bohemians) 1
Whittaker, R. 1959 (Chelsea) 1
Williams, D. S. 2018 (Blackburn R) 3
Williams, J. 1938 (Shamrock R) 1
Williams, S. 2018 (Millwall) 3
Wilson, M. D. 2011 (Stoke C, Bournemouth) 25

BRITISH AND IRISH INTERNATIONAL GOALSCORERS 1872–2020

Where two players with the same surname and initials have appeared for the same country, and one or both have scored, they have been distinguished by reference to the club which appears *first* against their name in the international appearances section.
Bold type indicates players who have scored international goals in season 2019–20.

ENGLAND

Player	Goals
Abraham, K. O. T. (Tammy)	**1**
A'Court, A.	1
Adams, T. A.	5
Adcock, H.	1
Alcock, C. W.	1
Alexander-Arnold, T. J.	1
Allen, A.	3
Allen, R.	2
Alli, B. J. (Dele)	3
Amos, A.	1
Anderson, V.	2
Anderton, D. R.	7
Astall, G.	1
Athersmith, W. C.	3
Atyeo, P. J. W.	5
Bache, J. W.	4
Bailey, N. C.	2
Baily, E. F.	5
Baines, L. J.	1
Baker, J. H.	3
Ball, A. J.	8
Bambridge, A. L.	1
Bambridge, E. C.	11
Barclay, R.	2
Barkley, R.	**6**
Barmby, N. J.	4
Barnes, J.	11
Barnes, P. S.	4
Barry, G.	3
Barton, J.	1
Bassett, W. I.	8
Bastin, C. S.	12
Beardsley, P. A.	9
Beasley, A.	1
Beattie, T. K.	1
Beckham, D. R. J.	17
Becton, F.	2
Bedford, H.	1
Bell, C.	9
Bent, D. A.	4
Bentley, R. T. F.	9
Bertrand, R.	1
Bishop, S. M.	1
Blackburn, F.	1
Blissett, L.	3
Bloomer, S.	28
Bond, R.	2
Bonsor, A. G.	1
Bowden, E. R.	1
Bowers, J. W.	2
Bowles, S.	1
Bradford, G. R. W.	1
Bradford, J.	7
Bradley, W.	2
Bradshaw, F.	3
Brann, G.	1
Bridge, W. M.	1
Bridges, B. J.	1
Bridgett, A.	3
Brindle, T.	1
Britton, C. S.	1
Broadbent, P. F.	2
Broadis, I. A.	8
Brodie, J. B.	1
Bromley-Davenport, W.	2
Brook, E. F.	10
Brooking, T. D.	5
Brooks, J.	2
Broome, F. H.	3
Brown, A.	4
Brown, A. S.	1
Brown, G.	5
Brown, J.	3
Brown, W.	1
Brown, W. M.	1
Buchan, C. M.	4
Bull, S. G.	4
Bullock, N.	2
Burgess, H.	4
Butcher, T.	3
Byrne, J. J.	8
Cahill, G. J.	5
Campbell, S. J.	1
Camsell, G. H.	18
Carroll, A. T.	2
Carter, H. S.	7
Carter, J. H.	4
Caulker, S. A.	1
Chadwick, E.	3
Chamberlain, M.	1
Chambers, H.	5
Channon, M. R.	21
Charlton, J.	6
Charlton, R.	49
Chenery, C. J.	1
Chivers, M.	13
Clarke, A. J.	10
Cobbold, W. N.	6
Cock, J. G.	2
Cole, A.	1
Cole, J. J.	10
Common, A.	2
Connelly, J. M.	7
Coppell, S. J.	7
Cotterill, G. H.	2
Cowans, G.	2
Crawford, R.	1
Crawshaw, T. H.	1
Crayston, W. J.	1
Creek, F. N. S.	1
Crooks, S. D.	7
Crouch, P. J.	22
Currey, E. S.	2
Currie, A. W.	3
Cursham, A. W.	2
Cursham, H. A.	5
Daft, H. B.	3
Davenport, J. K.	2
Davis, G.	1
Davis, H.	1
Day, S. H.	2
Dean, W. R.	18
Defoe, J. C.	20
Devey, J. H. G.	1
Dewhurst, F.	11
Dier, E. J. E.	3
Dix, W. R.	1
Dixon, K. M.	4
Dixon, L. M.	1
Dorrell, A. R.	1
Douglas, B.	11
Drake, E. J.	6
Ducat, A.	1
Dunn, A. T. B.	2
Eastham, G.	2
Edwards, D.	5
Ehiogu, U.	1
Elliott, W. H.	3
Evans, R. E.	1
Ferdinand, L.	5
Ferdinand, R. G.	3
Finney, T.	30
Fleming, H. J.	9
Flowers, R.	10
Forman, Frank	1
Forman, Fred	3
Foster, R. E.	3
Fowler, R. B.	7
Francis, G. C. J.	3
Francis, T.	12
Freeman, B. C.	3
Froggatt, J.	2
Froggatt, R.	2
Galley, T.	1
Gascoigne, P. J.	10
Geary, F.	3
Gerrard, S. G.	21
Gibbins, W. V. T.	3
Gilliatt, W. E.	3
Goddard, P.	1
Goodall, J.	12
Goodyer, A. C.	1
Gosling, R. C.	2
Goulden, L. A.	4
Grainger, C.	3
Greaves, J.	44
Grovesnor, A. T.	2
Gunn, W.	1
Haines, J. T. W.	2
Hall, G. W.	9
Halse, H. J.	2
Hampson, J.	5
Hampton, H.	2
Hancocks, J.	2
Hardman, H. P.	1
Harris, S. S.	2
Hassall, H. W.	4
Hateley, M.	9
Haynes, J. N.	18
Hegan, K. E.	4
Henfrey, A. G.	2
Heskey, E. W.	7
Hilsdon, G. R.	14
Hine, E. W.	4
Hinton, A. T.	1
Hirst, D. E.	1
Hitchens, G. A.	5
Hobbis, H. H. F.	1
Hoddle, G.	8
Hodgetts, D.	1
Hodgson, G.	1
Holley, G. H.	8
Houghton, W. E.	5
Howell, R.	1
Hughes, E. W.	1
Hulme, J. H. A.	4
Hunt, G. S.	1
Hunt, R.	18
Hunter, N.	2
Hurst, G. C.	24
Ince, P. E. C.	2
Jack, D. N. B.	3
Jagielka, P. N.	3
Jeffers, F.	1
Jenas, J. A.	1
Johnson, A.	2
Johnson, D. E.	6
Johnson, E.	2
Johnson, G. M. C.	1
Johnson, J. A.	2
Johnson, T. C. F.	5
Johnson, W. H.	1
Kail, E. I. L.	2
Kane, H. E.	**32**
Kay, A. H.	1
Keane, M. V.	1
Keegan, J. K.	21
Kelly, R.	8
Kennedy, R.	3
Kenyon-Slaney, W. S.	2
Keown, M. R.	2
Kevan, D. T.	8
Kidd, B.	1
King, L. B.	2
Kingsford, R. K.	1
Kirchen, A. J.	2
Kirton, W. J.	1
Lallana, A. D.	3
Lambert, R. L.	3
Lampard, F. J.	29
Langton, R.	1
Latchford, R. D.	5
Latheron, E. G.	1
Lawler, C.	1
Lawton, T.	22
Lee, F.	10
Lee, J.	1
Lee, R. M.	2
Lee, S.	2
Lescott, J.	1
Le Saux, G. P.	1
Lindley, T.	14
Lineker, G.	48
Lingard, J. E.	4
Lofthouse, J. M.	3
Lofthouse, N.	30
Hon. A. Lyttelton	1
Mabbutt, G.	1
Macdonald, M.	6
Maguire, J. H.	1
Mannion, W. J.	11
Mariner, P.	13
Marsh, R. W.	1
Matthews, S.	11
Matthews, V.	1
McCall, J.	1
McDermott, T.	3
McManaman, S.	3
Medley, L. D.	1
Melia, J.	1
Mercer, D. W.	1
Merson, P. C.	3
Milburn, J. E. T.	10
Miller, H. S.	1
Mills, G. R.	3
Milner, J. P.	1
Milward, A.	3
Mitchell, C.	5
Moore, J.	1

Moore, R. F.	2
Moore, W. G. B.	2
Morren, T.	1
Morris, F.	1
Morris, J.	3
Mortensen, S. H.	23
Morton, J. R.	1
Mosforth, W.	3
Mount, M. T.	**1**
Mullen, J.	6
Mullery, A. P.	1
Murphy, D. B	1
Neal, P. G.	5
Needham, E.	3
Nicholls, J.	1
Nicholson, W. E.	1
Nugent, D. J.	1
O'Grady, M.	3
Osborne, F. R.	3
Owen, M. J.	40
Own goals	33
Oxlade-Chamberlain, A. M. D.	**7**
Page, L. A.	1
Paine, T. L.	7
Palmer, C. L.	1
Parry, E. H.	1
Parry, R. A.	1
Pawson, F. W.	1
Payne, J.	2
Peacock, A.	3
Pearce, S.	5
Pearson, J. S.	5
Pearson, S. C.	5
Perry, W.	2
Peters, M.	20
Pickering, F.	5
Platt, D.	27
Pointer, R.	2
Quantrill, A.	1
Ramsay, A. E.	3
Rashford, M.	**10**
Revie, D. G.	4
Redknapp, J. F.	1
Reynolds, J.	3
Richards, M.	1
Richardson, K. E.	2
Richardson, J. R.	2
Rigby, A.	3
Rimmer, E. J.	2
Roberts, F.	2
Roberts, H.	1
Roberts, W. T.	2
Robinson, J.	3
Robson, B.	26
Robson, R.	4
Rooney, W. M.	53
Rowley, J. F.	6
Royle, J.	2
Rutherford, J.	3
Sagar, C.	1
Sancho, J. M.	**2**
Sandilands, R. R.	3
Sansom, K.	1
Schofield, J.	1
Scholes, P.	14
Seed, J. M.	1
Settle, J.	6
Sewell, J.	3
Shackleton, L. F.	1
Sharp, J.	1
Shearer, A.	30
Shelton, A.	1
Shepherd, A.	2
Sheringham, E. P.	11
Simpson, J.	1
Smalling, C. L.	1
Smith, A.	1
Smith, A. M.	2
Smith, G. O.	11
Smith, Joe	1
Smith, J. R.	2
Smith, J. W.	4
Smith, R.	13
Smith, S.	1
Sorby, T. H.	1
Southgate, G.	2
Southworth, J.	3
Sparks, F. J.	3
Spence, J. W.	1
Spiksley, F.	5
Spilsbury, B. W.	5
Steele, F. C.	8
Stephenson, G. T.	2
Sterling, R. S.	**12**
Steven, T. M.	4
Stewart, J.	2
Stiles, N. P.	1
Storer, H.	1
Stone, S. B.	2
Stones, J.	2
Sturridge, D. A.	8
Summerbee, M. G.	1
Tambling, R. V.	1
Taylor, P. J.	2
Taylor, T.	16
Terry, J. G.	6
Thompson, P. B.	1
Thornewell, G.	1
Tilson, S. F.	6
Townley, W. J.	2
Townsend, A. D.	3
Trippier, K. J.	1
Tueart, D.	2
Upson, M. J.	2
Vardy, J. R.	7
Vassell, D.	6
Vaughton, O. H.	6
Veitch, J. G.	3
Viollet, D. S.	1
Waddle, C. R.	6
Walcott, T. J.	8
Walker, W. H.	9
Wall, G.	2
Wallace, D.	1
Walsh, P.	1
Waring, T.	4
Warren, B.	2
Watson, D. V.	4
Watson, V. M.	4
Webb, G. W.	1
Webb, N.	4
Wedlock, W. J.	2
Welbeck D. N. T. M.	16
Weller, K.	1
Welsh, D.	1
Whateley, O.	2
Wheldon, G. F.	6
Whitfield, H.	1
Wignall, F.	2
Wilkes, A.	1
Wilkins, R. G.	3
Willingham, C. K.	1
Wilshaw, D. J.	10
Wilshere J. A.	2
Wilson, C.	1
Wilson, G. P.	1
Winckworth, W. N.	1
Windridge, J. E.	7
Winks, H. B.	**1**
Wise, D. F.	1
Withe, P.	1
Wollaston, C. H. R.	1
Wood, H.	1
Woodcock, T.	16
Woodhall, G.	1
Woodward, V. J.	29
Worrall, F.	2
Worthington, F. S.	2
Wright, I. E.	9
Wright, M.	1
Wright, W. A.	3
Wright-Phillips, S. C.	6
Wylie, J. G.	1
Yates, J.	3
Young, A. S.	7

NORTHERN IRELAND

Anderson, T.	4
Armstrong, G.	12
Bambrick, J.	12
Barr, H. H.	1
Barron, H.	3
Best, G.	9
Bingham, W. L.	10
Black, K.	1
Blanchflower, D.	2
Blanchflower, J.	1
Boyce, L.	1
Brennan, B.	1
Brennan, R. A.	1
Brotherston, N.	3
Brown, J.	1
Browne, F.	2
Brunt, C.	3
Campbell, J.	1
Campbell, W. G.	1
Casey, T.	2
Caskey, W.	1
Cassidy, T.	1
Cathcart, C. G.	2
Chambers, J.	3
Clarke, C. J.	13
Clements, D.	2
Cochrane, T.	1
Condy, J.	1
Connor, M. J.	1
Coulter, J.	1
Croft, T.	1
Crone, W.	1
Crossan, E.	1
Crossan, J. A.	10
Curran, S.	2
Cush, W. W.	5
Dallas, S. A.	3
Dalton, W.	4
D'Arcy, S. D.	1
Darling, J.	1
Davey, H. H.	1
Davis, S.	12
Davis, T. L.	1
Dill, A. H.	1
Doherty, L.	1
Doherty, P. D.	3
Dougan, A. D.	8
Dowie, I.	12
Dunne, J.	4
Elder, A. R.	1
Elliott, S.	4
Emerson, W.	1
English, S.	1
Evans, C.	2
Evans, J. G.	**4**
Feeney, W.	1
Feeney, W. J.	5
Ferguson, S. K.	1
Ferguson, W.	1
Ferris, J.	1
Ferris, R. O.	1
Finney, T.	2
Gaffkin, J.	4
Gara, A.	3
Gaukrodger, G.	1
Gibb, J. T.	2
Gibb, T. J.	1
Gibson, W.	1
Gillespie, K. R.	2
Gillespie, W.	13
Goodall, A. L.	2
Griffin, D. J.	1
Gray, P.	6
Grigg, W. D.	2
Halligan, W.	1
Hamill, M.	1
Hamilton, B.	4
Hamilton, W. R.	5
Hannon, D. J.	1
Harkin, J. T.	2
Harvey, M.	3
Healy, D. J.	36
Hill, C. F.	1
Hughes, A.	1
Hughes, M. E.	5
Humphries, W.	1
Hunter, A. (Distillery)	1
Hunter, A. (Blackburn R)	1
Hunter, B. V.	1
Irvine, R. W.	3
Irvine, W. J.	8
Johnston, H.	2
Johnston, S.	2
Johnston, W. C.	1
Jones, S. (Distillery)	1
Jones, S. (Crewe Alex)	1
Jones, J.	1
Kelly, J.	4
Kernaghan, N.	2
Kirwan, J.	2
Lacey, W.	3
Lafferty, K.	20
Lemon, J.	2
Lennon, N. F.	2
Lockhart, N.	3
Lomas, S. M.	3
Magennis, J. B. D.	**7**
Magilton, J.	5
Mahood, J.	2
Martin, D. K.	3
Maxwell, J.	2
McAdams, W. J.	7
McAllen, J.	1
McAuley, G.	9
McAuley, J. L.	1
McCann, G. S.	4
McCartney, G.	1
McCandless, J.	2
McCandless, W.	1
McCaw, J. H.	1
McClelland, J.	1
McCluggage, A.	2
McCourt, P.	2
McCracken, W.	1
McCrory, S.	1
McCurdy, C.	1
McDonald, A.	3
McGarry, J. K.	1
McGrath, R. C.	4
McGinn, N.	4
McIlroy, J.	10
McIlroy, S. B.	5
McKenzie, H	1
McKnight, J.	2
McLaughlin, C. G.	1
McLaughlin, J. C.	6
McMahon, G. J.	2
McMordie, A. S.	3
McMorran, E. J.	4
McNair, P. J. C.	**3**
McParland, P. J.	10

McWha, W. B. R. 1
Meldon, P. A 1
Mercer, J. T. 1
Millar, W. 1
Milligan, D. 1
Milne, R. G. 2
Molyneux, T. B. 1
Moreland, V. 1
Morgan, S. 3
Morrow, S. J. 1
Morrow, W. J. 1
Mulryne, P. P. 3
Murdock, C. J. 1
Murphy, N. 1

Neill, W. J. T. 2
Nelson, S. 1
Nicholl, C. J. 3
Nicholl, J. M. 1
Nicholson, J. J. 6

O'Boyle, G. 1
O'Hagan, C. 2
O'Kane, W. J. 1
O'Neill, J. 2
O'Neill, M. A. 4
O'Neill, M. H. 8
Own goals 10

Paterson, M. A. 3
Patterson, D. J. 1
Patterson, R. 1
Peacock, R. 2
Peden, J. 7
Penney, S. 2
Pyper, James 2
Pyper, John 1

Quinn, J. M. 12
Quinn, S. J. 4

Reynolds, J. 1
Rowland, K. 1
Rowley, R. W. M. 2
Rushe, F. 1

Sheridan, J. 2
Sherrard, J. 1
Sherrard, W. C. 2
Shields, D. 1
Simpson, W. J. 5
Sloan, H. A. de B. 4
Smith, M. 1
Smyth, P. 1
Smyth, S. 5

Spence, D. W. 3
Sproule, I. 1
Stanfield, O. M. 11
Stevenson, A. E. 5
Stewart, I. 2

Taggart, G. P. 7
Thompson, F. W. 2
Torrans, S. 1
Tully, C. P. 3
Turner, A. 1

Walker, J. 1
Walsh, D. J. 5
Ward, J. J. 4
Washington, C. J. 4
Welsh, E. 1
Whiteside, N. 9
Whiteside, T. 1
Whitley, Jeff 2
Whyte, G. 1
Williams, J. R. 1
Williams, M. S. 1
Williamson, J. 1
Wilson, D. J. 1
Wilson, K. J. 6
Wilson, S. J. 7
Wilton, J. M. 2
Young, S. 1

N.B. In 1914 Young goal should be credited to Gillespie W v Wales

SCOTLAND

Aitken, R. (Celtic) 1
Aitken, R. (Dumbarton) 1
Aitkenhead, W. A. C. 2
Alexander, D. 1
Allan, D. S. 4
Allan, J. 2
Anderson, F. 1
Anderson, W. 4
Andrews, P. 1
Anya, I. 3
Archibald, A. 1
Archibald, S. 4
Armstrong, S. 2

Baird, D. 2
Baird, J. C. 2
Baird, S. 2
Bannon, E. 1
Barbour, A. 1
Barker, J. B. 4
Battles, B. Jr 1
Bauld, W. 2
Baxter, J. C. 3
Beattie, C. 1
Bell, J. 5
Bennett, A. 2
Berra, C. D. 4
Berry, D. 1
Bett, J. 1
Beveridge, W. W. 1
Black, A. 3
Black, D. 1
Bone, J. 1
Booth, S. 6
Boyd, K 7
Boyd, R. 2
Boyd, T. 1
Boyd, W. G. 1
Brackenridge, T. 1
Brand, R. 8
Brazil, A. 1
Bremner, W. J. 3
Broadfoot, K. 1
Brown, A. D. 6
Brown, S. 4
Buchanan, P. S. 1
Buchanan, R. 1
Buckley, P. 1
Buick, A. 2
Burke, C. 2
Burke, O. J. 1
Burley, C. W. 3
Burns, K. 1

Cairns, T. 1
Caldwell, G. 2
Calderwood, C. 1
Calderwood, R. 2
Caldow, E. 4
Cameron, C. 2
Campbell, C. 1
Campbell, John (Celtic) 5
Campbell, John (Rangers) 4
Campbell, J. (South Western) 1
Campbell, P. 2
Campbell, R. 1
Cassidy, J. 1
Chalmers, S. 3
Chambers, T. 1
Cheyne, A. G. 4
Christie, A. J. 1
Christie, R. 1
Clarkson, D. 1
Clunas, W. L. 1
Collins, J. 12
Collins, R. Y. 10
Combe, J. R. 1
Commons, K. 2
Conn, A. 1
Cooper, D. 6
Craig, J. 1
Craig, T. 1
Crawford, S. 4
Cunningham, A. N. 5
Curran, H. P. 1

Dailly, C. 6
Dalglish, K. 30
Davidson, D. 1
Davidson, J. A. 1
Delaney, J. 3
Devine, A. 1
Dewar, G. 1
Dewar, N. 4
Dickov, P. 1
Dickson, W. 4
Divers, J. 1
Dobie, R. S. 1
Docherty, T. H. 1
Dodds, D. 1
Dodds, W. 7
Donaldson, A. 1
Donnachie, J. 1
Dougall, J. 1
Drummond, J. 2
Dunbar, M. 1
Duncan, D. 7
Duncan, D. M. 1
Duncan, J. 1
Dunn, J. 2
Durie, G. S. 7

Easson, J. F. 1
Elliott, M. S. 1
Ellis, J. 1

Ferguson, B. 3
Ferguson, J. 6
Fernie, W. 1
Findlay, S. J. 1
Fitchie, T. T. 1
Flavell, R. 2
Fleming, C. 2
Fleming, J. W. 3
Fletcher, D. 5
Fletcher, S. K. 10
Forrest, J. 5
Fraser, M. J. E. 3
Fraser, R. 1
Freedman, D. A. 1

Gallacher, H. K. 23
Gallacher, K. W. 9
Gallacher, P. 1
Galt, J. H. 1
Gemmell, T. (St Mirren) 1
Gemmell, T. (Celtic) 1
Gemmill, A. 8
Gemmill, S. 1
Gibb, W. 1
Gibson, D. W. 3
Gibson, J. D. 1
Gibson, N. 1
Gillespie, Jas. 3
Gillick, T. 3
Gilzean, A. J. 12
Goodwillie, D. 1
Gossland, J. 2
Goudie, J. 1
Gough, C. R. 6
Gourlay, J. 1
Graham, A. 2
Graham, G. 3
Gray, A. 7
Gray, E. 3
Gray, F. 1
Greig, J. 3
Griffiths, L. 4
Groves, W. 4

Hamilton, G. 4
Hamilton, J. (Queen's Park) 3
Hamilton, R. C. 15
Hanley, G. C. 1
Harper, J. M. 2
Hartley, P. J. 1
Harrower, W. 5
Hartford, R. A. 4
Heggie, C. W 4
Henderson, J. G. 1
Henderson, W. 5
Hendry, E. C. J. 3
Herd, D. G. 3
Herd, G. 1
Hewie, J. D. 2
Higgins, A. (Newcastle U) 1
Higgins, A. (Kilmarnock) 4
Highet, T. C. 1
Holt, G.J. 1
Holton, J. A. 2
Hopkin, D. 2
Houliston, W. 2
Howie, H. 1
Howie, J. 2
Hughes, J. 1
Hunter, W. 1
Hutchison, D. 6
Hutchison, T. 1
Hutton, J. 1
Hyslop, T. 1

Imrie, W. N. 1

Jackson, A. 8
Jackson, C. 1
Jackson, D. 4
James, A. W. 4
Jardine, A. 1
Jenkinson, T. 1
Jess, E. 2
Johnston, A. 2
Johnston, L. H. 1
Johnston, M. 14
Johnstone, D. 2
Johnstone, J. 4
Johnstone, Jas. 1
Johnstone, R. 10
Johnstone, W. 1
Jordan, J. 11

Kay, J. L. 5
Keillor, A. 3
Kelly, J. 1
Kelso, R. 1
Ker, G. 10
King, A. 1
King, J. 1
Kinnear, D. 1
Kyle, K. 1

Lambert, P. 1
Lambie, J. 1
Lambie, W. A. 5
Lang, J. J. 2
Latta, A. 2
Law, D. 30
Leggat, G. 8
Lennie, W. 1
Lennox, R. 3
Liddell, W. 6
Lindsay, J. 6
Linwood, A. B. 1
Logan, J. 1
Lorimer, P. 4
Love, A. 1
Low, J. (Cambuslang) 1
Lowe, J. (St Bernards) 1

Macari, L. 5
MacDougall, E. J. 3
MacFarlane, A. 1
MacLeod, M. 1
Mackay, D. C. 4
Mackay, G. 1
MacKenzie, J. A. 1
Mackail-Smith, C. 1
Mackie, J. C. 2
MacKinnon, W. W. 5
Madden, J. 5
Maloney, S. R. 7
Marshall, H. 1
Marshall, J. 1
Martin, C. H. 3
Mason, J. 4
Massie, A. 1
Masson, D. S. 5
McAdam, J. 1
McAllister, G. 5
McArthur, J. 4
McAulay, J. D. 1
McAvennie, F. 1
McCall, J. 1
McCall, S. M. 1
McCalliog, J. 1
McCallum, N. 1
McCann, N. 3
McClair, B. J. 2
McCoist, A. 19
McColl, R. S. 13
McCormack, R. 2
McCulloch, D. 3
McCulloch, L. 1
McDougall, J. 4
McFadden, J.* 15
McFadyen, W. 2
McGhee, M. 2
McGinlay, J. 4
McGinn, J. 7
McGregor, J. 1
McGrory, J. 6
McGuire, W. 1
McInally, A. 3
McInnes, T. 2
McKie, J. 2
McKimmie, S. 1
McKinlay, W. 4
McKinnon, A. 1
McKinnon, R. 1
McLaren, A. 4
McLaren, J. 1
McLean, A. 1
McLean, K. 1
McLean, T. 1
McLintock, F. 1
McMahon, A. 6
McManus, S. 2
McMenemy, J. 5
McMillan, I. L. 2
McNeill, W. 3
McNiel, H. 5
McPhail, J. 3
McPhail, R. 7
McPherson, J. (Kilmarnock) 7
McPherson, J. (Vale of Leven) 1
McPherson, R. 1
McQueen, G. 5
McStay, P. 9
McSwegan, G. 1
Meiklejohn, D. D. 3
Millar, J. 2
Miller, K. 18
Miller, T. 2
Miller, W. 1
Mitchell, R. C. 1
Morgan, W. 1
Morris, D. 1
Morris, H. 3
Morrison, J. C. 3

Morton, A. L. 5
Mudie, J. K. 9
Mulgrew, C. P. 3
Mulhall, G. 1
Munro, A. D. 1
Munro, N. 2
Murdoch, R. 5
Murphy, F. 1
Murray, J. 1

Napier, C. E. 3
Narey, D. 1
Naismith, S. J. 10
Naysmith, G. A. 1
Neil, R. G. 2
Nevin, P. K. F. 5
Nicholas, C. 5
Nisbet, J. 2

O'Connor, G. 4
O'Donnell, F. 2
O'Hare, J. 5
Ormond, W. E. 2
O'Rourke, F. 1
Orr, R. 1
Orr, T. 1
Oswald, J. 1
Own goals 21

Parlane, D. 1
Paul, H. McD. 2
Paul, W. 5
Pettigrew, W. 2
Phillips, M. 1
Provan, D. 1

Quashie, N. F. 1
Quinn, J. 7
Quinn, P. 1

Rankin, G. 2
Rankin, R. 2
Reid, W. 4
Reilly, L. 22
Renny-Tailyour, H. W. 1
Rhodes, J. L. 3
Richmond, J. T. 1
Ring, T. 2
Rioch, B. D. 6
Ritchie, J. 1
Ritchie, M. T. 3
Ritchie, P. S. 1
Robertson, A. (Clyde) 2
Robertson, A. 3
Robertson, J. 3
Robertson, J. N. 8
Robertson, J. T. 2
Robertson, T. 1
Robertson, W. 1
Russell, D. 1
Russell, J. S. S. 1

Scott, A. S. 5
Sellar, W. 4
Shankland, L. 1
Sharp, G. 1
Shaw, F. W. 1
Shearer, D. 2
Simpson, J. 1
Smith, A. 5
Smith, G. 4
Smith, J. 1
Smith, John 13
Snodgrass, R. 7
Somerville, G. 1
Souness, G. J. 4
Speedie, F. 2
St John, I. 9
Steel, W. 12
Stein, C. 10
Stevenson, G. 4
Stewart, A. 1

Stewart, R. 1
Stewart, W. E. 1
Strachan, G. 5
Sturrock, P. 3

Taylor, J. D. 1
Templeton, R. 1
Thompson, S. 3
Thomson, A. 1
Thomson, C. 4
Thomson, R. 1
Thomson, W. 1
Thornton, W. 1

Waddell, T. S. 1
Waddell, W. 6
Walker, J. 2
Walker, R. 7
Walker, T. 9
Wallace, I. A. 1
Wark, J. 7
Watson, J. A. K. 1
Watt, F. 2
Watt, W. W. 1
Webster, A. 1
Weir, A. 1
Weir, D. 1
Weir, J. B. 2
White, J. A. 3
Wilkie, L. 1
Wilson, A. (Sheffield W) 2
Wilson, A. N. (Dunfermline Ath) 13
Wilson, D. (Liverpool) 1
Wilson, D. (Queen's Park) 2
Wilson, D. (Rangers) 9
Wilson, H. 1
Wylie, T. G. 1

Young, A. 5

WALES

Allchurch, I. J. 23
Allen, J. M. 2
Allen, M. 3
Astley, D. J. 12
Atherton, R. W. 2

Bale, G. F. 33
Bamford, T. 1
Barnes, W. 1
Bellamy, C. D. 19
Blackmore, C. G. 1
Blake, D. 1
Blake, N. A. 4
Bodin, P. J. 3
Boulter, L. M. 1
Bowdler, J. C. H. 3
Bowen, D. L. 1
Bowen, M. 3
Boyle, T. 1
Brooks, D. R. 1
Bryan, T. 1
Burgess, W. A. R. 1
Burke, T. 1
Butler, W. T. 1

Chapman, T. 2
Charles, J. 1
Charles, M. 6
Charles, W. J. 15
Church, S. R. 3
Clarke, R. J. 5
Coleman, C. 4
Collier, D. J. 1
Collins, J. 3
Cotterill, D. R. G. B. 2
Crosse, K. 1
Cumner, R. H. 1
Curtis, A. 6
Curtis, E. R. 3

Davies, D. W. 1
Davies, E. Lloyd 1
Davies, G. 2
Davies, L. S. 6
Davies, R. T. 9
Davies, R. W. 6
Davies, Simon 6
Davies, Stanley 5
Davies, W. 6
Davies, W. H. 1
Davies, William 5
Davis, W. O. 1
Deacy, N. 4
Doughty, J. 6
Doughty, R. 2
Durban, A. 2
Dwyer, P. 2

Earnshaw, R. 16
Eastwood, F. 4
Edwards, D. A. 3
Edwards, G. 2
Edwards, R. I. 4
England, H. M. 4
Evans, C. 2
Evans, I. 1
Evans, J. 1
Evans, R. E. 2
Evans, W. 1
Eyton-Jones, J. A. 1

Fletcher, C. 1
Flynn, B. 7
Ford, T. 23
Foulkes, W. I. 1
Fowler, J. 3

Giles, D. 2
Giggs, R. J. 12
Glover, E. M. 7
Godfrey, B. C. 2
Green, A. W. 3
Griffiths, A. T. 6
Griffiths, M. W. 2
Griffiths, T. P. 3

Harris, C. S. 1
Hartson, J. 14
Hersee, R. 1
Hewitt, R. 1
Hockey, T. 1
Hodges, G. 2
Hole, W. J. 1
Hopkins, I. J. 2
Horne, B. 2
Howell, E. G. 3
Hughes, L. M. 16
Huws, E. W. 1

James, D. O. 2
James, E. 2
James, L. 10
James, R. 7
Jarrett, R. H. 3
Jenkyns, C. A. 1
Jones, A. 1
Jones, Bryn 6
Jones, B. S. 2
Jones, Cliff 16
Jones, C. W. 1
Jones, D. E. 1
Jones, Evan 1
Jones, H. 1
Jones, I. 1
Jones, J. L. 1
Jones, J. O. 1
Jones, J. P. 1
Jones, Leslie J. 1
Jones, R. A. 2
Jones, W. L. 6

Keenor, F. C. 2

* *The Scottish FA officially changed Robson's goal against Iceland on 10 September 2008 to McFadden.*

King, A. P. 2
Koumas, J. 10
Krzywicki, R. L. 1

Lawrence, T. M. 3
Ledley, J. C. 4
Leek, K. 5
Lewis, B. 4
Lewis, D. M. 2
Lewis, W. 8
Lewis, W. L. 3
Llewelyn, C. M 1
Lovell, S. 1
Lowrie, G. 2

Mahoney, J. F. 1
Mays, A. W. 1
Medwin, T. C. 6
Melville, A. K 3
Meredith, W. H. 11
Mills, T. J. 1
Moore, G. 1
Moore, K. R. F. 2
Morgan, J. R. 2
Morgan-Owen, H. 1
Morgan-Owen, M. M. 2
Morison, S. 1
Morris, A. G. 9
Morris, H. 2
Morris, R. 1
Morris, S. 2

Nicholas, P. 2

O'Callaghan, E. 3
O'Sullivan, P. A. 1
Owen, G. 2
Owen, W. 4
Owen, W. P. 6
Own goals 14

Palmer, D. 3
Parry, P. I. 1
Parry, T. D. 3
Paul, R. 1
Peake, E. 1
Pembridge, M. 6
Perry, E. 1
Phillips, C. 5
Phillips, D. 2
Powell, A. 1
Powell, D. 1
Price, J. 4
Price, P. 1
Pryce-Jones, W. E. 3
Pugh, D. H. 2

Ramsey, A. J. 16
Reece, G. I. 2
Rees, R. R. 3
Richards, R. W. 1
Roach, J. 2
Robbins, W. W. 4
Roberts, C. R. J. 1
Roberts, J. (Corwen) 1
Roberts, Jas. 1
Roberts, P. S. 1
Roberts, R. (Druids) 1
Roberts, W. (Llangollen) 2
Roberts, W. (Wrexham) 1
Roberts, W. H. 1
Robinson, C. P. 1
Robinson, J. R. C. 3
Robson-Kanu, T. H. 5
Rush, I. 28
Russell, M. R. 1

Sabine, H. W. 1
Saunders, D. 22
Savage, R. W. 2
Shaw, E. G. 2
Sisson, H. 4
Slatter, N. 2
Smallman, D. P. 1
Speed, G. A. 7
Symons, C. J. 2

Tapscott, D. R. 4
Taylor, G. K. 1
Taylor, N. J. 1
Thomas, M. 4
Thomas, T. 1
Toshack, J. B. 12
Trainer, H. 2

Vaughan, D. O. 1
Vaughan, John 2
Vernon, T. R. 8
Vizard, E. T. 1
Vokes, S. M. 11

Walsh, I. 7
Warren, F. W. 3
Watkins, W. M. 4
Wilding, J. 4
Williams, A. 1
Williams, A. E. 2
Williams, D. R. 2
Williams, G. E. 1
Williams, G. G. 1
Williams, W. 1
Wilson, H. 3
Woodburn, B. 2
Woosnam, A. P. 3
Wynn, G. A. 1

Yorath, T. C. 2
Young, E. 1

REPUBLIC OF IRELAND

Aldridge, J. 19
Ambrose, P. 1
Anderson, J. 1
Andrews, K. 3

Barrett, G. 2
Bermingham, P. 1
Bradshaw, P. 4
Brady, L. 9
Brady, R. 8
Breen, G. 7
Brown, J. 1
Browne, A. J. 1
Burke, G. D. 1
Byrne, D. 1
Byrne, J. 4

Cantwell, N. 14
Carey, J. 3
Carroll, T. 1
Cascarino, A. 19
Christie, C. S. F. 2
Clark, C. 2
Coad, P. 3
Coleman, S. 1
Collins, J. S. 1
Connolly, D. J. 9
Conroy, T. 2
Conway, J. 3
Cox, S. R. 4
Coyne, T. 6
Cummins, G. 5
Curtis, D. 8

Daly, G. 13
Davis, T. 4
Dempsey, J. 1
Dennehy, M. 2
Doherty, G. M. T. 4
Doherty, M. J. 1
Donnelly, J. 4
Donnelly, T. 1
Doyle, K. E. 14
Duff, D. A. 8
Duffy, B. 1
Duffy, S. P. M. 3
Duggan, H. 1
Dunne, J. 13
Dunne, L. 1
Dunne, R. P. 8

Eglington, T. 2
Elliott, S. W. 1
Ellis, P. 1

Fagan, F. 5
Fahey, K. 3
Fallon, S. 2
Fallon, W. 2
Farrell, P. 3
Finnan, S. 2
Fitzgerald, P. 2
Fitzgerald, J. 1
Fitzsimons, A. 7
Flood, J. J. 4
Fogarty, A. 3
Foley, D. 2
Fullam, J. 1
Fullam, R. 1

Galvin, A. 1
Gavin, J. 2
Geoghegan, M. 2
Gibson, D. T. D. 1
Giles, J. 5
Givens, D. 19
Gleeson, S. M. 1
Glynn, D. 1
Grealish, T. 8
Green, P. J. 1
Grimes, A. A. 1

Hale, A. 2
Hand, E. 2
Harte, I. P. 11
Haverty, J. 3
Healy, C. 1
Hendrick, J. P. 2
Holland, M. R. 5
Holmes, J. 1
Hoolahan, W. 3
Horlacher, A. 2
Houghton, R. 6
Hourihane, C. 1
Hughton, C. 1
Hunt, S. P. 1
Hurley, C. 2

Ireland, S. J. 4
Irwin, D. 4

Jordan, D. 1
Judge, A. C. 1

Kavanagh, G. A. 1
Keane, R. D. 68
Keane, R. M. 9
Kelly, D. 9
Kelly, G. 2
Kelly, J. 2
Kennedy, M. 4
Keogh, A. 2
Keogh, R. J. 1
Kernaghan, A. N. 1
Kilbane, K. D. 8
Kinsella, M. A. 3

Lacey, W. 1
Lawrence, L. 2
Lawrenson, M. 5
Leech, M. 2
Long, K. F. 1
Long, S. P. 17

Maguire, S. P. 1
Mancini, T. 1
Martin, C. 6
Martin, M. 4
McAteer, J. W. 3
McCann, J. 1
McCarthy, M. 2
McClean, J. J. 10
McEvoy, A. 6
McGeady, A. G. 5
McGee, P. 4
McGoldrick, D. J. 1
McGrath, P. 8
McLoughlin, A. F. 2
McPhail, S. J. P. 1
Miller, L. W. P. 1
Mooney, J. 1
Moore, P. 7
Moran, K. 6
Morrison, C. H. 9
Moroney, T. 1
Mulligan, P. 1
Murphy, D. 3

O'Brien, A. A. 1
O'Brien, A. J. 1
O'Callaghan, K. 1
O'Connor, T. 2
O'Dea, D. 1
O'Farrell, F. 2
O'Flanagan, K. 3
O'Keefe, E. 1
O'Leary, D. A. 1
O'Neill, F. 1
O'Neill, K. P. 4
O'Reilly, J. (Brideville) 2
O'Reilly, J. (Cork) 1
O'Shea, J. F. 3
Own goals 14

Pearce, A. J. 2
Pilkington, A. N. J. 1

Quinn, N. 21

Reid, A. M. 4
Reid, S. J. 2
Ringstead, A. 7
Robinson, C. J. 1
Robinson, M. 4
Rogers, E. 5
Ryan, G. 1
Ryan, R. 3

St Ledger-Hall, S. 3
Sheedy, K. 9
Sheridan, J. 5
Slaven, B. 1
Sloan, J. 1
Squires, J. 1
Stapleton, F. 20
Staunton, S. 7
Strahan, J. 1
Sullivan, J. 1

Townsend, A. D. 7
Treacy, R. 5
Touhy, L. 4

Waddock, G. 3
Walsh, D. 5
Walsh, M. 3
Walters, J. R. 14
Ward, S. R. 3
Waters, J. 1
White, J. J. 2
Whelan, G. D. 2
Whelan, R. 3
Williams, D. S. 1
Williams, S. 1
Wilson, M. D. 1

SOUTH AMERICA

COPA SUDAMERICANA 2019

FIRST STAGE – FIRST LEG

Montevideo Wanderers v Sport Huancayo	2-0
Bahia v Liverpool	0-1
Independiente v Binacional	4-1
Rionegro Aguilas v Oriente Petrolero	1-1
Argentinos Juniors v Estudiantes de Merida	2-0
Deportivo Municipal v Colon	0-3
Union Espanola v Mushuc Runa	1-1
UTC v Cerro	1-1
Deportivo Santani v Once Caldas	1-1
Universidad Catolica v Colo-Colo	0-1
River Plate v Santos	0-0
Macara v Guabira	2-1
Royal Pari v Monagas	2-1
Mineros v Sol de America	1-0
Union La Calera v Chapecoense	0-0
Deportivo Cali v Guarani	1-0
Nacional Potosi v Zulia	0-1
Corinthians v Racing	1-1
Independiente v La Equidad	0-0
Fluminense v Deportes Antofagasta	0-0
Union v Independiente del Valle	2-0
Botafogo v Defensa y Justicia	1-0

FIRST STAGE – SECOND LEG

Match	Score	*(agg)*
Sport Huancayo v Montevideo Wanderers	1-1	1-3
Liverpool v Bahia	0-0	1-0
Binacional v Independiente	1-2	2-6
Oriente Petrolero v Rionegro Aguilas	1-1	2-2
Rionegro Aguilas won 3-0 on penalties		
Estudiantes de Merida v Argentinos Juniors	1-0	1-2
Colon v Deportivo Municipal	2-0	5-0
Mushuc Runa v Union Espanola	1-1	2-2
Union Espanola won 6-5 on penalties		
Cerro v UTC	3-1	4-2
Once Caldas v Deportivo Santani	0-2	1-3
Colo-Colo v Universidad Catolica	0-1	1-1
Universidad Catolica won 3-0 on penalties		
Santos v River Plate	1-1	1-1
River Plate won on away goals		
Guabira v Macara	0-3	1-5
Monagas v Royal Pari	2-1	3-3
Royal Pari won 4-2 on penalties		
Sol de America v Mineros	1-0	1-1
Sol de America won 4-3 on penalties		
Chapecoense v Union La Calera	1-1	1-1
Union La Calera won on away goals		
Guarani v Deportivo Cali	1-0	1-1
Deportivo Cali won 4-1 on penalties		
Zulia v Nacional Potosi	0-1	1-1
Zulia won 2-0 on penalties		
Racing v Corinthians	1-1	2-2
Corinthians won 5-4 on penalties		
La Equidad v Independiente	0-0	0-0
La Equidad won 4-3 on penalties		
Deportes Antofagasta v Fluminense	1-2	1-2
Independiente del Valle v Union	2-0	2-2
Independiente del Valle won 4-2 on penalties		
Defensa y Justicia v Botafogo	0-3	0-4

SECOND STAGE – FIRST LEG

La Equidad v Deportivo Santani	2-0
Independiente del Valle v Universidad Catolica	5-0
Fluminense v Atletico Nacional	4-1
Union Espanola v Sporting Cristal	0-3
Argentinos Juniors v Deportes Tolima	1-0
Montevideo Wanderers v Cerro	0-0
Universidad Catolica v Melgar	6-0
Union La Calera v Atletico Mineiro	1-0
Sol de America v Botafogo	0-1
Rionegro Aguilas v Independiente	3-2
Corinthians v Deportivo Lara	2-0
River Plate v Colon	0-0
Zulia v Palestino	2-1
Deportivo Cali v Penarol	1-1
Liverpool v Caracas	1-0
Royal Pari v Macara	1-0

SECOND STAGE – SECOND LEG

Match	Score	*(agg)*
Deportivo Santani v La Equidad	1-2	1-4
Universidad Catolica v Independiente del Valle	3-2	3-7
Atletico Nacional v Fluminense	1-0	2-4
Sporting Cristal v Union Espanola	3-0	6-0
Deportes Tolima v Argentinos Juniors	0-0	0-1
Cerro v Montevideo Wanderers	0-1	0-1
Melgar v Universidad Catolica	0-0	0-6
Atletico Mineiro v Union La Calera	1-0	1-1
Atletico Mineiro won 3-0 on penalties		
Botafogo v Sol de America	4-0	5-0
Independiente v Rionegro Aguilas	2-0	4-3
Deportivo Lara v Corinthians	0-2	0-4
Colon v River Plate	3-1	3-1
Palestino v Zulia	0-1	1-3
Penarol v Deportivo Cali	2-0	3-1
Caracas v Liverpool	2-0	2-1
Macara v Royal Pari	3-2	3-3
Royal Pari won on away goals		

ROUND OF 16 – FIRST LEG

Royal Pari v La Equidad	1-2
Caracas v Independiente del Valle	0-0
Penarol v Fluminense	1-2
Zulia v Sporting Cristal	1-0
Colon v Argentinos Juniors	0-1
Corinthians v Montevideo Wanderers	2-0
Independiente v Universidad Catolica	1-0
Botafogo v Atletico Mineiro	0-1

ROUND OF 16 – SECOND LEG

Match	Score	*(agg)*
La Equidad v Royal Pari	2-1	4-2
Independiente del Valle v Caracas	2-0	2-0
Fluminense v Penarol	3-1	5-2
Sporting Cristal v Zulia	3-2	3-3
Zulia won on away goals		
Argentinos Juniors v Colon	0-1	1-1
Colon won 4-3 on penalties		
Montevideo Wanderers v Corinthians	1-2	1-4
Universidad Catolica v Independiente	3-2	3-3
Independiente won on away goals		
Atletico Mineiro v Botafogo	2-0	3-0

QUARTER-FINALS – FIRST LEG

Atletico Mineiro v La Equidad	2-1
Independiente v Independiente del Valle	2-1
Corinthians v Fluminense	0-0
Zulia v Colon	1-0

QUARTER-FINALS – SECOND LEG

Match	Score	*(agg)*
La Equidad v Atletico Mineiro	1-3	2-5
Independiente del Valle v Independiente	1-0	2-2
Independiente del Valle won on away goals		
Fluminense v Corinthians	1-1	1-1
Corinthians won on away goals		
Colon v Zulia	4-0	4-1

SEMI-FINALS – FIRST LEG

Colon v Atletico Mineiro	2-1
Corinthians v Independiente del Valle	0-2

SEMI-FINALS – SECOND LEG

Match	Score	*(agg)*
Atletico Mineiro v Colon	2-1	3-3
Colon won 4-3 on penalties		
Independiente del Valle v Corinthians	2-2	4-2

COPA SUDAMERICANA FINAL 2019

Asuncion, Saturday 9 November 2019

Independiente del Valle (2) 3 *(Leon 24, Sanchez 41, Dajome 90)*

Colon (0) 1 *(Olivera 88)*

Independiente de Valle: Pinos; Landazuri, Leon, Schunke, Segovia, Pellerano, Dajome, Franco, Mera (Garces 79), Sanchez (Cabeza 74), Torres (Corozo 85).
Colon: Burian; Vigo (Ortega 65), Ortiz, Olivera, Escobar (Esparza 69), Bernardi (Chancalay 76), Lertora, Zuqui, Estigarribia, Rodriguez, Morelo.
Referee: Raphael Claus (Brazil).

COPA LIBERTADORES 2019

▪ *Denotes player sent off.*

THIRD STAGE – FIRST LEG

Defensor Sporting v Atletico Mineiro	0-2
Melgar v Caracas	2-0
Libertad v Atletico Nacional	1-0
Talleres v Palestino	2-2

THIRD STAGE – SECOND LEG

		(agg)
Atletico Mineiro v Defensor Sporting	0-0	2-0
Caracas v Melgar	2-1	2-3
Atletico Nacional v Libertad	1-0	1-1
Libertad won 5-4 on penalties		
Palestino v Talleres	2-1	4-3

GROUP STAGES

GROUP A

Palestino v Internacional	0-1
Alianza Lima v River Plate	1-1
Internacional v Alianza Lima	2-0
River Plate v Palestino	0-0
Palestino v Alianza Lima	3-0
Internacional v River Plate	2-2
Internacional v Palestino	3-2
River Plate v Alianza Lima	3-0
Palestino v River Plate	0-2
Alianza Lima v Internacional	0-1
River Plate v Internacional	2-2
Alianza Lima v Palestino	1-2

Group A Table	P	W	D	L	F	A	GD	Pts
Internacional	6	4	2	0	11	6	5	14
River Plate	6	2	4	0	10	5	5	10
Palestino	6	2	1	3	7	7	0	7
Alianza Lima	6	0	1	5	2	12	–10	1

GROUP B

Huracan v Cruzeiro	0-1
Deportivo Lara v Emelec	0-0
Emelec v Huracan	0-0
Cruzeiro v Deportivo Lara	2-0
Emelec v Cruzeiro	0-1
Deportivo Lara v Huracan	2-1
Cruzeiro v Huracan	4-0
Emelec v Deportivo Lara	2-2
Deportivo Lara v Cruzeiro	0-2
Huracan v Emelec	1-2
Cruzeiro v Emelec	1-2
Huracan v Deportivo Lara	3-0

Group B Table	P	W	D	L	F	A	GD	Pts
Cruzeiro	6	5	0	1	11	2	9	15
Emelec	6	2	3	1	6	5	1	9
Deportivo Lara	6	1	2	3	4	10	–6	5
Huracan	6	1	1	4	5	9	–4	4

GROUP C

Godoy Cruz v Olimpia	0-0
Universidad de Concepcion v Sporting Cristal	5-4
Olimpia v Universidad de Concepcion	1-1
Sporting Cristal v Godoy Cruz	1-1
Universidad de Concepcion v Godoy Cruz	0-0
Sporting Cristal v Olimpia	0-3
Olimpia v Godoy Cruz	2-1
Sporting Cristal v Universidad de Concepcion	2-0
Universidad de Concepcion v Olimpia	3-3
Godoy Cruz v Sporting Cristal	2-0
Olimpia v Sporting Cristal	0-1
Godoy Cruz v Universidad de Concepcion	1-0

Group C Table	P	W	D	L	F	A	GD	Pts
Olimpia	6	2	3	1	9	6	3	9
Godoy Cruz	6	2	3	1	5	3	2	9
Sporting Cristal	6	2	1	3	8	11	–3	7
Universidad de Concepcion	6	1	3	2	9	11	–2	6

GROUP D

San Jose v Flamengo	0-1
LDU Quito v Penarol	2-0
Flamengo v LDU Quito	3-1
Penarol v San Jose	4-0
San Jose v LDU Quito	3-3
Flamengo v Penarol	0-1
Penarol v LDU Quito	1-0
Flamengo v San Jose	6-1
LDU Quito v Flamengo	2-1
San Jose v Penarol	3-1
Penarol v Flamengo	0-0
LDU Quito v San Jose	4-0

Group D Table	P	W	D	L	F	A	GD	Pts
Flamengo	6	3	1	2	11	5	6	10
LDU Quito	6	3	1	2	12	8	4	10
Penarol	6	3	1	2	7	5	2	10
San Jose	6	1	1	4	7	19	–12	4

GROUP E

Atletico Mineiro v Cerro Porteno	0-1
Zamora v Nacional	0-1
Nacional v Atletico Mineiro	1-0
Cerro Porteno v Zamora	2-1
Cerro Porteno v Nacional	1-0
Atletico Mineiro v Zamora	3-2
Cerro Porteno v Atletico Mineiro	4-1
Nacional v Zamora	1-0
Atletico Mineiro v Nacional	0-1
Zamora v Cerro Porteno	2-1
Nacional v Cerro Porteno	1-1
Zamora v Atletico Mineiro	1-2

Group E Table	P	W	D	L	F	A	GD	Pts
Cerro Porteno	6	4	1	1	10	5	5	13
Nacional	6	4	1	1	5	2	3	13
Atletico Mineiro	6	2	0	4	6	10	–4	6
Zamora	6	1	0	5	6	10	–4	3

GROUP F

Melgar v San Lorenzo	0-0
Junior v Palmeiras	0-2
Palmeiras v Melgar	3-0
San Lorenzo v Junior	1-0
San Lorenzo v Palmeiras	1-0
Melgar v Junior	1-0
San Lorenzo v Melgar	2-0
Palmeiras v Junior	3-0
Junior v San Lorenzo	1-0
Melgar v Palmeiras	0-4
Palmeiras v San Lorenzo	1-0
Junior v Melgar	0-1

Group F Table	P	W	D	L	F	A	GD	Pts
Palmeiras	6	5	0	1	13	1	12	15
San Lorenzo	6	3	1	2	4	2	2	10
Melgar	6	2	1	3	2	9	–7	7
Junior	6	1	0	5	1	8	–7	3

GROUP G

Deportes Tolima v Athletico Paranaense	1-0
Jorge Wilstermann v Boca Juniors	0-0
Boca Juniors v Deportes Tolima	3-0
Athletico Paranaense v Jorge Wilstermann	4-0
Athletico Paranaense v Boca Juniors	3-0
Deportes Tolima v Jorge Wilstermann	2-2
Athletico Paranaense v Deportes Tolima	1-0
Boca Juniors v Jorge Wilstermann	4-0
Jorge Wilstermann v Athletico Paranaense	3-2
Deportes Tolima v Boca Juniors	2-2
Boca Juniors v Athletico Paranaense	2-1
Jorge Wilstermann v Deportes Tolima	0-2

Group G Table	P	W	D	L	F	A	GD	Pts
Boca Juniors	6	3	2	1	11	6	5	11
Athletico Paranaense	6	3	0	3	11	6	5	9
Deportes Tolima	6	2	2	2	7	8	–1	8
Jorge Wilstermann	6	1	2	3	5	14	–9	5

GROUP H

Libertad v Universidad Catolica	4-1
Rosario Central v Gremio	1-1
Gremio v Libertad	0-1
Universidad Catolica v Rosario Central	2-1
Universidad Catolica v Gremio	1-0
Libertad v Rosario Central	2-0
Universidad Catolica v Libertad	2-3
Gremio v Rosario Central	3-1
Libertad v Gremio	0-2
Rosario Central v Universidad Catolica	1-1
Gremio v Universidad Catolica	2-0
Rosario Central v Libertad	2-1

Group H Table	P	W	D	L	F	A	GD	Pts
Libertad	6	4	0	2	11	7	4	12
Gremio	6	3	1	2	8	4	4	10
Universidad Catolica	6	2	1	3	7	11	–4	7
Rosario Central	6	1	2	3	6	10	–4	5

ROUND OF 16 – FIRST LEG

River Plate v Cruzeiro	0-0
Godoy Cruz v Palmeiras	2-2
Emelec v Flamengo	2-0
LDU Quito v Olimpia	3-1
Athletico Paranaense v Boca Juniors	0-1
Nacional v Internacional	0-1
Gremio v Libertad	2-0
San Lorenzo v Cerro Porteno	0-0

ROUND OF 16 – SECOND LEG

		(agg)
Cruzeiro v River Plate	0-0	0-0
River Plate won 4-2 on penalties		
Palmeiras v Godoy Cruz	4-0	6-2
Flamengo v Emelec	2-0	2-2
Flamengo won 4-2 on penalties		
Olimpia v LDU Quito	1-1	2-4
Boca Juniors v Athletico Paranaense	2-0	3-0
Internacional v Nacional	2-0	3-0
Libertad v Gremio	0-3	0-5
Cerro Porteno v San Lorenzo	2-1	2-1

QUARTER-FINALS – FIRST LEG

River Plate v Cerro Porteno	2-0
Gremio v Palmeiras	0-1
Flamengo v Internacional	2-0
LDU Quito v Boca Juniors	0-3

QUARTER-FINALS – SECOND LEG

		(agg)
Cerro Porteno v River Plate	1-1	1-3
Palmeiras v Gremio	1-2	2-2
Gremio won on away goals		
Internacional v Flamengo	1-1	1-3
Boca Juniors v LDU Quito	0-0	3-0

SEMI-FINALS – FIRST LEG

River Plate v Boca Juniors	2-0
Gremio v Flamengo	1-1

SEMI-FINALS – SECOND LEG

		(agg)
Boca Juniors v River Plate	1-0	1-2
Flamengo v Gremio	5-0	6-1

COPA LIBERTADORES FINAL 2019

Lima, Saturday 23 November 2019

Flamengo (0) 2 *(Gabriel Barbosa 89, 90)*

River Plate (1) 1 *(Borre 14)*

Flamengo: Diego Alves; Rafinha, Rodrigo Caio, Mari, Filipe Luis, Willian Arao (Vitinho 65), Gerson (Diego 65), Everton Ribeiro, De Arrascaeta (Da Motta 90), Bruno Henrique, Gabriel Barbosa■.
River Plate: Armani; Montiel, Martinez L, Pinola, Casco (Diaz 76), Perez, Fernandez (Alvarez 68), Palacios■, De La Cruz, Borre (Pratto 74), Suarez.
Referee: Roberto Tobar (Chile).

RECOPA SUDAMERICANA 2019

FINAL – FIRST LEG

Independiente del Valle v Flamengo	2-2

FINAL – SECOND LEG

		(agg)
Flamengo v Independiente del Valle	3-0	5-2

NORTH AMERICA

MAJOR LEAGUE SOCCER 2019

**After extra time.*

EASTERN CONFERENCE

	P	W	D	L	F	A	GD	Pts
New York City	34	18	6	10	63	42	21	64
Atlanta United	34	18	12	4	58	43	15	58
Philadelphia Union	34	16	11	7	58	50	8	55
Toronto	34	13	10	11	57	52	5	50
DC United	34	13	10	11	42	38	4	50
New York Red Bulls	34	14	14	6	53	51	2	48
New England Revolution	34	11	11	12	50	57	–7	45
Chicago Fire	34	10	12	12	55	47	8	42
Montreal Impact	34	12	17	5	47	60	–13	41
Columbus Crew	34	10	16	8	39	47	–8	38
Orlando City	34	9	15	10	44	52	–8	37
FC Cincinnati	34	6	22	6	31	75	–44	24

WESTERN CONFERENCE

	P	W	D	L	F	A	GD	Pts
Los Angeles	34	21	4	9	85	37	48	72
Seattle Sounders	34	16	10	8	51	49	2	56
Real Salt Lake	34	16	13	5	45	41	4	53
Minnesota United	34	15	11	8	52	42	10	53
LA Galaxy	34	16	15	3	56	55	1	51
Portland Timbers	34	14	13	7	49	48	1	49
FC Dallas	34	13	12	9	48	46	2	48
San Jose Earthquakes	34	13	16	5	51	52	–1	44
Colorado Rapids	34	12	16	6	57	60	–3	42
Houston Dynamo	34	12	18	4	45	57	–12	40
Sporting Kansas City	34	10	16	8	49	67	–18	38
Vancouver Whitecaps	34	8	16	10	37	58	–21	34

EASTERN CONFERENCE FIRST ROUND

Atlanta United v New England Revolution	1-0
Toronto v DC United	5-1*
Philadelphia Union v New York Red Bulls	4-3*

WESTERN CONFERENCE FIRST ROUND

Seattle Sounders v FC Dallas	4-3*
Real Salt Lake v Portland Timbers	2-1
Minnesota United v LA Galaxy	1-2

EASTERN CONFERENCE SEMI-FINALS

New York City v Toronto	1-2
Atlanta United v Philadelphia Union	2-0

WESTERN CONFERENCE SEMI-FINALS

Seattle Sounders v Real Salt Lake	2-0
Los Angeles v LA Galaxy	5-3

EASTERN CONFERENCE FINAL

Atlanta United v Toronto	1-2

WESTERN CONFERENCE FINAL

Los Angeles v Seattle Sounders	1-3

MLS CUP FINAL 2019

Washington, Sunday 10 November 2019

Seattle Sounders (0) 3 *(Leerdam 57, Rodriguez 76, Ruidiaz 90)*

Toronto (0) 1 *(Altidore 90)* 69,274

Seattle Sounders: Frei; Leerdam, Torres, Kee-hee, Smith (Rodriguez 61), Svensson, Roldan, Jones, Lodeiro, Morris (Delem 85), Ruidiaz (Arreaga 90)
Toronto: Westberg; Auro, Mavinga, Gonzalez, Morrow, Delgado, Bradley, Osorio (Laryea 77), Endoh (DeLeon 62), Pozuelo, Benezet (Altidore 68).
Referee: Allen Chapman.

UEFA YOUTH LEAGUE 2019–20

CHAMPIONS LEAGUE PATH

GROUP A

Club Brugge v Galatasaray	3-2
Paris Saint-Germain v Real Madrid	1-2
Real Madrid v Club Brugge	3-0
Galatasaray v Paris Saint-Germain	1-5
Galatasaray v Real Madrid	0-1
Club Brugge v Paris Saint-Germain	2-0
Paris Saint-Germain v Club Brugge	0-4
Real Madrid v Galatasaray	2-4
Galatasaray v Club Brugge	2-1
Real Madrid v Paris Saint-Germain	6-3
Club Brugge v Real Madrid	2-2
Paris Saint-Germain v Galatasaray	1-0

Group A Table	P	W	D	L	F	A	GD	Pts
Real Madrid	6	4	1	1	16	10	6	13
Club Brugge	6	3	1	2	12	9	3	10
Paris Saint-Germain	6	2	0	4	10	15	–5	6
Galatasaray	6	2	0	4	9	13	–4	6

GROUP B

Olympiacos v Tottenham H	1-1
Bayern Munich v Red Star Belgrade	0-0
Tottenham H v Bayern Munich	1-4
Red Star Belgrade v Olympiacos	2-1
Tottenham H v Red Star Belgrade	9-2
Olympiacos v Bayern Munich	0-4
Bayern Munich v Olympiacos	6-0
Red Star Belgrade v Tottenham H	2-0
Tottenham H v Olympiacos	1-0
Red Star Belgrade v Bayern Munich	1-1
Olympiacos v Red Star Belgrade	0-1
Bayern Munich v Tottenham H	3-0

Group B Table	P	W	D	L	F	A	GD	Pts
Bayern Munich	6	4	2	0	18	2	16	14
Red Star Belgrade	6	3	2	1	8	11	–3	11
Tottenham H	6	2	1	3	12	12	0	7
Olympiacos	6	0	1	5	2	15	–13	1

GROUP C

Shakhtar Donetsk v Manchester C	1-3
Dinamo Zagreb v Atalanta	1-0
Atalanta v Shakhtar Donetsk	2-2
Manchester C v Dinamo Zagreb	2-2
Shakhtar Donetsk v Dinamo Zagreb	1-1
Manchester C v Atalanta	1-3
Atalanta v Manchester C	1-0
Dinamo Zagreb v Shakhtar Donetsk	1-0
Atalanta v Dinamo Zagreb	2-0
Manchester C v Shakhtar Donetsk	5-0
Shakhtar Donetsk v Atalanta	1-2
Dinamo Zagreb v Manchester C	1-0

Group C Table	P	W	D	L	F	A	GD	Pts
Atalanta	6	4	1	1	10	5	5	13
Dinamo Zagreb	6	3	2	1	6	5	1	11
Manchester C	6	2	1	3	11	8	3	7
Shakhtar Donetsk	6	0	2	4	5	14	–9	2

GROUP D

Atletico Madrid v Juventus	0-4
Bayer Leverkusen v Lokomotiv Moscow	2-2
Lokomotiv Moscow v Atletico Madrid	2-3
Juventus v Bayer Leverkusen	4-1
Juventus v Lokomotiv Moscow	1-2
Atletico Madrid v Bayer Leverkusen	2-0
Lokomotiv Moscow v Juventus	0-1
Bayer Leverkusen v Atletico Madrid	0-2
Lokomotiv Moscow v Bayer Leverkusen	1-3
Juventus v Atletico Madrid	2-1
Bayer Leverkusen v Juventus	0-5
Atletico Madrid v Lokomotiv Moscow	3-0

Group D Table	P	W	D	L	F	A	GD	Pts
Juventus	6	5	0	1	17	4	13	15
Atletico Madrid	6	4	0	2	11	8	3	12
Bayer Leverkusen	6	1	1	4	6	16	–10	4
Lokomotiv Moscow	6	1	1	4	7	13	–6	4

GROUP E

Napoli v Liverpool	1-1
Red Bull Salzburg v Genk	1-1
Genk v Napoli	3-1
Liverpool v Red Bull Salzburg	4-2
Genk v Liverpool	0-2
Red Bull Salzburg v Napoli	7-2
Napoli v Red Bull Salzburg	1-5
Liverpool v Genk	0-1
Genk v Red Bull Salzburg	0-2
Liverpool v Napoli	7-0
Napoli v Genk	0-0
Red Bull Salzburg v Liverpool	2-3

Group E Table	P	W	D	L	F	A	GD	Pts
Liverpool	6	4	1	1	17	6	11	13
Red Bull Salzburg	6	3	1	2	19	11	8	10
Genk	6	2	2	2	5	6	–1	8
Napoli	6	0	2	4	5	23	–18	2

GROUP F

Internazionale v Slavia Prague	4-0
Borussia Dortmund v Barcelona	2-1
Slavia Prague v Borussia Dortmund	1-0
Barcelona v Internazionale	0-3
Slavia Prague v Barcelona	0-4
Internazionale v Borussia Dortmund	4-1
Barcelona v Slavia Prague	2-3
Borussia Dortmund v Internazionale	2-1
Slavia Prague v Internazionale	4-1
Barcelona v Borussia Dortmund	1-2
Internazionale v Barcelona	2-0
Borussia Dortmund v Slavia Prague	5-1

Group F Table	P	W	D	L	F	A	GD	Pts
Internazionale	6	4	0	2	15	7	8	12
Borussia Dortmund	6	4	0	2	12	9	3	12
Slavia Prague	6	3	0	3	9	16	–7	9
Barcelona	6	1	0	5	8	12	–4	3

GROUP G

Lyon v Zenit St Petersburg	4-2
Benfica v RB Leipzig	2-1
Zenit St Petersburg v Benfica	1-7
RB Leipzig v Lyon	1-3
RB Leipzig v Zenit St Petersburg	1-1
Benfica v Lyon	1-2
Zenit St Petersburg v RB Leipzig	0-2
Lyon v Benfica	2-3
Zenit St Petersburg v Lyon	3-1
RB Leipzig v Benfica	0-3
Lyon v RB Leipzig	1-0
Benfica v Zenit St Petersburg	1-0

Group G Table	P	W	D	L	F	A	GD	Pts
Benfica	6	5	0	1	17	6	11	15
Lyon	6	4	0	2	13	10	3	12
RB Leipzig	6	1	1	4	5	10	–5	4
Zenit St Petersburg	6	1	1	4	7	16	–9	4

GROUP H

Ajax v Lille	4-0
Chelsea v Valencia	3-3
Valencia v Ajax	3-5
Lille v Chelsea	2-0
Lille v Valencia	1-0
Ajax v Chelsea	0-1
Valencia v Lille	1-2
Chelsea v Ajax	1-1
Lille v Ajax	1-2
Valencia v Chelsea	2-1
Ajax v Valencia	1-1
Chelsea v Lille	1-1

Group H Table	P	W	D	L	F	A	GD	Pts
Ajax	6	3	2	1	13	7	6	11
Lille	6	3	1	2	7	8	–1	10
Chelsea	6	1	3	2	7	9	–2	6
Valencia	6	1	2	3	10	13	–3	5

DOMESTIC CHAMPIONS PATH

FIRST ROUND – FIRST LEG

APOEL v Gabala	1-1
Shkendija Tirane v Sheriff	1-2
MTK Budapest v Zrinjski Mostar	1-1
Real Zaragoza v Korona Kielce	1-0
FC Minsk v Derby Co	0-2
Elfsborg v Midtjylland	1-2
Sogndal v FC Honka	3-1
IA Akranes v FCI Levadia	4-0
Bohemians v PAOK	1-1
Rennes v Brodarac	2-1
Young Boys v Rangers	3-3
Porto v FK Liepaja	4-2
Viitorul Constanta v Domzale	0-0
Slovan Bratislava v Ludogorets Razgrad	1-0
Dynamo Kyiv v Shkendija	8-0
Astana v Maccabi Petah Tikva	1-0

FIRST ROUND – SECOND LEG

		(agg)
Gabala v APOEL	0-1	1-2
Sheriff v Shkendija Tirane	1-0	3-1
Zrinjski Mostar v MTK Budapest	2-0	3-1
Korona Kielce v Real Zaragoza	1-4	1-5
Derby Co v FC Minsk	7-2	9-2
Midtjylland v Elfsborg	1-0	3-1
FC Honka v Sogndal	1-1	2-4
FCI Levadia v IA Akranes	1-12	1-16
PAOK v Bohemians	1-0	2-1
Brodarac v Rennes	0-0	1-2
Rangers v Young Boys	2-2	5-5
Rangers won on away goals.		
FK Liepaja v Porto	0-3	2-7
Domzale v Viitorul Constanta	2-0	2-0
Ludogorets Razgrad v Slovan Bratislava	1-0	1-1
Slovan Bratislava won 4-2 on penalties.		
Shkendija v Dynamo Kyiv	2-2	2-10
Maccabi Petah Tikva v Astana	4-0	4-1

SECOND ROUND – FIRST LEG

Sheriff v Sogndal	2-0
Real Zaragoza v APOEL	5-0
Midtjylland v Zrinjski Mostar	3-1
IA v Derby Co	1-2
Porto v Domzale	2-2
Dynamo Kyiv v PAOK	3-0
Rangers v Slovan Bratislava	2-0
Rennes v Maccabi Petah Tikva	2-0

SECOND ROUND – SECOND LEG

		(agg)
Sogndal v Sheriff	3-1	3-3
Sheriff won on away goals.		
APOEL v Real Zaragoza	0-4	0-9
Zrinjski Mostar v Midtjylland	0-0	1-3
Derby Co v IA	4-1	6-2
Domzale v Porto	0-3	2-5
PAOK v Dynamo Kyiv	2-2	2-5
Slovan Bratislava v Rangers	1-2	1-4
Maccabi Petah Tikva v Rennes	0-1	0-3

PLAY-OFFS

Derby Co v Borussia Dortmund	3-1
Porto v Red Bull Salzburg	1-1
Red Bull Salzburg won 7-6 on penalties.	
Real Zaragoza v Lyon	1-3
Dynamo Kyiv v Dinamo Zagreb	0-0
Dinamo Zagreb won 4-3 on penalties.	
Sheriff v Red Star Belgrade	0-0
Red Star Belgrade won 4-2 on penalties.	
Rangers v Atletico Madrid	0-4
Midtjylland v Lille	1-1
Midtjylland won 7-6 on penalties.	
Rennes v Club Brugge	1-1
Rennes won 5-3 on penalties.	

KNOCKOUT STAGE

ROUND OF 16

Bayern Munich v Dinamo Zagreb	2-2
Dinamo Zagreb won 6-5 on penalties.	
Ajax v Atletico Madrid	0-0
Ajax won 6-5 on penalties.	
Atalanta v Lyon	3-3
Lyon won 5-3 on penalties.	
Red Bull Salzburg v Derby Co	4-1
Internazionale v Rennes	
Postponed	
Benfica v Liverpool	4-1
Red Star Belgrade v Midtjylland	0-3
Juventus v Real Madrid	
Postponed	

QUARTER-FINALS

Internazionale v Real Madrid	0-3
Red Bull Salzburg v Lyon	4-3
Midtjylland v Ajax	1-3
Dinamo Zagreb v Benfica	1-3

SEMI-FINALS

Benfica v Ajax	3-0
Red Bull Salzburg v Real Madrid	1-2

UEFA YOUTH LEAGUE FINAL 2019–20

Nyon, Tuesday 25 August 2020

Benfica (0) 2 *(Goncalo Ramos 47, 57)*

Real Madrid (2) 3 *(Rodriguez 26, Henrique Jocu 45 (og), Gutierrez 50)*

Benfica: Kokubo; Cruz (Brito 46), Morato, Araujo T (Neto 90), Ferreira, Dantas, Jocu (Camara 46), Araujo H, Ramos,
Embalo (Lopez 63).
Real Madrid: Lopez; Santos, Ramon, Chust, Gutierrez (Carrillo 66), Blanco, Park (Sintes 65), Arribas, Morante (Aranda 73), Dotor (Peter 73), Rodriguez (Jordi 30).
Referee: Chris Kavanagh (England).

ENGLAND C 2019–20

Caernarfon, Tuesday 24 March 2020

Wales C v England C

(Postponed due to the COVID-19 pandemic)

Aldershot, Monday 25 May 2020

England C v Nepal

(Postponed due to the COVID-19 pandemic)

UEFA UNDER-19 CHAMPIONSHIP 2018–19

FINALS IN ARMENIA

GROUP A
Armenia v Spain 1-4
Italy v Portugal 0-3
Portugal v Spain 1-1
Armenia v Italy 0-4
Portugal v Armenia 4-0
Spain v Italy 2-1

Group A Table	P	W	D	L	F	A	GD	Pts
Portugal	3	2	1	0	8	1	+7	7
Spain	3	2	1	0	7	3	+4	7
Italy	3	1	0	2	5	5	0	3
Armenia	3	0	0	3	1	12	–11	0

GROUP B
Norway v Republic of Ireland 1-1
Czech Republic v France 0-3
Czech Republic v Norway 0-0
Republic of Ireland v France 0-1
Republic of Ireland v Czech Republic 2-1
France v Norway 1-0

Group B Table	P	W	D	L	F	A	GD	Pts
France	3	3	0	0	5	0	+5	9
Republic of Ireland	3	1	1	1	3	3	0	4
Norway	3	0	2	1	1	2	–1	2
Czech Republic	3	0	1	2	1	5	–4	1

SEMI-FINALS
Portugal v Republic of Ireland 4-0
France v Spain 0-0*
Spain won 4-3 on penalties.

FINAL
Yerevan, 27 July 2019
Portugal (0) 0 **Spain (1) 2** *(Torres 34, 51)* 7150
Portugal: Biai; Costinha, Loureiro, Cardoso, Capitao, Mario (Gouveia 57), Ferreira (Costa 64), Ramos, Vieira (Silva 75), Correia (Gomes 76), Tavares.
Spain: Tenas; Gomez V, Miranda, Guillamon, Blanco, Torres (Chust 90), Moha (Mollejo 87), Ruiz (Marques 90), Gomez S (Barrenetxea 80), Garcia E, Gill (Orellana 80).
Referee: Sergey Ivanov (Russia).

UEFA UNDER-19 CHAMPIONSHIP 2019–20

QUALIFYING ROUND

GROUP 1 (TURKEY)
Montenegro v Bulgaria 1-3
Turkey v Armenia 4-1
Bulgaria v Armenia 3-0
Turkey v Montenegro 2-1
Armenia v Montenegro 3-3
Bulgaria v Turkey 1-2

Group 1 Table	P	W	D	L	F	A	GD	Pts
Turkey	3	3	0	0	8	3	5	9
Bulgaria	3	2	0	1	7	3	4	6
Montenegro	3	0	1	2	5	8	–3	1
Armenia	3	0	1	2	4	10	–6	1

GROUP 2 (SERBIA)
Spain v Lithuania 2-0
Romania v Serbia 1-1
Serbia v Lithuania 8-0
Spain v Romania 1-0
Lithuania v Romania 1-0
Serbia v Spain 0-4

Group 2 Table	P	W	D	L	F	A	GD	Pts
Spain	3	3	0	0	7	0	7	9
Serbia	3	1	1	1	9	5	4	4
Lithuania	3	1	0	2	1	10	–9	3
Romania	3	0	1	2	1	3	–2	1

GROUP 3 (SCOTLAND)
Germany v Andorra 3-0
Belarus v Scotland 2-2
Scotland v Andorra 2-0
Germany v Belarus 9-2
Andorra v Belarus 0-2
Scotland v Germany 1-0

Group 3 Table	P	W	D	L	F	A	GD	Pts
Scotland	3	2	1	0	5	2	3	7
Germany	3	2	0	1	12	3	9	6
Belarus	3	1	1	1	6	11	–5	4
Andorra	3	0	0	3	0	7	–7	0

GROUP 4 (BELGIUM)
Iceland v Belgium 0-3
Greece v Albania 5-1
Belgium v Albania 2-1
Greece v Iceland 2-5
Albania v Iceland 2-4
Belgium v Greece 1-0

Group 4 Table	P	W	D	L	F	A	GD	Pts
Belgium	3	3	0	0	6	1	5	9
Iceland	3	2	0	1	9	7	2	6
Greece	3	1	0	2	7	7	0	3
Albania	3	0	0	3	4	11	–7	0

GROUP 5 (WALES)
Wales v Poland 3-0
Russia v Kosovo 1-1
Poland v Kosovo 4-1
Russia v Wales 2-2
Kosovo v Wales 0-2
Poland v Russia 0-4

Group 5 Table	P	W	D	L	F	A	GD	Pts
Wales	3	2	1	0	7	2	5	7
Russia	3	1	2	0	7	3	4	5
Poland	3	1	0	2	4	8	–4	3
Kosovo	3	0	1	2	2	7	–5	1

GROUP 6 (ITALY)
Cyprus v Slovakia 1-2
Italy v Malta 2-0
Slovakia v Malta 3-0
Italy v Cyprus 2-0
Malta v Cyprus 0-2
Slovakia v Italy 0-3

Group 6 Table	P	W	D	L	F	A	GD	Pts
Italy	3	3	0	0	7	0	7	9
Slovakia	3	2	0	1	5	4	1	6
Cyprus	3	1	0	2	3	4	–1	3
Malta	3	0	0	3	0	7	–7	0

GROUP 7 (CZECH REPUBLIC)
Azerbaijan v Norway 0-1
Czech Republic v San Marino 6-0
Norway v San Marino 8-1
Czech Republic v Azerbaijan 4-0
San Marino v Azerbaijan 0-2
Norway v Czech Republic 1-1

Group 7 Table	P	W	D	L	F	A	GD	Pts
Czech Republic	3	2	1	0	11	1	10	7
Norway	3	2	1	0	10	2	8	7
Azerbaijan	3	1	0	2	2	5	–3	3
San Marino	3	0	0	3	1	16	–15	0

GROUP 8 (DENMARK)
France v Faroe Islands 5-0
Finland v Denmark 2-1
France v Finland 2-0
Denmark v Faroe Islands 2-0
Faroe Islands v Finland 1-1
Denmark v France 1-0

Group 8 Table	P	W	D	L	F	A	GD	Pts
Denmark	3	2	0	1	4	2	2	6
France	3	2	0	1	7	1	6	6
Finland	3	1	1	1	3	4	–1	4
Faroe Islands	3	0	1	2	1	8	–7	1

GROUP 9 (SWEDEN)

Ukraine v Estonia 4-0
Slovenia v Sweden 2-2
Sweden v Estonia 4-0
Ukraine v Slovenia 1-1
Estonia v Slovenia 0-7
Sweden v Ukraine 1-2

Group 9 Table	P	W	D	L	F	A	GD	Pts
Ukraine	3	2	1	0	7	2	5	7
Slovenia	3	1	2	0	10	3	7	5
Sweden	3	1	1	1	7	4	3	4
Estonia	3	0	0	3	0	15	–15	0

GROUP 10 (AUSTRIA)

Switzerland v Republic of Ireland 2-1
Austria v Gibraltar 14-0
Republic of Ireland v Gibraltar 13-0
Austria v Switzerland 2-1
Gibraltar v Switzerland 1-16
Republic of Ireland v Austria 0-2

Group 10 Table	P	W	D	L	F	A	GD	Pts
Austria	3	3	0	0	18	1	17	9
Switzerland	3	2	0	1	19	4	15	6
Republic of Ireland	3	1	0	2	14	4	10	3
Gibraltar	3	0	0	3	1	43	–42	0

GROUP 11 (NORTH MACEDONIA)

North Macedonia v Bosnia-Herzegovina 0-0
England v Luxembourg 4-0
Bosnia-Herzegovina v Luxembourg 1-0
England v North Macedonia 5-0
Luxembourg v North Macedonia 0-3
Bosnia-Herzegovina v England 1-4

Group 11 Table	P	W	D	L	F	A	GD	Pts
England	3	3	0	0	13	1	12	9
North Macedonia	3	1	1	1	3	5	–2	4
Bosnia-Herzegovina	3	1	1	1	2	4	–2	4
Luxembourg	3	0	0	3	0	8	–8	0

GROUP 12 (LATVIA)

Netherlands v Moldova 5-0
Latvia v Israel 0-0
Israel v Moldova 2-0
Netherlands v Latvia 8-2
Moldova v Latvia 0-6
Israel v Netherlands 0-2

Group 12 Table	P	W	D	L	F	A	GD	Pts
Netherlands	3	3	0	0	15	2	13	9
Latvia	3	1	1	1	8	8	0	4
Israel	3	1	1	1	2	2	0	4
Moldova	3	0	0	3	0	13	–13	0

GROUP 13 (HUNGARY)

Croatia v Kazakhstan 3-0
Hungary v Georgia 2-4
Georgia v Kazakhstan 3-1
Croatia v Hungary 2-0
Kazakhstan v Hungary 0-5
Georgia v Croatia 2-0

Group 13 Table	P	W	D	L	F	A	GD	Pts
Georgia	3	3	0	0	9	3	6	9
Croatia	3	2	0	1	5	2	3	6
Hungary	3	1	0	2	7	6	1	3
Kazakhstan	3	0	0	3	1	11	–10	0

ELITE ROUND

The Elite Round was due to take place between 25 March 2020 and 31 March 2020, but due to the COVID-19 pandemic it was postponed by UEFA until further notice.

QUALIFYING TEAMS

Group 1: Turkey, Bulgaria
Group 2: Spain, Serbia
Group 3: Scotland, Germany
Group 4: Belgium, Iceland
Group 5: Wales, Russia
Group 6: Italy, Slovakia
Group 7: Czech Republic, Norway
Group 8: Denmark, France, Finland (best 3rd-placed)
Group 9: Ukraine, Slovenia
Group 10: Austria, Switzerland
Group 11: England, North Macedonia
Group 12: Netherlands, Latvia
Group 13: Georgia, Croatia

ELITE ROUND DRAW

GROUP 1 (WALES)
Austria, Wales, Germany, Serbia

GROUP 2 (SPAIN)
Spain, Belgium, Bulgaria, North Macedonia

GROUP 3 (FRANCE)
Georgia, Scotland, France, Russia

GROUP 4 (DENMARK)
England, Ukraine, Denmark, Latvia

GROUP 5 (ITALY)
Italy, Norway, Iceland, Slovenia

GROUP 6 (CROATIA)
Portugal, Turkey, Croatia, Slovakia

GROUP 7 (NETHERLANDS)
Netherlands, Czech Republic, Switzerland, Finland

Each group winner will qualify to join hosts Northern Ireland in the finals.

FINAL TOURNAMENT (NORTHERN IRELAND)

The finals were due to take place between 13 July 2020 and 26 July 2020, but due to the COVID-19 pandemic they were postponed by UEFA until further notice.

UEFA UNDER-17 CHAMPIONSHIP 2019–20

QUALIFYING ROUND

GROUP 1 (POLAND)

North Macedonia v Poland 2-3
Belgium v Liechtenstein 12-0
Belgium v North Macedonia 3-1
Poland v Liechtenstein 11-0
Liechtenstein v North Macedonia 0-4
Poland v Belgium 2-2

Group 1 Table	P	W	D	L	F	A	GD	Pts
Belgium	3	2	1	0	17	3	14	7
Poland	3	2	1	0	16	4	12	7
North Macedonia	3	1	0	2	7	6	1	3
Liechtenstein	3	0	0	3	0	27	–27	0

GROUP 2 (LUXEMBOURG)

Northern Ireland v Turkey 0-4
Italy v Luxembourg 6-0
Turkey v Luxembourg 4-1
Italy v Northern Ireland 2-0
Luxembourg v Northern Ireland 0-7
Turkey v Italy 0-4

Group 2 Table	P	W	D	L	F	A	GD	Pts
Italy	3	3	0	0	12	0	12	9
Turkey	3	2	0	1	8	5	3	6
Northern Ireland	3	1	0	2	7	6	1	3
Luxembourg	3	0	0	3	1	17	–16	0

GROUP 3 (REPUBLIC OF IRELAND)

Montenegro v Israel 0-1
Republic of Ireland v Andorra 6-0
Israel v Andorra 0-1
Republic of Ireland v Montenegro 3-1
Andorra v Montenegro 0-2
Israel v Republic of Ireland 2-4

Group 3 Table	P	W	D	L	F	A	GD	Pts
Republic of Ireland	3	3	0	0	13	3	10	9
Montenegro	3	1	0	2	3	4	–1	3
Israel	3	1	0	2	3	5	–2	3
Andorra	3	1	0	2	1	8	–7	3

GROUP 4 (SWEDEN)

Faroe Islands v Denmark 1-6
Sweden v Lithuania 4-2
Denmark v Lithuania 6-1
Sweden v Faroe Islands 2-0
Lithuania v Faroe Islands 4-1
Denmark v Sweden 5-1

Group 4 Table	P	W	D	L	F	A	GD	Pts
Denmark	3	3	0	0	17	3	14	9
Sweden	3	2	0	1	7	7	0	6
Lithuania	3	1	0	2	7	11	–4	3
Faroe Islands	3	0	0	3	2	12	–10	0

GROUP 5 (CYPRUS)

Cyprus v Slovakia 0-3
France v Gibraltar 8-0
Slovakia v Gibraltar 9-1
France v Cyprus 2-0
Gibraltar v Cyprus 0-3
Slovakia v France 0-2

Group 5 Table	P	W	D	L	F	A	GD	Pts
France	3	3	0	0	12	0	12	9
Slovakia	3	2	0	1	12	3	9	6
Cyprus	3	1	0	2	3	5	–2	3
Gibraltar	3	0	0	3	1	20	–19	0

GROUP 6 (BELARUS)

Serbia v Latvia 1-2
Belarus v Hungary 0-0
Hungary v Latvia 3-0
Serbia v Belarus 2-1
Latvia v Belarus 0-1
Hungary v Serbia 0-0

Group 6 Table	P	W	D	L	F	A	GD	Pts
Hungary	3	1	2	0	3	0	3	5
Serbia	3	1	1	1	3	3	0	4
Belarus	3	1	1	1	2	2	0	4
Latvia	3	1	0	2	2	5	–3	3

GROUP 7 (SCOTLAND)

Iceland v Croatia 2-3
Scotland v Armenia 2-0
Croatia v Armenia 4-0
Scotland v Iceland 2-1
Armenia v Iceland 1-0
Croatia v Scotland 2-1

Group 7 Table	P	W	D	L	F	A	GD	Pts
Croatia	3	3	0	0	9	3	6	9
Scotland	3	2	0	1	5	3	2	6
Armenia	3	1	0	2	1	6	–5	3
Iceland	3	0	0	3	3	6	–3	0

GROUP 8 (PORTUGAL)

Georgia v Ukraine 0-2
Portugal v Albania 4-0
Ukraine v Albania 2-0
Portugal v Georgia 0-0
Albania v Georgia 0-0
Ukraine v Portugal 0-0

Group 8 Table	P	W	D	L	F	A	GD	Pts
Ukraine	3	2	1	0	4	0	4	7
Portugal	3	1	2	0	4	0	4	5
Georgia	3	0	2	1	0	2	–2	2
Albania	3	0	1	2	0	6	–6	1

GROUP 9 (GREECE)

Germany v Kazakhstan 5-0
Azerbaijan v Greece 1-6
Germany v Azerbaijan 2-0
Greece v Kazakhstan 5-1
Kazakhstan v Azerbaijan 2-0
Greece v Germany 2-0

Group 9 Table	P	W	D	L	F	A	GD	Pts
Greece	3	3	0	0	13	2	11	9
Germany	3	2	0	1	7	2	5	6
Kazakhstan	3	1	0	2	3	10	–7	3
Azerbaijan	3	0	0	3	1	10	–9	0

GROUP 10 (ROMANIA)

Russia v San Marino 7-0
Romania v Switzerland 0-1
Switzerland v San Marino 7-0
Russia v Romania 0-1
San Marino v Romania 0-6
Switzerland v Russia 1-2

Group 10 Table	P	W	D	L	F	A	GD	Pts
Russia	3	2	0	1	9	2	7	6
Switzerland	3	2	0	1	9	2	7	6
Romania	3	2	0	1	7	1	6	6
San Marino	3	0	0	3	0	20	–20	0

GROUP 11 (FINLAND)

Bosnia-Herzegovina v Moldova 3-0
Finland v Czech Republic 0-0
Bosnia-Herzegovina v Finland 1-2
Czech Republic v Moldova 0-0
Moldova v Finland 0-3
Czech Republic v Bosnia-Herzegovina 4-1

Group 11 Table	P	W	D	L	F	A	GD	Pts
Finland	3	2	1	0	5	1	4	7
Czech Republic	3	1	2	0	4	1	3	5
Bosnia-Herzegovina	3	1	0	2	5	6	–1	3
Moldova	3	0	1	2	0	6	–6	1

GROUP 12 (NETHERLANDS)

Wales v Slovenia 1-0
Netherlands v Kosovo 1-1
Slovenia v Kosovo 2-0
Netherlands v Wales 2-1
Kosovo v Wales 1-4
Slovenia v Netherlands 0-1

Group 12 Table	P	W	D	L	F	A	GD	Pts
Netherlands	3	2	1	0	4	2	2	7
Wales	3	2	0	1	6	3	3	6
Slovenia	3	1	0	2	2	2	0	3
Kosovo	3	0	1	2	2	7	–5	1

GROUP 13 (NORWAY)

Austria v Malta	6-0
Bulgaria v Norway	1-2
Austria v Bulgaria	4-1
Norway v Malta	8-0
Malta v Bulgaria	0-4
Norway v Austria	0-1

Group 13 Table	P	W	D	L	F	A	GD	Pts
Austria	3	3	0	0	11	1	10	9
Norway	3	2	0	1	10	2	8	6
Bulgaria	3	1	0	2	6	6	0	3
Malta	3	0	0	3	0	18	−18	0

ELITE ROUND

The Elite Round was due to take place between 25 March 2020 and 31 March 2020, but due to the COVID-19 pandemic it was cancelled by UEFA.

QUALIFYING TEAMS
Group 1: Belgium, Poland
Group 2: Italy, Turkey
Group 3: Republic of Ireland, Montenegro, Israel (best 3rd-placed)
Group 4: Denmark, Sweden
Group 5: France, Slovakia
Group 6: Hungary, Serbia, Belarus (best 3rd-placed)
Group 7: Croatia, Scotland
Group 8: Ukraine, Portugal, Georgia (best 3rd-placed)
Group 9: Greece, Germany
Group 10: Russia, Switzerland, Romania (best 3rd-placed)
Group 11: Finland, Czech Republic
Group 12: Netherlands, Wales
Group 13: Austria, Norway.

Spain and England received a bye to the Elite Round.

ELITE ROUND DRAW

GROUP 1 (TURKEY)
Greece, Ukraine, Turkey, Belarus

GROUP 2 (POLAND)
Italy, Poland, Wales, Montenegro

GROUP 3 (ISRAEL)
Spain, Croatia, Switzerland, Israel

GROUP 4 (SCOTLAND)
Republic of Ireland, Slovakia, Scotland, Czech Republic

GROUP 5 (AUSTRIA)
Austria, Netherlands, Germany, Portugal

GROUP 6 (BELGIUM)
England, Belgium, Romania, Georgia

GROUP 7 (RUSSIA)
Denmark, Finland, Russia, Serbia

GROUP 8 (HUNGARY)
France, Norway, Sweden, Hungary

FINAL TOURNAMENT (ESTONIA)

The finals were due to take place between 21 May 2020 and 6 June 2020, but due to the COVID-19 pandemic they were cancelled by UEFA.

UEFA UNDER-21 CHAMPIONSHIP 2019–21

QUALIFYING ROUND

All matches scheduled to be played between 25 March 2020 and 31 March 2020 have been postponed by UEFA due to the COVID-19 pandemic. For matches scheduled to be played from 3 September 2020 actual dates are to be confirmed.

GROUP 1

Republic of Ireland v Luxembourg 3-0
Iceland v Luxembourg 3-0
Republic of Ireland v Armenia 1-0
Iceland v Armenia 6-1
Sweden v Republic of Ireland 1-3
Italy v Luxembourg 5-0
Republic of Ireland v Italy 0-0
Armenia v Luxembourg 2-0
Sweden v Iceland 5-0
Armenia v Italy 0-1
Iceland v Republic of Ireland 1-0
Luxembourg v Sweden 0-3
Armenia v Republic of Ireland 0-1
Italy v Iceland 3-0
Republic of Ireland v Sweden 4-1
Italy v Armenia 6-0
Armenia v Sweden P-P
Republic of Ireland v Iceland P-P
Luxembourg v Italy P-P
Armenia v Iceland P-P
Italy v Sweden P-P
Luxembourg v Republic of Ireland P-P

Group 1 Table	*P*	*W*	*D*	*L*	*F*	*A*	*GD*	*Pts*
Republic of Ireland	7	5	1	1	12	3	9	16
Italy	5	4	1	0	15	0	15	13
Iceland	5	3	0	2	10	9	1	9
Sweden	4	2	0	2	10	7	3	6
Armenia	6	1	0	5	3	15	–12	3
Luxembourg	5	0	0	5	0	16	–16	0

GROUP 2

Liechtenstein v Azerbaijan 1-0
Georgia v Liechtenstein 4-0
Azerbaijan v Slovakia 2-1
Azerbaijan v Georgia 0-3
Liechtenstein v Switzerland 0-5
Liechtenstein v Slovakia 2-4
France v Azerbaijan 5-0
Switzerland v Georgia 2-1
Azerbaijan v Switzerland 0-1
Slovakia v France 3-5
Azerbaijan v Liechtenstein 1-0
France v Georgia 3-2
Slovakia v Georgia 3-2
Switzerland v France 3-1
Georgia v Slovakia P-P
Liechtenstein v France P-P
Switzerland v Azerbaijan P-P
France v Switzerland P-P
Slovakia v Liechtenstein P-P

Group 2 Table	*P*	*W*	*D*	*L*	*F*	*A*	*GD*	*Pts*
Switzerland	4	4	0	0	11	2	9	12
France	4	3	0	1	14	8	6	9
Georgia	5	2	0	3	12	8	4	6
Slovakia	4	2	0	2	11	11	0	6
Azerbaijan	6	2	0	4	3	11	–8	6
Liechtenstein	5	1	0	4	3	14	–11	3

GROUP 3

Albania v Turkey 1-2
Andorra v Albania 2-2
Andorra v Kosovo 0-4
Turkey v Albania 2-2
Kosovo v Turkey 3-1
Andorra v Austria 1-3
Turkey v England 2-3
Albania v Austria 0-4
England v Kosovo 2-0
Austria v Turkey 3-0
Albania v Kosovo 2-1
England v Austria 5-1
Austria v Kosovo 4-0
Albania v England 0-3
Andorra v Turkey 2-0
England v Andorra P-P
Kosovo v Albania P-P
Austria v Andorra P-P
England v Turkey P-P

Group 3 Table	*P*	*W*	*D*	*L*	*F*	*A*	*GD*	*Pts*
England	4	4	0	0	13	3	10	12
Austria	5	4	0	1	15	6	9	12
Kosovo	5	2	0	3	8	9	–1	6
Albania	6	1	2	3	7	14	–7	5
Andorra	4	1	1	2	5	9	–4	4
Turkey	6	1	1	4	7	14	–7	4

GROUP 4

San Marino v Lithuania 0-3
Greece v San Marino 5-0
Scotland v San Marino 2-0
Czech Republic v Lithuania 2-0
Greece v Lithuania 1-0
Croatia v Scotland 1-2
Czech Republic v Greece 1-1
Scotland v Lithuania 0-0
Czech Republic v Scotland 0-0
San Marino v Croatia 0-7
Lithuania v Croatia 1-3
Czech Republic v San Marino 6-0
Scotland v Greece 0-1
Croatia v Czech Republic 1-2
Greece v Czech Republic P-P
Lithuania v San Marino P-P
Scotland v Croatia P-P
Greece v Scotland P-P
Croatia v Lithuania P-P

Group 4 Table	*P*	*W*	*D*	*L*	*F*	*A*	*GD*	*Pts*
Czech Republic	5	3	2	0	11	2	9	11
Greece	4	3	1	0	8	1	7	10
Scotland	5	2	2	1	4	2	2	8
Croatia	4	2	0	2	12	5	7	6
Lithuania	5	1	1	3	4	6	–2	4
San Marino	5	0	0	5	0	23	–23	0

GROUP 5

Estonia v Bulgaria 0-4
Latvia v Poland 0-1
Russia v Serbia 1-0
Poland v Estonia 4-0
Serbia v Latvia 1-1
Bulgaria v Russia 0-0
Russia v Poland 2-2
Bulgaria v Serbia 0-1
Estonia v Latvia 2-1
Latvia v Bulgaria 0-0
Poland v Serbia 1-0
Estonia v Russia 0-5
Russia v Latvia 2-0
Bulgaria v Poland 3-0
Serbia v Estonia 6-0
Serbia v Russia 0-2
Poland v Latvia P-P
Bulgaria v Estonia P-P
Latvia v Serbia TBC
Russia v Bulgaria TBC
Estonia v Poland TBC
Poland v Russia TBC
Serbia v Bulgaria TBC
Latvia v Estonia TBC
Bulgaria v Latvia TBC
Serbia v Poland TBC
Russia v Estonia TBC
Latvia v Russia TBC
Poland v Bulgaria TBC
Estonia v Serbia TBC

Group 5 Table	*P*	*W*	*D*	*L*	*F*	*A*	*GD*	*Pts*
Russia	6	4	2	0	12	2	10	14
Poland	5	3	1	1	8	5	3	10
Bulgaria	5	2	2	1	7	1	6	8
Serbia	6	2	1	3	8	5	3	7
Estonia	5	1	0	4	2	20	–18	3
Latvia	5	0	2	3	2	6	–4	2

GROUP 6

Faroe Islands v Kazakhstan	1-3
Montenegro v Kazakhstan	1-2
Kazakhstan v Spain	0-1
Montenegro v Faroe Islands	3-0
Kazakhstan v Israel	1-2
North Macedonia v Faroe Islands	7-1
Spain v Montenegro	2-0
Montenegro v North Macedonia	1-2
North Macedonia v Kazakhstan	1-1
Israel v Faroe Islands	3-1
Montenegro v Spain	0-2
Israel v Montenegro	0-0
Spain v North Macedonia	3-0
Israel v Spain	1-1
North Macedonia v Israel	P-P
Faroe Islands v Spain	P-P
Faroe Islands v Montenegro	P-P
Spain v Kazakhstan	P-P
Israel v North Macedonia	P-P
Faroe Islands v North Macedonia	P-P

Group 6 Table	*P*	*W*	*D*	*L*	*F*	*A*	*GD*	*Pts*
Spain	5	4	1	0	9	1	8	13
Israel	4	2	2	0	6	3	3	8
Kazakhstan	5	2	1	2	7	6	1	7
North Macedonia	4	2	1	1	10	6	4	7
Montenegro	6	1	1	4	5	8	–3	4
Faroe Islands	4	0	0	4	3	16	–13	0

GROUP 7

Cyprus v Gibraltar	1-0
Belarus v Gibraltar	10-0
Portugal v Gibraltar	4-0
Norway v Cyprus	2-1
Belarus v Portugal	0-2
Netherlands v Cyprus	5-1
Belarus v Norway	1-1
Netherlands v Portugal	4-2
Cyprus v Belarus	1-1
Norway v Netherlands	0-4
Gibraltar v Netherlands	0-6
Cyprus v Norway	1-2
Norway v Portugal	2-3
Gibraltar v Belarus	0-2
Portugal v Cyprus	P-P
Netherlands v Belarus	P-P
Gibraltar v Norway	P-P
Gibraltar v Cyprus	P-P
Portugal v Netherlands	P-P

Group 7 Table	*P*	*W*	*D*	*L*	*F*	*A*	*GD*	*Pts*
Netherlands	4	4	0	0	19	3	16	12
Portugal	4	3	0	1	11	6	5	9
Belarus	5	2	2	1	14	4	10	8
Norway	5	2	1	2	7	10	–3	7
Cyprus	5	1	1	3	5	10	–5	4
Gibraltar	5	0	0	5	0	23	–23	0

GROUP 8

Ukraine v Finland	0-2
Northern Ireland v Malta	0-0
Ukraine v Malta	4-0
Finland v Northern Ireland	1-1
Denmark v Romania	2-1
Denmark v Northern Ireland	2-1
Finland v Malta	4-0
Romania v Ukraine	3-0
Finland v Denmark	0-1
Romania v Northern Ireland	3-0
Romania v Finland	4-1
Ukraine v Denmark	2-3
Denmark v Malta	5-1
Northern Ireland v Romania	0-0
Malta v Ukraine	P-P
Malta v Finland	P-P
Ukraine v Northern Ireland	P-P
Romania v Denmark	P-P

Group 8 Table	*P*	*W*	*D*	*L*	*F*	*A*	*GD*	*Pts*
Denmark	5	5	0	0	13	5	8	15
Romania	5	3	1	1	11	3	8	10
Finland	5	2	1	2	8	6	2	7
Ukraine	4	1	0	3	6	8	–2	3
Northern Ireland	5	0	3	2	2	6	–4	3
Malta	4	0	1	3	1	13	–12	1

GROUP 9

Bosnia-Herzegovina v Moldova	4-0
Wales v Belgium	1-0
Wales v Germany	1-5
Belgium v Bosnia-Herzegovina	0-0
Moldova v Wales	2-1
Bosnia-Herzegovina v Germany	0-2
Belgium v Moldova	4-1
Germany v Belgium	2-3
Wales v Bosnia-Herzegovina	1-0
Wales v Moldova	P-P
Bosnia-Herzegovina v Belgium	P-P
Germany v Wales	P-P

Group 9 Table	*P*	*W*	*D*	*L*	*F*	*A*	*GD*	*Pts*
Belgium	4	2	1	1	7	4	3	7
Germany	3	2	0	1	9	4	5	6
Wales	4	2	0	2	4	7	–3	6
Bosnia-Herzegovina	4	1	1	2	4	3	1	4
Moldova	3	1	0	2	3	9	–6	3

ENGLAND UNDER-21 RESULTS 1976–2020

EC *UEFA Competition for Under-21 Teams*

Bold type indicates matches played in season 2019–20.

Year	*Date*		*Venue*		
			v ALBANIA	*Eng*	*Alb*
EC1989	Mar	7	Shkoder	2	1
EC1989	April	25	Ipswich	2	0
EC2001	Mar	27	Tirana	1	0
EC2001	Sept	4	Middlesbrough	5	0
EC2019	**Nov**	**15**	**Shkoder**	**3**	**0**
			v ANDORRA	*Eng*	*And*
EC2017	Oct	10	Andorra la Vella	1	0
ec2018	Oct	11	Chesterfield	7	0
			v ANGOLA	*Eng*	*Ang*
1995	June	10	Toulon	1	0
1996	May	28	Toulon	0	2
			v ARGENTINA	*Eng*	*Arg*
1998	May	18	Toulon	0	2
2000	Feb	22	Fulham	1	0
			v AUSTRIA	*Eng*	*Aus*
1994	Oct	11	Kapfenberg	3	1
1995	Nov	14	Middlesbrough	2	1
EC2004	Sept	3	Krems	2	0
EC2005	Oct	7	Leeds	1	2
2013	June	26	Brighton	4	0
EC2019	**Oct**	**15**	**Milton Keynes**	**5**	**1**
			v AZERBAIJAN	*Eng*	*Az*
EC2004	Oct	12	Baku	0	0
EC2005	Mar	29	Middlesbrough	2	0
2009	June	8	Milton Keynes	7	0
EC2011	Sept	1	Watford	6	0
EC2012	Sept	6	Baku	2	0
			v BELARUS	*Eng*	*Bel*
2015	June	11	Barnsley	1	0
			v BELGIUM	*Eng*	*Belg*
1994	June	5	Marseille	2	1
1996	May	24	Toulon	1	0
EC2011	Nov	14	Mons	1	2
EC2012	Feb	29	Middlesbrough	4	0
			v BOSNIA-HERZEGOVINA	*Eng*	*B-H*
EC2015	Nov	12	Sarajevo Canton	0	0
EC2016	Oct	11	Walsall	5	0
			v BRAZIL	*Eng*	*Bra*
1993	June	11	Toulon	0	0
1995	June	6	Toulon	0	2
1996	June	1	Toulon	1	2
			v BULGARIA	*Eng*	*Bul*
EC1979	June	5	Pernik	3	1
EC1979	Nov	20	Leicester	5	0
1989	June	5	Toulon	2	3
EC1998	Oct	9	West Ham	1	0
EC1999	June	8	Vratsa	1	0
EC2007	Sept	11	Sofia	2	0
EC2007	Nov	16	Milton Keynes	2	0
			v CHINA PR	*Eng*	*CPR*
2018	May	26	Toulon	2	1
			v CROATIA	*Eng*	*Cro*
1996	Apr	23	Sunderland	0	1
2003	Aug	19	West Ham	0	3
EC2014	Oct	10	Wolverhampton	2	1
EC2014	Oct	14	Vinkovci	2	1
EC2019	June	24	Serravale	3	3
			v CZECHOSLOVAKIA	*Eng*	*Cz*
1990	May	28	Toulon	2	1
1992	May	26	Toulon	1	2
1993	June	9	Toulon	1	1
			v CZECH REPUBLIC	*Eng*	*CzR*
1998	Nov	17	Ipswich	0	1
EC2007	June	11	Arnhem	0	0
2008	Nov	18	Bramall Lane	2	0
EC2011	June	19	Viborg	1	2
2015	Mar	27	Prague	1	0
			v DENMARK	*Eng*	*Den*
EC1978	Sept	19	Hvidovre	2	1
EC1979	Sept	11	Watford	1	0
EC1982	Sept	21	Hvidovre	4	1
				Eng	*Den*
EC1983	Sept	20	Norwich	4	1
EC1986	Mar	12	Copenhagen	1	0
EC1986	Mar	26	Manchester	1	1
1988	Sept	13	Watford	0	0
1994	Mar	8	Brentford	1	0
1999	Oct	8	Bradford	4	1
2005	Aug	16	Herning	1	0
2011	Mar	24	Viborg	4	0
2017	Mar	27	Randers	4	0
2018	Nov	20	Esbjerg	5	1
			v EQUADOR	*Eng*	*Eq*
2009	Feb	10	Malaga	2	3
			v FINLAND	*Eng*	*Fin*
EC1977	May	26	Helsinki	1	0
EC1977	Oct	12	Hull	8	1
EC1984	Oct	16	Southampton	2	0
EC1985	May	21	Mikkeli	1	3
EC2000	Oct	10	Valkeakoski	2	2
EC2001	Mar	23	Barnsley	4	0
EC2009	June	15	Halmstad	2	1
EC2013	Sept	9	Tampere	1	1
EC2013	Nov	14	Milton Keynes	3	0
			v FRANCE	*Eng*	*Fra*
EC1984	Feb	28	Sheffield	6	1
EC1984	Mar	28	Rouen	1	0
1987	June	11	Toulon	0	2
EC1988	April	13	Besancon	2	4
EC1988	April	27	Highbury	2	2
1988	June	12	Toulon	2	4
1990	May	23	Toulon	7	3
1991	June	3	Toulon	1	0
1992	May	28	Toulon	0	0
1993	June	15	Toulon	1	0
1994	May	31	Aubagne	0	3
1995	June	10	Toulon	0	2
1998	May	14	Toulon	1	1
1999	Feb	9	Derby	2	1
EC2005	Nov	11	Tottenham	1	1
EC2005	Nov	15	Nancy	1	2
2009	Mar	31	Nottingham	0	2
2014	Nov	17	Paris	2	3
2016	May	29	Toulon	2	1
2016	Nov	14	Bondoufle	2	3
EC2019	June	18	Cesena	1	2
			v GEORGIA	*Eng*	*Geo*
EC1996	Nov	8	Batumi	1	0
EC1997	April	29	Charlton	0	0
2000	Aug	31	Middlesbrough	6	1
			v GERMANY	*Eng*	*Ger*
1991	Sept	10	Scunthorpe	2	1
EC2000	Oct	6	Derby	1	1
EC2001	Aug	31	Frieburg	2	1
2005	Mar	25	Hull	2	2
2005	Sept	6	Mainz	1	1
EC2006	Oct	6	Coventry	1	0
EC2006	Oct	10	Leverkusen	2	0
EC2009	June	22	Halmstad	1	1
EC2009	June	29	Malmo	0	4
2010	Nov	16	Wiesbaden	0	2
2015	Mar	30	Middlesbrough	3	2
2017	Mar	24	Wiesbaden	0	1
EC2017	June	27	Tychy	2	2
2019	Mar	26	Bournemouth	1	2
			v EAST GERMANY	*Eng*	*EG*
EC1980	April	16	Sheffield	1	2
EC1980	April	23	Jena	0	1
			v WEST GERMANY	*Eng*	*WG*
EC1982	Sept	21	Sheffield	3	1
EC1982	Oct	12	Bremen	2	3
1987	Sept	8	Ludenscheid	0	2

			v GREECE	*Eng*	*Gre*
EC1982	Nov	16	Piraeus	0	1
EC1983	Mar	29	Portsmouth	2	1
1989	Feb	7	Patras	0	1
EC1997	Nov	13	Heraklion	0	2
EC1997	Dec	17	Norwich	4	2
EC2001	June	5	Athens	1	3
EC2001	Oct	5	Ewood Park	2	1
EC2009	Sept	8	Tripoli	1	1
EC2010	Mar	3	Doncaster	1	2

			v GUINEA	*Eng*	*Gui*
2016	May	23	Toulon	7	1

			v HUNGARY	*Eng*	*Hun*
EC1981	June	5	Keszthely	2	1
EC1981	Nov	17	Nottingham	2	0
EC1983	April	26	Newcastle	1	0
EC1983	Oct	11	Nyiregyhaza	2	0
1990	Sept	11	Southampton	3	1
1992	May	12	Budapest	2	2
1999	April	27	Budapest	2	2

			v ICELAND	*Eng*	*Ice*
2011	Mar	28	Preston	1	2
EC2011	Oct	6	Reykjavik	3	0
EC2011	Nov	10	Colchester	5	0

			v ISRAEL	*Eng*	*Isr*
1985	Feb	27	Tel Aviv	2	1
2011	Sept	5	Barnsley	4	1
EC2013	June	11	Jerusalem	0	1

			v ITALY	*Eng*	*Italy*
EC1978	Mar	8	Manchester	2	1
EC1978	April	5	Rome	0	0
EC1984	April	18	Manchester	3	1
EC1984	May	2	Florence	0	1
EC1986	April	9	Pisa	0	2
EC1986	April	23	Swindon	1	1
EC1997	Feb	12	Bristol	1	0
EC1997	Oct	10	Rieti	1	0
EC2000	May	27	Bratislava	0	2
2000	Nov	14	Monza*	0	0
2002	Mar	26	Valley Parade	1	1
EC2002	May	20	Basle	1	2
2003	Feb	11	Pisa	0	1
2007	Mar	24	Wembley	3	3
EC2007	June	14	Arnhem	2	2
2011	Feb	8	Empoli	0	1
EC2013	June	5	Tel Aviv	0	1
EC2015	June	24	Olomouc	1	3
**Abandoned 11 mins; fog.*					
2016	Nov	10	Southampton	3	2
2018	Nov	15	Ferrara	2	1

			v JAPAN	*Eng*	*Jap*
2016	May	27	Toulon	1	0

			v KAZAKHSTAN	*Eng*	*Kaz*
EC2015	Oct	13	Coventry	3	0
EC2016	Oct	6	Aktobe	1	0

			v KOSOVO	*Eng*	*Kos*
EC2019	**Sept**	**9**	**Hull**	**2**	**0**

			v LATVIA	*Eng*	*Lat*
1995	April	25	Riga	1	0
1995	June	7	Burnley	4	0
EC2017	Sept	5	Bournemouth	3	0
EC2018	**Sept**	**11**	**Jelgava**	**2**	**1**

			v LITHUANIA	*Eng*	*Lith*
EC2009	Nov	17	Vilnius	0	0
EC2010	Sept	7	Colchester	3	0
EC2013	Oct	15	Ipswich	5	0
EC2014	Sept	5	Zaliakalnis	1	0

			v LUXEMBOURG	*Eng*	*Lux*
EC1998	Oct	13	Greven Macher	5	0
EC1999	Sept	3	Reading	5	0

			v MALAYSIA	*Eng*	*Mal*
1995	June	8	Toulon	2	0

			v MEXICO	*Eng*	*Mex*
1988	June	5	Toulon	2	1
1991	May	29	Toulon	6	0
1992	May	25	Toulon	1	1
2001	May	24	Leicester	3	0
2018	May	29	Toulon	0	0
2018	June	9	Toulon	2	1

			v MOLDOVA	*Eng*	*Mol*
EC1996	Aug	31	Chisinau	2	0
EC1997	Sept	9	Wycombe	1	0
EC2006	Aug	15	Ipswich	2	2
EC2013	Sept	5	Reading	1	0
EC2014	Sept	9	Tiraspol	3	0

			v MONTENEGRO	*Eng*	*Mon*
EC2007	Sept	7	Podgorica	3	0
EC2007	Oct	12	Leicester	1	0

			v MOROCCO	*Eng*	*Mor*
1987	June	7	Toulon	2	0
1988	June	9	Toulon	1	0

			v NETHERLANDS	*Eng*	*N*
EC1993	April	27	Portsmouth	3	0
EC1993	Oct	12	Utrecht	1	1
2001	Aug	14	Reading	4	0
EC2001	Nov	9	Utrecht	2	2
EC2001	Nov	13	Derby	1	0
2004	Feb	17	Hull	3	2
2005	Feb	8	Derby	1	2
2006	Nov	14	Alkmaar	1	0
EC2007	June	20	Heerenveen	1	1
2009	Aug	11	Groningen	0	0
EC2017	Sept	1	Doetinchem	1	1
EC2018	Sept	6	Norwich	0	0
2019	**Nov**	**19**	**Doetinchem**	**1**	**2**

			v NORTHERN IRELAND	*Eng*	*NI*
2012	Nov	13	Blackpool	2	0

			v NORTH MACEDONIA	*Eng*	*M*
EC2002	Oct	15	Reading	3	1
EC2003	Sept	5	Skopje	1	1
EC2009	Sept	4	Prilep	2	1
EC2009	Oct	9	Coventry	6	3

			v NORWAY	*Eng*	*Nor*
EC1977	June	1	Bergen	2	1
EC1977	Sept	6	Brighton	6	0
1980	Sept	9	Southampton	3	0
1981	Sept	8	Drammen	0	0
EC1992	Oct	13	Peterborough	0	2
EC1993	June	1	Stavanger	1	1
1995	Oct	10	Stavanger	2	2
2006	Feb	28	Reading	3	1
2009	Mar	27	Sandefjord	5	0
2011	June	5	Southampton	2	0
EC2011	Oct	10	Drammen	2	1
EC2012	Sept	10	Chesterfield	1	0
EC2013	June	8	Petah Tikva	1	3
EC2015	Sept	7	Drammen	1	0
EC2016	Sept	6	Colchester	6	1

			v PARAGUAY	*Eng*	*Par*
2016	May	25	Toulon	4	0

			v POLAND	*Eng*	*Pol*
EC1982	Mar	17	Warsaw	2	1
EC1982	April	7	West Ham	2	2
EC1989	June	2	Plymouth	2	1
EC1989	Oct	10	Jastrzebie	3	1
EC1990	Oct	16	Tottenham	0	1
EC1991	Nov	12	Pila	1	2
EC1993	May	28	Zdroj	4	1
EC1993	Sept	7	Millwall	1	2
EC1996	Oct	8	Wolverhampton	0	0
EC1997	May	30	Katowice	1	1
EC1999	Mar	26	Southampton	5	0
EC1999	Sept	7	Plock	1	3
EC2004	Sept	7	Rybnik	3	1
EC2005	Oct	11	Hillsborough	4	1
2008	Mar	25	Wolverhampton	0	0
EC2017	June	22	Kielce	3	0
2019	Mar	21	Bristol	1	1

			v PORTUGAL	*Eng*	*Por*
1987	June	13	Toulon	0	0
1990	May	21	Toulon	0	1
1993	June	7	Toulon	2	0
1994	June	7	Toulon	2	0
EC1994	Sept	6	Leicester	0	0
1995	Sept	2	Lisbon	0	2
1996	May	30	Toulon	1	3
2000	Apr	16	Stoke	0	1
EC2002	May	22	Zurich	1	3
EC2003	Mar	28	Rio Major	2	4
EC2003	Sept	9	Everton	1	2

				Eng	Por
EC2008	Nov	20	Agueda	1	1
2008	Sept	5	Wembley	2	0
EC2009	Nov	14	Wembley	1	0
EC2010	Sept	3	Barcelos	1	0
2014	Nov	13	Burnley	3	1
EC2015	June	18	Uherske Hradiste	0	1
2016	May	19	Toulon	1	0

v QATAR

				Eng	Qat
2018	June	1	Toulon	4	0

v REPUBLIC OF IRELAND

				Eng	RoI
1981	Feb	25	Liverpool	1	0
1985	Mar	25	Portsmouth	3	2
1989	June	9	Toulon	0	0
EC1990	Nov	13	Cork	3	0
EC1991	Mar	26	Brentford	3	0
1994	Nov	15	Newcastle	1	0
1995	Mar	27	Dublin	2	0
EC2007	Oct	16	Cork	3	0
EC2008	Feb	5	Southampton	3	0

v ROMANIA

				Eng	Rom
EC1980	Oct	14	Ploesti	0	4
EC1981	April	28	Swindon	3	0
EC1985	April	30	Brasov	0	0
EC1985	Sept	10	Ipswich	3	0
2007	Aug	21	Bristol	1	1
EC2010	Oct	8	Norwich	2	1
EC2010	Oct	12	Botosani	0	0
2013	Mar	21	Wycombe	3	0
2018	Mar	24	Wolverhampton	2	1
EC2019	June	21	Cesena	2	4

v RUSSIA

				Eng	Rus
1994	May	30	Bandol	2	0

v SAN MARINO

				Eng	SM
EC1993	Feb	16	Luton	6	0
EC1993	Nov	17	San Marino	4	0
EC2013	Oct	10	San Marino	4	0
EC2013	Nov	19	Shrewsbury	9	0

v SCOTLAND

				Eng	Sco
1977	April	27	Sheffield	1	0
EC1980	Feb	12	Coventry	2	1
EC1980	Mar	4	Aberdeen	0	0
EC1982	April	19	Glasgow	1	0
EC1982	April	28	Manchester	1	1
EC1988	Feb	16	Aberdeen	1	0
EC1988	Mar	22	Nottingham	1	0
1993	June	13	Toulon	1	0
2013	Aug	13	Sheffield	6	0
EC2017	Oct	6	Middlesbrough	3	1
2018	June	6	Toulon	3	1
EC2018	Oct	16	Edinburgh	2	0

v SENEGAL

				Eng	Sen
1989	June	7	Toulon	6	1
1991	May	27	Toulon	2	1

v SERBIA

				Eng	Ser
EC2007	June	17	Nijmegen	2	0
EC2012	Oct	12	Norwich	1	0
EC2012	Oct	16	Krusevac	1	0

v SERBIA-MONTENEGRO

				Eng	S-M
2003	June	2	Hull	3	2

v SLOVAKIA

				Eng	Slo
EC2002	June	1	Bratislava	0	2
EC2002	Oct	11	Trnava	4	0
EC2003	June	10	Sunderland	2	0
2007	June	5	Norwich	5	0
EC2017	June	19	Kielce	2	1

v SLOVENIA

				Eng	Slo
2000	Feb	12	Nova Gorica	1	0
2008	Aug	19	Hull	2	1
2019	**Oct**	**11**	**Maribor**	**2**	**2**

v SOUTH AFRICA

				Eng	SA
1998	May	16	Toulon	3	1

v SPAIN

				Eng	Spa
EC1984	May	17	Seville	1	0
EC1984	May	24	Sheffield	2	0
1987	Feb	18	Burgos	2	1
1992	Sept	8	Burgos	1	0
2001	Feb	27	Birmingham	0	4
2004	Nov	16	Alcala	0	1
2007	Feb	6	Derby	2	2
EC2009	June	18	Gothenburg	2	0
EC2011	June	12	Herning	1	1

v SWEDEN

				Eng	Swe
1979	June	9	Vasteras	2	1
1986	Sept	9	Ostersund	1	1
EC1988	Oct	18	Coventry	1	1
EC1989	Sept	5	Uppsala	0	1
EC1998	Sept	4	Sundvall	2	0
EC1999	June	4	Huddersfield	3	0
2004	Mar	30	Kristiansund	2	2
EC2009	June	26	Gothenburg	3	3
2013	Feb	5	Walsall	4	0
EC2015	Jun	21	Olomouc	1	0
EC2017	June	16	Kielce	0	0

v SWITZERLAND

				Eng	Swit
EC1980	Nov	18	Ipswich	5	0
EC1981	May	31	Neuenburg	0	0
1988	May	28	Lausanne	1	1
1996	April	1	Swindon	0	0
1998	Mar	24	Brugglifeld	0	2
EC2002	May	17	Zurich	2	1
EC2006	Sept	6	Lucerne	3	2
EC2015	Nov	16	Brighton	3	1
EC2016	Mar	26	Thun	1	1

v TURKEY

				Eng	Tur
EC1984	Nov	13	Bursa	0	0
EC1985	Oct	15	Bristol	3	0
EC1987	April	28	Izmir	0	0
EC1987	Oct	13	Sheffield	1	1
EC1991	April	30	Izmir	2	2
1991	Oct	15	Reading	2	0
EC1992	Nov	17	Orient	0	1
EC1993	Mar	30	Izmir	0	0
EC2000	May	29	Bratislava	6	0
EC2003	April	1	Newcastle	1	1
EC2003	Oct	10	Istanbul	0	1
EC2019	**Sept**	**6**	**Izmit**	**3**	**2**

v UKRAINE

				Eng	Uk
2004	Aug	17	Middlesbrough	3	1
EC2011	June	15	Herning	0	0
EC2017	Nov	10	Kiev	2	0
EC2018	Mar	27	Sheffield	2	1

v USA

				Eng	USA
1989	June	11	Toulon	0	2
1994	June	2	Toulon	3	0
2015	Sept	3	Preston	1	0

v USSR

				Eng	USSR
1987	June	9	Toulon	0	0
1988	June	7	Toulon	1	0
1990	May	25	Toulon	2	1
1991	May	31	Toulon	2	1

v UZBEKISTAN

				Eng	Uzb
2010	Aug	10	Bristol	2	0

v WALES

				Eng	Wal
1976	Dec	15	Wolverhampton	0	0
1979	Feb	6	Swansea	1	0
1990	Dec	5	Tranmere	0	0
EC2004	Oct	8	Blackburn	2	0
EC2005	Sept	2	Wrexham	4	0
2008	May	5	Wrexham	2	0
EC2008	Oct	10	Cardiff	3	2
EC2008	Oct	14	Villa Park	2	2
EC2013	Mar	5	Derby	1	0
EC2013	May	19	Swansea	3	1

v YUGOSLAVIA

				Eng	Yugo
EC1978	April	19	Novi Sad	1	2
EC1978	May	2	Manchester	1	1
EC1986	Nov	11	Peterborough	1	1
EC1987	Nov	10	Zemun	5	1
EC2000	Mar	29	Barcelona	3	0
2002	Sept	6	Bolton	1	1

BRITISH & IRISH UNDER-21 TEAMS 2019–20

▪ *Denotes player sent off.*

ENGLAND

UEFA UNDER-21 CHAMPIONSHIPS 2019–21

Izmit, Friday, 6 September 2019

Turkey U21 (1) 2 *(Sinik 25, Muldur 51)*

England U21 (1) 3 *(Nketiah 4, 74, Nelson 75)* 11,500

Turkey U21: (4231) Bayindir; Muldur, Turkmen, Tagir, Sertel; Ozcan (Oktay 45), Ozdemir (Yuksel 81); Kutucu, Kokcu, Sinik (Atakan Uner 71); Dervisoglu.
England U21: (433) Ramsdale; Aarons, Guehi, Panzo, Sessegnon S (Greenwood 59); Davies, Chalobah, Gibbs-White (Godfrey 81); Foden, Nketiah, Nelson (Brewster 78).
Referee: Luis Godinho.

Hull, Monday, 9 September 2019

England U21 (1) 2 *(Foden 25, 90)*

Kosovo U21 (0) 0 15,258

England U21: (352) Ramsdale; Guehi, Chalobah, Godfrey; Aarons (Justin 80), Gibbs-White (Cantwell 61), Davies, Foden, Sessegnon S; Nketiah (Brewster 76), Nelson (Greenwood 61).
Kosovo U21: (352) Smakiqi; Mema (Muja 34), Xhemajli, Kolgeci; Lirim Kastrati, Abedini, Hajrizi, Zekaj, Gashi (Baftiu 65); Daku (Mustafa 46), Lirim Kastrati.
Referee: Kristoffer Karlsson.

Milton Keynes, Tuesday, 15 October 2019

England U21 (4) 5 *(Hudson-Odoi 12, 45, Nketiah 28, 39, 79)*

Austria U21 (0) 1 *(Baumgartner 66)* 11,772

England U21: (352) Ramsdale; Justin, Guehi, Kelly; Aarons (Sessegnon S 60), Willock (Skipp 74), Davies, Foden, McNeil (Brewster 61); Nketiah (Surridge 86), Hudson-Odoi (Gallagher 86).
Austria U21: (4231) Ehmann; Malicsek, Danso, Maresic, Friedl; Demaku (Muller 69), Lovric (Halper 81); Arase (Grull 54), Baumgartner, Meister (Lema 80); Raguz (Schmidt 69).
Referee: Michael Fabbri.

Shkoder, Friday, 15 November 2019

Albania U21 (0) 0

England U21 (2) 3 *(Foden 22, Gallagher 43, Nelson 90)* 1050

Albania U21: (433) Hoxha; Maloku, Bajrami, Mersinaj, Pellumbi; Mala (Zejnulai 46), Kallaku (Imeri 86), Cokaj (Shehu 86); Kolaj, Xhixha (Qardaku 76), Sula (Tuci 61).
England U21: (433) Ramsdale; James, Guehi, Godfrey, Panzo (Justin 64); Willock (Nelson 64), Davies, Gallagher; Foden (Eze 81), Brewster (Sessegnon R 72), Greenwood.
Referee: Lionel Tschudi.

FRIENDLIES

Maribor, Friday, 11 October 2019

Slovenia U21 (0) 2 *(Pertovic 82, Pisek 90)*

England U21 (1) 2 *(Nketiah 39 (pen), Surridge 70)*

Slovenia U21: (442) Frelih; Rogelj, Zec, Zalatel, Celar (Stor 59); Mlakar, Valencic (Horvat 68), Sever (Pertovic 46), Stojinovic; Kryeziu (Pisek 67), Rom.
England U21: (442) Ramsdale; Aarons (Justin 46), Panzo, Kelly (Richards 62), Davies; Hudson-Odoi (Brewster 46), Willock (Gallagher 62), Nketiah (Surridge 46), Foden (Skipp 62); Guehi, McNeil (Wilmot 46).

Doetinchem, Tuesday, 19 November 2019

Netherlands U21 (1) 2 *(Sierhuis 23, Dilrosun 90)*

England U21 (0) 1 *(Greenwood 75)*

Netherlands U21: (442) Scherpen; Zeefuik, Schuurs (Doekhi 46), van Drongelen, Wijndal (Malacia 46); Reis (Kadioglu 88), Dilrosun, Koopmeiners (Harroui 46), Sierhuis (Gakpo 66); de Wit, Kluivert (Chong 79).
England U21: (433) Ramsdale; Aarons (James 62), Chalobah, Justin, Guehi; Foden (Willock 79), Skipp, Diangana (Sessegnon R 76); Gallagher (McNeil 62), Brewster (Greenwood 62), Eze (Nelson 62).

SCOTLAND

UEFA UNDER-21 CHAMPIONSHIPS 2019–21

Paisley, Thursday, 5 September 2019

Scotland U21 (2) 2 *(Tosi 21 (og), Middleton 28)*

San Marino U21 (0) 0 1542

Scotland U21: (433) Robby McCrorie; Magennis, Ross McCrorie, Johnston, Reading (Harvie 87); Campbell, Gilmour (Maguire 88), Ferguson (McAllister 72); McLennan (Smith 64), Middleton (Scott 72), Holsgrove.
San Marino U21: (4141) De Angelis; Conti (Franciosi 86), Moretti, Cevoli, Tosi (Liverani 55); Michelotti (Nanni 86); Pancotti, Ceccaroli, Cecchetti (Quaranta 73), Raschi; Babboni (Dolcini 55).
Referee: Vitaliy Romanov.

Sibenik, Tuesday, 10 September 2019

Croatia U21 (1) 1 *(Kulenovic 10)*

Scotland U21 (0) 2 *(McLennan 81, 89)* 2134

Croatia U21: (442) Semper; Hujber, Kalaica (Soldo 83), Sutalo, Sosa; Ivanusec, Moro, Nejasmic, Majer (Cuze 78); Bradaric (Marin 69), Kulenovic (Bistrovic 83).
Scotland U21: (433) Doohan; Ross McCrorie, Johnston, Porteous, Harvie; Magennis, Campbell, Reading (Middleton 78); Ferguson (McLennan 78), Hornby, Holsgrove (Maguire 84).
Referee: Michal Ocenas.

Tynecastle, Thursday, 10 October 2019

Scotland U21 (0) 0

Lithuania U21 (0) 0 1084

Scotland U21: (433) Doohan; Ross McCrorie, Porteous, Johnston, Harvie; Ferguson (McLennan 58), Campbell (Henderson 87), Gilmour; Magennis (Kelly 64), Hornby, Middleton.
Lithuania U21: (442) Krapikas; Stockunas, Kloniunas, Uzela, Milasius; Sesplaukis, Antanavicius, Megelaitis, Jankauskas (Sirvys 89); Marazas (Banevicius 73), Dubickas.
Referee: Krzysztof Jakubik.

Uherske Hradiste, Monday, 14 October 2019

Czech Rep U21 (0) 0

Scotland U21 (0) 0 5187

Czech Rep U21: (4231) Jedlicka; Holik, Chalus, Plechaty, Granecny; Janosek, Sadilek; Vanicek (Bucha 63), Matousek (Havelka 70), Hlozek; Sasinka.
Scotland U21: (433) Robby McCrorie; Ross McCrorie, Porteous, Johnston, Harvie; Gilmour, Middleton (Maguire 63), Campbell; Magennis, Hornby, Reading.
Referee: Alain Durieux.

Tynecastle, Friday, 15 November 2019

Scotland U21 (0) 0

Greece U21 (0) 1 *(Nikolaou 90 (pen))* 1284

Scotland U21: (433) Doohan; Brandon, Maguire, Johnston, Harvie; Ferguson, Campbell, Gilmour; Kelly (Middleton 70), Hornby, Holsgrove (McLennan 85).
Greece U21: (4231) Siampanis; Natsos, Evangelou, Nikolaou, Katranis; Retsos■, Balogiannis (Oikonomidis 30); Ntaviotis, Bouzoukis (Diamantis 77), Papanikolaou; Kampetsis (Ioannidis 54).
Referee: Bojan Pandzic.

NORTHERN IRELAND

UEFA UNDER-21 CHAMPIONSHIPS 2019–21

Ballymena, Friday, 6 September 2019

Northern Ireland U21 (0) 0

Malta U21 (0) 0 723

Northern Ireland U21: (433) Hazard; Balmer, Toal, Burns, Thompson; McClean (McCann L 78), McCalmont (Galbraith 71), Dunwoody; Gordon (Palmer 71), Parkhouse, Boyd-Munce (Gallagher 88).
Malta U21: (442) Vella; Borg, Shaw, Pulis, Grech; Friggieri (Tanti 81), Sansone, Camilleri, Beerman; Busuttil (Xuereb 70), Brincat (Elouni 90).
Referee: Ferenc Karako.

Oulu, Tuesday, 10 September 2019

Finland U21 (1) 1 *(Valakari 4)*

Northern Ireland U21 (1) 1 *(Thompson 35)* 3666

Finland U21: (352) Jaaskelainen; Halme, Pikkarainen, Sundman; Soisalo (Assehnoun 90), Hyvarinen, Lingman, Kairinen (Oksanen 66), Ylatupa (Fagerstrom 66); Kallman (Vertainen 90), Valakari.
Northern Ireland U21: (433) Hazard; Thompson (McClean 46), Balmer, Toal, Burns (Marron 90); Galbraith, McCalmont, Dunwoody; Gordon (Scott 70), McCann L (Ferris 76), Boyd-Munce (Palmer 70).
Referee: Julian Weinberger.

Aalborg, Thursday, 10 October 2019

Denmark U21 (1) 2 *(Poulsen 30, Odgaard 86)*

Northern Ireland U21 (0) 1 *(Dunwoody 57)* 647

Denmark U21: (451) Christensen; Anyembe, Nelsson, Sorensen, Poulsen (Madsen M 79); Skov Olsen, Hjulmand (Andersen 69), Nartey, Holse (Odgaard 69), Laursen (Madsen N 90); Bruun Larsen.
Northern Ireland U21: (352) Hazard; Marron (Palmer 78), Toal, Balmer; Gordon (O'Mahony 88), McCann A, McCalmont, Boyd-Munce (McClean 71), Thompson; Parkhouse (McCann L 71), Dunwoody (Galbraith 88).
Referee: Donatas Rumsas.

Voluntari, Monday, 14 October 2019

Romania U21 (0) 3 *(Baluta 48, Mihaila 59, Ciobanu 67)*

Northern Ireland U21 (0) 0 4067

Romania U21: (433) Vlad; Ratiu (Velisar 63), Pascanu, Chindris, Boboc; Oaida, Baluta (Grigore 79), Ciobanu; Man (Neicutescu 69), Petre (Ganea 69), Mihaila (Dragus 69).
Northern Ireland U21: (4231) Hazard■; Balmer, Toal, Brown, Graham (Thompson 74); McCalmont (Boyd-Munce 74), McCann A; Gordon (Parkhouse 74), Dunwoody (Palmer 61), Galbraith (Hughes 38); Lavery.
Referee: Nejc Kajtazovic.

Ballymena, Tuesday, 19 November 2019

Northern Ireland U21 (0) 0

Romania U21 (0) 0 1641

Northern Ireland U21: (442) Gartside; Gordon (Palmer 30), Marron, Toal, Balmer; Burns, McCann A, Dunwoody (Galbraith 84), McCalmont; Boyd-Munce (Thompson 84), Parkhouse.
Romania U21: (442) Vlad; Vladoiu, Pascanu, Chindris■, Grigore; Oaida, Marin (Olaru 72), Morutan (Ciobotariu 82), Man (George-Cristian 90); Petre, Mihaila (Ciobanu 71).
Referee: Kai Erik Steen.

FRIENDLY

Ballinamallard, Thursday, 14 November 2019

Northern Ireland U21 (0) 1 *(McCalmont 78)*

Hungary U21 (1) 1 *(Szoke 37)*

Northern Ireland U21: (442) Hughes; Toal, Graham, Marron, Gallagher; Scott, Gordon, Boyd-Munce, McCann A (McCalmont 65); Galbraith, Parkhouse.
Substitutes all used: Gartside, Burns, Balmer, Dunwoody, McCalmont, O'Neill, Thompson, Palmer, Robinson.

WALES

UEFA UNDER-21 CHAMPIONSHIPS 2019–21

Wrexham, Friday, 6 September 2019

Wales U21 (1) 1 *(Johnson 3)*

Belgium U21 (0) 0 304

Wales U21: (442) Ratcliffe; Coxe, Cabango, Poole, Norrington-Davies; Evans J (Stirk 86), Burton, Mooney (Cooper O 76), Harris; Johnson, Cullen.
Belgium U21: (442) Svilar; Sardella (Vanzeir 70), Bornauw, Faes, De Smet; Saelemaekers, Sambi Lokonga (Verreth 89), Rigo (Doku 70), Verstraete (Peeters 81); Amuzu, Openda.
Referee: Danilo Grujic.

Wrexham, Tuesday, 10 September 2019

Wales U21 (0) 1 *(Harris 48 (pen))*

Germany U21 (4) 5 *(Hack 19, 24, 29, Eggestein 41, Fein 50)* 841

Wales U21: (4231) Ratcliffe; Coxe, Poole, Cabango, Norrington-Davies; Burton, Evans J (Stirk 66); Cullen (Lewis A 66), Harris, Mooney (Cooper B 86); Johnson (Clifton 76).
Germany U21: (4141) Schubert; Baku R, Kilian, Chabot, Schlotterbeck (Handwerker 70); Janelt; Eggestein, Fein (Burnic 59), Dorsch (Ozcan 59), Hack (Baku M 70); Serra (Nmecha 59).
Referee: Tomasz Musial.

Orhei, Friday, 11 October 2019

Moldova U21 (1) 2 *(Belousov 41, 48 (pen))*

Wales U21 (1) 1 *(Broadhead 24)* 350

Moldova U21: (4231) Straistari; Boico, Craciun, Furtuna, Ursu■; Turcan, Dros; Belousov, Nihaev (Berco 56), Stina; Cojocaru.
Wales U21: (442) Przybek; Coxe (Lewis J 67), Cooper B, Cabango, Norrington-Davies; Levitt, Evans J, Burton (Evans K 67), Johnson; Broadhead, Harris (Vale 85).
Referee: Umit Ozturk.

Wrexham, Tuesday, 19 November 2019

Wales U21 (0) 1 *(Cullen 71)*

Bosnia-Herzegovina U21 (0) 0 1282

Wales U21: (442) Ratcliffe; Lewis A, Cooper B, Cabango, Norrington-Davies; Burton (Stirk 73), Evans J, Johnson (Taylor 60 (Mooney 90)), Broadhead; Cullen, Harris.
Bosnia-Herzegovina U21: (442) Kovacevic; Serbecic, Mujakic, Milicevic, Beganovic; Mustedanagic (Celikovic 87), Bojo (Coko 79), Cavar, Danilovic; Demirovic, Catic (Hadzic 72).
Referee: Georgios Kominis.

REPUBLIC OF IRELAND

UEFA UNDER-21 CHAMPIONSHIPS 2019–21

Dublin, Friday, 6 September 2019

Republic of Ireland U21 (1) 1 *(Parrott 31)*

Armenia U21 (0) 0 3658

Republic of Ireland U21: (4231) Kelleher; O'Connor L, Masterson, O'Shea, Leahy; Molumby, Coventry; Kilkenny (Elbouzedi 65), Parrott (Afolabi 82), Connolly (Knight 89); Idah (Mandroiu 66).
Armenia U21: (4231) Aslanyan; Ghubasaryan, Khachumyan, Nazaryan, Grigoryan; Mkrtchyan, Nadiryan (Vardanyan 81); Melkonyan, Bichakhchyan (Khamoyan 76), Nahapetyan (Tsaturyan 81); Kurbashyan (Movsisyan 69).
Referee: Fyodor Zammit.

Kalmar, Tuesday, 10 September 2019

Sweden U21 (1) 1 *(Svanberg 19)*

Republic of Ireland U21 (0) 3 *(Parrott 69, 90, Masterson 87)* 4078

Sweden U21: (442) Dahlberg; Beijmo, Andersson, Hadzikadunic, Poppler-Isherwood (Cajuste 62); Kulusevski, Ingelsson (Hussein 81), Svanberg, Hansson (Larsson 62); Mbunga-Kimpioka (Gyokeres 67), Irandust (Froling 80).
Republic of Ireland U21: (442) Kelleher; O'Connor L, Masterson, O'Shea, Leahy; Mandroiu (Parrott 51), Coventry, Molumby, Elbouzedi (Kilkenny 73); Connolly, Afolabi (Idah 82).
Referee: Rade Obrenovic.

Dublin, Thursday, 10 October 2019

Republic of Ireland U21 (0) 0

Italy U21 (0) 0 7231

Republic of Ireland U21: (352) Kelleher; Masterson, O'Shea, Scales; O'Connor L, Ronan (Knight 62), Coventry, Molumby (Kilkenny 85), Elbouzedi (Obafemi 68); Parrott■, Idah.
Italy U21: (433) Carnesecchi; Del Prato, Bastoni, Marchizza (Adjapong 23), Pellegrini; Locatelli, Tonali, Carraro (Sottil 68); Frattesi, Pinamonti (Cutrone 46), Scamacca (Kean■ 46).
Referee: Sascha Stegemann.

Reykjavik, Tuesday, 15 October 2019

Iceland U21 (1) 1 *(Gudjohnsen 29 (pen))*

Republic of Ireland U21 (0) 0 228

Iceland U21: (4141) Gunnarsson P; Gunnarsson H, Leifsson, Olafsson (Palmason 79), Sampsted; Porsteinsson (Willumsson B 90); Willumsson W, Hauksson, Pordarson (Hafsteinsson 77), Finnsson; Gudjohnsen (Ingimundarson 77).
Republic of Ireland U21: (352) Kelleher; O'Connor L■, Masterson, O'Shea; Ledwidge, Mandroiu (Drinan 86), Coventry, Molumby, Elbouzedi; Obafemi (Kilkenny 75), Idah.
Referee: Dumitri Muntean.

Yerevan, Thursday, 14 November 2019

Armenia U21 (0) 0

Republic of Ireland U21 (0) 1 *(Elbouzedi 63)* 270

Armenia U21: (442) Aslanyan; Geghamy, Nazaryan, Khachumyan, Grigoryan; Melkonyan, Harutyunyan (Khamoyan 66), Hovhannisyan (Movsisyan 78), Nahapetyan (Portugalyan 57); Bichakhchyan, Mkrtchyan.
Republic of Ireland U21: (442) Bazunu; McNamara, O'Shea■, Coventry, Elbouzedi; Idah (Keena 86), Ronan (Scales 77), Knight, Collins; Kilkenny (Taylor 81), O'Connor L.
Referee: Antti Munukka.

Dublin, Tuesday, 19 November 2019

Republic of Ireland U21 (0) 4 *(O'Connor L 50, Idah 63, Parrott 73, Elbouzedi 87)*

Sweden U21 (1) 1 *(Gyokeres 18)* 2760

Republic of Ireland U21: (3421) Bazunu; Masterson (Scales 46), Collins, O'Connor T; O'Connor L, Knight (Taylor 90), Molumby (Ronan 46), Coventry; Elbouzedi, Parrott (Kilkenny 86); Idah (Keena 90).
Sweden U21: (442) Dahlberg; Beijmo, Ahmedhodzic, Hadzikadunic, Bjorkengren; Larsson (Mbunga-Kimpioka 74), Erlingmark, Cajuste, Ingelsson (Hansson 84); Irandust, Gyokeres.
Referee: Karim Abed.

BRITISH UNDER-21 APPEARANCES 1976–2020

Bold type indicates players who made an international appearance in season 2019–20.

ENGLAND

Aarons, M. J. 2020 (Norwich C) 5
Ablett, G. 1988 (Liverpool) 1
Abraham, K. O. T. (Tammy) 2017 (Chelsea) 26
Akpom, C. A. 2015 (Arsenal) 5
Adams, N. 1987 (Everton) 1
Adams, T. A. 1985 (Arsenal) 5
Addison, M. 2010 (Derby Co) 1
Afobe, B. T. 2012 (Arsenal) 2
Agbonlahor, G. 2007 (Aston Villa) 16
Albrighton, M. K. 2011 (Aston Villa) 8
Alexander-Arnold, T. J. 2018 (Liverpool) 3
Alli, B. J. (Dele) 2015 (Tottenham H) 2
Allen, B. 1992 (QPR) 8
Allen, C. 1980 (QPR, Crystal Palace) 3
Allen, C. A. 1995 (Oxford U) 2
Allen, M. 1987 (QPR) 2
Allen, P. 1985 (West Ham U, Tottenham H) 3
Allen, R. W. 1998 (Tottenham H) 3
Alnwick, B. R. 2008 (Tottenham H) 1
Ambrose, D. P. F. 2003 (Ipswich T, Newcastle U, Charlton Ath) 10
Ameobi, F. 2001 (Newcastle U) 19
Ameobi, S. 2012 (Newcastle U) 5
Amos, B. P. 2012 (Manchester U) 3
Anderson, V. A. 1978 (Nottingham F) 1
Anderton, D. R. 1993 (Tottenham H) 12
Andrews, I. 1987 (Leicester C) 1
Ardley, N. C. 1993 (Wimbledon) 10
Armstrong, A. J. 2018 (Newcastle U) 5
Ashcroft, L. 1992 (Preston NE) 1
Ashton, D. 2004 (Crewe Alex, Norwich C) 9
Atherton, P. 1992 (Coventry C) 1
Atkinson, B. 1991 (Sunderland) 6
Awford, A. T. 1993 (Portsmouth) 9

Bailey, G. R. 1979 (Manchester U) 14
Baines, L. J. 2005 (Wigan Ath) 16
Baker, G. E. 1981 (Southampton) 2
Baker, L. R. 2015 (Chelsea) 17
Baker, N. L. 2011 (Aston Villa) 3
Ball, M. J. 1999 (Everton) 7
Bamford, P. J. 2013 (Chelsea) 2
Bannister, G. 1982 (Sheffield W) 1
Barker, S. 1985 (Blackburn R) 4
Barkley, R. 2012 (Everton) 5
Barmby, N. J. 1994 (Tottenham H, Everton) 4
Barnes, H. L. 2019 (Leicester C) 4
Barnes, J. 1983 (Watford) 2
Barnes, P. S. 1977 (Manchester C) 9
Barrett, E. D. 1990 (Oldham Ath) 4
Barry, G. 1999 (Aston Villa) 27
Barton, J. 2004 (Manchester C) 2
Bart-Williams, C. G. 1993 (Sheffield W) 16
Batty, D. 1988 (Leeds U) 7
Bazeley, D. S. 1992 (Watford) 1
Beagrie, P. 1988 (Sheffield U) 2
Beardsmore, R. 1989 (Manchester U) 5
Beattie, J. S. 1999 (Southampton) 5
Beckham, D. R. J. 1995 (Manchester U) 9
Berahino, S. 2013 (WBA) 11
Bennett, J. 2011 (Middlesbrough) 3
Bennett, R. 2012 (Norwich C) 2
Bent, D. A. 2003 (Ipswich T, Charlton Ath) 14
Bent, M. N. 1998 (Crystal Palace) 2
Bentley, D. M. 2004 (Arsenal, Blackburn R) 8
Beeston, C 1988 (Stoke C) 1
Benjamin, T. J. 2001 (Leicester C) 1
Bertrand, R. 2009 (Chelsea) 16
Bertschin, K. E. 1977 (Birmingham C) 3
Bettinelli, M. 2015 (Fulham) 1
Birtles, G. 1980 (Nottingham F) 2
Blackett, T. N. 2014 (Manchester U) 1
Blackstock, D. A. 2008 (QPR) 2
Blackwell, D. R. 1991 (Wimbledon) 6
Blake, M. A. 1990 (Aston Villa) 8
Blissett, L. L. 1979 (Watford) 4
Bond, J. H. 2013 (Watford) 5
Booth, A. D. 1995 (Huddersfield T) 3
Bothroyd, J. 2001 (Coventry C) 1
Bowyer, L. D. 1996 (Charlton Ath, Leeds U) 13
Bracewell, P. 1983 (Stoke C) 13
Bradbury, L. M. 1997 (Portsmouth, Manchester C) 3
Bramble, T. M. 2001 (Ipswich T, Newcastle U) 10
Branch, P. M. 1997 (Everton) 1
Bradshaw, P. W. 1977 (Wolverhampton W) 4
Breacker, T. 1986 (Luton T) 2
Brennan, M. 1987 (Ipswich T) 5
Brewster, R. J. 2020 (Liverpool) 6
Bridge, W. M. 1999 (Southampton) 8
Bridges, M. 1997 (Sunderland, Leeds U) 3
Briggs, M. 2012 (Fulham) 2
Brightwell, I. 1989 (Manchester C) 4
Briscoe, L. S. 1996 (Sheffield W) 5
Brock, K. 1984 (Oxford U) 4
Broomes, M. C. 1997 (Blackburn R) 2
Brown, M. R. 1996 (Manchester C) 4
Brown, W. M. 1999 (Manchester U) 8
Bull, S. G. 1989 (Wolverhampton W) 5
Bullock, M. J. 1998 (Barnsley) 1
Burrows, D. 1989 (WBA, Liverpool) 7
Butcher, T. I. 1979 (Ipswich T) 7
Butland, J. 2012 (Birmingham C, Stoke C) 28
Butt, N. 1995 (Manchester U) 7
Butters, G. 1989 (Tottenham H) 3
Butterworth, I. 1985 (Coventry C, Nottingham F) 8
Bywater, S. 2001 (West Ham U) 6

Cadamarteri, D. L. 1999 (Everton) 3
Caesar, G. 1987 (Arsenal) 3
Cahill, G. J. 2007 (Aston Villa) 3
Callaghan, N. 1983 (Watford) 9
Calvert-Lewin, D. N. 2018 (Everton) 17
Camp, L. M. J. 2005 (Derby Co) 5
Campbell, A. P. 2000 (Middlesbrough) 4
Campbell, F. L. 2008 (Manchester U) 14
Campbell, K. J. 1991 (Arsenal) 4
Campbell, S. 1994 (Tottenham) 11
Cantwell, T. O. 2020 (Norwich C) 1
Carbon, M. P. 1996 (Derby Co) 4
Carr, C. 1985 (Fulham) 1
Carr, F. 1987 (Nottingham F) 9
Carragher, J. L. 1997 (Liverpool) 27
Carroll, A. T. 2010 (Newcastle U) 5
Carroll, T. J. 2013 (Tottenham H) 17
Carlisle, C. J. 2001 (QPR) 3
Carrick, M. 2001 (West Ham U) 14
Carson, S. P. 2004 (Leeds U, Liverpool) 29
Casper, C. M. 1995 (Manchester U) 1
Caton, T. 1982 (Manchester C) 14
Cattermole, L. B. 2008 (Middlesbrough, Wigan Ath, Sunderland) 16
Caulker, S. R. 2011 (Tottenham H) 10
Chadwick, L. H. 2000 (Manchester U) 13
Challis, T. M. 1996 (QPR) 2
Chalobah, N. N. 2012 (Chelsea) 40
Chalobah, T. T. 2020 (Chelsea) 3
Chamberlain, M. 1983 (Stoke C) 4
Chambers, C. 2015 (Arsenal) 22
Chaplow, R. D. 2004 (Burnley) 1
Chapman, L. 1981 (Stoke C) 1
Charles, G. A. 1991 (Nottingham F) 4
Chettle, S. 1988 (Nottingham F) 12
Chilwell, B. J. 2016 (Leicester C) 10
Chopra, R. M. 2004 (Newcastle U) 1
Choudhury, H. D. 2018 (Leicester C) 7
Clark, L. R. 1992 (Newcastle U) 11

Clarke, P. M. 2003 (Everton) 8
Clarke-Salter, J. L. 2018 (Chelsea) 12
Christie, M. N. 2001 (Derby Co) 11
Clegg, M. J. 1998 (Manchester U) 2
Clemence, S. N. 1999 (Tottenham H) 1
Cleverley, T. W. 2010 (Manchester U) 16
Clough, N. H. 1986 (Nottingham F) 15
Clyne, N. E. 2012 (Crystal Palace) 8
Cole, A. 2001 (Arsenal) 4
Cole, A. A. 1992 (Arsenal, Bristol C, Newcastle U) 8
Cole, C. 2003 (Chelsea) 19
Cole, J. J. 2000 (West Ham U) 8
Coney, D. 1985 (Fulham) 4
Connolly, C. A. 2018 (Everton) 4
Connor, T. 1987 (Brighton & HA) 1
Cook, L. J. 2018 (Bournemouth) 14
Cooke, R. 1986 (Tottenham H) 1
Cooke, T. J. 1996 (Manchester U) 4
Cooper, C. T. 1988 (Middlesbrough) 8
Cork, J. F. P. 2009 (Chelsea) 13
Corrigan, J. T. 1978 (Manchester C) 3
Cort, C. E. R. 1999 (Wimbledon) 12
Cottee, A. R. 1985 (West Ham U) 8
Couzens, A. J. 1995 (Leeds U) 3
Cowans, G. S. 1979 (Aston Villa) 5
Cox, N. J. 1993 (Aston Villa) 6
Cranie, M. J. 2008 (Portsmouth) 16
Cranson, I. 1985 (Ipswich T) 5
Cresswell, R. P. W. 1999 (York C, Sheffield W) 4
Croft, G. 1995 (Grimsby T) 4
Crooks, G. 1980 (Stoke C) 4
Crossley, M. G. 1990 (Nottingham F) 3
Crouch, P. J. 2002 (Portsmouth, Aston Villa) 5
Cundy, J. V. 1991 (Chelsea) 3
Cunningham, L. 1977 (WBA) 6
Curbishley, L. C. 1981 (Birmingham C) 1
Curtis, J. C. K. 1998 (Manchester U) 16

Daniel, P. W. 1977 (Hull C) 7
Dann, S. 2008 (Coventry C) 2
Dasilva, J. R. 2018 (Chelsea) 13
Davenport, C. R. P. 2005 (Tottenham H) 8
Davies, A. J. 2004 (Middlesbrough) 1
Davies, C. E. 2006 (WBA) 3
Davies, K. C. 1998 (Southampton, Blackburn R, Southampton) 3
Davies, T. 2018 (Everton) 17
Davis, K. G. 1995 (Luton T) 3
Davis, P. 1982 (Arsenal) 11
Davis, S. 2001 (Fulham) 11
Dawson, C. 2012 (WBA) 15
Dawson, M. R. 2003 (Nottingham F, Tottenham H) 13
Day, C. N. 1996 (Tottenham H, Crystal Palace) 6
D'Avray, M. 1984 (Ipswich T) 2
Deehan, J. M. 1977 (Aston Villa) 7
Defoe, J. C. 2001 (West Ham U) 23
Delfouneso, N. 2010 (Aston Villa) 17
Delph, F. 2009 (Leeds U, Aston Villa) 4
Dennis, M. E. 1980 (Birmingham C) 3
Derbyshire, M. A. 2007 (Blackburn R) 14
Diangana, G. G. 2020 (West Ham U) 1
Dichio, D. S. E. 1996 (QPR) 1
Dickens, A. 1985 (West Ham U) 1
Dicks, J. 1988 (West Ham U) 4
Dier, E. J. E. 2013 (Sporting Lisbon, Tottenham H) 9
Digby, F. 1987 (Swindon T) 5
Dillon, K. P. 1981 (Birmingham C) 1
Dixon, K. M. 1985 (Chelsea) 1
Dobson, A. 1989 (Coventry C) 4
Dodd, J. R. 1991 (Southampton) 8
Donowa, L. 1985 (Norwich C) 3
Dorigo, A. R. 1987 (Aston Villa) 11
Dowell, K. O. 2018 (Everton) 17
Downing, S. 2004 (Middlesbrough) 8
Dozzell, J. 1987 (Ipswich T) 9
Draper, M. A. 1991 (Notts Co) 3
Driver, A. 2009 (Hearts) 1
Duberry, M. W. 1997 (Chelsea) 5
Dunn, D. J. I. 1999 (Blackburn R) 20
Duxbury, M. 1981 (Manchester U) 7
Dyer, B. A. 1994 (Crystal Palace) 10
Dyer, K. C. 1998 (Ipswich T, Newcastle U) 11
Dyson, P. I. 1981 (Coventry C) 4

Eadie, D. M. 1994 (Norwich C) 7
Ebanks-Blake, S. 2009 (Wolverhampton W) 1
Ebbrell, J. 1989 (Everton) 14
Edghill, R. A. 1994 (Manchester C) 3
Ehiogu, U. 1992 (Aston Villa) 15
Ejaria, O. D. 2018 (Liverpool) 1
Elliott, P. 1985 (Luton T) 3
Elliott, R. J. 1996 (Newcastle U) 2
Elliott, S. W. 1998 (Derby Co) 3
Etherington, N, 2002 (Tottenham H) 3
Euell, J. J. 1998 (Wimbledon) 6
Evans, R. 2003 (Chelsea) 2
Eze, E. O. 2020 (QPR) 2

Fairclough, C. 1985 (Nottingham F, Tottenham H) 7
Fairclough, D. 1977 (Liverpool) 1
Fashanu, J. 1980 (Norwich C, Nottingham F) 11
Fear, P. 1994 (Wimbledon) 3
Fenton, G. A. 1995 (Aston Villa) 1
Fenwick, T. W. 1981 (Crystal Palace, QPR) 11
Ferdinand, A. J. 2005 (West Ham U) 17
Ferdinand, R. G. 1997 (West Ham U) 5
Fereday, W. 1985 (QPR) 5
Fielding, F. D. 2009 (Blackburn R) 12
Flanagan, J. 2012 (Liverpool) 3
Flitcroft, G. W. 1993 (Manchester C) 10
Flowers, T. D. 1987 (Southampton) 3
Foden, P. W. 2019 (Manchester C) 15
Ford, M. 1996 (Leeds U) 2
Forster, N. M. 1995 (Brentford) 4
Forsyth, M. 1988 (Derby Co) 1
Forster-Caskey, J. D. 2014 (Brighton & HA) 14
Foster, S. 1980 (Brighton & HA) 1
Fowler, R. B. 1994 (Liverpool) 8
Fox, D. J. 2008 (Coventry C) 1
Froggatt, S. J. 1993 (Aston Villa) 2
Fry, D. J. 2018 (Middlesbrough) 11
Futcher, P. 1977 (Luton T, Manchester C) 11

Gabbiadini, M. 1989 (Sunderland) 2
Gale, A. 1982 (Fulham) 1
Gallagher, C. J. 2020 (Chelsea) 4
Gallen, K. A. 1995 (QPR) 4
Galloway, B. J. 2017 (Everton) 3
Garbutt, L. S. 2014 (Everton) 11
Gardner, A. 2002 (Tottenham H) 1
Gardner, C. 2008 (Aston Villa) 14
Gardner, G. 2012 (Aston Villa) 5
Gascoigne, P. J. 1987 (Newcastle U) 13
Gayle, H. 1984 (Birmingham C) 3
Gernon, T. 1983 (Ipswich T) 1
Gerrard, P. W. 1993 (Oldham Ath) 18
Gerrard, S. G. 2000 (Liverpool) 4
Gibbs, K. J. R. 2009 (Arsenal) 15
Gibbs, N. 1987 (Watford) 5
Gibbs-White, M. A. 2019 (Wolverhampton W) 3
Gibson, B. J. 2014 (Middlesbrough) 10
Gibson, C. 1982 (Aston Villa) 1
Gilbert, W. A. 1979 (Crystal Palace) 11
Goddard, P. 1981 (West Ham U) 8
Godfrey, B. M. 2020 (Norwich C) 3
Gomez, J. D. 2015 (Liverpool) 7
Gordon, D. 1987 (Norwich C) 4
Gordon, D. D. 1994 (Crystal Palace) 13
Gosling, D. 2010 (Everton, Newcastle U) 3
Grant, A. J. 1996 (Everton) 1
Grant, L. A. 2003 (Derby Co) 4
Granville, D. P. 1997 (Chelsea) 3
Gray, A. 1988 (Aston Villa) 2
Gray, D. R. 2016 (Leicester C) 26
Grealish, J. 2016 (Aston Villa) 7
Greening, J. 1999 (Manchester U, Middlesbrough) 18
Greenwood, M. W. J. 2020 (Manchester U) 4
Griffin, A. 1999 (Newcastle U) 3
Grimes, M. J. 2016 (Swansea C) 4
Guehi, A. K. M.-I. (Marc) 2020 (Chelsea) 6

Gunn, A. 2015 (Manchester C, Southampton) 12
Guppy, S. A. 1998 (Leicester C) 1

Haigh, P. 1977 (Hull C) 1
Hall, M. T. J. 1997 (Coventry C) 8
Hall, R. A. 1992 (Southampton) 11
Hamilton, D. V. 1997 (Newcastle U) 1
Hammill, A. 2010 (Wolverhampton W) 1
Harding, D. A. 2005 (Brighton & HA) 4
Hardyman, P. 1985 (Portsmouth) 2
Hargreaves, O. 2001 (Bayern Munich) 3
Harley, J. 2000 (Chelsea) 3
Harrison, J. D. 2018 (Manchester C) 2
Hart, C. J. J. (Joe) 2007 (Manchester C) 21
Hateley, M. 1982 (Coventry C, Portsmouth) 10
Hause, K. P. D. 2015 (Wolverhampton W) 10
Hayden, I. 2017 (Newcastle U) 3
Hayes, M. 1987 (Arsenal) 3
Hazell, R. J. 1979 (Wolverhampton W) 1
Heaney, N. A. 1992 (Arsenal) 6
Heath, A. 1981 (Stoke C, Everton) 8
Heaton, T. D. 2008 (Manchester U) 3
Henderson, D. B. 2018 (Manchester U) 11
Henderson, J. B. 2011 (Sunderland, Liverpool) 27
Hendon, I. M. 1992 (Tottenham H) 7
Hendrie, L. A. 1996 (Aston Villa) 13
Hesford, I. 1981 (Blackpool) 7
Heskey, E. W. I. 1997 (Leicester C, Liverpool) 16
Hilaire, V. 1980 (Crystal Palace) 9
Hill, D. R. L. 1995 (Tottenham H) 4
Hillier, D. 1991 (Arsenal) 1
Hinchcliffe, A. 1989 (Manchester C) 1
Hines, Z. 2010 (West Ham U) 2
Hinshelwood, P. A. 1978 (Crystal Palace) 2
Hirst, D. E. 1988 (Sheffield W) 7
Hislop, N. S. 1998 (Newcastle U) 1
Hoddle, G. 1977 (Tottenham H) 12
Hodge, S. B. 1983 (Nottingham F, Aston Villa) 8
Hodgson, D. J. 1981 (Middlesbrough) 6
Holding, R. S. 2016 (Bolton W, Arsenal) 5
Holdsworth, D. 1989 (Watford) 1
Holgate, M. 2017 (Everton) 6
Holland, C. J. 1995 (Newcastle U) 10
Holland, P. 1995 (Mansfield T) 4
Holloway, D. 1998 (Sunderland) 1
Horne, B. 1989 (Millwall) 5
Howe, E. J. F. 1998 (Bournemouth) 2
Howson, J. M. 2011 (Leeds U) 1
Hoyte, J. R. 2004 (Arsenal) 18
Hucker, P. 1984 (QPR) 2
Huckerby, D. 1997 (Coventry C) 4
Huddlestone, T. A. 2005 (Derby Co, Tottenham H) 33
Hudson-Odoi, C. J. 2020 (Chelsea) 2
Hughes, S. J. 1997 (Arsenal) 8
Hughes, W. J. 2012 (Derby Co) 22
Humphreys, R. J. 1997 (Sheffield W) 3
Hunt, N. B. 2004 (Bolton W) 10

Ibe, J. A. F. 2015 (Liverpool) 4
Impey, A. R. 1993 (QPR) 1
Ince, P. E. C. 1989 (West Ham U) 2
Ince, T. C. 2012 (Blackpool, Hull C) 18
Ings, D. W. J. 2013 (Burnley) 13
Iorfa, D. 2016 (Wolverhampton W) 13

Jackson, M. A. 1992 (Everton) 10
Jagielka, P. N. 2003 (Sheffield U) 6
James, D. B. 1991 (Watford) 10
James, J. C. 1990 (Luton T) 2
James, R. 2020 (Chelsea) 2
Jansen, M. B. 1999 (Crystal Palace, Blackburn R) 6
Jeffers, F. 2000 (Everton, Arsenal) 16
Jemson, N. B. 1991 (Nottingham F) 1
Jenas, J. A. 2002 (Newcastle U) 9
Jenkinson, C. D. 2013 (Arsenal) 14
Jerome, C. 2006 (Cardiff C, Birmingham C) 10
Joachim, J. K. 1994 (Leicester C) 9
Johnson, A. 2008 (Middlesbrough) 19
Johnson, G. M. C. 2003 (West Ham U, Chelsea) 14
Johnson, M. 2008 (Manchester C) 2
Johnson, S. A. M. 1999 (Crewe Alex, Derby Co, Leeds U) 15
Johnson, T. 1991 (Notts Co, Derby Co) 7
Johnston, C. P. 1981 (Middlesbrough) 2
Jones, D. R. 1977 (Everton) 1
Jones, C. H. 1978 (Tottenham H) 1
Jones, D. F. L. 2004 (Manchester U) 1
Jones, P. A. 2011 (Blackburn R) 9
Jones, R. 1993 (Liverpool) 2
Justin, J. M. 2020 (Leicester C) 5

Kane, H. E. 2013 (Tottenham H) 14
Keane, M. V. 2013 (Manchester U, Burnley) 16
Keane, W. D. 2012 (Manchester U) 3
Keegan, G. A. 1977 (Manchester C) 1
Kelly, L. C. 2019 (Bournemouth) 6
Kelly, M. R. 2011 (Liverpool) 8
Kenny, J. 2018 (Everton) 16
Kenny, W. 1993 (Everton) 1
Keown, M. R. 1987 (Aston Villa) 8
Kerslake, D. 1986 (QPR) 1
Kightly, M. J. 2008 (Wolverhampton W) 7
Kilcline, B. 1983 (Notts C) 2
Kilgallon, M. 2004 (Leeds U) 5
King, A. E. 1977 (Everton) 2
King, L. B. 2000 (Tottenham H) 12
Kirkland, C. E. 2001 (Coventry C, Liverpool) 8
Kitson, P. 1991 (Leicester C, Derby Co) 7
Knight, A. 1983 (Portsmouth) 2
Knight, I. 1987 (Sheffield W) 2
Knight, Z. 2002 (Fulham) 4
Konchesky, P. M. 2002 (Charlton Ath) 15
Konsa, E. 2018 (Charlton Ath, Brentford) 7
Kozluk, R. 1998 (Derby Co) 2

Lake, P. 1989 (Manchester C) 5
Lallana, A. D. 2009 (Southampton) 1
Lampard, F. J. 1998 (West Ham U) 19
Langley, T. W. 1978 (Chelsea) 1
Lansbury, H. G. 2010 (Arsenal, Nottingham F) 16
Lascellas, J. 2014 (Newcastle U) 2
Leadbitter, G. 2008 (Sunderland) 3
Lee, D. J. 1990 (Chelsea) 10
Lee, R. M. 1986 (Charlton Ath) 2
Lee, S. 1981 (Liverpool) 6
Lees, T. J. 2012 (Leeds U) 6
Lennon, A. J. 2006 (Tottenham H) 5
Le Saux, G. P. 1990 (Chelsea) 4
Lescott, J. P. 2003 (Wolverhampton W) 2
Lewis, J. P. 2008 (Peterborough U) 5
Lingard, J. E. 2013 (Manchester U) 11
Lita, L. H. 2005 (Bristol C, Reading) 9
Loach, S. J. 2009 (Watford) 14
Loftus-Cheek, R. I. 2015 (Chelsea) 17
Lookman, A. 2018 (Everton) 11
Lowe, D. 1988 (Ipswich T) 2
Lowe, J. J. 2012 (Blackburn R) 11
Lukic, J. 1981 (Leeds U) 7
Lund, G. 1985 (Grimsby T) 3

McCall, S. H. 1981 (Ipswich T) 6
McCarthy, A. S. 2011 (Reading) 3
McDonald, N. 1987 (Newcastle U) 5
McEachran, J. M. 2011 (Chelsea) 13
McEveley, J. 2003 (Blackburn R) 1
McGrath, L. 1986 (Coventry C) 1
MacKenzie, S. 1982 (WBA) 3
McLeary, A. 1988 (Millwall) 1
McLeod, I. M. 2006 (Milton Keynes D) 1
McMahon, S. 1981 (Everton, Aston Villa) 6
McManaman, S. 1991 (Liverpool) 7
McNeil, D. J. M. 2020 (Burnley) 3
McQueen, S. J. 2017 (Southampton) 1
Mabbutt, G. 1982 (Bristol R, Tottenham H) 7
Maddison, J. D. 2018 (Norwich C, Leicester C) 9
Maguire, J. H. 2012 (Sheffield U) 1
Maitland-Niles, A. C. 2018 (Arsenal) 4
Makin, C. 1994 (Oldham Ath) 5
Mancienne, M. I. 2008 (Chelsea) 30

March, S. B. 2015 (Brighton & HA) 3
Marney, D. E. 2005 (Tottenham H) 1
Marriott, A. 1992 (Nottingham F) 1
Marsh, S. T. 1998 (Oxford U) 1
Marshall, A. J. 1995 (Norwich C) 4
Marshall, B. 2012 (Leicester C) 2
Marshall, L. K. 1999 (Norwich C) 1
Martin, L. 1989 (Manchester U) 2
Martyn, A. N. 1988 (Bristol R) 11
Matteo, D. 1994 (Liverpool) 4
Mattock, J. W. 2008 (Leicester C) 5
Matthew, D. 1990 (Chelsea) 9
Mawson, A. R. J. 2017 (Swansea C) 6
May, A. 1986 (Manchester C) 1
Mee, B. 2011 (Manchester C) 2
Merson, P. C. 1989 (Arsenal) 4
Middleton, J. 1977 (Nottingham F, Derby Co) 3
Miller, A. 1988 (Arsenal) 4
Mills, D. J. 1999 (Charlton Ath, Leeds U) 14
Mills, G. R. 1981 (Nottingham F) 2
Milner, J. P. 2004 (Leeds U, Newcastle U, Aston Villa) 46
Mimms, R. 1985 (Rotherham U, Everton) 3
Minto, S. C. 1991 (Charlton Ath) 6
Mitchell, J. 2017 (Derby Co) 1
Moore, I. 1996 (Tranmere R, Nottingham F) 7
Moore, L. 2012 (Leicester C) 10
Moore, L. I. 2006 (Aston Villa) 5
Moran, S. 1982 (Southampton) 2
Morgan, S. 1987 (Leicester C) 2
Morris, J. 1997 (Chelsea) 7
Morrison, R. R. 2013 (West Ham U) 4
Mortimer, P. 1989 (Charlton Ath) 2
Moses, A. P. 1997 (Barnsley) 2
Moses, R. M. 1981 (WBA, Manchester U) 8
Moses, V. 2011 (Wigan Ath) 1
Mount, M. T. 2019 (Chelsea) 4
Mountfield, D. 1984 (Everton) 1
Muamba, F. N. 2008 (Birmingham C, Bolton W) 33
Muggleton, C. D. 1990 (Leicester C) 1
Mullins, H. I. 1999 (Crystal Palace) 3
Murphy, D. B. 1998 (Liverpool) 4
Murphy, Jacob K. 2017 (Norwich C) 6
Murray, P. 1997 (QPR) 4
Murray, M. W. 2003 (Wolverhampton W) 5
Mutch, A. 1989 (Wolverhampton W) 1
Mutch, J. J. E. S. 2011 (Birmingham C) 1
Myers. A. 1995 (Chelsea) 4

Naughton, K. 2009 (Sheffield U, Tottenham H) 9
Naylor, L. M. 2000 (Wolverhampton W) 3
Nelson, R. L. 2019 (Arsenal) 10
Nethercott, S. H. 1994 (Tottenham H) 8
Neville, P. J. 1995 (Manchester U) 7
Newell, M. 1986 (Luton T) 4
Newton, A. L. 2001 (West Ham U) 1
Newton, E. J. I. 1993 (Chelsea) 2
Newton, S. O. 1997 (Charlton Ath) 3
Nicholls, A. 1994 (Plymouth Arg) 1
Nketiah, E. K. 2018 (Arsenal) 8
Nmecha, L. 2018 (Manchester C) 3
Noble, M. J. 2007 (West Ham U) 20
Nolan, K. A. J. 2003 (Bolton W) 1
Nugent, D. J. 2006 (Preston NE) 14

Oakes, M. C. 1994 (Aston Villa) 6
Oakes, S. J. 1993 (Luton T) 1
Oakley, M. 1997 (Southampton) 4
O'Brien, A. J. 1999 (Bradford C) 1
O'Connor, J. 1996 (Everton) 3
O'Hara, J. D. 2008 (Tottenham H) 7
Ojo, O. B. (Sheyi) 2018 (Liverpool) 1
Oldfield, D. 1989 (Luton T) 1
Olney, I. A. 1990 (Aston Villa) 10
O'Neil, G. P. 2005 (Portsmouth) 9
Onomah, J. O. P. 2017 (Tottenham H) 8
Onuoha, C. 2006 (Manchester C) 21
Ord, R. J. 1991 (Sunderland) 3
Osman, R. C. 1979 (Ipswich T) 7
Owen, G. A. 1977 (Manchester C, WBA) 22
Owen, M. J. 1998 (Liverpool) 1
Oxlade-Chamberlain, A. M. D. 2011 (Southampton, Arsenal) 8

Painter, I. 1986 (Stoke C) 1
Palmer, C. L. 1989 (Sheffield W) 4
Palmer, K. R. 2016 (Chelsea) 6
Panzo, J. W. 2020 (Monaco) 3
Parker, G. 1986 (Hull C, Nottingham F) 6
Parker, P. A. 1985 (Fulham) 8
Parker, S. M. 2001 (Charlton Ath) 12
Parkes, P. B. F. 1979 (QPR) 1
Parkin, S. 1987 (Stoke C) 5
Parlour, R. 1992 (Arsenal) 12
Parnaby, S. 2003 (Middlesbrough) 4
Peach, D. S. 1977 (Southampton) 6
Peake, A. 1982 (Leicester C) 1
Pearce, I. A. 1995 (Blackburn R) 3
Pearce, S. 1987 (Nottingham F) 1
Pearce, T. M. 2018 (Leeds U) 2
Pennant, J. 2001 (Arsenal) 24
Pickering N. 1983 (Sunderland, Coventry C) 15
Pickford, J. L. 2015 (Sunderland) 14
Platt, D. 1988 (Aston Villa) 3
Plummer, C. S. 1996 (QPR) 5
Pollock, J. 1995 (Middlesbrough) 3
Porter, G. 1987 (Watford) 12
Potter, G. S. 1997 (Southampton) 1
Powell, N. E. 2012 (Manchester U) 2
Pressman, K. 1989 (Sheffield W) 1
Pritchard, A. D. 2014 (Tottenham H) 9
Proctor, M. 1981 (Middlesbrough, Nottingham F) 4
Prutton, D. T. 2001 (Nottingham F, Southampton) 25
Purse, D. J. 1998 (Birmingham C) 2

Quashie, N. F. 1997 (QPR) 4
Quinn, W. R. 1998 (Sheffield U) 2

Ramage, C. D. 1991 (Derby Co) 3
Ramsdale, A. C. 2018 (Bournemouth) 7
Ranson, R. 1980 (Manchester C) 10
Rashford, M. 2017 (Manchester U) 1
Redknapp, J. F. 1993 (Liverpool) 19
Redmond, N. D. J. 2013 (Birmingham C, Norwich C, Southampton) 38
Redmond, S. 1988 (Manchester C) 14
Reeves, K. P. 1978 (Norwich C, Manchester C) 10
Regis, C. 1979 (WBA) 6
Reid, N. S. 1981 (Manchester C) 6
Reid, P. 1977 (Bolton W) 6
Reo-Coker, N. S. A. 2004 (Wimbledon, West Ham U) 23
Richards, D. I. 1995 (Wolverhampton W) 4
Richards, J. P. 1977 (Wolverhampton W) 2
Richards, M. 2007 (Manchester C) 15
Richards, M. L. 2005 (Ipswich T) 1
Richards, O. T. C. 2020 (Reading) 1
Richardson, K. E. 2005 (Manchester U) 12
Rideout, P. 1985 (Aston Villa, Bari) 5
Ridgewell, L. M. 2004 (Aston Villa) 8
Riggott, C. M. 2001 (Derby Co) 8
Ripley, S. E. 1988 (Middlesbrough) 8
Ritchie, A. 1982 (Brighton & HA) 1
Rix, G. 1978 (Arsenal) 7
Roberts, A. J. 1995 (Millwall, Crystal Palace) 5
Roberts, B. J. 1997 (Middlesbrough) 1
Robins, M. G. 1990 (Manchester U) 6
Robinson, J. 2012 (Liverpool, QPR) 10
Robinson, P. P. 1999 (Watford) 3
Robinson, P. W. 2000 (Leeds U) 11
Robson, B. 1979 (WBA) 7
Robson, S. 1984 (Arsenal, West Ham U) 8
Rocastle, D. 1987 (Arsenal) 14
Roche, L. P. 2001 (Manchester U) 1
Rodger, G. 1987 (Coventry C) 4
Rodriguez, J. E. 2011 (Burnley) 1
Rodwell, J. 2009 (Everton) 21
Rogers, A. 1998 (Nottingham F) 3
Rosario, R. 1987 (Norwich C) 4
Rose, D. L. 2009 (Tottenham H) 29
Rose, M. 1997 (Arsenal) 2
Rosenior, L. J. 2005 (Fulham) 7

Routledge, W. 2005 (Crystal Palace, Tottenham H) 12
Rowell, G. 1977 (Sunderland) 1
Rudd, D. T. 2013 (Norwich C) 1
Ruddock, N. 1989 (Southampton) 4
Rufus, R. R. 1996 (Charlton Ath) 6
Ryan, J. 1983 (Oldham Ath) 1
Ryder, S. H. 1995 (Walsall) 3

Samuel, J. 2002 (Aston Villa) 7
Samways, V. 1988 (Tottenham H) 5
Sansom, K. G. 1979 (Crystal Palace) 8
Scimeca, R. 1996 (Aston Villa) 9
Scowcroft, J. B. 1997 (Ipswich T) 5
Seaman, D. A. 1985 (Birmingham C) 10
Sears, F. D. 2010 (West Ham U) 3
Sedgley, S. 1987 (Coventry C, Tottenham H) 11
Sellars, S. 1988 (Blackburn R) 3
Selley, I. 1994 (Arsenal) 3
Serrant, C. 1998 (Oldham Ath) 2
Sessegnon, K. R. (Ryan) 2018 (Fulham, Tottenham H) 12
Sessegnon, Z. S. (Steven) 2020 (Fulham) 3
Sharpe, L. S. 1989 (Manchester U) 8
Shaw, L. P. H. 2013 (Southampton, Manchester U) 5
Shaw, G. R. 1981 (Aston Villa) 7
Shawcross, R. J. 2008 (Stoke C) 2
Shearer, A. 1991 (Southampton) 11
Shelton, G. 1985 (Sheffield W) 1
Shelvey, J. 2012 (Liverpool, Swansea C) 13
Sheringham, E. P. 1988 (Millwall) 1
Sheron, M. N. 1992 (Manchester C) 16
Sherwood, T. A. 1990 (Norwich C) 4
Shipperley, N. J. 1994 (Chelsea, Southampton) 7
Sidwell, S. J. 2003 (Reading) 5
Simonsen, S. P. A. 1998 (Tranmere R, Everton) 4
Simpson, J. B. 2019 (Bournemouth) 1
Simpson, P. 1986 (Manchester C) 5
Sims, S. 1977 (Leicester C) 10
Sinclair, S. A. 2011 (Swansea C) 7
Sinclair, T. 1994 (QPR, West Ham U) 5
Sinnott, L. 1985 (Watford) 1
Skipp, O. W. 2020 (Tottenham H) 3
Slade, S. A. 1996 (Tottenham H) 4
Slater, S. I. 1990 (West Ham U) 3
Small, B. 1993 (Aston Villa) 12
Smalling, C. L. 2010 (Fulham, Manchester U) 14
Smith, A. 2000 (Leeds U) 10
Smith, A. J. 2012 (Tottenham H) 11
Smith, D. 1988 (Coventry C) 10
Smith, M. 1981 (Sheffield W) 5
Smith, M. 1995 (Sunderland) 1
Smith, T. W. 2001 (Watford) 1
Snodin, I. 1985 (Doncaster R) 4
Soares, T. J. 2006 (Crystal Palace) 4
Solanke, D. A. 2015 (Chelsea, Liverpool, Bournemouth) 18
Sordell, M. A. 2012 (Watford, Bolton W) 14
Spence, J. 2011 (West Ham U) 1
Stanislaus, F. J. 2010 (West Ham U) 2
Statham, B. 1988 (Tottenham H) 3
Statham, D. J. 1978 (WBA) 6
Stead, J. G. 2004 (Blackburn R, Sunderland) 11
Stearman, R. J. 2009 (Wolverhampton W) 4
Steele, J. 2011 (Middlesbrough) 7
Stein, B. 1984 (Luton T) 3
Stephens, J. 2015 (Southampton) 8
Sterland, M. 1984 (Sheffield W) 7
Sterling, R. S. 2012 (Liverpool) 8
Steven, T. M. 1985 (Everton) 2
Stevens, G. A. 1983 (Brighton & HA, Tottenham H) 8
Stewart, J. 2003 (Leicester C) 1
Stewart, P. 1988 (Manchester C) 1
Stockdale, R. K. 2001 (Middlesbrough) 1
Stones, J. 2013 (Everton) 12
Stuart, G. C. 1990 (Chelsea) 5
Stuart, J. C. 1996 (Charlton Ath) 4
Sturridge, D. A. 2010 (Chelsea) 15
Suckling, P. 1986 (Coventry C, Manchester C, Crystal Palace) 10
Summerbee, N. J. 1993 (Swindon T) 3
Sunderland, A. 1977 (Wolverhampton W) 1
Surman, A. R. E. 2008 (Southampton) 4
Surridge, S. W. 2020 (Bournemouth) 2
Sutch, D. 1992 (Norwich C) 4
Sutton, C. R. 1993 (Norwich C) 13
Swift, J. D. 2015 (Chelsea, Reading) 13
Swindlehurst, D. 1977 (Crystal Palace) 1

Talbot, B. 1977 (Ipswich T) 1
Targett, M. R. 2015 (Southampton) 12
Taylor, A. D. 2007 (Middlesbrough) 13
Taylor, M. 2001 (Blackburn R) 1
Taylor, M. S. 2003 (Portsmouth) 3
Taylor, R. A. 2006 (Wigan Ath) 4
Taylor, S. J. 2002 (Arsenal) 3
Taylor, S. V. 2004 (Newcastle U) 29
Terry, J. G. 2001 (Chelsea) 9
Thatcher, B. D. 1996 (Millwall, Wimbledon) 4
Thelwell, A. A. 2001 (Tottenham H) 1
Thirlwell, P. 2001 (Sunderland) 1
Thomas, D. 1981 (Coventry C, Tottenham H) 7
Thomas, J. W. 2006 (Charlton Ath) 2
Thomas, M. 1986 (Luton T) 3
Thomas, M. L. 1988 (Arsenal) 12
Thomas, R. E. 1990 (Watford) 1
Thompson, A. 1995 (Bolton W) 2
Thompson, D. A. 1997 (Liverpool) 7
Thompson, G. L. 1981 (Coventry C) 6
Thorn, A. 1988 (Wimbledon) 5
Thornley, B. L. 1996 (Manchester U) 3
Thorpe, T. J. 2013 (Manchester U) 1
Tiler, C. 1990 (Barnsley, Nottingham F) 13
Tomkins, J. O. C. 2009 (West Ham U) 10
Tomori, O. O. (Fikayo) 2018 (Chelsea) 15
Tonge, M. W. E. 2004 (Sheffield U) 2
Townsend, A. D. 2012 (Tottenham H) 3
Trippier, K. J. 2011 (Manchester C) 2
Tuanzebe, A. 2018 (Manchester U) 1

Unsworth, D. G. 1995 (Everton) 6
Upson, M. J. 1999 (Arsenal) 11

Vassell, D. 1999 (Aston Villa) 11
Vaughan, J. O. 2007 (Everton) 4
Venison, B. 1983 (Sunderland) 10
Vernazza, P. A. P. 2001 (Arsenal, Watford) 2
Vieria, R. A. 2018 (Leeds U) 3
Vinnicombe, C. 1991 (Rangers) 12

Waddle, C. R. 1985 (Newcastle U) 1
Waghorn, M. T. 2012 (Leicester C) 5
Walcott, T. J. 2007 (Arsenal) 21
Wallace, D. L. 1983 (Southampton) 14
Wallace, Ray 1989 (Southampton) 4
Wallace, Rod 1989 (Southampton) 11
Walker, D. 1985 (Nottingham F) 7
Walker, I. M. 1991 (Tottenham H) 9
Walker, K. 2010 (Tottenham H) 7
Walker-Peters, K. L. 2018 (Tottenham H) 11
Walsh, G. 1988 (Manchester U) 2
Walsh, P. A. 1983 (Luton T) 4
Walters, K. 1984 (Aston Villa) 9
Walton, C. T. 2017 (Brighton & HA) 1
Wan Bissaka, A. 2019 (Crystal Palace) 3
Ward, P. 1978 (Brighton & HA) 2
Ward-Prowse, J. M. E. 2013 (Southampton) 31
Warhurst, P. 1991 (Oldham Ath, Sheffield W) 8
Watmore, D. I. 2015 (Sunderland) 13
Watson, B. 2007 (Crystal Palace) 1
Watson, D. 1984 (Norwich C) 7
Watson, D. N. 1994 (Barnsley) 5
Watson, G. 1991 (Sheffield W) 2
Watson, S. C. 1993 (Newcastle U) 12
Weaver, N. J. 2000 (Manchester C) 10
Webb, N. J. 1985 (Portsmouth, Nottingham F) 3
Welbeck, D. 2009 (Manchester U) 14
Welsh, J. J. 2004 (Liverpool, Hull C) 8
Wheater, D. J. 2008 (Middlesbrough) 11
Whelan, P. J. 1993 (Ipswich T) 3
Whelan, N. 1995 (Leeds U) 2
Whittingham, P. 2004 (Aston Villa, Cardiff C) 17

White, D. 1988 (Manchester C) 6
Whyte, C. 1982 (Arsenal) 4
Wickham, C. N. R. 2011 (Ipswich T, Sunderland) 17
Wicks, S. 1982 (QPR) 1
Wilkins, R. C. 1977 (Chelsea) 1
Wilkinson, P. 1985 (Grimsby T, Everton) 4
Williams, D. 1998 (Sunderland) 2
Williams, P. 1989 (Charlton Ath) 4
Williams, P. D. 1991 (Derby Co) 6
Williams, S. C. 1977 (Southampton) 14
Willock, J. G. 2020 (Arsenal) 4
Wilmot, B. L. 2020 (Watford) 1
Wilshere, J. A. 2010 (Arsenal) 7
Wilson, C. E. G. 2014 (Bournemouth) 1
Wilson, J. A. 2015 (Manchester U) 1
Wilson, M. A. 2001 (Manchester U, Middlesbrough) 6
Winks, H. 2017 (Tottenham H) 2
Winterburn, N. 1986 (Wimbledon) 1
Wisdom, A. 2012 (Liverpool) 10
Wise, D. F. 1988 (Wimbledon) 1

Woodcook, A. S. 1978 (Nottingham F) 2
Woodgate, J. S. 2000 (Leeds U) 1
Woodhouse, C. 1999 (Sheffield U) 4
Woodman, F. J. 2017 (Newcastle U) 6
Woodrow, C. 2014 (Fulham) 9
Woods, C. C. E. 1979 (Nottingham F, QPR, Norwich C) 6
Worrall, J. A. 2018 (Nottingham F) 3
Wright, A. G. 1993 (Blackburn R) 2
Wright, M. 1983 (Southampton) 4
Wright, R. I. 1997 (Ipswich T) 15
Wright, S. J. 2001 (Liverpool) 10
Wright, W. 1979 (Everton) 6
Wright-Phillips, S. C. 2002 (Manchester C) 6

Yates, D. 1989 (Notts Co) 5
Young, A. S. 2007 (Watford, Aston Villa) 10
Young, L. P. 1999 (Tottenham H, Charlton Ath) 12

Zaha, D. W. A. 2012 (Crystal Palace, Manchester U) 13
Zamora, R. L. 2002 (Brighton & HA) 6

NORTHERN IRELAND

Allen, C. 2009 (Lisburn Distillery) 1
Amos, D. 2019 (Doncaster R) 2
Armstrong, D. T. 2007 (Hearts) 1

Bagnall, L. 2011 (Sunderland) 1
Bailie, N. 1990 (Linfield) 2
Baird, C. P. 2002 (Southampton) 6
Ball, D. 2013 (Tottenham H) 2
Ball, M. 2011 (Norwich C) 5
Ballard, D. G. 2019 (Arsenal) 3
Balmer, K. 2019 (Ballymena U) 8
Beatty, S. 1990 (Chelsea, Linfield) 2
Bird, P. M. 2019 (Notts Co) 4
Black, J. 2003 (Tottenham H) 1
Black, K. T. 1990 (Luton T) 1
Black, R. Z. 2002 (Morecambe) 1
Blackledge, G. 1978 (Portadown) 1
Blake, R. G. 2011 (Brentford) 2
Blayney, A. 2003 (Southampton) 4
Boyd-Munce, C. S. 2019 (Birmingham C) 7
Boyce, L. 2010 (Cliftonville, Werder Bremen) 8
Boyle, W. S. 1998 (Leeds U) 7
Braniff, K. R. 2002 (Millwall) 11
Breeze, J. 2011 (Wigan Ath) 4
Brennan, C. 2013 (Kilmarnock) 13
Brobbel, R. 2013 (Middlesbrough) 9
Brotherston, N. 1978 (Blackburn R) 1
Brown, C. M. 2020 (Cardiff C) 1
Browne, G. 2003 (Manchester C) 5
Brunt, C. 2005 (Sheffield W) 2
Bryan, M. A. 2010 (Watford) 4
Buchanan, D. T. H. 2006 (Bury) 15
Buchanan, W. B. 2002 (Bolton W, Lisburn Distillery) 5
Burns, A. 2014 (Linfield) 1
Burns, R. (Bobby) 2018 (Glenavon, Hearts) 10
Burns, L. 1998 (Port Vale) 13

Callaghan, A. 2006 (Limavady U, Ballymena U, Derry C) 15
Campbell, S. 2003 (Ballymena U) 1
Camps, C. 2015 (Rochdale) 1
Capaldi, A. C. 2002 (Birmingham C, Plymouth Arg) 14
Carlisle, W. T. 2000 (Crystal Palace) 9
Carroll, R. E. 1998 (Wigan Ath) 11
Carson, J. G. 2011 (Ipswich T, York C) 12
Carson, S. 2000 (Rangers, Dundee U) 2
Carson, T. 2007 (Sunderland) 15
Carvill, M. D. 2008 (Wrexham, Linfield) 8
Casement, C. 2007 (Ipswich T, Dundee) 18
Cathcart, C. 2007 (Manchester U) 15
Catney, R. 2007 (Lisburn Distillery) 1
Chapman, A. 2008 (Sheffield U, Oxford U) 7
Charles, D. 2017 (Fleetwood T) 3
Clarke, L. 2003 (Peterborough U) 4
Clarke, R. 2006 (Newry C) 7
Clarke, R. D. J. 1999 (Portadown) 5

Clingan, S. G. 2003 (Wolverhampton W, Nottingham F) 11
Close, B. 2002 (Middlesbrough) 10
Clucas, M. S. 2011 (Preston NE, Bristol R) 11
Clyde, M. G. 2002 (Wolverhampton W) 5
Colligan, L. 2009 (Ballymena U) 1
Conlan, L. 2013 (Burnley, Morecambe) 11
Connell, T. E. 1978 (Coleraine) 1
Cooper, J. 2015 (Glenavon) 5
Coote, A. 1998 (Norwich C) 12
Convery, J. 2000 (Celtic) 4

Dallas, S. 2012 (Crusaders, Brentford) 2
Davey, H. 2004 (UCD) 3
Davis, S. 2004 (Aston Villa) 3
Devine, D. 1994 (Omagh T) 1
Devine, D. G. 2011 (Preston NE) 2
Devine, J. 1990 (Glentoran) 1
Devlin, C. 2011 (Manchester U, unattached, Cliftonville) 11
Dickson, H. 2002 (Wigan Ath) 1
Doherty, B. 2018 (Derry C) 4
Doherty, J. E. 2014 (Watford, Leyton O, Crawley T) 6
Doherty, M. 2007 (Hearts) 2
Dolan, J. 2000 (Millwall) 6
Donaghy, M. M. 1978 (Larne) 1
Donnelly, L. F. P. 2012 (Fulham, Hartlepool U, Motherwell) 23
Donnelly, M. 2007 (Sheffield U, Crusaders) 5
Donnelly, R. 2013 (Swansea C) 1
Dowie, I. 1990 (Luton T) 1
Drummond, W. 2011 (Rangers) 2
Dudgeon, J. P. 2010 (Manchester U) 4
Duff, S. 2003 (Cheltenham T) 1
Duffy, M. 2014 (Derry C, Celtic) 9
Duffy, S. P. M. 2010 (Everton) 3
Dummigan, C. 2014 (Burnley, Oldham Ath) 18
Dunne, D. 2019 (Cliftonville) 1
Dunwoody, J. 2017 (Stoke C) 12

Elliott, S. 1999 (Glentoran) 3
Ervin, J. 2005 (Linfield) 2
Evans, C. J. 2009 (Manchester U) 10
Evans, J. 2006 (Manchester U) 3

Feeney, L. 1998 (Linfield, Rangers) 8
Feeney, W. 2002 (Bournemouth) 8
Ferguson, M. 2000 (Glentoran) 2
Ferguson, S. 2009 (Newcastle U) 11
Ferris, C. 2020 (Portadown) 1
Finlayson, D. 2019 (Rangers) 1
Fitzgerald, D. 1998 (Rangers) 4
Flanagan, T. M. 2012 (Milton Keynes D) 1
Flynn, J. J. 2009 (Blackburn R, Ross Co) 11
Fordyce, D. T. 2007 (Portsmouth, Glentoran) 12
Friars, E. C. 2005 (Notts Co) 7
Friars, S. M. 1998 (Liverpool, Ipswich T) 21

Galbraith, E. S. W. 2019 (Manchester U) 8
Gallagher, C. 2019 (Glentoran) 4
Garrett, R. 2007 (Stoke C, Linfield) 14
Gartside, N. J. 2020 (Derry C) 2
Gault, M. 2005 (Linfield) 2
Gibb, S. 2009 (Falkirk, Drogheda U) 2
Gilfillan, B. J. 2005 (Gretna, Peterhead) 9
Gillespie, K. R. 1994 (Manchester U) 1
Glendinning, M. 1994 (Bangor) 1
Glendinning, R. 2012 (Linfield) 3
Gordon, S. M. 2017 (Motherwell, Partick Thistle) 9
Gorman, D. A. 2015 (Stevenage, Leyton Orient) 13
Gorman, R. J. 2012 (Wolverhampton W, Leyton Orient) 4
Graham, G. L. 1999 (Crystal Palace) 5
Graham, R. S. 1999 (QPR) 15
Graham, S. 2020 (Blackpool) 2
Gray, J. P. 2012 (Accrington S) 11
Gray, P. 1990 (Luton T) 1
Griffin, D. J. 1998 (St Johnstone) 10
Grigg, W. D. 2011 (Walsall) 10

Hall, B. 2018 (Notts Co) 3
Hamilton, G. 2000 (Blackburn R, Portadown) 12
Hamilton, W. R. 1978 (Linfield) 1
Hanley, N. 2011 (Linfield) 1
Harkin, M. P. 2000 (Wycombe W) 9
Harney, J. J. 2014 (West Ham U) 1
Harvey, J. 1978 (Arsenal) 1
Hawe, S. 2001 (Blackburn R) 2
Hayes, T. 1978 (Luton T) 1
Hazard, C. 2019 (Celtic) 8
Hazley, M. 2007 (Stoke C) 3
Healy, D. J. 1999 (Manchester U) 8
Hegarty, C. 2011 (Rangers) 7
Herron, C. J. 2003 (QPR) 2
Higgins, R. 2006 (Derry C) 1
Hodson, L. J. S. 2010 (Watford) 10
Holden, R. 2019 (Bristol C) 2
Holmes, S. 2000 (Manchester C, Wrexham) 13
Howland, D. 2007 (Birmingham C) 4
Hughes, J. 2006 (Lincoln C) 7
Hughes, L. 2020 (Celtic) 2
Hughes, M. A. 2003 (Tottenham H, Oldham Ath) 12
Hughes, M. E. 1990 (Manchester C) 1
Hunter, M. 2002 (Glentoran) 1

Ingham, M. G. 2001 (Sunderland) 4

Jarvis, D. 2010 (Aberdeen) 2
Johns, C. 2014 (Southampton) 1
Johnson, D. M. 1998 (Blackburn R) 11
Johnson, R. A. 2015 (Stevenage) 13
Johnston, B. 1978 (Cliftonville) 1
Julian, A. A. 2005 (Brentford) 1

Kane, A. M. 2008 (Blackburn R) 5
Kane, M. 2012 (Glentoran) 1
Kee, B. R. 2010 (Leicester C, Torquay U, Burton Alb) 10
Kee, P. V. 1990 (Oxford U) 1
Kelly, D. 2000 (Derry C) 11
Kelly, J. 2019 (Maidenhead U) 2
Kelly, N. 1990 (Oldham Ath) 1
Kennedy, B. J. 2017 (Stevenage) 8
Kennedy, M. C. P. 2015 (Charlton Ath) 7
Kerr, N. 2019 (Glentoran) 2
Kirk, A. R. 1999 (Hearts) 9
Knowles, J. 2012 (Blackburn R) 2

Lafferty, D. 2009 (Celtic) 6
Lafferty, K. 2006 (Burnley) 2
Lavery, C. 2011 (Ipswich T, Sheffield W) 7
Lavery, S. 2017 (Everton, Linfield) 11
Lawrie, J. 2009 (Port Vale, AFC Telford U) 9
Lennon, N. F. 1990 (Manchester C, Crewe Alex) 2
Lester, C. 2013 (Bolton W) 1
Lewis, J. 2017 (Norwich C) 1
Lindsay, K. 2006 (Larne) 1
Little, A. 2009 (Rangers) 6
Lowry, P. 2009 (Institute, Linfield) 6
Lund, M. 2011 (Stoke C) 6
Lyttle, G. 1998 (Celtic, Peterborough U) 8

McAlinden, L. J. 2012 (Wolverhampton W) 3
McAllister, M. 2007 (Dungannon Swifts) 4
McArdle, R. A. 2006 (Sheffield W, Rochdale) 19
McAreavey, P. 2000 (Swindon T) 7
McBride, J. 1994 (Glentoran) 1
McCaffrey, D. 2006 (Hibernian) 8
McCallion, E. 1998 (Coleraine) 1
McCalmont, A. J. 2019 (Leeds U) 8
McCann, A. 2020 (St Johnstone) 4
McCann, G. S. 2000 (West Ham U) 11
McCann, L. 2020 (Dunfermline Ath) 3
McCann, P. 2003 (Portadown) 1
McCann, R. 2002 (Rangers, Linfield) 2
McCartan, S. V. 2013 (Accrington S) 9
McCartney, G. 2001 (Sunderland) 5
McCashin, S. 2011 (Jerez Industrial, unattached) 2
McChrystal, M. 2005 (Derry C) 9
McClean, J. 2010 (Derry C) 3
McClean, K. 2019 (St Johnstone) 6
McClure, M. 2012 (Wycombe W) 1
McCourt, P. J. 2002 (Rochdale, Derry C) 8
McCoy, R. K. 1990 (Coleraine) 1
McCreery, D. 1978 (Manchester U) 1
McCullough, L. 2013 (Doncaster R) 8
McDaid, R. 2015 (Leeds U) 5
McDermott, C. 2017 (Derry C) 4
McDonagh, J. D. C. 2015 (Sheffield U, Derry C) 9
McEleney, S. 2012 (Derry C) 2
McElroy, P. 2013 (Hull C) 1
McEvilly, L. R. 2003 (Rochdale) 9
McFlynn, T. M. 2000 (QPR, Woking, Margate) 19
McGeehan, C. 2013 (Norwich C) 3
McGibbon, P. C. G. 1994 (Manchester U) 1
McGivern, R. 2010 (Manchester C) 6
McGlinchey, B. 1998 (Manchester C, Port Vale, Gillingham) 14
McGonigle, J. 2017 (Coleraine) 4
McGovern, M. 2005 (Celtic) 10
McGowan, M. V. 2006 (Clyde) 2
McGurk, A. 2010 (Aston Villa) 1
McIlroy, T. 1994 (Linfield) 1
McKay, W. 2009 (Leicester C, Northampton T) 7
McKenna, K. 2007 (Tottenham H) 6
McKeown, R. 2012 (Kilmarnock) 12
McKnight, D. 2015 (Shrewsbury T, Stalybridge Celtic) 5
McKnight, P. 1998 (Rangers) 3
McLaughlin, C. G. 2010 (Preston NE, Fleetwood T) 7
McLaughlin, P. 2010 (Newcastle U, York C) 10
McLaughlin, R. 2012 (Liverpool, Oldham Ath) 6
McLean, B. S. 2006 (Rangers) 1
McLean, J. 2009 (Derry C) 4
McLellan, M. 2012 (Preston NE) 1
McMahon, G. J. 2002 (Tottenham H) 1
McMenamin, L. A. 2009 (Sheffield W) 4
McNair, P. J. C. 2014 (Manchester U) 2
McNally, P. 2013 (Celtic) 1
McQuilken, J. 2009 (Tescoma Zlin) 1
McQuoid, J. J. B. 2009 (Bournemouth) 8
McVeigh, A. 2002 (Ayr U) 1
McVeigh, P. M. 1998 (Tottenham H) 11
McVey, K. 2006 (Coleraine) 8
Magee, J. 1994 (Bangor) 1
Magee, J. 2009 (Lisburn Distillery) 1
Magennis, J. B. D. 2010 (Cardiff C, Aberdeen) 16
Magilton, J. 1990 (Liverpool) 1
Magnay, C. 2010 (Chelsea) 1
Maloney, L. 2015 (Middlesbrough) 6
Marron, C. 2020 (Glenavon) 4
Marshall, R. 2017 (Glenavon) 1
Matthews, N. P. 1990 (Blackpool) 1
Meenan, D. 2007 (Finn Harps, Monaghan U) 3
Melaugh, G. M. 2002 (Aston Villa, Glentoran) 11
Millar, K. S. 2011 (Oldham Ath, Linfield) 11
Millar, W. P. 1990 (Port Vale) 1
Miskelly, D. T. 2000 (Oldham Ath) 10
Mitchell, A. 2012 (Rangers) 3
Mitchell, C. 2017 (Burnley) 10

Moreland, V. 1978 (Glentoran) 1
Morgan, D. 2012 (Nottingham F) 4
Morgan, M. P. T. 1999 (Preston NE) 1
Morris, E. J. 2002 (WBA, Glentoran) 8
Morrison, O. 2001 (Sheffield W, Sheffield U) 7
Morrow, A. 2001 (Northampton T) 1
Morrow, S. 2005 (Hibernian) 4
Mulgrew, J. 2007 (Linfield) 10
Mulryne, P. P. 1999 (Manchester U, Norwich C) 5
Murray, W. 1978 (Linfield) 1
Murtagh, C. 2005 (Hearts) 1

Nicholl, J. M. 1978 (Manchester U) 1
Nixon, C. 2000 (Glentoran) 1
Nolan, L. J. 2014 (Crewe Alex, Southport) 4
Norwood, O. J. 2010 (Manchester U) 11

O'Connor, M. J. 2008 (Crewe Alex) 3
O'Hara, G. 1994 (Leeds U) 1
O'Kane, E. 2009 (Everton, Torquay U) 4
O'Mahony, J. 2020 (Glenavon) 1
O'Neill, J. P. 1978 (Leicester C) 1
O'Neill, M. A. M. 1994 (Hibernian) 1
O'Neill, P. 2020 (Glentoran) 1
O'Neill, S. 2009 (Ballymena U) 4
Owens, C. 2018 (QPR) 2

Palmer, C. 2019 (Rangers) 8
Parkhouse, D. 2017 (Sheffield U) 14
Paterson, M. A. 2007 (Stoke C) 2
Patterson, D. J. 1994 (Crystal Palace) 1
Paul, C. D. 2017 (QPR) 3
Peacock-Farrell, B. 2018 (Leeds U) 1

Quigley, C. 2017 (Dundee) 2
Quinn, S. J. 1994 (Blackpool) 1

Ramsey, C. 2011 (Portadown) 3
Ramsey, K. 2006 (Institute) 1
Reid, J. T. 2013 (Exeter C) 2
Robinson, H. D. 2020 (Motherwell) 1
Robinson, S. 1994 (Tottenham H) 1
Rooney, L. J. 2017 (Plymouth Arg) 1
Roy, A. 2019 (Derry C) 2

Scott, J. 2020 (Wolverhampton W) 2
Scullion, D. 2006 (Dungannon Swifts) 8
Sendles-White J. 2013 (QPR, Hamilton A) 12
Sharpe, R. 2013 (Derby Co, Notts Co) 6
Shiels, D. 2005 (Hibernian) 6
Shields, S. P. 2013 (Dagenham & R) 2
Shroot, R. 2009 (Harrow B, Birmingham C) 4
Simms, G. 2001 (Hartlepool U) 14
Singleton, J. 2015 (Glenavon) 2
Skates, G. 2000 (Blackburn R) 4
Sloan, T. 1978 (Ballymena U) 1
Smylie, D. 2006 (Newcastle U, Livingston) 6
Smyth, P. 2017 (Linfield, QPR) 12
Stewart, J. 2015 (Swindon T) 2
Stewart, S. 2009 (Aberdeen) 1
Stewart, T. 2006 (Wolverhampton W, Linfield) 19
Sykes, M. 2017 (Glenavon) 10

Taylor, J. 2007 (Hearts, Glentoran) 10
Taylor, M. S. 1998 (Fulham) 1
Teggart, N. 2005 (Sunderland) 2
Tempest, G. 2013 (Notts Co) 6
Thompson, A. L. 2011 (Watford) 11
Thompson, J. 2017 (Rangers, Blackpool) 13
Thompson, L. 2020 (Blackburn R) 6
Thompson, P. 2006 (Linfield) 4
Toal, E. 2019 (Derry C) 8
Toner, C. 2000 (Tottenham H, Leyton Orient) 17
Tuffey, J. 2007 (Partick Thistle) 13
Turner, C. 2007 (Sligo R, Bohemians) 12

Ward, J. J. 2006 (Aston Villa, Chesterfield) 7
Ward, M. 2006 (Dungannon Swifts) 1
Ward, S. 2005 (Glentoran) 10
Waterman, D. G. 1998 (Portsmouth) 14
Waterworth, A. 2008 (Lisburn Distillery, Hamilton A) 7
Webb, S. M. 2004 (Ross Co, St Johnstone, Ross Co) 6
Weir, R. J. 2009 (Sunderland) 8
Wells, D. P. 1999 (Barry T) 1
Whitley, J. 1998 (Manchester C) 17
Whyte, G. 2015 (Crusaders) 7
Willis, P. 2006 (Liverpool) 1
Winchester, C. 2011 (Oldham Ath) 13
Winchester, J. 2013 (Kilmarnock) 1

SCOTLAND

Adam, C. G. 2006 (Rangers) 5
Adam, G. 2011 (Rangers) 6
Adams, J. 2007 (Kilmarnock) 1
Aitken, R. 1977 (Celtic) 16
Albiston, A. 1977 (Manchester U) 5
Alexander, N. 1997 (Stenhousemuir, Livingston) 10
Allan, S. 2012 (WBA) 10
Anderson, I. 1997 (Dundee, Toulouse) 15
Anderson, R. 1997 (Aberdeen) 15
Andrews, M. 2011 (East Stirlingshire) 1
Anthony, M. 1997 (Celtic) 3
Archdeacon, O. 1987 (Celtic) 1
Archer, J. G. 2012 (Tottenham H) 14
Archibald, A. 1998 (Partick Thistle) 5
Archibald, S. 1980 (Aberdeen, Tottenham H) 5
Archibald, T. V. 2018 (Brentford) 1
Arfield, S. 2008 (Falkirk, Huddersfield T) 17
Armstrong, S. 2011 (Dundee U) 20

Bagen, D. 1997 (Kilmarnock) 4
Bain, K. 1993 (Dundee) 4
Baker, M. 1993 (St Mirren) 10
Baltacha, S. S. 2000 (St Mirren) 3
Bannan, B. 2009 (Aston Villa) 10
Bannigan, S. 2013 (Partick Thistle) 3
Bannon, E. J. 1979 (Hearts, Chelsea, Dundee U) 7
Barclay, J. 2011 (Falkirk) 1
Bates, C. 2019 (Hamburg) 4
Beattie, C. 2004 (Celtic) 7
Beattie, J. 1992 (St Mirren) 4
Beaumont, D. 1985 (Dundee U) 1

Bell, D. 1981 (Aberdeen) 2
Bernard, P. R. J. 1992 (Oldham Ath) 15
Berra, C. 2005 (Hearts) 6
Bett, J. 1981 (Rangers) 7
Black, E. 1983 (Aberdeen) 8
Blair, A. 1980 (Coventry C, Aston Villa) 5
Bollan, G. 1992 (Dundee U, Rangers) 17
Bonar, P. 1997 (Raith R) 4
Booth, C. 2011 (Hibernian) 4
Booth, S. 1991 (Aberdeen) 14
Bowes, M. J. 1992 (Dunfermline Ath) 1
Bowman, D. 1985 (Hearts) 1
Boyack, S. 1997 (Rangers) 1
Boyd, K. 2003 (Kilmarnock) 8
Boyd, T. 1987 (Motherwell) 5
Brandon, J. 2019 (Hearts) 2
Brazil, A. 1978 (Hibernian) 1
Brazil, A. 1979 (Ipswich T) 8
Brebner, G. I. 1997 (Manchester U, Reading, Hibernian) 18
Brighton, T. 2005 (Rangers, Clyde) 7
Broadfoot, K. 2005 (St Mirren) 5
Brophy, E. 2017 (Hamilton A, Kilmarnock) 3
Brough, J. 1981 (Hearts) 1
Brown, A. H. 2004 (Hibernian) 1
Brown, S. 2005 (Hibernian) 10
Browne, P. 1997 (Raith R) 1
Bryson, C. 2006 (Clyde) 1
Buchan, J. 1997 (Aberdeen) 13
Burchill, M. J. 1998 (Celtic) 15
Burke, A. 1997 (Kilmarnock) 4

Burke, C. 2004 (Rangers) 3
Burke, O. J. 2018 (WBA) 9
Burley, C. W. 1992 (Chelsea) 7
Burley, G. E. 1977 (Ipswich T) 5
Burns, H. 1985 (Rangers) 2
Burns, T. 1977 (Celtic) 5
Burt, L. 2017 (Rangers) 5

Cadden, C. 2017 (Motherwell) 12
Caddis, P. 2008 (Celtic, Dundee U, Celtic, Swindon T) 13
Cairney, T. 2011 (Hull C) 6
Caldwell, G. 2000 (Newcastle U) 19
Caldwell, S. 2001 (Newcastle U) 4
Cameron, G. 2008 (Dundee U) 3
Cameron, K. M. 2017 (Newcastle U) 3
Campbell, A. 2018 (Motherwell) 20
Campbell, R. 2008 (Hibernian) 6
Campbell, S. 1989 (Dundee) 3
Campbell, S. P. 1998 (Leicester C) 15
Canero, P. 2000 (Kilmarnock) 17
Cardwell, H. 2014 (Reading) 1
Carey, L. A. 1998 (Bristol C) 1
Carrick, D. 2012 (Hearts) 1
Casey, J. 1978 (Celtic) 1
Chalmers, J. 2014 (Celtic, Motherwell) 2
Christie, M. 1992 (Dundee) 3
Christie, R. 2014 (Inverness CT, Celtic) 9
Clark, R. B. 1977 (Aberdeen) 3
Clarke, S. 1984 (St Mirren) 8
Clarkson, D. 2004 (Motherwell) 13
Cleland, A. 1990 (Dundee U) 11
Cole, D. 2011 (Rangers) 2
Collins, J. 1988 (Hibernian) 8
Collins, N. 2005 (Sunderland) 7
Connolly, P. 1991 (Dundee U) 3
Connor, R. 1981 (Ayr U) 2
Conroy, R. 2007 (Celtic) 4
Considine, A. 2007 (Aberdeen) 5
Cooper, D. 1977 (Clydebank, Rangers) 6
Cooper, N. 1982 (Aberdeen) 13
Coutts, P. A. 2009 (Peterborough U, Preston NE) 7
Crabbe, S. 1990 (Hearts) 2
Craig, M. 1998 (Aberdeen) 2
Craig, T. 1977 (Newcastle U) 1
Crainey, S. D. 2000 (Celtic) 7
Crainie, D. 1983 (Celtic) 1
Crawford, S. 1994 (Raith R) 19
Creaney, G. 1991 (Celtic) 11
Cummings, J. 2015 (Hibernian) 8
Cummings, W. 2000 (Chelsea) 8
Cuthbert, S. 2007 (Celtic, St Mirren) 13

Dailly, C. 1991 (Dundee U) 34
Dalglish, P. 1999 (Newcastle U, Norwich C) 6
Dargo, C. 1998 (Raith R) 10
Davidson, C. I. 1997 (St Johnstone) 2
Davidson, H. N. 2000 (Dundee U) 3
Davidson, M. 2011 (St Johnstone) 1
Dawson, A. 1979 (Rangers) 8
Deas, P. A. 1992 (St Johnstone) 2
Dempster, J. 2004 (Rushden & D) 1
Dennis, S. 1992 (Raith R) 1
Diamond, A. 2004 (Aberdeen) 12
Dickov, P. 1992 (Arsenal) 4
Dixon, P. 2008 (Dundee) 2
Docherty, G. 2017 (Hamilton A) 4
Dodds, D. 1978 (Dundee U) 1
Dods, D. 1997 (Hibernian) 5
Doig, C. R. 2000 (Nottingham F) 13
Donald, G. S. 1992 (Hibernian) 3
Donnelly, S. 1994 (Celtic) 11
Doohan, R. 2018 (Celtic) 8
Dorrans, G. 2007 (Livingston) 6
Dow, A. 1993 (Dundee, Chelsea) 3
Dowie, A. J. 2003 (Rangers, Partick Thistle) 14
Duff, J. 2009 (Inverness CT) 1
Duff, S. 2003 (Dundee U) 9
Duffie, K. 2011 (Falkirk) 6
Duffy, D. A. 2005 (Falkirk, Hull C) 8
Duffy, J. 1987 (Dundee) 1
Durie, G. S. 1987 (Chelsea) 4
Durrant, I. 1987 (Rangers) 4
Doyle, J. 1981 (Partick Thistle) 2

Easton, B. 2009 (Hamilton A) 3
Easton, C. 1997 (Dundee U) 21
Edwards, M. 2012 (Rochdale) 1
Elliot, B. 1998 (Celtic) 2
Elliot, C. 2006 (Hearts) 9
Esson, R. 2000 (Aberdeen) 7

Fagan, S. M. 2005 (Motherwell) 1
Ferguson, B. 1997 (Rangers) 12
Ferguson, D. 1987 (Rangers) 5
Ferguson, D. 1992 (Dundee U) 7
Ferguson, D. 1992 (Manchester U) 5
Ferguson, I. 1983 (Dundee) 4
Ferguson, I. 1987 (Clyde, St Mirren, Rangers) 6
Ferguson, L. 2019 (Aberdeen) 7
Ferguson, R. 1977 (Hamilton A) 1
Feruz, I. 2012 (Chelsea) 4
Findlay, S. 2012 (Celtic) 13
Findlay, W. 1991 (Hibernian) 5
Fitzpatrick, A. 1977 (St Mirren) 5
Fitzpatrick, M. 2007 (Motherwell) 4
Flannigan, C. 1993 (Clydebank) 1
Fleck, J. 2009 (Rangers) 4
Fleck, R. 1987 (Rangers, Norwich C) 6
Fleming, G. 2008 (Gretna) 1
Fletcher, D. B. 2003 (Manchester U) 2
Fletcher, S. 2007 (Hibernian) 7
Forrest, A. 2017 (Ayr U) 1
Forrest, J. 2011 (Celtic) 4
Foster, R. M. 2005 (Aberdeen) 5
Fotheringham, M. M. 2004 (Dundee) 3
Fowler, J. 2002 (Kilmarnock) 3
Foy, R. A. 2004 (Liverpool) 5
Fraser, M. 2012 (Celtic) 5
Fraser, R. 2013 (Aberdeen, Bournemouth) 10
Fraser, S. T. 2000 (Luton T) 4
Freedman, D. A. 1995 (Barnet, Crystal Palace) 8
Fridge, L. 1989 (St Mirren) 2
Fullarton, J. 1993 (St Mirren) 17
Fulton, J. 2014 (Swansea C) 2
Fulton, R. 2017 (Liverpool, Hamilton A) 11
Fulton, M. 1980 (St Mirren) 5
Fulton, S. 1991 (Celtic) 7
Fyvie, F. 2012 (Wigan Ath) 8

Gallacher, K. W. 1987 (Dundee U) 7
Gallacher, P. 1999 (Dundee U) 7
Gallacher, S. 2009 (Rangers) 2
Gallagher, P. 2003 (Blackburn R) 11
Galloway, M. 1989 (Hearts, Celtic) 2
Gardiner, J. 1993 (Hibernian) 1
Gauld, R. 2013 (Dundee U, Sporting Lisbon) 11
Geddes, R. 1982 (Dundee) 5
Gemmill, S. 1992 (Nottingham F) 4
Germaine, G. 1997 (WBA) 1
Gilles, R. 1997 (St Mirren) 7
Gillespie, G. T. 1979 (Coventry C) 8
Gilmour, B. C. 2019 (Chelsea) 12
Glass, S. 1995 (Aberdeen) 11
Glover, L. 1988 (Nottingham F) 3
Goodwillie, D. 2009 (Dundee U) 9
Goram, A. L. 1987 (Oldham Ath) 1
Gordon, C. S. 2003 (Hearts) 5
Gough, C. R. 1983 (Dundee U) 5
Graham, D. 1998 (Rangers) 8
Grant, P. 1985 (Celtic) 10
Gray, D. P. 2009 (Manchester U) 2
Gray, S. 1987 (Aberdeen) 1
Gray S. 1995 (Celtic) 7
Griffiths, L. 2010 (Dundee, Wolverhampton W) 11
Grimmer, J. 2014 (Fulham) 1
Gunn, B. 1984 (Aberdeen) 9

Hagen, D. 1992 (Rangers) 8
Hamill, J. 2008 (Kilmarnock) 11

Hamilton, B. 1989 (St Mirren) 4
Hamilton, C. 2018 (Hearts) 3
Hamilton, J. 1995 (Dundee, Hearts) 14
Hamilton, J. 2014 (Hearts) 8
Hammell, S. 2001 (Motherwell) 11
Handling, D. 2014 (Hibernian) 3
Handyside, P. 1993 (Grimsby T) 7
Hanley, G. 2011 (Blackburn R) 1
Hanlon, P. 2009 (Hibernian) 23
Hannah, D. 1993 (Dundee U) 16
Hardie, R. 2017 (Rangers) 8
Harper, K. 1995 (Hibernian) 7
Hartford, R. A. 1977 (Manchester C) 1
Hartley, P. J. 1997 (Millwall) 1
Harvie, D. 2018 (Aberdeen, Ayr U) 10
Hastie, J. 2019 (Motherwell) 1
Hegarty, P. 1987 (Dundee U) 6
Henderson, E. 2020 (Celtic) 1
Henderson, L. 2015 (Celtic) 9
Hendrie, S. 2014 (West Ham U) 3
Hendry, J. 1992 (Tottenham H) 1
Henly, J. 2014 (Reading) 1
Herron, J. 2012 (Celtic) 2
Hetherston, B. 1997 (St Mirren) 1
Hewitt, J. 1982 (Aberdeen) 6
Hogg, G. 1984 (Manchester U) 4
Holsgrove, J. 2019 (Reading) 5
Holt, J. 2012 (Hearts) 7
Hood, G. 1993 (Ayr U) 3
Horn, R. 1997 (Hearts) 6
Hornby, F. D. I. 2018 (Everton) 13
House, B. 2019 (Reading) 1
Howie, S. 1993 (Cowdenbeath) 5
Hughes, R. D. 1999 (Bournemouth) 9
Hughes, S. 2002 (Rangers) 12
Hunter, G. 1987 (Hibernian) 3
Hunter, P. 1989 (East Fife) 3
Hutton, A. 2004 (Rangers) 7
Hutton, K. 2011 (Rangers) 1
Hyam, D. J. 2014 (Reading) 5

Iacovitti, A. 2017 (Nottingham F) 4
Inman, B. 2011 (Newcastle U) 2
Irvine, G. 2006 (Celtic) 2

Jack, R. 2012 (Aberdeen) 19
James, K. F. 1997 (Falkirk) 1
Jardine, I. 1979 (Kilmarnock) 1
Jess, E. 1990 (Aberdeen) 14
Johnson, G. I. 1992 (Dundee U) 6
Johnston, A. 1994 (Hearts) 3
Johnston, F. 1993 (Falkirk) 1
Johnston, G. 2019 (Liverpool, Feyenoord) 7
Johnston, M. 1984 (Partick Thistle, Watford) 3
Johnston, M. A. 2018 (Celtic) 7
Jones, J. C. 2017 (Crewe Alex) 4
Jordan, A. J. 2000 (Bristol C) 3
Jules, Z. K. 2017 (Reading) 3
Jupp, D. A. 1995 (Fulham) 9

Kelly, L. A. 2017 (Reading) 11
Kelly, S. 2014 (St Mirren) 1
Kelly, S. 2020 (Rangers) 2
Kennedy, J. 2003 (Celtic) 15
Kennedy, M. 2012 (Kilmarnock) 1
Kenneth, G. 2008 (Dundee U) 8
Kerr, B. 2003 (Newcastle U) 14
Kerr, F. 2012 (Birmingham C) 3
Kerr, J. 2018 (St Johnstone) 6
Kerr, M. 2001 (Kilmarnock) 1
Kerr, S. 1993 (Celtic) 10
Kettings, C. D. 2012 (Blackpool) 3
King, A. 2014 (Swansea C) 1
King, C. M. 2014 (Norwich C) 1
King, W. 2015 (Hearts) 8
Kingsley, S. 2015 (Swansea C) 6
Kinniburgh, W. D. 2004 (Motherwell) 3
Kirkwood, D. 1990 (Hearts) 1
Kyle, K. 2001 (Sunderland) 12

Lambert, P. 1991 (St Mirren) 11
Langfield, J. 2000 (Dundee) 2
Lappin, S. 2004 (St Mirren) 10
Lauchlan, J. 1998 (Kilmarnock) 11
Lavety, B. 1993 (St Mirren) 9
Lavin, G. 1993 (Watford) 7
Lawson, P. 2004 (Celtic) 10
Leighton, J. 1982 (Aberdeen) 1
Lennon, S. 2008 (Rangers) 6
Levein, C. 1985 (Hearts) 2
Leven, P. 2005 (Kilmarnock) 2
Liddell, A. M. 1994 (Barnsley) 12
Lindsey, J. 1979 (Motherwell) 1
Locke, G. 1994 (Hearts) 10
Love, D. 2015 (Manchester U) 5
Love, G. 1995 (Hibernian) 1
Loy, R. 2009 (Dunfermline Ath, Rangers) 5
Lynch, S. 2003 (Celtic, Preston NE) 13

McAllister, G. 1990 (Leicester C) 1
McAllister, K. 2019 (Derby Co, St Mirren) 2
McAllister, R. 2008 (Inverness CT) 2
McAlpine, H. 1983 (Dundee U) 5
McAnespie, K. 1998 (St Johnstone) 4
McArthur, J. 2008 (Hamilton A) 2
McAuley, S. 1993 (St Johnstone) 1
McAvennie, F. 1982 (St Mirren) 5
McBride, J. 1981 (Everton) 1
McBride, J. P. 1998 (Celtic) 2
McBurnie, O. 2015 (Swansea C) 12
McCabe, R. 2012 (Rangers, Sheffield W) 3
McCall, A. S. M. 1988 (Bradford C, Everton) 2
McCann, K. 2008 (Hibernian) 4
McCann, N. 1994 (Dundee) 9
McCart, J. 2017 (Celtic) 1
McClair, B. 1984 (Celtic) 8
McCluskey, G. 1979 (Celtic) 6
McCluskey, S. 1997 (St Johnstone) 14
McCoist, A. 1984 (Rangers) 1
McConnell, I. 1997 (Clyde) 1
McCormack, D. 2008 (Hibernian) 1
McCormack, R. 2006 (Rangers, Motherwell, Cardiff C) 13
McCracken, D. 2002 (Dundee U) 5
McCrorie, Robby 2018 (Rangers) 7
McCrorie, Ross 2017 (Rangers) 16
McCulloch, A. 1981 (Kilmarnock) 1
McCulloch, I. 1982 (Notts Co) 2
McCulloch, L. 1997 (Motherwell) 14
McCunnie, J. 2001 (Dundee U, Ross Co, Dunfermline Ath) 20
MacDonald, A. 2011 (Burnley) 6
MacDonald, C. 2017 (Derby Co) 2
MacDonald, J. 1980 (Rangers) 8
MacDonald, J. 2007 (Hearts) 11
McDonald, C. 1995 (Falkirk) 5
McDonald, K. 2008 (Dundee, Burnley) 14
McEwan, C. 1997 (Clyde, Raith R) 17
McEwan, D. 2003 (Livingston) 2
McFadden, J. 2003 (Motherwell) 7
McFadzean C. 2015 (Sheffield U) 3
McFarlane, D. 1997 (Hamilton A) 3
McGarry, S. 1997 (St Mirren) 3
McGarvey, F. P. 1977 (St Mirren, Celtic) 3
McGarvey, S. 1982 (Manchester U) 4
McGeough, D. 2012 (Celtic) 10
McGhee, J. 2013 (Hearts) 20
McGhee, M. 1981 (Aberdeen) 1
McGinn, J. 2014 (St Mirren, Hibernian) 9
McGinn, S. 2009 (St Mirren, Watford) 8
McGinnis, G. 1985 (Dundee U) 1
McGlinchey, M. R. 2007 (Celtic) 1
McGregor, A. 2003 (Rangers) 6
McGregor, C. W. 2013 (Celtic) 5
McGrillen, P. 1994 (Motherwell) 2
McGuire, D. 2002 (Aberdeen) 2
McHattie, K. 2012 (Hearts) 6
McInally, J. 1989 (Dundee U) 1
McIntyre, T. P. 2019 (Reading) 1
McKay, B. 2012 (Rangers) 4
McKay, B. 2013 (Hearts) 1

McKean, K. 2011 (St Mirren) 1
McKenna, S. 2018 (Aberdeen) 5
McKenzie, R. 2013 (Kilmarnock) 4
McKenzie, R. 1997 (Hearts) 2
McKimmie, S. 1985 (Aberdeen) 3
McKinlay, T. 1984 (Dundee) 6
McKinlay, W. 1989 (Dundee U) 6
McKinnon, R. 1991 (Dundee U) 6
McLaren, A, 1989 (Hearts) 11
McLaren, A. 1993 (Dundee U) 4
McLaughlin, B. 1995 (Celtic) 8
McLaughlin, J. 1981 (Morton) 10
McLean, E. 2008 (Dundee U, St Johnstone) 2
McLean, S. 2003 (Rangers) 4
McLeish, A. 1978 (Aberdeen) 6
McLean, K. 2012 (St Mirren) 11
McLennon, C. 2020 (Aberdeen) 4
MacLeod, A. 1979 (Hibernian) 3
McLeod, J. 1989 (Dundee U) 2
MacLeod, L. 2012 (Rangers) 8
MacLeod, M. 1979 (Dumbarton, Celtic) 5
McManus, D. J. 2014 (Aberdeen, Fleetwood T) 4
McManus, T. 2001 (Hibernian) 14
McMillan, S. 1997 (Motherwell) 4
McMullan, P. 2017 (Celtic) 1
McNab, N. 1978 (Tottenham H) 1
McNally, M. 1991 (Celtic) 2
McNamara, J. 1994 (Dunfermline Ath, Celtic) 12
McNaughton, K. 2002 (Aberdeen) 1
McNeil, A. 2007 (Hibernian) 1
McNichol, J. 1979 (Brentford) 7
McNiven, D. 1977 (Leeds U) 3
McNiven, S. A. 1996 (Oldham Ath) 1
McParland, A. 2003 (Celtic) 1
McPhee, S. 2002 (Port Vale) 1
McPherson, D. 1984 (Rangers, Hearts) 4
McQuilken, J. 1993 (Celtic) 2
McStay, P. 1983 (Celtic) 5
McWhirter, N. 1991 (St Mirren) 1
Mackay-Steven, G. 2012 (Dundee U) 3
Mackie, S. 2019 (Hibernian) 1
Magennis, K. 2019 (St Mirren) 5
Maguire, B. 2019 (Motherwell) 6
Maguire, C. 2009 (Aberdeen) 12
Main, A. 1988 (Dundee U) 3
Malcolm, R. 2001 (Rangers) 1
Mallan, S. 2017 (St Mirren, Barnsley, St Mirren) 9
Maloney, S. 2002 (Celtic) 21
Malpas, M. 1983 (Dundee U) 8
Marr, B. 2011 (Ross Co) 1
Marshall, D. J. 2004 (Celtic) 10
Marshall, S. R. 1995 (Arsenal) 5
Martin, A. 2009 (Leeds U, Ayr U) 12
Mason, G. R. 1999 (Manchester C, Dunfermline Ath) 2
Mathieson, D. 1997 (Queen of the South) 3
May, E. 1989 (Hibernian) 2
May, S. 2013 (St Johnstone, Sheffield W) 8
Meldrum, C. 1996 (Kilmarnock) 6
Melrose, J. 1977 (Partick Thistle) 8
Middleton, G. B. D. 2018 (Rangers) 11
Millar, M, 2009 (Celtic) 1
Miller, C. 1995 (Rangers) 8
Miller, J. 1987 (Aberdeen, Celtic) 7
Miller, K. 2000 (Hibernian, Rangers) 7
Miller, W. 1991 (Hibernian) 7
Miller, W. F. 1978 (Aberdeen) 2
Milne, K. 2000 (Hearts) 1
Milne, R. 1982 (Dundee U) 3
Mitchell, C. 2008 (Falkirk) 7
Money, I. C. 1987 (St Mirren) 3
Montgomery, N. A. 2003 (Sheffield U) 2
Morgan, L. 2017 (Celtic) 9
Morrison, S. A. 2004 (Aberdeen, Dunfermline Ath) 12
Muir, L. 1977 (Hibernian) 1
Mulgrew, C. P. 2006 (Celtic, Wolverhampton W, Aberdeen) 14
Murphy J. 2009 (Motherwell) 13
Murray, H. 2000 (St Mirren) 3
Murray, I. 2001 (Hibernian) 15
Murray, N. 1993 (Rangers) 16
Murray, R. 1993 (Bournemouth) 1
Murray, S. 2004 (Kilmarnock) 2

Narey, D. 1977 (Dundee U) 4
Naismith, J. 2014 (St Mirren) 1
Naismith, S. J. 2006 (Kilmarnock, Rangers) 15
Naysmith, G. A. 1997 (Hearts) 22
Neilson, R. 2000 (Hearts) 1
Nesbitt, A. 2017 (Celtic) 2
Ness, J, 2011 (Rangers) 2
Nevin, P. 1985 (Chelsea) 5
Nicholas, C. 1981 (Celtic, Arsenal) 6
Nicholson, B. 1999 (Rangers) 7
Nicholson, S. 2015 (Hearts) 8
Nicol, S. 1981 (Ayr U, Liverpool) 14
Nisbet, S. 1989 (Rangers) 5
Noble, D. J. 2003 (West Ham U) 2
Notman, A. M. 1999 (Manchester U) 10

O'Brien, B. 1999 (Blackburn R, Livingston) 6
O'Connor, G. 2003 (Hibernian) 8
O'Donnell, P. 1992 (Motherwell) 8
O'Donnell, S. 2013 (Partick Thistle) 1
O'Halloran, M. 2012 (Bolton W) 2
O'Hara, M. 2015 (Kilmarnock, Dundee) 2
O'Leary, R. 2008 (Kilmarnock) 2
O'Neil, B. 1992 (Celtic) 7
O'Neil, J. 1991 (Dundee U) 1
O'Neill, M. 1995 (Clyde) 6
Orr, N. 1978 (Morton) 7

Palmer, L. J. 2011 (Sheffield W) 8
Park, C. 2012 (Middlesbrough) 1
Parker, K. 2001 (St Johnstone) 1
Parlane, D. 1977 (Rangers) 1
Paterson, C. 1981 (Hibernian) 2
Paterson, C. 2012 (Hearts) 12
Paterson, J. 1997 (Dundee U) 9
Pawlett, P. 2012 (Aberdeen) 7
Payne, G. 1978 (Dundee U) 3
Peacock, L. A. 1997 (Carlisle U) 1
Pearce, A. J. 2008 (Reading) 2
Pearson, S. P. 2003 (Motherwell) 8
Perry, R. 2010 (Rangers, Falkirk, Rangers) 16
Polworth, L. 2016 (Inverness CT) 1
Porteous, R. 2018 (Hibernian) 11
Pressley, S. J. 1993 (Rangers, Coventry C, Dundee U) 26
Provan, D. 1977 (Kilmarnock) 1
Prunty, B. 2004 (Aberdeen) 6

Quinn, P. C. 2004 (Motherwell) 3
Quinn, R. 2006 (Celtic) 9
Quitongo, J. 2017 (Hamilton A) 1

Rae, A. 1991 (Millwall) 8
Rae, G. 1999 (Dundee) 6
Ralston, A. 2018 (Celtic) 5
Reading, P. J. 2020 (Stevenage) 4
Redford, I. 1981 (Rangers) 6
Reid, B. 1991 (Rangers) 4
Reid, C. 1993 (Hibernian) 3
Reid, M. 1982 (Celtic) 2
Reid, R. 1977 (St Mirren) 3
Reilly, A. 2004 (Wycombe W) 1
Renicks, S. 1997 (Hamilton A) 1
Reynolds, M. 2007 (Motherwell) 9
Rhodes, J. L. 2011 (Huddersfield T) 8
Rice, B. 1985 (Hibernian) 1
Richardson, L. 1980 (St Mirren) 2
Ridgers, M. 2012 (Hearts) 5
Riordan, D. G. 2004 (Hibernian) 5
Ritchie, A. 1980 (Morton) 1
Ritchie, P. S. 1996 (Hearts) 7
Robertson, A. 1991 (Rangers) 1
Robertson, A. 2013 (Dundee U, Hull C) 4
Robertson, C. 1977 (Rangers) 1
Robertson, C. 2012 (Aberdeen) 10
Robertson, D. 2007 (Dundee U) 4
Robertson, D. A. 1987 (Aberdeen) 7
Robertson, G. A. 2004 (Nottingham F, Rotherham U) 15

Robertson, H. 1994 (Aberdeen)	2
Robertson, J. 1985 (Hearts)	2
Robertson, L. 1993 (Rangers)	3
Robertson, S. 1998 (St Johnstone)	2
Roddie, A. 1992 (Aberdeen)	5
Ross, G. 2007 (Dunfermline Ath)	1
Ross, N. 2011 (Inverness CT)	2
Ross, T. W. 1977 (Arsenal)	1
Rowson, D. 1997 (Aberdeen)	5
Ruddy, J. 2017 (Wolverhampton W)	1
Russell, J. 2011 (Dundee U)	11
Russell, R. 1978 (Rangers)	3
Salton, D. B. 1992 (Luton T)	6
Sammut, R. A. M. 2017 (Chelsea)	3
Samson, C. I. 2004 (Kilmarnock)	6
Saunders, S. 2011 (Motherwell)	2
Scobbie, T. 2008 (Falkirk)	12
Scott, J. 2020 (Motherwell)	**1**
Scott, M. 2006 (Livingston)	1
Scott, P. 1994 (St Johnstone)	4
Scougall, S. 2012 (Livingston, Sheffield U)	2
Scrimgour, D. 1997 (St Mirren)	3
Seaton, A. 1998 (Falkirk)	1
Severin, S. D. 2000 (Hearts)	10
Shankland, L. 2015 (Aberdeen)	4
Shannon, R. 1987 (Dundee)	7
Sharp, G. M. 1982 (Everton)	1
Sharp, R. 1990 (Dunfermline Ath)	4
Shaw, O. 2019 (Hibernian)	2
Sheerin, P. 1996 (Southampton)	1
Sheppard, J. 2017 (Reading)	2
Shields, G. 1997 (Rangers)	2
Shinnie, A. 2009 (Dundee, Rangers)	3
Shinnie, G. 2012 (Inverness CT)	2
Simmons, S. 2003 (Hearts)	1
Simpson, N. 1982 (Aberdeen)	11
Sinclair, G. 1977 (Dumbarton)	1
Skilling, M. 1993 (Kilmarnock)	2
Slater, C. 2014 (Kilmarnock, Colchester U)	9
Smith, B. M. 1992 (Celtic)	5
Smith, C. 2008 (St Mirren)	2
Smith, C. 2015 (Aberdeen)	1
Smith, D. 2012 (Hearts)	4
Smith, D. L. 2006 (Motherwell)	2
Smith, G. 1978 (Rangers)	1
Smith, G. 2004 (Rangers)	8
Smith, H. G. 1987 (Hearts)	2
Smith, L. 2017 (Hearts, Ayr U)	12
Smith, L. 2020 (Hamilton A)	**1**
Smith, S. 2007 (Rangers)	1
Sneddon, A. 1979 (Celtic)	1
Snodgrass, R. 2008 (Livingston)	2
Soutar, D. 2003 (Dundee)	11
Souttar, J. 2016 (Dundee U, Hearts)	11
Speedie, D. R. 1985 (Chelsea)	1
Spencer, J. 1991 (Rangers)	3
Stanton, P. 1977 (Hibernian)	1
Stanton, S. 2014 (Hibernian)	1
Stark, W. 1985 (Aberdeen)	1
St Clair, H. 2018 (Chelsea)	3
Stephen, R. 1983 (Dundee)	1
Stevens, G. 1977 (Motherwell)	1
Stevenson, L. 2008 (Hibernian)	8
Stewart, C. 2002 (Kilmarnock)	1
Stewart, J. 1978 (Kilmarnock, Middlesbrough)	3
Stewart, M. J. 2000 (Manchester U)	17
Stewart, R. 1979 (Dundee U, West Ham U)	12
Stillie, D. 1995 (Aberdeen)	14
Storie, C. 2017 (Aberdeen)	2
Strachan, G. D. 1998 (Coventry C)	7
Sturrock, P. 1977 (Dundee U)	9
Sweeney, P. H. 2004 (Millwall)	8
Sweeney, S. 1991 (Clydebank)	7
Tapping, C. 2013 (Hearts)	1
Tarrant, N. K. 1999 (Aston Villa)	5
Taylor, G. J. 2017 (Kilmarnock)	14
Teale, G. 1997 (Clydebank, Ayr U)	6
Telfer, P. N. 1993 (Luton T)	3
Templeton, D. 2011 (Hearts)	2
Thomas, D. 2017 (Motherwell)	6
Thomas, K. 1993 (Hearts)	8
Thompson, S. 1997 (Dundee U)	12
Thomson, C. 2011 (Hearts)	2
Thomson, J. A. 2017 (Celtic)	1
Thomson, K. 2005 (Hibernian)	6
Thomson, W. 1977 (Partick Thistle, St Mirren)	10
Tolmie, J. 1980 (Morton)	1
Tortolano, J. 1987 (Hibernian)	2
Toshney, L. 2012 (Celtic)	5
Turnbull, D. 2019 (Motherwell)	1
Turner, I. 2005 (Everton)	6
Tweed, S. 1993 (Hibernian)	3
Wales, G. 2000 (Hearts)	1
Walker, A. 1988 (Celtic)	1
Walker, J. 2013 (Hearts)	1
Wallace, I. A. 1978 (Coventry C)	1
Wallace, L. 2007 (Hearts)	10
Wallace, M. 2012 (Hudderfield T)	4
Wallace, R. 2004 (Celtic, Sunderland)	4
Walsh, C. 1984 (Nottingham F)	5
Wark, J. 1977 (Ipswich T)	8
Watson, A. 1981 (Aberdeen)	4
Watson, K. 1977 (Rangers)	2
Watt, A. 2012 (Celtic)	9
Watt, E. 2018 (Wolverhampton W)	3
Watt, M. 1991 (Aberdeen)	12
Watt. S. M. 2005 (Chelsea)	5
Webster, A. 2003 (Hearts)	2
Whiteford, A. 1997 (St Johnstone)	1
Whittaker, S. G. 2005 (Hibernian)	18
Whyte, D. 1987 (Celtic)	9
Wighton, C. R. 2017 (Dundee)	6
Wilkie, L. 2000 (Dundee)	6
Will, J. A. 1992 (Arsenal)	3
Williams, G. 2002 (Nottingham F)	9
Williamson, R. 2018 (Dunfermline)	4
Wilson, D. 2011 (Liverpool, Hearts)	13
Wilson, I. 2018 (Kilmarnock)	7
Wilson, M. 2004 (Dundee U, Celtic)	19
Wilson, S. 1999 (Rangers)	7
Wilson, T. 1983 (St Mirren)	1
Wilson, T. 1988 (Nottingham F)	4
Winnie, D. 1988 (St Mirren)	1
Woods, M. 2006 (Sunderland)	2
Wotherspoon, D. 2011 (Hibernian)	16
Wright, P. 1989 (Aberdeen, QPR)	3
Wright, Stephen 1991 (Aberdeen)	14
Wright, Scott 2018 (Aberdeen)	5
Wright, T. 1987 (Oldham Ath)	1
Wylde, G. 2011 (Rangers)	7
Young, Darren 1997 (Aberdeen)	8
Young, Derek 2000 (Aberdeen)	5

WALES

Abbruzzese, R. 2018 (Cardiff C) 3
Absolom, K. 2019 (Ostersund) 1
Adams, N. W. 2008 (Bury, Leicester C) 5
Alfei, D. M. 2010 (Swansea C) 13
Aizlewood, M. 1979 (Luton T) 2
Allen, J. M. 2008 (Swansea C) 13
Anthony, B. 2005 (Cardiff C) 8

Babos, A. 2018 (Derby Co) 7
Baddeley, L. M. 1996 (Cardiff C) 2
Baker, A. T. 2019 (Sheffield W) 3
Balcombe, S. 1982 (Leeds U) 1
Bale, G. 2006 (Southampton, Tottenham H) 4
Barnhouse, D. J. 1995 (Swansea C) 3
Basey, G. W. 2009 (Charlton Ath) 1
Bater, P. T. 1977 (Bristol R) 2
Beevers, L. J. 2005 (Boston U, Lincoln C) 7
Bellamy, C. D. 1996 (Norwich C) 8
Bender, T. J. 2011 (Colchester U) 4
Birchall, A. S. 2003 (Arsenal, Mansfield T) 12
Bird, A. 1993 (Cardiff C) 6
Blackmore, C. 1984 (Manchester U) 3
Blake, D. J. 2007 (Cardiff C) 14
Blake, N. A. 1991 (Cardiff C) 5
Blaney, S. D. 1997 (West Ham U) 3
Bloom, J. 2011 (Falkirk) 1
Bodin, B. P. 2010 (Swindon T, Torquay U) 21
Bodin, P. J. 1983 (Cardiff C) 1
Bond, J. H. 2011 (Watford) 1
Bowen, J. P. 1993 (Swansea C) 5
Bowen, M. R. 1983 (Tottenham H) 3
Boyle, T. 1982 (Crystal Palace) 1
Brace, D. P. 1995 (Wrexham) 6
Bradley, M. S. 2007 (Walsall) 17
Bradshaw, T. 2012 (Shrewsbury T) 8
Broadhead, N. P. 2018 (Everton) 14
Brooks, D. R. 2018 (Sheffield U) 3
Brough, M. 2003 (Notts Co) 3
Brown, J. D. 2008 (Cardiff C) 6
Brown, J. R. 2003 (Gillingham) 7
Brown, T. A. F. 2011 (Ipswich T, Rotherham U, Aldershot T) 10
Burns, W. J. 2013 (Bristol C) 18
Burton, R. 2018 (Arsenal) 8
Byrne, M. T. 2003 (Bolton W) 1

Cabango, B. 2019 (Swansea C) 5
Calliste, R. T. 2005 (Manchester U, Liverpool) 15
Carpenter, R. E. 2005 (Burnley) 1
Cassidy, J. A. 2011 (Wolverhampton W) 8
Ċegielski, W. 1977 (Wrexham) 2
Chamberlain, E. C. 2010 (Leicester C) 9
Chapple, S. R. 1992 (Swansea C) 8
Charles, J. D. 2016 (Huddersfield T, Barnsley) 9
Charles, J. M. 1979 (Swansea C) 2
Christie-Davies, I. 2018 (Chelsea, Liverpool) 4
Church, S. R. 2008 (Reading) 15
Clark, J. 1978 (Manchester U, Derby Co) 2
Clifton, H. L. 2019 (Grimsby T) 3
Coates, J. S. 1996 (Swansea C) 5
Coleman, C. 1990 (Swansea C) 3
Collins, J. M. 2003 (Cardiff C) 7
Collins, M. J. 2007 (Fulham, Swansea C) 2
Collison, J. D. 2008 (West Ham U) 7
Cooper, B. J. 2019 (Swansea C) 6
Cooper, O. J. 2020 (Swansea C) 1
Cornell, D. J. 2010 (Swansea C) 4
Cotterill, D. R. G. B. 2005 (Bristol C, Wigan Ath) 11
Coyne, D. 1992 (Tranmere R) 7
Coxe, C. T. 2018 (Cardiff C) 13
Craig, N. L. 2009 (Everton) 4
Critchell, K. A. R. 2005 (Southampton) 3
Crofts, A. L. 2005 (Gillingham) 10
Crowe, M. T. T. 2017 (Ipswich T) 1
Crowell, M. T. 2004 (Wrexham) 7
Cullen, L. J. 2018 (Swansea C) 8
Curtis, A. T. 1977 (Swansea C) 1

Dasilva, C. P. 2018 (Chelsea, Brentford) 3
Davies, A. 1982 (Manchester U) 6
Davies, A. G. 2006 (Cambridge U) 6
Davies, A. R. 2005 (Southampton, Yeovil T) 14
Davies, C. M. 2005 (Oxford U, Verona, Oldham Ath) 9
Davies, D. 1999 (Barry T) 1
Davies, G. M. 1993 (Hereford U, Crystal Palace) 7
Davies, I. C. 1978 (Norwich C) 1
Davies, K. E. 2019 (Swansea C) 1
Davies, L. 2005 (Bangor C) 1
Davies, R. J. 2006 (WBA) 4
Davies, S. 1999 (Peterborough U, Tottenham H) 10
Dawson, C. 2013 (Leeds U) 2
Day, R. 2000 (Manchester C, Mansfield T) 11
Deacy, N. 1977 (PSV Eindhoven) 1
De-Vulgt, L. S. 2002 (Swansea C) 2
Dibble, A. 1983 (Cardiff C) 3
Dibble, C. 2014 (Barnsley) 1
Doble, R. A. 2010 (Southampton) 10
Doughty, M. E. 2012 (QPR) 1
Doyle, S. C. 1979 (Preston NE, Huddersfield T) 2
Duffy, R. M. 2005 (Portsmouth) 7
Dummett, P. 2011 (Newcastle U) 3
Dwyer, P. J. 1979 (Cardiff C) 1

Eardley, N. 2007 (Oldham Ath, Blackpool) 11
Earnshaw, R. 1999 (Cardiff C) 10
Easter, D. J. 2006 (Cardiff C) 1
Ebdon, M. 1990 (Everton) 2
Edwards, C. N. H. 1996 (Swansea C) 7
Edwards, D. A. 2006 (Shrewsbury T, Luton T, Wolverhampton W) 9
Edwards, G. D. R. 2012 (Swansea C) 6
Edwards, R. I. 1977 (Chester) 2
Edwards, R. W. 1991 (Bristol C) 13
Evans, A. 1977 (Bristol R) 1
Evans, C. 2007 (Manchester C, Sheffield U) 13
Evans, J. A. J. 2014 (Fulham, Wrexham) 6
Evans, J. M. 2018 (Swansea C) 12
Evans, K. 1999 (Leeds U, Cardiff C) 4
Evans, K. G. 2019 (Swansea C) 2
Evans, L. 2013 (Wolverhampton W) 13
Evans, O. R. 2018 (Wigan Ath) 3
Evans, P. S. 1996 (Shrewsbury T) 1
Evans, S. J. 2001 (Crystal Palace) 2
Evans, T. 1995 (Cardiff C) 3

Fish, N. 2005 (Cardiff C) 2
Fleetwood, S. 2005 (Cardiff C) 5
Flynn, C. P. 2007 (Crewe Alex) 1
Folland, R. W. 2000 (Oxford U) 1
Foster, M. G. 1993 (Tranmere R) 1
Fowler, L. A. 2003 (Coventry C, Huddersfield T) 9
Fox, M. A. 2013 (Charlton Ath) 6
Freeman, K. 2012 (Nottingham F, Derby Co) 15
Freestone, R. 1990 (Chelsea) 1

Gabbidon, D. L. 1999 (WBA, Cardiff C) 17
Gale, D. 1983 (Swansea C) 2
Gall, K. A. 2002 (Bristol R, Yeovil T) 8
Gibson, N. D. 1999 (Tranmere R, Sheffield W) 11
Giggs, R. J. 1991 (Manchester U) 1
Gilbert, P. 2005 (Plymouth Arg) 12
Giles, D. C. 1977 (Cardiff C, Swansea C, Crystal Palace) 4
Giles, P. 1982 (Cardiff C) 3
Graham, D. 1991 (Manchester U) 1
Green, R. M. 1998 (Wolverhampton W) 16
Griffith, C. 1990 (Cardiff C) 1
Griffiths, C. 1991 (Shrewsbury T) 1
Grubb, D. 2007 (Bristol C) 1
Gunter, C. 2006 (Cardiff C, Tottenham H) 8

Haldane, L. O. 2007 (Bristol R) 1
Hall, G. D. 1990 (Chelsea) 1
Harries, C. W. T. 2018 (Swansea C) 7
Harris, M. T. 2018 (Cardiff C) 17
Harrison, E. W. 2013 (Bristol R) 14

Hartson, J. 1994 (Luton T, Arsenal) 9
Haworth, S. O. 1997 (Cardiff C, Coventry C, Wigan Ath) 12
Hedges, R. P. 2014 (Swansea C) 11
Henley, A. 2012 (Blackburn R) 3
Hennessey, W. R. 2006 (Wolverhampton W) 6
Hewitt, E. J. 2012 (Macclesfield T, Ipswich T) 10
Hillier, I. M. 2001 (Tottenham H, Luton T) 5
Hodges, G. 1983 (Wimbledon) 5
Holden, A. 1984 (Chester C) 1
Holloway, C. D. 1999 (Exeter C) 2
Hopkins, J. 1982 (Fulham) 5
Hopkins, S. A. 1999 (Wrexham) 1
Howells, J. 2012 (Luton T) 5
Huggins, D. S. 1996 (Bristol C) 1
Huggins, N. 2019 (Leeds U) 1
Hughes, D. 2005 (Kaiserslautern, Regensburg) 2
Hughes, D. R. 1994 (Southampton) 1
Hughes, I. 1992 (Bury) 11
Hughes, L. M. 1983 (Manchester U) 5
Hughes, R. D. 1996 (Aston Villa, Shrewsbury T) 13
Hughes, W. 1977 (WBA) 3
Huws, E. W. 2012 (Manchester C) 6

Isgrove, L. J. 2013 (Southampton) 6

Jackett, K. 1981 (Watford) 2
Jacobson, J. M. 2006 (Cardiff C, Bristol R) 15
James, D. O. 2017 (Swansea C) 11
James, L. R. S. 2006 (Southampton) 10
James, R. M. 1977 (Swansea C) 3
Jarman, L. 1996 (Cardiff C) 10
Jeanne, L. C. 1999 (QPR) 8
Jelleyman, G. A. 1999 (Peterborough U) 1
Jenkins, L. D. 1998 (Swansea C) 9
Jenkins, S. R. 1993 (Swansea C) 2
John, D. C. 2014 (Cardiff C) 9
Johnson, B. P. 2020 (Nottingham F) 4
Jones, C. T. 2007 (Swansea C) 1
Jones, E. P. 2000 (Blackpool) 1
Jones, F. 1981 (Wrexham) 1
Jones, G. W. 2014 (Everton) 9
Jones, J. A. 2001 (Swansea C) 3
Jones, L. 1982 (Cardiff C) 3
Jones, M. A. 2004 (Wrexham) 4
Jones, M. G. 1998 (Leeds U) 7
Jones, O. R. 2015 (Swansea C) 1
Jones, P. L. 1992 (Liverpool) 12
Jones, R. 2011 (AFC Wimbledon) 1
Jones, R. A. 1994 (Sheffield W) 3
Jones, S. J. 2005 (Swansea C) 1
Jones, V. 1979 (Bristol R) 2

Kendall, L. M. 2001 (Crystal Palace) 2
Kendall, M. 1978 (Tottenham H) 1
Kenworthy, J. R. 1994 (Tranmere R) 3
King, A. 2008 (Leicester C) 11
Knott, G. R. 1996 (Tottenham H) 1

Law, B. J. 1990 (QPR) 2
Lawless, A. 2006 (Torquay U) 1
Lawrence, T. 2013 (Manchester U) 8
Ledley, J. C. 2005 (Cardiff C) 5
Lemonheigh-Evans, C. 2019 (Bristol C) 3
Letheran, G. 1977 (Leeds U) 2
Letheran, K. C. 2006 (Swansea C) 1
Levitt, D. J. C. 2020 (Manchester U) 1
Lewis, A. 2018 (Swansea C, Lincoln C) 9
Lewis, D. 1982 (Swansea C) 9
Lewis, J. 1983 (Cardiff C) 1
Lewis, J. C. 2020 (Swansea C) 1
Llewellyn, C. M. 1998 (Norwich C) 14
Lockyer, T. A. 2015 (Bristol R) 7
Loveridge, J. 1982 (Swansea C) 3
Low, J. D. 1999 (Bristol R, Cardiff C) 1
Lowndes, S. R. 1979 (Newport Co, Millwall) 4
Lucas, L. P. 2011 (Swansea C) 19

MacDonald, S. B. 2006 (Swansea C) 25
McCarthy, A. J. 1994 (QPR) 3
McDonald, C. 2006 (Cardiff C) 3
Mackin, L. 2006 (Wrexham) 1
Maddy, P. 1982 (Cardiff C) 2
Margetson, M. W. 1992 (Manchester C) 7
Martin, A. P. 1999 (Crystal Palace) 1
Martin, D. A. 2006 (Notts Co) 1
Marustik, C. 1982 (Swansea C) 7
Matondo, R. 2018 (Manchester C) 8
Matthews, A. J. 2010 (Cardiff C) 5
Maxwell, C. 2009 (Wrexham) 16
Maxwell, L. J. 1999 (Liverpool, Cardiff C) 14
Meades, J. 2012 (Cardiff C) 4
Meaker, M. J. 1994 (QPR) 2
Melville, A. K. 1990 (Swansea C, Oxford U) 2
Mepham, C. J. 2018 (Brentford) 4
Micallef, C. 1982 (Cardiff C) 3
Mooney, D. 2019 (Fleetwood T) 4
Morgan, A. M. 1995 (Tranmere R) 4
Morgan, C. 2004 (Wrexham, Milton Keynes D) 12
Morrell, J. J. 2018 (Bristol C) 8
Morris, A. J. 2009 (Cardiff C, Aldershot T) 8
Moss, D. M. 2003 (Shrewsbury T) 6
Mountain, P. D. 1997 (Cardiff C) 2
Mumford, A. O. 2003 (Swansea C) 4

Nardiello, D. 1978 (Coventry C) 1
Neilson, A. B. 1993 (Newcastle U) 7
Nicholas, P. 1978 (Crystal Palace, Arsenal) 3
Nogan, K. 1990 (Luton T) 2
Nogan, L. M. 1991 (Oxford U) 1
Norrington-Davies, R. L. 2018 (Sheffield U) 14
Nyatanga, L. J. 2005 (Derby Co) 10

Oakley, A. 2013 (Swindon T) 1
O'Brien, B. T. 2015 (Manchester C) 8
Ogleby, R. 2011 (Hearts, Wrexham) 12
Oster, J. M. 1997 (Grimsby T, Everton) 9
O'Sullivan, T. P. 2013 (Cardiff C) 15
Owen, G. 1991 (Wrexham) 8

Page, R. J. 1995 (Watford) 4
Parslow, D. 2005 (Cardiff C) 4
Partington, J. M. 2009 (Bournemouth) 8
Partridge, D. W. 1997 (West Ham U) 1
Pascoe, C. 1983 (Swansea C) 4
Pearce, S. 2006 (Bristol C) 3
Pejic, S. M. 2003 (Wrexham) 6
Pembridge, M. A. 1991 (Luton T) 1
Peniket, R. 2012 (Fulham) 1
Perry, J. 1990 (Cardiff C) 3
Peters, M. 1992 (Manchester C, Norwich C) 3
Phillips, D. 1984 (Plymouth Arg) 3
Phillips, G. R. 2001 (Swansea C) 3
Phillips, L. 1979 (Swansea C, Charlton Ath) 2
Pilling, L. 2018 (Tranmere R) 9
Pipe, D. R. 2003 (Coventry C, Notts Co) 12
Pontin, K. 1978 (Cardiff C) 1
Poole, R. L. 2017 (Manchester U, Milton Keynes D) 19
Powell, L. 1991 (Southampton) 4
Powell, L. 2004 (Leicester C) 3
Powell, R. 2006 (Bolton W) 1
Price, J. J. 1998 (Swansea C) 7
Price, L. P. 2005 (Ipswich T) 10
Price, M. D. 2001 (Everton, Hull C, Scarborough) 13
Price, P. 1981 (Luton T) 1
Price, T. O. 2019 (Swansea C) 1
Pritchard, J. P. 2013 (Fulham) 3
Pritchard, M. O. 2006 (Swansea C) 4
Pugh, D. 1982 (Doncaster R) 2
Pugh, S. 1993 (Wrexham) 2
Pugh, T. 2019 (Scunthorpe U) 2
Pulis, A. J. 2006 (Stoke C) 5
Przybek, A. 2020 (Ipswich T) 1

Ramasut, M. W. T. 1997 (Bristol R) 4
Ramsey, A. J. 2008, (Cardiff C, Arsenal) 12
Ratcliffe, G. 2019 (Cardiff C) 4
Ratcliffe, K. 1981 (Everton) 2
Ray, G. E. 2013 (Crewe Alex) 5
Ready, K. 1992 (QPR) 5

Rees, A. 1984 (Birmingham C) 1
Rees, J. M. 1990 (Luton T) 3
Rees, M. R. 2003 (Millwall) 4
Reid, B. 2014 (Wolverhampton W) 1
Ribeiro, C. M. 2008 (Bristol C) 8
Richards, A. D. J. 2010 (Swansea C) 16
Richards, E. A. 2012 (Bristol R) 1
Roberts, A. M. 1991 (QPR) 2
Roberts, C. 2013 (Cheltenham T) 6
Roberts, C. J. 1999 (Cardiff C) 1
Roberts, C. R. J. 2016 (Swansea C) 2
Roberts, G. 1983 (Hull C) 1
Roberts, G. W. 1997 (Liverpool, Panionios, Tranmere R) 11
Roberts, J. G. 1977 (Wrexham) 1
Roberts, N. W. 1999 (Wrexham) 3
Roberts, P. 1997 (Porthmadog) 1
Roberts, S. I. 1999 (Swansea C) 13
Roberts, S. W. 2000 (Wrexham) 3
Roberts, T. W. 2018 (Leeds U) 5
Robinson, C. P. 1996 (Wolverhampton W) 6
Robinson, J. R. C. 1992 (Brighton & HA, Charlton Ath) 5
Robson-Kanu, K. H. 2010 (Reading) 4
Rodon, J. P. 2017 (Swansea C) 9
Rowlands, A. J. R. 1996 (Manchester C) 5
Rush, I. 1981 (Liverpool) 2

Savage, R. W. 1995 (Crewe Alex) 3
Saunders, C. L. 2015 (Crewe Alex) 1
Sayer, P. A. 1977 (Cardiff C) 2
Searle, D. 1991 (Cardiff C) 6
Sheehan, J. L. 2014 (Swansea C) 12
Shephard, L. 2015 (Swansea C) 2
Slatter, D. 2000 (Chelsea) 6
Slatter, N. 1983 (Bristol R) 6
Smith, D. 2014 (Shrewsbury T) 3
Smith, M. 2018 (Manchester C) 5
Somner, M. J. 2004 (Brentford) 2
Speed, G. A. 1990 (Leeds U) 3
Spender, S. 2005 (Wrexham) 6
Stephens, D. 2011 (Hibernian) 7
Stevenson, N. 1982 (Swansea C) 2
Stevenson, W. B. 1977 (Leeds U) 3
Stirk, R. 2020 (Birmingham C) 3
Stock, B. B. 2003 (Bournemouth) 4
Symons, C. J. 1991 (Portsmouth) 2

Tancock, S. 2013 (Swansea C) 6
Taylor, A. J. 2012 (Tranmere R) 3
Taylor, G. K. 1995 (Bristol R) 4
Taylor, J. W. T. 2010 (Reading) 12
Taylor, N. J. 2008 (Wrexham, Swansea C) 13
Taylor, R. F. 2008 (Chelsea) 5
Taylor, T. 2020 (Wolverhampton W) 1
Thomas, C. E. 2010 (Swansea C) 3
Thomas, D. G. 1977 (Leeds U) 3
Thomas, D. J. 1998 (Watford) 2
Thomas, G. S. 2018 (Leicester C) 8
Thomas, J. A. 1996 (Blackburn R) 21
Thomas, Martin R. 1979 (Bristol R) 2
Thomas, Mickey R. 1977 (Wrexham) 2
Thomas, S. 2001 (Wrexham) 5
Thompson, L. C. W. 2015 (Norwich C) 2
Tibbott, L. 1977 (Ipswich T) 2
Tipton, M. J. 1998 (Oldham Ath) 6
Tolley, J. C. 2001 (Shrewsbury T) 12
Touray, M. 2019 (Newport Co) 3
Tudur-Jones, O. 2006 (Swansea C) 3
Twiddy, C. 1995 (Plymouth Arg) 3

Vale, J. 2020 (Blackburn R) 1
Valentine, R. D. 2001 (Everton, Darlington) 8
Vaughan, D. O. 2003 (Crewe Alex) 8
Vaughan, N. 1982 (Newport Co) 2
Vokes, S. M. 2007 (Bournemouth, Wolverhampton W) 14

Walsh, D. 2000 (Wrexham) 8
Walsh, I. P. 1979 (Crystal Palace, Swansea C) 2
Walsh, J. 2012 (Swansea C, Crawley T) 11
Walton, M. 1991 (Norwich C.) 1
Ward, D. 1996 (Notts Co) 2
Ward, D. 2013 (Liverpool) 6
Warlow, O. J. 2007 (Lincoln C) 2
Weeks, D. L. 2014 (Wolverhampton W) 2
Weston, R. D. 2001 (Arsenal, Cardiff C) 4
Wharton, T. J. 2014 (Cardiff C) 1
Whitfield, P. M. 2003 (Wrexham) 1
Wiggins, R. 2006 (Crystal Palace) 9
Williams, A. P. 1998 (Southampton) 9
Williams, A. S. 1996 (Blackburn R) 16
Williams, D. 1983 (Bristol R) 1
Williams, D. I. L. 1998 (Liverpool, Wrexham) 9
Williams, D. T. 2006 (Yeovil T) 1
Williams, E. 1997 (Caernarfon T) 2
Williams, G. 1983 (Bristol R) 2
Williams, G. A. 2003 (Crystal Palace) 5
Williams, G. C. 2014 (Fulham) 3
Williams, J. P. 2011 (Crystal Palace) 8
Williams, M. 2001 (Manchester U) 10
Williams, M. P. 2006 (Wrexham) 14
Williams, M. J. 2014 (Notts Co) 1
Williams, M. R. 2006 (Wrexham) 6
Williams, O. fon 2007 (Crewe Alex, Stockport Co) 11
Williams, R. 2007 (Middlesbrough) 10
Williams, S. J. 1995 (Wrexham) 4
Wilmot, R. 1982 (Arsenal) 6
Wilson, H. 2014 (Liverpool) 10
Wilson, J. S. 2009 (Bristol C) 3
Worgan, L. J. 2005 (Milton Keynes D, Rushden & D) 5
Wright, A. A. 1998 (Oxford U) 3
Wright, J. 2014 (Huddersfield T) 2

Yorwerth, J. 2014 (Cardiff C) 7
Young, S. 1996 (Cardiff C) 5

ENGLAND YOUTH GAMES 2019–20

▪ *Denotes player sent off.*

ENGLAND UNDER-16

ST GEORGE'S PARK TOURNAMENT

Burton, Sunday 18 August 2019

England (1) 2 *(Scarlett 1, 43)*

Denmark (0) 0 160

England: Stetford; Awe, Bryan-Waugh, Katongo, Parkes, Cannonier, Gyabi, Webster, Shoretire, Cho, Scarlett.
Substitutes: Collyer, Mabaya, Bynoe-Gittens, Soonsup-Bell, Irons, Murray-Jones, Earthy, Hughes, Hackford, McAdam.

Burton, Thursday 22 August 2019

England (2) 3 *(Bynoe-Gittens, Webster, Gyabi)*

Republic of Ireland (1) 3 *(Mullins, Quinn, Lonergan)*

England: Murry-Jones; Mabaya, McAdam, Awe (Earthy 41), Irons, Collyer, Hughes (Gyabi 41), Hackford, Webster, Bynoe-Gittens (Shoretire 41), Soonsup-Bell.
Republic of Ireland: Maguire; Curtis, Fogarty, Reilly, Ryan, Lonergan, Nzingo, Power, Agbaje, Ferguson, Quinn.

FRIENDLIES

Burton, Friday 25 October 2019

England (2) 2 *(Scarlett 19 (pen), Gordon 31)*

Norway (0) 1 *(Spencer 75)*

England: Hewitson; Winstanley, Murray, Collyer, Tarima, Awe, Bynoe-Gittens, Gyabi, Scarlett, Webster, Gordon.
Substitutes: Earthy, Knightbridge, Richards, Kaba.

Burton, Friday 25 October 2019

England 2 *(Mubama, Norton-Cuffy)*

Scotland 1 *(Brooks)*

England: Beadle; Quintyne, Hackett-Valton, Devine, Norton-Cuffy, Hughes, Hall, Weston, Mubama, Forson, Pennant.
Substitutes: Earthy, Knightbridge, Richards, Kaba, Gyabi, Bynoe-Gittens.
Scotland: Johnston; McPherson, Anderson, Strachan, Ewen H, Reid, Adam, Blaney, Andreucci, Brooks, Doak.
Substitutes: Ewen K, Letsoa, Mebude, McConnell, Semple, Flatman, Montgomery, Offord, Yeats.

SPORTCHAIN CUP, SPAIN

La Nucia, Spain, Monday 2 December 2019

Russia (0) 0

England (0) 0

England: Setford; Mabaya, Hughes, Awe, Chambers, Collyer, Gyabi, Baker-Boaitey (Mubama 59), Webster (Forson 59), Chrisene (Hall 67), Soonsup-Bell (Pennant 59).

Benidorm, Spain, Wednesday 4 December 2019

England (1) 5 *(Gyabi 39, Soonsup-Bell 45, Hall 56, Norton-Cuffy 72, Webster 78)*

Japan (0) 0

England: Whitworth; Norton-Cuffy, Jonas, Hughes, Hackett-Valton, Gyabi (Chrisene 59), Devine, Pennant (Webster 67), Hall, Forson (Mather 59), Soonsup-Bell (Mubama 59).

La Nucia, Spain, Friday 6 December 2019

Mexico (1) 1 *(Hernandez 30)*

England (0) 0

England: Maguire; Mabaya, Chambers, Collyer, Jonas, Awe, Mather, Webster, Mubama, Forson, Chrisene.
Substitutes: Setford, Norton-Cuffy, Devine, Hughes, Gyabi, Pennant, Soonsup-Bell, Baker-Boaitey, Hackett-Valton, Hall, Whitworth.

Benidorm, Spain, Sunday 8 December 2019

Spain (2) 3 *(Luzzi 21, 29, Alarcon 80)*

England (2) 3 *(Pennant 13, 23, Gyabi 73)*

England: Setford; Norton-Cuffy (Mubama 68), Chambers, Devine, Hughes, Awe, Pennant, Webster, Soonsup-Bell (Mabaya 68), Gyabi, Chrisene (Hall 50).

UEFA DEVELOPMENT TOURNAMENT (ST GEORGE'S PARK)

Burton, Wednesday 19 February 2020

England (1) 4 *(Mubama 6, Soonsup-Bell 8, 48, Pennant 61)*

Denmark (0) 0

England: Setford; Norton-Cuffy, Hughes, Collyer, Awe, Chrisene, Gyabi, Webster, Mubama, Gordon (Pennant 46), Soonsup-Bell.

Burton, Friday 21 February 2020

England (4) 4 *(Perkins (3), Pennant)*

USA (0) 1

England: Maguire; Ryan, Hackett-Valton, Perkins, Hughes, Collyer, Pennant, Hall, Kavanagh, Bynoe-Gittens, Lewis.
Substitutes: Setford, Norton-Cuffy, Gyabi, Webster, Soonsup-Bell, Chrisene, Gordon, Mubama, Awe.

Burton, Monday 24 February 2020

England (2) 3 *(Soonsup-Bell 10, 30, 70)*

Spain (1) 1 *(Alarcon 21)*

England: Setford; Norton-Cuffy, Hackett-Valton (Chrisene 60), Awe, Hughes, Gyabi, Pennant, Webster (Perkins 60), Soonsup-Bell (Kavanagh 80), Collyer (Lewis 80), Hall (Bynoe-Gittens 60).
England won the UEFA Development Tournament.

Due to the COVID-19 pandemic, all subsequent England Under-16 matches were postponed.

ENGLAND UNDER-17

SYRENKA CUP (POLAND)

Sulejowek, Poland, Friday 6 September 2019

England (2) 5 *(Musiala 38, Barry 44, 83, Bellingham 80, Simons 88)*

Finland (0) 0

England: Boyce-Clarke; Kenneh, Simons, Dobbin (Onyango 78), Barry, Musiala (Bellingham 71), Elliott, Raymond, Quansah, Monlouis, Samuels.

Zabki, Poland, Sunday 8 September 2019

England (3) 4 *(Richards 33, Delap 35, 70, Bellingham 42)*

Austria (1) 2 *(Coco 16, Omic 76)*

England: Richardson; Norris, Egan-Riley, Colwill, Bellingham (Simons■ 73), Burns, Iling-Junior, Onyango, Ramsey (Kenneh 88), Delap, Richards (Monlouis 90).

Warsaw, Poland, Tuesday 10 September 2019

Poland (2) 2 *(Cielemecki 30, Kozlowski 38)*

England (2) 2 *(Elliott 4 (pen), Musiala 9)*

England: Boyce-Clarke; Kenneh (Ramsey 69), Norris, Egan-Riley, Colwill, Bellingham, Barry (Dobbin 80), Musiala (Raymond 80), Elliott, Iling-Junior (Delap 69), Monlouis.
England won 3-1 on penalties and won the Syrenka Cup.

FRIENDLIES

Pinatar, Spain, Thursday 10 October 2019

England (1) 3 *(Diallo 27, Dobbin 55, Young-Coombes 90)*

Germany (3) 3 *(Gunther 6 (pen), Netz 12 (pen), 43)*

England: Oluwayemi; Baptiste (Kenneh 63), Norris, Patino, Egan-Riley (Fish 89), Colwill, Dembele (Iling-Junior 63), Dobbin, Musiala (Chukwuekema 85), Diallo (Young-Coombes 77), Onyango (Ramsey 63).

Pinatar, Spain, Saturday 12 October 2019

Germany (1) 2 *(Netz 11, Gunther 48)*

England (0) 1 *(Fish 90)*

England: Boyce-Clarke; Baptiste (Onyango 71), Ramsey, Badley-Morgan, Iling-Junior, Kenneh, Welch, Fish, Balagizi (Dobbin 64), Young-Coombes (Norris 76), Chukwuemeka (Musiala 71).

Pinatar, Spain, Monday 14 October 2019

Spain (1) 1 *(Rodriguez 90)*

England (1) 1 *(Dembele 26)*

England: Graczyk; Norris, Patino, Egan-Riley, Colwill, Dembele (Iling-Junior 65), Dobbin, Musiala, Diallo (Young-Coombes 75), Kenneh, Balagizi (Ramsey 65).

Alfreton, Friday 15 November 2019

England (0) 1 *(Dobbin 67)*

Denmark (1) 3 *(Kjaegaard 38, Faghir 47, Bredahl 59)* 453

England: Boyce-Clarke; Kenneh (Oyegoke 78), Egan-Riley, Badley-Morgan, Norris, Patino (Diallo 68), Simons (Robertson 46), Musiala, Dembele (Richards 78), Dobbin, Richardson (Barry 68).

Solihull, Tuesday 19 November 2019

England (2) 2 *(Robertson 30, 42)*

Czech Republic (0) 0 1151

England: Oluwayemi; Oyegoke, Monlouis, Fish, Colwill, Onyango, Ramsey, Robertson (Musiala 60), Richards (Dembele 71), Barry, Diallo (Dobbin 80).

UNDER-17S TOURNAMENT, MARBELLA

Marbella, Spain, Thursday 6 February 2020

England (0) 0

Ukraine (0) 0

England: Cox; Ross-Lang, Quansah, John (Vale 72), Abbey, Ingram, Ramsey, Dobbin, Musiala, Barry (Abdulmalik 84), Hutchinson (Diallo 72).

Marbella, Spain, Saturday 8 February 2020

England (0) 4 *(Vale 60, Diallo 78, Dobbin 80, Barry 90)*

Russia (0) 2 *(Gladyshev 46, Ermakov 76)*

England: Sharman-Lowe; Kenneh, Samuels, Vale (Dobbin 73), Abbey, Diallo, Abdulmalik (Barry 73), Sweet (Ramsey 73), Benarous (Hutchinson 73), Abu (Ingram 73), Mooney (Musiala 73).

Marbella, Spain, Monday 10 February 2020

England (2) 4 *(Barry 27, Dobbin 30, 67, Diallo 83)*

Ukraine (0) 0

England: Cox (Sharman-Lowe 46); Kenneh (Abbey 87), Samuels (Ingram 56), Ross-Lang, Quansah, John (Vale 56), Ramsey (Sweet 71), Dobbin (Mooney 71), Barry (Abdulmalik 71), Hutchinson (Benarous 71), Abu (Diallo 56).

Due to the COVID-19 pandemic, all subsequent England Under-17 matches were postponed.

ENGLAND UNDER-18

FOUR TEAM TOURNAMENT, ENGLAND

Leicester Road, Friday 6 September 2019

England (2) 3 *(Mighten 20, 36, 65)*

Australia (1) 2 *(Botic 4 (pen), Ostler 75)* 527

England: Moulden (Broome 46); Livramento, Wood, Simeu, Bondswell, Weir, Bate (Rogers 64), De Carvalho (Gelhardt 79), Knight (Musah 64), Stewart (Madueke 70), Mighten (Palmer 79).

Hednesford Town, Sunday 8 September 2019

England (1) 1 *(Musah 32 (pen))*

Brazil (0) 1 *(Magno 50)* 1800

England: Moulden; Livramento, Wood, Mengi, Roberts, Musah (De Carvalho 76), Azeez, Palmer (Weir 65), Madueke (Mighten 65), Gelhardt (Stewart 88), Rogers.

Alfreton Town, Tuesday 10 September 2019

England (2) 2 *(Palmer 25, Madueke 36)*

Korea Republic (0) 0 792

England: Trafford; Livramento, Roberts, Mengi (Simeu 46), Madueke, Musah (Weir 46), Gelhardt (De Carvalho 61), Palmer, Bondswell (Wood 80), Bate (Azeez 46), Mighten (Stewart 61).

FRIENDLIES

Opole, Poland, Friday 11 October 2019

Poland (1) 2 *(Bialek 7, Hyjek 71 (pen))*

England (3) 5 *(Mruk 9 (og), Tetek 23, Gelhardt 30 (pen), 47, Madueke 89)* 2500

England: Trafford; Matheson (Musah 78), Bondswell (Roberts 78), Azeez, Wood, Gelhardt (Greenwood 78), Palmer (Carvalho 85), Rogers (Madueke 78), Dorsett, Tetek (Weir 62), Sarmiento (Mighten 62).

Senec, Slovakia, Monday 14 October 2019

Slovakia (0) 0

England (0) 1 *(Greenwood 64)* 300

England: Trafford; Matheson (Azeez 78), Bondswell (Mengi 89), Roberts, Wood, Madueke (Sarmiento 89), Musah (Tetek 89), Weir, Mighten (Rogers 78), Greenwood (Gelhardt 84), Carvalho (Palmer 78).

Leobersdorf, Austria, Wednesday 16 October 2019

Austria (1) 2 *(Zimmerman 21, Braunoder 56)*

England (2) 3 *(Gelhardt 1, Musah 42, Sarmiento 77)*

England: Broome (Cartwright 46); Roberts, Musah (Wood 90), Gelhardt (Greenwood 46), Rogers (Madueke 46), Dorsett, Weir, Mengi, Tetek (Palmer 46), Mighten (Sarmiento 46), Carvalho (Azeez 46).

FOUR TEAM TOURNAMENT, SPAIN

Pinatar, Spain, Thursday 14 November 2019

England (2) 5 *(Madueke 9, Greenwood 45, Palmer 48, Rogers 84, Mighten 86))*

Russia (0) 2 *(Kozhedub 54, Shchetinin 63)*

Broome; Matheson (Azeez 72), Cirkin (Wilson-Esbrand 87), Dorsett, Wood, Madueke (Sarmiento 85), Greenwood (Stansfield 85), Palmer (McAtee 85), Rogers (Mighten 85), Weir, White (Musah 72).

Pinatar, Spain, Saturday 16 November 2019

England (1) 4 *(McAtee 42, 61, Greenwood 85 (pen), Azeez 90)*

Norway (2) 4 *(Sundberg 11, Aarstad 38, Geelmuyden 57, 86)*

England: Bosworth; Azeez, Wood, Musah (White 90), Wilson-Esbrand (Matheson 72), Weir, Simeu, Sarmiento (Madueke 72), Mighten (Rogers 72), Stansfield (Greenwood 72), McAtee (Palmer 72).

Pinatar, Spain, 18 November 2019

England (1) 1 *(Madueke 36)*

Czech Republic (0) 0

England: Graczyk; Matheson, Cirkin (Wood 84), Dorsett, Madueke (Sarmiento 46), Musah (Weir 84), Simeu, White (Azeez 46), Mighten (Rogers 46), Stansfield (Greenwood 46), McAtee (Palmer 46).

Due to the COVID-19 pandemic, all subsequent England Under-18 matches were postponed.

ENGLAND UNDER-19

FRIENDLIES

Burton, Thursday 5 September 2019

England (1) 3 *(Adshead 28, Edmondson 60, Doyle 74 (pen))*

Greece (1) 1 *(Vrakas 4)*

England: Jeacock (Dewhurst 46); Mumba, Thomas, Doyle, Harwood-Bellis, Alese, Adshead (Saka 60), Sibley (Mola 73), Edmondson (Jones 60), Ramsey, Gordon (John-Jules 60).

Haiger, Germany, Monday 9 September 2019

Germany (1) 1 *(Tauer 25)*

England (0) 0 3397

England: Ashby-Hammond; Daley-Campbell, Saka, Maghoma (Doyle 70), Williams, Binks, Whittaker (Thomas 65), Mola, John-Jules, Anjorin (Gordon 70), Jones (Edmondson 82).

Marbella, Spain, Wednesday 9 October 2019

France (1) 3 *(Eneme Ella 3, 72 (pen), Providence 83)*

England (0) 1 *(Garner 71 (pen))*

England: Ashby-Hammond (Bycroft 46); Daley-Campbell, Buchanan, Garner, Harwood-Bellis, Mola, Whittaker (Appiah 62), Maghoma (Hilton 83), Edmondson (Duncan 62), Jones (Ramsey 83), Gordon.

Marbella, Spain, Saturday 12 October 2019

Belgium (1) 2 *(Vertessen 23, Essabri 62)*

England (2) 4 *(Franky 6 (og), Duncan 45, 66, Lawrence 54)*

England: Jeacock (Ashby-Hammond 46); Lawrence, Williams, Alese, Thomas, Hilton, Garner (Maghoma 46), Ramsey, Appiah, Duncan, Gordon (Jones 46).

2020 EUROPEAN UNDER-19 CHAMPIONSHIP (QUALIFYING)

GROUP 11 (NORTH MACEDONIA)

Skopje, North Macedonia, Wednesday 13 November 2019

England (3) 4 *(Harwood-Bellis 7, Duncan 29, 32, Amaechi 75)*

Luxembourg (0) 0

England: Ashby-Hammond; Doyle (Garner 62), Harwood-Bellis (Laird 62), Anjorin, Saka (Gordon 71), Maghoma, Amaechi, Duncan, Alese (Mola 46), Livramento, Buchanan.

Skopje, North Macedonia, Saturday 16 November 2019

North Macedonia (0) 0

England (1) 5 *(Doyle 41, Gordon 54, Garner 72, 79, Saka 86)*

England: Ashby-Hammond; Laird, Thomas, Doyle (Maghoma 77), Harwood-Bellis, Mola, Appiah (Amaechi 59), Garner, John-Jules, Gordon (Saka 77), Hilton (Duncan 63).

Skopje, North Macedonia, Tuesday 19 November 2019

Bosnia-Herzogovina (0) 1 *(Djokanovic 48)*

England (2) 4 *(Anjorin 24, Laird 38, Harwood-Bellis 69, Gordon 70)*

England: Dewhurst; Laird, Doyle, Harwood-Bellis, Mola, Garner (Maghoma 73), Anjorin (Hilton 64), Gordon, Amaechi (John-Jules 17), Duncan, Buchanan.

Due to the COVID-19 pandemic, all subsequent England Under-19 matches were postponed.

ENGLAND UNDER-20

UNDER 20 ELITE LEAGUE

Shrewsbury, Thursday 5 September 2019

England (0) 0

Netherlands (0) 0 2578

England: Bursik, Lamptey, Williams, Gallagher, Latibeaudiere, Tanganga, Bolton, Dozzell, Leko (Clarke 66), Gomes, Giles (Loader 66).

St Jakob, Switzerland, Monday 9 September 2019

Switzerland (0) 0

England (0) 1 *(Clarke 90)* 1000

England: Bursik (McGill 46); Lamptey (Tanganga 63), Williams, Tavernier, Ferguson, Gibson, Thomas (Bolton 84), Shackleton (Dozzell 76), Loader (Giles 84), Slattery (Gomes 76), Clarke.

Parma, Italy, Thursday 10 October 2019

Italy (1) 2 *(Frabotta 39, Postanova 49 (pen))*

England (2) 2 *(Gomes 23 (pen), 24)*

England: Bursik; Lamptey, Williams, Downes (Slattery 83), Latibeaudiere, Tanganga, Bolton (Giles 72), Dozzell, Loader (Leko 76), Gomes (Tavernier 83), Clarke (Poveda-Ocampo 72).

Peterborough, Monday 14 October 2019

England (0) 0

Czech Republic (0) 3 *(Hellebrand 51, 60, Husek 74)* 6296

England: Crellin (McGill 46); Lamptey (Latibeaudiere 85), Williams (Giles 65), Tavernier, Ferguson, Gibson, Poveda-Ocampo (Bolton 75), Dozzell (Downes 65), Leko (Loader 75), Slattery (Clarke 65), Gomes.

Agueda, Portugal, Thursday 14 November 2019

Portugal (0) 0

England (3) 4 *(Campbell 10, 17 (pen), Poveda-Ocampo 26, Smith-Rowe 63)*

England: Bursik; Lamptey (Bogle 72), Ferguson, Downes, Latibeaudiere, Tanganga (Lewis 80), Smith-Rowe (Cochrane 80), Dozzell (Tavernier 61), Campbell (Loader 72), Gomes (Longstaff 72), Poveda-Ocampo (Clarke 61).

FRIENDLY

Wycombe, Tuesday 19 November 2019

England (0) 3 *(Loader 50, Poveda-Ocampo 71, 73)*

Iceland (0) 0 1390

England: Crellin (Anang 79); Bogle (Lamptey 84), Cochrane (Ferguson 79), Longstaff (Downes 72), Latibeaudiere (Tanganga 72), Gibson, Bolton (Poveda-Ocampo 61), Tavernier (Dozzell 84), Loader (Campbell 79), Gomes (Smith-Rowe 61), Clarke.

Due to the COVID-19 pandemic, all subsequent England Under-20 matches were postponed.

SCHOOLS FOOTBALL 2019–20

BOODLES INDEPENDENT SCHOOLS FA CUP 2019–20

**After extra time.*

FIRST ROUND

ACS Cobham v Buckswood	2-2*
(Buckswood won 5-4 on penalties)	
Birkdale v Bury GS	2-2*
(Bury GS won 10-9 on penalties)	
Bootham v Merchant Taylors', Crosby	2-4
Box Hill v Bristol GS	0-5
Canford v Taunton	1-3
Colfe's v Marlborough	3-4
Lingfield College v Abingdon	1-2*
Rossall v Moorland	5-2
Sevenoaks v RGS Guildford	2-0
Stafford GS v Wolverhampton GS	4-3
Wellington v Bournemouth Collegiate	3-0

SECOND ROUND

Abingdon v Merchant Taylors', Crosby	3-1
Alleyn's v Bolton	7-0
Ardingly v St John's, Leatherhead	4-3
Bede's v King Edward's, Witley	6-0
Berkhamsted v Royal Russell	0-4
Brentwood v Dulwich College	2-0
Brighton College v Millfield	2-6
Brooke House v University College School	6-1
Bristol GS v Grange	4-5
Buckswood v St Bede's College (walkover)	
Bury GS v Hampton	0-12
Charterhouse v Taunton	4-0
Cheadle Hulme v Harrow	0-3
Chigwell v Westminster	0-0*
(Chigwell won 4-2 on penalties)	
Haberdashers' Aske's v City of London	1-5
Harrodian v Highgate	1-3
KCS Wimbledon v Aldenham	1-3
Kingston GS v Forest	2-3*
Lancing v Kimbolton	1-2*
Merchant Taylors', Northwood v Latymer Upper	0-1*
Newcastle School/Boys v King's School, Chester	3-0
Oldham Hulme GS v Eton	0-7
Repton v Sherborne	9-0
RGS Newcastle v Manchester GS	0-2
Rossall v Bradfield	0-3
Sevenoaks v Trinity	2-4
Shrewsbury v Grammar School at Leeds	5-2
Stafford GS v John Lyon	8-3
Tonbridge v Stockport GS	2-2*
(Stockport GS won 3-0 on penalties)	
Winchester v Queen Ethelburga's Collegiate	1-2
Wellington v Marlborough	0-1
Whitgift v Oswestry	4-2

THIRD ROUND

Brooke House v Alleyn's	4-2
Charterhouse v Repton	1-2
Grange v Forest	1-2
Hampton v Abingdon	4-1
Highgate v Aldenham	1-5
Kimbolton v Harrow	1-0
Manchester GS v Bede's	5-3
Marlborough v Chigwell	3-2
Newcastle School for Boys v Ardingly	1-2
Queen Ethelburga's Collegiate v Trinity	5-1
Royal Russell v Latymer Upper	10-0
Shrewsbury v City of London	1-0
Stafford GS v Brentwood	1-3
Stockport GS v Eton	0-2
St Bede's College v Bradfield	1-5
Whitgift v Millfield	0-5

FOURTH ROUND

Aldenham v Hampton	2-2*
(Aldenham won 4-2 on penalties)	
Ardingly v Millfield	3-4
Eton v Brentwood	2-3*
Forest v Bradfield	0-2
Manchester GS v Marlborough	6-1
Queen Ethelburga's Collegiate v Royal Russell	2-1
Repton v Brooke House	0-4
Shrewsbury v Kimbolton	5-0

FIFTH ROUND

Aldenham v Brooke House	0-3
Bradfield v Queen Ethelburga's Collegiate	0-2
Brentwood v Shrewsbury	3-5*
Millfield v Manchester GS	3-1*

SEMI FINALS

Brooke House v Millfield	0-1
Shrewsbury v Queen Ethelburga's Collegiate	1-3

BOODLES INDEPENDENT SCHOOLS FA CUP FINAL 2019–20

Milton Keynes Dons, Monday 9 March 2020

Millfield (2) 5 *(Kemsley 2, Hemingway (og), El Sheikh, McCallum)*

Queen Ethelburga's Collegiate (2) 4 *(Westhead 2, Hemingway, Abusin)*

Millfield: Pike C, Clatworthy D, Jones B, Heywood A, Kemsley A, Harding A, McCallum T, Edwards D, Pereira R, Teniente R, Ojo S.
Substitutes: El Sheikh H, Wood J, Green W, Prescott A, Grad H.

Queen Ethelburga's Collegiate: Johnson K, Ingoldsby D, McGrath J, Bostock R, Hemingway L, Mutch D, Kitchen S, Westhead S, Bingham K, Monteiro W, Colville H.
Substitutes: Chandar J, Jarvis L, Abusin L, Hammond A, Tweddle T.

aet.

Referee: Tom Nield.

UNIVERSITY FOOTBALL 2020

136th UNIVERSITY MATCH

(Sunday 15 March 2020, at The Hive, Barnet FC)

Oxford University v Cambridge University

(Match postponed due to COVID-19 pandemic)

Oxford have won 55 games (2 on penalties), Cambridge 53 games (4 on penalties) and 27 games have been drawn. Oxford have scored 215 goals, Cambridge 208 goals.

NON-LEAGUE TABLES 2019–20

The FA cancelled all Non-League football below National League level on 26 March 2020 due to the COVID-19 pandemic. The following League Tables are as they stood at that time.

NATIONAL LEAGUE SYSTEM STEP 3

BETVICTOR NORTHERN PREMIER LEAGUE – PREMIER DIVISION

			Home			Away			Total						
		P	W	D	L	W	D	L	W	D	L	F	A	GD	Pts
1	South Shields	33	10	3	4	11	3	2	21	6	6	64	34	30	69
2	FC United of Manchester	32	8	3	4	8	6	3	16	9	7	73	51	22	57
3	Warrington T	32	9	5	3	5	8	2	14	13	5	57	44	13	55
4	Basford U	32	10	3	5	6	4	4	16	7	9	49	39	10	55
5	Lancaster C	34	7	6	4	8	2	7	15	8	11	58	46	12	53
6	Nantwich T	31	9	1	4	6	6	5	15	7	9	55	39	16	52
7	Whitby T	31	6	6	4	8	2	5	14	8	9	54	42	12	50
8	Scarborough Ath	35	8	8	1	6	0	12	14	8	13	44	47	–3	50
9	Morpeth T	27	8	3	1	6	3	6	14	6	7	48	37	11	48
10	Hyde U	33	7	4	6	5	3	8	12	7	14	55	55	0	43
11	Gainsborough Trinity	32	6	4	6	5	5	6	11	9	12	53	50	3	42
12	Stalybridge Celtic	33	5	2	9	7	4	6	12	6	15	42	50	–8	42
13	Bamber Bridge	33	9	3	5	3	1	12	12	4	17	53	64	–11	40
14	Witton Alb	31	8	2	5	2	7	7	10	9	12	40	43	–3	39
15	Mickleover Sports	29	6	1	6	5	4	7	11	5	13	42	52	–10	38
16	Radcliffe	32	7	5	4	4	0	12	11	5	16	34	50	–16	38
17	Ashton U*	29	6	3	6	4	4	6	10	7	12	40	45	–5	36
18	Buxton	32	4	5	7	4	6	6	8	11	13	56	52	4	35
19	Grantham T	32	7	2	7	0	7	9	7	9	16	38	71	–33	30
20	Matlock T	28	4	4	7	4	1	8	8	5	15	36	43	–7	29
21	Atherton Collieries	26	6	1	6	2	3	8	8	4	14	36	49	–13	28
22	Stafford Rangers	33	3	8	6	1	3	12	4	11	18	29	53	–24	23

**Ashton U deducted 1pt for fielding an ineligible player.*

BETVICTOR SOUTHERN PREMIER LEAGUE – CENTRAL DIVISION

			Home			Away			Total						
		P	W	D	L	W	D	L	W	D	L	F	A	GD	Pts
1	Peterborough Sports	33	10	5	2	9	3	4	19	8	6	90	46	44	65
2	Tamworth	30	12	1	4	9	1	3	21	2	7	63	27	36	65
3	Royston T	30	12	3	1	7	3	4	19	6	5	62	28	34	63
4	Bromsgrove Sporting	32	7	4	6	10	2	3	17	6	9	80	43	37	57
5	Rushall Olympic	33	10	2	5	5	6	5	15	8	10	58	43	15	53
6	Stourbridge	32	8	3	4	8	2	7	16	5	11	53	52	1	53
7	Banbury U	32	10	3	4	4	7	4	14	10	8	48	31	17	52
8	Coalville T	30	7	4	5	7	5	2	14	9	7	51	32	19	51
9	Nuneaton Bor	33	8	4	4	6	4	7	14	8	11	57	46	11	50
10	Kings Langley	30	7	3	4	8	2	6	15	5	10	51	41	10	50
11	Rushden & Diamonds	30	9	2	3	5	5	6	14	7	9	50	45	5	49
12	Barwell	32	9	2	5	5	4	7	14	6	12	58	54	4	48
13	Needham Market	33	5	6	5	8	3	6	13	9	11	43	40	3	48
14	Hednesford T	32	7	2	6	7	3	7	14	5	13	50	44	6	47
15	Biggleswade T	30	8	0	5	5	4	8	13	4	13	45	46	–1	43
16	Lowestoft T	33	9	2	6	4	0	12	13	2	18	48	62	–14	41
17	Hitchin T	32	4	5	6	6	4	7	10	9	13	43	49	–6	39
18	Stratford T	33	6	2	8	2	2	13	8	4	21	42	74	–32	28
19	Leiston	32	2	5	10	4	3	8	6	8	18	39	87	–48	26
20	St Ives T	33	4	3	9	2	2	13	6	5	22	33	76	–43	23
21	Alvechurch	30	2	4	9	2	1	12	4	5	21	25	58	–33	17
22	Redditch U	33	2	2	13	1	1	14	3	3	27	24	89	–65	12

BETVICTOR SOUTHERN LEAGUE PREMIER – SOUTH DIVISION

			Home			Away			Total					
		P	W	D	L	W	D	L	W	D	L	F	A	GD	Pts
1	Truro C	31	10	3	2	11	1	4	21	4	6	65	30	35	67
2	Chesham U	33	13	2	2	8	1	7	21	3	9	70	44	26	66
3	Hayes & Yeading U	32	9	3	5	8	3	4	17	6	9	65	42	23	57
4	Swindon Supermarine	32	9	3	3	8	3	6	17	6	9	50	41	9	57
5	Tiverton T	29	7	4	3	9	3	3	16	7	6	69	41	28	55
6	Taunton T	31	11	2	2	4	6	6	15	8	8	63	53	10	53
7	Salisbury	30	11	3	3	3	6	4	14	9	7	57	42	15	51
8	Gosport Bor	33	8	6	2	5	4	8	13	10	10	35	32	3	49
9	Poole T	27	6	1	2	8	5	5	14	6	7	46	28	18	48
10	Weston-super-Mare	29	7	4	3	6	2	7	13	6	10	54	45	9	45
11	Metropolitan Police	30	6	3	8	7	1	5	13	4	13	46	48	−2	43
12	Farnborough	30	8	3	6	5	0	8	13	3	14	41	43	−2	42
13	Merthyr T	31	8	4	4	1	7	7	9	11	11	37	37	0	38
14	Hendon	31	7	3	6	3	5	7	10	8	13	47	51	−4	38
15	Wimborne T	33	7	3	6	3	4	10	10	7	16	39	52	−13	37
16	Hartley Wintney	27	3	3	4	7	3	7	10	6	11	38	39	−1	36
17	Harrow Bor	34	4	5	9	5	4	7	9	9	16	44	62	−18	36
18	Blackfield & Langley	31	6	6	5	2	3	9	8	9	14	33	50	−17	33
19	Yate T	31	6	2	7	2	3	11	8	5	18	38	56	−18	29
20	Walton Casuals	33	3	3	11	4	3	9	7	6	20	40	71	−31	27
21	Beaconsfield T	32	4	4	9	2	3	10	6	7	19	29	54	−25	25
22	Dorchester T	32	3	5	10	1	1	12	4	6	22	36	81	−45	18

BETVICTOR ISMITHIAN LEAGUE – PREMIER DIVISION

			Home			Away			Total					
		P	W	D	L	W	D	L	W	D	L	F	A	GD	Pts
1	Worthing	34	11	3	4	10	5	1	21	8	5	72	41	31	71
2	Cray W	33	8	7	3	10	3	2	18	10	5	63	45	18	64
3	Hornchurch	33	11	5	0	6	6	5	17	11	5	62	28	34	62
4	Folkestone Invicta	32	10	4	3	8	4	3	18	8	6	60	34	26	62
5	Carshalton Ath	34	11	4	3	7	4	5	18	8	8	59	38	21	62
6	Horsham	33	10	4	3	7	2	7	17	6	10	51	35	16	57
7	Enfield T	32	7	5	4	9	3	4	16	8	8	61	51	10	56
8	Bognor Regis T	33	7	2	5	9	4	6	16	6	11	58	46	12	54
9	Leatherhead	31	9	2	4	6	5	5	15	7	9	48	42	6	52
10	East Thurrock U	31	9	2	4	5	3	8	14	5	12	47	40	7	47
11	Kingstonian	31	5	7	3	6	7	3	11	14	6	42	36	6	47
12	Margate	33	5	6	6	6	4	6	11	10	12	47	54	−7	43
13	Potters Bar T	32	6	2	6	5	6	7	11	8	13	47	56	−9	41
14	Bowers & Pitsea	33	5	2	9	6	5	6	11	7	15	49	42	7	40
15	Haringey Bor	31	8	4	3	3	3	10	11	7	13	44	47	−3	40
16	Lewes	34	2	4	12	6	3	7	8	7	19	35	55	−20	31
17	Bishop's Stortford	33	4	3	11	4	2	9	8	5	20	37	63	−26	29
18	Brightlingsea Regent	38	3	9	7	2	5	12	5	14	19	24	62	−38	29
19	Cheshunt	32	4	3	9	4	1	11	8	4	20	39	59	−20	28
20	Corinthian-Casuals	31	4	4	7	2	4	10	6	8	17	33	44	−11	26
21	Wingate & Finchley	33	2	5	10	3	5	8	5	10	18	34	58	−24	25
22	Merstham	33	4	2	10	2	5	10	6	7	20	34	70	−36	25

NATIONAL LEAGUE SYSTEM STEP 4

BETVICTOR NORTHERN PREMIER LEAGUE – DIVISION ONE NORTH WEST

			Home			Away			Total					
		P	W	D	L	W	D	L	W	D	L	F	A	GD	Pts
1	Workington	31	13	3	0	9	2	4	22	5	4	77	25	52	71
2	Ramsbottom U	28	11	1	1	8	3	4	19	4	5	71	36	35	61
3	Marine	30	10	4	2	7	3	4	17	7	6	66	34	32	58
4	Pontefract Collieries	25	8	1	2	8	3	3	16	4	5	47	24	23	52
5	Marske U	26	10	3	0	5	3	5	15	6	5	50	25	25	51
6	Clitheroe	30	6	5	5	6	3	5	12	8	10	46	39	7	44
7	Mossley*	30	10	3	3	2	3	9	12	6	12	37	49	−12	41
8	Tadcaster Alb	27	5	5	4	6	2	5	11	7	9	40	30	10	40
9	Trafford	29	6	3	6	4	5	5	10	8	11	46	39	7	38
10	Runcorn Linnets	27	7	4	3	3	4	6	10	8	9	41	40	1	38
11	Brighouse T†	29	9	0	7	4	3	6	13	3	13	38	41	−3	38
12	Widnes	31	5	4	6	4	6	6	9	10	12	47	49	−2	37
13	Dunston UTS	28	5	6	2	4	2	9	9	8	11	41	45	−4	35
14	Prescot Cables	30	6	5	4	2	4	9	8	9	13	32	41	−9	33
15	Colne	25	3	2	6	4	7	3	7	9	9	31	31	0	30
16	Droylsden	30	4	4	7	3	2	10	7	6	17	28	75	−47	27
17	City of Liverpool‡	27	6	1	6	3	4	7	9	5	13	32	45	−13	26
18	Ossett U	28	4	5	6	1	2	10	5	7	16	38	57	−19	22
19	Kendal T	29	2	3	9	3	3	9	5	6	18	29	72	−43	21
20	Pickering T	30	4	3	7	0	1	15	4	4	22	37	77	−40	16

**Mossley deducted 1pt for fielding an ineligible player; †Brighouse T deducted 4pts for fielding an ineligible player; ‡City of Liverpool deducted 6pts for fielding an ineligible player.*

BETVICTOR NORTHERN PREMIER LEAGUE – DIVISION ONE SOUTH EAST

			Home			Away			Total						
		P	W	D	L	W	D	L	W	D	L	F	A	GD	Pts
1	Leek T	28	11	1	0	12	2	2	23	3	2	64	19	45	72
2	Stamford	29	13	0	2	9	4	1	22	4	3	74	27	47	70
3	Cleethorpes T	29	11	2	2	6	4	4	17	6	6	67	40	27	57
4	Belper T	26	6	3	4	8	4	1	14	7	5	44	29	15	49
5	Carlton T	26	6	3	4	8	3	2	14	6	6	52	33	19	48
6	Stocksbridge Park Steels	30	6	5	4	7	3	5	13	8	9	49	45	4	47
7	Sutton Coldfield T	28	8	2	4	5	3	6	13	5	10	45	34	11	44
8	Frickley Ath*	31	6	3	7	8	1	6	14	4	13	49	44	5	43
9	Ilkeston T	32	6	5	5	6	2	8	12	7	13	52	50	2	43
10	Kidsgrove Ath	27	5	4	5	6	2	5	11	6	10	42	31	11	39
11	Loughborough Dynamo	29	9	4	3	2	2	9	11	6	12	43	45	−2	39
12	Worksop T	32	5	0	11	7	2	7	12	2	18	41	55	−14	38
13	Sheffield FC	27	5	2	4	5	5	6	10	7	10	49	47	2	37
14	Glossop North End	30	3	5	7	5	4	6	8	9	13	36	45	−9	33
15	Chasetown	30	2	4	10	7	1	6	9	5	16	38	52	−14	32
16	Spalding U	30	3	4	7	5	4	7	8	8	14	33	53	−20	32
17	Newcastle T	30	2	2	11	6	2	7	8	4	18	42	55	−13	28
18	Lincoln U	29	4	2	11	4	1	7	8	3	18	30	60	−30	27
19	Market Drayton T	30	1	0	13	5	2	9	6	2	22	34	85	−51	20
20	Wisbech T	29	2	3	9	2	3	10	4	6	19	29	64	−35	18

**Frickley Ath deducted 3pts for fielding an ineligible player.*

BETVICTOR SOUTHERN LEAGUE – DIVISION ONE CENTRAL

			Home			Away			Total						
		P	W	D	L	W	D	L	W	D	L	F	A	GD	Pts
1	Berkhamsted	28	11	0	2	9	4	2	20	4	4	69	24	45	64
2	Halesowen T	27	11	0	2	9	3	2	20	3	4	72	19	53	63
3	Corby T	28	10	2	2	8	3	3	18	5	5	64	26	38	59
4	Welwyn Garden C	30	9	2	4	6	5	4	15	7	8	59	36	23	52
5	Aylesbury U	29	7	6	1	6	4	5	13	10	6	49	30	19	49
6	Barton R	30	9	4	3	4	2	8	13	6	11	65	55	10	45
7	Biggleswade	27	10	1	3	3	4	6	13	5	9	44	33	11	44
8	Yaxley	29	9	1	5	4	4	6	13	5	11	55	52	3	44
9	Bedworth U	27	8	3	4	5	2	5	13	5	9	46	43	3	44
10	North Leigh	27	7	2	4	6	1	7	13	3	11	50	50	0	42
11	Thame U	27	8	3	2	4	1	9	12	4	11	51	35	16	40
12	Bedford T	29	7	4	4	4	3	7	11	7	11	49	54	−5	40
13	Daventry T	28	6	2	6	6	2	6	12	4	12	42	48	−6	40
14	Coleshill T	28	6	5	4	4	1	8	10	6	12	50	47	3	36
15	AFC Dunstable	29	7	2	6	3	2	9	10	4	15	51	54	−3	34
16	Kidlington	28	7	5	2	2	1	11	9	6	13	32	48	−16	33
17	Didcot T	27	5	2	6	2	2	10	7	4	16	20	44	−24	25
18	St Neots T	28	4	1	9	2	2	10	6	3	19	33	59	−26	21
19	Kempston R	28	3	1	10	2	1	11	5	2	21	29	68	−39	17
20	Wantage T	28	1	1	10	0	0	16	1	1	26	16	121	−105	4

BETVICTOR SOUTHERN LEAGUE – DIVISION ONE SOUTH

			Home			Away			Total						
		P	W	D	L	W	D	L	W	D	L	F	A	GD	Pts
1	Thatcham T	27	10	1	3	8	3	2	18	4	5	66	28	38	58
2	Frome T	28	11	3	1	6	4	3	17	7	4	57	27	30	58
3	Larkhall Ath	27	8	5	1	6	2	5	14	7	6	45	37	8	49
4	Winchester C	27	7	3	2	7	3	5	14	6	7	53	37	16	48
5	Melksham T	28	7	3	5	7	2	4	14	5	9	58	51	7	47
6	Cirencester T	27	11	1	3	3	2	7	14	3	10	58	38	20	45
7	Paulton R	27	7	2	4	6	4	4	13	6	8	61	43	18	45
8	Cinderford T	26	8	1	4	5	3	5	13	4	9	59	45	14	43
9	Evesham U	28	6	5	3	5	3	6	11	8	9	52	50	2	41
10	Sholing	25	8	1	5	4	1	6	12	2	11	39	33	6	38
11	Bideford	28	8	3	3	2	4	8	10	7	11	49	50	−1	37
12	Slimbridge	26	7	0	7	4	2	6	11	2	13	54	53	1	35
13	Highworth T	28	5	0	8	3	8	4	8	8	12	36	41	−5	32
14	Willand R	24	8	0	3	2	2	9	10	2	12	32	37	−5	32
15	Bristol Manor Farm	27	3	4	6	5	2	7	8	6	13	31	44	−13	30
16	AFC Totton	27	3	5	5	4	3	7	7	8	12	39	53	−14	29
17	Mangotsfield U	29	5	4	5	3	0	12	8	4	17	46	65	−19	28
18	Moneyfields	25	4	6	2	3	0	10	7	6	12	37	50	−13	27
19	Basingstoke T*	27	4	2	7	1	2	11	5	4	18	34	76	−42	18
20	Barnstaple T	27	3	1	9	2	0	12	5	1	21	26	74	−48	16

**Basingstoke T deducted 1pt for fielding an ineligible player.*

BETVICTOR ISTHMIAN LEAGUE – DIVISION ONE NORTH

			Home			Away			Total						
		P	W	D	L	W	D	L	W	D	L	F	A	GD	Pts
1	Maldon & Tiptree*	26	10	2	2	12	0	0	22	2	2	65	20	45	65
2	Aveley	26	8	2	2	6	7	1	14	9	3	66	31	35	51
3	Tilbury	27	7	4	3	8	1	4	15	5	7	49	30	19	50
4	Heybridge Swifts	29	7	2	5	8	3	4	15	5	9	54	43	11	50
5	Bury T	29	9	3	4	6	2	5	15	5	9	49	41	8	50
6	Coggeshall T	26	8	3	2	4	7	2	12	10	4	40	24	16	46
7	Great Wakering R	29	4	3	7	9	2	4	13	5	11	45	36	9	44
8	Dereham T	29	4	5	5	7	3	5	11	8	10	52	43	9	41
9	Cambridge C	28	4	2	7	8	1	6	12	3	13	42	39	3	39
10	Canvey Island	27	5	3	7	6	2	4	11	5	11	49	54	–5	38
11	AFC Sudbury	26	7	2	4	4	2	7	11	4	11	42	42	0	37
12	Histon	28	6	3	6	4	3	6	10	6	12	40	53	–13	36
13	Soham Town Rangers	28	6	1	8	4	3	6	10	4	14	41	47	–6	34
14	Grays Ath	30	6	3	7	3	2	9	9	5	16	41	47	–6	32
15	Hullbridge Sports	31	2	3	8	5	8	5	7	11	13	33	53	–20	32
16	Witham T	29	3	4	8	5	2	7	8	6	15	36	63	–27	30
17	Brentwood T	28	4	2	8	3	3	8	7	5	16	41	54	–13	26
18	Felixstowe & Walton U	29	3	5	6	3	2	10	6	7	16	40	62	–22	25
19	Basildon U	26	3	4	4	3	2	10	6	6	14	29	47	–18	24
20	Romford	25	4	1	8	3	2	7	7	3	15	41	66	–25	24

**Maldon & Tiptree deducted 3pts for fielding an ineligible player.*

BETVICTOR ISTHMIAN LEAGUE – DIVISION ONE SOUTH CENTRAL

			Home			Away			Total						
		P	W	D	L	W	D	L	W	D	L	F	A	GD	Pts
1	Ware	30	9	6	1	10	1	3	19	7	4	81	44	37	64
2	Hanwell T	28	9	1	4	8	6	0	17	7	4	72	32	40	58
3	Uxbridge	29	6	5	3	10	2	3	16	7	6	59	35	24	55
4	Chertsey T	28	8	4	1	7	3	5	15	7	6	74	40	34	52
5	Westfield	28	7	4	3	8	3	3	15	7	6	65	32	33	52
6	Bracknell T	26	9	3	2	6	2	4	15	5	6	63	33	30	50
7	Waltham Abbey	29	8	0	5	7	5	4	15	5	9	68	52	16	50
8	Tooting & Mitcham U	27	7	1	5	7	4	3	14	5	8	53	29	24	47
9	Barking	29	8	2	4	6	2	7	14	4	11	51	45	6	46
10	Chipstead	28	6	3	4	7	3	5	13	6	9	53	40	13	45
11	Marlow	28	6	5	4	5	5	3	11	10	7	39	30	9	43
12	Bedfont Sports	29	6	4	6	4	5	4	10	9	10	42	44	–2	39
13	Chalfont St Peter	30	5	4	6	5	3	7	10	7	13	45	59	–14	37
14	Harlow T	29	6	3	6	4	1	9	10	4	15	42	57	–15	34
15	South Park	26	3	3	5	3	6	6	6	9	11	37	52	–15	27
16	Hertford T	29	4	2	10	2	2	9	6	4	19	39	81	–42	22
17	Ashford T (Middx)	29	2	1	11	3	4	8	5	5	19	30	70	–40	20
18	Northwood	29	4	1	11	2	1	10	6	2	21	34	81	–47	20
19	FC Romania	28	3	3	9	1	1	11	4	4	20	35	84	–49	16
20	Staines T	29	1	6	6	1	2	13	2	8	19	39	81	–42	14

BETVICTOR ISTHMIAN LEAGUE – DIVISION ONE SOUTH EAST

			Home			Away			Total						
		P	W	D	L	W	D	L	W	D	L	F	A	GD	Pts
1	Hastings U	28	13	1	1	5	7	1	18	8	2	53	21	32	62
2	Ashford U	30	8	1	5	11	1	4	19	2	9	75	41	34	59
3	Cray Valley PM	28	11	3	2	6	3	3	17	6	5	53	29	24	57
4	Whitehawk	28	11	3	1	5	5	3	16	8	4	61	33	28	56
5	Herne Bay	28	9	2	4	6	4	3	15	6	7	53	40	13	51
6	Chichester C	25	5	4	3	8	2	3	13	6	6	46	34	12	45
7	Whyteleafe	28	9	3	4	4	3	5	13	6	9	47	40	7	45
8	VCD Athletic	30	6	5	4	6	1	8	12	6	12	48	53	–5	42
9	Phoenix Sports	27	7	0	6	6	2	6	13	2	12	46	40	6	41
10	Sevenoaks T	29	6	5	3	5	3	7	11	8	10	43	37	6	41
11	Hythe T	29	7	3	3	4	4	8	11	7	11	34	37	–3	40
12	Haywards Heath T	27	7	3	4	3	6	4	10	9	8	37	33	4	39
13	Guernsey	28	3	4	6	6	5	4	9	9	10	39	47	–8	36
14	Whitstable T	28	5	6	3	4	2	8	9	8	11	38	41	–3	35
15	Burgess Hill T	27	6	1	6	3	3	8	9	4	14	47	60	–13	31
16	Sittingbourne	29	5	2	6	3	2	11	8	4	17	31	42	–11	28
17	Faversham T	30	6	6	4	1	1	12	7	7	16	30	51	–21	28
18	Ramsgate	30	3	3	9	1	5	9	4	8	18	35	68	–33	20
19	Three Bridges	29	1	2	11	4	1	10	5	3	21	35	68	–33	18
20	East Grinstead T	26	0	5	7	1	2	11	1	7	18	25	61	–36	10

THE BUILDBASE FA TROPHY 2019–20

**After extra time.*

EXTRA PRELIMINARY ROUND

Colne v Marske U 2-1
Cleethorpes T v Frickley Ath 1-0
Runcorn Linnets v Marine 1-0
City of Liverpool v Tadcaster Alb 1-1, 1-6
Ossett U v Widnes 1-0
Clitheroe v Sheffield 2-1
Daventry T v Kidsgrove Ath 1-1, 0-2
Lincoln U v Bury T 1-3
Chasetown v Spalding U 5-1
Dereham T v Halesowen T 1-2
Biggleswade v Bedford T 2-2, 0-1*
(0-0 at the end of normal time)
Carlton T v St Neots T 3-1
Kempston R v Wisbech T 0-1
Stamford v Loughborough Dynamo 5-1
Heybridge Swifts v Hertford T 4-1
Maldon & Tiptree v Felixstowe & Walton U 5-0
Ramsgate v Haywards Heath T 2-2, 0-1
Bracknell T v Coggeshall T 2-1
Chichester C v Three Bridges 2-1
Hullbridge Sports v Barton R 2-4
Harlow T v Hanwell T 1-1, 1-4
Welwyn Garden C v Canvey Island 1-4
Faversham T v Chertsey T 1-3
Chalfont St Peter v Whitstable T 0-1
Bristol Manor Farm v Moneyfields 7-1
Thame U v Kidlington 1-1, 2-1
Basingstoke T v North Leigh 4-3
Mangotsfield U v Slimbridge 1-2

PRELIMINARY ROUND

Tadcaster Alb (walkover) v Brighouse T
Pontefract Collieries v Glossop North End 2-0
Clitheroe v Prescot Cables 0-3
Pickering T v Stocksbridge Park Steels 1-1, 3-1*
(1-1 at the end of normal time)
Trafford v Runcorn Linnets 0-3
Ramsbottom U v Colne 1-3
Worksop T v Kendal T 2-1
Cleethorpes T (walkover) v Mossley
Dunston v Ossett U 3-2
Droylsden v Workington 1-1, 1-3
Soham Town Rangers v Bury T 3-0
Sutton Coldfield T v Yaxley 2-1
Newcastle T v Leek T 2-5
Evesham U v Halesowen T 1-1, 0-3
Chasetown v Coleshill T 3-0
Belper T v Stamford 0-3
Histon v Corby T 0-0, 1-4
Cambridge C v Market Drayton T 2-1
Kidsgrove Ath v Wisbech T 1-0
Carlton T v Bedford T 3-2
Bedworth U v Ilkeston T 3-1
Staines T v Heybridge Swifts 0-2
Aylesbury U v Sevenoaks T 2-2, 4-2
Grays Ath v Bedfont Sports 0-1
Tie ordered to be replayed
Whitehawk v Romford 2-1
Whitstable T v Ware 2-2, 0-1*
(0-0 at the end of normal time)
Hanwell T v AFC Dunstable 2-4
Brentwood T v Basildon U 2-3
Sittingbourne v South Park 1-0
Chipstead v FC Romania 2-1
VCD Ath v AFC Sudbury 1-4
Great Wakering R v Westfield 3-5
Uxbridge v Northwood 4-1
East Grinstead T v Aveley 0-5
Berkhamsted v Herne Bay 5-0
Whyteleafe v Tooting & Mitcham U 1-3
Burgess Hill T v Phoenix Sports 0-2
Barton R v Chichester C 4-2
Ashford U v Witham T 2-2, 2-0*
(0-0 at the end of normal time)
Barking v Guernsey 2-1
Hythe T v Hastings U 1-2
Maldon & Tiptree v Cray Valley (PM) 5-2
Tilbury v Waltham Abbey 6-2
Ashford T (Middlesex) v Canvey Island 1-1, 0-5
Haywards Heath T v Bracknell T 2-1
Marlow v Chertsey T 1-0
Highworth T v Cinderford T 1-1, 1-2
Barnstaple T v Thatcham T 1-3
Paulton R (walkover) v Willand R
Slimbridge v AFC Totton 0-1
Melksham T v Wantage T 2-0
Frome T v Bideford 2-1
Didcot T v Larkhall Ath 0-2
Cirencester T v Basingstoke T 2-3
Winchester C v Thame U 3-3, 3-5
Sholing v Bristol Manor Farm 2-1

FIRST QUALIFYING ROUND

Buxton v Hyde U 3-2
Prescot Cables v Pickering T 0-0, 3-0
Whitby T v Worksop T 4-1
Lancaster C v Witton Alb 1-0
Nantwich T v Bamber Bridge 2-1
Atherton Colleries v Scarborough Ath 3-2
Morpeth T v Cleethorpes T 6-1
Runcorn Linnets v Pontefract Collieries 5-3
Tadcaster Alb v Workington 0-1
Warrington T v Ashton U 0-1
Dunston v Gainsborough Trinity 0-4
Radcliffe v FC United of Manchester 0-2
Kidsgrove Ath v Colne 0-1
Stalybridge Celtic v South Shields 0-2
Redditch U v Corby T 4-2
AFC Rushden & D v Banbury U 0-0, 2-1
Leek T v Chasetown 2-0
Halesowen T v Stamford 2-2, 3-0
Stourbridge v Nuneaton Bor 2-1
Peterborough Sports v Alvechurch 1-0
Biggleswade T v Bedworth U 2-1
Cambridge C v Needham Market 0-3
Carlton T v Matlock T 1-2
Lowestoft T v Coalville T 2-4
Basford U v Mickleover Sports 3-0
St Ives T v Soham Town Rangers 0-0, 0-3
Grantham T v Rushall Olympic 5-3
Tamworth v Leiston 4-0
Sutton Coldfield T v Stafford Rangers 2-1
Stratford T v Hednesford T 1-2
Bromsgrove Sporting v Barwell 2-7
Folkestone Invicta v Lewes 2-0
AFC Sudbury v Harrow Bor 2-0
Haywards Heath T v Aylesbury U 3-1
Carshalton Ath v Merstham 3-1
Uxbridge v Bognor Regis T 1-3
Westfield v Beaconsfield T 1-0
Hitchin T v Bedfont Sports 1-1, 1-1*
Bedfont Sports won 5-4 on penalties
Ashford U v Barton R 1-2
Hornchurch v Berkhamsted 3-1
Haringey Bor v Horsham 3-0
Maldon & Tiptree v Cray W 3-0
Bishop's Stortford v Enfield T 1-1, 2-4*
(1-1 at the end of normal time)
Heybridge Swifts v Potters Bar T 1-2
Brightlingsea Regent v Royston T 1-2
Metropolitan Police v Tilbury 4-3
Leatherhead v Ware 3-0
Aveley v Bowers & Pitsea 3-0
Sittingbourne v Tooting & Mitcham U 0-1
Chipstead v Canvey Island 3-3, 1-2
Whitehawk v Hendon 4-1
Barking v Margate 0-0, 0-2
Wingate & Finchley v Hayes & Yeading U 1-1, 1-2
Kingstonian v Corinthian Casuals 4-2
AFC Dunstable v Hastings U 0-4
Phoenix Sports v Kings Langley 3-5
Cheshunt v East Thurrock U 1-2
Basildon U v Chesham U 5-3
Worthing v Walton Casuals 2-1

Yate T v Tiverton T 3-3, 3-3*
Yate T won 4-1 on penalties
Melksham T v Basingstoke T 1-0
Truro C v Blackfield & Langley 1-1, 1-3
Poole T v Hartley Wintney 0-1
Thame U v Frome T 1-2
Marlow v Sholing 0-0, 0-2
Salisbury v Dorchester T 3-3, 3-0
Paulton R v Larkhall Ath 1-1, 3-1
Wimborne T v Taunton T 2-2, 1-4
Swindon Supermarine v Thatcham T 1-4
Gosport Bor v Farnborough 3-1
AFC Totton v Weston-super-Mare 3-2*
(1-1 at the end of normal time)
Cinderford T v Merthyr T 2-2, 5-4*
(4-4 at the end of normal time)

SECOND QUALIFYING ROUND
Halesowen T v Grantham T 2-1
Matlock T v Ashton U 1-0
Atherton Colleries v Morpeth T 2-1
Sutton Coldfield T v Hednesford T 1-5
Peterborough Sports v Whitby T 2-0
South Shields v AFC Rushden & D 4-0
Barwell v Redditch U 3-3, 2-3
Colne v Buxton 3-1
Runcorn Linnets v Prescot Cables 1-1, 2-1
FC United of Manchester v Basford U 3-1
Nantwich T v Coalville T 0-1
Leek T v Workington 1-3
Tamworth v Gainsborough Trinity 3-5
Stourbridge v Lancaster C 2-2, 2-1
Margate v Tooting & Mitcham U 0-4
Haringey Bor v Canvey Island 2-1
Yate T v AFC Totton 6-3
Royston T v Haywards Heath T 7-0
Bognor Regis T v East Thurrock U 3-1
Westfield v Hartley Wintney 1-1, 1-2
Basildon U v Hornchurch 1-6
Taunton T v Aveley 3-3, 1-2
Worthing v AFC Sudbury 1-4
Hastings U v Whitehawk 2-2, 2-1
Carshalton Ath v Frome T 5-3
Sholing v Barton R 2-1
Blackfield & Langley v Kingstonian 0-3
Maldon & Tiptree v Folkestone Invicta 4-3
Salisbury v Kings Langley 2-1
Hayes & Yeading U v Soham Town Rangers 4-2
Bedfont Sports v Paulton R 0-5
Enfield T v Thatcham T 5-0
Gosport Bor v Melksham T 4-2
Cinderford T v Potters Bar T 1-0
Needham Market v Leatherhead 1-2
Metropolitan Police v Biggleswade T 2-2, 0-1

THIRD QUALIFYING ROUND
Curzon Ashton v Kidderminster H 3-0
York C v Altrincham 0-1
Workington v Farsley Celtic 0-1
Hednesford T v Coalville T 2-1
Runcorn Linnets v FC United of Manchester 0-3
Darlington v Gainsborough Trinity 2-1
Gloucester C v Bradford (Park Avenue) 0-2
Blyth Spartans v Alfreton T 1-1, 3-1
Brackley T v Chester 0-1
Stourbridge v South Shields 1-1, 0-4
Guiseley v AFC Telford U 0-4
Matlock T v Redditch U 2-0
Colne v Southport 2-3
King's Lynn T v Hereford 0-0, 3-0
Atherton Colleries v Boston U 1-0
Peterborough Sports v Kettering T 0-3
Halesowen T v Gateshead 1-0
Leamington v Spennymoor T 2-1
Dulwich Hamlet v Chippenham T 2-2, 2-1
Bath C v Gosport Bor 0-0, 3-2*
(2-2 at the end of normal time)
Sholing v Paulton R 0-0, 2-1
Tonbridge Angels v Bognor Regis T 2-1
Weymouth v Hastings U 1-0
Chelmsford C v Hungerford T 2-1
Havant & Waterlooville v Cinderford T 3-1
Carshalton Ath v Tooting & Mitcham U 2-1
Enfield T v Maldon & Tiptree 4-3
Braintree T v Yate T 1-2
Biggleswade T v Aveley 1-4
Kingstonian v AFC Sudbury 2-1
Eastbourne Bor v Hartley Wintney 3-1
Leatherhead v Dorking W 0-3
Concord Rangers v Slough T 0-0, 3-2
Maidstone U v Dartford 2-2, 1-0
Haringey Bor v Hemel Hempstead T 1-4
Wealdstone v Royston T 2-3
Oxford C v Hornchurch 1-1, 4-4*
Hornchurch won 4-1 on penalties
Billericay T v Hampton & Richmond Bor 1-2
Welling U v St Albans C 3-1
Salisbury v Hayes & Yeading U 4-3

FIRST ROUND
Solihull Moors v Darlington 2-2, 0-1
South Shields v Southport 2-2, 1-3
Bradford (Park Avenue) v Halesowen T 2-2, 0-2
Harrogate T v Hartlepool U 3-2
Stockport Co v Blyth Spartans 4-2
Chesterfield v Notts Co 0-1
Hednesford T v Chester 0-0, 1-2
FC Halifax T v Wrexham 4-0
AFC Telford U v Leamington 0-5
Farsley Celtic v Altrincham 2-2, 2-1*
(1-1 at the end of normal time)
Matlock T v Chorley 2-2, 2-2*
Matlock T won 4-3 on penalties
FC United of Manchester v Kettering T 2-1
AFC Fylde v Curzon Ashton 1-0
Atherton Colleries v Barrow 2-2, 0-2
Yeovil T v Welling U 3-1
Hornchurch v Dulwich Hamlet 1-0
King's Lynn T v Dover Ath 2-2*
King's Lynn T won 4-2 on penalties
Carshalton Ath v Aveley 3-3, 0-2
Eastleigh v Yate T 6-1
Tonbridge Angels v Hampton & Richmond Bor 2-2, 0-2
Barnet v Weymouth 2-1
Kingstonian v Woking 3-1
Chelmsford C v Havant & Waterlooville 2-1
Enfield T v Ebbsfleet U 0-2
Eastbourne Bor v Salisbury 2-2, 0-1
Maidenhead U v Hemel Hempstead T 4-2
Sutton U v Dagenham & R 1-1, 2-3*
(1-1 at the end of normal time)
Maidstone U v Concord Rangers 2-3
Torquay U v Aldershot T 5-1
Bath C v Sholing 2-0
Dorking W v Bromley 3-0
Royston T v Boreham Wood 2-0

SECOND ROUND
Dorking W v Stockport Co 1-1, 4-0
Kingstonian v Leamington 1-1, 0-1
AFC Fylde v Southport 4-1
Royston T v Chester 3-0
Darlington v Harrogate T 0-2
Yeovil T v Hampton & Richmond Bor 4-0
Ebbsfleet U v King's Lynn T 1-0
Halesowen T v Maidenhead U 2-2, 3-1
Notts Co v Dagenham & R 2-1
Chelmsford C v Salisbury 4-0
Torquay U v FC Halifax T 1-2
Eastleigh v Matlock T 2-1
Concord Rangers v Bath C 1-1, 2-1
Farsley Celtic v Barnet 1-1, 0-2
Hornchurch v Aveley 1-2
Barrow v FC United of Manchester 7-0

THIRD ROUND
Ebbsfleet U v Royston T 0-2*
(0-0 at the end of normal time)
Concord Rangers v Leamington 2-2*
Concord Rangers won 4-3 on penalties
Harrogate T v Eastleigh 2-0
FC Halifax T v Halesowen T 0-1
Barnet v Barrow 3-0

Dorking W v AFC Fylde 2-4
Aveley v Chelmsford C 3-1
Yeovil T v Notts Co 1-2

FOURTH ROUND
Barnet v Halesowen T 1-2*
(1-1 at the end of normal time)
Notts Co v Aveley 5-0
Concord Rangers v Royston T 2-1*
(1-1 at the end of normal time)
AFC Fylde v Harrogate T 2-3*
(2-2 at the end of normal time)

SEMI-FINALS
Concord Rangers v Halesowen T 2-1
Notts Co v Harrogate T P-P
(to be played 15 September 2020)

THE BUILDBASE FA TROPHY FINAL 2019–20
Wembley Stadium, Sunday 27 September 2020
Concord Rangers v Notts Co or Harrogate T

THE BUILDBASE FA VASE 2019–20

**After extra time.*

FIRST QUALIFYING ROUND
Whitley Bay v Barnoldswick T 1-2
Birtley T v Jarrow 2-5
Harrogate Railway Ath v West Allotment Celtic 0-4
Willington v Albion Sports 0-2
Garstang v Sunderland West End 1-2
Northallerton T v Stokesley SC 7-0
Shildon v Tow Law T 3-0
Chester-le-Street T v Garforth T 1-2
Knaresborough T v Washington 2-1
Whitehaven v Billingham Synthonia 0-9
Billingham T v Heaton Stannington 2-1
Penrith v Guisborough T 0-1
Stockton T v Ashington 4-0
Thackley v Carlisle C 3-2
Crook T v Brandon U 2-1
Whickham v Squires Gate 1-2*
(1-1 at the end of normal time)
Nelson v Seaham Red Star 1-3*
(1-1 at the end of normal time)
AFC Blackpool v Redcar Ath 2-1
Padiham v Bedlington Terriers 5-0
Longridge T v Newcastle University 5-2
Newton Aycliffe v Silsden 2-1
Easington Colliery v Holker Old Boys 4-1
Eccleshill U v Thornaby 0-4
Yorkshire Amateur v Alnwick T 1-0
Esh Winning v Campion 3-2
Sunderland Ryhope CW v North Shields 2-0
Prestwich Heys v 1874 Northwich 1-0
Swallownest v Vauxhall Motors 0-2
Worsbrough Bridge Ath v Hall Road Rangers 5-6
Retford U v Daisy Hill 3-2
Skelmersdale U v New Mills 5-2
Handsworth v Shelley 4-0
Ashton Ath v AFC Darwen 3-2
Bacup Bor v Grimsby Bor 1-2
St Helens T v Rossington Main 1-2
Cammell Laird 1907 v Charnock Richard 2-3
Parkgate v Chadderton 2-3
Retford v Barton T 1-3
Wythenshawe T v Goole 5-2
Nostell MW v AFC Liverpool 4-1
Staveley MW v Cheadle T 2-5
Litherland Remyca v Glasshoughton Welfare 3-6*
(3-3 at the end of normal time)
Harworthy Colliery v Stockport T 1-3
Cheadle Heath Nomads v Ashton T 5-3
Maine Road v Maltby Main 5-2
AFC Emley v Burscough 1-1, 2-1
Brigg T v Armthorpe Welfare 2-0
Pilkington v Atherton LR 3-2*
(2-2 at the end of normal time)
Rylands v Athersley Recreation 6-0
Liversedge v Hallam 2-1
West Didsbury & Chorlton (walkover) v Egerton
Avro v Selby T 0-2
Abbey Hulton U v Tipton T 3-2
Boldmere St Michaels v Stourport Swifts 3-2
Heather St Johns v Hereford Pegasus 3-0
Bromyard T v Uttoxeter T 0-4
Stafford T v Tividale 1-3
Leicester Road v Dudley Sports 3-1
Racing Club Warwick v AFC Bridgnorth 4-0
FC Oswestry T v Bustleholme 4-0
Highgate U v Ellistown 11-1
Bewdley T v Alsager T 1-2
Malvern T v Pershore T 1-1, 2-0
Heath Hayes v Ashby Ivanhoe 1-2*
(1-1 at the end of normal time)
Eccleshall v Hanley T 2-3*
(2-2 at the end of normal time)
FC Stratford v Chelmsley T 3-2
Bolehall Swifts v Coventry Copsewood 0-5
GNP Sports v Littleton 3-2
Nuneaton Griff v Wellington Amateurs 5-3*
(3-3 at the end of normal time)
Stapenhill v Dudley T 0-2
St Martins v Shifnal T 0-3
Wolverhampton Casuals v Bilston T 2-1
Haughmond v Stone Old Alleynians 3-1
Gresley v Winsford U 1-0
Lichfield C v Romulus 5-2
Sandbach U v Wem T 13-0
Studley v Brocton 3-2
Wellington v Worcester C 0-5
Wolverhampton SC v Cradley T 3-0
Hinckley v Ellesmere Rangers 2-1
Coton Green v Shawbury U 0-3
Wednesfield v Droitwich Spa 0-2
Coventry Sphinx v AFC Wulfrunians 2-1
County Hall v Newark Flowserve 1-3
Radford v Cottesmore Amateurs S&S 1-3
Holbeach U v Lincoln Moorlands Railway 3-2
Bourne T v Sleaford T 4-2
Kirby Muxloe v Oakham U 3-2*
(2-2 at the end of normal time)
FC Bolsover v Long Eaton U (walkover)
Harrowby U v Belper U 3-1
Shirebrook T v Arnold T 3-2*
(2-2 at the end of normal time)
Quorn v Boston T 6-1
Horncastle T v Sherwood Colliery 0-2
Dunkirk v Oadby T 1-0
AFC Mansfield v Graham St Prims 1-0
Melton T v Gedling MW 2-4*
(2-2 at the end of normal time)
Barrow T v Friar Lane & Epworth 5-3
Pinxton v Birstall U 2-3
Hucknall T v Holbrook Sports 4-3*
(1-1 at the end of normal time)
Aylestone Park v Loughborough University 0-3
Holwell Sports v Heanor T 1-2
South Normanton Ath v Ollerton T 7-0
FC GNG v Clifton All Whites 0-9
Saffron Dynamo v Rainworth MW 0-2
Kimberley MW v Clipstone 2-1
Borrowash Vic v West Bridgford 1-2
Selston v Teversal 3-1
Newmarket T v Gorleston 2-1
Norwich CBS v March Town U 1-2
Downham T v Netherton U 0-4
Framlington T v Great Yarmouth T 1-1*
Great Yarmouth T won 4-2 on penalties
Fakenham T v Norwich U 0-4
Walsham Le Willows v Lakenheath 2-1
Mildenhall T v Swaffham T 2-0
Debenham LC v Wisbech St Mary 2-0
Diss T v Huntingdon T 1-3
Ely C v Peterborough Northern Star 4-6*
(3-3 at the end of normal time)
Park View v West Essex A-A, 1-4
First match abandoned after 87 minutes due to serious injury, 1-1

Wodson Park v Sawbridgeworth T 2-1
Holland v Baldock T 0-2
FC Broxbourne Bor v Barkingside 3-0
Clapton v Catholic U 1-6
New Salamis v Codicote 4-0
Hadleigh U v Stotfold 6-2
Hoddesdon T v Stanway R 1-2
Long Melford v Little Oakley 1-0
Cockfosters v Coggeshall U 1-2*
(1-1 at the end of normal time)
Woodford T v St Margaretsbury 1-2
Ilford v Enfield 1-2
Takeley v Burnham Ramblers 6-1
Halstead T v Haverhill Bor 1-3
FC Clacton v Southend Manor 3-0
Benfleet v Haverhill R 2-5
Wivenhoe T v Clapton Community 5-1
White Ensign v Cornard U 3-0
Colney Heath v London Lions 4-0
Lopes Tavares London v Harwich & Parkeston 2-0
London Colney v Brimsdown 3-1
Sporting Bengal U v Wormley R 0-1
Hackney Wick v May & Baker Eastbrook Community 6-3
Potton U v Frenford 0-6
Hashtag U v Leyton Ath 2-0
Ipswich W v Enfield Bor 0-3
Crawley Green v Ampthill T 4-2
Risborough Rangers v Easington Sports 6-0
Holmer Green v Raunds T 0-1
Irchester U v North Greenford U 0-3
Long Crendon v Langley 4-3
Wellingborough T v Wellingborough Whitworths 4-1
Bedford v Burton Park W 2-0
Burnham v Harborough T 2-4
Eynesbury R v Harpenden T 2-0
Winslow U v Rushden & Higham U 7-1
Chinnor v Broadfields U (walkover)
Rugby Bor v British Airways HEW 2-1
Leighton T v Bugbrooke St Michaels 3-0
Leverstock Green v Aylesbury Vale Dynamos 1-1, 1-3
Lutterworth T v Pitshanger Dynamo 7-1
Holyport v Unite MK 3-2
Ardley U v Northampton ON Chenecks 1-3
Chalvey Sports v Wembley 0-1
Flackwell Heath v Arlesey T 3-1
AFC Hayes v Dunstable T 3-1
Hanworth Villa v Marston Shelton R 5-1
St Panteleimon v Long Buckby 3-4
Bedfont & Feltham v Lutterworth Ath 5-0
Rothwell Corinthians v Desborough T 2-0
Hillingdon v Rayners Lane 5-1
NW London v Harefield U 0-2
Hillingdon Bor v Kensington & Ealing Bor 3-2
Amersham T v Thame Rangers 2-1
Ascot U v Fleet T 3-3, 3-1
Tytherington Rocks v Newent T 0-2
Shrivenham v Milton U 3-2
Cove v Fleet Spurs 0-1
Fairford T v Abingdon T 5-1
Frimley Green v Lydney T 3-1
Thornbury T v Cheltenham Saracens 6-2
Shortwood U v Tuffley R 5-0
New College Swindon v Royal Wootton Bassett T 0-7
Clanfield 85 v Sandhurst T 7-3
Wokingham & Emmbrook v Chipping Sodbury T 2-1*
(1-1 at the end of normal time)
Abingdon U v Eversley & California 1-0
Binfield v Virginia Water 1-0*
(0-0 at the end of normal time)
Malmesbury Vic v Woodley U 3-0
Banstead Ath v Greenwich Bor 2-2, 2-3
Little Common v K Sports 1-2
Egham T v FC Elmstead 3-2
Wick v Colliers Wood U 0-4*
(0-0 at the end of normal time)
Lydd T v Raynes Park Vale 5-5, 0-2*
(0-0 at the end of normal time)
Kent Football U v Snodland T 0-1*
(0-0 at the end of normal time)
Saltdean U v Lordswood 0-2
Tooting Bec v Walton & Hersham 2-4
Epsom & Ewell v Kennington 1-4
Molesey v Greenways 4-3*
(2-2 at the end of normal time)
Littlehampton U v Bexhill U 1-5

AFC Varndeanians v Loxwood 2-2*
Loxwood won 4-2 on penalties
Farnham T v Langney W 2-1
Sporting Club Thamesmead v Sutton Ath 3-2
Littlehampton T v Tunbridge Wells 0-4
Southwick v Billingshurst 1-2
Erith & Belvedere v Fire U Christian 3-0
Rochester U v Mile Oak 0-3
Ash U v Badshot Lea 1-2
Shoreham v Crowborough Ath 0-3
Holmesdale v Sheerwater 2-1
Crawley Down Gatwick v East Preston 5-4*
(4-4 at the end of normal time)
CB Hounslow U v Beckenham T 2-3
Bagshot v Broadbridge Heath 2-0
Bridon Ropes v Pagham 2-2*
Bridon Ropes won 4-3 on penalties
Meridian v Hassocks 0-2
Godalming T v Hailsham T 2-1
Storrington Community v Knaphill 0-6
Sheppey U v AFC Croydon Ath 2-0
Seaford T v Eastbourne U 2-1
Forest Hill Park v Westside 1-2*
(1-2 at the end of normal time)
Lingfield v Horley T 1-2
Guildford C v Glebe 0-3
Peacehaven & Telscombe v Steyning T 2-2, 3-0
Cobham v PFC Vic London 3-2
AFC Spelthorne Sports Club v Spelthorne Sports 1-4
Balham v Rushtall 1-2
Lancing v Chessington & Hook U 3-2
Erith T v Welling T 2-2, 0-2
Midhurst & Easebourne v Alfold 3-1
Punjab U v Selsey 5-0
Sidlesham v Stansfeld 1-1, 3-1
Lymington T v Fawley 5-2*
(1-1 at the end of normal time)
Fareham T v Whitchurch U 2-0
Folland Sports v East Cowes Vic Ath 0-1
Alton v Andover New Street 2-1
Hamble Club v Totton & Eling 4-0
Bashley v Bridport 3-0
Bemerton Heath Harlequins v Alresford T 1-2*
(1-1 at the end of normal time)
Solent University v Bradford T 2-7
United Services Portsmouth v Sherborne T 2-3
Calne T v Downton 1-3
New Milton T v AFC Portchester 1-4
Andover T v Westbury U 1-4
Swanage T & Herston v Dorchester Sports 0-1
Devizes T v Stockbridge 1-0
Cowes Sports v Shaftesbury 2-0
Ringwood T v Verwood T 1-1, 0-2
Amesbury T v Christchurch 1-4
Petersfield T v AFC Stoneham 1-0
Pewsey Vale v Laverstock & Ford 0-1
Clevedon T v Roman Glass St George 1-2
Almondsbury v Buckland Ath 2-4
Bishops Lydeard v Bodmin T 1-3
Shepton Mallet v Wellington 4-0
Bristol Telephones v Falmouth T 1-3
Ivybridge T v Bishop Sutton 4-1*
(1-1 at the end of normal time)
Cullompton Rangers v Newquay 2-0
St Blazey v Godolphin Atlantic 5-3
Elburton Villa v Saltash U 1-5
Keynsham T v Helston Ath 0-1
Tavistock v Hallen 4-1
Street v Crediton U 3-0
Hengrove Ath v Radstock T 0-1
Cadbury Heath v Longwell Green Sports 3-0
Wells C v Millbrook 5-3
Welton R v Newton Abbot Spurs 0-4
Bovey Tracey v Liskeard Ath 3-1
Porthleven v Callington T 7-0
Ilfracombe T v Torpoint Ath 1-2
Odd Down v Portishead T 1-2*
(1-1 at the end of normal time)
Launceston v Cheddar 0-2
Exmouth T v Brislington 3-2

SECOND QUALIFYING ROUND
Thornaby v Thackley 2-1
Steeton v Seaham Red Star 2-3
Durham C v Stockton T 0-2
Easington Colliery v Shildon 1-2

Ryton & Crawcrook Alb v Yorkshire Amateur 2-4
Esh Winning v Billingham T 2-3
Jarrow v Newton Aycliffe 2-1
Sunderland West End v Padiham 0-1
Albion Sports v Guisborough T 1-5
Northallerton T v Barnoldswick T 2-3
Squires Gate v West Allotment Celtic 1-4
Longridge T v AFC Blackpool 3-1
Billingham Synthonia v Knaresborough T 1-2
Garforth T v Sunderland Ryhope CW 0-2
Cleator Moor v Crook T 0-2
Skelmersdale U v Wythenshawe T 1-2
Ashton Ath v Liversedge 5-1
Chadderton v Brigg T 3-2
Runcorn T v West Didsbury & Chorlton 0-1
Cheadle Heath Nomads v Vauxhall Motors 1-2
Wythenshawe Amateurs v Selby T 1-3
Grimsby Bor v Dronfield T 3-2
Stockport T v Abbey Hey 1-2
Lower Breck v Pilkington 4-3
Handsworth v Glasshoughton Welfare 1-2
Hall Road Rangers v Maine Road 4-6
Nostell MW v Barton T 4-2
Retford U v Bottesford T 2-4*
(1-1 at the end of normal time)
Rylands v Rossington Main 4-2
Cheadle T v East Yorkshire Carnegie 4-0
Prestwich Heys v Charnock Richard 2-3*
(2-2 at the end of normal time)
AFC Emley v Winterton Rangers 0-2
Hinckley v Rocester 2-3
Shawbury U v Gornal Ath 3-0
Malvern T v NKF Burbage 5-2
Gresley v FC Oswestry T 3-2
Tividale v Droitwich Spa 1-2
Heather St Johns v Coventry Copsewood 5-2
Abbey Hulton U v Alsager T 2-2, 1-3
FC Stratford v GNP Sports 2-2*
GNP Sports won 4-3 on penalties
Black Country Rangers v Leicester Road 0-8
Whitchurch Alport v Nuneaton Griff 4-1
Atherstone T v Paget Rangers 3-1
Ashby Ivanhoe v Sandbach U 0-3
Boldmere St Michaels v Willenhall T 4-1
Worcester C v Highgate U 2-0
Uttoxeter T v Wolverhampton SC 1-0
Studley v Racing Club Warwick 1-2
Shifnal T v Haughmond 0-1
Coventry Sphinx v Hanley T 4-5
Lichfield C v Wolverhampton Casuals 4-2
Smethwick v Dudley T 0-1
Barrow T v St Andrews 3-2
Dunkirk v Anstey Nomads 2-1
Clifton All Whites v Holbeach U 1-3
Newark Flowserve v Skegness T 5-1
Loughborough University v Ingles 1-1, 2-1*
(1-1 at the end of normal time)
Quorn v Shirebrook T 5-0
Blaby & Whetstone Ath v Kimberley MW 0-2
Blidworth Welfare v Sherwood Colliery 0-5
AFC Mansfield v Rainworth MW 3-2
South Normanton Ath v Kirby Muxloe 2-1
Long Eaton U v Blackstones 3-0
West Bridgford v Selston 5-0
Clay Cross T v Gedling MW 2-2, 3-2
Heanor T v Birstall U 2-1
Bourne T v Hucknall T 1-2
Harrowby U v Cottesmore Amateurs S&S 1-2
Kirkley & Pakefield v Debenham LC 1-0
Huntingdon T v Mulbarton W 2-1
Netherton U v Wroxham 2-3
Thetford T v Peterborough Northern Star 0-5
March Town U v Walsham Le Willows 4-3*
(2-2 at the end of normal time)
Mildenhall T v Newmarket T 1-1, 3-3*
Mildenhall T won 7-6 on penalties
Great Yarmouth T v Norwich U 0-3
FC Clacton v Redbridge 4-1
Enfield v Enfield Bor 2-1
London Colney v Baldock T 2-4
West Essex v Brantham Ath 2-4
White Ensign v Newbury Forest 3-0
Coggeshall U v Long Melford 1-0
Langford v Hackney Wick 1-1*
Hackney Wick won 4-2 on penalties
Whitton U v St Margaretsbury 2-1

Takeley v Wormley R 3-0
Lopes Tavares London v Catholic U 3-1
New Salamis v Tower Hamlets 2-0
Frenford v Hashtag U 3-2
Hadleigh U v Haverhill Bor 5-2
Colney Heath v Haverhill R 2-0
FC Broxbourne Bor v Wivenhoe T 4-1
Stanway R v Wodson Park 7-1
Long Crendon v Leighton T 2-5
Bedford v Bedfont & Feltham 0-4
Broadfields U v Hanworth Villa 5-1
Harefield U v Rothwell Corinthians 1-3
Wembley v Risborough Rangers 1-3
Buckingham Ath v Hillingdon 6-0
Harborough T v Hillingdon Bor 3-3, 2-1
Northampton ON Chenecks v
Northampton Sileby Rangers 3-1
Cricklewood W v Long Buckby 1-4
Wellingborough T v Holyport 1-0
Raunds T v Flackwell Heath 1-2
Aylesbury Vale Dynamos v Rugby Bor 3-1
North Greenford U v Oxhey Jets 0-2
Edgware T v Eynesbury R 0-2
Lutterworth T v Amersham T 6-0
Crawley Green v Winslow U 4-0
AFC Hayes v London Tigers 2-0
Abingdon U v Reading C 3-1
Fairford T v Shortwood U 6-1
Wokingham & Emmbrook v Thornbury T 0-1
Frimley Green v Ascot U 0-3
Malmesbury Vic v Camberley T 2-1
Longlevens v Newent T 2-1
Milton Keynes Robins v Fleet Spurs 4-1
Shrivenham v Clanfield 85 2-2, 5-1
AFC Aldermaston v Binfield 1-3
Tadley Calleva v Royal Wootton Bassett T 1-0
Sidlesham v Kennington 2-4*
(2-2 at the end of normal time)
Crawley Down Gatwick v Mile Oak 4-6
Midhurst & Easebourne v Crowborough Ath 0-2
Hassocks v Horley T 1-6
Seaford T v FC Deportivo Galicia 2-0
Hollands & Blair v Deal T 1-2
Westside v Bexhill U 3-2
Molesey v Greenwich Bor A-A, 0-2
First match abandoned after 80 mins due to serious injury, 0-0
Erith & Belvedere v Oakwood 9-2
Sporting Club Thamesmead v Billingshurst 3-1
Knaphill v Tunbridge Wells 2-2, 1-5
Raynes Park Vale v Walton & Hersham 4-1
Beckenham T v Farnham T 6-0
Peacehaven & Telscombe v Spelthorne Sports 3-2*
(2-2 at the end of normal time)
Lancing v Worthing U 7-0
Arundel v Welling T 1-7
Croydon v Colliers Wood U 1-3
Punjab U v Loxwood 3-2
Cobham v Badshot Lea 2-4
Lordswood v Sheppey U 0-1
Redhill v Bagshot 4-3
Snodland T v Bridon Ropes 3-2
Rushtall v Godalming T 2-1
K Sports v Glebe 0-3
Holmesdale v Egham T 0-1
Corsham T v Romsey T 1-3
Bradford T v Hamble Club 1-0
Hythe & Dibden v AFC Portchester 2-3
Alton v Westbury U 1-2
Devizes T v Newport (IW) 1-3
Dorchester Sports v Christchurch 2-4
Bashley v Lymington T 1-4
Warminster T v Alresford T 2-1
East Cowes Vic Ath v Fareham T 3-2
Cowes Sports v Verwood T 7-3
Laverstock & Ford v Brockenhurst 0-4
Sherborne T v Petersfield T 2-2, 0-1
Downton v Wincanton T 2-1
Camelford v Ashton & Backwell U 2-1
St Blazey v Falmouth T 1-3
Cheddar v Tavistock 0-5
Shepton Mallet v Street 5-2
Cadbury Heath v Exmouth T 1-5
Radstock T v Bovey Tracey 2-3
Ivybridge T v Roman Glass St George 2-3
Sidmouth T v Cullompton Rangers 0-5

Bodmin T v Buckland Ath 0-4
Wells C v Newton Abbot Spurs 1-2
Torpoint Ath v Portishead T 4-1*
(1-1 at the end of normal time)
Saltash U v Porthleven 2-1
Helston Ath v Axminster T 2-0

FIRST ROUND
Jarrow v Vauxhall Motors 1-2*
(1-1 at the end of normal time)
Bottesford T v West Allotment Celtic 4-2*
(1-1 at the end of normal time)
Nostell MW v Wythenshawe T 0-2
Seaham Red Star v Yorkshire Amateur 1-3
Thornaby v Billingham T 4-0
Shildon v West Didsbury & Chorlton 2-0
Longridge T v Crook T 4-2
Knaresborough T v Stockton T 2-3*
(2-2 at the end of normal time)
Penistone Church v Bridlington T 1-2
Rylands v Bootle 3-0
Selby T v Cheadle T 5-1
Padiham v Bishop Auckland 0-1
Abbey Hey v Barnoldswick T 0-5
Sunderland Ryhope CW v Ashton Ath 2-0
Chadderton v Guisborough T 1-3
Winterton Rangers v Consett 2-5
Maine Road v Glasshoughton Welfare 4-2*
(2-2 at the end of normal time)
Charnock Richard v Lower Breck 2-5
Grimsby Bor v Hemsworth MW 4-0
Leicester Road v Walsall Wood 1-2*
(0-0 at the end of normal time)
Droitwich Spa v Whitchurch Alport 2-0
Newark Flowserve v Heather St Johns 2-1
GNP Sports v Malvern T 2-4*
(2-2 at the end of normal time)
Alsager T v Lutterworth T 1-2
South Normanton Ath v Holbeach U 1-0
Kimberley MW v Sherwood Colliery 0-4
Lichfield C v Dudley T 1-2*
(0-0 at the end of normal time)
Atherstone T v Sandbach U 3-1
Brackley T Saints v West Bridgford 2-3*
(2-2 at the end of normal time)
Shawbury U v Uttoxeter T 0-0, 0-4
Heanor T v Boldmere St Michaels 3-0
Gresley v Rugby T 0-1
Pinchbeck U v Worcester C 0-3
AFC Mansfield v Hanley T 2-1*
(1-1 at the end of normal time)
Haughmond v Loughborough University 1-3*
(1-1 at the end of normal time)
Dunkirk v Hucknall T 2-1
Racing Club Warwick v Long Eaton U 2-3
Clay Cross T v Cottesmore Amateurs S&S 3-1
Barrow T v Congleton T 1-2
Quorn v Rocester 5-3
New Salamis v Eynesbury R 1-6
March Town U v Rothwell Corinthians 0-1
Stansted v Aylesbury Vale Dynamos 5-1
Risborough Rangers v FC Clacton 0-2
Tring Ath v Woodbridge T 1-3
Broadfields U v Walthamstow 1-3
Mildenhall T v Crawley Green 4-1
Norwich U v Peterborough Northern Star 4-1*
(1-1 at the end of normal time)
AFC Hayes v FC Broxbourne Bor 1-3
Flackwell Heath v Colney Heath 2-3*
(2-2 at the end of normal time)
Leighton T v Hadleigh U 2-1
White Ensign v Buckingham Ath 4-1
Hadley v Milton Keynes Robins 0-2
Wroxham v Baldock T 6-2
Northampton ON Chenecks v Kirkley & Pakefield 2-3*
(1-1 at the end of normal time)
Whitton U v Long Buckby 1-3
Huntingdon T v Frenford 2-3*
(2-2 at the end of normal time)
Biggleswade U v Saffron Walden T 4-4, 1-5
Wellingborough T v Takeley 4-3
Oxhey Jets v Hackney Wick 7-0
Harborough T v Enfield 4-1
Coggeshall U v Brantham Ath 1-0
Lopes Tavares London v Stanway R 2-3
Southall v Tunbridge Wells 4-4, 3-1
Chatham T v Beckenham T 1-1, 2-2*
Chatham T won 7-6 on penalties
Egham T v Binfield 0-4
Raynes Park Vale v Horndean A-A, 2-2, 2-1
First match abandoned after 70 mins due to waterlogged pitch, 0-0
Sheppey U v Corinthian 0-2
Peacehaven & Telscombe v Glebe 3-5
Welling T v Erith & Belvedere 5-1
Westside v Deal T 3-4
Bedfont & Feltham v Colliers Wood U 3-1
Sporting Club Thamesmead v Ascot U 1-5
Fisher v Greenwich Bor 3-0
Kennington v Crowborough Ath 4-2
Punjab U v Newhaven 0-3
Mile Oak v Redhill 1-2
Seaford T v Horley T 1-0
Rushtall v Lancing 0-2
Sutton Common R v Snodland T 5-1
Eastbourne T v Horsham YMCA 4-2
Christchurch v Brimscombe & Thrupp 3-1
Bradford T v Lymington T 1-0
Cullompton Rangers v AFC Portchester 0-1
Newport (IW) v Bridgwater T 0-2
Westbury U v Badshot Lea 0-1
Malmesbury Vic v Roman Glass St George 3-5
Torpoint Ath v Saltash U 1-4
Tavistock v Shepton Mallet 4-1
Warminster T v East Cowes Vic Ath 3-2
Bitton v Tadley Calleva 6-1
Bournemouth v Petersfield T 1-2
Longlevens v Cowes Sports 1-0*
(0-0 at the end of normal time)
Romsey T v Plymouth Parkway 1-3
Bishop's Cleeve v Brockenhurst 2-3
Helston Ath v Falmouth T 1-5
Camelford v Buckland Ath 1-2
Bovey Tracey (removed) v Abingdon U 3-1
Downton v Thornbury T 0-4
Shrivenham v Fairford T 2-3
Exmouth T v Portland U 2-0
Newton Abbot Spurs v Westfields 0-8

SECOND ROUND
Bridlington T v Selby T 4-2
Bishop Auckland v West Auckland T 0-1*
(0-0 at the end of normal time)
Hebburn T v Sunderland RCA 3-0
Irlam v Consett 2-5
Congleton T v Maine Road 3-2
Stockton T v Barnoldswick T 2-0
Northwich Vic v Wythenshawe T 5-5, 1-2
Lower Breck v Shildon 2-1
Vauxhall Motors v Sunderland Ryhope CW 4-1
Yorkshire Amateur v Bottesford T 5-4
Newcastle Benfield v Guisborough T 4-0
Rylands v Grimsby Bor 0-1
Longridge T v Thornaby 6-4
Newark Flowserve v Rugby T 3-0
Lye T v Droitwich Spa 2-1
Wellingborough T v Dudley T 1-0
Malvern T v Loughborough University 5-4*
(4-4 at the end of normal time)
Lutterworth T v Eastwood Community 4-2*
(2-2 at the end of normal time)
AFC Mansfield v Long Buckby 3-1
Walsall Wood v Uttoxeter T 3-1
Leicester Nirvana v Westfields 1-2
West Bridgford v Heanor T 0-2
Sporting Khalsa v Quorn 3-1
Coventry U v Long Eaton U 1-0
Clay Cross T v Sherwood Colliery 3-1
Worcester C v Dunkirk 3-1
Harborough T v Atherstone T 1-6
Shepshed Dynamo v Cadbury Ath 4-1
Rothwell Corinthians v South Normanton Ath 1-3
White Ensign v Wroxham A-A, 2-5
First match abandoned 75 minutes due to floodlight failure, 0-3
Woodbridge T v Godmanchester R 5-2
Norwich U v Kirkley & Pakefield 1-2
Stansted v Mildenhall T 1-0
Newport Pagnell T v Coggeshall U 4-2
Saffron Walden T v FC Clacton 3-4
Leighton T v FC Broxbourne Bor 6-1
Deeping Rangers v Stanway R 1-3

Milton Keynes Robins v Eynesbury R 1-6
Colney Heath v Stowmarket T 0-1
Fisher v Glebe 1-2
Abbey Rangers v Ascot U 2-2, 0-7
Frenford v Lancing 1-3
Raynes Park Vale v Sutton Common R 0-4
Binfield v Redhill 3-1
Walthamstow v AFC Uckfield T 2-3
Corinthian v Canterbury C 2-0
Windsor v Eastbourne T 1-7
Deal T v Oxhey Jets 4-1
Southall v Seaford T 3-1
Welling T v Bedfont & Feltham 3-1*
(1-1 at the end of normal time)
Bearsted v Chatham T 0-1
Kennington v Newhaven 1-6
Warminster T v AFC Portchester 3-1
Baffins Milton R v Bradford T 2-3
Falmouth T v Longlevens 3-2*
(2-2 at the end of normal time)
AFC St Austell v Buckland Ath 0-1
Tavistock v Exmouth T 6-1
Saltash U v Bridgwater T 0-2*
(0-0 at the end of normal time)
Brockenhurst v Plymouth Parkway 0-3
Thornbury T v Cribbs 1-3*
(1-1 at the end of normal time)
Christchurch v Badshot Lea 2-1
Petersfield T v Roman Glass St George 1-2
Abingdon U v Hamworthy U 1-6
Bitton v Fairford T 4-0

THIRD ROUND
Bridlington T v Stockton T 1-4*
(1-1 at the end of normal time)
Vauxhall Motors v Newcastle Benfield 2-0
Lower Breck v Hebburn T 1-5
Wythenshawe T v Consett 1-1, 0-1
Congleton T v Longridge T 2-2, 0-2
West Auckland T v Yorkshire Amateur 2-1
Coventry U v Grimsby Bor 4-2
Westfields v Lutterworth T 1-3
Worcester C v Shepshed Dynamo 2-1*
(1-1 at the end of normal time)
Heanor T v Sporting Khalsa 2-4
Lye T v Walsall Wood 0-2
Malvern T v Atherstone T 3-3, 0-10
AFC Mansfield v Newark Flowserve 1-3
South Normanton Ath v Clay Cross T 2-1*
(1-1 at the end of normal time)
Newport Pagnell T v Kirkley & Pakefield 0-2
Wroxham v Wellingborough T 1-0*
(0-0 at the end of normal time)
Woodbridge T v Stanway R 1-1, 4-0
Stowmarket T v Stansted 4-0
FC Clacton v Eynesbury R 1-2
Chatham T v Welling T 1-0
Deal T v Southall 2-0
Glebe v Newhaven 1-0
Corinthian v Ascot U 2-1
Lancing v Sutton Common R 3-3, 0-1
Leighton T v Eastbourne T 2-1
Binfield v AFC Uckfield T 4-0
Bradford T v Bridgwater T 4-3*
(2-2 at the end of normal time)

Bitton v Cribbs 2-1
Hamworthy U v Plymouth Parkway 1-4
Christchurch v Falmouth T 2-1
Tavistock v Buckland Ath 1-2
Roman Glass St George v Warminster T 1-2

FOURTH ROUND
Worcester C v Coventry U 2-1
Stockton T v Atherstone T 0-1
Vauxhall Motors v Hebburn T 0-1
Longridge T v Newark Flowserve 5-1
Consett v Lutterworth T 3-1
West Auckland T v Walsall Wood 1-0
South Normanton Ath v Wroxham 1-3
Sporting Khalsa v Kirkley & Pakefield 2-0*
(0-0 at the end of normal time)
Stowmarket T v Glebe 3-0
Chatham T v Corinthian 1-2*
(1-1 at the end of normal time)
Eynesbury R v Leighton T 3-4
Deal T v Binfield 1-1, 3-3*
Deal T won 7-6 on penalties
Bitton v Warminster T 3-1
Woodbridge T v Plymouth Parkway 0-1
Buckland Ath v Bradford T 1-2
Christchurch v Sutton Common R 1-2

FIFTH ROUND
Corinthian v Sporting Khalsa 3-0
Bradford T v Leighton T 1-3
Consett v Deal T 2-0
Plymouth Parkway v West Auckland T 2-1
Longridge T v Hebburn T 0-1*
(0-0 at the end of normal time)
Wroxham v Stowmarket T 2-0
Bitton v Sutton Common R 2-1
Atherstone T v Worcester C 1-1, 1-1*
Atherstone T won 5-4 on penalties

SIXTH ROUND
Corinthian v Leighton T 4-3
Wroxham v Bitton 0-4
Atherstone T v Consett 1-3
Hebburn T v Plymouth Parkway 2-0

SEMI-FINALS
Consett v Bitton 1-0*
Hebburn T v Corinthian 2-2*
Hebburn T won 4-3 on penalties

THE BUILDBASE FA VASE FINAL 2019–20
Wembley Stadium, Sunday 27 September 2020
Consett v Hebburn T

THE FA YOUTH CUP 2019–20

After extra time.

PRELIMINARY ROUND
Carlisle C v Consett 3-3*
Carlisle C won 3-2 on penalties
Gateshead v South Shields 2-3
Chester-le-Street T v Stockton T 0-3
Penrith v Cleator Moor 9-0
Workington v Hebburn T 3-2*
(2-2 at the end of normal time)
Guisborough T v Morpeth T 0-11
North Shields (walkover) v Shildon
Bootle (walkover) v Abbey Hey
St Helens T v AFC Blackpool 0-2
Sandbach U v Witton Alb 6-2

Litherland Remyca v Garstang 4-1
Radcliffe v Skelmersdale U 8-1
West Didsbury & Chorlton v Cheadle T 2-5
Irlam v Mossley 10-0
Southport v Wythenshawe Amateurs 6-0
Ashton Ath v Prescot Cables 4-1
Ashton T v Vauxhall Motors 1-5
FC United of Manchester v Stalybridge Celtic 4-0
Altrincham v Curzon Ashton 2-2*
Curzon Ashton won 4-3 on penalties
City of Liverpool v Padiham 4-1
Egerton v Lancaster C (walkover)
Warrington T v Buxton 1-2
Retford v Frickley Ath 0-2
Stocksbridge Park Steels v Grimsby Bor 2-0

Hall Road Rangers v Selby T 1-3
Steeton v Handsworth 0-3
Silsden v Staveley MW 3-0
Brigg T v Scarborough Ath 4-1
Harrogate Railway Ath v Retford U 3-1
Sheffield v Rossington Main 7-1
Bradford (Park Avenue) v Brighouse T 1-4
Garforth T v Farsley Celtic 2-1
York C v Pontefract Collieries 3-0
Cleethorpes T v Guiseley 0-7
Bottesford T v Eccleshill U 1-1*
Eccleshill U won 2-1 on penalties
Dronfield T v Athersley Recreation 1-4
Dunkirk v Grantham T 2-2*
Grantham T won 3-0 on penalties
Bourne T v Leicester Nirvana 0-4
Stamford (walkover) v Belper T
Matlock T v Anstey Nomads 1-2
Mickleover Sports (walkover) v Harrowby U
Long Eaton U v Borrowash Vic 4-1
Deeping Rangers v Hinckley 7-2
Lincoln U v Blaby & Whetstone Ath 0-0*
Lincoln U won 4-3 on penalties
Eastwood Community v Lutterworth Ath 2-1
Leek T v Coleshill T (walkover)
Lye T v Ellesmere Rangers 3-1
Stafford Rangers v Leamington 2-1
Coton Green v Hednesford T 0-3
Coventry Sphinx v Newcastle T 5-6*
(3-3 at the end of normal time)
Alvechurch v Bedworth U 4-1
Lichfield C v Chelmsley T 6-0
Boldmere St Michaels v Paget Rangers 3-1
Atherstone T v Bromsgrove Sporting (walkover)
Rushall Olympic v Shawbury U 3-1
Bromyard T v Stratford T 0-5
Halesowen T v Tamworth 3-2
Bustleholme v Bilston T 4-0
Stourport Swifts v Tipton T 10-0
AFC Telford U v Hereford 2-3
Newport Pagnell T v Daventry T 0-5
St Neots T v Barton R 4-0
Bugbrooke St Michaels v Rothwell Corinthians 2-2*
Bugbrooke St Michaels won 3-0 on penalties
Brackley T v Wellingborough T 0-1
Biggleswade U v Leighton T (walkover)
Winslow U v Buckingham Ath 1-2
Netherton U v Hitchin T 1-4
Godmanchester R v Stotfold 1-2
Corby T v Royston T 1-9
Kettering T v Kempston R 4-2*
(1-1 at the end of normal time)
Rugby T v Wellingborough Whitworths 6-1
AFC Rushden & D v Peterborough Sports 2-3
Gorleston v Wroxham 2-1*
(1-1 at the end of normal time)
Hadleigh U v Wisbech St Mary 1-6
Ely C v Stowmarket T 4-2
Whitton U v AFC Sudbury 0-5
Walsham Le Willows v Framlingham T 2-1
Newmarket T v Dereham T 3-6
Mildenhall T v King's Lynn T 1-3
Cornard U v Bury T 0-6
Haverhill R v Ipswich W 8-2
Long Melford v Leiston 2-0
Fakenham T v Needham Market 0-15
Saffron Walden T v Lowestoft T 3-1
Histon v Lakenheath 1-2*
(1-1 at the end of normal time)
Cambridge C v Swaffham T 1-0
St Albans C v Aveley 1-2*
(1-1 at the end of normal time)
Harpenden T v Grays Ath 4-5*
(4-4 at the end of normal time)
Codicote v Hornchurch 1-8
Wodson Park v Ware (walkover)
Heybridge Swifts v Witham T 4-3*
(3-3 at the end of normal time)
Great Wakering R v Enfield T 0-3
St Margaretsbury v Ilford 1-0
Barkingside v Redbridge 1-3
Welwyn Garden C v Takeley 6-5
Stanway R v Sawbridgeworth T 3-2
Woodford T v FC Broxbourne Bor 2-0
Bowers & Pitsea v Cheshunt 7-1
Brightlingsea Regent v Brentwood T 1-3

Tilbury v Hertford T 0-5
Colney Heath v Chelmsford C 2-1
Bishop's Stortford v Romford 0-6
Wingate & Finchley v Cockfosters 2-2*
Wingate & Finchley won 4-2 on penalties
Barking v Braintree T 1-3
Hayes & Yeading U v Ashford T (Middlesex) 3-0
Spelthorne Sports v Hendon 3-2
London Tigers v Hampton & Richmond Bor 3-5
Uxbridge v Balham 1-0
Hanworth Villa v Harefield U 9-0
Staines T v Beaconsfield T 0-6
North Greenford U v Burnham 2-1
Edgware T v Chalfont St Peter 3-1
Wealdstone v CB Hounslow U 2-1
Cray W v VCD Ath 4-3
Carshalton Ath v K Sports 1-2
Hastings U v Punjab U 2-1*
(1-1 at the end of normal time)
Corinthian v Folkestone Invicta 3-1
East Grinstead T v Glebe 1-3
Eastbourne Bor v Eastbourne T 6-0
Tooting & Mitcham U v Dartford 0-8
Sittingbourne v AFC Croydon Ath 5-0
Maidstone U v Dulwich Hamlet 3-6
Phoenix Sports v Tonbridge Angels 0-1
Welling U v FC Elmstead A-A
Match abandoned after 85 minutes due to serious player and crowd disturbance, 6-5 – both teams removed
Ramsgate v Crowborough Ath 3-0
Tie awarded to Crowborough Ath – Ramsgate removed
Margate v Tower Hamlets 3-4*
(3-3 at the end of normal time)
Badshot Lea (walkover) v Welling T
Cray Valley (PM) v Bridon Ropes 2-1
Hollands & Blair v Whyteleafe 0-5
East Preston v Newhaven 1-0
Sutton Common R v Worthing 5-4*
(3-3 at the end of normal time)
Worthing U v Guildford C 3-0
Whitehawk v Walton Casuals 1-3
Steyning T v Godalming T 3-1
Chipstead v Arundel 2-1
Horley T v Shoreham 1-2
Chertsey T v Metropolitan Police 2-1
Redhill v Lewes 1-2
Abbey Rangers v Pagham 3-2*
(1-1 at the end of normal time)
Raynes Park Vale v Chichester C 4-3*
(3-3 at the end of normal time)
South Park v Bognor Regis T 1-1*
Bognor Regis T won 4-2 on penalties
Corinthian Casuals v Kingstonian 0-6
Leatherhead v Haywards Heath T 7-0
Lancing v Chessington & Hook U 2-0
Berkhamsted v Bracknell T 5-5*
Berkhamsted won 4-2 on penalties
Hungerford T v Tring Ath 1-1*
Hungerford T won 4-3 on penalties
Wokingham & Emmbrook v Thatcham T 3-2
Thame U v Easington Sports 1-2
Binfield v Camberley T 0-9
Farnborough v Kings Langley 0-3
Kidlington v Hemel Hempstead T 0-7
Fleet T v Aylesbury Vale Dynamos 1-2*
(0-0 at the end of normal time)
Reading C v Ardley U 4-1
Holmer Green v Tadley Calleva 1-2
Havant & Waterlooville v Winchester C 1-2
Basingstoke T v Dorchester T 0-1
Salisbury v Andover T 2-4
Bournemouth v Alton 0-6
Hamble Club v Ringwood T 7-1
AFC Totton (walkover) v Fareham T
AFC Portchester v Wimborne T 1-2
Brockenhurst v Pewsey Vale 15-1
Poole T v Moneyfields 1-2
Totton & Eling v Sholing 1-8
Slimbridge v Malvern T 3-2
Bishop's Cleeve v New College Swindon 3-4
Chippenham T v Gloucester C 3-0
Shrivenham v Cirencester T 0-4
Cinderford T v Tuffley R 3-1
Clanfield 85 (walkover) v Yate T
Wells C v Street 2-10
Bristol Manor Farm v Odd Down 2-1

Weston-super-Mare (walkover) v Radstock T
Bridgwater T (walkover) v Keynsham T
Clevedon T v Mangotsfield U 1-7
Paulton R v Brislington 1-3
Longwell Green Sports v Helston Ath (walkover)
Cribbs v Welton R 3-0
Portishead T v Bitton 1-2

FIRST QUALIFYING ROUND
Stockton T v North Shields 2-4*
(2-2 at the end of normal time)
Seaham Red Star v Darlington 2-1
Carlisle C v South Shields 0-10
Workington v Penrith 7-2
Spennymoor T v Morpeth T 1-3
Hyde U v Marine 3-3*
Marine won 5-4 on penalties
AFC Blackpool v Litherland Remyca 2-3
Sandbach U v Ashton Ath 2-3
Irlam v Southport 4-2
Nantwich T v FC United of Manchester 2-2*
Nantwich T won 4-3 on penalties
Radcliffe v City of Liverpool 3-9
Curzon Ashton v Vauxhall Motors 11-1
Cheadle T v Buxton 0-2
Clitheroe v Chester 1-4
Lancaster C v Bootle 4-1
Shelley v Athersley Recreation 0-4
Handsworth v Tadcaster Alb 0-1
AFC Emley v Frickley Ath 4-3
Eccleshill U v Brigg T 2-1
Harrogate Railway Ath v Harworthy Colliery 5-1
Sheffield v Stocksbridge Park Steels 4-2
Guiseley v Garforth T 2-0
Silsden v York C 0-5
Selby T v Brighouse T 1-0
Anstey Nomads v Leicester Nirvana 1-9
Mickleover Sports v Aylestone Park 5-0
Deeping Rangers v Harborough T 3-1
Basford U v Gresley 4-2*
(2-2 at the end of normal time)
West Bridgford v Eastwood Community 2-3
Long Eaton U v Boston U 5-2
Stamford v Lincoln U 6-0
Grantham T v Alfreton T 2-1
Stafford Rangers v Worcester C 2-1
Hednesford T v Lye T 1-2*
(1-1 at the end of normal time)
Alvechurch v Haughmond 1-2
Rushall Olympic v Bustleholme 3-2
Sutton Coldfield T v Bromsgrove Sporting 1-3
Romulus v Coleshill T 1-0
Racing Club Warwick v Newcastle T 3-1
Lichfield C v Boldmere St Michaels 2-0
Stourport Swifts v Stourbridge 0-1
Hereford v Stratford T 4-1
Kidderminster H v Halesowen T 2-2*
Halesowen T won 6-5 on penalties
St Ives T v Biggleswade T 4-2
Wellingborough T v Peterborough Northern Star 13-1
Rugby Bor v Daventry T 4-1
AFC Dunstable v Buckingham Ath 7-0
Hitchin T (walkover) v Eynesbury R
Stotfold v St Neots T 3-2*
(2-2 at the end of normal time)
Peterborough Sports v Kettering T 3-2
Leighton T v Rugby T 1-2
Bugbrooke St Michaels v Royston T 3-0
Felixstowe & Walton U v Cambridge C 1-0
AFC Sudbury v Woodbridge T 3-0
Norwich U v Gorleston 2-0
Lakenheath v Dereham T 2-7
King's Lynn T v Brantham Ath 6-2
Bury T v Wisbech St Mary 5-2
Saffron Walden T v Long Melford 4-0
Walsham Le Willows v Needham Market 4-5
Ely C v Haverhill R 7-1
Hornchurch v Haringey Bor 3-0
Ware v Grays Ath 7-1
Enfield T v Billericay T 6-1
Stanway R v Bowers & Pitsea 0-6
Braintree T v Welwyn Garden C 2-6
Romford v Aveley 0-4
Colney Heath v Heybridge Swifts 3-2
St Margaretsbury v Redbridge 0-3
Brentwood T v Wingate & Finchley 2-1
Hertford T v Concord Rangers 2-3
Walthamstow v Woodford T 2-7
Edgware T v Spelthorne Sports 6-1
Uxbridge v Brimsdown 10-0
North Greenford U v Hanworth Villa 0-5
Hanwell T v Hayes & Yeading U 1-0
Bedfont Sports v Windsor 3-2
Wealdstone v Northwood 4-1
Beaconsfield T v Hampton & Richmond Bor 3-4
Tower Hamlets v Hastings U 0-4
Glebe v Dartford 3-4*
(3-3 at the end of normal time)
Holmesdale v Faversham T 0-8
Badshot Lea v Whitstable T 2-3
Croydon v Whyteleafe 3-1
Fisher v Chatham T (walkover)
Hackney Wick (walkover) v Welling U
K Sports v Eastbourne Bor 2-0
Cray W v Ashford U 4-2
Dulwich Hamlet v Cray Valley (PM) 1-0
Tonbridge Angels v Sittingbourne 2-1
Crowborough Ath v Corinthian 0-4
Worthing U v Mile Oak 0-1
Walton Casuals v Sutton Common R 0-1
Chipstead v Walton & Hersham 5-2
Abbey Rangers v Kingstonian 0-1
Dorking W v Lewes 1-0
Burgess Hill T v East Preston 1-0
Knaphill v Steyning T 4-0
Shoreham v Chertsey T 1-3
Leatherhead v Ash U 4-1
Lancing v Raynes Park Vale 0-6
Three Bridges v Bognor Regis T 6-4*
(4-4 at the end of normal time)
Easington Sports v Hungerford T 4-3
Camberley T v Ascot U 5-1
Fleet Spurs v Cove 1-0
Leverstock Green v Tadley Calleva 5-0
Oxford C v Aylesbury Vale Dynamos 4-0
Kings Langley v Hartley Wintney 3-2
Wokingham & Emmbrook v Hemel Hempstead T 2-2*
Hemel Hempstead T won 4-2 on penalties
Berkhamsted v Reading C 1-6
Winchester C v Wimborne T 3-5
Dorchester T v Alton 4-0
AFC Totton v Brockenhurst 3-4
Sholing v Moneyfields 2-4
Andover T v Hamble Club 4-0
AFC Stoneham v Christchurch 8-0
Clanfield 85 v Chippenham T 0-4
Cinderford T v Evesham U 1-3
Slimbridge v New College Swindon 4-2
Cirencester T v Malmesbury Vic 3-0
Street v Helston Ath 1-1*
Helston Ath won 4-3 on penalties
Bristol Manor Farm v Bridgwater T 2-3
Brislington v Cribbs 3-0
Elburton Villa v Bitton 2-3*
(2-2 at the end of normal time)
Weston-super-Mare v Mangotsfield U 2-3*
(2-2 at the end of normal time)
Bath C v Frome T 5-0

SECOND QUALIFYING ROUND
Morpeth T v Workington 9-1
Seaham Red Star v Hartlepool U 0-7
South Shields v North Shields 3-1
Nantwich T v Ashton Ath 6-5*
(5-5 at the end of normal time)
Chorley v Chester 2-3*
(2-2 at the end of normal time)
Stockport Co v Irlam 3-2
AFC Fylde v Lancaster C 9-2
Marine v Curzon Ashton 3-7*
(3-3 at the end of normal time)
Litherland Remyca v City of Liverpool 3-1
Buxton v FC Halifax T 1-5
Harrogate Railway Ath v Selby T 4-3
Harrogate T v AFC Emley 8-3
Eccleshill U v Sheffield 0-7
York C v Guiseley 2-3
Athersley Recreation v Tadcaster Alb 2-0
Basford U v Grantham T 3-1
Chesterfield v Mickleover Sports 3-1
Deeping Rangers v Eastwood Community 2-1
Stamford v Long Eaton U 1-4

Notts Co v Leicester Nirvana	8-1
Haughmond v Stourbridge	2-0
Wrexham v Solihull Moors	5-2
Bromsgrove Sporting v Rushall Olympic	2-3
Romulus v Halesowen T	6-2
Stafford Rangers v Lye T	1-1*
Stafford Rangers won 3-1 on penalties	
Racing Club Warwick v Lichfield C	2-1
Stotfold v Ely C	4-2*
(2-2 at the end of normal time)	
St Ives T v AFC Dunstable	0-3
Hitchin T v Peterborough Sports	8-4
Bugbrooke St Michaels v Rugby T	0-5
Wellingborough T v Rugby Bor	2-5
AFC Sudbury v Felixstowe & Walton U	11-0
Saffron Walden T v Needham Market	0-5
King's Lynn T v Bury T	6-4
Dereham T v Norwich U	5-0
Bowers & Pitsea v Concord Rangers	4-2
Hornchurch v Dagenham & R	11-0
Aveley v Welwyn Garden C	2-1
Colney Heath v Woodford T	1-3
Ware v Enfield T	1-0
Redbridge v Brentwood T	0-9
Hanworth Villa v Hampton & Richmond Bor	3-0
Barnet v Edgware T	3-1
Uxbridge v Hanwell T	4-3
Wealdstone v Bedfont Sports	1-0
Tie ordered to be replayed	
Boreham Wood v Maidenhead U	0-3
Hackney Wick v Croydon	2-8
Dover Ath v Tonbridge Angels	2-2*
Dover Ath won 4-2 on penalties	
Dartford v Chatham T	5-4*
(3-3 at the end of normal time)	
Bromley v Corinthian	6-1
Faversham T v Cray W	1-2
Whitstable T v K Sports	1-4
Dulwich Hamlet v Hastings U	4-3
Kingstonian v Raynes Park Vale	7-1
Mile Oak v Sutton U	2-3
Burgess Hill T v Dorking W	0-4
Knaphill v Three Bridges	3-2
Sutton Common R v Chipstead	3-1*
(1-1 at the end of normal time)	
Chertsey T v Leatherhead	4-1
Camberley T v Easington Sports	5-1
Hemel Hempstead T v Reading C	1-6
Oxford C v Kings Langley	4-0
Leverstock Green v Fleet Spurs	4-0
Dorchester T v AFC Stoneham	0-5
Aldershot T v Yeovil T	2-6
Wimborne T v Brockenhurst	3-4
Andover T v Moneyfields	2-0
Eastleigh v Woking	3-3*
Eastleigh won 5-3 on penalties	
Bath C v Cirencester T	3-0
Evesham U v Hereford	0-4
Slimbridge v Chippenham T	2-0
Mangotsfield U v Bitton	5-0
Bridgwater T v Torquay U	2-1
Brislington v Helston Ath	0-5

THIRD QUALIFYING ROUND

Litherland Remyca v FC Halifax T	1-4
Stockport Co v Hartlepool U	0-6
Wrexham v Sheffield	3-2
Morpeth T v AFC Fylde	4-0
Athersley Recreation v Chester	2-8
Guiseley v Curzon Ashton	1-3
Harrogate Railway Ath v Nantwich T	2-3*
(1-1 at the end of normal time)	
South Shields v Harrogate T	5-1
Long Eaton U v Racing Club Warwick	4-1
Basford U v Notts Co	0-5
Romulus v Chesterfield	2-3*
(2-2 at the end of normal time)	
Deeping Rangers v Haughmond	0-6
Stafford Rangers v Rugby T	1-5
Rushall Olympic v Rugby Bor	4-2
Ware v Needham Market	4-1
Hitchin T v King's Lynn T	3-4
AFC Dunstable v Dereham T	0-1
Stotfold v Bowers & Pitsea	2-4
AFC Sudbury v Hornchurch	2-0
Woodford T v Brentwood T	5-5*
Brentwood T won 5-4 on penalties	
K Sports v Dulwich Hamlet	1-4
Reading C v Wealdstone	2-0
Dover Ath v Hanworth Villa	0-5
Barnet v Camberley T	4-1
Uxbridge v Knaphill	5-3
Sutton U v Croydon	2-3
Dorking W v Dartford	3-2
Sutton Common R v Leverstock Green	1-0
Maidenhead U v Cray W	6-2
Aveley v Bromley	1-1*
Aveley won 4-3 on penalties	
Chertsey T v Kingstonian	3-7
Bath C v Slimbridge	3-0
Mangotsfield U v Eastleigh	0-1
AFC Stoneham v Hereford	2-2*
Hereford won 4-2 on penalties	
Helston Ath v Brockenhurst	8-2
Yeovil T v Andover T	1-3
Bridgwater T v Oxford C	2-0

FIRST ROUND

South Shields v Morecambe	2-1
Morpeth T v Chester	1-0
Fleetwood T v FC Halifax T	5-0
Accrington Stanley v Hartlepool U	1-2
Bradford C v Rochdale	3-0
Salford C v Carlisle U	2-3
Sunderland v Tranmere R	3-1
Oldham Ath v Nantwich T	4-1
Curzon Ashton v Blackpool	2-1
Macclesfield T v Crewe Alex	2-3
Grimsby T v Rugby T	1-0
Shrewsbury T v Port Vale	1-0
Rushall Olympic v Lincoln C	0-4
Haughmond v Rotherham U	1-3
Long Eaton U v Wrexham	3-5
Chesterfield v Burton Alb	1-2
Mansfield T v Doncaster R	4-3
Coventry C v Walsall	1-2
Notts Co v Scunthorpe U	0-1*
(0-0 at the end of normal time)	
Milton Keynes D v Ware	0-2*
(0-0 at the end of normal time)	
Southend U v Cambridge U	1-2
Stevenage v Brentwood T	5-1
Ipswich T v King's Lynn T	6-1
Northampton T v Colchester U	1-2
Dereham T v Peterborough U	0-1*
(0-0 at the end of normal time)	
AFC Sudbury v Bowers & Pitsea	2-1
Sutton Common R v Uxbridge	1-3
AFC Wimbledon v Leyton Orient	5-0
Gillingham v Hanworth Villa	2-3
Reading C v Oxford U	0-1*
(0-0 at the end of normal time)	
Barnet v Dorking W	4-2
Maidenhead U v Kingstonian	2-1
Dulwich Hamlet (walkover) v Crawley T	
Croydon v Aveley	1-0
Cheltenham T v Eastleigh	3-2
Forest Green R v Helston Ath	5-0
Bridgwater T v Newport Co	0-1
Portsmouth v Hereford	5-1
Swindon T v Bristol R	1-3
Plymouth Arg v Exeter C	0-1
Bath C v Andover T	3-2*
(2-2 at the end of normal time)	

SECOND ROUND

Lincoln C v Wrexham	3-0
South Shields v Hartlepool U	3-2
Crewe Alex v Grimsby T	2-0
Mansfield T v Rotherham U	4-2*
(2-2 at the end of normal time)	
Scunthorpe U v Morpeth T	2-1
Burton Alb v Bolton W	1-1*
Bolton W won 3-1 on penalties	
Curzon Ashton v Oldham Ath	3-2
Carlisle U v Bradford C	2-3*
(2-2 at the end of normal time)	
Walsall v Fleetwood T	0-3
Shrewsbury T v Sunderland	2-5
Cheltenham T v Portsmouth	8-4
Croydon v Bath C	2-0

Ipswich T v Exeter C 2-1
Colchester U v Oxford U 3-4
Dulwich Hamlet v Forest Green R 1-9
Ware v Maidenhead U 1-3
Stevenage v Peterborough U 3-1*
(1-1 at the end of normal time)
Barnet v Cambridge U 3-2
Bristol R v AFC Sudbury 2-1
Hanworth Villa v AFC Wimbledon 1-5
Uxbridge v Newport Co 3-4

THIRD ROUND
Manchester C v Swansea C 3-0
Sunderland v Birmingham C 1-4
Cardiff C v Ipswich T 2-1*
(1-1 at the end of normal time)
Cheltenham T v Arsenal 0-0*
Arsenal won 4-2 on penalties
Stevenage v Aston Villa 0-0*
Aston Villa won 4-2 on penalties
Bradford C v Stoke C 3-3*
Bradford C won 5-4 on penalties
Manchester U v Lincoln C 2-0
Wigan Ath v Croydon 8-1
Preston NE v Bristol C 2-0
Sheffield U v AFC Wimbledon 2-1
Fulham v South Shields 10-1
Norwich C v Newcastle U 3-2
Bristol R v Southampton 1-3
Luton T v Sheffield W 2-3
Blackburn R v Newport Co 3-1
Chelsea v Huddersfield T 4-0
Mansfield T v QPR 3-1*
(1-1 at the end of normal time)
Reading v Crystal Palace 2-4
Wolverhampton W v Nottingham F 3-0
Fleetwood T v Watford 2-2*
Fleetwood T won 4-3 on penalties
Brighton & HA v Leicester C 3-2
Middlesbrough v Forest Green R 1-1*
Middlesbrough won 5-4 on penalties
Tottenham H v Liverpool 4-2
Leeds U v Hull C 3-1
Bolton W v Millwall 0-7
Crewe Alex v Barnsley 1-2
Oxford U v Maidenhead U 1-0
Bournemouth v Barnet 4-3
Curzon Ashton v Burnley 0-5
West Ham U v Charlton Ath 3-3*
Charlton Ath won 5-4 on penalties
Derby Co v Everton 1-0
WBA v Scunthorpe U 3-0

FOURTH ROUND
Norwich C v Manchester U 0-2
Leeds U v Sheffield W 2-2*
Leeds U won 5-4 on penalties
Bournemouth v Cardiff C 1-0
Arsenal v Southampton 1-0
WBA v Middlesbrough 4-1
Manchester C v Aston Villa 2-1
Blackburn R v Charlton Ath 1-0
Oxford U v Preston NE 0-2
Millwall v Fleetwood T 3-1
Wolverhampton W v Crystal Palace 2-1
Chelsea v Bradford C 5-0
Derby Co v Brighton & HA 1-2
Wigan Ath v Tottenham H 2-0
Birmingham C v Barnsley 2-1
Mansfield T v Burnley 0-3
Sheffield U v Fulham 1-2

FIFTH ROUND
Burnley v WBA 2-0
Bournemouth v Millwall 2-3
Blackburn R v Preston NE 4-2
Arsenal v Brighton & HA 4-3
Manchester C v Fulham 1-0
Wigan Ath v Birmingham C 4-0
Chelsea v Wolverhampton W 7-0
Manchester U v Leeds U 1-0

SIXTH ROUND
Blackburn R v Arsenal 4-1
Manchester C v Burnley 1-0
Manchester U v Wigan Ath 2-1
Chelsea v Millwall 1-0

SEMI-FINALS
Blackburn R v Manchester C P-P
Chelsea v Manchester U P-P
Due to the COVID-19 pandemic, the semi-finals were postponed

THE FA YOUTH CUP FINAL 2019–20

Due to the COVID-19 pandemic, the final due to be played on Friday 24 April 2020 was postponed

THE FA COUNTY YOUTH CUP 2019–20

**After extra time.*

FIRST ROUND
Northamptonshire v Durham 0-5
Staffordshire v East Riding 7-2
Westmorland v Shropshire 0-2
London v Devon 2-6
Kent v Guernsey 2-1
Gloucestershire v Bedfordshire 0-3
Cornwall v Jersey 0-2
Cheshire v Isle of Man 2-4*
(2-2 at the end of normal time)
Cumberland v West Riding 1-2*
(1-1 at the end of normal time)
North Riding v Northumberland 1-3
Amateur Football Alliance v Sheffield & Hallamshire 7-3
Middlesex v Berks & Bucks 5-2

SECOND ROUND
Isle of Man (walkover) v Manchester
Northumberland v Norfolk 0-4
Staffordshire v Durham 0-5
West Riding (walkover) v Shropshire
Bedfordshire v Sussex 0-1
Essex v Kent 4-1
Devon v Middlesex 7-2
Jersey v Amateur Football Alliance 1-2

THIRD ROUND
West Riding v Norfolk 1-3
Essex v Isle of Man 3-1
Sussex v Durham 8-1
Devon v Amateur Football Alliance 4-0

SEMI-FINALS
Devon v Sussex 0-1
Norfolk v Essex 2-1

THE FA COUNTY YOUTH CUP FINAL 2019–20
Sussex v Norfolk P-P

Due to the COVID-19 pandemic, the final due to be played on Monday 2 March 2020 was postponed

THE FA SUNDAY CUP 2019–20

**After extra time.*

FIRST ROUND

Billingham The Merlin v Witton Park Rose & Crown 1-5
Crossflatts Village v WHTDSOB 1-2
Newton Aycliffe Iron Horse v Boro Walkers 2-1
Dawdon Colliery Welfare v Greenside 1-5
Norton George & Dragon (walkover) v Stella Dons
Burradon & New Fordley v Peterlee Catholic Club 2-2*
Peterlee Catholic Club won 4-3 on penalties
Bransty Rangers v Blackhall Cricket Club (walkover)
Oyster Martyrs v Wellington Westgate 11-1
Mottram v HT Sports 2-6
Oakenshaw v Home Bargains 0-11
Kensington Fields v Mayfair 0-4
FC Walkers Hounds (walkover) v Leeds C R
Canada v BRNESC 3-2
Queens Park v Dock 2-4
Shepherds Arms v Bolton Woods 11-2
Lobster v Campfield 2-3
Dengo U v Linthwaite 1-3
The Brow v Allerton 3-0*
(0-0 at the end of normal time)
Pineapple v AFC Bull 4-3
Tie awarded to AFC Bull – Pineapple removed
Quarry Green v Main Line Social 4-4*
Main Line Social won 5-4 on penalties
Custys v Western Avenue 1-2
Armley CCFC v Kirkdale 1-3
FC Dovecot v LIV Supplies 6-2
Huyton Cons v West Bowling 6-0
Melling Vic v Kent 3-1
Rolls Royce v FC Lion 0-3
Messingham Junior Trinity (walkover) v Wigston Willow
Anstey Sports Bar v Phoenix Gedling 7-1
Joker (walkover) v Joeys Old Boys
Long Whatton v Attenborough Cavaliers 2-3
Oadby Ath v Long Eaton TNI 3-4
RHP Sports & Social v Crusader 0-5
Sporting Dynamo v AFC Dowhan 3-6*
(3-3 at the end of normal time)
FC Poplar v Sileby Ath 4-2
AFC Jacks v Austin Ex Apprentices 6-2*
(2-2 at the end of normal time)
Black Horse (Redditch) v Digby Rangers 2-1
Callow End v Sportsman 3-4
Waggon & Horses v Perrywood 0-5
Chaddesley Ravens v Codsall Legion Sundats 1-7
Hampton Sunday v OJM 0-5
Flaunden v Larkspur R 2-1
NLO (walkover) v FC Bentons
Heritage U v Old Southall 1-6
Shire U v Reed Rangers 3-0
Rectory R v AFC Links 4-4*
AFC Links won 9-8 on penalties
Global (Sunday) v Asianos 1-5
Lambeth All Stars v Priest Hill 5-0
Palmers (walkover) v Barnes Alb
Sauce v Mile End Baiteze Squad 0-7
Putney T v Portland 0-6
Harrow Sports v Hashtag U (Sunday) 4-2
Barnes v Sporting Club de Mundial (walkover)
Highgate Alb v Blacksmiths 3-2
Massie Warriors v Gym U 0-6
Bishops Stortford Swifts v Priory Sports 1-3
Brewery Tap v Broadwalk Pines U 1-4
Crawley Green (Sunday) v Caddington Social 2-1
Borussia Martlesham v Wixams W (walkover)
St Josephs (Luton) v Club Lewsey 2-1
Falcons v Skew Bridge 4-2
East Christchurch SSC (walkover) v Broadwater
AFC Portchester (Sunday) v Rudgwick Panthers SX 2-4
Talbot Rangers v Loch & Quay 3-2

SECOND ROUND

Greenside v Witton Park Rose & Crown 5-1
Peterlee Catholic Club v Messingham Junior Trinity 17-1
Dock v HT Sports 4-3*
(3-3 at the end of normal time)
Campfield v The Brow 2-0
Norton George & Dragon v FC Dovecot 3-6
Blackhall Cricket Club v Western Avenue 0-1*
(0-0 at the end of normal time)
WHTDSOB v Huyton Cons 3-2
Shepherds Arms v Kirkdale 4-3
Mayfair v Newton Aycliffe Iron Horse 2-1
FC Walkers Hounds (walkover) v AFC Bull
Home Bargains v Linthwaite 6-1
Canada v Oyster Martyrs 0-1
Melling Vic v Main Line Social 3-1
Perrywood v Attenborough Cavaliers 5-3*
(2-2 at the end of normal time)
Long Eaton TNI v AFC Dowhan 2-1
Birstall Stamford v AFC Jacks 1-5
OJM v Codsall Legion Sundats 5-1
Crusader v FC Poplar 7-0
Black Horse (Redditch) v Anstey Sports Bar 4-0
Joker v FC Lion 5-1
Broadwalk Pines U v AFC Links 8-1
Flaunden v Crawley Green (Sunday) 1-3
Priory Sports v Asianos 10-3
Lambeth All Stars v NLO 4-3
Highgate Alb v Palmers 5-2
Harrow Sports v Portland 1-2
Sporting Club de Mundial v Old Southall 6-1
Wixams W v Gym U 4-3
Falcons v St Josephs (Luton) 0-3
Shire U v Mile End Baiteze Squad 2-1
Rudgwick Panthers SX v
East Christchurch SSC (walkover)
Talbot Rangers v Sportsman 5-1

THIRD ROUND

WHTDSOB v Peterlee Catholic Club 2-4
Western Avenue v Melling Vic 0-2
FC Dovecot v Campfield 1-3
Oyster Martyrs v FC Walkers Hounds 8-0
Dock v Home Bargains 2-1
Mayfair v Greenside 3-1
Crusader v Shepherds Arms 3-8
AFC Jacks v Joker 2-1
Long Eaton TNI v Black Horse (Redditch) 0-2
Perrywood v OJM 3-5
Talbot Rangers v Shire U 1-0
Highgate Alb v East Christchurch SSC 5-1
St Josephs (Luton) v Lambeth All Stars 3-0
Broadwalk Pines U v Wixams W 1-2
Crawley Green (Sunday) v Portland 2-6
Sporting Club de Mundial v Priory Sports 2-0

FOURTH ROUND

Mayfair v Campfield 0-1
Peterlee Catholic Club v OJM 6-3*
(3-3 at the end of normal time)
Oyster Martyrs v Black Horse (Redditch) 0-1*
(0-0 at the end of normal time)
Shepherds Arms v Dock 1-2
Melling Vic v AFC Jacks 0-0*
AFC Jacks won 4-2 on penalties
St Josephs (Luton) v Sporting Club de Mundial 2-1
Talbot Rangers v Portland 0-1
Wixams W v Highgate Alb 2-2*
Wixams W won 4-3 on penalties

FIFTH ROUND

Portland v Dock 1-0
Wixams W v Peterlee Catholic Club 1-2
St Josephs (Luton) v Black Horse (Redditch) 4-1
AFC Jacks v Campfield 1-3

SEMI-FINALS

Peterlee Catholic Club v Campfield P-P
St Josephs (Luton) v Portland P-P
Due to the COVID-19 pandemic, the semi-finals were postponed

FA SUNDAY CUP FINAL 2019–20

Due to the COVID-19 pandemic, the final was postponed

PREMIER LEAGUE 2 2019–20

PREMIER LEAGUE 2 – DIVISION ONE

	P	W	D	L	F	A	GD	Pts
Chelsea	18	10	8	0	34	20	14	38
Leicester C	18	10	5	3	36	21	15	35
Brighton & HA	18	10	1	7	36	26	10	31
Derby Co	18	7	6	5	33	32	1	27
Liverpool	17	7	5	5	34	34	0	26
Arsenal	18	6	7	5	32	32	0	25
Everton	18	5	7	6	32	33	–1	22
Manchester C	18	6	3	9	30	29	1	21
Blackburn R	17	6	3	8	27	26	1	21
Tottenham H	18	6	3	9	31	34	–3	21
Southampton	18	4	3	11	23	47	–24	15
Wolverhampton W	18	2	5	11	21	35	–14	11

PREMIER LEAGUE 2 – DIVISION TWO

	P	W	D	L	F	A	GD	Pts
West Ham U	18	14	4	0	58	21	37	46
Manchester U	17	14	1	2	45	17	28	43
WBA	16	11	1	4	38	22	16	34
Stoke C	18	8	3	7	32	27	5	27
Middlesbrough	18	8	2	8	34	43	–9	26
Newcastle U	18	8	1	9	29	32	–3	25
Aston Villa	17	6	4	7	27	28	–1	22
Swansea C	17	6	3	8	22	32	–10	21
Reading	18	6	2	10	35	37	–2	20
Fulham	18	6	2	10	26	32	–6	20
Norwich C	17	5	2	10	23	35	–12	17
Sunderland	18	0	1	17	10	53	–43	1

PREMIER LEAGUE 2 LEAGUE CUP

**After extra time.* — **After extra time.*

QUALIFYING ROUND 1

Bristol R v Cambridge U	0-2
Southend U v Fleetwood T	4-1
Scunthorpe U v Shrewsbury T	2-0
Newport Co v Yeovil T	2-10

QUALIFYING ROUND 2

Huddersfield T v Oxford U	4-0
Cambridge U v Exeter C	0-2
Southend U v Scunthorpe U	1-3
Doncaster R v Portsmouth	1-0
Plymouth Arg v Yeovil T	2-0

GROUP STAGE

Group A Table	P	W	D	L	F	A	GD	Pts
Charlton Ath	6	3	1	2	14	10	4	10
Reading	6	2	4	0	10	8	2	10
Colchester U	5	1	2	2	5	8	–3	5
Swansea C	5	1	1	3	5	8	–3	4

Group B Table	P	W	D	L	F	A	GD	Pts
Everton	6	4	1	1	14	5	9	13
Fulham	6	3	0	3	13	11	2	9
Watford	6	2	1	3	7	11	–4	7
Plymouth Arg	6	1	2	3	6	13	–7	5

Group C Table	P	W	D	L	F	A	GD	Pts
WBA	6	4	0	2	8	4	4	12
Newcastle U	6	3	2	1	12	7	5	11
Hull C	6	2	2	2	7	6	1	8
Scunthorpe U	6	0	2	4	7	17	–10	2

Group D Table	P	W	D	L	F	A	GD	Pts
Exeter C	6	4	2	0	14	5	9	14
Doncaster R	6	4	1	1	12	5	7	13
Aston Villa	6	2	0	4	9	12	–3	6
Portsmouth	6	0	1	5	5	18	–13	1

Group E Table	P	W	D	L	F	A	GD	Pts
Bournemouth	6	4	1	1	11	5	6	13
Stoke C	6	3	3	0	12	4	8	12
Southampton	6	1	1	4	8	13	–5	4
Nottingham F	6	1	1	4	3	12	–9	4

Group F Table	P	W	D	L	F	A	GD	Pts
Liverpool	6	4	1	1	15	7	8	13
Wigan Ath	6	3	1	2	12	10	2	10
Huddersfield T	6	1	3	2	7	8	–1	6
Sunderland	6	1	1	4	5	14	–9	4

Group G Table	P	W	D	L	F	A	GD	Pts
Blackburn R	6	4	1	1	12	8	4	13
Middlesbrough	6	3	2	1	14	8	6	11
Burnley	6	1	3	2	7	8	–1	6
Crystal Palace	6	0	2	4	5	14	–9	2

Group H Table	P	W	D	L	F	A	GD	Pts
Derby Co	6	4	0	2	18	7	11	12
Wolverhampton W	6	2	3	1	10	10	0	9
Birmingham C	6	2	2	2	7	9	–2	8
Leeds U	6	0	3	3	5	14	–9	3

ROUND OF 16

WBA v Doncaster R	6-1
Derby Co v Middlesbrough	6-0
Everton v Reading	2-1
Charlton Ath v Fulham	1-2*
Blackburn R v WolverhamptonW	P-P
Exeter C v Newcastle U	P-P
Liverpool v Stoke C	P-P
Bournemouth v Wigan Ath	P-P

Due to COVID-19 pandemic, all remaining games cancelled.

PREMIER LEAGUE INTERNATIONAL CUP 2019–20

For Under-23 players; competition not UEFA-sanctioned.
**After extra time.*

GROUP STAGE

GROUP A
Dinamo Zagreb v Villarreal 2-1
Arsenal v Villarreal 3-0
Arsenal v Dinamo Zagreb 3-2
Leicester C v Villarreal 2-1
Arsenal v Leicester C 3-0
Leicester C v Dinamo Zagreb 2-1

Group A Table	P	W	D	L	F	A	GD	Pts
Arsenal	3	3	0	0	9	2	7	9
Leicester C	3	2	0	1	4	5	–1	6
Dinamo Zagreb	3	1	0	2	5	6	–1	3
Villarreal	3	0	0	3	2	7	–5	0

GROUP B
West Ham U v Valencia 1-0
Valencia v VfL Wolfsburg 0-4
West Ham U v VfL Wolfsburg 2-3
Brighton & HA v West Ham U 1-3
Brighton & HA v Valencia 0-0
Brighton & HA v VfL Wolfsburg 2-3

Group B Table	P	W	D	L	F	A	GD	Pts
VfL Wolfsburg	3	3	0	0	10	4	6	9
West Ham U	3	2	0	1	6	4	2	6
Brighton & HA	3	0	1	2	3	6	–3	1
Valencia	3	0	1	2	0	5	–5	1

GROUP C
Hertha Berlin v Benfica 1-2
Blackburn R v Hertha Berlin 0-2
Newcastle U v Benfica 1-1
Blackburn R v Benfica 1-2
Newcastle U v Hertha Berlin 3-1
Newcastle U v Blackburn R 2-3

Group C Table	P	W	D	L	F	A	GD	Pts
Benfica	3	2	1	0	5	3	2	7
Newcastle U	3	1	1	1	6	5	1	4
Hertha Berlin	3	1	0	2	4	5	–1	3
Blackburn R	3	1	0	2	4	6	–2	3

GROUP D
Swansea C v PSV Eindhoven 1-1
Swansea C v Porto 5-1
Everton v PSV Eindhoven 1-1
Porto v PSV Eindhoven 1-1
Everton v Porto 2-3
Everton v Swansea C 0-4

Group D Table	P	W	D	L	F	A	GD	Pts
Swansea C	3	2	1	0	10	2	8	7
Porto	3	1	1	1	5	8	–3	4
PSV Eindhoven	3	0	3	0	3	3	0	3
Everton	3	0	1	2	3	8	–5	1

GROUP E
Athletic Bilbao v Paris Saint-Germain 0-1
Wolverhampton W v Paris Saint-Germain 1-1
Wolverhampton W v Athletic Bilbao 1-1
Liverpool v Paris Saint-Germain 3-2
Liverpool v Athletic Bilbao 1-2
Wolverhampton W v Liverpool 2-2

Group E Table	P	W	D	L	F	A	GD	Pts
Liverpool	3	1	1	1	6	6	0	4
Paris Saint-Germain	3	1	1	1	4	4	0	4
Athletic Bilbao	3	1	1	1	3	3	0	4
Wolverhampton W	3	0	3	0	4	4	0	3

GROUP F
Derby Co v AS Monaco 2-0
AS Monaco v Feyenoord 3-1
Southampton v Feyenoord 1-2
Derby Co v Feyenoord 2-1
Southampton v AS Monaco 0-3
Derby Co v Southampton 3-1

Group F Table	P	W	D	L	F	A	GD	Pts
Derby Co	3	3	0	0	7	2	5	9
AS Monaco	3	2	0	1	6	3	3	6
Feyenoord	3	1	0	2	4	6	–2	3
Southampton	3	0	0	3	2	8	–6	0

KNOCKOUT STAGES

QUARTER-FINALS
Arsenal v AS Monaco 4-3
Derby Co v West Ham U 3-3*
West Ham U won 6-5 on penalties
Liverpool v VfL Wolfsburg P-P
Swansea C v Benfica P-P

Due to the COVID-19 pandemic, the remaining quarter-finals, semi-finals and final were postponed.

UNDER-18 PROFESSIONAL DEVELOPMENT LEAGUE 2019–20

UNDER-18 PREMIER LEAGUE

NORTH DIVISION

	P	W	D	L	F	A	GD	Pts
Manchester C	17	14	1	2	56	16	40	43
Liverpool	15	10	1	4	48	28	20	31
Everton	16	10	1	5	48	33	15	31
Derby Co	17	9	1	7	38	25	13	28
Stoke C	15	9	1	5	33	22	11	28
Manchester U	16	7	2	7	34	32	2	23
WolverhamptonW	15	6	3	6	22	23	–1	21
Middlesbrough	16	6	3	7	28	38	–10	21
WBA	16	6	2	8	34	42	–8	20
Newcastle U	16	4	3	9	23	38	–15	15
Blackburn R	15	4	2	9	24	35	–11	14
Sunderland	16	0	0	16	11	67	–56	0

SOUTH DIVISION

	P	W	D	L	F	A	GD	Pts
Fulham	17	12	4	1	53	24	29	40
West Ham U	17	11	4	2	51	28	23	37
Chelsea	16	11	3	2	44	21	23	36
Leicester C	18	8	3	7	44	35	9	27
Tottenham H	17	8	2	7	43	33	10	26
Brighton & HA	17	7	3	7	30	33	–3	24
Aston Villa	17	6	4	7	33	37	–4	22
Southampton	18	6	1	11	27	40	–13	19
Arsenal	16	4	5	7	28	34	–6	17
Reading	16	4	3	9	25	34	–9	15
Norwich C	16	1	8	7	32	48	–16	11
Swansea C	15	1	2	12	20	63	–43	5

UNDER-18 PROFESSIONAL DEVELOPMENT LEAGUE

NORTH DIVISION

	P	W	D	L	F	A	GD	Pts
Wigan Ath	24	18	3	3	65	29	36	57
Sheffield U	20	13	3	4	50	27	23	42
Barnsley	22	11	3	8	34	30	4	36
Burnley	23	10	4	9	36	39	–3	34
Nottingham F	23	8	5	10	30	36	–6	29
Crewe Alex	23	6	7	10	38	45	–7	25
Hull C	24	7	4	13	38	51	–13	25
Sheffield W	21	6	5	10	27	28	–1	23
Bolton W	22	6	4	12	37	62	–25	22
Leeds U	22	5	6	11	36	44	–8	21
Birmingham C	21	6	3	12	30	46	–16	21

SOUTH DIVISION

	P	W	D	L	F	A	GD	Pts
Millwall	19	14	1	4	61	23	38	43
Bristol C	22	12	4	6	53	41	12	40
Charlton Ath	20	11	6	3	42	21	21	39
Watford	20	11	4	5	47	37	10	37
Crystal Palace	19	10	4	5	45	25	20	34
Ipswich T	20	8	4	8	42	39	3	28
Cardiff C	21	5	7	9	43	45	–2	22
Coventry C	21	5	2	14	29	64	–35	17
Colchester U	18	4	4	10	33	55	–22	16
QPR	21	4	3	14	31	60	–29	15

Due to COVID-19 pandemic, all remaining games cancelled.

U18 PROFESSIONAL DEVELOPMENT LEAGUE CUP

**After extra time.*

GROUP STAGE

Group A Table	P	W	D	L	F	A	GD	Pts
Chelsea	3	3	0	0	7	3	4	9
Arsenal	3	1	0	2	6	5	1	3
Blackburn R	3	1	0	2	4	6	–2	3
WolverhamptonW	3	1	0	2	4	7	–3	3

Group B Table	P	W	D	L	F	A	GD	Pts
Reading	3	2	0	1	11	10	1	6
Aston Villa	3	1	1	1	9	9	0	4
Derby Co	3	1	1	1	8	8	0	4
Middlesbrough	3	1	0	2	7	8	–1	3

Group C Table	P	W	D	L	F	A	GD	Pts
Norwich C	3	2	1	0	7	1	6	7
Everton	3	2	0	1	5	6	–1	6
Fulham	3	1	1	1	8	5	3	4
Sunderland	3	0	0	3	0	8	–8	0

Group D Table	P	W	D	L	F	A	GD	Pts
Manchester C	3	3	0	0	13	1	12	9
Liverpool	3	2	0	1	6	8	–2	6
Swansea C	3	1	0	2	5	9	–4	3
Southampton	3	0	0	3	4	10	–6	0

Group E Table	P	W	D	L	F	A	GD	Pts
Newcastle U	3	2	0	1	10	6	4	6
Stoke C	3	2	0	1	9	6	3	6
Tottenham H	3	1	0	2	6	9	–3	3
West Ham U	3	1	0	2	4	8	–4	3

Group F Table	P	W	D	L	F	A	GD	Pts
Brighton & HA	3	2	1	0	8	3	5	7
Manchester U	3	1	2	0	8	7	1	5
WBA	3	1	0	2	4	8	–4	3
Leicester C	3	0	1	2	7	9	–2	1

QUARTER-FINALS

Brighton & HA v Manchester C 2-3
Newcastle U v Chelsea 0-2
Reading v Everton 3-2*
Stoke C v Norwich C 8-0

SEMI-FINALS

Stoke C v Chelsea 2-1*
Reading v Manchester C 2-5

FINAL

Manchester C v Stoke C 6-0

CENTRAL LEAGUE 2019–20

**After extra time.*

SOUTH	P	W	D	L	F	A	GD	Pts
Southend U	6	5	0	1	21	6	15	15
Plymouth Arg	5	2	1	2	10	8	2	7
Bristol R	6	2	1	3	11	14	–3	7
Peterborough U	3	2	0	1	7	4	3	6
Milton Keynes D	4	1	1	2	2	9	–7	4
Forest Green R	4	0	1	3	3	13	–10	1

NORTH WEST	P	W	D	L	F	A	GD	Pts
Huddersfield T	7	5	2	0	18	7	11	17
Fleetwood T	3	2	1	0	10	1	9	7
Morecambe	5	1	1	3	7	10	–3	4
Blackpool	4	1	0	3	5	11	–6	3
Tranmere R	5	1	0	4	5	16	–11	3

NORTH EAST	P	W	D	L	F	A	GD	Pts
Grimsby T	7	3	2	2	11	8	3	11
Mansfield T	5	3	1	1	8	5	3	10
Rotherham U	6	3	0	3	12	13	–1	9
Doncaster R	8	2	2	4	17	18	–1	8
Walsall	7	2	2	3	9	11	–2	8
Scunthorpe U	3	1	1	1	6	8	–2	4

CENTRAL LEAGUE CUP – NORTHERN

GROUP 1	P	W	D	L	F	A	GD	Pts
Huddersfield T	4	3	0	1	14	10	4	9
Doncaster R	4	3	0	1	11	7	4	9
Rochdale	4	2	0	2	9	10	–1	6
Rotherham U	4	1	0	3	8	11	–3	3
Shrewsbury T	4	1	0	3	5	9	–4	3

GROUP 2	P	W	D	L	F	A	GD	Pts
Wigan Ath	4	3	1	0	10	6	4	10
Carlisle U	4	2	1	1	9	3	6	7
Fleetwood T	4	1	2	1	7	7	0	5
Morecambe	4	1	1	2	6	10	–4	4
Blackpool	4	0	1	3	6	12	–6	1

GROUP 3	P	W	D	L	F	A	GD	Pts
WBA	4	4	0	0	14	6	8	12
Mansfield T	4	2	1	1	9	8	1	7
Peterborough U	4	1	1	2	14	9	5	4
Scunthorpe U	4	1	0	3	5	8	–3	3
Port Vale	4	1	0	3	4	15	–11	3

CENTRAL LEAGUE CUP – SOUTHERN

GROUP 4	P	W	D	L	F	A	GD	Pts
Cambridge U	4	4	0	0	9	4	5	12
Milton Keynes D	3	2	0	1	8	6	2	6
AFC Wimbledon	4	1	0	3	8	7	1	3
Leyton Orient	3	1	0	2	3	5	–2	3
Southend U	4	1	0	3	5	11	–6	3

GROUP 5	P	W	D	L	F	A	GD	Pts
Bournemouth	3	3	0	0	7	3	4	9
Portsmouth	3	1	1	1	5	5	0	4
Plymouth Arg	3	0	2	1	5	6	–1	2
Bristol R	3	0	1	2	4	7	–3	1

QUARTER-FINALS

WBA v Doncaster R 1-1*

Doncaster R won 9-8 on penalties

Due to COVID-19 pandemic, all remaining games cancelled.

EFL YOUTH ALLIANCE 2019–20

NORTH EAST	P	W	D	L	F	A	GD	Pts
Doncaster R	18	12	2	4	42	21	21	38
Rotherham U	16	7	6	3	39	28	11	27
Bradford C	17	8	1	8	33	29	4	25
Scunthorpe U	15	8	1	6	26	26	0	25
Huddersfield T	18	8	1	9	30	42	–12	25
Mansfield T	15	7	2	6	24	25	–1	23
Notts Co	17	7	1	9	31	28	3	22
Grimsby T	16	6	3	7	25	30	–5	21
Chesterfield	18	6	3	9	28	45	–17	21
Burton Alb	15	6	1	8	23	25	–2	19
Lincoln C	19	5	3	11	30	32	–2	18

NORTH WEST	P	W	D	L	F	A	GD	Pts
Salford C	17	14	0	3	65	21	44	42
Preston NE	17	12	1	4	50	22	28	37
Fleetwood T	15	12	1	2	35	8	27	37
Carlisle U	19	9	3	7	36	34	2	30
Accrington S	19	10	0	9	32	39	–7	30
Blackpool	18	9	2	7	36	37	–1	29
Walsall	16	8	2	6	37	26	11	26
Oldham Ath	18	7	4	7	31	36	–5	25
Tranmere R	18	6	2	10	42	40	2	20
Rochdale	15	4	1	10	27	38	–11	13
Shrewsbury T	16	4	1	11	18	29	–11	13
Morecambe	17	3	4	10	18	50	–32	13
Port Vale	15	1	1	13	14	61	–47	4
Bury	0	0	0	0	0	0	0	0

SOUTH EAST	P	W	D	L	F	A	GD	Pts
Peterborough U	20	15	3	2	55	24	31	48
Northampton T	20	14	2	4	74	34	40	44
AFC Wimbledon	20	11	4	5	58	22	36	37
Cambridge U	20	11	2	7	40	33	7	35
Southend U	20	9	3	8	46	43	3	30
Stevenage	20	9	1	10	45	45	0	28
Luton T	20	7	5	8	51	47	4	26
Gillingham	20	6	4	10	38	48	–10	22
Leyton Orient	20	7	1	12	37	65	–28	22
Barnet	20	6	2	12	36	58	–22	20
Milton Keynes D	20	1	1	18	22	83	–61	4

SOUTH WEST	P	W	D	L	F	A	GD	Pts
Bournemouth	20	14	4	2	71	22	49	46
Oxford U	20	13	3	4	58	26	32	42
Portsmouth	20	13	2	5	59	42	17	41
Exeter C	20	12	0	8	52	36	16	36
Swindon T	20	10	3	7	49	35	14	33
Yeovil T	20	10	2	8	43	45	–2	32
Forest Green R	20	6	3	11	33	48	–15	21
Bristol R	20	6	3	11	32	49	–17	21
Cheltenham T	20	5	2	13	30	55	–25	17
Plymouth Arg	20	4	3	13	33	61	–28	15
Newport Co	20	4	1	15	23	64	–41	13

MERIT LEAGUE 1	P	W	D	L	F	A	GD	Pts
AFC Wimbledon	4	3	0	1	6	3	3	9
Bournemouth	3	2	1	0	5	2	3	7
Cambridge U	3	2	1	0	7	5	2	7
Peterborough U	3	2	0	1	4	1	3	6
Oxford U	3	2	0	1	3	2	1	6
Swindon T	3	1	1	1	8	7	1	4
Yeovil T	2	1	0	1	4	3	1	3
Southend U	3	1	0	2	4	4	0	3
Northampton T	3	1	0	2	4	6	–2	3
Stevenage	4	1	0	3	4	8	–4	3
Portsmouth	3	0	1	2	0	3	–3	1
Exeter C	2	0	0	2	3	8	–5	0

MERIT LEAGUE 2	P	W	D	L	F	A	GD	Pts
Bristol R	2	2	0	0	7	0	7	6
Forest Green R	2	2	0	0	7	2	5	6
Luton T	2	2	0	0	8	6	2	6
Gillingham	1	1	0	0	2	0	2	3
Leyton Orient	1	1	0	0	2	1	1	3
Milton Keynes D	3	1	0	2	5	5	0	3
Plymouth Arg	2	0	0	2	3	5	–2	0
Newport Co	1	0	0	1	0	2	–2	0
Barnet	2	0	0	2	3	7	–4	0
Cheltenham T	2	0	0	2	1	10	–9	0

Due to COVID-19 pandemic, all remaining games cancelled.

IMPORTANT ADDRESSES

The Football Association: Wembley Stadium, PO Box 1966, London SW1P 9EQ. *0800 169 1863*

Scotland: Hampden Park, Glasgow G42 9AY. *0141 616 6000*

Northern Ireland (Irish FA): Chief Executive, Donegall Avenue, Belfast, Northern Ireland BT12 6LU. *028 9066 9458*

Wales: 11/12 Neptune Court, Vanguard Way, Cardiff CF24 5PJ. *029 2043 5830*

Republic of Ireland: National Sports Campus, Abbotstown, Dublin 15. *01 8999 500*

International Federation (FIFA): Strasse 20, P.O. Box 8044, Zurich, Switzerland. *00 41 43 222 7777. Fax: 00 41 43 222 7878*

Union of European Football Associations: Secretary, Route de Geneve 46, P.O. Box 1260, Nyon 2, Switzerland. *49 89 552608830*

THE LEAGUES

The Premier League: Richard Masters, 30 Gloucester Place, London W1U 8PL. *0207 864 9000*

The Football League: David Baldwin, EFL House, 10–12 West Cuff, Preston PR1 8HU. *01772 325 800. Fax 01772 325 801*

The National League: M. Tattersall, 4th Floor, Waterloo House, 20 Waterloo Street, Birmingham B2 5TB. *0121 643 3143*

FA Women's Super League: Wembley Stadium, PO Box 1966, London SW1P 9EQ. *+44 844 980 8200*

Scottish Premier League: Letherby Drive, Glasgow G42 9DE. *0141 620 4140*

The Scottish League: Hampden Park, Glasgow G42 9EB. *0141 620 4160*

Welsh Premier League: 11/12 Neptune Court, Vanguard Way, Cardiff CF24 5PJ. *029 2043 5830*

Northern Ireland Football League: Mervyn Brown Suite, National Stadium at Windsor Park, Donegall Avenue, Belfast BT12 6LW. *028 9560 7150*

Football League of Ireland: D. Crowther, National Sports Campus, Abbotstown, Dublin 15. *00 353 1 8999 500*

Southern League: J. Mills, Suite 3B, Eastgate House, 121–131 Eastgate Street, Gloucester GL1 1PX. *07768 750 590*

Northern Premier League: Ms A. Firth, 23 High Lane, Norton Tower, Halifax, W. Yorkshire HX2 0NW. *01422 410 691*

Isthmian League: Kellie Discipline, PO Box 393, Dartford DA1 9JK. *01322 314 999*

Combined Counties League: A. Constable, 3 Craigwell Close, Staines, Middlesex TW18 3NP. *01784 440 613*

Eastern Counties League: N. Spurling, 16 Thanet Road, Ipswich, Suffolk IP4 5LB. *01473 720 893*

Essex Senior League: Secretary: Ms. M. Darling, 39 Milwards, Harlow, Essex CM19 4SG. *07939 850627*

Hellenic League: John Ostinell, 2 Wynn Grove, Hazlemere HP15 7LY. *07900 081 814*

Midland League: N. Wood, 30 Glaisdale Road, Hall Green, Birmingham B28 8PX. *07967 440 007*

North West Counties League: J. Deal, 24 The Pastures, Crossens, Southport PR9 8RH. *01704 211 955*

Northern Counties East: Matt Jones, 346 Heneage Road, Grimsby DN32 9NJ. *07415 068 996*

Northern League: K. Hewitt, 21 Cherrytree Drive, Langley Park, Durham DH7 9FX. *07897 611640*

Spartan South Midlands League: M. Appleby, 15 Aintree Close, Bletchley, Milton Keynes MK3 5LP.

Southern Combination League: T. Dawes, 32 Reynolds Lane, Langney, Eastbourne BN23 7NW. *01323 764 218*

Southern Counties East League: D. Peck, secretary@scefl.com *07710 143 944*

United Counties League: Ms W. Newey, Nene Valley Community Centre, Candy Street, Peterborough PE2 9RE. *07890 5184577*

Wessex League: A. Hodder, leaguesecretary.wessexleague @gmail.com. *07780 496312*

Western League: A. Radford, 19 Longney Place, Patchway, Bristol BS34 5LQ. *07872 818 868*

OTHER USEFUL ADDRESSES

Amateur Football Alliance: Jason Kilby, Unit 3, 7 Wenlock Road, London N1 7SL. *0208 733 2613*

Association of Football Badge Collectors: K. Wilkinson, 18 Hinton St, Fairfield, Liverpool L6 3AR. *0151 260 0554*

British Olympic Association: 60 Charlotte Street, London W1T 2NU. *0207 842 5700*

British Blind Sport (including football): Plato Close, Tachbrook Park, Leamington Spa, Warwickshire CV34 6WE. *01926 424 247*

British Universities and Colleges Sports Association: Vince Mayne, Chief Executive: BUCSA, 20–24 King's Bench Street, London SE1 0QX. *0207 633 5080*

England Supporters Club: Wembley Stadium, PO Box 1966, London SW1P 9EQ. *0800 389 1966*

English Schools FA: 4 Parker Court, Staffordshire Technology Park, Stafford ST18 0WP. *01785 785 970*

Fields In Trust: Woodstock Studios, 36 Woodstock Grove, London W12 8LE. *0207 427 2110*

Football Foundation: 10 Eastbourne Terrace, Paddington, London W2 6LG. *0345 345 4555*

Football Postcard Collectors Club: PRO: John Farrelly, 163 Collingwood Road, Hillingdon, Middlesex UB8 3EW. Web: www.hobbyist.co.uk/pfcc

Football Safety Officers Association: Peter Houghton, Suite 5, Blackburn Rovers Enterprise Centre, Ewood Park, Blackburn BB2 4JF. *01254 841 771.*

Institute of Groundsmanship: 28 Stratford Office Village, Walker Avenue, Wolverton, Milton Keynes MK12 5TW. *01908 312 511*

League Managers Association: St George's Park, Newborough Road, Needwood, Burton on Trent DE13 9PD. *0128 357 6350*

National Football Museum: Urbis Building, Cathedral Gardens, Todd Street, Manchester M4 3BG. *0161 605 8200*

Professional Footballers' Association: 20 Oxford Court, Bishopsgate, Off Lower Moseley Street, Manchester M2 3WQ. *0161 236 0575*

Programme Monthly & Football Collectable Magazine: R. P. Matz, 11 Tannington Terrace, London N5 1LE. *020 7359 8687*

Programme Promotions: 21 Roughwood Close, Watford WD17 3HN. *01923 861 468*
Web: www.footballprogrammes.com

Referees' Association: 1A Bagshaw Close, Ryton-on-Dunsmore, Coventry CV8 3EX. *024 7642 0360*

Scottish Football Museum: Hampden Park, Glasgow G42 9BA. *0141 616 6139*

Sir Norman Chester Centre for Football Research: Department of Sociology, University of Leicester, University Road LE1 7RH. *0116 252 2741/5*

Sport England: 21 Bloomsbury Street, London WC1B 3HF.

Sports Grounds Safety Authority: 2–6 Salisbury Square, London EC4Y 8JX. *0207 930 6693*

Sports Turf Research Institute: St Ives Grove, Harden, Bingley, West Yorkshire BD16 1AU. *01274 565 131*

The Football Supporters' Federation: 1 Ashmore Terrace, Stockton Road, Sunderland, Tyne and Wear SR2 7DE. *0330 440 0044*

The Ninety-Two Club: Mr M. Kimberley, The Ninety-Two Club, 153 Hayes Lane, Kenley, Surrey CR8 5HP.

Walking Football Association: Kemp House, 160 City Road, London EC1V 2NX. *07517 033248*

Wheelchair Football Association: c/o Nottinghamshire FA, Unit 6b, Chetwynd Business Park, Chilwell, Nottingham NG9 6RZ.

FOOTBALL CLUB CHAPLAINCY

What does a football chaplain do?

It's a question that is often put to the football chaplains by individual fans or by a group of supporters.

The following may prove helpful to anyone who is genuinely interested. The role of a football chaplain is usually a supportive one (though most chaplains are also supporters of their clubs as well).

The injured or out of form star goalscorer; the bereaved player, fan or club official; the bitterly disappointed former youth team member who has learnt that his club is releasing him; the promising midfielder facing a career-threatening operation; the lonely new signing – these are all examples of football folk who have been glad (and appreciative) of the availability of a football club chaplain.

THE REV

OFFICIAL CHAPLAINS TO FA PREMIERSHIP AND FOOTBALL LEAGUE CLUBS

Aston Villa – Jon Grant
Barnsley – Peter Amos
Birmingham C – Kirk McAtear
Birmingham C Academy – Tim Atkins
Blackburn R – Ken Howles
Blackpool – Linda Tomkinson
Bolton W – Philip Mason
Bournemouth – Adam Parrett
Bradford C – Oliver Evans
Brentford – Stuart Cashman
Bristol C – Derek Cleave
Bristol R – Wayne Massey
Burnley – Barry Hunter
Burton Alb – Phil Pusey
Cambridge U – Leo Orobor
Cardiff C Academy – Bryon Castle
Carlisle U – Alun Jones
Charlton Ath – Matt Baker
Charlton Ath Academy – Gareth Morgan
Chelsea – Martin Swan
Cheltenham T – Malcolm Allen
Coventry C – Simon Betteridge
Crawley T – Steve Alliston
Crewe Alex – Phil Howell
Crystal Palace – Chris Roe
Derby Co – Tony Luke
Doncaster R – Barry Miller
Everton – Henry Corbett
Fleetwood T – George Ayoma
Fulham – Gary Piper
Gillingham – Chris Gill
Huddersfield T – Dudley Martin
Ipswich T – Kevan McCormack
Leeds U – Dave Niblock
Leyton Orient – Alan Comfort
Lincoln C – Canon Andrew Vaughan
Liverpool – Bill Bygroves
Luton T – David Kesterton
Macclesfield T – Chris Whiteley
Manchester C – Pete Horlock
Mansfield T – Kevin Charles
Millwall – Canon Owen Beament
Newport Co – Keith Beardmore
Northampton T – Haydon Spenceley
Norwich C – Jon Norman
Norwich C Academy – Tim Henery
Oldham Ath – John Simmons
Peterborough U – Richard Longfoot
Peterborough U Academy – Jonathan Greenwood
Plymouth Arg – Arthur Goode
Port Vale – John Hibberts
Portsmouth – Jonathan Jeffery and Mick Mellows
Preston NE – Chris Nelson
QPR – Joshua Baines
Reading – Steven Prince
Reading Academy – Charlie Baines
Rochdale – Richard Bradley
Rotherham U – Baz Gascoyne
Scunthorpe U – Alan Wright
Scunthorpe U Academy – David Eames
Sheffield U – Delroy Hall
Sheffield W – Baz Gascoyne
Sheffield W Wise Old Owls – David Jeans
Shrewsbury T – Phil Cansdale and Andy Ackroyd
Southampton – Jonny Goodchild
Southend U – Stuart Alleway and Mike Lodge
Sunderland – Father Marc Lyden-Smith
Swansea C – Kevin Johns
Swansea C Academy – Eirian Wyn
Swindon T – Simon Stevenette
Walsall – Lance Blackwood
Watford – Clive Ross
West Ham U – Alan Bolding
West Ham U Academy – Philip Wright
Wolverhampton W – David Wright
Wolverhampton W Academy – Steve Davies
Wycombe W – Benedict Mwendwa Musola

OTHER CHAPLAINS

EFL Offices London – Cameron Collington
EFL Offices Preston – Chris Nelson

The chaplains hope that those who read this page will see the value and benefit of chaplaincy work in football and will take appropriate steps to spread the word where this is possible. They would also like to thank the editors of the Football Yearbook for their continued support for this specialist and growing area of work.

For further information, please contact: Sports Chaplaincy UK, The Avenue Methodist Church, Wincham Road, Sale, Cheshire M33 4PL. Telephone: 0800 181 4051 or email: admin@sportschaplaincy.org.uk. Website: www.sportschaplaincy.org.uk

OBITUARIES

Junior Agogo (Born: Accra, Ghana, 1 August 1979. Died: Swiss Cottage, London, August 2019.) Junior Agogo was a pacy striker who signed for Sheffield Wednesday in October 1996, but made little impact during a four-year stay at Hillsborough, playing most of his football out on loan. He subsequently spent two years in the United States where he also developed a second career in modelling. On his return he had a brief spell as a non-contract player with Queens Park Rangers before moving on to Bristol Rovers where his career took off. He led the Pirates' scoring charts in 2004–05 and also enjoyed success with Nottingham Forest, helping them win promotion from League One as runners-up in 2007–08. He won 27 caps for Ghana and was a member of the squad that achieved third place in the African Cup of Nations finals in 2008.

Des Anderson (Born: Edinburgh, 9 January 1938. Died: 17 October 2019.) Des Anderson was a Scotland Schools international and went on to sign senior forms with Hibernian in September 1956. However, he managed just a couple of first-team appearances during a five-year stay at Easter Road before moving south to join Millwall. He enjoyed a couple of seasons of regular action at The Den, then played in the Southern League for a number of clubs including Dartford and Tonbridge. When his playing days were over he had a successful career as a coach working alongside Dave Mackay at Swindon Town, Nottingham Forest, Derby County and Walsall.

Jimmy Anderson (Born: Glasgow, 25 December 1932. Died: November 2019.) Wing-half Jimmy Anderson developed in Juvenile football with Partick Avondale and after being spotted playing for RAOC Hilsea during his National Service he was signed by Bristol Rovers in April 1953. A busy, bustling player, he never quite established himself with Rovers but fared much better during a three-year spell with Chester. He made 65 first-team appearances during his stay at Sealand Road before moving into non-league football with Rhyl.

Peter Anderson (Born: Devonport, 11 September 1932. Died: Torquay, 24 June 2019.) Peter Anderson was a traditional-style winger who joined Plymouth Argyle from local club Oak Villa in July 1950 and established himself in the first team in the 1954–55 season. After suffering a broken leg he fought back to full fitness and went on to make over 250 first-team appearances for Argyle, making a useful contribution to the team that won the Third Division title in 1958–59. He concluded his senior career with Torquay United before switching to non-league football with Bideford.

Raddy Antic (Born: Zitiste, Yugoslavia, 22 November 1949. Died: Madrid, 6 April 2020.) Radomir Antic was a sweeper who spent his best years in Yugoslavia with Partizan Belgrade before playing in turn for Fenerbahce, Real Zaragoza and Luton Town. He was 30 by the time he signed for the Hatters in July 1980 and was generally used in a midfield role, providing them with four years of fine service, the highlight coming in the final game of the 1982–83 season when he came off the bench to score a late winner thus preserving Luton's place in the top flight and relegating City. He later coached a number of top clubs including Real Madrid, Atletico Madrid and Barcelona. As a player he had been capped by Yugoslavia.

Mike Appleby (Born: Alnwick, Northumberland, circa 1954. Died: 21 April 2020.) Mike Appleby worked for the Football Association for over 30 years, retiring in November 2015. He was a key figure in the restructuring of the National League system in 2004–05 which resulted in the creation of the National North and South divisions. He is also credited with keeping the England C team fully funded and was involved in the creation of the UEFA Regions Cup. After retiring from the FA he became a director of the Spartan South Midlands League, serving as the competition's general secretary.

Bobby Ardrey (Born: Hammersmith, 18 October 1937. Died: West Molesey, Surrey, 2 April 2020.) Bobby Ardrey was a right-half who signed amateur forms for Chelsea after leaving school aged 14. He played for the junior and youth teams while at Stamford Bridge before moving on to Wimbledon in 1955. He went on to make 422 appearances for Wimbledon and was in the Dons team which won the FA Amateur Cup in 1963. He made 12 appearances for England Amateurs, captaining the team on four occasions, and also appeared in an Olympic qualifier for Great Britain.

Brian Arrowsmith (Born: Walney Island, Barrow, 2 July 1940. Died: 12 April 2020.) Brian Arrowsmith signed professional forms for Barrow in October 1961 and went on to feature regularly in the side for nine seasons. He initially played at full-back before switching to centre-half and made a club-record 378 Football League appearances for the Bluebirds. He left in the summer of 1971 for a three-year spell at Netherfield only to return to Holker Street where he remained for a further six seasons, including a spell as player-manager.

Dave Bacuzzi (Born: Islington, 12 October 1940. Died: Dublin, 21 April 2020.) Full-back Dave Bacuzzi was playing regularly for Eastbourne United as a 17-year-old and in March 1958 he signed amateur forms for Arsenal, turning professional 12 months later. Although generally a reserve at Highbury, he made 22 appearances in the 1961–62 season. He moved on to Manchester City towards the end of the 1963–64 campaign and was a regular in the line-up before returning south to sign for Reading. In May 1970 he became player-manager of Cork Hibernians, leading them to the League of Ireland title in his first season, 1970–71, and the FAI Cup in 1972 and 1973. Later he also won the FAI Cup with Home Farm for the only time in their history.

Ken Barclay (Born: 7 July 1949. Died: Whitehead, Co Antrim, 10 April 2020.) Ken Barclay was a goalkeeper who made over 200 first-team appearances for Linfield after making his debut in August 1972. He won two Irish League championship medals with Linfield and an Irish Cup winners' medal in 1978. He appeared for the Irish League representative team against the Scottish League in November 1978.

Chris Barker (Born: Sheffield, 2 March 1980. Died: Cardiff, 1 January 2020.) Chris Barker was an energetic left-back, strong in the tackle and a consistent performer throughout his career. A product of non-league football, he developed further with Barnsley before earning a move to Cardiff City. In his first season with the Bluebirds he was a member of the team that defeated Queens Park Rangers to win the Division Two play-off final. In total he made almost 600 senior appearances in a 15-year career, also playing for Queens Park Rangers, Plymouth Argyle and Southend United. He later had a brief spell as player-manager at Aldershot Town and at the time of his unexpected death was U18s manager at Forest Green Rovers.

Phil Barlow (Born: Shipley, 19 December 1946. Died: 27 November 2019.) Phil Barlow was a tall wing-half who joined Bradford City in the summer of 1966. He featured fairly regularly for the Bantams in the first half of the 1966–67 season but in the following summer moved on to Lincoln City where he appeared for the Imps in their 2-1 League Cup victory over Newcastle United. Later he enjoyed a lengthy association with Guiseley.

Graham Barnett (Born: Hanley, Stoke-on-Trent, 17 May 1936. Died: Bentilee, Stoke-on-Trent, 17 June 2019.) Graham Barnett was a goalscoring inside-forward who initially joined Port Vale as an amateur before turning professional in June 1956. He made something of a sensational start to his senior career, netting in his first three appearances, and he finished with 20 goals from 22 appearances as Vale won the Division Four title in 1958–59. He led the scoring charts the following season, but in March 1960 was sold to Tranmere Rovers for what was then a record fee for the Birkenhead club. He subsequently played for Halifax Town and Macclesfield Town before spending several years in Australia. On his return he resumed his links with Vale and joined the coaching staff, later running the youth team until 1985.

Albert Bateman (Born: Stocksbridge, 13 June 1924. Died: April 2020.) Albert Bateman was an outside-right who signed for Huddersfield Town at the beginning of the 1943–44 season and featured regularly for the club through to the end of the war. He retained his place when peacetime football resumed but then missed time following a cartilage operation before suffering a further knee injury in January 1949 which effectively ended his career. In total he made over 150 first-team appearances and was Huddersfield's oldest living player at the time of his death.

Mick Benning (Born: Watford, 3 February 1938. Died: 25 November 2019.) Mick Benning was a pacy winger who developed in local junior football before signing for Watford as a teenager. He missed just one game for the Hornets in their 1959–60 promotion season and went on to make over 100 appearances during his stay. In 1961–62 he helped Cambridge City win the

Southern League title and he went on to play for a number of clubs including Bedford Town. His son Paul Benning played in the Football League for Peterborough United.

John Bettany (Born: Laughton Common, Rotherham, 16 December 1937. Died: 23 October 2019.) John Bettany was a wing-half who was on Wolverhampton Wanderers' books as a junior before signing professional terms with Huddersfield Town. In almost five seasons at Leeds Road he was mostly a back-up player but came into his own when he moved on to Barnsley in March 1965. He was a near ever-present in the team that won promotion from the Fourth Division in 1967–68 and went on to make more than 200 appearances during his time at Oakwell. He wound down his career with spells at Rotherham United, Goole Town and Frickley.

Peter Billingham (Born: Pensnett, nr. Dudley, 8 October 1938. Died: 26 August 2019.) Peter Billingham was a lanky half-back who joined the groundstaff at Walsall on leaving school and went on to enjoy three seasons of regular first-team football with the Saddlers before being sold to West Bromwich Albion in the summer of 1960. However, he was unable to establish himself at The Hawthorns and quickly moved into non-league football with Worcester City. After retiring from football he became a well-known greyhound trainer in the West Midlands.

Sid Bishop (Born: Tooting, 8 April 1934. Died: April 2020.) Centre-half Sid Bishop developed with nursery club Chase of Chertsey before signing for Leyton Orient in June 1952. He went on to make his senior debut in February 1954 but it was not until the 1957–58 season that he established himself in the side. A tall, skilful defender, he was a fixture in the line-up for the next seven seasons and was an ever-present in the team that won promotion to the top flight in 1961–62. He left Brisbane Road at the end of the 1964–65 season having clocked up more than 300 first-team appearances and was later player-manager at Hastings United and Guildford City.

Micky Block (Born: Ipswich, 28 January 1940. Died: December 2019.) Winger Micky Block won England Youth international honours and was a member of the Chelsea team that reached the FA Youth Cup final in 1957–58. He never quite managed to establish himself at Stamford Bridge but enjoyed success in a four-year spell at Brentford, where he was a near ever-present in the team that won the Fourth Division title in 1962–63. He later wound down his career with spells at Watford and Chelmsford City.

Peter Bonetti (Born: Putney, 27 September 1941. Died: 12 April 2020.) Goalkeeper Peter Bonetti was one of the greatest players in the post-war history of Chelsea. As a youngster he starred for the Sussex Schools team and had a trial with Reading before joining the groundstaff at Stamford Bridge in July 1958. He made his first-team debut shortly before the end of the 1959–60 season when he was also a member of the Blues team that won the FA Youth Cup. A reliable and graceful goalkeeper nicknamed 'The Cat', he was first choice for the next 15 years and after a brief spell in the NASL with St Louis Stars he returned to Stamford Bridge where he remained until 1979. In total he made over 700 League and Cup appearances for Chelsea, with whom he won the European Cup Winners' Cup in 1971, the FA Cup (1970) and the Football League Cup (1965). He also won seven full caps for England. He later made a few appearances for Dundee United in the 1979–80 season before eventually turning to coaching.

Allan Boyd (Born: Dumbarton, 21 November 1929. Died: 25 October 2019.) Allan Boyd was a winger who made his debut for Queen's Park while still a pupil at Dumbarton Academy. He played in Scotland's first-ever youth international in October 1947 and went on to win representative honours for Scotland Amateurs and also Great Britain, for whom he appeared in the third-place play-off fixture against Denmark in the 1948 Olympic Games tournament. He later played for Aberdeen and East Fife, making a total of over 150 senior appearances.

Ray Brand (Born: Islington, 2 October 1934. Died: February 2020.) Ray Brand played for Hatfield Town as a youngster before signing professional forms for Millwall at the age of 17. He waited four years for his first-team debut but eventually established himself as a hard and uncompromising centre-half, making over 150 appearances during his stay at The Den. He briefly switched to centre-forward at the start of 1958–59, netting a hat-trick in a 4-0 home win over Aldershot, but he missed most of the remainder of the campaign due to kidney problems. He later spent a couple of seasons with Southend United before turning to Southern League football with Hastings United.

Eric Brookes (Born: Mapplewell, South Yorkshire, 3 February 1944. Died: January 2020.) Full-back Eric Brookes was a 16-year-old groundstaff boy when he made his Football League debut for Barnsley at Bradford City in September 1960. He went on to win England Youth honours and by the end of his first season at Oakwell he was established as a first-team regular. Signed up on professional forms at the age of 17, he went on to make over 350 appearances for the club, including a contribution to the 1967–68 promotion campaign. He subsequently concluded his senior career with spells at Northampton Town and Peterborough United before becoming player-manager of March Town United.

Bobby Brown (Born: Dunipace, Stirlingshire, 19 March 1923. Died: 15 January 2020.) Goalkeeper Bobby Brown was one of the all-time greats for Rangers for whom he made almost 300 peacetime appearances. He made his debut in senior football as a 17-year-old schoolboy for Queen's Park in April 1940. He went on to make 98 wartime appearances for Queens while serving in the Fleet Air Arm. He gained representative honours with the Royal Navy and played for Scotland in five wartime internationals. He made his full international debut in January 1946, and is the last amateur player to win a Scotland cap. In May 1946 he signed for Rangers and became an integral member of their 'Iron Curtain' defence, playing in every league game until April 1952, a run of 179 consecutive matches. He won three Scottish League titles, three Scottish Cups and two League Cups at Ibrox and after concluding his career as a player at Falkirk switched to management. He was manager of St Johnstone (1958 to 1967) and then the Scotland national team (1967 to 1971).

Bobby Brown (Born: Motherwell, 2 December 1931. Died: Workington, 19 June 2019.) Bobby Brown was a half-back who spent five years on the books of Motherwell where he was mostly used as cover and made just a handful of first-team appearances. In the summer of 1956 he moved south to sign for Workington. He quickly became a fixture in the line-up, initially at right-back before switching to centre-half during the 1962–63 season. He captained the Reds team that won promotion from Division Four in 1963–64 and stayed at Borough Park for over a decade, creating an all-time club record of 420 Football League appearances. His son Bobby also played in the Football League for Workington.

Charlie Brown (Born 18 September 1924. Died: 10 October 2019.) Charlie Brown was a centre- or inside-forward who developed in local Dumfries football with LMS Rovers before signing for Queen of the South at the start of the 1948–49 season. He spent five years on the books at Palmerston Park, mostly deputising for club legend Billy Houliston, before moving on to play for Tarff Rovers.

José Luis Brown (Born: Ranchos, Buenos Aires, 10 November 1956. Died: La Plata, Argentina, 12 August 2019.) José Luis Brown was a powerful central defender who was a member of the Argentina team that won the 1986 World Cup, scoring the first goal in the 3-2 win over West Germany in the final. It was the only goal he scored in his 36 appearances for Argentina. He played most of his club football for Estudiantes de La Plata and went on to a career in coaching once his playing days were over. He was assistant coach with the Argentina team that won the gold medal at the 2008 Olympic Games.

Bobby Buchan (Born: Kelty, Fife, 1 June 1929. Died: Heaton Moor, Yorkshire, 22 May 2019.) Bobby Buchan was a left-sided player who progressed from Secondary Juveniles Bayview YC to Lochgelly Violet Juniors and then on to Heart of Midlothian in July 1948. In four seasons at Tynecastle he made just two senior appearances, but then enjoyed two good seasons with Cowdenbeath where he played regular first-team football. He concluded his career at Raith Rovers where he stayed until the end of the 1957–58 campaign, although he was out of the game for 18 months during his time there due to illness.

Ray Byrom (Born: Blackburn, 2 January 1935. Died: 6 January 2020.) Ray Byrom was an outside-left who was on the books of Blackburn Rovers as an amateur before signing for Accrington Stanley, becoming a full-time professional with Stanley on completing his National Service. He received few opportunities at Peel Park, and in December 1958 followed his former manager Walter Galbraith to Bradford Park Avenue. He went straight into the first team and missed just one game during his stay with the club, making 73 League and Cup appearances, before suffering a broken leg in the home game with Chester in August 1960 which ended his career in senior football. His grandson Joel Byrom briefly played for Accrington Stanley and was on the books of Stevenage in 2019–20.

Jacky Butchart (Born: Dundee, 10 September 1923. Died: Dundee, 9 May 2020.) Jacky Butchart was an outside-right who made two appearances for Dundee United towards the end of the 1944–45 season. He also played as a trialist for Brechin City in March 1949, but otherwise featured for a number of Junior clubs in the Dundee area including Anchorage, Violet and Stobswell. At the time of his death he was Dundee United's oldest living player.

Les Cameron (Born: 24 September 1934. Died: Forres, 6 September 2019.) Les Cameron was a goalkeeper who had a spell on the books of Crystal Palace as an amateur while on National Service. On returning to Scotland he enjoyed regular first-team football with Forfar Athletic and Montrose in the early 1960s before switching to Junior football. In later life he played squash for Scotland at veteran level.

Les Campbell (Born: Wigan, 26 July 1935. Died: November 2019.) Winger Les Campbell was briefly on the books of Wigan Athletic but was sold to Preston North End in the summer of 1953. He served the two greatest wingers of the 1950s as a back-up: Tom Finney at Deepdale and Stanley Matthews at Blackpool. Les came into his own when he dropped down the divisions to play for Tranmere Rovers. He made over 100 first-team appearances during his time at Prenton Park before returning to non-league football with Wigan.

Alec Carson (Born: Clarkston, Glasgow, 12 November 1942. Died: April 2020.) Although born in Scotland, Alec Carson was brought up in Corby and after playing for Corby Town youth team he joined the groundstaff at Northampton Town. He progressed to a professional contract with the Cobblers but at the County Ground and in two years with Aldershot he made a total of just 13 Football League appearances. A hard-working wing-half, he later enjoyed a successful career in the Southern League with Cheltenham Town, Worcester City and Hereford United.

Brian Carter (Born: Dorchester, 17 November 1938. Died: Weymouth, 21 July 2019.) Brian Carter was a wing-half who joined Portsmouth from Weymouth in January 1956 and went on to make exactly 50 senior appearances during his stay at Fratton Park. He spent the 1961–62 season with Bristol Rovers, where he was mostly a reserve, before switching to Southern League football with Bath City.

Gerry Casey (Born: Birkenhead, 25 August 1941. Died: Birkenhead, 24 June 2019.) Gerry Casey was a hard and uncompromising central defender who first came to prominence with Ellesmere Port Town in the Cheshire League. After a brief spell with Holyhead he joined Tranmere Rovers in August 1967 on trial and despite being sent off on his Football League debut at Torquay he was offered a full contract. He went on to play over 50 games for the Birkenhead club before returning to non-league football with Ellesmere Port and Altrincham.

Sammy Chapman (Born: Belfast, 16 February 1938. Died: Wombourne, Staffordshire, 24 July 2019.) Sammy Chapman was on the books of Manchester United as a youngster but then went back to Ireland and was capped for Northern Ireland Amateurs at the age of 16. He eventually returned to the Football League, joining Mansfield Town from Shamrock Rovers in August 1956. He was second-top scorer for the Stags in 1957–58 which earned him a move to Portsmouth. However, he never really established himself for Pompey and in December 1961 he returned to Field Mill. He helped Mansfield win promotion in 1962–63, but then became involved in the match-fixing scandal that affected professional football at the time and received a lengthy ban. He eventually returned to the game and went on to play for Stafford Rangers and then coached at Crewe Alexandra before serving Wolverhampton Wanderers as manager between August and November 1985. His sons Campbell and Cavan both played for Wolves.

Charlie Chase (Born: Patcham, Sussex, 31 January 1924. Died: 3 February 2020.) Charlie Chase was recruited to Brighton & Hove Albion's newly formed junior team in 1940 and made his first team debut aged 16 when he played against Watford in June 1940. He made a number of wartime appearances for the Seagulls before moving on to Watford for the 1946–47 season. He was mostly a fringe player at Vicarage Road, but featured regularly in two seasons with Crystal Palace before retiring from football.

Roy Cheetham (Born: Eccles, Manchester, 21 December 1939. Died: 8 December 2019.) Roy Cheetham made his debut at right-half for Manchester City while still a teenager, but although he spent a total of 12 years at Maine Road he was rarely a first choice. He spent the summer of 1968 with Detroit Cougars then returned to England and after a trial period with Charlton Athletic he signed for Chester. He enjoyed regular first-team football at Sealand Road, making close to 150 first-team appearances.

Trevor Cherry (Born: Huddersfield, 23 February 1948. Died: 29 April 2020.) Defender Trevor Cherry was an apprentice with Huddersfield Town and went on to make over 100 appearances for the Leeds Road club, assisting them to promotion to the top flight in 1969–70. In the summer of 1972 he signed for Leeds United where he stayed for 10 years and played nearly 500 first-team games. In 1972–73 he gained runners-up medals in both the FA Cup and European Cup Winners' Cup and the following season he was a near ever-present in the team that won the Football League title. He was player-manager and then manager of Bradford City from December 1982 to January 1987 leading the club to the Third Division title in 1984–85, although the season ended tragically with the catastrophic fire at Valley Parade. He won 27 caps for England, captaining the side against Australia in May 1980.

Doug Clarke (Born: Bolton, 19 January 1934. Died: August 2019.) Winger Doug Clarke joined the professional ranks with Bury in February 1952 but was mostly a reserve during his time at Gigg Lane. Midway through the 1955–56 campaign he moved to Hull City where he enjoyed the best years of his career. He went on to make over 400 appearances for the Tigers and was a member of the team that won promotion to Division Two in 1958–59. He wound down his career at Torquay United where he featured regularly for three more seasons and was a near ever-present in the 1965–66 promotion campaign.

Brian Clifton (Born: Whitchurch, Hampshire, 15 March 1934. Died: Louth, Lincolnshire, 12 January 2020.) Brian Clifton was a versatile player who began at inside-forward and wing-half before switching to centre-half towards the end of his career. He signed for Southampton as a teenager, but missed two years on National Service. He enjoyed a good scoring record for Saints, netting in seven of the eight games he played in the 1959–60 season when the Third Division title was won, and a goal every three games during his time at The Dell. In October 1962 he moved to Grimsby Town where he evolved into a cultured defender and made over 100 appearances before switching to non-league football with Boston United.

John Collins (Born: Bedwellty, Monmouthshire, 21 January 1949. Died: Milford Haven, 14 April 2020.) John Collins was an apprentice at Tottenham Hotspur and then spent five years as a professional at White Hart Lane, making just two first-team appearances. A drop down a division to Portsmouth saw him feature more regularly and he went on to play for Halifax Town and Sheffield Wednesday before signing for Barnsley in December 1976. He enjoyed the best years of his career at Oakwell, making close on 150 appearances, mostly at full-back, and was an ever-present when the club won promotion from Division Four in 1979–80. As a youngster he won representative honours for Wales at U23 level.

Ernie Collumbine (Born: Carronshore, Falkirk, 20 December 1938. Died: 19 June 2019.) Ernie Collumbine was originally a wing-half with Stenhousemuir before signing for East Stirlingshire in November 1961. He captained the team that won promotion to the top flight in Scottish football in 1962–63 and continued to play for the club during its brief incarnation as ES Clydebank in 1964–65. During this time he switched to playing as a sweeper and is believed to be the first to appear in that role in the Scottish League. Later he played for both St Johnstone and Clydebank, taking his total of senior appearances beyond the 300-mark.

Joe Connelly (Born: 16 October 1946. Died: 12 July 2019.) Joe Connelly was a tall centre-forward who played a couple of games as a trialist with Forfar Athletic in the 1965–66 season before spending the following campaign with East Stirlingshire. His best season was 1967–68 when he featured regularly for Cowdenbeath and led the club's scoring charts. He subsequently returned to Junior football with Oakley United. He was the older brother of George Connelly of Celtic and Scotland.

Jimmy Conway (Born: Dublin, 10 August 1946. Died: Portland, Oregon, USA, 14 February 2020.) Jimmy Conway was a prodigious talent as a teenager, winning representative honours for the Republic of Ireland Amateur team and the League of Ireland before Fulham bought him from Bohemians in May 1966. He quickly established himself at first-team level and went on to make over 300 first-team appearances during a decade at Craven Cottage during which he helped the team win promotion in 1970–71. After a brief spell at Manchester City he signed for Portland Timbers of the NASL, remaining in the United States after he retired from playing. He won 20 full caps for the Republic of Ireland.

Charlie Cooper (Born: Farnworth, Lancashire, 14 June 1941. Died: Farnworth, May 2020.) Charlie Cooper was a full-back who signed for Bolton Wanderers in May 1959 but it was not until the 1965–66 campaign that he won a regular place in the first team. He made 90 senior appearances during his time at Burnden Park, then spent two years with Barrow where he made a further 65 appearances before leaving the game.

Paul Cooper (Born: Birmingham, 12 July 1957. Died: March 2020.) Full-back Paul Cooper joined Huddersfield Town as an apprentice on leaving school and was a member of the Terriers team that reached the FA Youth Cup final in 1973–74. He progressed to a professional contract but made just a couple of first-team appearances and then spent the 1977–78 season with Grimsby Town, although here too he was mostly a reserve. He returned to the West Midlands, signing for Mile Oak Rovers, and went on to play for a number of non-league clubs in the region.

Dave Corbett (Born: Marshfield, Gloucestershire, 15 May 1940. Died: 2020.) Dave Corbett was a traditional-style winger who made his first-team debut for Swindon Town as a teenager. He enjoyed a decent run in the first team in 1958–59 but thereafter was often in the reserves and in February 1962 he moved on to Plymouth Argyle. He enjoyed two good campaigns at Home Park but then injuries restricted his appearances, leading to his retirement from the game at the age of 26.

Laurie Craker (Born: Aylesbury, 1 March 1953. Died: 16 May 2020.) Laurie Craker was an apprentice with Chelsea, subsequently signing a professional contract in August 1970. However, he was never able to break into the first team at Stamford Bridge and after a spell in South Africa with Jewish Guild he returned to the UK in November 1972 and signed for Watford. During four seasons at Vicarage Road he made over 70 first-team appearances, and earned a reputation as a hard-tackling midfielder or defender. Thereafter he enjoyed a lengthy career as a player and then coach in the Home Counties non-league scene.

Paul Crooks (Born: Durham, 12 October 1966. Died: Tremadog, Gwynedd, 5 July 2019.) Paul Crooks was a trainee with Bolton Wanderers before moving to North Wales where he played for Caernarfon Town before signing a 12-month contract with Stoke City in August 1986. He scored regularly for the Potters' reserve team but his first-team experience was limited to three appearances as a substitute. He then moved on to Rhyl and played for a number of Welsh League clubs as well as having a spell in Finland.

Ian Cumming (Born: Aberdeen, 12 September 1947. Died: Aberdeen, 17 December 2019.) Inside-forward Ian Cumming was mostly a reserve during a six-year spell with Aberdeen having joined them as a provisional signing in June 1963. He made five starts and one appearance from the bench for the Dons before moving into the Highland League with Inverness Thistle. He became a legendary figure with Thistle and went on to become player-manager in the summer of 1977. He later had a spell as manager of Elgin City from November 1982.

Jimmy Dainty (Born: Coleshill, Warwickshire, 21 January 1954. Died: Coleshill, 15 July 2019.) Winger Jimmy Dainty made a handful of appearances for Walsall as a teenager before moving to Dundalk where he enjoyed seven seasons of first-team football. He was a member of the Lilywhites' team that won a double of the League of Ireland and the FAI Cup in 1978–79 having previously won the League title in 1975–76 and the FAI Cup the following season. He was League of Ireland Player of the Year in 1975–76 and 1976–77. He later played for Worcester City, Sligo Rovers and Waterford before returning to settle in the West Midlands.

Tom Daley (Born: Grimsby, 15 November 1933. Died: Grimsby, 23 January 2020.) Goalkeeper Tom Daley was attached to Grimsby Town while still at school and went on to sign professional forms for the Mariners. He made his first-team debut as a 17-year-old in a local derby match at Lincoln City and made good progress in his early years at Blundell Park before National Service intervened. When he eventually returned he managed just one more senior appearance before moving on to Huddersfield Town, where he was principally a reserve, and then West Bromwich Albion, where he failed to make the first team. From the 1959–60 season he switched to Midland League football, signing for Peterborough United.

Cyril Davies (Born: Circa 1926. Died: Llay, Clwyd, 22 July 2019.) Cyril Davies was an inside-forward who was a member of the Llay United team that won the Welsh Amateur Cup in 1949. He subsequently played for several seasons with Marine in the Lancashire Combination before returning to North Wales, where he was connected with the Llay Welfare club for more than 50 years. He was capped for Wales Amateurs against Scotland in March 1951.

Reg Davies (Born: Tipton, 10 October 1933. Died: 23 September 2019.) Goalkeeper Reg Davies joined the groundstaff at West Bromwich Albion on leaving school and went on to sign professional forms on reaching the age of 17. He found it difficult to gain a first-team place at The Hawthorns and moved on to Walsall in the 1955 close season. He was best known for a five-year spell at Millwall from May 1958, where he was a first-team regular, and was a near ever-present in 1961–62 when the Fourth Division title was secured. In later spells with Leyton Orient and Port Vale he was rarely a first choice and retired having made over 300 senior appearances.

Tom Dawson (Born: Inverkeithing, Fife, 11 July 1939. Died: May 2020.) Tom Dawson was on the books of Rangers as a youngster but it was only after he moved on to Cowdenbeath in October 1961 that he featured in first-team football. A wing-half and later centre-half, he made over 150 appearances during a five-year stay at Central Park, including an outing as an emergency goalkeeper at Forfar Athletic in October 1963. He later switched to Junior football with Lochore Welfare.

Geoff Denial (Born: Stocksbridge, 31 January 1932. Died: 2020.) Geoff Denial started out as a goalkeeper in schoolboy football, later signing professional forms for Sheffield United as an outfield player. He made 10 first-team appearances for the Blades at wing-half, mostly in the 1952–53 season, before eventually moving on to Southern League club Headington United (later to become Oxford United). He captained the U's and was their leading scorer in the 1959–60 season when he also set a club record by scoring in seven consecutive games. He stayed at the Manor Ground through to their first season in the Football League, making a handful of appearances before leaving for Rugby Town.

George Dewar (Born: 1937. Died: Kirkcaldy, 17 December 2019.) George Dewar was one of the all-time greats for East Fife and holds the club's scoring record for the post-war period. A product of local football in Fife, he joined the Methil club in November 1960 after scoring prolifically for St Andrew's United and once he had settled into Scottish League football continued in similar vein. He was regularly the club's leading scorer and in November 1963 netted six times in an 8-0 win over Alloa Athletic. He eventually retired in 1970 having scored 196 goals from 336 competitive appearances for the club. His grandson Luis Appéré is currently on the books of Dundee United.

John Dillon (Born: Coatbridge, 9 November 1942. Died: August 2019.) John Dillon was a winger who joined the groundstaff at Sunderland on leaving school, signing a professional contract when he reached the age of 17. He made a number of first-team appearances during his stay at Roker Park, then had brief spells with Brighton & Hove Albion and Crewe Alexandra before returning to Scotland. He signed for Albion Rovers in July 1964 where he spent five seasons as a first-team regular, making over 150 appearances. He was a useful goalscorer and netted four goals in a memorable 8-2 win over local rivals Airdrieonians in a League Cup tie in September 1965. He concluded his senior career with brief spells at Queen of the South, Stranraer and Hamilton Academical.

Matt Doherty (Born: Pennyburn, Derry 1940. Died: 16 July 2019.) Matt Doherty was an inside-forward who played in the Irish League for Derry City and Glentoran. He was a member of the Derry team that won the Irish Cup in 1964 and the Irish League in 1964–65. He also won three caps for the Irish League representative side and appeared for an Irish FA XI against the British Army in March 1961.

Peter Downsborough (Born: Siddal, Halifax, 13 September 1943. Died: Stainland, Halifax, 26 September 2019.) Goalkeeper Peter Downsborough made over 700 senior appearances in a career that spanned almost 20 years. He made his League debut for Halifax Town at the age of 16 and signed professional forms when he turned 17. In the summer of 1965 he moved on to Swindon Town where he was a key member of the team that defeated Arsenal in extra time to win the League Cup in March 1969, and he was also an ever-present that season as the club won the Division Three title. The following season he played in both legs of the Anglo Italian Cup Winners' Cup final victory over Roma. He concluded his career at Bradford City, helping the team win promotion from the Fourth Division in 1976–77.

Dickie Dowsett (Born: Chelmsford, 3 July 1931. Died: 19 April 2020.) Centre-forward Dickie Dowsett scored on his debut for Tottenham Hotspur in a 4-2 win over Aston Villa on the opening day of the 1954–55 season, but this was his only first-team opportunity at White Hart Lane. After spells with Southend United and Southampton he joined Bournemouth during the 1957 close season where he enjoyed the best years of his career. He was top scorer for the Cherries in both 1957–58 and 1961–62 and left the club with an impressive record of 83 goals from 184 League and Cup appearances. He concluded his senior career at Crystal Palace and then helped Weymouth win the Southern League title in 1965–66 before returning to Dean Court as commercial manager (1968 to 1983).

Tony Dunne (Born: Dublin, 24 July 1941. Died: June 2020.) Full-back Tony Dunne first came to prominence with League of Ireland team Shelbourne, winning Amateur international honours for the Republic of Ireland and gaining an FAI Cup winners' medal in 1959–60. Shortly before the end of the season he signed for Manchester United and went on to become of the best defenders in the club's history. He became a fixture in the line-up after the enforced winter break of the 1962–63 campaign and over the next four seasons rarely missed a match. During his time at Old Trafford he won two League Championships (1964–65 and 1966–67), the FA Cup in 1963, and the European Cup in 1968. In total he played over 500 first-team games for United before moving on to Bolton Wanderers where he played a further five seasons, helping them win the Second Division title in 1977–78. He ended his playing days with a season in the NASL with Detroit Express.

Dennis Edwards (Born: Slough, 19 January 1937. Died: Portsmouth, 13 September 2019.) Dennis Edwards was a big centre- or inside-forward who played for Slough Town and Wycombe Wanderers as a teenager and went on to win England Amateur international honours, scoring a hat-trick on his debut against Northern Ireland. After turning professional with Charlton Athletic in February 1959 he enjoyed a successful career in senior football for around a decade. He made close on 200 first-team appearances for the Addicks and also had spells with Portsmouth and Aldershot.

Bernard Evans (Born: Chester, 4 January 1937. Died: 24 July 2019.) Bernard Evans came up through the ranks at Wrexham and made his debut as a 17-year-old, scoring after 25 seconds in the 2-1 win over Bradford City. He found the net regularly during his time at the Racecourse Ground, and also at Queens Park Rangers after his transfer in October 1960. He was second-top scorer for the R's in 1961–62, but then lost his place in the team and later played for Oxford United and Tranmere Rovers. The later stages of his career were affected by a knee injury that eventually led to his retirement from the game.

John Ferguson (Born: Edinburgh, 14 June 1939. Died: 16 February 2020.) John Ferguson attracted attention from a number of senior clubs as a teenaged winger with Junior club St Andrew's United and in November 1956 he signed for Oldham Athletic. He made just one first-team appearance for the Latics, lining up at Bradford City in April 1957. He was later Manchester City's chief scout in Scotland for 50 years.

Mike Ferguson (Born: Burnley, 9 March 1943. Died: 27 August 2019.) Mike Ferguson was on the groundstaff at Plymouth Argyle as a youngster but was released at the end of the 1959–60 season and returned to the North West, signing for Accrington Stanley. He was just 17 when he made his senior debut and still a teenager when the club dropped out of the League although he played over 50 first-team games; he scored the club's final goal in a 1-1 draw at Doncaster Rovers. He then moved on to Blackburn Rovers where he enjoyed the best years of his career, making just short of 250 League and Cup appearances. Aston Villa played a club record fee to sign him in May 1968 and in total he went on to make over 550 senior appearances in English football. He later had a spell as manager of Rochdale (September 1977 to November 1978).

Archie Finlay (Born: Dundee, 12 November 1939. Died: St Andrews, Fife, 22 October 2019.) Defender Archie Finlay was capped for Scotland Schools and developed in the Juniors with St Andrew's United before signing for Dunfermline Athletic in May 1958. He spent a season with the Pars without breaking into the first team but featured regularly in 1959–60 for East Fife before being released and returning to St Andrew's United where he played until the mid-1960s.

Jimmy Fleming (Born: Glasgow, 7 January 1929. Died: August 2019.) Defender Jimmy Fleming joined Stirling Albion from Juvenile club Tollcross Clydesdale. His early career at Annfield was disrupted by National Service and it was not until the 1952–53 season that he featured regularly, contributing to the club's success in winning the B Division title that season. He went on to sign for Bill Shankly at Workington and spent four seasons with the Cumbrian club before returning to Scotland to conclude his career with Berwick Rangers.

Duncan Forbes (Born: Edinburgh, 19 June 1941. Died: Norwich, 23 October 2019.) Centre-half Duncan Forbes signed for Colchester United from Junior club Musselburgh Athletic at the age of 20. He established himself in the Essex club's line-up towards the end of the 1961–62 season and thereafter rarely missed a game, helping them to promotion from the Fourth Division in 1965–66. He was sold to Norwich City shortly after the start of the 1968–69 campaign and went on to become a legend at Carrow Road, making over 350 appearances and featuring in the side that won the Division Two title in 1971–72 as well as in two League Cup finals. In total he spent 33 years attached to the club: 13 as a player, seven as a member of the commercial team, and 13 as a scout.

Tommy Forgan (Born: Middlesbrough, 12 October 1929. Died: Perth, Australia, 15 December 2019.) Goalkeeper Tommy Forgan signed for Hull City in 1949 but his early career was disrupted by a spell of National Service in the RAF. He made a number of first-team appearances for the Tigers in the 1953–54 season before signing for York City in the summer of 1954 where he went on to become arguably the Minstermen's greatest-ever keeper. In his first season the club reached the FA Cup semi-final, only losing out to Newcastle United in a replay. He made over 400 senior appearances during his stay at Bootham Crescent before switching to non-league football with Gainsborough Trinity.

Alex Forsyth (Born: Falkirk, 29 September 1928. Died: March 2020.) Alex Forsyth was an old-fashioned winger who began his career with Albion Rovers before manager Bob Gurney signed him for Darlington at the start of the 1952–53 campaign. After a 12-month spell he returned to Scotland in the summer of 1953, signing for East Stirlingshire where he went on to make almost 100 first-team appearances before retiring from football through injury at the age of 27. In the 1960s he returned to East Stirling as a scout and then became a director of the club before stepping down in November 2006.

Dave Fraser (Born: Newtongrange, Midlothian, 6 June 1937. Died: 2019.) Dave Fraser was a winger who was capped for Scotland Schoolboys and played in the Juveniles for Broughton Star and then for Junior outfit Arniston Rangers before signing for Hull City. He scored twice on his debut for the Tigers at Rotherham and netted six times from six appearances at the end of the 1955–56 campaign. Thereafter he received few first-team chances and it was a similar tale when he moved on to Mansfield Town for the 1958–59 campaign. He spent the following season with Third Lanark then enjoyed a successful spell at Cowdenbeath, where he scored 49 goals in 94 appearances, before returning to East Yorkshire to play for Bridlington Town.

John Freebairn (Born: Stirling, 1938. Died: April 2020.) John Freebairn was a talented goalkeeper and athlete who competed in the decathlon in the 1958 AAA championships when he finished fifth. He lost his amateur status as an athlete when he signed part-time forms for Partick Thistle in October 1958, going on to make over 100 appearances for the Jags. Later he played for Portadown, Cowdenbeath, Albion Rovers and Hamilton Academical. He managed to combine his football with athletics as a professional, competing in the various Highland Games for 25 years and taking part in a wide range of events from caber tossing to pole vault and long jump. He won three caps for Scotland Amateurs.

Jim Fryatt (Born: Swaythling, Hampshire, 2 September 1940. Died: Henderson, Nevada, USA, 5 June 2020.) Jim Fryatt enjoyed a successful career between 1957 and 1975, scoring a total of 208 goals from 534 League and Cup appearances. He rarely stayed at his clubs for any length of time, mostly moving around the lower divisions where his ability in the air and his goalscoring talents were much appreciated. He played for 10 Football League clubs in total including two separate spells at Southport where he gained promotion twice. He also led the scoring charts for Oldham Athletic in 1970–71 when they were promoted to Division Three. He is widely credited with scoring the fastest goal in a Football League match when he netted for Bradford Park Avenue against Tranmere Rovers in April 1964 after just four seconds. In January 1973 he netted a hat-trick in 10 minutes as Southport beat Darlington 7-0. He later played in the NASL for a number of clubs, notably Philadelphia Atoms.

Allan Gauden (Born: Ashington, 20 November 1944. Died: 29 April 2020.) Allan Gauden was a clever winger who joined Sunderland from local junior football and went on to make his First Division debut at Aston Villa in September 1966, becoming the first-ever player to appear for the Black Cats as a substitute in the Football League. He went on to spend four seasons with Darlington before signing for Lawrie McMenemy at Grimsby Town in February 1972, assisting in the Mariners' success in winning the Fourth Division title that season. He wound down his senior career with spells at Hartlepool and Gillingham, taking his total of Football League appearances to over 300 before switching to non-league football with Blyth Spartans.

Ken Gilliland (Born: 3 October 1935. Died: 19 January 2020.) Full-back Ken Gilliland made over 500 appearances during a 16-year spell with Linfield; in total he won 25 medals during his stay, including five Irish League titles and the Irish Cup on three occasions. He was a member of the 1961–62 'Seven Trophy' team which monopolised the domestic trophies. He won a single cap for Northern Ireland Amateurs and appeared for the Irish League representative side on a number of occasions.

Jimmy Goodfellow (Born: Sunderland, 16 September 1943. Died: Newport, Gwent, 22 April 2020.) Inside-forward Jimmy Goodfellow was a member of the Crook Town team that won the FA Amateur Cup final at Wembley in 1964 before moving on to Bishop Auckland and then becoming a professional with Port Vale in the summer of 1966. After three seasons at Vale Park he was released and signed for Workington where he spent a further four seasons, during which time he made over 200 first-team appearances, rarely missing a match. In January 1974 he was sold to Rotherham United and the following season he was a near ever-present in the team that won promotion from the Fourth Division. After a brief association with Stockport County he turned to coaching with Newport County and then Cardiff City, where he was manager from March to September 1984. He later worked on the backroom staff at a number of clubs including Plymouth Argyle, Sunderland and Cardiff.

Harry Gregg MBE, OBE (Born: Magherafelt, Co Derry, 27 October 1932. Died: Coleraine, 16 February 2020.) Goalkeeper Harry Gregg won representative honours for the Irish League team and Northern Ireland Amateurs while with Coleraine, earning him a move to Doncaster Rovers in October 1952. It took him until January 1956 to establish himself in the Rovers line-up and within two years his performances had attracted the attention of Manchester United who paid a then record fee for a goalkeeper to sign him. In February 1958 he was on the plane carrying United back from Belgrade which crashed in the snow and ice at Munich. Harry was one of the heroes of the tragedy, pulling several passengers to safety including a number of his colleagues. He was back playing at Old Trafford within a fortnight and won an FA Cup runners-up medal that season. In total he played over 200 Football League games for United, but was increasingly affected by injuries. He ended his playing career with a brief spell at Stoke City and later managed a number of clubs – Shrewsbury Town, Swansea City, Crewe Alexandra and Carlisle United. In total he won 25 caps for Northern Ireland, and was a member of the team that reached the quarter-finals of the World Cup in 1958.

Pat Groome (Born: Nottingham, 16 March 1934. Died: 29 January 2020.) Full-back Pat Groome signed for Notts County from local football and was just 17 when he made his first-team debut for the Magpies. His early career was interrupted by National Service, but he returned to Meadow Lane and went on to make 41 senior appearances. He left the club at the end of the 1957–58 season, signing for Skegness Town.

Geoff Hamm (Born: Woking, 19 September 1930. Died: 14 October 2019.) Geoff Hamm was on Arsenal's books as a youngster, appearing for their nursery club, Chase of Chertsey, and also the Gunners' 'A' team. In 1950 he signed for Woking and developed into a skilful and creative inside-forward who was one of the stars of amateur football in the late 1950s and early '60s. He won 19 England Amateur caps and was a member of the FA squad that toured West Africa in the summer of 1958. He also won FA Amateur Cup winners' medals with Woking (1958) and Wimbledon (1963).

Ivan Hampton (Born: Kimberley, Nottinghamshire, 15 October 1942. Died: 2 September 2019.) Ivan Hampton developed in local junior football and joined Notts County as a centre-forward, signing professional forms towards the end of the 1959–60 season. It was not until 1962–63 that he began to establish himself as a regular in the line-up at Meadow Lane, featuring at full-back, and he went on to make over 150 appearances for the Magpies. He then enjoyed two decent seasons with Halifax Town before concluding his career with spells at Peterborough United and Matlock Town

Alan Harrington (Born: Penarth, 17 November 1933. Died: December 2019.) Alan Harrington was a wing-half who spent his entire career with Cardiff City for whom he made over 350 senior appearances. He broke into the first team at the beginning of 1953 and was a regular from 1954–55 onwards. He contributed to the Bluebirds' 1959–60 promotion campaign back into the top flight and remained at Ninian Park until the summer of 1966. He later had a spell as manager of Barry Town. He won 11 full caps for Wales.

Lol Harvey (Born: Loscoe, Derbyshire, 25 July 1934. Died: 24 April 2020.) Wing-half Lol Harvey was spotted in schoolboy football and came to Coventry City as a 15-year-old. After playing for the club's nursery side Modern Machine Tools he signed professional terms at the age of 17. He eventually established himself in the line-up in the 1954–55 season and was a key member of the team that won promotion from Division Four in 1958–59 when he missed just five games. A knee injury brought his career to a premature end in January 1961.

Martin Harvey (Born: Belfast, 19 September 1941. Died: 25 November 2019.) Martin Harvey won international honours for Northern Ireland Schools and joined Sunderland at the age of 16. He progressed to a professional contract at the age of 17 but it was not until the 1963–64 campaign that he established himself in the line-up at Roker Park. He made a useful contribution to the club's promotion that season and remained a regular choice for the next nine seasons, making over 300 first-team appearances at wing-half before injuries led to his retirement as a player. He stayed on at Sunderland on the coaching staff and enjoyed a successful career in that field serving, among others, Plymouth Argyle, Raith Rovers and Millwall, as well as having a spell as manager of Carlisle United (February to September 1980). He won 34 full caps for Northern Ireland.

John Haselden (Born: Doncaster, 3 August 1943. Died: March 2020.) John Haselden spent six seasons on the books of Rotherham United after signing for them in February 1962, but never firmly established himself in the side in any one position despite making over 100 appearances during his stay. He fared better when he joined South Yorkshire rivals Doncaster Rovers where he soon took over the number 6 shirt, making a significant contribution in his first season, 1968–69, when the Fourth Division title was secured. After retiring as a player in the summer of 1974 he turned to coaching with Mansfield Town and then Huddersfield Town (where he was manager from April to September of 1977), and later worked as a physio for a number of clubs including Reading and Nottingham Forest.

Sean Haslegrave (Born: Blurton, Stoke on Trent, 7 June 1951. Died: Preston, 22 November 2019.) Sean Haslegrave was a combative central-midfield player who began his career playing in the First Division with Stoke City. He went on to enjoy a successful career in the game, making over 600 senior appearances over two decades as a player. He won promotion with both Preston North End (1977–78) and York City (1983–84) before returning to Deepdale to work in the academy set-up. Later he coached the England Colleges team along with Gordon Staniforth.

Sam Hastings (Born: Kelloholm, Dumfriesshire, 18 February 1940. Died: 6 April 2020.) Tricky winger Sam Hastings was just 17 when he made his first-team debut for Hamilton Academical. In a seven-year stay at Douglas Park he made over 200

senior appearances scoring 84 goals before joining newly promoted Clyde for the start of the 1964–65 campaign. Here too he was a first-team regular, playing close on 300 games before concluding his career with brief spells at Alloa Athletic and Queen of the South.

Ray Hiron (Born: Gosport, 22 July 1943. Died: Fareham, 5 April 2020.) Ray Hiron was a tall, lanky centre-forward who first came to prominence when he scored the winner for Fareham Town as they knocked Hendon out of the FA Amateur Cup in January 1964. The following summer he signed professional forms for Portsmouth and became an established first-team player at Fratton Park towards the end of the 1965–66 campaign. He was Pompey's leading scorer three seasons in a row starting with 1968–69, and scored a total of 117 goals from over 350 appearances for the club. He later spent three seasons with Reading, dropping back to play as a central defender and occasional sweeper in the closing stages of his career.

Noel Hodgson (Born: Workington, 25 December 1938. Died: 23 March 2020.) Noel Hodgson was a talented rugby union player as a schoolboy and appeared at full-back in a trial for the England Schools team. However, he developed his career in soccer, signing as a part-time professional for Workington in August 1957. He spent six years on the club's books as an outside-right and although mostly a reserve he made over 50 first-team appearances during his stay. He later spent several years with Netherfield, helping them win the Lancashire Combination title in 1964–65.

Billy Hughes (Born: Coatbridge, 30 December 1948. Died: Derby, 20 December 2019.) Billy Hughes was an outside-left who joined Sunderland on leaving school and went on to become a member of the team that won the FA Youth Cup in 1966–67. After establishing himself in the Black Cats' line-up he went on to make over 300 first-team appearances, gaining an FA Cup winners' medal in 1973 when they defeated Leeds United in the final. He subsequently concluded his career with spells at Derby County and Leicester City. He was the brother of John Hughes (Celtic) and Pat Hughes (Darlington and St Mirren). He won a single cap for Scotland, appearing against Sweden in April 1975.

Ron Hughes (Born: Mold, Flintshire, 1 July 1930. Died: Wrexham, 30 July 2019.) Defender Ron Hughes signed amateur forms for Chester as a teenager, although it was not until September 1950 that he became a professional. He stayed on the books at Sealand Road for more than a decade, make a total of 399 Football League appearances, the second highest of any player in the club's history. A regular in the line-up for nine seasons, he was released on a free transfer in the summer of 1962 and signed for Oswestry Town.

Norman Hunter (Born: Eighton Banks, Co Durham, 29 October 1943. Died: 17 April 2020.) Defender Norman Hunter was one of the all-time greats for Leeds United and spent 15 years as a professional at Elland Road during the most successful time in the club's history. He was ever present in the team that won the Second Division title in 1963–64 and went on to win two Football League titles (1968–69 and 1973–74), as well as the FA Cup, Football League Cup and two Inter Cities Fairs Cups during his time at Elland Road. Renowned for his uncompromising style of play and ferocity in the tackle, he was also a very able footballer and was capped 28 times for England, as well as being the first winner of the PFA Player of the Year Award in 1974. He subsequently spent three years with Bristol City, then a top-flight club, before joining Barnsley as a player and then manager. He also had a spell as manager of Rotherham United.

Alex Jackson (Born: Glasgow, 28 November 1935. Died: 9 May 2020.) Centre-forward Alex Jackson made his name with Shettleston Juniors and was a Junior internationalist before heading south to sign for Birmingham City in April 1958. He had a successful run for the Blues in December 1957, scoring six goals in a run of four matches, but otherwise had few opportunities during his time at St Andrew's. He fared better on moving to Plymouth Argyle and had built a useful scoring record before suffering a broken leg in an FA Cup tie at West Bromwich Albion in January 1963. He made a brief return to first-team football the following season before joining Southern League club Weymouth. Later he had a spell as commercial manager of Torquay United.

Brian Jackson (Born: Walton on Thames, 1 April 1933. Died: 14 February 2020.) Brian Jackson was a winger who won international honours for England Schools and was playing regular first-team football for Leyton Orient as a 17-year-old. His form attracted attention from bigger clubs and in November 1951 he was sold to Liverpool. He scored on his Anfield debut against Bolton Wanderers and went on to make over 100 first-team appearances during his stay. Next stop in his career was Port Vale, where he was a regular in the team that won the Fourth Division title in 1958–59, and he went on to play for Peterborough United and Lincoln City, bringing his total of senior appearances beyond the 400-mark.

Freddie Jardine (Born: Edinburgh, 27 September 1941. Died: Luton, 7 October 2019.) Winger Freddie Jardine was a product of Edinburgh Juvenile club Edina Hearts, stepping up to the seniors as a 16-year-old when he signed for Dundee. A move south to Luton Town proved beneficial and after he established himself in the side in 1964–65 he went on to make over 200 appearances for the Hatters, missing just a single match in 1967–68 when the Fourth Division title was won. He later concluded his career with Torquay United.

Alan Jarvis (Born: Wrexham, 4 August 1943. Died: December 2019.) Wing-half Alan Jarvis joined Everton on leaving school and won representative honours for Wales Youth and Amateur teams as well as captaining the Central League side during his time at Goodison. He was released on a free transfer in the summer of 1964 and later enjoyed a successful seven-year spell with Hull City, helping them to promotion from the Third Division in 1965–66. He won three full caps for Wales before eventually moving on to Mansfield Town for a then record fee for the Stags. His career was ended prematurely by an eye injury.

Dale Jasper (Born: Croydon, 14 January 1964. Died: 30 January 2020.) Dale Jasper was a creative midfield player with excellent passing skills who developed in the Chelsea youth set-up before signing professional forms at the age of 18. He made a handful of first-team appearances at Stamford Bridge then spent two seasons with Brighton & Hove Albion, before moving on to sign for Crewe Alexandra in July 1988. He enjoyed the best years of his career at Gresty Road where he made over 100 first-team appearances and featured regularly in the team that won the Division Four title in 1988–89. He subsequently returned to Sussex, signing for Crawley Town, then members of the Southern League.

Rod Johnson (Born: Leeds, 8 January 1945. Died: December 2019.) Rod Johnson was a versatile forward who initially joined Leeds United on amateur forms, winning England Youth international honours and turning professional when he reached 17. He was carried off on a stretcher on his first-team debut at Swansea Town and was subsequently unable to win a regular place during five seasons at Elland Road. He fared much better when he dropped down to the lower divisions and won promotions with both Doncaster Rovers (1968–69) and Bradford City (1976–77), and also had a four-year spell at Rotherham United. In total he made 431 Football League appearances before joining Northern Premier League club Gainsborough Trinity.

Ken Jones (Born: Merthyr Tydfil, 11 October 1931. Died: 27 September 2019.) Ken Jones was a journalist who worked for Hayters Agency before joining the *Daily Mirror*. He was regarded as one of the finest writers of his era and subsequently worked for the *Sunday Mirror*, *Observer* and *Independent*. He was chairman of the Football Writers Association between 1975 and 1978. Ken was from a footballing family: his father Emlyn Jones had played for Southend United while uncles Bryn and Ivor won international honours for Wales, as did his cousin Cliff Jones.

Jim Keers (Born: Stanley, Co Durham, 10 December 1931. Died: April 2020.) Jim Keers was an outside-right who signed for Darlington from Northern League club Evenwood Town in March 1952. He went straight into the Quakers' first team, scoring on his debut at Barrow, and in three seasons at Feethams he made over 70 appearances. He later returned to non-league football, signing for Annfield Plain.

Albert Keetley (Born: Nottingham, 22 February 1930. Died: October 2019.) Full-back Albert Keetley was on the books of Nottingham Forest as a youngster and won international honours for the England NABC team. He signed as a professional for Bury towards the end of the 1949–50 season, but was principally a reserve during his time with the Shakers. He enjoyed plenty of first-team football with Bournemouth, where he was a regular in the line-up in 1953–54, and went on to play almost 100 games during his stay at Dean Court. He later had a spell at Weymouth and coached with Bradford City and Exeter City.

Doug Kelly (Born: Worsbrough, Barnsley, 30 May 1934. Died: August 2019.) Centre-forward Doug Kelly was a prolific scorer for Barnsley's junior teams and was just 18 when he made his first-team debut, scoring in a 3-2 home defeat to Everton. He never really established himself at Oakwell, but after dropping down a division to play for Bradford City he enjoyed a good run of first-team football. He concluded his senior career at Chesterfield before signing for Dodworth Colliery on their entry to the Yorkshire League for the 1958–59 season.

Ray Keogh (Died: Dublin, 26 August 2019.) Ray Keogh was a traditional-style outside-right who is believed to be the first black player to have appeared in the League of Ireland. He enjoyed a lengthy and successful career on both sides of the Irish border, turning out for Shamrock Rovers, Longford Town, Drumcondra, Ards, Portadown, Cork Hibs, and Drogheda. His best years were spent at Drumcondra (1960–1964) where he was a member of the team that won the League of Ireland title in 1960–61. He gained representative honours for both the Irish League and the League of Ireland.

Shay Keogh (Born: Dublin, 6 September 1934. Died: Rathfarnham, Dublin, 13 April 2020.) Centre-half Shay Keogh was a key figure in the successful Shamrock Rovers team of the 1950s with whom he won three League of Ireland titles as well as captaining the side that defeated Drumcondra to win the FAI Cup in 1955. He later played for Dundalk and St Patrick's Athletic. He won one full cap for the Republic of Ireland, featuring against Poland in October 1958, and also won representative honours for the Republic of Ireland B team and the League of Ireland.

Dudley Kernick (Born: Boscastle, Cornwall, 29 August 1921. Died: Solihull, 15 December 2019.) Dudley Kernick was a wing-half or inside-forward who was playing in Cornish junior football for Tintagel when given a trial by Torquay United in November 1938. He signed professional forms for the Gulls shortly afterwards and featured in the club's reserve team for the remainder of the 1938–39 season. He moved to live in Birmingham during the war and 'guested' for a number of clubs including Birmingham, Charlton Athletic, Walsall and Exeter City. When peacetime football resumed he returned to Plainmoor where he was a regular in the first post-war season. He subsequently had brief spells on the books of both Northampton Town and Birmingham City before switching to non-league football.

Martyn King (Born: Birmingham, 23 August 1937. Died: 25 December 2019.) Martyn King appeared for the FA Schools' XI against Scotland Schools in April 1956, then went on to Oxford University where he won his Varsity 'Blue'. He played for both Pegasus and Colchester United as an amateur before turning professional with the U's in September 1958. A prolific centre-forward, he formed a productive striking partnership with Bobby Hunt and the pair netted 68 goals between them in 1961–62 when promotion from the Fourth Division was secured. He established an all-time record of 130 Football League goals for the U's before moving to Wrexham and later played in the Welsh League North for Porthmadog before an injury led to his retirement from the game.

John Kirkwood (Born: Falkirk, 27 February 1932. Died: 8 December 2019.) Goalkeeper John Kirkwood joined Reading as a teenager from Junior club Blairhall Colliery and spent six years at Elm Park, partly disrupted by a period of National Service, featuring fairly regularly in the first team in 1952–53 and 1953–54. He subsequently played for several seasons in the Southern League, notably with Worcester City (1957–1962) for whom he was a member of the team that knocked Liverpool out of the FA Cup in January 1959.

Harry Knowles (Born: Hednesford, Staffordshire, 6 September 1932. Died: Truro, 20 January 2020.) Harry Knowles started his career as an outside-left, signing professional forms for Walsall at the age of 18 and going straight into the first team. He made 10 first-team appearances in two seasons at Fellows Park but was then given a free transfer and drifted into non-league soccer with Stourbridge. Spells with Kidderminster Harriers and Oswestry Town followed before he moved to Worcester City in the summer of 1956. Now transformed into a bustling centre-forward and a more than useful goalscorer, he starred in the FA Cup win over Liverpool in January 1959, the winning goal resulting from his cross. Soon afterwards he was sold to Cardiff City, but made just a handful of first-team appearances before returning to Worcester.

Denis Laughton (Born: Dingwall, 22 January 1948. Died: May 2020.) Defender Denis Laughton made his name playing in the Highland League for Ross County before being sold to Morton shortly after the start of the 1967–68 season. He did well during his stay at Cappielow where he played exactly 100 League and Cup games, and after impressing in a Texaco Cup game against Newcastle United he signed for the Magpies in October 1973. He was principally a reserve at St James' Park, playing as a sweeper or defensive midfielder. He featured in the second leg of the Texaco Cup final against Southampton in December 1974 but shortly afterwards suffered a bad ankle injury and this effectively ended his career.

Cyril Lawrence (Born: Ordsall, Lancashire, 12 June 1920. Died: Farnworth, Lancashire, 14 April 2020.) Inside-forward Cyril Lawrence was on Blackpool's books before the war and had progressed to the reserve team at the start of the 1939–40 season before football was suspended. He served in the Royal Navy during the hostilities, making two appearances for the Seasiders in the emergency competitions. When peacetime football resumed he returned to Bloomfield Road but was unable to break into the first team. In April 1947 he signed for Rochdale by which time he was playing at outside-right but he was never a regular at Spotland. He concluded his senior career at Wrexham before injury ended his career, just short of 100 senior appearances.

Davy Lawther (Died: 9 October 2019.) Davy Lawther was a versatile forward who played in the Irish League throughout the 1950s, turning out for a string of clubs including Bangor, Ards, Distillery, Cliftonville and Coleraine. He won an Irish Cup winners' medal for Ards in 1951–52 and an Irish League championship medal with the same club in 1957–58. He was capped six times for Northern Ireland Amateurs between 1955 and 1959.

Harold Lea (Born: Wigan, 14 September 1931. Died: Wigan, 16 April 2020.) Goalkeeper Harold Lea played for Horwich RMI and Wigan Athletic before signing as a part-time professional for Stockport County in May 1958. He was first-choice keeper at Edgeley Park in 1959–60 and 1960–61 and made 131 first-team appearances in total before leaving at the end of the 1963–64 season.

Billy Livingstone (Born: Kirkcaldy, 9 June 1936. Died: Kirkcaldy, 8 August 2019.) Billy Livingstone was a talented schoolboy footballer who represented Scotland Schoolboys three seasons in a row. He signed for Hibernian as a 15-year-old but failed to appear in the first team, with his only senior experience coming in 1952–53 when he was loaned out to C Division club Leith Athletic, for whom he made a handful of appearances. He later had spells with a number of clubs including Raith Rovers and St Johnstone but played no further first-team games.

John Lowey (Born: Manchester, 7 March 1958. Died: Brisbane, Australia, 5 August 2019.) John Lowey was a hard-working attacking player who signed as an associate schoolboy for Manchester United in September 1972. He progressed to a professional contract at Old Trafford at the age of 17, but 12 months later moved to the United States to play for Chicago Sting. On his return he eventually established himself at Sheffield Wednesday then moved on to Blackburn Rovers in November 1980. By this time he had become a goalscoring midfield player and he went on to make over 150 first-team appearances during his time at Ewood Park, before concluding his career with brief spells at Wigan Athletic, Preston North End and Chester City.

Dave Lyon (Born: Oldham, 21 November 1948. Died: 19 December 2019.) Dave Lyon was an inside-forward who was an apprentice with Bolton Wanderers and then played for a number of North West teams, including two spells with Macclesfield Town. He was a member of the Silkmen's team which won the inaugural FA Trophy final defeating Telford United 2-0 at Wembley in 1970, scoring his team's first goal. He was 27 when he finally made his Football League debut for Southport for whom he made 14 appearances in their penultimate season as League members. He later had a brief spell with Santa Barbara Condors in the ASL before continuing his career with Runcorn.

Peter McCall (Born: West Ham, 11 September 1936. Died: 9 February 2020.) Peter McCall was a cultured wing-half who joined Bristol City as a teenager and after suffering a broken ankle in an early appearance with the colts team he recovered to make his first-team debut in April 1958. In May 1962 he was transferred to Oldham Athletic where he was an ever-present in the team that won promotion from the Fourth Division in 1962–63. He went on to make over 100 appearances for the

Latics before returning to the West Country and signing for Hereford United, then members of the Southern League. After retiring from football he later took up bowls with some success. He represented the England international EBA team between 1984 and 1987 and also won the EBA national invitation singles title in 1984.

Danny McCarthy (Born: Abergavenny, 26 September 1942. Died: July 2019.) Danny McCarthy was a winger who came to prominence as a member of the successful Abergavenny Thursdays team that won the Welsh League in 1959–60. In July 1960 he signed professional forms for Cardiff City and stayed two seasons at Ninian Park, making nine first-team appearances. He subsequently returned to non-league football joining Merthyr Tydfil of the Southern League.

Peter McConnell (Born: Reddish, Stockport, 3 March 1937. Died: Leeds, 28 July 2019.) Peter McConnell joined Leeds United as an amateur on leaving school, signing professional forms when he reached the age of 17. An inside-forward or wing-half, he had to wait until December 1958 for his first-team debut and was just establishing himself in the side when Don Revie took over as manager. He moved on to Carlisle United in August 1962 and spent seven successful seasons at Brunton Park, captaining the side to successive promotions in 1963–64 and 1964–65 and making over 300 League and Cup appearances. Later he was with Bradford City before concluding his career with a season as player-manager of Scarborough.

Ian MacFarlane (Born: Lanark, 26 January 1933. Died: 17 June 2019.) Full-back Ian MacFarlane signed for Aberdeen in May 1954 but he was mostly a reserve during his time at Pittodrie, making just a dozen first-team appearances. He then moved south to sign for Chelsea in August 1956 and featured regularly for the Blues in his first season at Stamford Bridge before he moved on to Leicester City, linking up with former Dons manager David Halliday. He subsequently signed for Bath City where he went on to make more than 300 appearances and was a member of the team that won the Southern League title in 1959–60. After retiring as a player he embarked on a lengthy career as a coach, serving a number of clubs and he also had a spell as manager of Carlisle United (January 1970 to May 1972).

Jimmy McGhee (Born: Motherwell, 21 August 1930. Died: October 2019.) Jimmy McGhee was a centre-forward or winger who signed for Kilmarnock shortly after the start of the 1948–49 season. He scored twice on his senior debut against Alloa Athletic but was then required to undergo National Service, putting his career on hold. He was one of a number of Scots signed by manager Bob Gurney for Darlington for 1952–53, and went on to play for Barry Town, Newport County, Morton and Ballymena United, where he was a member of the team that won the Irish Cup in 1957–58.

Duncan MacKay (Born 14 July 1937. Died: Australia, 23 December 2019.) Duncan MacKay was an attacking full-back who signed for Celtic in April 1955. By the end of the 1958–59 season he was a first-team regular at Parkhead and had made his international debut against England. He captained the team that lost to Dunfermline Athletic in the Scottish Cup final of 1961 but otherwise had little to show in terms of domestic honours during his time at Parkhead. He moved on to Third Lanark shortly before Jock Stein returned to Celtic and then emigrated to Australia where he spent much of the remainder of his life. He won a total of 14 caps for Scotland.

George McLean (Born: Paisley, 16 September 1937. Died: 29 June 2019.) George McLean was a centre-forward who began his senior career with Rangers, breaking into the first team during 1960–61 when his contribution to the club's success in winning the Scottish League title that season included two goals in the 3-1 home win over Hearts. In March 1962 he moved south to sign for Norwich City, but he stayed only briefly at Carrow Road and made no first-team appearances. He did much better when signing for Grimsby Town, finding the net regularly and finishing as the Mariners' top scorer in 1962–63 and 1964–65. Thereafter he moved around, turning out for Exeter City, Workington and Barrow and taking his final Football League record to 77 goals from 218 appearances.

George McMillan (Born: Motherwell, 15 March 1930. Died: Peterborough, 25 December 2019.) George McMillan was an outside-left who progressed from Bridgeton Waverley to sign for Aberdeen but soon after his first-team debut he suffered a broken neck in his daytime job as an electrician. He recovered to sign for Wrexham, but his time at the Racecourse Ground was affected by injuries too, and he made just a single appearance. He returned to Scotland to make a useful contribution to the Brechin City team that won the Division C (North & East) title in 1953–54 and later spent a season with Montrose.

Maurice McVeigh (Born: Belfast, September 1928. Died: Antrim, 28 December 2019.) Maurice McVeigh was a skilful outside-left who spent more than a decade with Irish League club Glenavon. He was a member of the team that won the Irish League championship in 1951–52, making them the first team outside of Belfast to take the title. Chosen as Ulster Footballer of the Year in 1954–55, he won a second league title with Glenavon in 1956–57, as well as two Irish Cups (1957 and 1959). He featured regularly at Amateur international level between 1949 and 1957 and also played for the Irish League representative team against the Football League in October 1954.

Peter Madden (Born: Bradford, 31 October 1934. Died: April 2020.) Peter Madden was a big, powerful centre-half with a no-nonsense approach who signed for Rotherham United in October 1955. He won a regular place in the line-up from the start of the 1957–58 season and went on to make over 350 League and Cup appearances during his stay, featuring in both legs of the 1960–61 Football League Cup final when the Millers lost to Aston Villa. After winding down his career with spells at Bradford Park Avenue and Aldershot he was appointed player-manager of Midland League club Skegness Town in August 1970. He stayed two years before joining the backroom staff at Rochdale where he went on to become manager (August 1975 to October 1978). He also had a spell as manager of Darlington from January 1979 to March 1983.

Arthur Marsh (Born: Rowley Regis, West Midlands, 4 May 1947. Died: Bedfordshire, 31 March 2020.) Defender Arthur Marsh joined Bolton Wanderers as an apprentice on leaving school and after progressing to a professional contract he made his senior debut at Preston North End in February 1967. He was mostly a reserve during a six-year stay at Burnden Park, with the exception of 1969–70 when he featured regularly in the left-half position. He later had a three-year spell with Rochdale, where he made just short of 100 appearances, before concluding his career with a season at Darlington.

Dave Marshall (Born: Circa 1928. Died: Gateshead, 23 March 2020.) Dave Marshall was a right-back who was a member of the great Bishop Auckland team of the 1950s. He played in five FA Amateur Cup finals, gaining three winners' medals (1955, 1956 and 1957) and also won two caps for England Amateurs. Outside of football he was a school teacher whose former pupils included Paul Gascoigne.

Mike Marshall (Born: Buckhaven, Fife, 15 August 1942. Died: May 2020.) Mike Marshall was a winger who stepped up to the senior ranks with Alloa Athletic in the summer of 1965, having previously played for Glenrothes Juniors. He made 150 first-team appearances during two spells with the Wasps and in between spent a couple of seasons in the First Division with Falkirk. He later coached East Fife and Falkirk and had a brief spell as manager of the Methil club.

Allan Mason (Born: Hamilton, 25 July 1962. Died: April 2020.) Full-back Allan Mason featured as a trialist with both Clyde and East Stirlingshire from Blantyre Celtic in the early part of the 1985–86 season before joining the Firs Park club and making a number of appearances. Towards the end of the season he briefly returned to Clyde before spending the 1986–87 campaign back with East Stirling. He played a total of 47 League and Cup games before leaving senior football.

Joe Mason (Born: Kilmarnock, 17 August 1940. Died: Irvine, Ayrshire, 26 September 2019.) Centre-forward Joe Mason was playing in Ayrshire Junior football with Lugar Boswell Thistle when he signed for Kilmarnock at the age of 20. He scored regularly when selected for Killie, including a hat-trick in a 5-0 win at Clyde in November 1962, but played only a minor role in the team that won the Scottish League title in 1964–65. He later switched to Morton, helping the club to win the Scottish Second Division title in his first season with them. In that season (1966–67) he scored 34 goals in 36 League games and in total netted 43 League and Cup goals in 47 appearances. He signed for Rangers at the age of 32 but quickly switched to the backroom staff and during a decade at Ibrox he was involved in two treble-winning seasons as a coach.

Danny Masterton (Born: Ayr, 5 September 1954. Died: Falkirk, 5 January 2020.) Danny Masterton was a big, swashbuckling striker who joined Ayr United from Muirkirk Juniors in August 1975. He proved an effective attacking force for the Honest Men but did even better when he moved to Clyde for the 1980–81 season. He topped the club scoring charts in each of his first three seasons at Shawfield and his 23 goals in 1981–82 not only provided a major contribution to the club's success in winning the Second Division title, but also made him the Scottish League's leading scorer for the season. He began the 1984–85 campaign with Queen of the South but suffered an achilles injury early in the season which effectively ended his career.

Frank Mathews (Born: London, 7 January 1948. Died: December 2019.) Full-back Frank Mathews was an apprentice with Southend United before signing professional forms at the age of 18, but in two-and-a-half seasons at Roots Hall and a further season at Torquay United he was only a back-up player, deputising for injuries and unavailability. He had a trial with Reading in the summer of 1969 before leaving senior football.

Johnny Matthews (Born: Meriden, Warwickshire, 27 August 1946. Died: 25 December 2019.) Outside-left Johnny Matthews signed for Coventry City at the beginning of the 1964–65 season. He occasionally featured in the reserve team at Highfield Road but after recovering from a cartilage operation he moved on to Waterford in March 1966 and went on to become one of the leading scorers in League of Ireland football, netting more than 150 goals. He won five League titles with Waterford, and a further title with Limerick United. He also played three times for the League of Ireland representative team, scoring with a penalty in the 2-1 defeat by the Football League at Lansdowne Road in September 1971. He was the son of Horace Matthews, who played for Coventry in the 1945–46 season.

Baron Mawhinney of Peterborough (Born: Belfast, 26 July 1940. Died: 9 November 2019.) After a career as a Conservative MP and Cabinet Minister, Brian Mawhinney went on to serve as chairman of the Football League between January 2003 and March 2010 during which time he oversaw a series of significant changes. These included the reorganisation of the League structure and the introduction of the current divisional titles (Championship, League One and League Two), and a substantial programme of governance reforms that included the introduction of football's first 'Fit and Proper Person' test, sanctions for insolvent clubs, the publications of clubs' spending on agents' fees, and the monitoring of their tax affairs. He also oversaw the formation of the Football League Trust.

Kelvin Maynard (Born: Paramaribo, Surinam, 29 May 1987. Died: Amsterdam, Netherlands, 18 September 2019.) Kelvin Maynard was a right-back who had played in the Netherlands, Hungary and Belgium before signing for Burton Albion as a free agent during the 2014–15 season. He featured for Albion on a number of occasions as they went on to win the League Two title that season, but then suffered a serious injury in a pre-season match the following summer which ruled him out of the whole of the 2015–16 campaign. He subsequently returned to the Netherlands. His early death came when he was shot while driving his car in Amsterdam.

Christian Mbulu (Born: Newham, London, 6 August 1996. Died: Cottam, Lancashire, 26 May 2020.) Christian Mbulu was a defender who progressed from non-league football to a professional contract with Millwall in August 2015. He spent three seasons with the Lions without breaking into the first team and then spent the 2018–19 campaign with Motherwell. He made six appearances during his stay and also featured for the U20s in the Scottish League Challenge Cup. After trials with a number of clubs over the summer of 2019 he signed a short-term deal with Crewe Alexandra in October 2019 and added to his experience of senior football both here and at Morecambe, for whom he signed during the January transfer window.

Colin Meldrum (Born: Glasgow, 26 November 1941. Died: Fleetwood, 4 October 2019.) Colin Meldrum was a powerful defender who was on the books at Arsenal as a youngster before moving on to Watford midway through the 1960–61 season, but it was not until he signed for Reading that he played regularly in the first team. He made over 300 appearances during his stay at Elm Park and was twice voted as the club's Player of the Season. Later he played for Cambridge United where he had the distinction of scoring the club's first-ever goal in the Football League. After his playing career ended he was involved in coaching and management at a number of clubs including York City and Workington, where he was player-manager from December 1974 to April 1975.

Brett Mellor (Born: Huddersfield, 4 February 1960. Died: 11 July 2019.) Brett Mellor was a centre-half who came up through the ranks with Huddersfield Town, signing professional forms in February 1978. His only first-team appearance for the Terriers came shortly afterwards when he lined up for the home game with York City. He stayed at Leeds Road until the summer of 1980 and spent the following season at Barnsley, but was unable to add to his senior experience during his stay. He subsequently played in local football in the Huddersfield area.

Denis Miles (Born: Normanton, West Yorkshire, 6 August 1936. Died: 8 December 2019.) Denis Miles was a speedy winger who joined Bradford Park Avenue in September 1953 from West Yorkshire League outfit Snydale Athletic. He made his first-team debut in an FA Cup tie against Selby Town shortly afterwards and played a number of games in the 1954–55 season before moving to Southport in a player-exchange deal. His opportunities at Haig Avenue were restricted by his National Service commitments, but he made a total of 52 appearances during his time with the club before switching to non-league Boston United.

Sam Millar (Born: 2 January 1953. Died: 13 September 2019.) Sam Millar was a wing-half and occasional centre-forward who made over 150 appearances for Clyde between 1970 and 1976. The highlight of his career came when he helped the club win the Second Division title in 1972–73, scoring the winner in the penultimate fixture away to Clydebank which clinched the title. He later switched to Junior football, turning out for a number of clubs including Petershill (where he captained the team that reached the Scottish Junior Cup final in 1985), Shotts Bon Accord and Lesmahagow.

Kenny Mitchell (Born: Sunderland, 26 May 1957. Died: 4 September 2019.) Kenny Mitchell was a versatile player who was in Newcastle United's reserve team as a 16-year-old. He spent six years as a professional at St James' Park with his best season coming in 1978–79 when he featured in over half of the club's Second Division fixtures. After a season at Darlington he moved into non-league football with Workington then played for a number of clubs in Finland including Kuusysi Lahti for whom he featured in the European Cup.

Tommy Moffatt (Born: 30 September 1935. Died: Belfast, 24 December 2019.) Tommy Moffatt was a goalkeeper who enjoyed a successful career in Irish League football with Cliftonville, Ards and Linfield, separated by a three-year spell in South Africa. He was capped by Northern Ireland Amateurs against England in September 1956 and also appeared for the Irish League representative side.

Ricky Moir (Born Glasgow, 22 October 1945. Died: April 2020.) Ricky Moir was on Rangers' books as a youngster without making the grade and was then reinstated as a Junior player. He signed for Greenock Juniors and then Cumnock, where he was the star of their run to the quarter-finals of the Scottish Junior Cup in 1968–69. In March 1969 he moved south, joining the senior ranks with Shrewsbury Town and established himself in the line-up from the start of the following season. A hard-tackling and combative midfield player, he went on to make 165 Football League appearances for the Shrews then spent the 1974–75 campaign with Halifax Town before his career was ended by a hip injury.

Fred Molyneux (Born: Wallasey, 25 July 1944. Died: 1 October 2019.) Centre-half Fred Molyneux joined Liverpool on leaving school but he was unable to break into the first team in three years at Anfield. He signed for Southport shortly after the start of the 1965–66 campaign and went straight into the first-team line-up, retaining his place throughout the season. He featured for the Sandgrounders in 1966–67, although injury restricted his appearances, and the following season he was the club's Player of the Year. After a couple of seasons at Plymouth he returned to Merseyside, signing for Tranmere Rovers and then Southport once more, taking his career total of senior appearances to close on 350.

Mick Monaghan (Born: 28 June 1963. Died: January 2020.) Mick Monaghan was a goalkeeper best known for his four-year spell with Queen's Park between 1987 and 1991 when he made 138 appearances. Thereafter he moved around playing for Hamilton Academical, Dumbarton, Stirling Albion and Alloa Athletic although he never really established himself at any of these clubs. His career ended back at Queen's Park in the early part of the 1998–99 season.

Mick Morris (Born: Plaistow, 20 January 1943. Died: Stone, Staffordshire, 15 March 2020.) Mick Morris was a winger who joined Oxford United from Faversham in the summer of 1964 and in his first season at the Manor Ground helped the U's win promotion from the Fourth Division. After three seasons with Oxford he moved on to Port Vale where he quickly established himself. He made 200 senior appearances during his time at Vale Park and was a near ever-present in the side that secured promotion in 1969–70. Later he moved on to Stafford Rangers where he was a member of the team that reached the fourth round of the FA Cup in 1974–75 and were beaten finalists in the FA Trophy the following season.

Charlie Mortimore, MBE (Born: Gosport, 12 April 1928. Died: 10 September 2019.) Charlie Mortimore was a centre-forward who was one of the top English amateur players of the 1950s. He came to the fore playing for Aldershot in the old Division Three South and netted five goals in a 7-2 away win at Leyton Orient in February 1950. Later he played for many years for Woking, captaining the team that won the FA Amateur Cup final at Wembley in 1958. He won 19 caps for England Amateurs and was a member of the FA squad that visited Ghana and Nigeria in 1958.

Bert Mozley (Born: Derby, 23 September 1923. Died: Victoria, British Columbia, Canada, 28 October 2019.) Full-back Bert Mozley played for Nottingham Forest Colts and Shelton United during the war before joining Derby County as an amateur in the summer of 1945. He went on to become a first-team regular for the best part of eight seasons at the Baseball Ground, making more than 300 League and Cup appearances. He was capped three times for England, all in the autumn of 1949, and toured Canada with an FA squad the following summer. He later emigrated to Canada where he continued to play soccer and in August 1956 appeared for a Canada All Star XI against Lokomotiv Moscow. At the time of his death he was England's oldest international player.

John Murphy (Born: Wishaw, 6 December 1942. Died: Kilmarnock, 23 April 2020.) John Murphy was a solid, hard-tackling left-back who gained experience in the Juniors with Hurlford United and Darvel before signing for Ayr United in July 1963. Almost immediately he took possession of the left-back slot and he was first choice for almost all the 15 years he spent at Somerset Park. He made an all-time club record 585 competitive appearances and captained the side for several years. He featured in two promotion sides: the 1965–66 team that won the Second Division title and also in 1968–69 when Ayr were runners-up in the Second Division to Motherwell.

Tom Nekrews (Born: Chatham, 20 March 1933. Died: Perth, Australia, 30 October 2019.) Tom Nekrews was a centre-half who was on the books of Chelsea as a youngster without making the first team. He later spent five years as a professional with Gillingham, where he was mostly on the fringes of the first team with the exception of the 1956–57 season when he featured regularly throughout the campaign. He spent 1958–59 at Watford in the reserves, then switched to non-league football with Bexleyheath & Welling.

George O'Brien (Born: Dunfermline, 22 November 1935. Died: Southampton, 18 March 2020.) George O'Brien was a goalscoring inside-forward who was playing first-team football for Dunfermline Athletic at the age of 16. He made over 100 appearances for the Pars, despite his early career being interrupted by National Service, then moved south to sign for Leeds United. He never really established himself at Elland Road, but his career took off when he joined Southampton in the summer of 1959. His 23 goals helped the Saints win the Third Division title in 1959–60 and he enjoyed a tremendous scoring record at The Dell, netting 178 goals from just 277 League and Cup appearances and finishing top scorer on four occasions. He was sold to Leyton Orient shortly before Saints won promotion to the First Division and finished his career with a season at Aldershot.

John Ogilvie (Born: Motherwell, 28 October 1928. Died: Leicester, 2 May 2020.) John Ogilvie was a full-back who joined Hibernian from Junior club Thorniewood United shortly after the start of the 1946–47 season. It was not until 1950–51 that he began to establish himself at first-team level and he played in the League Cup final defeat by Motherwell in October 1950. The following March he had the misfortune to suffer a badly broken leg playing in the Scottish Cup semi-final and this put him out of action for some time. He was eventually released by Hibs and in October 1955 signed for Leicester City where he was the first choice at left-back in the team that won the Second Division title in 1956–57. He went on to conclude his senior career at Mansfield before moving to non-league club Bedworth United.

Les Onslow (Born: Swindon, 29 August 1926. Died: 31 March 2020.) Les Onslow was a wing-half who signed as a part-time professional for Swindon Town at the start of the 1945–46 campaign. Although principally a reserve during a six-year stay at the County Ground he played a handful of first-team games in 1945–46 and a further four Football League games when peacetime football resumed. His senior career was ended when he suffered a broken leg playing for the reserves in January 1950. He later played for Kidderminster Harriers. His younger brother Ken also appeared in League football for Swindon. At the time of his death Les was the club's oldest living player.

Glyn Pardoe (Born: Winsford, 1 June 1946. Died: 26 May 2020.) Glyn Pardoe was a bustling centre-forward when playing for England Schools, netting twice on his debut against Wales at Swansea. He went on to sign amateur forms for Manchester City, becoming the club's youngest-ever first-team player on making his debut against Birmingham City at the age of 15 years and 341 days. He continued to play an attacking role in the team that won the Division Two title in 1965–66 before switching to full-back the following season. He proved even better in this position and he played a key role in City's successes of the late 1960s, winning the European Cup Winners' Cup (1970), the Football League title (1967–68) and both the FA Cup (1969) and League Cup (1970). He scored the winning goal in the League Cup final victory over West Bromwich Albion in extra time at Wembley. A serious leg injury sustained at Old Trafford in December 1970 led to a lengthy spell on the sidelines and he was never quite the same player again. After retiring as a player he remained on the backroom staff at Maine Road for 16 years. His cousin Alan Oakes also played for Manchester City while his grandson Tommy Doyle made his first-team debut for City in October 2019.

Bobby Park (Born: Edinburgh, 3 July 1946. Died: 23 July 2019.) Bobby Park was a skilful midfield player who was an apprentice with Aston Villa, signing a professional contract at the age of 17. He made his first-team debut 12 months later but in six seasons at Villa Park he struggled to establish himself as a first-team regular with competition for places high. After dropping down a couple of divisions at Wrexham he fared much better, making over 100 first-team appearances and starring in the team that finished the 1969–70 campaign as runners-up in Division Four. A move to Peterborough United started brightly but he quickly lost his place following a change in manager, and he ended his senior career with spells at Northampton Town and Hartlepool.

Steve Parr (Born: Bamber Bridge, Lanarkshire, 22 December 1926. Died: 6 August 2019.) Steve Parr was a full-back who joined Liverpool in May 1948 but it was not until the summer of 1951 that he broke into the first-team squad, producing some fine displays during the club's tour of Sweden and retaining his place at the start of the 1951–52 season. However, he was never able to establish himself at Anfield and eventually moved on to Exeter City and then Rochdale, although he was mostly a reserve at both clubs. In July 1958 he was appointed player-coach of the Lancashire Combination club Burscough.

Norman Pavis (Born: Circa 1939. Died: 3 October 2019.) Norman Pavis was a tough-tackling defender who spent over a decade with Irish League club Crusaders. He won representative honours for Northern Ireland Amateurs and the Irish League XI during his time at the club and after his career was ended by injury he had spells as manager of both Carrick Rangers and Crusaders. His younger brother was Sammy Pavis (see below).

Sammy Pavis (Born: Belfast, 14 March 1943. Died: Belfast, 4 July 2019.) Centre-forward Sammy Pavis enjoyed a lengthy career in Irish League football during which time he won three League championships (one with Glentoran and two with Linfield) and two Irish Cup winners' medals (both with Linfield). He was the club's leading scorer in each of his five full seasons with Linfield. He also appeared for the Irish League representative side and won five caps for Northern Ireland Amateurs. He later became a top-class snooker player, winning the Northern Ireland Amateur Snooker Championship twice, and went on to become president of the Northern Ireland Billiards & Snooker Association. He was the younger brother of Norman Pavis (see above).

Arthur Perry (Born: Doncaster, 15 October 1932. Died: Hull, 27 October 2019.) Arthur Perry signed amateur forms for Hull City as a 14-year-old after scoring 10 goals in a schoolboy representative match for Rother Valley Boys. He played for the Tigers' junior and reserve teams for almost a decade, featuring in positions ranging from goalkeeper to outside left, but was unable to break into the first team. However, in two seasons with Bradford Park Avenue he featured regularly at left-back, making 63 first-team appearances, before moving to Rotherham United where he struggled to get in the team and was quickly transfer-listed.

George Petchey (Born: Whitechapel, 24 June 1931. Died: January 2020.) George Petchey was attached to West Ham United from an early age, appearing for their nursery team Corinthian Juniors and signing amateur forms in October 1947. He progressed to a professional contract with the Hammers 12 months later, but in five years at Upton Park he made just two first-team appearances. His career took off after he moved to Queens Park Rangers in the summer of 1953, initially playing at wing-half and occasionally at centre-forward. He scored a hat-trick in a 14-minute spell against Aldershot in January 1954 before settling down as a combative wing-half and going on to make over 250 appearances for the R's. He concluded his playing career with Crystal Palace where he featured prominently in the promotion teams of 1959–60 and 1963–64. After his playing career was ended by an eye injury he joined the backroom staff at Selhurst Park and later managed Leyton Orient (July 1971 to August 1977) and Millwall (January 1978 to November 1980).

Martin Peters, MBE (Born: Plaistow, 8 November 1943. Died: 21 December 2019.) Martin Peters was one of the most talented English players of the post-war period and one of the 11 'immortals' who won the World Cup in 1966. He was a supremely capable midfield player, famously described by Alf Ramsey in 1968 as being '10 years ahead of his time'. A former England Schoolboy international, he joined West Ham United where he graduated to the professional ranks on reaching his 17th birthday. He established himself for the Hammers in the 1962–63 season, but missed out on their 1964 FA Cup final win. He played in the team that won the Cup Winners' Cup in May 1965 but it was not until the following summer that he was called into the full England international squad. When the World Cup tournament started he had won just three caps, but after missing the opening game against Uruguay he played in all the remaining games and scored the second goal in the final against West Germany. At club level he enjoyed most success with Tottenham Hotspur where he won the Football League Cup twice and the UEFA Cup in 1971–72. Norwich City won promotion to the top flight in his first season at Carrow Road and he was twice the club's Player of the Year. He ended his senior career at Sheffield United before leaving football. He finished with a career total of 899 club appearances and also won 67 caps for England, scoring 20 international goals.

Peter Phoenix (Born: Urmston, 31 December 1936. Died: April 2020.) Winger Peter Phoenix had been on the books of Manchester City and Stoke City but it was not until he signed for Oldham Athletic in February 1958 that he made his debut in senior football. He was the Latics' top scorer in 1958–59, a remarkable feat for an outside-left, but increasingly he was used in different positions; in 1960–61 he wore five different shirt numbers during the season. After leaving Boundary Park he moved clubs quickly, playing for Rochdale, Exeter City, Southport and Stockport County before switching to non-league football.

Les Picking (Died: 8 April 2020.) Les Picking was a wing-half who was best known for the period he spent with Barnet (1960–67). He also had spells with Cheshunt, St Albans City and Hoddesdon Town, with whom he won the FA Vase in 1975. He won four caps for England Amateurs.

Brian Pilkington (Born: Leyland, Lancashire, 12 February 1933. Died: Adlington, Lancashire, 7 February 2020.) Brian Pilkington was a quick and skilful traditional-style winger who was spotted by Burnley playing in the Lancashire Combination for Leyland Motors. He became a fixture in the side at outside-left from the start of the 1953–54 campaign and went on to make 340 first-team appearances for the Clarets, winning a full England cap against Northern Ireland in October 1954. He missed just one game in 1959–60 when the club won the First Division title and he scored one of the goals in the decisive victory over Manchester City to clinch the trophy. Soon after netting twice in a European Cup tie against Hamburg he was sold to Bolton Wanderers in March 1961. He went on to play for Bury and then Barrow, where he featured in the side that won promotion from the Fourth Division in 1966–67.

Bobby Prentice (Born: Lanark, 27 September 1953. Died: 16 September 2019.) Bobby Prentice was a skilful winger who played his early football with Newtongrange Star, with whom he gained two caps for the Scottish Junior FA in 1971–72. He had already signed for Celtic by this time, but was unable to break into the first team and eventually moved on to Hearts, the club he had supported as a boy. He became something of a cult hero at Tynecastle, where he gained a Scottish Cup runners-up medal in 1976 and helped the team win promotion back to the top flight at the first attempt in 1977–78. Later he moved to North America, where he played in the NASL for Toronto Blizzard. He also won representative honours for Scotland U23s and the Scottish League.

Gerry Priestley (Born: Halifax, 2 March 1931. Died: January 2020.) Gerry Priestley signed for Nottingham Forest midway through the 1950–51 season after being spotted playing for his Army team in local football towards the end of his spell of National Service. However, in three seasons at the City Ground he was unable to break into the first team and he moved on to Exeter City where he made his Football League debut in the opening game of the 1953–54 season. His best years were spent at Grimsby Town where missed just a single game as the Mariners won the Division Three North title in 1955–56, before he closed his career with spells at Crystal Palace and Halifax Town.

Malcolm Pyke (Born: Eltham, 6 March 1938. Died: 13 February 2020.) Malcolm Pyke represented London Schools and was briefly signed by Wolverhampton Wanderers before joining the West Ham United groundstaff in January 1954. He progressed to a professional contract in March 1955 and went on to make his Football League debut for the Hammers at right-half against Bristol City in April 1957. The following season he made 15 appearances as the Second Division title was won but in the summer of 1959 he moved on to Crystal Palace. Later he switched to Southern League football, enjoying a lengthy spell with Dartford.

Stan Quinn (Born: Bridgeton, Glasgow, 15 April 1942. Died: 25 January 2020.) Stan Quinn was a tough and uncompromising centre-half who signed for Ayr United from Shettleston Juniors in June 1966. He created a piece of history early on in his Somerset Park career when he became the first substitute to be used by the club in a competitive fixture. He missed just one game in the 1968–69 promotion campaign and the following season was a member of the team that lost out to Celtic in a League Cup semi-final replay. After being chosen as the Supporters' Club Association Player of the Year in 1971–72 he departed for a brief spell at St Mirren 12 months later, before leaving the senior game.

Dave Quirke (Born: Ballina, Co Mayo, 11 January 1947. Died: 2019.) Dave Quirke was a powerful centre-half who developed with St Neots and Bedford Town before signing professional forms for Gillingham at the age of 19. He went on to make over 250 first-team appearances for the Gills and was a member of the team that finished as Division Four runners-up in 1973–74. He subsequently had a spell in South Africa with Durban United and later played for Chelmsford City, St Patrick's Athletic and Luleaa Sportklubb (Sweden).

Joe Rayment (Born: Hartlepool, 25 September 1934. Died: Stockton-on-Tees, 15 July 2019.) Joe Rayment was an England schoolboy trialist before signing for Middlesbrough and making his debut for Boro at Anfield at the age of 17. A talented winger, he never quite established himself at Ayresome Park and in July 1955 he joined Hartlepools. His time at the Victoria Ground was affected by National Service but after moving on to Darlington his career blossomed. He scored in the 3-2 League Cup win over West Ham United in October 1960 and went on to make close on 200 League and Cup appearances for the Quakers before leaving senior football to sign for North Regional League side Gateshead at the start of the 1965–66 season.

Brian Redfearn (Born: Bradford, 20 February 1935. Died: 10 August 2019.) Brian Redfearn was a tall, strong winger who was a member of the Bradford Boys team before going on to sign for Bradford Park Avenue. He made over 100 senior appearances for the club then briefly played for Blackburn Rovers before turning out for Darlington, Halifax Town and finally Bradford City. An ankle injury ended his playing career. His son Neil Redfearn enjoyed a very successful career as a midfielder in the 1980s and '90s.

Brian Richardson (Born: Sheffield, 5 October 1934. Died: May 2020.) Brian Richardson was a former Sheffield Boys player who developed in the ranks with Sheffield United before signing a professional contract at the age of 19. After making his first-team debut in December 1955 he established himself in the line-up during the 1957–58 campaign and went on to make over 300 League and Cup appearances for the Blades. A tough-tackling wing-half, he was a near ever-present in the team that won promotion from Division Two in 1960–61, but eventually lost his place in the side and moved on to Swindon Town in January 1966. He stayed only briefly at the County Ground, returning north to sign for Rochdale where he was appointed club captain. In November 1966 he suffered a fractured leg playing against Bradford City and this effectively ended his career.

Jim Richmond (Born: Blantyre, 13 October 1932. Died: Elgin, 2 November 2019.) Jim Richmond joined Hamilton Academical as a centre-half from Beith Juniors in the summer of 1954 and went on to enjoy a useful career in Scottish League football over the next 12 years. He played over 400 League and Cup games, also turning out for Falkirk, Kilmarnock and St Johnstone. His best years were spent at Rugby Park, where, by now a right-back, he made over 150 appearances and played in three losing Cup final teams (Scottish Cup 1960, League Cup 1961 and 1963). During this time he also appeared for the Scottish League representative team. After leaving St Johnstone he played and then managed in the Highland League with Lossiemouth and Rothes.

Fernando Ricksen (Born: Hoensbroek, Netherlands, 27 July 1976. Died: Airdrie, 18 September 2019.) Fernando Ricksen was a combative midfield player who played his early football in the Netherlands with Fortuna Sittard and AZ Alkmaar before his fellow countryman Dick Advocaat signed him for Rangers in the summer of 2000. He enjoyed six successful seasons at Ibrox, winning both the Scottish Cup and League Cup in 2001–02 and a domestic treble the following season, while in 2004–05 he captained the side that won the League Cup and the SPL title. He was also chosen as Rangers Player of the Year and was the joint winner of the SPFA Player of the Year award in 2004–05. He later linked up again with Advocaat at Zenit St Petersburg before ending his career back in the Netherlands with Fortuna. He won 12 caps for the Netherlands.

John Ridley (Born: Consett, 27 April 1952. Died: May 2020.) John Ridley was a defensive midfield player who won representative honours for England Universities before signing for Port Vale in August 1973. He was a first-team regular from March 1975 and the following season played in all 46 League games and was chosen as the club's Player of the Year. He spent the summer of 1978 with Fort Lauderdale Strikers in the NASL and then a season at Leicester City before joining Chesterfield. At Saltergate he was a member of the side that won the Anglo Scottish Cup in 1980–81 but he eventually returned to Vale Park where he was a regular in the team that won promotion from the Fourth Division in 1982–83. He retired from senior football having made close on 500 League and Cup appearances and joined non-league Stafford Rangers.

Walter Robertson (Born: Buckhaven, Fife, 28 November 1926. Died: April 2020.) Left-back Walter Robertson joined East Fife from local juvenile club Bayview Youth Club, but in six years as a professional with the Methil outfit he made just two first-team appearances, mostly featuring for the reserves in Division C. After being released in the summer of 1955 he spent a season with Forfar Athletic before injury ended his career. Later he coached at both Cowdenbeath and East Fife. His father had also played as a full-back for East Fife.

Cyril Robinson (Born: Nottingham, 4 March 1929. Died: Blackpool, 9 November 2019.) Wing-half Cyril Robinson represented the England NABC team in 1946–47 and went on to sign professional terms for Blackpool at the age of 19. Although mostly a reserve at Bloomfield Road he stepped in to replace the injured Hugh Kelly in the 'Matthews Cup Final' of 1953. After a season with Cheshire League club Northwich Victoria he returned to senior football with Bradford Park Avenue and Southport, captaining both teams and adding over 100 Football League appearances. He subsequently played for a number of non-league clubs as well as having spells in Canada and Australia.

Michael Robinson (Born: Leicester, 12 July 1958. Died: Madrid, 28 April 2020.) Michael Robinson was a hard-working forward who was effective at holding the ball up and pressurising opposition defenders. He made his debut in senior football for Preston North End while still an apprentice, and went on to win the club's Player of the Year award in 1978–79 before being sold to Manchester City for a then record fee for the Maine Road club. He led the scoring charts for City the following season and then went on to a three-year spell with Brighton & Hove Albion, where he gained an FA Cup runners-up medal in 1983. A brief association with Liverpool earned him winners' medals as a substitute in the European Cup final win over Roma and also in the League Cup. He subsequently played for Queens Park Rangers before signing for the Spanish club Osasuna. When his career was over he remained in Spain and became a successful television pundit. He won 24 full caps for the Republic of Ireland.

Bill Robson (Born: Whitehaven, 13 October 1931. Died: Whitehaven, 3 July 2019.) Inside-forward Bill Robson joined Workington as a part-time professional as they were about to embark on their first campaign of League football. It was not until the 1956–57 season that he became a regular in the side and he went on to score 57 goals from 132 League and Cup appearances during his stay at Borough Park. He played in the famous FA Cup tie against Manchester United in January 1958 and was the club's leading scorer in both 1957–58 and 1958–59. He later had a brief spell with Carlisle United before becoming player-manager of Netherfield, leading them to the Lancashire Combination title in 1964–65.

Doug Robson (Born: Washington, Co Durham, 20 July 1942. Died April 2020.) Defender Doug Robson spent three seasons on the books of Darlington in the mid-1960s, and although mostly a reserve he made a total of 35 first-team appearances. He later played for Stockton in the North Regional League.

John Rowlands (Born: Liverpool, 7 February 1945. Died: April 2020.) John Rowlands was a big powerful old-fashioned forward who enjoyed a 10-year career in the lower reaches of the Football League. Spotted by Mansfield Town manager Tommy Eggleston playing Sunday League football on Merseyside, he signed for the Stags in October 1967. He went on to play for a string of unfashionable clubs including Stockport County, Barrow, Workington, Crewe Alexandra and Hartlepool, making a total of more than 250 senior appearances. Towards the end of his career he played in the NASL with a number of clubs, notably Seattle Sounders and San Jose Earthquakes.

Bobby Russell (Born: Cambuslang, 5 August 1941. Died: 9 May 2020.) Goalkeeper Bobby Russell made his senior debut for Aberdeen as an 18-year-old before returning to the Juniors with Cambuslang Rangers. In April 1963 he was back in the Scottish League after signing for Stenhousemuir and in January 1965 scored his only League goal when he returned to the pitch as an outfield player after being injured in the game with Alloa Athletic. Later he played for both Third Lanark and Morton, for whom he appeared in a Fairs Cup tie with Chelsea, taking his career total of competitive appearances beyond the 150-mark.

Ron Saunders (Born: Birkenhead, 6 November 1932. Died: 7 December 2019.) Ron Saunders was an effective centre-forward who signed for Everton as a youngster where he proved to be a prolific goalscorer with the club's junior teams but received few first-team opportunities. It was only when he dropped down to play for Southern League club Tonbridge that he began to make an impact in adult football and he was quickly back in the Football League with Gillingham. In September 1958 he was sold to Portsmouth where he continued to score regularly: he remains the third highest goalscorer in the club's history, and topped the scoring charts in 1962–63 as they secured the Third Division title. After spells at Watford and Charlton Athletic he became player-manager of Yeovil Town. Thus began a second and even more successful career in the game, as he went on to manage Oxford United, Norwich City, Manchester City, Aston Villa, Birmingham City and West Bromwich Albion. He won a Division Two title with Norwich (1971–72) while at Villa he won the League Cup on two occasions and the League title in 1980–81, the first time in over 70 years that they had been champions.

Gerry Sharpe (Born: Gloucester, 17 March 1946. Died: Virginia Beach, Virginia, USA, 17 December 2019.) Gerry Sharpe was a winger who enjoyed a successful seven-year spell with Bristol City, making over 150 appearances before he suffered a broken leg in January 1971 which effectively ended his career. He later became youth-team coach at Ashton Gate and was briefly caretaker-manager before moving to the United States where he continued to coach for many years.

Jimmy Shields (Born: Derry, 26 September 1931. Died: 9 January 2020.) Jimmy Shields was a promising talent in Irish League football with Crusaders in the 1953–54 season. He appeared for the Irish League representative team against the Football League, won two Amateur caps and helped Crusaders win their first-ever trophy, the Ulster Cup. In March he was sold to Sunderland, but was unable to break into the first team in two seasons at Roker Park. He then moved to

Southampton where he enjoyed a productive campaign in 1957–58, netting 19 League and Cup goals, only to suffer a broken leg playing for the reserves at the start of the following season. This effectively ended his senior career and after a spell in the Southern League with Headington United he returned to the North East to sign for South Shields.

Paul Shrubb (Born: Guildford, 1 August 1955. Died: 28 May 2020.) Paul Shrubb was a versatile player who was an apprentice at Fulham, but after signing a professional contract he managed just one first-team appearance. After spending two years in South Africa with Hellenic he returned in March 1977, signing for Brentford. He made just short of 200 League and Cup appearances during his time with the Bees and was a near ever-present in the team that won promotion from the Fourth Division in 1977–78. He then moved on to Aldershot where in five seasons he wore each of the outfield shirts numbered 2 to 11, and also replaced injured goalkeeper David Coles during the match at Swindon in 1986. He later coached a number of clubs before returning to Aldershot Town in October 1992 where he played a number of games while on the backroom staff.

John Shuker (Born: Eccles, Manchester, 8 May 1942. Died: 29 December 2019.) Defender John Shuker was spotted by Oxford United playing junior football in the Manchester area, signing during their final season of Southern League football. In his early days at the Manor Ground he was a centre- or inside-forward before dropping back to wing-half and then full-back. He was a member of two promotion teams for the U's (1964–65 and 1967–68) and remained with the club for 17 years, establishing a club record of 478 Football League appearances which has yet to be beaten.

Archie Simpson (Born: Dundee, 8 June 1933. Died: Dundee, 28 July 2019.) Archie Simpson was capped for Scotland Schools and was a member of the Ashdale team that won the Scottish U16 Amateur Cup in 1948–49, by which time he had already joined the groundstaff at Dundee. He spent seven years at Dens Park, but his only first-team experience came when he was selected at inside-right at Clyde in January 1954. Surprisingly released in the summer of 1955, he spent a season with Newcastle United, where he featured in the reserves. He moved on to a three-year spell at Barrow making 80 first-team appearances, mostly at right-back, before returning to Scotland to conclude his career at East Fife and Brechin City.

Jordan Sinnott (Born: Bradford, 14 February 1994. Died: Sheffield, 25 January 2020.) Jordan Sinnott was a product of the Huddersfield Town Academy and after captaining the club's youth team he was signed on a professional contract. He made his senior debut for the Terriers in an FA Cup tie with Leicester City and remained with the club until February 2015, adding further appearances and also featuring in a loan spell with Bury. After a spell in non-league football he revived his senior career with Chesterfield in 2017–18 then moved on to Alfreton Town. At the time of his death, which occurred in very tragic circumstances, he was playing on loan for Matlock Town. He was the son of Lee Sinnott who played for a string of clubs, including Huddersfield Town, between 1982 and 1999.

Jimmy Small (Born: 7 July 1932. Died: Antrim, 20 November 2019.) Jimmy Small was a bustling centre-forward with an excellent goalscoring record in Irish League football in the 1950s and early '60s. He turned out for a number of clubs including Linfield, Larne, Ballymena United and Ards and won a single cap for Northern Ireland Amateurs against Scotland in February 1962.

Bobby Smith (Born: Barnsley, 20 June 1941. Died: August 2019.) Bobby Smith was a versatile player who featured at wing-half and on the wing in three senior appearances for Barnsley in the 1962–63 season before moving on to a successful career with Chelmsford City. He spent a decade with the New Writtle Street club, making over 400 appearances, mostly at left-half or full-back, and featured in the teams that won the Southern League title in 1967–68 and 1971–72.

Dick Smith (Born: Circa 1939. Died: 24 September 2019.) Dick Smith was a versatile player who joined East Fife towards the end of the 1962–63 season from Newburgh Juniors. Playing either at centre-forward or as a defender he made regular appearances in the 1963–64 season when the Methil club mounted an ultimately unsuccessful campaign for promotion from Division Two.

Fred Smith (Born: West Sleekburn, Northumberland, 25 December 1942. Died: Burnley, 2020.) Full-back Fred Smith won representative honours with Northumberland Schools before joining Burnley, initially as an amateur, signing professional terms shortly after his 17th birthday. Although never a regular for the Clarets, he made over 100 first-team appearances during a 10-year spell at Turf Moor. In July 1970 he moved to Portsmouth where he established himself in the line-up and was an ever-present in the side in 1971–72. After spending the summer of 1974 playing in the NASL with Dallas Tornado, he returned for a brief association with Halifax Town before leaving football.

Harry Smith (Born: Chester, 27 August 1930. Died: Chester, 22 April 2020.) Harry Smith was a wing-half or inside-forward who was on Liverpool's books as a youngster, going on to gain a Welsh Amateur Cup winners' medal with Connah's Quay Nomads in March 1953. Shortly afterwards he made his League debut for Chester, adding further senior appearances over the next couple of seasons, when he also won representative honours for the FA Amateur XI and appeared in an amateur international trial match for Northern Counties against Southern Counties. After failing to win a cap he became a part-time professional with Chester in August 1955. He remained at Sealand Road for a further three seasons, making a total of 73 Football League appearances before moving on to Flint Town

Jim Smith (Born, Sheffield, 17 October 1940. Died: 10 December 2019.) Jim Smith spent a lifetime in the game, starting out as a player with Sheffield United. Although he failed to make the first team at Bramall Lane, he earned a reputation as a solid wing-half in lower division football with Aldershot, Halifax Town and Lincoln City. After surprisingly being released by the Imps he turned to management, firstly as player-manager of Boston United. He turned the Pilgrims into one of the top non-league clubs in the country and this was the springboard which launched a highly successful career in management. He is one of the few men to have a record of over 1,000 games as a manager in British football and he won promotions with four of his clubs: Colchester United, Birmingham City, Oxford United and Derby County, taking Oxford to the top flight for the first time in their history. He continued to work in management until 2007, also having a brief spell as chief executive of the League Managers Association.

John Smith (Born: Circa 1942. Died: 5 October 2019.) John Smith became a director of Stirling Albion in the late 1980s and remained on the board until stepping down in 2010. He served as president of the Scottish Football League between 2002 and 2007 and also served on the Scottish FA Board for a number of years.

Dennis Sorrell (Born: Lambeth, 7 October 1940. Died: 10 November 2019.) Dennis Sorrell was a wing-half who signed for Leyton Orient from Woodford Town and featured regularly for the O's in the 1959–60 season but was mostly a reserve after this. In March 1962 he moved to Stamford Bridge in an exchange deal involving Gordon Bolland but he struggled to make an impact with his new club and returned to Brisbane Road shortly after the start of the 1964–65 season. He enjoyed two good seasons back at Orient and went on to play for Romford, assisting them to the Southern League title in 1966–67, and later had a brief spell in South Africa with Durban City.

Dave Souter (Born: 30 March 1940. Died: 11 March 2020.) Dave Souter was a full-back who developed in Junior football with Carnoustie Panmure before joining Arbroath in February 1959. He enjoyed a lengthy career in the Scottish game, also turning out for Berwick Rangers, East Fife, Clyde and Dundee before injury ended his career after more than 250 senior appearances. His best seasons were spent with Clyde, where he was a member of the team that finished in third place in the Scottish League and reached the semi-finals of the Scottish Cup before going down to Celtic in a replay in 1966–67.

Brian Sparrow (Born: Bethnal Green, 24 June 1962. Died: 6 December 2019.) Brian Sparrow was a full-back who signed professional forms for Arsenal at the age of 17. He made a number of senior appearances while out on loan and featured regularly for the Gunners' reserve team, but managed just two first-team appearances, both towards the end of the 1983–84 season. He was a regular for Crystal Palace in 1984–85 and later played for Enfield where he was a member of the team that won the FA Trophy final in 1988.

Charlie Stewart (Born: Circa 1937. Died: May 2020.) Charlie Stewart was a versatile forward who could play either at outside-left or centre-forward. He was best known for his two spells at Dumbarton (1957 to 1959 and 1960 to 1962) during which time he scored 62 goals from 127 League and Cup appearances. In between he had a season at Morton, where he was top scorer, and he later played for Stenhousemuir and for Irish League club Derry City.

Robbie Stewart (Born: Broxburn, West Lothian, 14 June 1971. Died: 25 December 2019.) Robbie Stewart was a midfielder who was a trainee with Doncaster Rovers. A member of the team that lost to Arsenal in the final of the FA Youth Cup in 1987–88, he was on the fringes of the first-team squad the following season. He made his Football League debut for Rovers at Stockport County in October 1988 and featured on the bench on a number of occasions, coming on twice in cup matches before being released.

Kevin Stonehouse (Born: Bishop Auckland, 20 September 1959. Died: 28 July 2019.) Kevin Stonehouse was a tall, slim striker who joined Blackburn Rovers in July 1979 from non-league Shildon. He made a handful of appearances that season as Rovers won promotion, scoring twice in his third game for the club. In total he scored 32 goals from 92 appearances for Rovers and went on to a lengthy career in the game, later playing for Huddersfield Town, Blackpool, Darlington and Rochdale. Later he returned to Darlington where he worked in the Football in the Community section and more recently he had been scouting for Newcastle United.

Gary Talbot (Born: Blackburn, 15 December 1937. Died: Chester, 22 December 2019.) Gary Talbot was a powerful centre-forward who was working as a press photographer before being spotted by Chester manager Peter Hauser. He scored in his first two senior games and topped the club's scoring charts in his first two seasons but then injuries restricted his appearances. He moved on to Crewe Alexandra, helping the Railwaymen win their first-ever Football League promotion in 1967–68, but was back at Sealand Road the following season, topping the scoring charts once more and setting a new club record for career goals scored. After his playing days were over he continued to work as a freelance photographer and for a time was the official photographer for Everton FC.

Steve Talboys (Born: Bristol, 18 September 1966. Died: Spain, 2019.) Steve Talboys was an energetic left-sided midfield player who developed in non-league football in Gloucestershire, joining Wimbledon from Gloucester City in January 1992. Although mostly on the fringes of the first team at Plough Lane, he made 26 appearances in the Premier League during his time at the club. In the summer of 1996 he signed for Watford, but here too he struggled to win a place in the side and after 18 months at Vicarage Road he moved on to Boreham Wood.

Stuart Taylor (Born: Bristol, 18 April 1947. Died: Bristol, 10 October 2019.) Stuart Taylor was a tall central defender who was comfortable on the ball. He played a few games for Hanham Athletic before signing for Bristol Rovers, where he established himself in the first team from the start of the 1967–68 season. He went on to establish a club record of 546 Football League appearances, which included a run of 207 consecutive games. In August 1972 he was a member of the team that defeated Sheffield United to win the Watney Cup, while he was ever present in 1973–74 when the Pirates won promotion to Division Two. Later he had a spell as player-manager of Bath City.

Ron Thompson (Born: Carlisle, 20 January 1932. Died: May 2020.) Ron Thompson developed in local football in the Carlisle area, signing professional forms for Carlisle United in July 1951. He was just 18 when he made his Football League debut and after winning a regular place in the side at left-half in 1954–55 he went on to make 373 League appearances, a club record for an outfield player. He missed just two games in 1961–62 when Carlisle won promotion from Division Four and stayed until the end of the 1963–64 season. Later, in 1975, he founded Carlisle City FC together with his fellow ex-player George Walker.

Hans Tilkowski (Born: Dortmund-Husen, 12 July 1935. Died: 5 January 2020.) Hans Tilkowski won 39 caps for West Germany and was his country's goalkeeper in the 1966 World Cup final when they lost to England in extra time. He played his club football with SC Westfalia Herne, Borussia Dortmund and Eintracht Frankfurt and was a member of the Dortmund team that won the DFB Cup in 1965 and the European Cup Winners' Cup in 1965–66 – the first German team to win a European club competition. Later in life he was involved with UNICEF and a number of charities. He was awarded the Federal Cross of Merit with ribbon in 1991 and the Federal Cross of Merit First Class in 2008.

Geoff Toseland (Born: Kettering, 31 January 1931. Died: 16 May 2019.) Winger Geoff Toseland was playing for Rothwell Town in the Leicestershire Senior League when he signed for Sunderland as a 17-year-old. He was mostly a reserve during his time at Roker Park, but managed a handful of first-team appearances during the 1952–53 season, scoring the winner on his debut against Derby County. He subsequently returned to Northamptonshire, signing for Kettering Town where he was a member of the team that won the Southern League title in 1956–57.

Gerardo Traverso (Born: Montevideo, Uruguay, 7 October 1975. Died: Asuncion, Paraguay, 16 May 2019.) Gerardo Traverso was a forward who spent most of his playing career in Paraguay where he had moved as a teenager to progress his career, although he also spent time in China, Mexico and Ecuador. During a brief attachment with Dundee towards the end of the 2001–02 season he made two substitute appearances totalling less than 45 minutes of football. His career ended in May 2004 after he was involved in a car accident that left him a paraplegic and this ultimately led to his early death.

Eric Tunstall (Born: Hartlepool, 21 November 1950. Died: 19 January 2020.) Eric Tunstall was a tall wing-half who developed with the juniors at Hartlepool, signing as a professional in November 1968. He made a solitary Football League appearance as a substitute, coming off the bench at Barnsley shortly after signing. He captained the Pools' youth team that knocked Newcastle United out of the FA Youth Cup and in January of 1969 was sold to the Magpies. However, he failed to make the first team at St James' Park and later returned to play in local football in the Hartlepool area.

Len Vallard (Born: Sherborne, Dorset, 6 July 1940. Died: Reading, 12 September 2019.) Full-back Len Vallard spent two years as an amateur with Portsmouth before returning to the West Country where he won representative honours for the England NABC team. He returned to senior football with Reading in May 1958 and featured regularly at left-back for the Biscuitmen in the first half of 1960–61. He later switched to Southern League football with Cambridge United and then Wisbech Town before becoming player-manager of League of Ireland club Sligo Rovers (September 1973 to August 1974).

Mick Vinter (Born: Boston, Lincs, 23 May 1954. Died: 20 January 2020.) Striker Mick Vinter was just 16 when he made his debut for Boston United in the Northern Premier League and he was quickly snapped up by Notts County. He spent seven seasons at Meadow Lane, winning a regular first-team place from the 1976–77 season and heading the scoring charts for the Magpies in three consecutive seasons; in 1977–78 he was the club's Player of the Year. Moving on to Wrexham in the summer of 1979, he gained experience in the European Cup Winners' Cup in his first season and went on to play for Oxford United, Mansfield Town and Newport County. He ended his career with a record of 114 goals from 422 Football League appearances.

Jimmy Wheeler (Born: Reading, 21 December 1933. Died: February 2020.) Jimmy Wheeler joined Reading from local side Huntley & Palmers and when promoted to the first team in April 1953 he scored on his debut against Shrewsbury Town. It was not until the 1955–56 season that he established himself in the side and he went on to play more than 400 games in a 16-year career at Elm Park. He finished top scorer three seasons in a row from 1958–59 and his total of 160 League and Cup goals is the third highest in the club's history. Towards the end of his playing career he became assistant manager, and he went on to become manager of Bradford City (June 1968 to September 1971), winning promotion in his first season at Valley Parade.

Johnny Wheeler (Born: Crosby, 26 July 1928. Died: 16 November 2019.) Johnny Wheeler was a wing-half who developed with Liverpool County Combination club Carlton before signing for Tranmere Rovers as a 17-year-old. He made a couple of appearances for Rovers at the end of the 1945–46 season but it was not until August 1948 that he returned to the first team. His performances at Prenton Park earned him a move to Bolton Wanderers where he gained an FA Cup runners-up medal in 1953 and was capped both by England and the Football League representative side, while he was also a member of the FA squad that toured West Africa in the summer of 1958. He concluded his senior career at Liverpool where he captained the side for a while and scored a remarkable hat-trick within five minutes against Port Vale in November 1956. In total he made 488 League and Cup appearances in a career that spanned the period 1946 to 1962.

Dennis White (Born: Hartlepool, 10 November 1948. Died: 2019.) Full-back Dennis White was a junior on the books of Hartlepools United and after making his senior debut as an amateur he signed as a part-time professional in November 1967. He stayed six seasons at the Victoria Ground making over 60 first-team appearances and was a regular in the side in 1969–70. He subsequently switched to non-league football with South Shields and then Bishop Auckland.

Tom White (Born: Musselburgh, East Lothian, 12 August 1939. Died: Blackpool, 17 December 2019.) Tom White was a centre-forward who signed professional forms for Raith Rovers at the age of 18. His career at Stark's Park was interrupted by National Service and it was only when he signed for Hearts that he began to show his true potential, scoring at a rate of almost a goal a game before being involved in a serious car accident which put him out of action for some time. During this time his brother John (of Tottenham Hotspur) was tragically killed in a lightning strike, and Tom moved on to Aberdeen and then south to Crystal Palace. The closing years of his career were spent with Blackpool, Bury and Crewe Alexandra although he was increasingly affected by injuries. He served for 12 years as a director of Blackpool and was briefly caretaker-manager of the club towards the end of the 1989–90 season

Peter Whittingham (Born: Nuneaton, 8 September 1984. Died: Cardiff, 19 March 2020.) Peter Whittingham was a product of the Aston Villa Academy and was a member of the team that won the FA Youth Cup in 2001–02. He signed professional forms at the age of 18, but although he regularly featured for England U21s he never established himself in the side at Villa Park. His career flourished after a move to Cardiff City in January 2007. He developed into a technically gifted midfield player with the knack of scoring spectacular long-range goals for the Bluebirds. In a decade with the club he made over 450 League and Cup appearances, gaining runners-up medals in the FA Cup (2008) and League Cup (2012) and assisting the team to promotion to the Premier League in 2012–13. He concluded his career with a brief spell at Blackburn Rovers.

Evan Williams (Born: Swansea, 12 October 1932. Died: 26 April 2020.) Left-back Evan Williams spent five seasons on the books of Cardiff City without breaking into the first team before moving on to sign for Exeter City in the 1954 close season. He made a solitary Football League appearance for the Grecians, lining up against Crystal Palace in December 1954. He was later on the books of Aldershot without adding to his experience of senior football.

Don Woan (Born: Bootle, 7 November 1927. Died: Yeovil, 24 April 2020.) Don Woan was an outside-right who joined Liverpool from Lancashire Combination club Bootle in October 1950. He made a couple of first-team appearances in January 1950 but was then sold to Leyton Orient in part-exchange for Brian Jackson. He was a member of the O's team that reached the fifth round of the FA Cup in 1951–52, then moved on to spells with Bradford City and Tranmere Rovers before joining Southern League club Yeovil Town. His younger brother Alan played for a number of Football League clubs including Norwich City, Northampton Town, Crystal Palace and Aldershot, while his nephew Ian made over 200 appearances for Nottingham Forest.

Alf Wood (Born: Macclesfield, 25 October 1945. Died: Worcester, 10 April 2020.) Alf Wood was an apprentice with Manchester City, moving on to a professional contract at the age of 17, by which time he had already made his Football League debut. In his early days he was a centre-half and he remained so on moving on to Shrewsbury Town. He became a fixture in the side at the heart of the defence before manager Harry Gregg switched him to centre-forward at the start of the 1971–72 campaign. The move was a great success and he finished the season with 35 Football League goals, making him the League's joint-top scorer; his total of 40 League and Cup goals was a new club record and included five in a 7-1 win over Blackburn Rovers. In the summer he was sold to Millwall where he continued to score regularly, before moving on to spells with Hull City, Middlesbrough and Walsall. On switching to non-league he scored both goals to give Stafford Rangers a Wembley win over Kettering Town in the 1979 FA Trophy final.

Phil Wood (Born: 6 February 1943. Died: 17 November 2019.) Phil Wood was a defender who made a total of 900 appearances for St Albans City over the period 1962 to 1984. He was a member of the Middlesex Wanderers team that toured Japan and South Korea in the summer of 1969 and won a single England Amateur international cap during a brief period spent with Enfield, featuring against Turkey in June 1973.

Billy Wright (Born: Blackpool, 4 March 1931. Died: 14 April 2020.) Winger Billy Wright began his career as understudy to the legendary Stanley Matthews at Blackpool, but received few first-team opportunities at Bloomfield Road and in August 1955 he moved on to Leicester City where he scored regularly for the reserves and made a useful contribution to the club's success in winning the Division Two title in 1956–57 with 10 goals from 17 appearances. He went on to play for Newcastle United, Plymouth Argyle and Millwall but the later stages of his career were affected by a series of injuries. After leaving senior football he played for Tonbridge in the Southern League.

Peter Wyer (Born: Coventry, 10 February 1937. Died: 13 November 2019.) Peter Wyer was an inside-forward who signed as a part-time professional for Coventry City at the age of 18. He was quickly promoted to the first-team squad and was given his League debut in October 1955. That was his only appearance that season and he moved on to Derby County, but in a two-year spell at the Baseball Ground he was again mostly a reserve. He returned to Highfield Road for a final season in senior football then played in the Southern League for Rugby Town and Nuneaton Borough.

Ron Wylie (Born: Glasgow, 6 August 1933. Died: April 2020.) Ron Wylie was a Scotland Schools internationalist who signed amateur forms for Notts County as a 16-year-old and was just 18 when he broke into the first team at Meadow Lane. He developed into a talented inside-forward who went on to make over 600 senior appearances in a career that spanned the best part of two decades. He left Notts after they were relegated to the basement division in 1958–59, signing for Aston Villa. It was here that he enjoyed his most successful years, featuring as a near ever-present in the team that won the Division Two title in 1959–60 and then gaining a League Cup winners' prize when Villa won the inaugural 1960–61 competition. After winding down his career as a player with Birmingham City he returned to Villa Park, joining the backroom staff. Later he was manager of West Bromwich Albion from July 1982 to February 1984.

Ian Young (Born: Neilston, Glasgow 21 May 1943. Died: 11 December 2019.) Ian Young was a tough-tackling right-back who developed in the Secondary Juveniles with Neilston Waverley before signing for Celtic at the age of 18. He played a part in the victory over Third Lanark in the Glasgow Cup final of May 1962 and went on to replace Duncan Mackay in the line-up. He made over 100 first-team appearances during his time at Parkhead, winning the Scottish Cup in 1964–65 and a double of the Scottish League and League Cup the following season. He later spent a couple of seasons with St Mirren then played for Beith Juniors before injury ended his career. He was capped for Scotland U23s.

Ian Nannestad

www.soccer-history.co.uk

THE FOOTBALL RECORDS

BRITISH FOOTBALL RECORDS

ALL-TIME PREMIER LEAGUE CHAMPIONSHIP SEASONS ON POINTS AVERAGE

	Team	*Season*	*P*	*W*	*D*	*L*	*F*	*A*	*Pts*	*Pts Av*
1	Manchester C	2017–18	38	32	4	2	106	27	100	2.63
2	Liverpool	2019–20	38	32	3	3	85	33	99	2.61
3	Manchester C	2018–19	38	32	2	4	95	23	98	2.58
4	Chelsea	2004–05	38	29	8	1	72	15	95	2.50
5	Chelsea	2016–17	38	30	3	5	85	33	93	2.45
6	Manchester U	1999–2000	38	28	7	3	97	45	91	2.39
7	Chelsea	2005–06	38	29	4	5	72	22	91	2.39
8	Arsenal	2003–04	38	26	12	0	73	26	90	2.36
	Manchester U	2008–09	38	28	6	4	68	24	90	2.36
10	Manchester C	2011–12	38	28	5	5	93	29	89	2.34
	Manchester U	2006–07	38	28	5	5	83	27	89	2.34
	Manchester U	2012–13	38	28	5	5	86	43	89	2.34
13	Arsenal	2001–02	38	26	9	3	79	36	87	2.28
	Manchester U	2007–08	38	27	6	5	80	22	87	2.28
	Chelsea	2014–15	38	26	9	3	73	32	87	2.28
16	Chelsea	2009–10	38	27	5	6	103	32	86	2.26
	Manchester C	2013–14	38	27	5	6	102	37	86	2.26
18	Manchester U	1993–94	42	27	11	4	80	38	92	2.19
19	Manchester U	2002–03	38	25	8	5	74	34	83	2.18
20	Manchester U	1995–96	38	25	7	6	73	35	82	2.15
21	Leicester C	2015–16	38	23	12	3	68	36	81	2.13
22	Blackburn R	1994–95	42	27	8	7	80	39	89	2.11
23	Manchester U	2000–01	38	24	8	6	79	31	80	2.10
	Manchester U	2010–11	38	23	11	4	78	37	80	2.10
25	Manchester U	1998–99	38	22	13	3	80	37	79	2.07
26	Arsenal	1997–98	38	23	9	6	68	33	78	2.05
27	Manchester U	1992–93	42	24	12	6	67	31	84	2.00
28	Manchester U	1996–97	38	21	12	5	76	44	75	1.97

PREMIER LEAGUE EVER-PRESENT CLUBS

	P	*W*	*D*	*L*	*F*	*A*	*Pts*
Manchester U	1078	666	236	175	2055	966	2234
Arsenal	1078	577	274	223	1901	1062	2011
Chelsea	1078	578	263	235	1839	1058	1997
Liverpool	1078	561	265	250	1859	1079	1948
Tottenham H	1078	462	268	346	1608	1353	1654
Everton	1078	390	306	380	1401	1367	1476

TOP TEN PREMIER LEAGUE APPEARANCES

1	Barry, Gareth	653	**6**	Speed, Gary	535
2	Giggs, Ryan	632	**7**	Heskey, Emile	516
3	Lampard, Frank	609	**8**	Schwarzer, Mark	514
4	James, David	572	**9**	Carragher, Jamie	508
5	Milner, James	538	**10**	Neville, Phil	505

TOP TEN PREMIER LEAGUE GOALSCORERS

1	Shearer, Alan	260	**6**	Henry, Thierry	175
2	Rooney, Wayne	208	**7**	Fowler, Robbie	163
3	Cole, Andrew	187	**8**	Defoe, Jermain	162
4	Aguero, Sergio	180	**9**	Owen, Michael	150
5	Lampard, Frank	177	**10**	Ferdinand, Les	149

SCOTTISH PREMIER LEAGUE SINCE 1998–99

	P	*W*	*D*	*L*	*F*	*A*	*Pts*
Celtic	819	606	122	91	1922	612	1940
Rangers	666	444	123	99	1373	555	1445
Aberdeen	819	328	189	304	1045	1049	1173
Hearts	781	300	197	284	1000	959	1082
Motherwell	819	292	172	355	1024	1228	1048
Kilmarnock	819	270	209	340	977	1172	1019
Hibernian	669	232	178	259	896	941	874
Dundee U	680	214	184	282	842	1021	823

Rangers deducted 10 pts in 2011–12; Hearts deducted 15 pts in 2013–14; Dundee U deducted 3 pts in 2015–16.

DOMESTIC LANDMARKS 2019–20

AUGUST 2019

6 Jude Bellingham became Birmingham City's youngest ever player at the age of 16 years 38 days when he started the EFL Cup first round tie at Portsmouth. Portsmouth won the tie 3-0.

9 Video Assistant Referee (VAR) was used for the first time in English football for the Liverpool v Norwich C Premier League match. Liverpool won 4-1 at Anfield and there were no high-profile decisions.

SEPTEMBER 2019

12 Peter Thomas became Rochdale's youngest ever player at 15 years and 22 days. Thomas was an 84th minute substitute in the Leasing.com Trophy Group F match against Manchester C Under-21s at Spotland. Manchester C Under-21s won the tie 2-0.

OCTOBER 2019

25 Leicester C broke the Premier League record for the biggest away league win when they defeated Southampton 9-0 at St Mary's.

DECEMBER 2019

18 Liverpool fielded their youngest ever team in the EFL Cup quarter-final at Villa Park. The side, at an average age of 19 years 182 days, lost the tie 5-0.

JANUARY 2020

12 Sergio Aguero became the highest overseas goalscorer in the Premier League. He reached 177 in Manchester City's 6-1 victory over Aston Villa at Villa Park breaking Thierry Henry's total of 175. In the same game Aguero scored his 12th Premier League hat-trick.

29 Liverpool broke the record for winning against every team in the Premier League in one season after defeating West Ham U 2-0 at the London Stadium. The victory meant that Liverpool had beaten every other team in the Premier League in their 24th game of the season, smashing the previous record of 31 held by Manchester C from the 2017–18 season.

FEBRUARY 2020

4 Curtis Jones became Liverpool's youngest ever captain at 19 years 5 days when he captained his side to a 1-0 victory over Shrewsbury T in the FA Cup 4th round replay at Anfield. The game also saw them field the youngest ever team again. At an average 19 years 102 days it was younger than the team who set the record on 18 December.

24 Liverpool broke the Premier League record of successive home wins when beating West Ham U 3-2 at Anfield. Manchester C held the record at 20, the Reds reached 21.

MARCH 2020

13 Professional football in England suspended until at least 4 April due to the COVID-19 pandemic.

19 Suspension of professional football in England extended until at least 30 April, with an agreement to extend the season indefinitely.

MAY 2020

19 Football players in England allowed to train in small groups with strict social distancing rules in place.

27 Premier League clubs vote unanimously to allow contact training.

28 Premier League clubs vote to restart the league on 17 June.

JUNE 2020

17 Premier League reopens ....

20 Bournemouth v Crystal Palace becomes the first Premier League game shown live on the BBC.

JULY 2020

1 Pierre-Emerick Aubameyang became Arsenal's fastest player to reach 50 goals for the club. He reached 50 goals in the 4-0 home victory against Norwich C in 79 games succeeding Thierry Henry who took 83 games to reach the same total.

1 Preston NE played their 5,000th league game in the EFL Championship match at home to Derby Co. Wayne Rooney scored the only goal of the game for Derby Co.

4 Leicester City's Jamie Vardy becomes the first player to score 100 goals for the club since Arthur Lockhead in 1933.

26 Kevin De Bruyne equalled the record for most assists in a season. His tally of 20 equalled that of Thierry Henry in the 2002–03 season.

EUROPEAN CUP AND CHAMPIONS LEAGUE RECORDS

MOST WINS BY CLUB

Real Madrid	13	1956, 1957, 1958, 1959, 1960, 1966, 1998, 2000, 2002, 2014, 2016, 2017, 2018.
AC Milan	7	1963, 1969, 1989, 1990, 1994, 2003, 2007.
Liverpool	6	1977, 1978, 1981, 1984, 2005, 2019.
Bayern Munich	6	1974, 1975, 1976, 2001, 2013, 2020.
Barcelona	5	1992, 2006, 2009, 2011, 2015.

MOST APPEARANCES IN FINAL
Real Madrid 15; AC Milan 11; Bayern Munich 11.

MOST FINAL APPEARANCES PER COUNTRY
Spain 29 (18 wins, 11 defeats)
Italy 28 (12 wins, 16 defeats)
England 22 (13 wins, 9 defeats)
Germany 18 (8 wins, 10 defeats)

MOST CHAMPIONS LEAGUE/EUROPEAN CUP APPEARANCES
181 Iker Casillas (Real Madrid, Porto)
174 Cristiano Ronaldo (Manchester U, Real Madrid, Juventus)
157 Xavi (Barcelona)
151 Ryan Giggs (Manchester U)
144 Raul (Real Madrid, Schalke)
143 Lionel Messi (Barcelona)
139 Paolo Maldini (AC Milan)
132 Andreas Iniesta (Barcelona)
131 Clarence Seedorf (Ajax, Real Madrid, Internazionale, AC Milan)
131 Gianluigi Buffon (Parma, Juventus, Paris Saint-Germain)
130 Paul Scholes (Manchester U)
128 Roberto Carlos (Internazionale, Real Madrid, Fenerbahce)
127 Xabi Alonso (Real Sociedad, Liverpool, Real Madrid, Bayern Munich)
124 Sergio Ramos (Real Madrid)

MOST WINS WITH DIFFERENT CLUBS
Clarence Seedorf (Ajax) 1995; (Real Madrid) 1998; (AC Milan) 2003, 2007.

MOST WINNERS MEDALS
6 Francisco Gento (Real Madrid) 1956, 1957, 1958, 1959, 1960, 1966.

BIGGEST WINS
European Cup
Real Madrid 8, Sevilla 0, 21.1.1958.
Champions League
HJK Helsinki 10, Bangor C 0, 19.7.2011 *(qualifier)*.
Liverpool 8, Besiktas 0, 6.11.2007.
Real Madrid 8, Malmo 0, 8.12.2015.

MOST SUCCESSIVE APPEARANCES
Champions League
Real Madrid (Spain) 23: 1997–98 to 2019–20.
European Cup
Real Madrid (Spain) 15: 1955–56 to 1969–70.

MOST SUCCESSIVE WINS IN THE CHAMPIONS LEAGUE
Barcelona (Spain) 11: 2002–03.

LONGEST UNBEATEN RUN IN THE CHAMPIONS LEAGUE
Manchester U (England) 25: 2007–08 to 2009 (Final).

MOST GOALS OVERALL
131 Cristiano Ronaldo (Manchester U, Real Madrid, Juventus).
115 Lionel Messi (Barcelona).
71 Raul (Real Madrid, Schalke).
68 Robert Lewandowski (Borussia Dortmund, Bayern Munich).
65 Karim Benzema (Lyon, Real Madrid).
60 Ruud van Nistelrooy (PSV Eindhoven, Manchester U, Real Madrid).
59 Andriy Shevchenko (Dynamo Kyiv, AC Milan, Chelsea, Dynamo Kyiv).
51 Thierry Henry (Monaco, Arsenal, Barcelona).
50 Filippo Inzaghi (Juventus, AC Milan).
49 Alfredo Di Stefano (Real Madrid).
49 Zlatan Ibrahimovic (Ajax, Juventus, Internazionale, Barcelona, AC Milan, Paris Saint-Germain).
47 Eusebio (Benfica).

MOST GOALS IN CHAMPIONS LEAGUE MATCH
5 Lionel Messi, Barcelona v Bayer Leverkusen (25, 42, 49, 58, 84 mins) (7-1), 7.3.2012.
5 Luiz Adriano, Shaktar Donetsk v BATE (28, 36, 40, 44, 82 mins) (0-7), 21.10.2014.

MOST GOALS IN ONE SEASON
17 Cristiano Ronaldo 2013–14
16 Cristiano Ronaldo 2015–16
15 Cristiano Ronaldo 2017–18
15 Robert Lewandowski 2019–20
14 Jose Altafini 1962–63
14 Ruud van Nistelrooy 2002–03
14 Lionel Messi 2011–12

MOST GOALS SCORED IN FINALS
7 Alfredo Di Stefano (Real Madrid), 1956 (1), 1957 (1 pen), 1958 (1), 1959 (1), 1960 (3).
7 Ferenc Puskas (Real Madrid), 1960 (4), 1962 (3).

HIGHEST SCORE IN A MATCH
European Cup
14 KR Reykjavik (Iceland) 2 Feyenoord (Netherlands) 12 *(First Round First Leg 1969–70)*
Champions League
12 Borussia Dortmund 8, Legia Warsaw 4 *(Group Stage 2016–17)*

HIGHEST AGGREGATE IN A MATCH
European Cup
Benfica (Portugal) 18, Dudelange (Luxembourg) 0 – 8-0 (h), 10-0 (a) *(Preliminary Round 1965–66)*
Champions League
Bayern Munich (Germany) 12, Sporting Lisbon (Portugal) 1 – 7-1 (h), 5-0 (a) *(Round of 16 2008–09)*

FASTEST GOALS SCORED IN CHAMPIONS LEAGUE

10.12 sec	Roy Makaay for Bayern Munich v Real Madrid, 7.3.2007.
10.96 sec	Jonas for Valencia v Bayer Leverkusen, 1.11.2011.
20.07 sec	Gilberto Silva for Arsenal at PSV Eindhoven, 25.9.2002.
20.12 sec	Alessandro Del Piero for Juventus at Manchester U, 1.10.1997.

YOUNGEST CHAMPIONS LEAGUE GOALSCORER
Ansu Fati for Barcelona v Internazionale 17 years 40 days in 2019–20.

OLDEST CHAMPIONS LEAGUE GOALSCORER
Francesco Totti for Roma v CSKA Moscow 38 years 59 days in 2014–15.

FASTEST HAT-TRICK SCORED IN CHAMPIONS LEAGUE
Bafetimbi Gomis, 8 mins for Lyon in Dinamo Zagreb v Lyon (1-7) 7.12.2011

MOST GOALS BY A GOALKEEPER
Hans-Jorg Butt (for three different clubs)
Hamburg 13.9.2000, Bayer Leverkusen 12.5.2002, Bayern Munich 8.12.2009 – all achieved against Juventus.

LANDMARK GOALS CHAMPIONS LEAGUE
1st Daniel Amokachi, Club Brugge v CSKA Moscow 17 minutes 25.11.1992
1,000th Dmitri Khokhlov, PSV Eindhoven v Benfica 41 minutes 9.12.1998
5,000th Luisao, Benfica v Hapoel Tel Aviv 21 minutes 14.9.2010

HIGHEST SCORING DRAW
Hamburg 4, Juventus 4, 13.9.2000
Chelsea 4, Liverpool 4, 14.4.2009
Bayer Leverkusen 4, Roma 4, 20.10.2015
Chelsea 4, Ajax 4, 5.11.2019

MOST CLEAN SHEETS
10: Arsenal 2005–06 (995 minutes with two goalkeepers Manuel Almunia 347 minutes and Jens Lehmann 648 minutes).

EUROPEAN CUP AND CHAMPIONS LEAGUE RECORDS – continued

CHAMPIONS LEAGUE ATTENDANCES AND GOALS FROM GROUP STAGES ONWARDS

Season	*Attendances*	*Average*	*Goals*	*Games*
1992–93	873,251	34,930	56	25
1993–94	1,202,289	44,529	71	27
1994–95	2,328,515	38,172	140	61
1995–96	1,874,316	30,726	159	61
1996–97	2,093,228	34,315	161	61
1997–98	2,868,271	33,744	239	85
1998–99	3,608,331	42,451	238	85
1999–2000	5,490,709	34,973	442	157
2000–01	5,773,486	36,774	449	157
2001–02	5,417,716	34,508	393	157
2002–03	6,461,112	41,154	431	157
2003–04	4,611,214	36,890	309	125
2004–05	4,946,820	39,575	331	125
2005–06	5,291,187	42,330	285	125
2006–07	5,591,463	44,732	309	125
2007–08	5,454,718	43,638	330	125
2008–09	5,003,754	40,030	329	125
2009–10	5,295,708	42,366	320	125
2010–11	5,474,654	43,797	355	125
2011–12	5,225,363	41,803	345	125
2012–13	5,773,366	46,187	368	125
2013–14	5,713,049	45,704	362	125
2014–15	5,207,592	42,685	361	125
2015–16	5,116,690	40,934	347	125
2016–17	5,398,851	43,191	380	125
2017–18	5,744,918	45,959	401	125
2018–19	5,746,629	45,973	366	125
2019–20	4,757,233	44,048	386	119

HIGHEST AVERAGE ATTENDANCE IN ONE EUROPEAN CUP SEASON

1959–60 50,545 from a total attendance of 2,780,000.

GREATEST COMEBACKS

Werder Bremen beat Anderlecht 5-3 after being three goals down in 33 minutes on 8.12.1993. They scored five goals in 23 second-half minutes.

Deportivo La Coruna beat Paris Saint-Germain 4-3 after being three goals down in 55 minutes on 7.3.2001. They scored four goals in 27 second-half minutes.

Liverpool three goals down to FC Basel in 29 minutes on 12.11.2002. They scored three second half goals in 24 minutes to draw 3-3.

Liverpool after being three goals down to AC Milan in the first half on 25.5.2005 in the Champions League Final. They scored three goals in five second-half minutes and won the penalty shoot-out after extra time 3-2.

MOST SUCCESSFUL MANAGER

Bob Paisley 3 wins, 1977, 1978, 1981 (Liverpool).
Carlo Ancelotti 3 wins, 2002–03, 2006–07 (AC Milan), 2013–14 (Real Madrid).
Zinedine Zidane 3 wins, 2015–16, 2016–17, 2017–18 (Real Madrid).

REINSTATED WINNERS EXCLUDED FROM NEXT COMPETITION

Marseille were originally stripped of the title in 1993. This was rescinded but they were not allowed to compete the following season.

INTERNATIONAL LANDMARKS 2019–20

JUNE 2019

28 Angel di Maria made his 100th international appearance for Argentina in the Copa America Quarter Final match against Venezuela. Goals from Lautaro Martinez and Giovani Lo Celso gave Argentina a 2-0 victory and a place in the semi-final.

SEPTEMBER 2019

6 David Ospina made his 100th international appearance for Colombia in their friendly international against Brazil in Miami. Casemiro opened the scoring for Brazil before Muriel equalised from the spot and then put Colombia ahead before half-time. Neymar equalised early in the second half and the match finished 2-2.

7 Emre Belozoglu made his 100th international appearance for Turkey in the European Championship Qualifying Group H match against Andorra. The former Newcastle United star was captain as his country won 1-0 with an 89th minute winner from Ozan Tufan.

OCTOBER 2019

10 Neymar made his 100th international appearance for Brazil in their friendly international with Senegal in Singapore. The match ended in a 1-1 draw with Liverpool's Roberto Firmino opening the scoring and Bristol City striker Famara Diedhiou scoring the equaliser from the penalty spot.

10 Andris Vanins made his 100th international appearance for Latvia in his country's 0-3 defeat to Poland in the European Championship Qualifying Group G. Robert Lewandowski scored all 3 goals for Poland.

NOVEMBER 2019

14 Maya Yoshida made his 100th international appearance for Japan in the Asian World Cup Group F Qualifier away to Kyrgyzstan. Japan consolidated top position in the group with a 2-0 win.

16 Bojan Jokic made his 100th international appearance for Slovenia in the European Championship Qualifying Group G match against Latvia. Slovenia won the game 1-0 thanks to an own goal in the 53rd minute.

17 The Women's Super League attendance record was broken when 38,262 watched Arsenal beat Tottenham 2-0 at the Tottenham Hotspur Stadium. The attendance beats the previous record of 31,213 set in the Manchester derby at the Etihad in September 2019.

DECEMBER 2019

10 Genk's goalkeeper Maarten Vandevoordt, at 17 years 287 days, became the youngest keeper to start a Champions League game in their Group E match against Napoli in Naples. Unfortunately for him the match ended 4-0 to Napoli.

JANUARY 2020

1 Real Madrid's Vinicius Junior became the youngest scorer in El Classico with a 71st minute goal against Barcelona at the Bernabeu. Los Blancos won the game 2-0 with a late Mariano Diaz strike sending them back to the top of La Liga.

FEBRUARY 2020

1 Jordan Sancho of Borussia Dortmund became the first teenager ever to score 25 goals in the Bundesliga.

22 Cristiano Ronaldo equalled Serie A's record of scoring in 11 consecutive matches. He scored the opening goal in a 2-1 away win at SPAL. It was also his 1,000th career game (including 2 matches played for Sporting Lisbon B).

MARCH 2020

10 Josip Ilicic became the oldest player to score an away hat-trick in the Champions League at the age 32 years 41 days. The Slovenian scored two penalties in the first half and then twice in the second half as Atalanta won 4-3 over Valencia at Mestalla in their round of 16 second leg match.

JUNE 2020

30 Lionel Messi scored the 700th goal of his career with a penalty in Barcelona's 2-2 draw against Atletico Madrid at the Nou Camp.

JULY 2020

30 Juventus goalkeeper Gianluigi Buffon set a Serie A record with his 648th appearance in his side's 4-1 victory over Torino in the Turin derby. In the same match Cristiano Ronaldo became the first player to score 25 goals in one season since 1961.

TOP TEN PREMIER LEAGUE AVERAGE ATTENDANCES 2019–20

1	Manchester U	72,726
2	Arsenal	60,279
3	West Ham U	59,896
4	Tottenham H	59,384
5	Manchester C	54,361
6	Liverpool	53,143
7	Newcastle U	48,251
8	Aston Villa	41,661
9	Chelsea	40,563
10	Everton	39,150

TOP TEN FOOTBALL LEAGUE AVERAGE ATTENDANCES 2019–20

1	Leeds U	35,321
2	Sunderland	30,118
3	Nottingham F	27,724
4	Derby Co	26,727
5	WBA	24,053
6	Sheffield W	23,733
7	Stoke C	22,828
8	Cardiff C	22,822
9	Bristol C	21,810
10	Huddersfield T	21,748

TOP TEN AVERAGE ATTENDANCES

1	Manchester U	2006–07	75,826
2	Manchester U	2007–08	75,691
3	Manchester U	2012–13	75,530
4	Manchester U	2011–12	75,387
5	Manchester U	2014–15	75,335
6	Manchester U	2008–09	75,308
7	Manchester U	2016–17	75,290
8	Manchester U	2015–16	75,279
9	Manchester U	2013–14	75,207
10	Manchester U	2010–11	75,109

TOP TEN AVERAGE WORLD CUP FINALS CROWDS

1	In USA	1994	68,991
2	In Brazil	2014	52,621
3	In Germany	2006	52,491
4	In Mexico	1970	50,124
5	In South Africa	2010	49,669
6	In West Germany	1974	49,098
7	In England	1966	48,847
8	In Italy	1990	48,388
9	In Brazil	1950	47,511
10	In Russia	2018	47,371

TOP TEN ALL-TIME ENGLAND CAPS

1	Peter Shilton	125
2	Wayne Rooney	120
3	David Beckham	115
4	Steven Gerrard	114
5	Bobby Moore	108
6	Ashley Cole	107
7	Bobby Charlton	106
	Frank Lampard	106
9	Billy Wright	105
10	Bryan Robson	90

TOP TEN ALL-TIME ENGLAND GOALSCORERS

1	Wayne Rooney	53
2	Bobby Charlton	49
3	Gary Lineker	48
4	Jimmy Greaves	44
5	Michael Owen	40
6	Harry Kane	32
7	Tom Finney	30
	Nat Lofthouse	30
	Alan Shearer	30
8	Vivian Woodward	29
	Frank Lampard	29

GOALKEEPING RECORDS

(without conceding a goal)

FA PREMIER LEAGUE
Edwin van der Sar (Manchester U) in 1,311 minutes during the 2008–09 season.

FOOTBALL LEAGUE
Steve Death (Reading) 1,103 minutes from 24 March to 18 August 1979.

SCOTTISH PREMIER LEAGUE
Fraser Forster (Celtic) in 1,215 minutes from 6 December 2013 to 25 February 2014.

MOST CLEAN SHEETS IN A SEASON

Petr Cech (Chelsea) 24, 2004–05

MOST CLEAN SHEETS OVERALL IN PREMIER LEAGUE

Petr Cech (Chelsea and Arsenal) 202 games.

MOST GOALS FOR IN A SEASON

		Goals	*Games*
FA PREMIER LEAGUE			
2017–18	Manchester C	106	38
FOOTBALL LEAGUE			
Division 4			
1960–61	Peterborough U	134	46
SCOTTISH PREMIER LEAGUE			
2016–17	Celtic	106	38
SCOTTISH LEAGUE			
Division 2			
1937–38	Raith R	142	34

MOST GOALS AGAINST IN A SEASON

		Goals	*Games*
FA PREMIER LEAGUE			
1993–94	Swindon T	100	42
FOOTBALL LEAGUE			
Division 2			
1898–99	Darwen	141	34
SCOTTISH PREMIER LEAGUE			
1999–2000	Aberdeen	83	36
2007–08	Gretna	83	38
SCOTTISH LEAGUE			
Division 2			
1931–32	Edinburgh C	146	38

MOST LEAGUE GOALS IN A SEASON

		Goals	*Games*
FA PREMIER LEAGUE			
1993–94	Andrew Cole (Newcastle U)	34	40
1994–95	Alan Shearer (Blackburn R)	34	42
2017–18	Mohamed Salah (Liverpool)	32	38
FOOTBALL LEAGUE			
Division 1			
1927–28	Dixie Dean (Everton)	60	39
Division 2			
1926–27	George Camsell (Middlesbrough)	59	37
Division 3(S)			
1936–37	Joe Payne (Luton T)	55	39
Division 3(N)			
1936–37	Ted Harston (Mansfield T)	55	41
Division 3			
1959–60	Derek Reeves (Southampton)	39	46
Division 4			
1960–61	Terry Bly (Peterborough U)	52	46
FA CUP			
1887–88	Jimmy Ross (Preston NE)	20	8
LEAGUE CUP			
1986–87	Clive Allen (Tottenham H)	12	9
SCOTTISH PREMIER LEAGUE			
2000–01	Henrik Larsson (Celtic)	35	37
SCOTTISH LEAGUE			
Division 1			
1931–32	William McFadyen (Motherwell)	52	34
Division 2			
1927–28	Jim Smith (Ayr U)	66	38

MOST FA CUP FINAL GOALS

Ian Rush (Liverpool) 5: 1986(2), 1989(2), 1992(1)

SCORED IN EVERY PREMIERSHIP GAME

Arsenal 2001–02: 38 matches

FEWEST GOALS FOR IN A SEASON

		Goals	*Games*
FA PREMIER LEAGUE			
2007–08	Derby Co	20	38
FOOTBALL LEAGUE			
Division 2			
1899–1900	Loughborough T	18	34
SCOTTISH PREMIER LEAGUE			
2010–11	St Johnstone	23	38
SCOTTISH LEAGUE			
New Division 1			
1980–81	Stirling Alb	18	39

FEWEST GOALS AGAINST IN A SEASON

		Goals	*Games*
FA PREMIER LEAGUE			
2004–05	Chelsea	15	38
FOOTBALL LEAGUE			
Division 1			
1978–79	Liverpool	16	42
SCOTTISH PREMIER LEAGUE			
2001–02	Celtic	18	38
SCOTTISH LEAGUE			
Division 1			
1913–14	Celtic	14	38

MOST LEAGUE GOALS IN A CAREER

FOOTBALL LEAGUE			
Arthur Rowley	*Goals*	*Games*	*Season*
WBA	4	24	1946–48
Fulham	27	56	1948–50
Leicester C	251	303	1950–58
Shrewsbury T	152	236	1958–65
	434	619	
SCOTTISH LEAGUE			
Jimmy McGrory			
Celtic	1	3	1922–23
Clydebank	13	30	1923–24
Celtic	396	375	1924–38
	410	408	

MOST HAT-TRICKS

Career
37: Dixie Dean (Tranmere R, Everton, Notts Co, England)

Division 1 (one season post-war)
6: Jimmy Greaves (Chelsea), 1960–61

Three for one team in one match
West, Spouncer, Hooper, Nottingham F v Leicester Fosse, Division 1, 21 April 1909
Loasby, Smith, Wells, Northampton T v Walsall, Division 3S, 5 Nov 1927
Bowater, Hoyland, Readman, Mansfield T v Rotherham U, Division 3N, 27 Dec 1932
Barnes, Ambler, Davies, Wrexham v Hartlepools U, Division 4, 3 March 1962
Adcock, Stewart, White, Manchester C v Huddersfield T, Division 2, 7 Nov 1987

MOST CUP GOALS IN A CAREER

FA CUP (pre-Second World War)
Henry Cursham 48 (Notts Co)

FA CUP (post-war)
Ian Rush 43 (Chester, Liverpool)

LEAGUE CUP
Geoff Hurst 49 (West Ham U, Stoke C)
Ian Rush 49 (Chester, Liverpool, Newcastle U)

GOALS PER GAME (Football League to 1991–92)

Goals per game	Division 1		Division 2		Division 3		Division 4		Division 3(S)		Division 3(N)	
	Games	Goals	Games	Goals	Games	Goals	Games	Goals	Games	Goals	Games	Goals
0	2465	0	2665	0	1446	0	1438	0	997	0	803	0
1	5606	5606	5836	5836	3225	3225	3106	3106	2073	2073	1914	1914
2	8275	16550	8609	17218	4569	9138	4441	8882	3314	6628	2939	5878
3	7731	23193	7842	23526	3784	11352	4041	12123	2996	8988	2922	8766
4	6229	24920	5897	23588	2837	11348	2784	11136	2445	9780	2410	9640
5	3752	18755	3634	18170	1566	7830	1506	7530	1554	7770	1599	7995
6	2137	12822	2007	12042	769	4614	786	4716	870	5220	930	5580
7	1092	7644	1001	7007	357	2499	336	2352	451	3157	461	3227
8	542	4336	376	3008	135	1080	143	1144	209	1672	221	1768
9	197	1773	164	1476	64	576	35	315	76	684	102	918
10	83	830	68	680	13	130	8	80	33	330	45	450
11	37	407	19	209	2	22	7	77	15	165	15	165
12	12	144	17	204	1	12	0	0	7	84	8	96
13	4	52	4	52	0	0	0	0	2	26	4	52
14	2	28	1	14	0	0	0	0	0	0	0	0
17	0	0	0	0	0	0	0	0	0	0	1	17
	38164	**117060**	**38140**	**113030**	**18768**	**51826**	**18631**	**51461**	**15042**	**46577**	**14374**	**46466**

Extensive research by statisticians has unearthed seven results from the early years of the Football League which differ from the original scores. These are 26 January 1889 Wolverhampton W 5 Everton 0 (not 4-0), 16 March 1889 Notts Co 3 Derby Co 5 (not 2-5), 4 January 1896 Arsenal 5 Loughborough 0 (not 6-0), 28 November 1896 Leicester Fosse 4 Walsall 2 (not 4-1), 21 April 1900 Burslem Port Vale 2 Lincoln C 1 (not 2-0), 25 December 1902 Glossop NE 3 Stockport Co 0 (not 3-1), 26 April 1913 Hull C 2 Leicester C 0 (not 2-1).

GOALS PER GAME (from 1992–93)

Goals per game	Premier		Championship/Div 1		League One/Div 2		League Two/Div 3	
	Games	Goals	Games	Goals	Games	Goals	Games	Goals
0	903	0	1251	0	1197	0	1218	0
1	1959	1959	2892	2892	2854	2854	2933	2933
2	2643	5286	3911	7822	3868	7736	3819	7638
3	2312	6936	3351	10053	3374	10122	3294	9882
4	1630	6520	2151	8604	2131	8524	2046	8184
5	815	4075	1142	5710	1144	5720	1070	5350
6	376	2256	509	3054	473	2838	435	2610
7	155	1085	176	1232	184	1288	178	1246
8	68	544	54	432	55	440	53	424
9	19	171	10	90	19	171	19	171
10	5	50	7	70	5	50	6	60
11	1	11	2	22	0	0	3	33
	10886	**28893**	**15456**	**39981**	**15304**	**39743**	**15074**	**38531**

New Overall Totals (since 1992)		Totals (up to 1991–92)		Complete Overall Totals (since 1888–89)	
Games	56720	Games	143119	Games	199839
Goals	147148	Goals	426420	Goals	573568
Goals per game	2.59		2.98		2.87

A CENTURY OF LEAGUE AND CUP GOALS IN CONSECUTIVE SEASONS

	League	Cup	Season
George Camsell			
Middlesbrough	59	5	1926–27
(101 goals)	33	4	1927–28

(Camsell's cup goals were all scored in the FA Cup.)

	League	Cup	Season
Steve Bull			
Wolverhampton W	34	18	1987–88
(102 goals)	37	13	1988–89

(Bull had 12 in the Sherpa Van Trophy, 3 Littlewoods Cup, 3 FA Cup in 1987–88; 11 Sherpa Van Trophy, 2 Littlewoods Cup in 1988–89.)

PENALTIES

Most in a season (individual)
Division 1 — *Goals* — *Season*
Francis Lee (Manchester C) 13 1971–72
Also scored 2 cup goals.

Most awarded in one game
5 Crystal Palace (1 scored, 3 missed) v Brighton & HA (1 scored), Div 2 1988–89

Most saved in a season
Division 1
Paul Cooper (Ipswich T) 8 (of 10) 1979–80

MOST GOALS IN A GAME

FA PREMIER LEAGUE

4 Mar 1995	Andrew Cole (Manchester U) 5 goals v Ipswich T
19 Sept 1999	Alan Shearer (Newcastle U) 5 goals v Sheffield W
22 Nov 2009	Jermain Defoe (Tottenham H) 5 goals v Wigan Ath
27 Nov 2010	Dimitar Berbatov (Manchester U) 5 goals v Blackburn R
3 Oct 2015	Sergio Aguero (Manchester C) 5 goals v Newcastle U

FOOTBALL LEAGUE

Division 1

14 Dec 1935	Ted Drake (Arsenal) 7 goals v Aston Villa

Division 2

5 Feb 1955	Tommy Briggs (Blackburn R) 7 goals v Bristol R
23 Feb 1957	Neville Coleman (Stoke C) 7 goals v Lincoln C

Division 3(S)

13 Apr 1936	Joe Payne (Luton T) 10 goals v Bristol R

Division 3(N)

26 Dec 1935	Bunny Bell (Tranmere R) 9 goals v Oldham Ath

Division 3

24 Apr 1965	Barrie Thomas (Scunthorpe U) 5 goals v Luton T
20 Nov 1965	Keith East (Swindon T) 5 goals v Mansfield T
16 Sept 1969	Steve Earle (Fulham) 5 goals v Halifax T
2 Oct 1971	Alf Wood (Shrewsbury T) 5 goals v Blackburn R
10 Sept 1983	Tony Caldwell (Bolton W) 5 goals v Walsall
4 May 1987	Andy Jones (Port Vale) 5 goals v Newport Co
3 Apr 1990	Steve Wilkinson (Mansfield T) 5 goals v Birmingham C
5 Sept 1998	Giuliano Grazioli (Peterborough U) 5 goals v Barnet
6 Apr 2002	Lee Jones (Wrexham) 5 goals v Cambridge U

Division 4

26 Dec 1962	Bert Lister (Oldham Ath) 6 goals v Southport

FA CUP

20 Nov 1971	Ted MacDougall (Bournemouth) 9 goals v Margate (*1st Round*)

LEAGUE CUP

25 Oct 1989	Frankie Bunn (Oldham Ath) 6 goals v Scarborough

SCOTTISH LEAGUE

Premier Division

17 Nov 1984	Paul Sturrock (Dundee U) 5 goals v Morton

Premier League

23 Aug 1996	Marco Negri (Rangers) 5 goals v Dundee U
4 Nov 2000	Kenny Miller (Rangers) 5 goals v St Mirren
25 Sept 2004	Kris Boyd (Kilmarnock) 5 goals v Dundee U
30 Dec 2009	Kris Boyd (Rangers) 5 goals v Dundee U
13 May 2012	Gary Hooper (Celtic) 5 goals v Hearts

Division 1

14 Sept 1928	Jimmy McGrory (Celtic) 8 goals v Dunfermline Ath

Division 2

1 Oct 1927	Owen McNally (Arthurlie) 8 goals v Armadale
2 Jan 1930	Jim Dyet (King's Park) 8 goals v Forfar Ath
18 Apr 1936	John Calder (Morton) 8 goals v Raith R
20 Aug 1937	Norman Hayward (Raith R) 8 goals v Brechin C

SCOTTISH CUP

12 Sept 1885	John Petrie (Arbroath) 13 goals v Bon Accord (*1st Round*)

LONGEST SEQUENCE OF CONSECUTIVE DEFEATS

FOOTBALL LEAGUE Division 2	*Team*	*Games*
1898–99	Darwen	18

LONGEST UNBEATEN SEQUENCE

FA PREMIER LEAGUE	*Team*	*Games*
May 2003–Oct 2004	Arsenal	49
FOOTBALL LEAGUE – League 1		
Jan 2011–Nov 2011	Huddersfield T	43

LONGEST UNBEATEN CUP SEQUENCE

Liverpool	25 rounds	League/Milk Cup	1980–84

LONGEST UNBEATEN SEQUENCE IN A SEASON

FA PREMIER LEAGUE	*Team*	*Games*
2003–04	Arsenal	38
FOOTBALL LEAGUE – Division 1		
1920–21	Burnley	30
SCOTTISH PREMIERSHIP		
2016–17	Celtic	38

LONGEST UNBEATEN START TO A SEASON

FA PREMIER LEAGUE	*Team*	*Games*
2003–04	Arsenal	38
FOOTBALL LEAGUE – Division 1		
1973–74	Leeds U	29
1987–88	Liverpool	29

LONGEST SEQUENCE WITHOUT A WIN IN A SEASON

FA PREMIER LEAGUE	*Team*	*Games*
2007–08	Derby Co	32
FOOTBALL LEAGUE Division 2	*Team*	*Games*
1983–84	Cambridge U	31

LONGEST SEQUENCE WITHOUT A WIN FROM SEASON'S START

FOOTBALL LEAGUE Division 4	*Team*	*Games*
1970–71	Newport Co	25

LONGEST SEQUENCE OF CONSECUTIVE SCORING (individual)

FA PREMIER LEAGUE

Jamie Vardy (Leicester C)	13 in 11 games	2015–16
FOOTBALL LEAGUE RECORD		
Tom Phillipson (Wolverhampton W)	23 in 13 games	1926–27

LONGEST WINNING SEQUENCE

FA PREMIER LEAGUE	*Team*	*Games*
2017–18	Manchester C	18
2019–20	Liverpool	18
FOOTBALL LEAGUE – Division 2		
1904–05	Manchester U	14
1905–06	Bristol C	14
1950–51	Preston NE	14
FROM SEASON'S START – Division 3		
1985–86	Reading	13
SCOTTISH PREMIER LEAGUE		
2003–04	Celtic	25

HIGHEST WINS

Highest win in a First-Class Match *(Scottish Cup 1st Round)*				
Arbroath	36	Bon Accord	0	12 Sept 1885
Highest win in an International Match				
England	13	Ireland	0	18 Feb 1882
Highest win in an FA Cup Match				
Preston NE *(1st Round)*	26	Hyde U	0	15 Oct 1887
Highest win in a League Cup Match				
West Ham U *(2nd Round, 2nd Leg)*	10	Bury	0	25 Oct 1983
Liverpool *(2nd Round, 1st Leg)*	10	Fulham	0	23 Sept 1986
Highest win in an FA Premier League Match				
Manchester U	9	Ipswich T	0	4 Mar 1995
Tottenham H	9	Wigan Ath	1	22 Nov 2009
Southampton	0	Leicester C	9	25 Oct 2019
Highest win in a Football League Match				
Division 2 – highest home win				
Newcastle U	13	Newport Co	0	5 Oct 1946
Division 3(N) – highest home win				
Stockport Co	13	Halifax T	0	6 Jan 1934
Division 2 – highest away win				
Burslem Port Vale	0	Sheffield U	10	10 Dec 1892
Highest wins in a Scottish League Match				
Scottish Premier League – highest home win				
Celtic	9	Aberdeen	0	6 Nov 2010
Scottish Division 2 – highest home win				
Airdrieonians	15	Dundee Wanderers	1	1 Dec 1894
Scottish Premier League – highest away win				
Hamilton A	0	Celtic	8	5 Nov 1988

MOST HOME WINS IN A SEASON

Brentford won all 21 games in Division 3(S), 1929–30

RECORD AWAY WINS IN A SEASON

Doncaster R won 18 of 21 games in Division 3(N), 1946–47

CONSECUTIVE AWAY WINS

FA PREMIER LEAGUE
Chelsea 11 games (2007–08 (3), 2008–09 (8)).
Manchester C 11 games (2016–17 (1), 2017–18 (10))

FOOTBALL LEAGUE
Division 1
Tottenham H 10 games (1959–60 (2), 1960–61 (8))

HIGHEST AGGREGATE SCORES

FA PREMIER LEAGUE				
Portsmouth	7	Reading	4	29 Sept 2007
Highest Aggregate Score England **Division 3(N)**				
Tranmere R	13	Oldham Ath	4	26 Dec 1935
Highest Aggregate Score Scotland **Division 2**				
Airdrieonians	15	Dundee Wanderers	1	1 Dec 1894

FEWEST WINS IN A SEASON

		Wins	*Games*
FA PREMIER LEAGUE			
2007–08	Derby Co	1	38
FOOTBALL LEAGUE **Division 2**			
1899–1900	Loughborough T	1	34
SCOTTISH PREMIER LEAGUE			
1998–99	Dunfermline Ath	4	36
SCOTTISH LEAGUE **Division 1**			
1891–92	Vale of Leven	0	22

MOST WINS IN A SEASON

		Wins	*Games*
FA PREMIER LEAGUE			
2017–18	Manchester C	32	38
2018–19	Manchester C	32	38
2019–20	Liverpool	32	38
FOOTBALL LEAGUE **Division 3(N)**			
1946–47	Doncaster R	33	42
SCOTTISH PREMIERSHIP			
2016–17	Celtic	34	38
SCOTTISH LEAGUE **Division 1**			
1920–21	Rangers	35	42

UNDEFEATED AT HOME OVERALL

Liverpool 85 games (63 League, 9 League Cup, 7 European, 6 FA Cup), Jan 1978–Jan 1981

UNDEFEATED AT HOME LEAGUE

Chelsea 86 games, Mar 2004–Oct 2008

UNDEFEATED AWAY

Arsenal 19 games, FA Premier League 2001–02 and 2003–04 (only Preston NE with 11 in 1888–89 had previously remained unbeaten away) in the top flight.

MOST POINTS IN A SEASON

(three points for a win)

		Points	*Games*
FA PREMIER LEAGUE			
2017–18	Manchester C	100	38
FOOTBALL LEAGUE **Championship**			
2005–06	Reading	106	46
SCOTTISH PREMIER LEAGUE			
2001–02	Celtic	103	38
SCOTTISH LEAGUE **League One**			
2013–14	Rangers	102	36

MOST POINTS IN A SEASON

(under old system of two points for a win)

		Points	*Games*
FOOTBALL LEAGUE **Division 4**			
1975–76	Lincoln C	74	46
SCOTTISH LEAGUE **Division 1**			
1920–21	Rangers	76	42

FEWEST POINTS IN A SEASON

		Points	*Games*
FA PREMIER LEAGUE			
2007–08	Derby Co	11	38
FOOTBALL LEAGUE **Division 2**			
1904–05	Doncaster R	8	34
1899–1900	Loughborough T	8	34
SCOTTISH PREMIER LEAGUE			
2007–08	Gretna	13	38
SCOTTISH LEAGUE **Division 1**			
1954–55	Stirling Alb	6	30

NO DEFEATS IN A SEASON

FA PREMIER LEAGUE
2003–04 Arsenal won 26, drew 12

FOOTBALL LEAGUE
Division 1
1888–89 Preston NE won 18, drew 4
Division 2
1893–94 Liverpool won 22, drew 6

SCOTTISH LEAGUE
Premiership
2016–17 Celtic won 34, drew 4
Division 1
1898–99 Rangers won 18
League One
2013–14 Rangers won 33, drew 3

ONE DEFEAT IN A SEASON

FA PREMIER LEAGUE		*Defeats*	*Games*
2004–05	Chelsea	1	38
2018–19	Liverpool	1	38
FOOTBALL LEAGUE			
Division 1			
1990–91	Arsenal	1	38
SCOTTISH PREMIER LEAGUE			
2001–02	Celtic	1	38
2013–14	Celtic	1	38
SCOTTISH LEAGUE			
Division 1			
1920–21	Rangers	1	42
Division 2			
1956–57	Clyde	1	36
1962–63	Morton	1	36
1967–68	St Mirren	1	36
New Division 1			
2011–12	Ross Co	1	36
New Division 2			
1975–76	Raith R	1	26

MOST DEFEATS IN A SEASON

FA PREMIER LEAGUE		*Defeats*	*Games*
1994–95	Ipswich T	29	42
2005–06	Sunderland	29	38
2007–08	Derby Co	29	38
FOOTBALL LEAGUE			
Division 3			
1997–98	Doncaster R	34	46
SCOTTISH PREMIER LEAGUE			
2005–06	Livingston	28	38
SCOTTISH LEAGUE			
New Division 1			
1992–93	Cowdenbeath	34	44

MOST DRAWN GAMES IN A SEASON

FA PREMIER LEAGUE		*Draws*	*Games*
1993–94	Manchester C	18	42
1993–94	Sheffield U	18	42
1994–95	Southampton	18	42
FOOTBALL LEAGUE			
Division 1			
1978–79	Norwich C	23	42
Division 3			
1997–98	Cardiff C	23	46
1997–98	Hartlepool U	23	46
Division 4			
1986–87	Exeter C	23	46
SCOTTISH PREMIER LEAGUE			
1998–99	Dunfermline Ath	16	38
SCOTTISH LEAGUE			
Premier Division			
1993–94	Aberdeen	21	44
New Division 1			
1986–87	East Fife	21	44

SENDINGS-OFF

SEASON
451 (League alone) 2003–04
(Before rescinded cards taken into account)

DAY
19 (League) 13 Dec 2003

FA CUP FINAL
Kevin Moran, Manchester U v Everton 1985
Jose Antonio Reyes, Arsenal v Manchester U 2005
Pablo Zabaleta, Manchester C v Wigan Ath 2013
Chris Smalling, Manchester U v Crystal Palace 2016
Victor Moses, Chelsea v Arsenal 2017
Mateo Kovacic, Chelsea v Arsenal 2020

QUICKEST
FA Premier League
Andreas Johansson, Wigan Ath v Arsenal (7 May 2006) and Keith Gillespie, Sheffield U v Reading (20 January 2007) both in 10 seconds
Football League
Walter Boyd, Swansea C v Darlington, Div 3 as substitute in zero seconds 23 Nov 1999

MOST IN ONE GAME
Five: Chesterfield (2) v Plymouth Arg (3) 22 Feb 1997
Five: Wigan Ath (1) v Bristol R (4) 2 Dec 1997
Five: Exeter C (3) v Cambridge U (2) 23 Nov 2002
Five: Bradford C (3) v Crawley T (2)* 27 Mar 2012
**All five sent off after final whistle for fighting*

MOST IN ONE TEAM
Wigan Ath (1) v Bristol R (4) 2 Dec 1997
Hereford U (4) v Northampton T (0) 6 Sept 1992

MOST SUCCESSFUL MANAGERS

Sir Alex Ferguson CBE
Manchester U
1986–2013, 25 major trophies:
13 Premier League, 5 FA Cup, 4 League Cup, 2 Champions League, 1 Cup-Winners' Cup.

Aberdeen
1976–86, 9 major trophies:
3 League, 4 Scottish Cup, 1 League Cup, 1 Cup Winners' Cup.

Bob Paisley – Liverpool
1974–83, 13 major trophies:
6 League, 3 European Cup, 3 League Cup, 1 UEFA Cup.

Bill Struth – Rangers
1920–54, 30 major trophies:
18 League, 10 Scottish Cup, 2 League Cup.

LEAGUE CHAMPIONSHIP HAT-TRICKS

Huddersfield T	1923–24 to 1925–26
Arsenal	1932–33 to 1934–35
Liverpool	1981–82 to 1983–84
Manchester U	1998–99 to 2000–01
Manchester U	2006–07 to 2008–09

MOST FA CUP MEDALS

Ashley Cole 7 (Arsenal 2002, 2003, 2005; Chelsea 2007, 2009, 2010, 2012).

MOST LEAGUE MEDALS

Ryan Giggs (Manchester U) 13: 1993, 1994, 1996, 1997, 1999, 2000, 2001, 2003, 2007, 2008, 2009, 2011 and 2013.

MOST SENIOR MATCHES

1,390 Peter Shilton (1,005 League, 86 FA Cup, 102 League Cup, 125 Internationals, 13 Under-23, 4 Football League XI, 20 European Cup, 7 Texaco Cup, 5 Simod Cup, 4 European Super Cup, 4 UEFA Cup, 3 Screen Sport Super Cup, 3 Zenith Data Systems Cup, 2 Autoglass Trophy, 2 Charity Shield, 2 Full Members Cup, 1 Anglo-Italian Cup, 1 Football League play-offs, 1 World Club Championship)

MOST LEAGUE APPEARANCES (750+ matches)

1,005 Peter Shilton (286 Leicester C, 110 Stoke C, 202 Nottingham F, 188 Southampton, 175 Derby Co, 34 Plymouth Arg, 1 Bolton W, 9 Leyton Orient) 1966–97
931 Tony Ford (355 Grimsby T, 9 Sunderland (loan), 112 Stoke C, 114 WBA, 68 Grimsby T, 5 Bradford C (loan), 76 Scunthorpe U, 103 Mansfield T, 89 Rochdale) 1975–2002
909 Graeme Armstrong (204 Stirling A, 83 Berwick Rangers, 353 Meadowbank Thistle, 268 Stenhousemuir, 1 Alloa Ath) 1975–2001
863 Tommy Hutchison (165 Blackpool, 314 Coventry C, 46 Manchester C, 92 Burnley, 178 Swansea C, 68 Alloa Ath) 1965–91
833 Graham Alexander (159 Scunthorpe U, 150 Luton T, 370 Preston NE, 154 Burnley) 1990–2012
824 Terry Paine (713 Southampton, 111 Hereford U) 1957–77
790 Neil Redfearn (35 Bolton W, 10 Lincoln C (loan), 90 Lincoln C, 46 Doncaster R, 57 Crystal Palace, 24 Watford, 62 Oldham Ath, 292 Barnsley, 30 Charlton Ath, 17 Bradford C, 22 Wigan Ath, 42 Halifax T, 54 Boston U, 9 Rochdale) 1982–2004
788 David James (89 Watford, 214 Liverpool, 67 Aston Villa, 91 West Ham U, 93 Manchester C, 134 Portsmouth, 81 Bristol C, 19 Bournemouth) 1988–2013
782 Robbie James (484 Swansea C, 48 Stoke C, 87 QPR, 23 Leicester C, 89 Bradford C, 51 Cardiff C) 1973–94
777 Alan Oakes (565 Manchester C, 211 Chester C, 1 Port Vale) 1959–84
774 Dave Beasant (340 Wimbledon, 20 Newcastle U, 133 Chelsea, 6 Grimsby T (loan), 4 Wolverhampton W (loan), 88 Southampton, 139 Nottingham F, 27 Portsmouth, 1 Tottenham H (loan), 16 Brighton & HA) 1979–2003
771 John Burridge (27 Workington, 134 Blackpool, 65 Aston Villa, 6 Southend U (loan), 88 Crystal Palace, 39 QPR, 74 Wolverhampton W, 6 Derby Co (loan), 109 Sheffield U, 62 Southampton, 67 Newcastle U, 65 Hibernian, 3 Scarborough, 4 Lincoln C, 3 Aberdeen, 3 Dumbarton, 3 Falkirk, 4 Manchester C, 3 Darlington, 6 Queen of the S) 1968–96
770 John Trollope (all for Swindon T) 1960–80†
764 Jimmy Dickinson (all for Portsmouth) 1946–65
763 Stuart McCall (395 Bradford C, 103 Everton, 194 Rangers, 71 Sheffield U) 1982–2004
761 Roy Sproson (all for Port Vale) 1950–72
760 Mick Tait (64 Oxford U, 106 Carlisle U, 33 Hull C, 240 Portsmouth, 99 Reading, 79 Darlington, 139 Hartlepool U) 1975–97
758 Ray Clemence (48 Scunthorpe U, 470 Liverpool, 240 Tottenham H) 1966–87
758 Billy Bonds (95 Charlton Ath, 663 West Ham U) 1964–88
757 Pat Jennings (48 Watford, 472 Tottenham H, 237 Arsenal) 1963–86
757 Frank Worthington (171 Huddersfield T, 210 Leicester C, 84 Bolton W, 75 Birmingham C, 32 Leeds U, 19 Sunderland, 34 Southampton, 31 Brighton & HA, 59 Tranmere R, 23 Preston NE, 19 Stockport Co) 1966–88
755 Jamie Cureton (98 Norwich C, 5 Bournemouth (loan), 174 Bristol R, 108 Reading, 43 QPR, 30 Swindon T, 52 Colchester U, 8 Barnsley (loan), 12 Shrewsbury (loan), 88 Exeter C, 19 Leyton Orient, 35 Cheltenham T, 83 Dagenham & R) 1992–2016
753 Andy Millen (71 St Johnstone, 111 Alloa Ath, 119 Hamilton A, 57 Kilmarnock, 51, Hibernian, 18 Raith Rovers, 60 Ayr U, 44 G Morton, 89 Clyde, 114 St Mirren, 19 Queen's Park) 1986–2012

† *record for one club*

CONSECUTIVE
401 Harold Bell (401 Tranmere R; 459 in all games) 1946–55

YOUNGEST PLAYERS

FA Premier League appearance
Harvey Elliott, 16 years 30 days, Wolves v Fulham, 4.5.2019

FA Premier League scorer
James Vaughan, 16 years 271 days, Everton v Crystal Palace 10.4.2005

Football League appearance
Reuben Noble-Lazarus, 15 years 45 days, Barnsley v Ipswich T, FL Championship 30.9.2008

Football League scorer
Ronnie Dix, 15 years 180 days, Bristol Rovers v Norwich C, Division 3S, 3.3.1928

FA Cup appearance (any round)
Andy Awford, 15 years 88 days as substitute Worcester City v Boreham Wood, 3rd Qual. rd, 10.10.1987

FA Cup goalscorer
George Williams, 16 years 66 days, Milton Keynes D v Nantwich T, 12.11.2011

FA Cup appearance (competition rounds)
Luke Freeman, 15 years 233 days, Gillingham v Barnet 10.11.2007

FA Cup Final appearance
Curtis Weston, 17 years 119 days, Millwall v Manchester U, 22.5.2004

FA Cup Final scorer
Norman Whiteside, 18 years 18 days, Manchester United v Brighton & HA, 1983

FA Cup Final captain
David Nish, 21 years 212 days, Leicester C v Manchester C, 1969

League Cup appearance
Connor Wickham, 16 years 133 days, Ipswich T v Shrewsbury T, 11.8.2009

League Cup goalscorer
Connor Wickham, 16 years 133 days, Ipswich T v Shrewsbury T, 11.8.2009

League Cup Final scorer
Norman Whiteside, 17 years 324 days, Manchester U v Liverpool, 1983

League Cup Final captain
Barry Venison, 20 years 7 months 8 days, Sunderland v Norwich C, 1985

Scottish Premier League appearance
Scott Robinson, 16 years 45 days, Hearts v Inverness CT, 26.4.2008

Scottish Football League appearance
Jordan Allan, 14 years 189 days, Airdrie U v Livingston, 26.4.2013

Scottish Premier League scorer
Fraser Fyvie, 16 years 306 days, Aberdeen v Hearts, 27.1.2010

OLDEST PLAYERS

FA Premier League appearance
John Burridge, 43 years 162 days, Manchester C v QPR, 14.5.95

Football League appearance
Neil McBain, 52 years 4 months, New Brighton v Hartlepools U, Div 3N, 15.3.47 (McBain was New Brighton's manager and had to play in an emergency)

Division 1 appearance
Stanley Matthews, 50 years 5 days, Stoke C v Fulham, 6.2.65

INTERNATIONAL RECORDS

MOST GOALS IN AN INTERNATIONAL

Record/World Cup	Archie Thompson (Australia) 13 goals v American Samoa	11.4.2001
England	Howard Vaughton (Aston Villa) 5 goals v Ireland, at Belfast	18.2.1882
	Steve Bloomer (Derby Co) 5 goals v Wales, at Cardiff	16.3.1896
	Willie Hall (Tottenham H) 5 goals v N. Ireland, at Old Trafford	16.11.1938
	Malcolm Macdonald (Newcastle U) 5 goals v Cyprus, at Wembley	16.4.1975
Northern Ireland	Joe Bambrick (Linfield) 6 goals v Wales, at Belfast	1.2.1930
Wales	John Price (Wrexham) 4 goals v Ireland, at Wrexham	25.2.1882
	John Doughty (Newton Heath) 4 goals v Ireland, at Wrexham	3.3.1888
	Mel Charles (Cardiff C) 4 goals v N. Ireland, at Cardiff	11.4.1962
	Ian Edwards (Chester) 4 goals v Malta, at Wrexham	25.10.1978
Scotland	Alexander Higgins (Kilmarnock) 4 goals v Ireland, at Hampden Park	14.3.1885
	Charles Heggie (Rangers) 4 goals v Ireland, at Belfast	20.3.1886
	William Dickson (Dundee Strathmore) 4 goals v Ireland, at Belfast	24.3.1888
	William Paul (Partick Thistle) 4 goals v Wales, at Paisley	22.3.1890
	Jake Madden (Celtic) 4 goals v Wales, at Wrexham	18.3.1893
	Duke McMahon (Celtic) 4 goals v Ireland, at Celtic Park	23.2.1901
	Bob Hamilton (Rangers) 4 goals v Ireland, at Celtic Park	23.2.1901
	Jimmy Quinn (Celtic) 4 goals v Ireland, at Dublin	14.3.1908
	Hughie Gallacher (Newcastle U) 4 goals v N. Ireland, at Belfast	23.2.1929
	Billy Steel (Dundee) 4 goals v N. Ireland, at Hampden Park	1.11.1950
	Denis Law (Manchester U) 4 goals v N. Ireland, at Hampden Park	7.11.1962
	Denis Law (Manchester U) 4 goals v Norway, at Hampden Park	7.11.1963
	Colin Stein (Rangers) 4 goals v Cyprus, at Hampden Park	17.5.1969

MOST GOALS IN AN INTERNATIONAL CAREER

		Goals	*Games*
England	Wayne Rooney (Everton, Manchester U)	53	120
Scotland	Denis Law (Huddersfield T, Manchester C, Torino, Manchester U)	30	55
	Kenny Dalglish (Celtic, Liverpool)	30	102
Northern Ireland	David Healy (Manchester U, Preston NE, Leeds U, Fulham, Sunderland, Rangers, Bury)	36	95
Wales	Gareth Bale (Southampton, Tottenham H, Real Madrid)	33	81
Republic of Ireland	Robbie Keane (Wolverhampton W, Coventry C, Internazionale, Leeds U, Tottenham H, Liverpool, Tottenham H, LA Galaxy)	68	146

HIGHEST SCORES

World Cup Match	Australia	31	American Samoa	0	2001
European Championship	San Marino	0	Germany	13	2006
Olympic Games	Denmark	17	France	1	1908
	Germany	16	Russia	0	1912
Olympic Qualifying Tournament	Vanuatu	46	Micronesia	0	2015
Other International Match	Libya	21	Oman	0	1966
	Abandoned after 80 minutes as Oman refused to play on.				
European Cup	KR Reykjavik	2	Feyenoord	12	1969
European Cup-Winners' Cup	Sporting Lisbon	16	Apoel Nicosia	1	1963
Fairs & UEFA Cups	Ajax	14	Red Boys Differdange	0	1984

GOALSCORING RECORDS

World Cup Final	Geoff Hurst (England) 3 goals v West Germany	1966
World Cup Final tournament	Just Fontaine (France) 13 goals	1958
World Cup career	Miroslav Klose (Germany) 16 goals	2002, 2006, 2010, 2014
Career	Artur Friedenreich (Brazil) 1,329 goals	1910–30
	Pele (Brazil) 1,281 goals	*1956–78
	Franz 'Bimbo' Binder (Austria, Germany) 1,006 goals	1930–50
World Cup Finals fastest	Hakan Sukur (Turkey) 10.8 secs v South Korea	2002

**Pele subsequently scored two goals in Testimonial matches making his total 1,283.*

MOST CAPPED INTERNATIONALS IN BRITAIN AND IRELAND

England	Peter Shilton	125 appearances	1970–90
Northern Ireland	Pat Jennings	119 appearances	1964–86
Scotland	Kenny Dalglish	102 appearances	1971–86
Wales	Chris Gunter	96 appearances	2007–2019
Republic of Ireland	Robbie Keane	146 appearances	1998–2016

THE PREMIER LEAGUE AND FOOTBALL LEAGUE FIXTURES 2020–21

All fixtures subject to change.

Community Shield

Saturday, 29 August 2020
Liverpool v Arsenal

Premier League

Saturday, 12 September 2020
Burnley v Manchester U (postponed)
Crystal Palace v Southampton
Fulham v Arsenal
Liverpool v Leeds U
Manchester City v Aston Villa (postponed)
Tottenham H v Everton
WBA v Leicester C
West Ham U v Newcastle U

Monday, 14 September 2020
Brighton & HA v Chelsea
Sheffield U v Wolverhampton W

Saturday, 19 September 2020
Arsenal v West Ham U
Aston Villa v Sheffield U
Chelsea v Liverpool
Everton v WBA
Leeds U v Fulham
Leicester C v Burnley
Manchester U v Crystal Palace
Newcastle U v Brighton & HA
Southampton v Tottenham H
Wolverhampton W v Manchester City

Saturday, 26 September 2020
Brighton & HA v Manchester U
Burnley v Southampton
Crystal Palace v Everton
Fulham v Aston Villa
Liverpool v Arsenal
Manchester City v Leicester C
Sheffield U v Leeds U
Tottenham H v Newcastle U
WBA v Chelsea
West Ham U v Wolverhampton W

Saturday, 3 October 2020
Arsenal v Sheffield U
Aston Villa v Liverpool
Chelsea v Crystal Palace
Everton v Brighton & HA
Leeds U v Manchester City
Leicester C v West Ham U
Manchester U v Tottenham H
Newcastle U v Burnley
Southampton v WBA
Wolverhampton W v Fulham

Saturday, 17 October 2020
Chelsea v Southampton
Crystal Palace v Brighton & HA
Everton v Liverpool
Leeds U v Wolverhampton W
Leicester C v Aston Villa
Manchester City v Arsenal
Newcastle U v Manchester U
Sheffield U v Fulham
Tottenham H v West Ham U
WBA v Burnley

Saturday, 24 October 2020
Arsenal v Leicester C
Aston Villa v Leeds U
Brighton & HA v WBA
Burnley v Tottenham H
Fulham v Crystal Palace
Liverpool v Sheffield U
Manchester U v Chelsea
Southampton v Everton
West Ham U v Manchester City
Wolverhampton W v Newcastle U

Saturday, 31 October 2020
Aston Villa v Southampton
Burnley v Chelsea
Fulham v WBA
Leeds U v Leicester C
Liverpool v West Ham U
Manchester U v Arsenal
Newcastle U v Everton
Sheffield U v Manchester City
Tottenham H v Brighton & HA
Wolverhampton W v Crystal Palace

Saturday, 7 November 2020
Arsenal v Aston Villa
Brighton & HA v Burnley
Chelsea v Sheffield U
Crystal Palace v Leeds U
Everton v Manchester U
Leicester C v Wolverhampton W
Manchester City v Liverpool
Southampton v Newcastle U
WBA v Tottenham H
West Ham U v Fulham

Saturday, 21 November 2020
Aston Villa v Brighton & HA
Burnley v Crystal Palace
Fulham v Everton
Leeds U v Arsenal
Liverpool v Leicester C
Manchester U v WBA
Newcastle U v Chelsea
Sheffield U v West Ham U
Tottenham H v Manchester City
Wolverhampton W v Southampton

Saturday, 28 November 2020
Arsenal v Wolverhampton W
Brighton & HA v Liverpool
Chelsea v Tottenham H
Crystal Palace v Newcastle U
Everton v Leeds U
Leicester C v Fulham
Manchester City v Burnley
Southampton v Manchester U
WBA v Sheffield U
West Ham U v Aston Villa

Saturday, 5 December 2020
Aston Villa v Newcastle U
Brighton & HA v Southampton
Burnley v Everton
Chelsea v Leeds U
Liverpool v Wolverhampton W
Manchester City v Fulham
Sheffield U v Leicester C
Tottenham H v Arsenal
WBA v Crystal Palace
West Ham U v Manchester U

Saturday, 12 December 2020
Arsenal v Burnley
Crystal Palace v Tottenham H
Everton v Chelsea
Fulham v Liverpool
Leeds U v West Ham U
Leicester C v Brighton & HA
Manchester U v Manchester City
Newcastle U v WBA
Southampton v Sheffield U
Wolverhampton W v Aston Villa

Tuesday, 15 December 2020
Arsenal v Southampton
Aston Villa v Burnley
Fulham v Brighton & HA
Leeds U v Newcastle U
Leicester C v Everton
Sheffield U v Manchester U
West Ham U v Crystal Palace
Wolverhampton W v Chelsea

Wednesday, 16 December 2020
Liverpool v Tottenham H
Manchester City v WBA

Saturday, 19 December 2020
Brighton & HA v Sheffield U
Burnley v Wolverhampton W
Chelsea v West Ham U
Crystal Palace v Liverpool
Everton v Arsenal
Manchester U v Leeds U
Newcastle U v Fulham
Southampton v Manchester City
Tottenham H v Leicester C
WBA v Aston Villa

Saturday, 26 December 2020
Arsenal v Chelsea
Aston Villa v Crystal Palace
Fulham v Southampton
Leeds U v Burnley
Leicester C v Manchester U
Liverpool v WBA
Manchester City v Newcastle U
Sheffield U v Everton
West Ham U v Brighton & HA
Wolverhampton W v Tottenham H

Monday, 28 December 2020
Brighton & HA v Arsenal
Burnley v Sheffield U
Chelsea v Aston Villa
Crystal Palace v Leicester C
Everton v Manchester City
Manchester U v Wolverhampton W
Newcastle U v Liverpool
Southampton v West Ham U
Tottenham H v Fulham

Saturday, 2 January 2021
Brighton & HA v Wolverhampton W
Burnley v Fulham
Chelsea v Manchester City
Crystal Palace v Sheffield U
Everton v West Ham U
Manchester U v Aston Villa
Newcastle U v Leicester C
Southampton v Liverpool
Tottenham H v Leeds U
WBA v Arsenal

Tuesday, 12 January 2021
Arsenal v Crystal Palace
Aston Villa v Tottenham H
Fulham v Manchester U
Leeds U v Southampton
Leicester C v Chelsea
Sheffield U v Newcastle U
West Ham U v WBA
Wolverhampton W v Everton

Wednesday, 13 January 2021
Liverpool v Burnley
Manchester City v Brighton & HA

Saturday, 16 January 2021
Arsenal v Newcastle U
Aston Villa v Everton
Fulham v Chelsea
Leeds U v Brighton & HA
Leicester C v Southampton
Liverpool v Manchester U
Manchester City v Crystal Palace
Sheffield U v Tottenham H
West Ham U v Burnley
Wolverhampton W v WBA

Tuesday, 26 January 2021
Brighton & HA v Fulham
Burnley v Aston Villa
Everton v Leicester C
Manchester U v Sheffield U
WBA v Manchester City

Wednesday, 27 January 2021
Chelsea v Wolverhampton W
Newcastle U v Leeds U
Southampton v Arsenal
Tottenham H v Liverpool
Crystal Palace v West Ham U

Saturday, 30 January 2021
Arsenal v Manchester U
Brighton & HA v Tottenham H
Chelsea v Burnley
Crystal Palace v Wolverhampton W
Everton v Newcastle U
Leicester C v Leeds U
Manchester City v Sheffield U
Southampton v Aston Villa
WBA v Fulham
West Ham U v Liverpool
WBA v Leeds U

Tuesday, 2 February 2021
Aston Villa v West Ham U
Burnley v Manchester City
Fulham v Leicester C
Leeds U v Everton
Sheffield U v WBA
Wolverhampton W v Arsenal
Manchester U v Southampton

Wednesday, 3 February 2021
Newcastle U v Crystal Palace
Tottenham H v Chelsea
Liverpool v Brighton & HA

Saturday, 6 February 2021
Aston Villa v Arsenal
Burnley v Brighton & HA
Fulham v West Ham U
Leeds U v Crystal Palace
Liverpool v Manchester City
Manchester U v Everton
Newcastle U v Southampton
Sheffield U v Chelsea
Tottenham H v WBA
Wolverhampton W v Leicester C

Saturday, 13 February 2021
Arsenal v Leeds U
Brighton & HA v Aston Villa
Chelsea v Newcastle U
Crystal Palace v Burnley
Everton v Fulham
Leicester C v Liverpool
Manchester City v Tottenham H
Southampton v Wolverhampton W
WBA v Manchester U
West Ham U v Sheffield U

Saturday, 20 February 2021
Arsenal v Manchester City
Aston Villa v Leicester C
Brighton & HA v Crystal Palace
Burnley v WBA
Fulham v Sheffield U
Liverpool v Everton
Manchester U v Newcastle U
Southampton v Chelsea
West Ham U v Tottenham H
Wolverhampton W v Leeds U

Saturday, 27 February 2021
Chelsea v Manchester U
Crystal Palace v Fulham
Everton v Southampton
Leeds U v Aston Villa
Leicester C v Arsenal
Manchester City v West Ham U
Newcastle U v Wolverhampton W
Sheffield U v Liverpool
Tottenham H v Burnley
WBA v Brighton & HA

Saturday, 6 March 2021
Aston Villa v Wolverhampton W
Brighton & HA v Leicester C
Burnley v Arsenal
Chelsea v Everton
Liverpool v Fulham
Manchester City v Manchester U
Sheffield U v Southampton
Tottenham H v Crystal Palace
WBA v Newcastle U
West Ham U v Leeds U

Saturday, 13 March 2021
Arsenal v Tottenham H
Crystal Palace v WBA
Everton v Burnley
Fulham v Manchester City
Leeds U v Chelsea
Leicester C v Sheffield U
Manchester U v West Ham U
Newcastle U v Aston Villa
Southampton v Brighton & HA
Wolverhampton W v Liverpool

Saturday, 20 March 2021
Brighton & HA v Newcastle U
Burnley v Leicester C
Crystal Palace v Manchester U
Fulham v Leeds U
Liverpool v Chelsea
Manchester City v Wolverhampton W
Sheffield U v Aston Villa
Tottenham H v Southampton
WBA v Everton
West Ham U v Arsenal

Saturday, 3 April 2021
Arsenal v Liverpool
Aston Villa v Fulham
Chelsea v WBA
Everton v Crystal Palace
Leeds U v Sheffield U
Leicester C v Manchester City
Manchester U v Brighton & HA
Newcastle U v Tottenham H
Southampton v Burnley
Wolverhampton W v West Ham U

Saturday, 10 April 2021
Brighton & HA v Everton
Burnley v Newcastle U
Crystal Palace v Chelsea
Fulham v Wolverhampton W
Liverpool v Aston Villa
Manchester City v Leeds U
Sheffield U v Arsenal
Tottenham H v Manchester U
WBA v Southampton
West Ham U v Leicester C

Saturday, 17 April 2021
Arsenal v Fulham
Aston Villa v Manchester City
Chelsea v Brighton & HA
Everton v Tottenham H
Leeds U v Liverpool
Leicester C v WBA
Manchester U v Burnley
Newcastle U v West Ham U
Southampton v Crystal Palace
Wolverhampton W v Sheffield U

Saturday, 24 April 2021
Arsenal v Everton
Aston Villa v WBA
Fulham v Tottenham H
Leeds U v Manchester U
Leicester C v Crystal Palace
Liverpool v Newcastle U
Manchester City v Southampton
Sheffield U v Brighton & HA
West Ham U v Chelsea
Wolverhampton W v Burnley

Saturday, 1 May 2021
Brighton & HA v Leeds U
Burnley v West Ham U
Chelsea v Fulham
Crystal Palace v Manchester City
Everton v Aston Villa
Manchester U v Liverpool
Newcastle U v Arsenal
Southampton v Leicester C
Tottenham H v Sheffield U
WBA v Wolverhampton W

Saturday, 8 May 2021
Arsenal v WBA
Aston Villa v Manchester U
Fulham v Burnley
Leeds U v Tottenham H
Leicester C v Newcastle U
Liverpool v Southampton
Manchester City v Chelsea
Sheffield U v Crystal Palace
West Ham U v Everton
Wolverhampton W v Brighton & HA

Tuesday, 11 May 2021
Brighton & HA v West Ham U
Burnley v Leeds U
Everton v Sheffield U
Manchester U v Leicester C
WBA v Liverpool

Wednesday, 12 May 2021
Chelsea v Arsenal
Newcastle U v Manchester City
Southampton v Fulham
Tottenham H v Wolverhampton W
Crystal Palace v Aston Villa

Saturday, 15 May 2021
Brighton & HA v Manchester City
Burnley v Liverpool
Chelsea v Leicester C
Crystal Palace v Arsenal
Everton v Wolverhampton W
Manchester U v Fulham
Newcastle U v Sheffield U
Southampton v Leeds U
Tottenham H v Aston Villa
WBA v West Ham U

Sunday, 23 May 2021
Arsenal v Brighton & HA
Aston Villa v Chelsea
Fulham v Newcastle U

Leeds U v WBA
Leicester C v Tottenham H
Liverpool v Crystal Palace
Manchester City v Everton
Sheffield U v Burnley
West Ham U v Southampton
Wolverhampton W v Manchester U

EFL Championship

Saturday, 12 September 2020
Barnsley v Luton T
Birmingham C v Brentford
Bournemouth v Blackburn R
Bristol C v Coventry C
Cardiff C v Sheffield W
Derby Co v Reading
Huddersfield T v Norwich C
Millwall v Stoke C
Preston NE v Swansea C
QPR v Nottingham F
Watford v Middlesbrough
Wycombe W v Rotherham U

Saturday, 19 September 2020
Blackburn R v Wycombe W
Brentford v Huddersfield T
Coventry C v QPR
Luton T v Derby Co
Middlesbrough v Bournemouth
Norwich C v Preston NE
Nottingham F v Cardiff C
Reading v Barnsley
Rotherham U v Millwall
Sheffield W v Watford
Stoke C v Bristol C
Swansea C v Birmingham C

Saturday, 26 September 2020
Barnsley v Coventry C
Birmingham C v Rotherham U
Bournemouth v Norwich C
Bristol C v Sheffield W
Cardiff C v Reading
Derby Co v Blackburn R
Huddersfield T v Nottingham F
Millwall v Brentford
Preston NE v Stoke C
QPR v Middlesbrough
Watford v Luton T
Wycombe W v Swansea C

Saturday, 3 October 2020
Blackburn R v Cardiff C
Brentford v Preston NE
Coventry C v Bournemouth
Luton T v Wycombe W
Middlesbrough v Barnsley
Norwich C v Derby Co
Nottingham F v Bristol C
Reading v Watford
Rotherham U v Huddersfield T
Sheffield W v QPR
Stoke C v Birmingham C
Swansea C v Millwall

Saturday, 17 October 2020
Barnsley v Bristol C
Birmingham C v Sheffield W
Blackburn R v Nottingham F
Bournemouth v QPR
Brentford v Coventry C
Derby Co v Watford
Luton T v Stoke C
Middlesbrough v Reading
Preston NE v Cardiff C
Rotherham U v Norwich C
Swansea C v Huddersfield T
Wycombe W v Millwall

Tuesday, 20 October 2020
Bristol C v Middlesbrough
Coventry C v Swansea C
Millwall v Luton T
Norwich C v Birmingham C
Nottingham F v Rotherham U
Reading v Wycombe W

Wednesday, 21 October 2020
Cardiff C v Bournemouth
Huddersfield T v Derby Co
QPR v Preston NE
Sheffield W v Brentford
Watford v Blackburn R
Stoke C v Barnsley

Saturday, 24 October 2020
Bristol C v Swansea C
Cardiff C v Middlesbrough
Coventry C v Blackburn R
Huddersfield T v Preston NE
Millwall v Barnsley
Norwich C v Wycombe W
Nottingham F v Derby Co
QPR v Birmingham C
Reading v Rotherham U
Sheffield W v Luton T
Stoke C v Brentford
Watford v Bournemouth

Tuesday, 27 October 2020
Barnsley v QPR
Blackburn R v Reading
Brentford v Norwich C
Middlesbrough v Coventry C
Swansea C v Stoke C
Wycombe W v Watford

Wednesday, 28 October 2020
Birmingham C v Huddersfield T
Bournemouth v Bristol C
Derby Co v Cardiff C
Luton T v Nottingham F
Preston NE v Millwall
Rotherham U v Sheffield W

Saturday, 31 October 2020
Barnsley v Watford
Bournemouth v Derby Co
Bristol C v Norwich C
Coventry C v Reading
Luton T v Brentford
Middlesbrough v Nottingham F
Millwall v Huddersfield T
Preston NE v Birmingham C
QPR v Cardiff C
Stoke C v Rotherham U
Swansea C v Blackburn R
Wycombe W v Sheffield W

Tuesday, 3 November 2020
Blackburn R v Middlesbrough
Brentford v Swansea C
Cardiff C v Barnsley
Huddersfield T v Bristol C
Norwich C v Millwall
Sheffield W v Bournemouth

Wednesday, 4 November 2020
Birmingham C v Wycombe W
Derby Co v QPR
Nottingham F v Coventry C
Rotherham U v Luton T
Watford v Stoke C
Reading v Preston NE

Saturday, 7 November 2020
Birmingham C v Bournemouth
Blackburn R v QPR
Brentford v Middlesbrough
Cardiff C v Bristol C
Derby Co v Barnsley
Huddersfield T v Luton T
Norwich C v Swansea C
Nottingham F v Wycombe W
Reading v Stoke C
Rotherham U v Preston NE
Sheffield W v Millwall
Watford v Coventry C

Saturday, 21 November 2020
Barnsley v Nottingham F
Bournemouth v Reading
Bristol C v Derby Co
Coventry C v Birmingham C
Luton T v Blackburn R
Middlesbrough v Norwich C
Millwall v Cardiff C
Preston NE v Sheffield W
QPR v Watford
Stoke C v Huddersfield T
Swansea C v Rotherham U
Wycombe W v Brentford

Tuesday, 24 November 2020
Barnsley v Brentford
Bournemouth v Nottingham F
Luton T v Birmingham C
Preston NE v Blackburn R
QPR v Rotherham U
Stoke C v Norwich C

Wednesday, 25 November 2020
Bristol C v Watford
Coventry C v Cardiff C
Middlesbrough v Derby Co
Millwall v Reading
Swansea C v Sheffield W
Wycombe W v Huddersfield T

Saturday, 28 November 2020
Birmingham C v Millwall
Blackburn R v Barnsley
Brentford v QPR
Cardiff C v Luton T
Derby Co v Wycombe W
Huddersfield T v Middlesbrough
Norwich C v Coventry C
Nottingham F v Swansea C
Reading v Bristol C
Rotherham U v Bournemouth
Sheffield W v Stoke C
Watford v Preston NE

Tuesday, 1 December 2020
Birmingham C v Barnsley
Bournemouth v Preston NE
Cardiff C v Huddersfield T
Derby Co v Coventry C
QPR v Bristol C
Rotherham U v Brentford

Wednesday, 2 December 2020
Blackburn R v Millwall
Luton T v Norwich C
Middlesbrough v Swansea C
Nottingham F v Watford
Sheffield W v Reading
Wycombe W v Stoke C

Saturday, 5 December 2020
Barnsley v Bournemouth
Brentford v Blackburn R
Bristol C v Birmingham C
Coventry C v Rotherham U
Huddersfield T v QPR
Millwall v Derby Co
Norwich C v Sheffield W
Preston NE v Wycombe W
Reading v Nottingham F
Stoke C v Middlesbrough
Swansea C v Luton T
Watford v Cardiff C

Tuesday, 8 December 2020
Coventry C v Luton T
Huddersfield T v Sheffield W
Millwall v QPR

Swansea C v Bournemouth
Watford v Rotherham U
Stoke C v Cardiff C

Wednesday, 9 December 2020
Barnsley v Wycombe W
Brentford v Derby Co
Bristol C v Blackburn R
Norwich C v Nottingham F
Preston NE v Middlesbrough
Reading v Birmingham C

Saturday, 12 December 2020
Birmingham C v Watford
Blackburn R v Norwich C
Bournemouth v Huddersfield T
Cardiff C v Swansea C
Derby Co v Stoke C
Luton T v Preston NE
Middlesbrough v Millwall
Nottingham F v Brentford
QPR v Reading
Rotherham U v Bristol C
Sheffield W v Barnsley
Wycombe W v Coventry C

Tuesday, 15 December 2020
Barnsley v Preston NE
Bournemouth v Wycombe W
Bristol C v Millwall
Nottingham F v Sheffield W
QPR v Stoke C
Watford v Brentford

Wednesday, 16 December 2020
Blackburn R v Rotherham U
Cardiff C v Birmingham C
Coventry C v Huddersfield T
Derby Co v Swansea C
Middlesbrough v Luton T
Reading v Norwich C

Saturday, 19 December 2020
Birmingham C v Middlesbrough
Brentford v Reading
Huddersfield T v Watford
Luton T v Bournemouth
Millwall v Nottingham F
Norwich C v Cardiff C
Preston NE v Bristol C
Rotherham U v Derby Co
Sheffield W v Coventry C
Stoke C v Blackburn R
Swansea C v Barnsley
Wycombe W v QPR

Saturday, 26 December 2020
Barnsley v Huddersfield T
Blackburn R v Sheffield W
Bournemouth v Millwall
Bristol C v Wycombe W
Cardiff C v Brentford
Coventry C v Stoke C
Derby Co v Preston NE
Middlesbrough v Rotherham U
Nottingham F v Birmingham C
QPR v Swansea C
Reading v Luton T
Watford v Norwich C

Tuesday, 29 December 2020
Birmingham C v Derby Co
Brentford v Bournemouth
Huddersfield T v Blackburn R
Luton T v Bristol C
Millwall v Watford
Norwich C v QPR
Preston NE v Coventry C
Rotherham U v Barnsley
Sheffield W v Middlesbrough
Swansea C v Reading
Wycombe W v Cardiff C
Stoke C v Nottingham F

Saturday, 2 January 2021
Birmingham C v Blackburn R
Brentford v Bristol C
Huddersfield T v Reading
Luton T v QPR
Millwall v Coventry C
Norwich C v Barnsley
Preston NE v Nottingham F
Rotherham U v Cardiff C
Sheffield W v Derby Co
Stoke C v Bournemouth
Swansea C v Watford
Wycombe W v Middlesbrough

Saturday, 16 January 2021
Barnsley v Swansea C
Blackburn R v Stoke C
Bournemouth v Luton T
Bristol C v Preston NE
Cardiff C v Norwich C
Coventry C v Sheffield W
Derby Co v Rotherham U
Middlesbrough v Birmingham C
Nottingham F v Millwall
QPR v Wycombe W
Reading v Brentford
Watford v Huddersfield T

Tuesday, 19 January 2021
Blackburn R v Swansea C
Derby Co v Bournemouth
Rotherham U v Stoke C
Sheffield W v Wycombe W
Watford v Barnsley
Reading v Coventry C

Wednesday, 20 January 2021
Birmingham C v Preston NE
Brentford v Luton T
Cardiff C v QPR
Huddersfield T v Millwall
Norwich C v Bristol C
Nottingham F v Middlesbrough

Saturday, 23 January 2021
Barnsley v Cardiff C
Bournemouth v Sheffield W
Bristol C v Huddersfield T
Coventry C v Nottingham F
Luton T v Rotherham U
Middlesbrough v Blackburn R
Millwall v Norwich C
Preston NE v Reading
QPR v Derby Co
Stoke C v Watford
Swansea C v Brentford
Wycombe W v Birmingham C

Saturday, 30 January 2021
Birmingham C v Coventry C
Blackburn R v Luton T
Brentford v Wycombe W
Cardiff C v Millwall
Derby Co v Bristol C
Huddersfield T v Stoke C
Norwich C v Middlesbrough
Nottingham F v Barnsley
Reading v Bournemouth
Rotherham U v Swansea C
Sheffield W v Preston NE
Watford v QPR

Saturday, 6 February 2021
Barnsley v Derby Co
Bournemouth v Birmingham C
Bristol C v Cardiff C
Coventry C v Watford
Luton T v Huddersfield T
Middlesbrough v Brentford
Millwall v Sheffield W
Preston NE v Rotherham U
QPR v Blackburn R
Stoke C v Reading

Swansea C v Norwich C
Wycombe W v Nottingham F

Saturday, 13 February 2021
Birmingham C v Luton T
Blackburn R v Preston NE
Brentford v Barnsley
Cardiff C v Coventry C
Derby Co v Middlesbrough
Huddersfield T v Wycombe W
Norwich C v Stoke C
Nottingham F v Bournemouth
Reading v Millwall
Rotherham U v QPR
Sheffield W v Swansea C
Watford v Bristol C

Tuesday, 16 February 2021
Bristol C v Reading
Luton T v Cardiff C
Middlesbrough v Huddersfield T
Preston NE v Watford
Wycombe W v Derby Co
Stoke C v Sheffield W

Wednesday, 17 February 2021
Barnsley v Blackburn R
Bournemouth v Rotherham U
Coventry C v Norwich C
Millwall v Birmingham C
QPR v Brentford
Swansea C v Nottingham F

Saturday, 20 February 2021
Bristol C v Barnsley
Cardiff C v Preston NE
Coventry C v Brentford
Huddersfield T v Swansea C
Millwall v Wycombe W
Norwich C v Rotherham U
Nottingham F v Blackburn R
QPR v Bournemouth
Reading v Middlesbrough
Sheffield W v Birmingham C
Stoke C v Luton T
Watford v Derby Co

Tuesday, 23 February 2021
Birmingham C v Norwich C
Derby Co v Huddersfield T
Luton T v Millwall
Middlesbrough v Bristol C
Rotherham U v Nottingham F
Wycombe W v Reading

Wednesday, 24 February 2021
Barnsley v Stoke C
Blackburn R v Watford
Bournemouth v Cardiff C
Brentford v Sheffield W
Preston NE v QPR
Swansea C v Coventry C

Saturday, 27 February 2021
Barnsley v Millwall
Birmingham C v QPR
Blackburn R v Coventry C
Bournemouth v Watford
Brentford v Stoke C
Derby Co v Nottingham F
Luton T v Sheffield W
Middlesbrough v Cardiff C
Preston NE v Huddersfield T
Rotherham U v Reading
Swansea C v Bristol C
Wycombe W v Norwich C

Tuesday, 2 March 2021
Cardiff C v Derby Co
Coventry C v Middlesbrough
Huddersfield T v Birmingham C
Millwall v Preston NE
Nottingham F v Luton T
Reading v Blackburn R

Wednesday, 3 March 2021
Bristol C v Bournemouth
Norwich C v Brentford
QPR v Barnsley
Sheffield W v Rotherham U
Watford v Wycombe W
Stoke C v Swansea C

Saturday, 6 March 2021
Barnsley v Birmingham C
Brentford v Rotherham U
Bristol C v QPR
Coventry C v Derby Co
Huddersfield T v Cardiff C
Millwall v Blackburn R
Norwich C v Luton T
Preston NE v Bournemouth
Reading v Sheffield W
Stoke C v Wycombe W
Swansea C v Middlesbrough
Watford v Nottingham F

Saturday, 13 March 2021
Birmingham C v Bristol C
Blackburn R v Brentford
Bournemouth v Barnsley
Cardiff C v Watford
Derby Co v Millwall
Luton T v Swansea C
Middlesbrough v Stoke C
Nottingham F v Reading
QPR v Huddersfield T
Rotherham U v Coventry C
Sheffield W v Norwich C
Wycombe W v Preston NE

Tuesday, 16 March 2021
Bournemouth v Swansea C
Cardiff C v Stoke C
Derby Co v Brentford
Luton T v Coventry C
Middlesbrough v Preston NE
Rotherham U v Watford

Wednesday, 17 March 2021
Birmingham C v Reading
Blackburn R v Bristol C
Nottingham F v Norwich C
QPR v Millwall
Sheffield W v Huddersfield T
Wycombe W v Barnsley

Saturday, 20 March 2021
Barnsley v Sheffield W
Brentford v Nottingham F
Bristol C v Rotherham U
Coventry C v Wycombe W
Huddersfield T v Bournemouth
Millwall v Middlesbrough
Norwich C v Blackburn R
Preston NE v Luton T
Reading v QPR
Stoke C v Derby Co
Swansea C v Cardiff C
Watford v Birmingham C

Friday, 2 April 2021
Barnsley v Reading
Birmingham C v Swansea C
Bournemouth v Middlesbrough
Bristol C v Stoke C
Cardiff C v Nottingham F
Derby Co v Luton T
Huddersfield T v Brentford
Millwall v Rotherham U
Preston NE v Norwich C
QPR v Coventry C
Watford v Sheffield W
Wycombe W v Blackburn R

Monday, 5 April 2021
Blackburn R v Bournemouth
Brentford v Birmingham C
Coventry C v Bristol C
Luton T v Barnsley
Middlesbrough v Watford
Norwich C v Huddersfield T
Nottingham F v QPR
Reading v Derby Co
Rotherham U v Wycombe W
Sheffield W v Cardiff C
Stoke C v Millwall
Swansea C v Preston NE

Saturday, 10 April 2021
Barnsley v Middlesbrough
Birmingham C v Stoke C
Bournemouth v Coventry C
Bristol C v Nottingham F
Cardiff C v Blackburn R
Derby Co v Norwich C
Huddersfield T v Rotherham U
Millwall v Swansea C
Preston NE v Brentford
QPR v Sheffield W
Watford v Reading
Wycombe W v Luton T

Saturday, 17 April 2021
Blackburn R v Derby Co
Brentford v Millwall
Coventry C v Barnsley
Luton T v Watford
Middlesbrough v QPR
Norwich C v Bournemouth
Nottingham F v Huddersfield T
Reading v Cardiff C
Rotherham U v Birmingham C
Sheffield W v Bristol C
Stoke C v Preston NE
Swansea C v Wycombe W

Tuesday, 20 April 2021
Birmingham C v Nottingham F
Brentford v Cardiff C
Norwich C v Watford
Preston NE v Derby Co
Sheffield W v Blackburn R
Swansea C v QPR

Wednesday, 21 April 2021
Huddersfield T v Barnsley
Luton T v Reading
Millwall v Bournemouth
Rotherham U v Middlesbrough
Wycombe W v Bristol C
Stoke C v Coventry C

Saturday, 24 April 2021
Barnsley v Rotherham U
Blackburn R v Huddersfield T
Bournemouth v Brentford
Bristol C v Luton T
Cardiff C v Wycombe W
Coventry C v Preston NE
Derby Co v Birmingham C
Middlesbrough v Sheffield W
Nottingham F v Stoke C
QPR v Norwich C
Reading v Swansea C
Watford v Millwall

Saturday, 1 May 2021
Birmingham C v Cardiff C
Brentford v Watford
Huddersfield T v Coventry C
Luton T v Middlesbrough
Millwall v Bristol C
Norwich C v Reading
Preston NE v Barnsley
Rotherham U v Blackburn R
Sheffield W v Nottingham F
Stoke C v QPR
Swansea C v Derby Co
Wycombe W v Bournemouth

Saturday, 8 May 2021
Barnsley v Norwich C
Blackburn R v Birmingham C
Bournemouth v Stoke C
Bristol C v Brentford
Cardiff C v Rotherham U
Coventry C v Millwall
Derby Co v Sheffield W
Middlesbrough v Wycombe W
Nottingham F v Preston NE
QPR v Luton T
Reading v Huddersfield T
Watford v Swansea C

EFL League One

Saturday, 12 September 2020
Accrington S v Peterborough U
Crewe Alex v Charlton Ath
Doncaster R v Milton Keynes D
Fleetwood T v Burton Alb
Gillingham v Hull C
Ipswich T v Wigan Ath
Lincoln C v Oxford U
Northampton T v AFC Wimbledon
Plymouth Arg v Blackpool
Portsmouth v Shrewsbury T
Sunderland v Bristol R
Swindon T v Rochdale

Saturday, 19 September 2020
AFC Wimbledon v Plymouth Arg
Blackpool v Swindon T
Bristol R v Ipswich T
Burton Alb v Accrington S
Charlton Ath v Doncaster R
Hull C v Crewe Alex
Milton Keynes D v Lincoln C
Oxford U v Sunderland
Peterborough U v Fleetwood T
Rochdale v Portsmouth
Shrewsbury T v Northampton T
Wigan Ath v Gillingham

Saturday, 26 September 2020
Accrington S v Oxford U
Crewe Alex v Milton Keynes D
Doncaster R v Bristol R
Fleetwood T v AFC Wimbledon
Gillingham v Blackpool
Ipswich T v Rochdale
Lincoln C v Charlton Ath
Northampton T v Hull C
Plymouth Arg v Shrewsbury T
Portsmouth v Wigan Ath
Sunderland v Peterborough U
Swindon T v Burton Alb

Saturday, 3 October 2020
AFC Wimbledon v Accrington S
Blackpool v Lincoln C
Bristol R v Northampton T
Burton Alb v Portsmouth
Charlton Ath v Sunderland
Hull C v Plymouth Arg
Milton Keynes D v Ipswich T
Oxford U v Crewe Alex
Peterborough U v Swindon T
Rochdale v Fleetwood T
Shrewsbury T v Gillingham
Wigan Ath v Doncaster R

Saturday, 10 October 2020
Accrington S v Rochdale
Crewe Alex v Wigan Ath
Doncaster R v Shrewsbury T
Fleetwood T v Hull C
Gillingham v Oxford U
Ipswich T v Charlton Ath
Lincoln C v Bristol R
Northampton T v Peterborough U
Plymouth Arg v Burton Alb
Portsmouth v Milton Keynes D

Sunderland v Blackpool
Swindon T v AFC Wimbledon

Saturday, 17 October 2020
AFC Wimbledon v Shrewsbury T
Bristol R v Burton Alb
Charlton Ath v Wigan Ath
Crewe Alex v Blackpool
Fleetwood T v Lincoln C
Ipswich T v Accrington S
Milton Keynes D v Gillingham
Peterborough U v Oxford U
Plymouth Arg v Northampton T
Portsmouth v Doncaster R
Rochdale v Hull C
Swindon T v Sunderland

Tuesday, 20 October 2020
Accrington S v Fleetwood T
Blackpool v Charlton Ath
Burton Alb v Rochdale
Gillingham v Portsmouth
Hull C v AFC Wimbledon
Lincoln C v Plymouth Arg
Northampton T v Swindon T
Oxford U v Milton Keynes D
Shrewsbury T v Bristol R
Sunderland v Crewe Alex
Wigan Ath v Peterborough U
Doncaster R v Ipswich T

Saturday, 24 October 2020
Accrington S v Bristol R
Blackpool v Milton Keynes D
Burton Alb v AFC Wimbledon
Doncaster R v Crewe Alex
Gillingham v Fleetwood T
Hull C v Peterborough U
Lincoln C v Ipswich T
Northampton T v Charlton Ath
Oxford U v Swindon T
Shrewsbury T v Rochdale
Sunderland v Portsmouth
Wigan Ath v Plymouth Arg

Tuesday, 27 October 2020
AFC Wimbledon v Blackpool
Bristol R v Hull C
Charlton Ath v Oxford U
Crewe Alex v Lincoln C
Fleetwood T v Shrewsbury T
Ipswich T v Gillingham
Milton Keynes D v Wigan Ath
Peterborough U v Burton Alb
Plymouth Arg v Doncaster R
Portsmouth v Northampton T
Rochdale v Sunderland
Swindon T v Accrington S

Saturday, 31 October 2020
Accrington S v Plymouth Arg
Burton Alb v Blackpool
Doncaster R v Lincoln C
Fleetwood T v Oxford U
Gillingham v Sunderland
Ipswich T v Crewe Alex
Milton Keynes D v AFC Wimbledon
Peterborough U v Shrewsbury T
Portsmouth v Charlton Ath
Rochdale v Bristol R
Swindon T v Hull C
Wigan Ath v Northampton T

Tuesday, 3 November 2020
AFC Wimbledon v Doncaster R
Blackpool v Wigan Ath
Bristol R v Peterborough U
Charlton Ath v Fleetwood T
Crewe Alex v Gillingham
Hull C v Accrington S
Lincoln C v Portsmouth
Northampton T v Milton Keynes D
Oxford U v Rochdale
Plymouth Arg v Swindon T
Shrewsbury T v Burton Alb
Sunderland v Ipswich T

Saturday, 14 November 2020
AFC Wimbledon v Wigan Ath
Blackpool v Ipswich T
Bristol R v Fleetwood T
Charlton Ath v Rochdale
Crewe Alex v Peterborough U
Hull C v Burton Alb
Lincoln C v Gillingham
Northampton T v Accrington S
Oxford U v Doncaster R
Plymouth Arg v Portsmouth
Shrewsbury T v Swindon T
Sunderland v Milton Keynes D

Saturday, 21 November 2020
Accrington S v Lincoln C
Burton Alb v Northampton T
Doncaster R v Sunderland
Fleetwood T v Plymouth Arg
Gillingham v Charlton Ath
Ipswich T v Shrewsbury T
Milton Keynes D v Hull C
Peterborough U v Blackpool
Portsmouth v Crewe Alex
Rochdale v AFC Wimbledon
Swindon T v Bristol R
Wigan Ath v Oxford U

Tuesday, 24 November 2020
Accrington S v Crewe Alex
Burton Alb v Charlton Ath
Fleetwood T v Sunderland
Gillingham v AFC Wimbledon
Ipswich T v Hull C
Milton Keynes D v Shrewsbury T
Peterborough U v Plymouth Arg
Portsmouth v Oxford U
Rochdale v Northampton T
Swindon T v Lincoln C
Wigan Ath v Bristol R
Doncaster R v Blackpool

Tuesday, 1 December 2020
AFC Wimbledon v Peterborough U
Blackpool v Portsmouth
Bristol R v Gillingham
Charlton Ath v Milton Keynes D
Crewe Alex v Swindon T
Hull C v Doncaster R
Lincoln C v Wigan Ath
Northampton T v Fleetwood T
Oxford U v Ipswich T
Plymouth Arg v Rochdale
Shrewsbury T v Accrington S
Sunderland v Burton Alb

Saturday, 5 December 2020
Accrington S v Milton Keynes D
AFC Wimbledon v Bristol R
Burton Alb v Crewe Alex
Fleetwood T v Blackpool
Gillingham v Swindon T
Northampton T v Doncaster R
Oxford U v Hull C
Plymouth Arg v Ipswich T
Portsmouth v Peterborough U
Rochdale v Lincoln C
Shrewsbury T v Charlton Ath
Sunderland v Wigan Ath

Saturday, 12 December 2020
Blackpool v Oxford U
Bristol R v Plymouth Arg
Charlton Ath v AFC Wimbledon
Crewe Alex v Northampton T
Doncaster R v Gillingham
Hull C v Shrewsbury T
Ipswich T v Portsmouth
Lincoln C v Sunderland
Milton Keynes D v Burton Alb
Peterborough U v Rochdale
Swindon T v Fleetwood T
Wigan Ath v Accrington S

Tuesday, 15 December 2020
Blackpool v Hull C
Charlton Ath v Bristol R
Crewe Alex v Plymouth Arg
Gillingham v Accrington S
Ipswich T v Burton Alb
Lincoln C v Shrewsbury T
Milton Keynes D v Peterborough U
Oxford U v Northampton T
Portsmouth v Fleetwood T
Sunderland v AFC Wimbledon
Wigan Ath v Rochdale
Doncaster R v Swindon T

Saturday, 19 December 2020
Accrington S v Blackpool
AFC Wimbledon v Crewe Alex
Bristol R v Oxford U
Burton Alb v Doncaster R
Fleetwood T v Wigan Ath
Hull C v Portsmouth
Northampton T v Lincoln C
Peterborough U v Ipswich T
Plymouth Arg v Milton Keynes D
Rochdale v Gillingham
Shrewsbury T v Sunderland
Swindon T v Charlton Ath

Saturday, 26 December 2020
Blackpool v Rochdale
Charlton Ath v Plymouth Arg
Crewe Alex v Fleetwood T
Doncaster R v Accrington S
Gillingham v Peterborough U
Ipswich T v Northampton T
Lincoln C v Burton Alb
Milton Keynes D v Bristol R
Oxford U v AFC Wimbledon
Portsmouth v Swindon T
Sunderland v Hull C
Wigan Ath v Shrewsbury T

Tuesday, 29 December 2020
Accrington S v Sunderland
AFC Wimbledon v Ipswich T
Bristol R v Portsmouth
Burton Alb v Wigan Ath
Fleetwood T v Doncaster R
Hull C v Lincoln C
Northampton T v Gillingham
Peterborough U v Charlton Ath
Plymouth Arg v Oxford U
Rochdale v Crewe Alex
Shrewsbury T v Blackpool
Swindon T v Milton Keynes D

Saturday, 2 January 2021
Accrington S v Portsmouth
AFC Wimbledon v Lincoln C
Bristol R v Blackpool
Burton Alb v Oxford U
Fleetwood T v Ipswich T
Hull C v Charlton Ath
Northampton T v Sunderland
Peterborough U v Doncaster R
Plymouth Arg v Gillingham
Rochdale v Milton Keynes D
Shrewsbury T v Crewe Alex
Swindon T v Wigan Ath

Saturday, 9 January 2021
Blackpool v Northampton T
Charlton Ath v Accrington S
Crewe Alex v Bristol R
Doncaster R v Rochdale
Gillingham v Burton Alb
Ipswich T v Swindon T
Lincoln C v Peterborough U

Milton Keynes D v Fleetwood T
Oxford U v Shrewsbury T
Portsmouth v AFC Wimbledon
Sunderland v Plymouth Arg
Wigan Ath v Hull C

Saturday, 16 January 2021
Accrington S v Gillingham
AFC Wimbledon v Sunderland
Bristol R v Charlton Ath
Burton Alb v Ipswich T
Fleetwood T v Portsmouth
Hull C v Blackpool
Northampton T v Oxford U
Peterborough U v Milton Keynes D
Plymouth Arg v Crewe Alex
Rochdale v Wigan Ath
Shrewsbury T v Lincoln C
Swindon T v Doncaster R

Saturday, 23 January 2021
Blackpool v Accrington S
Charlton Ath v Swindon T
Crewe Alex v AFC Wimbledon
Doncaster R v Burton Alb
Gillingham v Rochdale
Ipswich T v Peterborough U
Lincoln C v Northampton T
Milton Keynes D v Plymouth Arg
Oxford U v Bristol R
Portsmouth v Hull C
Sunderland v Shrewsbury T
Wigan Ath v Fleetwood T

Tuesday, 26 January 2021
Accrington S v Hull C
Burton Alb v Shrewsbury T
Fleetwood T v Northampton T
Gillingham v Crewe Alex
Ipswich T v Sunderland
Milton Keynes D v Charlton Ath
Peterborough U v Bristol R
Portsmouth v Lincoln C
Rochdale v Oxford U
Swindon T v Plymouth Arg
Wigan Ath v Blackpool
Doncaster R v AFC Wimbledon

Saturday, 30 January 2021
AFC Wimbledon v Milton Keynes D
Blackpool v Burton Alb
Bristol R v Rochdale
Charlton Ath v Portsmouth
Crewe Alex v Ipswich T
Hull C v Swindon T
Lincoln C v Doncaster R
Northampton T v Wigan Ath
Oxford U v Fleetwood T
Plymouth Arg v Accrington S
Shrewsbury T v Peterborough U
Sunderland v Gillingham

Saturday, 6 February 2021
Accrington S v Northampton T
Burton Alb v Hull C
Doncaster R v Oxford U
Fleetwood T v Bristol R
Gillingham v Lincoln C
Ipswich T v Blackpool
Milton Keynes D v Sunderland
Peterborough U v Crewe Alex
Portsmouth v Plymouth Arg
Rochdale v Charlton Ath
Swindon T v Shrewsbury T
Wigan Ath v AFC Wimbledon

Saturday, 13 February 2021
AFC Wimbledon v Rochdale
Blackpool v Peterborough U
Bristol R v Swindon T
Charlton Ath v Gillingham
Crewe Alex v Portsmouth
Hull C v Milton Keynes D
Lincoln C v Accrington S
Northampton T v Burton Alb
Oxford U v Wigan Ath
Plymouth Arg v Fleetwood T
Shrewsbury T v Ipswich T
Sunderland v Doncaster R

Saturday, 20 February 2021
Accrington S v Shrewsbury T
Burton Alb v Sunderland
Doncaster R v Hull C
Fleetwood T v Charlton Ath
Gillingham v Bristol R
Ipswich T v Oxford U
Milton Keynes D v Northampton T
Peterborough U v AFC Wimbledon
Portsmouth v Blackpool
Rochdale v Plymouth Arg
Swindon T v Crewe Alex
Wigan Ath v Lincoln C

Tuesday, 23 February 2021
AFC Wimbledon v Gillingham
Blackpool v Doncaster R
Bristol R v Wigan Ath
Charlton Ath v Burton Alb
Crewe Alex v Accrington S
Hull C v Ipswich T
Lincoln C v Swindon T
Northampton T v Rochdale
Oxford U v Portsmouth
Plymouth Arg v Peterborough U
Shrewsbury T v Milton Keynes D
Sunderland v Fleetwood T

Saturday, 27 February 2021
AFC Wimbledon v Hull C
Bristol R v Shrewsbury T
Charlton Ath v Blackpool
Crewe Alex v Sunderland
Fleetwood T v Accrington S
Ipswich T v Doncaster R
Milton Keynes D v Oxford U
Peterborough U v Wigan Ath
Plymouth Arg v Lincoln C
Portsmouth v Gillingham
Rochdale v Burton Alb
Swindon T v Northampton T

Tuesday, 2 March 2021
Accrington S v Ipswich T
Blackpool v Crewe Alex
Burton Alb v Bristol R
Gillingham v Milton Keynes D
Hull C v Rochdale
Lincoln C v Fleetwood T
Northampton T v Plymouth Arg
Oxford U v Peterborough U
Shrewsbury T v AFC Wimbledon
Sunderland v Swindon T
Wigan Ath v Charlton Ath
Doncaster R v Portsmouth

Saturday, 6 March 2021
Accrington S v Swindon T
Blackpool v AFC Wimbledon
Burton Alb v Peterborough U
Doncaster R v Plymouth Arg
Gillingham v Ipswich T
Hull C v Bristol R
Lincoln C v Crewe Alex
Northampton T v Portsmouth
Oxford U v Charlton Ath
Shrewsbury T v Fleetwood T
Sunderland v Rochdale
Wigan Ath v Milton Keynes D

Tuesday, 9 March 2021
AFC Wimbledon v Burton Alb
Bristol R v Accrington S
Charlton Ath v Northampton T
Crewe Alex v Doncaster R
Fleetwood T v Gillingham
Ipswich T v Lincoln C
Milton Keynes D v Blackpool
Peterborough U v Hull C
Plymouth Arg v Wigan Ath
Portsmouth v Sunderland
Rochdale v Shrewsbury T
Swindon T v Oxford U

Saturday, 13 March 2021
Blackpool v Fleetwood T
Bristol R v AFC Wimbledon
Charlton Ath v Shrewsbury T
Crewe Alex v Burton Alb
Doncaster R v Northampton T
Hull C v Oxford U
Ipswich T v Plymouth Arg
Lincoln C v Rochdale
Milton Keynes D v Accrington S
Peterborough U v Portsmouth
Swindon T v Gillingham
Wigan Ath v Sunderland

Saturday, 20 March 2021
Accrington S v Wigan Ath
AFC Wimbledon v Charlton Ath
Burton Alb v Milton Keynes D
Fleetwood T v Swindon T
Gillingham v Doncaster R
Northampton T v Crewe Alex
Oxford U v Blackpool
Plymouth Arg v Bristol R
Portsmouth v Ipswich T
Rochdale v Peterborough U
Shrewsbury T v Hull C
Sunderland v Lincoln C

Saturday, 27 March 2021
AFC Wimbledon v Northampton T
Blackpool v Plymouth Arg
Bristol R v Sunderland
Burton Alb v Fleetwood T
Charlton Ath v Crewe Alex
Hull C v Gillingham
Milton Keynes D v Doncaster R
Oxford U v Lincoln C
Peterborough U v Accrington S
Rochdale v Swindon T
Shrewsbury T v Portsmouth
Wigan Ath v Ipswich T

Friday, 2 April 2021
Accrington S v Burton Alb
Crewe Alex v Hull C
Doncaster R v Charlton Ath
Fleetwood T v Peterborough U
Gillingham v Wigan Ath
Ipswich T v Bristol R
Lincoln C v Milton Keynes D
Northampton T v Shrewsbury T
Plymouth Arg v AFC Wimbledon
Portsmouth v Rochdale
Sunderland v Oxford U
Swindon T v Blackpool

Monday, 5 April 2021
AFC Wimbledon v Fleetwood T
Blackpool v Gillingham
Bristol R v Doncaster R
Burton Alb v Swindon T
Charlton Ath v Lincoln C
Hull C v Northampton T
Milton Keynes D v Crewe Alex
Oxford U v Accrington S
Peterborough U v Sunderland
Rochdale v Ipswich T
Shrewsbury T v Plymouth Arg
Wigan Ath v Portsmouth

Saturday, 10 April 2021
Accrington S v AFC Wimbledon
Crewe Alex v Oxford U
Doncaster R v Wigan Ath
Fleetwood T v Rochdale

Gillingham v Shrewsbury T
Ipswich T v Milton Keynes D
Lincoln C v Blackpool
Northampton T v Bristol R
Plymouth Arg v Hull C
Portsmouth v Burton Alb
Sunderland v Charlton Ath
Swindon T v Peterborough U

Saturday, 17 April 2021
AFC Wimbledon v Swindon T
Blackpool v Sunderland
Bristol R v Lincoln C
Burton Alb v Plymouth Arg
Charlton Ath v Ipswich T
Hull C v Fleetwood T
Milton Keynes D v Portsmouth
Oxford U v Gillingham
Peterborough U v Northampton T
Rochdale v Accrington S
Shrewsbury T v Doncaster R
Wigan Ath v Crewe Alex

Tuesday, 20 April 2021
Accrington S v Doncaster R
AFC Wimbledon v Oxford U
Bristol R v Milton Keynes D
Burton Alb v Lincoln C
Fleetwood T v Crewe Alex
Hull C v Sunderland
Northampton T v Ipswich T
Peterborough U v Gillingham
Plymouth Arg v Charlton Ath
Rochdale v Blackpool
Shrewsbury T v Wigan Ath
Swindon T v Portsmouth

Saturday, 24 April 2021
Blackpool v Shrewsbury T
Charlton Ath v Peterborough U
Crewe Alex v Rochdale
Doncaster R v Fleetwood T
Gillingham v Northampton T
Ipswich T v AFC Wimbledon
Lincoln C v Hull C
Milton Keynes D v Swindon T
Oxford U v Plymouth Arg
Portsmouth v Bristol R
Sunderland v Accrington S
Wigan Ath v Burton Alb

Saturday, 1 May 2021
Accrington S v Charlton Ath
AFC Wimbledon v Portsmouth
Bristol R v Crewe Alex
Burton Alb v Gillingham
Fleetwood T v Milton Keynes D
Hull C v Wigan Ath
Northampton T v Blackpool
Peterborough U v Lincoln C
Plymouth Arg v Sunderland
Rochdale v Doncaster R
Shrewsbury T v Oxford U
Swindon T v Ipswich T

Saturday, 8 May 2021
Blackpool v Bristol R
Charlton Ath v Hull C
Crewe Alex v Shrewsbury T
Doncaster R v Peterborough U
Gillingham v Plymouth Arg
Ipswich T v Fleetwood T
Lincoln C v AFC Wimbledon
Milton Keynes D v Rochdale
Oxford U v Burton Alb
Portsmouth v Accrington S
Sunderland v Northampton T
Wigan Ath v Swindon T

EFL League Two

Saturday, 12 September 2020
Barrow v Stevenage
Bolton W v Forest Green R
Bradford C v Colchester U
Cambridge U v Carlisle U
Cheltenham T v Morecambe
Mansfield T v Tranmere R
Oldham Ath v Leyton Orient
Port Vale v Crawley T
Salford C v Exeter C
Scunthorpe U v Newport Co
Southend U v Harrogate T
Walsall v Grimsby T

Saturday, 19 September 2020
Carlisle U v Southend U
Colchester U v Bolton W
Crawley T v Scunthorpe U
Exeter C v Port Vale
Forest Green R v Bradford C
Grimsby T v Salford C
Harrogate T v Walsall
Leyton Orient v Mansfield T
Morecambe v Cambridge U
Newport Co v Barrow
Stevenage v Oldham Ath
Tranmere R v Cheltenham T

Saturday, 26 September 2020
Barrow v Colchester U
Bolton W v Newport Co
Bradford C v Stevenage
Cambridge U v Tranmere R
Cheltenham T v Grimsby T
Mansfield T v Exeter C
Oldham Ath v Crawley T
Port Vale v Harrogate T
Salford C v Forest Green R
Scunthorpe U v Carlisle U
Southend U v Morecambe
Walsall v Leyton Orient

Saturday, 3 October 2020
Carlisle U v Barrow
Colchester U v Oldham Ath
Crawley T v Southend U
Exeter C v Cambridge U
Forest Green R v Walsall
Grimsby T v Bradford C
Harrogate T v Bolton W
Leyton Orient v Cheltenham T
Morecambe v Port Vale
Newport Co v Mansfield T
Stevenage v Salford C
Tranmere R v Scunthorpe U

Saturday, 10 October 2020
Barrow v Leyton Orient
Bolton W v Grimsby T
Bradford C v Harrogate T
Cambridge U v Newport Co
Cheltenham T v Crawley T
Mansfield T v Stevenage
Oldham Ath v Morecambe
Port Vale v Carlisle U
Salford C v Tranmere R
Scunthorpe U v Forest Green R
Southend U v Exeter C
Walsall v Colchester U

Saturday, 17 October 2020
Bolton W v Oldham Ath
Carlisle U v Colchester U
Crawley T v Morecambe
Forest Green R v Stevenage
Harrogate T v Barrow
Leyton Orient v Grimsby T
Mansfield T v Bradford C
Newport Co v Tranmere R
Port Vale v Salford C
Scunthorpe U v Cambridge U
Southend U v Cheltenham T
Walsall v Exeter C

Tuesday, 20 October 2020
Barrow v Bolton W
Bradford C v Walsall
Cambridge U v Port Vale
Cheltenham T v Scunthorpe U
Colchester U v Forest Green R
Exeter C v Crawley T
Grimsby T v Harrogate T
Morecambe v Mansfield T
Oldham Ath v Carlisle U
Salford C v Southend U
Stevenage v Newport Co
Tranmere R v Leyton Orient

Saturday, 24 October 2020
Barrow v Walsall
Bradford C v Newport Co
Cambridge U v Bolton W
Cheltenham T v Mansfield T
Colchester U v Harrogate T
Exeter C v Scunthorpe U
Grimsby T v Carlisle U
Morecambe v Forest Green R
Oldham Ath v Port Vale
Salford C v Crawley T
Stevenage v Leyton Orient
Tranmere R v Southend U

Tuesday, 27 October 2020
Carlisle U v Morecambe
Crawley T v Tranmere R
Forest Green R v Grimsby T
Harrogate T v Stevenage
Leyton Orient v Exeter C
Mansfield T v Barrow
Newport Co v Colchester U
Port Vale v Cheltenham T
Scunthorpe U v Salford C
Southend U v Oldham Ath
Walsall v Cambridge U
Bolton W v Bradford C

Saturday, 31 October 2020
Barrow v Bradford C
Cheltenham T v Forest Green R
Crawley T v Cambridge U
Exeter C v Carlisle U
Leyton Orient v Bolton W
Mansfield T v Walsall
Newport Co v Harrogate T
Salford C v Oldham Ath
Scunthorpe U v Colchester U
Southend U v Port Vale
Stevenage v Grimsby T
Tranmere R v Morecambe

Tuesday, 3 November 2020
Bradford C v Southend U
Cambridge U v Salford C
Carlisle U v Newport Co
Colchester U v Stevenage
Forest Green R v Leyton Orient
Grimsby T v Barrow
Harrogate T v Tranmere R
Morecambe v Exeter C
Oldham Ath v Cheltenham T
Port Vale v Scunthorpe U
Walsall v Crawley T
Bolton W v Mansfield T

Saturday, 14 November 2020
Bolton W v Salford C
Bradford C v Exeter C
Cambridge U v Barrow
Carlisle U v Cheltenham T
Colchester U v Leyton Orient
Forest Green R v Mansfield T
Grimsby T v Newport Co
Harrogate T v Crawley T

Morecambe v Stevenage
Oldham Ath v Scunthorpe U
Port Vale v Tranmere R
Walsall v Southend U

Saturday, 21 November 2020
Barrow v Forest Green R
Cheltenham T v Walsall
Crawley T v Carlisle U
Exeter C v Oldham Ath
Leyton Orient v Harrogate T
Mansfield T v Colchester U
Newport Co v Port Vale
Salford C v Bradford C
Scunthorpe U v Morecambe
Southend U v Cambridge U
Stevenage v Bolton W
Tranmere R v Grimsby T

Tuesday, 24 November 2020
Barrow v Oldham Ath
Cheltenham T v Cambridge U
Crawley T v Grimsby T
Exeter C v Colchester U
Leyton Orient v Bradford C
Mansfield T v Harrogate T
Newport Co v Walsall
Salford C v Morecambe
Scunthorpe U v Bolton W
Southend U v Forest Green R
Stevenage v Port Vale
Tranmere R v Carlisle U

Tuesday, 1 December 2020
Bradford C v Cheltenham T
Cambridge U v Mansfield T
Carlisle U v Salford C
Colchester U v Crawley T
Forest Green R v Newport Co
Grimsby T v Exeter C
Harrogate T v Scunthorpe U
Morecambe v Barrow
Oldham Ath v Tranmere R
Port Vale v Leyton Orient
Walsall v Stevenage
Bolton W v Southend U

Saturday, 5 December 2020
Barrow v Salford C
Bolton W v Port Vale
Bradford C v Carlisle U
Cambridge U v Oldham Ath
Cheltenham T v Exeter C
Colchester U v Grimsby T
Harrogate T v Forest Green R
Mansfield T v Crawley T
Newport Co v Morecambe
Scunthorpe U v Leyton Orient
Stevenage v Southend U
Tranmere R v Walsall

Saturday, 12 December 2020
Carlisle U v Stevenage
Crawley T v Barrow
Exeter C v Tranmere R
Forest Green R v Cambridge U
Grimsby T v Mansfield T
Leyton Orient v Newport Co
Morecambe v Harrogate T
Oldham Ath v Bradford C
Port Vale v Colchester U
Salford C v Cheltenham T
Southend U v Scunthorpe U
Walsall v Bolton W

Tuesday, 15 December 2020
Cambridge U v Colchester U
Carlisle U v Mansfield T
Cheltenham T v Bolton W
Crawley T v Bradford C
Exeter C v Harrogate T
Morecambe v Leyton Orient
Oldham Ath v Walsall
Port Vale v Forest Green R
Salford C v Newport Co
Scunthorpe U v Barrow
Southend U v Grimsby T
Tranmere R v Stevenage

Saturday, 19 December 2020
Barrow v Cheltenham T
Bolton W v Tranmere R
Bradford C v Cambridge U
Colchester U v Morecambe
Forest Green R v Carlisle U
Grimsby T v Scunthorpe U
Harrogate T v Salford C
Leyton Orient v Crawley T
Mansfield T v Southend U
Newport Co v Oldham Ath
Stevenage v Exeter C
Walsall v Port Vale

Saturday, 26 December 2020
Cambridge U v Leyton Orient
Carlisle U v Bolton W
Cheltenham T v Stevenage
Crawley T v Newport Co
Exeter C v Forest Green R
Morecambe v Grimsby T
Oldham Ath v Harrogate T
Port Vale v Barrow
Salford C v Walsall
Scunthorpe U v Mansfield T
Southend U v Colchester U
Tranmere R v Bradford C

Tuesday, 29 December 2020
Barrow v Tranmere R
Bradford C v Port Vale
Colchester U v Cheltenham T
Forest Green R v Crawley T
Grimsby T v Oldham Ath
Harrogate T v Carlisle U
Leyton Orient v Southend U
Mansfield T v Salford C
Newport Co v Exeter C
Stevenage v Cambridge U
Walsall v Scunthorpe U
Bolton W v Morecambe

Saturday, 2 January 2021
Barrow v Exeter C
Bolton W v Crawley T
Bradford C v Morecambe
Colchester U v Tranmere R
Forest Green R v Oldham Ath
Grimsby T v Cambridge U
Harrogate T v Cheltenham T
Leyton Orient v Salford C
Mansfield T v Port Vale
Newport Co v Southend U
Stevenage v Scunthorpe U
Walsall v Carlisle U

Saturday, 9 January 2021
Cambridge U v Harrogate T
Carlisle U v Leyton Orient
Cheltenham T v Newport Co
Crawley T v Stevenage
Exeter C v Bolton W
Morecambe v Walsall
Oldham Ath v Mansfield T
Port Vale v Grimsby T
Salford C v Colchester U
Scunthorpe U v Bradford C
Southend U v Barrow
Tranmere R v Forest Green R

Saturday, 16 January 2021
Barrow v Scunthorpe U
Bolton W v Cheltenham T
Bradford C v Crawley T
Colchester U v Cambridge U
Forest Green R v Port Vale
Grimsby T v Southend U
Harrogate T v Exeter C
Leyton Orient v Morecambe
Mansfield T v Carlisle U
Newport Co v Salford C
Stevenage v Tranmere R
Walsall v Oldham Ath

Saturday, 23 January 2021
Cambridge U v Bradford C
Carlisle U v Forest Green R
Cheltenham T v Barrow
Crawley T v Leyton Orient
Exeter C v Stevenage
Morecambe v Colchester U
Oldham Ath v Newport Co
Port Vale v Walsall
Salford C v Harrogate T
Scunthorpe U v Grimsby T
Southend U v Mansfield T
Tranmere R v Bolton W

Tuesday, 26 January 2021
Barrow v Grimsby T
Cheltenham T v Oldham Ath
Crawley T v Walsall
Exeter C v Morecambe
Leyton Orient v Forest Green R
Mansfield T v Bolton W
Newport Co v Carlisle U
Salford C v Cambridge U
Scunthorpe U v Port Vale
Southend U v Bradford C
Stevenage v Colchester U
Tranmere R v Harrogate T

Saturday, 30 January 2021
Bolton W v Leyton Orient
Bradford C v Barrow
Cambridge U v Crawley T
Carlisle U v Exeter C
Colchester U v Scunthorpe U
Forest Green R v Cheltenham T
Grimsby T v Stevenage
Harrogate T v Newport Co
Morecambe v Tranmere R
Oldham Ath v Salford C
Port Vale v Southend U
Walsall v Mansfield T

Saturday, 6 February 2021
Barrow v Cambridge U
Cheltenham T v Carlisle U
Crawley T v Harrogate T
Exeter C v Bradford C
Leyton Orient v Colchester U
Mansfield T v Forest Green R
Newport Co v Grimsby T
Salford C v Bolton W
Scunthorpe U v Oldham Ath
Southend U v Walsall
Stevenage v Morecambe
Tranmere R v Port Vale

Saturday, 13 February 2021
Bolton W v Stevenage
Bradford C v Salford C
Cambridge U v Southend U
Carlisle U v Crawley T
Colchester U v Mansfield T
Forest Green R v Barrow
Grimsby T v Tranmere R
Harrogate T v Leyton Orient
Morecambe v Scunthorpe U
Oldham Ath v Exeter C
Port Vale v Newport Co
Walsall v Cheltenham T

Saturday, 20 February 2021
Barrow v Morecambe
Cheltenham T v Bradford C
Crawley T v Colchester U
Exeter C v Grimsby T
Leyton Orient v Port Vale

Mansfield T v Cambridge U
Newport Co v Forest Green R
Salford C v Carlisle U
Scunthorpe U v Harrogate T
Southend U v Bolton W
Stevenage v Walsall
Tranmere R v Oldham Ath

Tuesday, 23 February 2021
Bradford C v Leyton Orient
Cambridge U v Cheltenham T
Carlisle U v Tranmere R
Colchester U v Exeter C
Forest Green R v Southend U
Grimsby T v Crawley T
Harrogate T v Mansfield T
Morecambe v Salford C
Oldham Ath v Barrow
Port Vale v Stevenage
Walsall v Newport Co
Bolton W v Scunthorpe U

Saturday, 27 February 2021
Bolton W v Barrow
Carlisle U v Oldham Ath
Crawley T v Exeter C
Forest Green R v Colchester U
Harrogate T v Grimsby T
Leyton Orient v Tranmere R
Mansfield T v Morecambe
Newport Co v Stevenage
Port Vale v Cambridge U
Scunthorpe U v Cheltenham T
Southend U v Salford C
Walsall v Bradford C

Tuesday, 2 March 2021
Barrow v Harrogate T
Bradford C v Mansfield T
Cambridge U v Scunthorpe U
Cheltenham T v Southend U
Colchester U v Carlisle U
Exeter C v Walsall
Grimsby T v Leyton Orient
Morecambe v Crawley T
Oldham Ath v Bolton W
Salford C v Port Vale
Stevenage v Forest Green R
Tranmere R v Newport Co

Saturday, 6 March 2021
Barrow v Mansfield T
Bradford C v Bolton W
Cambridge U v Walsall
Cheltenham T v Port Vale
Colchester U v Newport Co
Exeter C v Leyton Orient
Grimsby T v Forest Green R
Morecambe v Carlisle U
Oldham Ath v Southend U
Salford C v Scunthorpe U
Stevenage v Harrogate T
Tranmere R v Crawley T

Tuesday, 9 March 2021
Carlisle U v Grimsby T
Crawley T v Salford C
Forest Green R v Morecambe
Harrogate T v Colchester U
Leyton Orient v Stevenage
Mansfield T v Cheltenham T
Newport Co v Bradford C
Port Vale v Oldham Ath
Scunthorpe U v Exeter C
Southend U v Tranmere R
Walsall v Barrow
Bolton W v Cambridge U

Saturday, 13 March 2021
Carlisle U v Bradford C
Crawley T v Mansfield T
Exeter C v Cheltenham T
Forest Green R v Harrogate T
Grimsby T v Colchester U
Leyton Orient v Scunthorpe U
Morecambe v Newport Co
Oldham Ath v Cambridge U
Port Vale v Bolton W
Salford C v Barrow
Southend U v Stevenage
Walsall v Tranmere R

Saturday, 20 March 2021
Barrow v Crawley T
Bolton W v Walsall
Bradford C v Oldham Ath
Cambridge U v Forest Green R
Cheltenham T v Salford C
Colchester U v Port Vale
Harrogate T v Morecambe
Mansfield T v Grimsby T
Newport Co v Leyton Orient
Scunthorpe U v Southend U
Stevenage v Carlisle U
Tranmere R v Exeter C

Saturday, 27 March 2021
Carlisle U v Cambridge U
Colchester U v Bradford C
Crawley T v Port Vale
Exeter C v Salford C
Forest Green R v Bolton W
Grimsby T v Walsall
Harrogate T v Southend U
Leyton Orient v Oldham Ath
Morecambe v Cheltenham T
Newport Co v Scunthorpe U
Stevenage v Barrow
Tranmere R v Mansfield T

Friday, 2 April 2021
Barrow v Newport Co
Bolton W v Colchester U
Bradford C v Forest Green R
Cambridge U v Morecambe
Cheltenham T v Tranmere R
Mansfield T v Leyton Orient
Oldham Ath v Stevenage
Port Vale v Exeter C
Salford C v Grimsby T
Scunthorpe U v Crawley T
Southend U v Carlisle U
Walsall v Harrogate T

Monday, 5 April 2021
Carlisle U v Scunthorpe U
Colchester U v Barrow
Crawley T v Oldham Ath
Exeter C v Mansfield T
Forest Green R v Salford C
Grimsby T v Cheltenham T
Harrogate T v Port Vale
Leyton Orient v Walsall
Morecambe v Southend U
Newport Co v Bolton W
Stevenage v Bradford C
Tranmere R v Cambridge U

Saturday, 10 April 2021
Barrow v Carlisle U
Bolton W v Harrogate T
Bradford C v Grimsby T
Cambridge U v Exeter C
Cheltenham T v Leyton Orient
Mansfield T v Newport Co
Oldham Ath v Colchester U
Port Vale v Morecambe
Salford C v Stevenage
Scunthorpe U v Tranmere R
Southend U v Crawley T
Walsall v Forest Green R

Saturday, 17 April 2021
Carlisle U v Port Vale
Colchester U v Walsall
Crawley T v Cheltenham T
Exeter C v Southend U
Forest Green R v Scunthorpe U
Grimsby T v Bolton W
Harrogate T v Bradford C
Leyton Orient v Barrow
Morecambe v Oldham Ath
Newport Co v Cambridge U
Stevenage v Mansfield T
Tranmere R v Salford C

Tuesday, 20 April 2021
Barrow v Port Vale
Bradford C v Tranmere R
Colchester U v Southend U
Forest Green R v Exeter C
Grimsby T v Morecambe
Harrogate T v Oldham Ath
Leyton Orient v Cambridge U
Mansfield T v Scunthorpe U
Newport Co v Crawley T
Stevenage v Cheltenham T
Walsall v Salford C
Bolton W v Carlisle U

Saturday, 24 April 2021
Cambridge U v Stevenage
Carlisle U v Harrogate T
Cheltenham T v Colchester U
Crawley T v Forest Green R
Exeter C v Newport Co
Morecambe v Bolton W
Oldham Ath v Grimsby T
Port Vale v Bradford C
Salford C v Mansfield T
Scunthorpe U v Walsall
Southend U v Leyton Orient
Tranmere R v Barrow

Saturday, 1 May 2021
Barrow v Southend U
Bolton W v Exeter C
Bradford C v Scunthorpe U
Colchester U v Salford C
Forest Green R v Tranmere R
Grimsby T v Port Vale
Harrogate T v Cambridge U
Leyton Orient v Carlisle U
Mansfield T v Oldham Ath
Newport Co v Cheltenham T
Stevenage v Crawley T
Walsall v Morecambe

Saturday, 8 May 2021
Cambridge U v Grimsby T
Carlisle U v Walsall
Cheltenham T v Harrogate T
Crawley T v Bolton W
Exeter C v Barrow
Morecambe v Bradford C
Oldham Ath v Forest Green R
Port Vale v Mansfield T
Salford C v Leyton Orient
Scunthorpe U v Stevenage
Southend U v Newport Co
Tranmere R v Colchester U

NATIONAL LEAGUE FIXTURES 2020–21

All fixtures subject to change.

Saturday, 3 October 2020
Altrincham v Weymouth
Barnet v Eastleigh
Dover Ath v Notts Co
FC Halifax T v Dagenham & R
Hartlepool U v Aldershot T
King's Lynn T v Yeovil T
Macclesfield T v Bromley
Sutton U v Maidenhead U
Torquay U v Stockport Co
Wealdstone v Chesterfield
Woking v Solihull Moors
Wrexham v Boreham Wood

Tuesday, 6 October 2020
Aldershot T v Sutton U
Boreham Wood v Macclesfield T
Bromley v Dover Ath
Chesterfield v Hartlepool U
Dagenham & R v Barnet
Eastleigh v Torquay U
Maidenhead U v King's Lynn T
Notts Co v Altrincham
Solihull Moors v Wrexham
Stockport Co v FC Halifax T
Weymouth v Woking
Yeovil T v Wealdstone

Saturday, 10 October 2020
Aldershot T v Macclesfield T
Boreham Wood v FC Halifax T
Bromley v Torquay U
Chesterfield v Woking
Dagenham & R v Wealdstone
Eastleigh v Altrincham
Maidenhead U v Hartlepool U
Notts Co v Barnet
Solihull Moors v King's Lynn T
Stockport Co v Dover Ath
Weymouth v Sutton U
Yeovil T v Wrexham

Tuesday, 13 October 2020
Altrincham v Solihull Moors
Barnet v Weymouth
Dover Ath v Aldershot T
FC Halifax T v Yeovil T
Hartlepool U v Bromley
King's Lynn T v Boreham Wood
Macclesfield T v Eastleigh
Sutton U v Notts Co
Torquay U v Chesterfield
Wealdstone v Stockport Co
Woking v Dagenham & R
Wrexham v Maidenhead U

Saturday, 17 October 2020
Altrincham v Bromley
Barnet v Hartlepool U
Chesterfield v Stockport Co
Dagenham & R v Yeovil T
Eastleigh v Aldershot T
Notts Co v Maidenhead U
Solihull Moors v Boreham Wood
Sutton U v Macclesfield T
Torquay U v Dover Ath
Wealdstone v Wrexham
Weymouth v King's Lynn T
Woking v FC Halifax T

Tuesday, 27 October 2020
Aldershot T v Torquay U
Boreham Wood v Woking
Bromley v Weymouth
Dover Ath v Eastleigh
FC Halifax T v Notts Co
Hartlepool U v Altrincham
King's Lynn T v Wealdstone
Macclesfield T v Chesterfield
Maidenhead U v Dagenham & R
Stockport Co v Solihull Moors
Wrexham v Barnet
Yeovil T v Sutton U

Saturday, 31 October 2020
Aldershot T v Notts Co
Boreham Wood v Dagenham & R
Bromley v Eastleigh
Dover Ath v Altrincham
FC Halifax T v Wealdstone
Hartlepool U v Torquay U
King's Lynn T v Woking
Macclesfield T v Barnet
Maidenhead U v Solihull Moors
Stockport Co v Weymouth
Wrexham v Sutton U
Yeovil T v Chesterfield

Saturday, 14 November 2020
Altrincham v Aldershot T
Barnet v Bromley
Chesterfield v Maidenhead U
Dagenham & R v Stockport Co
Eastleigh v Hartlepool U
Notts Co v Macclesfield T
Solihull Moors v FC Halifax T
Sutton U v King's Lynn T
Torquay U v Boreham Wood
Wealdstone v Dover Ath
Weymouth v Wrexham
Woking v Yeovil T

Tuesday, 17 November 2020
Aldershot T v Maidenhead U
Altrincham v Chesterfield
Barnet v King's Lynn T
Bromley v Boreham Wood
Dover Ath v Woking
Eastleigh v Wealdstone
Hartlepool U v Wrexham
Macclesfield T v FC Halifax T
Notts Co v Stockport Co
Sutton U v Dagenham & R
Torquay U v Solihull Moors
Weymouth v Yeovil T

Saturday, 21 November 2020
Boreham Wood v Altrincham
Chesterfield v Notts Co
Dagenham & R v Macclesfield T
FC Halifax T v Torquay U
King's Lynn T v Dover Ath
Maidenhead U v Bromley
Solihull Moors v Weymouth
Stockport Co v Eastleigh
Wealdstone v Sutton U
Woking v Barnet
Wrexham v Aldershot T
Yeovil T v Hartlepool U

Saturday, 28 November 2020
Aldershot T v Solihull Moors
Altrincham v Maidenhead U
Barnet v Yeovil T
Bromley v Wrexham
Dover Ath v Boreham Wood
Eastleigh v King's Lynn T
Hartlepool U v Stockport Co
Macclesfield T v Woking
Notts Co v Wealdstone
Sutton U v FC Halifax T
Torquay U v Dagenham & R
Weymouth v Chesterfield

Tuesday, 1 December 2020
Boreham Wood v Weymouth
Chesterfield v Aldershot T
Dagenham & R v Notts Co
FC Halifax T v Barnet
King's Lynn T v Bromley
Maidenhead U v Dover Ath
Solihull Moors v Hartlepool U
Stockport Co v Macclesfield T
Wealdstone v Torquay U
Woking v Sutton U
Wrexham v Altrincham
Yeovil T v Eastleigh

Saturday, 5 December 2020
Aldershot T v Dagenham & R
Altrincham v King's Lynn T
Barnet v Wealdstone
Bromley v Stockport Co
Dover Ath v Chesterfield
Eastleigh v Maidenhead U
Hartlepool U v Boreham Wood
Macclesfield T v Yeovil T
Notts Co v Woking
Sutton U v Solihull Moors
Torquay U v Wrexham
Weymouth v FC Halifax T

Tuesday, 8 December 2020
Aldershot T v FC Halifax T
Altrincham v Woking
Barnet v Stockport Co
Bromley v Yeovil T
Dover Ath v Solihull Moors
Eastleigh v Wrexham
Hartlepool U v King's Lynn T
Macclesfield T v Wealdstone
Notts Co v Boreham Wood
Sutton U v Chesterfield
Torquay U v Maidenhead U
Weymouth v Dagenham & R

Saturday, 12 December 2020
Boreham Wood v Aldershot T
Chesterfield v Barnet
Dagenham & R v Altrincham

FC Halifax T v Eastleigh
King's Lynn T v Torquay U
Maidenhead U v Macclesfield T
Solihull Moors v Bromley
Stockport Co v Sutton U
Wealdstone v Weymouth
Woking v Hartlepool U
Wrexham v Dover Ath
Yeovil T v Notts Co

Saturday, 26 December 2020
Aldershot T v Woking
Altrincham v Stockport Co
Boreham Wood v Barnet
Bromley v Sutton U
Dover Ath v Dagenham & R
Eastleigh v Weymouth
Hartlepool U v FC Halifax T
King's Lynn T v Notts Co
Maidenhead U v Wealdstone
Solihull Moors v Chesterfield
Torquay U v Yeovil T
Wrexham v Macclesfield T

Monday, 28 December 2020
Barnet v Maidenhead U
Chesterfield v King's Lynn T
Dagenham & R v Bromley
FC Halifax T v Altrincham
Macclesfield T v Solihull Moors
Notts Co v Hartlepool U
Stockport Co v Wrexham
Sutton U v Dover Ath
Wealdstone v Boreham Wood
Weymouth v Torquay U
Woking v Eastleigh
Yeovil T v Aldershot T

Saturday, 2 January 2021
Barnet v Boreham Wood
Chesterfield v Solihull Moors
Dagenham & R v Dover Ath
FC Halifax T v Hartlepool U
Macclesfield T v Wrexham
Notts Co v King's Lynn T
Stockport Co v Altrincham
Sutton U v Bromley
Wealdstone v Maidenhead U
Weymouth v Eastleigh
Woking v Aldershot T
Yeovil T v Torquay U

Saturday, 9 January 2021
Aldershot T v Barnet
Altrincham v Sutton U
Boreham Wood v Yeovil T
Bromley v Chesterfield
Dover Ath v Weymouth
Eastleigh v Notts Co
Hartlepool U v Wealdstone
King's Lynn T v FC Halifax T
Maidenhead U v Stockport Co
Solihull Moors v Dagenham & R
Torquay U v Macclesfield T
Wrexham v Woking

Saturday, 23 January 2021
Barnet v Altrincham
Chesterfield v Wrexham
Dagenham & R v King's Lynn T
FC Halifax T v Bromley
Macclesfield T v Dover Ath
Notts Co v Torquay U
Stockport Co v Boreham Wood
Sutton U v Eastleigh
Wealdstone v Aldershot T
Weymouth v Hartlepool U
Woking v Maidenhead U
Yeovil T v Solihull Moors

Tuesday, 26 January 2021
Aldershot T v Weymouth
Altrincham v Wealdstone
Boreham Wood v Chesterfield
Bromley v Woking
Dover Ath v Barnet
Eastleigh v Dagenham & R
Hartlepool U v Macclesfield T
King's Lynn T v Stockport Co
Maidenhead U v Yeovil T
Solihull Moors v Notts Co
Torquay U v Sutton U
Wrexham v FC Halifax T

Saturday, 30 January 2021
Altrincham v Macclesfield T
Barnet v Torquay U
Boreham Wood v Eastleigh
Bromley v Aldershot T
Dagenham & R v Chesterfield
FC Halifax T v Maidenhead U
Hartlepool U v Sutton U
King's Lynn T v Wrexham
Solihull Moors v Wealdstone
Weymouth v Notts Co
Woking v Stockport Co
Yeovil T v Dover Ath

Saturday, 6 February 2021
Aldershot T v King's Lynn T
Chesterfield v FC Halifax T
Dover Ath v Hartlepool U
Eastleigh v Solihull Moors
Macclesfield T v Weymouth
Maidenhead U v Boreham Wood
Notts Co v Bromley
Stockport Co v Yeovil T
Sutton U v Barnet
Torquay U v Altrincham
Wealdstone v Woking
Wrexham v Dagenham & R

Tuesday, 9 February 2021
Aldershot T v Chesterfield
Altrincham v Wrexham
Barnet v FC Halifax T
Bromley v King's Lynn T
Dover Ath v Maidenhead U
Eastleigh v Yeovil T
Hartlepool U v Solihull Moors
Macclesfield T v Stockport Co
Notts Co v Dagenham & R
Sutton U v Woking
Torquay U v Wealdstone
Weymouth v Boreham Wood

Saturday, 13 February 2021
Boreham Wood v Sutton U
Chesterfield v Eastleigh
Dagenham & R v Hartlepool U
FC Halifax T v Dover Ath
King's Lynn T v Macclesfield T
Maidenhead U v Weymouth
Solihull Moors v Barnet
Stockport Co v Aldershot T
Wealdstone v Bromley
Woking v Torquay U
Wrexham v Notts Co
Yeovil T v Altrincham

Saturday, 20 February 2021
Aldershot T v Wrexham
Altrincham v Boreham Wood
Barnet v Woking
Bromley v Maidenhead U
Dover Ath v King's Lynn T
Eastleigh v Stockport Co
Hartlepool U v Yeovil T
Macclesfield T v Dagenham & R
Notts Co v Chesterfield
Sutton U v Wealdstone
Torquay U v FC Halifax T
Weymouth v Solihull Moors

Tuesday, 23 February 2021
Boreham Wood v Bromley
Chesterfield v Altrincham
Dagenham & R v Sutton U
FC Halifax T v Macclesfield T
King's Lynn T v Barnet
Maidenhead U v Aldershot T
Solihull Moors v Torquay U
Stockport Co v Notts Co
Wealdstone v Eastleigh
Woking v Dover Ath
Wrexham v Hartlepool U
Yeovil T v Weymouth

Saturday, 27 February 2021
Aldershot T v Eastleigh
Boreham Wood v Solihull Moors
Bromley v Altrincham
Dover Ath v Torquay U
FC Halifax T v Woking
Hartlepool U v Barnet
King's Lynn T v Weymouth
Macclesfield T v Sutton U
Maidenhead U v Notts Co
Stockport Co v Chesterfield
Wrexham v Wealdstone
Yeovil T v Dagenham & R

Saturday, 6 March 2021
Altrincham v Dover Ath
Barnet v Macclesfield T
Chesterfield v Yeovil T
Dagenham & R v Boreham Wood
Eastleigh v Bromley
Notts Co v Aldershot T
Solihull Moors v Maidenhead U
Sutton U v Wrexham
Torquay U v Hartlepool U
Wealdstone v FC Halifax T
Weymouth v Stockport Co
Woking v King's Lynn T

Tuesday, 9 March 2021
Altrincham v Hartlepool U
Barnet v Wrexham
Chesterfield v Macclesfield T
Dagenham & R v Maidenhead U
Eastleigh v Dover Ath
Notts Co v FC Halifax T
Solihull Moors v Stockport Co
Sutton U v Yeovil T
Torquay U v Aldershot T
Wealdstone v King's Lynn T
Weymouth v Bromley
Woking v Boreham Wood

Saturday, 13 March 2021
Aldershot T v Altrincham
Boreham Wood v Torquay U
Bromley v Barnet

Dover Ath v Wealdstone
FC Halifax T v Solihull Moors
Hartlepool U v Eastleigh
King's Lynn T v Sutton U
Macclesfield T v Notts Co
Maidenhead U v Chesterfield
Stockport Co v Dagenham & R
Wrexham v Weymouth
Yeovil T v Woking

Tuesday, 16 March 2021
Boreham Wood v Notts Co
Chesterfield v Sutton U
Dagenham & R v Weymouth
FC Halifax T v Aldershot T
King's Lynn T v Hartlepool U
Maidenhead U v Torquay U
Solihull Moors v Dover Ath
Stockport Co v Barnet
Wealdstone v Macclesfield T
Woking v Altrincham
Wrexham v Eastleigh
Yeovil T v Bromley

Saturday, 20 March 2021
Aldershot T v Boreham Wood
Altrincham v Dagenham & R
Barnet v Chesterfield
Bromley v Solihull Moors
Dover Ath v Wrexham
Eastleigh v FC Halifax T
Hartlepool U v Woking
Macclesfield T v Maidenhead U
Notts Co v Yeovil T
Sutton U v Stockport Co
Torquay U v King's Lynn T
Weymouth v Wealdstone

Saturday, 27 March 2021
Boreham Wood v Dover Ath
Chesterfield v Weymouth
Dagenham & R v Torquay U
FC Halifax T v Sutton U
King's Lynn T v Eastleigh
Maidenhead U v Altrincham
Solihull Moors v Aldershot T
Stockport Co v Hartlepool U
Wealdstone v Notts Co
Woking v Macclesfield T
Wrexham v Bromley
Yeovil T v Barnet

Friday, 2 April 2021
Aldershot T v Stockport Co
Altrincham v Yeovil T
Barnet v Solihull Moors
Bromley v Wealdstone
Dover Ath v FC Halifax T
Eastleigh v Chesterfield
Hartlepool U v Dagenham & R
Macclesfield T v King's Lynn T
Notts Co v Wrexham
Sutton U v Boreham Wood
Torquay U v Woking
Weymouth v Maidenhead U

Monday, 5 April 2021
Boreham Wood v Hartlepool U
Chesterfield v Dover Ath
Dagenham & R v Aldershot T
FC Halifax T v Weymouth
King's Lynn T v Altrincham
Maidenhead U v Eastleigh
Solihull Moors v Sutton U
Stockport Co v Bromley
Wealdstone v Barnet
Woking v Notts Co
Wrexham v Torquay U
Yeovil T v Macclesfield T

Saturday, 10 April 2021
Aldershot T v Yeovil T
Altrincham v FC Halifax T
Boreham Wood v Wealdstone
Bromley v Dagenham & R
Dover Ath v Sutton U
Eastleigh v Woking
Hartlepool U v Notts Co
King's Lynn T v Chesterfield
Maidenhead U v Barnet
Solihull Moors v Macclesfield T
Torquay U v Weymouth
Wrexham v Stockport Co

Tuesday, 13 April 2021
Barnet v Dover Ath
Chesterfield v Boreham Wood
Dagenham & R v Eastleigh
FC Halifax T v Wrexham
Macclesfield T v Hartlepool U
Notts Co v Solihull Moors
Stockport Co v King's Lynn T
Sutton U v Torquay U
Wealdstone v Altrincham
Weymouth v Aldershot T
Woking v Bromley
Yeovil T v Maidenhead U

Saturday, 17 April 2021
Barnet v Aldershot T
Chesterfield v Bromley
Dagenham & R v Solihull Moors
FC Halifax T v King's Lynn T
Macclesfield T v Torquay U
Notts Co v Eastleigh
Stockport Co v Maidenhead U
Sutton U v Altrincham
Wealdstone v Hartlepool U
Weymouth v Dover Ath
Woking v Wrexham
Yeovil T v Boreham Wood

Saturday, 24 April 2021
Aldershot T v Wealdstone
Altrincham v Barnet
Boreham Wood v Stockport Co
Bromley v FC Halifax T
Dover Ath v Macclesfield T
Eastleigh v Sutton U
Hartlepool U v Weymouth
King's Lynn T v Dagenham & R
Maidenhead U v Woking
Solihull Moors v Yeovil T
Torquay U v Notts Co
Wrexham v Chesterfield

Saturday, 1 May 2021
Altrincham v Notts Co
Barnet v Dagenham & R
Dover Ath v Bromley
FC Halifax T v Stockport Co
Hartlepool U v Chesterfield
King's Lynn T v Maidenhead U
Macclesfield T v Boreham Wood
Sutton U v Aldershot T
Torquay U v Eastleigh
Wealdstone v Yeovil T
Woking v Weymouth
Wrexham v Solihull Moors

Monday, 3 May 2021
Aldershot T v Dover Ath
Boreham Wood v King's Lynn T
Bromley v Hartlepool U
Chesterfield v Torquay U
Dagenham & R v Woking
Eastleigh v Macclesfield T
Maidenhead U v Wrexham
Notts Co v Sutton U
Solihull Moors v Altrincham
Stockport Co v Wealdstone
Weymouth v Barnet
Yeovil T v FC Halifax T

Saturday, 8 May 2021
Altrincham v Eastleigh
Barnet v Notts Co
Dover Ath v Stockport Co
FC Halifax T v Boreham Wood
Hartlepool U v Maidenhead U
King's Lynn T v Solihull Moors
Macclesfield T v Aldershot T
Sutton U v Weymouth
Torquay U v Bromley
Wealdstone v Dagenham & R
Woking v Chesterfield
Wrexham v Yeovil T

Saturday, 15 May 2021
Aldershot T v Hartlepool U
Boreham Wood v Wrexham
Bromley v Macclesfield T
Chesterfield v Wealdstone
Dagenham & R v FC Halifax T
Eastleigh v Barnet
Maidenhead U v Sutton U
Notts Co v Dover Ath
Solihull Moors v Woking
Stockport Co v Torquay U
Weymouth v Altrincham
Yeovil T v King's Lynn T

Saturday, 22 May 2021
Aldershot T v Bromley
Chesterfield v Dagenham & R
Dover Ath v Yeovil T
Eastleigh v Boreham Wood
Macclesfield T v Altrincham
Maidenhead U v FC Halifax T
Notts Co v Weymouth
Stockport Co v Woking
Sutton U v Hartlepool U
Torquay U v Barnet
Wealdstone v Solihull Moors
Wrexham v King's Lynn T

Saturday, 29 May 2021
Altrincham v Torquay U
Barnet v Sutton U
Boreham Wood v Maidenhead U
Bromley v Notts Co
Dagenham & R v Wrexham
FC Halifax T v Chesterfield
Hartlepool U v Dover Ath
King's Lynn T v Aldershot T
Solihull Moors v Eastleigh
Weymouth v Macclesfield T
Woking v Wealdstone
Yeovil T v Stockport Co

THE SCOTTISH PREMIER LEAGUE AND SCOTTISH LEAGUE FIXTURES 2020–21

All fixtures subject to change.

SPFL Premiership

Saturday, 1 August 2020
Aberdeen v Rangers
Dundee U v St Johnstone
Hibernian v Kilmarnock
St Mirren v Livingston

Sunday, 2 August 2020
Celtic v Hamilton A

Monday, 3 August 2020
Ross Co v Motherwell

Saturday, 8 August 2020
St Johnstone v Aberdeen
Hamilton A v Ross Co
Livingston v Hibernian
Motherwell v Dundee U

Sunday, 9 August 2020
Rangers v St Mirren
Kilmarnock v Celtic

Tuesday, 11 August 2020
Dundee U v Hibernian

Wednesday, 12 August 2020
St Mirren v Celtic
Aberdeen v Hamilton A
Motherwell v Livingston
Rangers v St Johnstone
Ross Co v Kilmarnock

Saturday, 15 August 2020
Celtic v Aberdeen
Hamilton A v St Mirren
Kilmarnock v St Johnstone
Ross Co v Dundee U
Hibernian v Motherwell

Sunday, 16 August 2020
Livingston v Rangers

Saturday, 22 August 2020
Aberdeen v Livingston
Motherwell v Hamilton A
Rangers v Kilmarnock
St Mirren v Ross Co
Dundee U v Celtic

Sunday, 23 August 2020
St Johnstone v Hibernian

Saturday, 29 August 2020
Celtic v Motherwell
Kilmarnock v Dundee U
Livingston v Ross Co
St Johnstone v St Mirren
Hamilton A v Rangers

Sunday, 30 August 2020
Hibernian v Aberdeen

Saturday, 12 September 2020
Aberdeen v Kilmarnock
Livingston v Hamilton A
Motherwell v St Johnstone
Rangers v Dundee U
Ross Co v Celtic
St Mirren v Hibernian

Saturday, 19 September 2020
Aberdeen v Motherwell
Celtic v Livingston
Dundee U v St Mirren
Hibernian v Rangers
Kilmarnock v Hamilton A
St Johnstone v Ross Co

Saturday, 26 September 2020
Celtic v Hibernian
Hamilton A v Dundee U
Livingston v St Johnstone
Motherwell v Rangers
Ross Co v Aberdeen
St Mirren v Kilmarnock

Friday, 2 October 2020
Aberdeen v St Mirren
Dundee U v Livingston
Hibernian v Hamilton A
Kilmarnock v Motherwell
Rangers v Ross Co
St Johnstone v Celtic

Saturday, 17 October 2020
Celtic v Rangers
Dundee U v Aberdeen
Hamilton A v St Johnstone
Livingston v Kilmarnock
Ross Co v Hibernian
St Mirren v Motherwell

Saturday, 24 October 2020
Aberdeen v Celtic
Kilmarnock v Hibernian
Motherwell v Ross Co
Rangers v Livingston
St Johnstone v Dundee U
St Mirren v Hamilton A

Saturday, 31 October 2020
Celtic v St Mirren (PP)
Dundee U v Ross Co
Hamilton A v Aberdeen (PP)
Hibernian v St Johnstonen (PP)
Kilmarnock v Rangers
Livingston v Motherwell

Friday, 6 November 2020
Aberdeen v Hibernian
Motherwell v Celtic
Rangers v Hamilton A
Ross Co v Livingston
St Johnstone v Kilmarnock
St Mirren v Dundee U

Saturday, 21 November 2020
Dundee U v Hamilton A
Hibernian v Celtic
Kilmarnock v Ross Co
Livingston v St Mirren
Rangers v Aberdeen
St Johnstone v Motherwell

Saturday, 5 December 2020
Celtic v St Johnstone
Hamilton A v Kilmarnock
Livingston v Dundee U
Motherwell v Hibernian
Ross Co v Rangers
St Mirren v Aberdeen

Saturday, 12 December 2020
Aberdeen v Ross Co
Celtic v Kilmarnock
Dundee U v Rangers
Hamilton A v Hibernian
Motherwell v St Mirren
St Johnstone v Livingston

Saturday, 19 December 2020
Hibernian v Dundee U
Kilmarnock v Aberdeen
Livingston v Celtic
Rangers v Motherwell
Ross Co v Hamilton A
St Mirren v St Johnstone

Wednesday, 23 December 2020
Celtic v Ross Co
Dundee U v Kilmarnock
Hamilton A v Livingston
Hibernian v St Mirren
Motherwell v Aberdeen
St Johnstone v Rangers

Saturday, 26 December 2020
Aberdeen v St Johnstone
Dundee U v Motherwell
Hamilton A v Celtic
Kilmarnock v Livingston
Rangers v Hibernian
Ross Co v St Mirren

Wednesday, 30 December 2020
Celtic v Dundee U
Hibernian v Ross Co
Livingston v Aberdeen
Motherwell v Kilmarnock
St Johnstone v Hamilton A
St Mirren v Rangers

Saturday, 2 January 2021
Aberdeen v Dundee U
Hamilton A v Motherwell
Hibernian v Livingston
Kilmarnock v St Mirren
Rangers v Celtic
Ross Co v St Johnstone

Saturday, 9 January 2021
Aberdeen v Rangers
Celtic v Hibernian
Dundee U v St Johnstone
Kilmarnock v Hamilton A
Livingston v Ross Co
St Mirren v Motherwell

Saturday, 16 January 2021
Celtic v Livingston
Hamilton A v Dundee U
Hibernian v Kilmarnock
Motherwell v Rangers
Ross Co v Aberdeen
St Johnstone v St Mirren

Saturday, 23 January 2021
Aberdeen v Motherwell
Dundee U v Hibernian
Kilmarnock v St Johnstone
Livingston v Hamilton A
Rangers v Ross Co
St Mirren v Celtic

Wednesday, 27 January 2021
Celtic v Hamilton A
Dundee U v St Mirren
Hibernian v Rangers
Livingston v Kilmarnock
Ross Co v Motherwell
St Johnstone v Aberdeen

Wednesday, 3 February 2021
Aberdeen v Livingston
Hamilton A v Ross Co
Kilmarnock v Celtic
Motherwell v Dundee U
Rangers v St Johnstone
St Mirren v Hibernian

Saturday, 6 February 2021
Celtic v Motherwell
Hamilton A v Rangers
Hibernian v Aberdeen
Livingston v St Johnstone
Ross Co v Dundee U
St Mirren v Kilmarnock

Saturday, 13 February 2021
Aberdeen v St Mirren
Dundee U v Livingston
Motherwell v Hamilton A
Rangers v Kilmarnock
Ross Co v Hibernian
St Johnstone v Celtic

Saturday, 27 February 2021
Celtic v Aberdeen
Hamilton A v St Johnstone
Hibernian v Motherwell
Kilmarnock v Dundee U
Livingston v Rangers
St Mirren v Ross Co

Saturday, 6 March 2021
Aberdeen v Hamilton A
Dundee U v Celtic
Motherwell v Livingston
Rangers v St Mirren
Ross Co v Kilmarnock
St Johnstone v Hibernian

Saturday, 20 March 2021
Celtic v Rangers
Dundee U v Aberdeen
Hamilton A v St Mirren
Kilmarnock v Motherwell
Livingston v Hibernian
St Johnstone v Ross Co

Saturday, 3 April 2021
Aberdeen v Kilmarnock
Hibernian v Hamilton A
Motherwell v St Johnstone
Rangers v Dundee U
Ross Co v Celtic
St Mirren v Livingston

SPFL Championship

Saturday, 17 October 2020
Ayr U v Queen of the South
Dunfermline Ath v Inverness CT
Hearts v Dundee
Greenock Morton v Alloa Ath
Raith R v Arbroath

Saturday, 24 October 2020
Alloa Ath v Dunfermline Ath
Arbroath v Hearts
Dundee v Greenock Morton
Inverness CT v Ayr U
Queen of the South v Raith R

Saturday, 31 October 2020
Dundee v Raith R
Dunfermline Ath v Queen of the South
Inverness CT v Arbroath
Greenock Morton v Ayr U
Hearts v Alloa Ath (PP)

Saturday, 7 November 2020
Alloa Ath v Dundee
Arbroath v Queen of the South
Ayr U v Dunfermline Ath
Hearts v Inverness CT
Raith R v Greenock Morton

Saturday, 21 November 2020
Arbroath v Greenock Morton
Ayr U v Dundee
Dunfermline Ath v Hearts
Inverness CT v Raith R
Queen of the South v Alloa Ath

Saturday, 5 December 2020
Alloa Ath v Ayr U
Dundee v Arbroath
Greenock Morton v Hearts
Queen of the South v Inverness CT
Raith R v Dunfermline Ath

Saturday, 12 December 2020
Arbroath v Alloa Ath
Ayr U v Raith R
Dunfermline Ath v Greenock Morton
Hearts v Queen of the South
Inverness CT v Dundee

Saturday, 19 December 2020
Alloa Ath v Inverness CT
Arbroath v Ayr U
Dundee v Dunfermline Ath
Greenock Morton v Queen of the South
Raith R v Hearts

Saturday, 26 December 2020
Alloa Ath v Raith R
Dunfermline Ath v Arbroath
Hearts v Ayr U
Greenock Morton v Inverness CT
Queen of the South v Dundee

Tuesday, 29 December 2020
Ayr U v Greenock Morton
Dundee v Alloa Ath
Hearts v Arbroath
Inverness CT v Dunfermline Ath
Raith R v Queen of the South

Saturday, 2 January 2021
Alloa Ath v Greenock Morton
Arbroath v Inverness CT
Dundee v Hearts
Dunfermline Ath v Raith R
Queen of the South v Ayr U

Saturday, 9 January 2021
Ayr U v Alloa Ath
Hearts v Dunfermline Ath
Inverness CT v Queen of the South
Greenock Morton v Arbroath
Raith R v Dundee

Saturday, 16 January 2021
Alloa Ath v Hearts
Dundee v Ayr U
Greenock Morton v Dunfermline Ath
Queen of the South v Arbroath
Raith R v Inverness CT

Saturday, 23 January 2021
Arbroath v Dundee
Dunfermline Ath v Ayr U
Hearts v Raith R
Inverness CT v Alloa Ath
Queen of the South v Greenock Morton

Saturday, 6 February 2021
Alloa Ath v Queen of the South
Arbroath v Dunfermline Ath
Ayr U v Hearts
Dundee v Inverness CT
Greenock Morton v Raith R

Saturday, 13 February 2021
Alloa Ath v Arbroath
Dunfermline Ath v Dundee
Inverness CT v Greenock Morton
Queen of the South v Hearts
Raith R v Ayr U

Saturday, 20 February 2021
Arbroath v Raith R
Ayr U v Inverness CT
Dundee v Queen of the South
Dunfermline Ath v Alloa Ath
Hearts v Greenock Morton

Saturday, 27 February 2021
Ayr U v Arbroath
Inverness CT v Hearts
Greenock Morton v Dundee
Queen of the South v Dunfermline Ath
Raith R v Alloa Ath

Saturday, 6 March 2021
Alloa Ath v Inverness CT
Arbroath v Queen of the South
Hearts v Dundee
Greenock Morton v Ayr U
Raith R v Dunfermline Ath

Saturday, 13 March 2021
Dundee v Arbroath
Dunfermline Ath v Greenock Morton
Hearts v Ayr U

Inverness CT v Raith R
Queen of the South v Alloa Ath

Saturday, 20 March 2021
Alloa Ath v Dundee
Arbroath v Hearts
Ayr U v Raith R
Dunfermline Ath v Inverness CT
Greenock Morton v Queen of the South

Saturday, 27 March 2021
Alloa Ath v Ayr U
Dundee v Dunfermline Ath
Hearts v Queen of the South
Inverness CT v Arbroath
Raith R v Greenock Morton

Saturday, 3 April 2021
Arbroath v Alloa Ath
Ayr U v Dundee
Dunfermline Ath v Hearts
Greenock Morton v Inverness CT
Queen of the South v Raith R

Saturday, 10 April 2021
Ayr U v Dunfermline Ath
Dundee v Greenock Morton
Hearts v Alloa Ath
Queen of the South v Inverness CT
Raith R v Arbroath

Saturday, 17 April 2021
Alloa Ath v Raith R
Arbroath v Ayr U
Dunfermline Ath v Queen of the South
Inverness CT v Dundee
Greenock Morton v Hearts

Saturday, 24 April 2021
Ayr U v Queen of the South
Dundee v Raith R
Dunfermline Ath v Arbroath
Hearts v Inverness CT
Greenock Morton v Alloa Ath

Friday, 30 April 2021
Alloa Ath v Dunfermline Ath
Arbroath v Greenock Morton
Inverness CT v Ayr U
Queen of the South v Dundee
Raith R v Hearts

SPFL League One

Saturday, 17 October 2020
Airdrieonians v Peterhead
Clyde v Partick Thistle
Cove Rangers v East Fife
Forfar Ath v Dumbarton
Montrose v Falkirk

Saturday, 24 October 2020
Dumbarton v Clyde
East Fife v Montrose
Falkirk v Forfar Ath
Partick Thistle v Airdrieonians
Peterhead v Cove Rangers

Saturday, 31 October 2020
Clyde v Peterhead
Cove Rangers v Partick Thistle
Dumbarton v Airdrieonians
Falkirk v East Fife
Forfar Ath v Montrose

Saturday, 7 November 2020
Airdrieonians v Clyde
Cove Rangers v Forfar Ath
East Fife v Dumbarton
Montrose v Peterhead
Partick Thistle v Falkirk

Saturday, 21 November 2020
Clyde v Montrose
Falkirk v Cove Rangers
Forfar Ath v Airdrieonians
Partick Thistle v East Fife
Peterhead v Dumbarton

Saturday, 28 November 2020
Airdrieonians v Cove Rangers
Dumbarton v Falkirk
East Fife v Clyde
Montrose v Partick Thistle
Peterhead v Forfar Ath

Saturday, 5 December 2020
Clyde v Forfar Ath
Cove Rangers v Montrose
East Fife v Airdrieonians
Falkirk v Peterhead
Partick Thistle v Dumbarton

Saturday, 12 December 2020
Airdrieonians v Montrose
Clyde v Falkirk
Dumbarton v Cove Rangers
Forfar Ath v Partick Thistle
Peterhead v East Fife

Saturday, 19 December 2020
Cove Rangers v Clyde
East Fife v Forfar Ath
Falkirk v Airdrieonians
Montrose v Dumbarton
Partick Thistle v Peterhead

Saturday, 26 December 2020
Clyde v Airdrieonians
Dumbarton v East Fife
Falkirk v Partick Thistle
Forfar Ath v Cove Rangers
Peterhead v Montrose

Saturday, 2 January 2021
Airdrieonians v Dumbarton
Cove Rangers v Peterhead
East Fife v Falkirk
Montrose v Forfar Ath
Partick Thistle v Clyde

Saturday, 16 January 2021
Clyde v East Fife
Dumbarton v Forfar Ath
Falkirk v Montrose
Partick Thistle v Cove Rangers
Peterhead v Airdrieonians

Saturday, 23 January 2021
Airdrieonians v Partick Thistle
Dumbarton v Peterhead
East Fife v Cove Rangers
Forfar Ath v Falkirk
Montrose v Clyde

Saturday, 6 February 2021
Cove Rangers v Airdrieonians
Falkirk v Dumbarton
Montrose v East Fife
Partick Thistle v Forfar Ath
Peterhead v Clyde

Saturday, 13 February 2021
Airdrieonians v Falkirk
Clyde v Cove Rangers
Dumbarton v Montrose
East Fife v Partick Thistle
Forfar Ath v Peterhead

Saturday, 20 February 2021
Cove Rangers v Dumbarton
Falkirk v Clyde
Forfar Ath v East Fife
Montrose v Airdrieonians
Peterhead v Partick Thistle

Saturday, 27 February 2021
Airdrieonians v Forfar Ath
Clyde v Dumbarton
Cove Rangers v Falkirk
East Fife v Peterhead
Partick Thistle v Montrose

Saturday, 6 March 2021
Airdrieonians v East Fife
Dumbarton v Partick Thistle
Forfar Ath v Clyde
Montrose v Cove Rangers
Peterhead v Falkirk

Saturday, 13 March 2021
Clyde v Montrose
East Fife v Dumbarton
Falkirk v Forfar Ath
Partick Thistle v Airdrieonians
Peterhead v Cove Rangers

Saturday, 20 March 2021
Clyde v Peterhead
Cove Rangers v Partick Thistle
Dumbarton v Airdrieonians
Falkirk v East Fife
Forfar Ath v Montrose

Saturday, 27 March 2021
Airdrieonians v Peterhead
Cove Rangers v Forfar Ath
East Fife v Clyde
Montrose v Dumbarton
Partick Thistle v Falkirk

Saturday, 3 April 2021
Clyde v Partick Thistle
Dumbarton v Cove Rangers
East Fife v Montrose
Falkirk v Airdrieonians
Peterhead v Forfar Ath

Saturday, 10 April 2021
Airdrieonians v Clyde
Cove Rangers v East Fife
Forfar Ath v Dumbarton
Montrose v Falkirk
Partick Thistle v Peterhead

Saturday, 17 April 2021
Airdrieonians v Montrose
Clyde v Forfar Ath
Falkirk v Cove Rangers

Partick Thistle v Dumbarton
Peterhead v East Fife

Tuesday, 20 April 2021
Cove Rangers v Clyde
Dumbarton v Falkirk
East Fife v Airdrieonians
Forfar Ath v Partick Thistle
Montrose v Peterhead

Saturday, 24 April 2021
Airdrieonians v Cove Rangers
Clyde v Falkirk
East Fife v Forfar Ath
Montrose v Partick Thistle
Peterhead v Dumbarton

Saturday, 1 May 2021
Cove Rangers v Montrose
Dumbarton v Clyde
Falkirk v Peterhead
Forfar Ath v Airdrieonians
Partick Thistle v East Fife

SPFL League Two

Saturday, 17 October 2020
Albion R v Stenhousemuir
Brechin C v Edinburgh C
Cowdenbeath v Annan Ath
Stirling Alb v Queen's Park
Stranraer v Elgin C

Saturday, 24 October 2020
Annan Ath v Stranraer
Edinburgh C v Cowdenbeath
Elgin C v Brechin C
Queen's Park v Albion R
Stenhousemuir v Stirling Alb

Saturday, 31 October 2020
Albion R v Brechin C
Cowdenbeath v Stenhousemuir
Edinburgh C v Elgin C
Stirling Alb v Annan Ath
Stranraer v Queen's Park

Saturday, 7 November 2020
Annan Ath v Albion R
Brechin C v Stirling Alb
Elgin C v Queen's Park
Stenhousemuir v Edinburgh C
Stranraer v Cowdenbeath

Saturday, 21 November 2020
Cowdenbeath v Albion R
Edinburgh C v Stranraer
Queen's Park v Brechin C
Stenhousemuir v Annan Ath
Stirling Alb v Elgin C

Saturday, 28 November 2020
Albion R v Stirling Alb
Annan Ath v Edinburgh C
Brechin C v Stranraer
Elgin C v Cowdenbeath
Queen's Park v Stenhousemuir

Saturday, 5 December 2020
Cowdenbeath v Queen's Park
Edinburgh C v Albion R
Elgin C v Annan Ath
Stenhousemuir v Brechin C
Stranraer v Stirling Alb

Saturday, 12 December 2020
Albion R v Elgin C
Brechin C v Annan Ath
Queen's Park v Edinburgh C
Stenhousemuir v Stranraer
Stirling Alb v Cowdenbeath

Saturday, 19 December 2020
Annan Ath v Queen's Park
Cowdenbeath v Brechin C
Edinburgh C v Stirling Alb
Elgin C v Stenhousemuir
Stranraer v Albion R

Saturday, 2 January 2021
Albion R v Queen's Park
Brechin C v Elgin C
Cowdenbeath v Edinburgh C
Stirling Alb v Stenhousemuir
Stranraer v Annan Ath

Saturday, 16 January 2021
Annan Ath v Cowdenbeath
Elgin C v Edinburgh C
Queen's Park v Stranraer
Stenhousemuir v Albion R
Stirling Alb v Brechin C

Saturday, 23 January 2021
Albion R v Annan Ath
Brechin C v Queen's Park
Cowdenbeath v Stranraer
Edinburgh C v Stenhousemuir
Elgin C v Stirling Alb

Saturday, 30 January 2021
Albion R v Edinburgh C
Annan Ath v Elgin C
Queen's Park v Stirling Alb
Stenhousemuir v Cowdenbeath
Stranraer v Brechin C

Saturday, 6 February 2021
Brechin C v Stenhousemuir
Edinburgh C v Annan Ath
Elgin C v Stranraer
Queen's Park v Cowdenbeath
Stirling Alb v Albion R

Saturday, 13 February 2021
Annan Ath v Stirling Alb
Brechin C v Albion R
Cowdenbeath v Elgin C
Stenhousemuir v Queen's Park
Stranraer v Edinburgh C

Saturday, 20 February 2021
Albion R v Cowdenbeath
Edinburgh C v Brechin C
Queen's Park v Annan Ath
Stenhousemuir v Elgin C
Stirling Alb v Stranraer

Saturday, 27 February 2021
Annan Ath v Brechin C
Cowdenbeath v Stirling Alb
Edinburgh C v Queen's Park
Elgin C v Albion R
Stranraer v Stenhousemuir

Saturday, 6 March 2021
Albion R v Stranraer
Annan Ath v Stenhousemuir
Brechin C v Cowdenbeath
Queen's Park v Elgin C
Stirling Alb v Edinburgh C

Saturday, 13 March 2021
Edinburgh C v Albion R
Elgin C v Annan Ath
Queen's Park v Brechin C
Stenhousemuir v Stirling Alb
Stranraer v Cowdenbeath

Saturday, 20 March 2021
Annan Ath v Albion R
Brechin C v Stranraer
Cowdenbeath v Stenhousemuir
Edinburgh C v Elgin C
Stirling Alb v Queen's Park

Saturday, 27 March 2021
Albion R v Brechin C
Elgin C v Cowdenbeath
Stenhousemuir v Edinburgh C
Stirling Alb v Annan Ath
Stranraer v Queen's Park

Saturday, 3 April 2021
Brechin C v Stirling Alb
Cowdenbeath v Annan Ath
Edinburgh C v Stranraer
Elgin C v Stenhousemuir
Queen's Park v Albion R

Saturday, 10 April 2021
Albion R v Stirling Alb
Annan Ath v Edinburgh C
Cowdenbeath v Queen's Park
Stenhousemuir v Brechin C
Stranraer v Elgin C

Saturday, 17 April 2021
Albion R v Elgin C
Annan Ath v Stranraer
Brechin C v Edinburgh C
Queen's Park v Stenhousemuir
Stirling Alb v Cowdenbeath

Tuesday, 20 April 2021
Stenhousemuir v Annan Ath
Stranraer v Albion R
Cowdenbeath v Brechin C
Edinburgh C v Stirling Alb
Elgin C v Queen's Park

Saturday, 24 April 2021
Brechin C v Annan Ath
Cowdenbeath v Albion R
Queen's Park v Edinburgh C
Stenhousemuir v Stranraer
Stirling Alb v Elgin C

Saturday, 1 May 2021
Albion R v Stenhousemuir
Annan Ath v Queen's Park
Edinburgh C v Cowdenbeath
Elgin C v Brechin C
Stranraer v Stirling Alb

STOP PRESS

Arsenal win Community Shield ... Gareth Bale looking to leave Real Madrid? ... Messi to see out Barca contract ... Ronaldo hits 100th international goal for Portugal ... Manchester United sign van der Beek ... City owners buy Troyes ... Chelsea break record to sign Havertz from Bayer Leverkusen ... Chinese TV deal with Premier League terminated ... Crowds back at Cambridge ... Celtic through first qualifying round of Champions League but fall to Ferencvaros in second ... Aberdeen, Motherwell, The New Saints, Coleraine, Bala Town and Shamrock Rovers all through first qualifying round of Europa League ... England and Wales start Nations League campaigns with wins, Scotland, Northern Ireland and Republic of Ireland draws.

SUMMER TRANSFER DIARY 2020

Reported fees only, otherwise Free or Undisclosed.

27 July: **Daniel Harvie** Ayr U to Milton Keynes D; **Diallang Jaiyesimi** Norwich C to Swindon T; **Adam Lallana** Liverpool to Brighton & HA; **Dejan Lovren** Liverpool to Zenit St Petersburg – £10.9m; **Conor McGrandles** Milton Keynes D to Lincoln C; **Christopher Missilou** Oldham Ath to Northampton T; **Bali Mumba** Sunderland to Norwich C; **George Thomas** Leicester C to QPR; **Elliot Watt** Wolverhampton W to Bradford C.

28 July: **Fisayo Dele-Bashiru** Manchester C to Sheffield W; **Wes Hoolahan** Newcastle Jets to Cambridge U; **Josh Laurent** Shrewsbury T to Reading; **George Maris** Cambridge U to Mansfield T; **Luke McCormick** Swindon T to Plymouth Arg; **Rollin Menayese** Bristol R to Mansfield T; **Jordan Turnbull** Northampton T to Salford C.

29 July: **Jonah Ayunga** Havant & Waterlooville to Bristol R; **Ian Henderson** Rochdale to Salford C; **Matty Platt** Blackburn R to Barrow; **Joel Veltman** Ajax to Brighton & HA; **Andy Williams** Northampton T to Cheltenham T.

30 July: **Daniel Gyollai** Wigan Ath to Peterborough U; **Aiden O'Brien** Millwall to Sunderland.

31 July: **Craig Conway** Salford C to St Johnstone; **Grant Hall** QPR to Middlesbrough; **Ryan Jackson** Colchester U to Gillingham; **James Jones** Altrincham to Barrow; **Tyrone Marsh** Boreham Wood to Stevenage; **Erwin Mulder** Swansea C to Heerenveen; **Matty Taylor** Bristol C to Oxford U.

1 August: **Callum Camps** Rochdale to Fleetwood T; **Tony Craig** Bristol R to Crawley T; **Archie Davies** Brighton & HA to Crawley T; **Lewis Freestone** Brighton & HA to Cheltenham T; **Tyler Frost** Reading to Crawley T; **Liam Gordon** Dagenham & R to Bolton W; **Stephen Hendrie** West Ham U to Morecambe; **Joe Ironside** Macclesfield T to Cambridge U; **Mikael Mandron** Gillingham to Crewe Alex.

2 August: **Cameron Borthwick-Jackson** Manchester U to Oldham Ath; **Harry Davis** Grimsby to Morecambe; **Callum Gribbin** Sheffield U to Barrow; **Sido Jombati** Wycombe W to Oldham Ath; **Jason Lokilo** Crystal Palace to Doncaster R; **Carl Piergianni** Salford C to Oldham Ath; **Bailey Wright** Bristol C to Sunderland.

3 August: **Cameron Burgess** Scunthorpe U to Accrington S; **Josh Daniels** Glenavon to Shrewsbury T; **Ryan Edwards** Blackpool to Dundee U; **Aaron Jarvis** Luton T to Scunthorpe U; **Nat Knight-Percival** Carlisle U to Morecambe; **Rod McDonald** AFC Wimbledon to Carlisle U; **Kelsey Mooney** Aston Villa to Scunthorpe U; **Alex Newby** Chorley T to Rochdale; **Frank Nouble** Colchester U to Plymouth Arg; **Rekeil Pyke** Huddersfield T to Shrewsbury T; **Sean Raggett** Norwich C to Portsmouth; **Jordan Rossiter** Rangers to Fleetwood T; **Ricardo Santos** Barnet to Bolton W; **Lewis Spence** Ross Co to Scunthorpe U; **George Tanner** Manchester U to Carlisle U; **Zain Westbrooke** Coventry C to Bristol R; **Danny Whitehead** Salford C to Port Vale.

4 August: **Bobby Burns** Hearts to Barrow; **Neil Eardley** Lincoln C to Burton Alb; **Reiss Greenidge** Arendal to Bolton W; **Gethin Jones** Carlisle U to Bolton W; **Liam McAlinden** FC Halifax T to Morecambe; **Gavin Reilly** Bristol R to Carlisle U; **Liam Sercombe** Bristol R to Cheltenham T; **Ferran Torres** Valencia to Manchester C – £20.87m.

5 August: **Nathan Ake** Bournemouth to Manchester C – £40m; **Michael Bostwick** Lincoln C to Burton Alb; **Jordan Clark** Accrington S to Luton T; **Vadaine Oliver** Northampton T to Gillingham; **Joe Riley** Bradford C to Carlisle U; **Jay Spearing** Blackpool to Tranmere R; **Dru Yearwood** Brentford to New York Red Bulls.

6 August: **Jack Armer** Preston NE to Carlisle U; **Jake Caprice** Tranmere R to Exeter C; **Sean Clare** Hearts to Oxford U; **Nathan Delfouneso** Blackpool to Bolton W; **Danny Devine** Bradford C to Carlisle U; **Matt Gilks** Fleetwood T to Bolton W; **Jak Hickman** Coventry C to Bolton W; **Rory McArdle** Scunthorpe U to Exeter C; **Ethan Robson** Sunderland to Blackpool; **Alexis Sanchez** Manchester U to Internazionale; **Alex Woodyard** Peterborough U to AFC Wimbledon.

7 August: **Alex Baptiste** Doncaster R to Bolton W; **Liam Bridcutt** Nottingham F to Lincoln C; **Panutche Camara** Crawley T to Plymouth Arg; **Lewie Coyle** Fleetwood T to Hull C; **Josh Emmanuel** Bolton W to Hull C; **Morgan Fox** Sheffield W to Stoke C; **Magnus Norman** Fulham to Carlisle U; **Ollie Palmer** Crawley T to AFC Wimbledon.

8 August: **Joseph Mills** Forest Green R to Northampton T.

9 August: **Angel Gomes** Manchester U to Lille.

10 August: **James Chester** Aston Villa to Stoke C; **Ronnie Edwards** Barnet to Peterborough U; **Joe Gelhardt** Wigan Ath to Leeds U; **Otis Khan** Mansfield T to Tranmere R; **Jacob Mellis** Bolton W to Gillingham; **Ben Pringle** Gillingham to Morecambe; **Kostas Tsimikas** Olympiacos to Liverpool – £11.7m; **Elliott Whitehouse** Grimsby T to Forest Green R.

11 August: **Charlie Allen** Linfield to Leeds U; **Jack Colback** Newcastle U to Nottingham F; **Pierre-Emile Hojbjerg** Southampton to Tottenham H; **Rory Holden** Bristol C to Walsall; **Adam Jackson** Hibernian to Lincoln C; **Davis Keillor-Dunn** Wrexham to Oldham Ath; **Connor Kirby** Sheffield W to Harrogate T; **Kieran Sadlier** Doncaster R to Rotherham U; **Richie Smallwood** Blackburn R to Hull C; **James Vaughan** Bradford C to Tranmere R; **Kyle Walker-Peters** Tottenham H to Southampton.

12 August: **Ethan Chislett** Aldershot T to AFC Wimbledon; **Alex Dobre** Bournemouth to Dijon; **Alex Gilbey** Milton Keynes D to Charlton Ath; **Jordan Graham** Wolverhampton W to Gillingham; **Kane Hemmings** Dundee to Burton Alb; **Mohammed Salisu** Real Valladolid to Southampton – £10.9m; **Luke Varney** Cheltenham T to Burton Alb.

13 August: **Albian Ajeti** West Ham U to Celtic – £4.5m; **Brennan Dickenson** Exeter C to Carlisle U; **Cody Drameh** Fulham to Leeds U; **Chey Dunkley** Wigan Ath to Sheffield W; **Montel Gibson** Halesowen T to Grimsby T; **Ethan Hamilton** Manchester U to Peterborough U; **Bartosz Kapustka** Leicester C to Legia Warsaw; **Kelvin Mellor** Bradford C to Morecambe; **Kieffer Moore** Wigan Ath to Cardiff C – £2m; **Corey O'Keeffe** Birmingham C to Mansfield T; **James Perch** Scunthorpe U to Mansfield T; **Tom Walker** AFC Fylde to Harrogate T; **Joe Walsh** Milton Keynes D to Lincoln C; **Conor Washington** Hearts to Charlton Ath.

14 August: **Steven Fletcher** Sheffield W to Stoke C; **Dimitri Foulquier** Watford to Granada; **Fraser Horsfall** Macclesfield T to Northampton T; **Jack Iredale** Carlisle U to Cambridge U; **Kevin Lokko** Dover to Harrogate T; **Alex MacDonald** Mansfield T to Gillingham; **Jeremy Ngakia** West Ham U to Watford; **Will Norris** Wolverhampton W to Burnley; **Alhagi Touray Sisay** Aberystwyth T to Grimsby T; **Jan Vertonghen** Tottenham H to Benfica; **Willian** Chelsea to Arsenal.

15 August: **Tyler Blackett** Reading to Nottingham F; **George Friend** Middlesbrough to Birmingham C; **Angus MacDonald** Hull C to Rotherham U; **Lyle Taylor** Charlton Ath to Nottingham F.

17 August: **Luke Amos** Tottenham H to QPR; **David Cornell** Northampton T to Ipswich T; **Kyle Dempsey** Fleetwood T to Gillingham; **Paul Farman** Stevenage to Carlisle U; **Oli Hawkins** Portsmouth to Ipswich T; **Uche Ikpeazu** Hearts to Wycombe W; **Paul Lewis** Cambridge U to Tranmere R; **Lewis Macleod** Wigan Ath to Plymouth Arg; **Matheus Pereira** Sporting Lisbon to WBA; **David Silva** Manchester C to Real Sociedad; **Danny Ward** Cardiff C to Huddersfield T; **Stephen Ward** Stoke C to Ipswich T.

18 August: **Dylan Asonganyi** Milton Keynes D to Oxford U; **Joe Hart** Burnley to Tottenham H; **Conor McAleny** Fleetwood T to Oldham Ath; **Akin Odimayo** Reading to Swindon T; **Gime Toure** Hartlepool U to Carlisle U.

19 August: **Ben Chrisene** Exeter C to Aston Villa; **Lyndon Dykes** Livingston to QPR; **Charlie Goode** Northampton T to Brentford; **Aaron O'Driscoll** Southampton to Mansfield T; **Aaron Ramsdale** Bournemouth to Sheffield U – £18.5m.

20 August: **Joel Coleman** Huddersfield T to Fleetwood T; **Greg Docherty** Rangers to Hull C; **Dominik Frieser** LASK to Barnsley; **Wes Harding** Birmingham C to Rotherham U; **David Longe-King** St Albans to Newport Co; **Giles Phillips** QPR to Wycombe W; **Antonee Robinson** Wigan Ath to Fulham – £2m; **Ryan Taylor** Plymouth Arg to Newport Co; **Joe Williams** Wigan Ath to Bristol C.

21 August: **Cian Bolger** Lincoln C to Northampton T; **Marcus Dinanga** AFC Telford to Stevenage; **Morgan Feeney** Everton to Sunderland; **David Marshall** Wigan Ath to Derby Co; **Remi Matthews** Bolton W to Sunderland; **Robbie McKenzie** Hull C to Gillingham.

22 August: **Vaclav Hladky** St Mirren to Salford C; **Joe Murphy** Shrewsbury T to Tranmere R.

24 August: **Ryan Broom** Cheltenham T to Peterborough U; **Matt Butcher** Bournemouth to Accrington S; **Jeff Hendrick** Burnley to Newcastle U; **Jordan Hugill** West Ham U to Norwich C – £5m; **Jamie Mascoll** Wycombe W to Bolton W; **Theo Robinson** Southend U to Port Vale; **Jordan Williams** Rochdale to Blackpool.

25 August: **David Fitzpatrick** Macclesfield T to Port Vale; **Alex Fojticek** Manchester U to Blackpool; **Jason McCarthy** Millwall to Wycombe W; **Martin Montoya** Brighton & HA to Real Betis; **Tommy Smith** Sunderland to Colchester U; **Jon Toral** Hull C to Birmingham C.

26 August: **Fouad Bachirou** Malmo to Nottingham F; **Ben Chilwell** Leicester C to Chelsea – £45m; **Thomas Kaminski** Gent to Blackburn R; **Christian Maghoma** Arka Gdynia to Gillingham; **Scott Wagstaff** AFC Wimbledon to Forest Green R.

27 August: **Jonson Clarke-Harris** Bristol R to Peterborough U; **Donervon Daniels** Luton T to Crewe Alex; **Rhys Healey** Milton Keynes D to Toulouse; **Jamal Lowe** Wigan Ath to Swansea C – £800k; **Ivan Sanchez** Elche to Birmingham C; **Malang Sarr** Nice to Chelsea; **Dino Visser** Crewe Alex to Port Vale; **Ed Williams** Kidderminster to Doncaster R.

28 August: **Mason Bennett** Derby Co to Millwall; **Ovie Ejaria** Liverpool to Reading; **Eberechi Eze** QPR to Crystal Palace – £19.5m; **Dean Furman** SuperSport U to Carlisle U; **Shamal George** Liverpool to Colchester U; **Cameron John** Wolverhampton W to Doncaster R; **Jonathan Leko** WBA to Birmingham C; **Aaron Mooy** Brighton & HA to Shanghai SIPG; **Andres Prieto** Espanyol to Birmingham C; **Roberto** West Ham U to Real Valladolid; **Thiago Silva** Paris Saint-Germain to Chelsea; **David Tutonda** Barnet to Bristol R; **Tyler Walker** Nottingham F to Coventry C; **Callum Whelan** Watford to Oldham Ath.

29 August: **Myles Hippolyte** Yeovil T to Scunthorpe U; **Robin Koch** Freiburg to Leeds U; **Rodrigo** Valencia to Leeds U – £26m.

30 August: **Matt Doherty** Wolverhampton W to Tottenham H; **Harrison Reed** Southampton to Fulham.

31 August: **Ryan Loft** Leicester C to Scunthorpe U; **Henrikh Mkhitaryan** Arsenal to Roma; **Danny Rose** Swindon T to Grimsby T.

Compilers' one for the future: Maddie Langdon, Leam Lane Rangers U12 girls.